DICTIONARY OF
ENGLISH FURNITURE
MAKERS

1660–1840

DICTIONARY OF
ENGLISH FURNITURE
MAKERS
1660–1840

EDITED BY

GEOFFREY BEARD

AND

CHRISTOPHER GILBERT

ASSISTANT EDITORS

BRIAN AUSTEN   ARTHUR BOND

ANGELA EVANS

FURNITURE HISTORY SOCIETY

W. S. MANEY AND SON LTD

PUBLISHED IN 1986
ISBN 0 901286 18 4

PRINTED IN GREAT BRITAIN
BY W. S. MANEY AND SON LIMITED
HUDSON ROAD LEEDS LS9 7DL

CONTENTS

The engraving of 'The Cabinet-maker' is taken from *The Book of English Trades*, 1804
Endpapers from Thomas Sheraton's *Cabinet Dictionary*, 1803, plate 41

FOREWORD

From its foundation in 1964 the main concern of the Furniture History Society has been the publication of original research in its field, and its annual *Journal* has built up a high reputation over the years. Special issues such as Dr P. Eames's *Medieval Furniture* (1977) and Mr F. Bamford's *Dictionary of Edinburgh Furniture Makers* (1983) have surveyed important areas of study. The Hardwick Hall and Ham House inventories (1971 and 1980 respectively) and the facsimile of the *Cabinet-Makers' London Book of Prices 1793*, which the Society published in 1982, are good examples of its intention to make important source material available to scholars.

All this has been good work, of credit to the Society and especially to its Honorary Editors. There is no doubt, however, that the most important project yet undertaken by the Society is the *Dictionary* of furniture makers active in England in the years 1660–1840 and we have indeed been fortunate in having Dr Geoffrey Beard and Mr Christopher Gilbert as joint-editors. They were, each for ten years, the first and second editors of the Society's *Journal* and laid the foundations of its success. In the present work they planned and set going the system of regional research and then, with the help of three assistant editors, controlled the mass of information coming in as a result and imposed upon it their editorial discipline.

A special feature of the programme of research has been the large number of volunteers, members of the society and others, who have given to it their time and labour over this long period. Several hundreds of people have been involved in divers places under the supervision of some twenty-five regional organizers. Many have undertaken with ready enthusiasm tedious and repetitive tasks such as searching through long runs of trade directories, insurance registers, newspapers and periodical literature. Invaluable work has been done by members of the National Association of Decorative and Fine Art Societies. Others have worked at record offices and libraries and on collections of private records often travelling far to do so. The Society has conferred life membership on Arthur Bond, C.B.E. who freely gave many hours to the sorting and arranging of the blue record-cards which comprised the master index. Angela Evans and Brian Austen worked devotedly on converting the accumulated data into typescript and at proof reading. About ninety commissioned articles on notable furniture makers have been written by some thirty members, all expert in their subject.

As in every project finance has been a matter of concern, but the Society's Officers and other members of the Council have had good success in approaches to individuals and to charitable bodies for support.

The general impression, therefore, is of time and work and funds freely given by many people. But in recalling the help of all who have made the *Dictionary* a reality one's thoughts return inevitably to our two Editors. In their dedication to the planning of the work and in the determination to see the *Dictionary* successfully launched they have been the moving force behind all our effort. We offer them our admiration and thanks.

T. L. Ingram, PRESIDENT

ACKNOWLEDGEMENTS

This *Dictionary* represents a major step forward in our knowledge of London and provincial furniture makers in the years 1660–1840. It is by far the most ambitious co-operative effort ever undertaken by furniture historians and will stand for many years as a tribute to the enthusiasm and industry of a large number of people. It is the outcome of field work by over four hundred persons, organised by some twenty-five regional co-ordinators and all responsible to a central team. The scheme has been administered by two senior and three assistant editors (Geoffrey Beard, Christopher Gilbert; Brian Austen, Arthur Bond and Angela Evans) whose job it has been to plan, guide, take policy decisions and write most of the text. They have lived with the project in all of its stages for seven exhausting but exciting years of recording, checking and double-checking, sustained by mutual encouragement and selfless help. In the last stages the book itself was the object of intensive and caring attention by the Society's printer (and in this case its publisher).

Before the appearance of this book only one attempt had been made to examine the English furniture trade in biographical terms — the listing of some 2,500 London makers by Sir Ambrose Heal (1953). This work, whilst valuable, necessarily had to rely on the limited range of sources one person, however active, could check. It was decided that at least five years was the shortest period of diligent research by a large team in which a really worthwhile picture could be obtained. The central running of the scheme (equipment, salaries and expenses) has cost at least £20,000 partly met by various grants, listed below, and by careful application of the Society's limited reserves. This takes no account of the time spent on it voluntarily by the senior editors, co-ordinators and volunteers, or of the hundreds of hours expended freely by Arthur and Nora Bond in collating, consolidating and filing some seventy thousand record cards in alphabetical sequence.

Acknowledgements in the following pages will always seem an inadequate testimony to those who accomplished so much. The transfer by the Society of the *Dictionary* record cards (which have been kept at Temple Newsam House, Leeds) on permanent loan to the Department of Furniture and Interior Design at the Victoria and Albert Museum will allow researchers to check relevant facts against the master index when necessary. The Department, as part of its daily work, will continue to gather additional information of use in compiling a second edition, albeit one issued at some distant date. For the moment the present work is offered as one which will do much to extend understanding of furniture making in England.

It is a necessary and welcome task to accord special thanks to the Trusts and individuals who contributed money for research and to those who helped by co-ordinating it 'in the field'. Under the supervision of Sir Nicholas Goodison, the Honorary Treasurer, the day to day accounting has been carried out by Mrs Anne Law. The following donors contributed £500 or more to the *Dictionary* appeal. Their help was especially welcome, leading as it did to many smaller financial contributions:

ACKNOWLEDGEMENTS

Norman R. Adams Ltd.

The Baring Foundation

The British Academy

The British Antique Dealers' Association

The R. M. Burton Charitable Settlement

R. G. Cave & Sons (Antiques) Ltd

Christie, Manson & Woods Ltd

D. Copeland Esq.

Mrs C. M. Dawson

The Henry Francis Du Pont Winterthur
    Museum, Delaware

The Esmee Fairbairn Charitable Trust

The Marc Fitch Fund

Andrew Jenkins

Mr and Mrs G. Ll. Law

Mrs M. Miller

Florian Papp Inc., New York

The Pasold Research Fund

Mrs John Raven

Save & Prosper Education Fund

Mrs C. E. Smith

Sotheby & Co. (and their clients who
    responded to an appeal made by the firm)

H. Whitbread Esq.

Secondly, grateful thanks are accorded to the London research team, led by Simon Jervis (Victoria and Albert Museum) and to which invaluable assistance was given over several years by Janet Bird; Pamela Charlton; Frances Collard; Major T. L. Ingram; Linda Kramer; Catherine Norman; Treve Rosoman; Janey Spring; Mary Stirling; Nancy Trueblood and Vivienne Woolf.

Thirdly, the activities of the volunteer researchers was co-ordinated in over twenty regions of England by Pauline Agius; Dr Brian Austen; Elizabeth Drury; Robert Dukes; Dr Penelope Eames; Dr Ivan Hall; Helena Hayward; Anthony Howarth; The late Edward T. Joy; Alison Kelly; Dr Pat Kirkham; Dr Joan Lane; Mr and Mrs Robert Lewis; James Lomax; Sarah Medlam; Dr John Raine; Cyril Staal; Dr John Stabler; Dr Aubrey Stewart; Gillian Walkling; Karin M. Walton and Robert Williams.

A number of volunteer researchers were especially active, namely: Paul Aagaard; Enid Bassom; Susan Bourne; Martin Colman; June Dean; John Duxfield; Lilian Eaton; David Feather; Margaret Garbett; Robert and Helena Hewitt; David Jones; John Lord; John Malden; Sarah Nichols; Jeremy Pearson; Marjorie Ranft; Valerie M. Rickerby; Hugh Roberts; Ivan Sparkes; Anne Stevens; Diana Townsend; Stuart Turner and Charles Walford. Material was gathered in Scotland by Margaret Swain and Irene Grant.

EDITORS' EXPLANATION

Makers are entered in alphabetical order from Aaron to Zurn. When individuals bearing exactly the same name are recorded they are listed in chronological sequence. The name, sometimes with an alternative spelling in brackets, is printed in bold type, followed by an address or place of residence, where this is known; then, details of the person's trade are stated, and finally the date or time span when a maker was active is given in round brackets, e.g., (b. 1718–d. 1779). Next, any changes of address are noted, followed by the available details of apprenticeship, freedoms and relevant references in poll or rate books. Additional information such as the existence of a trade card, particulars gleaned from press notices, references to stamped or labelled furniture, any documentation and similar evidence is given in an orderly fashion. Sources are quoted in square brackets, usually at the end of entries. When dealing with well researched careers such as Thomas Chippendale or William Vile a biographical summary is followed by an account of the firm's commissions in date order.

County boundaries prevailing at the time have been adopted throughout, except in the case of London and its suburbs where the name of the capital instead of a county indicates the place lies within the present London postal district. The county in which towns and villages are located is stated unless this is self-evident such as Hereford, Lancaster or Lincoln and in the case of a few large urban centres including Manchester, Liverpool, Birmingham, Bristol and Newcastle-upon-Tyne. Ireland, Scotland and Wales have not been included in the present census (except for the quotation of English material found there) because of difficulties in placing the collection of information in these regions on a secure footing; the Isle of Man and the Channel Islands were also excluded.

It is well known that the compilers and printers of early trade directories were none too reliable when it came to spelling names or addresses correctly. We have, however, transcribed the information from these volumes faithfully, only making alterations where a suspected error can be proved by cross reference from another source.

All the main furniture trades are covered in our survey including specialist branches such as picture frame makers, clock and barometer case makers, box (dressing, knife, writing, etc.) makers, spinning-wheel makers, and inlayers. However, the following are only recorded in the *Dictionary* if there is evidence that they were actually involved in producing furniture: joiners, turners, carvers, japanners, auctioneers and appraisers. Furniture brokers or dealers have an entry if they identified their stock with a label or impressed mark. The following 'fringe' trades were deliberately ignored: trunk makers, bellow makers (usually industrial), coach builders, blind makers, French polishers, clock and musical instrument makers, timber merchants, makers of marble or scagliola table tops and suppliers of hardware to the cabinet trade. Furniture designers who were not trained as furniture makers are also excluded. The foregoing groups are not exhaustive but illustrate our guidelines. Some difficulty was experienced during the period 1660–c. 1715 when fashionable furniture makers were often described in accounts as 'joyners' —the context in which names occurred sometimes provided clues as to the nature of their craft.

Impressed and inscribed names were generally assumed to have belonged to makers, although they may have occasionally denoted owners. We realised that Victorian upholsterers quite often pencilled signatures on the frames of chairs they recovered; these were accordingly omitted. Punched initials frequently occur on seat furniture, particularly late Stuart caned walnut chairs, but also throughout the Georgian period. Such stamps, which have never been systematically studied, are referred to only in passing, although it is clear from the example of Thomas Rayner (q.v.) that they belong to journeymen.

The illustrations are intended to show the various ways in which firms and individuals identified their products and other sources of evidence for authorship. It would have been rewarding to feature more labelled or documented furniture, but we could not extend to a second volume. Hopefully a future generation of scholars will, by following up the copious references, compile a pictorial anthology of the work of many London and provincial firms. Virtually nothing is known about the majority of makers, although in due course some may emerge as rounded characters. The index records the names of various workmen mentioned in the text — often as apprentices — also members of partnerships who do not always have their own entries. Many of the former are likely to have been journeymen all their lives rather than masters. Users are therefore advised to check the index as well as the main alphabetical list when searching for a maker. We must admit, finally, that this *Dictionary* draws no conclusions about the organisation of the furniture industry or trade practices such as sub-contracting; it is in some ways a rather antiquarian compilation. However, students and collectors will find they can refer to the volume with confidence and we hope it will be judged by its achievement rather than its shortcomings.

SOURCES

It will be appreciated that this *Dictionary* is the result of collaboration by many people on a massive scale. The number of printed and manuscript sources checked during compilation was vast and since appropriate references are cited in the individual entries there seems little point in providing a consolidated list. It is hoped that the following summary indicating the main categories of source material and how thoroughly each area was covered will be found useful and acceptable.

Directories

Every effort was made to ensure that all Trade and Post Office Directories published in England before 1840 were fully trawled for relevant names and we believe that virtually complete coverage was achieved. Jane Norton's *Guide to the National and Provincial Directories of England and Wales, excluding London. Published before 1856* (Royal Historical Society 1950) proved invaluable, while for London holdings of Directories at the Guildhall Library, the Institute of Historical Research, Kensington Library, Westminster City Library and the Victoria and Albert Museum were collated and checked. One problem encountered, was the compiler's tendency to list joiners and cabinet makers under a single heading, which is why some tradesmen in the *Dictionary*, especially in northern towns and villages, are recorded as 'joiner/cm'.

Owing to the sheer multiplicity of references culled from Directories we decided to acknowledge all such information by the letter 'D' when citing the source. Full details of titles and dates are entered on cards in the master index.

Newspapers

It proved impossible to do more than sample London and provincial newspapers for press notices. The texts of trade advertisements are of capital interest and those which were traced are often quoted in full. However, a very fair coverage of Bath, Brighton, Bristol, Chester, Exeter, Hereford, Leeds, Liverpool, Newcastle and York papers was achieved while items were extracted from an art index of London papers covering the years 1735–55 kept in the Furniture Department at the Victoria and Albert Museum. In all 113 titles were sampled. The Symonds papers at the Henry Francis Du Pont Winterthur Museum, Delaware yielded a notable crop of transcripts from contemporary newspapers while some attempt was made by volunteers in the USA to supply particulars of furniture makers who emigrated to America and announced their recent arrival from England in the local press. The *Gentleman's Magazine* was fully scrutinised and the index to *The Times* partly so.

Trade Cards

Great pains were taken to trace these richly informative items of ephemera. Examples in the well known Banks, Heal, Fielden and Hodgkin collections at the British Museum were fully recorded, also the Landauer and Leverhulme collections at the Metropolitan Museum of Art, New York and significant holdings at the Victoria and Albert Museum, Guildhall Library, the Bodleian Library and the Westminster City Library. Many scattered groups in other Public Libraries and Record Offices were also located. Printed billheads proved another valuable source while detached labels (whether used as a docket and filed with estate papers, or harvested by furniture restorers) were always welcome discoveries.

Subscription Lists and Price Books

The lists of subscribers to furniture pattern books such as Thomas Chippendale's *Director*, 1754, Thomas Sheraton's *Drawing Book*, 1793 and his *Cabinet-Dictionary*, 1803 provided many index cards, although the information given is often bare. Volumes of architectural designs or engraved ornament, and various treatises published by subscription, and so likely to appeal to furniture tradesmen were also checked. Cabinetmakers' *Books of Prices* often named committees of masters and journeymen who drew up the piece-work rates on behalf of their colleagues; accordingly these too were examined.

Sale Catalogues

A systematic search of the furniture catalogues published by Christie's, Sotheby's and Phillips contributed rewarding evidence, particularly during the last thirty years when labels, stamps or available documentation are usually mentioned in lot descriptions. Several late Georgian catalogues of the stock-in-trade of cabinet makers sold by Christie's were discovered. In all sale catalogues issued by sixteen auctioneers yielded significant information.

Victoria and Albert Museum Furniture Archive

Prior to this project the only corporate effort to create an index of cabinet makers was attempted by the Department of Furniture at the Victoria and Albert Museum. Since about 1960 the staff had maintained a series of loose leaf binders containing green slips on which information about makers was recorded, often in a rather desultory way. Despite its shortcomings this index proved so useful as a supplement to Heal's *London Furniture Makers 1660–1840* and Jourdain and Edwards' *Georgian Cabinet-Makers* that it must be acknowledged as a major factor in inspiring the present venture. Needless to say the data it contained was meticulously carded for our own master index. The departmental files on individual country houses containing tear sheets from *Country Life*, photocopies of furniture bills, notes made on field trips to the houses, photographs etc. were thoroughly investigated and made a vital contribution to the present volume.

Personal Files

Members of the Furniture History Society and other well wishers, sadly with one exception, freely made available the contents of their own research files. These included museum curators, dealers, authors, lecturers, amateur collectors, antiquarians, local historians and genealogists. A special debt of gratitude is owed to Dr. Pat Kirkham who offered her considerable dossiers on the London furniture trade. The personal papers of the late Margaret Jourdain and of the late Edward Joy, both filed at the Victoria and Albert Museum, were searched thoroughly while a team of colleagues in America, aided by a generous grant from the Henry Francis Du Pont Winterthur Museum, Delaware, extracted information from the Symonds papers at that centre of learning.

Local, Corporate and Business Records

The coverage of this material was uneven; for example, few teams of volunteers found the time to check parish registers or rate books. However, freemens' rolls, apprenticeship registers and poll books were regarded as priority sources and, while gaps remain, no apology is necessary for the gatherings from these records. The Joiners' Company and Upholders' Company lists provided invaluable information, although it was not always easy to be certain that their members were involved in the furniture trades. The population census of 1841, the first regularly to state occupations, was ignored because it fell outside our time frame (except in the case of High Wycombe, a vitally important chairmaking centre for which other sources were extremely slender). Insurance records at the Guildhall Library provided one of the most fruitful and previously under researched blocks of material. A team concentrated on the Sun Fire Office policy registers and also combed some of those of the Hand in Hand company. Only limited use was made of bank ledgers — potential mines of information — owing to other pressures: it is hoped that funding will eventually become available for a computerised analysis of their contents. The Society of Genealogists very generously made their specialist indexes available to us.

Archives

Country house muniments are the most rewarding of all primary sources since they may offer the possibility of building bridges between documents and provenanced furniture. The leading London cabinet makers seldom identified their products with a label or impressed stamp so this avenue of research is frequently the only way of establishing an artistic biography. Many country house commissions have been investigated, especially since the last war when family papers became more generally accessible. Hopefully almost all published references to relevant bills, payments and correspondence were carded. Regrettably the survey of estate papers remains incomplete because some collections remain in private hands, others are unsorted and a few proved too voluminous to sift methodically. However, we are reasonably confident that most of the significant available material was studied in varying degrees of detail. A vigorous programme of exploration was directed at certain particularly rich but hitherto neglected archives such as the Badminton, Bedford, Croome Court, Chatsworth, Audley End, Egerton/Wilton, Monson, Ancaster and Strathmore papers. The Scottish Record Office was included in our survey while the Royal archives at Windsor and the Public Record Office were researched intensively. Occasionally two locations are cited for MS deposits where material has been moved recently to a different repository.

Periodical Literature

The main English language periodicals concerned with decorative art or antiques ranging from the *Burlington Magazine* to the *Antique Dealer and Collectors Guide*, plus associated Annuals and Year Books were explored. We did not check pre-1930 numbers of *Country Life* since documented or labelled furniture was little regarded before that time. Care was taken to use runs in which dealers' advertisements had been bound-in. Many journals published by learned societies and museums were also checked. The coverage of this material was impressively complete. References quoted in the *Dictionary* seldom cite authors of articles, only title and date or volume number and pagination of the periodical.

Modern Books

The carding of information from nineteenth and twentieth century books was a colossal undertaking. In view of the sheer bulk and repetitive nature of much of this data it was decided not to list all printed sources in a consolidated bibliography. Many books yielded only stray references and in such instances full details are given in the relevant entries. However, in the interests of space economy some books are cited in an abbreviated form. It was therefore considered essential to list these titles below in full, although the majority will be familiar to most users.

Bailey, William, *List of Bankrupts 1772–1793*, 1794

Bamford, Francis, *A Dictionary of Edinburgh Furniture Makers*, 1983

Beard, Geoffrey, *Georgian Craftsmen and their Work*, 1966

—— *Craftsmen and Interior Decoration in England*, 1981

Bellaigue, Geoffrey de, Harris, John and Millar, Oliver, *Buckingham Palace*, 1968

Bolton, Arthur T., *The Architecture of Robert and James Adam*, 2 vols, 1922

Chippendale, Thomas, *The Gentleman and Cabinet-maker's Director*, 1754

Claxton Stevens, Christopher and Whittington, Stuart, *Eighteenth Century Furniture: the Norman Adams Collection*, 1983

Clifford-Smith, H., *Buckingham Palace*, 1931

Coleridge, Anthony, *The Work of Thomas Chippendale and his Contemporaries in the Rococo Taste*, 1968

Colvin, Howard, *A Biographical Dictionary of British Architects 1600–1840* (rev. ed.) 1978

Edwards, A. C. (ed.), *The Accounts of Benjamin Mildmay, Earl Fitzwalter*, 1977

Edwards, Ralph, *The Dictionary of English Furniture*, 3 vols, 1954

Edwards, Ralph and Jourdain, Margaret, *Georgian Cabinet-Makers* (rev. ed.) 1955

Fastnedge, Ralph, *English Furniture Styles 1500–1830*, 1955

—— *Sheraton Furniture*, 1962

Fifth Hall Book of New Windsor (ed) South, R., Windsor Borough Historical Records Publication, 1974

Fitz-Gerald, Desmond, *The Norfolk House Music Room*, 1973

Fleming, John, *Robert Adam and his Circle*, 1962

Fowler, John and Cornforth, John, *English Decoration in the Eighteenth Century*, 1974

Gilbert, Christopher, *The Life and Work of Thomas Chippendale*, 2 vols, 1978

—— *Furniture at Temple Newsam House and Lotherton Hall*, 2 vols, 1978

Goodison, Nicholas, *English Barometers 1680–1860*, 1977

—— *Ormolu: the Work of Matthew Boulton*, 1974

Gunnis, Rupert, *Dictionary of British Sculptors 1660–1851* (rev. ed.) 1968

Harris, Eileen, *The Furniture of Robert Adam*, 1963

Harris, John, *Sir William Chambers*, 1970

Harris, M. & Sons, *Old English Furniture* (rev. ed.) 1938

Hayward, Helena and Kirkham, Pat, *William and John Linnell: Eighteenth Century London Furniture-Makers*, 2 vols, 1980

Heal, Ambrose, *The London Furniture Makers 1660–1840*, 1953

Hussey, Christopher, *English Country Houses: Early-Georgian* (rev. ed.) 1965

—— *English Country Houses: Mid-Georgian*, 1956

—— *English Country Houses: Late-Georgian*, 1958

Jervis, Simon, *Dictionary of Design and Designers*, 1984

Jourdain, Margaret, *The Work of William Kent*, 1948

—— *Regency Furniture*, (rev. by Fastnedge, R.) 1965

Jourdain, Margaret and Rose, F., *English Furniture the Georgian Period 1750–1830*, 1953

Joy, Edward, *English Furniture 1800–1851*, 1977

Loudon, John Claudius, *Encyclopaedia of Cottage, Farm and Villa Architecture and Furniture*, 1833

Malton, Thomas, *A Compleat Treatise on Perspective, in Theory and Practice on the True Principles of Dr. Brook Taylor*, 1775

Mayes, L. J., *The History of Chairmaking in High Wycombe*, 1960

Musgrave, Clifford, *Adam and Hepplewhite and other Neo-Classical Furniture*, 1966

—— *Regency Furniture*, 1961

Phillips, Hugh, *Mid-Georgian London*, 1964

Reade, Bryan, *Regency Antiques*, 1953

Robinson, Thomas, *The Long-Case Clock*, 1981

Sheraton, Thomas, *The Cabinet-Maker and Upholsterer's Drawing Book*, 1793

—— *The Cabinet Dictionary*, 1803

Stroud, Dorothy, *Henry Holland*, 1968

Symonds, Robert, *Furniture Making in Seventeenth and Eighteenth Century England*, 1955

—— *English Furniture from Charles II to George II*, 1929

Tomlin, Maurice, *Catalogue of Adam Period Furniture (V & A)* 1972

Ward-Jackson, Peter, *English Furniture Designs of the Eighteenth Century*, 1958

Watson, F. J. B., *Southill, a Regency House*, 1951

Wills, Geoffrey, *English Looking Glasses*, 1965

—— *English Furniture 1550–1760*, 1971

—— *English Furniture 1760–1900*, 1971

Wills at Chelmsford (ed.) Emmison, F. G., 3 vols, 1958–69

Wiltshire Apprentices and their Masters 1710–1760, (ed.) Dale, C., Wilts Arch and Nat. Hist. Soc. Record Series, vol. 17, 1961

ABBREVIATIONS

The abbreviations are printed in the type that is normally used for them.

app.	apprentice	cat.	catalogue
app. reg.	apprenticeship register	*Cf, cf*	*confer*, 'compare'
apps	apprentices	cm	cabinet maker(s)
Arch.	Archaeological	Co.	Company
Assoc.	Association	Coll.	Collection
Ave.	Avenue	Colvin	*A Biographical Dictionary of British Architects, 1600–1840* (rev. ed.) 1978
b.	born		
BADA	British Antique Dealers' Association	Comm.	Commission
		Conn.	*Connoisseur*
bapt.	baptised	Corp.	Corporation
Beds.	Bedfordshire	Cresc.	Crescent
Berks.	Berkshire	Ct	Court
bk	book	Cumb.	Cumberland
BL	British Library		
BM	British Museum	d.	died
Bucks.	Buckinghamshire	D	Directory/Directories
Burlington	*Burlington Magazine*	*DEF*	R. Edwards, *The Dictionary of English Furniture*, 3 vols (rev. ed.) 1954
c.	circa		
C. Life	*Country Life*	dept	department
Cambs.	Cambridgeshire	Derbs.	Derbyshire

DNB	*Dictionary of National Biography*	Mt	Mount
Ed.	Edited/edition	NACF	National Art-Collections Fund
e.g.	*exempli gratia*, 'for example'	Nat.	National
etc.	etcetera	Nat. Trust	National Trust
Exhib.	Exhibition	n.d.	no date
fl.	floruit, the period during which a person 'flourished'	no.	number
		Non-Conf.	Non-Conformist
Furn. Hist.	*Journal of the Furniture History Society*	Northants.	Northamptonshire
		Northumb.	Northumberland
		Notts.	Nottinghamshire
GCM	R. Edwards and M. Jourdain, *Georgian Cabinet-Makers*, (rev. ed.) 1955	NY	New York
		Oxon.	Oxfordshire
Gdn(s)	Garden(s)		
Gents Mag.	*Gentleman's Magazine* (1731–1840)	p.	page
		pa	per annum
GL	Guildhall Library	pp.	pages
Glos.	Gloucestershire	PCC	Prerogative Court of Canterbury (wills in PRO)
Gt	Great		
Gunnis	R. Gunnis, *Dictionary of British Sculptors, 1660–1851* (rev. ed., 1968)	Penn'a	Pennsylvania
		Perths.	Perthshire
		Pl.	Place/plate(s)
Hants.	Hampshire	*POD*	*Post Office Directory*
Heal	A. Heal, *The London Furniture Makers, 1660–1840*, 1953	PR	Parish Register
		PRO	Public Record Office, London
Herefs.	Herefordshire	Prob.	Probate
Herts.	Hertfordshire	pt	part
Hist.	*Historical/History*	publ.	published
Huguenot Soc.	*Proceedings of the Huguenot Society of London*	q.v.	*quod vide*, 'which see'
Hunts.	Huntingdonshire		
ie.	*id est*, 'that is'	RA	Royal Archives (Windsor)
illus.	illustrated	Rd	Road
ins	inches	Ref.	Reference
Inst.	Institute	reg.	register
IR	Inland Revenue	reg. of elect.	register of electors
		Rev.	Reverend/revised
Lancs.	Lancashire	RO	Record Office
LAC	*Leeds Arts Calendar*	RIBA	Royal Institute of British Architects
LC	Lord Chamberlain		
Leics.	Leicestershire	Salop	Shropshire
Lib.	Library	*sic*	To call attention to something anomalous in quotations
Lincs.	Lincolnshire		
Mass.	Massachusetts	Soc.	Society
Middlx	Middlesex	S of G	Society of Genealogists
Mkt	Market	Som.	Somerset
MMA	Metropolitan Museum	Sq.	Square
Mons.	Monmouthshire	St	Street/Saint
MS	manuscripts	Staffs.	Staffordshire

SPCK	Society for the Propogation of Christian Knowledge	viz	*videlicet*, 'namely'
Surtees Soc.	Surtees Society volumes	vol.	volume
		Warks.	Warwickshire
Terr.	Terrace	Westmld	Westmorland
Trans.	Transactions	Wilts.	Wiltshire
trans.	translated	Worcs.	Worcestershire
		Wren Soc.	*Wren Society*, 20 vols 1924–43
u	upholsterer(s)	*Walpole Soc.*	*Walpole Society*, vol. 1 1911 onwards
UBD	*Universal British Directory*		
Univ.	University		
USA	United States of America	YAS	Yorkshire Archaeological Society
		Yd	Yard
V & A	Victoria and Albert Museum	Yorks.	Yorkshire
V & A archives	files and indexes kept in the Dept. of Furniture and Interior Design		

COMMISSIONED ARTICLES

The following have provided signed contributions.

P.A.	Pauline Agius	S.J.	Simon Jervis
B.A.	Brian Austen	A.A.K.	Alison A. Kelly
G.B.	Geoffrey Beard	P.K.	Pat Kirkham
G. de B.	Geoffrey de Bellaigue	L.K.	Linda Kramer
C.C.	Charles Cator	C.E.L.-J.	Clare E. Lloyd-Jacob
F.C.	Frances Collard	S.R.	Simon Redburn
G.C.	Greer Crawley	W.R.	William Rieder
J.D.	June Dean	N.R.	Noël Riley
A.E.	Angela Evans	H.R.	Hugh Roberts
C.G.G.	Christopher G. Gilbert	T.R.	Treve Rosoman
J.G.	Judith Goodison	M.S.	Mary Stirling
I.H.	Ivan Hall	M.T.	Maurice Tomlin
J.H.	John Hardy	N.N.T.	Nancy N. Trueblood
H.H.	Helena Hayward	C.W.	Clive Wainwright
M.H.H.	Morrison H. Heckscher	R.W.	Robert Williams
J.D.H.	J. C. Davidson How	G.W.	Geoffrey Wills
G.J.-S.	Gervase Jackson-Stops	V.W.	Vivienne Woolf

PLATES

Illustrating various ways
in which furniture makers
identified their work

1. Impressed mark 'I [?] RICHARDS | 1746' on the
bottom of a mahogany cabinet

Florian Papp, Inc.

2. Mark of Frederick Walker, Rockley, Notts., struck
on the seat edge of a Windsor chair, *c.* 1840

Peter Brears

3. Label of Samuel Butt, pasted in the drawer of an early
eighteenth-century double chest of drawers

Phillips of Hitchin, Ltd

4. Label of John Belchier on a japanned bureau
cabinet, *c.* 1730. Small labels were often
favoured by furniture makers who worked in
the neighbourhood of St Paul's Church Yard

Christie's

5. Rare example of an inlaid maker's name featured on a pair of pilasters which decorate
the inside of a door enclosing the upper stage of an early eighteenth-century walnut
bureau cabinet

Victoria & Albert Museum

6

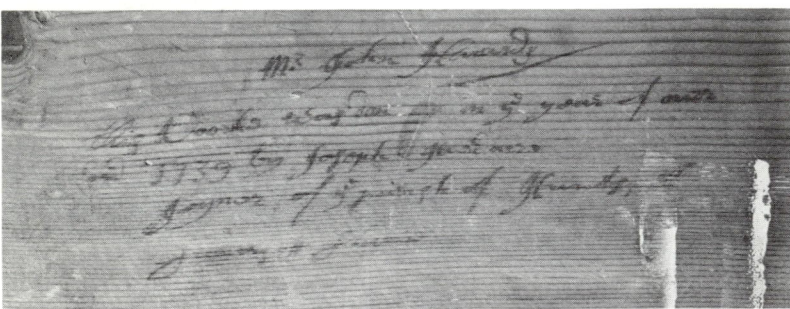

7

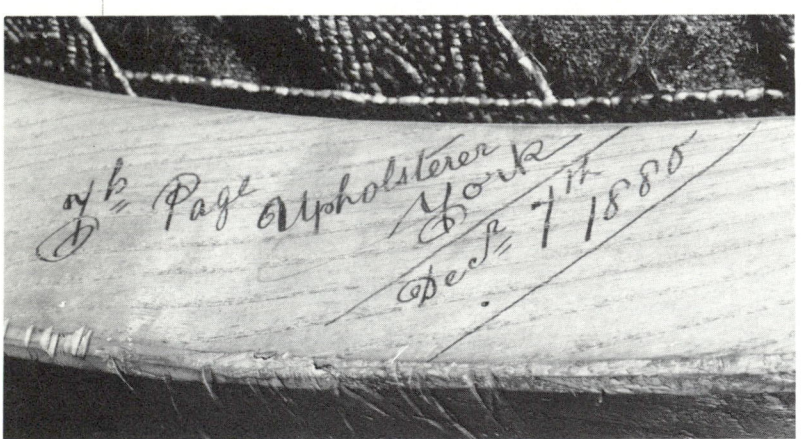

8

9

6. Incised and black-waxed inscription on a pine insert decorating the back-rail of a mahogany flap table

Temple Newsam, Leeds

7. Ink inscription on the drawer of a built-in painted pine cupboard in a cottage at Long Ashton, Somerset: 'Mr John Howarde | this Woorke was done in ye year of our | Lord 1739 by Joseph Hurdacre | Joyner of ye parish of Huntspill | Somersett Shire'

Bristol Museum and Art Gallery

8. Ink inscription on the under-brace of a Regency couch. It is quite common to find the names of Victorian journeymen who re-upholstered seat furniture on the frames

Temple Newsam, Leeds

9. Thomas Willson (*fl.* 1799–1829) was a broker or dealer in good quality secondhand furniture who stamped his stock. This mark occurs on the drawer-edge of a late eighteenth-century marquetry writing table

10

10. Mahogany dressing table supplied by Gillows to R. O. Gascoigne, Parlington Hall, Yorks in August 1811 at a cost of £6 16s 6d

Temple Newsam, Leeds

11. Punched stamp on the fore-edge of the central drawer

12. Signature on underside of the bottom right-hand drawer. The names of workmen are quite often found pencilled unobtrusively on Gillows furniture at this time

11

12

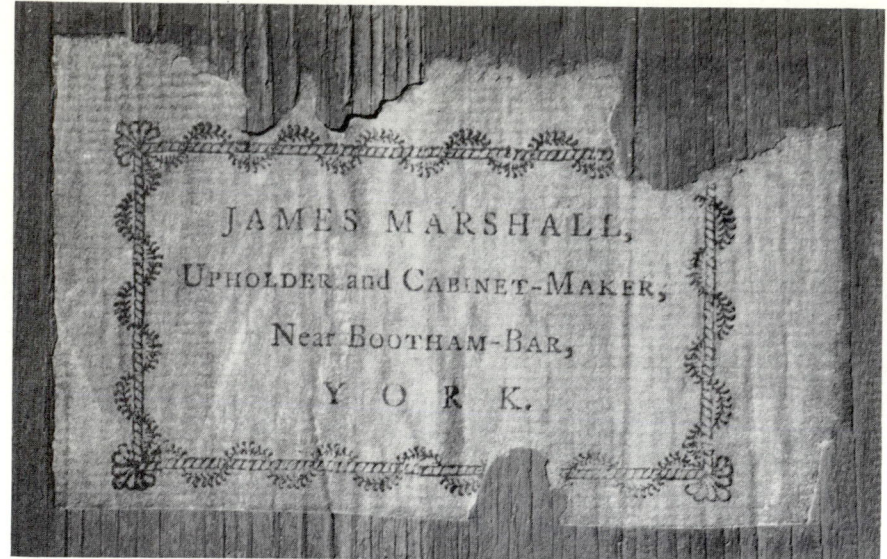

13

14

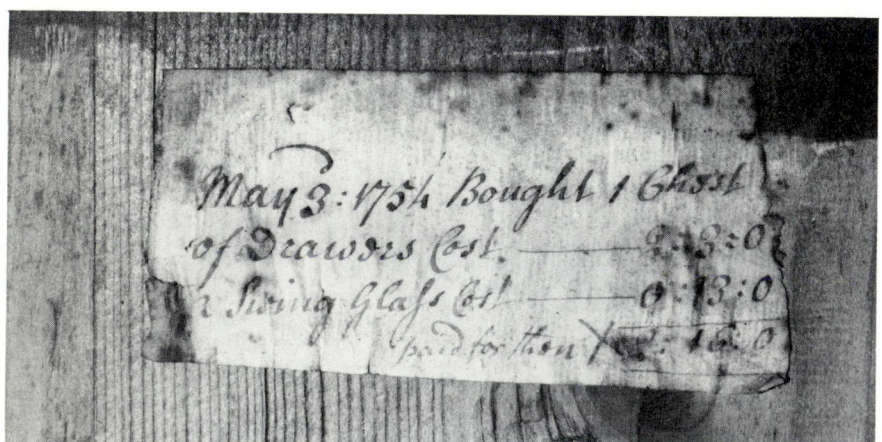

15

13. Label found on the back and top of the lower stage of a mahogany secretary and bookcase. The condition shows how prone labels in exposed positions are to damage

Florian Papp, Inc.

14. Label discovered beneath blue lining paper at the back of a small drawer below the platform of an elegant lady's spinning-wheel made *c.* 1800 for Mrs W. Rhodes of Armley House, Yorkshire

Temple Newsam, Leeds

15. Manuscript label on the back of a walnut chest of drawers. The date and price but not the maker are recorded

Robert Williams

16

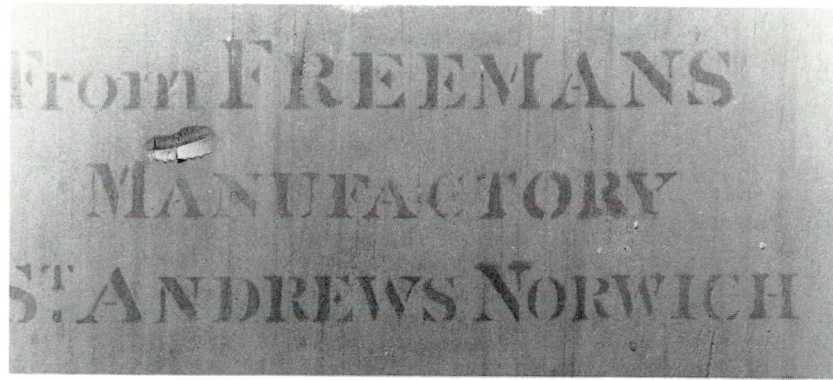

17

18

16. Label on a double chest of drawers, *c.* 1770. Typical of the ambitious professionally designed labels and trade cards favoured by some middling firms. Imprint: 'M. Darly Invt. & Sculp.'

Phillips of Hitchin, Ltd

17. Stencil on the back of a mahogany cupboard, *c.* 1840. Stencilled marks were seldom used before the Victorian period

Ralph & Bruce Moss

18. Label on the seat rail of a dining chair. According to directories Thomas Atkinson was trading at 38 & 39 Ludgate Hill only between 1823 and 24

J. A. Harrison

19. Tea chest
Thomas Sainsbury

20. Tea chest open showing label inside the recess designed to hold a glass sugar bowl

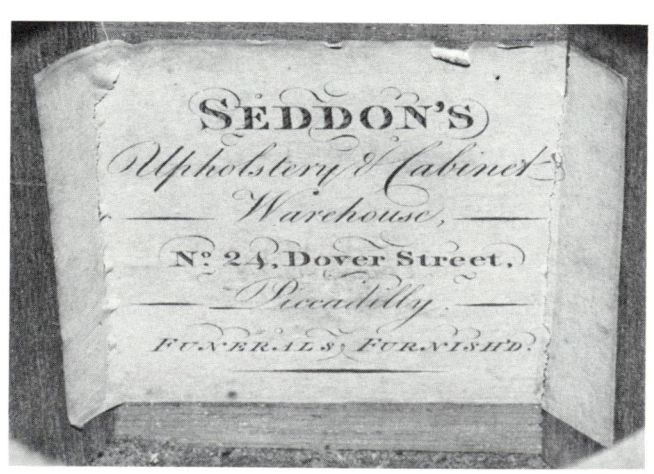

21. Detail of Seddon's label; the firm traded at 24 Dover Street only between 1793 and 1800

22

22. Lady's secretary and cabinet, satin wood and sabicu by George Simson. Based on a design dated 1794 in Sheraton's *Drawing Book*, pl. 64. The cabinetwork relates closely to a well known family of secretaire and dressing cabinets incorporating clocks from Weeks' Museum, permitting a cautious attribution of this group to Simson on the basis of stylistic analogy

Jeremy Ltd

23. Simson's label on the above piece

23

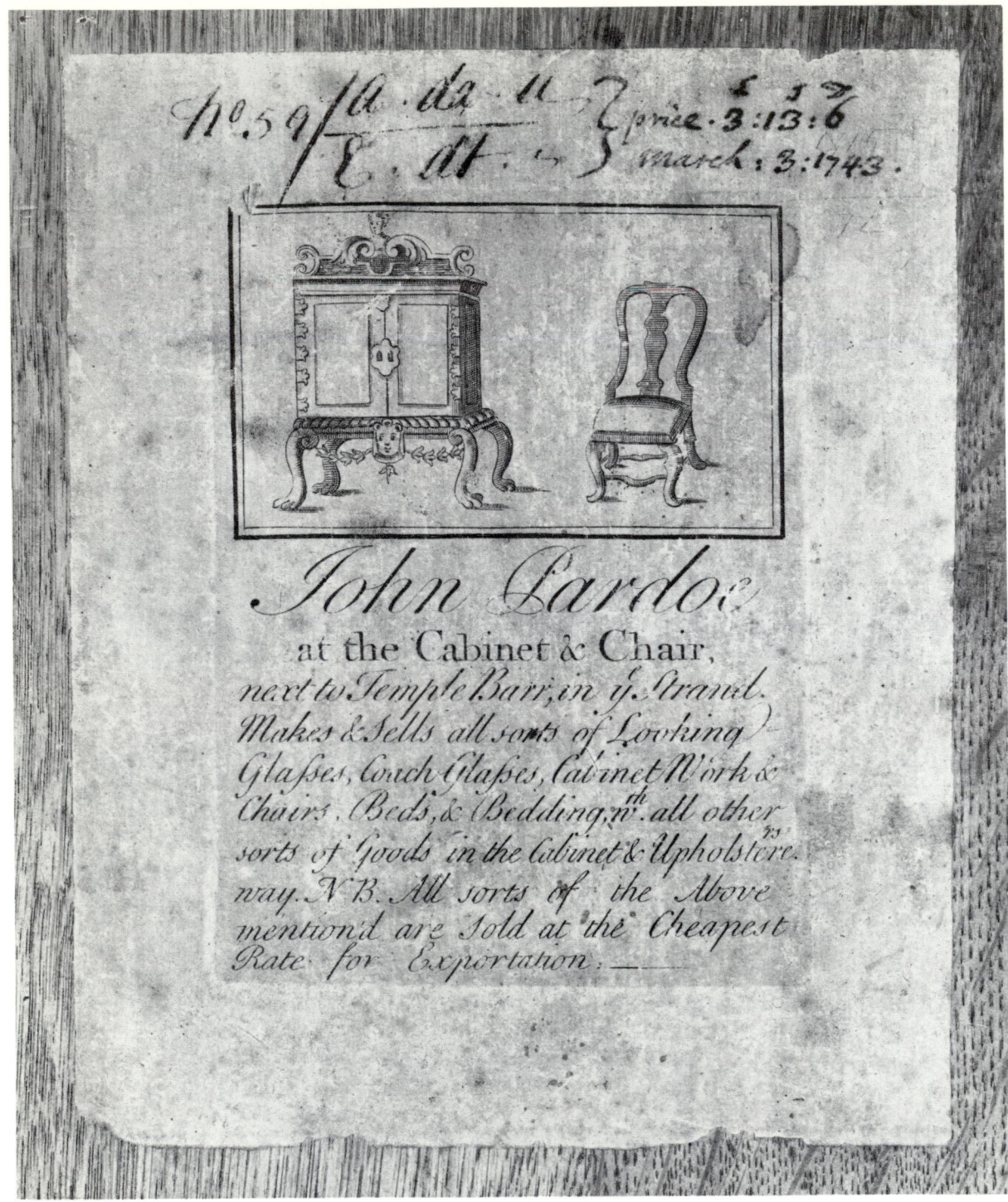

24. Label of John Pardoe on a mahogany bureau; the manuscript note, partly in code records the date and cost

Phillips of Hitchin, Ltd

JOHN BEST,

Cabinet-maker, Upholsterer, and Auctioneer,

St. COLUMB,

MAKES AND SELLS

THE FOLLOWING ARTICLES,

In the newest Taste, and on the most reasonable Terms:

(Viz)

MAHOGANY, wainscot, and other dining tables, either single or in sets, with octagon or circular ends

Ditto folding leaf, Pembroke, and card ditto

Ditto dressing, writing, and library ditto

Sideboards, with plain, serpentine, or circular fronts, with or without cellarets

Single and double chests of drawers

Wardrobes and bureaus

Secretories and book-cases

Square, circular, and enclosed wash-stands

Receptacles

Ladies' and Gentlemens' dressing stands

Mahogany framed and other chairs, with satin hair seats, loose seats, or brass nailed

A variety of painted and japan ditto

Dyed ditto with rush bottoms

Bed and easy ditto

Sofas and sociables

Conversation and dressing stools

Bedsteads with mahogany or stained pillars

Field, bureau, and press ditto

Plain and circular bed and window curtain cornices, to match the furniture

A variety of chintz, printed calicoes, and other bed furnitures

Bed lace, cotton line and tassels

Feather beds, mattresses, and London blankets

Quilts and counterpanes

Bed tick and sackings

Ovals, octagon, and round, mahogany tea trays and waiters

Ditto, ditto, japan ditto, with plain or gold borders

Tea urns and plate warmers

Bread baskets and bottle stands

Plain, inlaid, and varnished, tea caddees

Plated caddee shells

Oval and square swing looking-glasses

Ditto fixed on dressing boxes

Mahogany framed sconce glasses

Pier glasses in gilt frames, plain and ornamented

Mahogany or gilt frames put to old glasses

Mahogany portable desks

Black tambour top Spanish ditto

Black ebony ditto, with silver topped ink, sand, and wafer glasses

Gilt and black moulding for picture frames

A variety of fashionable paper hangings for rooms, both plain and glazed, with an elegant assortment of wide and narrow fancy borders

Blue paper for rooms

Brussels and Kidderminster carpets made to any size

Terry, Scotch, and Venetian stair and bed-side carpeting

Hearth rugs

Painted canvas for passages

Dutch matting

Rope and Venetian door mats, of different sizes

Register, Bath, Pantheon, and Rumfordized stoves

Sham ditto with black bars

Plain and urn head fire irons

Plain and hollow iron fenders

Bath, bow, and circular polished steel ditto

Green painted wire ditto, with plain or brass tops

Green canvas for window blinds

House bells and bell wire

Patent and plain bell cranks

Derbyshire spar and other bell pulls

Enamelled and brass cloak pins

A variety of curious brass locks for drawers, desks, and bureaus

Locks and hinges of all sorts

Brass handles and escutcheons for drawers

Oil and colours of all sorts, &c. &c.

Patterns of Paper Hangings, Carpets, Bed Furnitures, &c. sent to any Part of the County.

HOUSES FURNISHED ON SHORT NOTICE

Furniture appraised and sold on moderate Terms.

READY MONEY FOR FEATHERS.

25. Label of John Best, St Columb, Cornwall, placed under the lid of a simple mahogany lady's work table, *c.* 1805. The long list of stock is typical of a certain class of early nineteenth-century provincial trade label

Noël Riley

26. Robert Snowdon's printed bill head invoicing 'A Mahogany Moving Desk' supplied to Mr Hayes in September 1821 at a cost of £8 8s. This document is pasted under the lid of the davenport in illustration 28

27. Trade label in the well of the davenport in illustration 28

28. Davenport bearing Robert Snowdon's label and, exceptionally, the original bill dated 1821

Charles Lumb & Sons, Ltd

29. Scarlet japanned armchair from a very large set made by Giles Grendey for the Spanish export trade *c.* 1735–40

Temple Newsam, Leeds

30. Initials of a journeyman chairmaker struck on the pedestal at the base of the splat on the Grendey chair

31. Grendey's label under the seat rail; its intact state proves the caning is original

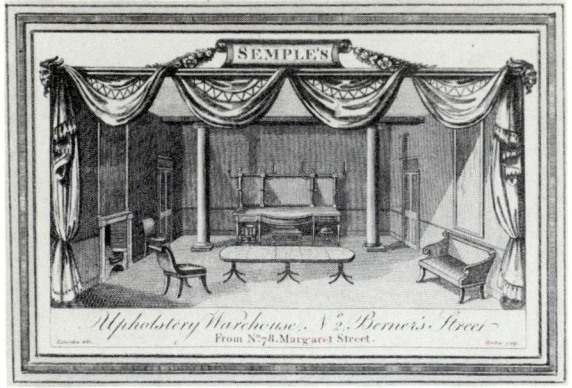

32. Trade card of J. & A. Semple, London, designed by Thomas Sheraton

London
Mr Wm Shadbolt To J & A Semple
1809
April 12 To a fine Kingwood
Sophatable with orangewood
borders 2 Drawers on solid turned
Standards & Rich Brass Lions Paws
Scroll Castors the whole superbly
ornamented with ormolu Moulding
Compleat — 22 0 0

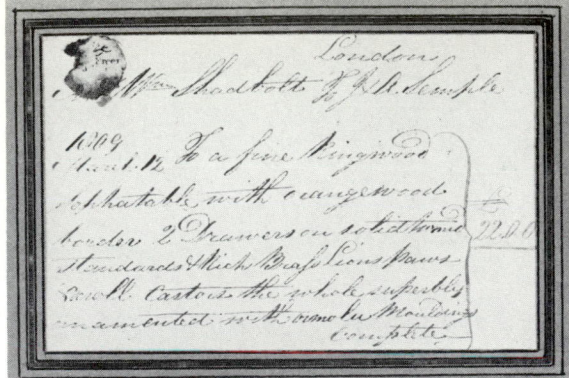

33. Bill on the back of Semple's trade card for 'a fine Kingwood Sophatable with orangewood borders' supplied to W. Shadbolt in 1809 at a cost of £22

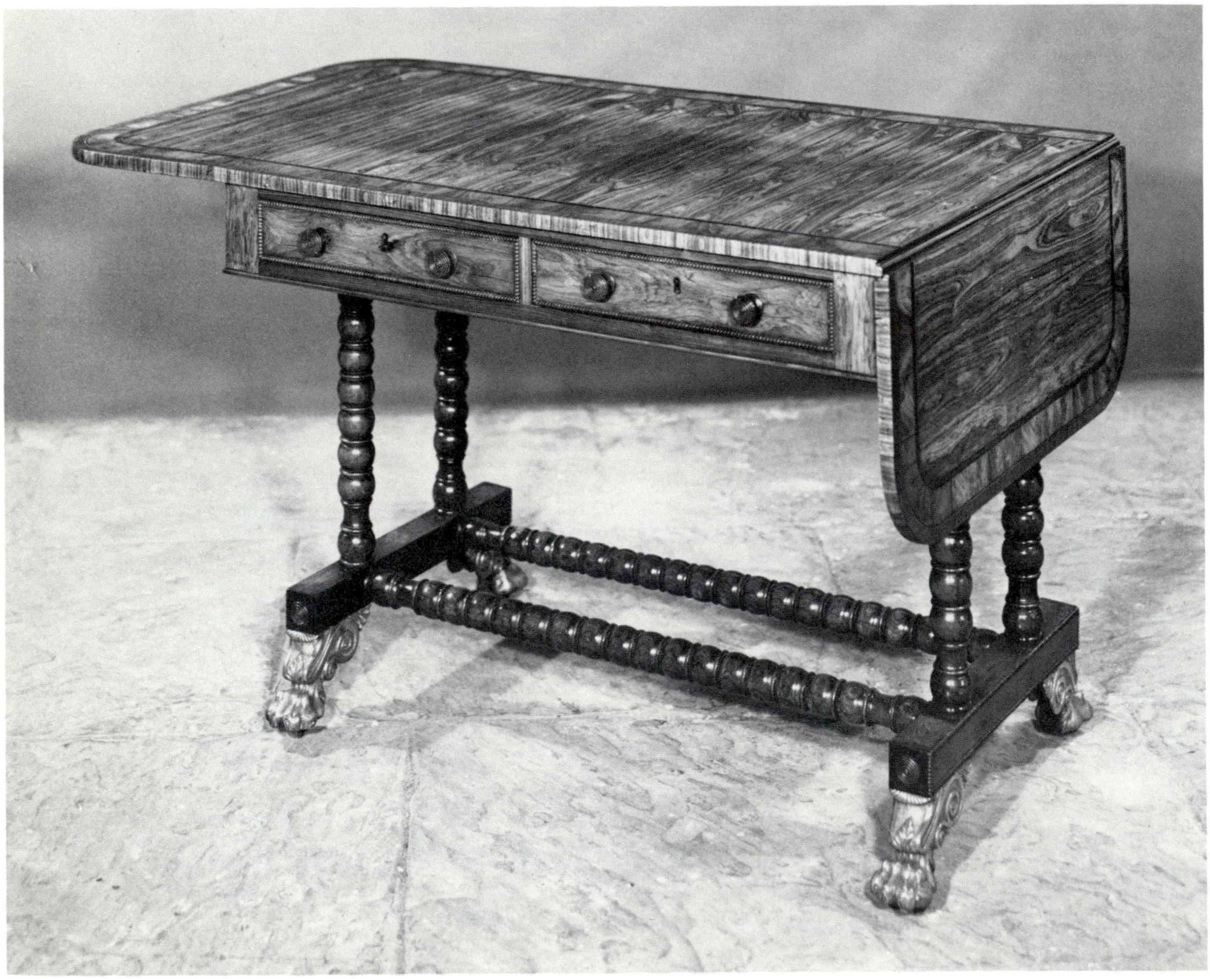

34. Sofa table made by J. & A. Semple in 1809. The original bill on tradesman's card, cheque paying it and receipt all survive

Temple Newsam, Leeds

35

36

37

38

35. Secretary and bookcase by George Speer, London, *c.* 1780
W. R. Harvey & Co. Ltd

36. Trade label discovered on the backboard of the desk drawer in the secretary and bookcase

37. One of twenty-eight documented dining chairs supplied by Elliott Smith of Cambridge to Trinity College in 1820 for £3 each
The Master and Fellows of Trinity College

38. Impressed mark found under the rear seat rail of eight of the chairs. The initials were almost certainly struck by Thomas Rayner, one of Elliott Smith's workmen

39

40

39. Trade card of Richard Wright and Edward Elwick, Wakefield

West Yorkshire Archives Service, Leeds

40. Detail of receipted account to a member of the Ingram family of Temple Newsam, Yorkshire on the back of Wright and Elwick's trade card

41. Documented green japanned clothes press supplied by Thomas Chippendale to Nostell Priory, Yorkshire in 1771

National Trust

42. Detail of the entry in Chippendale's bill under 8 April 1771 for the clothes press which cost £24

41

42

To A Cloaths press very neatly Japan'd green and Gold
with folding Doors and Drawers under, Sliding Shelves
lind with marble paper and bays Aprons, little Room,

43. Engraved brass tablet on a combined library steps and table made by John Meschain and Francis Hervé about 1785

Hotspur Ltd

A

Aaron, Randolph, Market Ct, Bow St, London, upholder (1706). [GL, Hand in Hand MS vol. 4, ref. 11781]

Abbey, Harry C., North St, York, joiner and cm (1787–1810). Died September 1810 aged 38; stock sold March 1811. [D; *York Courant*, 17 September 1810 and 18 March 1811]

Abbey, Jonathan, Queen St, Seven Dials, London, cm (1775). [GL, Sun MS vol. 242, p.551]

Abbey, Thomas, 11 Orange St and 15 Crooks Row, St Pancras, London, carver, gilder and joiner (1808–10). [GL, Sun MS vol. 443, ref. 825053]

Abbis, Thomas, Edmonton, London, upholder (1722–78). Son of Nicholas Abbis of Peckham, surgeon. App. to Wall Tidmarsh on 6 July 1715. Admitted freeman of the Upholders' Co. on 5 September 1722 by servitude. Took app. named Zachariah Clarke in 1728. [GL, Upholders' Co. records]

Abbot(t), David, Conduit St, Bedford, cm and u (1839). [D]

Abbot, Elizabeth, Park St, Leamington, Warks., cm (1830). [D]

Abbot, John, 4 Wilmot St, Russell Sq., London, cm and u (1829). [D]

Abbot, Joseph, Debenham, Suffolk, carpenter and cm (1824). [D]

Abbot, Mathew & Richard, Uppingham, Leics., chair turners (1790–98). [D]

Abbot, William, Preston, Lancs., u (1781–84). [D]

Abbot & Stidston, 137 Long Acre, London, u (1786–93). [D] See Philip Abbott & William Stidston.

Abbott, Andrin, Off Alley, Westminster, London, cm (1774). [Poll bk]

Abbott, Anthony, Liverpool, upholder (b. 1773/74–d. 1831). Recorded in 1796 at 14 Rainford's Gdn and subsequently at Davies St, Hackins Hey and Bolt St. In 1816 he had a warehouse at 3 Lower Spaling St. Advertised on 30 April 1813 that he had 'arrived from London with a selection of the newest patterns in upholstery & cabinet goods'. These included paper hangings, Brussels and Kidderminster carpets and 'Cabinet Goods in Rose, Zebra & other fancy woods'. Declared bankrupt in October 1819, and his stock was sold off by auction in the same month. Died in April 1831, aged 58. [D; *Liverpool Mercury*, 30 April 1813; 8 and 15 October 1819; 15 April 1831]

Abbot, Anthony & Sons, 32 Nelson St, Liverpool, u (1834–35). [D]

Abbott, Henry, 205 High St, Shoreditch, London, cm and u (1839). [D]

Abbot(t), James, Newgate St, Chester, cm (1778–97). Admitted freeman in 1778. Took apps named Edward Turner in 1778 and Thomas Walker in 1782. A cm of the same name is recorded at Watergate St, Chester in 1826. [D; Chester freemen rolls and app. reg.]

Abbott, John, London, carver and gilder (1765–68). Addresses in Dopping Alley, 1765, and Fleet Bridge, 1768. [GL, City Licence bks, vols 4 and 6]

Abbott, John, Cathedral Precincts, Canterbury, Kent, joiner and u (1782–86). Took out a Sun Insurance policy in 1782 for £300 on his utensils and stock. [GL, Sun MS vol. 299, p.2; vol. 304, p.585; Canterbury freemen rolls]

Abbott, John, Market Pl., Wellingborough, Northants., cm (1823–30). [D]

Abbott, John, 17 Judd St, Somerstown, London, cm and u (1839). [D]

Abbott, Nehemiah, 1 Spring Pl., Brownlow Lane, Chapel Hill, Liverpool, u (1834–37). [D]

Abbott, Philip, Coventry St (?), London, u (1777). See William Norton.

Abbot(t), Philip, St James, Westminster, London, upholder (1780). Declared bankrupt, *Gents Mag.*, November 1780.

Abbott, Philip & Charlton, John, 5 Princes St, Leicester Fields, London, upholders (1778–79). Took out a Sun Insurance policy in 1778 for £800 on his utensils and stock. [GL, Sun MS vol. 265, p.561; vol. 277, p.133]

Abbott, Philip & Stidston, William, 137 Long Acre, London, u and carpet warehousemen (1781). Took out a Sun Insurance policy in 1781 for £1,000 on their utensils and stock. [GL, Sun MS vol. 297, p.283] See Abbot & Stidston.

Abbott, Samuel, London, upholder (1712–c. 1754). Admitted freeman of the Upholders' Co. in October 1712. Took apps named John Underwood in 1714 and Richard Loveland in 1717. His son, William, admitted freeman of the Upholders' Co. on 4 July 1754 by patrimony. [GL, Upholders' Co. records]

Abbott, Samuel, Liverpool, u etc. (1834–39). Recorded at Birkett St in 1834 and at 34 Nelson St, St James's Sq. thereafter. [D]

Abbott, Stephen, Ramsgate, Kent, cm (1743). Took app. named Hooper in 1743. [S of G, app. index]

Abbott, Stephen, 3 King Ct, Lombard St, London, cm (1759–61). [D; GL, City Licence bks, vol. 2; Heal]

Abbott, Susanna, 61 Brill Row, Somerstown London, cm and u (1827–28). [D] See William Abbott.

Abbott, Thomas, Liverpool, u (1811–16). Trading at Thompson Ct, Back Bridport St in 1811, and at 28 Duncan St East in 1813. [D]

Abbott, Thomas, 118 Temple St, Bristol, sign and furniture painter (1828–33). [D]

Abbott, W., High St, Kensington, London, u and appraiser (1820). [D]

Abbott, William, 16 Bedford St, Covent Gdn, London, u (1791). [D] See Ann Ravald.

Abbott, William, Stamford, Lincs., chairmaker, cm and turner (1819–26). Trading at St Peter's Hill, 1819–22, and Beastmarket in 1826. [D]

Abbott, William, 60 and 61 Brill Row, Somerstown, London, cm and u (1832–37). [D] See Susanna Abbott.

Abbott, William, High St, Royston, Herts., cm and u (1824–39). His printed bill head decorated with miniature items of furniture states that he traded as 'Cabinet Maker, Upholsterer, paper hanger & manufacturer of Window Blinds' and stocked fire grates. [D]

Abbott, William, High St, Kensington, London, u (1826). [D]

Abbott, William, High St, Wem, Salop, joiner and cm (1840). [D]

Abbott & Siddons, 175 Long Acre, London, upholders (1784). [D]

Abegg, John Henry, parish of St Ann, Westminster, London, upholder (1757). Declared bankrupt, *Gents Mag.*, May 1757.

Abel, Anthony, 5 Upper Westwick St, Norwich, cm (1801). [D]

Abel, John, London, upholder (d. by 1748). Daughter Sarah admitted freeman of the Upholders' Co. by patrimony on 4 March 1748. [GL, Upholders' Co. records]

Abel, Samuel, Church Gate, Loughborough, Leics., cm, joiner, appraiser and auctioneer (1775–95). Took up auctioneering in 1786. Advertised for journeymen cm and chairmakers in 1775, 1789, 1791. [D; *Leicester Journal*, April 1775; 16 September 1786; 19 June 1789; 25 March 1791]

Abel, William, Bristol, cm (1818). [Evesham poll bk]

Abel, William, Pitt St, Norwich, cm (1839). [D]

Abell, W. C., 25 Sidmouth St, Gray's Inn Rd, London, u (1835). [D]

Abell, William, London, u and bed and mattress maker (1826–39). Trading at 22 Gt Eastcheap, 1826–35, and at 43 Fish St Hill in 1839. [D]

Abery, Christopher, Reading, Berks., upholder (1768). [Poll bk]

Abgood, William & Stevens, Edward, Gt Portland St, London, carvers (1783). Declared bankrupt, *Leicester Journal*, January 1783.

Abington, Leonard, 12 Plumtree St, Bloomsbury, London, carver and gilder (1819–25). [D]

Abraham, Abraham, London, cm (1829–39). Addresses at 142 St John's St in 1829, and at 57 St John's Sq. in 1837. In the latter year his trade is listed as fancy cm. [D]

Abraham, David, Searrett's Lane, Newport, Isle of Wight, Hants., chairmaker (1823–30). [D]

Abraham, Edm., West St, Fareham, Hants., cm, u and appraiser (1830). [D]

Abraham, Edward, High St, Gosport, Hants., appraiser and u (1839). [D]

Abraham, John, Long Acre, London, frame carver and gilder (1709). [Heal]

Abraham, Richard, 8 Bruton St, Bond St, London, carver, gilder and looking-glass frame maker (1835–39). [D]

Abrahams, J., 33 Red Cross St, Bow, London, u (1826). [D]

Abrahams, Nathaniel, Guildford St, Chertsey, Surrey, u (1839). [D]

Abrahams & Davis, 55 St John's Sq., Clerkenwell, London, cm (1837). [D]

Abram, John, 'The Sun', Long Acre, London, gilder (1714). [GL, Sun MS vol. 3, p.94]

Abram, William snr, High Wycombe, Bucks., chairmaker (1815–40).[PR]

Abram, William jnr, High Wycombe, Bucks., chairmaker (b.1816–41). [PR; 1841 Census]

Abrams, John & Robert, Oldham St, Manchester, with manufactories in Garden St and Major St, cm and u (1828–40). Recorded at 9 Oldham St in 1836 and 1840; nos 5 and 9, also with premises at Major St in 1838. [D]

Abram(s), William & John, Manchester, cm and u (1825–40). Addresses at 54 Back Piccadilly in 1825; Oldham St until 1840, no. 9 in 1829 and nos 5, 6 and 7 in 1832–33. [D]

Abrey, Henry, High St, Chelmsford, Essex, cm and u (1823–40). In November 1834 suffered a fire at his cabinet warehouse in New St, Chelmsford. [D; *Times*, 25 November 1834; Oxford RO, Misc. LR 1/9; Essex RO, Q/RJ/2/1]

Absell, James, 1 Cambridge Pl., Hackney Rd, London, chair stuffer (1835–39). [D]

Ackerley, John, Standishgate, Wigan, Lancs., cm (1834). [D]

Ackerman & Co., London, carvers, gilders and general repository of the arts (1796–1840). Trading at 101 Strand in 1796 and at 96 Strand from 1827. [D]

Ackers, James, 157 Dale St, Liverpool, cm and victualler (1780–81). [D; Liverpool RO, 352 CLE/REG 1/1]

Ackery, J., Bristol, cm and chair manufacturer (1834–40). Addresses at West St in 1834 and at 2 Jacob St from 1839. [D]

Ackroyd, Jane & Sons, 44 William St, Brighton, Sussex, French polishers and japanners (1829–39). [D; PR]

Ackworth, William, 86 High Street, Chatham, Kent, u and cm (1802–11). Took out a Sun Insurance policy in January 1802 for £3,200 of which stock and utensils accounted for £1,350. Trade label recorded on several respectable pieces of cabinet furniture including a Pembroke table, a secretaire and a bow-fronted chest of drawers sold at Bonham's on 18 October 1979, lot 55. His pictorial label states that he was able to supply 'Gentlemen of the Army and Navy' with 'Beds, Mattresses & Bedding'. Also traded as chairmaker, undertaker, appraiser and auctioneer. [D; poll bk; *C. Life*, 28 July 1977 (illus.); GL, Sun MS, vol. 43, ref. 728207]

Acres, Edward, 30 Gt Russell St, London, carver and gilder (1806–25). [D; GL, Sun MS vol. 493, ref. 991713]

Acret, John, 44 Wardour St, London, carver, gilder and picture frame maker (1778–93). [D; poll bk; GL, Sun MS vol. 264, p.519]

Acton, John, Salisbury, Wilts., cm (1759). App. to James Begbie, cm, on 1 June 1759. [*Wilts. Apps and their Masters*]

Acut, Charles Joseph, 16 Bath St, City Rd, London, cm and u (1839). [D]

Adair, John, London, carver and gilder (1749–69). Recorded at St Ann's Ct, Covent Gdn in 1749 but by 1763 was established at Wardour St, Soho. Worked at Shardeloes, Bucks., Croome Ct and the Church of St Mary Magdelene, Croome D'Abitot, Worcs. and Syon House, Brentford. [D; poll bk; *Conn.*, June 1981, p.145] Worked at Audley End, Essex, from September 1767 to February 1768 for Sir John Griffin Griffin, providing picture and mirror frames, mirror plates and gilt architraves, etc. The account of 1767 amounts to £25 18s. [Essex RO, D/DBy/A27/6] The accounts for work done at Shugborough, Staffs., submitted in 1763, amount to £65 16s 6d, and list carving capitals and making and regilding frames. Work under James Stuart's supervision continued until 1769. [Staffs. RO, Anson papers, D615E (H) 1/1; *C. Life*, 4 March 1954; *C. Life Annual*, 1965, p.54] Regarding work at Syon House, Brentford, a letter from the Duke of Northumberland, dated 4 November 1764, complained about 'those Carved Mouldings which have been so ill executed by Mr. Adair'. [*C. Life Annual*, 1965, p.54]

Adair, John & William, Wardour St, Soho, London, carvers and gilders (1769–77). The use of the same address and a reference to Adair & Co. show an association between John and William Adair in this period. In 1773 William Adair was described as joiner to HM's Privy Chamber, and Supplied 'two rich carved and gilded frames for Their Majesty's Pictures in whole Lengths'. [*DEF*] 'Adair Carver' worked at Hartwell House, Aylesbury, Bucks. in 1766 and 1778 supplying the frames for three tables in the drawing room, two mirrors 'and other ornaments in the room'. Recorded in Sir William Lee's account books. [Hartwell House Lib.; GCM] John Adair carried out carving work at Sir John Griffin Griffin's London house in New Burlington St for which he charged £41 in 1778. [Essex RO, D/DBy/A37/4] For Shelburne House, London, or Bowood, Wilts. Adair & Co. supplied goods and carried out work 'by order of Mr. Stuart', being paid between February and July 1775. [Bowood MS accounts bk] B.A.

Adair, William Robert, London, carver and gilder (1777–85). Initially carried on his business from 26 Wardour St, Soho, which had been earlier used by John Adair. In 1799 he was trading from 55 King St, Golden Sq., but by 1802 the business had transferred to 47 Brewer St, opposite Gt Pulteney St. A trade label with this address is attached to the back of a portrait of Ayscough Boucherett by Sir Thomas Lawrence (private coll.). On this label Adair describes himself as 'CARVER and GILDER to Their MAJESTIES'. In 1777 a policy was taken out with the Sun Insurance Office by Mary Adair of 'The Golden Head', Wardour St for £1,000 of which £330 was for 'utensils and stock in timbershop'. [D; GCM; DEF; GL, Sun MS vol. 256, p.205; V&A archives] Supplied picture frames and glass for Sir John Griffin Griffin for Audley End, Essex, amounting to £1 0s 3d in 1777 and was paid the following year. In 1788 an account for Lord Howard amounting to £5 14s 2d was issued in respect of picture and mirror frames, and a further account for 6s exists for 1791.

[Essex RO, D/DBy/A36/2, A46/7, A49/4] Adair also supplied items for Sir John Griffin Griffin's London home in New Burlington St. Accounts dated 1779 list picture and mirror frames, glazing, carving and gilding, amounting to £23 19s 9d. In 1789 a further amount of 13s was charged for similar work. [Essex RO, D/DBy/A37/3, A47/3] The Lord Chamberlain's accounts, 1799–1801 and 1805, list payments amounting to £268 for work done at St James's Palace, including repairs, regilding the state chair and two stools and regilding the railing round the throne. [PRO, LC11/7–9] In 1799 he supplied for the Queen's House, Buckingham Palace three large and '3 small sofas to go between the windows of the Great Saloon'. [H. Clifford Smith, *Buckingham Palace*, p. 92] His name appears in the Royal Household accounts in 1799, 1801 and 1805 for working at Windsor Castle, carving flowers on a pair of sofas and gilding them, making a large pier glass and repairing carving on a state chair. Plate glasses and chimney frames were supplied for the Duke of Cambridge's apartments. The total charge was £286 6s 6d. [PRO, LC11/7–9]

Adam, James, 16 Brownlow St, Soho, London, cm and plate case maker (1835–39). [D]

Adams, Benjamin, London, upholsterer (1710–18). App. to Thomas Rogers on 7 February 1710/11 and admitted freeman on 5 March 1717/18. [GL, MS 7142/1]

Adams, Charles, School Lane, Shrewsbury, Salop, cm (1825). Son of James Evan Adams and brother of Henry Adams. [Shrewsbury burgess roll]

Adams, Charles James, High St, Oxford, cm and u (1823–30). [D]

Adams, Daniel, Bury St, Stowmarket, Suffolk, cm, turner and chairmaker (1824–30). [D]

Adams, David, Liverpool, upholsterer's joiner (1724). In 1724 took app. named Wilcocks. [S of G, app. index]

Adams, Francis, Low Park St, Sheffield, Yorks., chairmaker and beer house owner (1837). [D]

Adams, George snr, cm (d. 1773). Small inlaid mahogany cabinet of *c.* 1750 by this maker belongs to University College, Oxford (on loan to the Museum of the History of Science).

Adams, George, London, u, cm, auctioneer and undertaker (1777–1828). Initially at 42 Haydon Sq., Minories, but from 1788 address changed to 122 Minories. Son of George Adams of Canterbury, innholder. App. to Joseph Merryman on 7 June 1769 and admitted freeman of the Upholders' Co. on 6 August 1777 by servitude. In that year he took out insurance with the Sun Office for £900 of which £520 accounted for utensils and stock. On 6 May 1801 his son Thomas was admitted freeman of the Upholders' Co. by patrimony. In 1802 the business is listed as George Adam & Son. Subscriber to Sheraton's *Cabinet Dictionary*, 1803. Several chairs, mostly in sets but including a single Windsor are known stamped 'ADAMS 122 MINORIES LONDON', or variants of wording. [D; GL, Upholders' Co. records; GL, Sun MS vol. 258, p. 28; Sotheby's, 16 April 1971, lot 177; Christie's, 8 May 1980, lot 24; *C. Life*, 3 December 1981, p. 54] Supplied several pieces of furniture to Uniacke House, Hants. Co., Canada, including a set of 12 mahogany hall chairs bearing George Adams's printed paper trade label inscribed 'George Adams, Upholder, Cabinet Maker, UNDERTAKER, Sworn Broker & Auctioneer, Corner of John Street MINORIES'. These items were supplied for the house which was built from 1813–15 for the Hon. Richard Uniacke who at the time was Attorney General for Nova Scotia. [*Material History Bulletin*, 1980, pp. 57–61]

Adams, George, London, cm (1817–32). Trading at 37 Long Alley, Moorfields in 1817. By 1832 the address had changed to 101 Long Alley. [D]

Adams, Henry, Castle Gates, Shrewsbury, Salop, cm (1830). Son of James Evan Adams and brother of Charles Adams. [Shrewsbury burgess roll]

Adams, J., London, cm (1824). Declared bankrupt on 27 November 1824. [*London Gazette*]

Adams, James, High St, Oxford, upholder (1782–1808). Took out a Sun Insurance policy in 1782 for £500 on his house. Trading as u and cm in 1808. [D; GL, Sun MS vol. 304, p. 27]

Adams, James Evan, Fish St, Shrewsbury, Salop, cm (1806). [Shrewsbury burgess roll]

Adams, James, London, cm, u and appraiser (1817–28). Trading at 49 and 67 Fore St, Cripplegate until 1822 when the address changed to 9 Pulteney St, Golden Sq. Between 1817 and 1823 traded as J. & G. Adams. [D]

Adams, James, Pavement, Moorfields, London, cm and u (1823–28). Declared bankrupt in November 1824. [D; *Brighton Gazette*, 2 December 1824]

Adams, James, High St, Staines, Middlx, cm (1823–32). Trading also as house agent in 1823 and furniture broker in 1832. [D]

Adam, James, 16 Brownlow St, Long Acre, London, cm (1837). [D]

Adams, James, Clarence St, Staines, Middlx, cm and u (1839). [D]

Adams, Job, London, u (1729). Son of Job Adams of Aldersgate, cooper. App. to William Cowthorpe on 4 August 1721. Admitted freeman of the Upholders' Co. on 5 March 1729. By 1732 in the United States. [GL, Upholders' Co. records]

Adams, John, Needham Mkt, Suffolk, chairmaker (1773). [Suffolk RO, FAA: 50/2/94–104]

Adams, John, Daventry, Northants., cm, shopkeeper and carver (1778–80). In 1778 took out a policy with the Sun Fire Office for £100 of which utensils and stock amounted to £20. By 1780 the cover had risen dramatically to £4,300 and £1,610 respectively. [GL, Sun MS vol. 289, p. 20]

Adams, John, Liverpool, cm (1810–23). Originally at 20–22 Tempest Hey but by 1816 had changed his address to 18 Standwick St. [D]

Adams, John, Cambridge, cm and u (1825–40). App. to Joseph Wentworth on 13 April 1825 and admitted freeman on 16 August 1833. Trading in Fair St in 1835, but at Rhadegond Building, Jesus Lane by 1837. Continued to trade from this address until 1850. [D; Cambs. RO, Corp. records]

Adams, John, Tipton, Dudley, Staffs., cm and u (1838–39). [D]

Adams, John, 48 Skinner St, London, cm and u (1839). [D]

Adams, John Atlie, Hog Lane, Woolwich, London, cm (1775–76). Took out insurance with the Sun Fire Office in 1775 for £500 of which utensils, stock and goods accounted for £90. In 1776 these figures were raised to £500 and £150. [GL, Sun MS vol. 242, p. 518; vol. 245, p. 421]

Adams, John & Robert, 5 and 9 Oldham St, Manchester, cm and u (1839). [D]

Adams, John & Son, 197 High St and 14 Market St, Lewes, Sussex, cm and u (1798–1839). In June 1838 the public were invited to 'inspect their newly erected and extensive showrooms . . . The Broking Department will be conducted in Market Street, communicating internally with the Premises in High Street'. The business may have continued in some form after 1839 as a Sarah Adams is shown in 1845 trading from School Hill, Lewes. [D; *Sussex Agricultural Express*, 2 June 1838]

Adams, Nathaniel, 1 Nassau St, London, u (1839). [D]

Adams, R., 169 Tottenham Ct Rd, London, upholder (1812). [D]

Adams, Richard A., 126 Thomas St, Bristol, cm and furniture warehouse owner (1838–40). Late J. & E. Knight. [D]

Adams, Richard James, High St, Chelmsford, Essex, u (1838). [Essex RO, Q/RJ/2/1]

Adams, Robert, Foregate St, Chester, cm and broker (1773–89). App. to Philip Presbury, cm, 29 May 1773 by his widowed mother Martha Adams. Sworn freeman on 3 October 1782. Took apps named John Nailor in 1782, John Henshaw in 1789 and Thomas Davenport. The latter absconded and was advertised for in August 1784. [D; Chester app. reg.; *Chester Chronicle*, 27 August 1784]

Adams, Robert & Co., 403 Oxford St and 2 Dean St, Soho, London, chair and sofa manufacturers, japanners and gilders (1801–16). Also traded under the style of Adams & Gray from 1801–04, and Adams, Graves & Co. from 1807–08. Had additional premises in Tottenham Ct Rd in 1808. Their trade card [BM] states that 'every article in the above Branches are Manufactured on the Premises under the immediate inspection of A. G. & Co.' and that 'an elegant assortment of the newest Patterns will be constantly kept in their Warerooms from Superb Drawing room & Parlour to the Common Bedroom Chair'. [D]

Adams, Thomas Price, 122 Minories, London, upholder (1801–07). Son of George Adams. Admitted freeman of the Upholders' Co. by patrimony on 6 May 1801. [GL, Upholders' Co. records]

Adams, Thomas, 8 and 9 Gt Pulteney St, Golden Sq., London, cm and u (1829–39). [D]

Adams, W., High St, Croydon, Surrey, carver and gilder (1822). [D]

Adams, W., 15 North Audley St, London u (1826). [D]

Adams, W., 11 Windmill St, Tottenham Ct Rd, London, u, cm and undertaker (1826–27). [D]

Adams, William, Prince's St, Westminster, London, upholder (1732). Declared bankrupt, *Gents Mag.*, July 1732.

Adams, William, Bridgnorth, Salop, cm (1741). Took app. named Taylor in 1741. [S of G, app. index]

Adams, William, Hampstead, London, upholder (1755–66). Son of William Adams of Welton, Northants. App. to William Parsons, merchant tailor, on 2 March 1742. Admitted freeman of the Upholders' Co. on 13 June 1755 by redemption. Took apps named Richard Godfree in 1755 and Josiah Turner in 1758. [GL, Upholders' Co. records]

Adams, William, St Paul's Churchyard, London, upholder (1764). [Essex RO, D/DQ 61/37]

Adams, William, 8 Cumberland St, Goodge St, London, chairmaker, cm and u (1809–39). [D]

Adams, William, 50 and 67 Fore St, Cripplegate, London, u (d. 1811). Death reported on 11 June 1811. [D; *Gents Mag.*]

Adams, William, 29 (from 1821, 17) New Surrey St, Blackfriars Rd, London, carver and gilder (1809–23). [D]

Adams, William, 34 Windmill St, Tottenham Ct Rd, London, u, cm and undertaker (1816–28). [D]

Adams, William, 9 Trippet Lane, Sheffield, Yorks., cabinet and portable desk manufacturer (1822). [D]

Adams, William, 28 Gt Pulteney St, Golden Sq., London, u and cm (1823–26). [D]

Adams, William, 2 Somerset Pl., Kennington, London, carver and gilder (1829). [D]

Adams, William, 25 Curtain Rd, London, cm (1832). [Shoreditch Ref. Lib., MS M3545, p. 41]

Adams, William L., 12 St James's Buildings, Clerkenwell, London, cm (1832). [D]

Adamson, H., 38 North Row, Grosvenor Sq., London, cm (1835). [D]

Adamson, John, 63 Fenchurch St, London, u (1803). Son of John Adamson of East Barnet, Herts. App. to Samuel Burton on 1 May 1793, and admitted freeman of the Upholders' Co. on 12 April 1803. [GL, Upholders' Co. records]

Adamson, Robert, Fenchurch St, London, cm, joiner and mahogany turner (1751–66). His trade card [Heal; MMA; NY] states that he 'Makes all sorts of Cabinet Looking Glasses and Mahogany Goods at the lowest Prices. NB. Funerals perform'd & Goods Appraised'. On 11 April 1766 supplied to Sir William Robinson of Newby Hall 'Blinds for windows . . . curiously painted on canvas, silk or wire'. [Temple Newsam Exhib., 1976, 21; GL, City Licence bks, vols 1 and 2]

Adamson, William, St Sepulchre Gate, Doncaster, Yorks., carver and gilder (1818). [D]

Adamson, William, 2 Upper Dorset Pl., Clapham, London, u and furniture dealer (1822–35). Recorded as cm and u in 1823. [D; GL, Sun MS vol. 493, ref. 997354]

Adanall, James, 41 Charing Cross, London, u (1784). [D]

Adcock, William, Catherine St, Birmingham, cm and timber dealer (1767). [D]

Adderley, Samuel, 2 Court, Branstone St, Birmingham, fancy box, case and caddy maker (1835). [D]

Adderton, John, 24 Greyhound Yd, Nottingham, chairmaker (1832–40). Recorded also at Chesterfield St and Derby Rd in 1840. [D]

Addey, William, Hull, Yorks., cm, undertaker and broker (1826–40). In 1826 listed at Valentine's Ct, Robinson Row, but by 1831 was at 13 Blackfriargate. He remained in this street being noted at 28 (1834), 30, and also 29 Queen St (1837) and 17 (1840). [D]

Addicot, Edward, Nottingham, u (1812–20). Trading at New St from 1812–14, but by 1820 had moved to New Yd, Paul St. [D; poll bk]

Addicot, John, Nottingham, cm and joiner (1823–30). App. in 1823 and admitted freeman in 1830. [Notts. RO, indices of apps and burgesses]

Addinall, James, 41 Charing Cross, London, u (1777–99). In 1777 took app. named Edward Cagill. Took out a Sun Insurance policy in 1781 for £500 on his house. [D; Westminster Ref. Lib., MS FH 309, p. 25; GL, Sun MS vol. 293, p. 439]

Addinet, —, London (?), upholder (1779–98). Recorded in the Longford Castle accounts are payments of £87 in 1779, and £20 14s in 1798. [V&A archives]

Addington, John, Stamford, Lincs., chairmaker (1840). [D]

Addison, John, Lancaster, cm (1784–1806). Admitted freeman in 1784. Married Mrs Redmayne, widow of Capt. Redmayne, on 25 January 1794. Took three apps between December 1790 and October 1806. [Lancaster app. reg. and freemen rolls; *Williamson's Liverpool Advertiser*, 27 January 1794]

Addison, John, Lancaster, chairmaker (1800–06). App. to Isaac Boulton in 1800. Admitted freeman in 1806, when stated 'of Skipton'. [Lancaster app. reg. and freemen rolls]

Addison, John, Clayton St, Colne, Lancs., chairmaker and turner (1816). [D]

Addison, John, Borwick, Lancs., cm ;1820). On 2 December 1820, at the age of 65, married Margaret Thompson, aged 25, at Warton. [*Liverpool Mercury*, 22 December 1820]

Addison, John, address unrecorded. Supplied a pair of 36 in. globes 'elegantly mounted in richly carved mahogany frames and the metallic parts made of mosaic gold' to George IV in November 1829 at a cost of £157 16s. [Windsor RA, 25447]

Addison, John, Richmond, Yorks., cm (1832). [PR (bapt.) 30 March 1832]

Addison, Richard, Preston, Lancs., u and auctioneer (1754–84). Took apps named Loxam in 1754, Foyle in 1756 and Edmondson in 1763. [D; S of G, apps index; *Manchester Mercury*, 15 April 1766]

Addison, Robert, London, cm (1774–76). Addresses given at Hanover St in 1774, and North Duke St, Grosvenor Sq.,

1775–76. Insured with the Sun Fire Office in 1775 for £800 of which £450 was for utensils and stock. Declared bankrupt, *Gents Mag.*, September 1776. [GL, Sun MS vol. 244, p. 62; poll bk]

Addison, Robert, 21 Fleet Mkt, London, upholder (1780). Admitted freeman of the Upholders' Co. by redemption on 6 December 1780. [GL, Upholders' Co. records]

Addison, Thomas, Lancster, cm (1753–84). Admitted freeman of Lancaster in 1753, when stated 'of London'. [Poll bk; Lancaster freemen rolls]

Addison & Davidson, address unrecorded (1772). Received 6s on 31 December 1772 for a looking-glass for Gibside, Co. Durham. [Durham RO, Strathmore MS D/St/V.995]

Aderne, Ralph Henry, High St, Southwark, London, cm (1830). Declared bankrupt on 30 November 1830. [*Chester Courant*]

Aderson, Thomas, Erick St, Newcastle, u (1838). [D]

Adey, Walter, Wednesfield, Staffs., cm (1839). [D]

Adin, John, Friar Gate, Derby, cm (1818–23). Trading at Willow Row, 1818–22, and also as a joiner at Friar Gate in 1823. [D]

Adler, George, St Bartholomew St, Newbury, Berks., cm and u (1840). [D]

Adlington, Thomas, Lancaster, joiner, house carpenter and cm (1787–94). Between 11 July 1787 and 26 March 1794 took six apps of whom two, Frederick Byam (18 November 1791) and Jonathan Hall (2 July 1792) were app. cm. [Lancaster app. reg.]

Adnum, John, 13 Dorrington St, Coldbath Fields, London, cm and u (1839). [D]

Adron, W. & C., New Rd, Fitzroy Sq., London, marble masons and scagliola workmen (1835). Repaired and polished scagliola and marble table tops and pedestals at Windsor. [RA, Lord Chamberlain's accounts, L56/12/3, 30 September 1835]

Adye, Thomas, London, carver and sculptor (1730–53). Responsible for the carved mahogany ballot box supplied in 1738 to the Society of Dilettanti for whom he had been appointed sculptor. In 1752 when the Mansion House was being furnished he submitted estimates for lamp stands, looking-glasses and carved brackets. [Gunnis; *DEF*]

Affiter, Thomas, Rochester, Kent, cm (1780). [Poll bk]

Affleck, James, Parliament St, Westminster, London, cm and corn chandler (1744–78). Subscriber to Chippendale's *Director*, 1754. In 1774 insured his stock in the yard in Derby Ct near his dwelling house for £100, and his house and contents for £600. [Poll bk; *London General Advertiser*, 15 January 1752; GL, Sun MS vol. 107, ref. 141999; vol. 262, p. 283]

Affleck, John, Darby Ct, London, upholder (1774). [Poll bk]

Affleck, Thomas, London, cm (1763–79). Later traded in Philadelphia, USA. [*Conn.*, March 1968, pp. 187–91]

Afflecks, —, Poult St, Westminster, London, cm and auctioneer (1751). [*London Advertiser*, 3 December 1751]

Agar, Edward, York, cm (1818). Son of Adam Agar, tailor, app. to John Middleton, cm, on 8 December 1807. Admitted freeman of York as a cm by order in 1818. [York freemen rolls]

Agar, P., 11 Old Round Ct, Strand, London, cm (1808). [D]

Agar, Robert, Whitby, Yorks., cm (1834). [D]

Agar, Samuel, London, carver (1747–63). A payment of £11 to a 'Mr. Agar' entered in John Cobb's bank account at Drummonds on 1 January 1760 may relate to Samuel Agar. Subscribed to Chippendale's *Director*, 1754. [Poll bk; GL, Sun MS vol. 110, ref. 145583]

Agar, Thomas, London, carver (1685–87). Surveyor General of Woods to Charles II and James II and carver in ordinary to Queen Catherine, 1685–87. [*Survey of London*, vol. 24, p. 385]

Agate, Peter, 3 Jewry St, Aldgate, London, cm (1832). [D]

Ager, Josiah, St Mary's St, Northampton, cm (1830). [Poll bk]

Agg, George, Bridge St, Evesham, Worcs., cm and u (1820). [D]

Aggio, Paul, Colchester, Essex, carver and gilder (1823–39). Trading at 12 Head St in the 1820s; at High St, also as a picture dealer, in 1832; and by 1839 at 37 High St. [D]

Agland, William, 4 Brydges Pl., Shoreditch, London, chairmaker (1823). Stock, utensils, goods in trust and dwelling house insured with the Sun Fire Office for £100. [GL, Sun MS vol. 494, ref. 1010925]

Agland, William, 49 Old St Rd, London, cm and u (1839). [D]

Aglen, George, 410 High St, Cheltenham, Glos., carver and gilder (1830). [D]

Aglen, George William, 26 Hustlegate, Bradford, Yorks., carver and gilder (1834–37). [D]

Aglen, J., 10 Providence Row, Finsbury Sq., London, carver and gilder (1804–08). [D]

Aglen, John jnr, Cheltenham, Glos., carver and gilder (1820–22). Trading at 19 High St and Crescent Pl. in 1820, and 2 Gyde's Terr. in 1822. [D]

Aglen, Thomas, 73 Paul St, Finsbury Sq., London, looking-glass manufacturer and picture frame maker (1817–35). [D]

Aglen & Co., 25 Little Britain, London, carvers, gilders and looking-glass manufacturers (1809). [D]

Agnew, Thomas & Zanetti, Vittore, Manchester, carvers and gilders (1810–40). Thomas Agnew (b.1794–d.1871), founder of the present firm of Bond St, London, fine art dealers, was app. to Zanetti in 1810 and made a partner in 1817. In partnership with Zanetti's son from 1825–34. The Dunham Massey papers record a payment on 10 January 1824 to 'Mr. Agnew carver & gilder £219'. The firm also supplied artists' materials, pictures, mirrors and barometers. They traded from 94 Market St in 1810, but in 1825 were listed at 25 Gartside St. By the next year the business was in Exchange St where they traded from number 10 and later from 18 (1832–33) and 14 (1836–40). [D; Goodison, *Barometers*] See Zan(n)etti & Agnew.

Ahrens, John, 37 Throgmorton St, London, dining room furnisher (1835). [D]

Aide, Robert, address unrecorded, chair frame maker (1722–36). Various payments occur in the accounts of the Duke of Northumberland. [V&A archives]

Aigby, Samuel, Liverpool, cm (1722). Took app. named Abbott in 1722. [S of G, app. index]

Aiken, James, 18 King St, Soho, London, carver and gilder (1790–93). [D]

Aikenhead, John, 2 Union Buildings, Leather Lane, London, carver and gilder (1829). [D]

Ainge, William, 5 Berkeley St, Lambeth, London, cm and undertaker (1832). [D]

Ainsley, John, Charlotte St, North Shields, Northumb., cm and joiner (1827). [D]

Ainsley, William, Northgate, Darlington, Co. Durham, joiner and cm (1827). [D]

Ainsworth, George, Preston, Lancs., cm (1758). Took app. named Edmondson in 1758. [S of G, app. index]

Ainsworth, John, High St, Stone, Staffs. chairmaker (1822). [D]

Ainsworth, John, Cricket Lane, Ashton-under-Lyne, Lancs., joiner and cm (1828). [D]

Ainsworth, Jos., Vauxhall, Lane End, Staffs., carver and gilder (1835). [D]

Ainsworth, Thomas, Colchester, Essex, chairmaker (1805–39). Initially traded from an address in Crouch St but in 1839 in Pelham St. [D]

Ainsworth & Milner, 24 Lichfield St, Soho, London, cm (1790–93). [D]

Airay, John, London, upholder (1712–17). Admitted freeman of the Upholders' Co. on 1 October 1712. [GL, Upholders' Co. records]

Airay, John, London, upholder (1724–34). In 1724 his business premises were situated near St Thomas's Hospital Gate, Southwark. On 7 February 1727 he took out cover with the Sun Fire Office for £500. By 1734 he had moved to Clerkenwell. [GL, Sun MS vol. 23, p. 391; Heal]

Airey & Bellingham, 3 Frederick Pl., Hampstead Rd, London, cm, carpenter and undertaker (1832–37). [D]

Aishford, Edmund, London, u (1756). App. to John Jeffries in 1756. [V&A archives]

Aislabie (or Aislaby), Michael, 54 Salthouse Lane, Hull, Yorks., cm and u (1840). [D]

Aitchison, George, 5 Hertford St, Fitzroy Sq., London, cm and u (1827–29). [D]

Aitken, Alexander, Walker's Ct, St Anne's, Soho, London, cm (1778). Declared bankrupt in February 1778. [Gents Mag.]

Aitken, Thomas, Langley St, Long Acre, London, cm (1760). Trade card illustrated in Heal states that he 'Makes and Sells all Sorts of Cabinet and Chair Work'.

Aitkin, John, 33 Gt Waterloo St, London, carver and gilder (1835). [D]

Aitkin & Son, 153 Swallow St, London, carvers and gilders (1784). [D]

Akam, John, 67 Myton Gate, Hull, Yorks., cm and u (1814–18). [D]

Akers, C., 12 Old Compton St, Soho, London, cm and upholder (1822). [D]

Akers, Edward, Burford, Oxon., carpenter, joiner and cm (1793). [D]

Akers, Edward, 30 Russell Ct, Covent Gdn, London, picture frame maker (1819–25). [D]

Akers, Mark, 12 Old Compton St, Soho, London, u and cm (1820–25). Bankruptcy announced, Brighton Gazette, 31 March 1825. [D]

Akers, William, 59 New Road, Woolwich, Kent, cm (1838–39). [D]

Akitt, John, Gt Dockray, near Penrith, Cumb., cm, joiner and u (1834). [D]

Akrill, George, Commercial Rd, Grantham, Lincs., turner and chairmaker (1835–40). [D]

Aland, John, 34 Little Pulteney St, Golden Sq., London, cm (1829). [D]

Aland, T. & J., 18 Gt Sutton St, Clerkenwell, London, water gilders (1835). [D]

Albert, Thomas, Berwick St, Westminster, London, u (1749). [Poll bk]

Albin, Joseph, Peter St, Bath, Som., cm and upholder (1793). [D]

Albina, Clementi, 14 Union Ct, Holborn, London, picture and looking-glass frame maker (1839). [D]

Albino, E. & Co., 14 Union Ct, Holborn, London, picture frame and birdcage manufacturers (1835). [D]

Albino, John, London, looking-glass and barometer makers (1837–40). Trading at 2 Beauchamp St in 1837, but by 1839 had moved to 47 St John St, West Smithfield where he continued to trade until 1849. [D; Goodison, Barometers]

Alchorne, James, 25 Evesham Buildings, Somerstown, London, carver and gilder (1808). [D]

Alcock, John, High St, Bishop Wearmouth, Co. Durham, u (1796–1827). Shop opened in October 1796. Undertook work for the Marquess of Londonderry at Wynyard Park, Co. Durham. [D; Durham RO, D/LO/E484; Newcastle Courant, 22 October 1796]

Alcock, Linney, Congleton, Cheshire, chairmaker (1744). Took app. named Copeland in 1744. [S of G, app. index]

Alcock, Samuel, Frederick St, Sunderland, Co. Durham, u (1828). [D]

Alcock, William, Chichester, Sussex, joiner and cm (1757). Took app. named Gray in 1757. [S of G, app. index]

Alcock, William Roscoe, 16 Percy St, Liverpool, cm (1822–39). App. to John Price in 1822. [D; Liverpool app. reg.]

Alden, Anne, Below the conduit, Exeter, Devon, u (1717–24). In 1717 took app. named Humphrey Wilcox who continued the business at the same address on her retirement in 1724. Between October and Christmas 1724 he disposed of her stock which consisted of 'standing beds, common curtains and vallince, Ticks made or unmade, Feathers, quilts, Ruggs, Blankets, Chairs, Fire Screens, fine or ordinary matts, Looking-Glasses, a Book-case, with arch'd Glass doors, mounted on a Buroe, single buroes, Scrutoires, Chests of Drawers, Tea-Tables, of all sorts, Dressing Tables, glass and gilded sconces, very large and fine Corner Cupboards, or ordinary ones, Haratines, China's printed stuffs, plain and striped stuffs, Bed laces and all sorts painted Linnen, Hangings'. [The Post Master or Loyal Mercury, 23 October 1724]

Alder, Brian, Canterbury and London, u and cm (1783–1808). Admitted freeman of Canterbury in 1783. In business at St Dunstan's, Canterbury the following year. Trading at 31 Leward St, Goswell St, London, from 1790; but in 1793, when he took out cover for £300 with the Sun Fire Office, £20 of this was in respect of utensils at the workshop of 'Mr. Seddon in Aldersgate Street'. By 1808 when he was at 6 Goswell St the insurance cover had been raised to £400. [D; GL, Sun MS vol. 397, p. 320; vol. 446, ref. 816360; poll bk]

Alder, Caleb, Newcastle, upholder (1753–87). Trading in 1753 at Burnt-house Entry, The Side, at which address he was receiving supplies of cloth from Philip Magee, linen bleacher. In 1781 he moved from Westgate St to Groat Mkt and in 1787 was trading from Nungate. [D; Newcastle Courant, 17 March 1753 and 30 June 1781]

Alder, John, Albion St, Cheltenham, Glos., cm and u (1820–40). Trading at no. 82 also as a paper hanger, in 1822. [D]

Alder, Joseph, St John's St, Clerkenwell, London, cm (1802). Declared bankrupt, Billinge's Liverpool Advertiser, 4 January 1802.

Alderman, J., 16 Soho Sq., London, inventor, patentee and manufacturer (c. 1830–40). Folding caned mahogany sedan chair with label [Sotheby's Belgravia, 16 November 1978, lot 25] and mahogany invalid's chair signed on hub caps [Phillips', 19 August 1969, lot 92] known. Label inscribed 'J. Alderman, Inventor, Patentee & Manufacturer, 16 Soho Square, London'.

Alderney, Daniel, London, cm (1757). Son of William Alderney of St Mary Aldermanbury, London, cm. App. to Henry Draper on 15 March 1749, and then to Thomas Brown, merchant tailor. Admitted freeman of the Upholders' Co. by servitude on 7 July 1757. [GL, Upholders' Co. records]

Alderney, William, see Daniel Alderney.

Aldersey, Thomas, London, glass grinder, cm and u (1754–81). In 1754 established at Addle St where he was employing one freeman as a chairmaker and one non-freeman as a glass seller. By 1761 he had moved to 20 Tooley St, Southwark at which address he was to remain until 1770. In 1767–68 the business was listed as 'Thomas Aldersey & James Cawdell'. From 1771 the address was given as Bridge Yd, Tooley St and from 1773 as 4 Bishopgate Without, when the style of the enterprise was given as 'Thomas Aldersey & Co.'. From 1779 the address was 17 Broker's Row, Moorfields. A mid 18th-century looking-glass with a mahogany frame is known with this maker's label. [D; GL, City Licence bks, vol. 1; *Antiques*, May 1968, p. 648]

Aldersmith, James, 27 Bond St, Hull, Yorks., carver and gilder (1831). [D]

Aldersmith, James, 79 Petergate, York, carver and gilder (1837–d. by 1840). Commenced business in January 1837, but dead by October 1840. [D; *York Gazette*, 28 January 1837; *Leeds Mercury*, 3 October 1840]

Alderson, John, Low-friar St, Newcastle, cm and carpenter (1790–94). Subscribed to Sheraton's *Drawing Book*, 1793. In April 1794 was paid £73 14s for household furniture for Gibside. Co. Durham. [D; Durham RO, D/St/V 998]

Alderson, John, Richmond, Yorks., cm (1818). [PR (bapt.)]

Alderson, Joseph, Durham, joiner and cm (1793). [D]

Alderson, Robert, Blackburn, Lancs., cm and joiner (1818–24). Addresses at Millgate in 1818 and Mill Lane in 1824. Continued to be listed in directories until 1834 but only as a joiner. [D]

Alderson, Thomas, 111 Pilgrim St, Newcastle, cm, u, carver and gilder (1827–34). From 1833 the business was styled Alderson & Turnbull and traded from 114 Pilgrim St. [D]

Alderton, Henry, Brighton, Sussex, cm and u (1826–40). Recorded at 12 Preston St in 1826 but by 1839 had moved to 1 Montpellier Rd. [D]

Alderton, J., 15 Upper Russell St, Brighton, Sussex, cm (1824). [D]

Alderton, Thomas, 23–24 St James's St, Brighton, Sussex, u, cm and undertaker (1816–23). [D; E. Sussex RO, PAR 255/1/2/2, 20 March 1816]

Alderton, William, High St, Lewes, Sussex, cm (1790). [Poll bk]

Alderton, WIlliam, 6 Little East St, Brighton, Sussex, cm and upholder (1793–d. 1822). Subscriber to Sheraton's *Drawing Book*, 1793. Death reported, *Brighton Gazette*, 12 December 1822. [D]

Alderton, William, Wood St, Brighton, Sussex, cm (1820–37). [E. Sussex RO, PAR 255/1/2/3, 6 December 1820; poll bk]

Aldis, J., Pimlico, London. Name stamped on late Regency writing desk.

Aldous, John, Beccles, Norfolk, cm and u (1824–39). Trading at Smallgate St in 1824 and 1839, but also recorded at Gentleman Walk in 1830 and New Market in 1839. [D]

Aldous, William, London, u, cm and undertaker (1816–32). Addresses at 54 Broad St, Golden Sq., 1816–21, and at 371 Oxford St from 1822. [D]

Aldred, John, Gt Yarmouth, Norfolk, cm (1795). App. to John Sewell. Admitted freeman in 1795. Changed his surname from Sallows. [Calendar of freemen]

Aldred, William, North Quay, Gt Yarmouth, Norfolk, cm chairmaker (1836–40). [D; poll bk]

Aldrich, Richard, Holton, Suffolk, chairmaker (1800–24). See Richard Aldridge. [Suffolk RO, FE1/32/11; *Ipswich Journal*, 7 October 1809]

Aldrid, John, West Wycombe, Bucks., chairmaker (b. 1801–41). Aged 40 at the time of the 1841 Census. [D]

Aldridge, Charles, 85 Bradford St, Birmingham, cm (1835). [D]

Aldridge, John, Beverley, Yorks., cm (1774). [Poll bk]

Aldridge, Richard, Holton, Suffolk, chairmaker (1761). Took app. named Copping in 1761. See Richard Aldrich. [S of G, app. index]

Aldridge, Robert, Reading, Berks., carver (1780–82). Insured his house with the Sun Fire Office for £300 in 1782. [GL, Sun MS vol. 306, p. 125; poll bk]

Aldridge, Simon, Liverpool, u (1704–06) In 1704 and 1705 supplied beds for Crosby Hall, Lancs. for Nicholas Blundell. The 'blew bed', ordered on 9 March 1704, was first set up in 'the Garden Chamber' and then transferred to 'the Blew Chamber'. This and a further bed ordered for his mother in February 1705 cost £27 2s 6d. [F. Tyrer (ed.), *The Great Diurnal of Nicholas Blundell*, vol. 1; Disbursement bk, Crosby Hall]

Aldridge, Thomas, London (?), upholder (1698). Admitted freeman of the Upholders' Co. on 17 August 1698. [GL, Upholders' Co. records].

Aldridge, Thomas, High St, Southampton, Hants., cm, u and auctioneer (1783–84). [D]

Aldwinckle, Henry, 18 Exmouth St, Spa Fields, London, bedstead maker and carpenter (1820–35). [D]

Alebon, John, Birmingham, u and cm (1816–35). Trading at Worcester St, 1816–18; Bromsgrove St in 1818; Worcester St in 1822; no. 62 in 1830; and Smallbrook St in 1835. [D]

Alexander, —, address unrecorded (1748). On 13 June 1748 £6 6s was paid by Mrs Bowes to 'Alexander for a pair of branches lackered'. [Durham RO, D/St/V1488–90]

Alexander, Francis, London, cm and u (1822–35). Trading at 1 Gt Charlotte St, Blackfriars from 1822, and also recorded at 72 Gt Surrey St. [D]

Alexander, Henry, 71 Gt Surrey St, Blackfriars Rd, London, u (1820). [D]

Alexander, J., 12 New Belton St, Long Acre, London, bedstead and chairmaker (1808). [D]

Alexander, James, 6 Prince's St, Drury Lane, London, broker and cm (1821). Took out insurance with the Sun Fire Office on 7 November 1821 for £450 of which £255 was for stock, utensils and goods in trust. [GL, Sun MS vol. 488, ref. 985173]

Alexander, John, Liverpool, cm (1781–1817). Admitted freeman on 4 January 1781. [Liverpool freemen reg.]

Alexander, John, Lancaster, joiner (1785–88). Named in the Gillow records. [Westminster Ref. Lib., Gillow vol. 344/94, p. 351]

Alexander, John, parish of St George Tombland, Norwich, cm (1807–30). App. to William Stevens and admitted freeman on 7 March 1807. [Norwich freemen reg. and poll bk]

Alexander, John, Ipswich, Suffolk, cm (1820). [Poll bk]

Alexander, John, Chelsea St, Haymarket, London, cm and u (1822). [D]

Alexander, John, Camden St, North Shields, Northumb., cm and joiner (1827). [D]

Alexander, John, 32 Newman St, London, cm and u (1829–39). [D]

Alexander, Mat, 10 Paradise St, Manchester Sq., London, cm (1835). [D]

Alexander, Samuel, London (?), upholder (1726–33). Son of Samuel Alexander, tanner of Norwich. App. to John Crouch on 1 August 1726. Admitted freeman of the Upholders' Co. on 5 September 1733. [GL, Upholders' Co. records]

Alexander, Thomas, Church St, Staines, Middlx., cm (1826). [D]

Alexander, William, Allend Ct, Westminster, London, cm (1784) [Poll bk]

Alferi, Charles, 31 Tib St, Manchester, picture frame and looking-glass manufacturer (1815). [D]

Alford, Aaron, Exeter, Devon, carver and gilder (1832–40). Trading in Paris St, 1832–39, then Blackboy Rd. Also recorded at 8 Brunswick Pl. in 1836. [*Exeter Pocket Journal*, 1836; PR (bapt.)]

Alford, J., 4 Redcross St, London, u (1826). [D]

Alford, James, Dale End, Birmingham, u (1767). [D]

Alford, Jock, Back of the Walls, Southampton, Hants., carver and gilder (1823–30). [D]

Alford, Robert jnr, Mint St, Southwark, London, cm (1820). [D]

Alford, Robert, Redcross St, Southwark, London, cm and u (1827). [D]

Algar, John, Cornwall St, Plymouth, Devon, chairmaker (d. 1827). Death reported, *The Alfred*, 30 October 1827.

Algar, Joseph, 9 King St, Holborn, London, upholder and broker (1821). On 30 May 1821 took out cover for £1,000 with the Sun Fire Office on his dwelling house at which it was stated there was 'no stove nor cabinet work done therein'. [GL, Sun MS, vol. 488, ref. 980500].

Algar, William & Son, 11 Cornwall St, Plymouth, Devon, Windsor and fancy chairmakers (1814–23). [D]

Alger, Mary, 33 Drury Lane, London, chair and sofa maker (1827). [D]

Alken, M., London, u (before 1785). Advertised in the *South Carolina Gazette,* 16 February 1785 that he was 'lately arrived from London' and was setting up his business at 80 King St. He stated that he was expecting 'a large assortment of goods from Europe'.

Alken, Martyn, Macclesfield St, Westminster, London, cm (1784). [Poll bk]

Alken, Oliver, London, carver (1766–68). Worked at St Mary's Lutheran Chapel, Savoy, from 1766–68 on architectural carving, brackets at the altar, branches at the altarpiece, etc. This was part of an extensive restoration surveyed by William Chambers. [Westminster Ref. Lib., MS 90/8/12, 14]

Alken, Sefferin, London, carver (1744–83). In 1744 his address was given as St James's, Westminster, and from 1760 he was at Dufour's Ct, Broad St, Golden Sq. Worked in both stone and wood and was active at Stourhead for Sir Richard Colt Hoare as early as 1744. In 1746 took app. named Lawrence (probably Richard Lawrence, 1760–95) who may subsequently have become his partner, as in 1763 the business is referred to as Alken & Lawrence. In 1760 took another app. named Engleheart (probably Thomas Engleheart, b.1745-d.1786). Alken subscribed to Chambers's *Designs for Chinese Buildings,* 1757, and *Treatise on Civil Architecture,* 1759. He was also a subscriber to Adam's *Spalato,* 1764. His son Samuel, born 22 October 1756, attended the Royal Academy Schools from 1769 and followed his father's profession as a carver. Sefferin may have died in 1783 as all payments after this date in connection with work being carried out at Somerset House are made to his son Samuel. Apart from these two talented craftsmen the Alken family was also renowned as sporting painters. [D; Gunnis; S of G, app. index; Beard, *Georgian Craftsmen*] Supplied furniture for Audley End, Essex, invoicing Sir John Griffin Griffin on 30 June 1770. The major part of the £16 total was for 'A Gothick Chair an Ornament at Top with foliage &c. 2 penicles at the Corners of the back with husks &c. 2 Boys heads at Elbows & Leaves' for which £13 was charged. The invoice was receipted on 10 April 1771 by Samuel Alken on behalf of his father. [Essex RO, D/DBy/A30/11] On 26 July 1778 'Mr. Alking' is recorded as providing for Blenheim Palace, Oxon., '4 Pier Glasses with Carved Frames Gilt in Burnish'd Gold' and also 'A large picture frame for the present family picture'. [V&A archives; *C. Life,* 23 January 1975] Worked as a carver at Cleveland House, London, 1746–52. [Raby Castle MS] In 1761 bills for work at Croome Court, Worcs. were approved by Robert Adam for the carving of garden chairs, the greenhouse pediment, two glass frames, table frames and two glass frames en suite for the dining room. In 1763–64 work involved the carving of bookcases, pediment etc. for the library and in 1765 furniture for the gallery. Sefferin was employed for carved work on chairs supplied by John Cobb and ten scroll end sofas supplied by Bradburn & France in this year. Much of the furniture was to designs by Robert Adam. Furniture from this commission is now at the V&A; the MMA, NY; Philadelphia Museum of Art; and Kenwood, London. Carving bills also exist for work at the Earl of Coventry's London house in Grosvenor Sq. dated 1761, 1767 and 1768 amounting to £39 11s 11d.

[V&A archives; Worcs. RO, Coventry papers; Harris, *Furniture of Robert Adam; Conn.,* January 1976 and June 1981] Worked at Kedleston Hall, Derbs., providing in 1759 five gilt picture frames for the Breakfast Room to Robert Adam's design. A letter from Adam to Lord Scarsdale dated 15 May 1761 stated that Alken had nearly finished making frames for the Painted Room. [V&A archives] Supplied to Marston House, Som., in 1754 'a richly carved pier-glass' for Lady Dungarvon, the daughter of Henry Hoare. [Gunnis] Carved work at Normanton Park, Rutland, including a chimney piece for Sir Gilbert Heathcote carried out in 1765–66. A part of this commission was for Sir Gilbert's London house in Grosvenor Sq. [Lincoln RO, 2 ANC 12/D/25] Carved work at Shardeloes, Amersham, Bucks. for William Drake to designs by Robert Adam. By 21 April 1763 the cost of this work amounted to £543 12s exclusive of the carving to be carried out on the mahogany doors. This additional work 'answerable to drawings delivered by Mr. Adam' amounted to £15 17s 2d, while carving 'one side of door next to drawing room' was charged at a further £11 13s 6d. [Bucks. RO, D/DR/5/14] Extensive work at Somerset House, Strand, London was carried out from 1777–83 by both Sefferin and Samuel Alken. This included a number of wooden chimney pieces. [PRO, AO 1/2495] A bill for work at Stourhead, Wilts., dated 24 May 1772, records the carving of an oval frame costing £29 10s and a 'rich flower for ceiling' at £3. A further charge of £9 9s 6d was made for joinery work. Between 1750 and 1770 no fewer than seven payments to Alken are recorded in Henry Hoare's account book. This included chimney pieces, 'Lady Boyle's Pier glass', £60, and a picture frame, £34 11s. Some of this work was in connection with a house that Henry Hoare was having built at Clapham, London. [Wilts. RO, 383/1, 383/6] Carved work at the Villa Marino, Lord Charlemont's seaside villa near Dublin. In a letter sent from Sir William Chambers to Lord Charlemont in 1767 regarding its furnishing it is recorded that 'Alkin has carved one of the little heads for the corner of the doors of the medal-cases. It is very fine, but as he tells me that he cannot do them under three guineas and a half a head, I have stopped his further progress till I hear from your Lordship'. [Hist. MS Commission, *Earl of Charlemont,* I, 283; cabinet sold, Christie's, 21–24 May 1984, lot 843, illus. in colour. See also *Burlington,* October 1985, pp. 693–94 and *Irish Arts Review,* summer 1984, pp. 23–7] Carried out work at Woburn Abbey, Beds. by order of William Chambers for the 4th Duke of Bedford and for Francis, Marquess of Tavistock at Houghton. This included a mahogany bookcase with the mouldings and drop ornaments representing music, war, painting and sculpture for which £27 9s 6½d was charged in 1764. Six chimney pieces, cornices, a bedhead and footboard, friezes etc. amounting to £36 3s 8d were paid for in 1769. A further sum of £117 9s 8d was paid in 1771 under the 4th Duke's executorship account for general carver's work at Woburn. [Bedford Office, London] The account of the Duke of Northumberland at Hoare's Bank records payments made to Alken between 1750 and 1768.
B.A.

Al(l)kin, Sampson, Cank St, St Martin's, Leicester, cm and u (1815–28). [D]

Al(l)kins, John, Church St, Uttoxeter, Staffs., chairmaker and turner (1818–34). [D]

Allam, James, Dovecot St, Stockton, Co. Durham, cm (1824). [D]

Allam, Joseph, High St, Chatteris, Cambs., cm and u (1830–39). [D]

Allam, Thomas, Maddox St, Westminster, London, u (1749–74). Fellow of the Society of Arts, 1760. [Poll bk]

Allam, Thomas, Market Deeping, Lincs., chairmaker and wood turner (1826–40). [D]

Allam, William, Market Deeping, Lincs., chair turner (1797). [D]

Allan, David, 6 Castle St, Leicester Sq., London, cm (1824). In 1824 took out cover for £100 with the Sun Fire Office in respect of household goods etc. 'in the now dwelling house of a turner'. [GL, Sun MS, vol. 499, ref. 1016092]

Allan, James, Market St, Chatteris, Cambs., u and carpenter (1839). [D]

Allan, John, Mock St, Wardour St, London, cm (1777–93). In 1777 took out insurance cover with the Sun Fire Office for £200 of which £30 covered utensils, stock and goods. Subscribed to Sheraton's *Drawing Book*, 1793. [GL, Sun MS vol. 257, p. 347]

Allan, John, Liverpool, cm (1804–39). Trading at 7 Back Jackson St in 1812 and in same street at no. 1 in 1837. Had moved to 7 Heath St, Toxteth Park by 1839. App. to William Harvey in 1804. Admitted freeman on 12 October 1812 but register which indicates trade as cm also states 'now mariner'. [D; Liverpool freemen reg.]

Allan, John, Wood St, Maryport, Cumb., joiner and cm (1828–34). [D]

Allan, Thomas, London, cm (1758). Freeman of York. May be the Thomas Allen, sedan chairmaker to the royal family, who was resident in Maddox St in the mid 1760s. [Poll bk; *C. Life*, 12 September 1960, p. 615]

Allan, Thomas, 12 Gibraltar Row, Lambeth, London, bedstead maker (1826). [D]

Allan, William, 52 London Rd, London, cm, u and bed and mattress maker (1837–39). [D]

Allard, John, Bristol, cm (1799–1818). Recorded at Old Mkt, 1799–1800, but by 1805 this address had been amplified to 91 Old Market St. [D]

Allanson, Thomas, Blake St, York, u (1777–d. 1784). Admitted freeman in 1777 and in this year he insured his utensils and stock in the Blake St premises for £800 with the Sun Fire Office. The York Minster fabric rolls record that he was paid £4 16s in 1781 for lining pews, and a further £3 1s 6d in 1783. In 1781 he was described as the successor to Joseph Reynoldson. Died in September 1784. [York freemen rolls; *York Chronicle*, 29 August 1777; *York Courant*, 7 September 1784; GL, Sun MS vol. 259, p. 111]

Allanson, William, 28 Clare St, Liverpool, cm and u (1839–40). Trading in 1839 but not sworn a freeman until 29 July 1840. [D; Liverpool freemen reg.]

Allars, Henry, London, cm and u (1832–39). Trading at 4 Cannon Pl., Whitechapel Rd in 1832 and at 32 Mile End Rd in 1839. [D]

Allatt, Christopher, 29 Silver St, Golden Sq., London, cm, upholder, turner, appraiser and sworn broker (1775–83). In 1775 insured his utensils, stock and goods with the Sun Fire Office for £200. Trade card in Banks Coll., BM. [GL, Sun MS vol. 243, p. 347]

Allatt, Richard, Barnsley, Yorks., cm and joiner (1793). [D]

Allatt, Thomas, Kirkgate, Wakefield, Yorks., cm and u (1837). [D]

Allatt, William, Kirkgate, Wakefield, Yorks., cm and u (1830). [D]

Allaway, George & James, 58 Minster St, Reading, Berks., cm and u (1803–40). Subscribed to Sheraton's *Cabinet Dictionary*, 1803. William Osmond was a partner in 1823. [D]

Allbritan, Samuel, 'on east side of Church land at Limehouse in the parish of St. Dunstan at Stepney', London, upholder (1715). On 25 July 1715 insured his house and another dwelling for £100 each with the Hand in Hand Fire Office. [GL, Hand in Hand MS vol. 14, p. 585]

Allcock, Charles, Mill St, Kidderminster, Worcs., cm and u (1822–35). [D]

Allcock, William, Little York St, parish of St Dunstan, Stepney, London, frame smith (1726). On 18 July 1726 insured property to the value of £300 with the Sun Fire Office. [GL, Sun MS vol. 23, p. 116]

Allcock, William, Leicester, cm (1773). App. to Thomas Tippler of Derby, cm. Admitted freeman in 1773. [Leicester freemen reg.]

Allcock, William, Blake Brook, Kidderminster, Worcs., cm and u (1835). [D]

Allden, Charles, 14 Well St, Oxford St, London, picture frame maker (1802–14). [D]

Alldridge, Charles, 85 Bradford St, Birmingham, cabinet case maker (1839). [D]

Alldridge, Edwin, Dean St, Birmingham, cm and clock case maker (1835). [D]

Allen, —, 'The White Swan', West Smithfield, London, u (d. 1704). Death reported, *Daily Courant*, 19 May 1704.

Allen's, —, 21 Little Eastcheap, London, u, cm and looking-glass maker (c. 1800). Trade card in Heal.

Allen, —, 12 Bell's Sq., Foster Lane, London, knife case maker (1809). [D]

Allen, Abraham, 61 Pall Mall, London, u, designer and manufacturer of 'furniture calicoes' (1809–21). Trade cards in BM, V&A and MMA, NY. Advertised that 'Elegant Specimens of made up Drapery for various purposes may be seen at the Warehouse'. In 1815 claimed to be 'Furniture designer & printer to HRH. the Princess Elizabeth', and in 1821 'Furniture designer and printer to His Majesty'. [D]

Allen, Andrew, St Michael's, Southampton, Hants., chairmaker (1725). On 16 November 1725 took out insurance cover of £300 with the Sun Fire Office for 'his dwelling house in Rumsey commonly known by the name of Cross Keys now in occupation of victualler'. [GL, Sun MS vol. 19, ref. 35174]

Allen, Anthony & Co., Hotwell Rd, Bristol, cm and u (1805–21). [D] See Allen & Foster.

Allen, Charles, London, u (before 1771). Advertised in *Penn'a Packet*, 3 October 1771 that he was lately from London and Paris and that he had learnt his trade from Mr Bradshaw and Mons. Fleuri respectively.

Allen, Charles, Load St, Bewdley, Worcs., u (1830). [D]

Allen, Charles, 32 Wharf St, Birmingham, cm and u (1835). [D]

Allen, Edward, Canterbury, Kent, u (1688). [Canterbury freemen rolls]

Allen, F., Esplanade, Dover, Kent, u (1838). [D]

Allen, Francis, 46 Hans Pl., Chelsea, London, cm and u (1823). [D]

Allen, George, York, u (1764). App. to George Marshall, u, on 19 November 1764. [York app. reg.]

Allen, George, Fenchurch St, London, u, cm and looking-glass manufacturer to the Bank of England (1800–20). Son and successor of John Allen. Admitted freeman of the Upholders' Co. by patrimony on 7 May 1800. For a brief period traded from his father's address at 50 Fenchurch St but by 1802 was at no. 158. Subscribed to Sheraton's *Cabinet Dictionary*, 1803. Maintained a carpet and paper-hanging warehouse, and acted as auctioneer, appraiser and undertaker. Trade card in BM. [D; GL, Upholders' Co. records]

Allen, George, 6 Bedford Pl., Commercial Rd, London, cm and u (1822–27). [D]

Allen, Henry, London (?), cm (1669–73). Supplied fourteen pieces of furniture to William, 5th Earl of Bedford at a cost of £66 16s. The main items were a walnut cabinet 'for my Lady's cabinet' supplied in 1669 at £17, a 31″ looking-glass in a walnut frame at £10, and a sleeping chair at £8 5s in 1672, and ten back stools at £6 10s in 1673. [Bedford Office, London]

Allen, Henry jnr, parish of St James, Bristol, carver (1774). [Poll bk]

Allen, J., address unrecorded. Name impressed on a Lancashire pattern spindle-back chair, c.1840 at Temple Newsam House, Leeds.

Allen, James, Thomas St, Bristol, architect and carver (1777–93). In 1777 insured his house with the Sun Fire Office for £300. [D; GL, Sun MS vol. 254, p. 567; poll bk]

Allen, James, Dovecot St, Stockton, Co. Durham, cm and joiner (1828). [D]

Allen, John, Fenchurch St, London, cm and u (1773–1800). Son of James Allen of Hereford, clerk. App. to Samuel Severn on 26 July 1752 and to John Trotter, joiner, on 15 July 1756. Admitted freeman of the Upholders' Co. on 7 April 1763 and master in 1799. Initially traded from 133 Fenchurch St but by 1782 was at no. 50. In 1780 insured with the Sun Fire Office with total cover of £700 of which £470 was for utensils and stock. Subscribed to Sheraton's *Drawing Book*, 1793. His son George took over the business c.1800 and in 1802 John was recorded living at Greenwich. Supplied furniture to Penrice Castle, Glam. [D; GL, Upholders' Co. records; GL, Sun MS vol. 287, p. 138; C. Life, 25 September 1975]

Allen, John, Romford, Essex, cm (1784). [D]

Allen, John, Torrington St, London, cm (1790–93). [D]

Allen, John, Dover, Kent, u (1792–93). [D]

Allen, John, Gt Charles St, Birmingham, gilder (1793). [D]

Allen, John, Lancaster, cm (1817–18). Admitted freeman, 1817–18, when stated 'of Liverpool'. [Lancaster freemen rolls]

Allen, John, Pride Hill, Shrewsbury, Salop, cm etc. (1822). [D]

Allen, John, 93 King Ct, Minories, London, u (1822). On 20 November 1822 took out insurance cover of £100 with the Sun Fire Office. [GL, Sun MS vol. 490, ref. 997891]

Allen, John, Blackheath Hill, Greenwich, London, cm etc. (1824–26). [D]

Allen, John, Hotwell Rd, Bristol, cm, u, appraiser and auctioneer (1828). [D]

Allen, John, London, cm (1829–35). Recorded at 3 King St, Goswell St in 1829 and at 64 Goswell St in 1835. [D]

Allen, John, 18 Gloucester St, Hoxton, London, cm and undertaker (1832–37). [D]

Allen, John, Gravesend, Kent, cm (1830). [Poll bk]

Allen, Joseph, Cheapside, Boston, Lincs., chairmaker and turner (1835). [D]

Allen, Moses, Silver St, Yeovil, Som., cm (1830). [D]

Allen, Nicholas, Bargate, Boston, Lincs., chair and wheel maker (1790–1835). Trading at Wide Bargate, 1819–35, in 1835 as cm. On 6 August 1790 advertised in the *Lincoln, Rutland and Stamford Mercury* for a 'journeyman pinchair and spinning wheel maker . . . A good Hand may have constant Employ, and good wages . . .'. [D]

Allen, Randolph, Newport Alley, parish of St Ann's, Westminster, London, upholsterer (1707). On 9 September 1707 took out insurance with the Hand in Hand Fire Office for £150 on his house, £200 on a rented house and £150 on two others. [GL, Hand in Hand MS vol. 5, ref. 14308]

Allen, Robert, Back St, Bristol, cm (1793–95). [D]

Allen, Samuel, High Wycombe, Bucks., chair turner (b. c.1796–1841). Aged 45 at the time of the 1841 Census.

Allen, Samuel, 5 Prince's St, Barbican, London, fancy cm (1835–39). In 1839 trade listed as portable desk, dressing case, work box and cabinet case maker. [D]

Allen, Silas, Rosemary Lane, Nottingham, cm (1832). [D]

Allen, Thomas, parish of St John, Bristol, cm (1721–22). [Poll bk]

Allen, Thomas, address unrecorded, u (1740). In 1740 he submitted an invoice to the Earl of Northumberland for cutting down chairs, mending hangings, etc. [V&A archives]

Allen, Thomas, Liverpool, cm and chairmaker (1810–35). Recorded at 23 Dale St in 1811 but in the next year at no. 32. No further entries appear in directories until 1834 when an address at 26 Heath St is listed, changing in the following year to 1 Red Ct, 57 Pool Lane, and shop at 7 Norfolk St. It is not certain whether the Thomas Allen trading in the 1830s was the same as the one active two decades earlier. [D]

Allen, Thomas, 9 Wandsworth Rd, London, bedstead maker (1829). [D]

Allen, William, London (?), u (1687–92). Supplied goods to the Royal Hospital, Chelsea, between 1687 and 1692 costing £8 14s 8d. [*Wren Soc.*, vol. 19, p. 85] Recorded in the Royal Household accounts in 1689 supplying upholstery work for the household staff rooms at Whitehall at a value of £43 16s. [PRO, LC9/279, pp. 542–56]

Allen, William, London, u (1712). Admitted freeman of the Upholders' Co. on 1 October 1712. [GL, Upholders' Co. records]

Allen, William, Saltford, Som., cm (1737–61). Took apps named Baker in 1737, and Thomson in 1761. [S of G, app. index]

Allen, William, Cannon St, London, upholder (1750). Admitted a member of the livery of the Upholders' Co. in 1750. [GL, Upholders' Co. records]

Allen (or Allan), William, London, upholder (1777–93). Trading initially at 129 New Bond St but in 1781 moved to 20 David St, and by 1790 was at 24 Davies St. His trade was probably fairly substantial, for as early as 1777 he carried an insurance cover of £500; by 1781 this had risen to £1,300 and by 1787 to £2,200. In 1785 he had a house on the north side of Berkeley Sq. [D; GL, Sun MS vol. 258, p. 522; vol. 328, p. 118; vol. 331, p. 555; vol. 342, ref. 532912]

Allen, William, Clarendon, St (or Rd), Leamington, Warks., cm (1828). [D]

Allen, William, Ludgate Hill, Birmingham, cm, u and broker (1830). [D]

Allen, William, West St, Nottingham, chairmaker (1832). [D]

Allen, William, 31 Ebury St, Pimlico, London, carver and gilder (1837–39). [D]

Allen & Doolan, 174 Borough, London, cabinet and chairmakers (1768–75). [D]

Allen & Foster, Hotwell Rd, Bristol, cm and u (1814–21). Traded before 1809 as Anthony Allen & Co. In 1821 Anthony Allen appears to have been the sole proprietor. [D]

Allett, John, Poland St, Carnaby Mkt, London, cm (1755). [*Public Advertiser*, 26 June 1755]

Alley, Christian, Moorfields, London, cm (1802). [PRO, C13 599/20]

Alley, H., 102 Goswell Rd, London, u etc. (1837). [D]

Alley, William, 56 St John St Rd, London, u etc. (1826). [D]

Allford, Edward, London, cm and u (1829–39). Addresses at 2 Mount Row, Kent Rd in 1829 and 5 Stafford Row, Pimlico in 1839. [D]

Allice, William, Newark, Notts., cm (1806). Admitted freeman of Lincoln in November 1806. [Lincoln freemen rolls]

Allin, William, Newark, Notts., cm (1770–88). Insured with the Sun Fire Office in 1776 for a total of £1,000 of which £400 was for utensils and stock. On 8 May he advertised his intention to discontinue trading and offered his stock to the public at 'considerably under Prime cost'. He stated that his stock consisted of 'a great Variety of large Pier, Chimney, Sconce, and Dressing Glasses, in carved, gilt, machee, japanned, painted, and plain Mahogany Frames; Tea Boards, Chests, Trays, and Caddies, plain or inlaid; Mahogany, Pembroke, Card or Tea Tables, Bason Stands, Knife Cases,

Backgammon Tables, Night Tables and Cribbage Boards; several Sets of Mahogany Chairs; Fire-Screens, Umbrellas, &c, &c. Also a large Quantity of Paper Hangings, of the newest Patterns'. [*Cambridge Chronicle and Journal*, 26 May 1770]

Allinson, John, Sunderland, Co. Durham, cm (1827–28). Recorded at Coronation St, Bishop Wearmouth in 1828, and High St in 1829. [D]

Alinson, Thomas, Briggate, Knaresborough, Yorks., joiner and builder (1828–37). [D]

Allison, John, Hull, Yorks., cm (1803–06). Trading in George St in 1803 but moved to St John's St in 1806. [D]

Allison, John, Mint Yd, York, cm (1823). [D]

Allison, Robert, London, cm (1793). Subscribed to Sheraton's *Drawing Book*, 1793.

Allison, Robert, Bridlington, Yorks., cm (1831–40). Trading in Market Pl. in 1831 and High St in 1840. [D]

Allison, Thomas, Southampton St, Camberwell, London, cm and u (1839). [D]

Allison, William, Hill's Lane, Shrewsbury, Salop, cm (1796). [Shrewsbury burgess roll]

Alliss, William, Hawton Rd, Newark, Notts., cm (1835). [D]

Allman, John, High St, Staines, Middlx, cm/carpenter (1823). [D]

Allnut, Charles, 193 Piccadilly, London, u and cm (1832–35). [D]

Allnutt, Francis, Southwark, London, cm (1742). Took app. named Hodges in 1742. [S of G, app. index]

Allott, David, May Day Green, Barnsley, Yorks., cm and u (1822). [D]

Allott, Richard, Barnsley, Yorks., cm (1814–30). Trading at Luke's Orchard in 1814 but by 1822 had moved to Clark's Yd, Market Pl. By 1828 he was back at the former address. [D]

Allport, James, High St, Stourbridge, Staffs., cm and u (1828–35). [D]

Allpress, James, 8 Union Pl., Lower Rd, Islington, London, cm (1832). Still trading from this address in 1835 when he is listed as a furniture broker. [D]

Allpress, John, Crown St, St Ives, Hunts., cm and u (1839). [D]

Allsop, William, George St, Tamworth, Staffs., cm and u (1822). [D]

Allsop, William, High St, Huntingdon, u and cm (1830–39). [D]

Allum, Thomas, London, cm (1832–39). Trading at 27 Arlington St, Clerkenwell from 1832–37, but by 1839 at 10 Upper Rosamon St, Clerkenwell. [D]

Allured, John, Gt Yarmouth, Norfolk, u (1790–98). App. to William Seaman. Admitted freeman of Gt Yarmouth in 1790. Declared bankrupt in 1798. [D; Gt Yarmouth freemen's calendar; *Billinge's Liverpool Advertiser*, 30 April 1798]

Allwood, Thomas, 35 Gt Russell St, London, carver and gilder (1772–93). [D] Carried out work at Bedford House, London for Gertrude, Dowager Duchess of Bedford, 1772–85, during the minority of her son Francis, 5th Duke of Bedford. This work concerned the making, mending and gilding of frames and cost £78 13s 3d. Between October 1792 and April 1793 work was carried out by Allwood for which the 5th Duke paid £594 14s. Allwood was also paid £218 12s 9d for furnishings for the Dowager Duchess's house at 112 Pall Mall, but the items are not specified. [Bedford Office, London] Employed at Carlton House, London, 1783–86, where the work amounted to £4,941 3s 3d and Henry Wood acted as examiner for his bills. [D. Stroud, *Holland*, p. 72; H. Clifford Smith, *Buckingham Palace*, p. 103] Worked for Sir Lawrence Dundas, submitting an undated estimate for making a glass frame for either 19 Arlington St, London or Moor Park, Herts. [N. Yorks. RO, ZNK 1/7/79] Carried out

work for Lord Monson in April 1782 amounting to £26 15s. [Lincoln RO, Monson 10/1/A/6] Worked for Sir John Nelthorpe, submitting an account on 8 July 1783 for carving and gilding a picture frame costing £4 13s. A further account, dated 8 April 1785, is 'to carving & gilding two frames for pictures by Mr. Stubbs', costing £1 4s 6d. [Lincoln RO, NEL 9/57/6, 9/7/29]

Allwood, Thomas, St George's, Tombland Churchyard, Norwich, cm (1830–39). [D]

Almand, Thomas, Hungate, York, cm (1823). [D]

Almond, Joseph, Liverpool, cm (1826). App. to John Armstrong in 1826. [Liverpool app. reg.]

Almond, Joseph, 1 Trentham St, Liverpool, carver (1827). [D]

Almond, Thomas, Castle St, Liverpool, cm (1749–50). On 21 March 1749–50 Thomas Livesley, apothecary, of Liverpool took out insurance amounting to £150 with the Sun Fire Office on a house occupied by Thomas Almond. [GL, Sun MS vol. 89, ref. 120437]

Almond, William, Brownlow St, London, carver and gilder (1739–66). On 16 April 1750 he was paid £5 10s for work carried out for the 3rd Earl of Burlington, £4 10s of this being in respect of Chiswick. A further sum of £4 15s was paid in March 1753 for gilding picture and table frames. [Chatsworth, Burlington papers, account bk] On 22 January 1765 authorisation was given at the weekly board meeting of the Middlx Hospital for payment for 'repairing and burnishng all over the large picture'. [Gilbert, *Chippendale*, p. 162] In the following year he acted as an arbitrator in a dispute concerning gilding work in the gallery at Moor Park between Sir Lawrence Dundas and Samuel Norman. [Gilbert, *Chippendale*, pp. 158–59] Took out insurance on his house in 1776 amounting to £100. [GL, Sun MS vol. 253, p. 43]

Alseabrooke, George snr, London, upholder (d. by 1719–20). [GL Upholders' Co. records]

Alseabrooke, George jnr, London, upholder (1719–20). Admitted freeman of the Upholders' Co. by patrimony on 13 January 1719–20. [GL, Upholders' Co. records]

Alsford, James, 23 Grove St, Commercial Rd, London, u and cm (1835). [D]

Alsop, Andrew, 28 Bedford St, Covent Gdn, London, upholder (1774–84). Insured with Sun Fire Office in 1783 for £700 cover of which £170 was for utensils, stock and goods. [D; GL, Sun MS vol. 319, p. 149; poll bk]

Alsop, Charles, Leeming St, Mansfield, Notts., cm (1832). [D]

Al(l)sop, Peter & Co., Mansfield, Notts., joiner, cm and u (1828–40). Trading at Nag's Head Yd in 1828; Westgate from 1832–40; and as Peter & Sons at Westgate and Cockpit in 1835. [D]

Alston, Thomas, Lancaster, cm (1812–20). App. to Leonard Redmayne in 1812 and admitted freeman in 1819–20. [Lancaster app. reg. and freemen rolls]

Alston, William, Chapel St, Garstang, Lancs., joiner and cm (1824–28). [D]

Alston, William, Ribchester, Lancs., cm and joiner (1825–34). [D]

Alton, John, 37 Piccadilly, Manchester, cm and u (1828–29). [D] John Cressell traded at this address

Alton, John, Market Pl., Bedale, Yorks., joiner and cm (1834). [D]

Alton, Mat(t)hew & John, 15 Piccadilly, Manchester, cm and u (1824–25). [D]

Alton & Atkinson, Masham, Yorks., joiners, cm and timber merchants (1834). [D]

Alvin, Charles, 60 Cromer St, Gray's Inn Lane Rd and Black Horse Yd, London, broker and cm (1821–23)). Insured with the Sun Fire Office for £200 in 1821 of which £40 was for stock and utensils. In 1823 these sums had risen to £350 of which £280 represented stock and utensils. It was stated that no carpenter's or cabinet work was done at the dwelling house but a workshop was mentioned in Black Horse Yd. [GL, Sun MS vol. 489, ref. 985974; vol. 496, ref. 1003518]

Aman, George, Newland, Northampton, cm (1820–30). [D]

Aman, Richard, Northampton, cm (1838). Declared bankrupt, *Sussex Agricultural Express*, 6 January 1838.

Amber, Francis, Paradise St, Key St, Rotherhithe, London, upholder (1722). Took out a Hand in Hand fire insurance policy in 1722 for £200. [GL, Hand in Hand MS vol. 26, p. 199]

Ambler, Thomas, 20 Mt Pleasant, Gray's Inn Rd, London, cm (1835). [D]

Ambridge, Harry, London, fancy cm (1809–32). Trading at 36 Ironmonger Rd, St Luke's in 1809, but by 1832 at 3 Ratcliff Grove, St Luke's. [D]

Ambrosoni, Francis, 4 Albion Pl., Clerkenwell, London, carver, gilder and looking-glass manufacturer (1839). [D]

Amery, Samuel, Liverpool, u (1761–c. 1812). Son of Thomas Amery, grocer. Admitted freeman of Liverpool on 12 March 1761 by patrimony. The 1812–17 freemen reg. listed him as debtor pauper, dead. [Liverpool freemen reg. and committee bk]

Ames, James, 1 Duke St, Manchester Sq., London, cm and u (1829–35). [D]

Ames, Samuel, 1 and 2 Rosamond Buildings, Islington, London, cm, u, furniture broker and appraiser (1822–39). [D]

Ames, Thomas, 17 Charles St, Goodge St, London, u (1820–32). [D]

Ames, Thomas, 60 Ellerton St, Hoxton, London, cm and u (1827). [D]

Ames, William, 15 Old Bailey, London, cm (1782). Took out a Sun fire insurance policy in 1782 for £100 on his house. [GL, Sun MS vol. 301, p. 186]

Ames, William, Vine Yd, Tooley St, London, cm (1812). On 20 February 1812 insured his stock and utensils with the Sun Fire Office for £150. [GL, Sun MS vol. 457, ref. 867783]

Amory, Jno., Long Sutton, Lincs., cm and builder (1825). [D]

Amos, John, Little Gonerby, Grantham, Lincs., Windsor chairmaker and turner (1814–d. 1842). Chairs known impressed on the seat edge or bottom near splat 'AMOS GRANTHAM'. There is an example at Temple Newsam House, Leeds. [D; *Furn. Hist.*, 1978]

Amos, Thomas, 25 Gloucester St, Hoxton, London, cm and undertaker (1832). [D]

Amphlett, Thomas, Worcester, carver and gilder (1830–35). Recorded at Spring Gdns in 1830 and Love's Grove in 1835. [D] See George Sterry.

Amry, George, Newcastle, cm (1827–38). In 1827 his address is given as Percy St, but by 1833 he was at Barrasbridge. In 1839 trading at 10 Pilgrim St. [D]

Anders, James, 32 Limekiln Lane, Liverpool, cm and butcher (1829). [D]

Anders, Jonathan, Liverpool, joiner and cm (1827–37). Addresses at 19 Strickland St in 1827; 39 Rose Pl. and 11 Wellington St in 1829; 26 Bevington Hill in 1834; 82 Limekiln Lane in 1835; and 19 Stanley St and 52 Limekiln Lane in 1837. [D]

Anderson, —, Long Acre, London, cm (1768). Theft of goods from shop reported in *Public Advertiser*, 2 March 1768.

Anderson, —, Windmill St, Tottenham Ct Rd, London, chairmaker (1803). Subscribed to Sheraton's *Cabinet Dictionary*, 1803.

Anderson, Alexander, London, cm (1793). Subscribed to Sheraton's *Drawing Book*, 1793.

Anderson, Alexander, Rothbury, Northumb., cm and joiner (1828–34). [D]

Anderson, Ambrose, 43 Mincing Lane, London, carver and gilder (1809). [D]

Anderson, Andrew, New Claypath Gates, Durham, u (1772). [*Newcastle Courant*, 4 July 1772]

Anderson, David, 4 Colvell Ct, Rathbone Pl., London, cm (1809). [D]

Anderson, Edward, Beverley, Yorks., cm (1752–90). Took app. named Milburn in 1752. [S of G, app. index; poll bk]

Anderson, George, Moorfields, London, upholder (1755). Admitted freeman of the Upholders' Co. on 5 April 1755. [GL, Upholders' Co. records]

Anderson, George, 17 Frith St, Soho, London, carver and gilder (1808). [D]

Anderson, George, 23 Everett St, Brunswick Sq., London, u and undertaker (1813–20). Business described at Anderson & Co. in 1819. [D]

Anderson, George, Witton St, Northwich, Cheshire, cm and chairmaker (1828–34). [D]

Anderson, Henry, 48 Castle St, Oxford Mkt, London, cm (1793–1808). Subscribed to Sheraton's *Drawing Book*, 1793, and *Cabinet Dictionary*, 1803. [D]

Anderson, J., Newcastle, joiner, cm, looking-glass, picture frame and composition ornament maker (1808–24). In 1808 he moved from Bigg-market to Westgate St. [D; *Newcastle Courant*, 12 November 1808, 17 June 1809]

Anderson, J. jnr, Newcastle, carver and gilder, looking-glass and picture frame maker (1823–33). On 7 June 1823 he announced in the *Durham County Advertiser* that he had opened a shop in Collingwood St 'adjoining the general Coach Office'. He claimed to have had experience 'both in London and Newcastle' and stated that he also executed ship carving. In 1833 his business address was 17 Mosley St and his house 9 Cumberland Row. He placed an advertisement in *Humble's Newcastle Directory*, 1824. [D]

Anderson, James, address unrecorded, cm (1754). Subscribed to Chippendale's *Director*, 1754.

Anderson, James, 96 Eastcheap (or Upper East Smithfield), London, cm (1789–93). [D]

Anderson, James & Robert, 36 Upper East Smithfield, London, brokers of household goods and cm (1808). On 18 July 1808 took out insurance cover on household goods, etc. for £100. [GL, Sun MS vol. 443, ref. 819492]

Anderson, James, Stafford St, Wolverhampton, Staffs., joiner and cm (1780). [D]

Anderson, James, Long Acre, London, cm (1808–27). Trade card in Heal Coll., BM. [D]

Anderson, James, 12 Broker's Alley, Drury Lane, London, bedstead maker (1839). [D]

Anderson, James, 71 Thomas St, Manchester, cm (1838–39). [D]

Anderson, John, Warrington, Lancs., cm (1717–24). In 1717 took app. named Okell and in 1724, Mather. [S of G, app. index]

Anderson, John, Liverpool, cm and carver (before 1746). In the *Maryland Gazette*, 21 October 1746 he announced that he made 'Chairs, Tables, Desks, Bureaus, Dressing Tables, Clock Cases and all kinds of Furniture'. He stated that he was 'late from Liverpool'.

Anderson, John, Little White Lion St, Seven Dials, London, cm (1781). Took out a Sun Insurance policy in 1781 for £100 on his house. [GL, Sun MS vol. 295, p. 602]

Anderson, John, Fanconbergh Ct, Westminster, London, cm (1784). [Poll bk]

Anderson, John, 4 Hanover St, Walworth, London, carver and gilder (1808). [D]

Anderson, John, address unrecorded, cm (1820). Mentioned in accounts for the furnishing of Wynyard Park, Co. Durham for the 4th Marquess of Londonderry. [Durham RO, D/LO/E484]

Anderson, John jnr, 32 Collingwood St, Newcastle, carver and gilder (1827). [D]

Anderson, John, Market St, Newcastle, carver and gilder (1838). [D] Possibly:

Anderson, John, Westgate St, Newcastle, cm and u (1827–38). Trading at Westgate St, 1827–34; 17 Moseley St in 1834; and Market St in 1838. [D]

Anderson, John, Knaresborough, Yorks., joiner, cm and builder (1828–37). Trading at Windsor Lane in 1828 but by 1837 his address had changed to High St. [D]

Anderson, John Wilson, 18 Ivegate, Bradford, Yorks., carver, gilder and artist (1834–37). [D]

Anderson, John, 59 Foregate St, Worcester, carver and gilder (1835–40). Trading as Jno. & Son in 1835. [D]

Anderson, Jonathan & Perry, Joshua, 59 Foregate St, Worcester, paper hangers, decorative house sign and furniture painters, carvers, gilders and frame makers (1820–33). Advertised themselves as successors to Mr Churchill (probably James Churchill, herald painter, of The Tithing, Worcester); and cleaned, repaired and varnished pictures, silvered looking-glasses and supplied paper hangings. An unusual George IV giltwood pier-glass is known with their trade label affixed which came from Elmley Castle, Worcester. [Christie's, 11 June 1981, lot 38] The business was carried on after 1835 under the style 'J. Anderson and Son'. [D] Carried out work at Westwood Park, Droitwich, Worcs., supplying picture frames to J. S. Pakington amounting to £9 17s 14d in 1828–29, and £19 4s 9d in 1831–32. The receipt for the latter amount indicates that it is due to 'the estate of Messrs. Anderson and Perry'. [Worcs. RO, 2309/705:380/56 and 380-56-V] Account for work done at Powick Court, Worcs., dated 6 April 1830, includes a picture frame supplied to J. S. Russell. This patron changed his name to Pakington on inheriting Westwood Park, near Droitwich, and subsequently became first Lord Hampton. [Worcs. RO, 2309/705:380/18(i)]

Anderson, Joseph, 19 George's Ct, Clerkenwell, London, water gilder (1808). [D]

Anderson, Ralph, Houghton-Le-Spring, Co. Durham, joiner, cm and auctioneer (1815–27). [D; Durham County Advertiser, 29 July 1815]

Anderson, Richard, Garratt Rd, Manchester, cm and u (1840). Father probably Robert Anderson of Preston. [D]

Anderson, Robert, Lancaster and Bradford, cm (1772–92). Admitted freeman of Lancaster in 1772, but in 1784 is recorded in the Lancaster poll bk as residing in Bradford. Named in the Gillow records, 1789–92. [Lancaster freemen rolls and poll bk; Westminster Ref. Lib., Gillow]

Anderson, Robert, Liverpool, cm (1811–23). Trading at 35 Frederick St in 1811, but by 1813 was at 6 Frederick St. [D]

Anderson, Robert, Preston, Lancs. and Manchester, u (1818–40). Son of Robert Anderson of Preston. Freeman of Preston. Trading at 8 Spring Gdns in 1818, but by 1828 was at 10 Alfred St and in 1834 at no. 19. By 1836 he had moved to Manchester and was trading from 40 Brook St, Chorlton-on-Medlock, and from no. 56 in 1838–40. His six sons included Richard and Robert, both u. [D; Preston Guild records]

Anderson, Robert, Carpenter St, South Shields, Co. Durham, carver and gilder (1827). [D]

Anderson, Robert, Twickenham, London, cm, u and paper hanger (1826–39). Recorded at Church St, 1826–32, and Back Lane in 1839. [D]

Anderson, Thomas, Carlisle, Cumb., u (1793). [D]

Anderson, Thomas, address unrecorded, cm (1803). Subscribed to Sheraton's Cabinet Dictionary, 1803.

Anderson, Thomas, 98 Dale St, Liverpool, carver and victualler (1810–11). [D]

Anderson, Thomas, Paradise St, Liverpool, u (1814–24). Successor to Mathew Gregson, u, whose foreman he had been before taking over the business in 1814. He had served Gregson for twelve years prior to this date. His number in Paradise St was 33 in 1814, but subsequently changed to 30 in 1816 and 35 in 1818. [D; Liverpool Mercury, 14 October 1814]

Anderson, Thomas, 10 Duke St, Liverpool, u (1827). [D]

Anderson, W., 44 Redcross St, London, cm (1826). [D]

Anderson, W. S., 22 Portland St, Hull, Yorks., cm (1838–40). [D]

Anderson, William, Louth, Lincs, cm (1754). Took app. named Foster in 1754. [S of G, app. index]

Anderson, William, Lancaster, cm (1779–1807). App. to A. Hudson in 1779. Admitted freeman in 1806–07. [Lancaster app. reg. and freemen rolls]

Anderson, William, 27 Circus St, Marylebone, London, cm and u (1820–39). [D]

Anderson, William, New Rd, Clitheroe, Lancs., joiner, cm and house builder (1824). [D]

Anderson, William, 24 Fleet St, London, writing desk and dressing case maker (1829). [D]

Anderson, William, 18 Bromsgrove St, Birmingham, maker of portable desks and dressing cases (1830). [D]

Anderson, —, Davies St, Liverpool, cm (1790). [D]

Anderson, —, Lancaster, carver (1816). Named in the Gillow records as carving trusses on bookcase. [Westminster Ref. Lib., Gillow vol. 344/100, p. 2006]

Anderton, —, Chesterfield Rd, Nottingham, chairmaker (1835). [D]

Anderton, Charles, 19 Paul St, Finsbury Sq., London, cabinet and chairmaker (1808). [D]

Anderton, Henry, Liverpool, cm and upholder (1811–19). In 1811 traded from 18 Sir Thomas Buildings and in the same year is recorded at 2 Marble St with a partner called Jamieson. An address at 52 London Rd is listed in 1813, but from the following year the Marble St address was used. Retired from business in 1819 and on 9 November that year an auction sale of his stock was held. This consisted of 'handsome Mahogany Trafalgar & other Chairs, Patent Dining, Card, Loo, Pembroke, Snap & other Tables, Secretaires, Bookcases, Chests of Drawers, Wardrobes, Sideboards, Sofas, Couches, a Spring Clock by Roskell, an Eight Day Ditto, Four-post & Camp Bedsteads, Hangings & Window Curtains, Prime Goose-feather Beds, Hair Mattresses, Paillasses, Children's Cribs, Night Chairs, Brussels, Kidderminster & other Carpets, Chimney Piece & Dressing Glasses, Chamber Articles, Polished Fire Irons etc.' Also on offer were 'about 400 Dozen Fancy WALL PAPERS & BORDERS'. On 17 November his stock of timber including 'fancy Hardwood Veneers', brasswork, benches, tools and stoves were also auctioned. Despite these sales which indicate a termination of trading, his name continues to be included in local directories until 1823. [D; Liverpool Mercury, 5 and 12 November 1819]

Anderton, John, 10 Elliot St, Liverpool, joiner and cm (1834). [D]

Anderton, Thomas, Liverpool, carver (1806–11). In 1806 in business at Bolton St but by 1811 at 9 New Johnson St. [D; Liverpool Chronicle, 28 May 1806]

Anderton, William, Liverpool, u and cm (b.1750–d.1812). Trading on his own account as early as 1777, in which year he was declared bankrupt. Had recommenced business by 1781 when he was trading from 17 Dale St. By 1790 had premises at 18 and 19 Paradise St. In 1796 his addresses are given as Harrington Park Rd, with a cabinet and paper warehouse at 41 Paradise St. In October of that year he was declared bankrupt for a second time and on 25 October his stock was sold by auction. It consisted mainly of upholstery materials, a quantity of timber and veneers and workshop equipment. He is once more recorded in trade in local directories by 1800 with an address at 68 Maguire St, Bevington Bush. This changed in 1803 to 7 Meadow St, Rose Pl., and the following year to Mile End, Scotland Rd, which may have been his house. His final address from 1806 was 3 Haymarket. In August of that year he announced in the press that he was recommencing business from that address. He stated that he had 'converted the apartment over his warehouse into a spacious room, which is in reserve for the reception of every description of goods intended to be sold by auction or otherwise (where an advance on deposits may be had if required)'. He also offered to use his best endeavours to dispose of land and buildings for clients. He died on 13 June 1812 at Mile End, aged 62. [D; *Gents Mag.*, May 1777; *Williamson's Liverpool Advertiser*, 6 June 1777; *Billinge's Liverpool Advertiser*, 17 and 24 October 1796, 16 July 1798; *Liverpool Chronicle*, 6 August 1806; *Liverpool Mercury*, 26 June 1812, 28 June 1816]

Anderton, William, Bromsgrove St, Birmingham, cabinet case maker (1835–39). Recorded at no. 18 in 1835. [D]

Andre, Edward, Brighton, Sussex, u and cm (1832–40). Recorded at 20 Devonshire Pl. in 1832, but the number had changed to 39 by 1839. [D]

Andre, Percy James, Beverley, Yorks., cm (1799). [Poll bk]

Andrew, Charles, High St, Royston, Herts., ironmonger and u (1838). [D]

Andrew, George, Prospect St, Bradford, Yorks., cm (1837). [D]

Andrew, John, Bourne, Lincs., carpenter, joiner and cm (1798). [D]

Andrew, John, Over, Middlewich, Cheshire, cm (1828). [D]

Andrew, John, Birmingham, cm and u (1828–35). Trading at 55 Edgbaston St in 1828 and Lombard St in 1835. [D]

Andrew, Joseph, Beverley, Yorks., cm (1774). [Poll bk]

Andrew, Nathaniel, Market Lane, Selby, Yorks., joiner, builder and cm (1831–37). [D]

Andrew, Philip, 33 Hart St, Manchester, cm (1808). [D]

Andrew, Thomas, Coggeshall, Essex, cm and u (1777–1824). Between 1777 and 1784 insured goods and stock with the Sun Fire Office for various sums ranging from £160 in 1777 to £300 in 1780. Owner of freehold property, 1780–83. In partnership with Bridge in 1823. Andrew's will is recorded in the following year. [D: GL, Sun MS vol. 254, p. 428; vol. 284, p. 293; vol. 324, p. 152; Essex RO, Q/RJ1/9, 10, 11; *Wills at Chelmsford*, vol. 3, p. 7]

Andrew, Thomas, 55 Edgbaston St, Birmingham, cm (1823). [D]

Andrew, William,, Spilsby, Lincs., cm and joiner (1835). [D]

Andrewes, Grace, 4 Colston's Pl., Milk St, Bristol, u (1831). [D]

Andrew(e)s, Mary, 25 Baldwin St, Bristol, cm (1819–26). Took over the business of her husband Thomas Andrews on his death. [D]

Andrewes, Thomas, 25 Baldwin St, Bristol, cm and upholder (1781–d.1819). In 1785 supplied a considerable quantity of fine inlaid furniture for the Mansion House, Queen's Sq. The cost of Andrewes's work amounted to £594 1s 9d. Although this building was destroyed in the riots of 1831 a few pieces of the furniture survive including one of a set of ten shield back chairs inlaid with the city arms now at the Georgian House Museum. Two pier tables from this commission similarly inlaid are in the present Mansion House. A fine inlaid cabinet

came on to the market in 1980 with a pencilled inscription indicating that it was made by 'Josh. N Slade apprentice to Thomas Andrewes' in 1811. His wife Mary took over the business in 1819 [D; poll bk; *Furn. Hist.*, 1976]

Andrews, —, Ipswich, Suffolk, cm (1793). Subscribed to Sheraton's *Drawing Book*, 1793.

Andrews, Anthony, 68 Fore St, London, cabinet founder (1784). [D]

Andrew(s), Christopher, Old Meeting Pl., Birmingham, carver and gilder (1828–39). Recorded at no. 13 in 1828; no. 12, 1830–35; and at 29 Exeter Row in 1839, also as picture frame and looking-glass manufacturer. [D]

Andrews, Edwin, West St, Exeter, Devon, cm (1833). On 18 June 1833 a son Edwin was bapt. at St Mary Major. [PR (bapt.)]

Andrews, George, 7 Charing Cross, London, carver, gilder, printseller and looking-glass manufactory owner (1806–15). Recommended in Duncan Macdonald, *The New London Family Book*, 1812. [D; Wills, *Looking-Glasses*]

Andrews, George, 36 Worcester St, Birmingham, cm and u (1839). [D]

Andrews, Henry, Norwich, cm (1762). Admitted freeman on 9 November 1762. His father, John Andrews, was a barber. [Norwich freemen reg.]

Andrews, Henry, Gt Castle St, Oxford Mkt, London, chair, sofa and invalid chair maker (1827–29). [D]

Andrews, John, Parish of St Stephen, Bristol, cm (1784). [Poll bk]

Andrews, John, Cambridge, carver and gilder (1808–12). Small payments recorded for gilding in Trinity College accounts.

Andrews, John, Birmingham, cm, u and clothes dealer (1816–30). Trading at Worcester St in 1816–18 but by 1830 had moved to 55 Edgbaston St. [D]

Andrews, John W., 6 Old Compton St, Soho, London, cm and u (1826–29). [D]

Andrew, Jonathan, Newport St, Worcester, cm (1818–35). Admitted freeman in 1818. [Worcester freemen rolls]

Andrews, Matthew, parish of St Nicholas, Bristol, cm (1774). [Poll bk]

Andrews, S., 3 London St, Fitzroy Sq., London, carver and gilder (1826–29). [D]

Andrews, Thomas, address unrecorded, u (1795). Supplied fabrics, wallpapers and furnished several bedrooms at Ammerdown. [*C. Life*, 16 February 1929, p. 222]

Andrews, Thomas Ward, Stamford, Lincs., cm and u (1813–34). Recorded 'opposite the Post Office', 1813–34, and in High Street, 1822. Admitted freeman in 1813. Trade card in Heal Coll., BM. [D; Stamford freemen rolls]

Andrews, William, 44 Worcester St, Birmingham, cm (1835). [D]

Andrews & Hilliam, High St, Stamford, Lincs., cm (1819). [D]

Angeir, Charles, Long Acre, London, carver (1749). [Poll bk]

Angel, John jnr, Fore St, Totnes, Devon, cm and u (1837–38). [D; poll bk]

Angel, Peter, 28 Gt Prescot St, Goodman's Fields, London, cm (1777). Insured with Sun Fire Office for £700 of which £50 covered utensils and stock. [GL, Sun MS vol. 256, p. 66]

Angell, Edward, Shoe Lane, London, cm (1792–96). Took out insurance with the Sun Fire Office for £300 on 3 November 1792. Subscribed to Sheraton's *Drawing Book*, 1793. Declared bankrupt on 4 April 1795. [GL, Sun MS, vol. 391, p. 343; *Billinge's Liverpool Advertiser*, 6 April 1795; 24 August and 5 September 1796]

Angell, Thomas, Red Cross St, Southwark, London, u and cm (1820). [D]

Angier, John, London, cm (1806). [Poll bk]

Angland, William, Star Ct, Westminster, London, chairmaker (1774). [Poll bk]

Angold, George, 7 Bencroft's Pl., Mile End, London, cm (1808). [D]

Angold, Henry, London, cm and u (1827–39). Recorded at 4 John St, Whitechapel in 1827 and 6 Cambridge Rd in 1839. [D]

Angold, John, London, cm, chairmaker and u (1827–35). Trading at 5 John St, Whitechapel in 1827 and at 2 Norfolk St, Goodge St in 1832. [D]

Angold, Samuel, 10 Sarah's Pl., Old St Rd, London, cm and u (1827). [D]

Angrove, William, Cornwall, cm (1783). Residuary beneficiary of William Angrove of St Columb. [Cornwall RO, DD. SHM. 648/1]

Angus, Abraham Cooke, Bigg Mkt, Newcastle, cm (1834). [D]

Angus, James, Shug Lane, Piccadilly, London, cm and upholder (1790–93). Subscribed to Sheraton's *Drawing Book*, 1793. [D]

Angus, John, 81 Newgate St and Low Friar St, Newcastle, cm (1827–28). [D]

Angus, Joseph, 18 Aldermanbury, London, looking-glass warehouse owner (1790). [Wills, *Looking-Glasses*]

Angus, Joseph, Strand, London, carver and gilder (1802). Declared bankrupt, *Billinge's Liverpool Advertiser*, 10 December 1802.

Angus, William, Groat Mkt, Newcastle, carver and gilder (1833–38). Trading at Fletcher's entry in 1834, and Low Friar St in 1838 as cm. [D]

Ankins, John, French Row, City Rd, London, carver and gilder (1808). [D]

Annely, John, parish of St Stephen, Bristol, upholder (1734). [Poll bk]

Annet, Thomas, Newcastle, joiner and cm (1767–78). In December 1767 moved from Silver St to Pilgrim St. [D; *Newcastle Courant*, 5 December 1767, 27 February 1773, 2 December 1775, 27 January 1776, 10 February 1776]

Annett, J., 3 George St, Sloane St, London, u (1820). [D]

Anning, John, Broad St, Lyme Regis, Dorset, cm and u (1829–40). Married a Miss Reader of Lyme in December 1829. Inscription recorded on drawer of mahogany bow-front toilet mirror: 'Mr. John Anning Cabinet maker Lyme 1833 Dorset'. [D; *Exeter Flying Post*, 10 December 1829]

Anning, Owen, parish of St Edmund, Exeter, Devon, cm (1829–32). [PR (bapt.), 8 February 1829; poll bk]

Anone, Francis, 26 High Holborn, London, carver, gilder, picture frame, barometer, print and painting dealer (1803). Insured on 10 November 1803 with the Sun Fire Office for £400 of which £200 was for stock and utensils. [GL, Sun MS vol. 430, ref. 754090]

Anott, George & Robert, Highgate, Beverley, Yorks., cm (1840). [D]

Ansell, John, Marylebone, London, carver and gilder (1780). Declared bankrupt in 1780. [Bailey's list of bankrupts]

Ansell, Robert, Edward St, Cavendish Sq., London, carver and gilder (1767–80). In 1777 insured his workshop in Edward St with utensils and stock with the Sun Fire Office for £600. Insured house in Margaret St, Cavendish Sq. in 1775 for £500. Subscribed to James Paine's *Noblemen's and Gentlemen's Seats*, 1767. Bankrupt November 1780. [GL, Sun MS vol. 243, p. 358; vol. 259, p. 313; *Leicester Journal*, 16 November 1780] Carried out minor work and supplied a picture frame to Audley End, Essex for Sir John Griffin Griffin, amounting to £2 2s 6d. [Essex RO, D/DBy/A38/21] Carried out work for Blenheim Palace, Oxon., where the account books list the following commissions. In September 1773, 'sent to Mr. Ansells 2 Octagon Marble Slabs'. In 1774,

'Sent to Mr. Ansells 2 Table frames came out of Winter Drawing Room to be gilt'. On 23 May 1774, 'Came from Mr. Ansells in 2 Large Cases 2 table frames Gilt with Burnish'd Gold; 3 Cornices Gold, for the Winter Drawing Room'. On 18 July 1774, 'Came from Mr. Ansells 2 Large Cases with Pier Glasses, frames for the winter drawing Room. A fine picture frame for Duchs of Richmond's picture'. On 9 December 1776 from Ansells — 5 palm freezes with wreaths of flowers gilt in Burnish'd Gold — 2 Ornaments with Medallions'. On 7 August 1778, 'Came from Mr. Ansells 4 leather covers for the tables in the Grand Cabinett'. [*C. Life*, 23 January 1975]

Ansell, Samuel, Birmingham, cabinet, dressing case and portable desk maker (1822–39). Recorded at Gt Charles St in 1822, no. 147, 1828–30; 28 Kenion St in 1835 as leather cabinet case maker; and Kenyon St in 1839. [D]

Ansell, William, Cambridge, cm (1815–40). On 21 April 1815 he advertised his intention of going into partnership with John Bedells, builder, but on 30 June he announced that the partnership was not going ahead and that he would open a shop in Petty Cury on 8 July. After 1834 he traded from Fitzwilliam St and Trumpington St. [D; *Cambridge Chronicle*, 21 April, 8 July 1815; poll bks]

Ansell, William, Fakenham, Norfolk, cm and u (1830–39). Trading at Norwich St, 1830–36, but by 1839 had moved to High St. [D]

Ansley, Thomas, Cheapside, Birmingham, cabinet case and inkstand maker (1805–08). [D]

Anslow, James, New St, Wellington, Salop, chairmaker (1835). [D]

Anslow, John, New St, Wellington, Salop, chairmaker (1822–28). Trading also as furniture broker in 1822. [D]

Anslow, Thomas, Market Sq., Shrewsbury, Salop, cm and u (1822–40). Recorded also at Wyle Cop in 1822 and Corn Mkt in 1828. A Thomas Anslow, chairmaker, was listed at Corn Mkt in 1822. On 15 February 1833 his wife Jane died aged 34. Declared bankrupt, *Chester Chronicle*, 11 September 1840. [D; *Chester Courant*, 26 February 1833]

Anson, G., Broadmead, Bristol, carver and gilder (before 1798). Ceased business in June 1798 when his stock and tools were sold by auction. The stock included 'a capital painting on plate glass, in a burnished-gold frame' and 'looking-glasses, in gilt and mahogany frames of various sizes'. Amongst his equipment was 'an exceedingly good silvering table complete'. [*Farley's Bristol Journal*, 16 June 1798]

Anson, George, 17 Bowling Green Lane, Clerkenwell, London, carver and gilder (1808). [D]

Anson, John, 'The Bell', Broadmead, Bristol, carver and gilder (1793–94). [D]

Anstel, William, 5 Adam St, West Portman Sq., London, u (1808). [D]

Anstey, George Thomas & Co., (after 1817 Anstey, Pearce & Co.), London, printed furniture warehouse owners (1801–20). Trading at 343 Strand in 1801 and at 24 Old Bond St in 1817. [D]

Anstice, William, Bristol, upholder (1799–1801). Recorded at Johnny Ball Lane, 1799–1800, and Kingstons buildings in 1801. [D]

Anstice, William, Bristol, u and undertaker (1818–26). Trading at Brunswick Sq. Burial Ground from 1818–20; 29 Marlborough St, 1821–22; and 11 Paul St, Kingsdown, from 1823. [D]

Anstie, Samuel, parish of St James, Bristol, cm (1784). [Poll bk]

Anston, Daniel, Sandwich, Kent, cm (1784). [D]

Anthony, Mark, London, cm (c. 1690). [Heal]

Anthony, William, 95 Sparling St, Liverpool, cm (1827). [D]

Antrobus, James, Manchester, cm (1725). Took app. named Dean in 1725. [S of G, app. index]

Anty, Joseph, Southgate, London, rustic chair manufacturer (1838). [D]

Anyon, John & Co., 17 Eaton St, Pimlico, London, carver and gilder (1839). [D]

Apletree, Frederick, 68 Bull St, Birmingham, cm and u (1830–39). Recorded at no. 68 in 1830, and no. 47, 1835–39, also with a house at Erdington Slade. [D]

Appleby, —, Stockton, Co. Durham, cm (1793). Subscribed to Sheraton's *Drawing Book*, 1793.

Appleby, John, Newcastle, u (1731–41). Admitted freeman on 30 July 1731 by servitude. [Newcastle freemen reg. and poll bk]

Appleby, John, Thistle Green, Stockton, Co. Durham, u and paper hanger (1827). [D]

Appleby, John, High St, Burton-on-Trent, Staffs., turner and chairmaker (1818–35). Trading in partnership with Joseph Appleby in 1834. [D]

Appleby, Joseph James, High St, Burton-on-Trent, Staffs., turner and chairmaker (1818–34). [D]

Appleby, Joseph jnr, Burton-on-Trent, Staffs., turner and chairmaker (1828–35). Trading at Cat St in 1828 and High St in 1835. [D]

Appleby, Robert, North Shields, Northumb., cm, joiner and u (1817–34). Declared bankrupt, *London Gazette*, 26 November 1817. Recorded at Clive St, 1817–34, and 66 Camden St in 1834. [D]

Appleby, W., Loft St, Grimsby, Lincs., joiner and cm (1831). [D]

Appleby, William, Lincoln, cm (1837). [Poll bk]

Appleton, C., Halifax, Yorks., cm (1793). Subscribed to Sheraton's *Drawing Book*, 1793.

Appleton, John, Oldham Ct, Oldham St with shop at 4 Richmond Row, Liverpool, cm (1829). [D]

Appleton, Samuel, Rock St, Bury, Lancs., joiner and cm (1816–18). [D]

Appleton, Thomas, 173 Drury Lane, London, turner and bedstead maker (1811–19). [D]

Appleton, William, Hull, Yorks., cm and u (1803–06). At Silver St, 1803–05, but by 1806 had moved to Whitefriarsgate. Subscribed to Sheraton's *Cabinet Dictionary*, 1803. [D]

Appleton, William, Pilgrim St, Newcastle, joiner and cm (1811). [D]

Appleton, William, Guisborough, Skelton, Yorks., joiner and cm (1828). [D]

Appletree, Charles, St Giles, London, u (1696). Married Jane Haynes at Holy Trinity Church in 1696. [PR]

Appletree, John, 8 Denmark St, Soho, London, cabinet and chairmaker (1809–17). [D]

Appletree, M., Bull St, Birmingham, cm, broker and u (1830). [D]

Appletree, Richard, London, upholder (1703). App. to Michael Brett, and admitted freeman of the Upholders' Co. by servitude on 1 December 1703. [GL, Upholders' Co. records]

Appley, Robert, Lancaster, cm (1749–54). App. to R. Thorney in 1749, and admitted freeman, 1753–54. Later moved to Leeds. [Lancaster app. reg. and freemen rolls]

Appley, Robert snr, Nottingham, cm (1784). Had a son, Robert, working in London as a cm. [Poll bk]

Appley, Robert jnr, London, cm (1784). Son of Robert Appley snr, cm of Nottingham. [Poll bk]

Appley, William, Lancaster, cm (1749–98). App. to R. Thorney in 1749 and admitted freeman, 1753–54. Moved to Nottingham where he was established by 1784. On 31 July of that year he advertised for a craftsman in *Nottingham Journal*. [D; Lancaster app. reg., freemen rolls and poll bk]

Appleyard, George, Church St, Conisbrough, Yorks., cm and u, paper hanger and decorator. Mahogany and satinwood

Davenport at Cusworth Hall Museum bears this maker's label.

Appleyard, Joseph, Conisbrough, Yorks., joiner and cm (1834). [D]

Appleyard, Thomas, Huddersfield, Yorks., cm etc. (1805). [D]

Appleyard, Thomas, 6 Hunt's Bank, Manchester, joiner, cm and builder (1825). [D]

Arabin, William, 21 Brill Cresc., London, u (1839). [D]

Aray, Robert, Sheffield, Yorks., carver (1755). Took app. named Kirk in 1755. [S of G, app. index]

Arber Stanton, Michael, 12 Little Newport St, London, cm (1785). On 25 June 1785 insured his household goods with the Sun Fire Office for £100 and his utensils and stock for an identical sum. [GL, Sun MS vol. 328, p. 595]

Arbuckle, Charles, St Alban's St, Pall Mall, London, u (1765–66). Fellow of the Society for Arts and Manufactures.

Arbunot, Jacob, London, cm and looking-glass manufacturer (1709–d. 1722). In 1709 his address is recorded as the south side of Long Acre. He then moved to near Hungerford Mkt, Strand, but in 1715 established himself at 'The Royal Cabinet' over against Church Ct, Strand. Almost immediately after moving he suffered a fire at this new premises. It was reported in *The Post Man*, 27 October 1715, that 'a great many of his Glasses have been broke, having had not time to move, the Fire being all round him, as well as many of his Household Goods'. He was dead by 21 February 1722 when his son and executor, James, was in charge. The business appears to have closed down in 1727 for an announcement in the *Daily Post* of 22 March refers to 'leaving off Trade' and the disposal of stock including pier-glasses. [Poll bk; GL, Sun MS vol. 5, ref. 6529; Heal; Wills, *Looking-Glasses*]

Arbuthnot, Philip, Villers St, Strand, London, cm, japanner and looking-glass seller (1702–27). One of the most fashionable furniture suppliers of the first decades of the 18th century. In June 1702 he was undertaking repairs to marquetry furniture and executing gilding at Drayton House, Northants., amounting to £52 9s 6d. In the period May to July of the following year he was engaged in 'making up an Indian Chest of yr. owne boards, finding locks & hindges and painting the 2 ends' for the same patron at a cost of £8 10s. His best known commission was probably executed at about the same time, for in 1703 he petitioned to be paid for 'two large sconces with double branches finely gilded, being three foot deep scoloped, diamond cutt and engraved embollished with crimson and gold Mosaic work with flowers on the bodys of the Glasses' which were executed as a present from Queen Anne for the Emperor of Morocco. These cost £12 7s. The sum of £500 insurance cover taken out in 1712 is probably indicative of the flourishing state of the business. On 14 January 1716 however an advertisement appeared in the *Daily Courant* giving notice that he intended to 'leave off his trade'. His stock included 'all Sorts of Looking Glasses Glass Pannels and sconces, Cabinets both English and Japan, Scrutores, Tables, Stands, Writing Desks, Book Cases, Card Tables, Dressing Suits and Chests of Drawers both of Japan and Wallnet-tree; likewise carved and Gilded Sconces, and all Sorts of China, Tea Tables, Screens and Fire-Screens, Oyl Pictures, Strong Boxes . . .'. Despite this announcement he continued to trade and in 1719 was supplying goods on a very grand scale to the Marquis of Annandale. One commission alone came to £222 9s while another account details the supply of mirrors with walnut and glass and gilt frames and 'a fine large pair of Sconces in glass & gold frames & carved as gold heads'. This latter item cost £24 alone and the total was £97 5s. His death was recorded in April 1727 and it was indicated that the premises that he occupied were available to let. [V&A archives; PRO, LC9/

282; GL, Hand in Hand MS vol. 10, ref. 784; *DEF*; Heal] B.A.

Arbuthnot, Thomas, King's Lynn, Norfolk, upholder (1723). Took app. named Saffery in 1723. [S of G, app. index]

Archard, Thomas, 6 Windmill St, Tottenham Ct Rd, London, cm and u (1839). [D]

Archbald, Adam, 3 Hatton Walk, Hatton St, London, joiner and bedstead maker (1787). On 12 July 1787 insured goods in his house and workshop for £400 with the Sun Fire Office. [GL, Sun MS vol. 346, p. 2971]

Archbald, E., 45 Greek St, London, u (1826). [D]

Archbell, John, Tadcaster, Yorks., joiner and cm (1834). [D]

Archbell, Thomas, Market Pl., Tadcaster, Yorks., joiner and/or cm (1837). [D]

Archer, Charles, Tewkesbury, Glos., cm (1822–39). Trading as cm, u and builder at Barton St in 1822; as cm and u at High St in 1830, and as cm and chairmaker there in 1839. [D]

Archer, Edward, Bradford, Yorks., cm and u (1830–37). In 1830 at 16 Cannon St and in 1837 at Chapel Lane. [D]

Archer, George, Barton St, Tewkesbury, Glos., cm and u (1830). [D]

Archer, Isaac, Without-the-Gate, Scarborough, Yorks., cm (1831). [D]

Archer, Jane, Cheapside, Liverpool, chairmaker (1805–07). At 68 Cheapside in 1805 but by 1807 the number had changed to 69. Successor to Ralph Archer. [D]

Archer, John, Chelmsford, Essex, cm (1826). [Maldon poll bk]

Archer, John, 64 Old Nichol St, Shoreditch, London, cm (1832–35). [D]

Archer, Ralph, Liverpool, chairmaker (1796–1803). At 1 Jewlers Ct, Chapel St in 1796, but by 1800 had moved to 68 Cheapside, Dale St. Jane Archer was his successor at this address. [D]

Archer, Robert, High St, Oxford, carver and gilder (1798–1808). Subscribed to Sheraton's *Cabinet Dictionary*, 1803. [D; poll bk]

Archer, Thomas, parish of St Saviour, York, cm (1808–20). Son of Margaret Archer. App. to Martha Doughty on 10 March 1808, and admitted freeman as a cm in 1820. [York app. reg. and freemen rolls]

Archer, Thomas, 25 St Sepulchre St, Scarborough, Yorks., cm (1830–40). [D]

Archer, Tristram, St Sepulchre St, Scarborough, Yorks., cm and u (1823–31). [D]

Archer, William, London, u (1793–1803). Subscribed to Sheraton's *Drawing Book*, 1793, and *Cabinet Dictionary*, 1803.

Archibald, Adam, Hatton Wall, Holborn, London, bedstead maker (1795–97). Declared bankrupt, March 1795. [*Billinge's Liverpool Advertiser*, 9 March 1795, 6 November 1797]

Archibald, Alex., 10 Little Duke St, Westminster, London, chair and sofa maker (1827). [D]

Ardean, John, Lymm, Altrincham, Cheshire, cm (1828). [D]

Arde(a)n, Thomas, King St, Knutsford, Cheshire, cm (1822–40). [D]

Arderne, Ralph Henry, 147 High St, Southwark, London, cm (1829–30). Declared bankrupt, November 1830. [D; *Liverpool Mercury*, 3 December 1830]

Ardran, Ann, 7 Lawrence St, Liverpool, u (1839). [D]

Are, Thomas, Oxford Rd, London, u (1809). [D]

Argall, William, Milford St, Salisbury, Wilts., carver and gilder (1839). [D]

Argent, John, 164 Tottenham Ct Rd, London, u and cm (1820–26). [D]

Arger, George, Philips Pl., Duckenfield St, Liverpool, cm (1834). [D]

Argles, Edward, Maidstone, Kent, then London, u and cm (1795–1813). Son of Thomas Argles. Traded from an address in High St, Maidstone until 1810. On 22 September 1804 took app. named George Johnson for seven years at a premium of £80. In *Maidstone Journal*, 29 May 1810, however, he asked for offers for his premises described as a 'freehold messuage with the Yard and Garden', and on 25 September of the same year an auction sale of his stock was advertised. The reason for selling up was 'his having taken the business of Dr BUTLER of Catherine-street in the Strand'. He was already in possession of the business of Thomas Butler in the following year. This extensive and fashionable business specialising in patent furniture was at 13 and 14, Catherine St, Strand. Argles must have taken over Butler's patrons who included many persons of consequence. To meet this fashionable demand Argles offered to execute designs 'in the Egyptian, Etruscan, Greek & Chinese manner'. He described himself as 'Upholsterer & Cabinet-maker to the King & Queen, their Royal Highnesses Prince, Princess & Princess Charlotte of Wales, Duke of York & Princesses'. While this assertion was probably made on the basis of past custom of Thomas Butler's business, Argles did attract Royal patronage. In 1811 he supplied the Prince of Wales with 'very elegant Royal Library Writing Tables made in fine Rosewood banded with Satin-wood, supported on brass pillars, fitted with draws, writing materials etc'. For this £38 15s 6d was charged, while a 'handsome leather cover' for the table cost £2 2s more. The extensive nature of the manufactory is reflected in the insurance cover of £4,500 taken out on 13 July 1812. This covered 'Stock & utensils in dwelling house being two houses with workshop, warehouse (no store for drying feathers)' amounting to £3,400 in value, £100 for the stock of glass and £1,000 for the 'stock, utensils in his upper woodyard Saxony'. As part of his business he undertook funerals, making his own coffins and shrouds. Argles's success in London was however short-lived. In 1813 he was declared bankrupt. His stock in trade was valued at £8,500 and his initial capital £1,000. [D; poll bk; RA 25328; *Maidstone Journal*, 29 May, 25 September 1810; S of G, app. index; GL, Sun MS vol. 455, ref. 871839; PRO, B/43] B.A.

Argles, Thomas, Week St, Maidstone, Kent, cm, auctioneer and upholder (1761–95). Father of Edward Argles and in the 1790s the business traded as T. Argles & Son. In the late 1780s employed a Thomas Greenstead as a yearly hired servant and on 1 January 1792 took app. named Samuel Larkin at a premium of £62. In 1784 insurance cover of £1,500 was taken out with the Sun Fire Office, £950 of this being in respect of utensils and stock suggesting a fairly large manufactory by provincial standards. [Poll bk; *Maidstone Journal*, 6 January 1795; GL, Sun MS vol. 324, p. 644; GL, P83/MRY1/869/1741]

Aris, John, Balscot, Oxon., cane chairmaker (d. 1761). [Bodleian Lib., index of wills, 19 May 1761]

Arkell, John, Burford, Oxon., cm (1802). [Oxford poll bk]

Arkell & Wheeler, 84½ High St, Cheltenham, Glos., cm (1839). [D]

Arkles(s), William, Evesham, Worcs., cm (1818–20). Recorded as joiner and cm at Vine St in 1820. [D; poll bk]

Arkwright, William, Clitheroe, Lancs., joiner, cm and house builder (1822–23). Trading at Wellgate in 1822 and New Rd in 1823. [D]

Arlidge, Abraham, 22 High St, Brompton, Kent, cm and u (1832–40). [D]

Armes, John, Aylsham, Norfolk, cm and u (1822). [D]

Armes, William, Westgate, Grantham, Lincs., cm and u (1819–28). Trading also as a paper hanger in 1826. [D]

Armes & Cranwell, High St, Grantham, Lincs., cm, u, paper hangers and undertakers (1835). [D]

Armisted, James, Lancaster (1795–99). Named in the Gillow records in connection with a press bed. [Westminster Ref. Lib., Gillow vol. 344/97, p. 1370]

Armitage, George, 175 Chapel St, Salford, Lancs., carver and gilder (1836). [D]

Armitage, John, 48 Long Acre, London, upholder and cm (1773–76). In 1775 insured his house with the Sun Fire Office for £300. Declared bankrupt, November 1776. [D; GL, Sun MS vol. 244, p. 57; *Sussex Weekly Advertiser*, 25 November 1776]

Armitage, John, London, upholder (1784–88). At 9 Poland St in 1784 but by 1786 had moved to 22 Silver St, Golden Sq. On 26 April that year he insured his household goods at the latter address for £200 and his utensils, stock and goods in trust for £500. In December 1788 he was declared bankrupt. [D; poll bk; GL, Sun MS vol. 336, p. 292; *Williamson's Liverpool Advertiser*, 29 December 1788]

Armitage, William, Leeds, Yorks., upholder, appraiser and cm (1769–79). In September 1769 announced that he had moved his shop from Kirkgate to 'the Back of the Shambles where Mr Joseph Wilson, Book seller lately dwells'. From the new address he offered a large assortment of paper hangings, fabrics, carpets and bedding. In May of the year following he stated that he had just returned from London and could offer from his shop 'Near the Town Hall' a wide selection of paper hangings, carpets and furniture. By 1773 he had moved once again to the sign of the 'Chest of Drawers and Chair' near the 'New Inn' in Briggate. Here he was able to offer 'Italian and Spring Blinds for Windows; Pier Looking Glasses, Mahogany, Rose and Swing ditto, Green and Gold, Blue and Gold and Black and Gold ditto for Ladies Toilets; Paper Machee Ornaments for Rooms and Chimney Pieces, etc. and Girandoles in Gold and ornamented Frames . . .'. He was patronised by Edwin Lascelles of Harewood House, Yorks., on several occasions. On 2 December 1771 he charged for fabrics, feathers, hair etc., £23 16s 7d; on 20 May 1774 for four stool frames with mahogany feet, £1; and on 6 November 1776 for 'a couch frame mahog'y with castors', mahogany pillars, tester ironwork and '2 chairs stuffed to Canvas', £5 4s. Some of the items were utilised by Thomas Chippendale's workmen. Armitage was declared bankrupt in July 1779. [*Leeds Mercury*, 12 September 1769, 29 May 1770, 11 May 1773, 25 May 1779; Leeds RO, Harewood MS 385, 386; *Furn. Hist.*, 1965; *Gents Mag.*, July 1779]

Armitage, William, Sheffield, Yorks., u (1798). [D]

Armitage, William, Hare St, Woolwich, London, cm (1823–24). [D]

Armitage, William George, Broadway, Deptford, London, cm (1832). [D]

Armitage, William, Heighington, Co. Durham, joiner and cm (1834). [D]

Armitrage, —, address unrecorded. Named in the Holkham Hall accounts, 1739, in connection with the supply of a dressing table 'for my Lord' at £2 12s 6d, and a mahogany 'voider & pail'. [V&A archives]

Armour, Henry, 3 Brompton Pl., Brompton, London, cm and u (1826). [D]

Armstrong, —, address unrecorded, u (1719). Received £9 13s from Lady Bowes on 19 February 1719 for upholsterer's work. [Durham RO, D/St/Box 352/1]

Armstrong, —, address unrecorded, u (1803). Subscribed to Sheraton's *Cabinet Dictionary*, 1803.

Armstrong, Charles, Gowthorpe, Yorks., joiner and cm (1826–37). [D]

Armstrong, Christopher, Church Lane, Selby, Yorks., joiner and cm (1826–37). [D]

Armstrong, Francis, Nottingham, cm (1711). [Notts. RO, index of burgesses]

Armstrong, John, Newcastle, u (1709–41). App. to Robert Webster, and admitted freeman of Newcastle on 12 April 1709. A further John Armstrong, u, was made a freeman of Newcastle in 1741 and may be a son. [Newcastle freemen reg. and poll bk]

Armstrong, John, 35 Piccadilly, London, upholder (1813). [D]

Armstrong, John, Liverpool, cm (1816–27). App. in 1808 to John Mears and sworn freeman on 10 June 1816. At 2 Sawney Pope St in 1824 but by 1827 had moved to 31 Standish St. In 1823 took Thomas McEbout and in 1816 Joseph Almond as apps. [D; Liverpool app. and freemen regs.]

Armstrong, John, Gowthorpe, Yorks., joiner and cm (1826–34). [D]

Armstrong, John, Market Pl., Wigton, Cumb., joiner and cm (1828). [D]

Armstrong, John, Hailgate, Howden, Yorks., cm (1828–31). [D]

Armstrong, Joseph, 21 Sherrard St, Golden Sq., London, cm and u (1826–40). [D]

Armstrong, Joshua, 12 Union Buildings, Union St, Hackney Rd, London, cm (1809). On 1 May 1809 took out cover with the Sun Fire Office for £300 in respect of goods in his dwelling house. [GL, Sun MS vol. 443, ref. 830518]

Armstrong, Lawson, Newcastle, u (1754). [Newcastle freemen reg.]

Armstrong, Michael, Widemarsh St, Hereford, carver in wood and stone, gilder and picture frame maker (1776). On 4 July 1776 advertised in *Pugh's Hereford Journal* that he was 'from London' and able to make 'Pier and Chimney-Glass frames, Girandoles, Sconces &c. gilt in oil or Burnish'd Gold, Chimney Piece, Brackets &c. &c.'. He also had barometers for sale, and offered to clean and repair paintings and silver glass.

Armstrong, Thomas, Newsham Pl., Sunderland, Co. Durham, joiner and cm (1828). [D]

Armstrong, Thomas, Cawood, Yorks., joiner and/or cm (1837). [D]

Armstrong, William, Bishop St, Stockton, Co. Durham, cm (1832–34). [D]

Armstrong, William, Hencoats St, Hexham, Northumb., joiner and cm (1834). [D]

Arnaboldi, Louis, 7 Watton Pl., Blackfriars Rd, London, carver and gilder (1829–35). Listed at 12 Gt Surrey St in 1832. [D]

Arnald, Mary, St Martin-in-the-Fields, London, upholder (1756). Declared bankrupt, *Gents Mag.*, August 1756.

Arne, Thomas, London, upholder (1690–d.1730). Initially traded at the 'George & White Lion', Great Piazza, Covent Gdn, but in 1698 announced a move to the 'George' in Bedford Ct, near Bedford St. By 1707 his address was the 'Two Crowns & Cushion' (sometimes referred to as the 'Crown') in King St, Covent Gdn, where he was to remain. On 9 May 1712 he took app. named Arthur Harris, son of Thomas Harris of Newport, Salop. He clearly carried on a successful and fashionable business. His house in King St was chosen as a lodging for four 'Indian Chiefs' who visited London in the reign of Queen Anne. In 1723 goods and merchandise 'in his dwelling house only and not elsewhere' were insured for £1,000. He had fashionable clients and between 1691 and 1710 undertook work at Felbrigg, Norfolk. Also between 1725–27 payments are recorded in the account books of Benjamin Mildmay, Earl Fitzwalter. These payments included arrangements for the funerals of the Lady Dowager Fitzwalter in 1726 and her son 'Schonberg' in 1727.

Thomas Arne was murdered on 2 March 1730. He is probably best remembered as the father of the composer Dr Arne and 'Mrs. Cibber', the actress. [Heal; Felbrigg papers, WKC 6/16, 6/23; A. C. Edwards, *The Accounts of Benjamin Mildmay, Earl Fitzwalter*; GL, Sun MS vol. 15, ref. 29153; *The Post Boy*, 15 December 1698; *The Monthly Remembrancer*, 1730]

Arnold, —, London, u (1680). Records of St Martin's Ludgate indicate payment of £10 8s in 1680. [*Wren Soc.*, vol. 19, p. 30]

Arnold, Daniel, Gloucester St, Cirencester, Glos., cm (1822). [D]

Arnold, David, 6 Cheapside, Dale St, Liverpool, cm (1796). [D]

Arnold, George, Middle St, Norwich, u (1817–36). App. to Charles Martin and Benjamin Row. Admitted freeman on 27 September 1817. In 1830 his address was recorded as Heigham, Norwich. [D; Norwich freemen reg. and poll bk]

Arnold, George W., 1 Michael's Pl., Brompton, London, cm and u (1826–40). [D]

Arnold, James, 16 Webber St, Blackfriars Rd, London, cm and u (1839). [D]

Arnold, John, 11 School Lane, Liverpool, cm (1823–24). [D]

Arnold, John, Cosford (or Gosford) St, Coventry, Warks., chairmaker and turner (1822–28). [D]

Arnold, John, Joyce Pool, Warwick, chairmaker and carpenter (1828–30). [D]

Arnold, Joseph, Tamworth St, Lichfield, Staffs., u (1834–35). [D; poll bk]

Arnold, Michael, York Buildings, Westminster, London, u (1739–50). Supplied goods and undertook work for Lord Monson. This included the funeral of Lady Georgina Ann Pierrepon in May 1739, the supply of a mahogany close stool chair costing £1 13s in 1749, and bedding, £8 15s in 1750. [Lincoln RO, Monson 12; poll bk]

Arnold, Richard, Bristol, carver (1715). [Poll bk]

Arnold, Richard, Moorfields, London, cm (1790). Freeman of Lincoln. [Lincoln poll bk]

Arnold, Samuel, Gracechurch St, London, upholder (1707–27). On 2 September 1709 took out insurance cover on a brick house 'situate on the west side of a yard on the south side of Haggs head Ct on the west side of Gracechurch St.'. In 1724 took out insurance on three further properties in the parish of St Dunstan, Stepney. [GL, Hand in Hand MS vol. 7, ref. 18917; vol. 28, ref. 33268; GL, Upholders' Co. records]

Arnold, Sturton, Devonshire St, London, upholder (1725). On 21 November 1725 took out insurance cover for £200 on goods and merchandise in his dwelling house and further cover of £100 for similar property at another house 'situate 2 doors from his own'. [GL, Sun MS vol. 20, ref. 37183]

Arnold, Thomas, 60 Allerton St, Hoxton, London, cm and u (1826–27). Also declared his trade to be that of a 'fancy cabinetmaker'. [D]

Arnold, Thomas, 3 King St, Clerkenwell, London, cm (1832–37). [D]

Arnold, William, 48 Aldermanbury, London, cm (1782–93). In 1782 insured his utensils and stock for £250 out of a total cover of £400. [D; GL, Sun MS vol. 298, p. 546]

Arnold, William, Oswestry, Salop, cm (1797). [D]

Arnold, William, Cross St, Oswestry, Salop, cm (1838). [D]

Arnold, William, 10 Gt Helens St, London, cm and u (1822). [D]

Arnold, William, Spon (or Spoon) St, Coventry, Warks., chairmaker and turner (1822). [D]

Arnold, William, High St, Canterbury, Kent, cm and broker (1824). [D]

Arnold, William, 2 Back Rd, St George's Sq., London, bedstead maker (1839). [D]

Arnoll, Eleanor, Southgate St, Exeter, Devon, u (1781). [*Exeter Flying Post*, 9 November 1781]

Arnot, William, High St, Canterbury, Kent, cm and furniture broker (1826–29). [D]

Arnott, George, Beverley, Yorks., cm (1790–1840). At Wednesday Mkt in 1826, and Highgate, 1831–40. His son, William Prince Arnott, was app. to John Stephenson, in March 1812. From 1826 in partnership with Robert Arnott. [D; poll bk; Hull app. reg.]

Arnould, Robert, Wallingford, Berks., u and milliner (1782). In 1782 insured his utensils and stock for £450 out of a total cover of £500. [GL, Sun MS vol. 300, p. 465]

Arrow, John Henry, 5 Cowley St, Westminster, London, cm and u (1820–39). On 9 March 1820 insured his house and workshop for £210 and stock, utensils and goods in trust for £150. In 1823 took an app. [D; GL, Sun MS vol. 483, ref. 964095; Westminster Ref. Lib., MS E3559]

Arrowsmith, —, Green End, Whitchurch, Salop, cm (1822). [D]

Arrowsmith, Henry, William & Arthur (late Henderson), London, carvers and gilders (1838–40). At 113 St Martin's Lane in 1838 but by the next year had moved to 80 New Bond St. Published in 1840 *The House Decorator and Painter's Guide*. Business continued after 1840, and in the Royal Accounts, 1846–51, they are described as 'Decorators to Her Majesty'. [D]

Arrowsmith, James, Market Pl., Richmond, Yorks., u (1811–40). On 2 July 1811 supplied wall paper and borders to the value of £2 17s 10d to the Duke of Leeds for Hornby Castle. [D; YAS archives]

Arrowsmith, John, 80 New Bond St, London, cm (d. 1759). Succeeded by John Hatt. [Heal]

Arrowsmith, John, Aldersgate St, London, joiner and cm (1760–61). Recorded 1760–61 employing non-freemen by licence. [GL, City Licence bks, vol. 2]

Arrowsmith, Simon, Manchester, u (1741). Took app. named Harris in 1741. [S of G, app. index]

Arrowsmith, Stephen, London, turner and cm (c. 1730–58). Born 26 December 1701 at Nantwich, Cheshire, his father being a skinner by trade. His address is variously given on trade labels as 'The Blue-Ball, in St. Martin's-le-Grand, near Aldergate' and the 'Blew Ball & Hartichoake in Aldersgate St'. At the former address he advertised that he 'sells all sorts of Mehogoney Tables, and all Sorts of Turners Work belonging to Joyners'. The other trade label mentions 'all sorts of Looking Glasses and Coach Glasses Chairs & Teabords'. His trade label is known on a two-door bureau cabinet. In 1758 he is recorded employing three non-freemen [V&A archives; GL, City Licence bks, vol. 2; Heal]

Arrowsmith, Thomas, Greenend, Whitchurch, Salop, cm and chairmaker (1822–35). [D]

Arrowsmith, Thomas, 12 Stanley St, Liverpool, gilder and household broker (1834). [D]

Arrowsmith & Son, Minster Yd, Ripon, Yorks., joiner, cm and u (1828). [D]

Arson, E. & Sons, Wakefield, Yorks., chairmakers (c. 1835). [V&A archives]

Arstall, Joseph, Altrincham, Cheshire, cm (1822–28). At Lymm, near Altrincham, in 1822 and at Well Lane in 1828. [D]

Artand, William, 13 Norton Pl., London, cm (1820). [D]

Artaud, William & Stephen, London, cm and u (1825–39). Between 1825–32 at 18 Queen Ann St, Cavendish Sq., but by 1837 have moved to 79 Wimpole St. [D]

Arthington, Joseph, 7 Cross St, Halifax, Yorks., cm (1837). [D]

Arthur, —, 45 Albany St, Regents Park, London, u and appraiser (1837). [D]

Arthur, John, Fleet St, London, cm (1790–93). [D]

Arthur, John, 68 Gt Queen St, Lincoln's Inn Fields, London, cm (1789–1811). Also listed as John Arthur & Co. [D]

Arthur, John, 71 Red Lion St, Holborn, London, cm and upholder (1817). [D]

Arthur, John, Arwinnick (or Arwenack) St, Falmouth, Cornwall, cm and u (1823–d. 1829). Death on 12 April 1829 reported in *Exeter Flying Post*, 16 April, but named in a directory of 1830. [D]

Arthur, William, 2 Church Lane, near Park Row, Bristol, cm and u (1817–23). [D]

Arthy, William, Lawford, Manningtree, Essex, cm (1826). [D]

Artingstall, J., Boughton, Cheshire, cm (1819). [Chester poll bk]

Arton, Isabella, Anne St, Osborn St, Hull, Yorks., u (1834). [D]

Artus, H., 52 Gt Sutton St, Clerkenwell, London, chair stuffer, etc. (1820). [D]

Arundale, W., 2 Castle St, Hastings, Sussex, carver and gilder (1837–40). Successor to G. Wooll. Arundale had previously been employed by Ackermann & Co., Strand, London. He advertised that he could offer carving and gilding 'in all its branches by competent workmen — Paintings cleaned and varnished'. The wide range of other goods offered for sale suggest that this business was organised as a general and fashionable repository of the arts. [D; *The Strangers Guide to Hastings,* c. 1839; *The Sussex Agricultural Express,* 4 February 1837, 24 March 1838]

Arundel, Charles, York, carver and gilder (1829–40). At Little Stonegate in May 1829 but by 1837 had moved to 5 St Helens Sq., and by 1840 to Ct, 5 St Helen's Sq. [D; *York Gazette,* 9 May 1829]

Arundel, Hannah, Eldon St, York, u (1837). [D]

Asals, Ann, 230 Whitechapel Rd, London, cm and u (1826–39). Also recorded at 224 Whitechapel Rd in 1827. [D]

Asals, James, Whitechapel Rd, London, cm (1808). [D]

Ash, Charles, Northampton, chairmaker (1820–26). At South Quarter in 1820 and Hobson's Yd in 1826. [Poll bk]

Ash, George, Wheelgate, Malton, Yorks., cm (1828). [D]

Ash, Hugh, Castle Cary, Som., cm (1793). [D]

Ash, James, Malton, Yorks, cm (1740). Took app. named Isherwood in 1740. [S of G, app. index]

Ash, James, 56 Gloucester St, Queen Sq., London, painter, writer and gilder (1812). [D]

Ash, Thomas, near the 'Thistle & Crown', Kingsland Rd, London, cm (1777). Insured his utensils and stock for £110 out of a total cover of £200 in 1777. [GL, Sun MS vol. 259, p. 468]

Ashalls, John, West Wycombe, Bucks., chairmaker (1798). [Militia Census]

Ashbourn(e), Ann, Stourbridge, Worcs., chairmaker (1818–20). Recorded at High St in 1818, and also as basket maker in 1820. [D]

Ashbridge, Thomas, London, looking-glass manufacturer (1815–20). At 72 Hatton Gdns in 1815 but by 1820 had moved to 163 Aldersgate St. Between 1817–19 the business is referred to as Ashbridge & Robertson. [D]

Ashburner, John, Keswick, Cumb., joiner and cm (1828). [D]

Ashburner, John Thomas, Brook St, Ulverston, Lancs., cm and u (1829–34). In 1829 the business is listed as Ashburner & Duke. [D]

Ashburner, Joseph, 11 Barbican, London, firescreen maker (1793). [D]

Ashby, James, Miles & Thomas, 11 Orange St, Red Lion Sq., London, carvers, gilders and joiners (1810). On 25 January 1810 insured stock utensils and glass for £300 out of a total cover of £600. [GL, Sun MS vol. 451, ref. 839652]

Ashby, John, 14 Old Compton St, Soho, London, carver and gilder (1837–39). In 1837 the business traded as Ashby & Sutton, looking-glass manufacturers, carvers and gilders. [D]

Ashby, John, 47 Dean St, Soho, London, carver and gilder (1839). [D]

Ashby, John, 17 West St, Swan Dials, London, u (1839). [D]

Ashby, Richard, Newgate Lane, Mansfield, Notts., joiner and cm (1832). [D]

Ashby, Thomas, 21 Red Lion St, Bermondsey St, London, cm (1776). Insured tenements for £200 in 1776. [GL, Sun MS vol. 244, p. 609]

Ashby, William, Peach St, Nottingham, joiner and cm (1832). [D]

Ashcroft, Joshua, St Ann's Terr., Liverpool, u (1827–39). In 1827 app. to Edward Beckerstaffe and sworn a freeman by servitude on 30 July 1839. In this year he was trading at the address above. [D; Liverpool app. and freemen regs.]

Ashcroft, Richard, Peter St, Chorley, Lancs., cm (1814–16). [D]

Ashelford, Joseph, Southwark, London, u and cm (1820–37). At 1 New St Maze (St Thomas St) between 1820–34, but at Dover St by 1837. [D]

Asher, William, Spilsby, Lincs., chairmaker (1790). [Lincoln poll bk]

Asheton, William, St Ann's Sq., Manchester, u (1781). [D]

Ashford, Charles, Shadwell St, Birmingham, clock case maker (1835). [D] Label giving trade as clock case manufacturer recorded on longcase clock by William Payne of Ludlow, Salop.

Ashford, John, Stockwell-gate, Mansfield, Notts., cm (1819). [D]

Ashford, John, West St, Havant, Hants., chairmaker, cm and shopkeeper (1823). [D]

Ashford, Thomas, Birmingham, chairmaker (1718). [Worcs. RO, 6088/705 : 739/101]

Ashford & Al(l)dridge, Shadwell St and Bath St, Birmingham, cabinet, dressing case and portable desk makers, clock case makers (1828–30). Trading at 67 Shadwell St in 1830. [D]

Ashforth, George, Duckingfield, Ashton-under-Lyne, Staffs., joiner and cm (1824). [D]

Ashley, George, Norwich, cm (1757–99). Son of Thomas Ashley, worsted weaver; admitted freeman on 25 June 1757. Lived in the following parishes: St Peter per Mountergate 1768; St Ethelbred 1780; St Julian 1784: St Michael at Thorn 1786–97; St Thomas Timberhill 1799. [Norwich freemen reg. and poll bk]

Ashley, John, Gloucester Pl., London, u, cm and paperhanger (1809–29). At 5 Gloucester Pl. and Islington Green in 1809 but by 1820 had moved to 7 Gloucester Pl. and was letting 5 to a stationer. On 8 November 1820 took out insurance cover for £500 of which half was for his dwelling house and workshop. [D; GL, Sun MS vol. 487, ref. 972880]

Ashlin, John, Brewer St, London, cm (1790). Freeman of Lincoln. [Lincoln poll bk]

Ashlin, Thomas, 3 Brewer St, London, cm and upholder (1779–90). A freeman of Lincoln. In 1779 insured his stock and utensils for £1,250 out of a total cover of £1,500. His house and workshop were insured in the same year for £1,000. By 1782 the insurance cover on utensils, stock and goods was only £400 out of a total of £1,100. [D; Lincoln poll bk; GL, Sun MS vol. 271, p. 348; vol. 278, p. 336; vol. 306, p. 261]

Ashlin, William, 6 Belton St, Long Acre and 68 Strand, London, carver, gilder and looking-glass maker (1789–1826). Initially trading solely from the Belton St address. By 1796 the Strand address was also in use and the business was referred to as Ashlin & Collings (or Ashlin & Co.). By 1821 the trading style had changed again to Ashlin, Collings & Ashlin. A pair of gilt tables bearing the trade label of Ashlin & Holland, Strand, London, sold at Sotheby's, NY on 13 December 1980 (lot 73) were almost certainly produced by this business. An earlier trade card of 1798 is in the Banks Coll., BM. [D] Submitted an estimate of £2,500 for work done at Carlton House, London, for the Prince of Wales. [H. Clifford Smith, *Buckingham Palace*, p. 104] Worked at Althorp, Northants., submitting an account on 2 October 1790 for repolishing a French plate, cutting a plate into bookcase door, and insurance amounting to £234 6s. A further sum of £10 12s was charged on 26 March 1791, which included £7 7s for an ebony dress frame inlaid with Prince's metal. [V&A archives] In August 1798 supplied Lord John Russell (later 6th Duke of Bedford) with a looking-glass in a burnished gilt frame at a cost of £28 19s. [Bedford Office, London] On 7 February 1811 an account for £121 9s 6d was submitted to Nicholas Pearse of Loughton, Essex, and Marylebone, London, for a mirror and frame. [Essex RO, D/DHt A1/3] The firm supplied items to the Royal Pavilion, Brighton, receiving £9,054 5s 7d between 1817–23 for plate and looking-glass. This included £701 17s for the chimney- glass in the Music Room, and £976 10s for those in the Banqueting Room. A further payment of £228 was made on 30 June 1826. [Wills, *Looking-Glasses*; RA, 35606] In 1821 the firm charged £2 12s 6d to Georgiana, Duchess of Bedford, for a looking-glass with a shaped frame with 'flannel to the back', for her dressing room at St James's Sq., London. [Bedford Office, London] B.A.

Ashman, John C., Lambeth, London, u (1826–29). At 16 Gibson St in 1826 but by 1829 the number had changed to 41. [D]

Ashmole, Benjamin, Derby, u (1820). Hon. burgess of Nottingham. [Index of burgesses]

Ashmole, David, Nottingham, cm (1820). Freeman. [Index of burgesses]

Ashmole, Richard, Derby, cm (1820). Hon. burgess of Nottingham. [Index of burgesses]

Ashmole, Thomas, Derby, cm (1820). Hon. burgess of Nottingham. [Index of burgesses]

Ashold, Amos, High Wycombe, Bucks., chairmaker (b. *c.* 1811–41). Daughter bapt. 1837. Aged 30 at the time of the 1841 Census.

Ashold, John, High Wycombe, Bucks., chairmaker and victualler (b. *c.* 1801–41). Three daughters bapt. between 1815 and 1821. Aged 40 at the time of the 1841 Census. [D]

Ashold, John, Oxford, u (1769). Married Elizabeth Hine at St Ebbe's, 13 November 1769. [Bodleian index of Oxf. marriage bonds]

Ashplant, John, Falmouth, Cornwall, cm (1804). Marriage to Mrs Hazlewood of Falmouth reported in *Exeter Flying Post*, 8 March 1804.

Ashton, A., 116 London Rd, Brighton, Sussex, u (1839). [D]

Ashton, Edward, Parade St, Rochdale, Lancs., cm (1825). [D]

Ashton, George, 3 Fontenoy St, Liverpool, cm and furniture broker (1835–37). [D]

Ashton, James, Liverpool, cm (1812–39). App. to Roger Reed in 1804, and admitted freeman on 6 October 1812. In business at 19 Comus St in 1827, but number subsequently changed to 27 (1829), 29 (1837) and 12 (1839). [D; Liverpool app. and freemen regs.]

Ashton, Jeremiah, Bridge St, Northampton, u (1830). [D; poll bk]

Ashton, John, Spalding, Lincs., chairmaker (1705). [Lincoln RO, INV 199/55]

Ashton, John, Old Horse Fair, Wisbech, Cambs., cm and u (1824). [D]

Ashton, John, Lough, Lincs., chairmaker (1819–28). Trading at Eastgate, 1822–26; and Butcher Mkt, also as a turner, in 1828. [D]

Ashton, John jnr, Bridge St, Warrington, Lancs., cm and u

(1828–34). Sarah, his wife, died on 5 October 1828 aged 32. On 16 February married again in Liverpool to Bridget Bates of that town. His father may have still played an active role in the business as late as 1828 as the business in that year was described as John Ashton & Son. [D; *Chester Courant and Anglo Welsh Gazette*, 23 February 1930]

Ashton, John, Northampton, cm (1823–30). Trading at Gold St in 1823 and Bridge St in 1830. [D; poll bk]

Ashton, John, Bridlesmith-gate, Nottingham, carver and gilder (1825). [D]

Ashton, John, Spilsby, Lincs., chair turner (1835). [D]

Ashton, Joseph, Coventry, Warks., u and cm (1828–35). Recorded at Smithford St, 1828–30, and Hertford St in 1835. [D]

Ashton, Peter, Chester, cm (1818–19). Admitted freeman on 18 May 1818. At William St in 1818; and Gorst Stacks and George St, 1819. [Chester freemen rolls and poll bks]

Ashton, Richard, Louth, Lincs., chairmaker and turner (1831–41). At Eastgate in 1831–35 but by 1841 had moved to Maiden Row. [D]

Ashton, Robert, Spilsby, Lincs., chair turner (1828–35). [D]

Ashton, Samuel, Louth, Lincs., chairmaker (1725). Took app. named Sheeles in 1725. [S of G, app. index]

Ashton, Samuel, Spilsby, Lincs., chairmaker (1826). [D]

Ashton, Simeon, Brighton, Sussex, cm and u (1826–27). At 25 Queens Rd in 1826 but by the next year at 28 London Rd. [D]

Ashton, Thomas, 4 Brewer St, Golden Sq., Westminster, London, upholder and cm (1784–93). [D; poll bk]

Ashton, Thomas, Horse Fair, Wisbech, Cambs., chair turner (1801). On 30 March 1801 insured his dwelling house and shop for £50 and his stock for £10. [GL, Sun MS vol. 39, ref. 716873]

Ashton, Thomas, Wormgate, Boston, Lincs., chairmaker (1819). [D]

Ashton, William, Worcester, cm (1758). App. to John Crump snr, cm, and admitted freeman by servitude on 21 August 1758. [Worcester freemen rolls]

Ashton, William, Alford, Lincs., chairmaker (1826–35). [D]

Ashton, William, Spilsby, Lincs., chairmaker (1822–40). Recorded as William & Son, 1826–40. [D]

Ashworth, James, Ulverston, Lancs., cm (1798). [D]

Ashworth, John, 19 Eastcheap, Hull, Yorks., joiner, cm and u (1826–31). [D]

Ashworth, John, Dobroyd, Todmorden, Yorks., cm (1828–37). [D]

Ashworth, T., York, turner and cm (1825). Declared bankrupt, *Brighton Gazette*, 16 June 1825. Working with D. Stones.

Ashworth, T., 1 Gt Tower St, Commercial Rd East, London, chairmaker, bedstead maker, cm and u (1829). [D]

Ashworth, Thomas, late of Clerkenwell Close, St James, Clerkenwell, London, cm and victualler (1761). Discharged from Debtors' Prison in 1761. [*London Gazette*]

Ashworth, Thomas, 2 Booth St, Spitalfields, London, cm and u (1827). [D]

Ashworth, William, Todmorden, Yorks., cm (1822). [D]

Askew, Edward, Lancaster. Named in the Gillow records in 1795 and 1797. [Westminster Ref. Lib.]

Askew, H., Elizabeth St, Workington, Cumb., joiner and cm (1811). [D]

Askew, John, 32 Rathbone Pl., London, carver and gilder (1839). [D]

Askew, Jonathan, Market Pl., Cockermouth, Cumb., cooper, turner and chairmaker (1829). [D]

Askew, William, London, cm (1749). Shown at Gt Pulteney St and also Knave's Acre, Westminster in this year. [Poll bk]

Askew, William, Lancaster. Named in the Gillow records in connection with a wardrobe in 1788. [Westminster Ref. Lib., Gillow vol. 344/94, p. 263]

Askwith, George, Lincoln, cm (1837). [Poll bk.]

Asling, William, Nottingham, joiner and cm (1819–28). App. in 1819, and admitted freeman in 1828. [Notts. RO, indices of app. and burgesses]

Aspinal, John, Otley, Yorks., cm (1798). [D]

Aspinall, Henry, Liverpool, cm (1840). Admitted freeman on 24 July 1840. [Liverpool freemen reg.]

Aspinall, James, 8 Derby St, Liverpool, cm and furniture broker (1821–24). In 1824 lived at a house at Edge Vale. [D]

Aspinall, James, 16 Hanover St, Hanover Sq., London, cm and u (1839). [D]

Aspinall, Robert, 6 Baptist St, Liverpool, chairmaker (1813). [D]

Aspinall, William snr, Liverpool, chairmaker (1806–d. 1826). Admitted freeman on 5 November 1806. At 6 Baptist St in 1811 and continued here until his death in March 1826. [D; Liverpool freemen reg.]

Aspinall, William jnr, Liverpool, chairmaker (1826–34). At 6 Baptist St in 1828 but the next year moved to 41 Harrison St and in 1824 was at 3 Sawney Pope St. [D]

Aspinall & Fearnley, Bradford, Yorks., cm and joiners (1818–22). [D]

Aspindle, Richard, Friargate, Preston, Lancs., chairmaker (1818). [D]

Aspinwall, James, 21 Princes St, Hanover Sq., London, cm (1825–39). Recorded at 16 Hanover St, Hanover Sq. in 1837. [D]

Aspinwall, John Francis, Manchester, cm and u (1822–40). At 1 Pool-fold in 1822; 14 Oldham St, 1824–33; and 27 Oldham St, 1836–40. [D]

Aspinwall, Thomas William, 152 Long Millgate, Manchester, u (1840). [D]

Aspinwall, Rhodes & Co., Church St, Preston, Lancs., joiners and cm (1818). [D]

Asplen, John, Birmingham, cm, broker, u and carpenter (1822–30). Trading at 42 John St in 1822 and Newton St, 1828–30. [D]

Asquith, Christopher, Leeds, Yorks., cm (d. 1788). [*Leeds Intelligencer*, 11 November 1788]

Asquith, James, Woodhouse Lane, Leeds, Yorks., cm and joiner (1837–40). Also had dwelling house at Wade St. [D]

Assals, Ann, 230 and 234 Whitechapel Rd, London, cm (1829). [D]

Assenden, Thomas, 8 St Ann's Pl., Commercial Rd, Limehouse, London, u, cm and furniture broker (1820–39). [D]

Assheton, Ralph, Manchester, u (1762–88). Admitted freeman of Preston, Lancs. in 1762. Brother to William Assheton of Preston, u. Had two other brothers, Richard and John, the latter a lawyer. Established at Market St Lane, Manchester by 1772 but in the next year had moved to 5 St Ann's Sq., Manchester at which address he was to remain. [D; Preston Guild records]

Assiter, Thomas, Rochester, Kent, Later London, cm and u (1776–90). In 1776 insured his storehouse, workshop and warehouse at Rochester for £1,050 with an additional £200 cover for utensils and stock. By June 1790 he was in London. [GL, Sun MS vol. 246, p. 267; Rochester poll bk]

Aster, William, Spilsby, Lincs., chairmaker (1790). [Lincoln poll bk]

Astle, Benjamin, 79 Islington Rd, St John's St, u and undertaker (1816–25). In 1819 the business was listed as Benjamin Astle & Co. [D]

Astle, John, Chester, cm (1766). App. to Mayor and admitted freeman, 9 September 1766. [Chester freemen rolls]

Astle, R., Macclesfield, Cheshire, cm (1789). [D]

Astle, Thomas snr, Eastgate St, Chester, cm (1743–d. 1782). Son of Edward Astle of Frodsham, Cheshire, yeoman. App. to John Dutton, joiner, 1738–40 and also to Edward Bromley, cm. Admitted freeman by servitude, 20 January 1745. Held the position of Sheriff, 1754–55, and Mayor, 1766–67. On 25 August 1749 took out insurance cover of £400 which included £100 on a workhouse and stable and £50 for stock. Although these sums appear fairly modest the business was probably substantial judging from the number of apps taken on. These commenced in 1743 with Wright. In 1750 three apps were accepted named Johnson, Bennet and Robert Hankey. Another, Richard Gorse Ogleby followed in 1775. Probably the 'Alderman Astle' listed at Eastgate St in 1781. Died on 15 February 1782. [Chester app. bks; freemen rolls; reg. of mayors and sheriffs; GL, Sun MS vol. 86, ref. 117513; S of G, app. index; poll bk]

Astle, Thomas jnr, Eastgate St, Chester, cm (1782–93). Took over the business following the death of his father and in March 1782 declared that 'He has now on hand a very extensive assortment of the most elegant and useful Mahogany Furniture; which for quality and cheapness, he can with confidence recommend to the attention and preference of the public — All manner of old glasses silvered and framed in the most elegant manner; all kinds of Coach and chaise Glasses sold'. He was sworn a freeman, 6 April 1784 and in this year took as app. Ralph Jackson. [D; Chester app. reg. and freeman rolls; *Chester Chronicle*, 29 March 1782]

Astley, Abraham, 'The Rising Sun', Harp Alley, Fleet Ditch, London, u and cm (c. 1720). Probably related to Isaac Astley who traded at the same address. A trade label has been recorded on a walnut veneered chest on stand of three long and three short drawers. The label states that he 'Maketh and Selleth all Sorts of Standing-Beds, Feather-Beds, Flock-Beds, Quilts, Rugs, Blankets &c. Also *Russia* Leather-Chairs, Chests of Drawers, Tables, and Looking-Glasses. He likewise Appraises, Buys and Sells all sorts of Household-Goods'. [*C. Life*, 13 October 1983]

Astley, Edward, 'The Clock Case', Wych St, Strand, London, cm (c. 1730). Trade card in Heal Coll., BM.

Astley, Isaac, 'The Ship and Rising Sun', Harp Alley, Fleet Ditch, London, u (c. 1753). Trade card [Heal Coll., BM] has text identical to that of Abraham Astley. Heal dates the card as 1753 and if this date is correct he may be the son of Abraham.

Astley, Thomas, Birmingham, cabinet case maker (1809–18). Recorded at Bordesley and Deritend, near Birmingham, in 1809, and at Cheapside, Birmingham, 1816–18, also as cm. [D]

Aston, Andrew, 90 Adam St, Bermondsey, London, cm and u (1839). [D]

Aston, John, 105 Suffolk St, Birmingham, cm (1823). [D]

Aston, John, 62 Navigation St, Birmingham, cm (1823). [D]

Aston, John, Dudley St, Birmingham, cm, broker and u (1828–30). Recorded at no. 14 in 1828. [D]

Aston, John, North St, Wolverhampton, Staffs., cm and u (1827–30). In 1828–30 listed as John Aston & Son. [D]

Aston, Joseph, bottom of Newhall St, Birmingham, chairmaker, spade and handle maker (1828–30). [D]

Aston, Thomas, 71 Cheapside, Deritend, Birmingham, cabinet case and black wood inkstand maker (1803). [D]

Aston, William, North St, Wolverhampton, Staffs., cm and u (1833—35). Possibly the son of John Aston. Trading also as auctioneer and appraiser in 1833. [D]

Astwick, John, Holme, Yorks., joiner and/or cm (1837). [D]

Astwick, Thomas, Honley, Yorks., cm (1822–37). [D]

Atherley, Francis, London, cm, u, chair and sofa maker, undertaker (1822–39). At 14 Richmond St, St Lukes, 1822–27 but by 1835 had moved to 64 Banner St. [D]

Atherton, —, A tallboy with secretaire drawer, a fall-front estcritoire, a tea table, and a number of chairs are known stamped 'ATHERTON'. These can be dated on the basis of style from *c.*1780 to *c.*1810 and are thought to be of north country origin. [V&A archives]

Atherton, Humphrey, Cambridge, carver (1793). [D]

Atherton, Humphrey, 132 Long Acre, London, carver and gilder (1808). [D]

Atherton, James, 10 Redman's Pl., Liverpool, cm (1780–1811). App. to Roger Reid and sworn freeman, 11 September 1780. [D; Liverpool app. and freemen regs.]

Atherton, James, Warrington, Lancs., cm and u (1814–22). Recorded at Bank (or Back) St, 1814–19, and Bridge St, as cm, in 1822. [D] Declared bankrupt, *Chester Guardian*, 20 April 1819.

Atherton, Joseph, Liverpool, cm (1835–39). At 18 Blake St, 1835–37, but by 1839 was at 24 Penrith St, Toxteth Park. [D]

Atherton, Thomas, Warrington, Lancs., cm, u and timber merchant (1798–1828). At Old Butter Mkt as cm only in 1808; Butter Market St, 1814–25; but in 1822–28 at Scotland Rd. [D]

Atherton, William, Liverpool, u (1774–77). At 31 Pool Lane in 1774 and 170 Dale St in 1777. [D]

Atherton, William, Liverpool, cm and chairmaker (1814–37). At 65 and 66 Lime St, 1814–23, but by 1827 the numbers are changed to 46, 69 and 70 and in 1829 to 79. By 1835 had moved to 70 Christian St and by 1837 the number had changed to 80. [D]

Athey, John, High St, Rotherham, Yorks., cm (1828). [D]

Athey, Joseph & William, Alnwick, Northumb., joiner and cm (1827–34). At Dispensary Lane in 1827 and Bondgate St from 1828. Recorded at 29 Narrowgate, also as u, in 1832. [D]

Athorn, John, Pontefract, Yorks., joiner and cm (1834). [D]

Atkin, Alexander, Wardour St, Westminster, London, upholder (1784). [Poll bk]

Atkin, Joseph, Louth Park, Louth, Lincs., cm and joiner (1835). [D]

Atkin, Moses, Louth Park, Louth, Lincs., cm and joiner (1835). [D]

Atkin(s), Samuel, Wormgate, Boston, Lincs., cm and chairmaker (1826–35). [D]

Atkins, —, 57 Gildengate, Norwich, cm (1783). [D]

Atkins, G. H., Ordnance Row, Portsea, Portsmouth, Hants., carver and gilder (1839). [D]

Atkins, Henry, 'The Three Crowns', St Paul's Churchyard, London, cane chairmaker (1723–24). Trade card in Banks Coll., BM. On 16 January 1723 covered goods and merchandise in his dwelling house only, and not elsewhere, for £500 with the Sun fire office. [GL, Sun MS vol. 16, ref. 30962] In October 1724 supplied to Chicheley Hall, Bucks., twelve chairs at £2 for Sir John Chester. [Bucks. RO, D/C/2/3 (ii)]

Atkins, James, London, upholder (1734). On 4 September 1734 his son Samuel was admitted freeman of the Upholders' Co. by patrimony. [GL, Upholders' Co. records]

Atkins, James, Portland St, Brighton, Sussex, cm, u and chairmaker (1832–40). The number in Portland St is variously given as 31, 32 and 33. [D]

Atkins, John, Oxford, cm (1744–68). On 19 May 1744 married Frances Richmond at the Church of St Mary Magdalen, Oxford. [Bodleian index of Oxf. marriage bonds; poll bk]

Atkins, John, Evesham, Worcs., cm (1818). [Worcs. RO, 6088/705:739/106]

Atkins, John, Uttoxeter, Staffs., chairmaker and turner (1824). [D]

Atkins, John, High St, St Neots, Hunts., chairmaker and turner (1830). [D]

Atkins, John, Oxford, cm and u (1823–32). Recorded at St Peter-le-Bailey in 1823 and Queen St, also as appraiser, in 1830. Declared bankrupt, 29 May 1832. [D; *Liverpool Mercury*, 1 June 1832]

Atkins, John, 56 Hill St, Birmingham, chairmaker (1835). [D]

Atkins, John, Paradise St, Birmingham, Windsor chairmaker (1835). [D]

Atkins, Joseph, London, cm and u (1820–39). At 10 Duke St, Spitalfields, 1820–22, but by 1826 had moved to 28 Fort St, Spitalfields, changed in the next year to no. 29. In 1832 the address was 9 Clarence Pl., Hackney Rd and in 1839 28 London Terr., Hackney Rd. [D]

Atkins, Richard, London, u (1820–39). At 51 Foley St, Portland Pl. in 1820 and on 20 December of that year took out insurance cover of £300 of which £250 was for his dwelling house in which it was stated there was 'no cabinet work nor stove'. Stock and utensils were insured for a mere £20. By 1835 he had moved to 6 Argyll Pl., Regent St at which address he continued in business. Thomas Atkins who traded at the Foley St address in 1817 was probably related. [D; GL, Sun MS vol. 483, ref. 974391]

Atkins, Richard, High Wycombe, Bucks., chairmaker (1839). Daughter bapt. 1839. [PR (bapt.)]

Atkins, Thomas, 51 Foley St, London, carpenter and upholder (1817). Probably related to the Richard Foley who traded at this address from 1820. [D]

Atkins, Thomas Illiff(e), Leicester and Northampton, u (1820–30). App. to Joseph Spencer of Belgrave Gate, Leicester, and admitted freeman in 1826. Trading at Mercer's Row, Northampton, 1823–30. A burr elm tripod table is known with a stenciled mark 'From Atkines, upholstery, paper hangings, cabinetwork house, Northampton'. [Northampton poll bks; Leicester freemen rolls]

Atkins, William, Park St, Westminster, London, carver (1749). [Poll bk]

Atkins, William, London, carver, gilder and picture frame maker (1784–1806). At 294 High Holborn in 1784, in which year his house was insured for £300. By 1790 an address at 41 Fenchurch St was being used in addition, and from 1793 this was the sole trade address. In the following year the business was trading as Atkins & Wallace. By 1799 the trading style had changed to Atkins & Nightingale (later Atkins & Co.) and the address was 143 Leadenhall St. [D; GL, Sun MS vol. 321, p. 365]

Atkins, William, High Wycombe, Bucks., chairmaker (1825–28). Three sons bapt. between 1825–28. [PR bapt.)]

Atkins, William, Thetford, Norfolk, cm (1836–39). At London Rd in 1836, but by 1839 had moved to St Mary's Lane. [D]

Atkinson, —, Aldersgate St, London, cm (1803). Subscribed to Sheraton's *Cabinet Dictionary*, 1803.

Atkinson, Bartholomew, Hull, Yorks., cm (1784). [Poll bk]

Atkinson, Benjamin, Ellerby Lane, Leeds, Yorks., cm (1822). [D]

Atkinson, Benjamin, Finkle St, Stockton-upon-Tees, Co. Durham, chair, clog and patten maker (1827). [D]

Atkinson, Caleb, address unrecorded. On 13 May 1763 supplied four wheel chairs for Burton Constable, Yorks. [Humberside RO, DDCC (2) vouchers]

Atkinson, Christopher, Gallgate, Barnard Castle, Co. Durham, cm and joiner (1834). [D]

Atkinson, Daniel, High St, Staines, Middlx, cm and u (1832–39). [D]

Atkinson, Edmund, Lancaster, cm (1774–84). From Kirby, Kendal, Westmld. App. to Wm. Bruce of Lancaster in 1774, and admitted freeman, 1783–84. [Lancaster app. reg., freemen rolls and poll. bk]

Atkinson, Edward, London, chairmaker (1789–1808). At Old

Fleet St in 1789 but by 1793 had moved to Old St Rd. In 1808 the address was 1 Crown Ct, Curtain Rd and the trade given as 'leather bottom chairmaker'. [D]

Atkinson, Edward, Sloane St, Chelsea, London, cm, u and undertaker (1817–35). At 177 Sloane St, 1817–20, but by 1826 at nos 26 and 170. By 1832 the business was styled Atkinson & Mackett and was trading from 26 Sloane St. In 1835 additional premises at 86 were being used. [D]

Atkinson, Francis, Leeds, Yorks., cm (1791). Named in the *Leeds Cabinet and Chair Makers' Book of Prices*, 1791, as a journeyman cm in basic sympathy with its contents.

Atkinson, Francis, Mount St, Salford, Lancs., chair bottomer (1818). [D]

Atkinson, Francis, Stricklandgate, Kendal, Westmld, cm and u (1829–34). [D]

Atkinson, George, Beverley, Yorks, cm (1790). [Poll bk]

Atkinson, George, Lancaster. Named in the Gillow records, 1790–1802, constructing various items of furniture, and 'making & moulding claws for dining tables'. [Westminster Ref. Lib.]

Atkinson, George & Somerville, William, London, cm (1805). Published a supplement with two plates to the 3rd edition of *The Cabinet-Makers' London Book of Prices*, 1805.

Atkinson, George, 26 Curtain Rd, Shoreditch, London, cabinet and chair manufacturer (1820). [D]

Atkinson, George, 17 Hackney Rd Cresc., London, cm and u (1822–28). [D]

Atkinson, George, Leeds, Yorks., cm (1826–37). At 2 Copenhagen St, 1826–30, but by 1834 had moved to a court at 4 Lowerhead Row, and was at Birch's Row in 1837. [D]

Atkinson, George, Flag Lane, Sunderland, Co. Durham, joiner and cm (1827–28). [D]

Atkinson, George, Lancaster, cabinet carver (1829–30). [Lancaster freemen reg.]

Atkinson, George, High St, Stockton-upon-Tees, Co. Durham, cm (1832). [D]

Atkinson, Henry, 45 Whitechapel, Liverpool, cm (d. by 1776). *Williamson's Liverpool Advertiser*, 22 March 1776, announced the sale by auction on 26 March of a 'Variety of CABINET GOODS of the BEST QUALITY The STOCK of the late MR. HENRY ATKINSON' at a 'Ware Room No. 45 White Chapel'.

Atkinson, James, Lancaster, joiner (1788–1820). [Westminster Ref. Lib., Gillow records, vol. 344/94, p. 459]

Atkinson, James, Back Ducie St, Strangeways, Manchester, cm (1817). [D]

Atkinson, John, Hull, Yorks., carpenter and cm (1790–1803). At Southend, High St in 1790, but by 1803 had moved to George St. [D]

Atkinson, John, Bishop Auckland, Co. Durham, cm (1793). [D]

Atkinson, John, Lancaster, furniture painter and japanner (1797–1801). [Westminster Ref. Lib., Gillow records]

Atkinson, John, Ledger St, Manchester, chairmaker (1800–02). [D]

Atkinson, John, Dockray, Penrith, Cumb., chairmaker (1811–34). [D]

Atkinson, John, Liverpool, cm (1820–37). App. to William Atkinson in 1812 and admitted freeman, 13 March 1820. In this year his address was recorded as 9 Basnett St, but by 1824 he was at 12 Leigh St. He was at 7 Lawton St between 1825–27, and from this address on 20 May 1825 advertised for four or five good journeymen cm. In 1827 he moved to 25 Ranelagh St, and the next year took John Jones as app. He remained at this address until at least 1829, but from 1834 is recorded in Gildart St. In 1834 the number was 9, but in the next year this had changed to 24 with an additional address at 9 Leigh St. In 1837 the numbers are 23 Gildart St and 17 Leigh

St. [D; Liverpool app. and freemen regs.; *Liverpool Mercury*, 20 May 1825]

Atkinson, John, Halton, Leeds, Yorks., cm (1822). [D]

Atkinson, John, Chipping, near Preston, Lancs., chairmaker (1834). [D]

Atkinson, John, 4 Chariot St, Hull, Yorks., cm (1838–39). [D]

Atkinson, John, Northallerton, Yorks., cm (1840). [D]

Atkinson, Joseph, 10 Medlock St, Chorlton Row, Manchester, cm (1825). [D]

Atkinson, Matthew, Penny-Bridge, Ulverston, Lancs., cm (1825). [D]

Atkinson, Peter, Liverpool, cm, joiner and umbrella maker (1827–29). At 87 Fontenoy St in 1827 and 9 Parker St in 1829. [D]

Atkinson, R., 1 Tower St, Seven Dials, London, picture frame maker (1802). [D]

Atkinson, R., 10 Rotherhithe St, London, carver (1835). [D]

Atkinson, Richard, Liverpool, cm (b.1792–d.1814). Married Miss Jane Hasan on 14 September 1812, and died on 10 February 1814 aged 22. [*Liverpool Mercury*, 18 September 1812; 18 February 1814]

Atkinson, Richard, York, carver and gilder (1819). Son of Richard Atkinson, musician. App. to Thomas Ferrand on 1 April 1819. [York app. reg.]

Atkinson, Richard, Finkell St, Richmond, Yorks., cm (1828). [D]

Atkinson, Robert, Manchester, chairmaker (1813–19). At 2 Lloyd St, Hulme in 1813, but by 1819 at 1 Mulberry Lane. [D]

Atkinson, Robert, Manchester, joiner and cm (1815–28). At 6 Lloyd St, Hulme in 1815 as chairmaker; Hargrave St, Manchester in 1818; 9 (or 4) Prime St, Hulme in 1825; and Queen St, Hulme in 1828. [D]

Atkinson, Robert, Bigg-market, Newcastle, joiner and cm (1824). [D]

Atkinson, Robert, 13 Queen St, York St, Manchester, cm (1840). [D]

Atkinson, Samuel, Lancaster. Named in the Gillow records in 1786 working on a table. [Westminster Ref. Lib., Gillow vol. 344/93, p. 372]

Atkinson, Thomas, London, cm, u and looking-glass maker (1748–76). Admitted a member of the Joiners' Co. on 5 July 1748. Subscribed to Chippendale's *Director*, 1754. Traded from an address at 'The Sun' on the south side of St Paul's Churchyard. On his trade card he claimed to be the successor 'to the late Mr. Belcher'. He offered 'all sorts of Cabinetwork, Chairs, Looking Glasses, Coach Glasses, Spring Curtains, Window Blinds, and all Sorts of Upholstery Goods', He is recorded in the City of London Licence bks employing non-freemen, the number permitted rising to 8 for the period 1764–76. In 1773 he was operating from 3 Broadway, Blackfriars, near Ludgate St while his house was being rebuilt. An account for the supply of two neat night tables costing £5 5s, dated 25 September 1755, is recorded at the BM. [D; V&A archives; Heal; GL, City Licence bks vols 3–9; Landauer Coll., MMA, NY]

Atkinson, Thomas, Beverley, Yorks., cm (1774–90). [Poll bks]

Atkinson, Thomas, Lancaster, cm (1784–1811). App. to William Blackburn in 1784 and admitted freeman, 1795–96. Named in the Gillow records, 1788–1811. [Lancaster app. reg. and freemen rolls; Westminster Ref. Lib., Gillow]

Atkinson, Thomas, London, cm (1793). Subscribed to Sheraton's *Drawing Book*, 1793.

Atkinson, Thomas, 9 Wynyate St, Islington Rd, London, cm (1808). [D]

Atkinson, Thomas, 38 and 39 Ludgate Hill, London, cm, u and undertaker (1820–24). Initially trading as Loader & Atkinson. The premises were at the corner of the 'Belle Sauvage', an important London coaching inn. A mahogany folding leaf table is known with their label. [Advert. in *Apollo*, February 1961] The practice of labelling furniture continued after 1823 when Atkinson was trading under his own name only, and a dining chair and a pedestal card table with D-shaped top are known (Fig. 18). [D; *Furn. Hist.*, 1978]

Atkinson, Thomas, Rawtenstall., Lancs., joiner and cm (1828). [D]

Atkinson, Thomas, Kirkby Stephen, Westmld, cm (1829). [D]

Atkinson, Thomas, 2 Moor Lane, Fore St, London, cm and undertaker (1832). [D]

Atkinson, Thomas, Staindrop, Co. Durham, cm and joiner (1834). [D]

Atkinson, Thomas, Easingwold, Yorks., cm and joiner (1834). [D]

Atkinson, William, Shoe Lane, London, u (1731–46). Fined in 1731, 1737, 1740 and 1746 for non-service at St Bride's. [GL, MS 6561, p. 54]

Atkinson, William, Grange, Lancs., cm (1752–74). In 1752 took app. named Kirby and two years later another named Clenny. A further app. named Clark was taken in 1774. [S of G, app. index]

Atkinson, William, Ripon, Yorks., cm (1779–93). Advertised in *York Courant*, 6 April 1779. Subscribed to Sheraton's *Drawing Book*, 1793.

Atkinson, William, 10 Little Litchfield St, Portland Chapel, London, cm (1781). Insured his house for £200 in 1781. [GL, Sun MS vol. 295, p. 600]

Atkinson, William, Lancaster (1790–1800). [Westminster Ref. Lib., Gillow records]

Atkinson, William, Liverpool, cm (1796–1840). App. to Edward Lowe and admitted freeman on 25 May 1796. Trading at 1 Derby St in 1804 and 58 Preston St, 1813–14. By 1818 he had obtained premises in Leigh St. These were numbered 11 (1818), 12 (1821–24 and 1835–37), 27 (1827–34) and 25 (1839). Addresses are also shown in Peter St (1824–39), Blake St (1834) and Williamson Sq. (1837). He is listed in a supplement to the *Liverpool Cabinet and Chair Prices*, 1805, on behalf of the journeymen. His apps included William Spencer in 1818 and Henry Harrison and John Hatton in 1825. Amongst his products were billiard tables which were of a sufficient quality for one to be listed by the maker in an auction advertisement in February 1820. His son William Greenhalgh Atkinson was admitted freeman of Liverpool on 28 July 1840. [D; Liverpool app. and freemen regs.; *Liverpool Mercury*, 4 February 1820]

Atkinson, William, address unrecorded, cm (1803). Subscribed to Sheraton's *Cabinet Dictionary*, 1803.

Atkinson, William, Bishop Lane, Hull, Yorks., cm and undertaker (1803). [D]

Atkinson, William, 336 High St, Lincoln, cm and u (1806–40). Freeman of Lincoln in November 1806. [D; poll bk]

Atkinson, William, Halton, Leeds, Yorks., cm (1822). [D]

Atkinson, Wilson, Priestgate, Workington, Cumb., joiner and cm (1829–34). [D]

Atle, Benjamin, 79 St John St Rd, Islington, London, u and undertaker (1820). [D]

Atlee, John, Windsor, Berks., u (1726). Admitted freeman of the borough on 8 June 1726. [S of G, hall bk]

Atlee, Samuel, Taunton, Som., upholder (1727). Took app. named Marshall in 1727. [S of G, app. index]

Atlee, William, London, u (1722–28). In 1722 he announced his move from 'York Buildings next to Mrs. Rochford's at the Upper Mews Gate to the corner of Duke Street, York Buildings'. In 1728 his address was given at the King's Arms Warehouse, Lincoln's Inn Pleas, on which he took out insurance cover for £500. [Heal; GL, Sun MS vol. 28]

Atley, William, London, u (1829–35). In 1829 at 2 Frederick Pl., Goswell Rd, and in 1835 at 102 Goswell Rd. [D]

Attenborough, George, Nottingham, joiner and cm (1820). Took William Peet as an app. in 1820. [Nottingham app. reg.]

Attenborough, Job, Rutland St, Nottingham, cm (1828). [D] See Job Atterbury.

Atterbury, James, High St, Burton-on-Trent, Staffs., cm and u (1828–35). Trading at New St in 1828 and High St, 1834–35. [D]

Atterbury, Job, Burton-on-Trent, Staffs., u and appraiser (1791–93). [D] See Job Attenborough.

Atterbury, Job, Rutland St, Nottingham, joiner and cm (1832). [D]

Atterbury, Michael, New St, Burton-on-Trent, Staffs., cm and u (1822). [D]

Atterbury, Michael, 1 St Michael's Cresc., Bristol, u, paper hanger and appraiser (1836). [D]

Atterbury & Dickinson, New St, Burton-on-Trent, Staffs., cm and u (1818). [D] See Michael Atterbury.

Attinwell, Robert, Strand on Green, London, upholder and cm (1808). [D]

Attiram, Francis, 1 Marsham St, London, cm (1782). Insured his utensils, stock and goods in 1782 for £100 out of a total insurance cover of £200. [GL, Sun MS vol. 303, p. 660]

Atto, William, High St, King's Lynn, Norfolk, cm (1793). [D]

Atto, William, High St, King's Lynn, Norfolk, cm (1836–39). At 27 in 1836 but in 1839 at 113. [D]

Atton, James, All Saints St, Stamford, Lincs., cm, u and pawnbroker (1840). [D]

Attree, Henry, Brighton, Sussex, upholder (1791). On 20 June 1791 took out insurance cover for £900, part of which was in respect of a warehouse, utensils and stock. [GL, Sun MS vol. 376, p. 620]

Attwater, James Thomas, High St, Sheerness, Kent, cm (1826–39). [D]

Attwater, W., 9 Drake St, Red Lion Sq., London, cm, u and undertaker (c. 1820). His trade card at the London Museum states that he manufactured 'every description of plain and sarcophagus Tea Chests, Knife Cases, Portable Desks, Dressing Cases, Ladies Work Tables and Baskets, Sofa and Pembroke Tables, Venetian Spring and Roller Blinds made and repaired. Furniture repaired on the most reasonable terms'.

Attwaters, Joseph, app. to James Begbie, cm of Salisbury, Wilts. on 5 August 1755. [*Wilts. Apps and their Masters*]

At(t)well, Thomas, Newport, Isle of Wight, Hants., cm and u (1823–39). Trading at Upper St James St in 1823, St James St in 1830 and Pyle St in 1839. [D]

Attwood, John, parish of St Philip and St Jacob, Bristol, cm (1781–84). [Poll bk]

Attwood, Thomas, 5 Fields, Chelsea, London, carver and gilder (1784). [Poll bk]

Atwell, Richard, Old Brentford, Middlx, cm (1809). [D]

Atwood, Thomas, Gt Russell St, Bloomsbury, London, carver and gilder to the Prince of Wales (1793). [D]

Aube, Peter, 5 Noel St, London, carver and gilder (1791). Took our insurance cover in 1791 for £200 which included £50 for stock and goods in a workshop behind. [GL, Sun MS vol. 373, ref. 580092]

Auby, —, address unrecorded, carver (1795), Bought bed linen from Kennet & Kidd, cm and u, New Bond St, London, in 1795. [PRO, C114/181, journal 3, p. 340]

Aucock, T., 18 Bond St, Brighton, Sussex, French polisher and japanner (1836–40). In February 1836 at the time of his daughter Jane's baptism he was living in Mulberry Sq. By 1843 his number in Bond St had changed to 13. [D; E. Sussex RO, PAR 255/1/2/10]

Audas, William, Wainfleet, Lincs., cm (1822–26). [D]

Audley, Edward, Gt Yarmouth, Norfolk, cm (1830). [Poll bk]

Audley, Erasmus, Bail, Lincoln, cm. Will proved in 1741. [Calendar of wills and administration, Lincoln]

Audley, William, London, u (1732–33). Paid £11 3s in the executors' accounts of Edward Barkham. [Bethlehem Hospital archives]

Audley, William, Nantwich, Cheshire, upholder and auctioneer (1781–84). [D]

Audley, William jnr & John, Newcastle-under-Lyme, Staffs., u, cm and auctioneers (1812–39). Initially at Lad Lane but by 1822 had in addition premises in the High St. In the period 1818–22 the business is referred to as William Audley & Sons. In 1834–39 William Audley appears to have been the sole proprietor and was trading from addresses at Iron Mkt and Bridge St. [D; poll bk] Advertised in *Cottrill's Directory*, 1836, as u, paper hanger and cabinet manufacturer with shop at 5 Ironmarket and manufactory and warehouse in Bridge St. He thanked customers for 'encouragement received by himself & his late brother over the last 20 years' and offered 'Beds and Window Curtains, of every description made and fitted up in the neatest manner. Carpets made up; Rooms, Halls and Passages papered in the first style of workmanship; and every article in the Cabinet busines repaired and made upon the most approved principle . . . He employs none but the best and most experienced workmen.' Audley offered his present stock at reduced prices, including 'Paper and Borders, suitable for parlours and bedrooms, Brussels, Kidderminster, Scotch and Venetian Carpeting; figured and plain Oil Cloths, Druggets and Matting; Moreens, Dimities and Chintz Furnitures; Fringes, Trimmings, Tassels, Lines and Bindings, Hair Seating, prime Goose Feathers and Ticking, Blankets and Mattresses of every description; Looking Glasses, Sofas and Chairs, Venetian, Shade, Spring and other Blinds together with a general assortment of Rosewood, Zebra, Mahogany, Oak and Painted Cabinet Furniture, Bedsteads &c. &c. Appraiser & auctioneer'.

Audley, William, Brunswick St, Hanley (or Shelton), Staffs., cm (1834–35). Trading in partnership with John Audley in 1834. [D]

Aughton, Richard, Preston, Lancs., joiner and cm (1818–25). In 1818 at Old Cock Yd, Church St but he moved in this year to William St. The numbers occupied in this street in 1824 were 4 and 19. [D]

Augier, Charles, Long Acre, London, carver (1749). [Poll bk]

Auls(ey)brook, John, King St, Southwell, Notts., joiner and cm (1822–28). [D]

Ault, John, 20 Apollo Buildings, Walworth, London, upholder (1803). Son of John Ault of Melbourne, Derbs., cm. Admitted freeman of the Upholders' Co. on 10 February 1803. [GL, Upholders' Co. records]

Ault, John, Melbourne, Derbs., cm (1803). [GL, Upholders' Co. records]

Aulton, Abraham, Park St, Walsall, Staffs., cm (1834–35). Recorded also at Bank St in 1834. [D]

Aungier, William snr, Ely, Cambs., turner and chairmaker (1790–1800). Took out insurance cover for £500 in 1790 which included £200 for his new dwelling house, shop and chamber over, £40 for his workshop, stock and utensils and £20 for a second thatched workshop, utensils and stock. In 1800 the business was taken over on his death by his son William. [GL, Sun MS ref. 571220; *Cambridge Chronicle*, 22 March 1800]

Aungier, William jnr, Ely, Cambs., turner and chairmaker (1800). On 22 March 1800 announced in *Cambridge Chronicle and Journal* that he was taking over the business of his late father, William.

Austen, —, St George's Spa, St George's Fields, London, chairmaker (1808). [D]

Austen, J., Rochester, Kent, cm (1806–07). In August 1830 living in London. [Poll bk]

Austen, John, 54 Queen St, New Ct, London, cm (1829). [D]

Auster, John, Worcester, upholder (1761). App. to William Ward, upholder, and admitted freeman on 19 March 1761. [Worcester app. and freemen regs.]

Auster, Roger, Birmingham, picture frame maker (1793–1818). At Brick Kiln Lane in 1793 but from 1812 was at Bristol St where the trade of brass founding was being carried on in addition and his son was assisting him in the business. [D]

Austin, Cornelius snr, Cambridge, joiner (c. 1660–1704). Cornelius Austin is better known for the fixed joinery work that is found in many of the Cambridge colleges such as King's Chapel, Emmanuel Chapel and the Wren Library at Trinity. He was employed regularly by St John's College from 1682, mainly for general joinery work but supplied such diverse articles as a candlebox (1697) to 'a medall case for ye Library £4 9. 2,' (1701). Most furniture supplied by him appears to have been part of the contract for the building or rooms he was employed in, as is the case of the Library at Emmanuel College where in 1679, Austin was employed to fit up wainscoting, supply new bookcases and the furnishings of eight tables and sixteen joyned stools. At least a dozen of the stools are still in use in the New Library. From the details given in the payments it is clear that he employed a small workforce. His name appears in the records of the parish of All Saints, although from 1670 he owned a large inn called 'The Cardinal's Hat' or 'Cap' in Trumpington St. [Archives of St John's College; Willis & Clark, *The Architectural History of the University of Cambridge*; All Saints' parish records, Cambs. RO, P20/8/1] R.W.

Austin, Cornelius jnr, Cambridge, joiner (c. 1698–d. 1729). It would appear that he worked for his father, although a few individual payments are recorded in his name, the earliest noted being in 1698 when Trinity College paid 'young Austin' for work in the Combination Room. From 1704 the payments made by St John's College are to 'Cornelius Austin jun', he presumably having taken over from his father. One of the first in that year was for '28 stools for ye scholars to kneel on in chappel . . . . £3. 3. 6.', which were upholstered by Thomas Moulder. Austin continued to work for the College up to his death in 1729 but the later payments give few details of the work undertaken. However in 1711 in partnership with Thomas Billups he altered the bookcases in the Library and supplied stools and tables. From December 1724 Austin was an Alderman of the Cambridge Corporation and on 29 September 1726 was sworn in as Mayor. He was buried in the parish of All Saints on 30 April 1729. [Archives of Trinity College and St John's College; Cambs. RO, Cambridge Corp. day books; All Saints parish records] R.W.

Austin, George, The Precints, Canterbury, Kent, carver and gilder (1823–29). [D]

Austin, J., Chester, chairmaker (1819). [Poll bk]

Austin, John, parish of Christchurch, Bristol, cm (1754). [Poll bk]

Austin, John, James St, Covent Gdn, London, u (1768). Declared bankrupt, *Williamson's Liverpool Advertiser*, 18 March 1768.

Austin, John, London, upholder (1773–c. 96). Son of John Austin of Sheerness, Kent, victualler. App. to Robert Phipps on 3 June 1762 and admitted freeman of the Upholder's Co. by servitude on 7 April 1773. His addresses were 29 Cannon St (1776–78), Gt Tower St (1781), Redman's Row, Mile End (1786) and 'The Stag', Brewhouse St, St Mary, Westminster (1796). [GL, Upholders' Co. records]

Austin, John, 46 East St, Portman Sq., London, cm and u (1839). [D]

Austin, Robert, 2 Keynshaw Terr., High St, Cheltenham, Glos., cm (1839). [D]

Austin, Samuel, 67 Charlotte St, Fitzroy Sq., London, portable desk maker (1817). [D]

Austin, Thomas, Petworth, Sussex, carpenter, builder and cm (1832–40). [D]

Austin & Gurney, 4 Old St, Goswell St, London, cm (1802). [D]

Autherton, Humphrey, 132 Long Acre, London, carver and gilder (1809). [D]

Auty, G., Lockwood, Yorks., cm (1823). [D]

Auty, George, Fall Lane Gate, Dewsbury, Yorks., cm (1822). [D]

Auty, Joseph, Southgate, Middlx, chairmaker (1839). [D]

Avant, Thomas, Queen St, Dawlish, Devon, cm and u (1810–30). On 26 April 1810 advertised in *Exeter Flying Post* for workmen. Supplied white and gold bookcases for the libraries at Powderham Castle in 1820. [D; *C. Life*, 18 July 1936]

Aveline, Frederick, High St, Stoney Stratford, Bucks., cm and u (1839). [D]

Avelin(e), George, High St, Leighton Buzzard, Beds., cm and u (1830–39). Trading also as paper hanger in 1839. [D]

Aven, Charles, Liverpool, u (1731–60). Took apps named Samuel Kirks in 1731, John Owen *c*.1750 and Campbell in 1755. His son Edward Aven petitioned freedom by patrimony in 1760. [Liverpool app. and freemen regs.; S of G, app. index]

Avery, Edward, Liverpool, chairmaker (1835–37). At 9 Cavendish St with shop in Standish St. The number of this shop was 79 in 1835 and 11 in 1837. [D]

Avery, Henry, address unrecorded, cm and u (1661–64). Account dated 5 January 1664 for the supply of various items of furniture and bedding to H. Morris & Partner at various dates between February and July 1661. [V&A archives]

Avery, John, Newcastle, carver and gilder (1833–38). Trading at Fighting-Cocks Yd with house at Trafalgar St in 1833; Erick St in 1834, and 48 Groat Mkt in 1838. [D]

Avery, William, Eagle and Child Alley, parish of St Andrew, Holborn, London, chairmaker (*c*.1750–60). Took app. named Joseph Smith. [GL, P83/MRYI(870/22]

Avery, William, Reading, Berks., upholder (1754). [Poll bk]

Avery & Dangar, 11 Gt Portland St, London, cm and u (1839). [D]

Aves, John, 3 Whitelion St, Chelsea, London, carver and gilder (1823–26). [D]

Aveson & Henry, Elland, Yorks., cm (1837). [D]

Aveyard & Buck, Leeds, Yorks., cm and joiners (1791–92). In 1791 took over the business of Isaac Croft by whom they had been employed for a number of years as journeymen. Advertised that they were selling 'The Cabinet Stock . . . at Prime Cost and under'. [*Leeds Intelligencer*, 13 September 1791; 27 February 1792]

Avington & Beckett, Swaffham, Norfolk, chairmaker (1828). Makers of a child's chair at a cost of 11 guineas for Robert John Steggles, son of Robert & Elizabeth Steggles, born on 4 March 1827. [*Eastern Daily Press*, 29 March 1975]

Avison, William, Carlton St, Nottingham, cm and u (1825). [D]

Avon, Charles, Liverpool, u (1730). Admitted freemen on 15 November 1730. [Liverpool freemen reg.]

Avon, Edward, Liverpool, u (1761). Admitted freeman on 9 February 1761. [Liverpool freeman reg.]

Avon, Margaret, 33 Chorley St, Water St, Liverpool, upholder (1796). [D]

Awty, Richard, 6 Rathbone St, Liverpool, cm (1814–23). [D]

Axton, Thomas, Manchester, carver, etc. (1755). Took app. named Baley in 1755. [S of G, app. index]

Aycliffe (or Ayliffe), George, Newport St, Covent Gdn, London, turner and chairmaker (1742–49). In 1742 he supplied Lord Monson with six Windsor chairs at 7s 6d each. May have been related to Thomas Aycliffe. [Lincoln RO, Monson 11/50; poll bk]

Aycliffe (or Ayliffe), Thomas snr, 'The Bathing Tubb', Newport St, London, turner (1713–15). Took an app. in 1713. [S of G, app. index; GL, Sun MS vol. 3, ref. 3745; vol. 4, ref. 5167]

Aycliffe (or Ayliffe), Thomas jnr, London, turner and chairmaker (1760–d.1805). 'Turner in Ordinary to his MAJESTY'. Originally at the corner of Gt Newport St but by 1762 had moved to 49 Wardour St which he used as ware rooms. He also occupied 'The King's Arms', Gerrard St, near Newport Mkt from this date. Married in October 1795 and died in April 1805 at Surbiton, Surrey. From 1767 the business is styled Aycliffe & Webb, and from 1783 Aycliffe & Gee. The term Aycliffe & Co. is used as an alternative name for these partnerships. In 1792 insurance cover of £500 was taken out 'on their utensils stock & goods in trust in their dwelling house and warehouse'. [D; V&A archives; *Gents Mag.*, October 1795; April 1805; GL, Sun MS vol. 382, ref. 505828] On 8 May 1762 submitted a bill to David Garrick for 'a Bed Waggon' costing 16s. [V&A archives] Supplied for Audley End, Essex, to the order of Sir John Griffin Griffin in November 1766 twelve small plain chairs, twelve garrett chairs, mats, etc. In 1775 'six forest stools' were supplied at £1 4s, and 2 clamp tables at 13s 6d. Two years later 12 'red moulded open back matted chairs' were supplied at 7s 6d each, six similar stools at 6s 6d each and two 'high Joint stools' at 6s. In 1783 a quantity of garden chairs and 'forest stools' were supplied totalling £10 9s. As Lord Howard de Walden, Sir John continued to patronise this firm from 1784. This included 12 further 'Red open back matted chairs'. An order for '12 japanned beach chairs with cane seats' was received in 1791. This patron also ordered '4 Beech matted chairs' for his London house in New Burlington St. [Essex RO, D/DBy/A27/4; A25/4; A36/3; A41/5; A42/8; A44/10; A49/5; A44/5] Supplied to Heaton Hall, Manchester, chairs costing £49 8s for Baron Grey de Wilton (later 1st Earl of Wilton). Believed to be for the Music Room. [Preston RO, bank deposit and accounts bks, DDEg] Small payments made, 1801–06, for work done at Madingley Hall. [Cambs. RO, 588/A45] B.A.

Ayerst, —, Ashford, Kent, upholder (1803–11). [D]

Ayles, Benjamin, Christchurch, Hants., chairmaker (1756). Took app. named Morris in 1756. [S of G, app. index]

Ayles, Charles, 4 King St, Holborn, London, carver, gilder, looking-glass and picture frame maker and paper hanger (1820–29). Trade card in Johnson Coll., Bodleian Lib., Oxford. In 1820 insured his house for £900, and in 1822 the household goods in it for £100. [D; GL, Sun MS vol. 483, ref. 972925; vol. 493, ref. 987900; vol. 498, ref. 1001006]

Aylett, Alfred, 8 Bloomfield St, Finsbury, London, u and cm (1826–27). [D]

Aylett, G., 21 Islington Row, Birmingham, carver and gilder (1823). [D]

Aylett, W., London, cm and u (1804–12). Had premises at 12 Broker Row but from 1807 had in addition addresses in New Bond St. The number was initially 19 but from 1811 25 was also used. [D]

Ayliffe, — See Aycliffe.

Ayling, James, Sloane St, London, cm and u (1808–26). At 151 Sloane St, 1808–09; 162 from 1813–23; and 195 from 1826. [D]

Ayling, James, 24 St George's Pl., Hyde Park Corner, Knightsbridge, London, cm, u, undertaker and carpet warehouseman (1828–39). In 1828 took on the lease of a manufactory at the back of Kinnerton St, St George, Hanover Sq. [D; Marylebone Lib., deed 134/15–16]

Ayling, T., 4 Middle Row, Knightsbridge, London, cm and u (1820). [D]

Ayling, Thomas, Andover, Hants., u (1762). Took app. named Spencer in 1762. [S of G, app. index]

Ayling, Thomas, Hants., u, cm and auctioneer (1784–93). At Farnham, 1784–92, and Gosport, 1793. [D]

Aynsley, John, King St, North Shields, Northumb., cm and joiner (1827). [D]

Aynsley, Robert, Newcastle, cm and mahogany dealer (1801–05). In 1801 moved his yard from Pandon to the Head of Manor Close. In 1805 at Big Mkt. [D; *Newcastle Courant*, 21 November 1801]

Ayre, George, South Biddick, Houghton-le-Spring, Co. Durham, joiner and cm (1827). [D]

Ayres, John snr, London, upholder (1698). On 29 September 1698 his son, John jnr, was admitted freeman of the Upholders' Co. by patrimony. [GL, Upholders' Co. records]

Ayres, John, Butcher Row, Exeter, Devon, cm (1822). [D]

Ayres, Mary, 5 Henrietta St, Covent Gdn, London, carver (1780). Insured utensils, stock and goods in 1780 for £50 out of a total cover of £450. [GL, Sun MS vol. 285, p. 351]

Ayres, Philip, 18 Sise Lane, Cannon St, London, writing desk and dressing case maker (1829). [D]

Ayres, Thomas, 28 Gt Bath St, Clerkenwell, London, fancy cm and u (1829–39). [D]

Aytell, Alfred, 8 Lower Moorfields, London, u (1825). [D]

Ayton, Jacob, 73 Berners St, London, carver, gilder and picture frame maker (1777). His trade card announced that he sold 'all sorts of Green & Gold Dressing Glasses, Pier Glasses, Girandoles, etc.'. Declared bankrupt, *Gents Mag.*, July 1777. [Heal]

B

Babel, Peter, near James's St, Long Acre, London, papier-mâché frames and ornaments maker (1763). [D]

Babin, Augustine, 3 New St, Old St, London, chair and sofa maker, invalid, recumbent, etc. (1839). [D]

Back, Stephen, Canterbury, Kent, cm (1826–39). Recorded in 1826 and 1830 in the parish of St Peter; in 1822–24, Monastery St; and 1838–39, Westgate St Without. [D; poll bks]

Back, William, St George's St, Canterbury, Kent, carver and gilder (1830–34). [D; poll bk]

Backhouse, Bartholomew, 36 Warren St, Liverpool, cm (1827). [D]

Backhouse, James, 21 John St, Liverpool, cm (1769–81). [D]

Backhouse, John, Liverpool, cm (1766–68). Trading at 36 King St from 1766–74, then at 21 John St by 1784. [D]

Backhouse, Richard, 1 Grimshaw St, Preston, Lancs., cm (1825). [D]

Backhouse, Robert, Silver St, Westminster, London, carver (1749). [Poll bk]

Backhouse, Thomas, Atherton St, Liverpool, cm (1787). [D]

Bacon, Charles, 31 Britannia St, City Rd, London, cm (1835). [D]

Bacon, Daniel, Norwich, cm (1825). App. to John Brunning; admitted freeman of Norwich 26 April 1825. A cm of the same name was also admitted on 3 May 1826. [Norwich freemen reg.]

Bacon, James, 6 New St Sq., Shoe Lane, London, cm (1778).

Took out a Sun Insurance policy for £200 of which utensils, stock and goods accounted for £100. [GL, Sun MS vol. 264, p. 100]

Bacon, James, address unrecorded, u (1803). Subscribed to Sheraton's *Cabinet Dictionary*, 1803.

Bacon, John, 'The Golden Fleece Inn', Colchester, Essex, u (1728). Took out a Sun Insurance policy for £1,200 of which stock in trade accounted for £400. [GL, Sun MS vol. 27, ref. 46355]

Bacon, John, Middle Row, Holborn, London, upholder (1763). [D]

Bacon, John, White Horse Yd, Coppergate, York, joiner, cm, undertaker etc. (1837). Advertised in *Yorkshire Gazette*, 7 January 1837.

Bacon, Mark, Nottingham, cm (1746). Will dated 29 June 1746. [Notts. RO, probate records]

Bacon, Richard, Colchester, Essex, u (1734). Probate dated 1734. [*Wills at Chelmsford*, vol. 3, p. 13]

Bacon, Samuel, Alfreton, Derbs., cm (1829). [D]

Bacon, Thomas, parish of St Mary, Rotherhithe, London, joiner and upholder (1706–20). Took out several insurance policies with the Hand in Hand Co. on a house 'on the north side of the street between Russells Mill and Globe Stairs' and 'divided into two tenements', for £100. [GL, Hand in Hand MS vol. 4, ref. 10988; vol. 12, p. 223; vol. 13, p. 445; vol. 22, p. 332]

Bacon, Thomas, Bridge St, Boston, Lincs., cm (1819–35). Recorded at no. 9 in 1819; also as an u in 1822; and as Bacon & Son, cm and chairmakers, 1826–35. [D]

Bacon, William, Ordnance Row, Portsea, Portsmouth, Hants., cm and upholder (1781–98). Took out a Sun Insurance policy in 1781 for £200 of which utensils and stock accounted for £140. [D; GL, Sun MS vol. 293, p. 41]

Badcock, Charles, Oxford, cm (1802–30). Polled of St Peter-le-Bailey in 1802, and listed in directories, 1823–30, as cm and u, of St Aldate's. See Martha Badcock.

Badcock, Francis, St Aldate's, Oxford, cm (1768). [Poll bk]

Badcock, John, St Clement's, Oxford, cm (1751). Married Martha Jones at Bloxham, 29 July. [Bodleian index of Oxf. marriage bonds]

Badcock, John, 31 and 34 New Bridge St, Exeter, Devon, cm (1830–40). [*Exeter Journal*]

Badcock, Martha, St Aldate's, Oxford, cm (1805–08). Presumably wife of John Badcock. [D]

Badcock, Richard, St Aldate's, Oxford, cm (1802). [Poll bk]

Badcock, Thomas, St Aldate's, Oxford, cm (1798–1802). [D; poll bk]

Badcock, Thomas, 95 Chapel St, Salford, Lancs., cm (1834). [D]

Baddely, Thomas, Uppingham, Rutland, cm (1732). Took app. named Freeman in 1732. [S of G, app. index]

Badge, —, 58 Princess St, Devonport, Plymouth, Devon, cm (1830). [D]

Badger, —, address unrecorded, cm (*c.* 1725–30). Named in the Chiswick account book as receiving £5 6s. [Chatsworth papers, ref. L166, vol. A, p. 170]

Badger, Ellen & Sons, 3 Bank St, Bolton, Lancs., cm and u (1814–34). [D]

Badger, James, Coleham, Shrewsbury, Salop, cm (1835). [Shrewsbury burgess roll]

Badger, Joseph, 25 Portobello, Sheffield, Yorks., carver and gilder (1822). [D]

Badger, Matthew, London, picture-frame maker (1761). Described as 'late of St. Andrew, Holborn' when discharged from Debtors' Prison. [*London Gazette*, 26 September 1761] A Mr Badger, carver, subscribed to Chippendale's *Director*, 1754.

Badger, Richard, Bolton-le-Moor, Lancs., cm and wheel maker

(1793). [D] A Mr Badger, cm of Battersley Moor, Lancs., subscribed to Sheraton's *Drawing Book*, 1793.

Badham, John (& Co.), Bristol, cm (1818–28). Trading 1818–19 at Clifton Pl.; 1820–21 at Clifton Pl. and Hotwell Rd; 1822–28 at 7–8 Clifton Pl. [D]

Badham, Richard, Boar Lane, Bedminster, Bristol, cm (1794). [D]

Badham, Thomas, 117 Redcliff St, Bristol, cm (1823–24). [D]

Bagg, Charles Johannes, Norwich, chairmaker (1806). Son of Charles Bagg, weaver, admitted freeman of Norwich 23 November 1806. [Norwich freemen rolls] A Charles Bagg, cm of Hoxton, London, is listed in the Norwich poll bks in 1818 and 1830.

Bagley, Edward, Tewkesbury, Glos., frame maker (1758). Took app. named Dudfield in 1758. [S of G, app. index]

Bagley, John, address unrecorded, joiner and carpenter (1733–37). Worked at Moulsham Hall, Essex, making garden furniture. [A.C. Edwards, *The Accounts of Benjamin Mildmay, Earl Fitzwalter*]

Bagnall, Walter, Blackheath, London, cm (1838–39). Recorded in 1838 at Tranquil Vale and in 1839 at South Vale. [D]

Bagnall & Sanderson, Green Dragon Yd, Worship St, London, cm (1832–34). [D]

Bagot, Thomas, Lancaster, cm (1767–84). App. to R. & R. Gillow and admitted freeman 1773–74. Took app. 6 April 1781. Named in the Lancaster poll bk in 1784. [Lancaster app. reg. and freemen rolls; poll bk]

Bagot, William, Liverpool, cm (1816). Admitted freeman 12 June 1816. [Liverpool freemen rolls] A William Bagott, cm of Liverpool, is recorded in 1821 at 41 Jordan St, in 1823 at 44 Jordan St, and in 1824 at 44 Bridgewater St. [D]

Bagott, Richard, Lancaster, cm (1799–1800). [Lancaster freemen rolls]

Bagott, Thomas, Liverpool, cm (1816–18). Recorded in 1816 at 2 Tarleton St, and in 1818 at 2 Morley's Ct, Bolton St. [D]

Bagshaw, John, 7 Parliament St, Nottingham, joiner and cm (1832–35). [D]

Bagshaw, Joseph, Dukinfield, Ashton-under-Lyne, Lancs., cm and joiner (1824). [D]

Bagshaw, Thomas, Chapel-en-le-Frith, Derbs., cm (1797–98). [D]

Bagshaw, William, Manchester, cm and furniture broker (1825–40). Recorded from 1825–32 at 14 Thomas St, and from 1833–40 at 33 Thomas St. [D]

Bagster, James, 20–21 Piccadilly, London, cm, upholder, looking-glass maker, tentmaker; carpet, bedding, cabinet warehouse manufactory owner (1782–1808). Trading from 1790–1808 at 20–21 Piccadilly, and in 1792 recorded as having a workshop at 7 Air St, Piccadilly. In 1791 he supplied furniture, including a carved and gilt looking-glass, to John Pinney of Bristol who considered this latter 'too crowded with ornaments' which he therefore removed. In 1794 he supplied 'A cushing stuft with fine wool etc.', costing £2 2s, to Mr Phillips of Langford Parsonage, near Maldon, Essex. Bagster subscribed to Sheraton's *Drawing Book*, 1793, and featured in Sheraton's list of master cabinet makers, 1803. He took out Sun Insurance policies in 1782 for £1,000 of which utensils, stock and goods accounted for £700; on 14 July 1792 for £500 of which utensils and stock in his workshop in a yard in Air St accounted for £250; on 9 July 1805 for utensils, stock and goods in trust in his shop and warehouse, for £1,000; and on 15 October 1806 on five houses in Baldwin's Gdn for £800. [D; poll bk; *Furn. Hist.*, 1976; Essex RO, D/D Sp. A5; GL, Sun MS vol. 301, p. 634; vol. 389, ref. 602691; vol. 434, ref. 777625; vol. 437, ref. 795474]

Bagster & Son, Richard & Jaspar, 20 Piccadilly, London, u and

tentmakers (1806–11). [D] An R. Bagster, u and tentmaker, is recorded at 35 Piccadilly, 1809–11. [D]

Baildon, Thomas, Blake St, Stonegate, York, u, appraiser, undertaker and auctioneer (1762–1798). Son of William Baildon, tailor, and Sarah Baildon. App. to Robert Barker jnr u, 1 May 1762. Admitted freeman 1785. Advertised 16 August and 11 October that he had been 'Fourteen years last past Foreman to Messrs. Haig & Chippendale, 60 St. Martin's Lane, London . . . purposes opening a shop in Blake St., York . . . where the upholstery business will be carried on in all its branches . . .' The sale of his effects is recorded in 1797. [D; York app. reg. and freemen rolls; *York Courant*, 16 August and 11 October 1785]

Baildon, Thomas, 2 Porter St, Newport Mkt, London, cm (1780–84). Took out a Sun Insurance policy in 1780 for his house for £200. Polled at Westminster, 1784. [GL, Sun MS vol. 287, p. 411]

Baildon, William, Porter St, Newport Mkt, London, u (1784). [D]

Bailes, John, 434 Oxford St, London, bedjoiner and carver (1780–1837). Took out Sun Insurance policies in 1780 for £400 of which utensils, stock and timbershop accounted for £160; in 1786 for £600 of which utensils accounted for £320; in 1791 for £500 for house and goods only; and in 1792 for £1,000 of which goods and stock accounted for £270. Partnered with William Bailes between 1806 and 1837. Subscribed to Sheraton's *Drawing Book*, 1793. [D; GL, Sun MS vol. 280, p. 641; vol. 338, p. 349; vol. 389, ref. 605474]

Bailes, Matthew, Pavement, York, u (1791). [D]

Bailes, Sarah, 343 Oxford St, London, bedstead maker (1829–1839). [D]

Bailes, William, 434 Oxford St, London, bedstead maker (1806–37). Took out Sun Insurance policies on 24 April 1807 for £300; and partnered with John Bailes on 17 October 1806 for £950 of which stock, utensils, workshop and sheds accounted for £550. Between 1809 and 1837 W. & J. Bailes are listed in London Directories. On 1 November 1810 William and Betsy Bailes took out a Sun Insurance policy for £350 for household goods. [D; GL, Sun MS vol. 440, ref. 802616; vol. 437, ref. 795490; vol. 453, ref. 850413]

Bailey, —, address unrecorded. In 1838 supplied new furniture for Stafford House, London, costing £226. [Staffs. RO, D593/R/126/8]

Bailey, Benjamin, West Gate St, Bath, Som., upholder (1805). [D]

Bailey, David, 52 St John's St, London, chairmaker (1809–11). [D]

Bailey, Edmund, 11 Gt Queen St, Lincoln's Inn Fields, London, cm and broker (1782). In partnership with Edward Johnson, with whom he took out a Sun Insurance policy for £200 of which utensils, stock and goods accounted for £180. [GL, Sun MS vol. 304, p. 531]

Bailey, Edward, Sheffield, Yorks., cm and u (1821–33). Recorded variously at 4, 1, and 29 Townhead Cross, 1821–25, Bow St in 1828 and Eyre St in 1833. [D]

Bailey, Edward, 13 and 14 Mount St, Grosvenor Sq., London, cm, u and undertaker (1809–40). In 1826 he endorsed the prefatory recommendation in Nicholson's *Practical Cabinet Maker* as 'Manufacturer to His Majesty', and is recorded in London directories between 1809 and 1840. He is frequently named in the Royal Household accounts as carrying out much general jobbing, cleaning, work on upholstery, blinds, carpets etc. at Carlton House, St James's Palace, King's Lodge, Windsor, and Carlton House Ride, between 1826 and 1831. In October 1829 he supplied furniture, including a patent recumbent chair, (presumably the model illustrated in the *Practical Cabinet Maker*, pl. 64), for the Royal Lodge,

Windsor, costing a total of £157. [Royal Household accounts, PRO, LC 11/53–74] Between 1832 and 1840 he performed similar work at the palaces of St James's, Kensington and Buckingham, and at Windsor Castle, and took an inventory of furniture at Stud House, Hampton Court. In 1833 he regilded the Royal Arms on top of the throne at St James's Palace, and in 1835 supplied two portable mahogany tables to Kew Palace.

The Lord Chamberlain's accounts for 1835–41 list furniture provided for the Store Tower, Windsor, being Her Majesty's Vice Chamberlain's apartments, including a 'Large Mahogany Wardrobe enclosed by folding doors panelled & veneered with Spanish on Honduras' costing £35. For the servants' rooms Bailey supplied '2 dressing tables japanned buff with shaped backs', '3 corner washhand stands japanned buff', '3–3ft. Japanned buff chests' and '18 black stained beech chairs with rush seats', for which the total bill was £142 16s. Bailey also provided curtains, locks and a bookcase for Clarence House, kneeling stools for the Chapel Royal, and undertook work at Kensington Palace for the Duke of Sussex's apartments. [PRO, LC 11/77–110] At the beginning of Queen Victoria's reign Bailey was re-appointed 'Upholsterer, Cabinet Maker, Undertaker, &c. to Her Majesty', as the bill-head for work done at the Coronation, totalling £7,154 2s 4½d, states. [PRO, LC 21/19] Bailey took out a Sun Insurance policy on 30 April 1823 for £2,000 [GL, Sun MS vol. 498, ref. 1003747] and in 1838 he took out a mortgage on 55 Green St, including household goods and furniture. [Marylebone Lib., deed 152/26]

Between 1817 and 1835 Edward Bailey is recorded as the partner of Richard Saunders (both having been partners with Thomas Tatham until Tatham's death in 1818). The firm of Bailey and Saunders received a lucrative commission from the Prince of Wales for furnishing Brighton Pavilion. In 1817 they provided for the Banqueting Hall two side tables of rosewood and satinwood supported by Chinese dragons, designed by Robert Jones costing £430 each. For work in the Music Room the firm were paid over £15,000, which included the chimney-glass at £857 11s, and 'four large chairs' superbly carved and gilded. They also provided a set of thirty-six japanned chairs, and in 1819 two 'Commodes Anglaise', copied from a French pair ordered for the Chinese Drawing Room in Carlton House. For the Saloon at Brighton Pavilion accounts of 1823 list velvet trimmings, lace tassels, draperies etc. and furniture made to the designs of Robert Jones, including a set of pier cabinets with Graeco-Indian ormolu enrichments, chairs, pole-screens and amboyna wood tables, totalling £2,757 18s 9d. Much of this furniture is still in the Royal Collection. [PRO, LC 11/41] The Royal Household accounts of 1819 cite general cleaning, alterations and upholstery work at Carlton House and Stud Lodge, totalling £705 5s 1d [PRO, LC 11/27] and between 1819 and 1823 furnishings for Royal Yachts, Carlton House, Brighton Pavilion, Kensington Palace and Hampton Court. [PRO, LC 11/20, 31–38] In 1824 the firm supplied a rosewood console and cabinet, and a mahogany writing table for the Red House, Carlton House, and a large mahogany chair for HM's bedroom. [PRO, LC 11/44, no. 74] In 1826 Messrs Bailey and Saunders were paid £1,413 12s 'in discharge of old claims as to Bills delivered to the Ld. Chamberlain'. [RA, 35606] A bill of 4 May 1820 for work done for John, 6th Duke of Bedford, is receipted by Edward Bailey, and one of November 1821, 'Richard Sanders for Bailey & self'. [Bedford Office, London] On 5 October 1835 Bailey and Saunders received orders for furniture for the Royal Library, Windsor, in the Elizabethan style. [D; *Conn.*, June 1977; *Apollo*, May 1975; Wills, *Looking-Glasses*; DEF; H. Clifford Smith, *Buckingham Palace*] See George Edward & William Marsh.

Bailey, Edward, Gloucester, cm (1833). Child bapt. at St John Baptist. [PR]

Bailey, Francis, 52 Warren St, Liverpool, u (1835). [D]

Bailey, George, High St, King's Lynn, Norfolk, cm and u (1784–1808). [D]

Bailey, Gilbert, Goosegate, Nottingham, cm, u, paper hanger and furniture broker (1832–41). [D]

Bailey, Henry, 29 Park Lane, Liverpool, cm (1790). [D]

Bailey, J., Worship Sq., Shoreditch, London, looking-glass frame maker (1790). [Wills, *Looking-Glasses*]

Bailey, J., Union Row, Torquay, Devon, cm and u (1838). [D]

Bailey, James & Boote, Alexander, Crown Ct, Soho, London, u (1778). Declared bankrupt, 28 February 1778. [*Leicester Journal*]

Bailey, James, 5 Margaret's Hill and 6 St Michael's Pl., Bath, Som., chairmaker (1826–33). [D]

Bailey, James, Horfield Rd and Lane, Bristol, cm (1793–94). [D]

Bailey, John, St Paul's Churchyard, Liverpool, cm, joiner, appraiser and auctioneer (1773–90). Trading in 1774 and 1787 at 5 Old Ropery, and in 1781 at 5 Fenwick Alley. [D] A Thomas Bailey was trading at 7 Fenwick Alley, 1766–74.

Bailey, John, Liverpool, cm (1778–1816). Recorded in 1804 at 9 Batchelor St, Dale St, and in 1816 at 6 Hawke St. Admitted freeman in 1778. His son, Robert Manners Bailey, cm and joiner, petitioned for freedom on his birthright in 1812. [D; Liverpool freemen committee bk]

Bailey, John, 46 Marshall St, Golden Sq., London, upholder and broker (1801–11). Took out Sun Insurance policies on 6 January 1801 for £900 of which utensils and stock accounted for £700; on 11 January 1805 for £1,000 of which utensils, stock and goods in trust accounted for £800; and on 10 December 1807 for £300. [D; GL, Sun MS vol. 419, ref. 712501; vol. 431, ref. 769997; vol. 440, ref. 809930]

Bailey, John, Belgrave Gate, Leicester, cm and broker (1828). [D]

Bailey, John jnr, Norwich, cm (1831). App. to John Kerry; admitted freeman 20 June 1831. [Norwich freemen reg.]

Bailey, Joseph, Spalding, Lincs., cm (1817–22). Recorded at Hall St, 1819–22. [D; Lincoln RO, subject index]

Bailey, Joseph, Liverpool, u (1820). Son of John Bailey, joiner, admitted freeman 11 March 1820. [Liverpool freemen reg.]

Bailey, Leonard, Duke St, Norwich, cm (1836). [D]

Bailey, Owen, 12–13 Speldhurst St, Burton Cresc., London, carver and gilder (1835–37). [D]

Bailey, Robert, Chard, Som., cm and joiner (1793). [D]

Bailey, Robert Manners, Liverpool, cm and joiner (b. 27 May 1788–1812). Petitioned for freedom on his birthright as son of John Bailey, cm, and admitted freeman, 12 October 1812. [Liverpool freemen's committee bk and reg.]

Bailey, Rodney, 9 Hawke St, Liverpool, u (1802–35). Admitted a freeman 8 July 1802 and thereafter until 1835 recorded several times in the freemen reg.

Bailey, Thomas, Liverpool, cm, builder and appraiser (1759–74). Trading at 7 Fenwick Alley from 1766–74. Married 19 April 1759 Mrs Bloodworth, 'housekeeper to Robert Cunliffe, Esq., Mayor', at the Old Church. In 1761 took app. named Cooper, whilst former apps Robert Fairhurst of London, and George Harper, were admitted freemen in 1761 and 1774 respectively. [D; Liverpool freemen's committee bk; *Liverpool Advertiser*, 20 April 1759] A John Bailey was trading at 5 Fenwick Alley in 1781.

Bailey, Thomas, address unrecorded, cm (1762–70). Cited in the account bk of the Earl of Ancaster on 30 May 1762 receiving £64 4s in full; and on 30 May 1770 £28 8s 6d in full for 'Beauro Library Table &c.' supplied in 1768. [Lincoln RO, 2ANC, 6/8; 6/13]

Bailey, Thomas, Conduit St, Hanover Sq., London, upholder and cm (1766–74). On 17 November 1766 he sent Mr Bennet a bill for 'a neat mahogany Pembroke table — £2 9s.' plus oddments totalling 2s 6d. A trade card of Vicars & Rutledge, upholders, in the Ponsonby Coll., states they are successors to Mr Bailey of Conduit St. [Poll bk; Heal Coll., BM]

Bailey, Thomas, North End, near Hampstead, London, upholder and cm (1777). Took out a Sun Insurance policy in 1777 for £300 of which utensils and stock accounted for £100. [GL, Sun MS vol. 257, p. 428]

Bailey, Thomas, 116 Aldersgate, London, carver and gilder (1835–37). [D]

Bailey, Thomas, Market Pl., Soham, Cambs., cm, u and carver (1839). [D]

Bailey, William, 177 Fleet St, London, u (1784). [D]

Bailey, William, Stoney Hill, Bristol, carver (1793–95). [D]

Bailey, William, Queen St, Shelton, Staffs., cm (1818–23). [D]

Bailey, William, Stowmarket, Suffolk, cm (1819–39). Addresses in Bury St from 1824–39, and in Market Pl. in 1830. Married in 1819. [D; Suffolk RO, calendar of marriage licence bonds, FAA: 50/2/118 p. 65]

Bailey, William, Camberwell Green, London, cm and u (1826). [D]

Bailey, William, 91 Great Titchfield St, London, bedstead maker (1829). [D]

Bailey, William, Birmingham, carver and gilder (1830–35). Trading at 10 Gough St in 1830 and 77 Navigation St in 1835. [D]

Bailey, William, Market Pl., East Harling, Norfolk, cm (1830–39). [D]

Bailey, William, 6 Leonard St, Shoreditch, London, cm (1832–34). [D]

Bailey, William, Belgrave Gate, Leicester, cm and broker (1828–35). [D]

Bailey, William, Brook End St, Ross-on-Wye, Herefs., cm (1835). [D]

Bailey, William, 15 Marshall St, Golden Sq., London, carver and gilder (1837). [D]

Bailey, William & Co., 102 Curtain Rd, and 1 and 2 Bateman's Row, London, cm and looking-glass manufacturer (1825–79). Established in 1825, the firm supplied 'Every description of gilt glasses, console and other tables, jardinières, fancy chairs, window cornices, picture frames etc.' wholesale and for export. [D]

Bailey, William, 30 New Gloucester St, Hoxton, London, looking-glass manufacturer and frame maker (1839). [D]

Bailey & Saunders, see George Elward & William Marsh.

Bailey & Archer, 61 Long Alley, Moorfields, London, cm and u (1827–28). [D]

Bailey & Jackson, 92 New Bond St, London, u (1839). [D]

Bailie, John, 23 Cow Cross, London(?), carpenter, joiner and cm (1782). Took out a Sun Insurance policy for £200 of which utensils, stock and goods accounted for £100. [GL, Sun MS vol. 299, p. 343]

Baillie, James, 4 Stephen St, Tottenham Ct Rd, London, cm (1808). [D]

Baily, John, Parish of St Augustine, Bristol, cm (1754). [Poll bk]

Baily, John, 39 Foster Lane, London, u (1773). [D]

Baily, John, St Mary Tower, Ipswich, Suffolk, cm (1788). Married in 1788. [Suffolk RO, calendar of marriage licence bonds, FAA: 50/2/108, 20 September]

Baily, Richard, Hill, Warks., chairmaker (1751). Took app. named Evins, in 1751. [S of G, app. index]

Bain, R., 11 King St, Clerkenwell, London, cm (1837). [D]

Bain, William, Bath, Som., cm (1761). Discharged from Debtors' Prison, 25 August 1761. [*London Gazette*]

Bainbridge, Henry, London, joiner (1702–16). Took out two insurance policies with the Hand in Hand Co. for a brick house on the north side of Gt Marlborough St in the parish of St James, Westminster, 'empty . . . and in his own possession', firstly on 11 July 1702 for £150, assigned to William Millman Esq. on 14 August 1703 and renewed on 5 March 1716; and secondly in 1706 for £500. [GL, Hand in Hand MS vol. 2, ref. 2939; vol. 4, ref. 12102]

Bainbridge, Thomas, Lancaster, trade unrecorded (1808–23). Named in the Gillow records making a bookcase in 1811. [Westminster Ref. Lib., vol. 344/99, p. 1902]

Bainbridge, Thomas, 176 High Holborn, London, carver and gilder (1813–16). [D]

Bainbridge, William, Gerard St, London, carver (1798). Declared bankrupt 1 January 1798. [*Liverpool Advertiser*]

Bainbridge, William, 5 Broad St, Carnaby Mkt, London, looking-glass manufacturer (1809–12). [D]

Bainbridge, William, 1 Gt Russell St, Bloomsbury, London, carver and gilder (1820). [D]

Baines, Abraham, 64 Gt Queen St, Lincoln's Inn Fields, London, cm and u (1808–11). [D]

Baines, Abraham & Son, Ludgate St, 1 St Paul's Churchyard, London, cabinet and upholstery warehousemen (1811–28). Named as Baines & Son in directories between 1822–28. The stamp of Baines & Son, 1 St Paul's, London, occurs on a circular monopodium rosewood table with a plaque underneath stating, in French, that Napoleon Bonaparte signed his abdication on it in 1814 at Fontainebleau. A set of four similated rosewood and gild dining chairs impressed 'BAINES & SON ST PAULS CHURCHYARD', and a sideboard bearing the inscription 'T. Baines London 1815' have been recorded. From 1823–27 Margaret or Margery Baines & Son, John, are listed at 1 St Paul's Churchyard. [D; V & A archives]

Baines, Edward & Henry, High St, Uppingham, Rutland, chairmakers and turners (1835). [D]

Baines, Francis Singleton, Lancaster, u (1817–18). [Lancaster freemen rolls]

Baines, Henry, Lancaster, joiner and cm (1739–84). Admitted freeman as a joiner, 1739–40, and took eighteen app. joiners and cm between 3 September 1744 and 15 October 1785. On account of his 'declining business', a sale of his stock in trade began on Monday 18 February 1782, and was 'to continue until the whole are sold'. The sale, which took place at 'a warehouse in Ranelagh Street', included 'a variety of elegant wardrobes, desks & book-cases, ladies toilets, French Commodes with toilets, ditto with writing tables . . . tea trays, corner cupboards, buffets, dining tables, snap, card, spider & Pembroke ditto, stands & wash stands . . . close-stool smoking chairs & clock cases . . . a great number of mahogany chairs . . . looking-glasses . . . Patterns of painted, stained & Windsor chairs may be viewed at the same time & place . . .' [D; Lancaster app. reg. and freemen rolls; *Williamson's Liverpool Advertiser*, 28 February 1782]

Baines, J., 46 Fleet St, London, upholstery and bedding warehouse owner (1835). [D]

Baines, James, 83 Well St, Oxford St, London, cm and u (1827–28). [D]

Baines, John, Littleworth, Uppingham, Rutland, chairmaker and turner (1835). [D]

Baines, John, Lutterworth, Leics., chairmaker and turner (1835). [D]

Baines, Joseph, St Peter's Sq., Leeds, Yorks., cm (1805). Placed advertisement in *Leeds Mercury*, 1 June 1805 in which he 'Returns thanks to his friends for past favours, and begs leave to inform them that having declined that business, various articles of new-made furniture . . . are to be disposed of at moderate prices . . . at his late shop, near St. Peter's Sq'.

Baines, Margaret & Son, 1 St Paul's Churchyard, London,

cabinet and upholstery warehouse, cabinet and carpet warehouse owners (1825–27). Margaret and John Baines, 1 St Paul's Churchyard, cm and u, took out Sun Insurance policies on 31 March 1823 'on warehouse, stable and workshops, Wheatsheaf Yard, Fleet Mkt' for £1,400, and on 'open shed and sawpit in yard' for £100; and on 'stock, utensils and goods in trust in warehouse, stable and workshops, live stock included' for £500, and 'in open shed and open yard', for £1,000. M. & J. Baines, London, u and cm, were declared bankrupt on 24 October 1826. [D; GL, Sun MS vol. 494, ref. 1003293 and ref. 1003294; *London Gazette*, 24 October 1826; *Liverpool Mercury*, 27 October 1826]

Baines, Robert, Littleworth, Uppingham, Rutland, chairmaker and turner (1835). [D]

Baines, Samuel, Stonechair, Shelf, Rishworth, Yorks., joiner and cm (1837). [D]

Baines, Thomas, Lancaster, cm (1768). Son of Henry Baines. [Poll bk] A Thomas Bains, cm of Lancaster, was admitted a freeman in 1766–67. [Lancaster freemen rolls]

Baines, Thomas, Lancaster, turner (1816–23). Named in the Gillow records. [Westminster Ref. Lib.]

Baines, Thomas, Northgate-Without, Canterbury, Kent, cm and broker (1824). [D]

Baines, William, Vicarage Lane, Kirkby Lonsdale, Westmld, cm and joiner (1829). [D]

Baines, William, Dean's Lane, Oakham, Leics., chairmaker (1835). [D]

Baines (or Baynes) & Dufill, 37 Fetter Lane, York, chairmakers (1828–40). [D]

Bains, James, Kirkby Lonsdale, Westmld, joiner and cm (1828–29). [D]

Baird, Thomas, Manor Chare, Newcastle, joiner and cm (1828). [D]

Bairsto, George, Selby, Yorks., joiner, builder and cm (1826–37). Trading from 1826–29 in Millgate, and from 1831–37 at Gowthorpe, near Selby. [D]

Baiston, James, Coach Lane, Leeds, Yorks., cm (1817–22). [D]

Baiston & Co., St Peter's Sq., Leeds, Yorks., joiners and cm (1790). [D]

Baiston & Hargill, Leeds, Yorks., cm (1793). Subscribed to Sheraton's *Drawing Book*, 1793.

Baivan, Edward, Liverpool, cm (1761). Report in *Williamson's Liverpool Advertiser*, 25 September 1761, concerned his imprisonment for debt in Lancaster Castle. Discharge from Debtors' Prison announced in *London Gazette*, 12 September 1761.

Baker, Amos, Much Part St, Coventry, Warks., chairmaker and turner (1822). [D]

Baker, Ann, Newgate St, Newcastle, working u (1827–34). Recorded at Court 15, Newgate St in 1827. [D]

Baker, Barnard, Covent Gdn, London, upholder and cm (1751–d. 1796). Trading in King St in 1776 and at 23 Bedford St, 1778–96. Son of John Baker of Shelley, Essex, farmer. App. to Elizabeth Hutt, widow of J. Hutt, clothworker. Admitted freeman of the Upholders' Co. 5 September 1751, and master of the Upholders' Co., 1785. Took apps named Thomas Greenwood between 1772–91, and Thomas Pickstone between 1777–84. In 1775 Baker supplied to the 2nd Earl of Shelburne goods 'to Mr Clerisseau's Account £100 15s', and from February to June 1776, goods to the value of £160s 1½d. The accounts of Robert Palmer, Executor to the late Thomas Tower of Weald Hall, South Weald, Essex, include payment to 'Mr Tower, £31 10s', on 21 December 1778. Several bills and receipts survive for furniture provided for Sir John Nelthorpe, Bart, including one

of 12 June 1784 for 'Ten neat arm chairs with cane seats and backs varnished, £10 10s'. Between 1784–95 Baker supplied 'A neat vase shape dress glass in mahg. compass frame & 3 drawers, £1 16s, and a 3ft. 3 wainscot chest drawers, £2 16s'. Another bill and receipt of 20 March 1793 lists 'a neat mahogany bottle carrier (for 2 bottles), a ditto small claw table, 15s, 2 large mahogany Berger chairs with hollow backs & seats caned, £5, and two (thin) cushions for ditto, 12s'

A shield-shaped dressing or shaving glass, c. 1790, with the label 'Barnard Baker, Upholder and Cabinet Maker, Bedford Street' in the drawer, is in the Du Pont Museum, Winterthur, Delaware. Died aged 69, January 1796. [D; GL, Upholders' Co. records; Bowood MS; Essex RO, D/DTw/A10; Lincoln RO, NEL 9/6/45–6; NEL VIII/92; NEL 9/15/13; *Antiques*, May, 1968; poll bk; *Gents Mag.*, January 1796]

Baker, Benjamin, 231 Whitechapel Rd, London, cm (1835). [D]

Baker, C. & W., 72 Margaret St, Cavendish Sq., London, u and cm (1820–37). [D] The firm of Baker & Webb was trading at this address from 1832–34. See William Baker at this address.

Baker, Charles, Laycock (Lacock), Wilts., chairmaker (1736). Recorded in the case of Thomas Fry, chairmaker of Laycock, called 'to appear and answer Charles Baker of Laycock, chairmaker, his master, concerning his assaulting and threatening to kill him'. Fry appeared and was discharged. [*Wiltshire Quarter Sessions and Assizes, 1736*, ed. J. P. M. Fowle]

Baker, Daniel S., Islington, London, cm and upholder (1793–1829). Recorded in Upper St, 1808–11, at 39 High St, 1822–23 and as D. S. at 39 Hedge Row in 1829. The firm of Baker & Co. was trading at this address, 1826–27. Subscribed to Sheraton's *Drawing Book*, 1793 and *Cabinet Dictionary*, 1803. In that year he declared his membership of the Freemasons, Lodge of Three Grand Principles, which met at the 'King's Head Tavern', Upper St, Islington. [D; GL, ref. MR/SF/283]

Baker, Edward, 40 Frankfort St, Plymouth, Devon, cm and u (1838). [D]

Baker, Edward, 10 Gildart's Gdns, Liverpool, cm (1839). [D]

Baker, Edward Jordan, Hotwell Rd, Bristol, cm (1810). See Thomas Baker and William Baker & Son, of Hotwell Rd. [D]

Baker, Emanuel, 28 Exmouth St, Commercial Rd, London, cm and u (1839). [D]

Baker, Gilbert, Folkestone, Kent, cm (1794). [D]

Baker, James, Bristol, u (1715–34). Polled of St Stephen's parish in 1715 and 1722, and of St Nicholas in 1734.

Baker, James, 7 Back Bittern St, Liverpool, cm (1834). [D]

Baker, James, 11 Shudehill and 33 Oldham Rd, Manchester, chairmaker (1836). [D]

Baker, John, address unrecorded, u (1710). Admitted freeman of the Upholders' Co., 26 April 1710. Recorded as having taken an app. on 5 October 1713. [GL, Upholders' Co. records]

Baker, John, Canterbury, Kent, upholder, appraiser and auctioneer (1760–1807). His trade label bears the address Birgate St, Canterbury, and his name occurs in directories and poll bks between 1784 and 1807. He is listed as a freeman in 1760 and 1796. [D; BM; V & A archives; poll bks; Canterbury freemen rolls]

Baker, John F., Sandwich, Kent, cm (b. 1728–d. 1809). Recorded in directories in 1798, 1803 and 1807. His wife, Anne, died aged 76 on 25 September 1808, and he died aged 81 on 26 October 1809. [D; *Gents Mag.*, November 1809]

Baker, John, Market St, Sandwich, Kent, cm (1823–39). [D; poll bks] Perhaps the son of John F. Baker of Sandwich.

Baker, John, Reading, Berks., cm (1768). [Poll bk]

Baker, John, Newcastle, cm (1803). Subscribed to Sheraton's *Cabinet Dictionary*, 1803.

Baker, John, Nantwich, Cheshire, cm and chairmaker (1812–40). Trading in Welsh Row, 1812–28, and High St in 1834. His daughter, Mary Astles, was bapt. 10 September 1812. [D; Chester RO]

Baker, John, Eastgate St, Gloucester, manufacturers of sofas and fancy chairs (1820). [D]

Baker, John, Church St, Woodbridge, Suffolk, cm (1839). [D]

Baker, John Luck & Olive, William, London, cm (1779–81). Trading at 59 Chiswell St in 1779 when they took a Sun Insurance policy for £200 of which utensils and stock accounted for £150. By 1781 their address is recorded as 13 Red Cross Sq., when Baker alone took out another Sun Insurance policy totalling £700 of which utensils and stock accounted for £400. [GL, Sun MS vol. 276, p. 416; vol. 294, p. 188]

Baker, Jonathan, Cockerton, Darlington, Co. Durham, spinning-wheel maker (1828). [D]

Baker, Joseph, Queen's Cross, Dudley, Worcs., cm (1820). [D]

Baker, M., 14 Museum St, Bloomsbury, London, u (1826–27). A William Baker, u, is recorded at this address in 1823. [D]

Baker, Mark, 9 George Yd, Hatton Wall, London, carpenter and picture and looking-glass frame maker (1835–39). [D]

Baker, Nicholas, Bath, Som., upholder (1731–41). Polled at Bristol in 1734, and took apps Arthur Trimnell in 1731 and Banbury in 1741. [Poll bk; S of G, app. index]

Baker, R., Bridewell Lane, Bristol, sign and furniture painter (1812–13). [D]

Baker, Richard, Bristol, carver and gilder (1784–94). Working in the parish of St Stephen in 1784, and at 15 Clare St in 1794. Declared bankrupt 23 February 1792. A William Baker, carver and gilder, is recorded in Clare St in 1784. [D; poll bk; *Exeter Flying Post*, 23 February 1792]

Baker, Richard jnr, St Clements, Ipswich, Suffolk, cm (1820). His name occurs in the calendar of marriage licence bonds, 1817–25. [Suffolk RO, FAA: 50/2/119, p. 87]

Baker, Richard, 8 Northgate St, Gloucester, cm (1839–40). [D]

Baker, Robert, 117 Long Acre, London, trunk and plate case maker (1801). [D]

Baker, Samuel, at the 'White Hart' on the north side of Monmouth St, in the parish of St Giles-in-the-Fields, London, upholder and broker (1733). Took out a Sun Insurance policy on 17 October 1733 'on household goods in trust in dwelling house in the parish aforesaid, £300'. [GL, Sun MS vol. 38, ref. 62132]

Baker, Samuel, Southwark, London, cm and u, carpet and upholstery warehouse owner (1803–08). Addresses at 40 Queen St in 1803, and at 144 High St from 1807–08. Took out a Sun Insurance policy on 17 August 1803, totalling £999 of which utensils and stock accounted for £700. [D; GL, Sun MS vol. 427, ref. 750994]

Baker, Thomas, Shrewsbury, Salop, joiner and cm (1720–21). Took app. named Rider in 1720, and is cited in the Shrewsbury burgess roll in 1721. [S of G, app. index]

Baker, Thomas, Hotwell Rd, Bristol, cm (1794). See Edward Jordan Baker and William Baker of Hotwell Rd. [D]

Baker, Thomas, 34 Snowhill, Birmingham, cm (1835). [D]

Baker, Thomas, 10 Union St North, Liverpool, u (1839). [D]

Baker, Thomas, 1 Christopher St, Hatton Wall, London, cm and u (1839). [D]

Baker, William, Shrewsbury, Salop, cm (1729). Took app. named Nicholas in 1729. [S of G, app. index]

Baker, William, East Retford, Notts., chairmaker (1752). [Notts. RO, probate records]

Baker, William, West Retford, Notts., cm (1757–58). Will dated 1757. Took app. named Hobson in 1758. [Notts. RO, probate records; S of G, app. index]

Baker, William, Clare St, Bristol, carver and gilder (1784). A Richard Baker carver and gilder, is recorded at 15 Clare St in 1794. [D]

Baker, William, address unrecorded, cm (1803). Subscribed to Sheraton's *Cabinet Dictionary*, 1803.

Baker, William, Hotwell Rd, Bristol, cm and u (1801–15). Recorded as W. B. & Son in 1810, and declared bankrupt in 1815. [D; *Exeter Flying Post*, 15 June, 1815] See Edward Jordan Baker and Thomas Baker both of Hotwell Rd.

Baker, William, 17 Church St, Lambeth, London, chairmaker (1809–11). [D]

Baker, William, Bailey St, Birmingham, 'Greecian & fancy chairmaker' (1818–22). [D]

Baker, William, Liverpool, chairmaker (1821–24). Trading at 31 Marlborough St from 1821–23, and at 23 Standish St in 1824. [D]

Baker, William, 14 Museum St, Bloomsbury, London, u (1823). [D] An M. Baker, u, is recorded at this address, 1826–27. [D]

Baker, William, 72 Margaret St, Cavendish Sq., London, u (1825). [D] See C. & W. Baker of the same address.

Baker, William, Windsor, Berks., and London, carver and gilder (1794–1840). Recorded in New Windsor between 1794–1806; at 9 Thames St, Windsor between 1824–30; and King St, Bloomsbury, London, 1835–40. Mentioned in the 5th hall book of the borough of New Windsor in connection with litigation brought against the Borough Council, (pp. 51–167, 1828–52). The Royal Household accounts refer to Baker as having carried out much jobbing work between 1831–40 at Windsor Castle, Hampton Court, Bushey Lodge and Buckingham Palace, including regilding, repairing and carving on chairs, sofas, picture and glass frames and door mouldings. On 30 June 1831 he was paid a total of £88 for such work, and in the same year was repairing and regilding the candelabras in the corridor and Dining Room of St George's Hall. He also supplied frames costing £65 18s 3d for Harrington House, and in 1832 carried out repairs to the 'Gothick pillars, Caps & Bases belonging to pedestal dining Tables'. In 1837 he was paid a total of £45 7s 7d for 94 days work repairing and regilding furniture 'throughout the principal suit of Apts.', no doubt in honour of Queen Victoria's accession. [D; poll bks; Royal Household accounts, PRO, LC 11/71, 74, 80–110; Joy, *English Furniture, 1800–1851*]

Baker, William, Redcross St, Southwark, London, cm and u (1827–28). [D]

Baker, William, Cannon St, Taunton, Som., cm (1830). [D]

Baker, William, Pipe Maker's Lane, Boston, Lincs., cm and chairmaker (1835). [D]

Baker, William, 27 High St, Bloomsbury, London, carver and gilder (1839). [D]

Baker & Bright, Newbury, Berks., turners and chairmakers (1798). [D]

Baker & Lyal, 243 High Holborn, London, cabinet manufacturers (1801–03). [D]

Bakestrom, William, Maiden Lane, parish of St Paul's, Covent Gdn, London, cm and looking-glass maker (1723). Took out a Sun Insurance policy on 28 May 1723 for £500 on goods and merchandise in his dwelling house only. [GL, Sun MS vol. 15, ref. 28099]

Bakewell, Mathew, Birmingham, inlayer and gilder (1712). Took app. on 9 July 1712. [PRO, app. reg.]

Bakewell, William, 'of Birmingham', cm (1826). App. to Job Hughes of Derby, cm, and admitted freeman of Leicester in 1826. [Leicester freemen rolls]

Balch, —, address unrecorded, frame maker (1770). The private accounts of Richard Hoare of Boreham House, Essex, include a payment to Balch of £6 11s on 2 December 1770. [Essex RO, D/DU 649/2]

Balch, Edward snr, West Ham, London, joiner and upholder (1769). By his will, dated 13 September 1769 and proved 18 December 1769, he left to his wife Hannah 'the shop & business of an Upholder to be carried on by my wife & grandson Edward Balch my apprentice'. [PRO, 953(406) p. 69]

Balcomb, James, Gillingham, Kent, cm and u (1839). [D]

Balders, William, Swaffham, Norfolk, cm, u and appraiser (1822–25). Will proved at Norwich in 1825. [D; Norfolk Record Soc., index of wills]

Baldie, John, 6 Meard's Ct, Dean St, Soho, London, cm (1809–11). [D] Possibly mis-spelling of Baldwin of this address.

Baldock, Edward Holmes, Hanway St, London, furniture dealer, restorer, etc. (b. 1777–d. 1845). Born on 14 May 1777. Married on 19 November 1811 Mary Goringe, the daughter of John and Sarah Goringe of Buxted, Sussex. They had two children: Edward Holmes (1812–75), who married the daughter of a Salopian baronet, Sir Andrew Corbet; Mary Frances (1814–42), who married a barrister of Lincoln's Inn, William Amos Starborough Westoby.

In 1805 Baldock's name first appears as the freehold owner of 7 Hanway St, London. Over the years he expanded his premises. By 1840 his property in this street comprised nos 1 and 2, both with back premises, and in addition he owned a yard (precise location unspecified) and no. 3, which he let. It was in 1 and 2 Hanway St that he carried on business up to 1843 when he retired, selling his stock and moving to a fashionable residential address, Hyde Park Pl. According to one 19th-century source the business was taken over by Frederick Litchfield's father. [Conn., June 1978, p. 102]

In 1805 he described himself as dealer in china and glass. By 1821 he was styled in the Post Office Directories as antique furniture and ornamental china dealer, and in 1826 he described his activities in a bill heading as 'buying, selling, exchanging and valuing China, Cabinets, Screens, Bronzes etc.'. Though Baldock's business consisted primarily in dealing in antique porcelain and furniture — largely foreign — he repaired, remodelled and altered existing furniture. He also produced designs for new pieces and had them made. Whether the furniture was actually manufactured on his premises is a matter of conjecture in the absence of documentary evidence.

References to alterations to furniture occur in the Lucy, Lowther and Buccleuch papers during the years 1836 to 1843. These involved the addition of mounts, the replacement of the interior fittings of secretaries and tables, the addition of doors to case furniture and the embellishment of other pieces with porcelain plaques. Baldock also supplied sofas and chairs made up in part or in whole of old pieces of carving. A large quantity of dismembered pieces of furniture, listed in Baldock's sale catalogues of May and July 1843, may well have been stocked for use in making up pieces. He evidently specialised in furniture in the Boulle manner, in French 17th-century style ebony cabinets and in oriental 17th-century style seat furniture of turned ebony and carved ivory.

In 1841 the Duke of Buccleuch was sent drawings of bedroom furniture as well as working drawings of an octagonal table, a bookcase and three stalls. A drawing of a Louis XV lean-to secretaire, which may have been supplied by Baldock, survives in the Buccleuch archives. It is not however clear whether it represents an existing piece or a design for a projected piece in the Louis XV style. The same doubt arises in the case of a design of a lectern in the Gothic revival style which was drawn on Baldock's premises (drawing now in Marylebone Lib.). On the other hand a design of a table in the Buccleuch papers which is annotated 'No. 3 Amboyna wood ground with coloured flowers' is almost certainly the preliminary sketch for a table which was later made.

A number of well constructed and, in some cases, finely inlaid pieces of furniture are known which are 19th-century in date and which are branded with Baldock's initials, 'EHB'. While some are pastiches of 18th-century French furniture others are in a contemporary English style. Whether these pieces were both designed by Baldock and made on his premises it is impossible to tell. The 'EHB' mark cannot be regarded as a maker's stamp in the accepted sense of the term as it is also struck on genuine French 18th-century furniture which merely passed through Baldock's hands.

[G. de Bellaigue, 'Edward Holmes Baldock', I and II, Conn., August 1975, pp. 290–99 and September 1975, pp. 18–25; C. G. Gilbert, Leeds Furn. Cat., no. 395, pp. 318–21]

Baldock's bills survive in the following archives: Windsor Royal Archives, George IV's papers, 1827–28; Staffs. RO, 1st Baron Hatherton papers, 1831; Warwick RO, George Lucy papers, 1826–37; Duke of Buccleuch and Queensbury's private archives, 5th Duke of Buccleuch papers, 1830–43; Cumbria RO, 2nd Earl of Lonsdale papers, 1836–41; Duke of Northumberland's private archives, 3rd Duke of Northumberland papers, 1824; Leeds archives dept, Harewood MS, Edward Lord Lascelles papers, 1807; Staffs. RO, Duke of Sutherland's papers, 1830; Lincoln RO, Lord Willoughby d'Eresby papers, (2nd Lord Gwydir), 1827–28; Herefs. RO, John Arkwright papers, 1832; Lord de Saumarez's private archives at Shrubland Hall, Sir William Middleton's papers, 1839–43.   G. de B.

Baldry, Foxale, St Clements, Ipswich, Suffolk, cm (1799). Marriage recorded in 1799. [Suffolk RO, calendar of marriage licence bonds, FAA: 50/2/111 p. 213]

Baldwin, David, George St, Derby, chairmaker and turner (1829–35). Recorded at no. 2 in 1835. [D]

Baldwin, John, 6 Meard's Ct, Dean St, Soho, London, cm (1808). [D] See John Baldie of this address.

Baldwin, Robert, Lancaster. Named in the Gillow records, 1807, working on a commode. [Westminster Ref. Lib., Gillow vol. 344/98, p. 1819]

Baldwin, Robert, Liverpool, cm (1809–27). Trading at 15 Scotland Rd in 1810, 5 Scotland Rd in 1811, and 35 Eldan St in 1827. Marriage reported in Liverpool Courier, 23 August 1809 'on monday last at St Ann's Church . . . to Miss Fletcher of Burscough'. [D]

Baldwin, Thomas, 21 Somerset Buildings, Bath, Som., cm and u (1826–33). [D]

Bale, James, Winchester, Hants., cm (1792–1805). Recorded in High St in 1805. [D]

Bale, Joshua, Bingley, Yorks., joiner and cm (1822). [D]

Bale, William Edward, Little Chapel St, St Margaret's, London, carver and gilder (1838). Took app. named John Wallace in 1838. [Westminster Ref. Lib., Grinsell's charity app. indentures]

Bales, Samuel, 36 Warren St, Fitzroy Sq., London, cm (1802). Took out a Sun Insurance policy on 15 July 1802 for £100. [GL, Sun MS vol. 423, ref. 732955]

Bales, Samuel, address unrecorded, cm (1803). Subscribed to Sheraton's Cabinet Dictionary, 1803.

Bales, Samuel, 36 Broad St, Golden Sq., London, cm and carver (1820). [D]

Bales, Samuel, Berwick St, Soho, London, cm and u (1822–29). From 1822–25 at 85, and in 1829 at 25 Berwick St when listed only as a carver. [D]

Bales, Simon, Norwich, cm (1793–1803). Subscribed to Sheraton's Drawing Book, 1793 and Cabinet Dictionary, 1803.

Baletti, Anthony, 13 Pottergate St, Norwich, frame maker (1802). [D]

Baliey, John, Meards Ct, London, cm (1784). [Poll bk]

Ball, Benjamin, 56 Port St, Manchester, joiner and cm (1794). [D]

Ball, David, 9 Anderson's Walk, Vauxhall, London, carver (1808). [D]

Ball, Edwin, 9 St Mary's St, Southampton, Hants., cm (1834–39). [D]

Ball, Elias, 4–5, Broad St, Golden Sq., London, cm and u (1826–29). [D]

Ball, G., 7 Castle Mill St, Bristol, cm and broker (1835). [D]

Ball, George, Downley, High Wycombe, Bucks., chairmaker (b. c. 1811). [Census 1841].

Ball, Henry, Downley, High Wycombe, Bucks., chairmaker (b. c. 1796–1840). Daughter's baptism recorded in 1816, and two sons in 1819 and 1824. [PR (bapt.); Census 1841]

Ball, Henry, 63 Gerard St, Liverpool, cm (1814–27). Indenture dated 1814. In 1822 he petitioned freedom on servitude to John Ward Turner and James Wainwright, cm, and was admitted freeman on 17 October 1827. [Liverpool freemen's committee bk]

Ball, James, Lee's Mews, North Audley St, London, cm and u (1839). [D]

Ball, James, 2 Beckford Pl., Walworth, London, chair and sofa maker (1839). [D]

Ball, John, 9 Princes St, Cavendish Sq., London, upholder (1808). [D]

Ball, John, 106 Gt Russell St, Bloomsbury, London, u (1809–11). [D]

Ball, John, Spilsby, Lincs., joiner and cm (1822–26). [D]

Ball, John, Hundleby, Lincs., cm and joiner (1835). [D]

Ball, John, Liverpool, cm (b. 1800–d. 1833). Indenture dated 1814. In 1821 he petitioned freedom on servitude to Thomas Dutton, and was sworn a freeman on 12 October 1826. Trading at 1 Leece St in 1827. Died on 9 April 1833 'after a short illness'. [D; Liverpool freemen's committee bk; *Liverpool Mercury*, 19 April 1833]

Ball, Jonathan, High St, Salisbury, Wilts., u (1839). [D]

Ball, Joseph, Bridgnorth, Salop, cm (1797–98). [D]

Ball, Mary, 2 Waring St, Gildarts Gdns, Liverpool, u (1837). [D] William Ball was trading in Gildarts Gdns in 1827.

Ball, Robert, Lancaster, joiner and cm (1747). Took app. named Edmondston, 1747. [S of G, app. index]

Ball, Robert, 31 St James's St, Portsea, Portsmouth, Hants., cm and u (1830). [D]

Ball, T., Union St, Ryde, Isle of Wight, Hants., cm and u (1839). [D]

Ball, Thomas, Vine St, St James's, London, u (1749–d. 1758). Polled at Westminster in 1749. Death reported on 29 May 1758: 'Last Friday died at his house in Vine Street... Mr Ball, upholsterer and deputy-master of the revels, under Solomon Dayrolles Esq.' [*London Chronicle*, 29 May 1758]

Ball, Thomas, Aldgate, London, cm and u (1824–29). Trading at 17 Mitre St from 1827–28, and at no. 34 in 1829. Took out a Sun Insurance policy on 5 July 1824 for £300. [D; Sun MS vol. 497, ref. 1017870]

Ball, W., Baxtergate, Loughborough, Leics., u and auctioneer (1800). Advertised on 7 March 1800 that he had 'just arrived from London' and was settling in Loughborough. [*Leicester Journal*, 7 March 1800]

Ball, William, Lancaster, joiner and cm (1751–65). Made free as a 'joyner', 1751–52. Took app. joiner and cabinet maker, 2 February 1765. [Lancaster freemen rolls]

Ball, William, Bull Inn Yd, Coventry, Warks., carpenter and cm (1776). Took out a Sun Insurance policy in 1776 for £200 of which utensils and stock accounted for £150. [GL, Sun MS vol. 244, p. 248]

Ball, William, Nottingham, joiner and cm (1798). App. to Samuel Dodd in 1798. [Notts. RO, app. list]

Ball, William, Liverpool, furniture and sign painter (1810–27). Addresses at 6 Brown St from 1810–11; at 13 Johnson St in 1818; at 34 Stanley St and 5 Carpenters Row in 1821; and at 24 Gildarts Gdns in 1827. [D] Mary Ball, u, was trading in Gildarts Gdns in 1837.

Ball, William, 76 Berwick St, Soho, London, cm and u (1822–39). [D]

Ball, William, Chichester, Sussex, chairmaker, turner and patten maker (1826–40). Recorded in St Pancras, 1826–28; Summers Town in 1832; and New Broyle in 1839. [D]

Ball, William, 26 Essex St, Birmingham, chairmaker (1835). [D]

Ball & Keating, Grosvenor Mews, Grosvenor Sq., London, cm (1832–39). [D]

Ballantine, David, Liverpool, joiner and cm (1834–39). Trading at 46 Norfolk St in 1834; 16 Sparling St in 1837; and 93 Sparling St in 1839. [D]

Ballard, Charles, 170 High St, Cheltenham, Glos., cm, u and paper hanger (1822). [D]

Ballard, Henry, Manchester, cm (1797–1808). Addresses at 35 Back Water St in 1797, and 4 Windmill St in 1808. [D]

Ballard, J., Nuneaton, Warks., plumber, glazier, house and sign painter, gilder and varnisher (c. 1760). A small mahogany toilet mirror has a trade label on the back describing Ballard's trade: 'Cleans, Repairs, or Varnishes old Paintings, & silvers Looking Glasses. House Painting and Paper Hanging Executed after the most Approved Methods on Reasonable terms'. The label has an oval Rococo border with easel, brushes and palette at top and bottom.

Ballard, Robert, Liverpool, cm (1761). Admitted freeman, 10 February 1761. [Liverpool freemen reg.]

Ballard, William, Hoxton, London, chairmaker and undertaker (1813–39). Trading at 7 Hoxton Mkt in 1813, and at 7 Britannia Row from 1837–39. Took out a Sun Insurance policy on 19 May 1813 for £100 of which household goods in his dwelling house, where no work was done, accounted for £70, and 'wearing apparel', £30. [D; GL, Sun MS vol. 463, ref. 881984]

Balld, Robert, Worcester, cm (1753). Took app. named Humphrys in 1753. [S of G, app. index]

Baller, Robert, Long Acre, St Martin-in-the-Fields, London, u (1671–74). Recorded in feuds between 1671–74 with George and Susannah Higgins, William Bursey and John Hales, Gent., relating to property in Long Acre, St Martin-in-the-Fields; Hart St, St Paul's, Covent Gdn; and Boonegate, Herts. [Marylebone Lib., deeds 176/4–10]

Balley, William, Spitalfields, London, cm and broker (1781–1816). Recorded at 42 Fashion St, 1781–84, and 190 Brick Lane, 1793–1816. Took out Sun Insurance policies in 1781 for £200 of which utensils and stock accounted for £100; and on 16 April 1803 for £1,000 of which utensils and stock accounted for £200. [D; GL, Sun MS vol. 291, p. 114; vol. 427, ref. 747111]

Balling, Timothy, St Ives, Hunts., chairmaker (1754). His son, William, was bapt. in 1754 at St Ives Independent Church. [Hunts. RO, Non-Con MF RG48]

Ballingal, John, address unrecorded, cm (1803). Subscribed to Sheraton's *Cabinet Dictionary*, 1803.

Ballon, John, Bedale, Yorks., joiner and cm (1840). [D]

Balls, John & Co., Bird St and Oxford St, London, cm, u and appraiser (1809–40). Addresses at 12–13 Bird St, Manchester Sq., 1809–37; George Yd, Grosvenor Sq., 1827–28; 170 Oxford St, 1835–40 and 26 Bird St in 1839. A Regency dwarf breakfront open bookcase bears the trade label of 'Balls &

Co., 170 Oxford St. . . . & 10,11,12, & 13 Bird St.' The bookcase, of rosewood inlaid with brass, has a frieze inlaid with scrolling foliage, and is raised on ebonized gadrooned feet. [Christie's, 28 April 1983, lot. 107] Recorded on a bill of 25 August 1840 as an orator with George Cossar, carpenter, of Walthamstow, Essex. An u named Balls, was paid 6s in June 1839 by 3rd Lord Braybrooke of Audley End, Essex. [D; PRO, C 13 417/16; Essex RO, D/DBy/A363]

Balls, Thomas, London, cm (1793). Subscribed to Sheraton's *Drawing Book*, 1793.

Balls & Hughes, 50 High St, Kensington, London, u (1826–27). [D]

Bally, —, 10 Milsom St, Bath, Som., cm and u (1793–1805). Subscribed to Sheraton's *Drawing Book*, 1793. [D]

Balmar, Adam, 30 Prudhoe St, Newcastle, cm (1828). [D]

Balme, Joshua, Main St, Bingley, Yorks., joiner and cm (1837). [D]

Balmer, Daniel, Liverpool, cm (1807–39). Recorded at 90 Gerard St in 1807, and at 63 Blackstock St in 1839. [D]

Balmer, James, Hungate, York, chairmaker (1828). [D]

Balmer, John, Greek St, Liverpool, cm (b. 1790–d. 1826). Sworn a freeman, 16 October 1812. Died, 12 June 1826, aged 36. [Liverpool freemen reg.; *Liverpool Mercury*, 23 June, 1826]

Balmer, Pexel, Sunderland St, Houghton-le-Spring, Co. Durham, joiner and cm (1827–34). [D]

Balmer, Thomas, Liverpool, cm (1829–39). Trading at 4 Whittle Ct in 1829, and Mill Pl., Shaw's Brow, 1835–39. [D]

Balmford, Simeon, 'Near the New Baths', Leeds, Yorks., joiner and cm (1822). [D] See Simeon Balmforth.

Balmforth, John & Sons, Dod Lee, Longwood, Huddersfield, Yorks., cm (1837). [D] See T. Balmforth and John Balmforth & Sons of Longwood.

Balmforth, Jos., Wakefield, Yorks., adjoining Vicarage, cm and u (1828–34). [D]

Balmforth, Simeon, Hotel Yd, Call Lane, Leeds, Yorks., 'Near the New Baths', joiner and cm (1817–22). [D] See Simeon Balmford.

Balmforth, T., Snow Lee, Longwood, Huddersfield, Yorks., cm (1837). [D] See John Balmforth & Sons and Thomas Balmforth of Longwood.

Balmforth, William, Fell Lane Gate, Dewsbury, Yorks., cm (1822). [D]

Balsam, John, Newton Abbot and Newton Bushel, Devon, cm (1838). [D] Possibly J. Balson of Newton Abbot, cm, who was declared bankrupt on 13 July 1837. [*Exeter Flying Post*]

Balshaw, Charles, Ormskirk, Lancs., cm (1822–25). Trading at Church St in 1825. [D]

Balshaw, John, Church St, Ormskirk, Lancs., cm, joiner and builder (1825–34). [D]

Baltis, Matthew, Norwich and London, cm (1803–18). Son of Matthew Baltis, bricklayer, admitted freeman of Norwich 25 June 1803, and polled at Norwich in 1806 and 1818. Subscribed to Sheraton's *Cabinet Dictionary*, 1803. [Poll bks; Norwich freemen reg.]

Bamber, George, Blackburn, Lancs., cm (1797–98). [D]

Bamber, Henry, Lancaster (1784–85). [Westminster Ref. Lib., Gillow records]

Bamber, James, Poulton St, Kirkham, Lancs., joiner and cm (1834). [D]

Bamber, Thomas, 44 Quay St, Manchester, cm, joiner and coffin maker (1797–1825). With Richard Bamber as cm and print block maker in 1825. [D]

Bamber, William, Cock Yd, Church St, Preston, Lancs., joiner and cm (1818–25). [D]

Bamber, William, Grange, Broughton, Westmld, cm (1829–34). [D]

Bamfield, William, Castle Ct, Strand, London, cm (1779). Took out a Sun Insurance policy in 1779 for £100 on his house. [GL, Sun MS vol. 273, p. 301]

Bamford, John, 50 Crickets Lane, Ashton-under-Lyne, Lancs., joiner and cm (1834). [D]

Bamford, John & Sons, Longwood, Huddersfield, Yorks., joiner and cm (1834). [D] See John Balmforth & Sons of Longwood.

Bamford, Thomas, Snowlee, Longwood, Huddersfield, Yorks., joiner and cm (1834). [D] See T. Balmforth of Longwood.

Bamforth, William, Daw Green, Dewsbury, cm (1828–34). [D]

Banbury, James, Bath, Som., u (1752). Declared bankrupt, July 1752. [*Gents Mag.*]

Banbury, William, 1 Smiths Rents, St John St, Clerkenwell, London, knife case maker (1778). Took out a Sun Insurance policy in 1778 for £100 of which utensils, stock and goods accounted for £20. [GL, Sun MS vol. 263, p. 608]

Bance, George, Croydon, Surrey, cm and u (1807–39). Addresses in Butcher Row, 1832 and High St, 1838–39. MS order book lists customers' addresses and breakdown of prices for work commissioned. [D; Potterton Books, catalogue 7, 1983, no. 2580]

Bancks, Adam, Westgate St, Newcastle, carver and gilder (1782). [D]

Bancks, Jacob, 78 Oldham St, Manchester, cm (1794). [D]

Bancroft, C., Manchester, chairmaker (1825). Worked with John Bancroft. [*Furn. Hist.*, 1981]

Bancroft, David, Dale St, Liverpool, chairmaker (1790–1800). [D; *Furn. Hist.*, 1981] J. & D. Bancroft were in Dale St, 1790, and Joseph Bancroft, 1804.

Bancroft, David, Salford, Lancs., chairmaker (1804–13). Trading in Collier St in 1804, and at 21 Bloom St from 1808–13. Partnered with John Bancroft in Chapel St, 1804–18. [D]

Bancroft, John, Chapel St, Salford, Lancs., chairmaker (1781–1825). Recorded at no. 126, 1797–1802; with David Bancroft there as fancy chairmakers in 1808; together at no. 141, 1804–18; and John alone there, 1821–25. There is a spindle-back chair at Temple Newsam House, Leeds, stamped 'J & D BANCROFT'. [D; *Furn. Hist.*, 1981]

Bancroft, John, Oldham, Lancs., joiner and cm (1828–34). Trading at Duke St, 1828 and Manchester St in 1834. [D]

Bancroft, Joseph, Liverpool, cm (1804–37). Recorded at 48 Vernon St, Dale St in 1804; 3 Trinket St in 1810; 3 Fox St, 1811–14; Clayton St, 1818–29; and London Rd, 1835–37. [D] The name 'I. BANCROFT', is stamped on a set of Regency chairs recorded in Liverpool. [V & A archives]

Bancroft, Sarah, 4 Back Falkner St, Manchester, u (1802). [D]

Bancroft, William, Manchester, u (1773–84). Addresses in Market St Lane, 1773, and Longmill Lane, 1781–84. [D]

Bandy, John, St Ann, London, gilder and carver (1761). Discharged from Debtors' Prison, 17 November 1761. [*London Gazette*]

Banfield, Edwin, 7 Sidney Pl., Commercial Rd, London, cm and u (1832–39). [D]

Ban(d)field, John, Som., cm (1830–40). Listed at Petherton in 1830; and as cm and u at High St, Chard, 1839–40. [D]

Banfill, Samuel, 20 Edward St, Cavendish Sq., London, cm and u (1822–34). [D]

Bangay, Samuel, 8 Brownlow St, Drury Lane, London, picture frame maker (1786). Took out a Sun Insurance policy on 1 April 1786 for £200 of which utensils accounted for £100. [GL, Sun MS vol. 336, p. 103]

Banister, George, 23 College St, Bristol, carver and gilder (1792–1800). [D]

Banister, John, Liverpool, cm (1761). Son of James Banister, polisher, sworn freeman 12 March 1761. [Liverpool freemen reg.]

Banister, Robert, Clayton St, Blackburn, Lancs., cm and joiner (1814–17). [D] Ann Bannister & Sons are recorded at this address, 1818.

Banister, Zachariah, Clipstone St, Fitzroy Sq., London, cm (1828). Reported on 1 August 1828 as insolvent with James Cook, cm. [*Chester Chronicle and North Wales Advertiser*, 1 August 1828]

Bankes, Margaret, Liverpool, u (1834–37). Trading at 24 Bevington Bush in 1834 and 77 Gerrard St, 1835–37. [D] The firm of Bankes & Fletcher, u, are recorded at 24 Bevington Bush in 1834. [D]

Bankes, William, 7 Gloucester St, Bloomsbury, London, fancy chairmaker (1808). [D]

Banks, —, address unrecorded (1750). Cited in the Holkham Hall accounts in 1750 as being paid £2 2s for a mahogany dining table, and £9 for a small wainscot table.

Banks, —, St Leonard St, Stamford, Lincs., cm and u (1835). [D] Probably either Thomas or William Banks.

Banks, Benjamin, 3 Lichfield St, Soho, London, cm and wine cooler maker (1801–27). Took out Sun Insurance policies on 6 July 1801 for £500 of which utensils and stock accounted for £440; and on 2 February 1813 for £500 'on house only in 10 High St. in tenure together with 50 Upper Thames (No stove therein)'. [D; C. *Life*, 30 April 1948, pp. 882–83; *DEF*; GL, Sun MS vol. 419, ref. 721125; vol. 462, ref. 889952]

Banks, Benjamin, Prescot, Lancs., cm and joiner (1814–34). Recorded in Fazakerley St, 1814–16; Toll Bar, 1818; and Fall Lane, 1834. [D]

Banks, Benjamin, Brierley, Yorks., joiner and cm (1837). [D]

Banks, Edward, Kingsgate St, St Giles-in-the-Fields, London, picture frame maker (1722). Took out Sun Insurance policies on 12 March 1722 for £500 on his house, goods and merchandise; and on 6 October 1722 for £300 on the same. [GL, Sun MS vol. 15, ref. 27953; vol. 14]

Banks, George, Hull, Yorks., cm (1768–84). [Poll bks]

Banks, Henry, Liverpool, cm (1812). On servitude to Thomas Burns, sworn a freeman 5 October 1812. [Liverpool freemen reg.]

Banks, James jnr, Bondgate, Selby, Yorks., turner, dish, bowl, chair and shovel manufacturer (1837). [D] A low back crinoline stretcher Windsor chair bears the stamp on the front corner of the seat in a triangle, 'J. BANKS SELBY'.

Banks, Joseph, Nottingham, joiner and cm (1710–13). Took apps named Clark in 1710 and Etherington in 1713. [S of G, app. index]

Banks, Thomas, London, cm (1793). Subscribed to Sheraton's *Drawing Book*, 1793.

Banks, Thomas, York, looking-glass maker (1809). Son of Christopher Banks, schoolmaster; app. to David Doeg, looking-glass maker, 12 August 1809. [York app. reg.]

Banks, Thomas, Finch St, Liverpool, cm (1812). Admitted freeman, 12 October 1812. [Liverpool freemen reg.]

Banks, Thomas, 13 New Dock Walls, Hull, Yorks., carver and gilder (1817–20). [D]

Banks, Thomas, Old Meeting St, Birmingham, carver and gilder (1822). [D]

Banks, Thomas, London, chairmaker (1835). Trading at 12 Smith Buildings, City Rd, and 31 Cross St, Islington. [D]

Banks, Thomas, 82 White Lion St, Pentonville, London, cm and u (1839). [D]

Banks, Thomas, Huntingdon St, St Neots, Hunts., cm and builder (1839–40). [D]

Banks, Thomas, Stamford, Lincs., cm and u (1831–40). [D; poll bk] See Banks, —.

Banks, W., High St, Lymington, Hants., u and cm (1839). [D]

Banks, William, Hull, Yorks., cm (1780). [Poll bk]

Banks, William, 10 Pavement, Moorfields, London, upholder (1778–88). Son of John Banks of Little Moorfields, Gent. App. to Mark Dawes on 5 August 1778, and admitted freeman of the Upholders' Co. by servitude on 19 August 1788. [GL, Upholders' Co. records]

Banks, William, St George's St, Stamford, Lincs., cm (1776–1835). App. to Wortley Searson of Stamford, u, in 1776; admitted freeman by servitude, 1789. Still alive in 1835. [Stamford app. and freemen reg.; poll bk] See Banks, —.

Banks, William, Hemsworth, Yorks., joiner and cm (1822–37). [D]

Banks, William, 1 St James Ct, Bath, Som., chairmaker (1826). [D]

Banks & Topping, Blackpool, Lancs., joiners, cm and timber dealers (1828). [D]

Bannard, John, Henrietta Pl., High Bridge, Hammersmith, Middlx, cm, u and furniture broker (1839). [D]

Banner, Francis, 113 Aldergate St, London, u (1791–1803). Took out Sun Insurance policies on 14 January 1791 for £3,000 of which workshops accounted for £300, counting house and warehouse, £100; and on 23 March 1791 for £1,000. Declared bankrupt, *Billinge's Liverpool Advertiser*, 3 September 1798. Subscribed to Sheraton's *Cabinet Dictionary*, 1803. [GL, Sun MS vol. 375, pp. 189 and 644] The firm of Banner & Bruce, cm, are recorded at the same address in 1799. [D]

Banner, J. L., 1 Hart St, Liverpool, cm and joiner (1827). [D]

Banner, Thomas, 3 St Thomas's Buildings, Liverpool, cm (1784). [D]

Banner, Thomas, Compton St, Clerkenwell, London, chairmaker (1808). [D]

Bannister, Ann & Sons, Clayton St, Blackburn, Lancs., cm and joiners (1818). [D] Robert Banister is recorded at this address, 1814–17.

Bannister, George, 10 Chamber St, Goodman's Fields, London, carver and gilder (1808). [D]

Bannister, John, Little Fish St, Worcester, chairmaker (1820–35). [D]

Bannister, William, 8 Pollen St, Hanover Sq., London, carver (1839–40). Took out a Sun Insurance policy in 1840. [D; GL, Sun MS ref. 134192]

Bansall, Richard, Brokers Row, Redcross St, Southwark, London, cm and carpenter (1835). [D]

Bant, William, Birmingham, cm (1816–22). Recorded at Bristol St in 1816 and 1822, and Suffolk St, 1817–18. [D]

Banter, Isaac, 14 Church Row, Bethnal Green, London, cm and u (1827–28). [D]

Banting, Thomas, 22 Pall Mall, London, cm and u (1823–40). See Banting, France & Co.

Banting, William, 27 St James's St, London, cm and u (1823–40). See Banting, France & Co.

Banting, France & Co., 27 St James's St, London, cm and u (1813–40). The intermesh of titles, France & Banting, Bantings, France & Banting, Banting, France & Co., and 'Thomas' and 'William' Banting serves to confuse the exact structure of this active firm. In one or other of its names it was active from the early 19th century. As Banting, France & Co. they worked for the Earl of Bristol at Ickworth from 9 August 1817. When Ickworth was completed in 1829 it too was furnished by Banting, and also the London house. The invoices totalled £5,177 12s 8d and were submitted from 27 St James's St. [Accounts: Bury St Edmunds and W. Sussex RO] As 'Thomas and William Banting' they were still at this address in 1840. [D] In 1834–36 the firm worked on London houses for the Gage family in Whitehall Yd and at 16 Arlington St, totalling £3,224 1s 9d. [Firle Pl. MS, copies V & A archives] It was however Royal commissions, seemingly inexhaustible, which were the firm's staple employment. They supplied furniture, moved and cleaned it, repaired and converted it in most royal houses over many years, 1825–36.

For the Belvedere, Banting estimated for Gothic furnishings, included a cellaret lined with lead, 4 side tables, 2 'mahogany conveniences for H.M.'s use, & polished tops, stuffed & covered with purple velvet'. [Windsor Royal Archives, Box 1, LC, item 17]

In June 1837 Willliam Banting made application from 27 St James's St to be appointed 'Upholsterer to Her Majesty' [PRO, LC5/22], noting '. . . the alteration of my premises as above will shortly be completed'. Pigot's *Directory*, 1838 shows Thomas Banting at 22 Pall Mall, and William at 27 St James's St. The entry was repeated in Pigot, 1839, but by 1840 they are both at 27 St James's St. [*POD*] A manuscript sketch-book for 'Banting & Son, 27 St James's Street' survives [MMA, NY, 36.28.5] and mentions clients such as Lord Bristol (Ickworth), one in Eaton Sq. (1838), and a client who 'died 1845'. The designs include beds, curtains and chairs with early examples of deep buttoning. [Joy, *English Furniture, 1800–1851*, pp. 197, 268; PRO, LC 1/12; 5/123; 10/14] The firm exhibited at the Great Exhibition of 1851 and as late as 1885 supplied furniture to Princess Beatrice at Windsor Castle.

KENSINGTON PALACE, London (Duke of Sussex). Supplied furniture in 1813 and had to wait three years for payment. [*Ickworth and the Hervey Family*; W. Sussex R.O.]

WINDSOR CASTLE (1825) A Handsome . . . Tambour Writing Desk on 4 turned legs with reeded & carved leaves on patent castors, 2 drawers in frame & 6 drawers in the inside with pigeonholes to the writing flap, lined with black morocco, 2 carved leaves for the handles, all of very fine Spanish mahogany, French polished £36. 10. 0.

2 Spanish Mahogany Boxes to slide on each side & Wood Knobs added to drawers, & fixing on the locks £7. 10. 8.

A very Handsome Stand made to match another for China dish on 4 standards & hollow-sided block, ornamented with brass, and French polished

(1826) A Mahogany Bookcase of Spanish wood to fill the recess, with divisions, and shelf in upper part and shelf in lower part enclosed by 2 pairs of folding Doors, to drawing £25. [Windsor Royal Archives, 25401–03] G. B.

Banton, T., Marylebone, London, cm (1830). [Norwich poll bk]

Baptist, Alexander, 5 Rankin's Yd, Newgate St, Newcastle, cm (1827). [D]

Baptist & Angus, Elliot's Ct, 29 Bigg Mkt, Newcastle, cm (1827–29). [D]

Barber, —, Piccadilly, London, upholder (1756). Announcement in *Public Advertiser*, 26 May 1756, read: 'Household Furniture to be sold . . . catalogues at Mr Barber'.

Barber, —, address and trade unrecorded (1803). Subscribed to Sheraton's *Cabinet Dictionary*, 1803.

Barber, Charles, parish of St Owen, Hereford, joiner and cm (1832). App. to Samuel Davies, carpenter and joiner of the parish of St Peter; admitted freeman, 1 July 1832. [Hereford freemen reg.]

Barber, Elias, 1 Minday's Ct, Carnaby Mkt, London, sedan chairmaker (1779). Took out a Sun Insurance policy in 1779 for £200 of which utensils, stock and goods accounted for £150. [GL, Sun MS vol. 277, p. 233]

Barber, George, Canterbury, Kent, cm (1780). [Canterbury freemen rolls]

Barber, J., 16 Cateaton St, London, desk and dressing case maker (1835). The firm of Barber, Son & Davey, writing desk and dressing case makers, are recorded at this address in 1829. [D]

Barber, Jacob, London, cm and u (1802–28). Trading at 37 Red Lion Sq., 1802–07, and at 18–20 Lamb's Conduit St, 1808–28. Cited in Sheraton's list of master cabinet makers, 1803. Took out a Sun Insurance policy on 2 March 1814 for £600 on a house, 66 Castle St East, Oxford St. [D; GL, Sun MS vol. 462] William Barber, u, is recorded at 18 Lamb's Conduit St in 1829.

Barber, James, Portugal St, Piccadilly, London, u (1746–49). John Forretts's account current with the 3rd Earl of Burlington lists payments to Barber, of London, on 6 May 1746, 10s 3d, and £72 11s 7d. [Poll bk; Chatsworth, Burlington papers, folio A/C BK, f.31, f.75]

Barber, James, 5 Artillery Ct, London, u (1776). Son of Joseph Barber, St Luke's, Middlx, Gent.; app. to Samuel Burton; admitted freeman of the Upholders' Co. by servitude, 3 April 1776. [GL, Upholders' Co. records]

Barber, James, Newark, Notts., cm (b. 1763–d. 1830). Addresses at Dry Bridge, 1788–98; Carter Gate, 1805–07; as cm, u and chair manufacturer there, 1819–22, and as James & Sons in 1828. Advertised, 9 May 1788, for two journeymen cm, stating: 'Good Workmen may find constant Employment by applying to JAMES BARBER . . . who begs leave to inform the Public that he has laid in a choice Assortment of the newest Patterns of Looking Glasses &c and every article in the Cabinet Business. His customers may be supplied with the best of Goods, on the Shortest Notice, and of the cheapest Terms. The Trade may be supplied with any quantity of the new fashioned hair covering for Chairs. NB. An Apprentice wanted.' Advertised again, 2 July 1790 for two journeymen cm who must apply to 'his Glass Warehouse on the Dry Bridge'. His death, aged 67 years announced in *Drakard's Stamford News*, 12 March 1830. [D; poll bk; *Lincoln, Rutland and Stamford Mercury*, 9 May 1788 and 2 July 1790]

Barber, John, London, cm (1755). Subscribed to Chippendale's *Director*, 1755.

Barber, John, Red Bank, Manchester, Windsor and Upton chair maker (1781–88). [D]

Barber, John, York(?), cm (1754). Subscribed to Chippendale's *Director*, 1754. A John Barber, York, was app. to Thomas Jackson, carpenter, in 1725 for 7 years. [York app. reg.]

Barber, John, Coney St, next to 'The Black Swan', York, turner, maker of ladies's spinning wheels, fire screens, writing tables etc. (1785–1806). Advertised in *York Courant*, 23 August 1785. Account with Mrs Woodhouse for 12 mahogany chairs and 2 with arms, paid on 13 May 1791, totalled £19 4s. [York archives dept] A John Barber, York, cm, is recorded taking apps named John Barker, 14 April 1790, William Fawbert, 10 October 1791; Henry Pullon, 1 November 1791; John Ward, 1 August 1794; Charles Scott, 14 October 1794; William Fawdington, 19 October 1801; and George Kelley, as toymaker and turner, 1 September 1806. [York app. reg.]

Barber, John, Chester, cm (1812). Admitted freeman, 7 October 1812. [Chester freemen rolls]

Barber, John, Lancaster, cm (1822–37). App. to Leonard Redmayne, 1822; admitted freeman, 1827–28. Named in the Gillow records, 1822–37. [Lancaster app. reg.; Westminster Ref. Lib., Gillow]

Barber, John, 133 Gt Suffolk St, Southwark, London, cm (1829). [D]

Barber, John Foster, Bargate, Newark, Notts., cm and u (1828). [D]

Barber, Joseph Foster, Bargate, Newark, Notts., cm and u (1835). [D]

Barber, Peter, Cartergate, Newark, Notts., cm and u (1832–41). [D]

Barber, Richard, Chester, joiner and cm (1753–54). Son of

Catherine Barber, widow; app. to John Welch, joiner and cm, 25 December 1753, 12 February 1754. [Chester app. reg.]

Barber, Robert, Brighton, Sussex, cm (1822–40). Addresses at 7 Portland St, 1822; Grenville Gdns, 1824; Mt Sion Pl., 1829–37; and in North St, 1840. Baptisms recorded of son, Thomas, 14 July 1822; daughter Jane, 27 June 1824; daughters Susannah, Elizabeth and Mary, 2 August 1829; son William Lane, 2 December 1832; daughter Ann, 16 April 1837; and son Robert Isaac, 2 February 1840. [D; E. Sussex RO, PR(bapt.)]

Barber, Samuel, 37 Shudehill, Manchester, cm (1804–08). [D]

Barber, Thomas, address unrecorded, cm (1773). The accounts of George Cooke for Dunham Massey, Cheshire, include a payment of £4 7s 6d for 'a Dail chest for Mr Worthington Room', 25 March 1773. [John Rylands Lib., Manchester]

Barber, Thomas, Brighton, Sussex, cm (1772–73). Advertised, 13 April 1772, for a journeyman cm 'WANTED immediately . . . Eleven Shillings per Week will be given, or if the Person chooses he may work by the Piece.' Advertised again, 12 July 1773, for a journeyman cm, 'One who is a compleat Master of his Trade, may have constant Employ . . .'. [*Sussex Weekly Advertiser*, 13 April 1772 and 12 July 1773]

Barber, Thomas, 28 Hanging Ditch, Manchester, cm (1772–1805). [D]

Barber, Thomas, 21 Regent Pl., Brighton, Sussex, cm (1822). [D]

Barber, Thomas, St Sidwell, Exeter, Devon, cm (1823). Baptism at St Sidwell's of son, Thomas Cooke, recorded 19 December 1823. [PR(bapt.)]

Barber, Thomas, Church Lane, Pontefract, Yorks., cm (1834–37). [D]

Barber, William, South St, Bishop's Stortford, Herts., cm (1823). [D]

Barber, William, 67 Leonard St, Shoreditch and 2 Leonard Sq., London, cm, u and fancy cm (1826–39). [D]

Barber, William, 18 Lamb's Conduit St, London, u (1829). Jacob Barber, cm and u, is recorded at 18 Lamb's Conduit St, 1808–28. [D]

Barber, William, 57 Upper Charlotte St, Fitzroy Sq., London, u (1839). [D]

Barberry, —, George St, Oxford Rd, London, cm (1803). Cited in Sheraton's list of master cabinet makers, 1803.

Barborough, Matthew, 24 Clowes St, Manchester, carver and gilder (1802). [D]

Barbour, Edward, address unrecorded, upholder (1708). Admitted freeman of the Upholders' Co., 5 May 1708. [GL, Upholders' Co. records]

Barclay, Jacob, Newcastle, u (1774). App. to Thomas Hunt; admitted freeman, 7 October 1774. [Newcastle freemen reg.]

Barden, Isaac, Gabriel's Hill, Maidstone, Kent, chairmaker (1805). [D]

Bardin, John, Worcester, spinning wheel maker (1747). App. to Thomas Bardin, spinning wheel maker; sworn freeman on 29 June 1747. [Worcester freemen admissions]

Bardin, Samuel, Worcester, upholder (1764). App. to Richard Meredith, upholder; admitted freeman on 24 September 1764. [Worcester freemen admissions]

Bardin, Samuel, Cornmarket, Oxford, upholder (1784). [D] Mentioned in *Jackson's Oxford Journal* between 1753–80.

Bardin, Samuel, Staines, Middlx, u (1802). Recorded in the Oxford poll bk of 1802 as not voting.

Bardin, Thomas snr, Worcester, turner and spinning wheel maker (1747–73). Took apps named John Bardin sworn free in 1747; Thomas Bardin jnr, sworn free in 1761; and William Bardin, sworn free in 1773. [Worcester freemen admissions]

Bardin, Thomas jnr, Worcester, turner and spinning wheel maker (1761). App. to father, Thomas Bardin, turner and

spinning wheel maker; admitted freeman, 2 March 1761. [Worcester freemen admissions]

Bardin, William, Worcester, spinning wheel maker (1773). App. to his uncle, Thomas Bardin, turner and spinning wheel maker; sworn freeman, 28 October 1773. [Worcester freemen admissions]

Bardolph, James, 11 Gt Chapel St, Soho, London, carver and gilder (1808). [D]

Bardsley, John, Town Lane, Dukinfield, Lancs., cm and joiner (1834). [D]

Bardswell, G., Liverpool, joiner and cm (1774–90). Trading at 76 Strand St in 1774; 33 Chapel St in 1777; and 65 Stanley St in 1790, as a household broker. [D]

Bardwell, Ann, 95 Fargate, Sheffield, Yorks., cm and u (1822–28). [D] Possibly wife or widow of:

Bardwell, Edward, 92 Fargate, Sheffield, Yorks., cm (1814–20). [D]

Bardwell, William, London, trade unrecorded (1840). The accounts of Glenstol House, Ireland, include regular and substantial purchases of furniture, glass, pictures, etc. from him. [V & A archives]

Barefoote, Josiah, London, cm and u (d. 1744). Sale of stock announced in *Daily Advertiser*, 19 May 1744: 'The Upholstery & Cabinet Goods of Mr Josiah Barefoote, deceas'd within Two Doors of Durham Yard in the Strand, viz. worsted Damask Beds, . . . settee Bedsteads, curtains, field bedsteads ditto, Easy chairs . . . fine french carpets, a small India cabinet, Mahogany & Walnut tree chairs, Leather seats'.

Barell & Robins, Westgate, Chichester, Sussex, cm and u (1823–26). [D]

Barfoot, B F., 47 New Gloucester St, Hoxton, London, cm (1835). [D]

Barfoot, Richard, 137 St John St, Clerkenwell, London, japanner and gilder (1821). Took out a Sun Insurance policy on 30 April 1821 for £400 of which stock, utensils and goods in trust accounted for £20. [GL, Sun MS vol. 486, ref. 980230]

Barfoot, William, Wimborne, Dorset, u (1798). [D]

Barford, Henry, London, cm and u (1768–83). Addresses in Pall Mall, 1768–70, 226 Piccadilly, 1773–80, and Covent Gdn Piazza, 1781–83. Fellow of the Society of Arts and Manufactures, 1768–70. [D]

Barford, Richard, next door to the Earl of Inchiquins, in Pall Mall, u (1747–48). [Heal]

Barford, Richard, Gt Yarmouth, Norfolk, u (1793). Recorded in the calendar of marriage licence bonds, 14 November 1793. [Suffolk RO, FAA: 50/2/108]

Barford & Pick, Piccadilly, London, cm and u (1776–77). [D]

Barfort, J., address and trade unrecorded, cm (1803). Subscribed to Sheraton's *Cabinet Dictionary*, 1803.

Barington, —, address unrecorded, u (1701). Supplied to Elizabeth, 4th Duchess of Bedford, bed and window curtains, cushions, window cornices and chairs costing a total of £42. [Bedford Office, London]

Barke, Thomas, High St, Shifnal, Salop, cm (1835–36). [D]

Barker, Mrs, Hall St, Spalding, Lincs., cm and u (1835). [D]

Barker, Charles, Hall St, Spalding, Lincs., cm, u, joiner and carpenter (1826). [D]

Barker, Edward, Leeds, Yorks., cm and joiner (1817–37). Trading in St Peter's Sq., 1817–30; Somerset St, 1834; and Albion Ct, Duke St, 1837. [D]

Barker, George, St George's parish, Southwell, and York, carver and gilder (1799). Son of Edward Barker, cornfactor; app. to John Staveley, carver and gilder, 24 June 1799. Admitted freeman of York, 1808. [York app. reg. and freemen rolls]

Barker, George, Leeds, Yorks., cm (1822–37). Addresses at 4

Providence Ct, Top Close, 1822; 46 Vicar Lane and 124 Kirkgate, 1826; and 124 Kirkgate, 1828–37. [D]

Barker, George, Wilsden, near Bradford, Yorks., joiner and cm (1830). [D]

Barker, Hugh, Sheffield, Yorks., cm and u (1825–33). Recorded in Division St, 1825; Baskes Pool, 1828–29; and Dronfield, 1833. [D]

Barker, James, Bedford, cm (1784). [D]

Barker, James, Newark, Notts., cm (1793). [D]

Barker, James, College St, Northampton, chairmaker (1820). [Poll bk]

Barker, James, King St, Hammersmith, Middlx, cm and u (1823–39).

Barker, John, Rowsley, Derbs., master joiner and architect (1700–02). Chatsworth accounts list payments on 30 October 1700 for 'Making & putting up Joyner's work of compass cornish with a coronet, Two eagles etc. and a head board, base and Balls for a bed over the Library', totalling £1 17s 4d; for making and putting up another 'Cornish' for a bed, assisted by Richard Holmes, for 18s; and 'To makeing and putting up mouldings about Hangings in ye Rooms next ye Upper Dining Rome', also for 18s. In 1702 he supplied an oval table frame for the arbour in the garden, with a marble top made by Samuel Watson, costing £6 7s 6d. [Chatsworth account bks, vols. 6 and 7]

Barker, John snr, Petergate, York, u (b. 1673–d. 1731). Son of Robert, blacksmith, bapt. 6 April 1673. Admitted freeman by patrimony in 1697. Married Jane Cobb, 20 November 1698 and had 7 children between 1701 and 1717, including William, John and Robert, who was his heir. Took apps named Smith in 1714, and Edward Wood, on 26 March 1716, for 8 years. Took out Sun Insurance policies on 31 October 1724 on a dwelling house in Thursday Mkt, St Sampson's parish, York, in occupation of Matthew Hall, attorney at law, at a premium of 2s; and on 24 June 1729 for £300 on two houses. Buried on 24 January 1731–32. [York app. reg.; PRO, 43/127, vol. 28, p. 5437; GL, Sun MS vol. 17, ref. 32568, vol. 28]

Barker, John jnr, York, u (1709–58). Son of John Barker bapt., 7 February 1709–10, at Holy Trinity (Christ Church) King's Sq. Admitted freeman, 1736. Polled in York in 1741 and 1758. [*York Parish Reg. Soc.*, vol. LXXXV; York freemen reg.; poll bks]

Barker, John, York, cm (1790). Son of John Barker, 'common brewer'; app. to John Barber, cm, 14 April 1790. [York app. reg.]

Barker, John, Nottingham, joiner and cm (1807). App. to Thomas Cullen, 1807. [Notts. RO, app. lists]

Barker, John, Northampton, chairmaker, chair turner (1820–30). Trading in Sheep St, 1820–23, and in Abingdon St, 1826–30. [Poll bks]

Barker, John, Chester, cm (1778–84). Recorded in Pepper St in 1784. App. to George Johnson, cm of Chester; sworn freeman, 9 May 1778. [Chester freemen rolls; poll bk]

Barker, John, Thomas Buildings, Chester, cm (1824). Sworn freeman, 21 October 1824. [Chester freemen rolls]

Barker, John, Windsor Pl., Chester, u (1840). [D]

Barker, John, Knightsbridge, London, cm (1821). Set up a furniture maker's shop but gave up after five months because of stagnation of trade and lost at least £100. [PRO, B3/438]

Barker, John, London, u (1820–35). Trading at 72 Gt Titchfield St, 1820–25; at 54 Dorset St, Manchester Sq., 1826–27; and at 31 Sloane St, Chelsea, 1835. [D]

Barker, John, Welch Row, Nantwich, Cheshire, chairmaker (1828). [D]

Barker, John, 123 Norfolk St, King's Lynn, Norfolk, cm and u (1830–39). [D]

Barker, John, Vine Lane, Northumberland St, Newcastle, cm and u (1833–38). [D]

Barker, John, Richmond, Yorks., cm (1838). [Richmond PR(bapt.), 9 March 1838]

Barker, Mary, 17–19 Cropper St, Liverpool, u (1810–37). [D]

Barker, Matthew, Pavement and Low Petergate, York, u, appraiser and undertaker (b. c. 1746–d. 1791). Son of Robert Barker, u of Pavement, Petergate, bapt. 20 September 1746 at Holy Trinity (Christ Church), King's Sq. Admitted freeman in 1778. Took over his late father's business in 1781 and opened his father's shop and warehouse in Petergate in 1782. Married twice, firstly in 1777, to Rosamund, daughter of Martin Croft, plumber and glazier; she had two children who both died in infancy, and died in childbed in 1780 aged 35. Married secondly, in 1781, Elizabeth Brabbs of Sheriff Hutton, who bore six children, all of whom died young. Matthew himself was buried on 14 November 1791, whilst his wife, Elizabeth died in 1816, aged 60. [D; York freemen rolls; *York Parish Reg. Soc.*, vol. LXXXV; poll bk; *York Courant*, 14 August 1781; *York Chronicle*, 14 March 1782; *York Gazette*, 31 August 1784]

Barker, Robert snr, at the 'Sopha Dome Beds', Petergate, York, u, appraiser and undertaker (b. 1706–d. 1781). Subscribed to Chippendale's *Director*, 1754. Son of John Barker, u of Petergate, bapt. 9 December 1707 at Holy Trinity (Christ Church), King's Sq. Admitted freeman by patrimony in 1731. Married twice, having, by the first marriage, four children who survived infancy, Robert jnr, his heir, bapt. 30 November 1734; Thomas, who became a clergyman, bapt. 12 March 1737–38; Noblet, who became a surgeon, bapt. 1 June 1742; and Matthew, who took over his father's business, bapt. 22 September 1746. Married secondly Mary Magdalene Devisnie of Escrick, on 10 July 1755, buried 15 March 1796, aged 75.

Took apps for £30 each: Robert Brennand, in 1744; Thomas Barker, in 1753; John Clarke, in 1742; Stephen Sagar, for £40 for 7 years in 1759; Joseph Wilson for 8 years in 1765; and Thomas in 1759.

Advertised on 13 October 1741, selling ass and foal, and on 16 November 1742, two geldings, and with John Barker of the same trade and address, on 12 October 1742, acting as agents for letting a house in Thursday Mkt and selling a house at the corner of Gillygate near Bootham Bar, inhabited by William Plowman, coach maker. They advertised together again on 25 January 1743 as agents selling a dwelling house in Thursday Mkt, and on 22 August 1749 selling 'all the genuine Household Furniture belonging to Capt. Graydon, at Fulford, near York . . .' from 4 September Robert and John both voted in parliamentary elections in 1741 and 1758, and Robert served as Sheriff of York, 1776–77, indicating his respectable status.

On 18 May 1756 Robert Barker submitted a bill totalling £35 14s to Daniel Lascelles for upholstery, beds, etc. and 6 Windsor chairs at 6s each. He is referred to several times in the York Assembly Rooms minute book between 1735–79, on 18 November 1735 concerning 'four Dozen Chaires according to the Pattern delivered in at 9s per Chaire with S.P. leather Bottom & Brass nailes . . .'. The Committee also 'Bargained with Mr Reynoldson and Mr Barker for four Quadrille Tables at £1 17s 6d each, each of them to make two according to this pattern now shown'. On 24 February 1736 the Committee 'Ordered that Mr. Barker's Bill for four Dozen chairs and 2 Quadrille Tables be discharged, £25 7s'. On 28 November 1739 Barker received a commission for two 'Mahogany Card Tables . . . for the use of the Card Assembly at £1 14s each', two more being supplied by Mr Reynoldson. On 28 January 1764 Barker was ordered to make four new card tables and recover four old ones and 'Twenty Four of the worst of the chairs with the new leather'. On 12 October 1776, a bill of £50 6s was discharged to Barker, and on 2 May 1779, another of £30 4s.

In 1781 he announced that he was declining business, and he died on 24 July, 1781, aged 75. His will, dated 18 June and proved 31 July, 1781, bequeathed to his wife Mary, a 'house in Petergate, divided into two tenements held on lease from the Corporation. Also the house part adjoining now or lately inhabited by Slingsby, Griffith & Gledding leased from the Vicars Choral. She to have for life, then to son, Noblet; also to wife her gold watch, 1 pair of silver candlesticks and her own jewels; £300 to his wife, . . . £100 to his son Robert, £20 to son Matthew, All else to Noblet & his mother.' His stock in trade was sold after his death, and the business was taken over by his son Matthew. [Surtees Soc. vol. 102, York freemen, p. 234; S of G, app. index; York City archives, D3–4; York Parish Reg. Soc., vol. 1, LXXXV; York Courant, 13 October 1741, 16 November 1742, 12 October 1742, 25 January 1743, 22 August 1749; poll bks; Furn. Hist., 1974; Leeds archives dept, Harewood MS 386; York Assembly Rooms, Directors' minute bk; York Courant, 6 March 1781, 16 August 1781, 14 August 1781; C. Life, 30 October 1974, pp. 932–33] A.E.

Barker, Robert jnr, at 'The Chinese Bed and Sopha', Coney St, Spurriergate, York, u, appraiser and undertaker (b. c. 1734–80). Eldest son of Robert snr, of Petergate, York, bapt. 30 November 1734. Admitted freeman by patrimony, 1758; polled in 1758, 1771 and 1774. On 29 June 1762 announced in York Gazette the opening of his shop in Coney St, but the business failed in 1765 when his assignees issued a notice to his creditors. [York Courant, 5 November 1765] His household furniture and stock were put up for sale shortly afterwards. [York Courant, 4 February 1766] Took out a Sun Insurance policy in 1765 totalling £1,000. [GL, Sun MS ref. 216066]

Three letters from Robert Barker to Sir Rowland Winn concern the furnishing of Nostell Priory, 1763–64, and include designs for bookcases. [Nostell archives, C3/1/5/1–6, 3–4; Furn. Hist., 1974, pls. 17 and 18A] In 1780 Robert Barker took an inventory of furniture etc. of C. S. Duncombe, Esq. [York freemen rolls; poll bks] Records do not always make it clear whether it is Robert snr or Robert jnr who is being referred to. A.E.

Barker, Robert, 43 Compton St, Soho, London, composition ornament maker and carver (1780–84). Took out a Sun Insurance policy in 1780 for £700 of which utensils and stock accounted for £550. [GL, Sun MS vol. 281, p. 296]

Barker, Robert, Shelf, Rishworth, Yorks., joiner and cm (1837). [D]

Barker, Thomas, Burslem, Staffs., turner and chairmaker (1798). [D]

Barker, Thomas, 41 Hanging Ditch, Manchester, cm (1800). [D]

Barker, William, Petergate, York, cm (1746). Advertised in the York Courant, on 14 October 1746. Possibly the son of John Barker and brother of Robert, bapt. 6 May 1714. William Barker of York and John Ellis took an inventory of Newby Park for Sir Tancred Robinson, c. 1750. [Leeds archives dept, Newby papers, 2789]

Barker, William, Lancaster, joiner and cm (1773–80). App. to Henry Baines, 1773 and admitted a freeman in 1779–80. Freemen rolls state he was 'of Wennington'. [Lancaster app. reg. and freemen rolls]

Barker, William, Black Burton, Yorks., cm (1784). Polled at Lancaster.

Barker, William, Leeds, Yorks., cm (1791). Named as a journeyman cm in the Leeds Cabinet and Chair Makers' Book of Prices, 1791.

Barker, William, London, u (1813). He altered and reupholstered six late 17th-century armchairs at Ham House, inscribing a new wooden member: 'this Chair was restufft at Kingston, but covered at the Time the Bed was done. April 13th 1813 William Barker from London'. [Furn. Hist., 1974]

Barker, William, Watton, Norfolk, cm and joiner (1822). [D]

Barker, William, Horse Mkt, Northampton, chairmaker (1823). [D]

Barker, William, 26 Edgware Rd, London, u (1839). [D]

Barker, William, 5 Middlesex Terr., London, chair and sofa maker (1839). [D]

Barker, William, 14 Elm St, London, cm and u (1839). [D]

Barkham, Thomas, Diss, Norfolk, cm, u, appraiser and brush maker (1822–39). Trading in Market Pl., 1830–39. [D]

Barkley, Alexander, at 'The Dukes Head', Monmouth Ct, Monmouth St, London, victualler and cm (1781). Took out a Sun Insurance policy in 1781 for £300 of which utensils, stock and goods accounted for £150. [GL, Sun MS vol. 288, p. 455]

Barkshire, Charles, Petworth, Sussex, chairmaker and turner (1826). [D]

Barkworth, John, Barton-upon-Humber, Lincs., cm (1793). Subscribed to Sheraton's Drawing Book, 1793. [D]

Barley, James & John, Market Pl., Harleston, Norfolk, cm (1839). [D]

Barley, John, Harleston, Norfolk, carpenter, cm and u (1830–39). [D]

Barloni, S.D., 6 Eyre St Hill, Clerkenwell, London, looking-glass and picture frame maker (1829). [D]

Barlow, Daniel, Wilmslow, Cheshire, chairmaker (1753). Took app. named Roylands, 1753. [S of G, app. index]

Barlow, Edward, 22 Market St Lane, Manchester, cm and sworn appraiser (1788–1819). Took out Sun Insurance policies on 18 August 1791, and on 18 June 1791 for £400 of which utensils, stock and goods in trust accounted for £350. [D; GL, Sun MS vol. 379, pp. 391 and 569]

Barlow, George, 52 Navigation St, Birmingham, cm (1816–22). [D]

Barlow, Henry, 6 Bloom St, Salford, Lancs., cm (1832–38). Trading as a chairmaker, 1836–38. [D]

Barlow, J., 107 Rea St, Birmingham, writing desk maker (1823). [D]

Barlow, John, Liverpool, cm (1790–1811). Addresses at 39 Matthew St in 1790; Dale St, Whitechapel in 1800; and 59 Circus St in 1811. [D]

Barlow, John, Back Queen St, Chester, cm (1831). Admitted freeman, 19 April 1831. [Chester freemen rolls]

Barlow, John, 21–24 New Richmond Rd, Pendlebury, Lancs., cm and u (1834–40). [D]

Barlow, Nathaniel, High St, Colchester, Essex, u (1780–84). [D; poll bks]

Barlow, T., 26 Rathbone Pl., Oxford St, London, cm (1820). [D]

Barlow, Thomas, Newington Causeway, London, chairmaker (1820). [D]

Barlow, Thomas, 1 Clover St, Princes Sq., London, chair and sofa maker (1827–28). [D]

Barlow, William, address unrecorded, upholder (1719–26). Son of Bartholomew Barlow, Boston, Lincs., baker; app. to Thomas Fidoe, 6 May 1719. Admitted freeman of the Upholders' Co. by servitude, 6 July 1726. [GL, Upholders' Co. records]

Barlow, William, Swallow St, London, carver (1745–51). Worked for William Kent at 44 Berkeley Sq. in 1745, and with James Richards at Henry Pelham's house in Arlington St. His 'Kentian' friezes with foliages, festoons, shells and flowers cost 48s each. Barlow's bill dated 1745–46 for work done at Berkeley Sq. includes a six-legged table with 'Raffle leaves, leather money & scal'd sides', possibly a writing table designed by Kent. Thomas Banks, the sculptor, worked as a young man for Barlow, an 'ornament carver'. Polled at Westminster in 1749, when he is recorded in Swallow St. In 1751 he was paid £220 by the 3rd Duke of Ancaster 'possibly for mirrors at Grimsthorpe, Lincs.' (Child's Bank). [Poll bk; *C. Life*, 13 September 1956; Beard, *Craftsmen and Interior Decoration*; *C. Life Annual*, 1965; *C. Life*, 28 May 1921, p. 645; *Conn.*, June 1981, p. 144]

Barlow, William, 30 Suffolk St, Birmingham, cm and u (1830–39). [D]

Barnaby, Edward Elden, Norwich, cm (1813–30). Recorded in the parish of St Peter, Permountergate, 1818, and St John, Timberhill, 1830. Edward Alden Barnaby app. to William Elden Earl, admitted freeman, 27 February 1813. [Poll bks; Norwich freemen reg.]

Barnard, J., Coleshill St, Birmingham, cm (1805–08). [D]

Barnard, J., 2 Green St, Bath, Som., cm and broker (1826–33). [D]

Barnard, James, 77 Broad Quay, Bristol, cm and u (1807). [D]

Barnard, James, 48 Upper Marylebone St, London, carver and gilder (1839). [D]

Barnard, John, London, carver and gilder (1781). On 29 April 1781 he supplied 'a pare tree frame two Edges Carv'd and gilt with board & glass to Ditto 2.6.', to the Hon. Mrs Henrietta Howard of South Audley St, London. Another similar account is dated 8 April 1781. [Essex RO, D/DP A190]

Barnard, John, Norwich, cm (1836–39). Trading in West Pottergate in 1836, and in Upper Mkt in 1839. [D]

Barnard, John, 29 Belton St, Long Acre, London, cm and u (1839). [D]

Barnard, P., 1 Leather Lane, London, picture frame and glass manufacturer (1809–11). [D] Possibly P. Barnarda or P. Barnaschina.

Barnard, Richard, Noel St, London, carver and gilder (1784). [Poll bk]

Barnard, Richard, 11 Francis St, Bedford Sq., London, carver and gilder (1809–11). [D]

Barnard, Robert, Rotherhithe, London, u, cm and broker (1775). Took out Sun Insurance policies in 1775 for £1,100 of which warehouse, utensils and stock accounted for £410; and for £1,100 of which utensils, stock and goods accounted for £280. [GL, Sun MS vol. 240, p. 59; vol. 245, p. 138]

Barnard, Thomas, 307 Holborn, London, upholder (1778–85). Son of Daniel Barnard, Dunmow, Essex, farmer; app. to Noah Chivers, 4 March 1778. Admitted freeman of the Upholders' Co. by servitude, 2 November 1785. [GL, Upholders' Co. records]

Barnard, William, St Mary's, Ely, Cambs., carpenter, joiner and chairmaker (1830). [D]

Barnarda, P., 22 West St, West Smithfield, London, barometer and looking-glass maker (1803–11). [D; Goodison, *Barometers*]

Barnaschina, Anthony jnr, New Rd, Gravesend, Kent, furniture broker and u (1832–39). [D]

Barnaschina, Anthony, 68 Leather Lane, London, wholesale picture and looking-glass frame maker (1839). [D]

Barnaschina, B., 68 Leather Lane, London, looking-glass frame maker (1837). [D]

Barnaschina, P., 4 Leather Lane, London, picture frame manufactory owner (1804–09). [D]

Barnasconi, Anthony, Manchester, looking-glass and picture frame maker (1836–39). Trading at 35 Swan St in 1836 and 116 Tite St in 1839. [D]

Barnby, Joshua (Wingfield), Hull, Yorks., cm and furniture broker (1826–39). Addresses at 4 Jackson St in 1826 and 26 Bridge St, 1835–39. [D]

Barnby, Timothy, Hull, Yorks., cm (1828–40). Addresses at 20

Wells St with res. at 6 St John's Sq., 1829–35; res. at 2 South St, 1838; 4 Wood's Pl., South St and Well's Yd, Waterworks St, 1839–40. [D]

Barndale, Josiah, Liverpool, cm (1750). Took app. named Lowe, in 1750. [S of G, app. index]

Barnes, George, Liverpool, cm (d. 1790). Died on 10 October 1790. [*Williamson's Liverpool Advertiser*, 18 October 1790]

Barnes, George, North High St, Bishop Wearmouth, Co. Durham, carver and gilder (1827). [D] The trade card of Barnes, looking-glass and picture frame maker, Sunderland, is in the Johnson Coll., Bodleian Lib., Oxford. [*Furn. Hist.*, 1974]

Barnes, J.H., 19 Pierpoint Row, Islington, London, u and auctioneer (1820). [D]

Barnes, James, Huntingdon, chairmaker (1793). App. to John Barnes of Huntingdon, basket maker and chairmaker, on 22 February 1793. [Hunts. RO, borough charity app. indentures, HB 13/10]

Barnes, James, 11 Castle St, Oxford Mkt, London, cm (1808). [D]

Barnes, James, 83 Well St, Oxford St, London, upholder and undertaker; carpenter and cm (1817–29). [D]

Barnes, John, Aldermanbury, London, cm (1750). Listed as a member of the Livery of the Joiners' Co. [GL]

Barnes, John, Warminster, Wilts., cm (1761–65). Took app. named Lewis, 1761. Declared bankrupt, June 1765. [S of G, app. index; *Gents Mag.*, June 1765]

Barnes, John, Huntingdon, basket maker and chairmaker (1780–93). Took app. named James Barnes of Huntingdon, 22 February 1793; and Robert Bird of Huntingdon, aged 14, 18 April 1780. [Hunts. RO, borough charity app. indentures, HB 13/10]

Barnes, John, Duke St, Bloomsbury, London, cm (1787). Took out a Sun Insurance policy on 2 July 1787 for £300 on household goods. [GL, Sun MS vol. 345, p. 264]

Barnes, John, address unrecorded, cm (1803). Subscribed to Sheraton's *Cabinet Dictionary*, 1803.

Barnes, John, 17 Frederick Pl., Tottenham Ct Rd, London, cm (1804). Took out a Sun Insurance policy on 10 July 1804 for £300 of which workshop accounted for £60, and utensils and stock, £40 [GL, Sun MS vol. 431, ref. 764303]

Barnes, John, 4 Poland St, Oxford St, London, cm (1809–11). [D]

Barnes, John, 2 Stangate, London, cm (1829). [D]

Barnes, John, Bristol, Windsor and fancy chairmaker, cm (1837–40). Recorded at Jacob St, 1837–38, and 60 Old Market St, 1839–40. [D]

Barnes, Jonathan, Stockwell St, Leek, Staffs., chairmaker (1816–28). [D]

Barnes, Joshua, Main St, Bingley, Yorks., joiner and cm (1837). [D]

Barnes, Robert, Manchester, u (1808–13). Trading at 5 Chatham St in 1808 and at 28 Broad St in 1813. [D]

Barnes, Robert, Sanvey Gate, Leicester, cm (1818–22). [D]

Barnes, Robert, 3 St Botolph St, Colchester, Essex, cm and u (1839). [D]

Barnes, Robert Wilkinson, 30 Great Underbank, Stockport, Cheshire, cm and u (1825–41). [D]

Barnes, Samuel, parish of St Augustine, Bristol, cm (1784). [Poll bk]

Barnes, Thomas snr, Preston, Lancs., cm (1742). Son of Richard Barnes, husbandman, recorded burgess in 1742. Uncle of Thomas Barnes jnr. [Preston Guild record of burgesses]

Barnes, Thomas jnr, Preston, Lancs., cm (1762). Nephew of Thomas Barnes snr. [Preston Guild record of burgesses]

Barnes, W., Wisbech, Cambs., cm (1839). Recorded in South End and Gt South St. [D]

Barnes, William, Leicester, cm (1788–96). App. to John Shipley in 1788; admitted freeman in 1796. [Leicester freemen rolls]

Barnes & Cook, 56 Queen St, Portsea, Portsmouth, Hants., carvers and gilders (1839). [D]

Barnescastle, John, London, cm (1796). [Norwich poll bk]

Barnet, John, Thorne, Yorks., cm (1780). [Hull poll bk]

Barnet, John jnr, Sunderland, Co. Durham, cm (1838). Reported bankrupt, *Sussex Agricultural Express*, 21 April 1838.

Barnett, C., Bridlesmithgate, Nottingham, upholder (1814). [D]

Barnett, Emanuel, May Fair, London, carver (1749). [Poll bk]

Barnett, F., 45 Castle St, Bristol, general furnishing iron-mongery and cutlery warehouse owner; manufacturer of iron bedsteads (1836–40). [D]

Barnett, George, 17 Market Pl., Derby, u and cm (1809–35). [D]

Barnett, George Frederick, 13 Duke St, Tooley St, London, cm, u and undertaker (1839). [D]

Barnett, Henry Mark, York, u (1826). Son of John Joseph Barnett; app. to John Milner, u, 13 April 1826. [York app. reg.]

Barnett, R., address unrecorded, cm(?) (1796). Supplied an ivory cabinet costing £4 14s 6d to the Hon. James Drummond of Perth, in 1796. [Scottish RO, GD 160/Box 46/XIV Bundle]

Barnett, T., 6 Chichester Pl., King's Cross, London, carver and gilder (1837). [D]

Barnett, Thomas, Liverpool, cm (1780–d. 1822). Admitted freeman on 11 March 1780. Died 3 June 1822. [Liverpool freemen reg.; *Gore's Paper*, 6 June 1822]

Barnett, Thomas, Goalgate St, Stafford, chairmaker (1828). [D]

Barnett, Thomas, London, carver (1829–35). Trading at 11 Tabernacle Row, City Rd in 1829, and 48 Upper North Pl., Gray's Inn Rd in 1835. [D]

Barnett, William, 47 Marshall St, Oldham Rd, Manchester, cabinet turner (1825). [D]

Barnfather, David, High St and George St, Wigton, Cumb., joiner, cm and chairmaker (1828–34). [D]

Barnham, James, Norwich, chairmaker (1751). Took app. named Blowfield in 1751. [S of G, app. index]

Barnham, James, parish of St Andrew, Norwich, carver (1812). [Poll bk]

Barnham, John, Norwich, carver and gilder (1799–1840). Addresses at St Martin's by Palace St in 1803, and St Stephen's Bank in 1830. [D; poll bks] A Mr Barnham of London, carver and gilder, polled at Norwich in 1796.

Barns, Edward, Temple St, Wolverhampton, Staffs., chair bottomer (1833). [D]

Barns, James, Back Lane, Ashford, Kent, cm, u and turner (1839). [D]

Barns, James, High St, Tenterden, Kent, cm and patten maker (1839). [D]

Barns, William, parish of All Hallows, Exeter, Devon, cm (1832). [Poll bk] W. Barns, u, is recorded at 14 Bartholomew St, Exeter, 1836–40. [*Exeter Pocket Journal*]

Barnsdall, Edward, 39 Warsergate, Nottingham, joiner, cm and paperhanger (1832). [D]

Barnsdall, Joseph, Nottingham, cm (1791–1835). Trading at Bottle Lane in 1799; Pilcher Gate in 1814, and Warsergate in 1835. Signed the *Nottingham Cabinet and Chair Makers' Book of Prices*, 1791, on behalf of the masters. [D]

Barnside, Edward, High St, Loughborough, Leics., joiner/cm (1822). [D]

Baron, Henry, Stoodley Bridge, Todmorden, Yorks., joiner and cm (1837). [D]

Baron, James, Market Pl., Plymouth, Devon, cm (1784). [D] See William Baron of Market St.

Bar(r)on, John, address unrecorded, upholder (1719–57). Son of Charles Barron, Brentwood, Essex, surgeon, app. to Arthur Osborn, 2 December 1719. Admitted freeman of the Upholders' Co. by servitude, 6 August 1729. Took app. named Charles Long, 1755–57. [GL, Upholders' Co. records]

Baron, John, 'Angel', Bread St, London, upholder (1750). Listed as a member of the Livery of the Upholders' Co. in 1750. [GL, Upholders' Co. records]

Bar(r)on, Randolph, Martletts Ct, Bow St, St Martin-in-the-Fields, London, upholder (1709–29). Advertised in press, 1712 and 1727. Took app. 16 December 1713. Took out a Hand in Hand Insurance policy on 19 October 1713, on his house in Martletts Ct for £150. His son, Thomas, admitted freeman of the Upholders' Co. by patrimony, 20 March 1728–29. [Heal; poll bk; GL, Hand in Hand MS vol. 12, p. 205; GL, Upholders' Co. records]

Baron, Robert, Newcastle, u (1760). App. to William Charnley; admitted freeman on 15 October 1760. [Newcastle freemen reg.] A Robert Barron of Alnwick polled at Newcastle in 1774.

Baron, Robert, Northgate, Blackburn, Lancs., cm (1834). [D]

Baron, Thomas, St Martin's Lane, London, upholder (1728–30). Son of Randolph Baron, u, admitted freeman of the Upholders' Co. by patrimony, 1728–29. Took out a Sun Insurance policy on 31 December 1730 for £300 on his household goods and goods in trade. [GL, Upholders' Co. records; GL, Sun MS vol. 33, ref. 52877]

Baron, Thomas, Bodmin, Cornwall, cm and u (1791–1805). Took out a Sun Insurance policy on 15 February 1791 for £300 of which £100 accounted for stock. Recorded in property deeds in 1784, 1798 and 1805. [D; GL, Sun MS vol. 374, ref. 580233; Cornwall RO, DD/RD/697; DD/CF/1255; DD/PH/66]

Baron, Thomas jnr, Bramhope, Yorks., cm (1822–30). [D]

Baron, William snr(?), Market St, Plymouth, Devon, cm, u and milliner (1785–1814). Took out a Sun Insurance policy on 21 March 1785 for £1,000 on utensils and stock. Fire 'raged for 7 hours' at his premises, 25 October 1798. [D; GL, Sun MS vol. 327, p. 482; *Exeter Flying Post*, 25 October 1798] A Mr Baron, u of Plymouth subscribed to Sheraton's *Cabinet Dictionary*, 1803. See James Baron of Market Pl.

Baron, William jnr, Whimple St, facing Broad St, Plymouth, Devon, cm, u, auctioneer, appraiser, undertaker, patent mangle and household furniture dealer (1822–26). Supplied bedding and household furniture to Major Carlyon at Tamar Terr., Stoke, on 9 May 1823, including a mahogany high bookcase 'enclosed by pannell doors . . . brass locks etc.', a lobby chest, supper tray, parrot hat stand, double lamp table, butler's tray, and two carved mahogany shell-backed hall chairs, totalling in all £27 2s 6d. Also recorded in the accounts of 14 August 1824 and 28 January 1826. [D; Cornwall RO, DD/CN/3445/1–18]

Baron & Mills, 72 and 73 Well St, Oxford St, London, cabinet founders and window blind makers (1835). [D]

Barr, James, London Rd, Twickenham, Middlx, cm and u (1832–38). [D]

Barr, John, Lancaster, japanner (1810). Named in the Gillow records working on a chair, 1810. [Westminster Ref. Lib., Gillow vol. 344/99, p. 1860]

Barr, John, St John's Bridge, Coventry, Warks., cm and u (1818–22). [D]

Barr, John, Hornsea, Yorks., cm and auctioneer (1834–40). [D]

Barr, Mary, Bristol, u (1829–31). Recorded at 20 Horfield Rd, 1829–30, and at 3 Duke St, King Sq. in 1831. [D]

Barr, T., Lechlade, Glos., cm, u and ironmonger. Undated trade card in Johnson Coll., Bodleian Lib., Oxford. [*Furn. Hist.*, 1974]

Barr, William, 29 Rose and Crown Ct, Moorfields, London, chair and sofa maker (1820–39). [D]

Barraclough, John, 107 Westgate, Bradford, Yorks., cm and joiner (1834–37). [D]

Barraclough, Richard, 60 King St, Manchester, cm and u (1814–18). [D] Also spelt Barrowclough (q.v.).

Barraclough, Thomas, Adwalton, Yorks., cm (1822). [D]

Barraclough, William, Holmfirth, Yorks., cm (1822). [D] Recorded in 1834 as Barrowclough.

Barracluff, J., High St, Leicester, cm (1815). [D]

Barralett, Anthony, 31 London Wall, London, cm and u (1822–23). [D]

Barrant, Thomas, Norwich, chairmaker (1750). Took app. named Gray, in 1750. [S of G, app. index]

Barrar, Beniah, Edbrook Rd, Kington, Herefs., carpenter, joiner and cm (1835). Beniah Barrell is recorded in Bridge St, Kington, in 1840. [D]

Barras, William, Newcastle, u (1782). App. to William Charnley. Admitted freeman 12 November 1782. [Newcastle freemen reg.]

Barrass, Cuthbert, address unrecorded, upholder (1733–42). Son of John Barrass of Wickham, Durham, yeoman; app. to Thomas Gardner, 25 September 1733. Admitted freeman of the Upholders' Co. by servitude, 5 May 1742. [GL, Upholders' Co. records] ·

Barratt, Wardour St, London. A Regency rosewood cabinet stamped 'BARRATT WARDOUR STREET' sold at Sotheby's, 15 June 1984, lot 131.

Barratt, George, Derby, u (1826–28). Recorded in the Chatsworth furnishing accounts as supplying goods to the value of £168 6s 11d in 1826; and £7 3s 9d in 1828. [Chatsworth papers, household ledger 1820–34]

Barratt, John Charles, 368 Strand, London, carver and gilder (1839). [D]

Barratt, Richard, 39 Northampton St, Clerkenwell, London, cm (1821). Took out a Sun Insurance policy on 29 January 1821 for £300 of which stock, utensils and goods in trust accounted for £100. [GL, Sun MS vol. 485, ref. 976309]

Barratt, Richard, High St, Bideford, Devon, cm and u (1823–26). [D] The marriage of the daughter of Mr Barrett, cm of Bideford, is reported in *The Alfred* 11 April 1826.

Barren, Thomas Richard, 3 Mary's Pl., Osborne St, Hull, Yorks., cm (1838–39). [D]

Barret, Benjamin, High St, Braintree, Essex, cm and u (1826–27). [D]

Barret, John, Dove Ct, Westminster, London, carver (1784). [Poll bk]

Barret, W., 13 Little Chapel St, Soho, London, chair and sofa maker (1809–11). [D]

Barret, William, Worcester, cm (1781). App. to Ely Crump, cm. Admitted freeman on 5 November 1781. [Worcester freemen admissions]

Barret, William, address unrecorded, u (1803). Subscribed to Sheraton's *Cabinet Dictionary*, 1803.

Barrett, — snr, 15 High St, Eton, Bucks., auctioneer, appraiser and u (1830). [D]

Barrett, Charles, 2 London St, Tottenham Ct Rd, London, cm and u (1839). [D]

Barrett, James, St John Timberland, Norwich, chairmaker (1768–80). [Poll bks] Mrs Barrett, widow, chairmaker, is recorded at 29 Timber-hill St, 1783–84. [D]

Barrett, James, Worcester, cm (1780). App. to Richard Morton, cm. Admitted freeman on 11 September 1780. [Worcester freemen admissions]

Barrett, James, 26 St Anne's Ct, Soho, London, chairmaker (1808). [D]

Barrett, John, Compton St, parish of St Ann, London, cm (1725). Took out a Sun Insurance policy on 5 January 1725, for £300. [GL, Sun MS vol. 22, p. 3]

Barrett, John, 49 Hounsditch, London, cm and dealer in china, glass and earthenware (1782). Took out a Sun Insurance policy in 1782 for £500 of which utensils and stock accounted for £250. [GL, Sun MS vol. 300, p. 522]

Barrett, John, 53–54 Wardour St, Soho, London, cm, bedstead maker, bedding warehouse owner (1789–1825). Recorded at 50 Wardour St, 1819–23, and 270 Strand, 1825. Took out a Sun Insurance policy on 15 July 1806 for £700 on 6 Meards St, Dean St, Soho, 'in tenure of a laceman'. [D; GL, Sun MS vol. 437, ref. 792303] See T. Barrett & G Wickstead, and Thomas Barrett.

Barrett, John, Moor Lane, Bolton, Lancs., chairmaker (1818). [D]

Barrett, John, Regent Rd, Eccles, Lancs., chairmaker (1834). [D]

Barrett, Robert, 70 Tooley St, Southwark, London, cm, broker and milkman (1782). Took out a Sun Insurance policy in 1782 for £300 of which utensils, stock and goods accounted for £140. [GL, Sun MS vol. 302, p. 242]

Barrett, Samuel, 8 Mansion House Pl., Camberwell, Surrey, u and cm (date unrecorded). Took out a Sun Insurance policy. [GL, Sun MS vol. 576, ref. 1335718]

Barrett, T. & Wickstead, G., 53–54 Wardour St, Soho, London, cabinet and bedstead manufacturers, chairmakers, bedding manufacturers (1803–15). Recorded at 50 Wardour St in 1811. Named in Sheraton's list of master cabinet makers, 1803. Succeeded by J. Ovenston. [D] John Barrett is recorded at this address, 1789–1820.

Barrett, Thomas, 270 Strand, London, cm and u (1826–28). A circular writing table is recorded bearing the label of Thomas Barrett, 270 Strand. [D; V & A archives] See John Barrett

Barrett, Thomas, 252 Tottenham Ct Rd, London, cm (1825–28). [D]

Barrett, Thomas, High Wycombe, Bucks., chairmaker (b. c. 1811–41). Daughter bapt. in 1834, sons in 1836 and 1840. Aged 30 at the time of the 1841 Census. [PR(bapt.)]

Barret(t), William, Liverpool, cm (1796–1819). Recorded at 17 Circus St in 1800. Petitioned freedom on birthright as son of Thomas Barrett, potter, paying 3s 4d. Admitted freeman, 25 May 1796. Death of his son, Richard, reported in *Liverpool Mercury*, 5 November 1819. [D; Liverpool freemen's committee bk and reg.]

Barrett, William, High Wycombe, Bucks., chairmaker (b. c. 1781–1841). Daughter bapt. in 1813, son in 1821, and daughter in 1831. Aged 60 at the time for the 1841 Census. [PR(bapt.)]

Barridger, Laurens, Sewer Lane, Hull, Yorks., wood clock maker (1790–91). [D]

Bar(r)iff, Thomas, 51 Charlotte St, Whitechapel, London, cm and u (1817–25). [D]

Barrington, James, 3 Greenland St, Liverpool, cm and u (1839). [D]

Barrington, John, 14 Dansie St, Liverpool, with shop at 5 Pembroke St, cm (1839). [D]

Barrington, Samuel B., 96 Wardour St, London, carver and gilder (1839). [D]

Barrington, William, Bridgwater, Som., cm (1778–80). Took out a Sun Insurance policy in 1778 for £200 on his house. [GL, Sun MS vol. 263, p. 542; poll bk]

Barrit, I., Summers Ct, Bishopsgate St Without, London, u etc. (1837). [D]

Barritt, James, Head Gate, Colchester, Essex, turner and cm (1823–39). Listed also as u in 1832. Took app. named John Winch in 1823. [D; Essex RO, D/DHt T337/5]

Barritt, James, 5 Fashion St, Spitalfields, London, cm and u (1839). [D]

Barritt, Samuel, 5 Fashion St, Spitalfields, London, carver and gilder, looking-glass and picture frame maker (1829–39). [D]

Barritt, Samuel, 8 High St, Camberwell, London, cm and u (1839). [D]

Barrnot, John, Cambridge, u (1711). Paid 19s 11d for work in the Masters' Lodge of St John's College.

Barron, —, London, u (1685–87). Named in the accounts of C. Blunt, u, as being paid 4s 6d in 1685–86, and £3 10s in 1686–87. [PRO, C114/164, pt.1]

Barron, —, 'The George', Bedford St, Covent Gdn, London, u (probably early 18th century). Mentioned in the Monson papers. [Lincoln RO, Monson 16/2/1/14]

Barron, A.F., 32 Pilgrim St, Newcastle, joiner, cm, furniture broker, u and carver. Early 19th-century trade card in Landauer Coll., MMA, NY.

Barron, Benjamin, over against Bond's Ct, Walbrook, London, u (1720–41). Son of Robert Baron of Mary Land, clerk, app. to John Osborn, 3 August 1720. Admitted freeman of the Upholders' Co. by servitude, 6 November 1728. Advertised in the press in 1732. Took app. named Christopher Appleby, 1732–41. [GL, Upholders' Co. records; Heal]

Barron, Elizabeth & Son, 35 Smithy Door, with house in Davenport Ct, 125 Deansgate, Manchester, cm (1808). [D] See John, Peter and Thomas Barron.

Barron, James, 28 Little Queen St, Lincoln's Inn Fields, London, upholder (1788–93). [D]

Barron, James, Oxford St, London and Lower Temple St, Birmingham, cm and u (1814). In 1814 he issued a 7 page catalogue with 68 plates, 65 in colour, entitled 'Modern & Elegant Designs of Cabinet & Upholstery Furniture', including drapery, furniture, roller and Venetian blinds, to be continued annually. [Copy at Du Pont Museum, Winterthur, Delaware]

Barron, John, Wood St, London, upholder (1747). Advertised in press, 1747. [Heal]

Barron, John, 35 Smithy Door, Manchester, cm and sworn appraiser (1788–97). [D] See Elizabeth Barron & Son, Peter and Thomas Barron.

Bar(r)on, John, Fore St, Lostwithiel, Cornwall, cm (1823–30). [D]

Barron, Peter, Manchester, cm, sworn appraiser and auctioneer (1800–04). Trading at 22 Market St Lane in 1800 and 35 Smithy Door in 1802–04. [D] See Elizabeth Barron & Son, John and Thomas Barron.

Barron, Richard, Liverpool, cm (1796). Petitioned freedom on birthright as son of Thomas Barron, silversmith, in 1796. [Liverpool freemen's committee bk]

Barron, Robert, Market Pl., Market Weighton, Yorks., cm (1840). [D]

Barron, Thomas, 35 Smithy Door, with house in Davenport Ct, 125 Deansgate, Manchester, auctioneer, sworn appraiser and cm (1808–09). [D] See Elizabeth Barron & Son, John and Peter Barron.

Barron, Thomas, Eccleston, Lancs., joiner and cm (1828). [D]

Barron & Golding, 24 Burr St, East Smithfield, London, cm (1807–11). [D]

Barroth, James, Norwich, chairmaker (1753). App. to Henry Nicholls; admitted freeman on 3 May 1753. [Norwich freemen reg.]

Barrow, James, Pilton, Som., cm (1810). On 19 April 1810 he announced that his wife Mary was now separated from him and he was not responsible for her debts. [*Exeter Flying Post*, 19 April 1810]

Barrow, John, Stamford, Lincs., turner and chairmaker (1773–1802). Admitted freeman in 1773 on payment of £5; took app. William Clapham, u, in 1802. [Stamford freemen reg.]

Barrow, John, Lancaster, cm (1791–1840). Admitted freeman, 1829–30. Named in the Gillow records, 1791–1840. [Westminster Ref. Lib., Gillow; Lancaster freemen rolls]

Barrow, John, 2 Rea St, Birmingham, cm (1822). [D]

Barrow, John, 68 Rahere St, Goswell Rd, London, fancy cm (1835–39). [D]

Barrow, Joseph, Edward St, Stockport, Lancs., cm (1825). [D]

Barrow, Lancelot, Bristol, u (1717–19). Took apps named Walker, 1717 and Hodges, 1719. [S of G, app. index]

Barrow, Margaret, 19 Richmond Fair, Liverpool, u (1827). [D]

Barrow, Nicholas, Lancaster, cm (1818–40). Admitted freeman in 1818–19. Named in the Gillow records between 1823–40 working on a washstand and table. [Westminster Ref. Lib., Gillow vol. 344/101, pp. 32–48, 3310; Lancaster freemen rolls]

Barrow, Richard, Liverpool, cm (1796–1811). Recorded at 33 Paul's Sq., 1810–11 as Sexton of St Paul's. Admitted freeman, 25 May 1796. [D; Liverpool freemen reg.] Possibly Richard Barron.

Barrow, Samuel, 4 Lombard St, Liverpool, cm (1790). [D]

Barrow, Thomas, address unrecorded (1670–71). Supplied chairs to Charles Stuart, Duke of Richmond. 1670–71. [Duke of Richmond papers, vol. 4: bills 1661–73, noted in Symonds papers, Winterthur, Delaware]

Barrow, Thomas, Lancaster, cm (1791–1800). App. to Isaac Greenwood, 1791. Admitted freeman, 1799–1800. [Lancaster app. reg. and freemen rolls]

Barrow, Thomas, Lancaster, cm (1825–26). Admitted freeman in 1825–26. [Lancaster freemen rolls]

Barrow, William, 3 Devonshire St, Queen Sq., London, carver and gilder (1785–92). Took out Sun Insurance policies on 22 June 1785 for £50 on utensils and stock; and on 13 September 1792 for £450 on his household goods. [GL, Sun MS vol. 329, p. 497; vol. 388, p. 575]

Barrow, William, Lancaster, cm (1799–1840). Admitted freeman, 1799–1800. Named in the Gillow records, 1800–40. [Westminster Ref. Lib., Gillow; Lancaster freemen rolls]

Barrow, William, Lancaster, cm (1829–37). App. to Leonard Redmayne, 1829. Admitted freeman on 28 October 1837. [Lancaster app. reg. and freemen rolls]

Barrow, William, 21 Evesham Buildings, Sommers Town, London, carver and gilder (1808). [D]

Barrow, William, 4 Little Suffolk St, Southwark, London, chair and sofa maker (1826). [D]

Barrowcliff, John, London, bed and mattress maker (1822–28). Trading at 40 Drury Lane in 1822 and 41 Regent St, Piccadilly in 1828. [D]

Barrowclough, John, 8 Back Spear St, Manchester, u (1821–22). [D]

Barrowclough, Richard, King St, Manchester, cm and u (1815–18). Listed at no. 61 in 1815 and 60 in 1818. [D]

Barrowclough, William, Nuneaton, Warks., u (1822). [D]

Barrows, Joseph, Chester, cm (1732). [Poll bk]

Barrows, Richard, Market End, Essex, cm and u (1780). Took out a Sun Insurance policy in 1780 for £200 on utensils and stock. [GL, Sun MS vol. 280, p. 91]

Barrs, Thomas, Birmingham, cm (1757). Took app. named Hodgkins in 1757. [S of G, app. index]

Barry, A., 7 Vere St, Oxford St, London, u (1801–03). Took out a Sun Insurance policy on 27 May 1801 for £450 of which utensils and stock accounted for £300. Named in Sheraton's list of master cabinet makers, 1803. [GL, Sun MS vol. 419, ref. 718602]

Barry, A., 1 Duke St, Grosvenor Sq., London, upholder (1807–17). [D]

Barry, Andrew, 16 Margaret St, Cavendish Sq., London, u (1820). [D]

Bar(r)y, Edward, Long Acre, London, u (1792). [Bailey's list of bankrupts]

Barry, Edward, Newington Causeway, London, u, undertaker and appraiser (1807–23). Addresses given at 58 in 1807–12, and 64 in 1815–23. The firm of E. Barry & Son, u and cm, is recorded at the second address, 1823–28. Trade card and bill-head in Heal Coll., BM. [D]

Barry, James, High St, Salisbury, Wilts., chairmaker (1830–39). [D]

Barry, Timothy, 60 Mortimer St, London, u (1839). [D]

Barry, William, 15 Junction Dock St, Hull, Yorks., cm, u, paper hanger and furniture broker (1831–40). Supplied furniture for Burton Constable on 29 July and 16 October 1838 comprising a press bedstead, £2, a French bedstead, £3, six painted chairs, 3s 6d each, six long backed chairs, 5s each and a 'pott cupboard', 10s. [D; Burton Constable vouchers]

Barry, William, High Wycombe, Bucks., chairmaker and French polisher (1840). [PR (marriage)]

Barshina, P. jnr, 4 Leather Lane, London, picture frame manufactory (1812–14). [D] See P. Barnaschina.

Barston, Thomas, Grantham, Lincs., ironmonger and cutler (1770). Advertised on 14 April 1770 that 'he has just laid in a fresh stock of London, Birmingham & Sheffield goods, mahogany tea boards, tea chests, looking glasses etc.' [*Cambridge Chronicle and Cambridge Journal*, 14 April 1770]

Barter, John, snr and jnr, Salisbury, Wilts., cm (1728). Took app. named Hallett in 1728. [S of G, app. index]

Barter, Robert, Exeter, Devon, cm (1754). Took app. named Bragg in 1754. [S of G, app. index]

Bartholomew, C., 38 Gt Pulteney St, Golden Sq., London, carver and gilder (1837). [D]

Bartholomew, J., London, cm, u and chair manufacturer (1837–39). Recorded at 4 Gray's Inn Rd in 1837 and 4 Upper North Pl., Gray's Inn in 1839. [D]

Bartholomew, J., Cheltenham, Glos., cm (1839–40). Trading at Gloucester Pl. in 1839. [D]

Bartholomew, Joseph, Derby, cm and u (1828–35). Trading at 28 St Mary's Gate in 1828 and no. 14 in 1835. Declared bankrupt, *Derby Gazette*, 13 March 1832. [D]

Bartholomew, William, Chichester, Sussex, chairmaker and turner (1826–39). Recorded in Somerstown in 1826 and South Pallant in 1832. [D]

Bartington, S., 95 Wardour St, Soho, London, carver and gilder (1837). [D]

Bartle, —, Market St, Ely, Cambs., chairmaker (1839). [D]

Bartleman, Robert, 76 Oxford St, London, chairmaker and u (1775–84). In partnership with William Fleming in Chandos St, 1775. [D]

Bartlett, Edward, Russell St, Drury Lane, London, cane chairmaker (1709). [Poll bk]

Bartlett, Frederick, 229 Whitechapel Rd, London, cm and u (1839). [D]

Bartlett, G., address unrecorded. In 1822 supplied chairs, curtains and carpet for Hampton Court Chapel. [PRO, LC11/35]

Bartlett, George, Old Jail Lane, Dorchester, Dorset, cm (1840). [D]

Bartlett, George Frederick, Lewes, Sussex, cm and u (1830–41). Trading in High St in 1830 and in St Mary's Lane in 1832. [D; poll bks]

Bartlett, Giles & Philip, 18 Blenheim St, Gt Marlborough St, London, gilders and chair japanners (1824–39). Took out a Sun Insurance policy on 16 February 1824 for £200 on stock, utensils and goods in workshop. [D; GL, Sun MS vol. 499, ref. 1013000]

Bartlett, Giles, 32 Drummond St, Euston Sq., London, cm and u (1839). [D]

Bartlett, Henry, Griffin Lane, Bristol, chair and couch maker (1838–40). [D] Possibly James Henry Bartlett, cm, of 2 Griffin Lane.

Bartlett, Henry, 18 New Rd, Brighton, Sussex, cm, u and furniture broker (1839). [D] See T. Bartlett.

Bartlett, James, Market Lavington, Wilts., cm (1730). Took app. named James Giddings on 29 August 1730 by Common Indenture and Counterpart, fee £10. [*Wilts. Apps and their Masters*]

Bartlett, James, Bristol, cm (1805–17). Addresses at 4 Broadmead in 1805 and Leek Lane, 1813–17. [D] The firm of Bartlett & Holland, cm and u, are recorded at 4 Broadmead in 1801 and 51 Castle St, 1799–1800. [D]

Bartlett, James Henry, 2 Griffin Lane, Bristol, cm (1831). [D] Possibly Henry Bartlett of Griffin Lane.

Bartlett, John, East St, Chichester, Sussex, cm, u and auctioneer (1793–1832). [D]

Bartlett, John, Church Passage, Weymouth, Dorset, cm, u and auctioneer (1823–24). [D]

Bartlett, Jonathan, 67 Aldersgate, London, cm (1780). Took out a Sun Insurance policy in 1780 for £400 on his house. [GL, Sun MS vol. 280, p. 135]

Bartlett, Robert, Newton Abbott, Devon, cm and shopkeeper (1780). Took out a Sun Insurance policy in 1780 for £600 of which utensils and stock accounted for £340. [GL, Sun MS vol. 287, p. 11]

Bartlett, Stephen, Upton-upon-Severn, Worcs., cm (1798). [D]

Bartlett, Susannah, Crewkerne, Som., chairmaker (1793). Took out a Sun Insurance policy on 8 January 1793 for £100. [GL, Sun MS vol. 392, p. 98] See W. Bartlett.

Bartlett, T., 18 New Rd, Brighton, Sussex, u (1839). [D] See Henry Bartlett.

Bartlett, W., Crewkerne, Som., chairmaker (1829). Fire on premises reported in *Exeter Flying Post*, 4 June 1829. See Susannah Bartlett.

Bartlett, William, Exeter, Devon, u (1798). Reported on 1 March 1798 that since 'Having been in Southgate prison for debt since June, his health has suffered.' Appeals for donations to pay the £15 for his release. [*Exeter Flying Post*, 1 March 1798]

Bartlett, William, Bromells Rd, Clapham, London, cm (1838). [D]

Bartlett, William, Stow-on-the-Wold, Glos., cm (1839). [D]

Bartlett & Co., 19 King St, Soho, London, japanners (1819). [D] Possibly Giles & Philip Bartlett.

Bartley, M. A., Vine Cottage, Ashley Pl., Bristol, u (1839). [D]

Bartlington, S., 95 Wardour St, Soho, London carver and gilder (1835). [D]

Barton, Edmond, High Wycombe, Bucks., cm (b. c. 1816–41). Aged 25 at the 1841 Census.

Barton, Frank, Nottingham, joiner and cm (1826–28). App. to John Chiswell, 1826–28. [Nottingham app. list]

Barton, George, Nantwich, Cheshire, cm (1794–98). Daughter bapt. and buried in 1794; son bapt. and buried in 1795; son bapt. in 1796. [D; Chester RO, PR(bapt.)]

Barton, George, John St, Meadow Lane, Leeds, Yorks., chairmaker (1828).

Barton, I., address unrecorded. Between 15 February and 10 March 1798 supplied a mahogany Pembroke table and four 'Camber' chairs, and cleaned 'the bookcase & bureau of ink etc', for Stourhead. [Wilts. RO, MS 383/5/1]

Barton, J., address unrecorded. Inlaid rosewood sofa table recorded signed 'J. Barton May 17 1822'. [C. *Life*, 12 June 1969, advert. of Meyrick Neilson, Tetbury]

Barton, Jacob, Eton, Bucks., u (1823–30). Trading also as an u in 1823; and also as appraiser and auctioneer in 1830 when his address is given at 40 High St. [D] See John Barton.

Barton, James, Liverpool, cm and joiner (1760–61). Petitioned his freedom on purchase, paying 6s 8d in 1760. Former apps Edward Sinclair and John Moncaster petitioned freedom in 1760 and 1761 respectively. Took out a Sun Insurance policy in 1761 for £400. [Liverpool freemen's committee bk; GL, Sun MS ref. 183970]

Barton, James, Blackburn, Lancs., u, cm and paper hanger (1818–34). Recorded at Northgate and New Sq. in 1818; 33 Fleming Sq., 1824–28; and Clayton St in 1834. Declared bankrupt, *Liverpool Mercury*, 19 October 1821. [D]

Barton, John, Smithy Door, Manchester, cm (1788). [D] Possibly John Barron.

Barton, John, address unrecorded, cm (1803). Subscribed to Sheraton's *Cabinet Dictionary*, 1803. 'Barton, Lincolnshire' subscribed to Sheraton's *Drawing Book*, 1793.

Barton, John, Horsefair, Rugeley, Staffs., cm (1818). [D]

Barton, John, 55 High St, Windsor, Berks., cm, u and appraiser (1824–40). [D; fifth hall book of the borough of New Windsor, pp. 109, 152, 159, 174, 183] See Jacob Barton.

Barton, Joseph, 18 Mint St, Southwark, London, u and appraiser (1820–27). [D]

Barton, Jos., Strand, Starcross, Devon, cm (1838). [D]

Barton, Miss Mary, 13 and 17 Shaw's Brow, Liverpool, u (1800–04). [D]

Barton, Matthew, 4 Short St, Spencer St, Hull, Yorks., cm (1838–39). [D]

Barton, Nathaniel, Colchester, Essex, u and cm (1775). Took out a Sun Insurance policy for £2,200 of which utensils, stock and warehouse accounted for £700. [GL, Sun MS vol. 242, p. 499]

Barton, Thomas, Liverpool, carver (1797–1835). Addresses at 51 Sparling St, Park Lane, 1800–05; 53 Sparling St with shop at 11 Wapping, 1807–10; 21 Wood St, 1811–14; 1 Williamson Sq., 1818–29; 1 Gregory Pl., Gerard St, 1829; and 11 Back Lime St, 1834–35. Marriage at St George's to Miss Elizabeth Case reported in *Liverpool Advertiser*, 6 March 1797. The firm of Barton & Bourne, carvers, is recorded at 12 Wapping, 1804–05. [D]

Barton, Thomas jnr, Green Ct, Green Lane, Pleasant St, Liverpool, carver (1835). [D]

Barton, Thomas, St Sepulchre Gate, Doncaster, Yorks., chairmaker (1830). [D]

Barton, Thomas, Manchester, cm (1808–17). Trading at 8–9 Water St, 1808–13 and 23 Bootle St in 1817. [D]

Barton, Thomas, Melton Mowbray, Leics., cm (1822). [D]

Barton, Thomas, 36 Lambert St, Sheffield, Yorks., chairmaker (1833). [D]

Barton, W., 2 Snow's Fields, Southwark, London, u (1809–11). [D]

Barton, W., Northgate St, Chester, cm (1819). [Poll bk]

Barton, William, Beverley, Yorks., cm (1774–91) [D; poll bk]

Barton, William, Southwark, London, u (1804–11). Trading at 17 Counter St in 1804 and 243 Borough, 1807–11. [D]

Barton, William, Prospect Pl., St George's Fields, London, u and cm (1809–11). [D]

Barton, William, Rochdale, Lancs., cm and chairmaker (1818–34). Recorded in Packer St, 1818–25 and South Parade in 1834. Advertised in *Liverpool Mercury*, 18 June 1824 for 'five or six CABINET MAKERS good workmen; will meet with constant employment and very liberal wages'. [D]

Barton, William, 3 and 5 Chaingate, Southwark, London, u and cm (1820). [D]

Barton, William, 20 St Saviour's Churchyard, London, u (1820–29). [D]

Barton, William, 4 Newington Causeway, London, upholder and cm (1823–35). Declared bankrupt, *Liverpool Mercury*, 17 May 1823. [D]

Barton, William, Hinderwell, near Whitby, Yorks., cm (1840). [D]

Barton & Bond, Longworth's Folly, Manchester, joiners and chest makers (1811). [D]

Bartram, Thomas, London, upholder (1761). [Maidstone poll bk]

Bartram, William, Nottingham(?), joiner and cm (1793). [D]

Bartrum, B., 10 Milsom St, Bath, Som., cm etc. (1826). [D]

Barwell, Robert, Maldon, Essex, cm and u (1826–32). [D]

Barwick, Benjamin, Catterick, Yorks., joiner and cm (1823). [D]

Barwick, Henry, Lancaster, chairmaker (1799–1800). Admitted freeman, 1799–1800, when stated 'of Broughton'. [Lancaster freemen rolls]

Barwick, James, Goosegate, Nottingham, chairmaker, cm and furniture broker (1812–32). Son of Samuel Barwick, app. by charity in 1812. Listed as burgess in 1821. Recorded at Paradise St in 1828 and Byron St, Snenton in 1835. [D; Notts. RO, list of charity app. indentures; index of burgesses]

Barwick, James, Market Pl., Broughton, Ulverston, Lancs., chairmaker (1829). [D]

Barwick, John, St Peter Mancroft, Norwich, cm (1734). [Poll bks]

Barwick, John, Lancaster, chairmaker (1799–1800). [Lancaster freemen rolls]

Barwick, John & James, Broughton-in-Furness, Lancs., chairmakers (1824–28). [D]

Barwick, Joseph, Lancaster, u (1837). Admitted freeman on 5 July 1837. [Lancaster freemen rolls]

Barwick, Thomas, Knottingley, Yorks., joiner and cm (1834). [D]

Barwick, William, Lancaster, u (1770–82). App. to Myles Pennington, 1770. Admitted freeman, 1781–82. [Lancaster app. reg. and freemen rolls]

Barwick, William, Liverpool, u and cm (1788–95). Trading at Renn's Gdn, 1790 and 26 Castle Ditch, 1794. Taken into partnership as u by the firm of Edmundson & Fayrer in 1788, but in 1791 the partnership was dissolved. Barwick started business on his own account but continued to share the old warehouse at 26 Castle Ditch with John Fayrer. Advertised together on 15 January 1791 as supplying 'Gentlemen, Merchants & others with goods of the best materials, either for exportation or their own houses, on the shortest notice & on the most reasonable terms'. Barwick declared bankrupt, 8 September 1794, and 4 May 1795. [D; *Williamson's Liverpool Advertiser*, 24 November 1788, 17 January 1791, 8 September 1794; Billinge's *Liverpool Advertiser*, 4 May 1795]

Barwick, William, 51 White Lion St, Pentonville, London, carver and gilder (1839). [D]

Barwood, William, North Walsham, Norfolk, cm (1798). [D]

Basan, John, Burlington Gdns, London, carver (before 1743). [Harris, *Old English Furniture*, p. 18]

Basendale, Lloyd, Liverpool, u (1760). Took app. named Fishwick in 1760. [S of G, app. index]

Basepool, Robert, Winchester, Hants., u (1783–84). [D]

Baserga, Louis, London, picture and looking-glass frame maker (1835–39). Recorded at 9 Back Hill, Hatton Gdns in 1835 and 9 Back Hill, Leather Lane in 1839. [D]

Basfield, John, York, cm (d. 1795). Death reported in *Gents Mag.*, March 1795, after having been 'retired some years'.

Basford, John, Wednesfield, Staffs., joiner and cm (1834). [D]

Baskerville, John, 22 Moor St, Easy Hill, Birmingham, japanner and papier mâché manufacturer (1706–75). Earliest recorded manufacturer of papier mâché, he supplied 'a selection of useful articles such as tea boards elegantly designed and finished'. [*Art Union*, 1846, p. 59; W. Hutton, *History of*

Birmingham, pp. 120–23; Jourdain & Rose, *English Furniture: the Georgian Period, 1750–1830*]

Baskerville, Thomas William, 4 Windmill St, Finsbury, London, furniture japanner and painter (1829–39). [D]

Baskett, J., Southampton Rd, Lymington, Hants., cm etc. (1839). [D]

Baskett, Joseph, York and Sheffield, carver and gilder (1784–95). Aged 14, of Wentworth, app. to Robert Blakesley, carver and gilder, on 19 June 1784. Of Sheffield, admitted freeman of York in 1795. [York app. reg. and freemen rolls]

Baslington, John, Spilsby, Lincs., joiner and cm (1826). [D]

Baslow, Samuel, 31 Duke St, Leeds, Yorks., cm (1830). [D]

Basnett, Edward, Liverpool, cm (1805–12). App. to Thomas Basnett, cm, in 1805. Admitted freemen on 6 October 1812. [Liverpool freemen's committee bk and reg.]

Basnett, Thomas, Liverpool, cm (1761). Admitted freeman on 10 February 1761. [Liverpool freemen reg.]

Basnett, Thomas P., Liverpool, cm and victualler (b. 1752–d. 1822). Trading at 17 Vernon St, 1781–90; no. 31 in 1796; 20 Key St, Tythebarn St in 1800; and Edmund St, 1803–22. Admitted freeman on 11 September 1780 on servitude to Edward Lowe. Son Thomas b. 22 June 1784, became a tailor. Took app. named Edward Basnett in 1805. Death reported on 7 June 1822, aged 70. [D; Liverpool freemen's committee bk and reg.; *Liverpool Mercury*, 7 June 1822]

Bass, Samuel, Gainsborough, Lincs., joiner and cm (1818). App. to William Rollett in August 1818. [Hull app. reg.]

Bass, Thomas, Exeter, Devon, cm (1767). Admitted freeman in 1767. [Exeter freemen rolls]

Basseler, —, address unrecorded, cm (1700). He was paid £1 3s 6d by the Executors of William, 1st Duke of Bedford, for unspecified work. [Bedford Office, London]

Bassett, Henry, Margate, Kent, cm, u and shop keeper (1777–81). Took out Sun Insurance policies in 1777 for £1,800 of which utensils and stock accounted for £300; and in 1781 for £1,800 of which utensils and stock accounted for £400. [GL, Sun MS vol. 257, p. 48; vol. 296, p. 513] Henry & Stephen Basset, cm, u and shopkeepers, are recorded in 1777 taking out a Sun Insurance policy for £1,000 of which stock, utensils, workshop and warehouse accounted for £380. [GL, Sun MS vol. 257, p. 49]

Bassett, Edward & Son, 64 Newington Causeway, London, cm and u (1827–28). [D]

Bassett, George, London, cm and u (1826–39). Addresses at 31 Judd Pl. West, New Rd, St Pancras, 1826–29, and at 17 and 22 York Terr. in 1839. [D]

Bassett, Stephen, address unrecorded, upholder (1703–04). Admitted freeman of the Upholders' Co. on 1 March 1703–04. [GL, Upholders' Co. records]

Bassett, Thomas, Steep Hill, Lincoln, carver and gilder (1835). [D]

Bassett, William, Back St, Leek, Staffs., chairmaker (1835). [D]

Bassick, A., Scarborough, Yorks., cm (1793). Subscribed to Sheraton's *Drawing Book*, 1793.

Bastable, Esarhaddon, Bristol, cm (1781–1827). Trading at Castle Mill St in 1792; Newgate St, 1793–95; Merchant St, 1799–1801; St Michael's Hill, 1805–06; Milk St, 1807–10; and Trenchard St, 1812–27. [D; poll bks] See Jonah and Jonathan Bastable.

Bastable, Jonah, Milk St, Bristol, carver (1792). [D]

Bastable, Jonathan, Bristol, upholder (1774–1812). Recorded in the parish of St Peter, 1774–81; parish of St James in 1784; and Milk St in 1812. [D; poll bks] Partnered with John Burge as carvers in Milk St in 1810 but both recorded alone by 1812. [D]

Bastard, John, Portsmouth, Hants., cm (1735). Took app. named Fitchett in 1735. [S of G, app. index]

Bastard, John & William, address unrecorded, cm (1756). Their account rendered to John, 4th Duke of Bedford on 30 July 1756 invoices nine small items: a tea board, coffee board, two trays, a plate basket, two punch ladles and a knife box, totalling £1 13s 3d, and is marked 'To go to Camp'. The Duke was in camp as a militia commander during the summer of 1756. The account also names George Rawson, personal servant to Francis, Marquess of Tavistock, the Duke's son, then aged 17 and probably in camp with his father. Some of the articles may have been for his use. [Bedford Office, London; G. Blakiston, *Woburn and the Russells*] Possibly the brothers John & William Bastard of Blandford, Dorset, better known as architects:

Bastard, John, Blandford, Dorset, cm (1740–52). Recorded in deeds of 19 May 1740 and 14 July, 1752. [*Dorset Nat. Hist. and Arch. Proceedings*, vol. LIII]

Bastard, Thomas, Sherborne, Dorset, carver and freeman (1761). Took app. named Painter in 1761. [S of G, app. index]

Baston, William, London, u (1835–39). Trading at 33 Marshall St, London Rd in 1835 and 28 Garden Row, Southwark in 1839. [D]

Bastow, Samuel, 31 Duke St, Leeds, Yorks., cm (1830). [D]

Batchellor, —, London, cm (1721). Sent a bill to the 1st Duke of Portland for 'what is due in London for Equipage, Furniture, workmanship &c to August 1721 — £288-0-9'. [Notts. RO, PW B90]

Batchelor, John, 5 Gt Quebec St, New Rd, London, cm (1809–11). [D] See William Batchelor.

Batchelor, Samuel, French St, Southampton, Hants., cm, broker, etc. (1811). [Southampton register] A Samuel Batchelor, cm, subscribed to Sheraton's *Cabinet Dictionary*, 1803.

Batchelor, Samuel, Silver St, Bradford-upon-Avon, Wilts., cm (1839). [D]

Batchelor, Walter, Bristol, cm, clock case and camp desk maker (1835–40). Recorded in Thomas St, Pugsley's Field in 1835 and at 3 Lower Montague St in 1839–40. [D]

Batchelor, William, High St, Chesham, Bucks., chairmaker (1830). [D]

Batchelor, William, 5 Gt Quebec St, Marylebone, London, cm (1820–39). Also recorded at 14 Gt Quebec St in 1820. [D] A William Batchelor, cm, subscribed to Sheraton's *Cabinet Dictionary*, 1803.

Batchelor, William & Thomas, 111 Crawford St, London, cm, u and undertakers (1839). [D]

Bate, —, Market Drayton, Salop, spinning-wheel maker (1797). [D]

Bate, George, Union St, Wolverhampton, Staffs., cm (1827). [D]

Bateman, George, Lancaster, u (1817–18). [Lancaster freemen rolls]

Bateman, John, 'The Golden Ball' by the Dytchside, Holborn Bridge, London, cm (date unrecorded). A walnut bureau is recorded bearing the label of John Bateman. [*C. Life*, 14 June 1962, p. 1420]

Bateman, John, St Luke, Middlx, chairmaker (1760). Took app. named Linney in 1760. [S of G, app. index]

Bateman, John, Lancaster (1816–33). Named in the Gillow records between 1816–33. A Regency mahogany teapoy with octagonal hinged top containing two boxes and spaces for two sugar bowls, on turned stem and four-cornered base, is recorded stamped 'Gillows Lancaster' and 'I. Bateman'. [Westminster Ref. Lib., Gillow; Christie's, 1 November 1976]

Bateman, John, Leicester, cm (1833). Admitted freeman in 1833. [Leicester freemen rolls]

Bateman, John, 8 John St, Marylebone, London, cm and u (1839). [D]

Bateman, Matthew, Lancaster, turner (1826–34). [Westminster Ref. Lib., Gillow records]

Bateman, Redman, Lancaster, cm (1751–73). App. to R. Bell in 1751. Admitted freeman, 1761–62. Recorded in partnership with William Blackburn in 1762 when he took app. named J. Crofts on 17 May; in partnership with William Blackburn and William Forrest in 1765 when he took app. named R. Russell on 25 February and in partnership with Forrest only in 1769 when he took app. named J. Hodgson on 6 November and in 1773 when he took app. named Thomas Cowper on 12 October. [Poll bk; Lancaster app. reg. and freemen rolls]

Bateman, William, Crewdson's Yd, Highgate, Kendal, Westmld, cm (1828–29). [D]

Bates, —, address unrecorded, cm (1774). Ralph Yates of Clerkenwell Close, Clerkenwell, London, carpenter, insured 'two houses only adjoining in the tenure of Bates, cabinet maker — £200'. [GL, Sun MS vol. 235, ref. 347657]

Bates, Edmund, 8 Wellington St, Leeds, Yorks., carver in wood, draughtsman and gilder. Early 19th-century trade card announces he is a member of the Yorkshire Architectural Society, and carves 'Models . . . for Architects, Silversmiths and Brass Founders', and executes 'every Description of Gilding and Bronzing . . . in a superior Style'. [Landauer Coll., MMA, NY]

Bates, George, Whitcombe St, Westminster, London, cm (1749). [Poll bk]

Bates, James, Bird Cage Alley, in the Mint, Southwark, London, cm (1785–87). Took out Sun Insurance policies on 8 July 1785 for £400 on houses only with Samuel Spicer, broker; and on 6 January 1787 for £800 on six houses in Southwark and a workshop. [GL, Sun MS vol. 331, p. 47; vol. 340, p. 496]

Bates, James, 20 London Rd, Southwark, London, cm and u (1809–19). [D] Possibly John James Bates.

Bates, James, 15 Southgate, Halifax, Yorks., cm and u (1830). [D] See Mary Ann Bates.

Bates, John, Gainsborough, Lincs., chairmaker (1760). [Lincoln RO, subject index]

Bates, John, 40 Newton St, Dale St, Manchester, with home at 2 Warwick St, Manchester, cm (1825). [D]

Bates, John, 7 Hardwick Pl., Commercial Rd, Whitechapel, London, cm etc. (1835). [D] See John Battes.

Bates, John James, London Rd, St George the Martyr, Southwark, London, u and cm (d. 1813). A bill of 26 October 1837 concerns his estate and gives the date of his will as 27 January 1813 and of his death as 31 January 1813. [PRO, C13 564] Possibly James Bates.

Bates, Mary, 14 Southgate, Halifax, Yorks., u (1837). [D] See James Bates.

Bates, Richard, 51 New Compton St, Soho, London, carver and gilder (1826–39). [D]

Bates, Samuel, Market Pl., Richmond, Yorks., painter, gilder and carver (1827). [D]

Bates, Thomas, London, cm (1784). [Norwich poll bk]

Bates, Thomas, London, mahogany knife case maker (1793). [D]

Bates, Thomas, Bolton St, Chorley, Lancs., cm and chairmaker (1828). [D]

Bates, William, Liverpool, cm and furniture broker (1835–39). Trading at 13 Stanley St in 1835; nos 5 and 43 in 1837; and nos 9, 76 and 80 in 1839. [D]

Bates, William, Bishop Wearmouth, Sunderland, Co. Durham, cm (1832). [D]

Bates, William Edward, 2 Black St, Horsely Down, London, carver and gilder (1839). [D]

Bateson, David, Lancaster and London, cm (1772–84). App. to J. Neill in 1772. Admitted freeman of Lancaster, 1782–83, when stated 'of Little Russel St., Bloomsbury, London'. Polled at Lancaster in 1784, with address in London. [Lancaster app. reg. and freemen rolls]

Bateson, David, 128 High Holborn, London, cm (1791–1821). Took out a Sun Insurance policy on 10 June 1791 for £400 of which utensils, stock and goods in trust and on commission accounted for £310. Named in Sheraton's list of master cabinet makers, 1803. [D; GL, Sun MS vol. 373, ref. 584247] See M. Bateson.

Bateson, James, Lancaster, cm (1799–1800). Admitted freeman of Lancaster in 1799–1800. Freemen rolls state 'of London'.

Bateson, M., 128 High Holborn, London, u and cm (1820). [D] See David Bateson.

Bateson, William, Bloomsbury, London, u and cm (1774–95). Recorded at Queen St in 1774; 13 Gt Russell St in 1782; 114 Gt Russell St from 1784–95 and no. 148 in 1789. Took out a Sun Insurance policy in 1782 for £1,000 of which utensils, stock and goods accounted for £200. [D; poll bk; GL, Sun MS vol. 300, p. 197]

Batger, Anthony, 159 Ratcliff Highway, London, u (1781–93). Son of John Batger, sugar refiner of St George in the East, Middlx. App. to Robert Phipps (d. 1775) then to Benjamin Soundy. Admitted freeman of the Upholders' Co. by servitude on 7 March 1781. [D; GL, Upholders' Co. records] The firm of Batger & Co. are recorded at the same address in 1789. [D]

Bath, John, 6 New Inn, Bateman's Row, Shoreditch, London, cm (1808). [D]

Bath, John, 3 Blossom St, Norton Falgate, London, cm (1820). [D]

Bath, John, London, fancy cm, portable desk, dressing case and cabinet case maker (1829–39). Trading at 7 Artillery St, Bishopsgate in 1829; 37 Jewin St in 1835; and 97 Cheapside in 1839. [D]

Bath, William, Sidney St, Cambridge, u (1829–32). Baptisms of two children, in 1829 and 1832, recorded in the parish of All Saints. [Cambs. RO]

Bather, Nathaniel, Foregate St, Chester, cm and furniture broker (1800–40). Son of James Batho of Chester, sworn freeman of Chester in June 1800 under the name of Batho. Took app. named Frederick Phillips in 1825. Recorded in the election for Sheriff of Chester in 1819. [D; poll bks; Chester freemen rolls and app. reg.]

Bather, Nathaniel, 2 Robert St, Clarence St, Liverpool, cm (1803). [D]

Bathgate, Archibald, 10 Trafford Lane, Liverpool, cm and victualler (1805–07). [D]

Batho, John, Bodingham, Suffolk, chairmaker (1730). Took app. named Cooper in 1730. [S of G, app. index]

Bathurst, Walter, address unrecorded, upholder (1766). Son of James Bathurst, Leominster, Herefs., farmer. Admitted freeman of the Upholders' Co. by redemption on 6 November 1766. [GL, Upholders' Co. records]

Batlerson, —, Berkeley Row, Berkeley Sq., London, cm and chairmaker (1744). Advertised in November 1744 as supplying 'wallnut tree chairs stuffed and covered with damask and spanish leather, matted bottom Beach chairs of all sorts'. [Harris & Sons, *The English Chair*]

Batley, Richard, Snaith, Yorks., cm (1831). [D]

Batley, William, 13 Brownlow St, Holborn, London, portable desk, dressing case, work box and pocket book manufacturer (1820–29). Recorded as Batey in 1820. [D]

Batley, William, Norwich, chairmaker and wholesale cm (1836–42). Addresses in St George's Plain in 1836 and Pitt St in 1842. [D]

Batt, John, 22 St James Parade, Bath, Som., u (1826). [D]

Battel, William, Mount St, Diss, Norfolk, cm and u (1830–39). [D]

Batten, Edward, Rochester, Kent, carver (1780). [Poll bk]

Batten, Edward, 14 Stepney Causeway, London, carver (1785). Took out a Sun Insurance policy on 26 May 1785 for £450 on household goods. [GL, Sun MS vol. 328, p. 363]

Batten, Elizabeth, Chatham, Kent, upholder (1784). [D]

Batten, John, St Margaret's Bank, Rochester, Kent, upholder, cm, appraiser and undertaker (1792–1839). Took out a Sun Insurance policy on 7 June 1792 for £3,300 of which utensils and stock accounted for £1,000, workshop and storehouse adjoining house for £300, utensils and stock therein, £200; cart house, stable and loft above, £70, utensils and stock therein, £30, and house in tenure of widow Batten, £485. Named as an orator in a bill of 13 June 1817. Trade card [Banks Coll., BM] advertises 'Gentlemens Cabbins, Wardrooms Marques &c. genteely fitted on the Shortest Notice' and 'Hair Trunks, Sea Chests, Cotts, Mattrasses, Bedding etc.' A bow front chest of drawers is recorded bearing the circular label of 'John Batten, Upholder, Rochester'. A Mr Batten, u, of Rochester, subscribed to Sheraton's *Drawing Book*, 1793. [D; GL, Sun MS vol. 387, p. 18; V & A archives; PRO, C13 710/29] See Latitia and T. Batten.

Batten, John jnr, High Wycombe, Bucks., chairmaker (1798). [Militia Census]

Batten, Latitia, St Margaret's Bank, Rochester, Kent, broker and upholder (1776–85). Took out Sun Insurance policies in 1776 for £1,800 of which utensils, stock and goods accounted for £100; in 1781 for £2,100 of which utensils, stock, workshop and storehouse accounted for £1,100; and on 8 October 1785 for £200 on various tenanted properties. [GL, Sun MS vol. 248, p. 553; vol. 297, p. 306; vol. 333, p. 108] See John and T. Batten.

Batten, T., St Margaret's Bank, Rochester, Kent, cm (1803). [D] See John and Latitia Batten.

Batten, William, High Wycombe, Bucks., chairmaker (1822–24). Daughter bapt. in 1822 and son in 1824. [PR(bapt.)]

Batten & Glover, Horse-Ferry, Rotherhithe, London, carvers. Early 19th-century trade card is in Landauer Coll., MMA, NY.

Battersby, —, Lancaster. Named in the Gillow records working on a bookcase in 1818. [Westminster Ref. Lib., Gillow vol. 344/100, p. 2065]

Battersby, John, Friar(gate) St, Lancaster, cm (1809–39). App. to John Hodgson in 1809. Admitted freeman in 1816–18. On 13 May 1826 Hodgson took into partnership 'his foreman, John Battersby, who has been many years in his service'. Between 18 May 1826 and 29 June 1839 took on 16 app. cm. [Lancaster app. reg. and freemen rolls; *Lancaster Gazette*, 13 May 1826]

Battersby, Robert, Lancaster, cm (b. 1790–d. 1827). Trading at Stonewell in partnership with Edward Lodge until 1826, and in Friar St in partnership with John Hodgson and his brother John Battersby as Hodgson & Battersbys. Died in August 1827 aged 37. [*Lancaster Gazette*, 13 May 1826 and 20 May 1826; *Liverpool Mercury*, 31 August 1827]

Battersby, Thomas, London, cm and joiner (1768). Petitioned freedom on servitude to Richard Copeland in 1768 paying 6s 8d. [Liverpool freemen's committee bk]

Battes, John, London, cm and u (1820–39). Trading at 82 Broad St, Ratcliff, 1820–29; 7 Hardwick Pl., Commercial Rd in 1835, and 3 and 4 Jamaica Terr., Commercial Rd East in 1839. [D] See John Bates.

Battey, William, 190 Brick Lane, Spitalfields, London, cm (1789). [D]

Battin, Isaac, Gloucester, cm (1822–29). Children bapt. between 1822–29 at St Nicholas's. [PR(bapt.)]

Battin, J., Suffolk Rd, Cheltenham, Glos., chair and sofa manufacturer (1839). [D]

Batting, Thomas, High Wycombe, Bucks., cm (1773). Named in the marriage register on 12 July 1773. [PR]

Battison, George, Ampthill, Beds., joiner (1835–36). Received commission for 50 double and 50 single beds from the Guardians of the new Union Workhouse, Ampthill, built in 1835, and was paid £58 6s 8d in February 1836. One survives, consisting of elm frame united by bed bolts, pine headboard and slats. [Exhib. cat., *Common Furniture*, Temple Newsam House, 1982]

Battison, William, Church St, Ampthill, Beds., cm (1839). [D]

Battistessa & Co, London and Edinburgh, carvers and gilders (1830–40). Recorded at 13 Baldwins Gdns, Gray's Inn Lane, London, 1830–35, whilst their undated trade card gives addresses at 106 Hatton Gdn, London, and Calton St, Edinburgh. It also describes services: 'Glasses Ground, Polished, Silvered, Paintings cleaned and repaired. Barometers, Thermometers & Optical Glasses Made & Repaired. Picture Frame Makers & Looking Glass Manufacturers.' The firm of Battistessa, Molteni & Guanziroli, carvers and gilders, was trading at 106 Hatton Gdn in 1839. [D; Goodison, *Barometers*; Landauer Coll., MMA, NY]

Battle, Joseph, Mews, back of Park St, Bristol, cm (1833). [D]

Battler, Mathew, York, cm (1754). Took app. named Leadly in 1754. [S of G, app. index]

Batton, Edward, St Mary, Rotherhithe, London, wood carver (1756). Took app. named Freeman in 1756. [S of G, app. index]

Batty, Edward, Lancaster, house carpenter and cm (1771–99). Between 20 June 1771 and 10 June 1799 took 12 apps. [Lancaster app. reg.]

Batty, John, 59 Hardman St, Manchester, cm (1838–40). [D]

Baty, William Lonsdale, Orchard St, Westminster, London, cm (1813). His father mortgaged the 'White Swan Inn', England St, Carlisle and died in 1768. [PRO, C13 683/28] Possibly related to:

Baty & Kirkbride, Carlisle, Cumb., cm and joiners (1828–34). Trading at Fisher St in 1829 and 17 Rosemary Lane in 1834. [D]

Baudvine (or Baudovin), Nicholas, London, u (1683–84). Recorded in the Royal Household accounts supplying 'a bed . . . 6 curtains, 3 cantoons, 3 bases, 1 coronidem, 2 cases for columns of the tester, 2 head panels, coverlet, 4 interior cantroons, 4 cups, 2 armchairs, 4 stools, all green silk, white interior etc. for Queen Mother, — £70. 9s. 0d'. The bill totalled £2,062 1s 5½d. [PRO, LC9/120, 277] See Podvine (or Paudevine).

Baugh, Francis, 146 Redcliff St, Bristol, basket and chairmaker (1799–1817). [D]

Baugh, Thomas, Scotland St, Ellesmere, Salop, cm and joiner (1822). [D]

Baugh, T. & G., Dudley, Worcs., chairmakers (1839). [D]

Baugham, William, 66 (New) Compton St, Soho, London, carver and gilder (1817–39). Took out a Sun Insurance policy on 2 October 1823 for £700. [D; GL, Sun MS vol. 498, ref. 1008441]

Bavin, James, 11 Market St, Borough St, London, chair and sofa maker (1832–39). [D]

Bavin, John, West Wycombe, Bucks., chairmaker (1798). [Militia Census]

Bavin, William, West Wycombe, Bucks., chairmaker and shopkeeper (1790–98). [D; Militia Census]

Bawcombe, Harry, Steyning, Sussex, cm (d. by 1778).

Advertisement 'asking all Persons indebted to the Estate of HARRY BAWCOMBE late of Steyning Cabinet-maker deceased to submit details of debts'. [*Sussex Weekly Advertiser*, 23 March 1778]

Bawden, J., 17 Lower Maudlin St, Bristol, ornamental and cabinet carver and cm (1834). [D]

Bawtry, Barnaby, next door to 'The Black Swan', Coney St, York, u (1717–41). Listed 'Master' in York reg. of app. indentures for Maurice Farnworth in 1717, Thomas Ubaine in 1722 and Joseph Metcalfe in 1731, all for 7 years. Took out Sun Insurance policies on 31 October 1724 on goods and merchandise in dwelling house only at a premium of 2s; and on 28 January 1728 for £300 on household goods and merchandise. His house is recorded for sale on 9 September 1740, but he was still in Coney St at the York poll of 1741. [GL, Sun MS vol. 17, ref. 32566; vol. 28, p. 36; *York Courant*, 9 September 1740; poll bk] Possibly the son of:

Bawtry, Joseph, York, u (1715). His son, Bernard, admitted freeman of York in 1715. [York freemen rolls]

Baxendale, Gamaliel, Liverpool, u (b. 1740–65). Son of Josiah Baxendale, petitioned to be free on birthright in 1765. [Liverpool freemen's committee bk] Possibly brother of Joseph Baxendale.

Baxendale, James, Manchester, chairmaker (1834–40). Recorded at 7 Ashley St, St Gee's Rd and 51 Thomas St in 1834; 7 Ashley St and 47 Thomas St in 1836; and 5 Ashley St in 1840. [D]

Baxendale, John, 10 Crown Lane, Manchester, chairmaker (1808–09). [D]

Baxendale, Joseph, Liverpool, cm (1750–52). Admitted freeman on 27 March 1750. Took apps named Finley and Leadbetter in 1752. [Liverpool freemen reg.; S of G, app. index]

Baxendale, Joseph, Liverpool, cm (1757). Petitioned freedom as free-born son of Josiah Baxendale, paying 3s 4d in 1757. Former app., Thomas Robinson, petitioned freedom in 1780. [Liverpool freemen's committee bk] Possibly brother of Gamaliel Baxendale, and possibly:

Baxendale, Joseph, Liverpool, cm (1766–74). Addresses in Oldhall St, 1766–73, and at 4 Peter's Lane in 1774. [D] A Joseph Baxendale of Liverpool, cm, was admitted a freeman of Lancaster in 1767–68. [Lancaster freemen rolls] Another is recorded in 1799 when his son, Josiah, petitioned freedom on birthright. [Liverpool freemen's committee bk] A 'Mr Baxendale of Liverpool' provided mahogany furniture for Sir Watkin Williams-Wynn in 1771. [Nat. Lib. of Wales, Wynnstay, R41]

Baxendale, Josiah, Liverpool, cm (1732–68). Admitted freeman of Lancaster, 1732–33, and of Liverpool on 8 September 1733. Took apps named Waller in 1735 and Ward in 1751. Former apps, Richard Waller and James Threlfall petitioned freedom in 1756; John Harvey and Leigh Sutton in 1757; and Thomas Potter, Thomas Ward and Edward Lowe in 1761. Recorded on 22 December 1758 concerning the sale by auction of the household goods of John Titley, Liverpool. Polled at Lancaster 1768. [Lancaster freemen rolls; S of G, app. index; *Liverpool Advertiser*, 22 December 1758; Liverpool freemen reg. and committee bk; poll bk]

Baxendale, Lloyd, 11 Oldhall St, Liverpool, u and cm (b. 1730/31–d. 1813/14). Recorded in West Derby in 1790. Admitted freeman of Liverpool on 26 October 1754 and of Lancaster, 1767–68. Took app. named Rosson in 1754. Former apps, Edward Fishwick, petitioned freedom in 1767, George Chesworth in 1774, Adam Cross in 1778 and Andrew Rosson in 1792. Reported in charge of the sale of a bankrupt's furniture on 25 September 1783 including 'an assortment of exceeding good mahogany goods in the present taste'.

Obituary notice of 7 January 1814 states 'Lately of London, aged 83 years'. [D; Lancaster freemen rolls; S of G, app. index; Liverpool freemen reg. and committee bk; *Liverpool Advertiser*, 25 September 1783; *Liverpool Mercury*, 7 January 1814]

Baxendale, Richard, 1 Moverley St, Salford, Lancs., chairmaker (1804). [D]

Baxendale, William, Blackburn, Lancs., chairmaker (1818–25). Trading at Penny St in 1818 and 17 Salford St, 1824–25. [D]

Baxland, Henry & Sons, London, cm (early 19th century). Employed by Sir John Soane to make furniture for the Bank of England in the Regency period. [R. A. Woods, *English Furniture in the Bank of England*]

Baxter, A., Duke St, Plymouth Dock, Devon, u and cm (1814). [D]

Baxter, Anthony Thomas, 'The Naked Boy', Henrietta St, Covent Gdn, London, cm and u(?) (1730–38). Letters to Baxter from Mrs Elizabeth Purefoy and her son Henry, of Shalstone, Bucks., discuss work he carried out for them from 1730–38. On 11 January 1735 Mrs Purefoy commissioned him for quilting patterns, whilst on 1 February 1735 her son wrote to Baxter, 'My mother would have one of the new fashioned low beds with 4 posts to them and a quilt to the same, she will endeavour to learn how many yards will do . . . If you have any freind an upholsterer let me know between this and next Saturday what quantity he thinks it requires . . .' Mrs Purefoy, however, 'is unwilling to give above 10s. a yard for the Quilting'. On 21 May 1738 she wrote to Baxter requesting 18 yards of chintz to make window curtains for a drawing room. [G. Eland, *The Purefoy Letters, 1735–53*; W. T. Whitley, *Artists and their Friends*; Heal]

Baxter, Elkanah, Bishopsgate St, London, upholder (1703–18). Son of Jeremy Baxter of Northowram, Yorks., clothier; app. to Robert Hall on 2 February 1703. Admitted freeman of the Upholders' Co. by servitude on 8 April 1718. In partnership with Jonathan Hall in Bishopsgate St. [GL, Upholders' Co. records]

Baxter, Francis, address unrecorded (1709–25). Carried out work at Chicheley Hall, Bucks., between 1709–25 supplying in August 1709 a Communion Table for the Church, and in April 1723 wainscotting 'little room with Elm', costing £10 15s. In April 1723 he set up 'ye great staircase' with W. Porden, together charging £90. Baxter's other assistants, Beale and Illison, are recorded in May 1723 carving and turning bannisters; G. Wolly in July 1724 for turning bannisters and columns for the pulpit stairs; and 'Ebrall' (Thomas Eborall) in December 1724 and September 1725 for joiner's work and wainscotting the Elm Room. [Bucks. RO, Sir John Chester's account bks, D/C/2/3(ii), 36(iii)]

Baxter, Francis, parish of St Peter, Bristol, cm (1784). [Poll bk]

Baxter, John, 112 Near Wapping, New Stairs, Wapping, London, cm and upholder (1776–93). Recorded at 114 Wapping, 1790–93. Took out Sun Insurance policies in 1776 for £400 of which £100 accounted for workshops and £250 for utensils, stock and goods; in 1782 for £400 of which utensils, stock and goods accounted for £250; on 13 October 1791 for a total of £900; on 27 September 1786 for £500 on his house; and on 18 July 1791 for a total of £700. Declared bankrupt in 1793. [D; GL, Sun MS vol. 249, p. 487; vol. 292, p. 555; vol. 381, p. 118; vol. 339, p. 465; vol. 379, p. 140; Bailey's list of bankrupts]

Baxter, John, Liverpool, cm (1790–d. by 1820). Admitted freeman on 20 June 1790. [Liverpool freemen reg.] Possibly son of Thomas Baxter, cm.

Baxter, Mary, 1 Ker St, Devonport, Plymouth, Devon, cm and u (1822–24). [D]

Baxter, Richard, Castle Foregate, Shrewsbury, Salop, cm and u (1840). [D]

Baxter, Samuel, Church St, Malpas, Cheshire, cm (1834). [D]

Baxter, Thomas, Liverpool, cm (1761–96). Recorded at 33 Crosshall St in 1796. Admitted freeman on 23 January 1761. His son John, trade unspecified but possibly cm, petitioned freedom on birthright in 1789 paying 3s 4d. [D; Liverpool freemen reg. and committee bk]

Baxter, Thomas, Norwich, cm (1800–18). Trading in the parish of St Peter per Mountergate in 1802, in the Close, 1806, Lakenham, 1807, and the parish of SS Simon and June, 1812. Son of Thomas Baxter, weaver; admitted freeman of Norwich on 4 October 1800. [Poll bks; Norwich freemen reg.]

Baxter, William, Cat St, Burton-on-Trent, Staffs., cm (1818). [D]

Bay, Thomas, Narrow St, Ratcliffe, London, cm (1767–68). Declared bankrupt, *Gents Mag.*, January 1767, and *Public Advertiser*, 11 April 1768.

Bay, Thomas, 17 Ships Alley, Wellclose Sq., London, carpenter and cm (1776). Took out a Sun Insurance policy in 1776 totalling £300 including cover for utensils and stock. [GL, Sun MS vol. 249, p457]

Bayfield, John Joachim, address unrecorded, cm(?), (1721). Name and date 'Aug. 1721' pencilled on carcase of early 18th-century walnut folding-top card table, private English coll.

Bayles, James, 14 Gt Suffolk St, Southwark, London, cm (1817). [D]

Bayles, Lucy, address unrecorded, cm and u (1745–46). Carried out work for Robert Nugent of Gosfield Hall, Essex, for his London house in Dover St. A long bill for cm and u sundries supplied, 1745–46, lists four items of furniture: on 22 October 1745 '8 very good Larch walnutry chairs with quilted backs . . . £14'; on 26 October 'a Large Chest', £3 15s; and on 18 March 1746 a mahogany table costing £2 8s and a mahogany 'standish with inck & sand glasses', costing 3s 6d. [Essex RO, D/DU 502/2, pp. 219–20]

Bayles, William, Market Pl., Barnard Castle, Co. Durham, joiner and cm (1827–39). A bill of 22 July 1839 lists items supplied for Wemmergill, North Yorks.: '2 swing glasses tray bott. with drawers' costing £2 8s and '6 staind cain bottom roswd chairs' costing £2 5s. [D; Durham RO, D/St/Box 208]

Bayless, James, 107 Bermondsey St, London, u (1819). [D]

Bayley, C., Market Pl., Abingdon, Oxon., cm and u (1823–30). [D]

Bayley, Daniel, at 'The White Bear', Aldermanbury, London, cm (1713–d. c. 1729). A bill of November 1713 paid by Mr Bempde(?) for Mr Child lists 'A Desk upon Drawers', costing £2 10s. [V & A archives; Harris, *Old English Furniture*]

Bayley, Francis Allen, Liverpool, u (1840). Son of Rodney Bayley, u, admitted freeman on 25 July 1840. [Liverpool freemen reg.]

Bayley (or Bayly), George, parish of St James, Bristol, cm (1774). [Poll bk]

Bayley, James, 11 Balsover St, London, u (1792). Took out a Sun Insurance policy on 24 December 1792 for £300. [GL, Sun MS vol. 389, ref. 609100]

Bayley (or Bayly), John, parish of St Augustine, Bristol, u (1754). [Poll bk]

Bayley, John, Liverpool, cm (1778–1802). Admitted freeman in 1778. In 1802 his son Rodney, u, petitioned freedom on his birthright. [Liverpool freemen's committee bk] Possibly grandfather of Francis Allen Bayley.

Bayley, John, James St, St Giles's, London, cm (1784). [D]

Bayley, John, Ashford, Kent, cm and auctioneer (1823–39). Recorded in High St in 1838. [D]

Bayley, Rodney, Liverpool, u (1802–35). Trading at 8 Hawke St from 1818–24; at 9 Tobin St from 1827–29 and 9 Hawke St in 1827; and at 10 Hawke St in 1835. Son of John Bayley, cm, admitted freeman on 8 July 1802. [D; Liverpool freemen reg.] An R. Bayley, u, of Liverpool married in 1808 Miss Jane Taylor of Castle St at St John's Church. [*Liverpool Courier*, 5 October 1808] See Francis Allen Bayley.

Bayley, Rubin, Liverpool, u (1840). Admitted freeman on 28 July 1840. [Liverpool freemen reg.]

Bayley, Samuel, 7 Park Pl., Carlisle Lane, Lambeth, London, cm (1823). Took out a Sun Insurance policy on 12 March 1823 for £200. [GL, Sun MS vol. 498, ref. 1001698]

Bayley, Thomas, 3 Hart Ct, Bridgewater Sq., London, convex mirror manufacturer (1808). [D]

Bayley (or Bailey), William, St Martin-le-Grand, Westminster, London, framemaker (1749). [Poll bk]

Bayley, William, London, upholder (1777–86). Trading at St Paul's Churchyard in 1780, Fleet St in 1781, and Gough Sq. in 1786. Son of James Bayley, app. to Joseph Graham on 2 January 1771. Admitted freeman of the Upholders' Co. by servitude on 5 April 1780. [GL, Upholders' Co. records and Livery lists]

Bayley, William, Rushall St, Walsall, Staffs., cm (1780). [D]

Bayley (or Bayly), (J.?) William, Lancaster, carver and gilder (1784–92). [Westminster Ref. Lib., Gillow records]

Bayley, Son & Blew, Cockspur St, London, cm (late 18th century). Satinwood writing or artist's cabinet recorded, bearing inside lid the label of 'Bayley, Son & Blew, Cockspur Street, London'. The cabinet contains wells, fitted compartments and bottles, and has a front falling to reveal four secret drawers. [Sotheby's, 3 March 1961, lot 150] The firm continued into the 19th century under the name of:

Bayley, Blew & Chapman, 17 Cockspur St, London, dressing case makers and Perfumers to His Majesty and HRH Duke of York (1829–35). The accounts of George IV of 1828 mention a rosewood writing desk edged with brass and a buhl border, patent lock, and flaps covered with green velvet; interior glass is mounted with silver. The cost of £15 12s included a solid leather travelling cover. A bill of 1835 in the Arundel Castle records for 3s has the heading: 'Bayley, Blew & Chapman, Dressing Case Makers, Perfumers to His Majesty, 17 Cockspur Street'. [D; RA 25433; Arundel Castle records, A2110]

Bayley, James & Boote, Alexander, Crown St, Soho, London, u and cm (1778–90). Declared bankrupt in February 1778, and again in May 1790. [*Gents Mag.*, February 1778; *Derby Mercury*, 27 May 1790]

Baylis, Thomas, address unrecorded, frame maker (1660). He provided five frames, gilded and burnished, for the 5th Earl of Bedford. [Bedford Office, London]

Bayliss, Joseph, against Thompson's Coffee House in George St, near Hanover Sq., London, cm (1719). Took out a Sun Insurance policy on 9 November 1719 on dwelling house, goods and merchandise. [GL, Sun MS vol. 10, ref. 15696]

Bayliss, Thomas, Walsall, Staffs., chairmaker (1813–18). Trading at George St, 1813–18, and High St in 1818. [D]

Bayliss, William, Woolwich, Kent, auctioneer and u (1792). Took out a Sun Insurance policy on 17 July 1792 for £1,000 of which household goods and utensils in stock accounted for £600 and utensils in shed, £100. [GL, Sun MS vol. 388, p. 249]

Bayliss, William, Bromsgrove, Worcs., cm (1831). [Poll bk]

Bayly, E., Shooters Hill, Cowes, Isle of Wight, Hants., u and cm (1839). [D]

Bayly, Richard, Bitton, near Bristol, cm (1774–81). [Poll bks]

Bayly, Richard Thomas, 22 Nassau Pl., London, cm, u and undertaker, furniture broker (1839). [D]

Bayly, Thomas, London, joiner or carver (1694). Signed a petition on 26 June 1694 presented by 'the Company of Joyners Carvers of London' to the City. [*Furn. Hist.*, 1974]

Bayly, Thomas, Maze Pond, parish of St Thomas, Southwark, London, turner (1712). Took out a Hand in Hand Insurance policy on 15 April 1712 on his dwelling house for £150. [GL, Hand in Hand MS vol. 10, ref. 22848]

Bayly, William, London, carver and gilder (1816–39). Trading at 15 Carnaby Mkt, Golden Sq., 1816–25, and at 15 Marshall St, Golden Sq., 1817–39. [D]

Bayman, Francis, Whitehorse Lane, Stepney, London, cm and u (1839). [D]

Baynard, John, Truro, Cornwall, cm (1808). Recorded concerning a lease dated 1 January 1808 of Sir William Lemon on part of Ryder's tenement in Lemon St. [Cornwall RO, DD WH 1220]

Bayne (or Boyne), George, London, upholder (1788–1802). Recorded at Irongate Wharf in 1797, and at Gloucester St, Whitechapel in 1802. Son of William Bayne of Tower Hill, tailor, app. to Richard Dennis on 2 January 1788. Admitted freeman of the Upholders' Co. by servitude on 5 April 1797. [GL, Upholders' Co. records and Livery list]

Baynes, George, Thaxted, Essex, cm (1798–1835). Probate dated 1835. [D; *Wills at Chelmsford*]

Baynes, Henry, Lancaster, cm (1759–62). Took apps named Whittingdale in 1759 and Lassells in 1762. [S of G, app. index]

Baynes, James, Lancaster, u (1811–12). [Lancaster freemen rolls]

Baynes, James, 24 Gt Mitchell St, Old St, London, cm (1812). Took out a Sun Insurance policy on 23 April 1812 for £300 of which stock, utensils and goods in trust accounted for £30, stock and utensils in workshop behind dwelling house, £70, and stock and utensils 'in Heathers shed in yard in Curtain Rd.', £150. [GL, Sun MS vol. 455, ref. 809700]

Baynes & Co, Jeremiah Finnis, 19 Blackman St, Southwark, London, u and cm, carvers and gilders, looking-glass manufacturers (1815). Took out a Sun Insurance policy on 30 January 1815 for £5,000 on stock, utensils and goods in trust in dwelling house, warehouses and workshops, sawpits and yards. [GL, Sun MS vol. 463. ref. 901849] See Baynes & Ireland.

Baynes, Richard & Duffield (Duffill or Druffil), 37 Fetter Lane, York, chairmakers and turners (1823–38). Baynes alone took app. named John Gill on 17 October 1823, whilst Baynes & Duffield took apps named George Johnson, 9 December 1824, Robert Lund, 1 January 1825, Anthony Smith, 1 September 1825, William Waggoner, 2 November 1825, George Brown, 17 March 1827, John Kettlewell, 26 May 1828, John Bellerby, 8 October 1833, John Baynes, 26 February 1834, James Jefferson and George Swalwell, 14 August 1835. [D; York app. reg.]

Baynes, Thomas, Lancaster, cm (1791–1800). App. to Isaac Greenwood in 1791. Admitted freeman in 1799–1800. [Lancaster app. reg. and freemen rolls]

Baynes & Ireland, 19 Blackman St, Southwark, London, looking-glass makers, carvers and gilders, carpenters, u and cm (1820–23). Took out a Sun Insurance policy on 26 February 1821 totalling £3,000 of which £800 accounted for warehouse, showroom and other buildings, £40 for household goods in dwelling house, warerooms, showrooms, gilding shop, glass room (no carpentry or cabinet work done therein) and three stores, £1,500 for stock, utensils and goods in trust, £150 for pictures and prints, £150 for stock, utensils and goods in trust in carpenters and cabinet manufactory in the yard next to Black Horse stables (a small stove therein), £160 for stock etc. in open shed and yard, and £200 for stable coachhouse and loft communicating with workshop above.

Insured the same buildings, stock, utensils and goods on 12 February 1823 for a total of £2,100. [D; GL, Sun MS vol. 486, ref. 978001; vol. 490, ref. 1001514] See Jeremiah Finnis Baynes & Co.

Baynham, J., 50 Collingwood St, Blackfriars Rd, London, carver (1829). [D]

Baynham, Thomas, Woodbridge, Suffolk, cm (1792). Recorded on 18 August 1792 in the calendar of marriage licence bonds. [Suffolk RO, FAA: 50/2/108]

Bayster, James, 20 Piccadilly, London, u (1788). [D]

Bazin, James, 24 Cumberland St, Tottenham Ct Rd, London, carver and gilder (1777). Took out a Sun Insurance policy in 1777 for £300 of which utensils, stock and goods accounted for £100. [GL, Sun MS vol. 255, p. 163, ref. 379289]

Bazin (or Basin), —, address unrecorded, carver (1787–88). Worked at Gorhambury, St Albans, Herts., sending bills on 24 May 1787 for 'carving capitols in library', £3 3s, on 1 January 1788 for carving a door, £6 3s, and on 5 June 1788 for door in music room, £11 12s. [Herts. RO, accounts bk XI, 71]

Bazive (or Bazine), Victor George, 125 Crawford St, London, carver and gilder (1835–37). [D]

Beach, George, Birmingham, cm (1760–62). Took apps named Kirk in 1760 and Lees in 1762. [S of G, app. index]

Beach (or Beech), Richard, 19 Straight, Lincoln, cm and u (1822–41). Recorded at Foot of the Hill in 1822, 19 Straight, 1826–41, and also High St in 1835. [D]

Beach, Robert, Crown Pl., Soho, London, chair and sofa maker (1839). [D]

Beach, William, Dorchester, Dorset, u (1803). Admitted freeman on 7 June 1803. [Dorchester freemen rolls]

Beach, William, 6 Providence Sq., Collier St, Hull, Yorks., cm (1838–39). [D]

Beach & Maschwitz, 30 Ann St and Lench St, Birmingham, cm (foreign furniture) (1835). [D]

Beachcroft, Samuel, London, upholder (1714–d. 1731). Recorded at 'the White Hart & Sun next St. Peter's Allye in Cornhill in the Parish of St. Peter's Cornhill' in 1714, and at 'The White Hart', Mark Lane, Fenchurch St, 1727–31. Took out a Sun Insurance policy on 6 May 1714 on goods in his dwelling house. Declared bankrupt in 1727 and died in 1731. [GL, Sun MS vol. 3, ref. 3928–29; Heal]

Beachcroft, Samuel, Marshall St, Westminster, London, upholder (1749). [Poll bk]

Beachcroft & Shepard, 4 Chandos St, Covent Gdn, London, upholders and cm (1805). Took out a Sun Insurance policy on 8 January 1805 for £1,300 of which £400 accounted for utensils and stock in workshop and warehouse, £400 for those in open yard, and £100 in sawpit and workshop above. [GL, Sun MS vol. 431, ref. 769948]

Beacock (or Beecock), John, Leeds, Yorks., cm (1828–39). Trading at 70 West St, 1828–34, at 115 West St, 1834–37, and 57 Savile St in 1839. [D]

Beadle & Perfect, Micklegate, York, house, sign and furniture painters (1823). [D]

Beagle, James, 29 Marshall St, London Rd, London, bedstead maker (1839). [D]

Beagle, James, 79 St George's Rd, Southwark, London, cm and u (1839). [D]

Beaker, Nicholas, address unrecorded, upholder(?) (1718–35). Son of Nicholas Beaker of Nettleton, Wilts.; app. to Athelstane Tindale (Tyndall), upholder, of Bristol on 11 August 1718 by common indenture and counterpart for the fee of £40. Took app. in 1735. [*Wilts. Apps and their Masters*; S of G, app. index]

Beal, —, London, cm (1793). Subscribed to Sheraton's *Drawing Book*, 1793.

Beal, Francis, Wainfleet, Lincs., joiner and cm (1822–26). [D]

Beal, George, York, cm and u (1806–40). Announced in *York Courant*, 18 August 1806 entering partnership with his uncle, Thomas Beale, and recorded in partnership at Stonegate in 1823 and 49 Coney St, 1837–40, no. 50 in 1828. Took apps named John Brown, 4 April 1807, John Webster, 5 October 1811, George Meynell, 17 October 1814, John Skilbeck, 8 March 1826, Henry Rhodes, 31 July 1828, John Chapman, 14 June 1835 and Edward Lund, 21 April 1836. [D; York app. reg.]

Beal, J., 70 West Smithfield, London, cooper and turner (1796). [D]

Beal, James, London, cm (1800–25). Recorded at 15 Albion Buildings, Bartholomew Close, 1800–11, and at 90 Gt Bartholomew Close, 1811–25. Took out Sun Insurance policies on 23 May 1800 for £200 on stock and utensils in his shop and adjoining warehouse; and on 11 March 1811 for £1,150 of which stock and utensils in dwelling house (no work done therein) accounted for £400, and stock and utensils in workshop, warehouse and store in Albion Buildings, £500. Took out further insurance policies on 2 February 1813 and 5 February 1814 each for £1,000 of which stock and utensils accounted for £750. [D; GL, Sun MS vol. 418, ref. 702756; vol. 452, ref. 854893; vol. 462, ref. 889986; vol. 462]

Beal(e) (or Beall), James, London, cm and u (1802–11). Addresses given at 4 Stephen St, Tottenham Ct Rd, 1802; 5 Old Bailey 1803–08; and 9 Commerce Row, St George's Rd, Blackfriars, 1807–11. Took out Sun Insurance policies on 3 August 1802 for £500 of which £450 accounted for utensils and stock; and on 20 January 1807 on household goods in dwelling house (no carpenter's or cabinet work done therein), £200; on stock, utensils and goods in trust, £600; on the same in open yard behind and on seasoning and open shed, £200; and on workshop, £100. Named in Sheraton's list of master cabinet makers, 1803. [D; GL, Sun MS vol. 423, ref. 735298; vol. 438, ref. 800040]

Beal, Nicholas, 22 Castle St East, Oxford Mkt, London, japan chairmaker (1817). [D]

Beal(e), Thomas, York, cm and u (1787–1838). Addresses at Micklegate Bar, 1787; Grape Lane, 1798; Minster Yd, 1809–11; Stonegate, 1818–23; and 49–50 Coney St, 1830. Announced in *York Courant*, 18 August 1806 taking nephew, George Beal, into partnership. Named in the account book of the Rev. John Firth on 23 June 1791 being paid £5 2s 4½d. [Mumby family papers] Advertised in *York Herald*, 29 July 1797, and *York Courant*, 26 July 1802. Subscribed to Sheraton's *Drawing Book*, 1793. [D; *York Courant*, 11 March 1816]

Beal, Thomas, Swinemarket, Pocklington, Yorks., cm (1840). [D]

Beale, Dan., Salisbury Sq., Shaftesbury, Dorset, chairmaker and cooper (1823–24). [D]

Beale (or Beall), George, London, carver (1745–49). Trading at Russell Ct, Westminster, 1749. Bill for carving carried out for 'the Honble. Mrs. Nugent' of Gosfield Hall, Essex, at her house in Dover St, London, dated 24 May 1745 refers to a chimney piece 'to hold China with a Basket in ye Midle', costing £12, '2 Glass frames Carvied for ye Dressing Room', £5, 'one Chimney Peices Car^d Round ye Marbel for ye Dresen Room', £5, '2 Trusses Carvid for the Indea Cabbinets', £2; and also 'Cleaning ye Carving in the Liberarey' and 'Maken good the Glass frame for ye Chimney'. [Essex RO, D/DU 502/2; poll bk]

Beale, George, Hull, Yorks., chairmaker (1837–40). Trading at 13 Leadenhall Sq., 1837–38, and at no. 14 and also in Guildhall Passage, 1840. [D]

Beale, J. H., 13 Westmoreland Pl., City Rd, London, cm, u and undertaker (1839). [D]

Beale, James, Maldon, Essex, cm (1839). [D]

Beale, John, 7 Rose St, Soho, London, cm (1793). Subscribed to Sheraton's *Drawing Book*, 1793.

Beale, John, 27 Joiner's Pl., St George's Fields, London, cm (1808). [D]

Beale, John, 7 Raven Row, Mile End Rd, London, cm and u (1826–28). [D]

Beale, John, Tunbridge Wells, Kent, cm (1836). Daughter Mary Anne bapt. on 13 December 1836. [Kent RO, DRb/RT2/371E/6]

Beale, Loyde, 15 Borough Rd, London, cm (1813–14). Took out Sun Insurance policies on 14 April 1813 and 1814, each for £1,050, of which stock, utensils and goods in trust accounted for £200 and £300 respectively. [GL, Sun MS vol. 462, ref. 893095; vol. 462]

Bealing, Richard, London, u (1672–1711). Named frequently in the Royal Household accounts between 1688–1711, supplying bedding, cushions, upholstered furniture, curtains etc. for the Houses of Parliament, Hampton Court, Kensington and Whitehall Palaces and Windsor Castle. Provided cases for 'St. Edward's Chair'. [PRO, LC9/279–282, LC11/5] A bill of December 1692 charged to 'her Matie' includes 'a fine carved Couch frame wth rounde ends of wallnuttre fully Carved at £3', with materials to upholster it including 'a thick squab Cushing . . . Gilt nailes and tax', and down-filled cushions covered with 'vellvett fringd and tassells'. The bill also listed an 'Easey Chaire frame wth eares and elbowes finely carvd at £1.15', upholstered and covered with velvet, edged with 'fine crimson Ingrane fring' and tassels. [Winterthur, Delaware, Symonds papers, 75 × 69, 27] In 1693, as Royal Upholsterer, Bealing supplied a 'very fashionable' Indian damask bed, and in the same year provided for Whitehall Palace a French bedstead, and 'Damaske hangings . . . finely fringed'. In 1696 he made for Kensington Palace a 'clothbed being finely done, and carved work', and in 1698 a 'scarlet & white damask bed, very fine, & covering all ye carving of ye tester, headboard & cornices & basemouldings', costing £30. [V & A archives] In that year he also supplied the State bed of William III now at Hampton Court. [*Conn.*, June 1977, pp. 138–39] In 1699 he made for Kensington Palace a 'crimson & gold velvett bed after ye newest fashion', and in 1699–1700 supplied to the groom of H M Bedchamber, Hampton Court, 'a fine flowered worsted Damask bed . . . and two elbow & four back chairs covered with the same fringed & done as the bed . . . £60'. [Winterthur, Delaware, Symonds papers] He also removed 'Ye Kings Bed and hangings' from Windsor to Hampton Court, set it up and supplied new bedding. He upholstered a canopy and chair of State, two walnut stools, four long forms of walnut etc. for the Privy Chamber at Hampton Court, the frames having been made by Thomas Roberts, joiner. In 1700–01 he was paid for upholstering two stools and an elbow chair made by Roberts for Hampton Court, and for upholstering 'four large sophas' and covering with green mohair 'laced with gold'. In 1711 he was still described as 'her Majesty's upholsterer'. [*DEF*; *Calendar of Treasury Papers*, 1708–11] A pair of carved walnut caned chairs, c.1685, featuring crowns and stamped 'RB' twice may be associated with this tradesman. [Gilbert, *Leeds Furn. Cat.*, vol. 1, 1978, p. 73; *Old Furniture*, vol. 2, pp. 16, 32; vol. 10, 1927] Bealing provided beds, chairs, curtains and wall-hangings for William, 5th Earl of Bedford at Woburn Abbey between 1672–82. Eight accounts exist in which 361 items are specified, totalling £556. Bealing also acted for the Earl at the auction sale in 1676 when he bought the crimson damask bed which had belonged to the Earl's sister, Margaret, Dowager Countess of Manchester. [Bedford Office, London]

Bealt, Francis, Chapel Lane, Hull, Yorks., cm (1790–99). [D]

Bean, Richard, Kirkgate, Leeds, Yorks., cm (1817). [D]

Bean, Samuel, Gillygate, York, joiner and cm (1816–18). [D]

Bean, Samuel, York, u (1823). Son of Elizabeth Bean, app to William Smith, u and cm, on 18 September 1823. [York app. reg.]

Bean, William, Edmund St, Birmingham, fancy gilder (1818). [D]

Beaney, Thomas, The Priory, Hastings, Sussex, cm and u (1832–39). T. Beaney listed as a turner at Pelham St in 1839. [D]

Bear, William, 54 Ashley Cresc., City Rd, London, cm and u (1839). [D]

Bear & Drew, Andover, Hants., cm (1823–24). [D]

Beard, Arabella, 157 Fenchurch St, London, cm and u (1787–1813). Named in Sheraton's list of master cabinet makers 1803. [D] See Geoffrey and Henry Beard.

Beard, Daniel, 51 Gloucester St, Liverpool, with shop at 10 Walnut St, cm (1839). [D]

Beard, David, Liverpool, cm (1780). Petitioned freedom on servitude to Lee (Leigh?) Sutton, who was admitted on the same terms as Robert Fairclough. [Liverpool freemen's committee bk]

Beard, Geoffrey, 157 Fenchurch St, London, cm and u (1803). [D] See Arabella and Henry Beard.

Beard, Henry, 157 Fenchurch St, London, upholder (1808). [D]

Beard, I., 4 Bearbinder Lane, Mansion Lane, London, brush maker and turner (1792). [D]

Beard, John, parish of St James, Bristol, carver (1774). [Poll bk]

Beard, John, Exeter, Devon, carver (1774). [Bristol poll bk]

Beard, T., address unrecorded, chairmaker (early 19th century). Spindleback chair of Herefs. type, impressed 'T. BEARD' on front seat rail is at Temple Newsam House, Leeds. Others of the same pattern recorded.

Beard, Thomas, Paignton, Devon, cm (1838). [D]

Beard, William, 32 Gloucester St, Queen's Sq., London, cm and u (1839). [D]

Beardmore, George, Market St, The Potteries, (Burslem), Staffs., cm (1818–34). Trading at Market St in 1818, also as a chairmaker; and Hanover St (or Sq.), 1822–34, also as joiner and builder in 1834. [D]

Beardwood, Henry, 24 Clare St, Liverpool, joiner and cm (1834). [D]

Bearman, Bartholomew & Hearsman, John, Moore St, London, cm (1779). Took out a Sun Insurance policy in 1779 for £200 of which utensils, stock and goods accounted for £140. [GL, Sun MS vol. 276, p. 73]

Bearne, Andrew, 5 Grafton St, Soho, London, cm and u (1820–39). Recorded as Bearne & Son, cm, u and undertakers in 1839. [D]

Bearsley, Samuel, Botolph St, Colchester, Essex, bedstead maker (1826–27). [D]

Beasley, George, Rugby, Warks., cm (1835). [D]

Beasley, Robert, Frankfort St, Plymouth, Devon, cm (1830). [D]

Beatie, —, address unrecorded, cm (1803). Subscribed to Sheraton's *Cabinet Dictionary*, 1803.

Beattie, William, 60 St Paul's Churchyard, London, cm and dealer in jewellery and hardware (1802–03). Took out Sun Insurance policies on 28 October 1802 for £990; and on 19 February 1803 for £999 of which utensils and stock accounted for £799. [GL, Sun MS vol. 427, ref. 740090]

Beattie (or Beaty), William & Son, Longtown, Carlisle, Cumb., joiner and cm (1811–29). [D] See George and John Beaty.

Beatty, Edward, Hungerford St, London, cm (1790–93). [D]

Beatty, Edward, Liverpool, joiner and cm (1823–27). Trading at 32 Vauxhall Rd in 1823; Walker Pl., Hatton Gdn in 1824; and 31 Warren St in 1827. [D]

Beatty, Thomas, Warwick, carver and gilder (1828–35). Addresses at Castle Hill, 1828–30 and Church St, 1831–35. [D; poll bk]

Beatty (or Beaty), William, Barnet, Herts., u and undertaker (1808–11). Recorded as Beatty in High St, 1808, and as Beaty in Wood St, 1809–11. [D]

Beatty, William, 8 Wellington St, Everton, Liverpool, cm (1835). [D]

Beaty, Francis, Hungerford Mkt, London, cm (1774–77). Took out a Sun Insurance policy in 1777 for £200 of which utensils, stock and goods accounted for £100. [GL, Sun MS vol. 257, p. 422; poll bk]

Beaty, George, Longtown, Carlisle, Cumb., joiner and cm (1828–29). [D] See William Beattie & Son, and:

Beaty, John, Longtown, Carlisle, Cumb., joiner and cm (1828–29). [D]

Beaty, William, St Clement Danes, London, upholder (1762). Declared bankrupt, *Gents Mag.*, January 1762.

Beauchamp, George, 18 St Paul's Churchyard, London, cm, u and joiner (1776–1814). Recorded at no. 31 in 1780. Took out Sun Insurance policies in 1776 for £700 on his house; in 1778 for £1,400 of which stock, utensils and goods accounted for £1,000; in 1779 for £600 on stock in warehouse near Chiswell St, Grub St; in 1780 for £1,000 of which utensils and stock accounted for £700; in 1781 for £2,000, utensils, stock and goods accounting for £1,300; in 1785 for £300 on utensils and stock in warehouse at 19 Grub St; in 1802 for £300; and in 1812 for £3,000, stock, utensils and goods in dwelling house accounting for £1,300. In 1777, 1779 and 1783 employed four non-freemen, licence renewed quarterly. Named in Sheraton's list of master cabinet makers, 1803. [D; GL, Sun MS vol. 244, p. 366; vol. 262, p. 520; vol. 272, p. 94; vol. 286, p. 491; vol. 292, p. 12; vol. 330, p. 114; vol. 423, ref. 727806; vol. 457, ref. 871558; GL, City Licence bks, vols. 9 and 10]

Beaumont, —, address unrecorded, carver and gilder (1785). Named in the Longford Castle, Wilts. accounts receiving payment of £8 8s in 1785. Possibly William Beaumont of the King's Arms, Leicester Sq., or of Mary-le-Bow-Fields. [V & A archives]

Beaumont, —, Baldwins Gdns, Gray's Inn Lane, London, cm (1789). James Pingay, carpenter, took out a Sun Insurance policy in 1789 on a brick house in Baldwins Gdns in the occupation of Beaumont for £200, and on timber workshop behind, £50. [GL, Sun MS vol. 363, ref. 556606]

Beaumont, —, London, carver and gilder (1809–11). The account bk of Edward, Lord Lascelles relating mainly to Harewood House, Hanover Sq., London, lists payment to Beaumont, carver and gilder, on 8 March 1809 for £62 12s, and on 7 February 1811 for £1 18s. [Leeds archives dept, Harewood MS 192] Possibly William Beaumont of 'The King's Arms', Leicester Sq., or of Mary-le-Bow-Fields, or Thomas Beaumont of 44 Poland St, Oxford St.

Beaumont, Charles, Old Kent Rd, London, cm and u (1826–37). Recorded at 2 Hanover Pl., 1826–28, and as C. Beaumont at 2 Wardour Pl. in 1837. [D]

Beaumont, George, 18 Gt Warner St, Coldbath Fields, London, cm (1808). [D]

Beaumont, George, 17 Eldon St, Finsbury, London, cm and u (1839). [D]

Beaumont, John, London, cm (1801–20). Addresses at 45 Beech St, Barbican, 1801–03; at no. 7, 1804–15; and 12 Cumberland St, Shoreditch in 1820. Named in Sheraton's list of master cabinet makers, 1803. [D]

Beaumont, John, Woolroad, Saddleworth, Yorks., cm and u (1822). [D]

Beaumont, John, 8 Bond St, Manchester, cm (1828). [D]

Beaumont, John D., Maidstone, Kent, u (1826). [Poll bk]

Beaumont, Joseph, Kirkgate, Wakefield, Yorks., cm (1816–18). [D]

Beaumont, Thomas, London, carver (1793). Subscribed to Sheraton's *Drawing Book*, 1793. Possibly:

Beaumont, Thomas, 44 Poland St, Oxford St, London, carver and gilder (1809–29). [D]

Beaumont, W., 13 Red Lion Sq., Spitalfields, London, cm (1820). [D]

Beaumont, William, Whitechapel, London, cm (1762). Took app. named Stapleton in 1762. [S of G, app. index]

Beaumont, William, 17 Wellclose Sq., London, cm (1777). Took out a Sun Insurance policy in 1777 for £400 on houses. [GL, Sun MS vol. 258, p. 227]

Beaumont, William, 'The King's Arms', 24 Leicester Sq., London, carver and gilder (1788–93). Trade card in Banks Coll., BM, dated 1788, shows classical female figure supporting oval frame with inscription 'Beaumont, CARVER & GILDER, Nephew & Successor to the late Mr. Vialls [Thomas Vialls] at the King's Arms, Leicester Square'. Took apps named Edward Bennet on 30 May 1791, and Robert Paul on 2 January 1792, both for £10. See Strawberry Hill accounts, p. 105. [D; PRO, 1R 1/36; Heal] Possibly:

Beaumont, William, Mary-le-Bow-Fields, London, carver and gilder (1791). Took app. named Harriet Du Flos in 1791. [Westminster Ref. Lib., St Martin-in-the-Fields PR]

Beaumont, William, 144 High St, Hull, Yorks. (1793). Advertised in *Hull Packet*, 1793, as a maker of tablets, friezes and chimney pieces.

Beaumont, William, 23 London Wall, opposite Carpenters' Hall, London, cm (1824). Took out a Sun Insurance policy on 5 April 1824 for £100 on household goods, and £500 on stock, utensils and stores in manufactory of Newnham Pl., Bishopsgate St Without. [GL, Sun MS vol. 494, ref. 1016206]

Beaumont, William, 23 Cable St, Manchester, chairmaker (1813). [D]

Beaumont, William, 147 Chapel St, Salford, Lancs., chairmaker (1816). [D]

Beauvais, Mrs, address unrecorded (1770). Named in the account bk of the Earl of Ancaster on 4 June 1770 receiving payment of £45 9s 10d for furniture purchased in France and brought over. [Lincoln RO, 2 ANC 6/3]

Beavan, George, Copse Cross St, Ross-on-Wye, Herefs., cm (1835). [D]

Beavan, James, 44 Lemon St, Whitechapel, London, cm (before 1826). Freeman of Hereford. His son, James Beavan, boot manufacturer, admitted freeman of Hereford by posthumous patrimony in 1826. [Hereford freemen admissions]

Beavan, Thomas, 3 Queen Lane, Thomas St, Bristol, cm (1799–1800). [D]

Beavan, William, Hereford, chairmaker (1734). [Poll bk]

Beavan, William, Bye St, Hereford, cm and u (1835–40). [D]

Beaver, George, Saddler St, Wells, Som., cm and u (1839). [D]

Beavit(t), George, Brownlow St, Drury Lane, St Martin's Lane, London, cm (1796–d. 1799). Foreman to Thomas Haig, who bequeathed him £100. [PRO, B 11/1394 fo. 536; PRO, C13 683/27]

Beazely & Sons, 92 Fenchurch St, London, trunk and chest maker (1804). [D]

Bebbington, Ralph, Salford, Lancs., cm (1804–33). Trading at 13 Union St in 1804; 15 Cook St in 1808; and 18 Cook St in 1813–33. [D]

Bebbington, Richard, 4 Back Fawcett St, Manchester, cm (1813). [D]

Beck,—, address and trade unrecorded (1768–87). Debts of £20 owed to Chipchase & Lambert between 1768–87. [PRO, C12, 2158/18]

Beck, Arnold Frederick, Glassonbury St, Long Acre, London, cm and musical instrument maker (1763–77). Insured his household goods and stock for £150 and wearing apparel for £50 on 2 August 1763. [GL, ref. 201685, p. 483] Possibly the maker of pianofortes (dated 1775 and 1777) trading at Broad St, Golden Sq., who is thought to have employed a cm in his firm to make instrument cases. He may, however, have gone to one of the specialist inlayers for some of the mahogany panels. Eight pieces are attributed to 'Beck's cabinet-maker', and three more bear marquetry medallions by 'the medallion marqueteur' who seems to have worked for him. Known pieces include a square piano in marquetry case by Frederick Beck at Lady Lever Gallery, Liverpool, and a pair of semi-circular commodes at Osterley Park, Middlx, bearing marquetry medallions. The central medallion of one, showing Diana seated with one of her hounds, is repeated on an unusual fall-front commode sold from the collection of Earl Temple, Sotheby's, 9 May 1941, lot 101. Lot 100 was a similar commode, probably from the same shop. Characteristic marquetry style of intricate contours of veneer and nervous engraved lines in draperies; fleurette-and-trellis marquetry. Beck piano illus. in *DEF*, 1st edn., vol. 2, p. 6, fig. 11. [C. Streeter, *Met. Museum Bulletin*, June 1971; *Burlington*, June 1980]

Beck, George, 20 Berwick St, London, cm (1787). Took out a Sun Insurance policy on 20 January 1787 for £200 on household goods, stock etc. [GL, Sun MS vol. 342, ref. 526789]

Beck, George, High St, Barton-upon-Humber, Lincs., joiner and cm (1835). [D]

Beck, J., Clerkenwell, London, journeyman cm (d. 1748). Death reported, *Penny London Post*, 1–4 July 1748: 'On Thursday about 6 o'clock, as Mr. Beck . . . was going through Red Lion Street, Clerkenwell, to his work, he was seized with a Apoplectick Fit, and, there not being any body present that could let him Blood, he expired in a few minutes'.

Beck, Joseph, 23 Plane St, Leeds, Yorks., cm (1826–30). [D]

Beck, Samuel, address unrecorded (1755). Worked for John Trotter, u. [PRO, LC9/211]

Beck, William, looking-glass manufacturer (1780). See Charles Walker. [GL, Sun MS]

Beckensall, W., East St Helen's St, Abingdon, Oxon., cm (1823–40). [D]

Becket, John, Lancaster, cm (1790–1836). Named in the Gillow records between 1790–1836, and in 1790 working on tables. Admitted freeman, 1806–07. [Westminster Ref. Lib., Gillow vol. 344/95, pp. 559, 609; Lancaster freemen rolls]

Becket(t), William, Lancaster, cm and joiner (1771–1800). App. to William Blackburn in 1771; admitted freeman, 1779–80, when stated 'of Wray'. Named in the Gillow records between 1786–1800 moulding claws. Possibly the maker of the large chest of drawers, mahogany veneer, oak carcase, bow-fronted, belonging to the late Edward Croft-Murray and traced to William Rawlinson of Ancoats Hall, which he rented from the Moseleys in the later 18th century. Inscriptions in black lead on underside of bottom of third drawer and on outside of back of third drawer: 'WILLIAM BECKET MAKER 1789'. [Poll bk; Westminster Ref. Lib., Gillow; Lancaster app. reg. and freemen rolls; V & A archives]

Beckett, Charles, Nantwich, Cheshire, cm (1822–37). Baptisms recorded of sons John, 31 July 1822, Henry, 16 January 1828, Edmund, 30 November 1829, and Henry, 10 February 1837. [Chester RO, PR(bapt.)]

Beckett, Henry, Wheelock St, Middlewich, Cheshire, cm and u (1834). Notice in the *Chester Courant and Advertiser for North Wales,* 1 April 1834 assigning 'all his stock in trade, household goods and furniture, books debts, personal estate and effects whatsoever unto William Hitchin of Newton, in the said county, timber merchant and Thomas Hitchin of Newton, aforesaid, cooper, in trust for the equal benefit of his creditors'. [D]

Beckett, John, St Ebbe's, Oxford, bedmaker (1802). [Poll bk]

Beckett, John, Kirkgate, Wakefield, Yorks., cm, u and auctioneer (1828–37). [D]

Beckett, John, 10 Leather Lane, Holborn, London, carver and gilder (1835–39). [D]

Beckett, Joseph, Chester, u (1772). Son of Joseph Beckett, innholder, admitted freeman on 1 January 1772. [Chester freemen rolls]

Beckett, Joseph, address unrecorded, u (1772–84). Worked at Erddig, Clwyd, submitting bills on 21 August 1772 for £24 10s 11d, paid on 29 June 1773, and on 27 October 1784. Probably a local man, as most of the other accounts are for work done by local craftsmen. [Erddig account bk]

Beckett, Samuel, Manchester, carver and gilder, looking-glass and picture frame maker (1825–38). Recorded at 14 Roger's Row in 1825–28; no. 11 in 1829; 22 Booth (or Bootle St), 1828–29; and 16 Bridge St, 1832–34. Recorded as Samuel and Sons, Booth St, 1838. [D]

Beckett, Thomas, Wenlock, Salop, plumber, glazier and cm (1822). [D]

Beckett, William, St Aldate's, Oxford, cm and u (1830). [D]

Becks, Andrew Berkley, Bath, Som., u (1828). Declared bankrupt with Edmund English, u, *Chester Chronicle and North Wales Advertiser,* 7 November 1828. See Andrew Berkley Beeks of Green St., London.

Becks (or Beeks), Frederick, Clifton, Bristol, cm and u (1833–40). Trading at Nelson Pl., 1833–36 and at Prince's Pl., 1837–40. [D]

Beckwith, Charlotte, 5 Rathbone Pl., Oxford St, London, u (1817–19). [D] See John Beckwith, and Beckwith & Hawksworth.

Beckwith, Henry, High St, Stockton-on-Tees, Co. Durham, cm and u (1784–1832). Subscribed to Sheraton's *Drawing Book,* 1793, and *Cabinet Dictionary,* 1803. Advertised in the *Liverpool Mercury,* 17 June 1825 wanting 'in an old established Cabinet & Upholstery Concern, a steady MAN, as FOREMAN in the Cabinet department. It is absolutely necessary that he should perfectly understand his business, & be fully competent to give proper directions to the workmen under his charge. The situation is permanent & would in every respect be found comfortable'. Probably the Henry Beckwith, cm, who supplied items of furniture to Wynyard Park, Co. Durham for the 4th Marquess of Londonderry in 1820. [D; Durham RO, Londonderry papers, D/LO/E 484, vol. 1829–41]

Beckwith, James, address unrecorded, cm (1814). Named in the Royal Household accounts on 5 January 1814 supplying new plate glass for dressing table in President's Room and blinds in Office Keeper's appartment, Council Office, Whitehall. Also provided Brussels carpet to St James's palace, making a total of £32 4s 7½d. [PRO, LC 11/15]

Beckwith, John, 5 Rathbone Pl., Oxford St, London, upholder and cm (1806–16). Also recorded at 8 Stangate St, Lambeth, in 1808. Trade card [Banks Coll., BM] shows Grecian sofa and elaborate draped window pelmet, and reads 'from St. Martin's Lane'. In 1806 worked at Hatfield House, Herts., and Hatfield town house, 'The Casino', Aldborough, carrying out repairs to upholstery and supplying, among other things, a large dumbwaiter costing £10. The Hatfield House town accounts record payments in 1811 for items provided and work done at 'The Casino', totalling £170 7s 9½d and including, on May 27, 'A large scrowl couch for bed; japanned bamboo and stuffed with best hair in fine canvas with squab, brass castors etc.' costing £17 8s. Between October and December 1811 Beckwith supplied items totalling £103 16s 11d, including, on 12 November 'a new white cover filled with your flock, tassled and quilted'; and on 12 December '2 deep moulding picture frames gilt on burnished gold with shells in the corners'. Named in partnership with Hawksworth, 1814–16, in the Hatfield town accounts carrying out repairs costing £67 15s 6d. [D; Hatfield House MS bills 604, 636] See Charlotte Beckwith.

Beckwith, Joseph, 4 Union St, Leeds, Yorks., carver (1837). [D]

Beckwith, Richard, Allhallowgate, Ripon, Yorks., joiner and cm (1834–37). [D]

Beckwith, Samuel, 101 and 105 St Martin's Lane, London, u (1774–1808). One of Thomas Chippendale's employees who receipted the Audley End account (1774) on behalf of the firm. At some point between 1774 and 1778 he left to take up a partnership with Edward France, and latterly William France jnr. *DEF,* I, p. 36 is in error in assuming this was with William France snr. Beckwith subscribed in 1791–94 to Sheraton's *Drawing Book,* and in 1795 supplied a 'neat mahogany worktable' to the Earl of Verulam at Gorhambury, Herts. [*DEF*] In 1804 he provided picture frames and did gilding, japanning and repairs charged to Lord Salisbury's town account. [Hatfield House MS, Bills 6/3, 1804, S.F.P. 6] However one 'Beckwith', u in St Martin's Lane, is noted among the deaths in *Gents Mag.,* April 1804. Holden's *Directory,* 1808 still records Samuel Beckwith as 'Upholsterer to His Majesty'.

Beckwith, Samuel, Duckinfield, Ashton-under-Lyne, Lancs., cm and joiner (1824–28). [D]

Beckwith, Thomas, Woodhouse Lane, Leeds, Yorks., carver and gilder (1830–37). Trading at no. 60 in 1830 and no. 61, 1834–37. [D]

Beckwith, William, 101 St Martin's Lane, London, cm and u (1789). A relative, possibly son of Samuel Beckwith. In 1789 they supplied 'a very neat Mahogany Horse-Shoe Reading Table made the same form as Her Majesty's at Kew' for the Queen's House (Buckingham House), at a cost of £4 14s 6d. [V & A archives] This large commission was however nominally in the hands of Beckwith and France as noted in the Wardrobe accounts. [PRO, LC 11/4]

Beckwith & France, 105 St Martin's Lane, London, cm and u (1774–1808). The partnership of Samuel Beckwith and various members of the France family — firstly Edward, and latterly William jnr — came into existence in the mid 1770s. Beckwith left Chippendale's firm after 1774. William France snr had died the year before and Edward France seems to have decided to go into partnership with Beckwith. By 1778 they had set up at 105 St Martin's Lane, London. The date and address is recorded on a print by James Donowell of the Steine, Brighton [Hove Museum of Art, Sussex] indicating it could be obtained from 'Messrs Beckwith and France'.

The earlier connections of William France snr with the Royal Wardrobe enabled the new partnership to take on work at St James's Palace, and at Buckingham House. [Royal Accounts, PRO, LC 11/4; Jourdain & Rose, *English Furniture: the Georgian Period,* 1750–1830]

The firm's principal private commission, 1781–90 was for work at Hatfield, Herts. (Lord Salisbury) and the town house. In 1781 this totalled over £4,778 and was above £1,000 in 1782 at both Hatfield and in 'Town'. [Hatfield House MS, Bills 151/23; *Burlington,* April 1967, pp. 201–09; the 1781–82 account is cited in *Apollo,* September 1967, p. 225]

Confirmation of the firm's St Martin's Lane address is provided by directories. [1789, *London Directory*; 1793 Supplement to *Patent London Directory*]

At this time the partnership continued with William France jnr. He however seems to have decided about 1810 to set up with a son (not named) as 'William France & Son'.   G. B.

Beckwys, Benjamin, 4 King St, Liverpool, u (1790). [D]

Beddard, James, 98 Holborn Hill, London, cm (1778–79). Took out Sun Insurance policies in 1778 for £500 of which utensils and stock accounted for £330; and in 1779 for £1,200 of which house and workshop accounted for £800. [GL, Sun MS vol. 270, p. 244; vol. 278, p. 508]

Beddine, David, 20 Back Lane, Radcliffe, London, cm and broker of household goods (1802). Took out a Sun Insurance policy on 27 April 1802 for £650 of which utensils and stock accounted for £220. [GL, Sun MS vol. 423, ref. 730769]

Beddine, David, London, cm and u (1809–35). Addresses given at 20 New Rd, St George's East, 1809–28, and 4 Wellclose Sq., 1829–35. [D]

Beddon (or Beddow), John, Manchester, chairmaker (1825–36). Addresses given at 71 Broad St in 1825 and at 68 London Rd, 1834–36. [D]

Bedell, John, Mint Lane, Bartholomew's Yd, Exeter, Devon, cm (1826–31). Daughter Elizabeth bapt. on 3 January 1826, and son John on 9 January 1831. [St Olave's PR(bapt.)]

Bedells, John, Trumpington St, Cambridge, cm and builder (1809–17). Announcements in the *Cambridge Chronicle and Journal*, 8 July 1809 dissolving partnership with James Metcalfe; 21 April 1815 declaring new partnership with William Ansell; 30 June William Ansell declining; 4 April 1817 declaring Bedells bankrupt.

Bedford, Benjamin, Pall Mall, London, upholder (1690–1709). Admitted freeman of the Upholders' Co. on 7 August 1700. Took out a Hand in Hand Insurance policy on 6 December 1703 for £500 on a house in Pall Mall 'being his now dwelling house & in his own possession for 7 years'. Notice in the *London Gazette*, 9 September 1709 that 'The Commissioners in a Commission of Bankrupt awarded against Benjamin Bedford, late of Pall Mall, Upholsterer, intend to meet . . .'. [GL, Upholders' Co. records; GL, Hand in Hand MS vol. 2, p. 674]

Bedford, Henry, New St, Chelmsford, Essex, cm and u (1839). [D]

Bedford, John, 22 Warwick St, Golden Sq., London, carver and gilder (1784–87). Took out Sun Insurance policies on his house in Butt Lane, Deptford, Kent, in 1784; and on 5 June 1787, for £200. [GL, Sun MS vol. 324, p. 452; vol. 346, p. 70]

Bedford, John, London, carver and gilder (1820–37). Addresses given at 28 Broad St, Golden Sq. and 9 Rosoman St, Clerkenwell, in 1820; and only the latter in 1837. [D]

Bedford, John, London, carver and gilder (1808–29). Addresses given at 56 Swallow St, Piccadilly in 1808; and at 13 Cross St, Golden Sq. in 1829. [D] See William Bedford.

Bedford, John & Son, 5 Mount St, Berkeley Sq., London, turner (1810). Between March and June 1810 provided for the 6th Duke of Bedford many items of hardware including clothes horses, totalling £34 3s 4d. [Bedford Office, London]

Bedford, John, High St, Bawtry, Yorks., cm (1832–37). Trading as Wilson & Bedford in 1832 in Notts. [D]

Bedford, P. snr, 23 Plumber St, City Rd, London, carver (1820). [D]

Bedford, Thomas, near 'The Star & Garter', Pall Mall, London, upholder (1704–15). Son of William Bedford of Shadbrooke, Suffolk, Doctor of Divinity, app. to Thomas Fe(?)wor on 12 December 1704. Admitted freeman of the Upholders' Co. by servitude on 10 April 1712. Took out Sun Insurance policies on 10 February 1714 on his dwelling house and on 25 March 1715 on goods and merchandise in his dwelling house. [GL, Upholders' Co. records; GL, Sun MS vol. 4, ref. 4492; vol. 4, p. 206]

Bedford, William, 56 Swallow St, Piccadilly, London, carver and gilder, picture frame maker (1809–20). [D] See John Bedford.

Bedford, William, Westgate, Ripon, Yorks., cm (1822). [D]

Bedford, William, Leeds Rd, Bradford, Yorks., cm (1830). [D]

Bedhouse, Thomas, 72 Gt Saffron Hill, London, water gilder (1835). [D]

Bedwell, James, London Rd, London, bed, mattress and bedstead manufacturer (1820–37). Trading at no. 116 from 1820–28, and at no. 52 in 1837, despite having been declared bankrupt on 18 January 1831, *London Gazette*. [D]

Bedwell, William, the Butter Mkt, Ipswich, Suffolk, joiner and cm (1723–42). As only joiner he took out a Sun Insurance policy on 6 January 1723 for £200 on his dwelling house in the parish of St Stephen. Advertised, *Ipswich Journal*, 8 September 1739, as joiner and cm who 'Maketh and Selleth all Sorts of Desks and Book-Cases, Chests of Drawers, Dressing-Tables, and Dining Tables, of all Sorts, of Mahogany Wallnutt-tree and Wainscott; all Sorts of Chairs, carved and plain; Tea-Trays and Waiters; Chimney-Glasses, Peer-Glasses, in Wallnut-tree Frames, or Gilt: Also buys old Glasses, and hangs Bells after the newest Fashion. A new Velvet or a Cloth Pall, and Cloaks, to be Lett'. Took app. named Henidge in 1742. [GL, Sun MS vol. 16, p. 234; S of G, app. index]

Bedwin, —, Oxford Rd, London, u (1747). [Heal]

Bee, Henry, High St, Leominster, Herefs., cm (1830). [D]

Bee, John jnr, Northleach, Glos., cm (1834). [D]

Beech, George, Market St, The Potteries, Staffs., cm (1818). [D]

Beech, James, Iron Mkt, Newcastle-under-Lyme, Staffs., joiner and cm (1822). [D]

Beech, Samuel, 18 Kingsgate St, Holborn, London, upholstery and mattress warehouse owner, bed and mattress maker (1823–28). Address given at no. 24, 1826–27. Took out a Sun Insurance policy on 12 February 1823 for £200 on dwelling house and offices (no store therein), £200 on household goods, £400 on stock and utensils, and £300 on house adjoining, no. 17, in tenure of a wax compo. doll maker. [D; GL, Sun MS vol. 489, ref. 1001422]

Beech, Thomas, Liverpool, cm (1806). Admitted freeman on 5 November 1806. [Liverpool freemen reg.]

Beechey, Thomas, 14 Mile End, London, cm (1809–11). [D]

Beedham, James, George St, Nottingham, cm (1835). [D]

Beedham, John, Fetter Lane, York, cm (1823). [D]

Beedham, William, Beedham's Yd, Skeldergate, York, joiner, cm, carpenter and house builder (1823). [D]

Beeger, Frederick, 7 West St, Seven Dials, London, cm (1780). Took out a Sun Insurance policy in 1780 for £200 of which utensils, stock and goods accounted for £100. [GL, Sun MS vol. 284, p. 43]

Beek, Elizabeth, Montpellier Arcade, Cheltenham, Glos., u (1839). [D]

Beeks, Andrew Berkley, Green St, Grosvenor Sq., London, upholder (1802). Declared bankrupt, *Billinge's Liverpool Advertiser*, 14 June 1802. See Andrew Berkley Becks of Bath.

Beeley, Edmund, Church St, Rotherham, Yorks., cm (1798–1814). [D]

Beeley, Joseph, Rotherham, Yorks., cm and u (1784). [D]

Beer, James, Market Pl., Dover, Kent, cm and u (1823–39). [D; poll bks]

Beer, John, Buckwell St, Plymouth, Devon, cm (1836). [D]

Beer, Samuel, 7 Chapel Row, Bath, Som., cm (1826). [D]

Beesley, John & Thomas, Garstang, Lancs., joiners and cm (1834). [D]

Beesley, Joshua, Northgate, Blackburn, Lancs., chairmaker (1818). [D]

Beesley, Nicholas, 1 Marybone, Liverpool, cm (1834). [D]

Beesley, Thomas, 46 Hill St, Birmingham, cm (1823). [D]

Beesley, William, Blackburn, Lancs., chairmaker (1818–34). Recorded at Lower Cock Croft St in 1818 and 4 North Gate in 1824–25. [D]

Beeson, Joseph, 3 Redman's Row, Whitechapel, London, cm and u (1839). [D]

Beeson, Joseph, St Augustine's Pl., Bristol, cm, u and undertaker (1821–22). Addresses given at no. 2 in 1821 and no. 15 in 1822. [D]

Beetham, Joseph, Liverpool, cm (1772–90). Addresses given at 10 Mason St from 1772–90; 9 Grayston St, 1781–84; and 3 Knight St, Berry St in 1790. [D]

Beetham, Joseph, 18 Waterhouse St, Halifax, Yorks., cm (1834–37). [D]

Beetham, Thomas, Liverpool, cm (1761–68). Took apps named Priest in 1761 and Wright in 1762. Admitted freeman of Lancaster, 1767–68. [S of G, app. index; Lancaster freemen rolls] A Thomas Beetham, timber merchant, is recorded at 19 Duke St, 1772–74, and 47 Duke St, 1781.

Beetham (or Beethom), William, Lancaster, cm (1761–68). As Beethom admitted freeman, 1761–62. As Beetham polled at Lancaster in 1768. [Lancaster freemen rolls]

Beethorn, Joseph, Liverpool, cm (1769–71). Took app. named Bryant Gorman, who wrote to his godfather in 1771 thanking him for placing him with Beethorn, 'such a good master'. [Berks. RO, D/EBt F29, 1–2; V & A archives]

Beeves, Josiah, West St, Brighton, Sussex, cm and u (1832–39). Trading at no. 55 in 1839, and as Beeves & Co., cm, u, interior decorators and furnishing undertakers, at no. 34. [D] See Thompson & Beeves.

Beevor, James, address unrecorded (c. 1780). Mahogany chest of drawers recorded with name 'JAMES BEEVOR' inscribed on underside of top.

Beezor, William, London, carver and gilder (1786). Polled at Norwich in 1786.

Begbie, James, Salisbury, Wilts., cm (1752–59). Took apps named George Brownjohn, 10 February 1752 for £21; Joseph Attwaters, 5 August 1755 for £30; John Kiddle, 2 February 1757 for 6 years for £26 5s; and John Acton, 1 June 1759 for £30. John Begbie, cm of Salisbury, perhaps misnamed, is recorded as having taken four apps between 1752–59. [Wilts. Apps and their Masters]

Begbie, Joseph, Salisbury, Wilts., cm (1755). Took app. named Attwaters in 1755. [S of G, app. index]

Beilby, John Alexander, York, cm (1818). Son of Jonathan Beilby, deceased, of North Grimston, app. to John Bellerby, cm and u, 14 September 1818. [York app. reg.]

Be(i)lby, Thomas, Cottingham, near Hull, Yorks., cm (1840). [D]

Belam, James, 3 Webber St, New Cut, London, carver and gilder (1829). [D]

Belcher, —, address unrecorded, cm and u (1775). Subscribed to Thomas Malton's *A Complete Treatise on Perspective*, 1775.

Belcher, Benjamin, Bridewell Lane, Bristol, cm, appraiser, auctioneer and undertaker (1792–1800). Trade card (Banks Coll., BM) shows Sheraton-style chair and table and classical figures. [D]

Belcher, Cathern, address unrecorded (1783–84). Repaired oval tea tray for Sir John Griffin Griffin of Audley End, Essex, for 3s. [Essex RO, D/DBy/A42/4]

Belcher, Charles, Cowick St, St Thomas, Exeter, Devon, cm (1820). Son Charles bapt. on 25 May 1820. [PR(bapt.)]

Belcher, Elisha, Gt Nelson St, Lime St, Liverpool, cm (1804). [D]

Belcher, John, 74 Earl St East, Lisson Grove, London, u (1839). [D]

Belcher, John, Thames St, Wallingford, Oxon., turner and cm (1840). [D]

Belcher, Joseph, Wallingford St, Wantage, Oxon., cm (1798–1824). [D]

Belcher, Thomas, 25 Gt Portland St, London, upholder and undertaker (1783). Took out a Sun Insurance policy in 1783 for £300 of which utensils and stock accounted for £213. [GL, Sun MS vol. 313, p. 403] Possibly the Thomas Belcher who supplied to Sir John Griffin Griffin of Audley End, Essex, for his London house in New Burlington St 'a Small Mahogany hand stand for 14 nozels to carrey candels in to light up the Drawing Room' and an 'Oval Teatray with brass hoops & wood handels & repairs to furniture', totalling £4 5s 6d, in 1783. [Essex RO, D/DBy/A41/6] Possibly the Belcher of:

Belcher & Gray, London, cm and u (1769–81). Addresses given at Brownlow St, Holborn, 1769–83, and Poultney St, Golden Sq., 1783–84. In 1779 supplied beds and bedding for Sir John Griffin Griffin's London house in New Burlington St. [Essex RO, D/DBy/A37/4] Sale of entire stock in trade on 21 November 1781 by Christie & Ansell, Pall Mall, including 'Elegant Mahogany Desk and Bookcases, Ditto Commodes, Wardrobes, Sideboards, Library Tables, Bureaus, Chests of Drawers, Dining and Card Tables, Two very Elegant TORTOISHELL Table Clock Cases, an Elegant Inlaid Secretary for a Lady, with a great Variety of Mahogany and Inlaid Articles of the Best Workmanship &c.' [D]

Belchier, John, 'The Sun', South side of St Paul's Churchyard, London, cm (1717–d. 1753). A craftsman whose surname might suggest a Huguenot origin. The earliest references to a John 'Belcher' are to be found in the accounts of Boughton House, Northants. Between 1687 and 1710 amounts totalling £3,880 are recorded for glass, solder, piping, lead etc., and as late as 1723 a receipt for £150 was given for money paid by the executors of the 1st Duke of Montagu. This tradesman may well have been the father of the John Belchier who traded at the St Paul's Churchyard address as cm. The latter was noted as a supplier of mirrors, and many of the bureau cabinets which bear his trade label are fronted with mirror glass. The St Paul's Churchyard address is first recorded on 26 July 1717 when insurance was effected 'for goods and merchandise in his said Dwelling House'. From 1720 he is recorded supplying furniture to Erddig, Clwyd, N. Wales. One of his trade bills indicates that he made and supplied 'All sorts of Cabinet Works,/ Chairs, Glasses, Sconces, & Coach-Glasses'. Another trade bill with different wording stated that he 'Grinds & Makes-up,/ all sorts of fine Peer & Chim/ney-Glasses and Glass Sconces,/ Likewise all Cabbinet Makers Goods'. He also indicated that he could offer 'Great choice of all Ready Made'. On 24 November 1741 he took as app. William Albrook, son of William Albrook snr, deceased, formerly an ivory turner. At this date Belchier was a member of the Joiners' Co. The death of John Belchier was announced in March 1753. He was nearly 70 years old at the time of his death and was described as 'for many years past a very eminent cabinetmaker'. He was also stated to be kinsman of William Belchier, one of the MPs for the borough of Southwark. His successor at the sign of 'The Sun', St Paul's Churchyard was Thomas Atkinson.

The most significant commission known to have been undertaken by Belchier was for John Meller at Erddig, Wales, a house which he acquired in 1716. He used Simon Yorke, his nephew, as his agent in London to order and supervise the furnishing of the house, which passed to him in 1723 on the death of his uncle. The most impressive piece of furniture in the house is the State Bed which was purchased in 1720. The bedframe with its carved and gilt gesso work is almost certainly by Belchier, the upholstery work being undertaken by a 'Mr Hunt', probably John Hutt, a tradesman whose workshops were also in St Paul's Churchyard. The hawks' heads on the tester of the bed closely compare with those on gilt pier glasses supplied in 1723 and 1726 at £36 and £50 respectively for the two best bedchambers. A pair of gilt girandoles with glass arms were supplied by Belchier on 25 August 1724 at a cost of £14 each. Apart from the bed and mirrors, a glass-topped table with the arms of John Meller supplied by Belchier on 6 June 1726 also survives in the house. These items are part of the substantial commissions placed with Belchier at this period. His bill covering November 1722 to January 1726 amounted to £262 12s. At the same period as he was working on furnishings for Erddig, he received orders for glass for St Paul's Cathedral. Accounts dated December 1724 to January 1725 record the supplying of 8 glasses 25 inches square at £8, and 27 others 25 by 18 inches at 16s each (£21 12s).

Regular customers in the 1730s and 40s were the Purefoy family of Shalston, Bucks. A letter survives from Elizabeth Purefoy dated 11 January 1735 regarding the supply of 'a glass in a gold frame'. The details provided suggest that this was a chimney glass which was still present in the house in 1950. It was charged at £3 16s. By a letter dated 8 February 1743 an order was sent for 'a round neat light mahogany folding table with four legs, two of them to draw out and hold up yᵉ ffolds'. Henry Purefoy, Elizabeth's son, recorded on 18 July 1749 the receipt of an artist's or architect's table for which £3 10s was paid. Of other commissions little is known. Two receipts survive written on trade bills and show that a varied trade was carried on. Items recorded on them include a 'tea box', 'a Claw table with two tops', 'A Round Board' and a mahogany chest of drawers.

Belchier labelled some of his furniture. Significantly, all the pieces known with labels are bureau cabinets veneered in walnut or japanned in red with gilt enrichment. All incorporate mirror glass in the door or doors. Some have a small round label specially made for this purpose worded 'made by/ John Bel Chier/ at Yᵉ Sun/in St Pauls Church/Yard' (Fig. 4). Some similar cabinets stamped with the impressed initials 'I. B.' may also be of his manufacture. The items marked with labels or stamped appear to be in style of the period to c. 1735, and it is possible that the practice was restricted to particularly prestigious pieces of case furniture and discontinued by the mid 1730s. [GL, Sun MS vol. 6, ref. 8806; Joiners' Co. records, bindings, vol. 5; BM, trade card coll.; V & A archives; *London Evening Post*, 24–27 March 1753; G. Eland (ed.), *The Purefoy Letters, 1735–53*, I, pp. 98, 107, 111; *Conn.*, vol. 125, pp. 85–86; *C. Life*, 10 June 1954, p. 1896, 11 February 1960, p. 264, 12 June 1969, supplement p. 57; 28 January 1971, supplement p. 162; 13 April 1978, pp. 971–73; *Apollo*, July 1978, pp. 46–55; *Wren Soc.*, vol. xv, p. 226; Heal; Christie's, 18 November 1982, lot 125; Sotheby's, 14 November 1980, lot 30]   B. A.

Belchier, Thomas, address unrecorded, cm (1754). Subscribed to Chippendale's *Director*, 1754.

Beley, Henry, 7 Clarendon St, Leamington, Warks., carver and gilder (1835–37). Trading at Regent Grove in 1835 and 7 Clarendon St in 1837. [D]

Belfield, Thomas, 3 Hunt St, Birmingham, cm, u and bedstead maker (1830). [D]

Belfour, Alexander, London, cm (1793). Subscribed to Sheraton's *Drawing Book*, 1793.

Belk, John, Hall Gate, Doncaster, Yorks., cm and u (1830–37). [D]

Belk, Vincent, Hall Gate, Doncaster, Yorks., cm and u (1818–34). Submitted bill for furniture and upholstery supplied to G. Wentworth of Woolley Hall, Yorks., between April and November 1825, totalling £48 7s 4d. [D; YAS, Wentworth papers, MD 272/2]

Bell, —, address unrecorded, cm (c. 1750–75). Mahogany Master's armchair with full padded back, surmounted by shield with bacchus head, scrolled arms, and cabriole leg with scroll foot recorded from Vintners' Hall, London. [V & A archives]

Bell, —, address unrecorded, cm (1803). Subscribed to Sheraton's *Cabinet Dictionary*, 1803.

Bell, Alexander, 9 Angel Ct, Windmill St, Haymarket, London, cm (1777–84). Took out a Sun Insurance policy in 1777 for £100 on his house. [Poll bk; GL, Sun MS vol. 254, p. 242]

Bell, Allan, High St, Wigton, Cumb., joiner and cm (1828–29). [D]

Bell, Anthony, Thorngate, Barnard Castle, Co. Durham, joiner and cm (1827–29). [D]

Bell, Augustus, East St, Fareham, Hants., carver and gilder (1839). [D]

Bell, Clement, Askrigg, Yorks., joiner and cm (1840). [D]

Bell, Daniel, London, joiner (1721–23). Took app. named John Harden on 21 November 1721 for seven years, but turned him over to Daniel Cooke on 20 October 1723. [GL, MS 8051/3] Possibly:

Bell, Daniel, London, cm and u (1725–31). Supplied furniture and upholstery to the Duke of Montrose between 1725–29 including a large mahogany oval table and frame, £6 15s, six walnut chairs with scarlet lace seats, £10 4s, a mahogany tea table, a large walnut couch and 15 yards of red shalloon for the Duchess of Montrose; 2 large walnut quadrille tables with folding frames, £8 8s, a mahogany pier table, a walnut 'necessary square stool with black leather feet'; 2 large walnut elbow chairs with stuffed backs and red linen seats, and a walnut couch frame. In 1731 he supplied 'mahogany drawers and a wainscot table' to the Duchess of Montrose's apartment, costing £5 11s 6d. [Scottish RO, GD 220/6/1349/46; 1251/18; 1371/32; 1373/30; 31/P610] Possibly:

Bell, Daniel, St Martin's Lane, London, cm (1724–34). Took out a Sun Insurance policy on 11 May 1728 for £1,800 on his dwellings, stock in trade and merchandise, fortunately, since on 13 October that year 'a violent fire broke out at a Mr. Currier's [or a Currier's] in Rose Street near Long Acre, which consumed his house and 3 others . . . & Mr. Bell, an eminent cabinetmaker's house that lay backward towards St. Martin's Lane, with the workhouses belonging thereunto, and a great quantity of valuable foreign wood lying in his yard for carrying on his business at which he employed several scores of people every day, so that this loss alone is reckoned to amount to some thousands of Pounds'. [*Daily Post*, 14 October 1728] The *Daily Journal* of 15 October however, reported that the fire started at Mr Negus's, a Leather Dresser's in Rose St, and consumed nine houses, Mr Bell, away in Brompton at the time, proving 'the greatest sufferer'. The *Ipswich Journal* of 12 October further sensationalised by adding that 'Mr. Bell had the Misfortune some Time ago to break his Leg into Splinters, and was then in the Country dangerously Ill'. After the fire 'Several Men were employ'd in removing his Looking Glasses and other Furniture sav'd out of the Fire; but the Damage in Walnut-Tree Plank only, amounts to £500'. A few days after the fire he announced in the *Daily Journal*, 17 October, 'I have taken a convenient House and Work Shops opposite to my late Dwelling-House, where all Business in Trade will go forward without the least Hinderance of Time and where I shall be in Person to give Attention, and receive proper Orders'.

In 1726 took app. named John Showbridge, who served for seven years. In 1734 he was appointed cm and chairmaker to the Royal Household. Heal considers it very possible that Bell was the originator of the business in St Paul's Churchyard carried on by Henry, Elizabeth and Philip Bell later in the 18th century.

Recorded in partnership with Thomas Moore as early as 1724 when the firm supplied goods to Benjamin Mildmay, Earl Fitzwalter for Moulsham Hall between 1724–34. On 13 December 1732 they received payment for 'a large Glass & dining chairs with Blew Leather, ten in no.' costing £33 6s; on 2 May, £10, and on 26 February 1734, £5 15s, 'To a Walnut-Tree Desk with 4 Drawers'. [A. C. Edwards, *The Accounts of Benjamin Mildmay, Earl Fitzwalter*, p. 104]

In December 1733 Bell & Moore were paid in full for various items supplied between September 1731–December 1733 to a Captain Hall. [PRO, C111 195] Their bill to the 'Hon. Counsellor Rider' of 1734, totalling £39 14s 6d included 'a large carved and guilt sconce, pediment frame', 'an eagle frame with top carved and guilded in burnished gold, and ten walnut chairs with rich carved fore feet with Lyons' faces on ye knees and Lyons' Paws'. This set, originally costing £27 10s is preserved at Sandon Hall, Staffs. [GL, Sun MS vol. 26, p. 161; *DEF*; Wills, *Looking-Glasses*; *GCM*; Strange, *Old Furniture*, vol. 4, pp. 48–51; *Conn.*, June 1933, pp. 379–80; Westminster Ref. Lib., St Martin's settlement records, ref. F/5037] A.E.

Bell, Edmund Hurst, Peacock St, Norwich, cm (1825–30). Son of William Bell, weaver, admitted freeman of Norwich on 13 August 1825. [D; poll bk; Norwich freemen reg.] See Edward Bell.

Bell, Edward, Young's Lane, Carlisle, Cumb., carver and gilder (1834). [D]

Bell, Edward, Peacock St, Norwich, Norfolk, cm and u (1839). [D] See Edmund Hurst Bell.

Bell, Elizabeth, 'The White Swan', against the South Gate, St Paul's Churchyard, London, cm (1740–c. 1758). Successor to Henry Bell at this address and almost certainly his widow. The trade labels that she used are identical to those of Henry Bell with the exception of the name. Most of the bills name the business as Elizabeth Bell & Son, the son probably being Philip who was in charge of the business by 1758. Following the practice of Henry Bell, Elizabeth appears to have frequently labelled furniture. Such pieces include a walnut bureau and a walnut kneehole chest, a black lacquer dwarf chest-on-chest, a mahogany chest-on-chest with slide and a mahogany card or tea table with rectangular top on cabriole legs. [V & A archives; *Antiques*, March 1966, p. 346; *C. Life*, 9 June 1966, p. 1467; *Conn.*, May 1980, p. 6; J. Kirk, *American Furniture and the British Tradition to 1830*, p. 1377; Christie's, 11 April 1985, lot 25] B. A.

Bell, Elizabeth, 9 Little Peter St, Knot Mill, Manchester, u (1813). [D]

Bell, Elizabeth, 35 Worcester St, Birmingham, u (1830). [D]

Bell, Enniskillen & Cavan, address unrecorded, cm and u. Yew sofa table recorded bearing trade label showing Regency period furniture. [V & A archives]

Bell, Francis, Little Russell Ct, Drury Lane, London, cm and broker (1787). Took out a Sun Insurance policy on 17 April 1787 for £800 on his house and goods. [GL, Sun MS vol. 342, ref. 529983]

Bell, Francis, Hotwell Rd, Bristol, cm (1805–06). [D]

Bell, G., 10 Wellington St, City Rd, London, looking-glass and picture frame maker (1829). [D]

Bell, George, London, carver and gilder (1817–39). Addresses at 55 Little Sutton St, Clerkenwell, 1817–29, and 4 Clerkenwell Green, 1835–39. [D]

Bell, George, Humshaugh, Simonburn, Northumb., joiner and cm (1827). [D]

Bell, George, Walkergate, Louth, Lincs., cm and joiner (1828). [D]

Bell, George, Union Rd, Southport, Portsea, Portsmouth, Hants., carver and gilder (1830). [D]

Bell, George, 6 East St, Hoxton Old Town, London, looking-glass and picture frame maker (1837). [D]

Bell, George, 36 Chester St, Birkenhead, Cheshire, cm (1839). [D]

Bell, George, Askrigg, Yorks., joiner and cm (1840). [D]

Bell, Henry, 'The White Swan', against the South Gate, St Paul's Churchyard, London, cm (1736–d. 1740). Successor to Coxed & Woster at this address. The death of Woster was announced in 1736 and it was probably in this year that Henry Bell commenced trading here. His trade card indicates that he made and sold 'all Sorts of ye finest Cabinet Goods, all sorts of Looking Glasses, Coach Glasses & Chairs of all sorts'. He offered to alter old looking-glasses to the latest fashion. Following the practice of Coxed & Woster he used his trade label to identify products from his workshops. This trade label has been recorded on a walnut chest of drawers, a walnut bureau and a walnut chest of drawers. Died 1740 and his successor at this address, Elizabeth Bell, was almost certainly his widow and Philip Bell his son. [Heal; V & A archives] See Daniel Bell. B. A.

Bell, J., north side of the Square, Stockton-on-Tees, Co. Durham, carver and gilder (1824). Advertised in the *Durham County Advertiser*, 3 April 1824 'that he has just returned from London with a selection of the best materials used in his art which can be procured, he trusts, by the superior method of finishing work which he possesses, combined with a determination to spare no exertion to give satisfaction to those who may favour him with their orders to merit a continuance of public patronage & support . . . Executes in the most fashionable manner, Mirrors, Chimney & Pier Glasses, bordering for Rooms, Bed & Window Cornices. Needle Work, Paintings, Drawings, Prints etc. framed; Old Frames re-gilded, & Prints varnished etc. NB. Ornamental Frames executed, Figures bronzed, & Paintings cleaned with care'.

Bell, J. W., Westgate, Rotherham, Yorks., cabinet manufacturer and u. Trade card noted at Grosvenor House Antiques Fair, 1985. Probably James William Bell.

Bell, James, Windsor, Berks., u (1757–58). Took app. named Massey in 1758. [S of G, app. index; poll bk]

Bell, James, Lancaster, u (1806–07). [Lancaster freemen rolls]

Bell, James, Westgate, Sheffield, Yorks., cm (1833). [D]

Bell, James, Liverpool, u (1831). App. to John Pemberton in 1831. [Liverpool app. reg.] Possibly:

Bell, James, 50 Hotham St, Liverpool, cm (1839). [D]

Bell, James William, High St, Rotherham, Yorks., cm (1834–37). [D] See J. W., John, Jonathan & Son, and Thomas Bell.

Bell, John & Pick, Robert, address unrecorded, cm. Mahogany breakfront bookcase, c. 1750, known bearing two of their labels. [V & A archives]

Bell, John, Petergate, York, cm (1771–d. 1786). Advertised in the *York Courant*, 2 March and 7 July 1771. Polled at York, 1774. Sale of stock after death announced in the *York Courant*, 31 October 1786.

Bell, John, 3 French Row, Old St, London, turner in general (1808). [D]

Bell, John, York, carver and gilder (1813). Son of Christopher Bell; app. to Robert Tomlinson, carver and gilder on 6 September 1813. [York app. reg.]

Bell, John, Westgate, Rotherham, Yorks., cm (1814–20). [D]
See James, Jonathan & Son and Thomas Bell.

Bell, John, Haggersgate, Whitby, Yorks., carver and gilder
(1823). [D]

Bell, John, Norwich, Norfolk, cm and chairmaker (1822–39).
Recorded in Goat Lane, 1822–30; and in Middleton's Ct,
with house in Gregory St, 1836–39. [D]

Bell, John, Dundas St, Hungate, York, cm (1823). [D]

Bell, John, Walworth St, Sunderland, Co. Durham, turner and
bed post carver (1827). [D]

Bell, John, Thorngate, Barnard Castle, Co. Durham, joiner and
cm (1827). [D] Possibly the John Bell, carpenter of Barnard
Castle who made new pews for the church in 1813. [Durham
RO, D/St/V612]

Bell, John, High St, Stockton-on-Tees, Co. Durham, joiner and
cm (1827–32). [D]

Bell, John, Main St, Cockermouth, Cumb., joiner and cm
(1829). [D]

Bell, John, New Rd, St Ann's, Newcastle, cm (1834). [D]

Bell, John, Old Market Pl., Barton-upon-Humber, Lincs., joiner
and cm (1835). [D]

Bell, John, Liverpool, cm (1835–39). Addresses at 3 St John's
Village, 1835, and at no. 6, and 31 Duncan St East, 1837–39.
[D]

Bell, John, 3 Berkeley St, London, water gilder (1835). [D]

Bell, John Thomas, 17 Old St, London, picture and looking-
glass frame maker (1835–39). Trading also at 5 Hatfield St in
1839. [D]

Bell, Johnson, Harrington, Workington, Cumb., cm and joiner
(1829–34). [D]

Bell, Jonas, Rastrick, Halifax, Yorks., joiner and cm (1834). [D]

Bell, Jonathan & Son, Westgate, Rotherham, Yorks., cm
(1822). [D] See James, John and Thomas Bell.

Bell, Joseph A., 32 Horsefair, Birmingham, cabinet carver and
chairmaker (1835). [D]

Bell, Lawrence, 31 Old Compton St, London, upholder (1790–
93). [D]

Bell, M., Ropemaker's Alley, Moorfields, London, cm
(1760–61). Philip Roscoe, a non-freeman at M. Bell's was
employed for 3 months each year by John Arrowsmith. [GL,
City Licence bks, vol. 2, pp. 231, 253, 310, 353]

Bell, M., 41 Eagle St, Red Lion Sq., London, cm and dealer in
mahogany (1790–93). [D]

Bell, Marchant M., King St, Richmond, Yorks., veneer and cm
(1813–30). Recorded in the Richmond PR(bapt.) in 1813. [D]

Bell, Michael, 6 Marchmont St, near Russell Sq., London, cm
(1807). Took out a Sun Insurance policy on 13 November
1807 for £300. [GL, Sun MS vol. 441, ref. 809797]

Bell, Philip, St Paul's Churchyard, London, cm and upholder
(1758–74). Successor to Elizabeth Bell and almost certainly
her son. His father was probably Henry Bell who also traded
at the same address. For a time he traded in partnership with
Elizabeth Bell but appears to have been in sole charge by
1758. Initially he used the trade sign of 'The White Swan' as
his predecessors had done, but it was in his period of trading
that numbering was introduced to this part of London.
Initially the premises appear to have been numbered 18 St
Paul's Churchyard but this was soon changed to 23. He was a
member of the Vintners' Co., but there is no evidence to show
that he adopted any other trade than that of cm. In 1758,
1761 and 1764 he took out licences to employ limited
numbers of non-freemen, never more than three. The trade
labels used by Henry and Elizabeth were considered out-dated
and he employed Matthias Darly to engrave a new one which
reflected the Rococo taste of the age. This featured
illustrations of a fine cabinet in the Chinese Chippendale taste,
an upholstered chair and a pole screen. The text indicated that

he performed funerals (Fig. 16). These labels were used to
identify products of his workshops and have been found on a
wide range of furniture. One such label is endorsed 'Removed
to No 9 Paternoster Row, Near Cheapside' though no other
reference to such a move has been noted and he appears to
have been still trading from 23 St Paul's Churchyard until
1774 when Henry Kettle took over, proclaiming himself to be
Bell's successor. Philip Bell took as app. William King, 1766–
74.

By the period that Philip Bell occupied the St Paul's
Churchyard address the centre of the fashionable furniture
trade had moved west to the St Martin's Lane and Soho areas.
The labelled pieces of furniture known are in the main
serviceable rather than highly fashionable and there is little
evidence of important commisions for the gentry and
aristocracy. The notebooks of Nathaniel Ryder, 1st Lord
Harrowby of Sandon Hall, Staffs. record payments to 'Bell'
between 27 March 1762 and 23 July 1774 but none of the
amounts are large. The total for the seven payments made is
only £52 8s 6d and the only items specified are a dressing glass
and three chests of drawers, two of these being noted as 'for
Shiplake'. Labelled pieces are mostly of mahogany and
include chests of drawers, a clothes press, tallboys, a secretaire
tallboy, a Pembroke table, a medicine chest, a bureau
bookcase, a tripod reading stand and a toilet mirror on a base
of three drawers. Limited acknowledgements of mid
18th-century fashion were made. One chest of drawers with
canted corners had these carved with blind fret, while a
tallboy with restrained Gothic decoration is known. [D; DEF;
GCM; Heal; Harrowby MS Trust, Notebooks; GL, Upholders' Co. records; City Licence bks, vols 2, 4; Conn., vol. 88,
p. 169, April 1969, p. 243, July 1977, p. 22; Apollo, May
1966, p. 405; Antique Collector, 1935, p. 275, September
1974, p. 71; Antique Collector's Guide, January 1973, p. 36;
J. Kirk, American Furniture and the British Tradition to
1830, pl. 1451; Christie's, 10 October 1968, lot 56; 9 July
1970, lot 87; 19 January 1978, lot 11; 23 October 1980,
lot 29; Parke-Bernet, NY, 19 February 1966, lot 134; Phillips', 31 July 1973, lot 83; Sotheby's, 31 July 1964, lot 410;
10 January 1969, lot 157; 20 November 1970, lot 154;
26 May 1972, lot 28]   B. A.

Bell, Richard, New St, St Ann's, Newcastle, joiner and cm
(1832–38). An R. Bell of Newcastle was declared bankrupt,
Chester Courant and Advertiser for North Wales, 17 July
1832. [D]

Bell, Richard, George Lane, Botolph Lane, London, cm and u
(1839). [D]

Bell, Robert, Lancaster, joiner and cm (1727–51). Admitted
freeman as a joiner, 1727–28. Took app. as joiner and cm on
9 May 1738 and on 27 May 1751. [Lancaster freemen rolls
and app. reg.]

Bell, Robert, 29 Minories, London, cm and u (1788–1804).
Recorded at 22 Minories in 1789. Named in Sheraton's list of
master cabinet makers, 1803. [D]

Bell, Stephen, Northgate, Darlington, Co. Durham, joiner and
cm (1827–34). [D]

Bell, Thomas, Stone Cutter's St, parish of St Bride, London, cm
(1729). Took out a Sun Insurance policy on 9 July 1729 for
£300 of which stock in trade in dwelling house accounted for
£100. [GL, Sun MS vol. 29, ref. 48160]

Bell, Thomas, Kingsland Rd, London, cm (1808). [D]

Bell, Thomas, Richmond, Yorks., cm (1823). [PR(bapt.)]

Bell, Thomas, Tynemouth, North Shields, Northumb., u
(1827). [D]

Bell, Thomas, Westgate, Rotherham, Yorks., cm (1830). [D] See
James, John and Jonathan Bell & Son.

Bell, Thomas, York, cm (1829). Son of Hannah, wife of

Edmund Palphraman; app. to Isaac Pape, cm and u, on 2 February 1829. [York app. reg.]

Bell, Thomas, Cartergate, Nottingham, cm (1835). [D]

Bell, Wallis, Beverley, Yorks., cm and auctioneer (1784–99). Trading in Graburn Lane, 1791, and Laregate, 1792. [D; poll bks]

Bell, William, near Stockbridge, Northumb., and Newcastle, joiner and cm (1787–1811). Recorded near Stockbridge, 1787–1801, and at Old Flesh-market, Newcastle, in 1811. [D]

Bell, William, Market Rasen, Lincs., cm, chairmaker and joiner (1813). App. to Henry Wakelin of Market Rasen in July 1813. [Hull app. reg.]

Bell, William, Newgate St, Barnard Castle, Co. Durham, joiner and cm (1827–34). [D]

Bell, William, 26 Gt Winchester St, London, cm and u (1839). [D]

Bell, William Worthington, 158 Fleet St, London, water gilder (1776). Took out a Sun Insurance policy in 1776 for £500 on a house in Northampton. [GL, Sun MS vol. 253, p. 114]

Bell & Moore, see Daniel Bell.

Bellamy, —, address unrecorded (1734). Named in the Holkham Hall accounts in 1734 supplying a large gilt frame for Lord Thanet's picture costing £6, and 2 picture frames costing £6 6s. [V & A archives]

Bellamy, Henry, Solihull, Staffs., chairmaker (1755). Took app. named Taylor in 1755. [S of G, app. index]

Bellamy, John, Sanvey Gate, Leicester, carpenter, turner and joiner (1767–75). Took app. named William Hall in 1767. Announced auction of stock in trade, including 'Claw tables, set, of chairs etc', *Leicester Journal*, 1775. [Leicester freemen rolls]

Bellamy, Joseph snr, London, upholder (d. by 1731). His son Joseph admitted freeman of the Upholders' Co. by patrimony on 13 July 1731. [GL, Upholders' Co. records]

Bellard, Henry, Windmill Yd, Manchester, cm (1800–02). [D]

Bellard, Robert, Liverpool, cm (1760). Petitioned freedom as freeborn son of Edward Bellard, cow keeper, paying 3s 4d. [Liverpool freemen's committee bk]

Bellatti, Charles, High St, Burton-on-Trent, Staffs., carver and gilder (1818). [D]

Bellat(t)i & Son, G., Stodman St, Newark, Notts., carver and gilders (1832–41). [D]

Bellchambers, Stephen, 8 Union St, Walcot Pl., London, chair and sofa maker (1827–28). [D]

Bellerby, John snr, Micklegate, York, u, cm and undertaker (b. 1782–d. 1827). App. and journeyman to William Hawkin. Freeman by 1811. [*York Courant*, 1 July 1811; 20 November 1815] Advertised in *York Gazette*, 3 July 1819. Death reported in *York Gazette*, 16 June 1827 aged 45 at 14 Micklegate. Successor, Thomas Hands, announced, *York Gazette*, 30 June 1827. He took John Bellerby jnr as app. Bellerby snr took apps named Joseph Waterhouse, 12 August 1809; John Blakey, 25 July 1811; Richard Carter, 1 June 1814; John Alexander Beilby, 14 September 1818; and Marmaduke Maw, 26 April 1826. [D; York freemen rolls and app. reg.]

Bellerby, John jnr, York, cm (1827–30). Recorded at 118 Walmgate in 1830. Son of John Bellerby, cm, deceased; app. to Thomas Hands, cm and u, on 6 July 1827. [D; York app. reg.]

Bellerby, John, York, chairmaker (1833). Son of George Bellerby; app. to Richard Baynes & Francis Duffill, chairmakers, on 8 October 1833. [York app. reg.]

Bellerby, Thomas, 2 Bishop Hill, York, joiner and cm (1823–38). [D]

Bellerby, William, Clifton, York, joiner and cm (1830–38). [D]

Bellet, A., Old Town, Plymouth, Devon, cm (1814). [D] Possibly Anthony Belletti.

Bellett, John, London, upholder's warehouseman (1768–83). Recorded at 22 Leadenhall St, 1770–78; at 12 St Mary Axe, 1780–81, in partnership with William Bellett (a former app.); and alone at 13 St Mary Axe in 1783. Admitted freeman of the Upholders' Co. by redemption on 3 August 1768. Recorded in Ireland, 1794–1802. [D; GL, Upholders' Co. records and Livery lists]

Bellett, William, St Mary Axe, London, upholder's warehouseman (1778). Son of Hugh Bellett of Sampford Arundell, Somerset, app. to John Bellett. Admitted freeman of the Upholders' Co. by servitude on 4 February 1778. In partnership with John Bellett at 12 St Mary Axe, 1780–81. [D; GL, Upholders' Co. records]

Belletti, Anthony, Treville St, Plymouth, Devon, cm (1822). [D]

Belletti, Joseph, London, cm and u (1826–29). Addresses given at 50 Long Alley, Finsbury Circus, 1826–27; 51 Long Alley, Moorfields, 1827–28; and 40 Skinner St, Finsbury Mkt, 1829. [D]

Bellhouse, David jnr, Garratt Rd, Manchester, cm (1840). [D]

Bellingham, —, address unrecorded, u (19th century). Name inscribed under a set of chairs and sofa also stamped 'JS' at Felbrigg, Norfolk.

Bellingham, Edward, High St, Maidstone, Kent, u (1832–37). [Poll bks]

Bellingham, John, St Ann, Soho, London, cm (1761). Discharge from Debtors' Prison announced in *London Gazette*, 12 September 1761.

Bellingham, William, address unrecorded, upholder (1749–56). Son of William Bellingham of Christ Church, Spitalfields, victualler; app. to William Jones jnr on 1 June 1749. Admitted freeman of the Upholders' Co. by servitude on 1 July 1756. [GL, Upholders' Co. records]

Bellino, John & Co., Dale St, Liverpool, carvers, gilders, print sellers and looking-glass manufacturers (1805–07). [D]

Bellion, James, Bread St, Birmingham, cabinet case maker (1818). [D]

Bellis, Edward, Chester, cm (1747). [Poll bk]

Bellison, —, Newark area, Notts., cm (1774). The Newark Town Hall account books of 1774 record a commission 'to make 4 mahogany card tables at 30/– a piece according to pattern produced'.

Bellwood, John, 11 Rupert St, Haymarket, London, cm (1821–23). Took out Sun Insurance policies on 26 September 1821 for £150 on household goods in private dwelling house, no cabinet work done therein; and on 7 November 1823 for £200. [GL, Sun MS vol. 488, ref. 983507; vol. 498, ref. 1010061]

Bellwood, William, Heighington, near Darlington, Co. Durham, joiner and cm (1828). [D]

Bellworthy, John, London, u (1826–38). Recorded also as cm at 5 and 6 Queen's Buildings in 1826, and also as appraiser at 5 Newland Pl. in 1838. [D]

Bellys, Benjamin, Liverpool, u (1780). Admitted freeman on 13 September 1780. [Liverpool freemen reg.]

Belongaro (or Bolongaro), Dominic, Manchester, carver, gilder, print seller, ladies' repository for fancy painting, barometer and looking-glass maker (1817–40). Trading at 2 Old Millgate, 1817–32; 32 Market St in 1839; and 14 Market St in 1840. A Banjo barometer and thermometer of mahogany with satinwood marquetry of conches and paterae, and inscribed 'DOMINIC BOLONGARO 2 OLD MILL GATE MANCHESTER' is owned by Manchester City Art Gallery. [D]

Belotti & Gugeri, Andrew, London, barometer, thermometer, looking-glass and picture frame manufacturers (1823–36).

Addresses at 15 Upper Union Ct, Holborn Hill, 1823–29, and 16 Charles St, Hatton Gdn, 1830–36. [D; Goodison, *Barometers*]

Belshaw, Edmund jnr, Liverpool, cm (1802–05). Admitted freeman on 8 July 1802. Took app. in 1802 named Samuel Sharrat, who petitioned freedom in 1818. Recorded in partnership with William Belshaw, 1803–04 in Commerce Ct, Lord St, with shop and manufactory in Whitechapel, Liverpool, in 1805. Firm declared bankrupt and sale of stock announced, *Liverpool Chronicle*, 30 January and 3 April 1805. Stock comprised 'mahogany chairs, card & dining Tables, wardrobes, Lady's Do. with Book-case, Desks, Chest of Drawers with Basins, Stands, Clock-cases, Clocks & Cases, painted Chairs, Bedsteads etc. . . . All the STOCK, TIMBER, etc., Consisting of mahogany Planks, Boards, & Veneers, Feather do. Oak, Ash, Maple, Birch, Deal Planks & Boards; Chests of Tools, Turners' Lathe & Tools, Benches etc.'. [D; Liverpool freemen's committee bk and reg.]

Belshaw, William, Liverpool, cm (1796–1812). Indenture dated 1796–97. In 1806 and 1812 he petitioned freedom on servitude to Samuel Chubbard, but each application was rejected, not having served his whole term. [Liverpool freemen's committee bk]

Belshaw, William, 22 Chester St, Birkenhead, Cheshire, cm (1834–39). [D]

Belson, White, George St, Gt Yarmouth, Norfolk, cm and chairmaker (1830). [D]

Beltshire, Thomas, 4 Harrow St, Lant St, Southwark, London, carver (1835). [D]

Belton, William, Northgate, Darlington, Co. Durham, joiner and cm (1834). [D]

Benbow, Thomas, 20 Holiday Yd, Creed Lane, London(?), frame maker (1779). Took out a Sun Insurance policy in 1779 for £100 on his house. [GL, Sun MS vol. 270, p. 376]

Bence, George, High St, Wells, Som., cm (1830). [D]

Bence, John, 2 College St, Southampton, Hants., cm (1836). [D]

Bendall, John, Strutton Ground, Westminster, London, cm (1774). [Poll bk]

Bendall, Mathew, Old Bethlem, London, upholder (1772–80). Son of Mathew Bendall; app. to Edward Shipman on 4 November 1772. Admitted freeman of the Upholders' Co. by servitude on 5 July 1780. [GL, Upholders' Co. records]

Benge, Samuel, 19 Devreux Ct, Strand, London, u (1776–79). Took out Sun Insurance policies in 1776 for £200 on his house; and in 1779 for £200 on 38 Essex St, Strand. [GL, Sun MS vol. 249, ref. 369903; vol. 272, p. 525]

Benham, Harvey, Church St, Whitchurch, Hants., chairmaker etc. (1830). [D]

Benifold, —, Chatham, Kent, u (1807). [*Maritime Imperial Guide*]

Benifold, John, Chatham, Kent, cm (1790). [Poll bk] John Bennifold, cm and u, took out a Sun Insurance policy in 1783 for £1,100 of which utensils, stock and workshop accounted for £650. [GL, Sun MS vol. 317, p. 385] See John Bonifold.

Benifold, Thomas, Chatham, Kent, u and cm (1793). [D]

Benifold, W., St Margaret's Bank, Rochester, Kent, cm (1803). [D]

Benifold, W., 25 High St, Chatham, Kent, cm and u (1806). Sale of stock by auction announced, *Maidstone Journal*, 12 August 1806, of 'Home Manufactured CABINET & UPHOLSTERY FURNITURE' of 'Mr. W. Benifold . . . leaving that line of business . . . Purchasers may be given 3 months credit at interest on puchases over £50'.

Benison, E., 1 Devonshire St, Queen Sq., London, japan furniture manufacturer (1813). [D]

Benjamin, Abraham, 30 Minories, London, u (1820). [D]

Bennel, Henry, King St, St James's, London, cm (1749). [Poll bk]

Bennell, James, Colchester, Essex, carver and gilder (1830–32). Recorded at East Hill in 1832. [D; poll bks]

Bennet, Henry, London Rd, Spalding, Lincs., cm and u (1835–41). [D]

Bennet, J., Camberwell Green, London, cm and u (1822–23). [D]

Bennet, John, address unrecorded, cm (1803). Subscribed to Sheraton's *Cabinet Dictionary*, 1803.

Bennet, John, Liverpool, u (1835). App. to Bartholomew Tyrer in 1835. [Liverpool app. reg.]

Bennet(t), Joseph, Dale St, Liverpool, cm (1800–04). Recorded at 1 Stanley St in 1800 and 2 Batchelor St, 1800–03. Relinquished his business in favour of Sharples & Rainford, cm and u, of 4 Haymarket, who had 'extensive knowledge & practice . . . in the finest houses in London'. [D; *Liverpool Chronicle*, 22 February 1804]

Bennet, Richard, Fore St, Topsham, Devon, cm (1838). [D]

Bennet, Samuel, London, trade unrecorded (1779). The accounts of Hafod House, N. Wales, July 1779, record payment for a table of £1 16s 4d. [Twiston-Davies & Lloyd Johnes, *Welsh Furniture*, p. 6]

Bennet, Stephen, Bristol, carver (1715–39). Trading in Castle Precincts, 1721–22; parish of St Stephen in 1734; and parish of St James in 1739. [Poll bks]

Bennet, Thomas, London, cabinet app. (1756). App. to Charles Tutop of St Margaret, Westminster in 1756 for £15 15s. [V & A archives]

Bennet(t), Thomas, Belford, Northumb., cm, u and bell hanger (1827–34). [D]

Bennet(t), Thomas, Totness, Devon, cm and u (1830–38). Recorded at Lower Main St in 1830 and Fore St, 1837–38. Headed invoice showing Regency period furniture and trees framing an inscribed oval is preserved at the MMA, NY. [D; voters' list]

Bennet(t), William, South Shields, Co. Durham, cm and joiner (1827–34). Trading at E. King St in 1827. [D]

Bennett, Charles, 29 Broad St, Ramsgate, Kent, carver and gilder (1838). [D]

Bennett, David, 22 Garden Row, London Rd, London, cm (1808). [D]

Bennett, David, 58 Blackman St, London, furniture broker, u and cm (1819–25). [D]

Bennett, Edward, Chapel-en-le-Frith, Derbs., cm (1797–98). [D]

Bennett, Edward, London, carver, gilder, looking-glass and picture frame manufacturer (1809–39). Recorded at 28 Northampton St, Clerkenwell, 1809–11; 28 St John's St Rd, 1809; and 6 St John's St, 1816–39. Took out a Sun Insurance policy on 17 April 1809 for £200. [D; GL, Sun MS vol. 446, ref. 830227]

Bennett, George, Gloucester, cm (1740). Took app. named Goldsmith in 1740. [S of G, app. index]

Bennett, George, St Philip and Jacob, Bristol(?), cm (1742). Took app. named Harris in 1742. [S of G, app. index]

Bennett, George, Clarence Terr., London Rd, Tunbridge Wells, Kent, Tunbridge-ware manufacturer (1838–40). [D]

Bennett, Henry, Bow St, Bloomsbury, London, carver (1783). Took out a Sun Insurance policy in 1783 for £100 on his house. [GL, Sun MS vol. 313, p. 353]

Bennett, J., 9 Wyndham St, New Rd, Marylebone, London, carver and gilder (1835). [D]

Bennett, James, 4 Gt Marlborough St, London, u (1808). [D]

Bennett, James, 10 Broker Row, Moorfields, London, u (1814–15). [D]

Bennett, James, 106 Fore St, Exeter, Devon, u and auctioneer (1816–24). [D]

Bennett, John, Newgrove, Mile End, London, upholder

(1794–1801). Son of Charles Bennett of Wellclose Sq., London, hair dresser; app. to John Preston on 2 April 1794, and then to Thomas Savile on 7 February 1798. Admitted freeman of the Upholders' Co. by servitude on 6 May 1801. [GL, Upholders' Co. records]

Bennett, John, 5 Chapel Path, Sommers Town, London, clockcase and cm (1808). [D]

Bennett, John, 77 Broad Quay, Bristol, cm and u (1809). Declared bankrupt, *Exeter Flying Post,* 9 November 1809. [D]

Bennett, John, 62 Crosshall St, Liverpool, cm (1823). [D]

Bennett, Jonathan, Fore St, St Austell, Cornwall, cm and u (1823–24). [D]

Bennett, Joseph, Boston, Lincs., chairmaker (1761). Took app. named Melton in 1761. [S of G, app. index]

Bennet(t), Joseph, 164 Tottenham Ct Rd, London, upholder, cm and chairmaker (1804–17). Took out Sun Insurance policies on 19 July 1804 for £350 of which utensils and stock accounted for £250; and on 6 July 1809 for £500 of which stock and utensils accounted for £250, and open shed, stock and utensils in open yard, £150. [D; GL, Sun MS vol. 431, ref. 764331; vol. 448, ref. 832636]

Bennett, Joseph, London, cm, u and mathematical instruments maker (1808–39). Recorded at East Harding St in 1808; 4–5 Goldsmith Row, Gough Sq., 1822–23 and 1829; and 10 East Harding St, 1823–35. Took out Sun Insurance policies on 17 April 1822 for £400 on his dwelling house only; on 6 June 1822 for £400 of which stock and utensils accounted for £160; on 24 August 1820 for £300 of which stock and utensils accounted for £110; and on 10 February 1823 for £400 on new dwelling house only and £400 on household goods, stock and utensils. [D; GL, Sun MS vol. 487, ref. 970735; vol. 489, ref. 993315; vol. 490, ref. 991355; vol. 492, ref. 1001259, 1001260]

Bennett, Joseph, 35 Major St, Manchester, cm (1817). [D]

Bennett, Joseph, Bilston, Staffs., chairmaker (1818–34). Trading at Crown St in 1818. [D]

Bennett, Joshua, 17 Little Windmill St, London, cm and u (1822–23). [D] See Thomas Bennett.

Bennett, Peter, Mariner's Ct, Sykes St, Hull, Yorks., cm (1839). [D]

Bennett, Richard, 6 Portland Pl., Brighton, Sussex, chairmaker (1823–33). Son George Kenwood bapt. on 7 December 1823, and daughter Ellen on 3 March 1833. [D; E. Sussex RO, PR(bapt.)]

Bennett(s), Richard, Devonport, Devon, painter, glazier, carver, gilder, picture frame maker and victualler (1826). Sued as Richard Bennett, and listed under Court for relief of insolvent debtors, 13 June 1826, *The Alfred.* Case for insolvency adjourned to next circuit, *Exeter Flying Post,* 13 July 1826.

Bennett, Robert, Lee Crescent, Birmingham, Windsor and fancy chairmaker (1839). [D]

Bennet(t), Samuel, 'at the Sign of the Cabinet', Lothbury, London, cm (c. 1695–d. 1741). The name of this accomplished craftsman and the words 'LONDON FECIT' are found inlaid on two high-quality bureau-bookcases, on the pilasters framing the doors (Fig. 5). One of these, formerly in the Donaldson Coll. is veneered in burr elm, and the lower stage is 'bombé' in the Dutch style. The other, now in the V & A, is veneered in burr walnut and decorated with arabesque marquetry. A label found in the drawer of a third walnut bureau at HM Legation to the Holy See in Rome reads: 'This cabinet was made by Samuel Bennett at the Sign of the Cabinet in Lothbury. He Maketh and Selleth all kinds of Fine Cabinet-Work and Looking-Glasses, at Reasonable Rates'. A china cabinet veneered with oyster walnut and laburnum, c. 1695, inlaid on the inside doors 'SAMUEL

BENNETT' and 'MONMOUTH SQUARE' is recorded in the collection of Viscount Rothermere. [Cescinsky & Gribble, *English Furniture and Woodwork,* p. 276] Took out Sun Insurance policies on 30 September 1723 for £300 on goods and merchandise in 'The Cabinetmaker's' warehouse in Paul's Alley, Red Cross St, and in the yard; and on 10 October 1729 for £1,000 on stock in trade in his dwelling house. [DEF; GCM; V & A archives; *Conn.,* vol. 141, 1958, p. 83 (illus.); Fastnedge, *English Furniture 1500–1830,* p. 296; Wills, *English Furniture 1550–1760,* p. 191, pl. 24; p. 185; *C. Life,* 23 January 1942, p. 169; GL, Sun MS vol. 17, ref. 29950; vol. 29, ref. 48902]

Bennett, Samuel, Gloucester, cm (1757). Took app. named Williams in 1757. [S of G, app. index]

Bennett, Samuel, 29 Lamb St, Bristol, cm (1775). [D]

Bennett, Thomas, Chester, u (1721). Son of Joseph Bennett of Chester, surgeon, defunct; admitted freeman on 12 October 1721. [Chester freemen rolls]

Bennett, Thomas, London, upholder (1726–86). Trading at 2 St Anne's Passage, Noble Ct, 1778–86. Son of Thomas Bennett, barber; app. to William Kemp on 23 August 1726. Admitted freeman of the Upholders' Co. by servitude on 5 February 1746–47. Took app. named James Birt, 1757–69. [GL, Upholders' Co. records and Livery lists]

Bennett, Thomas, 133 Long Acre, London, cm (1774). [D]

Bennett, Thomas, 50 Lower East Smithfield, London, cm and u (1814). Took out a Sun Insurance policy on 12 May 1814 for £1,000 of which stock, utensils and goods in trust accounted for £700. [GL, Sun MS vol. 462, ref. 893786]

Bennett, Thomas, Norwich, u (1819–39). Addresses at Livingstone's Ct, Market Pl., 1830; Broad St, St Giles, 1836; and St Giles St, St Peter Mancroft, 1839. App. to John Ling and admitted freeman on 30 May 1819. [D; Norwich freemen reg.]

Bennett, Thomas, Load St, Bewdley, Worcs., cm (1820). [D]

Bennett, Thomas, Little Windmill St, London, bedstead maker (1820–27). Recorded at no. 17 in 1820, and no. 18, 1826–27. [D] See Joshua Bennett.

Bennett, W. C., Durdham Down, Bristol, turner and cm (1835–40). [D]

Bennett, William, Wokingham, Berks., cm (1777–98). Took out a Sun Insurance policy in 1777 for £200 of which £100 accounted for stock. [D; GL, Sun MS vol. 255, p. 490]

Bennett, William, Liverpool, cm (1803–34). Trading at Temple St, Dale St in 1804 and 166 Upper Frederick St in 1834. [D]

Bennett, William, Gorst Stacks, Chester, cm (1818–26). Admitted freeman on 13 May 1818. [Chester freemen rolls; poll bks]

Bennett, William, Stamford St, Ashton-under-Lyne, Lancs., painter, gilder, joiner, builder, auctioneer and appraiser (1824). [D]

Bennett, William, Merton(?), Devon, cm and window blind manufacturer (1826). [D]

Bennett, William, London, carver and gilder (1829–39). Addresses given at 2 Fisher St, Red Lion Sq. in 1829, and 8 Princes St, Bedford Row, 1835–39. [D]

Bennett, William, Deptford, Kent, featherbed maker and furniture broker (1838). [D]

Bennett & Co., 3 Jamaica Terr., Limehouse, London, cm (1820). [D]

Bennetto, Edward, High St, Falmouth, Cornwall, cm and u (1830). [D]

Bennington, George, Hull, Yorks., cm (1799). [Beverley poll bk]

Bennington, George, 5 Sarah Rd, Old St Rd, London, carver in wood, cm (1839). [D]

Bennington, Henry, address unrecorded (1765–69). Supplied a bedstead for Burton Constable, Yorks. [Humberside RO, DDC/40/4, day bk]

Bennington, Michael, Cambridge, chairmaker (1755). Eldest son of Michael Bennington, chairmaker. Admitted freeman in 1755. [Cambs. RO, Corp. day bk, p. 656]

Bennington & Co., address unrecorded, lampmakers (1832). On 13 August 1832 supplied 24 ornamental double branch socket lights for lustres in Library and Drawing Room for Windsor Castle, costing £29 6s. [PRO, LC 11/77]

Bennion, George, Chester, cm (1747–84). Trading in Windmill Lane, 1771, and Gorse Stacks, 1784. App. to Thomas Calkin of Chester, cm. Admitted freeman on 14 July 1747. [Chester freemen rolls; poll bks]

Bennion, Joseph, Manchester, cm (1825–28). Recorded at Old Bridge St with house at 3 Brown's Pl., Salford in 1825; and Paulden's Ct, Salford in 1828. [D]

Bennison, John, 9 Stable St, Manchester, cm (1794). [D]

Bennison, Thomas, 8 Devon(shire) St, Queen Sq., London, japan furniture manufacturer (1806–20). [D; *C. Life*, 23 April 1964, p. 1004]

Bennison, William, Baxtergate, Whitby, Yorks., cm (1823). [D]

Benois, F., address unrecorded. On 10 October 1814 supplied to the Prince Regent 2 cabinets ornamented with Florentine marble, mounted in ormolu, costing £1,000, another costing £500, and a small toilette box, £50. Another bill of the same date includes one small japanned screen, costing £8. [Royal Household accounts, PRO, LC 11/18]

Bensley, John, High St, Maidenhead, Berks., cm (1830). [D]

Bensley, Thomas, Montague Close, Southwark, London, glass grinder (1770). Took out a Hand in Hand Insurance policy in 1770 for £400 on warehouses. [GL, Hand in Hand MS vol. 110, p. 23]

Benson, —, London, cm (1793). Subscribed to Sheraton's *Drawing Book*, 1793.

Benson, Abram, 24 Peter's Lane, Liverpool, cm (1813–14). [D]

Benson, Jabez, 39 Warwick St, Golden Sq., London, looking-glass and picture frame maker (1819–39). [D]

Benson, James, Gainsborough, Lincs., cm (1823–41). App. to William Rollett in February 1823. Recorded at Bridge St in 1841. [D; Hull app. reg.]

Benson, John, High St, Knaresborough, Yorks., joiner and cm (1834–37). [D]

Benson, Joseph, St John St, Clerkenwell, London, japan furniture manufacturer (1803–25). Trading at no. 202, 1803–08 and no. 132, 1819–25. Recorded as 'Benson & Co., Royal Japan Manufacturers' in 1820. Took out a Sun Insurance policy on 11 May 1805 for £3,000 of which utensils in painting workshop accounted for £2,000, in cabinet workshop, £500, and in open shed and drying room, £500. Took out another policy on 17 October 1808 for £400 on household goods, including musical instruments, pictures and prints. [D; GL, Sun MS vol. 426, ref. 747602; vol. 444, ref. 821767]

Benson, Joseph, Temple St, Birmingham, cabinet case maker (1816–18). [D]

Benson(e), Obadiah, E. side of Corbett's Ct, N. side of Brown's Lane, Spittalfields, London, turner (1707–16). Took out Hand in Hand Insurance policies on 12 April 1707 and on 14 May 1716 each for £100 on the above rented house. [GL, Hand in Hand MS vol. 5, ref. 12958; vol. 16, p. 212]

Benson, Thomas, Gelderd's Yd, Highgate, Kendal, Westmld, chairmaker and turner (1805–29). [D]

Benson, Thomas, York, chairmaker (1820). Admitted freeman in 1820. [York freemen rolls]

Benson, Thomas, York, cm (1828). Son of Joseph Benson, glass cutter; app. to William Wilson, Sarah Carlton, Job Clarke and William Mowbray, cm, on 17 September 1828. [York app. reg.]

Benson, Thomas, 23 Greenfield St, Whitechapel, London, looking-glass manufacturer (1839). [D]

Benson, W., Christchurch, Hants., joiner and cm (1793). [D]

Benson, William, Cross Lane, Long Acre, London, cm (1740–74). App. to Richard Wood of York from 1 May 1740–47, very possibly meeting Chippendale as co-app., and later becoming his foreman in London. Benson was blamed for neglecting the firm's business in October 1768 owing to the death of his wife and brother, which took him into Yorkshire for six weeks. Subscribed to Chippendale's *Director*, 1754. A 'Benson commode' is recorded in the V & A archives. [Gilbert, *Chippendale*, p. 25; York app. reg.; poll bks; Heal]

Benson, William, Liverpool, cm (1796–1800). Trading at 1 Sir Thomas Ct, Dale St in 1796, and 25 Highfield St in 1800. [D]

Benson, William, Fisher St, Knaresborough, Yorks., joiner and/or cm (1837). [D]

Benstead, James, Northampton St, Cambridge, cm (1834–40). Child bapt. in 1834. [Cambs. RO, St Clement's PR(bapt.); poll bks]

Benstone, Daniel, Dudley St, Wolverhampton, Staffs., cm and chairmaker (1770). [D]

Bent, Daniel, Kingswinford, Staffs., cm and u (1834). [D]

Bent, Daniel, Brierly Hill, Stourbridge, Worcs., cm and u (1835). [D]

Bent, Joseph, 27 Drury Lane, London, cm and broker (1783). Took out a Sun Insurance policy in 1783 for £400 of which utensils, stock and goods accounted for £240. [GL, Sun MS vol. 313, ref. 478475]

Bent, Thomas, opposite Bridewell Bridge, Fleet Ditch, London, bed-joiner (1749–c. 1760). Trade card c. 1760, shows ponderous scrolls, tassells and finials surrounding inscription. [Banks Coll., BM; London rate bk]

Bent, William, 2 Court, Bristol St, Birmingham, cm (1835). [D]

Bentham, Joshua, Lancaster, chairmaker (1787–96). App. to J. Tyson in 1787 and admitted freeman, 1795–96. [Lancaster app. reg. and freemen rolls]

Bentle, James, Norwich, Norfolk, chairmaker (1756). App. to Isaac Hoyle of Norwich, chairmaker, for 5s in 1756. [V & A archives]

Bentley, James, Bow St, Hanley, Staffs., cm (1822). [D]

Bentley, James, High St, Stoke-on-Trent, Staffs., cm and u (1834–35). [D]

Bentley, James, Selby, Yorks., cm (1822). App. to George Brook of Selby in October 1822. [Hull app. reg.]

Bentley, James, 41 Mason St, Hull, Yorks., with home at 17 Charlotte St., joiner and cm (1838). [D]

Bentley, John, Ipswich, Suffolk, cm, toyman and turner (1805–39). Addresses given at Buttermarket, 1805–07, and Falcon St, 1839. [D]

Bentley, John, Dean's Gate, Newcastle-under-Lyme, Staffs., u and tailor (1822). [D]

Bentley, John & Joseph, Bury Lane, Bury, Lancs., cm (1834). [D]

Bentley, Michael, Knottingley, Yorks., joiner and cm (1832). [D]

Bentley, Richard, Tottenham Ct Rd, London, cm, u and original French polish maker (1820–28). Trading at no. 71, 1820–23, and no. 194, 1826–28. [D]

Bentley & Booth, Caroline St, Stayley Bridge, Lancs., cm, joiners and timber merchants (1825). [D]

Bentley & Co., 69 Tottenham Ct Rd, London, cm (1823). [D]

Benton, Charles, Market Rasen, Lincs., joiner and cm (1822–26). Trading at Oxford St in 1826. [D]

Benton, Edward, 19 Providence Row, Finsbury, London, bedstead maker (1835–39). [D]

Benton, J., 19 Holywell Row, Shoreditch, London, bedstead maker (1822–23). [D]

Benwell, —, address unrecorded, upholder. In June 1801 the account books of 2nd Lord Braybrooke of Audley End, Essex, mention payment to Benwell of £1 18s. [Essex RO, D/DBy/A376]

Benwell, Charles, Reading, Berks., cm, u and auctioneer (1784–1826). Took out a Sun Insurance policy in 1784 for £2,000. Trading in Minster St in 1820 and Friar St in 1826. Subscribed to Sheraton's *Drawing Book*, 1793. [D; poll bks; GL, Sun MS vol. 321, ref. 490180]

Benwell, Thomas, Southampton, Hants., cm, u and auctioneer (1823–39). Recorded at 57 High St, 1823–24; no. 56 in 1830; and Bernard St, 1834–39. [D]

Benyon, John, Founders' Hall Ct, Lothbury, London, cm and u (1839). [D]

Benyon, Joseph, Old Bridge St, Manchester, cm (1822). [D]

Benyon, Richard, Manchester, upholder (1781–88). Trading in Canon St, 1781, and Back King St, 1788. [D]

Benzie, James, London and Tenterden, Kent, cm (1801–39). Recorded at 1 Baker St, North Portman Sq., London in 1801; 1 Charlotte St, Rathbone Pl. in 1808; and High St, Tenterden, 1838–39. Took out a Sun Insurance policy on 21 May 1801 for £300. Polled at Maidstone, Kent in 1831. [D; GL, Sun MS vol. 419, ref. 718382] A Mr Benzie, cm, subscribed to Sheraton's *Cabinet Dictionary*, 1803.

Berberry, T., 10 King St, Bryanston Sq., London, cm (1822–23). [D]

Berbouse, Matthew, 32 Chandos St, London, cm (1790–93). [D]

Beresselaer, John, at 'The Three Crowns', in the Strand against Southampton St, London, cm (d. 1733). [Heal]

Berkley, William, West End, Kirbymoorside, Yorks., joiner and cm (1840). [D]

Bernard, Abraham, Wood St, Stratford-upon-Avon, Warks., cm (1828). [D]

Bernard, Arthur, Back Parliament St, Manchester, cm (1817). [D]

Bernard, Charles, Shrewsbury, Salop, u (1754). Took app. named Roe in 1754. [S of G, app. index]

Bernard, John, London, u (1697–1701). In 1697 supplied to St Paul's, London, '12 high fine Russia Leather Chaires, 1 Great Chaire, 50 velvet cushions, 2 great Chaires, frames of walnut finely carved', the bill totalling £129 12s 6d. Further bills survive, for £63 18s, £11 9s for curtains etc.; and £32 0s 8d in 1698–99 for 'one great chair' and 12 caned chairs. [*Wren Soc.*, vol. xv, pp. 36–37, 42, 48] Acted as third party in the lease of a messuage in Latchford in 1701. [Oxford RO, Misc. A1 I/1]

Bernard, John, Liverpool, u (1710). Admitted freeman on 19 January 1710. [Liverpool freemen reg.]

Bernard, John Cowley, Park St, Chester, cm (1812–18). Admitted freeman on 3 October 1812. [Chester freemen rolls and poll bk]

Bernardeau, Daniel, at 'Ye Golden Coffee Mill' in St Martin's Ct, near Leicester Fields, London, hardwood turner and oval frame maker (c. 1750–53). His trade card, embellished with a frame of foliate scrolls, flower swags, and trellis centring on a mask, reads, 'Dan¹. Bernardeau, Late Apprentice to Mr. Storer at Snow Hill — Makes all Sorts of Fine Bowling Green Bowls of which he has great Choice at his Shop at ye GOLDEN COFFEE-MILL . . . NB. Likewise Makes all Sorts of Fine Mahogany Stands for China Dishes & Turns all Sorts of Oval Frames &c.' [Heal] Mr Bernardeau, turner, carried out work at Felbrigg, Norfolk, being paid £2 12s 6d on 11 January 1753. [Norfolk RO, Felbrigg papers, WKC 6/37]

Bernardi (or y), Peter, London, picture frame maker, looking-glass silverer and weather-glass maker (1792–1800). As Bernardy of the Castle or Gt Saffron Hill he took out a Sun Insurance policy on 17 July 1792 for £100 of which utensils and stock accounted for £52. As Bernardi of 22 Chick Lane, West Smithfield, he took out insurance for £300. [GL, Sun MS vol. 388, p. 246; vol. 418, ref. 700434]

Bernardin, Joseph, 12 Little Carter Lane, London, u (1835–39). [D]

Berridge, William, 6 St Thomas's Tents(?), St Thomas's, London, cm (1793). Took out a Sun Insurance policy on 18 July 1793 for £150. [GL, Sun MS vol. 395, p. 534]

Berridge, —, St George's Row, St George's Fields, London, cm (d. 1803). Suicide and coroner's verdict of lunacy reported, *Gents Mag.*, June 1803.

Berrington, James F., Chester, cm (1818–26). Addresses at Frodsham St, 1818–19, and Love St, 1826. [Poll bks]

Berrington, John, Liverpool, cm and victualler (1813–34). Addresses at 2 Preston St in 1816, no. 3 in 1818, no. 5, 1821–23, and 5 Sydney St, St James's in 1834. [D]

Berrington, William, Chester, cm (1812–19). Recorded at Cow Lane in 1818; and St. Martin's Pl. and Bowling Green in 1819. [Poll bks]

Berrington, William, Chester, cm (1816–28). Recorded at Werburgh Lane in 1816 and Werburgh St, 1818–28. [D]

Berrisford, John, Newcastle-under-Lyme, Staffs., upholder (1784) [D]

Berrow, Henry, London, upholder (1699–d. by 1723). Recorded in 1714 having removed from 'The George & Mitre' in King St to 'The Crown' in Bow St. Admitted freeman of the Upholders' Co. on 5 July 1699. Dead by 1723. [GL, Upholders' Co. records; Heal]

Berrow, John, London, u (1718–29). Trading in Bucklersbury, St Stephen Walbrook, 1729. Son of Richard Berrow, Rector of Blanham, Beds. App. to William Ventris on 5 June 1718 and admitted freeman of the Upholders' Co. by servitude on 23 March 1726/27. Took out a Sun Insurance policy on 13 August 1729. [GL, Upholders' Co. records; GL, Sun MS vol. 28]

Berrow, Lancelot, parish of St Nicholas, Bristol, u (1721–22). [Poll bk]

Berry, —, Dover St, London, cm (1772). Supplied furniture to Sir J. Stanley, Bart, costing £82 2s 1d in 1772. [V & A Lib., MS 86B96]

Berry, E., address unrecorded (1776). Provided Henry Hoare with velvet chairs costing £24 3s 6d on 1 March 1776. [Hoare's Bank, London, private accounts]

Berry, Edward, Liverpool, carver (1839). App. to Alexander Wells in 1839. [Liverpool app. reg.]

Berry, George, Church St, Hackney, London, carver and gilder (1839). [D]

Berry, Henry, 5 Edgware Rd, Paddington, London, cm and broker (1820–22). Recorded at 5 Paddington Buildings in 1821. Took out Sun Insurance policies on 2 February 1820 for £100 of which stock, utensils and goods in trust accounted for £80; on 27 June 1820 for £200, stock, utensils and goods in trust accounting for £150; on 12 March 1821 for £300 of which stock, utensils and goods in trust accounted for £150 and workshop, £70; and on 13 March 1822 for £400, stock and utensils accounting for £150 and workshop, £100. [GL, Sun MS vol. 483, ref. 962841; vol. 483, ref. 968277; vol. 487, ref. 978278; vol. 493, ref. 989385]

Berry, James, Bristol, picture frame maker (1819–37). Addresses given at Mardyke, Hotwells, 1819–24; 47 Mardyke, 1825–28; and 11 Rosemary St, 1832–37. [D]

Berry, John, London, upholder (1761). [Canterbury freemen rolls]

Berry, John, 84 Castle St, Bristol, u (1775–84). [D; poll bks]

Berry, John, 129 Oxford St, London, carver and gilder (1789). [D]

Berry, John, 131 Fleet St, London, sworn upholder and carpet warehouse owner (1799–1803). Son of Edward Berry of Newland, Oxon., 'Narrow weaver', admitted freeman of the Upholders' Co. by redemption on the recommendation of 'Mr. Deputy Herring' on 6 March 1799. Subscribed to Sheraton's *Cabinet Dictionary*, 1803. [GL, Upholders' Co. records and Livery lists]

Berry, John, 3 Ryley's Gdn, Liverpool, u (1834–35). [D]

Berry, Joseph, St Michael's Hill, Bristol, furniture japanner (1814). [D]

Berry, Robert, Rotherham, Yorks., cm (1814–20). Trading at Westgate in 1814, and Bridge St, 1818–20. [D]

Berry, Thomas Henry, Clarence St, Cheltenham, Glos., cm, u and appraiser (1830). [D]

Berry, Thomas, Market Sq, Aylesbury, Bucks., cm and u (1830–39). [D]

Berry, Thomas, Church St, Romsey, Hants., cm and auctioneer (1840). [GL, Sun MS vol. 269, ref. 1340368]

Berry, William, Tunbridge Wells, Kent, cm (1821). Daughter Sarah Ann bapt. on 29 April 1821. [Kent RO, PR(bapt.)]

Berry, William, Chester, cm (1826–40). Trading at Bridge St in 1826 and Oulton Pl. in 1840. [D; poll bk]

Bersselaer, John, at 'The Three Crowns', over against Southampton St in the Strand, London, cm (1712–d. 1733). Took out Sun Insurance policies on 25 December 1712 'for his good', and on 4 October 1728 for £600, £400 on his premises and £200 on his glass in trade. Took app. named John Rylance on 4 July 1717. In 1733 he died and his goods were sold. [GL, Sun MS vol. 2, p. 150; vol. 27, ref. 45497; PRO, IRI/5; Harris, *Old English Furniture*]

Bertell, —, Gt Russell St, London, cm (1759). Mentioned in *Public Advertiser*, 11 January 1759 regarding the sale of a house, particulars to be had from Mr Bertell.

Bertie, William, 68 Norfolk St, Sheffield, Yorks., carver and gilder (1837). [D]

Bertie & Nichols, 79 Norfolk St, Sheffield, Yorks., carvers and gilders (1833). [D]

Bertin, James Charles, 39 Holywell Lane, Shoreditch, London, chair and sofa maker (1829–39). [D]

Berles, Rob., Nottingham (1791). Signed the *Nottingham Cabinet and Chair Makers' Book of Prices*, 1791, on behalf of the masters.

Bertram, C., 8 Devonshire Buildings, Gt Dover St, London, u (1839). [D]

Bertram, William, 100 Dean St, Soho, London, u (1839). [D] Brass-inlaid mahogany kneehole desk in French style recorded in private collection with stamped name and address on edge of central drawer. Marquetry side cabinet with serpentine front, pair of drawers enclosing shelves, short ormolu-mounted cabriole legs, and inlaid on satinwood ground with urns, flowers and military trophies is also recorded. [Sotheby's, 10 May 1968, lot 165]

Berwick, Anthony, Scarborough, Yorks., raff merchant and cm (1781). [D]

Besfield, R. & J., Pottergate St, St Gregory's, Norwich, Norfolk, cm, u and mahogany merchants (1822). [D]

Besley, Robert, Plymouth, Devon, cm and u (1812–36). Addresses given in Market Pl., 1814, and Exeter St, 1823–24. [D]

Bessant, —, address unrecorded (1755). The Holkham Hall accounts record payment of £4 14s 6d for 4 walnut drawers in 1755. [V & A archives]

Besset, John, Broker's Row, Moorfields, London, cm (1780–81). Trading at no. 5 in 1780 and no. 24 in 1781. Took out Sun Insurance policies in 1780 for £700 on houses, and in

1781 for £200, £150 on utensils and stock. [GL, Sun MS vol. 285, p. 16; vol. 294, p. 282]

Best, Mrs, address unrecorded (1718). Mentioned in the private accounts of the Countess of Jersey on 17 June 1718 supplying 'a Dutch Stoole' costing 3s. [PRO, C111/54, pt. 1]

Best, —, address unrecorded (1734). Provided 'a wainscot pair of chests of drawers' costing £1 8s for Holkham Hall in 1734. [V & A archives]

Best, —, address unrecorded, u (1803). Subscribed to Sheraton's *Cabinet Dictionary*, 1803.

Best, Charles Frederick, 60 Berner's St, Oxford St, London, upholder, estate and house agent (1815–37). [D]

Best, George, Beverley, Yorks., cm (1740). Supplied two dozen chairs in 1740 for Burton Constable, Yorks. [C. *Life*, vol. CLIX, pp. 1476–80]

Best, George, George St, Richmond, Surrey, carpenter, cm, u, paper hanger and undertaker (1822–34). Trade card shows Regency period furniture and drapes framing inscription. [D; Landauer Coll., MMA, NY]

Best, John, St Columb Major, Cornwall, cm, u, general furnishing warehouse, auctioneer and agent to the Royal Exchange Fire Office (1798–1839). Advertised in the *Royal Cornwall Gazette*, 29 August 1801 for 'a sober, steady footman' who 'must understand breweing etc.' In that year he purchased 'several dwelling houses & premises' for £235. [Cornwall RO, DDCF 988/1–2] Advertised again in the *Royal Cornwall Gazette*, 31 July 1802. He may be the 'Mr. Best, upholsterer' who subscribed to Sheraton's *Cabinet Dictionary*, 1803. On 10 March 1806, he advertised in the *Sherborne and Devon Mercury* 'To be Let by Private Contract' his 'large front shop, neatly fitted up with circular windows, two parlours, kitchen, and other offices, with six good bedrooms and several closets. And if required the tenant may be accomodated with a large range of workshops and lofts'. Best does not seem to have given up trading, since his name occurs in directories in 1824 and 1830, and a pair of late Regency mahogany turned daybeds bear the words 'John Best 1816 Columb', hand written in pencil on the rails. There may, however, be a John Best jnr, since a cm of that name married Sarah Trevesso Carbis on 29 June 1839. [Cornwall RO, DDCF 992] A mahogany veneered work table with cross-banded borders and stringing is in the Noël Riley Coll. and has John Best's long and informative trade label pasted underneath the lid (Fig. 25). [D; *Furn. Hist.*, 1976, pls 36B and 37]

Best, Joseph, 19 Upper Temple St, Birmingham, cm and u (1828–30). [D]

Best, Martin, Mason's Ct, Stockton-upon-Tees, Co. Durham, joiner and cm (1827). [D]

Best, Samuel, St Stephen's, Norwich, cm and u (1822). [D]

Best, William, at 'The Cabinet', Fleet Ditch near Holborn Bridge, parish of St Andrew, Holborn, London, cm (1722). Took out a Sun Insurance policy on 25 July 1722 for £500, house accounting for £150, and goods, £350. [GL, Sun MS vol. 14, ref. 25983]

Best, Read & Co., Lionel St, Birmingham, cabinet, dressing case and portable desk makers (1830). [D]

Bestall & Wildey, Pelham St, Nottingham, u (1834). [D]

Beswick, Anthony, Pickering, Yorks., cm (1834). [D]

Beswick, Matthew, Manchester, u (1814–25). Addresses given at 215 Deansgate, 1814–15; 67 Portland St, 1816–18; and 19 Garden Ct, Lower Byron St, 1825. [D]

Bethall, Richard, 3 Rotten Row, London, cm (1780). Took out a Sun Insurance policy in 1780 for £100 on his house. [GL, Sun MS vol. 88, p. 313]

Bethel, John & E., 13 Union St, Ancoats, Manchester, cm (1836). [D]

Bethell, James, Tewkesbury, Glos., cm (1817–22). Recorded as chairmaker at High St in 1820, and as James T. H. Bethell at Sun Yd in 1822. [D; PR]

Bethell, Joseph, 8 East Row, Scott Rd, Hoxton, Newtown, London, cm (1814). Took out a Sun Insurance policy on 4 May 1814 for £100, £40 on his house and £40 on stock. [GL, Sun MS vol. 462]

Betion, George, Jesus Lane, Cambridge, turner (1819). Child bapt. in the parish of All Saints in 1819. [Cambs. RO, PR(bapt.)]

Betjeman, Gilbert, 18 White St, Long Lane, London, cm and u (1839). [D]

Betley, Samuel, Redcross St, Southwark, London, u (1803–08). Took out Sun Insurance policies on 19 August 1803 for £200, and on 26 October 1803 for £700, stock and utensils accounting for £500. Insurance did not cover the drying of feathers. [D; GL, Sun MS vol. 426, ref. 752012; vol. 430, ref. 754090]

Betson, John, Sheridan St, Nottingham, chairmaker (1840). [D]

Betteley, Henry, Liverpool Rd, Burslem, Staffs., cm and u (1828). [D]

Betteley, John, Market St, Hanley, Staffs., cm and u (1828–35). Recorded at Market Sq. in 1834. [D]

Betteley, Thomas, Market Lane, Newcastle-under-Lyme, Staffs., chairmaker (1822). [D]

Betteley, William, Wem, Salop, chairmaker (1822). [D]

Betterton, Joseph, 21 Aldersgate St, London, house, sign and ornamental carver and gilder (1820–29). [D]

Bettison, William, Newark, Notts., cm (1767–90). Advertised in the *Cambridge Chronicle and Journal*, 28 March 1767, for two journeymen cm. Polled at Newark in 1790.

Bettison, William, Castlegate, Grantham, Lincs., cm, u and paper hanger (1819–28). Trading also as a paper hanger in 1826. [D]

Betton, Charles, address unrecorded, cm (1803). Subscribed to Sheraton's *Cabinet Dictionary*, 1803.

Betton, Richard, Wyle Cop, Shrewsbury, Salop, u (1796). [Shrewsbury burgess roll]

Bettoney, John, Oadby, Leicester, carver and gilder (1835). [D]

Bettridge, Josh., 'Worcester Wharf, top of Severn St, Birmingham, English and Foreign Timber Merchant, Mahogany and Rose Wood Veneers, Wood Turner, Carver Bedstead Pillar Manufacturer' (1838). Thus reads the heading of a bill dated 19 April 1838 for deal timber supplied to G. Webb of Astwood Court, near Droitwich, Worcs. [Worcs. RO, Vernon papers 7335/705:7/25/622]

Betts, Charles, 10 Gibson St, Lambeth, London, carver and gilder (1829). [D]

Betts, David jnr, 1 Charles St, Grosvenor Sq., London, u (1835–37). [D] See George Betts.

Betts, Edward, Butt lands, Wells, Norfolk, chair and cm (1839). [D]

Betts, George, 1 Charles St, Grosvenor Sq., London, u, cm and undertaker (1817–34). Declared bankrupt, *London Gazette*, 25 February 1834. [D] See David Betts.

Betts, J., Winchester, Hants., cm (1833–34). Declared bankrupt, *Liverpool Mercury*, 29 November 1833 and 21 March 1834.

Betts, James, Colebrooke St, Winchester, Hants., u (date unrecorded). [GL, Sun MS vol. 269, ref. 1343945]

Betts, James, St Swithun's St, Winchester, Hants., auctioneer, appraiser and u (1839). [D]

Betts, James, 5 Porter St, London(?), picture frame maker and hair weaver (1782). Took out a Sun Insurance policy in 1782 for £100, utensils, stock and goods accounting for £20. [GL Sun MS vol. 304, p. 563]

Betts, James, 53 Stanhope St, Clare Mkt, London, frame maker and gilder (1809–11). [D]

Bettys, Benjamin, Liverpool, u (1780–1811). Trading at back 22 Pool Lane in 1790; 24 School Lane, Paradise St, 1800–03; and 22 School Lane, 1807–11. Admitted freeman on 13 September 1780. [D; Liverpool freemen reg.]

Bevan, Edward, Liverpool, cm (1761–d. by 1780). Admitted freeman on 13 March 1761. [Liverpool freemen reg.]

Bevan, Edward, Air St, Piccadilly, London, carpenter and blind maker (1778). He was granted a patent for 'his new and peculiarly constructed Venetian Blinds' for which he charged at the rate of one shilling per sq. ft. So reads the heading of a bill dated 1778 to Sir Humphrey Morice, Comptroller to the Household of George II. [Heal]

Bevan, George, Oundle, Northants., cm (1840). [D]

Bevan, James, Kidderminster, Worcs., cm (1818–20). Trading at Barns St in 1818. [D]

Bevan, James, Load (or Lord) St, Bewdley, Worcs., cm, u and trunk maker (1822–35). [D]

Bevan, James, Hart St, Henley-on-Thames, Oxon., cm and u (1830). [D]

Bevan, John, 5 Little Hermitage St, London, cm (1784). [D]

Bevan, John, Bristol, cm (1794–95). Recorded at Merchant St, 1794, and Milk St, 1795. [D]

Bevan, Richard, parish of St James, Bristol, carver and gilder (1784). [Poll bk]

Bevan, Thomas, Liverpool, cm (1761). Admitted freeman on 23 January 1761. [Liverpool freemen reg.]

Bevan, William, Shrewsbury, Salop, chairmaker (1741–61). [Hereford poll bks]

Bevan, William, 130 Piccadilly, London, paper hanging manufacturer, decorator, carver and gilder (1825–29). Bill of 1827–28 for wallpapers and painting carried out for Lord Gwydir, London, has the heading: 'William Bevan, paper hanging manufacturer & dealer in plate glass, ornamental & house painter, carver & gilder, pictures cleaned back lined & restored with the greatest care'. [D; Lincoln RO, 2 ANC 6/202/67, stock account]

Beven, William, 122 Digbeth, Birmingham, cm (1770). [D]

Beverley, George, Malton, Yorks., cm (1823–40). Recorded at Yorkersgate in 1840. [D]

Bevil, John, Wandsworth Rd, London, carver and gilder (1829). [D]

Bevill, J., 39 Harleyford Pl., Kennington Common, London, carver and gilder (1837). [D]

Beville, Charles, Old Town, Clapham, London, cm and u (1826–32). Declared bankrupt, *London Gazette*, 16 September 1831, but listed in a directory of 1832. [D]

Beville, Francis, 48 Wells St, Oxford St, London, u (1813–39). Four late 17th-century armchairs and three reproductions at Ham House were covered in blue and gold velvet by Beville whose label, inscribed 'Francis Beville June 8th 1813', was discovered tucked into the webbing of one. He may have made the copies. [D; *Furn. Hist.*, 1974, pl. 3]

Beville, Francis, Town's-end, Kingston, Surrey, u, cm and paper hanger (1822–39). [D]

Bevin, William, 3 Market St, 3 George's Fields, London, chairmaker (1808). [D]

Bevington, Fletcher, Cow Lane, Chester, cm (1818). Admitted freeman on 18 May 1818. [Chester freemen rolls]

Bevington, Henry, Liverpool, cm (b. 1753–d. 1830). Son of Thomas Bevington, admitted freeman on 14 September 1780. Death reported, aged 77, *Liverpool Mercury*, 15 October 1830. [Liverpool freemen reg.]

Bevins, —, 122 Digbeth, Birmingham, cm (1777). [D]

Bevins, John, New St, Oundle, Northants., cm/joiner (1823). [D]

Bevis, John, Peterborough, Northants., u (1723–59). Took out Sun Insurance policies on 19 April 1723 on his dwelling house for £500, and on 13 September 1725 for £500, his house accounting for £300, and kitchens, wool chamber above, stable, wool house and feather chamber, £200. Declared bankrupt, *Gents Mag.*, August 1748, but trading again by 1752 when he took app. named Wilkinson, and in 1759, Aveling. [GL, Sun MS vol. 15, ref. 28227; vol. 21, ref. 36689; S of G, app. index]

Bew, Josiah, Lambourn, Berks., cooper and turner (1830). [D]

Bewdley, —, Fountain Ct, Strand, London, cm (b. c. 1777–d. 1802). Suicide, aged c. 25, recorded, *Gents Mag.*, October 1802.

Bewes, John, Lancaster (1815–40). [Westminster Ref. Lib., Gillow records]

Bewick, William, Blackwellgate, Darlington, Co. Durham, u (1827). [D]

Bewsher (or Bewster), William, Manchester, cm (1818–25). Addresses given at 19 Church St, 1818–25, and 3 Dale St in 1825. [D]

Bexfield, J., Norwich, cm (1812). [Gt Yarmouth poll bk]

Bexfield, James, Norwich and London, cm (1818–39). Recorded in London, 1830, and at Golden Ball St, Norwich, 1836–39. Enrolled as freeman of Norwich on 3 May 1821. [D; poll bks; Norwich freemen rolls]

Bexfield (or Baxfield), John, Norwich and London, cm (1818–31). Stated of Norwich in Gt Yarmouth poll bk of 1818, and of London, 1820 and 1830–31.

Bexfield, Joseph, Norwich, cm and u (1818–39). Trading at 103 Pottergate St, 1830–39. Admitted freeman of Norwich, not by apprenticeship, on 30 May 1821. A Joseph Bexfield is also recorded enrolling as a freeman on 24 February 1831. Former app. George Kew, admitted freeman on 3 May 1834. [D; poll bks; Norwich freemen rolls]

Bexfield, Joseph jnr, Norwich, cm (1830). Admitted freeman of Norwich, not by apprenticeship, on 24 July 1830. [Norwich freemen reg.]

Bexfield, Richard, Norwich, cm (1783–1830). Addresses given at 'The Goat', 14 Upper Goat Lane, 1801–02; Pottergate St, 1810; and Heigham, 1830. App. to Samuel Bream and admitted freeman of Gt Yarmouth in 1783. Polled at Norwich and Gt Yarmouth between 1790–1831. [D; poll bks; Gt Yarmouth freemen's calendar]

Bexfield (or Baxfield), William, Norwich and London, cm (1818–31). Stated of Norwich in Gt Yarmouth poll bks. of 1818, 1826, 1830–31, and of London in 1820.

Beydaels, Philibert, Brompton Pl., London, gilder and leather painter (1669). Advertised in 1669. [Harris, *Old English Furniture*]

Beyer, James, 13 Broad St, Carnaby Mkt, London, cm and u (1776–93). Took out Sun Insurance policies in 1776 for £1,400, utensils, stock and goods accounting for £800; in 1781 and 1783, each for £2,000, utensils, stock, goods and workshop accounting for £1,500. Probably the James Beyer who provided 'a Corner Cobert with a Shleid door' costing £1 1s, to Sir John Griffin Griffin of Audley End, Essex, in 1772; and 'a neat Rich Inlaid fire Screen' costing £3 3s in 1775. [Essex RO, D/DBy/A30/7, A33/12] Possibly the Mr Beyer, cm, named in the Longford Castle accounts in 1775, being paid £7 17s 6d. [D; V & A archives; GL, Sun MS vol. 246, p. 446; vol. 290, p. 561; vol. 313, p. 131]

Beyer, James, Gt Portland St, London, cm (1787). Declared bankrupt, *Gents Mag.*, 1787.

Beyer, James, Shayer St, Manchester Sq., London, u (1796). Declared bankrupt, *Billinge's Liverpool Advertiser*, 26 December 1796.

Beynon, Rowland, Manchester, u (1781–88). Addresses given at Canon St in 1781 and Back King St in 1788. [D]

Bezilley, George, Sandgate, Newcastle, cm and/or carpenter (1788). [D]

Bianchi, John, 16 Tib St, Manchester, carver and gilder (1825). [D]

Bianchi, Nicholas, High St, Braintree, Essex, carver and gilder (1839). [D]

Bianchi, Peter, 263 Bradford St, Birmingham, picture frame and looking-glass maker (1839). [D]

Bibby, George, Liverpool, cm (1794–1805). Recorded at both 11 Powell Sq. and Dale St in 1805. App. to John Eden in 1794 and Edward Myers in 1795. In 1802 he petitioned freedom on servitude to Eden, and by assignment to Myers, paying 6s 8d. Admitted freeman on 7 July 1802. [D; Liverpool freemen's committee bk and reg.]

Bibby, Hannah, Hanover St, Liverpool, upholder (1796–1827). Recorded variously at nos 27–32. [D]

Bibby, Harriet, 28 Hanover St, Liverpool, upholder (1816). [D]

Bibby, John, 7 Hanging Bridge, Manchester, cm (1825). [D]

Bibby, Thomas, Prince's St, Dale St, Liverpool, cm (b. 1747–d. 1830). Recorded at no. 23, 1790–1804; no. 21 in 1805; no. 20, 1807–10; and no. 23, 1811–21. App. to Joseph Harling and admitted freeman on servitude on 11 September 1780. Death reported, aged 83, *Liverpool Mercury*, 29 January 1830. [D; Liverpool freemen reg.]

Bick, Mrs, Cheltenham, Glos., u (1839–40). [D]

Bick, John, Upton-upon-Severn, Worcs., cm (1798). Declared bankrupt, *Billinge's Liverpool Advertiser*, 11 June 1798.

Bickadike (Bickerdike or Bickersdike), John, Newcastle, cm (1734–59). Supplied many items to Gibside, Co. Durham, between 18 July 1734 and 31 December 1759, including mahogany chairs, tables, wainscotting, 'hand boards', 'walnut tree chairs, wainscotte Tables and Drawers', 'Beech Plank bought for ye kitchen table', 'a small glass', and various repairs to furniture. Took app. named Mastermann in 1741. [Durham RO, Strathmore MS, D/St/V986; S of G, app. index]

Bickerdike, John, Gateshead, Co. Durham, cm (1751–56). Took apps named Thompson in 1751 and Hamilton in 1756. [S of G, app. index]

Bickers, John William, 107 Old St, St Luke's, London, cm and chairmaker (1820–37). [D]

Bickerstaff(e), Edward, Liverpool, u (1839). App. to William Bickerstaffe. Admitted freeman on 30 July 1839. [Liverpool freemen reg.]

Bickerstaff, John, 102 Wardour St, London, japanner and gilder (1823). [D]

Bickerstaff(e), William, Liverpool, cm, u and cabinet wood turner (1820–39). Recorded at 56 Whitechapel and 23 Thomas St in 1823; the former only from 1824–29; 18 Leece St in 1834; and 10 Whitechapel in 1839. App. to James Gill and admitted freeman on 9 March 1820. As an u he took apps named Edward Bickerstaffe and John Webster in 1823, John Fogg in 1825, Joseph Cuddy, Sidney Heskin and Joshua Ashcroft in 1827, and William Hayes in 1830. As a cabinet wood turner, he took John Jones jnr in 1827. [D; Liverpool freemen reg. and committee bk]

Bickerstaff, William, 2 Little Vere St, Piccadilly, London, carver and gilder (1829). [D] Possibly the Bickerstaff of 2 Little Vine St, Piccadilly, whose trade card reads: 'CARVER & GILDER, PICTURE CLEANER, FURNITURE JAPANNER and ORNAMENTAL PAINTER, Chairs, Sofas, Commodes, Cornices, India Cabinets re-japanned or repaired. Looking Glass & Picture Frames made to order, old ones re-gilt. Varnishing & polishing. House painting. Graining &c. on lowest terms'. [V & A Print Dept, Box GG65, 12875. 3]

Bickley, D., Devonport, Devon, cm (1839). Declared bankrupt, *Exeter Flying Post*, 24 October 1839.

Bickley, John, Rugeley, Staffs., cm (1741). Took app. named Lea in 1741. [S of G, app. index]

Bickley, John, London, u, cm and gilder (1770). Carried out composition and gilding work at Chatsworth House, Derbs. in the mid 1770s, and in 1777 was paid for furniture and upholstery totalling £1813 10s 6d, including 'the Bookcase in the Great Apartment', costing £34 17s. [Chatsworth papers, accounts, p. 276; *Burlington*, June 1980, p. 416]

Bickley, John, Theobald's Row, London, upholder (1784). [D]

Bickley, William, Exeter, Devon, u (1754). Took app. named Grant in 1754. [S of G, app. index]

Bickley, William, Worcester St, Wolverhampton, Staffs., chairmaker and turner (1780). [D]

Bickmore, John, 7 Friar's St, Gt Surrey St, London, carver and gilder (1832). [D]

Biddell, Thomas, Load St, Bewdley, Worcs., cm (1830). [D]

Bid(d)en & Moorey, Ormond Row (or Pl.), Richmond, Surrey, cm and u (1826–39). [D]

Bidgood, John, Bristol, cm and undertaker (1831–40). Trading at 23 Limekiln Lane, 1831–34, and 24 College St, 1835–40. [D]

Bidman, Joseph, Lancaster, (1797). Named in the Gillow records in 1797 working on a wardrobe. [Westminster Ref. Lib., Gillow vol. 344/97, p. 1340]

Bielby (or Beilby), Matthew, Bridlington, Yorks., cm and u (1823–40). Recorded in High St, 1823–34; Queen St, 1828–40; and Quay St in 1840. [D]

Bielby, Richard, 32 Roper St, Hull, Yorks., cm (1838–39). [D]

Bielby (or Beilby), William, St John's Gate, Bridlington, Yorks., cm and u (1823–34). [D]

Bielby (or Beilby), William, Willow Gate, Pickering, Yorks., cm and joiner (1828–30). [D]

Bielefield & Haselden, London, papier mâché furniture and looking-glass makers (1833–40). [Loudon's *Encyclopaedia*, p. 343; Westminster Ref. Lib., H. 845, pp. 22–23; BM, 786m 28, 1 and 2]

Biers & Stringer, 13 Broad St, Soho, London, cm, u and undertakers (1839). [D]

Biffin, James, St Pancras, Chichester, Sussex, chairmaker and turner (1826–32). In partnership with John and Charles Biffin in East Gate in 1832. [D] Chair of imitation bamboo, c. 1800, recorded inscribed 'J. BIFFIN'. [V & A archives]

Bigbie, James, Salisbury, Wilts., cm (1757). Took app. named Kiddle in 1757. [S of G, app. index]

Bigelston (or Biggleston), William, 19 King St, Soho, London, chair japanner (1805–11). Took out a Sun Insurance policy on 17 June 1805 for £300 on household goods. [D; GL, Sun MS vol. 434, ref. 777142]

Bigg, Thomas, Smith, John & Samuel, James, Peterborough Ct, Fleet St, London, cm and chairmakers (1739). Took out a Sun Insurance policy on 17 March 1739 for £600. [GL, Sun MS vol. 54, p. 342]

Biggam (or Bigham), William, Plumb St, King St, Liverpool, with shop in Brunswick St, cm (1800–14). [D]

Bigger, William, London, u (1793). Subscribed to Sheraton's *Drawing Book*, 1793.

Biggin, William, Liverpool, cm (d. 1814). Death on 22 June 1814 reported, *Liverpool Mercury*, 5 August.

Biggins, George, Liverpool and Wrexham, Wales, u (1747–71). Polled at Chester in 1747 'of Liverpool', and in 1771 'of Wrexham' and non-resident of Chester.

Biggins, Griffith, Chester, u (1732). Son of John Biggins of Chester, 'innholder defunct'; admitted freeman on 14 September 1732. [Chester freemen rolls]

Biggins, Samuel, Liverpool, cm (1790). Admitted freeman on 24 June 1790. [Liverpool freemen reg.]

Biggs, —, Gt Portland St, Oxford Mkt, London, cm and chairmaker (1761). Published statement regarding working conditions, *Lloyd's Evening Post and British Chronicle*, 30 September to 2 October and 9–12 October 1761; reply to announcement, *British Chronicle*, 14–16 October 1761.

Biggs, Abraham, Greenwich, London, u (1761). Discharge from Debtors' Prison reported in *London Gazette*, 26 September 1761.

Biggs, Ambrose, 11 Fontenoy St, Dale St, Liverpool, chairmaker (1790). [D]

Biggs, John, 93 Tottenham Ct Rd, London, auctioneer and cm (1811). [D]

Biggs, John, 67–68 Milk St, Bristol, carver and gilder (1826–39). [D]

Biggs, John, Holloway Pl., Holloway, London, u etc. (1838). [D]

Biggs, Joseph, 16 and 18 Castle St, Birmingham, cm and joiner (1767–81). [D]

Biggs, Richard, High Wycombe, Bucks., chairmaker (b. c. 1801–41). Seven children bapt. between 1824–36. Aged 40 at the time of the 1841 Census. [PR(bapt.)]

Biggs, Thomas, 57 Rathbone Pl., Oxford St, London, cm, portable desk manufacturers (1820–29). [D]

Biggs, Thomas, West Wycombe, Bucks., chairmaker (b. c. 1821–41). Aged 20 at the time of the 1841 Census.

Biggs, William, Lyncombe and Widcombe, Som., carver (1784). [Poll bk]

Biggs, William, 31 Conduit St, 30 Ward's Row, London, furniture carver and gilder (1839). [D]

Biggs & Armstrong, 74 Gt Titchfield St, Oxford Mkt, London, cm and u (1820–37). [D]

Bigmore, Job, 1 White St, London, stained wood, japanned and Windsor chairmaker (1839). [D]

Bignall, Thomas, 1 Robert Terr., Commercial Rd East, London, cm and u (1839). [D]

Bigrave, John, address unrecorded, upholder (1707–18). Son of Thomas Bigrave, Cardington Cotton end, Beds., yeoman. App. to John Howard on 6 August 1707. Admitted freeman of the Upholders' Co. by servitude on 5 February 1717–18. [GL, Upholders' Co. records]

Bilby, Thomas, Cadogan Mews, Chelsea, London, cm and u (1823). [D]

Biles & Co., Ambrose, Blandford, Dorset, joiners and cm (1732). Took out a Sun Insurance policy on 9 June 1732 for £700, of which £100 accounted for a house in Salisbury St, £100 for workshops and chambers, £50 for household goods, and £450 for stock in workshop. [GL, Sun MS ref. 58077]

Bill, Richard & George, 12, 13 and 14 Summer Lane, Birmingham, with depot at 17 Ave Maria Lane, London, papier mâché and japan works (1818–39). Trade card reads: 'Japanners & manufacturers of Paper Trays of all shapes, Cabinet Toilette, work & Card Boxes, Tables, Table Tops, Pole & Hand Screens, Tea Chests, Caddees, Quadrille Pools. Card Racks, Snuff Boxes, Pannels of miniature Frames & Veneering & every other Description of Article in Papier Mache'. [Bodleian Lib., Oxf., Johnson Coll.; *Furn. Hist.*, 1974] Advertised in Pigot's *Nat. and London Directory*, 1839, 'their most splendid specimens of articles . . .'.

Billam, Edward, Nesham Sq. and Coronation St, Sunderland, Co. Durham, cm (1827). [D]

Billerby, John, Micklegate, York, cm, u and undertaker (1823). [D]

Billes, J., 13 Providence Building, New Kent Rd, London, cm and chairmaker (1837). [D]

Billing, George, opposite Exeter Exchange in the Strand, London, broker and upholder (1753). Took out a Sun

Insurance policy on 12 October 1753 for £500, £180 accounting for utensils and stock in trade, and £20 for wearing apparel. [GL, Sun MS vol. 102, ref. 137896]

Billing, J. S., 5 St Mary's Hill, cm, u and undertaker. Label recorded on oak low boy, c. 1760.

Billings, John, Drury Lane, Westminster, London, upholder (1774–76). Probably the 'Billings London Drury Lane' included in a list of fashionable furniture makers compiled by the Duchess of Northumberland, c. 1776. [Gilbert, *Chippendale*, p. 154; poll bk]

Billinghurst, Edward, Brighton, Sussex, cm and u (1837–39). Trading at King St in 1837 and 125 Western Rd in 1839. [D; poll bk]

Billington, George, Chester, cm (1819). Admitted freeman on 20 October 1819. [Chester freemen rolls]

Billington, John, Southgate, Wakefield, Yorks., cm, u, joiner, builder, architect (1830–37). [D] See William Billington.

Billington, Thomas, Stepney, London, cm (1757–61). Declared bankrupt, *Gents Mag.*, June 1757. Discharge from Debtors' Prison announced, *London Gazette*, 7 April 1761.

Billington, Thomas, High St, Manchester, cm (1788). [D]

Billington, William, Southgate, Wakefield, Yorks., cm and u (1828–37). [D] See John Billington.

Billis, Joseph, London, cm and u (1839). [D]

Billson, G., 10 Blenheim St, Manchester Sq., London, cm (1826–27). [D]

Bil(l)son, 26 Marshall St, Golden Sq., London, cm and u (1827–39). [D]

Billson, George, 26 King St, Argyle Pl., London, cm and u (1839). [D]

Billson, Thomas, 16 Blenheim St, Oxford St, London, cm (1809–11). [D]

Billson, Thomas, London, carpenter and cm (1835–39). Addresses given at 346 Oxford St in 1835, 7 Gt Titchfield St, 1837 and 4 Little Charlotte St, 1839. [D]

Billson, William, 28 Rupert St, Haymarket and 4 Mead St, London, cm and u (1829–39). [D]

Billups, Thomas, Cambridge, joiner (1670–1723). Possibly the son of William Billups, he is recorded in the accounts of Christ's College. In partnership with Cornelius Austin in 1711 undertook for St John's College the altering of the bookcase in the Library and the supplying of stools and tables. [Archives of Christ's and St John's Colleges]

Billups, William, Cambridge, joiner (1664–1688). William Billups is first recorded when, with his father Richard and Cornelius Austin, he signed a contract on 10 January 1664 with Pembroke College to undertake the wainscoting and joinery work for the interior of the new Chapel. Payments are recorded in the accounts of Christ's College to William Billups between 1682–88. Most are for general joinery work but on 23 January 1682/83 he was paid £5 10s for a 'dozen and a half Chair frames for ye College Parlour, and for one great Chair frame and for new Tables there'. The chairs were upholstered in leather by Thomas Peters. The tables would appear to have been 'Four Spanish tables' listed in the Parlour in an inventory of 1688. [Willis & Clark, *Architectural History of the University of Cambridge*; archives of Christ's College; *Cambridge Royal Commission on Historical Monuments*] See Thomas Peters. R. W.

Billyard, William, Beardsall's Row, Retford, Notts., cm (1832). [D]

Bilston, William, Chester, cm (1824–28). Trading at Trinity St in 1824 and St Werburgh St in 1828. Admitted freeman on 9 October 1824. [D; poll bk; Chester freemen rolls]

Bilton, Peter, Kay's Entry, Blanket Row, Hull, Yorks., cm (1839). [D]

Bilton, Ralph, parish of St Oswald, Durham, spinning-wheel

maker (1718). Daughter bapt. on 24 March 1718. [PR (bapt.)]

Binchs, J. D., 40 Willington St, Woolwich, London, cm and u (1838). [D]

Bincks, Andrew, address unrecorded, upholder (1719). Admitted freeman of the Upholders' Co. by patrimony on 14 October 1719. [GL, Upholders' Co. records]

Binder, William, Marylebone Rd, London, cm and u (c. 1830). Upholstered easy chair with simulated bamboo frame recorded bearing label.

Bindon, Stephen, Eastbourne, Sussex (c. 1750). Mahogany kneehole desk recorded with the words 'Stephen Bindon, Eastbourne' inlaid in ivory on the centre drawer. Possibly name of owner rather than maker. [*Collector's Guide*, January 1951]

Binel, Samuel, address unrecorded, cm (1803). Subscribed to Sheraton's *Cabinet Dictionary*, 1803.

Binge, John, 4 Paradise Sq., Sheffield, Yorks., cm and u (1797–98). [D]

Bingham, Daniel, Cirencester, Glos., cm (1793–1833). Trading at Park St, 1822–23. Children bapt. in 1830 and 1833. [D; PR(bapt.)]

Bingham, David, Cirencester, Glos., cm and u (1822–30). Trading at Park St in 1822 and Black Jack St in 1830. [D]

Bingham, Davis, Newport St, Covent Gdn, London, carver (1749). [Poll bk]

Bingham, John, Leeds, Yorks., journeyman cm (1791). Listed in the *Leeds Cabinet and Chair Makers' Book of Prices*, 1791.

Bingham, William, Atherstone, Warks., cm, grocer and tea dealer (1793). [D]

Bingham, William, 3 Henrietta St, Cheltenham, Glos., cm, u and paper hanger (1820–22). [D]

Bingley, —, Chester(?), u (1720). Supplied items to Erddig, Clwyd, being paid £1 17s on 13 June 1720 'for blew Damask & Double Tick'; 1s 6d on 5 December for 'two or three parcells from Chester'; and £1 17s 9d on 21 July 'for Ruggs etc.' May have been Phillip Hunt's man sent to fix upholstery. [V & A archives] Probably either Ralph or Randle Bingley.

Bingley, Gabriel, Salop, u (1732–47). [Chester poll bks]

Bingley, Ralph, Chester, u (1719–34). Son of John Bingley of Chester; admitted freeman on 20 October 1719. Took apps named Edward Dodd in 1723, John Bridge, 1730, and John Elrington, 1734. Former app. William Broadbent admitted freeman in 1746. [Poll bk; Chester freemen rolls and app. reg.] Probably brother of:

Bingley, Randle, Chester, u (1697–1722). Son of John Bingley of Chester, chandler, and app. to Abner Scholes, u of Chester. Admitted freeman on 13 July 1697. Took apps named Hawkins in 1712 and Bennett in 1722. Mayor of Chester, 1719–20. [Chester freemen rolls; S of G, app. index]

Bings, John, Sheffield, Yorks., cm (1793). Subscribed to Sheraton's *Drawing Book*, 1793.

Binigan, George, Chester, cm (1747). [Poll bk]

Bining, William, Bolt Lane, Gloucester, cm and chairmaker, u and hardware dealer (1820–23). [D]

Binkley, George, 28–30 Clumber St, Nottingham, cm, u and furniture broker (1832–41). Recorded also at no. 2 as cm, u and paper hanger, in 1835. [D]

Binks, Arthur, Sunderland St, Houghton-le-Spring, Co. Durham, joiner and cm (1827). [D]

Binks, Francis, 13 Crescent Jewin St, and 12 Cripplegate, London, cm and undertaker (1817–23). [D]

Binks, John, 28 Mason St, Hull, Yorks., cm, u and paper hanger (1826–29). [D]

Binks, Joseph David, London, cm and u (1832–39). Addresses given at Green End St, Woolwich in 1834, and Wellington St in 1839. [D]

Binks, Thomas, Catterick, Yorks., joiner and cm (1823). [D]

Binnall, James, 473 Strand, London, frame maker (1786). [D]

Binnington, Christopher, Church St, Hull, Yorks., with home at Raikes St, Dry Pool, joiner and cm (1826–29). [D]

Binninton, Foster, High St, Bridlington, Yorks., cm (1840). [D]

Binnington, James, York, carver and gilder (1801–08). Son of Caroline Binnington; app. to William & John Staveley, carvers and gilders, on 14 August 1801. Admitted freeman by order in 1808. [York app. reg. and freemen rolls]

Binnington, James, Sculcoates, Hull, Yorks., app. cm (1822). App. to Richard Binnington in May 1822, not his father. [Hull app. reg.]

Binnington, Richard, Hull, Yorks., cm and broker (1803–31). Recorded at 8 Wellington Mart and 5 Newton St in 1826, and 7 Broadley Sq. in 1831. App. to John & George Chapman of Hull on 14 March 1803 as cm and paper hanger. Trading as Binnington & Shepherd at Newton St, 1821–23, with home at Leadenhall Sq. Took app. named James Binnington, not his son, in May 1822. [D; Hull app. reg.]

Binns, —, address and trade unrecorded (late 18th century). Set of 14 dining chairs stamped 'BINNS' under the seat rails sold Christie's, 29 November 1984, lot 35 (illus.).

Binns, Edward, Middle St, Cloth Fair, Aldersgate, London, cabinet inlayer (1776). Took app. in 1776. [PRO, IRI/37; *Burlington*, June 1980, p. 416]

Binns, Edward, London, joiner, cm and carver (1772–84). App. to J. Wakefield in 1772. Admitted freeman of Lancaster, 1782–83 when stated of London. Polled at Lancaster in 1784, resident of London. [Lancaster app. reg. and freemen rolls]

Binns, Edward, Mount St, Grosvenor Sq., London, cm, u and appraiser (1791–1820). Recorded at 1 Burden St with shop at Mount St in 1791; 99 Mount St, 1803–11; and no. 102, 1810–20. Took out Sun Insurance policies on 13 January 1791 for £200, £50 accounting for utensils, stock and goods in trust, £48 for stock in shop in Burden St and £50 for utensils and stock in shop in Mount St; on 17 April 1805 for £1,050, utensils, stock and goods in trust accounting for £450, a house at 10 Mount St in tenure, £100, wareroom behind, £50, and utensils, stock and goods in trust, £50. Took out further policies on 2 April 1807 for £1,050, utensils and stock accounting for £550; and on 14 April 1810 for £2,400, of which house, workshops and goods accounted for £1,800, houses at 103–04 Mount St, £500, and warehouse behind, stock, utensils and goods, £100. Submitted a bill in November 1816 for furnishing a house for Lady Viscountess Kirkwale. Subscribed to Sheraton's *Drawing Book*, 1793, and named in his list of master cabinet makers, 1803. [D: Sun MS ref. 579092; vol. 434, ref. 775615; vol. 440, ref. 800956; vol. 453, ref. 844451; PRO, C13 710/33]

Binns, Edward & George, 35 Grafton St, London, cm and u (1822–23). [D] See Samuel & George Binns.

Binns, J., London, cm (1827–29). Trading at Crown Row, Mile End Rd, 1827–28, and 4 High St, Stepney, 1829. [D] See Nimrod Binns.

Binns, John, Cowling, near Colne, Yorks., cm (1822). [D]

Binns, John, Nantwich, Cheshire, cm (1827–36). Son Thomas bapt. on 31 March 1827, and George on 14 December 1836. [PR(bapt.)]

Binns, Joseph, Sunderland, Co. Durham, cm (1745). Took app. named Richardson in 1745. [S of G, app. index]

Binns, Joseph, London, cabinet inlayer, shell and stringing maker, buhl manufacturer (1776–1829). Addresses given at 24 Duke St, 1792–1811; 6 Albion Buildings, Bartholemew Close in 1788; and 5 Goswell Rd, Frederick Pl., 1813–29. Specialised in inlaying, playing a part in the revival of buhl work in London after c. 1822. Trade card, c. 1795, reads 'Oval Shell & Stringing Maker, Dyed Woods of Different Colours, Oval Inlay'd Tea Trays &c.' [Heal Coll., BM] Took apps named Richard Barnes on 2 April 1788, and Thomas Gosling on 12 May 1796, for eight years at £10. [PRO, IRI/37] Subscribed to Sheraton's *Drawing Book*, 1793, and named in his list of master cabinet makers, 1803. [D; *Burlington*, June 1980, p. 416] A Joshua Binns, cabinet inlayer, perhaps mis-named, is also recorded at Albion Buildings in 1793.

Binns, Nimrod, Stepney, London, cm and carpenter (1822–39). Trading at 4 High St, 1822–24, and Ocean Rd, 1835–39. Took out Sun Insurance policies on 26 August 1822 for £350, of which £150 accounted for shop, stock and utensils; and on 1 March 1824, for £400. [D; GL, Sun MS vol. 489, ref. 995504; vol. 497, ref. 1014522] Probably Nimrod Burns.

Binns, Samuel & George, 35 Grafton St East, 243 High Holborn, and 6 Devonshire St, London, cm, chair and sofa makers and u (1826–39). Declared bankrupt, *London Gazette*, 24 June 1826. [D]

Binns, Thomas, Sunderland, Co. Durham, u (1765). Declared bankrupt, *Gents Mag.*, March 1765.

Binns, Thomas, Church Passage, New Compton St, London, cm and chairmaker (1786–93). Took out Sun Insurance policies on 23 May 1786 for £100, utensils etc. accounting for £40; and on 24 June 1791 for £300, utensils, stock and goods in trust accounting for £190. Subscribed to Sheraton's *Drawing Book*, 1793. [GL, Sun MS vol. 337, p. 346; vol. 373, ref. 584771]

Binns, Thomas, St Giles, London, cm (1790). Took app. named George C. Herbert on 23 February 1790. [PRO, IRI/34]

Binsted, John, High St, Alton, Hants., u and cm (1839). [D]

Binste(a)d, Peter, Winchester, Hants., cm and u (1775–79). Recorded as Binsted, cm of Winchester in 1775, and as Binstead, u of Winton in 1779. Took out Sun Insurance policies in 1775 for £300 on a house, and in 1779 for £200. [GL, Sun MS vol. 236, p. 267; vol. 274, p. 125]

Binstead, William, North St, Chichester, Sussex, cm and u (1822–39). [D]

Bintcliff, Charles, Rastrick, Yorks., joiner and cm (1834). [D]

Bintliff, George, 173 Stamford St, Ashton-under-Lyne, Lancs., cm and joiner (1834). [D]

Birch, —, Duke St, London, cm (1741). Death of daughter reported, *Daily Post*, 7 October 1741.

Birch, Charles, 15 Mercer St, London, carver (1774–82). Took out a Sun Insurance policy in 1782 for £300 on a house. [GL, Sun MS vol. 303, p. 647; poll bk]

Birch, Charles, Manchester, cm (1802–22). Addresses given at 38 John St, Salford in 1802, 11 Bridge St, Manchester, 1814–18, and no. 19, 1821–22. [D] See Thomas Birch.

Birch, Francis, Uppingham, Rutland, cm (d. 1791). Death reported, *Gents Mag.*, March 1790.

Birch, Geof., Cannock, Staffs., cm, u, paper hanger and manufacturer of 'the German sprung matresses' (c. 1820–30). Trade card shows sofa, chairs, table, cabinet and domed bed. [Heal Coll., BM]

Birch, George, 1 Lower Pershore St, Birmingham, cm and chairmaker (1839). [D]

Birch, John, Long Acre, London, carver (1774). [Poll bk]

Birch, John, 3 Back Ridgefield, Manchester, cm and billiard table maker (1825). [D]

Birch, John, Shrewsbury, Salop, u and cm (1825–28). Recorded at Belmont in 1825 and Castle St, 1828. [D; Shrewsbury burgess roll]

Birch, Joseph, Church St, Birmingham, gilder (1818). [D]

Birch, Josiah & Son, address unrecorded, u (1785). Supplied items to Mr Jackson, Nassau St, Soho, London in March 1785. [PRO, C107/67]

Birch, Thomas, Farnham, Surrey, cm (1811). [D] See William Birch.

Birch, Thomas, 20 and 26 Bridge St, Manchester, cm (1824–29). [D] See Charles Birch

Birch, William, Nantwich, Cheshire, cm (1829). Married Elizabeth Capper on 13 April 1829. [Chester RO, PR]

Birch, William, Castle St, Farnham, Surrey, cm and u (1838–39). [D] See Thomas Birch

Birchall, Daniel, 4 Sweeting St, Liverpool, cm (1830). App. to John O'Neill. Admitted freeman on 18 November 1830. [Liverpool freemen reg.]

Birchall, James, 33 Strand, London, carver, gilder, print seller and dealer in glass (1780). Took out a Sun Insurance policy in 1780 for £1,400 of which utensils and stock accounted for £500. [GL, Sun MS vol. 284, p. 119] Possibly:

Birchall, James, 473 Strand, London, carver, gilder, frame maker and print seller (1783–89). Trade card shows two classical figures supporting oval frame with text, in which Birchall offers German glasses for large prints and drawings. [D; Banks Coll., BM]

Birchall, Sophia, 2 Hartlam St, Liverpool, u (1834). [D]

Birchall, Thomas, Liverpool, carver and gilder (1807–14). Addresses given at 47 Gascoigne St in 1807; 29 Leeds St, 1810; 27 Leeds St, 1811; and 6 Scotland Rd, 1813–14. [D]

Birchall, William, address unrecorded, upholder (1746–60). Son of John Birchall, Carshalton, Surrey, gardener; app. to William Witton on 5 February 1756, and to Thomas Ridgeway, 'Skynner', on 11 January 1752. Admitted freeman of the Upholders' Co. on 8 July 1760 by servitude. [GL, Upholders' Co. records]

Birchall, William, Queen Sq., Bath, Som., u and cm (1770–93). Took out a Sun Insurance policy in 1775 for £1,400, of which utensils, stock and goods accounted for £1,010. [D; GL, Sun MS vol. 242, p. 613] See Thomas Bird. Advertised in *Bath Chronicle*, 25 January 1770 that he was from London and had just set up business. In December 1777 he was employed by Bath Corporation to make a pattern settee for others to follow and in 1778 was paid £68 13s 6d for settees he covered in crimson check. [Bath Corp. records] See Thomas Bird.

Birchall, William, Shaw's Brow, Liverpool, u (1818–21). Recorded at no. 9 in 1818 and no. 55 in 1821. [D]

Birchell (Birchall?), —, address unrecorded, u (1780–81). Carried out work at Corsham Court, being paid £125 on 23 October 1780, and £44 on 29 December 1781. [Wilts. RO, Paul Methuen's Day Bk, 1760–95]

Birchnall, James, Leicester, cm, carver and gilder (1829–40). Trading in the parish of St Nicholas, 1829–35, and at West Bridge, 1840. [D]

Bird, Benjamin, Downham, Norfolk, cm and auctioneer (1793). [D]

Bird, Benjamin, 9 Bateman Row, Shoreditch, London, cm and u (1839). [D]

Bird, George, address unrecorded, upholder (1714–21). Son of George Bird, clothier of Holdridge, Devon. App. to John Staples on 21 July 1714. Admitted freeman of the Upholders' Co. by servitude on 6 December 1721. [GL, Upholders' Co. records]

Bird, George, St Paul's Sq., Birmingham, cm (1835). [D]

Bird, Henry, 56 Burgate St, Canterbury, Kent, cm and broker (1823–38). [D]

Bird, Isaac, Penrith, Cumb., cm (1798–1811). Trading at Old Post Office Lane in 1811. [D]

Bird, James, address unrecorded, cm and u (1779–80). Carried out upholstery work, furniture repairs and supplied items for Mrs Harper in October and November 1779, totalling £4 8s 6d, including 'a Toilett Table', 6s 6d, and three

mahogany window blinds, 12s. [Worcs. RO, Palfrey Coll., 3762/6866:31, vol. 1]

Bird, John, Hull, Yorks., cm (1784–90). [Beverley poll bks]

Bird, John, 247 Whitechapel Rd, London, chairmaker (1809–11). [D]

Bird, John, St John's, Worcester, cm (1835). Admitted freeman on 1 December 1835. [Worcester freemen rolls]

Bird, John Soale & Taylor, James, Bath, Som., cm (1832). Declared bankrupt, *Liverpool Mercury*, 13 January 1832.

Bird, Joseph, London, cm, u and undertaker (1826–39). Trading at 8 Crombies Row, Comrel Rd, 1826–27, and 24 New North St, Finsbury, 1839. [D]

Bird, Peter, High St, Stourbridge, Worcs., cm, u and gilder (1818–22). [D]

Bird, Richard, Risbygate St, Bury St Edmunds, Suffolk, cm (1836). [Poll bk]

Bird, Robert, Huntingdon, chairmaker (1780). App., aged 14, to John Barnes of Huntingdon on 18 April 1780. [Hunts. RO, HB 13/10]

Bird, Robert, Rowcliffe Lane, Nether End, Penrith, Cumb., joiner and cm (1828–34). [D]

Bird, Samuel, Liverpool, upholder (1737). Son of Joseph Bird, yeoman. App. to Thomas Hale for eight years in 1737. [Liverpool app. reg.]

Bird, Stephen, Redcliff St, Bristol, cm and broker (1795). [D]

Bird, Stephen, Castle St, Bristol, mangle press maker, auctioneer and broker (1799–1800). [D]

Bird, Stephen, 11 Little Russell St, Drury Lane, London, cm, broker and auctioneer (1802). Took out a Sun Insurance policy on 20 May 1802 for £500 of which £400 accounted for utensils and stock. [GL, Sun MS vol. 424, ref. 732103]

Bird, Thomas, Bath, Som., upholder, auctioneer and undertaker (1784–94). Trading in Queen Sq., 1784, and 34 Broad St, 1794. Declared bankrupt, *Williamson's Liverpool Advertiser*, 14 December 1789, but trading again by 1794, the date on his trade card which reads 'T. BIRD . . . from Mr. Birchalls, No. 34 Broad Street, Bath', within a Rococo cartouche embellished with items of furniture. [Banks Coll., BM] See William Birchall of Bath.

Bird, Thomas, 67 Bromsgrove St, Birmingham, carver (1823). [D]

Bird, Thomas, Ryland's Rd, Edgbaston, Birmingham, u (1835). [D]

Bird, Thomas, 106 Wardour St, Soho, London, with workshop at Hollan St, Blackfriars, cm and u (1839–40). Took out a Sun Insurance policy in 1840. [D; GL, Sun MS ref. 1335128]

Bird, William, at 'The Rocking Horse', just without Newgate, London, turner (1724). [Heal]

Bird, William, High St, Dudley, Worcs., cm and u (1830–40). [D]

Bird, William jnr, New St, Dudley, Worcs., cm and u (1840). [D]

Bird, William Edward, Nottingham, joiner and cm (1786). [Notts. RO, index of burgesses]

Birdsall, Thomas, York, cm (1819). Son of Thomas Birdsall, deceased. App. to Hugh Rusby, cm, on 22 March 1819. [York app. reg.]

Birket(t), Henry, Lancaster, cm (1768–86). Took apps on 4 August 1769 and 14 April 1772. Son admitted freeman, 1785–86. [Poll bk; Lancaster freemen rolls]

Birket(t), Thomas, Lancaster and Manchester, cm (1759–1801). Admitted freeman of Lancaster 1759–60. Polled at Lancaster in 1768 as Thomas snr, so that it is presumably either snr or jnr who is named in the Gillow records between 1786 and 1801, in 1786 working on a chest, and in 1799 as 'from Manchester'. [Poll bks; Lancaster freemen rolls; Westminster Ref. Lib., Gillow vol. 344/93, p. 380; 98, p. 1534]

Birkett, Edmundson, Liverpool, u (1818–39). Addresses given at 60 St Thomas Buildings in 1821; 5 Spring Pl., Springfield St, 1823; Upper Bear St, 1824; 32 Hunter St, 1827; 30 Circus St, 1835; 13 Roscoe Lane, 1837; and 20 Bittern St, 1839. App. to George Philander Lyon, and admitted freeman on 11 June 1818. [D; Liverpool freemen reg.]

Birkett, Henry, 5 Old Hall St, Liverpool, u (1772–77). [D]

Birkett, John, Keswick, Cumb., cm and joiner (1834). [D]

Birkett, Thomas, Boroughgate, Appleby, Westmld, cm (1829). [D]

Birkett & Co., 91 Leather Lane, London, looking-glass makers (1825). [D]

Birkhead, Philipson, Henley-upon-Thames, Oxon., (1781), and Reading, Berks., cm (1803). Married Elizabeth Turpin at Rotherfield Greys on 29 November 1781, when he was aged 23. Took out a one-year lease on a property in Watlington. [Bodleian index of Oxf. marriage bonds; Oxford RO, Misc. Cha 1/2]

Birkit, —, Halles St, Clare Mkt, London, cm (1776). Straight-fronted chest of five drawers in two contrasting woods, with top formed as a secretaire recorded, inscribed with name, address and date. [V & A archives]

Birkit, Richard, King St, Golden Sq., London, cm (1803). Named in Sheraton's list of master cabinet makers, 1803.

Birkit, Richard, 24 Dover St, London, upholsterer's foreman (1811). Foreman to John Blease, successor to Seddon, he had lived in Blease's house for over 10 years. [PRO, B3/274]

Birkmayer, Joseph, Liverpool, carver and gilder (1834–37). Trading at 51 Brownlow Hill, 1834–35, and no. 47 in 1837. [D]

Birks, Joseph, Price St, Birmingham, picture frame maker (1800–03). [D]

Birks, Richard, 7 Downing St, Chorlton Row, Manchester, cm, joiner and builder (1825). [D]

Birmingham, Fernando, Chipping Norton, Oxon., joiner and cm (1775). Took app. named Robert Birmingham for seven years in 1775. [Oxford RO, Woot. PC, IX/iii/10]

Birsch, August, 10 Lambs Conduit Passage, Red Lion Sq., London, cm (1785). Took out a Sun Insurance policy on 2 July 1785 for £50 on his house and £30 on utensils and stock in trade. [GL, Sun MS vol. 331, p. 182]

Birt, James, Silver St, Wood St, London, jeweller (1757–82). Son of John Birt, peruke maker of Leominster, Herefs. App. to Thomas Bennett on 7 July 1757. Admitted freeman of the Upholders' Co. by servitude on 5 April 1769. Took app. named Richard Dennis, 1774–82. [GL, Upholders' Co. records and Livery lists]

Birt, John, Queen St, Oxford Rd, London, u (1774). [Poll bk]

Birt, John, 19 Oxford St, London, u and cm (1785–87). Took out a Sun Insurance policy on 16 July 1785 on household goods, £200, utensils, stock and goods in trust, £600, and on two houses communicating in Portman St, household goods and utensils, £360. Declared bankrupt, *Gents Mag.*, September 1787. [GL, Sun MS vol. 331, p. 285]

Birtchnall, James, St Nicholas St, Leicester, cm (1828). [D]

Birtchnall, James, Westbridge, Leicester, carver and gilder (1835). [D]

Birtchnall, John, Friar Lane, Leicester, cm (1835). [D]

Birtes, William, Swinton, Yorks., joiner and cm (1789). [D]

Birtill, Joseph, Clare St, Bristol, carver and gilder (d. by 1785). Sale of stock in trade after death announced, *Bonner and Middleton's Bristol Journal*, 25 June 1785, 'consisting chiefly of modern Glasses in the neatest stile, Gerondoles, a Quantity of Plate Glass, Mahogany Goods, &c. compleat Implements for Silvering and other necessary Fixtures. The House is exceedingly well calculated for the cabinet or Carving Business or both . . .'.

Birtle, —, address unrecorded (1728–29). Named in the Holkham Hall accounts supplying in 1728 a mahogany bureau, £1 8s; 2 mahogany tables and 2 screens, £10 18s; and in 1729, a mahogany writing table, £6 6s, and a wainscot dumbwaiter, £1 8s. [V & A archives]

Birtles, Robert, Bottle Lane, Nottingham, joiner and cm (1793–99). [D]

Birtwistle, Daniel, Padiham, Whalley, Lancs., joiner and cm (1825). [D]

Birtwistle, James, Padiham, Whalley, Lancs., joiner and cm (1825). [D]

Birtwistle, William, Burnley, Lancs., cm, u and joiner (1814–24). Recorded at Market St in 1814, New Rd, 1816–22 and 5 Market St, 1824. [D]

Bisbrown(e), Cuthbert, Liverpool, cm and builder (1762–77). Trading at Paradise St in 1766, with wareroom at Temple St, and timber yard at Park Lane, Tythe Barn St. Took app. named Nernon in 1762. Sale of stock after bankruptcy announced, *Williamson's Liverpool Advertiser*, 24 October 1766, consisting of bricks, wood, 'and other Articles suitable for Builders, Joiners, Cabinet Makers etc. . . . A large Quantity of Cabinet Furniture, Braziery Goods etc: Belonging to the Estate of Cuthbert Bisbrowne, Printed Catalogues containing the particular Kind of Goods, Quantities and Qualities will be timely dispersed . . .'. *Williamson's Liverpool Advertiser*, 22 July 1768 announced that his premises in Park Lane 'have been exposed to public Sale Three Times' but as no purchasers had appeared at the appointed times, 'it will consequently occasion great delay in the settlement of his affairs'. By 1773 he was trading again, but now as a land surveyor in Back Jordan St, and in 1777 at 1 Bridgewater St. [D; S of G, app. index]

Bisham (or Bispham), John, 30 Windmill St, St Peter's, Manchester, billiard table maker (1840). [D]

Bishop, —, Aldersgate St, London, cm (1767). Report that he had been attacked appeared in *Public Advertiser*, 26 June 1767.

Bishop, —, Long Acre, London, 'from Edinburgh', gilder and carver (late 18th century). Hepplewhite-style oval mirror recorded bearing label which states that he 'performs carving & gilding in all its branches, viz. chimney pieces, bed posts, chairs, girandoles, ornaments, looking glass frames, picture frames, gilt mouldings for rooms, prints, needlework, framed with fancy glass & maps neatly mounted. Orders expeditiously answered'.

Bishop, —, Houndsditch, London, cm (1793). Subscribed to Sheraton's *Drawing Book*, 1793.

Bishop, —, address unrecorded, cm (1812). Paid £2 6s on 4 January 1812 for making tables for Sir John Geers Cotterell, Bart, of Garnons, near Hereford, and Hertford St, London. [Herefs. RO, Garnons papers, W69/III/183] Possibly William Bishop of Hereford.

Bishop, —, Black Horseyard, Tottenham Ct Rd, London, carver (1835). [D]

Bishop, David, 49 Baldwin's Gdns, Leather Lane, London, cm and broker of household goods (1811–14). Took out Sun Insurance policies on 24 January 1811 for £1,100 of which household goods and workshop accounted for £450, stock and utensils, £250, and houses at 12 Baldwin's Gdns and 2 Leopard's Ct, £400; and on 10 February 1814 for £700, dwelling house and workshop accounting for £300, stock and utensils, £250. [GL, Sun MS vol. 449, ref. 852738; vol. 463, ref. 891180]

Bishop, George, 12 Corner of Queen Sq., Broker Row, Moorfields, London (furniture warehouse), cm, u, appraiser, auctioneer and undertaker (18th century). Trade card states that he 'Keeps ready made all kinds of Household Furniture, both new & second hand in great Variety, on the most reasonable Terms. NB. Money immediately advanced for any quantity of Goods intended for public or private Sale'. [Landauer Coll., MMA, NY]

Bishop, Eli, South St, Crewkerne, Som., cm and u (1839–40). [D]

Bishop, James, 6 Phoenix St, London, chairmaker (1791). Took out a Sun Insurance policy on 21 November 1791 for £100, of which finished goods in dwelling house accounted for £50, and wearing apparel, £50. [GL, Sun MS vol. 382, ref. 591778]

Bishop, John, Bedminster, Bristol, cm (1795). [D]

Bishop, John, South St, Crewkerne, Som., cm (1822–30). [D]

Bishop, John, Aston Rd, Birmingham, cm, u and carver (1828–30). Recorded also at 34 Bradford St in 1830. [D]

Bishop, John, High St, Lewes, Sussex, chair bottomer (1830). [Poll bk]

Bishop, John, Paradise Row, Maidstone, Kent, cm (1834–38). [Voters' reg. and poll bk]

Bishop, John, 1 Tudor Pl., London, cm and u (1839). [D]

Bishop, Samuel, Bristol, cm (1739–54). Recorded in the parish of St Thomas, 1739, and Clifton, 1754. [Poll bks]

Bishop, Samuel, St Michael's, Oxford, u (1768). [Poll bk]

Bishop, Thomas, Stamford, Lincs., cm (b. 1726–d. 1801). Took app. named Pulford in 1759. Death, aged 75, reported, *Gents Mag.*, March 1801. [S of G, app. index]

Bishop, Thomas, 183 Church St, Bethnall Green, and 27 Duke St, St James's, London, cm, broker and carpenter (1808). [D]

Bishop, Thomas, Market Pl., Chippenham, Wilts., cm etc. (1839). [D]

Bishop, William, Hereford, cm (1818). [Poll bk]

Bishop, William, 67 James St and 7 Emanuel's Buildings, James St, Devonport, Devon, carver and gilder (1830–38). Recorded in Ker St, 1838. [D]

Bishop, William Henry, 16 Ann St, Birmingham, cm, u, carpet dealer and paper hanger (1828–35). Mahogany table reputedly from Sion House, Clent, Worcs. and designed by A. W. N. Pugin, bears Bishop's label. [D; auction at Lawrence's, Crewkerne, Som., 29 September 1983]

Bishop (& Terry), High St, Maidstone, Kent, u and auctioneer (1805–11). [D]

Bishoprick, Xerxes, Beverley, Yorks., cm (1805). App. to John Stephenson in April 1805. [Hull app. reg.]

Bispham, Edward, Liverpool, cm (1761–74). App. to Nicholas Cross and admitted freeman on 7 April 1761. [Liverpool freemen reg.] Possibly the Edward Bispham who was paid 14s 9d on 4 August 1773 for repairing tables at Dunham Massey, and £14 14s on 24 March 1774 for one mahogany chest and '3 dail chests' [John Rylands Lib., Manchester Univ., George Cooke's accounts]

Bissell, Benjamin, address unrecorded, upholder (1722–30). Son of William Bissell, mercer of Hereford. App. to John Bissell on 1 January 1722–23, and admitted freeman of the Upholders' Co. by servitude on 7 January 1729/30. [GL, Upholders' Co. records]

Bissell, John, Towre St, London, upholder (1721). Admitted freeman of the Upholders' Co. by order of the Court of Aldermen on 23 May 1721. [GL, Upholders' Co. records]

Bissell, John, Camomille St, London, freeman sadler, by trade carver and coach carver (1763–68). Employed nine non-freemen for several months each between 1763–68. [GL, City Licence bks, vols 3–6] See Rachell Bissell.

Bissell, Joseph, Liverpool, cm and household broker (1821–29). Addresses given at 17 Hatton Gdn in 1821; 91 Dale St in 1823; 75 Duke St in 1824; and 74 Dale St, 1827–29. [D] See Thomas Bissell.

Bissell, Rachell, Camomile St, London, freeman sadler, by trade

a coach carver (1770). Employed one non-freeman for three months in 1770. [GL, City Licence bks, vol. 7] See John Bissell

Bissell, Roger, Dolphin Inn Yd, Bishopsgate St Without, London, freeman sadler, by trade a carver (1774–75). Took out a Sun Insurance policy on 4 November 1774 for £300 of which utensils and stock accounted for £35 and wearing apparel £80. In 1775 employed one non-freeman for six weeks. [GL, Sun MS vol. 235; GL, City Licence bks, vol. 9]

Bissell, Thomas, Liverpool, carver (1827–35). Addresses given at 74 Dale St in 1827 and no. 77, 1830–35. Admitted freeman on 15 November 1830. [D; Liverpool freemen reg.] See Joseph Bissell.

Bisset(t) (or Birset), John, London, cm, cabinet and upholstery warehouseman, sworn appraiser and undertaker (c. 1760–93). Trade card, c. 1760 [Banks Coll., BM] gives address at 'Ye Chair & Coffin', Lower Moorfields, and states 'stocks in Trade And Household Goods of all Sorts Bought, Sold or Appraised'. Card has Rococo embellishments and shows Chippendale-style chair and later secretaire. In 1790 warehouse recorded at Brokers Row, Moorfields. [D]

Bissett, Thomas, Liverpool, carver (1819–30). App. to John Summer in 1819, petitioned freedom paying 6s 8d in 1827, and admitted freeman in 1830. [Liverpool freemen's committee bk]

Bissix, C. & Co., 171 High Holborn, London, bed and mattress maker (1822–23). [D]

Bissoll, —, Worcester, u (17th century). Wing armchair recorded bearing label. [*Apollo*, June 1975, p. 110]

Bithell, Joseph, Hospital St, Nantwich, Cheshire, chairmaker (1830–37). Married Sarah Williamson on 9 November 1830. Daughter Anne bapt. on 27 February 1833, Mary on 2 February 1837, and son George on 27 March 1837. [Chester RO, PR(bapt.)]

Bitterton, George, Southampton St, Camberwell, London, u (1839). [D]

Bittleston, George, Gravel Lane, Southwark, London, cm and upholder (1820). [D]

Bitton, William, parish of St James, Norwich, cm (1830–31). [Gt Yarmouth and Norwich poll bks]

Bivet, —, address unrecorded, cm (1803). Subscribed to Sheraton's *Cabinet Dictionary*, 1803.

Blaber, —, 12 Boyces St, Brighton, Sussex, cm and u (1822). [D] Possibly:

Blaber, Oliver, Brighton, Sussex, cm (1818–24). Recorded at Middle St in 1818, and 1 Regent Hill, 1822–24. Daughter Ann bapt. at St Nicholas on 3 May 1818. [D; E. Sussex RO, PR(bapt.)]

Blaby, Richard, Banbury, Oxon., cm (1774–75). Marriage recorded, *Jackson's Oxford Journal*, 19 June 1774, to the eldest daughter of William Barker of the 'Red Lion'. Same journal, 5 October 1775, recorded sale of 'freehold estate of 8 stone houses in John Street, two large ones let to Blaby & Knowles'.

Blachford, Robert, High St, Salisbury, Wilts., cm and u (1822–30). [D]

Black, Algernon, London, cm (1793). Subscribed to Sheraton's *Drawing Book*, 1793.

Black, Henry, Teddington, Middlx, turner (1770). Took out a Hand in Hand Insurance policy in 1770 for £100, renewed in 1777 by Elizabeth Black. [GL, Hand in Hand MS vol. 110; p. 27]

Black, James, Leeds, Yorks., journeyman cm (1791). Named in the *Leeds Cabinet and Chair Makers' Book of Prices*, 1791.

Black, John, London, cm (1793). Subscribed to Sheraton's *Drawing Book*, 1793.

Black, John, Broad St, Nottingham, cm (1828–35). [D]

Black, John, 33 Ernest St, Regent's Park, London, carver and gilder (1839). [D]

Black, R., London, cm (1793). Subscribed to Sheraton's *Drawing Book*, 1793.

Black, R., 8 Steven St, Tottenham Ct Rd, London, cm (1835). [D]

Black, Robert, 15 Bateman's Buildings, Soho, London, cm (1809–11). [D]

Black, Thomas, 18 Greek St, Soho, London, looking-glass manufactory owner (1809–11). [D]

Blackall, B., 16 Bath St, City Rd, London, bed-pillar manufacturer (1820–27). [D]

Blackborne, Edward, Lancaster and Liverpool, cm (1801–07). App. to I. Greenwood in 1801. Admitted freeman, 1806–07, when stated 'of Liverpool'. [Lancaster app. reg. and freemen rolls] Possibly Edward Blackburn(e)

Blackbourne, William, Lancaster, cm (1794). Marriage reported, *Billinge's Liverpool Advertiser*, 18 August 1794, to Miss Jolly of Mythop at Kirkham. Possibly William Blackburn, d. 1803.

Blackburn, Christopher, York, u (1767). Nephew of Edward Smith; app. to Jeremiah Smith & Matthew Hearon, u and appraisers, 19 January 1767. [York app. reg.]

Blackburn(e), Edward, Liverpool, cm and shopkeeper (1811–14). Trading at 1 Bean St in 1811 and 32 Hill St, Harrington, 1813–14. [D]

Blackburn, James, Albion Sq., Leeds, Yorks., cm (1822). [D]

Blackburn(e), John, Liverpool, u (1772–83). Trading at Fenwick St, in 1772, with warehouse at 12 High St, 1773–74; and Pownall Sq., 1781–83. Admitted freeman on 23 July 1772. Advertised, *Williamson's Liverpool Advertiser*, 17 June 1774, that 'from an indisposed State of Health, he finds it indispensibly necessary to retire from Business & reside in the Country . . . and . . . he is determined to disperse of his Stock in Trade on exceeding low Terms; consisting of all Sorts of Bed Furniture, Bed Ticks, Superfine Dantzig Feathers, Blankets, Counterpanes, Wilton & Scotch Carpets, Elegant Pier Glasses & Girandoles in Gilt Frames, Pier Glasses in Mahogany Frames, Dressing Glasses in Japan & Mahogany Frames, great variety of Paper Hangings, Fringes . . . all of which are entirely fresh & new & of the best Qualities'. He also offered his house and shop with 15 year lease, 13½ of which were unexpired. Trading again by 1781. [D; Liverpool freemen reg.]

Blackburn, John, 41 Coalpit Lane, Sheffield, Yorks., chairmaker (1821–22). [D]

Blackburn, Joseph, West Melton, Yorks., cm (1837). [D]

Blackburn, R., 7 Green St, Leicester Sq., London, cabinet and case maker (1817). [D]

Blackburn, Richard, Lancaster, cm (1750–68). App. to Henry Baines in 1750, and admitted freeman, 1765–66. [Lancaster app. reg. and freemen rolls; poll bk]

Blackburn, Richard, Delph, Saddleworth, Yorks., cm and u (1822). [D]

Blackburn, Robert, 73 Kirkgate, Leeds, Yorks., chairmaker (1814). [D]

Blackburn (or Blakeburn), Thomas, St Mary's Gate, Manchester, cm (1771–73). Recorded at no. 14 in 1773. Announced in *Prescott's Manchester Journal*, 21 December 1771 'that he has enter'd on the shop late of Mr. Watkinson's, in St. Mary's Gate, where he intends carrying on the said Business in all its Branches, in the most fashionable Taste and the newest Patterns . . . [He] . . . has on sale A Choice Quantity of Mahogany, both log and plank, Oak Billets, Deal and a parcel of good black Ebony, now lying in a Yard behind the Old Windmill in Deansgate'. [D]

Blackburn, Thomas, Lancaster, (1788–1804). [Westminster Ref. Lib., Gillow records]

Blackburn, Thomas, Liverpool, cm (1802–22). Named in the Preston Guild record of burgesses as son of Edward Blackburn late of Preston, shopkeeper, and as having a son, Edward.

Blackburn, Thomas, Liverpool, cm (1832). App. to Thomas Blackburn in 1832. [Liverpool app. enrolment bk]

Blackburn, William snr, Lancaster, cm (b. 1727–d. 1793). Admitted freeman, 1764–65. By 1788 his son William the younger had entered the business. Tombstone in Lancaster Priory churchyard records that he died on 3 December 1793, aged 66. [Lancaster freemen rolls and app. reg.; poll bk]

Blackburn, William jnr, Lancaster, cm (b. 1767–d. 1803). Son of William, cm of Lancaster, admitted freeman in 1782–83. In business with his father in 1788 when Robert Toulmin was taken as app. on 23 July. Tombstone in Lancaster Priory churchyard records that he died on 3 July 1803, aged 36. [Lancaster freemen rolls and app. reg.]

Blackburn, William, London, u (1793). Subscribed to Sheraton's *Drawing Book*, 1793.

Blackburn, William, 14 Dean St, Soho, London, chair and sofa maker (1827–28). [D]

Blackburn, William, Strong's Yd, Wigton, Cumb., joiner and cm (1828–29). [D]

Blackburn, William, Bristol, coach and cabinet carver (1836–40). Trading at 9 Brandon St, 1836–37, and 5 Old Park Hill, 1838–40. [D]

Blackburne, Elizabeth, Cable St, Lancaster, cm (1808). [D]

Blackburne, Elizabeth, 32 Clayton St, Liverpool, u (1813–14). [D]

Blackburne, Margaret, 1 Langhorne Pl., Clayton St, Liverpool, u (1821–23). [D]

Blacket, John, Sunderland, Co. Durham, cm (1803). Subscribed to Sheraton's *Cabinet Dictionary*, 1803.

Blacketer, Thomas, 2 Wych St, Strand, London, frame maker (1839). [D]

Blackett, Henry, Tubwell Row, Darlington, Co. Durham, turner and chairmaker in wood and metal (1827). [D]

Blackett, S., 9 Aldgate High St, London, turner (1796). [D]

Blackhurst, Robert, Preston, Lancs., cm (1816–25). Addresses given as Roe St, 1816; Cock Yd, Church St, 1818; and 45 Tythebarn St, 1825. [D]

Blackley, John, Liverpool, cm (1780). Petitioned freedom on servitude to Joseph Parke in 1780 paying 6s 8d. [Liverpool freemen's committee bk]

Blacklock, —, 79 Park St, London, cm and undertaker (1793). Subscribed to Sheraton's *Drawing Book*, 1793.

Blacklock, J., Upper Borough Walls, Bath, Som., cm and upholder (1833). [D]

Blacklock (or Blaiklock), Musgrave, 14–15 North Audley St, London, u and cm (1803–25). Recorded as Blaiklock in Sheraton's list of master cabinet makers, 1803; and in directories as H.M. Blacklock after 1817, but as H. & M. Blacklock in 1820.

Blackman, James, Mermaid St, Rye, Sussex, cm, u, paper hanger and patten maker (1823–26). [D]

Blackman, John, 16 Green St, Leicester Sq., London, case and cabinet manufacturer (1837). [D] See Sarah and Robert Blackman.

Blackman (or Blackmore), Sarah, 7 Green St, Leicester Sq., London, cm, case and cabinet manufacturer (1820). [D]

Blackman, Robert, 7 Green St, Leicester Sq., London, case and cm (1808–28). Took out a Sun Insurance policy on 15 November 1821 with John Benjamin Osborne, and mentioned in other policies taken out in 1823. [D; GL, Sun

MS vol. 488, ref. 98515; vol. 499, refs 1010727 and 1010709]

Blackmoor, John, Westgate, Rotherham, Yorks., cm (1833–37). [D]

Blackmore, James, May-Fair, London, u (1749). [Poll bk]

Blackmore, Thomas, 85 Fleet Mkt, London, upholder and cm (1797–1803). In 1797 acted as 4th party in a one year lease of property in Berks. Took out a Sun Insurance policy on 10 November 1803 for £850, of which utensils and stock in dwelling house accounted for £200, and a house at 14 Royal Row, Lambeth in tenure, £400. [D; Oxford RO, Wi I/iii/25; GL, Sun MS vol. 430, ref. 754730]

Blacknell, John, Snowsfields, St Saviour's, Southwark, London, upholder (1760). Took out a Hand in Hand Insurance policy in June 1760 for £200. [GL, Hand in Hand MS vol. 94, p. 49]

Blackshaw, Mary, Flagen Row, Deptford, Wilts., cm (1832–34). [D]

Blackstock, Peter, London, cm and u (1780–1808). Addresses given at Littlelark St, Seven Dials in 1780; at the Gridiron, Castle St, Long Acre, 1792–96; and 24 Knightsbridge, 1808. In 1780 took out a Sun Insurance policy with Robert Duncan for £600 on houses, and on 26 July 1792 insured stock in two houses communicating in Castle St for £800. Subscribed to Sheraton's *Drawing Book*, 1793. Declared bankrupt, *Billinge's Liverpool Advertiser*, 26 December 1796, but trading again by 1808. [D; GL, Sun MS vol. 281, p. 307; vol. 389, ref. 603087]

Blackwell, Charles, Stratton, Cirencester, Glos., cm (1830). [D]

Blackwell, E. & J., 59 Union St, Stonehouse, Plymouth, Devon, carvers and gilders (1830). [D] See F. S. Blackwell.

Blackwell, Edward, Silver St, Cirencester, Glos., cm (1820–22). Trading at Silver St in 1820 and Castle St in 1822. [D]

Blackwell, F. S., 59 Union St, East Stonehouse, Devon, carver and gilder (1838). [D] See E. & J. Blackwell.

Blackwell, James, Dyers Yd, Wicker, Sheffield, Yorks., cm (1821). [D]

Blackwell, John, address unrecorded, upholder (1727–35). Son of Samuel Blackwell, baker of July St, Southwark, London. App. to Edward Hiller on 20 August 1727, and then to James Maulden on 2 April 1729. Admitted freeman of the Upholders' Co. by servitude on 5 February 1734/35. [GL, Upholders' Co. records] Possibly:

Blackwell, John, King St, Snowsfields, St Saviour's, Southwark, London, upholder (1760–81). Took out a Hand in Hand Insurance policy in June 1760 for £200, renewed on 1 June 1767, 28 June 1774 and 1781. [GL, Hand in Hand MS vol. 94, p. 49; vol. 106, p. 42; vol. 116, ref. 79676]

Blackwell, W, Belvoir St, Leicester, cm (1815). [D]

Blackwell, William, London (1790). On 5 October 1790 received payment of £65 17s 6½d for mahogany tables and chairs supplied to Mount Stewart, N. Ireland. [Mount Stewart papers]

Blackwell, William, Castle St, Cirencester, Glos., cm (1830). [D]

Blackwell, William, 34 Long Row, Nottingham, u (1832). [D]

Blackwell, William & Henry, Long Row, Nottingham, cm, u and brokers (1834–40). Trading at no. 3 in 1835; and Long Row and Derby in 1840. [D]

Blackwell & Son, Long Row, Nottingham, u (1825). [D]

Blackwell, Norgrove & Smagge, address unrecorded, (c. 1725–30). Supplied chairs for Sherborne House, Glos. [Glos. RO, D678, A/C 1790]

Blades, Thomas, London, cm and u (1774–1822). Trading in St James's Mkt, 1774; 114 Jermyn St, 1790–93; and 177 Piccadilly, 1804–22. In partnership with his son from 1799–1802, and with Palmer, 1803–22. Took out a Sun Insurance policy in 1780 for £800, utensils, stock and goods accounting for £300, and workshop for £200. Subscribed to

Sheraton's *Drawing Book*, 1793, and named with Palmer in Sheraton's list of master cabinet makers, 1803. [D; poll bk; GL, Sun MS vol. 287, p. 73] Trade label of 'BLADES & SON, PICCADILLY' recorded on a George III satinwood drop-leaf 'bonheur-du-jour' veneered in rosewood and mahogany with tulip wood banding. [Phillips', 29 July 1975, lot 100; *Antique Collecting*, September 1975] Portable water closet in mahogany cabinet by Blades & Palmer, c. 1810, recorded with directions for use. [*Antique Collecting*, April 1979]

Bladwell, John, Bow St, Covent Gdn, London, u, cm and chairmaker (1724–68). These dates possibly cover two related tradesmen. On 7 December 1724 took out a Sun Insurance policy for £500 on goods and merchandise in his house 'four doors above the Buck's Tavern in Bow St.', the street where he is recorded in the Westminster poll of 1749, and directories of 1763–67. Earliest commission known is for furniture supplied for the Senate House, Cambridge University, his account dated 1 July 1730 totalling £17 11s 9d, and including two large walnut chairs upholstered in Genoa velvet and 'Blew Turkey Leather', and a carpet. [Cambridge Univ. Lib., Vice Chancellor's vouchers, 14(3)] Bladwell's chief patron appears to have been the 4th Duke of Bedford of Woburn, Beds., whom he supplied with various items of upholstery and furniture from 1732–54. Bills of 1752 include 'five neat mahogany chairs carved after Lady Holderness's pattern with elbows' at £1 17s each. A later account of 1752 describes '6 neat mahogany carved chairs in the Dutch pattern', £12 6s, 'six neat Chinese chairs, walnut tree, the seats cane', £6 12s, and 'six neat strong mahogany Pembroke chairs . . . the seats caned', £7 16s. [D; G. Scott-Thomson, *Family Background*, 1949, pp. 49, 52–54; *GCM*; *DEF*; *Apollo*, January 1956, pp. 10–12, pls xi, xiii; December 1965, pp. 449, 452] In March 1752 Bladwell provided for the Duchess of Bedford's bedchamber at Woburn, 'a wainscot bedstead with yellow linen head and tester', and other furniture including French chairs and sofas. In 1753–54 he supplied further items of bed and seat furniture for Woburn. An account of 1767 shows that he also worked for Francis, Marquess of Tavistock. [Bedford Office, London] Other commissions known are for Felbrigg, Norfolk, where account books record payment in full to Bladwell on 7 July 1756 of £448. [V & A archives] Received several payments from Sir Matthew Featherstonhaugh of Uppark from March 1758 to January 1767, totalling £810 6s. [*Conn.*, November 1967, pp. 160–61] Possibly the Bladwell named in the account bks of Sir John Dutton of Sherborne House, Glos., 1728–29, as being paid several hundred pounds for making up beds, curtains, putting up hangings, supplying sets of chairs, a couch bed, screens, bedding etc. [Glos. RO, Sherborne Muniments D 678 (acc. 1790)] Possibly the Bladwell or Bleedwell who worked at Holkham Hall in 1748, supplying a couch bed and mattress, and in 1750, eight rush bottom chairs and couch and repairing furniture. [V & A archives] Bladwell, u, is recorded on 6 July 1768 in the accounts of Richard Hoare of Boreham House, Essex, being paid £126 13s. [Essex RO, D/DU 649/2]

Blagburn, William, 42 Collingwood St, Newcastle, auctioneer and u (1833–34). [D]

Blagden, William, Nether-Green, near Sheffield, Yorks., cm, wheelwright and carpenter (1822). [D]

Blain, Arthur, Liverpool, cm (c. 1835). Five late Regency-style mahogany chairs recorded bearing stamps on rails, deeply impressed, 'A. BLAIN, LIVERPOOL', the maker, and faintly, 'C. CHATHAM', possibly the firm for which he worked. A mahogany Canterbury, c. 1835, recorded stamped 'T.& A. BLAIN, LIVERPOOL', possibly relates to Thomas Blain, who was in partnership with A.T. Blain, 1835–37. [D]

Blain, Joshua, 8 Denmark St, Soho and 10 Little Earl St, Seven Dials, London, turner and bedstead maker (1820–39). [D]

Blain, Thomas, Liverpool, u and carpet warehouse owner (1816–37). Address given at 55 Mt Pleasant, 1816–34; 18 Paradise St, 1827–37; in partnership with Arbuthnot at 3 Manesty St with shop at 17 Paradise St, 1834–35; and in partnership with A. T. Blain at 15 Paradise St, 1835, and no. 18 in 1837. Advertised, *Liverpool Mercury*, 4 July 1828, his 'CARPET, FLOOR-CLOTH, BED & BEDDING WARE-HOUSE, UPHOLSTERY FURNITURE & CABINET ROOMS', where he has ready 'an extensive stock of BRUSSELS, KIDDERMINSTER & VENETIAN CARPETS of the newest patterns & best fabric, which he is Determined to sell, for cash, at as low rates as any house in the trade. Ship's Cabins fitted up, & Passengers supplied with every Article in the Bed & Bedding line, on moderate terms. N.B. A YOUTH of responsible connexions wanted as an APPRENTICE to the UPHOLSTERY BUSINESS'. Mahogany Canterbury *c.* 1835, recorded stamped 'T.& A. BLAIN, LIVERPOOL', possibly refers to Arthur Blain. [D]

Blair, James, London, cm (1808–39). Addresses given at 8 Little St, St Martin's Lane, 1808–20, with workshop at 22 Queen St; and 32–33 King St, Holborn, 1821–39. Took out a Sun Insurance policy on 30 December 1808 for £300 on household goods at 8 Little St, no work done therein, and £100 on stock, utensils and store in workshop at Queen St. On 7 November 1821 insured his dwelling house at 32 King St for £800. [D; GL, Sun MS vol. 445, ref. 823991; vol. 484, ref. 985313]

Blair, Thomas, 7 Wood St, Exmouth St, Spitalfields, London, chair and sofa maker (1829). [D]

Blair & Sons, Liverpool, cm (*c.* 1800). Small kneehole desk recorded bearing stamp. Made of solid padoukwood presumably imported into Liverpool about the turn of the century and made to the owner's specification. [*Antiques Trade Gazette*, 1 January 1983]

Blake, Benjamin, 8 Mint St, Southwark, London, cm, u and broker (1820–39). [D]

Blake, Benjamin, Bridge St, Southampton, Hants., cm and chairmaker (1839). [D]

Blake, Edward, Well St, Buckingham, cm (1823). [D]

Blake, George, Ordnance Row, Portsea, Portsmouth, Hants., cm, u, chairmaker and auctioneer (1823–39). Recorded at no. 24, 1823–30. [D]

Blake, Henry, The Square, Winchester, Hants., cm (1839). [D]

Blake, James, 12 Berwick St, London, cm and upholder (1816–23). Took out Sun Insurance policies on 23 January 1823 for £400, and on 12 March 1823 for £300, utensils and stock accounting for £150. [D; GL, Sun MS vol. 498, ref. 999634; vol. 498, ref. 1001910]

Blake, James, Newlands, Pershore, Worcs., cm (1840). [D]

Blake, John, London St, Greenwich, London, 'Cabinet Maker & Upholsterer, to Her Royal Highness the Princess of Wales & the Duchess of Brunswick. Paper Hanger, Appraiser, Auctioneer & Undertaker' (1802–24). So reads his trade card embellished with the Prince of Wales feathers. [D; Landauer Coll., MMA, NY; Heal Coll., BM]

Blake, John, 29 Tottenham Ct Rd, London, u (1829–35). [D]

Blake, John, High St, Croydon, Surrey, cm and u (1809–39). In partnership with William Blake, 1809–22. [D]

Blake, Richard, Chester, cm (1831). Admitted freeman on 21 April 1831. [Chester freemen rolls]

Blake, Richard, Chapel St, Marlow, Bucks., carver and gilder (1839). [D]

Blake, Robert, 11 King St, Snowsfields, London, picture frame maker and gilder (1784). [D]

Blake, Robert, 8 Stephen St, Tottenham Ct Rd, London, cm and buhl manufacturer (1826–39). [D]

Blake, Samuel, Church St, Pershore, Worcs., cm (1840). [D]

Blake, William, Gt St Andrew's St, Seven Dials, London, cm (1784). [Bristol poll bk]

Blake, William, Ryder's tenement, Lemon St, Truro, Cornwall, cm (1800). Lease on above property from Sir William Lemon dated 25 March 1800 when Blake was 'about 45 yrs.', and was to build a good substantial house faced with Ashlar stone and make a garden of 'Shoot Close'. [Cornwall RO, DD WH 1201]

Blake, William, High St, Croydon, Surrey, broker and u (1793–1826). Address given at London St in 1808. Recorded in partnership with John Blake as cm, u, auctioneers and house agents, 1809–26. Probably the William Blake, cm, who subscribed to Sheraton's *Cabinet Dictionary*, 1803. [D]

Blakeley, George, London, bed and mattress maker (1822–37). Addresses given at 133 Bishopsgate Without, 1822–28, and 26 Acorn St, 1835–37. [D]

Blakeman, Solloman, 'The Barber's Pole', Harthorn's Lane, Strand, London, tablemaker (1712). Took out a Sun Insurance policy on 3 July 1712 'for his goods'. [GL, Sun MS vol. 2, p. 55]

Blaker, Joseph, address unrecorded, upholder (1705). Admitted freeman of the Upholders' Co. on 1 August 1705. [GL, Upholders' Co. records]

Blakesl(e)y (or Blaksley), Robert, York, carver, gilder and composition maker (1770–87). Recorded in Coney St in 1787. Admitted freeman by order in 1776. Took apps named Robert Tomlinson, admitted freeman in 1789; Mark Barfe, freeman in 1784; John Hunsley, later turned over to Robert Tomlinson, freeman in 1795; and Joseph Baskett, freeman of Sheffield in 1795. Much employed by John Carr for ornamental carving and composition work including '3 window cornices carved & gilt with burnished gold at £5.15s.6d.' [York app. reg. and freemen rolls; Chatsworth papers, voucher 77, 5/12/85]

Blakesly, William, Micklegate, York, carver and gilder (1781). [D]

Blakeway, Robert, Cornmarket, Shrewsbury, Salop, upholder (1796). [Shrewsbury burgess roll]

Blakey, George, Bishop Wearmouth, Sunderland, Co. Durham, cm (1832). [D]

Blakey, John, Gray's Inn Passage, London, cm (1784). [D]

Blakey, John, York, cm (1811–30). Trading in Tanner Row, 1823. Son of Elizabeth Blakey, widow, of Moreby. App. to John Bellerby, cm and u, on 25 July 1811. Admitted freeman in 1820. [D; York app. reg. and freemen rolls]

Blakey, John, Keighley, Yorks., cm and u (1834–37). Trading in North St, 1837. [D]

Blakey, Thomas, Chester-le-Street, Co. Durham, cm and joiner (1834). [D]

Blakey, Joseph, Hull, Yorks., cm (1822). App. to William Silbon in November 1822. [Hull app. reg.]

Blame, John, 11 Bell Yd, Temple Bar, London, carver and gilder (1784–93). [D]

Blamer, Thomas, Liverpool, u (1834). App. to George Philander Lyon in 1834. [Liverpool app. enrolment bk]

Blamey, J., New Rover Ct, Strand, London, carver, gilder and painter (1808). [D]

Blanch, Samuel, Compton St, Soho, London, cm and u (1749). [Poll bk; Heal]

Blanch, Thomas, Reading, Berks., u (1735–40). Took apps named Blanch in 1735 and Peeres in 1740. [S of G, app. index]

Blanchard, Andrew, Cornhill, London, cm (1707). Known to be active from advertisements. [Harris, *Old English Furniture*, p. 19] See Samuel Blanchard.

Blanchard, Francis, 10 Goodge St, London, cm and upholder (1839). [D]

Blanchard, James, Wimborne, Dorset, chairmaker and turner (1823). [D]

Blanchard, James, Bell St, Shaftesbury, Dorset, chairmaker (1830). [D]

Blanchard, James, 32 Peter St, Liverpool, cm (1837). [D]

Blanchard, Richard, address unrecorded. App. of William Jackson, he received payment for chairs supplied to the 5th Earl of Bedford by Jackson in 1677. [Bedford Office, London]

Blanchard (or Blarchard), Samuel, Cornhill, London, cm (1705–13). [Heal] A Samuel Blarchard of London was declared bankrupt, *London Gazette,* 13 March 1706. See Andrew Blanchard.

Blanchard, W., 15 Wish St, Southsea, Hants., cm and u (1839). [D]

Blanchard, William, Exeter, Devon, cm (1819–31). Addresses at Holloway St in 1819, and Magdalen St in 1824. Baptisms recorded of daughter Mary Jane, 12 September 1819, son William, 21 March 1824, and daughter Susanna, 13 November 1831, at Holy Trinity. [PR(bapt.)]

Bland, Charles, London, cm and u (1672–80). Named in the Royal Household accounts as a cm to Charles II. In 1672 he supplied to the King 'a bed of needlework richly wrought with silver trimmed with silver and gold fringes, with all other necessaryes thereunto belonging bought by His Majesty's especiall command for the service of her Grace the Duchess of Monmouth'. At the same time he also supplied 'two large elbow-chaires of needleworke richly wrought of blew and gold, the other of silver and pinke'. In 1680 the king purchased from him a 'barber's case, covered with purple velvet, and edged with a gold gallone, with scissors and razors tipt with silver, fine ivory, and tortoiseshell combs, horn with a gilt lock'. [DEF; PRO, Great Wardrobe Accounts; *Conn.,* February 1934]

Bland, Edward, London, cm (1812–20). [Colchester poll bks]

Bland, Henry Nicholas, King St, Hammersmith, London, cm and upholder (1832–39). [D]

Bland, Isaac, Kirkland, Kendal, Westmld, letter case maker (d. 1800). Death reported, with obituary, in *Gents Mag.,* August 1800.

Bland, James, Sheffield, Yorks., cm and case maker for knives razors etc. (1787–88). Trading in Queen St, 1787, but declared bankrupt in 1788. [D; Bailey's list of bankrupts]

Bland, James, Liverpool, cm (1810–29). Addresses given at 12 Crosshall St, 1810–11; Circus St, 1818–24; and Christian St, 1827–29. [D]

Bland, John, Hanover Sq., St Martin-in-the-Fields, London, cm (1754–65). Subscribed to Chippendale's *Director,* 1754. Took app. named Joseph Elms in 1761 for £5 5s. Took out a Sun Fire policy in 1765 for £1,000. [S of G, app. index; GL, Sun MS ref. 221916]

Bland, John, 31 Suffolk St, Birmingham, cm (1823). [D]

Bland, John, West Mill Rd, Ware, Herts., cm and u (1839). [D]

Bland, Matthew, Halifax, Yorks., cm (1793–1837). Trading at 2 Broad St in 1837. Probably the Bland, cm of Halifax, who subscribed to Sheraton's *Drawing Book,* 1793. [D]

Bland, William, Low Bridge, Knaresborough, Yorks., joiner, cm and builder (1828–29). [D]

Blandford, William, 29 Bouverie St, London, carver and gilder (1839). [D]

Blaney (or Blayney), Thomas, Liverpool, cm (1802–12). Admitted freeman on servitude to Thomas Savage Tyrer, paying 6s 8d, on 14 October 1812. [Liverpool freemen's committee bk and reg.]

Blass, Daniel, 430 Oxford St, London, upholder (1835). [D]

Blatch, Benjamin, 2 Denmark St, St Giles, London, cm (1808). [D]

Blatchford, Thomas, 50 Redcliff St, Bristol, u and broker (1826). [D]

Blatchley, William, 5 Abbey Green, Bath, Som., fancy cm (1833). [D]

Blaxell, William, 10 James St, Devonport, Devon, cm (1838). [D]

Blaxland, Henry, London, upholder (b. 1738–d. 1816). Addresses given at Pigg St, near the Royal Exchange, 1770, 1778–86; 71 Old Broad St, 1775–1811, and no. 72 by 1813. Son of John Blaxland, farmer of Goodenstree, Kent; app. to William Elliot on 5 August 1762. Admitted freeman of the Upholders' Co. by servitude on 7 February 1770, and master in 1798. Took apps named John T. Deeble, 1770–77; John Priestland, 1773–81; John Kemp, 1785–1800; and Edward Crispe, 1791–99. Took son Thomas as app. on 3 September 1794, admitted freeman of the Upholders' Co. by servitude in 1802. Son George admitted freeman in 1808. Trading as Blaxland & Son, 71–72 Old Broad St, 1803–13. Took out Sun Insurance policies in 1778 for £5,000, utensils and stock accounting for £500; and in 1783 for £900, utensils and stock accounting for £450. Subscribed to Sheraton's *Cabinet Dictionary,* 1803. Death at Camberwell reported in *Gents Mag.,* May 1816, with obituary stating he was 'deputy of the ward of Broad Street ... He was for 36 years an active and highly respected Member of the Common Council, and executed the duties of many important offices in the City of London with the strictest integrity.' [D; GL, Upholders' Co. records; GL, Sun MS vol. 270, p. 189; vol. 306, p. 448]

Blaxland, Thomas, London, cm and upholder (1794–1827). Trading at 72 Old Broad St, 1817–27. Son of Henry Blaxland, u of London. App. to his father on 3 September 1794, and admitted freeman of the Upholders' Co. by servitude on 2 February 1802. [D; GL, Upholders' Co. records]

Blaxley, John, High St, Towcester, Northants., cm/joiner (1823). [D]

Blaxley, William, High St, Towcester, Northants., cm and u (1830). [D]

Blazeby, James, parish of St Stephen, Norwich, cm (1830). [Poll bk]

Blazeby, John, Norgate Ct, Norwich, cm (1818–39). [D; poll bks] Possibly the John Blazeby snr, chairmaker of Norwich, whose will was proved in 1840. [Norfolk Record Soc., index of wills]

Blea, —, Swerford, Oxon., 'Cabinet Maker, Upholsterer, Carver Gilder, Sign Decoration Painter' (c. 1830–40). So reads heading of bill which continues 'Projecting Word Letters carved, Brass Door Plates etc. Neatly Engraved'. [Private coll.]

Blears, Joseph, Nantwich, Cheshire, cm (1805–12). Son Joseph bapt. on 10 July 1805, and daughter Frances on 16 April 1812. [Chester RO, PR(bapt.)]

Blease, Peter, Liverpool, cm (1812). Admitted freeman on 14 October 1812. [Liverpool freemen reg.]

Bledwell, —, Covent Gdn, London, u (1739). Appointed by Dean of Bedford as Church Warden of St Paul's, Covent Gdn, *Read's Weekly Journal or British Gazetteer,* 28 April 1739.

Blenkhorne, James, Eldon St, Tuxford, Notts., joiner and cm (1832). [D]

Blenkinsop, Alexander, Leeds, Yorks., cm (1822–34). Trading at Mill Hill in 1822 and Basinghall St after 1826. [D]

Blenkinsop(p) (or Blenkinshop), Peter jnr, Durham, u (1754–62). Recorded in Market Pl. before 1762, and Sadler St from 1762. Worked at Gibside for Mrs Bowes, whose accounts record payments on 13 November 1754 of £8 1s 11½d for upholsterer's work; on 8 October 1756 'for a mahogany close stool', £1 4s 2d; on 4 June 1757 for bed tick, coverlets, blankets etc., £2 8s; on 15 March 1759 for materials for a new bed, £5 10s 4d; and on 11 December 1759, £6 4s 6d. Probably the Peter 'Blankinsop' who subscribed to Chippendale's *Director*, 1754. Published notice of remorse, *Newcastle Courant*, 20 February 1762, and declared bankrupt, *Gents Mag.*, December 1762. [Durham RO, Strathmore MS, Gibside, D/St/V 1488–90]

Blenkinsop, Thomas, Newcastle, cm, carpenter and joiner (1757–1801). Trading in Ballist Hills, 1778, and Pilgrim St, 1790–1801. Took app. named Haddock in 1757. [D; S of G, app. index]

Blennerhasset(t), Robert, 9 Windmill St, Finsbury Sq., London, and later 13 Bridport Pl., New North Row, upholder and cabinet warehouse owner (1803–35). Subscribed to Sheraton's *Cabinet Dictionary*, 1803. [D]

Blent, Charles, High St, Bromsgrove, Worcs., chairmaker (1835). [D]

Bletsoe, James snr and jnr, Oxford, cm and u (fl. until 1759). Partnership of father and son. [Harris, *Old English Furniture*]

Bletsor, William, Oxford, cm (1746). Took app. named Smith in 1746. [S of G, app. index] Probably:

Blettsoe, William, Oxford, cm (d. 1763). Probate of will dated 15 March 1763. [Bodleian Lib., index of wills]

Blick, Nicholas, Bolton St, St Martin-in-the-Fields, London, freeman joiner and by 1713 upholder (1703–13). Took out Hand in Hand Insurance policies on houses in Bolton St on 14 July 1703 for £250 on two tenanted houses in possession of the Countess of Rolliement(?), for seven years; on 18 October 1703 on two tenanted houses for £250 each for seven years; in 1706, £800 on brick houses, let; on 1 March 1706 on three houses for £300 each, one being let; and on 23 September 1713 on four houses for £300 each. Possibly the Blick paid on 20 November 1697 for supplying the Earl of Rockingham with two picture frames and mending an old one. [GL, Hand in Hand MS vol. 2, p. 539; vol. 2, p. 631; vol. 4, ref. 11817; vol. 5, ref. 12634; vol. 12, p. 148; Lincoln RO, Monson, 10/1/A/19]

Blin, Joshua, 25 St Thomas St, Weymouth, Dorset, cm and u (1840). [D]

Blinkhorn, George, Liverpool, u (1811–20). Indenture dated 1811. Petitioned freedom on servitude to George Philander Lyon, paying 6s 8d in 1820. [Liverpool freemen's committee bk]

Blinkhorn, James Gleed, Northampton St, Cambridge, cm (1840). [Poll bk]

Bliss, William, Bristol, cm (1775–81). Trading at 29 Horse St in 1775, and in the parish of St Augustine, 1781. Took out a Sun Insurance policy in 1776 for £300 on his house. [D; poll bk; GL, Sun MS vol. 248, p. 343]

Blissart, —, address unrecorded, turner (1794). Named in the Royal Household accounts on 5 January 1794 being paid 13s. [Windsor Royal Archives, RA 88837] Possibly Edward Blisset.

Blissatt, James, St Dunstan's in the West, London, upholder (1766–74). Son of James Blissatt, farmer of Thatcham, Berks. App. to Edward Rowley, 2 October 1766, and admitted freeman of the Upholders' Co. by servitude on 3 August 1774. [GL, Upholders' Co. records]

Blisset, Edward, 209 Piccadilly, London, turner and toyman (1789). [D]

Blissett, —, Marylebone St, Piccadilly, London, u and cm (1790–1803). Partnered with Mackenzie at no. 57, 1790–96, and no. 34, 1790–1803. Subscribed together to Sheraton's *Cabinet Dictionary*, 1803. [D]

Bliz(z)ard, A. & R., 42 Everett St, Brunswick Sq., London, upholstery and cabinet manufacturers, undertakers (1813–20). [D] Possibly Allen Blizzard.

Blizard, Richard, Stow-on-the-Wold, Glos., cm (1839). [D]

Blizard & Co., James, 10 New Cavendish St, London, u, cm and undertaker (1816–39). [D] Possibly father and son of same name.

Blizzard, Allen, 39 Judd St, Brunswick Sq., London, cm (1820). [D] Possibly of A. & R. Bliz(z)ard.

Blizzard, Robert, 7 Guildford Pl., Spitalfields, London, cm (1820). [D]

Block, R., Aldborough, Suffolk, carpenter and chairmaker (1839). [D]

Block, W., 36 Horse St, Bath, Som., chair and cm (1819). [D]

Bloer, William, 14 Dengell St, Clare Mkt, London, cm (1808). [D]

Blofeld, —, Turn-again-Lane, near Littlegate, Oxford, chairmaker (d. 1772). Sale of furniture 'at late Blofeld's' advertised, *Jackson's Oxford Journal*, 12 November 1772.

Blofeld (or Blofield) & Co. Thomas, Red Lion St, Banbury, Oxon., u, cm and auctioneers (1772–76). Advertised opening of warehouse in *Jackson's Oxford Journal*, 25 April 1772. Notice on 14 October 1774 of sale of stock of Blofield & Co. on dissolving of partnership; and on 28 March of sale of stock and goods of Thomas Blofield, bankrupt.

Blomfield, Anne, Cambridge, u(?) (1694). Named in St John's College account bks being paid £1 3s 2d for '11 yds. of Holland for Curtains for the Masters Lodge and for rings, tape and making'.

Blomfield, John, Baker's Rd, Norwich, cm (1818–36). App. to Thomas Smith, and admitted freeman on 14 July 1818. Took app. named Thomas Nelson jnr, admitted freeman on 21 September 1830. [D; poll bk; Norwich freemen reg.]

Blomley, Robert, Manchester, cm (1728). Took app. named Johnson in 1728. [S of G, app. index]

Blood, Robert, Swan St, Loughborough, Leics., joiner/cm (1822). [D]

Bloomfield, J., Walsall, Staffs., u (1839). [D]

Bloomfield, John, St Nicholas St, Ipswich, Suffolk, cm and u (1830). [D]

Bloomfield, William, Bury St, Stowmarket, Suffolk, cm (1830). [D]

Bloomfield, William, Clarence Cottage, 37 Clarence Pl., Brighton, Sussex, u (1826–40). Polled at Maldon, Essex, in 1826. Daughter Mary married Richard George Ward on 20 October 1840. [D; poll bks; E. Sussex RO, PAR 225/1/3/13]

Bloore, John, 20 Charterhouse St, London, cm (1791). Took out a Sun Insurance policy in 1791 for £200 on utensils and stock. [GL, Sun MS vol. 370]

Bloore, Samuel, Colmore Row, Birmingham, appraiser, auctioneer, u and cm (1816–35). Recorded at no. 27, 1822–35. [D]

Blossom, George, 92 Portland St, Liverpool, gilder (1835). [D]

Blott, John, London, paperhanger and u (1764–66). Advertised that he had arrived from London to Charleston, USA, *South Carolina Gazette*, 7 January 1764, 20 April and 29 June 1765, 18 February and 22 October 1766.

Blow, John, parish of St Clement Danes, London, carver (1727–28). Appointed assignee of the estate of Thomas England, joiner and chairmaker of the parish of St Ann's, Westminster, bankrupt, *London Gazette*, 9–12 March 1727–28.

Blower, J., 40 George St, London, carver and gilder (1835–39). [D] See T. Blower.

Blower, John, Pride Hill, Shrewsbury, Salop, cm and u (1840). [D]

Blower, Richard, St John's St, Lewes, Sussex, chairmaker and chair bottomer (1830–37). [Poll bks]

Blower, T., 40 George St, Portman Sq., London, carver and gilder (1837). [D] See J. Blower

Blowers, Mark, Charlotte St, Gt Yarmouth, Norfolk, cm and u (1830–39). [D; poll bks]

Bloxham, Samuel, 1 Brown Pl., Brown St, Liverpool, cm (1837). [D]

Bludwell, John, Bow St, London, u (1749). [Poll bk]

Blugrove, Ann, 'Nonburry' (Newbury, Berks.?), cm (1730). Named in the Stowe MS being paid £3 10s for a writing desk in 1730. [Huntington Lib., California, MS ST 82, p. 261]

Blumfield, James, St Martin's at Oak, Norwich, cm and u (1830). [D]

Blumley, —, Doncaster, Yorks., cm (1757). Took app. named Lee in 1757. [S of G, app. index]

Blundall, John, address unrecorded, upholder (1709). Admitted freeman of the Upholders' Co. on 27 January 1709. [GL, Upholders' Co. records]

Blundell, Ellis, Bridge St, Warrington, Lancs., u (1805–07). [D]

Blundell, John, Ormskirk, Lancs., cm (1752). Took app. named Lyon in 1752. [S of G, app. index]

Blundel(l), Richard, 'The Royal Bed', Paternoster Row, parish of St Faith, London, u (1710–14). Advertised to be 'sold or let on any sudden Occasion, fine stitched Quilts and Bed Gowns at reasonable Rates', *The Post Man*, 3 January 1710. Took out Sun Insurance policies on 3 April 1714 'for his Goods'; and on 19 October 1714 'for his goods and merchandizes in his house in Stanhope court next the Divill Tavern in Spring garden comm. Middx. No papers.' [GL, Sun MS vol. 3, ref. 43833; vol. 4, p. 103]

Blundell, Thomas, Southampton, Hants., cm (1836–39). Trading at King St in 1836 and St George's Pl., Houndwell, in 1839. [D] Probably the Thomas Blundel, cm, who subscribed to Sheraton's *Cabinet Dictionary*, 1803.

Blundell, William, London, frame maker (1829–35). Trading at 21 Little St Andrew St, Seven Dials in 1829 and at 9 Mead St, Soho in 1835. [D]

Blunt, Charles, Brook St, near Holborn Bars, London, u (1685–1705). Advertised sale, *London Gazette*, 20 March 1690, of 'A Fine large Tent lined with a bedstead and six large Russia Leather Stools, a good Marquee, and two French Tents, a handsome carriage cover'd with Leather and four Harnesses all New'. His accounts mention in 1687–88 a gilt frame sold to Mr Graves for 15s. In 1705 he wrote to his cousin, possibly Sir John Blunt of the South Sea Co. in the Bay of Bengal, to bring the finest muslins from abroad. Charles Blunt's accounts, 1686–92, name his patrons including Sir Robert Clarke, Sir Francis Blundell, Dowager Countess of Mountrath, Lady Ellsmore, Lady Ellis, Sir John Champentaire, Sir Henry Ingolsby and Lady E., Lord Abercorn, Sir Ralph Verney, Countess of Portland, Lady Vera Wilkinson, Sir Charles Fielding, Sir John Wilkinson, Lady Porthscourt, Lady Sadler, Earl of Mulgrave, and Squire Robert of Radnorshire. [PRO, C114/164, pt 1] Named in the accounts of Hoare's Bank, Fleet St receiving £48 in 1703 and £48 6s 8d in 1705. [Ledger nos 5/327, 7/243, 16/195]

Blunt, Charles, Worcester St, Bromsgrove, Worcs., chairmaker (1820). [D]

Blunt, J., 10 Coppice Row, Clerkenwell, London, cm, fancy cm and u (1826–39). [D]

Blunt, Robert, address unrecorded, leather case maker (1833–34). Supplied 'For Her Majesty's Own Use' two solid leather cases with partitions for paper and folding doors, leather cover for despatch box, and twelve black leather skins for chair covers, totalling £17 1s. [PRO, LC80; LC11/86]

Blunt, Thomas & William, London, u and furniture brokers (1825–27). Addresses given at Broker's Row, Mint in 1825, and 15 Redcross St, Southwark, 1826–27. [D]

Blunt, William, 10 Portsmouth St, Clare Mkt, London, carver and gilder (1808). [D]

Blyde, Charles, London, cm, u, appraiser and undertaker (c. 1760–84). Trading at 'The Chair and Tea Chest', c. 1760, the address given on his trade card framed by foliated Rococo scrolls, which states he was 'Late foreman to Messrs. Gally & Baker', and supplied blankets and carpets etc. [Heal] Recorded at Oxford St in 1773, when declared bankrupt; and in Berwick St, 1784. [Bailey's list of bankrupts; poll bk]

Blyth(e), Andrew, St Catherine's St, London, cm (1808–09). Took out Sun Insurance policies on 6 February 1808 for £1,650; and on 27 April 1809 in association with Alexander Mitchell, cm. [GL, Sun MS vol. 441, ref. 814238; vol. 447, ref. 830380]

Blyth, Samuel, Colchester, Essex, cm (1820–30). [Poll bks]

Blythe, Clarke, Colchester, Essex, cm (1755). Took app. named King in 1755. [S of G, app. index]

Blythe, Richard, Hull, Yorks., cm (1808–39). Recorded at Myton, near Hull, in 1808, and Jackson St, Neptune St, 1838–39. App. to Edward Dickon of Hull in October 1808. [D; Hull app. reg.]

Blythe, Thomas, 123 East St, Leeds, Yorks., cm (1826). [D]

Boaler, James Box, Tarleton St, Liverpool, cm (1837–39). Trading at no. 7 in 1837 and no. 13 in 1839. [D]

Board, Hannah, Blackfriars, St James's, Bristol, u (1832–34). [D]

Board, James, Bristol, cm and u (1837–40). Addresses given at 3 Bedminster Causeway in 1837 and 16 Griffin Lane 1838–40. [D]

Board, Nathaniel, Ipswich, Suffolk, cm (1756). Took app. named Turner in 1756. [S of G, app. index]

Board, W. & H., 11 Barton, Bristol, cm, u and undertakers (1835–40). [D]

Boardley, William, Lancaster, cm (1776–80). App. to Henry Baines in 1776 and admitted freeman in 1779–80. [Lancaster app. reg. and freemen rolls] Possibly:

Boardley, William, Slyne, Lancs., cm (1784). [Poll bk]

Boardman, Henry, 1 Bond St, Liverpool, u and cm (1837). [D]

Boardman, Thoephicks, Well Lane, Altrincham, Cheshire, cm (1822–28). [D]

Boardman, Thomas, 2 Queen St, Blackburn, Lancs. (home), u (1824–25). [D]

Boardman, William, Liverpool, cm (1760–84). Former apps named William Wilkinson and Daniel Gibbons petitioned freedom in 1760 and 1784 respectively. [Liverpool freemen's committee bk]

Boarsmith, Samuel, Bury St Edmunds, Suffolk, cm (1707). Probate inventory dated 1707. [Suffolk RO, (Bury), 592/34/28]

Boatwright, W., 41 Bury St, St James's, London, cm etc. (1820–28). [D]

Bobbitt, William, 29 Crown St, Soho, London, with workshop at 10 Sutton St, picture frame maker (1791). Took out a Sun Insurance policy on 16 March 1791 for £100, £30 accounting for utensils and stock in workshop. [GL, Sun MS vol. 373, ref. 580679]

Boddy, John, Dunkirk St, Bradford, Yorks., cm (1830). [D]

Boddy, William, York, cm (1784). Son of William Boddy, whitesmith; app. to William Hawkins, cm, on 16 February 1784. [York app. reg.]

Boddy & Wharrie, Canal Rd, Bradford, Yorks., joiners and cm (1830). [D]

Bodell, Christopher, Lancaster, house carpenter and cm (1789–90). [Lancaster freemen rolls]

Boden, —, Tiverton, Devon, cm (1824). Marriage to Miss M.

Rossiter of Tiverton reported, *Exeter Flying Post*, 22 July 1824.

Boden, William, Derby, cm (1741). [Poll bk]

Bodenham, George, 317 Cheapside, Birmingham, cm (1835). [D]

Bodham, Philip, 'The Three Chairs', Bartholomew Close, West Smithfield, London, u (1719–24). 'Was partner with the late Mr. John Hibbert, is now remov'd to the next door', as above. [Heal] Took out a Sun Insurance policy on 13 July 'for his goods and merchandise in his dwelling house only'. [GL, Sun MS vol. 9, p. 357] Known to have supplied carpets, 1720–23. [Scottish RO, GD 220/6/1201/6; GD 220/6/1240/30] In 1724 P. Bodham & Co. provided Robert Walpole with 'Twelve Wallnut wood chairs with India backs & seates veneer'd at 13/– each'. [*C. Life*, 15 January 1921, p. 66]

Bodington & Thorp, Red Lyon St, Clerkenwell, London, cm (1794). [D]

Bodle, John, Canterbury, Kent, cm (1747). [Canterbury freemen rolls]

Bodley, John, Canterbury St, Devonport, Devon, cm (1822). [D]

Bodovine, Rene, King St, London, u (Charles II). [Heal] See Paudevin.

Bodwell, James, London Rd, St George's, London, bed and bedstead maker (1831). Declared bankrupt, *Liverpool Mercury*, 21 January 1831.

Boeger(t) (or Bogaert, or Boeges), **Frederick**, address unrecorded, cm and carver (1795). Supplied furniture to the Prince of Wales, claiming £6 9s by bill for work ordered. [V & A archives; C. Musgrave, *Regency Furniture*, p. 48]

Boen, F., 24 Greville St, Hatton Gdn, London, looking-glass manufacturer (1820). [D]

Bogaert(s) (or Bogeart), **Peter**, London, carver, gilder, u etc. (1792–1819). Trading at 142 Tottenham Ct Rd in 1792, and as Bogaerts & Co. at 23 Air St, Piccadilly, 1809–19. [D; Westminster Ref. Lib., poor rate bk, D135] Took out Sun Insurance policies on 10 July 1792 for £100; and on 18 October 1809 for £300 on household goods. An earlier policy of 1809 refers to Paul Storr, the celebrated silversmith for whom he may have produced the models for making silver castings. [GL, Sun MS vol. 389, ref. 602642; vol. 448, refs 836376 and 836378] Bogaerts and Storr submitted a bill to the Prince of Wales on 17 December 1807 for supplying to Carlton House two carved and gilt candelabra for nine lights each, nine ft high, 'to stand one on each side of the Throne', £410. [RA 25282] On 1 February 1809 'Bogart carver' was paid £8 11s 6d by Edward, Lord Lascelles, probably for work at Harewood House, Hanover Sq., London. [Leeds archives dept, Harewood MS 192] A Peter Bogaerts, carver of St James's, Westminster, took app. named John Newbury on 6 April 1805 for £50. [PRO, IRI/40 and HO/107/1475]

Bogg, William, Boston, Lincs., joiner and cm (1793). [D]

Boggle, Thomas, St Dunstan's, London(?), cm (1758). Took app. named Davis in 1758. [S of G, app. index]

Bogle, John, Holborn, London, carver (1722). Took out a Hand in Hand Insurance policy in 1722 for £75 'on a brick house, empty'. [GL, Hand in Hand MS vol. 26]

Bogue, John, 4 Gerrard St, Soho, London, cm and upholder (1790–93). [D]

Boire, Joseph, St George's, Queen Sq., London, cm and carver (1755). Recorded going abroad in 1755. [Westminster Ref. Lib., Middlx session bk, 1116, p. 25]

Bois, Lazere Des, 'The Clock Case, Northside of Farmers Buildings', High St, St Giles-in-the-Fields, London, cm (1730). Took out a Sun Insurance policy on 10 August 1730 for £300, £50 accounting for goods and utensils in trade in a timber shed behind his house. [GL, Sun MS vol. 37, ref. 58396]

Bolam, James, London, carver and gilder (1808–27). Addresses given at 23 Lambeth Marsh in 1808, and 27 Lower Marsh, Lambeth, 1826–27. [D]

Bolam, John, Newcastle, joiner and cm (1827–34). Trading at 20 Butcher Bank in 1827 and 41 Bigg Mkt in 1833. [D]

Bolam, John, 23 Hillgate, Gateshead, Co. Durham, joiner and cm (1833–34). [D]

Bolam, Ralph, Castle-garth, Newcastle, cm and chairmaker (1824). [D]

Bolam, Robert, Newcastle, cm and joiner (1784). Took out a Sun Insurance policy in 1784 for £200, utensils and stock accounting for £140. [GL, Sun MS vol. 324, p. 417]

Bolam, William, Newcastle, cm (1827–38). Addresses given at 5 Prudhoe St, 1827–29; 11 Lisle St and 60 Northumberland St in 1834; and 5 Blackett St, also as u and joiner, in 1838. [D]

Bolar (or Boler), **Samuel**, London, cm (1724–37). Much employed by Lady Fitzwalter before and after her marriage to Fitzwalter, supplying items for Moulsham Hall or Schomberg House, Pall Mall, London. Between 1724–37 he was paid a total of £934 15s, 15% of all payments on furniture and fittings during these years. No details of his commissions survive, but his patronage bears witness to his quality, despite the fact he was relatively inexpensive. [Essex RO, Moulsham House archives; A. C. Edwards, *The Accounts of Benjamin Mildmay, Earl Fitzwalter*]

Boldison, Mark, Knaresborough, Yorks., joiner and cm (1834). [D]

Boler, John, 16 St James's St, Leeds, Yorks., cm and u (1826–30). [D]

Boler (or Bolder, or Bolar), **Richard**, Leeds, Yorks., cm (1816–37). Recorded at Woodhouse Bar, 1816–20, and Woodhouse Lane, 1821–37, no. 51 in 1830. Recorded also at 16 St James's St, as cm and u, in 1830. [D]

Boles, Peter, Nantwich, Cheshire, cm (1798). [D]

Boley, John, parish of St James, Bristol, cm (1774–84). [Poll bks]

Boley, Robert, Bristol, carver and gilder (1781). [Poll bk]

Bollam (or Bollom), **Robert**, Newcastle, cm, joiner and carpenter (1778–1801). Trading at Bankside, Castle Yd in 1778; Castle, Castle Yd in 1782; and Painter-heugh, 1787–1801. [D]

Bollam, Thomas, See Thomas Bolland.

Bolland, John William Joseph, Nantwich, Cheshire, cm (1833–35). Married Anne Birch on 17 February 1833. Daughter Elizabeth bapt. on 3 July 1835. [Chester RO, PR]

Bolland, Ralph, Foregate St, Chester, cm (1814). [D]

Bolland (or Bollard, or Bollam), **Thomas**, Liverpool, cm (1805–39). Recorded as Bollam at 10 Norfolk St in 1805, and no. 11 in 1807; as Bolland at no. 10 in 1810; no. 9 in 1811, and 30 Castle St in 1813–14; as Bollard at 12 Duncan St in 1816; 18 Pitt St, with joiner's shop at no. 16 in 1818; 46 London Rd in 1821; and as Bolland at 3 St Mary's Pl., Duckinfield, 1834–39. [D]

Bolland, Thomas, Liverpool, cm (1840). Admitted freeman on 21 April 1840. [Chester freemen rolls]

Bolland, William, Chester, joiner, carver and turner (1702). Master to William or Thomas Roberts in 1702. [Chester app. bks]

Bollans, Francis, Petergate, York, cm and u (1818–23). [D]

Bolongaro, Dominic, Manchester, carver, gilder, barometer and looking-glass maker, picture frame maker (1817–40). Addresses given at 2 Old Millgate, 1817–30; 14 Market St, 1832–33; no. 32, 1834–40. [D; Goodison, *Barometers*]

Bolson, Barker, Leeds, Yorks., carver (1750). Took app. named Spence in 1750. [S of G, app. index]

Bolt, Thomas, 28 Margaret St, Cavendish Sq., London, cm (1837–38). Letters and bills dated 8 December 1837 for items supplied to George Lucy at Charlecote Park, Warks., list '22

Antique Oak chairs for Dining Room' at £5 18s each, and '2 very handsome large elbow chairs — carved', £17 14s; bill totalled £158 13s 6d. [Warwick RO, L6/1118; V & A archives] Presumably Thomas Bott.

Bolte, Adrian, London, cm (1660–75). Cm to Charles I, he applied for re-appointment to the office under Charles II. Named in the Great Wardrobe Accounts early in his reign, supplying in 1668 a great press. [State Papers of Charles II; *DEF*] On 16 January 1670 provided a 'Great Cabinet' for the use of the Privy Council of Scotland. [Scottish RO, E28/74/1/1; *Conn.*, February 1977, p.127] Probably the 'Adrianne Boltee', cm of St George's, Southwark, who died in 1675. [PCC Wills, Index Lib., IX, p.23]

Bolter, James, London, cm and u (1760–92). Addresses given at 45 Bishopsgate Without, 1778–81, and Dorset St, Spitalfields, 1786–92. Son of Thomas Bolter, husbandman of Little Chiveron(?), Wilts.; admitted freeman of the Upholders' Co. by redemption on 15 June 1760. Took out a Sun Insurance policy in 1778 for £800, utensils and stock accounting for £400. Declared bankrupt, *Leicester Journal*, 7 July 1781. [D; GL, Upholders' Co. records; GL, Sun MS vol. 264, p. 298]

Bolter & Dawes, 1 Moorfields, London, u (1772–78). [D]

Bolton, Barker, Leeds, Yorks., cm (1762). Notice in the *Leeds Intelligencer*, 23 March 1762 stated that Bolton required evidence of identification of Isabella Grimslaw who had eloped.

Bolton (or Boulton), Benjamin, Fetter Lane, London, freeman joiner, by trade cm and chairmaker (1759–72). Employed two non-freemen for three months in 1759, and one in 1761. [GL, City Licence bks, vol. 2] Declared bankrupt in 1772. [Bailey's list of bankrupts] Possibly the B. Boulton of St Dunstan-in-the-West, declared bankrupt, *Gents Mag.*, September 1770.

Bolton, Ed., Thomas & Son, King St, New Bermondsey Rd, London, chair and sofa makers (1832–39). Trading as Thomas & Son, 1827–28. [D]

Bolton, George, King St, Shelton, Staffs., cm (1818). [D]

Bolton, George, Haxby, York, cm(?) (1824). Mahogany tea table with tapering turned legs and reeded edges to flaps recorded, signed underneath and dated 30 June 1824.

Bolton, George, High St, Witney, Oxon., cm and u (1830). [D]

Bolton, George J., London, upholder and undertaker (1826–39). Addresses given at 79 Charlotte St, Rathbrone Pl., 1826–27; 65 High St, Marylebone in 1835; and no. 85, 1837–39. [D] Possibly George Boulton, admitted freeman of the Upholders' Co. by redemption in 1798. [GL, Upholders' Co. records]

Bolton, James, Silver St, London, cm (1774). [Poll bk]

Bolton, Jeremiah, St Martin-in-the-Fields, London (1711–18) and Richmond, Surrey (1725), carver. Took out Hand in Hand Insurance policies on rented houses in Princes St, parish of St James, on 14 August 1711 for £100 on one house; renewed on 16 August 1718; and on 31 May 1712 for £150 each on two houses. Took out a Sun Insurance policy on 2 December 1725 for £500 on one house occupied by a silversmith. [GL, Hand in Hand MS vol. 9, p. 211; vol. 10, ref. 250; vol. 19, p. 113; Sun MS vol. 21, ref. 37480]

Bolton, John, Liverpool, cm (1747). Took app. named William Short in 1747. [Liverpool app. enrolment bk] Probably:

Bolton, John, Liverpool, cm (1780). His son, John Bolton, tailor, petitioned freedom by birth in 1780. [Liverpool freemen's committee bk]

Bolton, John, 9 Silver St, Liverpool, cm (1827–29). [D]

Bolton, John, New Elvet, Durham, cm and joiner (1828–34). [D]

Bolton, Joseph, Baildon, Yorks., cm (1822). [D]

Bolton, Ralph, Castlegate, Newcastle, cm (1827). [D]

Bolton, Richard, York, cm (1777). Of Fossgate, allowed four days to take freedom of city, 3 October 1777. [York freemen rolls]

Bolton, Richard, Higher Hillgate, Stockport, Cheshire, cm (1818–20). [D]

Bolton (or Boulton), Robert, Higher Hillgate, Stockport, Cheshire, cm (1816–28). [D]

Bolton, Samuel, High St, Chatteris, Cambs., cm, u and paper hanger (1839). [D]

Bolton (or Boulton), Thomas, 6 Windmill St, Tottenham Ct Rd, London, cm, upholder and undertaker (1818–28). [D]

Bolton, Thomas & Son, King St, New Bermondsey Rd, London, chair and sofa makers (1827–28). [D] See Ed. & Thos. Bolton & Son.

Bolton, Thomas, Princess St, Wigan, Lancs., u (1834). [D]

Bolton (or Boulton), William, London, cm and upholder (1809–29). Trading at 7 Chapel St, Grosvenor Sq., 1809–11; 30 Broad St, Carnaby Mkt in 1811; and 1 Mount Row, Berkeley Sq., by 1829. [D]

Bolton, William, Margaret St, Cavendish Sq., London, u etc. (1820–27). Trading at no. 8 in 1820, and in partnership with Elizabeth Sparrow at no. 7–8, 1820–27. In June 1825 the premises of Bolton & Sparrow were 'in part destroyed and greatly injured by fire'. [D; PRO, B3/504]

Boltz, Thomas, Heigham, Norwich, cm (1828–30). Son of John Boltz, gardener, admitted freeman on 27 February 1828. [Norwich freemen rolls and admissions reg.; poll bk]

Bolus, Henry, Worcester, u (1745–46). App. to his father Samuel Bolus, u, and admitted freeman on 18 January 1745–46. [Worcester freemen rolls]

Bolus, Samuel, Worcester, u (1740–58). Former apps admitted freemen: George Stephens in 1740, Henry Bolus in 1745–46, Richard Meredith in 1754, and Susanna Bolus in 1758. [Worcester freemen rolls]

Bolus, Susanna, Worcester, u (1758). App. to Samuel Bolus, u, admitted freeman on 13 March 1758. [Worcester freemen rolls]

Bolwell, Sarah, 9 St Michael's Hill, Bristol, carver and gilder (1832–35). [D]

Bolwell, William, 9 St Michael's Hill, Bristol, carver and gilder (1817–31). [D]

Bomer, Abraham, Bedfordbury, Covent Gdn, London, looking-glass maker (1709). [London rate bks; Wills, *Looking-Glasses*]

Bomery, James, address unrecorded, cm(?) (1770). Bill of 24 May 1770 for £3 3s for a chest of drawers submitted to the Earl of Winterton. [V & A archives]

Bon, George, 6 Mansfield Pl., Kentish Town, London, cm (1822). Took out a Sun Insurance policy on 30 January 1822 for £400, £50 accounting for stock and utensils in his house. [GL, Sun MS vol. 493, ref. 987851]

Bon, Mary, 6 Mansfield Pl., Kentish Town, London, cm (1824). Took out a Sun Insurance policy on 29 January 1824 for £300 on her new dwelling house, household goods, etc. [GL, Sun MS vol. 499, ref. 1012635]

Bonce, George, address unrecorded, cm (1803). Subscribed to Sheraton's *Cabinet Dictionary*, 1803.

Boncroft, John, address unrecorded, cm (1803). Subscribed to Sheraton's *Cabinet Dictionary*, 1803.

Bond, Benjamin, 24 Ratcliffe Highway, London, cm, chairmaker and furniture broker (1782–1827). Took out Sun Insurance policies in 1782 for £300, £225 accounting for stock and goods; 18 December 1801 for £600; and 10 October 1811 for £800, £50 on household goods and workshops, £650 on stock and utensils inside, £50 on stock china and glass; and £50 on stock and utensils in the open yard, with no stores for drying feathers. Named in Sheraton's list of master cabinet makers, 1803. [D; GL, Sun MS vol. 307, p. 72; vol. 423, ref. 725550; vol. 457, ref. 862383] See E., and John & James Bond & Son.

Bond, E., 24 Ratcliffe Highway, London, cm and chairmaker (1837). [D]

Bond, Edward, Lancaster, cm (1825–26). [Lancaster freemen rolls]

Bond, Edward, 176 Oxford St, London, cm (1840). Took out a Sun Insurance policy in 1840. [GL, Sun MS ref. 1339076]

Bond, Henry, 176 Drummond Cresc., Euston Sq., London, cm (1824). Took out a Sun Insurance policy on 8 April 1824 for £350 on household goods etc. at his dwelling house only, no work done therein. [GL, Sun MS vol. 499, ref. 1016085]

Bond, J. H. B., Langland St, Poole, Dorset, cm and u (1840). [D]

Bond, John, Bartholomew Close, St Bartholomew the Gt, London, chairmaker (1722). Took out a Sun Insurance policy for £500 on goods and merchandise in his house only. [GL, Sun MS vol. 14, p. 139]

Bond, John, James & Son, 24 Ratcliffe Highway, London, cm and u (1829–39). [D] See Benjamin and E. Bond.

Bond, Joseph or Joshua, Lancaster (1822–23). Named in the Gillow records working on a table in 1822. [Westminster Ref. Lib., Gillow vol. 344/100, p. 3171]

Bond, Matthew, Hedon, Yorks., cm and joiner (1828–29). [D]

Bond, Richard, 54 Seymour St, Euston Sq., London, cm, upholder and furniture broker (1835–39). [D]

Bond, S. G., 50 Dean St, Soho, London, cm etc. (1820). [D] See Stephen Griffith Bond.

Bond, S. E., 11 Knightsbridge, London, upholder and cm (1826–39). [D] See Stephen Griffith Bond.

Bond, Stephen, 18 Church St, Soho, London, broker and upholder (1812). Took out a Sun Insurance policy on 4 November 1812 for £300, £70 accounting for books and wearing apparel, and £200 for stock, utensils and goods in trust. [GL, Sun MS vol. 459, ref. 875623]

Bond, Stephen Griffith (or Griffyth), London, cm, u and undertaker (1826–38). Addresses given at 11 Dorcas Buildings, Hammersmith in 1832; 11 Knightsbridge in 1826; and Dorcaster, Hammersmith Rd, Hammersmith in 1838. [D]

Bond, T., 10 James St, Bath, Som., cm (1819). [D]

Bond, William, London, (1753). Son of William Bond of Godalming, Surrey, innholder, app. to William Linnell, cm on 26 June 1753 for £50. [GL, Joiners' Co. records]

Bond, William, Vine St, Piccadilly, London, carver and gilder (1774). [Poll bk]

Bond, William, Haymarket, London, carver and gilder (1778). Took out a Sun Insurance policy for £800 in 1778 with William Crawford, upholder, and Thomas Noble, proprietors of the Casino in Marlborough St. [GL, Sun MS vol. 267, p. 356]

Bond, William, High St, Marlow, Bucks., cm, joiner and builder (1823). [D]

Bone, Barnabas, Greenwich, London, cm (1822–39). Addresses given at Royal Hill, 1824–26; London St in 1834; and High St, Deptford, Kent in 1839. [D] See Samuel Bone.

Bone, Charles, Arundel, Sussex, chairmaker and turner (1826–39). Trading at Tarrant St, 1826–32, and High St in 1839. [D]

Bone, Henry, Truro, Cornwall, then Plymouth, Devon, carver and worker in wood (1755–72). Carved and inlaid the pulpit in St Mary's Church, Truro, which was incorporated in the present Truro Cathedral and forms St Mary's aisle, where the pulpit, slightly cut-down, still stands. It is polygonal with veneered sides inlaid with representations of the Saviour's life, and has a curiously German or N. Italian appearance. Bone's son of the same name was app. to Richard Champion, china manufacturer, on 20 January 1772, and became the well-

known enamel-painter. [G. C. Boase, *Collectanea Cornubiensis*, 1890, col. 88; Lake's *Complete Parochial History of . . . Cornwall*, vol. 4, (1872) p. 253; Pountney, *Old Bristol Potteries*, p. 312]

Bone, James, Montpelier Vale, Lewisham, London, cm and u (1826–38). Recorded in partnership with William Bone, cm, in 1838. [D]

Bone, John, Norwich and London, cm (1790–1818). Recorded in the parish of St Ethelred, Norwich, 1794; parish of St Julian, 1796–99; and London, 1802–1818. [Norwich poll bks] Polled at Ipswich, Suffolk in 1790.

Bone, Samuel, 8 Royal Hill, Greenwich, London, cm (1838–39). [D] See Barnabas Bone.

Bone, Thomas, 127 Fenchurch St, London, cm and upholder (1808–11). [D]

Bone, William, Montpelier Vale, Blackheath, London, cm (1838). [D] See James Bone.

Bonella, —, 2 Worship St, Finsbury, London, cm and u (1839). [D]

Bonella, Alexander, 5 Worship Sq., London, carver (1829). [D]

Bonella, William, 107 Whitechapel Rd, London, cm, chairmaker, u, bedstead maker and undertaker (c. 1800). Trade card shows Sheraton-style chair and desk framed by swags of drapery. [Heal]

Bones, John, King's Lynn, Norfolk, cm (1724/25). Took app. named Row in 1724/25. [S of G, app. index]

Bonham, William, 15 Gerrard St, Soho, London, cm and upholder (1839). [D]

Bonifold, John, address unrecorded, chairmaker (1791–92). In 1791 the account books of the Governors of the Hospital of Sir John Hawkins, Chatham, record the purchase of eight mahogany elbow chairs of Hepplewhite design with finely carved interlaced shield backs and moulded frames on tapered legs, costing £16. In the same ownership until 1944, when they fetched £640 at Sotheby's. On 6 April 1792 Bonifield was paid £6 0s 6d, the remainder of his bill for chairs and table supplied for the Council Room; and on 27 April £8 18s 6d for chairs and table. [Heal; *Conn.*, June 1931; Sotheby's, 29 July 1929] See John Benifold.

Boning, Thomas, Little St Mary's Lane, Cambridge, cm (1832–40). [Poll bks]

Bonnel(l), Henry, Lancaster, cm (1821–28). Second son of Jabez Bonnell, wheelwright and joiner of Lancaster; app. to J. Hodgson in 1821 and admitted freeman, 1827–28. Married on 30 January 1828 Betsy, youngest daughter of George Loxam of Lancaster. [Lancaster app. reg. and freemen rolls; *Liverpool Mercury*, 8 February 1828]

Bonnel(l), Thomas, 133 Long Acre, London, upholder and cm (1744–d. 1782). In partnership with William Simmon(d)s, cm, St Martin-in-the-Fields, when declared bankrupt, *Gents Mag.*, April 1744. Sale announced in *Daily Advertiser*, 14 March 1744, of 'All the entire genuine Stock in Trade of those ingenious and eminent Cabinet Makers, Mess. Bonnell and Simmonds, consisting of several curious pieces of Work in Mahogany, Walnut-Tree, Amboyna and other Woods, viz. Buroes, Cabinets, Bookcases and Tables, with many other pieces of Furniture, finish'd in the most elegant Taste . . .'. Death reported in *Gents Mag.*, 9 March 1782, stating he was 'many years a cabinet-maker in Long Acre, and lately retired from business'. [D; poll bk] Probably the Bonnell of London named in the St John's College, Cambridge, account bk in 1748 supplying 'chairs for the Lodge', totalling £19 13s 6d. Probably also the Bonnel who was paid £18 0s 6d in 1771 for work at Longford Castle. [V & A archives]

Bonnell, — jnr, Long Acre, London, cm (1768). Death of his wife at her lodgings near Hampstead reported in *Public Advertiser*, 1 August 1768.

Bonnet, Adrian, King's Head Ct, Petticoat Lane, Stepney, London, u (1724). Took out a Sun Insurance policy on 25 March 1724 for £500 on goods and merchandise in his house only. [GL, Sun MS vol. 16, ref. 31468]

Bonnett, John, 63 Green Lane, Sheffield, Yorks., cm (1822). [D]

Bonney, John, 71 Pembroke St, Devonport, Devon, cm (1838). [D]

Bonney, Richard P., Liverpool, Lancs., cm (1767–96). Son of John Bonney; admitted freeman on 2 December 1767. Recorded at Canal Side, Vauxhall Rd in 1796. [D; Liverpool freemen reg.]

Bonnin, James, 15 Exeter St, Brampton, Cumb., cm (1809–11). [D]

Bonnington, —, 12 George Ct, Clerkenwell, London, clock-case maker (1810). Took out a Sun Insurance policy on 26 April 1810 in association with Joseph Warren, Gent. and Gibbs, cm of 11 George Ct. [GL, Sun MS vol. 452, ref. 844194] Possibly:

Bonnington, George, Red Lion Sq., Clerkenwell, London, clock-case maker (1812). Took out a Sun Insurance policy on 26 November 1812 for £300 on household goods. [GL, Sun MS vol. 457, ref. 877090] Trading as:

Bonnington, George & Thorp(e), George, 21–22 Red Lion St, later no. 6, Clerkenwell, London, and 42 Tavistock St, 'BENT GLASS MANUFACTORY, Likewise Clock Case & Cabinet Makers . . . GLASS CASES AND OVAL SHADES Made of the finest White Glass to any given Dimensions to preserve Gilt or any other ornaments of Clocks, Girandoles, Vases, Figures, where may be had Bent, Round, Convex, Convex & Concave Mirrors with or without Frames, from 4 to 4 ever, Finished in the most elegant style, Also Glasses for Windows & Coach Lanterns.' (1793–1814). Subscribed to Sheraton's *Drawing Book*, 1793. Took out a Sun Insurance policy on 27 April 1809 for £1,700, £950 on dwelling house and shops behind, £200 on George Thorpe's household goods, and £400 on stock and utensils in open yard behind. [D; trade card, MMA, NY; GL, Sun MS vol. 447, ref. 830361]

Bonsall, Richard, Bull's Head Ct, Newington Causeway, Newington Butts, London, carpenter and cm (1801–02). Took out Sun Insurance policies on 22 December 1801 for £200, £50 accounting for utensils and stock; and on 11 February 1802 for £300, £130 on stock and utensils. [GL, Sun MS vol. 423, ref. 725579; vol. 424, ref. 727721]

Bonsall, Richard, 4 Broker's Row, Red Cross St, London, cm (1835–37). [D]

Bonsal(l), Thomas, Blackman St, Southwark, London, cm and upholder (1792). Took out a Sun Insurance policy on 12 November 1792 for £800. Declared bankrupt that year. [GL, Sun MS vol. 389, ref. 606465; Bailey's list of bankrupts]

Bonsor, Henry, Castlegate, Nottingham, u and paper hanger (1835). [D]

Bonynge, —, address unrecorded, upholder (1795). Two of a set of six painted beechwood armchairs signed 'BONYNGE UPHOLDER 1795', exhibited by D. Drey, Antique Fair, Grosvenor House, 7–22 June 1962. [*Conn.*, June 1962, p. 126] Inscription is similar in date and character to that handwritten in ink found on a satinwood urn table, which reads 'M. GREGSON, LIVERPOOL', paper-hanger, stationer and u, possibly the dealer who received Bonynge's furniture from elsewhere. [V & A archives]

Boocock, Benjamin, York, cm (1796–97). On 2 April 1796 was paid £52 4s 9d for bedsteads, tables, chairs etc. supplied to The Retreat Quaker Asylum, York. Other bills are dated August 1796 and February 1797. [Borthwick Institute, York, Retreat MS H/1]

Boocock, S. C., 65 Queen St, Cheapside, London, cm (1826–27). [D]

Booden, Thomas snr and jnr, London, upholder (1713–56).

Trading at Fenchurch St in 1727 and Seething Lane, 1750. Thomas snr was son of John Booden, clothworker of London; app. to Edward Wood on 4 July 1713. Admitted freeman of the Upholders' Co. by servitude on 6 July 1720, and recorded as a member of the Livery in 1750. His son, Thomas Booden, was admitted freeman by patrimony on 5 April 1750. Either snr or jnr took app. named Thomas Old, 1754–56, but then left London for Charleston, USA, where his arrival was reported in *South Carolina Gazette*, 28 October and 16 December 1756. [Poll bk; GL, Upholders' Co. records and Livery lists]

Booker, Thomas, Pownall Sq., Liverpool, gilder (1794). [D]

Booker, William, 8 Porter St, Soho, London, cm (1822). Took out a Sun Insurance policy on 21 February 1822 for £300, £250 accounting for stock, utensils and goods in trust. [GL, Sun MS vol. 493, ref. 989098]

Booker, William, 14 Lower Seymour St, Portman Sq., London, cm and u (1826–39). [D]

Boon, J., 7 Southampton Ct, Queen's Sq., London, upholder (1835). [D]

Boon(d), John, Greenhead, Burslem, Staffs., joiner, cm, chairmaker and builder (1818). [D]

Boon, John, 9 Duke St, Liverpool, with shop at 1 Waterloo Pl., Church St, cm and u (1827). Declared bankrupt, *Liverpool Mercury*, 25 May 1827. Sale of stock in trade announced, same paper, 18 May, 'consisting of two elegant Four-post Bedsteads, tastefully fitted up with French Gray & Blue Morine Furniture, excellent Hair Mattresses, Feather Beds, etc: several pieces of Brussels Carpets & Hearth Rugs, of modern patterns, seven pieces of rich Blue Silk Damask, Striped Cotton, Sundry Fringes, etc: two sets of Mahogany Chairs, handsome Card Tables, Lady's Work Ditto, Cabinet, Chests of Drawers, Dressing Glasses, Portable Desks, imitation Rosewood framed Couch, covered with Morine, thirteen pairs of Mahogany Bedposts, a quantity of two-inch Maple Planks, four Cabinet-makers Benches etc.'. [D]

Boone, Samuel Joseph, London, upholder (1787–96). Recorded with his brother, Thomas, at Drury Lane in 1796. Son of Robert Boone, butcher of Chandos St. App. to John Smith of Union St on 1 August 1787, and admitted freeman of the Upholders' Co. by servitude on 2 March 1796. [GL, Upholders' Co. records]

Boone, Samuel, London, chair and sofa manufacturer (1829–39). Trading at 101 Gt Guildford in 1829, 9 West St, Soho in 1835 and 15 Gravel Lane, Southwark in 1839. [D]

Boone, Thomas, London, upholder (1784–94). Recorded at John Smith's, Union St, Southwark in 1794, and with his brother, Samuel Joseph, at Drury Lane in 1796. Son of Robert Boone, butcher of Chandos St, Covent Gdn. App. to John Smith on 7 January 1784, and admitted freeman of the Upholders' Co. by servitude on 5 February 1794. [GL, Upholders' Co. records]

Boone, Thomas, 17 Moore St, Soho, London, chair and sofa maker (1820). [D]

Boone, Thomas, 46 King St, Seven Dials, London, upholder (1826–27). [D]

Boone, William, Seven Dials, London, u (1820). [D]

Boons, Richard, Cambridge, cm (1730). Took app. named Flack in 1730. [S of G, app. index]

Boor(e), John, Pool Lane, Liverpool, u and auctioneer (1804–05). Addresses given at no. 35 in 1804 and no. 36 in 1805. Marriage reported, *Liverpool Chronicle*, 9 October 1805, to Mrs Sarah Sherwood of John St. [D]

Boor(e), Charles snr, 34 High St, Lewes, Sussex, cm (1774–1826). [D; poll bks]

Boore, Charles jnr, Sun St, Lewes, Sussex, possibly home address, with trade address at 34 High St, journeyman cm

(1816–18), cm, u and furniture broker (1823–39). Recorded in partnership with Edward Boore at 34 High St, 1832–39. [D; poll bks] Sale of stock in trade, possibly on bankruptcy, of Messrs. C. & E. Boore, 'Cabinet makers, Chair manufacturers and General Furnishers . . . upwards of 50 years', announced, *Sussex Agricultural Express*, 20 April 1839. Goods to be sold at 'a very considerable REDUCTION IN PRICE . . . as the whole must be cleared by Midsummer next . . .'. Sale re-advertised, 1 June 1839, and public auction by Verral & Son announced, 8 and 15 June 1839.

Boore, Edward, Lewes, Sussex, cm (1818–37). Addresses given at New St in 1818, as journeyman cm, and at West St, probably his home, in 1837. In partnership with Charles Boore jnr, 1832–39. [D; poll bks]

Boore, Frederick, Sun St, Lewes, Sussex, journeyman cm (1816–37). [Poll bks] See Samuel Boore.

Boore (or Bore), Sam(p)son, Brighton, Sussex, cm (1822–37). Addresses given at Carlton Hill before 1822; Ship St Ct in 1822; Richmond Hill, 1829; and Cavendish Pl. North, 1837. Another address, possibly for trade, given at 5 Cavendish St, date unspecified. [D; poll bks] Baptisms recorded of Harriet, daughter of Samson and Harriet Bore; Jane, daughter of Samson and Frances Bore, 22 December 1822; Edward, 22 March 1829; and Eliza, 25 June 1837. [E. Sussex RO, PR(bapt.)]

Boore, Samuel, North St, Lewes, Sussex, journeyman cm (1826–30). [Poll bks] See Charles, Edward and Frederick Boore.

Boosey, Abraham & Son, 53 Bermondsey St, London, cm and upholder (1839). [D]

Boot, Aaron, Nottingham, app. turner and chairmaker (1824). [Nottingham app. list]

Boote, Alexander, Crown St, Soho, London, u (1778). [*Gents Mag.*, February 1778] See James Bayley.

Booth, —, address unrecorded (1771). Named in the Earl of Ancaster's account book, 25 August 1771, supplying a commode chest of drawers etc., totalling £13 1s. [Lincoln RO, 2 ANC 6/14]

Booth, Benjamin, at 'The Rocking Horse', near Serjeant's Inn, Fleet St, London, turner (1749–75). [Heal; V & A archives; GL, trade cards]

Booth, Cath., Salthouse Ct, Salthouse Lane, Hull, Yorks., upholstress (1838–39). [D]

Booth, Henry, Blackfriars, London, gilder (1713). Took app. on 31 August 1713. [PRO, app. reg.]

Booth, James, 148 Chapel St, Salford, Lancs., cm (1800). [D]

Booth, James, Brightholmlee, Ecclesfield, Sheffield, Yorks., cm (1837). [D]

Booth, John, Leek, Staffs., chairmaker (1797–98). [D] See William Booth.

Booth, John, Liverpool, cm (1807–39). Trading at 19 Pall Mall, 1807–18; 53 Stanley St, 1827; and 6 Whitemill St, 1839. [D] See Nathan Booth.

Booth, John, Raistrick, Yorks., joiner and cm (1834). [D] See Jonas Booth.

Booth, John, 9 Cross St, Stalybridge (Stalbridge), Dorset, cm and joiner (1834). Presumably of Booth & Sykes, cm and joiners, Stalybridge. [D]

Booth, John, Sparrow Hill, Loughborough, Leics., cm (1835–40). [D]

Booth, John Henry, 65 Charles St, Sheffield, Yorks., cm (1833–37). Recorded also at 65 Eyre St in 1837. [D]

Booth, John, Stamford, Lincs., cm (1784). Son of Richard Booth, butcher and freeman burgess; admitted freeman in 1784. [Stamford freemen rolls]

Booth, Jonas, Raistrick, Yorks., cm (1822). [D] See John Booth.

Booth, Nathan, 73 Stanley St, Liverpool, cm etc. (1834–37). [D] See John Booth.

Booth, Nathan, 8 North Parade, Bradford, Yorks., cm (1837). [D]

Booth, Nathaniel, Ct 76, Newgate St, Newcastle, joiner and cm (1827). Recorded also as a grocer in Heron St, with house at 5 Stowell St. [D]

Booth, Ralph, Salford, Lancs., cm (1800–17). Trading at Nightingale Sq. in 1800 and 4 Caygill St in 1817. [D]

Booth, Samuel, Warrington, Lancs., chairmaker (1828–34). Trading in Riding St, 1828, and Horse Market St, 1834. [D]

Booth, Stephen & J., 43 Lower Marsh, Lambeth, London, chair and sofa makers (1820–39). [D]

Booth, Thomas, 1 Back Blakeley St, Manchester, cm (1804–17). [D]

Booth, William, Scotland St, Ashton-under-Lyne, Lancs., cm and joiner (1828). [D]

Booth, William, Spout St, Leek, Staffs., chairmaker and turner (1816–35). [D]

Booth, William Aspinall, 29 Young St, Quay St, Manchester, cm and u (1840). [D]

Bootham, Joseph, Glayson St, Liverpool, cm and mortgager (1781). Took out a Sun Insurance policy in 1781 for £300 on houses. [GL, Sun MS vol. 294, p. 296]

Boothby, Henry, Eastgate, Louth, Lincs., cm/joiner (1822). [D]

Boothby, John, at 'The Golden Head', Norfolk St, Strand, London, u, sworn appraiser and undertaker. Mid 18th-century trade card framed by elaborately scrolled and foliated bedstead with drapes and tester, states that he 'Makes and Sells all Sorts of Upholstery Goods, Cabinets, Chairs, and Looking Glasses, &c.' [Leverhulme Coll., MMA, NY; Westminster Ref. Lib., Gardener Coll., 63–31B] Mahogany drop-leaf dining table exhibited by John McMaster, c. 1970, revealed in a secret compartment a letter from the maker, John Boothby, to its original owner, Mrs Norton of Leics., dated Christmas Eve, 1743. It reads, 'Madam. — I hope these 2 tables will please. I do Ashure you thay are very good tables, the longer thay are worn the better thay will look, with a little Rubbing. I Coud have sent tables of the same size for 6s. A table Cheaper, but as to promise I have them Good, the Scarborough Rock is a Name I never Heard.' [9th Spring Antiques Fair, Chelsea Old Town Hall]

Boothman, John, 47 Blackley St, Manchester, cm (1797). [D]

Bootland, George, 29 Hampstead Rd North, London, cm and upholder (1839). [D]

Bootle, Henry, 40 Newman St, London, carver (1829). [D]

Bootley, William, York, cm (1831). Son of William Bootley, joiner; app. to William Greenwood, cm, on 21 November 1831. [York app. reg.]

Bore, Robert, Norfolk, cm (1793–1807). Recorded in the parish of St Saviour, Norwich, 1796; Swaffham, Norfolk, 1799–1802; and King's Lynn in 1807. Son of John Bore, cobbler; admitted freeman on 28 September 1793. Subscribed to Sheraton's *Drawing Book*, 1793. [Poll bks; Norwich freemen reg.]

Borini, Peter, Birmingham, carver, gilder, picture frame, looking-glass, barometer and thermometer manufacturer (1816–35). Trading at 89 Bull St in 1816; Snowhill in 1818; Bull St, 1821–35, no. 46 in 1822, and no. 40, 1823–35. [D; Goodison, *Barometers*]

Bo(o)rman, William, High St, parish of St Lawrence, Winchester, Hants., cm and upholder (1763–98). Son of Rev. Daniel Borman, clerk of Winchester; app. to Edward Polhill on 31 August 1763, and admitted freeman of the Upholders' Co. by servitude on 3 July 1771. Took out Sun Insurance policies in 1775 for £300 on utensils and stock; in 1781 for £500 on shop, utensils and stock; in 1782 for £500 on his house; in

1783 for £400, £300 on utensils and stock; and on 19 July 1791 for £1,000, utensils and stock accounting for £300. Mahogany serpentine chest of drawers recorded bearing label. [D; GL, Upholders' Co. records; GL, Sun MS vol. 238, p. 470; vol. 295, p. 19; vol. 303, p. 59; vol. 314, p. 153; vol. 379, p. 160; V & A archives]

Borne (or Boorne), Robert, over against George Yd, Lombard St, London, cm (d. by 1727). [Heal; Harris, *Old English Furniture*, p. 19]

Borough, —, London, cm (1793). Subscribed to Sheraton's *Drawing Book*, 1793.

Borough, John, Leeds, Yorks., cm and u (1802–06). Announced his move from Burley Bar to Kirkgate, *Leeds Mercury*, 27 February and 13 March 1802. Advertised, *Leeds Mercury*, 5 April and *Leeds Intelligencer*, 24, 31 March and 7 April 1806, his proposal to practice as appraiser and auctioneer, claiming that 'a person in the constant Practice of making every Article in [that] business must be the best judge of its value'.

Borron, James, 28 Little Queen St, London, broker and cm (1790–93). [D]

Borrows, David, Lincoln, cm (1837). [Poll bk]

Borrows, William, 72 Frederick St, Liverpool, carver (1781). [D]

Borsman, John, Tonbridge, Kent, u (1784). [D]

Borwick, William, Lancaster, cm (1799–1800). Admitted freeman, 1799–1800, when stated 'of Liverpool'. [Lancaster freemen rolls]

Bosden, Henry, 206 St John St, Clerkenwell, London, u (1793). Took out a Sun Insurance policy on 30 March 1793 for £200, £100 on household goods in house of Pearce, baker, and £50 on utensils and stock. [GL, Sun MS vol. 386, p. 234]

Boseley, John, address unrecorded, freeman turner (1742–49). Took out a Hand in Hand Insurance policy on 1 April 1742 for £125, renewed in 1749. [GL, Hand in Hand MS vol. 62, ref. 53643]

Bosens, Samuel, Daniel's Row, Burslem, Staffs., chairmaker (1822). [D]

Bosfield, Thomas, Banbury, Oxon., upholder (1776). Declared bankrupt, *Gents Mag.*, April 1776.

Boshell, Henry, 61 Byron St, Leeds, Yorks., cm and joiner (1837). [D]

Bosley, James snr, London, upholder (d. by 1725). His son, James Bosley, admitted freeman of the Upholders' Co. by patrimony in 1725. [GL, Upholders' Co. records]

Bosley, James jnr, London, upholder (1725). Son of James Bosley, upholder of London, admitted freeman of the Upholders' Co. by patrimony on 21 April 1725. [GL, Upholders' Co. records]

Bosley (or Boseley), John, St Bride's, London, cm and joiner (1712–39). Addresses given at 'The Crown', Fleetditch, 1712–19, and Ditch Side, 1717–39. Took out insurance policies as a joiner on 16 August 1712 with the Hand in Hand Co. for £150 on his house; with the Sun Co. on 3 October 1713; the Hand in Hand Co. on 22 September 1718 for £150 on his house and two others; and with the Sun Co. on 9 July 1719 on his warehouse and four houses adjoining in tenure. As cm, served at St Bride's as Questman in 1717, Sidesman in 1720, and Churchwarden in 1739. [GL, Hand in Hand MS vol. 10, ref. 23629; vol. 19, p. 165; GL, Sun MS vol. 3, p. 65; vol. 9, p. 353; GL, MS 6561, p. 28]

Boson, John, London, carver (1720–d. 1743). When John Boson died in April 1743 he had become one of a select group of craftsmen closely connected with the designs of William Kent. Vertue said of Boson that he was 'a man of great ingenuity and undertook great works in his way for the prime

people of quality and made his fortune well in the world'. [*Walpole Soc.*, vol. XXII, p. 116] It is possible that his death at a relatively young age — Vertue says 'an age not considerably above middle age' — robbed Boson of his place in furniture history, letting contemporaries such as Benjamin Goodison take more of the limelight.

The date of Boson's birth is uncertain, but was probably about 1705. It is also probable that he served his apprenticeship as a ship's carver based near the naval ship-yards at Deptford, for by the 1720s he had a yard at Greenwich. His name first appears working as a carver on St George's Bloomsbury between 1720–30. In 1725 his first domestic work is recorded when he made carvings for 4 St James's Sq., London. At the same time he was also one of the craftsmen employed to build the Fifty New Churches. Other churches that Boson worked on included a screen and organ gallery for Westminster Abbey in 1729, and a reredos for Canterbury Cathedral in 1732.

He did not neglect the secular market, working on East India House, Leadenhall St in 1730 with a partner at this time, John How. Together they were responsible for all the carved woodwork on the facade and the chimney-pieces inside. Chimney-pieces may have been one of Boson's specialities for there are others recorded, for example in 1735 when the Hon. Francis Godolphin paid £61 for the 'Great room' chimney-piece at Baylies, Stoke Poges, Bucks. and another example for Sir Michael Newton's seat, Culverthorpe, Lincs. He also signed an interesting monument, sculptured by Guelfi (and may therefore only have erected it) to Anne, Duchess of Richmond, c. 1730, Deene Church, Northants.

The 1730s were Boson's years of greatest success. From 1732 onwards he regularly carried out work for Frederick, Prince of Wales on his houses at Leicester Fields, Kew Palace and Cliveden, Bucks. In 1738 Boson carved the taffrail, or stern-board, of a barge for the Prince and even after Boson's death the Prince owed a considerable sum, subsequently paid to the executors. Only seven pieces remain complete with their receipts: a pair of pier tables and matching glasses, a pair of candlestands and the stand for the 'Pope's Cabinet' at Stourhead. The pier glasses and tables are decorated with the owl crest and were made for Lady Burlington, wife of the 3rd Earl, and installed in her Garden Room at Chiswick. Designed by William Kent, the carved and gilt glasses cost £15 and the two leather-topped mahogany tables with gilt-wood enrichments, £20. The receipt is signed by Boson and dated 11 September 1735. Included on this receipt was a pair of candle-stands with 'Boys heads' for which Boson charged £5 each but deducted £1 16s for the woodwork of the stands which was to be paid to 'Mr Davis the Joiner'. In 1742 Henry Hoare II commissioned Boson to make a mahogany stand in the form of a Roman Triumphal Arch to carry an important piece of 16th-century Italian *pietre-dura* work known as 'The Pope's Cabinet'. In October 1738 Boson had charged Sir Richard Hoare £10 5s for making a mahogany bed.

Another facet of John Boson's business included the making of picture frames. For example, in 1746 Boson's executors put in a bill of £328 11s 4d to the Prince of Wales for work on his house at Leicester Fields. This included two large frames for 'Battle Pieces painted by Mr Wooton', two frames in 'the French Manner' as well as several hundred feet of enriched mouldings.

Apart from working for people in Burlington's circle, such as Lord Charles Somerset (later 4th Duke of Beaufort) and Lord Guilford, Boson also subscribed to a number of important books: Leoni's *Alberti*, 1726 and Isaac Ware's *Palladio*, 1738. John Boson often worked on his own, but he did however share the work on East India House with John

How, and Benjamin Goodison also worked with Boson at Leicester Fields.

In March 1733/34 Boson took a long lease from Lord Burlington on a plot in Savile Row. The house was probably designed by William Kent and was finished in 1735. Boson lived there with his wife until his death in 1743. He also had a country house at St Anne's Hill, Chertsey, Surrey. In his will, made in April 1740, Boson left amongst various bequests £10 to his foreman Thomas Nicholls the elder, and the Chertsey house and its contents to Mary Norman, daughter of Barak Norman, a musical instrument maker of St Paul's Church-yard. Boson's executors were the painter George Lambert, James Horne the architect, and thirdly John Thornhill of St Martin-in-the-Fields.

ST GEORGE'S CHURCH, Bloomsbury, London. Between 1720–30 carried out carved work. [Lambeth Palace Lib., papers: Fifty New Church, MS 2728, f55]

4 ST JAMES'S SQ., Westminster, London. In 1725 payments for carving work made to Boson by the Duke of Kent are recorded in his account at Hoare's Bank. [Survey of London, vol. 29, p. 90, addendum]

ST JOHN'S CHURCH, Smith Sq., Westminster, London. In 1727 petitioned for payment for carving work. [Lambeth Palace Lib., papers, Fifty New Churches, MS 2728, f55]

ST LUKE'S CHURCH, Old St, London, Between 1727–33 carried out carved work. [Gunnis]

ST JOHN HORSELEYDOWN, Southwark, London. Between 1728–33 carried out carved work. [Gunnis]

WESTMINSTER ABBEY. In 1729 worked on the screen and organ gallery for £33. [Westminster Abbey archives]

EAST INDIA HOUSE, Leadenhall St, London. In 1730 he was paid £189 19s for 'carvers work' in association with John How. [Mildred Archer, 'The East India Co. and British Art', Apollo, November 1965, p. 405]

CLEY (A house of the Duke of Montrose). In 1732 payments were made to John Boson for the decoration of the dining room and stairs totalling £33 3s. [Scottish RO, GD 220/6/31/p. 640, Montrose papers: cash bk, 1732]

CANTERBURY CATHEDRAL. In 1732 charged £242 for the reredos. [Fabric account bk, Cathedral Lib.]

HOLKHAM HALL, Norfolk (1st Earl of Leicester). In 1732 the accounts for the 4th quarter record payments to Boson of £19. [V & A archives]

KEW PALACE, Surrey (Frederick, Prince of Wales). In 1732 carried out various carved work for the Prince, receiving £100 (vol. 2, pp. 291–92) and £20 (vol. 3, p. 261). In 1733 carried out further carving work costing £30 (vol. 3, p. 265). Additional work included a chimney piece and terms at £177 (vol. 4, p. 238). In 1734 Boson received £16 0s 4d (vol. 4, pp. 262, 273d). In 1745 payment of £1 9s was made by the Prince of Wales to Boson's executors. [Household accounts of Frederick, Prince of Wales, Duchy of Cornwall archives, vol. 15, pp. 312, 347]

BAYLIES, Stoke Poges, Bucks. (Hon. Francis Godolphin). In 1735 Boson was paid £61 for a chimney piece to fit the 'Great room'. [YAS, Duke of Leeds papers]

CHISWICK HOUSE, Middlx (3rd Earl of Burlington). Bill of 1735 for two 'Rich Glas frames', two 'Mahogany Tables with Tearmes' (now at Chatsworth, cf. Rosoman article cited below, pl. 15) and two 'Stands with Boys heads' (Rosoman, pl. 7) costing £43 4s, was signed by Boson on 11 September, and payment received from 'Right Honble the Countess of Burlington'. [Burlington papers; Chatsworth archives, no. 247:1; T. Rosoman, 'The Decoration and use of the Principal Apartments of Chiswick House, 1727–70', Burlington, October 1985]

ST JAMES'S PARK, Westminster (Frederick, Prince of Wales).

In 1735 carried out various carved work for the Prince costing £233 19s 5½d. [Household accounts of Frederick, Prince of Wales, Duchy of Cornwall archives, vol. 4, pp. 269, 273]

CULVERTHORPE HALL, Lincs. (Sir Michael Newton). Supplied a chimney-piece in 1736. [C. Life, vol. LIV, pp. 350, 386]

FREDERICK, PRINCE OF WALES. Boson received payment for 'service to Christmas 1736 £10 – 16 – 2d and £1 – 1s – 0' (vol. 19, pp. 165–66). In 1738 carved frames costing £24 5s (vol. 19, p. 167). Worked on the barge for the Prince of Wales, submitting a bill for carving the taffrail or stern-board, and other ship decoration costing £10 10s on 12 December 1738 (Vouchers Bk, vol. 7). [Household accounts of Frederick, Prince of Wales, Duchy of Cornwall archives]

SIR RICHARD HOARE. Bill for carving a mahogany bedstead at £10 5s is signed and dated 10 October 1738. [V & A Lib., MS 86, NN 3, no. 12]

ST OLAVE'S CHURCH, Southwark, London. In 1739 Boson attended a meeting concerning the building of the church where he produced designs and costs and also specimens of his work. Accordingly he was asked 'to perform the said work for £50'. [The Builder, 1844, p. 253]

LORD CHARLES SOMERSET. In 1740 Boson submitted a bill for carving chimney mouldings, table frames and oval sconces at £71 5s 7d. This may have been for work at Badminton House, Glos. but this is not certain. [Badminton House, Muniment Room, Correspondence, Drawer 32]

LORD GUILFORD, 1st Earl of. In 1740 payment was made to 'Mr Booson' of £94. This money may have been for work on Guilford's London house, 50 Grosvenor Sq. [Bodleian Lib. MS, North C 58, F99; Survey of London, vol. L, p. 164]

WESTMINSTER ABBEY. In 1741 received £95 for an organ case. [Westminster Abbey archives]

STOURHEAD, Wilts. (Henry Hoare II). In 1742 commission to make a stand for the 'Pope's Cabinet'. [Nat. Trust guide to Stourhead]

LEICESTER HOUSE, London (Frederick, Prince of Wales). Between 1742–43 various carving work for the Prince included frames for two pictures by John Wooton. Boson also gilded some furniture, and appears to have worked with Benjamin Goodison on some of the State rooms. [Survey of London, vol. 34, 1966]

LEICESTER HOUSE, London (Frederick, Prince of Wales). A detailed account was rendered on 1 August 1746 by John Boson's executors to the Prince. Included are hundreds of feet of enriched mouldings and architraves, columns and capitals, a chimney-piece and a coat of arms. The total was for £328 11s 4d. [Ibid. vol. 15, pp. 373–74]   T. R.

Bossen, Samuel, Chell St, Hanley, Staffs., chairmaker (1834). [D]

Bostock, Edward, Liverpool, cm (1780). Admitted freeman on 8 September 1780 on servitude to John Jones. [Liverpool freemen reg.]

Bostock, Edward, Middle-gate, Newark, Notts., cm and u (1822). [D]

Bostock, James, at 'The Rising Sun', Wich St, parish of St Mary le Savoy, London, upholder (1718). Took out a Sun Insurance policy on 22 January 1718 on goods and merchandise. [GL, Sun MS vol. 7]

Bostock, James, at 'The Two Black and White Balls', Holborn Row, Lincoln's Inn Fields, London, u (1727–35). [Heal; M. A. Steer, Index of London Tradesmen]

Bostock, Mary, 1 Brown St, Salford, Lancs., u (1825). [D]

Boston, J., 10 Potter St, Soho, London, chair and sofa maker, broker (1826–39). [D]

Bosvera, Henry, St Anne's Ct, London, cm (1749). [Poll bk]

Boswell, William, Norwich, carver and gilder (1831). Admitted freeman on 20 June 1831. [Norwich freemen rolls]

Bosworth, James, Hereford, cm and u (1830–35). Ten bills dated 1830–35 from Bosworth to Capt. N. L. Pateshall, RN of Hereford, list upholstery, bedding, carpets, and furniture supplied, including a wardrobe, £2 2s; chimney glass, £6 10s; mahogany table, £4 10s; dressing table, 18s; music stool, 15s; side board, £4; mahogany library table, £4 4s; bedstead and hangings, £6 10s; and 6 mahogany trafalgar chairs, £6 12s the set. Other items supplied by the versatile Mr Bosworth include '19 Gallons Cyder at 1/– a gallon', bottles, saucepans, fire irons, ivory-handled knives, and brooms. [Herefs. RO, F60/202, 208, 218, 226, 257, 271, 290, 302, 513 and 540]

Bosworth, Joseph, Edgbaston St, Birmingham, cm and joiner (1777–80). [D]

Bosworth, Robert, Market Harborough, Leics., u (1791). [D]

Botamley, William, Gainsborough, Lincs., chairmaker (1690–91). [Lincoln RO, subject index, Inv 189/196]

Botcherby, Robert, Darlington, Co. Durham, cm (1793–1803). Subscribed to Sheraton's *Drawing Book*, 1793, and *Cabinet Dictionary*, 1803. [D]

Botham (or Bothman), John, Leicester, cm (1826). App. to Joseph Green, cm; admitted freeman in 1826. [Leicester freemen rolls]

Botham, Robert, Friargate, Derby, cm and u (1823–35). Recorded also at 3 Brookside in 1828 and 17 Friargate in 1835. [D]

Botham, William, Gloucester, cm (1813–19). Children bapt. in 1813, 1815 and 1819 at St Michael's. [PR(bapt.)]

Bott, Samuel, 59 York St, Westminster, London, cm and upholder (1839). [D]

Bott, Thomas, London, cm and u (1816–39). Addresses given at 10–11 Gt Portland St, Oxford St 1816–31, and 28 Margaret St, 1832–39. [D] Supplied furniture to Streatlam Castle, Co. Durham, receipts for which are dated July 1829 and January 1830. An estimate of 10 July 1829, totalling £67 4s, refers to 'A French Bedstead with Solid Ends & Sweep etc. Sideboards neatly Japaned in colors of chintz hangings ... Handsome chintz hangings for ditto lined thro' blue & white stripe — Teaster cloth & full valence finished twine fringes bound silk lace ...'. [Durham RO, Strathmore MS D/St/64] Received substantial commission from John Arkwright of Hampton Court, Leominster, Herefs., being paid a total of £230 10s 6d in May 1830. His bill covers extensive redecoration, including the repair of furniture, supplying of new furniture, curtain and roller-blind making, and paper hanging, prior to rebuilding of Hampton Court, 1834–42. Bott sent Arkwright another bill on 6 November 1834 for items supplied in 1832, including principally eight mahogany dining room chairs covered in red Morocco leather and costing £23 4s. An accompanying letter asks for payment of outstanding amount as he has 'experienced several disappointments latterly'. [Herefs. RO, Arkwright papers, A63/161] Account dated 9 October 1830 lists furniture made for Thomas Vernon of Hanbury Hall, near Droitwich, Worcs. His bill, totalling £137 18s 6d, describes a handsome suite of furniture in rosewood, including 12 chairs costing £39 12s, a sofa £22 10s, and two elbow chairs, £10 each, all being 'stuffed and covered purple morocco finish gold colour silk netted Buttons and gimp', an occasional table, and a circular table 'on Neat Turned and carved Pillars triangular block feet and castors.' Vernon also commissioned Bott for a suite of mahogany bedroom furniture, including a carved four-post bedstead with cornices, bedding and chintz hangings, washstand, dressing table and two wardrobes. His bill, totalling £208 6s 4d, was paid on 5 April 1831, and also listed a rosewood tea poy and Davenport desk, and making window

curtains. [Worcs. RO, Vernon papers, 7335/705:7/8ii 39–40; 77v 30 and 45] Worked for the Lucy family at Charlecote Park, Warks., submitting a bill on 8 December 1837 totalling £158 13s 6d for twenty-two antique oak dining chairs and two matching elbow chairs with turned supports and upholstered in Genoa velvet. [Nat. Trust guide to *Charlecote Park*, p. 27; Joy, *English Furniture, 1800–1851*, p. 121] Presumably Thomas Bolt.

Bott, William, London, cm (1806). Admitted freeman of Lincoln in November 1806. [Lincoln freemen rolls]

Botterell, Thomas & Sons, 37 Northumberland Pl., Commercial Rd, London, upholders (1826–39). [D]

Botterill, William Houghton, 37 Northumberland Pl., Commercial Rd, London, u (1840). [GL, Sun MS ref. 1335024]

Bottom, Henry, 9 Silver St, Golden Sq., London, u and cm (1785). Took out a Sun Insurance policy on 28 March 1785, £50 on utensils and stock and £50 on household goods. [GL, Sun MS vol. 327, p. 511]

Bottom, Henry, 39 Wardour St, London, upholder (1790–93). [D]

Bottom, Joseph, London, upholder (1773). Son of Joseph Bottom, app. to Richard Gomm of Clerkenwell, and admitted freeman of the Upholders' Co. on 7 April 1773. [GL, Upholders' Co. records]

Bottom, Joseph, 39 Gt Queen St, Lincoln's Inn Fields, London, upholder (1776). Took out a Sun Insurance policy in 1776 for £600, £350 accounting for utensils, stock and goods. [GL, Sun MS vol. 248, p. 373]

Bottomley, John, Honley, near Huddersfield, Yorks., cm (1830–37). [D]

Bottomley, John, Holme, Yorks., joiner and/or cm (1837). [D]

Bottomley, Thomas, Liverpool, u (1811–27). Trading at 57 Circus St in 1811; 17 Paradise St in 1818; 60 Gloucester St, 1821; 88 London Rd 1823; and 2 Devon St, 1827. [D]

Bottrell, John, 20 Bridge St, Leeds, Yorks., cm (1822). [D]

Botts, George, parish of St Mary, Chelmsford, Essex, cm (1777). Son Thomas bapt. on 2 February 1777. [Essex RO, PR(bapt.)]

Bouch, Thomas, Wells, Norfolk, cm (1777–1839). Recorded at Freeman St, 1830–39. App. to James Lyther, joiner and cm, and admitted freeman of King's Lynn, 1777–78. [D; King's Lynn poll bks and freemen's calendar]

Bouch, William, Wells St, London, cm (1793). Subscribed to Sheraton's *Drawing Book*, 1793.

Boucher, Daniel, St George's Pl., Cheltenham, Glos., cm and u (1820–30). Trading at nos 9–11 in 1830. [D] See Thomas Boucher.

Boucher, George, 14 Henrietta St, Cheltenham, Glos., cm and u (1830). [D]

Boucher, John, 15 Chesterfield St, Marylebone, London, cm (1791). Took out a Sun Insurance policy on 27 September 1791 for £250. [GL, Sun MS vol. 379, p. 631]

Boucher, John, 9 St George's Pl., Cheltenham, Glos., cm and u (1822). [D]

Boucher, Thomas, Cheltenham, Glos., cm and u (1820–30). Recorded at 8 Henrietta St, in 1820; nos 8 and 9, also as paper hanger and appraiser in 1822; and Bath Rd in 1830. [D]

Bough, Thomas, Swine Market St, Ellesmere, Salop, joiner/cm (1822). [D]

Boughey, George, Nantwich, Cheshire, turner (1789–92). Burial of daughter Ellin by his wife Hannah recorded, 20 November 1789; of daughter Ann, 26 March 1791; and baptism of Sarah, daughter by his wife Anna, 12 March 1792. [Chester RO, PR(bapt.)]

Boughey, Samuel, Nantwich, Cheshire, turner (1824). Married on 20 January 1824. [Chester RO, PR]

Boughtflower, Benjamin, address unrecorded, cm (1803). Subscribed to Sheraton's *Cabinet Dictionary*, 1803.

Boughton, George, Nantwich, Cheshire, turner (1782). Son Richard bapt. on 3 October 1782. [Chester RO, PR]

Boulderson, William, Falmouth, Cornwall, u, linen and woollen-draper (1783–84). [D]

Boulnois, —, 14 Charlotte St, Rathbone Pl., London, u (c. 1830). Address on label recorded on chair of transitional Sheraton-Victorian type. [V & A archives] Label also found on a music Canterbury at Birthwaite Hall, Yorks. Probably the Boulnois who worked for the 3rd Lord Braybrooke, supplying furniture either for Audley End, Essex, Billingbear, Berks., or his London house, being paid £6 2s in December 1835; £12 16s in June 1837; and £69 9s 7d in June 1839. [Essex RO, D/DBy/A363] Probably:

Boulnois, John, 44 South Moulton St, London, u (c. 1830–39). Address in directories, 1837–39, and on labels found on set of fourteen William IV mahogany dining chairs and armchair, with curved top rails, rectangular backs, seats covered in buttoned scarlet leather on reeded tapering legs. [Christie's, 22 March 1979, lot 8] Label also recorded on pieces in various sets of varnished oak chairs, upholstered in green leather, at Penrhyn Castle, Wales. [V & A archives]

Boulter, Henry, Leicester, turner (1839). [Leicester freemen rolls]

Boulter, William, 5 Skinner St, Bishopsgate, London, chair and moulding manufacturer (1820). [D]

Boulton, B., St Dunstan-in-the-West, London, cm (1770). Declared bankrupt, *Gents Mag.*, September 1770. Possibly Benjamin Bolton.

Boulton, Charles, Chester, cm (1789–1856). Addresses given in Eastgate St, 1812–22, and Lower Row, Bridge St, 1828. Probably the Charles Boulton app. to Richard Hawkins, cm, on 30 November–3 December 1789. Admitted freeman on 7 November 1811. Took apps named John Cross in 1814, John Todd in 1826, Charles Leatwood in 1830 and Joseph Boulton, his son, in 1856. Declared bankrupt, *Chester Guardian and Cambrian Intelligence*, 20 May 1819, having 'assigned over his Estate and Effects for the equal benefit of such of his creditors . . .'. [D; poll bks; Chester freemen rolls and app. bks] See Joseph Boulton.

Boulton, Charles, Chester, cm (1831). Admitted freeman on 27 April 1831. [Chester freemen rolls]

Boulton, Charles, Bevington Hill, Liverpool, Lancs., cm (1835–37). Trading at no. 8 in 1835 and no. 2 in 1837. [D]

Boulton, George, Charing Cross, London, upholder (1798–1802). Son of George Boulton, agent, of Golden Cross, Charing Cross. Admitted freeman of the Upholders' Co. by redemption in 1798. [GL, Upholders' Co. records and Livery lists] Possibly George Bolton of Charlotte St and High St, London.

Boulton, George, Wood St, Hanley, Staffs., cm (1822). [D]

Boulton, Isaac, Lancaster, chairmaker (1788–1810). App. to Joseph Tyson, chairmaker, in 1788, and admitted freeman, 1795–96. Took apps on 19 March 1800, 26 June 1805 and 22 February 1810. [Lancaster app. reg. and freemen rolls]

Boulton, John snr, 48 Threadneedle St, London, upholder, auctioneer and undertaker (1761–d. 1798). Son of John Boulton, freeman weaver of London; app. to J. Shard armourer, on 16 November 1749, and to William Jones on 6 August 1752. Admitted freeman of the Upholders' Co. on 15 December 1757, and master in 1793. Took apps named William White, 1761–68, and Sterry Marks, 1771–74. His son, John Boulton, admitted freeman in 1794. Died in 1798, but his name occurs in directories at 48 Threadneedle St, 1801–02, referring presumably to his son. Small bow-fronted mahogany chest-of-drawers with his label sold at Sotheby's, 19 November 1948. [D; GL, Upholders' Co. records; Heal]

Boulton (or Bolton), John jnr, 109 St Martin's Lane, London, u (1794–1803). Son of John Boulton of Threadneedle St, upholder, admitted freeman of the Upholders' Co. on 2 July 1794. Named in Sheraton's list of master cabinet makers, 1803. Declared bankrupt, *Billinge's Liverpool Advertiser*, 30 August 1802. [D; GL, Upholders' Co. records and Livery list]

Boulton, Joseph, Eastgate St, Chester, cm (1827). Admitted freeman on 16 October 1824. [Chester freemen rolls] See Charles Boulton.

Boulton, William, Peterborough, Northants., carver (1775). Took out a Sun Insurance policy in 1775 for £1,500, £230 accounting for warehouses and timbersheds. [GL, Sun MS vol. 238, p. 481]

Boulton, William, Queen's Sq., Lancaster, chair and bedstead maker (1816–34). Addresses given at King St in 1816–18, and Queen Sq., 1822–34. [D]

Bounsall (or Bounfall), A., 8 Middle Row, Holborn, London, japanned chair manufacturer (1802–04). Named in Sheraton's list of master cabinet makers, 1803. [D]

Bourke, James, address unrecorded, upholder (1711). Admitted freeman of the Upholders' Co. on 2 May 1711. [GL, Upholders' Co. records]

Bourlet, William, London, carver and gilder (1808–29). Trading at 26 Chad's Row, Gray's Inn Rd, 1808, and 45 London St, Fitzroy Sq., 1829. [D]

Bourn (or Bourne), George, Liverpool, carver and gilder (b. 1763–d. 1823). Recorded as Bourne at 18 Tarleton St in 1810–11 and as Bourn at Renshaw St in 1823. Death aged 60 on 6 July 1823 reported, *Liverpool Mercury*, 25 July. [D]

Bourn, James, 6 Case St, Liverpool, carver and gilder (1827–37). [D]

Bourne, John, 2 New Cut, Lambeth, London, carver and gilder (1826–27). [D]

Bourne, Lancelot, Newcastle, u (1792). App. to John Hudson, admitted freeman on 12 July 1792. [Newcastle freemen reg.]

Bourne, Peter, 56 Sparling St, Liverpool, joiner and cm (1835). [D]

Bourne, William, London, cm and u (1816–39). Addresses given at 25 Bun St, Low E. Smithfield and 2 New St, St Catherine's, 1816–19; 13 Hereford Pl., Commercial Rd, 1820; and Devonshire Pl., Commercial Rd East, by 1839. [D]

Bouskell, George, 17 Amwell St, Spitalfields, London, cm (1829). [D]

Boustead, James, Over Darwen, near Blackburn, Lancs., joiner and cm (1824–25). [D]

Bouvrier, Thomas, Liverpool, cm (1759). Petitioned freedom on servitude to William Leech, deceased, paying 6s 8d in 1759. [Liverpool freemen's committee bk]

Boveri (or Bouveri), Francis, 9 Eyre St Hill, London, barometer, thermometer, looking-glass, crown glass and picture frame maker (1830–41). [D; Goodison, *Barometers*]

Bow, Charles, 24 Harcourt St, Marylebone, London, cm (1826–39). [D]

Bow, Robert, 10 Homer St, Marylebone, London, upholder (1826–27). [D]

Bowcher (or Boucher), John, Exeter, Devon, cm and u (1826–38). Addresses given at High St in 1826; Goldsmith St, 1828–30; and 20 Magdalen St, 1838. Son John Spark bapt. at St Martin's on 22 September 1826, and George John at All Hallows on 3 November 1828. [D; PR(bapt.)]

Bowcock, William, 5 Bond St, Manchester, painter and gilder (1797). [D]

Bowd, Charles, 44 Old Compton St, London, ironmonger and cm (1793). [D]

Bowden, —, Fore St, Tiverton, Devon, cm (1823–24). [D]

Bowden, —, Chester, cm (1831). Account bks at Erddig, Clwyd, list two rosewood trays costing 7s 6d supplied to Mrs Yorke in 1831.

Bowden, Andrew, Exeter, Devon, cm (1776). [Exeter freemen rolls]

Bowden, E., Cowick St, St Thomas's, Exeter, Devon, u (1838). [D]

Bowden, George, London, cm and upholder (1820–39). Addresses given at 10 New Inn Sq., Shoreditch, 1820–21; 51 Featherstone St, City Rd, 1822–28; and 4 White Lion St, Norton Falgate, 1837–39. Took out a Sun Insurance policy on 30 November 1820 or 1821 for £600, £50 on shop behind house, and £350 on stock and utensils in shop, open yard, and workshop behind 129 Curtain Rd. Another policy of 14 January 1822 for £850, included £500 on stock and utensils in warehouse, open yard, and manufactory behind warehouse; and £150 on a house and shop at 10 New Inn Sq. in tenure of a cm. Took out a further policy on 1 April 1824 for £800. [D; GL, Sun MS vol. 486, ref. 974240; vol. 489, ref. 987580; vol. 497, ref. 1016183]

Bowden, James, Witton St, Northwich, Cheshire, joiner and cm (1822). [D]

Bowden, John, corner of May's Buildings, Bedfordbury, London(?), cm (1775). Took out a Sun Insurance policy in 1775 for £100, £30 accounting for utensils, stock and goods. [GL, Sun MS vol. 242, p. 621]

Bowden, John, West Wycombe, Bucks., chairmaker (b. c. 1791–1841). Aged 50 at the time of the 1841 Census.

Bowden, Jos., Chesham, Bucks., seedsman and chairmaker (1793). [D]

Bowden, Joseph, 15 Elder St, Norton Falgate, London, chairmaker (1817). [D]

Bowden, Joseph, 17 Lower Maudlin St, Bristol, ornamental and cabinet carver (1832–33). [D]

Bowden, Joshua, 12 Spicer St, Spitalfields, London, chair manufacturer (1820). [D]

Bowden, William, Fore St, Totnes, Devon, cm and u (1838). [D]

Bowden, William, 62 Bridport St, Hoxton, London, cm (1839). [D]

Bowdige, Samuel, Axminster, Devon, cm and u (1808). Advertised, *Exeter Flying Post*, 16 June 1808, for two cm.

Bowditch, George, address unrecorded, upholder (1754–62). Son of John Bowditch, clothier of Swinsham, Somerset, app. to William Jones jnr on 5 December 1754, and then to Richard Hearne on 7 February 1759. Admitted freeman of the Upholders' Co. by servitude on 4 February 1762. [GL, Upholders' Co. records]

Bowen, George, Corve St, Ludlow, Salop, cm and u (1822). [D]

Bowen, Henry, 9 Salter's Ct, Hull, Yorks., cm (1838–39). [D]

Bowen, Matthew, Bristol, u (1715–18). Trading at Wine St in 1717. Took apps named Elliot in 1715 and Whitfield in 1718. Took out a Sun Insurance policy on 4 June 1717 on his house. [Poll bk; S of G, app. index; GL, Sun MS vol. 6, p. 267]

Bowen, Thomas, London and Pembrokeshire, upholder (1778–1802). Recorded in Ludgate St, London, 1778–86, and Milford, Pembrokeshire, 1794–1802. Son of Thomas Bowen of Pembrokeshire, Gent.; app. to William Fassett and admitted freeman of the Upholders' Co. by servitude on 6 October 1773. [GL, Upholders' Co. records]

Bower, Benjamin, 3 Bow St, Sheffield, Yorks., carver and gilder (1830). [D]

Bower, Charles, Paternoster Row, Sheffield, Yorks., cm (1821). [D]

Bower, Charles, 50 Chichester Pl., Gray's Inn Rd, London, carver and gilder (1837). [D]

Bower, Charles, Nine Elms, London, cm and upholder (1839). [D]

Bower, J. D., London, upholder (1797). [D]

Bower, Joseph, 5 Stewart's Rents, Drury Lane, London, cm (1775). Insured his house with the Sun Co. for £200 in 1775. [GL, Sun MS vol. 243, p. 27]

Bower (or Borver), Joseph, London, cm, upholder and broker (1778–96). Trading at 12 Old Round Ct, Strand, 1778–93, with timber workshop adjoining in Vine St, Covent Gdn in 1792; and 64 Gt Queen St, Lincoln's Inn Fields, by 1796. Took out Sun Insurance policies in 1778 for £400, of which £200 accounted for utensils and stock ; on 13 July 1786 for £1,200, £730 on utensils etc.; and on 30 June 1792 on utensils, stock and goods in the Vine St timber workshop. Subscribed to Sheraton's *Drawing Book*, 1793. [D; GL, Sun MS vol. 267, p. 350; vol. 339, p. 146; vol. 389, ref. 602222]

Bower(s), Robert, High Wycombe, Bucks., chairmaker (1798). [Militia Census]

Bower, Thomas, 4 Mill Pl., Shaw's Brow, Liverpool, cm (1834). [D]

Bowerbank & Bamber, Fishergate, Preston, Lancs., joiners and cm (1814–16). [D] See Walmsley & Bowerbank of Preston.

Bowers, John & Thomas, 241 Oxford St, London, carvers and gilders (1802–23). [D]

Bowers, Robert, Chester, u (1754). Master to John Denson, 1754. [Chester app. bks]

Bowers, Robert, Aylsham, Norfolk, carver and gilder (1830–39). Trading at Whitehart St in 1830 and Cromer Rd in 1839. [D]

Bowers, William, Russell St, Bedford, cm (1839). [D]

Bowes, George, Moore St, London, cm (1784). [Poll bk]

Bowes, George, Kingston, Surrey, cm and undertaker (1794). [D]

Bowes, John, West Cowes, Isle of Wight, Hants., cm (1757–61). Took apps named Parkman in 1757, Cox in 1759, Wise in 1760 and Smyth in 1761. [S of G, app. index]

Bowes, Philip, Cowes, Isle of Wight, Hants., cm (1777–78). Took out Sun Insurance policies in trust for John Lewis in 1777 for £100 and 1778 for £200; and in 1777 insured utensils and stock for £110 out of a total of £200. [GL, Sun MS vol. 260, p. 233; vol. 265, p. 499; vol. 261, p. 147]

Bowes, Thomas, 'a timber house, S. side Hand Alley, E. side Bishopsgate St.', London, turner (1717). Took out a Hand in Hand insurance policy on 24 October 1717 on his house for £150. [GL, Hand in Hand MS vol. 17, p. 333]

Bowes, Thomas, St Oswald's parish, Durham, cm (1746–48). Son's baptism registered on 30 April 1746, and others recorded until 1748. [PR(bapt.)]

Bowhill, John, Berwick-upon-Tweed, Northumb., cm (1827–34). Trading at Church St in 1827 and Western Lane 1828–34. [D]

Bowker, John, London, upholder, carpet, u and bedding warehouse owner (1757–1811). Addresses given at Leather Lane, Holborn in 1772; 127 Holborn in 1774; 29 Cannon St in 1779; 128 Leadenhall St, 1781–84; and 3 Postern Row or Rd, Tower Hill by 1793–1810. An address at 25 Duke St, St James's also given, date unspecified. Son of John Bowker, tanner, Yaxley, Hunts.; app. to Nicholas Parkes, draper, on 6 April 1757, and admitted freeman of the Upholders' Co. on 6 March 1766. Took out Sun Insurance policies on utensils and stock in 1779 for £750 out of a total of £1,000; in 1781 for £1,630 out of £2,000; and on 21 February 1810 for £1,650 out of £2,000. Probably the John Bowker, upholder of St Andrew's, Holborn, declared bankrupt, *Gents Mag.*, June 1772, and July 1784. [D; GL, Upholders' Co. records and Livery lists; GL, Sun MS vol. 276, p. 379; vol. 289, p. 19; vol. 451, ref. 841330]

Bowker, Thomas, 19 Fairhurst St, Cheapside, Liverpool, gilder (1790). [D]

Bowler, Charles, West Wycombe, Bucks., chairmaker

(b. *c*.1811–41). Aged 30 at the time of the 1841 Census.

Bowler, George, Nantwich, Cheshire, u (1713). Daughter Mary bapt. on 26 January 1713. [Chester RO, PR(bapt.)]

Bowler, James, West Wycombe, Bucks., chairmaker (b. *c*.1821–41). Aged 20 at the time of the 1841 Census.

Bowler, Samuel, London, upholder (1723–31). Son of Charles Bowler, freeman hatbandmaker; app. to James Maulden on 5 March 1723 and admitted freeman of the Upholders' Co. by servitude on 5 May 1731. [GL, Upholders' Co. records]

Bowler, William, High St, Lymington, Hants., cm etc. (1839). [D]

Bowles, Bernard, parish of St Peter, Hungate, Norwich, cm (1802–07). App. to William Elden Earl, and admitted freeman on 13 April 1802. [Poll bks; Norwich freemen reg.]

Bowles, George, 5 Little Chapel St, Soho, London, carver and gilder (1829). [D]

Bowles, John S., Middle St, Norwich, cm and u (1830). [D]

Bowles, Thomas, 153 Leadenhall St, London, frame maker (1796). [D]

Bowles, William, 52 Old St Rd, London, bedstead maker (1839). [D]

Bowley, John, 26 Bridges St, Covent Gdn, London, upholder and auctioneer (1807). Took out a Sun Insurance policy on 12 May 1807 for £400, of which £130 accounted for utensils and stock in trust. [GL, Sun MS vol. 440, ref. 802699]

Bowling, John, Hatfield, near Doncaster, Yorks., joiner and cm (1834). [D]

Bowling, John, Otley, Yorks., joiner and cm (1834). [D]

Bowling, John, Thorne, Yorks., joiner and cm (1834). [D]

Bowling, Robert, Porter St, Covent Gdn, London, cm (1749). [Poll bk]

Bowling, Thomas, Sheffield, Yorks., chairmaker, turner and beerhouse owner (1833–37). Trading at 69 Norfolk St, 1830–33, and 8 New Church St, 1837. [D]

Bowlt, William, Hillgate, Gateshead, Co. Durham, joiner and cm (1787–95). [D]

Bowlt, William, 192 High St, Gateshead, Co. Durham, cm and joiner (1838). [D]

Bowman, Edmund, Baston, Cumb., cm (1751). Took app. named Bateman in 1751. [S of G, app. index]

Bowman, Frederick, 9 Old Bond St, London, cm (1839). [D]

Bowman, George, Northampton St, Cambridge, cm (1832). [Poll bk]

Bowman, Isaac, Liverpool, cm (1816–21). Addresses given at 24 Pellew St in 1816, no. 29 in 1818, and 55 Copperas Hill in 1821. [D]

Bowman, James, 27 Whitechapel, Liverpool, cm (1790). [D] See Thomas Bowman.

Bowman, John, 15 Hatfield St, Blackfriars, London, cm (1793–1808). [D] Probably the John Bowman, cm of London, who subscribed to Sheraton's *Drawing Book*, 1793.

Bowman, John, Sandgate, Penrith, Cumb., joiner and/or cm (1829). [D]

Bowman, Kemp, 7 Bayn's Row, Clerkenwell, London, cm and u (1839). [D]

Bowman, R., Blackfriar's St, Carlisle, Cumb., joiner and/or cm (1811). [D]

Bowman, Robert, Liverpool, cm (1772–96). Trading at 13 Argyle St, 1772–74; 24 Paradise St in 1777; no. 22 in 1781; 41 Atherton St and 2 Murray's Ct, 40 Atherton St in 1790; with shop at 5 Park Lane in 1796. [D]

Bowman, Robert, Wardour St, Soho, London, cm and upholder (1821–29). Recorded at no. 113, 1821–23, and no. 110 by 1829. Took out Sun Insurance policies on 7 February 1821 for £300, of which £200 accounted for stock and utensils in

house and workshop; on 4 October 1821 for £400, £200 on stock and utensils in house and parlour, and £100 on those in workshop behind 8 Portland St; on 15 November 1821 at 6 Portland St in association with William Keatinge; on 7 October 1822 for £400, £200 on stock, utensils and goods in trust in house, and £100 on those in workshops behind 4 Portland St; and on 7 November 1823 for £600, £500 on utensils and stock. [D; GL, Sun MS vol. 488, refs 976086, 893575 and 985449; vol. 493, ref. 997020; vol. 498, ref. 1010049]

Bowman, Robert, 85 St Mary St, Weymouth, Dorset, carver and gilder (1823). [D]

Bowman, Robert, 50 East St, Brighton, Sussex, carver, gilder and looking-glass maker (1833–40). [D] See William Bowman at this address.

Bowman, Thomas, 27 Whitechapel, Liverpool, cm (1790). [D] See James Bowman.

Bowman, Thomas, Scruton, near Bedale, Yorks., u (1840). [D]

Bowman, William, Liverpool, cm (1788). Drop-front secretary desk with panels of black lacquer and set with K'ang Hsi *famille verte* porcelain cut from plates, etc., signed in red paint on the back of the inside of the secretary section, 'WB 1788', and written in pencil, 'WILLIAM BOWMAN LIVERPOOL AUG. 19TH 1788'. [Sold by Hotspur Ltd, 1968; *Conn.*, June 1969]

Bowman, William, London, cm (1793). Subscribed to Sheraton's *Drawing Book*, 1793.

Bowman, William, Lancaster and Manchester, cm (1794–99). App. to T. Lister in 1794. Lancaster freemen rolls state 'of Manchester'. Named in the Gillow records, 1798–99. [Lancaster app. reg. and freemen rolls; Westminster Ref. Lib., Gillow] Possibly:

Bowman, William, Manchester, cm and u (1808–25). Trading at 13 Richmond St, 1808–13, and 3 Lever St, 1815–25. [D]

Bowman, William, 50 East St, Brighton, Sussex, carver, gilder and looking-glass manufacturer (1821–32). Recorded at no. 48 in 1831. Advertised, *Brighton Gazette*, 20 December 1821, 'BOWMAN'S GLASS WAREHOUSE AND PICTURE FRAME MANUFACTORY'. [D] See Robert Bowman at this address.

Bowmer, Michael, Front St, Gateshead, Co. Durham, joiner and cm (1824). [D]

Bownd, John, East St, Southampton, Hants., cm (1811). [D]

Bowran (or Bouran), William, London, and Bank St, Boar Lane, Leeds, Yorks., cm and u (1803–05). Advertised in *Leeds Mercury*, 8 October 1803, describing himself as 'from London', and thanking 'those Ladies and Gentlemen who have liberally honoured him with their commands'. He begs leave 'to inform them and the public in general, that he has now upon Hand an Elegant Assortment of articles in the above business . . .'. Advertised in *Leeds Intelligencer*, 8 April 1805 his 'extensive assortment of chairs in the most modern style of fashion', and again in *Leeds Mercury*, 20 and 27 April 1805.

Bowring, Moses, Launceston, Cornwall, shopkeeper and cm (1782). Took out a Sun Insurance policy in 1782 for £400, of which £370 accounted for utensils and stock. [GL, Sun MS vol. 298, p. 662]

Bowtcher, William, parish of Holy Trinity, Exeter, Devon, sedan chairmaker (1832). [Poll bk]

Bowther, Laurence, parish of St Augustine, Bristol, cm (1784). [Poll bk]

Bowyer, C. R., 33 Store St, Bedford Sq., London, carver and gilder (1829). [D]

Bowyer, Edward, St John St, Clerkenwell, London, chair carver (1775–76). Trading at no. 211 in 1775, and no. 208 in 1776. Took out Sun Insurance policies in 1775 and 1776 for £300,

£50 on stock, utensils and goods. [GL, Sun MS vol. 238, p. 460; vol. 247, p. 256]

Bowyer, Thomas, east side of Queen St, near Cheapside, Pancras Lane, London, upholder (1702–14). Insured his brick house for £300 for seven years on 3 February 1702 with the Hand in Hand Co., renewed on 21 May 1714. Took app. on 16 March 1714. [GL, Hand in Hand MS vol. 2, ref. 2448; PRO, app. reg.]

Box, George, 22 Union St, Maidstone, Kent, cm and u (1826–38). [D; poll bks] See James Box.

Box, Henry, address unrecorded, cm (1803). Subscribed to Sheraton's *Cabinet Dictionary*, 1803.

Box, James, Union St, Maidstone, Kent, cm and u (1838–39). Trading at no. 18 in 1838 and no. 17 in 1839. [D] See George Box.

Box, John, London, carver and gilder (1826–39). Addresses given at 25 Downing St, Westminster, 1826–27; no. 24 in 1837; and 2 Gt Smith St, 1838–39. Took app. in 1838 under Grinsell's Charity. [D; Westminster Ref. Lib., MS E 3559, app. indentures]

Box, Philip, address unrecorded, upholder (1720–30). Son of Philip Box, Gent. of South Newington, Oxford; app. to Robert North on 2 November 1720, and admitted freeman of the Upholders' Co. by servitude on 11 November 1730. [GL, Upholders' Co. records]

Box, Thomas, George St, Grosvenor Sq., London, carpenter, joiner and undertaker (*c*. 1790). [Trade card, Heal Coll., BM]

Boxall, Benjamin, St Pancras, Chichester, Sussex, cm (1839). [D]

Boxall, G., address unrecorded (1813 or 15). Pair of Regency parcel gilt cross-framed stools recorded, one bearing signature and date on under-frame. [Sotheby's, 1 March 1983, lot 123; Michael Norman Antiques, Brighton, July 1983]

Boxall, William, Brighton, Sussex, cm, u and carpenter (1823–39). Trading at 7 Bond St, 1823–27; 23 East Cliff in 1832; Greville Pl., 1837; and 10 Western Rd, 1839. Daughter Eliza bapt. on 1 June 1825. [D; poll bk; E. Sussex RO, PR(bapt.)]

Boxall, William, High St, Guildford, Surrey, cm and u (1830–39). Recorded at no. 42 in 1838. [D; poll bks]

Boyce, J., 13 Hampton Row, Bath, Som., cm (1833). [D]

Boyce, John, Garlick Hill, London, cm (1724). [Heal]

Boyce, John, parish of St Stephen, Bristol, carver (1722–39). [D]

Boyce, John jnr, Cash St, St James's, London, cm (1750). [GL, Joiners' Co. Livery list] Possibly son of John Boyce of Garlick Hill.

Boyce, John, 9 Essex St, Strand, adjacent to the Temple, London, carpenter, builder, cm etc. (*c*. 1800). Pedestal writing table, *c*. 1800, bears his label which adds, 'Chambers Offices etc. fitted up with neatness & dispatch. NB. Blinds Made and repaired'. [Christie's, January 1966; V & A archives]

Boyce, John, Southampton, Hants., cm (1811–39). Recorded 'opposite the Rooms' in 1811; West Pl. in 1830; in St Michael Sq., 1836–39; and also West Quay in 1839 as John Boyce snr, cm and chairmaker. [D]

Boyce, John, Birmingham, cm, joiner etc. (1816–30). Addresses given in Stafford St, 1816–18, and Bath St, 1818–30. [D]

Boyce, R., 22 Charlotte St, Fitzroy Sq., London, u etc. (1802–03). Named in Sheraton's list of master cabinet makers, 1803. [D]

Boyce, William, 7 Moore St, Seven Dials, London, cm and upholder (1839). [D]

Boyd, —, 53 Gt Marylebone Ct, London, cm (1835). [D]

Boyd, Archibald, 5 Upper Marylebone St, London, cm and upholder (1837–39). [D]

Boyd, Robert Barton, Liverpool, cm (1826). App. to William John Roberts in 1826. [Liverpool app. enrolment bk]

Boyd, Robert, Liverpool, cm (1840). Admitted freeman on 20 July 1840. [Liverpool freemen reg.]

Boyd, William, Peter St, London, cm (1784). [Poll bk]

Boyden, John, Clair Ct, Drury Lane, London, carver (1775). Insured his house for £100 with the Sun Co. in 1775. [GL, Sun MS vol. 236, p. 411]

Boyes, John, Epworth, Lincs., cm and joiner (1835–41). [D]

Boyle, Esther, near the Turnpike, Tottenham Ct, London, carver and gilder (1780). Took out a Sun Insurance policy in 1780 for £400, of which £100 accounted for utensils and stock. [GL, Sun MS vol. 289, p. 57]

Boyle, James, at 'The Golden Eagle', Gt Pulteney St, Golden Sq., London, carver and gilder (1763–78). Trade card framed by asymmetrical Rococo foliated scrolls states that he undertook 'all manner of CARVEING in the Italian, French, Gothick & Chiniese tastes Either in Wood or Stone'. [Heal] Between 20 June and 14 October 1768 supplied 'Picture and Glass Frames, Gilding Etc.', costing £187 7s 6d to Shelburne House, Berkeley Sq., London. [Bowood MS] The Earl of Shelburne's accounts record payments to Boyle, *c*. 1771, of £100, £150 and £91 for carving at Lansdowne House, London. [A. T. Bolton, *The Architecture of Robert and James Adam*, vol. 2, p. 314] Sir Richard Hoare's private accounts refer on 3 July 1773 to '2 Gilt Frames (Angelica) £8.8.–', provided by Boyle. [Hoare's Bank, London] Took out a Sun Insurance policy in 1778 for £200, of which £50 accounted for his shop. [D; poll bk; GL, Sun MS vol. 268, p. 307]

Boylin, Caesar, 20 Copper St, Sheffield, Yorks., chairmaker (1833). [D]

Boynton, James, 43 Brewer St, London, painter and gilder (1790). Insured his house and goods for £900 on 13 October 1790 with the Sun Co. [GL, Sun MS ref. 575108]

Boys, John jnr, New Park St, Devizes, Wilts., cm and chairmaker (1839). [D]

Boyse, Peter Paul, London(?), carver (1686). Worked for Sir William Bruce at Kinvour, 1686. See Cornelius Vanerba.

Brabant, Rob., Atherstone, Warks., cm (1749). Took app. named Bliss in 1749. [S of G, app. index]

Brabazon, Edward, 1 Pleasant View, Kirkdale, Liverpool, cm (1839). [D]

Braben, J., 'Shop goods at an house over against Burley-Street-end by Exeter Exchange in the Strand', London, cm (d. 1714). [V & A archives]

Brabner, Samuel, 32 Strand St, Liverpool, cm (1811). [D]

Brabs, William, London and York, u (1783–96). Son of John Brabs, farmer of Haughton; app. to Matthew Barker, u, on 12 August 1783. In 1796, from Rose St, Covent Gdn, London, admitted freeman of York. [York app. reg. and freemen rolls]

Brabs, William, 21 Gt May's Buildings, St Martin's Lane, London, upholder (1812). Took out a Sun Insurance policy on 20 February 1812 for £300 on a house in Tabernacle Walk, Moorfields, in private tenure. [GL, Sun MS vol. 457, ref. 867744]

Brace, —, Lower College Lane, Gloucester, cm (1802). [D]

Brace, Henry, Church St, Birmingham, gilder in general (1818). [D]

Bracebridge, George, Lincoln, u (1716). On 3 February 1716 insured his house and one in the occupation of John Holland, framer, and Peter Smith, with the Sun Co. [GL, Sun MS vol. 5, ref. 6251–52]

Braceby, William, Lincoln, u (1715). On 2 May 1715 insured his house, goods and merchandise with the Sun Co. [GL, Sun MS vol. 5, p. 8]

Bracey, Jay, Gt Yarmouth, Norfolk, u (1795–98). Son of William Bracey, deceased, admitted freeman in 1795 by patrimony. [D; poll bk; Gt Yarmouth freemen's calendar]

Brac(e)y, William, Gt Yarmouth, Norfolk, u (1754–d. by 1795). Took apps named Godbold in 1754, Simons in 1775, and Denew in 1759. His sons, William and Jay, u, admitted freemen by patrimony in 1754 and 1795 respectively. Former app., John Brown, u, admitted freeman by servitude in 1775. Declared bankrupt, *Gents Mag.*, April 1757. [Poll bk; S of G, app. index; Gt Yarmouth freemen's calendar]

Bracey, William, Norwich, upholder (1781). App. to Paul Colombine, upholder; admitted freeman on 14 April 1781. [Norwich freemen reg.]

Bracey, William, Bristol, furniture painter (1818–32). Trading at 8 Limekiln Lane, 1818–22; 3 Pipe Lane, 1823; no. 4, 1824–30; 24 Trenchard St and Limekiln Lane, 1831; and 24 Trenchard St and Brandon Hill Steep, 1832. [D]

Brachcroft, Samuel, Carnaby Mkt, London, u (1749). [Poll bk]

Bracher, Eleanor, (widow), 1 Primrose St, London, turner, cm and maker of telescope cases (1821). Took out Sun Insurance policies on 7 June 1821 for £500, of which stock and utensils accounted for £300, and musical intruments, £10; and on four houses, 63–66 Wentworth St, Spitalfields, in private tenure, for £600. [GL, Sun MS vol. 487, refs 980950–51]

Bracher, T., 29 Broad St, Golden Sq., London, cm and upholder (1820). [D]

Bracken, —, London(?), u (1778). Immediately put in charge of the hasty refurnishing of Thorndon Hall by Lord Petre for the visit of George III in October 1778, first proposed by the King on 22 September. Lord Petre's summary account of the visit describes the rooms 'entirely new furnished', including the King's Dressing Room furnished with 'Green Damask, large glasses, Gild chairs, Lustres'; the Bedchamber with furniture of 'Red and White Damask, the Bed of the same which was made in every respect as to beding the same as their Majestys at Buckenham House. The Tables, commodes and every other piece of furniture made use of in the above apartment were all new. To this may be added great number of beds Tables & commodes for other apartments & fifty damask stools, for the company to sit on who had the honour of dining with the King and Queen. Their Majestys only being seated on chairs . . .'. The accounts, including food and new silver, totalled £1,001 7s 2d. [Essex RO, D/DP F322/2–37A]

Bracken, Henry, York, carver and gilder (1761). Son of Edward Bracken, clerk; app. to George Gibson, carver and gilder, on 6 November 1761. [York app. reg.]

Bracken, John & Saunders, Ann, Charlotte St, Bloomsbury, London, upholders (1775). Insured a house for £600 in 1775 with the Sun Co. [GL, Sun MS vol. 244, p. 71]

Brackett, William Bury, Tombland, Norwich, cm and u (1830). [D]

Brackston, Charles, Lymington, Hants., cm (1784). [D]

Bradbear, Richard, 4 Hoxton Mkt, London, cm (1840). Insured his workshop on property of Elisha Milward in 1840 with the Sun Co. [GL, Sun MS ref. 1339528]

Bradbear, William, 33 Essex St, Hoxton, London, carpenter, cm and undertaker (1808). Took out a Sun Insurance policy on 7 September 1808 for £150, of which stock and utensils in workshop and open yard accounted for £70. [GL, Sun MS vol. 443, ref. 821051]

Bradbear, William, 11 Lamb St, Spitalfields, London, carpenter and cm (1820). Took out a Sun Insurance policy in July 1820 for £200, of which stock and utensils in a house other than that in Lamb St accounted for £100. [GL, Sun MS vol. 485, ref. 968889]

Bradbear, William, 123 Curtain Rd, London, cm and upholder (1826–37). Recorded concerning sale of lease in 1832. [D; Rose Lipman Lib., Shoreditch archives, MS M3545]

Bradbear, William, Lower Ward, Tottenham, London, cm (1832). [D]

Bradbeer, A., 17 York St, Bath, Som., wheelchair maker (1819–24). [D]

Bradbridge, John, Canterbury, Kent, u (1734). [Canterbury freemen rolls]

Bradbridge, John, Dover, Kent, u (1784–93). Trading on the Quay in 1784. [D]

Bradburn(e), John, London, cm, u, appraiser, undertaker (1750–d. 1781). Bradburne held the Royal Warrant of 'Upholsterer to his Majesty and Cabinet-Maker to the Great Wardrobe' and was responsible for supplying considerable quantities of furniture and furnishings to the Royal House-hold between 1764 and 1777. His name first appears in the Royal Household accounts in 1764, when he succeeded William Vile, but he is credited with having produced some of the finely carved furniture provided during the 1750s and early 1760s by the firm of Vile & Cobb, cm and u, of 72 St Martin's Lane. Several payments to him are noted in Cobb's account at Drummond's Bank between 1759 and 1763. On the 24 August 1763 he was also mentioned in William Vile's will. However a codicil was added to the will on 9 November 1764 stating that if Bradburne was no longer a 'servant' to Vile, the £20 legacy was to go instead to Mrs Vile.

Bradburne was established in Hemmings Row, off Long Acre, in 1758 and during the 1760s owned three houses in the street. In 1764 he went into partnership with William France and their joint names first appear on a billhead dated 13 July 1764 sent to Sir Lawrence Dundas for work done at his house in Arlington St, London. The following year France paid the rates on premises at 8 Long Acre, which some years previously had been occupied by William Linnell, and after France's death in 1767 Bradburne continued to pay the rates there until 1776. Bradburne is noted at this address in Lowndes *London Directory* for 1773 and 1775. William France's branch of the business was continued by Edward France, who later went into partnership with Samuel Beckwith. Bradburne was responsible for supplying much furniture for the Royal residences betwen 1764 and 1777, and in particular for Buckingham House, which had been acquired by George III in 1761. In her Journal for 1768 Lady Mary Coke noted 'Bradburn, the King's upholster has been with me this morning and tells me that he has been at the Queen's Palace'. [*Letters and Journals*, 1756–74, vol. II, p. 264] Apart from George III and Queen Charlotte, he also worked for other members of the Royal Household such as Lady Charlotte Finch.

None of Bradburne's designs have been identified, but he charged £1 10s in 1767 for drawing a mahogany glass case to stand on top of the Queen's 'Secretary' which had been supplied by William Vile in 1762. [G. de Bellaigue *Buckingham Palace*, p. 112] He worked to the architect Robert Adam's designs when providing sofas for the 6th Earl of Coventry in 1765 and pier tables billed to Sir Lawrence Dundas in 1765. His account for supplying a glass case for one of George III's clocks in 1766 included an extra charge of £1 10s for 'extraordinary trouble and attention in blowing the glass according to His Majesty's direction'.

As late as 1773 Bradburne receipted payment for an account headed 'John Chute Esq For the executors of my late partner William France and all demands on their account and mine'. When he retired from business in 1776 Bradburne vacated Long Acre and after his resignation in July 1777 the Royal Warrant of Cabinet-maker to the throne was granted to William Gates. Bradburne's death was recorded in the *Gents Mag.*, 6 October 1781 where it was stated that he was 'Formerly Upholsterer to his Majesty, but had retired some years'. The will of 'John Bradburne . . . of the Parish of Wandsworth in Surrey . . . Gentleman' is dated 19 August

1780. A mourning ring and £50 each were bequeathed to his mother Margaret, his wife Elizabeth and his 'good friends' James Ely of the Lord Chamberlain's Office, Thomas Knight the Elder, glass grinder of Soho, and Samuel Naylor, Attorney at Law of Gt Newport St. 'My son Thomas Bradburne . . . my daughter Ann Holloway, my daughter Mary Hinchcliffe . . . my son George, my daughter Charlotte and son Samuel Bradburne when they arrive at the full age of twenty one years £500 stock . . . unto my grandson John Bradburne lawful son of my aforesaid son Thomas £200 stock . . . to my nephew Thomas Bradburne . . . he worked at White Fryers glass house some years ago but at present do not know where he is . . . my sister Sarah Bod residing at Boyle in Ireland . . .'. [PRO, Prob. 11/Webster 462, p. 15]

CROOME COURT, Worcs. (George William, 6th Earl of Coventry). Bill dated 28 December 1763 to 15 September 1764 totalling £343 13s 2d was made out to Wm France and John Bradburn and receipted on 4 January 1765 'For me Wm France'. Amongst the entries for supplying or repairing furniture and furnishings is one dated January 1764 'For altering the crimson velvet church furniture to Mr. Lamb's directions'. A large bed with 'corinthian capital' foot posts and a dome is itemised in July 1764. A second bill dated 4 March 1765 totalling £352 16s 6d is receipted by Jno Bradburn 'for partner and self'. It concerns the fitting up of various bedrooms and the supply of mahogany chairs for the Eating Room. There is also a reference to the moving of a bed to the London House in Piccadilly. A third bill dated 1765 for various items of furniture, includes ten mahogany 'scrole' sofas, which were executed to a design billed by Robert Adam in February 1765 and carved by Sefferin Alken. (A sofa is now at Kenwood House). There is also an entry for the cornice of the Library window, which was 'prepared for Mr Alkin to carve'. [Worcs. RO, 4025/r970.5.73]

106 PICCADILLY, London (George William, 6th Earl of Coventry). Bill dated 25 May 1765 totalling £69 12s 6d made out to Wm. France and John Bradburn was receipted by Bradburn 'for partner and self'. Includes the hire of furniture and supplying a gilt 'Sideboard table' and window cornices for the Eating Room. In addition there is a charge of £1 5s for a pattern hall chair 'left with Mr Adams for determination'. [Worcs. RO, 4025/r970.5:73]

RICHMOND LODGE (George III). In 1764 Bradburne charged £7 7s 0d for a book desk' to lye upon a table'. [PRO, LC 9/293]

BUCKINGHAM HOUSE, London (George III and Queen Charlotte). Between 1764 and 1777 Bradburne is mentioned in most quarterly bills for furnishings for the Royal residences and in particular for Buckingham House, referred to as the Queen's House or Palace. [PRO, LC 9/293, 294, 316–24] Amongst the various items are a tent frame supplied in 1764 for the Queen's House, St James's [PRO, LC 9/293] and a 'breakfast table' and 'A neat inlaid cabinet with drawer and neat wrought brass ornaments and gilt curious locks . . . £31.5.0.' in 1765. It has been suggested [G. de Bellaigue Buckingham Palace, pp. 158, 220] that Bradburne supplied the case for an astronomical clock for which Eardley Norton was paid in July 1765 and for which Bradburne charged £38 15s for supplying a gilt bracket in the 'Antique' style, when it was put in George III's Dressing Room in 1766. Bradburne also supplied a glass case for the clock and charged £1 10s for 'extraordinary trouble and attention in blowing the glass according to His Majesty's Direction.

In 1766 Bradburne supplied a 'Very grand organ case' carved with a 'variety of ornaments viz. satyr boys, musical instruments, drapery curtains, foliage, palms, festoon of husks etc'. [GCM] In the same year a carved 'chimney glass'

with '21 plates of glass and 48 brackets for china' was supplied for the Queen's closet.

During 1767 Bradburne supplied a mahogany tea board with a 'rich cutt work border and black and white mosaick work on the edge of it . . . £1.13.0', 'An extraordinary neat mahogany round table' for the Queen's Library in the North Wing [H. Clifford Smith, Buckingham Palace, p. 76] and a 'Mahogany octagon pillar and claw table neatly carved, on castors and covering the top in needlework in being . . . £6.6.0.'. [Clifford Smith, p. 91; GCM, fig. 68] Two gilded candlestand 'terms' with marble tops were supplied for Queen Charlotte for £55 15s together with two 'girandoles with silvered nossels'. [PRO, LC 9/294] A number of items were supplied for Mrs Kroms, the Princess Royal's governess, including a mahogany 'cloaths press' and a 'Mahogany corner beaufet'. Bradburne also paid a visit to Richmond Lodge to show the Queen a 'Drawing' of a 'Mahogany glass case' to stand on top of her 'Secretary'. He charged £1 10s for the drawing and £24 10s for the 'Neat mahogany glass case', [PRO, LC 9/314, 61, quarter to Midsummer 1767; G. de Bellaigue, pp. 113–14, repr.]

In 1768 Bradburne altered cabinets for recesses in the Mathematical Room or Gallery and supplied 'A neat mahogany piece of work for papers' for the King's New Dressing Room. A mahogany chamber horse was delivered for the 'Nursery at the Queen's House . . . to carry 4 children at once . . . £10.15.0.'. [Clifford Smith, p. 90]

In 1770 he supplied 'A neat mahogany press for Linnen . . . with extra good guarded tumbler locks and 2 Dutch bow'd keys . . . £84.10.0.'. [Coleridge, Chippendale Furniture, pl. 388] and a 'Mahogany case with glass doors for 'India figures . . . £7.7.0.'.

In 1774 the Princess Royal was supplied with 'A neat mahogany secretary with drawers in front and a writing drawer made to draw forward, and a neat bookcase at top with looking glass doors . . . £20.0.0.'. [Coleridge, Chippendale Furniture, fig. 387]

19 ARLINGTON ST, London (Sir Lawrence Dundas). An account dated 13 July 1764 to December 1765 totalling £990 12s 11½d is detailed in a bound notebook for 'House furniture . . . furnished to Arlington Street and Moor Park'. It is headed 'To Wm France and Jno Bradburn' and is the first occasion that Bradburne's name is included in the work that France was carrying out for Sir Lawrence Dundas. An entry for 12 January 1765 for a 'Circular Frame for a Marble Table richly carv'd with ramsheads . . . and gilt in burnished gold . . .' at £37 10s was executed to a design by Robert Adam. A second table to the same design was invoiced again at £37 10s by France & Bradburne on 30 December 1765. [Apollo, September 1967, p. 204, fig. 1; Christie's, 26 April 1934, lot 77; Christie's NY, 28 March 1981, lot 213; N. Yorks. RO, Zetland archive, ZNK x 1/730]

NORMANTON PARK, Rutland (Sir Gilbert Heathcote). Five large accounts survive for furniture supplied during 1765–66 by France & Bradburne. [Lincoln RO, Ancaster MS 8/8]

CHARLES ST, London (John Chute). Bill headed 'To John Bradburne and the Executors of the late Mr Wm France' for furnishings supplied between March 1765 and January 1767 totalled £1,052 4s 1½d. The items include hall chairs, a gilt chandelier, 'a shed in the yard for hens', a pair of 'half circle sideboard tables' [Coleridge, Chippendale Furniture, fig. 391] and a set of three mahogany 'sophas' and eight armed chairs [Coleridge, fig. 390] The nineteen-page bill is preserved in a book, which was annotated in 1884: 'The bill must have been chiefly for the London House in Charles Street but the hangings and mirrors were probably moved to the Vyne'. [Hants. RO, 31 M57/634]

THE VYNE, Hants. (John Chute). 1765–67. See entry for Charles St, London. [*C. Life*, 1963, pp. 214–16]

PRINCESS AUGUSTA. Bill from Bradburne totalling £21 13s for a 'Mahog. case for a turning machine with drawers etc.' was receipted on 8 February 1769. [Windsor accounts for Dowager Princess of Wales, RA 55539] Bill of 1770–71 totalled £241 5s 3d. [Duchy of Cornwall, Household accounts, Princess Augusta, LVII (1) 1770–71]

2 GROSVENOR SQ., London (Marquis of Carmarthen). Bill survives from 'John Bradburne, Cabinet-maker, Upholder, Appraiser, Undertaker etc.' totalling £2,576 3s 9d and receipted in November 1775 for fitting out entire house between June 1774 and March 1775. The furnishings included curtains, carpets, pier glass, 'hollow splat' back chairs, painted tables, a marble topped mahogany 'commode table', two tulip wood corner commodes, French back-stool chairs, 'cabriolet' chairs, a 'confident' and a mahogany stand for bird cages. [YAS, Duke of Leeds papers, DD5/Box 136/22]

KEW (Prince Ernest). In 1777 Bradburne charged £4 for a 'Mahogany hanging shelf with four shelves for books, the end cut through like Chinese rales, a drawer at the bottom'. [V & A archives]

ST JAMES'S PALACE, London (Lady Charlotte Finch). Bradburne charged 4s 6d 'for 2 brass hooks to hang Lady Charlotte's watch and fixing do. by the side of the chimney with brass plates and long gilt nails'. [DEF] J. H.

Bradburn, John, Whitechapel, Liverpool, upholder and block-maker (1800–07). Recorded at no. 50 in 1800, and also no. 46 with Mary Bradburn, mattress maker; no. 52 in 1805; and no. 4 in 1807. [D]

Bradburn, John, 5 Rosemary St, Bristol, bedstead, chair and sofa frame maker, wholesale and retail (1831–32). [D]

Bradburn, William, King St, Burslem, Staffs., joiner, builder and cm (1834). [D]

Bradbury, Bob, Liverpool and Royal Row, Westminster, London, cm and 'celebrated clown' (b. 1774–d. 1831). Death, aged 57 on 21 July 1831 reported, *Chester Courant and Anglo-Welsh Gazette*, 2 August 1831. Originally a cm in Liverpool, had become 'a celebrated clown', and 'well known eccentric', author of the *Itinerant*, and lessee of the Liverpool Theatre.

Bradbury, Jn, 8 Eltham Rd, Kent Rd, London, cm and upholder (1822–23). [D]

Bradbury (or Bradbery), John, St Gregory's Churchyard, Norwich, cm and u (1819–30). Admitted freeman on 30 May 1819, not by servitude [D; poll bk; Norwich freemen reg.]

Bradbury, John, 103 Risbygate St, Bury St Edmunds, Suffolk, u and cm (1839). [D]

Bradbury, Richard, Liverpool, cm and victualler (1807–10). Trading at 5 Tempest Hey in 1807; Springfield St, 1810; and no. 4, 1813–14. [D]

Bradbury, Robert, 10 Leaf St, Hulme, Manchester, cm (1834). [D]

Bradbury, Samuel, Strand, London, u (1774). [Poll bk]

Bradbury, Samuel, Butcher Row, Temple Bar, London, carpet and upholder warehouse owner (1778). [D]

Bradbury, Thomas, Livery St, Birmingham, gilder (1780). [D]

Bradbury, Thomas, Liverpool, cm (1814–23). Trading at 10 Redman Pl. in 1814. [D]

Brade, John, Lancaster, cm (1817–18). Admitted freeman in 1817–18 when stated 'of Preston'. [Lancaster freemen rolls] Possibly of Brade & Storey.

Brade, Lawrence, Lancaster, cm (1803–16). App. to T. Lister in 1803, and admitted freeman, 1815–16. [Lancaster app. reg. and freemen rolls]

Brade & Storey, Preston, Lancs., (1799). Signed the *Preston*

Cabinet Makers' and Chair Makers' Book of Prices, 1799, on behalf of the masters.

Brader, John, 5 Holland St, Soho, London, cm (1808–11). [D]

Bradfield, Charlotte, Middle-gate, Newark, Notts., cm and u (1822). [D]

Bradfield (or Brafield), Edward, 169 Tottenham Ct Rd, London, cm, u and bedstead maker (1817–25). [D]

Bradfield, John, Newark, Notts., cm (1819–22). Trading at Middlegate in 1819. [D; Notts. RO, probate records]

Bradford, George, Turner's Pl., Ramsgate, Kent, cm (1838). [D]

Bradford, James, 'The Angel', at the corner of Poppins Alley, Fleet St, London, cm (1714). [Heal]

Bradford, John, 'Printing-House-Yard in Black-Friers', London, cm (c. 1674–75). Walnut parquetry cabinet or chest of drawers with compass stringing recorded, one drawer of which is lined with cancelled MS accounts of 1674–75. Label inside reads: 'Cabinets, Escreutors, Desks, Tables, Burows; Likewise Glasses, Peirs, Chimney-Glasses, Sconces. And all manner of Cabinet, or Joyner's Work Made or Mended by me . . .'. [Heal; Symonds papers, Winterthur, Delaware]

Bradford, John, Beverley, Yorks., cm (1784–1829). Recorded at Fryer Lane in 1823 and Charity Lane, 1826–29. [D] Possibly it was an older John Bradford who polled at Beverley in 1784 and 1790.

Bradford, John, address unrecorded, cm (1813). Made officers' furniture costing £1 13s for Sir John Geers Cotterell, Bart, of Garnons, near Hereford, and Hertford St, London, being paid on 7 January 1813. [Herefs. RO, Garnons MS W69/III/183]

Bradford, John snr and jnr, Doncaster, Yorks., cm and u (1818–37). John snr was trading at Church Yard, 1818–20, and Frenchgate, 1822–29; in partnership with John jnr at Frenchgate in 1830, and in Cleveland St, Cornmarket in 1837. [D]

Bradford, Samuel, Sotwell, Berks., u (1795). Declared bankrupt, *Billinge's Liverpool Advertiser*, 8 June 1795.

Bradford, Thomas, Doncaster, Yorks., u(?) (1777–84). Former app. Robert Coupland, advertised in *Leeds Intelligencer*, 11 and 18 March 1777. Bradford declared bankrupt, *Gents Mag.*, July 1784.

Bradgate, Elisa, address unrecorded, u(?) (1725–26). Submitted a bill to Madam Monson on 11 November 1725 totalling £14 4s 4d and paid on 24 January 1726, describing 'a fine scane cradle raised head & carved feet', bedding, 'rich pillong satten' for 'counterpain, curtings & vallance', and 'Quilting ye cradle in a fine diamond'. [Lincoln RO, Monson 12]

Bradick, William, 10 West St, Seven Dials, London, bedstead maker (1837–39). [D]

Bradley, —, address unrecorded, upholder (1805). Named in the Longford Castle accounts in 1805 receiving £1 7s 6d. [V & A archives]

Bradley, Arthur, Market Pl., Malton, Yorks., u (1840). [D]

Bradley, Benjamin, South St, Ponder's End, Middlx, cm (1791–1803). Took out Sun Insurance policies on 22 November 1791 for £400; and on 11 February 1803 for £200. [GL, Sun MS vol. 381, p. 564; vol. 427, ref. 743995]

Bradley, Benjamin, 4 Ely Pl., Dog and Duck Rd, London, cm (1804). Took out a Sun Insurance policy on 7 May 1804 for £200, £100 accounting for house and workshop, and £100 for a private house at 2 Ely Pl., with no store for drying feathers. [GL, Sun MS vol. 430, ref. 762332]

Bradley, Charles, Cirencester, Glos., cm (1830–37). Children bapt. in 1830, 1834 and 1837. [PR(bapt.)]

Bradley, Daniel, Chelsea, London, u (1758). Declared bankrupt, *Gents Mag.*, February 1758.

Bradley, Francis, 144 Moore St, Birmingham, mahogany case maker (1777–80). [D]

Bradley, Francis, London, upholder and cm (1803–28).

Addresses given at 2 Newman St, Oxford Rd, 1803–16; 5 King St in 1817; variously at 11, 16, 18 and 19 Old Cavendish St, 1817–23; Crawford St in 1825; and 2 Henrietta St, Cavendish Sq., 1826–28. Subscribed to Sheraton's *Cabinet Dictionary*, and named in his list of master cabinet makers, 1803. [D]

Bradley, George, York, u (1771). Son-in-law of William Benson of Otley; app. to Jeremiah Smith and Matthew Browne, u and appraisers, on 24 June 1771. [York app. reg.]

Bradley, Henry, Billesdon, Leicester, cm (1780–85). Took out a Sun Insurance policy on 1 June 1785, shop accounting for £10, and utensils and stock in house and shop, £148. Presumably the Henry Bradley, joiner and cm of 'Rolleston', Leics., who announced in *Leicester Journal*, 26 February 1780, that 'he has made up capital pieces of furniture in mahogany . . . book cases cabinets etc. — embellished with ivory — subscriptions invited'. [GL, Sun MS vol. 328, p. 416]

Bradley, Henry, Peascod St, Windsor, Berks., cm, u and undertaker (1824–38). Recorded in 1837–38 in connection with a lease. [D; fifth hall book of the borough of New Winsor, pp. 51, 61, 63–64]

Bradley, J., New St, Worcester, chairmaker (1820). [D]

Bradley, James jnr, Lancaster, cm (1779–1800). Admitted freeman in 1779–1800, when stated 'of Manchester'. [Lancaster freemen rolls] Possibly:

Bradley, James, back of 127 Deansgate, Manchester, cm (1794–1802). [D]

Bradley, James, 4 Spa Pl., Somerstown, London, carver and gilder (1808). [D]

Bradley, James, New St, Worcester, fancy chairmaker and turner (1820). [D]

Bradley, John, Beverley, Yorks., cm (1720–54). Son of William Bradley, app. to William Hunter, 'pin & cabnt £5', in 1720. Took app. named Kirby in 1754. [V & A archives]

Bradley, John, Church Lane, London, carver (1774). [Poll bk]

Bradley, John, Lancaster, cm (1799–1800). Admitted freeman, 1799–1800, when stated 'of Manchester'. [Lancaster freemen rolls]

Bradley, Jn, 6 Old Round Ct, Strand, London, cm and broker (1808). [D]

Bradley, John, 125 Blackman St, Southwark, London, upholder and undertaker (1817). [D]

Bradley, John D., 4 Old St Rd, London, cm (1827–35). [D]

Bradley, Lawrence, 18 King St, Preston, Lancs., chairmaker (1825). [D]

Bradley, Richard, Horsemarket, Warrington, Lancs., cm (1796–1808). Witnessed a will in 1796. Good quality mahogany bow-fronted secretaire bookcase, c. 1800, with four drawers and two glazed doors, inlaid with ivory, now at Warrington Museum and Art Gallery; stamped twice 'R. BRADLEY, WARRINGTON', referring to either Richard or Robert. [D; NACF, Exhib., *Eighty Years On*, Manchester City Art Gallery, 1983] Possibly the father of Robert Bradley.

Bradley, Richard, Grantham, Lincs., cm and u (1819–22). Recorded at Church pavement in 1819 and High St, 1822–26, also as a paper hanger in 1826. [D]

Bradley, Robert, Horsemarket, Warrington, Lancs., cm and u (1805–48). Declared bankrupt, *Liverpool Mercury*, 27 June 1817, but trading again from 1818–48; recorded wrongly as 'Beadley' in 1818. Secretaire bookcase, c. 1800 at Warrington Museum and Art Gallery stamped 'R. BRADLEY, WAR-RINGTON', referring either to Richard or Robert. Possibly the son of Richard Bradley. [D; NACF Exhib., *Eighty Years On*, Manchester City Art Gallery, 1983]

Bradley, S., London, cm (1793). Subscribed to Sheraton's *Drawing Book*, 1793.

Bradley, T., address unrecorded (c. 1820). Rosewood chairs with cane seats, c. 1820, recorded stamped 'T. BRADLEY'. [V & A archives]

Bradley, Thomas, Lancaster, cm (1799–1800). Admitted freeman in 1799–1800. [Lancaster freemen rolls]

Bradley, Thomas, Liverpool, cm (1813–39). Trading at 10 Redman Pl., 1813–14; 5 Springfield St, 1816–18; 127 Richmond Row, 1835; no.130 in 1837; and 34 Roscommon St with shop at 58 Richmond Row in 1839. [D]

Bradley, Thomas, Horsemarket, Warrington, Lancs., cm and u (1816–18). [D]

Bradley, Thomas, High St, Deptford, London, bed and mattress maker (1826–27). [D]

Bradley, W., Belgrave, Leicester, cm (1795). Advertised for a journeyman cm, *Leicester Journal*, 3 April 1795.

Bradley, William, Lancaster, cm (1817–18). Admitted freeman, 1817–18, when stated 'of Liverpool'. [Lancaster freemen rolls]

Bradley, William, 45 Mill St, Leeds, Yorks., cm (1837). [D]

Bradley, William, Windmill Lane, Chester, cm (1840). [D]

Bradley, William, Widemarsh St, Hereford, musical instrument warehouse owner, cm and u (1840). [D]

Bradshaw, —, London, cm (1735). Supplied the Earl of Ancaster with chair frames and tables costing £129 4s in 1735. [Lincoln RO, ANC 6/32] Probably either George Smith Bradshaw or William Bradshaw

Bradshaw, —, Soho Sq., London, u (1739). Mentioned in a letter from Richard Bateman to Mr Fallowes, his agent, at Shobdon Ct, near Leominster, Herefs., of 5 November 1739: 'My brother Jemmy has desired me to inquire of you whether you have sent up to Mr. Bradshaw in Sohoe Square a yellow Cloth bed of his with the bedding that came from Bath.' [Herefs. RO, Bateman letters, G39/III/E/5] Probably either George Smith Bradshaw or William Bradshaw.

Bradshaw, —, address unrecorded, cm and u (1775). Subscribed to Thomas Malton's *A Compleat Treatise on Perspective*, 1775. Probably either George Smith Bradshaw or William Bradshaw.

Bradshaw, —, address unrecorded, cm and u (1777). The Blenheim accounts mention '18 pieces of green flock paper' supplied on 26 February, and '2 four post bedsteads with purple flowered Cotton furn. each; 2 Window Curtains, 6 Chairs and 2 Elbow Chairs cover'd as before', on 17 April 1777. [V & A archives] Probably:

Bradshaw, George Smith, London, cm, u and tapestry maker (b. 1717–d. 1812). Addresses given at Greek St, Soho, 1737–59; no. 59 from 1755 (previously the workshop of William Bradshaw); at 80 Dean St with store room at Sutton St, Soho Sq. in 1755; Dean St, 1759–93; at Crown Ct, Dean St, 1769–87; as Bradshaw, Smith & Son at 69 Dean St, 1784–95; and no. 91 in 1795. The last of the Soho tapestry makers, either he or William was probably the 'Mr. Bradshaw tapestry weaver in Soho Square' mentioned in the note book of John, brother of Robert Adam, on his visit to London in 1748. [Fleming, *R. Adam*] G. S. Bradshaw was in partnership with Paul Saunders as Smith Bradshaw & Saunders, probably from 1751. Together they supplied tapestry panels of 'Pilgrimage to Mecca', dated 1756 and 1758, to Holkham Hall, Norfolk. In 1755 a fire occurred at the firm's workshop, reported in the *Public Advertiser*, 8 February 1755; presumably the same Messrs. Bradshaw & Co. whose workshop and house adjoining 'in Hog Lane, St. Giles, was consumed by fire'. [*Gents Mag.*, February 1755] In that year Bradshaw and Saunders took out a Sun Fire policy for £2,500, £2,000 on stock in warehouse and sheds, and £500 on that in store room at Sutton St, Soho Sq. [GL, Sun MS vol. 110, ref. 148000] The partnership between Bradshaw and Saunders was dissolved on 15 October 1758 [*London Gazette*] with Bradshaw continuing in Greek St, and Saunders trading from Soho Sq. at the corner of Sutton St, with William Ince, whose later partner, John Mayhew, was app. to Bradshaw and in his service in 1756. An enterprising and apparently fairly wealthy tradesman, Bradshaw acquired a number of sites in what is now Carlisle St in 1756, rebuilding houses and workshops there in 1757, and moving in in 1758, having left 59 Greek St and 80 Dean St. Probably to pay for this rebuilding, he mortgaged all his property to William Bradshaw (for whom he was to act as executor and trustee of estates) and Robert Andrews of Hanover Sq. on 25 March 1758. He was able to assign it back on 23 November 1763, and he was again buying up leases and rebuilding houses in Carlisle St between 1764–74. He took out insurance policies in 1765 on his house, warehouses and stock of wood for £3,600, and on 5 July 1786 for £2,800, of which utensils accounted for £2,200. [GL, Sun MS vol. 337, p. 652] In 1766 he was involved in a matter of arbitration between Lawrence Dundas and Samuel Norman, the upholder. In 1768–69 he was admitted freeman of Lancaster.

In 1795, aged 78, he retired to Pershore, Worcs., but was still purchasing property in 1799 at 1 Crown Ct from the Duke of Portland. In 1812, at the grand age of 95, he died leaving two sons and two daughters, all legitimate; £1,500 to his eldest son, John Bradshaw Smith, and £2,500 to his second son, and perhaps successor, George Smith Bradshaw. The firm of G. S. Bradshaw & G. Smith worked for the Rt Hon. Mrs Leigh, 1791–92, supplying carpet, hanging curtains and bed curtains, and calico cases for furniture at Grove House, Stoneleigh, Warks. [Shakespeare Birthplace Trust, DR 18/5, Leigh papers] Otherwise little is known about Bradshaw's furniture or commissions, with the exception of furniture supplied between 1764–74 to the 1st Lord of the Admiralty [D; *Survey of London*, vol. 34, 238F; Lancaster freemen rolls, Heal; *GCM*; *DEF*; Wills, *English Furniture 1760–1900*, p. 62; Coleridge, *Chippendale Furniture*, pp. 137–38; Gilbert, *Chippendale*, pp. 158–59] A.E.

Bradshaw, Isaac, Lancaster, cm (1826–40). App. to John Battersby in 1826 and admitted freeman on 28 October 1837. Named in the Gillow records, 1836–40. [Lancaster app. reg. and freemen rolls; Westminster Ref. Lib., Gillow]

Bradshaw, James snr, Liverpool, cm (1790–98). Admitted freeman on servitude to Robert Fairhurst on 20 April 1790. Father of James Bradshaw jnr, cm, born 1 November 1794, who petitioned freedom on his birthright in 1816; and of Thomas Bradshaw, tailor, born 3 February 1798. [Liverpool freemen's committee bk and reg.]

Bradshaw, James jnr, Liverpool, cm (b. 1794–1839). Probably it was James jnr who is recorded at 17 Milton St, 1823–29, and 6 St Stephen's St, 1834–39. Son of James Bradshaw snr, cm; admitted freeman on 8 June 1816. [D; Liverpool freemen reg.]

Bradshaw, James, 63 Darwen St, Blackburn, Lancs., cm, joiner and house-builder (1824). [D]

Bradshaw, John, Market St (or Pl.), Chorley, Lancs., cm (1828–34). [D]

Bradshaw, Joseph, address unrecorded, upholder (1754–61). Son of Hannah Bradshaw, Walthamstow, London, and brother of Thomas Bradshaw, upholder, of Aldgate. App. to Thomas Nickalls on 5 April 1754, and admitted freeman of the Upholders' Co. by servitude on 6 August 1761. [GL, Upholders' Co. records]

Bradshaw, Matthew, Hull, Yorks., cm (1814–31). Addresses given at Parade St, 1814–20, and 11 Junction Dock St, 1831. [D]

Bradshaw, Michael, address unrecorded, upholder (1710–66). Son of John Bradshaw, ironmonger of London; app. to Richard Bradshaw on 7 September 1710 and admitted

freeman of the Upholders' Co. by servitude on 7 May 1718. Resigned as Assistant of the Co. in October 1766 after suffering great losses in supporting his son-in-law. Took apps named Hugh Hughes, 1722–30; Paul Saunders, 1738–51, William Rogers, 1753–62; and Isaac Solly, 1756–64. [GL, Upholders' Co. records]

Bradshaw, Michael, London, cm and u (1750–63). Trading in Bridge or Budge Row in 1763. Member of the Livery of the Upholders' Co. in 1750. On 4 September 1760 was paid £31 for curtains, seven chairs and cases supplied to Charles Rogers of Laurence Pountney Lane, London. [D; GL, Upholders' Co. records and Livery lists; *Apollo*, December 1960, pp. 196–98; Plymouth City Museum and Art Gallery, Cottonian Coll., Charles Rogers' accounts]

Bradshaw, Richard, address unrecorded, upholder (1710–18). Admitted freeman of the Upholders' Co. on 6 September 1710. Took apps named Christopher Robinson, 1710–17, and Michael Bradshaw, 1710–18. [GL, Upholders' Co. records]

Bradshaw, Samuel, Liverpool, cm (1834–35). Trading at 17 Brown St in 1834 and 121 Upper Frederick St in 1835. [D]

Bradshaw, Thomas, 10 St Paul's Churchyard, London, upholder and cm (1754–75). [D] Subscribed to Chippendale's *Director*, 1754. Label found on Chippendale-style mahogany bureau bookcase with scrolled fretted pediment, Chinoiserie frieze and bracket feet. [Sold at Worsfold's, Canterbury, 15 November 1979] Declared bankrupt, *Gents Mag.*, November 1772. Probably the Thomas Bradshaw of London who provided Sir John Griffin Griffin with 'a neat gressing [sic] glass wth deal case & packing' costing £2 2s, for Audley End, Essex, in 1772. [Essex RO, D/DBy/A30/4]

Bradshaw, Thomas, London, upholder (1759–1802). Addresses given at Fox's Lane, Shadwell, 1778; 'Saracen's Head', near Aldgate, 1781; Aldgate, 1783; and Gracechurch St, 1792–1802. Son of Hannah Bradshaw, Walthamstow, London, and brother of Joseph Bradshaw, upholder. App. to Edward Stanton, grocer, on 6 March 1759, and then to Thomas Nicholls in March 1761. Admitted freeman of the Upholders' Co. on 4 September 1766. Recorded being 'in distressing circumstances' in 1791. [D; GL, Upholders' Co. records]

Bradshaw, Thomas, 6 James St, Covent Gdn, London, picture frame maker (1774–84). Took out Sun Insurance policies in 1778 for £600 on his house; and in 1783 for £1,000, £180 accounting for utensils, stock and goods. [Poll bks; GL, Sun MS vol. 265, p. 187; vol. 313, p. 328]

Bradshaw, Thomas, 4 Coventry St, Haymarket, London, carver and gilder (1789–93). [D]

Bradshaw, Thomas, 57 Rathbone Pl., London, frame maker (1809–11). [D]

Bradshaw, Thomas, corner of New Market Pl., Bolton, Lancs., cm (1824). [D]

Bradshaw, William, St Ann's West, London(?), u (1735). Took apps named Rid. Poole, son of Ric., of Newport, Bucks., for £100; and William Roberts, son of Ric., of St James's West, for £35. [V & A archives]

Bradshaw, William, London, cm, u and 'tapissier' (1728–d. 1775). Workshops at Frith St, 1728–32; the 'Gr. House', 27 Soho Sq. and 59–60 Greek St, 1732–47; 60 Greek St, 1748–51; no. 59, 1752–55; and Princes St, Hanover Sq., 1756–62. Recorded in Frith St, at premises previously occupied by Joshua Morris, in 1730 with the artist Tobias Stranover. They were possibly partners at this time, since a tapestry on a settee from Belton House, Lincs., supplied to Lord Brownlow, is signed by both of them. It is part of a suite of walnut furniture, c. 1720, with six chairs on cabriole legs with club feet, covered with Fulham tapestry. [Christie's,

14 March 1929, lot 78; F. Lenygon, *English Furniture, 1660–1760*] Bradshaw and Stranover may have worked together on the Watteau tapestries for the Cabal Room at Ham House, Richmond, London, but as they are signed by W. Bradshaw only, the two craftsmen appear to have separated by 1732. [*C. Life*, 26 December 1931; Marillier, *English Tapestries of the Eighteenth Century*, 1930] On the separation, Bradshaw moved to 27 Soho Sq., with back premises at 59–60 Greek St, probably workshops. He may have been the 'Mr. Bradshaw tapestry weaver in Soho Square' mentioned in the notebooks of John, brother of Robert, Adam, on his visit to London in 1748; but it possibly refers rather to George Smith Bradshaw, since in 1747 William gave up his house in Soho Sq., although retaining the premises at 60 Greek St, 1748–51, and no. 59, 1752–54. [Fleming, *R. Adam*] In 1755 no. 59 was taken over by George Smith Bradshaw & Co. with his partner, Paul Saunders. Both George Smith and Saunders may have been partners with William before this date. He was probably the 'William Bradshaw Esq.' who subscribed to Chippendale's *Director*, 1754. He retired to Halton, Lincs., which he purchased in 1743. George Smith Bradshaw was named as one of his executors, and trustee of his several estates, which included Damyns Hall, Upminster, Essex; but he and William were probably not closely related since the estate was left in trust to the son of William's niece. [D; poll bk; *Survey of London*, vol. 34, pp. 517–19; *C. Life*, 20 and 27 September 1946]

In a lawsuit in the 1740s William Bradshaw was described as being 'in a large way of Trade as an upholsterer', and several important commissions are documented:

CHEVENING, Kent, for the 2nd Earl of Stanhope. In 1736–37 Bradshaw's bill for furniture, totalling £1,200, included joiner's, painter's and japanner's work, subcontracted. It possibly includes the gilt chairs, settees and other furniture still at the house. Bradshaw received a further £38 3s on 19 October 1737, and was supplying items in 1751. [*Old Furniture*, vol. 6, p. 129; Kent RO, MS U1590, A20A; Coleridge, *Chippendale Furniture*, p. 137; *DEF*; Washington, *The Treasure Houses of Britain*, 1985, no. 179]

CLIVEDEN, Bucks., accounts, for the Prince of Wales, Duke of Cornwall's London house in St James's Sq. In 1737 Bradshaw received £1,312 for carrying out repairs, alterations and furnishings. [V & A archives]

EARL OF BRISTOL's Expense Book records small payments to Bradshaw, 1738–39; and the Earl's diary, p. 156, mentions a table, bed and lining carpet bought from him. [*GCM*]

LONGFORD CASTLE, Wilts., for Lord Folkestone. From 1737–50 Bradshaw co-operated with Benjamin Goodison, providing furniture and carpets, and hanging tapestries. In 1737 he supplied a tapestry carpet for £26, and in 1750 was paid £12 15s for putting up a tapestry made by 'Monsieur Neprune à Bruxelles'. [*C. Life*, 26 December 1931, p. 716]

HOLKHAM HALL, Norfolk, for the 1st Earl of Leicester. In 1740 Bradshaw received £185 for furniture made for the attic and rustic floors; and £85 for 'mending tables, cabinet work and furnishing Mr. Coke's apartment in the London House' (Thanet House). Furniture provided between 1740–47 included a Dutch tea chest, two large leather chairs, a mahogany dining table, and eighteen chairs with leather seats for the library and dining room at London. In 1742 he received £429 14s for furniture supplied to Holkham. Bradshaw is recorded as late as 1773 by M. Brettingham, completing an unfinished series of tapestries 'hung in Mr. Coke's bedchamber', executed by Vanderbank, from designs by F. Albini, 'excepting the 2 door pieces (Venus, Vulcan & Cupids) which additions were manufactured by the late Mr. Bradshaw'. This refers to William, d. 1775, and not George

Smith, who also worked at Holkham, d. 1812. [Holkam Hall accounts, V & A archives]

DEENE PARK, Northants., and DOVER HOUSE, London, for the 4th Earl of Cardigan (or Cadogan). Bradshaw's bill of 1741, totalling £70 9s 5d includes 'making up a sett of blue Damask hangings 2 pair of Window Curtains, 14 chairs and a safoy sofa with all materials except Damask as p. estimate £63.2.10.' [*DEF*]

DUKE OF GORDON paid Bradshaw £50 in 1741–42 for furniture including two bedsteads on castors, and a mahogany couch 'stuffed in linen with squabb crimson damask and linen'. [Scottish RO, GD 44/51/295]

ALSCOT PARK, Warks., for Mr James West. Bradshaw submitted a bill on 28 September 1745 for '6 Manchineel pembroke chairs with Check Cases', costing £7 10s. In July 1748 he was paid £29 for furniture supplied the previous year, including '12 Pembroke Chairs with Check Cases', £14 8s and '6 Wallnuttree Library stools wth carved roses and painted', £3 15s. [Alscot Park file, V & A archives]

BROOK ST, London house of George Bowes. Bradshaw was responsible for hiring out and supplying furniture from January 1746–June 1751, including on 10 February 1748, 'a blue and mixt Damask bed with quilt etc. and a Bed Carpet', costing £64. [Durham RO, Strathmore MS D/St/247; D/St/V1488–90; V1497; D/St/327c]

MOULSHAM HALL, Chelmsford, Essex or SCHOMBERG HOUSE, Pall Mall, London, for Benjamin Mildmay, Earl Fitzwalter. Bradshaw is recorded in the accounts receiving a total of £529 11s 8½d between 1746–51. On 15 May 1753 he provided 'an easie-chair and 6 matted ones', costing £3 18s, and on 16 November a Turkey carpet, £10. [A. C. Edwards, *The Account Books of Benjamin Mildmay, Earl Fitzwalter*, pp. 99–113; Essex RO]

ROBERT GILLOW of Lancaster sent £30 to 'William Bradshaw Esqr. in Soho Square London' on 6 February 1746–47. [V & A archives]

NEWBY PARK, Yorks., for William Robinson. Bradshaw's bills, 1749–50, total £272, and include bedsteads and bedding, curtains, '2 neat Mahogany Dressing Tables', £2 12s; '2 Mahogany Streight Legged Elbow Chairs on Castors', £4 8s and 'Mosaick Carpeting', £9 15s for the Dining Room; and '8 Mahogany Fann Back Chairs Covered with black leather and Brass Nail'd', £8 8s, with a matching elbow chair, £2 15s. [Leeds archives dept, Newby MS NH 2277/29/2; NH 2277/20/4]

CHISWICK VILLA and BURLINGTON HOUSE, London, for the 3rd Earl of Burlington. Bradshaw provided three couch beds on 15 December 1750 for £13; on 15 January 1751 for £12; and on 5 August 1751 for £17. [Chatsworth papers, Burlington accounts]

CLEVELAND HOUSE, London. Listed in the accounts 1750–52, as an u. [V & A archives, Raby Castle MS] A.E.

Bradshaw, W., Langley, Kent, cm (1807). [Rochester poll bk]

Bradshaw, W., Maidstone, Kent, cm (1830). [Rochester poll bk]

Bradshaw, William, London, cm (1790). [Rochester poll bk]

Bradshaw, William, Shambles, Preston, Lancs., chairmaker (1818). [D]

Bradwell, David jnr, St Andrew's St, Cambridge, carver and gilder (1830). [D]

Brady, Philip, Hull, Yorks., cm (1812). Son of an East Riding militiaman; app. to Robert Waugh of Hull in February 1812. [Hull app. reg.]

Braess, W. C. J., 4 Crawford, London, cm and upholder (1820–39). [D]

Bragg, John, Whitehaven, Cumb., cm (1798). [D] See William Bragg.

Bragg, Nathaniel, Warrior's Gate, St Leonards, Sussex, cm (1839). [D]

Bragge, Nathaniel, 103 High St, Hastings, Sussex, cm and u (1839). [D]

Bragg, William, Marlborough St, Whitehaven, Cumb., painter and chair manufacturer (1811). [D] See John Bragg.

Braillwaite, John, Stockton, Co. Durham, joiner and cm (1720). Took app. named Warwood in 1720. [S of G, app. index]

Brailsford, J. W., Sheffield, Yorks., u (1783). Supplied window curtains to Hardwick Hall in 1783, costing £4 1s 11½d. J. and W. (William) Brailsford, u and cm of Sheffield, provided brass frames costing £7 10s for the Great Ballroom at Buxton Assembly Room, Derbs., in 1784. [Chatsworth account bks] See Thomas and William Brailsford.

Brailsford, Joseph Hill, 3 George St, Sheffield, Yorks., cm and u (1817–33). Address given at Machin Bank in 1822. [D]

Brailsford, Thomas, Sheffield, Yorks., cm and u (1774–1814). Recorded with William Brailsford at High St in 1774; alone there in 1787; and at George St, 1797–1814, no. 3 in 1797. T. & W. Brailsford were employed at Chatsworth in the mid 1770s. [*Burlington*, June 1980, p. 413] Thomas took out a Sun Insurance policy on 19 July 1792 for £400, of which £300 accounted for utensils and stock. [GL, Sun MS vol. 387, p. 342] T. Brailsford, cm of Sheffield, subscribed to Sheraton's *Drawing Book*, 1793. [D]

Brailsford, William, Sheffield, Yorks., cm and u (1774–1837). Trading with Thomas Brailsford at High St in 1774; alone at Norfolk St in 1787; at 3 Market St in 1797; at 3 George St in 1837. [D] Subscribed to Sheraton's *Drawing Book*, 1793. Employed at Chatsworth, Derbs., by the 5th Duke of Devonshire, supplying furniture, carpets, and carved mouldings. On 12 April 1774 the accounts list two wainscott four-poster beds with hangings and bedding, Wilton and other carpets, chests of drawers, tables, backstools, mahogany swing-frame looking-glasses; servant's furniture and bedding; wall-paper, 'verditer blue furniture paper & border for Chintz Bed Chamber', and '32 pieces of Rich pea green furniture paper', £14 8s, with border, £1 14s 8d. In January 1775 Brailsford fitted up the Dining Room with Turkey and Persia carpets, festoon window curtains, '4 open cut & moulded cornices covered wᵗʰ superfine green morine', £4; '36 Dining Room Chairs with Curved Backs, moulded feet and compass seats stuffed over the rails with curly hair in two liners well quilted down to secure to seats afterwards covered with hair seating tyed down and finished with a double row of best burnished nails', £56 14s; a mahogany 'Slab Frame' ornamented with 'a festoon of husks elegantly carved'; '4 Girandoles in white richly carved with double branches to each and best Silvered Glass Plates', £13; and a 'Mahogany Oval cistern hooped with brass and made to fit into the marble cistern'. Brailsford also provided carved window, door and architrave mouldings, including '73 feet of Rich Carved Waterleaf to go round Doors' in the Duke's room. Further sumptuous pieces are described, such as '4 Bergère Arm'd Chairs with Compass seats and oval — Richly Carved and moulded Stuffed in the best manner with Curl'd hair and afterwards coverd with Green flowered Silk Mantua and finished with best Burnished nails complete', £5 10s; and a pair of terms on triangular pedestals supported on lion paws and surmounted by volutes and wreaths, the sides 'with other Ornament richly carved and inlaid the whole completed in a masterly mannr', £91. On 7 February 1782 Brailsford was paid for taking a plan of the Drawing Room to be sent to London; and in 1783 supplied dressing tables, drawer and glass. [Chatsworth papers, *Green Vellum Copy Book*]
Lord Rockingham of Wentworth Woodhouse, Yorks. ordered a carpet from Brailsford, sent on 6 September 1781.

With J. Brailsford, William supplied brass frames for the Great Ballroom at Buxton Assembly Rooms, Derbs., on 11 January 1784. [Chatsworth papers, Buxton Crescent and Stables building account bk; *Burlington*, June 1980, p. 413]

Brailsford, William, Doncaster, Yorks., upholder (1785). [Bailey's list of bankrupts]

Braim, Thomas, 4 Park Lane, Leeds., Yorks., cm (1826–34). [D]

Braime, William, Methley, Yorks., cm (1822). [D]

Brain, John, Bitton, Glos., cm (1784). [Poll bk]

Brain, John, Kingston's Buildings, Bristol, cm (1795). [D]

Braine (or Brown), James, address unrecorded, u (1769–1772). The private accounts of Richard Hoare of Boreham House, Essex, record payments on 15 April 1769 of 18s 6d, and on 15 January 1772, £2 18s 6d. [Essex RO, D/DU 649/2]

Brainsby, Fraser, Double St, Spalding, Lincs., woodturner and chairmaker (1826). [D]

Braint, Andrew, Piazza, Covent Gdn, London, upholder (1743–72). Son of Joseph Braint, Gent. of Hendon; app. to Richard Freelove on 3 August 1743, and admitted freeman of the Upholders' Co. by servitude on 2 March 1758. [D; GL, Upholders' Co. records]

Braithwaite, Benjamin, Southwark, London, upholder (1723). [Heal]

Braithwaite, Christopher, 34 Blue Anchor Alley, Bunhill Row, London, frame maker and gilder (1808). [D]

Braithwait(e) (or Brathwait(e), Ebenezer, Cornhill, London, u (1717–55). Trading at the 'Ship and Anchor', 1727–32. Son of Samuel Braithwaite, cheesemonger of Westminster, possibly brother of Samuel, cm and u of Holborn. App. to William Jones on 3 April 1717, and admitted freeman of the Upholders' Co. by servitude on 7 December 1726. Took out a Sun Insurance policy on 2 November 1729 for £300 on household goods and stock in trade in his house. He submitted a bill in May 1730 to William Cotesworth, general treasurer of the Court at Hicks Hill(?), for 'an elbow chair for the chairman of this court, stuff'd and covered with black Spanish leather, and gilt nails . . . a common velvet squob cushion, trimmed with crimson silk lace, and filled with swan's feathers and downe', and 'green cloth for the table in the court'. [Winterthur, Delaware, Symonds Papers] Declared bankrupt, *Gents Mag.*, March 1734, and was described as a 'Prisoner for Debt', *London Gazette*, 27–31 May 1755. [D; GL, Upholders' Co. records; GL, Sun MS vol. 24, ref. 43211]

Braithwaite, F., Store St, Bedford Sq., London, upholder (1809–11). [D]

Braithwaite, Francis, London, cm (1784). [York poll bk]

Braithwaite, John, York, cm (1774–58). Trading in Davygate in 1774. [Poll bks]

Braithwaite, John, York, carver and gilder (1771–84). Trading in Micklegate in 1784. Son of Thomas Braithwaite, staymaker; app. to James Officer, carver and gilder, on 9 October 1771. [Poll bk; York app. reg.]

Braithwaite, John, Oxford, carver and gilder (b. c. 1802–30). Aged c. 21 he married Eliza Giles of Oxford at St John Baptist on 2 January 1823. [Bodleian index of Oxf. marriage bonds] John Braithwaite, carver, gilder and printseller, is listed in directories at High St in 1830.

Braithwaite, Matthew, Gaunless Chare, Bishop Auckland, Co. Durham, joiner and cm (1827). [D]

Braithwaite, R. & J., 120 Curtain Rd, London, frame maker and looking-glass manufacturer (1809–17). [D]

Bra(i)thwaite, Samuel, London, u, cm, auctioneer, appraiser and undertaker (1757–1811). Addresses given at 315 High Holborn, 1772–92; 145 Cheapside, 1779 and 13 High Holborn, 1781–87. Trade card [Heal Coll., BM] gives address 'between Southampton Buildings and Chancery Lane in Holborn', and states that he 'Makes and Sells all Sorts of

Cabinet and Upholstery Goods in the newest Taste & on the most reasonable Terms'. Son of Samuel Braithwaite, cheesemonger of St Andrew's, Holborn, possibly brother of Ebenezer, u of Cornhill. App. to Thomas Cooke, 'skynner', on 5 July 1757, and admitted freeman of the Upholders' Co. on 6 July 1768. Took apps named Joseph Robins, 1770–80; Thomas Tucker, 1775–88; and William Robins, 1781–88. Took out a Sun Insurance policy on 31 July 1787 for £800 on his dwelling house, counting house and warehouse. [D; GL, Upholders' Co. records and Livery lists; GL, Sun MS vol. 345, p. 455; Heal]

Braithwaite, Thomas, Lancaster, cm (1799–1823). Named in the Gillow records, 1799–1822. Admitted freeman, 1822–23. [Westminster Ref. Lib., Gillow; Lancaster freemen rolls]

Braithwait(e) (or Brathwaite), William, London, upholder (1713–24). Recorded at 'a house situate on the south side of Cornhill in the parish of St Michael', 1714–22. Took app. on 3 December 1713. [PRO, app. reg.] Took out Hand in Hand Insurance policies in 1714 and 1722 for £250 on his house. Polled in 1724. [GL, Hand in Hand MS vol. 13, p. 337; vol. 26, p. 54; Heal]

Brakes, Mary, 4 Shorts Gdns, London, cm and coach joiner (1807). Took out a Sun Insurance policy on 15 December 1807 for £300 of which £150 accounted for utensils and stock. [GL, Sun MS vol. 440, ref. 809944]

Brakes, Simon, 4 Shorts Gdns, London, cm and coach joiner (1805). Took out a Sun Insurance policy on 9 January 1805 for £140 of which £50 accounted for utensils, stock and goods in his workshop at 177 Drury Lane. [GL, Sun MS vol. 431, ref. 7699062]

Bramah, J. & Sons, west end of Piccadilly, London, 'Patent Engine Lock & Water Closet Manufacturer' (1807–23). Between 21 August 1817–17 February 1823 provided the Royal Household with travelling and dressing cases, 'Morocco Soufflet' writing boxes, and ink stands, totalling £593 2s. [Windsor Royal Archives, RA 35513; 35521; –27; –39; –47; –60] Two trade labels found on a mahogany portable toilet box of rectangular design, brass-bound with sunk handles at the sides; interior of lid lined with red gilt-tooled leather and opening on a central tumbler to reveal a blue gilt-tooled leather interior and a removable easel mirror framed in ebony and silver. Removable fittings in red leather, with three glass wells all with silver and ebony lids and four glass stoppered bottles. The silver lids are marked 'LONDON 1807', with the maker's mark, 'T.H.', Thomas Holland. Lock stamped 'I. BRAMAH PATENT'. [Sotheby's, 23 November 1973, lot 41] Two portable mahogany water-closets recorded, one with directions for use, both in the form of a chest of drawers with five dummy drawers, the lid and top three drawers lifting to reveal a porcelain receiver, and brass-handled plunger. [Sotheby's, 27 June 1969, lot 103; 18 July 1975] Possibly of Bramah & Prestage.

Braman, William, London, upholder (1700–13). App. to Abraham Ashley, blacksmith, and admitted freeman of the Upholders' Co. on 17 September 1700. Took apps named Samuel Marriot, 1703–15, John Whittle on 13 November 1711, and Henry Coward on 28 September 1713, both for £35. Took out a Hand in Hand Insurance policy on 28 July 1712 on a rented house on the east side of Warwick Lane, parish of St Faith, next to the Bell Inn, for £225. [GL, Upholders' Co. records; PRO, IRI/1–2; GL, Sun MS vol. 10, ref. 8517]

Bramant, William, Strand, London, u (1709). [London rate bks]

Bramble, Humphrey, Basinghall St, London, joiner and cm (1750–55). Member of the Livery of the Joiners' Co. in 1750. Employed two non-freemen for three months in 1754 and

1755. [GL, Joiners' Co. records and Livery lists; GL, City Licence bks, vol. 1]

Brame, Benjamin, St Peter's, Ipswich, Suffolk, cm (1788). Named in the calendar of marriage licence bonds on 27 September 1788. [Suffolk RO, FAA: 50/2/108]

Bramley, John, New Jerusalem Pl., Manchester, cm (1797). [D]

Bramley, R.H., 99 London Wall, London, looking-glass manufacturer (1829). [D]

Brammich, Thomas, Suffolk St, Birmingham, cm, u and broker (1803–30). Recorded at no. 30, 1823–28. [D]

Brampton, Samuel, Horsemarket, Kettering, Northants., cm and u (1830). [D]

Brancroft, J. & D., 141 Chapel St, Salford, Lancs., chairmakers (1815). [D]

Brand, —, address unrecorded, carver (1754). Subscribed to Chippendale's *Director*, 1754.

Brand, Benjamin, Sudbury, Suffolk, cm (1824–30). Trading at Market Hill in 1830. [D] See John Brand.

Brand, George, Petticoat Lane, London, cm (d. by 1761). [Harris, *Old English Furniture*]

Brand, George snr, 'late of St. Mary's, Whitechapple, Middx.', cm (1771). His son, George Brand, admitted freeman of the Upholders' Co. in 1771. [GL, Upholders' Co. records]

Brand (or Brants), George jnr, London, cm, upholder and auctioneer (1764–1829). Recorded at Church Row in 1771; 37 Houndsditch, 1790–93; and 8 Nassau St some time between 1790–1829. Son of George Brand, cm, late of St Mary's, Whitechapel; app. to John Kent on 3 April 1764, and admitted freeman of the Upholders' Co. by servitude on 1 May 1771. Employed six non-freemen for six months in 1793, and took app. named Samuel Daniel, 1780–1801. [D; GL, Upholders' Co. records and Livery lists; GL, City Licence bks, vol. 10]

Brand, George, 7 Suffolk Mews, Middlx Hospital, London, cm and chair manufacturer (1820). [D]

Brand, John, Southgate, Sleaford, Lincs., chairmaker and wood turner (1826). [D]

Brand, John, Church St, Sudbury, Suffolk, cm and chairmaker (1830–39). [D] See Benjamin Brand.

Brand, Thomas, address unrecorded, cm (1757). Subscribed to Sir W. Chambers's *Designs of Chinese Buildings*, 1757, for four sets.

Brand, Thomas, St James's Ct, Hanway Yd, Hanway, London, cm (1802). Only son and legatee, named in will dated 6 July 1802, of Thomas Brand, d. 1795, which left £600 in 3% consolidated annuities, to be passed to his son on his mother's death. [PRO, C13 23/38]

Brander, Alexander, London, cm and u (1817–25). Trading at 3 Ave Maria Lane, Ludgate St from 1817; and 1 Bridge or Budge Row and 17 Tower Royal by 1820. [D]

Brander, E., 87 Minories, London, u and cabinet warehouse owner (1820). [D]

Brander, Edward, London, upholder (1786–1802). Recorded at 22 St Paul's Churchyard in 1802. Son of Normand Brander, cooper of Savage Gdns, Tower Hill; app to Thomas Saville on 5 July 1786, and admitted freeman of the Upholders' Co. by servitude on 2 June 1802. [GL, Upholders' Co. records]

Branford, J., 10 Adam & Eve Ct, Oxford St, London, cm (1809–11). [D]

Brandreth, Charles, Liverpool, cm (1809–18). App. to Thomas Savage Tyrer, who d. 1811, when Brandreth continued to serve Bartholomew Tyrer, his executor, for the remainder of his term. Petitioned freedom in 1818, paying 6s 8d. [Liverpool freemen's committee bk]

Brandreth, Robert, Liverpool, cm (1804–23). Addresses given at 16 Johnson St, Dale St in 1804; 7 Dickson St in 1810; and 18 Bolton St, 1821–23. [D]

Brandreth, Thomas, Johnson St, Liverpool, cm (1818–39). Trading at no. 49 in 1818; no. 55, 1829–34; no. 49 in 1835; no. 51 in 1837; and no. 22 in 1839. Admitted freeman on 15 October 1818. [D; Liverpool freemen reg.]

Brands, Peter, address unrecorded, cm (1803). Subscribed to Sheraton's *Cabinet Dictionary*, 1803.

Branet, —, address unrecorded (1772). Named in the Earl of Ancaster's account bks on 6 June 1772 supplying a picture frame costing £4 10s. [Lincoln RO, 2 ANC 6/15]

Bran(d)t, Charles, London, carver and gilder (1814–31). Trading at 16 Bow St, Bloomsbury in 1814; Compton House, 53 Old Compton St, Soho, 1816; 33 Theobalds Rd, Bedford Row, 1818; no. 32 in 1819; 145 Regent St, 1823–24; 14 Shaftesbury Terr., Pimlico, 1825; and 22 Upper Belgrave Pl., Pimlico, 1828. Recorded in the Royal Household accounts, 1814–31, restoring candelabra, ormolu ornaments and mounts on furniture and chimney pieces at Carlton House, and mending silver-gilt objects and china. In June 1830 he was paid £29 10s for making and gilding the mountings of a 'large glass shade to cover crystal coffer in the small drawing room'. Supplied 12 'Black Stained Chairs' at 6s 6d in September 1831. [PRO, LC11/15, 18, 21, 24, 27, 41–71]

Brannagan, William, Lydia Ann St, Liverpool, cm (1818–35). Trading at no. 9, 1818–21, and no. 16 before 1835. Son of William Brannagan, shipwright; admitted freeman on 15 June 1818. [D; Liverpool freemen reg.]

Brannan, —, Thos. St, Gros Sq., London, carver and gilder (1835). [D] Possibly:

Brannan, Henry, 13 Duke St, and 30½ Thomas H. Oxford St, London, carver and gilder (1839). [D]

Brannon, James, 153 Rotherhithe, London, cm (1829). [D]

Bransby, Robert, St Bartholomew-the-Great, London, u (1668–74). One of the agents in Britain for the tapestry firm of Michiel and Philip Wauters, Antwerp. He is mentioned in a letter of 17 March 1668 from the Earl of Lauderdale to the Privy Council of Scotland concerning a set of tapestries, 'The Story of Cyrus', for Holyrood, Edinburgh, for which he was paid £160 10s. [Scottish RO, GD90/2/93; 128/74/1/1; *Conn.*, April 1977] Bransby also worked for Anabel, Dowager Countess of Kent, of Wrest Park, Beds., his account totalling £84 10d between 9 July 1673–27 June 1674. His bill of 27 June describes 'a rich ash colour morella bed made up complete and lined with incarnadine Florence sarsnet, with a rising roof and ... headposts inside embroidered with fringes, gilt knobs carved and feet agreeable with 4 silk spriggs.' He also supplied two armchairs and six back chairs of walnut covered in morella silk to match the bed, and a French bedstead; the whole totalling £76. [Bedford Office, London, L28/14] He is recorded supplying landscape hangings, a French bedstead, and 'a bed of rich morella mowhayr embroidered on the inside with cyphers and corronetts', on 15 June 1674. [Nat. Lib. of Scotland, Tweedale MS 7106/108]

Bransby, Samuel, Daggels Ct, parish of St Leonard, Shoreditch, London, cm (1761). Named in settlement records on 29 January 1761 having got Elizabeth Holland pregnant. [GL, P91/LEN]

Branston, —, address unrecorded, cm (1840–41). Mentioned in a bill of Edward Bailey as a cm working at Buckingham Palace with five other cm, and being paid a total of £65 7s 4d for 182 days and 5 hours work. [Windsor Royal Archives, Lord Chamberlain's accounts]

Branston, Abram, 36 Peter's Lane, Liverpool, cm (1816). [D]

Branston, Thomas, 11 opposite the Charterhouse Wall in Goswell St, London, carver and broker (1775). Took out a

Sun Insurance policy in 1775 for £400, £230 accounting for utensils, stock and goods. [GL, Sun MS vol. 239, p. 574]

Branston, William, 25 White Cross Alley, Wilson St, Moorfields, London, chair painter (1803). Took out a Sun Insurance policy on 30 July 1803 for £500 of which £250 accounted for utensils and stock. [GL, Sun MS vol. 426, ref. 750737]

Branston, William, Crown St, London, cm, chairmaker, u, joiner and japanner (1807–35). Trading at no. 6 by 1816; no. 18 in 1817; and nos 4 and 18 from 1820. [D] Presumably the 'William Augustus Branstore', u of 6 Crown St, who took out a Sun Insurance policy on 29 October 1807 for £1,200. [GL, Sun MS vol. 441, ref. 809476]

Brant, William, London, bedstead maker (1823–39). Trading at 5 Baldwin's Gdns, Gray's Inn Lane in 1823; and 31 Gray's Inn Lane, 1835–39. Took out a Sun Insurance policy on 10 September 1823 for £200, of which £170 accounted for stock and utensils. [D; GL, Sun MS vol. 494, ref. 1008274]

Brasgirdule, John, Manchester, cm (1756). Took app. named Fanshaw in 1756. [S of G, app. index]

Brash, John, Leeds, Yorks., cm (1793). Subscribed to Sheraton's *Drawing Book*, 1793.

Brassington, Stephen, Bird St, Lichfield, Staffs., cm etc. (1818–35). Recorded also as a furniture broker, 1828–35. [D; poll bk]

Bratherton, Thomas, Warrington, Lancs., cm (1769). Marriage to Miss Langam of Warrington reported, *Williamson's Liverpool Advertiser*, 12 May 1769.

Bratherton, William, 2 Lawton St, Liverpool, chairmaker (1790). [D]

Braton, Frank & Ernest, High St, Chelmsford, Essex, carvers and gilders (1839). [D]

Bratt, Sm., Rose & Crown Ct, Moorfields, London, cm and u (1808). [D]

Bratt, William, Birmingham, cm (1778–82). Recorded at Spicull St in 1778, 16 Spicer St in 1780, and Church St in 1782. Took out Sun Insurance policies in 1778 for £200 on utensils and stock; and in 1782 for £200, of which £50 accounted for utensils, stock and shop. [D; GL, Sun MS vol. 268, p. 243; vol. 299, p. 452]

Brattan (or Bratton), Edward, Northwich, Cheshire, cm, u, dealer and chapman (1822–34). Addresses given at Witton St in 1822; Castle St in 1828; and High St in 1834. Declared bankrupt and sale of stock announced, *Chester Courant and Anglo-Welsh Gazette*, 7 and 21 September, 5 and 12 October 1830. [D]

Brattan, James, 32 Gascoyne St, Liverpool, cm (1837). [D]

Brattan, James, 23 Market St, Birkenhead, Cheshire, cm (1839). [D]

Bratton, Richard, Wyle Cop, Shrewsbury, Salop, cm and u (1822–35). [D]

Bratton, Thomas, Wyle Cop, Shrewsbury, Salop, cm (1830). [Shrewsbury burgess roll]

Bravery, Henry, Courthouse St, Hastings, Sussex, cm and u (1832). [D]

Bravington, Joseph, High Wycombe, Bucks., turner (1841). [Census]

Brawder, Edw., 87 Little Tower Hill, London, upholder (1808). [D]

Brawley, Alexander, 8 Torbock St, Liverpool, cm (1837). [D]

Bray, —, Marlborough St, Devonport, Plymouth, Devon, cm (1822). [D]

Bray, Benjamin, Holbeach, Lincs., joiner, cm, u and furniture broker (1819–41). [D]

Bray, Caleb, Temple parish, Bristol, cm (1754). [Poll bk]

Bray, Charles, Lissington, Lincs., cm and chairmaker (1810). App. to Henry Wakelin in March 1810. [Hull app. reg.]

Bray, Charles, Norfolk St East, Wisbech, Cambs., turner and chairmaker (1830). [D]

Bray, Frederick, Market Pl., Wisbech, Cambs., u and cm (1839). [D] Mahogany toilet mirror recorded bearing his label.

Bray, George, 4 Cross Parish, Leeds, Yorks., 'dressing case, workbox maker & fancy stationer' (1819). Advertised in *Leeds Intelligencer*, 20 September 1819.

Bray, H., Norfolk St, Wisbech, Cambs., cm (1839). [D]

Bray, James, Timber Mkt, Wisbech, Cambs., cm and u (1824). [D]

Bray, James, Redruth, Cornwall, cm (1830). [D]

Bray, Jeremiah, address unrecorded, upholder (1773–83). App. to Edward Richardson on 1 December 1773, and admitted freeman of the Upholders' Co. by servitude on 5 November 1783. [GL, Upholders' Co. records]

Bray, John, Bourne, Lincs., turner and chairmaker (1826). [D]

Bray, Joseph, address unrecorded, cm (1729–30). The accounts of Temple Newsam House, Leeds, Yorks., record payments for furniture from 5 March 1729 to 6 October 1730, including 'a larg wallnuttree Chest upon a frame', £8 8s, a 'mahogony Tray with Draw under it and a Piller and Claw', £1 10s, 'wallnutree chears', £4 4s, and 'a wallnutree stouel with the top to oupen and coufer with sclat Leass with a putter pan in it', £1 6s. [*Furn. Hist.*, 1967]

Bray, Thomas, East St, Horncastle, Lincs., cm and furniture broker (1835). [D]

Bray & Winder, Preston, Lancs. Signed the *Preston Cabinet Makers' and Chair Makers' Book of Prices*, 1799, on behalf of the masters.

Brayman, —, Fleet St, London, u (d. by 1736). Death of his widow announced, *Daily Post*, 16 March 1736. A former u of Fleet St, he was reputedly worth £20,000.

Brayman, Thomas, address unrecorded, u (1701–02). Carried out upholstery work in Scotland for Dalkeith Palace for thirty-nine weeks from July 1701 to March 1702, amounting to £28 16s 4d. [Scottish RO, Buccleuch MS GD 224 Box 28]

Brayshew, William, Kirkby Lonsdale, Westmld, joiner and cm (1834). [D]

Brazier, James, Rye, Sussex, carpenter, turner and chairmaker (1761). Advertised as a journeyman chair turner in *Sussex Weekly Advertiser*, 17 August 1761.

Brazier, William, parish of St George the Martyr, London, cm (1744–64). App. to William Linnell in 1744 for seven years for £42. Took Vincent Rice as app. on 12 July 1764 for £50. [GL, Joiners' Co. records; PRO, IR1/24]

Brazier, William, Red Lion Sq., London, cm (1766–68). At first in very good business, by 1766 it was declining, and in 1768 Brazier went to the West Indies. [Westminster Ref. Lib., Middlx session bk, p. 49; V & A archives]

Brazier, William, Rye, Sussex, cm (1780–98). Took out Sun Insurance policies in 1780 for £600, £330 accounting for warehouse, utensils, stock and workshop; and in 1783 for £400, £230 on utensils, stock and workshop. [D; GL, Sun MS vol. 283, p. 467; vol. 314, p. 116]

Brazier, William Henry, Leeds, Yorks., u, appraiser and auctioneer (1775–1805). Trading in Briggate, 1775; Call Lane 1783; and Kirkgate, 1793–1805. Advertised frequently in *Leeds Mercury*, on 18 and 25 April 1775 as 'late an Apprentice to Mr. William Armitage, just returned from London, where he has laid in a good and fresh assortment of different articles belonging to the upholstery business . . . An apprentice is immediately wanted.' Advertised again on 30 January, 6 February and 23 April 1776 his stock of goods, 'the newest and most fashionable . . . from the most capital warehouse'; on 14 and 21 October, 18 and 25 November and 2 December 1777, sale of entire stock announced; on 3 June 1783, 25 January 1785, and 11 May 1793 claimed that he

'continues to Appraise and Sell Household Furniture, Plate etc. . . . He still continues the Upholstery business'. He frequently advertised auctions and furniture sales until 1803. [D]

Brazier, Blundell & Tutt, Rye, Sussex, u, chairmakers and cm (1826). [D] Possibly William Brazier.

Bready, James, 13 Hatton Wall, London, carver and gilder (1791). Took out a Sun Insurance policy on 31 March 1791 for £100 on his house and goods. [GL, Sun MS vol. 376, p. 79]

Breakhill, Thomas, Liverpool, cm (1767). Petitioned freedom by birthright as son of Thomas Breakhill, staymaker, in 1767, paying 3s 4d. [Liverpool freemen's committe bk]

Bream(e) (or Braem), Jasper, London, inlayer and cm (1684–d. c. 1696). Trading in St Clement Danes parish before 1696. Worked at Windsor Castle, 1684–86, 'inlaying ye step under her highness ye Dutchess of York's Bed done with several coloured woods in Resemblance of flowers, leaves etc. & for Inlaying ye step at ye foot of ye said Bedd, done with walnutt', for which he was paid £33 6s 8d. [W.H. St John Hope, *Windsor Castle*; V & A archives] Between 1689–92 he rendered three bills to the 5th Earl of Bedford, totalling £45 17s 6d for repairing and supplying furniture including three tables 'of Gernobel wood' (French walnut), costing £7 15s, three other walnut tables; 'a black table 4 foot', £9 10s; and a 34 inch glass in a walnut frame, £5 5s. On 3 July 1688 Bream was paid 'for a Walnutt Tree Table & Stands &c.'; and on 8 August 1689, for 'Wares delivered and Workmanship done', including 'a Wainscott Table for the Dyneing Roome'. [Bedford Office, London; Bedford Inventory, 1585] His will is dated 1696. [PCC, Wills, Index Lib., 12, p. 51, ref. 1696f.4]

Bream, Samuel, Gt Yarmouth, Norfolk, cm and chairmaker (1774–1807). Addresses given at the 'Tea-Chest', Charlotte St in 1776; Blind Middle St, 1779–80; and near the New Hall on the Quay, 1780–87. Advertised in *Norfolk Chronicle*, 10 August 1776, 'that he has now finish'd several Pieces of elegant Inlaid Furniture, (which is now the Taste in London) and proposes to sell them at a much lower Price, than Goods of the same Quality are usually sold there'. [*Conn.*, June 1956; Symonds, *Furniture-making in 17th and 18th Century England*, p. 131] Announced his removal from Charlotte St to the Quay in *Norfolk Chronicle*, 18 March 1780. Took out Sun Insurance policies in 1779 for £1,100, £640 accounting for utensils, stock and warehouse; in 1780 for £1,300, £470 on utensils and workshops; on 20 April 1787 for £1,000 on household goods, stock, warehouse and utensils; on 10 February 1791 for £200; and on 17 July 1792 for £550 on utensils and stock in workshop and woodyard. [GL, Sun MS vol. 273, p. 590; vol. 283, p. 41; vol. 344, p. 497; vol. 375, p. 426; vol. 388, p. 300] Former apps admitted freemen: Jacob Furrance, 1774; Samuel Crisp, 1777; John Browne, 1780; Richard Baxfield, 1783; and Edmund Stolworthy, cm, London, 1796. Subscribed to Sheraton's *Drawing Book*, 1793. [D; poll bks; Gt Yarmouth freemen's calendar] There may have been two Samuel Breams snr and jnr.

Breamer, William, address unrecorded, upholder (1700). Admitted freeman of the Upholders' Co. on 4 September 1700. [GL, Upholders' Co. records] Possibly William Breman.

Brearley, William, 2 New Hampton St, Liverpool, cm (1829). [D] Possibly William Breerly.

Brecher, J., 29 Broad St, London, cm and appraiser (1817). [D]

Breckell (or Brekell), William, Liverpool, chairmaker (1807–35). Addresses given at 37 Stanley St, 1807; 20 Matthew St, 1810; 35 Stanley St, 1811; no. 39, 1813–14; 21 Matthew St, 1823; 1 Derby St, 1824; no. 2, 1827–29; and 44 Circus St, 1834–35. Daughter Ellen's marriage to Peter

Lundy at St Phillip's Church recorded, *Liverpool Mercury*, 17 November 1826. [D]

Breckels (or Breckles), Francis, London, cm and bedstead maker (1825–26). Trading at Little George St, Grange Walk, 1825; and 19 King St, Southwark, 1826. [D]

Breckels, Sam., London, bedstead maker (1826–39). Addresses given at 21 Paul St, Finsbury; 49 King St, Southwark; 5 Fleur de Lis St, Norton Falgate; 243 High St, Southwark; 265 High St; and 64 King St. [D]

Breckels, Thomas, Listergate, Nottingham, cm (1832). [D]

Breckels, Thomas, Eastthorpe, Southwell, Notts., cm and u (1832–41). Recorded at Eastgate, Southwell, as cm and bedstead maker in 1835. [D]

Breckels (or Breckles), William, Long Alley, Moorfields, London, cm, u and bedstead maker (1820–39). Recorded at no. 124, 1820–37, and also at no. 134, date unspecified. [D]

Breckin, Ralph, Bedale, Yorks., joiner and cm (1828–29). [D]

Breckin (or Brecklin), Thomas, Northallerton, Yorks., cm and u (1828–30). [D]

Brecknock, Benjamin, against James St, Piccadilly, London, upholder (1720). Took out a Sun Insurance policy on 15 February 1720 on goods and merchandise in his house. [GL, Sun MS vol. 10, ref. 16623] Probably Benjamin Brocknock.

Breedford, Henry, New St, Chelmsford, Essex, cm and u (1832). [D]

Breer, John, Liverpool, cm (b. 1794–1822). Aged 28 in 1822 when named in the account of leases granted by Corp. of Liverpool. [Liverpool RO]

Breerly (or Brerely), William, 10 Roscoe Lane, Liverpool, cm (1827). [D] Possibly William Brearley.

Brees, Sam., 7 Warwick Ct, Holborn, London, gilder (1835). [D]

Breet, James, Portsea, Portsmouth, Hants., cm (1792–98). [D]

Bregazzi, C. & S., New Parliament Row, Hanley, Staffs., carvers and gilders. Trade card reads: 'Carvers, Gilders, Picture frame & Looking Glass Manfrs. Barometer & Thermometers of every description; Old Glasses Repolished & Silvered, Old Paintings cleaned & varnished'. [Johnson Coll., Bodleian Lib., Oxf.; *Furn. Hist.*, 1974]

Bregazzi, Charles Sebastino, High St, Hanley, Staffs., carver and gilder (1835). [D]

Bregazzi, Innocent & Peter, High Pavement, Nottingham, carvers, gilders, barometer and thermometer makers, looking-glass and picture frame makers (1825–35). [D; Goodison, *Barometers*] Trading at Bridlesmith Gate, 1834–42 the address on Peter Bregazzi's trade card. [MMA, NY]

Bregazzi, Samuel, Derby, carver, gilder and barometer maker (1818–35). Addresses given at Jury St in 1818, Saddlergate in 1822, 38 Queen St, 1828–29; and Cheapside in 1835. [D]

Brekell, John, Liverpool, cm (1767). Admitted freeman on 7 December 1767. [Liverpool freemen reg.]

Breman, William, Strand, London, u (1712–15/16). Recorded next to the Tunn Tavern in 1712; and at the corner of York Buildings in 1715/16. Took out Sun Insurance policies on 13 June 1712 'for his goods'; and on 17 January 1715/16 for goods and merchandise at his dwelling house. [GL, Sun MS vol. 2, p. 39; vol. 5, p. 170] Possibly William Breamer.

Brembridge, Jn, 20 Hatton Wall, London, cm and upholder (1808–12). [D]

Brenes, James, Church Lane, Bocking, Essex, cm and u (1839). [D]

Brenson, Abram, Liverpool, cm (1814–18). Recorded at 24 St Peter's Lane in 1814, with shop at 16 College Lane in 1818. [D]

Brent, Ann, 65 Thomas St, Liverpool, upholsteress (1790). [D]

Brent & Lowe, address unrecorded. Mentioned in bills for Stourhead, Wilts., in 1754. [V & A archives]

Brenton, Thomas, parish of St Thomas, Winton (Winchester), Hants., upholder (1777). Took out a Sun Insurance policy in 1777 for £1,800, of which stock and utensils accounted for £1,500. [GL, Sun MS vol. 256, p. 243]

Brereton, James, Old Priory, Shrewsbury, Salop, cm and u (1840). [D]

Brereton, Thomas, High St, Winchester, Hants., cm (1784). [D]

Bresbury, Philip, Chester, cm (1761). Took app. named Harden in 1761. [S of G, app. index]

Breteuil(e), John, 14 Bond St, Soho, London, upholder (1790–94). Named in Henry Holland's accounts for work carried out at Woburn Abbey, Beds., 1790–92, being paid £197 2s 7d on 24 December 1791, and £398 6s 9d a year later for unspecified upholstery work. [D; Bedford Office, London]

Bretherton, William, Ben Jonson St, Liverpool, chairmaker (1810). [D]

Bretland, Benjamin, Addle St, London, (1711). Received 'eleven pounds in full for a large looking glass and all accts' from 'My Lady Heathcote' on 11 October 1710. [Lincoln RO, 2 ANC 12/D/5]

Bretland, George, Carlton St, Nottingham, cm, u and paper hanger (1834–35). [D]

Bretland, Samuel, 'at the Looking Glass in Gracechurch Street near Cornhill', and 'at the Looking Glass in Threadneedle Street near the South Sea House', London, 'sells all sorts of Looking Glas's, Cabinettwork & Chairs' (c. 1740–60). Two identically designed trade cards with George I style mirror each bear one of the above addresses. [Banks Coll., BM; Heal]

Brett, J., 4 Spencer St, Shoreditch, London, cm (1826). [Maldon poll bk]

Brett, James & Eastman, John, Portsea, Portsmouth, Hants., cm and upholders (1781). Took out a Sun Insurance policy in 1781 for £300 on utensils and stock. [GL, Sun MS vol. 296, p. 503]

Brett, Jn, 58 Compton St, Clerkenwell, London, cm and upholder (1839). [D]

Brett, Thomas, 24 Church St, Spitalfields, London, cm and upholder (1826–29). [D]

Brett, William, Bristol, cm (1807–37). Trading at Horsefair, 1807–09; Nelson St, 1810–12; 1 Tippet's Ct, Horsefair, 1816–18; 24 Trenchard St, 1829–30; Upper Maudlin St, 1831; as W. B. & Son in Upper Maudlin St, 1832–34; St James's Sq., 1835 and 49 Park St, 1836–37. [D]

Brett, William, High St, Margate, Kent, cm (1824–39). Trading at no. 119 in 1824, and no. 48, 1831–39. [D]

Brett, William, Jesus Lane, Cambridge, picture frame maker (1828). Child bapt. parish of All Saints, 1828. [Cambs. RO, PR(bapt.)]

Brett, William, 27 Guildford Pl., Clerkenwell, London, cm (1835–39). [D]

Brettell, —, address unrecorded, u (1757). Named in the Holkham Hall, Norfolk, accounts in 1757 providing a bed, window curtain etc. costing £4 8s 9d; two mattresses, three blankets and a quilt, £9 2s 4d; four chairs for Mr Cauldwell's room, £1 4s; and repairing furniture, £2 1s 6d. [V & A archives]

Brettell, James, Dudley, Worcs., joiner and cm (1793). [D]

Brettel(l), Nathan, 122 High Holborn, London, upholder (1773–95). Recorded alone, 1773–92; and in partnership with William Brettel(l), 1777–95. Took out a Sun Insurance policy alone in 1776 for £400 on his house. [D; GL, Sun MS vol. 248, p. 422]

Brettel(l), William Guidott, 122 High Holborn, London, u and cm (1777–95). Recorded alone and in partnership with Nathan Brettel(l). Took out Sun Insurance policies alone in

1777 for £1,000, £700 on utensils and stock; in 1781 for £400 on his house; in 1782 for £400 on his workshop; and on 5 October 1793 for £300. [D; GL, Sun MS vol. 260, p. 208; vol. 292, p. 630; vol. 303, p. 358; and vol. 397, p. 103]

Brettingham, Matthew & Lillie, James, London. Between 1756–59 the architect Brettingham and the carver and joiner Lillie worked together at Holkham Hall, Norfolk. Brettingham (surprisingly) himself charged for 'carving 35 chairs, 4 Sophas, 4 Settees, 4 Picture Frames' in 1759. Lillie worked in various rooms from 1753. [Holkham Estate Office, family deeds 66, quoted Beard, *Craftsmen and Interior Decoration*, p. 183; C. *Life*, February 1980, pp. 427–31]

Brettingham, Robert, Norfolk, upholder (1795–1812). Son of John Brettingham; admitted freeman of Norwich on 18 July 1795. Recorded in the parish of St Giles, Norwich, 1806; parish of St Benedict, 1799; and Gt Yarmouth, 1807–12. [Norwich poll bks and freemen reg.]

Bretton, Stephen, Miller's Lane, Cambridge, cm and auctioneer (1832). Advertised on 14 September 1832 in *Cambridge Chronicle and Journal* that he was late app. to John Swan of Cambridge and starting business as cm and auctioneer.

Brew, John, Liverpool, cm (1821–37). Addresses given at 34 Gloucester St, 1821–24; 16 Roscoe Lane, 1827; 7 Pontack Lane, 1829; and Joplin Ct, 67 Christian St, 1837. [D]

Brew, Thomas, Liverpool, carver and chairmaker (1829–39). Trading at 6 Rainford Gdns, 1829 as a carver; and at 7 St John's Lane, 1839 as a chairmaker. [D]

Brew, Thomas, Barker St, Shrewsbury, Salop, carver and gilder (1840). [D]

Brew, William, Liverpool, carver and cm (1821–39). Trading at 45 Lime St in 1821; no. 44 and also Hart Ct, Rathbone St, 1823–24; Hardman Buildings, Williamson St, 1827; Hartcourt, Rathbone St, 1829; 3 Rathbone St, 1837; and no. 5, 1839. [D]

Brewen, Francis, East Harling, Norfolk, u (d. 1837). Will proved at Norwich in 1837. [Norfolk Record Soc., index of wills]

Brewen, James, Highgate, London, cm (1823–26). [D]

Brewer, —, Broad Capuchin Lane, Hereford, turner (1779). Advertised in *Hereford Journal*, 18 March 1779, for a journeyman turner and chairmaker: 'a good hand will meet with constant employment, and every encouragement due to his merit'.

Brewer, Francis, 69 Chancery Lane, London, cm (1808). [D] See Francis Brewin.

Brewer, Francis, Brighton, Sussex, turner and chairmaker (1822–27). Trading at 25 Queen's Rd in 1822; Prospect Pl., 1823; 6 Queen's Rd, 1824; and 21 Devonshire Pl., 1826. [D] See Joseph Brewer.

Brewer, Francis, Worcester and Hereford, chairmaker (1826–35). Polled at Hereford in 1826 and trading at Union St, Hereford in 1835. Eldest son of Francis Brewer of Tewkesbury; admitted freeman of Hereford on 14 June 1826, when stated of Worcester. [D; poll bk; Hereford freemen rolls]

Brewer, Francis, 53 Cannon St, London, frame maker (1839). [D]

Brewer, James, Tewkesbury, Glos., chairmaker (1750). Took app. named Bevan in 1750. [S of G, app. index]

Brewer, James, London, carver and gilder, looking-glass manufacturer (1779–1804). Addresses given at 33 Snow Hill, 1779–84; and 126 Newgate St some time between 1786–1804. Took out Sun Insurance policies in 1779 for £2,600 on houses; and in 1781 for £200. [D; GL, Sun MS vol. 276, p. 329; vol. 297, p. 49; Wills, *Looking-Glasses*, p. 148] See Willoughby Brewer. Possibly:

Brewer, James Jupp Norris, Newport St, London, carver and gilder (1801). Married daughter of a carpenter in 1801. [PRO, C13 2/15]

Brewer, James, Dyer St, Cirencester, Glos., cm, chairmaker and basket maker (1813–23). Children bapt. in 1813, 1815 and 1823. [D; PR(bapt.)]

Brewer, John, Cirencester, Glos., chairmaker (1780–93). Brewer and his wife, Elizabeth, acknowledged receipt of £100 legacy given by Richard Norman in 1780. [D; Oxford, RO, Rob II/iii/4]

Brewer, John, High St, Arundel, Sussex, chairmaker and turner (1826–32). [D]

Brewer, Joseph, Brighton, Sussex, cm and u (1815–26). Recorded in parish reg. as u at Russell Row in 1815; as cm at Russell St, 1818; Granville Pl., 1821; and in directories at 20 Devonshire Pl., 1824–26. Children bapt. at St Nicholas's Church: Martha Eliza, daughter of Joseph and Sarah, 17 February 1815; Mary, daughter of Joseph and Jane, 25 February 1818; and Josephine, daughter of Joseph and Sarah, 17 August 1821. Possibly two tradesmen of the same name. See Francis Brewer.

Brewer, Nathan & C., 37 Duke St, London, carver and gilder (1825). [D]

Brewer, Richard, Cow Lane, London, joiner and carver (1762–63). Employed five non-freemen for three months in 1762, and three licence renewed quarterly, in 1763. [GL, City Licence bks]

Brewer, Willoughby, London, carver, gilder and looking-glass manufacturer (1778–94). Trading at 7 Aldersgate St, 1778–79; 33 Snow Hill some time between 1779–89; and 67 Red Lion St, Clerkenwell, 1792–94. Took out Sun Insurance policies on 17 October 1774 for £500, £200 accounting for utensils, stock and goods in trust, and £10 on printed books; and in 1780 for £1,000, £300 on utensils and stock. [D; GL, Sun MS vol. 235; vol. 287, p. 502; Wills, *Looking-Glasses*] See James Brewer.

Brewin, Francis, 69 Chancery Lane, London, upholder and cm (1804). Took out a Sun Insurance policy on 21 September 1804, £300 on household goods in his house where no cabinet work done, £600 on utensils and stock goods in trust, and £50 on workshop behind. [GL, Sun MS vol. 431, ref. 767021] See Francis Brewer.

Brewin, Francis, the corner of Orange St, Kingsgate St, London, upholder (1805). Took out a Sun Insurance policy on 15 October 1805 for £800 on his dwelling house. [GL, Sun MS vol. 434, ref. 781404]

Brewin, J., Southgate St, Leicester, turner (1822). [D]

Brewster, George, Hurworth, Co. Durham, cm (1828–29). [D]

Brewster, John, Lowestoft, Suffolk, cm (1824–30). [D]

Brewster, Robert, High St, Lowestoft, Suffolk, cm and paper hanger (1839). [D]

Brexley, —, address unrecorded, cm (1803). Subscribed to Sheraton's *Cabinet Dictionary*, 1803.

Brian, Peter, 50 Myton Gate, Hull, Yorks., cm and broker (1831). [D]

Brian, Samuel, Lancaster, cm (1793). Marriage on 21 June 1793 reported, *Billinge's Liverpool Advertiser*, 24 June.

Brice, Benjamin, Silver St, London, cm (1774). [Poll bk]

Brice, Edward, Bristol, cm, u and undertaker (1823–33). Trading at Old King St, 1823–31, with cabinet factory at St James's Sq., 1825–31; and at 2 St James's Barton with manufactory at 10 St James's Sq., 1833. Probably the E. Brice, cm of Bristol, declared bankrupt, *Chester Courant and North Wales Advertiser*, 1 May 1832. [D]

Brice, Mary, 5 Gloucester St, St Paul's, Bristol, upholsteress (1835–40). [D]

Brice, Rob., 22 New St, Covent Gdn, ironmonger and cabinet founder (1817–19). [D]

Brickley, John, Rugeley, Staffs., cm (1753). Took app. named Perkin in 1753. [S of G, app. index]

Brickwell, John, High Wycombe, Bucks., chairmaker (1798). [Militia Census]

Brickwell, Thomas, High Wycombe, Bucks., chairmaker (1798). [Militia Census]

Bridge, John, Chester, u (1730). Son of Thomas Bridge, feltmaker; app. to Ralph Bingley, u, 5–24 March 1830/31. [Chester app. bks] Possibly:

Bridge, John, Chester, u (1732–47). Son of Thomas Bridge, feltmaker of Chester; admitted freeman on 1 September 1732. [Chester freemen rolls; poll bk]

Bridge, Stephen, Coggeshall, Essex, cm etc. (1826–27). [D]

Bridge, Susannah, Market Hill, Coggeshall, Essex, cm, u and furniture broker (1839). [D]

Bridge, Walter snr, Poland St, Manchester, cm (1834). [D]

Bridge, William, 70 Scotland Rd, Liverpool, cm and u (1835). [D]

Bridge, William, New Romney, Kent, cm and u (1839). [D]

Bridgen, —, 15 Irongate, Derby, cm and u (1835). [D] Of Gamble & Bridgen.

Bridges, Charles, 49 Wardour St, London, Chairmaker and Turner to His Majesty (1825–35). Successor to John Gee at above. [D; Heal]

Bridges, Joseph, East side of Mars St, parish of St John, Hackney, London, turner (1718). Took out a Hand in Hand Insurance policy on 19 April 1718 for £100 on a rented building at above, and £50 each on two other rented buildings. [GL, Hand in Hand MS vol. 18, p. 273]

Bridgewater, —, address unrecorded, cm (1720). Mentioned in *The Diary of Humfrey Wanley*, ed. E.C. & R.C. Wright, 1966, under 5 and 19 April 1720.

Bridgewater, James, Downley, High Wycombe, Bucks., chairmaker (b.c.1796–1841). Aged 45 at the time of the 1841 Census.

Bridgewater, Thomas, London, carver (1725). Supplied pulpit, various brackets and columns, reader's desk and communion table for St Martin-in-the-Fields Church in November 1725. [Westminster Ref. Lib., MS 419/311]

Bridgewater, Thomas, 17 Swinegate, York, cm (1838). [D]

Bridgewater, William, High Wycombe, Bucks., chairmaker (1798–1830). [D; Militia Census]

Bridgewater, William jnr, Downley, High Wycombe, Bucks., chairmaker (1823–44). [D]

Bridgford, John, New George St, Smithfield, Manchester, cm, u and furniture broker (1834–36). [D]

Bridgman, Jonathan, King's Lynn, Norfolk, u (1674–75). [King's Lynn freemen's calendar]

Bridgman, Thomas, address unrecorded, u (1768). In March 1768 he was paid £80 by the 4th Duke of Bedford for chintz furniture for a bedchamber at Woburn Abbey, Beds., consisting of a bed, four window curtains, twelve chairs with backs and two armchairs. In the same month he was paid £27 6s for furniture including 'an Indian commode' at 16 guineas. [Bedford Office, London]

Bridgwater, Thomas, address unrecorded (1713). Worked for Samuel Tufnell of Middle Temple, London, and, from 1710, of Langleys, Gt Waltham, Essex, receiving from him in May 1713 'three pounds in full for framing ye Battles of Alexander & a case'. [Essex RO, D/DTu 276]

Brierley, Abraham, Heckmondwike, Yorks., cm (1822). [D]

Brierley, John, Manchester, u and cm (1808–38). Trading at 13 Fountain St, 1814–18; 72 Market St, 1821–24; also no.74, 1821–22; 23 Market St, 1828–29; 45 Market St, 1832–33; and 5 Lever St, 1834–36. [D]

Brierley, John, Baildon, Yorks., cm (1822). [D]

Brierley, William, Liverpool, cm (b.1791–1812). Petitioned freedom on birthright as son of William Brierley, shipwright, paying 3s 4d in 1812. [Liverpool freemen's committee bk] Possibly:

Brierley, William, 4 Hampton St, Toxteth Park, Liverpool, cm (1816). Admitted freeman on 10 June 1816. [Liverpool freemen reg.]

Briggs, Abraham, High Wycombe, chairmaker (b.c.1781–1841). Daughters bapt. in 1818 and 1820, and son in 1822. Aged 60 at the time of the 1841 Census. [PR(bapt.)]

Briggs, Amos, 10 Fontenoy St, Dale St, Liverpool, chairmaker (1796). [D]

Briggs, Constantine, London, cm and upholder (1808–37). Addresses given at 6 Broadway from 1808, and 58 Tooley St some time before 1820; at Newington Causeway in 1820, and 19 Bridgehouse Pl. in 1837. [D]

Briggs, E., 19 Bridge St, London, cm and upholder (1825). [D]

Briggs (or Brigg), George, Dalton-in-Furness, Lancs., joiner and cm (1829–34). [D]

Briggs, James, 11 Saville Green, Halifax, Yorks., cm (1822). [D]

Briggs, James, St Augustine St, Norwich, cm and u (1817–30). App. to Holden Gray; admitted a freeman on 27 September 1817. [D; poll bk; Norwich freemen reg.]

Briggs, James, Back St, Reedham, Norfolk, cm and chairmaker (1830–39). [D]

Briggs, John, York, cm (1809). Son of John Warrilow; app. to John Middleton, cm, on 1 May 1809. [York app. reg.]

Briggs, John, Holloway, London, u (1826). [D]

Briggs, Joseph, Longwood, near Huddersfield, Yorks., joiner and cm (1822). [D]

Briggs, Joseph, 11 Nelson St, Halifax, Yorks., cm and joiner (1818–30). [D]

Briggs, Luke, Wisbech, Cambs., cm, chairmaker and u (1822). [D]

Briggs, Ralph, Gisburn, Yorks., joiner and cm (1822). [D]

Briggs, Samuel, Hunslet, Leeds, Yorks., cm (1817–34). [D]

Briggs, Samuel, Moor St, Birmingham, cm, u and broker (1830). [D]

Briggs, Sarah, Greenwich, London, u (1791). [D]

Briggs, Thomas, address unrecorded (1692). He was paid £3 6s by the 5th Earl of Bedford for a frame for a picture and case in 1692. [Bedford Office, London]

Briggs, Thomas, London, cm, writing desk and dressing case maker (1819–35). Addresses given at 20 Newington Causeway, 1819–23, and 27 Piccadilly, 1829–35. [D]

Briggs & Brown, Bradford St, Birmingham, cm and u (1830). [D]

Brigham, George, Beverley, Yorks., cm and u (1818–40). Trading at Norwood in 1818; at Tollgavel, 1831–14; and Butcher Row, 1840. [D]

Brigham, Nicholas, York, u (1739–46). Son of Roger Brigham, Gent., deceased; app. to George Reynoldson, u, on 7 February 1739. Listed on 11 October 1745 amongst papists recognizances, and granted licence to travel as popish recusant with Henry Smith to Barnborough for twenty-one days, on 22 February 1746; and alone to Weighton for seven days on 29 April 1746. [York City Archives, app. reg.; Quarter sessions bk, E/41B]

Brigham, Thomas, Irish Lane, Leytonstone, Essex, cm (1831). [Leyton Census]

Bright, —, London, mattress maker (1768). Received £6 6s on 8 November 1768 for supplying two mattresses to Shelburne House, Berkeley Sq., London. [Bowood MS]

Bright, George, Liverpool, joiner and cm (1835–39). Trading at 13 Fletcher's Gdn, Birkett St in 1835, with shop at 19 King St, Soho; at 10 Peover St, with shop at 15 King St, Soho, in 1837; and 19 Peover St with shop at 30 Wilson St in 1839. [D]

Bright, Jerome Denny & Co., Saxmundham, Suffolk, cm, watch and clock maker (1839). Circular mahogany table on a central pillar leading to a circular platform above curled feet recorded bearing label, c. 1840. [D]

Bright, John, Colchester, Essex, u (1697). Date of probate. [*Wills at Chelmsford*]

Bright, Joseph, Bull Ring, Coventry, Warks., cm (1830). [D]

Bright, Thomas, 3 Brick Lane, Old St, London, cm and upholder (1839). [D]

Bright, W., 16 Queen St, Upper Brook St, London, carver and gilder (1826–27). [D]

Bright, William, 'The Crown Inn', Thomas St, Bristol, ornamental carver (1835). [D]

Brighton, T. W., Cheltenham, Glos., cm (1839–40). [D]

Brighton & Co., 7 Providence Villas, Cheltenham, Glos., cm and u (1839). [D]

Brimelow, Zachary, Bolton, Lancs., cm (1824–28). Trading in Chapel St, 1824, and at 123 Bradshawgate, 1828. [D]

Brimmacombe, William, Northernhay, Exeter, Devon, carver and gilder (1815). Daughters Frances Grace and Rosina bapt. on 10 September 1815 at St David's Church. [PR(bapt.)] Possibly:

Brimmacombe (or Brimmanscombe), William, London, carver and gilder (1820–37). Addresses given at 8 Swan Yd, Strand in 1820 and 17 Holywell St, 1835–37. [D]

Brinkley, Peter, 24 Tooley St, London, cm and upholder (1781–1808). Took out a Sun Insurance policy in 1781 for £400, of which £200 accounted for utensils and stock. [D; GL, Sun MS vol. 289, p. 438]

Brinkworth, Luke, 1 French Row, Peerless Pool, Old St, London, fancy chair manufacturer (1808). [D]

Brinley, Caroline, Exeter, Devon, upholsteress (1827–40). Recorded at Paris St, 1827; Sidwell St, 1828–30; North St, 1831–34; and King St, 1836–40. Featured regularly in *Exeter Journal*, 1827–40.

Brinsley, John, Hill St, Stoke-on-Trent, Staffs., cm and u (1835). [D]

Brinsley, Richard, Church St, Stoke-on-Trent, Staffs., cm and u (1834–35). Trading at Church St in 1834 and Welch St in 1835. [D]

Brinton, Joseph, 4 Castle St, Leicester Fields, London, upholder (1777–93). Took out Sun Insurance policies in 1777 for £300, of which £200 accounted for utensils and stock; and in 1780 for £500, £400 on utensils and stock. [D; GL, Sun MS vol. 262, p. 280; vol. 288, p. 283]

Brion, Charles, High Wycombe, Bucks., chairmaker (b. c. 1824–1841). Aged 17 at the time of the 1841 Census.

Brion, Richard, High Wycombe, Bucks., cabinet turner (b. c. 1821–41). Married in 1840, and aged 20 at the time of the 1841 Census. [PR]

Brisband, Roger, Birmingham, joiner, cm and mortgager (1779). Took out a Sun Insurance policy in 1779 with John Smallwood for £200 on houses. [GL, Sun MS vol. 276, p. 244]

Brisco(e), Joseph, Wigton, Cumb., joiner and cm (1811–34). Trading at Allonby Rd, 1811 and 1829; and West St, 1828–34. [D]

Briscoe, Peter, Lancaster (1778–1821). App. to Gillow in 1778, and admitted freeman, 1795–96. Named in the Gillow records, 1784–1821. [Westminster Ref. Lib., Gillow; Lancaster app. reg. and freemen rolls]

Brisco(e), Richard, London, u (1705–27). Recorded at 'The Golden Lion', corner of Blackmoor St, Drury Lane, London, 1721; and in St Clement Danes, 1727. Son of John Brisco of Crofton, Northumb., app. to James Gronous on 29 September 1705, and admitted freeman of the Upholders' Co. on 4 November 1724 by servitude. [Heal; GL, Upholders' Co. records]

Briscoe, Thomas, Lancaster. Named in the Gillow records, 1784–98. [Westminster Ref. Lib.]

Briscoe, W., 8 Fountain Buildings, Bath, Som., u and cm (1826). [D]

Briscoe, William, Lancaster, cm (1781–98). App. to Gillow in 1781, and named in the Gillow records as 'making claws', 1784–98. [Westminster Ref. Lib., Gillow; Lancaster app. reg.]

Briscoe, William, 111 Fleet St, Ashton-under-Lyne, Lancs., cm and joiner (1834). [D]

Brisenden, Thomas, Tunbridge Wells, Kent, cm and u (1832–39). Recorded at Park Pl. in 1839. Daughter Ann Maria bapt. on 13 June 1832; son Thomas Samuel on 18 December 1833; and son Samuel George on 20 July 1836. [D; PR(bapt.)] Possibly of:

Brissenden & Hodges, Russell Pl., Tunbridge Wells, Kent, cm and u (1832–37). Notice in *Sussex Agricultural Express*, 29 July 1837 concerned the auction sale of 'all those several extensive Business Premises, Dwelling House, Warehouses, and Shops, large Cellarage and Domestic Offices situate immediately facing the weekly Corn Market House and Kentish Hotel, Tunbridge Wells, known as Russell Place (late in the occupation of Messrs. BRISSENDEN and HODGES cabinet makers and upholsterers and others)'. [D]

Brissenden (or Brissender), William, 203 High Holborn, London, u, cm, auctioneer and appraiser (1777–92). Trade card, c. 1780, shows a furnished interior including carpet and ceiling plasterwork. [Banks Coll., BM] Took out a Sun Insurance policy in 1777 for £900, of which £750 accounted for utensils and stock. [GL, Sun MS vol. 258, p. 510] Declared bankrupt, *Williamson's Liverpool Advertiser*, 29 October 1792.

Bristow, George, Peterborough, Northants., cm and u (1822–30). Recorded at Long Causeway, 1822–30 and 'near the Church' in 1823. [D]

Bristow, J. M., address unrecorded. Undated chair recorded bearing impressed stamp 'J. M. BRISTOW' on leg. [V & A archives]

Bristow, James, 10 Narrow Weir, Bristol, chairmaker (1831). [D]

Bristow, John, London, upholder (1711). Son of Lionel Bristow, late freeman blacksmith of London; app. to William Humphrey on 7 November 1711 for £53 15s. [PRO, IR1/1]

Bristow, J., St Martin-in-the-Fields, London, u (1765). Declared bankrupt, *Gents Mag.*, October 1765. Possibly:

Bristow, John, St Martin-in-the-Fields, London, u and cm (1768). Declared bankrupt, *Williamson's Liverpool Advertiser*, 2 December 1768.

Bristow, John, St Alban's St, Pall Mall, London, u, cm and undertaker (1791). Trade card, marked 1791 in pencil, shows earlier Rococo-style furniture. [Banks Coll., BM]

Bristow, John, Peterborough, Northants., cm and u (1822–30). Trading at Broad Bridge St in 1822 and Cumbergate in 1830. [D]

Bristow, William Henry, 81 Pearson St, Kingsland Rd, London, cm and upholder (1839). [D]

Bristow, William, Downley, High Wycombe, Bucks., chairmaker (b. c. 1811–41). Aged 30 at the time of the 1841 Census.

Britain, Richard, Wapping, London, upholder (1790–1802). Recorded at 5 New Cutt in 1798, and Anchor Rope, 1802. App. to Isaac Vizard on 7 July 1790, and admitted freeman of the Upholders' Co. by servitude on 3 January 1798. [GL, Upholders' Co. records]

Britisle, James, Norwich, cm (1784). Former app., George Darking, admitted freeman on 24 February 1784. [Norwich freemen reg.]

Brittain, G., 2 Woburn St, and 2 Streatham St, Bloomsbury, London, carver and gilder (1837). [D] Possibly:

Brittain, George, address unrecorded, carver and gilder (1835). [D]

Brittain, H., 39 Grafton St East, Tottenham Ct Rd, carver (1829). [D]

Brittain, Thomas, Duke St, Grosvenor Sq., London, cm and undertaker (1780). Took out a Sun Insurance policy in 1780 for £300 on his house. [GL, Sun MS vol. 282, p. 92]

Britten, Daniel, Mare St, Hackney, London, carver, gilder and toy dealer (1823). [D]

Britten, Sam, 5 Baynes Row, Clerkenwell, and 23 Red Lion Sq., London, cabinet and morocco case maker (1809–29). [D]

Britten, James, 32 Thomas St, Bath, Som., chairmaker (1833). [D]

Britton, Thomas, 8 Five Foot Lane, Bermondsey St, London, cm and upholder (1777–99). [D]

Brix, Robert, 22 Queen's Buildings, Knightsbridge, London, cm and upholder (1809–11). [D]

Broad, —, address unrecorded, 'Carvers & Gilders, Picture Frame & Looking Glass Manufacturers, Etc.' Pair of gilded George II-style console tables from Linton Park recorded bearing label. [Christie's, 2–3 October 1961, lot 134]

Broad, Charles William, 6 Bench St, Dover, Kent, carver and gilder (1824–39). [D; Dover and Canterbury poll bks]

Broad, John Abel, 8 St Martin's St, London, cm and upholder (1839). [D]

Broad, Robert, 14 Walcot Buildings, Bath, Som., cm, u and broker (1826). [D]

Broad, William, Goodramgate, York, joiner, cm and u (1828–30). Recorded at no. 86 in 1828 and no. 66 in 1830. [D]

Broadbent, Joseph jnr, Liverpool, cm (1822). App. to Joseph Roberts in 1822. [Liverpool app. reg.]

Broadbent, Samuel, Liverpool, cm (1810–11). Trading at 2 St Stephen St in 1810 and 6 Cartwright Pl. in 1811. [D]

Broadbent, William, Chester, upholder (1746–47). Son of John Broadbent, silk stocking weaver, late of Nantwich; app. to Ralph Bingley, embroiderer and upholder of Chester; Admitted freeman in January 1746. [Chester freemen rolls; poll bk]

Broadbent, William, Hipperholme, Halifax, Yorks., joiner and cm (1834). [D]

Broadbent & Wright, 53 Wigmore St, Cavendish Sq., London, upholders (1817). [D]

Broadbrook, Edward, 18 Dorrington St, Cold Bath Fields, London, cm and upholder (1794). Took out a Sun Insurance policy on 16 April 1794 for £300, £50 on utensils and stock. [GL, Sun MS vol. 397, ref. 626933]

Broadbrook, Edward, Broad St, London, u (1798). Declared bankrupt, *Billinge's Liverpool Advertiser*, 30 April 1798.

Broadbrook, Ed., 88 Gt Saffron Hill, London, cm (1809–11). [D]

Broadfield, Benjamin, 4 Court, Breat St, Birmingham, cabinet case maker, portable desk and dressing case maker (1830). [D]

Broadhead, Benjamin, Holmfirth, Yorks., joiner and cm (1834). [D]

Broadhurst, George, Nottingham, cm (1802–20). Trading at Wheelgate in 1820. Listed as app. in 1807 and burgess in 1814. [Notts. RO, indices of app. burgesses; poll bk]

Broadhurst, George, Churchyard, Chesterfield, Derbs., cm (1818–22). [D]

Broadhurst, John, Bridge St, Warrington, Lancs., chairmaker (1822–34). [D]

Broadhurst, John, Lichfield St, Hanley, Staffs., joiner, builder and cm (1834). [D]

Broadhurst, Joseph, Congleton, Cheshire, cm (1793). [D]

Broadhurst, Joshua (or Josiah), Manchester, cm (1794–1825). Addresses given at 97 Portland St in 1794; 41 Croft St, 1797; 41 Travis St, 1800–04; no. 46 in 1808; and 2 London Rd, 1811–25. [D]

Broadhurst, Samuel, 6 Cartwright's Pl., Liverpool, cm (1818). [D]

Broadhurst, Thomas, Chester, joiner and cm (1794). Declared bankrupt, *Williamson's Liverpool Advertiser*, 2 June 1794.

Broadstock, William, address unrecorded, u (1668). Recorded in the Royal Household accounts in 1668 providing bullrush mats costing £4 15s. [PRO, LC9/271, p. 75]

Broadwood, Matthew, 20 Oxendon St, Haymarket, London, carver and gilder (1829–39). [D]

Broadwood, Robert, 20 Oxendon St, Haymarket, London, carver and gilder (1826–37). [D]

Brobie, William, address unrecorded, cm (1803). Subscribed to Sheraton's *Cabinet Dictionary*, 1803.

Brock, James, Camberwell Green, London, cm and upholder (1839). [D]

Brock, John, Chester, u (1747). [Poll bk]

Brock, John, Oldham (or Old Hall) St, Hanley, Staffs., chairmaker and turner (1834–35). [D]

Brock, R., 10 Stephen St, Tottenham Ct Rd, London, picture framer and blind maker (1820). [D]

Brockband, George, Blackburn, Lancs., cm (1797–98). [D]

Brockbank, Ellwood, Carlisle, Cumb., cm (1834). [D] Possibly of:

Brockbank & Edmondson, Castle St, Carlisle, Cumb., u and cm (1829). [D]

Brockbank, John, 191 Pilgrim St, Newcastle, cm (1834). [D]

Brockbridge, Henry, 6 Little Suffolk St, Southwark, London, cm and carver (1832–34). [D]

Brockbridge, Thomas, Green Walk, Holland St, London, bedstead and chair manufacturer (1808–20). Trading at no. 3 in 1808 and no. 7 in 1820. [D]

Brocklebank, David, 47 Coney St, York, carver, gilder and looking-glass maker (1829–d. 1849). Advertised in *York Gazette*, 4 April 1829. Took C. Arundel (late five years with Mr Terry, Davygate) into partnership in October 1829, and recorded in partnership with him in 1830. Moved to 32 Stonegate on 3 November 1832. Declared bankrupt, *York Gazette*, 15 November 1834, and died in July 1849. [D]

Brocklebank, John jnr, Soutergate, Ulverston, Lancs., chairmaker (1834). [D]

Brocklebank, Joseph, Stonegate, York, carver and gilder (1818–d. 1819). Death, aged 30, reported, *York Gazette*, 10 July 1819. [D]

Brocklehurst, Joseph, Saville St, Sheffield, Yorks., cm (1821). [D]

Brockwell, John, 50 Rahere St, City Rd, London, clock-case maker (1839–40). [D]

Brocknock, Benjamin, Portugal St, London, upholder (1712). Took out a Sun Insurance policy on 18 April 1712 'for his goods'. [GL, Sun MS vol. 2, p. 21]

Broderick, Henry, 97 Bedford St, North Shields, Northumb., carver and gilder (1834). [D]

Broderip & Wilkinson, 13 Haymarket, London, cm. Label recorded on early 19th-century piece of patent furniture.

Brodie, George, 24 Gloucester St, Queen Sq., London, cm (1835). [D]

Brodie, George, 41 Eagle St, Red Lion Sq., London, cm (1837). [D]

Brodie, J., carver and gilder. Early 19th-century trade card is at MMA, NY.

Brodie, John, 18 Concert St, Liverpool, joiner and cm (1827). [D]

Brodstock, William, address unrecorded, u and cm to Charles II

(1667). First appears in the Royal accounts in February 1667, when he 'delivered unto his Maj^ies Great Wardrobe' a quantity of chairs and tables. His bills are mainly for small amounts. [Royal Household accounts; *DEF*]

Brogg, James, 1 Princes St, Red Lion Sq., London, picture frame maker (1820). [D] Probably of:

Broggi & Co., 1 Princes St, Red Lion Sq., London, carver and gilder (1829). [D]

Broham, Daniel, New St, St Bride's, London, cm (1761–72). Served as Constable at St Bride's in 1761, and Collector for the Poor in 1771–72. [GL, MS 6561, p. 97]

Broitehall(?), Henry, Norwich, u (1829). App. to John Cox; admitted freeman on 6 June 1829. [Norwich freemen reg.]

Broley, Alexander, Liverpool, cm (1827–35). Trading at Heaton Ct, Knight St in 1827 and 8 Torbock St, 1834–35. [D]

Bromage, William, Richmond, Surrey, carver and gilder (1822–26). Recorded at Upper Hill St in 1822 and Hill St in 1826. [D]

Bromage, William, Twickenham, Middlx, carver and gilder (1823–38). Recorded at London Rd in 1823 and Twickenham Green in 1838. [D]

Bromely, John, 23 Tuble St, Manchester, cm (1804). [D]

Bromfield, —, Lombard St, Liverpool, cm and joiner (1765). Death of his wife reported, *Williamson's Liverpool Advertiser*, 29 March 1765.

Bromfield, —, d. c. 1804. See James (John) & Playfair.

Bromfield, Francis, 8 Leather Lane, Dale St, Liverpool, chairman (1700–96). [D]

Bromfield, Mary Ann, Brad St, West Bromwich, Staffs., u (1830). [D]

Bromford, Rob., 51 New Bond St, London, trunk maker to His Majesty (1796). [D]

Bromhead, —, address unrecorded (1727). Named in the Holkham Hall accounts supplying '4 Russia chairs and 2 settees etc.' costing £11, in 1727. [V & A archives]

Bromhead, Thomas Boyall, Stamford, Lincs., carver, gilder, picture frame maker and paper hanger (1829–d. by 1848). Trading in St Michael's parish, 1832 and St Mary's St, 1835. Admitted freeman by right of birth in 1829. Bill heads of 1842, and in his widow's name of 1848, give address and trade details. [Poll bk; Stamford freemen rolls; Stamford Town Hall Lib., ref. T22, file 2]

Bromley, Edward, Chester, cm and silverer of glass (1715–45). Son of Edward Bromley, baker of Chester; admitted freeman on 17 January 1715. Took app. named John Davies in 1726. Former app., Thomas Astle, admitted freeman in 1745. [Chester freemen rolls and app. reg.]

Bromley (or Brumley), Ed., Wilmott St, Brunswick Sq., London, upholder and cm (1809–13). Recorded as Brumley, cm, at no. 11, 1809–11; and as Bromley, u, at no. 20, 1811–13. [D]

Bromley, John, address unrecorded, upholder (1698). App. to William Tilley, skinner, and admitted freeman of the Upholders' Co. on 19 August 1698. [GL, Upholders' Co. records]

Bromley, Robert, 24 Hatton Wall, Hatton Gdn, London, cm and chairmaker (1787–93). Took out a Sun Insurance policy on 6 February 1787 for £200 on his dwelling, workshop, goods and utensils. [D; GL, Sun MS vol. 344, p. 61]

Bromley, Thomas, Colchester, Essex, cm (1806–44). Probate dated 1844. [Poll bks; *Wills at Chelmsford*]

Bromley, William, Derby, cm (1820). Named as Hon. Burgess in 1820. [Notts. RO, index of burgesses]

Brompton, John, Ludlow, Salop, saddler and u (1714). Took app. named Howton in 1714. [S of G, app. index]

Bromridge, —, George Yd, Hatton Gdn, London, cm (1793). Subscribed to Sheraton's *Drawing Book*, 1793.

Bromwell, John, New Palace Yd, Westminster, London, upholder (1725). [Heal]

Bromwich, Henry, Gt Russell St, Bloomsbury, London, frame maker (1779). Took out a Sun Insurance policy in 1779 for £600, £120 accounting for timber workshop, utensils, stock and goods. [GL, Sun MS vol. 274, p. 213]

Bromwich, Thomas, at 'The Golden Lyon', Ludgate Hill, London, paper stainer and u (1748–d. 1787). Trade card, dated 1748, states that he 'Makes and Sells all manner of Screens, Window Blinds, and Covers for Tables, Cabins, Stair-Cases, &c. Hung with Guilt Leather, or India Pictures, Chints's, Callicoes, Cottons, Needlework, & Damasks Matched in Paper; to the utmost exactness, at Reasonable Rates'. [*Conn.*, vol. 112, 1943, p. 38] Master of the Painter-Stainers' Co. in 1761, and appointed 'Paper-hanging Maker in Ordinary to the Great Wardrobe' in 1763. In 1754 he supplied 'the new furniture wallpaper' to Horace Walpole, [Strawberry Hill accounts]; and between July 1766– 29 September 1768 provided 'Paper, Colours, Papie Mache etc.' to Shelburne House, Berkeley Sq., London, receiving £195 11s. [Bowood MS] Worked for Lord Darnley of Cobham Hall, Kent, being paid £26 on 23 February 1773 for India paper 'for my Lady's Dressing Room & paper for the two nurseries'. The Chinese paper supplied by Bromwich is still 'in situ' at Cobham Hall. He also made a surviving papier-mâché ceiling at Dunster Castle. [*C. Life*, 10 May 1983, pp. 568–71] Thomas Bromwich is named in Paul Methuen's Day Book for items supplied to Corsham Court, Wilts., 1770–73, including marble tables costing £67 3s 6d on 29 February 1772; and a 'glass & new gilding the frame', £23 13s on 17 February 1773. The firm of Thomas Bromwich & Co. was paid £40 12s on 17 June 1773 by Edward Morant of Brokenhurst Park, Hants. [Morant accounts, Roydon Manor, Hants.] Thomas Bromwich is recorded in partnership with Leonard Leigh at 'The Golden Lyon', 1758–65; as Bromwich and Isherwood in 1766; and Bromwich, Isherwood and Bradley, 1769–88. [Heal] This last firm supplied wallpaper and borders, a fire screen and '3 Pair Small Tree Gerandoles with Single Branches in Burn^d Gold' to Charles Long of Saxmundham, Suffolk, receiving a total of £6 on 10 June 1769. [Suffolk RO, HA 18/EC/S]

Bromwich, Thomas, 24 Suffolk St, Birmingham, cm (1800). [D]

Brook, Benjamin, Bristol, cm (1774). [Poll bk]

Brook, Charles, Birstal, Yorks., joiner and/or cm (1830–37). [D]

Brook, Emanuel, Rastrick, Yorks., joiner and cm (1834). [D]

Brooks, George, Hull and Selby, Yorks., cm, u, paper hanger and broker (1814–29). Recorded at 27 Blackfriargate, Hull, 1814; Finkle St, Selby, 1822; and Edgar St, Hull, 1828–29. Took app. named Daniel England of Sutton in July 1814 until December 1817 when assigned to Robert Waugh; assigned Thomas Johnson from George Chapman, deceased, in March 1815; assigned William Gibson from John Levett in January 1819; took James Lowther of Sculcoates in May 1819; and James Bentley of Selby in October 1822. [D; Hull app. reg.]

Brook, I, address unrecorded. Set of four undated mahogany chairs, yoke-back with brass strings stamped 'I. BROOK', recorded in Wakefield, Yorks.

Brook(e), John snr, Briggate, Leeds, Yorks., cm and u (1783–d. c. 1804). [D] Address also given at Wormald Yd in 1798. Advertised in *Leeds Mercury*, 18 February 1783, that '. . . he makes and sells all sorts of Cabinet and Upholstery goods in the best and newest Taste, and on the most reasonable Terms. NB. Three journeymen in the cabinet and chair Branch wanted immediately, who may depend on constant Employment and Wages according to Merit'. Announced in *Leeds Intelligencer*, 21 and 28 July 1789 his removal 'into a house in the late Mrs. Lee's Yard, nearly opposite the hotel in

Briggate'. Advertised for journeymen, *Leeds Mercury*, 18 May 1790, and *Leeds Intelligencer*, 1 June 1790, 'wages from 12s. to 16s. a week, and allowed to work overtime throughout the year'. Brook was one of the few Masters called to sign an agreement with the journeymen in the *Leeds Cabinet and Chair Makers' Book of Prices*, 1791. Advertised for six cm in *Leeds Mercury*, 4 December 1802, and mentioned in *Leeds Intelligencer*, 23 March 1807. Subscribed to Sheraton's *Cabinet Dictionary*, 1803. Dead by 1804, when his son, John Brook jnr announced continuation of trading on the same premises after his father's death, *Leeds Mercury*, 15 December 1804. Brook snr worked at Harewood House, Yorks. between 1783–1801, being paid about £275 for furniture including, in 1796, '2 large Round end Dining Teble (sic)'. [Leeds archives dept, Harewood MS 189, 190–91, 211; *Furn. Hist.*, 1965, 1971 and 1974]

Brook, John jnr, Leeds, Yorks., cm and u, dealer and chapman (1804–17). Trading in Briggate from 1808–16, and at Wormald's Yd in 1817. Announced in *Leeds Mercury*, 15 December 1804 continuation of trade at the same premises in Briggate after the death of his father. Advertised in *Leeds Intelligencer*, 29 September and 6 October 1808 for a 'Person to act as Foreman in a shop where a number of Hands are employed'. Declared bankrupt, *Leeds Mercury*, 24 December 1814, and 29 April 1815; and *Leeds Intelligencer*, 2 January 1815, but trading again by 1817. [D]

Brook, John, Node Hill, Newport, Isle of Wight, Hants., cm and u (1830). [D]

Brook, Joseph, 10 Aldersgate St Buildings, Aldersgate St, London, cm (1785). Took out a Sun Insurance policy on 13 April 1785 which included £100 on household goods in the dwelling of Jonathan Binns, cm. [GL, Sun MS vol. 328, p. 72]

Brook, Joseph & John, High-Town, near Dewsbury, Yorks., cm (1822). [D]

Brook, Richard, Ossett, Yorks., cm (1822–30). [D]

Brook(e)(s), Robert, London, cm and upholder (1764–1802). Trading at 1 Budge Row, 1774–93; and Bell Yd, Temple Bar, 1794–1802. Son of John Brooke, clothworker of London; app. to Dan. Holbrow on 2 August 1764, and William Rogers on 7 March 1765. Admitted freeman of the Upholders' Co. on 7 August 1771. In 1785 employed two non-freemen for three months. Marriage to Miss Brewer reported, *Gents Mag.*, September 1787. In 1789 the firm of Brook & Shotter, upholders and cm, recorded at Bridge Row (a common misnaming of Budge Row). [D; GL, Upholders' Co. records; City Licence bks, vol. 10]

Brook, Thomas, Bowling, Bradford, Yorks., cm (1822). [D]

Brook, Thomas, Heckmondwike, near Dewsbury, Yorks., cm (1822). [D]

Brook, William, Breadeston, Norfolk, u (1780). [Norwich Poll bk]

Brook, William, High-Town, near Dewsbury, Yorks., cm (1822). [D]

Brook, William, Joseph & John, Liversedge, Yorks., joiner and cm (1830). [D]

Brookbank, Joseph, Ainsworth St, Blackburn, Lancs., cm and joiner (1816–18). [D]

Brooke, Daniel, Thorpe, Essex, cm and u (1839). [D]

Brooke (or Brooks), Francis, St Peter Mancroft, Norwich, u (1745–68). App. to Timothy Money and admitted freeman on 24 February 1745. Former app., William Smith, u, admitted freeman on 2 May 1753. Brooke elected Sheriff on 26 July 1766. [Poll bk; Norwich freemen rolls] See William Brooke.

Brooke, John, St Dunstan's, London, chairmaker (1722). Took app. named Stanbridge in 1722. [S of G, app. index]

Brooke, Joseph, St John St, Bromsgrove, Worcs., cm (1820). [D]

Brooke, R. & William, 19 Wellclose Sq., London, looking-glass manufacturer, cm (1775–88). [D]

Brooke, Robert, 14 King St, Whitehaven, Cumb., carver and gilder (1834). [D]

Brooke, Thomas, Market Pl., Boston, Lincs., carver and gilder (1826). [D]

Brooke(s) (or Brooks), William, White Lion Lane, Norwich, u (1776). Trade card, *c*. 1770, states that he 'Executes all Kinds of Upholstery Work, In the newest Taste & on yᵉ lowest Terms. NB. Variety of Paper-Hangings, Carpets & Beds ready standing'. [Norwich local history Lib.] Supplied beds, curtains and carpets to the Rev. James Woodforde, Rector of Weston Longwith, Norfolk, in June 1776; and sent him 'a fine Hind Quarter of London Lamb, prodigious fine' on 25 December 1776. [*The Diary of James Woodforde, The First Six Norfolk Years*, ed. R. L. Winstanley, 1981]

Brooke, William, St Peter's Mancroft, Norwich, u (1777). Insured his house for £300 in 1777 with the Sun Co. [GL, Sun MS vol. 259, p. 168] See Francis Brooke.

Brooke, William, Norwich, cm (1799). Son of Daniel Brooke, baker; admitted freeman on 1 June 1799. [Norwich freemen reg.]

Brooke(s), William, 19 Wellclose Sq., London, cm, glass-grinder, looking-glass warehouseman (1775–88). Took out a Sun Insurance policy in 1778 for £500 of which £430 accounted for utensils and stock. Recorded with R. Brooke, 1775–88. [D; GL, Sun MS vol. 268, p. 396]

Brooke, William, London, cm (1802). [Norwich poll bk]

Brooker, George, Trinity St, Cambridge, carver and gilder (1839). [D]

Brooker, James, 1 King St, Commercial Rd, London, carver and gilder (1824). Took out a Sun Insurance policy on 5 January 1824 for £300. [GL, Sun MS vol. 497, ref. 1012429]

Brooker, James, Cheltenham, Glos., carver and gilder (1830–40). Trading at 8 Clarence St in 1830 and 8 Clarence Colonnade in 1839. [D]

Brooker (or Brocker), John, 5 Southampton Row, London, carver and gilder, picture frame and looking-glass maker, picture dealer (1820–39). Took out Sun Insurance policies on 31 January 1821 for £2,200 of which stock, utensils and workshop accounted for £650; and on 17 April 1822 for £2,450, of which stock, utensils and workshop accounted for £450, and pictures and prints as stock, £250. [D; GL, Sun MS vol. 485, ref. 976383; vol. 490, ref. 991380] Letter recorded, dated 1 May 1830, informing that J. Brooker & Son of 5 Southampton Row had established a branch in Market Hill, Cambridge, where they had gilt looking-glasses, frames and plate glass.

Brooker, Thomas, 36 Gloucester St, Queen's Sq., London, carver and gilder (1817). [D]

Brookes, Margaret, 10 Bow St, Bloomsbury, London, cabinet founder (1819–25). [D]

Brookes, William, Brighton, Sussex, carver and gilder (1824–26). Trading at 83 Church St in 1824 and 22 North St in 1826. [D]

Brookes, William, 14 Gt Queen St, London, carver and gilder, looking-glass frame maker (1835–39). [D]

Brooking, John, Stoke Damerell, Devon, cm (1759). Took app. named Holman in 1759. [S of G, app. index]

Brooks, —, address unrecorded, cm (1803). Subscribed to Sheraton's *Cabinet Dictionary*, 1803.

Brooks, Andrew, Baldertongate, Newark, Notts., u (1835). [D]

Brooks, Charles & Co., High St, Southampton, Hants., cm and u (1823). [D]

Brooks, Elias, 14 Charlotte St, London, cm and upholder (1827–28). [D]

Brooks, George, Blackheath Hill, Greenwich, London, u (1838–39). [D]

Brooks, Henry, Queen's Head Ct, London, carver (1774). [Poll bk]

Brooks, Henry, Coventry St, London, carver and gilder (1790). [D]

Brooks, James, Kirby St, Hatton Gdn, London, upholder (1774–77). [D]

Brooks, James Philip, Portsea, Portsmouth, Hants., cm and u (1823–30). Addresses given at 79 North St in 1823 and 6 Charlotte St, Southport in 1830. [D]

Brooks, John, at the 'White Balcony', Maiden Lane, parish of St Paul, Covent Gdn, London, chairmaker (1723). Took out a Sun Insurance policy on 2 July 1723 for £200 on goods and merchandise in his house. [GL, Sun MS vol. 15, ref. 29044]

Brooks, John, London, cm (1776). [Cambridge poll bk]

Brooks, John Bobbett (or Boffett), New Market, Beccles, Suffolk, u and agent for the County Fire and Provident Life Office (1820–39). Named in the calendar of marriage licence bonds in 1820. [D; Suffolk RO, FAA: 50/2/119, p. 78]

Brooks, Joseph, Walsall, Staffs., u (1770–80). Trading at New St in 1770 and Church St in 1780. [D]

Brooks, Jos., 15 King's Head Ct, Holborn, London, gilder (1808). [D]

Brooks, Stephen, Littleworth, High Wycombe, Bucks., chairmaker (b. c. 1814–41). Aged 27 at the time of the 1841 Census.

Brooks, Thomas, Hull, Yorks., cm, carver, gilder and looking-glass manufacturer (1778–1840). Addresses given at 1 North Dockside in 1803; 50 Whitefriargate, 1806–14; no. 16, 1817–26; 48 Savile St, Osborne St, 1831–34; and no. 50, 1835–40. Also trading as a stationer, 1817–22; comb warehouse owner, 1821–23; 'British Plate glass manufacturer', 1823–35; and tea dealer in 1823. Worked at Burton Constable House, Yorks., supplying in 1839 carved and japanned tables with shelves; two cabinets; two stools bearing trade labels; carved dragons for the Chinese room; gilt stands for the upper staircase; and a gilt frame for John Brown's sketches. Carried out much work at Burton Constable after 1840. [D; Humberside RO, DDCC; C. Life, June 1976, pp. 1622–24] See William Brooks.

Brooks, Thomas, 101 Mary St, Hampstead Rd, London, chair and sofa manufacturer (1839). [D]

Brooks, William, Gt Yarmouth, Norfolk, cm (1784). [Poll bk]

Brooks, William, Hull, Yorks., cm (1826–40). Trading at 27 Lower Union St in 1826; 28 Bridge St, 1831; Anne St, Osborne St, 1834; 50 Osborne St, 1838; Anne St, 1839; and 50 Osborne St, 1840. [D] See Thomas Brooks.

Brooks, William, 7 Lower Elizabeth St, Eaton Sq., London(?), (1835). [D]

Brooksbank, Timothy, Nottingham, joiner and cm (1828). [Nottingham app. reg.]

Brookshaw, Ann, All Saints St, Bristol, cm (1826). [D]

Brookshaw, George, All Saints St, Bristol, cm (1825). [D]

Brookshaw, George, 48 Gt Marlborough St, London, cm, commode maker, 'Peintre-Ebéniste par Extraordinaire' (1783–86). Employed at Carlton House, 1783–86, when his bill totalling £55 15s 6d was examined by Henry Holland. This sum included £50 for supplying the Prince of Wales in 1783 with 'an elegant commode highly finished with a basket of flowers painted in the front of the body and sprays of jasmine all over the top, and ditto on the front, the body with carved and gilt mouldings and legs'. Gilt wood armchair with original covers of silk damask recorded, stamped with the initials 'G.B.' for George Brookshaw. [Windsor Royal Archives, RA 25051; DEF; GCM; H. Clifford Smith,

Buckingham Palace, p. 103; Nat. Trust Exhib., Edinburgh, August 1952]

Broom, Francis, Marlborough, Wilts., upholder (1765). Declared bankrupt, Gents Mag., April 1765.

Broom, John, Mint St, Southwark, London, cm (1770–85). Took his son, John Broom, as app. for ten months only, when due to the father's declining health the son transferred for six months, and then went to sea. [GL, P83/MRY/869/98]

Broom, John, Liverpool, cm (1796–1839). Trading at 35 Roscoe Lane in 1839. Admitted freeman on 27 May 1796. [D; Liverpool freemen reg.]

Broom, John & Herbert, Saville House, Leicester Sq., London, upholders and carpet warehousemen (1806–10). Took out Sun Insurance policies on 2 January 1806 for £4,500 on utensils, stock and goods in trust; and in partnership with John Harrys on 12 January 1810 for £7,000 on stock and utensils in house and communicating warehouse. [GL, Sun MS vol. 434, ref. 785057; vol. 453, ref. 839799]

Broom, Robert, Davies Ct, Gt Crosshall St, Liverpool, turner (1827). Admitted freeman on 17 October 1827. [Liverpool freemen reg.]

Broome, David, 20 Duke St, Liverpool, cm (1818). [D]

Broome, Samuel, Baldwin St, Bristol, chairmaker and cane worker (1832). [D]

Broomes, John & Sons, Small hall table recorded inscribed 'John Broomes & Sons, token to His Majesty & Princess, Priny Street, Golden Sq., London.' [V & A archives]

Broomhall, John, Newcastle-under-Lyme, Staffs., cm (1837). [Poll bk]

Broomhead, George, Saffron St., Saffron Hill, London, cm (1775). Took out Sun Insurance policies in 1775, one for £100 on utensils and stock, and one for £200. [GL, Sun MS vol. 240, p. 298; vol. 243, p. 114]

Broomhead (or Bromhead), John, Worksop, Notts., cm (1784). [D]

Broomhead, William, 20 Robert St, Bedford Row, London, cm (1829). [D]

Broster, William, Castle St, Liverpool, cm and toyman (1766–69). Announced in Williamson's Liverpool Advertiser, 10 April 1767 that he was declining trade as cm, proposing 'only to follow the Toy & Hardware Business', and 'to open a large commodious AUCTION ROOM at his own House, where all Manner of Goods will be taken upon Commission, which will be sold to the Highest Bidder'. Sale of household goods and stock in trade advertised in the same paper on 11 September 1767, comprising 'Some exceeding good Household Goods & Hardware Goods & Brass Foundry Goods; with some Jewellry Goods, Toys, & a large Quantity of Scotch Carpets.' [D]

Brotherhood, Samuel, Nottingham, joiner and cm (1816). [Nottingham app. reg.]

Brothers, Benjamin, 65 Long Row, Nottingham, u (1782–1841). Addresses also given at Carrington St (house) in 1834 and High St in 1840. Took out a Sun Insurance policy in 1782 for £600 on his house. Will dated 26 October 1810 and proved 27 November 1812. Named in the index of Nottingham burgesses in 1829. Clearly there were two Benjamin Brothers. [D; GL, Sun MS vol. 302, p. 66; Notts. RO, probate records] See Mary Brothers.

Brothers, George, Coventry, Warks., cm (1756). Took app named Wooton in 1756. [S of G, app. index]

Brothers, John, Leicester, joiner, turner and cm (1710–c. 1733). Admitted freeman as a joiner in 1710 and classed as cm in 1722. Took a number of apps. [Leicester freemen rolls]

Brothers, Mary, Long Row, Nottingham, upholder (1814–25). Listed as cm and u in 1825. [D] See Benjamin Brothers.

Brotherton, Charles, 13 St John's Lane, Liverpool, cm and victualler (1827). [D]

Brotherton, Thomas, 42 Walkinson St, Liverpool, cm (1835). [D]

Brotherton, William, 6 and 11 Shaw's Brow, Liverpool, chairmaker (1800). [D]

Brougall, James, Church St, Oswestry, Salop, cm (1822). [D]

Brough, Mrs, George St, Nottingham, u (1834). [D]

Brough, John, Lancaster. Named in the Gillow records, 1818–25. [Westminster Ref. Lib.]

Brough, William, 6 Fontenoy St, Dale St, Liverpool, cm (1804). [D]

Broughton, Christopher, Norfolk St, Strand, London, upholder (1699–d. by 1749). Took app. named William Wimpenny, 1699–1714. Took out Hand in Hand Insurance policies on 1 July 1707 and 9 June 1714 for £550 on 2 houses. Advertised in *The Post Man*, 1 November 1709, 'A Large House in Norfolk Buildings with a Coach-house and Stables to be Let, Furnished to Unfurnished'. His son, Francis, admitted freeman of the Upholders' Co. by patrimony in 1749. [GL, Hand in Hand MS vol. 5, ref. 13670; vol. 13, p. 370; GL, Upholders' Co. records]

Broughton, Francis, London, upholder (1749). Son of Christopher Broughton, upholder; admitted freeman of the Upholders' Co. by patrimony on 8 June 1749. [GL, Upholders' Co. records]

Broughton, Henry, address unrecorded, upholder (1754–63). Son of Thomas Broughton, Gent. of Thetford, Norfolk; app. to William Merrifield, merchant tailor, on 2 October 1754, and John Iliffe on 10 May 1759. Admitted freeman of the Upholders' Co. by servitude on 3 February 1763. [GL, Upholders' Co. records]

Broughton, John, St Michael's parish, Stamford, Lincs., cm (1832). [Poll bk]

Broughton, Thomas, Preston, Lancs., u (1755). Took app. named Crookie in 1755. [S of G, app. index]

Broughton, William, St Michael's parish, Stamford, Lincs., cm (1832). [Poll bk]

Broumhead, Rob., St Paul's Churchyard, at the 'Red Lyon', London, chairmaker(?) (1730). On 17 July 1730 he was paid £1 4s for 'a Windsor chair with 4 seats' supplied to Earl Fitzwalter at Moulsham Hall. [A. C. Edwards, *The Accounts of Benjamin Mildmay, Earl Fitzwalter*, p. 102]

Brounton, J., London, carver and gilder (1835–39). Trading at 19 Alfred Pl., Newington Causeway, 1835–37, and 11 Bridgehouse Pl., 1839. [D]

Browell, John, Coronation St, Sunderland, Co. Durham, joiner and cm (1828–29). [D]

Brower, James, 7 Aldersgate St, London, carver and gilder, looking-glass manufacturer (1787). [D]

Browett, Joseph, Butcher Row, Coventry, Warks., cm and u (1835). [D]

Browless, James, Liverpool, cm (1796–1812) App. to Mathew Newall in 1796 and assigned to John Parry in 1797. Petitioned freedom on servitude in 1812, paying 6s 8d. [Liverpool freemen's committee bk]

Brown, —, St Paul's Churchyard, London, chair and cm (1747). 'An eminent Chair & Cabinet Maker' he was 'declared a common council man of Faringdon Ward within, on a majority of fifteen in the scrutiny . . .', *Penny London Post*, 13–16 March 1747. Possibly either James or John Brown.

Brown, —, address unrecorded (1757–58). Named in the Holkham Hall, Norfolk, accounts supplying six Windsor chairs, costing £1 16s in 1757; and five compass-back chairs, £1 16s, in 1758. [V & A archives]

Brown, —, York(?), upholder (1791). He was paid £90 5s 9d in August 1791 by the Rev. John Finch. [Mumby family papers]

Brown, —, London, cm (1793). Subscribed to Sheraton's *Drawing Book*, 1793.

Brown, —, Newcastle, u (1793). Subscribed to Sheraton's *Drawing Book*, 1793.

Brown, —, Bury, Lancs., cm (1793). [D]

Brown, —, Twickenham, Middlx, u (1797). Marriage of daughter recorded, *Gents Mag.*, June 1797. Possibly Henry Brown.

Brown, —, address unrecorded, cm (1803). Subscribed to Sheraton's *Cabinet Dictionary*, 1803.

Brown, —, Littleham, Exmouth, Devon, cm (1827). Marriage to Jane Stacey of Exmouth reported, *The Alfred*, 22 May 1827. Possibly John Brown.

Brown, Absalom, Newport St, Barton-on-Humber, Lincs., joiner and cm (1835). [D]

Brown(e), Adam, Vine St, London, u (1774–84). Recorded at no. 16 in 1784. [Poll bks]

Brown, Anthony, King St, Maryport, Cumb., joiner and cm (1829–34). Trading with George and Thomas Brown in 1834. [D]

Brown, Benjamin, Worksop, Notts., turner (1749). Worked for Henrietta Cavendish Holles, Countess of Oxford, of Welbeck Abbey, Notts., being paid £1 17s on 27 November 1749. [Notts. RO, DD 5P 14/1]

Brown, Benjamin, Boston, Lincs., cm (1806). Admitted freeman in November 1806. [Lincoln freemen rolls]

Brown, Benjamin, London, cm and chairmaker (1808–11). Trading at Carlisle Lane, Lambeth in 1808 and 8 Gt Pulteney St, 1809–11. [D]

Brown, Benjamin, 5 Duke St, Adelphi, London, chair manufacturer (1825). [D]

Brown, Charles, Chelmsford, Essex, upholder (1766). Named in the sessions book on 7 October 1766. [Essex RO, Q/5 Mg20]

Brown, Charles, Cambridge St, Birmingham, builder and cm (1818). [D]

Brown, Charles, 28 Chapel St, Holywell Mt, London, sofa and chair manufacturer (1826–28). [D]

Brown, Charles, Southampton, Hants., cm and chairmaker (1834–39). Addresses given in West St (or Quay), 1834 and 1839; and also at the 'Bell Inn', Bell St, and 2 French St in 1836–39. [D]

Brown, Christian, Farnham, Surrey, u (1838). [D]

Brown, Christopher, Cheke Lane, Exeter, Devon, carver and gilder (1828–36). Children bapt. at St Sidwell's, Exeter; daughters Georgina on 16 April 1828, and Sarah Margaret on 28 March 1830; sons Christopher James on 18 January 1832, Edward Turton on 29 November 1833, and John Jolly on 20 April 1836. [PR(bapt.)]

Brown, Christopher, Bideford, Devon, cm (1830–38). Trading at Mill St in 1830 and High St in 1838. [D]

Brown, David, 'at Mr. Marshall's, no. 189 Oxford Street', London, upholder (1772–79). Son of Nathaniel Brown, Gent., of Berwick St, Soho; app. to James Marshall on 3 June 1772, and admitted freeman of the Upholders' Co. by servitude on 2 July 1779. [GL, Upholders' Co. records]

Brown, David & Edward, 25 St Martin's Lane, London, upholders (1789–93). [D]

Brown(e), Ebenezer, Bristol, cm (1774–81). Recorded at 30 Lamb St in 1775. [D; poll bks]

Brown, Edward, 403 Oxford St, London, cm (1820). [D] See George Brown at this address.

Brown, Edwin, Castle St, Shrewsbury, Salop, carver and gilder (1840). [D]

Brown, Elizabeth, 22 Hackins Hey, Liverpool, u (1790). [D]

Brown, F. S., Conduit St, Chelmsford, Essex, carver and gilder (1839). [D]

Brown, Francis, Castle St, Saffron Walden, Essex, cm (1811). [Census]

Brown, Frederick snr, 179 Wardour St West, 'late 32 Charlotte St.', London, 'Practical Carver, Gilder & Picture framer' (c. 1825). Regency carved giltwood convex mirror with elaborate carved foliage and eagle recorded bearing label.

Brown, George, Newcastle, u (1774). [Poll bk]

Brown, George, Shug Lane, London, carpenter, cm and undertaker (1777). Took out a Sun Insurance policy in 1777 for £400 of which £90 accounted for utensils and stock, and £50 for timbershop. [GL, Sun MS vol. 256, p. 182]

Brown, George, Manchester, cm (1794–97). Trading at 23 Hanover St in 1794 and Garden Lane, St Mary's in 1797. [D]

Brown, George, Bishop Wearmouth, Sunderland, Co. Durham, cm (1798). [D]

Brown, George, address unrecorded, cm (1803). Subscribed to Sheraton's *Cabinet Dictionary*, 1803.

Brown, George, London, u and cm (1808–28). Addresses given at 13 Broad St, Soho, 1808–11; 403 Oxford St, 1820–21; and 4 Regent St by 1824. Took out Sun Insurance policies on 28 March 1810 for £4,750, £3,500 accounting for stock, utensils and goods; on 10 May 1810 for £600 on stock and utensils in feather warehouse and timber store behind 2 New St, Broad St; on 13 March 1811 for £4,750, £1,200 on house, warehouse and workshops, and £3,550 on stock, utensils and goods in trust; on 2 February 1820 for £1,250, £950 on stock, utensils and goods in house and workshop at Dean St, part in tenure of a basket maker; and on 12 March 1821 for £1,000, £700 on stock, utensils and goods and a further policy of £400 on stock in workshops in Pittnay Sq., Perry Pl., Oxford St. Probably the G. Brown, u, of Regent St, declared bankrupt, *Brighton Gazette*, 12 August 1824. [D; GL, Sun MS vol. 449, ref. 841703; vol. 451, ref. 844704; vol. 449, ref. 854962; vol. 483, ref. 962837; vol. 488, ref. 978124–25] See Edward Brown.

Brown, George, Crosby St, Maryport, Cumb., joiner and cm (1811–29). [D] See Anthony Brown.

Brown, George, Sheffield, Yorks., cm (1817–33). Addresses given at Wicker in 1817; Lady's Bridge, 1825; and 1 Stanley St, 1833. [D] Possibly:

Brown, George, Sheffield, Yorks., cm (1828–37). Addresses given at Bridge St, 1828–29, and Nursery St with house at Woodside in 1837. [D]

Brown, George, 5 Grosvenor Pl., Duckenfield St, Liverpool, cm (1818). Admitted freeman on 13 June 1818 on servitude to William Harvey. [Liverpool freemen reg.]

Brown, George, York, chairmaker (1827). Son of Thomas Brown; app. to Richard Baynes & Francis Duffill, chairmakers, on 17 March 1827. [York app. reg.]

Brown, George, King's Sq., York, joiner and cm (1828). His succession by William Groves reported, *York Gazette*, 14 June 1828. [D]

Brown, George, 5 Hanover Buildings, Southampton, Hants., cm (1839). [D]

Brown, Gregory, Norwich, u (1726). Took app. named Sayer in 1726. [S of G, app. index]

Brown, Henry, Bristol, upholder (1774–81). [Poll bks]

Brown, Henry, Twickenham, Middlx, cm and u (1797–1825). [D] Trading at London Rd in 1823. Probably the H. Brown, cm of Twickenham, declared bankrupt, *Brighton Gazette*, 19 May 1825.

Brown, Henry Carey, 82 High St, Winchester, Hants., carver and gilder, builder (1830–39). [D]

Brown, Isaac, Newbottle Rd, Houghton-le-Spring, Co. Durham, joiner and cm (1827–29). [D]

Brown, J., Saffron Walden, Essex, u (1793). Worked for Lord Howard de Walden of Audley End, Essex, supplying bedstead and furniture, bed bolster, pillow and mats for the cook's room, totalling £6 19s. [Essex RO, D/DBy/A51/5]

Brown, J., 38 Little Pulteney St, at the corner of Crown Ct., London, u etc. (1794). [D]

Brown, J., 5 Mount St, Lambeth, London, chair and sofa maker (1809–34). [D] See William Brown at this address, 1806–25.

Brown(e), J. H., Frankfort Pl., Plymouth, Devon, u (1814–22). As Browne, recorded in Drake St, 1814. [D]

Brown, J. J., 22 Castle St, Oxford St, London, chair, sofa and couch maker (1816). [D]

Brown, J., Atherstone, Warks., cm (1822). [D]

Brown, J., 37 Minories, London, u and chairmaker (1837). [D] Possibly Joseph Brown of 7 Church St, Minories.

Brown, J., address unrecorded, plate-glass and looking-glass manufacturer (1838–40). Worked at Buckingham Palace, providing a 'chimney glass frame with ornamental carved top and sides, finished in bevelled burnished gilt', for the Duchess of Kent's Dressing Room; '4 new silvered plates . . . for doors of two cabinets' for the Queen's Dressing Room; '8 silvered plates . . . , mahogany tray swings', costing £30; and 'Looking glasses furnished for the accommodation of Prince Albert', totalling £244 18s, prior to the Royal Wedding on 10 February 1840. [PRO, LC11/99; 104; 107] Possibly John James Brown of 6 Gt Queen St, London.

Brown, J., Lower St, Dartmouth, Devon, cm and u (1838). [D]

Brown, J., St John St, Bridlington, Yorks,. cm (1840). [D]

Brown, Jacob, Newcastle, joiner, cm and house carpenter (1795–1801). [D]

Brown, Jacob jnr, 10 Portland Pl., Newcastle, cm and joiner (1838). [D]

Brown, James, parish of St Paul, Covent Gdn, London, upholder (d. 1742). Known only from his will dated 19 May 1742 which left all his estate to his sister Elizabeth Sergeant. One of his executors was Woolhouse Lambe, an u of St James's, Westminster. [PRO, C108/367]

Brown, James, St Paul's Churchyard, London, u and cm (1747–96). Traded initially at the sign of 'The King's Arms' on the south side of St Paul's Churchyard which had been previously used by Christopher Gibson. When numbering was introduced this became 29 St Paul's Churchyard. He was a member of the Joiners' Co., and a trade card [BM] dating from the earlier part of his career indicates the nature of his trade at this date. It states that he made and sold 'all Sorts of the best & most Fashionable Chairs, either Cover'd, Matted or Can'd, Likewise all sorts of Cabinet Work, with Sconces, Pier-Glasses, Mahogany & other Tables, Blinds for Windows made & curiously painted on Canvas, Silk or Wire'. He took out licences to employ non-freemen at various periods from 1755–58 but never more than two men at a time and on a short term basis only. The business must have been substantial by 1779 in which year he took out insurance cover for £2,000 of which £1,400 was for utensils and stock. Directories record the business from 1768–96 and in 1793 he subscribed to Sheraton's *Drawing Book*. The long length of time during which the business traded suggests that more than one James Brown was involved, possibly a father and son.

The business attracted some patronage from wealthy members of the artistocracy and gentry. As early as 1747 he was supplying the Duke of Gordon, though the sums involved could not be deemed substantial. Supplied were two 'compas elbow chairs Spanish leather £2.14s' and a mahogany 'bewrow dressing chest £2.10s'. His name also appears in the Croome Court accounts as the supplier under 23 June 1781 of six green and white japanned rout chairs at £4 2s 6d and in 1785 a mahogany tea chest with canisters, £3 6s. He appears to have marked some of his furniture by the use of trade labels though only one instance is so far recorded, a mahogany side table on slender cabriole legs of c. 1780. [D; Heal; PRO, C107/109; GL, City Licence bks, vols 1, 2; Sun MS vol. 276, p. 122; Scottish RO, GD44/33/29; Crome Court MS; V & A archives]   B. A

Brown(e), James, Portugal St, Lincoln's Inn Fields, London, cm, broker and auctioneer (1769–72). [D]

Brown, James, Clare Mkt, London, upholder (1772). [Bailey's list of bankrupts]

Brown, James, Bedford St, Covent Gdn, London, cm and u (1791). [D]

Brown, James, Bridgnorth, Salop, cm (1797–98). [D]

Brown, James, 14 West Lane, Walworth, London, paper hanger and upholder (1800). Insured his house, goods and stock for £500 on 7 March 1800 with the Sun Co. [GL, Sun MS vol. 418, ref. 700467]

Brown, James, Nottingham, joiner and cm (1813). Son of John Brown, joiner and cm of Newark; app. in 1813. [Nottingham app. reg.]

Brown, James, Blackfriars Rd, London, cm and u (1820–23). Recorded at 9 Green St in 1820 and 9 Lower Green St, 1822–23. [D]

Brown, James, Charles St, St Margaret, London, upholder (1825). Took app. named Mary Ann Farr in 1825. [Westminster Ref Lib., MS E3559, Grinsell's charity app. indentures]

Brown, James, Liverpool, cm, dealer and chapman (1826–29). Declared bankrupt, *Liverpool Mercury*, 3 March and 6 October 1826, and 7 August 1829.

Brown, James, York, u (1828). Son of James Brown, u; app. to James Brown, u, on 10 October 1828. [York app. reg.] Perhaps the son of:

Brown, James, York, u and cm (1828–40). Trading as James & Co. at 19 Castlegate in 1828; alone there in 1830; at 3 Lendal St in 1838; and 7 St Martin's Ct in 1840. [D]

Brown, James, 39 Bloom St, Manchester, chairmaker (1836). [D]

Brown, James & Son, Whitefriargate, Hull, Yorks., feather merchants, u and carpet warehousemen (1826–35). Recorded at no. 11, with house at 8 George Yd in 1826; no. 40 in 1831; and no. 25 in 1835. [D] See Samuel Brown.

Brown, James, 46 Cheapside, London, writing and dressing case maker (1829). [D]

Brown, James, Dewsbury, Yorks., cm and joiner (1834–37). Trading at Westgate in 1837. [D]

Brown, James, Falkner Pl., Falkner St, Liverpool, cm (1837–39). Recorded at no. 4 in 1837 and no. 1 in 1839. [D]

Brown, John, St Paul's Churchyard, London, cm and u (1718–68). Son of Richard Brown of Chipping Norton, Oxon., tallow chandler. App. to John James on 28 March 1718 and free of the Upholders' Co. by servitude, 6 October 1725. About 1728 he took over the premises in St Paul's Churchyard at the sign of 'The Walnut Tree' formerly occupied by William Rodwell. The trade carried on by Rodwell was similar to that adopted by Brown, and in January 1727 the former advertised as one of his specialities his range of window blinds. When Brown took over he changed the trade sign to that of 'The Three Cover'd Chairs and Walnut Tree' probably to emphasise the fact that chairmaking was a major element in his trade. Rodwell's sign of 'The Walnut Tree' might suggest that cabinet making was the major element of his trade. Examples of Brown's trade bills exist [GL and MMA, NY] and show that he made and sold 'all sorts of the best & most fashionable Chairs, either Cover'd, Matted or Can'd', cabinet goods, glasses and blinds. The text is identical to that on the trade card of James Brown who traded at 'The King's Arms',

also in St Paul's Churchyard, suggesting some connection between the two makers. The trade card of John Brown is illustrated with engravings of mirrors and splat back and upholstered chairs. His range of blinds is fully described in a newspaper advertisement of 1729. These were 'of all sorts, painted in Wier, Canvas Cloth and Sassenet, after the best and most lasting manner ever yet done so that if ever so dull and dirty they will clean with sope and sand and be like new'. He also offered in the same advertisement 'new fashion Walnut Tree Window seat cases to slip off and on, very much approved of beyond stuff seats'. The business premises first occupied were on the east side of St Paul's Churchyard near the School, but in 1730 he advertised a move to another building close at hand formerly occupied by Robert 'Garridge' (Gammage) chairmaker and lately trading as 'The Crown Tavern'. This was 'two doors above the School nearer Cheapside'. In this year he was offering 'ALL SORTS OF WINDSOR GARDEN CHAIRS, of all Sizes, painted green or in the Wood'. This is the earliest known public advertisement for this type of chair though they may not be of his manufacture. He evidently marked some of his furniture for a walnut framed toilet mirror of c. 1730 is known with a circular label indicating him as the supplier.

From 1761 the business is listed in directories at 43 St Paul's Churchyard. From 1763 it is shown as John Brown & Son. The son may possibly have been the John Brown who in 1750 was shown in a Livery list as a member of the Joiners' Co. The address of James Brown at this period was 29 St Paul's Churchyard. [D; Heal; GL, Upholders' Co. records; Joiners' Co. records, list of Liverymen, 1750; *Furn. Hist.*, 1979; M. Harris & Sons, *The English Chair*, 1937, p. 173; C. *Life*, 7 July 1966, pp. 47–48]   B. A

Brown, John, St Martin's Lane, London, cm (1749). [Westminster poll bk]

Brown, John, St Mary's parish, Chelmsford, Essex, u (1763). Son Charles bapt. on 14 August 1763. [Essex RO, PR(bapt.)]

Brown, John snr, Gt Yarmouth, Norfolk, u (1760–90). Recorded in Broad Row, 1784. Took app. named True in 1760. Took out a Sun Insurance policy in 1776 for £200. [D; poll bks; S of G, app. index; GL, Sun MS vol. 244, p. 527] A John Browne of London polled at Gt Yarmouth in 1790.

Brown, John, Gt Yarmouth, Norfolk, u (1775). App. to William Bracey; admitted freeman in 1775. [Gt Yarmouth freemen's calendar]

Brown, John jnr, Gt Yarmouth, Norfolk, u (1784–96). Trading in Market Pl., 1784, where Ann Brown, milliner and haberdasher, was also in business. App to John Browne; admitted freeman in 1784. [D; poll bk; Gt Yarmouth freemen's calendar]

Brown, John, Lancaster, cm (1767–68). Admitted freeman in 1767–68 when stated 'of Liverpool'. [Lancaster freemen rolls]

Brown, John, Lancaster. Named in the Gillow records in 1807 working on a bidet. [Westminster Ref. Lib., Gillow vol. 344/99, p. 1813]

Brown, John, address unrecorded, gilder (1774). Worked at Harewood House, Yorks., and possibly on an organ case (1766) at Kedleston, Derbs. [Beard, *Craftsmen and Interior Decoration*, p. 248]

Brown, John, London, picture frame maker (1777). In 1777 he was paid £2 3s by Alexander Wedderburn. [Scottish RD, GD 164/Box 20/177/2 and 3]

Brown, John, York, cm (1774–d. 1784). Recorded in Fossgate and Foss Bridge, 1774; and Walmgate Bar, 1784. Dead in 1784 when his son. William, admitted freeman. [Poll bks; York freemen rolls]

Brown, John, York, cm (1807). Son of Thomas Brown; app. to George Beal, cm, on 4 April 1807. [York app. reg.]

Brown, John, York, cm (1826). Son of William Brown; app. to John Cluderoy, cm, on 6 November 1826. [York app. reg.]

Brown, John, York, cm (1833). Son of Henry Brown, innkeeper; app. to William Wilson & Sarah Carlton & William Mowbray, cm and u, on 4 November 1833. [York app. reg.]

Brown, John, Bristol, carver and gilder (1792–1807). Addresses given at 43 Old Mkt, 1792–93; Church St, St Stephen's, 1793–94; and St Stephen's Ave, 1795–1807. [D]

Brown, John, Margate, Kent, cm (1794). [D]

Brown, John, 8 Dean St, Newcastle, u, auctioneer and appraiser (1796). Advertised, *Newcastle Courant*, 31 December 1796, that he had commenced the business of auctioneer and appraiser.

Brown, John, High Wycombe, Bucks., chairmaker (1798). [Militia Census]

Brown, John, Liverpool, cm (1804–37). Addresses given at 5 Trueman St, Dale St, 1804; 1 Duke St Lane, 1821; and 55 Gt George St with shop at 21 College Lane, 1837. [D] See Mary Brown.

Brown, John, Carlisle, Cumb., journeyman chairmaker (d. 1807). Death at the workshop of his master, Edmund James, reported, *Gents Mag.*, March 1807.

Brown, John, 15 Wynatt, Islington, London, carver and gilder (1808). [D]

Brown, John, Hull, Yorks., cm (1780). Declared bankrupt, *Gents Mag.*, March 1780.

Brown, John, Hull, Yorks., cm, carver and gilder (1803–40). Addresses given at Bridge St, 1803–10, and no. 28, 1826–40. [D]

Brown, John, Hull, Yorks., cm (1837–40). Addresses given at 53 Osborne St and 24 Humber Dock St, 1837–38; 34 Osborne St and Ann's Pl., Osborne St, 1839; and Osborne St, 24 Humber Dock St and 23 Machell St, 1840. [D]

Brown, John, London, cm, u and bedstead maker (1817–39). Trading at 2 Church Lane, 1817–19; no. 3, 1821–23; no. 9, 1822; no. 2, 1825; and 6 Cambridge Rd, Mile End, 1839. [D]

Brown, John, London, cm (1818). [Gt Yarmouth poll bk]

Brown, John, 223 Tottenham Ct Rd, London, u (1820). [D]

Brown, John, Stepcote Hill, Exeter, Devon, cm (1820). Son John James bapt. on 25 December 1820 at St Mary Steps, Exeter. [PR(bapt.)]

Brown, John, Blucher St, Exeter Rd, Birmingham, builder, cm etc. (1823). [D]

Brown, John, 150 Friargate, Preston, Lancs., cm (1825). [D]

Brown, John, 7 Nelson Pl., Old Kent Rd, London, cm and u (1826–29). [D]

Brown, John, Kenilworth, Warks., chairmaker and turner (1828). [D]

Brown, John, Grantham, Lincs., cm, u and paper-hangers (1826–35). Trading at Spittlegate, 1826–28, and High St in 1835. [D]

Brown, John, Haltwhistle, Northumb., joiner and cm (1828–29). [D]

Brown, John, Boroughbridge, Yorks., joiner and cm (1828–34). [D]

Brown, John, St John's parish, Stamford, Lincs., cm (1830–32). [Poll bks]

Brown, John, Exmouth, Devon, cm (1830–38). Trading in the Strand in 1830 and Sheppard's Walk, 1838, also as u. [D]

Brown, John, Westgate, Otley, Yorks., joiner and cm (1828–37). [D]

Brown, John, Butcher's Row, Exeter, Devon, cm (1831–37). Children bapt. at St Olave's: daughters Charlotte, on 17 May 1831 and Matilda, 7 July 1833; son George on 10 May 1835;

and daughter Isabella Thomasina on 3 March 1837. [PR(bapt.)]

Brown, John, 111 Rea St, Birmingham, cm (1835). [D]

Brown, John, Charing Cross, Norwich, cm (1836). [D]

Brown, John, Spring Gdns, Skipton, Yorks., joiner and cm (1837). [D]

Brown, John, 56 Gt Queen St, London, carver and gilder (1839). [D] Possibly John James Brown of 6 Gt Queen St.

Brown, John, Upgate, Louth, Lincs., carver and gilder (1840). [D]

Brown, John Cossons, Market Pl., Blandford, Dorset, cm, u and designer (1836–40). Took app. named Cornelius Weaver Doe in 1836 for five years at a charge of £95 including food and lodging. Early Victorian rosewood folding card table recorded bearing label, 'J. C. BROWN FROM BLAND-FORD', dated 1840. [D; Dorset RO, MK/713; V & A archives]

Brown, John James, 6 Gt Queen St, Lincoln's Inn Fields, London, plate-glass and looking-glass manufacturer, carver and gilder (1808–11). [D] Possibly John Brown of 56 Gt Queen St.

Brown, Jonathan, Howden, Yorks., cm (1774). [York poll bk]

Brown, Joseph, Poland St, Westminster, London, u (1714). Took out a Sun Insurance policy on 29 January 1714. [GL, Sun MS vol. 3, p. 105]

Brown, Joseph, address unrecorded, cm (1754). Subscribed to Chippendale's *Director*, 1754.

Brown, Joseph, 9 Lord St, Liverpool, cm (1765–74). Former apps John Sharp, petitioned freedom in 1765, and John Kenyon in 1768. [D; Liverpool freemen's committee bk]

Brown, Joseph, parish of St James, Bristol, cm (1784). [Poll bk]

Brown, Joseph, 52 Paul St, Finsbury Sq., London, cm and upholder (1808). [D]

Brown, Joseph, 5 Bury St, Salford, Lancs., cm (1813). [D]

Brown, Joseph, High Wycombe, Bucks., chairmaker (1823). Daughter baptised. [PR(bapt.)]

Brown, Joseph, 22 Gloucester St, Red Lion Sq., London, carver and gilder (1826–27). [D]

Brown, Joseph, Whitechapel, London, cm and u (1827–29). Trading at 23 Back Church Lane, 1827–28, and 7 Church St, 1829. [D]

Brown, Joseph, 163 Tooley St, London, upholder (1829). [D]

Brown, Joseph, 52 Broad St, Golden Sq., London, carver and gilder (1829). [D]

Brown, Joseph, High St, Sunderland, Co. Durham, joiner and cm (1828–29). [D]

Brown, Joseph, 7 Church St, Minories, London, chairmaker (1835–39). [D]

Brown, Joseph, 120 Upper Seymour St, Euston Sq., London, carver and gilder (1835). [D]

Brown, Joshua, Southwell, Notts., joiner and cm (1822–32). Trading at Easthorpe in 1822. [D]

Brown, Lucy, Gt Marlborough St, parish of St Ann, Westminster, London, u (1723). Took out a Sun Insurance policy on 8 November 1723 for £500 on goods and merchandise in her house. [GL, Sun MS vol. 16, ref. 30342]

Brown, Mary, Liverpool, cm (1834–37). Addresses given at 15 Upper Stanhope St with shop at 7 Norfolk St in 1834; 54 Gt George St with shop as above in 1835; and 65 Gt George St, with shop as above in 1837. [D] See John Brown at 55 Gt George St in 1837.

Brown(e), Matthew snr, Ousegate, York, cm and u (b. 1741–d. 1829). Recorded at High Ousegate in 1808. Son of Matthew Brown, gardener; app. to Richard Farrer, u, on 15 November 1756 and admitted freeman in 1772. Advertised in *York Courant*, 25 November 1766, that he was succeeding to Farrer's business and setting up shop in High

Ousegate with Jeremiah Smith, another former employee of Farrer. With Smith he took apps, George Bradley on 24 June 1771; and alone, William Halfpenny on 3 April 1778; William Smith, 28 February 1787; Reuben Williamson, 1 April 1793; and John Duffill (Duffield), 27 July 1809. Took son, William, into partnership [*York Herald*, 10 October 1801] but son died aged 25. [*York Courant*, 1811] Decline of business and sale of stock announced, *York Chronicle*, 1818. Died aged 88 at his house 'Without Micklegate Bar', 1829. [D; poll bk; York app. reg. and freemen rolls]

Brown, Matthew, Chester, u (1762). Son of Matthew Brown, innholder; admitted freeman on 14 January 1762. [Chester freemen rolls]

Brown, Matthew, Liverpool, carver and gilder (1800–37). Addresses given at 62 Cheapside in 1811; 43 Cable St, 1818; 19 Redmund Pl., 1829; and Vaughan Buildings, Old Haymarket, 1835–37. Marriage to Miss Kewley of Liverpool at St Ann's Church reported, *Billinge's Liverpool Advertiser*, 23 June 1800. [D]

Brown, Matthew, New Elvet, Durham, cm (1817). Declared bankrupt, *Durham County Advertiser*, 14 June 1817.

Brown, Matthew, 185 Pilgrim St, Newcastle, cm and furniture broker (1834). [D]

Brown, Matthew, Chapel Row, Bishop Auckland, Co. Durham, cm (1834). [D]

Brown, Matthew, Shildon, Co. Durham, joiner and cm (1835). Declared bankrupt, *Durham Advertiser*, 12 June 1835.

Brown, Mathew, North St, Colchester, Essex, cm and u (1839). [D]

Brown, Michael, London, cm (1793). Subscribed to Sheraton's *Drawing Book*, 1793.

Brown, Pedigrey, Gt Yarmouth and Norwich, upholder (1719–21). On 11 August 1719–20 insured his goods and merchandise with the Sun Co. Moved from Yarmouth to the parish of St John, Norwich, on 10 January 1720; and to the parish of St Peter on 2 May 1721. [GL, Sun MS vol. 10, ref. 14844]

Brown, Peter, 4 Gt Warner St, Coldbath Sq., Clerkenwell, London, japan chair and sofa maker (1809–28). [D]

Brown, Peter, Farnham, Surrey, cm and u (1826–31). Declared bankrupt, *Chester Courant and Anglo-Welsh Gazette*, 22 February 1831. [D]

Brown, Peter, East Dereham, Norfolk, cm and joiner (1822–30). Trading at Baxter Row in 1830. [D]

Brown, Peter, St Benedict St, Norwich, cm and u (1839). [D]

Brown, Philip, Hertford, victualler and u (1783). Took out a Sun Insurance policy in 1783 for £200 of which £130 accounted for utensils and stock. [GL, Sun MS vol. 319, p. 95]

Brown(e), Philip, Curtain Rd, London, cm, u, bedstead maker, broker of household goods and undertaker (1820–37). Addresses given at 3 Susannah Pl., Curtain Rd in 1820; 1–4 Curtain Rd in 1822; no. 3 only, 1826–37; and as P. & E. Browne at 3–4 Curtain Rd, 1835. Took out Sun Insurance policies on 6 November 1822 for £650, £300 on his house, £100 on a house at 33 Howard's Green, City Rd; £100 on two houses at Reeves Pl., Hoxton; and £150 on 2 houses at 4–5 Collingwood St, Bethnell Green. A second policy included £1,000 on his houses at 1–4 Curtain Rd; £800 on stock and utensils; £100 on houses at 17 and 133 Old St Rd, where no work was done; £150 on two houses near 'The Ship', Cock Lane, Bethnell Green; £100 on a house in Nelson St; and £200 on a house at 4 New Inn Yd. [D; GL, Sun MS vol. 492, ref. 997522 and 997528] In 1832 Messrs. Brown of 1–2 Curtain Rd, 'who for 24 years carried on the business of cabinet makers & upholsterers', sold the lease which included their warehouse at 3 and 4 Curtain Rd; but P. Brown was still trading at no. 3 in 1837. [Shoreditch Lib.]

Brown, R., St Margaret's Church, Leicester, cm (1796). Advertised for an app., *Leicester Journal*, 13 January 1796.

Brown, R., Eastern Lane, Berwick-upon-Tweed, Northumb., cm (1806). [D]

Brown, Ralph, Newcastle, u (1768–1808). Trading at 'The Royal Tent, Foot of the Side', 1768–1792; and Dean St, no. 8 from Mosley St, 1792–1808. Trade card of elaborate Rococo design shows tent, sofa and French chair in the Chippendale style. [Banks Coll., BM] Advertised in *Newcastle Courant*, 19 November 1768, that he was journeyman to William France, 'and wrought at several of his Majesty's Palaces . . . and is becoming partner of Mrs. Elizabeth Webster'. Announced in same paper, 29 February 1772 that partnership was dissolved. Advertised again, 14 February 1778, and 14 April 1781; and gave notice of his removal to Dean St, 14 April 1792. Worked for Lord Strathmore at Gibside, Co. Durham, between 18 June 1791 and 20 November 1801, receiving a total of £166 5s ¾d supplying items including 'bed sacking', 'check coverlids', 'Fashionable Bell Ropes, Chintz Tassels', and 'Nailing Down Wilton Carpets'. [Durham RO, Strathmore MS D/St/ Box 206; D/St.v.998–9; 350/7 and 9a] Declared bankrupt, *Billinge's Liverpool Advertiser*, 26 March 1798. [D; R. W. Symonds, *Furniture Making in 17th and 18th Century England*, p. 31]

Brown, Richard, London. In 1766 he was involved in a matter of arbitration between Sir Lawrence Dundas and the upholder, Samuel Norman, over the latter's charges for gilding the gallery at Moor Park. [Gilbert, *Chippendale*, pp. 158–59]

Brown, Richard, Grishe St, St Pancras, London, carver and gilder (1780). Declared bankrupt, *Leicester Journal*, 18 November 1780. Probably the R. Brown, carver, gilder and picture frame maker whose trade card *c.* 1780, is embellished by a Neo-classical mirror frame. [Banks Coll., BM]

Brown, Richard, Old Market, Bristol, cm (1793–1800). Trading at no. 62, 1795–1800. [D]

Brown, Richard, address unrecorded. In 1805 patented a method of expanding dining tables. [Fastnedge, *Sheraton Furniture*]

Brown, Richard, 13 Lune St, Preston, Lancs., joiner and cm (1814–25). [D]

Brown, Richard, St George's Pl., Walworth, London, cm (1817). [D]

Brown, Richard, Dalston, Carlisle, Cumb., joiner and cm (1828–29). [D]

Brown, Richard, 196 Walmgate, York, working u (1830–40). [D]

Brown, Richard, Chester, u (1838). Son of John Brown, tanner of Chester; app. to John Edwards, cm and u, for 7 years on 30 November 1838. [Chester app. reg.]

Brown, Richard, Mr Clarke's Yd, Cumberland St, Church St, Hull, Yorks., carver (1838–39). [D]

Brown, Richard, High Wycombe, Bucks., chairmaker (1824–38). Daughters bapt. in 1824, 1826, 1829 and 1831; and son in 1838. [PR(bapt.)]

Brown, Robert, Preston, Lancs., u (1732–42). In 1732 he was assessed for Poor Tax of 6d monthly, and in 1742 named as a burgess. [Regulation of poor pay, Preston, Harris Museum, Preston]

Brown, Robert, address unrecorded, cm (1754). Subscribed to Chippendale's *Director*, 1754.

Brown, Robert, Beverley, Yorks., cm (1774–84). [Poll bks]

Brown, Robert, Bedford St, Covent Gdn, London, cm and u (1790–1803). Recorded at 24 Bedford Ct in 1798; and as Brown & Co. in Bedford St, 1790–93. [D]

Brown, Robert, Hunslet, Leeds, Yorks., cm (1793). See James Mitchell of Hunslet.

Brown, Robert, Frenchgate Head, Richmond, Yorks., joiner and cm (1827–39). Child bapt. on 4 November 1839. [D; PR(bapt.)]

Brown, Robert, York, cm (1828). Son of Richard Brown, confectioner; app. to Joseph Marsh, cm, on 4 June 1828. [York app. reg.]

Brown, Robert, Atherstone, Warks., cm (1835). [D]

Brown, Samuel, Baldwin St, Bristol, chairmaker and cane worker (1828). [D]

Brown, Samuel, 25 Whitefriargate, Hull, Yorks., with house at Cottingham, cm, u, feather merchant and carpet warehouse-man (1826–40). Worked at Burton Constable, Yorks., providing in 1833 a 'biddett'; in 1834 a french bedstead, mattress and 'Napkin Horses'; in 1839, a mahogany stand and two French bedsteads; and in 1840 an Ottoman chair bedstead, three tray glasses, a chest of drawers, a Pembroke table, and another French bedstead. [D; Humberside RO, DDCC, Burton Constable papers] See James Brown & Son.

Brown, Sarah, 43 Chapel St, Lisson Grove, London, carver and gilder (1839). [D]

Brown, Thomas, Leadenhall St, London, upholder (1756). 'Catalogues for sale of stock in trade of George Clarke, watchmaker of Leadenshall St to be had at Thomas Brown's'. [*Public Advertiser*, 22 May 1756]

Brown, Thomas, Newcastle, u (1757–82). Admitted freeman in 1757. Advertised in *Newcastle Courant*, 18 April 1767. Son Richard admitted freeman by patrimony in 1777. Former app., Thomas Churnside, admitted freeman on 7 October 1782. [D; poll bk; Newcastle freemen reg.]

Brown, Thomas snr, Aldgate High St, London, upholder (1761–87). Took app. named William Darby in 1761. Brown's Son, Thomas, admitted freeman of the Upholders' Co. in 1787. [GL, Upholders' Co. records]

Brown, Thomas, London, merchant tailor, by trade u (1761). Master of William Darby until 1761. [GL, Upholders' Co. records]

Brown, Thomas, 41 Cannon St, London, upholder (1762–83). Trading as Brown & Read, 1769–83. [D]

Brown, Thomas, St Mary's parish, Chelmsford, Essex, u (1765–81). Child bapt. on 26 July 1765. Declared bankrupt, *Leicester Journal*, 10 March 1781. [PR(bapt.)]

Brown, Thomas, London, upholder (1766–78). Addresses given at St James's, Westminster and Windmill Stable Yds, 1766–73, and Carnaby St, 1767–78. Took out Hand in Hand Insurance policies in 1766, renewed in 1773, for £500 on two houses in Windmill St with coach houses under them, and £100 on three stables with lofts in Windmill Stable Yd. A further policy of 1767, renewed in 1778, was for £550 on two houses in Carnaby St. [GL, Hand in Hand MS vol. 105, p. 16; vol. 106, p. 177]

Brown, Thomas, 50 Edmund St, Birmingham, cm and joiner (1770). [D]

Brown, Thomas, Newcastle, u (1774). App. to William Charnley; admitted freeman on 22 August 1774. [Poll bk; Newcastle freemen reg.]

Brown, Thomas, Little Poulteney St, London, upholder (1774–84). [Poll bks]

Brown, Thomas & Pyner, James, 30 Cow Lane, West Smithfield, London, cm and brokers (1777–79). Took out Sun Insurance policies in 1777 for £1,100, £1,000 accounting for utensils, stock and goods; and in 1779 for £1,000, £860 on utensils and stock at Holborn Hill. [GL, Sun MS vol. 263, p. 25; vol. 274, p. 392]

Brown, Thomas, 33–34 New St Sq., Street Lane, London, water gilder (1778). Took out a Sun Insurance policy in 1778 for £500 of which £140 accounted for utensils, stock and goods. [GL, Sun MS vol. 267, p. 219]

Brown, Thomas, Liverpool, cm (1780). Petitioned freedom on servitude to Robert Copeland in 1780, and admitted 'on same terms as Robert Fairclough'. [Liverpool freemen's committee bk]

Brown, Thomas, Liverpool, cm (1784). Admitted freeman on 5 April 1784. [Liverpool freemen reg.]

Brown, Thomas, Prince's St, Leicester Sq., London, and 11 Brewer St, u, cabinet and case maker (1784). Trade card of Brown of 11 Brewer St in Banks Coll., BM. [D; poll bk]

Brown, Thomas jnr, London, upholder (1772–93). Trading at 14 Cullum St, Fenchurch St, 1787–93. Son of Thomas Brown, upholder, of Aldgate High St; app. to John Constable on 2 September 1772, and admitted freeman of the Upholders' Co. by servitude on 7 March 1787. [D; GL, Upholders' Co. records]

Brown, Thomas, Liverpool, cm (1796–1822). Admitted freeman on 31 May 1796 on birthright as son of Richard Brown, peruke maker. Recorded at Bevington Bush in that year. His son, John Brown, cooper, b. 13 May 1800, petitioned freedom on birthright in 1822. [Liverpool freemen's committee bk and reg.]

Brown, Thomas, Maryport, Cumb., joiner and cm (1811–29). Addresses given at King St in 1811, and Back Row in 1829. [D]

Brown, Thomas, Chester, chairmaker (1812). Admitted freeman on 13 October 1812. [Chester freemen rolls]

Brown, Thomas, 32 Salford, Blackburn, Lancs., cm and joiner (1816–28). [D]

Brown, Thomas, 167 Fleet St, London, backgammon table maker (1819). [D]

Brown, Thomas, Silver St, Thorne, near Doncaster, Yorks., chairmaker (1826–31). [D]

Brown, Thomas, Gt Hampton St, Birmingham, cm and u (1830–35). Trading at no. 67 in 1835. [D]

Brown, Thomas, 13 Friars St, Gt Surrey St, London, carver and gilder (1832–34). [D]

Brown, Thomas, King St, Derby, cm and u (1829–35). Trading at no. 27 in 1835. [D]

Brown, Thomas, 67 Buttesland St, City Rd, London, cm and upholder (1839). [D]

Brown, Thomas, 7 Boyces St, Brighton, Sussex, cm and u (1839–43). [D]

Brown, Thomas Richardson, Pudding St, Hartlepool, Co. Durham, joiner and cm (1834). [D]

Brown, W., Carlisle Lane, Lambeth, London, chairmaker (1803–11). Named in Sheraton's list of master cabinet makers, 1803. [D]

Brown, W., 6 Gt George St, Liverpool, cm and u (1832–34). Advertised in *Liverpool Mercury*, 18 May 1832, that he 'has removed from 41 St. James Street to No. 6 Great George Street'. Sale of stock announced, same paper, 2 May 1834, 'of Mr. W. Brown who is removing from the Premises [at Gt George St] comprising excellent Mahogany Articles, in sets of Chairs, Sofas, & modern Couches, Secretaires, Cabinets, & Cheffioneers, Loo, Card, Pembroke, & Snap Tables, Ladies' Work Tables, Chests of Drawers, Toilet Tables, & Wash-stands, Hat Stands, Hall Chairs, etc. Modern Rosewood Card, Loo & Sofa Tables, Cabinet & Ladies' Work Tables — Set of ten Oak Chairs, Loo Table & Cabinet to correspond, several painted Dressing Tables & Washstands, Chests of Drawers etc: the whole of the best materials & workman-ship'.

Brown, W., 10 Norway Pl., Hackney Rd, London, cm and u (1839). [D]

Brown, W., York, furniture broker, ironmonger, cm etc. (1840). Advertised in *York Gazette*, 16 May 1840, his removal from 19 Fossgate and High Ousegate to 30 Parliament St.

Brown, William, London, upholder (1748–58). Son of John Brown, printer of Aldersgate St; app. to Samuel Phene, stationer, on 22 February 1748. Admitted freeman of the Upholders' Co. on 1 June 1758. [GL, Upholders' Co. records]

Brown, William, Lancaster and London, cm (1749–84). App. to Thomas Walker in 1749, and admitted freeman, 1767–68, when stated 'of London'. Polled at Lancaster in 1768 and 1784, living in London. [Lancaster app. reg. and freemen rolls]

Brown, William, at 'The Cross Keys and Star', the corner of Spittle Sq., Spittalfields, London, upholder, sworn appraiser and funeral furnisher. Trade card, c. 1750–60, has frame of Rococo foliated scrolls. [Banks Coll., BM]

Brown, William, address unrecorded, upholder (1766–74). Son of William Brown, woolcomber pf Coggeshall, Essex; app. to Thomas Brown, merchant tailor, on 3 September 1766, and admitted freeman of the Upholders' Co. by servitude on 2 February 1774. [GL, Upholders' Co. records]

Brown, William, 41 Cannon St, London, upholder (1770–83). Recorded in partnership as Brown & Read, 1770–83; with John Nicholson in 1777; and alone, 1778–82. Declared bankrupt with John Nicholson, Gents Mag., October 1777; and alone, Leicester Journal, 15 August 1778. [D]

Brown, William, Leeds area(?), Yorks., u (1772). On 21 January 1772 received payment of 14s 6d for work done for Daniel Lascelles of Plompton Hall, near Knaresborough, Yorks. [Leeds Archives Dept, Harewood papers, MS 188]

Brown, William, address unrecorded, cm and upholder (1775–82). Took out Sun Insurance policies in 1775 and 1782 in association with Walter Wilson of the Strand.

Brown, William, 2 Founder's Ct, Lothbury, London, upholder and cm (1775–82). Recorded, probably wrongly, at 22 Founder's Ct in 1776. Took out Sun Insurance policies in 1775 for £400 of which £260 accounted for utensils, stock and goods; and in 1776 for £600, £400 on utensils, stock and goods. [D; GL, Sun MS vol. 236, p. 392; vol. 244, p. 530]

Brown, William, Gainsborough, Lincs., cm (1790). [Lincoln poll bk]

Brown, William, Liverpool, cm (b. 1784–d. 1834). Recorded at Kaye Pl., 1802; and 8 Fleet St, 1813–14. Indenture dated 1792. Petitioned freedom on servitude to John Parry in 1802, paying 6s 8d, and admitted freeman on 5 July 1802. Death, aged 50, reported Liverpool Mercury, 10 May 1834. [D; Liverpool freemen's committee bk and reg.]

Brown(e), William, Liverpool, cm (1808–37). Addresses given at 11 Oak St, 44 Cable St, and 14 Houghton St in 1816; 15 Houghton St in 1818; Lawton Ct, Lawton St and 51 Ranelegh St in 1821; 11 Pleasant St with shop at 7 Lawton St in 1823; 91 St James St and 7 Lawton St, with veneer sawmill at Norfolk St in 1824; 91 St James St, 1827; no. 94 and 7 Charters St, 1829; and 9 Roscoe St 1837. Indenture dated 1808. Petitioned freedom on servitude to William Harvey in 1816, paying 6s 8d, and admitted freeman on 8 June 1816. [D; Liverpool freemen's committee bk and reg.] Possibly there are two William Browns here.

Brown, William, 10 Little Moorfields, London, upholder (1808). [D]

Brown, William, 28 Widegate St, Bishopsgate Without, London, 'Leather Backgammon Table, and Dice Box Maker' (c. 1810). [Trade card, MMA, NY]

Brown, William, Workington, Cumb., joiner and cm (1811–34). Trading at Washington St, 1811; Jane St, 1829; and Washington St, 1834. [D]

Brown, William, 5 Mount St, Lambeth, London, chairmaker (1806–25). Recorded at 5 Mount Row in 1806. Took out Sun Insurance policies on 12 November 1806, including £450 on stock, utensils and workshop; and on 12 January 1810 for £1,000 of which £500 accounted for stock, utensils and workshop. [D; GL, Sun MS vol. 437, ref. 795907; vol. 453, ref. 839468]

Brown, William, 30 Gt Titchfield St, London, carver and gilder (1810). Took out a Sun Insurance policy on 30 May 1810 for £300, £100 on stock and utensils, and £50 on pictures and prints. [GL, Sun MS vol. 453, ref. 844656]

Brown, William, 127 Edward St, and 89 St James's St, Brighton, Sussex, cm and builder (1820–27). Probably home address also given at Mulberry Sq. in 1820. Sale of 'the remaining part of Mr. Brow's stock' advertised, Brighton Herald, 14 July 1827, including 'Rose-wood, Zebra wood and Spanish Mahogany Veneers'. [D; E. Sussex RO, PR(bapt.)]

Brown, William, 31 Gray's Inn Rd, London, bedstead maker (1824–29). [D]

Brown, William, 14 Brook St, Lambeth, London, cm and upholder (1827–28). [D]

Brown, William, 1 Tower St, Westminster Rd, London, cm and upholder (1827–28). [D]

Brown, William, Brighton, Sussex, cm and u (1836–39). Trading at 23 Dorset Gdns, 1836, and 4 Richmond Rd, 1839. Large mahogany cabinet recorded, the upper section with moulded cornice and four panelled doors divided by columns, the lower section similar; bears trade label of 'W. Brown, maker, 23 Dorset Gdns, 1836'. [D; Christie's, 13 June 1974, lot 171]

Brown, William, Swinegate, Grantham, Lincs., cm, u and paper hanger (1826). [D]

Brown, William, Ct 16, High Bridge, Newcastle, wood turner and spinning wheel maker (1827). [D]

Brown, William, New Elvet, Durham, cm (1827–29). [D]

Brown, William, Market Pl., Pickering, Yorks., cm and joiner (1828–40). [D]

Brown, William, Chancery Lane, Skipton, Yorks., joiner and cm (1830). [D]

Brown, William, 78 Colebrook St, Winchester, Hants., chairmaker (1830). [D]

Brown, William, 13 Steelhouse Lane, Birmingham, cm and u (1828–30). [D]

Brown, William, 26 Aston St, Birmingham, cm (1835). [D]

Brown, William, Millgate, Newark, Notts., cm (1828–35). [D]

Brown, William, Low Skellgate, Ripon, Yorks., joiner and cm (1834). [D]

Brown, William, George's Pl., Gt Waterloo St (Rd), London, (1835–37). [D]

Brown, William, Dartmouth St, Westminster, London, chair manufacturer (1835–37). Recorded at no. 32 in 1835 and no. 2 in 1837. [D]

Brown, William, 62 Prospect St, Hull, Yorks., with house at 2 Beverley Rd, cm (1840). [D]

Brown & Co., York, cm and u (1834). [D] Possibly either James or Samuel.

Brown & Jennings, Chester-le-Street, Co. Durham, cm and joiners (1828–34). [D]

Brown & Lamont, Chester, cm and u (1820s). Trade label recorded on three-drawer writing table in the Gothic style from Eaton Hall, Cheshire. [V & A archives]

Brown & Pattendon, 190 Oxford St, London, japanned chairmakers (1808–11). [D]

Brown & Pyner, 63 Holborn Hill, London, upholders (1782–83). [D]

Brown & Ring, 45 St Paul's Churchyard, London, cm (1770). [D]

Brown & Son, 17 Old St Rd, London, u and appraiser (1820–23). [D]

Brown & Wilson, Long Acre, London, cm (1763). [D]

Brownbill, James, Stretford, near Manchester, cm (1825). [D]

Brownbill, Jonathan, Liverpool, cm (1761). Admitted freeman on 13 March 1761. [Liverpool freemen reg.]

Browne, Benjamin, address unrecorded, upholder (1733–40). Son of John Browne, clerk, of Highgate, London; app. to Samuel Skelton on 6 June 1733, and admitted freeman of the Upholders' Co. by servitude on 3 December 1740. [GL, Upholders' Co. records]

Browne, Benjamin, St John St, Colne, Lancs., cm (b. c. 1816–41). [1841 Census]

Browne, G., 15 Wood St, Princes St, Chelsea, London, 'Carver, Gilder, & Mounter, Looking glass & picture frame Manufacturer' (c. 1830). Label recorded, Mentmore Sale, Sotheby's, lot 3082.

Browne, George, 22 East Pl., Lambeth, London, upholder and cm (1808). [D]

Browne, J. E., Marlborough St, Devonport, Plymouth, Devon, cm and u (1822). [D]

Browne, James, St Paul's Churchyard, London, upholder (1791). Declared bankrupt, 1791, in Bailey's list of bankrupts.

Browne, John, King's Lynn, Norfolk, chairmaker (1680–81). Son and app., Oliver Browne, chairmaker, admitted freeman by patrimony, 1680–81. [King's Lynn freemen's calendar]

Browne, John, London, joiner or carver (1694). On 26 June 1694, as one of the warders of 'The Company of Joyners Carvers of London', he signed a petition presented by that Company to the City of London. [*Furn. Hist.*, 1974]

Browne, John, address unrecorded (1738). Invoice for two large corner cabinets, costing £15 6s dated 13 September 1738. [V & A archives]

Browne, John, Gt Yarmouth, Norfolk, cm (1780–90). App. to Samuel Bream; admitted freeman by servitude in 1780. [Gt Yarmouth poll bk and freemen's calendar]

Browne, John & Co., 2 Charles St, Grosvenor Sq., London, upholders and furniture agents (1814). [D]

Browne, John, Blucher St, Birmingham, builder and cm (1818). [D]

Browne, Jonas, Norwich, u (1825–26). Son of Charles Browne, hairdresser; admitted freeman on 26 April 1825/26. [Norwich freemen rolls] Possibly:

Browne, Jonas, London, upholder (1830). [Norwich poll bk]

Browne, Joshua, Norwich, cm (1832). App. to Joseph Gray; admitted freeman on 27 September 1832. [Norwich freemen rolls]

Browne, Matthias, Norwich, cm (1798). [D]

Browne, Oliver, King's Lynn, Norfolk, chairmaker (1678–79 or 1680–81). Son and app. of John Browne, admitted freeman 1678–79 or 1680–81, by patrimony. [King's Lynn freemen's calendar]

Browne, Peregrine, Norwich, u (1721–23). Admitted freeman, not by apprenticeship, on 3 May 1721. Took app. named Harewood in 1723. [Norwich freemen rolls; S of G, app. index]

Browne, T., Middlx, picture frame maker (1826). Declared bankrupt, *London Gazette*, 18 March 1826.

Browne, Thomas, 30 King St, Snow Hill, London, upholder (1778). Son of Samuel Browne, wine merchant of Ludlow, Salop; admitted freeman of the Upholders' Co. on 4 March 1778. [GL, Upholders' Co. records]

Browne, Thomas, 316 High Holborn, London, cm and upholder (1783–86). Took out Sun Insurance policies in 1783 in association with Joseph Harkness; and in 1784 with the Earl of Radnor for £500. [D; GL, Sun MS vol. 322, p. 623]

Browne, William, Fountain Ct, London, cm (1774). [D]

Browne & Co., 53 University St, Fitzroy Sq., London, scagliola works (1835–39). In June 1839 supplied twenty-two scagliola pedestals with Ravaccione marble bases, costing £264, for the Sculpture Gallery at Buckingham Palace. Lamp candelabra with scagliola columns illustrated in *Loudon's Encyclopaedia*, p. 1072. [D; RA Box 1, item 2]

Browne & Gregson, London and Liverpool, u and cm (1816–20). Addresses given at Duke St, Liverpool, 1816–18; also 2 Charles St, Grosvenor Sq., London in 1818; and the latter alone in 1820. [D]

Brownfoot, Samuel, 110 East St, Leeds, Yorks., cm (1837). [D]

Brownhill, James, Alport St, Manchester, cm (1788). [D]

Brownhill, James, Leeds, Yorks., cm and joiner (1830–37). Trading at 6 North Row in 1830 and 21 Mill Hill in 1837. [D]

Brownhill, Johnathon, Liverpool, joiner and cm (1761). Petitioned freedom on servitude to William Leech, paying 6s 8d in 1761. [Liverpool freemen's committee bk]

Browning, —, at 'The Royal Tent', Threadneedle St, London, upholder and appraiser (1747). [M. A. Steer, *Index of London Tradesmen*; Heal]

Browning, —, Peter's Lane, Cowcross, West Smithfield, London, carver and gilder (1829). [D]

Browning, George, 'In the East Pawn, over the Royal Exchange, up the great Stair-case in Cornhill, London', upholder, appraiser and auctioneer (c. 1760). Trade card inscribed: 'Houses Compleatly fitted up with all kinds of Furniture Viz. Beds & Beding, Carpets of all Sorts, Chairs, Looking-Glasses Variety of Cabinet-Work, both for home or Abroad Wholesale or Retail. Ready Money given for all Manner of Household Goods, Plate, China, Books. Funerals Perform'd To any part of Great Britain.' [Heal]

Browning, George, 30 Cornhill, London, auctioneer and upholder (1780–83). [D]

Browning, J. H., 4 Ship Alley, Wellclose Sq., London, cm etc. (1820). [D]

Browning, John, Market Pl., Cheadle, Staffs., u (1818). [D]

Browning, John, 60 Sun St, Bishopsgate, London, upholder (1826–28). [D]

Browning, Samuel, Well Hill, Minchinhampton, Glos., cm (1839). [D]

Browning, William, Long Melford, Suffolk, cm (1757). Took app. named Wood in 1757. [S of G, app. index]

Browning & Hopkins, 26 High Holborn, London, Tunbridge-ware manufacturers (1813). [D]

Brownjohn, George, Salisbury, Wilts., cm (1752–98). App. to James Begbie, cm of Salisbury, on 10 February 1752 for £21. [D; *Wilts. Apps and their Masters*]

Brownjohn, James, London, cm, u and undertaker (1817–23). Addresses given at 22 Castle St, Gt Oxford Mkt in 1817; and 37 Gt Titchfield St, 1819–23. [D]

Brownlem, Thomas, 35 Ogle St, Fitzroy Sq., London, cm and upholder (1822–35). [D]

Brownless, James, Liverpool, cm (1812–16). Trading at 27 Shaw's Brow in 1812, and 3 Weale St, 1816. Admitted freeman on 12 October 1812. [D; Liverpool freemen reg.]

Brownnut, John, 23 Friars St, Gt Surrey St, London, chair and sofa maker (1832–34). [D]

Brownrigg, Samuel, Cross St, Whitehaven, Cumb., joiner and cm (1811). [D]

Brownrigg, William, Lancaster. Named in the Gillow records in 1787 working on a table. [Westminster Ref. Lib., Gillow vol. 344/94, p. 17]

Brownrigg, William, 176 Oxford St, London, cm (1805–08). Took out Sun Insurance policies on 14 October 1805 for £700 on a private house at 7 Bedford St, Bedford Row; on 26 October 1805 for £500, £100 on two adjoining houses at ½ East Lane, Greenwich, and £200 on six houses in tenure, three in Mowbray Ct; and on 17 October 1808 for £1,400, £800 on a private house at 7 Bedford St, £800 on no. 9 in tenure, £140 on private houses at 1–2 East Lane, Greenwich, and £260 on six houses in tenure in Mowbray Ct. [GL, Sun MS vol. 434, ref. 781285; vol. 445, refs 823077–78]

Brownsgrave, Arthur, Northampton, upholder (1784–92). Took out Sun Insurance policies in 1784 for £200 on houses; and on 24 October 1792 for £100 on three tenements adjoining the Green, possibly tenanted. [GL, Sun MS vol. 324, p. 13; vol. 391, p. 204]

Brownson, William, Noble St, Foster Lane, London, upholder (1782). Insured houses for £300 in 1782 with the Sun Co. [GL, Sun MS vol. 302, p. 533]

Bruce, Adam, Hunslet, Leeds, Yorks., cm and u (1816–30). Recorded in Hunslet Lane, 1828. [D]

Bruce, Charles, Leicester(?), u and auctioneer (1779). Announced in *Leicester Journal*, 1779 that he was starting business as an auctioneer but still continuing as an u.

Bruce, D., address unrecorded, u (1809). Named in the account books of Nicholas Pearse of Loughton, Essex, and London, receiving £27 6s on 31 August 1809. [Essex RO, D/DHt A1/4] Possibly:

Bruce, David, Aldersgate St, London, cm and u (1792–1823). Recorded at no. 110 in 1792 and no. 113, 1800–23. [D] Took out Sun Insurance policies on 12 July 1792 for £300 of which £40 accounted for utensils and stock; on 21 January 1802 for £100; on 13 August 1810 and 27 June 1811 for £5,000 on his house, warehouses and workshops 'parts of which extend to Long Lane'; and on 22 August 1811 for £5,700 on house, warehouses, sawpits, sheds, utensils and stock. [GL, Sun MS vol. 388, p. 240; vol. 423, ref. 727217; vol. 452, ref. 848124; vol. 451, ref. 858596; vol. 457, ref. 860763] Named in Sheraton's list of master cabinet makers, 1803. Bill of 4 May 1813 survives from Bramston to Bruce regarding money due 'for his Tythes' of his house, workshop and warehouse in Aldersgate St. [PRO, C13 525] In 1809 he supplied 'twenty mahogany trellis chairs, the back legs reeded and fluted, the seats covered with best leather' for the Governor's Room at the Bank of England. The chairs were 84s each, and the elbow chairs, 98s. A similar set is in the Dining Room at the Soane Museum and a set of similar chairs was sold at Sotheby's on 13 October 1967, lot 108. [C. Life, 3 October 1947; DEF; V & A archives]

Bruce, Elizabeth, Leicester, chairmaker (1815–27). Trading at St Nicholas St in 1815 and Coventry St, 1818–27. [D] Possibly the wife of John Bruce. chairmaker.

Bruce, Henry, 307 Holborn, London, u (1790–93). Subscribed to Sheraton's *Drawing Book*, 1793. [D]

Bruce, Henry, 29 Little Queen St, Lincoln, upholder and cm (1793–94). Took out a Sun Insurance policy on 8 June 1793 for £1,000, of which utensils and stock accounted for £500. [GL, Sun MS vol. 395, ref. 615581] In partnership as Bruce & Robinson in 1794. [D]

Bruce, J. H., Cambridge, cm and u (1826). Declared bankrupt, *Liverpool Mercury*, 27 January 1826.

Bruce, James, 6 Water St, Bridewell Precinct, London, upholder (1790–93). [D]

Bruce, John, Leicester, chairmaker (1800). [Leicester freemen rolls] Possibly the husband of Elizabeth Bruce, chairmaker.

Bruce, Robert, 12 Store St, Bedford Sq., and Alfred Pl., London, cm and u (1817–29). [D]

Bruce, William, Lancaster, cm (1766–d. 1792). Admitted freeman, 1766–67. Took five apps between 1770–82. Death reported, *Liverpool Advertiser*, 21 May 1792. [Lancaster freemen rolls and app. reg.; poll bk]

Bruce, William, 8 Russell St, Covent Gdn, London, upholder and cm (1790–95). [D]

Bruffell, Thomas, Liverpool, chair bottomer (1840). Admitted freeman on 24 July 1840. [Liverpool freemen reg.]

Bruf(f)ord, Charles, London, cm (1808–39). Trading at

26 Gloucester St, Hoxton, from 1808; 47 Wellclose Sq. by 1837; and nos 46–48 before 1839. [D]

Bruford, George, 16 Gloucester Terr., Vauxhall Rd, London, cm and u (1839). [D]

Bruggerman, Henry, 140 Whitechapel Rd, London, cm and u (1827–39). [D]

Bruin, Samuel, Leicester, turner and gilder (1826). [Leicester freemen rolls]

Brumby, John, High St, Lincoln, cm and u (1835–41). Recorded at no. 174 in 1841. [D]

Brumby, Joseph, Union St, Boston, Lincs., chairmaker and turner (1835). [D]

Brum(m)ell, George, Newcastle, cm, glass grinder and carpenter (1754–1801). Trading at 'The Foot of the Side', 1763; and Pilgrim St, 1778–1801. [D] Subscribed to Chippendale's *Director*, 1754, and James Paine's *Noblemen's and Gentlemen's Seats*, 1767. Took apps named John Bell in 1757 and Hubberthorn in 1761. [V & A archives; S of G, app. index] Advertised in *Newcastle Courant*, 19 November 1763, his stock of 'carv'd-gilt, white & plain frames, also Postchaise and plain Glasses of all Dimensions'. Recorded in partnership with Dunn, 1790–98. Subscribed to Sheraton's *Drawing Book*, 1793. Possibly of:

Brumel & Miller, address unrecorded, cm (1807). Received payment of £129 13s on 28 November 1807 for work done at Gibside, Co. Durham, for Lord Strathmore. [Durham RO, Strathmore MS D/St/349/17]

Brumfield (or Bro(o)mfield), Philip, London, carver and gilder to the Crown (1661–67). Recorded in the Royal Household accounts between 1662–67 supplying furniture for Hampton Court and Whitehall Palace, including 'sixe Sheilds all Gilt with burnish gold'; 'Stooles Crimson and gould gilt with burnish gold'; 'very Large Stands richly carved & gilt with burnish gold'; and numerous carved gilt sconces and 'X gilt Brannches'. [PRO, LC 5/39–40; Conn., January 1934, p. 22; April 1934, p. 226; September 1938, p. 125; R. W. Symonds, *Furniture-making in 17th and 18th Century England*, p. 142]

Brumfitt, Edward, Skipton, Yorks., cm (1827–37). Addresses given at Chancery Lane in 1822; Market Pl., 1828–29; and High St, 1837. Named in the Holy Trinity Church PR in 1827. [D] The firm was reputedly founded in 1790, and there is a late Regency couch at Broughton Hall, Yorks., bearing their label.

Brumfitt, John, Manchester, cm (1825–38). Addresses given at 29 Blackfriars St, Salford, 1825–33; 51 Hanover St in 1834; and 27 Gartside St, Manchester, 1838. [D]

Brumfitt, William, Chancery Lane, Skipton, Yorks., cm and u (1828–34). Named in the Holy Trinity Church PR in 1828. [D]

Brumidgham (or Brumingham), James Rule, London, cm (1776). [Cambridge poll bk]

Brumley, Robert, 1 Orange St, off Swallow St, London, chairmaker (1780). Took out a Sun Insurance policy for £100 on his house in 1780. [GL, Sun MS vol. 284, p. 133]

Brumwell, Herbert Walwin, address unrecorded, upholder (1745–56). Son of John Brumwell, upholder; app. to John Brumwell on 3 August 1745, and admitted freeman of the Upholders' Co. by servitude on 11 November 1756. [GL, Upholders' Co. records]

Brumwell, John, London, upholder (1712–86). Recorded at Morden College, 1778–81, and Morden Wall, 1786. Son of John Brumwell, surgeon of Wapping, Middlx; app. to Daniel Woodroffe on 10 April 1712, and admitted freeman of the Upholders' Co. by servitude on 1 May 1723. Took apps named Thomas Eyre, 1731–38, and Herbert Walwin Brumwell, 1745–56, the latter admitted freeman of the

Upholders' Co. in 1756. [GL, Upholders' Co. records and Livery lists]. See John Brunwell.

Brumwell, Jonathan, Newcastle, joiner and cm (1787–1811). Trading Without Pilgrim Street Gate in 1787; Northumberland St, 1795; and Blackett St, 1811. [D]

Brundrett, William, Manchester, cm (1808–17). Addresses given at 37 Lomax St in 1808; 13 Bond St, 1811; 8 Abingdon St, 1813; and 4 Williamson's Buildings, Salford. [D]

Brune, George, Petty Cury, Cambridge, carver and gilder (1839). [D]

Brun(n)ing, William, Suffolk, cm (1748–60). As Bruning of Melford took app. named Herrington in 1748; and as Brunning Mitford took app. named Buskell in 1760. [S of G, app. index]

Brunning, John, Grout's Passage (or Ct), St John's, Timberhill, Norwich, cm and u (1817–42). App. to Elden Earle; admitted freeman on 16 June 1817. Former apps, Daniel Bacon, cm, admitted freeman on 26 April 1825; and Moses Samuel Watts, 19 June 1826. [D; poll bks; Norwich freemen reg.]

Bruntnell, William, Broomsgrove, Nottingham, cm (1835). [D]

Brunton, J. P., London, carver and gilder (1802). [Norwich poll bk]

Brunton, James, Norwich, u (1780–1802). Recorded in St Laurence's parish in 1780; St Stephen's, 1784–86; and St Giles's, 1794–1802. [Poll bks]

Brunton, James, London, cm (1793). Subscribed to Sheraton's *Drawing Book*, 1793.

Brunton, James, 23 Chapel Sq., Pentonville, London, cm (1808). [D]

Brunton, Thomas Page, Norwich, carver (1799). Son of James Brunton, woollen draper; admitted freeman on 17 June 1799. [Norwich freemen rolls]

Brunton, Thomas, London, carver and gilder (1806). [Norwich poll bk]

Brunton, Thomas, 8 Oxford Mkt, London, carver and gilder (1820). [D]

Brunwell, John, address unrecorded, upholder (1750). Named as a member of the Upholders' Livery in 1750. [GL, Upholders' Co. Livery lists] See John Brumwell.

Brushfield (or Broshfield), William, Car(e)y St, London, upholder (1720–76). Son of Thomas Brushfield, Gent. of St Martin-in-the-Fields, Middlx; app. to Richard Farmer on 1 March 1720, and admitted freeman of the Upholders' Co. by servitude on 3 September 1729. Named as a member of the Upholders' Livery in 1750. Took app. named William Chaplin, 1768–76. Polled at Westminster in 1749 and 1774. [GL, Upholders' Co. records and Livery lists] Two tradesmen must be concerned here, since the death of 'Mr Brushfield, jun. Upholder in Carey-street, Lincoln's inn' was reported in *Public Advertiser*, 2 June 1768: 'he was to have been married on Sunday last'.

Brussells, Thomas, Liverpool, chair bottomer (1840). Son of Thomas Brussell, bricklayer; admitted freeman on 24 July 1840. [Liverpool freemen reg.]

Brutnell, William, Radford, Notts., joiner and cm (1832). [D]

Bryan, I. (or J.) T., 17 Rosoman (or Rosamund) St, Clerkenwell, London, fancy cm (1817–20). [D]

Bryan, John, Painswick, Glos., carver (1760). Took app. named Millard in 1760. [S of G, app. index]

Bryan, Joshua, address unrecorded, upholder (1707/08). Admitted freeman of the Upholders' Co. on 3 March 1707/08. [GL, Upholders' Co. records]

Bryan, Mark, Bearward St, Northampton, chair turner (1830). [Poll bk]

Bryan, Peter, 43 Bolton St, Copperas Hill, Liverpool, cm (1839). [D]

Bryan, William, Gravel Lane, Southwark, London, mahogany

turner (c. 1760). Trade card states that he 'makes & sells all sorts of mahogany tea boards, bottle stands, waiters, china dish stands . . . Likewise turns all sorts of iron moulds for casting shott, and patterns for iron & brass founders . . .'. [MMA, NY]

Bryant, Adam, Gore Hedge, Frome, Som., cm (1839). [D]

Bryant, Francis, Mitchell St, Old St, London, cm (1787). Took out a Sun Insurance policy on 1 February 1787 for £200. [GL, Sun MS vol. 343, p. 55]

Bryant, Francis, 1 Berkeley St, Red Lion St, Clerkenwell, London, cm (1794). Took out a Sun Insurance policy on 17 April 1794 for £450 of which £220 accounted for utensils and stock. [GL, Sun MS vol. 397, p. 483]

Bryant, James, London, upholder (1772–86). Recorded in China Row, Lambeth, 1778; and Westham Abbey, Stratford, 1781–86. Son of Abraham Bryant; admitted freeman of the Upholders' Co. by redemption on 7 October 1772. [GL, Upholders' Co. records and Livery lists]

Bryant, John, at 'The Royal Bed. Mkt Pl'., Bath, Som., upholder (1753–69). Sworn freeman, 1753. Advertised in *Bath Chronicle*, December 1760 that he had just laid in a fresh stock of upholstery goods to be sold on the lowest terms. His stock and services offered are described in detail. Declared bankrupt, *Gents Mag.*, August 1769.

Bryant, John, High Wycombe, Bucks., chairmaker (b. c. 1814–41). Aged 27 at the time of the 1841 Census.

Bryant, Matthew & Sophia, 17 Gardener St, Brighton, Sussex, chairmakers (1826). [D]

Bryant, Mathew, 21 New St, Brighton, Sussex, cm (1832). [D]

Bryant, William, Risbygate St, Bury St Edmunds, Suffolk, cm (1836). [Poll bk]

Bryant, William, West Wycombe, Bucks., chairmaker (b. c. 1816–41). Aged 25 at the time of the 1841 Census.

Bryce, David, Liverpool, cm (b. c. 1777–d. 1831). Addresses give at 11 Back Lime St with shop at 2 Tobin St, Copperas Hill, 1823–24; 106 and 97 Copperas Hill in 1827; and 13 Caxton Buildings, Bolton St, 1829. Declared bankrupt, *Liverpool Mercury*, 2 August 1827; and death, aged 54, reported, same paper, 28 January 1831. [D]

Bryce, Peter, 56 New Church St, Portman Mkt, London, cm and upholder (1839). [D]

Bryde, Thomas, Liverpool, cm and timber dealer (1805–16). Trading at 8 Whitechapel in 1805; 11 White St with timberyard in Cornwallis St, 1810–14; and as a timber dealer at 11 St James St in 1816. [D]

Bryde, William, Liverpool, cm (b. 1777–d. 1823). Addresses given at 9 Hatton Gdns, 36 Harrington St, 1811; 35 Circus St, 1813–14; and 34 and 51 Circus St, 1816–23. Death reported, aged 46, 'after a painful illness of sixteen months', *Liverpool Mercury*, 31 January 1823. [D]

Bryden, Andrew, London, silverer and polisher, carver and gilder (1825–29). Trading at 15 Jewry St from 1825 and 12 George St, Minories by 1839. [D]

Bryden (or Brydon), John, 7 Charing Cross, London, carver, gilder, printseller and looking-glass manufacturer (1784–90). [D; Wills, *Looking-Glasses*] See John Brydon.

Bryden, Michael, 86 Finch St, Liverpool, cm (1837). [D]

Bryden, Nicholas, 22 Finch St, Liverpool, cm (1839). [D]

Brydon, John, 48 Brewer St, London, carver and gilder (1780). Took out a Sun Insurance policy in 1780 for £500 of which utensils and stock accounted for £100. [GL, Sun MS vol. 289, p. 62] Possibly John Bryden.

Brydone, Charles, Leicester, carver and gilder (1822–30). Trading at Gallowtree Gate, 1822–28; also as a restorer of paintings in 1828. Declared bankrupt, *Chester Courant and Anglo-Welsh Gazette*, 1 June 1830. [D]

Brydone & Son, Middle Pavement, Nottingham, carver and gilder (1814). [D]

Bryer, John, 6 Upper Boro Walls, Bath, Som., cm (1819). [D]

Bryer, Robert, 6 John St, Bath, Som., cm (1824). [D]

Bryer, Robert, St James St, Taunton, Som., cm (1830). [D]

Bryer, Thomas, North Lane, Brighton, Sussex, French polisher, japanner and cm (1839). [D]

Bryers, Charles W., Angel Ct, Gt Windmill St, London, upholder and cm (1817–20). Recorded at no. 7 in 1820. [D]

Bryham, Simon, Lancaster, cm (1791–1811). App. to J. Wakefield in 1791; freemen rolls state 'of London'. Named in the Gillow records working on a bookcase in 1811. [Westminster Ref. Lib., Gillow vol. 344/99, p. 1893; Lancaster app. reg. and freemen rolls]

Bryling (or Bryning), Robert, Cheapside, Liverpool, cm (1834–39). Trading at no. 28, 1834–37; and no. 65 in 1839. [D]

Bryson, G., address unrecorded. Set of mahogany Regency dining chairs recorded, with well-shaped sabre legs, reeded frame and concave top rail; stamped 'G. BRYSON' on the loose seat and inner frame; but one chair is stamped 'W.B.' Similar chairs illus. in M. Jourdain, *Regency Furniture*, figs 90 and 94. [V & A archives]

Bryson, James, 38 Newhall St, Liverpool, cm and victualler (1823). [D]

Bryson, Robert, Southend, Morpeth, Northumb., joiner and cm (1827). [D]

Brytam, S., London, cm (1793). Subscribed to Sheraton's *Drawing Book*, 1793.

Bubb, John, Southwark, London, toy and cabinet manufacturer (1809–37). Trading at 39 White St in 1809 and 7 White Cross St, 1837. Took out a Sun Insurance policy on 17 July 1809 for £200 of which stock and utensils accounted for £120. [D; GL, Sun MS vol. 447, ref. 832782]

Bubkrook, Thomas, Surrey Pl., Walworth, London, cm and u (1839). [D]

Buchan, Henry, Little Walsingham, Norfolk, cm (1756). Took app. named Harrison in 1756. [S of G, app. index]

Buchan, Henry, High St, Southampton, Hants., carver and gilder (1824–30). Trading at no. 159 in 1830. Advertised in *Southampton Herald*, 8 March 1824.

Buchan & Slodden, 159 High St, Southampton, Hants., carvers and gilders (1836–39). Advertised in *Fletcher's Southampton Directory*, 1836: 'Decorative House Painters, Paper Hangers, carvers & gilders … Rooms Decorated with Ornamental Pannels, Landscapes, &c. &c. Also Plain House Painting, Glazing, & Plumbing, at the usual Trade Prices. Workmen sent to all Parts of the Country.'

Buchanan, P., address unrecorded (c. 1810–20). Stamp of 'P. BUCHANAN' found on mahogany armchair with drop in horsehair seat, sabre back legs, turned front legs, scrolled back upright enclosing both top and centre back rail, both additionally veneered; and serpentine, square-sectioned arms curving down to turned supports. [Bowes Museum, Barnard Castle, Co. Durham] Possibly:

Buchanan, Peter, 45 Back Piccadilly, Manchester, cm (1817). [D]

Buchanan, William, 2 Whitcomb St, London, cm (1808). [D]

Buchanan, William, 53 Berner's St, London(?), cm (1837). Sold a magnificent wardrobe of inlaid wood, costing £50, to Charlecote Park, Warks. in 1837. [Warwick RO, L6/1118 and 1120]

Buchannan, John, Liverpool, cm (1821–29). Trading at 93 Gloucester St, 1821–24, and 62 Copperas Hill, 1829. [D]

Bucherfield, John, Oldbury, Tewkesbury, Glos., cm (1823). Child bapt. in 1823. [PR(bapt.)]

Buchop, Johan George, near Red Lion St, Holborn, London, musical instrument and cm (1778). Took out a Sun Insurance policy in 1778 for £100 of which utensils and stock accounted for £40. [GL, Sun MS vol. 269, p. 66]

Buck, Ann, at 'The Queen's Head', Holborn, near Hatton Gdn, London, dealer in furniture and upholstery (1741–50). Trade card showing Queen Anne's bust framed by Rococo scrolls states that she 'Buys and Sells Beds, Bedding, Buroes, Book-Cases Chairs, Glasses, China, and all Sorts of Household Furniture New & Old. NB. Quilts, Blankets, Tickens, Harrateens & Cheneys Sold, Wholesale and Retale'. [Heal; GL, trade card coll.] Joy considers that Ann set up business after the death of her husband, Henry Buck of St Paul's Churchyard in 1750, but she was trading earlier since her signature is on a receipted bill dated 2 June 1741, for two mahogany chests of drawers costing £4. [BM Coll.] In 1748 she advertised the sale of 'Buck's Views', a well-known series of topographical engravings by S. & N. Buck, from the above address. [Heal]

Buck, Avery, 69 St Thomas St, Weymouth, Dorset, cm and u (1840). [D]

Buck, Edward Jonathan, Leamington, Warks., cm and u (1835–37). Trading at 29 Grove St in 1835 and Wellington St in 1837, also as a house agent. [D]

Buck, Henry, at 'The Hand, Crown & Star', on the south side of St Paul's Churchyard, removed from 'The Hand & Crown' at the East end of St Paul's, London, cm and chairmaker (1731–d. 1750). Trade card, c. 1741, states that he 'Makes and Sells all sorts of Chairs, Tables, Cabinet Work, Looking Glasses, and Window Blinds &c. at Reasonable Rates — for both Sea and Land'. In partnership with Richard Farmer at 'The Hand & Crown', 1732–47, when Farmer died. [Heal] Together they supplied chairs, costing £3 15s to Sir Richard Hoare of Stourhead, 1732–33; and on 20 November 1732 Henry Buck is recorded receiving £7 1s. [Hoare's Bank, London, private accounts] Named as a Liveryman of the Joiners' Co. in 1750. [GL, Joiners' Co. records] Probably the 'Mr. Buck, a wealthy Cabinet Maker in St Paul's Churchyard', who died 'of the Gout in his Stomach', in 1750. [*London Evening Post*, 15–17 November 1750; *Notes and Queries*, 24 January 1942]

Buck, John, address unrecorded, cm (1751–55). Admitted freeman of the Joiners' Co. by patrimony on 2 July 1751, and named as Liveryman on 31 October 1755. Subscribed to Chippendale's *Director*, 1754. [GL, Joiners' Co. records and Livery lists]

Buck, Peter, Knaresborough, Yorks., cm and u (1822–37). Trading at High St, 1822 and Savage Yd, 1828–29. [D]

Buck, Stephen, London, cm (1831). [Colchester poll bk]

Buck, William, Beccles, Suffolk, u, auctioneer and appraiser (1806–39). Recorded in Smallgate St, 1824 and 1839; and at Theatre Plain, 1830. Named in the calendar of marriage licence bonds in 1806. [D; Suffolk RO, FAA, 50/2/113, p. 31]

Buckerfield, John, Birmingham, cm (1826). [Leicester freemen rolls]

Buckerfield, Thomas, 180 Park St, Birmingham, cm (1800–03). [D]

Bucket, Joseph, Salisbury, Wilts., cm (1754). App. to John Green, cm of Salisbury, on 28 December 1754 by indenture, for £17 10s. [*Wilts. Apps and their Masters*]

Buckingham, —, address unrecorded, cm (1803). Subscribed to Sheraton's *Cabinet Dictionary*, 1803.

Buckingham, H., the Mint, London, japanned chair manufactory (1803–15). Recorded in Old St, 1803, and Old George St, 1802–20. Named in Sheraton's list of master cabinet makers, 1803. [D]

Buckingham, Henry, Southwark, London, chair and sofa manufacturer (1827–39). Addresses given at Bridge Rd, 1827–35; no. 20 in 1829; and 2 Windsor Pl., 1839. [D]

Buckingham, Michael, High Wycombe, Bucks., chairmaker (1798). [Militia Census]

Buckingham, William, Thorofare, Woodbridge, Suffolk, cm (1803). Announced in *Ipswich Journal*, 8 January 1803, that his shop was being taken over by Edmund Cross.

Buckingham, William, St Clement's, Ipswich, Suffolk, cm, u and slop seller (1804–09). Trading at Butter Mkt, 1805–08. Notices in *Ipswich Journal*, 15 January 1804 and 11 March 1809. [D]

Buckingham, William jnr, Brook St, Ipswich, Suffolk, cm, u and auctioneer (1824). [D]

Buckingham, William, 39 South Audley St, London, cm (1809). Took out a Sun Insurance policy on 14 October 1809 for £200, £10 accounting for stock and utensils and £30 on chest of tools in workshop of Gillow, cm in George St. [GL, Sun MS vol. 448, ref. 834977]

Buckingham, William, 26 Adam St, Manchester Sq., London, cm (1823). Took out a Sun Insurance policy on 17 November 1823 for £550 of which £34 accounted for chest of tools in manufactory of Ferguson & Co. in Providence Ct, North Audley St, Grosvenor Sq.; and £300 on houses at 1–3 Hague Pl., and 10–11 Sale St, Bethnal Green. [GL, Sun MS vol. 494, ref. 1010493]

Buckland, G., Fore St Hill, Exeter, Devon, cm (1816). [D] See William Buckland.

Buckland, Henry, 8 Circus St, Lisson Grove, London, cm and u (1839). [D]

Buckland, R., Shaftesbury, Dorset, joiner and cm (1798). [D]

Buckland, W., Exeter, Devon, cm (1814–16). Report in *Exeter Flying Post*, 21 July 1814 that his app., John Glanfield, had run away, describing him as 'about 5 feet 5 inches high, fair complexion and slight made. Whoever harbours or employs him after this notice will be prosecuted'. [Poll bks]

Buckland, William, Exeter, Devon, u (1743). Married Elizabeth Bear of Newton Abbot on 1 September 1743. [Exeter marriage bonds]

Buckland, William, Fore St Hill, Exeter, Devon, cm (1822). [D] See G. Buckland.

Buckland, William, Shaldon, Devon, cm and u (1830). [D]

Buckle, George, address unrecorded, upholder (1709–16). Son of Stephen Buckle, button maker of York; app. to Remey George on 5 August 1709, and admitted freeman of the Upholders' Co. by servitude on 5 September 1716. [GL, Upholders' Co. records]

Buckle, Joseph, address unrecorded, upholder (1734–42). Son of Joseph Buckle, goldsmith of York; app. to John Underwood on 5 March 1734, and admitted freeman of the Upholders' Co. by servitude on 5 May 1742. [GL, Upholders' Co. records]

Buckle, Oswald, at 'The Chair Royal', Bury St, St James's, London, u (1725). Insured his goods and merchandise for £500 on 17 June 1725 with the Sun Co. [GL, Sun MS vol. 21, ref. 36101; *Notes and Queries*, 24 January 1942]

Buckle, William Glazby, parish of St James, Bristol, upholder (1781–84). [D]

Buckler, Elizabeth (or Eli), Birmingham, cm, tool chest and cabinet case maker (1816–35). Addresses given at Vale St in 1816 and 1818; 33 Worcester St, 1817–22; 38 Constitution Hill in 1830; and at no. 35½ in 1835. [D]

Buckler, Powell, 10 Queen St, Cheapside, London, upholder (1769–82). Son of Humphrey Buckler of Warminster, Wilts., woolstapler; app. to Daniel Langton on 7 June 1769 with whom he lived at above address, continuing there until 1782. Admitted freeman of the Upholders' Co. by servitude on 3 July 1776. [D; GL, Upholders' Co. records)

Buckley, Ann, Old St, Ashton-under-Lyne, Lancs., cm (1816–18). [D]

Buckley, Samuel, Ashby-de-la-Zouch, Leics., cm (1775). Report in *Leicester Chronicle*, 8 July 1775, that he had deserted his family.

Buckley, William, 28 King St, Southwark, London, furniture maker (1839). [D]

Buckman, Edward, Church St, Lambeth, London, chair and sofa manufacturer (1822–39). Recorded at no. 8, 1822–35, and no. 20 in 1839. Trading as a chairmaker in 1835. [D]

Buckman, James, 24 and 26 Red Cross St, London, dyed and japanned chair manufacturer (1808–11). [D]

Buckman, James, 30 Mint St, Southwark, London, chairmaker (1813). Took out a Sun Insurance policy on 30 September 1813 for £400, of which £150 accounted for stock and utensils in his house, warehouse and open yard. [GL, Sun MS vol. 463, ref. 885790]

Buckmire (or Burkmire), William, London, upholder (1762–86). Recorded at 37 Lombard St in 1779, and Jermyn St, 1786. Son of William Buckmire (or Burkmire), Denby; app. to Francis Pyner on 6 May 1762, and admitted freeman of the Upholders' Co. by servitude on 4 August 1779. Recorded 'drowned in the Serpentine River' after 1786. [GL, Upholders' Co. records]

Bucknall, William, Leicester, u (1827–35). Trading at Townhall Lane, 1827–35, also as a paper hanger in 1835. [D]

Bucknall, William, Bristol, cm and u (1830–36). Trading at 12 Bridewell Lane, 1830–31; 33 Broad St, 1832–33; and St John's Bridge, 1834–36. [D]

Bucknell, John, Chancery Lane, Thrapston, Northants., cm/joiner (1823). [D]

Bucktrout, Benjamin, London, cm. Emigrated to America and advertised his business in Williamsburg in *The Virginia Gazette*, 25 July 1765. A Masonic chair bearing his stamp is in the Colonial Williamsburg collection. [W. B. Gusler, *Furniture of Williamsburg and Eastern Virginia*, 1979, pp. 63–66]

Buckwell, George, 10 Crown St, Hoxton, London, cm (1808). Possibly George Buckwell, pianoforte maker of 30 Hackney Rd, 1826–27. [D]

Budd, Charles, 5 West St Lane, Brighton, Sussex, cricket-bat and cm (1800–05). [D]

Budd, John, Emsworth, Hants., cm and u (1830). [D]

Budd, Joseph, at 'The Rising Sun', Chancery Lane, parish of St Dunstan's-in-the-West, London, u (1716–19). Took out a Sun Insurance policy on 16 August 1717 for goods and merchandise in his house. [GL, Sun MS vol. 6, p. 353; Heal]

Budd, Joseph, Wine Office Ct, Fleet St, London, u (1726). Took out a Sun Insurance policy on 10 October 1726 for £500. [GL, Sun MS vol. 22, p. 381]

Budd, Joseph, High Wycombe, Bucks., chairmaker (b. c. 1819–41). Aged 22 at the time of the 1841 Census.

Budd, William, Bristol, cm, u and undertaker (1816–19). Addresses given at Hanmer's Buildings, Park St, 1816–19, and also College Pl., 1818–19. [D]

Budden(n), Robert, Portsmouth, Hants., u (1778–84). Took out Sun Insurance policies in 1778 for £200 on tenements; and in 1781 for £800 on his house. [D; GL, Sun MS vol. 269, p. 346; vol. 294, p. 279]

Budge, Thomas, Plymouth, Devon, cm and u (1814–24). Recorded as T. Budge in Pembroke St, 1814; Mr Budge in Fore St, Stonehouse, 1822; and Thomas at 15 High St, Stonehouse, 1823–24. [D]

Bugg, Thomas, Newark, Notts., joiner and cm (1793–1807). Trading at Carter Gate in 1805. [D]

Buggs, James, address unrecorded, upholder (1750–60). Son of Peter Buggs, labourer, of Brockham, near Dorking, Surrey; app. to John Huggett on 21 January 1750, and admitted freeman of the Upholders' Co. by servitude on 3 April 1760. [GL, Upholders' Co. records]

Buhl, John, London(?). Named in the accounts of Lord Shelburne in 1771 for furnishing Landsdowne House, receiving £373 19s. [A. T. Bolton, *The Architecture of Robert and James Adam*, vol. 2, p. 314]

Buist, David, London, cm (b. *c.* 1806–46). Trading at George St, Hanover Sq., 1829; and 13 Smith Sq., 1846. Second son of William Buist, of 10 Queen St, Grosvenor Sq., and bapt. in 1806 at the Scots Church, Crown Ct, Russell St. His own daughter was bapt. on 22 March 1829. Presumably the D. Buist of 13 Smith Sq. who reported the death of Henry Seaton Buist in 1846.

Buist, Henry Seaton (or Seton), London, cm and pianoforte maker (b. *c.* 1804–d. 1846). Addresses given at 6 Hudson's Terr., Westminster, 1834; 23 Vauxhall Bridge Rd, 1836–38; and 13 Smith Sq., Westminster, 1846. Eldest son of William Buist, cm, of 10 Queen St, Grosvenor Sq., and bapt. on 5 June 1804 at the Scots Church, Crown Ct, Russell St. His own children were bapt. in 1834, and 1836–38, at St John the Evangelist, Smith Sq., Westminster. He died, aged 42, on 13 August 1846, of 'ulceration of the wind pipe'. [PR(bapt.); death certificate from General Reg. Office, London]

Buist, William, London, cm (1801–09). Recorded at Davies St, Mayfair, 1801–02; and Queen St, Grosvenor Sq., 1804–09. Children bapt. between 1804–06 at the Scots Church, Crown Ct, Russell St, including David and Henry Seaton, cm. [D; PR(bapt.)]

Bulbrook, Charles, Southwark, London, chair and sofa maker (1832–39). Addresses given at 55 Land St, 1832–34; no. 17 Lant St and 13 Garden Row, 1839; and just the latter in 1835. [D]

Bulbrook, J., Brewhouse Lane, Southampton, Hants., carver (1839). [D]

Bul(l)brook, Thomas, London, cm and u (1820–35). Trading at Kent Rd in 1820; 10 Northampton Pl., Old Kent Rd, 1826–28; and 13 Garden Row, London Rd, 1835. [D]

Bulbrooke, Thomas, 10 Market St, Borough Rd, London, chair and sofa maker (1839). [D]

Bulcock, Thomas, Limbrick, Blackburn, Lancs., joiner and cm (1824–25). [D]

Bulkley, —, address unrecorded. Supplied furniture to Denton House, Yorks. in 1770, costing £5 3s. [*Furn. Hist.*, 1968]

Bull, —, St Paul's Churchyard, London, cm (d. 1743). Death reported, *London Evening Post*, 24–26 March 1743, when he was described as a 'wealthy cabinet maker & one of the People call'd QUAKERS'.

Bull, Ebenezer, St James's St, Northampton, cm (1830). [Poll bk]

Bull, George, Mount East St, Nottingham, cm (1835). [D]

Bull, Henry, 152 Kent St, Southwark, London, chairmaker (1808). [D]

Bull, Henry, Magdalen St, Norwich, u and paper hanger (1822). [D]

Bull, James, address unrecorded, upholder (1717–49). Son of Samuel Bull, clerk of Westhall, Suffolk; app. to William Brathwaite on 13 November 1717, and admitted freeman of the Upholders' Co. by servitude on 7 May 1735. Took app. named George Taylor, 1735–49. [GL, Upholders' Co. records]

Bull, James, 2 Hackney Rd, London, bedstead maker (1822–27). [D] See O. Bull.

Bull, Joseph, Ringwood, Hants., cm (1747–49). Took apps named Eastman in 1747 and Wright in 1749. [S of G, app. index]

Bull, Joseph, Princess St, in the Park, Southwark, London, cm (1768). Declared bankrupt, *Gents Mag.*, May 1768.

Bull, Joseph, Bristol, chairmaker (1815–16). Trading at 33 Redcliff St, 1815, and 2 Countership, 1816. [D]

Bull, O., 2 Hackney Rd, London, bedstead and bed cornice maker (1820–29). [D] See James Bull.

Bull, Obadiah, 127 Shoreditch, London, bedstead maker (1807–08). Took out a Sun Insurance policy on 24 January 1807, £220 on a house at 7 Widegate St in tenure; £140 on a house at the corner of Savage Ct in tenure; and £540 on six other houses there, all in tenure. Took out another policy on 11 January 1808 for £1,050, of which £900 accounted for houses, and £50, stock and utensils. [GL, Sun MS vol. 438; vol. 442, ref. 812463]

Bull, Sarah, 3 Artillery St, Bishopsgate, London, cm and u (1839). [D]

Bull, William, Mount East St, Nottingham, cm (1828). [D]

Bull, William, Duke St, Chelmsford, Essex, cm and u (1826–39). Trading as Bull & Son in 1839. [D]

Bull, William, Market St, Lichfield, Staffs., cm and chairmaker (1834–39). Declared bankrupt, *Sussex Agricultural Express*, 11 May 1839. [D; poll bk]

Bull, William, 76 Berwick St, Soho, London, cm (1835). [D]

Bulla Grassi & Pontana, 134 Fore St Hill, Exeter, Devon, looking-glass and barometer makers (1830). [D]

Bullard, F., 7 Tottenham Ct Rd, London, cm (1835). [D]

Bullard, Henry, Windmill Yd, Manchester, cm (1804). [D]

Bullas, Thomas, Barnsley, Yorks., cm (1743). Took app. named Hawkesworth in 1743. [S of G, app. index]

Bullen, —, Preeson's Row, Liverpool, cm and u(?) (1800–d. *c.* 1810). Born at Bury St Edmunds, Suffolk, where he served as app. to his father. Entered into partnership with Mathew Gregson, cm and u, on 1 March 1800, but left on 1 September 1806 due to ill health. Retired to Leicester as a 'wood factor', and died, 1809–10. [D; Liverpool RO, 920 GRE 1/3, 44 and 47]

Bullen, Ann, Jonathan & Thomas, Market Pl., Bury St Edmunds, Suffolk, u and cm (1795). Ann, widow of Henry, advertised in *Bury and Norwich Post*, 2 September 1795, their business of 'UPHOLSTERY and CABINET-MAKING', to be 'carried on in all its branches by herself and two of her sons, the elder of whom is just returned from London, where he has had an opportunity of gaining a thorough knowledge of his employment. The AUCTIONEERING AND APPRAIS-ING will be punctually attended to, as usual, by J. & T. BULLEN and EDWARD BUSHELL, the latter of whom has been for more than 20 years her husband's assistant.'

Bullen, Henry, Bury St Edmunds, Suffolk, upholder, cm and mortgager (1768–d. 1796). [D] Trading in Butter Mkt, 1784. Advertised sales of furniture and estates in *Cambridge Chronicle and Journal*, June 1760, 24 June 1769, and 26 May 1770. Listed as an upholder, same paper, 9 October 1784, and named as a member of the Common Council, 10 August 1782. Signed lease for property in Cook Row on 1 July 1789. [Suffolk RO, 742/2–3] Took out Sun Insurance policies in 1777 and 1781 for £300 on houses. [GL, Sun MS vol. 261, p. 253; vol. 297, p. 495] *Norwich Chronicle*, 27 November 1783, announced that 'at Mr. Henry Bullen's, Upholder' may be seen a specimen of 'Cast-Iron Covering for Houses invented by Ransomes and Co., Founders, in Norwich'. Named in the accounts for Ickworth, Suffolk, from April 1778 to April 1779, receiving a total of £22 10s. Messrs. Lanchester & Bullen appraised the stock at Ickworth, charging £21 6s. Bullen is named in the Essex Estate accounts on 4 March 1780, receiving £10 9s. [PRO, C 103/174] On 11 May 1791, Henry Bullen presented the Headmaster of King Edward VI School at Bury St Edmunds, Rev. Michael Becher, with a mahogany tambour cylinder writing desk, as an act of gratitude for the education of his son. Letter of thanks, dated 12 May 1791, survives. [R. W. Elliott, *The Story of King Edward VI School*, 1963, p. 90, illus. pp. 128–29] died in 1796. [Suffolk RO, Corp. index] See Thomas, and Thomas George Bullen.

Bullen, James, Bridge St, Bristol, cm (1793–94). [D]

Bullen, Mary, Beast Mkt, Bury St Edmunds, Suffolk, cm (1824). [D]

Bullen, Thomas, St Austell, Cornwall, cm (1798). [D]

Bullen, Thomas, Bury St Edmunds, Suffolk, upholder (1811–d. 1817). Elected a Common Councillor on 3 May 1811, and died in 1817. Father of Thomas George Bullen. [D; Suffolk RO, Corp. index]

Bullen, Thomas George, Bury St Edmunds, Suffolk, u, cm, auctioneer and estate agent (b. 1803–d. 1850). Trading at Market Pl., 1830; Butter Mkt, 1836; and no. 20, 1839. Son of Thomas Bullen, educated at the King Edward VI School, Bury St Edmunds. Elected a Common Councillor on 29 June 1830, and died in 1850. [D; poll bk; Suffolk RO, Corp. index]

Buller, John, Downley, High Wycombe, Bucks., chairmaker (b. c.1821–41). Aged 20 at the time of the 1841 Census.

Buller, Jonathon, King St, Liverpool, u (1803). [D]

Buller, Philip, Middle Row, Holborn, London, cm (d. by 1752). Sale of stock in trade of Philip Keeler and Philip Buller, cm, both deceased, announced, *General Advertiser*, 11 May 1752.

Buller, William, Downley, High Wycombe, Bucks., chairmaker (b. c.1791–1841). Aged 50 at the time of the 1841 Census.

Bullidge, William, Norwich, chairmaker (1765). Son of William Bullidge, carpenter; admitted freeman on 23 March 1765. [Norwich freemen rolls]

Bullin, F., St Aubyn St, Plymouth Dock, Devon, cm and u (1814). [D]

Bullin, Thomas, Plymouth Dock, Devon, cm (1810). On 8 February 1810 signed a contract to purchase trees at St Mellion, Cornwall, 133 cherry and 143 oak, for £70 5s. [Cornwall RO, DD Cy, 5888]

Bullivant, John, London, chair and sofa maker (1827–39). Trading at 10 Gt Waterloo St, 1827–28 and 28 High St, Southwark, 1839. [D]

Bul(l)man, Robert, Leeds, Yorks., cm, u, undertaker and patent mangle maker (1783–1848). Addresses given 'Opposite Old Bank', Briggate in 1783; no. 21, 1805–1818; as Robert Bullman & Sons at 27 Commercial St in 1808; 21 Briggate in 1816–17; 5 Commercial St from 1819; no. 27, 1820–34; and no. 31, 1830–37, with works in Bond St in 1830. [D] App. in Bath, he then set up business in Leeds in 1783. Robert Bullman & Son announced their move from Briggate to 5 Commercial St in *Leeds Intelligencer*, 19 April 1819, where 'they propose carrying on as usual the Upholstery, Cabinet & general furnishing business' which they claimed had been going for 40 years. Advertised, same paper, 24 March 1825 for 'two clever carvers accustomed to carving mahogany and rosewood. Also an experienced Turner and a few experienced journeymen cabinet makers'. Bullman & Son of Leeds advertised in *Liverpool Mercury*, 18 April 1828, with full description, their patent 'IMPROVED CABINET MANGLE . . . greatly superior to Mangles in the usual construction . . . allowed by the best Mechanics to be one of the most perfect pieces of Machinery yet produced'. Marble rosewood sideboard c.1810, recorded signed 'BULLMAN & SON, LEEDS'. [*C. Life*, vol. CLXXII, supplement p. 32c] There is a large bookcase in Wakefield Town Hall with secret drawer containing documents stating the bookcase was made by Messrs Bullman of Leeds, c.1820–30, for Richard Mellin, dyer, of Wakefield, at a cost of £90. Worked at Broughton Hall, Yorks., for Sir Charles Tempest, Bart, where 3 bills, a letter and a sketch survive for furniture supplied between 1840–42. Bill of 29 October 1841 totalled £203 0s 4½d. [Broughton Hall MS] Provided furniture for local Yorks.

families, such as the Gotts and the Tempests which seems to have been for the servant's quarters and less fashionable rooms. [Joy, *English Furniture, 1800–1851*, p. 234] Firm taken over by G. W. England c. 1848. [D]

Bullock, Ebenezer, Hamersley Lane, High Wycombe, Bucks., chairmaker (b. c.1796–1841). Aged 45 at the time of the 1841 Census.

Bullock, George, Liverpool and London, cm (b. 1777/78–d. 1818). Bullock's place of birth is unknown though at some stage he certainly lived in London: 'August 27 1798 Mr Bullock the young artist who gained such great repute in Birmingham . . . returning to London, the statue business not answering his expectation. He now intends giving his whole attention to the modelling and painting of likenesses . . . his age does not exceed twenty'. [J. W Langford, *A Century of Birmingham Life*, vol. II, 1868, p. 118] There is no further record of his early career other than a superb wax depicting a figure seated in an interior in the collection of Leeds Art Galleries. This depicts Henry Blundell of Ince and is signed 'G. Bullock 1801'. In 1804 Bullock showed at the Royal Academy a marble bust of Blundell. A portrait by Joseph Allen of a very Byronic looking Bullock includes a plaster model of this bust. The portrait and bust are in the Walker Art Gallery, Liverpool. [*Walker Art Gallery, Merseyside Painters, People and Places*, 1978, pp. 19–20]

Bullock re-emerges in Liverpool in 1804: 'Bullock, George, Modeller and Sculptor, Lord Street'. [*Gore's Liverpool Directory*, 1804] His brother William who was to become the celebrated Museum promoter, was already established there as 'Museum, Jeweller and China Dealer, Church Street'. [*Gore*, 1804] Also in Church St was 'William Stoakes, Looking Glass Manufactory'. [*Gore*, 1803] By 1805 George was in partnership with Stoakes and had moved in with him: 'Bullock & Stoakes Cabinet Makers, General Furnishers and Marble Workers 48 Church Street'. [*Gore*, 1805] Bullock advertised his 'Grecian Rooms at Mr Stokes Looking Glass Manufactory . . . this day re-opened where are the most extensive collection of Bronze and Bronzed Figures . . . Marble Tables, Chimney Pieces . . . see the Rich Gothic Furniture, Armour &c which he has designed and executed for . . . Cholmondeley Castle'. [*Liverpool Chronicle*, 4 September 1805] This is the first furniture known to have been designed and made by Bullock. The armour was probably ancient and supplied by William Bullock.

Bullock continued to practice as a sculptor and showed busts at both the Liverpool Academy and the Royal Academy. In 1804 he showed one of William Roscoe the celebrated Liverpool virtuoso and scholar. Roscoe certainly helped Bullock's career, for Thomas Johnes of Hafod wrote to Roscoe on 15 March 1808: 'a protege of yours Mr Bullock a very clever fellow who is to fit up my home . . .'. [Liverpool Public Lib., Roscoe papers 398] In 1810 he showed nine busts in the Liverpool Academy of which he was founding President from 1810–12.

By June 1807 Bullock's partnership was over, for he advertised that his partnership with 'Mr Stoakes . . . has been dissolved . . . Bullock has removed his Grecian Room from Church Street to No 23 Bold Street'. [*Liverpool Chronicle*, 3 June 1807] But from 1809–10 he was again in partnership, this time with Soane's celebrated assistant J. M. Gandy who took with him to Liverpool as a pupil Soane's eldest son. The firm was styled 'Bullock, George & Joseph Gandy, architects, modellers, sculptors, marble masons, cabinet makers and upholsterers 55 Church Street'. [*Gore*, 1810] The firm did not prosper for Gandy wrote to Soane from Liverpool on 1 September 1810: 'The affair of the Liverpool Academy . . . took a serious turn a few days after you left us, my partner insisting . . . that the partnership interest was most deeply hurt by my refusal of joining with him as one of the numbers of the Liverpool Academy . . . the result was to separate publicly on the 22 Sept 1810'. [A. T. Bolton, *The Portrait of Sir John Soane*, p. 126]

By 1810 William Bullock had moved to London to create his famous museum in the Egyptian Hall in Piccadilly. In 1812 George sold the contents of his premises: 'Fashionable Modern Furniture . . . of Mr George Bullock who is going to reside in London'. [*Liverpool Mercury*, 28 August 1812] He was however still included in the Liverpool directories for 1813 and 1814 so it is possible that he maintained premises there. He was first listed in London in 1813: 'Bullock, George, upholsterers, Grecian Rooms, Egyptian Hall Piccadilly'. [*Post Office Annual Directory London*, 1813] He was not listed in 1814 but by 1815 was established as 'Sculptor, 4 Tenterden Street, Hanover Square, Mona Marble and Furniture Works, Oxford Street'. [*POD*, 1815] These were his premises until his death on 1 May 1818. At Christmas 1817 were insured 'George Bullock and Charles Fraser of the Mona Marble Works Oxford Street Cabinet makers and Upholders . . . £3,800'. [GL, Sun MS vol. 471, ref. 925754]

After this brief sketch of Bullock's career several other points need to be made. It is obvious from many of the sources that Bullock used a wide range of exotic woods and marbles in his furniture designs and for the chimney pieces. Later in his career however he made a particular virtue of using native British woods and marbles. There were strong commercial and patriotic reasons for this during the Napoleonic wars, but interestingly a similar move towards native woods also took place in France. In a geological lecture in Liverpool a Mr Bakewell described Mona marble as 'a beautiful Green Stone which is found in a part of the island of Angelsea the property of Mr George Bullock'. [*Liverpool Mercury*, 30 August, 1811] Bullock also used Scottish marbles. In 1985 two oak boxes to Bullock's design were sold by the London dealer J. Harris. They both contained samples of various marbles and one had the words 'Mona Marble' inlaid into its top: were these samples perhaps shown to customers by Bullock? Mona marble chimney pieces are illustrated along with Bullock's furniture in Ackermann's *Repository* during his lifetime.

Bullock's furniture was far more assertive in its character than was usual in his day, and the ornament both in the form of its finely modelled metal mounts and the Boulle and marquetry of various woods and metals is highly stylized and dramatic. His use of native woods and marbles was often commented upon: 'British Oak Furniture — This novel article first brought to a degree of perfection by Mr Bullock'. [*Times*, 1 July 1819]

Whilst most of his furniture was Neo-classical in style, some was Gothic, Elizabethan and Jacobean and he developed these styles far beyond other designers of his day. How much he designed himself is unknown as no records of his firm survive beyond a book of designs for furniture, interiors and metalwork entitled 'Tracings by Thomas Wilkinson from the designs of the late Mr. George Bullock 1820'. [Birmingham Museum and Art Gallery] This title cannot be wholly accepted, as some of these designs are certainly by Richard Bridgens who was involved with Bullock as a designer in London and Liverpool. At Abbotsford Bridgens was closely involved, and to judge from his work after Bullock's death specialized in the Gothic and Rennaisance styles. [*Furn. Hist.*, 1979] It would also seem likely that Gandy designed furniture during the partnership.

Many questions remain to be answered: what were Bullock's links with Matthew Boulton; who was Bullock's partner Colonel Charles Fraser of whom Bullock sculpted a bust in 1813; what other houses did he work in; and did he commit suicide? He certainly had a magnetic personality which enabled him to achieve a great deal before his early death at about 40. He made many friends including Sir Walter Scott who was shocked by his sudden death. Scott's letters throw light upon his life. Daniel Terry, a London friend of Bullock and Scott, wrote to Scott on 15 May 1818: 'I do not see how the large concern which owed its existence its conduct & its peculiar excellence entirely to the personal talent and activity of poor Bullock can be continued longer than the impetus which he had given . . . George's fate was something accelerated by . . . the fantastic, damnable conduct of the monied partner Colonel Frazer, an old crackbrained East Indian Jackass'. [Nat. Lib. of Scotland, MS 3889, f 94]

The artist Benjamin Robert Haydon wrote in December 1818: 'George Bullock was one of those extraordinary beings who receive great good fortune & are never benefitted by it, & suffer great evils, and are never ruined, always afloat but never in harbour, always energetic, always scheming'. [*The Diary of Benjamin Robert Haydon*, W. B. Pope (ed.), II, p. 209]

Bullock's stock was sold in 1819 . . . *The Superb Furniture and Sculptured Articles of Beautiful Mona Marble . . . The whole of the finished stock of that highly ingenious artist . . . By Mr Christie on the premises No 4 Tenterden Street Hanover Square on Monday the 3d of May 1819 and two following days . . .* [A. Coleridge, 'The work of George Bullock cabinet maker in Scotland', *Conn.*, vol. CLVIII, 1965, pp. 249–252 and vol. CLIX, 1965, pp. 13–17; R. Edwards, 'George Bullock as a sculptor and modeller', *Conn.*, July 1969, pp. 172–173; V. Glenn, 'Regency Furnishing Schemes', *Furn. Hist.*, 1979, pp. 54–67; E. T. Joy, 'A Modernist of the Regency', *C. Life*, vol. CXLIV, 1968, pp. 456–57, 507–08; E. T. Joy 'Identifying a Regency Cabinet', *C. Life*, vol. CLXVIII, 1980, pp. 646–48; E. T. Joy, *English Furniture 1800–1851*; B. Reade, *Regency Antiques*; 'The Late George Bullock', *Annals of The Fine Arts*, vol. III, 1819, pp. 321–22]

CHOLMONDELEY CASTLE, Cheshire (Lord Cholmondeley). In 1805 supplied 'Gothic furniture, armour &c'. [*Liverpool Chronicle*, 4 September 1805]

BOLTON HALL, Yorks, (John Bolton). Gandy restored this house 1806–1810 for the Liverpool merchant John Bolton. So this Bullock/Gandy design — possibly unexecuted — must date from 1809–1810. [Wilkinson tracings]

HAFOD, Cardiganshire (Thomas Johnes). In 1808 mentioned as 'Mr Bullock a very clever fellow who is fitting up my home'. [Liverpool Public Lib., Roscoe papers 398]

EDMUND RUNDELL. Designed an 'Oak cabinet Nov 30 1810', possibly not executed. [Wilkinson tracings]

THORNHILL, Birmingham (James Watt). Between 1808–1818 supplied a wide range of furniture and fittings, some of which Watt took to Aston Hall in 1819. [*Furn. Hist.*, 1979]

SCONE PALACE, Perthshire (Earl of Mansfield). Several pieces of furniture c. 1803–12, attributed to Bullock, although no bills survive. [Coleridge]

SPEKE HALL, Liverpool. 'Just finished in great taste . . . the furniture . . . executed by and under the direction of George Bullock', state the sale particulars of Speke Hall, 1812. [*Liverpool Mercury*, 14 August 1812, p. 53]

BLAIR CASTLE, Perthshire (Duke of Atholl). Bills for furniture date between 1814–19. [Blair archives: Coleridge]

ARMADALE CASTLE, Isle of Skye (Lord Macdonald). Designed furniture and furnishings, possibly not executed, 1814–18. [Wilkinson tracings]

BIEL, East Lothian (W. Nisbet). Designed furniture and furnishings, possibly not executed, 1815–17. [Wilkinson tracings]

ABBOTSFORD, Roxburghshire (Sir Walter Scott). Between 1816–19 supplied furniture and fittings. [C. Wainwright, 'Walter Scott and the furnishings of Abbotsford', *Conn.*, vol. CXCIV, 1977, pp. 3–15]

BATTLE ABBEY, Sussex (Sir G. Webster). Between 1816–18 supplied furniture and fittings. [Wilkinson, Webster archives, E. Sussex RO]

MRS BARRON. Designed 'Oak book commode Aug 1816' and 'Mahogany commode Sep 1816', possibly not executed. [Wilkinson tracings]

MRS FERGUSSON. Design for 'Table April 1817', possible not executed. [Wilkinson tracings]

LORD ABERCORN. Design for 'Cabinet May 1817' possibly not executed. [Wilkinson tracings]

MR SONE. Designed furniture, possibly not executed. [Wilkinson tracings]

LADY SPENCER. Designed 'Table April 1818', possibly not executed. [Wilkinson tracings]

MRS DOWKING. Designed furniture, possibly not executed. [Wilkinson tracings]

LADY ORMOND. Designed furniture, possibly not executed. [Wilkinson tracings]

SIR H. BUNBURY. Designed furniture, possibly not executed. [Wilkinson tracings]

WILLIAM ROSCOE, Liverpool. Two ebony cabinets inlaid with brass designed by Bullock for Roscoe are now is the Walker Art Gallery, Liverpool. [H. Roscoe, *Life of William Roscoe*, vol. II, 1833, p. 378]

SHRUBLAND PARK, Suffolk (W. F. Middleton). Designed furniture, possibly not executed. [Wilkinson tracings]

WARLEY HALL, Worcs. (H. Galton). 'Design for living room', possibly not executed. [Wilkinson tracings]

THORNHILL, Birmingham (Miss Boulton). Designed furniture, possibly not executed. [Wilkinson tracings]

C. W.

Bullock, George, Bristol, cm (1792–95). Trading at King St, 1792–93, and 28 Redcliff St, 1793–95. [D]

Bullock, James, 15 Holywell Row, Worship St, Shoreditch, London, cm and u (1835–39). Trading as Bullock & Simpson in 1839. [D]

Bullock, Jeremiah, London, u (1743–d. 1784). Trading in New Bond St, 1778–84, at no. 64 in 1784. Son of John Bullock of Andover, Hants., tailor; app. to Sandys Jones on 4 May 1743, and admitted freemen of the Upholders' Co. by servitude on 1 December 1763. Took app. named Alexander Swinley, 1764–71. [D; poll bk; GL, Upholders' Co. records]

Bullock, John, Turnham Green, Surrey, chairmaker (1778–79). Took out Sun Insurance policies in 1778 for £300 on his house; in 1778 with William Pilton for £300 on workshops, utensils and stock; and in 1779 for £500. [GL, Sun MS vol. 268, pp. 77–78; vol. 272, p. 69]

Bullock, Richard, London, cm and u (1790–93). Married in 1790 at St George's, Hanover Sq. Subscribed to Sheraton's *Drawing Book*, 1793. [PR]

Bullock, Robert, Market Pl., Rugeley, Staffs., cm and u (1818–35). Recorded also as a builder in 1828. [D]

Bullock, William, London, cm (1793). Subscribed to Sheraton's *Drawing Book*, 1793.

Bullock, William, Shifnal, Salop, cm (1797–98). [D]

Bullock, William, 118 Upper Frederick St, Liverpool, cm (1834). [D]

Bullock & Stoakes, 48 Church St, Liverpool, cm, general furnishers and marble workers (1805). [D]

Bullon, J. G., Bury St Edmunds, Suffolk, cm (1833). Supplied the base of a chess table in the Drawing Room at Ickworth in 1833. [Nat. Trust guide to *Ickworth*, p. 15; Joy, *English Furniture, 1800–1851*, illus. p. 213]

Bullough, John, Barnsley, Yorks., cm (1834–37). Trading in Sheffield Rd, 1837. [D]

Bullrock, James, 73 French St, Southampton, Hants., carver and gilder (1836). [D]

Bullymore, —, address unrecorded, carver (1673–75). Employed at Ham House, Surrey, where he received, between 1673–75 £102. [O. Hill & J. Cornforth, *English Country Houses: Caroline*, p. 74]

Bullman, Christopher, St Cuthbert's Lane, Carlisle, Cumb., joiner and cm (1829–34). [D]

Bulman, Hesilrigg, Middle St, Newcastle, cm or carpenter (1778). [D]

Bulmer, —, Newcastle, cm (1793). Subscribed to Sheraton's *Drawing Book*, 1793. Probably either George or Joseph Bulmer.

Bulmer, Benjamin, Boston, Lincs., joiner and/or cm (1834). [D]

Bulmer, Blackett, 293 Strand, London, painter, u, floorcloth manufacturer and undertaker (1779). Took out a Sun Insurance policy in 1779 for £1,000 of which utensils, stock and goods accounted for £510. [GL, Sun MS vol. 275, p. 199]

Bulmer, George, Northumberland St, Newcastle, joiner and cm (1801). [D] See Joseph Bulmer.

Bulmer, James, Hungate, York, chairmaker (1828). [D]

Bulmer, John, York, chairmaker (1797–1812). Son of Stephen Bulmer; app. to George Stones, chairmaker, on 24 June 1797. Admitted freeman in 1712. [York app. reg. and freemen rolls]

Bulmer, Joseph, Northumberland Pl., Newcastle, cm and carpenter (1790). [D] See George Bulmer.

Bulmer, Mary, Hull, Yorks., cm and broker (1810–18). Trading at 18 Posterngate, 1810–14. [D]

Bulmer, Robert, Prospect St, Hull, Yorks., cm (1806). [D]

Bulmer, Samuel, 19 Commercial St, Leeds, Yorks., carver and gilder (1828). [D]

Bulmer, William, Wetherby, Yorks., joiner and/or cm (1837). [D]

Bulmer, William, 13 Silver St, Halifax, Yorks., carver and gilder (1837). [D]

Bulstrode, Charles or Christopher, 50 Paddington St, Marylebone, London, cm and u (1820–39). Christopher was trading there in 1829 and 1839. [D]

Bult, Robert, Bridgwater, Som., cm (1793). [D]

Bunage, Thomas, Ipswich, Suffolk, cm (1790). [Poll bk]

Bunce, John, Shoe Lane, St Bride's, London, cm (1753). Served as Scavenger at St Bride's in 1753. [GL, MS 6561, p. 87]

Bunce, Robert, 7 St Mary's Butts, Reading, Berks., cm and u (1830–40). [D; poll bk]

Bunce, Thomas, 9 Gt Russell St, Covent Gdn, London, cm (1809–11). [D]

Bunce, William, 11 Duke's Ct, Bow St, London, upholder (1779). Took out a Sun Insurance policy in 1779 for £100 of which £10 accounted for utensils, stock and goods. [GL, Sun MS vol. 279, p. 396]

Bunce, William, 8 Russell St, Covent Gdn, London, cm and u (1789–1812). Took out a Sun Insurance policy on 26 January 1786 for £500 of which utensils etc. accounted for £300. Named in Sheraton's list of master cabinet makers, 1803. [D; GL, Sun MS vol. 335, p. 347]

Bunce, William, Chester, cm (1831). Admitted freeman on 25 April 1831. [Chester freemen rolls]

Bunch, James, upholder — See Elizabeth Maynard.

Buncher, W., 27 High St, Brighton, Sussex, u (1839). [D]

Bunderson, George, Back 54 Shaw's Brow, Liverpool, cm (1790–96). [D]

Bundock, Jonathan, 29 Palace St, Canterbury, Kent, cm and furniture broker (1826–34). [D]

Bundock, William, 53 Gt Russell St, Bloomsbury, London, u, cm and undertaker (1807–15). Bill to Mr Harris, dated

16 March and 3 October 1810 totalled £23 2s, and included a 'field Bedstead with sweepd laths' costing £2 10s, and bedding totalling £23 2s. Bill shows engravings of sofa and chair beds in a style similar to that of Morgan & Sanders. [D; GL, print dept] See W. E. Caldecott.

Bundy, Charles, 48 Watling St, London, cm (1775). Took out a Sun Insurance policy in 1775 for £400, utensils and stock accounting for £300. [GL, Sun MS vol. 245, p. 197]

Bun(ler), John, High Wycombe, Bucks., chairmaker (b. c. 1796–1841). Aged 45 at the time of the 1841 Census.

Bunn, Henry, 95 Curtain Rd, Shoreditch, London, cm and u (1822–37). [D]

Bunn, J. & W., 12 Spicer St, Spitalfields, London, cm (1835–37). [D]

Bunn, John Henry, Spicer St, Spitalfields, London, cm (1838). Declared bankrupt, *Chester Courant and North Wales Advertiser*, 30 January 1839.

Bunnell, William, Colchester, Essex, cm etc. (1784–93). Trading in High St in 1784. Subscribed to Sheraton's *Drawing Book*, 1793. [D]

Bunnett, Jacob jnr, 102 High St, King's Lynn, Norfolk, cm and u (1839). [D]

Bunnett, R., Sedgford Lane, King's Lynn, Norfolk, cm (1839). [D]

Bunnett, S., Holt, Norfolk, cm and joiner (1822). [D]

Bunnett, W. & A., 4 Newington Causeway, London (wholesale) and 82 Lombard St (retail), 'Manufacturers of all Kinds of Sun Shades, Patent Wire & Transparent Blinds, also of SUPERIOR PAINTED BAISE FOR TABLE AND OTHER COVERS AND INDIA JAPANNED FURNITURE In Screens, Chairs, Cheffoniers, Tables &c.' (c. 1820). [Trade card, B. Austen]

Bunney, Thomas, Mint Sq., Southwark, London, bed and mattress manufacturer (1820). [D]

Bunning, James, Doncaster, Yorks., cm and u (1830–37). Trading at St George's Gate in 1830 and French Gate, 1837. [D]

Bunny, Jacob, Andover, Hants., cm (1758). Took app. named Macmin in 1758. [S of G, app. index]

Bunny, Joseph, 6 Leigh St, Red Lion Sq., London, cm (1775–76). Took out Sun Insurance policies in 1775 in association with John Marshall; and in 1776 for £200, £100 on utensils, stock and goods. [GL, Sun MS vol. 253, p. 622]

Bunyan, —, Thrift St, Soho, London, cm (1761). Signed statements regarding working conditions of journeyman cm in *Lloyd's Evening Post and British Chronicle*, 9–12 October 1761. Related notices in same paper, 30 September– 2 October, and 14–16 October 1761. Conditions include working no longer than from 6 a.m. to 7 p.m., except Saturdays, and the raising of the price of piece-work.

Bunyan, Robert, Royston, Herts., u, cm and brazier (1763–98). Advertised auction sales of furniture in *Cambridge Chronicle and Journal*, 17 September 1763; 25 October 1766; 18 February, 30 September and 25 November 1769. Took out Sun Insurance policies in 1775 for £200 on his house; and on 27 March 1786 for £800. [D; GL, Sun MS vol. 243, p. 336; vol. 336, p. 73]

Bunyan (or Bunyard), William, London, cm (1768–1812). Polled at Colchester, Essex, 1768–1812, as Bunyard, 1784– 1812.

Bunyard, William, 89 George Inn Passage, Snowhill, London, looking-glass frame maker (1775). Took out a Sun Insurance policy in 1775 for £100, £50 on utensils and stock. [GL, Sun MS vol. 238, p. 617]

Burall, Paul, Camborne, Cornwall, cm (1786). Married by licence to Grace Jennings at Illogan on 31 May 1786. [PR]

Burbage, Grain, St Andrew St, Cambridge, cm, u and paper hanger (1830–48). Will dated 1848. [D; Cambridge Univ. Lib., AR3:216]

Burbage, Joseph, Leicester, joiner and cm (1754–68). App. to John Shipley in 1754, and admitted freeman in 1768. [Leicester freemen rolls]

Burberow, Matthew, London, carver, gilder and frame maker (c. 1800–29). Addresses given at 32 Chandler St, c. 1800; 16 Oakley St, Lambeth, 1826; and no. 58, 1827–29. [D; trade card, Heal Coll., BM]

Burbery, T., 11 King St West, Edgware Rd, London, cm and u (1820–23). [D]

Burbery (or Burbury), Thomas, George St, Oxford Rd, London, cm (1803–20). Trading at no. 6 in 1820. Subscribed to Sheraton's *Cabinet Dictionary*, and named in his list of master cabinet makers, 1803. [D]

Burbidge, William, address unrecorded, upholder (1749–57). Son of William Burbidge, Gent., of Raisby, Lincoln; app. to Thomas Dobyns on 5 May 1749, and admitted freeman of the Upholders' Co. by servitude on 3 February 1757. [GL, Upholders' Co. records]

Burbridge, John, 8 Tysoe St, Spitalfields, London, fancy cm (1829–37). [D]

Burbun, John, Tufton St, London, frame maker (1749). [Poll bk]

Burbury, —, London, cm (1793). Subscribed to Sheraton's *Drawing Book*, 1793. Probably Thomas Burbery (or Burbury).

Burby, James, address unrecorded, cm (1754). Subscribed to Chippendale's *Director*, 1754. [DEF]

Burch, James, Maidstone, Kent, turner and chairmaker (1826– 39). Addresses given at 72 High St 1826–27, and Bank St 1834–39. [D; voters list]

Burch, Stephen, Mark St, Dover, Kent, cm and u (1838). [D]

Burch, Thomas, Strood, Kent, chairmaker (1798). [D]

Burch & Tyndal, Bristol, u (1736). Inventory of John Burch and Mr Tyndal taken on 2 May 1736 lists the contents of three separate buildings including a 'Large house in the Square'. [*Furn. Hist.*, 1979]

Burchall, Roger, address unrecorded, upholder (1716–29). Son of Robert Burchall, Gent., of Wooden Bassett, Wilts.; app. to Thomas Kingsman, merchant tailor, and George Carter, on 5 September 1716. Admitted freeman of the Upholders' Co. by servitude on 6 August 1729. [GL, Upholders' Co. records]

Burchall, William, Nicholas Lane, London, upholder (1764). Employed a non-freeman for six weeks in 1764. [GL, City Licence bks, vol. 4]

Burcham, Henry, Walsingham, Suffolk, cm (1752). Took app. named Mitchel in 1752. [S of G, app. index]

Burcham, Peter, Norwich, carver (1742). Son of Thomas Burcham, weaver; admitted freeman on 25 September 1742. [Norwich freemen rolls]

Burcham, Peter, London, carver, cm, chairmaker, undertaker and appraiser (1754–63). Trading at the Cabinet Warehouse, Fleet Mkt, 1755–63, and also near Holborn Bridge, 1763. Trade card with Rococo frame states that he 'Makes and Sells all Sorts of Looking Glasses, Chairs, & Cabinet Work &c. in ye neatest Manner Wholesale & Retail'. [Heal] Subscribed to Chippendale's *Director*, 1754, and named as a Liveryman of the Joiners' Co. on 22 September 1749. Pair of early 19th-century mahogany card tables recorded, with rectangular tops crossbanded in satinwood and rosewood, on turned legs, partly ebonised; one stamped 'BURCHAM'. [D; Sotheby's, 22 March 1968, lot 193]

Burchby, Francis, Nottingham, upholder (1741). Married on 1 May 1741. [Notts. RO, marriage licences index]

Burchby, Thomas, Clumber Park, Notts., cm (1832). [D]

Burchen, W., 19 St Augustine's Pl., Bristol, u (1828). [D]

Burden, Anne, Long Row, Nottingham, u (1762). Advertised in

Leicester Journal, 1762, that she 'hangs rooms with newest patterns . . . upholstered goods at lowest rates'.

Burden, Richard, Coventry, Warks., chairmaker (1747). Married Mary Thacker of Hook Norton at Bloxham on 22 August 1747, aged *c.* 22. [Bodleian index of Oxf. marriage bonds]

Burden, Robert, Nottingham, u (1754). Will dated 24 March 1754. [Notts. RO, probate records]

Burden, Thomas, Christchurch, Hants., chairmaker (1745–57). Took apps named Seymour in 1745 and Froud in 1757. [S of G, app. index]

Burdett, James, 6 Turville St, Bethnal Green, London, looking-glass and picture frame maker (1829). [D]

Burditt, David, High St, Market Harborough, Leics., cm and u (1828–35). [D]

Burdon, Matthew & F. & G., Claypath, Durham, cm and furniture brokers (1827–37). Recorded as Burdon & Son in 1834. Notice in the *Durham Advertiser*, 16 January 1837 returning thanks to 'their numerous Friends for the patronage so long & so extensively conferred on the late Firm of MATTHEW BURDON & SON, & to inform them & the Public that the Business will be further carried on under the Style & Firm of F. & G. BURDON, who will continue to keep on hand a large & fashionable assortment of NEW & SECOND-HAND FURNITURE & to furnish Houses for Hire at moderate rates.' [D]

Bure, William, Lancaster, cm (1768). [Poll bk]

Burford, John, on the Pavement, St Martin's Lane, London, carver and gilder (1763). [D]

Burford, William, Somerton, Som., cm (1730). Took app. named Pounsett in 1730. [S of G, app. index]

Burgan (or Burgon), Benjamin, Doncaster, Yorks., upholder (1782). Declared bankrupt, *Gents Mag.*, April 1782, and Bailey's list of bankrupts.

Burge, John, Milk St, Bristol, carver and dealer in spirits (1805–22). Trading in Mills's Pl., Milk St, 1805–09; 6 Milk St 1812–14; and no. 7, 1819–22. Recorded as Bastable & Burge in 1810. [D]

Burge, Richard, 19 Lamb's Conduit Passage, London, cm and u (1839). [D]

Burges, B., 84 St George's Rd, Southwark, London, chairmaker (1835). [D]

Burges, Isaac, address unrecorded, upholder (1738). Son of Obadiah Burges, Marlborough, Wilts., Gent.; app. to Thomas Ward, and admitted freeman of the Upholders' Co. on 4 October 1738. [GL, Upholders' Co. records]

Burgess, Edw., 8 Percival St, Clerkenwell, London, cm (1837–40). [D]

Burgess, Henry, Mersey St, Liverpool, cm (1772–96). Recorded at no. 37 in 1781; nos 49 and 36 in 1790; and no. 41 in 1796. [D]

Burgess, James, Blunt St, Frome, Som., cm (1830). [D]

Burgess, John, High St, Northwich, Cheshire, cm and chairmaker (1828). [D]

Burgess, Joseph, Nantwich, Cheshire, chairmaker (1809). Married on 15 May 1809. [Chester RO, PR]

Burgess, Robert, Stokenchurch, Oxon.(?), chairmaker (1825). Third party in a deed for property in Chinnor. [Oxford RO, Li II/iii/b/4]

Burgess, Thomas, Coventry, Warks., joiner and cm (1793). [D]

Burgess, William, Nantwich, Cheshire, chairmaker (1820). Daughter Mary Ann by his wife Mary bapt. on 30 August 1820. [PR(bapt.)]

Burgess, William, 9 Green St, Leicester Sq., London, cm and chairmaker (1823). Took out a Sun Insurance policy on 2 January 1823 for £150 on utensils and stock. [GL, Sun MS vol. 498, ref. 999456]

Burgh, —, address unrecorded, u (1660–62). Worked for the Earl of Salisbury at Hatfield House in 1660, charging a total of £66 2s 2d, including £1 10s for a 'French bedstead lath bottom'. In 1662 he worked at the Earl's London stables supplying '12 Rushee leather chairs for steward's dining room', costing £5. [Hatfield House MS bills 262 and 269]

Burgh, James, 19 Edward St, Hampstead Rd, London, carver and gilder (1839). [D]

Burghers, John, address unrecorded, upholder (1705). Admitted freeman of the Upholders' Co. on 4 July 1705. [GL, Upholders' Co. records]

Burgin, Richard, 'King's Head Inn', near Market Sq., St Neots, Hunts., carpenter and cm (1839). [D]

Burgis, William, 5 Hollen St, Wardour St, Soho, London, cm, u, chair and sofa maker and undertaker (1827–39). [D]

Burgiss, William, High St, Uxbridge, Middlx, carver and gilder (1826). [D]

Burgoine, Aaron, Plymouth, Devon, cm (1826). Marriage to Miss Elizabeth Collins of Plymouth at Charles Church on 14 February 1826 reported in *The Alfred*.

Burgoine (or Burgoyne), John, Plymouth, Devon, cm (1814–38). Addresses given at Colmer's Lane, 1814–22; 2 Colmore Lane, 1823–24; 15 Park St, 1830; no. 55 in 1836; and no. 32 in 1838. Report in *Exeter Flying Post*, 18 September 1834, that his workshops in Park St had been destroyed by fire on 13 September but there had been little wind at the time, so the damage was not extensive. [D]

Burgoine, Thomas, Hare Lane, Gloucester, cm and chairmaker (1820). [D]

Burgon, Benjamin, Derby, u (1792). Advertised in *Derby Mercury*, 22 November 1792, sale of 'Household furniture, China, Glass, Delph and Linen . . . Night Tables, Mahogany and Stain'd Chairs, Stands, Trays, Tea Board, Tea Chests . . .'.

Burgon, Benjamin, 5 New Ormond St, London, upholder (1808). [D]

Burham, John jnr, 69 Walnut St, Liverpool, with shop at 9 Post Office Lane, ivory turner and carver (1839). [D]

Burke, Thomas, High St, Shifnall, Salop, cm and u (1835). [D]

Burkett, Thomas, 16 Rogers Row, Manchester, cm (1808). [D]

Burkitt, William, Kendal, Westmld, cm (1834). [D]

Burland, John, Hargreaves Ct, Hanley St, Liverpool, u (1829). [D]

Burland, Thomas, Liverpool, cm (1821–37). Addresses given at Rupert St, 1821–24; 15 Collingwood St with shop at 2–3 Tyrer St, 1827; 29 Collingwood St with shop as above in 1829; and shop at Tyrer St, 1834–37. [D] See William Burland.

Burland, Thomas, Rock Ferry, Birkenhead, Cheshire, with shop at 5 Tyrer St, Birkenhead, cm (1839). [D]

Burland, William, Liverpool, carver and gilder (1823–39). Addresses given at 1 Tyrer St with shop at 64 Church St, 1823; 1 Tyrer St and Cash's Buildings, Church St, 1824; 8 Clarence St with shop at 66 Church St, 1827–29; 4 South Hunter St with shop at 65 Church St, 1834; 8 Harmony St, Gt Richmond, 1835; shop at 67 Church St, 1837; and no. 36 in 1839. [D] See Thomas Burland.

Burleigh, James, late of Hog Lane, St Giles in the Fields, London, cm and chairmaker (1761). Discharge from Debtors' Prison on 15 September 1761 announced in *London Gazette*.

Burleigh, Thomas, Shrewsbury, Salop, u (1721). [Shrewsbury burgess roll]

Burley, James, address unrecorded, upholder (1717–24). Son of Moses Burley, Gent. of Reading, Berks.; app. to Joseph Pluckrose on 23 May 1717 and turned over to Major William Beton, skinner, on 11 July 1723. Admitted freeman of the

Upholders' Co. by servitude on 12 December 1724. [GL, Upholders' Co. records]

Burley, Thomas, Otley, Yorks., cm (1822–37). Trading in Boroughgate, 1822–30 and Bondgate in 1837. [D]

Burlingham, Charles, Bridge St, Evesham, Worcs., u (1828–40). [D; Sheriffs' poll bk]

Burlingham, John, 2 High St, Mile Town, Sheerness, Kent, cm and u (c. 1820–39). Trade card reads: 'J. BURLINGHAM, Cabinet, Upholstery, Looking Glasses &c. CARPET WARE-HOUSE . . . BELL and PAPER HANGING -COACH and HEARSE KEPT'. [D; Kent RO, U36/21]

Burlison, Isaac, South Shields, Co. Durham, cm and joiner (1834). [D]

Burlison, William, Jarrow, Co. Durham, joiner and cm (1828). [D]

Burman, James, Gt Yarmouth, Norfolk, cm (1795–1841). Trading at 40 Row in 1836. [Poll bks]

Burman, John, Louth, Lincs., cm and joiner (1828–35). Trading at Maiden Row in 1828 and Eastgate in 1835. [D]

Burman, William, London, cm (1831). [Gt Yarmouth poll bk]

Burn, George, Newbiggin, Richmond, Yorks., cm (1840). [D]

Burn, Isaac, Hull, Yorks., cm (1818). App. to Edward Dickon in January 1818. [Hull app. reg.]

Burn, John, 5 Little Hermitage St, London, cm (1784). [D] See Thomas Burn.

Burn, John, Tweedmouth, Berwick-upon-Tweed, Northumb., cm (1827–34). [D]

Burn, Thomas, London, cm and u (1778–93). Addresses given at 38 Wapping in 1778; 5 Little Hermitage St, 1782–89; and no. 1 in 1793. Took out Sun Insurance policies in 1778 and 1782 for £400 in trust for minor, Sarah Kilbington; and in 1781 for £800, £550 accounting for utensils, stock and goods. [D; GL, Sun MS vol. 263, p. 163; vol. 299, p. 538; vol. 292, p. 171] See John Burn.

Burn, Thomas, Rothbury, Northumb., cm and joiner (1834). [D]

Burn, William, Whitby, Yorks., cm and u (1823–40). Trading in Church St, 1823–34; and Flowergate in 1840, as cm and chairmaker. [D]

Burn, William, Wearmouth Green, Bishop Wearmouth, Co. Durham, u (1827). [D]

Burn, William, Prospect Pl., Exeter, Devon, cm (1839). Son William bapt. at St Mary Major on 13 April 1839. [PR(bapt.)]

Burn & Kerr, Rose St, Soho and 21 Clipstone St, London, chairmakers and glass paper manufacturers (1835). [D]

Burnaford, Thomas, Exeter, Devon, chairmaker (1751). Took app. named Spear in 1751. [S of G, app. index]

Burnaford (or Bunaford), Thomas, Bristol, cm (1792–1800). Trading at Denmark St, 1792–94, and Bridewell Lane, 1799–1800. [D]

Burnand, Richard, Newcastle, u (1686). [Newcastle freemen rolls]

Burnard, Robert, High St, Sheffield, Yorks., u and cm (1805–08). [D]

Burnell, C. & Fox, John, London, cm, upholders, appraisers and undertakers, successors to William Lamb (1809–25). Trading at 9–10 Jewin St, Cripplegate, 1809–19; and 46–47 Newgate St, 1820–25. Supplied John Gibbard of Sharnbrook, near Bedford, in 1817 with 'a set of cotton 4-post bed furniture with full inside and outside valances lined all through and turned over in drab calico and full bias; together with other cotton furnishings, French fringes etc.', costing £14 16s 4d. In 1818 he provided 'a pair of mahogany pole fire screens, with round corner mounts covered with green silk fluted in front with balance lead weights covered', costing £3 10s; and 'Twelve new large elbow chair cushion covers lined with white calico bordered with chintz', at £5 2s. [D; Bedford Office, London]

Burnet, Mr, Strand, London, upholder (1748). Catalogues for auction of deceased's furniture to be had from Mr. Burnet. [*General Advertiser*, 7 June 1748]

Burnet, Alfred, High Wycombe, Bucks., chairmaker (b. c. 1816–41). Aged 25 at the time of the 1841 Census.

Burnet, Samuel, at 'The Rose & Crown', Russell St, St Paul's, Covent Gdn, London, gilder (1722). Took out a Sun Insurance policy on 9 March 1722 for £500 on goods and merchandise in his house. [GL, Sun MS vol. 15, ref. 27929]

Burnet, William, High Wycombe, Bucks., chairmaker (b. c. 1806–41). Aged 35 at the time of the 1841 Census.

Burnet & Painter, Bristol, cm (1793). Subscribed to Sheraton's *Drawing Book*, 1793.

Burnett, Andrew, Lisle St, Leicester Sq., London, upholder, cm and undertaker (1808–39). Addresses given at no. 30, 1808–15; no. 13, 1816–23; no. 14, 1824–28; and 10 Gerrard St, Soho and 48 King St, 1829. Took out a Sun Insurance policy on 24 February 1808 for £1,000, of which £640 accounted for workshop, stock, utensils and goods in trust. [D; GL, Sun MS vol. 445, ref. 814434]

Burnett, Charles, Drury Lane, London, cm (1770). Declared bankrupt, *Gents Mag.*, July 1770.

Burnett, Christopher, Laceby, Lincs., cm and u (1802). App. to John & George Chapman of Hull in July 1802. [Hull app. reg.] Possibly:

Burnett, Christopher, 6 Chapel St, Hull, Yorks., cm (1837–40). [D]

Burnett, D., 24 Garden Row, St George's Fields, London, cm (1809–15). [D]

Burnett, Emanuel, South St, London, carver (1749). [Poll bk]

Burnett, George, York, u (1797). A Blue Coat boy; app. to James Marshall, u, on 14 March 1797. [York app. reg.]

Burnett, George, Liverpool, cm (1813–37). Addresses given at 3 Rupert St, 1813–14; 1 Rupert St., 1824; 25 Brownlow Hill and 2 Russell St, 1827; 2 Russell St, 1829–35; and 24 Gt Newton St, with shop at 50 Copperas Hill, 1837. [D]

Burnett, Gilbert, Strand, London, u (1753–75). Trading at 16 Strand in 1774, and 16 or 167, 1773–75. App. to Thomas Burnett in 1753, and in partnership with him, 1747–74. [D; Children Apprenticed by the Sons of the Clergy] See Thomas and Gilbert Burnett.

Burnett, Henry, North St, Gosport, Hants., turner and chairmaker (1781–93). Took out a Sun Insurance policy in 1781 for £600 of which utensils, stock, workshop and warehouse accounted for £200. [D; GL, Sun MS vol. 291, p. 521]

Burnett, James, St Martin-in-the-Fields, London, carver (1754). App. to Rob. Parker, carver, in 1754 for £20. [V & A archives]

Burnett, R., Rochester, Kent, cm (1806–07). [Poll bks]

Burnett, Thomas, Strand, London, u and cm (1744–74). Recorded at 'The King's Arms, against the New Church in the Strand', 1747–66, and no. 61 Strand, 1760–74. [D] In partnership with Gilbert Burnett, 1747–74. Named as a Fellow of the Society for Arts and Manufactures, 1761–68. Marriage to Miss Jenny Parker, with a fortune of £10,000 reported, *Read's Weekly Journal*, 11 May 1751. Probably the Mr Burnett, upholder in the Strand, who advertised an auction sale, *Daily Advertiser*, 21 February 1744, of furniture and stock of a goldsmith at 'The Golden Acorn', over against the New Church in the Strand. Advertised in *General Advertiser*, 18 December 1750; and *London Evening Post*, 21–23 February 1749 regarding the let of a house. Two long bills survive for work done for Peter Du Cane of Braxted Park, Essex, for his London house in St James's Sq., 1748–49.

Furniture supplied included 'Five beech 4 post bedsteads on Castors', £6 17s 6d; 'a wainscot Toylett table', 17s; '2 large handsome carv'd drapery Window Cornishes', £4 4s; 'two French Elbow chairs, quilted in Linnen on Casters and check cases', £4 4s; 'two Mohog. Soffoy frames Carv'd after the Chinese Manners stufft and Quilted in Linnen on Castors', £12; '9 Mahogany Elbow Chairs'; £25 17s 6d; 'a walnuttree closestool stufft and covered with black leather', £1 12s 6d; and 'an Ovall Glass in a carvd and painted frame', £1 15s. Almost all the seat furniture was provided with red check case covers. Further bills for work done, 1750–51 and 1756, total £413. [Essex RO, D/Dc A80, A13, folio 59] Named in the Holkham Hall accounts in 1755 receiving £7 16s 6d for a 'chair quilted & covered with green stuff', backgammon tables and dice, counters, and a Cyprus chest. [V & A archives] Between 1764–66 he supplied furniture to Lord Leigh for Stoneleigh Abbey, Warks., receiving £3,536. [Hussey, *English Country Houses: Early Georgian*, p. 40; *Conn.*, 1947, vol. 119, p. 19; Shakespeare Birthplace Trust, Leigh receipts, DR 18/5] His association with Gilbert Burnett, to whom he was app. from 1753, spanned the years 1747–74. Together they advertised in *Daily Advertiser*, 5 September 1747, and 3 March 1749, and their names occur in directories from 1760–74. They are described as upholstery, cabinet and carpet warehousemen, undertakers, appraisers and marquee makers. Sir John Griffin Griffin of Audley End, Essex, bought two mahogany writing tables from them in 1766, costing £7 7s. In 1768–69 they carried out miscellaneous upholstery work and furniture repairs charging a total of £11 11s 5d. [Essex RO, D/DBy/A24/11; A27/2] They may have been responsible for a commode with drawers, shaped front and straight sides which has been recorded. [V & A archives] See Gilbert Burnett, and Chillingworth & Burnett.

Burnett, William, Hotwell, Rd, Bristol, cm (1795). [D]

Burnett, William, Market Pl., Horncastle, Lincs., joiner/cm (1822). [D]

Burney, Alexander, 8 Gt Pulteney St, Golden Sq., London, (1805–08). Took out a Sun Insurance policy on 20 August 1805 for £700, £300 on his house and shop, £300 on utensils and stock, and £100 on household goods. [D; GL, Sun MS vol. 434, ref. 779149]

Burney, Andrew, 8 Gt Pulteney St, Golden Sq., London, cm and u (1809–11). [D]

Burney, Joseph, 6 (?) St, Red Lion Sq., London, cm (1776). Took out a Sun Insurance policy in 1776 for £100 on his house and goods. [GL, Sun MS vol. 246, p. 63]

Burnie, Charles, London, cm (1793). Subscribed to Sheraton's *Drawing Book*, 1793.

Burningham, William, Downing St, Farnham, Surrey, cm etc. (1839). [D]

Burniston, John, York, cm and u (1816–23). Trading in Walmgate, 1816–17 and 1823, and in Fossgate, 1818–20. [D]

Burnley, Thomas, Canterbury, Kent, u (1655–79). [Canterbury freemen rolls]

Burnley, William, Bartholomew Close, London, upholder (1711–13). [Heal]

Burns, James, 70 Cable St, Liverpool, gilder (1749). [D]

Burns, Nimrod, 4 High St, Stepney, London, cm (1821). Took out a Sun Insurance policy in association with David Vines on 12 July 1821 for £350, £200 accounting for his house, £50 on shop behind, and £100 on stock and utensils. [GL, Sun MS vol. 487, ref. 981417] Probably Nimrod Binns.

Burns, Thomas, Liverpool, cm (b. 1763–d. 1837). Addresses given at Tythebarn St, 1805–07; Marylebone, 1810–11; Gildart's Gdns, 1821; 5 All Saints Lane, 1823–24; and Collingwood St, Scotland Rd, 1831. App. to Henry Banks, and admitted freeman on 30 May 1796. Death of his wife, Martha, reported, *Liverpool Mercury*, 22 July 1831; and his own death on 17 August 1837 aged 74 recorded in the account of lives in lease granted by Corp. of Liverpool. [D; Liverpool freemen reg.]

Burns, Thomas, Belford, Northumb., cm (1834). [D]

Burns & Bayne, 16 Gate St and 1 Whetsone Park, Lincoln's Inn Fields, London, cm (1816–20). [D]

Burnup, Cuthbert, Barrasbridge, Northumb., cm, carpenter, cartwright and wheelwright (1790–d. 1803). Death reported, *Newcastle Courant*, 29 January 1803. [D]

Burnyeat, Jonathan, 28 Chapel St, Whitehaven, Cumb., joiner and cm (1829–34). [D]

Burr, James, High St, Bedford, cm and u (1830–39). Described as 'late Lilley & Co.' [D]

Burr, John, 3 Hammond Pl., Chatham, Kent, cm and u (1826–29). [D] See Robert Burr

Burr, John, Horseley, Glos., cm (1839–40). [D]

Burr, Robert, Rochester, Kent, cm (1780). [Poll bk]

Burr, Robert, Chatham, Kent, u, cm appraiser and auctioneer (1779–1839). Recorded at '108 opposite Room Lane', c. 1792; 108 High St, 1805–07; Hammond Pl., 1823–24; no. 3, 1832–34; no. 5, 1838–39; and as 'Burr-Junior' at no. 3 in 1811. [D] Trade card, c. 1792, embellished with Neo-classical drapery swags and oval medallions, Windsor chair, Pembroke table and French bed, states: 'All sorts of Household Goods in the newest taste. Retail & for Exportation. Gentlemen's Cabbins fitted out in the neatest manner & on the shortest Notice. Sea Chests, Sea-Bedding &c.' [Landauer Coll., MMA, NY; Banks Coll., BM] Took out Sun Insurance policies in 1779 for £400, utensils and stock accounting for £300; in 1781 for £500 on utensils, stock and workshop; and on 16 May 1787 for £400 on his house, goods, workshop and utensils. A further undated policy is recorded, with £305 on utensils and stock, £200 on warehouse and gallery, and £100 on workshop, utensils, and stock. [GL, Sun MS vol. 276, p. 535; vol. 296, p. 311; vol. 346, p. 22; vol. 386, p. 363] See John Burr.

Burr, Robert, Manchester Sq., London, u, cm and invalid chairmaker (1829–39). Trading at 25 Thayer St, 1829; Bentinck St, 1835–39; and no. 18 in 1837. With Charles Burr declared bankrupt, *Liverpool Mercury*, 28 October 1831. [D]

Burr, Thomas, City Repository, High St, Rochester, Kent, u and undertaker (1839). [D]

Burrage, John, Norwich, cm (1806). Son of Thomas Burrage, gardener; admitted freeman on 20 September 1806. [Norwich freemen reg.]

Burrage, John, Downham Mkt, Norfolk, u (1812). [Norwich poll bk]

Burrage, John Calvin, London, dyed chairmaker (1810). Recorded at 13 Lant St, Southwark, with manufactory in White Horse Stable Yd, 69 Blackman St. Took out Sun Insurance policies on 2 July 1810 for £100 on stock and utensils in his manufactory; and on 27 August 1810 for £300 of which £150 accounted for stock and utensils in his manufactory. [GL, Sun MS vol. 451, ref. 846362; vol. 449, ref. 848376]

Burrage, Thomas, Ipswich, Suffolk, cm (1790). [Poll bk]

Burranston, G. W., 4 Chapman's Pl., Gt Dover St, London, cm and u (1839). [D]

Burrard, John, 109 High Holborn, London, carver and gilder (1809–11). [D]

Burrell, Benjamin, Leeds, Yorks., cm, joiner and builder (1817–34). Trading at St George's St, 1817; Turner's Yd, 1822; and Fountain St, Upper Albion St from 1826. [D]

Burrell, Charles, London, u and auctioneer (1775–1802). Trading at 157 Fenchurch St in 1782; 56 Leadenhall St,

1790–97; and Throgmorton St, 1802. Son of William Burrell; app. to Richard Wright and Samuel Burton on 1 February 1775. Admitted freeman of the Upholders' Co. by servitude on 2 October 1782. Took app. named Joseph Pullen, 1788–95. Took out Sun Insurance policies on 11 February 1786 for £1,000 of which £500 accounted for utensils and stock; and on 25 September 1792 for £2,100 including £100 on utensils and goods in stock, £300 on those in trust, and £300 on his warehouse. Declared bankrupt, *Billinge's Liverpool Advertiser*, 6 June 1796 and 7 August 1797; and certificate declared on 20 March 1797. [D; GL, Upholders' Co. records and Livery lists; GL, Sun MS vol. 335, p. 499; vol. 388, p. 615]

Burrell, Jane, Herald Office, Pavement, York, u (1828). [D]

Burrell, Samuel, Cowgate, Newcastle, carver and gilder (1790). [D]

Burrell, W., Westgate, Chichester, Sussex, u (1824). Death of wife reported, *Brighton Gazette*, 11 March 1824.

Burrey, James, Claremont Hill, Shrewsbury, Salop, u (1837). [Shrewsbury burgess roll]

Burrey & White, Shrewsbury, Salop, cm and u (c. 1810–40). Early 19th-century mahogany wine table at Powis Castle, with base curtain rail, double decanter stand and bottle net, is signed 'BURREY & WHITE, SHREWSBURY'. [D; Nat. Trust guide to *Powis Castle*, p. 9]

Burrington, Carter, Exeter, Devon, u (1786). Took out a Sun Insurance policy on 11 August 1786 for £800 of which utensils, stock and goods in trust accounted for £350. [GL, Sun MS vol. 339, p. 246]

Burrington, Thomas, near Palace Gate, Exeter, Devon, u (1767–87). Admitted freeman in 1767. Notice in *Exeter Flying Post*, 26 April 1784 offering reward for the return of his lost son; and on 10 May 1787 reporting that his son had been found drowned in the Exe near Lime Kilns.

Burrough(s) (or Borough(s)), John, at 'Ye Looking Glass', Cornhill, London, cm and looking-glass maker (1662–c. 1690). An account dated 17 June 1662 survives, totalling £60 11s, made out to 'Mr. Clayton and Mr. Morris' for a 'large cabinett', £56 18s and other items. Clayton was knighted Sir Robert in 1671, and made Lord Mayor in 1679; John Morris (Alderman) was in partnership with Clayton as a 'moneye scrivener' at the Flying Horse in Cornhill. [Heal Coll., BM] Burrough was in partnership with William Farnb(o)rough, as cm to Charles II and William and Mary, 1677–c. 1690. Burrough and Farnbrough figure in the Lord Chamberlain's Royal Household accounts, Farnbrough much more frequently than his partner, who is not mentioned until 1677, when they both supplied for 'his Majesty's service at Windsor' two large glass tables and stands, one being flowered, — that is, decorated with floral marquetry — and the other carved and gilt, at a cost of £50 each. In about 1670 they supplied 'a glass & table of Wallnutt' costing £4 to Charles II's yacht, 'The Charlotte'. [*C. Life*, 8 April 1956, p. 1029; Wills, *Looking-Glasses*; Fastnedge, *English Furniture Styles, 1500–1830*, p. 296] Burrough and Farnbrough are named in the Hatfield House accounts in April 1688, providing a walnut escritoire costing £7, and a walnut table, £1 5s. [Hatfield House MS bills 325] Either Burrough or Thomas Strawbridge may have been responsible for a set of four William and Mary black japanned side chairs from Stoneleigh Abbey, Warks., with narrow, tall padded backs, arched and scrolled crestings pierced with foliage; scalloped seat rails on square columnar legs joined by arched and pierced front stretchers on fluted scrolled feet, the frames decorated with sprays of foliage and flowers in gilt with scarlet details, upholstered in contemporary polychrome leather. Either craftsman may also have made a second set of six William and Mary black japanned side chairs, also from

Stoneleigh, upholstered in crimson damask. The chairs may possibly be some of the '10 chear frames japaned with gold', upholstered in damask, now re-covered, referred to in a bill of Burroughs of 6 December 1709, totalling £209 3s 8d. As this date is rather late for the chairs, they are perhaps instead those referred to in a bill of Thomas Strawbridge, 30 August 1691, as '4 black stooles & 2 elbow chayes . . . black varnished', £7 10s, upholstered in crimson damask. [Christie's, 15–16 October 1981, lots 100–01]

Burrough, Thomas, Wet Dock, Rotherhithe, London, carver (1780). Took out a Sun Insurance policy in 1780 for £500 of which £25 accounted for utensils and stock. [GL, Sun MS vol. 287, p. 309]

Burroughes, Thomas, Nantwich, Cheshire, cm (1779). Married on 20 January 1779. [Chester RO, PR]

Burroughs, R., 7 St George's Pl., Walworth, London, cm (1826–27). [D]

Burroughs, Samuel Adolphus, Bristol, u (1812–40). Trading at 38 Wine St, 1812; no. 31, 1813–15; no. 38, 1816; and 37 Castle Green, 1817–40. [D]

Burroughs & Watts, 19 Soho Sq., London, billiard table maker (1839). Billiard table at Mersham-le-Hatch, Kent, recorded in the inventory of 1926. [D]

Burrow, John, Grange, Lancs., cm (1784). [Lancaster poll bk]

Burrow, John, Lancaster, cm (1829–30). Admitted freeman in 1829–30 when stated 'of Grange in Cartmel'. [Lancaster freemen rolls]

Burrow, Richard, Bolton-le-Moors, Lancs., cm (1784). [Lancaster poll bk]

Burrow, William, Otley, Yorks., joiner and/or cm (1834). [D]

Burrowclough, William, Nuneaton, Warks., u (1822). [D]

Burrow(e)s, Joseph, Chester, cm (1720–58). Son of Joseph Burrowes; app. to Edward Turnbrooke, joiner and cm, 13 January 1720–23 December 1726. Admitted freeman in 1727. Took app. named Thomas Woodworth, 1749–55. Former apps, John Edwards, admitted freeman in April 1744, and George Fothergill, July 1758. [Poll bk; Chester app. bks and freemen rolls]

Burrows, Francis, Coalpit Lane, Nottingham, cm (1835). [D]

Burrows, George & James, Tunbridge Wells, Kent, Tunbridge-ware manufacturers (1828–40). James Burrows was a partner of William Burrows in 1827 but in the following year this was dissolved and a fresh partnership with George Burrows established. They had their manufactory at Hanover Lodge, Hanover Rd, but also had retail outlets on the Parade (the Pantiles) and at Gibraltar Cottage on the Common. James Burrows is credited with being the first producer of inlaid turnery wares (stickware) in Tunbridge Wells. He was probably also the originator of the miniature parquetry wares, using in the main triangular units, which are a common feature of Tunbridge-wares from the late 1820s. The claim that he was the inventor of the popular tessellated mosaic wares which form the bulk of the industry's production from the mid 1830s is not however established. He was however one of the earliest makers to exploit the techniques, and a local guide of 1840 credits him with the introduction of designs featuring butterflies and birds. Although undoubtedly one of the largest manufactories of this period, none of the partner's wares have been identified with certainty. [D; Kent RO, tithe award; Clifford, *The Tunbridge Wells Guide*, 1837; Phippen, *Colbran's New Guide*, 1840] B. A.

Burrows, Henry, 38 Adlington St, Liverpool, gilder and japanner (1835). [D]

Burrows, Humphrey snr, Jordan House, London Rd, Tunbridge Wells, Kent, Tunbridge-ware manufacturer (c. 1800–33). A number of members of the Burrows family had been involved in the manufacture and sale of Tunbridge-ware in the 18th century and it is reputed that a James Burrow took over Jordan House *c*. 1740. Humphrey Burrows snr is first recorded in 1803 when he paid a fine of 10s to avoid militia service. Jordan House during the period that he was working there is featured in prints depicting the young Princess Victoria riding on the Common and these may well have been published by Burrows. The house prominently displayed a board inscribed 'Original Manufactory of Tunbridge Ware'. His son Humphrey jnr was bapt. on 4 January 1812 and in 1833 leased Jordan House from his father though he continued to live there and remained active in the business. A Tunbridge-ware block featuring Eridge Castle, Sussex, now in the Tunbridge Wells Museum, bears on the reverse a contemporary inscription stating 'This was the last work of Mr. Humphrey Burrows the Elder at Jordan Place, Tunbridge Wells in the year 1844'. [D; PR (bapt.)]

Burrows, Humphrey jnr, Jordan House, London Rd, Tunbridge Wells, Kent, Tunbridge-ware manufacturer (b. 1811/12–40). Son of and successor to Humphrey Burrows snr. Bapt. on 4 January 1812. Took over the business which he leased from his father from 1833. Carried out extensive alterations at Jordan House. None of his work has been identified. [D; *Sussex Agricultural Express*, 21 and 28 October 1837]

B. A.

Burrows, John, King St, Westminster, London, upholder (1784). [Poll bk]

Burrows, John, 18 High St, Kensington, London, cm (1808–09). [D]

Burrows, John, 12 Bradley St, Manchester, cm (1817). [D]

Burrows, John, Liverpool, cm (1816). Son of Ralph Burrows, tailor; admitted freeman on 8 June 1816. [Liverpool freemen reg.]

Burrows, Richard, Saffron Walden, Essex, cm and u (1777–87). Named in the accounts for Audley End, Essex, where he supplied Sir John Griffin Griffin with '12 Stained Chairs @ 4/10 for Steward's Room', in 1777. In 1783 he received 4s 6d for 'alltring a Mahog^y Clockcase for Mrs. Wheeler', and working on curtains and mattresses. He supplied three wainsccott desks, chest of drawers and bedside stand in 1786; totalling £11 8s 6d; and in 1787 '12 best dyed Chairs for Stewards Rooms @ 5/6' and '4 hart wood walnuttree Chairs', totalling £6 1s 4d. [Essex RO, D/DBy/A35/8; A41/6; A44/7; A445/8] On 22 May 1787 he insured his house, workshop, goods and farmhouse at Little Sampford, Essex, for £100 with the Sun Co. [GL, Sun MS vol. 345, p. 74] Notice in *Cambridge Chronicle and Journal*, 8 February 1806, that he had been appointed agent for the Union Fire Office of London.

Burrows, Samuel, 52 Barleymow Passage, Clothfair, London(?), chair and sofa manufacturer (1829). [D]

Burrows, Thomas, The Parade, Tunbridge Wells, Kent, turner and Tunbridge-ware manufacturer (1782–1808). Paid rentals for business premises in 1808. [Kent RO, U747/E15–9]

Burrows, Thomas, Havannah Buildings, Whitchurch, Salop, cm and chairmaker (1822–35). [D]

Burrows, William & James snr, The Parade, Tunbridge Wells, Kent, Tunbridge-ware manufacturers (1820–28). Took out a 21-year lease for property on the Parade; paid rental for shop in 1828; and recorded concerning the Speldhurst poor rate. [Kent RO, U785/T10; U749/E20; P344/11/1]

Burrup, Richard, Gloucester, u and auctioneer (1784–1802). Recorded in Upper West St, 1802. [D]

Burrup, Thomas, Westgate St, Gloucester, cm and chairmaker, u, auctioneer and appraiser (1820–23). [D]

Bursill, W., 12 Duke St, Manchester Sq., London, u (1826–27). [D]

Burt, —, address unrecorded, cm (1803). Subscribed to Sheraton's *Cabinet Dictionary*, 1803.

Burt, —, address unrecorded (1836). Lawrence of Lancaster bought a four-leaved blue and gold leather screen, costing £4 from Burt on 15 December 1836. [Cornwall RO, DD LR 114]

Burt, Charles William, 9 Strand, Torquay, Devon, cm and u (1838). [D] See Burts, —.

Burt, David, Hay Hill, Norwich, u and auctioneer (1805–10). Recorded as Burt & David in 1805, 1808 and 1810, but as David Burt, 1805–07. [D]

Burt, James, Exeter, Devon, cm (1828). Advertised sale of large amount of stock by auction on declining the cabinet branch of his business; and removal from Fore St Hill to St David's Hill where 'he will display his matchless clock and collection of rare old china and pictures'. [*Exeter Flying Post*, 24 July 1828]

Burt, John, Andover, Hants., cm and carpenter (1778). Took out a Sun Insurance policy in 1778 for £400 of which shop and stock accounted for £120. [GL, Sun MS vol. 266, p. 86]

Burt, John, Bristol, upholder (1799–1817). Trading at 35 Castle Green, 1799–1800; Lower Castle St, 1807–10; and 13 Norfolk St, 1813–17. [D]

Burt, Richard, 6 Moor St, Birmingham, cm and joiner (1770–77). [D]

Burt, William, Basinghall St, London, freeman plaisterer, by trade a cm (1763). Employed three non-freemen for three months in 1763. [GL, City Licence bks, vol. 3]

Burt, William, Norwich, upholder, auctioneer and appraiser (1784–1824). Addresses given at 1 Rampant Horse St in 1784; St Peter Mancroft, 1786 and 1802; St Stephen's, 1790–96; and 11 Brigg's Lane, 1801–02. Admitted freeman as an upholder, not apprenticed, on 24 February 1784. Former app., John Cox, upholder, admitted freeman on 21 March 1812. His own sons, John Toll Burt, Gent., and William Burt jnr, brewer, admitted freemen on 24 April 1821 and 16 June 1824 respectively. [D; poll bks; Norwich freemen reg.]

Burt, William Charles, Park St, Dawlish, Devon, cm, u and undertaker (1830). [D] Possibly the Burt, cm, of Dawlish whose name appears in the list of creditors of John Bulkeley, watchmaker, of Dawlish, *Exeter Flying Post*, 6 April 1815.

Burtenshaw, Richard, 18 Duke St, Brighton, Sussex, cm (1822–39). Children by his wife Sarah bapt.: Caroline on 15 November 1822; Henry, 18 March 1824; and Sarah on 21 May 1828. Occurs in directories in 1822 and 1839. [D; E. Sussex RO, PR(bapt.)]

Burtenshaw, Thomas, Marine Pl., Worthing, Sussex, cm and u (1839). [D]

Burt(t)on, —, address unrecorded, upholder (1685–86). Named in the accounts of C. Blunt, upholder, receiving £9 14s in 1685–86. [PRO, C114 1164, pt. 1]

Burton, —, Chandos St, London, cm (1761). Signed statement regarding working conditions, *Lloyds Evening Post and British Chronicle*, 30 September–2 October, 9–12 October and 15–16 October 1761. See Bunyan of Thrift St.

Burton, —, address unrecorded. Named in the Massingberd account book, February 1768, supplying 'green chairs', costing £2 2s. [Lincoln archives, MM 9/9]

Burton, —, Stamford, Lincs., carver and gilder (c. 1826–32). Trade card reads: 'CARVER, GILDER, Looking Glass and Picture Frame Maker, Bookbinder &c. Glasses polished and silvered. Frames made to Pattern. Old Frames Regilt. Pictures Cleaned and Repaired. Composition Ornaments in great variety. Accompt Books to Pattern. Black Japan. Varnishing and Bronzing. Printseller. Copper Plate Printer.' [V & A Print Dept] Probably either Edwin or Frederick Thomas Burton.

Burton, Christopher, Wormgate, Boston, Lincs., cm and joiner (1826). [D]

Burton, Charles, Enville St, Stourbridge, Worcs., chairmaker (1828–30). [D]

Burton, Edwin, St John's parish, Stamford, Lincs., carver and gilder (1830–32). [Poll bks] Possibly son of Frederick Thomas Burton.

Burton, Frederick Thomas, St Mary's St, Stamford, Lincs., carver and gilder (1819–35). [D] Possibly father of Edwin Burton.

Burton, George, 13 Edge St, Manchester, chairmaker (1825). [D]

Burton, George, 18 George Leigh St, Manchester, chairmaker (1824–25). [D]

Burton, George, John St, Meadow Lane, Leeds, Yorks., chairmaker (1830). [D]

Burton, George, 28 Burgess St, Sheffield, Yorks., chairmaker (1830). [D]

Burton, George, Fox's Yd and New Church St, Sheffield, Yorks., chairmaker (1833). [D]

Burton, Henry, London, cm (1808–14). Trading at 11 Blenheim St in 1808 and 67 Welbeck St, 1812–14. [D]

Burton, James snr, Lancaster, cm (1779–98). Admitted freeman, 1779–80; polled at Lancaster, 1784; and named in the Gillow records in 1798 working on a secretaire. [Lancaster freemen rolls; Westminster Ref. Lib., Gillow vol. 344/97, p. 1456]

Burton, James, Lancaster, cm (1794–96). Recorded as a Gillow app. in 1794, and admitted freeman, 1795–96. [Lancaster app. reg. and freemen rolls]

Burton, James, 77 Bunhill Row, London, carver, cm etc. (1826–37). [D]

Burton, James, 18 Charles St, Manchester Sq., London, cm, u and chairmaker (1835–39). [D]

Burton, James, Middleward, Tottenham, Middlx, cm (1839). [D]

Burton, John, Crooked Lane, London, u (1778). Declared bankrupt, *Leicester Journal*, 12 September 1778.

Burton, John, Lancaster, cm (1795–96). [Lancaster freemen rolls]

Burton, John, Townhead Cross, Sheffield, Yorks., cm and case maker (1814–18). Trading at no. 4 in 1818. [D]

Burton, John, London, bedstead maker (1816–29). Addresses given at 110 Wardour St, Soho, 1816–20, and 29 Holywell Row, Shoreditch, 1825–29. [D] See Joseph and Joshua Burton.

Burton, John, Liverpool, cm (1835–39). Trading at Lambeth Pl., Lambeth in 1835 and 2 Jubilee St, 1837–39. [D]

Burton, Joseph, Wolverhampton, Staffs., chairmaker (1816–38). Recorded at Salop St in 1816, no. 112 in 1818. [D]

Burton, Joseph, 29 Holywell Row, Chapel St, Curtain Rd, London, bedstead maker (1821). Took out a Sun Insurance policy on 10 May 1821 for £300 of which stock and utensils accounted for £180. [GL, Sun MS vol. 487, ref. 980336] See John and Joshua Burton.

Burton, Joshua, 29 Holywell Row, Shoreditch, London, bedstead maker (1820). [D]

Burton, Langley, Burton End, Melton Mowbray, Leics., cm (1840). [D]

Burton, M. & J., 55 Skinner St, London(?), u (1835). [D] John and Ann Burton, furniture brokers, at this address in 1839.

Burton, Martin Charles, 18 Brownlow St, Holborn, London, cm and u (1820–39). Took out Sun Insurance policies on 12 June 1820 for £600, £550 on his house and £50 on shed behind; and on 14 May 1821 for the same. Recorded as M. C. & J. Burton, 1826–27 and 1839. [D; GL, Sun MS vol. 486, ref. 968472; vol. 484, ref. 980559]

Burton, Mevil, Leicester, cm and joiner (1764). App. to John Shipley, cm, in 1764. [Leicester freemen rolls]

Burton, Robert, Nottingham, joiner and cm (1826). Son of John Burton, victualler, of Wollerton; app. in 1826. [Nottingham app. reg.]

Burton, Sam., parish of All Saints, Cambridge, joiner (1665–75). Recorded in the account bks of Trinity College, 1665–68, mending forms, seats, table and desk; and in 1667 supplying 'a new table for the Upper Buttry', 15s. Carried out joinery work at St John's College, 1668–75, and in 1672 received 5s 6d for '2 Boxes for ye use of ye Vestry'.

Burton, Samuel snr, London, u, cm, auctioneer and undertaker (1765–d. 1801). Addresses given in St Mary Axe, near Leadenhall St, *c*.1765; 13 Houndsditch, 1768–83; no. 15, 1778–86; no. 11, 1782–83; and no. 8, 1782–1801. Recorded as Samuel Burton & Son, 1799; and Burton & Son, 1800–01. Trade card, *c*.1765, has inscription embellished with whimsical columns, Rococo scrolls, Chippendale-style Rococo chair and Chinoiserie table. Card states that he 'Makes & Sells all Sorts of Cabinet & Upholstery Goods in the genteelest & newest fashion in Silk and Worsted Damask Furniture, Mohair, Morine, and Cotton ditto, with all Sorts of Cheque, Harrateen, &c., Feather Beds, hair & flock Matrasses, Counterpanes, Cotton Quilts, Blankets, &c. Chests of Drawers, Desk & Book Cases, Wardrobes, Dining Tables, Card dittos and Commode Dressing Tables, Chairs, Looking Glasses &c. Turkey, Wilton & other Carpets for Home use or Exportation. Variety of Paper Hangings.' [Heal; *C. Life*, 11 February 1960, p. 275] App. to Thomas Ridgway, 'skynner'; admitted freeman of the Upholders' Co., 7 February 1765. Recorded as Senior Warden of the Upholders' Co. in 1800. Took apps named James Barber, 1766–76; William Chaplin, 1768–76; Charles Burrell, 1775–82; John Fletcher, 1776–84; Edward Rickett, 1783–89; and John Anderson, 1793–1803. This last may have been app. to Samuel Burton jnr, since Samuel snr died in 1801. [D; GL, Upholders' Co. records and Livery lists] See William Burton of Houndsditch.

Burton, Samuel jnr, 133 Leadenhall St, London, upholder (1796). Son of Samuel Burton, upholder, and brother of William. Admitted freeman of the Upholders' Co. by patrimony on 5 October 1796. [GL, Upholders' Co. records]

Burton, T., Lancaster. Named in the Gillow records in 1789 working at a commode. [Westminster Ref. Lib., Gillow vol. 344/95, p. 513]

Burton, Thomas, Melton Mowbray, Leics., cm (1781–1822). Advertised in *Leicester Journal*, 1781, his stock of mirrors, waiters and trays; and on 30 October 1789 and 7 October 1791 for journeyman cm. Took app named Zachary Wragg. [D]

Burton, Thomas, Burton End, Melton Mowbray, Leics., cm (1828–35). [D]

Burton, Thomas, Whitehaven, Cumb., u (1791–d. 1821). Trading in Lowther St in 1811. Advertised concerning sale of stock and let of premises after death, *Liverpool Mercury*, 13 April 1821: 'The Stock consists of an extensive Assortment of the best & most fashionable Paper Hangings, Carpetings, Moreens, Oil Cloths, & every other Article belonging to the Trade of an Upholsterer . . . the above concern has been established & successfully carried on for upwards of 30 years, & is the only one of the kind in Whitehaven or its vicinity . . '. [D]

Burton, Thomas, Westgate, Wakefield, Yorks., cm (1816–18). [D]

Burton, Thomas, Church St, Sheffield, Yorks., cm (1817). [D]

Burton, Thomas, 5 Galway St, City Rd, London, cm and u (1827–39). [D]

B(l)urton, Venables, Market Pl., Uttoxeter, Staffs., clock case maker, u and cm (1828–35). [D]

Burton, William, 8 Houndsditch, London, upholder (1799). Son of Samuel Burton, upholder, and brother of Samuel. Admitted freeman of the Upholders' Co. by patrimony on 7 August 1799. [GL, Upholders' Co. records]

Burton, William, London, u and chair manufacturer (1803–39). Addresses given at 62 Cheapside, 1803; 62 Cornhill, 1808–11; 203 Oxford St, St Giles, 1807–23; and 28 King St, Soho, 1839. Took out a Sun Insurance policy on 13 April 1807 for £800 of which utensils and stock accounted for £400. Trading as Burton & Vennor, u, at 62 Cornhill in 1808. [D; GL, Sun MS vol. 440, ref. 802413]

Burton, William, Chester, cm (1818). Admitted freeman on 13 June 1818. [Chester freemen rolls]

Burton, William, Manchester, chairmaker (1825–28). Addresses given at 27 Oldham Rd, 1825 and Edge St, 1828. [D]

Burton, William, Staithes, Yorks., joiner and cm (1834). [D]

Burton, William, Scarborough, Yorks., cm (1828–40). Trading at Low Conduit St, 1828–29; Quay St, 1834; and Sand Side, 1840. [D]

Burton, Wilson, 12 Downe St, Liverpool, chairmaker (1839). [D]

Burton & Co., 18 Chiswell St, London, cm (1825). [D]

Burton & Watson, Liverpool, chairmakers (1827–39). Trading at 7 Parr St in 1827 and London Rd, 1835–39. [D]

Burts, —, Torquay, Devon, cm and u (c. 1820). Regency rosewood marble-top table with anthemion pillars and concave base recorded bearing label of 'BURTS, Cabinet Maker & Upholstery Manufacturer TORQUAY'. Possibly Charles William Burt.

Bury, George, address unrecorded, inlayer (1713). Described his craft as that of inlayer rather than cm when he took app. in 1713. [PRO, IR 1/2; Burlington, June 1980, p. 415]

Busbridger, Richard, 8 Crown St, Finsbury Ct, London, broker and cm (1804). Took out a Sun Insurance policy on 9 May 1804 for £600, £300 on his house and workshop, £200 on stock, utensils and household goods; and £50 on stock in open yard and sheds. [GL, Sun MS vol. 430, ref. 762360]

Busby, A., address unrecorded. Set of six Regency mahogany rail back chairs with wide satinwood back panels, reeded frames and drop-in seats on sabre legs recorded, stamped 'A. BUSBY'. [Dreweatt, Watson & Barton auction, 26 January 1983]

Busby, Joseph, address unrecorded, u (1721). Worked at Streatlam, near Darlington, Co. Durham, for Lady Elizabeth Bowes, receiving £20 on 30 November 1821 for items supplied for a funeral; on 22 December 1721, £8 17s 'for upholstering at Streatlam before death'; and on 23 January 1721–22, £13. [Durham RO, Strathmore MS D/St/Box 352/2, Lady Bowes's cash bk]

Busendon, James, Maidstone, Kent, turner and chairmaker (1794). [D]

Bus(s)field, John, York, cm (1756–74). Trading in Petergate, 1756 and Swinegate, 1774. Listed as 'Master' cm in the York app. reg. for John Lofthouse, carpenter, joiner and cm, app. for seven years in 1756. Busfield was succeeded by John Sanderson. [Poll bk]

Busfield, Josh. (or Joseph), Union St, Southwark, London, chair and sofa manufacturer (1827–39). Trading at no. 64, 1827–39; and no. 139, 1837–39. [D]

Bush, Henry, Roach's Ct, Fisher Lane, Norwich, cm (1836). [D]

Bush, John, Bristol, u (1774–92). Polled at Bristol 'of Bath' in 1774, and of the parish of St James, Bristol in 1784. Trading in Beauford's Ct, Bristol, 1792. [D; poll bks]

Bush, Richard, Saffron Walden, Essex, turner (1794). Worked for Lord Howard de Walden of Audley End, Essex, receiving 8s 10d in 1794 for turning chair posts, and pillars and tops for tables. [Essex RO, D/DBy/A52/11]

Bush, Robert, Norwich and London, u (1828–30). Son of John Bush, cordwainer; admitted freeman on 22 October 1828. Polled at Norwich 'of London' in 1830. [Norwich freemen rolls and poll bk]

Bush, Thomas, 245 Whitechapel, London, u and cm (1784–93). [D]

Bush, Thomas, Sheppard's Pl., City Rd, London, u (1809–11). [D]

Bush, William, opposite St Mary's, High St, Oxford, upholder (1765–66). Advertised in Jackson's Oxford Journal, 13 April 1765 opening of his shop; and on 8 May 1766 that his shop was to let.

Bush, William, 31 Theobald's Rd, Red Lion Sq., London, cm and u (1815–19). [D]

Bush & Cheppett (or Chippett), St James's Churchyard, Bristol, carvers and gilders (1812–14). Trading at no. 3 in 1812. [D]

Bushell, William, Worcester, cm and u (1799). App. to John Timmings, cm and u; admitted freeman on 9 September 1799. [Worcester freemen rolls]

Bushell, William, 23 Church St, Manchester, cm and hat manufacturer (1808). [D]

Bushnell, John, 1 Bishopsgate St Within, London, cm and upholder (1758–1802). Recorded in Wallingford, Berks., 1794–1802. Son of Benjamin Bushnell, farmer of Blewbury, Berks.; app. to Stephen Abbott, wheelwright, on 28 February 1758. Admitted freeman of the Upholders' Co. on 2 May 1765, and master in 1800. Trading as Bushnell & Savill, 1792–94. [D; GL, Upholders' Co. records and Livery lists]

Buskin (or Bushen), S., W. & W. S., London, looking-glass manufactory (1796–1811). Trading at 19 Wellclose Sq., 1796–1801; and 14 Church St, Spitalfields, 1804–11. [D]

Buskin, William, London, freeman draper, by trade a carver and gilder; looking-glass manufacturer (1756–90). Addresses given at Aldermanbury, 1756–62; in partnership with Michael Dunn(s) at 63 Snowhill, 1774–77; and alone at Wellclose Sq. by 1790. In 1756 Buskin employed two non-freemen for three months; in 1762, one only; and in 1776, twelve for six months. Advertised end of partnership with Dunn, London Gazette, 28 March 1780. [D; GL, City Licence bks, vols 1, 3 and 9; Wills, Looking-Glasses] Presumably of S., W. & W. S. Buskin.

Buskins, —, Moorfields, London, chairmaker (1792). Mentioned in a Sun Insurance policy of 8 August 1792 taken out by John Emmett jnr. [GL, Sun MS vol. 387, p. 442]

Busley, Henry, address unrecorded, cm (1803). Subscribed to Sheraton's Cabinet Dictionary, 1803.

Bussell, Henry, 89 Golden Lane, London, cm, tobacconist, snuffmaker and chandler (1787). Insured his house, books, stock and goods for £500 on 1 January 1787 with the Sun Co. [GL, Sun MS vol. 340, p. 481]

Bussel(l), Joseph, Plymouth, Devon, cm and u (1783–99). Advertised in Exeter Flying Post, 7 August 1783, sale of mahogany in plank, board or log, and requesting eight good cm. Death of wife reported, 6 August 1784. Sale of house, furniture and stock in trade on his retirement announced, 20 November 1788, successor to be John Wills. Stock consisted of 'Beds with mahogany fluted pillars and elegant cornices. Wardrobe chest of drawers, secretaries, Prince's-metal nailed and other chairs, mahogany childrens' chairs, circular-end dining tables, drawing room set of twelve chairs and sofa, wash-hand stands, pier and swing glasses'. Despite retirement, either this tradesman or one of the same name is recorded dissolving his partnership with George James of Plymouth, Exeter Flying Post, 21 March 1799; and J. Bussel occurs in directories in 1798.

Bussey, Samuel, Knaresborough, Yorks., joiner and cm (1834). [D]

Bussey, William, 1 Castle St, Sheffield, Yorks., cm and u (1828–29). [D]

Bust, James, Coleman St, London, stuffman and upholder (1721–37). Admitted freeman of the Upholders' Co. by redemption on 8 February 1721–22. Took son, Thomas Bust, as app., 1723–37, when admitted freeman. [GL, Upholders' Co. records]

Bust, Thomas, London, upholder (1723–37). App. to his father, James Bust, upholder, of London, on 3 March 1723; admitted freeman of the Upholders' Co. by servitude on 6 July 1737. [GL, Upholders' Co. records]

Buswell & Scarott, Digbeth, Birmingham, cm and chairmakers (1818). [D]

Butcher, George, Framlingham, Suffolk, cm (1839). [D]

Butcher, Henry, Stamford, Lincs., u (1724). Admitted freeman by birthright between 1663–1721. Insured goods and merchandise in his house for £500 on 29 September 1724. [Stamford freemen rolls; GL, Sun MS vol. 19, ref. 33217] Possibly son of John Butcher, u.

Butcher, James, 81 Long Lane, Smithfield, London, cm and u (1839). [D]

Butcher, John, Stamford, Lincs., u. Admitted freeman by birthright between 1663–1721. [Stamford freemen rolls] Possibly father of Henry Butcher, u.

Butcher, John, Nottingham, u and cm (1786). Took William Stephenson as app. in 1786. Took out an undated Sun Insurance policy for £200 on utensils and stock. [Nottingham app. reg.; GL, Sun MS vol. 336, p. 276]

Butcher, Michael, 190 Long Lane, Southwark, London, cm and u (1839). [D]

Butcher, Philip, 21 Winchester St, Pentonville, London, gilder (1808). [D]

Butcher, Philip, Silver St, Trowbridge, Wilts., carver and gilder (1822). [D]

Butcher, Thomas, Epsom, Surrey, carpenter, builder, auctioneer and cm (1822). [D]

Buth, W., Theobald's Row, Bedford Row, London, cm, u and paper hanger (1815). [D] Possibly William Bush.

But(t)ler, —, Preston, Lancs., — see Walker (Salthouse) & Butler.

Butler, Abraham, Bolton-le-Moors, Lancs., cabinet and machine maker (1793). [D]

Butler, Benjamin, Bolton-le-Moors, Lancs., cabinet and machine maker (1793). [D]

Butler, Edmund, north side of Broad St, parish of St James West, London, gilder (1710). Insured his house for £250 on 13 April 1710 with the Hand in Hand Co. [GL, Hand in Hand MS vol. 7, ref. 4123]

Butler, Edwin, Tipton, Dudley, Worcs., cm and u (1838–39). [D]

Butler, G., 56 George St, Blackfriars Rd, London, cabinet stringing maker (1809). [D] See John Butler at this address.

Butler, Hester, 59 Lewins Mead, Bristol, u (1775). [D]

Butler, J., Deptford Bridge, London. A folio trolly in the Codrington Lib., Oxford, has a brass tablet engraved with this maker's name.

Butler, Jacob, Cambridge(?) (1758–60). Named in the St John's College lists supplying chairs for the lodge, costing £2 8s.

Butler, James, 4–5 New St Hill, London, chairmaker (1775). On 9 January 1775 John Dawes of Canonbury House, Islington, insured the above houses in tenure of Butler and Thomas Routledge, glazier, for £900 each. Jonathan Farlam and Francis Richardson were also associated with this policy. [GL, Sun MS vol. 236, ref. 348496]

Butler, James, 4 Grafton St, Soho, London, cm (1817). [D]

Butler, James, Back Bow St, Leeds, Yorks., cm (1837–80s). [D]

Butler, Jeremiah, 24 or 29 Bowling Green Lane, Clerkenwell, London, chair carver (1808–11). [D]

Butler, John, Preston, Lancs., joiner and cm (1742–62). Admitted to the Guild of Burgesses in 1742 on payment of £4 4s, and present at the Preston Guild in 1762. [Preston Guild record of burgesses]

Butler, John, Birmingham, manufacturer of miniature frames, shaving cases, ladies work boxes etc. (1812–18). Trading at Gt Hampton St in 1812, and Regent Pl., Harper's Hill, 1818. [D]

Butler, John, George St, Blackfriars Rd, London, cabinet stringing maker, cabinet inlayer (1813–28). Recorded at no. 56, 1814–15, and no. 41, 1813–28. [D] See G. Butler.

Butler, John, 16 Allerton St, Hoxton, London, cabinet inlayer (1839). [D]

Butler, Jos., Tattenhall, Cheshire, cm (1814). Signed and dated in marquetry the door of an oak housekeeper's cupboard with marquetry inlay, now at the Grosvenor Museum, Chester.

Butler, Martin, 4 Junction Dock St, Hull, Yorks., cm and furniture broker (1840). [D]

Butler, Matthias, Micklegate, York, cm (1758–d. 1763). Death and sale of stock announced, November 1763. [Poll bk]

Butler, Nicholas, High Holborn, London, u (1759). Declared bankrupt, *Gents Mag.*, June 1759.

Butler, Robert, St Martin-in-the-Fields, London, carver (1771). Took app. named William Thompson in 1771. [Westminster Ref. Lib., PR, MS F4309, p. 9]

Butler, Robert, Lancaster. Named in the Gillow records between 1814–25, working on a bookcase in 1814, and a bedstead in 1819. [Westminster Ref. Lib., Gillow vol. 344/99, p. 1967; 100, p. 3015]

Butler, Robert, Derby Rd, Nottingham, joiner and cm (1832–35). [D]

Butler, Robert, Chester, cm, u, dealer and chapman (1840). Declared bankrupt, *Chester Chronicle, Cheshire and North Wales Advertiser*, 14 August 1840.

Butler, Thomas, formerly of Clothfair, West Smithfield, late of Wardour St, Soho, London, chair carver (1761). Discharge from Debtors' Prison announced, *London Gazette*, 20 June 1761.

Butler, Thomas, Stewerton, Berks., cm, upholder and shopkeeper (1778). Took out a Sun Insurance policy in 1778 for £300 of which utensils and stock accounted for £240. [GL, Sun MS vol. 267, p. 108]

Butler, Thomas, Staines, Middlx., cm (1798). [D]

Butler, Thomas, London, cm and u (1787–1814). Initially took employment as an attorney's clerk and was a part-time nonconformist minister at a chapel in Hitchin, Herts. Prior to 1787 he was in partnership with a person named Johnson trading as upholders and cm at 146 Strand. His partner was probably Edward Johnson, upholder and cm who in 1784 took out insurance cover of £600 on 14 Catherine St, Strand. The partnership had been dissolved by mutual consent by March 1787 and the stock was sold on 28 March 1787 by Christie. The auction catalogue bears a note that 'THE BUSINESS will be carried on for the future by Mr. BUTLER in Catherine Street'. Seven days before the sale Butler had taken out insurance cover of £1,100 on the Catherine St property. Initially he may have traded only from 14 Catherine St but the numbers 13 and 14 are frequently listed as addresses. By January 1800 he was claiming the patronage of the King and Queen, the Prince of Wales and the Duke of York but he was not one of the regular suppliers to the Royal Household. He did however supply the Prince of Wales in November 1802 with 'Two Elegant mahogany Library Writing Tables of curious fine wood richly inlaid with different curious woods' for which £39 10s was charged.

Late in 1800 Butler decided to dispose of this business and two of his employees, Thomas Morgan and Joseph Sanders expressed an interest in purchasing it. To their great annoyance Butler sold it to Thomas Oxenham of Oxford St, and Morgan and Sanders promptly set up business close at hand at 16 and 17 Catherine St in bitter opposition. Oxenham soon tired of the Catherine St premises and had moved the manufacture of furniture to his Oxford St address by April 1802. Thomas Butler therefore once more set up production at his old address and in 1803 was included in the list of master cabinet makers in Sheraton's *Cabinet Dictionary*. In 1804 he had a timber yard at Pegasus Yd, Savoy. By this date the business that Butler was conducting in Catherine St was of substantial size and utilised not only 13 and 14 but the properties behind at 4 to 7 Helmet Ct. Insurance cover was for £3,500 of which £2,000 was for utensils and stock. In 1810 Butler retired for the second time selling the business to Edward Argles who had previously traded as a cm and u in Maidstone, Kent. Argles was however declared bankrupt in 1813 and Butler once more commenced business in Catherine St late in that year. He offered existing stock at trade prices and especially mentioned 'a very superb and truly elegant Temple Book Case suitable for one of the first Libraries, considered worth £250 will be sold under its value'. He may have been merely disposing of Argles's stock for in September 1814 he had ceased business finally and by April 1816 Morgan & Sanders were able to advertise that they had taken 'a considerable part of Mr. Butler's late Ware-rooms'.

Butler's speciality was the production of patent furniture. He took out no patents of his own but exploited that granted to Thomas Waldron of 11 Catherine St on 4 June 1785 (patent 1483). This concerned the construction of bedsteads without the use of screws or nuts and bolts, to facilitate easy assembly. Butler marked such patent furniture with brass plates in common with other makers in this line. These have been found on a number of extending dining tables, on bedsteads and chairs that converted into bedsteads. He claimed that his bedsteads were 'admired for their absolute Prevention of Vermin' and stated that his beds and bedding were 'calculated for the East and West Indies. Ships Cabins furnished. Articles particularly adapted for travelling and for exportation'. [D; BM, Banks 28–26, 28–27; GL, Sun MS vol. 342, ref. 528300; vol. 419, ref. 718867; vol. 431, ref. 769048; vol. 445, ref. 823984; vol. 448, ref. 832048; Windsor Royal Archives, RA 25119, RA 88919; *Conn.*, November 1974, pp. 180–91; Sotheby's, 20 October 1972, lot 109, 18 May 1973, lot 105, 4 April 1975, lot 89; Christie's NY, 17 October 1981, lot 107] B. A.

Butler, Thomas, Little Pancras St, Tottenham Ct Rd, London, carver in wood, cm etc. (1839). [D]

Butler, W., Warwick St, Leamington, Warks., carver and gilder (1837). [D]

Butler, William, address unrecorded, upholder (1703). Admitted freeman of the Upholders' Co. on 3 November 1703. [GL, Upholders' Co. records]

Butler, William, address unrecorded, cm (1754–60). Admitted freeman of the Joiners' Co. by redemption on 2 April 1754, and named as Liveryman on 19 September 1760. Subscribed to Chippendale's *Director*, 1754. [GL, Joiners' Co. records]

Butler, William, 27 Coppin Row, Clerkenwell, London, cm, chairmaker and carver (1775). Took out a Sun Insurance policy in 1775 for £600 of which utensils, stock and goods accounted for £320. [GL, Sun MS vol. 237, p. 277]

Butler, William, Cambridge, carver and gilder (1824–d. 1837).

Trading in Rose Yd, 1824. Died in the parish of St Giles, 1837. [D; Cambridge Univ. Lib., Will WR20:263]

Butler Brothers, Birmingham, coffin furniture, picture frame and looking-glass frame makers (1800–06). Trading at 1 Mary Ann St, 1800–03, and Lionel St in 1806. [D]

Butler & Co., address unrecorded, upholders (1802). Named in the accounts of 2nd Lord Braybrooke of Audley End, Essex receiving £21 in July, and £12 16s in October 1802. [Essex RO, D/DBy/A357]

Butler & Heppel, 14 Catherine St, Strand, London, upholders etc. (1790). [D] See Thomas Butler at this address.

Butlin, Thomas, Melton Mowbray, Leics., turner(?) (1840). [D]

Butson, H., 3 Blenheim St, London, cm (1809–11). [D]

Butt, —, address unrecorded (1838). Supplied 'new furniture' for Stafford House, London, costing £322, in 1838. [Staffs. RO, D/593/R/1/26/8]

Butt, Alexander, 97 Leather Lane, Holborn, London, looking-glass manufacturer (1839). [D]

Butt, John, High St, Tewkesbury, Glos., chairmaker (1814–15). [PR(bapt.)]

Butt, John, 7 New St, Cheltenham, Glos., cm and u (1820). [D]

Butt, Robert, Bridgwater, Som., cm (1784). Insured his house for £200 in 1784 with the Sun Co. [GL, Sun MS vol. 321, p. 390]

Butt, Samuel, 'at the Greyhound and Hat, on the East End of St. Paul's Church-Yard, near Cheapside corner, Makes and Sells all sorts of the Best Cabinet and Looking Glass Work at the cheapest Rates' (c. 1700–10). So reads label in drawer of walnut tallboy of two tiers, four drawers in the lower section and six above, on later bun feet (Fig. 3). [Phillips of Hitchen (Antiques) Ltd, 1980, Exhib. of beds and bedroom furniture, 1700–1830; V & A archives refs N6083, F3004; C. *Life*, 3 December 1981, supplement, p. 74; *Conn.*, May 1981, p. 74; *Burlington*, June 1980; *Antique Collecting*, May 1980, p. 27, fig. 23]

Butten, John, St Margaret's Bank, Rochester, Kent, cm (1803–26). [D] Probably John Batten.

Butter, John, parish of St John Sepulchre, Norwich, chairmaker (1818). [Poll bk]

Butter, William, 204 Whitecross St, London, furnishing ironmonger and brazier (1801). [D]

Butte(r)feild, James, address unrecorded, upholder (1718–25). Son of John Buttefield, mercer, of Buckingham; app. to Daniel Cooper on 3 December 1718, and admitted freeman of the Upholders' Co. by servitude on 8 December 1725. Took app. named James Short 1738–46. [GL, Upholders' Co. records] Possibly:

Butterfield, James, at 'The Black Lyon', Compton St, parish of St Ann, Westminster, London, upholder (1727). Took out a Sun Insurance policy on 31 May 1727 for £300 on stock in trade in his house. [GL, Sun MS vol. 24] Possibly:

Butterfield, James, Princes St, London, u (1749). [Poll bk]

Butterfield, John, Dawson Weir, Todmorden, Yorks., cm (1822–30). [D]

Butterfield, Richard, address unrecorded, upholder (1752–60). Son of Edward Butterfield, Gent. of Hemel Hempstead, Herts.; app. to Robert Phipps on 21 August 1752, and admitted freeman of the Upholders' Co. by servitude on 7 August 1760. [GL, Upholders' Co. records]

Butterfield, Richard, Southampton, Hants., upholder (1774). [Poll bk]

Butterfield, Thomas, address unrecorded, upholder (1759). Son of James Butterfield, u; admitted freeman of the Upholders' Co. by patrimony on 19 January 1759. [GL, Upholders' Co. records]

Butters, John, Walkergate, Louth, Lincs., chairmaker (1822). [D]

Butterworth, James, Bury, Lancs., cm (1793). [D]

Butterworth, John, Back 48 Thomas St, Liverpool, upholder (1796). [D]

Butterworth, John, 10 Fletcher St, Manchester, chairmaker (1836). [D]

Butterworth, Joseph, 7 Northumberland St, Marylebone, London, upholder (1808). [D]

Butterworth, Samuel, Bury, Lancs., cm (1793). [D]

Buttery, John, address unrecorded. In October 1687 he received £2 9s 2d from the 5th Earl of Bedford, for expenses of a two-day journey, probably from Woburn, to London and back during the summer. This sum included 3s 8d for 'four blag [sic] bottom chairs for Mrs Rachalls [sic] chamber', and 'two bells and a line', 2s. [Bedford Office, London]

Buttery, Robert, 1 Union Row, Willmot St, Bethnal Green, London, chairmaker (1810). Took out a Sun Insurance policy on 1 January 1810 on 3 houses in Fleet St, Bethnal Green, in tenure, for £400. [GL, Sun MS vol. 447, ref. 839238]

Buttifant, John, parish of St Paul, Norwich, cm (1820–30). App. to B. P. Fitter, cm; admitted freeman on 16 March 1820. [Poll bk]

Buttifant, Jonathan, Lakenham, Norwich, chairmaker (1830). [Poll bk]

Buttifant, Thomas, Princes St, Norwich, cm and u (1822–30). Admitted freeman, not by servitude, on 24 February 1825, although trading in 1822. [D; poll bk; Norwich freemen reg.]

Buttler, —, address unrecorded. Named in the Holkham Hall, Norfolk accounts in 1755 silvering and framing glasses for £3 9s, and supplying four mahogany dressing tables with drawers, £2 16s. [V & A archives]

Buttler, C. H., 20 Little Portland St, Marylebone, London, cm (1820). [D]

Button, Jane, Liverpool, u (1835–39). Addresses given at 78 Gt Howard St in 1835; no. 49 in 1837; and no. 123 in 1839. [D]

Button, John, London, glass grinder and cm (1761–1802). Addresses given at 33 Crooked Lane, 1769–81; and River-head, Kent, 1786–1802. Son of John Button, grazier, of Peasmarsh, Sussex; admitted freeman of the Upholders' Co. by redemption on 6 August 1761. Took son, William Button, as app., 1768–93; and John Joad, 1771–79/80. Declared bankrupt, *Gents Mag.*, September 1778. [D; GL, Upholders' Co. records and Livery lists]

Button, John, Cornhill, London, cm (1765–66). Named as Fellow of the Society of Arts and Manufactures.

Button, Lago & Co., 15 Brown St, Bryanston Sq., Edgware Rd, London, cm and u (1829–39). [D]

Button, William, Paternoster Row, London, upholder (1768–1802). Trading at no. 24 in 1793. App. to his father, John Button, upholder, in 1768. Admitted freeman of the Upholders' Co. by servitude on 6 March 1793. [GL, Upholders' Co. records and Livery lists]

Button, William, Norwood, Beverley, Yorks., cm (1791). [D]

Button (or Budden), William, Gundry's Lane, Bridport, Dorset, cm (1830–40). [D]

Buxton, Charles, Watton, Norfolk, u (1839). [D]

Buxton, German, address unrecorded, upholder (1699–1700). Admitted freeman of the Upholders' Co. on 7 February 1699–1700. [GL, Upholders' Co. records]

Buxton, Thomas, St Matthew's, Ipswich, Suffolk, chairmaker (1751–52). Named in the calendar of marriage licence bonds on 27 April 1751–52. [Suffolk RO, FAA 50/2/89–93]

Buy, George, St Mary-le-Strand, London, inlayer (1712–13). Took app. on 7 January 1712–13. [PRO, app. reg.]

Buzzacott, A., North Gdns, Brighton, Sussex, cm and u (1839). [D]

Buzzard, John, 109 High Holborn, London, carver, gilder, paper hanger and looking-glass dealer (1801–25). Recorded at no. 100 in 1820, and at 109 as Buzzard & Son, 1823–25. Took out Sun Insurance policies on 7 April 1801 for £1,900, utensils and stock accounting for £900; on 4 September 1823 for £2,000; and on 19 May 1824 for £2,000, £1,000 accounting for stock, utensils and workshop. [D; GL, Sun MS vol. 419, ref. 715894; vol. 497, ref. 1008057; vol. 496, ref. 1017175]

Bye, George, 25 Queen's Row, Pimlico, London, u (1835–39). [D]

Bye, Jacob, 25 Queen's Row, Pimlico, London, cm and u (1822–28). [D]

Byer, —, address unrecorded (1801). Name and date inscribed in ink on set of ten Sheraton-style dining chairs. [V & A archives]

Byer, Thomas, Cheltenham Pl., North Lane, Brighton, Sussex, cm, u and French polisher (1832). [D]

Byfeld, H., address unrecorded, carver and gilder (1823–24). Named in the Royal Household accounts on 4 March 1823 receiving £155 16s. [Windsor, RA 35579] Possibly misreading of 'T' for Thomas Byfield.

Byfield, James, London, carver and gilder (1777–1829). Recorded at the corner of Holland St in Wardour St, 1777; in partnership with Thomas Byfield at 16 Wardour St, Soho, in 1793; and at 37–39 Old Compton St, Soho, 1808–29, where Thomas was trading, 1809–25. Took out a Sun Insurance policy in 1777 for £400, utensils and stock accounting for £100. [D; GL, Sun MS vol. 254, p. 249]

Byfield, James, 9 Richmond Buildings, Soho, London, carver and gilder (1837). [D]

Byfield, Thomas, Soho, London, carver and gilder (1793–1827). Recorded in partnership with James Byfield at 16 Wardour St in 1793 and alone at 39 Old Compton St, 1809–25. As carver and gilder to His Majesty, recorded in the Royal Household accounts between 1808–27 supplying frames for portraits of Their Majesties to ambassadors to foreign courts, e.g. the Duke of Wellington, Ambassador to the Court of Paris; and carving and gilding several sets of state canopies, chairs, stools and footstools. In 1808 he provided a set 'for Lord Strangeforth's Embassy', and pier and chimney glasses for the Queen's nursery. [PRO, LC 11/10, 18, 21, 24, 41–56] See H. Byfeld.

Byles, Henry, Henley, Oxon., draper, mercer and u (1763–71). Advertised sales in *Jackson's Oxford Journal*.

Byles, John, Henley, Oxon., cm, u or furniture dealer (1753–80). Mentioned in *Jackson's Oxford Journal*.

Byng, Finnis D., Dover, Kent, cm (1826). [Poll bk]

Byng, Henry, Union Terr., Commercial Rd, London, cm (1835). [D]

Byng, Lawrence, address unrecorded, upholder (1712). Admitted freeman of the Upholders' Co. on 24 October 1712. [GL, Upholders' Co. records]

Byrne, C., Buckingham Pl., Fitzroy Sq., London, u and cm (1835). [D]

Byrne, Edmund, 40 Queen St, Southwark, London, looking-glass manufacturer (1809–11). [D]

Byrne, James, 6 Bowling Green Lane, Clerkenwell, London, cm (1808). [D]

Byrne, John, London, One of Chippendale's employees who receipted a small account on behalf of the firm in 1761. [Gilbert, *Chippendale*, p. 25]

Byrne, John, Carnaby Mkt, London, cm (1774). [Poll bk]

Byrom, Patrick, 43 Leeds St, Liverpool, u and shopkeeper (1805). [D]

Byron, T., Liverpool, cm (1834). Marriage on 17 April 1834 to Miss E. Stringfellow, eldest daughter of Mr J. Stringfellow of Preston Brook, reported, *Liverpool Mercury*, 25 April 1834.

Bytham, Henry, Margate, Kent, cm (1831). [Sandwich poll bk]

Byewater, George, Kirkgate, Wakefield, Yorks., cm (1814–30). [D]

Bywater, John, Grosvenor St, Bond St, London, cm and u to His Majesty (1803–39). Recorded at 70 Lower Grosvenor St, 1812–39; as Bywater & Goodbarne at no. 10 in 1835, and no. 70, 1836–37; and as Bywater & Co. at no. 70, 1829–39. Took out a Sun Insurance policy on 27 January 1812 for £3,900 of which £3,000 accounted for stock, utensils, warerooms and workshops, and £200 for warehouse and sawpit in Grosvenor Mews. [D; GL, Sun MS vol. 459, ref. 867039] Signed prefatory recommendation to P. & M. A. Nicholson's *Practical Cabinet Maker*, 1826. Fire in premises adjoining Bywater's private dwelling reported in *The Times*, 7 February 1835. Worked for Lord Crewe, probably at his London house rather than Crewe Hall, Cheshire, between 1819–26, receiving a total of £3,437 17s 7d. [Chester RO, Crewe Hall papers, DCR/47, boxes 4–5] As u to His Majesty, Bywater carried out general jobbing work for the royal yachts. M. (Mr?) Bywater is recorded working on *The Royal Sovereign* yacht in 1827, and also repairing chair and sofa cases, and supplying a mahogany chest, £7 7s, japanned candlesticks and snuffer, and campstools covered in carpet. Named in the Royal accounts with Goodbarne, 1832–45, in June 1836 being paid £3 3s for 'attending at Windsor Castle to examine furniture, writing out a statement on the quality and workmanship and reporting thereon'; and £1 for 'inspecting furniture in Mount Street'. [D; PRO, LC 11/56; 3031; 92] Probably the Bywater, u of London, named in the accounts of Lord Stamford of Dunham Massey, 15 May 1817. [Dunham Massey papers] Probably the John Bywater, cm, who subscribed to Sheraton's *Cabinet Dictionary*, 1803.

Bywater(s), John, Hull, Yorks., u (1823–42). Trading at 6 Waltham St, 1823–26; 19 Anne St, Osborne St, 1831; and Anne St, 1837–40, no. 7, 1837–38. [D]

C

Cable, —, (1766–76). Payments made by Nathaniel Ryder, 1st Lord Harrowby of Sandon Hall, Staffs. to 'Cable Cabt. Maker' of £13 1s on 30 July 1766 and £9 7s on 15 January 1776, in the latter instance for 'a Table for M. de Chabrauseut'. [Harrowby MS Trust, Notebooks vols 330 and 337]

Caborne, Thomas, 3 Grub St, London, bedstead maker, broker, smith and butcher (1821). [GL, Sun MS vol. 487, ref. 980343]

Cacket, Thomas, Northgate, Canterbury, Kent, cm (1830). [Poll bk]

Cadby, Joel, parish of St Mary, Devizes, Wilts., cm (1761). On 22 August 1761 discharged from Debtors' Prison. [*London Gazette*]

Caddey, John, 'The Cabinet', King St and Wood St, London, cabinet and looking-glass maker (1724–27). On 5 June 1725 took out insurance cover 'on goods and merchandise in dwelling house only' for £500. [GL, Sun MS vol. 21, ref. 36035; Heal; Wills, *Looking-Glasses*]

Cade, Robert, Beverley, Yorks., cm (1790). [Poll bk]

Cadman, John, Manchester, chairmaker, upholder and cm (1772–93). At Shudehill from 1772 to 1788 and in the latter year was advertising his business as a 'stain'd chair warehouse'. In the next year he was trading from 31 Swallow St, Piccadilly and by 1793 his number had changed to 81. On 10 November 1788 he was paid £7 13s by George Cooke for twelve chairs supplied to Dunham Massey. [D; John Rylands Lib., Manchester Univ., George Cooke's accounts]

Cadman, Rebecca, 26 Shudehill, Manchester, chairmaker (1797). Probably the widow of John Cadman. [D]

Cadwell, William, London, upholder (1729). Son of William Cadwell of Peterborough, apothecary. App. to Samuel Kempster 2 May 1706 and admitted freeman of the Upholders' Co. by servitude, 3 December 1729. [GL, Upholders' Co. records]

Cadwell, William, Maidstone, Kent, u (1802). [Poll bk]

Cadow, Matthew, Stanley St, Liverpool, joiner, cm and dealer in household goods (1778). In 1778 insured his stock for £700 [GL, Sun MS vol. 268, p. 72]

Caffyn, Henry, 13 Egremont Pl., Brighton, Sussex, u (1839). [D]

Caffyn, John Benjamin & Charles, Brighton, Sussex, carvers and gilders (1839–40). In 1839 John Benjamin was trading from addresses at 32 Marine Parade and 51 and 53 East St. The business was sometimes referred to as John Benjamin Gaffyn & Co. On 2 January 1840 he was married to Mary Ann Hudson and his address was then listed as 7 Market St. [D; E. Sussex RO, PAR 255/1/3/12]

Cafrani, Lewis, Liverpool, carver and gilder (1811–13). At 18 Pitt St in 1811 but two years later the number is listed as 28. [D]

Cain, Henry, 16 Rathbone St, Liverpool, cm (1839). [D]

Cain, James, King St, Richmond, Surrey, carver and gilder (1822–39). [D]

Cain, John, 29 Wilson St, Finsbury, London, cm (1835). [D]

Cainey, James, opposite Gravel Lane, Ratcliff Highway, London, cm and broker (1777). In 1777 insured his stock and goods for £650 out of a total cover of £1,200. [GL, Sun MS vol. 255, p. 129]

Caird, James, address unrecorded, cm (1803). Subscribed to Sheraton's *Cabinet Dictionary*, 1803.

Caird, James, 20 King St, Golden Sq., London, cm and u (1827). [D]

Caird, W., 20 King St, Golden Sq., London, cm (1827). [D]

Cairncross, William, Soho, London, cm (1784–1825). In 1784 at Greek St, but by 1795 had moved to Wardour St. After 1786 his usual trade address is given as 11 Hollen, St, but he seems to have retained the Wardour St building (no. 17) which was possibly his dwelling house. No. 11 Hollen St was his manufactory and had in the yard behind a 'sawpit and loft over'. He also appears to have occupied the yard behind no. 5 Hollen St. His total insurance cover in 1805 was £500 but this had risen to £800 by 1810. Declared bankrupt in 1795 which may well explain the change of address from Greek to Wardour St. Listed in Sheraton's, *Cabinet Dictionary*, 1803. [D; GL, Sun MS vol. 431, ref. 769989; vol. 437, ref. 787080; vol. 453, ref. 844466; vol. 459, ref. 873587; Westminster poll bk; Heal; *Liverpool Advertiser*, 16 February 1795]

Caistor, Thomas, Nottingham, cm (1790). [Poll bk]

Caistor, Thomas, Newark, Notts., cm (1806). Admitted freeman of Lincoln, November 1806. [Lincoln freemen rolls]

Caistor, Thomas, High St, Boston, Lincs., cm, joiner and u (1826). [D]

Caistor, William, Nottingham, cm (1790). [Poll bk]

Caitcheon, John, carver and gilder (1758). Recorded in the Blair Castle accounts 13 November 1758 for work on balusters, carved details and gilding picture frames and a bust. [V & A archives]

Caiton, William, Cambridge, joiner (1670–d. c. 1723). William Caiton is first recorded in the Trinity College, Junior Bursar's account bks from 1670 and received regular payments up to his death c. 1723. Although at this period the work undertaken included general joinery, he seems to have been almost a specialist furniture maker as most of the payments are for the supply or repair of furniture, a large percentage being for tables, chairs and stools, which would make up the majority of a Colleges furnishings. However they include 'a table turned and polished in the Masters Gallery 6s. 6d.' (1676), the Masters bedstead (1677), 'a spanish table to Joyn to ye Bursars table 12s. od.' (1679), 'for new feet turned and screw cut by hand for ye Quadrant 8s. od.' (1682), 'for an oval table in the Library' (1685), 'for 2 new frames for ye great globes in ye Library 15s. od.' (1702). William Caiton rented from Trinity College a property in the parish of St Mary the Great from 1696–1723, at which date it is listed in the names of Susan and Jane Caiton. [Archives of Trinity College]

R. W.

Cakebread, William, Royston, Herts, chairmaker (1732). In 1732 took app. called Broughton. [S of G, app. index]

Calam, Richard, 31 Scale Lane, Hull, Yorks., cm (1799–1814). Recorded in Beverley, Yorks. poll bk of 1799 and was possibly trained in that town, though by this date he was already living in Hull. [D; Beverley poll bk]

Calar, William, York Rd, Nottingham, joiner, cm and carpenter (1778–1805). His apps included Thomas Milligan (1778), George Pearson and Robert Lamb (1785), William Collinson (1800), George Wightman (1802) and John Eden (1805). On 31 July 1784 he advertised in the *Nottingham Journal* for craftsmen. All of this suggests an extensive business. [D; Notts. RO, app. list]

Calbreath, Robert, Newcastle, u (1777). App. to William Charnley and admitted freeman 20 January 1777. [Newcastle freemen reg.]

Calcott, Arthur, London, u (1709–22). In 1709 his address was New South St, St Martin's Lane but by 1720 he had moved to the Black-Moor Head upon the Pavement in St Martin's Lane and on 18 July of that year insured with the Sun Fire Office. [GL, Sun MS vol. 12, ref. 19052; Heal]

Caldcleugh, Robert, Silver St, Durham, u and cm (1839). On 29 November 1839 a notice was inserted in *Durham Advertiser* by John Tiplady, solicitor requiring claims from creditors to be lodged with him within two months.

Caldcleugh, Thomas, Framwellgate, Durham, joiner and cm (1827). [D]

Caldecott, William Edward, 53 Gt Russell St, Bloomsbury, London, u, cm and undertaker (1815–40). Successor to W. Burdock. By 1820 he had developed an extensive business and in December insured his dwelling house and the adjacent one, no. 54 which he was also using, for £2,800. Additional cover of £600 was taken out for the workshops in the yard behind. A further policy covered his stock in the two houses for £1,650 and those in a warehouse behind 7 Duke St for £300. He also owned a house at 4 Crescent Pl., Burton Cresc. which was let to a tenant and valued with the contents at £1,100. Similar cover was maintained in 1824 with his insurers. Several of Caldecott's commissions have been traced: On 3 July 1819 he invoiced furniture to J. H. Leigh amounting to £37 8s 3d which included 'a fine rosewood sofa table' at 12 guineas. [Shakespeare Birthplace Trust, Leigh receipts, DR 18/5] On 3 May 1821 Nicholas Pearse of Loughton, Essex and London settled his account for a night stool £1 11s 6d. [Essex RO, D/DHt A1/4] On 24 March 1827 and 28 March 1828 bedding to the value of £22 16s was invoiced to Sir William Fraser. [Lincoln RO, Monson 11/51] The business was still trading in the early 1840s and two bills of this period are in the V & A archives. [D; GL, Sun MS vol. 483, refs 974317, 974366, 974367, 962867; vol. 498, ref. 999605; vol. 499, ref. 1014217; Heal]

Calder, John, 8 St George's Pl. (1826) and 4 James St, (1833), Bath, Som., cm. [D]

Calder, John, Broad St, Worcester, cm (1833–35). Admitted freeman 1833. Noted in Worcester freemen rolls, 1 December 1835.

Calder, Robert, New Glass-house Bridge, North Shields, Northumb., cm, joiner and carpenter (1790–98). In 1798 his address is listed simply as Newcastle-upon-Tyne but this does not necessary imply that he had moved from North Shields. [D]

Caldwell, Elizabeth, 12 Wigmore St, Cavendish Sq., London, cm and u (1808). Possibly the widow of William Caldwell. [D]

Caldwell, William, Wigmore St, Cavendish Sq., London, cm and u (1783–c. 1805). In 1783 at Wigmore St which he insured for £800 of which £300 was for utensils, stock and goods. In 1791 took out a joint insurance policy with Robert Stone, an ironmonger of 13 Oxford St on a property at 32 Welbeck St, which was tenanted by a Mr Wells. [GL, Sun MS vol. 313, refs 485226 and 583072]

Caldwell, William, London, cm and u (1809–35). Successor and possibly the son of William and Elizabeth Caldwell. Initially traded from 12 Wigmore St, Cavendish Sq. and in 1811 the business is referred to as Caldwell & Co. By this date the trade had changed from cm to u. In 1826 at 4 Dorset St, Manchester Sq. but in 1835 the number had changed to 2. [D]

Caleborne, Thomas, Bennett St, Bath, Som., upholder, auctioneer and undertaker (1784). [D]

Cales, Charles, The Square, Winchester, Hants., carver and gilder (1839). [D]

Calken, Thomas, Liverpool, cm (1747–71). May be related to the Thomas Calkin who was in business as a cm in Chester from 1732–42, as he was also a freeman of Chester. In 1771 his address is listed as Wavertree. [Chester poll bks]

Calkin, Thomas, Eastgate St, Chester, cm (1725–d. by 1742). App. to Edward Twanbrooke, cm, 5 November 1725 and admitted freeman on 26 January 1732. On 9 June 1742 *Adam's Weekly Courant* carried an announcement that the stock of the late Thomas Calkin was to be sold off. [Chester app. bks; freemen rolls; poll bk]

Call, James, 29 Barnes St, Bunhill Row, London, carver and gilder (1808). [D]

Callan & Booth, Mesdames Westgate St, Bath, Som., cm and upholders (1805–19). [D]

Callcott, William, parish of St Ebbe's, Oxford, cm (1772). On 20 April 1772 married Jane Carpenter. [Bodleian index of Oxf. marriage bonds]

Calldicolt, —, address unknown (1736). In October 1736 submitted to Edward Monnington of Sarnesfield Court near Kington, Herefs., an account for 19s 6d for 'making a box for a clock' and 'altering ye Great Table in ye Dyning Room' amongst other work. [Herefs. RO, P94/32]

Callen, Charles Coombes, Southampton, Hants., carver and gilder (1830–39). Trading at 21 Union Terr. in 1830 and 101 High St in 1839. [D]

Callen, John, 11 St Mary's St, Southampton, Hants., carver and gilder (1839). [D]

Callendar, Alexander, Bishopgate St, London, chairmaker (b. 1760–d. 1838). Death at the age of 78 reported in *Gents Mag.*, May 1838 where he was described as the philosophical chairmaker.

Callenio, C., Coldbath Sq., London, looking-glass manufacturer (1825). [D]

Callon, James, St Helens, Lancs., joiner and cm (1818–34). At Bridge St in 1818 and 1834, but in 1828 his address is listed as Moorflat. [D]

Callow, Martin, Melton Mowbray, Leics., u (1823). Honorary freeman of Leicester 1823. [Leicester freemen rolls]

Callow, Martin, 3 High St, Bordesley, Birmingham, u and paper hanger (1835). [D]

Calloway, Felix, Bond St, London, u (1749). [Westminster poll bk]

Calloway, Henry, New Bond St, London, u (1710/11). Admitted a freeman of the Upholders' Co., 3 January 1710/11. [GL, Upholders' Co. records]

Calloway, John, Hanover Sq., London, u (1727–34). [Heal]

Calloway, John, New Bond St, London, u and undertaker (1789–1820). At 64 New Bond St from 1789–1809 when the number changed to 69. [D]

Calloway, John, 3 Howland St, Fitzroy Sq., London, chair carver (1835). [D]

Callowey, R., Salisbury, Wilts., u (1797). In March 1797 Richard Cox of Quarley, Hants. settled an account of £6 9s from R. Callowey. [Lloyds Bank archives]

Calow (or Callow), John, Southwark, London, manufacturer of japan chairs and furniture (1820–39). In 1820 at 44 Gt Dover St, but by 1835 had moved to 62 Kent St. [D]

Calthrop, —, address not known (1775). Paid £22 4s in connection with the furnishing of Denton Park, Yorks. [*Furn. Hist.*, 1968]

Calver, James, Lion Walk, Colchester, Essex, carver and gilder (1839). [D]

Calver, William, parish of St Lawrence, Ipswich, Suffolk, u (1790–1800). [Poll bk; Suffolk RO, calendar of marriage licence bonds]

Calvert, —, 'The Raven', Cornhill, London, u (1693). [Heal]

Calvert, Matthew, London, u (1793). Subscribed to Sheraton's *Drawing Book*, 1793.

Calvert, Nathaniel, Swainson's Yd, Market Pl., Lancaster, cm (1811–18). Freeman of Lancaster 1811–12. [D; freemen rolls]

Calvert, Rupert, Castle St, Uttoxeter, Staffs., cm (1828). [D]

Calvert, Thomas, Goodramgate, York, joiner and cm (1760–80). In 1760 took app. named Marshall. Advertised in *York Courant*, 4 March 1777. Insured his house for £300 in 1780. [S of G, app. index; *Furn. Hist.*, 1971; GL, Sun MS vol. 285, p. 453]

Calvert, William, Liverpool, cm (d. 1797). Died in New York aged 25. Mother living in Chapel St, Liverpool at the time of his death. [*Billinge's Liverpool Advertiser*, 15 May 1797]

Calvert, William, Lancaster, u (1811–12). [Lancaster freemen rolls]

Calvert William, Leeds, Yorks., cm and u (1814–40). At Mill Hill in 1814 and listed at no. 9, 1828–30. By 1837 at Butler's Ct, Kirkgate. [D]

Cambridge, John, London, cm (1775–78). At 12 Ranelagh St, Pimlico in 1778 when he insured his utensils, stock and goods for £250 out of a total cover of £500. Three years later his address was opposite Mays Buildings, St Martin's Lane and his insurance cover had been increased to £400 and £700 respectively. [GL, Sun MS vol. 238, p. 381; vol. 266, p. 379]

Came, J., Marlborough St, Plymouth, Devon, cm (1822). [D]

Cameron, Charles, 107 St John's St and 3 Dorrington St, Clerkenwell, London, Tunbridge-ware manufacturer (1826–35). From 1834 at Dorrington St only. [D]

Cameron, George, Hollyhill, Jarrow, Co. Durham, cm (1828). [D]

Camfield, John Thomas, 5 Upper Clifton St, Finsbury, London, cabinet wood carver (1839). [D]

Caminada, Francis, 13 Bond St, Manchester, cm (1832). [D]

Cammegh, John, 217 Whitechapel Rd, London, u, cm and undertaker (1814–39). From 1825 the business is listed as John Cammegh & Son. In 1839 the number was changed to 216 Whitechapel Rd and for the first time he was recorded as cm instead of u. [D]

Camotta, Richard, Halifax, Yorks., carver, gilder, optician and thermometer and barometer maker (1830–40). In 1830 at

14 Bull Green but by 1837 the number had changed to 12. [D.; Goodison, *Barometers*]

Camms, James, Hog Hill, Norwich, cabinet and chairmaker (1805). [D]

Camory (or Camery), James, Castle St, Westminster, London, cm (1749). [Poll bk]

Camozi, James, 37 Gt Saffron Hill, London, billiard table and backgammon board maker (1832). [D]

Campbell, A., London, cm (1793). Subscribed to Sheraton's *Drawing Book*, 1793.

Campbell, Daniel, address unknown (1743). On 7 April 1743 he was paid £13 10s for 'Dressing Beds' for Gibside, Co. Durham. [Durham RO, Strathmore MS D/St/V989]

Campbell, Edward, Old Church Yd, Preston, Lancs., cm (1818). [D]

Campbell, George, Grosvenor St, London upholder (1764–76). Insured his house in 1776 for £500. [Heal; Westminster poll bk; GL, Sun MS vol. 248, p. 421]

Campbell, George, Market St, Northampton, cm (1823). [D]

Campbell, John, 140 High Holborn, London, u (1774–1801). The house in High Holborn included ware rooms and workshops. From 1785 he maintained additional workshops at Dumbs Alley, Holborn. Other property owned by John Campbell included houses in Hart St, Bloomsbury and in 1793 a house, offices, stables and other buildings in Mile End Rd let to Abraham Hall and insured alone for £1,800. He was clearly a man of some considerable affluence for the total insurance cover on his properties amounted to £5,900 in 1790 and reached £6,200 two years later. By the early 1790s he was probably living at 2 Lyon St, Holborn. Subscribed to Sheraton's *Drawing Book*, 1793. Between 1783–86 he was employed at Carlton House and his bills amounted to £663 14s 9d. [D; GL, Sun MS vol. 255, p. 266; vol. 276, p. 604; vol. 293, p. 65; vol. 294, p. 302; vol. 329, p. 64; vol. 370, p. 278; vol. 386, p. 461; vol. 392, p. 230; H. Clifford Smith, *Buckingham Palace*]

Campbell, John, 5 Rosemary St, Bristol, 'beach chair' and bedstead maker (1822–30). From 1829 his address changed to 4 Old King St. [D]

Campbell, John, Gainsborough, Lincs., chairmaker and turner (1831). [D]

Campbell, Richard, Horse-fair, Bristol, cm and joiner (1794). [D]

Campbell, Robert, London, u and cm (1754–80). At Porter St near Newport Mkt from the 1750s until the late 1780s when he moved to 33 Marylebone St, Piccadilly. Subscribed to Chippendale's *Director*, 1754, his copy now being in the British Library. A trade card of this period in a Chinoiserie style survives. [MMA, NY, print dept] It states that Robert Campbell 'Makes and Sells all sort of Household Furniture, Useful & Ornamental in the Newest Fashion, at the most Reasonable Rates. NB. Rooms Neatly Paper'd & all sorts of Goods . . . for Exportation'. In 1761 he signed statements regarding the working conditions of journeymen cabinet and chairmakers which were published in *Lloyds Evening Post and British Chronicle*. In this year he took John Finnis as an app.

Robert Campbell was a man of considerable ingenuity and his business flourished, diversifying away from the purely upholstery side of the trade. In 1774 he took out a patent on sets of library steps which could be 'contained in tables . . . chairs or stools' when not in use. The first set was stated to have been made for George III. The practical nature of this piece of furniture had a strong appeal and a number of examples are known of sets of library steps enclosed in tables which bear Robert Campbell's trade label. One of these sets of steps enclosed in a mahogany Pembroke table is in the Library at Saltram, Devon and was supplied to John Parker in 1777 at a cost of £6 10s. Thomas Sheraton thought this item of furniture of sufficient merit to illustrate and describe it in his *Drawing Book*, 1793.

By the 1780s Robert Campbell was attracting patronage of the very highest order and his firm was described as 'Upholsterers to their Majesties' and 'Cabinet maker to the Prince of Wales'. He produced an estimate for furniture required for Carlton House in 1789 amounting to £10,500 and subsequently was employed there on upholstery work. Chinoiserie chairs for the Chinese Drawing Room, Carlton House (illustrated by engravings dated 1793 in Sheraton's *Drawing Book*) were made by François Hervé but upholstered in plain yellow satin and brocaded satin by Robert Campbell. A set of four chairs at the Nieborow Palace, near Warsaw, owned formerly by the Radziwill family, are labelled 'Robt. Campbell . . . upholders & cabinetmakers . . . to his Royal Highness the Prince of Wales on the west side of Leicester Square London. Makes all Kinds of useful & ornamental furniture in the newest taste'.

In 1785 he took out insurance cover on his dwelling house and workshop amounting to £1,500 with a further £750 for utensils, stock and goods in trust. He owned other property and in 1791 insured a house at 28 Gt Ormond St tenanted by James Buckley Esq. He subscribed to Sheraton's *Drawing Book*, 1793. From 1784 the business is usually described as Robert Campbell & Son. [D; GL, Sun MS vol. 330, p. 247; ref. 585598; S of G, app. index; Westminster poll bk; V & A archives; *DEF*; *Burlington*, September 1967] B.A.

Campbell, Robert, Windsor, Berks., u (1780–84). [D; poll bk]

Campbell, Robert, 3 Broker's Row, Moorfields, London, upholder (1808). [D]

Campbell, Samuel, Liverpool, u (1812–39). Son of William Campbell, breeches maker. Sworn freeman 5 October 1812. At 7 Clayton Sq., 1813–14 but in 1816 was at 2 Trafalgar St with a shop at 18 Church St. From 1835–39 in School Lane. [D; Liverpool freemen reg.]

Campbell, Samuel, Market St, Bolton, Lancs., u (1824). [D]

Campbell, Theodore, London, cm and broker (1793–94). Recorded at both 24 Fore St and 24 Barbican in 1793. Bankrupt 1794. [D; *Liverpool Advertiser*, 23 June 1794]

Campbell, William, London, u (1726–49). In 1726 his address was listed as within 3 doors of the 'Dog & Duck' on the south side of new Bond St, near Hanover Sq. but in the next year as Grosvenor St. In 1745 a payment of £150 was made by the Earl of Stair for 'part of his bill for furniture' to Campbell. In the following year further payments were made to 'Messrs. Campbell & Bruce'. [Heal; Westminster poll bk, 1749; Scottish RO, GD 135/Box 51/2/1–2; Box 55/31]

Campbell, William jnr, Pedley St, upper end of Bond St, London, upholder (1753). Took out insurance on 27 January 1753 for household goods and furniture in a house 'near opposite the Coach & Horses in Conduit Street in Occupation of Barlow Esqre'. [GL, Sun MS vol. 98, ref. 134090]

Campe, James, London, upholder (1720). Son of John Campe of Chipping Ongar, Essex, clerk. App. to Richard Chambers 2 May 1711 in trust for William Wood, girdler 'who neglected to turn him over'. Admitted freeman of the Upholders' Co. by redemption 7 December 1720. [GL, Upholders' Co. records]

Camper-Harris, James, Sampson Gdns Hermitage by Worship Ct, Worship St, Moorfields, London cm (1787). On 12 May 1787, together with James Patterson, insured utensils, stock, goods and 'Mr Patterson's household goods' for £400. [GL, Sun MS vol. 345, p. 30]

Campfield, Richard, Old Palace Yd, Westminster, London, upholder (1700–12). Admitted freeman of the Upholders'

Co., 28 September 1700. Took an app. 22 December 1711. Between 1705 and 1712 took out insurance cover on three houses immediately to the west of Westminster Abbey to the extent of £1,000. [GL, Upholders' Co. records; Hand in Hand MS vol. 4, p. 17; vol. 12, refs 9128–30; S of G, app. index]

Campfield, Richard, King St, St James's, London, upholder (1712–24). [Heal]

Campfield, Robert, Duke St, St James's, London, upholder (1712). [GL, Sun MS vol. 2, p. 27]

Campini & Capella, 8 Court, Digbeth, Birmingham, picture frame makers (1839). [D]

Campion, George, 23 Union St, Bishopsgate, London, cm, u and carpenter (1808–16). In 1808 took out insurance cover on his house in Bishopsgate St for £450 and another at 31 Skinner St for £350. [D; GL, Sun MS vol. 444, ref. 819529]

Campion, Thomas, Bridge St, Northampton, cm (1830). [D]

Campion, Thomas, Hull, Yorks., cm (1831–42). At 3 Burke's Sq. in 1831, but by 1838 had moved to 4 James Sq., Myton St at which address he continued in trade until 1842. [D]

Campion & Watkins, London, billiard and backgammon table makers (1829–39). At 13 Henrietta St, Covent Gdn in 1829 but by 1835 the partnership had ended and Arthur Campion was trading from 10 Adele St, Cheapside. By 1839 the address had changed to 5 Princes St, Gate St. [D]

Camplin, William, East Moor, Wakefield, Yorks., cm and u (1828). [D]

Campsall, John, Hull, Yorks., carver and gilder (1723). [Poll bk]

Canes, William, Painter's Row, Exeter, Devon, builder and cm (1822–25). [D]

Canham, Peter, Bridewell St, Wymondham, Norfolk, cm (1839). [D]

Canham, William, Norwich, cm (1713). Took app. named Melchior. [S of G, app. index]

Cann, James, 35 Timberland, Norwich, cm (1801–18). Admitted freeman of Norwich 24 February 1804 (not by apprenticeship). [D; freemen reg.; poll bks]

Cann, John, Norwich, cabinet and chairmaker (1798). [D]

Cann, Peter, Finkle St, Stockton, Co. Durham, cm and winnowing machine maker (1832). [D]

Cannaway (or **Canneway** or **Caneway**), **Walter**, Head of Flesh-market, Newcastle, carver and gilder (1778–98). On 28 February 1778 advertised in *Newcastle Courant* that he was capable of 'carving up marble, wood or stone. Old square glasses are cut to any oval and framed to any taste'. [D]

Cannell, Hugh, Henry St, Liverpool, cm (1802–27). Admitted freeman on 5 July 1802 after app. to William Smith. Took apps named William Dyer in 1822 and Daniel Waddle in 1823. After 1821 frequently changed his address being located at 33 King St in that year, 7 Roscoe Lane in 1823 and 20 Coopers Row in 1827. [D; Liverpool freemen reg. and app. enrolment bk]

Canning, Joseph, 8 Little St Andrews St, Seven Dials, London, cm and u (1839). [D]

Cannings, William, Bath, Som., u (1831). Bankrupt 4 November 1831. [*Liverpool Mercury*, 11 November 1831]

Cannon, Charles, High Wycombe, Bucks., chairmaker (1827–40). [D; PR (bapt.)]

Cannon (or **Canon**), **Edward**, 109 High Holborn, London, papier mâché manufacturer and looking-glass warehouse (1771–93). An address at 17 Crutched Friars is listed in directories in 1775 only. Business continued after 1793 as Cannon & Buzzard. [D; Wills, *Looking-Glasses*]

Cannon & Buzzard, 109 High Holborn, London, carvers, gilders and paperhangers (1793–1829). [D]

Cannon, George, Tylers Green, High Wycombe, Bucks., chairmaker (1834–41). Aged 25 at the time of the 1841 Census. [PR (bapt.)]

Cannon, John, High Wycombe, Bucks, chair manufacturer (b. c. 1781–1841). Mentioned in Militia Census 1798. Three daughters and two sons bapt. between 1814 and 1824. Aged 60 at the time of the 1841 Census. [PR (bapt.)]

Cannon, Joseph, High Wycombe, Bucks, chairmaker, (1815–26). Three daughters and a son bapt. 1815–26. [PR (bapt.)]

Cannon, Mary, Tylers Green, High Wycombe, Bucks., chair bottomer (b. c. 1806–41). Aged 35 at the time of the 1841 Census.

Cannon, Thomas, 58 Shadwell High St, London, broker and cm (1781). Took out insurance on his utensils, stock and goods for £150. [GL, Sun MS vol. 298, p. 159]

Cannor (or **Connor**), **Charles**, Wycombe Marsh, High Wycombe, Bucks., chairmaker (b. c. 1781–1841). Aged 60 at the time of the 1841 Census.

Canns, James, Hoghill, Norwich, cabinet and chair manufacturer (1805). [D]

Cansick, Robert, Bradford, Yorks., cm (1840). Bankrupt January 1840. [*Leeds Mercury*, 1 February 1840]

Cant, James, High St, Uppingham, Rutland, chairmaker and turner (1835). [D]

Cant, Robert James, High St, Uppingham, Rutland, chairmaker and turner (1840). [D]

Cant, William, North St, Ripon, Yorks., cm (1822). [D]

Cant & Collins, London, cabinet and cornice maker and u (1820–26). Shown at 11 Brook St, New Rd in 1820 and 1826, but at 1 Gt Brook St, Fitzroy Sq. in 1822. [D]

Canter, William, Ixworth, Suffolk, cm (1839). [D]

Canton, James, Church St, Hackney, London, carver and gilder (1808). [D]

Cantrill, Joseph, Market Pl., Blandford, Dorset, cm, u and auctioneer (1823–30). [D]

Canway, John, Lancaster, cm (1779–80). [Lancaster freemen rolls]

Cape, John, Lancaster, cm (1792–93). Named in the Gillow records as a maker of bookcases. [Westminster Ref Lib., vol. 344/96, pp. 883 and 938]

Cape, Thomas, Liverpool, cm (1813–37). At 34 Stanley St, 1813–16, but address changed to 3 Norris St, 1835–37. [D]

Cape, William, Main St, Cockermouth, Cumb., cm and joiner (1829). Subsequently traded as William & George Cape. Address in 1829 also recorded as Cocker Bridge End. [D]

Cape, William & George, Main St, Cockermouth, Cumb., cm, joiners and builders (1834). [D]

Capel(l), James, Watford, Herts., cm (1832–39). [D]

Caple, Robert, Edward St, Carnaby Mkt, London, cm (1749). [Poll bk]

Capon, George, London, u and cm (1811–39). In 1811 at 7 Theobalds Rd, Red Lion Sq., but by 1813 at 13 Greek St, Soho, at which address he remained until at least 1815. In 1820 he was trading from 1 Nassau St, Middlx Hospital, and in the next year from 388 Oxford St. From this date the trade in the directories is changed from u to cm. In November 1824 he was declared bankrupt but despite this continued to trade from the same address until at least 1826. In 1835 the address is recorded as 54 Poland St, Oxford St and in 1839 as Woodstock St. A John Capon is recorded at 388 Oxford St in the 1825 edition of Kent's *London Directory* but this may be an error. [D]

Capon, J., Bury St Edmunds, Suffolk, u (1732). Bankruptcy announced in *Gents Mag.*, May 1732.

Capon, William, Newport Pagnell, Bucks., cabinet and chairmaker (1780–98). In 1780 insured his utensils and stock for £50 out of a total insurance cover of £200. [D; GL, Sun MS vol. 288, p. 27]

Capp, Dennis, 46 Foley St, London, carver and gilder (1820–37). [D]

Capp, James, Holbeach, Lincs., joiner and cm (1822–26). Trading also as an ironmonger in 1822 and paperhanger in 1826. [D]

Capprani (or **Caprini**), **Antonio**, 110 Tib St, Manchester, carver, gilder, looking-glass, picture frame and barometer maker (1836–40). [D]

Caprani, John B., 29 Pitt St, Liverpool, carver and gilder (1827–39). [D]

Caprani, Lewis, 28–29 Pitt St, Liverpool, carver and gilder (1814–23). Succeeded by John B. Caprani. [D]

Caprani & Sanderson, 30 Pitt St, Liverpool, carvers and gilders (1835). [D]

Capson, John, Bury St Edmunds, Suffolk, u (1725). In 1725 took app. named Cross. [S of G, app. index]

Capstack (or **Capstick**), **James**, Market St, Lancaster, cm (1798–1812). A cm of this name is recorded in the Gillow records for the periods 1798–99, 1800 and 1812–14. He may, or may not, be the same person as the James Capstick whose household and business goods were put up for sale in April 1811. Apart from his household furniture, much of which was mahogany, carpets, looking-glasses, etc, he had a stock consisting of 'new-made mahogany writing desks, wardrobes, chests of drawers, clock-cases, washstands, night-chairs, tables, pier and swing looking glasses', eight work benches, mahogany and oak in planks and boards and mahogany veneers. In the same year a James Capstick was made freeman of Lancaster as a cm. [Westminster Ref. Lib., Gillow vol. 344/98, p. 1600; *Lancaster Gazette*, 27 April 1811, 25 April 1812; freemen rolls]

Capstick, Thomas, Lancaster, cm (1817). Son of James Capstick 'late of Lancaster'. Made a freeman of Lancaster, 1817–18, when stated 'of Preston'. [Lancaster freemen rolls]

Capstick, Thomas, Liverpool, cm (1824–29). From 1823–24 at 187 Vauxhall Rd but by 1827 had moved to 13 Grafton St and two years later was at Academy Pl., Gore St. [D]

Capstick, Thomas, Caldcoats, Carlisle, Cumb., cm and joiner (1828–34). [D]

Carbanati, Joseph, 37 Southampton St, Strand, London, looking-glass manufacturer (1835). [D]

Carberry, Christopher & Cubett, Benjamin, 17 Cow Lane, West Smithfield, London, cm (1783–84). Insurance on stock, goods and utensils in 1783 was £60 out of a total cover of £100. [D; GL, Sun MS vol. 314, p. 300]

Carbery, Christopher, 24 Red Lion Ct, Saffron Hill, London, cm (1787–92). Insurance cover on utensils and stock was £200 in 1787 rising to £300 for the period 1790–92. [GL, Sun MS vol. 344, p. 628; vol. 370, July 1790; vol. 388, p. 124]

Carbinall, William, St Catherine's New Court, St Catherine's, London, cm (1782–91). Out of a total insurance cover of £1,000 in 1782 only £50 was in respect of utensils, stock and goods. Declared bankrupt by 1791 when described as 'late of St Catherine's Court'. [GL, Sun MS vol. 300, p. 622; *Williamson's Liverpool Advertiser*, 4 April 1791]

Carbon, John, 6 High St, Brighton, Sussex cm (1824). [D]

Carby, William, 53 Cannon St, Ratcliffe, London, carver and gilder (1817). [D]

Card, C. H., West St, Wareham, Dorset, cm and u (1840). [D]

Card, Edward, West St, Wareham, Dorset, u (1823–30). [D]

Carden & Stoddard, Jew St, Brighton, Sussex, cm and u (1832). [D]

Carder, Thomas, Fore St, Teignmouth, Devon, cm and dealer in earthenware (1823–32). By 1832 was bankrupt and in this year appeared before the court for the relief of insolvent debtors. Afer leaving Teignmouth he moved to the parish of St Sidwell, Exeter and then to Dawlish, Devon before dwelling in

Goldsmith St, Exeter and finally at a college in the precinct of the Cathedral Close. [D; *Exeter Flying Post*, 16 February 1832]

Cardiff, Hester, Edmonds Ct, Dead Wall, London, u (1723). Took out insurance cover of £150 on her dwelling house, and the goods and merchandise in it were covered for a similar sum. [GL, Sun MS vol. 16, ref. 29703]

Cardinal, Roger, Bridge End, Saffron Walden, Essex, cm (1811). [Census in possession of the Town Clerk, Saffron Walden]

Careless, Henry, Richmond, Surrey, u (1738). Took app. named Perkins in 1738. [S of G, app. index]

Careless, Thomas, London, upholder (1712 d. by 1732). Admitted freeman of the Upholders' Co., 1 October 1712. [GL, Upholders' Co. records]

Careswell, John, St Alkmund's Churchyard, Shrewsbury, Salop, u (1796). [Freemen rolls]

Carey, John, 8 East Ascent, St Leonards, Sussex, u and cm (1839–40). [D]

Carey, Peter, 'The Golden Lyon', Bridges St, Covent Gdn, London, u (1720). [GL, Sun MS vol. 11, 11 April 1720]

Carhill, George & Joseph, 45 Whitefriargate, Hull, Yorks., cm (1837). [D]

Cark, John, Blackman St, Southwark, London, carver (1784). [Bristol poll bk]

Carkeel, N., 4 Albion St, Blackfriars Rd, London, u and cm (1809). [D]

Carkeet, Nathaniel, Truro, Cornwall and London cm and u (1797–1820). Initially at West Bridge St, Truro, from which address he advertised in December 1798 that he could supply 'Japan chairs, sofas, fire-screens' of his own manufacture together with a 'a very large & handsome assortment of Chintz Bed Furniture, Feather Beds, Carpets etc.' He offered to take old furniture in part exchange. By March 1801 he had moved to Lemon St and was once again making a feature of japanned 'Modern & Rich drawing-room chairs'. In addition to his cabinet and upholstery stock he was offering tea for sale in July 1803. During 1806 and 1807 he continued to use the local press to feature 'paper hangings of the newest patterns from one of the first houses in London' together with fabrics and japanned and mahogany furniture. He constantly emphasised his knowledge of the latest London fashions and his ability to match goods made in the capital. In June 1807 for instance he was offering to furnish drawing rooms and beds 'on a new principle according to the present London method.'

The claim that he had an intimate knowledge of the London fashions and was importing into Cornwall the most elegant fashions of the capital may not have been an idle boast. He clearly had London connections and in August 1807 indicated his intention of moving his business there. His stocks were offered at prime cost or below. In the same year he established himself at 49 Skinner St, London. As foreman for his London manufactory he obtained the services of a Mr Hixon who had previously been employed by 'Mr. Stephen's business in Piccadilly', and that of 'Mr Smith of Grosvenor St. Grosvenor Square, each of whom are employed by the Royal Family'. In order to benefit from his previous Cornish connections he sent Mr Hixon to the county in the summer of 1809 'to fix an assemblage of handsome furniture' for a client in the Lostwithiel area, and announced that he would be prepared to call on any 'gentlemen in Devonshire or any other County' on his way back to London. Two of his trade cards from this London period are in the Banks Coll., BM, and feature an elaborately draped window and a Grecian sofa. They also reflect the frequent changes of address that this business underwent in its latter years. It remained at 49 Skinner St, Snow Hill until at least 1812, but by 1814 was at 5 Lisle St, Leicester Sq. In the

next year the business was at 17 Tavistock St, Covent Gdn at which it continued until 1819, but by the next year it was at 23 New Bond St.

Nathaniel Carkeet appears to have been a Non-Conformist and his signature is recorded on the trust deed of the Dissenting Meeting House, Bull Hill, Fowey, Cornwall dated 29 September 1798. [D; Cornwall RO, D.D. CF. 1255; *Sherborne Mercury*, 10 December 1798; *Royal Cornwall Gazette*, 7 March 1801, 26 December 1801, 30 July 1803, 3 May 1806, 6 June 1807, 24 June 1809] B.A.

Carkman, Robert, John St, Dale St, Liverpool, cm (1796–1803). Recorded at 14 John St in 1796 and no. 8 from 1800. [D]

Carkman, Thomas, 6 Chapel St, Liverpool, cm (1767–1803). The number of the business premises in Chapel St was constantly changing. By 1777 it was 51; in 1781, 39; and in 1790 it was 40. After 1796 the business was conducted from 4 Lord St. In 1781 Carkman advertised himself as a cabinet and trunk maker. [D]

Carlaw, William, 55 Davies St, Berkeley Sq., London, cm (1808). [D]

Carle, Charles, London, carver and gilder (1817–39). At 11 Kent St, Southwark 1817–20, but by 1829 had moved to 2 Cumberland Pl., Newington, and recorded at no. 3 in 1837. [D]

Carlean, John, address unknown, cm (1717–28). Received small payments from the Duke of Northumberland in 1712, 1714, 1717, 1727 and 1728, the largest sum being £8 15s in the latter year. [V & A archives]

Carleton, —, Ludgate Hill, London, maker of travelling and other writing cases (1763). [D]

Carley, Jesse, 37 George St, Brighton, Sussex, cm and u (1826–28). Daughter Sarah bapt. 2 April 1828. [D; E. Sussex RO, PR (bapt.)]

Carley, Stephen, 66 North St, Brighton, Sussex, bed and mattress manufacturer, (1826). [D] See S. and Stephen Carly.

Carlill, George & Joseph, 45 Whitefriargate, Hull, Yorks., cm, u and undertakers (1838–40). This partnership took over from the former one of Thomas & George Carlill trading from the same address. Apart from the business address directories show also a residence at 36 Dock St in their occupation, 1838–39. [D]

Carlill, Thomas & George, Whitefriargate, Hull, Yorks., cm, u and undertaker (1810–35). The number of the business premises in Whitefriargate is variously given as 42 (1810), 45 (1814 and 1821–35) and 43 (1817). The partnership was succeeded by that of George & Joseph Carlill trading from the same address. [D]

Carlton, John, York, cm (1823–30). Address given as Pavement in 1823, but by 1828 had moved to 8 Coppergate and trading as John & Co. After 1830 the business continued at this address as Sarah Carlton & Co. [D]

Carlton, Samuel, Beeston, Leeds, Yorks., cm (1817–22). [D]

Carlton Sarah & Co., 8 Coppergate, York, cm and u (1830–34). Successor to John Carlton. [D]

Carly, Cornelius, 7 Bolingbroke Row, Walworth, London, u, bed and mattress maker (1822–39). [D]

Carly, J., Edward St, Brighton, Sussex, cm and u (1827). [D]

Carly, James, East St, Kent Rd, London, bed and mattress maker (1822). [D]

Carly, James, All Saints St, Hastings, Sussex, bed and mattress maker (1826). [D]

Carly, S., North St, Brighton, Sussex, cm and u (1827). [D] See Stephen Carley and Stephen Carly.

Carly, Samuel, 13 Ship St, Brighton, Sussex, u (1822–24). [D]

Carly, Stephen, 14 Ship St, Brighton, Sussex, u (1823). [D]

Carmichael, John, address unknown but possibly Newcastle, joiner and cm (1774). Advertised in the *Newcastle Courant*,

26 February 1774 that he was continuing his father's business 'in the trade of shop-keeping . . . has laid in fresh assortment of all kinds of linen drapery, haberdashery, hosiery & teas; & also executes, in the neatest manner, all sorts of household furniture in the cabinet & upholstery branches'.

Carnaby, John, Low Friar St, Newcastle, cm (1838). [D]

Carnaby, Ralph, Newcastle, cm (1808–34). In March 1808 the *Newcastle Courant* carried an announcement that W & R. Carnaby 'cabinet-makers from London' had commenced business at Green-court, Newgate St. The partnership was obviously unsuccessful for in April of the next year Ralph was advertising that he had never had any trading connection with his brother, William, who had already by this date set himself up in opposition at 3 Collingwood St. Ralph continued to trade from the Newgate St premises until 1812. In May of that year he advertised his move to 21 Low Friar St at which address he continued to trade until 1834. In 1827 he was also shown to have had a house in Gallowgate. [D; *Newcastle Courant*, 5 March 1808, 22 April 1809, 2 September 1809, 9 May 1812]

Carnaby, Robert, Newcastle, cm (1752). On 25 January 1752 announced in *Newcastle Courant* that he had moved his business from the foot of Butcher-bank to 'his house near Pardon-gate'. His stock included 'lead, tea & bottle boards'.

Carnaby, William, Newcastle, cm (1808–24). Before setting up in business in partnership with his brother Ralph he had been employed in London as foreman to W. D. Watson of Parliament St. The partnership with Ralph at 1 Green-court, Newgate St, was short-lived and by 1809 he was trading on his own account at 3 Collingwood St. In 1813 however he moved back to 1 Green-court which in May 1812 had been vacated by his brother when he moved to Low Friar St. [D; *Newcastle Courant*, 5 March 1808, 29 April 1809, 12 August 1809; *Newcastle Chronicle*, 27 February 1813]

Carnley, John, Hull, Yorks., cm (1828–31). At 3 King St in 1828 but by 1831 had moved to 12 Prince St. [D]

Carp, Plenty, High St, Southampton, Hants., joiner and cm (1783). [D]

Carpenter, Abraham, parish of St Nicholas, Bristol, upholder (1754). [Poll bk]

Carpenter, Andrew, Westminster, London, carver (1696–1730). Married Ann Billingsley at Holy Trinity Church in 1696 when he was described as being resident in the parish of St Ann, Westminster. In 1730 his address was St George's, Hanover Sq. He is almost certainly the Carpenter who was paid on 9 May 1701 for carved work 'in his Majesties garden at Kensington'. The entry appears in a Garden account bk, 1696–1702, for the royal gardens of William III, kept for the Earl of Portland by Caspar Frederick Henning. [Marriage reg; Lincoln RO, 3ANC 8/19; Worcs. RO, 2252/705: 366/2]

Carpenter, Benjamin, 11 Gt Titchfield St, London, carver and gilder (1815). [D]

Carpenter, Conyngesby, London, upholder (1711). Son of William Carpenter, Gent. of Mawden, Herefs. App. to Thomas Few(?) on 17 August 1704. Admitted a freeman of the Upholders' Co. by servitude, 24 August 1711. [GL, Upholders' Co. records]

Carpenter, Jabez, 147 High St, Bromley, Kent, cm and u (1826–d. 1847). [D; Bromley Ref. Lib., Baxter, *Itinerary of Bromley*, p. 38]

Carpenter, James, 3 Gt Bath St, Clerkenwell, London, cm and u (1825). [D]

Carpenter, John, carver (1741). Listed in York poll bk with an address given as 'Hilton Castle' which may be Hylton Castle, near Sunderland, Co. Durham.

Carpenter, John, 12 Hanover St, Bristol, carver and gilder (1819–21). [D]

Carpenter, John, 3 Gt Bath St, Clerkenwell, London, cm and u (1820–26). [D]

Carpenter, John, Back St, Exeter, Devon, cm (1838). A son, George, bapt. at the Church of St Mary Minor on 12 April 1838. [PR (bapt.)]

Carpenter, Joseph, Birmingham, cabinet case maker (1830–35). Trading at 10 Court, Lancaster St in 1830 and 6 York St in 1835. [D]

Carpenter, Robert, Westgate St, Bath, Som., carver, gilder and frame maker (1785–91). [D]

Carpenter, Samuel, High St, Lambeth, London, cm and u (1827). [D]

Carpenter, Stephen, Bryanston, Dorset, carver (1759). Took an app. called Noyes. [S of G, app. index]

Carpenter, Stephen, Blandford, Dorset, cm, builder and joiner (1771–1816). On 16 April 1771 took an app. John Tucker for 7 years. A contract of 1816 exists between John Austen of Spethisbury, clerk, and Stephen Carpenter for the erection of a dwelling house at Tarrant Keyneston. [D; Dorset RO, B5; D81, E2]

Carpenter, Thomas, Marylebone St, London, chairmaker (1734–49). Recorded commissions for Lady Monson (1734 and 1745) and the Earl of Hertford (1741) suggest that his main trade was that of sedan chair maker. [Lincoln RO, Monson 12; V & A archives (Duke of Northumberland's accounts); Westminster poll bk]

Carpenter, William, East St, Southampton, Hants., cm (1793–1811). [D]

Carr, — (widow), 53 Colehill St, Sutton Coldfield, Warks., u (1767–77). [D]

Carr, Adam, Fenkle St, Alnwick, Northumb., cm (1828–34). Recorded also at Coming's Yd in 1834 as cm and joiner. [D]

Carr, Andrew Henry, 13 St Michael's Sq., Southampton, Hants., cm and u (1811–36). Business continued by George Carr at the same address. [D]

Carr, Ann, High Wycombe, Bucks., chairmaker (b. c. 1806–41). Aged 35 at the time of the 1841 Census.

Carr, George C., Newcastle, u (1784). App. to Thomas Hunt, and admitted freeman of Newcastle 15 April 1784. [Freemen rolls]

Carr, George, 13 St Michael's Sq., Southampton, Hants., and cm and chairmaker (1839). Successor to Andrew H. Carr. [D]

Carr, James, Holt, Norfolk, cm and joiner (1822). [D]

Carr, James, 6 Clipstone St, London, chair and sofa manufacturer (1827). [D]

Carr, John, London, upholder (1731–37). Son of William Carr of Lambeth, surgeon. App. to Ezra Doughty on 14 July 1721. Admitted freeman of the Upholders' Co. by servitude, 3 February 1731. Took as app. Charles Maynard in 1737. [GL, Upholders' Co. records]

Carr, John, Lancaster, u (1767–68). [Lancaster freemen rolls]

Carr, John, Leicester, cm (1772). App. to John Shipley in 1761 and admitted freeman in 1772. [App. and freemen rolls]

Carr, John, New St, Broad St, London, cm (1775). Took out insurance cover of £300, £100 being in respect of utensils and stock. [GL, Sun MS vol. 238, p. 265]

Carr, John, Woolmarket, Berwick-upon-Tweed, Northumb., cm (1806). [D]

Carr, John E., Grimsby, Lincs., joiner and cm (1819–40). At St Mary's Gate in 1826, but by 1831 had moved to Bethlem St where he advertised in addition that he was a builder. Trading at Baxtergate in 1835 as joiner and cm. [D]

Carr, John, Thomas St, Cirencester, Glos., cm (1830). [D]

Carr, Thomas, 20 High St, Birmingham, u (1767–80). [D]

Carr, Thomas, Sunderland, Co. Durham, cm (1784). [D]

Carr, Thomas, Clayport St, Alnwick, Northumb., cm and joiner (1828–34). [D]

Carr, Thomas, Market Pl., Pontefract, Yorks., cm (1834–37). [D]

Carr, William, 12 St James St, King's Lynn, Norfolk, carver, gilder and painter (1836–39). [D]

Carrack, John, Leeds, Yorks., cm and u (1816–34). His address initially is variously described in directories as near Bank (1816), Rear Bank (1818) and Far Bank (1817 and 1822). From 1826–30 he was trading from 1 Cavalier St and in 1834 at The Calls. [D]

Carrall, Richard jnr, Hull, Yorks., cm (1826–40). App. to Joseph Hick in January 1817. Trading at 20 Bishop Lane in 1826. By 1838 he had moved to 18 George's Pl., Mytongate. The business continued to trade until 1848. [D; Hull app. reg.]

Carraway, —, Margate, Kent, upholder and cm (1803–39). Initially traded as an upholder but from the 1820s was describing himself solely as a cm. At Union Cresc., 1823–26, and this address re-appears in a directory entry of 1839. His main place of business after 1831 however appears to have been 4 Cecil St. [D]

Carrick, George, Lawrence Pouteney Lane, London, upholder, paper hanger and cm (1778–83). The number of the business premises is listed as 39 in 1778 but from 1781 as 17. He also appears to have owned another house at 20 in 1778. Insurance cover on his business premises amounted to £800 including £400 for stock, goods and utensils in 1778; and £1,000 with £700 for stock in 1782. A George Carrick of 73 Lombard St who was admitted a freeman of the Upholders' Co. by redemption on 4 November 1778 may be the same person. [D; GL, Sun MS vol. 263, p. 176; vol. 270, p. 189; vol. 298, p. 318; GL, Upholders' Co. records]

Carrick, Mark, Skelton, Guisborough, Yorks., joiner, cm and wheelwright (1828–34). [D]

Carrier, John, London, upholder (1726). Son of John Carrier of the parish of St Botolph Without, Bishopgate, tailor. App. to John Newton and admitted a freeman of the Upholders' Co. by servitude on 4 May 1726. [GL, Upholders' Co. records]

Carrington, Benjamin, Lincoln, cm, u and furniture broker (1819–35). Trading at 'Strait', 1819–22; 29 'Straight' in 1826; and High St in 1835. [D]

Carrington, Joseph, 28 Snow Hill, Birmingham, cm (1777–80). [D]

Carrington, Richard, High St, Colchester, Essex, cm and u (1790–93). May well be the Richard Carrington who is recorded as residing in London in the 1784 Colchester poll bk and declared his trade as upholder. May well have returned from London in 1790 when he took out insurance cover for £500 on property in the High St described as a 'new house, shops & ware room'. [D; GL, Sun MS 1790, ref. 572493]

Carrington, William, London, u (1763–93). On 12 April 1763 married Mary Smeaton of Stanlake, Oxon. at Stanlake. His address is recorded as Marylebone, London. In 1776 took out insurance cover of £200 on a property on the corner of Castle St in Hanover St, Long Acre which he was using as business premises. Of this £60 was to cover utensils, stock and goods. By the next year he had moved to 8 Little St Martin's Lane which he was to occupy until 1793. The insurance cover taken out in 1775 on this new property was £300 of which £160 was for utensils, stock and goods. [D; Bodleian index of Oxf. marriage bonds; GL, Sun MS vol. 237, p. 223; vol. 249, p. 76]

Carrivon (or **Carrivor**), **Mr**, Wapping, London, cm (1774). An insurance policy in respect of a beer and wine merchant's premises near King Edward Stairs, Wapping mentions insurance on goods 'in a cellor under the Dwelling House of Mr Carrivon, Cabinetmaker'. [GL, Sun MS vol. 235, ref. 347634]

Carroll, Andrew, Nottingham, u and mattress maker (1834–40). Trading at Plat(t) St, 1834–35, and 4 Parliament St in 1840. [D]

Carrs, Henry, High Wycombe, Bucks., chairmaker (b. c. 1819–41). Aged 22 at the time of the 1841 Census.

Carruthers, Reginald, Spring Gdn Lane, Carlisle, Cumb., joiner and cm (1811). [D]

Carse, Samuel, King's Lynn, Norfolk, cm and u (1830–39). At 38 High St in 1830, but by 1836 the number had changed to 72. His trade label is known applied to a bow-fronted chest of drawers of early 19th-century date sold by Sotheby Bearne in November 1981. [D]

Carsey, James, Gt Yarmouth, Norfolk, cm (1836). [Poll bk]

Carsey, William, Gt Yarmouth, Norfolk, cm (1826–32). [Poll bks]

Carson, W., 19 Lambs Conduit Passage, London, bedstead maker (1829). [D]

Carstairs, George, 64 King St, Argyle Pl., London, cm and u (1839). [D]

Carter, Mr, Piccadilly, London, 'eminent Carver' (d. 1756). [*Public Advertiser*, 30 August 1756]

Carter, Adcock, address unknown (1833). Payments made in February 1833 by 3rd Lord Braybrooke of Audley End for a music stool (7s) and a picture frame (2s). [Essex RO, D/DBy/A358]

Carter, Andrew & John, 8 Market Pl., Preston, Lancs., carvers and gilders (1825). [D]

Carter, Anthony, 349 Rotherhithe St, London, cm and u (1827). [D]

Carter, Anthony, Brickhouses, Keighley, Yorks., cm and u (1830). [D]

Carter, B., Exeter, Devon u (1816). [Election Squibs]

Carter, Burrington, Fore St, Exeter, Devon, u and cm (1777–87). In 1777 insured his utensils, and stock for £500 out of a total insurance cover of £600. In the next year however the figures were reduced to £250 and £300 and total cover was still £300 in 1787. [GL, Sun MS vol. 256, p. 640; vol. 269, p. 152; vol. 344, pp. 380]

Carter, David & Sons, Berrycroft, Honley, near Huddersfield, Yorks., joiner and cm. (1837). [D]

Carter, Edward, 58 Exmouth St, Spitalfields, London, carver and gilder (1829–39). [D]

Carter, Elias, Exeter, Devon, u (1803–24). Address given in the 1803 Militia Census as St Stephen. May have traded as Carter & Son, High St (1809–17). At 25 High St from 1819. In November 1824 a decision appears to have been made to operate solely as an auctioneer and appraiser. [*Exeter Flying Post*, 18 February 1819, 4 November 1824]

Carter, Gabriel, Camberwell, London, cm (1718). [GL, Sun MS vol. 8, ref. 12787]

Carter, George, at the George in Hays St, against St Ann's Church, parish of St James, Westminster, London, upholder (1717–18). Probably the u who was paid £3 3s on 6 December 1718 for appraising the Goods 'at Squerries'. [GL, Sun MS vol. 9, p. 73; PRO, private accounts, Countess of Jersey, C 111/54 pt 1]

Carter, Henry, Wilbar's Yd, High St, Lewes, Sussex, chair manufacturer and turner (1839–40). [D]

Carter, J., 20 Hanway St, Oxford St, London, u (1821–25). [D]

Carter, James, 62 Leadenhall St, London, carver, gilder and dealer in pictures (1808–09). [D]

Carter, James, 8 St John's St, Brick Lane, London, carpenter and cm (1820). [D]

Carter, James, 37 Friargate, Preston, Lancs., cm (1825). [D]

Carter, James, London, carver and gilder (1829–37). At 9 Little

Vine St, Piccadilly in 1829 but by 1837 had moved to 65 Berwick St, Soho. [D]

Carter, James, Norwich, cm (1830). Son of John Carter, hotpresser. Admitted freeman of Norwich 14 August 1830. [Freemen rolls]

Carter, John, Dean St, Westminster, London, cm (1713). [GL, Sun MS vol. 3, ref 3054]

Carter, John, High St, Poplar, London, cm (1820–39). In 1820 at 67 High St but from 1837 the business is styled John Carter & Sons, u and cm and the address is changed to 67 High St. [D]

Carter, John, Beastmarket, Gainsborough, Lincs., chairmaker (1819–26). [D]

Carter, John, Liverpool, chairmaker (1818–34). At 3 Trueman St in 1818 but between 1823 and 1827 at Gildart's Gdn. By 1834 the address had changed again to Cheapside. [D]

Carter, John, 2 Stone Buildings, Clifton, Bristol, 'painter, plumber, tiler, plasterer, builder, carpenter, cm, undertaker, house agent, licenced maltster and dealer in hops' (1832–39). [D]

Carter, John, 60 Powis St, Woolwich, London, cm and u (1838–39). [D]

Carter, Joseph, Hull, Yorks., cm and chairmaker (1821–31). App. to Thomas Ross of Cottingham near Hull in February 1806. In business by June 1821 when he in turn took John Todd of Cottingham as his app. The business continued at Cottingham until 1826. In 1831 however the address is shown as 51 Wincolmlee, Hull and the trade is changed from cm to chairmaker. [D; Hull app. reg.]

Carter, Joseph, Portland Sq., Workington, Cumb., joiner and cm (1829). [D]

Carter, Joseph, Westgate, Otley, Yorks., joiner and/or cm (1837). [D]

Carter, Richard John, Devonport, Devon, cm (1830). [Rochester poll bk]

Carter, Richard, York, cm (1834). Son of Thomas Carter of the parish of St John, York. App. to John Bellerby, cm and u of the parish of St Martin-cum-Gregory, 1 June 1814. In business on his own behalf in 1834. [D; York RO, D15 f287]

Carter, Robert, Lancaster, cm (1753–68). App. to David Wright of Lancaster 1753 and free 1767–68. [Lancaster app. reg., freemen rolls and poll bk]

Carter, Robert, Rainsford's Gdns, Liverpool, cm (1790–96). At 25 Rainsford's Gdns in 1790 but by 1796 the number had changed to 27. [D]

Carter, Robert, parish of St Mary Major, Exeter, Devon, cm (1803). [Militia Census]

Carter, Robert, Friernhay St, Exeter, Devon, u (1816–19). Son William Faithful bapt. 22 June 1816 and further son Thomas Fortescue on 29 March 1819. [PR (bapt.)]

Carter, Robert Burgess, Barnstaple, Devon, cm and u (1823–30). At High St in 1823 but by 1830 at Baker's Ct. [D]

Carter, S., Wellclose Sq., London, cabinet manufacturer (1820). [D]

Carter, Samuel, Richmond, Surrey, cm (1798). [D]

Carter, Samuel, St George's Pl., Cannon St Rd and 12 New Rd, St George's East, London, cm (1817). [D]

Carter, Samuel, Church Rd, Camberwell, London, cm and u (1822). [D]

Carter, Thomas, 12 Wardour St, London, cm (1776). Took out insurance cover for £600, half of which was for his workshop, utensils, stock and goods. [GL, Sun MS vol. 245, p. 552]

Carter, Thomas, 3 Withy Grove, Manchester, cm (1788–1833). Listed in a directory of 1788 and then there is a considerable gap until 1804. The 1804 entry is for Robert Carter but this may be an error. Regular and frequent listings begin in 1814. In 1818–21 the business is listed as Thomas Carter & Sons

but this style is not used thereafter. Recorded also at Water St in 1824 and at 13 Bond St only in 1833. [D]

Carter, Thomas, Stone St, Maidstone and Blue Town, Sheerness, Kent, cm, u, tin man and brazier (1790–1834). The earliest reference to this business occurs in the *Maidstone Journal*, 27 July 1790. The business was trading as Carter & Palmer and offered a wide range of goods and services. They acted as auctioneers and sworn appraisers. They offered to supply 'Bath, Pantheon and all kinds of STOVES with Wind-up and other Kitchen ranges'. 'Hair Trunks and Caravan Boxes' were included in their stock. They offered to re-silver mirrors and dealt in second hand furniture, as well as keeping large stocks of paper hangings. They could 'lay Oast and Malt Kilns with Iron-plate' and offered to purchase old metal or take it in exchange. They also stated they required two apps for whom premiums would be required. The size of the business is reflected in the insurance cover that they carried which included £400 for a house and offices, £500 for stock and utensils at Maidstone, and a further £200 for premises at Sheerness, with £600 for stock and utensils. From 1803–09 the business traded as Thomas Carter & Son but the Sheerness side is not mentioned after 1803. In 1810 the firm was styled Carter & Morris and was offering stock 'in fashion and workmanship inferior to none in London and at Prices considerably lower'. They offered to supply country shop-keepers with their range of goods. The firm continued to trade as Carter & Morris until 1829 though from 1823 their address was given as Week St, Maidstone. A Thomas William Carter with house and premises in Stone St is however listed in the 1834 poll bk. [D; *Maidstone Journal*, 27 July 1790, 27 February 1810; GL, Sun MS vol. 37, ref. 713331]

Carter, Thomas, London, cm, u and paperhanger (1802–15). At 8 Hanover St, Hanover Sq. from 1802–07 when the address changed to 141 Oxford St. In 1808 supplied to Farnley Hall, Otley, Yorks. '10 Grecian chairs stained to imitate ebony' at £22 10s and '2 large Grecian couches to accord with above' at £15 15s. This suite is still at Farnley Hall. The business continued to trade in Oxford St until at least 1811 but in 1814 was at New Bond St. [D; Farnley Hall papers]

Carter, Thomas, Greengate St, Stafford, cm (1822). [D]

Carter, Timothy, King St, Hammersmith, London, Windsor chairmaker (1804–08). He is probably the 'Carter' who was paid £3 3s 6d in May 1804 for 'rustic chairs', the transaction being recorded in the Heathcote account book. [D; Lincoln RO, 3 ANC 6/380]

Carter, William, Newgate St, London, case maker. Trade card, c.1760, in MMA, NY.

Carter, William, London, carver (1761). Discharged from Debtors' Prison, 13 June 1761. Described as being 'formerly of St Ann, late of Bedfordbury, St Martin in the Fields'. [*London Gazette*, , 1761, p.11]

Carter, William, 30 Cross St, Hatton St, London, carver (1794). Insured his utensils and stock for £20 out of a total cover of £100. [GL, Sun MS vol. 321, p. 126]

Carter, William, 17 Willow, Shoreditch, London, carver and gilder (1808). [D]

Carter, William, Beastmarket, Gainsborough, Lincs., chairmaker (1822). [D]

Carter, William, 172 Pilgrim St, Newcastle, cm and wood turner (1827). [D]

Carter, William, 34 East St, Leeds, Yorks., cm (1837–40). [D]

Carter, William, Middle St, Gt Driffield, Yorks., cm (1840). [D]

Carter, Wright John, Lancaster, chairmaker (1806–07). Admitted freeman 1806–07, when stated 'of Liverpool'. [Freemen rolls]

Carter & Crane, 92 New Bond St, London, upholders and cm (1812–13). In 1813 listed as Crane & Co. wholesale u. [D]

Carter & Morris, Maidstone, see Thomas Carter of Maidstone.

Carter & Son, High St, Exeter, Devon, u and cm ((1809–17). In July 1807 advertised for good workmen as journeymen cm. By 1816 a decision had been taken to dispose of the business and they advertised in July that they were willing to offer possession of the shop and manufactory at Christmas. This may not have produced a satisfactory response immediately but in April of the following year they organised an auction sale of household furniture 'mostly brought from the country for the convenience of sale' and announced at the same time that the premises had been let to Messrs Holman & Shufflebotham. The relationship of this business with the Elias Carter who traded from 25 High St from 1819 but was resident in Exeter as early as 1803 is unclear. [D; *Exeter Flying Post*, 20 July 1809, 3 April 1817; *Western Luminary*, 9 September 1816]

Cartledge, N., Boughton, Cheshire, cm (1819). [Chester poll bk]

Cartlich (or **Cartlick**), **Thomas**, 43 Sadlergate (or Sadler St), Derby, cm and u (1835). [D]

Cartner, Isaac, Middlegate, Penrith, Cumb., u (1834). [D]

Carto, David, 'The Dripping Pan, between New Broad St. and Little Moorgate in Moorfields, London', cm, undertaker and sworn appraiser (1745). Trade card states that he 'buys and sells all sort of Household Goods' and his trade may have been more that of a broker than a cm. [Heal]

Carto, Nicholas, 'The King's Arms', over against Bride Lane, Fleet St, London cm (1725). [Heal]

Cartwright, Mr, address unknown (1764). Paid for 'the Pulpit & Library Ladder £20' for Rousham House, Oxon. [Account bk of Sir Charles Cottrell Dormer (kept at the house)]

Cartwright, —, London carver (1793). Subscribed to Sheraton's *Drawing Book*, 1793.

Cartwright, —, Ipswich, Suffolk, cm (1793). Subscribed to Sheraton's *Drawing Book*, 1793.

Cartwright, —, Newcastle-under-Lyme, Staffs., turner and chairmaker (1798). [D]

Cartwright, —, Cross St, Leamington, Warks., joiner and cm (1822). [D]

Cartwright, Elizabeth, Manchester, u (1817–29). At 4 Halliwell St in 1814 but by 1829 had moved to 1 Welling St. Recorded also at 1 Wellington St, Salford, in 1829. [D]

Cartwright, F. & R., High St and Back Castle St, Bridgnorth, Salop, cm (1829). [D]

Cartwright, Francis, Back Castle St, Bridgnorth, Salop, cm (1835). [D]

Cartwright, Jane, 2 Old Shambles, Manchester, u (1825). [D]

Cartwright, John, Chester, cm (1812–26). Admitted freeman 5 October 1812 at which time he was living in Cow Lane. From 1818 living at Frodsham St. [Chester freemen rolls and poll bks]

Cartwright, John, 35 Barter St, Liverpool, cm (1837–39). [D]

Cartwright, Joseph, Birmingham, cm and u (1823–30). Trading at 22 Smallbrook St in 1823 and 22 Digbeth, 1828–30. [D]

Cartwright, Joseph, Richmond Row, Liverpool, cabinet-case maker (1837–39). At 67 Richmond Row in 1837 and 141 in 1839. [D]

Cartwright, Richard, 8 Duke Court, Bow St, Covent Gdn, London, cm (1822). Insured 'household goods etc in new dwelling house' for £100. [GL, Sun MS vol. 492, ref. 999176]

Cartwright, Richard, High St, Bridgnorth, Salop, cm (1835). [D]

Cartwright, Thomas, Bryanston, Dorset, carver (1755). Took app. named Walker. [S of G, app. index]

Cartwright, Thomas, Manchester, u (1794–1802). At 2 Bever Yd in 1794 and 12 Old Mill Gate in 1797. Bankrupt 1802. [D; *Billinge's Liverpool Advertiser*, 27 December 1802]

Cartwright, Thomas, Chester, cm (1818–40). Admitted freeman 12 May 1818 at which date he was living at George St.

An address in Frodsham St is also recorded for the same year. From 1819 at King's St. [D; Chester freemen rolls and poll bks]

Cartwright, William, High St, Bridgnorth, Salop, cm (1822–28). Recorded at High St or High Town in 1822 and Castle St in 1828. [D]

Carus, Edward, 6 Everton Gdns, Preston, Lancs., u and paper hanger (1834). [D]

Carver, Richard, Plymouth, Devon, carver (1750–61). Took the following apps: Olives (1750), Spry (1755), Kingston (1759) and Bryant (1761). [S of G, app. index]

Carver, Thomas, Weobley, Herefs., builder, cm etc. (1835). [D]

Cary, John, Wyre St, Colchester, Essex, chairmaker (1832). [D]

Cary, John, St Andrews St, Hertford, carver and gilder (1838). [D]

Cary, Robert, 33 Dukenfield St, Liverpool, u (1829). [D]

Casartelli, Lewis, 133 Duke St, Liverpool, carver and gilder (1835–39). [D]

Casbert, John, address unknown, u (1660–76). Supplied furnishings for royal palaces during the reign of Charles II on a very extensive scale. These included upholstered chairs, some chairs of estate with the associated stools and cushions, bedsteads, canopies of state and hangings and curtaining. Much of the material used was of fine quality and included Turkey work, crimson velvet and scarlet satin. Gold and silver fringe is frequently mentioned. Typical of the type of furniture supplied is an entry in the royal accounts for May 1674 for 'a French chaire Hollow in ye back and quilted with two Stooles suitable of crimson Damaske with border and bayes and silke Fringe and cases of Serge' for which £1 was charged. One 'rich bed of Crimson Velvett' supplied to Hampton Court was charged at £30. The Palace of Whitehall, Windsor Castle and Somerset House were likewise supplied by Casbert. He also appears to have been responsible for the fitting up the the royal yachts *Monmouth*, *Cleveland* and *Henrietta* and in September 1668 made a charge of £13 'for going and coming by water to the *Monmouth* Yacht fowre severall tymes, and carriage of Goodes'. [Heal; PRO, LC5/39–40, LC9/271–75; *Conn.*, vol. 43, pp. 15, 19, 86, 89; *C. Life*, 8 April 1954, p. 1028, 9 June 1977, p. 1620; *DEF*]

Case, George, Eastgate St, Gloucester, carver and gilder (1830). [D]

Case, John, Bristol, carver and gilder (1805–10). At 37 Milk St, 1805–07 but in 1810 at Lower Maudlin St. [D]

Case, John, Eastgate St, Gloucester, carver, gilder and picture frame maker (1820–22). [D]

Case, Matthew, Ulverston, Lancs., cm (1825–29). At King St in 1825 but from 1828 at Duke St. [D]

Case, Peregrine, Banbury Ct, Westminster, London, cm (1749). [Poll bk]

Case, Richard, 163 Brick Lane, Whitechapel, cm and u (1822). [D]

Casebow, William, High St, Downham Market, Norfolk, cm (1839). [D]

Casement, Evans, address unknown, cm (1803). Subscribed to Sheraton's *Cabinet Dictionary*, 1803.

Casement, William, address unknown, cm and designer of furniture (1793). Contributed three plates to *The Cabinet Makers' London Book of Prices*, 1793. Subscribed to Sheraton's *Drawing Book*, 1793. Heal states that a dining table bearing his label exists at Clarence House.

Casser, Thomas, Long Acre, London, frame maker (1692). In June 1692 fined as a papist for refusing the oath of fidelity. [Westminster Ref. lib., Middlx session bk, 498 pp. 76–79]

Cash, Charles, Liverpool, cm (1794–1827). In 1794 at 2 Jordan St but the number changed to 5 in 1803 and 8 in 1805. After

1810 at Sparling St for a number of years before moving to Pellow St by 1818 and 1 Pembroke St by 1824. [D]

Cash, George, 4 Pembroke St, Liverpool, cm (1823). [D]

Cash, William, Mansfield, Notts., joiner and cm (1828–35). Trading at Tenter Lane in 1828 and Portland Sq., 1832–35. A Samuel Cash is shown at the same address in 1841. [D]

Cashen, Charles snr, 55 Paradise St, Liverpool, carver and gilder (1796–d. 1829). Trade card in Banks Coll., BM. Took an app. John Steele jnr in 1824. [Liverpool app. enrolment bk; freemen reg.]

Cashen, Charles jnr, Liverpool, gilder (1818–39). Admitted freeman 17 June 1818. At 13 Jarvis St in 1821. In 1837 at 31 Shaws' Bow and 3 Adelaide Buildings, 124 Mt Pleasant, but in 1839 at 32 Shaws' Bow only. [D; freeman reg.]

Cashen, Christopher, 122 Duke St, Liverpool, carver and gilder (1823–24). App. to William Cashen and admitted freeman 5 September 1823. Took an app. Edward John Williams in 1823 and in May of the following year was advertising for two good journeyman carvers and gilders and an app., stating 'one from the country would be preferred'. In the advertisement the business is referred to as Christopher Cashen & Co. [D; freemen reg.; app. enrolment bk; *Liverpool Mercury*, 28 May 1824.]

Cashen, David, 15 Greenfield St, Liverpool, carver and gilder (1827). [D]

Cashen, Edward, 124 Adelaide Buildings, Mount Pleasant, Liverpool, carver, gilder and cm (1830–39). Son of William Cashen. Admitted freeman 22 November 1830. Initially in partnership with his brother Henry under the style Henry & Edward Cashen, but the arrangement was dissolved in November 1833. Thereafter he traded on his own account as a cabinet-maker. [D; freemen reg.; *Liverpool Mercury*, 8 November 1833]

Cashen, Ellen, Paradise St, Liverpool, carver and gilder (1834–39). At 88 Paradise St in 1834 but subsequently at 10, 87 and 90. [D]

Cashen, Henry, Liverpool, carver and gilder (1827–35). Son of William Cashen. Admitted freeman, 19 February 1827. Address initially 77 Whitechapel, but by 1832 in partnership with his brother Edward at Adelaide Buildings, Ranelagh Pl. The partnership declared that they were in a position to supply 'Chimney Glasses, Mirrors & Dressing Glasses, of all sizes & of every description; Ornamental, Gilt & rosewood Pier Tables, Window Cornices, Picture Frames & Gilt Mouldings for Rooms'. The services offered included picture cleaning and restoration, the re-silvering of glass and the re-gilding of frames. The trade and ship's captains were invited to patronise their services. They also advertised for two journeyman gilders. The partnership was however short-lived and was dissolved in November 1833. John Richardson was taken as app. in 1831 and Hugh O'Donnell in the following year. An address at 30 Bold St was being used in 1834. [D; freemen reg.; app. enrolment bk; *Liverpool Mercury*, 10 February 1832, 8 November 1833]

Cashen, James, 87 Paradise St, Liverpool, gilder (1830). Son of William Cashen, gilder. Admitted freeman 10 November 1830. [Freemen rolls]

Cashen, Philip, Liverpool, gilder (1818–29). Son of William Cashen, carver and gilder. Admitted freeman 17 June 1818 and trading at 51 Ranelagh St in that year. In 1821 and 1824 shown at 9 White Mill St but from 1827 at 60 Copperas Hill. [D; freemen rolls]

Cashen, Thomas, Liverpool, carver and gilder (1827–39). At 15 Sydney Pl., Edgehill in 1827 but by 1829 had moved to 39 St Anne's St. In 1834 and 35 at 2 Kensington Pl. but by 1839 had moved once again at Frederick Buildings, 4 Back Queen Anne St. [D]

Cashen, William snr, Liverpool, gilder (1796–1824). Admitted freeman 31 May 1796. Initially in business in Paradise St where his number is shown as 55 (1796), 65 (1800), 67 (1804), 86 (1805), 85 (1807–10 and 1814), 81 (1811) and 84 (1813 and 1816–18). Between 1821–24 the business address was 90 Paradise St and in addition 53 Byron St in 1821. His apps were James Smart (indenture 1793, free 1802), Harry Wilson (indenture 1800, free 1812), John Davies (indenture 1804, free 1812), William Kenyon (indenture 1814, free 1822) and William Smith (indenture 1824, free 1831). [D; freemens' committee bk]

Cashen, William jnr, 90 Paradise St, Liverpool, carver and gilder (1818–d. 1829). Second son of William Cashen snr. Sworn freeman 17 June 1818. Took as apps Thomas Hardman in 1826 and William Miles Walters in 1831 according to the app. enrolment bk. As he is recorded dying on 16 December 1829 'after a lingering illness' the existence of a third William Cashen would seem likely. [D; Liverpool freemen reg.; *Liverpool Mercury*, 25 December 1829]

Casimir, Josiah, Nag's Head Ct, Gracechurch St, London, u (1714–24). [Heal]

Caspall, James Austen, Snargate St, Dover, Kent, cm (1832–37). [Poll bks]

Cassell, J. H., 47 High St, Whitechapel, London, cm etc. (1835). [D]

Cassera, Charles, Dudley, Worcs., cm and u (1838–40). Trading at High St in 1840. [D]

Casson, John, Sandside Low Quarter, Broughton, Westmld, cm (1829). [D]

Casson, John, Corn Mkt, Wigton, Cumb., cm and joiner (1834). [D]

Casson, Thomas, Lancaster. Craftsman named in the Gillow records between 1814–40. [Westminster Ref. Lib.]

Cassteel(?), Lewis, London(?), carver and gilder (1702). Sums amounting to £8 paid by Samuel Tufton of Middle Temple, London for gilt frames. [Essex RO, D/DTu 276]

Castairs, J., 64 King St, Golden Sq., London, cm (1837). [D]

Castell, James, cm (1803). Subscribed to Sheraton's *Cabinet Dictionary*, 1803.

Castell, John, 43 King St, Clerkenwell, London, cm (1835–37). [D]

Castell, Peter, 4 Lewis Pl., Duncan St East, Liverpool, carver and gilder (1829). [D]

Castille, Nathaniel, London, carver and gilder (1829–39). At 25 Charlotte St (1829) but between 1835 and 39 at 6 Chapel St, Tottenham Ct Rd. [D]

Castle, Daniel, Canterbury and London, u (1757–96). Sworn freeman of Canterbury 1757 and whilst in that city took app. named Hampton in 1758 and another named Homersham in 1760. In 1796 shown at Windmill St, Middlx. [Canterbury freemen rolls and poll bk; S of G, app. index]

Castle, John, 73 Chiswell St, Finsbury Sq., London, cabinet manufacturer (1816–17). [D]

Castle, Richard, Middle St, Deal, Kent cm (1813–19). [D; Sandwich poll bks]

Castle, Samuel, Hull, Yorks., cm (1780). [Poll bk]

Castle, Thomas, parish of St Michael, Bristol, carver and gilder (1715–34). [Poll bks]

Castle, Thomas, Canterbury, Kent and Portsmouth, Hants., cm (1767–1826). Sworn freeman of Canterbury 1767. At Portsmouth in 1796 but by 1818 had moved back to Canterbury where he was living in Love Lane. [Canterbury freemen rolls and poll bks; Dover poll bk]

Castle, William, London, cabinet and chair maker, knife case manufactory (1796–1823). Initially at 38 Smithfield but by 1802 had moved to 65 Aldersgate St where he was to remain in business until 1823. His trade card [Johnson Coll.,

Bodleian Lib., Oxford] states that he made 'Knife cases, Portable Desks and every article in the Cabinet Line — carpentry of every description'. [D]

Castleman, Richard, Gosport, Hants., cm (1792–93). [D]

Castley, William, Shap, Westmld, joiner and cm (1828). [D]

Castoll, John Soames, Norwich, cm (1791). Son of Richard Castoll, grocer. Admitted freeman, 12 March 1791. [Norwich freemen reg.]

Caston, Thomas, 7 York Pl., Lambeth, London, cm and u (1827). [D]

Caswell, Thomas & W., 71 Lower Sloane St, Chelsea, London, cm and u (1823).[D]

Cataneo, Evangelista, Liverpool, carver and gilder (1820). Declared bankrupt, *Liverpool Mercury*, 31 March 1820.

Catchmead, John, Canterbury, Kent, u (1674). [Canterbury freemen rolls]

Catchpole, Thomas, 44 Cannon St Rd, London, cm and u (1839). [D]

Catchpool, John, Sittingbourne, Kent, cm and u (1832). [D]

Catear, Jewell, Plymouth, Devon, cm (1815). Appears in a list of creditors of the cm Thomas Smith of Plymouth. [*Exeter Flying Post*, 2 March 1815]

Cater, Andrew, Stapleton, Glos., u (1715–39). [Bristol poll bks]

Cater, David & Son, Berry Croft, Holme, Yorks., joiner and/or cm (1837). [D]

Cater, J., Higher Broad St, Plymouth, Devon, cm and u (1814). [D]

Cater, John Wyatt, Stapleton, Glos., carver (1784). [Bristol poll bk]

Cater, William Charles, London, u and cm (1811–39). At 95 Wardour St, 1811–16, and then 45 London St, Fitzroy Sq. until 1828. An entry for 1839 however shows the address as 38 Newman St. [D]

Catesby, Frederick, 99 High St, Marylebone, London, japanner and gilder (1837–39). [D]

Catesby, Jekel & Spencer, Alexander, 62 Castle St East, Oxford Mkt, London, chair painters (1805). Took out insurance cover on their workshop behind 122 Wardour St, which contained a stove, for £100. Both Catesby and Spencer each took out similar cover on their dwelling houses and household goods. [GL, Sun MS vol. 434, ref. 781705]

Catherick, Henry, 74 Charlotte St, Tottenham Ct Rd, London, cm and u (1839). [D]

Cathery, Desbrough, Poole, Dorset, cm (1823–30). At Long Fleet in 1823 but by 1830 had moved to High St. [D]

Cathrall, William, Bunbury, Cheshire, cm (1818). On 16 November married Miss Martha Peacock of Denham. [*Chester Guardian*, 21 November 1818]

Cathrow, Thomas, Minories, London, upholder (1768–82). Son of James Cathrow of Tottenham, London, gardener. App. to Elizabeth Dawson, 1 May 1760 and admitted freeman of the Upholders' Co. by servitude on 1 June 1768. Took apps John Harris (1771–78) and James H. Kirby (1778–82). [GL, Upholders' Co. records]

Catignou, James. Supplied many sconces for Kensington Palace, c. 1795. [*Conn.*, vol. 57, p. 90]

Catley, James, Factory Lane, Doncaster, Yorks., carver and gilder (1830).

Catley, James, 21 Waterhouse Lane, Hull, Yorks., wood turner and carver (1831). [D]

Caton, John Varley, Lancaster, u (1806–07). [Lancaster freemen rolls]

Catt, Benjamin, Buttermarket, Ipswich, Suffolk, cm and auctioneer (1782–1807). In 1782 insured his house for £200. [GL, Sun MS vol. 301, p. 4]

Cattall, Samuel, Cow Lane, Daventry, Northants., joiner,

carpenter and cm (1792). Insured his house, workshop and stable for £300. [GL, Sun MS vol. 388, p. 200]

Cattaneo, Charles, London, carver, gilder and look-glass maker (1826–39). Initially at 30 Guildford Pl., Bagnigge Wells Rd, but by 1835 he was trading as Charles Cattaneo & Co., 'looking glass manufacturer to His Majesty' at 377 Strand. [D]

Cattaneo & Co., E., 66 Hanover St, Liverpool, opticians, barometer, thermometer and looking-glass manufacturers (1818). In November 1818 advertised that they had recently moved from London and set up a business that stocked a wide range of scientific equipment, 'Foreign & English Toys, Ladies' French Fancy Baskets etc. Sheffield & Birmingham good of all kinds, Umbrellas, Parasols' etc. They could supply 'Concave & Convex Glasses & Mirrors' and 'Looking Glasses of all sizes & kinds'. They also offered to re-silver mirrors and frame and glaze pictures and needlework and re-gild frames. [*Liverpool Mercury*, 13 November 1818]

Cattaneo, Pasqual, High St, Croydon, Surrey, carver and gilder (1839). [D]

Catter, Charles, 22 Warwick St, Golden Sq., London, carver, gilder and housepainter (1809). [D]

Catterall, John, Liverpool, carver (1796–1816). Sworn freeman 31 May 1796. At 12 Edgar St in 1807 but by 1810 had moved to Brooks Alley where his number was 7 from 1810–11, 11 in 1813–14 and 8 in 1816. [D; freemen reg.]

Catterall, William, Liverpool, cm (1796–d. by 1820). Sworn freeman 27 May 1796. [Freemen reg.]

Cattle, Enoch, 9 Gloucester St, St John's St Rd, London, fancy cm and u (1837–39). [D]

Cattle, William, 65 Aldersgate St, London, knifecase maker (1821). [D]

Cattrall, John, 31 Prince Edward St, Edgehill, Liverpool, carver (1796). Sworn freeman 31 May 1796. [Freemen reg.]

Cattrall (or Catherall), William, Liverpool, cm (1818–40). Son of Jonathan Cathrall, pot maker. App. to Ralph Magill in 1806 and free, 17 June 1818. By 1827 he was in partnership with Thomas Whittingham and trading from 3 Hood St. In July 1831 the partners advertised that they had to let in Gt Charlotte St 'an excellent WORKSHOP, with an OFFICE & STORE ROOM, a good STOVE & roomy YARD; together with a very convenient DWELLING HOUSE adjoining' suitable for 'JOINERS CABINET MAKERS etc'. Subsequently the business was carried on from 6 Leigh St North (1835) and Westmorland Pl. with a shop at 6 and 11 Brooks Alley. The business took the following apps: Neil NcNabb (1822), Joseph Mitchell (1823), Frances Underwood (1823), Joseph Davies (1825), Thomas Pike (1825), Robert Pawlett (1827), Thomas Wakefield (1830), John Maybreck (1832), and Thomas Thompson (1834). [D; *Liverpool Mercury*, 1 July 1831; freemen reg.; app. enrolment bks]

Caudby, —, Lancaster, japanner (1819). Named in the Gillow records. [Westminster Ref. Lib., Gillow vol. 344/100, p. 3015]

Caulton, Edward, Leicester, u (1695–98). App. to Ann Sherwin. Had two sons John and Richard. [Freemen reg.]

Caulton, Edward, Nottingham, u (1703). [Freemen reg.]

Caulton, John, Leicester, u (1726). Son of Edward Caulton of Leicester, u. Free 1726. [Freemen reg.]

Caulton, Richard, Leicester, u (1734). Son of Edward Caulton of Leicester, u. Freeman 1734. [Freemen reg.]

Caunce, John, 7 Barnes St, Manchester, cm (1804). [D]

Caunce, William, 12 Blake St, Liverpool, cm and u (1829). [D]

Causby, John, 46 Noble St, Goswell St, London, bedstead and chair carver (1808–09). [D]

Cauty, William, London, cm and u (1748–80). Established initially at the sign of 'The Chair & Curtains' at the west end of Somerset House, Strand. His trade card from this period states that he was able to supply 'Chairs, Tables and Glasses of all sorts, neat Mahogany Bedsteads & Cloaths-Presses, with the greatest variety of nice Tea-Tables, Trays and Chests.' In 1755 he subscribed to the second edition of Chippendale's *Director*. Although a number of commissions executed from the late 1740s would suggest a successful and fashionable business he nevertheless was declared bankrupt in March 1757. In the same month however he was advertising in the *London Chronicle* offering 'Mahogany and walnut-tree corner chairs, reading chairs, shaving chairs, compass seat chairs and dressing chairs.' He also stated that his 'Bedsteads, Sophas and Chairs' were 'finished so that no vermin of any denomination can possibly exist in either', a claim that he was to repeat on subsequent trade cards. He was supplying furniture from the same address in 1757 and the interruption of the business by the bankruptcy may therefore have been minimal. From 1769–70 he is recorded as a Fellow of the Society of Arts. By this date he had however moved his business to King St, corner of Bury St, St James's St where he carried on a similar trade. He used his trade bills both for issuing invoices for goods supplied and marking his furniture. One is recorded on a mahogany chest of drawers made in the 1770s. By 1780 however the business must have hit hard times for in the Westminster rates bk of this year his failure to pay is recorded with the marginal remark 'poor. Give him time'.

Cauty's earliest recorded commission was on 21 July 1748 when he invoiced two mahogany card tables at £4 10s each, two girandoles and a mahogany tea table to a 'Mr West'. This was the Hon. James West of Alscot Park, Warks. who also purchased from him in July 1751 'twelve Nova Scotia walnut chairs' at £1 7s 6d each. In the same year he supplied to John Dalrymple of Stair '6 Large French Chairs stuffed in canvas with mahogany frames' and 'check cases' for them, amounting with cartage to £8 8s 6d. An account written on his trade bill in the Heal Coll. records the supply in 1757 of a mahogany bookcase for which £26 5s was charged. [*DEF*; Heal; *Gents Mag.*, March 1757; *C. Life*, 7 July 1966, p. 48; poll bks; *GCM*; Scottish RO, GD 135/Box 42/7/6; V & A archives] B.A.

Cavallier, William, Whitby, Yorks., cm and u (1823–40). At 'West end of the Bridge' in 1823 but by 1828 at Old Market Pl. In 1840 at Flowergate as cm, chairmaker and undertaker. [D]

Cave, George, Old Market, Wisbech, Cambs., cm and auctioneer (1830–39). [D]

Cave, Henry, 69a Gravel Lane, Manchester, cm, joiner and builder (1825). [D]

Cave, James, High St, Oakham, Rutland, cm (1840). [D; GL, Sun MS vol. 268, ref. 1340270]

Cave, John, London, chair and sofa maker (1826–37). In 1826 the address is recorded as 9 Richmond St, St Luke's but by 1837 this had changed to 9 Bartholomew Sq., St Luke's. [D]

Cave, Robert, Jewin St, Cripplegate, London, cm and broker (1793). [D]

Cave, William, 7 College St, Worcester, cm and u (1830). A Richard Cave, cm, u and chairmaker, was trading at College St, date unspecified. [D]

Cave, William, Pump St, Worcester, cm and u (1830). [D]

Cavel, George, 26 Bridge House Pl., Newington Causeway, London, chair and sofa maker (1820–39). [D]

Cavey, James, 73 Pitt St, Liverpool, carver and gilder (1821). [D]

Cawdle, —, address unknown. Recorded on the Holkham Hall, Norfolk accounts in 1728 working on a bed and repairing furniture for which £1 5s was paid. [V & A archives]

Cawley, Edward & Joseph, High St, Poole, Dorset, cm and u (1840). [D]

Cawley, James, Exeter and Budleigh Salterton, Devon, cm (1791–d. 1832). Trading at Mary Arches Lane, Exeter in 1791 and Fourth St, Exeter in 1796. He is recorded in the Exeter Militia list for 1803 in the parish of St Mary Major. On 1 March 1810 he advertised the sale of cabinet and upholstery furniture and plank mahogany prior to his removal to Budleigh Salterton. His life at this new location was however to take a dramatic turn, for in November of the same year two newly built houses belonging to him with all their furniture were swept out to sea as a result of severe flooding. He died at Budleigh Salterton in June 1832. [D; *Exeter Flying Post*, 1 March 1810, 15 November 1810; *The Alfred*, 5 June 1832]

Cawley, James, West St, Bridport, Dorset, cm, u and auctioneer (1823–30). In 1830 the business is recorded as James Cawley & Son. [D]

Cawley, James, 144 High St, Poole, Dorset, cm (1830). [D]

Cawley, William Bale, High St, Huntingdon, builder, u and cm (1830–40). [D; Cambs. RO (Hunts), HB 12/4]

Cawood, Benjamin, Pinfold, Knaresborough, Yorks., joiner, cm and builder (1828–34). [D]

Cawood, Henry, Green Hammerton, near Boroughbridge, Yorks., cm (1822). [D]

Cawston, James, 27 Burlington Arcade, Piccadilly, London, dressing case and writing desk maker (1829–35). Recorded on the 1830 voters list for Petersfield, Hants. although living and working in London at this period. [D]

Cawthorn, John, Red Cross St, London, cm (1790–93). [D]

Cawthorn, William, 1 Upper James St, Golden Sq., London, cm (1809–26). [D]

Cawthorne (or **Cawthorpe**), **William**, Mardol, Shrewsbury, Salop, cm and u (1828). [D]

Cawthorne, William, 36 Finch St, Liverpool, cm (1839). [D]

Cayford, James, London, cm and u (1790–1819). In the period 1790–93 recorded at 31 Fetter Lane but in 1795 the address changed to 31 Bartlet's Building, High Holborn. From 1809 the number is changed to 13. [D]

Cayley, William, London, cm, u and undertaker (1820–39). Initially at 137 Upper St, Islington but by 1826 the number had changed to 123. By 1835 the number had changed again to 122 and the business was styled W. Cayley & Son and in 1839, Cayley & Sons. [D]

Cayzer, James, St Columb, Cornwall, u (1827–30). [D; Cornwall RO, DD/CF 999/1–2]

Cazzanigha, F. & Co., 3 Spring Gdns, Manchester, looking-glass and picture frame makers (1804). [D]

Ceely, William, Aldersgate St, London, cm (1774–84). [Bristol poll bks]

Cerne, John, Middlesex Ct, St Martin-in-the-Fields, London, cm (1749). [Westminster poll bk]

Cetta, John, London, looking-glass and barometer maker, picture and looking-glass frame maker (1838–40). At 7 Union Ct, Black Hill, Holborn in 1838, but by the next year had moved to 15 Brook St. [D]

Cetti, John & Co., 25 Red Lion St, London, looking-glass and barometer makers (1820–40). [D; Goodison, *Barometers*]

Cetti, Isaac & Co, 55 Red Lion St, London, carver and gilder (1839). [D]

Cetti, Joseph & Co., Red Lion St, London, looking-glass manufacturer (1813–35). At 54 Red Lion St in 1813 but by 1817 the number had changed to 25. [D]

Ceulas, Marmaduke, St Augustine's Back, Bristol, upholder. Trade card in MMA, NY.

Chabanel, —, New Broad St Buildings, London, u and company merchant (1775). [D]

Chabot, Robert, 31 Leadenhall St, London, looking-glass manufacturer (c. 1790). [Wills, *Looking-Glasses*]

Chaddock, Charles, 'The Red Hart', Red Cross St, The Mint, Southwark, London, broker, cm and undertaker (1786). Took out insurance cover of £400 on utensils and stock on 3 January 1786. [GL, Sun MS vol. 334, p. 164]

Chadley, James, Frogmore-ward, High Wycombe, Bucks., cm and u (1823). [D]

Chadley, Robert & George, London, cm and u (1821–25). Successors to Proctor & Chadley who had traded in Albemarle St, 1818–20. Also referred to as Chadley & Co. At 28 Albemarle St, Piccadilly in 1821 when insurance cover of £2,200 was taken out on stock, utensils and goods in trust in warerooms and workshops, an open shed under the workshops and an open yard. A further £200 cover was taken out on china and glass. Such figures suggest a very substantial business. After 1822, however, the address used was 42 Jermyn St, a dwelling house. In the insurance policy it was stated that there was 'no stove nor cabinet work done therein' and cover was for £650 with £100 extra for china and glass and £25 for stock, utensils and goods in trust. It is possible that by this date the partnership had been dissolved though the evidence is not entirely clear. [D; GL, Sun MS vol. 488, ref. 976759; vol. 493, ref. 989375]

Chadwell, —, Oxford. In 1756 received £1 4s from All Souls College for two reading desks. [MS DD c. 257]

Chadwell, Robert, Wivelscombe, Som., cm (1755). In 1755 took app. named Tymewell. [S of G, app. index]

Chadwick, Benjamin, King's Lynn, Norfolk, u (1774). App. to John Chadwick and free 1774–75. [Freemen rolls]

Chadwick, Jeremiah, Batley Carr, Dewsbury, Yorks., cm (1830–37). [D]

Chadwick, John, King's Lynn, Norfolk, u (1759–75). App. to Asty Harwick and free 1759–60. In the freemen rolls he is described as John Chadwick jnr. Took app. Benjamin Chadwick, probably his son, who was made free 1774–75. [Freemen rolls; poll bk]

Chadwick, Joseph, Standish Gate, Wigan, Lancs., cabinet and chair maker (1825). [D]

Chadwick, Joseph, Liverpool, cm (1835–39). At 41 Wood St, Toxteth in 1835 and 13 Shannon St in 1839. [D]

Chadwick, Richard, Liverpool, joiner and cm (1790). Took an app. John Whitby who was made free 1790. [Freemen's committee bk]

Chadwick, William Henry, Manchester, carver and gilder, looking-glass and picture frame maker (1825–40). At 15 Exchange St in 1825; 22 Fountain St, 1828–29; 75 Fountain St in 1832–33; 21 Ridgefield, 1834–38 and 9 King St, 1840. [D]

Chaffe, Stephen, Yealmpton near Plymouth, Devon, chairmaker and carpenter (1819–23). [PR; *Furn. Hist.*, 1976]

Chaffer, Benjamin, Burnley, Lancs., cm (1834–38). At 7 Goodham Hill, 1834 and in partnership with Wm. C. Chaffer at Howe St in 1838. [D]

Chaffer(s), William, Burnley, Lancs., cm, chairmaker, cooper, u, constable and appraiser (1792–1838). Initially at Hill Top, and still there in 1822; but by 1818 also recorded at Church St. Also recorded living near the 'Bull Inn' in Market St and tenant of the New Sparrow Hawk by the church in 1824. Paid £50 p.a. c. 1835 as 'deputy constabale' which by 1838 had risen to £65. [D; Bennett, *History of Burnley*, vol. 3, pp. 208 ff, 213]

Chaffin, Charles, London, cm and u (1809–35). At Gt Somerset St, Aldgate in 1809 but after 1813 at 9 Somerset St, Whitechapel. One directory entry of 1820 however gives the address as 3 Swan St, Minories. [D]

Chalk, Charles, London, cm (1812–20). At 18 Gt Sutton St,

Clerkenwell 1812–13, but by the next year had moved to 19 Goswell St at which address he continued till 1820. [D]

Chalk, James T., 18 Gt Sutton St, Clerkenwell, London, cm (1809–11). Succeeded at this address by Charles Chalk. [D]

Chalk, Thomas, 49 Little Eastcheap, London, cm (1794–95). [D]

Chalk, Thomas, High St, Lincoln, cm (1805–08). [D]

Chalker, George, 29 St Mary St, Maiden St, Weymouth, Dorset, cm and u (1840). [D]

Challand, W., Arnold, Notts., joiner and cm (1832). [D]

Challen, William, 17 Gt Saffron Hill, London, chairmaker (1790–97). [D; Heal]

Challenor, J., 2 Bath Rd, Cheltenham, Glos., carver and gilder (1839). [D]

Challice, Richard, Spillers Lane, Exeter, Devon, carver (1826). Baptism of daughter Sarah, 8 October 1826. [PR(bapt.)]

Challiner, Thomas, Chester, cm (1811). Sworn freeman 12 June 1811. [Freemen rolls]

Challis, Charles, 3 Noel St, Berwick St, London, cm (1787). On 25 June 1787 took out insurance cover on goods for £200. [GL, Sun MS vol. 342, ref. 532032]

Challis, John, London, u (1793). Subscribed to Sheraton's *Drawing Book*, 1793.

Chalmer, Charles, 78 Berwick St, Soho, London, cm (1808–09). [D]

Chalmers, James, 1 Milk Alley, Wardour St, London, chairmaker and carver (1780). In 1780 took out insurance cover of £100 which included £40 for utensils and stock. [GL, Sun MS vol. 280, p. 638]

Chalmers, T., 9 Charlotte St, Fitzroy Sq., London, u (1815). [D]

Chamber, Samuel, Southampton, Hants., cm (1793). [D]

Chamberlain, Charles, London, cm (1774–76). Bankruptcy recorded November 1774. In 1776 he took out insurance cover of £200 of which £100 was for utensils, stock and goods. The addresses recorded are Somerset Yd, Strand in 1774 and corner of Durham St, Strand in 1776. [*Gents Mag.*, November 1774; GL, Sun MS vol. 244, p. 597]

Chamberlain, Charles, Bridge St, Norwich, cm (1839). [D]

Chamberlain, Dixon, Sun St, Bernwell, Cambridge, turner and chairmaker (1830). [D]

Chamberlain, J & T., 19 Newington Causeway, London, cm etc. (1820). [D]

Chamberlain, John, corner of Crown Ct, Knave's Acre, London, cm and broker (d. 1743). In March 1743 the sale of his stock by auction was announced. The stock consisted of 'Desks and Bookcases, Desks, Tables, Chests of Drawers, Cloaths Chests, Scrutores etc in Walnut-Tree, Wainscot, and Mahogany, Pier and Chimney Glasses, Sconces, Chairs, Carpets, Standing Beds . . . with divers other Goods in the Cabinet, Chair and Upholstery way'. It is possible that John Chamberlain may have been the Mr Chamberlain, u who supplied chairs and upholstery work for the Earl of Rockingham in September 1692 and August 1696. [*Daily Advertiser*, 4 March 1743; Lincoln RO, Monson 10/1/A/19]

Chamberlain, John, parish of St Edmund, Exeter, Devon, cm (1803–10). Recorded in Militia list 1803, and may in 1810 have occupied a house in Newbridge as a tenant. [*Exeter Flying Post*, 8 November 1810]

Chamberlain, John, 15 Sherborne Lane, Lombard St, London, billiard table maker (1810–22). In May 1810 took out insurance cover for £500 of which £300 was for household goods and £200 for stock and utensils. May be the John Chamberlain recorded as dying at Poplar in March 1835. [D; GL, Sun MS vol. 451, ref. 844707; PR, St Mary Abchurch (bapt. and burial)]

Chamberlain, John, 28 Western Rd, Brighton, Sussex, cm (1832–40). Births of two sons and two daughters recorded between 1832 and 1840. [D; E. Sussex RO, PAR 255/1/2/10–12]

Chamberlain, T., Ipswich, Suffolk, cm (1793–1801). Subscribed to Sheraton's *Drawing Book*, 1793. [*Ipswich Journal*, 10 January 1801]

Chamberlain, William, Colegate St, St George's, Norwich, cm and u (1822–40). [D]

Chamberlayne, James, Barnstable, Devon, cm and maltster (1793). [D]

Chambers, —, address not known, u (1814). Paid £3 in July 1813 by 2nd Lord Braybrooke for Audley End, Essex or Billingbear, Berks. [Essex RO, D/DBy/A376]

Chambers, Andrew, 13 Turnstile Alley, Drury Lane, cm and broker (1782). Took out insurance of £200 of which half was for utensils, stock and goods. [GL, Sun MS vol. 300, p. 176]

Chambers, George, Woolshops, Halifax, Yorks., carver, gilder and painter (1837). [D]

Chambers, Henry, Yealmpton, near Plymouth, Devon, chairmaker (1832). [*Furn. Hist.*, 1976]

Chambers, James, Lancaster, turner and chairmaker (1797–1813). App. to J. Tyson 1797 and free 1806–07. Mentioned in Gillow records 1797–1813. [App. and freemen regs; Westminster Ref. Lib., Gillow]

Chambers, James, St Mary's, Ely, Cambs., carpenter, joiner and cm (1830). [D]

Chambers, James, 71 Sloane St, London u (1835). [D]

Chambers, Joseph, 15 Panton St, London, cm and u (1839). [D]

Chambers, Peter, 147 Whitechapel Rd, London, u (1814–37). [D]

Chambers, Richard, Throgmorton St, London upholder (1706–34). Admitted freeman of Upholders' Co. on 3 July 1706. [GL, Upholders' Co. records; Heal]

Chambers, Richard, Wokingham, Berks., cm (1823). [D]

Chambers, Samuel, Milk St, London, u (1709–68). Son of Abraham Chambers of Selling, Kent, yeoman. App. to Henry Winton, 10 March 1709/10 and free of the Upholders' Co. by servitude, 7 May 1718. Master of the Upholders' Co., 1746. In 1768 trading as Chambers & Lynes and on 22 October of that year supplied 'bed furniture etc' for Shelburne House, Berkeley Sq. amounting to £22 14s. A further account dated 19 November of that year for 'Crimson Nassau Damask' amounted to £36 15s. [GL, Upholders' Co. records; Heal; Bowood MS]

Chambers, Samuel, Coventry, Warks., carver and gilder (1818–30). At Hertford St, 1818–28 and Little Park St, 1822–30. [D]

Chambers, Samuel, 80 Bull St, Birmingham, fancy box, case and caddy maker (1835). [D]

Chambers, Thomas, London, cm and upholder (1784–87). At 99 Upper East Smithfield in 1784 when he took out insurance cover for £2,000 which included £320 for utensils, stock, goods and workshop. In 1787 he insured thirteen houses in Nightingale Lane, Upper East Smithfield, for a total of £900. [GL, Sun MS vol. 319, p. 419; vol. 340, p. 522]

Chambers, Thomas, Yealmpton, near Plymouth, Devon, chairmaker (1815). [*Furn. Hist.*, 1976]

Chambers, Tristram, Cary St, near Lincoln's Inn Playhouse, London, u (1749). [Heal; poll bk]

Chambers, William, Raistrick, near Halifax, Yorks., cm and valuer (1822–28). [D]

Chambers, William, Brighouse, Halifax, joiner/cm (1834). [D]

Chambers & Lynes, see Samuel Chambers, London.

Champ, George, 9 Upper Baker St, New Rd, Marylebone, London, carver, gilder etc. (1809–37). [D]

Champion, John, Sheffield, Yorks., cm (1821–22). At Duke St in 1821 and 7 Ramsden's Ct, High St the following year. [D]

Champion, John, London, cm and u (1835–39). At St James's in 1835 and 1 Richmond St, Soho in 1839. [D]

Champion & Watkins, 13 Henrietta St, Covent Gdn, London, billiard and backgammon table makers (1829). [D]

Champman & Son, 31 Market Pl., Hull, Yorks., u (1805). [D]

Champness, Thomas, London, turner and chairmaker (1761). Discharged from Debtors' Prison 26 September 1761. His address was stated to be 'formerly of Holborn and late of Old Bailey'. [*London Gazette*, September 1761, p. 5]

Champney, Robert Nelson, Prebend Row, Darlington, Co. Durham, joiner and cm (1834). [D]

Champneys, Edmund, Trim St, Bath, Som., u and auctioneer (1783–91). [D]

Chance, James & Henry, 84 Charlotte St, Fitzroy Sq., London, carvers and gilders (1839). [D]

Chandle, Thomas, 19 Bow Lane, Cheapside, London, cm, u and chairmaker (1827). [D]

Chandler —, 144 Sloane St, Chelsea, London, cm and u (1823). [D]

Chandler, Charles, Fairview Pl., Cheltenham, Glos., cm (1839). [D]

Chandler, Edward, 7 Queen's Row, Pimlico, upholder (1814). [D]

Chandler, George Loudon, Worcester, cm (1835). App. to James Mason and free 26 January 1835. [Freemen reg.]

Chandler, John, Shoreham, Sussex, carver (1742). In 1742 took app. named Chatfield. [S of G, app. index]

Chandler, John, New St, Westminster, London, carver (1749). [Poll bk]

Chandler, John, Kingston, Surrey, cm (1796). [Canterbury poll bk]

Chandler, John, Cambridge, turner, chairmaker and cm (1820–40). At Petty Cury (1823–24), Red Heart Yd (1830), Willow Pl. (1832–35) and Fitzroy St in 1837. On 29 September 1820 claimed freedom as first born son of Thomas Chandler, freeman. [D; poll bks; Cambs. RO, Corp. records] See Chandler & Hazelwood.

Chandler, John, 7 Oyle Mews, London, chairmaker and cm (1840). [GL, Sun MS ref. 133065]

Chandler, Richard, Paul St, Exeter, Devon, u (1835). [D]

Chandler, Thomas, Cambridge, cm, joiner, broker and turner (1788–1845). On 31 March 1788 he was bound app. to Edward and Thomas Yorke of Cambridge, cm and joiners, for a fee of 10s. He claimed his freedom of the Corporation of Cambridge through his apprenticeship on 29 September 1798. In June 1806 he is listed as one of the Bailiffs of the Corporation and in September of the same year a Common Councillor. Poll bks list him at various addresses: in 1818, Sparrow Lane; in 1832 Hobson St; in 1834, Willow Pl.; and from 1837–40, Fitzroy St. Accounts submitted by him to the Corporation survive for the years 1820–24, and are mostly for general joinery work although the repair of furniture is mentioned. He appears to have worked with his son John, as both are named in the apprenticeship of Thomas Legge. Many of the poll bks also list him at the same addresses. His apps were William Swan from 15 May 1810 for a fee of £20, Thomas Legge jnr from 4 February 1822 for a fee of £20 and Joseph Rutherford from 3 January 1831 for an undisclosed fee. By 1822 his son John Chandler was active in the business. [Cambs. RO, Cambridge Corp. day bks and app. lists] See Chandler & Hazelwood. R. W.

Chandler, Thomas, Bristol, cm (1818–40). At 6 St John's Bridge (1818–19), Upper Maudlin St (1820), 6 Barrs St (1822), Merchants St (1823–24), College Pl. (1825), 4 Limekiln Lane (1826–28), 17 Redcliff Hill (1829–31) and 6 Sussex Pl. (1833–40). [D]

Chandler & Hazelwood, Brazenwell George Yd, Cambridge,

turner and chairmakers (1839). [D] Presumably John Chandler and Thomas Hazelwood who are both recorded in 1830 at Red Hart Yd.

Chandlor, Thomas, 9 Colville Ct, Rathbone Pl., London u (1809). [D]

Channon, Atho, Exeter, Devon, cm (1742). In 1742 he took app. named Thomas Parker for a consideration of £15. [S of G, app. index] Possibly the same person as Otho Channon, chairmaker.

Channon, George, St Martin's Lane, London, cm (1749). [Westminster poll bk]

Channon, John, 109 St Martin's Lane, London, cm (b. 1711–d. c. 1783). In the 18th century there were many Channons living in Exeter and Tiverton, and it is not always possible to establish their precise relationship to each other. However, it is likely that John was the younger brother of Otho, an Exeter chairmaker, and that both were the sons of Otho Channon who on 8 October 1697 married Anne Sone and who appears in the Exeter poor rate bk between 1699 and 1732 wherein he is described as innkeeper, 1714 and 1719, and as a serge maker 1725–26. Otho Channon snr lived in the parish of St Sidwell, the baptism of his son Otho being listed in the church register on 4 November 1698 and of his son John on 21 May 1711. In 1726, at the age of fifteen, John was app. to his elder brother Otho 'of Exeter joiner' for a consideration of £8. [PRO, IR 1/13/155, vol. 6, p. 1012] He would have completed his training in 1733 and is next heard of in London in 1737 when he set up a cabinet making business at premises 'upon the Pavement' on the west side of St Martin's Lane, later numbered 109. His name first appears in the Westminster poor rate bk for the last quarter of 1737. He lived in the house until 1783 when he was succeeded by Hugh Channon who vacated it after a year. The church registers of St Martin-in-the-Fields record the baptism and subsequent burial of five children born to John Channon and his wife Martha between 1758 and 1771.

No trade card or label issued by Channon has been recorded, but it is possible that his shop sign was 'The Golden Fleece' since the inner hinge plate of a cabinet on stand in the V & A [W. 7-1964] which has been attributed to him is engraved with a ram pendant from twisted snakes and it is known that, in 1742 and 1747 one house 'on the Pavement' in St Martin's Lane displayed the sign of 'The Golden Fleece'. However it is not mentioned in the following advertisement which appeared in *The Craftsman*, 24 July 1742: 'This is to give Notice, that Furbur's Collection of Twelve Monthly Flower Prints are now reprinted, and to prevent the Public being imposed upon, by spurious Copies sold about Town, the original Prints are Sixteen inches and a Quarter by Twelve, with a Handsome Title Plate of the Subscriber's Names, and under each Plate is engrav'd these words, From the Collection of Robert Furbur, Gardener at Kensington, design'd by P. Cassteels, and engrav'd by H. Fletcher; and now sold colour'd for Two Guineas a Set by Samuel Sympson, Engraver and Print Seller, in Maiden-Lane, Covent Garden; John Channon, Cabinet maker and Frame Maker, in St Martin's Lane and George Lacy who colours the said Flowers, in Red-Lion Court, Long-Acre. NB At the above Places are sold Mr. Furbur's Collection of Fruit Pieces'. Another notice mentioning Channon appeared in the *Daily Advertiser*, 23 November 1742: 'Mr Eade having left off his publick school in St. Martin's Lane, continues to teach (only abroad) some few Persons Writing, Arithmetick and Merchants' Accounts, in a very short and easy Method. His Lodgings are at Mr. Channon's, a Cabinet-Warehouse, upon the Pavement in St. Martin's Lane'.

John Channon's fire insurance policy dated 9 January 1760 gives the following values: on household goods, utensils and stock in trade in dwelling house £500; glass in trade £100; household goods, utensils and stock in trade in a house behind £150; wearing apparel £50; glass therein not exceeding £50; utensils, stock in trade in shop only in the yard behind £150. Total £1,000. [GL, Sun MS vol. 130, p. 283] In 1741 in the app. records John Channon is described as a joiner, but in 1752 when he took app. named Rowland Jackson, as a cm. He required a fee of £25 and £15 respectively on these occasions, but when in 1762 Edward Henry Williamson was taken as app. the sum of £50 was charged. [S of G, app. index]

The only signed or labelled pieces of furniture by John Channon are a spectacular pair of bookcases at Powderham Castle, near Exeter, Devon, bearing brass tablets engraved 'J Channon Fecit 1740'. In 1965–66 John Hayward published a group of furniture which, on account of design, type and quality of wood, manner of construction, similarities in brass inlay decoration and ormolu mounts appeared to come from the same workshop. He attributed them all to John Channon on the evidence of stylistic analogy and technical parallells with the Powderham bookcases. [V & A Bulletin, January 1965 and April 1966] John Channon's furniture displays a strong continental influence in the association of brass inlay with Boulle-work, the use of tortoiseshell veneer on arched pediments, refined gilt brass mounts and vigorous serpentine shapes which show an affinity with German furniture. In addition to engraved brass inlay, pieces attributed to Channon exhibit the following characteristics. The wood is not ordinary Cuban mahogany but is particularly richly figured, often with rosewood cross banding. Drawer linings are frequently mahogany and when oak is employed the bottoms may be of framed panel construction. Cabinets have brass cock beads, mouldings and stringing, the latter sometimes precisely engraved with very fine bordering lines. The inlay work on many pieces differs from the familiar Boulle technique of veneering sheets of worked brass onto a carcase; instead, decorative brass elements are inset directly into the mahogany or rosewood surface. The locks on several cabinets and boxes are fitted with an unusual hinged keyhole cover, released by a concealed spring. Two writing cabinets have a desk drawer that pulls forward on divided front corner trusses. Channon's distinctive repertoire of flamboyant ormolu mounts include satyr and nereid masks, elaborate cartouche-shaped handle and keyhole plates and elaborate foot mounts. His decorative brass inlay work is curiously old fashioned, almost Bérainesque in character compared with the progressive Rococo mounts. The principal items attributed to John Channon are:

Pair of bookcases signed and dated 1740 (Powderham Castle, Devon)
Cabinet on stand (V & A, No. W. 7–1964)
Bureau cabinet (V & A, No. W. 37–1953)
Writing table (V & A, No. W. 44–1947)
Armchair (V & A, No. W. 32–1959)
Bureau (Kenwood House, London)
Bureau cabinet, stamped 'J.GRAVELY' (Hayward, 1965, p. 15)
Library desk (V & A, No. W. 4–1956)
Library desk, companion to above (Sotheby's, 12 February 1965, lot 88)
Medal cabinet (Bristol City Art Gallery)
Commode (Temple Newsam House, Leeds)
Commode (Fitzwilliam Museum, Cambridge)
Writing cabinet, made for the Murray family of Ochtertyre, Scotland (Temple Newsam House, Leeds)
Writing cabinet, ex. Leverhulme Coll. (C. Life, 13 January 1950, p. 104, fig. 2)

Cabinet on stand (*C. Life*, 18 October 1956, p. 893)
Tea caddy (V & A, No. W. 11–1956)
Tea caddy (*V & A Bulletin*, October 1966, p. 146)
Supper table (V & A, No. W. 22–1962)
Bureau cabinet (*C. Life*, 3 June 1962, p. 1620)

The Germanic personality of some of the pieces ascribed to Channon's workshop raises the question as to whether he may have been German or have employed German craftsmen. The name Otho recurs in the family, certainly over three generations, while his mother's name Anne Sone, could be an Anglicised version of Anne Sohn or Sonne. Peter Thornton and Desmond Fitz-Gerald have explored a possible link with the great Abraham Roentgen who came to London about 1733 and worked for several different masters over a number of years. Their hypothesis rests on certain similarities between furniture made by Roentgen after his return to Germany and pieces thought to have been produced in the Channon workshop. The items of furniture listed above all date from about 1740–55. It may be that John and his elder brother Otho were both involved in the business since the subscribers to Chippendale's *Director*, 1754 include '–Channon, Senr.', and '–Channon, Jnr.' If this is so, Otho's death in 1756 coincided with a change in the firm's style to conform more with routine fashions, which explains why Channon's later products are not readily distinguishable from others working at the time.

POWDERHAM CASTLE, Devon (Sir William Courtenay). A massive and very richly styled pair of rosewood library bookcases with fine engraved brass inlay work and gilt carving, each bear a brass plaque inscribed 'J. Channon Fecit 1740' (the initial was originally misread 'T'). The Powderham Castle papers [Ledger 1, f.104] record under 29 April 1741 'Cash to John Channon part on acct — £50'. The entry presumably refers to these bookcases. The bookcases, now in the ante-room on the ground floor, were commissioned for the library on the first floor of the north east wing, created 1739–46. The room still retains its original chimney piece, possibly by Otho Channon.

HORNBY HALL, Lancs. (Mrs Anne Fenwick). A bill, some letters and a receipt spanning the years 1766–69 survive. The account dated 18 June 1766 totals £6 8s 5½d and itemises '2 pictures in carved and gilt, frames £5. 5.0.' and 'a small pair of garrendoles painted flack white with brass norsels, hold fasses and screws 15s 6d'. [Preston RO, RCHy 2/6/8] At the bottom of this bill Channon wrote: 'If you have a Desire for any Perticular Picture or Pictures please to lett me know what will sute for it Offon falls in my way to Meet with Some Very Good I shall take A pleasure to Oblege you Without any fee or Reward'. In a further letter to Mrs Fenwick, (4 August 1766), written by Martha Channon, John's wife, it is stated that 'Mr Channon has been in pursuit of some Vast Curious and Valuable pictures which at last he has purchased its our Bless.d Savour and Six of his Apostles Supposed by the best Judges to be done by Raphel Urbin the Size of the pictures and frames together is 19 by 14 in neat Carv.d frames the price is thirteen Guineas in all probability worth three times the Money but Mr. Channon was Requested by you he would take no Advantage and if you please to Desire it they shall be sent Down for you to see and if you dont like them Mr. Channon will keep them himself he Coud not Get them to Send without Buying them and their being a great bargain he will take them if Dislik.d by you'. The seven pictures were sent up to Hornby, but were returned. Friendly relations evidently continued since there is also a receipt dated 19 December 1769 for £7 worth of Channon's lottery tickets.

HENRIETTA ST, Covent Gdn, London (Richard Crosse, miniature painter). [V & A Lib., R. Crosse accounts. Shelf

mark 86.GG.23] 1773 June 20: To Repaireing a Mahog.y Clock case head a New frett to D.o. Cleaning & Lackering the Capitles & bases & varses & polishing D.o. alover Screwes & c
0 – 6. 6
To Repaireing a Serpentine teatable a New frett to D.o. scrapeing & polishing D.o. Alover
0 5.6
July 12: To a 5f.t. Bedstead Stout Mahog.y Pillers fine Wood Car.v on Strong Castors the best Double horsecloath Ticking bottom & Laceing line Compas rod & base latts & a Scerpintain Cutt cornis &c Compleate
6 – 16 – 6
To 55y.ds . . . of the best Crimsen Moreene at 2.s 9.p. Yard
7 – 11 – 3
To 102y.ds of the best Cover.d, lace
1 – 9 – 3
To 8y.ds of brown hesings to Back line the head & teaster
0 – 10 – 6
To 2 Torsels
0 – 3 – 0
Buckram to back line the Vallens & Bases & tamme to back line D.o.
0 – 17 – 0
Brass Rings Silk tape thread Studs tax &c
– 10 – 6
To Makeing the Furniture and Covering the Cornishses
2 – 12 – 6
To 3 Men & fixing up the bedstead & furniture at Y.r House tax &c
0 – 5 – 0
Cash paid for a Bedwrinch left at Y.r House
0 – 2 – 0
To a paper case to the teaster of Cateredge paper 0 – 2 – 0
Octo.br 18 1773   £21 – 11 – 6
Rec.d, the Contents in full & all Demands
John Channon

[John Hayward, 'Brass-inlaid Furniture', *V & A Bulletin*, January 1965, pp. 10–23 and 'The Channon family of Exeter and London, chair and cabinet makers', *V & A Bulletin*, April 1966, pp. 64–70; Peter Thornton and Desmond Fitz-Gerald, 'Abraham Roentgen "englische kabinetmacher" and some further reflections on the work on John Channon', *V & A Bulletin*, October 1966, pp. 137–147; Coleridge, *Chippendale Furniture*; Gilbert, *Leeds Furn. Cat.*, pp. 177–78; Christopher Claxton Stevens and Stuart Whittington, *Eighteenth Century Furniture: The Norman Adams Collection*, 1983, pp. 182–86, Mark Girouard, 'Powderham Castle, Devon 1', *C. Life*, 4 July 1963, pp. 18–21; *Rococo Art and Design*, exhib. cat., V & A, 1984 (L2)]   C.E.L.-J.

Channon, John, 12 Poland St, Oxford St, London, cm and u (1827–39). [D]

Channon, Joseph, address unknown, cm (1769). Supplied furniture, probably for a London house in 1769. [Scottish RO, Polesworth papers, box 4, household accounts]

Channon, Otho, Exeter, Devon, and London? chairmaker (b. 1698–1756). The eldest son of Otho Channon of the parish of St Sidwell, Exeter and elder brother of John Channon the celebrated cm of St Martin's Lane, London. Otho was app. in 1714 to William Culme, joiner, of Exeter for a consideration of £8 [PRO, IR 1 46/155, vol. 6, p. 1012] and in 1726 his younger brother John was app. to him. The subscription list to Chippendale's *Director*, 1754 lists '–Channon, senr, cabinet maker' and 'Channon, jun, cabinet maker'; it is likely that Otho is the former, John the latter. In 1729 Otho took on an app. Charles Morgan of Exeter for a fee of £10. His only known commission was for Sir William Courtenay at Powderham Castle, Devon where the account books record: 24 March 1743 'Pd Otho Channon in full of all demands £27 13'; 12 October 1748 'To cash paid him in full £14 5'; 23 August 1751 'To cash, paid him full for a mahogany table and chairs £33 10'. Some of these payments may relate to the library which was decorated between 1739 and 1746 and contained two bookcases made by John Channon in 1740. [J. Hayward, 'The Channon family of

Exeter and London', *V & A Bulletin*, No. 2 (April 1966), pp. 64–70; *C. Life*, 4 July 1963, pp. 18–21]

Channon, T., (fictitious). Misreading by Heal and Edwards, *DEF*, of initial letter J on engraved brass maker's tablets on the Powderham bookcases.

Channon, Thomas, Taunton, Som, cm and shopkeeper (1757–58). Insured his house, household goods and stock, etc. in January for £300, the stock accounting for £50. In 1758 he took on an app. Richard Tucker. [GL, Sun MS vol. 118, p. 155; S of G, app. index]

Chantler, John, 9 Water St, Bridge St, Manchester, cm (1815–17). Trading at 9A Water St in 1815 and no. 9 in 1817. [D]

Chantler, Joseph, London, u (1820–37). At Layton's Buildings, Southwark in 1820 but after 1829 at 12 Alfred Pl., Newington Causeway. [D]

Chantler, William, Foregate St, Chester, chairmaker (1797). [D]

Chantrell, Jane, Liverpool, u (1833–39). Initially at Torbock St but by 1837 was at 9 King St, Soho and in 1839 at Wilton St. [D]

Chapell, Daniel, London, upholder (1712–33). App. to Joseph Green on 7 October 1704 and free of the Upholders' Co. by servitude, 2 April 1712. Took app. George Heath, 1725–33. [GL, Upholders' Co. records]

Chapelow, Thomas, 297 Newton St, Manchester, joiner and cm (1811). [D]

Chaplain, Robert, Woodbridge, Suffolk, cm (1783). Married on 26 September 1783. [Suffolk RO, FAA: 50/2/105]

Chaplin, James, Long Melford, Suffolk, cm (1762–84). In 1762 took app. named Burning. [S of G, app. index]

Chaplin, John, Tiverton, Devon, u (1810). On 13 December 1810 married Miss Mary Ann Worthy of Exeter. [*Exeter Flying Post*, 13 December 1810]

Chaplin, John, High St, Exeter, Devon, carver and gilder (1825). Son Johnathan bapt. at St Martin's 10 May 1825. [PR (bapt.)]

Chaplin, Joseph, Clifton, Bristol, cm, u, house agent and auctioneer (1815–35). Between 1815–23 at York House, and from 1824–35 at 5 Gloucester Row. [D]

Chaplin, William, Eversly, Southampton, Hants, chairmaker (1719–37). In 1719 took app. named Clarke and in 1737 another named May. [S of G, app. index]

Chaplin, William, London, upholder (1768–76). Son of Richard Chaplin of Sudbury, Suffolk, merchant. App. to William Brushfield and Samuel Burton 4 May 1768 and free by servitude 3 April 1776. [GL, Upholders' Co. records]

Chaplin, William, John's Lane, John's St, London, cm (1787). On 12 February 1787 insured goods, utensils and stock in the house of John Gill, cm, for £200. [GL, Sun MS vol. 344, p. 81]

Chaplin, William, Wymondham, Norfolk and Ipswich, Suffolk, cm (1790–1805). By 1800 he had moved from Wymondham to Ipswich, and in 1805 was trading from an address in Tacket St as a cm and broker [D; Ipswich poll bk; *Ipswich Journal*, 12 July 1800]

Chaplins & Co., Hotwell Rd, Bristol, cm and u (1810–13). [D]

Chapman, Mr, Coleman St, London, 'eminent Upholder' (1748). Death of his wife reported in *General Advertiser*, 25 March 1748.

Chapman, —, Ipswich, Suffolk, u (1793). Subscribed to Sheraton's *Drawing Book*, 1793. It is possible that this is an erroneous entry and that the subscriber was William Chaplin of Ipswich.

Chapman, —, Oldbury, Glos., chairmaker, (1839). [D] Probably John Chapman of Old Bury, Tewkesbury.

Chapman, C., Church St, Basingstoke, Hants., cm and u (1839). [D]

Chapman, Charles, 130 Pottergate St, Norwich, u (1754–99). Son of Benedict Chapman, grocer. Admitted a freeman

23 October 1756. His own sons John Charles and Benedict, both described as clerks, were admitted freemen 27 July 1799. Took apps named Ireland in 1754 and Parson in 1760. Appears to have been concerned with the furnishings of Holkham Hall, Norfolk, and also was paid £89 for carpets and upholsterers' work carried out at Felbrigg Hall, Norfolk. This, combined with the long period during which the business traded, suggests an extensive and important provincial establishment. [D; poll bks; freemen reg.; S of G, app. index; V & A archives]

Chapman, Charles, Newmarket, Suffolk, cm and u (1830). [D]

Chapman, Charles, 1 Exeter St, Sloane St, London, cm and u (1839). [D]

Chapman, Edward, address unknown, cm (1723). A receipt signed by Edward Chapman for £5 5s and dated 17 May 1723 exists for goods supplied to Paul Foley Esq., of The Temple and Little Ormond St, London, and Newport House, Almeley, Herefs. The goods supplied were a marble table costing £3 10s with its frame at £1 15s. [Herefs. RO, F/AIII/55]

Chapman, Edward, 1 and 20 Princess St, Mason St, Hull, Yorks., joiner and cm (1826–38). In 1838 the number is changed to 6 Princess St. Edward Chapman was also a beer retailer from 1835 and in 1838 is shown, additionally, as trading from 'The King's Arms'. [D]

Chapman, Edward, St Matthews's, Ipswich, Suffolk, cm and u (1839). [D]

Chapman, Elizabeth, London, upholder (1747). Daughter of William Chapman of Highgate, London, clerk. Sister of Sarah Chapman to whom she was app. 25 November 1738. Free of the Upholders' Co. by servitude 10 October 1747. [GL, Upholders' Co. records]

Chapman, Francis, High St, Tewkesbury, Glos., chairmaker (1820–30). Recorded at no. 98 in 1820. [D]

Chapman, George & John, 31 Market Pl., Hull, Yorks., u and cm (1776–1815). John Chapman, the founder of the business was the son of Thomas Chapman of York, a painter. John took the freedom of York as an u in 1776 and in the same year established himself in a shop and house in the Market Pl. at Hull. This he insured for £600, with an additional £250 cover for utensils and stock, and £100 for warehouse stock. In February 1793 he insured a 'house, shop & warehouse in one building on the East side of Market Place Yard, on the W. side of Tinkle Street' with two tenements adjoining at £500. The tenements may have been used as a lodging house as he advertised this aspect of his business from 1791. By 1803 his son George was assisting with the business which was styled John Chapman & Son. The father is however no longer named after 1807 and had probably died by this date, or certainly retired from the business. George took the freedom of York as an u in 1810. He followed a similar line of trade to his father and included paper hanging and paper staining in his activities. He died in 1815.

Apps of the business included Thomas Hallam of Rotherham, May 1802; Christopher Burnett of Laceby, Lincs., July 1802; Richard Binnington of Hull, March 1803; Charles Hart; Thomas England of Sutton near Hull, October 1806; Thomas Marshall of Hull, January 1807; Thomas Dobson of Hull, May 1807; Edward Gainer of Hull, May 1810; Thomas Johnson of Sculcoates near Hull, January 1812 and William Collison, James Hill and Charles Robinson, all of Hull, July 1813. The death of George Chapman in 1815 forced the assignment of Edward Gainer to a new master, Robert Waugh and Thomas Johnson to George Brook both in March 1815; and James Hill was also assigned to Robert Waugh, March 1818. A number of commissions undertaken by the business are recorded in the Hull Corp. archives. These included work on the Corporation pews in Holy Trinity Church in November 1798, and upholstery work including blinds, curtaining and recovering 8 cabriole chairs, 1814–15, amounting to £43 3s. The painting of 4 small and two arm chairs 'blue striped with white' cost an additional £1 4s. [D; poll bk; York freemen rolls; Hull app. reg.; Hull Corp. accounts bks; GL, Sun MS vol. 392, p. 291; vol. 248, ref. 369067] B.A.

Chapman, George, Snettisham, Norfolk, cm (1836). [D]

Chapman, George, Northallerton, Yorks., cm (1840). [D]

Chapman, George, Durham St, Middlesbrough, Yorks., joiner and cm (1840). [D]

Chapman, Henry, London (1771). Son of Cludd Chapman of Houndsditch, tallow chandler. App. to Joseph Merryman 4 June 1761 and free of the Upholders' Co. by servitude 5 June 1771. [GL, Upholders' Co. records]

Chapman, J., Spalding, Lincs., joiner and cm (1792). On 27 March 1792 advertised for two journeymen joiners and cm offering from twelve to fifteen shillings a week each as wages. He also indicated the diverse nature of his business which included the stocking of 'Dry and Ground Colours of all Sorts, Linseed Oil, Turpentine, and every Kind of Paint of the *first Quality*, for House-painting, ready prepared for the Brush'. He also kept 'A large Quantity of Grave-stones, curiously carved . . . which will be lettered and finished in a masterly Manner'. [*Lincoln, Rutland and Stamford Mercury*, 30 March 1792]

Chapman, James, 51 High St, Southampton, Hants., chairmaker (1803–11). [D]

Chapman, James, Suffolk, u and clothes dealer (1817–24). [D; *Cambridge Chronicle and Journal*, 20 June 1817]

Chapman, James, Northallerton, Yorks., cm (1828). [D]

Chapman, John, Hull. See George & John Chapman.

Chapman, John, Newcastle, joiner, cm and house carpenter (1778–1811). From 1778 to 1801 at Bigg-market but in 1811 at Queen St. [D]

Chapman, John, Canterbury, Kent, cm (1779–1830). At Longport in 1790, parish of St George in 1826 and Canterbury Lane in July 1830. [Poll bks]

Chapman, John, 7 Peter St, Saffron Hill, London, chairmaker (1808). [D]

Chapman, John, 62 Red Lion St, Clerkenwell, London, japan chairmaker (1817–25). [D]

Chapman, John, 6 Red Lion St, Clerkenwell, London, clock case maker (1823). [D]

Chapman, John, 95 Cromer St, Brunswick Sq., London, cm and u (1822). [D]

Chapman, John, North end, Gt Yarmouth, cabinet and chairmaker and u (1822). [D]

Chapman, John, Yorkshire St, Oldham, Lancs., joiner and cm (1825). [D]

Chapman, John, Gt Aycliffe, near Darlington, Co. Durham, joiner and cm (1828). [D]

Chapman, John, Norwich, cm (1829). App. to John Ling and free 21 September 1829. [Freemen reg.]

Chapman, John, Old Bury, Tewkesbury, Glos., chairmaker, (1830–40). [PR (bapt.)] See Chapman, —.

Chapman, John, Staithes, Yorks., joiner/cm/cartwright (1834). [D]

Chapman, John, Snow Hill, Stafford, chairmaker (1828–35). Recorded at Union Buildings in 1834. [D]

Chapman, John, Chingswell St, Bideford, Devon, cm and u (1838). [D]

Chapman, John, 28 Berwick St, Oxford St, London, chair and sofa maker (1839). [D]

Chapman, John, 2 Pitt St, Fitzroy Sq., London, picture and looking-glass frame maker (1839). [D]

Chapman, John, Cheveley Rd, Newmarket, Suffolk, cm (1839). [D]

Chapman, R., 6 Red Lion St, Clerkenwell, London, clock and dial case maker (1820). See also John Chapman, carrying on a similar trade at this address in 1823. [D]

Chapman, Sarah, London, upholder (1716–38). Daughter of William Chapman of Highgate, London, clerk. App. to Joseph Williams 20 December 1716 and free of the Upholders Co. by servitude 6 July 1737. Took her sister Elizabeth as app. 25 November 1738. [GL, Upholders' Co. records]

Chapman, Thomas, Little Brickhill, Bucks., upholder (1727). Took out insurance cover on 5 October 1727 of £500 which included £300 for a dwelling house and brewhouse, £50 for a barn and stable, £50 for a tenement and £100 for household goods and stock in trade. [GL, Sun MS vol. 25, ref. 42661]

Chapman, Thomas, Old Bethlem, London, cm and bedsteadmaker (1748–83). App. to John Price, upholder of London, in September 1741 for seven years. Subscribed to Chippendale's *Director*, 1754. Already trading on his own account by 1758 when he was licensed to employ four non-freemen for six months. From this date until 1775 he was a frequent employer of such labour and in 1760 was using as many as thirteen non-freemen in his business. Initially his address was 17 Old Bethlem (or Bedlam) but by 1787 the number had changed to 13. In 1779 his workshop, utensils and stock were insured for £375, out of an entire insurance of £700. The nature of his trade is well described on his trade card [Heal Coll., BM] which states that he made and sold 'Mahogany Tea & Dining Tables, Chamber-Tables, Tea Boards, Waiters, and Tea-Chests'. He was also able to undertake 'Bed Carving and Joyners Work on Bed Cornishes, Window Cornishes, Teastors and Head Boards, Settees, Beauroes and Field Beds'. [D; GL, Sun MS vol. 275, p. 11; City Licence bks, vols 2, 8; Heal]

Chapman, Thomas, Bishopsgate Without, London, carver (1782). Bankruptcy announced in *Gents Mag.*, April 1782.

Chapman, Thomas, Yorkshire St, Oldham, Lancs., joiner and cm (1825). [D]

Chapman, Thomas, 8 Denmark St, Soho, London, u and cm, patent invalid furniture (1835–39). In 1835 his works were described as an 'invalid bed, chair & sofa manufactory', the words 'By Appointment' being added. Advertised in the 1839 edition of Pigot's *Directory*. [D]

Chapman, Thomas, Leeds, Yorks., cm (1837–39). At 18 Lands Lane, in 1837 and 44 George's St in 1839. [D]

Chapman, Thomas, Brighton, Sussex, cm and u (1837–40). At Grenville Pl. in 1837 but by 1839 had moved to 9 Duke St. [D; poll bks]

Chapman, Walter, Bristol and London, upholder (1774–84). Living in Temple parish, Bristol in 1774 but by 1781 had moved to Ludgate Hill, London. In 1784 at Bennet's St, Oxford Rd, London. [Bristol poll bks]

Chapman, William, 43 Coleman St, corner of Lothbury, London, u (1748–1820). The long time span involved might suggest a father and son of the same name. Heal cites a Chapman, christian name unspecified, at Coleman St in 1748. The next recorded reference is in 1774 when William Chapman was summoned to be made free of the Upholders' Co. under the terms of the 1750 Upholders' Act. He paid £15 15s to be excused and declared himself a freeman of the Armourers and Braziers' Co. In 1785 he insured his utensils and stock for £1,000. He probably had additional warehouse premises in Coleman St at Coleman St Buildings, since in 1789, Brough Maltby, Gent. of 73 Basinghall St, insured some of his household goods at the warehouse of Mr Chapman at this address. He is only infrequently listed in London directories, listings of 1781, 1789 and 1820 being recorded. In 1789 the business was named as Chapman & Sons and their trade included that of auctioneer, carpenter and undertaker. [D; GL, Upholders' Co. records; GL, Sun MS vol. 331, p. 612; vol. 362, p. 439]

Chapman, William, Castle Precincts, Bristol, upholder (1754). [Poll bk]

Chapman, William, 41 Berwick St, London, cm (1782). Insured his house at the above address for £300. [GL, Sun MS vol. 302, p. 196]

Chapman, William, Pottergate St, opposite Lower Goat Lane, Norwich, upholder etc. (1802–03). [D]

Chapman, William, 59 King St, Southwark, London, cm and Venetian shade maker (1803). On 30 July 1803 took out insurance cover of £1,100 of which £400 was for stock and utensils. [GL, Sun MS vol. 426, ref. 750772]

Chapman, William, Norwich, cm (1829). Admitted freeman 21 September 1829. [Freemen rolls]

Chappell, Job, Cirencester, Glos., cm (1793). [D]

Chappell, Daniel, 39 Temple St, Bristol, carpenter, builder, cm, appraiser and undertaker (1827–29). [D]

Chappell, Thomas, London, bedstead maker (1820–37). At 8 Bowling St, Westminster in 1820 though by 1826 the number had changed to 5. From 1835 the business was conducted from Gt Smith St, Westminster, first at no. 17, and by 1839 at no. 28. [D]

Chapple, Charles, Exeter, Devon, cm (1819–24). At St Thomas in 1819 when the death of his wife was recorded. By 1822 at North St and in the following year at 26 Holloway St. It was at this address that in January 1824 his stock was sold by auction together with his household furniture 'under a distress for Rent & an execution from the Sheriff'. The stock was said to be well manufactured. It was principally of mahogany, but satinwood, birch and chestnut are also mentioned. [D; *Exeter Flying Post*, 8 July 1819; *The Alfred*, 20 January 1824]

Charles, Charles, 60 Stanley St, Liverpool, cm (1735–87). Sworn freeman 17 October 1735. He took apps: George Chares, John Orme, Richard Fleetwood, Richard Tyrer and George Wainwright. Charles petitioned freedom in 1760, Orme in 1765, Fleetwood and Tyrer in 1780 and Wainwright in 1790. In September 1778 he advertised his dwelling house and large workshop in Stanley St as available for letting. Despite this the business continued to trade in Stanley St. [D; freemen reg. and committee bk; *Williamson's Liverpool Advertiser*, 1 September 1778]

Charles, Edward, Liverpool, cm (b. c. 1750–d. 1820). Son of Charles Charles. Free 11 September 1780 and by 1790 in trade at 18 Bold St. Another directory of the same year gives the address as 43 Bold St with a shop at 44, and subsequently 42–44 Bold St is the address used to 1803. From then until 1811 the business traded from 9 Commutation Row, Shaw's Brow and between 1816 and 1818 was at Bridgport St. In 1796 Edward married Miss Elizabeth Skillicorn, possibly the sister of his app. Robert Skillicorn whom he had taken on the previous year and was made free 1803. He also took as apps Ralph Summers and Edward Dillart in 1802, and both became free 1812. His death is recorded on 24 February 1820 aged 70. [D; freemen's committee bks and reg.; *Billinge's Liverpool Advertiser*, 4 April 1796; *Liverpool Mercury*, 10 March 1820]

Charles, Edward, High St, Thrapston, Northants., cm and u (1823). [D]

Charles, George, Batchelor St, Liverpool, cm (1760–74). Petitioned freedom in 1760 after serving as app. to Charles Charles. In 1774 a tenant of John Forrest, also of Batchelor St, marble cutter. [Freemen's committee bk; GL, Sun MS vol. 235, 15 November 1774]

Charles, Michael, Gardeners Lane, Petty France, London, carver (1749). [Westminster poll bk]

Charles, Robert, 9 Fisher St, Red Lion Sq., London, carpenter, chairman and cm (1809). On 1 May 1809 took out insurance cover of £100. [GL, Sun MS vol. 443, ref. 830553]

Charles, Walter, Allonby, Maryport, Cumb., joiner and cm (1828–34). [D]

Charles, William, Uttoxeter, Staffs., chairmaker and turner (1818–34). Trading at Balance St in 1818 and High St in 1834. [D]

Charleton, John, Liverpool, u (1767). App. to Samuel Kirks for seven years. Petitioned for freedom 1767. [Freemen's committee bk]

Charley, Josiah, Crown St, parish of St Ann, Westminster, London, looking-glass maker (1714). Took out insurance cover on two adjoining buildings in Crown St at £100 each on 30 December 1714. [GL, Hand in Hand MS vol. 13, p. 638]

Charlton, Mr, 'near the Haymarket', London, 'eminent Upholsterer' (d. 1767). Death 'at his lodgings near Vauxhall' reported in *Public Advertiser*, 18 June 1767.

Charlton, Charles, 9 Friday St, London, u (1738–8?). Frequently described as wholesale u after 1768. [D]

Charlton, John, Wardour St, London, u (1784). [Westminster poll bk]

Charlton, John, 44 Upper Rathbone Pl., London, cm (1809). [D]

Charlton, John, 39 Windmill St, Tottenham Ct Rd, London, cm, u and firescreen manufacturer (1820–25). [D]

Charleton, John, Levett's Sq., Hodgson St, Hull, Yorks., cm (1823). [D]

Charlton, John, Union St, Morpeth, Northumb., joiner and cm (1827). [D]

Charlton, John, Smith St, Stockton, Co. Durham, cm (1832). [D]

Charlton, John, Hexham, Co. Durham, joiner/cm (1834). [D]

Charlton, Michael, Gainford, near Darlington, Co. Durham, joiner and cm (1827). [D]

Charlton, Samuel, Coventry St, London, chairmaker (1749). [Westminster poll bk]

Charlton, Samuel, Glasshouse St, London, upholder (1749). [Westminster poll bk]

Charlton, Sarah & Co., Coppergate, York, cm and u (1830–40). At 8 Coppergate 1830–34, but from 1837–40 at no. 10. [D]

Charlton, Thomas, Newcastle, joiner, cm and furniture broker (1833–38). Shown at 14 Cloth-market in 1833, but in the same year moved to High-bridge. Listed there at no. 47 in 1834, but at 14 Cloth-market again in 1838. [D]

Charlton, William, 38 Moxon St, Hull, Yorks., cm (1838–40). [D]

Charlwood, Joseph, 127 High Holborn, London, u (1799). [D]

Charman, Samuel, 9 Fisher St, Red Lion Sq., London, cm (1809). Appears to be associated with Robert Charles who also occupied this address in 1809. [D]

Charmbury, Daniel, Blandford, Dorset, builder, cm and u (1809). In May 1809 advertised that his property and business were for sale as he was giving up the business because of 'ill-health brought on by over exertion'. Succeeded by Penning & Charmbury. [*Sherborne Mercury*, 15 and 22 May 1809]

Charnley, Alexander, corner of Duke St and Queen St, the Mint, Southwark, London, cm, bedstead maker and broker (1775). Took out insurance cover of £1,100 in 1775 of which £480 was for utensils and stocks, £75 for similar items in the cabinet-making shop and £75 for those in the bedstead-making shop. [GL, Sun MS vol. 243, p. 112]

Charnley, Jane, 9 Chapel Yd, Preston, Lancs., u (1825). [D]

Charnley, Richard, 58 Friargate, Preston, Lancs., cm (1825). [D]

Charnley, Richard, Chapel St, Little Bolton, Lancs., cm (1834). [D]

Charnley, William, Newcastle, u (1753–82). In early 1760s also described himself as a tinplate worker and stationer. Took apps named Robert Baron, 15 October 1760; Thomas Saint, 26 March 1761; David Crool, 6 October 1763; James Mitchell, 12 October 1767; James Rayson, 23 February 1771; Robert Walton, 31 October 1771; Thomas Brown, 22 August 1774; Robert Rumney, 4 October 1774; Robert Calbreath, 20 January 1777; Anthony Douthwaite, 16 September 1780 and William Barras, 12 November 1782. [Freemen reg.; poll bks]

Charnock, John, Thomas St, Bristol, picture frame maker (1795). [D]

Charnock, John, 3 Back Pickup St, Liverpool, u (1814–23). [D]

Charnock, Robert, 6 Horseferry Rd, Westminster, London, u (1782–1808). Freeman of Preston, Lancs., in both 1782 and 1802 but living in London. [D; freemen reg.]

Charnock, Thomas, Liverpool, cm (1767). App. to William Quin and free 2 December 1767. [Freemen reg.]

Charpentier, Benjamin, London, carver, gilder and picture frame maker (1775–1825). In 1775 at 430 Oxford St and from 1778–87 at 24 Cumberland St, Tottenham Ct Rd. After 1808 at 11 Gt Titchfield St. In 1775 the house in Oxford St was insured for £200 and in 1778 a total insurance cover of £300 was taken out on the Cumberland St address, which included £200 on the utensils, stock and goods. The cover was the same in 1787 but by 1808 had increased to £500 which included £300 for household goods in the dwelling house, £100 for the workshop behind and £100 for utensils and goods in trust. His trade card is dated 1783. [Banks Coll., BM] He appears to have developed an extensive and widespread patronage. In 1794 a frame was supplied to Alexander Wedderburn at a cost of £6 10s and in 1816 an account was rendered to Adam Cottam of Whalley, Lancs. through James Northcote, the artist, for a frame for the painting 'Christ in the Garden' for Whalley Church at a cost of £8 10s and £5 10s for the packing case. [D; GL, Sun MS vol. 243, p. 531; vol. 266, p. 613; vol. 342, ref. 527551; vol. 445, ref. 823745; Scottish RO, GD 164/Box 20/AA/2–3; Preston RO, DDX 3361, 31]

Charrington & Henning, 23 Leicester Sq., London, cm and u (1790–93). [Heal]

Chart, William, London, cm and u (1822–29). At Charlotte Pl. in 1822, Upper Kennington Lane in 1827 and 8 Hollen St, Soho in 1829. In 1827 the business is recorded as William Chart & Mason. [D]

Charter, Charles, 57 Stanley St, Liverpool, upholder (1784). [D]

Charters, John, 37 Stanley St, Liverpool and shop 9 Back Leeds St, cm (1834). [D]

Chartres, David, Hyde (or Hide) Hill, Berwick-upon-Tweed, Northumb., cm and u (1806–34). [D]

Chartres, Francis, Church St, Berwick-upon-Tweed, Northumb., cm (1827). [D]

Chase, Edward, London, upholder (1762). Son of Edward Chase of Sunbury, Middlx, Gent. App. to Timothy Goulding 20 February 1755 and free by servitude 1 April 1762. [GL, Upholders' Co. records]

Chassereau, —, High St, Lewes, Sussex, carver and gilder (1805). [D]

Chater, Thomas, Salisbury, Wilts., chairmaker (1798). [D]

Chater, William, 5 Sans St, Bishop Wearmouth, Sunderland, Co. Durham, cm (1827–28). [D]

Chatfield, Thomas & Joseph, Small Silver St, Uttoxeter, Staffs., cm (1818). [D]

Chatfield, Thomas, Bridge St, Uttoxeter, Staffs., chairmaker and turner (1834). [D]

Chatfield, Thomas, Silver St, Uttoxeter, Staffs., cm (1828–35). [D]

Chatham, Charles, 9 Nash Grove, shop at 46 Limekiln Lane, Liverpool, cm (1814–21). Later in partnership with A. Blain. A set of chairs with the impressed mark 'C CHATHAM' and 'A BLAIN' is known. [D]

Chatham, Thomas, 15 Roscoe Lane, Liverpool, carver (1837). [D]

Chatterton, Richard, Lichfield, Staffs., cm and upholder (1780–95). In 1780 took out insurance cover of £400 of which £30 was for his workshop. His wife died in February 1795. [GL, Sun MS vol. 289, p. 257; *Staffordshire Advertiser*, 28 February 1795]

Chatterton, Richard, Dam St, Lichfield, Staffs., carver and gilder (1818). [D]

Chatterton, Thomas, 101 Digbeth, Birmingham, cm (1770). [D]

Chaunder, Thomas, Romsey, Hants., cm (1792). [D]

Chawner, William, Cank St, Pump Lane, Leicester, gilder and japanner (1796–1822). Opened trading in April 1796 as a furniture painter and gilder, but not made a freeman until 1807. [D; *Leicester Journal*, 1 April 1796; freemen reg.]

Chead, Joseph, 1 Brimble's Ct, Bath, Som., cm (1826). [D]

Cheale, Charles, Southover, Lewes, Sussex, cm and u (1823–40). [D]

Cheary, William, 1 St James's Back, Bristol, cm (1775). [D]

Cheater, John jnr, Easterton, Wilts., chairmaker (1751). Took an app. named Gifford Draper in 1751. [*Wilts Apps and their Masters*]

Cheater, Sara, 6 Rose St, Soho, London, chair and sofa maker (1835–39). [D]

Cheater, William, 7 Sutton St, Soho Sq., London, chair and sofa maker (1829). [D]

Cheatham, J., Eagle Ct, Clerkenwell, London, cm (1793). Subscribed to Sheraton's *Drawing Book*, 1793.

Chebsey, John, 'The Hand & Chair', first shop from Ludgate St, St Paul's Churchyard, London, chair and cm (c. 1710–36). A kneehole desk veneered in figured walnut, c. 1710, with a trade label pasted inside the frieze drawer is known. This features his trade sign showing a chair of early Georgian character, as does his invoice for a 'Wall^tre wisk table & lined with Green Cloth' dated 1 March 1735/36. The card table was charged at £3 3s and was for Paul Foley of the Temple and Little Ormond St, London and Newport House, Almeley, Herefs. [Herefs. RO, Foley MS, F/AIII/55]

Checketts, John, Wolverhampton, Staffs., cm (1830–40). At 8 Queen St in 1830 and Red Lion St, 1833–34. [D]

Chedsey, Mathew, Donyatt, Som., chairmaker (1743). In 1743 took app. named Cape. [S of G, app. index]

Cheere, Sir Henry, St Margaret's, Westminster, London, carver (b. 1703–d. 1781). For details of the work of this noted sculptor in stone see Gunnis. Amongst the Blackett accounts for Fenham Hall, Northumb. is an entry of 14 December 1751 for two oval looking-glasses at £16 10s and two carved table frames, both painted, one costing £16 7s 6d and the other £21 7s. These accompanied two Sienna marble table tops charged at £27. [V & A archives]

Cheeseman, Charles, 21 French Row, Aldersgate St, London, cm and Tunbridge-ware maker (1809). [D]

Cheesewright, Joshua, 7 Percival St, Clerkenwell, London, cm and u (1822). [D]

Cheesewright, Samuel, Aldersgate St, London, cm (1774). In 1774 given a licence to employ two non-freemen for three months. [GL, City Licence bks, vol. 8]

Cheesman, Samuel George, 4 Weymouth St, New Kent Rd, London, chair and sofa maker (1829). [D]

Cheesman, Thomas, Brighton, Sussex, Tunbridge-ware maker and turner (1818–c. 1835). Lived at Richmond Row between

1818–23, at which time he was probably in the employment of Morris's, one of the major Brighton Turnbridge-ware manufacturers. At Alban St in 1825 but does not feature in directories until 1832 when he was at Riding School Lane. A rosewood tea caddy and a rosewood workbox, both decorated with perspective cube parquetry and bearing trade labels of this maker are known. These however feature an address at 9 Cranbourn St not recorded in directories. On the trade label he indicates his ability to supply 'Every description of Ladies' Work Boxes, Fire Screens &c.'. [D; E. Sussex RO, PAR 255/1/2/1, 255/1/2/4, 255/1/2/5]

Cheesman, Thomas, 7 George St, Blackfriars Rd, London, u (1821). [D]

Cheetham, Joseph, Eagle St, St John's St, London, cm (1809). [D]

Cheetham, Joshua, 7 Percival St, Goswell Rd, London, cm (1820). [D]

Cheltman, John, 10 Shorts Buildings, Clerkenwell, London, cm and u (1777). Insured a house for £100 in 1777. [GL, Sun MS vol. 256, p. 630]

Chenery, Benjamin, near the Cornhill, Ipswich, Suffolk, carver (1743–59). Moved from London and in 1743 advertised his ability to carve 'all Sorts of Chimney Pieces, Picture-Frames, Glass Frames, Sconces, Table-Frames for Marble Slabs . . . in the newest Taste'. Married 22 February 1756. Took app. named Goodchild in 1759. [*Ipswich Journal*, 22 October 1743; Suffolk RO, 50/2/89–93; S of G, app. index]

Chenery, William, London, u and cm (1777–93). Successor to Thomas Phipps. In Leadenhall St from 1777 to c. 1790, the number being variously given as 83 (1777), 81 (1784) and 84 (1786). About 1790 declared bankrupt but was in business again at 57 Crutched Friars from 1790–93. [D; *Williamson's Liverpool Advertiser*, 26 November 1792; Heal Coll., BM]

Chenery, William, 6 Swithins Lane, Cannon St, London, upholder (1780). Son of Joseph Chenery of Lambourn, Essex, innholder. App. first to David Langton on 4 December 1771 and then to J. Shephard, feltmaker and upholder, on 3 March 1773. [GL, Upholders' Co. records]

Cheney, William, Aldersgate St, London, cm (1785). [Bailey's list of bankrupts]

Cheppett, Elias, Walcot, Som., cm (1819). Declared bankrupt, *Exeter Flying Post*, 11 March 1819.

Cherington, Pettit & Oliver, 19 New Bond St, London, u (1814–15). [D]

Cherrington, Edward, 13 Tottenham Ct Rd, New Rd, London, cm (1829). [D]

Cherrington & Henning, Leicester Sq., London, u (1784–93). At 23 Leicester Sq. 1784–90, from then at 22. [D]

Cherry, David, 12 and 18 Bridewell Lane, Bristol, auctioneer and cm (1774–75). [D; poll bk]

Cherry, Henry Granger, Bristol, cm (1821–24). In 1821 at 8 Redcross St but by the following year had moved to 19 Montague St where he was to remain until 1824. [D]

Cherry, J. L., Bristol, cm (1818–20). In Cannon St in 1818 but by the following year had moved to 22 North St. [D]

Cherry, James, Cross Cheaping, Coventry, Warks., carver and gilder (1818–31). Trading at High St in 1828. Bankrupt by January 1831. [D; *London Gazette*, 18 January 1831]

Cherry, John, Bristol, cm (1774–84). In the parish of St Michael in 1774, St James in 1781 and St John in 1784. [Poll bks]

Cherry, William, 81 John's St, London, cm and undertaker (1808). [D]

Cherry, William, Pithay, Bristol, cm (1814–16). [D]

Cheshire, John, Coleham, Shrewsbury, Salop, cabinet carver (1835). [Freemen rolls]

Cheshire, Stanbridge, West St, Dunstable, Beds., cm and u (1839). [D]

Cheshire, Thomas, Albion St, Rugeley, Staffs., cm and u (1828–34). Recorded also as a builder in 1828. Trading at Albion St in 1834. [D]

Cheshire, William, Oxford Rd, Bilston, Staffs., cm and u (1828–30). [D]

Chessey, Robert, London, upholder (1764–99). Son of William Chessey of Ware, Herts., yeoman. App. to William Woodward, draper 14 April 1756. Admitted freeman under the 1750 Upholders' Act, 15 November 1764. Recorded in Moorfields 1778–86 and at 54 Houndsditch 1794–99. [D; GL, Upholders' Co. records]

Chesson, William, London, u and auctioneer (1744–74). Initially traded from 'The Three Chairs', Grocer's Alley, Poultry but by 1753 was installed at 157 Fenchurch St, from which address the business traded for the remainder of its existence. After 1767 the business was styled Chesson & Bathurst. In 1756 involved with Thomas Humphreys in selling by auction the stock of Stephen Theodore Janssen of York Pl., Battersea (the enamel works). He was one of the furniture makers employed in the furnishing of the Mansion House, 1752–53, and in February 1764 was paid £76 1s for 'furniture and upholsterer's work' at East India House, Leadenhall St. [D; Heal; *Apollo*, November 1965, p. 405; *Conn.*, December 1952, p. 181; *Antique Collector*, June 1953, p. 126; GL, City Licence bks, vols 2 and 3]

Chester, E., 4 Mount St, Lambeth, London, u (1835). [D]

Chester, John jnr, Fetter Lane, Hull, Yorks., cm and joiner (1840).

Chester, Joseph, 7 Gloucester Pl., Islington Green, London, cm and u (1839). [D]

Chester, Joshua, 209 High Holborn, London, u (1835). [D]

Chester, Nicholas, London, cm (1767–1808). At 9 Butcher Row, Ratcliff Cross until 1789 when the number changed to 12. After 1799 at White Horse St, Ratcliff. From 1788 the business is referred to as Nicholas Chester & Son. [D]

Chester, Robert, Stanley St, Liverpool, cm and household broker (1824–39). Initially at 23 Stanley St but from 1835 the number changed to 21 and in 1839 it is shown as 45–47. [D]

Chesters, Charles, Chester, cm (1759). App. to John Croughton of Chester, cm and free 10 February 1759. [Freemen rolls]

Chesters, James, 34 Stanley Pl., Liverpool, cm and furniture broker (1835–37). [D]

Chesters (or Chester), John snr and jnr, Liverpool, cm (1806–39). John Chesters snr was app. to Edward Lowe and free 31 October 1806. His first recorded trade address was 24 Harrington St in 1811. Subsequent addresses are 32 Addison St in 1816, 3 Mathew St in 1818, 9 Nash Grove in 1821 and 37 Stanley St in 1823. The latter address is also recorded in the period 1834–37 as a shop. Additionally the address 1 Chester Pl., Marquis St appears from 1827–37. In 1839 the number in Stanley St was 73. John Chesters jnr was app. to his father in 1817 and free 17 October 1827. Other apps taken were John Mercer (1811 and free 1818), William Chesters (1819 and free 1827), William Gerrard (1820), Robert Musker (1823), Adam Wilkinson Orierie (1828), George Johnson (1828 and free 1835) and Thomas Blackburn (1832). [D; app. enrolment bks]

Chesters, Thomas, Nantwich, Cheshire, u, undertaker and paper hanger (1829–34). Opened his business in Pillory St in January 1829. By 1834 had moved to Welsh Row. [D; *Chester Chronicle*, 6 February 1829]

Chesters, William, Albion Pl., Upper Birkett St, Liverpool, cm (1827). App. to John Chesters snr in 1819 and free 17 October 1827. [Freemen reg.]

Chesterton, George, 50 Gloucester St, Queen's Sq., London, cm (1820). [D]

Chesworth, George, Liverpool, u (1774). App. to Lloyd Baxendale and free 8 December 1774. [Freemen reg.]

Chesworth, William, 17 Hanover St, Long Acre, London, u (1808). [D]

Chesworth, William, 27 Edmund St, Liverpool, u (1811). [D]

Chettee, William, Oxford, cm (1730). Took app. named Dewell in 1730. [S of G, app. index]

Chevers, Philip, Piccadilly, London, upholder (1780). [Bailey's list of bankrupts]

Cheverton, John, High St, Newport, Isle of Wight, Hants., chairmaker and patten maker (1823–39). [D]

Chew, John, Liverpool, u and cm (1787–1811). In 1787 shown at Ormond St, where his trade was listed as upholder and victualler. He is recorded at both 18 York St and 3 George's St in 1790. Thereafter he traded from addresses in Lord St, first at no. 10 (1792–1803) and then no. 12. In April 1792 he announced the ending of a partnership with Robert Smith and the opening of 'a commodious SHOP opposite the Post Office in Lord-street'. In April of the following year he announced that he had just returned from London 'with an assortment of the most fashionable articles in the UPHOLSTERY BUSINESS'. He was also seeking an app. Although the directories show no change of address, he advertised in January 1798 that he had moved 'six doors higher than his late shop'. His trade card survives in both the Banks Coll., BM, and Leverhulme Coll., MMA, NY. On it he declares himself u and cm to 'His Royal Highness Prince William Frederick of Gloucester'. The business continued to trade after 1811 initially as Chew & Son and then under the sole control of his son William. [D; *Williamson's Liverpool Advertiser*, 9 April 1792, 1 April 1793; *Billinge's Liverpool Advertiser*, 8 January 1798.]

Chew, William, 12 Lord St, Liverpool, u and cm (b. 1784–d. 1824). Initially traded in partnership with his father John Chew under the style 'Chew & Son'. In November 1811 it was announced that they were agents for 'patent adjusting bedsteads for the relief of sick, lame & infirm persons' devised by Messrs Parker and Cluley of Sheffield. An example of this patent bedstead was shown in their shop. William Chew may have been involved in the business long before 1811 however as he is recorded as a subscriber to Sheraton's *Cabinet Dictionary*, 1803 at which date he was aged 19. The period when the business was in his sole charge was however brief. In July 1815 he informed the public that because of his ill-health he was retiring from trade and his stock was offered to the public 'at prime cost'. The stock was said to consist of 'large and Brilliant Looking Glasses, cut glass Lustres, Lights and Mirrors, Lamps for Halls, Passages &c. Chairs, Tables, and a variety of Cabinet Goods in Satin, Mahogany and other Woods, Ladies' Work, Console and Pier Tables, superfine Kidderminster, Venetian and Brussels Carpets, with Imperial Hearth Rugs to match, elegant Four-post Bedsteads, with Cotton, Morine, Calico and other Hangings, with Window Curtains to match, a variety of Paper Hangings, with Fancy Borders to match, a few sets of handsome Mahogany Dining-room Chairs and Tables, quite new, with every other Article in the above business'. The unsold stock and the supplies of materials in his workshops were sold by auction in two sales conducted by Charles Chester jnr of Lord St on the 10 and 24 November 1815. William Chew retired from Liverpool to Holt Hill, Cheshire and in April 1816 his household furniture was also auctioned by Charles Chester at William Chew's house, no. 6 Maryland St. His death at the age of 40 'after a short illness' was announced in May 1824. [D; *Liverpool Mercury*, 22 November 1811, 14 July 1815, 27 October 1815, 24 November 1815, 26 March 1816, 7 May 1824] B.A.

Chewter, Thomas, London, upholder (1724). Son of Thomas Chewter of London, tallow chandler. App. to Giles Bly 14 February 1716/17. Free by servitude 7 October 1724. [GL, Upholders' Co. records]

Cheyney, William, 81 Leadenhall St, London, u (1784). [D]

Chick, Thomas, 7 Mount Row, Liverpool Rd, London, cm and u (1839). [D]

Chickley, Richard, Chatham and Rochester, Kent, carver (1732–61). Recorded at Chatham in 1732 when he took app. named Sarjant. In 1736 at Rochester when he took app. named Whitfield and in 1742 another app. of the same name. In 1761 at Chatham when he took app. named Munton. [S of G, app. index]

Chidwick, William, 14 and 15 Red Cross Sq., London, cm (1784–90). In 1784 licenced to employ three non-freemen for six weeks. Took out insurance cover in May 1790 of £500 which included £50 for utensils and stock in his workshop, and £150 for utensils and stock in an open yard. [GL, City Licence bks, vol. 10; Sun MS ref. 570026]

Chiffen, William, Whitechapel, London, upholder (1763). [D]

Chignall, Charles, Botolph St, Colchester, Essex, cm and u (1832–39). [D]

Chilcot, Jos., 16 Rawstone St, Goswell Rd, London, cm (1826). [D]

Child, George, 6 Rotten Row, Old St, London, cm (1802). In October 1802 took out insurance cover of £100 of which £50 was for utensils and stock. [GL, Sun MS vol. 426, ref. 738934]

Child, I., High St, Shaftesbury, Dorset, cm and u (1830–40). Initially traded in partnership as Child & Sweet, but by 1840 I. Child was the sole proprietor. [D]

Child, John, 37 Ludgate St, London, upholder (1791–93). Admitted freeman of the Upholders' Co. by redemption 16 November 1791. Subscribed to Sheraton's *Drawing Book*, 1793. In the same year in partnership with Pearce at the Ludgate St address. [D; GL, Upholders' Co. records]

Child, John, Birmingham, picture frame maker (1812–18). At Deritend in 1812 and in the same year moved to Cheapside were he was to remain until 1818. [D]

Child, Michael, Cross Lane, St Martin-in-the-Fields, London, bedstead maker (1774). Declared bankrupt *Gents Mag.*, February 1774.

Child, Richard, 38 Albert Pl., Bedford Sq., London, u (1835). [D]

Child, Richard, 70 Berners St, Oxford St, London, u etc. (1837). [D]

Child, Robert, address unknown, cm (1794). Payment of £2 9s made by Edward, Lord Harewood in respect of Harewood House, Hanover Sq., London, to Robert Child on 10 June 1794. [Leeds archives dept, Harewood MS 212]

Child, Thomas, Dudley, Worcs., cm (1818–19). Trading at High St in 1818. [D]

Child(e) & Walker, Dudley St, Woverhampton, Staffs., u and cm (1802–09). Recorded at 41 High Green in 1802 and Dudley St, 1805–09. [D; rate bk]

Childerhouse, Charles, Attleborough, Norfolk, cabinet and chairmaker (1822). [D]

Childs, William, Brighton, Sussex, Tunbridge-ware manufacturer and toyman (1832–40). At 4 East Cliff, 1832–33, but in 1839 at 53 King's Rd. [D]

Chilevier, —, 30 Brunswick St, Blackfriars, London, cm (1808). [D]

Chiles, Edward & Gumbrett, John, Richmond, Surrey, carpenters and u (1802). Declared bankrupt, *Billinge's Liverpool Advertiser*, 22 November 1802.

Chillingworth, Robert & Burnett, Thomas, London, cm, u and appraisers, (1724–44). In 1724 the firm was trading at the sign of 'The King's Arms', near Harp Alley, Fleet Ditch (now New Bridge St). About 1740 they moved to a position opposite the newly built church of St Mary-le-Strand, at the east end of the Strand. The partnership dissolved in 1741 and Chillingworth set up at this address on his own. His business had ceased by 1744 when the shop was taken by Dominic Hornon, a grocer. Thomas Burnett was however trading from this address or a shop adjacent from 1747. [V & A archives; Heal; Phillips, *Mid-Georgian London*, 1964, p. 172]

Chilton, John, Lewes, Sussex, cm and auctioneer (1796). [Poll bk]

Chilton, Thomas, High Wycombe, Bucks., chairmaker. (b. *c.* 1807–41). Aged 34 at the time of the 1841 Census.

Chilver, Robert, Queen St, Ipswich, Suffolk, cm and u (1839). [D; poll bk]

Chinn, Charles, Honey Hill, Cambridge, cm (1840). [Poll bk]

Chinn, Frederick, Milford St, Salisbury, Wilts., cm and u (1839). [D]

Chinnock, Charles, 219 Tottenham Ct Rd, London, cm and u (1835–39). For part of the period of the existence of this business Chinnock had a partner named Lorimer. In 1835 the business was described as Chinnock & Son. The partnership with Lorimer was dissolved in January 1839. [D; *Chester Courant*, 30 January 1839]

Chinnock, Frederick, 18 Duke St, Grosvenor Sq., London, cm and u (1837–39). In 1837 the business was styled Chinnock & Son. [D]

Chipchase, Robert & Lambert, Robert, London, cm and u (1767–88). At 2 Beak St, Golden Sq., 1767–75 when the address became 28 Warwick St, Golden Sq. The Beak St address was still being used by Robert Chipchase as late as 1787. About 1788 the partnership was dissolved and Robert Lambert formed a new partnership in Beak St known as Lambert & Turner. Robert Chipchase took his son Henry into partnership and moved to 39 Dover St. Insurance records provide additional information about the business. The Beak St premises are called a house, and only household goods appear to have been insured there. By February 1787 however a workshop in North Bruton Mews, Bruton St was being used and utensils, stock and goods there were covered for £700, indicating an extensive trade. One of the firm's workmen, John Robertson insured his tools in their workshop in 1779 for £20. Robert Chipchase subscribed in 1775 to Thomas Malton's *Treatise on Perspective*. Several important commissions carried out by the firm are known.

AUDLEY END, Essex. On 18 May 1768 Chipchase & Lambert submitted their account to Lord Howard de Walden for a state bed. The four-page invoice added to a total cost of £398 0s 4d. A further invoice of 28 June 1786 amounting to £160 11s 1d was concerned with the making and hanging of curtains, putting up tapestry hangings, covering chairs etc. Much of this work, in the state bedroom, ante room and dressing room survives, including the state bed itself. [Essex RO, D/DBy/A45/3, A44/5; V & A archives; *Conn.*, June 1977, p. 143]

BLAIR CASTLE, Tayside, Scotland. Chipchase & Lambert were working for the 3rd Duke of Atholl as early as 1767 undertaking repair work to carpets and curtains and supplying and cleaning bedding. In the next year they submitted an account for 'a sett of mahog. Dining tables to join together making 20 feet in length, of very fine wood with the best brass fastnings' at a cost of £21, and 20 mahogany dining chairs at 28s each, six of which still survive. A much more important commission was carried out in 1783 for twelve giltwood chairs and a pair of sofas in a restrained Neo-classical manner which are still in the State Drawing Room. [*Conn.*, February 1966; V & A archives]

NEW BURLINGTON ST, London. Furniture was supplied and work carried out 1783–84 for the London house of Sir John Griffin Griffin (later Lord Howard de Walden and 1st Lord Braybrooke). The main item recorded was the supply of a pair of satinwood painted pier tables in 1784 at a cost of £21. [Essex RO, D/DBy/A41/11, A42/1, A42/5]

OTHER COMMISSIONS. The Stanhope papers record a payment of £12 8s in 1775 for a chest of drawers and a 3ft mahogany bed. [Kent RO, U590 A61/7] In 1777 the Earl of Stair was supplied with a mahogany Pembroke table at £4 10s, a mahogany clothes press at £9 10s and four secondhand settees and two elbow chairs for which £10 10s was charged. A further account amounting to £25 14s was settled in 1785. [Scottish RO, GD 135/Box 59/34/5, Box 54/4/15] B.A.

Chipchase, Robert & Henry, 39 Dover St, London, cm and u (1788–1809). Successors to Chipchase & Lambert. The business is also styled Chipchase & Son. The first mention of the use of the Dover St premises was in April 1787 when household goods, stock etc. were insured for £2,400. The firm is recorded by Sheraton in his list of master cabinet makers, 1803. The Dover St address was a dwelling house tenanted by the Chipchase family and their workshops appear to have been adjacent to the house in Berkeley St. These consisted of a stable, warehouse, workshop over and a workroom and with utensils and goods which were insured for £3,500 alone in 1791. Property in Albemarle St variously described as 22(1791), 14(1792), 17(1806), 12 and 22(1809) and 14(1810) was also insured. During this period many important commissions were undertaken, several being those served formerly by the Chipchase & Lambert partnership.

BLAIR CASTLE, Tayside, Scotland. In 1805 Robert & Henry Chipchase supplied the 4th Earl of Atholl with 'six strong mahogany elbow chairs with loose seats covered with your Grace's Needlework' at £14 2s and 'Three shell back chairs japanned black' also at £14 2s. Other items supplied were three stools, and two fine Wilton carpets for the Drawing Room and Billiard Room which cost £51. A further carpet for the State Dining Room costing £34 12s 9d was supplied in 1808. Chipchase's appear to have been heavily involved in the supply of carpeting to which there are many references in the Blair Castle accounts of this period. An account of 1807 in respect of furniture for Blair Castle and Dunkeld House, Perthshire, included 'two very large sofas with scrole heads' charged at £84 and 'Two large Indulgent chairs' at £18. [*Conn.*, February 1966]

GORHAMBURY, St Albans, Herts. In 1796 supplied furniture to the value of £100. [Herts. RO, account bk XI 74]

KENWOOD, Highgate, London. In 1795 Chipchase & Co. were paid £14 9s by Hoare & Co., Lord Mansfield's bankers. [V & A archives]

LONGFORD CASTLE, Wilts. Payment of 18s in 1804. [V & A archives]

PORTMAN SQ., London, the town house of the Earl of Athol. Chipchase & Son appear to have been responsible for the cleaning and maintenance of the house in the absence of the Earl and acting as the Earl's agents for its supervision when let to others. They even supplied resident caretakers for the Earl, and accounts for 1809 included sums of £4 'to porter for wages and board in charge of the house' and £11 for 'the man and woman in charge of the house . . . 11 weeks'. [*Conn.*, February 1966]

OTHER COMMISSIONS. An account dated 5 May 1797 survives recording the hire of a sofa for 19 weeks at 19s, and general repairs and maintenance to furniture and wall coverings amounting to £4 13s 6d. [Lincoln RO, NEL 9/19/10] B.A.

Chipchase & Proctor, Albemarle St, London, cm and u (1809–18). As the business was styled R. & H. Chipchase & Proctor in 1809 this suggests that both father and son were still active. Little is known about Proctor but it has been suggested that he may have been the firm's manager, and his full name appears to have been William Grosvenor Proctor. No. 27 (later 28) Albemarle St appears to have been the centre of production with an insurance cover of £2,000 for stock and utensils and a further £200 for similar items in an open yard. A further cover of £800 in 1810 for household goods suggests that a part was being used as a dwelling. From 1812 however Robert and Henry Chipchase appear to have lived at 29 Albemarle St. Few commissions of this period are recorded though there is no reason for thinking that their trade had changed from that conducted earlier. Two invoices made out to James Henry Leigh exist, presumably for work at Stoneleigh, Warks. One dated 19–26 July 1813 is largely in respect of furniture and amounts to £132 13s 6d. The main item was a brass inlaid rosewood loo table costing £36 12s. A further invoice dated 4 April 1814 lists a similar table at £36 12s and 'a Handsome four post bedstead the posts carved & japanned in imitation of Bamboo' for the 'India Bed room' costing £16 7s. The total of the invoice is £154 19s 6d. This document also shows that an account had been rendered for £235 5s 3d of which £200 had been settled on 16 June 1814 in cash. [Shakespeare Birthplace Trust, Leigh receipts, DR 18/5] By 1818 Robert & Henry Chipchase appear to have been no longer active in the business which briefly traded as Proctor & Chadley before these partners broke away in 1820 to trade independently as William Grosvenor Proctor at 29 Argyle St and Robert & George Chadley at the Albemarle St address. [D; Westminster poll bks; GL, Sun MS vol. 238, p. 299; vol. 247, p. 95; vol. 273, p. 105; vol. 296, p. 576; vol. 342, refs 527977, 529377, 574941 and 580662; vol. 389, ref. 606428; vol. 434, refs 781258, 785055; vol. 445, refs 819006, 825222; vol. 448, ref. 830825; vol. 453, refs 839918, 841517, 839918, 841517; vol. 459, refs 867002, 864798, 864799, 864800, 867001; Heal] B.A.

Chipendale, John, Park St, London, cm (1774). [Westminster poll bk]

Chipp, Jane, Aldersgate St, London, cm (1768–69). Licenced in 1768 to employ twelve non-freemen and in the following year ten and then fourteen. [GL, City Licence bks, vol. 6]

Chippendale, A., Boston and Thorpe Arch, Yorks., cm (1837). [D]

Chippendale, Benjamin, Bondgate, Otley, Yorks., joiner, builder and cm (1822–34). [D]

Chippendale, John, Bondgate, Otley, Yorks., cm (1822). [D]

Chippendale, Thomas snr, London, cm (b. 1718–d. 1779). Enjoys an international reputation as author of *The Gentleman and Cabinet-Maker's Director* and is often described as 'the Shakespeare of English furniture makers': his career and achievements have been researched in depth and his name is now freely used as a convenient generic label to describe all *Director*-style furniture. Thomas Chippendale, the son of a joiner, was bapt. in the Yorkshire market town of Otley on 5 June 1718. Hardly anything is known about his early life or craft training, although it is likely that after serving a family apprenticeship he spent some time in the workshop of Richard Wood, a York joiner and cm. He may have received his artistic education from Matthias Darly, a professional designer, engraver and drawing master, the two men were certainly on friendly terms; but prior to his marriage in 1748 to Catherine Redshaw at St George's Chapel, Mayfair, Chippendale is a very shadowy figure.

At Christmas 1749, shortly after the birth of his eldest son, Thomas, who was to inherit the business, Chippendale took a house in Conduit Ct, a small enclave off Long Acre on the fringes of a fashionable furniture making district. At midsummer 1752 he moved to more respectable premises in Somerset Ct adjoining the Earl of Northumberland's palatial residence. Throughout 1753 Thomas Chippendale and Matthias Darly were collaborating on the *Director* plates, and a smart address from which to solicit subscriptions for his ambitious pattern book was obviously an advantage. It is difficult to gauge the extent of Chippendale's commercial activities at this time, but it is likely that he was serving the London cabinet trade as a free-lance designer and making small quantites of furniture on a sub-contract basis for established firms rather than dealing directly with private clients.

In 1754 Chippendale moved to spacious new premises in St Martin's Lane, formed an alliance with a financing partner named James Rannie and issued his celebrated volume of furniture designs titled *The Gentleman and Cabinet-Maker's Director* which clearly benefited his trade, for all known commissions to supply furniture date from after its appearance. This folio volume, published by subscription, contained 161 superbly engraved plates portraying a wide range of fashionable household furniture. It was reprinted in 1755 and a third enlarged edition featuring progressive Neo-classical elements was issued in parts between 1759 and 1762. Chippendale's popular reputation is largely founded on this distinguished collection of designs which exerted a powerful influence on contemporary styles. He stated in the preface that 'Persons of Distinction' and 'Eminent Taste' had encouraged him to publish the *Director*, one of whom may have been Lord Burlington whose private account book contains the intriguing entry under 13 October 1747 'to Chippendale in full £6.16.0.'. The first two editions were dedicated to the Earl of Northumberland, a notable patron of the arts, while the third was dedicated to H R H Prince William Henry: both commissioned furniture from the author. Many titled individuals ordered copies of the *Director*, which was marketed through London and provincial newspaper advertisements, however the majority of subscribers were practicing tradesmen.

Chippendale and Rannie called their new establishment at nos 60–62 St Martin's Lane 'The Cabinet and Upholstery Warehouse' and adopted a chair as their shop sign. They issued a trade card featuring a chair at about this time, although it was never applied as a label to identify their products. In 1755 the property was rated at £124 and Chippendale arranged fire cover with the Sun Insurance Office for £3,700. Several early policies (1755 (2), 1756 and 1767) and a highly instructive plan showing the layout of the premises was attached to Chippendale, the Younger's, 1803 schedule. The firm suffered a setback in April 1755 when fire ravaged the cabinet shop destroying the chests of 22 journeymen: £847 was paid in compensation and the partners helped to organise a public appeal to replace their employees tools. Ceasar Crouch, a cm living on the South Side of St Paul's was one of the people nominated to receive donations, he had subscribed to the *Director* and Chippendale designed an ornamental invitation card for him which displays such striking affinities to several trade cards engraved by Darly, that it is likely Chippendale was in demand as a designer of decorative surrounds.

James Rannie was a Scotsman with relatives living in Edinburgh which doubtless explains the firm's early success in attracting patrons such as the Earls of Dumfries and Morton, Lord Arniston and the Duke of Atholl, who lived north of the border. Rannie died in January 1766 and the next month press notices appeared announcing the dissolution of the partnership and that the 'Trade will for the future be carried on by Mr Chippendale on his own account'. Faced with a pressing need for ready money to satisfy Rannie's executors who were intent on withdrawing his capital, a well publicised auction of 'The entire genuine and valuable Stock in Trade of Mr Chippendale and his late Partner Mr Rannie . . . also all the large unwrought Stock consisting of fine mahogany and other woods, in Plank, Boards, Vanier and Wainscot' was held on the premises in March and April. The acute financial strains that this crisis imposed on the firm are vividly reflected in Chippendale's letters to Sir Rowland Winn; he feared he would be arrested for debt, ruined or driven out of his mind by money problems. These troubles were aggravated by the dilatoriness of many patrons in settling their accounts and in 1771, to stave off bankruptcy, Rannie's book keeper Thomas Haig who had remained with the firm, and another executor Henry Ferguson each bought a third share in the business. This injection of funds seems to have paved the way for a period of relative prosperity.

Although Chippendale's business career is impressively documented little is known about his private life. His first wife Catherine Redshaw bore five boys and four girls. She died in 1772 and in 1777 he married Elizabeth Davis. They had three children, but only four of his offspring survived until 1784. Chippendale died of consumption at Hoxton and was buried in the graveyard of St Martin-in-the-Fields on 13 November 1779. In the absence of a will administration was granted to his widow. A probate inventory suggests that the couple lived quite simply.

Most of our information about Chippendale's activities comes from the firm's surviving bills and two collections of letters associated with his work at Nostell Priory and Mersham-le-Hatch. In his day he was regarded merely as a successful tradesman and did not enjoy the social status of fashionable architects or artists, so it is hardly surprising that few references to his affairs occur in diaries or journals and no obituary notice appeared. Diligent searches have revealed the identity of some sixty-five patrons (with a significant concentration in Yorkshire) although in many cases only bills, payments for unspecified work in ledgers or entries in bank accounts remain, the furniture having been dispersed. Even so, significantly more furniture from Chippendale's workshop has been identified — about 700 items — than from any of his rivals. Chippendale therefore fulfils the most important requirement of any major artistic figure: he has left a substantial body of high quality work that displays a steady development from an early through a middle to a late style.

Obviously Chippendale did not personally make the furniture recorded in his bills; in fact it is highly unlikely that he ever worked at the bench after setting up in St Martin's Lane, although the prefatory notes to the *Director* plates confirm that he received a sound practical training as a cm. It would, however, be unfair to regard him merely as an entrepreneur — the managing director of a successful company employing a team of up to 50 specialist tradesmen — because he certainly conceived his own designs, selected materials and supervised workshop production: he remained responsible to his patrons for artistic and quality control. It should be stressed that Chippendale did not possess a monopoly of the most skilled craftsmen and was only one of several elite London furniture makers. Chippendale's special achievement was as an inspired and innovative designer.

Unless a piece of furniture carries a maker's label, and Chippendale never used this form of advertisement, the only sure way of identifying the author is by tracing the original bill or equivalent documentation. Even if an item corresponds exactly to one of Chippendale's published designs this does not amount to proof since many practicing cm bought the *Director* in order to copy the engravings. If, however, superlative 'post-Director' furniture displaying striking stylistic and technical affinities with the firm's proven work for other patrons is discovered at a house — such as Newby or Brocket — where Chippendale is known to have worked, an attribution is acceptable, even if the itemized bills do not survive.

Chippendale was patronised by the Royal Family, wealthy members of the nobility, gentry and connoisseurs who lived in the highest style of elegance; one therefore naturally associates him with luxurious furnishings. However, in addition to equipping state apartments the partners provided a complete house furnishing service supplying everything from the most opulent beds, mirrors and cabinets to cheap domestic wares for the staff quarters. The firm regularly provided curtains, carpets, wall papers, chimney-pieces, loose covers and bell systems; undertook repairs, removals, hired out furniture, and were even prepared to direct and furnish funerals for respected customers.

Chippendale often furnished interiors designed by Robert Adam who laid great stress on stylistic continuity, but he is only known to have executed one of the latter's furniture designs (for Sir Lawrence Dundas in 1765). It is a myth to believe they formed a partnership with Adam supplying, and Chippendale carrying out, designs provided by the architect. On the contrary, when an owner did not require Adam to produce furniture drawings he appears frequently to have recommended Chippendale as the most accomplished exponent of Neo-classical furniture who could safely be trusted to equip his most elegant interiors with decorum. Architects of course expected to be consulted about schemes for rooms they had designed and Sir William Chambers insisted in a rather highhanded manner on vetting Chippendale's proposals for the principal apartments at Melbourne House, Piccadilly.

Chippendale's versatility is underlined by the fact that in addition to furniture he was prepared to design wallpapers, carpets, needlework, cast-iron stoves, silverware, decorative ormolu, trade cards and complete room schemes. He is known to have visited Paris in 1768 and in 1769 was apprehended at the Customs while attempting to import illegally 60 unfinished French chair frames. This episode raises the question of sub-contracting. From our knowledge of the infrastructure of the London cabinet trade it is likely (but not, as yet, proven) that at busy times Chippendale farmed out work involving specialist skills such as marquetry, carving and gilding or brass work to other firms — to be executed according to his designs. It is also probable that he bought-in and merely invoiced to customers common 'backstairs' articles and sometimes sophisticated items such as the combination backgammon and chessboard supplied to Ninian Home in 1774 and the French tortoiseshell and brass inlaid commode listed in his Dumfries House account.

Many of Chippendale's original manuscript designs survive in two major and several minor holdings. In 1920 the MMA, NY acquired two albums of drawings formerly owned by the Foley family, which include nearly all Chippendale's drawings for the first edition of the *Director*, plus a fair number prepared for the third edition and a scattering of unpublished designs. To these can be added an unprovenanced portfolio of 144 furniture drawings ascribed to Chippendale purchased by the V & A in 1906 and 7 *Director* designs which survive in the archive of Matthias Lock, bought by the same institution in 1862. The presence of Chippendale material amongst the Lock sketches prompted speculation in the 1920s that Lock and his associate Copland had ghosted the *Director* plates, but since then abundant evidence in the form of letters and drawings in country house archives has confirmed that Chippendale was perfectly capable of producing his own furniture designs.

From the catalogue of Chippendale's known commissions the following may be singled out as pre-eminent owing to the abundance of elite documented furniture which survives for the most part in its original setting. His finest ensemble of 'Director' period furniture is at Dumfries House with a smaller anthology at Wilton; Nostell Priory and Aske Hall contain the best collections of pieces illustrating Chippendale's transition to Neo-classical ideals of taste, while Harewood, despite post-war sales, still retains the largest and most outstanding concentration of masterpieces in his mature 'Adam' manner. Paxton House and Mersham-le-Hatch deserve a special mention for their repertoire of well made but not overtly ambitious mahogany furniture expressing a very English character which illustrates Chippendale 'manor house' rather than palatial style. Much of the green and white japanned furniture enchantingly decorated in the Chinese taste ordered by David Garrick for his villa on the Thames at Hampton has been identified, it conveys a gay, lighthearted spirit appropriate to a rural retreat. Other notable Neo-classical suites survive at Newby Hall, Brocket Hall and Burton Constable, while no fewer than three beds complete with their original cut velvet hangings are to be found at Petworth. The most complete Chippendale archives are associated with his Nostell, Mersham and Harewood commissions. [O. Brackett, *Thomas Chippendale*, 1924; A. Coleridge, *Chippendale Furniture*; Gilbert, *Chippendale*]

BURLINGTON HOUSE (?) London (3rd Earl of Burlington) 1747. His private account bk records under 13 October 1747 'to Chippendale in full £6 16s 0d'. [Chatsworth papers, account bk 1747–51]

BULLER, JAMES. Account 29 January 1757 for £8 11s 0d. [Cornwall RO, Buller papers, bundle 337]

STOWE HOUSE, Bucks. (Earl Temple). A bill of 14 February 1757 for a library table costing £13 13s. [Huntington Lib., California, Stowe MS, STG. 144, 1756 bundle]

ARNISTON HOUSE, Midlothian, Scotland (Lord Arniston). Minor ledger entries 2 April 1757 encourage speculation that a fine 'Director' pattern dressing table now in the Lady Lever Art Gallery may be by the firm. [Arniston papers, House bk 1757, p. 125]

EAST SUTTON PARK, Kent (Sir John Filmer). Ten ledger payments 1757–73 total £598 14s 10d. [Kent RO, no. VI 736 A1]

CALTHORPE, JAMES. His pocket book notes on 13 March 1758 an appointment with Chippendale. [Chippendale Soc.]

BLAIR CASTLE, Perthshire, Scotland (Duke of Atholl). A bill of 8 May 1758 invoices a surviving firescreen and pair of candlestands. [Blair Castle papers]

DUMFRIES HOUSE, Ayrshire, Scotland (5th Earl of Dumfries). The main bill May/July 1759 amounting to £647 14s 1d is followed by lesser accounts of 1763 and 1766. Nearly all the furniture survives, it is of elite quality and forms easily the best documented collection illustrating Chippendale's 'Director' style. [Dumfries House papers, 34/49–54–56–68]

DALMAHOY, Midlothian, Scotland (14th Earl of Morton). A prefatory note in the *Director*, 1762 states the Earl had ordered the bed featured on pl. xxxix

LONDON, 26 Soho Sq. and Glasshouse St (Sir William Robinson). Two large accounts of 1759–60 for £469 9s 1d and 1763–65 for £208 7s 9d together with four smaller bills provide a record of goods supplied and services performed when Sir William moved his London home. An inventory compiled by Chippendale for his patron but no furniture

survives. [Leeds archives dept, NH. 2785A; 2277/27; 2277/29/2–3]

WILTON HOUSE, Wilts. and **PEMBROKE HOUSE**, London (Earl of Pembroke). The Earl is named in a prefatory note to pl. xlvi in the *Director*, 1762. Receipts 1763–73 total £1,500. Three magnificent bookcases, a library table and two drawings for torchères at Wilton can be ascribed to the firm. [Wilton Estate Office, Pembroke papers]

ALSCOT PARK, Warks. (James West). Two bills of 1760 and 1767 survive; the latter documents a pair of side tables costing £44 0s 8d.

HESTERCOMBE HOUSE, Som. (Coplestone Warre Bampfylde). A pier glass in 'the Chippendale albums' at the MMA, NY is annotated 'for Cop Warr Bampfylde Esq'r at Hestercombe'. This design can probably be associated with a pair dispersed at the Hestercombe sale in 1872. [MMA, Acc. No. 20. 40. 1,2 — No. 83]

CRANFORD PARK, Middlx (Countess of Berkeley). Bank ledgers record that in 1761 she paid Chippendale £130 3s. [Royal Bank of Scotland, Drummonds Branch]

WOLVERLEY HOUSE, Worcs. (Edward Knight jnr). Two note books record minor payments 1763–69 totalling £195 which may relate to certain pieces which have descended in the family. [Kidderminster Lib., Knight MS Notebooks 283 and 287]

SANDON HALL, Staffs. (Earl of Harrowby). Various ledgers record minor payments mostly for unspecified work 1763–77. [Sandon Hall papers, vols 324, 326, 330, 337, 338]

NORTHUMBERLAND HOUSE (?), London (1st Duke of Northumberland). Chippendale dedicated his *Director* to Hugh, Earl of Northumberland (created Duke in 1766) but the only proof of his patronage is an isolated payment dated June 1763 'Mr. Chippendale for Writing table £24' — it has not been identified. His name also occurs in two lists of fashionable cm drawn up *c.* 1767 and a memorandum in Lady Northumberland's notebooks. [Alnwick papers, U.1.42; 121/60, p. 344 and 121/63]

ASKE HALL, Yorks. and 19 Arlington St, London (Sir Lawrence Dundas). A bill of 1763–66 lists luxurious furniture costing £1,123 1s 6d; many of the finest pieces are now at Aske, including part of a suite of seat furniture designed by Robert Adam and made by Chippendale in 1765. [N. Yorks RO, ZNK X 1/7/19]

GOODNESTONE, Kent (Sir Brook Bridges). A cash note book records one payment in 1765 for £177 2s. [Kent RO, U373/A2]

CARLISLE HOUSE, Soho Sq., London (Theresa Cornelys). When in 1772 Madam Cornelys, owner of the fashionable assembly rooms at Carlisle House, was declared bankrupt, Chippendale was amongst her creditors. [PRO, B1, vol. 59, pp. 164–69]

MIDDLESEX HOSPITAL, London. A notice in the *Gazeteer and New Daily Advertiser*, 28 November 1767 states that Chippendale 'designed and executed' an elegant frame for R. E. Pine's (surviving) portrait of the Duke of Northumberland. The Governor's minute books record that Samuel Hayworth was paid for the frame, so Chippendale presumably supplied it on a sub-contract basis. [Middlx Hospital archives]

GLOUCESTER HOUSE, London (H R H Prince William Henry, 1st Duke of Gloucester). An account book records payments to Chippendale 1764–66 totalling £134 15s 6d. He had dedicated the 3rd Edition of his *Director* to the Prince in 1762. [Royal Archives, Duke of Glos. accounts 1764–67]

ROUSHAM HOUSE, Oxon. (Sir Charles Cotterell-Dormer). A pocket account book records small payments in 1764. [Rousham papers]

BADMINTON HOUSE, Glos. (Duchess of Beaufort). A red leather bound book entitled 'Bills & Receipts The Duchess of Beaufort' includes a bill dated 3 March 1764 'for a mahogany frame 10s 6d'. [Badminton papers]

CROOME COURT, Worcs. and 29 Piccadilly, London (Earl of Coventry). Four small bills 1764–70 exist; the earliest documents a box on frame sold at Christie's, 30 November 1978, lot 58; the last invoices a looking-glass plate to fit a frame designed by Robert Adam for the Earl's London house. [Worcs. RO, Croome papers]

CHRIST CHURCH, Oxford. On 21 July 1764 Chippendale was paid £38 15s 0d for library stools; they were of X-frame design and are still in use. [Christ Church Lib., MS 373 f 26]

FOX-STRANGWAYS, Lady Susan. Before emigrating to New York in 1764 Lady Susan bought goods to the value of £247. [Ilchester (ed.), *The Life and Letters of Lady Susan Lennox*, 1901.i. pp. 148–49]

FOREMARK HALL, Derbs. (Sir Robert Burdett). Account books 1766–74 record payments of £510. [Reading archives dept, D/EUB A8/2–A/8/3–A9/1]

CLAYDON HOUSE, Bucks. (Earl Verney). Two obscure references to Chippendale and his first partner James Rannie occur in 1771 and 1766 respectively. There are also three drawings for library bookcases possibly from Chippendale's hand. [Claydon House papers]

NOSTELL PRIORY, Yorks. and 11 St James's Sq., London (Sir Rowland Winn). This highly important commission initiated in 1766 is impressively documented by letters, estimates, memoranda, accounts and drawings. Much of the furniture survives *in situ* (Figs 41–42). [Nostell Priory papers]

BURLINGTON HOUSE, London (Duke of Portland). A ledger records under 1 November 1766 'Chippendale for Girandoles £48 10s 0d' [Notts. RO, Portland MS DD SP 3/1]

LANGTON HALL, Yorks. (Thomas Norcliffe). A scrappy note of articles ordered from Chippendale in 1767. [Scunthorpe Museum]

BOYNTON HALL, Yorks. (Sir George Strickland). Account book payment, June 1767 of £16 7s 0d. [Mrs L. Strickland]

HAREWOOD HOUSE, Yorks. (Edwin Lascelles). This commission was the most notable of Chippendale's career. One bill amounting to £6,838 19s 1d survives, but the final figure probably exceeded £10,000. There is a Day Work Book 1769–76 recording how the firm's outworkers spent their time, also many ledger payments, relevant letters and a group of drawings at large provided for local tradesmen. Despite some sales, the collection still illustrates a full range of Chippendale's pre-eminent Neo-classical furniture. [Leeds archives dept, Harewood papers]

MERSHAM LE HATCH, Kent (Sir Edward Knatchbull). A major commission to equip a new Adam house; documented by letters, estimates memoranda and bills. Comparatively little furniture has been identified. [Kent RO, Knatchbull–Bradbourne MS U957 A/18/14–33]

BOREHAM HOUSE, Essex (Richard Hoare). An account book lists four modest payments 1767–76. [Essex RO, D/DU 649/2]

CANNON HALL, Yorks. (John Spencer). His diary records a visit to Chippendale's shop in 1768. [Sheffield archives dept, Spencer–Stanhope MS 60633–19/JS (3)]

GARRICK, DAVID. Between 1768 and 78 Chippendale furnished three houses for Garrick — 27 Southampton St and 5 Royal Adelphi Terr., London and a villa on the Thames at Hampton. The Adelphi bill totals £931 but only a pair of bergère chairs has been identified. Documentation of the Hampton commission is slighter but many pieces of white and green japanned furniture from this house survive — mostly at the V & A. [V & A Lib., RC Q20; 86NN 4–iii, iv and VIII]

NORMANTON PARK, Rutland; BROWNE'S HOUSE, Fulham and GROSVENER SQ., London (Sir Gilbert Heathcote). Five accounts span 1768–79; no furniture can be positively identified, but a bill for Lady Bridget Heathcote's funeral is of capital interest since the coffin was photographed in 1972 and the hardware is now owned by the Chippendale Soc. [Lincoln RO, Ancaster papers]

LANDSDOWNE HOUSE, London (Earl of Shelburne). A bill of 1768–69 amounts to £428 13s 0d together with two lesser accounts of 1770 and 1772, no furniture has been identified. [Bowood MS]

KENWOOD HOUSE, Middlx (Earl of Mansfield). In 1769 Chippendale contracted to supply looking-glass plates for two mirrors in the library; the frames were made by William France to Adam's design. [Scottish RO, Mansfield papers]

THANET, 8th Earl. His bank account records under 12 April 1769 a payment of £66. [Hoare's Bank, London]

BROCKENHURST PARK, Hants. (Edward Morant). His 1769 notebook records a payment of £8 18s 6d. [Morant papers]

THORESBY PARK, Notts. (Duke of Kingston). His bank account records two payments in 1770 totalling £300. [Hoare's Bank, London]

SALTRAM HOUSE, Devon (Lord Boringdon). In 1771 Chippendale received three payments amounting to £225 which relate to gilt chairs and sofas in the saloon. [Saltram papers]

GOLDSBOROUGH HALL, Yorks. (Daniel Lascelles). Chippendale and his foreman William Reid made several trips to Goldsborough to supervise work between 1771–76. [Leeds archives dept, Harewood MS 492]

CLEVELAND COURT, London (George Selwyn). In 1772 he ordered a flower pot stand costing £1 16s 0d. [Castle Howard papers]

ROCHFORD, Earl of. His bank account records payments of £68 11s 0d and £75 to Chippendale in 1772 and 1773. [Coutt's Bank, L58, L59]

BROCKET HALL, Herts. and MELBOURNE HOUSE, Piccadilly, London (Viscount Melbourne). Both houses were furnished c. 1771–76; documentation exists in the form of letters between his Lordship and Sir William Chambers and in the Journal of Thomas Mouat. Magnificent furniture survives. [BM, Add MS 41135]

NEWBY HALL, Yorks. (William Weddell). A major but thinly documented commission of c. 1772–76. The Tapestry Room is one of several expensively furnished interiors. [Leeds archives dept, Harewood MS 490, 492; Newby MS 2980

MANOR HOUSE, Beckenham, Kent (Henry Hoare jnr). An account at Hoare's Bank records a payment on 2 January 1773 of £63 8s 6d.

SHERBORNE CASTLE, Dorset (Earl Digby). A note of expenditure dated 1774 lists a payment of £14 6s 0d. [Sherborne Castle papers]

TEMPLE NEWSAM HOUSE, Yorks. (Viscount Irwin). A bill dated 10 February 1774 totals £8. [Leeds archives dept, TN EA 12/5]

PAXTON HOUSE, Berwick, Scotland (Ninian Home). One account of 1774 totals £405 6s 10d; this extensive commission is also documented in later letters. Numerous furnishings survive. [Paxton House papers]

AUDLEY END, Essex (Sir John Griffin Griffin). An account of 30 May 1774 records the purchase of a tripod table. [Essex RO, D/DBy A/32/9]

BURTON CONSTABLE, Yorks. and MANSFIELD STREET, London (William Constable). Between 1768 and 79 Chippendale provided costly furniture for both houses which survives; the saloon suite at Burton Constable is sumptuous. [Hull University archives dept, Burton Constable papers]

THOMAS MOUAT, Shetland Isles, Scotland. On a visit to London in 1775 he purchased a set of mahogany chairs. [*Furn. Hist.*, 1975]

APPULDURCOMBE HOUSE, Isle of Wight (Sir Richard Worsley). Bank ledgers record that 1776–78 Chippendale was paid £2,638. Eight library chairs now at Brocklesby, Lincs relate to these payments. [Hoare's Bank, London]

CASTLE HOTEL ASSEMBLY ROOMS, BRIGHTON, Sussex (Samuel Shergold). Two letters of 1777 from J. Crunden, architect, to the proprietor refer to the purchase of furniture. [Brighton Public Lib.]

WIMPOLE HALL, Cambs. (Earl of Hardwicke). Bank books record that in 1777 Chippendale was paid £14 4s od. [Herts. RO, E/ECd F82]

DALTON HALL, Yorks. (Sir Charles Hotham-Thompson). A bank ledger records under 21 November 1777 the payment of £84. [Coutt's Bank: L.69 f 676]

PETWORTH HOUSE, Sussex and other properties (Earl of Egremont). A bill of 1777–78 in four sections headed 'Petworth/Shortgrove/Newmarket/Town acc' invoices goods amounting to £764 19s 1od; documented furniture at Petworth includes three bed with their original hangings. [W. Sussex RO, Petworth papers No. 6611]

DENTON HALL, Yorks. (Sir James Ibbetson). An undated (*c.* 1778) summary of money spent on furniture includes 'Chippendale's Bill £551'; a marquetry commode and a pair of pier tables survive. [Chippendale Soc.]

CLIFFORD, Lord. The general accounts of the executors of the Rt Hon. Lord Clifford January 1778–June 1779, vol. 1, include under the heading 'Funeral charges' payments dated 20 January 1778 'for Lord Clifford £279' and 5 December 1778 'for Master Southwell £47.8'. [Badminton papers]

CORSHAM COURT, Wilts. (Paul Methuen). A day book records under 1 November 1779 a payment 'for the Library Table £18 16s od'. [Wilts. RO, Corsham Papers]   C. G. G.

Chippendale, Thomas jnr, London, cm (b. 1749–d. 1822). The eldest of his illustrious father's children, was bapt. at St Paul's, Covent Gdn on 23 April 1749. He was brought up to assist in the family business, the earliest known letter from him (in the Nostell archive) being dated 5 August 1767. Thereafter young Thomas became increasingly involved in running the firm, assuming a major share of artistic control following his father's second marriage in 1777. The cm George Smith spoke of him posthumously as possessing 'a very great degree of taste, with great ability as a draughtsman and designer'. His earliest finished drawing is, rather surprisingly, an elegant Neo-classical cartouche on a survey of the High St, Hull executed in 1772 — a date that coincides with the father's commission at neighbouring Burton Constable. In 1779 he published a modest suite of eight decorative designs on five plates titled *Sketches of Ornament* inscribed 'T. Chippendale, Jun'r inv et ex.' He exhibited five genre scenes at the Royal Academy between 1784 and 1801 and in Regency days filled a small book with drawings of fashionable French furniture. The existence of this volume (formerly in the Ralph Bernal collection) described as *Sketches by Tho. Chippendale at various times* was reported by Margaret Jourdain, but its whereabouts is unknown. Other evidence of his artistic ability is provided by an accomplished 'exploded' drawing room scheme in pen, ink and watercolour prepared for William Weddell's town house in Upper Brook St, about 1787 and preserved amongst the Newby Hall papers; he also purchased numerous lots at a Christie's sale held on 31 December 1794 devoted to a collection of prints and drawings by Cipriani, Bartolozzi and others, which suggests that he may have dealt in fine art engravings. He subscribed to four pattern books by George Richardson, Robert Adam's chief draughtsman.

After his father's death in 1779, Chippendale continued the business with Thomas Haig who became the senior partner until his retirement in 1796, the firm trading as Haig & Chippendale. A Fire Insurance policy of 1796 shows that the dwelling house and personal belongings of Thomas Chippendale, 62 St Martin's Lane, Gent., were covered for £1,200. [GL, Sun MS vol. 407, ref. 655620] There is some evidence that during the 1780s and 90s the partners transacted business with Gillows whose archive includes a sketch and estimate for a secretary desk and bookcase (1794) inscribed 'No. 30433 Mr Chippindale London made by Jno Crookall'; a similar entry relates to a guardawine made in 1789. [Westminster Ref. Lib., Gillow vol. 344/96, p. 1047 and 344/95, p. 525]

On his death in 1803 Haig bequeathed over £10,000 to various friends and relatives, directing that the legacies were to be paid out of 'monies secured to me on several bonds of Thomas Chippendale, my successor in business.' Regretfully his late partner, unable to meet these obligations, was declared bankrupt in 1804. The trustees disposed of Chippendale's assets, which included 'many articles of great taste and of the finest workmanship' at four public auctions devoted to manufactured stock in trade; holdings of timber and veneers; upholstery materials and finally his household goods. The advertisements for these sales [*Morning Chronicle*, 23, 27, 31 July 1804] yield important information about Chippendale's business and his private circumstances. Another valuable item of evidence from this time is an annotated plan of Chippendale's premises in St Martin's Lane attached to his Sun Fire Insurance policy taken out in 1803 which provides an excellent record of the workshop layout.

Chippendale survived this setback, for in Holden's *Directory* for 1805 he is still entered at 60 St Martin's Lane as 'upholsterer and cabinet-maker to the Duke of Gloucester.' The bankruptcy does not reflect adversely on Chippendale's status as one of the leading cm of his day; such mishaps were common and he continued to receive lucrative commissions. According to poor rate bk entries [Westminster Ref. Lib.] he remained at 60 St Martin's Lane until Michaelmas 1813 when he moved to 17 Haymarket, then in 1818 he took up residence at 42 Jermyn St which he vacated in 1821. His will, dated 22 December 1822, is addressed from 61 Regent St. [PRO, Prob. 11/1665, 17101] He died a bachelor, leaving the whole of his personal property to Sarah Wheatley of Regent St who presumably nursed him in his last illness. Although less charismatic than his father, Thomas Chippendale, the Younger, was perhaps commercially more successful, while both in design and quality his furniture compares favourably with the great tradition of the firm he inherited. The major commissions, where documented furniture survives, are at Stourhead, Harewood and Paxton. [D; Gilbert, *Chippendale*; *Furn. Hist.*, 1975, 1981]

APPULDURCOMBE, Isle of Wight and STRATFORD PL., London (Sir Richard Worsley Bt). Largely furnished 1776–78 but settlement of the accounts dragged on into the next decade, including a payment in 1781 of over £300 for work for the town house. [*Burlington*, May 1968, pp. 352–55]

HAREWOOD HOUSE, Yorks. and HAREWOOD HOUSE, Hanover Sq. London (Lord Harewood). The firm of Chippendale was deeply involved from 1767 onwards. A bill of 5 August 1796 totalling £564, 15s 2d lists furniture ordered for the newly acquired London house and the Yorkshire residence; identifiable pieces include the Gallery pier tables and a large mahogany press. The White Drawing Room and the Gallery were equipped during the 1780s; the last recorded payment on 28 June 1799 was for £42 19s but some extant

Regency furniture may also be by the firm. [Leeds archives dept, Harewood MS 210 and 211]

WIMPOLE HALL, Cambs. (Earl of Hardwicke). His bank bks record three payments in 1779, 1780 and 1784 totalling £662 8s 0d. [Herts. RO, D/Ecd F82 and 83]

SCAWBY HALL, Lincs. (Sir John Nelthorpe). An account dated 13 June 1780 totals £19 7s 7d. [Lincoln RO, NEL 1X/1/68]

LANSDOWNE HOUSE, Berkeley Sq., London (Earl of Shelburne). Following a major commission in the 1770s there is an account of 12 February 1780 for a bidet costing £2 15s 0d. [Bowood MS, Bundle 11B.3.7]

AUDLEY END, Essex (Sir John Griffin, Lord Howard de Walden). Two minor accounts of 1780 and 1790 total £5 16s; both are receipted by John Peareth. [Essex RO, D/DBy/A38/9 and A/49/6]

NORMANTON HALL, Rutland, **NORTH END**, Fulham; houses in Richmond, Surrey, and Grosvener Sq., London (Sir Gilbert and Dowager Lady Heathcote, etc.). The family patronised the firm of Chippendale for over half a century. Two bills of 1782 total £203 11s 1d and £49 12s 7d; an invoice dated 1800 amounts to £807 6s 9d, another of 1804 is for £144 16s 1d, while an account bk lists payments between 1815–21 totalling £1,665 11s 0d. No furniture has been traced. [Lincoln RO, 2 ANC 12/D/35– 36– 45– and 3 ANC 6/30a]

WREST PARK, Beds. (Lady Polworth). A letter advising on the rent of her house survives, dated 28 February 1782. [Beds. RO, L30/11/126]

SOANE, Sir John. His notebooks contain four references to Chippendale between July and September 1782. [Sir John Soane's Museum]

BURTON CONSTABLE, Yorks. (William Constable). As a post-script to their main commission of 1778–79 worth £1,100 the firm received in 1782 £48 7s 9d, possibly for 4 small sofas in the saloon. [Hull University archives dept, Burton Constable MS]

NEWBY HALL, Yorks. (William Weddell). Chippendale compiled an inventory of Newby in 1792; there is also a splendid 'exploded' room scheme of c. 1785 for Weddell's house in Upper Brook St, London. [Leeds archives dept, N.H 2800; drawings coll. at Newby]

CORSHAM COURT, Wilts. (Paul Methuen). A day book records payments 1785–87. [C. Life, 12 March 1938]

NOSTELL PRIORY, Yorks. (Sir Rowland Winn). An invoice of 1785 lists surviving parade furniture for the saloon and drawing room 'now in hand' valued in its 'present and unfinished state' £570. There is also a letter from Haig dated 10 July 1781 requesting payment and the immediate return of some silk patterns. The firm was also involved in furnishing the town house. [Nostell Priory papers, C.3.1.5.3.49 and C.3.1.5.3.35]

HAM COURT, Glos. (John Martin). His bank account records a payment on 8 May 1786 to 'Haigh and Co. £23 7s 0d'. [Christie's, 19 June 1980, lot 140]

NEWBY PARK, Yorks. (Lord Grantham). A statement of receipts and payments in 1786 contains 'Chippendale, Cabinet maker £24 18s 3d.' [Leeds archives dept, N H 2797A]

DALTON HALL, Yorks. (Sir Charles Hotham-Thompson Bt). Several passing references to work in London and Yorkshire occur in drafts and copies of letters of 1788–94; the correspondence includes one Chippendale autograph letter. [Hull University archives dept, DD HO/4/23; 13/11; 4/27]

PAXTON HOUSE, Berwick, Scotland (Ninian Home). Fourteen copy letters to Haig & Chippendale 1789–91 document an extant suite of drawing room furniture. [Conn., August 1972, pp. 254–66]

BARR CONVENT, York. A ledger records payments under 5 December 1789 for minor items costing £38 12s 6d. [Barr Convent MS 7B2]

BURWOOD PARK, Surrey (Sir John Frederick Bt). A long bill of 1790–92 headed 'Town Account' totals £723 10s 0d. [Surrey RO, 183/34/10c]

RICHMOND PARK, Surrey (Earl of Pembroke). Two bills dated 1790–91 total £151 6s 4d. [Wilton Estate Office]

STOURHEAD, Wilts. (Sir Richard Colt Hoare). Chippendale, the Younger's, most celebrated commission. Fifteen bills of 1795–1820 amounting to over £3,500 and associated material document an impressive array of progressive Regency furniture. [Wilts. RO, Stourhead MS VRO 381/1; private household accounts 4, 1801–38; 383/4/63; National Trust Year Book, 1975–76, pp. 93–102]

LONDON, 13 College St, Westminster (John Bruce). Furnishing bill of 1795 amounting to £252 5s 10d. [Scottish RO, GD 152/216/2]

LUSCOMBE CASTLE, Devon (Charles Hoare). Between 1796 and 1808 the firm was paid £1,434. [K. Woodbridge, Landscape and Antiquity, 1970, pp. 147–53]

BROWN B. His notebook refers under 24 April 1799 to a patent writing box seen at Chippendale's shop. [Birmingham Assay Office, memorandum bk II, p. 210]

AYNHO PARK, Northants. (William Cartwright). In 1804 Chippendale was paid £41 9s 6d for a bed. [C. Life, 16 July 1953, p. 205]

GRANGE, Yorks. (Sir John Lister Key). In 1817 he ordered from Mrs Coade by Mr Chippendale '2 statues of lamps Vestal and Sybil' to be bronzed £65 19s. [PRO, C 111/106]

RAYNHAM HALL, Norfolk (Marquis of Townshend). In 1819 Chippendale was paid £1,200. [Conn., VII, 1903, p. 219]

CARLTON HOUSE, London (The Prince Regent). In 1820 John Children commissioned an elaborate commemorative armchair for the Prince from the wood of the famous elm tree from the battlefield of Waterloo. [Furn. Hist., 1978]

C. G. G.

Chippendale, William, Farnley, Yorks., joiner (1735–70). Second cousin to Thomas Chippendale snr. In 1767–68 erected a second storey over the school house at Burnt Yates, Yorks. and in 1770 made the Trustees of Admiral Long's School 'A strong wooden Chest well secured with iron clamps and three locks and Keys . . . wherein to deposit the Deeds and other writings and papers relating to the trust £1.11s.6d.'. [Temple Newsam House, Leeds, exhib., 'Town & Country Furniture', 1972; C. Life, 3 October 1974]

Chippett, —, St James's Churchyard, Bristol, carver and gilder (1812–16). Listed as Bush & Chippett 1812–14. [D]

Chippett, E., 5 St Margaret's Buildings, Bath, Som., cm (1819). [D]

Chippett, John, Priest's Row, Wells, Som., carver and gilder (1839). [D]

Chippindale, Edmund, Aighton Bailey and Chaigley in the parish of Mitton, Lancs., chairmaker and bobbin turner (1815). Sustained loss in fire 19 September 1815. [Furn. Hist., 1981]

Chippindale, Mark, Aighton Bailey and Chaigley in the parish of Mitton, Lancs., chairmaker and bobbin turner (1815). Sustained loss in fire 19 September 1815. [Furn. Hist., 1981]

Chippindale, William, Boroughgate, Otley, Yorks., joiner and cm (1834–37). [D]

Chippindall, Richard, 59 Watling St, London, cm and brass founder (1783). In 1783 insured his utensils and stock for £900 out of a total insurance cover of £1,000. [GL, Sun MS vol. 313, p. 258]

Chisholm, Charles, Long Ditton, Surrey, rustic chairmaker (1839). [D]

Chisholm, George, 2 Portsmouth St, Lincoln's Inn Fields, London, cm, billiard table and backgammon board maker (1808–28). In 1809 insured his own house for £300 and no. 3 adjoining, let to Kennett, a box maker, for £200. Also appears to have owned property in Kingland Rd (1813) and Union St, Somers Town (1821). [D; GL, Sun MS vol. 443, ref. 836161; vol. 463, ref. 887361; vol. 488, ref. 985401]

Chisholm, William, Gt Newport St, London, carver (1749). [Westminster poll bk] Probably the 'Mr Chisolm', picture frame maker of Gt Newport St who advertised in *General Advertiser*, 1 April 1747. See William Chissham.

Chisholme, Thomas, 7 Gt Pulteney St, London, cm (1773–93). Subscribed to Sheraton's *Drawing Book*, 1793. Probably the Chisholme who supplied two cabriole sofas, four cabriole arm chairs and twelve cabriole back stools for the Drawing Room at Drayton House, Northants. [D; Westminster poll bk; *C. Life*, 3 June 1965, p. 1350]

Chislome, William, address unknown, cm (1803). Subscribed to Sheraton's *Cabinet Dictionary*, 1803.

Chisman, John, Skinnergate, Darlington, Co. Durham, joiner and cm (1827–34). [D]

Chissham, William, Newport St, Covent Gdn, London, carver (1749). [Westminster poll bk] See William Chisholm.

Chissholm, John, 36 Old Compton St, Soho, London, cm (1809). [D]

Chiswell, Jock, Hockley, Nottingham, cm (1828). [D]

Chiswell, John, Drury Hill, Nottingham, joiner and cm (1832). [D]

Chisworth, William, address not known, u (1803). Subscribed to Sheraton's *Cabinet Dictionary*, 1803.

Chittenden, George, Maidstone, Kent, cm (1834–39). At Pudding Lane, 1834–35 and 1839 but in 1837 at Stone St. The Pudding Lane address appears to have been a dwelling house. [D; poll bks]

Chitty, John, Rose & Crown Ct, Moorfields, London, u (1779). Insured his house for £100 in 1779. [GL, Sun MS vol. 279, p. 292]

Chivers, James, Bristol, cabinet and ivory turner (1832–40). At 1 Baldwin St, 1832–35 but from 1836 at 12 Horse fair. [D]

Chivers, John, High St, Calne, Wilts., cm and u (1822–30). [D]

Chivers, Matthew, High St, Calne, Wilts., cm and u (1822–39). Recorded also at Market Pl. in 1830. [D]

Chivers, Noah, High Holborn, London, u and cm (1770–93). Son of Thomas Chivers of Warminster, Wilts., farmer. App. to Thomas Humphreys 5 August 1762, then James Grange 5 June 1765. Free of the Upholders' Co. by servitude 4 April 1770. Trading from 290 High Holborn, 1772–75. He moved to 308 High Holborn in 1776; from 1783 the number changed to 307. His trade card [BM] describes him as an upholder, cm, undertaker and auctioneer. He appears to have attracted some important customers though their known purchases are for small items only. The Croome Court accounts of the Earl of Coventry record the supply of a mahogany tea chest at 18s on 27 June 1776. On 23 May 1776 Edward Knight of Wolverley House, Worcs., paid £16 14s for a mahogany commode. In the following year a fire screen costing £1 was supplied to Alexander Wedderburn. Chivers used his trade label to identify some of his furniture, and it has been noted on a harewood and satinwood Pembroke table offered for sale in 1968. By 1794 he had probably retired from the business and in this year and in 1802 he is recorded living in Bath. [D; GL, Upholders' Co. records; V & A archives; Kidderminster Lib., Knight MS; Scottish RO, GD 164/Box 20/AA/2 & 3; *Antique Collector's Guide*, May 1968, p. 40]

Chivers, Philip, 219 Piccadilly, London, u (1778–80). Took out insurance cover for £1,900 in 1778 of which £1,400 was for utensils, stock and goods. In 1779 the total was the same but the cover for utensils, stock and goods was raised to £1,500. The business thus appears to have been of substantial size. Its life was however short for its bankruptcy was announced in January 1780. [GL, Sun MS vol. 264, p. 532; vol. 276, p. 69; *Gents Mag.*, January 1780]

Chivers, William, London, u, cabinet warehouseman and auctioneer (1794–1803). Brother of Noah Chivers. App. to Robert Herring on 5 January 1785 and free of the Upholders' Co. by servitude on 5 March 1794. At that date his address is given as Salisbury Ct, Fleet St. He is first recorded in London directories in 1797 at 137 Salisbury Sq., Fleet St which may be the same address. He remained here until 1799 but in 1801 was trading from 15 Newgate St. He was still at the address in 1803 but in the previous year an address in Wilstead St, Sommers Town is listed which may have been his dwelling house. [D; GL, Upholders' Co. records]

Choat, George, Maldon, Essex, cm and u (1832). [D]

Cholerton, Matthew, 2 Brookside, Derby, cm and u (1829–35). [D]

Choles, Joseph, Wandsworth, London, chairmaker and turner (1777). In 1777 insured his goods for £200 out of a total cover of £300. [GL, Sun MS vol. 254, p. 146]

Chopping, Mat., 85 Upper St, Islington, London, japanner and cm (1835). [D]

Chorley, James, Market St, Chorley, Lancs., cm and joiner (1818). [D]

Chorley, John, Newcastle, joiner and cm (1794). In June 1794 announced that his former partnership with Peter Foreman had been amicably dissolved and that he was setting up on his own. [*Newcastle Courant*, 7 June 1794]

Chorlton, James, Back of Nile St, Leeds, Yorks., cm (1822). [D]

Chowis, Thomas, Stangate Mews, Stang St, London, cm (1837). [D]

Chowles, Charles, North Audley St, London, u and cm (1775–1814). Recorded in 1775 as a subscriber to Thomas Malton's *Compleat Treatise on Perspective*. At North Audley St by 1784, and shown at no. 21 in 1793 when he subscribed to Sheraton's *Drawing Book*. The number changed to 16 in 1797, and from 1809 to 17. An additional address of 3 Lower North Row, Oxford St is shown in 1809 but this may have been his dwelling house. Bankrupt October 1794. In the last years of trading the business is listed as Charles Chowles & Son, and it was his son George who took over the enterprise in 1814 on his father's retirement. A number of commissions have been identified. In 1777 two mahogany dumb waiters of 'Jamaica wood' were supplied to Sir John Griffin Griffin at Audley End, Essex for which £3 3s was charged. In the period 1780–81 the same patron paid 6s 6d for repairs to a cabinet and two dumb waiters. [D; Westminster poll bk; *Derby Mercury*, 16 October 1794; Essex RO, D/DBy/A35/4, A39/5]

Chowles, George, 17 North Audley St, London, u (1814–37). Son of Charles Chowles to whose business he succeeded. Declared bankrupt *London Gazette*, 20 November 1829. [D]

Chowles, Henry, London, cm (1829–39). At 32 Hackney Rd in 1829 and 16 Hertford St, Kingsland Rd in 1839. [D]

Chowne, John, 8 Rose St, Soho, London, carver and gilder (1839). [D]

Choyce, Christopher, 18 George Yd, Old St, London, cabinet and portable desk maker (1808). [D]

Chreiman, Olive, Albion St, Cheltenham, Glos., carver and gilder (1839). [D]

Chrichley, Hugh, 34 Whitechapel, Liverpool, u (1781). [D]

Chrippis (or Chripps), Thomas, Back St, Petworth, Sussex, cm and u (1826–39). [D]

Crisp, William, London, portable desk and dressing case maker (1814–37). At 39 Cockspur St in 1814 but by 1820 the number had changed to 34. From 1829 the address of 49 New

Bond St is used in directories. An invoice of June 1831 however records both addresses and indicates that writing cases, ink stands and work boxes were also items he could supply. The business was also that of a silversmith and cutler. The invoice referred to concerned the repair of a Russian leather dressing pouch for Sir John Packington, later 1st Lord Hampton of Westwood Park near Droitwich, Worcs. [D; Worcs. RO, 2309/705: 380/18(i)]

Christian, John, Nook St, Workington, Cumb., joiner/cm (1811). [D]

Christian, John Houghton, Liverpool, u (1836). App. to George Philander Lyon and free 29 July 1836. [Liverpool freemen reg.]

Christian, Thomas, London, u (1793). Subscribed to Sheraton's *Drawing Book*, 1793.

Christian, Thomas, 3 Marsh St, Queen's St, Liverpool, joiner and cm (1804). [D]

Christie, —, 83 Craven St, near Oxford Mkt, London, cm (1767). [*Survey of London*, vol. 18, p. 131]

Christie, —, London, cm (1793). Subscribed to Sheraton's *Drawing Book*, 1793.

Christie, Charles, 14 Brewer St, Golden Sq., London, upholder and auctioneer (1786–92). [D]

Christie, J., High Cross, Tottenham, London, u (1838). [D]

Christie, James, Castle St, Cavendish Sq., London, upholder (1764–68). Fellow of the Society of Arts, 1764–68.

Christie, James, London, u (1829–39). At 5 Gt Portland St in 1829 and Middle Ward, Tottenham, London in 1839. [D]

Christie, John, London, cm (1789–1808). At 2 Queen's St, Bartholomew Close 1789–93 and in 1808 at 38 Silver St, Golden Sq. [D]

Christie, John, 4 Warwick St, Golden Sq., London, chairmaker. In Sheraton's list of master cabinet makers in his *Cabinet Dictionary*, 1803.

Christie, Robert, London, cm (1780–93). At 4 Little Pulteney St in 1780 when he took out insurance cover of £200, half of which was for utensils and stock. By 1790 he was at 2 Newman St and in 1793, whilst at this address, subscribed to Sheraton's *Drawing Book*. By this period his insurance cover had risen to £700, all but £100 of which was in respect of property and stock used in connection with his trade. [D; GL, Sun MS vol. 280, p. 162; vol. 339, p. 396]

Christmas, Erasmus, Norwich, cm (1831). [Gt Yarmouth poll bk]

Christmas, Joseph, Cley, Norfolk, joiner and cm (1822). [D]

Christmas, William, Liverpool, chairmaker (1807–29). At 72 Brownlow Hill in 1807 and 15 Shaw's Bow in 1829. [D]

Chrystall, D., Paddington, London, cm (1808). [D]

Chub, Stephen, Exeter, Devon, carver (1686). (Freemen rolls)

Chubb, William, New Rd, Newcastle, cm and joiner (1838). [D]

Chubb, William, 37 High Holborn, London, cm and u (1839). Supplier of patent night commodes. [D]

Chubbard, Samuel, Liverpool, carver, gilder and glass grinder (b. 1741–d. 1807). From the 1780s also referred to as a cm on a number of occasions. Initially at Williamson St but in 1774 at 16 Liver St where he remained until 1781. He then moved to 17 Lord St staying here until at least 1787. His address in 1796 was however 44 Harrington St with a warehouse at 3 Lord St. He took the following apps: William Turner (1784 and free 1802), George Smith (1789 and free 1796), Thomas Hignett (1797 and free 1806), Edward Jones (1797 and free 1806), Hugh Jones (1796 and free 1806) and William Belshaw (1797 and free 1807). He died in February 1807 aged 66 at his house in Kensington, London Rd, Liverpool. [D; Liverpool freemen reg.; *Liverpool Chronicle*, 11 February 1807]

Chubbe, Robert, Chester, cm (1818). Sworn freeman 13 June 1818. [Freemen reg.]

Chuck, John, London, cm, u, appraiser and furniture broker (1822–39). At 18–19 Shoe Lane from 1822–29. By 1835 at 154 High Holborn. One directory of 1839 gives this latter address and indicates that the business was then trading as John & Joseph Chuck. Another directory of the same year gives the address as 90 Shoe Lane and mentions John Chuck only. An invoice dated 22 June 1822 made out to a Mr Wilson in respect of 'four bordered mattresses in brown Holland & tick borders' charged with carriage at £5 1s 6d exists in the collection of the GL. The billhead indicates that the business is a 'NEW & SECONDHAND FURNITURE WAREHOUSE' with 'Household Furniture Bought Sold or Exchanged' and 'Rents Legally Recovered'. A trade card is in the Landauer Coll., MMA, NY. [D]

Chudley, John, Hatherleigh, Devon, joiner and cm (1830). [D]

Chupain, Elijah, 'The Crown', King St, Bloomsbury, London, chair and cabinet maker (d. 1739). Died early in 1739 and on 27 July his household goods and stock were listed for sale by auction. They consisted of 'large glass Sconces in carv'd and gilt Frames, a large Quantity of Mahogany, Walnut-Tree and other Work, as fine Desks and Bookcases with Glass Doors: Mahogany and Walnut-Tree double Chests, with a Desk in them or without; quadrille Tables, fine Writing-Tables, Spring Tables, dining, Box, Right, Corner, Square and other Tables; a large quantity of Mahogany or Walnut-Tree Chairs, cover'd or uncover'd'. Chupain was described as 'eminent in his Profession for his many new and beautiful designs in the Cabinet Way'. [*London Daily Post and General Advertiser*, 27 July 1739]

Church, Christopher, Norwich, u (1660). His son Robert made a freeman in 1660. [Freemen reg.]

Church, G., address unknown. Paid £21 for library tables for Felbrigg, Norfolk on 19 December 1756. [Norfolk RO, WKC 6/453]

Church, George, Somerset St, Bristol, musical instrument and cm (1834). [D]

Church, Robert, Norwich, u (1660). Son of Christopher Church, admitted freeman in 1660. [Freemen reg.]

Church, Thomas, Hull, Yorks., u (1749–74). Took the following apps: Addinhall and Johnson (1749), Jolland (1755) and Ellis (1757). Charged £26 1s 3d on 6 September 1769 for work in connection with furnishing and upholstering the Chintz Bedroom at Burton Constable, Yorks. [S of G, app. index; poll bk; *C. Life*, 3 June 1976, p. 1476]

Church, Thomas, Gt Yarmouth, Norfolk, u (1755). Declared bankrupt, *Gents Mag.*, March 1755.

Churcher, J. M., Bishops Waltham, Hants., cm, u and agent for the Crown Life Assurance Office (1839). [D]

Churchill, Frederick, Epsom, Surrey, u and paper hanger (1838–39). [D]

Churchill, George, 58 Hanover St, Portsea, Portsmouth, Hants., cm and u (1830). [D]

Churchill, James, 29 Charlotte St, Old St Rd, London, fancy cm and u (1835–39). [D]

Churchill, John, New Woodstock, Oxon., cm (1772–85). Married Elizabeth Turner of Blenheim Park at Woodstock 6 January 1772. Party in a lease of property at Kidlington, Oxon. in 1780. Insured tenanted property for £300 in 1785. [PR (marriage); Oxford RO, U1/pl10; GL, Sun MS vol. 329, p. 106]

Churchill, John, 15 Tib St, Manchester, chairmaker (1813–24). [D]

Churchill, John, Church St, Sidmouth, Devon, cm, u and auctioneers (1830). [D]

Churchill, John, Market Pl., Warminster, Wilts., cm and u (1830–39). [D]

Churchill, Nichols & Kelly, 29, 30 and 31 Charlotte St, London, cm (1832). Sold lease. [Rose Lipman Lib., Shoreditch archives]

Churchward, George, Paris St, Exeter, Devon, cm (1832). Daughter Elizabeth bapt. 26 December 1832 at St Sidwell's, Exeter. [PR (bapt.)]

Churchward, John, St George's Sq., Exeter, Devon, cm (1832). His son, Leonard William Goading, bapt. at St George's, Exeter 18 January 1832. [PR (bapt.)]

Churchward, Robert, Exe Lane, Exeter, Devon, cm (1839). His son, Robert Henry, bapt. at St David's, Exeter, 1 September 1839. [PR (bapt.)]

Churchyard, John, Long Melford, Suffolk, cm (1830). [D]

Churley, William, 19 Islington Row, Birmingham, cm (1835). [D]

Churnside, Thomas, Newcastle, u (1782). App. to Thomas Brown and free 7 October 1782. [Freemen reg.]

Churton, William, High St, Whitchurch, Salop, and Foregate St, Chester, cm, u, chairmaker, auctioneer and appraiser (1822–40). William Churton started his business in Whitchurch but in 1833 took his sons into the firm and expanded, taking over the premises formerly occupied by Joseph Cliffe in Foregate, Chester. From this date the business is styled Churton & Sons. Cliffe's remaining stock in trade was offered 'at very reduced prices'. The business was still operating from both towns in 1840 when in addition to an 'Extensive Assortment of CABINET FURNITURE' they stocked Brussels carpets and offered to execute orders for 'British Plate glass' with punctuality. [D; *Chester Courant*, 9 December 1833]

Clack, Henry, 49 George St, Portman Sq., London, cm and u (1835–39). [D]

Clackson, William, Oxford, u (1673–98). Married Mary Such of Oxford 7 June 1673. Marriage settlement between Benjamin Howes and Mary Clackson, William Clackson's daughter 1698. [Bodleian index of Oxf. marriage bonds; Oxford RO, Dash XIV/V/14–16]

Clackson, William, Ditch Side, St Bride's, London, u (1709–15). Supplied furniture for St Paul's Cathedral in 1709 amounting to £12 13s and in 1713 also supplied 30 Spanish leather chairs, a footstool and a 'fine armed chair' for the Chapter House, £78 17s 1d. A further bill in 1713 amounted to £43 1s 9d. In 1715 fined for non-service, St Bride's. [*Wren Soc.*, XV; GL, MS 6561/7]

Clair, John, address unknown, cm (1754). Subscribed to Chippendale's *Director*, 1st edn.

Clancy, John, 7 New Turnstile, Holborn, London, broker and cm (1809–21). In February 1821 took out insurance cover of £600 of which £330 was in respect of stock and utensils in his dwelling house in New Turnstile. Supplied furniture to Nicholas Pearse of Loughton, Essex and Marylebone, London, consisting of a kidney shape writing table in November 1809 costing £8 8s, and further items in May 1813, £52 7s 9d and March 1815 £31 15s 6d. [GL, Sun MS vol. 488, ref. 976421; Essex RO, D/DHt A1/3]

Claney, Daniel, 20 Shire Lane, Temple Bar, London, cm (1790–93). [D]

Clansey, Michael, 8 Orange St, Liverpool, cm (1818–21). [D]

Clapcott, Henry, Bedford St, Holborn, London, bedstead and cm (1753–57). Declared bankrupt early in 1753. In June 1757 listed as a 'fugitive for debt'. [*Gents Mag.*, February–March 1753; *London Gazette*, 14–17 June 1757]

Clapham, Charles, York, carver (1752). Took app. named Marshall in 1752. [S of G, app. index]

Clapham, Edward, Lindum Rd, Lincoln, cm and u (1835). [D]

Clapham, George, London, cm, timber merchant and broker of household goods (1797–1811). Declared bankrupt 1797. In 1808 he was trading from 12–13 Orange St, Loman's Pond, Southwark, but the following year his address is recorded in directories as 11 Norfolk St, Southwark. He took out insurance cover on the Orange St premises to the extent of £900 in 1808. Stock and utensils were valued at £350 with an additional £100 each for the workshop behind no. 16 and items in the open yard behind. Trade card in MMA, NY. [D; *Liverpool Advertiser*, 17 April 1797; GL, Sun MS vol. 446, ref. 821985]

Clapham, John, parish of St Sepulchre, Norwich, chairmaker (1816–39). Son of Charles Blundell, carpenter. Free 7 December 1816. [D; poll bks; freemen rolls]

Clapham, Richard, Halesworth, Suffolk, cm (1830). [D]

Clapham, Samuel, parish of St John Timberhill, Norwich, chairmaker, (1830). [Poll bk]

Clapham, William, Norwich, cm (1816). Son of Charles Blundell Clapham and brother of John Clapham. Free 20 March 1816. [Freemen reg.]

Clappen, F., Cricklade St, Cirencester, Glos., cm and u (1839). [D]

Clapton, William, High St, Stamford, Lincs., chairmaker and turner (1802–26). App. to John Barrow, chairmaker and free 1802. Recorded also at St Paul's St, 1819–22. [D; freemen rolls]

Clarchtrue, —, address unknown, cm (1803). Subscribed to Sheraton's *Cabinet Dictionary*, 1803.

Clare, Elizabeth, Sheep Green, Rossendale, Lancs., joiner and cm (1828). [D]

Clare, Francis, parish of St Martin-in-the-Fields, London, carver (1741). Three polices totalling £300 5s cover taken out 25 February 1741. [GL, Hand in Hand MS vol. 62, refs 42961, 42962, 67497]

Clare, Francis, Tottenham Ct Rd, London, u (1784). [D]

Clare, F. Knight, London, cm and u (1816–39). From 1816–19 at 33 Aylesbury St, Clerkenwell where his trade is listed as cm. The business continued under the style of Clare & Son in the 1820s from 33 Rosamon St, Clerkenwell trading as cm; and from 1835 as u, when the former style was once more reverted to. [D]

Clare, G. & W., Mount St, London, trade unknown (1826). Signed the prefatory recommendation to P. & M. A. Nicholson's *Practical Cabinet Maker*, 1826.

Clare, James, 18 Northampton Row, Spitalfields, London, cm (1808–29). In 1808 referred to as a chairmaker. [D]

Clare, John, Mayfair, London, cm (1749). [Westminster poll bk]

Clare, John, Handbridge, Chester, cm (1812). [Poll bk]

Clare, John, 64 West St, Hull, Yorks., cm and u (1814). [D]

Clare, John, Liverpool, cm and household broker (1821–24). At Walker Pl., Hatton Gdn in 1821. In 1824 the address is recorded as 23 Hatton Gdns. [D]

Clare, Richard, Birmingham, cm (1731). In 1731 took app. named Clarson. [S of G, app. index]

Clare, Sarah, 38 Holloway Head, Birmingham, u (1839). [D]

Clare, Thomas, Gothic St, Cambridge, carver and gilder (1837). [Poll bk]

Clare, William, Haslingden, Lancs., cm, joiner and house builder (1822–24). Trading at Chapel St, Sheep Green in 1824. [D]

Clare, William, 8 Clerkenwell Close, London, bed and mattress maker (1822–27). [D]

Clarebrough, Joseph, Ackworth, Yorks., cm (1822). [D]

Claridge, Robert, London, u, cm and undertaker (1790–1817). At Orchard St, Portman Sq., 1790–93 but by 1795 was at 185 Oxford St. This latter address continued to be used until 1815 when the firm moved to 2 Upper Montague St, Montague Sq. Included in Sheraton's list of London master cabinet makers, 1803. In June 1795 the 1st Earl of Harewood paid a small invoice amounting to £2 5s no doubt concerned with goods supplied to, or for work undertaken at, Harewood House, Hanover Sq., London. [D; Heal; Leeds archives dept, Harewood MS 212]

Claris, William, Canterbury, Kent, cm (1793). [D]

Clark, —, 'The Lyon and Lamb', James St, Covent Gdn, London, u (1707–48). [Heal]

Clark, —, Suffolk Pl., Hackney Rd, London, chair and cabinet maker (1820). [D]

Clark, Alexander, 30 Lincoln's Inn Fields, London, upholder and cm (1792–93). In 1793 listed as Clark & McKinnon. [D]

Clark, Arthur, Lancaster, u (1792). On 28 July 1792 married Miss Cotham of Lancaster. [*Billinge's Liverpool Advertiser*, 6 August 1792]

Clark, Charles, High Wycombe, Bucks., chairmaker (b. c. 1806–1841). Two sons and two daughters bapt. 1833–39. Aged 35 at the time of the 1841 Census. [PR (bapt.)]

Clark(e), Cornelius, Kirkbymoorside, Yorks., joiner, cm and auctioneer (1823–40). At Crown Sq. in 1823. Addresses given as Market Pl. in 1828 and West end in 1840. [D]

Clark, D., 27 Gloucester St, St John's St Rd, London, cm (1835–37). [D]

Clark, George, Durham, u (1744–84). In 1744 took app. named Shaffield and in 1762 one named Clarke. In 1756 acted as an agent in connection with the sale of furniture for Sir Richard Hylton. Sir Richard was not the only member of the local gentry to use his services for between 1743–47 he is frequently mentioned in connection with the furnishing of Gibside, Co. Durham. On 18 June 1743 he was paid £14 5s 2½d for hanging rooms, putting up beds and for two carpets and paper. A sum of £11 11s was paid on 20 July 1749 for two beds and further sums of £11 9s and £20 1s were paid on 25 November 1751 and 15 November 1752. Ticking and crimson harrateen were paid for in April 1751 and further harateen, tape and a 'coverlid' supplied in 1753. [D; S of G, app. index; *Newcastle Courant*, 24 July 1756; Durham RO, D/St/v. 989, D/St/325, D/St/V1488–90, D/St/330/3, D/St/326/a, D/St/v. 995]

Clark, George, Deal, Kent, upholder and cm (1784). [D]

Clark, George, Bedale, Yorks., joiner and cm (1828–40). [D]

Clark, George, Somerset Pl., Ripon, Yorks., joiner/cm (1834–37). [D]

Clark, George, High Wycombe, Bucks., chairmaker (1831). Daughter bapt. 1831. [PR (bapt.)]

Clark, George, foot of Pilgrim St, Newcastle, cm (1838). [D]

Clark, Henry, 41 Lavender St, Brighton, Sussex, chairmaker (1823). [D]

Clark, Henry, 15 South Row, New Rd, London, cm (1835). [D]

Clark, Henry, 9 Merchant St, Bristol, furniture broker and cm (1836–37). [D]

Clark, J., London, u (1793–1803). Subscribed to Sheraton's *Drawing Book*, 1793 and *Cabinet Dictionary*, 1803.

Clark, J., Church St, Croydon, Surrey, cm (1838). [D]

Clark, James, 'The Three Black Lyons', Paternoster Row, parish of St Michael le Quern, London, upholder and undertaker (1719–32). On 9 October 1725 took out insurance cover of £1,000 of which £750 was in respect of goods and merchandise in his dwelling house and £250 for those in his shop. [Heal; GL, Sun MS vol. 10, 25 December 1719; vol. 20, ref. 36949]

Clark, James, 54 Broad St, Carnaby Mkt, London, u, cm and carpet warehouse (1809–13). In 1808 took out insurance cover of £1,000 of which £780 was for stock, utensils and goods in trust. This was increased to £1,300 in the following year, the addition being in respect of a workshop in Portland Mews. A further £100 was added in 1810 but by 1812 the cover had been reduced to £500 with £300 in respect of stock, utensils and goods in trust. [D; GL, Sun MS vol. 445, ref. 819332; vol. 448, ref. 825837; vol. 453, ref. 846208; vol. 459, ref. 873028]

Clark, James, Bristol, u (1815–25). At 17 Lower Maudlin St, 1815–16; 18 Union St 1819; 3 St James's Parade, Churchyard, 1819–21; and 13 St James's Parade, Churchyard, 1822–25. [D]

Clark, James, 13 Henrietta St, Covent Gdn, London, cm and u (1820–25). In 1822 listed as Clark & Manchett. Trade card in BM. [D]

Clark, James, Botesdale, Suffolk, cm and chairmaker (1824). [D]

Clark, James, 14 Upper East St, Southampton, Hants., cm and u (1824). [*Southampton Herald*, 12 April 1824]

Clark, James, High Row, Darlington, Co. Durham, turner and chairmaker (1827–28). [D]

Clark, James, London, bedstead maker (1829–35). At 11 Lower Marsh in 1829 and 48 Guildford Pl., Kennington in 1835. [D]

Clark, James, Portingscale, near Keswick, Cumb., cm/joiner and machine maker (1834). [D]

Clark, James, 18 City Terrace Rd, London, chair and sofa maker (1839). [D]

Clark, John, 'The Crown and Cabinet', Fleet Ditch near Holborn Bridge, London, joiner and cm (1720–24). In 1720 served as a Constable for the parish of St Bride and in 1724 as a Collector for the Poor. In the same year he insured goods and merchandise in his dwelling house for £500. [GL, MS 6561/30; Sun MS vol. 17, p. 330]

Clark, John, Gerrard St, Covent Gdn, London, u (1749). [Westminster poll bk]

Clark, John, Bristol and London, carver and gilder (1774–81). In 1774 shown in the parish of St Augustine, Bristol and in the following year at 9 Denmark St. By 1781 he was residing at Blackman St, St George's, Southwark, London. [D; Bristol poll bks]

Clark, John, Durham, u (1793–1827). Recorded in the Streatlam household accounts in 1814 and in the South Durham Estate accounts, 1814–17, supplying furniture including a sofa bed. In 1827 trading as Clark & Robson at Old Elvet, Durham. [D; Durham RO, D/St/V612, S/St/V308]

Clark, John, 20 Duke St, Brighton, Sussex, turner and chairmaker (1779–1800). [D]

Clark, John, Hull, Yorks., joiner, cm and paper hanger (1814–17). In February 1814 took an app. called Joseph Sharp of Sculcoates near Hull. William Gibson, also of Sculcoates became his app. in January 1815. John Clark's business may have ceased trading in 1817 for in June of that year William Gibson was assigned to John Levett. [Hull app. reg.]

Clark, John, 13 Henrietta St, Covent Gdn, London, upholder and undertaker (1817). [D]

Clark, John, Kirkbymoorside, Yorks., joiner, cm, toy dealer and ironmonger (1823). In 1823 in Crown Sq. A mahogany tea caddy, cross banded, with brass paw feet and ring handle was sold by Phillips (Leeds), 20 October 1982. In style it looked c. 1820 and bore the trade label of this maker featuring engravings of a pair of Regency chairs and table and a toilet mirror. The text read 'J. CLARKE/ CABINET MAKER/ AND / IRONMONGER/ KIRBY MOORSIDE/ Bar Rod Hoop & Plate Iron/ Birmingham & Sheffield Goods in Great Variety/ Wedding Rings Jewellery &c.'. [D]

Clark, John, Leeds, Yorks., cm (1825–30). Recorded as bankrupt August 1825. At 6 Lonsdale Gdns the following year and from 1828–30 at Bramley's Yd. [D; *Brighton Gazette*, 25 August 1825]

Clark, John, 21 White Hart Row, Kennington, London, cm and u (1827). [D]

Clark, John, York St, Leicester, cm (1828). [D]

Clark, John, King St, Leicester, carver and gilder (1835). [D]

Clark, John, Islington, London, cm and turner (1835). Recorded in one directory of 1835 at Lower St and at Cross St in another. [D]

Clark, John, St Andrew St, Hertford, cm and u (1838–39). [D]

Clark, Joseph, parish of St James, Bristol, cm (1754). [Poll bk]

Clark, Joseph, London, carver, gilder and picture frame maker (1784–93). At 51 Fetter Lane in 1784 and 92 Fenchurch St. 1790–93. [D]

Clark, Joseph, 16 Wellclose Sq., London, u (1803). [D]

Clark, Joseph, High Wycombe, Bucks., chairmaker (b. c. 1815–1841). Two sons and two daughters bapt. 1835–40. Aged 26 at the 1841 Census. [PR (bapt.)]

Clark, Josiah, Abington St, Northampton, cm (1830). [Poll bk]

Clark, Lancelot, Gateshead, Co. Durham, cm and carpenter (1778–82). At Silver St in 1778 and Bottle-Bank in 1782. [D]

Clark, Morris, 31 St Thomas St, Weymouth, Dorset, cm, u and auctioneer (1823). [D]

Clark, Peter, 9 Soho Sq., Collier St, Hull, Yorks., cm (1838–39). [D]

Clark, Phineas, Willenhall, Staffs., joiner/cm (1834). [D]

Clark, Richard, 168 Ratcliff Highway, London, cm and u (1775). In 1775 took out insurance cover for £700 of which £500 was for utensils and stock. [GL, Sun MS vol. 240, p. 605]

Clark, Richard, Bond St, Weymouth, Dorset, cm and u (1823–30). Also auctioneer in 1830. [D]

Clark, Richard, 9 Hillgate, Gateshead, Co. Durham, joiner and cm (1833). [D]

Clark, Richard, Blomberg Terr., Vauxhall Bridge Rd, London, cm (1835–39). [D]

Clark, Rob., 19 Crooked Lane, Cannon St, London, carver and gilder (1808). [D]

Clark, Robert, parish of St Sidwell, Exeter, Devon, cm (1815). His son Charles Gardener bapt. 1 October, 1815. [PR (bapt.)]

Clark, Robert, 7 West St, Seven Dials, Soho, London, cm (1829–37). [D]

Clark, Samuel, North St, Bedminster, Bristol, chairmaker (1818–23). [D]

Clark, Thomas, 5 Broker Row, Moorfields, London, u (1789–93). [D]

Clark, Thomas, 11 New Inn Yd, Shoreditch, London, cabinet and chairmaker (1810–13). In October 1810 took out insurance cover on his dwelling house for £150, a similar cover on 12 New Inn Yd and cover for the same sum on a workshop behind. [D; GL, Sun MS vol. 449, ref. 848957]

Clark, Thomas, Fleur-de-Lis St, Spitalfields, London, carver and gilder (1820). [D]

Clark, Thomas, 21 Mount St, Berkeley Sq., London, cm (1829). [D]

Clark, Thomas, High Wycombe, Bucks., chairmaker (1814–40). Three sons and two daughters bapt., 1814–38. Recorded at 'Canal' in 1839. [D; PR (bapt.)]

Clark, Thomas, High Wycombe, Bucks., cm (1835–37). A daughter bapt. 1835 and a son 1837. [PR (bapt.)]

Clark, W., Stockton, Co. Durham, cm (1793). Subscribed to Sheraton's Drawing Book, 1793.

Clark, William, Birmingham, cm (1762). In 1762 took app. named Sandford. [S of G, app. index]

Clark, William, 109 Whitechapel Rd, London, cm (1786). In 1786 took as app. Elizabeth Poole. [PR, St Clement Danes]

Clark, William, High St, Hull Yorks., carver and gilder (1790–d. 1793). In 1792 in partnership with Dring. [D; Hull Packet, May 1793]

Clark, William, 4 Warwick St, Golden Sq., London, cm and upholder (1817). [D]

Clark, William, High Wycombe Bucks., chairmaker (1815–18). Daughter bapt. in 1815 and sons in 1816 and 1818. [PR (bapt.)]

Clark, William, 6 and 7 Clerkenwell Green, London, cm (1820). On 29 May 1820 took out insurance cover which included £800 for his dwelling house and workshops at 6 Clerkenwell Green and a similar sum for no. 7 which was in his tenure. Cover of £1,500 was taken out for utensils and goods in trust with a further £150 for china and glass and £150 for household goods. Two of the policies were issued jointly with Samuel Garnon. [GL, Sun MS vol. 485, refs 968317, 968319–20]

Clark, William, Allen St, Sheffield, Yorks., cm and u (1828). [D]

Clark, William jnr, Hull Yorks., cm and u (1828–40). At 37 Bridge St, 1828–31; by 1834 at 17 Humber Dock St, and from 1835–40 at no. 21. [D]

Clark, William, Newcastle, u and cm (1833–38). Recorded at 28 Arcade with house in Dean Ct, 1833; and Royal Arcade, 1834–38. [D]

Clark, James & Thomas, Philip, 11 New Inn Yd, Shoreditch, London, cm (1810). In October 1810 took out insurance cover on 11 and 12 New Inn Yd and a workshop behind amounting to £450. This is identical in amount to that taken out by Thomas Clark on the same property, also in October 1810. [GL, Sun MS vol. 449, ref. 848957]

Clark & Wyatt, 5 Digbeth, Birmingham, cm, u and broker (1830). [D]

Clarke, Mr, near Beaufort Buildings, Strand, London, 'many years an eminent Cabinet-maker' (d. 1768). Death reported, Public Advertiser, 16 April 1768.

Clarke, Anthony, Lancaster and London, u (1806–07). App. to J. Roberts 1785. Free 1806–07. Freemen rolls state 'of London'. [Lancaster app. reg.]

Clarke, Daniel, 95 Sparling St, Liverpool, carver and gilder (1821). [D]

Clarke, Edward Gillborn, London, upholder (1767). Son of Zachariah Clarke of London, upholder. Admitted a freeman of the Upholders' Co. patrimony 1 January 1767. [GL, Upholders' Co. records]

Clarke, Elizabeth, Castle St, Long Acre, London, upholder and broker (1810). Took out insurance cover for £500 on 7 November 1810. Stock and utensils were covered for £400. GL, Sun MS vol. 453, ref. 850604]

Clarke, Elizabeth, High St, Staines, Middlx, cm/carpenter (1823). [D]

Clarke, Francis, parish of St Peter Mancroft, Norwich, cm (1813–30). App. to Thomas Smith of Norwich and free 3 May 1813. [Freemen reg.; poll bk]

Clarke, Henry, 'The sign of the Harrow and Crooked Billett', Cumpton St, Clerkenwell, London, upholder (1700–22). Admitted freeman of the Upholders' Co. on 1 May 1700. Between 1712 and 1719 insured his own house 'situate on the south side of Cumpton St. in Woods Close in the parish of St. James Clerkenwell' for £100 and another house on the 'North side of Northampton St. in Woods Close . . . known by the sign of the Cheshire Cheese' for a similar sum. In 1722 insured for £300 a house in the possession of Thomas Brownjohn 'on the south side of Ormond St'. [GL, Upholders' Co. records; GL, Hand in Hand MS vol. 9, p. 524; vol. 19, p. 329; vol. 26, p. 135]

Clarke, Henry, Midhurst, Sussex, cm and (1794). [D]

Clarke, Henry, London, cm (1806). Included in election roll of the freemen of Lincoln, November 1806.

Clarke, Henry, Clapham Common, London, cm and u (1822–39). [D]

Clarke, Henry, 50 Fuller St, Bethnal Green, London, cm and u (1839). [D]

Clarke, James, Newbury, Oxford, cm (1802). [Oxford poll bk]

Clarke, James, Green Walk, Blackfriars Rd, London, chair-maker (1808). [D]

Clarke, James, High Wycombe, Bucks., chairmaker (b. c. 1807–1841). Sons bapt. in 1834 and 35. Aged 34 at the time of the 1841 Census. [PR (bapt.)]

Clarke, James & Son, 33 Rosamond St, Clerkenwell, London, cm and upholders (1820). [D]

Clarke, Joab, York, fancy chairmaker (d. 1830). [York Gazette, 3 April 1810]

Clarke, John & Yardley, Samuel, Coventry, Warks., u, cm, joiners, cider merchants, brickmakers and farmers (1777–83). In 1777 insured house and workshops for £100 and utensils and stock for £730 out of an entire insurance cover of £2,200. By 1781 insurance cover had fallen to £850 of which £280 was for utensils and stock. Corresponding figures for 1782 are £700 and £360 and for 1783 £700 and £170. In 1783 only John Clarke is named on the insurance records and his address is given as Smithford St. [GL, Sun MS vol. 257, p. 595; vol. 292, pp. 354–55; vol. 302, p. 267; vol. 314, p. 72]

Clarke, John, corner of Round Ct, Chandos St, London, upholder (1779). In 1779 insured his house for £400. [GL, Sun MS vol. 278, p. 331]

Clarke, John, 8 Gardeners Row, Bevington Bush Lane, Liverpool (1790). Son of William Clarke, plasterer. Sworn freeman 24 June 1790. [D; freemen reg.]

Clarke, John, Hinckley, Leicester, cm (1791). [D]

Clarke, John, 1 Castle St, Long Acre, London, u (1794–1812). After 1806 occupied both 1 and 2 Castle St. In 1794 insured the utensils and stock in his dwelling house at 1 Castle St for £600. Included in Sheraton's list of master cabinet makers in his Cabinet Dictionary, 1803. [D; GL, Sun MS vol. 401, ref. 628026]

Clarke, John jnr, Nottingham, carver and gilder (1820). [Freemen reg.]

Clarke, John, Blandford St Mary, Dorset, cm and u (1823–30). [D]

Clarke, John, New Chapel St, Guildford, Surrey, cm (1826–40). [D; poll bks]

Clarke, John, Leicester, cm (1829–35). In 1829 at York St and in 1835 at Hotel St. [D]

Clarke, Joseph, Loughborough, Leics., joiner and cm (1719). In 1719 took app. named Ray. [S of G, app. index]

Clarke, Joseph, Chapel St, Westminster, London, carver (1749). [Poll bk]

Clarke, Joseph, Preston, Lancs., u (1818–34). In 1818 at 3 Old Cock Yd and in 1834 at 122 Church St. [D]

Clarke, Joseph, Benton End, Hadleigh, Suffolk, cm (1830–39). [D]

Clarke, Massey, Market Pl., Wisbech, Cambs., furniture broker, u and paper hanger (1830). [D]

Clarke, Michael, Leicester, joiner and cm (1723–d. 1754). Free 1723 as a joiner. Took on several apps [Freemen reg.]

Clarke, Morley, Guisborough, Yorks., joiner and cm (1828–40). In Market Pl. in 1829 but by 1840 had moved to Westgate. [D]

Clarke, R., 'The Royal Billiard Table', under the Piazza, Covent Gdn, London, billiard table maker (1759). [Public Advertiser, 3 November 1759]

Clarke, Robert, opposite St Clement's, Norwich, cm and u (1822). [D]

Clarke, Robert, High Pavement, Nottingham, cm and u (1834–40). [D]

Clarke, Samuel, Cheapside, London, exchange and stockbroker and cm (1765–72). Address given as 'facing Bow Church' in 1765 and as 104 Cheapside subsequently. Complained about furniture smuggling to the Commissioners of Customs. [D; Apollo, August 1965, p. 114]

Clarke, Samuel, Coventry, Warks., cm (1793). [D]

Clarke, Samuel, Pershore, Worcs., cm (1818). [Evesham poll bk]

Clarke, Stephen, Smallgate St, Beccles, Suffolk, cm (1839). [D]

Clarke, Thomas, 'The Crown' within Bishopsgate, London, upholder (1719–d. 1746). On 29 September 1719 insured a dwelling house at Havant, Hants. Master of the Drapers' Co. [GL, Sun MS vol. 10, ref. 15250; Penny London Post, 24–26 February 1746]

Clarke, Thomas, 'The Three Black Lyons', Paternoster Row, London, u (1733). On 31 July 1733 took out insurance cover of £100 on a house at 5 Crane Ct, Fleet St 'at present empty'. [GL, Sun MS vol. 38, ref. 61496]

Clarke, Thomas, Liverpool, cm (1764). App. to George Parker and free 20 December 1764. [Freemen reg.]

Clarke, Thomas, parish of St Giles, Norwich, cm (1818). [Poll bk]

Clarke, Thomas, Windmill Row, Camberwell, London, cm and u (1822). [D]

Clarke, Thomas, 4 Hatton Wall, London, cm (1829). [D]

Clarke, Thomas, Charles St, Wolverhampton, Staffs., cm (1834–38). [D]

Clarke, Thomas Hardeman, 5 Digbeth, Birmingham, cm and chairmaker (1835). [D]

Clarke, Thomas M., Botesdale, Suffolk, chair and cabinet maker (1830–39). [D]

Clarke, W. D., 10 Trinity St, Southwark, London, upholder (1835). Recorded as W. & D. Clarke at this address in 1837. [D]

Clarke, William, London, u (1688–1707). Mentioned in the Hatfield House MS, 1688–91, supplying 'a new damask bed with chairs and other appertinences' at £177, a 'set of new chairs for Turkey Work; for rugs bedding and other new goods' £98, and for 'disfurnishing at Salisbury House and setting new goods up' and 'unfurnishing house in St Martin's Lane' at a cost of £147. In 1690 Clarke advertised 'Several Fair Tents well lined and little used, whereof one large Tent for a Colonel with chairs and Camp Beds'. At this period his address is given as 'next Bedford House in the Strand'. By 1707 he had moved to the sign of 'The Lyon and Lamb in Jame-street, Covent Garden'. [Hatfield MS, bills 472; Heal: London Gazette, 3 February 1690; Daily Courant, 8 February 1707]

Clarke, William 'Painter', Ansford, Som., furniture maker, tailor, undertaken and auctioneer (1760). Friend of the family of the Rev. James Woodforde. [R. L. Winstanley, ed., The Ansford Diaries of James Woodforde, vol. 1, p. 103]

Clarke, William, corner of Cross St, Long Acre, London, broker and cm (1808). Took out insurance cover of £1,500 of which £1,000 was in respect of utensils and goods in trust in a warehouse communicating with the workshop of Godsal & Co., coachmakers. Further stock and utensils in a workshop opposite accounted for £350. [GL, Sun MS vol. 445, ref. 821289]

Clarke, William, 79 St John St Rd, London, u (1823). Took out insurance cover of £300 on a house at 11 Vine St, Hatton Wall in the tenure of Fleetwood, broker. [GL, Sun MS vol. 491, ref. 1001726]

Clarke, William, 10 Gt Mount St, Manchester, u and paper hanger (1825). [D]

Clarke, William, 40 School Lane, Liverpool, carver and gilder (1827). [D]

Clarke, William, 7 Broad St, Golden Sq., London, carver and gilder (1829). [D]

Clarke, Zachariah, London, upholder (1734–c. 1760). Son of Zachariah Clarke of Southgate, Middlx. App. to Thomas

Abbis on 14 July 1728 and free of the Upholders' Co. by servitude, 1 August 1734. His son Edward Gillborn Clarke was admitted a freeman by patrimony in 1767 by which date his father was dead. [GL, Upholders' Co. records]

Clarke & Wyatt, 136 Digbeth, Birmingham, u (1828). [D]

Clarkson, Edward, Windmill St, Finsbury, London, cm and u (1825–27). At 33 Windmill St in 1825 and no. 4 in 1827. [D]

Clarkson, George, Bristol, carpenter, joiner, cm, corn machine maker, auctioneer, appraiser and undertaker (1799–1817). At 2 Frog Lane and 24 Park St in 1799. In 1801 and 1810–13 at 2 Frog Lane only, and from 1805–07 and 1814 at 1 Park St, though from 1815–17 the number changed to 2. Declared bankrupt 1809. Activities as an auctioneer, appraiser and undertaker date from 1810. [D; *Exeter Flying Post*, 15 June 1809]

Clarkson, George, Aughton St, Ormskirk, Lancs., cm (1828). [D]

Clarkson, John, London, upholder (1714). Son of Anthony Clarkson of Abingdon, maltster. App. to Thomas Cooke on 24 July 1705. Free of the Upholders' Co. by servitude on 7 April 1714. [GL, Upholders' Co. records]

Clarkson, John, Middleham, Yorks., joiner/cm (1834). [D]

Clarkson, Mary, 32 Pitt St, Liverpool, u (1813). [D]

Clarkson, Robert, Lancaster (1784–1800). Free 1784–85. Named in Gillow records, 1788–1800. [Westminster Ref. Lib. Gillow; Lancaster freemen rolls]

Clarkson, Thomas, 3 Charles St, Hoxton, London, cm (1808). [D]

Clarkson, Thomas, 2 Turnham Pl., London, cm (1809). [D]

Clarkson, Thomas, Liverpool, cm (d. 1819). Died 31 January 1819, aged 63. [*Liverpool Mercury*, 5 February 1819]

Clarkson, William, Liverpool, cm (1760). App. to William Quin and petitioned freedom in 1760. [Freemen's committee bk]

Clarkson, William, 'The King's Head', corner of Old Bedlam, Moorfields, London, upholder, appraiser, cm and undertaker (c. 1760). His trade card states that he 'Makes & sells all Sorts of Upholstery, Cabinet Goods viz. Four Post & other Bedsteads, wth Damask, Mohair, Moreen, Harratteen, Cheney, Cotton & Check Furnit[r], Feather Beds, Blankets, Quilts, Matresses, Counterpanes, Coverlids and Rugs, Desks & Bookcases, Chests of Drawers &c., Chairs, Din[g] Card & other Tables in Mahogany & Walnuttree. Looking Glasses in Carv'd, Gilt & other Frames, wth Carpets & Paper Hang[gs] of all sorts'. He also offered to sell estates, stocks in trade and household furniture on commission. [Heal]

Clarkson, William, Little Pulteney St, London, cm (1784). [Westminster poll bk]

Clarkson, William, 39 Highfield St, Liverpool, cm (1803). [D]

Clarkson, Knight & Pratt, Kingston-upon-Thames, Surrey, drapers, mercers, undertakers, u etc. (1794–96). Supplied for Garrick House, Hampton, Middlx on 28 May 1794 hangings for a four poster bed, deal tables, rush seat chairs and recovered a sofa etc. at a total cost of £60 1s 6d. In June and July 1796 supplied beech chairs, a mahogany low night table, bookcase, bedstead etc. amounting to £12 16s 6d. [V & A archives]

Claron, —, Plymouth, Devon, cm (1803). Subscribed to Sheraton's *Cabinet Dictionary*, 1803.

Clarridge, —, address unknown, cm (1802). The Heathcote account book records the supply of a sofa table on 27 July at a cost of £12 12s. [Lincoln RO, 3 ANC 6/380]

Clater, John, 6 Castle St, Long Acre, London, cm and undertaker (1808). [D]

Claus, William, 1 Exeter St, Strand, London, cm and u (1839). [D]

Claverie, John, 2 Bullet, Goswell St, London, cm and u (1827). [D]

Clawson, Joshua, High St, Southampton, Hants., cm and u (1783–93). [D]

Claxton, Samuel, Wisbech, Cambs., cm, chairmaker, u, auctioneer and appraiser (1807–24). In April 1807 he advertised that his shop had been taken over by H. Norton. In August 1818 he was advertising for a good cabinet and chairmaker to act as manager possibly because he wished to develop the auctioneering and appraising side of the business. [D; *Cambridge Chronicle and Journal*, 25 April 1807, 7 August 1818]

Claxton, Thomas, Norwich, cm and u (1830–39). In 1830 the address is given as Orford Hill but 1836–39 it was Back of the Inns. [D]

Claxton, William, 'The Golden Lyon', Fleet Ditch, London, (1711–d. 1718). Accidentally killed on Shrove Tuesday 1718. [Heal; *Weekly Packet*, 22 February 1718]

Claxton, William, Hog Lane, Westminster, London, cm (1749). [Poll bk]

Clay, Henry, Birmingham and London, japanner and papier–mâché manufacturer (1772–d. 1812). App. to John Baskerville of 22 Moor St, Birmingham from 1740–49. He then became a printer, but the wealth and fame that he subsequently achieved was based upon a patent taken out on 20 November 1772 for a 'new Improved Paper-ware'. This involved pasting sheets of paper together and then oiling, varnishing and stove-hardening them. This process produced panels suitable for coaches, carriages, sedan chairs and furniture. It was claimed that the material could be 'sawn, planed, dove-tailed or mitred in the same manner as if made in wood'. The trade in this new material developed rapidly with smaller furniture wares such as teatrays, waiters, caddies and dressing cases finding particular favour. These were japanned and decorated with painted scenes and classical (Etruscan) and Chinoiserie subjects; and in some items Wedgwood cameos were employed. The wares that emerged from his works at 19 New Hall St, Birmingham found favour with the rich and influential, and in 1790 his status was such that he was appointed High Sheriff of Warks. He employed as his London agent Thomas Eagles of Bedford St. At this early phase his wares may bear the impressed mark 'CLAY PATENT' with sometimes a crown over the name.

About 1785 Clay transferred his business to London, trading from 18 King St, Covent Gdn, though production continued in Birmingham until at least 1801. He had been reported in 1781 as producing 'Several pieces of superb furniture which now adorn the royal residences' and King George III seemed happy in expressing his utmost approbation. In 1792 he claimed the title of 'Japanner to His Majesty' and by 1803 was incorporating in his billhead the words 'Japanner in ordinary to His Majesty and to His Royal Highness the Princes of Wales'. Clay died in 1812 reputably worth £80,000, all made from his papier mâché manufactures. The business was however continued in London at his King St address until 1822, and also under the style of W. Clay & Sons at an address in Fenchurch St with showrooms in Haymarket. Clay's patent had expired in 1802 however, and a number of rival producers set up including Jennens & Bettridge who opened up in 1816 in Henry Clay's former Birmingham works. Wares by Clay produced in this London phase are found with the impressed mark 'CLAY, KING STREET, COVENT GARDEN'. Large pieces are frequently so marked, but smaller items are less likely to be.

Clay's commissions for the Royal family, the nobility and gentry are well documented. As early as 1776 Boulton & Fothergill reported him as making japanned knife cases [Goodison, *Ormolu*, p. 135]; and in 1778 Horace Walpole purchased two waiters, a card rack, a tea caddy and a table decorated by Paul Sandby, from him. By 1787–88 Clay was supplying waiters, tea boards etc. to Carlton House for the Prince of Wales, and in June 1800 supplied him with four large paper tea trays finely painted with four views of the Landgrau of Hessen-Cassel at a cost of 25 guineas each.

On 27 May 1793 Queen Charlotte accepted a sedan chair decorated with copies of Guido paintings, and console tables similarly finished. A japanned mahogany Pembroke table in the Etruscan Room at Osterley Park, Middlx, is identified in a 1782 inventory as originating from Clay's manufactory; and the doors in the Hall at Kedleston, Derbs., were decorated by him. Clay's name appears in the Longford Castle accounts, 1778–86, and the Stoneleigh Abbey accounts in 1790. Other known patrons included Lady Howard de Walden (1785), Lady Grenville (1794), Sir Thomas Baring (1798), 6th Duke of Bedford (1803–18), Lord Braybrooke (1810), and the Duke of Northumberland. [D; Heal; *DEF*; *Antique Dealer and Collector's Guide*, November 1970, p. 72; V & A archives; MMA, NY, trade card; Windsor, RA 25103; Cornwall RO, D DF (4) 114/27; Shakespeare Birthplace Trust, Leigh receipts, 1, DR 10/5; Essex RO, D/DBy/A43/7, A376; Whitten, *Nollekens and his Times*; Warner's *Northern Tour*, vol. 2, 1802, pp. 222–23; Tomlin, *Catalogue of Adam Furniture*, 1972, p. 82; Goodison, *Ormolu*, pp. 135 and 200] B.A.

Clay, Samuel, 5 Bowl Alley Lane, Hull, Yorks., cm and broker (1828–31). [D]

Clay, William, Coventry, Warks, cm (1744). Took app. named Clay in 1744. [S of G, app. index]

Clay, William Hopper, 2 Todd's Entry, Silver St, Hull, Yorks., cm (1831). [D]

Clayford, J., London, u (1802–03). The address is given as either 31 Barlett's Buildings, Holborn or 31 Boulter's Buildings, Holborn. Included in Sheraton's list of master cabinet makers in the *Cabinet Dictionary*, 1803. [D]

Clayson, William, St Edmund's Terr., Northampton, u (1830). [Poll bk]

Clayton, Dennis, London, cm (1812). [Colchester poll bk]

Clayton, Henry, 3 Francis St, Tottenham Ct Rd, London, cm (1781). Insured his house in 1781 for £300. [GL, Sun MS vol. 289, p. 368]

Clayton, James, Cheapside, Deritend, Birmingham, picture frame maker (1793–1800). [D]

Clayton, John, Haye's Ct, Leeds, Yorks., cm (1822). [D]

Clayton, John, Drighlington, near Bradford, Yorks., cm (1822). [D]

Clayton, Theophilus, parishes of St Michael-at-Plea and St Stephen, Norwich, u (1720–34). Son of Mark Clayton. Admitted freeman 22 March 1720. In 1722 took app. named Church and in 1730 another named Leeds. Bankrupt 1733. [Freemen reg.; poll bks; S of G, app. index; *Gents Mag.*, July 1733]

Clayton, Theophilus, New Palace Yd, Westminster, London, u (1749). [Poll bks]

Clayton, Thomas, Newgate St, Chester, u (1819–d. 1820). Freeman 20 October 1819; d. 11 December 1820. [Freemen reg.; poll bks; *Chester Guardian*, 14 December 1820]

Clayton, William, Crab Lane, St Helens, Lancs., cm and joiner (1825). [D]

Clayton, William, 4 High St, Newington Causeway, London, carver and gilder (1829–39). [D]

Cleare, Thomas, 'The Indian Chair', south side of St Paul's Churchyard, London, cm (1724). His trade label has been recorded on a walnut kneehole writing desk sold at Sotheby's on 26 March 1976, lot 47. The label illustrates an early Georgian chair, with central shaped splat, framed by an ornate carved mirror. The text states that he 'makes and sells all Sorts of Cabinet Work and Looking Glasses, as Sconces, and Corner Cupboards. Likewise Blinds for Windows of all Sorts, painted on Wier or Canvass and all Sorts of Chairs of the newest and best Fashion, Wholesale or Retail and Reasonable Prices'. He is probably the same person as the Thomas Cleare of the parish of St Giles-in-the-Fields who declared his trade as 'joyner' and on 17 March 1724 insured a house on the north side of Holborn, in the parish of St Giles for £150. [GL, Hand in Hand MS vol. 28, ref. 8674]

Cleare, William, London, carver (c. 1660–70). Collaborated with John Wratton and Whitting in building a triumphal arch for Charles II's coronation in 1661. Recorded 1663–65 in the accounts of the 6th Duke of Richmond and Lennox during the building programme at Cobham Hall, Kent. [Colvin, ed., *History of King's Works*, V, pp. 252, 278, 284, 289, 330] Probably William Cleer(e).

Clearson, James, 125 Strand, London, carver and gilder (1799). [D]

Clearson, Samuel, 125 Strand, London, carver and gilder (1800). [D]

Cleator, George, Liverpool, cm (1767–82). At 7 Atherton St, 1767–81 according to directory entries but in 1782, the year of his retirement, he was in Lord St. By this year he also had a partner Thomas Potter whose death was the occasion for the termination of the business. Their stock of furniture was sold on 7 January 1782 and consisted of 'mahogany chairs, tables, desks, chests of drawers, bedsteads, a very good mahogany wardrobe, looking-glasses etc.'. On 14 January 1782 the stocks of timber were auctioned consisting of 'about seven thousand feet of mahogany in boards & plank, & a quantity of very fine veneers; together with some walnut, oak, deal etc.' [D; *Williamson's Liverpool Advertiser*, 3 and 10 January 1782]

Cleaver, Richard, 164 Tottenham Ct Rd, London, cm (1819–25). [D]

Cleaver, Samuel, Hungerford Mkt, London, cm (1830). Declared bankrupt, 24 August 1830. [*Chester Courant*, 31 August 1830]

Cleere, George, 'The Chair', Castle St, near Long Acre, London, cm (1788). His trade card [GL] states that he 'sells all Sorts of household Goods at reasonable Rates N.B. Funerals decently performed'. The Rococo frame of the trade card might suggest an earlier period of operation, but it bears the manuscript date 29 July 1788.

Cleer(e), William, London, carver and joiner (1668–90). Cleere worked at Badminton (1668), the Sheldonian Theatre, Oxford, many London City Churches, and on the Great Model of St Paul's Cathedral. Payments of £147 and £60 are recorded in the Vice-Chancellor's accounts for 1669-70 in respect of joiner's work done on the Divinity School by Cleere 'and his brother the carver', possibly Richard Cleere. [Beard, *Georgian Craftsmen*, p. 251] Probably William Cleare.

Cleets, J., 4 Little Compton St, Soho, London, carver, gilder, looking-glass and picture frame maker (1814). [Trade card, Banks Coll., BM]

Clegg, Andrew, Failsworth, near Manchester, cm (1825). [D]

Clegg, George, Hebden Bridge, Yorks., cm (1837). [D]

Clegg, James, Liverpool, cm (1777–90). App. to George Parker and free 6 November 1777. In this year shown at 126 Dale St, but by 1790 at 27 Vernon St, Dale St. [D; freemen reg.]

Clegg & Bowes, Swan Bank, Congleton, Cheshire, gilders, sign painters and furniture painters (1828). [D]

Cleland, Alexander, London, cm (1792–1825). Initially at 28 Peter St, Soho, where on 18 May 1792 he took out insurance cover of £200, the utensils and stock in the house and workshops accounting for £180 of this. He subscribed to Sheraton's *Drawing Book*, 1793. By 1802 he had moved to

14 Charles St, Middlx Hospital, at which address he was to remain until 1825. From 1812 in certain years directories list him as an u. In 1803 he was included in the list of master cabinet makers in Sheraton's *Cabinet Dictionary*. At this period and in the years that followed the business increased in size, and in 1810 insurance cover amounted to £1,100. This included £500 for stock, utensils and goods in trust in his dwelling house, in the women's workroom, warehouse and cabinet workshop, and a further £400 for similar items in a warehouse behind and above it, and in an open shed and yard. Despite this high level of activity he was declared bankrupt early in 1811. [D; GL, Sun MS vol. 453, ref. 848524; *Sussex Weekly Advertiser*, 4 March 1811]

Clemapon, George, Mugwell St, Cripplegate, London, cm (1743). In 1743 a George Siddon (or Seddon) was app. to him at a premium of £16. [Heal]

Clemence, Thomas, Truro, Cornwall, cm (1827). Bankrupt 9 February 1827. [*Exeter Flying Post*, 15 February 1827]

Clemenson, Joseph, Whitehaven, Cumb., cm (1798). [D]

Clement, —, 22 New Kent Rd, London, carver and gilder (1820). [D]

Clement, Henry, East St, Chichester, Sussex, upholder (1717–23). Also owned a house in Alingborne near Chichester, leased to a John Barcher, which with its outbuildings was insured for £500 in 1723. [GL, Sun MS vol. 6, p. 208; vol. 15, ref. 28733]

Clement, John, Dover, Kent, cm and auctioneer (1792–93). [D]

Clementia, Samuel, 13 Stafford Pl., Richmond Row, Liverpool, cm (1834). [D]

Clements, George, Leicester, cm (1834). [Freemen reg.]

Clements, George, Plaxtol, near Wrotham, Kent, u (1838). [D]

Clements, James, Liverpool, carver and gilder (1816–39). The main place of business for the entire period of operation was in Richmond Row but the number seems to have changed frequently. Between 1816–27 it was 18 and 19, in 1829 it was 95, in 1834 no. 121, 1835 no. 26, 1837 no. 29 and in 1839 no. 60. Apart from these addresses a workshop was maintained in Myrtle St from 1829–37, but in 1839 the workshop was at 3 Holly St, St Anne's St. [D]

Clements, John, George St, Devonport, Plymouth, Devon, cm and u (1822–30). In 1823 at 8 George St. The business was in financial difficulties by the mid 1820s. In July 1826 it was declared that John Clements was entitled to the benefit of the act for the relief of insolvent debtors and it was ordered that he be discharged. He re-established his business by 1830 and was trading from 83 George St. [D; *Exeter Flying Post*, 13 July 1826]

Clements, John snr, Southgate St, Leicester, chairmaker (1808–15). In 1808 took John Townsend as an app. [D; freemen reg.]

Clements, John jnr, High Cross St, Leicester, chairmaker (1826–40). App. to his father John Clements snr, and free 1826. [D; freemen reg.]

Clements, John, Norwich, cm and u (1836–40). At Dove St in 1836 but by 1839 had moved to 81 St Giles St. [D]

Clements, Joseph, Market end, Bicester, Oxon., cm and u (1830). [D]

Clements, Joseph, High Cross St, Leicester, turner and chairmaker (1834–40). Second son of John Clements snr. Free 1834. [D; freemen reg.]

Clements, Robert, 5 Fashion St, Spitalfields, London, cm and looking-glass frame maker (1808–22). In January 1808 took out insurance cover of £1,800 which included £50 for stock and utensils in his dwelling house, £250 for his workshop behind, £350 for stock and utensils therein, and £200 for stock and utensils in an open yard which also included a sawpit. A further £200 of the total was for no. 6 Fashion St. By January 1822 the cover had been increased to £2,000 of which £770 was for the two houses which included a warehouse and manufactory and £550 for stock, utensils and goods in trust. [GL, Sun MS vol. 442, ref. 812488; vol. 491, ref. 987781]

Clements, Valentine, Gt Yarmouth, Norfolk, cm (1832). Will proved at Norwich in 1832. [Norfolk Record Soc., index of wills]

Clements, W. George, 15 Bartholomew Close, London, carver, gilder and picture frame maker (1790–93). [D]

Clements, William, Monmouth St, parish of St Giles in the Fields, London, cm (1712). In 1712 insured his own dwelling house for £100 and three other houses in Monmouth St leased to others for £100, £100 and £50 respectively. [GL, Hand in Hand MS vol. 10, ref. 23068]

Clements, William, 9 Mitchell St, St Luke's, London, cm (1809). [D]

Clements, William, 16 New St, Old St, London, cm (1817). [D]

Clementson, Thomas, Broad St, Westminster, London, cm (1784). [Poll bk]

Clemesha, Samuel, Liverpool, cm (1827–39). At 46 Lime St in 1827 but two years later the number had changed to 51. By 1835 he had moved to 13 Stafford Pl., Richmond Row and from 1837–39 he was at 7 Back Rathbone St. [D]

Clemetshaw, Thomas, Little Lane, Easingwold, Yorks., joiner and cm (1828–34). [D]

Cleminshaw, John, Henry St, Bury, Lancs., joiner and cm (1816). [D]

Clemman, J., 3 Worship St, Finsbury, London, u (1826). [D]

Clemmans, James & Son, Holywell, Shoreditch, London, u, auctioneers and appraisers (1835–37). At 21 Holywell Row in 1835 but in 1837 were occupying 17 and 18. John Clemmans was the son. [D]

Clemmans, William, 2 Cross St, Bethnal Green, London, bedstead maker (1829). [D]

Clemmy, William, Lancaster (1828–32). Named in Gillow records. [Westminster Ref. Lib.]

Clennell, George, Sunderland St, Houghton-le-Spring, Co. Durham, joiner and cm (1827–28). [D]

Cleugh, George, Salmon Lane, Limehouse, London, cm and u (1839). [D]

Clewes, Jacob, Nantwich, Cheshire, u (d. 1733). Buried 21 June 1733. [PR (burial)]

Clewlow, William, Flint St, Lane End, Staffs., chairmaker (1818). [D]

Clewlow, William, Stockwell St, Leek, Staffs., joiner and cm (1818). [D]

Clewly, George, 11 Market St, Borough Rd, London, chair and sofa maker (1839). [D]

Clews, James, Shropshire St, Market Drayton, Salop, cm (1835–36). [D]

Cliff, —, London, u (1793). Subscribed to Sheraton's *Drawing Book*, 1793.

Cliff, George, High St, Nantwich, Cheshire, u (1828–38). In partnership with Joseph Cliff, 1828–34. Three daughters bapt. 1834–36. Possibly the son of Washington Cliff and if so born 1801. [D; PR (bapt.)]

Cliff, James, Hanley, Staffs., cm (1828–35). Trading at Tontine St in 1828, Miles Bank in 1834 and Piccadilly, Shelton in 1835. [D]

Cliff, Joseph, High St, Nantwich, Cheshire, u (1828–34). In partnership with George Cliff. Possibly the son of Washington Cliff and if so b. 1797. [D; PR (bapt.)]

Cliff, J. Needham, Nantwich, Cheshire, u (1799–1802). A son born 1799 and a daughter 1802 to his wife Mary. [PR (bapt.)]

Cliff, Washington, High St, Nantwich, Cheshire, u (1797–1823). Married to Mary who gave birth to a son Joseph Dutton in 1797, daughter Mary in 1799 and son

George in 1801. Supplied furniture and furnishings to Lord Crewe of Crewe Hall 1822–23. These included three 'Handsome Mahogany Biddets with turned legs' at £1 3s each on 18 August 1822 and a 'A Handsome piece of Mahogany Furniture with 6 deep drawers, wardrobe cupboard, sliding shelves in centre, large turned black feet' at £9 10s on 27 August 1822. In June of the following year £30 13s 3d was paid for various items including a carpet. [D; PR (bapt.); Cheshire RO, DCR/47/11a]

Cliffe, Charles, 34 Watergate St Row, Chester, cm and u (1822–d. 1833). Died on 24 November 1833. [D; *Chester Courant*, 26 November 1833]

Cliffe, John, Harp Alley, near Fleet Mkt, London, u (1780). Declared bankrupt, *Gents Mag.*, November 1780.

Cliffe, Joseph, Chester, u, cm, auctioneer and appraiser (1823–33). in 1818–19 recorded at Bold St but at this period he was probably employed in the business of his uncle Samuel Davies in Foregate St. He was in his uncle's employ for 17 years. In 1829 he set up his own business in Bridge St Row which he described as an upholstery warehouse. Here he offered 'an assortment of CARPETS, PAPER HANGINGS, FLOOR CLOTHS and every other article in the UPHOLSTERY BUSINESS'. An unusual commission came his way in June 1829 when he provided 'A bed of peculiar construction' which enabled Chief Justice Warren, who had been detained at the Judge's Lodgings by an indisposition, to 'return by easy stages to London . . . without experiencing any inconvenience'. Joseph Cliffe also appears to have specialised at this stage in the disposal of carriages and equipment. The death of his uncle in 1829 gave him the chance of taking over his premises in Foregate St and he opened there on 25 March 1830. His stock included a 'new assortment of Brussels, Kidderminster and Venetian carpets, printed druggets, floor cloths, paper hangings, chimney and dressing glasses, sofas, chairs and every other article of the upholstery business'. He did not carry on the upholstery business for very long and in December 1833 he advised the public that he had gone into partnership with his brother C. Cliffe and was going to concentrate on the auctioneering and appraising side of the business. He disposed of his stock in the upholstery and cabinet-making lines to Churton & Sons whom he named as his successors. [D; poll bks; *Chester Chronicle*, 26 June 1829, 28 August 1829, 25 September 1829, 2 October 1829, 16 October 1829, 30 March 1830, 9 December 1833] B.A.

Clifford, Mrs, 25 College Green, Bristol, u (1831–36). Successor to Mrs Green. [D]

Clifford, Francis, 15 John St, Oxford St, London, u (1839). [D]

Clifton, Joseph, Galegate, Barnard Castle, Co. Durham, joiner and cm (1827–28). [D]

Clifton, Thomas, Market Pl., Bingham, Notts., joiner and cm (1832). [D]

Clifton, William, Gt St Helen's, near Bishopsgate, London, u (1729). [Heal]

Clifton, William jnr, Minories, London, u (1795). [D]

Climpson, Edward, Wilden St, Amersham, Bucks., chairmaker (1830). [D]

Clinch, John, Tunbridge Wells, Kent, cm (1836). On 10 February 1836 baptism of Emma Daughter of John and Philadelphia Clinch. [PR (bapt.)]

Clinch, Thomas, 'The Clock Case', Long Alley, Moorfields, London, clock case maker and japanner (c. 1730). A handwritten label on the door of a longcase clock states that he 'sells all sortes of lackquard work for clock cases, all sortes of varnish'. The existence of a longcase clock in a black lacquer case with 'Thomas Clinch, London' on the dial might suggest that he also sold complete clocks. [*Antique Collector*, June 1952, p. 113]

Clipsham, John, Westgate, Sleaford, Lincs., joiner, builder and cm (1826). [D]

Clipsham, William, Kettering, Northants., cm and u (1823–30). Recorded near Market Pl. in 1823 and at Park-Stile Lane in 1830. [D]

Clipsham, William, Spilsby, Lincs., cm and joiner (1835). [D]

Clive, —, London, cm (?) (c. 1680). In a letter from the East India Co. to 'The Chief and Factors of Tonquin' dated 26 September 1684 concerning 'some quantity of Joyners ware to be Lackred there', it was suggested that the advice be sought of a Mr Clive, the purser of the 'Dragon'. It was stated that he had formerly been a cabinetmaker 'and kept a great Shop of Such Wares in this City'. [*Conn.*, May 1934, p. 287]

Clive, Mr, Oxford(?) (mid 1740s). Supplied 'Two Oriental Jasper Tables' to Sir James Dashwood of Kirtlington Park. [*Apollo*, January 1980]

Cloak, Elizabeth, 24 Old Bethlem, London, carpenter, cm and upholder (1808–10). Also listed as a dealer in shop fittings and a japanner. Took out insurance cover of £1,650 in October 1808 of which £320 was for stock and utensils at 24 Old Bethlem and £400 for a warehouse, workshop and stock and tools kept there. In 1809 the total cover was £1,600 but in the next year it fell to £1,400. [GL, Sun MS vol. 446, ref. 821916; vol. 444, ref. 836274; vol. 449, ref. 852193]

Cloak, Jacob, London, upholder and broker (1771–94). Admitted freeman of the Upholders' Co. by redemption by an order of the Court of Alderman 3 April 1771. His address at this date was Moorfields. In 1780 he was at 30 Old Bethlem where he took out insurance cover of £200, half of which was for utensils and stock. By 1786 the insurance cover had risen to £500 of which £200 was for utensils and stock. In this year he was at 24 Old Bethlem, the address subsequently occupied by Thomas and Elizabeth Cloak. In 1794 at 87 Old Bethlem. [GL, Upholders' Co. records; Sun MS vol. 282, p. 530; vol. 335, p. 235]

Cloak, James, York, looking-glass maker (1812). Son of Nicholas Cloak of Penzance, Cornwall. App. to David Doeg, looking-glass maker on 7 April 1803. Free 1812. [Freemen reg.]

Cloak, Thomas, London, u, cm, u, undertaker, appraiser and auctioneer (1784–1809). The addresses given for this maker in trade directories and cards may well be variations of the same location. Initially 4–6 Lower Moorfields is used but later this becomes 4–6 Broker's Row, Moorfields. In the 1790s 24 and 30 Old Bethlem are used. Existing trade cards suggests that the business was concerned as much if not more in the buying and selling of secondhand furniture as new items. New items were available 'Ready-Made'. Thomas was the son of Jacob Cloak and was admitted a member of the Upholders' Co. by patrimony 3 January 1798. He is included in the list of master cabinet makers in Sheraton's *Cabinet Dictionary*, 1803. [D; Heal; GL Upholders' Co. records]

Clode, William, Exeter, Devon, cm (1825–40). The baptism of six sons and one daughter are recorded in the registers of St Sidwell's between 1835–40. In 1829 an address in Spiller's Lane is given, but he was trading from an address in Sidwell St, 1838–40. [D; PR (bapt.)]

Close, William, Kirkby Stephen, Westmld, cm (1829–34). [D]

Closs, Thomas, opposite 'The Drum' in Snowfields, London, cm and broker (1775). In 1775 took out insurance cover of £300 of which £100 was for stock and utensils. [GL, Sun MS vol. 236, ref. 350203]

Closs, Thomas, London, u, cm, auctioneer and appraiser (1808–22). At 68 Tooley St in 1808 but from 1820 at 9 Borough High St. On 25 September 1822 took out insurance cover of £700 in respect of this address which was stated to be a 'dwelling house and warehouse (no cabinet work done therein) or pipe stove or store for drying feathers'. Stock, utensils and goods in trust accounted for £400. [D; GL, Sun MS vol. 491, ref. 995893]

Closson, Joseph, Portsea, Portsmouth, Hants., cm (1760). In 1760 took app. named Struggnell. [S of G, app. index]

Closson, Josiah, Portsmouth Common, Hants., cm (1774). Declared bankrupt, *Gents Mag.*, March 1774.

Clough, Jemima, 68 Gt George Pl., Liverpool, u (1839). [D]

Clough, Ralph Burnell, 25 North St, Hull, Yorks., cm (1831). [D]

Clover, Edward, 110 Rotherhithe, London, carver (1793). [D]

Clow, Alexander, Hemming's Row, Westminster, London, cm (1774). [Poll bk]

Clow, Mark, 40 Goodge St, London, picture and looking-glass manufacturer (1839). [D]

Clowes, Daniel & Samuel, Paradise St, Birmingham, hardwood and bone turners, brush and cm (1816–23). Recorded at no. 37 in 1823. [D]

Clowes, John, London, u (1822). Son of John Clowes. Freeman of Preston, Lancs. [Preston freemen reg.]

Clowes, Joseph, London, upholder (1783–1802). Son of Richard Clowes of Fenchurch St, Gent. App. to Robert Hernig 5 June 1776 and free by servitude 2 July 1783. From this date until 1795 at 13 Winchester St but in 1802 at 15 Pentonville Row, Walworth. In 1786 took out insurance cover for £100 solely for household goods and clothes. [D; GL, Upholders' Co. records; GL, Sun MS vol. 339, p. 435]

Cloyde, John, St Pancras, Chichester, Sussex, cm and u (1826). [D]

Clubb, John, Richmond, Surrey, chairmaker (1798). [D]

Clubbe, Robert, Chester, cm (1791–1819). Son of John Clubbe. App. on 1 March 1787 to William Henderson, cm, and free 21 May 1791. At Foregate St in 1818 and Cross St the following year. On 11 August 1818 his son George Taylor Clubbe was app. to John Moss, cm. The boy was described as 'a poor boy of St. Michael's parish'. [Freemen records]

Clube, Ann, Romford, Essex, cm (1832–39). Recorded as cm and u at Market Pl. in 1832. [D]

Club(s), John, Market Pl., Romford, Essex, cm (1823–26). [D]

Cluderay, John, 12 Aldwark, York, joiner and cm (1830–38). [D]

Clugston, James, 18 Rose Pl., St Anne's, Liverpool, chairmaker (1800–03). [D]

Cluit, William, 10 Rose St, Soho, London, cm (1785). On 18 June 1785 took out insurance cover not exceeding £25 on utensils. [GL, Sun MS vol. 329, p. 503]

Cluley, —, Sheffield, Yorks., maker of patent bedsteads (1811). In partnership with a man named Parker. Their Liverpool agents were Chew & Sons. [*Liverpool Mercury*, 22 November 1811]

Clunes, Duncan, 44 Goodge St, London, cm and u (1811–25). On 12 December 1824 his wife Betty took out insurance cover amounting to £2,700 on 26 houses in Lambeth, Locks Fields, Bedford St, Nelson Pl., Newington Butts etc. In 1825 Duncan Clunes declared bankrupt. [D; GL, Sun MS ref. 1014131; *Brighton Gazette*, 26 May 1825]

Clutterbuck, Obadiah, Gloucester, cm (1828–32). Children bapt. at St Michael's 1828–32. Trading at Barton St, also as an u, in 1830. [D; PR (bapt.)]

Clyatt, Henry, New Rd, St George's in the East, London, upholder (1791). Son of Henry Clyatt of St Paul's Shadwell, London, Gent. App. to Henry Clyatt 7 January 1784 and Mark Dawes 11 May 1784. Free by servitude 8 January 1791. [GL, Upholders' Co. records]

Clyma, Catherine, 55 Kenwyn St, Truro, Cornwall, u (1830). [D]

Coade, Eleanor and her successors, London (1769–c. 1840).

Eleanor Coade (b. 1733—d. 1821) made an artificial stone at Narrow Wall, Lambeth, which so successfully imitated natural limestone that it has been mistaken for it ever since. The firm began in 1769, and it is possible that her mother, also called Eleanor (d. 1796) was involved, but as she was over 60 in 1769 it seems probable that the daughter ran the firm from the beginning. Daniel Pincot, who also made some form of artificial stone, was her manager at first, but he was sacked in 1771, and John Bacon, the sculptor, then at the beginning of his career, was appointed manager a few weeks later. The firm owed much to his elegant figure designs and, no doubt, to the admiration shown by George III for his sculpture, which led to a number of royal Coade commissions.

At first, Coade pieces were stamped 'COADE', or, for a period in the 1780s to 1790s, 'COADE'S LITHODIPYRA'. In 1799 she took on as partner her cousin John Sealy, and the firm became Coade & Sealy until his death in 1813. She then appointed William Croggon, a remote relation, to be her manager. His work books from 1813–21 survive. [PRO, C.111/106] The firm's stamp, which had been 'COADE & SEALY', reverted to being 'COADE'. On Eleanor's death in 1821, William Croggon bought the business and traded successfully, doing much work for Buckingham Palace, until 1833. He then went bankrupt, probably through £20,000-worth of work left unpaid by the Duke of York, and died in 1835. His son Thomas John refounded the firm which survived until the early 1980s. Very little more Coade stone was made, however, and no pieces dated later than 1840 have been found, though the moulds were not sold until 1843. Mark Blanchard, of Blackfriars Rd advertised as late as 1855 that he had been trained at the Coade factory and was their successor, using the Coade formula. Several pieces of Coade design and apparently of the Coade medium, but marked Blanchard, are known; but he later followed the Victorian fashion for red and yellow terracotta.

In 1784, a catalogue of more than 700 items was published. Engravings were made of these from time to time, and booklets of prints were assembled, probably after 1784, of which three in various formats exist. [British Library, GL, and Sir John Soane's Museum] Further information about the firm's designs comes from the handbook, published in 1799, of the exhibition gallery opened by Coade and Sealy at Pedlar's Acre, near the Surrey end of Westminster Bridge.

After he took over, William Croggon opened premises in the New Rd (Euston Rd — Marylebone Rd). These must have been showrooms to take advantage of the well-to-do public now establishing itself in the New Regent's Park residential district. The Pedlar's Acre gallery must have closed as its elaborate sculptured frontispiece seems to have been taken to the New Rd. The factory remained on the old site, but changed its address as the winding lane of Narrow Wall was straightened to become Belvedere Rd.

The main part of Mrs Coade's production took advantage of the fact that her material was weatherproof, and therefore particularly suitable for gardens. In 1784 she offered a garden seat for £3 10s. But she also made a number of pieces suitable for interior use; the catalogue offers a clock stand and a dining room group consisting of a pair of pedestals surmounted by urns, and a wine cooler to go underneath a table between them. She also had a very large range of swags, festoons, griffins, urns, flowers, paterae etc. in low relief (many of them costing only a few pence) which could be stuck on a wood background for chimney-pieces and furniture. When painted in with the background, these motifs successfully imitated hand carving, and offered an alternative to the metal or composition ornaments sold by other manufacturers.

No furniture decorated in this way has been traced so far,

but a fine pair of seats, or more properly thrones, in Coade stone survives at Parham Park, Sussex. These copy exactly a Roman throne drawn by C. H. Tatham in the Vatican in 1799. The arms of these thrones are sphinxes whose wings sweep up to meet the tops of the backs. Thomas Hope's *Household Furniture*, 1807 portrays an identical pair of thrones in his Picture Gallery in Duchess St. In the text, they are described as being of stone; unfortunately the provenance of the Parham seats is not known, so it is not possible to be certain if these are Hope's own seats, or duplicates. In the same illustration there is a tripod table consisting of three lion-faced monopodia, copied from a table in the House of the Cervi, Herculaneum. Mrs Coade had already made a copy of this classical piece for Sir John Griffin Griffin at Audley End, Essex, in 1783, and it still survives there. If Hope had wanted another, the moulds would have existed at Lambeth, and Mrs Coade could have made him another copy of this catalogue number: unfortunately we have no evidence that his tripod table was made by her and not by his regular cabinetmaker.

Pedestals for lamps or sculpture were also made, and a fine set of four, consisting of three classically draped girls linked by garlands, survives at West Wycombe Park, Bucks. In an inventory of 1781 they are described as '4 Composition therms Designed and Executed in a Masterly Stile'. They hold round tables or abaci on their heads which now support a set of four sculptures by Delvaux. Another similar pair, though with the figures having their arms raised, were sold from Godmersham Park, Kent, in June 1983 for £32,000. Candelabra were also made in the style of the great Classical pieces several feet high in the Vatican collection. One example, bronzed, is at Tatton Park, Cheshire, and another, with the Coade stone left in its natural state, and thought to have come from the house of Sir George Beaumont, is now in a private collection. These could be used to hold candelabra or lamps. The range of Coade classical figures, mainly designed for ornament, could also make themselves useful by holding candle-branches in their hands. A number of orders for them appear in Croggon's order book, and they were made earlier as well, as a set of ten Sibyls, holding lamps in their hands, survive in the Chapel at Burghley House, Northants., and were *in situ* before 1799.

The bulk of Mrs Coade's pieces were based on Classical models, but she sometimes worked in a Gothic style. For the conservatory of Carlton House, Thomas Hopper in 1810 ordered a set of ten great Gothic candelabra. They are strange pieces, 7ft high with their bases consisting of bat-winged creatures perhaps supposed to be Welsh dragons. The shafts and tops are decorated with pointed arches and other Gothic details. Plate 1 of Pyne's *Royal Residences*, 1819 shows these pieces, described in the text as being 'enriched with devices most tastefully designed and curiously modeled which support elegant lamps of six burners each'. (The lamps are not shown on the plate). These candelabra were taken to Windsor and then lost sight of. In the 1970s some of them, or a duplicate set, were sold at Christie's. Another specimen is now in the garden at Athelhampton, Dorset.

During the Regency period, Mrs Coade and Croggon embarked on the manufacture of scagliola. Most of the pieces were columns, but a number of slabs were made for furniture dealers or individual customers, and details of them are in Croggon's work books. They were usually narrow, and their front and side edges were polished, suggesting that they were for console tables. Such slabs were supplied to Seddon of Aldersgate St, Ferguson of Oxford St and John Mullane of Palace Row, New Rd. A similar slab was supplied to Miss Johnes of Portman Sq. Scagliola pedestals were made for General Phipps of Mount St, Mr Blacquier of Dublin and Earl Grosvenor of Upper Grosvenor St. Sir John Langham, of Langham House, Portland Pl. had a set of pedestals with his arms on them, though how this was contrived in the scagliola is not clear. Eight small pedestals, perhaps the bases for clocks, were made for Justin Vulliamy of Pall Mall. Most of these orders date from 1820–21, and as Croggon's work books end in that year and he went on making scagliola through the 1820s, it is likely that there were other examples of which no information survives.   A. A. K

Coake, John, Chester, cm (1786). Took app. named Griffith in 1786. [Chester app. bk]

Coape, —, address unknown, cm (1691). On 16 January 1691 the Earl of Rockingham paid £9 3s to 'Mr Coape' for a chest of drawers. [Lincoln RO, Monson 10/1/A/19]

Coates, Daniel, King's Lynn, Norfolk and Southampton, Hants., cm (1817-26). App. to James Oldmeadow of King's Lynn, cm, and free by servitude, 1817–18. Recorded at King's Lynn (1822) and South Lynn (1824) but by 1826 had moved to Southampton. [King's Lynn freemen records; King's Lynn poll bks]

Coates, Edward, Newcastle, u (1738–81). Free 1738. Took apps Henry Marr (free 17 June 1774), William Jopling (free 11 October 1774), Joseph Henry Spooner (free 11 October 1774), William Story (free 5 July 1771) and Joseph Lamb (free 15 January 1781). His son John was made free by patrimony 13 January 1777. [Freemen reg.]

Coates, Edward, Rake St, Hull, Yorks., cm (1817). [D]

Coates, George, 4 King's Head Yd, Salford, Lancs., u (1824). [D]

Coates, Henry, Hull, Yorks., cm (1768). [Poll bk]

Coates, John, Skipton, Yorks., cm (1839). [PR Holy Trinity]

Coates, John, Stokesley, Yorks., joiner and cm (1840). [D]

Coates, William jnr, parish of St Lawrence, Norwich, cm (1808–18). Free 24 February 1808 (not by servitude). [Freemen reg.; poll bks]

Coates, William, Tanner Row, York, joiner and cm (1816). [D]

Coates & Girdley, Swaffham, Norfolk, upholders and cm (1784). [D]

Coats, J., London, cm (1793). Subscribed to Sheraton's *Drawing Book*, 1793.

Coatsforth, John, Newcastle, u (1722). Free 16 March 1721/22 by servitude. [Freemen reg.]

Coatsworth, Hugh, Newcastle, u (1741). [Poll bk]

Coatsworth, John, Newcastle, and Chester-le-Street, Co. Durham (1734–80). At Newcastle 1734 but subsequent Newcastle poll bks give the addresses W. Bowden (1774), Whitehouse (1777) and Scot's House (1780). His name appears in the Bowes estate accounts, Barnard Castle, Co. Durham 1745–66 where his address is given as Whitehouse near Chester-le-Street. His son John was made freeman of Newcastle 12 October 1774 and another son Ralph 20 April 1784, both by patrimony. [Newcastle freemen reg.; Newcastle poll bks; Durham RO, D/St/239]

Coatsworth, Robert, Newcastle, u (1741). [Poll bk]

Cobb, Henry, London, 'joyner' (1697–1703). On 28 September 1697 he was paid £14 15s in connection with the furnishing of Chatsworth, Derbs. This was for 'cases for yᵉ japan chests, china . . . pictures, Tables, Stands, Glasses, carved works, statues, beds etc. sent to chatsworth'. His name appears in the Duchess of Norfolk's account (Drayton 2452) for work in connection with Drayton House for which £13 was paid. [V & A archives]

Cobb, John, 72 St Martin's Lane, London, u and cm (c. 1715–78). John Cobb was presumably the one of that name put app. in 1729 to Tim Money, a Norwich u, for £45. [GL, Boyd's app. lists, vol. VI, p. 1155] Some support for a Norfolk origin appears in Cobb's will [PRO, Prob. 11/1044, f. 314] in which, in a codicil of August 1778 he leaves interest on money to 'William Cobb, infant boy, grandson of William Cobb at Wallingford in Norfolk'. Nothing further is known of John Cobb until he entered into partnership with William Vile in 1751. Having come out of his apprenticeship about 1736 he may have continued as a journeyman until some chance brought the contact with the slightly older Vile.

It has been usual to assume that as Cobb trained as an u he cared for this side of the business, and Vile dealt with the cabinet making. This may well be part of the pattern, but late in life Cobb showed himself to be a very capable cm, or more correctly of having the knowledge to oversee cabinet work of very high quality. In later years, when he was renowned especially for marquetry furniture, Hester Thrale (Mrs Piozzi) describing, in 1775, the inlaid floors at Sceaux for her journal (*Observations and Reflections . . . through France, Italy and Germany*, 1789) noted that 'the floor of every Chamber is finished like the most high prized Cabinet which Mr Cobb can produce to captivate the Eyes of his Customers'.

Apart from the participation in the successful partnership with Vile, John Cobb was also a son-in-law of the very competent maker Giles Grendey. On 31 March 1755 he had married Sukey Grendey. [*General Evening Post*, 1 April 1755] At Sukey's death it is true that he married again: his second wife, Mary, outlived him, and also married again. [*Gents Mag.*, I, III, pt 2, p. 804] There was perhaps some advantage in the connections the first marriage brought, but little to condone the 'singularly haughty character' as 'one of the proudest men in England' which Cobb assumed. J. T. Smith in *Nollekens and his Times*, 1829, II, p. 243, recorded how Cobb 'in full dress of the most superb and costly kind, strutted 'through his workshops giving orders to his men'. Smith also relates George III's placing of Cobb in second place through annoyance at his pomposity and imperious delega-tion of duties to his man Jenkins. [*GCM*]

When Vile retired in 1764 (three years before his death) Cobb continued in business for a further thirteen years. He had long since abandoned any work at the bench and concerned himself, presumably, with design, quality control, and administration of the business. In this he was served ably on the large Croome commission by his foreman Samuel Reynolds. Mindful of the upsurge in Neo-classical taste he introduced work in woods other than mahogany. This is apparent in particular in a series of commodes and other pieces, veneered, and incorporating marquetry of excellent quality. There was probably a need to do this to withstand the competition from, in particular, Ince & Mayhew.

Seminal to this late style is the inlaid commode and pair of satinwood pedestals, 1772–74 supplied to Paul Methuen (still at Corsham Court, Wilts.). In 1772 Cobb was implicated with others, including James Cullen, in the smuggling of furniture from France by the use of the diplomatic bag of the Venetian Resident, Baron Berlindis and the Neapolitan Minister, Count Pignatelli, thereby intending to evade import duty. [G. Wills, *Apollo*, August 1965, pp. 112–17; *Journal of the House of Commons*, 1773, vol. 34, p. 297; Report and Appendix, pp. 349–59] It is however unwise to speculate if this furniture (which was seized by the Customs) gave him ideas about style and technique. He had in any case started several years previously to design in a French way, making the lower drawer or part of his commodes to form the apron, rather than in the usual English way of incorporating the apron as part of the carcase. This feature can be noted on a wide group of commodes attributed to Cobb (e.g. *GCM*, pls 70–71; Sotheby's, 6 October 1967, lot 227), including that at Alscot Park (Commissions, 1766), and one similar to that at Corsham (*Conn.*, September–December 1964, illus.).

They usually incorporate tulipwood banded in kingwood, inlaid with natural and green-stained fruitwoods, and having gilt-metal mounts including cabochons and berried leaves continuing in twisted ribbon to pierced scroll and cabochon feet. We may never know the respective roles Cobb and Vile took in the firm. There is some evidence of Cobb taking apps to himself within the partnership years, and he may have had the arrangement to deal with some kinds of furniture, particularly upholstered items, for certain customers. We would need to know much more about the terms of the arrangement made for backing from William Hallett snr, although this was offered to Vile as the principal partner.

There is some parallel in stylistic outlook and the seizing of opportunity, between Vile & Cobb and their successful rival, and near-neighbour, Thomas Chippendale. However with great acumen Chippendale both took on board the prevailing Rococo and Chinese styles for the first edition of the *Director* 1754, changing to Neo-classical observance by the 3rd edition 1762, when of the two partners it was only the younger Cobb who then had the energy and flair to follow. Vile was a superb craftsman at creating carved mahogany furniture. However could the inlays of Queen Charlotte's jewel cabinet (1762) have been incorporated at Cobb's suggestion presaging his own development? In any case Vile was about to retire in 1764, the year Cobb created the important early Neo-classical chairs for the 6th Earl of Coventry. In these later years Cobb was assisted by the experienced Samuel Reynolds and by John Graham (?–1808) who went on to receive money on his master's behalf at Audley End (1772). He also signed an affidavit at his master's death (together with William Hallett snr) that he knew him well. Graham then entered into partnership with one Litchfield, as 'Litchfield and Graham' and continued to supply furniture from Cobb's old address at 72 St Martin's Lane to Croome Court until c. 1785.

In 1777 Cobb had insured this property together with stock, utensils and goods for £6,550 in a total insurance of £9,000. [GL, Sun MS vol. 259, p. 617; see also vol. 236, p. 511 and vol. 239, p. 508] However the best guide to his success is his will noted above. He had his dwelling house in St Martin's Lane, a house at Highgate, a chariot, horses, and a large fortune to leave to Mary Cobb. Probate was granted to his wife on 21 August 1778, and as noted, Hallett snr and John Graham signed to their knowledge of the deceased. A subsequent notice in the *Gents Mag.*, 6 September 1783 recorded that Cobb was 'formerly partner with the late Mr Hallett of Cannons', a fact well attested by the financial arrangement between himself, Vile and the third partner of 'for Self & Co.'

Commissions by Vile and Cobb are listed under Vile. The following are in Cobb's name only, and normally date from about 1764 onwards. Exceptions are the first two entries.

BOYNTON HALL, Yorks. (Sir George Strickland) 1754 and 1767–73. (a) 1 March 1754, a bill to Mr Cobb £3 2s. 17 November 1754, a bill to Mr Cobb £6 6s. (b) In 1767–73 a further three payments were made to Cobb, that of 4 May 1767 being for £251 17s. Some of this furniture may be at Temple Newsam House, Leeds, through acquisition at the Boynton Hall sale, November 1950, e.g. No. 327, sideboard table, almost identical one at National Gallery of Australia; No. 347, sideboard pedestal and urn; both illus. Gilbert, *Leeds Furn. Cat.*, pls 337, 347.

MADINGLEY HALL, Cambridge (Sir John Hinde Cotton). 1757 28 May: 'upholder, Cobb, on account £200'. [Cambs. RO, S88/A 33]

UPPARK, Sussex (Sir Matthew Featherstonhaugh). 1764 1 January 'Paid Mr Cobb in full for Gouty Chairs £5. 13s. 0d.'. [*Conn.*, November 1967, p. 160]

HOLME HALL, Yorks. (Lord Langdale)
1765 7 November: 'For Repairing the frames of three Arm'd Chairs with an Addition of new Canvas, Brass Nails &c. 3 Setts of Strong Brass Castors to Ditto Compleat £1. 11. For Repairing the frame of a french arm'd chair Putting a new Back to Ditto and new Burnish'd Nailes &c Compleat — 4s. 6d.
[Reverse of bill] Lord Langdale, Golden Square £1. 15. 6.
Receipted on Cobb's behalf on 9 December 1765 by George Day. [V & A Lib., 86 N.N. Box II]

BURTON HALL, Lincs (2nd Lord Monson) 1765–66 and 1769–71. (a) 3 pp. bill including hanging India paper; painting papier-mâché border 'gilt in burnish'd gold'; repairing window frames; 'For a large pier Glass in a pediment gilt frame, and fixing Do Compleat £14'; '. . . For 4 men's Time taking down Glasses & Gerrondoles and Sundry other jobs . . .'. (b) 8 pp. bill totalling £730 13s 11d including: 'A Large handsome frontispiece for a Chimney Carv'd & Gilt in Burnish Gold with Borders in Compartmts with Double branches for Candles Wrot leaf Nossels & pans', (£47 5s); 'For 2 Paper Mache Girandoles Gilt in Burnish'd Gold with branches for Candles wrot leaf Nossels & Pans, brass plates &c Compleat' (£5 10s); 'For 2 Large Handsome Oval Glasses Carvd & Gilt in Burnish'd Gold with Ribbons & Husks at Top Brass plates Screws &c Compleat' (£41); 'For 2 Mahog Circular Tables Cross banded with Carved Bracketts &c Compleat' (£13); 'For 4 India Pictures of basketts & flower Potts for Chimney Boards' (£4 4s). [Lincoln RO, Monson MS 7/45; 11/58]

AUDLEY END, Essex (Sir John Griffin Griffin Bt)
1 May 1765–74: 'For 2 Large Mahogany night tables the top parts made to open with Catch Locks and the one with a Biddoc [bidet?] all Compleat made to turn out on Castors and the other with a Close Stool all Compleat & brass handles to the sides. £11 For 2 Cases, Battens, Screws, nails & paper Cover &c to pack Ditto 10s.
1776: 'Feby 18. For a Solid Mahogany Dineing Table, the top made to fold as a Card Table £3. 16s.
Bill amounting to £29 7s 6d receipted 29 November 1766 by Samuel Reynolds (see Croome Court, below).
Further bills 1769–72 including: 1769 3 October, 'For a large Book Backgammon table', £1 5s; 24 January 1772, 'For a Mahog Clothes Horse', 10s; 16 September, 'For a neat Inlaid table on a Mahog frame. 6. 6s. Packing 6s. 6d.' Bill receipted 20 November 1772 by John Graham (one of the executors of Cobb's will). [Essex RO, D/DBy A24/11; A30/11; A32/2; A34/2; A205 p. 229]

CROOME COURT, Worcs. (6th Earl of Coventry). 1765–73 Vile and Cobb's most extensive commission (cf. Vile). However the following bills are in Cobb's name only (numbers in parentheses relate to the xerox copy of the Croome archive, V & A archives).
(29) 1765: 16 items (£202 9s 6d) including: July, 'For 8 Mahogany Armd Chairs the Seats Stuffd & Coverd with blue Morrocco Leather and finishd with burnish'd nails and Carving, all the Arms and 2 front feet, all the rest Carvd by Mr Alkin, £30'. (The chairs are owned by the Croome Court Trustees, and are a fascinating example of collaboration between Cobb and the carver Sefferin Alken who did the splats; illus. Musgrave, *Adam and Hepplewhite Furniture*, pl. 58; Coleridge, *Chippendale*, pl. 38).
(29) 1766 26 February: 'For a Large Mahogany Wardrobe, 26 Drawers and 13 Sliding Shelves in the middle part with Pannel Doors before the Drawers and Shelves in bottom and top part, a Dental Cornice and 4 Terms in front and a frett in

the Attic part, and fixing on all the Carv'd Ornaments on the pannel &c. Extra good Locks to lock twice, and a Master Engrav'd Key and fixing up the whole in the Roome Compleate 129 — —
For Lineing the shelves with Baize and Baize Flaps to ditto 3 12 —
(The money was received on Cobb's behalf on 23 June 1766 by Samuel Reynolds.)
(34) 1766–67 25 July: 'For a Extra neate & Large Mahogony Shaveing Stand with a Glass to rise & 2 Drawers and on Castors 4 15 —
For a Mahogoney Child's Chairs, the seate Stuff'd and Coverd with Hair Cloth 1 5 —
Aug. For a neate India Cedar work Box with a brass handle at Top & a Good Lock & Key to Do. — 16 —
Oct. For a neate Mahogany Carv'd Pillar & Claw Table on Castors 1 15 —
(40) 1767–68
1767 24 June: For an Hovanah wood Cloths press, with 6 shelves with Baize Flaps and Drawers at Bottom 9 10 —
23 July: For Carving a pattern Top and Rail, for a Chair — 6 —
12 Sept.: For Wood, Holdfasts, Screws, Nails, & 2 Men's Time putting Batterns round the doors & Chimneys in three Rooms in Order to fasten the Hangings too 1 15 —
For 329 yds of strong Cloth, thread and sewing do to go under the damask Hangings of the Dressing Room, Drawing and antichamber at 6d 8 4 6
For 40 Quires of Carteridge Paper, tax [tacks], paste and Men's Time putting up the Canvas and paper 11 — —
For strong Waintscott downrights, screws, nails and Men's time Making and putting up do in the Corners of the 3 rooms to fasten the Damask hangings too 4 15 —
To Men & Women's Time Cutting making and putting up the Crimson silk damask hangings in the 3 rooms 24 — —
For Making your Crimson Silk damask into 2 festoon Window Curtains lin'd and Fring'd &c 1 8 —
(The account included various charges for fringes, brackets, thread, tape etc.)
1768 January: For 8 french pattern arm'd Chairs Carv'd and gilt in burnish'd gold, with hollow backs, stuff'd & quilted in Linnen, finding stuff to the backs, gilt nails, all small Materials & Covering do Compl. with your Crimson silk Damask 46 — —
For 7 Sattinwood arm'd Chairs on Castors with fluted arms, varnish'd and stuff'd in Linnen . . . Covering do with your Crimson silk Damask 25 11 —
For 7 red & white Turkey Cotton Check Cases to the Sattinwood Chairs, thread, tape &c. 4 11 —
For 8 do Cases to the Gilt Chairs to hang to the ground 6 8 —
(Money received for Cobb 'by a draft on Mr Child' by Samuel Reynolds, 2 July 1768.)
(50) 1768–69 January: For the use and double porteridge of the mahogy Cloaths press 18 months 2 2 —
24 Dec For two french Sofas, stuff'd and quilted in Linnen with a Bolster at each end, the frame Carvd and gilt in burnish'd gold 23 8 —
For Covering the 2 Sofas with the Crimson silk Damask finish'd Compleat with ye gilt nails 2 — —
For 2 Check Cases to do. 5 4 —
For Carteridge paper Covers to the Gerrondoles & Vauses and Serge Bags to the bell Tossells — 5 6
(Money received by Samuel Reynolds, 13 June 1769.)
(57) 1769: For the use and porterage of a Mahog Dineing table — 4 —

Mar. For a Crimson Silk tossell and a Man's time putting Do to a bell   – 5 6
Apr For 3 brown Damask'd Leather Spotts for Candlesticks   – 3 –

(Money received by Samuel Reynolds, 2 July 1770.)

(62) 1770–72 July 7: For 4 brown Damaskd Leather Covers to 4 tables (Various other small tasks of hanging, repairs, hiring 'Lew tables', mahogany bowls etc. £37 14s 6d received by Samuel Reynolds, 4 July 1772.)   4 18 –

(66) 1773: One item only, a breakfast table, £4 7s. [The Croome commission, overall is described by J. Parker and others, *Decorative Art in the Metropolitan Museum...*, 1964.]

ALSCOT PARK, Warks. (James West) 1766: For an 'Extra fine wood Commode chest of drawers with large Handsome wrought Furniture, good brass locks &c to do'. £16. [*C. Life*, 15 May 1958, fig. 5] An almost identical commode was sold Sotheby's, 5 March 1971, lot 165 [*Burlington*, 1971, p. 283, fig. 60]. [Warwick RO, Box 42/8, Alscot Park MS, copies V & A archives]

1769: Includes, 24 March, 'For 2 extra neat carv'd Pillars and Claws, and straining Frames, and mounting yr 2 Pieces of Tapstry & Silk for fire screens', £6 10s; 'For a neat Japann'd Teaboard', £1 1s; he also charged for the use of a 'Lew Table' and 2 mahogany card tables. Bill receipted 9 May 1771 by Samuel Reynolds. [Alscot Park MS]

HAMPTON, Middlx (David Garrick). 1766–72: An explanation of Garrick's patronage of Chippendale and others at Hampton, 5 Royal Adelphi Terr. and 27 Southampton St, London is given in Gilbert, *Chippendale*, pp. 236–48. Cobb provided brass lanterns, a 'manilla wood Tea Chest with 3 Tinn Canisters', £1 15s; in 1768 a plate warmer, bottle tray and dish tray, £11 8s 6d; and in 1772 a 'Box to Contain 8 Bottles with Ground Stoppers and 4 Glass Tumblers with a Lock Comp', £22. [V & A archives, 86 NN 4(1), xerox copies]

CAMPSALL HALL, Doncaster, Yorks. 1768: Cobb wrote on 28 July 1768 to say that he was 'much put to it for money at this time' and asking for settlement of his account for unspecified work. [Sheffield archives dept, MS BFM 1322/35]

CANNON HALL, Yorks. (John Spencer). 1768: Spencer refers in his diary to visiting Cobb's workshop or showroom. There are a number of payments for unspecified work. [Sheffield archives dept, MS 60633–19. Diary vol. 3]

COBHAM HALL, Kent. 1768: An account was closed in September in the 3rd Earl of Darnley's account book. [*C. Life*, 10 March 1983, p. 570]

SAXMUNDHAM, Suffolk (Charles Long). 1769 11 June:

a mahogy flowerstand	12s.
a mahogy Candlestand	6s.
a Dressing Glass in a mahogy frame	18s.
	£1. 16s.
Discount	– 1s.
	£1. 15s.

[Suffolk RO, HA 18/EC/5]

SANDON HALL, Staffs. (1st Lord Harrowby):

1 June 1769. To Cobb Cabt maker	£1. 4. 6.
26 July 1770. To Cobb Cabinet maker	£9. 8. 6.
23 July 1774. To Cobb Cabt maker for a Present to Mr de l'Andre	£9. 14. 6.

[Harrowby MS Trust, Sandon, vol. 334]

CORSHAM COURT, Wilts. (Paul Methuen): '30 April 1770. Pd Cobb's bill for a Screen etc. £3. 8. 8'. 1772: 'Extra neat Inlaid Commode ... with brass Ornaments, your Coat of Arms inlaid in the ends ... £63. 5. 3'. 1774: Two vase stands. The commode and stands are among Cobb's finest achievements. The pieces are veneered in satinwood, and the side panels of the commode as indicated in the bill have Methuen's arms quartered with that of his wife Catherine Cobb (seemingly no relation to John Cobb). At Corsham they stand beneath and flank an Adam pier mirror. The Adam drawing at Corsham (almost identical to one at the Soane Museum, see E. Harris, *Furniture of Robert Adam*, p. 80) has the pencil outline of the Cobb commode and stands substituted for the table. [Wilts. RO, Corsham archives, Paul Methuen's Day Book; furniture illus. GCM, pls 71–72 and *in situ*, C. Life, 7 October 1954, p. 1156; C. Hussey, *English Country Houses: Early Georgian*, pl. 424] For a similar commode and related items see E. T. Joy, *Conn.*, September/December 1984; GCM, p. 56; C. Streeter, *Furn. Hist.*, 1974, pp. 52–53; Christie's, NY, 30 January 1982, lot 170 etc.

CUSWORTH HALL, Yorks. (John Battie). 1770: 'Mr Cobb upholster £31. 9. 0.' was recorded following a bill of 19 November 1768 for £21 19s. The 'Cusworth suite' of 2 arm and 6 side chairs with original upholstery, water-gilt nailing and silk fringeing was illus., *Apollo*, December 1971 and attributed c. 1760 to Vile & Cobb on the basis of the later payments (above) to Cobb. The similarity to the work of Paul Saunders was however noted. The usual hazards of attribution are ever-present. [Leeds archives dept, Battie Wrightson MS A165, 166]

SOUTH AUDLEY ST, London (Hon. Mrs Henrietta Howard). 1770: One page bill including: 'For a Mahog Cabriole Settee with arms, made with Back & Seat loose to take out, stuf'd in Linnen & Cover'd with your Needlework, finding Tammy Back & All Materials, to make do Compleat, £8. 16s.'. The bill (£17 16 3d) was receipted 26 March 1772 by Wm. Eversley (who had been mentioned in Vile's will). [Essex RO, D/DPA. 189]

STRAWBERRY HILL, Middlx (Horace Walpole). 1770: 'Cobb's bill for furnishing the Round Room, Tapestry chairs for the Cottage, carpet for ditto. £99. 8s. 6d.'. [Paget Toynbee (ed.), *Strawberry Hill Accounts*, 1927, pp. 129–30, 133]

FOREMARK HALL, Derbs. (Sir Robert Burdett). 1771 21 June: 'To Mr Cobb for a japan tea tray, £1. 12. 0. and a Mahogy —£1. 7. 0.' (£2 19s) — 'for ye countrey'. [Berks. RO, D/E BU A/8/2]

9th VISCOUNT IRWIN. 1773 1 April:

For 3 Mohogy Pole Glasses at 8/6	1. 5. 6.
Discount	0. 1. 0.
	£1. 4. 6.

Rec'd May 7, 1773 the Contents in full for Mr Cobb, — Joseph Dennison. [Leeds archives dept, TN/EA/12/5]

HATFIELD PRIORY, Essex (John Wright). 1774 Paid £26 to 'Mr Cobb'. [Hoare's Bank, London, vol. 90, f. 287]

G. B.

Cobb, Nathaniel, 19 Head St, Colchester, Essex, cm, u and undertaker (1839). [D]

Cobb, Samuel jnr, High St, Newport, Salop, cm, u and carpet warehouseman (1835–40). In 1891 it was stated that the business had been in the hands of the family for sixty years and that the trade had been carried on in the same premises for 100 years. [D; *Industries of Shropshire Business Review*, 1891]

Cobb, Thomas, Strand, London, u (1749). [Westminster poll bk]

Cobb, Thomas, Hull, Yorks., cm, u, joiner and builder (1823–31). At 21 George Yd, 170 High St, 1823–26. In 1826 his residence was at Providence Pl., Drypool and he was still living there in 1831. [D]

Cobb, W., St Martins Lane, London, cm (1776). In 1776 Samuel Reynolds took out insurance cover of £300 for items at W. Cobb's and William Richardson £100 for items at W. Cobb's 'timbershop, Round Court'. [GL, Sun MS vol. 244, p. 512]

Cobb, William, York, cm (1784–d. 1813). In Hungate in 1784, Great Shambles in 1798 and Peter Lane in 1800. [D; poll bk; *York Herald*, 17 May 1800; *York Courant*, 25 October 1813]

Cobb & Ellisdon, Head St, Colchester, Essex, cm and u (1832). [D]

Cobbett, Edward, 21 Gt Newport St, London, carver and gilder (1835–39). [D]

Cobbett, Pitt & Son, address unknown, japanners (1833). In June 1833 carried out work at the Stud House, Hampton Court, Middlx, which included japanning 43 wash-hand-stands and dressing tables and painting and staining a large Gothic sideboard. [PRO, LC11/80]

Cobbett, William, 72 Drummond St, Euston Sq., London, cm (1835–37). [D]

Cobley, J., 6 Carlisle St, Soho, London, glass frame maker (1835). [D]

Cochran, William, 20 Nassau St, Middlx Hospital, London, cm (1823). On 30 April 1823 took out insurance cover of £2,100 of which £2,000 was for utensils and stock. [GL, Sun MS vol. 498, ref. 1003754]

Cock, J., 11 Grange St, Bloomsbury, London, carver and gilder (1816). [D]

Cock, J., 23 James St, Devonport, Plymouth, cm (1830). [D]

Cock, James, Ashton-under-Lyne, Lancs., cm (1816–28). At 14 Old St, 1816–24 but by 1828 had moved to Mill Lane. [D]

Cock, James, Norwich, u (1823). Son of Joseph Cock, cooper. Admitted freeman 26 May 1823. [Freemen reg.]

Cock, Samuel, Brentford, Middlx, cm (1793). [D]

Cock, William, 9 Berwick St, Soho, London, upholder (1790–1820). Mentioned in Sheraton's *Cabinet Dictionary*, 1803 as a master craftsman. [D]

Cock, William, 77 Wood St, Cheapside, London, cm (1792). Took out insurance cover of £200 on 16 April 1792. [GL, Sun MS vol. 386, p. 248]

Cock, William, Hillgrove St, Bristol, cm (1792–93). [D]

Cock, William, Marsh Lane, Leeds, Yorks., cm (1793). On 30 May 1793 took out insurance cover for £900 of which £250 was in respect of utensils and stock. [GL, Sun MS vol. 395, p. 249]

Cock, William, Bristol, cabinet and clockcase maker, camp writing desk inventor and manufacturer (1816–40). At Hillgrove St, 1816–17, when clockcase making was the main activity. Between 1818–19 at Bush St, Hillgrove St and 1820–39 at Cock's Buildings, Hillgrove St. In 1840 at Lower Cheltenham Pl. A brass-bound mahogany folding desk with this maker's label is known. [D]

Cock, Wiltshire, 23 James St, Devonport, Plymouth, Devon, cm and u (1823). [D]

Cockbain, Joseph, Keswick, Cumb., joiner/cm (1829–34). [D]

Cockcroft, John, Hebden Bridge, Yorks., joiner/cm (1834). [D]

Cocke, George, Town St, Thaxted, Essex, cm and u (1839). [D]

Cockerell, G. W., 59 Blackman St, Southwark, London, u and auctioneer (1817–20). [D]

Cockerell & Clarke, 47 Blackman St, Southwark, London, u (1837–39). [D]

Cockerill, Edward & James, 1–3 Curtain Rd, Finsbury Sq., and 203 Oxford St, London, japanned chairmakers (1790–1804). It is not clear whether a partnership existed in connection with this business. Directories in some years list Edward and in others James with very considerable overlap. The business may well have been commenced before 1790 for in an advertisement of 1797 it was claimed that it had been carried on 'upwards of 40 years at No 1, Curtain-road'. They had on sale 'the greatest variety of Drawing, Parlour, and Bedroom Japanned chairs; sofas, Bed and Window Cornices to match, and, Pembroke, and Toilet Tables, and every other article in the Japanned Line'. They claimed to sell at 30% below their rivals and offered to renovate japanned furniture. The business was carried on at the same address in Curtain Rd after 1804 by Mary Cockerill. Both James and Edward Cockerill are included in the list of master furniture makers in Sheraton's *Cabinet Dictionary*, 1803. [D; Heal; *Times*, 22 November 1797]

Cockerill, Henry, Ambrosden, Oxon., u and paperhanger (1765). Son of the late Rev. Thomas Cockerill, vicar of Ambrosden. In June 1765 announced the commencement of his business. [*Jackson's Oxford Journal*, 8 June 1765]

Cockerill, John, North Bar Without, Beverley, Yorks., cm and u (1814–40). [D]

Cockerill, Mary, 1–4 Curtain Rd, Finsbury Sq., London, japanned chairmaker (1806–08). [D]

Cockerill, Robert, Parson's St, Banbury, Oxon., cm and u (1839). [D]

Cockering, Francis, 17 Gresse St, Rathbone Pl., London, cm (1808). [D]

Cockersole, Sampson, Newcastle-under-Lyme, Staffs., cm (1812). [Poll bk]

Cocket, Nicholas, 33 Chapel St, Curtain Rd, London, bedstead maker (1807–08). On 12 October 1807 took out insurance cover for £500 all but £20 of which was in respect of utensils and stock in a workshop, warehouse and yard. [D; GL, Sun MS vol. 442, ref. 806996]

Cockfield, George, Finkle St, Ripon, Yorks., cm (1822–37). [D]

Cockhill, John, West Side Old Dock, Hull, Yorks., turner and carver (1840). [D]

Cockin, —, near 'The Golden Fleece', Pavement, York, mercer, draper and u (1748). Announced a sale of stock in *York Courant*, 12 January 1748.

Cockin, William, Middlegate, Penrith, Cumb., cm (1798–1811). [D]

Cockin, John, Middlegate, Penrith, Cumb., joiner and cm (1828–34). [D]

Cocking, Joseph, Cannon St, Taunton, Som., cm (1822–39). [D]

Cocking, Robert, Norfolk St, Sheffield, Yorks., cm and u (1828–37). At 30 Norfolk St in 1828 but by 1830 at 23 Norfolk St and Watson Walk. [D]

Cocking, William & Robert, Hartshead, Sheffield, Yorks., cm (1822–25). [D]

Cocking, William, Sheffield, Yorks., cm and u (1828). Shown at both Furnival St and Union St in 1828. [D]

Cockney, Mary, Liverpool, u (1827). Married John Cannon, painter, at St Philip's Church. [*Liverpool Mercury*, 2 March 1827]

Cockrell, Edward, Withy Grove, Manchester, chairmaker (1773). [D]

Cockrill, Mark, Rake Foot, Rossendale, Lancs., joiner and cm (1834). [D]

Cocks, Francis, 16 Charles St, Manchester Sq., London, carver and gilder (1835–39). [D]

Cocks, George C., Bristol, portable desk maker (1825–35). At 3 Lower Montague St, 1825–29, 2 Denmark St, 1830–32, and Upper Maudlin St, 1833–35. In 1832 declared himself to be the 'manufacturer of the Beautiful Polyanthus Wood and all other kinds of British Woods, also Manufacturer of Portable Desks, Dressing & Travelling Cases, Bagatelle Tables, Beer Engines, Clock and Spring Cases, Fire Screens

&c. Manufacturer of Tea Caddies and other Fancy articles in Tortoiseshell, Hard Wood & Ivory turner, Glass bender &c.'. His label is pasted to the inside of a clock case in Bristol Art Gallery collection. [D]

Cocks, James, Gloucester, cm (1818–27). Children bapt. 1818 and 1827 at the church of St John the Baptist. [PR (bapt.)]

Cocks, John, Dog Lane, Shrewsbury, Salop, cm (1812). [Freemen rolls]

Cocks, John, New Rd, Gravesend, Kent, carver and gilder (1826–29). [D]

Cocks, John, St Augustine St, Norwich, cm and u (1830). [D]

Cocks, Thomas, Gloucester, cm (1822). Child bapt. 1822 at church of St John the Baptist. [PR (bapt.)]

Cocksedge, H., 8 Chapel St, Holywell Mt, London, carver (1829). [D]

Cockshut, Martin, Bradford, Yorks., cm and joiner (1805–08). [D]

Cod(d)ington, John, Church Lane, Gainsborough, Lincs., chairmaker (1819–31). In 1831 listed as a cm and furniture broker. [D]

Code, A., Harford St, St James's, Bristol, cm (1837–40). Successor of Richard Code. [D]

Code, Richard, Bristol, cm (1817–36). At Lewin's Mead 1817–19, Harford St, St James's 1820–35 and 36 Redcliff St in 1836. [D]

Codlin, Thomas, 7 Junction Dock St, Hull, Yorks., cm (1840). [D]

Codlin, William, Hull, Yorks., cm (1818–38). At Milk St, 1818; 11 Bond St Mews, 1823; 28 Bond St, 1826; 7 Paragon Pl, 1831; and 2 Wellington Mart, 1834–38. [D]

Codlin & Hick, 7 Junction Dock St, Hull, Yorks., cm etc. (1840). [D]

Codling, George, Swift Ct, 11 Castle St, Liverpool, joiner and cm (1839). [D]

Coe, Anthony Stephen, Ipswich, Suffolk, u (1790). [Poll bk]

Coe, Charles, Southwark, London, chairmaker and japanner (1820–39). At 5 Redcross St, 1820; 46 Lant St, 1835; and 124 Gt Suffolk St, 1839. [D]

Coe, David, Bridgegate, Rotherham, Yorks., cm (1818–37). [D]

Coe, John, Middle Westwick, near St Laurence's Church, Norwich, cm (1810). [D]

Coffee, George, 181 High Holborn, London, carver and gilder (1793). [D]

Coffin, Edmund, Holloway St, Exeter, Devon, carver (1761–91). In 1761 took app. named Reynell. [D; S of G, app. index]

Cogan, John, Bath, Som., cm (1774). [Bristol poll bk]

Cogger, John George, Clapham Rise, Clapham, London, cm, u and furniture broker (1832). [D]

Coghlan, John, Gt Crosshall St, Liverpool, carver and gilder (1810). [D]

Coghlan, T., Liverpool, carver and gilder (1808). In March 1808 he announced his intention of declining his business 'on or before the 12th of April'. He declared that he was selling off his stock which consisted of 'fashionable Pier & Chimney Looking Glasses, Convex Mirrors, Engravings, framed & unframed etc at considerably reduced prices'. He also had available 'Glasses, Composition Beads, Strap Leaf, Corinthian & Ionic Capitals etc. etc.'. At this stage he was trading from an address at 39 Whitechapel. On 25 May 1808 an auction sale was advertised to take place on 30 May which included 'An Elegant Assortment of fashionable PIER & CHIMNEY LOOKING GLASSES, HOUSEHOLD FURNITURE, consisting of Chairs, Tables, Beds, Bedding etc.'. His retirement from the trade was however short for on 17 June he advertised that he was once more setting up in the same trade at 45 Gt Crosshall St with the addition of an auctioneering department. [*Liverpool Courier*, 23 March 1808, 4 May 1808, 25 May 1808, 17 June 1808]

Cohen, Alexander, 120 Gravel Lane, Houndsditch, London, clock case maker (1839–40). [D]

Cohen, J., Middlx, u and picture dealer (1826). Declared bankrupt, *Liverpool Mercury*, 25 August 1826.

Cohen, Jacob, London, chairmaker (1808–28). At 9 Little Somerset St, Whitechapel in 1808 and 45 Gt Prescott Rd, Goodman's Fields, 1817–28. From 1822 he added the trades of u, cm and appraiser to his existing business. [D]

Cohen, Jacob, Chelmsford, Essex, cm etc. (1826–39). At Conduit St, 1826–32 and King St in 1839. [D]

Coke, T. & J., 2 Colonnade, Cheltenham, Glos., cm and u (1820). [D]

Colbatch, George, Bristol, cm (1781). [Poll bk]

Colbatch, Harry, St Philip Out-parish, Bristol, cm (1784). [Poll bk]

Colbeck, John, 4 Holdgate, York, cm (1830). [D]

Colbeck, William, York and London, cm (c. 1795–1818). Son of Christopher Colbeck of Askham Bryan, Yorks., labourer. App. to John Sanderson, 26 June 1787. Granted freedom of York as a cm 1818 and at that date in Cavendish Sq., London. [York app. and freemen reg.]

Colborn, W., London, cm (1793). Subscribed to Sheraton's *Drawing Book*, 1793.

Colborne, Benjamin, Walcot, Som., carver and gilder (1832). Bankrupt 15 May 1832. [*Liverpool Mercury*, 18 May 1832]

Colborne, Joseph, 26 Worcester St, Birmingham, cm and u (1830). [D]

Colbourne, James, Twyford, Berks., cm (1830). [D]

Colbourne, Thomas, 47 Worcester St, Birmingham, cm and u (1830). [D]

Colbron, William, 10 New St, Brighton, Sussex, u (1799–1805). Recorded in the Royal archives seven times between July 1801 and January 1804 in connection with the supply of goods and services for the Royal Pavilion. The total amounts paid to the firm were £98 2s 3d. In the Royal archives the business is referred to as 'Corbron & Co.'. [D; Windsor Royal Archives, RA, 88883, 88886, 88894, 88898, 88902, 88912, 88919]

Colby, James, Norwich, u (1799). App. to James Sudbury and free 5 May 1799. [Freemen reg.]

Colby, Rouse, Gt Yarmouth, Norfolk, cm (1826–38). [Poll bks]

Colchester, Benjamin Russel, Needham Market, Suffolk, u (1814). Married 1814. [Suffolk RO, FAA: 50/2/117, pp. 89–90]

Colclough, James, Scotch Common, Sandbach, Cheshire, cm and joiner (1828). [D]

Colder, James, 76 New Summer St, Birmingham, u (1835). [D]

Coldicott, —, address unknown, u (1834). In March 1834 he was paid £1 2s 3d in connection with the 3rd Lord Baybrooke's London house (or Billingbear, Berks.). [Essex RO, D/DBy/A363]

Coldwell, Benjamin, Wadsley, Sheffield, Yorks., cm (1834). [D]

Coldwell, Robert, 15 Gt Mays Building, London, portable desk, dressing case, work box and cabinet case maker (1839). [D]

Cole, Charles, 270 High St, Exeter, Devon, carver and gilder (1816–40). The business was also styled Cole & Co. from 1816–20, and from 1830 was in partnership with John Gendall. On 3 August 1819 they announced their appointment as agents for the sale of Crease & Co.'s washable paper hangings. Charles Cole appears to have had a house in Eastgate, Exeter, and this address is given in connection with the baptism of his two sons, James Henry on 26 April 1823 and James Jarvis on 29 April 1825. A curtain rod at Moditonham House, Cornwall has been noted with a label of this maker stating: 'LOOKING GLASS, MIRRORS, MOULDINGS, etc. executed in the neatest manner'. The partnership with Gendall was unsuccessful and the bankruptcy of the partners was announced in August 1832. [D; PR (bapt.); election squibs, 1816; *Western Luminary*, 3 August 1819, 28 September 1819; *Liverpool Mercury*, 17 August 1832]

Cole, Cornelius, address unknown, cm to William III (c. 1690). [Harris, *Old English Furniture*, p. 11]

Cole, Edward, Reading, Berks., u (1731–68). In 1731 took app. named Bartholomew and in 1737 another named Shirley. [S of G, app. index; poll bks]

Cole, George, Golden Sq., London, u (1747–74). Supplied goods and carried out work at Corsham Court, Wilts. between 1761 and 1774. Some of the sums paid were substantial, such as £130 14s on 10 March 1761 and £101 8s on 30 April 1763. In 1773 alone £505 5s was paid in the first six months. There is little indication of the nature of the goods supplied and work done, but the payment of £34 11s 6d made on 17 April 1769 was stated to be 'for upholstery goods sent to Corsham House being furniture for the Great Room' (i.e. the Picture Gallery). On 29 April 1773 £5 5s was paid for 'Mr West's small ebony cabinet'. Both a Cole snr and jnr are mentioned in the accounts. Commissions were also carried out for the Duke of Atholl's Scottish houses. In 1761 a pier-glass was supplied to Dunkeld House and two years later three pier-glasses and associated tables were provided for Blair Castle. The three tables were charged at £43 and the glasses at £168. A resemblance between these items and the designs of Thomas Johnson has been noted, and it has been speculated that Cole may have employed Johnson to supervise these Scottish commissions for him. [Heal; poll bks; Wills, *Looking-Glasses*; *Conn.*, December 1960, pp. 252–56]

Cole, James, Market Pl., and Long Causeway, Peterborough, Northants., u, cm, chairmaker and appraiser (1768–92). In 1770 he advertised that he could supply furniture in mahogany, walnuttree and wainscot; and three years later, when seeking two journeyman chairmakers, stated that 'none need apply but what are good hands, as their work will be chiefly in mahogany'. Total insurance cover was £600 in 1779, £700 in 1782 and £1,400 in 1792 of which utensils, stock, goods, warehouse and workshop accounted for £320, £400 and £500 respectively. [*Cambridge Chronicle*, 24 September 1768, 24 February 1770, 13 November 1773; GL, Sun MS vol. 271, p. 497; vol. 299, p. 565; vol. 388, p. 552]

Cole, James, Kemp's Ct, Berwick St, London, chairmaker (1774). [Poll bk]

Cole, James, James St, Golden Sq., London, upholder (1774). [Poll bk]

Cole, James, Merchant St, Bristol, broker and bed joiner (1799–1801). [D]

Cole, James, Narrow Lane, Bristol, clock case maker (1806–13). [D]

Cole(s), James, Wendover, Bucks., chairmaker (1823–30). Trading at Aylesbury St, also as a timber dealer, in 1830. [D]

Cole, James, Blackheath Hill, Lewisham, London, cm and u (1832). [D]

Cole, John, St James's, Westminster, London, cm (1706). [*London Gazette*, 3 March 1706]

Cole, John, Exeter(?), carver and gilder (1825). Lay-vicar at the Cathedral. Victim of an assault by a labourer residing in the College. [*The Alfred*, 31 May 1825]

Cole, John, Marske, Yorks., joiner/cm (1834). [D]

Cole, Jonathan, London, u (1777–92). In 1777 at 52 Chiswell St but in 1786 the number is shown as 32. By 1792 at 29 Windmill St, Moorfields. Total insurance cover in 1777 was £300 of which half was for utensils and stock. This would suggest a small scale of operation but nevertheless he could insure five houses in Southwark for £700 in 1786 and £1,000

in 1792. [GL, Sun MS vol. 255, p. 582; vol. 336, p. 4; vol. 386, p. 221]

Cole, Thomas, parish of St Sidwell, Exeter, Devon, carver and gilder (1814–18). Son Thomas bapt. 4 November 1814 and daughter Louisa 23 July 1818. [PR (bapt.)]

Cole, Thomas, Bartholomew Ct, Birmingham, chairmaker (1835). [D]

Cole, W., Middle St, Yeovil, Som., cm (1839). [D]

Cole, William, Newark, Notts., chairmaker and turner (1712–15). In 1712 took app. named Hilton and in 1715 one named Shackleton. [S of G, app. index]

Cole, William, Newbiggin, Thaxted, Essex, chairmaker (1798–1839). Recorded as William Cole jnr, cm, in 1832. [D]

Cole, William, 206 Whitechapel Rd, London, cm (1826). [D]

Cole, William, Market Hill, Cambridge, u (1830–32). [D; poll bk]

Cole, William, Worcester, cm and u (1830–37). Trading at 11 Pump St in 1835 and 11 Mealcheapen St in 1837. [D]

Cole, William, 60 St Peter's St, Derby, cm and u (1835). [D]

Cole, William, London, carver and gilder (1835–39). Between 1835–37 he was at 25 St John St Rd, Clerkenwell but by 1839 had moved to 16 Pierpont Row, Islington. [D]

Cole, William, 40 Park St, Birmingham, chairmaker (1839). [D]

Coleborne, Thomas, Bennet St, Bath, Som., u, auctioneer and undertaker (1783). [D]

Coleburn, Isaac, West Hampton, carver (1762). In 1762 took app. named Morris. [S of G, app. index]

Coleby, James, The Close, Norwich, u (1812). [Poll bk]

Coleclough, William, Nine Houses, Chester, cm (1812). Son of John Coleclough. App. 30 June 1790 and 24 February 1792 to William Henderson, cm. Free 20 October 1812. [App. bks; freemen reg.; poll bk]

Coleman, —, Middlx, upholder (1755). In May 1755 imprisoned for debt. [*London Gazette*, 27–31 May 1755]

Coleman, —, 65 Davies St, Bulkeley St, London, cm etc. (1820). [D]

Coleman, Edward, 9 Upper Maudlin St, Bristol, cm (1835). [D]

Coleman, Francis, Millgate, Newwark, Notts., u (1835). [D]

Coleman, James, Wymondham, Norfolk, cabinet and chairmaker (1830–39). At Bridewell St in 1830 and Fairland St in 1839. [D]

Coleman, John, 9 King St, Derby, carver and gilder (1828–35). Trading at no. 9, 1828–29, and no. 3 in 1835. [D]

Coleman, Robert, 'The King's Arms', Houndsditch, Aldgate, London, cm and undertaker (1714–27). In 1723 insured house in Woolsack Alley in Houndsditch, divided into three tenements, for £300. [GL, Sun MS vol. 4, ref. 427; vol. 16, p. 252; vol. 23, p. 320]

Coleman, Robert, Blackheath Hill, London, carver and gilder (1826). [D]

Coleman, Thomas, 'The Ship' on London Bridge, London, u and appraiser (1733–37). Son of Thomas Coleman of White Chappell, Middlx, Gent. App. to Ambrose Pearman 7 April 1725 and admitted a freeman of the Upholders' Co. by servitude 5 December 1733. On his trade card he stated that he made and sold 'all Sorts of Upholstery Goods wholesale or retail viz. Fashionable Beds, Feather Beds, Quilts, Ruggs, Blankets, Coverlets, Flanders & English Ticking, also Leather, Cane & Matted Chairs'. He was made bankrupt early in 1737. [GL, Upholders' Co. records; Banks Coll., BM; *Gents Mag.*, May 1737]

Coleman, William, 45 Curzon St, Mayfair, London, u (1804–25). Subscribed to and included in the list of master cabinet makers in Sheraton's *Cabinet Dictionary*, 1803. On 30 April 1808 Sir John Geers Cotterell of Garnons near Hereford and Hertford St, London settled an account amounting to £8 17s. [D; Herefs. RO, W69/III/182]

Coleman, William, 4 Haymarket, London, writing desk and dressing case maker (1829). [D]

Coleman, William, 42 St Paul's Sq., Birmingham, cm (1835). [D]

Coleman, William, Caudwell St, Bedford, cm and u (1839). [D]

Colemark, —, St Martin's Lane, London, u (1768). [V & A archives]

Coleridge, James, Bitten St, Teignmouth, Devon, cm and u (1838). [D]

Coles, Benjamin, parish of St Mary Redcliffe, Bristol, carver (1834). [Poll bk]

Coles, Charles, 3 Gt Minster St, Winchester, Hants., carver and gilder (1830). [D]

Coles, David, 67 Charlotte St, Tottenham Ct Rd, London, upholder (1777). In 1777 insured his house for £500. [GL, Sun MS vol. 256, p. 348]

Coles, David, 91 Aldersgate St, London, cm (1785). On 14 February 1785 took out insurance cover of £300 which included £50 for utensils and stock. [GL, Sun MS vol. 327, p. 326]

Coles, F. E., Assembly Rooms, Blandford, Dorset, cm (1840). [D]

Coles, Francis, Hendford, Yeovil, Som., cm and u (1830). [D]

Coles, G., 15 Gt Mays Buildings, St Martin's Lane, London, dressing case maker (1835). [D]

Coles, John, parish of St James, Bristol, cm (1784). [Poll bk]

Coles, John, Market Pl., Chard, Som., u (1830). [D]

Coles, Robert, Cross House, Southampton, Hants., cm (1811). [Poll bk]

Coles, Roger jnr, Ansford, Som., cm (1763–64). Worked for Rev. James Woodforde 3 November 1763 on 'a small writing Table with a Drawer & Lock' for which 8s was charged. On 19 and 23 December 1764 working with his boy, Bob Chaffin making a 'Desk Table' and a 'new round Table for common uses'. [R. L. Winstanley, ed., *The Ansford Diary of the Revd. James Woodforde*, vol. 2, p. 78]

Coles, William, Watlington, Oxon., cm (1791). On 8 December 1791 married Diana Barnett of Brightwell. [Bodleian index of Oxf. marriage bonds]

Collambell, Thomas, 2 River St, Derby, cm and u (1835). [D]

Collens, George, Maidstone, Kent, cm (1832–37). In 1832–35 at Week St, but in 1837 at Market St. [Poll bks]

Collet, R., Wakefield, Yorks., joiner and cm (1798). [D]

Collett, James, 138 High Holborn, London, u (1811–19). [D]

Collett, James, King's Rd, Chelsea, London, cm and u (1823). [D]

Collett, John, 138 High Holborn, London, cm and u (1808–23). In August 1810 took out insurance cover of £2,000 which included £1,200 for his dwelling house and workshop behind and £500 for stock and utensils. [D; GL, Sun MS vol. 452, ref. 848112]

Collett, John, Liverpool, cm (1829–39). From 1829–34 at 9 Tyren St but thereafter at 21 Leigh St. [D]

Collett, Jonas, 19 Maiden Lane, Covent Gdn, London, carver and gilder (1808). [D]

Collett, Jonathan, 'The King's Arms', opposite Pall Mall, Charing Cross, London, glass cutter (1769–86). On 18 May 1769 supplied a 'pair of two light Girandolles, richly ornamented' at £9 9s for Alscot Park, Warks. A payment of £3 19s 6d to 'COLLETT Glass man' is recorded in the account book of Sir George Cornewall of Moccas Court, near Hereford. [V & A archives; Herefs. RO, Moccas papers, J56/IV/4]

Collett, Samuel, Upper Slaughter, Glos., builder and carpenter(?) (1765–66). In 1766 made a bookcase including drawers for James Leigh for which £4 0s 6d was charged.

[Shakespeare Birthplace Trust, Leigh receipts, household accounts box 2, bundle 2 DR 18/8/5]

Collett, Thomas, Gloucester(?), carpenter (1761–62). In 1761 made a bookcase for James Leigh for his study at a cost of £18 5s. In March of the following year a table with one leaf was charged at 18s and 3s charged for '2 men making a sideboard for the parlour at the Parsonage'. [Shakespeare Birthplace Trust, Leigh receipts, household accounts, box 2, bundle 2 DR 18/8/5]

Colley, James, Cartway, Bridgnorth, Salop, chairmaker (1822). [D]

Colley, John, 21 Fleet St, Liverpool, joiner and cm (1790). Also had workshop at 5 Manesty's Lane. [D]

Colley, Joseph, Broseley, Salop, chairmaker (1840). [D]

Colley, Richard, address unknown, cm and u (1830–32). Work undertaken for J. S. Russell (changed name to J. S. Pakington on inheriting property) 1830–32 for High Park and Westwood House, near Droitwich, Worcs. The work was mainly furniture repairs, removal work, carpentry but did include upholstery work such as fixing curtains, moving and remaking bedsteads. [Worcs. RO, 2309/705:380/56/ii and iv]

Colley, Thomas, Dudley, Worcs., chairmaker (1820). [D]

Collier, Brooks, Queen St, Oxford, cm and u (1823). [D]

Collier, Francis, Stafford, cm (1778). A Queen Anne style walnut chair with a solid splat back and cabriole legs with a drop-in seat is known stamped 'F. COLLIER'. Bankruptcy announced, *Leicester Journal*, 7 March 1778.

Collier, Francis, 7 Artillery St, Bishopsgate St, London, cm (1808). [D]

Collier, George, parish of St Matthew, Ipswich, Suffolk, u (1810). Married in 1810. [Suffolk RO, FAA: 50/2/115, pp. 83-84]

Collier, James, 9 Cable St, Ratcliff, London, cm (1808). [D]

Collier, John, 4 Gerrard St, London, carver and gilder (1792). On 10 October 1792 took out insurance cover of £300. [GL, Sun MS vol. 389, ref. 606726]

Collier, Joseph, 188 Chapel St, Salford, Lancs., carver and gilder (1821). [D]

Collier, Stephen, High St, Romford, Essex, cm and u (1823–39). [D]

Collier, Thomas, 3 Eldon Pl., Liverpool, cm (1827). [D]

Collin, George, 43 Upper Marylebone St, London, picture frame maker (1840). [GL, Sun MS ref. 1333459]

Colling, Edward, 28 Basnett St, Liverpool, carver and gilder (1827). [D]

Colling, George, Ryton, near Gateshead, Co. Durham, joiner and cm (1827). [D]

Colling, William K., 33 Phythian St, Liverpool, carver and gilder (1829). [D]

Colling & Hargreaves, 106 Bold St, Liverpool, carvers and gilders (1829). [D]

Collingridge, Thomas, Buckingham, cm (1760). In 1760 took app. named Finch. [S of G, app. index]

Collings, John, 12 George St, Gt Portland St, London, chair and sofa maker (1805–39). Insurance records show a cover of £300 in 1805, £550 in 1808 and £600 in 1810 of which utensils, stock and goods in trust accounted for £100, £300 and £500 respectively. There is mention of a 'workshop behind' and in 1810 of 'the open shed under workshop behind 74 Great Titchfield St'. [D; GL, Sun MS vol. 434, ref. 779797; vol. 445, ref. 819983; vol. 453, ref. 844420]

Collings, William, Plymouth, Devon, cm (1762). Took app. named Sluggett in 1762. [S of G, app. index]

Collings, William, address unknown, cm (1803). Subscribed to Sheraton's *Cabinet Dictionary*, 1803.

Collings, William, Belton St, Long Acre, London, carver and gilder (1809). Mortgage of 3 Chapel St, St Anne, Soho. [Marylebone Lib., deed 10/287]

Collingwood, Robert, 26 Grafton St, Liverpool, chairmaker (1823). [D]

Collins, —, Red-Cross St, Southwark, London, cm (1738). Reported to have died 'in an odd frightful manner'. [*Daily Post*, 13 July 1738]

Collins, Aaron, Market Pl., Boston, Lincs., cm and u (1835). [D]

Collins, Caleb Welch, 119 Fleet St, London, horse hair weaver and cm (1782–91). Son of George Collins of St Martin le Grand, knife case maker. App. to Richard Thurgood, cutler 31 December 1782. Admitted freeman of the Upholders' Co. by order of the Court of Assistants 7 July 1790. On 14 September 1791 took out insurance cover of £2,200 of which £2,000 was for utensils and stock. [GL, Upholders' Co. records; Sun MS vol. 379, p. 547]

Collins, Charles, London, upholder (c. 1725–54). Son of John Collins of London, yeoman. App. to Jeremiah Poole, freeman upholder for seven years on 17 August 1715. No premium paid. [V & A archives]

Collins, Edward, 9 Regent Hill, Brighton, Sussex, cm and u (1823–26). Sons William Alfred and Henry bapt. 15 June 1823. [D; PR (bapt.)]

Collins, Edward, Palace St, Canterbury, Kent, cm and broker (1824). [D]

Collins, Edward, 38 Bond St, Brighton, Sussex, cm (1832–40). Son Edwin Albert bapt. 3 March 1833. [D; PR (bapt.)]

Collins, Francis, Wokingham, Berks., upholder (1745–61). Took app. named Martin in 1745 and one named Jewer in 1761. [S of G, app. index]

Collins, George, Molemaker Row, Westminster, London, cm (1774). [Poll bk]

Collins, George, St Martin's le Grand, London, knife case maker (1790). His son Caleb admitted a freeman of the Upholders' Co. 7 July 1790. [GL, Upholders' Co. records]

Collins, George, Whickham, Co. Durham, joiner/carpenter/cm (1834). [D]

Collins, H., 31 Cockspur St, Charing Cross, London, carver, gilder and picture dealer (1820–29). [D]

Collins, Hⁿ., Northumberland House Repository, 147 St Martin's Lane, London, picture frame maker, carver and gilder (1808). Trade card in Banks Coll., BM. Stated to be late of 45 Old Compton St, Soho. Card shows royal coat of arms but no claim of royal patronage made in the text.

Collins, Isaac, 23 White Queen St, Lincoln's Inn Fields, London, carver and gilder (1826). [D]

Collins, James, Queen St, Ipswich, Suffolk, cm and u (1839). [D; poll bk]

Collins, James, Downley, High Wycombe, Bucks., chairmaker (b. c. 1821–41). Aged 20 at the time of the 1841 Census.

Collins, John, 18 Frogmore St, Bristol, cm, u and undertaker (1837). [D]

Collins, Joseph, Littleworth, High Wycombe, Bucks., chairmaker (b. c. 1821–41). Aged 20 at the time of the 1841 Census.

Collins, Matthew, 'Ye Half Moon', Cheapside, corner of Soper Lane, London, u (c. 1669). [Heal]

Collins, Pendlebury, Chester and Liverpool, cm (1732). Son of Pendlebury Collins of Chester, wet glover. Sworn freeman of Chester 9 September 1732. [Chester freemen rolls]

Collins, Philip Alford jnr, Chard, Som., casemaker (1777). Insured house in 1777 for £100. [GL, Sun MS vol. 254, p. 117]

Collins, Richard, London (1774). Supplied Sir Watkin Williams Wynn at 20 St James's Sq., London, in 1774 with 'two Bookcases Extraordinary to a design of Messrs. Robt and James Adam £15.18.7¼'. They were of 'rich mahogany' with

'12 ovall Patterae let into the Legs' and '130 Small (Patterae) let into the Pannells of the Doors'. [Nat. Lib. of Wales, Wynnstay MS 115/17/10; designs at the Soane Museum]

Collins, Robert, 1 Brook St, New Rd, Marylebone, London, cm and bedstead maker (1835–39). In 1839 listed as Collins & Son. [D]

Collins, Samuel, late of King St, St Anne, Westminster, London, u (1761). In August 1761 discharged from Debtors' Prison. [*London Gazette*, 22 August 1761]

Collins, Samuel, 131 Tooley St, London, cm (1793). [D]

Collins, Samuel, Downley, West Wycombe, Bucks., chairmaker (b. c. 1795–1834). Born c. 1795 at Chargrove, Oxon. Married on 5 August 1816 at West Wycombe. Son Samuel born in 1834 and subsequently chairmaker. Daughters Sarah and Ann born in 1832. Not in 1841 Census. [PR (bapt. and marriage)]

Collins, T., High St, Southwark, London, bedstead maker (1829). [D]

Collins, Thomas, Bread St, London, upholder (1719). Son of Thomas Collins of St Ives, Hunts., clerk. App. to Thomas Phill, freeman upholder, 22 June 1709. Free of the Upholders' Co. 4 November 1719. [V & A archives]

Collins, Thomas, 17 Cannon St Rd, St George's in the East, London, cabinet and chairmaker (1817). [D]

Collins, William, Lichfield, Staffs., carver and gilder (1802). At Shugborough, Staffs. in 1802 where he charged £4 16s for gilding a large window cornice. [Staffs. RO, Anson papers, D615 E(H)/2/6]

Collins, William, Tothill Fields, London, (1812–23). The suite of gilt furniture presented to Greenwich Hospital in 1813 by John Fish of Kempton Park, Middlx, in memory of Nelson includes a lamp or torchère, the plinth of which is signed 'William Collins, London fecit'. This has led to speculation that Collins was a cabinet-maker and responsible for the entire suite which is currently on display at the Royal Pavilion, Brighton. A pair of gilt bronze five branch gas lights originally made for Bath House, Piccadilly by William Collins and dated 1823 in the Bowes Museum collection would however suggest that Collins was a supplier of lighting equipment not a cabinet-maker. [V & A archives]

Collin(s), William, Kensington, London, u (1823–26). Listed at Newland Terr. in 1823 and 5 Newland Pl. in 1826. [D]

Collins, William, Tenterden, Kent, u (1838). [D]

Collins, William, 3 Gloucester St, St John's St Rd, London, u (1839). [D]

Collins, William, Downley, High Wycombe, Bucks., chairmaker (b. c. 1796–1841). Aged 45 at the time of the 1841 Census.

Collins & Clearson, 125 Strand, London, frame makers and glass grinders (1789–94). Also listed in some directories from 1790 as carvers and gilders. [D]

Collins & Co., Sun St, Bishopsgate, London, cm (1800). [D]

Collinson, Benjamin, Bridlington, Yorks., joiner and cm (1793). [D]

Collinson, David, Gt George St, Pocklington, Yorks., cm and joiner (1834). [D]

Collinson, Enoch, London, carver and gilder (1829–39). In 1829 at 82 Curtain Rd and in 1839 at 2 New Rd, Whitechapel. [D]

Collinson, George, 53 Frith St, Soho, London, cm (1808). [D]

Collinson, George Croyson, London, cm and u (1820–37). Initially in business at Kendrick Pl., Chenies St, Bedford Sq., and this address appears to have been retained for the whole life of the concern. In 1833 however their billheads gave an address at 61 Conduit St, Regent St and stated 'From Chenies House, Bedford Square'. In the early 1820s the firm traded as Collinson, Potts & Collinson but by 1826 was listed in directories as George Collinson & Son, suggesting the departure of Mr Potts. In 1837 the business is listed as G. Collinson jnr, indicating the death or retirement of the father. The enterprise was in 1820 on a substantial scale with a fire insurance cover of £4,000. There was a counting house, warehouse and workshop in which was a stove (not for drying feathers), sheds and a coach house and stables. All the insurance cover was in respect of utensils, stock and goods in trust. The only known commission was in 1833 and contained in a bill in the Stowe archives. The sum was £6 os 6d and was in respect of hanging curtains and carrying out repairs to furniture (some in servants' rooms). [D; GL, Sun MS vol. 483, ref. 968249; vol. 498, ref. 1001378; Huntington Lib., California, ST Box 148]

Collinson, John, Nottingham, u (1689–d. 1705). [Freemen records; Notts. RO, probate inv. 12/9/1705]

Collinson, Leonard, Grimsby Lane, Hull, Yorks., cm (1790–91). [D]

Collinson, William, Tonge's Building, Chorlton Row, Manchester, cm (1824–28). [D]

Collip, John, London, upholder and undertaker (1803–29). At 122 Gt Portland St from 1803–07, though also recorded at John St, Oxford Rd in 1803 only. From 1816–29 at 75 Titchfield St, Fitzroy Sq. Subscriber to Sheraton's *Cabinet Dictionary*, 1803 and included in his list of master cabinet makers. [D]

Collis, Barnard, 32 Brownlow St, Drury Lane, London, carpenter and cm (1807). On 21 August 1807 took out insurance cover of £200. [GL, Sun MS vol. 440, ref. 806251]

Collis, George, 2 North St, Bristol, ornamental screen and card rack manufacturer (1827–31). By 1828 trading also as a stationer; and in 1830 also as a varnisher. [D]

Collis, Mrs H., 2 North St, Bristol, ornamental screen and card rack manufacturer (1826). [D]

Collis, William, London, upholder (1724). Son of Joseph Collis of Cambridge, tallow chandler. App. to William Hayes on 3 June 1713 and free of the Upholders' Co. by servitude on 6 May 1724. [GL, Upholders' Co. records]

Collishaw, Charles, Wyche St, St Clement Danes, London, cm (1802). Declared bankrupt, *Billinge's Liverpool Advertiser*, 19 July 1802.

Collison, George, 8 Cambridge St, Soho, London, cm and u (1839). [D]

Collison, Sarah, 2 Junction Dock St, Hull, Yorks., cm etc. (1840). [D]

Collison, Thomas, 55 Southampton Row, Bloomsbury, London, u (1811). [D]

Collison, William, Canterbury, Kent, cm (1805–30). At Jewry Lane, 1805–26 but in 1830 at St Mary Bredman. [D; poll bks]

Collison, William Gilbank, 2 Junction Dock St, Hull, Yorks., cm and u (1834–40). App. to George Chapman of Hull July 1813. In 1835 listed as a broker. Succeeded by Sarah Collison. [D; Hull app. reg.]

Collumbell, Thomas, 2 River St, Derby, cm and u (1835). [D]

Collyer, —, 44 Fore St, near Moorgate, London, u. Late 18th-century trade card in the Landauer Coll., MMA, NY, states that Collyer offered not only 'all sorts of Upholstery Goods' wholesale and retail, but also 'Cabinet Furniture' and 'Paper Hangings &c.'.

Collyer, John, London, carver and gilder (1811–39). At 8 Constitution Row, Gray's Inn Rd, 1811–15 but by 1827 at 63 Frith St at which address he continued to trade until 1839. [D]

Colman, William, Oak St, Fakenham, Norfolk, cabinet and chairmaker (1822–30). [D]

Colombine, Paul, Norwich, u (1721–86). Son of Francis Colombine of Norwich, physician. App. to William Braithwaite of London 8 April 1714 and admitted a freeman of the Upholders' Co. by servitude on 2 August 1721. Admitted a freeman of Norwich 19 June 1727 but was already trading in Norwich before this date. An insurance policy taken out on 8 October 1726 for £500 included £400 in respect of stock. The address on the policy is listed as parish of St Simon though by 1735 he had moved to the parish of St Peter Mancroft. In 1745 he took an app. named Richer; in 1751 another named Withers; and in 1754 one named Marks. Other apps were Isaac Hoyle (free 3 May 1753), William Notloy (free 3 May 1760) and William Bracey (free 14 April 1781). Hoyle was taken app. jointly with Woodhouse Harmer which might suggest some form of business relationship at this period. Colombine is mentioned in the Holkham Hall, Norfolk accounts. In 1743 he was paid £1 8s for a mahogany chair with leather seat, £1 1s for a dressing glass and also supplied another mahogany chair, rush seated, and some curtains. In 1757 he was again involved at Holkham on upholstery work. [GL, Upholders' Co. records; GL, Sun MS vol. 22, p. 377; Norwich freemen reg.; S of G, app. index; V & A archives; *C. Life*, 14 February 1980, p. 427; poll bk]

Colsey, William, London, cm (1802–29). In 1802 at 19 Hatton Wall where he took out insurance cover for £300. In 1808 he was at 18 Charles St, Hatton Gdn, and in 1817 at 28 Charlotte St, Old St Rd. His trade at this period was mainly in small case furniture, and his trade card described him as a 'Knife case, portable desk and tea caddy maker'. From 1825–29 he was at 11 George St, Mansion House and in 1829 was simply described as a cm. [D; Hackney archives dept, 332 TDE/22]

Colsey, William, 'The Three Jolly Butchers', Boot St, Hoxton, London, victualler and cm (1812). Took out insurance cover of £2,000 on 13 October 1812 of which £450 was for stock, utensils and goods in trust. [GL, Sun MS vol. 455, ref. 875158]

Colshaw, Thomas, Great White, Ramsey, Hunts., carpenter, joiner and cm (1839). [D]

Colson, William, Southampton, Hants., cm (1811–23). Trading at 'Above Bar' in 1811 and Orchard St in 1823. [D; poll bk]

Colston, Daniel Edward, London, cm and u (1822–39). At 8 Edward Pl., St John's St Rd in 1822 and at Peel Pl., Kennington in 1839. [D]

Colston, David, 1 Duncan Pl., City Rd, London, u (1820). [D]

Colter, Thomas, Windsor, Berks., upholder (1780). [Poll bk]

Coltman, George, High Wycombe, Bucks., japanner (b. c. 1816–1841). Aged 25 at the time of the 1841 Census.

Coltman, Robert, Blackheath Hill, Greenwich, London, carver and gilder (1824). [D]

Coltman, Thomas, Bottlebank, Gateshead, Co. Durham, joiner and cm (1790–95). [D]

Colton, Arthur, London, upholder (d. by 1717). Son Thomas admitted freeman of the Upholders' Co. 1717. Father already dead by this date. [GL, Upholders' Co. records]

Colton, Richard, Newark, Notts., cm (1790–98). [D; poll bk]

Colton, Thomas, London, upholder (1700–07). Admitted freeman of the Upholders' Co. 23 April 1700. [GL, Upholders' Co. records]

Colton, Thomas, London, upholder (1707–17). Son of Arthur Colton, London, upholder. App. to Jonathan Halley 29 July 1707 and free by servitude 9 January 1716/17. [Upholders' Co. records]

Colton, William, 4 Heston Pl., King's Cross, London, furniture broker, carver and gilder (1839). [D]

Columbani, Placido, 33 Dorset St, Portman Sq., London, carver and gilder (1795). Supplied two gilt frames, one new, for 11s to Lord Howard of Audley End. Also seems to have carried out architectural design work and surveying for this patron; also did plasterwork at Mount Clare, Surrey; Ickworth,

Suffolk; and Downhill, Co. Antrim, N. Ireland. [Essex RO, D/DBy/A53/12; Hussey, *English Country Houses: Mid-Georgian*, p. 240; *C. Life*, 6 January 1950]

Colwell & Co., 33 Leicester Sq., London, u (1811). [D]

Combe, John, 'The Bunch of Grapes', Silver St, parish of St Olave, Silver St, London, upholder (1704–14). Admitted freeman of the Upholders' Co. 1 November 1704. On 30 May 1714 insured his 'goods & merchandize' in his 'dwelling house', amount of cover not specified. [GL, Upholders' Co. records; GL, Sun MS vol. 3, ref. 3974]

Combee, Peter, St Giles without Cripplegate, London, carver (1712). Took an app. in 1712. [S of G, app. index]

Comber, George, 35 Ratcliff Highway, London, cm and u (1839). [D]

Comery, James, 'The Golden Eagle', Castle St, Long Acre, London, cm and broker (1749–74). His trade card [Heal coll., BM] states that he 'Appraiseth and Buyeth & Selleth all manner of Household Goods at Reasonable Rates'. Also owned a property in Brownlow St, Drury Lane on which he paid insurance cover of £400 from 1760–74. [Heal; poll bk; GL, Hand in Hand MS vol. 94, p. 28; vol. 106, p. 36; vol. 116, ref. 23693]

Comfort, H., 20 St Stephen's St, Tottenham Ct Rd, London, chair caner (1835). [D]

Comfort, John, 8 Wells Row, Islington, London, u (1835–39). [D]

Comings, Matthew, Dorchester, Dorset, joiner and cm (1732). On 9 December 1732 insured his dwelling house, outhouse, shop, workshop, 'timber house' and cellar with his household goods and stock therein for £200. [GL, Sun MS vol. 37, ref. 59502]

Commell, George, Newport, Salop, cm (1797). [D]

Commins, Richard, St Mary St, Weymouth, Dorset, cm and u (1830–40). At no. 85 in 1830 and no. 95 in 1840. [D]

Compston, John, Abbey St, Carlisle, Cumb., chairmaker (1810). [D]

Compton, Richard, Barton St, Tewkesbury, Glos., cm and chairmaker (1839). [D]

Compton, Robert W., Greenwich Rd, Greenwich, London, cm (1838–39). [D]

Compton, William, High Wycombe, Bucks., chairmaker (b. c.1779–1841). Aged 62 at the time of the 1841 Census.

Comroy, John, Bentford St, Exeter, Devon, cm (1819). Daughter Harriet Caroline bapt. at St Stephen's, 11 July 1819. [PR (bapt.)]

Comte, Henry, 176 Church St, Shoreditch, London, cabinet and chairmaker (1820–22). [D]

Compte, Henry, 41 Union St, Whitechapel Rd, London, cm and u (1839). [D]

Conder, Samuel, Sutton Ct, Threadneedle St, London, upholder (1714–27). App. to Robert Roades of York, upholder. Admitted freeman of the London Upholders' Co. 3 February 1713/14 by purchase. On 14 December 1714 took out insurance on his house for £450. Took app. John Goodchild 1719 (free 1726–27). [GL, Upholders' Co. records; Hand in Hand MS vol. 13, p. 622]

Conder, Samuel, Market Pl., Biggleswade, Beds., cm and u (1830–39). [D]

Conigrave, James, London, cm (1817–37). At 3 St John's St Rd, St John's St, 1817–29. From 1823–26 traded as Conigrave & Son and in 1829 as B., J. & J. Conigrave. From this year they also advertised themselves as upholsterers. One directory in 1829 however lists James Conigrave at 13 Whiskin St, Spitalfields. By 1835 the business had moved to 33 Aldersgate St but still retained premises in St John's St Rd. The business was in this year described as B. & J. Conigrave, u, undertakers, house estate agents. On 13 August 1821

insurance cover of £700 was taken out on a 'dwelling house and workshops (no pipe stove therein)' at 3 St John's St Rd. Another policy for £600 was taken out in respect of household goods (£100) and stock, utensils and goods in trust, some of which was kept at 44 Upper St, Islington. [D; GL, Sun MS vol. 487, ref. 983176]

Coningsby, Bennet & Barnes, Elizabeth, Duke St, Bloomsbury, London, cm (1725). On 8 October 1725 took out insurance cover of £500 most of which was in respect of property at 'Weberly in Hereford' (i.e. Weobley). Elizabeth Barnes was described as a spinster. [GL, Sun MS vol. 20, ref. 36927]

Conk, John, 4 Bartholomew Close, London, cm and u (1827). [D]

Conkerton, Alexander, 29 Bishop Lane, Hull, Yorks., joiner and cm (1838–39). Also listed in 1838 as a printer and in 1839 as a machine ruler. [D]

Conlan & Nicholson, 2 Hilton St, Manchester, carvers and gilders (1834). [D]

Conley, John, 9 Bridge Pl., Haggeston, London, cm and u (1839). [D]

Conn, P., Stockton-on-Tees, Co. Durham, cm (1827–37). In August 1837 advertised for sale 'a large quantity of WHITE & GREY GOOSE FEATHERS & FEATHER BEDS. Also Bedsteads, Tables, Chairs, Drawers, Sofas & Loo Tables, Gilt Pier & Dressing Glasses, 8 Days' & 30 Hours' Clocks, Hearth Rugs, Yard-wide & Stair Carpets etc.'. [D; *Durham County Advertiser*, 18 August 1837]

Connard, Edward, 21 East St, Brighton, Sussex, 'Brighton ware manufacturer' and fancy japanner (1822). [D]

Connell, James, 55 Roper St, Whitehaven, Cumb., joiner and cm (1828). [D]

Connell, William, Virgil St, Liverpool, cm (1823). [D]

Conner, Michael, address unknown, carver and gilder (d. 1819). Died 24 April 1819 at Wigan 'of a decline'. [*Liverpool Mercury*, 30 April 1819]

Connibeare, George, Gloucester, u (1784). [D]

Con(n)ibeare, R., Lower North St, Gloucester, u (1802). [D]

Connop, John, London, carver, gilder, looking-glass and picture frame maker and undertaker (1808–25). At 10 St Ann's Lane, Aldersgate St, 1808–20, and his trade card from this period is in the Banks Coll., BM. In 1825 at 6 Lombard St. [D]

Connor, Daniel, Liverpool, cm (1837–39). At 34 Hodson St, in 1837 and 11 Pellew St in 1839. [D]

Connor, James, Smithford St, Coventry, Warks., carver and gilder (1835). [D]

Consilt, John, York, joiner and cm (1772). In 1772 moved from Thursday Mkt to Pavement. [*York Courant*, 7 July, 22 November 1772]

Constable, Henry, address unknown, u (1754). Subscriber to Chippendale's *Director*, 1754.

Constable, John, London, upholder (1758–1802). Son of John Constable, freeman harberdasher of London. App. to William Boulter, freeman basket maker 26 October 1750. Free of the Upholders' Co. under the 1750 Upholders' Act, 29 December 1758. At Gravil Lane, Houndsditch in 1772 and Bell-alley, Coleman St in 1778. He is first recorded in directories in 1782 at 14 Cullum St and continued at this address until 1788. In 1794 and 1802 recorded at Northampton. Took apps Thomas Brown (1772–87) and Thomas Peirson (1778–94). [D; GL, Upholders' Co. records]

Constable, Thomas, London, u (1761). Said to be formerly of Turnagain Lane, Snow Hill and late of Lombard St. Discharged from Debtors' Prison, August 1761. [*London Gazette*, 22 August 1761]

Constance, William, Fakenham, Norfolk, cm and ironmonger (1794). Bankrupt August 1794. [*Williamson's Liverpool*

Advertiser, 18 August 1794; *Billinge's Liverpool Advertiser*, 29 March 1796, 4 April 1796]

Constantine, Benjamin, New Shop, Stansfield Township, Todmorden, Yorks., joiner/cm (1837). [D]

Constantine, William, Salford, Lancs., cm (1817–40). At 22 Booth St in 1817 and 89 Greengate in 1840. [D]

Constantine, William & Co., 3 South Parade, Leeds, Yorks., cm and u (1834–40). The autobiography of Thomas Wilkins records that his brother was employed as foreman carver by Constantine from the mid 1830s at 28s a week. By the early 1840s the firm was employing about a hundred workers including fifteen carvers. On 27 January 1837 they supplied for the Oxford Pl. Methodist Chapel, Leeds a pair of 'Handsome Ottoman Stools for Altar Table, covered with Brussels Carpets, on Spanish Mahogany Frames'. These with their brown Holland covers were charged at £4. [D; Leeds archives dept, OP/35]

Consterdine, William, 135 Chapel St, Salford, Lancs., cm (1797–1802). [D]

Conty, David, 92 Ratcliff Highway, London, broker and cm (1808). [D]

Conway, C., London, carver and gilder (1820–39). At 41 Kennington Lane in 1820, 20 White Hart Pl., Kennington in 1829 and 12 Commerce Pl., Brixton 1837–39. [D]

Conway, Charles, 16 West St, Seven Dials, London, carver and gilder (1835–39). [D]

Conway, Henry, 24 Waterloo Rd, Lambeth, London, carver and gilder (1832). [D]

Conway, John, see Fletcher & Conway.

Conway, Phillip, Fore St, Wellington, Som., cm and u (1822). [D]

Conyeare, Joseph, address unknown, cm (1754). Subscribed to Chippendale's *Director*, 1754.

Conyer, George, address unknown, cm (1793). Subscribed to Sheraton's *Drawing Book*, 1793.

Cook, —, 17 John St, Gt Portland St, Oxford St, London, carver, gilder, printseller, glass and girandole supplier (1801). Trade card in Banks Coll., BM.

Cook, Absalom, London, carver, gilder and looking-glass manufacturer. (1826–39). In 1826 at 12 Brook St, New Rd, Marylebone where he was carrying on the trade of chairmaker. In 1829 at 20 Marylebone St, as a looking-glass manufacturer. In 1839 the number changed to 54. [D]

Cook, Betsey, 17 Little Common St, Birmingham, u (1835). [D]

Cook, Daniel, Halesworth, Suffolk, cm (1804). [*Ipswich Journal*, 29 September 1804]

Cook, Edward, Cow Cross, Smithfield, London, cm (1793). Subscribed to Sheraton's *Drawing Book*, 1793.

Cook, Elizabeth, Cannon St, Birmingham, u (1828–30). Trading at no. 28 in 1828 and 29 in 1830. [D]

Cook, Frederick, Heavitree, Exeter, Devon, cm and u (1838). [D]

Cook, G., 7 Wellington Buildings, Bath, Som., chairmaker (1819). [D]

Cook, George, Debenham, Suffolk, chairmaker and cooper (1718). In 1718 took app. named Reeve. [S of G, app. index]

Cook, George, Cirencester, Glos., cm (1827). Birth of child 1827. [PR (bapt.)]

Cook, Gregory, Norwich, u (1724). App. to Robert Osborn and admitted freeman 3 May 1724. In the same year himself took an app. [Freemen reg.; S of G, app. index]

Cook, Harriet, 8 Denmark St, Soho, London, bedstead maker (1823). Took out insurance cover of £150 of which £50 was in respect of utensils and stock. [GL, Sun MS vol. 498, ref. 1005370]

Cook, Henry, Russell St, Covent Gdn, London, patent furniture maker (1790–93). [D]

Cook, Henry, 8 Denmark St, Soho, London, cm (1826). Successor to Harriet Cook at the same address. [D]

Cook, Henry, Painswick, Glos., chairmaker (1839). [D]

Cook, Isaac, Walket, Glos., u (1757). Took app. named Austin in 1757. [S of G, app. index]

Cook, Isaac, 24 Charlotte St, Blackfriars, London, cm, u, portable desk maker and undertaker (1813–39). [D]

Cook, J., 53 Gt Marylebone St, London, u (1819). [D]

Cook, J., London, looking-glass and picture frame maker (1829–39). At 10 Mitchell St, St Luke's 1829–35. In 1835 moved to 2 Feather Lane, Holborn and in 1839 was at Eyre St Hill. [D]

Cook, James, Camomile St, London, carver (1766–67). Member of the Blacksmiths' Co. In 1766 licenced to employ three non-freemen for three months and in the following year held a licence to employ two to five freemen. [GL, City Licence bks, vol. 5]

Cook, James, 85 Old Market St, Bristol, looking-glass manufacturer (1805–09). [D]

Cook, James, Clipston St, Fitzroy Sq., London, cm (1828). Bankruptcy of James Cook and Zachariah Banister announced in *Chester Chronicle*, 1 August 1828.

Cook, Jeremiah, Colchester and London, u and chairmaker (1793–1839). Subscribed to Sheraton's *Drawing Book*, 1793. In London by 1806 when he was living in Lambeth. In 1828 at 230 Kent Rd, Southwark as a chair and sofa maker and in 1839 at 26 Church Rd, St George's in the East. [D; Colchester poll bks]

Cook, John, Stamford, Lincs., u (1735–d. 1762). Freeman of Stamford by purchase 1735. In 1762 it was announced by Robert Tymperon, cm of Stamford, that he had purchased the stock of Cook, deceased. [Freemen records; *Cambridge Chronicle*, 24 December 1762]

Cook, John, Mortlake, Surrey, shopkeeper and cm (1785–90). On 1 August 1785 took out insurance cover of £230 on his utensils and stock. In 1790 the figure was £150 out of a total sum insured of £500. [GL, Sun MS vol. 330, p. 387; ref. 570212]

Cook, John, Marsh (or March) Lane, Leeds, Yorks., joiner and cm (1798). [D]

Cook, John, Cirencester, Glos., u (1826–35). Children born 1826, 1828 and 1835. [PR (bapt.)]

Cook, John, Wincolmlee, Hull, Yorks., cm (1834–35). At 26 Wincolmlee in 1834 and no. 30 in 1835. [D]

Cook, John, 48 Kent St, Southwark, London, chair and sofa maker (1839). [D]

Cook, Joseph, London, cm (1793). Subscribed to Sheraton's *Drawing Book*, 1793.

Cook, Joseph, 59 Margaret St, Cavendish Sq., London, u (1813). [D]

Cook, Jos., Northgate, Sleaford, Lincs., joiner, builder and cm (1826). [D]

Cook, Robinson, High St, near the Exchange, Liverpool, u (1746–67). Free 2 May 1746. On 19 September 1747 took out insurance cover of £600 which included stock in trade. In 1754 subscribed to Chippendale's *Director*. Took an app. John Wood in 1757, and two other of his apps are recorded as petitioning for freedom: William Litherlad in 1761 and William Woods in 1767. [Freemen rolls; GL, Sun MS vol. 81, ref. 109496; S of G, app. index]

Cook, S., Star Corner, Bermondsey, London, bedstead maker (1820). [D]

Cook, Samuel, 19 Martletts Ct, Bow St, Covent Gdn, London, portable desk maker (1809). Took out insurance cover of £150 on his household goods, stock and utensils on 20 March 1809. [GL, Sun MS vol. 448, ref. 828684]

Cook, Samuel, 27 Little Alie St, Goodman's Fields, London, u

(1814–29). Until 1827 traded with a number of partners. Between 1814–17 the business is listed as Cook, Jenkins & Howard and in 1816 as Cook & Goring. In 1826 the title was yet again different with Cook & Judson being adopted. In June 1829 Cook was declared bankrupt. [D; *London Gazette*, 26 June 1829]

Cook, Samuel, Bennett's Ct, Bridewell Lane, Bristol, bedstead maker (1828). [D]

Cook, Samuel, 39 Aldermanbury, London, cm (1835). [D]

Cook, Thomas, Liverpool, chairmaker (1816). Married Miss Margaret Bentley, Vauxhall Rd, at St Nicholas Church 2 September 1816. [*Liverpool Mercury*, 6 September 1816]

Cook, Thomas, 6 Twisters Alley, Bunhill Row, London, cm and u (1839). [D]

Cook, Thomas Aquilas, 90 Hatton Gdn, London, carver and gilder (1839). [D]

Cook, Thomas, Adam & Eve St, Market Harborough, Leics., turner and chairmaker (1840). [D]

Cook, Vincent, Lowesmoor, Worcester, cm and u (1840). [D]

Cook, Walter, Close, Newcastle, joiner and cm (1811–27). [D]

Cook, William, Lancaster, gilder (1785–92). Named in Gillow records in 1785, 1787 and 1792. [Westminster Ref. Lib., Gillow vol. 344/96, p. 829; 344/94, p. 101]

Cook, William, London, cm (1793). Subscribed to Sheraton's *Drawing Book*, 1793.

Cook, William, Chelmsford, Essex, cm (1798). Baptism of son Richard 13 June 1789. [PR (bapt.)]

Cook, William, 28 Berwick St, Soho, London, cm and tea-chest maker (1808–20). [D]

Cook, William, 8 Denmark St, St Giles, London, cm and u (1822). [D]

Cooke, Charles, Nantwich, Cheshire, chairmaker (1756). Baptism of daughter Catherine 31 October 1756. [PR (bapt.)]

Cooke, Charles, Cirencester, Glos., cm (1829–36). Children bapt. 1829, 1831, 1833, 1836. [PR (bapt.)]

Cooke, Edward, Carlisle St, Soho Sq., London, chair and cabinet-maker (1809–28). Listed at 5 Carlisle St except for 1822 when number is given as 6. In 1822 trade listed as chair and sofa maker. [D]

Cooke, George, London, upholder (1739). Son of Thomas Cooke, freeman upholder. Free of the Upholders' Co. by patrimony on 5 April 1739. [GL, Upholders' Co. records]

Cooke, George, Lincoln, cm (1806). Free November 1806. [Freemen rolls]

Cooke, George, London, chair and sofa maker (1829–37). At 17 Cleveland St, Fitzroy Sq. in 1829. At this date also bedstead maker, and appears to have been in partnership with Thomas Cooke. By 1835 had moved to 5 Upper Marylebone St. [D]

Cooke, George, Town St, Thaxted, Essex, cm (1832). [D]

Cooke, Henry, High St, King's Lynn, Norfolk, cm and u (1822). [D]

Cooke, Henry, 36 New St, Birmingham, carver and gilder (1835). [D]

Cooke, Isaac, London, upholder (1722–38). Son of Abraham Cooke, freeman blacksmith. App. to George Friend 18 November 1715. Free by servitude 5 December 1722. Took app. John Holmes 1727 (free 1738). [GL, Upholders' Co. records]

Cooke, Isaac, Bath, Som., u and cm (1765–1778). Employed by John, 4th Duke of Bedford. Presented account for £30 in June 1765 in respect of work carried out for the Duke at Bath. Between June and August 1765 supplied goods and carried out work amounting to £578 2s 9d. Included in the bill were bedsteads, ash chairs, deal tables, night tables, toilet tables, mattresses, pillows, blankets, two dining tables, twelve French chairs, six French elbow chairs, a walnut bureau, cherry tree chairs and frames, and glasses for two pictures. Another bill dated November 1766 was for cherry tree chairs and deal stools and tables amounting to £86. Between 1766–70 Cooke continued to carry out work for the Duke, repairing furniture and textiles but on a much reduced scale with only £16 being charged for the whole period. [Bedford Office, London] In 1777–78 he supplied Bath Town Hall with a pattern table, three dozen chairs, two armchairs and set of thirty chairs. [Bath Corp. records]

Cooke, Isaac, Norwich, u (1766). Son of John Cooke, worsted weaver. Admitted freeman 30 November 1766. [Freemen reg.]

Cooke, J., Lancaster, trade unknown (1789). Named in the Gillow records. [Westminster Ref. Lib., Gillow vol. 344/95, p. 510]

Cooke, J., 4 Broad St, Bath, Som., u and auctioneer (1819–26). [D]

Cooke, Jacob, 'The Three Chairs', Little Tower Hill, London, u (d. 1748). Death of 'Mr Cooke, an eminent Upholster in the Minories, near Tower-Hill' reported in *General Advertiser*, 21 November 1748. His widow, 'Mrs Mary Cooke at the Three Chairs on Little Tower Hill . . . Mr Jacob C. being deceased', advertised in the same paper on 31 January 1749, stating: 'a good Upholsterer's shop, that has been so for nearly sixty years' was to be let and stock to be sold. [Heal]

Cooke, John, Chester, cm (1765–89). Free 18 February 1765 after serving as app. under Philip Prestbury of Chester, cm. By 1771 had set up in business in Eastgate St. Took apps named John Formstone and Thomas Latchford (free 1784) and James Gardner (free 1790); also Edward Williams from 1775. The business continued at the Eastgate St address until March 1782 when John Cooke announced that his shop had been disposed of to a person in a different line of trade necessitating the sale of his stock. This was disposed of in a three day sale at 'The Mitre' in Eastgate St. The stock to be auctioned without reserve consisted of 'Mahogany Wardrobes, Desks and Book-cases with Glass & Inlaid Doors; double chests with and without Desk-drawers; Mahogany Bureaus and Chests-of-drawers; neat inlaid commode Side-boards; Cisterns upon frames with brass hoops and handles; Mahogany Dining Tables in sets, with round and square ends; Single ditto; Card Tables, lined and plain; Tea Tables and Kitchen Stands; Ladies' Toilets; Gardevines of different sizes, with white square bottles; Neat inlaid Caddies and Tea-chests; Mahogany Knife-cases; Fire-Screens of different sorts; Bason-stands; Mahogany and japanned Tea-trays; Gentlemen's shaving-tables; Mahogany Night-tables and Chairs; Large Exercise Chairs, in Mahogany Frames and Springs; Tent, Camp and Settee Bedsteads with check furniture; Large easy Chairs; a large quantity of Mahogany Chairs with strip'd and plain bottoms; ditto Sofas; all kinds of Pier and Dressing Glasses, in oval and square frames; Clocks in Mahogany Cases; and a compleat Electrical Machine'. In October 1782 a further sale was held at Cooke's timber yard at the upper end of Werburgh Lane, where he also appears to have had a 'ware room'. Apart from mahogany in planks and veneers he had supplies of oak, elm and cherry wood. Other items offered included 'Bed-posts and Coffin Boards' and 'several Benches and Working tops'. A quantity of finished furniture was included in the sale, presumably the residue of the March auctions. Despite these sales Cooke did not retire from the trade but continued to carry on his business from his house in St John's St. He was already back in business in 1782 and continued for a further seven years. He also retained his yard and workshop in Werburgh Lane. In September 1789 the sale of his household furniture and goods 'consisting of every useful article essential for a large house' was announced, together with the yard and workshop. [D; poll bks; app. bks; freemen rolls; *Chester Chronicle*, 8 March 1782, 4 October 1782, 25 September 1789] B.A.

Cooke, John, 20 New St, Birmingham, carver, gilder, looking-glass and picture frame maker (1816–30). Listed also at 36 New St in 1828. [D]

Cooke, Joseph, Nantwich, Cheshire, cm (1806). Daughter Ann bapt. on 23 January 1806. [PR (bapt.)]

Cooke, Joseph, 40 Lower Brook St, London, u (1816). [D]

Cooke, Joseph, 53 Gt Marylebone St, London, u etc. (1820). [D]

Cooke, Joseph, 26 Major St, Manchester, cm (1825). [D]

Cooke, Joseph, 40 Manchester St, London, u (1835). [D]

Cooke, Joseph, 1 New St, Dorset Sq., London, cm (1837–39). [D]

Cooke, Joseph, Cambridge, cm (1839–40). At York St in 1839 but by the next year in King St. [D; poll bks]

Cooke, Joshua, London, cm and u (1762–79). Son of Caleb Cooke of Compton, Dorset. App. to Thomas Cooke, skinner, and admitted freeman of the Upholders' Co. under the 1750 Upholders' Act on 5 August 1762. His address in 1762 is given as Holborn but in the next two years he was in Shoe Lane. In 1766 at Little Moorgate which may be the same address as 3 Broker's Row, Moorfields which he occupied from 1769–75. In 1773 however an alternative address of 21 Pavement, Moorfields is listed. Moved in 1775 to 22 Cheapside and in 1778 was at 80 Holborn Bridge. Between 1762 and 1769 licenced to employ non-freemen. In 1763 and 1764 he held licences to employ fourteen non-freemen for six weeks each, but for other periods the number was fewer and from 1766 only two non-freemen were licenced. Took as app. Charles Morgan 1767–74. The business was ultimately unsuccessful and in November 1779 he is recorded as 'a poor Member' of the Upholders' Co. and a pensioner. [D; GL, Upholders' Co. records; City Licence bks, vols 3–6]

Cooke, Richard, Humberstone Gate, Leicester, cm (1828–29). [D]

Cooke, Robert, Gt Sutton St, Clerkenwell, London, cm (1780). In 1780 took app. named Mary Walker. [Westminster Ref. Lib., MS F 4309]

Cook(e), Robert & Thomas, Haymarket, Leicester, cm and u (1815–22). [D]

Cooke, Robert jnr, High St, Guildford, Surrey, cm and u (1818–26). [D; poll bk]

Cooke, Robert, Humberstone Gate, Leicester, u (1828). [D]

Cooke, Samuel, Manchester, timber dealer and cm (1832). Bankrupt 6 March 1832. [*Liverpool Mercury*, 9 March 1832]

Cooke, Samuel, Shambles, Worcester, chairmaker (1840). [D]

Cooke, Thomas, Fletching, Sussex, chairmaker (1673). Supplied two rush-bottomed chairs to Giles Moore, Rector of Horstead Keynes, Sussex on 29 March 1673. [R. Bird, ed., *The Journal of Giles Moore*, 1971, p. 16]

Cooke, Thomas, 'The Golden Key', Fleet Ditch, St Andrews, Holborn, London, u (1700–17). Free of the Upholders' Co. on 1 May 1700. Took apps named John Clarkson 1705–14 and John Heath 1706–17. He took another app. in 1713. Father of George Cooke (free 1739). [GL, Upholders' Co. records; S of G, app index]

Cooke, Thomas, Bewdley, Worcs., joiner and cm (1742). Took an app. in 1742. [S of G, app index]

Cooke, Thomas, London, cm and u (1746–64). In 1746 at 'The Crown & Cushion', Gt Queen St, Lincoln's Inn Fields. From this address he announced his intention of selling up his stock and going into partnership with 'Mr Nash at the Royal Bed, Holbourn-Bridge'. His stock and household furniture, sold by auction in September 1746, consisted of a 'Variety of Work in Walnut Tree and Mahogany, viz. Desks and Bookcases, Buroes, Chests of Drawers, a large Sortment of Tables, Chairs, Cloaths Chests, Pier-Glasses, Sconces and Chimney Glasses, Turky Carpets, Feather beds, Blankets etc.'. By 1753 he was trading on his own behalf at the Holborn Bridge address but from 1759–63 the business is listed as Thomas Cooke & Co. and from 1763 as Thomas & Joshua Cooke. The Joshua Cooke was probably a relative. He came from Compton in Dorset and was app. to Thomas Cooke. Thomas Cooke was licenced to employ five non-freemen for five months in 1762. He was one of two cm employed 1752–53 to furnish the new Mansion House. His billhead, used to invoice 'a neat square mahogany fly table', £1 12s to a Mrs Hucke, is in the Museum of London collection. In 1764 T. & J. Cooke were declared bankrupt. Thomas Cooke's name continues to appear at the Holborn address in London directories until 1768 but this may be an oversight of the publishers. Joshua Cooke established his own business and traded from various London addresses in the 1760s and 70s. [D; *General Advertiser*, 5 September 1746; GL, City Licence bks, vol. 3; *Conn.*, December 1952, p. 181; Museum of London, A15191; *Gents Mag.*, May 1764]

Cooke, Thomas, Cheltenham, Glos., cm and u (1818–30). In 1818 advertised that he had warerooms at Portland Passage and declared himself 'cabinet & upholstery manufacturer to his Highness, Duke of Gloucester'. His trade card [Banks Coll., BM] also makes this claim but lists the address as 2 Colonnade. By the 1820s he was in partnership with John Cooke but the business was declared bankrupt on 21 December 1824. Trading again in 1830 at 1 Bedford Buildings, also as 'manufacturer of patent elastic stuffing'. [D; *Liverpool Mercury*, 31 December 1824]

Cooke, Thomas & John, 2 Colonnade, Cheltenham, Glos., cm and u (1822). [D]

Cooke, Thomas, Hereford, carver and gilder (1822–35). At Wye Bridge St in 1822 and in St John St, 1830–35. A receipt exists for £1 8s, dated 23 August 1826 paid by Capt. N. L. Pateshall RN, for 'framing etc. a carved Picture'. [D; Herefs. RO, F60/33]

Cooke, Thomas, Manor Row, Tower Hill, London, cm (1826–28). [D]

Cooke, Thomas, 5 Duke St, Brighton, Sussex, chairmaker and turner (1826–27). [D]

Cooke, Thomas, Leicester, cm and u (1828–35). Trading at Eastgate in 1828 and Cank St in 1835. [D]

Cooke, Thomas, Liverpool, chairmaker (1829–35). At 53 Marylebone in 1829 and 1 Musker Ct, Bevington Bush in 1835. [D]

Cooke, Thomas, St Marygate North, Grimsby, Lincs., joiner and cm (1835). [D]

Cooke, William, 'The Two Trees', the lower end of Devonshire St, near St George's Chapel, London, u (1712). [Heal]

Cooke, William, London, upholder (1726–33). Son of John Cooke of Warwick, weaver. App. to Purbeck Savage 2 December 1718 and turned over to J. Sanderson, freeman draper, 11 May 1720. Free of the Upholders' Co. by servitude, 5 October 1726. Probably the William Cooke concerned in a Chancery suit against Thomas Jobber of Aston, Salop, in 1732–33. [GL, Upholders' Co. records; *Furn. Hist.*, 1979]

Cooke, William, Oxford, cm and u (1802–30). In 1802 listed in the parish of St Peter's in the East. From 1805–30 trading in the High St. In the accounts of Lincoln College are recorded payments of £99 in 1815, £50 on account in 1815–16 and £50 as the final balance on furnishings for the Common Room in 1816–17. [D; poll bk]

Cooke & Co., Albion St, Cheltenham, Glos., cabinet turner (1839). [D]

Cooke & Sutton, 40 Lower Brook St, London, u (1814–15). [D]

Cookes, William, Warwick and Leamington, cm and u (1816–35). In business at Warwick in 1816 and in 1828 his address is recorded as Low Church St. From 1822–30 at Ranelagh St, Leamington. Trading as Cookes & Sons at 34 Warwick St, Leamington, in 1834. [D]

Cookman, —, Ashen Tree Ct, Whitefriars, London, u (1689–90). In February 1690 it was stated that he had 'a Colonel's Tent and a Captain's Tent to be sold'. [Heal; *London Gazette*, 27 February 1690]

Cookman, Giles, Castle St, Salisbury, Wilts., cm and u (1839). [D]

Cookman, Henry, Parkstone, Poole, Dorset, cm and u (1840). [D]

Cooknall, John, London, chairmaker and victualler (1761). Said to be formerly of Tothill Fields, Westminster and late of Mint St, Southwark at the time of his discharge from Debtors' Prison on 18 April 1761. [*London Gazette*]

Cooks, James, St Aldgate's St, Gloucester, cm and chairmaker (1820). [D]

Cooks, Thomas, Gloucester, cm (1820). Child bapt. in 1820. [PR (bapt.)]

Cooks & Sons, 34 Warwick St, Leamington, Warks., cm and u (1837). [D]

Cookson, James, Blackpool, Lancs., joiner and cm (1834). [D]

Cookson, John, Liverpool, cm (1827–39). Son of Thomas Cookson, clockmaker. Free 16 October 1827. At 18 Upper Pitt St in 1835 but in 1837 the number is recorded as 26 with additional premises at 23 Lambert St. In 1839 only the Lambert St address is listed. [D]

Cookson, Richard, Lytham, Lancs., joiner and cm (1825). [D]

Cooling, William, Holywell, Oxford, upholder (1802). [Poll bk]

Coolridge, William, Windsor St, Chertsey, Surrey, cm and paperhanger (1839). [D]

Coombe, J., Butcher Row, Exeter, Devon, cm (1791). [D]

Coombes, J. J., 49 Holywell St, Strand, London, carver and gilder (1839). [D]

Coombes, Stephen, James St, Southampton, Hants., cm (1839). [D]

Coombes, William, Load St, Bewdley, Worcs., cm (1822). [D]

Coomes & Son, 15 Charlotte St, Fitzroy Sq., London, u, appraiser and undertaker (1811–27). [D]

Cooper, —, Chatsworth, Derbs., u (1699–1704). The Chatsworth accounts show an u named Cooper working on an extensive scale from 1699–1704. The accounts mention an annual wage of £30 in 1704 suggesting that Cooper was probably resident during this period and concentrating all his efforts on the Chatsworth commissions. The earliest entries are for 28 September 1699 when Cooper was paid £35 for a 'skreen' and £43 14s for '2 bills for the new bed'. In 1701 several payments were made for making and altering furniture and he is recorded working in conjunction with other craftsmen. Payment was made in July 1702 to 'Mr Buxton for Silk thread, galloone etc. for Mr Cooper upholsterer' and Cooper's expenses for travelling to London were met. Matthew and Robert Carver were paid for 59 days at 9d per day for assisting 'Mr Cooper to make up furniture'. The next year Cooper travelled to Manchester at the Duke of Devonshire's expense 'to buy Manchester goods' which included 300 yards of baize for covering for chairs costing £15 5s 9d. In 1704 he was varnishing and gilding chair frames, cleaning and mending locks and supplying blue and red silk lace 'to finish Chapel closet'. [Chatsworth papers, account bks]

Cooper, —, address unknown, cm (1754). Subscribed to Chippendale's *Director*, 1754. The identification with Joseph Cooper at 'The Crown & Bowl', Snow Hill, London, would seem unlikely as he was a turner and not involved with cabinet or upholstery work.

Cooper, —, London, cm (1793). Subscribed to Sheraton's *Drawing Book*, 1793. Might be either Benjamin Cooper of Warner St, Cold Bath St or John Cooper of 3 St Michael's Alley.

Cooper, Mrs, Plymouth, Devon, cm (1798). [D]

Cooper, Benjamin, London, cm etc. (1789–93). In 1789 at 6 Little Warner St, Cold Bath St where he was described as a cm and fret cutter. Between 1792 and 93 he was at 101 Goswell St but is also shown in 1793 at 1 Warner St, Cold Bath St. [D]

Cooper, C., Lancaster, trade not recorded (1827). [Westminster Ref. Lib., Gillow vol. 344/102, p. 3618]

Cooper, Daniel snr, London, upholder (1706–23). Father of Daniel Cooper jnr, who served under him as an upholder, 1716–23. In 1714 took out insurance cover of £300 on his newly built dwelling house situated on the west side of Littlewood St in the parish of St Alban, Wood St. In July 1721 however he was insuring for a similar sum a house on the south side of Cornhill. He was paid £16 10s in 1706 for repairs at St Michael's, Queenhithe, London. [GL, Upholders' Co. records; Hand in Hand MS vol. 13, p. 215; vol. 24, p. 56; *Wren Soc.*, Vol. XIX, p. 43]

Cooper, Daniel jnr, London, upholder (1723). Son of Daniel Cooper snr, freeman and member of the Upholders' Co. App. to his father 25 March 1716 and free by servitude 2 October 1723. [GL, Upholders' Co. records]

Cooper, Edward, London, clock case maker (1776–90). In 1776 at Sun Ct, Cloth Fair and in this year insured his utensils and stock for £50 out of an entire insurance cover of £300. Between 1779 and 1790 at Gt Sutton St, Clerkenwell. Here in 1779 he took out insurance cover of £500 of which £150 was in respect of utensils and stock and £50 for his workshop. [GL, Sun MS vol. 279, p. 311]

Cooper, Edward, Lancaster, cm (1799–1836). Free 1799–1800. Named in Gillow records between 1812–36. [Westminster Ref. Lib., Gillow]

Cooper, Edward jnr, Lancaster, trade not known (1835). Named in Gillow records. [Westminster Ref. Lib., Gillow vol. 344/103, p. 5009]

Cooper, Francis, Wolverhampton, Staffs., joiner and cm (1833–38). Listed at Lichfield St in 1833. [D]

Cooper, Francis, Woodridge Rd, Ipswich, Suffolk, cm and u (1839). [D]

Cooper, George, Stratford-upon-Avon, Warks. (1759). Mulberry wood tea caddy commemorating Shakespeare, signed and dated sold by Christie's, NY, 31 January 1981, lot 74.

Cooper, George, London, carver and gilder, glass grinder and looking-glass manufacturer (1784–1839). At 8 Lombard St in 1784 but by 1785 the number had changed to 82. In 1809 moved to 12 George Ct, Piccadilly and subsequently shown at 42 Piccadilly 1811–14, 43 Piccadilly 1815–20 and 36 Piccadilly 1821–39. In 1811 referred to as Cooper & Co. and it is likely because of the long duration of the business that more than one George Cooper was involved. The firm's trade label is known [Symonds papers, Winterthur, Delaware] from the 82 Lombard St address. This states, 'Looking glasses and all sorts of frames with carving and gilding by George Cooper, real manufacturer . . . Coach and sash glasses on the shortest notice, old looking glasses new silvered, or the full value given for them'. A pair of shield-shaped gilt mirrors, one labelled, was included in the Parke-Bernet sale 13 May 1954, lot 481. During the 1830s the firm was involved with work at Windsor Castle. This commenced in 1831 when re-japanning, graining and varnishing several items of furniture was charged at £9 19s 9d. In September 1832 the gilding of a large chimney glass and the painting and varnishing of old bedsteads ends and further furniture renovation is listed. In December 1837 a payment of £30 10s is recorded for two composition and gold screens to display pieces of needlework. A further payment was made on 30 June 1839 for staining and varnishing oak furniture, preparing, painting and varnishing chiffoniers, bookcases, a press and bedsteads. Cooper also supplied goods and carried out work at Panshanger, Herts., 1835–36. Amongst the items supplied was a 'richly ornamented gilt chimney glass frame' costing £30. He was also paid £7 10s 6d by the 3rd Lord Braybrooke of Audley End, Essex in December 1833. [D; Wills, *Looking-Glasses*; PRO, LC11/77, 11/98; RA, box 1/2; Herts. RO, Panshanger papers, box 56; Essex RO, D/DBy/A358, A363]

Cooper, George, Blackfriargate, Hull, Yorks., cm (1790–91). [D]

Cooper, George, 32 Brick Lane, Old St, London, cm (1820–29). In 1820 listed as a caddy maker. [D]

Cooper, George, Carlisle St, St Anne, Soho, London, u (1834). [Marylebone Lib., deed 15/45]

Cooper, H. W., address unknown, (c. 1785). A Hepplewhite-style oval backed mahogany armchair at Temple Newsam House, Leeds, has this name impressed on the seat rail. [Gilbert, *Leeds Furn. Cat.*, vol. 1, pp. 93–95; V & A archives]

Cooper, Henry, London and Canterbury, Kent, u (1818–30). In London in June 1818, but in the parish of St Martin, Canterbury, June 1830. Freeman of Canterbury. [Canterbury poll bks]

Cooper, Henry, East St, Horsham, Sussex, chairmaker and turner (1832–39). [D]

Cooper, Henry, Parliament St, Nottingham, carver and gilder (1835). [D]

Cooper, Henry, 14 Grindlegate, Sheffield, Yorks., cm and broker. (1837). [D]

Cooper, Henry L., 93 Bishopsgate St Within, London, cm, u, carver and gilder, estate agent and undertaker (1828–30). An ambitious maker whose advertisements in the local press matched his claim to wait upon families 'in any part of the United Kingdom'. His advertisements have been recorded in London, Brighton, Chester, Southampton and Liverpool newspapers. His stock and skills appear to have embraced every field of house furnishing and other fields as well. His upholstery department featured 'the improved Elastic Steel Stuffing for Carriage Cushions, Chairs, Sofas, Mattresses &c. in addition to a handsome assortment of Bedstead Furniture, Window Cornices, Curtains &c.'. Cabinet goods were produced of 'the first quality and Materials' and 'Solid Furniture' supplied 'for Foreign Climates'. Cabins of ships were fitted up 'with Elegance and Despatch'. Carpets, looking-glasses, carving and gilding, paper hanging and painting all came within Henry Cooper's sphere. Services offered included funerals, a house agency, sales and appraisements, the collection of rents and the warehousing of furniture. He claimed the patronage of 'some of the first Families in the Kingdom' and stated that 'for style and price' his stock 'challenges competition with any respectable establishment'. The short duration of the business might however suggest that it was not the great success that its proprietor assumed. [D; *Brighton Herald*, 23 February, 19 August, 3 May, 28 June, 12 July 1828; *Liverpool Mercury*, 17 October 1828; *Chester Chronicle*, 9 May 1829; *Southampton Advertiser*, October 1829; *Court Guide to London*, 1830]

Cooper, J., Sevenoaks, Kent, chairmaker (1803). [D]

Cooper, J., Chester, upholder (1819). [Poll bk]

Cooper, J., 1 Lucklom Buildings, Bath, Som., chair and couch maker (1826). [D]

Cooper, J., 23 Little Russell St, Bloomsbury, London, carver (1829). [D]

Cooper, James, London, upholder (1710). Admitted freeman of the Upholders' Co., 1 March 1709/10. [GL, Upholders' Co. records]

Cooper, James, Shrewsbury, Salop, cm and u (1786–1835). At Wyle Cop from 1786 to 1814. In 1835–36 at Princes St. The long span of trading might suggest that there was more than one James Cooper. [D; freemen rolls]

Cooper, James, High Wycombe, Bucks., chairmaker (b. c. 1796–1841). Two sons and three daughters bapt. 1825–34. Aged 45 at the time of the 1841 Census. [PR (bapt.)]

Cooper, James, Market Pl., Hitchin, Herts., carver and gilder (1839). [D]

Cooper, James Winter, 30 West St, Hull, Yorks., cm (1838–40). Listed also at no. 82 in 1840. [D]

Cooper, John, Bedford St, London, picture frame maker (1723). A receipt exists for the supply of sixteen peartree frames with gold edges which were charged at 7d a foot for the 112 ft of framing used. Possibly for Montrose. [Scottish RO, GD 129/Box 10/35/25]

Cooper, John, London, upholder and cm (1768–1798). Son of Cooper of St Clement, East Cheap, freeman joiner. App. to Charles Greenwood on 1 December 1768 and admitted freeman of the Upholders' Co. by servitude, 6 December 1775. In 1776 he is recorded at 20 Gt East Cheap and in 1778 at Rood Lane. The following year his address was Clements Lane. He first appeared in London directories in 1784 at 3 St Michael's Alley, Cornhill and traded at this address until his bankruptcy in April 1798. In 1802 he was shown living at 38 Cornhill. Insurance records show a business of moderate size with £500 cover (£250 stock and utensils) in 1777 and £700 (£400 stock and utensils) in 1780. [D; GL, Sun MS vol. 255, p. 75; vol. 285, p. 130; Upholders' Co. records]

Cooper, John, Boston, Lincs., cm and u (1786–87). In December 1786 he announced that he had just opened his business after a period in the trade in London. He claimed to have 'a large quantity and great variety of mahogany, satin, purple, king and tulip woods: all kind of stain'd woods, stringing and shells'. He also advertised for 'Three or Four Hands' and an app. In July 1787 he once more advertised for staff stating that he required immediately 'Six Journeyman CABINET MAKERS and CHAIR CARVERS' who were offered permanent employment at London rates. He also needed an app. and a turner 'who is handy at making Chairs and Wheels, and everything in that Branch'. Next month he advertised that he required immediately 'Eight Journeymen Cabinet-makers' and 'A Pair of SAWYERS, that is used to Sawing Mahogany Veneers &c.'. [*Lincoln, Rutland and Stamford Mercury*, 22 December 1786, 20 July, 17 August 1787]

Cooper, John, parish of St Mary, Bungay, Suffolk, cm (1787). Married in 1787. [Suffolk RO, FAA: 50/2/107]

Cooper, John, Maidenhead, Berks., carpenter and cm (1791). On 21 February 1791 took out insurance cover for £800. [GL, Sun MS vol. 374, ref. 580403]

Cooper, John, High Wycombe, Bucks., chairmaker (1798). [Militia Census]

Cooper, John, Lancaster, cm (1813–18). Named in Gillow records 1813 and 1815. Free 1817–18. [Westminster Ref. Lib., Gillow; freemen rolls]

Cooper, John, Brook(e) St, Derby, cm and u (1818–22). [D]

Cooper, John, 11 Cross St, Newington, London, bedstead maker (1820–26). [D]

Cooper, John, Stoney St, Nottingham, cm and u (1822). [D]

Cooper, John & Son, Bell St, Henley-on-Thames, Oxon., cm and u (1823–30). [D]

Cooper, John, Nottingham, carver and gilder (1828–32). Listed at Parliament St in 1828 and 19 Broad St in 1832. [D]

Cooper, John, 3 London Rd, Southwark, London, u (1835). [D]

Cooper, Joseph, Cornhill, London, u (1728–31). Received £6 in March 1729, £95 in November 1729 and £23 12s in July 1730 for 'upholsterer's work' at East India House, London. [Heal; *Apollo*, November 1965, p. 405]

Cooper, Joseph, 'The Crown & Bowl', facing St Sepulchre's Church, Snow Hill, London, wood and ivory turner (c. 1760). Trade Card in Heal Coll., BM. Included amongst his wares were 'Powder Boxes, Tea Boards, Dressing Boxes & Tea Chests of the most Curious English & Foreign Woods'. [Heal]

Cooper, Joseph, London, carver, gilder, looking-glass maker, cm and u (1761–1828). From 1761 to 1797 at 20 Noble St, Foster Lane. In 1761 he was licenced to employ three non-freemen for three months and took out further licences to employ two non-freemen in 1762–63 and 1767. First mentioned in directories in 1763. In 1777 shown to have additional premises at 9 Fitchet Ct. Up to 1795 appears to have been solely a carver and gilder and as such concerned with the manufacture of looking-glasses. In 1795 for the first time cabinet wares are mentioned. In 1802 moved to 107 Bishopgate Within and after 1820 the number changed to 93. It was in this period that the trading style of the business changed. From 1814 the business was called Cooper & Co. and certainly by 1817 he had a partner called Elliott, hence the use of the name Cooper, Elliott & Co. The partnership may not have lasted long for by 1822 the business was trading as Joseph Cooper & Son. A trade card from the 93 Bishopsgate address is in the Towneley papers. Their stock included a 'Variety of Solid Portable Furniture, Improved Light Beds for the East & West Indies, An elegant assortment of Brussels and Turkey Carpeting, Floor Cloth etc.'. They also advertised themselves as Appraisers, Undertakers and Paper-hangers. The trade card shows an engraving of their business premises consisting of a double fronted shop with central doorway and above three stories. [D; GL, City Licence bks, vols 2, 3 and 5; Preston RO, Towneley papers, box 10]

Cooper, Joseph, Birmingham, cm (1761–93). At 26 High St, 1764–80 and in Summer Lane, 1770 and 1793. In 1761 took app. named Lemon. [S of G, app. index]

Cooper, Joseph, 37 Bishopsgate Within, London, u and cm (1786–96). Free of the Upholders' Co. under the 1750 Upholders' Act, 22 November 1786. Subscribed to Sheraton's *Drawing Book*, 1793. [D; GL, Upholders' Co. records]

Cooper, Joseph, Derby, cm, joiner and u (1783–95). In 1783 in the parish of St Peter where he took out insurance cover for £200 of which £100 was in respect of utensils and stock. In April 1795 announced that he had moved from this address and was now at St Mary's Gate in the parish of All Saints. He was also adding upholstery to the work that he undertook and in this connection had 'engaged a person from London, duly qualified to execute that business in all its branches'. In 1793 he is recorded as a subscriber to Sheraton's *Drawing Book*. [D; GL, Sun MS vol. 313, p. 170; *Derby Mercury*, 16 April 1795]

Cooper, Osborn, Guanock Terr., King's Lynn, Norfolk, cm (1836). [D]

Cooper, Philip, Chester, carver (1704). Son of Richard Cooper of Chester, gardener. App. to Thomas Davies, carver, and free 6 May 1704. [Freemen rolls]

Cooper, Richard, Trippet, Hull, Yorks., joiner, cm and victualler (1826). As a victualler maintained the 'Wellington', Witham. [D]

Cooper, Richard, William St, Stockton-on-Tees, Co. Durham, cm (1832). [D]

Cooper, Robert, Lancaster, cm (1779–84). App. to J. Wakefield in 1768 and free 1779–80. [Lancaster app. reg.; freemen reg.; poll bk]

Cooper, S., 9 Knightsbridge, London, carver, gilder and looking-glass maker to His Majesty. Early 19th-century trade card in Banks Coll., BM.

Cooper, Samuel, Cox and Stoole Row, Nottingham, haberdasher and cm (1732). On 24 November took out insurance cover of £100. [GL, Sun MS vol. 37, ref. 59431]

Cooper, Samuel, Lancaster, trade not known (1787–1822). Named in Gillow records 1787–1811 and 1816–22. [Westminster Ref. Lib., Gillow]

Cooper, Samuel, 55 Lothbury, London, carver, gilder and looking-glass maker (1819–20). [D]

Cooper, Samuel, Ringwood, Hants., cm (1839). [D]

Cooper, Stephen, 10 Grindlegate, Sheffield, Yorks., cm and furniture broker (1833). [D]

Cooper, T., Arundel, Sussex, cm and auctioneer (1839). [D]

Cooper, Thomas, London, upholder (1733–41). Son of John Cooper of Holmes Chapel, Chester, 'finer of iron'. App. to William Spurreet on 18 October 1733 and admitted freeman of the Upholders' Co. by servitude, 4 March 1741. [GL, Upholders' Co. records]

Cooper, Thomas, address unknown, u (1750–d. by 1754). On 15 July 1754 the Countess of Oxford paid £260 9s to the executors of Thomas Cooper, deceased, for wages and upholsterer's work. Payments in 1750 of £48 6s 1½d and £14 8s 6d by the same patroness are recorded. [Notts. RO, DD 5P, 14/1–2]

Cooper, Thomas, Chandos St, Westminster, London, cm (1774). [Poll bk]

Cooper, Thomas, High Wycombe, Bucks., chairmaker (1798–1817). Recorded in the Militia Census, 1798. Daughter bapt. in 1817. [PR (bapt.)]

Cooper, Thomas, Gildengate, Norwich, cm and house broker (1805). [D]

Cooper, Thomas, King's Lynn, Norfolk, u (1810). App. to James Oldmeadow, u, and free 1810–11. [Freemen reg.]

Cooper, Thomas, 25 Russell St, Bloomsbury, London, carver (1820). [D]

Cooper, Thomas, Broad St, Reading, Berks., cm (1820). [Poll bk]

Cooper, Thomas, Helmsley Gate, Yorks., joiner and cm (1823). [D]

Cooper, Thomas, High St, Halstead, Essex, cm (1823–39). [D]

Cooper, Thomas, Lancaster, carver (1824–25). [Freemen reg.]

Cooper, Thomas, 4 Haddon Pl., Gt Waterloo St, London, bed and mattress maker (1827). [D]

Cooper, Thomas, address unknown, japanner (1831–32). Employed at Windsor 1831–32. In June 1831 received payment for re-japanning old chests of drawers, wash hand stands, sundry old chairs and painting and graining shelves for which £10 18s 6d was paid. For similar work £21 17s 6d was paid on 30 September 1831. On 31 December 1832 he received 3s 6d for painting and varnishing a flower stand. Also employed at Hampton Court varnishing and cleaning walnut stools, chairs, fire screens etc. for which £2 3s was paid. [Windsor Royal Archives]

Cooper, Thomas, Newport, Salop, cm (1835). [PR (bapt.)]

Cooper, Thomas, London Rd, near the Blind School, London, bed and mattress maker (1837). [D]

Cooper, William, Lancaster (1801–35). Named in Gillow records 1801, 1806–07, 1810, 1812–29 and 1831–35. [Westminster Ref. Lib., Gillow]

Cooper, William, Dyer St, Blackfriars Rd, London, cm (1808). [D]

Cooper, William, High Wycombe, Bucks., chairmaker (b. c. 1791–1841). Three daughters and two sons bapt.

1814–23. Aged 50 at the time of the 1841 Census. [PR (bapt.)]

Cooper, William, Newcastle-under-Lyme, Staffs., cm (1823–32). [Poll bks]

Cooper, William, 6 Gt Shaw St, Preston, Lancs., cm (1825). [D]

Cooper, William, Henley-on-Thames, Oxon., u (1834). [Oxford RO, Mercer III/iii/10–11]

Cooper & Son, Wyle Cop, Shrewsbury, Salop, cm etc. (1822). [D]

Coopland, Richard, Liverpool, cm (1759). In 1759 took app. named Breckett. [S of G, app. index]

Cooqus, John, address unknown, u (c. 1670–80). Worked for the court. Maker of Nell Gwyn's bed, the largest piece of silver furniture made in England. [Conn., November 1934]

Coote, Benjamin, 104 Tottenham Ct Rd, London, cm and u (1839). [D]

Coote, John, Cheping (or Chipping) Hill, Witham, Essex, cm and u (1832–39). [D]

Coote, R., Petworth, Sussex, turner and chairmaker (1729). An inventory of his shop stock included sixteen chairs valued at 15s 4d. [Sussex Arch. Collections, 1960, p. 102]

Coote, William, parish of St Giles, Cambridge, clockcase maker (d. 1831). [Cambridge Univ. Lib., WR 19:410]

Cootes, I. C., 104 Tottenham Ct Rd, London, u and house agent (1837). [D]

Cope, Edward, Market St, Lane End, Staffs., cm (1822). [D]

Cope, Francis, 3 Cope St, Oxford Mkt, London, u and undertaker (1817). [D]

Cope, Henry, Crown St, St Ives, Hunts., u (1839–40). [D]

Cope, James, Milton St, Nottingham, cm (1832–40). [D]

Cope, Joseph, Husband St, Westminster, London, cm (1784). [Poll bk]

Cope, Richard & Gray, Alexander, 10 King St, Bloomsbury, London, upholders and cm (1782–1811). In 1782 took out insurance cover for £300 of which £200 was in respect of utensils, stock and goods in trust. Four years later the figures were £700 and £500 respectively. Listed by Sheraton amongst the master cabinet makers in his Cabinet Dictionary, 1803. [D; GL, Sun MS vol. 298, p. 389; vol. 338, p. 470]

Cope, Thomas, 3 Norris St, Liverpool, cm (1834). [D]

Cope, William, London, upholder (1712–25). Admitted freeman of the Upholders' Co., 13 February 1711/12. Took app. also named William Cope, on 2 February 1725. Master of the Upholders' Co. 1750. [GL, Upholders' Co. records; S of G, app. index]

Cope, William, London, upholder (1735–86). Son of Henry Cope of Langer, Notts., grazier. App. to William Cope 2 February 1725 and free of the Upholders' Co. by servitude 4 February 1735. Took as apps Thomas Scott, 1746–54; Samuel Garton 1756–69; James Porter, 1761–86; and Thomas Williams in 1761. Master of the Upholders' Co. 1770. [GL, Upholders' Co. records]

Cope, William, Market St, Lane End, Staffs., cm (1822). [D]

Copeland, Charles, York, carver and gilder (1756–84). Son of Charles Copeland, paver. App. to Charles Mitley, carver and gilder, 26 March 1749. Shown at Beddern in 1758, Newby in 1774 and Monk Bar in 1784. [York app. reg.; poll bks]

Copeland, James, Upgate, Louth, Lincs., cm, joiner and builder (1826–28). [D]

Copeland, Joseph, Whitehaven, Cumb., (1798). [D]

Copeland, Richard snr, Liverpool, cm (1741–54). In 1741 took app. named Southworth and in 1754 another named Marsh. [S of G, app. index]

Copeland, Richard jnr, Liverpool, joiner and cm (1761–d. 1779). Free on 9 February 1761. Took apps Thomas Battersby (free 1768) and Samuel Holland (free 1768), both from London. Died 1779 and his stock was sold

by auction on 29 September at 'BANNER's GREAT ROOM, the Fleece in Dale-Street'. A total of 108 lots were put up for sale, many of which were sets of chairs both walnut and mahogany. Some case furniture was included comprising dressing chests, desks and night tables etc. Many small cabinet wares were also on offer with a range of 'beautiful MACHEE Square and Oval TRAYS, WAITERS, TEA CADIES, &c.'. [Freemen reg. and committee bk; Liverpool RO, Gregson papers, 920 GRE 3/1 13]

Copeland, Robert, Liverpool, cm (1766–d. 1796). Initially traded from an address in High St but by 1772 had moved to 36 Lord St. The number in Lord St from 1781 was 32. He was probably associated for part of the period that he was trading with a Richard Copeland. In 1772–73 he is shown living also at 36 Lord St and trading as a house painter. A directory of 1781 lists the business as Richard & Robert Copeland and another in 1783 as Robert Copeland & Co. Robert Copeland took as apps Thomas Brown (free 1780) and William Hughes (free 1786). In January 1780 advertised that he was receiving details of outstanding debts of the late Richard Copeland to whom he must have been closely related. A month later he advertised for letting a house at 37 Lord St together with 'a large timber yard, saw-pit, & work shops at the back thereof, convenient for a Joiner or Cabinet-maker, now occupied by R. Copeland. Likewise the HOUSE, No. 36, next adjoining the above mentioned House'. The reason for letting is not clear, for although in the next year he is found at 31 and 32 Lord St, this may be a re-numbering rather than an actual move. The business continued to trade until 1791 when Robert Copeland announced that he was 'declining business'. An auction sale was arranged for 5 and 6 May 1791 at the Great Room at the Hotel, Lord St, where there was on sale 'A LARGE and CAPITAL ASSORTMENT OF Inlaid and Plain MAHOGANY FURNITURE'. A few pier and other glasses were included. On 23 May an auction sale of his timber stock and equipment was held at his yard in Lord St. Amongst the items offered were 'MAHOGANY in planks & boards; a great variety of valuable Veneers; Oak & Deal Boards of different thicknesses; Maple Plank & Boards, Bed-stuff of Different sorts; Some Cardivines & Chests for the Guinea trade, Windsor Chairs ready to put together; Some new & old six & four panelled Doors, some old sash frames & sashes with glass; framed saws etc. belonging to the saw pit; Work Benches, Iron Cramps, Screws etc'. Died December 1796. [D; freemen's committee bks; Williamson's Liverpool Advertiser, 28 January 1780, 18 February 1780, 2 May 1791, 16 May 1791; Billinge's Liverpool Advertiser, 19 December 1796; Liverpool RO, Gregson papers, 920 GRE 3/1, 14] B.A.

Copeland, Thomas, Burslem (or The Potteries), Staffs., cm and chairmaker (1818–28). Listed at Market Pl., 1818–22, and Queen St in 1828. [D]

Copeland, William, Darwen's Wient, Liverpool, cm (1767–69). [D]

Copeland, William, Queen St, Burslem, Staffs., chairmaker (1834–35). [Gatini]

Copini, Gatini, London, carver, gilder and looking-glass and barometer maker (1829–40). At 217 High St, Shoreditch, 1829–39 but in 1839 took additional premises at 280 High Holborn. [D; Goodison, Barometers]

Copland, Henry, Gutter Lane, Cheapside, London, engraver and designer (1720–d. 1753). Trained as a silver engraver. App. to goldsmiths in 1720 and 1724. His engraved work popularised the Rococo style. In 1746 he published in conjunction with Bucksher A New Book Of Ornaments. Much better known is his liason with Matthias Lock, the carver and designer. In 1752 they co-operated in the publication of an important design book under the same title as that used for the 1746 book. The only subsequent publication known of interest to furniture historians is the inclusion in Robert Manwaring's *The Chair-Maker's Guide*, 1776, of designs by Copland for hall chairs (pls 58A–59C). [*Furn. Hist.*, 1979; V & A, *Rococo Exhib.*, 1984, D29, p. 323, fn.20]

Coplep, John, Burton-upon-Trent, Staffs., u (1839). Declared bankrupt, *Liverpool Mercury*, 13 February 1829.

Copley, Charles, 33 Hatton Wall, London, cm and u (1827). [D]

Copley, John, Burton-upon-Trent, Staffs., u and cm (1828–29). Trading at High St in 1828. Declared bankrupt, *Chester Chronicle*, 13 February 1829.

Copley, Samuel, Leicester, cm (1782–90). App. to John Shipley in 1782, and admitted freeman, 1790. [Freemen reg.]

Copley, William, 20 Storey St, Southwark, London, cm and u (1839). [D]

Coppard, Lawrence, Brighton, Sussex, carver, gilder and looking-glass maker (1832–40). At 143 North St, 1832–39, then at 160. Daughter, Fanny, bapt. on 23 October 1833, and son Charles Lawrence on 18 May 1836. [D; PR (bapt.)]

Coppell, James, 19 Ben Jonson St, Liverpool, chairmaker (1821). [D]

Coppell, John, 44 Addison St, Liverpool, chairmaker (1816). [D]

Coppell, Richard, Liverpool, cm (1780–c. 1820). App. to John Eden and free 13 September 1780. [Freemen reg.]

Copple, Richard, Penketh, Warrington, Lancs., cm (1825). [D]

Corben, John, 8 Little James St, Bedford Row, London, chair and sofa maker (1826–27). [D]

Corben, Thomas, Broad St, Brighton, Sussex, cm (1837). [Poll bk]

Corbett, Alexander, High St, Southwark, London, cm (1784). [Bristol poll bk]

Corbett, Edward, Cooken St, Worcester, cm (1818–35). Free 1818. [Freemen rolls]

Corbett, George, London, upholder (1742). Son of George Corbett of the parish of St Martin-in-the-Fields, London, Gent. App. to Thomas Dobyns on 5 February 1734 and free of the Upholders' Co. by servitude, 2 June 1742. [GL, Upholders' Co. records]

Corbett, John, Chetwynd End, Newport, Salop, cm and u (1828). May also have kept the Bridge Tavern, Newport. [D]

Corbett, Thomas, 198 St John St, Clerkenwell, London, cm (1803). [D]

Corbett, Thomas, Bye St, Hereford, u (1830). Admitted freeman 1 February 1830. Married Ann, widow of James Woakes of Hereford, u and freeman. [D; freemen reg.]

Corbett, William, London, upholder (1771). Son of Matthias Corbett of Hampton, Middlx., baker. App. first to John Francklin and then to Thomas Silk, upholder and freeman. Free of the Upholders' Co. by servitude, 5 June 1771. [GL, Upholders' Co. records]

Corbett, William, West St, Oundle, Northants., cm and joiner (1823). [D]

Corbet(t), William, 8 Garratt Rd, Manchester, cm (1836–38). [D]

Corbin, John, Brighton, Sussex, cm (1827–39). At Cavendish Sq., in 1827, Meeting House Lane in 1831 and 21 Russell Sq., in 1839. By November 1839 had moved again to Union Pl. Son Henry bapt. on 26 August 1827 and Charles, 13 November 1831. [D; PR (bapt.)]

Corbitt, John, Bilston, Staffs., joiner and cm (1793). [D]

Corcorine, Philip, 43 Lumber St, Liverpool, joiner and cm (1834). [D]

Cordell, Thomas, Stamford, Lincs., u (late 17th century). Freeman of Stamford by servitude. [Freemen reg.]

Cordelle, Thomas, 111 Houndsditch, London, broker and cm

(1785). Took out insurance cover of £130 on his utensils and stock. [GL, Sun MS vol. 330, p. 401]

Corden, John, Duck Lane, Edward St, Westminster, London, bed-joiner (1791). Took app. named Sarah Banham. [Westminster Ref. Lib., MS F4309, p. 72]

Cording, J. & W., 231–32, Strand, London, writing desk makers and jewellers (1801–03). [D]

Cordingley, David, Skircoat, near Halifax, Yorks., joiner and cm (1822). [D]

Cordon, J., Parliament St, Nottingham, joiner and chairmaker (1814). [D]

Cordy, William, London, carver and gilder (1790–93). In 1790 moved from 24 Cannon St to Bride Lane, Bridge St, Blackfriars and in that year declared bankrupt. In January 1791 he was living in Cornhill but by 1792 had re-commenced business at 3 Essex St, Strand. [D; Heal; *Williamson's Liverpool Advertiser*, 3 January 1791]

Corfield, B., 10 Mount St, Grosvenor Sq., London, cm (1825). [D]

Corfield, John, 10 Mount St, Grosvenor Sq., London, writing desk and dressing case maker (1829–35). A Regency rosewood artist's table with an envelope top enclosing a leather tray, lidded boxes, a palette and drawing instruments, on a fluted stem and four cornered base (15″ sq.) was included in auction by Christie's, 1 November 1976, lot 66. This table had Corfield's trade label affixed. [D]

Corfield, Mary, 10 Mount St, Berkeley Sq., London, dressing case maker (1837). Successor to John Corfield. [D]

Cork, John, 17 Stephen St, Tottenham Ct Rd, London, chairmaker (1808–20). [D]

Cork, Joseph, Ling Yd, Magdalen St, Norwich, cm (1826). [D]

Cork, William, Warwick St, Golden Sq., London, cm (1803). Included by Sheraton in the list of master cabinet makers in his *Cabinet Dictionary*, 1803.

Cork & Goring, Gt Alice St, Goodman's Fields, London, cm and u (1818). Bankrupt 1818 and their stock sold by auction October 1818. This consisted of 'rose wood sofa card and loo tables, mahogany chests of drawers, dressing stands, bed steps, ship sideboard, sets of dining, card and Pembroke tables, mahogany and japanned chairs of various descriptions, fire screens, numerous 4-post tent and other bedsteads, with mahogany pillars, cornices &c., feather beds, matresses and blankets, Brussels and Kidderminster carpets, mahogany in boards and veneers, a large assortment of brass work, ten work benches, unfinished cabinet work and other effects'. [*Times*, 10 October 1818]

Corke, William, Tonbridge, Kent, chairmaker (1832). [D]

Corkham, Joshua, Canterbury, Kent, u (1700). [Freemen reg.]

Corkhill, Thomas, 5 Brunswick St, Liverpool, joiner and cm (1835–37). [D]

Corkwell, William, Nantwich, Cheshire, cm (1837). Daughter Mary bapt. 3 July 1837. [PR (bapt.)]

Corlass, John, 5 Low St, Keighley, Yorks., joiner/cm (1837). [D]

Corless, James, Crosshall St, Liverpool, cm (1806–39). Free on 31 October 1806. At 20 Crosshall St in 1829, 19 in 1835 and 35 in 1839. [D; freemen reg.]

Corless, John, Copperas Hill, Liverpool, u and cm (1816–d. 1819). At 25 Copperas Hill in 1816 but at 24 in 1818. Died in 1819 but business insolvent at time of death. [D; *Liverpool Mercury*, 14 January 1820]

Corless, Joseph, 22 Trueman St, Liverpool, cm (b. 1791–c. 1830). Son of Roger Corless, cm, and born on 15 September 1791. Free, 5 October 1812. Lived at the same address as Samuel Corless, clockmaker. [Freemen reg.]

Corless, Roger, Dale St, Liverpool, cm (1784–d. c. 1818). App. to Roger Reid and free by servitude, 1 April 1784. Father of Roger Corless, born 15 September 1791 and free as cm in

1812; and Samuel Corless, born 3 January 1802 and free as clockmaker, 1823. At 115 Dale St in 1804 but in the next year at 125. At 122 Dale St in 1800, 115 in 1804, 125 in 1805, 132 in 1807, 3 Wykes Ct, Dale St in 1810 and 5 Wykes Ct in 1811. Died c. 1818. [D; freemen's committee bks]

Corlett, Edward, London, cm (1793). Subscribed to Sheraton's *Drawing Book*, 1793.

Corlett, Edward, 4 Macquire St, Liverpool, cm (1818–d. 1819). Died on 6 January 1819 'after a long and painful illness'. [D; *Liverpool Mercury*, 22 January 1819]

Corlett, Edward, 2 Newington Bridge, Liverpool, cm (1823–24). In 1823 also a tea dealer and in 1824 also a small ware dealer. [D]

Corlett & Owen, 1 Hood St, Lord St, Liverpool, cm (1805–11). [D]

Corley, Roger, Liverpool, cm (1790–96). In 1790 at 61 High-field St, Liverpool but in 1796 shown at both 26 Fairhurst St, Cheapside as a cm and victualler and 48 Dale St as a cm and broker. [D]

Cormel, —, address unknown, cm (1803). Subscribed to Sheraton's *Cabinet Dictionary*, 1803.

Corner, Mat., Chester-le-Street, Co. Durham, joiner and cm (1793). [D]

Corner, William & Son, Newcastle and Gateshead, Co. Durham (1790–1803). In 1790 at the West end of High-bridge, Newcastle, but in 1801 at High Church St, Gateshead. In 1803 subscribed to Sheraton's *Cabinet Dictionary* when their address is given as Newcastle. [D]

Corner, William, Dovecot St, Stockton-on-Tees, Co. Durham, cm (1832). [D]

Corney, William & Hodson, Richard, 4 Broad St, Soho, London, cm and u (1791–93). [D]

Cornfoot, John, Morpeth, Northumb., cm (1784). [D]

Cornforth, William, London, cm (1808–20). At 19 Elder St, Norton Falgate in 1808 but by 1813 had moved to 24 White Lion St. He stayed at this address until 1819 but in the next year the business was styled William Cornforth & Son and was trading from 15 Broker Rd, Moorfields as cm and u. [D]

Cornish, Charles, Southampton, Hants., cm (1805–36). At East St, 1805–08, but from 1811 at 3 St Georges Pl. [D]

Cornish, Samuel, French St, Southampton, Hants., cm (1792–1808). [D]

Cornish, Thomas, Kingston, Yeovil, Som., cm and u (1830). [D]

Cornish, William, Bristol, cm, u and undertaker (1834–40). From 1834–36 at 24 Philadelphia St but in 1837 moved to St Augustine's Back. [D]

Cornish & Monday (or Mondey), Bridge St, Southampton, Hants., cm and u (1823–30). Listed at 10 Bridge St in 1823 and no. 106 in 1830. [D]

Cornock, Thomas, Bristol, carver (1715). [Poll bk]

Corns, Joseph, 19 Smallbrook St, Birmingham, cm (1835). [D]

Cornthwaite, George, Milnthorpe, Westmld, cm (1829). [D]

Cornwell, James, London, joiner and u (1782). Freeman of Preston, Lancs. [Preston freemen rolls]

Corp, William, Weymouth, Dorset, joiner and cm (1775–98). In 1775 occupied premises in the Melcombe Regis part of the borough, on which he took out insurance cover for £200, half of which was for utensils and stock. [D; GL, Sun MS vol. 239, p. 100]

Corral, Charles Prow, St Margaret's Bank, Rochester, Kent, carver and gilder (1824–28). Declared bankrupt, *London Gazette*, 7 March 1828. [D]

Corrall, Charles, 44 Lamb's Conduit St, London, carver and gilder (1835–39). [D]

Corran, Henry, Liverpool, cm (1816). App. to William Longworth Walker and free by servitude on 6 June 1816. [Freemen reg.]

Corran, John, 36 Ormond St, Liverpool, cm (1796). [D]

Corrin, Robert, Liverpool, cm (1806). App. to Isaac Marsh and free by servitude 31 October 1806. Addresses shown are Hanover Ct, Finch St, and Bakehouse Lane, Stanley St. [Freemen reg.]

Corrin, Robert jnr, Bartock St, Liverpool, cm (1830). Son of Robert Corrin. Free 19 November 1830. [Freemen reg.]

Corrington, John, Church St, Gainsborough, Lincs., cm and u (1834). [D]

Corrington, William, Ormskirk, Lancs., cm (1813). In August 1813 married Miss Mary Meadows of Ormskirk. [*Liverpool Mercury*, 6 August 1813]

Corroll, Richard, 20 Bishop Lane, Hull, Yorks., cm (1828). [D]

Corry, William, Preston, Lancs., joiner, cm and builder (1801–02). Freeman of Preston. In August 1801 married a Mrs Parker, widow and proprietor of the 'George Inn'. [Freemen reg.; *Billinge's Liverpool Advertiser*, 17 August 1801]

Corvall, Charles, 31 Gt Ormond St, Queen Sq., London, carver and gilder (1840). [GL, Sun MS ref. 1333477]

Cory, George, Gt Yarmouth, Norfolk and London, u (1802–10). Bankrupt June 1802. By 1807 in London and in 1810 at 148 High Holborn where he took out insurance cover for £500 of which £300 was in respect of stock, utensils and goods in trust. [Gt Yarmouth poll bk; *Billinge's Liverpool Advertiser*, 28 June, 13 September, 23 October 1802; GL, Sun MS vol. 453, ref. 839930; *Monthly Magazine*, 1803, p. 480]

Cory, Thomas, Hartland, Devon, cm (1830). [D]

Corzens, John, London, upholder (1709). Admitted freeman of the Upholders' Co., 21 November 1709. [GL, Upholders' Co. records]

Cosens, Hannah, Bristol, clock case finisher (1818–30). From 1818–29 at Temple back but in 1830 at Charles St. [D]

Cosham, William, Ringmer, Sussex, cm (1839). [D]

Cosier, Henry, High St, St Albans, Herts., cm and u (1823–39). [D]

Cosier & Seager, High St, Chatham, Kent, u and cm (1838–40). At 104 High St in 1838 but in the next year the number was 85. [D]

Cosins, William, Newark, Notts., chairmaker (1790). [Poll bk]

Cosser, Andrew, 22 Bridge Rd, Lambeth, London, cm, u, builder and carpenter (1820). [D]

Cossway, George, Milverton, Som., cm (1839–40). Listed at Sand St in 1840. [D]

Cossway, Philip, High St, Wellington, Som., cm and u (1839). [D]

Cost, Warneris, London, cm (1778). In 1778 took out insurance cover of £200 on utensils, stock and goods kept at W. W. Duffs, cm at 4 Husband St. [GL, Sun MS vol. 265, p. 27]

Costar, Henry, Salisbury, Wilts., organ builder, harpsichord and cabinet maker (1784–1803). The Longford Castle, Wilts. accounts record payments of £2 2s in 1798, £6 15s 6d in 1799, £20 6s 6d in 1801 and £9 in 1803. [D; V & A archives]

Cotesforth, Hugh, Newcastle, u (1740). [Freemen reg.]

Cotesforth, John, Newcastle, u (1740). [Freemen reg.]

Cottesforth, Robert, Newcastle, u (1740). [Freemen reg.]

Cotman, Robert Sargent, Blackheath Hill, Lewisham, London, carver and gilder (1832–39). [D]

Cottam, John, West Bradford, near Clitheroe, Yorks., joiner and chairmaker (1822). [D]

Cottam, William, Hull, Yorks., cm (1784). Freeman of Lancaster. [Lancaster poll bk]

Cotte(e), Benjamin, Witham, Essex, cm and u (1823–39). Trading as Benjamin & Son in 1832. [D]

Cotte, James, Maldon, Essex, cm (1839). [D]

Cotte(e), John & Co., Witham, Essex, cm and u (1823–39). In 1839 the business is styled John & George Cotte. [D]

Cottee, Joseph, Witham, Essex, cm (1798–d. 1814). Probate granted on will 1814. [D; *Wills at Chelmsford*]

Cottee, William, Maldon, Essex, cm and u (1832). [D]

Cotten, Henry, 3 Whitcomb St, London, cm and box maker (1808). On 8 November 1808 took out insurance cover of £300, half of which was in respect of stock and utensils. [GL, Sun MS vol. 445, ref. 821842]

Cotter, William, 24 Burr St, Wapping, London, cm (1790–1808). From 1790–92 trading as Cotter & Morton. Subscribed to Sheraton's *Drawing Book*, 1793 and included in the list of master cabinet makers in his *Cabinet Dictionary*, 1803. [D]

Cotterell, Richard, London, cm, u and undertaker (1808–28). In 1808 he moved from Essex St, Whitechapel to 19 Primrose St, Shoreditch at which address he stayed until at least 1822. In 1827 at 51 Charlotte St, Whitechapel Rd. No mention of an upholstery or undertaking side to the business until 1822. [D]

Cotterell, Samuel & Co., Manchester, cm (?) (1762). In 1762 took app. named Barlow. [S of G, app. index]

Cotterell, Thomas, Birmingham, cm (1731–54). In 1731 took app. named Clement; in 1735, Hodgkins; in 1752, Chamberlain; and in 1754, Masefield. On 16 January 1734 he was paid £3 4s by William, Baron Dudley, Ward of The Grange, Halesowen, Salop (now Worcs.) for 'three Close Stools and two Dressing Glasses'. Another receipt exists dated 3 September 1751 for 'a Mahogany Table and silvering and repairing a Glass' for a Mrs Rock at a cost of £1 1s. [S of G, app. index; Worcs. RO, 2422/705:122/26]

Cottingham, Richard, Bridge St, Chester, cm (1730–71). Took apps named Nicholls in 1730, Richards in 1742 and Lindsey in 1753. [S of G, app. index; poll bks]

Cottle, J., 12 Hampton Row, Bath, Som., cm (1833). [D]

Cotton, Anne, 32 Corn St, Bristol, upholder (1792–99). [D]

Cotton, Benjamin, Bristol, u (1774–84). Shown in 1774 in the parish of St Philip and St Jacob and in 1775 in the parish of St Werburgh. By 1775 at 33 Corn St. [D; poll bks]

Cotton, Joseph, Leg Alley, Westminster, London, carver (1749). [Poll bk]

Cotton, Mary, 32 Corn St, Bristol, u (1793–94). [D]

Cotton, Samuel, George St, Tamworth, Staffs., cm and u (1822–28). [D]

Cotton, Thomas Barnett, 42 Fenchurch St, London, carver, gilder and picture frame maker (1773–1808). Freeman and member of the Joiners' Co. in 1773 licenced to employ a non-freeman for three months and in 1779 a similar licence was issued. In 1782 took out insurance cover of £1,900 of which £850 was in respect of utensils, stock and goods. His trade card [Landauer Coll., MMA, NY] states that he made and sold 'all sorts of Gold, Black & Oval Frames for Prints, Drawings, Paintings &c, Looking Glass Frames & Girandoles Carved & Gilt in the modern taste, Cleans, lines & repairs Old Paintings & new Gilds old Frames on the shortest notice . . . N.B. Mouldings of different Patterns & lengths for conveniency of Cabinet Makers in the Country, likewise Buys & Sells all sorts of Pictures, also Paintings, for Chimney Pieces. Printseller. Wholesale, Retail & for Exportation'. [D; GL, City Licence bks, vols 8 and 9; Sun MS vol. 301, p. 541]

Cotton, William, Lancaster and Birmingham, cm (1767–68). Free 1767–68. By 1768 living in Birmingham. [Freemen rolls; Lancaster poll bk]

Cotton, William, 32 Corn St, Bristol, cm and upholder (1799–1800). [D]

Cotton, William, London, u and cm (1806–23). At 80 Stones End (or Newington Causeway), Southwark 1806–15 but from 1817 at 52 Blackman St, Southwark. The cm side of the business first mentioned 1809, and between this date and 1811 the business was styled Cotton & Cobb. [D]

Cotton, William, Worcester St, Bromsgrove, Worcs., cm (1820). [D]

Cottrell, J. F., 21 Barton St, Bristol, cm and u (1840). [D]

Cottrell, Richard, Worcester, joiner and cm (1776). App. to William Dawson, joiner and cm, and free by servitude 1 April 1776. [Freemen reg.]

Cottrell, Richard, 13 Crosbie St, Liverpool, cm (1810). [D]

Cottrell, Samuel, Birmingham, cm (1823–30). Listed at Bradford St in 1823 and at Alcester St, also as a dressing case and portable desk maker, in 1830. [D]

Cottway, —, London(?), u (1703). On 6 March 1703 he was paid 6s for assisting in making the Duke of Leeds's 'easy chair'. [YAS, DD5/39]

Couch, William, 30 Crouch St, Colchester, Essex, cm and u (1839). [D]

Couchman, Edward, 109 Goswick St, London, cm (1820). [D]

Couchman, Henry, Montpelier Rd, Blackheath, London, cm and u (1839). [D]

Couchman, Richard, 23 Gabriel's Hill, Maidstone, Kent, cm (1837–39). [D; poll bks]

Couchman, William, High Wycombe, Bucks., cm (1837). Son and daughter bapt. in 1837. [PR (bapt.)]

Coulam, Henry, Eastgate, Louth, Lincs., cm, u and joiner (1835). [D]

Coulam, Richard & Henry, Eastgate, Louth, Lincs., cm, joiners and builders (1826–40). [D]

Coulam (or Cowlam), William, Water Lane, Louth, Lincs., cm/joiner (1819–22). [D]

Coulam (or Cowlam), William, Eastgate, Louth, Lincs., cm, joiner and u (1819–40). [D]

Coulbourn, Richard, Freckleton, Lancs., joiner and cm (1828). [D]

Couldwell, Roger, Bartholomew Close, London, u (1709). Said to have removed from his lodgings in Bartholomew Close with '8 yards of Rich Sky-colour'd Red Damask, large Figure, cut out for use, with Silk lace'. John Mitchell offered to redeem the goods if they had been pawned and offered in addition a reward of 10s. [*Daily Courant*, 8 January 1709]

Coules, Marmaduke, Bristol, upholder (1754–81). In the parish of St Augustine in 1754 and at both 13 St Augustine's back and 31 Clifton Hill in 1775. Took app. named Cottle in 1756. Bankrupt 1777. His trade card is in the Leverhulme Coll., print dept, MMA NY. [D; poll bks; S of G, app. index; *Gents Mag.*, March 1777]

Coulling, Robert, 253 Oxford St, London, u (1808). [D]

Coulsher, Thomas, Ramsey, Hunts., cm (1839). [D]

Coulson, Joseph, Kirkgate, Thirsk, Yorks., chairmaker (1823–40). [D]

Coulson, Ralph, 30 Duke St, Lincoln's Inn Fields, London, cm (1832). In 1832 took app. named Bruce Gillchrist. [Westminster Ref. Lib., MS 4310]

Coulson, Thomas, Pilgrim St, Newcastle, glazier, japanner, house-painter and gilder (1802–05). Included in his stock were japanned chairs 'in gold or colours', fire-screens, bed and window cornices and flower pot stands. In August 1802 advertised that he had taken into his employ a new foreman who was 'a proper Herald Painter and Japanner, and who has been employed in the first Shops in the Metropolis'. Apart from the japanning of chairs, tea trays and other items of furniture Coulson claimed that he could japan ironwork 'as at the Birmingham manufactories'. He also dealt in old paintings, drawings and portraits. In November 1805 he claimed that there was a conspiracy amongst his rival tradesmen to ruin his business by bribing his workmen to neglect their duty and pass trade information on their techniques to them. He threatened to prosecute should further action of a similar nature take place. [*Newcastle Courant,*

6 January, 21 August 1802, 20 August 1803, 11 November 1805]

Coulson, Thomas, Horse Mkt, Northampton, chairmaker and turner (1830). [D]

Coulsting, James, parish of St Mary Redcliffe, Bristol, cm (1754). [Poll bk]

Coulstone, Richard, Lancaster, cm (1756–58). App. to R. Gillow of Lancaster 'joyner and cabinet maker' and free 1756–57 by servitude. In November 1758 took an app. [App. reg.; freemen rolls]

Coultart, Francis, Liverpool, cm (1810–35). At 16 Cuncliffe St in 1810 and 18 Cuncliffe St, 1813–18. At 9 Lawrence St in 1827 but two years later the number is given as 8. In 1834–35 was at 9 Garden Lane (or Limekiln Lane) with a shop at 2 Poynton St. [D]

Coultart, Richard, London, carver (1767–78). In parish of St George's Hanover Sq., in 1767 and in 1774 at Park St, Grosvenor Sq., Westminster. By the next year however he had moved to 14 John St, Tottenham Ct Rd where he took out insurance cover of £400 of which £100 was in respect of utensils and stock. [Marylebone Lib., deed 1249; poll bk; GL, Sun MS vol. 264, p. 496; vol. 240, p. 548]

Coulthirst, Robert, address unknown, joiner and chairmaker (1691). On 1 July 1691 supplied four beds and six chairs for Temple Newsam House, Leeds at a cost of £8 5s. [*Furn. Hist.*, 1967]

Counsel, —, London, u (1793). Subscribed to Sheraton's *Drawing Book*, 1793.

Counzes, Vidall, 6 New Lisle St, London, carver and gilder (1809). On 7 February 1809 took out insurance cover of £700 which included £200 for stock and utensils and £100 for timber in a workshop. [GL, Sun MS vol. 448, ref. 828310]

Coupland, Charles, Newby, Yorks., carver (1774). [York poll bk]

Coupland, James, Up-gate, Louth, Lincs., cm/joiner (1819). [D]

Coupland, Richard, Lancaster, u (1829–30). [Lancaster freemen rolls]

Coupland, Robert, Leeds, Yorks., u (1777–80). App. to Thomas Bradford of Doncaster, Yorks. In 1777 advertised that he had recently returned from London 'with all kinds of Most Fashionable upholstery goods' which he intended to make up and sell from his shop in Briggate, formerly occupied by the late John Lambert. In the following year the address is given as 'near the Cross', at the shop formerly occupied by Messrs Horsfell & Richardson. Also in this year he advertised for a journeyman u to assist him in his business. In 1780 he described himself as an appraiser and distiller. [*Leeds Intelligencer*, 18 March 1777; 9 January 1778, 25 August 1778, 22 April 1780]

Coupland, Thomas, 11 Sewer Lane, residence Anne St, Osborne St, Hull, Yorks., furniture painter (1831). [D]

Coupland, William, Up-gate, Louth, Lincs., cm/joiner (1822). [D]

Coupland, William, Spilsby, Lincs., joiner and cm (1826). [D]

Courrant, Peter, 'The Cabinet', Wardour St, Westminster, London, cm and joiner (1728). On 27 December 1728 insured his dwelling house for £200 and his household goods and stock in trade for £100. [GL, Sun MS vol. 27, ref. 46392]

Court, Charles, Under the Bank and Host St, Bristol, cm (1812–20). Formerly a partner of William Court but from 1812 trading on his own account. Supplied furniture etc. to Col. Henry Knight of Tythegston Court, Glam., in 1818. In 1820 the business is shown at the addresses above but was being conducted by Esther Court. [D; *Furn. Hist.*, 1976; *C. Life*, 5 October 1978, p. 1029]

Court, David snr, Redmans Row, Mile End, London, upholder

(1782). Insured his house for £100 in 1782. [GL, Sun MS vol. 302, p. 618]

Court, Esther, Under the Bank and Host St, Bristol, cm (1820). Probably the widow of Charles Court. [D; *Furn. Hist.*, 1976]

Court, George, 9 Adam St East, Portman Sq., London, u, carver and gilder (1839). [D]

Court, James, 53 Castle St, Bristol, cm and u (1799–1807). [D]

Court, James, High St, Godalming, Surrey, cm (1838–39). [D]

Court, John, Bristol, joiner and cm (1759–d. 1806). In 1775 had a cabinet warehouse at 12 Horse St but in 1784 recorded at Back Horse St. In 1759 took app. named Evans. Retired in 1791 and passed the business to his sons William and Charles. [D; poll bks; S of G, app. index; *Furn. Hist.*, 1976]

Court, Philip, 31 Wincolmlee, Hull, Yorks., cm (1828). [D]

Court, William & Charles, Under the Bank and Host St, Bristol, cm (1791–1812). Sons of John Court whose business they continued. Subscribed to Sheraton's *Drawing Book*, 1793. On 21 May 1791 supplied a white and gold communion table with a mahogany top to Christchurch, Bristol, for which £21 was charged. In 1791–92 they supplied furniture for John Pinney for his house at 7 Gt George St, Bristol (now the Georgian House Museum) for which £360 was charged. Pinney paid a further sum of £7 8s for a 'Mah^y bason' in 1795. After 1812 the business was continued by Charles Court alone. [D; *Furn. Hist.*, 1976]

Courtenay, Hercules, London, carver and gilder (before 1769). App. to Thomas Johnson and in August 1769 in Front St, Philadelphia, USA. He stated that he was 'from London'. [*Penn'a Chronicle*, 14 August 1769; M. Heckscher, *American Furniture in the MMA*, 1985, p. 24]

Courthope, William, London, upholder (1700–29). Freeman 4 September 1700. Took apps named Thomas Smith, 1710–21, and Job Adams, 1721–29. [GL, Upholders' Co. records] Possibly:

Courthorp, William, London, upholder (1724–37). Freeman. At the 'Rose & the Star', Paternoster Row, 1724–30, but in 1734 at Newgate St. [Heal]

Courtnay, J., 54 Gt Wild St, Lincoln's Inn Fields, London, cm (1829). [D]

Cousens, Cooper William, London, cm (1826–31). Freeman of Gt Yarmouth, Norfolk. [Gt Yarmouth poll bks]

Cousens, Thomas, London, cm and u (1820–29). At 7 Gt Russell St, Bloomsbury, 1820–28. In 1820 the business was described as a sofa and chair manufactory. In 1829 moved to 14 Little Charlotte St, Rathbone Pl. [D]

Cousin, Peter, address unknown, picture and mirror frame maker (1690–1701). Possibly a relative of Antonio Verrio's gilder, René Cousin. In 1690 he supplied a picture frame for Petworth House, Sussex; and in 1701 produced 'four large looking glass frames guilt in gold' for the new building, Hampton Court, Middlx. [PRO, S/32; *Wren Soc.*, vol. XVIII, pp. 160–61; *C. Life*, 4 September 1980]

Cousin, René, address unknown (1675–94). A French carver and gilder in England by 1675. Antonio Verrio's chief gilder at Burghley, Stamford, Lincs., and Windsor. Also worked at Petworth House, Sussex. [Croft-Murray, *Decorative Painting in England*, I, p. 246; *Apollo*, May 1977]

Cousins, John, Bethlem St, Grimsby, Lincs., turner and chairmaker (1822). [D]

Cousins, John, Ambleside, Westmld, cm (1834). [D]

Coussins (or Cossins), Robert, Crewkerne, Som., cm (1830–40). Listed at Orchard St in 1830 and Market Pl. in 1840. [D]

Couty, David jnr, London, upholder, cm, undertaker, appraiser and auctioneer (1823–35). At 4 Nassau Pl., Commercial Rd, 1823–28. Insurance cover amounted to £600 in 1823 and £650 in the following year of which utensils and stock amounted to £220 and £180 respectively. By 1835 had moved to 16 Alfred Pl., Newington Causeway. [D; GL, Sun MS vol. 490, ref. 1001556; vol. 494, ref. 1012579]

Couzens, Thomas, 8 Woburn Ct, Bloomsbury, London, cm and u (1827). [D]

Couzins, George, Wardour St, Westminster, London, cm (1784). [Poll bk]

Covell, John, 11 Harrow Rd, Edgware Rd, London, bedstead maker (1835). [D]

Coventon, Joseph, 60 Red Lion St, Clerkenwell, London, clock case maker (1837–40). [D]

Coventry, Edward jnr, Liverpool, cm (1802–d. 1824). Free 5 July 1802. At 10 Brooke's St in 1810 but in the following year at St Paul's Sq. Also acted as clerk of St Paul's Church and 'looker' in the Customs. Died 8 April 1824. In 1825 when his son Edward Coventry, watchmaker tried to gain freedom by patrimony this was refused as his father was not free at the time of his son's birth. [D; freemen reg.]

Coventry, John, 9 Wycombe Pl., Kent St, Southwark, London, chairmaker (1800). On 19 June 1800 took out insurance cover on his own newly built dwelling house and five others totalling £300. [GL, Sun MS vol. 418, ref. 704012]

Coventry, John, London, chair and sofa maker (1826–40). At 134 Kent St, Southwark, 1826–29, but by 1832 at 8 Parogem Pl., New Kent Rd and in 1840 at 'Three Colts', Old Ford, Middlx. [D; GL, Sun MS vol. 575, ref. 1341185]

Coventry, Thomas, Liverpool, chairmaker (1812–d. by 1835). Son of Hugh Coventry, sailmaker. Free 5 October 1812. [Freemen reg.]

Cowan, Alexander, Plymouth Dock, Devon, u (1789–98). In 1789 leased a house at Fowey, Cornwall for a year. [D; Devon RO, DDTF. 1383/1–2]

Cowan, David, 63 Close and New Rd, Newcastle, joiner and cm (1824–33). [D]

Coward, Henry, Green Hammerton, York, joiner and cm (1834). [D]

Coward, John, 4 Tower St, Seven Dials, London, carver (1766–89). On 1 November 1766 he received £88 10s from the Duke of Portland for work at Burlington House, London and in July of the following year received £88 10s for work undertaken at Welbeck Abbey, Notts. He modelled shapes and supplied drawings for Josiah Wedgwood, c. 1768–69. In 1789 Joseph Richards, cm, took out insurance cover of £60 on household goods kept at Coward's house in Tower St. [Notts. RO, DD5P 3/1, DD5P 3/4; Finer & Savage, *Wedgwood, Selected Letters*, p. 71; GL, Sun MS vol. 363, ref. 555671]

Coward, John, Tottenham Ct Rd, London, carver and gilder (1808–23). At 13 Tottenham Ct Rd 1808 but from 1816 at 253. Also owned or used 245 Tottenham Ct Rd which was empty in 1821 when he took out insurance cover of £700 on it with a further £100 for the stable behind. [D; GL, Sun MS vol. 485, ref. 976388]

Coward, Michael Godman, Swaffham, Norfolk, cm and u (1822–d. 1823). Will proved at Norwich in 1823. [D; Norfolk Record Soc., index of wills]

Coward, William, Coward's Yd, Highgate, Kendal, Westmld, joiner/cm (1829). [D]

Cowd, Joseph, Salterton, Devon, cm (1830). [D]

Cowdall, Samuel, 5 Little Cheapside and Sun St, Finsbury Sq., London, chair stuffer (1808). [D]

Cowderay, William, parish of St Clement, Oxford, cm (1768). [Poll bk]

Cowdry, Richard, Farnham, Surrey, cm (1740–48). In 1740 took app. named Barnard and in 1748 another named Cook. [S of G, app. index]

Cowdry, Samuel, 78 Leather Lane, Holborn, London, chair and bedstead manufacturer (1820). [D]

Cowell, Daniel, 95 High St, Worcester, cm and u (1817–37).

Admitted freeman 1817 and by 1820 was already trading from the High St address. He declared himself to be the successor of Mr Timings, and was agent for the Phoenix Fire Assurance Co. of London. He also appears to have had a partner, for the business is described as Cowell & Cartwright (late Timings) in an 1820 directory though an advertisement placed in the same publication is in the name of Daniel Cowell only. From 1828–37 the business was named Daniel & William Cowell, though William Cowell was not a freeman of Worcester until 1831. In 1834 John Henry Hall, app. to Daniel Cowell, was admitted a freeman. Between 1829–31 this business supplied various items and carried out work for J. S. Packington of Westwood, near Droitwich, Worcs. amounting in total to £80 7s 5d. Payment was however slow in coming and on 4 January 1833 a request was made for payment of this sum and interest on £73 13s 5d being the amount owing since Christmas 1830. The debt was settled in April 1833 but without the payment of the interest requested. [D; freemen rolls; Worcs. RO, 2309/705; 380/56/iii, vi]

Cowell, William, 95 High St, Worcester, cm and u (1840). [D]

Cowen, David, New Rd, St Ann's, Newcastle, cm (1834–38). Trading also at 66 Close in 1834. [D]

Cowen, Thomas, 30 Townhead St, Sheffield, Yorks., cm, u and furniture broker (1833). [D]

Cowham & Clark, Hull, Yorks., carvers and gilders (1787). Both partners were app. to Jeremiah Hargrave. In August and September 1787 supplied two oval and two square gilt frames to Burton Constable, Yorks. at a total cost of £1 3s 6d. [Humberside RO, DDCC vouchers]

Cowie, John, Bedford Ct, Bedford St, Covent Gdn, London, cm and broker (1776–77). In 1776 took out insurance cover of £600 of which £350 was in respect of utensils, stock and goods. Bankrupt early in 1777. [GL, Sun MS vol 245, p. 533; *Gents Mag.*, May 1777]

Cowin, J., London, cm (1793). Subscribed to Sheraton's *Drawing Book*, 1793.

Cowles, David, Howland St, London, cm (1777). In 1777 insured a house in Grafton St. for £500. [GL, Sun MS vol. 262, p. 259]

Cowley, —, Liverpool, cm (1793). Subscribed to Sheraton's *Drawing Book*, 1793.

Cowley, J., Whitby, Yorks., u (1798). [D]

Cowley, William, address unknown, joiner (1736). In November 1736 received £11 15s for work carried out at Chatsworth, Derbs., which included making two bedsteads and a leaf for a dining room table. [Chatsworth vouchers]

Cowling, T., Townsend St, Cheltenham, Glos., carver and gilder (1839). [D]

Cowparthwaite, William, Bullstake, Sheffield, Yorks., cm (1774). [D]

Cowper, John, 'The Three Blackbirds', Cornhill, London (1693). [Heal]

Cowper, Simon, parish of St Martin, Ludgate, London, cm (1687). [PCC Wills]

Cowper, William, 'Angel', Grove St, London, cm (1784). [Westminster poll bk]

Cowperthwaite, William, Manchester, cm (1797–1817). At 21 Back Water St, 1797–1813 but by 1817 at 7 Christchurch Sq., Hulme. [D]

Cowsthorpe, William, London(?), u (1713). In 1713 took an app. [S of G, app. index]

Cowthron, William, Mardol, Shrewsbury, Salop, cm and u (1835). [D]

Cowx, John, Liverpool, cm (before 1819). On 24 August 1819 the widow of John Cowx died aged 35. [*Liverpool Mercury*, 10 September 1819]

Cowx, Thomas, Liverpool, cm (1804–29). At 15 Charles St,

Whitechapel 1804–07 and in 1804 had a shop at 13 Pool Lane. From 1810 shown in Whitechapel at no. 32 (1810), no. 29 (1811) and from 1812 at no. 30 with a shop at 2 Dawson St. [D]

Cox, Cabel, High St, Chesham, Bucks., cm (1839). [D]

Cox, Comfort, 39 Adam St West, London, u (1839). [D]

Cox, Edward, Rood Lane, parish of St Gabriel's, Fenchurch St, London, u (1722). Jointly with Thomas Gardiner took out insurance cover on goods and merchandise in his dwelling house for £500 on 6 November 1722. [GL, Sun MS vol. 14, ref. 26792]

Cox, Edward, St James's, Westminster, London, carver (1745). Declared bankrupt, *Gents Mag.*, November 1745.

Cox, Edward, Northampton, carpenter and cm (1776–98). In 1776 took out insurance cover of £55 for his stock and in 1779 insured his house for £400. Subscribed to Sheraton's *Drawing Book*, 1793. [D; GL, Sun MS vol. 247, p. 494; vol. 274, p. 293]

Cox, Edward, Brentwood, Essex, auctioneer and cm (1801). Probate granted on will, 1801. [*Wills at Chelmsford*]

Cox, Edward Treslove, London, u and cm (1807–21). At 104 St Martin's Lane, 1807–11, 13 Haymarket St 1811–20 and 6 Northumberland Ave., 1821. In July 1819 he advertised that he was in a position to manufacture oak furniture for gentlemen 'having curious specimens'. He stated that 'this novel article . . . brought to a degree of perfection by the late Mr Bullock' could now be manufactured by him into 'various beautiful articles of furniture, according to the late Mr Bullock's designs some of which may be seen at E. T. Cox's cabinet-maker 13, Haymarket, who has engaged several of the late Mr B's workmen.' [D; *Times*, 1 July 1819]

Cox, Francis, Hampstead Marshall, Berks., u (d. 1698). Will proved 1698. [Berks. RO, W Inv 58/34]

Cox, George, London, cm, broker and appraiser (1808–11). At Old St Rd in 1808 and 2 City Rd and 89 Old St, 1809–11. [D]

Cox, George, London, u (1835–39). At 58 Cirencester Pl., 1835–39, but in 1839 moved to Little Portland St. [D]

Cox, James, Gloucester and Tetbury, Glos., cm and u (1820–40). In 1820 living in the parish of St Aldgate, Gloucester where a child was baptised. By 1822 at Market Pl., Tetbury at which address the business continued, and was listed at Cirencester St in 1839. [D; PR(bapt.)]

Cox, James Valentine, Norwich, upholder (1835). Son of John Cox of Norwich, u. Admitted freeman of Norwich 29 April 1835. [Freemen reg.]

Cox, James, Wellington Ct, Hastings, Sussex, chairmaker, turner and town crier (1835–40). [D]

Cox, James, High Wycombe, Bucks., chairmaker (b. c. 1814–41). Aged 27 at the time of the 1841 Census.

Cox, John, London, u (1713–49). In the period 1713–18 at the 'Iron Balcony', next door to Lord Craven's in Drury Lane, but by 1734 had moved to The Piazza, Covent Gdn. As early as 1713 he took an app. and by the 1730s had built up a substantial business serving influential and wealthy clients. In 1734 he is recorded subscribing two guineas annually to St George's Hospital, Hyde Park Corner, London. His earliest known commission was in 1728 when he was paid £10 16s 6d for papering 'corniches', lining curtains and making covers for chairs. The client was possibly the Duke of Montrose. In 1734 he was paid £200 for a state bed and a matching set of backstools for Belhus, Essex (now at Christchurch Mansion, Ipswich). On 5 November 1735 Earl Fitzwalter paid Cox £5 16s for a large Turkey carpet for Moulsham Hall, Essex, and in 1738 six mahogany chairs costing £4 19s were supplied to Holkham Hall, Norfolk. Various small amounts for taking down beds, hanging curtains and making a wainscot bedstead (£2 5s) were paid, 1739–41, by Robert and Anne Nugent of

Gosfield Hall, Essex, the work being for their London house in Dover St. Cox also manufactured tents and one costing £23 15s was supplied to Lord Charles Gordon 1748–49. [D; poll bk; GL, Sun MS vol. 4, ref. 4066; Heal; S of G, app. index; St George's Hospital Minute bk, p. 117; Scottish RO, GD 220/6/1373, GD 44/51/288/1/46; V &A archives; A. C. Edwards, *The Accounts of Benjamin Mildmay, Earl Fitzwalter*, p. 106; Essex RO, D/DU 502/2]

Cox, John, Stratford, London, u (1763). Fellow of the Society of Arts in this year only.

Cox, John, London, cm (1776–85). At 32 Oxford St in 1776 when he took out insurance cover of £100 on his utensils and stock. In 1785 at 21 Rupert St and on 18 July of that year took out cover of £200 'on his utensils & stock in his timberyard in the Savoy'. [GL, Sun MS vol. 246, p. 103; vol. 330, p. 326]

Cox, John, Clare, Suffolk, cm, u, appraiser and auctioneer (1796–1803). On 4 May 1796 advertised that he had moved to 'a more comodious situation near the Cock Inn, where he has enlarged his stock, and added thereto a fashionable assortment of Register and Pantheon Stoves, Kitchen Ranges, polished Fender and Fire-irons, Tea Urns, Steel Patent and other Snuffers, Prince's Metal Candlesticks, &c.'. He also advertised that he received 'a regular assortment of new Paper Hangings twice a year,' and offered to install house bells. [*Bury and Norwich Post*, 4 May 1796; *Ipswich Journal*, 26 February 1803]

Cox, John, Oxford, cm (1798). [D]

Cox, John, 6 Queen St, Bank Pl., Tombland, Norwich, u and cm (1812–40). App. to William Burt, upholder, and free by servitude, 21 March 1812. His apps Henry Broitehall and William English, were made free on 6 June 1829 and 24 February 1835 respectively. His two sons John Edmund Cox, an under-graduate of All Souls, Oxford, and James Valentine Cox were made freemen 29 April 1835. [D; freemen reg.]

Cox, John, Garland St, Bury St Edmunds, Suffolk, cm (1824). [D]

Cox, John, 8 Adam St West, Bryanston Sq., London, cm (1826). [D]

Cox, Joseph, London, upholder (1755). Son of Japez Cox of Moorfields, broker. App. to William Guidot 4 May 1748 and free by servitude 5 June 1755. [GL, Upholders' Co. records]

Cox, Joseph, Round Ct, St Martin le Grand, London, frame maker and gilder (c. 1760). Trade card [Heal Coll., BM] states that he made and sold 'all Sorts of Carv'd and Gilt Frames for Looking Glasses; Also Lacker'd and Black Frames for Paintings or Prints; Likewise Old Glasses New Silver'd & put into the Newest Fashion, Gilt Sconces.' [Heal]

Cox, Joseph, from London, u (1756). Traded in New York, 1756–73. [M. Heckscher, *Antique Furniture in the MMA*, 1985, pp.137–38]

Cox, Joseph, London, u and cm (before 1773). On 27 September 1773 advertised from the 'Royal Bed and Star', Wall St, New York USA, a long list of articles in the cabinet and upholstery branches and claimed to be 'from London'. [*New York Gazette*, 27 September 1773]

Cox, Joseph, High Wycombe, Bucks., chairmaker (1798). [Militia Census]

Cox, Joseph, Birmingham, cm and u (1820 or 28–35). Listed at Deritend Bridge in 1820 or 28 and Cheapside in 1835. [D]

Cox, Joseph, Colmore Row, Birmingham, cabinet, dressing case and table desk maker, u (1830). [D]

Cox, Philip, High St, Ledbury, Herefs., cm (1830–35). [D]

Cox, Robert, London, upholder (1719–23). Son of Richard Cox of Westminster, baker. App. to Henry Heasman on 2 June 1708 and free by servitude, 26 October 1719. In 1720 at the 'Three Pillars', Piccadilly but in 1723 moved to Maddox St, near Hanover Sq. [GL, Upholders' Co. records, Sun MS vol. 12, ref. 19044]

Cox, Samuel, 39 Gray's Inn Lane, London, u etc. (1819–23). [D]

Cox, Samuel, Worcester St, Birmingham, chairmaker (1830). [D]

Cox, Stephen, 10 and 11 Gt Portland St, London, u (1803–15). Included in the list of master cabinet makers in Sheraton's *Cabinet Dictionary*, 1803. Supplied furniture to Caldecott Hall in 1806. [D; V & A archives]

Cox, Thomas, Liverpool, chairmaker (1790–96). At 4 Wright Ct, Batchelor St in 1790 and back of 19 Orange St in 1796. [D]

Cox, Thomas, Sherborne, Dorset, builder and cm (1809–30). In *Sherborne Mercury*, 25 December 1809 advertised for a cm and a joiner. [D]

Cox, Thomas Jupeth, 5 Hatton Gdn, Liverpool, cm (1816–18). On 26 August 1816 married Miss Elizabeth Reilly. [D; *Liverpool Mercury*, 30 August 1816]

Cox, Thomas, Cheap St, Frome, Som., cm (1822). [D]

Cox, Thomas, Worcester, cm and u (1830–40). Trading at Lowes Moor in 1830 and 25 High St, 1835–40. [D]

Cox, Thomas, Tipton, Staffs., cm and u (1838). [D]

Cox, William, Northampton and Daventry, Northants., carver and painter (b. 1717–d. 1793). Born 29 June 1717. Worked in London for part of his early career but most of his recorded work is in the county of Northants. In 1768 at Cock Lane, Northampton but also had property at Cow Lane, Daventry where he insured utensils and stock for £20 out of a total of £100 cover in 1778. Most of his work was probably in stone. [Gunnis; Northampton poll bk; GL, Sun MS vol. 265, p. 48]

Cox, William, Bordesley and Deritend, Birmingham, upholder and cm (1800–09). Trading at 1 Warwick St, Deritend, also as an umbrella maker, in 1800. [D]

Cox, William, High St, Warminster, Wilts., cm and u (1822). [D]

Cox, William, 50 Union St, City Rd, London, cm (1826). Freeman of Maldon, Essex. [Maldon poll bk]

Cox, William Farmer, Birmingham, cm, u and chairmaker (1828–39). Listed at 52 Worcester St in 1828; nos 51 and 52 in 1830; 12 Exeter Row in 1835, and 6 Court, Bromsgrove St in 1839. [D]

Cox, William, High St, Berkhampstead, Herts., French polisher and painter (1839). [D]

Cox, Zachariah, Tonbridge, Kent, cm and Tunbridge-ware maker (1815–23). Daughters Harriet and Eliza bapt. 19 July 1815 and 26 October 1817 respectively. Father's trade stated to be cm but by 1823 listed as Tunbridge-ware maker. [D; PR(bapt.)]

Cox & Abbott, Wilmot St, Brunswick Sq., London, cm and u (1825–26). At 5 Wilmot St in one 1825 directory but another gives the number as 4. [D]

Coxbrooke, —, address unknown, cm (1803). Subscriber to Sheraton's *Cabinet Dictionary*, 1803.

Coxed, John and G., and **Woster, Thomas**, cm of 'The White Swan', St Paul's Churchyard, London, (1700–36). A number of desks, bureaux, bureau cabinets, secretaire cabinets and chests of drawers dating from the period 1700–30 have been found with the trade labels of John Coxed and G. Coxed & T. Woster (e.g. Colonial Williamsburg). Typically, they are veneered in walnut, mulberry or burr elm (sometimes stained to resemble tortoiseshell), and some pieces are embellished with kingwood crossbanding and pewter stringing. This metal line inlay was almost certainly due to the influence of Gerrit Jensen who introduced such fashionable Continental habits into England in the late 17th century. The earliest examples — all bureau or secretaire cabinets dating from

c. 1700–10 — are labelled 'John Coxed, At the *Swan* in St *Paul*'s Church-Yard, London, makes and sells Cabinets, Book Cases, Chests of Drawers, Scrutoires and Looking-glasses of all sorts'. John Coxed was the second in a long succession of cm known to have occupied 'The Swan' in St Paul's Churchyard. By *c.* 1710 he seems to have been replaced at this address by G. Coxed and T. Woster, whose fullest known trade label reads 'G. Coxed and T. Woster At the *White Swan*, against the South-Gate in St *Paul*'s Church Yard, *London*, Makes and Sells Cabinets, Scrutoires, Desks and Book-Cases, Buro's Chests of Drawers, Wisk, Ombre, *Dutch* and *Indian* Tea-Tables; All sorts of Looking-Glasses, Large Sconces, Dressing Sets and Wainscot-Work of all sorts, at Reasonable Rates. Old Glasses New polished and Made up fashionable.'

The distinctive nature of this furniture has naturally led to speculation that other, similar, pieces were the products of the same workshop. As well as these important burr-veneered cabinet pieces, Coxed & Woster clearly made other types of furniture and carried out more ordinary 'Wainscot-Work'. In 1723 Thomas Woster was paid £2 5s by 'Mad^me Rudge' for a writing table, and in 1725 the same lady paid £2 12s 6d for a card table [Lincoln RO, Monson, 12], while in April 1735 Woster sent a bill to Richard Hoare of Barn Elms (later of Stourhead) for a 'strong wainscot table' and a 'large wainscot press' at a total cost of £9 12s 6d. In December the same year he sent a bill to Hoare for strong wainscot tables at a total cost of £1 12s 6d. [V & A Lib., English Manuscripts, 147] In September 1724 Thomas Woster, cm, had taken out insurance on three houses in Chiswell St and two in Sword Bearer Alley with two sheds, to the value of £800. [GL, Sun MS vol. 19] His death was recorded in *Daily Post*, 14 December 1736: 'Mr. Woster, a Cabinet-maker in St Paul's Church-yard, the Foreman of the London Jury, dy'd suddenly in the Session-house about Twelve o' clock the same day: He complain'd of a Pain in his Stomach and drank a Glass of Mountain, and afterwards desired a Glass of Sack, but expir'd before it could be brought to him'. [*Apollo*, January 1936, p. 22] Coxed & Woster were followed at 'The White Swan' by Henry Bell and his successors. [*GCM*; Heal; *Apollo*, November 1941; *C. Life*, 20 August 1948, pp. 384–85] N. R.

Coxeter, Charles, 73 St Paul's Churchyard, London, upholder (1771–72). Bankrupt 1772. [D; *Gents Mag.*]

Coxeter, William, London and Oxford, u and cm (1767–81). Son of John Coxeter of Witney, Oxon., blanket maker. App. to Charles Westwood of London, upholder, 3 July 1760 and free of the Upholders' Co. by servitude, 6 August 1767. In the following year he was living in the parish of St Michael's, Wood St and on 2 November 1768 married Elizabeth Marriatt of Witney at that town. By September 1774 he had established himself in Oxford and had a cabinet manufactory in New Inn Hall Lane. On 5 July 1776 he announced from this address the sale of the furniture and instruments of Richard Church. In October of that year a serious fire occurred at his workshop which was partially burnt down. His foreman had to be sent to the Radcliffe Infirmary with burns, and Coxeter estimated the loss of goods and tools at £300. In addition, property owned by a London victualler, Thomas Dawson, to the value of £254 was also destroyed. Neither were insured and a subscription list was opened which by the end of November had brought in £185 9s 3d. With this Coxeter was able to reimburse his workmen, William Whitmore, Daniel Shepherd, Edward Evans, Lewis Lewis and George Breakspear for their personal losses. The partially burnt out property was sold by auction in February 1777. Coxeter obviously learnt a lesson from this disaster and immediately took out insurance on his new premises in the High St near the

New Market. In both 1776 and 1777 cover of £500 was taken out of which £350 and £450 respectively were in respect of utensils, stock and goods. In August 1778 he moved his workshops back to New Inn Hall Lane, and gave up the High St premises. Apart from his furniture manufacturing he appears to have been involved with the sale of house property. Bankrupt in late 1781. [GL, Upholders' Co. records; Sun MS vol. 253, p. 337; vol. 259, p. 573; Bodleian index of Oxf. marriage bonds; *Jackson's Oxford Journal*, 3 September 1774, 5 July 1776, 21 October 1776, 7 February 1777, 7 January 1778, 26 August 1778, 10 April 1779, 16 April 1780; *Gents Mag.*, December 1781]

Coxford, William, Wendover, Bucks., cm (1839). [D]

Coxhead, Robert, Bath, Som., cm (1771). The Bath Corporation Furnishing Committee ordered in June 1771 6 mahogany round tables, chairs, tea and card tables, screens, trays, teaboards, knife boxes, a toilet/glass, etc. from this maker [Bath Corp. records]

Coxhead, William, Hungerford, Berks., cm and haberdasher (1779). Took out insurance cover of £200 of which £170 was in respect of utensils and stock. [GL, Sun MS vol. 270, p. 571]

Cozens, James, Gt Yarmouth and Sustead, Norfolk and London, cm (1807–31). Freeman of Gt Yarmouth but shown at Sustead, near Cromer in 1812 and in 1830–31 in London. [Gt Yarmouth poll bks]

Cozens, John jnr, 6 York St, Queen Ann St East, London, carver and gilder (1809). [D]

Cozens, William, Gt Yarmouth, Norfolk, cm (1818–40). [Poll bks]

Crabb, B., 15 King St, Southwark, London, coach and looking-glass manufacturer (1804–25). [D]

Crabb, Isaac, 4 Baldwin's Gdns, Gray's Inn Lane, London, cm (1808). [D]

Crabb, John, parish of St Maurice, Winchester, Hants., upholder (1778). In 1778 insured a house for £500. [GL, Sun MS vol. 267, p. 238]

Crabb, T. R., Gt Suffolk St, Southwark, London, carver and gilder (1820–37). At 49 Gt Suffolk St, 1820–21. From 1823–25 the number was 2½ and after 1829 it was 140. [D]

Crabb, Thomas, 74 Redcross St, Southwark, London, carver and gilder (1808). [D]

Crabtree, Benjamin, Bradford, Yorks., u (1834–37). Listed at Bowling Lane in 1834 and Halifax Rd in 1837. [D]

Crabtree, Edward, Charlotte St, Gt Yarmouth, Norfolk, cm (1818–36). [D; poll bks]

Crabtree, James, London(?), u (1775–77). Account for small upholstery jobs totalling 8s 6d settled by Mrs Howard for either her London house in South Audley St or Thorndon Hall, Essex. [Essex RO, D/DP A 189/6]

Crabtree, John, Mill Lane, Ashton-under-Lyne, Lancs., cm and joiner (1828). [D]

Crace, Frederick & Son, London, painters, gilders and japanners (1821–40). Listed in the Royal Household accounts as early as 1821 when an account for £223 was settled. At this period the firm was described as Frederick & Henry Crace and was trading from an address at 60 Gt Queen St, presumably that used by their father's firm. To what extent they had taken over their father's business by this date is not clear as payments were still being made to John Crace as late as 1826. Henry appears to have left the business and by the late 1830s Frederick was in sole charge. At this period they were trading from 14 Wigmore St. From 1838 furniture was being supplied to Buckingham Palace which included ten rosewood chairs 'inlaid with ornaments in gold and varnished' charged at £15. Tables of various kinds and pole screens were also supplied. In the quarter to December 1839 goods supplied and work carried out amounted in total to £359 18s 11d. Work here continued on into the early 1840s. [PRO, LC11/31; Windsor Royal Archives]

Crace, John & Sons, London, painter, gilders and decorators (1802–26). Initially at 158 Drury Lane but by 1808 had moved to 59 Gt Queen's St, Lincoln's Inn Fields. The firm is particularly associated with materials provided, and work carried out, at the Royal Pavilion, Brighton, both for the original Chinoiserie interior scheme from 1802 and the later extensions and re-decoration under John Nash from c. 1815. Detailed accounts and designs exist covering the period 1802–23. In 1802 and 1803 Crace & Son supplied many pieces of oriental furniture imported from China including 'Japan lacquer' cabinets, 'very handsome Sophas' and chairs and stools of bamboo. Large quantities of porcelain, banners, models of junks and costumes were also supplied to provide an 'authentic' decor. In January 1803 an account for £317 16s 6d was submitted and in 1804 a further one for £441. The greatest expense, however, was for the large collection of oriental ware specially purchased in China by Dr James Garrett for which £2,090 was asked. Chinese items were also purchased for Carlton House. For the work carried out from c. 1817 the principal designer was John Crace's son Frederick. He received the assistance of artists of talent like Robert Jones and a man named Lambelet who executed Frederick's grand concepts with great talent. Payments were again substantial amounting to £440 2s on account in 1824 and £173 in 1836. [D; Musgrave, *Royal Pavilion*; Windsor Royal Archives, RA 25135, RA 25131, RA 25158, RA 25181, RA 25184, RA 25186, RA 25172, RA 35583, RA 35606] B.A.

Crackerode, John, 'The Tea Table', Henrietta St, Covent Gdn, London, cm (1722–24). On 6 October 1722 took out insurance cover of £500 on goods and merchandise in his dwelling house. This would seem to suggest a business of considerable proportions but its life may well have been short. In December 1724 his stock was sold by auction. It was said to be all new and consisted of 'Peer-Glasses, Chimney-Glasses, and Sconces, India Skreens and Chests, Tea-Tables, Hand-Boards, Bottle-Stands, Burows, Tables of several Sorts both Wallnut-tree and Mahogany, Lanthorns for Halls and Stair-Cases.' [Heal; GL, Sun MS vol. 14, ref. 26583; *Daily Courant*, 3 December 1724]

Crackles, John, 64 West St, Hull, Yorks., cm and u (1814). [D]

Crackles, Richard, Hull, Yorks., cm and broker (1803–31). In 1803 at Steeple Entry with a shop in Trippett St but in 1806 at Myton Walls. By 1810 at 16 Blackfriargate and in 1816 at 7 Waterworks St. From 1823 addresses in Chariot St are used, first no. 28 and from 1826 no. 27. The last recorded address in 1831 is Garden Pl., Sykes St, the same location as Robert Crackles who was probably his successor. [D]

Crackles, Richard Slack, 28 Humber St, Hull, Yorks., carver and gilder (1834–40). [D]

Crackles, Richard, 4 Dorset St, Manchester Sq., London, u and cm (1835–37). The dates allow the possibility that this is the Richard Crackles previously recorded as working in Hull. [D]

Crackles, Robert, 13 Garden Pl., Sykes St, Hull, Yorks., cm (1839). Possibly the successor of Richard Crackles recorded at this address in 1831. [D]

Cracknell, George, Witham, Essex, upholder (1712–34). Son of Aawron Cracknell of Witham, Gent. App. to Edward Warren of London, upholder, 26 September 1705 and free of the London Upholders' Co. by servitude 9 October 1712. In 1734 recorded as a freeholder at Witham. [GL, Upholders' Co. records; Essex RO, Q/RJ 1/1]

Cracknell, William Francis, Eden St, Cambridge, cm (1840). [Poll bk]

Cradleton, Thomas, Whitecross St, Barton-on-Humber, Lincs., joiner and cm (1835). [D]

Cradock, Robert, Canterbury, Kent, u (1691–1716). Freeman of Canterbury in 1691. Took app. named Juss in 1716. [Freemen reg.; S of G, app. index]

Craft, William, Hexham, Northumb., joiner and cm (1827–34). At Hall Garth, 1827–28, but in 1834 in Fore St. [D]

Crafter, Edward, London, bedstead maker (1835–39). In 1835 at Horton Old Town and in 1839 at 51 Kingsland Rd. [D]

Crafter, Richard, 2 Booth St, Spitalfields, London, bedstead maker (1839). [D]

Cragg, James, London, cm (1793–1835). Recorded as a subscriber to Sheraton's *Drawing Book*, 1793 but not listed in directories until 1808. In that year he is shown at 1 Holland St, Soho, but before the end of the year had moved to 88 Tottenham Ct Rd. He stayed here until at least 1811 but in 1813 was at no. 188. The business continued here until 1825 but in the next year was at 27 Francis St, Tottenham Ct Rd, where the trade is listed as u. Last recorded in 1835 but by 1837, John Cragg was trading from the same address. [D]

Cragg, John, 27 Francis St, Tottenham Ct Rd, London, u (1837–39). [D]

Cragg, Leonard, London, cm (1793). Subscribed to Sheraton's *Drawing Book*, 1793.

Cragg & Maxwell, Duke St, Whitehaven, Cumb., joiner/cm (1811). [D]

Craggs, John, 2 Maxwell Ct, Old Brokers Row, Moorfields, London, carver, gilder and chandler (1779). In 1799 insured his house for £100. [GL, Sun MS vol. 277, p. 76]

Craggs, Thomas, 5 Feasgate, York, baker and cm (1830). [D]

Craig, Andrew, Newcastle, cm and bellows maker (1801–38). From 1801–06 at Postern. At this stage bellow making was an important part of the business and in 1803 he advertised 'bellows for forgers, smelt-mills, anchor-smiths, black and white smiths'. At the same time however he advertised for a turner and four cm, suggesting that this side of the business was also very active. In 1811 at Old Flesh Market and from 1824–38 at Forth St. From 1824 the business is described as cm and mahogany merchant. By 1833 his son had joined him in the business and it is described as Andrew Craig & Son. [D; *Newcastle Courant*, 23 April 1803, 29 March 1806]

Craig, Colton, parish of SS Philip and Jacob, Bristol, carver (1754). [Poll bk]

Craig, James, 9 Gt Saffron Hill, London, clock-case and cabinet makers. Late 18th-century trade card [Banks Coll., BM] states that he made 'all sorts of Dial Cases and Stands for Time Pieces' but illustrates no furniture.

Craig, John, address unknown, cm (1803). Subscribed to Sheraton's *Cabinet Dictionary*, 1803.

Craig, John, 45 Groat Mkt, Newcastle, cm and joiner (1838). [D]

Craigall, Francis, 2 Rose St, Soho, London, cm (1808). [D]

Craister, William, Court, 123 Kirkgate, Leeds, Yorks., cm (1837). [D]

Crake, —, 21 South Molton St, Oxford Rd, London, carver and gilder. Card, c.1800, recorded by Heal. May be the John Crake trading in Oxford St as a painter and gilder in 1807.

Crake, John, Lower Brook St, Westminster, London, carver (1774). [Poll bk]

Crake, John, 18 Quebec St and 258 Oxford St, London, painter and gilder (1807–08). [D; Heal]

Crakeplace, Henry, Wilson St, Workington, Cumb., cm and joiner (1828–34). [D]

Cramp, Enoch, Deal, Kent, cm, upholder and auctioneer (1784–93). On 25 January 1787 insured household goods for £500. [D; GL, Sun MS vol. 343, p. 2]

Cramp, James, Strand, London, u (1830). Freeman of Canterbury. [Canterbury poll bk]

Cramp, Thomas, 6 Duke St, Lincoln's Inn Fields, London, upholder (1776). In 1776 took out insurance cover of £600 of which £400 was in respect of utensils and stock. [GL, Sun MS vol. 246, p. 430]

Cramp & Tolputt, 115 Long Acre, London, upholders (1790–93). Subscribers to Sheraton's *Drawing Book*, 1793. [D]

Crampton, Ellis, 130 Digbeth, Birmingham, u (1828). [D]

Crampton, James, Aswell Lane, Louth, Lincs., cm, joiner and builder (1826–40). [D]

Crane, Benjamin, 19 Glanville St, Rathbone Pl., London, cm (1786). On 2 August 1786 took out insurance cover of £300 of which £20 was in respect of utensils and stock in shop. [GL, Sun MS vol. 338, p. 239]

Crane, Benjamin, 68 Tottenham Ct Rd, London, u, cm, broker and appraiser (1803–15). On 2 December 1807 took out insurance cover of £1,000 of which £450 was in respect of utensils and stock. [D; GL, Sun MS vol. 440, ref. 809908]

Crane, Edward, 43 London Lane and repository 127 Pottergate St, Norwich, upholder and auctioneer (1775–98). Freeman of Preston, Lancs. where he probably spent his early life. App. to Henry Withers of Norwich and free by servitude 3 May 1775. In 1780 insured his house for £600. [D; Preston freemen rolls; Norwich freemen reg.; GL, Sun MS vol. 280, p. 547]

Crane, George, 32 Glanville St, London, upholder (1783). In 1783 insured his house for £300. [GL, Sun MS vol. 313, p. 392]

Crane, Joseph, 55 Southampton Row, Russell Sq., London, cm, upholder, appraiser and undertaker (1817–29). Trade card in Landauer Coll., MMA, NY. [D]

Crane, Peter, Bristol, cm (1781–1801). At Cathay, 1792–95, and Lawrence Hill 1799–1801. [D; poll bks]

Crane, William, address unknown, cm (1757). On 27 May 1757 received £5 5s for stands made for Felbrigg, Norfolk. [Norfolk RO, Felbrigg MS WKC 6/454]

Crane, William, Brighton, Sussex, carver and gilder (1822–40). At 1 Milton Pl., Upper Russell St in August 1822 when his daughter Rose Falmer was bapt. He remained at this address until 1824 but in the next year was at Cottage Gdns. From 1839 his address was 21 Portland St. [D; PR(bapt.)]

Crane, Jeremiah, Shipwright St, Rotherhithe, London, carver (1762–74). In 1762 took app. named Porter. On 12 December 1774 took out insurance cover of £300 of which £150 was in respect of houshold goods in his house and timber. [S of G, app. index; GL, Sun MS vol. 235, ref. 347289]

Cranford, William, High Holborn, London, upholder (1779). Insurance cover of £500 taken out in 1779 with Jacob Fletcher, in trust for creditors of William Cranford. [GL, Sun MS vol. 274, p. 567]

Crankshaw, Edward, Windy Bank, Colne, Lancs., carpenter, joiner and cm (b. 1792–1841). Son Richard aged 21 at the time of the 1841 Census. [D]

Cranston, George, Christchurch, Hants., u (1839). [D]

Cranston, George, Ringwood, Hants., u (1839). [D]

Cranston, John C. snr, Ringwood, Hants., u and ironmonger (1767–82). In 1767 appointed guardian of Ann Cranston, his wife, for the administration of her former husband's will. In 1775 took out insurance cover for £300 which was increased to £500 in 1778 and £800 in 1782. Of this utensils and stock accounted for £80 in 1775, £250 in 1778 and £300 in 1782. [S of G, Winchester Guardianships; GL, Sun MS vol. 242, p. 143; vol. 267, p. 315; vol. 306, p. 214]

Cranston, John jnr, Ringwood, Hants., u, cm and auctioneer (1823–39). In 1823 the business was described as Cranston & Sons but thereafter as John Cranston jnr. Listed at High St and West St in 1830. He appears to have adopted a policy of labelling his furniture and examples are known of a mahogany extending dining table, a rosewood table with a penwork top and a pair of rosewood card tables, all of Regency date, so marked, and of good quality. [D; V & A archives; *Antique Dealer's and Collector's Guide*, January 1956]

Cranston, John, Castle St, Christchurch, Hants., u (1830). [D]

Cranwell, Robert, 33 Edward St, Portman Sq., London, cm and u (1839). [D]

Crasby, —, 33 Clerkenwell Close, London, chairmaker (1809). [D]

Craske, James, Norwich, u (1826). Admitted freeman 19 August 1826. [Freemen rolls]

Craskel, John, Lancaster, cm (1799). Named in the Gillow records in connection with the making of a wardrobe. [Westminster Ref. Lib., Gillow vol. 344/98, p. 1520]

Crastay, —, London, cm (1793). Subscribed to Sheraton's *Drawing Book*, 1793.

Craven, Ambrose, Calverley-cum-Farsley, Yorks., cm (1837). [D]

Craven, George, Hull, Yorks., cm (1774–80). [Poll bks]

Craven, John, Northgate, Blackburn, Lancs., cm and joiner (1814). [D]

Craven, John, Leeds, Yorks., cm and u (1834–39). At 8 Commercial Rd (or St), in 1834, 1 Central Market Buildings and Lands Lane in 1837 and 3 Bank St in 1839. [D]

Craven, John, Skyeshead, Keighley, Yorks., joiner/cm (1837). [D]

Craven, Joseph, Hull, Yorks., cm (1774). [Poll bk]

Craven, William, Finkle St, Hull, Yorks., cm (1792–93). In 1793 took out insurance cover on his house and household goods for £300. [D; GL, Sun MS vol. 392, p. 548]

Craven & Smith, Leeds, Yorks., cm and u (1834). [D]

Craven & Worswick, Ebenezer St, Leeds, Yorks., cm and u (1798). [D]

Craw, Thomas, 57 Thomas St, Manchester, cm and chairmaker (1834–40). [D]

Crawford, George, 1 King St, Westminster, London, carver and gilder (1820). [D]

Crawford, George, 129 Queen St, Whitehaven, Cumb., cm (1828–29). [D]

Crawford, James, 22 Bridge St, Westminster, London, carver and gilder (1823–29). [D]

Crawford, John, Sunderland, Co. Durham, cm (1827–28). At 3 George St in both 1827 and 28, but shown also at High Villers St in 1828. [D]

Crawford, W., Chester, cm (1812–19). At Handbridge St in 1812 but by 1818 at Northgate St. [Poll bks]

Crawford, William, 228 High Holborn, London, cm and u (1768–83). In 1778 with William Bond, carver and gilder, and Thomas Noble, proprietors of the Casino in Marlborough St, took out insurance cover for £800. In 1770 supplied furniture to Sir Edward Knatchbull of Mersham le Hatch, Kent. This included a mahogany Gothic four post bedstead at £24, a 'common' mahogany clothes press at £5, a mahogany commode table with a dressing drawer at £5, a basin stand at 10s 6d and a dressing table at £11 5s. An account for £62 for 'Bed, bedding & other furniture for ye Girls room' was settled in October 1770. [D; GL, Sun MS vol. 267, p. 256; Kent RO, U951 A18/66, A19/2]

Crawley, Gerard, 'The Coffee Mill and Nimble Ninepence', Cornhill, London, turner (1743–68). Although a turner he dealt with and made items of furniture. In 1743 he supplied to Sir James Dashwood of Kirtlington Park, Oxon., 'a pair of Roman tables' costing £43. His trade card [Heal Coll., BM] indicates that he made 'Tea Chests, Mahogany Waiters, Tea Boards, Voiders, Tables &c.' Other items of stock included floor coverings, coffee mills, nine pins, bottle and ink stands and washball boxes. [Heal; *Apollo*, January 1980]

Crawshaw, Charles, Sheffield, Yorks., cm (1756–58). In 1756 took two apps named Hildyard and Wood, and in 1758 another named Emborough. [S of G, app. index]

Crawson, William, Sedgford Lane, King's Lynn, Norfolk, cm (1839). [D]

Crawston, William, North Walsham, Norfolk, cm (1798). [D]

Cray, T., address unknown, chairmaker (c. 1805). A pair of beechwood japanned chairs in the Indianapolis Museum of Art and a set of twelve mahogany dining chairs sold by Phillips on 29 March 1983, lot 64, were stamped 'T CRAY'.

Crayer, Benjamin, 132 Golden Lane, London, carver (1777). In 1777 took out insurance cover of £400 of which £200 was in respect of utensils and stock. [GL, Sun MS vol. 257, p. 376]

Crayne, Thomas, Derby, joiner and cm (1793–1806). Subscribed to Sheraton's *Drawing Book*, 1793. On 27 April 1806 suffered from a fire. [Gents Mag., May 1806]

Crayton, William, King St, St Ann's, London, cm (1791). Took out insurance cover of £100 in 1791. See James Nelson.

Creak, William, 48 Northampton St, Clerkenwell, London, cm (1809). [D]

Creasy, James, Exe Lane, Exeter, Devon, cm (1839). Daughter Jane bapt. on 1 September at St David's Church. [PR (bapt.)]

Creasy, Thomas, Bargate, Boston, Lincs., cm (1805–08). [D]

Creech, James, London, upholder (1710). Free of the Upholders' Co., 19 October 1710. [GL, Upholders' Co. records]

Creed, John & Co., Gt Yarmouth, Norfolk, cm (1755). In 1755 took app. named Cooper. [S of G, app. index]

Creed, Samuel, Beccles, Suffolk, upholder (1784). [D]

Creed, William, Gt Yarmouth, Norfolk, joiner and cm (1777). In 1777 insured his house for £500 with Thomas Davy, Gent. and mortgager. [GL, Sun MS vol. 257, p. 500]

Creed, William, address unknown, cm (1803). Subscribed to Sheraton's *Cabinet Dictionary*, 1803.

Creed, William, Albion St, Cheltenham, Glos., cm (1839). [D]

Creer, Gilbert B., 18 Lime St with shop at 71 Lime St, Liverpool, u and cm (1835). [D]

Creighton, Adam, Liverpool, japanner and cm (1835–37). In 1835 at Hill St with a shop at 18 Park Pl., but in 1837 shown at 19 Park Pl. only. [D]

Creighton, James, Carlisle, Cumb., joiner/cm (1811–34). In 1811 at Keay's Lane, Scotch St but from 1829 at 40 Lowther St. [D]

Crellin, John, shop at 4 Riding St, Liverpool, cm (1837). [D]

Cremer, John, London, upholder (1714–27). Son of John Cremer of Grimston, Norfolk, clerk. App. to Bladwell Peyton on 6 October 1714 and admitted freeman of the Upholders' Co. by servitude, 4 January 1726/27. [GL, Upholders' Co. records]

Crerar, John, 25 Gt New St, Fetter Lane, London, cm and timber merchant (1792). On 12 July 1792 took out insurance of £800 on the utensils and stock in his open yard, millhouse, sheds and sawpits communicating. [GL, Sun MS vol. 387, p. 267]

Cressall, John, 5 Whitechapel Rd, London, upholder and undertaker (1791). On 15 April 1791 took out insurance cover of £1,800 of which £400 was in respect of utensils and stock in his workshop. [GL, Sun MS vol. 376, p. 203]

Cresshall (or Cresshull), James, Birmingham, cm and u (1818–30). in 1818 at the Square; in 1828 at 2 Coleshill St; and in 1830 shown at both Coleshill St and 18 Back St. [D]

Cresswell, Henry, Huddersfield, Yorks., cm and u (1822–37). At Cross Church St, 1822–30 but from 1830 shown at 39 New St. [D]

Cresswell, James, Steelhouse Lane, Birmingham, cm and u (1818). [D]

Cresswell, John, Manchester, cm and u (1829–40). At 37 Piccadilly in 1829, 25 Abrahams Ct, also as carver and gilder, in 1832–33; 6 Blackfriars, 1834–36; and 83 Portland St, 1836–40. Bankrupt 26 June 1829. [D; *Liverpool Mercury*, 3 July 1829] See John Alton, carver and gilder at 37 Piccadilly.

Cressy, George, 6 Gt Earl St, Seven Dials, London, bedstead maker (1826–29). [D]

Cressy, Sarah, 6 Gt Earl St, Seven Dials, London, bedstead maker (1837–39). Successor to George Cressy and probably his widow. [D]

Crew, Arthur, Plymouth, Devon, upholder (1719). In 1719 took app. named Treffry. [S of G, app. index]

Crew, Edward, Abingdon, Berks., upholder (1718–34). Insured his dwelling house in 1718 the premium being paid through a Mr Crew of St Clements Lane, Lombard St, London. Freeman of Abingdon. [GL, Sun MS vol. 8, ref. 11184; poll bk]

Crew, Milburn, Silver St, Tetbury, Glos., cm and u (1822). [D]

Crew, Robert, Abingdon, Berks., u (1752–84). In 1752 took app. named Davis. [D; poll bk; S of G, app. index]

Crew, Samuel, Falmouth, Cornwall, u (1709). In December 1709 advertised that he made 'all sorts of Field-Beds, Where all Gentlemen that go by the Packets for Portugal or Spain may be furnish't as in London'. [*The Post Boy*, 21 December 1709]

Crew, Samuel, High St, Congleton, Cheshire, cm (1822–28). [D]

Crew, William snr, 6 Christmas St, Bristol, cm and broker (1817–27). [D]

Crew, William jnr, Bristol, cabinet and chairmaker (1823–34). Operated from various addresses in Thomas St, 1823–31, these being no. 118 (1823), no. 129 (1824–25), no. 25 (1826–28) and no. 140 (1829–31). In 1833 at 25 Temple St and in 1834 at 3 Merchant St. [D]

Crews, C., Newton Abbot, Devon, cm (1814). Agent for Swift & Co.'s state lottery. [*Exeter Flying Post*, 6 January 1814]

Creyghton, Matthew, London, u (1749–61). In 1749 at Bedford St, Westminster. Announced in *General Advertiser*, 31 March 1750 that he had 'removed from Bedford-street, Covent Garden to Duke-street, York Buildings, the house that was late general Barrel's, a Busto of King Charles is in the Front'. Discharge from Debtors' Prison reported in *London Gazette*, 26 September 1761, when stated as 'late of St Mary's parish, Lambeth'. [Poll bk]

Cribb, Robert, High Holborn, London, carver, gilder and print seller (1790–1834). Virtually all sources record his address as 288 High Holborn, near Gt Turnstile, but in 1790 an insurance policy gives the number as 200 and one directory entry for 298 occurs. These may be errors. After 1806 his son was assisting him in the business and the trading style changed to Robert Cribb & Son. In 1790 insurance cover of £1,000 was taken out, half of which covered goods and utensils in his dwelling house, counting house and workshops used in connection with the business. In 1785 however cover on utensils, stock and goods in trust was only £300. His trade card [Heal Coll., BM] indicates that he made looking-glass and picture frames, offered to re-gild old frames and re-silver mirror plates. Pictures were cleaned, lined and repaired and Venetian window blinds and paper hangings stocked. A different card in the Banks Coll., BM displays the Prince of Wales' feathers and reads: 'Carvers and gilders to H.R.H. the Prince of Wales'. Royal commissions were received and in July 1810 £6 11s 10d was paid to the firm for work undertaken. Other important clients were served. Sir Joshua Reynolds used a frame maker by the name of Cribb who may be this maker. A gilt side table in the manner of William Kent at Chatsworth is signed and dated 'R. Cribb fecit 1834'. Three other tables of the same type, although not signed, are undoubtedly from the same source. Some of his furniture was marked by the application of paper trade labels. A pair of painted pier glasses so labelled and dated in manuscript 21 June 1805 were included in the Sotheby's sale of 2 June 1967, lot 118. [D; GL, Sun MS vol. 370; vol. 328, p. 576; Heal; Windsor Royal Archives, RA 89007]

Cribb, William, London, carver and gilder (1812–40). At 13 Tavistock St, Covent Gdn, 1812–20, but by July 1820 at 34 King St, Covent Gdn at which address he remained. On 4 November 1812 took out insurance cover of £1,600 on his dwelling house alone. This amount of cover was repeated at his new King St house with an addition of £400 for stock and utensils and £100 for pictures, prints and glass. His trade cards [GL and Westminster Ref. Lib.] indicate that he undertook house painting, the manufacture of looking-glasses, the framing of pictures and prints, which he also sold. [D; GL, Sun MS vol. 459, ref. 875619; vol. 483, ref. 970065]

Crichton, David, 28 King St, Soho, London, cm and looking-glass maker (1774–81). Appears to have attracted important patrons. In July 1777 submitted an account to the Duke of Dorset for goods supplied and work carried out in connection with his London house at 38 Grosvenor Sq. The total sum involved came to £520 0s 5d of which the most expensive item was 'a very large pier glass with a Top plate in a neat carved & gilt frame' which was charged at £45. In January 1781 John Parker of Saltram, Devon paid him £40 for a looking-glass and in October of the same year £42 for a pier glass. In 1782 for the same house he supplied sheets for the servants and china dessert dishes. Succeeded at this address by William Crichton. [Heal; V & A archives]

Crichton, Jeremiah, London, cm, u, auctioneer, appraiser, house and estate agent (1820–28). At 2 High St, Newington Butts (opposite the Church) 1820–28, but one directory of 1826 gives the address as Norwood, Surrey. [D]

Crichton, Joseph, 17 Kennington Lane, Lambeth, London, upholder and undertaker (1817). An u of the same name was in 1841 trading from an address at 7 Keppel Terr., King's Rd, Chelsea, London and could be the same man. [D; V & A archives]

Crichton, William, 28 King St, Soho, London, u (1784–1808). Successor of David Crichton at this address. In 1795 supplied furniture including cabinets, screens, beds and a sofa, to the Rt Hon. Lord Grenville, amounting to £400 16s 7d. His name is included in the list of master cabinet makers in Sheraton's *Cabinet Dictionary*, 1803. [D; Heal; Cornwall RO, Fortescue papers]

Crichton, William jnr, 3 George's Buildings, Old St Rd, London, chair and sofa maker (1839). [D]

Crichton & Pitchford, address unknown, cm (1759). Submitted accounts in 1759 for work carried out for Kedleston, Derbs. [V & A archives]

Crickmar, Robert, King's Quay St, Harwich, Essex, cm (1823–39). Listed at King St in 1832. [D]

Crine, John, 87 Bartholomew Close, London, upholder and cm (1803–09). In July 1803 took out insurance cover of £1,900 of which £1,050 was in respect of utensils and stock. [D; GL, Sun MS vol. 427, ref. 750321]

Crine, John Henry, 25 Cannon St Rd, London, carver, gilder and looking-glass and picture frame maker (1839). [D]

Cripps, John, address unknown, garden furniture supplier (1838–40). Recorded from February 1838 supplying rustic furniture and metalwork for the gardens at Buckingham Palace. In the quarter to September 1839 he supplied 'two Swiss Pattern Garden Chairs' at £1 1s, a rustic garden table with drawers and varnished at £2 12s 6d, and eight 'Improved Pattern Windsor Chairs' for which £2 16s was charged. Also prepared a mahogany parrot stand, supplied flower stands and boxes and firescreens. [Windsor Royal Archives, RA, box I, item 2; Lord Chamberlain's accounts]

Crish, Jos., Silver St, London, cm (1743). Advertised that his app. Samuel Higgs had absconded and warned other makers not to employ him. [*Daily Advertiser*, 29 January 1743]

Crisp, Samuel, Gt Yarmouth, Norfolk, cm (1777–95). App. to Samuel Bream and free by servitude 1777. At this date or before may have lived at Bungay, Suffolk. [Poll bk; freemen records]

Crisp, Samuel, Colchester, Essex, cm (1793). [D]

Crisp, Samuel, London, cm (1796–1807). Freeman of Gt Yarmouth and probably the same cm who was resident in that town 1777–95. [Gt Yarmouth poll bks]

Crisp, Thomas, King's Lynn, Norfolk, u and cm (1777–80). In 1777 took out insurance of £900 of which £500 was in respect of utensils and stock. By 1780 the insurance cover was only £300 of which £100 was for a kitchen and workshop. [GL, Sun MS vol. 256, p. 138; vol. 281, p. 47]

Crisp, Thomas, London, upholder (1781–83). In 1781 at 3 New Bond St which he insured for £300. Two years later he was at 19 Castle St, Leicester Fields, and took out a similar amount of insurance cover of which £30 was in respect of utensils, stock and goods. [GL, Sun MS vol. 291, p. 167; vol. 314, p. 549]

Crisp, William, London, portable desk and dressing case manufacturer (1817–37). At 34 Cockspur St, Charing Cross, 1817–20 but by 1823 had moved to 49 New Bond St. [D]

Crispe, Edward, 22 Southampton Buildings, London, upholder (1799). Son of John Crispe of Sutton Valence, Kent, Gent. App. to Henry Blaxland on 5 October 1791 and free of the Upholders' Co. by servitude, 2 October 1799. [GL, Upholders' Co. records]

Crispe, John, Maidstone, Kent, cm (1832–39). At High St in 1832–35 but by 1837 had moved to King St. [D; poll bks]

Crispin, William, 12 Spicer St, Spitalfields, London, cm and u (1827). [D]

Criswick, J. jnr, London, carver, gilder and picture and looking-glass frame makers (1829–39). At 46 Greek St, Soho 1829–37 but by 1839 at 6 New Compton St, Soho when the firm was trading as Criswick & Ryan. [D]

Critchell, John, Kingstone, Yeovil, Som., cm and u (1822–30). [D]

Critchley, Cornelius, Shropshire St, Market Drayton, Salop, cm (1835). [D]

Critchley, George, 3 Carlton Pl., Ardwick, Manchester, u (1836–40). [D] See George Critchlow.

Critchley, Hugh, Preston, Lancs. and Liverpool, u (1780–82). In 1780 at Liverpool where he insured a house for £100. He was described as a u and mortgager. He was however a freeman of Preston and probably worked for some time in that town. [GL, Sun MS vol. 283, p. 283; Preston freemen records]

Critchley, John, Chester, u (1687). Free 26 October 1687. [Freemen rolls]

Critchley, John, 38 Cock St, Wolverhampton, Staffs., cm and u (1818). [D]

Critchley, John, Liverpool, cm (1835–37). At 6 Brown St, Rupert St in 1835 and 14 Back Blake St in 1837. [D]

Critchley, Richard, Rochester, Kent, carver (1743). In 1743 took app. named Batten. [S of G, app. index]

Critchley, Thomas, 1 Cow Lane, Liverpool, cm (1818–21). [D]

Critchlow, Esther, 4 Carlton Pl., Manchester, u (1825). [D]

Critchlow, George, 3–4 Carlton Pl., Downing St, Ardwick, Manchester, u (1832–36). Successor to Esther Critchlow. [D] See George Critchley.

Critchlow, Henry, 4 Brook St, Chorlton Row, Manchester, u (1825). [D]

Critchlow, John, 25 London Rd, Manchester, u (1808). [D]

Crocker, John, North Parade, Penzance, Cornwall, cm etc. (1823–30). [D]

Crockett, Charles, London, cm (1793–1809). Subscribed to Sheraton's *Drawing Book*, 1793. At 42 Berwick St, Oxford St in 1802 when he took out insurance cover for £100. By 1809 he was at 2 Norton St where the insurance on the house contents was £170 out of a total of £200. It was stated that no work was carried out there. [GL, Sun MS vol. 423, ref. 730118; vol. 448, ref. 830826]

Crockett, John, 7 Snow Hill, London, water gilder (1766–79). Received £60 in 1766 for work carried out for the Duke of Northumberland. In 1775 insured his house for £200 which was increased to £300 in 1779. [GL, Sun MS vol. 276, p. 379; vol. 240, p. 602; V & A archives]

Crockett, Joseph, Market Pl., Devizes, Wilts., cm and u (1830–39). Trading as Joseph & Son in 1839. [D]

Crockett, William, Wolverhampton, Staffs., cm (1818–22). Recorded at High-green in 1822. [D]

Crockford, Jon., 12 Hammond Pl., Chatham, Kent, cm and u (1824–40). In 1832 the directory entry is in the name of John Crockford jnr, and it is possible that this indicates the transfer of the business from father to son. [D]

Croft, —, London(?), u (1676). Received £8 for beds and bedding in 1676. [Lincoln RO, Monson 10/1/A/14 — C. Wren's account bk]

Croft, Isaac, Leeds, Yorks., cm and joiner (1791–93). Succeeded by Aveyard & Buck in 1792. They had previously been employed by him as journeymen. Subscribed to Sheraton's *Drawing Book*, 1793. [*Leeds Intelligencer*, 13 September 1791]

Croft, James, Sheffield, Yorks., cm and u (1828–37). In 1828 at 19 Burgess St, in 1833 at 47 Rockingham St and from 1837 at Hereford St and Porter St. [D]

Croft, John, 17 Pall Mall, Tithebarn St, Liverpool, chairmaker (1796). May have moved to 11 Pownall St in 1796. [D]

Croft, Joseph, Lancaster and Preston, Lancs. cm (1762–84). App. to W. Blackburn and R. Bateman of Lancaster 1762 and free by servitude, 1772–73. Recorded trading in Preston, 1781–84. [D; Lancaster app. reg. and freemen rolls]

Croft, Joseph, Downe St, Richmond Row, Liverpool, u and cm. App. to Mathew Gregson in 1795 and free by servitude, 7 September 1806. In partnership with another craftsman named Lowe he undertook work on behalf of Mathew Gregson, 1807–08. [Freemen reg.; Liverpool RO, Gregson papers, 920 GRE 1/27]

Croft, Joseph, St George St, Sheffield, cm (1838). [D]

Croft, Nicholas, Lancaster and London, cm (1768). App. to G. Rawes in 1749 and free by servitude, 1767–68. Then moved to London. [Freemen rolls; Lancaster poll bk]

Croft, Robert, Liverpool, chairmaker (1781–90). Recorded in 1781 at 6 East Side, St Peter's Church, and in 1787 at Lord St. In 1790 once again at 6 Church Alley, St Peters. [D]

Croft, Samuel, Battle, Sussex, carpenter, joiner, cm and looking-glass maker (1773–77). In October 1773 Croft described his business as 'old-accostomed' and he may well have been trading for several years before this date. The object of the advertisement he issued in that month was to obtain a foreman for the carpentry and joinery side of the business and he stated that if the applicant was well-qualified he would have no objection to taking him as a partner. He stated that he could undertake all sorts of cabinet making and could re-silver glasses. In April 1777 Croft declared that he was retiring from business and offered to let his carpenter's and joiner's shop, dwelling house, gate-way, yard and large garden. He had in stock at this time a quantity of cabinet and upholstery goods that could be taken at 'a fair Appraisment'. [*Sussex Weekly Advertiser*, 25 October 1773, 14 April 1777]

Croft, Samuel & Son, 4 Water Lane and Meadow Lane, Leeds, Yorks., cm and joiner (1837). [D]

Croft, Simon, Liverpool, cm (b. 1755–d. 1833). At 11 Pownall Sq., Highfield St, in 1803 and at 7 Pownall Sq., 1805–10. In 1811 Croft moved to Richmond Row which he used as his address up to the time of his death in 1833. He signed the Supplement to the *Liverpool Cabinet and Chair Prices*, 1808, on behalf of the masters. His wife died in December 1818 in her sixtieth year and Simon Croft died on 5 February 1833 aged 78. [D; *Liverpool Mercury*, 25 December 1818; 22 February 1833]

Croft, William, Bath, Som., cm and joiner (1753–61). App. to George Davis in 1753, free 1761. [Bath app. reg. and freemen rolls]

Croft, William, Little Queen St, Holborn, London, cm (1784). [D]

Croft, William, 27 Chapel St, Liverpool, cm (1821). [D]

Crofton, J. S., 145 Aldersgate St, London, u (1837). [D]

Crofton, Philip, London, cm and u (1823–28). In 1823 at 1 Joseph St, Brunswick Sq. where he took out insurance cover for £300 of which £160 was in respect of utensils and stock. In 1826 at 113 Cromer St, Brunswick Sq. as a cm and broker. Although directory entries at this address continue until 1829 it is likely that trading ceased a year earlier for Crofton was listed as a bankrupt in August 1828. He appears to have also acted as an appraiser and house agent. [D; GL, Sun MS vol. 498, ref. 1005087; *Liverpool Mercury*, 29 August 1828]

Crofts, Dudley, Princes St, Leicester Sq., London, u (1779–93). Between 1786 and 89 listed as an 'upholstery & carpet warehouse'. In 1779 took out insurance cover of £2,000 of which £1,400 was in respect of utensils, stock and goods. [D; GL, Sun MS vol. 279, p. 378]

Crofts, Henry, London. In 1718 supplied four marble tables costing £10 to the Duke of Montrose for his London house in Bond St. [Scottish RO, GD 220/6/28/P85]

Crofts, John, New Bridge, Exeter, Devon, carver (1827). Daughter Mary Eliza bapt. at St Edmund's Church on 13 May 1827. [PR (bapt.)]

Crofts, William, Stamford, Lincs., u (late 17th century). Freeman of Stamford by purchase. Two William Crofts appear to be recorded on the freemen rolls at this period.

Crofts, William, Chester, cm (1747). [Poll bk]

Crohan, Edward, 18 Kings-gate St, High Holborn, London, bed and mattress maker (1822). [D]

Cromack, John, Gowthorpe, Selby, Yorks., cm (1822). [D]

Crompton, Ellis, 3 No. 2 Court, Lomax St, Manchester, u (1817). [D]

Crompton, John, Liverpool, u (1714). Free 3 September 1714. [Freemen reg.]

Crompton, John, London, upholder (1773–1804). Son of Benjamin Crompton of Cockspur St. In 1773 admitted a freeman of the Upholders' Co. under the terms of the 1750 Upholders' Act. He recorded his address as Cockspur St in 1778 and 1781 and was probably at this period assisting in the family business. Between 1786 and 1794 living at Church St, St Ann's, Soho and in 1802 at Percy St. On the death of his father, his brother James appears to have succeeded to the business in Cockspur St and it is possible that John decided to retire from active participation in the trade. He was however made master of the Upholders' Co. in 1804. [GL, Upholders' Co. records]

Crompton, John, 41 Digbeth, Birmingham, u (1835–39). [D]

Crompton, Joseph, 32 Worcester St, Birmingham, u (1830). [D]

Crompton, Robert, 17 Johnson St, Salford, Lancs., u, mattress and cushion maker by machinery (1832–33). [D]

Crompton, Ellis, 15 Snow Hill, Birmingham, u (1822–30).

Listed at 80 Digbeth, also as a mattress maker, in 1822; and at 15 Snow Hill in 1830. [D]

Crompton, James, Cockspur St, Charing Cross, London, paper hanging manufacturer and u (1795–d. by 1799). Successor to Benjamin Crompton at the same address. James Crompton was probably dead by 1795, and certainly was by 1799 at the time of his wife's death. [D; *Gents Mag.*, March 1799]

Crompton, Samuel, London, u (1753–93). First associated with a partnership named Crompton & Spinnage trading from Charles St, St James's Sq., in 1753. This business described itself as upholders and paper hangings manufacturers. About 1753 the partners moved to Cockspur St, Charing Cross, an address which was to be used until the termination of the business in the 1790s. In the late 1760s the original partnership appears to have broken up. The business continued at the Cockspur St address as Benjamin Crompton & Son. Benjamin Crompton had two sons, John and James, both u. The matter is, however, complicated by the appearance at about the same time of a partnership calling itself Crompton & Hodgson, and trading from Castle St, corner of Bear St, Leicester Sq., as paper stainers. Its life appears to have been brief. Crompton & Son, however, appear to have flourished, trading as upholders, paper hangings manufacturers and carpet dealers. In 1782 they took out insurance cover on their utensils, stock and warehouses of £6,000, and although this dropped to £3,800 in 1784 the sum is still substantial. The firm comes to notice supplying the household of the 6th Earl of Coventry at Croome Court, Worcs., in 1761. They were paid £60 14s 3½d for items supplied to the Earl of Egremont at Petworth, Sussex, in 1774–75. Also in 1775 they received payments in connection with Chevening, Kent, which included work on a green and white bed for the house. They also appear to have taken commissions in connection with the Stanhope's town house. Total payments were £148 17s 4½d. The firm also supplied to the Royal Household of George IV. An interesting side line appears to have been the supplying of chamber horses and stands. As many as three of these appear to have been supplied to Charles Long of Saxmundham, Suffolk, 1768–69, and another to William Constable at Burton Constable, Yorks., in 1772. [D; Heal; GL, Sun MS vol. 298, p. 363; vol. 324, p. 281; V & A archives; Kent RO, U590 A 61/7; Suffolk RO, HA18/EC4–5; Nat. Lib. of Wales, Wynnstay MS, 115/7 (wallpaper only); H. Clifford Smith, *Buckingham Palace*, p. 277; *C. Life*, 6 May 1982]

Crompton, Thomas, 49 and 50 Essex St, Strand, London, cm and u (1800–13). In 1803 took out insurance cover of £999 and in 1810, £900. In the latter year £750 was in respect of stock, utensils and goods in trust. No. 50 Essex St is never recorded in trade directories and is not mentioned initially in the fire insurance records. He was however using both addresses by 1810. [D; GL, Sun MS vol. 427, ref. 747707; vol. 453, ref. 850160]

Crompton, William, London, turner (1735). Supplied Frederick, Prince of Wales in 1735 with a 'Windsor Chair Civer'd [Covered] with Royal Mat' for which 18s 6d was charged. The chair was for the Prince's house in St James's Park. [*Furn. Hist.*, 1979]

Cronk, John, 4 Bartholomew Close, Little Britain, London, u and appraiser (1809–39). In 1820 took insurance cover of £1,400 of which £400 was in respect of stock and utensils. [D; GL, Sun MS vol. 484, ref. 968720]

Crook, Benjamin snr, 'The George & White Lyon', south side of St Paul's Churchyard, London, joiner and cm (1732–50). Although he was not elected freeman of the Joiners' Co. until 13 September 1734 it is clear that he was trading earlier than this date. On 30 December 1732 he took out insurance cover of £300 which included not only his household goods but also his stock in trade. On 2 May 1748 he announced an auction of his stock without reserve, the reason being his wish to retire from the trade. The stock on offer consisted of 'Pier and Chimney Glasses, Sconces and Dressing Glasses, in carv'd, gilt, Mahogany and Walnut Tree Frames, great Variety of Desks and Bookcases with Glass Doors, and Buroes, several sorts of Chairs, Mahogany Tables, Cloathes Chests, Chests of Drawers, and all other sorts of Cabinet Work in Mahogany and Walnut Tree, and other Woods'. A further advertisement of 5 May 1748 added 'Dining Tables, Card Tables, Buroes Tables, Dressing Tables and Claw Tables, Dumb Waiters, Bason Stands, Beaufets and Corner Cupboards, Tea Boards, Tea Chests'. Despite the finality of this announcement a 'Mr Crooke, Cabinet maker in St. Paul's Church yard' was concerned in a court case involving stolen property in December 1750. It is possible however that this was his son, Benjamin Crook jnr, who appears to have continued his father's business at the same address. After his retirement Benjamin Crook snr, appears to have been active still in the affairs of the Joiners' Co. and in 1757 he was elected Upper Warden.

Crook's only patron to have been identified is the Duke of Montrose who in 1733 paid £7 15s 6d for some chairs and a table for Cley. Crook did however follow a policy of labelling his furniture and this enables an estimate to be made of the type and quality of his wares. The labelled pieces recorded include a walnut card table on cabriole legs with ball and claw feet (Percival Griffiths Coll., sold Christie's 10 May 1939, lot 202; Sotheby's, 16 May 1952, lot 128 — illustrated Heal, p. 239; R. W. Symonds, *English Furniture from Charles II to George II*, figs 25, 139, 217; Wills, *English Furniture, 1550–1760*, p. 208). Other items noted are a wainscot bureau (Heal, p. 238), a walnut bureau, a walnut bureau cabinet with mirror fronted doors (advertisement Jeremy Ltd., *Conn.*, November and December 1973) and a walnut tea caddy (Harrogate Antiques Fair, 1977). [GL, Joiners' Co. records; Sun MS vol. 36, ref. 59662; *General Advertiser*, 2 May 1748; *London Evening Post*, 25 December 1750; Scottish RO, GD 220/6/31/647]

Crook, Benjamin jnr, 'The George & White Lyon', south side of St Paul's Churchyard, London, cm (1752–71). Free of the Joiners' Co. by patrimony on 3 October 1752. In 1771–72 together with Henry Banner and John Horne signed a protest against the legality of the election of officers. [GL, Joiners' Co. records]

Crook, Charles, High St, Newport, Isle of Wight, Hants., u (1839). [D]

Crook, James, High St, Portsmouth, Hants., cm and upholder (1793–1803). In February 1793 took out insurance cover of £500 which included £170 in respect of utensils and stock. Subscribed to Sheraton's *Cabinet Dictionary*, 1803. [GL, Sun MS vol. 392, p. 400]

Crook, James, 125 High St, Gosport, Hants., u (1823–30). Polled at Petersfield, Hants. in 1830. [D]

Crook, Joseph, Princes Risborough, Bucks., chairmaker (1839). [D]

Crook, Richard, Exeter and Barnstaple, Devon, cm and u (1815–38). Daughter Matilda bapt. at St Paul's Church, Exeter in 1815. Left Exeter soon after and by 1823 was trading from Boutport St, Barnstaple. [D; PR (bapt.)]

Crook, Robert, Newport, Isle of Wight, Hants., cm and u (1823–39). Trading at High St, 1823–30 and Pyle St in 1830. [D]

Crook, William, Liverpool, cm etc. (1834–39). At 6 Roscoe Lane with a shop at 26 Duke St in 1834. In 1839 at 4 Houghton St. [D]

Crookall, John, Lancaster, cm (1785–99). Free 1785–86. Named in Gillow records 1787–99. [Freemen rolls; Westminster Ref. Lib., Gillow]

Crookbain, Henry, 13 Bell Lane, Spitalfields, London, cm (1808). [D]

Crookham, John, Gage St, Lancaster, cm (1834). [D]

Crool, David, Newcastle, u (1763). App. to William Charnley and free by servitude, 6 October 1763. [Freemen reg.]

Cropland, Richard, Scotland St, Sheffield, Yorks., cm (1817). [D]

Cropper, James, Sleaford, Lincs., joiner and cm (1798). [D]

Crosby, Benjamin, address unknown, (1808). Patentee of a revolving bookcase 1808. [*DEF*]

Crosby, John, Spofforth, Yorks., cm (1759–76). In 1759 took app. named Smith. Probably the craftsman who made furniture for Harewood House, Yorks. in the 1770s, including two tables and a mahogany stand for which £2 was charged; and in 1776 twenty-four rout chairs which cost with carriage £8 8s. [S of G, app. index; *Furn. Hist.*, 1965; Leeds archives dept, Harewood MS 248, 249, 383]

Crosby (or Crosbie), John, The Calls, Leeds, Yorks., cm (1834–40). May perhaps be identified with the John Crosby app. to Martha Doughty of York on 20 April 1812. His father, John was a coachmaker. [D; York app. bk]

Crosby, Robert, Case St with shop in Lime St, Liverpool, cm, u and joiner (1829–39). The address in Case St is given as 15 (1829 and 37), 16 (1835) and 8 (1839). The Lime St number is listed as 52 (1835), 34 (1837) and 66 (1839). [D]

Crosby, Samuel, Chester, cm (1831). Free 23 April 1831. [Freemen rolls]

Crosby, Thomas, Newcastle and London, u (1765–74). App. to William Hudson of Newcastle, u, and free 24 August 1765. In London in 1774. [Freemen reg.; Newcastle poll bk]

Crosby, Thomas, 4 Princes Sq., Wilson St, Moorfields, London, painter and japanner (1821–25). In 1821 took out insurance cover of £300 which included £100 in respect of stock and utensils in a workshop in the yard behind his dwelling house. A stove was allowed. [D; GL, Sun MS vol. 486, ref. 976582]

Crosby, Thomas, Cow fair, Banbury, Oxon., chairmaker (1830–41). [D]

Crosby, William, Birmingham, chairmaker (1830–35). Listed at 6 Court Rea St in 1830 and 100 Rea St in 1835. [D]

Crosier, —, Leadenhall St, London, cm (1740). His app. was drowned in July 1740. [*London Evening Post*, 24 July 1740]

Crosier, John, Pickering, Yorks., cm (1834). [D]

Croskell, Thomas, Liverpool, u, cm and window blind manufacturer (1806–39). Freeman of Lancaster 1806–07, but moved to Liverpool almost immediately. In business by 1811 as an u and victualler at 27 Upper Milk St. In 1813 the number changed to 31 and in June he advertised the opening of a cabinet, chair and upholstery warehouse at 25 Shaw's Brow. In the advertisement he claimed to have had experience in the trade 'in London and other towns'. The number in Shaw's Brow was subsequently listed as 27 (1821–28), 30 and 31 (1827–29), 30 only (1834–37) and 63 (1839). In 1837–39 he had an additional address at Bootle Marsh, probably his dwelling house. In the late 1820s he seems to have specialised in window blinds and in October 1828 advertised that his were superior not only because of the use of the best materials but because of the advantageous prices achieved by 'the saving of labour by the use of steam'. Croskell also reminded the public of his cabinet wares 'manufactured from the best seasoned wood'. [D; Lancaster freemen rolls; *Liverpool Mercury*, 18 June 1813, October 1828]

Croskey, John, Rye, Sussex, turner and chairmaker (1826–32). At Mermaid St in 1826 and Market St 1832. [D]

Crosland, Andrew, Silver St, Thorne, Yorks., joiner and cm (1828–34). [D]

Crosland, Mess(?), Leen Side, Nottingham, joiner and cm (1799). [D]

Crosland, Richard, Sheffield, Yorks., cm (1798–1816). At Grindlegate in 1814 and 108 Scotland St in 1816. [D]

Crosley, James, Newark, Notts., chairmaker (d. 1815). Probate on will granted 21 June 1815. [Notts. RO, probate records]

Crosoer, Francis, Strand St, Sandwich, Kent, cm (1823–38). [D; poll bks]

Cross, Adam, Liverpool, cm (1780–1827). App. to Lloyd Baxendale and free by servitude, 12 September 1780. At this date living in Gill St. Trading by 1790 at Hakins Hay and remained at this address until 1804. In the period 1823–27 at 14 Richmond Row. [D; freemen reg.]

Cross, Aubery, London, cm (1793). Subscribed to Sheraton's *Drawing Book*, 1793.

Cross, Charles, Bridge St, Northampton, cm and u (1820–26). [Poll bks]

Cross, Edmund, Colchester, Essex, joiner and cm (1742–72). Took apps named Fridge in 1750, Thomas in 1755 and Holland in 1761. Examples of patronage to him by the local gentry are known. He supplied furniture and undertook repairs and alterations for Peter Creffield of Ardleigh, Essex 1742–47. The new items included a looking-glass in a carved frame on 19 October 1747 for which £3 13s 6d was charged and a wainscot chest supplied on 15 March of the same year which cost £4 4s. In 1772 Peter du Cane of Braxted Park, Essex, settled an account for a table and four chairs charged at £2 7s. [S of G, app. index; Essex RO, D/DRc F23, D/DDC A22 folio 15]

Cross, Edmund, Thorofare, Woodbridge, Suffolk, cm (1803). In *Ipswich Journal*, 8 January 1803 announced that he was taking over the shop of William Buckingham.

Cross, Edmund, Magdalene St, Colchester, Essex, cm (1829). [D]

Cross, Edward, London, cm and upholder (1806–26). With exception of the last year of its trading life this business operated from 123 Aldersgate St. Initially it was a partnership known as Cross & Wood but nothing is heard of the latter after 1807. In 1826 the business was at 6 Rose & Crown Ct, Finsbury Circus, and described as that of cabinet making and broking. In 1810 the 2nd Lord Braybrooke of Audley End, Essex paid £9 7s to the firm of Cross & Co., which is probably this business. [D; Essex RO, D/DBy/A376]

Cross, Edward, 57 Barbican, London, cm, upholder, auctioneer, appraiser and undertaker (1808–09). Trade card in Heal Coll., BM. [D]

Cross, George, Gainsborough, Lincs., and Newark, Notts., cm and u (1767–70). In March 1767 Cross announced that he had set up in Little Church Lane, Gainsborough in succession to the late Mr Silverwood. In May 1770 he indicated that in addition he had set up a warehouse in the Shambles, Newark. [*Cambridge Chronicle*, 21 March 1767, 19 May 1770]

Cross, George, Hull, Yorks., cm (1784). Freeman of Beverley, Yorks. [Beverley poll bk]

Cross, James, Shrewsbury, Salop, u (1712–19). Freeman of Shrewsbury. Took apps named Norgrave in 1712 and Ekin in 1717. [S of G, app. index; freemen rolls]

Cross, James, Grange Ct, Cary St, London, cm (1774–80). Took out insurance cover of £700 in 1780 of which £330 was in respect of utensils, stock and workshop. [GL, Sun MS vol. 281, p. 275; Westminster poll bk]

Cross, James, 19 Bell Alley, Goswell St, London, carpenter and cm (1820). On 16 August 1820 took out insurance cover of £100 which included £20 for stock and utensils. [GL, Sun MS vol. 486, ref. 970689]

Cross, James, High Wycombe, Bucks., chairmaker (1837). Witness at his daughter's wedding in 1837. [PR (marriage)]

Cross, John, parish of St James, Bristol, picture frame maker (1774). [Poll bk]

Cross, John, 18 Warwick St, Golden Sq., London, upholder and undertaker (1808). [D]

Cross, John, Exeter, Devon, cm (1830–32). Living in the parish of All Hallows on the Walls when his son Charles Henry was bapt. at St Sidwell's Church on 25 December 1830. Two years later Cross was living in Fore St when on 29 July 1832 a further son, Frederic John, was bapt. at St George's [PR (bapt.)]

Cross, John Wainwright, 107 High St, Colchester, Essex, cm and u (1839). [D]

Cross, Joseph, St Helen's Lane, Colchester, Essex, cm and u (1790). On 16 August 1790 took out insurance cover of £300 on his house, shop, warerooms and office. [GL, Sun MS ref. 572773]

Cross, Joseph, 149 Goswell St, London, cm and u (1802). On 28 January 1802 took out insurance cover of £400 of which £250 was in respect of utensils and stock. [GL, Sun MS vol. 424, ref. 727475]

Cross, Joseph, 87 Bartholomew Close, London, u and cm (1793–1803). Probably the Joseph Cross who subscribed to Sheraton's *Drawing Book*, 1793. In 1802 took out insurance cover of £999 of which £549 was for utensils and stock. In 1803 the insurance cover rose substantially to £1,900 of which £1,050 was for utensils and stock. [GL, Sun MS vol. 426, ref. 740181; vol. 427, ref. 750321]

Cross, Nathaniel, 23 Gt Bell Alley, Coleman St, London, upholder (1773–75). [D]

Cross, Nicholas, 10 Pool Lane and 4 Thomas's St, Liverpool, cm (1754–d. 1780). In 1762 also referred to as a glass grinder. Took apps named Mosson in 1754, Thomas Holmes 1755 (free 1762), William Rigby and Edward Bispham (free 1759), Robert Wilding (free 1761), James (app. 1761), and James Ackers (free 1780). His son John was made free by patrimony 1777 when he was trading as a timber merchant. At the time of his death in 1780 Nicholas Cross was also in partnership with a Joseph Harling operating as timber merchants, and it is probable that John was assisting in this side of the business. After 1780 this part of the enterprise was continued with Harling in partnership with John Cross. They had yards in Pack Lane and Redcross St and were able to offer 'FIR TIMBER of all kinds, MAHOGANY, OAK, WALNUT, BEECH etc'. This part of the business was still trading in 1790 from 37 Park Lane and Mercer's Ct, Redcross St. John Cross and his partner attempted to sell the cabinet-making business and stock as a whole in February 1780, but failing to find a buyer they offered the goods in March for retail sale at much reduced prices. The stock was stated to be of 'the best Jamaica or Hispaniola mahogany' and consisted of 'dining tables; piece, fly, snap & round tables; side-board table; writing desks; desk & bookcase; wardrobes, cloths press; chests of drawers; tea chests; butler & knife trays; cardivines, looking-glasses etc'. [D; S of G, app. index; freemen's committee bks; *Williamson's Liverpool Advertiser*, 17 November 1775, 18 February 1780; 10 March 1780]

Cross, Peter, Colchester, Essex, cm (1793). [D]

Cross, Ralph, Uttoxeter, Staffs., clock case maker and cm (1834–35). Listed at Bridge St in 1834 and Spiceal St in 1835. [D]

Cross, Richard, Exeter, Devon, cm (1821–26). From 1821–23 at Paris St but in 1826 Friernhay St. The baptisms of a daughter Caroline Reed on 12 April 1821, and sons Henry on 1 November 1824 and Frederick on 25 June 1822, are recorded. [D; PR (bapt.)]

Cross, Richard, High Wycombe, Bucks., chairmaker (1821–40). Sons bapt. 1821, 1831, 1837 and daughters 1838 and 1840. [PR (bapt.)]

Cross, Simon, 90 Richmond Row, Liverpool, cm (1814). [D]

Cross, T., near the Foundry, Rugeley, Staffs., chairmaker (1818). [D]

Cross, Thomas, Liverpool, furniture painter (1818). App. to Richard Nickson, painter, and free 11 June 1818. Addresses at Upper Frederick St and 4 Berry St are recorded. [Freemen reg.]

Cross, William, Nottingham, u (1693). [Nottingham freemen reg.]

Cross, William, Chester, cm (1747). Son of John Cross of Chester, barber. Free 13 June 1747. [Freemen rolls]

Cross, William, Porters Block, St John St, London, cm (1782). Took out insurance cover of £300 of which £260 was in respect of utensils, stock, workshop and a shed. [GL, Sun MS vol. 299, p. 367]

Cross, William, Milsom St, Bath, Som., upholder, auctioneer and undertaker (1771–84). A reference in the Massingberd account bks mentions a payment to a Mrs Cross, upholder at Bath in 1782. [D; Lincoln RO, MM 9110] In 1771–72 supplied Bath Corporation with furnishings costing £280 and in January 1778 with a mahogany library table £12 12s. [Bath Corp. Records]

Cross, William, 17 Gt Surrey St, Blackfriars Rd, London, cm and upholder (1790–97). Subscribed to Sheraton's *Drawing Book*, 1793. His trade card [Heal and Banks Colls, BM] shows a lady mourning by an urn flanked by a chair in the Sheraton style and a dressing chest. In 1795 the business was listed as Cross & Sons. [D]

Cross, William, Birmingham, cm and u (1803–30). At Smallbrook St, 1803–18; Horse fair in 1822, no. 36 in 1823; and Constitution Hill, 1828–30. [D]

Cross, William, Exe Island, Exeter, Devon, cm (1837–40). [D]

Crossgrove, Barnard, 26 Hosier Lane, West Smithfield, London, chairmaker (1789). [D]

Crosshawe, John, Leadenhall St, London, looking-glass maker (1738). [D]

Crosskey, William, Rye, Sussex, chairmaker and turner (1832–40). At Cattle Mkt in 1832 and Market St, 1839. [D]

Crossland, Richard, Sheffield, Yorks., cm (1818–22). At 108 Scotland Rd in 1818 and 20 Grindlegate in 1822. [D]

Crossley, John Mather, Manchester, cm and u (1825–40). In 1825 at Windmill St, St Peter's but by 1828 at 50 Bridge St. From 1822–33 at 14 Police St. By 1834 at 22 St Ann's St though from 1836–40 the number is 14. Also listed at 23 Old Millgate in 1840. [D]

Crossley, William, Manchester, cm (1794–1817). At 29 Toad Lane 1794; 5 Back Irwell St, 1800–04; White Cross Bank, Salford, 1808; 115 Chapel St, Salford, 1811; 12 William St, Salford, 1813; and Broker Bank, Salford, 1817. [D]

Crosthwaite, Jonathan, Market Pl., Whitehaven, Cumb., cm (1811). [D]

Crosty, James, Blackheath Rd, Greenwich, London, cm and u (1823–38). [D]

Crosty, Robert, Blackheath Rd, Greenwich, London, cm (1839). Successor to James Crosty at the same address. [D]

Crouch, Ceasar, 'The Black Swan', south side of St Paul's, London, trade unknown (1754–67). Free of the Joiners' Co. by consent, 3 October 1755. Had already subscribed to Chippendale's *Director* in the previous year and when in 1755 the latter's workshops were damaged by fire he helped to organise an appeal for funds to replace the workmen's tools. Thomas Chippendale designed an engraved invitation card for him. In 1767 he subscribed to Paine's *Plans . . . of Noblemen's and Gentlemen's Seats*. His connection with the furniture trade is however uncertain. [Gilbert, *Chippendale*, 2, pl. 12]

Crouch, George, Salisbury, Wilts., carver and gilder (1798). [D]

Crouch, John, Crown Ct, Gracechurch St, London, upholder (b. 1668–d. 1748). Free of the Upholders' Co., 1698 and master, 1732. His dwelling house was insured for £350 in 1706 and £600 in 1718, falling to £200 in 1721. He also appears to have owned other properties in Hoxton and Stepney. He died in 1748 aged 80 and was described as a wholesale upholder who had acquired a plentiful fortune and had retired some years previously. By religious persuasion Crouch was a Quaker. [GL, Upholders' Co. records; Sun MS vol. 4, ref. 4498; Hand in Hand MS vol. , ref. 11663; vol. 17, ref. 33350; vol. 19, ref. 7418; vol. 12, p. 479; vol. 23, ref. 7420 11663; *London Evening Post*, 20–23 February 1748]

Crouch & Jones, 31 Old Compton St, London, u and warehousemen (1811). [D]

Crouchley, Henry, Liverpool, joiner and cm (1790). Son of William Crouchley, shipwright. Free by patrimony 1790. [Freemen's committee bk]

Croughton, John, Bridge St, Chester, cm (1747–84). Son of Henry Croughton of Chester, Glover. Free 15 July 1747. Took apps Charles Chester (free 1759), Thomas Johnson (free 1767) and John Key (free 1784). [Freemen rolls; poll bk]

Crouzet, Joseph, Gt Titchfield St, Fitzroy Sq., London, carver and gilder (1817–37). At no. 107 in 1817 but by 1820 at no. 11. On 5 February 1823 Crouzet took out insurance cover on this latter address for £1,000 of which £300 was for stock. In 1827 carried out work in the Gallery or New Corridor at Windsor Castle. He submitted an estimate of £719 13s for work on picture frames and was employed to broaden and enrich the frames of seventy-two Italian paintings which had been acquired in 1762 by George III. [D; *Furn. Hist.*, 1972; GL, Sun MS vol. 498, ref. 1001090]

Crow, Augustin, Bartholomew Close, near Smithfield, London, u (d. by 1689). Successor to Alderman William Crow. Augustin Crow was already dead by April 1689 when his stock was disposed of. This consisted of 'all manner of rich Household Goods . . . as Damask, Mohair and Camlet Beds, Tapestry Hangings, Feather beds, Chairs, Carpets and other Furniture'. [Heal; *London Gazette*, 25–29 April 1689]

Crow, Charles, London, cm (1793). Subscriber to Sheraton's *Drawing Book*, 1793.

Crow, Charles, King St, Gt Yarmouth, Norfolk, cabinet and chairmaker (1805–d. 1834). Will proved 1834. [D; probate (Norwich)]

Crow, Edward, Boar Lane, Newark, Notts., cm and u (1822). [D]

Crow, James, Newcastle, u (1674). Free 1674 as an u. [Freemen reg.]

Crow, John, Gt Yarmouth, Norfolk, cm (1805–38). At Broad Row in 1805, Charlotte St in 1822 and Howard St, 1830–38. [D; poll bks]

Crow, John, Norwich, cm and u (1838–40). In 1839 moved from Lower St, Lawrence St to 2 Surrey St. Might be the John Crow working at Gt Yarmouth prior to 1838. [D]

Crow, John, 2 Crown Terr., Mile End Rd, London, carver and gilder (1835–39). [D]

Crow, Robert, London, u (1784–1820). Not shown in any of the directories. On 10 December 1784 paid £18 14s 7d in connection with work at Mount Stewart, Ulster, Ireland. In 1820 working on the furnishing of Wynyard Park, Co. Durham for Charles William Vane, Marquess of Londonderry. [Mount Stewart papers, D654/41/59; Durham RO, D/LO/E 484]

Crow, Robert, High St, Bishop Wearmouth, Sunderland, Co. Durham, cm (1827). [D]

Crow, William, St Bartholomew's, Bartholomew Close, London, u (1659–68). Alderman of the City of London. Mentioned in Samuel Pepys's Diary no fewer than ten times between 1660–68. Pepys records purchasing from him in 1668 a set of tapestries featuring the Apostles for £83. These were probably based on the famous Raphael cartoons of the Acts of the Apostles which were reproduced by the Mortlake factory. The low price paid might suggest that the set purchased by Pepys were either secondhand or painted or stained cloths in imitation of tapestries. Crow died in 1668 and was succeeded by Augustin Crow, probably at the same address. [Heal]

Crow, William, Broad Row, Gt Yarmouth, Norfolk, carver, gilder, chairmaker and cm (1776–98). In 1776 advertised that he was 'from London' and had engaged the services of a John Smethurst to assist in the business. He mentioned his ability at ship carving and the framing of looking-glasses 'in the newest Taste'. In 1777 he insured jointly with Thomas Wright, Gent. a house for £200. In 1786 the same cover was taken out 'on a house & shop' in his tenure. In the policy he is named as William Crow jnr. He was succeeded at the Broad Row address by John Crow. [D; *Norfolk Chronicle*, 18 May 1776; GL, Sun MS vol. 258, p. 297; vol. 336, p. 276]

Crow, William, Newark, Notts., cm, appraiser and auctioneer (1789–98). An advertisement of 1789 concentrates on the auctioneering and estate agency side of the business. In it Crow also offers to buy household furniture at a fair appraisement. This might suggest that actual cabinetmaking was a small part of the business. [D; *Lincoln, Rutland and Stamford Mercury*, 12 June 1789]

Crowcroft, John, Finkle St, Thorne, Yorks., joiner and cm (1830). [D]

Crowder, James, Chapel St, Marlow, Bucks., chair manufacturer (1839). [D]

Crowder, Samuel, Loft St, Grimsby, Lincs., joiner and cm (c. 1823–31). Originally from Hull. App. to Joseph Scholey of Grimsby March 1816. In business by 1831. [D; Hull app. reg.]

Crowder, William, Hull, Yorks., cm and broker (1817–23). At 1 Dagger Lane in 1817 and 10 New Dock St, 1821–23. [D]

Crowder, William, 32 King Cross Lane, Halifax, Yorks., cm and u (1830). [D]

Crowdson, John, Lancaster, joiner and cm (1779–99). Free 1779–80 and stated to be of Haslingden, Lancs. Named in the Gillow records as a joiner, 1785–99. [Lancaster freemen rolls; Westminster Ref. Lib., Gillow vol. 344/94, p. 459]

Crowdy, Richard, 78 Leather Lane, Holborn, London, cm and u (1808–29). In 1821 took out insurance with James and Charles Leigh of £400 with stock and utensils separately listed at £300. The property was declared to be a dwelling house and it was stated that no work was done there. In the next year the same house was insured for £250 with stock and utensils therein additionally insured for £100. Items in a workshop were seperately listed at £100. A separate policy for £450 in the name of Crowdy and James Henry and Charles Leigh mentions Richard Crowdy's dwelling house at £350 and a workshop at £100. A Samuel Crowdy listed in one directory in 1817 at this address is probably an incorrect entry. [D; GL Sun MS vol. 489, ref. 985962, 985963; vol. 489, ref. 999239, 999240]

Crowley, John, 5 Liman St, Goodman's Fields, London, cm (1812). In 1812 took out insurance cover of £500, of which £300 was in respect of stock and utensils. [GL, Sun MS vol. 455, ref. 875742]

Crowley, Thomas, 22 Vere St, Clare Mkt, London, carver, gilder and looking-glass and picture frame maker (1817–37). [D]

Crowshaw, John, Leadenhall St, London, looking-glass maker (1736–45). [D]

Crowson, Elizabeth, 71 High St, King's Lynn, Norfolk, cm and u (1836–39). [D]

Crowson, John, 71 High St, King's Lynn, Norfolk, cm and u (1822–30). Succeeded by Elizabeth Crowson at this address, probably his widow. [D]

Crowson, William, King's Lynn, Norfolk, cm and u (1830–36). At 41 Norfolk St in 1830 and 116 Norfolk St in 1836. [D]

Crowther, Ely, Skinner Lane, Leeds, Yorks., cm and joiner (1837).

Crowther, Hannah, 35 Bull Green, Halifax, Yorks. See William & Hannah Crowther.

Crowther, Joseph, Bennet Thorp, Doncaster, Yorks., cm and u (1830). [D]

Crowther, William & Hannah, Halifax, Yorks., cm, turner, watch and clock maker (1793–1840). Subscribed to Sheraton's *Drawing Book*, 1793. Regularly recorded in directories from 1822 initially at Kings Cross Lane and after 1830 Bull Green and/or 32 Hopwood Lane as cm and u. Their trade card offered 'All kinds of Framing for Samplers, Pictures &c. in Oil or Burnish'd Gold' and stated that 'Boarding Schools supplied with Cases for Filligree Work'. [D; Bodleian Lib., Johnson Coll.]

Croxford, Francis, London, chair and cabinetmaker (1733). Croxford was described in 1733 as a furniture maker 'eminent in his profession for his many new and beautiful designs, neatness of workmanship, etc.'. The only firm fact known about his career is that in July 1733 his stock was advertised for sale by Jeremiah Surman at his salerooms in Soho Sq. No reason is given for the sale but it would appear likely that Croxford gave up the cabinetmaking business in this year. The stock was said to consist of 'magnificent large and noble glass sconces, and chimney glasses in rich carved and gilt Frames, made after his own design, and several fine walnut-tree, mahogany, mehone and other desks and bookcases with glass doors, and several fine mahogany clothes chests ornamented with brass, mahogany, walnut-tree and pigeon wood quadrille tables, fine mahogany dining tables of all sizes, and dressing glasses and dressing tables of several sorts, walnut-tree, mahogany and other desks, fine walnut-tree chests upon chests and about one hundred dozen of chairs of several sorts'. [*Daily Post*, 12 July 1733]

Croxton, George, 27 Smithy Door, Manchester, cm, joiner and builder (1825). [D]

Croxton, Thomas, Chester, u (1661). Free 10 July 1661. [Freemen rolls]

Croxton, William, Chester, (1687–d. 1727). Free 11 April 1687. On 12 May 1690 received 19s 3d for five days work at Chirk Castle, Clwyd, for 'setting up ye bedds & furniture att the Castle which came from Newhall &c'. At the time of his death in 1727 he was living in St Oswald's parish, Chester. [Myddelton, *Chirk Castle Accounts*, 1931, p. 245]

Croydon, Elizabeth, Fore St, Totnes, Devon, carver and gilder (1838). [D]

Croydon, William N., Ashburton and Totnes, Devon, carver and gilder (1830–38). In 1830 at West St, Ashburton but in 1838 at Fore St, Totnes, an address at which Elizabeth Croydon is also recorded in that year operating in the same trade. [D]

Crozier, James, 1 City Rd, London, carver and gilder (1809). [D]

Crozier, John, 14 Air St, Piccadilly, London, u (1787). On 19 June 1787 took out insurance cover of £100 on goods. [GL, Sun MS vol. 342, ref. 531494]

Cruden (or Crunden), Thomas, 21 New Rd, Brighton, Sussex, cm, u and furniture broker (1839–40). [D]

Crudge, Thomas, Exeter and Exmouth, Devon, cm and u (1813–38). On 7 October 1813 Crudge was married at Littleham Church, Devon to Miss Floyde, the daughter of a brandy merchant. In March 1821 he announced that he had commenced business in Friernhay St, Exeter, and was also acting as an undertaker, general auctioneer and appraiser. In the same year his only daughter Elizabeth died of burns when her clothes caught fire. Her father also suffered from burns through his attempts to try to save his child by extinguishing the flames. His address was given as North St, Exeter. The following year was marked in May by the baptism of a son, Charles at St Mary Steps. He was then living in Bridge St, Exeter. Later in life he appears to have returned to the area in which he lived in his youth for in 1838 he is recorded trading at Johnson's Walk, Exmouth. [D; *Exeter Flying Post*, 7 October 1813, 6 September 1821; *The Alfred*, 13 March, 20 March 1821; PR (bapt.)]

Crump, Benjamin, High St, Kington, Herefs., turner and cm (1830). [D]

Crump, Charles Collins, Worcester, cm (1812). On 6 October 1812 admitted freeman by patrimony. Eldest son of Richard Crump, cm. [Freemen rolls]

Crump, Daniel, Stone Cutter St, St Bride's, London, chairmaker (1749–52). In 1749 and 1752 fined for non-service at St Bride's. [GL, MS 6541, p. 83]

Crump, Edward, Pentonville, London, cm (1798). [D]

Crump, Ely, High St, Worcester, cm and upholder (1776–d. 1782). Took apps William King, free 1776, Thomas Phillips, free 1777 and William Barret, free 1781. Took his son, Robert, as app., but died soon after on 22 April 1782 of 'asthmatic consumption'. Robert Crump was however declared free in October 1786 by servitude. Crump had taken out insurance cover of £1,100 in 1779 of which £300 was in respect of 'workshops, utensils & stock'. [Freemen rolls; GL, Sun MS vol. 277, p. 24; *Berrow's Worcester Journal*, 22 April 1782]

Crump, Francis, 4 Tower St, Seven Dials, London, upholder (1820). [D]

Crump, J., 5 Goswell St Rd, London, u etc. (1820). [D]

Crump, James, King St, Westminster, London, cm (1749). [Poll bk]

Crump, James, Worcester, u and cm (1784–1808). App. to John Crump snr, and free by servitude 29 March 1784. He was already in business by that year. In 1803 subscribed to Sheraton's *Cabinet Dictionary*. Took John Crump III as app. and he was made free by servitude 1808. [D; freemen reg.]

Crump, John snr, parish of St Swithin, Worcester, cm (1747–84). Took the following apps: William Ashton (free 1758), Nicholas Field (free 1760), John Crump jnr (free 1773), Finch Collins (free 1776), Richard Crump (free 1780), William Crump (free 1780) and James Crump (free 1784). Undertook commissions for the Lechmere family of Severn End, Hanley Castle, Worcs. [Poll bk; freemen reg.; Worcs. RO, 1531/705: 134/65]

Crump, John jnr, Worcester, upholder and cm (1773–77). Free by servitude to John Crump snr, 22 March 1773. In 1775 took out insurance cover of £700 of which £500 was in respect of utensils and stock. In 1777 insured tenements and a stable for £400 and a house for the same sum. [Freemen reg.; GL Sun MS vol. 236, p. 291; vol. 259, p. 383; vol. 260, p. 12]

Crump, John III, Worcester, cm (1808). App. to James Crump of Worcester and free by servitude 6 June 1808. [Freemen reg.]

Crump, Richard, High St, Worcester, cm and u (1780–1820). Listed at no. 83, 1794–97. App. to his father John Crump snr, and free by servitude, 11 September 1780. Took as apps

Thomas Mason (free 1802), and Charles Collin Crump (free 1812). About 1802 a bill of complaint was issued by Richard Crump against Ann Lyle and Elizabeth Lyde, defendants, relating to the 'Sign of the Three Neats Tongues', Strand, London. [D; freemen reg.; Marylebone Lib., deed 152–103]

Crump, Richard, Walsall, Staffs., u (1798). [D]

Crump, Robert, Worcester, cm and u (1786–96). Trading at Bridge St in 1794. App. to his father Ely Crump (d. 1782) and free by servitude 23 October 1786. Took as app. John Vernal, free 27 June 1796. [Freemen reg.]

Crump, William, Worcester, u (1796). Bankrupt 1796. [*Billinge's Liverpool Advertiser*, 18 April, 4 July 1796, 7 July 1797]

Crump, William, Guiting, Glos., cm (1747). [Worcester poll bk]

Crump, William, Ledbury, Herefs., cm (1757–62). Took apps named Yarnold in 1757 and Hill in 1762. [S of G, app. index]

Crump, William, Worcester, cm (1780). Free 13 September 1780 by servitude to John Crump snr. [Freemen reg.]

Crump & Timmings, High St, Worcester, cm, u and auctioneers (1788–94). Listed at no. 94 in 1794. [D]

Crumpton, —, Liverpool, u (1718–26). Supplied goods and carried out work for Nicholas Blundell of Crosby Hall, Lancs. between 1718–26. On 1 April 1718 he went there to dine and to discuss the work needed, and on the 21st his man was undertaking work to repair the cornice of the bed in the 'Parlour Chamber'. Work in 1718 amounted to £8 4s and included the supply of curtains and vallances for the windows in the Gallery, and covering ten cushions and a squab and repairing beds. In the following year an easy chair was covered at a cost of 18s. No further work is recorded until late in 1722 when making up furniture for the Parlour was charged at £10 13s. In 1723 work centred round a new Red Bed for the Garden Chamber and 'new vamping' the Green Bed in the Parlour Chamber. A sum of £67 4s 11d was paid to Crumpton for work in this year. New green curtains and a valance for the Back Parlour are mentioned in December 1725 and this with other work was settled in the next year for £4 with a further 10s 4d for a window curtain for his daughter's room and covering a cushion. [Tyrer, *Great Diurnal of Nicholas Blundell*, 2 and 3; Disbursement bk at Crosby Hall]

Crumpton, Aaron, Broadwall, Gt Surrey St, London, carver and cornice maker (1826). [D]

Cruse, Catherine, Newark, Notts., u and cm (1793–98). Successor and probably the widow of William Cruse. [D]

Cruse, Daniel, Exeter, Devon, carver and gilder (b. c. 1804–d. 1838). In 1837 at North Bridge but in 1838 moved to St David's Hill and there died in that year aged 34. [*Exeter Pocket Journal*, 1837–38; *Exeter Flying Post*, 4 October 1838]

Cruse, Gabriel, Devizes, Wilts., u and cm (1752–79). Took as apps Sarah Sulivan 8 April 1752, James Stockham 23 July 1752, John Sullivan 11 July 1754 and John Holdenby Langley 5 December 1758, two as u and the others as cm. In 1779 insured his house with Thomas Cripps for £300. In August and October 1766 undertook work and supplied goods to the 2nd Earl of Shelburne for Bowood Park, Wilts. amounting to £62 10s 9d. Of the items supplied the most significant were six mahogany chairs, 'Stuff'd Backs and seats in canvis' at £7 10s and 99 yds of Wilton Carpet and ten bedside carpets which together came to £29 14s. [App. bks; GL, Sun MS vol. 272, p. 159; Bowood MS]

Cruse, William, Newark, Notts., cm (1790–92). Probate granted on his will April 1792. [Poll bk; Notts. RO, probate records]

Cruse, William, East St, Newton Abbot, Devon, cm (1830). [D]

Crusoe, Charles, King's Lynn, Norfolk, upholder (1782–1811). Son of Robinson Crusoe of King's Lynn, upholder. Made freeman of Norwich 29 November 1782. His sons John M., a mariner, and Robinson, an auctioneer were made free of Norwich on 23 November 1809 and 14 December 1811 respectively. [Norwich poll bks; Norwich freemen reg.]

Crusoe, Robinson, High St, King's Lynn, Norfolk, upholder and cm (1754–86). App. to Asty Hardwick u, and free 1754–55. Took as apps George Mathyson Vincent (free 1770–71), James Oldmeadow (free 1778–79) and Charles Crusoe (free 1782–83). Charles, his son, was also admitted freeman of Norwich on 29 November 1782. In 1781 he insured his house for £300 and in 1783 took out insurance amounting to £700 of which £300 was for utensils and stock. [D; poll bks; King's Lynn freemen rolls; Norwich freemen reg.; GL, Sun MS vol. 291, p. 519; vol. 317, p. 287]

Crussett, James, 27 East St, Red Lion Sq., London, u (1809). [D]

Crutchley, Cornelius, Shropshire St, Market Drayton, Salop, cm (1828). [D]

Crutchley, Henry, Stafford, joiner and cm (1737–52). Took apps named Brett in 1737, Hatton in 1741 and Bull in 1752. [S of G, app. index]

Crutchley, John, Bewdley, Worcs., cm (1761). Discharged from Debtors' Prison on 31 October 1761 and said to be 'late of Bewdley'. [London Gazette]

Crutchley, John, High Green, Wolverhampton, Staffs., u and auctioneer (1780–1820). Listed also at Cock St, as cm and u, in 1816. [D]

Crutchley, Sarah, 8 Cock St, Wolverhampton, Staffs., u (1802). [Rate bk]

Crye, Robert, 57 Stanley St, Liverpool, furniture broker, appraiser and cm (1839). [D]

Cryer, Anthony, 32 Moor Lane, Bolton, Lancs., cm (1824). [D]

Cryer, John, Chapel Lane, Bingley, Yorks., joiner/cm (1837). [D]

Cryer, John, Millgate, Selby, Yorks., joiner/cm (1837). [D]

Crystall, Alexander, 27 Wardour St, Soho, London, cm (1809). [D]

Crystall, William, London, cm (1793). Subscriber to Sheraton's Drawing Book, 1793

Cubett, Benjamin, see Christopher Carberry & Benjamin Cubett.

Cubbin, William, 35 Fishergate, Preston, Lancs., carver and gilder (1825–30). [D]

Cubit, Thomas, parish of All Saints, Norwich, cabinet and chairmaker (1780–d. 1804). Will proved at Norwich 1804. [Poll bks; Norfolk Record Soc., index of wills]

Cubitt, —, London, cm (1793). Subscriber to Sheraton's Drawing Book, 1793.

Cubitt, Jonah, Mill's Pl., Milk St, Bristol, upholder (1801). [D]

Cubitt, Richard, Norwich and London, cm (1804–18). Son of Samuel Cubbitt, woolcomber and made free 26 May 1804. In 1818 in London. [Freemen reg.; Norwich poll bk]

Cubitt & Pettitt, 4 Archer St, Gt Windmill St, London, cm and u (1839). [D]

Cuckson, Francis, 78 West Bar Green, Sheffield, Yorks., cabinet and chairmaker (1822). [D]

Cudbart, John, Whitby, Yorks., cm (1793–8). Subscribed to Sheraton's Drawing Book, 1793. [D]

Cudden, James, Olland St, Bungay, Suffolk, cm, chairmaker, paper hanger and ironmonger (1813–39). Married at St Mary's Church, Bungay, 1 February 1813. [D; Suffolk RO, FAA: 50/2/116]

Cudden, John, Beccles, Suffolk, chairmaker (1782). Married 8 June 1782. [Suffolk RO, FAA: 50/2/105]

Cuddon, John, Beccles, Suffolk, chairmaker (1757). Took app. named Fletcher in 1757. [S of G, app. index]

Cuddy, Joseph, 15 Turner's Buildings, St James St and shop 7 and 13 Norfolk St, Liverpool, u (c. 1834–39). App. to

William Bickerstaff 1827. Had opened his own business at the addresses above by 1827. [D; app. bk]

Cudworth, Thomas, London, upholder (1775). Son of William Cudworth of Marylebone, London, schoolmaster. App. to Robert Fowler on 3 October 1765 and free by servitude, 1 February 1775. [GL, Upholders' Co. records]

Cuenot, John Antoine, Warwick St, Golden Sq., London, carver (1744–62). Although included in Mortimer's London Directory of 1763 he had probably died the year previously and the John Cuenot at this address in 1763 was his son. Employed at Cleveland House in 1752 and in the same year provided a picture frame for the Duke of Northumberland costing £4 13s 9d. His best known commission is in connection with Norfolk House, St James's Sq., London for the Duke of Norfolk between 1753–56. Although the house no longer survives several interior features do. The most significant of these is the Music Room now displayed at the V & A. Cuenot was involved with the production of the carved work in connection with this interior (some of it to the design of G. B. Borra), and employed both French and English craftsmen to assist him. Work on the Music Room alone came to £645 7s 3d, the most expensive item being '6 Trophies to go in the pannels with laurels & oak branches' for which £60 5s was charged. Two of the 'monkey' doors from the Great Drawing Room still exist, one in the V & A and the other in the Untermyer Collection in New York. The four doors of this room were charged by Cuenot at £104 15s 1d. One of the doorcases from the Green Damask or Flowered Velvet Room is now in the Art Institute of Chicago. Cuenot's account for this amounted to £12 11 3½d. Apart from wall panelling and door cases Cuenot also produced a pair of lanterns for the staircase hall at £29 17s 6d, four pier tables 'decorated with masks of Mercury' to be placed between the windows of the Green Damask Room at £48 12s and pier glasses and overmantels for the same room. On 25 October 1756 Cuenot received £1,000 in payment as 'part of the money due . . . from his Grace', the total cost eventually amounting to £2,643 3s 8½d. A carved diptych by him survives at Arundel Castle, Sussex. Further small commissions of 1759 from the Duke of Northumberland and the Duke of Montagu, are known. Another John Cuenot is recorded in connection with a carved model for a cornice for the Duchess's dressing room at Chatsworth, Derbs., in the mid 1770's. This could not be John Cuenot jnr as he is known to have died in 1764. [D; V & A archives; Fitz-Gerald, The Norfolk House Music Room; Arundel Castle Records, MD 18, pt. II; Burlington, June 1980, p. 403; J. Martin Robinson, The Dukes of Norfolk] B.A.

Cuer, —, Haymarket, London, u (1733). In 1733 the death of the wife of Cuer occurred. She was the daughter of Sir George Hampton. [Gents Mag., November 1733]

Cuff, Thomas, 4 Curzon St, London, sadler (1804–08). Described as sadler to their Royal Highnesses the Prince of Wales and the Dukes of York, Clarence, Cumberland and Cambridge. In 1804 supplied twenty six skins of Russian leather for lining wardrobes at Brighton, the cost being £44 6s 6d. Carried out similar commissions in 1805, 1807 costing £96 18s 11d and 1808 at £22 18s 4d. [Windsor Royal Archives, RA 25162, 88941, 88956, 88968]

Cuffians, John, 102 High St, Marylebone, London, u (1815). [D]

Cugnett, Peter, 1 Thorney St, Bloomsbury, London, upholder (1781). In 1781 took out insurance cover of £200 for his house. [GL, Sun MS vol. 290, p. 281]

Cuisset, James, address unknown, u (1803). Subscribed to Sheraton's Cabinet Dictionary, 1803.

Cuisset, John, 28 East St, Red Lion Sq., London, u (1809). [D]

Cull, James, High St, Ramsgate, Kent, cm, u, auctioneer and undertaker (1807–29). His trade card [Banks Coll., BM] shows a bed in the Sheraton style, a broken branch and mourners. From 1826–29 the business is described as James Cull & Son and was trading from 60 High St. The son was almost certainly Thomas Cull who is shown trading from this address in 1832. [D]

Cull, James, Church St, Tewkesbury, Glos., cm and u (1830). [D]

Cull, Robert, 60 High St, Ramsgate, Kent, cm and undertaker (1838–39). Successor of Thomas Cull trading at this address in 1832. [D]

Cull, Thomas, 60 High St, Ramsgate, Kent, cm and undertaker (1832). Successor of James Cull trading at this address from 1807 and almost certainly his son. In partnership with his father from 1826. [D]

Cullen, Daniel, 30 Gt Albert St, Goswell St, London, cm (1811). Took out insurance cover of £200 on 19 September 1811, half of which was for stock and utensils and the other half for household goods in his residence. [GL, Sun MS vol. 455, ref. 860972]

Cullen, James, 56 Greek St, Soho, London, u and cm (1754–79). Listed in London directories between 1765 and 1779. Nothing is known of his background before 1754 when, together with 'several of the principal wrights in Edinburgh' he advertised the formation of the Edinburgh Upholstery, Joiner and Mirror Glass Co., which offered upholstery, cabinet joinery, mirror glass work and all the necessaries for funerals, plus many textiles, quilts, blankets, carpets, wallpapers, leather and mattresses. [*Edinburgh Evening Courant*] A few pieces of furniture inscribed with his name have been recorded, but it is likely that he retailed the work of other tradesmen as a middleman rather than maintaining a major workshop. He appears in fact to have operated as a high level entrepreneurial interior decorator and house furnisher who supplied textiles, designs, furnishings and advice on a consultancy basis. Presumably his reputation and livelihood was made on the services he provided for clients which included Earl Waldegrave, the Duke of Abercorn and Mr Launderdale (besides those listed below). He was energetic in travelling to solicit custom, commissioned drawings from leading designers such as Matthias Lock, placed orders with elite craftsmen such as Samuel Norman and obtained competitive estimates. For the convenience of Lord Hopetoun he supplied a pattern chair with different enrichments on the seat rails for local tradesmen to copy His Lordship's choice of fashionable patterns. [F. Bamford, *A Dictionary of Edinburgh Furniture Makers*, pl. 30] Like other cm of the time, Cullen accepted law-breaking as a legitimate risk. He was involved in selling textiles illegally imported by foreign diplomats. [*Apollo*, August 1965 and September 1970] Cullen was declared bankrupt in 1777, not through his furnishing business, but as a result of having assumed management of The Ladies' Club, or Coterie, in Arlington St, London.

HOPETOUN HOUSE, West Lothian (Earl of Hopetoun). James Cullen's accounts for furniture supplied to Hopetoun have virtually all disappeared, but numerous letters, memoranda and lists of items required exist showing that he provided drawings, estimates and advice to his patron between 1753 and 1773. Cullen appears to have co-ordinated the furnishing schemes, obtaining designs and co-ordinating the commission rather than actually making the furniture which was probably sub-contracted; Matthias Lock and Samuel Norman were certainly involved in the project. The following selective abstract of the documentation indicates his role.

1 February 1755: Note of dimensions of marble tables for the dining room and drawing room.

3 December 1755: Calculation of damask required for the North Apartments estimated to cost £348.

13 October 1758: Memo of furniture needed for the great apartments. February 1763: Payment of £198 for furniture.

4 & 18 February 1766: Letters from Cullen re- damask.

22 May 1766: Letter and estimate about enclosing a new design for Drawing Room glasses (finally despatched 26 June 1768).

13 February 1767: Letter concerning papier-mâché borders for damask hangings.

January/February 1768: Letters concerning the state Bed and a looking-glass state enclosed drawings are 'designed by Mr Matt Lock, lately deceased' and refer to 'Mr Norman'. They also allude to designs for commodes and a toilet table.

1773: Bill for a travelling bottle case £2 4s a crib bedstead £1 3s and a mahogany tea box £1 4s.

The documentation permits a fair number of pieces surviving at Hopetoun House to be associated with Cullen including the state bed, a pair and a set of four looking-glasses, three commodes, a pair of pier tables and several suites of seat furniture. [Scottish RO, Hopetoun papers; A. Coleridge, *Chippendale Furniture*, pp. 160–69; A. Coleridge, 'James Cullen, cabinet maker at Hopetoun House', *Conn.*, November and December 1966]

FLAP TABLE, mahogany with frieze drawer and fluted legs. The back rail is inset with a boxwood plaque inscribed: 'Jas Cullen Londini, Soho, fecit 1769'. Now at Temple Newsam House, Leeds (Fig. 6).

BLAIR CASTLE, Perthshire (3rd Duke of Atholl). An account dated 20 December 1770 totalling £116 16s includes entries for the following: 'Men putting 2 large plates of glass in the piers in the Drawing Room; 2 elegant pier glass frames carved and gilt with 3 light branches; cabinet in 3 parts, the middle part shaped, with drawers and writing conveniences; polishing . . . a temple cabinet; 4 carved settees with Chinese backs; 2 elbow chairs to match the above; 6 cushions'. None of these pieces appears to have survived. [Blair Castle archives]

CARLISLE HOUSE, Soho Sq., London. 'James Cullen, upholsterer' was named as one of the principal creditors of the estate of Madame Cornelys proprietor of a fashionable assembly room in Soho Sq. in bankruptcy proceedings, 1773. [C. Gilbert, *Chippendale*, p. 161]

NORTHUMBERLAND HOUSE, London (1st Duke of Northumberland). In the mid 1770s Cullen supplied a suite of gilt seat furniture comprising armchairs and settees in the newly-fashionable French Style for the Glass Drawing Room at Northumberland House. The set is now at Syon House; one chair is signed inside the rear rail in a copper plate hand 'J. Cullen.' [*Apollo*, September 1970, pp. 206–09]   P. A.

Cullen, James, Nottingham, joiner and cm (1818–25). Son of James Cullen of Nottingham, joiner. App. 1818 to Thomas Cullen of Parliament St, Nottingham, and free by 1825. [App. and freemen regs.]

Cullen, Thomas, parish of St Paul, Canterbury, Kent, cm and upholder (1782–94). [Poll bks]

Cullen, Thomas, 4 Parliament St, Nottingham, joiner and cm (1784–1832). Advertised in July 1784 for craftsmen to assist him in his business. Took as apps John Barker (1807), James Cullen (1818), Samuel Cullen (1820–22), John Cullen (1823) and Charles Cullen (1826). Signed the *Nottingham Cabinet and Chair Makers' Book of Prices*, 1791 on the behalf of the masters. [D; *Nottingham Journal*, 31 July 1784; app. reg.]

Cullen, William, parish of St Paul, —, Kent, cm (1803). On 14 March 1793 took out of insurance cover of £1,000 of which £100 was in respect of utensils and stock kept in a hop oast and stable. [GL, Sun MS vol. 392, p. 475]

Culler, Thomas, 8 Dove Lane, Norwich, upholder (1802). [D]

Culley, John, London Lane, Norwich, cm and chairmaker (1801–03). Admitted freeman of Norwich on 24 February 1803, not by servitude. Traded from 43 London Lane, 1801–02, but in 1802 moved to 10 London Lane. [D; freemen reg.]

Culligan, Mary, 12 Sparling St, Liverpool, u (1839). [D]

Cullimore, Daniel, 9 Orchard St, Bath, Som., u (1819). [D] Probably same as:

Cullimore, Daniel, London, u (1822–39). At 2 John's Pl., Gray's Inn Rd, 1822–24, where he took out insurance cover of £300, half this sum being in respect of stock, utensils and goods in trust. In 1824 he moved to 22 Ray St, Clerkenwell and on 8 April of that year took out insurance cover of £600 of which £350 was in respect of stock, utensils and goods in trust. He was still at this address in 1827. By 1835 however he had moved to 63 North Pl., Gray's Inn Rd. [D; GL, Sun MS vol. 490, ref. 989228; vol. 497, ref. 1014088; vol. 494, ref. 1016264]

Cullimore, Thomas, Exeter, Devon, cm (1777). [Freemen rolls]

Cullingford, William, 40 George St, Portman Sq., London, invalid chair etc. maker (1829). [D]

Cullington, Robert, parish of St Lawrence, Norwich, upholder (1818). [Poll bk]

Cully, David, High St, Marlborough, Wilts., carver and gilder (1839). [D]

Culm, John jnr, Eastgate St, Chester, cm (1771). [Poll bk]

Culverwell, Charles, 70 Union St, Stonehouse, Plymouth, Devon, carver and gilder (1823–38). Death of his wife recorded in August 1826. [D; *The Alfred*, 29 August 1826]

Culverwell, Robert, 204 Tooley St, Southwark, London, cm (1778). In 1778 insured his utensils, stock and goods for £100 out of a total cover of £300. [GL, Sun MS vol. 271, p. 137]

Culverwell, Robert, Bridgwater, Som. and Exeter, Devon, carver (1774–81). In 1774 at Bridgwater and in 1781 at Exeter. [Bristol poll bks]

Culyer, Thomas, Lakenham, Norwich, chairmaker (1818–30). Son of Henry Cullyer, worsted weaver. Free 25 April 1818. [Freemen reg; poll bk]

Culyer, William, Norwich, cm and chairmaker (1811–18). Son of Henry Culyer, worsted weaver. Free 16 February 1811. [Freemen reg.; poll bks]

Cumber, Peter, 'The Golden Boy', Chiswell St, parish of St Giles, Cripplegate, London, picture frame maker, dealer in pictures and undertaker (1724–28). Insurance cover on goods and stock amounted to £300 in 1728. [GL, Sun MS vol. 16, ref. 31719; vol. 29, ref. 47080]

Cumine, Francis, 2 Bowling Green, 63 King St, Snowfields, London, cm (1779–80). Insured his utensils and stock for £100 out of a total of £200 cover. [GL, Sun MS vol. 274, p. 545; vol. 285, p. 310]

Cumming, Alexander, London, cm (1765–75). Shown at Bartholomew Close for the entire period of operation, though in 1770 an address at Maiden Lane, Covent Gdn is recorded. It was in December of that year that his bankruptcy was announced and he was said to be of Covent Gdn. [D; *Gents Mag.*, December 1770]

Cumming, John, 8 Nicholas St, Liverpool, u (1835). [D]

Cummings, James, London, chair and bedstead maker (1792–1808). In July 1792 at 3 Calender Yd, Long Alley, Moorfields where he took out insurance cover of £200 which included £40 for utensils and goods in stock and £60 for utensils and goods in yard. In 1808 at 10 Little Cheapside, Sun St, Finsbury Sq. [D: GL, Sun MS vol. 388, p. 245]

Cummings, John, Redcross St, Bristol, looking-glass manufactory (1792–1806). [D]

Cummings & Barrow, Prussia St, Liverpool, joiners and cm (1810). [D]

Cummins, Andrew, 7 Gt Pulteney St, Westminster, London, cm (1784). [Poll bk]

Cummins, Charles, parish of St James, Bristol, cm (1784). [Poll bk]

Cummins, Charles, 1 Pithay, Bristol, cm and u (1825–30). [D]

Cummins, Peter, London, carver and gilder (1820–35). In 1820 at 5 Hertford St but when in 1822 he took an app. he was in Titchfield St, Marylebone. From 1829 his address is recorded as 55 Upper Marylebone St, Portland Pl. [D; Westminster Ref. Lib. MS E3559]

Cummins, Philip, 55 Upper Marylebone St, London, carver, wood and cabinet etc. (1839). [D]

Cummins, R., 55 Upper Marylebone St, London, carver (1835). Successor to Peter Cummins at this address. [D]

Cummins, Thomas, Bristol, carver and gilder (1812–40). In 1812–13 at Ellbroad St and from 1814–18 at 6 Syms's Alley. After this period remained at 13 Broadmead and from 1838 also claimed to be a cm. [D]

Cummins, William, Liverpool, cm (1810–14). In 1810 at Hurst Pl. and 1813–14 at 14 Harrington St. [D]

Cummins, William, Liverpool, cm (1812). App. to John Gaston of Liverpool and free by servitude, 5 October 1812. [Freemen's committee bk]

Cumpston, John, Carlisle, Cumb., chairmaker (1810–34). At Abbey St, 1810–11, but by 1829 at Old Grapes Lane. By 1834 had moved again to 70 Castle St. [D]

Cumpsty, Thomas, Lancaster, (1784–1824). Named in the Gillow records 1784–86, 1807, 1809, 1816, 1818, 1821–24. [Westminster Ref. Lib., Gillow]

Cumpsty, William, Lancaster (1784–86). [Westminster Ref. Lib., Gillow records]

Cundale, Thomas, Kirkgate, Ripon, Yorks., cm (1822–37). [D]

Cundall, William, Ogleforth, York, cm and auctioneer (1823). [D]

Cundall, William, Otley, Yorks., joiner, cm and builder (1828–37). At Northgate in 1828–34 but by 1827 had moved to Bridge St. [D]

Cundell, Joseph, Northgate, Darlington, Co. Durham, cm and joiner (1828). [D]

Cunliffe, Henry, Siddal's Lane, Derby, cm and u (1828–35). [D]

Cunningham, John & James, Bridge St, Warrington, Lancs., u (1828–34). In 1834 only John Cunningham is recorded. [D]

Cunningham, Vincent, Stratford, London, upholder (1736). Recorded as bankrupt, *Gents Mag.*, June 1736.

Cure, George, London, upholder (1691–1718). In 1709 in Haymarket but in 1718 in King St, St Ann, Westminster. Recorded in the Royal Household accounts for 1691 working on a substantial order. This was for '20 caned bottom chairs with banister backs and carved, 20 cushions of crimson damask for the chairs, squabs, valences, floor mats for St. James's House'. These goods were charged at £43 9s 8d. In 1718 took out insurance cover of £400 on his rented house in King St. [Heal; GL, Hand in Hand MS vol. 19, p. 94; PRO, LC9/280]

Cure, George, the 'Three Golden Chairs', Haymarket, London, u (1721–d. 1759). Probably the son and successor of the George Cure working in London in the same trade, 1691–1718. The business operated by George Cure jnr was of a substantial nature. As early as June 1725 he took out insurance cover for the goods and merchandise in his dwelling house for £1,000. His recorded commissions appear to be entirely for Frederick Louis, Prince of Wales, and he may well be entitled to a place with other better known craftsmen such as Benjamin Goodison who were similarly employed at this period. Between 1731 and 1747 he provided bedding, bolsters, blankets, cushions etc. for his royal patron and was responsible for moving furniture between the various places of residence of the Prince such as Kew, Norfolk House, Carlton House and Leicester House. On 13 November 1738 it was announced in the press that 'Mr Cure, upholsterer to His Royal Highness the Prince of Wales has received orders from Bath to get Norfolk House in St James's Square in readiness by the beginning of December'. In 1740 he was referred to as Keeper of the Wardrobe with responsibility for disbursements for repairs, cleaning and porterage. When in 1737 the Company of Upholders at Exeter Exchange furnished mourning at Norfolk House at a cost of £191 11s it was George Cure who appears to have been responsible on behalf of the Company. He appears to have played a part in the decoration and fitting out of the state barge designed by William Kent for the Prince of Wales and built 1731–32. On 12 December 1737 he supplied for the barge chintz window curtains with the necessary rods, green cloth for the table in the cabin and carpets for which £42 14s 4d was charged. In this year alone £132 16s 2d was paid to Cure.

In 1739 the Prince of Wales leased Cliveden, Bucks., from Lady Orkney and lived there in great style until his death in 1751. Cure was frequently employed to undertake work and after the Prince's death his position in the household continued with his appointment as Wardrobe Keeper to Her Royal Highness Princess Augusta, wife of the Prince. For this position he received a salary of £50 a year.

Typical entries for Clivedon recorded in the Duchy of Cornwall records include:

'7 May 1742 For 2 Green Lutestring curtains for a Night Table 17s
For 2 Large Wainscott table bedsteads with Double Sack bottoms for the footmen £3.10s
For a half Canepy hoop tester, with a compass rod, nutts & screws & plates £1
For 17 yds ½ blew harrateen for a Curtain & Cover the Teaster £1.15s
For blew lace to trim it, Rings, thread, silk & tape 11s.6d
Making the Curtain Gathered with a head and cover the canepy 12s
May 21 1743 For a Windsor Chair for Lord Carnervon 11s
For a fine large Turkey Carpitt for the Rooms where the young Princes Dine in, by Ordr £7.7s
For a fine Large Hanin blankitt bound with white Ribbon for Prince George £1.7s
For 3 Large Green Sherge coushions fil'd with flox for the Doggs £1.3s
For cuttong out & Makeing 2: crimson Lutstring cases for 2: Easy Chairs & Coushions for their Royall Highness to Dine on £1.4s
Oct 1744 Payd a man to go to Cliffden to mend furnetr aboutt the House, mend 2 paper skreens, and Doe severall things about the House, Passage ther & Back £2
Aug 18 Payd a cart to carry the large Couch & top etc to Cliffden £1
Payd a Man to Goe to Cliffden to put up the Couch, umbrellas & other things, Expenses etc 19.6d'

George Cure died in 1759 and letters of administration concerned with the goods and chattels were issued to John Cope guardian to George and Capel Cure who were minors at the time of the death. [Heal; poll bk; GL, Sun MS vol. 21, ref. 36144; Duchy of Cornwall Office LX(2), p. 29, p. 159, vouchers vi(i) 1735–37, p. 264, v p. 262, household accounts,

I to XX; *London Daily Post*, 13 November 1738; V & A archives] B.A.

Curle, Thomas & Son, carpenters (1800–03). Undertook work for the Royal Family. Accounts for work amounted to £69 9s 9d in 1800 and in 1803 £18 14s. The latter work consisted of supplying mahogany boxes, painting and japanning basin stands and a table, the making of an elm confectionary block and 'Painting & fitting 4 brass castors & 2 glass eyes to Horse in Armoury and making the figure of a man for the horse'. [Windsor Royal Archives, RA 88867, 25137]

Curles & Harris, 4 Clare St, Bristol, carvers and gilders (1830–40). [D]

Curme, Charles, High St, Dorchester, Dorset, cm, u, auctioneer and builder (1823–30). In 1830 recorded in partnership with John Acres at High West St. [D]

Curme, H., Bridport, Dorset, cm (1837–40). In 1837 listed as insolvent but by 1840 back in business at West St. [D; *Exeter Flying Post*, 23 May 1837]

Curme, Thomas, Dorchester, Dorset, cm (1786–93). In July 1786 insured his house for £60 and his utensils and stock for £260. In 1791 insured his goods, utensils and wearing apparel for £1,400. [D; GL, Sun MS vol. 339, p. 103; vol. 376, p. 657]

Curnock, Thomas, London, carver (1754). Freeman of Bristol. [Bristol poll bk]

Curr, Samuel, London, upholder (1730). Son of William Curr of 'Adbury', Hants., yeoman. App. to Nathaniel Spindler 22 July 1723 and James King, freeman and draper 18 February 1725. Free of the Upholders' Co. by servitude, 7 October 1730. [GL, Upholders' Co. records]

Curran, Robert, Liverpool, cm (1804–35). At 4 Little Harford St, Mount Pleasant in 1804 and Carver Ct, 28 Stanley St in 1835. [D]

Currer, Thomas, Madeley, Salop, cm (1840). [D]

Currey, William, Norwich, cabinet and chairmaker (1836–39). At Field Sq. in 1836 and St Stephen's Gate in 1839. [D]

Currie, Archibald, 24 Denmark St, Soho, London, cm (1786–1813). On 3 April 1786 took out insurance cover of £200 of which £50 was for utensils etc. Executor of the will of James Reid, cm, proved 6 March 1800. Not recorded in trade directories until 1808. On 18 April 1809 took out insurance cover on a house at 14 Gloster Pl., Camden Town for £200 with a further £200 for household goods. The house was said to be in 'his own tennure'. Despite this the business continued to operate from the Denmark St premises. [D; GL, Sun MS vol. 448, ref. 830691; vol. 336, p. 108]

Currie, Samuel, 9 Bakehouse Lane, Stanley St, Liverpool, cm (1790). [D]

Currie, William, Longtown, Cumb., cm and ironmonger (1811). [D]

Currie & Gibson, Westgate, Newcastle, cm and joiners (1838). [D]

Curry, —, Lancaster, u (1798–1803). [Westminster Ref. Lib., Gillow records]

Curry, Abraham, 32 Theobald's Rd, Red Lion Sq., London, upholder and undertaker (1789–93). Some directories record the Christian name as Andrew and in 1792 the address is stated to be 30 Theobalds Rd. Bankrupt 1791, a dividend being paid in 1795. [D; Bailey's list of bankrupts; *Derby Mercury*, 29 January 1795]

Curry, John, 87 Leather Lane, Holborn, London, u (1812). In 1812 married Elizabeth Lucy, late wife of John Clark, late of Kingston, Surrey, Gent. [PRO, C13/139/12]

Curry, Joseph, Butcher Bank, Newcastle, u (1778). [D]

Curry, Joseph, Turner's Pl., St James' St, Liverpool, cm (1834). [D]

Curry, Robert, Newcastle, u (1723–41). Free 30 October 1723. [Freemen reg.; poll bks]

Curry, Robert, Darlington, Co. Durham, u (1774–77). Freeman of Newcastle. [Newcastle poll bks]

Curry, Robert, Newcastle, u (1782–88). At Scale Cross in 1782 but by 1787 at the foot of Side where he had a shop. Thomas Eden, u, took over the business at this address in March 1788. [D; *Newcastle Courant*, 22 March 1788]

Curry, William, Union St, Cheltenham, Glos., cm (1839). [D]

Curtis, Anthony, Essex, cm (1832–39). Recorded at Manningtree in 1832 and Misterley in 1839. [D]

Curtis, Augustine snr and jnr, Norwich, carvers (1661–1732). Augustine Curtis snr was born 1661 and died 1731. His son, born 1701, was his app. and made free, 18 August 1722. The nature of their work is uncertain and Gunnis records only their own memorial in St John Maddermarket, Norwich, the son only surviving his father by a year. [Gunnis; freemen rolls]

Curtis, Benjamin, 3 St James' St, Liverpool, cm and broker (1834). [D]

Curtis, C. W., address unknown. A George IV pollard elm pedestal table with the label of this maker included in Christie's sale of 16 July 1981, lot 41.

Curtis, Cornelius, Wells, Som., cm (1784). Freeman of Bristol. [Bristol poll bk]

Curtis, Henry, Norwich, chairmaker (1753–55). Took apps named Bartell in 1753 and Yeomans in 1755. He was however not free himself until 3 May 1755 (not by servitude). [Freemen reg.; S of G, app. index]

Curtis, Henry, parish of St John Maddermarket, Norwich, cm (1779–80). Son of John Curtis, joiner. Free 11 December 1779. [Freemen reg.; poll bk]

Curtis, Hipsley, Chewton, Som., u (1734). Freeman of Bristol. [Bristol poll bk]

Curtis, James, Lewes, Sussex, cm, u and furniture broker (1823–40). Initially in South St but by 1832 had moved to 39 High St, Cliffe. [D; poll bks]

Curtis, James, 113 Wardour St, Soho, London, carver and gilder (1835). [D]

Curtis, John, Wisbech, Cambs., cm, u and chairmaker (1768–1824). An advertisement in the *Cambridge Chronicle and Journal* of 8 October 1768, gives details of property for sale in Wisbech, including 'a Shop or Shed . . . near to Roper's Fields, now in the Occupation of John Curtis, chairmaker'. The poll bks of 1780 and 1802 also record him in Wisbech. Advertised for a chair turner and an u, *Lincoln, Rutland and Stamford Mercury*, 12 March 1790. The *Cambridge Chronicle and Journal*, 14 May 1796 carried an advertisement for two experienced journeymen cm to apply 'to John Curtis at his Chair, Cabinet and Upholstery Manufactury in the Beast Market, Wisbech'. There was also a vacancy for an app. and 'A spinning wheel maker . . . who can do the Job Turning in a cabinet shop'. Another advertisement appeared in the *Cambridge Chronicle and Journal*, 17 April 1812, addressed to journeymen chair and cm: 'Two or three good workmen in the above branches may have constant employ, by the Norwich book of prices, and the late advances theron, by applying immediatly to Mr. John Curtis's Chair, Cabinet and Upholstery Manufactory near the Corn Exchange, Wisbech St. Peters, Cambridgeshire'. Curtis again advertised in *Cambridge Chronicle and Journal*, 26 April 1818 for two further workmen. Pigot's directory of 1823–24 lists the firm of John Curtis & Son in Wisbech. The business was probably fairly substantial and as early as 1777 utensils, stock and workshop were insured for £400. Some furniture appears to have been labelled and one piece inscribed in manuscript 'John Curtis/Fecit 1774/Wisbich' is known. The label is on the inner carcase of a 17th-century marquetry cabinet which had

been extensively rebuilt and altered in the 18th century to form a chest of drawers. [D; GL, Sun MS vol. 263, p. 97]
R. W.

Curtis, John, Wisbech, Cambs., cm and u (1839). Recorded at North Brink, Wisbech, and possibly the 'son' from John Curtis & Son above. [D]

Curtis, John, London Lane, Reigate, Surrey, cm, turner and u (1826–39). [D]

Curtis, John, 11 Oxford St, Leeds, Yorks., cm (1839–40). [D]

Curtis, Joseph, 23 Pithay, Bristol, carpenter and cm (1775). [D]

Curtis, Joseph, Otley, Yorks., cm (1822–37). At Rotten Row in 1822, Westgate in 1830, but in 1837 at Kirkgate. [D]

Curtis, Joseph Digby (or Digley), Newark, Notts., carver, gilder and painter (1805–35). Trading at Castlegate in 1805–08, and Lombard St, 1828–35. [D]

Curtis, P., 17 Peter St, Bishopsgate, London, cm and u (1835–39). [D]

Curtis, Robert, London, cm (1830–31). Freeman of Gt Yarmouth, Norfolk. [Gt Yarmouth poll bk]

Curtis, Thomas, Wisbech, Cambs., chairmaker, cm and u (1798–1830). Recorded in a 1798 directory as an u. From 1806–19 the address is given as 'near the Church' but from 1830 as Market Pl. Advertised for an app. in August 1806 and March 1819. [D; *Cambridge Chronicle*, 30 August 1806, 5 March 1819]

Curtis, William, Worcester, upholder (1775–98). Trading at 6 Goose Lane in 1797. App. to Richard Meredith and free by servitude 6 March 1775. [D; freemen rolls]

Curtis, William jnr, Billericay, Essex, cm, u, appraiser and house agent (1823–38). At the time of his death in 1853 he was also listed as a farmer, brickmaker and carpenter but the date on which he added these activities is not known. [D; Maldon poll bk., jurors' bk; *Wills at Chelmsford*]

Curtis, William, High St, St Mary's, Lincoln, cm and u (1835). [D]

Curtis, William, Dorking, Surrey, cm (1826–39). [D]

Curtis & Drake, 2 Elm Hill, Norwich, cm (1783–84). [D]

Curtois, Charles, Lincoln, cm (1805–22). Trading at New St, 1805–06, New Rd in 1819 and Silver St in 1822 also as an u. [D; poll bk]

Curtois, Mary, New Rd, Lincoln, u and cm (1819). [D]

Curtois, William, bottom of New Rd, Lincoln (1805). Trade card [Banks Coll., BM] shows three pieces of furniture in the Sheraton style and two looking-glasses. [D]

Curwin, John, Leeds, Yorks., cm (1791). Listed in the *Leeds Cabinet and Chair Makers Book of Prices*, 1791 as a journeyman in sympathy with the intentions of its compilers.

Cushen, Edward, East St, Tichfield, Hants., cm and u (1830). [D]

Cushen, William, 55 Paradise St, Liverpool, carver and gilder (1794). [D]

Cushing, Charles, Lawrence Lane, St Laurence, Norwich, carver and gilder (1835–40). Son of John Cushing, bookbinder and free 10 January 1835. In business by 1839. [D; freemen reg.]

Cushing, James M., Gt Yarmouth, Norfolk, cm (1774). Took as app. John George (free 1774). [Freemen rolls]

Cushing, John William, Norwich, cm (1827). Son of John Cushing, bookbinder. Free 3 February 1837. [Freemen reg.]

Cushing, Robert Harley, Norwich, carver and gilder (1799). Son of Samuel Cushing, carver and gilder. Free 26 October 1799. [Freemen reg.]

Cushing, Samuel snr and jnr, Norwich, carvers and gilders (1770–1840). Samuel snr was app. to Benjamin Jagger and free by servitude, 21 September 1770. Already trading on his own behalf by 1776 at St Giles Broad St, the number being initially 10 but was changed to 9 about 1800. In 1776 advertised that he could execute articles 'as cheap as in London' and specified his products as 'Ornaments for Chimney Pieces, Glass Frames, Girandoles and Picture Frames of all Kinds, in the present Taste, Prints fram'd and glaz'd. oval or square, and every other Article in the Carving Business'. He also pointed out that his wood carvings were 25% cheaper than work carried out in lead; and three years later claimed in an advertisement that he had devised 'a Method of strengthening light Ornaments, which renders them free from any Danger of breaking'. His only recorded app. was William Dansie who was free 24 February 1793 but as he had two sons to assist in the business outside assistance was probably less necessary. His eldest son Samuel was made free by 1796 and Robert Harley on 26 October 1799. Samuel Cushing snr probably died between 1812 and 1818 and after that his eldest son continued the business at the same address. By 1830 however the address was changed to Bethel St and from 1836 to Surrey St. [D; freemen reg.; poll bks; *Norfolk Chronicle*, 3 August 1776, 17 July 1779]

Cushing, T. jnr, Marylebone, London, cm (1830). Freeman of Norwich. [Norwich poll bk]

Cussans, John, 102 High St, Marylebone, London, u (1812–14). [D]

Cussans, Leonard, 47 Gray's Inn Rd, London, mattress and bed maker (1820). [D]

Cussons, George, 115 Wardour St, London, cm (1781). In 1781 insured his utensils and stock for £100 out of a total cover of £200. [GL, Sun MS vol. 292, p. 55]

Cust, George & Cox, John, Strand, parish of St Clement Danes, London, upholders (1741–48). Insured the Upholders' Co. building, as above, in their own possession for £2,000. [GL, Hand in Hand MS vol. 62, ref. 4332]

Custance, John Miles, London, broker, upholders and undertaker (1786–1802). At 40 Brewer St, Golden Sq. in 1786 when he took out insurance cover of £800 on his house and workshop and £300 on his utensils, stock and goods in trust. In 1793 the number is recorded as 41. He also appears to have had additional premises at 32 Bishopsgate 1790–93. He was admitted a member of the Upholders' Co. by redemption on 5 May 1802. At the time he was living at 31 Bow Lane, Cheapside and declared his trade as 'auctioneer & appraiser'. [D; Heal; GL, Sun MS vol. 337, p. 154; Upholders' Co. records]

Custance, King's Lynn, Norfolk, u (1787–88). On 9 February 1787 insured his goods for £500. In January of the following year his marriage to Miss Holman of Downham Market, Norfolk was announced. [GL, Sun MS vol. 343, p. 103; *Gents Mag.*, January 1788]

Custance, William, Fakenham, Norfolk, cm (1794). Bankruptcy announced in 1774, and from 6 October of that year his stock was sold by auction. It consisted of 'several very handsome mahogany double and single chests of drawers, two mahogany bureaus, wardrobes, several mahogany voiders, set of dining tables, with circular ends, handsome secretary and bookcase, with glazed gothic doors, staircase and other carpets, pier and dressing glasses in burnished gold and mahogany frames, tea caddies, very handsome bason stands, wardrobe bedstead, about 12 dozen mahogany chairs with hair and other seats and a great variety of other articles of useful furniture'. His stock of timber was also offered for sale consisting of 'upwards of TEN THOUSAND FEET of FINE DRY MAHOGANY, in boards and planks, 6000 feet of wainscot in boards, a very large quantity of fine dry deals, dyed woods, veneers, walnuttree and elm planks, two fine cedar logs' together with 'a good timber drug, and two carts'. [*Bury and Norwich Post*, 24 September 1794]

Custance, William, parish of St Michael at Plea, Norwich,

upholder (1788–90). App. to Henry Withers, upholder, and free by servitude 3 May 1788. [Freemen reg.; poll bk]

Cutbush, Edward, Rochester, Kent, carver (1771). [Poll bk]

Cuthbert, James, London, upholder (1780–97). Free of the Upholders' Co. under the 1750 Upholders' Act on 7 June 1780. It is probable that at this date he was already trading as his address is shown as 123 Fleet St which was used for the business up to 1793. In 1780 he took out insurance cover for £600, half of which was in respect of utensils and stock. In 1790 he was declared bankrupt and in the same year fined £9 for non-service at St Bride's Guildhall. Business was not interrupted for long however, for by 1792 Cuthbert was once again trading from the Fleet St address in partnership with his son. In 1795 the address was changed to 79 Islington Rd. [D; GL, Sun MS vol. 284, p. 104; Upholders' Co. records; MS 6561, p. 118; Bailey's list of bankrupts]

Cuthbertson, Daniel, Newcastle, u (1746). Free 1746. His son John was also declared free on 14 January 1762 by patrimony. [Freemen reg.]

Cuthbertson, J. W., 86 Percy St, Newcastle, u (1838). [D]

Cuthbertson, John, Brighton, Sussex, u and cm (1822–26). At 10 Cumberland Pl. in 1822 but from the next year at 46 Edward St. [D]

Cuthey, Samuel, Regent St, Newark, Notts., carver and gilder (1835). [D]

Cutler, Richard, High Wycombe, Bucks., chairmaker (1798). [Militia Census]

Cutler, Samuel, 11 Clarence St, Liverpool, u etc. (1837). [D]

Cutler, Thomas, Norwich, u and paper hanger (c. 1790–1830). His trade card in the Norwich Lib. gives his address as St Andrew's and shows a draped shield with the Prince of Wales's feathers. This must be dated by style to c. 1790. Cutler is first mentioned in local directories in Rampant Horse St. Took an app. Ambrose Gedge who was made free, 7 December 1818. In 1822 the business was listed as Cutler & Tomlinson but no mention of Tomlinson occurs in an 1830 directory entry. [D; poll bks, freemen reg.]

Cutler, William, Market Pl., Warminster, Wilts., cm and u (1839). [D]

Cutsforth, Thomas, Hull, Yorks., u and cm (1790–1823). At Land of Green Ginger, 1790–99, but from 1803 at 57 Whitefriargate. [D]

Cuttell, Stephen, 99 Berwick St, London, cm (1779–84). In 1779 insured his house for £100. [GL, Sun MS vol. 271, p. 355, poll bk]

Cutter, Charles, Warwick St, Golden Sq., London, carver and gilder and painter (1805–18). Trading from 22 Warwick Sq. by July 1806 when he took out insurance cover of £550 which included £250 in respect of stock, utensils and goods in trust. The cover for stock was the same in 1810 though that on his house rose to £700 with an additional cover of £650 for household goods. In 1817 Cutter was in partnership with a man named Brown, but this must have been the last year of trading, for in January 1818 his stock was sold by auction 'by the direction of trustees'. The Warwick St premises were described as being a 'Leasehold dwelling house, and a large shop' and was said to have been used for the trade of carver and gilder for 'upwards of Thirty Years'. The stock offered for sale consisted of 'A NOBLE PIER GLASS 62 by 31, ONE 42 by 24, AND SEVENTY OTHER PLATES OF GLASS, ORIGINAL DRAWINGS, By Hogarth, Walmsley, Craig, Gainsborough &c. PICTURES, STAINED GLASS AND PAINTINGS ON GLASS, Elegantly carved and gilt Pier Tables, with Marble Tops; carved Brackets, pair of beautifully carved Dogs, Antique carved and Modern Picture Frames, A BUHL CLOCK, Marble Slabs, 5 feet by 2 feet, Eight richly carved Chairs, covered with Damask, and a variety of carved Work'. Several of Cutter's customers are known and indicate a flourishing and fashionable trade. In 1805 five gilt picture frames and three others in black and gold were supplied to James Brogden, MP, costing £17 17s 6d. At the same period he was working for Edward Lascelles of Harewood House, Yorks. supplying items mainly for his London house in Hanover Sq. On 24 April 1805 £2 10s was paid to 'J. Cutler framemaker' and on 15 July 1806 a further payment of £85 was made. In March 1806 he charged £7 14s for gilding the cornice in the Library at Gorhambury, near St Albans, Herts. A further £13 0s 6d was paid in March of the following year for 'gilding and bronzing the border in the Drawing Room'. The 2nd Lord Braybrooke paid him £7 7s in 1810 for picture frames etc. and in June and December 1813 £2 11s for picture frames and £5 5s for carving and gilding. These commissions were for Audley End, Essex and his London house. [D; GL, Sun MS vol. 437, ref. 792102; vol. 453, ref. 846764; vol. 453, ref. 839489; V & A archives; Essex RO, D/D Se 8; D/DBy/A376, Leeds archives dept, Harewood MS 192; Herts. RO, accounts bk XI 77] B.A.

Cutter, William Biggs, London St, Reading, Berks., carver and gilder (1820). [Poll bk]

Cutting, John, 42 London St, Tottenham Ct Rd, London, cm and u (1839). [D]

Cutting, William, Smallgate St, Beccles, Suffolk, u (1839). [D]

Cymington, James, address unknown, cm (1803). Subscribed to Sheraton's *Cabinet Dictionary*, 1803.

D

Dabine, Josiah, Wells, Som., u (1798). [D]

Dacie, Robert, Exeter, Devon u (1740). [Exeter freemen rolls]

Dacre, Benjamin, Long St, Easingwold, Yorks, joiner and/or cm (1830). [D]

Dacre, Benjamin, Wetherby, Yorks., joiner and/or cm (1837). [D]

Dacre, William jnr, Wharton Lane, Wetherby, Yorks., cm (1830). [D]

Dadd, Isaac, Chatham, Kent, carver and gilder (1832–38). Trading at 2 High St, 1832–34, and Hammond Pl. in 1838. [D]

Dadd, Robert, 15 Suffolk St, Pall Mall East, London, French gilder, water gilder (1838–40). Trade label in the Windsor Royal Archives states that he was 'Successor to A. PICNOT, French Gilder, Clock Case Maker & Bronzist'. The accounts for Windsor Castle and Buckingham Palace record him in 1840 gilding mounts for inkstands, fenders and furniture, and lacquering and making mounts for a chess table. [D; PRO, LC 11/107]

Dadd, Thomas, 14 Clarence Pl., Hackney Rd, London, cm (1838). [D]

Dady, James, Norwich and Bury St Edmunds, Suffolk, upholder (1795–1830). Recorded in Norwich, 1796–97; Bury St Edmunds, 1802–12; and Heigham, Norwich, 1830. Son of George Dady, weaver; admitted freeman of Norwich on 24 January 1795. [Poll bks; Norwich freemen reg.]

Daft, David, Leicester, cm (1826). [Leicester freemen rolls]

Daggett, John, 33 King St, Worship St, Hull, Yorks., cm (1831). [D]

Daggett, John, 13 Leading Post St, Scarborough, Yorks., cm (1834). [D]

Daggitt, Robert, Peck's Entry, 57 Mytongate, Hull, Yorks., cm (1826). [D]

Daglish, Anthony, Newgate St, Morpeth, Northumb., joiner and cm (1827). [D]

Daglish, William, Portsea, Portsmouth, Hants., cm and undertaker (1792–98). [D]

Daglish, William, Gateshead and Newcastle, joiner and u (1782–1838). Addresses given below Tollbooth, Gateshead, 1782–90; Cooper's-entry, 1795–1811; and Westgate St, Newcastle, 1824–34, no. 35, 1834–38. Advertised his stock in *Newcastle Courant*, 6 February 1808, including 'lobby chests, American birch bedsteads, desk beds, press beds'. Announced that he was commencing trade as an auctioneer, same paper, 4 February 1809. [D]

Dagnall, Thomas, Liverpool, cm (1761). Admitted freeman on 12 March 1761. [Liverpool freemen reg.]

Daguerre, Dominique, Sloane St, Chelsea, London, cm (1789–d. 1796). A refugee French dealer who fled to London in 1793. He was purveyor of furniture to Louis XVI and styled 'Marchand privilégé de la Cour', his shop in Paris being at the sign of the 'Couronne d'Or', Rue St Honoré. He is mentioned in D'Oberkirch's *Memoirs* as having there a fine sideboard, which was to be sent to the Duke of Northumberland. In 1785 he supplied furniture to the 2nd Earl Spencer at Althorp. [D. Stroud, *Henry Holland*, 1966, pp. 145–46] In 1789 he sent in a bill to the English Crown for £1,659 for 'carving and gilding done by S. Nelson by order of Mr. Dagare'. After his arrival in London he entered into partnership with another Frenchman, M. E. Lingereux, at a shop in Sloane St. From there the firm supplied a large quantity of costly furniture for Carlton House, including some gilt armchairs and sofas, which are still in the Royal Collection and bear Daguerre's label. He claimed £15,000 in the proceedings of the Commissioners for the settlement of the Prince's debts. [*DEF*; H. Clifford Smith, *Buckingham Palace*, pl. 169–70; Salverte, *Les Ebénistes du XVIIIe Siècle*; Jourdain, *Regency Furniture*; G. de Bellaigue, *Waddesdon Catalogue*, II, pp. 858–59] Daguerre is named in Henry Holland's accounts for furniture supplied to Woburn Abbey, Beds., costing £107 5s 6d. Items included four lamps with two burners for the Billiard Room, £12, and two writing tables for the Dressing Room of the East Apartment. [Bedford Office, London; Beds. RO, Russell Estate papers] Lord Palmerston purchased girandoles and a clock from Daguerre for Broadlands in 1790. [*C. Life*, 5 February 1981]

Daken, William, Church St, Uttoxeter, Staffs., cm and clock case maker (1828). [D]

Dakor (?), James, Berwick St, London cm (1784). [Poll bk]

Dalby, Edward, 8 Minories, London, carver, gilder, paper hanging and looking-glass manufacturer (1809–14). Trade label recorded: 'Houses & Rooms Papered in Town or Country in a New & Superior Style. Every Allowance made to Builders & Dealers. Stationary & Paper Hangings for Exportation. Pictures, Needlework &c. neatly Fram'd and Glaz'd'. [D]

Dalby, George, 33 Upper North Pl., Gray's Inn, London, u and cm (1815–21). [D]

Dalby, Michael, Thorner, Yorks., cm (1822). [D]

Dalby, William, Cambridge, cm (1813–23). Three children bapt. at St Andrew the Great between 1813–19. Took app. named Joseph Ling on 14 August 1823. [PR (bapt.); Cambridge app. reg.]

Dalby, William, York, carver and gilder (1826). Son of David Dalby, animal painter; app. to William Fawcett Dodgson, carver and gilder, on 11 September 1826. [York app. reg.]

Dale, Charles, Andover, Hants., cm and u (1830–39). Listed at Market Pl. in 1830 and High St in 1839. [D]

Dale, George, address unrecorded, upholder (1720–29). Son of George Dale, innholder, of Kingston-upon-Thames, Surrey; app. to James Gronous on 6 July 1720, and admitted freeman of the Upholders' Co. by servitude on 3 December 1729. [GL, Upholders' Co. records] Possibly:

Dale, George, at 'The Black Lyon', Wich St, London, u (1733). Took out a Sun Insurance policy on 14 September 1733 for £300 on household goods and stock in trade in his house. [GL, Sun MS vol. 38, ref. 61796] Possibly:

Dale, George, near Slaughter's Coffee House, the Upper End of St Martin's Lane, London, upholder and cm (d. by 1747). Meeting of creditors of the late George Dale called, *Daily Advertiser*, 28 July 1747.

Dale, John, Wyaston, Derby, cm (1726–54). Took app. named Thomas Wainwright of Tulbury, Staffs., in 1726 for £5. Subscribed to Chippendale's *Director*, 1754. [V & A archives]

Dale, John, Liverpool, joiner and cm (1821–29). Addresses given at Livesty Pl., Shaw's Brow, 1821–23; and 25 Norton St, 1827–29. [D]

Dale, John, Newgate St, Chester, cm (1840). [D]

Dale(s), Joseph, 4 Broad St, Golden Sq., Carnaby Mkt, London, cm, chairmaker, u and broker (1809–19). Recorded at no. 2 in 1816. Took out a Sun Insurance policy on 11 July 1809 for £800 of which stock, utensils and goods in trust accounted for £600. [D; GL, Sun MS vol. 448, ref. 832694] Possibly Joseph Dales of Wardour St.

Dale, Samuel, Chester, cm (1827). Son of John Dale, yeoman of Chester; assigned over from Richard Gorst, cm, to William Podmore, cm, for the rest of his apprenticeship for seven years, on 8 September 1827. [Chester app. indentures] Possibly:

Dale, Samuel, Chester, cm (1831). Admitted freeman on 28 April 1831. [Chester freemen rolls]

Dale, Samuel, Framlingham, Suffolk, cm and furniture broker (1839). [D]

Dale, Thomas, 81 Shude Hill, Manchester, chairmaker (1794). [D]

Dale, Thomas, 9 Clarence Pl., Hackney Rd, London, cm (1808). [D]

Dale, William, near Mr Button's Coffee House, over the Corner of the Piazza, Covent Gdn, London, u (1709–24). His dwelling house was on the south side of Russell St and the east side of the little Piazza in March 1709 when he insured it for £400. The insurance cover on this property had risen to £600 by October 1717. Although nothing is known about his business or its customers it was probably of some importance. By 1720 he had accumulated sufficient wealth and had sufficient confidence to invest in the shares of the South Sea Co. The rapid rise of these shares enabled Dale to purchase from the Earls of Islay and Bute the Kenwood estate at Highgate for £3,150. Dale may have made further investments in property on the strength of the ever rising value of his shares for the *York Mercury*, 12 December 1720 announced that 'Mr. Dale, an upholsterer of Covent Garden has purchased the estate which belonged to the late Viscount Bolingbroke for £50,000'. The South Sea Co. shares which at their height had sold for £1,050 per £100 share had by 29 September 1720 tumbled to £150 and Dale, seriously over-extended, desperately tried to stave off his creditors. On 15 October 1720 he had mortgaged Kenwood to the Earl of Islay for £1,575. Neither the interest nor the capital appear to have been repaid and the Earl complained that Dale was trying to raise income by ruthless felling of the timber. On 29 October 1724 judgement to foreclose was given against Dale and the estate reverted to the Earl of Islay. [Heal; GL, Hand in Hand MS vol. 6, ref. 2510; vol. 17, p. 287; *Survey of London*, XVII, pp. 129–30]　　　B. A.

Dales, George, Goosepool, Louth, Lincs., cm and joiner (1826–31). [D]

Dales, John, Beverley, Yorks., cm (1774). [Poll bk]

Dales, John, Beverley, Yorks., cm (1828–31). Trading in Walkergate, 1828–29, and Norwood, 1831. [D]

Dales, Joseph, Wardour St, London, cm, u, undertaker, chairmaker and broker (1807–39). Recorded at no. 12, 1807–09, and no. 26 in 1839. Took out Sun Insurance policies on 13 May 1807 for £900, £350 on utensils and stock; and on 12 July 1808 for £800, £600 on stock and utensils in workshop. [D; GL, Sun MS vol. 440, ref. 802907; vol. 445, ref. 819384] Possibly Joseph Dale of Broad St.

Dales, Joseph, Kidgate, Louth, Lincs., cm, joiner and builder (1826–41). [D]

Dales, Sam., Limekiln Hill, Louth, Lincs., cm and joiner (1826). [D]

Dalkin, Joseph, King St, Barnard Castle, Co. Durham, joiner and cm (1828–29). [D]

Dall, Joseph, York, cm and u (1804–40). Trading at 91 Petergate, 1830–38, and 31 Colliergate in 1840. Son of Robert Dall; app. to William Smith, u and cm, on 10 October 1804. Admitted freeman in 1811. [D; York app. reg. and freemen rolls]

Dallain, Abraham, Berwick St, London, carver and gilder (1774). [Poll bk]

Dallain, Isaac, London, carver and gilder (1768–82). Recorded in partnership with R. Harding at 7 Berwick St in 1782 as 'successors to Mr. Gossett'. Dallain worked for Sir Gilbert Heathcote between 1768–72, 'gilding 7 frames in Oyl Gold', £3 6s; supplying '2 Glass frames for North End, Fulham', £30; 'a large pier Glass frame to the End of the Great Room', £66, possibly at Normanton Park; 'gilding 4 festoons between the windows'; and providing looking-glasses totalling £429 8s. On 22 July 1782 Dallain & Harding received 12s for 'two small ovals in burnish gold with glasses'; and on 9 October, £2 17s for 'a frame with a Frett 2½ wide burnish gold' with a plate glass. [Lincoln RO, 2 ANC/D/30 and 35]

Dallas, John, 19 Gt Bell Alley, Coleman St, London, cm (1784). [D]

Dallas, Robert, Broadway, Southwark, London, cm (1837). [D]

Dallman, —, address unrecorded, cm (1803). Subscribed to Sheraton's *Cabinet Dictionary*, 1803.

Dallman, Charles, 3 Princes St, Holborn, London, carver and gilder (1839). [D]

Dalrimple, —, 5 New St, Carnaby Mkt, London, cm (1809). [D] Probably Hugh Dalrymple.

Dalrimple, H., 10 Broad St, Soho, London, cm and upholder (1811–15). [D] Probably:

Dalrymple, Hugh, London, upholder and undertaker (1809–17). Trading at 90 Charlotte St, Rathbone Pl. in 1817. [D] In 1809 he supplied Earl Spencer of Althorp, Northants. with 'a Mah-y Cabinet of Fine Wood on castors ornamented w[t]. Black Moulding w[t]. a Rising Top to d[o]. cover'd w[t]. Russia Leather w[t]. a Black à la Grec Border Round the edge of d[o].; the inside fill'd with cedar Trays engraved & lind w[t]. green silk cushions stuff'd with cotton for Books', costing £58. The cabinet was designed to hold a set of Shakespeare's historical plays illuminated by Margaret, Countess of Lucan. [Althorp archives; *Apollo*, October 1968, pp. 266–77] Probably the Dalrymple, u, who received £7 19s from Lord Braybrooke of Audley End, Essex, in September 1810. [Essex RO, D/DBy/A376]

Dalrymple, James, Liverpool, cm (1834–37). Addresses given at 73 St Andrew's St in 1834; no. 13 in 1835; and 50 Gloucester St, 1837. [D]

Dalrymple, William, 10 Castle St, Long Acre, London, cm (1782). Insured his house for £200 with the Sun Co. in 1782. [GL, Sun MS vol. 299, p. 420]

Dalrymple, William, New Inn Yd, Kendal, Westmld, turner (1829). [D]

Dalston, John, Carlisle, Cumb., u (1793). [D]

Dalston, Jonathan, Scotch St, Carlisle, Cumb., u (1810–11). [D]

Dalton, Christopher, 25 Goodramgate, York, u (1840). [D]

Dalton, John, St Martin's Ct, Bear St, London, carver and gilder (1790–93). [D]

Dalton, John, Pickering, Yorks., cm (1834). [D]

Dalton, Robert, address unrecorded, chairmaker (1803). Subscribed to Sheraton's *Cabinet Dictionary*, 1803.

Dalton, Thomas, Hungate, Pickering, Yorks., cm and joiner 1828–29). [D]

Dalton, Thomas, London, writing desk and dressing case maker (1829–39). Trading at 31 Percival St, Clerkenwell in 1829 and 6 Gt Ormond St, 1839. [D]

Dalziel, —, at 'The Chair', the corner of Wych St, facing Drury Lane, London, cm (c. 1770). Trade card shows octagonal and oval cisterns and Chippendale-style Rococo chair framed by Rococo scrolls; it states that he 'Makes & Sells all Sorts of Mahogany Cisterns & Pails'. [Heal; *C. Life*, December 1955, p. 1383]

Dalziel(l) (or Dalzeel), William F., Bedford Row, London, cm and u (1803–39). Trading at 4 Chapel St, 1803–11; 24 Gt James St, 1814–39, and also no. 23, 1820–21. Took out Sun Insurance policies on 12 June 1820 and 24 September 1821 for £2,200, of which two houses with warehouses, workshops and counting houses accounted for £520; pictures and prints, £25; and stock, utensils and goods in trust, £1,235. Named in Sheraton's list of master cabinet makers, 1803. The majority of designs in J. C. Loudon's *Encyclopaedia of Cottage, Farm & Villa Architecture & Furniture*, 1833, were supplied by Dalziel. Dalziel, cm of Gt James St was mentioned in correspondence with the Royal Society of Arts in 1817 concerning mahogany. [D; GL, Sun MS vol. 486, ref. 968438; vol. 487, ref. 983639; Heal]

Damer, William James, 6 Shepperton Pl. North, North Rd, London, cm (1839). [D]

Damget, —, address unrecorded. Secretaire cabinet recorded impressed 'DAMGET 1753'. [Sotheby's, 18 November 1982]

Danby, J., Lancaster. Named in the Gillow records working on a pulpit in 1801. [Westminster Ref. Lib., vol. 344/98, p. 1667]

Danby, T., 3 Wardour St, near Oxford St, London, upholder, cm and undertaker. Late 18th-century trade card shows Neo-classical urn, chair and serpentine-fronted chest. [Banks Coll., BM]

Danby, Thomas, 7 Green St, Leicester Fields, London, upholder (1778). Took out a Sun Insurance policy in 1778 for £200 of which utensils, stock and goods accounted for £90. [GL, Sun MS vol. 264, p. 656]

Dancaster, George, 28 St James's St, Brighton, Sussex, cm and u (1823). [D]

Dancaster, Henry, West St, Alresford, Hants., auctioneer, cm and u 1830–39). [D]

Dance, Edward, Vauxhall Bridge Rd, London, cm and u (1827–28). [D]

Dancer, Thomas J., 6 Wentworth Buildings, City Rd, London, carver in wood, cm (1829–39). [D]

Dandy, James, Church St, Preston, Lancs., joiner cm and timber merchant (1814–25). [D]

Dandy, James, Tarleton, Cheshire, cm (1825). [D]

Danell, James, Jermyn St, London, cm (1774). [Poll bk]

Danes, Richard, 48 Conduit St, Hanover Sq., London, cm (1787). On 5 March 1787 insured utensils and stock in his workshop for £200 with the Sun Co. [GL, Sun MS vol. 342, ref. 528221]

Daniel, Edward, address unrecorded, upholder (1746–55). Son of John Daniel, Gent. of St Anne's, Soho; app. to Peter Deschamps on 14 August 1746, and admitted freeman of the Upholders' Co. by servitude on 16 December 1755. [GL, Upholders' Co. records]

Daniel, George, 2 Reeves Pl., Hoxton, London, cm and undertaker (1808). [D]

Daniel, George T., London cm (1818). [Gt Yarmouth poll bk]

Daniel, John, Deansgate, Manchester, joiner and cm (1772–73). [D]

Daniel, Samuel, London, cm (1793). Subscribed to Sheraton's *Drawing Book*, 1793.

Daniel, Samuel, London, upholder (1780–1801). Trading at 59 York St, Westminster, in 1801. Son of Samuel Daniel, leather breeches maker of King St, Westminster; app. to George Brand on 11 November 1780, and admitted freeman of the Upholders' Co. by servitude on 2 December 1801. [GL, Upholders' Co. records]

Daniel, Samuel, King St, Westminster, London, u and cm (1804–27). Recorded at no. 6, 1821–27. Took out a Sun Insurance policy on 26 March 1804 for £400 of which stock, utensils and goods in trust accounted for £200. [D; GL, Sun MS vol. 431, ref. 760540]

Daniel, Samuel, 54 Princes St, Leicester Sq., London, cm and u (1808–20). [D]

Daniel, Thomas, Long Acre, London, cm (1709). [London rate bks]

Daniel, William, Cannon St, Eastcheap, London, u and wholesaler (1763). Delcared bankrupt, *Gents Mag.*, December 1763. [D]

Daniel, William, London, u (1785). Carried out upholstery work at Mount Stewart, N. Ireland, receiving £6 13s 5d on 5 February 1785. [Mount Stewart papers, D654/41/1, p. 72]

Daniel, William, 143 Chapel St, Salford, Lancs., cm and u (1840). [D]

Daniell, —, 42, 44 and 46 Wigmore St, London, cm. Trade label recorded on mahogany writing table of George III style, with rectangular leather-lined top and three frieze drawers carved with fluting and roundels, on square tapering legs carved with acanthus. [Christie's, 14 February 1980, lot 97]

Daniell, —, Clerkenwell, London, clockcase, cabinet and chairmaker (1796–c. 1800). Trading as Daniell & Co. at 18 Coppice Row, 1796–97; and at 1 St James's St c. 1800. [D; Heal]

Daniell, George, Tayspill, London, cm (1806–12). Polled at Colchester, Essex, of Somerstown, Middlx in 1806; and of London in 1812. Possibly George T. Daniel.

Daniell, Peter, address unrecorded, upholder (1710–26). Son of Peter Daniell, Gent., of Sawbridgeworth, Herts.; app. to Henry Calloway on 12 January 1710, and admitted freeman of the Upholders' Co. by servitude on 2 March 1725/26. [GL, Upholders' Co. records]

Daniels, George, Chapel St, Marlow, Bucks., cm and joiner (1823). [D]

Daniels, Thomas, Stanley St, Bury, Lancs., cm (1834). [D]

Danks, John, Gt Bridge, West Bromwich, Staffs., cm and u (1830–34). [D]

Dannatt, John, 4 Constable's Buildings, English St, Hull, Yorks., cm (1838–39). [D]

Dansie, William, Norwich and London, carver and gilder (1793–1806). App. to Samuel Cushing; admitted freeman of Norwich on 24 February 1793. Polled at Norwich, of London, 1796–1806. [Norwich freemen reg.; poll bks] Possibly:

Dansie, William, 34 Evesham Buildings, Somerstown, London, gilder (1808). [D]

Danson, Edward, Liverpool, cm and turner (1824–37). Addresses given at Old Haymarket in 1824; 13 Gt Crosshall St with shop at 41 Clayton St, 1827–29; 12 Clayton St, 1835;

and 18 Lime St, 1837. Marriage to Miss Margaret Duckworth, 'Lancaster Arms', Gt Crosshall St, reported, *Liverpool Mercury*, 5 November 1824. [D] See Richard and Robert Danson.

Danson, George, Lancaster, cm (1838–39). Admitted freeman in 1838 and named in the Gillow records in 1839. [Lancaster freemen rolls; Westminster Ref. Lib., Gillow vol. 344/104, p. 5249]

Danson, James, 7 Chestnut St and 71 Mulberry St, Liverpool, cm, flour dealer and beer shop (1835–37). [D]

Danson, Myles, London, cm (1774–93). Trading at King St, Golden Sq. in 1774; no. 44 in 1779; and Norfolk St, 1790–93. Took out a Sun Insurance policy in 1779 for £300 of which utensils, stock and goods accounted for £30. [D; poll bks; GL, Sun MS vol. 273, p. 102]

Danson (or Dawson), Richard, Haymarket, Liverpool, chairmaker (1796–1827). Addresses given at 13 Batchelor St, Dale St, and Haymarket, 1796; St John's Lane, Haymarket, 1804; behind 7 Haymarket, 1805–07; and various numbers in Haymarket, 1810–27. Notices in *Liverpool Mercury*, 8 October 1819 and 7 March 1823, concerned the sale of Danson's shop and extensive workshops in Old Haymarket. [D] See Edward and Robert Danson.

Danson, Robert, 6 Old Haymarket, Liverpool, furniture and house painter (1827). [D]

Danson, Stephen, Cable St, Liverpool, cm and victualler (1774–77). Trading at no. 80 in 1774 and no. 78 in 1777. [D]

Danson, Thomas, Chester St, Birkenhead, Cheshire, cm (1834). [D]

Danvers, Margaret, 13 Wood St, Liverpool, u (1827). [D]

Darby, John, St Mary, London, freeman joiner, by trade a carver (1765–66). Employed three to four non-freemen for six months in 1765, and six for three months in 1766. [GL, City Licence bks, vol. 4]

Darby, Samuel jnr, 12 Haye's Entry, Chapel Lane, Hull, Yorks., cm (1838–42). [D]

Darby, Thomas, address unrecorded, upholder (1713–20). Son of John Darby, maltster, of Chipping Norton, Oxon.; app. to Wall Tidmarsh on 9 September 1713, and admitted freeman of the Upholders' Co. by servitude on 5 October 1720. [GL, Upholders' Co. records]

Darby, Thomas, London, cm and upholder (1698–1734). Recorded as cm, next door to 'The Castle Tavern', Fleet St, 1698; as upholder in Princes St, Stocks Mkt, 1727; and Blackfriars, 1734. Advertised that he was declining trade in March 1698. [Poll bks; Harris, *Old English Furniture*, p. 20]

Darby, Thomas, White St, Little Moorfields, London, carver and gilder (1779). Took out a Sun Insurance policy in 1779 for £200 of which utensils and stock accounted for £25. [GL, Sun MS vol. 274, p. 313]

Darby (or Derby), Thomas, 25 Blackman St, Southwark, London, carver and gilder (1789–1811). [D]

Darby, William, at 'The Bear & Crown', 12 Aldermanbury, London, u, appraiser and undertaker (1750–70). Son of John Darby, 'baymaker', of Witham, Essex; app. to Thomas Brown, freeman merchant tailor, by trade upholsterer. Admitted freeman of the Upholders' Co. on 1 October 1761. Trade card, c. 1760–65, shows Chippendale-style chair, tripod table, chest of drawers and tallboy framed by Rococo foliated scrolls. Inscription lists stock of upholstery and cabinet goods, fabrics, bedding, carved and gilt looking-glasses, carpets, window blinds and paper hangings. [Banks Coll., BM] Declared bankrupt, *Gents Mag.*, December 1769, but trading again in 1770. [D; GL, Upholders' Co. records]

Darbyshire, G. G., 45 Whitecross St, London, cm and u (1839). [D] See John Darbyshire at this address.

Darbyshire, John, Church St, Liverpool, cm (1766–67). [D]

Darbyshire, John, Liverpool, joiner and cm (1784). Former app., William Smith, petitioned freedom in 1784. [Liverpool freemen's committee bk]

Darbyshire (Derbyshire or Derbishire), John, 145 White Cross St, London, chair and sofa maker, cm (1792–1837). Recorded at no. 45 in 1803 and 1828; and no. 245 in 1837. [D] Took out Sun Insurance policies on 5 May and 9 June 1792 for £1,000 of which utensils, stock and workshops accounted for £850; on 21 September 1803 for £700; on 8 November 1820 for £1,200 and £1,000, £700 on stock and utensils; and on 7 June 1821 for £1,800 on two houses and shops in tenure. Named in Sheraton's list of master cabinet makers, 1803. [D; GL, Sun MS vol. 383, p. 485; vol. 388, p. 3; vol. 426, ref. 752450; vol. 487, ref. 980952] See G. G. Darbyshire. Possibly:

Darbyshire, John, Anchor Ct (or Yd), off Brew House, Old St, London, cm and turner (1821). Took out Sun Insurance policies on 29 March 1821 for £700 of which stock and utensils accounted for £400; and on 12 April 1821 for £800 on house, offices and shops in tenure. [GL, Sun MS vol. 485, ref. 978586; vol. 487, ref. 978813]

Darbyshire (or Derbyshire), Thomas, Liverpool, cm and chairmaker (1814–39). Shop at 32 Tythebarn St, 1816–23. Addresses also given at 2 Pall Mall in 1818; no. 3 in 1821 and 1824–29; no. 4 in 1823 and 1837; no. 2 in 1827; no. 55 in 1813; and no. 9 in 1839. [D]

Dare, Barnard, Exeter, Devon, cm (1832). [Reg. of elect.]

Dare, George, London, cm (b. 1740–1773). Emigrated to Virginia in December 1773 aged 33. [V & A archives]

Dare, George, 4 Car(e)y Lane, Foster Lane, London, ivory and hardwood turner, Tunbridge-ware maker (1796–1804). [D] Trade card, c. 1780, cited in Heal.

Dare, John, Exeter, Devon, cm (1827–40). Trading in South St, 1827–38; Magdalen St, 1839; and Quay Lane, 1840. Advertised every year between 1827–40 in *Exeter Journal*. [Reg. of elect.]

Dare, Samuel, Minories, London, upholder (1771). Son of Gideon Dare, farmer of St Mary Ottery, Devon; admitted freeman of the Upholders' Co. by redemption on 6 March 1771. Declared bankrupt, *Gents Mag.*, December 1771. [GL, Upholders' Co. records]

Darenson, —, address unrecorded, cm (1803). Subscribed to Sheraton's *Cabinet Dictionary*, 1803.

Darg, William, 33 Banner St, Bunhill Row, London, haberdasher and cm (1808–13). Took out a Sun Insurance policy on 30 August 1813 for £400 of which £200 accounted for stock and utensils. [D; GL, Sun MS vol. 461, ref. 885441]

Daring, John, 23 Queen St, Seven Dials, London, cm and u (1839). [D]

Dark, John, 8 Leathersellers Buildings, Bell Alley, London, cm (1822–37). Took out a Sun Insurance policy on 31 May 1824 for £500 of which stock and utensils accounted for £280. [D; GL, Sun MS vol. 494, ref. 1017415]

Dark(e), John, London Wall, London, cm and u (1827–39). Trading at no. 44, 1827–28, and nos 34 and 36 in 1839. [D]

Dark(e), Richard, Bedford St, Covent Gdn, London, u (1754–68). Subscribed to Chippendale's *Director*, 1754. Declared bankrupt, *Liverpool Advertiser*, 28 October 1768. [D]

Dark, Thomas, 23 Redman's Row, Mile End, London, carver and gilder (1808). [D]

Darker, John Lomas, Nottingham, u (1824). [Nottingham index of burgesses]

Darkin, George, Norwich, cm (1784–1818). App. to James Britisle, cm; admitted freeman on 24 February 1784. Former app., John Flood, admitted freeman on 24 February 1800. [Poll bks; Norwich freemen reg.]

Darkin, James, Norwich, cm (1799–1829). App. to Edward

Sharpe, cm; admitted freeman on 21 September 1799. His son, James, iron founder, admitted freeman on 6 May 1829. [Poll bks; Norwich freemen reg.]

Darkin, Robert, Norwich, upholder (1812). [Poll bk] Possibly:

Darkins, Robert, Norwich, cm (1803). Admitted freeman, not by servitude, on 24 February 1803. [Norwich freemen reg.]

Darley, Henry, Ringwood, Hants., chairmaker (1823–39). [D]

Darley, Robert, 11 Somers Pl., Westminster, London, cm, u and undertaker (1827–28). [D]

Darling, Philip, 16 St Saviourgate, York, cm (1838). [D]

Darling, William, Hull, Yorks., cm and appraiser (1810–34). Trading at 36 St John's St in 1810; 2 Brown's Ct, Brook St, 1817; Kirkus's Buildings, Lowgate, 1823; 12 Manor Alley with home at 43 Garden St, 1826; and 49 Garden St, 1831–34. [D] See Webster & Darling.

Darnby, John, York, chairmaker (1812). App. to George Stones, toy and chairmaker; admitted freeman in 1812. [York freemen rolls]

Darnell, John, 28 Leonard St, Shoreditch, London, cm and u (1827–28). [D]

Darnell, William, 10 Rose & Crown Ct, Finsbury, London, carver and gilder (1829–39). [D]

Darnton, Frederick, Manchester, carver and gilder (1808–40). Addresses given at 8 Hampson (or Hampton) St, Salford 1808–15; 8 Thompson St, 1817; 3 Jones St, Salford, 1825; 23 Portland St, 1834; as Frederick jnr at 3 Caygill St, Chorlton-upon-Medlock in 1836 and 5 Garratt Rd, 1838; 44 York St, Chorlton-upon-Medlock in 1839; and 51 Rusholme Rd, 1840. [D] These entries probably refer to two related tradesmen of the same name, snr and jnr.

Darnton, George, 3 Dean St, Manchester, carver and gilder (1800–02). [D]

Darnton, John, Manchester, u (1828–34). Trading at 1 Downing St in 1828 and 108 Portland St, 1834. [D] See Foulkes & Darnton.

Darsey, Robert, 11 Sommers New Rd, St Pancras, London, cm (1826–27). [D]

Dart, Richard, Park Pl., Kennington Cross, London, cm and u (1826–39). Recorded at no. 30, 1826–39, and no. 20, 1837. [D]

Dartch, Benjamin, 13 Artillery Pl., Bishopsgate St, London, cm and broker (1831). Took app. named Redburn in 1831. [Westminster Ref. Lib., MS F4310, St Martin-in-the-Fields PR]

Darter, John, 2 Hartshorn Ct, Basing Lane, London, chair and sofa maker (1839). [D]

Dartnall, William, Cheltenham, Glos., cm and u (1839–40). Listed at 12 Clarence St in 1839. [D]

Darvell, W., Townfield Yd, Chesham, Bucks., cm (1839). [D]

Darvil, William, High Wycombe, Bucks., chair manufacturer (1824). Daughter bapt. in 1824. [PR (bapt.)]

Darwen, Thomas, Lancaster. Named in the Gillow records between 1799–1804. [Westminster Ref. Lib.]

Darwent, A., 6 Myer's St, Edgehill, Liverpool, cm (1829). [D]

Darwent, Andrew, Yarm, Yorks., cm (1828–29). [D]

Darwent, Henry, Yarm, Yorks., joiner and cm (1827). [D]

Darwin, Eubulus Thorold, Lincoln, joiner and cm (1757–61). Son of William Darwin, yeoman of Caythorpe; app. to William Johnson of Lincoln on 6 September 1757, and assigned to his son, Thomas Johnson, on 14 March 1761. [Lincoln app. reg.]

Darye, William, Burnley, Lancs., cm (1814–24). Trading in Market St, 1814–18; St James St, 1818; and Bay Horse Yd, 1824. [D]

Dashwood, Henry, Lingley (or Lugley) St, Newport, Isle of Wight, Hants., cm (1839–40). [D; GL, Sun MS vol. 267, ref. 1332124]

Date, Richard, Bridgwater, Som., upholder (1754–80). Polled at Bristol, 1754 and 1774; and Bridgwater, 1754 and 1780.

Dattman, Robert, North Quay, Gt Yarmouth, Norfolk, turner (1805–07). [D]

Dauber, Thomas, 3 Crofton's Ct, Dale St, Liverpool, cm and joiner (1790–1805). [D]

Daulby, George, Liverpool, cm (1830–39). Trading at 56 Stanley St, 1830; and 63 Cumberland St, 1839. Admitted freeman on 13 November 1830. [D; Liverpool freemen reg.]

Daulby, Robert, Liverpool, u (1827–37). Addresses given at 3 Back Leece St in 1827 and 20 Cumberland St, 1829–37. [D]

Dausell, John, College Green, Gloucester, cm (1839–40). [D]

Davenish, Joseph, Thames St, Garlicheath, London, upholder (1702). Took out a Hand in Hand fire insurance policy on 6 March 1702 on the above house, empty and in his possession for seven years. [GL, Hand in Hand MS vol. 2, p. 416]

Davenish, T. C., Villers St, Strand, London, cm (1784). [D]

Davenny, James, High Wycombe, Bucks., chairmaker (b. c. 1786–1841). Aged 55 at the time of the 1841 Census.

Davenport, —, address unrecorded, chairmaker (1803). Subscribed to Sheraton's *Cabinet Dictionary*, 1803.

Davenport, George, Barton St, Gloucester, carver and gilder (1822–23). [D]

Davenport, J. O., Westgate St, Gloucester, coach, sign and furniture painter (1820). [D]

Davenport, James, Parade St, Rochdale, Lancs., cm (1798–1825). [D]

Davenport, James, Parade St, Rotherham, Yorks., cm (1816). [D]

Davenport, John, Chester, u (1784–1819). Addresses given at Nine Houses, 1784; Duke St, 1812; and Love St, 1818–19. App. to John Stringer, u of Chester. Admitted freeman on 31 March 1784. [Poll bks; Chester freemen rolls]

Davenport, Thomas, Manchester cm (1804–17). Trading at 92 Deansgate in 1804; 32 Thomas St, 1808; and 14 Turner St in 1817. [D]

Davenport, Uriah, Derby St, Leek, Staffs., joiner and cm (1816–18). Listed at Black's Head Yd, Derby St in 1818. [D]

Davenport, William, Market St, Ashby-de-la Zouch, Leics., cm and u (1822–35). [D]

Davenport, William, Bedward Rd, Chester, u (1838). Admitted freeman on 28 July 1838. [Chester freemen rolls]

Davey, David, Paul St, Exeter, Devon, cm (1832). Son James bapt. at St Paul's, Exeter on 24 April 1832. [PR (bapt.)]

Davey (or Davy), John, Cullompton, Devon, cm (1823–38). Recorded in Fore St, 1825. House advertised for sale in *The Alfred*, 29 March 1825. [D]

Davey, John, Upton, Norfolk, joiner and cm (1836). [D]

Davey (or Davy), Robert, London, carver and gilder (1817–29). Addresses given at 16 Wardour St, 1817–23 and 83 Newman St, 1823–39. Took out Sun Insurance policies on 14 December 1820 for £800 of which stock, utensils and goods in trust accounted for £200; and on 21 June 1821 for £800 on his house. [D; GL, Sun MS vol. 483, ref. 974355; vol. 488, ref. 980758]

Davey, Samuel, address unrecorded, cm (1803). Subscribed to Sheraton's *Cabinet Dictionary*, 1803.

Davey, William, Chesham, Bucks., chairmaker (1718). Took app. named Grove in 1718. [S of G, app. index]

Davey & Davis, 33 Ogle St, Middlx Hospital, London, cm (1829). [D]

David, Henry, Bride Lane, London, cm (1769). Served as Constable for St Bride's in 1769. [GL, MS 6561, p. 102]

David, Thomas, Lancaster, cm (1758–68). App. to Gillows in 1758 and admitted freeman in 1767–68. [Lancaster app. reg. and freemen rolls]

David, William Heron, Haymarket, Norwich, u and paper hanger (1804–30). Trading at the top of Bridewell Alley in 1830. App. to John Horth, upholder; admitted freeman on 21 September 1804. [D; poll bks; Norwich freemen reg.]

Davids, Charles, High St, Eton, Bucks., bookseller, carver and gilder (1830). [D]

Davidson, A., 39 Windmill St, Tottenham Ct Rd, London, cm and chairmaker (1837). [D]

Davidson, Alexander, address unrecorded, chairmaker (1803). Subscribed to Sheraton's *Cabinet Dictionary*, 1803.

Davidson, Alexander, 21 Norton St, London, chair and sofa maker (1826–39). [D]

Davidson, Alexander, 37 Lower Thornhaugh St, London, cm and u (1827–28). [D]

Davidson, Charles, Falcon Yd, Cambridge, turner, chairmaker and carver (1830). [D]

Davidson, Cornelius, Old Round Ct, Strand, London, u (1784). [D]

Davidson, John, 37 Foley St, Portland Pl., London, upholder and undertaker (1817–19). [D]

Davidson, John, Tomkinson Pl., Thurlow St, Liverpool, cm and u (1829). [D]

Davidson, John, Blyth, Northumb., joiner and/or cm (1834). [D]

Davidson, Peter, address unrecorded, upholder (1755–63). Son of John Davidson, sadler of London; app. to Francis Say on 3 September 1755 and admitted freeman of the Upholders' Co. by servitude on 3 March 1763. [GL, Upholders' Co. records]

Davidson, Thomas, Sandgate-gate, Newcastle, cm and carpenter (1778). [D]

Davidson, Thomas, Liverpool, cm (1813–24). Trading at 13 Dance St, 1813–14, and Mitchell Pl., Ranelagh St, 1824. [D]

Davidson, Thomas, Allhallowgate, Ripon, Yorks., chairmaker (1830). [D]

Davidson, William, Berwick-upon-Tweed, Northumb., cm (1759–61). Took apps named Gallimore in 1759 and Menzie in 1761. [S of G, app. index]

Davidson, William, 6 Peover St, Liverpool, with shop at 18 Mansfield St, joiner and cm (1834–39). [D]

Davie, Ben & Sarah, his wife, Bristol, upholders (1722). Took app. named Curtis in 1722. [S of G, app. index]

Davie, Jurdison, Nesham Sq., Sunderland, Co. Durham, cm (1827). [D]

Davies, —, address unrecorded, cm (1695–1706). Named in the Chatsworth accounts in 1695 receiving £10 for a clock case; and in 1706, £15 for a 'large Wainscot Bedsted with . . . a large carved Tester and a carved set of cornishes, and a large Carved Head board, and a Set of Moulded Piedestalls Stumps and Backs'. [V & A archives] Possibly Roger or Thomas Davies, or William Davis.

Davies, —, York (?), cm (1791). Noted in the account bk of the Rev. John Firth on 22 June 1791 as receiving £6 6s. [Mumby family papers] Possibly Peter Davies.

Davies, —, Shrewsbury, Salop u (1798). [D] Possibly Peter or William Davies.

Davies, —, address unrecorded. Late Regency-style folding bagatelle table, c. 1830–40, recorded, mounted on a table with end supports; top edge impressed four times 'DAVIES'.

Davies, Adam, Castle Gates, Shrewsbury, Salop, cm (1840). [Shrewsbury burgess roll]

Davies, Catherine, 75 Chester St, Birkenhead, Cheshire, u (1837). [D]

Davies, David, Holywell Rd (or Row), Shoreditch, London, cm, u, billiard table and backgammon board maker (1826–29). Recorded at no. 20, 1826–28, and no. 29, 1829. [D]

Davies, David, 15 Chestnut St, Liverpool, with shop at 2 Back Knight St, joiner and cm (1839). [D]

Davies (or Davis), Edward, King St, Golden Sq., London, cm and upholder (1784–1811). Recorded at no. 86, 1790–93. [D; poll bk]

Davies, Edward, Union Pl., Shelton, Staffs., cm (1818). [D]

Davies, Edward & Thomas, 5 Old Bridge St, Manchester, cm and u (1824). [D]

Davies, Edward, Mathew St, Liverpool, cm (b. c. 1795–d. 1828). Death aged 33 reported, *Liverpool Mercury*, 6 June 1828.

Davies, Edward, 8 Back Strickland St, Liverpool, cm (1839). [D]

Davies, Evan, John & Henry, London, cm and u (1822–37). Trading at 18 Middle St, Cloth Fair in 1822; at 45 Little Bartholomew Close, 1823–37; and also at no. 42 in 1829. Recorded as Davis & Co., 1827–28; and as I. & F. Davies in 1835. The firm took out Sun Insurance policies on 4 July 1822 for £300, £280 accounting for stock, utensils and goods in trust in warehouse and workshops; and on 31 March 1823 for £700 on their house. Evan Davies alone took out a policy for £400 on 8 January 1824. [D; GL, Sun MS vol. 491, ref. 993652; vol. 495, ref. 1003315; vol. 497, ref. 1012464]

Davi(e)s, Evan, Pride Lane (or Hill), Shrewsbury, Salop, carver and gilder (1835). [D]

Davies, George, 1 Market St, Finsbury Sq., London, chair and sofa manufacturer (1829). [D]

Davies, George, 1 Mansfield St, Liverpool, cm (b. c. 1797–d. 1833). Trading at the above address in 1829. Death on 10 June 1833, aged 36, reported, *Liverpool Mercury*, 28 June. [D]

Davies, George, 33 Williamson St, Liverpool, (warehouse), cm (1839). [D]

Davies, Henry, Worcester, cm, u, undertaker and paper hanger (1822–28). Listed at Leach St in 1822 and 1 High St, 1828. Trade label gives address at 1 High St. [D; BM]

Davies, Henry, Friar St, Worcester, u (1825–35). Admitted freeman in 1825, and named in the Worcester freemen rolls in 1835.

Davies, Henry, 8 Cropper St, Liverpool, cm (1827). App. to William Harvey; admitted freeman on 18 October 1827. [Liverpool freemen reg.]

Davies, Henry, Aldersgate St, London, cm, manufacturer and u (1834). Declared bankrupt, *Liverpool Mercury*, 17 January 1834.

Davies, Horatio David, 6 Sun St, Bishopsgate, London, billard table, backgammon board and bagatelle maker (1832–34). [D]

Davi(e)s, Hugh, Manchester, cm (1825–40). Addresses given at 12 Captenter's Lane in 1825; no. 2 in 1828; and 64 Jib (or Tib) St, 1839–40. [D]

Davies, Hugh, Manchester, cm (1840). Admitted freeman of Chester on 17 June 1840. [Chester freemen rolls]

Davies, Humphrey, St Martin's Fields, London, u (1711/12). Took app. on 11 March; and another named Anton, son of John Witherington, victualler of St Paul's, on 12 February for £10. [PRO, IRI/1] Possibly Humphrey Davis.

Davies, J. jnr, 76 Minories, London, cm, chair and bedstead maker (1825).

Davies (or Davis), James, 9 Hanover Ct (or St), Grub St, London, cm (1778–1808). Took out Sun Insurance policies in 1778 for £800 on utensils and stock, and workshops, £200; and in 1782 for £1,500 of which utensils and stock accounted for £1,440. [D; GL, Sun MS vol. 266, pp. 464 and 479; vol. 304, p. 284]

Davies (or Davis), James, Ormskirk, Lancs., cm (1787–98). [D]

Davies (or Davis), James, Gt Carter Lane, Doctors' Commons, London, cm and vintner (1774–93). Recorded at no. 23 in 1784, and no. 13, 1789–93. In 1774 and 1775 he employed eight non-freemen for three months [D; GL, City Licence bks, vol. 8]

Davies, James, College Pl., Bristol, cm and chairmaker (1820). [D]

Davies, James, Church St, Hereford, cm and u (1822–40). [D; poll bks]

Davies, James, Manchester, cm (1825–40). Addresses given at 361 Oldham Rd, 1832–33; no. 157 in 1836–38; and 44 Oxford St, 1840. [D]

Davies, James Swithen, 87 Redcliff St, Bristol, cm (1820–21). [D] Probably:

Davies, James Smithers,, Belle Vue Mews, Clifton Hill, Bristol, cm and chairmaker (1822). [D]

Davies, John, address unrecorded, upholder (1708). Admitted freeman of the Upholders' Co. on 6 October 1708. [GL, Upholders' Co. records]

Davies, John, Chester, cm and glass silverer (1726). Son of Sarah Davies, widow; app. to Edward Bromley, cm, on 5 November 1726. [Chester app. bks]

Davies, John, Hereford, chairmaker (1741). [Poll bk]

Davies, John, 3 Gt Chapel St, Soho, London, carver (1780). Took out a Sun Insurance policy in 1780 for £300 on his house. [GL, Sun MS vol. 287, p. 54]

Davies, John, 9 King's Gate St, Holborn, London, japanner, painter and gilder (c. 1800). Trade card shows two female Classical figures examining a picture on an easel. [Banks Coll., BM]

Davies, John, 15 Gt Richmond St, Liverpool, gilder (1807). Admitted freeman on 6 May 1807. [D; Liverpool freemen reg.]

Davies, John, Newington Causeway, Newington Butts, London, chairmaker (1808). Took out a Sun Insurance policy on 22 September 1808 for £800 of which stock, utensils, timber, timber yard and workshop accounted for £500. [GL, Sun MS vol. 444, ref. 821142]

Davies, John, Liverpool, gilder (1812–29). Trading at 18 Parr St in 1827 and 17 Manchester St in 1829. App. to William Casher; admitted freeman on 5 October 1812. [D; Liverpool freemen reg.] Possibly:

Davies, John, Parr St, Liverpool, cm (1835–39). Recorded at no. 21, 1835–37, and nos 37 and 39 in 1839. [D]

Davies, John, Wells, Som., cm (1818). Declared bankrupt, *Exeter Flying Post*, 1 January 1818. Probably the John Davis, cm and u listed at High St in 1839. [D]

Davies, John, 19–20 St James's Walk, Clerkenwell, London, cm and upholder (1820–28). [D]

Davies, John, St Martin's St, Hereford, cm, appraiser, u, timber merchant and joiner (1822–40). Also trading at Bridge Wharf in 1840. [D]

Davies, John, Bristol, cabinet and clock-case maker (1827–40). Addresses given at 42 Marlborough St in 1827; Horfield Rd, 1832–40, no. 5 1832–36; and trading as Davies & Hayman, 1837–40. [D]

Davies, John, 13 Thomas St, Manchester, cm and u (1829). [D]

Davies, John Austin, 10 King St and Hulme St, Brazenose St, Manchester, carver and gilder (1832–40). Recorded at 15 Brazenose St, 1834–38. [D] Possibly John Austin Davis of Stockport.

Davies, John, 8–9 Fontenoy St, Liverpool, chairmaker and furniture broker (1835–37). [D]

Davies, John, Castle St, Ludlow, Salop, cm and u (1840). [D]

Davies, Joseph, Grub St, Cripplegate, London, cm (1820). [D]

Davies, Joseph, Liverpool, cm (1825). App. to Cattrall & Whittingham in 1825. [Liverpool app. enrolment bk]

Davies, Margaret, 38 Gerard St, Liverpool, u (1839). [D]

Davies, Peter, Shrewsbury, Salop, u (1747–54). Took apps named Jones in 1751 and Grant in 1754. [Poll bk; S of G, app. index; Shrewsbury burgess roll]

Davies, Peter, York and London, cm (1783–1818). Polled in York, of London, in 1784. Trading in Coney St, York, 1805–18. Son of Richard Davies, mariner, deceased; admitted freeman of York in 1783. Former apps admitted freemen: George Williamson in 1796; James Mitchell in 1806; John Ellison, 1809; and John Stout, 1819. [D; York freemen rolls] Possibly of Davies & Wilson.

Davies, Richard, Hulme St, Little Bolton, Lancs., cm (1828). [D]

Davies, Robert, Liverpool, joiner and cm (1835–39). Addresses given at 8 Cumberland St, with shop at 118 Dale St in 1835; 111 Dale St, 1837; and no. 116, 1839. [D]

Davies, Roger, address unrecorded, 'Master Joyner' (1687–1709). Worked for the 1st Duke of Montagu at Boughton House, Northants., carrying out general carpenter's and joiner's work, furniture repairs, and making routine furniture. Between 1691–1709 he was paid £2,727 7s 8d of £3,174 17s 11¼d owed him. Another account dated between 1687–92 totalled £1,546. [V & A archives]

Davies, Samuel, Chester, carver (1696). App. to Thomas Davies, carver; admitted freeman in October 1696. [Chester freemen rolls]

Davies (or Davis), Samuel, Chester, u, cm and auctioneer (b. c. 1770–d. 1829). Trading in Eastgate St, 1797–1805; Foregate St, 1812–30; and no. 132 in 1828; in partnership with Cliffe in 1822. Admitted freeman on 23 January 1798. From 1796–98 Davies supplied furniture to John Leicester of Tabley Hall, Cheshire, totalling £170, including, in 1796, '2 Neat Painted Flower-stands'; and on 23 January 1798 '12 Handsome Mahog. Chairs Carv'd Reeded Pillars and feet, red morroco & brass-nailed', £33 12s; two sets of ten 'Neat Painted' chairs, four large painted elbow chairs, and several screens. Davies's bill of 1 June to 3 October 1798 lists nine sofas and two long wondow stools upholstered in 'fine canvas and Best Hair with squab seats', totalling £70 3s 6d. Took out a Sun Insurance policy on 16 January 1802 for £900, of which stock and utensils in St Werburgh's Churchyard, Old Yorkshire Hall, accounted for £100. Announced in *Chester Courant*, 2 June 1815, 'his willingness to accept customers following the death of Joseph Powell', u of Chester. Named in *Chester Chronicle and North Wales Advertiser*, 1 May 1829, as subscriber of 5s to a gold cup for the Chester Races of 1829. Death, aged 59, reported in the same paper, 31 July 1829, when described as 'universally esteemed by all who knew him as an upright, honest man'. On 28 August 1829 his widow announced her husband's chosen successor to be James Whittingham. On 16 March 1830 the sale of Davies's stock was advertised, consisting of 'mahogany dining room and parlour chairs, two sofas, several sets of imitation rosewood and black chairs, chimney, peir and dressing glasses, Kidderminster and Venetian carpeting, chests of drawers, mahogany celleret, lounging chairs, tea chests . . .' [D; Chester freemen rolls; GL, Sun MS vol. 43, ref. 728048; Chester RO, Leicester papers]

Davies, Samuel, Hanover Ct, Grub St, London, cm and timber merchant (1804). Took out a Sun Insurance policy on 4 August 1804 for £1,000 on stock in his yard and open sheds. [GL, Sun MS vol. 430, ref. 76460]

Davies, Samuel, Bewall St, Hereford, joiner, cm and u (1822). App. to Thomas Gwillyam, joiner and cm of Hereford; admitted freeman on 23 May 1822. [D, Hereford freemen reg.]

Davies (or Davis), T. & Griffin, Warwick and Newhall St, Birmingham, carver and gilders (1769–70). The firm advertised in the *Birmingham Gazette*, 4 September 1769, as 'CARVERS in STONE and WOOD, at their Shops in

Warwick and Birmingham' who 'perform all Sorts of Monuments, Chimney-Pieces and all Branches of Household-Furniture Ornaments, Ornamental Vases and Terms, in the Greek and Roman Taste, for Halls, Gardens, Walks etc'. In the advertisement Davies claims he is 'well satisfied with the great Preference given to those Things I have executed in the Town to any other Person's, which may be seen at several Gentlemen's Houses in Birmingham and the Country, as well as my Shops...'. He also challenges his rival carver, E. Grubb, to a competition. Davies refers to 'the Box I was carving for the Corporation to be presented to Mr. Garrick...', the celebrated Shakespearean actor, by the Stratford-upon-Avon Corp. Bills show that the box was probably made by the joiner Thomas Taylor, then carved by Davies with four emblematic and theatrical scenes, one showing Garrick as King Lear during the storm, framed by Rococo scrolls. [D; *British Museum Quarterly*, vol. XXIV, no. 3–4, pp. 104–06] Possibly the gilder, Thomas Davies, who worked at Syon, or Thomas Davis, at Gibside.

Davies, T., 5 Grange Rd, Bermondsey, London, bedstead and cm (1820). [D]

Davies, Thomas, Chester, joiner and carver (1681-d. by 1716). Applied for freedom in 1681, but rejected; admitted in 1682. Former apps Samuel Davies and John Tiltson admitted freemen in 1696; Joseph Rylands in 1697; and Philip Cooper in 1704. In 1697–98 Davies provided surety for R. Warmington, tailor; in 1699, petitioned for reimbursement for security on timber transactions; in 1700, offered to provide timber for Dee navigation; in 1702, elected council man; and in 1702–04, signed various petitions concerning debts. [Chester freemen rolls and city records]

Davies, Thomas, London (?), cm (1709–18). Named in the accounts of Samuel Tufnell of Middle Temple, London, who bought Langley's, Gt Waltham, Essex in 1710. On 7 December 1709 he received 5s for glasses; on 12 May 1714, 20s for a pair of gilt sconces; and on 18 April 1716, £7 17s 3d for cabinet work. He is probably the Davis who received £6 on 10 December 1718 for a chest of drawers supplied to Rebecca Tufnell. [Essex RO, D/DTu 276 and 278]

Davies, Thomas, London, cm (1711–12). Worked for Lord Leigh of Stoneleigh, Warks., receiving a total of £40 2s for looking-glasses and sconces, including a 'very fine large Glass', costing £22 10s; 'a fine Glass in a narrow Glass frame & joints cover'd with silver', costing £3 10s; and also a 'princewood strong box' and 'a very fine Japan'd table', costing £5 7s 6d. [Shakespeare Birthplace Trust, Leigh receipts, DR 18/5]

Davies, Thomas, address unrecorded, cm (1715–29). The accounts of Edward Harley, 2nd Earl of Oxford, record a bill from Davies for furniture supplied to Wimpole Hall, Cambs., between 23 April 1715 and 13 December 1716, totalling £220 15s. Davies was also paid £618 2s 6d on 25 July 1729. [British Lib., Portland loan, 29/388]

Davies (or Davis), Thomas, address unrecorded, gilder (1758–65). In 1765 he gilded the gallery at Syon House, Middlx., 'at 2/6 pr. sq. ft.', for the Duke of Northumberland. Probably the Davis, gilder, named in the Hoare accounts receiving £50 in 1758, £1,500 in 1764, and £200 in 1765. [Duke of Northumberland's accounts, V & A archives]

Davies (or Davis), Thomas, Liverpool, cm (1790–1811). Addresses given at 11–12 Fontenoy St, Dale St, 1790; Shaw's Brow, 1794–1811, nos 37 and 43, 1794–96; and no. 45 in 1796. [D]

Davies, Thomas, Gorst Stacks, Chester, cm (1812). Admitted freeman on 8 July 1812. [Chester freemen rolls and poll bk]

Davies, Thomas, Chester, cm (1818). Admitted freeman on 12 May 1818. [Chester freemen rolls]

Davies, Thomas, (St) John St, Chester, cm (1818–26). [Poll bks] Presumably one of the above.

Davies, Thomas, Manchester, cm and u (1817–28). Trading at 57 Gt Ancoat's St in 1817; Hughes St, Chorlton Row, 1818; and 3 Lever St, 1828. [D]

Davies, Thomas & Edward, 4 Old Bridge St, Salford, Lancs., u (1825). [D]

Davies, Thomas, Liverpool, cm (1823). App. to William Harvey in 1823. [Liverpool app. enrolment bk]

Davies, Thomas, Green St, Theobalds Rd, London, cm and u (1827–28). [D]

Davies, Thomas, Bristol, cm (1832–35). Trading at 5 Queen St, 1832–34, and 5 St Michael's Steps in 1835. [D]

Davies, Thomas, 33 Chester St, Birkenhead, Cheshire, u (1835). [D]

Davies, Thomas & Son, Wyle Cop, Shrewsbury, Salop, cm and u (1840). [D]

Davies, William, Tottenham Ct, London, carver (1765). Insured a building for £730 in March 1765 with the Hand in Hand Co. [GL, Hand in Hand MS vol. 164, ref. 87537]

Davies, William, Shrewsbury, Salop, u (1767). Son of Peter Davies, u; named in the Shrewsbury burgess roll in 1767. Possibly:

Davies, William, Shrewsbury, Salop, u (1786–1822). Trading at Kiln Lane, 1786–96, and Princess St in 1822. [D]

Davies, William, Hereford, cm and u (1822–35). Trading in Church St, 1822; High St, 1830; and Packers' Lane, 1835. [D]

Davies, William, 6 Union St, Lambeth, London, chair and sofa maker (1826–28). [D] See Edward Davis.

Davies, William, Liverpool, cm (1827–35). Recorded at 6 Peover St in 1835. Admitted freeman on 18 October 1827. [D; Liverpool freemen reg.]

Davies (or Davis), William, Newbury, Berks., cm and u (1798–1830). Trading in Northbrook St, 1823–30. Declared bankrupt, *London Gazette*, 3 July 1830. [D]

Davies, William, Church Row, Greenwich, London, chairmaker (1832–34). [D]

Davies, William, Bull Ring, Ludlow, Salop, cm and u (1835). [D]

Davies, William Woodburn, Liverpool, cm (1807). Admitted freeman on 6 May 1807. [Liverpool freemen reg.]

Davies, William Woodburne, Redmayne Ct (or Edmund Ct), Upper Milk St, Liverpool, cm (b. 1788–1812). Son of Walter Davies, painter; admitted freeman on 5 October 1812. [Liverpool freemen reg.]

Davies & Wilson, York, cm (1793). Subscribed to Sheraton's *Drawing Book*, 1793. Possibly Peter Davies.

Davis, —, at 'The Hen & Chickens', Gt Queen St, London, cm (1709–10). Advertised in *Daily Courant*, 5 December 1709–10, offering reward for return of a gold watch-case 'Lost from a Lady's Side at the Chappel in G. Queen St'. Worked at Rousham, Oxon. [Heal; V & A archives] See Peter Hazard.

Davis, —, address unrecorded, cm (1803). Subscribed to Sheraton's *Cabinet Dictionary*, 1803.

Davis, —, Pilgrim St, Newcastle, carver and gilder (1811). [D]

Davis, —, address unrecorded. Supplied Lord Braybrooke with a book-case costing £28 19s in June 1834, for Audley End, Essex, Billingbear, Berks., or his London house. [Essex RO, D/DBy/A358 and A363]

Davis, Benjamin, Bristol, upholder (1715–22). Took app. named Savage in 1717. [S of G, app. index; poll bks]

Davis, Benjamin, Whitchurch, Salop, cm (1797). [D]

Davis, Benjamin, Liverpool, carver and gilder (1813–15). Recorded at 7 Hanover St, 1813–14; and Duke St, 1815. Declared bankrupt, *Liverpool Mercury*, 22 September 1815. [D]

Davis, Benjamin, London, cm (1818). [Evesham poll bk]

Davis, Benjamin, High St, Fulham, London, cm, u, carver and gilder (1838–39). [D]

Davis, Benjamin, 114 Edward St, Brighton, Sussex, carver and gilder (1839). [D]

Davis, Bingham, Gt Newport St, London, carver (1749). [Poll bk]

Davis, C., 8 Palace Row, New Rd, London, cm (1835). [D]

Davis, Charles, Bristol, cm and upholder (1792–1832). Addresses given at St Augustine's Back, 1792–1801; 14 Alfred Pl., 1807–17; 19 Somerset St, 1819; 'Cloisters', 1829–31; and 19 Orchard St, 1832. [D] See Mary Davis.

Davis, Charles, 29 Panton St, Haymarket, London, cm, broker and dealer in curiosities (1820–23). Took out a Sun Insurance policy on 6 April 1820 for £1,000 of which jewels, pictures, china, glass and curios accounted for £350, and stock, untensils and goods in trust, £500. [D; GL, Sun MS vol. 483, ref. 964970] Possibly:

Davis, Charles, London, cm and u (1822–28). Recorded at 48 Strand in 1822; no. 486, 1823–28; and 6 Warwick Pl., Bedford Row, 1823. Took out Sun Insurance policies on 12 June 1822 for £1,200 of which jewels, musical instruments, prints and pictures accounted for £150, stock and utensils, £800; on 24 July 1823 for £950, £500 on utensils and stock in workshops in Hudson's Ct, Strand; on 1 December 1823 for £500 on stock and utensils in trust and £150 on stock in his workshop in Hudson Ct; and on 25 March 1824, for £1,250, £900 on stock and utensils. [D; GL, Sun MS vol. 493, ref. 993052; vol. 499, ref. 101714; vol. 498, ref. 1006232; vol. 499, ref. 1014688]

Davis, Christopher, 16 Southampton Row, London, u and undertaker (1816–17). [D]

Davis, D., 43 Rathbone Pl., London, u and auctioneer (1825). [D]

Davis, David, address unrecorded, carver and gilder (1813–15). Worked at the 6th Duke of Bedford's house in Hamilton Pl., London, and was paid £57 13s in December 1815. The work included the provision of plate glass in the back Drawing Room, and a circular looking-glass in a black and gold frame; 500 yards of gilt moulding for doors and shutters; 246 feet of gilt cornice cleaned and repaired; 'ornaments of 19 pilasters for the staircase', and regilding the railings. [Bedford Office, London]

Davis, Edward, Marshall St, Carnaby Mkt, London, cm (1774). [Poll bk]

Davis, Edward, 5 Union St, Lambeth, London, chairmaker (1808). [D] See William Davies.

Davis, Edward & Thomas, 5 Old Bridge St, Manchester, cm and u (1824). [D]

Davis, Francis & Co., Lancaster, cm (1760). Took app. named Wilson in 1760. [S of G, app. index]

Davis, George, Orange Grove, Bath, Som., cm (1740–53). Took apps named Penny in 1740, Morris in 1744 and Croft in 1753. [S of G, app. index and Bath app. reg.]

Davis, George, 8 Worship St, Finsbury, London, u, mattress maker etc. (1826–29). [D]

Davis, George, Skinner St, Bishopsgate, London, cm and japanner (1835–39). [D]

Davis, Henry David, 17 Artillery Lane, Bishopsgate, London, cm and u (1839). [D]

Davis, Henry Hart, 40 Gerrard St, Soho, London, auctioneer and upholder (1840). [GL, Sun MS ref. 1341922]

Davis, Humphry, Whitehart Yd, Drury Lane, London, u (1725). Took out a Sun Insurance policy on 11 May 1725 for £500 on goods and merchandise in his house. [GL, Sun MS vol. 20, ref. 35716]

Davis, Isaac, Merchant St, Bristol, carver and gilder (1820–21). [D]

Davis, J., next door but one to 'The Golden Sugar Loaf', on the Terrace in St Martin's Lane, London, u (1705). Advertised in *The Post Man*, 24 February 1705, his business 'where Gentlemen may be furnished with Tents and Field-beds to their satisfaction, and at very reasonable Prices, likewise Bells and Cases, for Colours and Drums'. Worked at Rousham, Oxon. [V & A archives]

Davis, J., 406 Oxford St, London, u (1835). [D]

Davis, J., 5 Queen's Row, Pimlico, London, u and cm (1835). [D]

Davis, J., 58 Redcliff St, Bristol, carver and gilder (1838–40). [D]

Davis, John, address unrecorded, upholder (1711). Admitted freeman of the Upholders' Co. on 4 July 1711. [GL, Upholders' Co. records]

Davis, John, Bath, Som., frame maker (1722). [Bristol poll bk]

Davis, John, Minster Yd, York, cm (1741). Advertised, *York Courant*, 22 December 1741 that he 'furnishes Gentlemen with Cloth Cushions, Pockets, Brass Masts, Balls, Queus, Sconces and printed Orders, and Looking Glass, and side Lanterns, Cabinet and Chair Work, China and Earthenware at Reasonable Rates . . .'. He also advertised for sale 'Two New Billiard Tables and 'till they are disposed of, Attendance is given to play the Game'.

Davis, John, Lancaster. Named in the Gillow records between 1789–94. [Westminster Ref. Lib.]

Davis, John, Worcester, cm and u (1799). App. to Abraham and Isaac Fluke, cm and u; admitted freeman on 17 June 1799. [Worcester freemen rolls].

Davis, John, 15 Hatton Wall, London, bedstead maker (1806). Took out a Sun Insurance policy on 16 December 1806 for £400 of which stock, utensils and workshop accounted for £200. [GL, Sun MS vol. 438, ref. 798178]

Davis, John, 16 Gt Portland St, London, broker and upholder (1810). Took out a Sun Insurance policy on 17 January 1810 for £750 of which stock, utensils and goods in trust in a house at 20 Mortimer St accounted for £400. [GL, Sun MS vol. 453, ref. 839934]

Davis, John, 16 Russell St, Bloomsbury, London, upholder (1820–21). Took out a Sun Insurance policy on 10 May 1821 for £1,000 of which stock, utensils and goods in trust accounted for £600. [D; GL, Sun MS vol. 488, ref. 980177] Possibly:

Davis (or Davies), John, 66 Gt Russell St, Bloomsbury, London, cm, u, auctioneer, appraiser and house agent (1817–25). Receipt dated 15 March 1819 totals £35, and includes '1 Rosewood Conversation Table', '1 Basin Stand with Rising Glass', 'two Mah^y- Night tables', 'three Hearth Rugs', and '1 Small Pembrook Work table'. Took out a Sun Insurance policy on 30 April 1723 for £1,000 of which utensils and stock accounted for £600. [D; GL, trade card coll.; GL, Sun MS vol. 498, ref. 1003774]

Davis, John, 43 Rathbone Pl., London, u and auctioneer (1823). [D]

Davis, John, 20 Lower Brook St, Grosvenor Sq., London, cm and u (1820–27). Recorded at no. 29 in 1823. Supplied furniture for Lord Belgrave's house in Grosvenor Sq., 1823–24. [D; London rate bks; V & A archives]

Davis, John, 27 Soho Sq., London, u (1826–29). [D]

Davis, John, Davies Mews, Oxford St, London, cm and u (1827–28). [D]

Davis, John, 278 High Holborn, London, u (1839). [D]

Davis, John, 1 Tottenham Ct Rd, London, cm and u (1839). [D]

Davis, John, Church St, Fulham, London, cm and u (1838–39). [D]

Davis, John, 10 Finkle St, Hull, Yorks., cm (1837–40). [D]

Davis, John Austin, 8 Little Underbank, Stockport, Cheshire, carver and gilder (1834). [D] Possibly John Austin Davies of Manchester.

Davis, John Giles, Fore St, Bridgwater, Som., cm, u and agent for the Exchange Assurance (1839–40). [D]

Davis, Jonathan, near Corve St Gate, Ludlow, Salop, cm (1789). Mentioned under the insurance record for James Goodwin, farmer, as tenant of above house. [GL, Sun MS vol. 362, p. 586]

Davis, Marks, Milsom St, Bath, Som., cm (1748–85). Son of George Davis, cm and joiner; app. to Thomas Bishop, cm of Bath, in 1748; free 1756. Took app. named Sylvester in 1759. [S of G, app. index] In 1763, 1773, 1776, 1783 and 1785 leased premises in Milsom St, Union Passage; Stall St and Orange Grove from Bath Corporation. Advertised in the *Bath and Bristol Chronicle*, 1 February 1770 with his partner Bartlett to inform their friends and public 'that they have this day opened their Upholstery and Cabinet, Chair, Carpet and Paper Hanging warehouse in Union Passage. N.B. Goods let on hire, appraised and Funerals completely furnished'. [Bath app. reg.]

Davis, Mary, St Augustine's Back, Bristol, upholder and cm (1794). [D] See Charles Davis.

Davis, N., 16 Giltspur St, Smithfield, London, u (1803). Named in Sheraton's list of master cabinet makers, 1803. See William Davis at this address.

Davis, Nathaniel, 'Warde Arms', Westerham, Kent, cm and u (1839). [D]

Davis, Owen, Bridgnorth, Salop, chairmaker (1797–d. 1805). Death reported, *Gents Mag.*, January 1805, with anecdotes of his long drinking life. [D]

Davis (or Davies), Peter, Lime St, Liverpool, u, feather bed and mattress maker (1822–37). Trading at 9 Lime St, 1822–27, with manufactory at 30 Cable St, 61 Lime St, 1827–29; no. 69, 1832–34; and no. 57, 1837. [D] Advertised the opening of his feather bed warehouse in *Liverpool Mercury*, 8 November 1802; and on 25 February 1825 announced that he had 'lately made considerable improvements in the mode of STOVING FEATHERS', making his goods 'perfectly sweet & clean'. He advertised his re-dressing service for old beds, and his stock of 'prime DANZIG, IRISH & LINCOLN-SHIRE GOOSE & POULTRY FEATHERS'. Advertised again, 5 May 1826; and on 11 May 1827 his removal to 61 Lime St. On 15 June announced that he had 'engaged some first-rate hands in the UPHOLSTERY line, who have been accustomed to work in London' and described his stock of beds, cabinet and upholstery goods, bedding, feathers and cabin furniture. On 21 September 1827 advertised that he had 'lately opened a connexion with several manufacturers of FRINGES, BELL ROPES, BLIND CORDS & every description of BED FURNITURE LACES'. His expansion into the household removal business, using 'Cart on Springs', was announced on 27 March 1829; and a 'newly invented ELASTIC METAL SPRING BED' which 'supersedes the use of Feather Bed, Mattress & Paillasse', suitable particularly for invalids and emigrants to hot climates, was advertised on 29 June 1832. Announced on 21 February 1834 that he was declining 'all connexion with the Upholstery business', intending to confine himself to 'his original Business of FEATHER BED & MATTRESS MANUFACTURER'.

Davis, Philip, High St, Oxford, printseller, carver and gilder (1830). [D]

Davis, Richard, Salisbury, Wilts., u (1798). [D]

Davis, Robert, 18 Southampton Row, Russell Sq., Bloomsbury, London, painter, glazier, dealer in writing desks, work boxes, cutlery and toys (1820–23). Trading as Davis & Horwood, ladies' work box makers, in 1820. Took out a Sun Insurance policy alone on 25 April 1823 for £800 of which utensils and stock accounted for £400. [D; GL, Sun MS vol. 498, ref. 1003493] See Christopher Davis.

Davis, Robert, Bristol, chairmaker (1831–40). Trading at 4 Redcliff Back, 1831–36; and 36 Redcliff St, 1837–40. [D]

Davis, Robert, 203 Lent St, London, turner (1835). [D]

Davis, Simon, 10 Gt Surry St, St George's Rd, London, upholder (1793). Took out a Sun Insurance policy on 18 October 1793 for £1,000 on utensils and stock in a house in Charles St, Covent Gdn. [GL, Sun MS vol. 397, p. 127]

Davis, Simon, 29 King St, Covent Gdn, London, upholder (1799). [D]

Davis, Simon, 2 Little St Martin's Lane, London, u and cm (1802–09). Named in Sheraton's list of master cabinet makers, 1803. [D]

Davis, Simon, 8 Gt Newport St, London, cm, auctioneer and upholder (1811–23). [D]

Davis, T. & Beamish, George, Whitechapel, Liverpool, carvers and gilders, looking-glass and picture frame makers (1787). Notice in *Williamson's Liverpool Advertiser*, 12 March 1787 concerned the dissolving of their partnership, and announced that Davis was to continue the business in Whitechapel.

Davis, T., 50 Park St, Dorset Sq., London, cm (1835). [D]

Davis, T. H., 27 Stockbridge (?), Pimlico, London, carver and gilder (1837). [D]

Davis, Thomas, address unrecorded, carver and gilder (?) (1757–62). Named in the accounts for Gibside, Co. Durham, on 6 June 1759, supplying 'new gilt frames for the pictures', costing £19; and on 24 March 1762 'gilding etc. the frame of a large Picture at Gibside of the Rape of the Sabines', £4 17s 6d. [Durham RO, D/St/v1510] See T. Davies & Griffin.

Davis, Thomas, address unrecorded, upholder (1768–75). Son of John Davis, wall painter of Allhallows, London; app. to John Evans, cook and upholder, on 8 May 1768. Admitted freeman of the Upholders' Co. by servitude on 7 June 1775. [GL, Upholders' Co. records]

Davis, Thomas, Lancaster, cm (1768). [Poll bk] Possibly:

Davis, Thomas, Lancaster. Named in the Gillow records, 1784–86. [Westminster Ref. Lib., Gillow vol. 344/93, p. 284]

Davis, Thomas, Draper's Lane, Leominster, Herefs., cm (1776). Advertised in *Pugh's Hereford Journal*, 14 March 1776, that he was 'lately from London (where he served his apprenticeship, and had upwards of twenty years practice) has now opened a shop in Drapers Lane, Leominster, where he makes and sells every article in the Cabinet and Upholstery Way . . . N.B. A sober young man, of good character, is wanted as an apprentice'.

Davis, Thomas, Farthing Alley, Barnaby (or Bermondsey) St, Southwark, London, chairmaker, carver and cm (1779–80). Insured houses for £400 and £200 in 1779; and for £400 in 1780. [GL, Sun MS vol. 276, p. 93; vol. 277, p. 203; vol. 285, p. 301]

Davis, Thomas, London, cm (1806). Admitted freeman of Lincoln in November 1806. [Lincoln freemen rolls]

Davis, Thomas, Bristol, cm, chairmaker, pantile lath manufacturer and earthenware dealer (1817–30). Addresses given at Bedminster, near the Turnpike, 1817–19; Redcliff Hill, 1820–26; no. 14, 1827–29; and no. 15 in 1830. [D]

Davis, Thomas, Barton St, Gloucester, cm and chairmaker (1820). [D]

Davis, Thomas, 65 Minories, London, chair manufacturer, cm and u (1826–28). [D]

Davis, Thomas, 16 Princes St, Holborn, London, cm and u (1827–28). [D]

Davis, Thomas, 17 Houndsditch, London, cm (1829–35). [D]

Davis, Thomas, Smallbrook St, Birmingham, cm and u (1830–35). Listed at no. 16 in 1830 and no. 15 in 1835. [D]

Davis, Thomas, 24–25 Liverpool St, Finsbury, London, cm (1835–37). [D]

Davis, Thomas H., 30 Queen's Row, Pimlico, London, carver and gilder (1839). [D]

Davis, William, Corn Mkt, Louth, Lincs., carver, gilder, printseller, looking-glass and picture frame maker (c. 1800). [Trade card in Johnson Coll., Bodleian Lib., Oxford]

Davis, William, address unrecorded, carver (early 18th century). Worked with Joel Lobb and Samuel Watson at Chatsworth, Derbs. [V & A archives]

Davis, William, London, upholder, cm and auctioneer (1784–1828). Son of James Davis of Hanover Ct, Cripplegate; app. to James Senols on 7 January 1784, and admitted freeman of the Upholders' Co. by servitude on 29 October 1796. Recorded at Giltspur St, Smithfield, 1796–1828, no. 16, 1802–28. [D; GL, Upholders' Co. records] See N. Davis.

Davis, William, the Quay, Bristol, carver and gilder (1792). [D]

Davis, William, Bristol, cm and chairmaker (1812–33). Recorded at Temple St, 1812; Temple Back, 1813–20; 31 Montague St, 1824–31; 50 St Michael's Hill, 1832; and Tankard's Close, 1833. [D]

Davis, William, 3 Park St, Bristol, u (1830). [D]

Davis, William, Lancaster, cm (1794–1807). App. to J. Sowerby in 1794, and admitted freeman in 1806–07. [Lancaster app. reg. and freemen rolls]

Davis, William, London, cm (1818). [Worcester poll bk]

Davis, William, 43 Seward St, Goswell St, London, cm (1820). [D]

Davis, William, Gt Carlisle St, Edgware Rd, London, bed and mattress maker (1827–28). [D] Possibly of Davis & Newton.

Davis, William, Castle St, Northampton, cm (1830). [Poll bk]

Davis, William, 21 Aston St, Birmingham, cm and u (1830). [D]

Davis, William, 22 King St, Bartholomew Sq., London, cm and u (1839). [D]

Davis, William, Shire Lane, Dorchester, Dorset, cm (1840). [D]

Davis, William, 7 Walker Sq., Hull, Yorks., cm and u (1840). [D]

Davis, William, North Parade, Frome, Som., cm and u (1840). [D]

Davis & Co., address unrecorded, frame makers (1763–68). Named in the accounts of Henry Hoare of Stourhead, Wilts., on 17 December 1763, receiving £15 6s for two gold frames; on 31 January 1764 for two more; and on 19 March 1768, £57 11s. [V & A archives] Possibly Thomas Davies (or Davis).

Davis & Elliot, 97 New Bond St, London, upholders (1776–83). The accounts of Sir Thomas Egerton, later 1st Earl of Wilton, record payment of £3 14s 6d to Davis & Elliot for a bed carpet on 2 November 1776. [D; Preston RO, DDEg] See Charles Elliot, London.

Davis & Griffin, Birmingham, carvers and gilders (1769–70). See T. Davies & Griffin.

Davis & Newton, 21 Carlisle St, Soho, London, cm etc. (1821). [D] Possibly William Davis.

Davis & Sargent, 104, Bishopsgate Within, London, glass grinders and cm (1767–79). [D]

Davison, Barnard, St Martin's Lane, London, cm (1796). Thomas Haig bequeathed £100 to Barnard Davison 'my foreman' in his will dated 1796.

Davison, George Canham, High St, London, carver (1778). Insured his house for £100 in 1778 with the Sun Co. [GL, Sun MS vol. 271, p. 190]

Davison, George, 4 Foley St, Foley Pl., London, u (1839). [D]

Davison, Joseph, High St, Bishop Wearmouth, Sunderland, Co. Durham, cm (1827–32). [D]

Davison, Richard, address unrecorded, chairmaker (1803). Subscribed to Sheraton's *Cabinet Dictionary*, 1803.

Davison, S., New Bridge St, Exeter, Devon, u (1816–25). Advertised in *Exeter Pocket Journal*, 1816, 1822 and 1825. [D]

Davison, Sibella & Deacon, Thomas, London, cm (1783). The Forbes family accounts, possibly for Callendar House, Scotland, record purchases in 1783 of a double writing desk and three stools, £1 11s 6d; a walnut dressing table, 4s, four ash chairs, 4s, and a wooden clock, 2s 6d. [Scottish RO, GD171/Box 54]

Davison, Thomas, Chichester, Sussex, cm (1761). Took app. named Hoskins in 1761. [S of G, app. index]

Davison, Thomas, Church St, Gainsborough, Lincs., joiner and/or cm (1823). [D]

Davison, Thomas, Bland's Cliff, Scarborough, Yorks., cm (1840). [D]

Davison, W., London, cm (1793). Subscribed to Sheraton's *Drawing Book*, 1793.

Davison, W., 34 Wells St, Oxford St, London, u and undertaker (1809–20). Trading as Davison & Sons in 1820. [D]

Davison, William, York, cm (1754–56). Subscribed to Chippendale's *Director*, 1754. Took app. named John Copeland in 1756 for £7. [V & A archives]

Davy, John, Pound St, Halesworth, Suffolk, cm (1830–39). [D]

Davy, William, Exeter, Devon, cm (1803). [Militia Census]

Davy, William, London, cm (1830). [Norwich poll bk]

Davye, William, Burnley, Lancs., cm and joiner (1814–24). Trading in Market St, 1814; Market Pl. in 1822; and Bay Horse Yd, 1824. [D]

Daw, —, Fetter Lane, London, u (1751). Notice in the *General Advertiser*, 20 November 1751.

Daw, —, Cheapside, London. Label recorded on Regency sarcophagus-shaped tea caddy, c. 1810, with canted corners, ring handles at ends, and four gilt paw feet; veneered in tortoiseshell and containing two compartments with tortoiseshell veneered lids and sugar bowl.

Daw, William, Brewood, Staffs., joiner and/or cm (1834). [D]

Daw(e), William, Exeter, Devon, cm (1827–35). Recorded at Union Terr. in 1829 and Coombe St, 1833–35. Marriage to Miss Sarah Youd of Exeter at St Sidwell's Church reported in *The Alfred*, 9 January 1827. Son James Youd bapt. at St Sidwell's on 18 January 1829; and daughters Elizabeth, on 29 September 1833 and Jane, on 25 October 1835, at St Mary Major. [PR (bapt.)]

Daw(e), William, 6 Theberton St, Islington, London, cm and u (1835–39). [D]

Dawes, —, Duke St, Bloomsbury Sq., London, u (d. by 1833?). Report in *Chester Courant and North Wales Advertiser*, 8 October 1833, that Mrs Elizabeth Dawes was caught stealing a boa from a shop in Oxford St. 'Her husband was an upholsterer residing in Duke St., Bloomsbury Sq'.

Dawes, —, address unrecorded, u (1786–91). Recorded in Paul Methuen's Day Book working at Corsham Ct, Wilts., being paid £29 6s 6d on 7 June 1786; £25 15s on 20 April 1790; and £55 10s 6d on 22 January 1791. [V & A archives]

Dawes, —, address unrecorded, u (1809). Supplied upholstery goods to Lord Braybrooke for his Berkshire house, Billingbear, in June 1809, totalling £4 18s. [Essex RO, D/DBy/A376]

Dawes, Ann, Bold St, Liverpool, carver and gilder (1837–39). Recorded at no. 38 in 1837 and no. 126 in 1839. [D] See John Dawes.

Dawes, B., Soho Sq., London, u (1832). Provided patent sunshades and curtains costing £22 for Hopetoun House, Lothian, Scotland, in 1832. [Scottish RO, bundle 264] Probably:

Dawes, Bartholomew, 20 Carlisle St, Soho, London, u, cm and undertaker (1826–39). Worked for Lord Viscount Lowther in July 1838, 'Reframing a Gilt Cabriole Sofa thoroughly repairing Do. and making good the carving', for £2 15s. From 2–14 July he supervised moving and repairing furniture, taking down, repairing and replacing blinds, taking up, brushing and laying down 'druggets' and carpets; 'papering up the Furniture', 'scouring & glazing the Brown holland coverings of the Staircase', and 'Making up a Table cover of your Embroidered Velvet lined throughout with fine green bevill'd merino bound with silk lace and fringed all round'. [D; V & A archives] See Thomas Dawes, 'inventor of the patent sun shades'.

Dawes, George, Dartmouth St, London, u (1774). [Poll bk]

Dawes, John & Noyes, Edward, near the 'Feathers Inn', Bridge St Row, Chester, carvers, gilders, picture dealers and looking-glass manufacturers (1828–30). Advertised in *Chester Chronicle and North Wales Advertiser,* 28 August 1829, that they 'manufacture all kinds of MODERN and ANTIQUE PICTURE FRAMES, CHIMNEY and PIER GLASSES, of the largest dimensions, made to order in the most fashionable style and on the most moderate terms. Antique and modern CARVING to match any work. A large assortment of Chimney, Pier and mahogany Cheval and Box Dressing Glasses, constantly on Sale . . . N.B., Gentlemen wishing to have their Picture-frames regilt or Pictures cleaned can have them done at their own houses, to prevent the possibility of damage on removing'. Dissolving of partnership announced, *Chester Courant and Anglo-Welsh Gazette,* 31 August 1830, the business to be carried on by Edward Noyes jnr & Co.

Dawes, John, 53 Bold St, Liverpool, carver and gilder (1835). [D] See Ann Dawes.

Dawes, Mark, London, upholder (1773–96). Trading at 1 Broker Row, Moorfields, 1778–86; and 86 Little Tower Hill, 1791–96. App. to Henry Hall; admitted freeman of the Upholders' Co. by servitude on 7 July 1773. On 4 August 1779 he was excused serving as steward of the Co., having suffered 'great losses in Trade'. Took apps named William Banks, 1778–88; William Wilson, 1780–87; and Henry Clyatt, 1784–91. Took out a Sun Insurance policy on 21 May 1791 for £400 on his goods. Declared bankrupt, *Billinge's Liverpool Advertiser,* 15 February and 9 May 1796. [D; GL, Upholders' Co. records and Livery lists; GL, Sun MS vol. 376, p. 495]

Dawes, Richard, 51 Conduit St, London upholder and undertaker (1783–84). Took out a Sun Insurance policy in 1783 for £1,900 of which utensils, stock, goods and wareroom accounted for £1,400. [GL, Sun MS vol. 317, p. 112; poll bk]

Dawes, Richard, address unrecorded. Supplied furniture to Lord Howard of Audley End, Essex in 1786 totalling £24 17s, including '2 Cabriole Arme Chairs fancy backs Japannd black painted in Colours', '4 Neate fancy back Chairs stuft Seats', '46yᵈ of Printed Cotton', and 'a Cabriole Settee to Match Chairs'. [Essex RO, D/DBy/A44/11]

Dawe(s) (or Daws), Robert, 17 Margaret St, Cavendish Sq., London, cm, u and recumbent chair manufacturer (1820–39). Trading at 33 Edgware Rd in 1839. Also listed at Harlington, Middlx in 1838. [D] Patented his 'Improved Recumbent Chair' in 1827, and advertised it in *Liverpool Mercury,* 1 August 1828, describing the mechanics: 'By elevating a spring beneath the arm of the chair, where the hand rests, it may be converted into a couch, & any required inclination given to the back & arms; & by drawing out a sliding panel beneath, the length may be increased'. One such chair, covered in claret morocco, was bought for £14 on 17 September 1831 by Edward Hurt of 34 Dorset Sq., London, to be sent to Miss Hoskins at Claremont House, Gloucester. [Herefs. RO, Arkwright papers, A63/161] Daws made several variants of the chair, examples being illustrated

in Loudon's *Encyclopaedia,* 1833 and 1839. Several survive, and are generally of oak or mahogany, with out-scrolled, adjustable backs, padded arms carved with Gothic or lotus leaves; baluster, reeded or octagonal legs on brass castors; and upholstered in leather. Some have pull-out leg supports or adjustable book-rests. The chairs are generally stamped with the maker's name and address, and bear labels dated 1833–34 with instructions. One label, dated January 1833, reads: 'respecting the permanence of the principle of this chair, but little need be said, since R. Dawes is willing to make OATH that the least derangement has not to his knowledge averaged one in FIVE HUNDRED during five years'. Probably the maker of the mahogany arm chair at Heveningham Hall, Suffolk, stamped 'DAWES PATENT GR'. [*Antique Collecting,* February 1979, p. 13; *C. Life,* 7 February 1963, supplement, p. 18; *Apollo,* August 1965, November 1975, p. 104; *Conn.,* December 1979, p. 260; Sotheby's 5 July 1968, lot 249; 13 November 1970, lot 247; 10 July 1970, lot 74; 20 October 1972, lot 106; 12 July 1974, lot 135; 11 October 1974, lot 145; 25 July 1975, lot 184; 22 April 1977, lot 155; Christie's 15 May 1975, lot 31; 19 January 1978, lot 24; 10 May 1984, lot 22; V & A archives]

Dawes, Thomas, address unrecorded, u (1687–92). Supplied fifty-two beds and other upholstery wares to the Royal Hospital, Chelsea, costing £170 2s 6d. [*Wren Soc.,* vol. XIX, p. 85]

Dawes, Thomas, near Portland St, Berwick St, London, cm (1775). Took out a Sun Insurance policy in 1775 for £400, utensils and stock accounting for £150. [GL, Sun MS vol. 240, p. 453]

Dawes, Thomas, London, cm, u and 'inventor of the patent sun shades' (1783–1825). Recorded at 26–28 Dean St, 1783–99; nos 68–69, 1798–1824; and 48 Conduit St, 1803–04; in partnership with Newton (or Neton), 1812–17, at no. 59 Dean St in 1820; also 20–21 Carlisle St, 1808–25. [D] Subscribed to Sheraton's *Drawing Book,* 1793 and *Cabinet Dictionary,* 1803. Named in his list of master cabinet makers, 1803. Took out Sun Insurance policies on 11 April 1791 for £1,800 on his house and goods; and on 28 March 1804 for £2,400 on household goods as 33 Michael Pl., Brompton, in tenure. Daws jnr, cm of Dean St, subscribed to Sheraton's *Cabinet Dictionary,* 1803. [GL, Sun MS ref. 582000; vol. 431, ref. 760558] See Bartholomew Dawes.

Dawes, Thomas, 3 Southampton Ct, Southampton Buildings, Holborn, London, manufacturer of portable desks, cases, tea caddies etc. (1812). [D]

Dawes, Thomas, 5 Upper Southampton St, Pentonville, London, cm and u (1839). [D]

Dawes, Thomas, 8 Upper Northern Pl., Gray's Inn Lane, London, cm (1819–20). [D]

Dawes, Thomas, 15 Millman St, Bedford Row, London, cm and u (1826–35). [D]

Dawes (or Daws), William, 57 Red Lion St, Clerkenwell, London, cm (1801–08). [D]

Dawes, William, 48 Sutton St, Clerkenwell, London, cm (1808). [D]

Dawes, William, 10 Hull St, London, cm (1808). [D]

Dawes & Grimes, 10 St John's Lane, Smithfield, London, cm (1789–93). [D]

Dawes & White, Queen St, Westminster, London, u (1780–81). [D]

Dawkins, John, Churchgate, Loughborough, Leics., cm (1835). [D]

Dawre, George, Bristol, u and paper hanger (1834–40). Recorded at Old Park Hill, 1834–35; no. 20, 1836–37; and 2 St Michael's Hill, 1838–40. [D]

Daws, Edward, 44 King St, Soho, London, cm (1822). Insured his house for £800 on 10 October 1822 with the Sun Co. [GL, Sun MS vol. 493, ref. 995783]

Daws, Edward, 59 Quadrant, Regent St, London, writing desk and dressing case maker (1829). [D]

Daws, Thomas, Snowfields, Southwark, London, cm (1791–92). Declared bankrupt, *Williamson's Liverpool Advertiser*, 31 October and 5 December 1791; and 8 June 1792.

Daws, William, 56 Lower Marsh, Lambeth, London, cm (1822). Took out a Sun Insurance policy on 25 April 1822 for £150, of which £30 accounted for a chest of tools in workshop of Kilvington, cm, 9 Newman Mews, Castle St East, Oxford Mkt. [GL, Sun MS vol. 493, ref. 991184]

Dawson, Mrs, address unrecorded. Named in the accounts of Benjamin Mildmay, Earl Fitzwalter, of Moulsham Hall, supplying 'Two Japan Boards for tea, chocolate, etc.' costing £1 4s, on 28 February 1738. [Ed. A. C. Edwards]

Dawson, —, address unrecorded. Provided three japan tea boards, costing £2 6s, to Holkham Hall, Norfolk in 1740. [V & A archives]

Dawson, A., 6 Walks (1819) and 19 York St, Bath, Som., wheelchair maker to HM. [D]

Dawson, Benjamin, Hull, Yorks., cm etc. (1823–40). Trading at 8 Dibb's Yd, Scott St, 1823; and Harcourt St, 1826–40, no. 1, 1826–37. [D]

Dawson, Bryan, Knaresborough, Yorks., joiner and/or cm (1834). [D]

Dawson, Elizabeth, address unrecorded, upholder (1758–68). Daughter of Thomas Dawson; admitted freeman of the Upholders' Co. by patrimony on 2 February 1758. Took apps named Thomas Cathrow, 1760–68 and William Chancellor, 1766–68. [GL, Upholders' Co. records]

Dawson, Elizabeth, Rochester, Kent, u, cm etc. (1838–39). trading at 125 Eastgate, 1838 and Star Hill, 1839. [D] See John Dawson at this address.

Dawson, Francis, Hull, Yorks., cm (1768–74). [Poll bks]

Dawson, James, Penrith, Cumb., cm (1798). [D]

Dawson, James, Green St, Blackfriars Rd, London, upholder and undertaker (1817). [D]

Dawson, James jnr, Westgate, Otley, Yorks., cm (1822–37). [D] See William Dawson at this address.

Dawson, John, Millbank, Westminster, London, carver (1749). [Poll bk]

Dawson, John, Market Pl., Kingston, Surrey, u (1822–32). [D] Recorded in partnership with Huxley in 1822.

Dawson, John, Eastgate, Rochester, Kent, cm and u (1826–34). [D] See Elizabeth Dawson at this address.

Dawson, John, 15 Williams Buildings, Old St Rd (?), London, cm (1835–39). [D]

Dawson, Joseph, address unrecorded, upholder (1718–36). Son of Joseph Dawson, warehouseman, late of London; app. to William Brown on 21 March 1718. Admitted freeman of the Upholders' Co. by servitude on 8 September 1736. [GL, Upholders' Co. records]

Dawson, Nathaniel, 117 Aldersgate St, London, cm (1790–93). [D]

Dawson, Perry, Chester, cm (1794). Son of Perry Dawson, skinner, deceased; admitted freeman on 3 July 1794. [Chester freemen rolls]

Dawson, Robert, Fair St, Horncastle, Lincs., joiner and cm (1835). [D]

Dawson, Robert, 51 Charlotte St, Old St Rd, London, bedstead maker (1839). [D]

Dawson, Samuel, Norwich, chairmaker (1780–95). [Poll bks]

Dawson, Samuel, 26 Lloyd St, Manchester, cm (1836–40). [D]

Dawson, Samuel, 7 Roger's Row, Jackson's Row, Manchester, cm (1840). [D]

Dawson, Thomas, address unrecorded, upholder (1705–27). Admitted freeman of the Upholders' Co. on 1 August 1705. Took apps named John Warren, 1707–15; John Hibberdine, 1712–23; James Maudlin, 1715–23; and Cleave Harrison, 1719–27. [GL, Upholders' Co. records] Possibly:

Dawson, Thomas, at 'The Black Lyon', Houndsditch, Without Aldgate, London, upholder (1712). Insured his house for £200 on 23 July 1712 with the Hand in Hand Co. [GL, Hand in Hand MS vol. 10, ref. 23501]

Dawson, Thomas, Houndsditch, London, carpenter and carver (1764). Employed six non-freemen for three months in 1764. [GL, City Licence bks, vol. 4]

Dawson, Thomas, 26 Oxford St, London, cm and u (1754–93). Subscribed to Chippendale's *Director*, 1754. Took an app. in 1754 for £21. Took out Sun Insurance policies in 1782 for £700 of which utensils, stock and goods accounted for £480; with Richard Dawson on 2 January 1786 for £1,000, £600 on utensils, stock and goods in trust; and on 8 January 1787 for £800. Possibly the Thomas Dawson, cm, of Long Acre, involved in bankruptcy proceedings with Chippendale and others in March 1773, declared in *British Chronicle*, 21–24 September 1759. [D; GL, Sun MS vol. 304, p. 564; vol. 335, p. 134; vol. 342, ref. 526271]

Dawson, Thomas, Lancaster, cm (1795–96). [Lancaster freemen rolls]

Dawson, Thomas, Portland St, Cheltenham, Glos., chairmaker (1820–22). [D]

Dawson, Thomas, Toll Sq., North Shields, Northumb., cm and u (1827). [D]

Dawson, W., address unrecorded, cm (mid 18th century). Name impressed on high quality mahogany Rococo card table with concertina action.

Dawson, W. T., address unrecorded, cm (1830). [Rochester poll bk]

Dawson, William, 'a stranger working in Leicester', upholder (1734). [Leicester freemen rolls]

Dawson, William, address unknown. Mahogany 'cockfighting' chair dated 1773, with original ink bottles, spurs, leather castors and covered in russet leather, recorded. [*Antiques*, December 1965, p. 750]

Dawson, William, 7 Langley St, Long Acre, London, upholder (1775). Insured his house for £100 in 1775 with the Sun Co. [GL, Sun MS vol. 239, p. 638]

Dawson, William, Worcester, joiner and cm (1776). Former app. Richard Cottrell admitted freeman in 1776. [Worcester freemen rolls]

Dawson, William, 73 Wardour St, London, cm and upholder (1780–84). Took out a Sun Insurance policy in 1780 for £500 of which £370 accounted for utensils, stock and goods. [D; poll bk; GL, Sun MS vol. 283, p. 358]

Dawson, William, Nottingham. Signed the *Nottingham Cabinet and Chair Makers' Book of Prices*, 1791, on behalf of the Masters.

Dawson, William, 1 Britannia Row, Islington, London, cm (1808–11). [D]

Dawson, William, Market Pl., Horncastle, Lincs., chairmaker (1819–22). [D]

Dawson, William, Islington, London, cm (1825). Recorded concerning deed dated 24–25 February 1825. [Surrey RO, deed BR/T/2048]

Dawson, William, Market Pl., Romford, Essex, cm (1823–24). [D]

Dawson, William, 8 Market Pl., Halifax, Yorks., cm (1830). [D]

Dawson, William, Westgate, Otley, Yorks., joiner and/or cm (1834–37). [D] See James Dawson at this address.

Dawson, William, Mate's Sq., and/or 6 Pond St, Sheffield, Yorks., cm (1837). [D]

Day, —, Chipping Norton, Oxon., cm, u or furniture dealer (1753–80). [*Jackson's Oxford Journal*]

Day, —, 64 Kennington St, Newington, London, carver and gilder to His Majesty (*c.* 1815). Trade card reads: 'Chimney and Pier Glasses Manufactured. Old Frames Re-gilt. Picture Frames to any dimensions. Prints and Needle Work framed & Glazed. All sorts of Gilt Work Manufactured'. [GL, trade card coll.]

Day, Anthony, Gloucester Lane, Bristol, cm (1792–94). [D]

Day, Charles, Cambridge, cm, u, joiner and auctioneer (1762–d. 1805). The work undertaken by Charles Day covers a fairly wide field, from a payment made to him by the Cambridge Corporation in 1766 for making a ducking chair to erecting the new Cambridge Guildhall in 1782. He was noted as an eminent cm when in 1769 the Mayor made him his honorary freeman. Advertisements for auction sales in the *Cambridge Chronicle* between 1762–65 give his address as 'near the Market Hill'. The newspaper for 14 August 1773 carried announcement that he was going to sell or let his premises 'consisting of a large front shop, and a Parlour behind the same . . . A large Work shop, and Shed, 14 Feet high, under the same, a back Kitchen, and Yard. All the Premises have been new built within these seven years'. It goes on to say that he has taken 'the House late the Tuns Tavern in Cambridge . . . for the better Convenience of carrying on the above business'. He is known to have taken three apps: Josiah Marshall from 25 June 1770 for a fee of £30, John Stamford Moore from 18 September 1770 for a fee of £20 and Sir John Swan who is recorded as already being an app. in 1769. The newspaper reported on 21 December 1805 that 'died in his 77th year, Mr. Charles Day, senior common councilman of the Corporation of Cambridge, and late a surveyor of Taxes in this County'. Probably the Charles Day, u and cm of Cambridge who took out a Sun Insurance policy in 1778 for £900, £200 on utensils and stock, and £50 on workshop. [C. H. Cooper, *Annals of Cambridge*, 1852, p. 340; Cambs. RO, Corp. day bks and archives; poll bk; GL, Sun MS vol. 264, p. 113]   R. W.

Day, Daniel, Mendlesham and Stoneham, Suffolk, chairmaker and carpenter (*c.* 1790). Thought to have lived and worked at a house in Fore St, and began trading as a wheel-wright. Credited with the Mendlesham pattern of Windsor chair, perhaps leading a Day 'dynasty' of chairmakers in Mendlesham. [V & A archives; Fastnedge, *Sheraton Furniture*, pl. 14; C. *Life*, 24 September 1959, p. 376; *Apollo*, November 1935] See Richard Day.

Day, James, address unrecorded, upholder (1709). Admitted freeman of the Upholders' Co. on 26 March 1709. [GL, Upholders' Co. records]

Day, James, Fleet St, London, upholder (1727). [Poll bk]

Day, James, address unrecorded, upholder (1735–42). Son of J. Day, carpenter of Edmonton; app. to Joseph Welsh on 3 September 1735, and admitted freeman of the Upholders' Co. by servitude on 1 December 1742. [GL, Upholders' Co. records]

Day, John, 34 St John's Sq., Clerkenwell, London, cm and u (1826–28). [D]

Day, John Joseph, 5 President St West, London, cm and u (1839). [D]

Day, Michael, Oxford, upholder (1784). [D] Possibly of Day & Parker.

Day, Peter, 2 Burleigh St, Strand, London, printer and carver (1784). Took out a Sun Insurance policy in 1784 for £300 of which utensils and stock accounted for £50. [GL, Sun MS vol. 321, p. 548]

Day, Phillip, Poppings Ct, London, carver (1781). Fined for non-service at St Bride's in 1781. [GL, MS 6561, p. 111]

Day, Philip, 67 Cheapside, London, carver and gilder, glass manufacturer (1782–89). Took out a Sun Insurance policy in 1782 for £1,000, £450 accounting for utensils and stock. Declared bankrupt, *Liverpool Advertiser*, 19 January 1789. [D; GL, Sun MS vol. 300, p. 23]

Day, Philip, Newgate St, London, carver, gilder and looking-glass manufacturer (1790–93). Recorded at no. 5 1790–91; and no. 3, 1790 and 1793. [D; Wills, *Looking-Glasses*]

Day, Philip, 24 Worcester St, Southwark (?), London, carver and gilder (1808). [D]

Day, Richard, Mendlesham, Suffolk, cm and chairmaker (b. 1785–d. 1838). Recorded in Market St, now Front St, until 1839. Bapt. on 25 May 1785; death certificate dated 10 December 1838, aged 55; buried on 14 December. [D; PR; *Furn. Hist.*, 1978] See Daniel Day.

Day, Robert, 14 Well St, Oxford St, London, u (1819–25). [D]

Day, Samuel, St. Loy(e)s St, Bedford, carver and gilder (1839). [D]

Day, Theophilus, London, carver and gilder, looking-glass manufacturer (1808–29). Addresses given at 4 Three Tuns Ct, Southwark, 1808; and Black Prince Row, Walworth, London, 1812–29. Associated with a Sun Insurance policy of 13 July 1812 as a trustee of property. [D; GL, Sun MS vol. 455, ref. 871833]

Day, Thomas, Stoney Stratford, Bucks., cm, ironmonger and painter (1798). [D]

Day, Thomas, 64 Kensington St, Walworth, London, carver and gilder (1839). [D]

Day, W., 353 Strand and 12 Charing Cross, London, trunk and portable bed manufacturer (*c.* 1820). Trade card announces him to be 'BY HIS MAJESTY'S ROYAL LETTERS PATENT . . . OF THE EXPANDING AND PRESS TRUNKS & PORTMANTEAUS, Trunk Maker to HRH the DUKES OF YORK & SUSSEX. Sole Inventor of the Imperial Double Trunk & Trunk Canteen at his PORTABLE BEDSTEAD AND CAMP EQUIPAGE Manufactories'. William IV military oak chest of drawers recorded bearing trade label. [GL, trade card coll.; Phillips', 12 November 1963, lot 99]

Day, William, Marlborough, London, cm (1777–79). Took out a Sun Insurance policy in 1779 for £100 on his house. [D; GL, Sun MS vol. 271, p. 425]

Day, William, 33 Banner St, Bunhill Row, London, cm (1808). [D]

Day, William, 17 City Terr., City Rd, London, cm and auctioneer (1817–20). [D]

Day, William, High St, Maidstone, Kent, cm and u (1832–39). Recorded at no. 23 in partnership with Stanger, 1838–39. [D; poll bks; reg. of elect.]

Day, William, Church St, Mansfield, Notts., joiner and cm (1828–41). [D]

Day, William, 15 Mint St, Southwark, London, bedstead maker (1837). [D]

Day, William & Son, 8 Crouch St, Colchester, Essex, cm and u (1839). [D]

Day & Parker, Oxford, upholders (1798). [D] Possibly Michael Day.

Daymond, Edward James, 25 Wardour St, Soho, London, cm (1807). Took out a Sun Insurance policy on 11 November 1807 for £300 of which utensils and stock accounted for £60. [GL, Sun MS vol. 441, ref. 809762]

Daymond, Sophia, 26 Wardour St, Soho, London, cm (1816). [D]

Dayns, Jos., at 'The Rising Sun', Lower Moorfields, London, turner (1718). Insured his house for £150 on 5 December 1718. [GL, Hand in Hand MS vol. 19, p. 268]

Deacon, —, address unrecorded, cm (1803). Subscribed to Sheraton's *Cabinet Dictionary*, 1803.

Deacon, C., 2 Berners St, Oxford St, London, u and auctioneer (1837). [D] See John Deacon.

Deacon, Edward, Bodmin, Cornwall, cm (1830). [D]

Deacon, Henry, 7 Riding House Lane, Gt Titchfield St, London, cm (1821–23). Took out Sun Insurance policies on 24 September 1821 for £300 on household goods; and on 5 November for £400. [GL, Sun MS vol. 487, ref. 983627; vol. 497, ref. 1010235] See John and T. & B. Deacon.

Deacon, J., 71–72 Margaret St, Cavendish Sq., London, cm (1806–11). [D] See S. Deacon.

Deacon, James, Smithford St, Coventry, Warks., cm, u and paper hanger (1818–35). Listed also at Cross Cheaping in 1822. [D]

Deacon, John & Sons, 7 Riding House Lane, Portland Rd (or St or Pl.), cm, u and chairmaker (1811–28). Subscribed to Sheraton's *Cabinet Dictionary*, 1803. Took out Sun Insurance policies on 25 July 1822 for £3,700, of which stock, utensils and goods accounted for £3,500, and warehouses in Titchfield St in tenure of a carpenter, £200; and on 3 March 1824 for £500, £460 on household goods in the Pulteney Hotel, Piccadilly, in tenure of a hotel keeper. [D; GL, Sun MS vol. 493, ref. 993821; vol. 499, ref. 1014289] See T. & B. and Henry Deacon.

Deacon, John, 18 Eyre St (Hill), Hatton Gdn, London, cm, u, chair and sofa maker (1822–28). [D]

Deacon, John, 2 Berners St, London, cm and u (1831–35). Deacon & Co. are named in the Royal Household accounts, 1831–32, receiving £53 10s for a 'very handsome Spanish mahogany map table on stand and ends — carved & french polished. Inside fitted up with brass work & rollers for maps'. The accounts of December 1833 refer to the same, or another similar map table costing £151 15s. [D; Windsor Royal Archives, Lord Chamberlain's accounts; RA, 17, Box 1] See C. Deacon.

Deacon, John Charles, 240 Regent St Circus, Oxford St, London, cm and u (1827–28). [D]

Deacon, Joseph, 41 Lambeth Rd, London, chairmaker (1809–12). [D]

Deacon, Richard, Portsmouth, Hants., cm (1749). Took app. named Thresher in 1749. [S of G, app. index]

Deacon, S., 72 Margaret St, Cavendish Sq., London, upholder and undertaker (1817). [D] See J. Deacon.

Deacon, Samuel, 22 Wardour St, Soho, London, cm (1803). Subscribed to Sheraton's *Cabinet Dictionary*, 1803.

Deacon, Samuel, 7 Air St, Piccadilly, London, cm (1808–16). [D]

Deacon, Samuel, 135 Oxford St, London, cm (1817–23). [D]

Deacon, T. & B., 7 Riding House Lane, Gt Portland St, London, chairmaker (1812–14). [D] See Henry & John Deacon.

Deacon, Thomas, — See Sibella Davison & Deacon.

Deacon, William, Newport, Isle of Wight, Hants., chairmaker (1726). Took out a Sun Insurance policy on 13 January 1727 for £300 of which utensils and stock accounted for £75. [GL, Sun MS vol. 23, p. 302]

Deacon, Zephania, St Michael's Hill, Bristol, cm and joiner (1794). [D]

Deacon & Davis, Piccadilly, London, u and cm (1819–21). Recorded at no. 35 in 1819 and no. 27 in 1821. [D]

Deadman, James, Hoxton Mkt, Shoreditch, London, joiner and cm (1780s). App. to his brother, Samuel Deadman, joiner and cm, and served for three years, when Samuel Deadman's business declined and he went to Scotland, giving up his claim to the apprenticeship. James's oldest child was twelve, so his apprenticeship was probably in the 1780s. [GL, P83/MRY1/872/45]

Deadman, Samuel, Hoxton Mkt, Shoreditch, London, joiner and cm (1780s). See James Deadman.

Deake, Richard, 20 New Compton St, London, upholder (1778). Took out a Sun Insurance policy in 1778 for £100 of which utensils, stock and goods accounted for £20. [GL, Sun MS vol. 268, p. 455]

Deake, Richard, 26 Broad St, Carnaby Mkt, London, upholder and dealer in musical instruments (1787). On 12 March 1787 insured his household goods and printed books for £100. [GL, Sun MS vol. 342, ref. 528249]

Deakin, John, Steels Yd, Uttoxeter, Staffs., cm (1818). [D]

Deakin, Thomas, High St, Birmingham, cm and upholder (1793). [D]

Deals, Joseph, 6 Hollen St, Soho, London, cm (1808). [D]

Dean, Henry, 4 Cockcroft, Northgate, Blackburn, Lancs., chairmaker (1824–25). [D]

Dean, Isaac, Yd 73, Kirkgate, Bradford, Yorks., cm (1830). [D]

Dean, John, Nantwich, Cheshire, cm (1772). Son Samuel bapt. on 16 December 1772. [PR (bapt.)]

Dean, John, Eastgate St, Chester, cm (1775–81). Admitted freeman of Chester on 8 July 1775. [D]

Dean, John, Macclesfield, Cheshire, cm, u, paper hanger and agent for the sale of fringes (1818–28). Listed at Sunderland St in 1818 and Park Green, 1822–28. [D]

Dean, John, Bingley, Yorks., joiner and/or cm (1822–37). Trading at Main St in 1822 and the Wharf in 1837. [D]

Dean, John, King St, Market Rasen, Lincs., joiner and cm (1826). [D]

Dean, John, Magdalen St, Exeter, Devon, cm (1826). Daughter Mary Ann bapt. on 30 November 1828 at Holy Trinity Church. [PR (bapt.)]

Dean, John & Sons, 8 Wilmot St, Russell Sq., London, cm and carvers in wood (1839). [D]

Dean, Joseph, Sheffield, Yorks., joiner and cm (1784). Took out a Sun Insurance policy in 1784 for £300, workshop, utensils and stock accounting for £70. [GL, Sun MS vol. 321, p. 529]

Dean, Joseph, Hull, Yorks., cm, broker, appraiser and auctioneer (1806–23). Trading at 35 St John's St, with auction room at Saville St, 1806–14; and 45 Market Pl., 1823. [D]

Dean, Thomas, address unrecorded, cm (1754). Subscribed to Chippendale's *Director*, 1754.

Dean, Thomas, Manchester, chairmaker (1781–1815). Addresses given in Long Millgate, 1781; no. 158 in 1794; 17 Swan St, 1797–1804; 28 Lower Swan St, 1814–15; and 24 Swan St in 1815. [D]

Dean, Thomas, 5 Stonecutter St, Fleet Mkt, London, u (1808). [D]

Dean, Thomas, Liverpool, joiner and cm (1822–29). Recorded at 18 Roscoe St in 1827; and 44 Russel St with shop at 17 Roscoe St in 1829. App. to Thomas Dutton in 1822. [D; Liverpool app. enrolment bk]

Dean, William, Market Pl., Cockermouth, Cumb., joiner and cm (1828–29). [D]

Dean, William, New St, Keighley, Yorks., cm, u and auctioneer (1828–37). Trading at 10 New Bridge St in 1837. [D]

Dean, William, Broadmarsh, Nottingham, u (1822–40). Listed at Broad St in 1828. In 1834 both William Dean snr and jnr were trading at Broadmarsh, and in 1840 William jnr was there alone. [D]

Dean & Jackson, Pilgrim St, Newcastle, cm, u, appraisers and auctioneers (1815). Advertised in *Durham County Advertiser*, 16 September 1815.

Dean & Steele, 71 Shudehill, Manchester, chairmakers (1815). [D]

Deane, John, Horseferry, Narrow St, Limehouse, London, carver (1781). Took out a Sun Insurance policy in 1781 for £200, utensils, stock and goods accounting for £70. [GL, Sun MS vol. 295, p. 483]

Deane, Richard, Limehouse, London, carver (1741). Took app. named Perry in 1741. [S of G, app. index]

Dear, Charles & Son, Old Brentford, Middlx, cm, chairmaker and furniture broker (1839). [D]

Dear, John, 143 Long Lane, Southwark, London, carver and gilder (1832–34). [D]

Dear, W. B., London, cm (1835–37). Trading at 21 Broad Ct, Long Acre in 1835 and John St, Tottenham Ct Rd in 1837. [D]

Dearden, James, Bolton-le-Moors, Lancs., cabinet and machine maker (1793). [D]

Deare, John, address unrecorded, upholder (1716–24). Son of George Deare, shoemaker of Chichester, Sussex; app. to Robert North on 6 February 1716, and admitted freeman of the Upholders' Co. by servitude on 4 November 1724. [GL, Upholders' Co. records]

Deare, F. & Son, King's Mead St and Queen Sq., Bath, Som., carvers, gilders and picture frame makers (1787–91). [D]

Dearl, Robert, 7 Gower's Row, Goodmansfields, London, gilder (1808). [D]

Dearnley, William, Morley, Yorks., cm (1837). [D]

Dearsley, Samuel, Wyre St, Colchester, Essex, chairmaker (1823–24). [D]

Death, James, 23 Upper St Martin's Lane, London, carver and gilder, picture and looking-glass frame maker (1839). [D]

Deavey, William, West Holborn, South Shields, Co. Durham, cm and joiner (1828–34). [D]

Deavin, Samuel, address unrecorded, upholder (1721–29). Son of Joseph Deavin; app. to William Braithwaite and J. Elliot, draper, on 3 May 1721. Admitted freeman of the Upholders' Co. by servitude on 27 August 1729. [GL, Upholders' Co. records]

Debond, Charles, 2 Gt St Andrews St, London, carver and gilder (1807). Took out a Sun Insurance policy on 7 December 1807 for £150. [GL, Sun MS vol. 440, ref. 809919]

De Caix, Alexander, 15 Rupert St, Coventry St, London, water gilder and burnisher (1791–1819). Submitted a bill to the Prince of Wales on 4 November 1791 for £195 15s, of which £162 15s accounted for two years and seven months wages, at sixty guineas a year; and the rest for repairs, including soldering and gilding chandeliers. Another bill, dated 19 July 1792, totals £46 12s for cleaning and repairing furniture, vases, ornaments and chimney pieces, carried out from 20 March to 28 June, at Carlton House and Kempshott. A further bill of 5 January 1801 describes him as a 'bronze and ormolu manufacturer'. Carried out 'or moulu gilding' for Henry Holland at Woburn Abbey, Beds., receiving £6 10s 9d in December 1791. Took app. named Jane McCaddon in 1806. [D; Windsor RA, 25093, 25097–99; 25105; Bedford Office, London; Westminster Ref. Lib., MS F4310, St Martin-in-the-Fields PR]

De Caux, David, King's Lynn, Norfolk, cm (1794–1802). App. to William De Caux, cm; admitted freeman of Norwich on 16 June 1794. Polled at Norwich in 1799 and Lyme Regis, Dorset in 1802. [Norwich freemen reg.]

De Caux, William, Norwich, cm and u (1771–d. 1841). Addresses given at Cook St, 1784; 14 Fyebridge St, c. 1802–03; SS Simon and Jude in 1808; and Madder St, 1839. Admitted freeman on 1 March 1771. Former app., David De Caux, cm, admitted freeman on 16 June 1795, and William Proctor Hatch, cm, on 24 September 1808. Will proved in 1841. [D; poll bks; Norwich freemen reg.; Norfolk Record Soc., index of wills]

Deckard (or Deikard), Henry, St Martin-in-the-Fields, London, cm (1713–14). Took apps named George, son of John Hollinshed, cm, on 5 January 1712, for £8; and John, son of John Davidson, Gent. deceased, on 30 March 1714 for £10.

[Westminster Ref. Lib., MS F4310, St Martin-in-the-Fields PR]

Decker, Henry, Moseley St, Birmingham, cabinet case maker (1839). [D]

Dedhart, —, Keere Hill, Lewes, Sussex, chairmaker (1830). [Poll bk]

Deeble(s) (or Debble), John Thurston, London, upholder (1770–1802). Recorded at Old Fish St, 1777; 85 Cannon St, 1782–93; no. 82, 1791–97; and Sun St, Bishopsgate Without, 1802. Son of Thomas Deeble, Gent., of Old Fish St; app. to Henry Blaxland on 2 May 1770, and admitted freeman of the Upholders' Co. by servitude on 2 July 1777. Took app. named William Withers, 1782–89. On 28 April 1787 insured household goods for £600 with the Sun Co. Declared bankrupt, *Williamson's Liverpool Advertiser*, 7 March 1791 and *Billinge's Liverpool Advertiser*, 11 December 1797. [D; GL, Upholders' Co. records; GL, Sun MS vol. 343, p. 584]

Deebles, I., 19 Riding House Lane, Gt Portland St, London, chair and sofa maker (1820). [D]

Deeker, James, Aylesham, Norfolk, cm (1760). Took app. named Cooke in 1760. [S of G, app. index] Possibly:

Deeker (or Decker), James, Norwich, cm (1773). Declared bankrupt, *Gents Mag.*, and Bailey's list of bankrupts, September 1773.

Deeker (or Decker), James, 59 Berwick St, Soho, London, cm and backgammon and billiards table maker (1780–81). Trade cards show E. O. table flanked by figures of Hope and Chance, and state that Deeker 'makes E. O. tables on a new construction, Billiard, King and Queen, Trow Madame and Backgammon tables in the latest manner'. There is an E. O. table, in a room apparently specially designed for it, at Alnwick Castle, Northumb. Took out a Sun Insurance policy in 1781 for £100 of which utensils and stock accounted for £50. [GL, Sun MS vol. 288, p. 454; Banks Coll., BM]

Deekes, John, Halesworth, Suffolk, cm (1759). Took app. named Ellis in 1759. [S of G, app. index].

Deeks, George, 15 Nassau St, London, cm, u and bedstead maker (1835–39). [D]

Deering, —, London, cm (1767). Worked at Tythegston Court, Glam. in 1767. [C. Life, 5 October 1978, p. 1024]

Deering, Samuel, address unrecorded, picture frame gilder (1780–81). Named in Paul Methuen's Day Book for gilding picture frames at Corsham Court, from 4 March 1780 to 19 March 1781 costing a total of £126 1s. [V & A archives]

Deering, William, Gt Newport St, Long Acre, London, Venetian blind and game table maker and retailer (1769). Advertised in *Middlesex Journal*, 16 May 1769, as the 'original maker of Venetian blinds. Tables of a new invention, are likewise made and sold at the above place, which are very convenient for playing at backgammon, draft, chess, cribbage, or hazard, with every conveniency for writing, reading desk, or breakfast table &c'.

Defriez, Richard, 137 Pennington St, Ratcliff, London, cm (1782). Took out a Sun Insurance policy in 1782 for £200 of which utensils and stock accounted for £50. [GL, Sun MS vol. 298, p. 637]

Deggitt, John, address unrecorded, cm and chairmaker (1821). App. to Francis Ross of Cottingham, Yorks. in September 1821. [Hull app. reg.]

De Guidice, Anthony, 50 Broadmead, Bristol, carver, gilder and looking-glass maker (1830–31). [D]

De Hoare, —, London, carver (1749). Report that he had been 'knock'd down in St Margaret's Church-yard, Westminster, by two Fellows' appeared in *General Advertiser*, 30 January 1749.

Dekin, George, Mottram in Longdendale, Lancs., cooper and chairmaker (1825). [D]

De Labertauche(s) (or De La Tauche), Stephen, Noel St, Soho, London, cm, u and mattress maker (1808–28). Recorded at no. 4 in 1808–20; and no. 3, 1827–28. [D] See Stephen Delavertauche.

De Labertauche, T. U., 3 Noel St, Soho, London, u (1829). [D]

De Labertauche, W., 4 Noel St, Soho, London, upholder and undertaker (1817). [D]

Delabourd, John & Jacob, London, carvers and gilders (1715). Took app. named Isaac Delaunay in 1715. [Boyd's index to IR app. reg.]

Delabrière, Louis A., Tenterden St, London, decorative furnisher (1795–1816). Employed by Henry Holland at Carlton House, his name appears in the Prince of Wales's Debt Book in July 1795, when he was established in Tenterden St. He may be the 'Louis Andre Delabièse of Sherrard Street', who worked at Carlton House, or the Louis Alexandre Delabrière who, before the Revolution, was 'Architect à Mgr. le Comte d'Artois', later Charles X; or perhaps a relation of this architect. He was responsible for the painted decoration of the ceilings and overmantel in the boudoir at Southill, Beds.; and the panels of a pair of rosewood parcel gilt pole screens in the house are stated in the inventory of 1816 to be 'painted by Delabrière'. The decoration of a pair of 'Round Seat Chairs with painted Tablet backs' may also be assigned to him. [*DEF*; H. Clifford Smith, *Buckingham Palace*, p. 109; F. Watson, *Southill, the Furniture and Decoration*, p. 26]

Del(l)afield, Erasmus & Matthews, Timothy, 'at the Royal Bed & Rising Sun', by Fleet Ditch, London, u (1723–50). Took out a Sun Insurance policy on 15 November 1723 for £1,000 on goods and merchandise in dwelling house. Mentioned in newspapers of 1742. Erasmus Dellafield, upholder, of Ditch Side, was fined for non-service at St Bride's in 1726 and 1739; and served as a Questman and Collector for the poor in 1735. Delafield retired from partnership with Matthews in 1750. [Heal; GL, Sun MS vol. 17, ref. 30414; GL, MS 6561, p. 45] See Matthews & Delafield.

Delaforce, Samuel, 10 Queen St, in the Park, London, cm, chairmaker and pawnbroker (1776). Took out two Sun Insurance policies in 1776, both for £600 of which utensils, stock and goods accounted for £435. [GL, Sun MS vol. 245, p. 294; vol. 253, p. 530]

Delamere, Abraham, St Martin-in-the-Fields, London, cm (1718). Put app. to James Riorto in 1718. [Boyd's index to IR app. reg.]

Delaney, Dennis, Maddox St, London, upholder (1780–84). Took out Sun Insurance policies in 1780 for £800, £150 on his shop; and in 1782 for £1,900 on houses. [GL, Sun MS vol. 286, p. 402; vol. 306, p. 265; poll bk]

Delap, John, High St, Gravesend, Kent, u and shopkeeper (1780–81). Took out Sun Insurance policies in 1780 for £2,200, £740 on warehouses and stock; and in 1781 for £1,900, £540 on warehouses, utensils and stock. [GL, Sun MS vol. 280, p. 336; vol. 298, p. 172]

Delap, John, Newcastle and Gateshead, joiner, house carpenter and cm (1787–1824). Trading at High-church Chair, Newcastle in 1787, and Battle-bank, Gateshead in 1824. [D]

Delasson, Peter, 11 Duke St, Grosvenor Sq., London, cm (1776). Insured his house for £200 in 1776. [GL, Sun MS vol. 248, p. 278]

Delaunay, Isaac, London, carver and gilder (1715). Put app. to John & Jacob Delabourd in 1715. [Boyd's index to IR app. reg.]

Delavertauche, Stephen, 17 Cromer St, London, cm (1829). [D] Probably Stephen De Labertauche.

Dell, —, 62 French St, Southampton, 'Oval and Round Turner, Picture Frame Maker & Gilder' (*c.* 1825–30). So states label on gilded frame containing silk-work landscape picture, *c.* 1825–30. Label continues: 'GLASS FRAMES of all sorts, and GOLD BORDERING for Rooms. NEEDLEWORK neatly framed & Glazed. All sorts of FACE SCREENS. Frames fresh gilt & repaired'.

Dell, Benjamin, Moorfields, London, bedstead maker (1749–1802). Trade card, *c.* 1763–92, gives address 'next Door to the Sash, middle Moorfields'; and Heal also gives Christopher's Alley, Moorfields. A 1763 directory gives Punch Bowl Alley, Lower Moorfields. Trade card with Rococo frame states that he 'Makes & Sells all Sorts of Four Post, Turnup & Standing Bedsteads. Desk & Table Bedsteads of all sorts in Mahogany, Wainscot, Beach, etc. ... NB. Bedsteads Dyed in yᵉ- neatest manner'. Son of Francis Dell, publican, of Reading, Berks.; app. to Richard Wright on 4 May 1749, and admitted freeman of the Upholders' Co. by servitude on 3 August 1758. Took apps, Thomas Robinson, until 1771, and Neal Young, 1764–76. [D; Heal; GL, Upholders' Co. records and Livery lists]

Dell, Nathan, Snowhill, London, turner (1748). Declared bankrupt, *Gents Mag.*, March 1748.

Dell, Nathaniel, 43 Colegate St, Norwich, cm (1802–03). [D]

Dell, Tom, address unrecorded, cm (1697). Received £19 5s in 1697 from Sir Richard Temple of Stowe, Bucks. [Huntington Lib., California, MS ST155, p. 7]

Della Torre, Jos. & Co., 9 Lamb's Conduit St, London, carvers, gilders and looking-glass makers (1829–39). Trading in partnership with Barelli in 1839. [D]

Dellier (or Delwer), Desire & Emanuel, 58 Berner's St, London, u and cm (1835–39). [D]

Delo, William H., Rosemary Lane, Canterbury, Kent, u (1830). [Poll bk]

Del Vecchio, —, 26 Westmorland St, and 187–88 Gt Brunswick St, London, 'PRINT, LOOKING-GLASS, STATUARY, PLAISTER OF PARIS, & ROMAN CEMENT MANUFACTURER, TO HIS MAJESTY KING GEORGE IV AND TO THE BOARD OF WORKS' (1831). So reads label on the back of a miniature, stating that he makes and sells the 'greatest variety of Prints, Pier, Chimney, Dressing Glasses, Mirrors'. George IV marble-topped and mirror-backed side table recorded, with pierced vine-frieze and eagle monopodia legs; back signed in bold script, 'Del Vecchio, Westmorland St, 5 February 1831'. [V & A archives]

Demaine, Christ., Sheep St, Skipton Yorks., cm (1822). [D]

Demar, Mr, 'late of Castle-street, near Leicester–Fields', printseller, carver and gilder (d. by 1748). Sale of 'Patterns, Tools and other Utensils in the carving and gilding Business together with his Prints in Frames' on his death announced in *General Advertiser*, 14 December 1748.

Demar(s), James, West St, over against the French chapel, by Grafton St, Soho, London, carver and gilder (1723–27). Named in the Montrose papers in 1723 and 1725 supplying carved and gilt table frames; a frame for 'Montrose's Great Grandfather', James, 2nd Marquis in 1723; and a 'Rich carved & gilt picture frame', costing £13, in 1726. [Scottish RO, GD220/6/1249/39; GD220/5/858/16; GD220/6/1364/77]

Demay, Joseph, 52 Broad St, Golden Sq., London, upholder (1806–11). Took out Sun Insurance policies on 9 July 1806 for £800, £600 on stock, utensils and goods in trust; and on 5 July 1809 for £1,400, £1,000 on stock, utensils and goods in trust. [D; GL, Sun MS vol. 437, ref. 792128; vol. 448, ref. 832629] Possibly:

Demay, Joseph, Duke St, London, cm and decorative u (1810–29). Trading at no. 6, 1810–20; and no. 10, 1821–29. Took out a Sun Insurance policy on 21 November 1810 for £4,000, house, workshop and warehouse accounting for £200, stock and utensils, £400. [D; GL, Sun MS vol. 453, ref. 850683]

Demee, Daniel, address unrecorded, upholder (1728–61). Son of James Demee, Gent. of Norwich; app. to John Goodchild on 18 December 1728, and admitted freeman of the Upholders' Co. by servitude on 19 December 1735. Took apps named Richard Hudson, 1736–44, and William Rogers, 1745–61. [GL, Upholders' Co. records]

Dempsey, John, 43 Russell St, Liverpool, upholder (1813–14). [D]

Dempsey, William, Bristol, upholder (1784). [Poll bk]

Dempster, Anthony, 3 Mint Yd, York, joiner and cm (1816–30). [D]

Dempster, James, Westminster, London, chairmaker (1748). Took app. named Balden in 1748. [S of G, app. index]

Dempster, Thomas, 16 Stonegate, York, cm (1838). [D]

Dempsy, Charles, address unrecorded, upholder (1731). Admitted freeman of the Upholders' Co. by redemption, on 7 April 1731. [GL, Upholders' Co. records]

Denby, Edward, Sidmouth, Devon, cm and u (1830–38). Trading in Market Pl., 1830, and Prospect Pl., 1838. Advertised as agent of sale of the Villa Verde, Sidmouth, in *Exeter Flying Post*, 14 June 1832. [D]

Denby, John, Marsh, Huddersfield, Yorks., cm and u (1822). [D]

Dench, Charles, 65 Seymour St, Portman Sq., London, u (1839). [D]

Dench, Henry, 58 Seymour Pl. (or St), Bryanston Sq., London, u (1826–39). Declared bankrupt, *Chester Courant and Anglo-Welsh Gazette*, 16 March 1830, but in trade directories, 1835–39. [D]

Denew, —, London (?), u (1820). With Francis & Elliot, u, appraised furniture for sale after the death of the Duke of Kent. [PRO, LC1/22]

Denham, James, London, bed-joiner (1703–d. 1758). Took app. named William Shepherd in 1703 for seven years. Died on 10 January 1758. [GL, St Leonard, Shoreditch settlement records, P91/LEN]

Denham, James, Brighouse, Halifax, Yorks., joiner and/or cm (1834). [D]

Denham, Robert William, 10 Wyndham St, London, u (1839). [D]

Denham, Thomas, address unrecorded, upholder (1735–42). Son of Thomas Denham, Gent. of London; app. to Thomas Hathaway on 2 April 1735; and John Howard on 2 April 1741. Admitted freeman of the Upholders' Co. by servitude on 7 April 1742. [GL, Upholders' Co. records]

Denham, William, Tweedmouth, Northumb., joiner and cm (1834). [D]

Denison, John, The Calls, Leeds, Yorks., joiner and cm (1821–22). [D]

Denison, Joseph, Kirk Ings Wharf, Leeds, Yorks., cm and joiner (1826). [D]

Dennant, Michael, Framlingham, Suffolk, cm (1821–24). Named in the calendar of marriage licence bonds in 1821. [D; Suffolk RO, FAA: 50/2/119, p. 87]

Denne (or Deane), Ambrose, 4 King St, Deal, Kent, cm and u (1838–39). [D]

Denne, John, Sandwich, Kent, cm (1824–39). Probably of Pott & Denne, Margaret St, 1824–39; and Denne & Hicks, cm, u and brokers, Market St, 1832–34. [D; poll bk]

Denne, William, Stone St, Maidstone, Kent, cm (1832–39). [D; poll bk; reg. of elect.]

Dennelle, H., 12 Newman St, London, carver and gilder (1829). [D]

Dennett, Malcolm, address unrecorded, cm (1803). Subscribed to Sheraton's *Cabinet Dictionary*, 1803.

Dennett, Thomas, High Wycombe, Bucks., chairmaker (1824–26). Sons bapt. in 1824 and 1826. [PR (bapt.)]

Dennett, William, Princes St, Liverpool, joiner and cm (1781). [D]

Denney, John, West End, Kirbymoorside, Yorks., cm and joiner (1840). [D]

Denney, Joseph, West End, Kirbymoorside, Yorks., cm and joiner (1834–40). [D]

Denning, Henry, Military Rd, Chatham, Kent, furniture broker and chairmaker (1826–27). [D]

Dennis, Benjamin, 74 Maid Lane, Southwark, London, cm (1808). [D]

Dennis, Charles, 53 Frogmore St, Bristol, cm and chairmaker (1822). [D]

Dennis, J., Sandford St, Lichfield, Staffs., cm (1818). [D]

Dennis, James, Sneinton St, Nottingham, joiner and cm (1832). [D]

Dennis, John, Penzance, Cornwall, cm and joiner (1773). Recorded on 1–2 May 1773 concerning the lease and release of property and mortgage transactions from 21 October 1765. [Cornwall RO, DD ML, 103]

Dennis, John, Westgate, Grantham, Lincs., carver and gilder (1822). [D]

Dennis, John, Kirby's bank, North Shields, Northumb., cm and joiner (1827). [D]

Dennis, John, Leicester, u and cm (1827–35). Recorded at Granby St in 1827 and London Rd, 1828–35. [D]

Dennis, Richard, London, upholder (1774–1802). Trading in Cheapside, 1794–1802. App. to James Birt of 5 Silver St, Wood St, on 5 December 1774. Admitted freeman of the Upholders' Co. by servitude on 13 November 1782. Took app. named George Bayne, 1788–97. [GL, Upholders' Co. records]

Dennis, Thomas, Lichfield, Staffs., cm (1834). [D]

Dennis, Thomas, Gainsborough, Lincs., joiner, carpenter and/or cm (1828–40). Trading in Church St, 1828–29 and Bellmangate, 1840. [D]

Dennis, William, Newcastle, joiner and cm (1801–29). Recorded in Ouseburn, 1801–29 and Ballast Hills East, 1824. [D]

Dennis, William, East Bridgford, Notts., cm (1825). Will dated 19 February 1825. [Notts. RO, probate records]

Dennison, James, High Cross Ward, Tottenham, London, cm (1832–39). [D]

Dennison, John, address unrecorded, upholder (1726). Son of John Dennison, mariner, of London; app. to John Newton, and admitted freeman of the Upholders' Co. on 4 May 1726. [GL, Upholders' Co. records]

Dennison, T., Devonshire St, Queen Sq., London, japan furniture manufacturer (1807–25). Trading at no. 8 and later no. 1. [D]

Dennison, William, North Bar St Without, Beverley, Yorks., cm (1826–29). [D]

Dennis, William, 14 Fletchergate, Nottingham, joiner and cm (1832). [D]

Dennitts, Thomas, Sandford St, Lichfield, Staffs., cm and cabinet case maker (1834). [D]

Denny, Henry, Ipswich, Suffolk, cm (1832). [Poll bk]

Denny, Joseph, Percy End, Kirbymoorside, Yorks., cm and joiner (1830). [D]

Denny, William, Eye, Suffolk, cm and u (1824–30). Trading at Castle St in 1830. [D]

Denson, Elizabeth, Dufour's Pl., Carnaby Mkt, London, upholder (1786). [D]

Denson, John, 1–2 Dufour's Pl (or Ct), Carnaby Mkt, London, upholder (1776–84). Took out Sun Insurance policies in 1776 for £900 of which utensils and stock accounted for £500; and in 1780 for £400, utensils, stock and goods accounting for £240. [D; GL, Sun MS vol. 246, p. 538; vol. 282, p. 106]

Denson, John, Chester, u (1781). App. to Robert Bowers, u, and assigned to Thomas Powell, u. Admitted freeman on 11 September 1781. [Chester freemen rolls]

Denson, Richard, Handbridge, Chester, cm (1818–26). Admitted freeman on 18 May 1818. [Poll bks; Chester freemen rolls]

Denston(e), Thomas, Dam St, Lichfield, Staffs., carver and gilder (1818–22). [D]

Dent, Henry, 27 Little Castle St, London, cm (1793). Subscribed to Sheraton's *Drawing Book*, 1793.

Dent, John, 45 Ernest St, Regent's Park, London, cm and u (1839). [D]

Dent, Joseph, Bethnal Green, London, orchell maker (1796). [D]

Dent, Robert, 43 Turner St, Manchester, cm (1817). [D]

Dent, Thomas, Carlisle, Cumb., joiner and/or cm (1811–29). Recorded in Blackfriars St, 1811 and White Lion Yd, 1829. [D]

Denton, John, 7 Yeate's Ct, Carey St, London, cm and u (1839). [D]

Denton, Octavius J., Canal Row, Wisbech, Cambs., carver and gilder (1830–39). [D]

Denton, William, New Mkt, Huddersfield, Yorks., cm (1818). [D]

Denton, William, 34 Pitt St, Liverpool, u and paper hanger (1823–24). [D]

Denton, William S., Lowther St, Carlisle, Cumb., joiner and/or cm (1829). [D]

Denyer, William, Littlehampton, Sussex, furniture painter (1836). Commissioned by the Earl of Surrey at Littlehampton in 1836 to paint furniture, including eleven bedroom chairs, and graining a book stand and table to simulate rosewood; also stripping and varnishing eleven tables and stands, totalling £3 19s ½d. [Arundel Castle records, A2006]

De Perway, Daniel, Castle St East, London, gilder (1709). [Westminster Ref. Lib., St Martin's poor rate]

Derbyshire, Edward, res. at Union Ct, Gibralter Row, Liverpool, cm (1835). Admitted freeman on 31 July 1835. [Liverpool freemen rolls]

Derecourt, James Greaves, Tower St, Dudley, Worcs., cm and u (1840). [D]

Derecourt, John, Dudley, Worcs., cm and u (1838). [D]

Derignee (Devignee or Derique(e)), Robert, carver and gilder (1691–1707). Supplied carved and gilt furniture for the Royal palaces in the reign of William and Mary. In 1691 he made for Kensington Palace, at a cost of £20, 'a great wainscott frame for a glass 10 feet long and seven feet wide in her Mat.ˢ-closett, carved with figures and gilt gold'. In 1694 Robert Deuguée is recorded supplying 'three frames for Pictures Richly carved with flowers'. In 1699 he charged £30 for carving two sconces 'with ffestoones, fflowers and other ornaments' for the late Queen's Gallery, Kensington; also for Kensington, two tables, two pairs of stands and two looking-glass frames, 'all enriched with fine carved work', costing £70. This furniture was later gilded by John Pelletier, another refugee French craftsman. Payment was made in 1707 to Derignee for carver's work for the 1st Duke of Montagu and recorded in the notebook of the Duke's man, Marc Antoine. [*DEF*; Royal Household accounts, PRO, LC9/280; *C. Life*, 12 June 1958]

Dermer, William, address unrecorded, cm or dealer (1796). Provided the Hon. James Drummond of Perth with 'A Capital Tortoise-shell Cabinet' for £42; and 'A pair of old Raised Japanned Tables', £10. On 18 March 1796 he received £52 10s for a 'curio Cabinet' supplied to Croome Court, Worcs. [Scottish RO, GD160/box 46, bundle 14; V & A archives]

Dermott, Dominick, 23 St James's St, Portsea, Portsmouth, Hants., carver and gilder (1823). [D]

Dermott, Henry, Southampton, Hants., carver and gilder (1823–39). Listed at 36 High St in 1823 and East St in 1839. [D]

Derrett, Nathaniel, Moorfields, London, u (1706). Declared bankrupt, *London Gazette*, 6 January 1706.

Derring, —, London, cm (1767). Received payments from Henry Knight of Tythegston Court, Glam., in 1767. [*C. Life*, 5 October 1978, p. 1024]

Derry, William, Newark, Notts., cm (1793–98). [D] Marriage to Miss Kirk reported, *Gents Mag.*, November 1794.

Dervey (or Devey), John, Wolverhampton, Staffs., upholder (1795–96). Declared bankrupt, *Billinge's Liverpool Advertiser*, 8 June 1795 and 20 February 1796.

Desbois, Lazaire, at 'The Clock case and Cabinet', Compton St, London, cm (1723). Heal notes him in insurance co. records.

Deschamps, Francis, London, upholder (1715–93). Recorded at 23 Wardour St, 1774–93; and no. 21, 1779–84. Son of James Deschamps of Curry in Poistou, France. App. to Susanna Deschamps on 3 October 1715, and admitted freeman of the Upholders' Co. by servitude on 1 October 1729. His son, James Deschamps, admitted freeman in 1758. Married Sussanah, sister of Anne Protin. who married the silversmith and porcelain manufacturer Nicholas Sprimont in 1742. Insured a house in High Row, Knightsbridge for £1,000 in 1779; for £200 in 1781; and £400 in 1784. Francis and Sussanah are buried in Petersham Churchyard, Surrey. [D; poll bks;, GL, Upholders' Co. records; GL, Sun MS vol. 278, p. 487; vol. 297, p. 444; vol. 324, p. 586; *Antique Collector*, 1937, p. 214]

Deschamps, Isaac, address unrecorded, upholder (1712–d. by 1727). Wife named as Susanna, and sons as John and Peter, upholders. Took app. named Alexander Watson on 14 January 1712 for £10. [GL, Upholders' Co. records; PRO, IRI/1]

Deschamps, James, address unrecorded, upholder (1745–58). Son of Francis Deschamps, upholder of London; app. to John Deschamps on 14 August 1745, and admitted freeman of the Upholders' Co. by servitude on 7 September 1758. [GL, Upholders' Co. records]

Deschamps, John snr, address unrecorded, upholder (1727–48). Son of Isaac Deschamps, upholder; admitted freeman of the Upholders' Co. by patrimony on 26 April 1727. Took his son, John Deschamps jnr, as app., 1741–48, admitted freeman in 1748; and James Deschamps, 1745–58. [GL, Upholders' Co. records]

Deschamps, John jnr, address unrecorded, upholder (1741–48). Son of John Deschamps snr, upholder of London. App. to his father on 4 November 1741, and admitted freeman of the Upholders' Co. on 4 November 1748. [GL, Upholders' Co. records]

Deschamps, John, Knaves Acre, London, upholder (1736–52). Son of Peter Deschamps, upholder of London; app. to his father on 3 November 1736, and admitted freeman of the Upholders' Co. by servitude on 6 February 1752. [GL, Upholders' Co. records]

Deschamps, John, 29 Eaton St, Pimlico, London, u and cm (1778). Took out a Sun Insurance policy in 1778 for £600 of which utensils and stock in the house of Thomas Leaf, carpenter at 75 Haymarket, accounted for £400. [GL, Sun MS vol. 264, p. 132]

Deschamps, Peter, London, upholder (1710–49). Trading in Greek St, Soho, 1747, and Compton St, 1749. Son of Isaac Deschamps, upholder, and Susanna Deschamps. App. to his father on 1 August 1710, and admitted freeman of the Upholders' Co. by servitude on 3 November 1725. Took apps named Thomas Heath and Edward Daniel, 1746–55; and his son, John Deschamps, 1736–52, admitted freeman in 1752. [GL, Upholders' Co. records; poll bk; Heal]

Desessarts, Henry, Marylebone, London, gilder (*c.* 1680–1740). On 7 March 1740/41 he applied to enter the French Protestant Hospital, London. Died at an unknown date, aged 74. [*Huguenot Soc.*, Quarto Series, vol. 111 (1977)] Possibly Henri Dessases.

Desmoulins, Paul, London, cm (1698). Offered reward to anyone discovering Benjamin Goode, probably his app., who was sent 'to the Brew-House' on 28 April 1698, 'and has not been heard of since . . . and . . . it is supposed he was stolen away'. [*Post Man and the Historical Account*, 28–30 April 1698]

Desnoy, Edward, 85 Charlotte St, Rathbone Pl., London, chair manufacturer (1826–27). [D]

Dessases, Henri, London, carver (1688–89). Married Anne Heywood of Oxford on 22 February 1688/89. [Bodleian index of Oxf. marriage bonds] Possibly Henry Desessarts.

De Steffani, William, 33 Exmouth St, Spitalfields, London, looking-glass maker, barometer and thermometer maker (1829–37). [D]

Dethick, Ann, Sherwood Pl., Charlotte St, London, u (1835). [D]

Devell, James, Diglake, Stafford, u (1835). [D]

Devenish (or Devinish), Joseph, London, upholder (1707–22). Recorded in King St, St Paul's, Covent Gdn, 1707–14; and St Martin-in-the-Fields, 1722. Took out Hand in Hand fire policies on 9 December 1707 for £550 on a rented house in King St, on 14 July and 18 December 1710 for £200 on a house in Thames St, and £1,500 on a house in High St. Insured his dwelling house in Kensington Sq. for £400 on 6 October 1711; a house in King St for £550 on 4 December 1714; and a tenanted house for £1,500 in 1722. Named in newspapers, 1712. [GL, Hand in Hand MS vol. 5, ref. 14965; vol. 8, refs 3854 and 9875; vol. 9, p. 315; vol. 13, p. 565; vol. 26, p. 243; Heal]

Devenish, Thomas, Villiers St, Strand, London, u and cm (1756–1808). Recorded at no. 32, 1756–67; as Messrs Devenish, 1768–1805; and nos 33–34, 1784–1805. [D; *Survey of London*, vol. 18, p. 133]

Deverell, Joseph, Bristol, cm (1784). [Poll bk]

Deverell, Joseph, 16 Ratcliffe City Rd, London, cm (1808). [D]

Devereux, T., Queen Sq., Finsbury, London, French polisher (1835). [D]

Devey, James, Shrewsbury, Salop, upholder (1802). Declared bankrupt, *Billinge's Liverpool Advertiser*, 11 January 1802.

Devey, James, King St, Wolverhampton, Staffs., upholder (1805–09). [D]

Devey, John, Wolverhampton, Staffs., upholder (1798). [D]

Devey, John, Snow Hill, Wolverhampton, Staffs., cm (1816). [D]

Devey, John, Paradise St, Liverpool, u (1803). [D]

Devey, John, Woburn, Beds., u, cm and chair manufacturer (1822). Named in the Leigh accounts, supplying furniture for Stoneleigh, Warks., namely 'A Large highly finished Flower Stand yellow deal & painted green wth Elm inside box upon large ball feet', costing £9 9s; and 'making a Coromandale [sic] reading frame finish'd on wainscot & Beech. French polish'd', £2 8s. [Shakespeare Birthplace Trust, Leigh receipts DR 18/5] See T. S. Devey. Probably:

Devey, John Spencer, High St, Woburn, Beds., cm and u (1830–39). Trading also as appraiser and auctioneer in 1839. [D]

Devey, R. C. & W., 3 Shoe Lane, Fleet St, London, founders and closet makers (1820). [D]

Devey, T. S., High St, Woburn, Beds., u (1839). [D] See John Devey of Woburn.

Devis, Anthony, Lancs., joiner and cm (b.*c.* 1692–1742).

Recorded in Cockerham, date unrecorded; and Church St, Preston, 1712. App. to a cm, possibly James Verscragen, in Preston, *c.* 1701. Named in the Preston Court Leet records as a juror, and as having completed his apprenticeship in 1708. In 1714 he was elected burgess, and in 1729 and 1742, a town councillor. Son, Arthur Devis, the portrait painter, b. 1712, when the family lived in Church St. His five other sons included Bartholomew and William, watchmakers of London. Recorded as 'joyner' in 1722, but made furniture for Hoghton Tower, near Preston. [Preston Guild record of burgesses; Preston RO, Hoghton Tower accounts; *Polite Society, by Arthur Devis*, Preston Exhib. cat., 1983, pp. 19 and 49]

Devonshire, Abraham, Banbury, Oxon., u (1800). Administrator of will of his father, deceased, in 1800. [Oxford RO, BB 38/ii/9]

Devonshire, John, Falmouth, Cornwall, joiner and cm (d. by 1814). Deed, dated 8 January 1814, assigned property near Cross Lanes and Rope Walk Field to his widow, Jane, sons, John, Charles and George, and others. [Cornwall RO, 263/14]

Dew, Thomas, Cley, Norfolk, joiner and cm (1822–39). [D]

Dew, William, 219 Piccadilly, London, cm (1784–86). [D; poll bk]

Dewar, David, Francis St, London, u (1794–1811). Trading at no. 4, 1794–99, and no. 12, 1806–11. [D]

Dewberry, Daniel, Pinfold St, Loughborough, Leics., joiner and cm (1822). [D]

Dewberry, Thomas, Mill St, Loughborough, Leics., turner (1840). [D]

Dewdney, Francis, Woodstock, Oxon., cm (1798). [D]

Dewe, J., Lambwell, St Mary's Butts, Reading, Berks., cm (1820–26). [D; poll bks] Presumably of:

Dewe, Musgrove & Quelch, Reading, Berks., cm and u (1826–30). [D]

Dewell, Robert, Hunmanby, Yorks., cm (1840). [D]

Dewer, James, 4 Terrace, Tottenham Ct Rd, London, u (1808). [D]

Dewer, Peter, Liverpool, cm (1834–39). Addresses given at 6 Robert St, Clarence St, 1834; no. 9, 1835–37; and 11 Franceys St, Clarence St, 1839. [D]

Dewerson, John, Birmingham, cm, carver and gilder (1828–30). Trading at 2 King St, in 1828 and 2 Dudley St in 1830. [D]

Dewey, William, London, cm (1760). App. to Ince & Mayhew in 1760 for £63. [*Furn. Hist.*, 1974]

Dewey, William, Bourne, Lincs., cm and joiner (1826). [D]

Dewhurs, Ralph, Church St, Preston, Lancs., u (1805). [D]

Dewhurst, James, 46 Brook St, Chorlton-upon-Medlock, Manchester, u (1836). [D]

Dewhurst (or Dewhirst), John, Liverpool, cm and timber merchant (1766–99). Recorded in Thomas St, 1766–73. App. to James Robinson, joiner; admitted freeman on 19 November 1767. Son, Charles Dewhurst, b. 1776, sail-maker, petitioned freedom on birthright in 1799. [D; Liverpool freemen reg. and committee bk]

Dewhurst, John, Blackburn, Lancs., cm (1797–98). [D]

Dewhurst, Roger & Gerrard, Peter, Liverpool, cm (1761). Former app., John Fisher, petitioned freedom in 1761. [Liverpool freemen's committee bk]

Dewhurst, Thomas, Preston, Lancs., joiner and cm (1814–17). Trading in Water St, 1814 and Roe St, 1816. [D]

Dewick, George, Hull, Yorks., wood turner, carver and bedpole manufacturer (1831–40). Addresses given in Queen St, with res. at 40 Spencer St, 1831; 30 Queen St, and West End Old Dock, 1834; 52 Queen St, 1835–40, and res. at Adelaide St, 1838–40. [D]

Dewick, John, Hull, Yorks., cm, wood turner and furniture broker (1823–40). Addresses given at Old Dock End, 1823; 31 Queen St with res. at 12 Neptune St, 1826; 15 William's Pl., 1831; 52 Queen St, with res. in Anne St, 1835; and 26 Junction Dock St, 1837–40. [D]

Dewick, John, Hessle, near Hull, Yorks., cm (1830). [D]

Dewick, William, Hull, Yorks., cm and u (1831–40). Recorded at 42 Spencer St, 1831 and 63 Lowgate, 1838–40. [D]

Dewing (or Dueing), Francis, London and King St, Boston, Massachusetts, engraver and carver (1716). Advertised in *Boston City Directory* as engraver on copper and silver plate (carver and calico printer), King Street — lately of London. 'He likewise cuts neatly in wood'.

Dewson, James, Gt Charles St, Birmingham, miniature picture frame maker (1818). [D]

Dewson, James, 127 Norfolk St, King's Lynn, Norfolk, cm (1822–39). [D]

Dexter, Christopher, Gretton, Northants., cm and undertaker (1716–24). Worked for Lord Rockingham between July 1716–April 1724, receiving £66 19s 1d for mending chairs and tables, supplying wainscoting and window shutters, painting boards and providing a coffin. [Lincoln RO, Monson 28B/14/1; 10A/1]

Dexter, John, St Ives, Cornwall, draper and u (1765–66). Recorded in Bridge St, *Cambridge Chronicle*, 21 December 1765. Sale of stock announced, 4 January 1766; and home to let, 25 October 1766. See Thomas Dexter.

Dexter, John Charles, Commercial St, Northampton, cm (1826). [Poll bk]

Dexter, Robert, Loughborough, Leics., cm (1794). Advertised for a journeyman cm, *Leicester Journal*, 12 September 1794.

Dexter, Thomas, Godmanchester, Hunts., cm or u (?) (1766). Advertised home to be let, *Cambridge Chornicle*, 25 October 1766. See John Dexter.

Dey, Peter, 42 Port St, Manchester, furniture broker and cm (1838–40). [D]

Deykin, Thomas, 26 Mercer's St, Long Acre, London, coach and cabinet founder (1817–20). [D]

Dias, George, Old Bethlem, London, broker and cm (1793). [D]

Diason, John, Chester, cm (1732). Son of Samuel Diason, glover of Chester, deceased; admitted freeman on 4 October 1732. [Chester freemen rolls]

Dibb, James, 28 (or 38) Downing St, Chorlton-on-Medlock, Manchester, cm and u (1838). [D]

Dibble, Andrew, Long Acre, London, turner and cm (1765). Employed four non-freemen for three months in 1765. [GL, City Licence bks, vol. 4]

Dibble, Andrew, Hosier Lane, West Smithfield, London, cm and dealer in wood (1778). Took out a Sun Insurance policy in 1778 for £500 of which utensils, stock and goods accounted for £350. [GL, Sun MS vol. 265, p. 209]

Dibble, Andrew, 20 Gt Pearl St, Spitalfields, London, cm (1801–08). Took out a Sun Insurance policy on 8 December 1801 for £300 of which £50 accounted for utensils and stock. [GL, Sun MS vol. 424, ref. 725383]

Dibble, J., 29 Little Pearl St, Spitalfields, London, cm (1809–11). [D]

Dibon, Charles, address unrecorded, upholder (1704–19). Son of James Dibon, weaver, of Spitalfields, London; app. to Mark Anthony Pigou on 12 February 1704. Admitted freeman of the Upholders' Co. by servitude on 4 March 1718/19. [GL, Upholders' Co. records]

Dick, —, London, cm (1793). Subscribed to Sheraton's *Drawing Book*, 1793.

Dicken, Francis, Stowe St, Lichfield, Staffs., cm (1826–35). [Poll bks]

Dickens, William, 13 Gt Chesterfield St, Marylebone, London, cm (1829). [D]

Dickens, William, 23 Norton St, Fitzroy Sq., London, cm and u (1835–39). [D]

Dickenson (or Dickison), Henry, 138 Long Millgate, Manchester, cm (1832–33). [D]

Dickenson, J., London St, Swaffham, Norfolk, chair bottom maker (1839). [D]

Dickenson, John, Cross Cheaping, Coventry, Warks., cm and paper hanger (1822–28). [D]

Dickenson, Jonathan, Marble St, with auction room (late Mr Berry's) in Market Pl., Manchester, cm, appraiser and auctioneer (1788). [D]

Dickenson, Thomas, 9 North St, Tottenham Ct, London, cm and upholder (1780). Took out a Sun Insurance policy in 1780 for £200 of which utensils, stock and goods accounted for £110. [GL, Sun MS vol. 281, p. 508]

Dickenson, Thomas, Greek St, London, cm (1784). [Poll bk]

Dickenson, Thomas, 5 Church Lane, Liverpool, cm and timber measurer (1790). [D]

Dickenson, Timothy, Butter Mkt, Ipswich, Suffolk, gilder (1805). [D]

Dickenson, William, 16 Red Bank, Manchester, cm (1808). [D]

Dicker, R., Crediton, Devon, cm (1836–38). Fire at his dwelling house reported, *Exeter Flying Post*, 20 October 1836. [D]

Dickerson, James, Plymouth, Devon, master carver in the dock yard (1798–1830). Recorded at 20 Morice Sq., Devonport in 1830. [D]

Dickerson, John, 46 Norfolk St, King's Lynn, Norfolk, working u (1836–39). [D]

Dickinson, David, Whitehaven, Cumb., cm (1793–d.1800). Subscribed to Sheraton's *Drawing Book*, 1793. Will proved, 24 June 1800. [Deanery of Copeland, Cumb., death duty reg.]

Dickinson, Edward, Hull, Yorks., cm (1819). App. to Edward Dickon in November 1819. [Hull app. reg.]

Dickinson, H., address unrecorded, cm (c. 1790). Mahogany wardrobe, c. 1790, with unusual arrangement of small cupboard and fourteen drawers in lower half, recorded as made by H. Dickinson. [*Collector's Guide*, August 1948, Drury & Drury, London, advert.]

Dickinson, John, Hawk St, Sandbach, Cheshire, cm (1834). [D]

Dickinson, Matthew, Leeds, Yorks., cm (1779–84). Son of John Dickinson, labourer; admitted freeman of York in 1779. Polled at York in 1784. [York freemen rolls]

Dickinson, Richard, Nottingham, joiner and cm (1824). Son of Richard Dickinson, joiner of Sneinton; app. in 1824. [Nottingham app. list]

Dickinson, Stephen, Huddersfield, Yorks., cm (1834). [D]

Dickinson, Thomas, Lancaster and London, cm (1742–68). App. to R. Thorney in 1742; admitted freeman, 1767–68, when stated 'of London'. Polled at Lancaster, of London, in 1768. [Lancaster app. reg. and freemen rolls]

Dickinson, Thomas, London, cm (1784). [York poll bk]

Dickinson, Thomas, Liverpool, cm (1789–96). Appointed as 'appraiser & measurer', *Williamson's Liverpool Advertiser*, 30 November 1789. Declared bankrupt, *Billinge's Liverpool Advertiser*, 19 September 1796.

Dickinson, Thomas, 32 Bold St, Liverpoool, carver and gilder (1837). [D]

Dickinson (or Dickenson), William, York, cm (1823–30). Recorded in High Jubbergate, 1823, and 10 St Saviour Gate, 1830. [D]

Dickinson, William, Snaith, Yorks., cm (1831). [D]

Dickinson (or Dickenson), William, Market Pl., Pontefract, Yorks., cm (1834–37). [D]

Dickinson & Chaloner, Bedford St, Covent Gdn, London, upholstery warehouse (1765). [D]

Dickison, John, Cross Cheaping, Coventry, Warks., cm and u (1822–35). [D]

Dickison, William, 38 Clipstone St, London (?), cm and broker (1807). Took out a Sun Insurance policy on 8 July 1807 for £600 of which utensils and stock accounted for £480. [GL, Sun MS vol. 440, ref. 804705]

Dickon (or Dickin), Edward, Hull, Yorks., cm and joiner (1803–38). Trading at 80 Mytongate, 1803–31; and no. 72, with res. at 20 English St in 1838. Took apps named James Gleadow in July 1808; Richard Blythe of Myton, October 1808; John Woodward, July 1813; Thomas Metcalfe, April 1814; John Clappison, July 1815; James Smith, August 1815; George Thairlwall, May 1817; Isaac Burn, January 1818; Thomas Smith, July 1819; Edward Dickinson, November 1819; and John Cherry, November 1822, all of Hull. [D; Hull app. reg.]

Dickon, John, Hull, Yorks., cm and u (1802–42). Trading at Mytongate, 1802; 19 St John's St, 1810–23; 41 Savile St, 1826; 13 Humber Dock St, 1831; Junction Dock St and North Side Old Dock, 1834–40; with res. at 4 English St, 1838–40. Took apps named Robert Waugh of Stoneferry, October 1802; John Hinsley, April 1808; Joseph Purdon, March 1810; James Yeall Grover, May 1812; William Sunley, April 1814; William Luddington Hunter, March 1818; and John Samuel Redfearn, July 1819, all of Hull. [D; Hull app. reg.]

Dicks, Joseph, High St, Thrapstone, Northants., cm/joiner (1823). [D]

Dicks, William Andrew, High St, Oxford, cm and u (1830). [D]

Dickson, Abraham, Bevington Hill, Liverpool, with shop at Crofton Ct, Cheapside, cm (1804–05). [D]

Dickson, Elizabeth, south side of Castle St, Long Acre, London, broker and cm (1801). Took out a Sun Insurance policy on 10 July 1801 for £550. [GL, Sun MS vol. 419, ref. 721403] See James and John Dickson.

Dickson, George, Kirkham, Lancs., cm (1754). Took app. named James Brown in 1754 for £10. Subscribed to Chippendale's *Director*, 1754. [S of G, app. index]

Dickson, George, 21 Upper Harrington St, Liverpool, cm (1834–39). [D]

Dickson, James, Lancaster, cm (1766–84). App. to H. Baines in 1766, and admitted freeman in 1767–68. Polled at Lancaster in 1784. [Lancaster app. reg.]

Dickson, James, the corner of Castle St, Hanover St, Long Acre, London, cm and u (1791–1804). Took out Sun Insurance policies on 13 June 1791 for £700 on his house in tenure of Smart, staymakers; and on 23 February 1794 for £960, utensils and stock in trade accounting for £750. Named in Sheraton's list of master cabinet makers, 1803. [D; GL, Sun MS vol. 373, ref. 584280; vol. 382, ref. 597060] See Elizabeth and John Dickson.

Dickson, James, Liverpool, joiner and cm (1790–1803). Addresses given at 5 Renshaw St, 1790–96; 52 Crosshall St, 1796–1803; and also 3 Clayton St, 1790–1800. [D] See Robert Dickson.

Dickson, James, Lancaster, cm (1793–95). App. at Gillows in 1793, and admitted freeman, 1794–95. [Lancaster app. reg. and freemen rolls] Possibly James Dixon.

Dickson, James, 16 Bedford St, Covent Gdn, London, u (1796–99). [D]

Dickson, John, south side of Castle St, Long Acre, London, broker and cm (1801). Took out a Sun Insurance policy on 11 July 1801 for £550. [GL, Sun MS vol. 419. ref. 721403] See Elizabeth and James Dickson.

Dickson, John, Earl St, Horseferry Rd, Westminster, London, joiner (1838–41). Submitted bills for work done at Buckingham Palace, September 1838 to 30 June 1841, which totalled £1,142 5s 3¼d, and included altering wardrobes, fitting up the library, and supplying '3 Deal supper Tables with back

jointed & folding legs'; and '2 Octagon deal pedestals prepared to raise the orchestra & steps for the same'. [Windsor Royal Archives, Lord Chamberlain's accounts, RA Box 1/2]

Dickson, Robert, 22 Renshaw St, Liverpool, cm (1834). [D] See James Dickson.

Dickson (or Dixon), Thomas, Sculcoates, Hull, Yorks., cm and u (1801). App. to Thomas Shakels of Hull on 10 July 1801. [Hull app. reg.]

Dickson, Thomas, 13 London St, Fitzroy Sq., London, carver and gilder (1835–39). [D]

Dickson, W. H., 18 Lower Kensington Lane, London, chair and sofa manufacturer (1829). [D] Possibly William H. Dickson.

Dickson, William, address unrecorded, cm (1803). Subscribed to Sheraton's *Cabinet Dictionary*, 1803.

Dickson, William, Eccleston St, Prescot, Lancs., joiner and cm (1816). [D]

Dickson, William H., 172 Long Lane, London, chair and sofa maker (1826–32). [D] Possibly W. H. Dickson.

Dickson, William, 55 Newington Causeway, London, cm (1835). [D]

Digby, James, York, cm (1793). Subscribed to Sheraton's *Drawing Book*, 1793.

Digby, Joseph, 97 Queen St, Portsea, Portsmouth, Hants., cm, u and chairmaker (1830–39). [D]

Dillart, Edward, Liverpool, cm (1812). App. to Edward Charles; admitted freeman on 14 November 1812. [Liverpool freemen reg.]

Dillart, Edward, 50 Howland St, Fitzroy Sq., London, chair and sofa manufacturer (1822–23). [D] Possibly:

Dillart, Edward, 21 Judd St, Brunswick Sq., London, chair and sofa manufacturer (1829). [D]

Dillart, Edward, Lewes, Sussex, cm and u (1832–41). Recorded at 98 High St, 1837 and Mt Pleasant, 1837–41. [D; poll bks]

Diller, C. & J., 5 Charlotte St, Covent Gdn, London, manufacturer of dressing boxes, cases, buhl work. Label recorded on dressing box, probably pre-1840, inlaid with mother-of-pearl, pewter etc.

Diller, D. & J., 5 Chandos St, Covent Gdn, London, travelling, writing desk and dressing case manufacturers (1837–41). Trade card lists 'Ladies Work & Jewel Boxes, Ebony Inlaid & Buhl Inkstands, Copying Machines, Tea Chests, Liquor Cases & Medicine Chests'. The Royal accounts of September 1837 show the firm supplying six ebonized ink stands, seven rosewood and three ebony tray stands; whilst bills of 30 June 1840 and 25 June 1841 include sycamore and mahogany trays. Gentlemen's travelling mahogany toilet box recorded, with hinged, leather-lined lid enclosing mirror, phials, trays, boxes, an inkwell and shaving fittings. [Windsor Royal Archives, Lord Chamberlain's accounts, RA Box 1/2; PRO, LC11/98-110; Sotheby's, 29 July 1983, lot 147] See George Christian Diller.

Diller, Frederick, 8 Little Russell St, Bloomsbury, London, writing and dressing case maker (1840). [GL, Sun MS ref. 1339914]

Diller, George Christian, 5 Chandos St, Covent Gdn, London, cm and u, portable desk, writing desk and dressing case maker (1819–37). [D] See D. & J. Diller

Dillon, James, 16 Green St, Leicester Fields, London, u (1785–79). Took out Sun Insurance policies in 1779 for £500 on his house; and on 17 June 1785 for £200 on utensils, stock and goods in trust, and £210 on those in house behind 16 Green St. [GL, Sun MS vol. 279, p. 484; vol. 328, p. 465]

Dillon, Joseph, address unrecorded, chairmaker (1701). In October 1701 he was paid £4 6s by 2nd Duke of Bedford for six walnut backstools and four walnut elbow chairs, all with stuffed backs, and two walnut round stools. [Bedford Office, London]

Dillow, William H., Canterbury, Kent, cm (1826). [Poll bk]

Dillworth, Edward, Durham Yd, Westminster, London, u (1749). [Poll bk]

Dilworth, Daniel Large, Liverpool, carver (1823–39). App. to John Skillicorn in 1823, and trading at 65 Shaw's Brow, 37 Mill Lane in 1839. [D; Liverpool app. reg.]

Dilworth, Richard, Broker's Alley, London, upholder (1774). [Poll bk]

Dimmock, John, High Wycombe, Bucks., chairmaker (b. c. 1806–41). Aged 35 at the time of the 1841 Census.

Dimoline, Abraham snr, Lincoln, cm (1806). [Lincoln freemen rolls]

Dimoline, Abraham, High St, Lincoln, cm (1819). [D]

Dimoline, Abraham, 34 Villiers St, Strand, London, cm and u (1822–23). [D]

Dimpline, John, 5 Percy Mews, Rathbone Pl., London, cm (1826–27). [D]

Ding, Daniel, Gt Yarmouth, Norfolk, cm (1820–41). [Poll bks]

Ding, John, Norwich and London, cm (1830–41). Polled at Gt Yarmouth, of Norwich, 1830, 1838–41; and of London in 1831.

Dingle, Alexander, London, cm and chairmaker (1749). [Poll bk]

Dingle, Daniel, Exeter, Devon, cm (1826–40). Trading in Cowick St, 1831–34; 3 Bridge St, 1833; and New Bridge St, 1836–40. Son William bapt. at St Thomas's Church on 16 July 1826. Advertised in *Exeter Flying Post*, 12 December 1833, 'A Rising Library Table Desk . . . The pigeon holes are raised by means of machinery, and when lowered form a most secure deposit for cash or important documents'. [D; list of voters; PR (bapt.)]

Dingle, John, 9 Gt Pultney St, Golden Sq., London, cm and chairmaker (1803–16). Named in Sheraton's list of master cabinet makers, 1803. [D]

Dingle, Joseph, Plymouth Dock, Devon, cm (1811). Declared bankrupt, *Sussex Weekly Advertiser*, 18 March 1811.

Dingwall, Alexander, Leicester Fields, Charing Cross, London, upholder and cm (1749–74). Polled at Westminster in 1749. Declared bankrupt, *Gents Mag.*, May 1753; and sale of stock in trade announced, *Public Advertiser*, 20 June 1753, consisting of '4 Post Mahog. Bedsteads with Printed Cotton furnishings & water-closets, Pier & Sconce glasses in carved & gilt frames, mahog. Bureaus, Clothes Presses, Tables, Chests, & several other sorts of Cabinet Goods, all furnished in the neatest & best manner'. Took app. named Hen. Restell for £20 in 1754, in which year he subscribed to Chippendale's *Director*. Worked for the Duke of Gordon between 1749–55, buying furniture 'at Mr. Joseph Thorpe's sale', furnishing and carrying out repairs at the Duke's London house in Upper Grosvenor St. Furniture supplied included 'A Neat Mahogany tea board', 'A strong solid walnut tree chest', a cradle, beds floorcloths, and '5 strong Marlborough chairs with leather seats', totalling £133 15s 9d. An additional account for March to June 1752 records payment for repairs, and plates of silvered and Venice glass with 'Dale' and japanned frames. On 12 October 1752 Dingwall was paid for putting up curtains and providing the Duchess of Gordon with 'a strong wainscot mouse cage'. The Duke died in August 1752, and Dingwall helped with the funeral arrangements, suppling drapes with the Duke's arms, and '2 Outside mourning frames, covered with black bayes', fixed at the late Duke's houses in London and Enfield. The new Duke continued to patronize Dingwall, who carried out repairs to furniture in 1754, and provided the Duke, then twelve years old, with a

fully equipped tool box in December 1755. Polled in 1774. [V & A archives; Scottish RO, GD 44/51/306–09]

Dingwall, Patrick, 68 Charing Cross, London, upholder (1785). Took out a Sun Insurance policy on 4 April 1785 for £500 of which utensils and stock accounted for £200. [GL, Sun MS vol. 327, p. 565]

Dinn, Robert, London, chairmaker (1784–86). [Norwich poll bks]

Dinning, William, 11 Trenchard St, Bristol, Windsor and fancy chairmaker (1817–18). Trading in partnership with Holebrook in 1817. [D]

Dinnwol (?), John, Berwick St, London, cm (1784). [Poll bk]

Diplock, Thomas, High St, Tonbridge, Kent, carpenter and u (1832–39). [D]

Discombe, Richard, Exeter, Devon, carver and gilder (1813). Daughter Urith Gale bapt. at St Sidwell's Church on 6 June 1813. [PR (bapt.)]

Dishon, John Baptist, address unrecorded, gilder (1759). Gilded the state bed designed by Borra for Stowe, Bucks., now in the Lady Lever Art Gallery, Port Sunlight, Liverpool.

Disney, John, York or Wakefield, cm (c. 1760). In the archives of Nostell Priory, Yorks., there is a design for a console table with caryatid supports inscribed on the back 'John Disney — £4.10.0.' The somewhat naive perspective and unsatisfactory scale of the female heads suggests a local cm. [*Furn. Hist.*, 1974, pl. 14B]

Ditchburn, Richard Nightingale, High St, Bishop Wearmouth, Sunderland, Co. Durham, cm (1827–32). [D]

Ditchfield, John, Newcastle-under-Lyme, Staffs., cm (1830). [Poll bk]

Ditchfield, William, 23 New St, Manchester, chairmaker (1808). [D]

Ditchfield, William, Spring St, Sheffield, Yorks., chairmaker (1821). [D]

Dix, Robert, Cock Yd, Swaffham, Norfolk, cm (1836). [D]

Dix, William, 34 New St, Gravesend, Kent, cm (1839). [D]

Dix, William, Chepping Wycombe, High Wycombe, Bucks., chairmaker (1798). [Militia Census]

Dixey, George, High Wycombe, Bucks., chairmaker (1833). Son bapt. in 1833. [PR (bapt.)]

Dixon, —, Shrewsbury, Salop, frame maker (1757). Named in the Congreve correspondence supplying looking-glasses in 1757: 'the largest frame & glass was 15s, the two upper ones 12s a piece'. [William Salt Lib., Stafford, 217/47/6]

Dixon, —, London, cm (1793). Subscribed to Sheraton's *Drawing Book*, 1793. This entry appears twice in the list.

Dixon, —, Lancaster. The Dixon family are named in the Gillow records, 1796–1822, and working on a bookcase, date unspecified. [Westminster Ref. Lib., Gillow, vol. 344/98, p. 1576]

Dixon jnr, Lancaster. Named in the Gillow records working on a bookcase in 1814. [Westminster Ref. Lib., Gillow, vol. 344/99, p. 1949]

Dixon, Mrs, 79 Byrom St, Liverpool, cabinet and upholstery warehouse owner (1821). Advertised in *Liverpool Mercury*, 4 May 1821, that she was continuing her late husband's business 'in all its various branches for the support of herself & children, assuring those who may favour her with their commands that They may rely upon being served with the very best articles on the most moderate terms. NB. Orders for Exportation executed on the shortest notice'. See James Dixon.

Dixon, Barnard, Newgate St, London, turner (1712). Insured his house for £300 on 19 July 1712. [GL, Hand in Hand MS vol. 10, ref. 23435]

Dixon, Charles, 107 Tottenham Ct Rd, London, bed and mattress maker (1827–28). [D]

Dixon, Charles, 86 Crown Ct, Blackfriars, London, cm and upholder (1839). [D]

Dixon, Christopher, Lancaster. App. to R. Gillow of Lancaster for £10 on 30 July 1766. [V & A archives]

Dixon, Christopher, Silver St, York, cm (1774). [Poll bk]

Dixon, David, Grantham, Lincs., cm, u and joiner (1835–41). Trading at High St in 1835 and Wharf Rd in 1841. [D]

Dixon, Frederick, Middlx, feather bed and mattress manufacturer (1824). Declared bankrupt, London Gazette, 21 December 1824. Possibly:

Dixon, Frederick, Oxford St, London, u (1829). Declared bankrupt, London Gazette, 5 May 1829.

Dixon, George, at 'The Four Coffins', Warwick St, Golden Sq., London, cm and undertaker (1748–93). Advertised in newspapers in 1748, and polled at Westminster in 1749. Notice in Public Advertiser, 8 January 1753, concerned sale of household furniture at a house in Silver St, for which further details were to be obtained from George Dixon's, 'where all sorts of merchandise or household goods are bought and sold by commission'. Subscribed to Sheraton's Drawing Book, 1793. [Heal]

Dixon, George, 29 Bradshawgate, Bolton, Lancs., cm and u (1824–28). [D]

Dixon, Ger(r)ard, Blackburn, Lancs., cm (1828–34). [D]

Dixon, Henry, address unrecorded, upholder (1709–17). Son of Thomas Dixon, blacksmith of London; app. to William Burnley on 1 February 1709/10. Admitted freeman of the Upholders' Co. by servitude on 3 April 1717. [GL, Upholders' Co. records]

Dixon, Henry, address unrecorded, cm (1803). Subscribed to Sheraton's Cabinet Dictionary, 1803.

Dixon, Henry, 42 Newman St, Oxford St, London, carver and gilder (1829–39). [D]

Dixon, Henry, 108 Fleet St, London, desk, dressing case, work box and cabinet case manufacturer (1839). [D]

Dixon, Henry, 4 Crown St, Walworth, London, cm and u (1839). [D]

Dixon, Henry, King St, Quay, Bridlington, Yorks., cm (1831–40). [D]

Dixon, Hervey, Lancaster, cm (1767–68). Admitted freeman, 1767–68, when stated 'of London'. [Lancaster freemen rolls]

Dixon, Hugh, 3 Covent Gdn, Liverpool, cm (1774–77). [D]

Dixon, Isaac, Middlegate, Penrith, Cumb., u (1834). [D]

Dixon, J., 4 Herberts Buildings, Gt Waterloo St, London, chair and cabinet carver (1835). [D]

Dixon, James, Lancaster. Named in the Gillow records, 1792–1817. [Westminster Ref. Lib.] Possibly James Dickson.

Dixon, James, Byrom St, Liverpool, chairmaker (1810–d. c. 1821). Trading at no. 80 in 1810; no. 69, 1811; and no. 78, 1813–21. Died c. 1821, when his widow continued the business. [D] See Mrs Dixon.

Dixon, James, 3 Parade, St James's Churchyard, Bristol, u (1827–28). [D]

Dixon, Jarrat, 27 King St, Blackburn, Lancs., cm, joiner and house builder (1824). [D]

Dixon, John, address unrecorded, upholder (1708). Admitted freeman of the Upholders' Co. on 7 April 1708. [GL, Upholders' Co. records]

Dixon, John, Stamford, Lincs., carpenter (1748–80). Admitted freeman in 1748. In April 1780 he was commissioned by the town Corp. to make removable seats and other 'proper woodwork' in the Town Hall, at a cost of £25. [Stamford Hall Bk, 2A/1/4]

Dixon, John, Hull, Yorks., cm (1768–84). [Poll bks]

Dixon, John, Louth, Lincs., cm (1774). [Hull poll bk]

Dixon, John, Lancaster, cm (1784–1811). App. to E. Batty as a charity boy in 1794 and admitted freeman, 1801–02, when stated 'of Manchester'. Named in the Gillow records, 1784–99. A dressing table supplied by Gillows to R. O. Gascoigne of Parlington, Yorks, in 1811 is inscribed in pencil 'J. Dixon'. [Lancaster app. reg. and freemen rolls; Westminster Ref. Lib., Gillow] Possibly:

Dixon, John, Manchester and Salford, cm (1808–13). Trading at 68 Hart St, Manchester in 1808, and 14 Hadson St, Salford, 1813. [D]

Dixon, John, Cumwhitton, Carlisle, Cumb., joiner and/or cm (1829). [D]

Dixon, John, 3 Gray's Inn Lane Terr., London, cm and u (1839). [D]

Dixon, John Henry, Lancaster, cm (1806–07). Admitted freeman, 1806–07, when stated 'of London'. [Lancaster freemen rolls]

Dixon, Joseph, Lancaster, cm (1767–68). Admitted freeman, 1767–68, when stated 'of London'. [Lancaster freemen rolls]

Dixon, Joseph, 21 Chiswell St, London, cm, chairmaker and upholder (1776). Took out a Sun Insurance policy in 1776 for £300 of which utensils, stock and goods accounted for £150. [GL, Sun MS vol. 244, p. 530]

Dixon, Joseph, Doncaster, Yorks., cm (1784). [D]

Dixon, Leonard, Skelton, Gainsborough, Lincs., joiner, cm or cartwright (1834). [D]

Dixon, Moses, Carey's Yd, Nottingham, u (1832). [D]

Dixon, P. J., 26 Ward's Row, Bethnal Green Rd, London, cm and u (1839). [D]

Dixon, Peter, Liverpool, cm (1831). App. to William John Roberts in 1831. [Liverpool app. enrolment bk]

Dixon, Richard, Lancaster. Named in the Gillow records, 1799–1803, as brother of Thomas. [Westminster Ref. Lib., Gillow vol. 344/98, p. 1684]

Dixon, Richard, 31 Marsden's Buildings, Bootle St, Manchester, cm (1813). [D]

Dixon, Robert, address unrecorded, upholder (1709–10). Admitted freeman of the Upholders Co. on 1 February 1709/10. [GL, Upholders' Co. records]

Dixon, Robert, Twinside Lodge, Keswick, Cumb., cm, joiner and/or cartwright (1834). [D]

Dixon, Samuel, 1 Lascelles Pl., Broad St, Bloomsbury, London, carver and gilder (1809–11). [D] Possibly:

Dixon, Samuel, 12 Gt Portland St, Oxford St, London, carver and gilder (1820–39). Trading as chair and sofa maker, 1822–23. [D]

Dixon, Samuel, 2 Crown Ct, Crown St, Finsbury London, bedpost and chair carver (1823). Took out a Sun Insurance policy on 12 March 1823 for £200 of which stock and utensils accounted for £50. [GL, Sun MS vol. 492, ref. 1003118]

Dixon, T., Bath, Som., cm (1825). Declared bankrupt, Brighton Gazette, 18 August 1825.

Dixon, Thomas, — See John Hibbert.

Dixon, Thomas, Bartholomew Close, London, upholder (1709–24). Recorded in the accounts of Felbrigg Hall, Norfolk, receiving on 21 July 1709 £70 'in full of Europa'; on 13 August 1709, £46; and on 1 March 1710, £12. [Poll bks; Norfolk RO, Felbrigg papers, WKC 6/23]

Dixon, Thomas, Lancaster, cm (1795–1802). App. to R. Mashiter in 1795, and admitted freeman, 1801–02, when stated 'of Tatham'. [Lancaster app. reg. and freemen rolls]

Dixon, Thomas snr, Lancaster, cm (1794–1835). Admitted freeman in 1806–07. Named in the Gillow records, 1794–1835, in 1814 working on a bookcase, and in 1823, a desk. Brother of Richard Dixon. [Lancaster freemen rolls; Westminster Ref. Lib., Gillow vol. 344/99, p. 1949; 101, p. 3240]

Dixon, Thomas jnr, Lancaster. Named in the Gillow records, 1813–22, and in 1822 working on bedsteads. [Westminster Ref. Lib., Gillow vol. 344/101, pp. 3180 and 3184]

Dixon, Thomas, 11 Hodson St, Salford, Lancs., cm (1808–13). [D]

Dixon, Thomas, Deal St, Salford, Lancs., cm (1808–13). Trading at no. 12, 1808–11, and no. 17, 1813. [D]

Dixon, Thomas, 18 Friargate, Preston, Lancs., chairmaker (1818–25). [D]

Dixon, Thomas, Grantham, Lincs., cm, u and paper hanger (1826–41). Recorded in Castlegate, 1826–28 and Walkergate, 1835–41. [D]

Dixon, Thomas, Stepney, Hull, Yorks., u (1838–39). [D]

Dixon, Thomas Post, Fitzroy St, Cambridge, cm (1840–41). [Poll bks]

Dixon, William, Chapel St, London, cm (1784). [Poll bks]

Dixon, William, Liverpool, cm (1804–24). Recorded in Highfield St, 1804 and 44 Johnson St, 1824. [D]

Dixon, William, Temple Pl., London, cm (1820–27). Trading at no. 15 in 1820 and 1827, and no. 16 in 1821. Took out a Sun Insurance policy on 16 May 1821 for £300 on household goods. [D; GL, Sun MS vol. 484, ref. 980600]

Dixon, William, Silver St, Durham, joiner and cm (1827). [D]

Dixon, William K., 13 Jane St, Commercial Rd, London cm (1839). [D]

Dixon & Waters, Flesh Mkt, Newcastle, cm (1790–95). [D]

Dixwell, —, London, cm (1793). Subscribed to Sheraton's *Drawing Book*, 1793.

Dobb, Thomas, Liverpoool, cm (1760–80). Addresses given in Frog Lane, 1766–67; Williamson Sq., 1768–69; Lord St, 1768–77; and as 'Gent.' at no. 30 in 1777. Petitioned freedom on servitude to Thomas Gatliff in 1760, paying 6s 8d, and admitted freeman on 11 February 1761. Announced in *Williamson's Liverpool Advertiser*, 17 June 1768, that he was taking Henry Hadkinson, his late foreman, into partnership in his business 'of Cabinet-making Chests & Cases for the African Trade, with the Addition of all Kinds of House Joiner & Capenter's Work . . . at their shop in Williamson Square'. Sale of Dobb's stock in his former Lord St shop announced in the same paper, 3 June 1768; stock consisted of clocks in mahogany cases, chairs, tables, cupboards, tea chests, watches and cloth. Former apps John Parry and James Rimmer admitted freemen in 1780. [Liverpool freemen reg. and committee bk]

Dobbins, —, address unrecorded, u (1739). Recorded in the daybooks and ledgers of Thomas Wagg on 15 September 1739. [PRO, C 109/25, part 1]

Dobbinson, Richard, 41 Ironmonger Row, London, u (1809–11). [D]

Dobbs, —, Tottenham, London, u and paper hanger (d. 1799). Death by drowning 'in Tottenham Marsh' reported, *Gents Mag.*, August 1799.

Dobbs, Thomas, Market Pl., Horncastle, Lincs., cm (1819). [D]

Dobbs, Thomas, 32 Sims Croft, Sheffield, Yorks., cm (1822). [D]

Dobey (or Doby), John, Litchfield St, London, cm (1749). [Poll bk] Possibly John Doby of Swallow St.

Dob(b)ing, Anthony, High St, Stockton-upon-Tees, Co. Durham, u and cm (1820–32). Involved in the furnishing of Wynyard Park, Co. Durham, for the Marquis of Londonderry, 1820–40. [D; Durham RO, Londonderry papers, D/LO/E 484, vol. 1829–41]

Dobinson, Arthur, at 'The Bed', on London Bridge, London, upholder and hosier (1724). Insured goods and merchandise in his house for £500 on 7 May 1724. [GL, Sun MS vol. 17, ref. 31818]

Doninson, James, North Shields, Northumb., u (1827–34). Trading at Church Way in 1827 and 15 Saville St in 1834. [D]

Dobinson, Mark, Wolsingham, Co. Durham, joiner and cm (1828–29). [D]

Doblett, George, 48 Swain St, London, cm (1809–11). [D]

Dobson, Christopher, London, cm (1793). Subscribed to Sheraton's *Drawing Book*, 1793.

Dobson, Hardon (or Harden), Woodhouse Lane, Leeds, Yorks., carver and gilder (1822–28). [D]

Dobson, Henry, 41 Creech (?) Lane, Cannon St, London, upholder (1790–99). Son of William Dobson, victualler, of Gamlingay, Cambs.; app. to James Porter on 1 September 1790, and admitted freeman of the Upholders' Co. by servitude on 6 March 1799. [GL, Upholders' Co. records]

Dobson, Isaac, New Dock St, Hull, Yorks., cm (1817). [D]

Dobson, James, Lancaster, cm (1812–16). App. to T. Lister in 1812, and admitted freeman 1815–16. [Lancaster app. reg. and freemen rolls]

Dobson, James, Gowthorpe, Yorks., joiner and cm (1826–34). [D]

Dobson, John, St Martin's Ct, Westminster, London, cm (1749). [Poll bk]

Dobson, John, Newcastle, u, cm, carver and japanner (1792–1816). Addresses given at 16 Dean St, 1792–96; and 7–8 Mosley St, 1796–1816. Subscribed to Sheraton's *Drawing Book*, 1793. Advertised in *Newcastle Courant*, 19 May 1792 that he had commenced in the upholstery business, and 'is not only at present Master of the French and Turkish mode of fitting up Furniture as now used in London, but assures his friends, the least change of fashions cannot take place, but he will have it sent down immediately'. On 7 May 1796 he announced his removal to 'more extensive and commodious Premises in Mosley Street'; and advertised again on 19 April 1800, showing the Prince of Wales Feathers. On 13 April 1803 announced that he was 'Back from the South with new stock . . . Houses furnished throughout, from a cottage to the first mansion . . . American black birch for sale, a good substitute for mahogany', at 'THE TEMPLE OF TASTE', no. 7 Mosley St. On 23 April 1808 he claimed that 'The whole of the fashionable work is executed under his own roof & the greatest part of the new patterns are manufactured solely for himself'. Further advertisements of 20 May 1809 concerned curing feathers; on 24 April 1813, a patent mangle; on 16 April 1814, enlargement of warerooms and stock of transparent blinds 'on which are painted gentlemen's seats, parks or pleasure grounds'. On 12 and 19 November 1814 he announced his return from Paris 'with a very great Variety of Beautiful Designs'; and on 28 September 1816 a sale of stock. Probably the John Dobson, u, named in the Strathmore papers on 23 December 1808 receiving £43 13s; and on 14 September 1810, £7 7s 7d. [D; Durham RO, Strathmore MS, D/St/349/21 and 24]

Dobson, John, Kidderminster, Worcs., u and cm (1805–22). Recorded at Worcester St, 1818–22. [D]

Dobson, John, Lofthouse, Yorks., joiner, cm or cartwright (1834). [D]

Dobson, Lawrence, Liverpool, carver (1813). Marriage to Miss Goodacre of Liverpool at St Thomas's Church reported, *Liverpool Mercury*, 17 December 1813.

Dobson, Lawrence, Manchester, wood carver (1825–34). Trading at 12 Camp St, 1825, and 2 Fetter Lane, 1834. [D]

Dobson, Moses, address unrecorded, chairmaker (1733–41). Supplied chairs to Gibside, Co. Durham, between 26 July 1733 and 21 August 1741, totalling £7 18s. [Durham RO, Strathmore MS, D/St/v.986–87]

Dobson, Robert, 32 Brownlow St, Drury Lane, London, carpenter and cm (1807). Took out a Sun Insurance policy on 21 August 1807 for £200. [GL, Sun MS vol. 440, ref. 80251]

Dobson, Robert, 5 New (or Junction) Dock St, Hull, Yorks., cm, u and furniture broker (1817–35). [D]

Dobson, Thomas, Lancaster, carver and gilder (1794–1802). [Westminster Ref. Lib., Gillow records]

Dobson, Thomas, 35 Chiswell St, Finsbury Sq., London. Pair of slope-top knife boxes, *c.* 1800, at Came House, Dorset, both bear maker's label inside lid.

Dobson, Thomas, Hull, Yorks., u and cm (1807). App. to John and George Chapman of Hull in May 1807. [Hull app. reg.]

Dobson, Thomas, Church St, Whitby, Yorks., cm (1823). [D]

Dobson, William, Strand, London, 'HARDWAREMAN, STATIONER, &c., Dealer in fine Cutlery, Manufacturers of Pocket Books, Writing Desks, Shaving, Dressing, Cases &c.' (1797–1847). Recorded at no. 165, 1797–1805; no. 166, 1805–25; nos 16 and 38 in 1820; and no. 162, 1826–47. Mahogany artist's (?) box with brass corner plates, corner bands and brass plate with sunk handle engraved 'J. Cheap', recorded bearing label giving address at 166 Strand, and trade details above. Stock includes Reeves's colour cases, ivory and toothpick cases, ebony ink stands, inlaid Tunbridge-wares, and patent letter copying machines and air ventilators. [Private coll.] Same label also found on a portable writing desk with a drawer containing gentlemen's toilet requisites. [BBC, TV, *Antiques Show*, 4 April 1982] and on a plain, brass-banded writing desk. [Bannister's, Haywards Heath, 29 April 1982; D; trade cards in Heal and Banks Colls., BM]

Dobson, William, Liverpool, cm (1824–39). Addresses given at 1 Bean Lane, Bean St, 1824–29; 9 Audley St, 1834–37; no. 26 in 1839; and shop at 1 Back Commutation Row, 1834–39. [D]

Dobson, William Fawcett, 23 Boar Lane, Leeds, Yorks., carver and gilder (1828). [D]

Doby, John, Swallow St, London, upholder (1772). [Bailey's list of bankrupts] Possibly John Dobey of Litchfield St, or John Dobyns of Swallow St.

Dobyns, Edward Harris, London, upholder (1758–65). Son of John Dobyns, late of Salisbury Ct, London, printer; app. to Thomas Dobyns on 6 April 1758, and admitted freeman of the Upholders' Co. by servitude on 4 July 1765. Brother of John Dobyns. [GL, Upholders' Co. records]

Dobyns, John, London, upholder (1752–78). Recorded at Swallow St in 1778. Son of John Dobyns, printer of Blackfriars; app. to Thomas Dobyns on 6 August 1752, and admitted freeman of the Upholders' Co. by servitude on 6 September 1759. Brother of Edward Harris Dobyns. Declared bankrupt, *Gents Mag.,* December 1770. [GL, Upholders' Co. records and Livery lists] Possibly John Doby, or:

Dobyns, John, warehouse at Conduit St, Hanover Sq., London, u and undertaker (1771). Sale of stock by Christie's on bankruptcy held on 21–22 January 1771, consisting of 'A Variety of Cabinet and Upholstery Goods, in Four-Post Bedsteads, Tables, Wilton and Scotch Carpeting, some very elegant Pier Glasses, Pictures, Stoves, some Plate and white Copper Candlesticks'; also wallpaper, feathers and funeral palls.'

Dobyn(s), Thomas, London, upholder (1722–d. 1765). Trading at George St, Hanover Sq., 1734–65. Son of Thomas Dobyns, vintner of Ruislip, Middlx; app. to Robert Webb on 23 June 1722; admitted freeman of the Upholders' Co. by servitude on 4 February 1729/30; and master in 1758. Named as a Fellow of the Society for Arts and Manufactures in 1761. Took apps named Harry Skinner, 1732–33; George Corbett, 1734–42; William Burbridge, 1749–57; John Dobyns, 1752–59; Joseph Knight, 1752–59; Edward H. Dobyns 1758–65; John West, 1758–65; and John Hewitt, 1760–67. On 10 May 1731 insured household goods and stock in trade for £300 with the Sun Co. Probably the Thomas Dobyn who was paid £10 10s on 28 September 1747 for a mahogany chair, cabinet,

dressing bureau and writing table supplied to Alscot Park, Warks. [V & A archives] Probably also the Dobyn who advertised sale of 'several dozen chairs from 2/2d to £3 per chair', in *London Advertiser,* 1751. On 17 May Thomas Dobyns received £65 19s for an octagonal library table bought by the Earl of Ancaster. [Lincoln RO, 2 ANC 6/6] Thomas Dobyn of George St wrote to James Leigh of Stoneleigh, Warks. on 31 July 1755, acknowledging receipt of payment in full, and apologising for some mistake in the delivery of a sofa. [Shakespeare Birthplace Trust, Leigh receipts DR 18/5] Dobyn, upholder of George St placed a notice in *General Advertiser,* 29 January 1748 and *Gazetteer and London Daily Advertiser,* 28 August 1756. Died in 1765. [Poll bks; GL, Upholders' Co. records; GL, Sun MS vol. 32, ref. 53988; Heal]

Docker, Henry, 43 Moseley St, Birmingham, cabinet case maker (1835). [D]

Docker, John, 228 Kent St, Southwark, London, chairmaker and japanner (1808). [D]

Dockray, Richard, address unrecorded, upholder (1713). App. to Nicholas Clarke, and 'lived greate p'te of his time with Charles Williams'. Admitted freeman of the Upholders' Co. by servitude on 10 November 1713. [GL, Upholders' Co. records]

Dodd, Edward, Chester, u (1722–32). Son of Thomas Dodd, maltster and brewer; app. to Ralph Bingley, u, 18–19 March 1722/23. Admitted freeman on 9 October 1732. Possibly the Edward Dod, upholder, of London, who polled at Chester, 1732. [Chester app. bks and freemen rolls]

Dodd, Edward, address unrecorded, u (1731). Named in John, 2nd Duke of Argyll's accounts on 29 May 1731 receiving £86 2s 2d. [Coutts Bank archives, ledger]

Dodd, Edward, Hanover Sq., London, upholder (1734). Took out a Sun Insurance policy on 5 April 1734 for £500 on goods in a dwelling house in Mount St. [GL, Sun MS vol. 38, ref. 63390]

Dodd, George, 52 Myddleton St, Spitalfields, London, carver and gilder (1835). [D]

Dodd, George, 1 St James's Pl., Hampstead Rd, London, carver (1835). [D]

Dodd, Isaac, 9 Hammond Pl., Chatham, Kent, carver and gilder (1839). [D]

Dodd, James, 151 Tottenham Ct Rd, London, u and cabinet merchant (1816). [D]

Dodd, James, 56 Marchmont St, Burton Cresc., Brunswick Sq., London, carver and gilder (1817–39). [D]

Dodd, James, Clapham Common, London, carver and gilder (1832). [D]

Dodd, John, 10 Crown St, Halifax, Yorks., carver and gilder (1830). [D]

Dodd, John, 12 New Inn Yd, Shoreditch, London, cm and u (1839). [D]

Dodd, Joseph, 12 Roe St and 86 Fontenoy St, Liverpool, u (1827). [D]

Dodd, Joseph, 75 High St, Gateshead, Co. Durham, cm and joiner (1838). [D]

Dodd, Robert, 15 Suffolk St, Pall Mall East, London, water gilder (1835). [D]

Dodd, Samuel, Nottingham, joiner and cm (1779–1804). Son of Thomas Dodd, plasterer of Nottingham; app. in 1779. Took apps named John Pinkney in 1790; James Hall in 1791; John Misson in 1802; Ben Fleuritt (Flewitt?) in 1803; and John Farrands in 1804. Signed the *Nottingham Cabinet and Chair Makers' Book of Prices,* 1791, on behalf of the masters. Subscribed to Sheraton's *Drawing Book,* 1793; and *Cabinet Dictionary,* 1803. Marriage on 11 May 1794 to Miss Smart of

Redmill, Leics., reported in *Derby Mercury*, 22 May. [D; Nottingham app. list]

Dodd, Samuel, 4 Fetter Lane, Manchester, cm (1808–09). [D]

Dodd, Thomas, St Andrew, Middlx, cm (1758). Took app. named Frazer in 1758. [S of G, app. index]

Dodd, Thomas, Cunliffe St, Liverpool, cm (1805–11). Recorded at no. 26 in 1805 and no. 9, 1810–11. [D]

Dodds, Matthew, Winston, Co. Durham, joiner and cm (1828). [D]

Dodds, Thomas, 6 Stephen St, Rathbone Pl., London, cm and organ builder (1777). Took out a Sun Insurance policy in 1777 for £400 of which utensils, stock and goods accounted for £240. [GL, Sun MS vol. 261, p. 370]

Dodds, Thomas, Tattershall Rd, Horncastle, Lincs., joiner/cm (1822). [D]

Dodds, William, opposite Cecil St, St Martin's Lane, London, cm (1775–76). Took out Sun Insurance policies in 1775 and 1776 for £500 and £600 respectively, of which utensils, stock and goods accounted for £340. [GL, Sun MS vol. 238, p. 291; vol. 246, p. 213]

Dodds, William, London, carver, gilder and glass grinder (1790–1808). Trading at 51 St Martin's Lane, 1790–93, and 72 Oxford St, 1799–1808. [D] Worked for Sir John Nelthorpe, Bart, from 30 June 1792–6 July 1795, receiving a total of £22 5s 6d, for supplying and repairing frames 'in burnish'd gold', including on 11 July 1794 '1 Frame 4 in. moulding 6ft. 8 at 4s 6d. with black insides and gilt on burnished gold', £1 13s; and on 6 July 1795, '1 fluted frame in best burnish gold', £5 5s. [Lincoln RO, NEL 9/14/35; 8/13/19; 9/16/9] In October 1792 he was paid £1 8s by Gertrude, Dowager Duchess of Bedford, for providing two looking-glasses, one in a black frame with gilt edges, costing 4s 6d, and the other in a frame of 'burnish gold, £1 3s 6d. These were probably for her London house, 112 Pall Mall. [Bedford Office, London]

Dodds, William, Sunderland, Co. Durham, cm (1827–29). Trading in York St, 1827–28 and High St, 1828–29. [D]

Dodge, John, Honiton, Devon, cooper and cm (1784). Took out a Sun Insurance policy in 1784 for £100, utensils and stock accounting for £50. [GL, Sun MS vol. 322, p. 316]

Dodge, Robert, Market Pl., Stockport, Cheshire, cm (1784–93). Declared bankrupt, *Derby Mercury*, 15 August 1793. [D]

Dodge, Thomas, Fore St, Exeter, Devon, u (1743–84). Listed as a freeman of Exeter in 1743. [D]

Dodge, William, address unrecorded, upholder (1705/06). Admitted freeman of the Upholders' Co. on 2 January 1705/06. [GL, Upholders' Co. records]

Dodge, George, Main St, St Martin's, London, cm (1784). [Poll bk]

Dodgson, George, 18 Broker's Row, Moorfields, London, cabinet and upholstery warehouse man (1790–93). [D]

Dodgson, George, 3 Sheritt St, Salford, Lancs., cm (1808). [D]

Dodgson (or Dodson), George, Brook St, Ulverston, Lancs., cm (1822–28). [D]

Dodgson, George, address unrecorded. William IV mahogany library chair recorded, of eccentric design with saddle-shaped seat and rounded back of Windsor influence, twisted spindle splats, shaped toprail and cabriole legs; stamped George Dodgson. [Sotheby's, 6 December 1963, lot 139]

Dodgson, Henry, Blackfriar's St, Carlisle, Cumb., innkeeper and cm (1811). [D]

Dodgson, John, Ulverston, Lancs., cm (1781–98). Took out a Sun Insurance policy in 1781 for £200 of which utensils and stock accounted for £60. [D; GL, Sun MS vol. 288, p. 543]

Dodgson, John, Sedbergh, Yorks., joiner and cm (1830). [D]

Dodgson, William Fawcett, Coney St, York, carver and gilder (1816–25). Recorded at no. 3 in 1823. Partnership with

Thomas Ferrand dissolved in 1816. Admitted freeman in 1818. Took son William as app. on 28 January 1825. [D; York app. reg. and freemen rolls]

Dodgson, William, York, carver and gilder (1825). Son of William Fawcett Dodgson, carver and gilder; app. to his father on 28 January 1825. [York app. reg.]

Dodgson, William, Wood St, Wakefield, Yorks., carver and gilder (1830–37). [D]

Dodman, W., London, cm (1793). Subscribed to Sheraton's *Drawing Book*, 1793.

Dods, Andrew, Broad St, Soho, London, cm (1786). Subscribed to George Richardson's *Treatise on the Four Orders of Architecture*, published in 1787.

Dods, Archibald, Church Lane, Banbury, Oxon, cm and u (1835–41). [D]

Dods, James, 34 Broad St, Carnaby Mkt, London, cm (1793). Subscribed to Sheraton's *Drawing Book*, 1793.

Dods, James, 46 Brewer St, Golden Sq., London, u (1795–1803). [D]

Dod, Peter, King St, Golden Sq., London, cm (1774). [Poll bk]

Dodsley (or Dodssley) & Weston, Nottingham, joiners and cm (1793–99). Trading at Barker Gate in 1799. [D]

Dodson, George, Colchester, Essex, cm and chairmaker (1790–93). Polled at Canterbury in 1790. Subscribed to Sheraton's *Drawing Book*, 1793. [D]

Dodson, George, 41 Hart St, Manchester, cm (1813). [D]

Dodson, William, Lancaster, cm (1830–31). [Lancaster freemen rolls]

Dodsworth, J., Thornton Pl., Bryanston Sq., London, cm (1835). [D]

Dodsworth, Richardson, Bullring, Gt Grimsby, Lincs., joiner and cm (1826). [D]

Dodsworth, Thomas, Ripon. Yorks., cm. Sofa table, c. 1805, at Newby Hall, Yorks., signed by him. [*C. Life*, 3 October 1974]

Doe, Aaron, Newbury, Berks., cm (1798). [D]

Doe, Cornelius Weaver, Blandford, Dorset, cm, u and designer (1836). App. to John Conons Brown, cm, u and designer of Blandford, for five years, his father, George Doe paying £95. [Dorset app. indenture]

Doe, John, Northbrook St, Newbury, Berks., cm and u (1823–42). [D]

Doeg, David, York, carver and gilder, looking-glass maker (1798–1817). Recorded at Stonegate in 1814 and Spurriergate, 1816. Son of Thomas Doeg, linen draper; admitted freeman in 1798. Took apps named George Thompson on 8 November 1798, admitted freeman in 1806; Charles Ward Strawder on 28 May 1802, freeman in 1809; James Cloak on 7 April 1803, freeman in 1812; and Thomas Banks on 12 August 1809. [D; York app. reg. and freemen rolls]

Dogan, James, Long Acre, London, u (1749). [Poll bk]

Dogget, Henry, 16 Little Cheapside, Sun St, Finsbury Sq., London, chairmaker (1808). [D]

Doggett, Henry, London, chair and bedstead maker (1820–37). Trading at 13 Somerset St, Whitechapel in 1820 and 12 Skinner St, Bishopsgate, 1837. [D]

Doggett, Thomas, 12 Chapel Lane, Whitechapel, London, chair, sofa and bedstead maker (1827–28). [D]

Doke, Samuel, 24 Redmund Pl., with shop at 16 Christian St, Liverpool, chairmaker (1835). [D]

Dolby, Edward, 24 Bridge House Pl., Newington Causeway, London, chair and sofa maker (1827–28). [D]

Dolby, George, 71 Newington Causeway, London, cm (1820). [D]

Dolby, John, Saracen's Head Yd, Leeds, Yorks., cm (1826). [D]

Dolby, John, Farnsfield, Southwell, Notts., cm (1835). [D]

Dollain, Abraham, Berwick St, London, carver and gilder (1784). [Poll bk]

Dolland, —, Chester, cm (1819). [Poll bk]

Dollen, Thomas, Taunton, Som., cm (1748). Declared bankrupt, *London Evening Post*, 3–6 September 1748.

Dollett (Dollitt or Dol(l)iff), George, Minories, London, cm, u and joiner (1767–1812). Recorded in Swan St, 1776; and 48 Minories, 1780–1812. Possibly the George Dollitt, joiner who insured property for £250 on 1 June 1767 with the Hand in Hand Co. George Dolliff, cm, of the Minories was declared bankrupt, *Gents Mag.*, July 1770. Took out Sun Insurance policies in 1776 and 1780 both for £600, utensils, stock and goods accounting for £410 and £350 respectively. Named in Sheraton's list of master cabinet makers, 1803. [D; GL, Hand in Hand MS vol. 106, p. 30; GL, Sun MS vol. 248, p. 265; vol. 283, p. 474; Heal]

Dollman, Thomas, Burton-upon-Trent, Staffs., chair and basket maker (1793). [D]

Dolman, Frederick, London, carver and gilder (1819–41). Addresses given at 8 Kent Rd as Dolman & Co., 1819–20; 37 Upper Berkeley St, 1835–39; and 261 Oxford St, 1839–41. Declared bankrupt, 1840–41. [D; Marylebone Lib., deeds 122/1–18]

Dolman, Frederick & Son, Oxford Rd, Newtown, Bilston, Staffs., chairmakers (1828). [D]

Dolman, George, London St, Greenwich, Kent, carver and gilder (1824–39). [D]

Dolton, William, 5 Church St, Kensington, London, u (1826). [D]

Doman, Sophia, 26 Wardour St, Oxford St, London, u (1819). [D]

Domer, Robert, Limekiln Lane, Bristol, chairmaker (1799–1800). [D]

Donald, Robert, 78 Margaret St, Cavendish Sq., London, cm and upholder (1780). Took out a Sun Insurance policy in 1780 for £900 of which utensils, stock and goods accounted for £600. [GL, Sun MS vol. 284, p. 452] Possibly Robert Donard.

Donald, Robert, address unrecorded, frame maker (1783). Supplied a glass frame, costing £5 9s to Lord Monson on 4 June 1783. [Lincoln RO, Monson 10/1/A/6]

Donald, Robert, 78 Oxford St, London, u (1784). [D]

Donald, Robert, Grosvenor St, London cm (1793). Subscribed to Sheraton's *Drawing Book*, 1793.

Donaldson, D. A., 2 Devonshire St, Queen Sq., London, u (1835). [D]

Donaldson, David, 8 Denmark St, London, cm and chairmaker (1793–1817). Recorded in partnership with Bruce, 1793–1815; and with Appletree, 1803–17. Donaldson & Bruce subscribed to Sheraton's *Drawing Book*, 1793; and Donaldson of Gt Denmark St, chairmaker, is named in Sheraton's list of master cabinet makers, 1803. [D]

Donaldson, F., address unrecorded, cm. George III mahogany tripod table recorded, with circular tray top, spiral baluster stem, and legs carved with acanthus leaves with later brass feet; stamped 'F. DONALDSON'. [Sotheby's, 26 June 1970, lot 154]

Donaldson, James, Cowes, Isle of Wight, Hants., cm and u (1823). [D]

Donaldson, John, St Chad's Hill, Shrewsbury, Salop, carver and gilder (1828). [D]

Donaldson, Peter Evans, High St, Shrewsbury, Salop, u (1837). Son of Thomas Donaldson. Named in the Shrewsbury burgess roll, 1837.

Donaldson, Robert, London, cm and u (1808–27). Trading at nos 1 and 10 Castle St, Strand, in 1808; 12 Castle Ct, 1817; no. 11, 1820–23; and 14 Rathbone Pl., Oxford St, 1826–27. [D]

Donaldson, Thomas, High St, Shrewsbury, Salop, joiner, carver

and gilder (1803–35). [D] Recorded at St Chad's Hill in 1822. Named in the Shrewsbury burgess roll, 1806, in which year his son James was born; he too became a carver and gilder. Supplied items to Lord Berwick for Attingham Park, Salop: in 1806, pier glasses and tables for the Drawing Room; and in 1811 a pair of coromandel side tables with marble tops and gilt chimera supports for the Picture Gallery. These survive *in situ*. T. J. Howell in *The Stranger in Shrewsbury*, 1816, described Attingham, noting 'the rich and costly carvings and ornamental furniture ... executed by Mr. Donaldson of Shrewsbury, whose correct taste in that fine art is too well appreciated to need any eulogium here'. [Nat. Trust guide to *Attingham Park*, pp. 8 and 13]

Donaldson, William, Newcastle, u (1784). App. to Henry Reed and admitted freeman on 20 April 1784. [Newcastle freemen reg.]

Donally, John, Earl's Ct, Duke's Ct, London, chairmaker (1749). [Poll bk]

Donard, Robert, Margaret St, Cavendish Sq., London, u (1784). Declared bankrupt, *Gents Mag.*, July 1784. Possibly Robert Donald of Margaret St.

Donegan, Peter & Co., 7 Union Ct, Holborn, London, picture framers (1805). [Goodison, *Barometers*]

Donery, —, address unrecorded, cm (1803). Subscribed to Sheraton's *Cabinet Dictionary*, 1803.

Donkin, Lewis, Hillgate, Gateshead, Co. Durham, joiner and cm (1795). [D]

Donkin, William, Newcastle, cm (1827–38). Recorded at Scafe's Ct, Pilgrim St, 1827–38; Stamfordham Pl., Percy St in 1834; and Blenheim St in 1838. [D]

Donnald, Thomas, High Wycombe, Bucks., chairmaker (1826–28). Daughters bapt. in 1826 and 1828. [PR (bapt.)]

Donne, George J., Hoxton, London, carver and gilder (1826–37). Addresses given at 26 Pitfield St, 1826–27; 6 Charles Sq., 1829; and Queen St, 1835–37. [D]

Donne, George, 9 Eldon St, Finsbury, London, carver, gilder and looking-glass manufacturer (1835–39). [D]

Donne, James, Brighton, Sussex, cm and u (1830–36). Addresses given at North Gdns in 1830; 4 Middle St in 1832; and Rose Hill, 1836. Son James bapt. on 5 December 1830, and Richard on 11 November 1832; and daughter Elizabeth on 14 August 1836. [D; E. Sussex RO, PR (bapt.)]

Donne, Thomas, King's Lynn, Norfolk, u (1667–68). App. to Pope, u; admitted freeman in 1667–68. [King's Lynn freemen's calendar]

Donnithorne, Issac, Stafford St, Wolverhampton, Staffs., cm (1816). [D]

Donovan, Daniel, Bristol, cm, u and undertaker (1814–18). Trading at Eugene St, 1814–15, and 8 Lower Montague St, 1816–18. [D]

Doody, Joseph, Yarpole, Salop, cm (1760). Took app. named Twitty in 1760. [S of G, app. index]

Doody, Joseph, Leominster, Herefs., cm (active before 1777). 'Late an eminent cabinet maker of Leominster', his appointment to the rank of Colonel in the Provincial Army was reported in *Hereford Journal*, 10 April 1777.

Dooks, Thomas, Greenwich, London, cm (1791). [D]

Doolan, John, London, upholder (1767). [Canterbury freemen rolls]

Doolan & Co., Southwark, London, u (1769–70). Sold goods at the annual Stirbitch Fair held in September just outside Cambridge, 1769–70. [*Cambridge Chronicle and Journal*]

Dooley & Son, name recorded punched on a three pedestal dining table, c. 1810.

Doran, John, London, cm (1831). [Sandwich poll bk]

Dore, Frederick, 179 Borough, Southwark, London, cm and u (1809). [D]

Dore, Samuel, Bristol St, Birmingham, cm, u and broker (1828–30). Recorded at no. 163 in 1828. [D]

Dorling, Peter, Millgate, Wigan, Lancs., cm (1834). [D]

Dormer, Thomas, High Wycombe, Bucks., chairmaker (b. c. 1791–1841). Daughters bapt. in 1814, 1816 and 1822. Aged 50 at the time of the 1841 Census. [PR (bapt.)]

Dorney, William, North St, Brighton, Sussex, cm and u (1832–39). Addresses given at no. 66 in 1832 and no. 70 in 1839. Son William Thomas bapt. on 27 December 1832; Charles Champion on 4 January 1835; and Alfred, 11 November 1838. [D; poll bk; E. Sussex RO, PR (bapt.)]

Dornings, Peter, Bradshawgate, Bolton, Lancs., cm and u (1834). [D]

Dorrel (or Dorril), Thomas, Yates Ct, Clements Lane, London, upholder (1724–49). [Poll bks]

Dorrington, William, High St, Epping, Essex, cm (1822–24). Named in the account bks of Nicholas Pearse of Loughton, Essex, and Marylebone, London, on 27 July 1822, supplying furniture costing £1 1s. [D; Essex RO, D/DHt A1/3]

Dorsey, Robert, Carr Lane, Hull, Yorks., cm (1839). [D]

Dossor, R., Toll-Gavel, Beverley, Yorks., cm and chairmaker (1826). [D]

Dotchin, James, 67 Westgate St, Newcastle, cm and u (1838). [D]

Dotchin, Thomas & James, 67 Westgate St, Newcastle, cm and u (1834). [D]

Dotchin, Thomas, Marshall's Ct, Newgate St, Newcastle, cm and u (1838). [D]

Doubleday, George, Chatham St, Newark, Notts., cm (1835). [D]

Doughty, Ezra, address unrecorded, upholder (1708–d. by 1748). Son of Ezra Doughty, weaver of London; app. to William Whale on 16 August 1708, and admitted freeman of the Upholders' Co. by servitude on 11 July 1716. Took apps named William Kemp, 1716–24; John Carr, 1721–31; and James Underwood, 1723–32. [GL, Upholders' Co. records]

Doughty, George, York, cm (1828). Son of Isabella Doughty, widow; app. to William Wilson, Sarah Carlton, Job Clarke and William Mowbray, cm, on 24 May 1828. [York app. reg.]

Doughty, Henry, Charles St, London, carver (1774). [Poll bk]

Doughty, John, High St, Grantham, Lincs., cm and u (1822). [D]

Doughty, Joseph & Martha, Minstergate and 6 Coney St, York, turners, toymen and cm (1755–1824). Born in 1755, Joseph continued his father's business in Minstergate selling fishing tackle and ivory, bone and wooden 'toys'. Admitted freeman in 1795, when he opened a shop at 6 Coney St in partnership with Marshall. Advertised their 'new invented spinning wheel'. A wheel in the Castle Museum, York, is inscribed 'Doughty, York'. Doughty died in 1801, and his widow, Martha, announced her intention of carrying on the business in York Courant, 8 March 1802. Further advertisements in 1805 and 1807 show her trading as a 'Toy, Tunbridge & Cabinet Manufacturer'; and on 28 March 1814 appears as 'M. MARSHALL, (Late Doughty)', having either married Doughty's partner or reverted to her maiden name. In Yorkshire Gazette, 8 May 1824 she announced sale of business to John Hardy, and expressed thanks for favours conferred upon her during the last thirty years. [Furn. Hist., 1978, pl. 29B]

Doughty, Thomas, address unrecorded, upholder (1715–33). Son of Thomas Doughty, gunsmith of London; app. to Joseph Hudson on 6 April 1715, and admitted freeman of the Upholders' Co. by servitude on 5 September 1733. [GL, Upholders' Co. records]

Doughty, Thomas, Oldham St, Manchester, cm and joiner (1788). [D]

Doughty, William, Gibraltar St, Sheffield, Yorks., chairmaker (1817). [D]

Doughty, William, York, cm (1825). Son of Joseph Doughty, servant, of Kilnwick Percy; app. to John Ellison, cm, on 14 November 1825. [York app. reg.]

Douglas, —, London, chairmaker (1793). Subscribed to Sheraton's Drawing Book, 1793.

Douglas, —, London. Supplied a set of dining tables to Alexander Wedderburn costing £25 4s in 1794. [Scottish RO, GD 164/Box 20/177/2–3]

Douglas, —, address unrecorded, cm (1803). Subscribed to Sheraton's Cabinet Dictionary, 1803.

Douglas, Adam, Egypt St, Liverpool, cm and u (1835–39). Trading at no. 3 in 1835; no. 7 in 1837; and no. 13 in 1839. [D]

Douglas, Archibald, Clerkenwell, London, cm (1776). Insured houses for £1,000 with Thomas Richardson, carpenter, in 1776. [GL, Sun MS vol. 248, ref. 368905]

Douglas, Daniel, Bedford Ct, Bedford St, London, cm (1782). Took out a Sun Insurance policy in 1782 for £200 of which utensils, stock and goods accounted for £100. [GL, Sun MS vol. 301, p. 611]

Douglas, Daniel, 19 Mercer St, London, cm (1782). Took out a Sun Insurance policy in 1782 for £200 of which utensils, stock and goods accounted for £100. [GL, Sun MS vol. 298, p. 312]

Douglas, George, Clothmarket, Newcastle, cm and joiner (1838). [D]

Douglas, J., 9 Bedford Pl., Southampton, Hants., carver and gilder (1834–39). [D]

Douglas (or Dugler), John, Leicester, cm and joiner (1761–69). The John Dugler app. to Joseph Johnson, cm and joiner of Leicester, from 10 October 1761 is probably the John Douglas, admitted freeman on 17 June 1790. Mahogany bureau recorded bearing the words 'John Douglas, Leicester, January 17th 1769' written in pencil on the bottom. [Leicester freemen rolls; Furn. Hist., 1976, pl. 36A]

Douglas, John, Northampton, cm (1784–98). Recorded in Bridge St in 1784 and Sheep St, 1796. [D; poll bks]

Douglas, John, London, chairmaker, cm and upholder (1809–28). Trading at 5 King St, Old St, Islington, 1809–11; 50 Paddington St, Marylebone, 1817–19; and 8 Richmond St, Old St, Islington, 1820–28. [D]

Douglas, John, Whitehaven, Cumb., cm (1828–34). Trading at 6 Church St, 1828–29, and George St, 1829–34. [D]

Douglas, Joseph, 3 Little Peter St, Westminster, London, carver and gilder (1820). [D]

Douglas, Joseph, 9 Bedford Pl., Southampton, Hants., carver and gilder (1830–39). [D]

Douglas, William, 42 Little Sutton St, Clerkenwell, London, chair and sofa manufacturer (1829). [D]

Douglass, Daniel, Hart St, London, cm (1774). [Poll bk]

Douglass, Francis, Portsea, Portsmouth, Hants., cm and upholder (1775). Took out a Sun Insurance policy in 1775 for £1,300 of which utensils and stock accounted for £400. [GL, Sun MS vol. 238, p. 164]

Douglass, James, Claypath, Durham, joiner and cm (1816). Announcement concerning end of partnership with Hopper and continuation of business alone, Durham County Advertiser, 16 March 1816. Added that 'he now has a choice assortment of mahogany dining & claw tables, a variety of chairs & an excellent wardrobe to dispose of.'

Douglass, Robert, Newport, Isle of Wight, Hants., chairmaker (1722). Took app. named Swaine in 1722. [S of G, app. index]

Dounton, S., Kidderminster, Worcs., cm and u (1818–20). [D] Probably Samuel Downton.

Douse, Daniel, at 'The Blue Ball & Star', Snow Hill, London, turner (1724). Named in insurance company records. [Heal]

Douthwaite, Anthony, Newcastle and Bishop Wearmouth, u (1780). App. to William Charnley; admitted freeman on 16 September 1780. Polled at Newcastle of Bishop Wearmouth in that year. [Newcastle freemen reg.]

Douthwaite, Edward, St Gilesgate, Durham, cm (1827). [D]

Douthwaite, John, Finkle St, Malton, Yorks., cm and u (1823). [D]

Douthwaite, William, Smithfield, Stockton-on-Tees, Co. Durham, cm (1832). [D]

Dove, —, 4 Mount Row, Lambeth, London, cm and chair manufacturer (1820). [D]

Dove, Arthur, Pavement, York, cm, u and ironmonger (1823). [D]

Dove, Daniel, Hull, Yorks., cm and chairmaker (1826–39). Trading at 56 Dock St, 1826–31. [D]

Dove, David, 33 Sykes St, Hull, Yorks., cm (1838). [D]

Dove, John, York, carver and gilder (1792–1800). Son of John Dove, musician; app. to William & John Staveley, carvers and gilders, on 26 May 1792. Admitted freeman in 1800. [York app. reg. and freemen rolls]

Dove, Stephen, Charterhouse St, London, cm, u and undertaker (1808–20). Recorded at no. 13 in 1808, and no. 18, 1816–19. [D]

Dover, Charles, 7 Duke St, Bloomsbury, London, carver (1829). [D]

Dover, J., address unrecorded. Provided Nichaolas Pearse of Loughton, Essex, and London, with a music stool, receiving £1 5s on 16 November 1815. [Essex RO, D/DHt A1/4] See W. Dover.

Dover, P. E., 36 Gt Russell St, Bloomsbury, London, auctioneer, u and cm (1837). [D]

Dover, W., address unrecorded. Provided Nicholas Pearse of Loughton, Essex, and Bloomsbury, London, with two hall chairs, receiving £2 15s on 26 April 1814. [Essex RO, D/DHt A1/4] See J. Dover.

Dover, William, 6 Newman's Row, Lincoln's Inn Fields, London, cm (1817). [D]

Doverton, George, 7 Percy Mews, Rathbone Pl., London, cm and u (1827–28). [D]

Doveston, George, 106 King St, Manchester, cm and u (1832–40). Listed also at 19 Oxford Rd, 1832–33, with works at Zara St, 1836–40. [D]

Dovey, John, Tallow Hill, Worcester, cm (1812–35). App. to John Timmings cm and u; admitted freeman on 5 October 1812. Named in the Worcester freemen rolls in December 1835.

Dovey, Samuel, Pershaw, Worcs., u and cm (1784). [D]

Dovey, William, St John's, Worcester, with res. at Wick Episcopi, near Worcester, cm (1831). [Poll bk]

Dowbiggen, John, Lancaster, cm (1783). App. to Richard Gillow of Gillow & Co., cm, on 24 September 1783 for £7 10s. [PRO, IRI/32]

Dowbiggin, John, Lancaster, cm (1783–84). [Lancaster freemen rolls, poll bk]

Dowbiggin, Francis, Lancaster, cm (1782–1818). Admitted freeman, 1782–83, and named in the Gillow records, 1787–1818. [Lancaster freemen rolls; Westminster Ref. Lib., Gillow]

Dowbiggin, Thomas, Lancaster, cm and varnisher (b. 1738–d. 1811). Polled at Lancaster in 1784. Named in the Gillow records, 1800–09, as a varnisher and working on a wardrobe in 1809. Admitted freeman, 1806–07. Death aged 73 reported, *Liverpool Mercury*, 4 October 1811. [Lancaster freemen rolls; Westminster Ref. Lib., Gillow vol. 344/98,

p. 1621; 99, p. 1857] Probably two craftsmen of the same name, one of which may have been:

Dowbiggin(g) (or Dowbiggen), Thomas, Mount St, London, Royal cm and u (b. 1788–d. 1854). After long neglect, Dowbiggin has at last come to light as probably the most highly reputed and successful cm of the 2nd quarter of the 19th century. He headed a celebrated and prosperous furniture, decorating and building business, and was a pioneer in establishing Mount St as the most fashionable cm centre of Victorian London. He was patronized by the Royal Household and some of the most important families of the country; and was succeeded by another successful Victorian firm, Holland & Sons, who collaborated with him during his final years and eventually leased his premises in 1851. The two firms continued to act independently, but Dowbiggin's increasing age and lack of a direct successor in the family encouraged the close association with Holland's firm, which by Dowbiggin's death in 1854 was absorbing and settling the older firm's commitments. Dowbiggin's reputation was such that Holland & Sons are listed in directories under Dowbiggin's name until as late as 1895. 'Holland, late Dowbiggin' can be found in later Victorian references. It was even used on the furniture bills connected with the opening of Parliament in 1901 and the Coronation of Edward VII in 1902. Dowbiggin's origins are obscure. Frederick Litchfield in his *Illustrated History of Furniture*, 1892, states that 'Dowbiggin, founder of the firm of Holland & Sons, was an apprentice of Richard Gillow', but this assertion is not backed by evidence from the Gillow records. The earliest firm date is 1816, when London directories give Dowbiggin's name and address at 128 Mount St. He is listed at no. 12 in 1821, and nos 22, 23 and 25 from 1823–39, and remained at no. 23 until his retirement, c. 1852–54. In association with Holland & Sons, Dowbiggin leased property in Adam Mews, Hanover Sq., from the Earl of Grosvenor in 1821. This reversionary lease, preserved amongst other related legal documents in the V & A Museum, was for fifty-two years. In 1830 Dowbiggin renewed his lease of the Mount St premises from the Earl. Sun Insurance policies show that the premises in Adam Mews were a workshop and warehouse. Dowbiggin insured stock, utensils and goods there on 10 February 1820 for £2,200; on 14 February 1821 for £2,700; on 27 December 1821 for £3,000; and on 24 January 1822 for £5,000. He insured his house and goods for £1,490 on 5 June 1822. Clearly prospering financially, Dowbiggin's reputation was also flourishing. In 1831 he was recommended with Gillow by the Select Committee appointed by Parliament to investigate the excessive charges of Morel & Seddon, the firm responsible for the refurnishing of Windsor Castle for George IV. Dowbiggin and Gillow were to give a 'fair trade price' for the furniture. Dowbiggin declined the invitation, but was paid for his trouble. His prosperity is witnessed by his purchase, in 1833, of Bute House in the fast-growing fashionable area of Brompton. Bute House had been built in the Italian taste by James, brother of Robert Adam, for his own occupation. Sold in 1782, it was later owned by the 1st Marquis of Bute between 1795–c. 1804, hence its name. Dowbiggin may have lived in the house himself for a time, but by 1841 it was occupied by Viscount Ingestre, and demolished, 1845–46. Dowbiggin laid out Bute St in its grounds between 1846–48; and between 1843–50 was engaged on other building projects in the Grosvenor Sq. area. A much respected figure, Dowbiggin was appointed an adviser on furniture and upholstery for the Great Exhibition, 1851. Both he and Holland exhibited, separately, and were awarded medals for their novel furniture using unusual new timbers and painted china decoration. Dowbiggin appears to have spent his last years at Abercorn Lodge, St John's Wood, since payments by him for upholstery work there are recorded in Holland's Sales Journal, 1849–54. He died in 1854, and his obituary in the March issue of the *Gents Mag.* read: 'January 6. At Abercorn Lodge, St. John's Wood, aged 65, Thomas Dowbiggin, Esq., head of the late eminent firm of Dowbiggin and Son, cabinet makers and upholsterers, Mount-street, Grosvenor Square'. [D; E. T. Joy, unpublished notes at the V & A; *Burlington*, May 1910, p. 349, and 1954, p. 393; *Furn. Hist.*, 1970, pp. 43–45, 1972, p. 7, note 60, and p. 9, note 78; GL, Sun MS vol. 483, ref. 962849; vol. 488, ref. 976465; vol. 493, refs 987146, 987497 and 993006; *Survey of London*, vol. 38, pp. 16–17] Holland's Sales Journal, 1849–54, lists some of Dowbiggin's clients, including Lady Cardigan, Lord Winchelsea and Lord Casterleagh, but details of work are not given. Documented commissions are as follows:

BURTON CONSTABLE, Yorks. Dowbiggin's name appears among the firms engaged on the refurnishing, after Sir Clifford Constable's succession to the house in the early 1820s. Other well-known London firms engaged in the house were Miles & Edwards and Charles Hindley. [*Furn. Hist.*, 1972]

APSLEY HOUSE, London. From 1825 Dowbiggin was in charge of refurnishing Apsley House, during its alteration by Benjamin Dean Wyatt, for the Duke of Wellington. A bill from Dowbiggin for work there is preserved in the Wellington archives at Stratfield Saye, the Duke's country seat in Hampshire. Dated 1826, it totals £1,553 1s 11d and lists a considerable amount of cleaning, repairing, decorating and varnishing, as well as the supply of furniture and upholstery. Upholstery accounted for most of the bill, and some expensive materials were used, such as 470 yards of gold silk costing £152 15s. On 30 October 1829 Benjamin Wyatt wrote to the Duke: 'Mr. Dowbiggin has mentioned to me what Your Grace desired him to say concerning three large looking-glasses. I certainly think they would be a great acquisition to the Room [Waterloo Gallery] with frames in character with the rest of the decorations. Mr. Dowbiggin also mentioned to me that Your Grace had some idea of hanging the walls of the Gallery with yellow damask.' Dowbiggin continued working for the Duke at Apsley House until the early 1850s, and, with Holland, undertook the Duke's funeral in 1852. The bulk of the arrangements, however, seem to have been handled by Holland's, who by 1853 had taken over completely Dowbiggin's position as cm to the Duke. [Hist. MS Commission Report, Ashburnham 1000, bk f46, 1085–91]

WYNYARD PARK, Co. Durham. Dowbiggin & Co. are named in the accounts of 1820 regarding furnishing the new hall for the Marquis of Londonderry. [Durham RO, D/LO/E484, 1 vol. 1829–41]

DRUMMOND CASTLE, Tayside, Scotland. Lord Gwydir, Lord Willoughby de Eresby, appears to have been one of Dowbiggin's most notable patrons, buying much clearly sumptuous furniture from him between 1823–31, some of which was for Drummond Castle, and some for Grimsthorpe, Lincs. Bills do not always specify, however, where work was done. In July 1823 the firm fitted a mahogany staircase for £59 12s, and supplied 'A Mahogany French Bedstead with Stuffed Ends, Reeded Legs & Castors, French Polished', costing £5 18s. In March 1825 they received £43 1s 2d for fitting silvered-glass plates into Drawing Room doors. A bill of February–October 1825 specified that items were to be sent to Drummond Castle, and included 'A Mahogany Escarte Table of fine Woods, French Polished, Lined with Crimson Cloth', and looking-glasses in carved frames 'gilt in matt and burnished gold'.

A long bill of 1826 totalling £341 14s 7d is for repairs, alterations and making window drapes, and lists green silk, leather and velvet; also 'Yellow Gros de Naples' drapes with Parisian fringe 'for piers in the ante room'. Other items on the bill include 'A Handsome Carved Frame Gilt in Matt and Burnished Gold for Plate', with a richly carved and gilt pediment, costing £67 19s; and 'A Montague Chair with Carved Legs, Japan'd White & Burnished Gold', covered in green silk and costing £11 0s 7d.

Between May and June 1829 Dowbiggin worked for Lord Willoughby 'for Piccadilly', submitting a bill totalling £55 1s 6d. Items described included Italian walnut chairs, 'Montague' chairs with white and gold legs, covered with crimson 'taffety' and finished with silk cord; and 'A Large Handsome Sofa with Richly Carved Elbows and Legs Finished White and Gold Stuffed in the Best Manner in Fine Linen', costing £23. Lord Willoughby's accounts, specified for Grimsthorpe, from 3–6 June 1829 total £335 17s 1d and record payments to Dowbiggin for two chests of drawers, £50; and various wall hangings including 'Blue India Silk Damask for the Drawing Room Walls', £63; and 'Gold Coton India Damask for the Duchess of Suffolks Bedroom', £57. A set of Spanish mahogany dining tables 'of Fine Wood on Sliding Frames, Reeded Legs' cost £64. The accounts for 4 July–17 October 1829 describe further notable purchases made for Drummond Castle, including 'A Handsome Mahogany French Bedstead Richly Carved of Fine Wood', £26 12s; walnut conversation chairs, richly-carved mahogany elbow chairs, various ottomans, three 'with Mahogany Pedestal Ends of Fine Wood French Polished Stuff'd in the Best Manner & Covered with your Persian Carpet, the Bolsters with Green Morocco and Fine Green Cloth Border', £39; '2 Handsome Mahogany Wash Tables with Shaped Tops and Legs Richly Carved & French Polished' with marble slabs, £41; and on 6 October 'An Antique Bedstead with Carved Footboard & Turned Foot Pillars, Strong Tester Frame and Large Cornice Covered with Crimson Velvet', £39 10s. The last known bill from Dowbiggin to Lord Willoughby is for June–July 1831, and includes 'A Large Chinese Commode Mounted with Brass, 3 Drawers Enclosed by Doors with Marble Slab on the Top', costing £10; and an ottoman covered with blue silk damask, £20 6s. During the years 1823–31 Lord Willoughby bought furniture from Dowbiggin totalling in the region of £1,300. [Lincoln RO, 2 ANC 6/202/45–46 and 59;

AUDLEY END, Essex, **BILLINGBEAR**, Berks., or Lord Braybrooke's London house. In October 1827 Dowbiggin received £8 4s for a screen. [Essex RO, D/DBy/A 361]

STAFFORD HOUSE, London. In 1838 Dowbiggin supplied 'new furniture' costing £95. [Staffs. RO, D593/R/1/26/8]

WREST PARK, Beds. Much furniture provided for Earl de Grey in 1839. [*C. Life*, 2 July 1970, p. 21]

ASHBURNHAM PLACE, Sussex, and the Earl of Ashburnham's London house in Upper Grosvenor St. Three sets of accounts, now in the E. Sussex RO, show that the firm carried out cleaning, repairing, painting, woodworking, plumbing and bricklaying, as well as supplying furniture and fitting carpets and curtains, between July 1837 and December 1840. The first bill, for work done between July 1837 and July 1838, amounted to £722 12s 6d (receipted 17 September 1838). The second bill, covering January 1839 to December 1814, came to £200 0s 11d (receipted 5 May 1842). These two bills are almost entirely concerned with work in the London house. The third and largest bill, amounting to £1,236 13s 5d (not receipted) was for work at Ashburnham Place between May and August 1840. There seem to be few pieces of exceptional cost or importance among the furniture in the bills. The most expensive single item is a wainscot bookcase of five compartments made for Ashburnham Place in 1840 for £89. Items such as a 'couch with scroll ends' and a 'Grecian couch' suggest that the furniture was generally in the late Regency 'Grecian' classical style. The earliest bill gives more details of furniture than the other two, and shows that the firm followed the prevailing fashion of using woods which were considered particularly 'suited to the purpose to which each apartment is intended', as Henry Whitaker expressed it in his *Treasury of Designs*, 1847. Two bedrooms described in detail rang the changes on mahogany, oak and birch. The 'Back Drawing Room' was furnished in mahogany. In the Library, most of the furniture was in fashionable oak, which Whitaker described as 'the most quiet wood' for the room which 'should have an air of quiet and repose'. In the Dining Room mahogany predominated, while the Drawing Room had practically all rosewood, with mention of some satinwood and zebrawood. The third bill refers to the graining of wood, which had been growing in fashion since the early years of the century when the French wars seriously disrupted timber imports and encouraged methods of imitating woods. In the Library at Ashburnham Place, £23 was charged for '92 yds windows, doors, lining etc. 5 oils grained oak and twice varnished with copal @ 5s.' Two guineas were charged for oak-graining six dozen sash frames; and £8 for '32 yds to painting outside of Bookcase 4 times in oil, grained Oak and twice varnished', in the Small Dining Room. One specialist grainer was apparently employed. The grained oak of the Ashburnham accounts was most probably imitation pollard oak which became very fashionable according to the most important trade manual of the time, Nathaniel Whittock's *The Decorative Painter and Glazier's Guide*, first published in 1827, and reissued in 1828, 1832 and 1841. A red damask bed, window curtains, pelmet cornice, valances and a sofa supplied by Dowbiggin to Ashburnham are now at Basildon House, Berks. [E. Sussex RO, ASH 1085, 1087, 1089; *C. Life*, 19 May 1977]

WINDSOR CASTLE & BUCKINGHAM PALACE. Dowbiggin's name appears among the seven firms which submitted tenders for supplying furniture in the Louis XV style for the Ball Room at Windsor for George IV. [*Furn. Hist.*, 1972] Dowbiggin received commissions from the Queen at the beginning of her reign, and had the distinction of making the State Throne in 1837 at a cost of £1,187. The firm supplied furniture to Windsor Castle and upholstery for Buckingham Palace between 1837–50; and from about 1845 the names of the firms of Dowbiggin and Holland are first found linked together in connection with the furnishing of Osborne House, Isle of Wight, for the Queen. At the same period Dowbiggin was working alone at Holkham Hall, Norfolk, showing that the two firms were still independent at this time. The last reference to Dowbiggin in the Lord Chamberlain's accounts of work done for the Royal family is in 1853. [H. Clifford Smith, *Buckingham Palace*, p. 147]   A. E.

Dowden, Andrew, 24 New Church Ct, London, cm and u (1827–28). [D]

Dowden, Robert, Wincanton, Som., cm (1798). [D]

Dowel, Richard, Sunderland, Co. Durham, cm (1803–29). Recorded at George St, 1828–29. Subscribed to Sheraton's *Cabinet Dictionary*, 1803. [D] Possibly of:

Dowel & Renwick, Sunderland, Co. Durham, cm (1798). [D]

Dowglass, Joseph, Angel Ct, Strand, London, carver and gilder 1781). Took out a Sun Insurance policy in 1781 for £200 of which utensils, stock and goods accounted for £40. [GL, Sun MS vol. 289, p. 361]

Dowing, James, Charlotte Row, Gt Yarmouth, Norfolk, furniture warehouseman (1805). [D]

Dowler, John, Church St, Leamington, Warks., cm (1828–37).

Recorded at Church St, 1828–30, and Regent Pl., Bath St, 1835–37. [D]

Dowler, John, Brook St, Warwick, u (1831). [Poll bk]

Dowler, William, Brook St, Warwick, cm and u (1828–35). Recorded also at Woodhouse St, 1831. Vote tendered in Warwick poll of 1831, but disallowed. [D]

Dowler & Son, High St, Warwick, cm (1822). [D]

Dowling, John, 24 Portpool (or Pierpool) Lane, Hatton Gdn, London, upholder, cm and carpenter (1770–93). Trading as Dowling & Sons from 1781. Took out a Sun Insurance policy in 1782 for £1,200, utensils and stock accounting for £260. [D; GL, Sun MS vol. 302, p. 604]

Down(e), William, Truro, Cornwall, cm and carpenter (1797). Took app. named Peter Burd, aged *c.* 14, on 10 June 1797 for £40. [Cornwall RO, DDGR 715]

Down & Delatouche, 34 Redcliff Hill, Bristol, cm (1827). [D]

Down & Stone, 125 Gt Portland St, London, cm and u (1839). [D]

Downard (or Donnard), Henry, Mt Pleasant Terr., Tunbridge Wells, Kent, u (1838–39). [D]

Downes, —, 88 Curtain Rd, Shoreditch, London, carver and gilder (1820). [D]

Down(e)s, Edward, Bridgnorth, Salop, cm (1759–98). Took app. named Bubb in 1759. [D; S of G, app. index] Possibly:

Downes, Edward snr, High St (or High Town), Bridgnorth, Salop, cm (1822–28). [D]

Downes, Edward William, 18 Chenies St, Bedford Sq., London, carver and gilder (1835–39). [D]

Downes, J.(?), 20 Flower and Dean St, Spitalfields, London, bedstead maker (1839). [D]

Downes, Sarah, 6 Manor Row, Little Tower Hill, London, turner (1808). [D]

Downham, Joseph, Bury, Lancs., joiner and cm (1816–34). Addresses given in Millgate, 1816; Bury Lane, 1818; and Union St, 1834. [D]

Downie, Alexander, Groat Mkt, Newcastle, cm (1824). [D]

Downie, Robert, 26½ Crescent St, Euston Sq., London, cm and u (1839). [D]

Downing, —, address unrecorded. On 5 September 1812 supplied a pair of dressing tables, costing £5 5s to Erddig, Clwyd. [V & A archives]

Downing, —, address unrecorded, cabinet manufacturer (1830). Named in the Royal Archives, Windsor in April 1830 being paid £36 for a Belvedere.

Downing, Amos, 2 Duke St, Devonport, Devon, carver and gilder (1838). [D]

Downing, E., 48 Lambeth Marsh, London, chairmaker (1817). [D] See William Downing.

Downing, George R., Bridewell Lane, Bristol, carver and gilder (1823–24). [D]

Downing, Henry Shuckforth, Market Pl., Stowmarket, Suffolk, cm and toy dealer (1830). [D]

Downing, J., Stowmarket, Suffolk, cm (1809). Notice in *Ipswich Journal*, 17 June 1809. Possibly:

Downing, James, Market Pl., Stowmarket, Suffolk, cm and furniture broker (1830). [D]

Downing, John, 37 New Montague St, Brick Lane, London, chair and sofa maker (1839). [D]

Downing, Jos., Norwich, chairmaker (1787). App. to William Rullidge; admitted freeman on 3 May 1787. [Norwich freemen reg.]

Downing, Joseph, Freeth St, Oldbury, near Birmingham, cm, u and joiner (1830). [D]

Downing, William, Gibraltar St, Sheffield, Yorks., chairmaker (1797–1820). Recorded at no. 41, 1797–1817, and no. 38, 1818–20. [D]

Downing, William, 46 Lower Marsh, Lambeth, London, cm (1817–29). [D] See E. Downing.

Downs, Michael, Piccadilly, London, u (d. 1798). Death reported, *Gents Mag.*, April 1798.

Downs, Richard, Shaftesbury, Dorset, cm and builder (1823–40). Trading at Bimport in 1823 and High St, 1830–40. [D]

Downton, Samuel, Kidderminster, Worcs., cm and u (1818–35). Trading at High St, 1818–22 and Coventry St, 1828–35. Probably S. Dounton.

Dowsett, John, Conduit St, Chelmsford, Essex, cm (1839). [D]

Dowsing, J., Low Barclay St, Ipswich, Suffolk, chair and sofa manufacturer (1839). [D]

Dowsing, William, 2 St Anne's Ct, Bath, Som., cm (1826). [D]

Dowthwaite, John, Howe End, Kirbymoorside, Yorks., cm and joiner (1840). [D]

Dowthwaite, William, New Malton, Yorks., cm (1789). Son of John Dowthwaite, deceased; admitted freeman in 1789. [York freemen rolls]

Dowyer, —, address unrecorded, carver (1730–32). Worked for Benjamin Mildmay, Earl Fitzwalter, receiving £101 9s 4d on 11 November 1730; £10 10s for carving at Moulsham Hall on 1 May 1731; and £6 12s on 19 January 1732. [A. C. Edwards, *The Accounts of Benjamin Mildmay Earl Fitzwalter*] Possibly:

Dowyer, John, next to 'The Castle Tavern', Drury Lane, London, carver (1720). Insured goods and merchandise in his house on 27 January 1720 with the Sun Co. [GL, Sun MS vol. 10, ref. 16460]

Doyle, Mrs, 68 Bridgewater St, Liverpool, u (1829). [D]

Doyle, Charles, 36 Vauxhall Rd, Liverpool, cm (1813–14). [D]

Doyle, James, 32 Tabernacle Row, City Rd, London, chair and sofa maker (1839). [D]

Doyle, Michael, London, bedstead maker (1829–35). Trading at 15 Berwick St, Soho in 1829 and 12 Broad St, Golden Sq., 1835. [D]

Doyle, Robert, 3 Grenville St, Liverpool, cm (1807). [D]

Doyle, William, Beverley, Yorks., cm (1784). [Poll bk] Probably:

Doyle, William, Hull, Yorks., cm (1790). [Beverley poll bk]

Doyle, William, 31 Betts St, Ratcliff, London, cm and u (1839). [D]

Doyley, —, address unrecorded, u (1696). Named in the Earl of Rockingham's accounts in August 1696 receiving 18s 5d for a bed and quilt. [Lincoln RO, Monson 10/1/A/19]

Drabble, James, Carlton in Lindrick, Notts., cm and joiner (1832). [D]

Dracot, James, Lambeth Rd, St George's Fields, London, carver and gilder (1808). [D]

Dracott, Joseph, George St, Hastings, Sussex, carver and gilder (1823). [D]

Dracott, Jos., 13 Gibson St, Lambeth, London, carver and gilder (1826–27). [D]

Drake, H., 102 Hanover St, Bristol, cm (1838–40). [D]

Drake, Henry Robert, 6 Margaret Pl., Hackney Fields, London, cm and u (1839). [D]

Drake, John, Ripon, Yorks., cm (1798). [D]

Drake, John, 54 Upper North Pl., Gray's Inn Rd and 25 Chichester Pl., London, cm and u (1839). [D] Probably J. Drane.

Drake, Joseph, Snaith, Yorks., cm (1798). [D]

Drake, Joseph, 45a Queen Anne St, Cavendish Sq., London, cm and broker (1823). Took out a Sun Insurance policy on 21 August 1823 for £700 of which utensils and stock accounted for £500. [GL, Sun MS vol. 498, ref. 1006716]

Drake, Richard, address unrecorded, u (1671). Worked for the 5th Earl of Bedford being paid in December 1671 for 'Five bed ticks without the bolster', £4 15s; and 'For filling the five beds', 5s. [Bedford Office, London]

Drake, Richard, Bedford St, Covent Gdn, London, u (1768). Declared bankrupt, *Gents Mag.*, September 1768.

Drake, Richard, Taunton, Som., carver and gilder (1798). [D]

Drake, Richard, 2 St Andrew's Chancery St, Norwich, cm (1798–1803). [D]

Drake, Thomas, Petergate, York, cm (1774–84). [Poll bks]

Drake, Thomas, 7 Club Row, Church St, Bethnal Green, London, carpenter, cm and broker (1821). Took out a Sun Insurance policy on 24 May 1821 for £300 of which utensils and stock accounted for £150. [GL, Sun MS vol. 485, ref. 980651]

Drakeford, John & Price, Richard F., Birmingham (1815–21). Signed and dated a leather-covered pinewood work or jewellery box with stamped gilt metal mounts. [*Apollo*, April 1961, p. 100, illus.]

Drakeford, John, Most Row, Birmingham, cabinet case maker (1839). [D]

Drane, J., 25 Chichester Pl., Gray's Inn Rd, London, cm (1835). [D]. Probably John Drake.

Drape, Thomas, Lancaster (1789–1804). App. at Gillows in 1789, and admitted freeman, 1795–96. Named in the Gillow records, 1790–1804. [Lancaster app. reg. and freemen rolls; Westminster Ref. Lib., Gillow records]

Drape, Thomas, Thomas St, Salford, Lancs., cm (1808–09). [D]

Draper, Giffard, Easterton, Wilts., chairmaker (1751). Son of William Draper; app. to John Cheater jnr, chairmaker of Easterton, on 7 October 1751 for £1. [*Wilts. Apps and their Masters*]

Draper, James, 17 St John's Lane (or Sq.), West Smithfield, London, carver and gilder (1789–93). [D]

Draper, James, Sherrard St, Middlx, cm (1802). Declared bankrupt, *Billinge's Liverpool Advertiser*, 11 December 1802.

Draper, John, at 'The Duke of Marlborough', Wendover, Bucks., victualler and u (1724). Insured his goods and merchandise for £300 on 10 July 1724 with the Sun Co. [GL, Sun MS vol. 17, ref. 32396]

Draper, John, Lombard St, Chelsea, London, cm and broker (1777). Took out a Sun Insurance policy in 1777 for £300 of which £200 accounted for utensils, stock and goods. [GL, Sun MS vol. 254, p. 536]

Draper, John, corner of Queen St, Redcross St, Southwark, London, cm and broker (1777). Took out a Sun Insurance policy in 1777 for £300, utensils, stock and goods accounting for £100. [GL, Sun MS vol. 263, p. 119]

Draper, John, Bridge St, Deritend, Birmingham, carver and gilder (1793). [D]

Draper, Thomas & Co. Lower Moorfields, London, u, cm, appraiser and undertaker (1752–1811). Recorded at 'The Key & Plow', corner of Dagget's Ct, 1769–71; no. 25 Broker's Row, 1784–1804; nos 23–24, 1806–11; and Broker Row, Finsbury, 1802–03. Son of Thomas Draper, clothier of London; app. to William Guidott on 15 March 1752 and admitted freeman of the Upholders' Co. by servitude on 5 April 1759. Invoices sent to a Mr Gordon, dated 19 December 1769 for a mahogany desk, £7 17s 6d, and 10 November 1771 for a writing desk and stool, £1 7s 6d, are on the reverse of his trade card which reads: 'THOMAS DRAPER, Cabinet-maker, Upholder and Appraiser; AT THE KEY and PLOW, the Corner of Daggets-Court in Lower Moorfields, LONDON. BUYS, SELLS, and APPRAISES all kinds of Household Furniture, Second-hand and New. LIKEWISE Executes all ORDERS respecting the UPHOLSTERY and CABINET Branches, in a genteel MANNER with DISPATCH . . .'. He also sold musical instruments and furnished funerals. [BM; GL, trade card coll.] Took out a Sun Insurance policy in 1781 for £200 on his house. Probably the Draper, u, of Broker Row named in Sheraton's list of master cabinet makers, 1803. [D; GL, Upholders' Co. records; GL, Sun MS vol. 296, p. 509]

Draper, Thomas, 4 Queen St, Southwark, London, chairmaker and japanner (1802–37). Named in Sheraton's list of master cabinet makers, 1803. [D]

Drawbridge, David, Lewes, Sussex, u (1832–39). Addresses given at 71 High St, 1832; St Mary's Lane, 1837; and 69 High St, 1839. [D; poll bks]

Draycon, James, Globe Lane, Chatham, Kent, cm (1838). [D]

Draycon, Robert, Globe Lane, Chatham, Kent, cm and u (1839). [D] Probably Robert Drayton.

Draycott, —, address unrecorded, u (1773). Named in the private accounts of Richard Hoare of Boreham House, Essex on 12 October 1773 receiving £1 12s 6d. [Essex RO, D/Du 649/2]

Draycott, Frederick, 27 Duke St, Bloomsbury, London, carver and gilder (1835–39). [D]

Draycott, James, 329 Oxford St, London, u (1790). [D]

Draycott, John, 8 St Martin's Lane, London, cm (1776). Took out a Sun Insurance policy in 1776 for £300 of which utensils, stock and goods accounted for £200. [GL, Sun MS vol. 244, p. 503]

Draycott, John, 39 Oxford St, London, cm (1776–84). Took out a Sun Insurance policy in 1776 for £900 of which utensils, stock and goods accounted for £500, workshop and sawpit, £200. [GL, Sun MS vol. 249, p. 75; poll bk] Possibly:

Draycot(t), John, 329 Oxford St, London, cm and u (1781–94). James Draycott recorded at this address in 1790. [D]

Draysdale, Elias, Old Gath, Old Foundry, Hull, Yorks., veneer cutter (1838–39). [D]

Drayson, John, Sittingbourne, Kent, cm (1824). [D]

Drayton, Edmund, London, upholder, cm and undertaker (1790–1808). Trading at 46 Rotherhithe St, 1790–93; 368 King Stairs, Rotherhithe, 1803; and 130 Fenchurch St, 1808. Took out a Sun Insurance policy on 23 March 1791 for £1,000 of which £200 accounted for utensils and stock. [D; GL, Sun MS vol. 375, p. 634]

Drayton, Richard, 9 St Mary Rotherhithe, London, upholder (1765). Took out a Hand in Hand Insurance policy in February 1765 for £225. [GL, Hand in Hand MS vol. 102]

Drayton, Robert, Globe Lane, Chatham, Kent, cm and u (1840). [D] Probably Robert Draycon.

Drew, Daniel, 94 Shoe Lane, London, cm (1824). Took out a Sun Insurance policy on 25 March 1824 for £100. [GL, Sun MS vol. 497, ref. 1016160]

Drew, Daniel, London, cm and u (1835–39). Trading at 11 Orange St, Red Lion Sq. in 1835, and 134 St John St Rd, 1839. [D]

Drew, James, Exeter, Devon, carver and gilder (1820). Son James bapt. at St David's Church on 31 January 1820. [PR (bapt.)]

Drew, John, Little Poulteney St, London, bedjoiner (1774). [Poll bk]

Drew, John, 43 Lignorpond St, London, upholder (1790). [D]

Drew, John, Sims's Alley, Bristol, carpenter, joiner and cm (1805–07). [D]

Drew, Robert, Andover, Hants., cm and u (1830–39). Recorded at Market Pl. in 1830 and High St in 1839. [D]

Drew, Samuel, Wakefield, Yorks., cm and/or u (1834–37). Trading in partnership with Richard Drew in Westgate, 1837. [D] See William Drew.

Drew, William, Poole, Dorset, joiner, cm and auctioneer (1777–98). Took out a Sun Insurance policy in 1777 for £300 of which utensils and stock accounted for £160. [D; GL, Sun MS vol. 260, p. 401]

Drew, William, Bawtry, Notts., cm (1788). Probate dated 17 July 1788. [Notts. RO, probate records]

Drew, William, Wakefield, Yorks., cm and u (1794–1837). Recorded in Northgate, 1794–96; Westgate, 1798–1837. Submitted three bills for small articles, upholstery and jobbing work to Godfrey Wentworth of Woolley Hall, Yorks., in 1794 for £17 15s 6d; in 1795 for £98 1s 3d; and in 1796 for £78 6s 5½d, including £16 for 'A Mahogany Warde Robe', and £6 16s 6d for 'A Large size 4 poster Bed Stead'. [D; YAS, Wentworth papers, MD 272/2] See Samuel Drew.

Drewett, William, Petworth, Sussex, cm and stationer (1784). [D]

Drewey, John, Hull, Yorks., upholder (1780–84). [Poll bks]

Drewry (or Drewery), Benjamin, Nottingham, joiner and cm (1822–39). Trading at Warsergate in 1828 in partnership with William Drewery; and at 17 Plumtree St in 1832. Joint master with John and William Drewry of Edward Killingley, 1822–25; Richard Lowater, 1825; and Joseph Beardsley, 1839. [D; Nottingham app. list]

Drewry, John, Nottingham, joiner and cm (1822–39). See Benjamin Drewry.

Drewry, Jonathan, Cockermouth, Cumb., joiner and cm (d. by 1808). Named in death duty registers relating to wills, 12 December 1808. [Deanery of Copeland, Cumb.]

Drewry (or Drewery), William, Nottingham, joiner and cm (1822–39). Trading at Plumtree St in 1828, no. 17 in 1832. [D] See Benjamin Drewry.

Dricey, George, High Wycombe, Bucks., chairmaker (1835). Son bapt. in 1835. [PR (bapt.)]

Dring, Draper, Hull, Yorks., and London, carver and gilder (1792–1802). Recorded at High St, Hull, 1792–93; and polled at Hedon, Yorks., of London, in 1802. [D; poll bk] See William Clark & Dring.

Dring, Samuel, address unrecorded, cm (1803). Subscribed to Sheraton's *Cabinet Dictionary*, 1803.

Dringwall, Patrick, Charing Cross, London, upholder (1784). [D]

Drinkwater, Eliza, 37 Portland St, Manchester, u (1840). [D]

Drinkwater, George, Over, Middlewich, Cheshire, cm (1828–34). [D]

Drinkwater, James, Dyre's St, Hulme, Manchester, u (1817). [D]

Drinkwater, James, Birkenhead, Cheshire, cm (1839–40). Trading at 59 Chester St in 1839. Marriage to Miss Robinson of Liverpool on 28 July 1840 reported in *Chester Chronicle and North Wales Advertiser*, 31 July. [D]

Driver, John, Thomas St, Bristol, cm, u and furniture broker (1810–40). Trading at no. 131 in 1810; as John & Matthew at nos 16 and 128–30 from 1812–21; alone at nos 128–30, 1822–23; nos 128–32 from 1824–40; with factory at no. 118 from 1830–40. [D]

Driver, Richard, Thomas St, Bristol, cm, u, broker and carpet maker (1793–1810). Trading at no. 16 when he advertised in *Farley's Bristol Journal*, 17 March 1798, thanking the public for their 'very liberal support received . . . for a series of years'. Announced that 'his STOCK of UPHOLSTERY, CABINET and CARPET GOODS is comparatively extensive, and superbly good and elegant; the whole of which will be disposed of . . . at very reduced prices . . .'. [D]

Driver, Sam., Norwich, u (1759). App. to Isaac Hoyle, u of Norwich, in 1759 for £30. [Norwich app. reg.]

Driver, Thomas, address unrecorded, cm (1748). On 11 May 1748 he supplied the Duke of Gordon with '2 Setts of Mahogany Chaina Dish Stands of Nine in a Sett', costing £2 10s. [Scottish RO, GD 44/33/29/61]

Driver, Thomas, Thornton, Bradford, Yorks., cm (1822–37). [D]

Driver & Satterthwaite, Wellgate, (or Well-fold) Clitheroe, Lancs., joiners, cm, housebuilders etc. (1822–24). [D]

Drummond, James, 29 Russel Ct, St Martin-in-the-Fields, London, cm (1781–91). Declared bankrupt, *Gents Mag.*, December 1781. Took out Sun Insurance policies on 12 April 1787 for £500 on his house, goods and stock; and on 8 April 1791 for £1,100, including £200 for stock and goods in trust at Russel Pl., and a sum on a house at 5 Kennington Pl. [GL, Sun MS vol. 342, ref. 529941]

Drummond, Robert, 120 Long Lane, Bermondsey, London, chair and sofa maker (1826). [D]

Drury, Edmund, Norwich, chair turner (1828). App. to William Hubbard; admitted freeman on 24 February 1828. [Norwich freemen reg.]

Drury, Edward, 41 Church St, Sheffield, Yorks., joiner and cm (1797). [D]

Drury, George, High St, Guildford, Surrey, cm and u (1832–41). Recorded at no. 142 in 1838. [D; poll bks]

Drury, Henry Carey, 15 Smith Buildings, City Rd, London, cm (1824). Took out a Sun Insurance policy on 27 May 1824 for £600 of which utensils and stock accounted for £250. [GL, Sun MS vol. 497, ref. 1017263]

Drury, James, Golden Lion Yd, Leeds, Yorks., cm and joiner (1837). [D]

Drury, James, 8 South Colonade, St Leonards, Sussex, cm (1839). [D]

Drury, John, Tenterden, Kent, cm (1824). [D]

Drury, Joseph, Chatham and Maidstone, Kent, cm (1818–31). Polled at Gt Yarmouth, Norfolk, of Chatham, 1818 and 1820; and of Maidstone, 1831.

Drury, Thomas, London, upholder and cm (1776–93). Trading at 21 St Paul's Churchyard, 1776–77; and 33 Red Lion St, Bloomsbury, 1790–93. [D]

Drury, Thomas, 83 Newgate St, London, cm (1779). Took out a Sun Insurance policy in 1779 for £100, utensils and stock accounting for £5. [GL, Sun MS vol. 275, p. 513]

Drury, Thomas, 97 Arundel St, Sheffield, Yorks., cm (1837). [D]

Dry, Samuel, Smithford St, Coventry, Warks., cm and u (1822–35). [D]

Dry, Thomas, 11 Union Ct, Church Lane, Hull, Yorks., cm (1838–39). [D]

Dry, William, 5 Youls Pl., Old Kent Rd, London, cm and u (1820–28). [D]

Dryden, John, address unrecorded, carver and gilder (1801–07). [DEF; C. Life, 30 April 1948, p. 882]

Dryhurst, James, address unrecorded, carver (1725–62). Worked at Stowe, Bucks., carving the capitals for the summer house in 1725, for which he was paid £62. [Huntington Lib., California, MS ST82, p. 179] For other carving commissions see Beard, *Craftsmen and Interior Decoration*, p. 257.

Drysdale, Daniel, 16 Charles St, Manchester Sq., London, cm etc. (1817–19). [D]

Drysdale, H., 24 Theobalds Rd, London, cm and undertaker (1820). [D]

Drysdale, Henry, 4 Lamb's Conduit St, London, u and cm (1826–39). [D]

Drysdale, John, London, cm (1786). Subscribed to George Richardson's *Treatise on the Five Orders of Architecture* in 1786, to be published the following year.

Drysdale, William, Upper Sans St, Sunderland, Co. Durham, joiner and cm (1828–29). [D]

Duane, Matthew, Lincoln's Inn, London, cm (1773). Made a medal cabinet for Mr Grimston of Yorkshire in 1773. [E. Ingram, *Leaves from a Family Tree*, p. 63]

Dubini, Joseph, at 'The Ship', Little Turnstile, London, picture frame maker (1805). Took out a Sun Insurance policy on 9 January for £200, utensils and stock accounting for £80, and house in tenure of a victualler, £80. [GL, Sun MS vol. 431, ref. 769974]

Dubois, Julian, 22 King St, Soho, London, cm (1790–93). [D]

Du Bois, Lazare, at 'The Clockcase & Cabinet', Compton St, London, cm (1723). Insured goods and merchandise in his house for £500 on 19 August 1723 with the Sun Co. [GL, Sun MS vol. 16, ref. 29683]

Dubourdieu, A. & Clark, Z., at 'The Three Chairs', Cannon St, near the London Stone, London, u, appraisers and undertakers (c. 1740). Trade card shows three cabriole-legged chairs with splat backs, and states that the firm made and sold 'all sorts of Upholsterers goods at the most reasonable Rates. Likewise all sorts of Turky and Persian carpets'. [Banks Coll., BM]

Dubourgh, John, Long Acre, London, carver (1749). [Poll bk]

Duburge, George, 83 Long Acre, London, carver and gilder (1790–93). [D]

Duchemin, George, 7 Fore (or High) St, Exeter, Devon, carver and gilder (1816–26). Retirement and succession in business by J. Fisher announced in *The Alfred*, 4 July 1826. [D]

Duchemin, J., 4 Long Acre, London, carver, gilder and looking-glass manufacturer (1817–19). [D]

Du Chemin, John, Exeter St, Salisbury, Wilts., carver and gilder (1830). [D]

Duchemin, Peter, London, carver, gilder and looking-glass manufacturer (c. 1790–1815). Trade cards of 'Du Chemin' give addresses at 3 Gt Russell St, Bloomsbury, c. 1790, and 130 Long Acre; and directories, 4 Long Acre, 1802–15. Trading at Peter & Son after 1806, and as J. Duchemin after 1817. Three Neo-classical trade cards recorded. [D; Banks Coll., BM; Heal]

Du Chesne, Gideon, address unrecorded, carver (1703–06). Listed as creditor after the death of the 1st Duke of Montagu in 1706, being owed £120 5s 6d for work done at Boughton House, Northants. between 1703–05. Much of this was architectural carving. [V & A archives]

Duchesne, John & Thomas, Camomile St, Bishopsgate, London, cm, u, auctioneers, appraisers and undertakers (1824–28). John recorded at no. 2 in 1824; and with Thomas at no. 21, 1823–28. John took out a Sun Insurance policy on 31 May 1824 for £1,500, stock and utensils in his house accounting for £900. In 1826 he supplied a Mr Angier with a mahogany pedestal sideboard, four-post bedstead and 'skeleton case'. [D; GL, Sun MS vol. 494, ref. 1017416; information from R. A. Moss, Herts.]

Duck, John, 26 Fashion St, Spitalfields, London, cm, u and mathematical case maker (1826–28). [D]

Duckett, William, Norwich, cm (1780–1812). Son of John Duckett, weaver; admitted freeman on 5 February 1780. [Norwich freemen reg.; poll bks]

Duckett, William, Liverpool, cm (1837–39). Trading at 27 Park Rd in 1837 and 19 Jones St, 1839. [D]

Duckitt, Christopher, Gisburn, Yorks., joiner and cm (1816–22). Worked for Lord Ribblesdale, receiving £11 4s 9d in 1816, part of which was for a coffin for Lady Ribblesdale; and £2 2s 9d in 1820. [D; YAS, archives deposit]

Duckworth, Richard, Liverpool, carver and gilder (1837–39). Trading at Albion Pl., Birkett St, 1837, and 5 St Anne's Buildings, 17 Gt Richmond St, 1839. [D]

Duckworth, Thomas, Montague St, Blackburn, Lancs., cm (1834). [D]

Ducroy, Lewis, London, upholder (1741–1802). Recorded in Fleet Mkt, 1778–1802. Son of Lewis Ducroy, victualler of Spitalfields; app. to Samuel Simpson on 22 April 1741, and admitted freeman of the Upholders' Co. by servitude on 5 April 1750. [GL, Upholders' Co. records]

Dudley, Charles, Willow Row, Derby, chairmaker/turner (1829). [D]

Dudley, Francis, Foregate St, Stafford, cm (1818–22). [D]

Dudley, James, Stafford, cm and u (1818–34). Recorded at Pig Mkt, 1818–22 and Vine St in 1834. [D]

Dudley, John, Ct 3, Weaman St, Birmingham, portable desk, cabinet case maker, copying machines (1818–23). [D]

Dudley, John, 4 Prospect Pl., Kingsland Rd, London, chair and sofa maker (1839). [D]

Dudley, Nathaniel, Birmingham, cm (1761–81). Addresses given at 1 New Meeting St, 1767–70; 69 High St, 1773–77; and 8 New St, 1780–81. Took app. named Mase in 1761. On 27 June 1774 commissioned by Boulton & Fothergill, silversmiths, to make a chest for silver objects. On 25 May 1776 the firm supplied Dudley with two sets of mounts for knife cases, and in November 1779 and July 1780 with further mounts. [D; S of G, app. index; Birmingham Lib., Boulton MS letter bk. G, p. 147; ledger 1776–78, p. 103; day bk, 1779–81, p. 28; letter bk 1, p. 611]

Dudley, Thomas, King St, Soho Sq., London, metal ornament and bell-hanging manufactory (1817–20). Trading at no. 34 in 1817 and no. 36 in 1820. Named in the Royal Household accounts on 10 October 1817 supplying an inkstand in bronze and ormolu in the form of the Royal Mortar, costing £37 10s. Regency rosewood Davenport recorded, with pierced gallery; front embellished with a figure of Mercury flanked by two amboyna columns with brass capitals and bases; heavily carved gadrooned base and paw feet; inscribed 'T. DUDLEY, 36 KING ST., SOHO, MARCH 1820'. [PRO, LC11/24; Sotheby's, Los Angeles, 24–27 May 1982, lot 241]

Dudman, John, 37 Temple St, Brighton, Sussex, cm and u (1839). [D]

Duesbery, William, Ct 14, Posterngate, Hull, Yorks., cm (1826). [D]

Dufaur, John, 7 Bell Yd, Temple Bar, London, carver and gilder (1826–27). [D]

Dufautey, Charles, Southampton, Hants., cm and u (1792–1811). Recorded at no. 132, 1792–93. [D]

Duffield (or Duffill), Francis, York, chairmaker (1805–53). Resident at Seagrave's Ct, Micklegate, in 1823. Son of Francis Duffield; app. to George Stones, spindle chairmaker, on 2 May 1805. Admitted freeman in 1814. Recorded in partnership with Richard Baynes, 1824–53, together taking apps named George Johnson on 9 December 1824; Robert Lund, 1 January 1825; Anthony Smith, 1 September 1825; William Waggoner, 2 November 1825; George Brown, 17 March 1827; John Kettlewell, 26 May 1828; John Bellerby, 8 October 1833; John Baynes, 26 February 1834; William Richardson, 3 March 1834; James Jefferson, 14 August 1835; and George Swalewell, 14 August 1835. [D: York app. reg. and freemen rolls] See James & John Duffill.

Duffield (or Duffill), Henry, Portugal St, London, cm (1749). [Poll bk]

Duffield, Thomas, London, cm (1818). [Norwich poll bk]

Duffill, James, res. at St Clement's Pl., York, chairmaker (1837). [D]

Duffill, John, York, u (1809–18). Son of Francis Duffill, chairmaker; app. to Matthew Browne, u, on 27 July 1809. Admitted freeman in 1818. [York app. reg. and freemen rolls]

Diffill, John, 9 Caroline St, Leeds, Yorks., working u (1834–37). Recorded also at 9 Crescent St and West St in 1837. [D]

Duffill, Miles, London, u (1829–37). Addresses given at 17 Wyndham St, Bryanston Sq., 1829; 11 Gt Quebec St, 1835; and 8 Agar St, Strand, 1837. [D]

Duffour, Joseph, London, frame maker, carver and gilder (1737–57). Recorded at Berwick St in 1752. Took app. named Cook in 1743. In 1737 supplied Frederick, Prince of Wales, with a set of twelve frames, costing £97 7s. Provided carved and gilt picture frames to Petworth House, Sussex, between 1752–57. [S of G, app. index; Duchy of Cornwall office, Prince of Wales accounts, vol. 7, pp. 195–96; *Apollo*, May 1977, p. 362; *C. Life*, 25 September 1980, p. 1030] Possibly the predecessor of William Duffour. See René and William Duffour.

Duffour, René, Berwick St, London, carver and gilder. Supplied picture frames for Felbrigg, Norfolk, and Stourhead, Wilts. [*C. Life*, 25 September 1980, p. 1030] Possibly the 'Dufour, frame maker' named in the Felbrigg papers receiving £25 on 29 March 1756. [Norfolk RO, Felbrigg papers, WKC 6/453] Probably René Stone, successor to Duffour.

Duffour, William, Berwick St, London, carver, gilder and papier-mâché maker (c. 1760–84). William and Marrianne Duffour took out a Sun Insurance policy in 1777 for £600, utensils, stock and goods accounting for £200. Polled at Westminster in 1784. [GL, Sun MS vol. 254, p. 632] Almost certainly the W. Duffour whose trade label is recorded on a looking-glass, c. 1775, giving address at 'The Golden Head', 30 Berwick St. [*Antiques*, May 1968, p. 648; *Furn. Hist.*, 1966] Rococo trade label, c. 1760, of Duffour at this address is recorded. Duffour was succeeded by René Stone, probably René Duffour. [Heal] Duffour supplied frames to Longford Castle, Wilts., at about £4 each. [*C. Life*, 26 December 1931, p. 717] Probably the William Duffour who supplied the Duke of Beaufort, for Badminton House, Glos. with 'Two rich Italian picture frames, Two smaller do'. costing £5 17s, on 5 and 28 April 1778. [Badminton papers: account bks]

Du Fort, John, 92 Silk St, Manchester, gilder (1813). [D]

Dugdale, Joseph, Liverpool, carver (1826). App. to John Skillicorn in 1826. [Liverpool app. enrolment bk]

Dugdale, Richard, Blandford Forum, Dorset, cm (1753–55). Took app. named Tiffin in 1753, and Filham in 1755. [S of G, app. index; PRO, 20/89, p. 1925, vol. 10]

Dugdale, Robert & Co., North Rd, Preston, Lancs., carver and gilder (1825). [D]

Dugdello, Abraham, St Martin-in-the-Fields, London, looking-glass maker (1715). Insured a house in Castle St, fronting Green St for £200 on 13 July 1715. [GL, Hand in Hand MS vol. 14, p. 567]

Dugelby, Robert, Jubbergate, York, joiner and cm (1816–26). Took son Robert as app. on 27 January 1826. [D; York app. reg.]

Duggan, John snr and jnr, Kirkgate, Leeds, Yorks., cm and u (1786–d.c. 1794). John snr took out a Sun Insurance policy on 3 April 1786 for £100 on his house and shop, and £400 on utensils, stock and goods in trust and in his warehouse. Advertised in *Leeds Mercury*, 27 June 1786 for cabinet makers who must be 'Sober Men who can work neat', in a business where 'all the different Branches . . . are executed in the neatest manner'. Declared bankrupt, *Derby Mercury*, 29 May 1790; and *Williamson's Liverpool Advertiser*, 18 June 1792. Presumably retired or dead by 1794, when his son, John Duggan jnr advertised, *Leeds Mercury*, 19 April 1794, 'that he has entered the premises lately occupied by his father . . . and has also entered into the Appraising and Auctioneering Line', which aspect is given more emphasis in later advertisements. [GL, Sun MS vol. 337, p. 90]

Duke, Bartholomew, Chester, cm (1784). Son of Thomas Duke, wetglover; admitted freeman on 1 April 1784. Polled as resident of Linnen Hall St in 1784. [Chester freemen rolls]

Duke, Henry & Simpson, 14 Hanley St, Liverpool, chairmakers (1839). [D]

Duke, John, Liverpool, cm (1823–39). Addresses given at

14 McKee St, 1823; no. 5 in 1827; 15 Epworth St, 1829; 21 Gt Charlotte St, 1834; 48 Devon St, 1834–35; 6 Parr St, 1837; and 23 Clare St, with shop at 49 Hatham St, 1839. [D]

Duke, Robert, Harwich, Essex, cm (1758). Took app. named Knights in 1758. [S of G, app. index]

Duke, Robert, Church St, Gateshead, Co. Durham, joiner and cm (1811). [D]

Duke, William, Lancaster. Named in the Gillow records in 1818–19 working on bookcases. [Westminster Ref. Lib., Gillow vol. 344/100, pp. 2084 and 3020]

Duke, William, Soutergate, Ulverston, Lancs., cm and u (1834). [D]

Duke & Ashburner, Brook St, Ulverston, Lancs., cm (1829). [D]

Dukes, John, 11 Barr St, Birmingham, fancy box, case and caddy maker (1835). [D]

Dulley, Henry, Wooburn, Bucks., chairmaker (1830). [D]

Dummer, Robert, 120 Long Lane, London, chair and sofa maker (1827–28). [D]

Dunbabin, John, Liverpool, chairmaker (1790–1822). Addresses given at Grenville St North, and Scotland Rd in 1790; 162 Dale St in 1796; 59 Tythebarn St, 1805; and 3 Milk St, 1807. Son of Daniel Dunbabin, potter; admitted freeman on 20 June 1790. Sons John Hulker Dunbabin, brushmaker, born on 5 August 1790, petitioned freedom on birthright in 1812; Samuel Dunbabin, tobacconist, born on 31 July 1796, petitioned freedom in 1818; and Daniel Dunbabin, stonemason, born on 11 May 1801, petitioned freedom in 1822. [D; Liverpool freemen reg. and committee bk]

Dunbabin, William, Liverpool, cm (b. 1808–39). Trading at 22 Mansfield St in 1839. Petitioned freedom in 1830. [D; Liverpool freemen's committee bk]

Dunbar, John, Chester, cm (1747). [Poll bk]

Dunbar, Robert, Aldermanbury, London, (1738–40). Named in the accounts of the Duchy of Cornwall in 1738 supplying paper hangings for Cliveden, Berks.: '134 ps white ground green popie Chince', £26 16s; and '12 ps of green on white borders', £7 4s. In 1740 he submitted a bill to Lord Cardigan for putting up wallpapers. [V & A archives; *DEF*]

Dunbar, William, Angel Meadow, Manchester, joiner and cm (1788). [D]

Duncalfe, Henry, Digbeth, Walsall, Staffs., cm and u (1828–30). [D] Possibly:

Duncalfe, Henry, High St, Wednesbury, Staffs., cm and u (1830). [D]

Duncan, George, South Shields, Co. Durham, cm (d. 1774). Sale of stock after death announced in *Newcastle Courant*, 2 April 1774; consisting of 'A large quantity of cabinet goods, made and unfinished, with all the stock of mahogany, walnut tree, wainscot boards, deals etc. . . . also the tools, benches, and many other articles in that business'.

Duncan, John, Newman St, Oxford St, London, chair and sofa manufacturer (1817–29). Trading at no. 46, 1817–23, and no. 55 1827–29. [D]

Duncan, Robert, Russell Ct, Drury Lane, London, cm (1780). Took out Sun Insurance policies in 1780 for £300 of which utensils and stock accounted for £180; and for houses in association with Peter Blackstock. [GL, Sun MS vol. 281, p. 307]

Duncan, William, Newcastle, cm (1794–95). Declared bankrupt, *Williamson's Liverpool Advertiser*, 24 March 1794; and *Billinge's Liverpool Advertiser*, 27 April 1795.

Duncan, William, 27 Middle St, Newcastle, cm and furniture broker (1827). [D]

Dunch, James, London, upholder (1784–1806). Addresses given at 18 Norfolk St in 1784; Sheppard St, Hanover Sq., 1785–1806; and no. 12, 1802–06. Took out a Sun Insurance policy on 4 April 1785 for £600 of which utensils and stock

accounted for £100. Named in Sheraton's list of master cabinet makers, 1803. [D; poll bk; GL, Sun MS vol. 327, p. 562]

Duncley, John, 14 Dickenson St, Liverpool, joiner and cm (1796). [D]

Dunckley, Richard, address unrecorded, upholder (1721–29). Son of Thomas Dunckley, apothecary of Towcester, Northants.; app. to John Thorold on 3 January 1721, and admitted freeman of the Upholders' Co. by servitude on 5 February 1728/29. [GL, Upholders' Co. records]

Duncombe, John, 32 Curistor St, Chancery Lane, London, cm (1808). [D]

Duncombe, John, 9 Middle Row, Holborn, London, cm (1809–11). [D]

Duncombe, Joseph, Gt Garden St, Whitechapel, London, cm (1793–97). Trading as Duncomb & Thompson at no. 4, 1794–96. Subscribed to Sheraton's *Drawing Book*, 1793. Declared bankrupt, *Liverpool Advertiser*, 31 July 1797. [D]

Duncombe, M., London, cm (1793). Subscribed to Sheraton's *Drawing Book*, 1793.

Duncombe, Richard, Bedford Ct, Covent Garden, London, u, cm and chairmaker (1772–85). Supplied furniture to Croome Court, Worcs., including in 1775 a mahogany night table and reading desk, costing £2 18s 6d, a mahogany folding table, £2 9s, and a wardrobe and camp table, £14 5s. In 1778 he charged £3 12s for six mahogany camp stools covered with black leather; and in 1783 provided a mahogany folding table. [D; V & A archives]

Dunderdale, John, Lancaster cm (1801–02). Admitted freeman in 1801–02 when stated of Chorley, Lancs. [Lancaster freemen rolls]

Dunford, James, 16 Gt Newport St, London, carver and gilder (1826–27). [D]

Dungate, S., Larkhall Lane, Clapham, London, cm (1838). [D]

Dunge(r)y, Thomas, Redruth, Cornwall, cm and u (1830). [D]

Dunham, Richard, Uxbridge Moor, Uxbridge, Middlx, cm, u and furniture broker (1839). [D]

Dunkley, John, Market Sq., St Neots, Hunts., cm (1839). [D]

Dunkley, Thomas, 20 Joiner's Pl., St George's Fields, London, dyed and japanned chairmaker (1808). [D]

Dunkley, Thomas, 17 Tower St, Westminster Rd, London, chair and sofa manufacturer and undertaker (1827–35). [D]

Dunkley, Thomas, 16 Eltham Pl., Old Kent Rd, London, chairmaker (1835). [D]

Dunkley, William, Market Sq., St Neots, Hunts., chairmaker and turner (1830). [D]

Dunkley, Thomas, 2 Ellecton St, Hoxton New Town, London, cm and u (1827–28). [D]

Dunlin, William, 23 Ann St, Osborne St, Hull, Yorks., u (1831). [D]

Dunlop, Conyers, London, cm (1748). Supplied the Duke of Gordon with 'A Large Month Clock in a Wallnut-tree case', costing £15 15s, and charged for 'sending on board ship'. [Scottish RO, GD 44/33/29/67]

Dunlop, George, 54 Wapping, London, cm (1777–82). Took out Sun Insurance policies in 1777 for £400, £150 on utensils and stock, £50 on his workshop; and in 1779 and 1782 for £700, utensils, stock and goods accounting for £250. [GL, Sun MS vol. 257, p. 129; vol. 274, p. 24; vol. 300, p. 328]

Dunlop, John, 6 Grafton St, London, cm (1779–87). Declared bankrupt, *Gents Mag.*, February 1779. Took out Sun Insurance policies in 1781 for £400, utensils, stock, goods and workshop accounting for £300; and on 15 January 1787 for £500 on household goods and workshop. [D; poll bk; GL, Sun MS vol. 292, p. 616; vol. 342, ref. 526756]

Dunn, —, 60 Castle St, Southwark, London, cm (1808). [D]

Dunn, —, address unrecorded, u (1825–37). Worked for 3rd

Lord Braybrooke of Audley End, Essex between 1825–37, receiving small monthly payments, the most being £24 17s 6d. One entry is 'for Carved work'. [Essex RO, D/DBy/A376, A358 and A361] Possibly either Hannibal or Henry of Saffron Walden, Essex.

Dunn, Charles, address unrecorded, upholder (1768). Son of James Dunn, glover of London; admitted freeman of the Upholders' Co. by patrimony on 14 June 1768. [GL, Upholders' Co. records]

Dunn, Charles, 25 Back Church Lane, Whitechapel, London, cm, u and undertaker (1826–28). [D]

Dunn, E., 107 Titchfield St, Fitzroy Sq., London, carver and gilder (1816). [D]

Dunn, Edward, Market Sq., Bromley, Kent, cm and u (1774–1818). Successor of John and William Dunn, and succeeded by his daughter, Sarah. [Bromley Local Hist. Lib., Dunn family archives]

Dunn, Edward E., Market Sq., Bromley, Kent, cm and u (1818–61). Successor to Sarah Dunn, probably his elder sister. Dining chair with upholstered seat still in possession of the family is said to be an app. piece. [D; Bromley Local Hist. Lib., Dunn family archives] See Edward, George, John, Sarah and William Dunn.

Dunn, Edward, 8 China Walk, Lambeth, London, chair and sofa maker (1839). [D]

Dunn, George, Bromley, Kent, cm and undertaker (1826–27). [D]

Dunn, Hannibal, Market St (or Pl.), Saffron Walden, Essex, cm and u (1826–39). [D]

Dunn, Henry, Market St, Saffron Walden, Essex, u (1838). [Essex RO, jurors' bk, Q/RJ/2/1]

Dunn, Isaac, Richmond, Yorks., cm (1814). [PR (bapt.)]

Dunn, James, Liverpool, carver and gilder (1830–39). Addresses given at 35 Christian St, 1834–37, and no. 69 in 1839. Marriage to Anne Smith at St David's Church reported, *Liverpool Mercury*, 21 September 1830. [D]

Dunn, John, Market Sq., Bromley, Kent, u (1710–21). In 1710 he founded the firm which spanned the 18th and 19th centuries and was only recently taken over by Heal. The business seems to have been continued in John's name by William, his son (1721–74), since a bill of January 1774 to the parish of Hayes for a bed and bedding is signed John Dunn. [D; Bromley Local Lib., Dunn family archives] See Edward, Edward E., George, Sarah and William Dunn. It is not known whether or not he was a relative of the following John Dunn of Bromley.

Dunn, John, Bromley, Kent, upholder (1771–93). App. to William Chesson, haberdasher and upholder; admitted freeman of the Upholders' Co. on 3 April 1771. Took app. named George Wilkins, 1773–79. [GL, Upholders' Co. records] Declared bankrupt, *Leicester Journal*, 6 May 1780 and named in directories, 1793.

Dunn, John, Newcastle, cm (1793–1834). Subscribed to Sheraton's *Drawing Book*, 1793. Trading at Dog Bank, also as a furniture broker, in 1834. [D]

Dunn, John, 25–26 Kent St, Liverpool, u (1805–07). [D]

Dunn, John, 27 Gt Pulteney St, Golden Sq., London, carver and gilder (1808–11). Named in the Bad Debts book of Herries, Farquhar & Co., private bankers, London, on 7 October 1809, owing £35 to Michael Flynn, u of Wardour St. [Lloyds Bank archives, bk 2036]

Dunn, John, Lambeth, London, chair and sofa maker (1808–35). Recorded at Lambeth Walk in 1808 (?); 3 China Rd, 1832–34; and 39 Gibson St, 1835. [D]

Dunn, John, 9 Orange St (?), Kennington London, cm and u (1822–23). [D]

Dunn, John, Chestergate, Macclesfield, Cheshire, chairmaker (1828). Made rush seated spindle and ladder back chairs. [D; V & A archives]

Dunn, John, King St, South Molton, Devon, cm (1830). [D]

Dunn, John, Church St, Warwick, u (1831). [Poll bk]

Dunn, John, 5 Brunswick St, Blackwall, London, cm (1835–37). [D]

Dunn, Joseph, 28 Skinner St, Bishopsgate, London, sofa and bedstead maker (1820–21). [D]

Dunn, Joseph, London, Rd, Twickenham, Middlx, cm and u (1832–39). Trading also as a paper hanger in 1832. [D]

Dunn, Lawson, Stockton-upon-Tees, Co. Durham, carver and gilder (1798). [D]

Dunn, Martin, Church Walk, Gateshead, Co. Durham, cm and joiner (1838). [D]

Dunn, Michael, York, u (1762–67). Son of George Dunn, brewer, of Blaydon, Co. Durham; app. to George Reynoldson, u, on 7 December 1762. Probably the Michael Dunn, app. u, resident for three years in St Michael-le-Belfrey parish in the 1767 Census of Roman Catholics. [York app. reg.; *Catholic Recusancy in York*] See William Buskin.

Dunn, Michael, Charlotte St, Bloomsbury, London, upholder and cm (1784–93). [D]

Dunn, Michael, address unrecorded, u (1786). Between January and November 1786 he undertook repairs to curtains and minor pieces of furniture, cleaned beds and laid carpets for Gertrude, Dowager Duchess of Bedford, presumably for her house, 112 Pall Mall, into which she moved when her son, the 5th Duke, came of age. [Bedford Office, London]

Dunn, Richard, Castle Garth, Newcastle, cm (1762). Took app. named Laing in 1762. [S of G, app. index]

Dunn, Richard, Scruton, Yorks., joiner and cm (1840). [D]

Dunn, Richard, Pennistone, Windsor, Berks., cm and u (1838–40). Named in the fifth hall book of the borough of New Windsor on 2 January 1838 and 1839 being appointed cm to the Windsor Corp. for the year.

Dunn, Sarah, Market Sq., Bromley, Kent, cm and u (1832–39). Her trade card, undated, reads: 'SARAH DUNN, (Successor to her late Father Edward Dunn) Cabinet Maker, Upholsterer, Appraiser, Paper Hanger & Undertaker. MARKET PLACE, BROMLEY, KENT. House and Estate Agent, Trunks, Portmanteaus, Carpet Bags &c'. Leased property in Market Sq. in 1838. She is said to have been entrusted with the arrangements for William IV's visit to Bromley. Succeeded by Edward E. Dunn (1818–61), probably her younger brother. [D; Bromley Local Hist. Lib., Dunn family archives] See Edward, Edward E., George, John and William Dunn.

Dunn, Thomas, 29 Berkeley St, Lambeth, London, chair and sofa maker (1832–34). [D]

Dunn, William, Market Sq., Bromley, Kent, cm (1721–74). Carried on the business of his father, John Dunn, possibly in his name. Succeeded by Edward Dunn, 1774–1818. [Bromley Local Hist. Lib., Dunn family archives] See Edward, Edward E., George, John and Sarah Dunn.

Dunn, William, 59 Chandos St, London, u (1790). Insured his house and contents for £200 on 7 October 1790. [GL, Sun MS ref. 574915]

Dunn, William, Hornsby's Chare, Quayside, Newcastle, builder, joiner, cm and ship joiner (19th century). House at Stepney, Ouseburn, Newcastle. [Landauer Coll., MMA, NY] Possibly:

Dunn, William, Stepney Sq., Newcastle, cm and joiner (1838). [D]

Dunning, H., 5 Queen St, Hoxton St, London, wood turner (1835). [D]

Dunning, Henry, High St, Stroud, Glos., chair manufacturer (1805–24). [D]

Dunning, Henry, St Margaret's Bank, Rochester, Kent, chair-maker and furniture broker (1832–39). [D]

Dunning, James, address unrecorded, cm (1746). Receipt dated 15 September 1746 for a chest and desk 'and all demands', totalling £10 10s, submitted to Mr West for Alscot Park, Warks. [V & A archives]

Dunning, John, Driffield, Yorks, cm (1793). [D]

Dunning, Thomas, St Benedict's Gates, Norwich, carver and gilder (1839). [D]

Dunning, William, York, cm (1818). App. to Joseph Hick in November 1818. [Hull app. reg.] Possibly:

Dunning, William, Hull, Yorks., cm and u (1831–40). Addresses given at 30 Waterworks St, 1831–34; no. 26, 1835–38; and 12 Chariot St, 1839–40. [D]

Dunning, William, 5 Bridge St, Southampton, Hants, chair-maker (1830). [D]

Dunnings, George W., Bermondsey, London, cm (1830). [Rochester poll bk]

Dunnitt, William, 3 Cheapside, London, cm (1839). [D]

Dunno, James, Westminster, London, cm (1740). Took out a Sun Insurance policy for £500 in 1740. [GL, Sun MS vol. 55, p. 93] Possibly James Durno.

Dunsbye, Richard, Wells-next-the-Sea, Norfolk, u (1778). Insured houses for £350 in 1778. [GL, Sun MS vol. 269, p. 421]

Dunstone, John, Lewes, Sussex cm (1830–39). Recorded as a journeyman cm in High St in 1830; and as cm in Fisher St 1835–39. [D; poll bks]

Dunstone, Thomas, 163 High St, Lewes, Sussex, cm and u (1812–39). [D; poll bks]

Dunton, —, King St, Covent Gdn, London, u (1764). Described in newspapers of 1764 as 'an eminent upholsterer'. [Heal]

Dunton, James, St Albans St, London, upholder (1778). Insured his house for £800 in 1778. [GL, Sun MS vol. 270, p. 50]

Dunton, John jnr, London u (1705–24). Trading at 'The Wheatsheaf', Bedford St, Covent Gdn, 1722–23. Son of John Dunton, yeoman of Ryslip, (Ruislip) Middlx, and brother of William Dunton. App. to Benjamin Powell on 3 July 1705, and admitted freeman of the Upholders' Co. by servitude on 7 January 1715. Took his brother as app. 1715–24. Took out a Sun Insurance policy on 2 March 1722 for £500 on goods and merchandise in his house. A further policy of 1723 is known. [GL, Upholders' Co. records; GL, Sun MS vol. 15, ref. 278640; Heal]

Dunton, William, London, cm and u (1715–d. 1764). Trading in Bedford St, Covent Gdn in 1733. Son of John Dunton, yeoman, of Ryslip, (Ruislip) Middlx, and brother of John Dunton, jnr, to whom he was app. on 7 March 1715/16. Admitted freemen of the Upholders' Co. by servitude on 4 March 1723/24, and master in 1756. Took app. named Daniel Louth, 1727–34. Took out a Sun Insurance policy on 13 December 1733 for £600 on goods in trust and utensils in warehouse, yard and storerooms. William Dunton & Co. are named in the accounts of Benjamin Mildmay, Earl Fitzwalter of Moulsham Hall, on 27 January 1743 supplying chair and settee frames costing £15 15s, and on 31 March, a walnut settee for the 'Drawing Room above-stairs London', £3 5s. [GL, Upholders' Co. records; GL, Sun MS vol. 38, ref. 62539; A. C. Edwards, *The Accounts of Benjamin Mildmay, Earl Fitzwalter*, p. 110]

Duperey, James, 10 Dorrington St, London, carver and gilder (1829). [D]

Duplex, George jnr & Bowring, Francis, 6 Ropemaker St, Finsbury, London, cm and brokers of household goods (1821). Insured stock and utensils in their house for £100 on 18 April 1821. [GL, Sun MS vol. 484, ref. 976991] See John Duplex. Possibly:

Duplex, George, 23 Ropemaker St, Finsbury, London, cm and u (1820–39). [D]

Duplex (or Dupless), John, 44 Grubb St, London, cm (1786). Took out a Sun Insurance policy on 22 March 1786 for £70 on utensils, stock and goods. [GL, Sun MS vol. 337, p. 8]

Duplex, John, 6 Ropemaker Alley (or St), Chiswell St, London, chairmaker (1791–94). Took out Sun Insurance policies on 4 July 1791 for £100, £50 on utensils and stock; and on 8 July 1794 for £300, £120 on utensils and stock. [GL, Sun MS vol. 379, p. 38; vol. 379, p. 591] See George Duplex.

Dupont, Richard, Sudbury, Suffolk, cm (1798). [D]

Dupree, James, 11 Daggetts Ct, Broker Row, Moorfields, London, upholder (1781). Took out a Sun Insurance policy in 1781 for £200 of which utensils, stock and goods accounted for £40. [GL, Sun MS vol. 290, p. 617] Possibly:

Dupree, James, London, upholder and furniture warehouseman (1784–1808). Trading at 27 Middle Moorfields, 1784–1802; and 26–28 Wilson St, Finsbury, 1803–08. [D]

Duprey, William, Kemps Ct, Berwick St, London, carver (1777). Took out a Sun Insurance policy in 1777 for £100, £20 on utensils, stock and goods. [GL, Sun MS vol. 255, p. 382]

Dupuys, John, 11 Upper Rathbone Pl., London, upholder and mattress maker (1791). Took out a Sun Insurance policy on 24 May 1791 for £600, utensils, stock and goods in trust accounting for £200. [GL, Sun MS ref. 583754]

Durand, George, 8 Catherine St, Strand, London, carver and gilder, picture frame maker and printseller (1778). Took out a Sun Insurance policy in 1778 for £500 including £180 on utensils and stock. Trade card recorded. [GL, Sun MS vol. 264, p. 394; Heal]

Durant, I., address unrecorded. Three late 18th-century part-gilt cabriole chairs in the French taste from Newton Park, Bristol, recorded bearing stamp of 'I. DURANT' on seat rails. [Sotheby's 9 May 1941, lot 145]

Durant, Thomas, Blenheim St, Marble St, London, cm (1774). [Poll bk]

Durant, Thomas, Waltham Green, London, cm and undertaker (1808). [D]

Durant(e), William, Liverpool, cm (1823–30). App. to John O'Neill in 1823 and admitted freeman on 18 September 1830. [Liverpool app. enrolment bk and freemen reg.]

Durbar, John, Chester and Budeley, cm (1732–47). Admitted freeman of Chester on 12 October 1732. Polled at Chester, of Budeley, in 1732; of Chester in 1747. [Chester freemen rolls]

Durden, Francis, 36 Gresse St, Rathbone Pl., off Tottenham Ct Rd, London, fancy cm and u (1827–37). [D]

Durden, M. A., 36 Gresse St, Rathbone Pl., off Tottenham Ct Rd, London, cm and u (1839). [D]

Durham, Edward, Exeter, Devon, cm (1803). [Militia Census]

Durham, John, York, u (1786–93). Of Lendal, app. to Thomas Baildon, u, undertaker and appraiser of Blake St, York, on 3 July 1786. Admitted freeman in 1793. [York app. reg. and freemen rolls]

Durham, John, 79 Gray's Inn Lane, London, carver, gilder and paper hanger (1808). [D]

Durham, John, London, cm and u (1821–35). Trading at 16 Catherine St, Strand, 1823–28; and 16 Rupert St, Haymarket, 1829–35. Stock consisted of varieties of folding, camp and field beds, combined settee, couch and cabinet beds. As Messrs Durham, furniture makers and retailers, successor to Morgan & Sanders, they illustrated a secretaire bookcase in Ackermann's *Repository of Arts*, September 1822. Took out a Sun Insurance policy on 26 April 1821 for £2,000, stock, utensils and goods in trust accounting for £1,750. Declared bankrupt, *Brighton Gazette*, 30 December 1826. [D; GL, Sun MS vol. 488, ref. 978784; C. Musgrave, *Regency Furniture*, p. 121]

Durham, Robert, New Sleaford, Lincs., chairmaker (1721). Took app. named Baker in 1721. [S of G, app. index]

Durham, Robert, address unrecorded, u (1791). Supplied items to Lord Howard of Audley End, Essex for his London house in Burlington St. His bill totalled £7 18s and listed blankets, curtains, a stump bedstead and four chairs. [Essex RO, D/DBy/A49/3]

Durham, Thomas, Paradise Row, Warwick, cm (1831). [Poll bk]

Durie, Sand, address unrecorded, chairmaker (1803). Subscribed to Sheraton's *Cabinet Dictionary*, 1803.

Durley, John, 84 Wells St, Oxford St, London, cm and u (1822–39). [D]

Durley, John, 16 Adam & Eve Ct, Oxford St, London, u (1835–39). [D]

Durling, George, Salisbury Ct, Fleet St, London, looking-glass grinder and frame maker (1729). Insured his house, goods, utensils and stock for £500 on 11 August 1729. [GL, Sun MS vol. 28]

Durnford, John, Shrewsbury, Salop, u (1806–35). Named in the Shrewsbury burgess roll, 1806. Trading at Shoplatch in 1806–22, and Wyle Cop, 1828–35. [D]

Durno, James, Jermyn St, Westminster, London, cm (1749). [Poll bk] Possibly James Dunno.

Durrant, John, London, upholder (1790–98). Recorded at 6 Osborne Pl., Whitechapel in 1789. Son of John Durrant, Gent, of Doggetts Ct, Moorfields. App. to William Wood on 4 August 1790, and admitted freeman of the Upholders' Co. by servitude on 6 June 1798. [GL, Upholders' Co. records]

Durrant, Thomas snr, Norwich and London, chairmaker and cm (1754–1830). Recorded in Norwich from 1754, but had moved to London by September 1768, and polled at Norwich, of London, until 1830; and of Fulham in 1802 and 1830. Later entries may refer to his son of the same name. App. to Stephen Howlett, and admitted freeman of Norwich on 24 February 1756. Took app. named Starling in 1754. Former app. John Stocking, chairmaker, admitted freeman on 3 May 1770. Son Thomas Durrant jnr admitted freeman on 2 September 1780. [Poll bks; Norwich freemen reg.; S of G, app. index]

Durrant, Thomas jnr, Norwich, chairmaker (1780). Son of Thomas Durrant, chairmaker and cm; admitted freeman on 2 September 1780. [Norwich freemen reg.]

Durrant, Thomas, 28 Gee St, Goswell St, London, turner (1835). [D]

Durrant, William, 10 Fazakerley St, Liverpool, cm (1830). Admitted freeman on 18 November 1830. [Liverpool freemen reg.]

Durrett, William, Gloucester, cm (1823). Child bapt. at St John Baptist's Church in 1823. [PR (bapt.)]

Dury, Andrew, address unrecorded. In 1772 he charged £21 3s for 'a Screen of Maps' and 'fitted up 2 sheets Maps' for Sir John Griffin Griffin of Audley End, Essex. [Essex RO, D/DBy/A30/5]

Duryer, Henry Robert, 16 Dean St, Holborn, London, upholder (1814). Took out a Sun Insurance policy on 24 December 1814 for £550 of which stock and utensils accounted for £100. [GL, Sun MS vol. 463, ref. 99330]

Duryer (or Duryor), John, Dean St, London, u and appraiser (1790–1830). Recorded at no. 16, 1790–1808, and no. 15 in 1817. Polled at Canterbury in 1796 and 1830. [D] Probably John Dwyer.

Dusautoy, Charles, High St, Southampton, Hants., upholder (1805–08). [D]

Duthoit, James, London, upholder, cm and auctioneer (1777–1817). Addresses given at 9 Old Broad St, 1789–1804; 1 Bridge (or Budge) Row, 1803–12; Watling St, 1806–17; and also 17 Tower Royal, 1807–12. Son of James Duthoit, baker of Brick Lane, Spitalfields; app. to Charles Greenwood on 2 April 1777, and after 1783 to his widow. Admitted freeman of Canterbury in 1782; and of the Upholders' Co. by servitude on 2 March 1785. Took app. named James Toplis, 1790–98. Named in Sheraton's list of master cabinet makers, 1803. Submitted invoice [GL, print dept] for church furnishings dated 14 August 1807 for three hassocks, 8s 6d; and 27 February 1812 for curtains, £7 7s. Invoice gives addresses at 1 Budge Row and 17 Tower Royal. [D; GL, Upholders' Co. records; Canterbury freemen rolls]

Dutton, Alexander, Bury St Edmunds, Suffolk, journeyman cm (1775). Letter from a Norwich newspaper dated 1775 recorded on the back of a chest of drawers stating that Dutton, from Norwich, had left employment at Bury. See John Oldfield.

Dutton, Edward, Southwell, Notts., cm (1728). Took app. named Leigh in 1728. [S of G, app. index]

Dutton, G. M., address unrecorded, cm. Two-drawer commode with ormolu mounts, c. 1750–75, in Royal Collection is signed 'G. M. DUTTON'. [V & A archives]

Dutton, H. (or M.), address unrecorded, inlayer (c. 1770). Signed a marquetry panel on a commode attributed to P. Langlois. [*Burlington*, June 1980, p. 416]

Dutton, John, Broadhurst, address unrecorded, upholder (1755–63). Son of Joseph Dutton of St Sepulchre's, London. App. to Richard Walker on 5 June 1755, and admitted freemen of the Upholders' Co. by servitude on 1 December 1763. [GL, Upholders' Co. records]

Dutton, John, Crooked Lane, London, u (1778). Declared bankrupt, *Williamson's Liverpool Advertiser*, 14 August 1778.

Dutton, John, Liverpool, cm (1816–24). Addresses given at 9 Lumb St in 1818; no. 57 in 1821; and with Joseph Dutton at 24 Cornwallis St and 63 Bridgewater St in 1824. App. to Thomas Gorton, and admitted freeman on servitude on 10 June 1816. [D; Liverpool freemen reg.] See Joseph, Nathan, Nathaniel and Thomas Dutton.

Dutton, Joseph, Liverpool, cm (1810–35). Addresses given at 4 Oldham St with shop at Seel St, 1810–11; 63 Bridgewater St, 1813–29, with shop at Fleet St, 1813–14; in 1816 he moved from Seel St to 24 Cornwallis St, and is recorded there with John Dutton in 1824; shop addresses given at 24–25 Cornwallis St and 53 Frederick St, 1827–29; 66 Bridgewater St in 1834; and 7 Nelson St in 1835. Announced his removal to 24 Cornwallis St in *Liverpool Mercury*, 29 March 1816, 'where an Assortment of Furniture of every description, of the most modern & approved Patterns, is now ready for inspection . . . Orders for the East & West Indies, America and other foreign parts, carefully & expeditiously executed'. Import duties for 1816 given as 22% on japanned wares of all kinds, and 35% on cabinet wares and all manufactures of woods. Named in 1822 in the account of lives in leases granted by the Corp. of Liverpool, as having a daughter aged nine and a son, Joseph, aged 18 in 1822. Advertised in *Liverpool Mercury*, 4 June 1824, for '6 or 8 good CABINET MAKERS — Men of Sober habits will meet with constant employ at the late advance of wages, which far exceeds any former period. Likewise 2 or 3 good MAHOGANY CHAIR-MAKERS'. [D]

Dutton, Joseph, Hospital St, Nantwich, Cheshire, chairmaker (1803–34). Daughter Mary bapt. on 17 April 1803; Ann on 21 July 1805; Eliza on 17 May 1807; Elizabeth on 16 June 1810; son Joseph on 18 May 1813; Jonathan on 28 May 1816; daughter Anne on 9 July 1820; Sarah on 8 May 1822; and son Thomas on 24 May 1826. [D; PR (bapt.)]

Dutton, Maria, 10 Ormond St, Chorlton Row, Manchester, u (1825). [D]

Dutton, Mathew, 148 Fleet St, London, u (1839). [D]

Dutton, Nathan, Liverpool, cm and u (1818–39). Trading at 7 Nelson St, 1835–37;. at 27 Cornwallis St in 1835 with Joseph, and in 1837 with Thomas Dutton. N. & T. Dutton are recorded at 24 Nelson St in 1839. Nathan was app. to Bartholomew Tyrer in 1818. [D; Liverpool app. enrolment bk] See John, Joseph & Thomas Dutton. Possibly:

Dutton, Nathaniel & Son, 66 Bridgewater St, Liverpool, with shop at 7 Cornwallis St, cm and u (1834). [D]

Dutton, Robert, 10 Birchin Lane, London (?), upholder (1799–1802). Son of Robert Dutton, Gent., Bretton Hall, Hawarden, Flint, Wales. Admitted freeman of the Upholders' Co. by redemption on 19 September 1799. [GL, Upholders' Co. records]

Dutton, Robert, Chester, cm (1809–12). Admitted freeman on 7 June 1809. [Chester freemen rolls; poll bk]

Dutton, Thomas, Liverpool, cm (1790–1837). Trading at Union St, Old Hall, St, with shop at Thomas St, Pool Lane in 1790; 11 Russell St, 1800–07; Russell St, Fairclough St and Ranelagh St, 1810–11; Fairclough St, 1813; 8 Cheapside, 1814–27; 7 Nelson St, 1824; and 7 Cornwallis St, 1835–37. App. to John Eden, and admitted freeman on servitude on 20 June 1790. Took app. named Thomas Jebson in 1802, who petitioned freedom in 1812; Luke Plunkett in 1808, petitioned freedom in 1816; John O'Neill in 1807, petitioned in 1816; Thomas Morgan in 1810, petitioned in 1818; and John Ball in 1814, petitioned in 1821. Took apps named Maurice Powers and John Murray in 1819; and Thomas Dean in 1822. Father of John Dutton, broker, born on 13 November 1800, who petitioned freedom on birthright in 1822. [D; Liverpool app. enrolment bk, freemen reg. and committee bk] See John, Joseph, Nathan, Nathaniel & William Dutton.

Dutton, Thomas, London, cm (1793). Subscribed to Sheraton's *Drawing Book*, 1793.

Dutton, William, 6 Union St, Old Hall St, Liverpool, cm (1800). [D]

Dutton, William, York St, Chester, cm (1812–26). [Poll bks]

Duval, L. C., 12 Museum St, Bloomsbury, London, water gilder (1835). [D]

Du Vige, Isaac, London, cm (1681). Described by the Threadneedle St Relief in September 1681 as a 'jeune gentilhomme', the son of a recently converted Catholic, arrived from Paris 'last Lord's Day'. He was given £2 2s 6d to buy clothes, and 3s 6d to app. him to a cm. [*Hogarth Soc.*, 1949, pp. 13 and 85]

Duxfield, Ralph, Duxfield's Ct, Northumberland St, Newcastle, cm (1834–38). [D]

Dwyer, John, 16 Dean St, Holborn, London, u (1809–11). [D] Probably John Duryer.

Dybill, Daniel, 44 London Wall, London, cm (1826–27). [D]

Dycher, John, address unrecorded. Chair said to have been made by him in 1794 sold at Sotheby's, May 1965.

Dye, James, Holt, Norfolk, cm (1830–39). [D]

Dye, Joseph, Holt, Norfolk, cm (1839). [D]

Dyer, Adolphus, Plymouth, Devon, cm and u (1830–38). Trading in King St, 1830, and Union St, 1836–38. [D]

Dyer, Benjamin, Tunbridge Wells, Kent, Tunbridge-ware manufacturer (1832–39). Trading in Market Pl., 1832, and Bedford Pl., 1839. [D]

Dyer, J., 1 Frederick Pl., Borough Rd, London, cm (1837). [D]

Dyer, John, 4 Frederick Pl., Borough Rd, London, bedstead maker (1829–39). [D]

Dyer, Leonard, formerly of New St, Cloth Fair, late of Cable St, Wellclose Sq., London, woolcomber and carver (1761).

Discharge from Debtors' Prison announced, *London Gazette*, 12 August 1761.

Dyer, Nicholas, 32 North St, Brighton, Sussex, cm and u (1822–26). [D] Possibly of Dyer & Gates.

Dyer, William, Wallingford, Berks., cm (1798–1830). [D]

Dyer, William, Liverpool, cm (1822). App. to Hugh Cannell in 1822. [Liverpool app. enrolment bk]

Dyer, William & Co., Maldon, Essex, cm and u (1823–27). [D]

Dyer & Gates, 27 North St, Brighton, Sussex, cm (1805). [D] Possibly Nicholas Dyer.

Dyke, William, 13 St James's Back, Bristol, cm (1837–40). [D]

Dymond, Thomas, Lower North St, Exeter, Devon, u (1836). Daughter Eliza bapt. at St David's Church on 7 September 1836. [PR (bapt.)]

Dyson, Edmund, Kirkburton, Yorks., joiner and cm (1834). [D]

Dyson, Gibson, Manchester, cm and furniture broker (1825–36). Addresses given at 77 St George's Rd in 1825; 439 Oldham Rd in 1829; and no. 88 in 1836. [D]

Dyson, Hugh, London, cm (1732). [Chester poll bk]

Dyson, James, address unrecorded, u (?) (1709). Submitted a bill to Temple Newsam House, Yorks., 'For Bottoming 12 Chaires with Cayne'. [*Furn. Hist.*, 1967]

Dyson, John, Birkby, Yorks., cm (1785). Announced dissolution of partnership with Benjamin Scholes, *Leeds Mercury*, 22 February 1785.

Dyson, Joseph, Skircoat, Yorks., joiner and cm (1822). [D]

Dyson, Jos., Islington, London, cm and u (1826–35). Trading at 62 St John's St, 1826–28; and 30½ Cumberland Row, 1835. [D]

Dyson, Roger, Skipton Rd, Colne, Lancs., joiner and cm (1818). [D]

Dyson, Samuel Pagett, Gt Yarmouth, Norfolk, cm (1830). [Norwich poll bk]

Dyson, Thomas, South St, Chesterfield, Derbs., cm and u (1818–35). Trading at Beetwell St in 1818 and South St, 1822–35). [D]

Dyson, William, 5 Mount St, Manchester, cm and joiner (1804–17). [D]

Dyson, William, Kirkburton, Yorks., joiner and cm (1834). [D]

E

Eaches (Eachus?) Peter, Wheelock, Sandbach, Cheshire, cm (1822–34). [D]

Eade, Henry, London, carver (1779–80). Insured his house at 109 Gt Portland St for £200 in 1779 with the Sun Co. Of 3 Deans Pl., near the Turnpike in the New Road, Tottenham Ct Rd, London, insured his house for £200 in 1780. [GL, Sun MS vol. 277, p. 231; vol. 284, p. 393]

Eade & Saunders, 10 Gt Castle St, London, carvers and gilders (1784).

Eades, James, 2 Eades Buildings, Bath, Som., cm (1826). [D]

Eadon, George, Sheffield, Yorks., carver, gilder and looking-glass maker (1821–37). Addresses given at 2 Flat St in 1822; 2 George St, 1825–30; also no. 9 in 1825; and 'The Repository', 91 Fargate, 1833–37. [D]

Eadon & Son, address unrecorded. Set of twelve early 19th-century mahogany dining chairs recorded, with central armorial device of three crossed swords on curved top rails; horizontal splats and sabre legs; some stamped 'EADON & SON', others, 'G. D. HEELEY', 'G. TAYLOR', and 'W. J. CAULT'. [Phillips', 23 August 1983, lot 52]

Eadson, Joseph, Worthing, Sussex, cm and u (1823–39).

Trading at 11 Warwick St, 1823–26, Ann St, 1832–39, with house at 3 Warwick St, 1839. [D]

Eady, Charles, 20 Goswell St, London, water gilder (1808). [D]

Eagle, James, 2 Warwick Row, Blackfriars Rd, London, looking-glass and picture frame maker (1829). [D]

Eagle, John, 33 Oxford St, Manchester, cm (1840). [D]

Eagle, Lot, 62 Old Market St, Bristol, turner and chairmaker (1801–05). [D]

Eagle(s), Thomas, Bedford, turner and chairmaker (1785–1830). Recorded at Silver St in 1823 and Old Market Pl. in 1830. [D]

Eagle, William, Perkins Rents, London, chairmaker (1749). [Poll bk]

Eagles, T. F., 18 King St, Covent Gdn, London, manufacturer of paper tea trays to their Majesties and the Royal Family (1813–25). Eagles succeeded to the premises and business of Henry Clay between 1810–13. He continued to provide for the 6th Duke of Bedford at Woburn, St James's Sq., and Endsleigh, Devon, trays and teapot stands of similar decoration and price as his predecessor had done in the previous decade. In the last quarter of 1821 the paper tea tray 'sent to Woburn for His Grace's exclusive use' cost £3 10s; and at the same time he supplied '5 iron Japan trays for Woburn, £8 18s'. Another item supplied in 1818 and 1820 was paper bread baskets. A curious item for Endsleigh in 1817 was '2 setts paper Indian Card pools' which, together with seven red India paper tea trays and two teapot stands, cost £19 19s including packing. Altogether during the period the nine extant invoices show twenty-four entries totalling £90 11s. [D; Bedford Office, London]

Eagles, Thomas, Cheltenham, Glos., cm and u (1820–30). Trading at 8 Albion St in 1820 and 21 Corpus St in 1830. [D]

Eagles, William, 169 Hockley Pl., Gt Hampton St, Birmingham, cm (1835). [D]

Eaglesfield, Charles, Catherine St, Maryport, Cumb., joiner and/or cm (1829–34). [D]

Eagleso (or Eggleso), Peter, London, carver (1774–81). Trading at Aylesbury St, Clerkenwell in 1774 and Brick Lane, Old St, 1781. [Bristol poll bks]

Eales, James Thomas, Exeter, Devon, cm (1828). Son Walter Stephen bapt. at St Sidwell's on 12 February 1828. [PR(bapt.)]

Eeales, William, Exeter, Devon, cm (1822–36). Recorded at Blackboy Rd in 1831. Children by his wife Mary bapt. at St Sidwell's: Edwin on 21 April 1822, James Thomas on 26 January 1825, Hercules Stevens on 2 February 1831, and Hannah on 7 February 1836. [PR(bapt.)]

Eeales, William Henry, Russell St, Exeter, Devon, cm (1840). Daughter Mary Jane by his wife Sarah bapt. at St Sidwell's on 6 July 1840. [PR(bapt.)]

Eames, John & Robert, Bristol, carpenters, cm and undertakers (1823–40). Trading at Lower Portland Pl., Clifton, 1823–24 and 1840; and 27 Nelson Pl., 1839. [D]

Eames, Robert, Portland Pl., Clifton, Bristol, cm and carpenter (1831–37). [D]

Eames, Samuel, Shillington, Beds., u and auctioneer (1767–71). Advertised auctions of furniture in *Cambridge Chronicle and Journal*, 6 June 1767 and 12 January 1771.

Eames, William, Margaret St, Cavendish Sq., London, carver and gilder (1837–39). Recorded at no. 21 in 1837 and no. 23 in 1839. [D]

Eamonson, John, 281 Oxford St, London, u (1839). [D]

Eardley, Samuel, Well St, Tunstall, Staffs., cm and u (1834–35). [D]

Earing, Casper, 12 Old George St, near the Mint, London, cm (1808). Took out a Sun Insurance policy on 25 March 1808

for £100 of which household goods accounted for £60. [GL, Sun MS vol. 442, ref. 816688]

Earl, Charles, Over, Middlewich, Cheshire, cm (1834). [D]

Earl, Elden, 13 Rampant Horse St, Norwich, cm and chairmaker (1796–1817). Former apps John Brunning and Samuel Nockolds admitted freemen on 16 June 1817. [D; poll bks; Norwich freemen reg.] See William Elden Earl.

Earl, Elijah, Town St, Shepton Mallet, Som., cm (1830). [D]

Earl(e), George, 14 Duke St, Grosvenor Sq., London, u, appraiser and broker (1817–20). [D]

Earl, James, West St, Farnham, Surrey, cm etc. (1839). [D]

Earl, Samuel, Limekiln Dock, Bristol, cm (1832). [D]

Earl, Thomas, at 'The Walnut Tree', Long Acre, London, turner (1722). Named in insurance records in 1722. [Heal]

Earl(e), William, Farnham, Surrey, cm and u (1756–94). Took app. named Slow in 1756. Took out a Sun Insurance policy on 7 July 1791 for £600 of which utensils and stock accounted for £150. [D; S of G, app. index; GL, Sun MS vol. 377, p. 516]

Earl, William Elden I, 6 Rampant Horse St, Norwich, cm and chairmaker (1762–1802). App. to Wright Smith, and admitted freeman on 18 June 1762. [D; poll bks; Norwich freemen reg.]

Earl, William Elden II, Norwich, cm and mahogany merchant (1788–1825). Recorded at Red Lion St in 1810. App. to William Elden Earl I, and admitted freeman on 24 February 1788. Former apps admitted freemen cm: Barnard Bowles on 13 October 1802; Edward Alden Barnaby on 27 February 1813; William Pearse on 7 December 1818; and James Sharwood on 21 September 1825. [D; poll bks; Norwich freemen reg.] See Elden Earl.

Earle, Thomas, Norwich, chairmaker (1752). Son of Arthur Earle, cordwainer; admitted freeman on 4 October 1752. [Norwich freemen reg.]

Earle, Thomas, Lewes, Sussex, u (1763). Declared bankrupt, *Gents Mag.*, March 1763.

Earnshaw & Heptonstall, Kirkburton, Yorks., joiner and cm (1834). [D]

Eason, John, 20 Tottenham Ct Rd, London, carver (1810). Took out a Sun Insurance policy on 13 January 1810 for £2,600 of which stock and utensils accounted for £2,000. [GL, Sun MS vol. 451, ref. 839620]

East, Benjamin, 105 Curtain Rd, Shoreditch, London, cm and u (1827–28). [D]

East, Edward, 30 Chapel St, Holywell Mt, London, cm (1829). [D]

East, John, address unrecorded, upholder (1707–54). Son of Robert East, grocer of London; app. to Samuel Arnold on 21 August 1707. Admitted freeman of the Upholders' Co. by servitude on 5 September 1716, and master in 1754. [GL, Upholders' Co. records]

East, John, All Hallows the Great, London, upholder (1720). Took out a Hand in Hand Insurance policy on 31 May 1720 for £150 on a house in Dowgate Dock. [GL, Hand in Hand MS vol. 22, p. 64]

East, John, St Leonard, Eastcheap, London, upholder (1724–27). Took out a Hand in Hand Insurance policy on 12 March 1724 for £300 on a house in Gracechurch St. [Poll bk; GL, Hand in Hand MS vol. 28, p. 240]

East, John, Exeter, Devon, then Bodmin, Cornwall, cm and chairmaker (1784). Notice in *Exeter Flying Post*, 5 March 1784 stated that he had absconded with the proceeds from an illegal sale of furniture of John Salisbury, cm of Exeter, after having moved from Exeter to Bodmin.

East, John & Co., 8 Old Bond St, London, cm and u (1795–96). [D]

East, John, 1 Maria St, Thomas St, Hackney Rd, London, cm and u (1839). [D]

East, Samuel, High Wycombe, Bucks., chairmaker (b. *c.* 1821–41). Aged 20 at the time of the 1841 Census.

East, T., 3 Stall St, Bath, Som., fancy cm (1819). [D]

East, William, Newton Abbot, Devon, cm (1787–89). Announcement in *New Exeter Journal*, 12 February 1789 that on 25 March 1787 East left two chests of cabinet tools in a cellar; if he did not pay the cellarage by 25 February 1789 the chests were to be sold by auction.

East, William, High Wycombe, Bucks., chairmaker (b. *c.* 1778–1841). Daughters bapt. in 1813, 1821 and 1822; sons in 1815 and 1818. Aged 63 at the time of the 1841 Census. [PR (bapt.)]

East, William, Lower Marsh, High Wycombe, Bucks., chairmaker (b. *c.* 1806–41). Aged 35 at the time of the 1841 Census.

Easten, James, Ct 14, Old Butcher Mkt, Newcastle, joiner and cm (1827–34). [D]

Easter, William, Norwich, cm (1827–30). Admitted freeman on 3 May 1827. [Poll bk; Norwich freemen rolls]

Easterbrook, William, Boot Lane, Devonport, Plymouth, Devon, u and cm (1822). [D]

Eastern, James, Dog Bank, Newcastle, cm and furniture broker (1834). [D]

Eastgate, Charles, London, cm (1820–29). Addresses given at 1 Gt Russell St, Bloomsbury in 1820, and 1 Little Russell St in 1829. [D]

Eastham, James, Castle St, Clitheroe, Lancs., joiner, cm, housebuilder etc. (1822–24). [D]

Eastham, John, London, u (1722). [Preston Guild record of burgesses]

Easthope (or Easthorpe), George, Cock St, Wolverhampton, Staffs., upholder and cm (1816–35). Trading at Old Church Yd in 1816 and Cock St, 1822–35. Named in the accounts of Josiah Hinckes of Tettenhall Wood, near Wolverhampton, receiving 12s 2d on 29 March 1819. [D; Herefs. RO, Foxley papers, B47/S40]

Eastman, Benjamin, 4 Smiths Ct, Barbican, London, dyed and japan chair and sofa maker (1827–28). [D]

Eastman, James, Portsea, Portsmouth, Hants., cm (1792–98). [D]

Eastman, John, — See James Brett.

Eastman, Thomas, opposite St George's Chapel, Portsea, Portsmouth, Hants., cm (1787). Took out a Sun Insurance policy on 20 July 1787 with his partner, George Whitbread, on household goods, a house in Butcher St, and £1,100 on stock and utensils. [GL, Sun MS vol. 345, p. 413]

Eastman, Thomas S., 79 St George's Sq., Portsea, Portsmouth, Hants., cm, u and auctioneer (1823). [D]

Eastmure, J., London, cm (1807). [Gt Yarmouth poll bk]

Eastoe, William, Baxter Row, East Dereham, Norfolk, cm and u (1836–39). [D]

Easton, —, Chatham, Kent, carver and gilder (1807). [D]

Easton, George, Dog Bank, Newcastle, cm and furniture broker (1827). [D]

Ea(s)ton, John, 38–39 High St, Hastings, Sussex, cm and u (1823–39). [D]

Easton, Robert, Liverpool, cm (1819–37). Trading at 9 Clayton St, 1827–29, and no. 11 in 1837. Marriage to Miss Hannah Lobley at St Anne's Church reported in *Liverpool Mercury*, 26 November 1819. [D]

Eastop, Roger, Bow St, London, u (1749). [Poll bk]

Eastwood, Jonas, Holmfirth, Huddersfield, Yorks., joiner and/or cm (1834–37). Trading at Dean House, Honley in 1837. [D]

Eastwood, Thomas, Honley, near Huddersfield, Yorks., joiner and/or cm (1837). [D]

Eaton, James, King St, Hammersmith, Middlx, furniture broker, appraiser, cm and u (1839). [D]

Eaton, John, Liverpool, cm (1777–84). Addresses given at 55 Ranelegh St and Stanley St, 1777; and 29 School Lane, 1781–84. [D]

Eaton, John, King St, Derby, cm (1829). [D]

Eaton, Peter, address unrecorded, cm (1803). Subscribed to Sheraton's *Cabinet Dictionary*, 1803.

Eaton, Thomas, Castle St, The Potteries, Staffs., cm (1818). [D]

Eaton, Thomas, St John's Sq., Burslem, Staffs., joiner and cm (1822). [D]

Eaton, Thomas, Navigation Rd, Burslem, Staffs., cm and u (1834). [D]

Eaves, James, Trumpington St, Cambridge, joiner and cm (b. *c.* 1753–d. 1800). Death aged 47 reported in *Cambridge Chronicle and Journal*, 8 March 1800.

Eaves, Richard, Liverpool, late of Blackburn, Lancs., cm (1782). Named in the Preston Guild record of burgesses in 1782 as son of William Eaves, carrier of Preston, deceased.

Ebbs, Nathaniel, London, cm (1821–23). Trading at 13 Red Lion St, Clerkenwell in 1821, and 177 Piccadilly, 1823. [D]

Ebditch, —, London, cm (1793). Subscribed to Sheraton's *Drawing Book*, 1793.

Eccles, Bowyer, Market Lane, Newcastle-under-Lyme, Staffs., joiner and cm (1818). [D]

Eccles, Edward, 15 Lill's Ct, Preston, Lancs., chair-bottomer (1818). [D]

Eccles, Henry, Manchester, cm, carver and gilder (1800–36). Addresses given at 65 Shude Hill in 1800; 35 Wood St in 1802; 7 Mulberry Ct in 1808; 37 Wood St in 1817; 20 Kennedy St in 1818; no. 29, 1819–20; 1 Hulme St, Ridgefield, with res. at 3 Gore St, Salford in 1825; 14 Broker Bank in 1829; 26 Deal St, 1832–33, no. 25 in 1834–36 and as John Henry Eccles at no. 25 in 1836. [D]

Eccles, James, New Market Pl., Bolton, Lancs., carver and gilder (1824–34). [D]

Eccles, Thomas, Manchester, carver and gilder (1813–40). Addresses given at 14 Mulberry St, 1813–17; no. 12 in 1818; 62 King St, 1821–25; 9 Back King St, 1828–29; 12 Mulberry St, 1832–33; and 32 Princess St, 1838–40. [D]

Eccles, William, Henderson Ct, Back Chester St, Liverpool, cm (1829). [D]

Echlers, Richard, Liverpool, cm (1830–40). Indenture dated 1830. Admitted freeman on servitude to William John Roberts in 1840. [Liverpool freemen's committee bk]

Eckford, Charles & John, 45 Fleet St, London, picture cleaners, restorers and frame makers (1792–1840). Advertised in *Art Union*, 1840, p. 47, stating the firm had been established in 1792. [D]

Eckford, John, 17 Water St (or Lane), Bridewell Precinct, London, carver and gilder, dealer in paintings (1814–29). Took out Sun Insurance policies on 12 September 1814 for £700 of which stock, utensils and goods in trust accounted for £300; on 21 September 1818 for £300 on a let house in Crosby Row, Walworth; and on 14 December 1820 for £650, including £450 on houses in tenure at 7 Crown Ct, Dorset St, and 4 George Row; and £200 on a private house at 8 George Row. [D; GL, Sun MS vol. 461, ref. 897352; vol. 480, ref. 946122; vol. 487, ref. 974492]

Eckford, John, 48 Lothbury, London, carver and gilder (1826–27). [D]

Eckhardt, Anthony George, London, cm (1771–98). Trading at Hans Pl., Chelsea in 1798. In 1771 he patented for fourteen years a portable table 'with Double or Single Folding Flaps and Folding Feet, and also a New Portable Chair, so Contrived as to Answer all the Purposes of the common Tables and Chairs, and at the same Time to Lay in the

Compass of a Small Box.' In 1798 he took out another patent for his 'Improved Method of Making Chairs, Sofas, Stools, Benches, &c., &c., Adapted for Rooms or Carriages with Backs and Seates, or Cushions fixed in such a Manner as instantly to Change or Shew Two Different Surfaces in One . . .'. [V & A archives; *DEF*]

Eddy, John, Fore St, Kingsbridge and Dodbrook, Devon, cm (1838). [D]

Ede, George, Chapel Rd, Worthing, Sussex, cm and u (1832–39). Recorded at no. 6, with furniture warehouse at South St in 1839. [D]

Ede, Joseph, High St, Dorking, Surrey, cm (1801). Took out a Sun Insurance policy on 13 April 1801 for £300 of which £250 accounted for his house, where no work was done; and £50 for washroom, warehouse and workshop. [GL, Sun MS vol. 39, ref. 717207]

Eden, Christopher, Liverpool, carver and gilder (1821–39). Addresses given at Duncan St East, 1821–24; no. 24, and also 23 Sidney St in 1824; 30 Bridport St, 1829–30; and 6 Spencer Buildings, Hunter St, with shop in Williamson St, 1834–39. [D]

Eden, Francis, at the Foot of the Butcher-Bank, Newcastle, joiner and cm (1768). Advertised in *Newcastle Chronicle*, 14 May 1768 that he 'Makes and sells all Sorts of Cabinet Goods, Chairs, Tables, &c. on reasonable Terms.'

Eden, Francis, George's Stairs, Newcastle, cm and/or carpenter (1778). [D]

Eden, Francis, Pilgrim St, Newcastle, cm (1805–08). [D]

Ed(d)en, John jnr, Liverpool, cm (1760–d. 1802). Addresses given in partnership with Ellen Rigg, cm, at Newmarket in 1765, and Derby Sq., 1766–67; recorded alone at 11 Derby Sq. in 1769; 55 Ranelegh St with warehouse at 5 Harrington in 1777; Lord St, 1778–87; no. 33, 1784–87; warehouse at 5 Islington and workshop at Back 34 Lord St in 1790; Folly Lane, 1794; and 3 Upper Islington, 1796. In 1760 he petitioned freedom on birthright as son of Thomas Eden, shoemaker, paying 3s 4d. Admitted freeman on 30 May 1761. Former apps petitioned freedom: Richard Coppell and John Walker in 1780; Thomas Dutton in 1790; Samuel Nelson in 1802, indenture dated 1790; and George Bilby in 1802, indenture dated 1794. Son, John Eden, Gent., petitioned freedom on birthright in 1802. On 25 October 1765 Ellen, widow of Edward Rigg, cm, announced in *Williamson's Liverpool Advertiser* her intention of carrying on business and entering into partnership with Eden, 'who has been several Years in some of the principal Shops in London'. Eden alone took out a Sun Insurance policy in 1778 for £500, utensils and stock accounting for £200. Probably the J. Eden, cm of Liverpool, who subscribed £1 1s to the Mayor's fund for the relief of soldiers and their dependants in the American war [*Williamson's Liverpool Advertiser*, 17 November 1775]; and who acted as agent in a sale of stock, same paper, 10 January 1782. [D; Liverpool freemen reg. and committee bk; GL, Sun MS vol. 264, p. 537] Probably John Edon.

Eden, John, Nottingham, joiner and cm (1805). Son of William Eden, farmer of Breaston, Derbs.; app. to William Calar in 1805. [Nottingham app. list]

Eden, Michael, 17 Grenada Pl., Commercial Rd, Limehouse, London, u and cm (1826–39). [D]

Eden(s), Michael, 9 City Rd, London, u (1823–25). [D] See Thomas Eden(s). Possibly:

Eden, Mitchell, 9 City Rd, London, bed and mattress maker (1822–23). [D]

Eden, Thomas, Newcastle, u and furniture broker (1788–1801). Addresses given at 'The Sofa, Foot of the Side', 1788–91; 21 Dean St, 1791–94; no. 18, 1794–95; and Groat Mkt, 1801. Advertised in *Newcastle Courant* several times for

apps; and on 22 March 1788 that he had begun business in the shop 'late Mr. Robert Curry's', and had 'been in some of the first shops in London'. On 12 April he announced the arrival from London of 'a large assortment of Paper Hangings'. Advertised an assortment of stained chairs on 31 May 1789, and for an app. on 16 January 1790. His notice of 15 January illustrated a Hepplewhite-style sofa, and advertised 'stain'd chairs, from eight shillings down to four and sixpence'. On 24 December 1791 he announced his removal from 'his Shop at the Foot of the Side, to a more eligible situation, No. 21, Foot of Dean-street'. On 28 April and 3 November 1792 he advertised his 'Great variety of French and English Sofas with folding beds to them, extremely convenient in large families'. Sale of upholstery goods announced, 22 June 1793 'by order of the Trustees', F. Elden & Son, so he is presumably the Thomas Weatherburn Eden, u of Newcastle, declared bankrupt, *Williamson's Liverpool Advertiser*, 13 May 1793. He was trading again by 16 May 1794 when he advertised his business at 18 Dean St. On 29 August 1795 his advertisement declared he was 'sensible of the liberal support he had for these eighteen years experienced . . . He wishes at the same time to inform the gentlemen of the Army that he has at present by him, a handsome foulding Camp Sofa Bed, on a new Construction, German Beds for Foreign Service . . . Cott Beds, Mahogany folding tables, Looking Glasses, Camp stools . . . he also makes the MARQUE and TENTS on the newest Construction without any Centre Poles.' [D]

Eden(s), Thomas, City Rd, London, u and mattress maker (1809–28). Trading at no. 12, 1809–11, and no. 9, 1816–28. [D] See Michael and Mitchell Eden.

Eden, William, Nottingham, joiner and cm (1823–32). Trading at Derby Rd in 1832. App. to John Addicott in 1823. [D; Nottingham app. list]

Edgar, James, 170 Pilgrim St, Newcastle, cm and furniture broker (1834). [D]

Edgcombe, George, Scotland St, Ellesmere, Salop, cm (1822). [D]

Edgcome, William, High St, Penryn, Cornwall, joiner and cm (1802–10). Advertised in *Royal Cornwall Gazette*, 24 and 31 July 1802 that he was commencing business as a sworn appraiser and auctioneer for sale of lands, merchandise, furniture etc. Signed lease, dated 24 June 1810, on a house with gardens, backhouse and orchard in High St. [Cornwall RO, AD 201/14/2]

Edge, Joseph, 19 Church St, Blackburn, Lancs., carver and gilder (1828). [D]

Edge, Richard, 94 Portland St, Manchester, cm (1824–25). [D]

Edge, Samuel, Witton St, Northwich, Cheshire, cm (1822). [D]

Edge, Samuel, Over, near Middlewich, Cheshire, cm (1834). [D]

Edgecombe, Handy, High St, Tewkesbury, Glos., cm (1798–1830). Child bapt. in 1824. Declared bankrupt, *Liverpool Mercury*, 25 January 1826. [D; PR(bapt.)]

Edgecombe, Richard F., Tewkesbury, Glos., cm and builder (1798). [D]

Edgecombe, William, High St, Tewkesbury, Glos., cm and u (1820). [D]

Edgecumbe, Mrs, High St, Tewkesbury, Glos., cm, u and builder (1822). [D]

Edgerly, Thomas, High Wycombe, Bucks., chair caner (b. c.1791–1841). Daughter bapt. in 1825, sons in 1829, 1831 and 1834; daughter in 1837. Aged 50 at the time of the 1841 Census. [PR(bapt.)]

Edghill, Henry, 1 Anderson's Buildings, City Rd, London, cm and u (1839). [D]

Edie, James, London, cm (1793). Subscribed to Sheraton's *Drawing Book*, 1793.

Edisforth, William, Canterbury, Kent, upholder (1663). [Canterbury freemen rolls]

Edkins, Thomas, 34 Ebury St, Chelsea, London, carpenter, cm and u (1808). [D]

Edleston (Edels(t)on or Edlisden), James, 40 Drury Lane, London, cm (1789–1811). [D]

Edleston, James, 9 Rosamon (or Rosomond) Buildings, Islington, London, cm and appraiser (1820–37). [D]

Edlin, Edward C., New Bond St, London, turner and toyman by appointment to His Majesty (1796–1832). Recorded at no. 34, 1798–1808; and no. 31, 1831–32. Bills in the Arundel Castle records dated December 1831 for a backgammon table, and September 1832 for a doll, have the heading which reads: 'Turnery in all its Branches, Foreign Toys and Tunbridge Ware. Juvenile Publications.' [D; Arundel Castle records, A 2094]

Edlyn, John & Chappell, address unrecorded. In 1778 supplied a bookcase with sash doors, costing £1 2s 6d to Croome Court, Worcs. [V & A archives]

Edmett, Thomas, Maidstone, Kent, cm and u (1810–39). Recorded at Middle Row, 1832–38, and High St, 1834. Advertised in *Maidstone Journal*, 29 May 1810 that he was formerly app. to Edward Argles who is 'now on the eve of leaving Maidstone, for a large and extensive concern in the Metropolis'. Argles took over the business of Thomas Butler in Catherine St, Strand. [D; poll bks; reg. of elect.]

Edmonds, —, address unrecorded, 'inventor' (1744). Notice in *Daily Advertiser*, 23 April 1744 concerned the sale 'by Order of the Creditors of Mr. Edmonds the Inventor' of 'That curious Piece of Machinery, call'd the Temple of Arts and Sciences . . . This most valuable Structure of Mahogany, in form of a Roman Temple, neatly carved and gilt, finely embellish'd with emblematical figures . . .' painted and carved, representing geography, astronomy, night, music, mathematics and painting. The contraption incorporated 'a moving Picture, representing Mount Parnassus, where Clouds break away, and Apollo appears with the Muses while the Most sublime Pieces of Mr. Handel's Musick are perform'd by the Machine . . .'.

Edmonds, George, West Wycombe, Bucks., chairmaker (b. c. 1804–41). Aged 37 at the time of the 1841 Census.

Edmonds, Henry, Camomile St, London, carver and sadler (1763–79). Employed one non-freeman for three months in 1763, and one for six weeks in both 1764 and 1765. Insured his house at 9 Camomile St for £300 in 1779 with the Sun Co. [GL, City Licence bks, vols 3 and 4; GL, Sun MS vol. 272, p. 608]

Edmonds, John, 16 Church St, Soho, London, upholder (1786). On 22 July 1786 insured his house and offices adjoining for £300 with the Sun Co. [GL, Sun MS vol. 339, p. 129]

Edmonds, John, 6 Old Compton St, Soho, London, cm and u (1796–1839). Named in Sheraton's list of master cabinet makers, 1803. Took out a Sun Insurance policy on 7 July 1804 for £500 on his house at 1 Kemps Row, Chelsea, in tenure. Referred to in Whitten's *Nollekens and His Times*. Probably the maker of an oval mahogany Pembroke table at Temple Newsam House, Leeds, stencilled under the drawer, 'J. EDMONDS'. [D; GL, Sun MS vol. 431, ref. 764049; Gilbert, *Leeds Furn. Cat.*, vol. 2, p. 349]

Edmonds, John, 1 Monkwell St, Cripplegate, London, turner etc. (1835). [D]

Edmonds, John, 3 Meredith St, Clerkenwell, London, cm, u and dressing case maker (1835–39). [D]

Edmonds, Joseph, 13 Court, Gt Hampton St, Birmingham, carver and gilder (1835). [D]

Edmonds, Robert, Lowestoft, Suffolk, cm and u (1830). [D]

Edmonds (or Edmunds), Samuel(l), London, upholder (1713–25). Recorded as Edmonds in James St, near Golden Sq. in 1720. Son of Samuel Edmunds, plumber of London; app. to John Rose(?) and admitted freeman of the Upholders' Co. by servitude on 3 March 1713/14. Took out a Sun Insurance policy on 25 March 1720 on goods and merchandise in his house. In 1725 he received £4 11s for 'upholstery work of a blue cloth bed', probably carried out for the Duke of Montrose. [GL, Upholders' Co. records; GL, Sun MS vol. 11, p. 77; Scottish RO, GD 220/6/1256/47]

Edmonds, Thomas, London, upholder (1742–56). Son of William Edmonds, upholder of London; app. to his father on 3 November 1742, and admitted freeman of the Upholders' Co. by servitude on 4 November 1756. [GL, Upholders' Co. records]

Edmonds, Thomas, Northbrook St, Newbury, Berks., cm and u (1823–42). [D]

Edmonds, William, address unrecorded, upholder (1711–56). Son of John Edmonds, yeoman of Maningford, Wilts. App. to William Cope on 5 March 1711, and admitted freeman of the Upholders' Co. by servitude on 7 December 1737. Took son, Thomas Edmonds, as app., 1742–56, admitted freeman in 1756. [GL, Upholders' Co. records]

Edmonds, William, Oxford, then Burford, joiner, cm, carpenter and chairmaker (1775–79). Opened a shop in High St, near All Saints on 21 October 1775. Sale of stock in trade on the take-over of Edmonds's business by Mr Linsell announced in *Jackson's Oxford Journal*, 18 September 1779. Edmonds was 'going to keep the Mermaid at Burford; where he intends carrying on the Carpenter's, Joiner's, and Cabinet Business, as usual'. Stock for sale consisted of beds and bedding, 'Mahogany and Walnut-tree Chairs, Tables, Bureaus, Chests of Drawers, Pier and Swing Glasses, Tea-Boards, Trays, Chests, China &c.'

Edmonds, William, Silver St, Northampton, cm (1830). [Poll bk]

Edmondson, James, Lancaster, cm (1817–18). Admitted freeman, 1817–18, when stated 'of Liverpool'. [Lancaster freemen rolls] Possibly James Edmundson of Liverpool.

Edmondson, Matthew, 64 Lombard St, London, upholder (1778–83). Admitted freeman of the Upholders' Co. by redemption on 2 December 1778. Took out a Sun Insurance policy in 1778 for £700 of which utensils and stock accounted for £550. [D; GL, Upholders' Co. records; GL, Sun MS vol. 269, p. 16]

Edmondson, Matthew, 28 Haymarket, Piccadilly, London, upholder (1783). Took out a Sun Insurance policy in 1783 for £1,700 of which £1,400 accounted for utensils, stock and goods. [GL, Sun MS vol. 317, p. 542]

Edmondson, Matthew, 9 Dean St, Soho, London, u and furniture warehouseman (1809–11). [D]

Edmondson, Peter, Liverpool, chairmaker (1827–35). Addresses given at 38 Hodson St, 1823–29; no. 35 in 1827; shop at 26 Hart St, 1834–35; and Woodward Sq., Lawrence St in 1835. [D]

Edmondson, Peter & Sons, 12 Bold St, Liverpool, u and cm (1827). [D]

Edmondson, Richard, Lancaster, cm (1817–18). [Lancaster freemen rolls] See Richard Edmundson.

Edmondson, Robert I, Lancaster, cm (1767–84). Admitted freeman, 1767–68, polled at Lancaster in 1768, and named in the Gillow records in 1784. [Lancaster freemen rolls; Westminster Ref. Lib., Gillow]

Edmondson, Robert II, Lancaster, cm (1779–84). Admitted freeman, 1779–80. [Lancaster freemen rolls and poll bk]

Edmondson, Robert III, Lancaster, cm (1817–18). Admitted freeman in 1817–18, when stated 'of Liverpool'. [Lancaster freemen rolls]

Edmondson (or Edmundson,) Robert, Liverpool, cm and u (1816–24). Addresses given at 26 Clarence St with cabinet manufactory at 2 Marshall St in 1816; Toxteth Park in 1823; and 5 Pack Rd in 1824. [D] See Richard Edmundson.

Edmondson, Samuel, Lancaster, carver (1830–31). [Lancaster freemen rolls]

Edmondson, Thomas, Lancaster, cm (1806–24). App. to J. Hodgson in 1806 and admitted freeman, 1817–18. Named in the Gillow records, 1815–24. [Lancaster app. reg. and freemen rolls; Westminster Ref. Lib., Gillow]

Edmondson, William, Netherend, Penrith, Cumb., cm, u and joiner (1834). [D]

Edmondson & Creighton, 36 Castle St, Carlisle, Cumb., carvers, gilders, u and paper hangers (1834). [D]

Edmonson, Matthew, 48 Wimpole St, London, upholder (1794). Took out a Sun Insurance policy on 8 July 1794 for £950, with the addition of £45 on house, utensils and stock. [GL, Sun MS vol. 401, ref. 630170]

Edmund, James, East Walls, Carlisle, Cumb., chairmaker (1811). [D]

Edmund, Platt, address unrecorded, carver and gilder (1775). Subscribed to Thomas Malton's *Compleat Treatise on Perspective*, 1775.

Edmunds, —, Dean St, London(?) u (1785). Named in A. T. Smith's *A Book for a Rainy Day*, 1842, pp. 91–92.

Edmunds, Isaac, High St, Worcester, cm (1794–98). Recorded at 5 Corn Mkt in 1794 and High St, 1797–98, no. 51 in 1797. [D]

Edmunds, John, Liverpool, furniture painter (1807–18). Recorded at Sir Thomas's Buildings in 1807; 25 Vernon St, 1810–11; and no. 47, 1813–18. Marriage to Miss Chritchley of Rainford's Gdns at St Nicholas's Church, reported in *Liverpool Chronicle*, 17 June 1807. [D]

Edmunds, Richard, 41 Gt Alice St, London, picture and looking-glass frame maker (1826). [D]

Edmundson, —, Liverpool, cm (1793). Subscribed to Sheraton's *Drawing Book*, 1793.

Edmundson, J., Moor Lane, Lancaster, chairmaker (1811). Advertised in *Lancaster Gazette*, 7 September 1811, that he was continuing his business 'in all its branches'.

Edmundson, James, 2 Oldham St, Liverpool, u (1827–39). [D] Possibly James Edmondson of Lancaster.

Edmundson, Rachel & Sons, Liverpool, cm and u (1816–39). Recorded at 2 Oldhall (probably Oldham) St, 1816–35, and Marshall St, 1817–23. Announced changes of address from Marshall St to 11 Bold St in *Liverpool Mercury*, 11 February 1820; and on 10 December 1830 from 12 Bold St (where directories list the firm from 1827–29) to no. 52, 'which they are now fitting up to suit the convenience of their Business. As they intend to open their new establishment with a modern & fashionable assortment of UPHOLSTERY & CABINET FURNITURE they have commenced selling their stock at very reduced prices.' Recorded at 62 Bold St, 1834–35, no. 63 in 1837 and no. 112 in 1839. Supplied furniture to Liverpool Town Hall between 1817–23, totalling £2,057. [D; *Furn. Hist.*, 1970] Clearly connected with:

Edmundson, Richard, Liverpool, cm and u (1779–1839). Admitted freeman of Lancaster, 1779–80, when stated 'of Liverpool', and polled at Lancaster in 1784. Addresses given in partnership with Robert Edmundson at Castle Ditch in 1781; as Edmundson & Fayrer at 26 Castle Ditch, 1785–91; as Edmundson, Fayrer & Barwick at no. 26 in 1788, and no. 21 in 1790; alone at 50 and 55 Paradise St in 1790; at 49 Paradise St, 26 Castle Ditch, with yard at Dale St in 1791; from February 1791 at 62 Castle St; no. 60 in 1794, with shop and timberyard at 2 Holden St, Renshaw St in 1796; 2 Marshall St, Lord St with shop and timberyard at 2 Oldham St, Renshaw St, 1800–18; as Edmundson & Son, 1813–17; at 2 Oldham St, 1827–37; 12 Bold St in 1829; and 3 Oldham St in 1839. Edmundson & Fayrer announced the opening of their warehouse at 26 Castle Ditch in *Williamson's Liverpool Advertiser*, 14 November 1785, and listed stock including library book cases, billiard tables, bureau writing tables, sideboard tables with vase and pedestals, cylinder desks, wine cisterns, cabriole chairs and sofas, and camp chairs and tables. The firm announced the addition of an upholstery branch to the business on 24 November 1788. They had also taken another partner, William Barwick, and now stocked mattresses, bedsteads, mosquito nets and sofas, and appraised household furniture. Dissolution of the partnership was announced on 17 January 1791, sale of stock to be held on 24 January 1791. Edmundson advertised on 7 February 1791 that he was continuing business 'as usual on his own account in a large & convenient shop, no. 62 CASTLE-STREET . . . which will be ready to open in a few weeks . . .'. Took out a Sun Insurance policy on 3 December 1792 for £2,600, £200 on his new house and shop in Castle St, £1,250 on utensils and stock; £1,000 on those in his warehouse and workshop communicating in Spitalfields; and £100 on his workshop and sawpit in Thomas's Buildings. In *Liverpool Chronicle*, 18 November 1805 Edmundson offered thanks for 'the very kind & spirited exertions made for suppressing the Fire in his Workshop in Oldham-Street'. [D; GL, Sun MS vol. 391, p. 502] Possibly two tradesmen of the same name are concerned here.

Edmundson, Robert, 23 North St, Dale St, Liverpool, cm (1796). [D] See Robert Edmondson.

Edmundson, Thomas, 51 Stanley St, Liverpool, cm (1790). [D]

Edney, James, Emsworth, Hants., chairmaker (1839). [D]

Edney, John, Witney, Oxon., cm (1718). Took app. named Smart in 1718. [S of G, app. index]

Edney, William, Chapel St, Tottenham Ct Rd, London, cm (1835–39). Recorded at no. 12 in 1835 and no. 9 in 1839. [D]

Edon, —, Newcastle, cm (1793). Subscribed to Sheraton's *Drawing Book*, 1793. Probably either Francis or Thomas Eden.

Edon, John, Liverpool, cm (1761). Admitted freeman on 30 January 1761. [Liverpool freemen reg.] Possibly John Eden.

Edridge, William, Canterbury, Kent, u (1706). [Canterbury freemen rolls]

Edsall, Henry, Milford St, Salisbury, Wilts., chairmaker (1839). [D]

Edson, John, London, chairmaker, cm and u (1794–1819). Trading at 28 Berwick St, 1794–96, and 74 Titchfield St, Fitzroy Sq., 1806–19. Possibly the maker of a set of ten parcel gilt and white painted chairs with caned seats, tapering 'bamboo' legs, and X-shaped stretchers; attributed in design to James Wyatt, and stamped 'I.E.' or 'J.E.' [D; Sotheby's, 2 April 1971, lot 76]

Edward, George, 115 Long Acre, London, upholder (1776). Took out a Sun Insurance policy in 1776 for £1,100 of which £1,000 accounted for utensils and stock. [GL, Sun MS vol. 248, ref. 369807]

Edwardes & Har(mibe), address unrecorded. Mahogany sofa table has this firm's name written in ink with the date 1826. [V & A archives]

Edwards, —, Glean Alley, Coleman St, London, cm (d. 1750). Report in *General Advertiser*, 15 June 1750 that Edwards had fallen down 'in an Apoplectick Fit in his House, & died instantly.'

Edwards, —, London, carver (1767). Received payments from Henry Knight of Tythegston Court, Glam., in 1767 for picture frames. [*C. Life*, 5 October 1978]

Edwards, —, 15 John St, Pentonville, London, carver and gilder (1808). [D]

Edwards, —, address unrecorded. Extending mahogany dining table, 1820, noted with lazy-tongs underframe action; end standards each bear small die stamped octagonal tablet featuring the Royal Coat of Arms and Motto with 'EDWARDS PATENT'. Possibly David Edwards of 21 King St, London.

Edwards, —, address unrecorded, frame maker (1824). In March 1824 received £30 2s for picture frames, and in December 1824, 6s 7d for 'frame-cartoon' supplied to Nicholas Pearse of Loughton, Essex, and Marylebone, London. [Essex RO, D/DHt A1/3] See J. and R. Edwards, and Edwards & Son.

Edwards, Abraham, Lewes, Sussex, u (1734). [Poll bk]

Edwards, Adam, 70 Whitechapel, London, carver, gilder, looking-glass manufacturer and paper hanger (1809–25). [D] See William Edwards at this address.

Edwards, Alexander, 11 Richmond Terr., Richmond Row, Liverpool, cm (1839). [D]

Edwards, Anthony, 201 Bradford St, Birmingham, Grecian and fancy chairmaker (1835). [D]

Edwards, Charles, 10 Berkeley St, Clerkenwell, London, clock-case maker (1809–11). [D]

Edwards, Charles, 1 Gloucester St, Bristol, cm (1835–40). [D]

Edwards, David, 21 King St, Bloomsbury Sq., London, writing and dressing case maker to the Royal Family, inventor of the patent military travelling cases (1813–d. 1848). Addresses also given at 84 St James's St, 1813–14, and 5 Orange St in 1817. [D] Submitted bill dated 22 July 1813 to Robert Clavering Savage of Gloucester Pl., Portman Sq., London, and Elmley Castle, near Worcester, for a total of £11 13s 6d for a kingwood jewel case, and repairs to an old jewel case. Receipt dated 23 March 1814 is signed by J. Bacon. Bill heading lists stock which includes writing, dressing, plate and canteen cases, combs, brushes, cut glass and cutlery. [Worcs. RO, 4600/705: 505/763/3] Named in the Royal Household accounts on 19 December 1823 receiving £72 6s. For items supplied between 21 July 1824 and 1 May 1825 he was paid £78 11s 6d; and between 1824–27, £54 12s. [Windsor Royal Archives, RA35570, 35591, 89520] Submitted a bill, dated 18 December 1832, to John Arkwright of Hampton Court, Leominster, Herefs., for a rosewood tea chest costing £4 4s. On Edwards's death in 1848, his solicitors or creditors wrote to Arkwright requesting settlement of his account, £16 2s having been owed 'some years.' [Herefs. RO, Arkwright papers, A63/161] Portable writing desk of brass-bound rosewood recorded bearing inside the trade label of 'EDWARDS, 21 KING STREET, HOLBORN'. Label also found on portable brass inlaid kingwood-veneered writing box containing two silver-stoppered glass containers with hallmarks for 1828. [Sotheby's, 10 July 1970, lot 17; 3 June 1977, lot 81] See Thomas Edwards, cm of London.

Edwards, David, Birmingham, Grecian, Windsor and fancy chairmaker (1816–30). Trading at 5 Rea St, 1816–22, and Bradford St, 1828–30. [D]

Edwards, David, Cambridge, cm (1830). Child bapt. on 14 February 1830 at St Clement's Church. [PR(bapt.)]

Edwards, Edward, London, furniture designer (b. 1738–d. 1806). Born in London, the son of a chairmaker and carver native of Shrewsbury. Aged fifteen he was app. to work with his father in the shop of William Hallett, the well-known cm and u of Long Acre, and among the chief exponents of the Gothic and Chinese styles. Remaining there for three years Edwards 'drew patterns for furniture' and 'sought every opportunity of looking at works of art'. In 1759 he became a student in the Duke of Richmond's Academy, and in 1760,

opened an evening school in Compton St, Soho, to support his widowed mother and sister. Here he taught drawing to 'several young men who either aimed to be artists, or to qualify themselves to be cabinet, or ornamental furniture makers'. In 1769 he became a student of the Royal Academy and in 1773 was elected an Associate. Two years later he went to Italy to study art, but mediocre as a painter, he returned to furniture designing. On his return 'he was soon engaged by the honourable Horace Walpole at Strawberry Hill', as his master, Hallett, had been. He received commissions from Walpole until 1784, in which year he designed a cabinet in the Gothic style. He was appointed Teacher of Perspective at the Academy in 1788, where he frequently exhibited. An antiquarian, he studied and etched Newcastle topography, and painted scenery for a Newcastle theatre in 1787. He wrote *Anecdotes of Painters*, published posthumously in 1808, and containing a brief autobiography. The V & A has a portfolio of his sketches of old furniture, architectural details, glass and silverware. Edwards died on 19 December 1806. [DEF; C. Life, 7 June 1930, pp. 848–50]

Edwards, Edward, Gorst Stacks, Chester, cm (1812). [Poll bk]

Edwards, Edward, Birmingham, victualler and chairmaker (1816–22). Recorded at Rea St in 1816 and Digbeth, 1818–22. [D]

Edwards, Edward, Ironbridge, Salop, cm (1822–35). [D]

Edwards, Edward, Upper Burgess St, Grimsby, Lincs., joiner and cm (1835). [D]

Edwards, Francis, 4 Crown St, Soho, London, cm and u (1839). [D]

Edwards, George, 6 St James's St, Bristol, cm (1754–84). [Poll bks]

Edwards, George Barrister, Liverpool, u (1824–29). Trading at 31 New Scotland Rd in 1824 and 41 Milton St, 1827–29. [D]

Edwards, George, 46 Milk St, Bristol, carver and gilder (1833). [D]

Edwards, George, Church St, Warminster, Wilts., cm and u (1839). [D]

Edwards, Hannah, Riding's Yd, Warrington, Lancs., u (1822). [D]

Edwards, Henry, Rotten Row, Old St, Cripplegate, London, joiner, cm and broker (1727). Took out a Sun Insurance policy on 1 April 1727 for £500 of which goods and stock accounted for £200. [GL, Sun MS vol. 23, p. 510]

Edwards, Henry, Exeter, Devon, freeman cm (1832). [Voters list]

Edwards, J., address unrecorded. In 1810 repaired and gilded three picture frames for Nicholas Pearse of Loughton, Essex, and London. [Essex RO, D/DHt A1/4] See R. Edwards, and Edwards & Son.

Edwards, J., 33 Mount St, Grosvenor Sq., London, carver and gilder (1835). [D]

Edwards, I. or J., 13 Bedford Pl., Commercial Rd, London, cm (1837). [D]

Edwards, James, Cannon St, Nicholas Lane, London, turner (1717). Insured his house for £250 on 13 November 1717. [GL, Hand in Hand MS vol. 18, p. 25]

Edwards, James, 46 Ewer St, Southwark, London, cm (1809–11). [D]

Edwards, John, Chester, cm (1744–47). Son of John Edwards, Gent., deceased; app. to Joseph Burrows, cm, and admitted freeman on 19 April 1744. [Chester freemen rolls; poll bk]

Edwards, John, Chester, cm (1755). App. to Philip Presbury, cm, 1 March to 1 April 1755. [Chester app. bks]

Edwards, John, High St and St Mary's Lane, Lewes, Sussex, u (1774–90). [Poll bks; T. Woollgar, *Spicilegia Sive Collectanea ad Historiam et Antiquitates Lewensis, c. 1790*]

Edwards, John, Peterborough, Northants., u (1806). [Lincoln freemen rolls]

Edwards, John, Liverpool, cm (1824–39). Addresses given at 4 Cable St in 1824; 4 Tarleton St, 1827–32; Williamson St with shop at 4 Parker St in 1835; 3 Riding St and 59 Lime St in 1837; 2 Stanhope St with shop at 32 Lime St, and 7 Parker St with shop at 24 Williamson St in 1839. Two tradesmen may be involved here, since a John Edwards is also recorded in directories at 11 Vine St in 1832. [D] John Edwards submitted bills to George Holt of Rake Lane, Liverpool, dated 14 and 21 January 1832. The first totalled £153 18s 4d and included '14 Rosewood Antique Chairs', £49; 'a Circular Rosewood Table', £18 18s; 'a Pair of Card Tables', £18 18s; '2 Rosewood Couches', £28; silk gimp for curtaining, gilt cornices; supervising the fixing of blinds and curtains, making bolsters, pillow, chair, chandelier and embroidered table covers; cleaning and polishing furniture. The second bill records payment of £57 3s 6d for a looking-glass and 'blind frame'; and £61 16s 9d 'to a large Chimney Glass in Gold frame Fitted up Complete'. [Liverpool RO, 920 HOL 3/1]

Edwards, John, 3 Black Swan Ct, Bath, Som., chairmaker (1826). [D]

Edwards, John, Chester, cm and u (1828–47). Addresses given in Northgate St in 1828; 82 Watergate St, 1829–33; and 29 Watergate Row with res. in Watergate St, 1840. Advertised as agent in sale of the Manor House in Gt Boughton, near Chester, in *Chester Chronicle, Cheshire and North Wales Advertiser*, 11 December 1829. Announced in *Chester Courant and Advertiser for North Wales*, 19 and 26 March 1833, that 'he has taken a licence to act as an appraiser and auctioneer' and 'flatters himself that his long experience in the cabinet and upholstery business will enable him to fix a just and fair valuation on goods and furniture.' Advertised in the *Chester General Directory*, 1840, that he sold 'Paper hangings, carpets, hearth rugs, fringes, laces, bell pulls, floor cloths, and every other article connected with his respective trades.' Took apps named Richard Brown in 1838, Thomas Carline in 1839, Thomas Marshall in 1841, and William, son of Thomas Edwards, in 1842. Elected councilman in 1839 and 1847. [D; Chester app. bks]

Edwards, John, 25 Thomas St, Bristol, cm, broker, trunk and band-box maker (1834–40). [D]

Edwards, John, Paris St, Exeter, Devon, carver and gilder (1835). His son John Kelly bapt. at St Sidwell's on 17 May 1835. [PR(bapt.)]

Edwards, John, 17 Shepherd's Mkt, London, carver and gilder (1835). [D]

Edwards, John, 4 Cannon Pl., Whitechapel Rd, London, bedstead maker (1837). [D]

Edwards, John, High St, Ellesmere, Salop, cm (1840). [D]

Edwards, John Holland, Holyrood St, Chard, Som., cm (1840). [D]

Edwards, Joseph, 6 Richmond St, Whitechapel, Liverpool, joiner and cm (1790). [D]

Edwards, Joshua, King's Lynn, Norfolk, u (1732–47). Admitted freeman by patrimony, 1732–33. Will proved at Norwich in 1747. [King's Lynn freemen's calendar; Norfolk Record Soc., index of wills]

Edwards, Luke, London(?), carver (1701). The Annandale accounts record payment to Edwards in 1701 of £13 10s for '1 fine carved tester headboard', and £2 5s for '1 large set carved cornices for case curtains'. [Hopetoun papers, NRA (s) 888/637]

Edwards, Oliver, London, upholder (1706–d. 1742). Recorded in Bartholomew Close, 1724–34. Son of Oliver Edwards, Gent. of Devizes, Wilts.; app. to James Parke on 5 June 1706. Admitted freeman of the Upholders' Co. by servitude on

5 December 1716, and master in 1742, in which year he died. [GL, Upholders' Co. records; poll bks]

Edwards, P., Gt Waterloo St, Lambeth, London, cm and u (1823–37). Trading at no. 5, 1826–27, and no. 99, 1827–35. [D]

Edwards, Peter, 5 Hyde St, Bloomsbury, London, cm (1781). Took out a Sun Insurance policy in 1781 for £100, utensils, stock and goods accounting for £25. [GL, Sun MS vol. 297, p. 472]

Edwards, R., address unrecorded, carver and gilder (1811–21). Named in the account bk of Nicholas Pearse of Loughton, Essex, and London, between 1811–21. Typical payments include on 6 June 1811, £3 for picture frames, and in May 1819, £2 8s for gilding picture frames. [Essex RO, D/DHt A1/4] See J. Edwards, and Edwards & Son. Possibly:

Edwards, Richard, 10 Ann St, Pentonville, London, carver and gilder (1790–1811). Worked for Lord Spencer at Althorp, Northants., carving glass frames and dado rails in Lady Spencer's Dressing Room, for which he submitted a bill for £64 18s 3d in June 1790. A receipt dated 10 May 1791 is for £1 9s 5d. [D; V & A archives]

Edwards, Richard, 12 Ossulton St, Somerstown, London, carver and gilder (1837). [D]

Edwards, Robert, Yoxford, Suffolk, cm (1792). Named in the calendar of marriage licence bonds on 5 November 1792. [Suffolk RO, FAA: 50/2/108]

Edwards, Samuel, 7 Cambridge Rd, London, furniture japanner (1830–39). [D]

Edwards, Samuel, Chester, cm (1831). Admitted freeman on 20 April 1831. [Chester freemen rolls]

Edwards, Samuel, Ironmarket, Newcastle-under-Lyme, Staffs., cm (1832). [Poll bk]

Edwards, Samuel, 7 Devonshire Buildings. Gt Dover St, London, joiner and cm (1832–45). [D; Lord Chamberlain's Royal accounts]

Edwards, Samuel, 40 Redcross St, Southwark, London, cm (1835–37). [D]

Edwards, Samuel, Holywell Row, Worship Sq., London, cm and u (1839). [D]

Edwards, Samuel, 13 Cannon St Rd, London, bedstead maker (1839). [D]

Edwards, Sarah, 11 Coach Yd, Bull St, Birmingham, u (1830). [D]

Edwards, Saul, 5 Gt Waterloo St, London, cm and u (1827–28). [D]

Edwards, Thomas, King's Lynn, Norfolk, joiner and cm (1713). Took app. named Farthing in 1713. [S of G, app. index]

Edwards, Thomas, Chandos St, Westminster, London, cm (1749). [Poll bk]

Edwards, Thomas, 131 Ratcliffe Highway, Upper East Smithfield, London, carver, gilder and paper hanger (1817–18). Took out a Sun Insurance policy on 31 December 1818 for £400 on goods in his new house. [D; GL, Sun MS vol. 480, ref. 948931]

Edwards, Thomas, Ironmarket, Newcastle-under-Lyme, Staffs., cm, u, appraiser and auctioneer (1818–39). Trading at no. 56, 1836–39, and as Thomas & Sons in 1839. [D]

Edwards, Thomas, High St, Bromsgrove, Worcs., carpenter and cm (1820). [D]

Edwards, Thomas, London, cm (1832–39). Sent account dated 23 August 1839 to John Arkwright of Hampton Court, Leominster, Herefs., for articles supplied in 1832–33. His bill, totalling £16 2s, included a rosewood tea chest costing £4 4s, and a mahogany dressing box, £3 13s 6d. [Herefs. RO, A63/161] See David Edwards of 21 King St, London.

Edwards, Thomas, Cambridge, cm and u (1832–47). Trading in Sussex St in 1832, and Market St, 1834–47. [D; poll bks]

Edwards, Thomas, Hanley, Staffs., cm and u (1834–35). Listed at York St and Stafford Row in 1834, and Market Pl. in 1835. [D]

Edwards, Thomas, Duckinfield St, Liverpool, cm (1835–39). Trading at no. 55, 1835–37; no. 12, and also 82 Chatham St in 1839. [D]

Edwards, Thomas, 21 King St, Holborn, London, workbox, desk and dressing case maker (1839). [D] See David Edwards.

Edwards, Thomas, 7 Beswick Row, Miller St, Manchester, chairmaker (1840). [D]

Edwards, W., Beatrice St, Oswestry, Salop, cm and joiner (1828). [D]

Edwards, William, Norwich, u (1692). App. to Sam Reeve on 24 February 1692. [Norwich app. reg.]

Edwards, William, address unrecorded, carpenter and joiner (1753–56). Worked at Norfolk House, London, in 1753 preparing the pier glasses and frames for Cuenot to carve for the Music Room. Supplied furniture, mainly for minor rooms, and carried out repairs. [V & A archives; Arundel Castle records, MD18, part 1]

Edwards, William, Bristol, cm (1754). [Poll bks]

Edwards, William, Wosbury, Salop, chairmaker (1755). Took app. named Davis in 1755. [S of G, app. index]

Edwards, William, 5 Hart St, London, upholder (1784). Son of William Edwards, barber of Hart St; app. to John Evans, and admitted freeman of the Upholders' Co. by servitude on 7 July 1784. [GL, Upholders' Co. records]

Edwards, William, 12 Cooper's Row, Crutched Friars, London, upholder (1806–16). [D]

Edwards, William, Stamford, Lincs. and Peterborough, Northants., cm and u (1806–32). Admitted freeman of Lincoln in 1806. Recorded in High St, Stamford, 1822–31, and in both Stamford and Peterborough in 1832. Listed at Long Causeway, Peterborough, 1822–30. Advertised sale of stock in *Cambridge Chronicle and Journal*, 14 September 1832, on giving up his Stamford shop. [D; Lincoln freemen rolls; poll bks]

Edwards, William, 70 Whitechapel, London, carver and gilder (1809–11). [D] See Adam Edwards at this address.

Edwards, William, High Petergate, York, carver, gilder and looking-glass maker (1823). [D]

Edwards, William, 201 Bradford St, Birmingham, Windsor and fancy chairmaker (1830). [D]

Edwards, William, Monks Dyke, Louth, Lincs., cm and joiner (1835). [D]

Edwards, William, 40 High St, Camden Town, London, cm and u (1838–39). In 1838 described as cm 'for Natural History'. [D]

Edwards, William, 60 Wentworth St, Whitechapel, London, cm and u (1839). [D]

Edwards, William, St Martin's St, Birmingham, cabinet and coffin maker (1839). [D]

Edwards & Son, address unrecorded. On 14 March 1820 the firm received £1 10s 6d for picture frames supplied to Nicholas Pearse of Loughton, Essex, and London. [Essex RO, D/DHt A1/4]

Edwards & Webster, 251 Strand, London, carvers and gilders (1784). [D]

Edwin, Thomas, address unrecorded, cm (1803). Subscribed to Sheraton's *Cabinet Dictionary*, 1803.

Edwin, Thomas, 151 St John's St, London, cm (1809–11). [D]

Edy, George jnr, 19 Limekiln Lane, Bristol, cm and undertaker (1828–33). [D]

Eedy, John, Broad St (or Row), Gt Yarmouth, Norfolk, carver and gilder (1805–08). [D]

Eeling, —, Star Ct, Butcher Row, near Temple Bar, London, cm (1747). Named in contemporary newspapers. [Heal]

Effery, Henry, Souldern, Oxon., cm and u (1780). Advertised for an app. in *Jackson's Oxford Journal*, 25 November 1780.

Egerton, George, Cash St, Kennington, London, chairmaker (1826). Named on 14 November 1826 as having got Elizabeth Egerton pregnant. [GL, P83/MRY1/877/41]

Egerton, John, Middlewich, Cheshire, cm (1782–84). [D]

Eggett, George, Melbourne St, King's Lynn, Norfolk, u (1839). [D]

Egginton, Josiah, Meeting St, Stroud, Glos., cm and chairmaker (1815–23). [D; PR(bapt.)]

Eggitt, Frances, South Clough Lane, King's Lynn, Norfolk, working u (1836–39). [D]

Eggless, William, Gloucester, carver (1752). Took app. named Woodall in 1752. [S of G, app. index]

Eggleston, William, Kew Rd, Richmond, Surrey, cm (1838). [D]

Egglestone, William, Belton St, London(?), carver and gilder (1775). Insured his house for £100 in 1775. [GL, Sun MS vol. 238, p. 327]

Eginton, Francis, Ashted Row, Birmingham, engraver, print seller, picture frame maker, painter and glass stainer (1800–12). [D]

Eginton, Mary, 20 Camden St, Walworth, London, chair and sofa maker (1839). [D]

Egleston, Thomas, Burton, Staffs.(?), u (1762). Took app. named Fretwell in 1762. [S of G, app. index]

Eglin & Gregory, 17 Shude Hill, Manchester, cm (1794). [D]

Eglington, Richard, Manchester, u and cm (1788–1817). Addresses given at Brown St in 1788, and 13 St Mary's Gate, 1794–1815. [D]

Ehlers, Richard, Liverpool, cm (1840). Admitted freeman on 31 July 1840. [Liverpool freemen reg.]

Ehrliholtzer, Felix, Plastow, Essex, tambour manufacturer (1776). [D]

Eichel, George, 20 John's St, Tottenham Ct Rd, Fitzroy Sq., London, carver and gilder (1802–25). [D]

Eichel, John, John St, Tottenham Ct Rd, London, carver (1786). Subscribed to George Richardson's *Treatise on the Five Orders of Architecture*, 1787.

Eilbeck, John, Egremont, Whitehaven, Cumb., joiner and/or cm (1829). [D]

Eilbeck, Robert, 20 Duke St, Whitehaven, Cumb., joiner and/or cm (1828–34). [D]

Ekins, Shadrach S., High St, Hampstead, London, and Harlow, Essex, cm, u and wire worker (1839). [D]

Elam, William, 3 Onslow St, near Vine St, Saffron Hill, London, bedstead maker (1785–93). Named in a court case, reported in *Williamson's Liverpool Advertiser*, 8 February 1790. Took out a Sun Insurance policy on 9 June 1785 for £1,000 on three houses. [D; GL, Sun MS vol. 328, p. 495]

Eland, John, Hutton, Yorks., cm (1823). [D]

Elborough, William, Cirencester, Glos., cm (1839). [PR(bapt.)]

Elcock, John, Compton St, Soho, London, cm (1786). Subscribed to George Richardson's *Treatise on the Five Orders of Architecture*, 1787.

Elcock, Jos., Warrington, Lancs., chairmaker (1743). Took app. named Cooper in 1743. [S of G, app. index]

Elden, William, Red Lion St, Norwich, cm and u (1822). [D]

Elder, Alexander, 2 St Paul's Pl., Walworth Common, London, cm and u (1839). [D]

Elder, John, Manchester and Salford, cm (1828–36). Trading at 36 Chester Rd, Hulme, Manchester in 1828; no. 28 in 1829; Green Bank, Salford in 1834; and 40 St Steven's St, Salford, in 1836. [D]

Elder, Peter, 486 Strand, London, carver, gilder and looking-glass manufacturer (1800–11). Took out a Sun Insurance policy on 17 October 1800 for £1,500 of which utensils and stock accounted for £800. [D; GL, Sun MS vol. 419, ref. 709334]

Elderton, William, Salisbury, Wilts., carver (1759). App. to Richard Langley, carver of Salisbury, on 7 April 1759 for £21. [*Wilts. Apps and their Masters*]

Eldon, Earl W., London, cm (1793). Subscribed to Sheraton's *Drawing Book*, 1793. Possibly William Elden Earl.

Eldrick, Stephen, 4 Noel St, Soho, London, u (1820). [D]

Eldridge, Charles, Woodstock, Oxon., cm (d. 1839). Will probated, 1839, in which all property was left to his wife. [Oxford RO, ROB II/9/3]

Eldridge, Henry, 7 Moon St, Soho, London, cm (1791). Took out a Sun Insurance policy for £100, of which £20 accounted for utensils, stock and goods in trust in the house of Rolfe, bedstead maker, 3 Stacey St. [GL, Sun MS vol. 382, ref. 593114]

Eldridge, Thomas, Stable Tower or Rampart, Southampton, Hants., cm and u (1774–92). Named concerning a lease on 26 September 1777. Insured his house for £300 in 1778 with the Sun Co. [D; poll bk; Southampton Corp. leases, ref. SC4/3/766b; GL, Sun MS vol. 268, p. 136]

Eldridge, Thomas, Northampton, u (1779). Insured his house for £800 in 1779. [GL, Sun MS vol. 272, p. 173]

Eldridge, Thomas, 34½ High St, Hastings, Sussex, cm and u (1839). [D]

Eldson, John, Lancaster, house carpenter and cm (1771–80). App. to E. Batty in 1771, and admitted freeman, 1779–80. [Lancaster app. reg. and freemen rolls] Possibly John Elsdon.

Eley, John, Nottingham, joiner and cm (1792). Joint master of Thomas Walker. [Nottingham app. list]

Elfe, —, Garlic Hill, London(?), cm (1723–24). Supplied items to Longford Castle: in 1723 a card table costing £3, and a sconce with a large glass, £7 7s; and in 1724 a pair of sconces costing £6 6s. [V & A archives]

Elfe, George, London, cm (1750). Death of William Elfe on 27 February 1750 at his seat in Warham, Herefs., reported in *Gents Mag.*, March 1750. Immensely rich, his estate was to be left to George Elfe, his heir at law.

Elford, Lawrence, South St, Dorchester, Dorset, cm and u (1823–30). [D]

Elford, Samuel, 60 Union St, Portsea, Portsmouth, Hants., cm and u (1830). [D]

Elgar, —, Folkestone, Kent, u (1807). [D]

Elgar, Richard, Queen's Pl. (or Sq.), Folkestone, Kent, cm and furniture broker (1823–34). [D]

Elgar, Thomas, Folkestone, Kent, u (1794). [D]

Elgee (or Elgie), Edward, Commercial St, Darlington, Co. Durham, joiner and cm (1827–34). [D]

Eling, James, Maze Pond, Southwark, London, carpenter and cm (1753). Sale of stock on declining business announced in *Public Advertiser*, 23 March 1753, consisting of oak, fir and deal, walnut veneers, cabinets, chairs and looking-glasses.

Elkin, Samuel, Waterloo, London, chair and sofa maker (1832–39). Recorded at 19 Henney St, 1832–34, and Franby St(?) in 1839. [D]

Elkins, Charles, Catherine St, Salisbury, Wilts., cm and u (1839). [D]

Elkins, Edmund, Charterhouse Sq., London(?), cm (1791). [Bailey's list of bankrupts]

Elkins, George, High St, Ware, Herts., cm and u (1839). [D]

Elkins, George, Back St, Ware, Herts., cm, u and wire worker (1839). [D]

Ellam, Peter, Welch St, Hereford, cm (1733). Took app. named Price in 1733. [S of G, app. index]

Ellam, Peter, St Clement Danes, London, cm (1727–39). Receipts survive for items supplied to Mrs Frances Heathcote. One dated 9 May 1727 is for a table costing £1 10s, and one of

1 April 1728 is for a dressing table, £2 18s. [Lincoln RO, 2 ANC 12/D/18] Declared bankrupt, *London Daily Post and General Advertiser*, 1739.

Ellam, William, Ormond St, Manchester, cm, joiner and builder (1825). [D]

Ellams, William, 18 Jenkinson St, Chorlton Row, Manchester, cm (1824–25). [D]

Ellender, Daniel, Rochester, Kent, u (1818). [Canterbury poll bk]

Ellender, Philip, Canterbury, Kent and London, cm (1818–30). Recorded in North Lane, Canterbury in 1818, and Edmonton, London, in 1830. [Poll bks]

Elleray, Roger & Sons, Bowness, Cartmel, Westmld, cm (1829). [D]

Ellerbeck, John, London, cm (1793). Subscribed to Sheraton's *Drawing Book*, 1793.

Ellerby, Bartholomew snr, 21 New Dock St, Hull, Yorks., cm (1823). [D]

Ellerby, Bartholomew jnr, Hull, Yorks., cm and broker (1823–40). Addresses given at 2 New John St in 1823; 20 Wellington Mart, 1826; 16 Blackfriargate, 1831–39; 13 Junction Dock Walls in 1835; and 12 and 24 Junction Dock St, 1837–40. [D]

Ellerker, John, Hull, Yorks., cm (1754–74). [Poll bks]

Ellershaw, James, Lancaster, cm (1806–07). Admitted freeman of Lancaster, 1806–07, when stated of London. [Lancaster freemen rolls]

Ellet(t), Samuel, 9 Charterhouse Lane, London, cm, u, undertaker and case maker (1839). [D]

Elle(t)son, Daniel, 109 St Martin's Lane, London, upholder (1792–1801). [D]

Ellett, James, Lowestoft, Norfolk, chairmaker (1743). Took app. named Mayers in 1743. [S of G, app. index]

Ellett, James, Gt Yarmouth, Norfolk, cm (1796–1831). [Poll bks]

Elleys, Thomas, Beccles, Suffolk, cm (1812). [Gt Yarmouth poll bk]

Ellick, —, Cheshire area(?), u (1770). Named in Lady Caroline Fleming Leicester's account bk in February 1770 receiving £33 10s. [Chester RO, Tabley Hall vouchers DLT/D46/2]

Elliot, Charles, High St, Cheadle, Staffs., chairmaker and turner (1834–35). [D]

Elliot(t), David, Paternoster Row, Spitalfields, London, cm and u (1808–16). Recorded at no. 8, 1808–16; nos 5 and 28, 1809–11. [D]

Elliot, David, 39 Cavendish St, Liverpool, cm (1829). [D]

Elliot, James, Liverpool, u (1827–29). Trading at 35 St James's St in 1827, and Bowyers Pl., Head St, Hart, in 1829. [D]

Elliot(t), James, Workington, Cumb., cm and/or joiner (1828–34). Trading at Harrington Harbour in 1834. [D]

Elliot, John, Netherend, Penrith, Cumb., cm and joiner (1834). [D]

El(l)iot, Richard, at 'The Golden Head', corner of Queen St, Cheapside, London, carver and gilder. Rococo trade card states 'Paintings, Looking Glasses, or Prints are Fram'd or Sold, Pictures Carefully Clean'd and Repair'd, & Window Blinds done in the neatest manner.' [Heal]

Elliot, Richard, Wooler, Northumb., cm and joiner (1828–34). [D]

Elliott, —, 6 St James's Buildings, Rosomand St, Clerkenwell, London, carver and gilder. Undated trade card states: 'Prints, Drawings, Needlework Framed & Glazed.' [Bodleian Lib., Johnson Coll.; *Furn. Hist.*, 1974]

Elliott, —, Grafton St, London, cm (1792–1813). Named in the Longford Castle accounts between 1792–1813 receiving over £3,000. [V & A archives]

Elliott, —, College Sq., Bristol, fancy chairmaker (1817). [D]

Elliott, —, 14 St Martin's St, Leicester Sq., London, cm and joiner (1820). [D] Possibly W. Elliott.

Elliott, Benjamin, London, carver, gilder and picture frame maker (1808–29). Trading in Hosier Lane, Smithfield in 1808; 20 St John's St, 1809–11; and no. 19, 1816–29. [D] Trade card reads: 'Pictures neatly and elegantly framed. OLD GLASSES MODERNISED OR TAKEN IN EXCHANGE. FRAMES REGILT, GLASSES Polished and Silvered.' [D; Finsbury Lib., archives dept, L6/19]

Elliott, Charles, London, cm and u (1752–d. 1832) and successors. Charles Elliott was one of the chief London cm of the late 18th century. He held royal appointments from 1783–c. 1810, and was succeeded as royal cm and u by William Francis, his brother-in-law and partner. The firm continued in the royal service until the end of Victoria's reign. Elliott was a descendent of the Elliots of Liddesdale, famous in legends of the Scottish border. His father, outlawed for his part in the 1715 uprising, lived in Java where he worked for the Dutch East India Co. After his return to Britain he became the local Searches and Tidewater Officer in H M Customs at Burnham-on-Crouch in 1742. Charles was born there in 1752, one year before the death of his father. Heal, p. 53 notes 'The Elliotts were an old cabinet-making family probably dating back to one William Elliott of Shenley, Herts., 1655–1730. His brother John was working in London and died in 1729. The one who is best known was Charles Elliott . . .'.

In 1770 Elliott arrived in London 'with a shilling in his pocket'. In 1774 he became a partner in the firm of Davis and Elliott and was listed in Lowndes London Directory, 1775. The same year he married the daughter of Rev. Dr Sherman, Sarah Ann, at St George's, Hanover Sq., and by 1783 they had five children, all bapt. at the same church. During these years the business greatly prospered. In the mid 1770s carpets were supplied to Chatsworth; in 1775 he insured a house on Shepard St with the Sun Insurance Co. for £500. Also insured in 1775 were the firm's utensils, stock, goods, etc. for £1,100. In 1779 the firm's insurance was increased to £2,500, and Elliott, now successful, had his portrait painted by John Russell. In December 1781, George and Joseph Weston (alias Samuel Watson and William Johnson) were supplied with furniture, cutlery and plate for the Friars, Winchelsea, E. Sussex. The firm's insurance was further increased that year to £3,200.

Elliott became the sole proprieter of the firm in 1783, and is listed in various London directories from 1784–1808. In 1783 he received his first appointment as 'Royal Upholsterer and Cabinetmaker'. From the beginning of his appointment he was the only royal furniture maker who was also employed as a general contractor and decorator, receiving a fixed salary of £157 10s 5d every quarter in addition to quarterly bills for furniture, mirrors, upholstery, carpets, etc. The contract work included 'cleaning, renewing & fixing furniture' at St James's, the House of Lords and Buckingham House, 'washing, mending and making up of cushions, carpets, stools, sconces, curtains and tapestry' for the Houses of Lords and of Commons, and also in 1791 the 'use of a dozen Japan'd chairs and porterage to and from the Queen's house for the King's private apartment'. This contract work was continued by Elliott, Son & Francis as the firm was called after 1805. They charged, in 1810, the sum of £606 for re-upholstering the House of Commons, including 'ripping out the whole of the leather cushions from the seats of the House entirely to pieces'.

Descriptions of furniture in the Lord Chamberlain's accounts indicate the versatility of Elliott's work. In 1783 he completely furnished Swindley Lodge including 'mahogany cabriole chairs covered with crimson silk damask' and 'festoon window curtains' as well as a folding camp bedstead and 'wainscott night stool and pan'. He provided 'a very large mahogany sideboard table with 12 cellarets for 10 bottles; very fine wood and cross-banded and strong', £17 10s, for the dining room at Newmarket Palace in 1784.

In 1787 a dispute arose between Elliott and the Prince of Wales over a £1,745 bill for various articles of upholstery and other furnishings. A committee of three u arbitrated the matter and found in favor of Elliott. The accounts show that a substantial part of Elliott's work for the crown was upholstery — curtains, carpets, etc. Elliott, Son & Francis also provided both upholstery work and furniture for the Speaker's new Gothic Rooms: 'two superb Gothic sofa tables on rich carved and socket claws, octagon molded pillars . . . partly gilt in burnished gold and picked in with polished black to look like ebony, the drawer fronts enriched with Gothic ornaments' were provided in 1807.

In May 1784 Elliott's wife died, and a year and half later he married Eling Venn, whose father Rev. Henry Venn was one of the most important figures in the Evangelical movement in the Church of England. Elliott may have visited France or was involved in obtaining French furniture, as indicated in Venn correspondence, and the memoirs of Elliott's great-grand-daughter, who described him as 'the first importer of French furniture to London'. A 1784–86 cash book records a payment of £171 15s to Elliott although it is not known for whom he did the work. About this time William Francis, his brother-in-law, joined the firm. The insurance on the New Bond St premises was renewed for £3,200 in 1787. He had subscribed to the first edition of Sheraton's Drawing Book, as 'upholsterer to his Majesty and Cabinetmaker to the Duke of York' and acquired a 'charming country villa at Paddington' in 1792. He answered Pitt's appeal to the nation for finances with a loan in 1796; that year or the next the Elliotts moved to Clapham, retaining the Bond St premises.

Elliott was employed by William Tufnell of Langleys, Essex in 1797–98 to redecorate and provide furniture for several rooms. A surviving bill provides the only positive identification of Elliott's furniture. The bill is endorsed 'part of the furniture of the drawing room; besides this the stoves in both rooms, chairs and tables in the green drawing room, windows and carpets in do., girandoles bronze, figures and two pier glasses'. Furniture which can be identified includes a satinwood Gothic back chair, a Pembroke table, a rectangular commode and an overmantle mirror. Also described in the bill is a pot cupboard, now in the bedroom, which is en suite with the rest of the furniture in that room, now attributed to Elliott. All the furniture at Langleys by Elliott is of fine quality. In addition to furniture the bill specifies 'pumice stoning & sizeing the walls of the drawing room, 12 pieces of yellow satin ground paper, paste, hanging and panelled, 380 feet gilt molding'.

In 1798 no. 96 (103) New Bond St, also owned and usually rented out by Elliott, was occupied by Nelson after the Battle of St Vincent and 'it was here that he dealt with the bill for his amputation'. At the formation of the Church Missionary Society in 1799 Elliott was elected to serve on the committee. He was a member of a host of other religious organizations as well as the Clapham Sect. In 1800 the premises in New Bond St were insured for only £1,000. Elliott and Co. appears in Sheraton's 1803 list of master cabinet makers. A minor commission was for Edward, Lord Lascelles in April 1801 for Harewood House, Hanover Sq., London. Elliott was paid £23. [Leeds archives dept, Harewood MS 101] It is not clear exactly when Elliott retired but from 1805–19 the firm was called Elliott, Son, and Francis. In 1808 William Francis, the brother-in-law, was promoted to a partnership. From about

1819–27 the firm was known as Elliott & Francis and by 1821 the Elliotts were living mostly in Brighton. Elliott, Son & Francis is listed in various directories from 1806–27. In addition to work for the Royal Household a bill exists to the Hon. Mrs Leigh for a 'circular japanned bamboo wash-hand stand' for £2 10s in 1818. [Shakespeare Birthplace Trust, Leigh receipts, DR 18/5] In 1826 Charles Elliott purchased the Chapel of St Mary in Brighton for £10,000 and presented the living to his son Henry who presumably left the firm about that time. From 1827 William Francis continued the business in his name alone and is listed in various London directories from 1827–39. In 1828 he assigned a lease to 17 Portland Pl. [Deed 1092, Marylebone Lib.] He continued working for the Royal Household until 1839–40. Due to the complexity of the various names under which Elliott traded, as set out in this article it is not possible to be specific about the range of activity in each period. See however the entry under William Francis for work in the 19th century. [PRO, LC 9/331–39, LC 11/1–27; GL, Sun MS vol. 236, p. 490; vol. 240, p. 368; vol. 273, p. 83; vol. 299, p. 176; vol. 342, ref. 528260; vol. 419, ref. 706221; *GCM*; N. Barton, 'Rise of a Royal Furntiure Maker', *C. Life*, 10 February 1966, pp. 293–95; 17 February 1966, pp. 360–62; 'Charles Elliott, Cabinetmaker', *Antiques*, October 1958, p. 450; 'Documented Furniture at Langleys, Essex', *C. Life*, 7 August 1942, pp. 264–65; R. Fastnedge, *Sheraton Furniture*, p. 37; C. Harper, *Half Hours with the Highwaymen*, pp. 330–31; I. Hall, 'A neo-classical episode at Chatsworth', *Burlington*, June 1980, pp. 400–14; C. Hussey, 'Langleys, Essex', *C. Life*, 9, 16 and 23 January 1942; E. T. Joy, 'Charles Elliot, Royal Cabinetmaker', *Conn.*, June 1959, pp. 34–39; Joy, *English Furniture, 1800–1851*, pp. 183–84, 223; M. Jourdain, *Regency Furniture*, p. 101; 'Langleys, Great Waltham, Essex', *Antique Collector*, January/February 1948, p. 10, March/April 1948, pp. 42–43; L. G. G. Ramsey, 'Langleys', *Conn.*, December 1957, pp. 210–17] See Davis & Elliot.

L. K.

Elliott, Daniel, Horniglow St, Burton-on-Trent, Staffs., chairmaker and turner (1818). [D]

Elliott, David, Norwich, upholder (1805). App. to John Horth, upholder; admitted freeman on 21 September 1805. [Norwich freemen reg.] Possibly:

Elliott, David, London, upholder (1818). [Norwich poll bk]

Elliott, Ebenezer, Low Friar St, Newcastle, cm and u (1824–29). [D]

Elliott, Francis, 12 Fleur de Lis St, Norton Falgate, London, cm (1808). [D]

Elliott, Francis, Nottingham, cm (1823). Master of William Barnes. [Nottingham app. list]

Elliott, George, 6 Northbrook St, Newbury, Berks., cm and u (1840). [D]

Elliott, John, High St, Leicester, cm, chairmaker, joiner and turner (b. 1713 — emigrated to America 1753). Elliott, a Quaker, was born 8 August 1713 in Bolton, Lancs, and after being app. to Jehu Sutton, cm in 1726 and Thos Hands of Oakham in 1731 he was made a freeman of Leicester in 1739. He took several apps before emigrating to Philadelphia in 1753. His English background, career in America and that of his son, are the subject of a student thesis by Mary Ellen Hayward (1972) at Winterthur, Delaware. A simple cabriole leg oak dressing table, acquired by Colonial Williamsburg in 1973 bears the label 'John Elliott, Cabinet-maker, Joyner and Turner; AT the Sign of the [torn] Coffins, opposite the King's Arms in the High-street; LEICESTER: Makes and sells all sorts of Goods in the above mention'd Branches, in Mahogany, Walnut-tree &c, Intirely new, and as cheap as in LONDON. He also hangs the new Fashion Spring Bells in

Gentleman's Houses, in the same manner as done in LONDON. NOTE Looking-glasses Silver'd and Fram'd at reasonable Rates'. C. G. G.

Elliott, John, London, cm (d. 1729). [Heal] See William Elliott of 2 Clements Lane, London.

Elliott, John, London, u (1728–d. 1768). Recorded in Clements Lane, Lombard St in 1728; and Poland St, 1749. Insured his house and goods for £500 on 1 November 1728 with the Sun Co. [Poll bk; GL, Sun MS vol. 26, p. 507; Heal] See William Elliott of Clements Lane.

Elliott, John, Nottingham, joiner and cm (1792). Son of James Elliott; app. in 1792. [Nottingham app. list]

Elliott, John, New Bond St, London, upholder (1803). Subscribed to Sheraton's *Cabinet Dictionary*, 1803.

Elliott, John, 13 Nichols Croft, Manchester, cm (1808–09). [D]

Elliott, John, 43 Chapel St, Devonport, Plymouth, Devon, cm and u (1823–24). [D]

Elliott, John, 49 Drummond St, London, cm and u (1827–28). [D]

Elliott, Michael Cooke, Leicester, cm (1768). Son of Thomas Elliott, cm of Leicester; admitted freeman in 1768. [Leicester freemen reg.]

Elliott, O., St Albans Row, Weymouth, Dorset, cm and u (1840). [D]

Elliott, Paul, Chippenham, Wilts., cm and u (1822). [D]

Elliott, R., Cheltenham, Glos., cm (1839–40). [D]

Elliott, Richard, Newgate St, London, carver (1793). [D]

Elliott, Robert, Stowmarket, Suffolk, cm (1798). [D]

Elliott, Thomas, Nottingham, joiner, cm and u (1803–28). Addresses given at Pelham St, 1805–18; George St and New Sneinton in 1820; George St in 1822 (as Thomas jnr); and St James's St, 1825–28. Subscribed to Sheraton's *Cabinet Dictionary*, 1803. Took apps named Thomas Elliott in 1811; Charles Lloyd and John Harrison in 1823. Listed as a freeholder in 1812, and burgess in 1818. [D; poll bks; Nottingham burgess index and app. list]

Elliott, Thomas, Nottingham, joiner, cm and u (1811). Son of William Elliott, silk throwster of Nottingham; app. to Thomas Elliott in 1811. [Nottingham app. list]

Elliott, W., 14 St Martin's Lane, London, cm (1820). [D]

Elliott, Walter, Newcastle, u (1731–34). Trading at 1 Low Friar St in 1733. Admitted freeman on servitude on 12 February 1731–32. [D; Newcastle freemen reg.]

Elliott, Walter, 1 Low Friar St, Newcastle, cm and u (1834–38). [D]

Elliott, William, Castle Precincts, Bristol, u (1734–39). [Poll bks]

Elliott, William, 220 St John's St, London, carver and gilder (1808). [D]

Elliott, William, Penrith, Cumb., joiner and/or cm (1828–29). Trading at Bridge Lane, 1828–29, and Nether End in 1829. [D]

Elliott, William, 2 Clement's Lane, Lombard St, London, u (1746–92). Recorded at various addresses: 2 Clement's Lane, 1778–81; Sonning, near Reading, Berks., 1782–86; and St Albans, Herts. in 1791. Son of Samuel Elliott, Hereford, Gent.; app. to John Elliott, draper on 23 October 1746; admitted freeman of the Upholders' Co. in 1756 and elected master, 1792. [GL, Upholders' Co. records] Took apps named Henry Blaxland, 1762–70 and George Oakley, 1773–82. Elliott was in partnership with Thomas Rutt, u, after about 1779. [S of G, app. index]

Elliott & Davies, Elliot & Co., Elliott & Francis, see Charles Elliott.

Elliott & Rutt, see William Elliott of 2 Clements Lane, London.

Elliotts, James, 35 Northbrook St, Newbury, Berks., cm and u (1840). [D]

Ellis, —, address unrecorded, cm (*c.* 1775). Supplied furniture to Denton Park, Yorks., *c.* 1775, totalling £22 4s. [*Furn. Hist.*, 1968] Perhaps John Ellis of York.

Ellis, B., London, carpenter (1804–07). Carried out repairs and made furniture for Bedford House and St James's Sq., London. In 1804 he made 'a stong kitchen table', costing £10, for the stables at St James's. Later that year, by order of the Duchess of Bedford he made 'a cabinet for coin' for her stepson, the fourteen-year-old Marquess of Tavistock. In 1807 he made two large linen presses for the housekeeper's room and the garret, and carried out repairs; his bill totalled £116 6s 1d. [Bedford Office, London]

Ellis, Benjamin, York, cm (1789). Son of Francis Ellis, farmer; app. to William Hawkins, cm, on 8 February 1789. [York app. reg.]

Ellis, Benjamin, 67 Upper Ebury St, Pimlico, London, cm, u and undertaker (1839). [D]

Ellis, Burton, Market Pl., Bridlington, Yorks., cm (1831–40). [D]

Ellis, Charles, London, cm (1793). Subscribed to Sheraton's *Drawing Book*, 1793.

Ellis, Charles, London, cm (1818–31). [Gt Yarmouth poll bks]

Ellis, Evan, Liverpool, cm and furniture broker (1829–39). Addresses given at 2 Derby Pl. in 1829; 23 Matthew St in 1834; no. 25 in 1835; 23 Derby Pl., Matthew St, in 1837; and 75 Stanley St in 1839. [D]

Ellis, Francis, Spurriergate, York, u (1784–1814). Son of John Ellis, u and undertaker; app. to John Ellis on 4 March 1784, and later assigned to James King. Admitted freeman of York in 1793. On 30 January 1814 Ellis wrote to the widow and executors of Robert Clavering Savage of Gloucester Pl., Portman Sq., London, and Elmley Castle, near Worcester, concerning a debt, which he requested should be paid 'with interest as for the Table and Dresser'; and also a debt of £10 10s owed to Daniel Curling & Co., furniture printers, of 18 Cheapside, London, [D; York app. reg. and freemen rolls; Worcs. RO, 4600/705:550/763/3]

Ellis, G., 1 Old Orchard, Bath, Som., u (1819). [D]

Ellis, G. T., Gt Yarmouth, Norfolk, cm (1818–20). [Poll bks]

Ellis, George, address unrecorded, upholder (1709–17). Son of George Ellis, clerk of Over Worton, Oxon.; app. to Samuel Kempster on 4 May 1709, and admitted freeman of the Upholders' Co. by servitude on 20 March 1716/17. [GL, Upholders' Co. records]

Ellis, J., Newark, Lincs., turner (1792). Advertised for a journeyman chair turner in *Lincoln, Rutland and Stamford Mercury*, 21 September 1792.

Ellis, James, Bideford, Devon, cm (1793). [D]

Ellis, John, York, u (1776–84). Son of William Ellis, grocer, formerly brazier, deceased; admitted freeman in 1776. Trading at Pavement in 1784. [York freemen rolls; poll bk] See Ellis, —.

Ellis, John, Baldwin St, Bristol, basket and chairmaker (1805–36). Trading as Walter & John Ellis, 1805–06; alone from 1807; and at 4 Baldwin St, 1815–36. [D] See Judith and Walter Ellis.

Ellis(s), John, Sheffield, Yorks., cm (1814–29). Addresses given at 26 Pinstone Lane in 1817; 4 Pinstone St in 1821; and Fargate, 1828–29. [D]

Ellis, John, Long St, Wotton-under-Edge, Glos., cm and chairmaker (1820–25). Child bapt. in 1825. [D; PR(bapt.)]

Ellis, John, Liverpool, cm (1827–39). Trading at 31 Leigh St in 1827; 11 Spring St in 1835; 56 Renshaw St, 1837; and no. 28 in 1839. App. to John Otty in 1827, and admitted freeman on 18 July 1835. [D; Liverpool app. enrolment bk and freemen reg.]

Ellis, John, 1 Oxford Rd, Manchester, cm (1829). [D]

Ellis, John, Chester, cm and u (1831). Admitted freeman on 20 April 1831. [Chester freemen rolls]

Ellis, John, Longroyd Bridge, Huddersfield, Yorks., cm and/or u (1837). [D]

Ellis, Joseph, the Minories, London, carver and gilder (1808–11). Trading at 16 Little Heydon Sq. in 1808, and 56 Church St, Little Minories, 1809–11. [D] See William Ellis.

Ellis, Joseph, Armley, near Leeds, Yorks., cm (1822). [D]

Ellis, Joseph, Fulneck, Yorks., cm (1828–30). [D]

Ellis, Joseph, Fall Lane, Dewsbury, Yorks., cm (1837). [D]

Ellis, Jos., 19 Tower St, Seven Dials, London, bedstead maker (1837). [D]

Ellis, Judith, 4 Baldwin St, Bristol, basket and chairmaker (1837). [D] See John and Walter Ellis.

Ellis, Matthew, Chester, u (1671). Admittted freeman on 2 February 1671. [Chester freemen rolls]

Ellis, Michael, 95 Bold St, Liverpool, u (1839). [D]

Ellis, Moses, London, freeman joiner, cm, stationer, backgammon table maker and turner (1769–1804). Recorded in Westharding St, 1769–72; Fenchurch St in 1773; Westharding St, 1775–79; and Fetter Lane, 1780–83. Trading at 110 Fetter Lane, 1802–04. Employed one non-freeman for three months in both 1769 and 1772; five for three months in 1773; between three and six annually, 1775–79, their licence renewed quarterly; and between four and six annually, 1780–83, licence renewed quarterly. [D; GL, City Licence bks, vols 6 and 8–10]

Ellis, Richard, London, upholder, auctioneer and undertaker (1807–29). Addresses given at 16 Billiter Lane, 1807–13; 16 Callum St, Fenchurch St, 1809–11; and 36 Fenchurch St, 1814–29. [D]

Ellis, Richard, Liverpool, cm (1828–35). App. to John Otty in 1828, and admitted freeman on 18 July 1835. [Liverpool app. enrolment bk and freemen reg.]

Ellis, Robert Stephen, York, cm (1791). Son of Joseph Ellis, grocer; app. to John Thompson, cm, on 4 July 1791. [York app. reg.]

Ellis, S., 3 Sheffield St, London, cm (1835). [D]

Ellis, Samuel, 27 Chandos St, Covent Gdn, London, cm (1826–27). [D]

Ellis, Thomas, 32 Worcester St, Birmingham, cm (1777). [D]

Ellis, Thomas, Gt Yarmouth, Norfolk, cm (1807). [Poll bk]

Ellis, Thomas, Long St, Sherborne, Dorset, cm and builder (1823–30). [D]

Ellis, Thomas, Daw Green, Dewsbury, Yorks., cm (1828–30). [D]

Ellis, Thomas, 104 James St, Devonport, Devon, cm and u (1830–38). [D]

Ellis, Thomas, Pickering, Yorks., cm and u (1834). [D]

Ellis, Thomas, 25 Berry St, Liverpool, cm (1835). [D]

Ellis, Walter, Bristol, basket and chairmaker (1799–1806). Trading at Baldwin St and Somerset Pl., with manufactory at Countership, 1799–1801; and with John Ellis in Baldwin St, 1805–06. [D] See Judith and John Ellis.

Ellis, Wilfred, Peter Lane, York, cm and u (1828–30). Trading at no. 22 in 1828, and no. 5 in 1830. [D]

Ellis, William, Bell Alley, Petticoat Lane, London, cm (1766). Insured his utensils, stock and clothes for £200 in 1766. [GL, Sun MS vol. 168]

Ellis, William, Fenchurch St, London, cm and u (1771–99). Trading at no. 126, 1774–99. Admitted freeman of the Upholders' Co. on 6 March 1771. Insured his house for £100 on 13 March 1787 with the Sun Co. [D; GL, Upholders' Co. records; GL, Sun MS vol. 343, p. 232]

Ellis, William, Bristol, carver, gilder, printseller and

looking-glass manufacturer (1774–75). Trading at 11 Clare St in 1775. [D; poll bk]

Ellis, William, Chester, carver and gilder (1781–89). Addresses given near Eastgate, 1781–82, and Queen St, 1789. [D]

Ellis, William, address unrecorded, carver and gilder (1789). Took app. named John Matthews as carver and gilder in 1789. [Goldsmiths' Hall, app. and freemen index]

Ellis, William, the Minories, London, carver and gilder (1789–1808). Addresses given at 16 Haydon Sq., 1789–93; 8 Little Minories, 1799; and 56 Church St, Little Minories, 1808. [D] See Joseph Ellis.

Ellis, William, 34 Rupert St, Piccadilly, London, carver and gilder (1823–25). [D]

Ellis, William, Lower Rd, Deptford, London, cm and furniture broker (1823–27). [D]

Ellis, William, Allhalland St, Bideford, Devon, cm (1830). [D]

Ellis, William, 5 Petergate (or Peter Lane), York, cm and u (1830). [D]

Ellis, William, 9 Templar Terr., 11 Gt George St, Liverpool, cm (1839). [D]

Ellis & Co., 19 Phoenix St, Soho, London, cm and u (1839). [D]

Ellis & Rusby, Micklegate, York, cm and u (1814). [D]

Ellisdon, Joseph, Eld Lane, Colchester, Essex, cm and u (1839). [D]

Ellishaw, James, St James St, Liverpool, chairmaker (1818–39). Trading at no. 13 in 1818; no. 14, 1821–27; no. 16, 1827–29; no. 20 in 1834; no. 18 in 1835; no. 21 in 1837; and no. 43 in 1839. [D]

Ellison, Edward, Liverpool, cm (1761). Admitted freeman on 28 January 1761. [Liverpool freemen reg.]

Ellison, Edward, Preston, Lancs., cm (1798). [D]

Ellison, James, Skipton, Yorks., joiner and cm (1822–37). Recorded at New Market St in 1822 and 1837; and Hole in the Wall Yd in 1830. [D]

Ellison, John, York, cm (1802–09). Son of John Ellison, ostler of York; app. to Peter Davies, cm, on 12 January 1802. Admitted freeman in 1809. [York app. reg. and freemen rolls]

Ellison, John, Mason's Lane, South Shields, Co. Durham, cm and joiner (1828–29). [D]

Ellison, John, Cawood, Yorks., joiner and/or cm (1837). [D]

Ellison, T., Liverpool, u and cm (1768–72). Recorded at the corner of Whitecross St in 1768. Advertised sale of stock in *Williamson's Liverpool Advertiser*, 16 September 1768, at 'his Wholesale & Retail UPHOLSTERY, CABINET & LOOKING-GLASS WAREHOUSE'. Stock consisted of a 'great Variety of GLASSES, of all sorts & sizes, in Elegant Frames, Carved & Gilt, in Burnish'd Gold, MAHOGANY, Paper MACHEE in White & JAPAN Frames, from Three Shillings a Dozen to Thirty Pounds the Pair, with GERANDOLES & BRACKETS to match the GLASSES & other Ornaments . . . in the New, Neatest & Genteelest Taste & in a Workmanlike manner . . .'. In the same paper on 25 December 1772, T. Ellison, cm and u of Liverpool announced that he was selling off stock on declining the upholstery business and entering new employment. He had for sale 'all sort of upholstery & some few cabinet goods, of the newest & best construction, according to the present taste; great variety of paper, all or greatest part this years patterns, furniture of all sorts, & the largest & greatest assortment of glasses not to be met with at any other house except one, in London, where his was made . . .'. Probably:

Ellison, Thomas, Liverpool, u (1767–96). Addresses given in High St, 1767–73; 22 Sparling St, 1787; and no. 39 in 1796. [D] Advertised a lottery of his furniture at Sparling St in *Williamson's Liverpool Advertiser*, 13 September 1790. The chief 'specimen of his abilities' was a bed of state, with window curtains, chairs etc.: 'The bed consists of a fine whited corded dimity, with variegated purple white silk and cotton fringe, with most superb French tassels, to match the cornices, carved with three figures, two of them the Seasons, and the other a Venus, with Medallions in burnished gold, bedposts of sattin wood, painted and embellished with flowers. On the top of the dome stands a plumage of real Ostridge feathers, and the window curtains in the height of taste, taken from the Dutchess of Devonshire, and part of the bed, from his Royal Highness the Prince of Wales, which the proprietor had the honor of conducting.' Other items in the lottery were 'A set of neat French mahogany cabriole Chairs, which are well adapted for a small drawing-room or tea-room, and will come lower than the vulgar carved mahogany-back ones, are more suitable for the purpose, and always made use of in genteel families; also several sets of choice Paper Hangings, mahogany Tables and Thairs [sic] of different constructions, and Beds and Hangings in different Stiles, &c.' Ellison advertised on 29 November 1790 requesting payment for lottery tickets, certain patrons having put him off 'with evasive answers'; otherwise 'he shall be under the disagreeable necessity of inserting their names in the public papers', and failing this, taking them to court.

Ellison, Thomas, Liverpool, u (1775). Admitted freeman on servitude to Samuel Kirke on 30 March 1775. [Liverpool freemen reg.]

Ellison, Thomas, Liver St, Liverpool, u (1784). Advertised sale of household furniture and stock in *Williamson's Liverpool Advertiser*, 11 March 1784, probably on bankruptcy, having assigned over all his estate. Stock consisted of 'a large assortment of fashionable PAPER & CARPETS etc . . .'.

Ellison, Thomas, East Holborn, South Shields, Co. Durham, cm and joiner (1828–29). [D]

Ellison, Thomas, 13 Meredith St, Clerkenwell, London, billiard table maker (1839). [D]

Ellison, William, Liverpool, u (1827). App. to John Pemberton in 1827. [Liverpool app. enrolment bk]

Ellison, William, Wharton's Yd, Skipton, Yorks., joiner and/or cm (1837). [D]

Ellison & Co., Preston, Lancs. Signed the *Preston Cabinet Makers and Chair Makers Book of Prices*, 1799, on behalf of the masters. Possibly Edward Ellison.

Elliston, A., Stall St (1819), 1 Abbey Gate (1826), 1 Claverton Pl. (1833), Bath, Som., cabinet and wheel chair maker. [D]

Elliston, Henry, 3 Buckle St, Red Lion St, Whitechapel, London, cm (1808). [D]

Ellorshaw, John, 10 Queen St, Golden Sq., London, cm (1809–11). [D]

El(l)rington, John, Chester, u (1734–47). Son of Charles Elrington, Gent. of Parkgate; app. to Ralph Bingley, u, on 22 June 1734. [Poll bk; Chester app. bks]

Ellrington, John, Chapel Alley, London, carver (1749). [Poll bk]

Ellrington, William, Bar St, Beverley, Yorks., cm (1840). [D]

Ells & Co., 59 Brook St, Grosvenor Sq., London, cm and u (1839). [D]

Ellson, William, 14 Beaufort Buildings, Strand, London, cm (1808). [D]

Ellwood, John, Lancaster, carver (1829–30). [Lancaster freemen rolls]

Ellwood, Joseph, High Wycombe, Bucks., chairmaker (b. 1766–1841). Named in the Militia Census, 1798, and aged 75 at the time of the 1841 Census.

Elmer, Samuel, Ipswich, Suffolk, cm (1832–39). Recorded in Queen St, 1835–39. [Poll bks]

Elmes, Thomas, address unrecorded, upholder (1727–36). Son of Thomas Elmes of Chiselhurst, Kent; app. to John Osborn on 29 September 1727, and admitted freeman of the

Upholders' Co. by servitude on 4 August 1736. [GL, Upholders' Co. records]

Elms, D. F., 16 Grafton St, London, cm (1826–27). [D]

Elmsley, Alexander, 4 Red Cross Sq., Jewin St, London, cm (1782). Insured his house for £200 in 1782. [GL, Sun MS vol. 301, p. 492]

Elph, Thomas T., East Dereham, Norfolk, cm (1830). [Poll bk]

Elsdon, John, Lancaster, cm (1784). [Poll bk] Possibly John Eldson.

Elsdon, John, Boar's Head Yd, Westgate, Newcastle, turner and spinning wheel maker (1827). [D]

Else, George, late of Threadneedle St, London, cm (1739). Declared bankrupt, *Daily Post*, 5 November 1739.

Elsey, William, Parliament St, Nottingham, cm (1828). [D]

Elsmere, —, Lord St, Liverpool, u (1774). Sale of stock for benefit of creditors, presumably on bankruptcy, announced in *Williamson's Liverpool Advertiser*, 25 February 1774. Stock consisted of 'Beds & Bedsteads, Ticks, Counterpanes, Quilts, Bed Furniture, both Moreen & Harrateen, of different Colours, Check, Variety of Laces, Papers, Carpeting, & other Upholstery Goods of Various Sorts.'

Elsmore, Henry, address unrecorded, upholder (1761–66). Son of Henry Elsmore of Sevenoaks, Kent; app. to Thomas Ridgway, skinner, on 2 June 1761, and admitted freeman of the Upholders' Co. on 6 November 1766. [GL, Upholders' Co. records]

Elsom (Elsam or Elison), John, Boston, Lincs., cm (1819–35). Recorded as Elison at Wide Bargate in 1819; as Elsam at Market Pl., 1822; and as Elsom at Mill Hill, Bargate, in 1835. [D]

Elstob, Jonathan, Sunderland St, Houghton-le-Spring, Co. Durham, cm (1827). [D]

Elston, —, Petergate, York, joiner and billiard table maker (1775). Advertised in *York Courant*, 2 May 1775, sale of 'A new complete BILLIARD TABLE, mahogany Frame, Feet and Cushion Mouldings, Mouldings carved round the low edge of the Frame, Oak Leaf, with superfine Broad Cloth.'

Elston, Robert, Lancaster, chairmaker (1811–12). [Lancaster freemen rolls]

Elston, William, Liverpool, cm (1784–1822). Trading at Lewis's Ct, Queen St in 1790. Admitted freeman on 5 April 1784. Father of John Elston, slater and plaisterer, born on 29 November 1801, who petitioned freedom in 1822. [D; Liverpool freemen reg. and committee bk]

Elsworth, Israel, 15 Cheapside, Liverpool, u (1834). [D]

Elsworthy, Mary, 2 Anderson Buildings, City Rd, London, chair and sofa maker (1827–28). [D]

Elsworthy, Richard, Plummers Row, City Rd, London, cm (1811–19). [D]

Eltoft, Joseph Green, Leeds, Yorks., carver, gilder and joiner (1834–37). Trading at 2 Mill Hill in 1834 and 19 Upperhead Row in 1837. [D]

Eltoft & Proctor, 27 Park Row, Leeds, Yorks., cm (1837). [D]

El(s)ton, Thomas, Liverpool, cm (1816). Admitted freeman on 10 June 1816 as son of John Elton, cooper. [Liverpool freemen reg.]

Eltringham, John, Newcastle and Lancaster, u (1780). App. to William Hudson; admitted freeman of Newcastle on 12 September 1780, in which year he polled at Newcastle and was stated to be 'of Lancaster'. [Newcastle freemen reg.]

Elvee (or Elver), Robert, Rochester, Kent, cm (1798–1807). [D; poll bks]

Elvey, Elizabeth, 9 New Bond St, London, pocket book, dressing case and desk maker to the Royal Family, the King of Prussia and his Serene Highness the hereditary Prince of Orange (1806–24). Trade card [Johnson Coll., Bodleian Lib., Oxf.] gives above details, and a directory of 1808 adds HRH the

Duke of Sussex to her patrons. J. and E. Elvey supplied items for Hatfield House, Herts. in 1806: J. Elvey, two pocket books on 25 July; and E. Elvey, a mahogany writing desk costing £6 6s 6d, receipt dated 4 August 1806. [Hatfield House MS, bills 618] Elizabeth submitted bills to Lord Crewe of Crewe Hall, Cheshire, dated 24 March 1820 and April 1821, for repairing furniture, supplying large leather portfolios, and a dressing case with bottles; bills totalled £13 2s. A billhead dated 17 August 1831 states that Mrs Elvey was succeeded by her nephew, George Lawrence. [D; Chester RO, Crewe papers, DCR/47/box 5; Suffolk RO (Bury), 941/73/16; *Furn. Hist.*, 1974, pl. 43]

Elvin (or Elwin), Charles, London, cm (1784–1818). [Norwich poll bks]

Elvin, Isaac, Market Pl., Louth, Lincs., joiner and cm (1831). [D]

Elvin, Robert, Norwich, u (1831). Admitted freeman on 24 February 1831. [Norwich freemen rolls]

Elvius, Sarah, 1 Rand Ct, London(?), ornamental clock-case maker (1778). Took out a Sun Insurance policy in 1778 for £100, utensils, stock and goods accounting for £50. [GL, Sun MS vol. 268, p. 281]

Elward, George & Marsh, William, succeeded by Elward, Marsh & Bailey; Elward, Marsh & Tatham; Marsh & Tatham; Tatham & Bailey; Tatham, Bailey & Saunders; Bailey & Saunders; Edward Bailey; Mount St, near Charles St, London, cm and u (1774–1840).

WILLIAM MARSH. The earliest record of his name that has appeared so far is an entry for insurance cover of £1,500 in 1774 [GL, Sun MS vol. 236, ref. 348625] where he is described as 'upholder . . . near Charles Street in Mount Street'. He is also listed as cm and u among the subscribers to Thomas Malton's *Complete Treatise on Perspective*, 1775 and seems to have acquired aristocratic clients early in his career since he supplied the Hon. Mrs Howard, mother of Lady Petre, with new upholstery work for two screens in 1777. [Essex RO, D/DP A189/8] His bankruptcy [*Gents. Mag.*, November 1780] probably prompted his partnership with George Elward which is first recorded in rate bks in 1785.

GEORGE ELWARD. Elward had also been working in Mount St since at least 1780 when he insured his property near Charles St in Mount St for £1,600. He subsequently insured a workshop in South Audley St for £200 in 1780 when his address was given as 14 Mount St and his occupation as upholder and cm. [GL, Sun MS vol. 286, ref. 435669; vol. 290, ref. 440745]

ELWARD & MARSH; ELWARD, MARSH & BAILEY; ELWARD, MARSH & TATHAM. Although it is not certain just where in Mount St the partnership began it was Elward's premises at no. 14 which were given in trade directories as the firm's address from 1790, changing to 13 Mount St, Grosvenor Sq. in insurance records when a dwelling house with warehouse in the yard behind and the contents were insured for a total of £5,800. [GL, Sun MS vol. 389, ref. 606749] This address remained the same for the firm through all subsequent changes of partnership up to 1840. Elward & Marsh were joined by Edward Bailey in 1793 [D] and by Thomas Tatham in 1798 [rate bks] and the firm was known as Elward, Marsh & Tatham until 1803 when Elward is no longer listed in trade directories.

MARSH & TATHAM, TATHAM & BAILEY, TATHAM, BAILEY & SAUNDERS, BAILEY & SAUNDERS, EDWARD BAILEY. From 1803–11 Marsh & Tatham are listed in trade directories although Tatham & Bailey appear in the rate bks from 1807–10 and these two partners took out insurance in 1808, suggesting that William Marsh had retired by then. The insurance policy was for a dwelling house, warehouse and workshop and their contents, value £3,000, and the firm had at that time three other polices with different companies, for £8,000, £5,000 and £3,000 respectively, suggesting a large and prosperous business. The premises apparently included a number of workrooms and storerooms, including a sawpit, drying places for timber, and veneering rooms, while the shop had a new shopfront designed by John Linnell Bond. The confusion over the title of the firm continues with Tatham & Bailey listed in some trade directories up to 1820 while the rate bks list Richard Saunders with Tatham and Bailey as partners. Thomas Tatham died in Brighton in 1818 [*Gents Mag.*, January 1818] and Bailey & Saunders continued as partners until 1827 when Edward Bailey took over until at least 1840.

Although the firm was associated from the 1780s with the group of distinguished craftsmen working for the Prince of Wales and other important patrons like Samuel Whitbread II, it is not clear who provided the designs for their furniture. Henry Holland was certainly closely involved in the work for the Prince of Wales at Carlton House and at Brighton and for his other patrons, but his employment of Charles Heathcote Tatham as an assistant from 1788 suggests a requirement for additional help. Charles Heathcote, who was Thomas Tatham's borther, would presumably have had close contacts with his brother's firm but it is through C. H. Tatham's publication of his drawings of Roman antiquities as models for cabinet makers and other craftsmen, particularly *Etchings of Ancient Ornamental Architecture*, 1st edition 1799, that he was most influential. C. H. Tatham is known to have been employed by the Prince and in contact with the Prince's circle of friends like Sir Harry Fetherstonhaugh after Holland's downfall and is quite likely to have supplied ideas for his brother, particularly for the large amount of furniture demanded by their royal patron. Certain pieces supplied by Marsh & Tatham for Carlton House are either taken directly from C. H. Tatham's designs, like the carved and gilded Council chairs, or are very reminiscent of his refined style like the set of library bookcases supplied in 1806.

Right through its existence and many changes of title, the firm established by William Marsh and George Elward remained one of the most important and influential cabinet making businesses of the late 18th and early 19th centuries. From their highly stylish pieces in the Anglo-French taste produced for Southill in the 1790s, through the japanned furnishings for Brighton Pavilion in 1801, the distinguished Grecian library furniture for Carlton House of 1806, to the rich and elaborate furniture produced for the final phase at Brighton *c.*1820, the firm's surviving pieces present a distinguished and important record of their output.

THE ROYAL FAMILY. 1783–89. Wm. Marsh & Co.: Among debtors of the Prince of Wales listed on his marriage in 1795 as having supplied £373 of furniture, probably for Carlton House. [H. Clifford-Smith, *Buckingham Palace*, pp. 107–09]
1799 Elward, Marsh & Co.: Bill, Duchy of Cornwall papers.
1801 Elward, Marsh & Co.: Payments in arrears. [Windsor Royal Archives 88874, 88890]
1801–02 Elward, Marsh & Tatham: Bills for work at Carlton House and Brighton including '36 carved bamboo japanned chairs £100.16.0' for the 1801 Eating Room, Brighton(?). [Windsor RA 25123–32]
1806 Marsh & Tatham: Furniture, furnishings and bedding for Brighton totalling £401 18s 6d, including some pieces in the Chinese taste, japanned.
1806 Marsh & Tatham: Furniture and furnishings for Carlton House totalling £5,964 16s 6d including ebony and ivory veneered library furniture [*Conn.*, June 1977] and ebony inlaid yewtree bookcases with bronze antique heads for

£680 (one now V & A; one sold Christie's, 21 November 1985, lot 96). [Windsor RA 25205–09]
1806 Marsh & Tatham: Furniture, furnishings and fittings for Carlton House totalling £7,387 5s, the most costly items being 4 cut-glass lustres with bronze fittings £1,812. [Windsor RA 25223–26]
22 June 1808: Letters from Thomas Tatham saying that the cost of the works already executed for Carlton House totalled over £30,000. [Windsor RA 31528–29]
1808 Tatham & Bailey: Bill for work for the Prince of Wales for furniture and furnishings totalling £616 19s 9d including alterations to Gothic bookcases and decoration of Military Tent Room.
1809 Tatham, Bailey & Saunders: Furniture and furnishings totalling £1,423 16s 6d including number of japanned pieces such as chest of drawers japanned to correspond with two Oriental panels, £155. [RA 25251–53, 25300–01]
1811 Tatham, Bailey & Saunders: Furniture for Carlton House including four large candelabra for the Saloon £680 and five tripods for alabaster vases £715, mahogany horse 'to beat clothes on' £2 66s, two green and black painted flower boxes for the Conservatory £6, and alterations to the Hervé seat furniture from the Chinese Drawing Room. Total £3,157 5s.
1811 Tatham, Bailey & Saunders: Carlton House, repairs and cleaning (including Hervé seat furniture) and new furniture (including couch to match that in Lower Dining Room £45 10s). Total £706 18s. [RA 25329–30, 25341–43]
1811 Tatham & Co.: Bill for four tripods at £143 each which may be those in Jutsham's Carlton House Ledger June 1811 with crane figures. [G. de Bellaigue, J. Harris, O. Millar, *Buckingham Palace*, p. 154]
1813 Tatham, Bailey & Saunders: '60 Antique chairs' at £502 8s which may be those shown by Pyne in the Gothic Dining Room at Carlton House, 1818, and afterwards moved to the North Drawing Room, Brighton Pavilion. [G. de Bellaigue etc., *Buckingham Palace*, p. 137]
1813 Tatham & Co.: '2 very large Antique Elbow chairs' £587 12s which may be the carved and gilt pine and beech council chairs, after designs by C. H. Tatham shown in Pyne's view of the Throne Room, Carlton House, 1818. [G. de Bellaigue, *Buckingham Palace*, p. 195]
1814 Tatham, Bailey & Saunders: Seven bookcases of rosewood and gilt bronze for the Gold Drawing Room, Carlton House. [Pyne, *Royal Residences*, vol. 3, 1817, pl. 27]

The firm continued to be mentioned in the Royal Household accounts 1813–18 [PRO, LC 11/15–24] and worked at Brighton, Carlton House and Stables, Red House and Stud Lodge, Hampton Court, Windsor Cottage, Cumberland Lodge and on the 'Royal George' yacht. The work at Brighton included furnishings for the Banqueting Room (set of 36 chairs and 2 armchairs of lacquered beech with applied gilt ornaments for £669 12s and set of rosewood sideboards with carved and gilt dragons and ornaments for £4,129 3s). They also provided furniture and furnishings for the Music Room (set of chairs £1,517) for the Saloon (total £2,415) and made copies in 1819 of the original side tables made by Adam Weisweiler for the Chinese Drawing Room, Carlton House, for all four to be used in the North Drawing Room. [H. D. Roberts, *The Royal Pavilion Brighton*, 1939; J. Dinkel, *The Royal Pavilion Brighton*, 1983] Edward Bailey & Son continued to work for the Royal Household at least until 1840, providing, for example, furniture in the best bedrooms and servant's rooms in the Vice-Chamberlain's Apartments, Windsor Castle 1835, and the chair of state for Queen Victoria's wedding in 1840. [Windsor RA, Box I item 17, Estimates; Joy, *English Furniture, 1800–1851*]

COMMISSIONS FOR OTHER CLIENTS. 1777 William Marsh: Bill for 14s for work for Hon. Mrs Howard, mother of Lady Petre. [Essex RO, D/DP A189/8]

1787–88 Marsh: Furniture for Viscount Grimston. [Gorhambury accounts, *DEF*, vol. II, p. 299]

1790–93 Elward & Marsh, Elward Marsh & Bailey: Furnishing of 112 Pall Mall, London, for Dowager Duchess of Bedford — Total £250 0s 6d and regular repairs and maintenance thereafter. [Bedford Office, London]

1796–c.1807 Marsh & Tatham: Furnishing of Southill for Samuel Whitbread II. [*Southill, A Regency House* with introduction by Major S. Whitbread, 1951]

1797 Tatham: Payment £28 6s for work at the Berkeley Sq. house. [Lord Jersey's accounts, Williams & Glyn's Bank, Child's Branch]

1797–99 Elward Marsh & Tatham, Marsh & Tatham: Work at Croome Court, Worcs. [V & A archives, copies of Croome Court accounts]

1797–99 Elward Marsh & Tatham: Payment for £3,000 for work at Powderham Castle including probably the white and gold seat furniture in the 2nd Library and the suite of seat furniture with dolphin arms in the Music Room. [M. Girouard, 'Powderham Castle', III, *C. Life*, 18 July 1963, pp. 140–43]

1801 Elward Marsh & Tatham: Payment for furniture, £172 10s in account book of Edward, Lord Lascelles relating mainly to Harewood House, London. [Leeds archives dept, Harewood MS 190]

1801–03 Elward Marsh & Co.: Payments totalling £605 10s for 2nd Lord Braybrooke but not specified whether for Audley End, Billingbear or his London house. [Essex RO, D/DBy/A357]

1804 Marsh & Tatham: Payment for furniture, £715, for Lord Villiers, later Earl of Jersey. [Osterley Park accounts, Earl of Jersey]

1804 Marsh & Tatham: In December received payment of £395 6s from 6th Duke of Bedford 'being the amount of a Bill delivered for Cabinet and Upholstery Work'. Earlier that year Arthur Young, the agriculturalist, had noted at Woburn that 'several appartments were newly furnished . . .'. [G. Blakiston, *Woburn and the Russells*, 1980, p. 178]

1806 Marsh & Tatham: Bill for £6 12s for mahogany caned bergère with cushion supplied to Nathaniel Bond, East Holme, Dorset. [Dorset RO, D367/F2]

c.1805–10 Tatham & Bailey: Furniture and furnishings supplied for Sir Henry Harpur, Calke Abbey, including gilt furniture and mirrors for the Drawing Room and library tables, steps, chairs and map fitting for the Library. [H. Colvin, *Calke Abbey, Derbyshire*, 1985, pp. 109, 111]

c.1806–10 Marsh & Tatham (attributed): Suite of ebony and ivory dining room furniture inset with 'pietra dure' including pair of pedestals, firescreen, centre table and jardinière, supplied to Sir Harry Fetherstonhaugh, Uppark. Cf. suite of library furniture supplied to Carlton House in 1806 by Marsh & Tatham. [C. Wainwright, 'The Furnishing of The Royal Library, Windsor', *Conn.*, June 1977, pp. 104–09]

1807 Tatham & Bailey: Payment for £27 15s. [3rd Earl of Mansfield's domestic account bks, Kenwood]

1807 Tatham & Bailey: Payment £13 2s 6d for bath chair. [V & A archives, copies of Petworth accounts]

c.1808 Tatham & Bailey: Provided '6 bamboo chairs, japanned as Botany Bay wood' for The Thornery, Woburn. [C. Aslet, 'Park and Garden Buildings at Woburn', I, *C. Life*, 31 March 1983, pp. 772–75]

1809–11 Tatham & Bailey: Various sums, maximum £25 7s 10d, in the account bks each December for Lord Braybrooke but not specified for a particular house. [Essex RO, D/DBy/A376]

1811 Marsh & Tatham: Payment of £65 7s 6d in account bk of Edward Lord Lascelles relating mainly to work at Harewood House, London. [Leeds archives dept, Harewood MS 192]

1810–13 Tatham Bailey & Saunders: Undertook move of 6th Duke of Bedford from Stanhope St to Hamilton Pl., Piccadilly, London in 1810 and furnishing of new house. Bill of 1813 for 393 items, total £5,575 10s 2d. Thereafter regular repairs and maintenance.

1820 Bailey & Saunders: Undertook move of the Duke to a house on the west side of St James's Sq. and the furnishing — bill dated May 1820 for 129 items at a cost of £660 18s. In 1820 the Duke also bought for his wife a house on Campden Hill, Kensington, London, and had built for her a house at Endsleigh, Devon, furniture for both being provided by Bailey & Saunders until at least 1825. [Bedford Office, London]

c.1812–c.1814 Tatham Bailey & Saunders (attributed): Various alterations made by the Dowager Marchioness of Downshire at Ombersley Court, Worcs., including redecoration of room in Chinese taste with imitation bamboo furniture, very similar to that provided by Elward & Marsh for Brighton Pavilion from 1802. [*C. Life*, 16 January 1953, pp. 153–55]

1815–23 Richard Saunders: Furniture and upholstery, total £327, supplied for Colonel Henry Knight, Tythegston Court, Glam. [*C. Life*, 5 October 1978, pp. 1024, 1027, 1029]

H. Clifford-Smith, *Buckingham Palace*, 1931; G. de Bellaigue, J. Harris, O. Millar, *Buckingham Palace*, 1968; H. D. Roberts, *The Royal Pavilion Brighton*, 1939; J. Dinkel, *The Royal Pavilion Brighton*, 1983; Major S. Whitbread (introduction to) *Southill A Regency House*, 1951; C. Wainwright, 'The Furnishing of the Royal Library Windsor', *Conn.*, June 1977, pp. 104–09 See Edward Bailey. F. C.

Elwick, Edward snr, Northgate, Wakefield, Yorks., cm and u (1745–d. 1771). See Richard Wright & Edward Elwick.

Elwick, Edward jnr & Son, Northgate, Wakefield, Yorks., cm and u (1771–d. 1787). See Richard Wright & Edward Elwick.

Elwick, John & Robinson, John, Northgate, Wakefield, Yorks., cm and u (1788–1816). See Richard Wright & Edward Elwick.

Ely, —, Nottingham (1791). See Shelton & Ely.

Ely, James, 5 College St, Bury St Edmunds, Suffolk, cm and u (1830–39). [D]

Ely, Joseph, Bury St Edmunds, Suffolk, cm (1793). [D]

Ely, Robert, St Mary Stoke, Ipswich, Suffolk, chairmaker (1798). [Suffolk RO, calendar of marriage licence bonds, FAA:50/2/111, p. 207]

Emans, William, Queen St, London, upholder (1766). Insured a house at Twickenham for £150 in 1766. [GL, Hand in Hand MS vol. 105, p. 120]

Emanuel, —. See Toun & Emanuel.

Emanuel, E., Portsmouth, Hants., cm (1840–41). Supplied a table costing £13 13s to Charlecote Park, Warks., in 1840–41. [Warwick RO, L6/1118]

Ember, Francis, Paradise St, near King St, Rotherhithe, London, freeman upholder (1715). Took out a Hand in Hand Insurance policy on 23 August 1715 for £200 on his house, and £200 on a house nearby. [GL, Hand in Hand MS vol. 14, ref. 16862–63]

Emberry, Thomas, St Martin's St, London, chairmaker (1749). [Poll bk]

Embleton, John, Ouseburn, Newcastle, joiner and cm (1801). [D]

Embley, Samuel, 38 Horse Fair, Bristol, picture frame maker (1775–93). [D]

Embley, William, Horse Fair, Bristol, picture frame maker (1793–1801). [D]

Emerick, John, 8 Coburg Pl., Clerkenwell, London, clock-case maker (1839). [D]

Emerson, George, Spittal Hill, Louth, Lincs., joiner and cm (1831–41). [D]

Emerson, Joseph, 44 Merchant St, Bristol, cm (1815–17). [D]

Em(m)erson, Robert, Sheep Mkt, Leek, Staffs., joiner and cm (1816–18). [D]

Emerson, T., 91 Newgate St, London, furnishing u (1837). [D]

Emerson, William, Upgate, Louth, Lincs., joiner and cm (1831). [D]

Emerton, Thomas, 36 Gloucester St, Queen Sq., London, upholder (1824). Took out a Sun Insurance policy on 26 February 1824 for £400 on household goods, including £50 on stock, utensils and goods. The name Thomas has been deleted and Mary substituted. [GL, Sun MS vol. 499, ref. 1014216]

Emery, Ann, 3 Carthusian St, London, cm (1835). [D] See James Emery.

Emery, D., 17 Union St, East Stonehouse, Plymouth, Devon, cm and u (1838). [D]

Emery, Edward, 16 Henrietta St, Covent Gdn, London, carver and gilder (1839). [D]

Emery, James, Bristol, cm and u (1805–12). Trading at 5 Clare St, 1805–06; Wine St and Baldwin St in 1809; and Alfred Hill, 1810–12. [D]

Emery, James, Carthusian St, Charterhouse, London, cm, u and chairmaker (1817–28). Recorded at no. 5 in 1817, and no. 3, 1820–28. Took out Sun Insurance policies on 6 July 1820 for £400 on a house at 3 Carthusian St, unfurnished; and on 1 December 1821 for £1,000 of which £180 accounted for stock, utensils and goods in trust in his house, where no work was done; and £100 on those in workshops and warehouse. [D; GL, Sun MS vol. 485, ref. 968870; vol. 486, ref. 981962] See Ann Emery.

Emery, Thomas, 54 Key St, Liverpool, cm (1805–07). [D]

Emery, William, Rotherhithe, London, house, ship and sign carver and cm (1826–34). Trading at 31 Clarence St in 1826, and 4 Stringers Row, 1832–34. [D]

Emes, J., 108 Gt Russell St, London, trunk and platecase manufacturer (1837). [D]

Emett (or Emmitt), Michael snr, Preston, Lancs., cm (1781–d. by 1802). Former app., George Hall, and his son Richard Emett and four brothers were admitted burgesses in 1782 on payment of the fine. Dead by 1802 when his son, Thomas and three other sons including Michael, 'late upholsterer' were named in the Preston Guild record of burgesses. [D]

Emett, Michael jnr, Preston, Lancs. and Liverpool, u (1802–22). Named in the Preston Guild record of burgesses in 1802 as 'late upholsterer son of . . . Michael deceased'; and in 1822 as 'of Liverpool formerly of Preston'.

Emett, Thomas, Preston, Lancs., cm, builder and joiner (1782–d. by 1842). Trading at 21 Lord St with office at Parks Ct and house at 2 Vicarage in 1818. Admitted burgess of Preston in 1782 as son of Michael snr and brother of Michael jnr. Named in the Preston Guild record of burgesses with his own son, Thomas, in 1802; and in 1822 with three sons. Both he and his son, Thomas, were dead by 1842 when his grandson, Thomas, with seven sons, were named as burgesses in 1842. [D]

Emmans, P., address unrecorded, cm (1814–17). Supplied furniture to Nicholas Pearse of Loughton, Essex, and London on 31 March and July 1814, and 28 March 1817, totalling £36 8s. [Essex RO, D/DHt A1/4]

Emmens, Thomas, 11 Gt Russell St, Bloomsbury, London, upholder and cm (1817–28). [D]

Emmens, Thomas, 22 Paget Pl., Gt Waterloo St, London, invalid chairmaker, chair and sofa maker (1835–39). [D]

Emmery, John, address unrecorded, cm (1725). Referred to in Penn'a Gazette, 8 July 1731, as having left England in 1725.

Emmes, Edward snr, Norwich, u (1677). His son, Edward jnr, was admitted freeman on 4 July 1677. [Norwich freemen reg.]

Emmes, Edward jnr, Norwich, u (1677). Son of Edward snr; admitted freeman on 4 July 1677. [Norwich freemen reg.]

Emmett, John jnr, 10 Britannia Gdns, Hoxton, London, chairmaker (1792). Took out a Sun Insurance policy on 8 August 1792 for £100 on his household goods in the house of Emmett snr, and his utensils in the house of Buskins, chairmaker, at Tenton (or Fenton) Timber Ground, Moorfields. [GL, Sun MS vol. 387, p. 442]

Emmett, John, 23 Dorset St, Spitalfields, London, chairmaker (1813). Took out a Sun Insurance policy on 19 May 1813 for £200 of which stock and utensils accounted for £40. [GL, Sun MS vol. 463, ref. 881981]

Emmett, Robert, Garden Row, Deptford, Kent, carver and gilder (1839). [D]

Emmett, W., 11 Upper St, Martin's Lane, London, wine cooler manufacturer (1835). [D]

Emmett, William, London, carver (b. 1641–93). Recorded by Vertue as successor to his uncle, Henry Phillips Emmett, as Sculptor to the Crown and predecessor to Grinling Gibbons. Known to have worked with William Morgan. Named in the Livery of the Joiners' Co. in 1666. Worked at Whitehall in December 1688 receiving £197 10s 6d for a picture frame 'with 2 inrichments oak leaves and husks and Italian moulding', for the Queen's Closet; and 'two scollop shells in the neeches' for the Privy Gallery. In March and August 1690 his bill for work at Hampton Court on the Water Gallery included 'large Italian picture fram'd mouldings . . . over the 2 chimneys in the Great Room', costing £8 8s 5d. In 1693 he was paid £220 for work done at Hampton Court. He also worked at Kensington Palace in 1790, Chelsea, and the City Churches. Temple Church has two capitals by him. [British Arch. Assoc. Journal, 1951, p. 4; Wren Soc., vol. XX; PRO, Works 5/42, 46 and 55]

Emmitt, William, 56 Aldersgate St, London, chairmaker (1785). Took out a Sun Insurance policy on 28 February 1785 for £100 on household goods and wearing apparel. [GL, Sun MS vol. 327, p. 399]

Emmorson, Peter, Liverpool, upholder (1716). Admitted freeman on 3 October 1716. [Liverpool freemen reg.]

Emmott, George, Mabgate, Leeds, Yorks., cm (1822). [D]

Emmott, James, Leeds, Yorks., cm (1817–39). Addresses given at Mabgate in 1817, and Gower St, 1826–29, no. 1 in 1826. [D]

Emmott (or Emmett), Thomas, 99 Marsh Lane, Leeds, Yorks., cm and u (1816–20). [D]

Emmott, William, Colne Lane, Colne, Lancs., cm (b. c. 1786–1841). Aged 55 at the time of the 1841 Census, and son, Robert, aged 30.

Empsall, Joseph, Hipperholme, Yorks., joiner and cm (1822). [D]

Empson, Henry, Liverpool, cm (1805–d. 1826). Recorded at 51 Byrom St with shop at 1 Hood St in 1818; 97 Copperas Hill with shop at 3 Hood St in 1821; 81 Byrom St in 1823; no. 79 in 1824; and Islington in 1826. Signed the Supplement to the Liverpool Cabinet and Chair Prices, 1805, on behalf of the journeymen. Recorded as clerk to St Stephen's Church in 1821. Death at Kirkdale reported in Liverpool Mercury, 16 June 1826. [D]

Empson, Thomas, 56 North St, Prospect St, Hull, Yorks., cm (1834–35). [D]

Emptage, Humphry, Dover, Kent, cm and broker (1792–1811). [D]

Emptage, John, Dover, Kent, cm (1826–37). Trading at Charlton Rd in 1832, and Charlton Cresc. in 1837. [Poll bks]

Emuss, James, High St, Droitwich, Worcs., cm (1835). [D]

Emuss, Thomas, Queen St, Birmingham, cm (1816). [D]

Emuss, William, Droitwich, Worcs., cm and u (1828–35). Trading at Hanbury St in 1835. [D; poll bk]

Endicott, John jnr, Holloway St, Exeter, Devon, cm, u, chairmaker, undertaker and builder (1819–24). Trading at no. 31 when he advertised sale of mahogany and other furniture and paper hangings in *Western Luminary*, 26 October 1819. [D]

Endicott, Joseph, St Mary Arches St, Exeter, Devon, cm (1836). Daughter Sarah Jane bapt. at St Olave's on 28 February 1836. [PR(bapt.)]

England, Daniel, Sutton and Hull, Yorks., cm, chairmaker, furniture broker and shopkeeper (1814–42). Recorded at Sutton in 1814; Witham, Hull, 1826–40; with res. at William St, Drypool, Hull in 1826. App. to George Brook in July 1814, and assigned to Robert Waugh in December 1817. [D; Hull app. reg.]

England, George, Nottingham, joiner and cm (1778–85). Grandson of Michael Skevington, Ilkeston, Derbs., Gent.; app. in 1778. Named as a burgess in 1785. [Nottingham app. list and burgess index]

England, John Frederick, Steelhouse Lane, Birmingham, cm, carver and gilder (1822). [D]

England, John, Nottingham, joiner and cm (1824–48). App. in 1824, becoming a master in 1838, when also named as a burgess. Took apps named John Henry Statham in 1838; Henry Roberts in 1844; and Walter Gamble in 1848. [Nottingham app. list and burgess index]

England, Matthew, Castleford, Yorks., cm (1822). [D]

England, Robert, High St, Birmingham, cm, chairmaker and cane worker (1816–18). Recorded also at Moat Row in 1816. [D]

England, Thomas, James St, London, cane chairmaker (1709). [London rate bks] Possibly the Thomas England, chairmaker, who provided six chairs and four 'banketts' for the 2nd Duke of Bedford in 1710. [Bedford Office, London]

England, Thomas, Newport St, Leicester Fields, London, cm (1727–28). Named in contemporary newspapers. [Heal]

England, Thomas, St Ann's, Westminster, London, joiner and cm (1728). On bankruptcy his estate was assigned to John Blow, carver. [*London Gazette*, 9–12 March 1727/28 and 6–10 August 1728]

England, Thomas, Sutton and Hull, Yorks., cm, paper stainer, undertaker, furniture broker, victualler and flour dealer (1806–42). Recorded at Sutton in 1806; Witham, Hull, in 1823; with res. at Gt Union St, 1817–40; listed as Thomas jnr, 1823–42. App. to George & John Chapman of Hull in October 1806. Acted as Constable of Sutton in 1831. [D; Hull app. reg.] Two tradesmen may be involved here.

England, Thomas, Tadcaster, Yorks., joiner and/or cm (1834). [D]

England, William, Hull, Yorks., cm and u (1821–31). Recorded at Drypool in 1821; and at Gt Union St in 1831. App. to Robert Waugh in June 1821. [D; Hull app. reg.]

Engleheart, Peter, 40 Castle St, Oxford Mkt, London, cm, u and undertaker (1793–1808). Subscribed to Sheraton's *Drawing Book*, 1793, and named in his list of master cabinet makers, 1803. Mahogany double pedestal writing table recorded bearing his label. [D; Sotheby's, NY, 21 November 1981, lot 254, illus.]

Engley, John, High St, Stroud, Glos., cm (1816–18). [PR(bapt.)]

Engley, John, 4 Perry Pl., Oxford St, London, chair carver (1821). Took out a Sun Insurance policy on 7 June 1821 for £150 of which stock, utensils and goods in trust accounted for £60. [GL, Sun MS vol. 488, ref. 980749]

Engley, John, 10 Commercial Pl., City Rd, London, chairmaker (1826–29). [D]

English, Edmund, Bath, Som., cm and u (1787–1828). Trading in Broad St in 1793. Declared bankrupt with Andrew Berkley Becks, *Chester Chronicle and North Wales Advertiser*, 7 November 1828. [D] Probably of English & Son.

English, Thomas, 5 Broad St, Soho, London, looking-glass manufacturer (1794–1801). [D]

English, William, Spring Gdn Lane, Sunderland, Co. Durham, joiner and cm (1828–29). [D]

English, William, Camberwell Grove, London, cm (1835). [D]

English, William, Norwich, u (1835). App. to John Cox; admitted freeman on 24 February 1835. [Norwich freemen rolls]

English & Son, 21 Milsom St, Bath, Som., u, cm, auctioneers, appraisers, undertakers, carvers and gilders, estate and house agents (est. 1751). Advertised sale of furniture on 20 November 1845. [V &A archives] In 1819 trading as English, English & Becks. [D] See Edmund English.

Ennis, Thomas, Liverpool, carver (1752). Took app. named Jones in 1752. [S of G, app. index]

Ensar, George, Tamworth, Staffs., turner (c. 1686). Mentioned in Plot's *History of Staffordshire*, 1686 as having 'contrived an engine to turne wreath work' (i.e., spiral turning) by which he was enabled to 'make not only of two but of three or four twists, and that in so little time that he can turn twenty of these while one is cut or raspt the only way they can make such at London and Oxford that I could by any means hear of.' [*DEF*]

Ensom, Jane, 14 Golden Lane, Barbican, London, cm, u and undertaker (1839). [D]

Ensom, Thomas, 14 Golden Lane, Barbican, London, turner (1835). [D]

Enston, Daniel jnr, Sandwich, Kent, cm (1798–1831). [D; poll bk]

Enstone, Daniel, Archbishop's Palace, Canterbury, Kent, chairmaker (1818). [Poll bk]

Entwistle, Mrs, address unrecorded. Between 1746–67 the account bk of Sir Matthew Featherstonhaugh of Uppark, Sussex, records substantial payments to Mrs Entwistle, or Entwishle, for household furniture amounting to £575 5s 3d. She was probably a widow carrying on a well-established business after her husband's death. [*Conn.*, November 1967, p. 158]

Entwisle [*sic*], Thomas, 37 Bishopsgate Within, London, cabinet founder (1776). [D]

Eplett, Charles, 2 College Sq., Bristol, cm and u (1831–32). [D]

Epps, Thomas, 33 Castle St, Canterbury, Kent, cm, furniture broker, chair and sofa maker (1832–34). [D]

Epps, Thomas, Dover, Kent, cm, u, carver and gilder, fancy turner and chair and sofa maker (1838–39). Trading at Biggin St, 1838, and 6 Church Pl., 1839. [D]

Epworth (or Epsworth), Joseph, 12 Little St Martin's Lane, London, cm (1793–96). [D]

Equillent, Francis, 2 Little Pulteney St, Golden Sq., London, tassel and fringe maker (1808). [D] See Ann Esquilant.

Erard, P., London, pianoforte and music stand maker (c. 1821–37). Trading at 17 Gt Marlborough St, 1826–27; and no. 18 and also 3–4 Little Portland St, Marylebone in 1837. Music stand recorded inscribed 'ERARDS, 18 Gt. Marlborough Strt. London.' [D; V & A archives]

Erlam, Peter, Liverpool, cm (1831). App. to John O'Neill in 1831. [Liverpool app. enrolment bk]

Erlington, John, Chester, u (1741). Admitted freeman on 1 February 1741. [Chester freemen rolls]

Errington, Thomas, Appleby, Westmld, joiner and/or cm (1828–34). [D]

Errington, Thomas, Goal St, Gt Yarmouth, Norfolk, carver and gilder (1839). [D]

Erskine, Thomas, 55 Castle St East, Oxford Mkt, London, carver and gilder (1817). [D]

Erskine, William, 55 Castle St East, Oxford Mkt, London, carver (1807–20). Took out a Sun Insurance policy on 11 February 1807 for £500 of which stock, utensils and goods in trust accounted for £10. [D; GL, Sun MS vol. 437, ref. 800184]

Erskine, William, 5 Hyde St, Bloomsbury, London, carver and chair carver (1826–29). [D]

Ersser, William, 33 Broad St, Golden Sq., London, furniture japanner (1835). [D]

Erwood, Alfred, 9 Brownlow St, Holborn, London, billiard and backgammon table maker (1815–34). Recorded in partnership with James Erwood at no. 3, 1815–25; and alone, at no. 9, 1829–34. Declared bankrupt, *Liverpool Mercury*, 10 July 1829. [D]

Erwood, James, 3 Brownlow St, Holborn, London, billiard table and backgammon board maker (1815–39). Recorded in partnership with Alfred Erwood, 1815–25; and alone, 1822–39. J. & A. Erwood, successors to the late Solomon Erwood, supplied Francis, Marquess of Tavistock of Oakley, Beds., with cues, maces, sets of balls, mainly 'for the Russian game', and framed rules for 'the pool of Russian games', the whole amounting to £8 19s. The firm submitted a bill to the 6th Duke of Bedford dated 16 October 1822 totalling £58 17s. Furniture supplied for Woburn Abbey, Beds., included a 'Full size Mahogany Table with Lion Claw Feet new Cloth Pockets, Brown Holland Cover, Maces Cues Balls etc. as agreed in Exchange for the old Table' and 'The 4 Rules at Bill^ds in black Frames'. The receipt is dated 8 October 1823. [D; Bedford Office, London]

Erwood, Solomon, 3 Brownlow St, Holborn, London, billiard table maker (b. 1741–d. 1813). Trade card [Landauer Coll., MMA, NY] reads 'Maces, Cues &c. on the shortest Notice.' Took out Sun Insurance policies in 1778 for £400 of which utensils and stock accounted for £200; and on 15 January 1808 for £800, £600 on utensils and stock. [GL, Sun MS vol. 270, p. 97; vol. 441, ref. 812556] Submitted a bill to Mr Hill on 21 December 1780 for eight billiard maces and case. [Shakespeare Birthplace Trust, Leigh receipts DR 18/5] In December 1791 Solomon Erwood was paid £27 16s 6d by the 5th Duke of Bedford by order of Henry Holland, the architect, presumably for a billiard table for Woburn. [Bedford Office, London] A billhead [Banks Coll., BM] is dated 24 June 1807. Death, aged 72, reported in *Gents Mag.*, March 1813. He was succeeded by James and Alfred Erwood.

Escolme, Thomas, Lancaster, cm (1779–95). Admitted freeman, 1779–80. Named in the Gillow records, 1787–95. [Lancaster freemen rolls; Westminster Ref. Lib., Gillow]

Eshelby, George, York, joiner, cm and u (1816–38). Recorded at High Ousegate, 1816–18; 7 Fetter Lane in 1830; and 96 Micklegate in 1838. [D]

Eskholme, Richard, Lancaster, cm (1784). [Poll bk]

Esplin, William, 1 New Shambles, Manchester, cm (1822). [D]

Esquilant, Ann, 16 Rathbone Pl., London, trimming manufacturer (1819). [D] See Francis Equillent.

Essex, C., Upper King St, Bloomsbury, London, writing desk manufacturer (1837). [D]

Essex, Charles, 19 Pantheon, London, manufacturer. Label recorded on rosewood bookrack, mahogany veneered, with turned spindle gallery, c. 1820. [V & A archives]

Estill, Thomas, Church St, Whitby, Yorks., cm and chairmaker (1834–40). [D]

Eston, Negus, addresss unrecorded. On two occasions in 1755 he provided furniture for the 4th Duke of Bedford at Woburn Abbey, Beds., the only items specified in the accounts being bedsteads, both four-post and tent, with their furnishings, at a cost of £33 14s 6d. In 1764 he made curtains for windows and beds, and chair covers, totalling £4. [Bedford Office, London]

Estwick, William, Market Pl., Hitchin, Herts., auctioneer, appraiser, cm and u (1838–39). [D]

Etchells, John, Stockport, Cheshire, joiner, cm and u (1816–34). Addresses given at Little Underbank, 1816–28, and Etchells St in 1834. Declared bankrupt, *Liverpool Mercury*, 10 October 1817. [D]

Etchells, Robert, Little Underbank, Stockport, Cheshire, cm and u (1816–41). Recorded at no. 29 in 1841. [D]

Etchells, William, Church Gate, Stockport, Cheshire, cm (1825–41). Recorded at no. 1 in 1834, and 31 St Peter's Gate in 1841. [D]

Ethell, Mary, Temple Row, Birmingham, cm (1822). [D]

Ethell, Stephen, Temple Row, Birmingham, cm, u and broker (1828–30). Trading at no. 33 in 1828. [D]

Ethell, Stephen & Ann, Ann St, Birmingham, cm, u and paper hangers (1830–39). Recorded at no. 9 in 1830, and no. 12, 1835–39, also as feather dealers in 1835. [D]

Ethell, Thomas, Bull Ring, Birmingham, cm and u (1816). [D]

Ethell, William, Birmingham, cm, u and chairmaker (1780–1822). Addresses given at 101 Digbeth, 1780; Moor St, 1793; 4 High St, 1800–05; as William & Sons at no. 3 in 1809; and Moor St, 1816–22. Trade card in Landauer Coll., MMA, NY. Took out Sun Insurance policies in 1782 and 1784 for £200, of which £120 accounted for utensils and stock. [D; GL, Sun MS vol. 302, p. 164; vol. 322, p. 210]

Etheredge, Thomas, 36 Bartholomew Close, London, cm (1790). Took out a Sun Insurance policy on 10 May 1790 for £100 on his house and wearing apparel. [GL, Sun MS ref. 569730]

Etheridge, E., 5 Bedford Pl., Southampton, Hants., cm (1834–36). [D]

Etheridge, Thomas, North St, City Rd, London, cm and u (1791–1802). Trading at no. 7 in 1791, and no. 46 in 1802. Took out Sun Insurance policies on 13 July 1791 for £200 of which utensils in Mr Seddon's warehouse in Aldersgate St accounted for £20; and on 20 July 1802 for £400 of which utensils and stock accounted for £240. [GL, Sun MS vol. 379, p. 92; vol. 424, ref. 735134]

Etheridge, Thomas, 10 Pelham St, Spitalfields, London, cm (1804). Took out a Sun Insurance policy on 20 January 1804 for £400, stock and utensils accounting for £240. [GL, Sun MS vol. 430, ref. 757655]

Etheridge, Thomas, Cambridge, carver and gilder (1830–41). Addresses given at Slaughterhouse Lane, 1830, and Trumpington St, 1832–41. [D; poll bks]

Etherington, Francis, Newton Lane, Manchester, cm (1788). [D]

Etherington, George, Middle St, Gt Driffield, Yorks., cm etc. (1823). [D]

Etty, John, (c. 1634–1708). Master builder and joiner who provided the reredos and altar-rail for St Michael-le-Belfry, York, 1708. [Beard, *Craftsmen and Interior Decoration*, p. 259]

Etty, William, York, carpenter (1694–d. 1734). Admitted freeman in 1694. Worked for City House by order of the Honourable Committee, supplying an oak table costing 12s, a 'binch', 6s, and 'A Oak Window Seate', £1 2s; account is dated 21 December 1729. [*Surtees Soc.*, vol. 102, p. 174]

Eules, John, Gt Yarmouth, Norfolk, u (1719). Took app. named Foster in 1719. [S of G, app. index]

Eules, Susanna & Co., Gt Yarmouth, Norfolk, u (1729). Took out a Sun Insurance policy on 10 April 1729 for £500 of which household goods and stock accounted for £200. [GL, Sun MS vol. 29, ref. 47402]

Eustace, —, address unrecorded, cm (1803) Subscribed to Sheraton's *Cabinet Dictionary*, 1803.

Eustace, Harrington, Aylesbury, Bucks., cm (1822–32). Named in a deed of 1822. Acted as 5th party in lease and mortgage in 1832. [Oxford RO, TA 4/8/c/4/1–3]

Eustace, William, 15 St Peter's Hill, Thames St, London, cm (1808). [D]

Eustace, William, Walton St, Aylesbury, Bucks., cm (1839). [D]

Euster, —, near Water Lane, Fleet St, London, (1807). On 21 August 1807 his premises were destroyed by a fire which started nearby. [*Gents Mag.*, August 1807]

Eustice, —, London, cm (1793). Subscribed to Sheraton's *Drawing Book*, 1793.

Evans, —, St Paul's Churchyard, London, cm (1744). Announced in *Daily Advertiser*, 6 December 1744 sale of 'a small and very Curious inlaid Cabinet, on a Frame, a proper Piece of Furniture for any elegant House, containing above One Hundred and Fifty Drawers contrived in the most useful Way, many of which are secret, fit for a Medallist or a Virtuoso. This Cabinet was many Years Making, and is not the least damag'd; the Back is ornamented with many fine Italian Stone Landscapes, and must be pleasing to any curious Eye for the Inspection only.' Probably Phineas Evans.

Evans, —, Chester, cm (1793). App. by indenture of assignment to James Gardner, cm, 27 June to 8 July 1793. [Chester app. bks]

Evans, —, Upper West St, Gloucester, carver and gilder (1802). [D]

Evans, A., address unrecorded, cm (1774). Small George II mahogany secretaire cabinet recorded, with double-fronted secretaire drawer containing drawers and pigeon-holes; four graduated drawers below, all with chased brass loop-handles, and raised on panelled bracket feet; two-tier lattice-work superstructure; signed 'A.EVANS, 1774'. [Sotheby's, 19 June 1980, lot 152; similar examples illus. in *DEF*, figs 60, 61]

Evans, Ambrose, Liverpool, upholder (1749–60). Recorded in Pool Lane, 1760. Admitted freeman on 12 May 1749. Former app., John Owen, petitioned freedom in 1760 after serving Evans for two years, and Charles Aven for five. [Liverpool freemen reg. and committee bk]

Evans, Ann, Little Underbank, Stockport, Cheshire, cm and u (1828–41). Trading as Ann & Co. at no. 27 in 1841. [D] See Edwards and William Evans.

Evans, Benjamin, Wheatsheaf Yd, Fleet Mkt, London, cm (1821–c.1825). Insured stock and utensils in his house and workshop for £300 on 18 July 1821 with the Sun Co. His trade card was cut up and used to make numbered tickets to ensure correct assembly of a set of window cornices *en suite* with a four-post bed (probably by Gillows) made for Clifton Castle, Yorks., c.1825, now at Temple Newsam House, Leeds. Card reads: 'B. EVANS, CABINET MAKER, 3 WHEATSHEAF YARD, RESPECTFULLY solicits . . . made to the PEDESTAL and other SIDEBOARDS . . . complete; also every description of TELESCOPIC . . . SINGLE FRAME DINING TABLES; and hopes . . . of the best seasoned materials, and select wood . . . patronage. The above Telescopic Frame constructed . . . ten feet and upwards, with only four . . . Loo, sofa and Card Tables, &c. . . . modern principles. PATENT FOUR POST BRASS . . . SOCKET BEDSTEADS, SOFA AND CHAIR . . .'. [GL,

Sun MS vol. 484, ref. 981648; Gilbert, *Leeds Furn. Cat.*, vol. 1, pp. 23–27]

Evans, Benjamin, London, cm and u (1824–39). Addresses given at 5 Clerkenwell Green, 1824–27; 3 St John's Lane, Clerkenwell in 1829; and 48 Myddleton St, Spitalfields, 1839. Took out a Sun Insurance policy on 5 March 1824 for £350 of which stock and utensils in house and offices accounted for £320. [D; GL, Sun MS vol. 494, ref. 1014715]

Evans, Cadwalader, address unrecorded, cm (1724–30). Carried out much jobbing and general repair work for the Monson family. Bills to Lady Mary Saunderson submitted between 1724–30 totalled £85 0s 11d, and refer generally to furniture repairs. He supplied a few items, however, including on 3 May 1825, an ebony picture frame costing 7s, and a gold one, £1 10s; and several lanterns, such as 'a Lanthorn with a silk Line & Tossil & a Golden Ball', costing £4 10s on 2 February 1729. Evans also carried out silvering and diamond cutting looking-glasses, lacquering and japanning. His bill for work done between 27 January and 28 March 1829–30 including 'putting up & Fitting of Indian Pictures Making an Addition to One', altering frames, repairing a walnut settee and a cedar table, putting up two silver sconces, re-lacquering a cabinet and cleaning the brass-work on the frame; shortening a stone table frame; fitting a 'new wainscott Claw to a Table'; 'Fastening a silver cock in a Fountain'; and providing 'Two Canvas Window Blinds Painted in Mahogany Frames.' On 10 November he was paid for further repairs, regilding furniture, 'covering of 8 seats with yr. own Velvet'; and on 20 November supplying a 'Walnut Quadrale Table & Cover', £3 5s. Evans also worked for Lady Margaret Monson between 1725–26, supplying on 9 December 1725 'a Horse to Dry Cloaths upon', and a 'Bed Table'; on 18 December an 'Indian Tea Board'; and on 21 December a 'Bed Chair Frame'. Evans also fitted up a bed, put up silver sconces, and carried out various repairs to furniture. Evans's bill to Sir John Monson for work done between 28 August and 15 January 1827 again records routine mending and cleaning of furniture. [Lincoln RO, Monson, 10, 1/A/16; 12]

Evans, Charles, at W. Mills, cm, opposite Slaughter's Coffee House, St Martin's Lane, London, cm (1775). Insured his household goods for £100 in 1775. [GL, Sun MS vol. 243, p. 531]

Evans, Charles, Manchester, chairmaker (1794–1838). Addresses given at 19 Brown St in 1794; Apple Mkt, 1818–22; 67 Thomas St, 1825–33; and no. 18, 1834–38. [D]

Evans, D. & S., 2 Wardour St, London, cabinet, chair and sofa manufacturer (1837). [D]

Evans, Daniel, Cirencester, Glos., u (1802). [Oxford poll bk]

Evans, David, St John's Lane, St John's St, London, bedstead and mattress maker (1820–28). Trading at no. 12 in 1820 and no. 18, 1827–28. [D]

Evans, David, 13 Guildford Pl., Bagnigge Wells, London, bedstead maker (1839). [D]

Evans, Edward, 11 Chichester Pl., King's Cross, London, cm, u and undertaker (1839). [D]

Evans, Edward, 113 Wardour St, London, cm and u (1839). [D]

Evans, Edwards, 27 Little Underbank, Stockport, Cheshire, cm (1834–41). [D] See Ann and William Evans.

Evans, F., 8 Bedford St, Bedford Row, London, furniture broker, cm and u (1835–39). [D]

Evans, Frederick, New St, Worcester, cm, u and chairmaker (1828). [D]

Evans, G. & H., address unrecorded. Name stamped on William IV rosewood Davenport with sloping leather-lined slide each side, a pen drawer and four graduated long drawers on the right, on columnar supports and concave-fronted base with paw feet. [Christie's, 16 July 1981, lot 47]

Evans, G., 13 Welsh Back, Bristol, chairmaker (1835). [D]

Evans, George, London, carver and gilder (1826–39). Trading at 47 Upper North Pl., Gray's Inn Rd, 1826–29; and 17 Chad's Row, 1837–39. [D]

Evans, George, Bristol, Windsor and fancy chairmaker, broker, tobacco and snuff dealer (1821–35). Addresses given at Ellbroad St, 1821–22; 11 Old Market St, 1823–26; 2 Lower Castle St, 1827–28; 54 Castle St, 1829–34; and no. 45 in 1835. [D]

Evans, George, 12 Back Lime St, Liverpool, cm (1829). [D]

Evans, H. Samuel, address unrecorded, joiner and chairmaker (1832–36). Named in the Royal Household accounts supplying strong deal dovetailed boxes from 1831–36; six strong splat-back chairs, tapered legs, and wainscott seats for the King's Footman's Apartments, costing £3 12s. Carried out much jobbing work at St James's and Hampton Court Palaces, and supplied various deal presses for Kensington Palace. Worked at the Stud Lodge, Hampton Court, re-framing and adding new legs to eleven chairs and repairing twelve long seats, 'movable on low wheels with hinged feet and back boards', all in the Conservatory and pleasure grounds. [PRO, LC11/77–92] Presumably Samuel Evans.

Evans, J., 70 Banner St, London, water gilder (1835). [D]

Evans, James, Queen St, Wolverhampton, Staffs., cm and timber dealer (1770). [D]

Evans, James, 27 Panton St, Haymarket, London, carver and gilder (1829). Heavy Rococo trade card also gives trade as glass and picture frame maker. [D; Banks Coll., BM]

Evans, James, Pembroke St, Oxford, cm (1830). [D]

Evans, James, 1 Gibson St and 5 Gt Waterloo St, Lambeth, London, carver and gilder (1835–37). [D]

Evans, John, address unrecorded, cm (d. 1689). App. to Robert Halford, of St Michael Royal, at the time of his death in 1689. [PCC Wills, vol. XI, p. 93]

Evans, John, address unrecorded, joiner (1720–21). Mentioned frequently in the general accounts of Erddig, Clwyd between 1720–21. On 14 July 1720 he received £2 7s 1½d 'for making two large tables'; and on 10 December £1 6s for 'work done by One of his Men for the Upholsterers'. [V & A archives]

Evans, John, Chester, cm (1747). [Poll bk]

Evan(s), John, Skynner St, Bishopsgate St, London, upholder (1768–84). Son of John Evan, cook of London, and brother of Thomas Evans, upholder. Admitted freeman of the Upholders' Co. on 6 November 1776. Took apps named Thomas Davis, 1768–75; William Wood, 1770–77; John Ranshall, 1771–78; John Knife, 1776–83; and William Edwards until 1784. [GL, Upholders' Co. records]

Evans, John, Broad Mead, Bristol, cm (1774–1801). Recorded at 44 Broad Mead in 1775. Supplied furniture for John Pinney's house, 7 Gt George St, Bristol (now the Georgian House Museum), being paid £1 18s in 1792; £50 in 1793; and £28 5s in 1795. The only recorded item was a tea caddy for 18s. A mahogany bureau-bookcase by Evans, now in the Georgian House, has inscribed on a secret door: 'B. Milward Keynsham, Jany 25 1787, Bought of Mr. Evans, Broad Mead, Bristol, Price £15–15–0.' The book case was in the Milward family until 1970. [D; poll bks; Bristol Univ. Lib., John Pinney's private cash bk; *Furn. Hist.*, 1976, pp. 61–62, illus.]

Evans, John, 9 Mill Lane, Shaw's Brow, Liverpool, chairmaker (1796). Son of Edward Evans, pilot; admitted freeman on 30 May 1796. [D; Liverpool freeman reg.]

Evans, John, 101 Aldersgate St, London. See Oakley & Shackleton.

Evans, John, Cumming St, Pentonville and St James, Clerkenwell, London, u (1816). Recorded concerning lease of premises in 1816. [Marylebone Lib., deed 35/30]

Evans, John, The Tything, Worcester, cm and u (1820–30). Recorded at no. 48 in 1830. [D]

Evans, John, Birmingham, Tunbridge-ware manufacturer (1821–35). Trading at Upper Temple St in 1821; 30 Colmore St, 1828; and 87 Hill St, 1835. [D]

Evans, John, Liverpool, cm (1822–35). Trading at 9 Finch St in 1835. App. to William Harvey in 1822. [D; Liverpool app. enrolment bk]

Evans, John, Cambridge, cm (1834). App. to Thomas Legge, cm of Cambridge on 1 April 1834 for £10. [Cambridge app. reg.]

Evans, Joseph, Liverpool, cm (1791–1821). Trading at 1 Sefton Ct, Stockdale St in 1821. App. in 1791 to Thomas Gorton, on whose death Evans served his widow. Petitioned freedom on servitude in 1816, and affidavit made; but application postponed pending information with regard to stamp and witnesses. [D; Liverpool freemen's committee bk]

Evans, Maurice Evan, 12 Holborn Bars, Holborn, London, u, cm and carpet dealer (1839–40). Evans & Co. recorded at this address in 1839. Took out a Sun Insurance policy in 1840. [D; GL, Sun MS vol. 57, ref. 1328772]

Evans, P., 13 Guildford(?) Pl., Spitalfields, London, bedstead maker (1835). [D]

Evans, Phineas, at 'The Fleece', St Paul's Churchyard, London, cm (1727–47). Submitted a bill to Burghley House, Stamford, dated 1727–28, for 'Three sconces Carved and Guilt in Gold with a Trebble Branch to each at £14.14s. per sconce — £44.2.0.' The three mirror sconces are still at Burghley, but the other seven items on the bill have not been identified. [*C. Life*, 29 August 1974, pp. 562–64] Advertised house to let, *Daily Advertiser*, 6 April 1744. Named in contemporary newspapers, 1744–47. [Heal]

Evans, Poynton, Wolverhampton, Staffs., cm (1818–20). [D]

Evans, Richard, 7 Weak St, Liverpool, carver and gilder (1821). [D]

Evans, Richard, 46 Hanover St, Manchester, carver and gilder (1832–33). [D]

Evans, Richard, Tylers Green, High Wycombe, Bucks., chair turner. [1841 Census]

Evans, Robert, 24 Cornwallis St, Liverpool, cm (1813–14). [D]

Evans, Robert snr, Madeley, Salop, cm (1828). [D]

Evans, Robert jnr, Madeley, Salop, cm (1828). [D]

Evans, Robert H., 93 Pall Mall, London, joiner or carpenter (1835). Named in the Lord Chamberlain's accounts in September 1835 for work done at Kensington Palace, making two deal presses with fitted shelves and 'moulded & rose panneled Doors', costing £20 14s and £17 5s for the wardrobe rooms of the Duchess of Kent and Baroness Lehzen. [Windsor Royal Archives]

Evans, Samuel, address unrecorded, joiner and chairmaker (1826–31). Carried out general jobbing work and repairs at St James's and Hampton Court Palaces, the Houses of Peers and Commons, Stud Lodge, the Queen's stable, Bushy, the Tower of London, and the *Royal Sovereign* yacht. He also supplied some furniture, the accounts of 10 October 1826 listing a high wainscott linenpress costing £23 3s, a deal cupboard, £6 15s, and a press bedstead, £15, all for St James's Palace. For the House of Commons he made an elbow chair frame 'with very large elbows', for the Speaker's seat, costing £5 8s, and a mahogany high chair frame 'for the principal clerk at the table', £1 17s. On 5 July 1827 he was paid £4 2s for a strong deal linen chest for the *Royal Sovereign* yacht. [Royal Household accounts, PRO, LC11/53–74] Presumably H. Samuel Evans.

Evans, Samuel Diamond, London, cm and u (1835–39). Trading at Black Horse Yd, High Holborn in 1835, and 2 Wardour St, Soho, in 1839. [D]

Evans, Tempest, 36 Broadwall, Blackfriars, London, chair-maker (1808). [D]

Evans, Thomas, Park St, London, carver (1749). [Poll bk]

Evans, Thomas, London, upholder (1753–69). Son of John Evans, cook of London, and brother of John Evans, upholder. App. to John Evans on 18 December 1753, and admitted freeman of the Upholders' Co. on 3 May 1769. [GL, Upholders' Co. records]

Evans, Thomas, 25 Cullum St, London, cm (1796–1800). [D]

Evans, Thomas, Camberwell Rd, London, cm and u (1809–11). [D]

Evans, Thomas, 3 Redcross St, Southwark, London, cm and broker (1820). [D]

Evans, Thomas, 8 Little Ryder St, London, cm and u (1823–28). [D]

Evans, Thomas, Wotton-under-Edge, Glos., cm (1827). [PR(bapt.)]

Evans, W. H., The Gardens, Charles St, Wolverhampton, Staffs., carpenter, cm and coffin maker (1833). [D] Possibly William Evans of Wolverhampton.

Evans, William, London, upholder and carpet warehouseman (1769–86). Recorded at Talbot Ct, Gracechurch St, 1769–82; no. 3, 1770–82; and Edmonton in 1786. Admitted freeman of the Upholders' Co. by redemption on 5 July 1769. In 1775 he employed a non-freeman for five months. In 1780 insured a house at 31 Queen's Row, Walworth, for £200. Named in contemporary newspapers, 1772–79. [D; GL, Upholders' Co. records; GL, City Licence bks, vol. 9; GL, Sun MS vol. 283, p. 110; Heal]

Evans, William, Bristol, cm (1774). [Poll bk]

Evans, William, London, upholder (1794–1806). Trading at 1 Budge Row, 1801–06. App. to Gawn Shotter on 1 January 1794, and admitted freeman of the Upholders' Co. by servitude on 7 January 1801. Named in Sheraton's list of master cabinet makers, 1803. [D; GL, Upholders' Co. records] See James Duthoit at the same address.

Evans, William, Richmond, Surrey, u (1798). [D]

Evans, William, 18 Silver St, Golden Sq., London, carver and gilder (1801–39). Recorded in partnership with John Nathaniel Jordan (or Jordaine), 1805–25. Took out Sun Insurance policies, alone on 21 August 1801 for £300 of which £100 accounted for utensils and stock; and in partnership with Jordan on 28 January 1805 for £500, utensils, stock and goods in trust in workshop and shop accounting for £200. [D; GL, Sun MS vol. 419, ref. 712742; vol. 431, ref. 772317]

Evans, William, Bowling Green Lane, Clerkenwell, London, chair and cm (1808–11). Recorded at no. 26 in 1808 and no. 32, 1809–11. [D]

Evans, William, Little Underbank, Stockport, Cheshire, cm and u (1816–25). [D] See Ann and Edwards Evans.

Evans, William, Bristol, cm and furniture broker (1816–27). Trading in Temple St, 1816–17, and 43 Merchant St, 1823–27. [D]

Evans, William, High St, Uttoxeter, Staffs., clockcase maker and cm (1818–35). [D]

Evans, William, Wolverhampton, Staffs., builder and cm (1827–38). Trading at Stafford St, 1833–34. [D] See W. H. Evans.

Evans, William, 24 Ann St, Birmingham, carver and gilder (1828–30). [D]

Evans, William, Underhill, Ross-on-Wye, Herefs., cm (1830). [D]

Evans, William jnr, 21 Blenheim St, Liverpool, cm (1839). [D]

Evans & Movette, 4 Sussex St, Manchester, carvers in wood and marble (1794). [D]

Evatt, Francis, Compton St, London, upholder (1776). Declared bankrupt, *Williamson's Liverpool Advertiser*, 27 December 1776.

Evatt, James, Westgate St, Bath, Som., upholder, auctioneer and undertaker (1784). [D]

Evatt, John, Bristol, u and cm (1810–18). Trading at St Vincent's Pl. in 1810, and Waterloo Pl., Clifton, 1818(?). [D]

Evatt, Richard, address unrecorded, upholder (1720–42). Son of Anthony Evatt, yeoman of Gazeley, Suffolk; app. to Francis Thorpe on 6 July 1720, and admitted freeman of the Upholders' Co. by servitude on 4 March 1729/30. Took app. named Matthew Jones, 1735–42. [GL, Upholders' Co. records]

Evatt, Richard, St Paul's, Covent Gdn, London, upholder and broker (1740). Took out a Sun Insurance policy on 29 March 1740 for £40. [GL, Sun MS vol. 54, p. 417]

Evatt, Richard, at 'The Turk's Head', Bedford St, Covent Gdn, London, u (1744–56). Named in newspapers, 1744–56. Polled at Westminster in 1749. [Heal]

Evatt, Richard, Westgate St, Bath, Som., cm and auctioneer (1761). Advertised in the *Bath Chronicle*, July 1761 that he had quitted business in London and was setting up in Westgate St, with an upholstery and carpet warehouse.

Eve, Thomas, 36 Tottenham Ct Rd, London, turner (1835). [D]

Everard, Richard, address unrecorded, chairmaker (1702–25). In 1702 he provided walnut chairs and a nursing chair for Wriothesley, 2nd Duke of Bedford, at a cost of £3 6s; and in 1709 twenty walnut chairs for £8. [Bedford Office, London] Submitted bills to Lady Mary Saunderson for items supplied between 7 June 1715 and 1 June 1725, costing a total of £46 3s. Furniture bought included, on 7 June 1715, '12 Fine Matted Chairs', costing £12 12s; on 2 January '2 Settees the Best Sort', £4 10s; two X-framed stools with 'French Feet'; and various chair frames. [Lincoln RO, Monson, 10 1/A/16] The account bk of the Earl of Rockingham records payments to Everard, chairmaker, of £4 2s for chairs, in April 1716; £2 8s for a settee frame on 28 May 1718; and £3 for two chairs on 20 October 1718. [Lincoln RO, Monson, 10 A/1]

Everidge, John, Gravel Lane, Southwark, London, looking and coach glass manufacturer (1775–88). [D; Wills, *Looking-Glasses*]

Everingham, John, Westgate, Wakefield, Yorks., cm (1814–20). [D]

Everingham, Richard & John, Wakefield, Yorks., joiner and cm (1798). [D]

Everingham, W., 76 Oxford St, London, cm and u (1796–99). [D]

Everingham, William, 24 Savile Row, Hull, Yorks., u (1821–23). [D]

Everitt (or Everett), Abraham, London, chairmaker (1806–31). [Colchester poll bks]

Everitt, Allen, Union St, Birmingham, picture framer and Artist's General Repository (b. 1759–d. 1851). Bapt. on 14 December 1759, one of a family of artists. He established an Artist's Repository in Union St, and was a drawing master as well as a framer of pictures, to the backs of which he added his trade card. Among pictures in the Birmingham Art Gallery framed by him are some by David Cox. [Birmingham Art Gall., trade card coll., ref. F105770, p. 66]

Everitt, John, High St, Doncaster, Yorks., carver and gilder (1830). [D]

Everitt, John, Bridlesmithgate, Nottingham, carver and gilder (1832). [D]

Everitt, Thomas, Aldborough, Suffolk, chairmaker (1776). Will proved at Norwich in 1776. [Norfolk Record Soc., index of wills]

Everitt, William, Keelby, Lincs., joiner and cm (1821). App. to

Joseph Scholey of Gt Grimsby, Lincs., in May 1821. [Hull app. reg.]

Evers, Benjamin, York, carver and gilder (1828–38). Trading at 9 St Helen's Sq., 1828–30, and 43 Stonegate, 1838. [D]

Evers, Charles, address unrecorded, upholder (1711–18). Son of Thomas Evers, Gent. of Westminster, London; app. to Remey George on 10 April 1711, and admitted freeman of the Upholders' Co. by servitude on 19 June 1718. [GL, Upholders' Co. records]

Eversedge, Thomas, Liverpool, cm (1816–18). Trading at 1 Birkett St, Soho in 1816, and 1 Prince's Pl., Clayton St, 1818. [D]

Eversley, W., 2 French Alley, Goswell St, London, cm (c. 1780). Trade card embellished with Classical figures and an urn states that he 'Makes and repairs all sorts of Household Furniture'. [Banks Coll., BM]

Every, Edward, 23 Cavendish St, Liverpool, chairmaker (1839). [D]

Every, Henry, 3 Virgil St, Liverpool, cm (1839). [D]

Every, James, 45 Marlborough St, Devonport, Devon, chairmaker (1838). [D]

Evill, Mark, Bath, Som., turner (1800). Advertised for journeymen, especially spinning wheel makers, in *Leicester Journal*, 17 January 1800.

Evill, William, Milsom St, Bath, Som., upholder (1805). [D]

Evins, James, St Aldgate's, Oxford, cm (1802). [Poll bk]

Evon, John, address unrecorded, cm (1803). Subscribed to Sheraton's *Cabinet Dictionary*, 1803.

Ewbank, James, King St, Barnard Castle, Co. Durham, joiner, cm and u (1827–29). [D]

Ewbank, John, Plough St, Whitechapel, London, chairmaker and carver (1778). Took out a Sun Insurance policy in 1778 for £200 of which utensils, stock and goods accounted for £100. [GL, Sun MS vol. 265, p. 235]

Ewbank, John, 47 Pennington St, London, cm and carver (1782). Took out a Sun Insurance policy in 1782 for £200 of which £40 accounted for utensils and stock. [GL, Sun MS vol. 301, p. 67]

Ewbank, John W., Yarm, Yorks., joiner and cm (1827). [D]

Ewbank, Thomas, York, u (1721). See Thomas Ubank.

Ewbank, Thomas Steel(e), Hull, Yorks., carver and gilder (1831–40). Trading at 49 English St in 1831 and 11 North Church Side (or St), 1838–40. [D]

Ewbank, William, Nether End, Penrith, Cumb., joiner and/or cm (1829). [D]

Ewell, Richard, London, cm (1831). [Sandwich poll bk]

Ewing, David, 34 Gt Charlotte St, Blackfriars Rd, London, looking-glass manufacturer (1835–39). [D]

Ewins, Daniel, 45 Hedge Rd, Islington, London, u (1839). [D]

Exley, William, Stockport, Cheshire, cm (1834–41). Trading at 97 Chestergate in 1834 and Queen St West in 1841. [D]

Exton, —, Newport, engraver, carver and gilder, looking-glass and picture frame maker. 19th-century trade card reads: 'Elegant Chimney Glasses &c. of the Newest London Patterns. ... Agent to the East of England Fire & Life Insurance Company, Exeter, Instituted 1807. Capital £600,000 Sterl. Property Insured of any amount of 2 pr. Cent Premium.' [Landauer Coll., MMA, NY] Probably:

Exton, Barnabas, South St, Newport, Isle of Wight, Hants., carver and gilder (1830). [D]

Exton, John, Medbourne, Leics., chairmaker (1840). [*Leicester Mercury*]

Eycott, William Powlett, Cirencester, Glos., cm (1796). Declared bankrupt, *Billinge's Liverpool Advertiser*, 1 February 1796.

Eyes, John, Liverpool, cm (1727). Took app. named Charles in 1727. [S of G, app. index]

Eykin (or Eykyn), James, Wolverhampton, Staffs., u (1770–78). Trading in High Green, 1770. Insured houses for £600 in 1778 with the Sun Co. [D; GL, Sun MS vol. 263, p. 605]

Eyles, Charles, 7 High St, Shadwell, London, bed manufacturer (1835). [D]

Eyles, James, 122 Wardour St, Soho, London, cm and fancy chairmaker (1805–23). Trading as J. & W. Eyles, 1815–16; and as Eyles & Yate, 1820–23. Took out a Sun Insurance policy on 1 November 1805 for £750, of which utensils, stock and workshop accounted for £600. [D; GL, Sun MS vol. 434, ref. 781704]

Eyles, Joseph, Christchurch, Pirewich, Hants., cm (1840). [GL, Sun MS vol. 267, ref. 1327576]

Eyles, T. G., Bath, Som., chairmaker. Supplied seating furniture for Bath Assembly Rooms, c. 1771. [V & A archives]

Eyles, Thomas, 36 St James St, Cheltenham, Glos., cm and u (1830). [D]

Eyles, William, Swindon, Wilts., u (1784). [D]

Eyles, William, Castle St, Cirencester, Glos., cm (1813–35). Children bapt. in 1813, 1831 and 1835. [D; PR(bapt.)]

Eyles, William, 42 Poland St, Oxford St, London, cm (1820). [D]

Eyles, William, London, cm, u, chair and sofa manufacturer (1823–39). Addresses given at 203 High Holborn, 1823–27, and 11 Brownlow St, Holborn, 1835–39. Took out Sun Insurance policies on 25 August 1823 for £1,050; and on 11 December 1823 also for £1,050 on his new house and adjoining workshop. [D; GL, Sun MS vol. 498, ref. 1006771; vol. 499, ref. 1010797]

Eyles, William, Rugby, Warks., cm (1835). [D]

Eyles, William Henry, 409 High St, Cheltenham, Glos., cm, u, chair and sofa manufacturer (1839). [D]

Eyos, John, Liverpool, cm (1727–d. by 1780). Admitted freeman on 16 October 1727. [Liverpool freeman reg.]

Eyos, James, Liverpool, cm (1750). Admitted freeman on 9 October 1750. [Liverpool freemen reg.]

Eyre, Charles, London(?). Recorded in 1715 as having supplied '12 armed chairs & 12 without, all blew japanned & gilt' for £65 to John Richards, a merchant in London. [*Proceedings of the Dorset Natural History & Antiquarian Field Club*, 1918, p. 28]

Eyre, Isaac & Thomas, 356 Oxford St, London, u (1784). [D]

Eyre(s), James & Thomas, 356 Oxford St, near the Pantheon, London, u and carpet manufacturers (1773–1815). Recorded at 358 Oxford St in 1773; as Thomas & Son, 1809–12; and as J. Eyre (perhaps the son of Thomas) in 1814–15. James alone took out a Sun Insurance policy on 3 January 1775 for £400 on the contents of a house in Jermyn St in tenure. Took out insurance policies with Thomas in 1776 and 1779, both for £2,600, £2,200 on utensils, stock and goods; and in 1777 for £800 on a house. The firm is named in Sheraton's list of master cabinet makers, 1803. Trade card or bill head recorded. [D; GL, Sun MS vol. 236, ref. 348640; vol. 248, p. 584; vol. 255, p. 392; vol. 271, p. 343; Heal] Possibly:

Eyre(s), James & Large, James, 226 Piccadilly, opposite 'The Black Bear Inn', London, carpet, bedding, cabinet warehouse and manufactory, undertakers (1777–99). Eyre is recorded alone at this address in 1799, and James Eyre (or Ayre) alone took out Sun Insurance policies in 1783 and 1784 for £1,500 and £2,100, utensils and stock accounting for £1,200 and £1,800 respectively. Eyres and Large took out insurance policies on 15 September and 31 December 1785, both for £2,450 on utensils and stock, and £160 and £340 respectively on those in a warehouse in Crown St, Soho. On 4 January 1787 Eyre and Aron Large, upholder, together insured a house in New Spring Gdns for £400; and insured goods and property for £3,900 with James Large on 9 June 1787. On 20 January 1761 Eyre and James Large insured household goods at 26 West Side, Golden Sq. for £400; and on 10 March a house and goods at 3 Barton St, Westminster, and house behind for £300. [D; GL, Sun MS vol. 313, p. 376; vol. 322, p. 307; vol. 331, p. 573; vol. 335, p. 128; vol. 342, ref. 526233; vol. 373, refs 579423 and 580648] Several bills and accounts survive for work done, including a payment to Eyre of Piccadilly of £16 6s 6d for work done between 1784–86; both patron and nature of the work are unrecorded. [Scottish RO, GD 157/815] Eyre & Large are mentioned in Lord Howard's accounts for items supplied to Audley End, Essex. Their bill of 1786 totalled £48 6s 3d and included '2 Large stained 4 post Bedsteads' costing £3 4s, 'A Square feet sweep Field Bedstead', £1 18s, and a large quantity of bedding and upholstery materials. In 1787 the firm provided 'A Field Bed with sacking, castors, brass caps & stripe furniture compleat', and bedding, totalling £10 12s 6d. [Essex RO, D/DBy/A44/10; A45/8] In 1788 Eyre & Large worked for the 5th Duke of Bedford at Bedford House, London, providing four four-post beech bedsteads with morine furniture, mattresses and blankets. [Bedford Office, London] A bill, dated 29 August 1793 and receipted 23 October by R. Styning(?), is in the Sawston Hall archives, and records payment of £1 7s 4d for a blanket and canvas [Cambs. RO]

Eyre, Joseph, Packer's Row, Chesterfield, Derbs., cm and u (1833–35). [D]

Eyre, Richard, 32 Minster St, Reading, Berks., cm (1823–42). [D; poll bk]

Eyre, Thomas, address unrecorded, upholder (1716–23). Son of Thomas Eyre, clerk of Staines, Middlx; app. to William Scrimshire on 17 May 1716, and admitted freeman of the Upholders' Co. by servitude on 4 December 1723. [GL, Upholders' Co. records]

Eyre, Thomas, address unrecorded, upholder (1731–38). Son of Thomas Eyre, victualler of London; app. to John Brumwell on 5 May 1731, and admitted freeman of the Upholders' Co. by servitude on 2 August 1738. [GL, Upholders' Co. records]

Eyre(s), Thomas, 356 Oxford St, near the Pantheon, London, carpet, cabinet and upholstery warehouseman, undertaker (1773–1814). Recorded in partnership with James Eyre, 1773–12, and as Thomas & Son, 1809–12; J. Eyre, perhaps his son, was trading in 1814–15. Took out Sun Insurance policies alone in 1780 for £2,600, £2,200 accounting for utensils, stock and goods; and on 11 January 1792 for £4,000, of which £3,630 accounted for utensils, stock and goods in trust or on commission in his house and warehouse. [GL, Sun MS vol. 280, p. 195; vol. 382, ref. 595345] Submitted a bill to Lady Anne Conolly on 2 February 1790 for a carpet, costing £3 16s 6d provided for Stretton Hall, Staffs. [V & A archives] See Isaac & Thomas and James & Thomas Eyre.

Eyre, William, 19 Cockspur St, Haymarket, London, portable desk manufacturer and trunk maker 'to their Royal Highnesses the Prince Regent and Prince Saxe Coburg' (1820). [D]

Eyres, John, North St, Exeter, Devon, chairmaker (1791). [D]

F

Fabb, Charles, Norwich, cm (1817). App. to Samuel Martin and admitted freeman on 24 February 1817. [Norwich freemen reg.]

Fabry, John George, Duke St, Bloomsbury, London, carver (d. 1794). At his death in 1794 he possessed several leasehold houses. A court case was held in 1801 concerning his estate. [PRO, C13 3/22]

Facey, —, London, u (1793). Subscribed to Sheraton's *Drawing Book*, 1793.

Facey, Edward Cox, 9 Banner St, London, cm and u (1839). [D]

Facey, John, 15 Mount St, Berkeley Sq., London, u etc. (1794). [D]

Facon, William, late of St Giles-in-the-Fields, London, carver (1761). Discharge from Debtors' Prison announced in *London Gazette*, 20 September 1761.

Fagin, Robert, 25 Tooley St, Southwark, London, upholder (1776). Admitted freeman of the Upholders' Co. on 7 February 1776. [GL, Upholders' Co. records]

Faherty, John, Lichfield St, Birmingham, builder and cm (1815). [D]

Fahetty, John, Berkley St, Birmingham, cabinet case maker (1839). [D]

Faiers, John, 42 Broad St, Golden Sq., London, u and cm (1835–39). [D]

Fair, William, Berwick-upon-Tweed, Northumb., cm (1793–1834). Recorded at Hyde Hill, 1806–34, no. 17 in 1834. Subscribed to Sheraton's *Drawing Book*, 1793. [D]

Fairbairn, —, 104 Titchfield St, Oxford Mkt, London, joiner, cm and undertaker (1784–87). Address also given at the 'Three Tuns', Portman Mews, Portman St in 1785. Took out Sun Insurance policies in 1784 for £400, utensils and stock accounting for £100; and on 11 March 1785 for £200, of which his house and adjoining workshop behind 104 Titchfield St accounted for £100. Trade card of 1787 bears inscription within oval Neo-classical frame with scrolls and husk chains flanked by vases. [GL, Sun MS vol. 321, p. 548; 11 March 1785, ref. 501793; Banks Coll., BM] Possibly John Ferbaern.

Fairbank(s), John, Orange St, London, cm (1749). [Poll bk]

Fairbank, John, York, carver and gilder (1757). Son of Christopher Fairbank, carver and gilder; app. to his father on 10 February 1757. [York app. reg.]

Fairbridge, Anthony, 55 South Audley St, London, cm and u (1820–30). Declared bankrupt, *London Gazette*, 18 May 1830. [D]

Fairbrother, Charles, Thomas St, Upper Stamford St, London, picture and looking-glass frame maker (1826). [D]

Fairchild, Charles, Stamford, Lincs., cm (1809–32). [Poll bks]

Fairchild, James, Rochford, Essex, u (1798). [D]

Fairchild, John, Stamford, Lincs., joiner and cm (1748–80). Admitted freeman as a joiner in 1748. Took John Brumhead as app. for seven years on 10 October 1776 for £31 10s; a John Brumhead, watchmaker, was admitted freeman in 1795. Took Thomas Marshall as app. for seven years on 20 July 1780 for £21. [Stamford app. reg. and freemen rolls]

Fairchild, Rowland, London, cm (1793). Subscribed to Sheraton's *Drawing Book*, 1793.

Fairclough, Henry, Ranelegh St, Liverpool, cm (1767). [D]

Fairclough, Henry, Highfield St, Liverpool, u (1824–39). Recorded at no. 66 in 1824; 60 in 1827; 67 in 1829; 69 in 1834–35; 60 in 1837; and 54 in 1839. [D]

Fairclough, Robert, Liverpool, cm (1780). Petitioned freedom on servitude to Samuel Nevitt in 1780. [Liverpool freemen's committe bk]

Fairclough, William, Liverpool, cm (1765–74). Recorded at Cases St, 1769–74. Petitioned freedom on servitude to Richard Wilcock and his assign, Richard Hayhurst, in 1765. Admitted freeman on 27 November 1767. [D; Liverpool freemen reg. and committee bk]

Fairclough, William, Liverpool, u and cm (1819–39). Trading at 16 Roscoe Lane, 1821–24; 25 Renshaw St, 1827–29; 120 Mt Pleasant, 1834; 20 Brownlow Hill, 1835; 13 Newington St,

1837; and no. 23 in 1839. Marriage on 13 June 1819 to Elizabeth Price, dressmaker, announced in *Liverpool Mercury*, 25 June. Declared bankrupt, same paper, 28 February 1834. [D]

Fairest, Jeremiah, 6 Workhouse Croft, Sheffield, Yorks., cm (1817–28). Recorded at no. 8 in 1825. [D] See Mary Fairest.

Fairest, Joseph, Wadsley, Sheffield, Yorks., cm (1834). [D]

Fairest, Joseph, Worral, Stannington, Yorks., picker and cm (1837). [D]

Fairest, Mary, Workhouse Croft, Sheffield, Yorks., cm and u (1828–29). [D] See Jeremiah Fairest.

Fairfax, Benjamin, Gt Hermitage St, Wapping, London, cm, u and undertaker (1825–28). [D]

Fairfax, William, Smith St, Warwick, cm and u (1835). [D]

Fairfoot, William, 46 Walmgate, York, joiner and cm (1830). [D]

Fairful, Thomas, 56 Gt Chart St, Hoxton, London, cm and u (1835–39). [D]

Fairhurst, Elizabeth, Winwick St, Warrington, Lancs., cm and u (1834). [D]

Fairhurst, John, Winwick St, Warrington, Lancs., cm and u (1822–28). [D]

Fairhurst, Robert, Liverpool, cm, appraiser and auctioneer (1761–d. by 1817). Addresses given in partnership with Luke Swain at 21 Union St, 1767–73; alone at this address, 1774–77; cabinet warehouse at 16 Union St in 1777; 10 Queen St, with cabinet warehouse at John St in 1781; Hackins Hey in 1787; 32 Chapel St with auction room at 15 Tempest Hey in 1790; 35 Chapel St in 1794; and 5 Cumberland St in 1796. Petitioned freedom on servitude to Thomas Bailey in 1761, paying 6s 8d. Dates of admission as freeman are recorded as 2 April 1761 and 2 April 1765, possibly implying two different craftsmen of the same name. Former apps, James Foster and James Bradshaw petitioned freedom in 1790. [D; Liverpool freemen's committee bk and reg.]

Fairlamb, Michael, Allendale, Northumb., joiner and cm (1834). [D]

Fairlamb, Nicholas, Allendale, Northumb., joiner and cm (1827–29). [D]

Fairman, Francis, Portsmouth, Hants., u (1796). [Canterbury poll bk]

Fairn, Robert, 3 Little Marybow St, Marybow, London, cm (1780). Insured his house for £200 in 1780. [GL, Sun MS vol. 281, p. 524]

Fairway, Charles, Sawbridgeworth, Herts., cm and auctioneer (1779–82). Took out Sun Insurance policies in 1779 for £100 on a house; and in 1782 for £400, of which £100 accounted for utensils and stock. [GL, Sun MS vol. 279, p. 412; vol. 302, p. 460]

Fairweather, George, address unrecorded, cm (1754). Subscribed to Chippendale's *Director*, 1754.

Fairweather, George, Stephenson St, North Shields, Northumb., cm and joiner (1827–29). [D]

Falciola, Barnard, 51 Edgbaston St, Birmingham, carver and gilder (1835). [D]

Falciola & Co., Benjamin, 3 Brunswick St, Liverpool, carvers, gilders, looking-glass and picture frame manufacturers (1799). Advertised in *Billinge's Liverpool Advertiser*, 30 September 1799 that they had 'just received from London an extensive assortment of elegant PRINTS, DRAWING BOOKS, CARICATURES etc: by the most eminent masters. Also a great variety of PICTURES for the American & African trade, & every other article in the above line . . .'.

Falciola, Benjamin, Hill St, Birmingham, carver and gilder (1830). [D]

Falck, Joakim (or Joachim), at 'The Four Coffins', St Saviour's Dock Head, Southwark, London, joiner (1727). Took out a Sun Insurance policy on 8 January 1727 for £500 on household goods, stock in trade, workhouse and wareroom. Walnut chest-on-chest recorded bearing label. [GL, Sun MS vol. 25, p. 493; Christie's NY, 28 March 1981, lot 159, illus.]

Falconer, Alexander, London, cm and upholder (1779–87). Recorded at Whitcomb St in 1779, and 13 Market St, St James's Mkt, 1787. Took out Sun Insurance policies in 1779 for £200 on his house; and in 1787 for £200, £120 accounting for utensils and stock. [GL, Sun MS vol. 276, p. 432; vol. 322, p. 291]

Faldo, George jnr, 177 Rotherhithe St, London, wood carver and cm (1832–35). [D]

Falkes, Thomas, 45 Adams St West, Upper Seymour St, London, upholder and cm (1817). [D]

Falkner, William, Nottingham, joiner and cm (1736–80). Recorded at Angel Row in 1774, and Chapel Bar in 1780. Son of John Falkner, husbandman of Sandiacre; app. in 1736 as a joiner. [Nottingham app. list and poll bks]

Fall, Jonathan, London, u (1753–92). Trading at Trump St, Cheapside, 1763; and as successor to J. Iliffe at 'The Blue Curtain', 5 St Paul's Churchyard, 1765–73. Trade Card states that he 'Makes and Sells all sorts of Beds and Bedding, Mohair, Silk, worsted and mix'd Damasks, And all Kinds of Upholder's Goods. Great Choice of English, French & Turkey Carpets; Screens of every kind. Rich Carved Sconces, Tables & Picture Frames, Brass Lanthorns and Arms, with All manner of Glass, Cabinet & Chair Work at Reasonable Rates. NB. Goods Appraised and Funerals Performed. Estates &c. BOUGHT & SOLD by Commission.' Recorded as a member of Upholders' Co. in Mile End Green, 1770–92. [D; Heal]

Fall, Jonathan, London, upholder (1770–94). Recorded in Islington, 1778–81; Bermondsey Spa in 1786; and Bencrafts' Alms Houses in 1794. Son of James Fall of Watford, Herts.; admitted freeman of the Upholders' Co. on 5 December 1770. [GL, Upholders' Co. records]

Fallet(t), Nicholas, near Red Lion Ct, Long Acre, St Martin-in-the-Fields, London, cm (1717–27). Took out Sun Insurance policies on 30 July 1717 on goods and merchandise in his house; and on 13 November 1727 for £500 on household goods, glass and stock in trade. [GL, Sun MS vol. 6, p. 336; vol. 25, ref. 43045]

Fallows, James, 14 Mangle St, Piccadilly, Manchester, cm (1794). [D]

Fallows, John, Liverpool, cm (1794–1823). Addresses given at Oldham St, 1794–96; 6 Lower Newington in 1800; no. 9 in 1803; 3 Oldham St, 1804–14; and 6 Head St in 1823. [D]

Fallows, John, Manchester, chairmaker (1808–38). Trading at 11 Cable St, 1808; near 'The Black Horse', Miles Platting in 1813; 161 Oldham Rd in 1817; 17 Thomas St in 1825; 35 Cable St in 1829; and no. 2, 1836–38. [D]

Fallows, Joseph, Liverpool, chairmaker (1835–39). Addresses given at 44 Cheapside in 1835; 41 Shaw's Brow, also a Temperance House, in 1837; and 83 Shaw's Brow in 1839. [D]

Fallows, Thomas, Well Lane, Birmingham, picture frame maker (1839). [D]

Fallshaw, John F., 2 St John's Ct, Snowhill, London, portable desk, dressing case, work box and cabinet case maker (1839). [D]

Famariss, Frederick, King St, Sandwich, Kent, cm and u (1838–39). [D]

Famariss, Robert, King St, Sandwich, Kent, cm and u (1823–34). [D]

Fancote, James, Nottingham, u (1830). [Nottingham burgess index]

Fancourt & Pratt, Clumber St, Nottingham, u (1840). [D]

Fane, William & Thomas, High St, Whitechapel, London, u (1796). Declared bankrupt, *Billinge's Liverpool Advertiser*, 26 December 1796.

Faner, Robert, York, u (1756). Took app. named Brown in 1756. [S of G, app. index]

Fanshaw, Edward, Bread St, London, upholder (1705–13). Named as a policy holder of the Society for Assurance of Widows and Orphans, 1705–07. Took app. on 22 April 1712/13. Carried out work for St Paul's, in 1708 supplying two chairs for the Dean and Residentiary's Lady's Seat costing £20; and in 1710, velvet curtains etc. for the Lord Mayor's and Bishop's seats, and nine leather chairs for the office. Possibly the tradesman reported in newspapers in 1717 as 'Mr. Fenshaw [sic] a relation of the Lord of that name [Featherstonehaugh?] an upholsterer in Bread St., taking a walk about Islington . . . died very suddenly.' [PRO, app. reg.; *Wren Soc.*, vol. xv, pp. 161 and 192; Heal] See Fenshaw, —.

Fantham (or Fanthom), James, Digbeth, Birmingham, cm (1816–18). Recorded at no. 50 in 1816. [D]

Faraday, Robert, address unrecorded, brass and lamp manufacturer (1838–40). Worked at Buckingham Palace, 1838–40, repairing music tables, desks, candelabra etc. [PRO, LC11/101 and 110]

Faradin, Abraham, address unrecorded, cm (1735). Supplied furniture to the Mohun family of Boconnoc, Lostwithiel, Cornwall, for which he was paid £12 2s on 14 April 1735. His bill lists a dressing table, carpet, card and writing tables, smoking chairs and a mahogany tea boat. [Cornwall RO, DD CF 3296/26]

Faris, Joseph, Tickhill, Yorks., joiner and cm (1822). [D]

Farlam, Isaac, Town End, Workington, Cumb., joiner and/or cm (1811). [D]

Farlam, Jonathan, Old Round Ct, Chandos St, Strand, London, cm and u (1774–75). His house, in tenure, was insured by John Dawes of Canonbury House, Islington, for £125 on 9 January 1775. [Poll bk; GL, Sun MS vol. 236, ref. 348496] See Francis Richardson and James Butler.

Farlam, Joseph, Brow Top, Workington, Cumb., joiner and/or cm (1828–29). [D]

Farley, G., 26 Clarges St, London, cm and u (1828–35). Submitted a bill to Sir John Geers Cotterell, Bart. of Hertford St, London and Garnons, near Hereford, for a total of £3 17s 2d, paid in 1835. The bill is for work done between 1828–30, and includes joinery, putting up curtains and drapery, and repairing furniture such as a bedstead for 12s 6d, a chair for 14s 6d, and a table for 9d. [Herefs. RO, Garnons MS W69/3/460]

Farley, James, Tilehurst, Berks., cm (1830). [D]

Farley, John, 45 Little Britain, London, picture frame maker and gilder (1784–85). Neo-classical trade card of 1785 shows frames containing pictures, and states that he 'Supplies country cabinet makers etc. with mouldings of any length or pattern . . .'. [D; Banks Coll., BM]

Farley, Moses, address unrecorded, upholder (1700). Admitted freeman of the Upholders' Co. on 23 April 1700. [GL, Upholders' Co. records]

Farley, Richard, Newent, Glos., cm (1798). [D]

Farley, Samuel, 35 New Bond St, London, carver and gilder (1793). [D]

Farlow, Richard, London, cm (1793). Subscribed to Sheraton's *Drawing Book*, 1793.

Farmborough (or Farnbrough), Hannah, London, u (1773–75). Widow of William Farmbrough, probably the cm of North Audley St, London, she continued to work for the Royal Household after her husband's death. Between 1773–75 she provided bases for a sofa, stuffed the seats of ten mahogany 'Gothic back' chairs, twelve 'banister back' chairs, and supplied carpeting and bedding for the palaces at St James's and Kew, and the Houses of Parliament. [PRO, LC9/320–23] See John Gilroy.

Farmborough, Thomas, London, cane chairmaker (1699). A collection of letters, dating from 1768–92 concerns land bought by Farmborough in Pennsylvania in 1699, and claimed by his descendants. Baptismal and Wedding certificates survive. [Beds. RO, How White Coll., 90]

Farmborough (Farnborough or Farnbrough), William, at 'Ye Looking Glass' on Cornhill, London, cm, glassman and inlayer (1672–1700). One of the foremost Royal tradesmen in the late 17th century, he is named in the Royal Household accounts betwen 1672–1700. He worked with John Burrough(s) in 1677, providing two large looking-glasses, tables and stands 'flowered carved & gilded', to Windsor Castle; and a looking-glass for the lodge at Richmond. For Charles II's new lodgings at Whitehall, late in the King's reign, Farnborough provided a looking-glass, dressing table and candle stands of prince's wood, costing a total of £22. On 2 October 1689 he supplied for Kensington Palace 'a large looking glasse, table & stands fine inlaid', costing £19. He continued to receive Royal patronage on the accession of William and Mary, in 1692 supplying the Queen with 'two corner cabonetts of Japan and carved frames.' Farnborough also supplied looking-glasses, tables and stands for the Houses of Parliament and the Royal Hospital, Chelsea, those for the latter costing £39 10s. He also worked for William, 5th Earl of Bedford, receiving £11 5s in March 1682 for two looking-glasses, tables and stands; and in December he provided 'a large looking-glass, table and stands walnut tree . . . for my lady', £7 5s, presumably Anne, Countess of Bedford. [PRO, LC9/273, 275–77, 279–80; LC11/5; Lord Chamberlain's Office, 5/41; *DEF*; Heal; Wills, *Looking-Glasses*, p. 151; Fastnedge, *English Furniture Styles*, p. 298; Harris & Sons, *Old English Furniture*, p. 12; V & A archives; *C. Life*, 13 March 1926; *Wren Soc.*, vol. xix, p. 85; Bedford Office, London]

Farmb(o)rough (Farnborough or Farnbrough), William, London, cm (1749–73). Recorded in North Audley St, 1749–55; and St George, Hanover Sq., 1754–61. Polled at Westminster in 1749. Subscribed to Chippendale's *Director*, 1754. Took apps named Lewis in 1752; Owen Farnham, Fearnan or Featham in 1754 for £10 10s; Garbutt in 1758; and an unnamed app. in 1761. Supplied furniture to Lord Irwin for Temple Newsam House, Leeds, in 1773, including a mahogany bedstead and trays of various types. His bill totalled £72 15s. Provided Sir John Griffin Griffin at Audley End, Essex, with two mahogany dumbwaiters costing £3. [S of G, app. index; *Furn. Hist.*, 1967; Essex RO, D/DBy/A28/3; Heal] Possibly the husband of Hannah Farmbrough.

Farmer, —, address unrecorded, cm (1813). On 9 June 1813 he was paid £1 6s for a writing desk sold to Sir John Geers Cotterell, Bart. of Garnons, near Hereford, and Hertford St, London. [Herefs. RO, Garnons MS W69/3/183]

Farmer, —, Lancaster, carver (1828–40). [Westminster Ref. Lib., Gillow records]

Farmer, Anthony, address unrecorded, cm (1803). Subscribed to Sheraton's *Cabinet Dictionary*, 1803.

Farmer, Benjamin, Eden Pl., Hoxton, London, cm and u (1839). [D]

Farmer, Edward, Bath St, Ashby-de-la-Zouch, Leics., turner and chairmaker (1822–40). [D]

Farmer, Henry, 2 Cannon St Rd, St George's East, London, carver and gilder (1826–29). [D]

Farmer, John, Willow St, Oswestry, Salop, cm (1835–36). [D]

Farmer, Richard, address unrecorded, upholder (1708–54). Son of Richard Farmer, clothworker of London; app. to Matthew Scrimshire on 6 October 1708, and admitted freeman of the Upholders' Co. by servitude on 2 May 1716. Recorded as Beadle of the Co. from 1744. Took apps named William Brushfield, 1720–29; John Shepherd, 1722–24; William Russell in 1751; George Thorne in 1753; and William Rhodes in 1754. [GL, Upholders' Co. records]

Farmer, Richard, London, upholder (1723–d. 1747). Poll bks record him at Holborn Hill, 1724–34, with country house at Pynest Green, Waltham, Essex. Contemporary newspapers and trade cards show him in partnership with Henry Buck as chairmakers at Holborn Hill, 1723–c. 1740; and also at 'The Hand & Crown', St Paul's Churchyard in 1723. Farmer is recorded there alone from 1744 until his death in 1747. Farmer and Buck insured goods and merchandise at 'The Hand & Crown' for £500 on 13 July 1723 with the Sun Co. Henry Buck left the partnership c. 1740 and set up at 'The Hand, Crown & Star', on the south side of St Paul's Churchyard, Farmer remaining at Holborn Hill; but the latter is recorded at 'The Hand & Crown', 1744–47. [Heal; Essex RO, freeholders' bk, Q/RJ 1/1; GL, Sun MS vol. 15, ref. 29205] See Buck & Farmer; Henry and Ann Buck.

Farmer, Richard, 20 Cow Cross, London, cm (1779). Insured his house for £100 in 1779 with the Sun Co. [GL, Sun MS vol. 276, p. 370]

Farmer, Richard, Newbury, Berks., cm (1790). Declared bankrupt, *Williamson's Liverpool Advertiser*, 6 September 1790.

Farmer, Richard, Loughborough, Leics., turner and chairmaker (1795). [D]

Farmer, Richard, Birmingham, cm and u (1803–35). Recorded at Hagley Row in 1803, Russell Row, Five-ways, 1816–18, and 11 New St in 1835. [D]

Farmer, Richard, Birmingham, u and cm (1818–30). Trading at Ladywood Lane, in 1818 and 2 Edgbaston St, 1830. [D]

Farmer, Thomas, 4 Bridgewater Gdns, Barbican, London, cm, chairmaker and undertaker (1808). [D]

Farmer, Thomas, Cumberland St, Liverpool, cm (1824–29). Trading at no. 5 in 1824 and 1829; and no. 3 in 1827. [D]

Farmer, W., 31 Belvedere, Bath, Som., cm (1833). [D]

Farmer, William, High St, Upton-on-Severn, Worcs., chairmaker (1798–1820). [D]

Farmery, —, address unrecorded. On 2 September 1724 he was paid £6 13s 6d for 'Chair & Japan' provided for Lady Mary Saunderson. [Lincoln RO, Monson 10/1/A/16]

Farnes, Martin, London, cm (1793). Subscribed to Sheraton's *Drawing Book*, 1793.

Farnes, Nicholas, Friars Walk, Lewes, Sussex, u (1790–96). [Poll bks; T. Woollgar, *Spicilegia Sive Collectanea ad Historiam et Antiquitates Lewensis*]

Farnham, Owen, address unrecorded. App. to William Farnbrough of St George, Hanover Sq., cm, for £10 10s in 1754. Also recorded as Fearnan and Featham. [V & A archives]

Farnham, William Earl, Surrey, joiner and cm (1782). Insured his utensils and stock for £300 in 1782. [GL, Sun MS vol. 301, p. 541] Probably William Earl of Farnham.

Farnsworth, Maurice, York, u (1717). Of Aldbrough, app. to Barnaby Bawtry, u, on 8 October 1717. [York app. reg.]

Farnworth, Samuel, Pavement, near Finsbury Sq., London, carver, gilder and picture frame maker (c. 1790). Bill head shows Neo-classical girandole with clock and mirror embellished by sphinxes and masonic signs. [Heal Coll., BM]

Farnworth, Samuel, Chester, carver and gilder (1814–22). Trading at the Exchange in 1814; Eastgate St in 1816; and Eastgate Row in 1822. [D]

Farnworth, Samuell, Welsh Row, Nantwich, Cheshire, carver and gilder (1834). [D]

Farquhar, John, 48 Conduit St, Hanover Sq., London, u and cm (1797). [D]

Farquharson, James, Villiers St, Strand, London, cm (1784). [D]

Farquharson, William, Villiers St, 3 York Buildings, Strand, London, cm and u (1769–81). Took out Sun Insurance policy in 1777 for £500 of which utensils, stock and goods accounted for £330. Declared bankrupt, *Gents Mag.*, February 1781. [D; poll bk; GL, Sun MS vol. 257, p. 423]

Farrah, John, Beverley, Yorks., cm (1784). [Poll bk]

Farrah, Richard, Beverley, Yorks., cm (1784–1814). Trading at Kitchin Lane in 1791 and Kelgate in 1792. [D; poll bks]

Farrah, William, Beverley, Yorks., cm (1790). [Poll bk] The Farrah family were trading until the 1830s.

Farrance, Thomas, 14 Bland Terr., Gt Dover St, Southwark, London, upholder (1835). [D]

Farrand, Jacob, 1 Silver St, Wood St, London, u, cabinet and case maker (1808–39). Trading as S. & J. Farrand, 1808–09. [D]

Farrand, Matthew, 152 Bermondsey St, Southwark, London, cm, chair and blind maker (1820). [D]

Farrand, Matthew, 15 Star Corner, London, cm and chairmaker (1823–25). [D]

Farrand, Matthew, Middleward, Tottenham High Cross, London, cm and undertaker (1823–26). [D]

Farrand, Roger, 25 Queen St, Manchester, cabinet turner (1825). [D]

Farrands, John, Nottingham, joiner and cm (1804). Son of John Farrands, farmer of W. Bridgford; app. to Samuel Dodd in 1804. [Nottingham app. list]

Farrant, Richard, High St, Sidmouth, Devon, cm and u (b. 1788–d. 1835). Trade card reads: 'Farrant, Upholsterer, and Cabinet Maker, High Street, Sidmouth, London Paper, Hangings, Floor Cloths &c., Transparent Blinds, Sofas, Chair Beds &c. Funerals Completely Furnished.' [Leverhulme Coll., MMA, NY] Advertised as agent in sale of Violet Bank Cottage in *The Alfred*, 19 September 1826; and of a house, in *Exeter Flying Post*, 3 July 1828. Death, aged 47 on 21 July 1835, reported on 30 July; and his Executor placed a notice in the same paper on 14 April 1836. Directories list a tradesman of the same name in 1838. [D]

Farrant, Thomas, Egham, Surrey, u (1830). Declared bankrupt, *Chester Courant and Anglo-Welsh Gazette*, 12 January 1830.

Farrar, Abraham, 37 Garden St, Marsh Lane, Leeds, Yorks., cm (1826). [D]

Farrar, Christopher, 37 Garden St, Marsh Lane, Leeds, Yorks., cm (1830). [D]

Farrar, Francis, address unrecorded, cm (1803). Subscribed to Sheraton's *Cabinet Dictionary*, 1803.

Farrar, Richard, Green Lane, Hellard's Yd, Hull, Yorks., cm (1823). [D]

Farrar, Simeon, 28 Nelson St, Leeds, Yorks., cm (1834–40). [D]

Farrell, James, John St, Bath, Som., carver and gilder (1781). [D]

Farrell, Luke, 20 Charles St, Curtain Rd, London, chair and sofa maker (1827–28). [D]

Farrell, Thomas, 14 Paradise St, Liverpool, cm (1839). [D]

Farren, —, address unrecorded. Noted in Matthew Boulton's diary in 1768 as a 'Gilt Chair Maker'. [Birmingham Lib., archives dept, Boulton MS]

Farrer, David, Northgate, Bradford, Yorks., cm (1830). Also recorded as Graham & Farrer. [D]

Farrer, Edwin, 8 Eldon St, Finsbury, London, cm etc. (1835–37). [D]

Farrer, Horatio, 15 Holywell Row, London, cm (1829). [D]

Farr(i)er, John, Gerrard St, Soho, London, cm and upholder (1782–84). Recorded at no. 4 in 1784. Took out Sun Insurance policies in 1782 for £1,300 of which utensils, stock and goods accounted for £850; and in 1784 for £1,000, utensils and stock accounting for £440. [D; GL, Sun MS vol. 299, p. 415; vol. 324, p. 605]

Farr(i)er, John, Leicester St, Leicester Sq., London, upholder (1790–99). Trading at no. 11, 1790–93. [D]

Farrer, John, Princes St, Leicester Sq., Soho, London, u, cabinet and upholstery warehouseman (1802–08). Trading at no. 5 in 1808. Named in Sheraton's list of master cabinet makers, 1803. [D]

Farrer, John, Curtain Rd, Shoreditch, London, cm (1829–37). Trading at no. 86 in 1829 and no. 116, 1835–37. [D]

Farrer, Richard, York, u (1722–d. 1780). Recorded in Spurriergate, 1735–41; Spurriergate and/or Coney St, 1742; and Coney St in 1758. Owned property in Micklegate Bar Without in 1763; let his house in Stonegate in 1766; and retired to Manchester in 1770. Son of Richard Farrer; app. to George Reynoldson, u, on 7 November 1722 for seven years, and admitted freeman in 1730. In 1733 he married Margaret Napier who, with two infant children, was presented in 1735 as a papist in Spurriergate. She bore Farrer six sons, most of whom died young: Richard, buried on 7 March 1736; Edward, 1 August 1740; James, 27 March 1746; Richard, 26 March 1756; Luke, who died in 1784 [*York Courant*, 20 July 1784] and their eldest son, John, who died in 1756, and whose business, unspecified, was to be 'continued by his surviving partners Messrs. Tasker & Routh.' [*York Courant*, 21 September 1756] A prominent civic figure, Richard Farrer was Chamberlain, 1736–37; and appointed to the Committee of Leases and to audit the Mayor's accounts, 1741–47. He was elected Sheriff in 1751, trustee of Wilson's Charity in 1752, Alderman in 1754, 1758 and 1763; and Lord Mayor in 1756 and 1769. His wife died in 1764, and in 1766 he let his house in Stonegate, selling his stock of upholstery and furnishings. He was succeeded by two of his former employees, Jeremiah Smith and Matthew Browne, who opened a shop in High Ousegate. [*York Courant*, 4 and 25 November 1766] He retired to Manchester in 1770, marrying Mrs Gorton, a wealthy widow from that city, on 6 December 1778. He died at Manchester on 15 July 1780, and was buried at St Michael-le-Belfrey Church, York. His will, made on 1 July 1779 and proved, 6 December 1780, left everything to his only remaining son, Luke. Farrer appears to have been most active as a tradesman in the 1740s, when he occasionally advertised in the *York Courant*: on 15 January 1740 and 17 February 1741 regarding the let of houses at Acomb and Holdgate; on 23 February 1742, 22 June 1742, and 29 April 1746, sales of household furniture; on 24 September 1745 as assignee in Caesar Wood's bankruptcy; and on 3 June 1746 the sale of a sedan chair. Took apps named Theophilus (William) Garencieres on 27 July 1744; William Cross on 1 November 1753; Matthew Brown on 15 November 1756; Hewson in 1761; and Michael Simpson of Leeds. Subscribed to Chippendale's *Director*, 1754. Little is known of his career as an upholder, but some furniture at Burton Constable is attributed to him, including frames for portraits of Alderman James Rowe (1707–72) and his wife, Mary (d. 1783) by Henry Pickering, commissioned for the Mansion House, York. [York app. reg. and freemen rolls; York City archives, B43/69, 96–97, 128, 233, 225, 488, 490; E94/53/b; poll bks; will at Borthwick Institute of Historical Research, York; *Catholic Recusancy in York*; Burton Constable Exhib. Cat., Hull, 1970; *C. Life*, 3 June 1976, p. 1476] A.E.

Farrer, Thomas, address unrecorded, upholder (1713). Son of Thomas Farrer, Gent. of London; app. to Arthur Osborn, and admitted freeman of the Upholders' Co. by servitude on 13 January 1713. [GL, Upholders' Co. records]

Farrier, George, New Rd, St Ann's, Newcastle, cm (1834). [D]

Farrier, Lawrence, Newcastle, joiner and cm (1827–38). Recorded at Dog Bank and St Anne's St, 1827–38, in partnership with Ann Farrier in 1833; and at New Rd in 1838. [D]

Farrier, Robert, New Rd, Newcastle, cm (1824–27). [D]

Farrimond, Thomas, Moira St, Liverpool, carver and gilder (1834–39). Trading at no. 3 in 1834, and no. 14, 1835–39. [D]

Farrington, John, Heath St, Hampstead, London, cm, u and furniture broker (1838–39). [D]

Farrington, Richard snr and jnr, Newcastle, carvers and gilders, cm and u (1778–1844). Recorded at Painter-heugh, 1778–87; Broad Chair, 1787–1806; Farrington's Ct, 8 Bigg Mkt, 1806–44; and also 10 Eldon Pl., 1833–44. Recorded as Richard Farrington & Brothers, 1834–38. [D] Richard Farrington snr advertised in *Newcastle Courant*, 30 May 1795 as 'Carver & Gilder . . . carving on Wood and Stone . . . also burnished Oil and Glass-gilding for Spandells in Frames, burnished Names, &c. . . . Figure Heads and Sterns of Ships carved in the most elegant Manner . . . Likenesses modelled in stained Wax, or carved on Marble.' A directory of 1793 has the annotation '3 sons' after Farrington's entry. By 1800, Richard was trading in partnership with John Farrington, when they advertised in *Newcastle Courant*, 25 January; and on 4 October 1806, when they announced the firm's expansion into cabinet making, and recruitment of cabinet and chairmakers. Further advertisements occur in the same paper on 25 October 1806; and on 29 July 1809 for Farrington's 'Fashionable Cabinet Furniture Manufactory and Exhibition Rooms'. Richard Farrington & Bros. appear to have run a most comprehensive business. The firm's label, *c.* 1810, headed by a grand engraving of putti carving classical busts, reads: 'FARRINGTONS, SHIP & HOUSE CARVERS, CABINET MAKERS, JOINERS, Looking Glass & Picture Frame Manufacturers & Gilders in General', and lists their stock which included marble chimney pieces, chairs, sofas, fire screens, cabinet furniture, '& a variety of other Ornaments Either Gilded, Bronzed, or Japanned, such as are not to be equalled at any other Manufactory in the North of England — Also an elegant Collection of Designs of FURNITURE finished in the Egyptian taste. Boarding Schools, Printsellers, Upholsterers, Cabinet Makers & Painters served as usual.' The label is under the lid of a mahogany cellaret in the Bowes Museum, Barnard Castle, Co. Durham. This is of sarcophagus form with lion monopodia in gilt wood; carved and painted on the front are the arms of Leyton-Blenkinsopp of Hoppyland Hall, near Hamsterley, Co. Durham. [*Furn. Hist.*, 1976, pl. 31 A&B] John Wilson Carmichael (1799–1868) was app. to Richard Farrington, who is recorded as having set up as a boat builder between 1810–20, after being a carver and gilder. [Tyne & Wear Co. Museum Exhib. Cat., 1982] A bill of 1822 survives, sent by Farrington to Cuthbert Ellison of Hebburn Hall, Co. Durham, and includes repairs to furniture and the making of an old library table into a dressing table. [Ellison papers, Gateshead Ref. Lib.] In 1824 Farrington & Bros., chairmakers of Newcastle, submitted a design for an oak chair for the President of the Society of Antiquaries of Newcastle. Described in the bill as '1 best finished elbow chair . . . elegantly carved and covered with Red morocco leather, silk Tufts &c.' it cost £8 8s and is now in Newcastle Castle. [*Archaeologia Aeliana*, vol. 8, pp. 177–78, p. 31, fig. 25] A.E.

Farrington, Thomas, Chorley, Lancs., cm and joiner (1818–22). Recorded at Pall Mall in 1818 and Fleet St in 1822. [D]

Farrington, William, Liverpool, carver and painter (1717–25). Took apps named Prescott in 1717, Grimbalstone in 1721, and Harrison in 1725. [S of G, app. index]

Farrist, Jeremiah, 6 Workhouse Croft, Sheffield, Yorks., cm (1818–20). [D]

Farrow, Benjamin, 141 Bowl Alley Lane, Hull, Yorks., cm and broker (1828–31). [D]

Farrow, Daniel, 5 Kirkle's Buildings, 7 Silver Lane, Hull, Yorks., cm (1828–29). [D]

Farrow (or Farron), Henry, Manchester, cm (1829–40). Trading at 15 Oak St in 1829; 30 (or 50) Thomas St, 1832–33; and no. 26 in 1840. [D]

Farrow, John, Gerrard St, London, cm (1784). [Poll bk]

Farrow, Richard, York, cm (1823). Son of Richard Farrow, yeoman of Clifton; app. to Joseph Marsh, cm, on 9 July 1823. [York app. reg.]

Farthing, John, King's Lynn, Norfolk, cm (d. 1770). Will proved at Norwich, 1770. [Norfolk Record Soc., index of wills]

Farthing, John H., Cornhill, London, writing desk, dressing case and work box maker (1808–39). Recorded at nos 43–44 in 1808, and no. 42, 1829–39. [D]

Fassett, —, 75 Shoreditch, London, u, cm appraiser and undertaker. Early 19th-century trade card continues: 'Paper Hangings and Old Furniture taken in Exchange for New.' [London borough of Hackney, archives dept, 332 TDE/30]

Fassett, Elias de Gruchy, Hoxton, London, upholder (1718–d. 1782). Trading at Hoxton Sq. in 1781. Son of John Fassett, tanner of Southton; app. to Robert Hall on 5 July 1718, and admitted freeman of the Upholders' Co. by servitude on 3 January 1733. Father of William Fassett, admitted freeman of the Upholders' Co. in 1757. [GL, Upholders' Co. records]

Fassett, William, 5–6 Leadenhall St, London, u (1787–1809). Son of Elias de Gruchy Fassett, chemist of Castle St, Oxford Mkt; app. to Joseph Robins on 6 June 1787; and Thomas Silk on 11 September 1788. Admitted freeman of the Upholders' Co. by servitude on 7 September 1796. [D; GL, Upholders' Co. records]

Fassnidge, James, Hillingdon End, Uxbridge, Middlx, cm, u and builder (1826–39). Trading at London St in 1826 and Hillingdon End, 1832–38. [D]

Fatnall, John, address unrecorded, u (1712). Took app. on 11 July 1712. [PRO, app. reg.]

Faucon, James, London, cm and glass-grinder (1731–32). An advertisement appeared 119 times in the *Daily Post*, between 16 February 1731 and 26 September 1732, announcing the sale of 'goods of the noted Mr. James Faucon at Surnam's Great House in Soho Square'. The goods included 'several dozen of the newest fashioned wallnut tree chairs covered with velvet, Damask and black Spanish leather', and various types of chairs, settees and chairbeds. [*Conn.*, February and June 1933, pp. 89–90; Harris, *Old English Furniture*, p. 21]

Faulding, R., Coventry St, Haymarket, London, looking-glass manufacturer (1812–37). Addresses given at no. 23 in 1837, and no. 26 on label on plain rectangular looking-glass at Kenwood House, London. [D]

Faulke, James, Norwich, cm (1818). Son of Robert Faulke; admitted freeman on 27 June 1818. [Norwich freemen reg.]

Faulkener, James, Gt Kirby St, London(?), cm (1736). Took app. named Cotton from Eaton, Bucks., in 1736. [S of G, app. index]

Faulkener, James, 109 Wardour St, Soho, London, cm (1777). Insured his house for £100 in 1777. [GL, Sun MS vol. 260, p. 280]

Faulker, Jos., Suffolk Pl., Hackney Rd, London, cm and u (1827). [D]

Faulkner (or Faulconer), Alexander, Whitcomb St, London, cm and upholder (1774–82). Took out a Sun Insurance policy in 1782 for £300 of which utensils, stock and goods accounted for £220. [Poll bk; GL, Sun MS vol. 299, p. 157]

Faulkner, Benjamin, London, turner (1707–18). Insured his dwelling house in Clare St, St Clement Danes, for £200 on 2 August 1707; an empty house in Hollis St, near Clare Mkt for £150 on 6 November 1717; and a house in Drury Lane for £150 on 17 November 1718. [GL, Hand in Hand MS vol. 5, ref. 13978; vol. 18, p. 19; vol. 19, p. 237]

Faulkner, Charles, Newcastle, cm (1813). Submitted a bill to Cuthbert Ellison of Hebburn Hall, Gateshead, in 1813 for furniture costing £33 19s 6d. [Gateshead Ref. Lib., Ellison papers; *Furn. Hist.*, 1976]

Faulkner, Hannah, 14 Stanley St, Liverpool, cm (1834). [D]

Faulkner, J., 17 Suffolk Pl., Hackney Rd, London, cm and chairmaker (c. 1800). [Heal Coll., BM]

Faulkner, James, Hughes Ct, Water Lane, Blackfriars, London, cm (1725). Insured goods and merchandise in his house for £500 on 20 May 1725. [GL, Sun MS vol. 20, ref. 35930]

Faulkner, Jeremiah, 25 Chapel Lane, Hull, Yorks., joiner and cm (1838–48). [D]

Faulkner, Joseph, 29 Old St Rd, London, cm (1829). [D]

Faulkner, M. & J., 137 High Holborn, London, u (1839). [D]

Faulkner, Thomas, 1 Back Thomas St, Manchester, chairmaker (1811–17). [D]

Faulkner, William, Newgate St, Chester, cm (1802–18). Admitted freeman on 10 July 1802. Took app. named James Roberts in 1801. [Poll bks; Chester freemen rolls and app. bk]

Faun(t)leroy, Thomas, Potter's-field(s), Tooley St, London, turner and dealer in hard wood (1780–92). [D]

Fauset, Nathaniel, Strand, London, u (1709). [Westminster rate bks]

Faux, Grey F., Thetford, Norfolk, grocer, draper, ironmonger, builder, cm and u (1798). [D]

Fawbert, William, York, cm, u, wood turner and toyman (1791–1823). Trading in Micklegate in 1801 and Stonegate, 1818–23. Son of Robert Fawbert, tailor; app. to John Barber, cm, on 10 October 1791. Admitted freeman in 1801. Took apps named Christopher Rawden on 18 January 1807; Robert Isaacson on 12 May 1809; William Catton on 28 September 1809; George Parker on 7 October 1812; and Robert Lamb on 28 September 1820. [D; York app. reg. and freeman rolls]

Fawcet, Peter, Mersey St, Liverpool, cm (1766). [D]

Fawcett, Christopher, Lancaster, cm (1826–27). [Lancaster freemen rolls]

Fawcett, Christopher, Lancaster, cm (1827). App. to J. Hodgson in 1827. [Lancaster app. reg.]

Fawcett, George, Church St, Dewsbury, Yorks., cm (1828–30). [D] See Thomas Fawcett.

Fawcett, George, Knaresborough, Yorks., joiner and/or cm (1834). [D]

Fawcett, James, 57 Prescott St, Low Hill, Liverpool, u (1839). [D]

Fawcett, John, 19 Oldham Rd, Manchester, chairmaker (1817–20). [D]

Fawcett, John, Brough, Westmld, cm (1829). [D]

Fawcett, John, Mellbecks, Kirkby Stephen, Westmld, cm (1828–34). [D]

Fawcett, Jos., London, cm and u (1826–35). Recorded at 10 Adams Row, Hampstead Rd, 1826–27; 10 Hampstead Rd, 1827–28; and no. 16 in 1835. [D]

Fawcett, Thomas, Dewsbury, Yorks., cm and joiner (1822–37). Trading near Church St in 1822; Union St in 1830; and Bond St in 1837. [D] See George Fawcett.

Fawcett, William, Boar Lane, Leeds, Yorks., carver and gilder (1786–1824). Recorded at no. 17 in 1817. Moved to new premises, also in Boar Lane, in 1820. Recorded at no. 21 in 1822. Advertised in *Leeds Mercury* between 1786–1807: in 1786 his stock of 'Glass & Picture frames, Girandoles etc. in burnished gold & also in black'; and in *Leeds Intelligencer*, 9 June 1789, that he 'makes chimney pieces, glass frames, girandoles — and also has in stock an elegant assortment of Burnished gold picture frame patterns which may be viewed by customers.' Other very descriptive advertisements occur on 2 October 1815, 15 April 1822, and in 1824. Announced change of premises in *Leeds Mercury*, 1820, offering thanks for thirty years patronage. His career included external carving in a stone-like composition, and the range of his internal carved and gilded work was certainly restricted. In later years he increasingly offered drawings and prints as well as frames. Probably the Fawcet of Leeds who supplied picture frames costing £32 4s 3d to Edward, Lord Lascelles, of Harewood House, on 20 December 1799. [D; Leeds archives dept, Harewood MS 191]

Fawcett, William, 36 Seymour Pl., London, u (1829). [D]

Fawcett & Walker, Westgate, Wakefield, Yorks., cm (1814–20). [D]

Fawconer, Jonathan, address unrecorded, upholder (1713–53). App. to John Harris at 'corner of ye old Jury', London; admitted freeman of the Upholders' Co. by servitude on 14 December 1713. Took apps named John Sutton, 1733–43; William Weare, 1739–53; and Samuel Maris, 1741–48. [GL, Upholders' Co. records]

Fawdington, William, York, cm (1808–20). Son of Robert Fawdington, carpenter, deceased; app. to John Barber, cm and turner, on 19 October 1801. Admitted freeman of York as cm of London in 1820. [York app. reg. and freemen rolls] Possibly:

Fawdington, William, 22 Warwick Sq., Newgate St, London, cabinet and pocketbook manufacturer (1820). [D]

Fawdry, Thomas, 17 Holloway Head, Birmingham, cm (1835). [D]

Fawkes, John, Guildford, Surrey, u (1754–57). Advertised in *Oxford Gazette and Reading Mercury*, 29 April and 3 June 1754; and on 2 May 1757 that he 'has continually fresh Goods coming in of the best of every Sort, being resolved to keep great Choice, and to supply his Customers as cheap as they can buy in London, viz. Standing Beds ready made up of all Sorts and Colours, as Red, Green, Yellow, Blue in Damasks, Harateens, Cheneys, and Linseys, with every Sort by the Piece or yard; also Flowered Linens, Checks, and Wrought Dimity Beds, Printed Paper, Bedsteads, Sacking Bottoms, a large Quantity of Goose, Duck, and Hen Feather Beds ready made, and fill'd with the best dried Feathers to lay on immediately, Ticken of all Sorts by the Yard or Bed, and Feathers of every Sort by the Pound; Quilts, Rugs, Coverlids, Counterpanes, Blankets of all Sorts and Sizes; Chairs, Clocks, Bureaus, Desks, Chests of Drawers, Tables, Glasses, Kitchen Furniture of all Sorts, Iron Pots, and Household Goods in general; where all Persons may be furnish'd at once. He also Buys any Sort of Household Goods, or Appraises and Sells for any Person.' On 2 May 1757 he added that he bought 'his Goods of the Makers . . .'.

Fawley, John, London, wholesale furniture manufacturer and transparent window-blind and decorative painter (1813–16). Trading at 20 Gt Surrey St, Blackfriars, 1813–16, and 20 Blackfriars Rd in 1815. [D]

Fawley & Ward, 43 Wardour St, Soho, London, japanned chair and furniture manufactory (1802–08). Recorded at no. 48 in 1804. Trading as Fawley, Ward & Co. in 1808. Named in Sheraton's list of master cabinet makers, 1803. [D; Fastnedge, *English Furniture Styles, 1500–1830*, p. 306]

Fawthorp, Richard, Leeds Rd, Huddersfield, Yorks., cm and u (1830). [D]

Fawthorp, Richard, George St, Bradford, Yorks., cm and joiner (1834–37). [D]

Fayle, William, Swallow St, London, u (1774). Declared bankrupt, *Gents Mag.*, April 1774.

Fayrer, Edmund, Lancaster, cm (1767–68). [Lancaster freemen rolls]

Fayrer, James, Lancaster, cm (1779–84). Admitted freeman, 1779–80. [Lancaster freemen rolls and poll bk]

Fayrer, John, Lancaster, joiner and cm (1770–84). Son of James Fayrer; app. to J. Wright in 1770, and admitted freeman, 1779–80. [Lancaster app. reg., freemen rolls and poll bk]

Fayrer, John, Union Sq., Lancaster, cm (1822). [D]

Fayrer, John, Liverpool, cm, coachmaker, appraiser and auctioneer (1787–96). Addresses given at Castle Ditch in 1787; no. 26 in 1790; 26 Church St, 1790–91 with yard at Dale St in 1791; Castle Ditch, near Lord St, 1793; and 28 Church St in 1796. [D] Sale of household furniture announced in *Williamson's Liverpool Advertiser*, 15 March 1790, including 'a very good Mahogany Counting house Desk', and a horse chaise. He also required an experienced journeyman u. In the same paper on 17 January 1791 was announced the dissolving of the partnership between Fayrer and Richard & Robert Edmundson, cm; and also that between Fayrer, Richard Edmundson and William Barwick, u. Fayrer, cm, and Barwick, u, were to continue trading in the old warehouse at 26 Castle Ditch, but separately: 'They will engage to supply Gentlemen, Merchants, & others with goods of the best materials, either for exportation of their own houses.' Sale of stock of cabinet goods and timber of Edmundson & Fayrer took place on 24 and 26 January 1791. In the same paper on 5 August 1793, John Fayrer announced his intention of giving up the cabinet making business and concentrating solely on coach making, which he had carried on for some time in co-partnership with his brother, Thomas. He now wished to sell 'the commodious warehouse, occupied by himself in Castle-ditch, near to top of Lord-Street, which is a very advantageous situation for business, & as an inducement, he will accommodate them with a choice, excellent & extensive assortment of fashionable articles, with tools, benches, saw-pits, wood & every other requisite upon reasonable terms. And in the meantime the goods are now selling at the Warehouse, at cheap & reduced prices.'

Fayrer, John T., London, cm and u (1826–39). Trading at 42 South Molton St, Oxford St, 1826–35; 6 Gray St, 1837–39, in partnership with William Fayrer in 1839. [D]

Fayrer, William, Lancaster, cm (1817–18). Admitted freeman, 1817–18, when stated 'of London'. [Lancaster freemen rolls]

Fear, W., Gascoyne Pl., (1819), 1 Abbey Gate (1826), 6 James St (1833), Bath, Som., cm. [D]

Fearby, Charles, York, cm (1834). [D]

Fearby, Thomas, 31 Fossgate, York, cm and u (1828–30). [D]

Fearenside, John, Lancaster, cm (1823–24). [Lancaster freemen rolls]

Fearn, John, 45 Long Acre, London, cm (1778). Insured his house for £200 in 1778. [GL, Sun MS vol. 266, p. 354]

Fearnley, Charles Bewstead, York, cm (1824). Son of Thomas Fearnley, turner; app. to John Lupton, cm, on 13 December 1824. [York app. reg.]

Fearnley, Henry, Mill St, Canal Rd, Bradford, Yorks., cm (1828–30). [D]

Fearnley, John, 'The Golden Head', Flesh Mkt, Newcastle, carver and gilder (1757–63). Advertised in *Newcastle Journal*, 11–18 June 1757 that he was from London, and made 'chimney-pieces in marble, wood and stone; frames for pictures, looking-glasses and marble slabs; chandeliers, girandoles, brackets &c. Likewise party-gilds ceilings, chimney-pieces, cornishes, windows, doors etc. and cleans, repairs and varnishes or new gilds old frames. Upholsters, cabinet-makers, joiners &c. may be furnished, with mouldings and ornaments in burnish gold, for walnut tree frames &c. The above work will be executed in the neatest & most approv'd taste, and gilt in oil or burnish gold to the utmost perfection on the most reasonable terms.' A similar advertisement of 30 July 1763 mentions that he also carved tombs and monuments, and 'has to dispose of a very good sign of the Queen's Head, with a bunch of grapes.'

Fearnley, John, Hipperholme, Halifax, Yorks., cm (1834). [D]

Fearnley, Matthew, Bootle St, Manchester, cm (1813). [D]

Fearnley, Peter, Lancaster. Named in the Gillow records, 1819–31. [Westminster Ref. Lib.]

Fearn(s)ley, Thomas, 8 Jubbergate, York, cm, u and wood turner (1830). [D]

Fearnside, Henry, 19 Bond St, Leeds, Yorks., carver and gilder (1834). [D]

Fearnside & Morton, 22 Commercial St, Leeds, Yorks., carvers, gilders and looking-glass manufacturers (1837). [D]

Fearon, John, Tangier St, Whitehaven, Cumb., joiner and/or cm (1811). [D] Possibly John Fearson.

Fearson, Elizabeth, Stamford, Lincs., u (1779). Took out a Sun Insurance policy in 1779 for £800 of which utensils and stock accounted for £500. [GL, Sun MS vol. 275, p. 232]

Fearson, John, Whitehaven, Cumb., cm (1798). [D] Possibly John Fearon.

Feast, John, Mill End, Chatteris, Cambs., carpenter and u (1839). [D]

Feather, John, Lidgate, Keighley, Yorks., joiner and/or cm (1837). [D]

Featherstone, Abraham, Brighton, Sussex, cm, boxmaker and u (1813–40). Addresses given at The Level, as boxmaker in 1813 and cm in 1816; at Oxford Pl., 1814, 1819 and 1823; Oxford St, 1825–28; and 3 Ditchling Terr., 1839–40. Children bapt. at St Nicholas's Church: Mary Anne by Sarah Featherstone on 29 August 1813; John Adams by Sarah on 28 December 1814; Abraham by Elizabeth Featherstone on 22 December 1816; Caroline by Sarah on 11 April 1819; Sarah Rebecca by Sarah on 1 June 1823; William Henry by Sarah on 7 August 1825; and Adam by Sarah on 8 March 1828. [D; E. Sussex RO, PAR 255/1/2/1–6]

Feen, William, 23 School Lane, Liverpool, cm (1834). [D]

Feetam, John, 9 Thornton Sq., Posterngate, Hull, Yorks., cm (1838–39). [D]

Feet(h)am, Thomas, Hull, Yorks., cm, u and undertaker (1810–40). Addresses given at 62 Mytongate, 1821–34; no. 29, 1835–40, and as Thomas & Co. in 1839. App. to Richard Meadley of Sculcoates in February 1810. Mahogany Davenport recorded stamped on edge of well: 'T. FEETAM HULL MAKER'. [D; Hull app. reg.]

Feetham, Elizabeth, Mill Hill, Leeds, Yorks., u (1822). [D]

Feetham, Mary, Leeds, Yorks., working u (1830–34). Recorded at 2 Bilton's Yd, 16 Mill Hill in 1830 and 5 Sandford St in 1834. [D]

Feetham, Mark, 11 Mill Hill, Leeds, Yorks., u (1826–30). [D]

Fehrenback, Henry, High Wycombe, Bucks., chairmaker (b. c. 1821–41). Aged 20 at the time of the 1841 Census.

Fehrenback, Joseph, High Wycombe, Bucks., chairmaker (b. c. 1811–41). Aged 30 at the time of the 1841 Census.

Feild, Abraham, St Margaret's, Westminster, London, frame-maker (1695). Married Jane Burton at Holy Trinity Church in 1695. [Westminster Ref. Lib., transcription of marriage reg., 929.3]

Feldgate, Andrew, Norwich, u (1735–68). App. to Timothy Ganning; admitted freeman on 21 September 1735. [Norwich freemen rolls and poll bks]

Fell, —, address unrecorded, cm and u (1775). Subscribed to Thomas Malton's *Compleat Treatise on Perspective,* 1775.

Fell, Benjamin, Rock St, Bury, Lancs., chairmaker (1824). [D]

Fell, George, Louth, Lincs., joiner, cm and u (1819–41). Trading in Walkergate, 1819–35, and Eastgate, 1841. [D]

Fell, James, Ulverston, Lancs., cm (1801–34). Trading in Soutergate in 1825–29, and Union St, 1834. Admitted freeman of Lancaster, 1801–02. [D; Lancaster freemen rolls]

Fell, Jane, Fountain St, Ulverston, Lancs., cm and u (1828). [D]

Fell, John, Lancaster, ironmonger (1789–1813). [Westminster Ref. Lib., Gillow records]

Fell, John, Manchester, cm (1811–13). Trading at 21 Kennedy St in 1811, and 11 Commerce St, 1813. [D]

Fell, Joseph, Half Moon Inn Yd, Bigg Mkt, Newcastle, cm (1816). Sale by Joseph Fell of stock of 'an eminent CABINET-MAKER' declining business, announced in *Durham County Advertiser,* 29 June 1816. Stock consisted of '40 mahogany & beech circular-front lobby, dressing and single chests of drawers; 30 mahogany dining, card, Pembroke & screen tables; & ditto pillar & claw tables; 6 sets of mahogany chairs; 12 sets of beech ditto; 2 bookcases & wardrobes; circular & square washstands; night tables, child's chairs, and foot stools; together with a variety of drawing room furniture . . .'.

Fell, Lawrence, London, cm (1766–97). In notable partnership with William Turton from c. 1770, and later with James Newton at 31 Compton St, 1781–84, and 63 Wardour St and 10 Bruton St in 1797. Little is known of the firm of Fell and Turton, but that they were important in their day is implied by documents concerning the prestigious patronage received from Sir Lawrence Dundas of Moor Park, Herts., and Arlington St, London. His account at the Royal Bank of Scotland, Drummonds Branch, shows that he paid Lawrence Fell over £5,000 between 1765–75 for work at Moor Park and Arlington St; but the seven surviving bills document only a fraction of this commission. Fell may have already carried out work for Dundas by 1764, as a bill of that date from France & Bradburn to Dundas suggests; but his first known bill is dated 1766, for supplying, repairing and regilding picture frames for a total of £86 1s. The next document is a receipt for £300 dated 31 December 1768. An undated document, c. 1770, bears a rough note in Dundas's hand of expenses for furnishing Moor Park, his house in Arlington St, and Aske Hall, Yorks., and reads: 'Fell before done £1,200'. On 12 October 1770 Fell submitted a bill for fixing paintings to 'straining' frames, and carving and gilding new frames to be shipped to Aske Hall. Another bill of 1770 for glass frames for pictures at Moor Park totalled £299 5s 5d, with £281 10s 6d for materials, labour and shipping. In September 1771 Fell and Turton, now in partnership, provided bed furniture for Dundas's trip abroad, costing £36 18s 6d; and received £104 5s 10½d for carrying out joiner's work, making carved and gilt cornices and festoon curtains at Arlington St. Fell and Turton's most outstanding commission from Dundas was for furnishing the famous Tapestry Room at Moor Park: the suite of carved and gilt furniture covered with tapestries executed by Jacques Neilson at the 'Manufacture Royale des Gobelins' between 1766–69, and delivered in 1771. Fell and Turton's account of 1771 for this suite records only two sofas, six chairs and two window stools, additional pieces (including a pair of fire screens) being supplied later. Their bill which totals £138 4s 6d invoices two sofas costing £50, two stools, £16, and six elbow chairs, £60, all 'Carved and gilt in Burnished gold, stuff'd with Best Curl'd hair and fine linnin', covered with tapestry, and supplied with paper cases. The tapestry suite is now split between the Philadelphia Museum of Art and Temple Newsam House, Leeds. A pair of side tables made by Fell & Turton, c. 1770, for the Gallery at Moor Park are now at Kenwood, London. [N. Yorks. RO, ZNK X 1/7/7–14; 22; *Apollo,* September 1967, pp. 186–88; Sotheby's, 26 May

1967, lot 178; Gilbert, *Leeds Furn. Cat.*, vol. 1, pp. 63–67; GLC Exhib. Cat., Kenwood, 1975]

By 1781 the partnership between Fell and Turton appears to have been dissolved, and Lawrence Fell is recorded with James Newton, 1781–97. At 31 Compton St they took out Sun Insurance policies in 1781 for £2,400, £1,800 on utensils, stock, goods and workshop; and in 1783 for £2,000, £1,750 on utensils, stock and goods. Fell and Newton carried out work at Burghley House, Stamford, 1788–97, including a state bed. [D; GL, Sun MS vol. 298, p. 136; vol. 306, p. 487; *C. Life*, 29 August 1974, pp. 562–64; 16 October 1975, p. 985] Lawrence Fell alone subscribed to George Richardson's *A Book of Ceilings*, 1776, and his *Iconology*, 1779–80, and polled at Westminster in 1784.   A.E.

Fell, Robert, Lancaster. Named in the Gillow records, 1789–95. [Westminster Ref. Lib.]

Fell, Thomas, Lancaster, cm (1795–1818). Named in the Gillow records, 1795–96. Admitted freeman, 1817–18, when stated of Leeds. [Westminster Ref. Lib., Gillow; Lancaster freemen rolls] Possibly:

Fell, Thomas, Back Nile St, Leeds, Yorks., cm (1822). [D]

Fell, Thomas, Ulverston, Lancs., cm and chairmaker (1800–34). Trading in King St, 1828–34, and Fountain St, 1822–25. Fell sent a letter to Gillows regarding mahogany in 1800. Admitted freeman of Lancaster, 1801–02, when stated of Ulverston. Marriage to Miss Jane Turner of Whitehaven reported in *Liverpool Mercury*, 5 July 1811. [D; Gillow letter bk, 1800, p. 296; Lancaster freemen rolls]

Fell, Valentine, Castlegate, Grantham, Lincs., cm and u (1835). [D]

Fell, William, Ulverston, Lancs., cm (1760–98). Took app. named Brockbank in 1760. [D; S of G, app. index]

Fell, William, Liverpool, joiner and cm (1824–39). Addresses given at 13 Crosshall St in 1824; 57 and 59 Byrom St with shop at 10 Gt Crosshall St in 1827; 36 Byrom St with shop at 6 Brook's Alley in 1829; 23 School Lane, 1835–37; and no. 45 in 1839. [D]

Felliot, Nicholas, Long Acre, London, cm (1709). [Westminster rate bks]

Fellows, Edward, Waterloo St, Kidderminster, Worcs., cm and u (1835). [D]

Fellows, Robert, 10 Hart St, Bloomsbury, London, carver and gilder (1787). Took out a Sun Insurance policy on 30 March 1787 for £100 on the household goods of Brockett, shoemaker. [GL, Sun MS vol. 342, ref. 528796]

Fellows, Robert, 22 Warwick St, Golden Sq., London, carver, gilder and printseller (1790–94). Took out a Sun Insurance policy on 22 August 1791 for £300, including £50 on utensils and stock and £50 on prints and drawings. Trade card or billhead recorded. [D; GL, Sun MS ref. 587669; Heal]

Fellows, Roger, London, looking-glass frame maker (1784). [Colchester poll bk]

Fellows, Thomas, 31 Court, Lancaster St, Birmingham, chairmaker (1835). [D]

Fells, John, Ash, Kent, cm (1839). [D]

Felt (or Felto(e)), John, Bristol, carver (1721–81). Recorded in Bristol, 1721–39, and Marshfield, Glos., 1754–81. [Bristol poll bks]

Felton, John, 41 Charles St, Fitzroy Sq., London, cm (1808). [D]

Felton, Joseph, Broad St, Ludlow, Salop, appraiser, cm and u (1822–35). [D]

Felton, Mary, Clare St, Liverpool, u (1827–34). Trading at no. 12 in 1827 and no. 16 in 1834. [D] See Patience Felton.

Felton, Michael, 47 Brick Lane, Spitalfields, London, cm, u, chair and sofa maker, undertaker (1817–28). Took out Sun Insurance policies on 12 April 1821 for £400 of which £300 accounted for stock and utensils; and on 18 November 1822

for £350, £200 on stock, utensils and goods in trust and in open yard. [D; GL, Sun MS vol. 487, ref. 978817; vol. 489, ref. 997634]

Felton, Patience, Liverpool, u (1814–29). Trading at 23 Bispham St, 1814–23, and 12 Clare St, 1824–29. [D] See Mary Felton.

Femaister, George, London, u (1793). Subscribed to Sheraton's *Drawing Book*, 1793.

Fenlaw, John, London(?), cm (1772). Complained about furniture smuggling to Commissioners of Customs in 1772. [*Apollo*, August 1965, p. 104]

Fenlyson, James, St Martin's St, Leicester Fields, London, cm (1774). [Poll bk]

Fenn, Robert, Norwich, picture frame maker (1798). [D]

Fenn, Thomas, address unrecorded, upholder (1719–27). Son of Samuel Fenn, Gent. of Bedford; app. to John Mercer on 5 August 1719, and admitted freeman of the Upholders' Co. by servitude on 1 February 1727. [GL, Upholders' Co. records]

Fenn, Thomas, 14 Little Chapel St, Wardour St, London, carver and gilder, carver in wood, cm (1835–39). [D]

Fenn, William, Shifnal, Salop, cm and u (1822–35). Recorded at High St in 1822, Shrewsbury Rd in 1828 and Salop St in 1835. [D]

Fenna, John, Nantwich, Cheshire, cm (1722–d. 1779). Married on 20 February 1772; buried on 18 March 1779. [Chester RO, PR]

Fenna, Mrs Mary, Nantwich, Cheshire, cm (1781–89). [D]

Fennell, J., 37 James St, Bath, Som., upholder (1819). [D]

Fenner, L., 216 East Room Gallery, Pantheon, London, fancy cm (*c.* 1830). Label recorded on small fancy cabinet consisting of a podium containing one drawer, and surmounted by a rosewood gallery. The cabinet is of rosewood and satinwood veneered in alternating bands on a cedarwood carcase.

Fenner, L., 20 Rawstorne St, Goswell Rd, London, fancy cm (1835). [D]

Fenner, Samuel, 11 Guildford St, East Spa Fields, London(?), picture frame and looking-glass maker (1824). Took out a Sun Insurance policy on 4 February 1824 for £300. [GL, Sun MS vol. 497, ref. 1014083]

Fenner, William, Tunbridge Wells, Kent, Tunbridge-ware manufacturer (1792–1840). Probably trading on the Walks (the Pantiles) by 1792 in which year he subscribed £5 5s towards their paving. His trade card, probably dating from 1796, indicates that he sold a considerable range of print-decorated wares 'in the TURNER or CABINET line' at his shop on the Walks. In 1797 went into partnership with James Nye who had been trading in Tunbridge-wares certainly since 1772 and probably from 1757. James Nye was dead by 1809 and a further partnership was formed with Edmund Nye, son of James Nye. This partnership absorbed the business formerly conducted by William Foley. The partners centred their production on the Chalet, Mount Ephraim and this manufactory was continued by William Fenner when the partnership broke up in 1817. Fenner was chosen by the inhabitants of Tunbridge Wells to produce a fine work and writing table for the Princess Victoria in 1826. A subscription of 25 guineas was raised by the people of the town to defray the cost. In the late 1830s the business traded as Fenner & Co. and tried to develop markets in London for its products. In 1840 Fenner advertised that he was offering wares 'at very reduced prices owing to the introduction of new machinery'. This was however the last year of trading.

A number of pieces produced in the last years of the business bear a trade label indicating that Fenner & Co. were 'Inlaid & Mosaic Wood Manufacturers to HER MAJESTY & THE ROYAL FAMILY'. These pieces use the miniature

parquetry work characteristic of the 1830s but no examples of tessellated mosaic from this manufactory are known. [D; Tunbridge Wells Museum, Sprange Coll.; Kent RO, u747/E20, P344/11/1; Britton, *Descriptive Sketches . . .*, 1832]
B.A.

Fennesy, Richard, Liverpool, cm and u (1837–39). Trading at 6 Bulton St in 1837 and 19 Rainford Gdns, 1839. [D]

Fenny, John, 57 Frith St, Soho, London, turner (1808). [D]

Fenshaw, —, Bread St, London, u (d. 1717). Newspapers of 1717 report that on 'Fryday Sennight Mr. Fenshaw, a Relation of the Lord of that Name, an Upholsterer in Bread-street, taking a Walk about Islington, was taken very ill, and returning to Town sate down by the Chappel at Aylesbury-house in St. Jones's; while he sate there, appearing to be indisposed, one of the inhabitants knowing him, invited him into his House, where continuing ill he fell a vomiting, soon asked for the necessary house, and he staying there longer than ordinary, they went after him, and found him dead upon the seat.' [Winterthur, Delaware, Symonds papers] Possibly Edward Fanshaw.

Fensom, George, 32 Wood St, Salford, Lancs., chairmaker (1828). [D]

Fenteman, Joseph, Beverley, Yorks., joiner and cm (1818). App. to John Grassam of Gt Driffield, Yorks., in July 1818. [Hull app. reg.]

Fenteman, Michael, Petergate, York, cm (1758). Son of John Fentiman, bricklayer; admitted freeman in 1758. [York freemen rolls and poll bk]

Fentham, Thomas, London, carver, gilder, glass grinder and picture frame maker (1774–1825). Trading at 49 Strand in 1777; no. 52, 'opposite Old Round Court', 1778–93; no. 51 in 1784; and 136 Strand, near Somerset House, 1794–1820. Recorded as Thomas & Co., 1807–21; and as C. T. Fentham & Co. in 1820. [D] Took out Sun Insurance policies on 23 July 1787 for £5,400 on household goods, utensils, shops, warehouses and offices; in 1779 for £200 on utensils, stock and goods in warehouse and workshop in St Martin's Lane; and in 1780 for £300 on his house. [GL, Sun MS vol. 346, p. 386; vol. 274, p. 234; vol. 287, p. 410] Polled at Westminster in 1774, and named as a Fellow of the Society of Arts and Manufactures, 1787–90. His trade label, found behind an oval carved and gilt Neo-classical looking-glass announced that he 'sells all sorts of picture, print, and looking-glass frames, of any colour to match rooms. Various sorts of dressing glasses, rich girandole and green and blue Venetian Window blinds.' [GCM; Wills, *Looking-Glasses*, pl. 163] Labels also found on various gilded looking-glasses, of round or architectural form, Neo-classical ornament, often convex, and surmounted by a carved eagle. [Parke-Bernet, 30 January 1942, lot 95, illus., and 31 March 1960, lot 89; Phillips', 8 September 1964, lot 64; Sotheby's, 29 March 1968, lot 226; *Antiques*, February 1976, p. 351, fig. 3, and January 1982, p. 122, illus.] The gilt pier tables in the Gallery at Erddig, Clwyd, are almost certainly by Fentham, whose label has survived on the back of a picture frame with similar decoration in the Chinese Room. He probably also supplied the stand for *The Ruins of Palmyra*, and for models by Elizabeth Ratcliffe, which may well account for the payment to him in 1775 of £15 12s 6d. Fentham is also known to have carried out work for the state bedrooms, completed by *c.* 1775. [Nat. Trust guide to *Erddig*; *Apollo*, July 1978, pp. 56–63, illus.; *C. Life*, 6 April 1978] Probably the T. Fentham of London who provided Lady Heathcote with '1 Square Frame with Spandle for a Picture of Mr. Folkstone', costing 16s, on 19 June 1779. [Lincoln RO, 2 ANC 12/D/34] Probably also the Thomas Fentum of London who was paid on 23 January 1782 for picture frames supplied to Charles

Towneley; and on 10 June 1785, £10 16s 'for the square glass and frame done in 1784.' [Towneley account bk in private archive]

Fentham, William, 54 Belvedere Pl., Southwark, London, carver, gilder and looking-glass manufacturer (1820–37). [D]

Fenton, Francis, address unrecorded, painter and gilder (1764–69). Recorded in James Paine's papers relating to work done at Worksop Manor for the Duke of Norfolk. In April 1764 he was gilding picture frames; and in December 1769, was paid 2s 6d 'To an Iron bedstead painting Mahogany', and painting other furniture. [Arundel Castle records, MD 18, pt. 2]

Fenton, Francis, High St, Colchester, Essex, cm, u and auctioneer (1816–d. 1848). Trading as Fenton & Son, 1823–24, and as Francis & Charles at 51 High St in 1839. Sent account to the Churchwardens of Wormingford, Essex, in 1816. Probate will dated 1848. [D; Essex RO, D/P/185/5/1; *Wills at Chelmsford*]

Fenton, George, Nelson Pl., Well St, Hanley, Staffs., gilder (1818). [D]

Fenton, John, address unrecorded, cm (1769–72). Worked at Gibside, Co. Durham, for the Earl of Strathmore. On 21 June 1769 he was paid £1 13s 10d; on 26 May 1770, £1 5s 'for a Chair for Lord Glamis'; on 9 November 1771, £27 17s 3d for a mahogany 'Buro Bed', feather bed, bolster, pillows and curtains; and on 6 July and 31 December 1772, a total of £14 6s for child's chairs, quilts and 'happins'. [Durham RO, Strathmore MS D/St/v1493; 352/9; v995; 286]

Fenton, Thomas, Leeds, Yorks., cm (1751). Took app. named Smith in 1751. [S of G, app. index]

Fenton, Thomas, 6 Meat Mkt, Bury St Edmunds, Suffolk, cm and u (1839). [D]

Fenton, William, Gt Suffolk St, Haymarket, London, cm (1744–49). Notice in *Daily Advertiser*, 21 February 1744 reads: 'Lost on Saturday last from Mr. Fenton, a Cabinet Maker at the lower end of Suffolk Street near the Haymarket, a white dog spotted all over with Black.' A notice of 15 May also concerns the lost dog, 'who answers to the name of Tyger: he belongs to a Gentlewoman that is blind, and is taught to lead her. Whoever brings him to Mr. Fenton's . . . shall receive half a Guinea.' Polled at Westminster in 1749.

Fenton, William, address unrecorded, u (1767–73). Between April 1767 and January 1773 received four payments totalling £559 for work done at Badminton House, Glos. for the Duke of Beaufort. [Badminton papers; account bks]

Fenwick, Edward, St Mary Woolchurch Hawe, London, u (1678–1708). [Heal gives no source but his list of sources includes 'Churchwarden's Records of St Mary Woolchurch Hawe']

Fenwick, Thomas, Quay Side, Blyth, Northumb., joiner and cm (1827–34). [D]

Fenwick & Pringle, Sunderland, Co. Durham, cm (1798). [D]

Ferbaern, John, Gt Titchfield St, London, cm (1784). [D] Possibly Fairburn, —.

Ferber, William, address unrecorded, u (1803). Subscribed to Sheraton's *Cabinet Dictionary*, 1803.

Fereday, Thomas jnr, Sedgley, Staffs., carpenter and/or cm (1833–38). Recorded at Gospel End in 1833. [D]

Ferely, Charles, 49 Hinton St, Brunswick Sq., London, cm (1816). [D]

Ferguson, Adam James, late of Union St, Liverpool, u and licensed victualler (1829). Declared bankrupt, *Liverpool Mercury*, 30 October 1829. Probably James Adam Ferguson.

Ferguson, Barnaby, 51 St John St, West Smithfield, London, chair japanner (1789–93). [D]

Fergusson, Duncan, North St, Prospect St, Dockside, Hull, Yorks., cm and chandler (1803–06). [D]

Ferguson, Henry, London (1771–79). A hawkish executor of Thomas Chippendale's first partner James Rannie who died in 1766; joined forces with his fellow Scotsman and co-executor Thomas Haig to rescue the firm from bankruptcy in 1771, both acquiring a one-third share in the business. He was not directly involved in the furniture making trade, although described in an accompaniment to Chippendale's probate inventory as 'Cabinet Maker'. After 1771 the firm traded as 'Chippendale, Haig & Co.', Ferguson being alluded to in the appended '& Co'. [C. Gilbert, *Chippendale*] C.G.G.

Ferguson, James Adam, 16 Union St, Liverpool, u and victualler (1827–29). [D] Probably Adam James Fergusson.

Ferguson, John, address unrecorded, cm or furniture dealer (1687–92). In 1690 he submitted an account for 'a very large fine japan looking glass and frame, table and stands bought by her Majesty's command'. In 1691 he provided for Kensington Palace 'a japan cabinett agreed by her Mat.ʸ for 50 guinneys'. Between 1687/88–1692 he supplied 'one dozen and a half chairs' to the Royal Hospital, Chelsea, costing £6 15s. [*DEF*; *Conn.*, vol. LVII, 1920, p. 90; PRO, LC9/280, p. 29; *Wren Soc.*, vol. XIX, p. 85] See Mary Ferguson.

Ferguson, John, Leeds, Yorks., cm (1791–1822). Trading at Gale's Yd, Call Lane, 1817–22. As a journeyman cm named in the list of journeymen in basic sympathy with the *Leeds Cabinet and Chair Makers' Book of Prices*, 1791. [D]

Ferguson, Mary, address unrecorded, cm or furniture dealer (1686). Supplied Kensington Palace 'a fine table stand and looking-glass frame £108.6.8.' In 1686 she presented a petition for the delivery to her of some 'white wood boxes, Tunbridge deskes, which had been sent by her to Holland to be laquered there'. A few days later, the Customs Commissioners delivered to her 'some cases of Dutch lacquer'. [*DEF* citing *Calendar of Treasury Books*, 8 December 1686; *Conn.*, vol. LVII, 1920, p. 90] Possibly the wife of John Ferguson.

Ferguson, Matthew, Chelsea, London, joiner and cm (1773). Declared bankrupt, *Gents Mag.*, November 1773.

Ferguson, Robert, Newcastle, cm (1824–27). Trading at Groat Mkt in 1824, and 38 Middle St, St Nicholas's Churchyard, in 1827. [D]

Ferguson, Thomas, 47 Edmund St, Liverpool, joiner and cm (1824). [D]

Ferguson, William James, Oxford St, London and Lancaster, cm and u (1794–1840). In 1794 he witnessed the indentures of Henry Whiteside to R. &. G. Gillow. Admitted freeman of Lancaster, 1817–18, 'on a gift of Mr. Redmayne, the late bailiff of the bretheren'. Recorded in partnership with Henry and Edward Whiteside and Leonard Redman (or Redmayne) and described as 'late Gillows' at 176–77 Oxford St, 1813–35; and no. 178 in 1839. Trading as Ferguson, Redmayne & Co. in 1835, and Ferguson & Co. in 1839. Ferguson, Whiteside & Redman took out Sun Insurance policies on 23 September 1813 for £2,000, of which £1,700 accounted for stock, utensils and goods in trust and on commission; and another policy in 1840. Ferguson, Whiteside & Co. signed the prefatory recommendation to P. & M. A. Nicholson's *Practical Cabinet Maker*, 1826. [D; Preston RO, DDX 1122/1/1; Lancaster freemen rolls; GL, Sun MS vol. 463, ref. 885720; ref. 1339076, 1840]

Ferguson, William, 10 Manchester St, London, cm (1803). Subscribed to Sheraton's *Cabinet Dictionary*, and named in his list of master cabinet makers, 1803.

Ferguson, William S., Exeter, Devon, carver and gilder (1822–38). Recorded as W. S. in Bartholomew St, 1822–28, and as William in Heavitree, 1838. [D]

Fern, Geoffrey, on Little Tower Hill, Aldgate, London, u (1723). Insured goods and merchandise in his house for £500 on 25 June 1723. [GL, Sun MS vol. 15, ref. 28981]

Fernall, James, address unrecorded, upholder (1710). Admitted freeman of the Upholders' Co. on 13 April 1710. [GL, Upholders' Co. records]

Ferneyhough, William, Stoke, Staffs., cm (1818). [D]

Fernihough (or Fernyhough), Robert, London, billiard table and backgammon board maker (1808–29). Addresses given at 72 New Rd, Sloane St in 1808, with workshop at Silver St, Golden Sq., 1808–12; 36 Silver St, 1822–29; and 55 Parliament St, Westminster, in 1829. Took out Sun Insurance policies on 11 October 1802 for £600 on stock and utensils in his workshop at Silver St; and on 16 November 1812 for £900, £300 on his workshop, and £600 on stock and utensils. [D; GL, Sun MS vol. 445, ref. 821891; vol. 459, ref. 875669]

Ferniough, James, Church St, Leek, Staffs., cm (1816–22). [D]

Fernot, William, Beverley, Yorks., cm (1790). [Poll bk]

Fernyhough, James, 2 London Bridge, Southwark, London, billiard and backgammon table maker (1829). [D]

Fernyhough, Robert, 76 Moor St, Birmingham, cm (1800). [D]

Ferraby (or Fernaby), George, 42 Long Acre, London, u and cm (1820–23). Took out Sun Insurance policies on 15 May 1820 for £700, stock, utensils and goods in trust accounting for £480; and on 29 January 1821 for £700, £200 on stock, utensils and goods, £400 on his workshop in Nash's livery stables yd at 72 St Martin's Lane. [D; GL, Sun MS vol. 483, ref. 966931; vol. 488, ref. 976035]

Ferraby, Thomas, Windmill St, Tottenham Ct Rd, London, u (1835–39). Trading at no. 4 in 1835; no. 1 in 1837; and no. 11 in 1839. [D]

Ferraby & Hanson, 28 Princes St, Leicester Sq., London, cm (1820). [D]

Ferrand, Thomas, York, carver, gilder and frame maker (b. 1786–d. 1852). Trading in partnership with William Dodgson in Coney St, 1814–16, when the partnership was dissolved. Ferrand is recorded alone in Stonegate in 1823; and at 7 Mount, 1828–30. [D] Son of William Ferrand, plane-maker of York; app. to Robert Tomlinson, carver and gilder, on 11 May 1802 for seven years, 'no consideration in money being given'. Admitted freeman in 1809. [York app. reg. and freemen rolls] Marriage to Miss Dove at St Martin's Church, London, on 31 May 1814 reported in *York Courant*, 6 June. Notice regarding the dissolution of partnership with William Dodgson occurred in *York Courant*, 24 June 1816, when Ferrand announced the continuation of the carving and gilding business opposite the 'George Inn', Coney St. Dodgson moved to a shop in Coney St 'lately occupied by Mr. Baker, Confectioner, where he will continue the business of CARVER and GILDER . . . N.B. An Apprentice wanted.' Ferrand was imprisoned twice as an insolvent debtor, and his discharge announced in *York Courant*, 28 July 1821 and 10 October 1829. On 15 March 1823 it was announced in the same paper that his shop in Stonegate had been taken over by a clock and watchmaker. Ferrand's death on 4 April 1852, aged 66, was reported in *Yorkshire Gazette*, 9 April. His trade label, with the Coney St address, is found on a pair of early Georgian-style looking-glasses on loan to the Philadelphia Museum of Art; and also on an Adam-style looking-glass of oval form framed by swagged husk chains and surmounted by a vase. [*Antiques*, May 1968, p. 648, illus.] Label also recorded on a painted satinwood cabinet, decorated with garlands, arched panels of Classical landscapes, flowers and foliate scrolls; containing drawers and compartments enclosed by a pair of doors, the stand raised on turned and reeded tapering legs with stretchers. [Phillips', 26 March 1963, lot 62]

Ferrari, Bernard, Fishpool St, St Albans, Herts., looking-glass manufacturer (1839). [D]

Ferraro, Peter, London, carver, gilder and looking-glass manufacturer (1813–39). Addresses given at 15 New Ct, Broad St, Golden Sq., 1813; 5 Lower James St, 1815–35; 67 Quadrant, Regent St, 1826–37; 7 Regent St in 1831; and 69 Quadrant in 1839. Named in the Royal Household accounts supplying on 10 October 1813 a frame for a portrait of the Prince Regent, costing £45; and on 5 January 1815, miscellaneous pedestals for china jars, 'richly ornamented and gilt in burnished gold', £27 10s. On 10 October 1823 he was paid a total of £253 10s which included '3 large ornaments to the design of Mr. Jones for tops of pilasters in the Saloon, £165.0.0., and various other work to Mr. Jones order, all in the Saloon' at Brighton Pavilion. On 5 April 1831 he was paid for regilding pier glasses and picture frames at St James's Palace. [D; PRO, LC11/15, 18, 41 and 71]

Ferrers, George, 26 Gt Pulteney St, London, bed and mattress maker (1827–28). [D]

Ferrers, Thomas, address unrecorded, u (1688–89). Recorded in the Royal Household accounts, 1688–89, carrying out upholstery work for rooms of maids of honour, servants etc., at St James's and Whitehall Palaces. [PRO, LC9/279] Possibly:

Ferrers, Thomas, Bolt Ct, Fleet St, London, upholder (1701). Took out Hand in Hand Insurance policies on 13 October 1701 for seven years for £100 on a brick house, and £500 on his dwelling house at 'The Helmet'. [GL, Hand in Hand MS vol. 2, ref. 2151–52] Possibly:

Ferrers, Thomas, at 'The Sun', Fleet St, London, u (1706–32). Named in newspapers in 1706. Took out a Sun Insurance policy on 7 February 1712/13 on his goods in Arlington St, 'now in possession of Baron Groot, Envoy of Hannover'; on his house in Jarman St, Westminster, 'now in the possession of the Rt. Hon. Earl of Blessington'; and on his goods in Newbrook House, St James's Park, 'now in possession of the Rt. Hon. Charles, Earl of Peterborough'. On 29 September 1715 he insured goods and merchandise in his house. A Thomas Ferrers of London, u, was declared bankrupt, *Gents Mag.*, September 1732. [GL, Sun MS vol. 2, p. 186; vol. 5, p. 86; Beresford Chancellor, *Annals of Fleet Street*, 1912; Heal] See also Woodrose, u, at this address in 1702.

Ferres, Samuel jnr, 11 Cross St, Leonard St, London, cm (1808). [D]

Ferrier, Richard, Bristol, upholder (1715–22). [Poll bks]

Ferrimond, Joseph, Bishop Wearmouth, Sunderland, Co. Durham, joiner and cm (1798). [D]

Ferris, J., Devizes, Wilts., cm (c. 1820). George IV rosewood whatnot recorded, with three-quarter gallery to each of the five tiers, on turned supports, above a single drawer bearing the maker's label. [Sotheby's, Torquay, 30 September–1 October 1981, lot 835, illus.] Probably:

Ferris, John, Devizes, Wilts., u and cm (1839). [D]

Ferris, Samuel, London, upholder (1771–78). Trading at 38 Holborn in 1778. Son of Henry Ferris, maltster of Warminster, Wilts.; app. to Samuel Martin on 1 May 1771, and admitted freeman of the Upholders' Co. by servitude on 3 June 1778. [GL, Upholders' Co. records]

Ferryhouse, William, Stoke, Staffs., cm (1798). [D]

Fersey, Francis, 11 Suffolk Pl., Hackney Rd, London, carver and gilder (1839). [D]

Fertel, —, 13 Well St, Oxford St, London, cm (1829). [D]

Few, Edward, 46 Oxford St, Chorlton-upon-Medlock, Manchester, cm and u (1836). [D]

Fewel(l), James, Carnaby Mkt (or St), London, cm (1749). [Poll bk]

Fewkes, Joseph, Leicester, turner (1784). App. to Richard Seal, spinning wheel maker; admitted freeman in 1784. [Leicester freemen rolls]

Fewkes, Joseph, Leicester, u (1837). [Leicester freemen rolls]

Fewkes, William, High St, Leicester, cm (1800). Advertised auction of contents of property in *Leicester Journal*, 25 April 1800.

Fewller, Samuel, 6 Chapel St, Liverpool, cm (1761–81). Petitioned freedom as son of John Fewler, and admitted freeman on 12 March 1761. [D; Liverpool freemen reg. and committee bk]

Fey, William, Plymouth, Devon, cm and u (1822–38). Addresses given at Lower Broad St in 1822; Cambridge St in 1836; and Bilbury St, 1836–38. [D]

Fice, William, 12 East St, Plymouth, Devon, cm and u (1838). [D]

Fiche, Peter, Denmark St, London, carver (1797). Declared bankrupt, *Billinge's Liverpool Advertiser*, 20 November 1797.

Fichel, George, 20 John St, Goodge St, London, carver and gilder (1820). [D]

Ficke, Peter, 46 Compton St, Soho, London, carver and gilder (1789). [D]

Fickling, R., 133 Bishopsgate Without, London, cm (1837). [D]

Fickus (or Finkus), Thomas, Taunton, Som., carver and gilder (1817–30). Declared bankrupt, *Exeter Flying Post*, 13 March 1817. Trading at East St, 1822–30. [D]

Fiddeman, James, Whitechapel Rd, London, cm (1825). [D]

Fiddeman, Robert, Norwich, cm (1829). App. to Edward Woolverton; admitted freeman on 24 July 1829. [Norwich freemen reg.]

Fidel, John & Son, James, Faringdon, Oxon., cm and u (1823–40). Trading as James and John in 1823; John & Son at Marlborough St in 1840; and James Fidel jnr at Market Pl., 1840. [D]

Fides, Benjamin, St John's, Worcester, cm and u (1830). [D]

Fidler, Harvey, Staindrop, near Barnard Castle, Co. Durham, u (1824). Son bapt. on 27 September 1824. [PR(bapt.)]

Fidler, Richard, Bullocksmity, Stockport, Cheshire, cm (1818). [D]

Fidler & Son, 25 Plumtree St, Bloomsbury, London, carvers and gilders (1790–93). [D]

Fidoe, Anthony, address unrecorded, upholder (1704–12). Son of William Fidoe, yeoman of Stanford, Worcs.; app. to Thomas Dixon on 6 December 1704, and admitted freeman of the Upholders' Co. by servitude on 19 September 1712. [GL, Upholders' Co. records]

Fidoe, Thomas, London, upholder (1708–31). Address given at 'The Three Golden Chairs', over against the Saddlers' Hall and Half Moon Tavern, in Cheapside, 1711–31. App. to Henry Winton, and admitted freeman of the Upholders' Co. on 1 September 1708. Took app. named William Barlow, 1719–26. Took out a Sun Insurance policy on 15 March 1714 on his goods. Advertised in *London Journal*, 20 May 1721, his stock of 'Beds ready made . . . made full fashionable and as well as if bespoke, from nine to thirteen foot high, more or less if required.' [GL, Upholders' Co. records; GL, Sun MS vol. 3, ref. 3771; *Apollo*, February 1960, p. 34; Heal; Harris, *Old English Furniture*, p. 21]

Fidoe, Thomas, at 'The Old Red Lyon Inn', Kingston, Surrey, upholder (1723). Took out a Hand in Hand Insurance policy on 26 June 1723 for £200 on a house on the west side of the market, £200 on house abutting, and £200 on a house nearby. [GL, Hand in Hand MS vol. 27, p. 183]

Field, Benjamin, 3 Union St, Bishopsgate St Without, London, upholder and appraiser (1802). Declared bankrupt, *Billinge's Liverpool Advertiser*, 11 October 1802. [D]

Field, Charles, 1 Bowling St, Westminster, London, u (1839). [D]

Field, H. W., 2 West Strand, London, miniature picture and looking-glass frame and case maker (1835–39). [D]

Field (alias Fearby), Henry, York, cm (1833). Son of Ellen Hick; app. to Thomas Walls, cm, on 18 December 1833. [York app. reg.]

Field, J., 21 Pitfield St, Hoxton, London, bed and mattress maker (1822–23). [D]

Field, James, at 'Ye Desk & Bookcase', Aldermanbury, London, cm (1727). Took out a Sun Insurance policy on 10 February 1727 for £300. [GL, Sun MS vol. 22, p. 550]

Field, James, Downton, Wilts., cm (1756). App. to Thomas How, cm, of Downton, Wilts., on 27 July 1756 for a fee of £15 15s. [*Wilts. Apps and their Masters*]

Field, John, Holborn, London, cm (1701). Took out a Hand in Hand Insurance policy in 1701 for £55 on a house, not his own, in Bermondsey; and four other similar policies. [GL, Hand in Hand MS vol. 1, ref. 1711–15]

Field, John, 1 New Meeting St, Birmingham, cm (1777–80). [D]

Field, John, Daventry, Northants., u (1786–93). Took out a Sun Insurance policy on 5 May 1786 for £100 of which utensils and stock accounted for £60. [D; GL, Sun MS vol. 336, p. 391]

Field, John, Brook End, Daventry, Northants., cm and u (1830). [D]

Field, John, 2 Backchurch Lane, London, cm (1821). Took out a Sun Insurance policy on 17 January 1821 for £100 of which household goods in the house of Leslie, cm, accounted for £60, and stock and utensils, £20. [GL, Sun MS vol. 484, ref. 976201]

Field, John, Wallingford, Oxon., cm (1823). [D]

Field, Joseph, London, cm (1793). Subscribed to Sheraton's *Drawing Book*, 1793.

Field, Matthew, 10 Court, Holloway Head, Birmingham, Windsor and fancy chairmaker (1839). [D]

Field, Nicholas, Worcester, joiner and cm (1760). App. to John Crump joiner and cm; admitted freeman on 26 May 1760. [Worcester freemen rolls]

Field, Robert, Wildness, St Bride's, London, cm (1767). Fined for non-service at St Bride's in 1767. [GL, MS 6561, p. 102]

Field, Robert, Stratton St Mary, Norfolk, cm (1839). [D]

Field, Thomas, 'next door to the Plaster Head', King St, Soho, London, carver (1749). Rococo trade card recorded. [Poll bk; Heal]

Field, Thomas, 'with Mr. Ladyman of Fleet Market', London, upholder (1772). Son of William Field; app. to J. Sturges, merchant tailor, and admitted freeman of the Upholders' Co. by servitude on 2 September 1772. [GL, Upholders' Co. records]

Field, Thomas, 6 Bath St, Cold Bathfields, London, cm and broker (1777–79). Took out Sun Insurance policies in 1777 and 1779 for £200 of which utensils and stock (in 1779 at 34 Bath St) accounted for £60. [GL, Sun MS vol. 261, p. 341; vol. 273, p. 540]

Field, Thomas, 5 Plumb Tree St, St Giles's, London, carver (1784). Took out a Sun Insurance policy in 1784 for £200 on a house at 3 St James St, Grosvenor Sq. [GL, Sun MS vol. 324, p. 114]

Field, Thomas, 12 Princes St, Cavendish Sq., London, carver and gilder (1804–08). Took out Sun Insurance policies on 8 December 1804 for £650, £200 on his house and workshop, and £50 on utensils, stock and goods in trust; and on 2 January 1806 for £750, £200 on his house and workshop, and £50 on utensils, stock and goods in trust. [D; GL, Sun MS vol. 431, ref. 769131; vol. 434, ref. 785060]

Field, Thomas, 57 Nelson St, Birmingham, joiner, cm and coffin maker (1839). [D]

Field, William, Cannon St Rd, St George's East, London, cm and u (1822–27). Trading at no. 41, 1822–23, and no. 43, 1826–27. [D]

Fielder, —, 8 Princes St, London, chairmaker (1803). Subscribed to Sheraton's *Cabinet Dictionary*, and named in his list of master cabinet makers, 1803.

Fielder, Richard, Portsmouth, Hants. cm (1739). Submitted an account to the Duke of Gordon in October 1739, which included '10 small Chaiers at 19s pr. Chaier — £9.10.0; 2 Elbow Chaiers at 27s pr. Chaier — £2.14.0; A Writing Chaier — £3.3.0' and 'A Tea Box — £1.1.0'. The account is accompanied by a note which reads: 'Plese your Grace I have sent the Goods According to your Grace's Order I hope the will come safe and Plese, the will be at the White Hart Inn in the Bourow South Wark Tomorrow Evening the 25 of this Instant: I hope your Grace will Rec^ve Them Safe and will be Plesd with the Bothoms It wass my Lord's Advice I did Them with French Carpiting, The Price Being but one Shilling pr. Chaier More: I have mead Bould according to your Grace's Desier to Draw on your Grace for the Under Menchend Goods Payable to Mr. Robert Shallett at the Black Boy near Temple Barr London . . .'. A note of 24 October 1739 requests payment of £17 2s to Robert Shallet from the Duke in Craven St, Strand. Receipt is dated 2 November 1739. [Scottish RO, GD 44/51 or 57/465/4/47]

Fielder, Thomas, Greek St, Soho, London, carver, gilder, looking-glass and picture frame manufacturer (1829–39). Recorded at no. 26 in 1829, and no. 3, 1835–39. Trade card in Landauer Coll., MMA, NY. [D]

Fieldhouse, Richard, Hollow Lane, Wolverhampton, Staffs., chest and bed maker (1770). [D]

Fielding, —, address unrecorded, carver and gilder (1825). Named in the Windsor Royal Archives on 21 May 1825 receiving £13. [RA 35591]

Fielding, O., 20 Mount St, Devonport, Plymouth, Devon, gilder (1823–24). [D]

Fields, J., address unrecorded, cm (1803). Subscribed to Sheraton's *Cabinet Dictionary*, 1803.

Fields, Simon Henry, Vine St, Evesham, Worcs., cm and u (1840). [D]

Fieldus, Peter, Otley, Yorks., joiner and/or cm (1834). [D]

Fife, George, Postern, Newcastle, cm (1782–1824). Subscribed to Sheraton's *Cabinet Dictionary*, 1803. Announced in *Newcastle Courant*, 6 May 1809, that he was moving 'to a smaller house the door above and will dispose of such a part of his furniture as he shall not have occasion for, by public auction', but indicated that he was continuing business. Supplied furniture to Cuthbert Ellison of Hebburn Hall, Gateshead, at some date between 1806–25. [D; Gateshead Ref. Lib., Ellison papers; *Furn. Hist.*, 1976]

Fifield, William, over against 'The George' Inn, Piccadilly, London, u (1714). Named in newspapers in 1714. [Heal]

Fildes, Benjamin, St John's, Worcester, cm and u (1828–40). Mentioned in connection with enquiry about bad debt customer, Jane Spicer, of Berwick, Lechmere & Co., bankers, Worcester. [D; Lloyds Bank archives, ref. 2081]

Fildes, George, 66 Lamb's Conduit St, London, cm (1835). [D]

Fildes, James, Shude Hill, Manchester, cm (1794–1800). Trading at no. 66 in 1794, and no. 65 in 1800. [D]

Fildes (or Fieldes), John, Lamb's Conduit St, London, cm and u (1807–28). Recorded at no. 20, 1807–23; nos 19–20, 1815–25; no. 26, 1819–25; and no. 19, 1826–28. [D]

Filliner, T. H., 34 Berners St, London, u, appraiser etc. (1835). [D] See H. & T. and Thomas Henry Filmer.

Fillingham, William, 64 Princes Rd, London, chair and sofa maker (1839). [D]

Filmer, H. & T., 34 Berners St, London, u (1837). [D] See T. H. Filliner.

Filmer, Thomas Henry, 34 Berners St, London, cm and u (1839). [D] See T. H. Filliner and H. & T. Filmer.

Finch, Gray, Newbury, Berks., cm (d. 1793). Will proved in 1793, which left £20 in cash, seven messuages, guns, shooting tackle and a chest of tools. [Berks. RO, DA1 156/42]

Finch, James, Holborn, London, cm (1776). Declared bankrupt, *Gents Mag.*, June 1776.

Finch, John, address unrecorded, upholder (1722–30). Son of John Finch, yeoman of Hawstead, Suffolk; app. to Cullum Wicks on 7 March 1722, and admitted freeman of the Upholders' Co. by servitude on 2 December 1730. [GL, Upholders' Co. records]

Finch, John, Little Armoury, Westminster, London, cm (1744). Declared bankrupt, *Gents Mag.*, August 1744.

Finch, John Williams, Excise Passage, High St, Exeter, Devon, u (1813). Son John Fisher and daughter Mary Ann bapt. at St Stephen's Church, All Hallows, Goldsmith St, on 10 January 1813. [PR(bapt.)]

Finch, Joseph, St Bartholomew St, Newbury, Berks., cm and u (1840–42). [D]

Finch, Stephen, 'Tunbridge', Kent, cm (1826). Daughter Elizabeth by Ann Finch bapt. in the parish of SS Peter and Paul, 3 December 1826. [PR(bapt.)]

Finch, Thomas, Birmingham, cm (1757). Took app. named Brazier in 1757. [S of G, app. index]

Finch & Smith, King St, Covent Gdn, London, carpet and upholstery warehousemen (1764). Named in the Petworth accounts on 30 May and 2 June 1764 for work done for the Earl of Egremont. [V & A archives]

Fincher, S., 11 Newton St, Holborn, London, japan chair manufacturer (1830). [D]

Fincher, William, Worcester, chairmaker (1747). [Poll bk]

Findlay, Alexander, Whitcomb Ct, Oxendon St, London, cm (1772–78). Signatory to 'The Real State of the Complaints of the Cabinet Makers as published & signed by the Committee', in *Gents Mag.*, June 1772. Took out a Sun Insurance policy in 1778 for £200 of which £30 accounted for utensils, stock and goods. [GL, Sun MS vol. 263, p. 337]

Findlay, William, Nightingale Lane, London, cm (1778–82). Trading at 4 Jones Ct in 1778, and 9 Three Tun Ct in 1782. Took out Sun Insurance policies in 1778 for £100, and in 1782 for £200 on houses. [GL, Sun MS vol. 271, p. 139; vol. 304, p. 276]

Findley, William, Upper Charles St, Leicester, cm and u (1835–42). [D]

Finer, James, London, u (1784–1812). [Colchester poll bks]

Finer, William, Tendring, Essex, cm (1780–81). [Colchester poll bks]

Finer(s), William & James, 19 Leadenhall St, London, cm and upholsters (1786–96). Admitted freemen of the Upholders' Co. by redemption in 1786, William on 6 September, James on 22 November. Took out Sun Insurance policies together on 18 July 1786 for £200, of which £150 accounted for utensils and stock; and on 10 July 1787 for £500 on house, utensils and stock. [D; GL, Upholders' Co. records; GL, Sun MS vol. 338, p. 160; vol. 345, p. 312]

Finer, William, Camomile St, Bishopsgate St, London, cm and u (1784–1821). Trading at no. 21, 1796–1819, and no. 24, 1816–19. Named in Sheraton's list of master cabinet makers, 1803. Took out Sun Insurance policies on 27 April 1808 for £1,000, stock and utensils accounting for £700; and on 26 April 1810 for £1,200, £700 on stock and utensils. [D; Colchester poll bks; GL, Sun MS vol. 446, ref. 816366; vol. 452, ref. 844192]

Finkle, —, London, carpenter (1721). Sent to 1st Duke of Portland 'An Account of what is Due in London for Equipage, Furniture, workmanship &c. to August 1721 — £664-7-5'. [Notts. RO, Pw B 90]

Finlay (or Findlay), John, Hull, Yorks., cm, tide waiter, painter and furniture broker (1826–46). Recorded at Marvel St, Drypool in 1826; 34 New George St, 1831; 57 Dock St, 1831–35; and Francis St, 1838–40. [D]

Finlayson, James, Midford Pl., Tottenham Ct Rd, London, cm and chairmaker (1786–1817). Recorded at no. 6, 1804–17. Took out Sun Insurance policies on 27 June 1786 for £300, utensils and stock accounting for £200; and on 5 July 1791 for £600 of which £580 accounted for two shops, sawpit, stock and goods. John and James Finlayson of Bedford Pl. took out insurance on 17 July 1809 for £800 of which workshop, stock, utensils and shop accounted for £600. Subscribed to Sheraton's *Drawing Book*, 1793, and named in the list of master cabinet makers, in his *Cabinet Dictionary*, 1803. [D; GL, Sun MS vol. 337, p. 626; ref. 585595; vol. 447, ref. 832770]

Finlayson, Jn, 45 Upper Baker St, New Rd, London, cm and u (1827–28). [D]

Finlayson, John, 20 Bernard St, Southampton, Hants., chairmaker (1834–39). [D]

Finn, Robert, London, cm (1793). Subscribed to Sheraton's *Drawing Book*, 1793.

Finnemore, James, 15 Sun Tavernfields, St George's East, London, cm and u (1827–28). [D]

Finney, Charles, Derby, joiner and cm (1728–52). Took app. named Capp in 1738. Advertised house in Cornmarket for letting, *Derby Mercury*, 6–13 October 1752. [S of G, app. index]

Finney, Charles, Derby, joiner and cm (1827). Declared bankrupt, *Liverpool Mercury*, 1 June 1827.

Finney, John, Derby, joiner and cm (b. 1738–d. 1804). Had two apps, John Ward of Derby in 1797, and Richard Humber. Death, aged 76 reported in *Gents Mag.*, August 1804. Succeeded by Charles Finney of Derby, perhaps his son.

Finnis, George, Hythe, Kent, cm (1823–24). [D] Possibly of Finnis & Ronalds.

Finnis, Henry, London, carver and gilder (1835–39). Addresses given at 16 Moor Pl., Kennington Rd, 1835–37, and 19 York Pl., Lambeth, 1839. [D]

Finnis, Jeremiah, Danehill, Margate, Kent, carver and gilder (1823–29). [D]

Finnis, Robert, Hythe, Kent, u (1768–1803). Trading in High St in 1803. Son of Robert Finnis, carpenter of Dover; app. to John Allen on 6 May 1768, and admitted freeman of the Upholders' Co. by servitude on 17 September 1781. Took out Sun Insurance policies on 18 February 1791 for £200; and on 2 February 1793 for £200 on a house with barn and stable at Sandgate, near Folkestone, and £100 on household goods. [D; GL, Upholders' Co. records; GL, Sun MS vol. 375, p. 468; vol. 392, p. 292] Possibly of Finnis & Ronalds.

Finnis, W., 2 St Thomas's Pl., Gt Dover St, London, carver, gilder and looking-glass manufacturer (1837). [D] See Finnis & Co.

Finnis, William, 8 Hall Pl., Lower Kennington Lane, London, carver and gilder (1829). [D]

Finnis & Co., London, carvers, gilders and looking-glass manufacturers (1804–39). Addresses given at 19 Blackman St, 1804–15 and 1820; 153 Half Moon Inn, Southwark, 1817; 153 High St, Southwark, 1819–25; no. 152 in 1825; 2 Thomas Pl., Gt Dover Rd in 1835; 111 Blackman St and 2 Dover Rd in 1837 and Thomas Pl. and 111 Blackman St in 1839. [D] See W. Finnis.

Finnis & Ronalds, Hythe, Kent, cm and auctioneers (1826–39). [D] See George and Robert Finnis.

Finschard(?), —, address unrecorded, upholder (1813). Named in the Longford Castle, Wilts. accounts in 1813 receiving £424 15s 6d. [V & A archives]

Finstwaite, Christopher, near 'The King's Arms' tavern at the west end of St Paul's, London, u (1715). Named in the newspapers of 1715. [Heal]

Fiora, J., Long Row, Nottingham, looking-glass maker (1814–15). [Goodison, *Barometers*]

Fipping, Benjamin, Stamford, Lincs., cm (1725). Took app. named Lindsey in 1725. [S of G, app. index]

Fipps, John, Petty France, London, u (1749). [Poll bk]

Firbank, Christopher, York, carver (1724–60). App. to Edward Raper, carver and mason, on 4 May 1724. Took his son, John Firbank, as app. in 1757; and Matthias Freer in 1760. [York app. reg.]

Firby, John, 78 Paradise Row, Chelsea, London, cm and u (1823). [D]

Firmage, W., Leicester, looking-glass maker (1791). Advertised in *Leicester Journal* in 1791 that he made girandoles, looking-glasses and picture frames in burnished gold.

Firman, Robert, Sible Hedingham, Essex, cm (1832). [D]

Firmin & Sutton, High Holborn, London, upholders (1767–68). [D]

Firth, G., address unrecorded. Stamp found on pair of mid Georgian mahogany open armchairs with shaped rectangular backs, pierced vertical splats between outcurved arm supports, upholstered seats, square fluted legs and stretchers. [Christie's, 15 February 1979, lot 84]

Firth, Gabriel, St James, Westminster, London, upholder (1742). Took out Hand in Hand Insurance policies on 1 April 1742 for £400, £250 (assigned to John Aldridge in 1746), and £250. [GL, Hand in Hand MS vol. 62, refs 13736, 67529, 67530]

Firth, James, York, cm (1830). Son of Henry Firth, carpenter of Allerton Park; app. to Edward Steward and Arthur Shores on 23 October 1830. [York app. reg.]

Firth, John, Todmorden, Lancs., cm (1822–37). Trading at Wood Shade in 1834, and Shade, Todmorden Chapelry, 1837. [D]

Firth, John, Thorne, Yorks., joiner and/or cm (1828–34). Recorded in Market Pl., 1828–29, and King St, 1831. [D]

Firth, Joseph, Dewsbury, Yorks., cm (1830–37). Trading in Daw Green in 1830, and Webster Hill in 1837. [D]

Firth, Thomas, 168 Borough High St, London, u (1783). [D] Possibly Thomas Fish.

Fischer, William, 3 Nottingham Ct, Castle St, Long Acre, London, cm and clothes dealer (1780). Took out a Sun Insurance policy in 1780 for £100 of which utensils, stock and goods accounted for £40. [GL, Sun MS vol. 284, p. 469]

Fish, George, Paull, Holderness, Yorks., joiner and cm (1812). App. to George Harper in April 1812. [Hull app. reg.]

Fish, John, Long Acre, London, cm (1749). [Poll bk]

Fish, John, Leeds, Yorks., journeyman cm (1791). Named in the *Leeds Cabinet and Chair Makers' Book of Prices*, 1791, among other journeymen in basic sympathy with its contents.

Fish, John, Gt Yarmouth, Norfolk, cm (1807–41). Recorded at Somerley (Somerleyton, Suffolk?) in 1807; and Howard St, Gt Yarmouth, 1818–39. [D; Gt Yarmouth poll bks]

Fish, Joseph, Stratton, Cornwall, cm (1836). Daughter Susannah born at Stratton and bapt. at the Wesleyan Church in Holsworthy, Devon, in 1836. [PR(bapt.)]

Fish, Peter, Hopton, Suffolk, cm (1744–d. 1788). Two walnut bureaux bear an inscription by Peter Fish. The earliest is veneered in walnut with two small and two long drawers and is decorated with two rows of chevron banding and crossbanding. The interior is fitted with a well and inlaid with a chequer pattern and a half compass medallion. Written in pencil underneath a drawer is 'Maker Peter Fish for Mrs. Verlander, Hopton, Suffolk. Decbr. 15th 1744'. The strengthening blocks of the feet are also stamped 'P.F.'. The second bureau is of similar pattern but with a single row of

chevron banding, the interior having a central cupboard door with columns either side and drawers and pigeon holes. On one of the pull-out columns is written 'Made by Peter Fish, Hopton, Suffolk, Janauary 1749'.

Hopton is a village approximately ten miles north-east of Bury St Edmunds and in the 1801 Census is listed with a population of 433. The parents of Peter Fish appear to have moved into the village after his birth as the first reference to the name Fish appears in the parish records in 1728. Peter Fish was married on 1 November 1748 and two sons are recorded as being bapt.: Peter in 1750 and Samuel in 1754. No other details of the family have been found in Hopton, possibly because they moved into the adjoining parish of Garboldisham as that is the place of residence given in his will which was proven on 13 August 1788. [*Furn. Hist.*, 1978; Christie's, 27 November 1980, lot 98] R.W.

Fish, Thomas, 168 Borough High St, London, u (1773–82). [D] Possibly Thomas Firth.

Fish, Thomas, 4 Bridewell Alley, Norwich, cm and carver (1801–03). [D]

Fish, William, Bude, Cornwall, cm and u (1839–44). [D]

Fisher, Benjamin, Heath, West Bromwich, Staffs., cm and u (1830). [D]

Fisher, Edward, 12 Beer Lane, Tower St, London, carver and gilder (1809–23). [D]

Fisher, Edward, 36 Leadenhall St, London, carver and gilder (1835–39). [D]

Fisher, Elizabeth, 5 Oxendon St, London(?), cm (1783). Took out a Sun Insurance policy in 1783 for £500 of which utensils, stock and goods accounted for £40. [GL, Sun MS vol. 306, p. 593]

Fisher, Evan, Preston, Lancs., wood throwster (1742). [Preston Guild record of burgesses]

Fisher, Francis, Lincoln, joiner and cm (1764). Son of Joseph Fisher; app. to Henry Stanley, cm and joiner. [Lincoln app. reg.]

Fisher, Hannah, Parliament St, Nottingham, cm (1835). [D]

Fisher, Henry, Birmingham, cm (1742–62). Named in the Preston Guild record of burgesses, 1742–1762. Took apps named Turner in 1757 and Gardner in 1761. [S of G, app. index]

Fisher, Henry, Michael Lane, Whitehaven, Cumb., joiner and/or cm (1811). [D]

Fisher, Jabez Henry, Exeter, Devon, carver and gilder (1826–30). In 1826 he succeeded to the business of Duchemin at 7 High St, adding stationery, art materials, pier tables, cornices, frames and lamps to the stock. [*Exeter Flying Post*, 29 July 1826] Moved to 253 High St, at the corner of Castle St in 1828. [*Exeter Flying Post*, 31 June] Declared bankrupt, same paper, 11 December 1828 (as James Henry Fisher, *Liverpool Mercury*, 12 December 1828). Moved to Cathedral Yd, 'recently Moll's Coffee House' in 1830. [*Exeter Flying Post*, 13 May] and also in that year recorded at 40 Paris St. [*Exeter Journal*, 1830] and in directories at 253 High St. In *The Alfred*, 29 July 1828 he advertised 'a superb assortment of every article in the GILDING & CARVING department, together with a splendid variety of fancy articles — paintings, pencil & other drawings — Chimney & pier glasses. Glasses polished & silvered — All descriptions of frames elegantly executed — Arms, Crests, seals engraved.' On 2 September 1828 he advertised 'for a respectable youth as an apprentice to the Business of CARVING & GILDING — He would be treated as one of the Family.' [D]

Fisher, Jacob, Bridge St, Workington, Cumb., joiner and/or cm (1829). [D]

Fisher, James, Bishopsgate St, London, freeman long-bow

maker, by trade a cm (1755). Employed one non-freeman for three months in 1755. [GL, City Licence bks, vol. 1]

Fisher, James, address unrecorded. In January 1796 he was paid £9 3s 9d for three bedsteads for the Retreat Quaker Asylum in York. [Borthwick Inst., Retreat MS H/1]

Fisher, James, 1 Paradise St, Marylebone, London, cm (1808). [D]

Fisher, James & Clarkson, Edward, 7 Gloucester St, Curtain Rd, London, cm (1821). Took out Sun Insurance policies on 25 July 1821 for £1,000 on house and workshop; and for £1,700, of which stock and utensils accounted for £1,500. [GL, Sun MS vol. 484, refs 981688–89]

Fisher, James, 23 Hare St, Bethnal Green, London, chair and sofa manufacturer (1829). [D]

Fisher, John, next door to 'The Peacock', Shoe Lane, London, gilder and cm (1722). Insured goods and merchandise in his house for £300 on 28 January 1722. [GL, Sun MS vol. 15, ref. 27568]

Fisher, John, London(?), upholder (1757–72). Recorded in Crutched Fryers in 1772. Son of Richard Fisher, maltster and farmer of Henley-on-Thames, Oxon. App. to Samuel Hibberdine on 13 December 1757, and admitted freeman of the Upholders' Co. by servitude on 7 February 1765. [GL, Upholders' Co. records]

Fisher, John, Liverpool, cm (1761). Petitioned freedom on servitude to Roger Dewhurst and Peter Gerrard, paying 6s 8d. Admitted freeman on 6 March 1761. [Liverpool freemen reg. and committee bk]

Fisher, John, 4 Queen St, Liverpool, cm (1787–90). [D]

Fisher, John, Lancaster, Named in the Gillow records, 1799–1803. [Westminster Ref. Lib.]

Fisher, John, Cumb., cm (1783–1811). Recorded at Curwen St, Workington in 1811. Supplied furniture to Workington Hall, receiving £12 5s 10d in August 1783; and £11 6s 4d on 26 June 1784, which included mending a chair, and supplying an oak camp bedstead, four toilet tables, a camp bedstead with turned posts, and a four-post bedstead in mahogany. [D; Cumbria RO, Curwen MS]

Fisher, John, 10 Michael St, Whitehaven, Cumb., joiner and/or cm (1829). [D]

Fisher, John, 79 Leonard St, Shoreditch, London, cm (1820). [D]

Fisher, John, Liverpool, cm (b. 1776–1827). Born on 28 December 1776. Petitioned freedom on birthright as son of Joseph Fisher, potter, paying 3s 4d. Admitted freeman in 1827. [Liverpool freemen's committee bk] Possibly:

Fisher, John, 24 Christian St, Liverpool, cm (1827). Admitted freeman on 17 October 1827. [Liverpool freemen reg.]

Fisher, John E., Hotwells Rd, Bristol, cm and u (1823–26). [D]

Fisher, John, Masham, Yorks., joiner and cm (1823–40). [D]

Fisher, John, Woodbridge, Suffolk, cm and u (1824–39). Trading in partnership with William Fisher in 1824; and alone at Bridewell St in 1830 and Bredfield St, 1839. [D]

Fisher, John, Liverpool, u (1832–39). App. to Bartholomew Tyrer in 1832, and admitted freeman on 31 July 1839. [Liverpool app. enrolment bk and freemen reg.]

Fisher, John, 32 (Little) Bartholomew Close, London, cm (1835–37). [D]

Fisher, John, 21 New St, Cloth Fair, London, cm (1835–37). [D]

Fisher, Joseph, in the open part of Tooley St, near 'The Ram's Head Tavern', Southwark, London, u and appraiser (1724). Named in newspapers in 1724. [Heal]

Fisher, Joseph, at 'The Black Lyon' in Houndsditch, near Aldgate Church, London, u, appraiser, undertaker and cm (c. 1740). Trade card gives long list of types of furniture made, including 'Buroe tables, chamber tables . . . pillar and claw tables, dining tables . . . in walnut tree, mahogany and wainscot.' [Banks Coll., BM]

Fisher, Joseph, address unrecorded, draper, by trade an upholder (1753). Master of John Waylett III, 1753. [GL, Upholders' Co. records]

Fisher, King, 17 Stubbs Buildings, West St, Hull, Yorks., cm (1838–39). [D]

Fisher, King, 2 Norman St, St Luke's, London, carver and gilder (1839). [D]

Fisher, Peter, 14 Newton St, Holborn, London, carver and gilder (1808). [D]

Fisher, Robert, Lancaster. Named in the Gillow records in 1799 working on a wardrobe. [Westminster Ref. Lib., Gillow vol. 344/98, p. 1523]

Fisher, Robert, Liverpool, cm (1835–39). Trading at St James's Terr., 81 Stanhope St in 1835; and 1 Back Chester St, Toxteth, 1837–39. [D]

Fisher, T., 5 Hollen St, Soho, London, chairmaker (1820). [D]

Fisher, Thomas, Newcastle Ct, Temple Bar, London, cm (1784). [Bristol poll bk]

Fisher, Thomas, Liverpool, cm (1795–d. by 1831). Trading at 23 Lionel St, Gerrard St, 1800–03. Admitted freeman on 9 November 1795. Marriage to Miss Faull at St Nicholas's Church reported in *Billinge's Liverpool Advertiser*, 19 January 1795. Dead by 1831 when the death of his widow, Ann Fisher, aged 56, was reported in *Liverpool Mercury*, 25 February 1831. [D; Liverpool freemen reg.]

Fisher, Thomas, Lancaster, Named in the Gillow records in 1800 working on a chest. [Westminster Ref. Lib., Gillow vol. 344/98, p. 1601 b]

Fisher, Thomas, York, cm (1804–12). App. to William Hawkin, cm, on 17 April 1804, and admitted freeman in 1812. [York app. reg. and freemen rolls]

Fisher, W. & H., Shambles, Preston, Lancs., chairmakers (1814–15). [D]

Fisher, William, York, cm (1783–84). Recorded in Fossgate in 1784. Son of Thomas Fisher, translator; admitted freeman in 1783. [York freemen rolls and poll bk]

Fisher, William, London, cm (1789–96). Admitted freeman of Canterbury in 1789, and polled there in 1796 when stated of Clerkenwell, London. [Canterbury freemen rolls and poll bk]

Fisher, William, Woodbridge, Suffolk, cm and u (1824–39). Trading in partnership with John Fisher in 1824; and alone in New St, 1830, and Brook St, 1839. [D]

Fisher, William, Liverpool, cm (1829–35). Recorded at 14 Portland St in 1829, and 14 Peach St, 1835. [D]

Fishpool, William, St Michael's Hill, Bristol, u and trunk maker (1820–36). Recorded at no. 8, 1820–29, and no. 49, 1832–36. [D]

Fishwick, Edward, Liverpool, u (1762–67). Petitioned freedom on servitude to Lloyd Baxendale, paying 6s 8d in 1767. Named in the Preston Guild record of burgesses in 1762. [Liverpool freemen's committee bk]

Fisk, Samuel, Market Hill, Woodbridge, Suffolk, u and cm (1830–39). [D]

Fisk, William, Debenham, Suffolk, cm and chairmaker (1830–39). [D]

Fiske, Robert, 2 Duke St, West Smithfield, London, cm (1807–17). [D]

Fitch, J., 15 Berwick St, Soho, London, cm and u (1817). [D]

Fitch, James, Chequer St, St Albans, Herts., cm, u and builder (1823). [D]

Fitch, John, 26 Chandler St, Grosvenor Sq., London, cm (1808). [D]

Fitch, William, 9 Oxford St, Brighton, Sussex, cm and u (1832). [D]

Fitchet(t), John, London, upholder (1710–d. 1744). Trading in Bartholomew Close in 1727. Son of William Fitchet(t), upholder of Westminster; app. to Robert North on 4 October

1710; admitted freeman of the Upholders' Co. by servitude on 11 June 1718. Took app. named John Woodward, 1721–29. Named in newspapers in 1727. [GL, Upholders' Co. records; Heal]

Fitchet(t), William, Westminster, London, upholder (1718). His son, John Fitchet(t) admitted freeman of the Upholders' Co. in 1718. [GL, Upholders' Co. records]

Fitt, James, London, dressing and morocco case maker (1829–35). Trading at 35 Coldbath Sq., Clerkenwell, 1829, and 12 King's Terr., Pentonville, 1835. [D]

Fitter, B. P., Norwich, cm (1820). Former app., John Buttifant, cm, admitted freeman on 16 March 1820. [Norwich freemen reg.]

Fitzgerrald, James, 98 High Holborn, London, cm (1789). [D]

Fitzhugh (or Fitzlugh), Samuel, Regent St, Leamington, Warks., cm and u (1835–37). Listed at no. 36 in 1835 and no. 50 in 1837. [D]

Fitzjohn, Daniel, St Ives, Hunts., cm and chairmaker (1770). Advertised in *Cambridge Chronicle and Journal*, 8 September 1770, for journeymen chairmaker and cm.

Fitzwalter, Francis, Nottingham, carver and gilder (1825–35). Recorded at Bridlesmith-gate in 1825, Toll St, 1828–35, and High Pavement in 1835 also as a fancy stationer. [D]

Fitzwalter, Fraser, Toll St, Nottingham, carver and gilder (1832). [D]

Fitzwalter, Joseph, Nottingham, carver and gilder (1798–d. 1804). Probate will dated 6 July 1804. Death of 'Fitzwalter — Carver of Nottingham' reported in *Gents Mag.*, 1804. [D; Notts. RO, probate records]

Fitzwalter, Joseph, Houndsgate, Nottingham, carver and gilder (1834). [D]

Fitzwalter, T., Nottingham, carver and gilder (1814–41). Recorded in Houndsgate in 1814 and at 29 Bridlesmith Gate, 1832–41. Trade card reads: 'T. Fitzwalter, Carver and Gilder, Bridlesmith-Gate, Nottingham, Old Frames regilt equal to new and Paintings cleaned and repaired.' [D; Landauer Coll., MMA, NY]

Fitzwalter, Thomas & Francis, Bridlesmith-gate, Nottingham, carvers and gilders (1818). [D]

Fitzwalter, Thomas snr, Houndsgate, Nottingham, carver, gilder and carver in wood, stone and marble (1822–28). [D]

Fitzwalter, Thomas jnr, Bridlesmith-gate, Nottingham, carver and gilder (1822–35). [D]

Fitzwalter, Thomas, Green St, St George's, Hanover Sq., London, carver (1749). [Poll bk]

Fitzwalter, Thomas, Rosemary Lane, Newcastle, carver and gilder (1787). [D]

Fitzwalters, —, Broad Lane, Nottingham, carver and gilder (1799). [D]

Flack, John, Shepherd St, Oxford Mkt, London, cm and u (1823–27). Trading at no. 17, 1823–25, and 19 Shepherd's Mkt, 1826–27. [D] See Richard Flack.

Flack, John, 81 Gt Saffron Hill, London, chair and sofa maker (1835–39). [D]

Flack, Richard, Shepherd St, Oxford St, London, cm and chairmaker (1820–35). Trading at no. 17 in 1820, and at 19 Shepherd's Mkt, 1835. [D] See John Flack.

Flack, Richard, 17 South Audley St, London, u (1839). [D]

Flack, Thomas, Little Chelsea, Chelsea, London, cm and u (1823). [D]

Flamston, Richard, 8 Eldon St, Finsbury Cresc., Moorfields or Finsbury, London, cm and u (1825–28). [D]

Flamston, Thomas, Broker Row, Moorfields, London, broker and upholder (1793). Took out a Sun Insurance policy on 18 September 1793 for £650 of which utensils and stock accounted for £350. [GL, Sun MS vol. 397, p. 59]

Flamstone, Thomas, Houndsgate, Nottingham, joiner and cm (1799). [D]

Flanegan, John H., Hereford, carver, gilder, picture frame and looking-glass manufacturer (1835–40). Recorded at St Owen St in 1840, the address given on his trade label. Submitted bills dated September 1835 and December 1836 to Captain N. L. Pateshall, RN of Hereford, for picture frames totalling 13s 9d and 9s 6d. [D; Hereford Lib., Pilley Coll., no. 2305, notebk 3; Herefs. RO, F60/543 and 632]

Flanner, James, Wisbech, Cambs., chairmaker (1718). Took app. named Knight in 1718. [S of G, app. index]

Flashman, George, St Mary Major, Exeter, Devon, cm (1803). [Militia Census]

Flashman, George, Dover, Kent, cm (1832–39). Trading at Last Lane, 1832–34; as George & Co. there in 1838; and at 8 Market Pl. and Castle St. in 1839. [D]

Flashman, Henry, Exeter, Devon, cm (1761–d. 1808). Trading in South St, 1791–95, and Fourth St, 1796. Took app. named Parnell in 1761. Took out a Sun Insurance policy in 1782 for £300 on utensils and stock. Notice in *Sherborne Mercury*, 28 March 1808 concerned 'demands on the state of the late Mr. Henry Flashman of the City of Exeter, cabinet maker, deceased 21 March 1808'. H. Flashman jnr, cm and chairmaker, of South St advertised in *Exeter Flying Post*, 17 March 1808 informing 'Friends of his Late Father and the Public in General that he has Commenced Business on his own Account'. [D; S of G, app. index; GL, Sun MS vol. 303, p. 57; Militia Census, 1803]

Flashman, Joseph, Berwick St, Soho, London, cm and u (1808). [D]

Flashman & Horne, Hythe, Kent, cm, auctioneers and appraisers (1832–34). [D]

Flather, E., 41 Duke St, Little Britain, London, cm etc. (1826–27). [D]

Flather, James, 41 Duke St, West Smithfield, London, portable desk, dressing case, work box and cabinet case maker and cabinet liner (1835–39). [D]

Flatt, London, cm (1727–44). Supplied six Windsor chairs costing £2 5s in 1727 to Holkham Hall, Norfolk. Notice in *Daily Advertiser*, 13 October 1744 concerned the theft 'out of the House of Mr. Flatt, a cabinet-maker in Red Lion Street, Holborn, a Man's Mazarine Blue Coat . . .'. [V & A archives]

Flavell, William, Lady Well Walk, Birmingham, cm (1839). [D]

Flaxman, Robert, London, cm, carpenter and joiner (1820–37). Recorded at 25 Fleur de Luce Ct, Fleet St in 1820, and 29 Fetter Lane in 1837. [D]

Flaxman, William, Woodbridge, Suffolk. Handwritten label found inside lid of mahogany writing box with inlaid decoration, one false and one frieze drawer. Label reads: 'William Flaxman made this box in June 1828 Aged 16 Years and 8 Months. Woodbridge Suffolk.' [M. Colman Coll.]

Fleck, Henry, Egremont, Whitehaven, Cumb., joiner and/or cm (1828–29). [D]

Fleet, Francis, North St, Chichester, Sussex, cm, broker, paper hanger, u and undertaker (1826). Trade card continues: 'A large assortment of seasoned Patent Floor Cloths.' [D; Johnson Coll., Bodleian Lib., Oxford; *Furn. Hist.*, 1974]

Fleet, James, North St, Chichester, Sussex, cm and u (1823). [D]

Fleet, Jos., West Cross, Tenterden, Kent, turner and chairmaker (1839). [D]

Fleet, Richard, Smarden, Kent, carver and gilder (1839). [D]

Fleetwood, Richard, Liverpool, cm (1780–1802). Petitioned freedom on servitude to Charles Charles in 1780, and admitted freeman on 11 September. In 1790 he took app. named Peter Kay, who petitioned freedom on 1802. Notice in *Williamson's Liverpool Advertiser*, 21 March 1782, concerned his wife, Martha's debts, which he refused to pay. [Liverpool freemen reg. and committee bk]

Fleetwood, Richard, 19 Judd St, Brunswick Sq., London, u and house agent (1835–39). Trading in partnership with Gairdner as cm and u in 1839. [D]

Fleming, E., 178 Queen St, Portsea, Portsmouth, Hants., cm and u (1839). [D]

Fleming, Hannah, 4 Chandos St, Covent Gdn, London, upholder and cm (1800). Took out a Sun Insurance policy on 30 October 1800 for £1,600 of which £980 accounted for utensils and stock. [GL, Sun MS vol. 419, ref. 709511] See William Fleming.

Flem(m)ing, John, Rose St, Covent Gdn, London, cm and u (1749). [Poll bk]

Fleming, John, Vere St, London, u (1774). [Poll bk]

Fleming, John, Rose Pl., Liverpool, cm (1811). [D]

Fleming, Jonah, Cocker Bridge End, Cockermouth, Cumb., cooper, turner and chairmaker (1829). [D]

Fleming, Joshua, Carlisle, Cumb., joiner and/or cm (1811–29). Trading at Scotch St in 1811, and Wings Arms Lane, 1829. [D]

Fleming, Matthias, Stafford Rd, Pimlico, London, u (1839). [D]

Fleming, Matth. J., Back Rd, St George's East, London, cm and u (1839). [D]

Fleming, Richard, 190 Sloane St, Chelsea, London, upholder (1817–20). [D]

Fleming, Richard, Ebury St, Pimlico, London, cm and u (1830–39). Recorded at no. 6 in 1835, and no. 37, 1839. Declared bankrupt, *Chester Courant and Anglo-Welsh Gazette,* 16 November 1830. [D]

Fleming, Robert, 76 Oxford St, London, upholder (1781). [D]

Fleming, Thomas, 12 Prospect Row, Devonport, Plymouth, Devon, cm (1838). [D]

Fleming, William, 4 Chandos St, Covent Gdn, London, cm and u (1775–1808). Trading in partnership with Robert Bartleman (or Ba(n)tleman), 1775–77, and in 1775 took out a Sun Insurance policy together for £1,300, of which utensils and stock accounted for £1,000. Recorded in partnership with Frederick Fleming, 1779–96; and with Shep(p)ard (or Shepherd), 1801–08. Fleming & Sheppard are named in Sheraton's list of master cabinet makers, 1803. William subscribed to Sheraton's *Drawing Book,* 1793, and *Cabinet Dictionary,* 1803. Probably the William Fleming of London who in 1775 supplied '2 mahogany medicine chests' to Hopetoun House, Lothian. [D; GL, Sun MS vol. 240, p. 566; Scottish RO, Hopetoun MS, Box 106–07] See Hannah Fleming.

Fleming, William, 31 Cherry St, Birmingham, cm and u (1809). [D]

Fleming, William, Queen St, Portsea, Portsmouth, Hants., cm, u and chairmaker (1823–39). Recorded at no. 185 in 1823 and no. 8, 1830–39. [D]

Flemming, James, York, cm (1758–74). Trading in Spurriergate in 1774. Admitted freeman in 1758. [York poll bk and freemen rolls]

Flemming, Lancelot, Liverpool, cm, provision dealer and joiner (1810–21). Addresses given at 1 Rose Pl. in 1810; 5 Edgar St with shop in Hunter St, 1816; and 18 New Scotland Rd with timber yd at 8 Hunter St in 1821. [D]

Flesher, Benjamin, 29 Albion St, Leeds, Yorks., cm and u (1828–37). [D]

Fleshman, Henry, Oxford, cm (1760). Took app. named Smith in 1760. [S of G, app. index]

Fletcher, —, Rose St, Soho, London, cm (1793). Subscribed to Sheraton's *Drawing Book,* 1793.

Fletcher, Mrs Ann, 12 Providence Sq., Osborne St, Hull, Yorks., u (1839). [D]

Fletcher, Benjamin, 49 Baldwins Gdns, Leather Lane, London, broker and u (1784). Took out a Sun Insurance policy in 1784 for £300 of which utensils and stock accounted for £240. [GL, Sun MS vol. 322, p. 272]

Fletcher, Charles, Deansgate, Marlow, Bucks., cm/joiner (1823). [D]

Fletcher, Edward, Chester, u (1824–26). Addresses given at Wellington Pl. in 1824 and Goss St, 1826. Admitted freeman on 16 October 1824. [Chester freemen rolls and poll bk]

Fletcher, Elizabeth, 21 High St, Knightsbridge, London, cm and u (1839). [D]

Fletcher, Ellen, 13 Bevington Bush, Liverpool, (1835). [D]

Fletcher, Henry, Liverpool, u (1761–d. between 1812–17). Petitioned freedom as son of Thomas Fletcher, cooper, in 1761, paying 3s 4d. Admitted freeman on 13 March 1761. [Liverpool freemen reg. and committee bk]

Fletcher, James, London, clockcase maker (1730–81). Recorded at Long Lane, West Smithfield in 1730; St Bartholomew the Great, 1741–49; and 36 Bartholomew Close in 1781. Took out a Sun Insurance policy on 27 February 1730 for £300 of which household goods and stock in trade accounted for £260. Took out Hand in Hand Insurance on 25 February 1741 for £125, renewed in 1749; and Sun Insurance in 1781 for £600, £150 on his shop, utensils and stock. Named as a Fellow of the Society of Arts and Manufactures, 1760–68. [GL, Sun MS vol. 32, ref. 53421; vol. 296, p. 114; Hand in Hand MS vol. 62, ref. 23902]

Fletcher, James, 3 Whitelion Passage, Wych St, London, chair and sofa maker (1827–28). [D]

Fletcher, James, London, cm and u (1835–39). Recorded as cm in Church St, Hackney in 1835, and as u in Back Lane, Lower Clapton, 1839. [D]

Fletcher, Jeremiah, London, upholder (1715–d. 1723). Recorded at 'The Lyon & Lamb', Strand, in 1720 when he took out a Sun Insurance policy on 14 March on goods and merchandise in his house. Rebecca Fletcher took out insurance after his death in 1723. In 1715 Jeremiah Fletcher supplied beds, now at Hampton Court, to the Prince of Wales. Named in the Royal Household accounts, 1716–18, with Thomas Phill, regarding the refurbishing of parts of the Houses of Parliament, Windsor and Hampton Court. [GL, Sun MS vol. 11, p. 37; PRO, LC9/286; *Conn.,* June 1977, p. 141]

Fletcher, John, Ormskirk, Lancs., cm (1756–98). Took app. named MacDonald in 1756. [D; S of G, app. index]

Fletcher, John, London, cm and u (1776–97). Addresses given at 11 Distaff Lane, 1784; 8 Houndsditch, 1790–97; and Fenchurch St, 1802. Son of Thomas Fletcher, ironmonger of Abingdon; app. to Richard Wright and Samuel Burton on 7 August 1776. Admitted freeman of the Upholders' Co. by servitude on 6 October 1784. Subscribed to Sheraton's *Drawing Book,* 1793. [D; GL, Upholders' Co. records]

Fletcher, John, Sheffield, Yorks., cm (1798). [D]

Fletcher, John, Hull, Yorks., carver and gilder (1816–26). Recorded at 17 New Dock Walls, 1816 and 1823; 10 and 18 Dagger Lane, 1817–23; and Robinson Row in 1826. [D]

Fletcher, John, Howden, Yorks., cm and joiner (1823–34). Addresses given at Bridgegate in 1823; Vicar Lane, 1826; Corn Mkt Hill, 1828–29; and Market Pl., 1831. [D]

Fletcher, Joseph, at 'The King's Arms', St Paul's Churchyard, London, leather gilder to His Majesty and u (1716–d. 1732). Advertised in *London Gazette,* 16 December 1716 that he 'Maketh & Selleth all sorts of hangings for Rooms and Staircases, settees and Screens, of the newest fashion'. On 19 December 1728 Fletcher was paid £1 7s for a gilt leather screen sent to Moulsham Hall for Earl Fitzwalter. In partnership with John Conway in 1732, when Fletcher died, and Conway continued the business under his own name until 1739. Fletcher's death reported in *Gents Mag.*, October 1732. [A. C. Edwards, *The Accounts of Benjamin Mildmay, Earl Fitzwalter*, p. 100; Heal citing Hilton Price, *Signs of Old London*]

Fletcher, Kay, Packer St, Rochdale, Lancs., chairmaker (1818–25). [D]

Fletcher, Peter, 92 Pitt St, Liverpool, u (1821). [D]

Fletcher, Peter, Main St, Cockermouth, Cumb., cooper, turner and chairmaker (1829). [D]

Fletcher, Richard, at 'The Golden Head', 50, corner of Tower Royal, Watling St, London, removed from 143 Fleet St, carver, gilder and picture frame maker (*c.* 1770). Rococo trade label found on back of picture at Freshford Manor, Bath, states that he 'Makes & Sells all Sorts of Carved Brackets, Sconces, Picture and Chimney Frames, Walnuttree & Mahogany ditto, with all manner of black Peartree & Deal Frames, for Maps, Prints or Drawings. Pictures carefully Clean'd & broken Paintings Mended: with Carvers & Gilders work in all its various branches expeditiously done after the neatest & newest Taste, at the lowest Prices. NB. Prints &c. Pasted Framed and Glazed very reasonable. I always keep by me Peartree & Deal Mouldings fit for Picture frames of any Breadth, ready to make up at a short warning or Sold as they are for Town or Country.' [Heal Coll., BM]

Fletcher, Richard, 9 Norfolk St, Middlx Hospital, London, carver and gilder (1835–39). [D]

Fletcher, Roun(d)cival, Hull, Yorks., carver, gilder and painter (1790–1826). Addresses given at High St, 1790–99; Castle Row, 1792; 25 Finckle St, 1803–14; 12 Castle St, 1817–22; 62 Mytongate, 1823; and 3 New Dock Walls, 1826. Named as Clerk to Holy Trinity Church in 1803. Took app. named James Waters of Hull in August 1799. One of a family of carvers, gilders and painters active in Hull in the second half of the 18th century. Bills from the Fletchers are recorded for carrying out painting at Burton Constable Hall, near Hull. [D; Hull app. reg.]

Fletcher, Sam., Gracechurch St, London, chairmaker (1775). Named in the calendar of marriage licence bonds of Suffolk on 31 May 1775. [Suffolk RO, FAA: 50/2/94–104]

Fletcher, Samuel, Harleston, Norfolk, cm (1786–96). [Norwich poll bks]

Fletcher, Samuel, Beccles, Suffolk, cm and chairmaker (1802–07). [Norwich poll bks]

Fletcher, Samuel, Liverpool, cm (1810–35). Addresses given at 79 Hanover St in 1810; no. 69 in 1811; no. 70 in 1813; 128 Duke St, 1816; no. 20, 1824–27; and no. 27 in 1835. [D]

Fletcher, Thomas, Chatham, Kent, carver (d. 1685). [PCC Wills, Index Lib., vol. 10, 1948, p. 123]

Fletcher, Thomas, Kirk, Thomas & Mower, William, 48 Brewer St, London, cm (1791). Took out a Sun Insurance policy on 18 March 1791 for £300 of which £250 accounted for utensils, stock and goods in trust in Rose St, Soho. [GL, Sun MS vol. 373, ref. 580689]

Fletcher, Thomas, Rock St, Bury, Lancs., cm and chairmaker (1824–34). [D]

Fletcher, Thomas, Leeds, Yorks., cm (1826–37). Trading in Brown's Yd, Mill Hill, 1826, and Cross Ct, 96 Briggate, 1834. [D]

Fletcher, William, London, cm (1786). [Norwich poll bk]

Fletcher, William, Norwich, cm (1790). [Norwich poll bk]

Fletcher, William, Bury, Lancs., chairmaker (1793–1818). Recorded in Millgate, 1818. [D]

Fletcher, William, New Dock St, Hull, Yorks., cm (1814). [D]

Fletcher, William, Queen St, Portsea, Portsmouth, Hants., cm, u and chairmaker (1830–39). Recorded at no. 125 in 1830 and no. 122 in 1839. [D]

Fletcher & Hollingsworth, Liverpool, cm (1800–05). Trading in Thomas St, 1800–03, and Hanover St, 1805. [D]

Fleuriot, Peter, address unrecorded, upholder (1726–33). Son of Peter Fleuriot, late of London, merchant; app. to John Hibberdine on 1 June 1726, and admitted freeman of the Upholders' Co. by servitude on 6 June 1733. [GL, Upholders' Co. records]

Fleuriot (or Flewriot), William, London, u (1784–1803). Recorded at 7 Little George St in 1784, and 7 Gt Tower St, 1797–1803. Son of Peter Fleuriot, merchant of London; admitted freeman of the Upholders' Co. by patrimony on 4 August 1784. Named in Sheraton's list of master cabinet makers, 1803. [D; GL, Upholders' Co. records]

Fleuriot, William & Russell, James, Hull, Yorks., cm (1780). Declared bankrupt, *Gents Mag.*, April 1780.

Fleuritt (or Flewitt), Benjamin, Nottingham, joiner and cm (1803). Son of William Flewitt, labourer of Basford; app. to Samuel Dodd in 1803. [Nottingham app. list]

Flewker, Rob., Old Malton Gate, Yorks., cm (1828–40). [D]

Flex(t)on, John, Orchard St, Portman Sq., London, cm and u (1823–39). Recorded at no. 22, 1823–28; no. 20, 1835–39; and as John and Henry, 1827–28. [D]

Flexon, W., 22 Orchard St, Portman Sq., London, cm (1825). [D]

Flight, B., Exeter-change, Strand, London, organ builder and mahogany case maker (1801). [D]

Flight, Benjamin & William, Exeter-change, Strand, London, organ builders and mahogany case makers (1781–87). [D]

Flight & Kelly, Exeter-change, Strand, London, organ builders and mahogany case makers (1788–96). Trading as Flight, Son & Kelly, 1791–94. [D]

Flinn, Henry, Stacey St, Seven Dials, London, carver and gilder (1835–37). Recorded at no. 3 in 1835, and no. 2 in 1837. [D]

Flinn, Robert, 4 Stacey St, Compton St, London, carver and gilder (1808–20). [D]

Flint, Abraham, Cross St, Cheadle, Staffs., cm (1822). [D]

Flint, Abraham, Birmingham, cabinet case and clock case maker (1828–35). Recorded at Gt Brook St, 1828–30, and 30 Hampton St in 1835. [D]

Flint, Alexander, St Martin's Lane, London, cm and u (1822–39). Trading at no. 67, 1827–39. Took out Sun Insurance policies on 21 October 1822 for £700 on 'workmens chest of tools included in Mr. Russell's workshops'; and on 31 March 1823 for £600, £300 on stock and utensils, and £300 on a steam engine in workshops. On that date he also insured stock, utensils and goods in trust in house and workshops in tenure of Russell, cm, in St Martin's Lane, for £200. On 19 November 1823 Flint insured stock and utensils in his house for £300. [D; GL, Sun MS vol. 490, refs 997221–22; vol. 494, refs 1003290, 1014754; vol. 496, ref. 1010626]

Flint, Charles, St Martin at Palace, Norwich, chairmaker (1768). [Poll bk]

Flint, Charles, Spilsby, Lincs., joiner and cm (1822–35). [D]

Flint, Edmund, West Bromwich, Staffs., joiner and cm (1834). [D]

Flint, Henry, Greek St, Soho, London, cm, u and undertaker (1792–1835). Trading at no. 17 in 1793; no. 13, 1798–1813; no. 14, 1807–15; and no. 15, 1819–35. Recorded as Flint & Thomas at no. 13, 1796–1803. Took out Sun Insurance policies on 2 August 1792 and 6 January 1807 for £600, of which £450 accounted for utensils and stock. Named with Thomas in Sheraton's list of master cabinet makers, 1803. [D; GL, Sun MS vol. 389, ref. 603531; vol. 437, ref. 798546]

Flint, T., 20 Charlotte St, Bloomsbury, London, cm and u (1813). [D]

Flint, Thomas, 107 Gt Russell St, Bloomsbury, London, cm (1820). [D]

Flint, William, Yorkersgate, Malton, Yorks., cm (1834–40). [D]

Flint & Co., Russell St, Bloomsbury, London, cm (1803). Subscribed to Sheraton's *Cabinet Dictionary*, 1803.

Flint & McLellan, 114 Gt Russell St, Bedford Sq., London, u and undertakers (1803–08). Named in Sheraton's list of master cabinet makers, 1803. [D] Possibly Thomas Flint.

Flintham, Robert, Heydon St, Westminster, London, cm (1749). [Poll bk]

Flintoff, William, 19 Bartholomew Close, London, bedstead maker and carver (1775–84). Took out Sun Insurance policies in 1775 for £600 of which utensils and stock accounted for £200; and in 1779 for £100. [D; GL, Sun MS vol. 278, p. 89; vol. 242, p. 78]

Flintoff, William, 67 West Smithfield, London, cm, u and feather bed maker (1790–1808). Took out a Sun Insurance policy for £1,400 on 26 July 1803, in which year he was named in Sheraton's list of master cabiner makers. Trade card or bill head recorded. [D; GL, Sun MS vol. 427, ref. 750660; Heal]

Flintof(f)t, James, 115 Wardour St, Soho, London, u and cm (1808–37). Trading as Flintoft & McDonald, plate-case makers and u, in 1837. Flintoff & McDonald, u, are named in the accounts of Charles William Vane, Marquess of Londonderry, regarding the furnishing of Wynyard Park, Co. Durham, c. 1829–41. [D; Durham RO, D/LO/E 484, vol. 1]

Flintoft, John, 115 Wardour St, Soho, London, cm and u (1839). [D]

Float, Thomas, 14 Long Lane, West Smithfield, London, gilder, turner and frame maker (1747–84). Named in newspapers in 1747. Employed one non-freeman for eight months in 1768. Took out a Sun Insurance policy in 1781 for £200 of which £100 accounted for utensils and stock. Trade card or bill head recorded. [D; GL, City Licence bks, vol. 6; GL, Sun MS vol. 293, p. 296; Heal]

Flock, Richard, 19 Shepherd's Ct, Mayfair, London, u (1829). [D]

Flockton, John, Huddersfield, Yorks., cm and u (1814–37). Addresses given at North Bar in 1814; North gate, 1818–29; Market Pl., 1828–30; and Battye's Yd, Market Pl., 1837. Trading as John & Son in Market Pl. and Cross Church St, 1830–37. [D]

Flodberg, —, Little St Martin's Lane, London, cm (c. 1776). Named in the list of furniture makers compiled by the Duchess of Northumberland, c. 1776. [Gilbert, *Chippendale*, p. 154]

Flood, James, Honiton, Devon, cm (1823–24). [D]

Flood, James, 8 Charles St, Middlx Hospital, London, u, cm and chairmaker (1824–39). Recorded in the Signature Book of Herries, Farquhar & Co., private bankers of 16 St James's St, London, in 1824. [D; Lloyds Bank archives, bk 2055]

Flood, John snr, Norwich, cm and chairmaker (1800–24). App. to George Darking, and admitted freeman on 24 February 1800. His son, John Flood jnr, cm, admitted freeman on 13 November 1824. [Poll bks; Norwich freemen reg.]

Flood, John jnr, Norwich, cm and u (1824–39). Recorded at Charing Cross in 1839. Son of John Flood snr, cm and chairmaker; admitted freeman on 13 November 1824. [D; poll bk; Norwich freemen reg.]

Flood, Patrick, 124 Gt Ancoats St, Manchester, cm (1817–19). [D]

Flook, John, Wimborne, Dorset, chairmaker and turner (1823). [D]

Flower, James, London, upholder (1778–1802). Trading at 64 Minories in 1786, and Crow Nest Wharf, Wapping in 1802. Son of Stephen Flower, cheesemonger of the Minories; app. to John Phillips and Thomas Savill on 2 December 1778. Admitted freeman of the Upholders' Co. by servitude on 4 January 1786. [GL, Upholders' Co. records]

Flower, John, Bath, Som., cm (1774). [Bristol poll bk]

Flower, Matthew, Northallerton, Yorks., cm (1840). [D]

Flower, Samuel, Newmarket St, Birmingham, framemaker (1818). [D]

Flower, Thomas, 17 Hayser St, New Kent Rd, London, bedstead maker (1839). [D]

Flowers, Henry, London, carver, gilder and looking-glass manufacturer (1820–39). Addresses given at Alfred Pl., Newington in 1820; 5 Mount Row, Kent Rd, 1826; 1 Durham Pl., Lambeth Rd, 1835; and 24 Gt Dover St, 1839. [D]

Floyd, Thomas, Chester, chairmaker (b. 1796–d. 1831). Death on 22 February 1831, aged 35, reported in *Chester Courant and Anglo-Welsh Gazette*, 1 March 1831.

Fluke (or Fluck), Abraham, Worcester, upholder and cm (1785–99). Trading at 11 High St, 1797–98. App. to Thomas Howton, upholder, and admitted freeman on 17 January 1785. Former app., Moses Rayer, admitted freeman in 1798; and John Davis, as app. of Abraham and Isaac Fluke, in 1799. [D; Worcester freemen rolls]

Fluke, Isaac, Manchester, cm (1795). Declared bankrupt, *Billinge's Liverpool Advertiser*, 9 March 1795.

Fluke, Isaac, Worcester, cm and u (1799). Former app. of Abraham and Isaac Fluke, John Davis, admitted freeman on 17 June 1799. [Worcester freemen rolls]

Fluriot, M., 23 Cannon St, London, cm (1808). [D]

Fly, William, at the 'Sign of the Three Chairs', Cannon St, London, u (1719). A bill in the Lincoln RO lists work done and items supplied between 5 August and 21 November 1719, totalling £4 12s 6d. He was paid for putting up and moving beds and hangings, making headcloths and testers, covering window cornices; and supplying 'a Bedsted with Wheels', 'a single raised Tester Cutt Headbord', and a 'Sett of Cornishes & Base Mouldings'. Receipt dated 5 December 1719. [Lincoln RO, 2 ANC 12/D/19]

Flynn, Michael, Wardour St, London, u (1809–13). Named in the Bad Debts book of Herries, Farquhar & Co., private bankers of 16 St James's St, London, being paid £35 by John Dunn, carver and gilder, 27 Gt Pulteney St on 7 October 1809; and standing in debt of one penny in 1813. [Lloyds Bank archives, bk 2036]

Foard, E., 63 High St, Brighton, Sussex, cm (1822–24). [D]

Focan, —, address unrecorded. Top of a marquetry commode in the Royal Collection attributed to Pierre Langlois. c. 1765, is inscribed 'FOCAN', presumably a specialist inlayer. [*Conn.*, vol. 179, 1972, p. 187]

Fodden, William, Dennison St, Liverpool, cm (1787). [D]

Foden, Henry, High St, Leicester, carver and gilder (1815). [D]

Fogarty, Edward, 13 Hart St, Bloomsbury, London, u and designer (1814–15). [D]

Fogden, John, Shrewsbury, Salop, cm (1796). [Shrewsbury burgess roll]

Fogg, Edward, 6 Comburg Pl., Old Kent Rd, London, cm, u and furniture broker (1839). [D]

Fogg, J., London, chinaman to His Majesty (1824–28). Trading at 150 Regent St, 1826–28. Submitted a bill to Lord Gwydir for work done between 2 March 1824 and 15 April 1826, totalling £177 15s 8d. In March 1824 he provided a large mahogany stand, repaired and cleaned furniture including a 'french cabinet inlaid and Stand' for £10 5s; a 'French Table Inlaid with Porcelaine', and a 'Marq.ᵉ Cabinet Inlaid with 2 pieces of China'. On 17 February 1824 Fogg supplied a large commode and two covers; and on 16 March 1825, a 'Pair of Sq.ʳ Walnut Tree Pedest.ˢ Richly Ornamented with Gilt Mountings', costing £20. Fogg was also paid for china, glass, marble, and for cleaning 'Stuff Birds'. [Lincoln RO, 2 ANC 6/202/33]

Fogg, John, Liverpool, u (b. 1809–30). Recorded at 136 Coopers Hill in 1830. Born on 12 May 1809, son of James Fogg, cooper. App. to William Bickerstaff in 1823, and admitted freeman on 15 November 1830. [Liverpool app. enrolment bk, freemen reg. and committee bk]

Fogg, Samuel, 20 Bixteth St, Liverpool, cm (1787–90). [D]

Foggin(s) (or Foggen), John, Gateshead, Co. Durham, joiner and cm (1787–1801). Recorded in partnership with William Foggin at the 'Red Lion', High Church-chair in 1787, and Below Tollbooth, 1790. John alone is recorded at Church-stairs in 1795, and Oakwellgate in 1801. [D]

Foggitt, Ann, 7 Museum St, Bloomsbury Sq., London, cm etc. (1820). [D]

Foggo, William, Fighting Cocks' Yd, Denton-chare, Newcastle, joiner and cm (1833–34). [D]

Fokard, William, near Butter Mkt, Ipswich, Suffolk, joiner and cm (1747). Advertised in Ipswich Journal, 29 August 1747, that he 'is removed from the house next door to Mr. Moore's, Clock-Maker, into the late Dwelling house of Mr. Hicks, near the Butter-Market in Ipswich. Makes and Sells all sorts of cabinet goods, viz. desks, desk and book-cases, chests of drawers, with all sorts of tables, tea-boards, tea-chests, dumb-waiters, chairs carv'd and plain. He buys walnut-tree in Trees or Planks. The aforesaid House is to be let at Michaelmas next, and a small Tenement in St. Matthew's Parish.'

Fold, James, 3 Carpenter's Row, Hurst St, Liverpool, carver (1804). [D]

Fold, John, 3 Carpenter's Row, Hurst St, Liverpool, carver (1800–03). [D] See John Folds.

Folds, James jnr, Liverpool, carver, now hairdresser (1790). Admitted freeman on 20 June 1790. [Liverpool freemen reg.]

Folds (or Fowles), John, Liverpool, carver (1759–96). Addresses given in Argyle St, 1766; 1 Henry St, 1769; 13 Cleveland Sq. with shop and warehouse at 5 Park Lane in 1777; as ship carver at Cornhill and Cleveland Sq. in 1787; at 3 Carpenter's Row, with shop and warehouse in Cornhill in 1790; also 34 South Dock in 1790; and 19 Mason St in 1796. John Folds & Nephew, carvers, are recorded at 21 Mason St, 1805–10. In 1759 petitioned freedom on servitude to William Mercer; admitted freeman on 16 August. Took apps named Anderton in 1761; and William Folds in 1788, admitted freeman in 1796. [D; Liverpool freemen reg. and committee bk; S of G, app. index] Possibly two tradesmen of the same name are concerned here.

Folds, John jnr, Elton Ct, Norfolk St, Liverpool, carver, hairdresser by 1820 (1790–1820). Admitted freeman on 20 June 1790. Took app. named John Sumner in 1798, who petitioned freedom in 1806. His sons, Phillip Hind Folds, painter, born 25 August 1791, and Henry Folds, shipwright, born 13 December 1794, petitioned freedom on birthright in 1816. [Liverpool freemen reg. and committee bk] Either of the two John Folds above may be those now listed:

Folds, John, Park Lane, Liverpool, carver (1790–1807). Recorded at no. 48 in 1790 and 1807; no. 50 with shop at 18 Mason St, Wapping, 1800–04; and 56 Park Lane in 1805. [D]

Folds, John, Shaw's Alley, Liverpool, carver (1796–1805). Recorded at 3 Grayson St in 1796; no. 8 in 1803; and 21 Shaw's Alley in 1805. [D]

Folds, John, Liverpool, carver (1816–21). Trading at 22 Hurst St in 1810; no. 24 in 1816; and 8 Norfolk St in 1821. [D]

Folds, William, Liverpool, carver (1788–1811). Addresses given at 20 Frederick St in 1796; 22 Hurst St, Mersey St, 1800–04; and 30 Hurst St with shop at no. 227, 1805–11. App. to John Folds in 1788; admitted freeman on 27 May 1796. [D; Liverpool freemen reg. and committee bk]

Foley, William, Mount Ephraim, Tunbridge Wells, Kent, Tunbridge-ware manufacturer (1792–1809). In 1792 he subscribed £5 5s towards the new paving of the Walks. Named in the poor rate bks of Speldhurst parish in 1809. [Kent RO, P344/11/1]

Foley, William, Liverpool, cm (1821). App. to John O'Neill in 1821. [Liverpool app. enrolment bk]

Folgham, John, London, cm, case and knife-case maker, dealer in silver and plated goods (c. 1750–1803). Trade card, c. 1760, gives address opposite the 'Castle Inn', Wood St; trade card and directories, c. 1750–77 and 118 Fetter Lane; and 81 Fleet St, 1778–1803. Trading in partnership with his son, Timothy, 1790–1803; and John Folgham jnr is also recorded in 1787. Trade card, c. 1760, shows knife and dressing cases, and lists stock which includes knife-cases and writing desks 'Mounted in silver or Plain'. Folgham & Son of 81 Fleet St are known to have advertised their stock of 'Cabinet-ware, Upholstery, Cutlery, Plated Goods, Japanned Goods, Clay's Papier Machee and Umbrellas'. [Landauer Coll., MMA, NY] John alone took out a Sun Insurance policy in 1777 for £3,000, of which £2,000 accounted for utensils, stock and goods. John and Timothy took out insurance for £2,000 on 15 October 1802. [GL, Sun MS vol. 261, p. 528; vol. 423, ref. 738508] John Folgham's daughter's marriage was reported in Gents Mag., June 1787. Folgham & Son are named in Sheraton's list of master cabinet makers, 1803. Several of John Folgham's bills survive. One is for items supplied to Croome Court, Worcs., on 23 April 1765, costing £4 12s 6d, and comprising 'a neat mahogany folding fire screen with 3 leaves covered in green canvas'; a '28 inch oval crimson striped Pontipool Tea Tray'; and a '13 in. round Db. waiter'. Receipt is dated 1785. [V & A archives] A bill submitted to Stourhead, Wilts., on 25 August 1781 includes 'A portable mahogany writing desk lin'd with green cloth flap inside Compt with a pr. Ink Squares £3.3.0.' In 1783 he provided 'a neat Brown Jappann'd Tea Urn', and 'a neat Satinwood Tea Chest banded with Tulipwood.' Between 31 March 1802 and 2 February 1803 Timothy and John Folgham, cm, u and hardwaremen, supplied further items to Stourhead, including '6 neat mahogany Biddets fiddle shape compl. with Earthen pans £12.12.6.' [Wilts. RO, MS 383.4.1; 383.5.1] A bill dated 22 August 1781 to the Rev. M. Moore of Stretton Hall, Staffs., is for a silver-mounted and engraved drinking horn, costing £7 15s 9d. [V & A archives] Another, of 19 April 1787, was sent to Sir John Nelthorpe for '1 Pair of Oval Flatt Candlesticks'; and '1 Pair of Plat.d Top Ink Squares', costing £2 6s 6d; receipted by Timothy on 19 April 1787. Nelthorpe also bought a mahogany case, cutlery and '1 pair of Sqr. Foot'd & Fluted Candlesticks' on 30 April 1787, costing £5 14s 6d, receipted on 2 May by John Folgham jnr. [Lincoln RO, NEL 9/9/20, 21, 26 and 27] On 26 February 1798 John Folgham & Son supplied to Hatfield House, Herts., 'A solid mahogany Folio Copying Machine with brass corners and patent lock', costing £12. [Hatfield MS bills 597]

Folgham, Timothy, Fleet St, London, u, cm, cabinet and knife-case maker, dealer in silver and plated goods (1787–d. 1805). Receipted a bill for his father, John in 1787, and trading in partnership with him, 1790–1803, at 81 Fleet St. Recorded alone there, presumably wrongly, 1804–08. In 1799 he was fined for non-service at St Bride's. Took out Sun Insurance policies with his father on 15 October 1802 for £2,000 and £750. Death reported Gents Mag., May 1805. [D; GL, MS 6561, p. 124; GL, Sun MS vol. 423, ref. 738508]

Folker, Samuel Sheppard, North St, Brighton, Sussex, cm, carver and gilder to His Majesty, looking-glass manufacturer and printseller (1819–31). Addresses given at no. 137, 1819–21; Royal Colonnade, North St, 1822–28; and 143 North St in

1831. Children by Susannah Folker bapt.: William Thorp on 26 December 1821; Sara Thorp on 21 May 1823; John Ambros on 24 June 1825; William Henry on 1 September 1826; Alfred on 16 September 1828; and Alfred Hanley on 11 June 1830. Trade card, c. 1825, incorporates Royal coat of arms, and reads: 'S.S. FOLKER, Carver, Gilder & Frame Maker To His Majesty, Royal Colonnade, North Street, Brighton. PLATE GLASS WAREHOUSE.' Announced the opening of his premises at 137 North St in *Sussex Weekly Advertiser*, 1 February 1819, having arrived from Messrs. Boydell & Co., 90 Cheapside, London. Advertised in *Brighton Gazette*, 22 February 1821; and also 6 May 1821, when he claimed 'A Drawing Desk has been invented by Mr. S.S. Folker, of the Royal Colonnade, by which a lady may be enabled to mount her own drawings, and which may also be used as a reading desk. It has a drawer for paints and brushes, and by means of moveable joints, the frame is adapted either for portraits or landscape painting; and it also has an ingenious contrivance for holding books, which answers the purpose of a T. square' Folker worked at Brighton Pavilion in November 1830, repairing and gilding eight 'Turned Ornaments' for £2 8s; and in January 1831, repairing and gilding a glass frame for £11. [D; E. Sussex RO, PR(bapt.); Windsor Royal Archives] Possibly:

Folker, S. S., 3 Bridge St, Westminster, London, carver and gilder etc. (1835). [D]

Folker, William, Oxford, u (1784–1808). Trading at Corn Mkt in 1808. Furnished the rooms of Lord William Russell, younger brother of the 5th and 6th Dukes of Bedford, at Christchurch, Oxford, where he was a student, 1784–87. In November 1784 Folker provided a tent bedstead with blue check furniture and mattress; a mahogany washhand stand; an oval glass in gilt frame; a mahogany two-flap dining table; a mahogany Pembroke table; a tea tray and tea caddy; and a bureau bedstead painted mahogany colour. The bill, including repairs to a bureau and chair, totalled £28 18s 3d. A consolidated payment of £27 2s 2d was made to Folker in April 1785 'for fitting up my Lord William's rooms', but the work is not specified. Thereafter there are four bills for small items, and for maintenance, including 'repairing servant's bed; that for servant's room', in February 1787, for 4s. [D; poll bks; Bedford Office, London]

Follows, John, 2 Cable St, Oldham Rd, Manchester, chairmaker (1836). [D]

Follows, Thomas, Stafford, chairmaker and turner (1828–35). Recorded at St Chad's St in 1828 and Diglake, 1834–35. [D]

Fone, Samuel, Bristol, cm (1774–81). [Poll bks]

Fontaine, George Daniel, Dorking, Surrey, cm (1822). [D]

Fontaine (or Fountaine), George David, London, cm, u and undertaker (1800–26). Neo-classical trade card with figures of Hope and Britannia gives address at 13, opposite Middle Row, Holborn. Recorded at 25 Gt Russell St, Covent Gdn, 1800–12; and Dorking, Surrey in 1826. Subscribed to Sheraton's *Cabinet Dictionary*, and named in his list of master cabinet makers, 1803. Took out Sun Insurance policies on 18 October 1805 for £1,000, of which £770 accounted for utensils and stock; and on 1 March 1809 for £800 on his house and workshop. [D; Banks Coll., BM; GL, Sun MS vol. 434, ref. 781440; vol. 448, ref. 828512]

Fontaine, Peter, St Amherst(?), cm (1713–14). Took app. on 8 February 1713/14. [PRO, app. reg.]

Fooks, Charles B., 31 St Thomas St, Weymouth, Dorset, cm and u (1830). [D]

Foord, George, Wardour St, Soho, London, carver and gilder (1829–39). Recorded at no. 53 in 1829, and no. 52, 1835–39. [D]

Foord, William, Cranbrook, Kent, cm and u (1824–39). Notice in *Sussex Agricultural Express*, 12 May 1838, informed cm and u that 'THE OLD-ESTABLISHED BUSINESS, for many years carried on by Wm. FOORD of Cranbrook, in the County of Kent, TO BE DISPOSED OF, in consequence of a declining state of health. The stock is now much reduced, and the rent moderate.' [D]

Foot, George, Bristol, carver and gilder (1784–1812). Trading in Brandon St, 1799–1812. [D; poll bk]

Foot, John, Dorchester, Dorset, cm (1793). [D]

Foot, John, Peterborough, Northants., cm (1798). [D]

Foot, T., Monmouth Pl., Bath, Som., bedstead maker (1819). [D]

Foot, William, Bristol, bed-joiner (1784). [Poll bk]

Foote, Richard, High Wycombe, Bucks., chairmaker (b. c. 1791–1841). Son bapt. in 1813. Aged 50 at the time of the 1841 Census. [PR(bapt.)]

Foote, Samuel, Sheffield, Yorks., cm, u and furniture broker (1833–37). Trading at 31 Eyre St in 1833, and 18 South St in 1837. [D]

Footner, James, Lymington, Hants., cm and u (1823–30). Trading at High St in 1830. [D]

Footner, R., High St, Lymington, Hants., u and cm (1839). [D]

Forbes, Robert, Little Windmill St, London, cm (1774). [Poll bk]

Forbes, William, 51 Swallow St, London, cm (1782). Took out a Sun Insurance policy in 1782 for £100, of which £20 accounted for utensils in workshop of Mr Allan, cm, in Grosvenor Mews. [GL, Sun MS vol. 298, p. 310]

Forbes, William, 1 Hanover St, Hanover Sq., London, cm (1783). Insured his house for £200 in 1783 with the Sun Co. [GL, Sun MS vol. 319, p. 224]

Forbes, William, 55 Tottenham Ct Rd, London, cm (1790–93). [D]

Forbes, William, 122 Gt Portland St, London, u (1811–13). [D]

Force, Charles, 193 High St, Exeter, Devon, cm (1831). Announced in *The Alfred*, 7 June 1831, public auction of his stock of cabinet and upholstery furniture and premises to let with possession. Stock included mahogany and painted sideboards, wardrobes, wash-stands and dressing tables; telescope dining tables; rosewood card tables and chiffoniers; hair seat, rosewood and mahogany chairs and sofas; looking-glasses, dresssing cases, cellarets and music stools. Stock also included well-seasoned Spanish and Honduras mahogany and rosewood. On 9 August 1831 Force announced he was relinquishing the London paper hanging business. His stock was bought up by Mr H. Force.

Force, Henry, Exeter, Devon, cm and u (1823–40). Addresses given at Gandy St, 1823–25; 209 High St, 1825–30; and North St, 1839–40. Children bapt.: Edwin at St Paul's on 9 December 1823; Mary Louisa on 12 April 1826; and Edmund Warwick on 4 September 1828, both at All Hallows, Goldsmith St. Announced in *Exeter Flying Post*, 24 November 1825 that he was purchasing the business of William Sandford at 209 High St, and required several good workmen. In the same paper on 22 October 1829 a Mrs Gregory, teacher of handwriting, advertised lessons at her appartments at 209 High St. Force was declared bankrupt, same paper, 14 October 1830. [D; PR(bapt.)]

Ford, —, address unrecorded. Set of four George III mahogany chairs including a pair of armchairs recorded, with rectangular panelled top rails, curved X-frame cross panels with reeded down-curved arms and baluster supports, and stuffed seats raised on turned legs: some are stamped 'FORD'. [Sotheby's, 7 May 1971, lot 169] One item in a set of five single and an armchair, c. 1820–30, with X-framed backs, reeded uprights and turned front legs, at the Bowes Museum, Barnard Castle, Co. Durham is stamped under the seat rail 'FORD'.

Ford, —, Derby, turner and chairmaker (1793). [D]

Ford, Benjamin, London, chairmaker (1728). Named in the S.P.C.K. Subscription Ledger and Cash Book on 30 July 1728 receiving £16 9s. [FT9/2]

Ford, George & William, 12 St Paul's Churchyard, London, cm and u (1777–96). [D] See James Ford at this address.

Ford, George, 25 King St, Covent Gdn, London, cm and u (1822–23). [D]

Ford, George, 160 Piccadilly, London, u (1835). [D]

Ford, George, 126 Piccadilly, London, cm (1837). [D]

Ford, Henry, High Wycombe, Bucks., chairmaker (b. c.1821–41). Daughter bapt. in 1840. Aged 20 at the time of the 1841 Census. [PR(bapt.)]

Ford, Humphrey, Leicester or Derby, cm (1766–73). App. to Thomas Tippler, cm of Derby; and admitted freeman of Leicester in 1773. [Derby app. reg.; Leicester freemen rolls]

Ford, James, Bull Ring, Birmingham, u (1767). [D]

Ford, James, 12 St Paul's Churchyard, London, cm and u (1775–95). Recorded, probably wrongly, at no. 21 in 1783. Took out a Sun Insurance policy on 30 June 1790 for £1,700 on his house and goods. Declared bankrupt, *Billinge's Liverpool Advertiser*, 27 April 1795. [D; GL, Sun MS ref. 570945, p. 187] See George & William Ford.

Ford, James, Hull, Yorks., cm, u and undertaker (1814–39). Addresses given at 4 Clarkson's Entry and 50 Blanket Row in 1814; 7 Land of Green Ginger, 1817–22; 4 New Dock St, 1823; 31 Bond St, 1826–31; 41 Spaldine Pl., 1831; and 17 Blackfriargate, 1834–39. [D]

Ford, James, Honiton, Devon, cm (1823–24). [D]

Ford, James, High St, Berwick-upon-Tweed, Northumb., cm (1827–34). [D]

Ford, John, Liverpool, joiner and cm (1790–1811). Trading at 19 Princes St in 1790; 11 Leece St, 1805–07; and 21 Ranelegh St, 1810–11. [D]

Ford, John, Lancaster, carver and gilder (1794–1825). [Westminster Ref. Lib., Gillow records]

Ford, John, Temple St, Bristol, cm and furniture broker (1813–38). Recorded at no. 14 in 1813; no. 84, 1814–15; no. 86, 1816–19; and no. 95, 1821–38. [D]

Ford, John, Reading, Berks., cm and u (1820–40). Trading at Market Pl., 1820–26; and Sydney Terr., 1837. J. Ford is recorded at 40 Market Pl., 1830–40. [D; poll bks]

Ford, John, Wellington Pl., Clifton, Bristol, cm (1821–25). Recorded at no. 3, 1821–23; and no. 2, 1824–25. [D]

Ford (or Foord), John, Richmond Spring, Clifton, Bristol, carpenter, cm and undertaker (1839–40). [D]

Ford, John, Hallgate, Cottingham, Yorks., cm (1834). [D]

Ford, John, Boal St, King's Lynn, Norfolk, cm (1836). [D]

Ford, Joseph, St John's Bridge, Coventry, Warks., cm, u and paper hanger (1818–22). [D]

Ford, Mary, Godalming, Surrey, cm and u (1826–32). [D] See William Ford.

Ford, Richard, 32 Gt Carter Lane, London, cm, u, undertaker and bedstead maker (1839). [D]

Ford, Richard, Downley, High Wycombe, Bucks., chairmaker (b. c.1811–41). Aged 30 at the time of the 1841 Census.

Ford, Samuel, London and Reading, Berks., u (1768–1836). Recorded at 77 New Bond St in 1780; and Reading, 1794–1836; as Samuel jnr at Market Pl., Reading, 1820–26; and as S. & Sons, cm, at no. 40, 1823–36. Samuel Ford snr was son of Samuel Ford of Reading; app. to James Grange on 11 April 1768, and admitted freeman of the Upholders' Co. by servitude on 2 August 1780. Took out a Sun Insurance policy on 8 May 1801 for £490 on a house in tenure of Mr Earles, broker. [D; poll bks; GL, Upholders' Co. records; GL, Sun MS vol. 40, ref. 717976] Apparently three generations of tradesmen are concerned here.

Ford, Samuel, High Wycombe, Bucks., carpenter and chairmaker (1822–26). Son bapt. in 1822; and daughters in 1824 and 1826. [PR(bapt.)]

Ford, T., 13 Half Moon Cresc., White Conduit Fields, London, cm (1835). [D]

Ford, Thomas, Barnstaple, Devon, cm (1793). [D]

Ford, Thomas, King St, Derby, basket and chairmaker, turner (1818–35). Recorded at no. 3, 1823–29 and no. 4 in 1835. [D]

Ford, W., Bristol, carver and gilder (c. 1750s). Took app. named Thomas Law. [GL, P83/MRY1/867/123]

Ford, William, Scarborough, Yorks., cm (1773–84). App. to Mark Robinson, cm, and admitted freeman of York in 1773. Polled at York in 1774 and 1784. [York freemen rolls]

Ford, William, 23 Half Moon St, Bishopsgate, London, bedstead maker (1813). Took out a Sun Insurance policy on 14 June 1813 for £100 of which £80 accounted for his house. [GL, Sun MS vol. 461, ref. 883291]

Ford, William, 28 Primrose St, Bishopsgate, London, bedstead maker (1820). [D]

Ford, William, Godalming, Surrey, cm (1822). [D] See Mary Ford.

Ford, William, 1 Chapel Row, Bath, Som., cm (1826). [D]

Ford, William, Navigation Rd, Burslem, Staffs., joiner, builder and cm (1834). [D]

Ford, William, 1 Chapel St, Derby, cm and u (1835). [D]

Forde, John, Carpenter's Row, Liverpool, carver (1787). [D]

Fordham, James, Carpenters' Hall, London Wall, near Moorgate, London, cm and u (1727–45). Trade card states that he 'Makes all sorts of Cabinet & Upholstry Worke in the best manner new finished.' [Johnson Coll., Bodleian Lib., Oxford] Took out a Sun Insurance policy on 8 December 1727 for £1,000 on household goods and stock in trade. Co-partnership between James Fordham snr and jnr ended by deed signed at Carpenters' Hall in 1744. [D; GL, Sun MS vol. 24, ref. 43353; *Furn. Hist.*, 1974; Harris, *Old English Furniture*, p. 21]

Fordham, Thomas, Essex, cm (1786). Took out a Sun Insurance policy on 12 August 1786 for £200, of which utensils and stock accounted for £100. [GL, Sun MS vol. 338, p. 616]

Fordham, Thomas jnr, Braintree, Essex, u (1783–d. 1813). Named in the freeholders' bk, 1783. Probate will dated 1813. [Essex RO, Q/RJI/11 (Hinekford Hundred); *Wills at Chelmsford*]

Fordred, Jacob, address unrecorded, upholder (1706–29). Son of William Fordred of Canterbury, Kent. App. to Richard Fettiplace on 4 December 1706, and admitted freeman of the Upholders' Co. by servitude on 7 May 1729. [GL, Upholders' Co. records]

Fore, Samuel, Bristol, cm (1774–81). [Poll bks]

Foreman, Francis, Orchard St, Newcastle, cm (1811). [D]

Foreman, Henry, Coronation St, Bishop Wearmouth, Sunderland, Co. Durham, cm (1827–29). [D]

Foreman, James, address unrecorded, joiner (1699). A bill dated 1699 lists '3 cases of Drawers, a chest of Drawers & new doors for Mr. Grosvenor's Closet', costing £1 18s. [Chatsworth papers, account bk 4, p. 21]

Foreman, Peter, Newcastle, cm and joiner (1794–1838). Trading in partnership with John Chorley before 1794; alone at Court 48, Groat Mkt, Fenkle St in 1827; at Morrisons Entry, Groat Mkt, 1828–29; and as Peter & Sons at 4 Fenkle St, 1833–38. Notice in *Newcastle Courant*, 7 June 1794, that the co-partnership between Peter Foreman and John Chorley had been amicably dissolved. [D]

Foreman, William, Court 4, Fenkle St, Newcastle, cm (1827). [D]

Fores, John, 19 Cannon St Rd, St George's East, London, cm and u (1820–23). [D]

Fores, John, King's Terr., Commercial Rd, London, cm, u and auctioneer (1826–39). [D]

Fores, Thomas, 18 Broker's Row, Southwark, London, cm and u (1839). [D]

Foresitt, John, Maiden Lane, London, carver and gilder (1784). [D] Probably John Forfeit

Forester, John Bruce, Groat Mkt, Newcastle, cm (1834–38). Listed at no. 48 in 1838. [D]

Forester, William, 6 Narrowgate, Alnwick, Northumb., cm and joiner (1834). [D] See William Forster.

Forfar (or Forfur), John, London, upholder (1759–1802). Addresses given at 41 Houndsditch in 1772; Leadenhall St in 1778; Little St Mary Axe in 1781; Fenchurch St in 1786; Garlick Hill in 1794; and Islington in 1802. Son of John Forfar, mariner of St George in-the-East. App. to William Guidott on 6 September 1759, and Thomas Brown, merchant tailor, on 5 August 1762. Admitted freeman of the Upholders' Co. by servitude on 6 November 1766. Took app. named Andrew Pratt, 1768–72. [GL, Upholders' Co. records]

Forfeitt, John, Maiden Lane, London, carver and gilder (1774). [Poll bk] Probably John Foresitt.

Forman, A., 48 Marshall St, Golden Sq., London, cm (1825). [D]

Forman, A., 3 King's Terr., Commercial Rd, London, chairmaker (1826–27). [D]

Forman, Archibald, 27 Walnut Tree Walk, Lambeth, London, cm and u (1839). [D]

Formstone, John, Chester, cm (1784). App. to John Cooke of Chester, cm; admitted freeman on 3 April 1784. [Chester freemen rolls and poll bk]

Forrest, James, Manchester, cm (1819–25). Trading at 28 Shude Hill in 1819, and 26 Bury St, Salford in 1825. [D]

Forrest, Jeremiah, Wetherby, Yorks., joiner and/or cm (1837). [D]

Forrest, Robert, London, u (1793). Subscribed to Sheraton's *Drawing Book*, 1793.

Forrest, Thomas, 4 Old St, London, cm (1808). [D]

Forrest, William, Lancaster, cm (1751–73). App. to R. Gillow in 1751 and admitted freeman, 1764–65. Recorded in partnership with William Blackburn and Redman Bateman in 1765 when they took R. Russell as app. on 25 February. In partnership with Bateman only in 1769 when they took J. Hodgson as app. on 6 November and Thomas Cowper on 12 October 1773. [Lancaster app. reg. and freeman rolls; poll bk]

Forrest, William, 3 Bolton Ct, Preston, Lancs., cm (1825). [D]

Forrester, John, 10 Scarlatt St, Mansfield St, Liverpool, cm (1839). [D]

Forrester, Samuel, St Dunstan's Ct, Fleet St, London, cm (1775–91). Took out Sun Insurance policies in 1775 for £200, of which £115 accounted for utensils, stock and goods at no. 88 St Dunstan's Ct; and in 1791 for £400, £140 on utensils and stock at no. 8. [GL, Sun MS vol. 244, p. 200; vol. 375, p. 163]

Forse, C., Little Warner St, Clerkenwell, London, chair and cm (1825). [D]

Forse, George, 20 Stone Cutter St, Fleet Mkt, London, carver (1820). [D]

Forse, George, 18 Tash St, Gray's Inn Rd, London, carver in wood and cm (1839). [D]

Forsey, John, 8 Norman St, Old St, London, carver and gilder (1820). [D]

Forshaw, Nathaniel, Moor St, Ormskirk, Lancs., cm and chairmaker (1825–34). [D]

Forster, Arthur, Newcastle, u (1726). Admitted freeman on servitude on 13 October 1726. [Newcastle freemen rolls]

Forster, Barnabas, Gilesgate, Durham, cm and joiner (1828–29). [D]

Forster, George & Thomas, Eyre Lane, Sheffield, Yorks., cm and u (1833). [D]

Forster, George, 16 Clipstone St, London, fancy cm and u (1839). [D]

Forster, James, 9 Gt Portland St, London, cm and u (1826–39). [D]

Forster, John, Carlisle, Cumb., joiner and/or cm (1811–34). Trading at Lowthian's Lane, English St in 1811 and Grey Goat Lane, 1834. [D]

Forster, John, Frodsham, Cheshire, cm and joiner (1822–34). [D]

Forster, John, Head of Elvet Bridge, Durham, u (1827). [D]

Forster, John, Swalwell, Co. Durham, joiner, carpenter and/or cm (1832). [D]

Forster, John, Brunswick Terr., Gateshead, Co. Durham, cm and joiner (1838). [D]

Forster, John, 189 Whitechapel Rd, London, cm and u (1839). [D]

Forster, Robert, 36 Adam St, London, cm (1826). Polled at Maldon, Essex, in 1826.

Forster, Thomas, York, chairmaker (1729). On 2 October 1729 supplied for the Mansion House sixteen chairs at 11s each, and two arm chairs, 16s each, costing a total of £10 16s. [York City archives]

Forster, W., Stockton-on-Tees, Co. Durham, builder, cm, u and undertaker. 19th-century trade card in Landauer Coll., MMA, NY.

Forster, William, address unrecorded, upholder (1700). Admitted freeman of the Upholders' Co. by order of the Court of Aldermen on 23 April 1700. [GL, Upholders' Co. records]

Forster, William, Alnwick, Northumb., cm (1834). [D] See William Forester.

Forster, William, 81 Gt Titchfield St, London, cm and u (1839). [D]

Forsyth, James, 83 North St, Leeds, Yorks., carver and gilder (1837). [D]

Forsyth, Margaret, 9 Elliot St, Liverpool, carver and gilder (1829). [D]

Forsyth, Samuel, Liverpool, carver and gilder (1813–35). Addresses given at 8 Shaw's Brow in 1813; 14 Pellew St with shop at 38 Lord St in 1816; at 59–60 Church St in 1821, when he also had a fruit warehouse; at 21 Limekiln Lane, with shop at 32 Lord St in 1823; 24 Limekiln Lane in 1824; 3 Elliot St in 1827; 34 Limekiln Lane in 1829; and 35 Ford St in 1835. [D] Two tradesmen of the same name must be concerned here, one of them being:

Forsyth, Samuel, Elliot St Liverpool, carver and gilder (b. 1774–d. 1828). Death aged 54 reported in *Liverpool Mercury*, 15 August 1828.

Forsyth, William, 10 Stanley St, Liverpool, cm (1834–37). [D]

Fort (or Forst), Alexander, London, joiner (c. 1645–1706). App. to Henry Phillips, 1659. Master Joiner in the Office of Works, 1678, but not able to take it up until 1688. Employed at Whitehall, St James's, Westminster, Hampton Court and with Henry Lobb at Kensington Palace in the reign of William III. In April 1689 he supplied 'Wainscott in her Maties new Bedchamber, drawing Room, Closett & passages', costing £67 4s, and '377 foot of Italian Moulding round the doors 5″ deep', for Hampton Court. In the same year he also supplied there 'a carved walnuttree table to sett flowers on', costing £2 10s. In 1691, as master joiner, he was paid for making a frame for a marble table, for Kensington Palace. [Royal tradesmen's accounts, Lord Chamberlain's Office; PRO,

Works, 5/55; *DEF*; *Conn.*, vol. 127, 1931, p. 87; Beard, *Craftsmen and Interior Decoration*, p. 259]

Forth, George, Ripon, Yorks., joiner and cm (1828–37). Trading at Beverley Bank, 1828–30; Kirkgate in 1834; and Beddern Bank in 1837. [D]

Forth, George jnr, St Agnesgate, Ripon, Yorks., joiner and/or cm (1837). [D]

Forth, Thomas, Market Pl., Bridlington, Yorks., cm (1830–40). [D]

Forth, William, Louth, Lincs., cm (1784). Insured his house for £200 in 1784 with the Sun Co. [GL, Sun MS vol. 324, p. 389]

Forton, Thomas, Lancaster, cm (1752–68). Admitted freeman, 1752–53. [Lancaster freemen rolls and poll bk]

Fortune, Timothy, at 'The Plough & Harrow', Witch St, behind St Clement's Church, Strand, London, upholder (1720–24). Insured goods and merchandise on 17 February 1720 with the Sun Co. Named in newspapers, 1721–24. [GL, Sun MS vol. 10; Heal]

Fosbrook(e), John, Townhall (or Townhill) Lane, Leicester, u and cm (1815). [D]

Fossett, —, 5–6 Leadenhall St, London, u (1803). Named in Sheraton's list of master cabinet makers, 1803.

Foster, —, Boston, Lincs. Impressed mark noted on longcase for clock by Bottomley, Boston, c. 1800–10.

Foster, Benjamin, Liverpool, cm (b. 1790–1818). Petitioned freedom on birthright as son of James Foster, cm, paying 3s 4d in 1818; admitted freeman on 15 June. [Liverpool freemen reg. and committee bk]

Foster, Edmund, Hull, Yorks., carver and gilder (c. 1762–1805). Rococo trade card, dating before 1784, gives address 'at the Golden Boy in the High Street'. Recorded in Lowgate from 1784–99; and North Church Side, 1803–05. He had branched out into bookselling by 1793. Trade card in the Castle Museum, York states that he 'Executes in the ancient and modern Taste Chimney pieces, Coats of Arms, Compartments, Monuments, Tombs & Head Stones, Frames for Looking Glasses, Pictures & Marble Slabs, Gerandoles, Chandeliers, Consoles, Ornaments of Architecture & every other Ornament pertaining to ye Businesss in Marble, Stone & Wood. OIL & BURNISH'D GILDING. N.B. He proposes to keep (as at present) a Shop furnish'd with an elegant Assortment of Glasses in Gold, in White Frames, Gerandoles &c. ready for Sale.' Foster was one of the leading carvers active in the East Riding during the second half of the 18th century. He supplied furniture to Burton Constable Hall, carved the splendid ornament in the Court Room of Beverley Guildhall, c. 1762–64, and executed, with other craftsmen, the organ-case in Beverley Minster designed by Thomas Lightoler in 1765. [D; Beverley poll bk; I. & E. Hall, *Historic Beverley*, pp. 25, and 49, figs 154–56] See James & Edward Foster.

Foster, Edmund, 75 Union St, Lambeth Walk, London, chair and sofa maker (1839). [D]

Foster, Edward, Hull, Yorks., carver and gilder (1784–1806). Trading in Lowgate in 1784, and North Church Side, 1803–06. [D]

Foster, Edward, Huddersfield, Yorks., carver and gilder (1830–32). Trading at New St in 1830. Declared bankrupt, *Chester Courant and Advertiser for North Wales*, 13 November 1832. [D]

Foster, Edward, Market Pl., Derby, carver and gilder (1835). [D]

Foster, Francis, Gerrard St, Soho, London, u (1770). Declared bankrupt, *Gents Mag.*, February 1770.

Foster, George, 16 Manor St, Little Bolton, Lancs., cm and joiner (1824). [D]

Foster, George, Union St and Church Way, North Shields,

Northumb., furniture broker and cm (1827–34). Recorded also at 39 Tyne St in 1834. [D]

Foster, Henry, Bristol, cm (1813–21). Addresses given at Clark St, Milk St, with warehouse at Broad Weir in 1813; Hotwells, 1814–15; Cumberland Buildings, Bathurst's Basin, Hotwells, 1816–17; and 13 Cumberland Buildings, 1819–21. [D]

Foster, James & Edward, Hull, Yorks., cm (1774). Supplied sidetables to Burton Constable Hall in 1774. [*C. Life*, vol. CLIX, no. 4118, pp. 1476–80] See Edmund and Edward Foster.

Foster, James, Liverpool, cm (1790–1835). Addresses given at 23 Cumberland St, 1800–03; no. 43 in 1804; 39 in 1805; 29, 1807–10; 30 in 1811 and 1814; 28 in 1813 and 1818; shop at 1 Cheapside Alley in 1821; 35 Cumberland St, 1823–27; and no. 37, 1834–35. Son of John Foster, labourer; petitioned freedom on servitude to Robert Fairhurst of Liverpool, paying 6s 8d in 1790; admitted freeman on 21 June 1790. Took app. named Samuel Foster in 1807, who petitioned freedom in 1816. Father of Benjamin Foster, cm, born 28 August 1790, petitioned freedom in 1818. [D; Liverpool freemen's committee bk]

Foster, James, 12 Gt Suffolk St, Southwark, London, broker and cm (1820). [D]

Foster, John, Chandler St, London, upholder and dealer in liquors (1778). Took out a Sun Insurance policy in 1778 for £300 of which £40 accounted for utensils and stock. [GL, Sun MS vol. 268, p. 436]

Foster, John, Lancaster, Named in the Gillow records, 1784–87, in 1785 working on a wardrobe. [Westminster Ref. Lib., Gillow vol. 334/93, p. 187]

Foster, John, Nottingham, joiner and cm (1814). Took app. named John Leighton in 1814. [Nottingham app. list]

Foster, John, Lancaster, u (1815–16). Admitted freeman, 1815–16, when stated 'of Thurnham'. [Lancaster freemen rolls]

Foster, John, Preston, Lancs., u (1822–25). Trading at 111 Fishergate in 1825. Named in the Preston Guild records in 1822 as son of John Towns Sergeant, deceased. [D]

Foster, John, Exeter, Devon, chairmaker and cm (1822–40). Addresses given at West Quarter, 1823–24 and 1830–37; Goldsmith St in 1829; Paul St, 1832–35; and Spicer's Ct, Fore St Hill, 1838–40. Marriage to Miss Salter of Exeter reported in *The Alfred*, 7 May 1822. Son William bapt. at All Hallows, Goldsmith St, on 17 May 1829. Children bapt. at St Paul's: Thomas on 26 February 1832; Thomas on 6 January and Charles on 25 January 1835. [D; PR(bapt.)] Possibly two tradesmen of the same name are concerned here.

Foster (or Forster), John Bruce, 48 Groat Mkt, Newcastle, cm (1824–34). Recorded at Morrison's Entry, 1828–29. [D]

Foster, John, Lairgate, Beverley, Yorks., cm (1831). [D]

Foster, John, Brighton, Sussex, cm (1831–34). Recorded at Western Rd in 1831; no. 83 in 1832; Norfolk Sq., 1832; and Grenville Pl. in 1834. Son Thomas by wife Catherine bapt. on 4 August 1831; and daughter Catherine on 16 March 1834. [D; E. Sussex RO, PR(bapt.)]

Foster, John, Wednesfield, Staffs., joiner and/or cm (1834). [D]

Foster, John, Willenhall, Staffs., joiner and/or cm (1834). [D]

Foster, John, 2 Andrew's Ct, Collier St, Hull, Yorks., cm (1838–39). [D]

Foster, Joseph, Liverpool, cm (1790–94). Addresses given at 16 Love Lane and 32 Atherton St in 1790, and 31 Atherton St, 1794. [D]

Foster, Nicholas William, Portsmouth and Southampton, Hants., cm (b. 1795–26). Born in Portsea; recorded in Portsmouth, 1819–21; and Southampton in 1826. Sons, also cm, bapt. at Portsmouth: William Henry on 5 August 1819, and Samuel on 21 December 1821. [PR(bapt.)]

Foster, Richard, Kidgate, Louth, Lincs., joiner and cm (1826–31). [D]

Foster, Robert, Westgate, Louth, Lincs., cm/joiner (1819–22). Trading as Robert Foster & Son, 1826–31. [D] See William Foster of Westgate, Louth.

Foster, Robert, 18 Witham, Hull, Yorks., furniture and house painter and paper hanger (1838–40). [D]

Foster, Thomas, address unrecorded, joiner (1663). On 26 February 1663 the 1st Viscount Irwin paid Foster £5 10s 'for one dozen & a halfe of chares' supplied to Temple Newsam House, Leeds. [*Furn. Hist.*, 1967]

Foster, Thomas, Liverpool, cm (1767–d. by 1817). Admitted freeman on servitude to John Walker on 5 November 1767. [Liverpool freemen reg. and committee bk]

Foster, Thomas, Pontefract, Yorks., joiner and/or cm (1834). [D]

Foster, Thomas, Market Pl., Luton, Beds., furniture broker, bedstead and chairmaker (1839). [D]

Foster, William, Gainsborough, Lincs., cm (1792–94). [D]

Foster, William, Hayes's Ct, Leeds, Yorks., carver and gilder (1822). [D]

Foster, William, Castle St East, Oxford St, London, u and cm (1820–28). Trading at no. 50 in 1820; no. 49 in 1823; 40 in 1825; and 50, 1827–28. [D]

Foster, William, 32 West St, Hull, Yorks., cm (1823). [D]

Foster, William, Boston, Lincs., cm (1826–35). Trading at St George's Lane in 1826, and Rosegarth St, 1835. [D]

Foster, William, 5 Winsley St, London, u (1829). [D]

Foster, William, Watergate, Carlisle, Cumb., joiner and/or cm (1829). [D]

Foster, William, Westgate, Louth, Lincs., joiner, cm and builder, u (1831–41). [D] See Robert Foster & Son.

Foster, William, 28 College St, Southampton, Hants., cm (1836–39). [D]

Foster, William, Milton, Kent, cm and carpenter (1838). [D]

Foster & Co., 13 Hackin's Hey, Liverpool, joiners and cm (1807). [D]

Fothergill, Christopher, Leeds, Yorks., journeyman cm (1791). Named in the *Leeds Cabinet and Chair Makers' Book of Prices*, 1791, among journeymen in basic sympathy with its contents.

Fothergill, Frederick & John, 42 Call Lane, Leeds, Yorks., carvers and gilders (1830). [D]

Fothergill, George, Chester, joiner and cm (1758–84). App. to Joseph Burrows, joiner and cm, and admitted freeman on 15 July 1758. Took apps named Thomas Saladine in 1760 and John Hall in 1774. Polled at Chester in 1784. [Chester app. bks and freemen rolls]

Fothergill, John H., Call Lane, Leeds, Yorks., carver and gilder (1834). [D]

Fothergill, Joseph, Correction house Yd, Alnwick, Northumb., cm and joiner (1834). [D]

Fotheringham, William, Rockley, near Retford, Notts., chairmaker (1840). [Retford Denman Lib., 942–52 Roc.]

Fouke, —, at 'The Goat', Barbican, London, u (1672). Named in newspapers in 1672. [Heal]

Foulds, Francis, Leicester, cm (1760). [Leicester freeman rolls]

Foulds, Thomas & William, Main St, Bingley, Yorks., joiner and/or cm (1837). [D]

Foulger, Lock^n, Walham Green, London, chairmaker (1773). Trade card shows Gothic and twig-work settees, a Windsor chair on wheels, a light carriage and a barrel or boat chair. It states that he 'Makes all sorts of Windsor Chairs, Garden Seats, Rural Settees etc.' [Banks Coll., BM]

Foulkes, Edward, 14 Piccadilly, Manchester, cm and u (1821). [D]

Foulkes, John, Stanley St, Liverpool, cm (1834–39). Addresses given at 55 Stanley St, 1834–37, and no. 52 in 1839. [D]

Foulkes, Richard, Castle Hill, Whitchurch, Salop, cm (1835–36). [D]

Foulkes, Richard, Prees, near Wem, Salop, joiner and cm (1840). [D]

Foulkes, Thomas, 10 Old Bailey, London, cm, u, auctioneer and undertaker (1822–23). [D]

Foulkes, Thomes Bennet, Castle St, Chester, u (1839). Admitted freeman on 3 June 1839. [Chester freemen rolls]

Foulkes & Darnton, 14 Piccadilly, Manchester, u (1818). [D] See John Darnton.

Foulsham, William, Town Green, Wymondham, Norfolk, cm (1839). [D]

Fountain, Daniel, High Wycombe, Bucks., chairmaker (1828). Son bapt. in 1828. [PR(bapt.)]

Fountain, Nathaniel, York, cm (1812). Son of Thomas Fountain; app. to Thomas Walls, cm, on 1 July 1812. [York app. reg.]

Fouracres, John, East St, South Molton, Devon, u and cm (1838). [D]

Fowell, Benjamin, 19 Old Thomas St, Birmingham, chairmaker (1830). [D]

Fowell, George, 3 Brickkiln St, Birmingham, cm and Windsor chairmaker (1828–35). Recorded at no. 3, 1830–35. [D]

Fowell, Thomas, Birmingham, ram rod and chairmaker in hardwood (1793–1830). Trading at Snow Hill in 1793, and 16–18 Stanley (or Slaney) St, 1816–30. [D; *Arms and Armour Soc. Journal*, vol. 10, no. 4]

Fowell, Thomas, 15 Snowhill, Birmingham, cm, u and chairmaker (1835–39). [D]

Fowl, William, 6 Carnaby St, Golden Sq., London, cm, chairmaker, furniture broker and u (1817–39). [D]

Fowler, —, Whitechapel, London, cm (1751). Notice in *London Evening Post*, 10–12 January 1751, that 'On Wednesday night Mr. Fowler, a Cabinetmaker, in Whitechapel, was attacked near Whitechapel Church by three fellows, but making resistance and several Persons coming to his Assistance they were pursued, and one of them taken in Red Lion Street and on Thursday committed to Newgate.'

Fowler, Benjamin, Liverpool, cm (1827). Took app. named John Pearson in 1827. [Liverpool app. enrolment bk]

Fowler, Benjamin, Exmouth St, Spitalfields, London, chair and sofa maker (1829–39). Recorded at 7 Wood St, Exmouth St, 1829–39; and 51 Exmouth St, 1835–39. [D]

Fowler, George, Cullompton, Devon, u and cm (1799–1803). Marriage to Miss Charlotte Martin, daughter of Mr James Martin, saddler and ironmonger, reported in *Exeter Flying Post*, 29 August 1799. Subscribed to Sheraton's *Cabinet Dictionary*, 1803.

Fowler, George, Tiverton, Devon, cm (1808). Auction on 10 May 1808 of entire stock of George Fowler, prior to his settling in London, advertised in *Exeter Flying Post*, 21 April 1808.

Fowler, Giles, London, cm (1793). Subscribed to Sheraton's *Drawing Book*, 1793.

Fowler, Giles, 10 Wilstead St, Somerstown, London, chairmaker (1808). [D] See James Fowler.

Fowler, Henry, Port St, Evesham, Worcs., cm and u (1840). [D]

Fowler, James, 57 Bull Row, Somerstown, London, chair and sofa maker (1827–28). [D] See Giles Fowler.

Fowler, John, York, u (1718–41). App. to George Reynoldson, u, on 25 March 1718. Admitted freeman of York in 1739. Polled at York as u at Long Newton in 1741. [York app. reg. and freemen rolls]

Fowler, John, North Shields, Northumb., cm (1778). Insured his stock for £200 in 1778 with the Sun Co. [GL, Sun MS vol. 264, p. 604]

Fowler, Joseph, Winchester, Hants., cm (1792). [D]

Fowler, Joseph, Portsmouth, Hants., cm (1798). [D]

Fowler, Joseph, High Wycombe, Bucks., chairmaker (b. c. 1816–41). Aged 25 at the time of the 1841 Census.

Fowler, R., 61 Mortimer St, Cavendish Sq., London, u etc. (1807–08). [D]

Fowler, Richard, address unrecorded, upholder (1755–63). Son of Richard Fowler, surgeon of Southwark; app. to Richard Walker on 8 February 1755, and admitted freeman of the Upholders' Co. by servitude on 1 December 1763. [GL, Upholders' Co. records]

Fowler, Richard, 41 James St, Lambeth Marsh, London, cm (1820–28). [D]

Fowler, Robert, address unrecorded, upholder (1752–75). Son of Leonard Fowler, merchant tailor of London; admitted freeman of the Upholders' Co. on 5 March 1752. Took app. named Thomas Cudworth, 1765–75. [GL, Upholders' Co. records]

Fowler, Samuel, Liverpool, cm (1761–d. by 1817). Admitted freeman on 6 March 1761. [Liverpool freemen reg.]

Fowler, Samuel, 32 Westbar, Sheffield, Yorks., broker and u (1797). [D]

Fowler, Thomas, Tiverton, Devon, maltster and cm (1798–1805). [D]

Fowler, Thomas, 6 (St) James's Buildings, Rosomon Buildings, Clerkenwell, London, cm (1835–37). [D]

Fowler, William, 28 Brewer St, London, upholder (1782). Took out a Sun Insurance policy in 1782 for £500 of which £150 accounted for utensils, stock and goods. [GL, Sun MS vol. 299, p. 145]

Fowler, William, address unrecorded, cm and/or joiner (1802–03). Submitted bills to Mr Colfox of Bridport, Dorset, on 30 August 1802 for a total of £22 8s 6d; and on 18 March 1803 for 'lessor table in kitchen', £1. [Dorset RO, D43 F4]

Fowler, William, Winterton, Lincs., cm (1819). [D]

Fowler, William, Sheffield, Yorks., cm (1821–37). Addresses given at 71 Pond St in 1821; West St, 1828–37, no. 11 in 1837. [D]

Fowler, William, 39 Fair St, Horsleydown, London, cm and upholder (1827–28). [D]

Fowles, Charles, Church St, Tetbury, Glos., cm and u (1822–40). [D]

Fowles, Jonathan, Witton St, Northwich, Cheshire, cm (1822). [D]

Fowles, Samuel, Church St, Tetbury, Glos., cm etc. (1839). [D]

Fowles, Sir Thomas, shop near Temple Bar, London. In *London Gazette,* 14–18 May 1691 a notice reads: 'There is a new silver table, stands, glass frame & top-piece all chased work, but the tops which are engraved to be disposed of at a Reasonable Price. They may be seen at Sir THOMAS FOWLES SHOP near Temple Bar.'

Fowles, Thomas, Compass Hill, Tetbury, Glos., cm and u (1822). [D]

Fox, B., address unrecorded, cm (1803). Subscribed to Sheraton's *Cabinet Dictionary,* 1803.

Fox, Benjamin, 12 Little St Martin's Lane, Long Acre, London, cm and u (1755–94). Subscribed to Chippendale's *Director,* 1754 and to T. Malton's *Treatise on Perspective,* 1778. Took out a Sun Insurance policy in 1781 for £800 of which £600 accounted for utensils, stock and goods. Probably the 'Fox Upholsterer' of London named in the Duke of Portland's account bk kept by his steward, John Hutchinson, on 3 July 1766, being paid £175 6s; and on 1 November, £281 1s 1d for work at Burlington House. [D; GL, Sun MS vol. 297, p. 441; Notts. RO, DD5P 3/1] See Fox, Hepworth & Raynes.

Fox, Benjamin, Fetter Lane (or St), Northampton, chairmaker and turner (1820–30). [D; poll bks]

Fox, Charles, Parsons Meadow Lane, Banbury, Oxon., chairmaker (1830–41). [D]

Fox, Charles, 7 Eldon St, London Wall, London, cm and u (1839). [D]

Fox, Christopher, Wardour St, London, cm (1784). [D]

Fox, Deveareux, address unrecorded, joiner, carver and gilder (1764). Commissioned by Lord Leigh of Stoneleigh, Warks., to make three chimney pieces. His bill for work done between 26 May and 9 June 1764 described them in detail. The first, costing £12 9s 9d, had an ogee cornice carved with three mouldings of 'leav'd grass', 'Eggs and tongs', and 'flowers and Double Tongs'. The 'tirms' were 'Work'd with scrolls foulladge leaves swags of fruit and flowers', and the 'Cove frezes Work'd with Husks and foulladge leaves and a swag of fruit and flowers.' The second, or 'Gilt Chimney Peice', costing £26 5s 6d, had freezes enriched with astragals, and 'tirms Work'd with scrolls foulladge leaves &c, the freze with a Floras Head in the Middle and Drapery with swags of fruit and flowers — To joiners Work Carving Gilding'. The third chimney piece, costing £14 16s 1d, had an ogee cornice enriched with '7 leav'd grass', flowers, and 'Tongs', 'the tirms Work'd with scrolls foulladge leaves flowers &c.' The freeze was 'Work'd 2 Boys in the Middle with a bird, and french work treework swags of fruit and flowers &c all According to Drawing.' The bill totalled £53 11s 4d, and was receipted on 6 August 1764 by Samuel Butler. [Shakespeare Birthplace Trust, Leigh receipts DR 18/5]

Fox, Edward, London, u and undertaker (1729–32). Recorded at St James's St in 1729; Bennet St, St James's, 1730; and Park Pl., St James's in 1731. Newspapers reported that he conducted the funeral of the Duke of Devonshire at Chatsworth in 1729. Also named in newspapers in 1730; and 1731–32, when he was appointed u to H R H Prince of Wales. [Heal; Harris, *Old English Furniture,* p. 21]

Fox, Edward, Hull, Yorks., cm (1780–84). [Poll bks]

Fox, Francis, Bennett St, St James's St, St Martin-in-the-Fields, London, upholder (1715–57). Took out Sun Insurance policies on 1 February 1715 on goods and merchandise in his house; and on 1 May 1823 for £500 on household goods and stock in trade. Named in 1757 concerning lease of house by James Gisborne of Staley, Derbs., to George Okeover, 'formerly in the occupation of Francis Fox, upholder.' [GL, Sun MS vol. 4, p. 164; vol. 27; Derbs. RO, Okeover deeds, 231 M/T, 692–93]

Fox, Francis, Northampton, u (1762–65). [PR(bapt.)]

Fox, Francis, Northampton, u (1766–d. 1802). Recorded at St John's Lane in 1768, and Bridge St, 1774–96. Children bapt. between 1766–84. Will dated 11 March 1802. [Poll bks; PR(bapt.); Northampton wills index]

Fox, George, Huntingdon(?), u, cm auctioneer and appraiser (1818). Advertised his stock of paper hangings, upholstery and cabinet wares, and requested a cm and u in 1818.

Fox, George, Brewood, Staffs., joiner and/or cm (1834). [D]

Fox, Henry, Rotherhithe, London, u (1805). App. to Robert Job in August 1805. [Hull app. reg.]

Fox, Henry Harris, 105 Hatton Gdn, London, u etc. (1835–37). [D]

Fox, Henry, 6 Bedford St, Bedford Row, London, u (1839). [D]

Fox, James, Richmond Hill, Leeds, Yorks., hair-seating manufacturer (1822). [D] See John Kendell & Co.

Fox, James & Charles, 27 Church St, Sheffield, Yorks., cm, carvers and gilders (1833). [D]

Fox, James, Bond St, Hull, Yorks., cm, u and undertaker (1834–40). Trading at no. 28 in 1834, and no. 40, 1835–40. [D]

Fox, John, address unrecorded, upholder (1708–44). Son of John Fox, Gent. of Burton Leonard, Yorks.; app. to Thomas Hatley on 1 May 1708, and admitted freeman of the Upholders' Co. by servitude on 16 May 1723. Took app. named William Mather, 1737–44. [GL, Upholders' Co. records]

Fox, John, Cambridge, joiner and cm (1713). Took app. named Draper in 1713. [S of G, app. index]

Fox, John, in the Green Dragon Ct, Southwark, London, upholder (1723). Took out a Sun Insurance policy on 30 December 1723 for £500 on goods and merchandise in his house. [GL, Sun MS vol. 16, ref. 30797]

Fox, John, Ludgate St, London, upholder (1734). Named in newspapers in 1734. [Heal]

Fox, John (snr and jnr?), St Ives and Huntingdon, cm, u, auctioneer and appraiser (1765–1817). Auction advertisements appeared in *Cambridge Chronicle*, 8 June 1765, and *Cambridge Chronicle and Journal*, 7 March 1766, 27 August, 19 September and 7 November 1767, and 18 March and 25 November 1769. Announced in the same paper on 5 April 1770 that he was taking over house and shop of the late Mr Nodes, cm, of Huntingdon, whilst continuing his own shop at St. Ives for the present. On 8 September 1770 a large advertisement for furniture appeared, and Fox stated that he 'continues his old booth in Gorlier[?] Row.' Took out Sun Insurance policies in 1778 for £400, £200 on utensils and stock; in 1781 for £300 on his house; in 1785 for £350 on his house and £50 on his warehouse etc.; and on 18 July 1787 for £700 on his house, brewery, workshop, stables, chaise-houses, goods and utensils. A notice in *Cambridge Chronicle and Journal*, 20 February 1796 asked anyone owing money to the 'late John Fox late of St. Ives' to forward it to John Fox, u and cm, of Huntingdon. Death, aged 67, announced, same paper, 24 January 1817, when a detailed inventory was made. Marriage of Miss E. Fox, daughter of the late John Fox, cm, to Mr Warne, reported on 2 February 1819. [GL, Sun MS vol. 269, p. 445; vol. 289, p. 613; vol. 330, p. 39; vol. 346, p. 357; Hunts. RO, inventories F]

Fox, John, Lancaster, cm (1779–1811). Admitted freeman, 1779–80. Named in the Gillow records in 1796 working on a folding screen, and in 1811 on a bookcase. [Lancaster freemen rolls; Westminster Ref. Lib., Gillow vol. 344/97, p. 1284; vol. 344/99, p. 1893]

Fox, John, Newgate St, London, cm, u, appraiser and undertaker, paper hanger, and 'transparent, Venetian & other blinds' maker (1822–39). Trading as Burnell & Fox, 46 Newgate St, 1822–23; alone at 46–47 in 1825; no. 47, 1826–29; and no. 14, 1837–39. In 1826 Fox supplied to John Gibbard of Sharnbrook, near Bedford, 'a suite of embossed scarlet moreen curtains for two windows' and 'a long window cornice japanned black with gold ornaments made in 2 parts with brass cornice ends', costing £16 8s. Declared bankrupt, *Liverpool Mercury*, 20 April 1832. [D; Beds. RO, GA 66]

Fox, John, 53 Jewin St, London, cm (1835). [D]

Fox, Joseph, Raistrick, Yorks., joiner and/or cm (1834). [D]

Fox, Joshua, Sheffield, Yorks., cm (1834–37). Trading at 27 Church St in 1837. [D]

Fox, Robert, Cross St, Newington Butts, London, cm, u and bedstead maker (1835–39). Trading at no. 4 in 1835, and no. 5, 1837–39. [D]

Fox, Samuel, Wells, Norfolk, cm and joiner (1822). [D]

Fox, Solomon, Wardour St, London, cm (1766–1808). Recorded at no. 38, 1790–93, and no. 33 in 1808. Took out Sun Insurance policies in 1777 for £800 on his house; and on 16 February 1786 for £400 on his house in Grafton St, Tottenham Ct Rd. Carried out work at Welbeck Abbey from June 1766 to January 1777 for which he was paid £281 1s 1d.

Probably the Solomon Fox who supplied items to Sir John Griffin Griffin of Audley End, Essex, 1780–83, including in 1780 'a long dressing table with looking glass and 4 Bolbels'(?) costing £3 13s 6d; in 1781 'New Mahogany boxes and new frames, and repairs to boxes and glasses & frames', costing £3 16s 3d for Sir John's London house in New Burlington St; and in 1782 was paid £10 3s for cleaning and repairing furniture, curtains and carpets. Between 1782–83 he received a total of £16 8s 9d for laying carpets, putting up curtains, carrying out further repairs, and on 14 February 1783 supplying a mahogany library table for Sir John's London house. For there Fox also supplied 'a small Picture frame in Burnish'd gold & a piece of plate glass to Dᵒ', costing £7 6s in 1783. As Lord Howard de Walden, Sir John Griffin Griffin continued to patronize Fox, who in June 1784 submitted a bill totalling £23 7s 3d, which included furniture repairs, providing two 4-post bedsteads 'All Stain'd & Polished'; bedding, pink and white cotton bed hangings, and a mahogany night stool with 'white Stoan Pann'. In 1785 Fox was paid for further furniture repairs and alterations; and in 1788, £17 6s for a 'nue glass cutt into a mahogany Fraim', and making two mahogany frames 'with Back feet'. In 1789 he supplied a 'stand for a screen on Pillar & Claws Japand holes through the stick & 2 Ivery Pins to Dᵒ' costing £8 6s. [D; GL, Sun MS vol. 335, p. 455; vol. 268, p. 8; Notts. RO, DD5 P3/4, Welbeck Abbey accounts; Essex RO, D/DBy/A38/9; A212; A39/5; A40/11; A41/5 and 11; A42/12; A43/6; A46/6; A47/3]

Fox, Thomas, Bridge St, Northampton, u (1796–1820). [Poll bks]

Fox, Thomas, 93 Bishopsgate St, London, 'Upholder by Appointment to the Hon. East India Company' (1839). So reads his advertisement in Pigot's *Directory*, 1839, and continues: 'True Economy is BEST CONSULTED BY AN INSPECTION OF THE Elegant Stock of CABINET & UPHOLSTERY FURNITURE AT THOMAS FOX'S ESTABLISHMENT, No. 93, BISHOPSGATE STREET WITHIN, LONDON, WHICH, IN COMBINATION OF QUALITY AND PRICE, CANNOT BE EXCELLED.' Advertised in *Sussex Agricultural Express*, 30 March, 11 May and 8 June 1839, his 'extensive, economical and elegant stock of Furniture suited to every style of residence, from the cottage to the mansion; among which is to be found Looking Glasses, varying from 18 inches to 120 inches in height in rich gilt frames, Carpets, Chintzes, and ornamented Glass in every variety. N.B. Every article delivered from this establishment will be found durable, as well as low in price.'

Fox, William, address unrecorded, upholder (1714–31). Son of Robert Fox, Gent. of London; app. to William Ventris on 1 September 1714, and admitted freeman of the Upholders' Co. by servitude on 7 July 1731. [GL, Upholders' Co. records]

Fox, William, Little Catherine St, Eagle Ct, St Martin-in-the-Fields, London, upholder (1760). Took out a Hand in Hand Insurance policy in June 1760 for £100 on his above premises. [GL, Hand in Hand MS vol. 94, p. 14]

Fox, William, 5 Gerrard St, London, cm (1775). Took out a Sun Insurance policy in 1775 for £500 of which £400 accounted for utensils, stock and goods. [GL, Sun MS vol. 236, p. 504]

Fox, William jnr, Castle St, St Marylebone, London, u (1777). Declared bankrupt, *Sussex Weekly Advertiser*, 6 January 1777. Probably the son of William Fox, admitted freeman of the Upholders' Co. in 1731.

Fox, William, Sheffield, Yorks., joiner and cm (1797–1833). Addresses given at 2 Gibralter St in 1797; Paradise Sq., 1814–20; 21 Fargate, 1822; 13 Workhouse Croft, 1825–29; and Bow St in 1830. [D]

Fox, William, Lytham, Lancs., joiner and cm (1825–28). [D]

Fox, **William**, 11 Kingsmead Terr., Bath, Som., cm (1826). [D]

Fox, **William**, Newcastle-under-Lyme, Staffs., chairmaker (1832–39). Recorded at Lower St, 1832–37; 16 Merrial St, 1836–39; and as an u at 16 Garden St in 1839. [D]

Fox & Grundy, or 'G. & F.', 25 St Ann's Sq., Manchester, barometer and looking-glass makers, carvers and gilders, picture frame makers (1828). [D] See John Clowes Grundy.

Fox, Hepworth & Raynes, Little St Martin's Lane, Long Acre, London, u (1788). [D] See Benjamin Fox.

Foxhall, —, address unrecorded. Furniture-maker to William Beckford, and recorded dining regularly at the steward's table. [*Burlington*, December 1980, p. 820]

Foxhall, —, address unrecorded, carver (1779–93). Employed by William Rhodes, u and cm, 127 Lower Holborn, London; and possibly made furniture for Drayton House, Northants. [*C. Life*, 3 June 1965, p. 1349]

Foxhall, —, address unrecorded (1805–09). Named in the account book of Lady Cotton of Madingley Hall, Cambridge, in January 1805 receiving £38 10s. 'for the use of Furniture by draft', and in July 1809, £20 5s for 'Tent bedstead white Dimity furniture', mattress, and hire of various articles of furniture for two years. [Cambs. RO, 588/A45]

Foxhall, Edward, London, carver (c. 1790). At Wimpole Hall, near Cambridge, Foxhall executed the carved work of the Yellow Drawing Room for Sir John Soane. [Nat. Trust guide to *Wimpole Hall*, p. 24]

Fox(h)all, Edward, & Fryer, Old Cavendish St, Cavendish Sq., London, u (1799–1816). Foxhall is recorded alone in Cavendish St in 1799; and in partnership with Fryer at 19 Old Cavendish St, 1802–07; and there as Foxhall & Co., 1808–16, at no. 29, 1807–09. Foxhall & Fryer are named in Sheraton's list of master cabinet makers, 1803. [D]

Foxhall, Marⁿ, at 'The Golden Head' in Great St Andrew's St, Seven Dials, London, carver and gilder (c. 1770). Rococo trade card reads: 'PICTURES Carefully Cleand, Lin'd & Fram'd, in the neatest manner. N.B. All sorts of Hosiery & Haberdashery Goods, with Checks and Irish Cloth, AT THE Lowest Prices.' [Heal]

Foxhall, Martin, Hotwell Rd, Bristol, carver and gilder (1794). [D]

Foxton, Dixon, Allhallow Gate, Ripon, Yorks., joiner and/or cm (1834). [D]

Foxton, James, North St, Ripon, Yorks., cm (1822). [D]

Foxton, John Dixon, Allhallow Gate, Ripon, Yorks., joiner and/or cm (1837). [D]

Foy, A., King St, Plymouth, Devon, cm and u (1838). [D]

Foy, Henry, York, cm and joiner (1725–58). Recorded in Davygate, 1741–58. Married Isabel Scott at Holy Trinity, Christ Church, King's Sq. on 1 January 1725. [PR] On 10 August 1737 it was 'Ordered — That Henry Foy, cabinet maker shall be admitted to the Freedom of this City upon his delivering so many Chairs and Chests of Drawers or other cabinet maker's work as my Lord Mayor shall think proper to the value of Five & Twenty pounds of the use of the Lord Mayor's House'. [T. P. Cooper, *The Mansion House*, vol. 40, pt. 2] Admitted freeman 'per ordinam' in 1739. [York freemen rolls] In December 1747 property in Davygate was assigned by Henry Foy and Thomas Bond, coachman, to Thomas Featherstone, Gent. [York City Archives, E93/196] Took his son, John, as app. cm on 1 May 1744 for seven years; and John Oliver as app. cm and joiner in 1755. [York app. reg.] On 17 December 1751 it was declared that Henry Foy have £25 of Sir Thomas White's gift 'to provide interest free loans of £25 for periods of 10 years to poor clothiers and other tradesmen and for deserving artisans'. [York City archives, B43/376, Victoria County History, *York*, p. 438] Subscribed to Chippendale's *Director*, 1754, and advertised

his cure for stammering and stuttering in *York Courant*, 20 May 1755. [Poll bks]

Foy, Henry, King St, Plymouth, Devon, cm (1836). [D]

Foy, Mary, 58 Humber St, Hull, Yorks., cm (1831). [D] See William Foy.

Foy, Thomas, Leeds, Yorks., cm and u (1834–39). Trading at 20 and/or 29 Lowerhead Row in 1834, and top Meadow Lane in 1839. [D]

Foy, William, Hull, Yorks., cm, chairmaker and broker (1803–29). Addresses given at High St, near Grimsby Lane in 1803; Bridge St in 1806; Drypool in 1810; 2 New Dock St in 1814; Cockpit Yd, 6 Castle St in 1823; and 58 Humber St, 1826–29. [D] See Mary Foy.

Foy, William, 56 Shoe Lane, Fleet St, London, cm and u (1820). [D]

Foyer, James, address unrecorded, cm (1771). Named in the private accounts of Richard Hoare of Boreham House, Essex, on 10 December 1771, receiving 7s 6d. [Essex RO, D/Du 649/2]

Fozard, John, Lands Lane, Leeds, Yorks., cm and joiner (1837). [D]

Fozzard, Jonathan, West Ardsley, Yorks., cm (1822). [D]

Fozzard, William, West Ardsley, Yorks., cm (1822). [D]

Fradin, Abraham, Haymarket, London, u and cm (1744). Auction announced in *Daily Advertiser*, 22 October 1744 of the 'Household Furniture, Stock in Trade and Lease of the late Dwelling-House of Mr. Abraham Fradin, Cabinet-maker, next Door to Mr. Ford's, the Upper End of the Haymarket, St. James's . . . consisting of Needlework, Mohair and other Beds, Chairs and Window Curtains, large Pier Glasses and Sconces, Marble Tables and Carpets, Bookcases, Cloaths Presses, Chests of Drawers, Tables and other useful Furniture in Walnut Tree and Mahogany, with some valuable Pictures . . .'. On 11 December another advertisement read: 'To all Housekeepers, and those who furnish Lodgings, this Day the 11th Instant will be sold by Hand cheap, all the remaining Sconces, Pier and Chimney Glasses . . . the useful Cabinets, Buroes, Chairs, Furniture . . . Marble Tables . . . belonging to the late shop of Mr. Abraham Fraden, Upholsterer and Cabinet Maker, Three Doors above Panton Street in the Haymarket . . .'.

Fram, Samuel, Sculcoates, Hull, Yorks., cm (1822). App. to William Guy in 1822. [Hull app. reg.]

Frame, John, Bridgegate, Rotherham, Yorks., cm (1814). [D]

Framingham, C., 2 York St, Bethnal Green, London, cm (1835). [D]

Framington, Christ., 2 York St, Bethnal Green, London, cm (1837). [D]

Frampton, William, 59 Fleet Mkt, London, chairmaker (1777). Insured his house for £100 with the Sun Co. in 1777. [GL, Sun MS vol. 254, p. 150]

France, —, 22 Pall Mall and 17 James St, Haymarket, London, cm (1832–34). See William France snr and jnr, and France & Banting.

France, Edward, 101 St Martin's Lane, Charing Cross, London, u and cm (1773–1803). Admitted freeman of Lancaster, 1773–74, when stated 'of Westminster'. In partnership with Samuel Beckwith when they supplied much of the fine furniture in Lord Mansfield's house, Kenwood, between 1768–71. The name of the firm appears in the Royal Household bills until the end of the century, and their trade card, 'France and Beckwith, Upholsterers and Cabinet makers to His Majesty, no. 101 St. Martin's Lane', is dated 1803. [D; Lancaster freemen rolls; Heal; Banks Coll., BM] Edward France & Co., upholders of London (possibly an early reference to France & Beckwith) were paid £12 12s on 3 July 1766 by the Duke of Portland for work done at Burlington

House. [Notts. RO, DD5P 3/1] Edward France alone is recorded, c. 1775, supplying furniture for the state rooms at Erddig Park, Clwyd. [*C. Life*, 6 April 1978, p. 909] See Edward Francis.

France, John, Lancaster, cm (1767–68). Admitted freeman, 1767–68, when stated 'of London'. [Lancaster freemen rolls]

France, Joseph, Westgate, Rotherham, Yorks., cm (1830). [D]

France, Richard, Pride Hill, Shrewsbury, Salop, cm (1786–98). [D; Shrewsbury burgess roll]

France, Richard jnr, Mardol, Shrewbury, Salop, cm (1812). [Shrewsbury burgess roll]

France, Robert, Soho, London, carver, gilder and frame maker (1808–35). Recorded at 9 Crown St in 1808; and Denmark St, 1820–35, no. 16 in 1835. [D]

France, Stephen, Hodnet, Market Drayton, Salop, cm (1840). [D]

France, T., Middlx, timber merchant and cm (1824). Declared bankrupt, *London Gazette*, 6 November 1824.

France, William snr, St Martin's Lane, London, cm and u (1734?–d. 1773). William France snr who had a distinguished patronage, and whose firm continued after his death in various titles (noted at end of entry), may have been born in 1734. One of that name was bapt. on 1 January 1734 at St Martin-in-the-Fields, London, [PR] son of Edmund and Elizabeth France. No record of France's apprenticeship has been traced, but by 1759 he was in the employment of William Vile and John Cobb. His name appears in Cobb's bank account, 19 February and 26 November 1759 and 22 July 1763, and in that of Vile (both Drummonds Bank), on 17 December 1760, and 14 August 1761. In work for the Royal Wardrobe by Vile & Cobb the Lord Chamberlain's accounts are often signed on their behalf by France (or John Bradburne). They signed for the last time on 11 October 1763. Vile and Cobb's short-lived warrant (1761) had come to an end — their last account was 11 April 1764 — and a fortnight later, 25 April, William France submitted his first account. The safe continuity of royal patronage, in succession to Gumley, Moore Goodison, Vile and Cobb was thus continued by the latter's former employees, France and Bradburne. [PRO, LC 9/214]

It was probably between May and July 1764 that Bradburne and France entered into partnership. This has been suggested [A. Coleridge, *Apollo*, September 1967, p. 214] on the basis of bills submitted to Sir Lawrence Dundas (noted below). Those of 16 April and 3 May 1764 are invoiced by William France, alone. A third account, dated 13 July 1764, is headed: 'To Wm. France and Jnº Bradburn'. There is further evidence in an account of 10 July 1764, as 'Ballanced, William France', with subsequent accounts being rendered by both partners.

With more work for the firm to undertake, a number of apps were taken on: 1766, 28 July, Edward France (William's son); 1768, 4 March, William Burnet, 6 April, Geo Thacker; 1769, 6 February (for 4 years), John Johnson. [PRO, IR1/25; 26] Their normal premiums ranged between £50 to £70. There seems to have been the usual division of activity between Bradburne and France, with the former acting mostly as a carver, whereas France had seemingly trained as an u. (He is not, however, listed among the freemen of the Worshipful Co. of Upholders. [*Furn. Hist.*, 1973]

Any cm in royal service carried out a variety of tasks, and in France's case this extended from 1764 to 1773. He died in 1773 and his last account for the small amount of £6 6s 6d was paid in 1774. The granting of probate to his will was noted by those keeping records on behalf of the Great Wardrobe. [PRO, LC 105, p. 108]

19 ARLINGTON ST, London (Sir Lawrence Dundas).

1761–65: June 1761, For altering Mrs Dundas's Bede by taking away the head, front rail, and sacking, and putting in new ones, and new Sacking, to make it full one foot wider, and polishing all over. 16s. 0d.
April–June 1764: 8 page bill, totalling £263 5s 6¾d.
April 16, 1764: 'For a neat Mahny Chair with a high Seat to sit on to write and seat stuffed and covered with Crimsome Morine. Bill receipted by Wm France. [N. Yorks. RO, Zetland archive]

1765: One of a pair of console tables, made by France and Bradburne to a Robert Adam design, 1765 was sold Christie's, NY, 28 March 1981, lot 213, illus. It was invoiced on 12 January 1765. Another table from the same design was invoiced on 30 December 1765, as previously, at £37 10s. [Coleridge, *Apollo*, September 1967, pp. 214–15]

MOOR PARK, Herts. (Sir Lawrence Dundas). 1764–67: 21-page bill, 3 May 1764 to July 1764, (source as above). France signed receipts on 22 May 1765 (£600) and 3 January 1767 (£247 16s 8d), both witnessed by James Wilson. Two extracts show the wide range of activity: 3 May 1764, 'For making hangings of your own blue Genoa Damask to fit the Bed Chamber, and Dressing Room compleatly, and 3 Gib Doors, and putting up to Do in the 2 Rooms, £19. 17. 0.' June 1764, 'For altering your Dining tables in the eating room to make the leaves take off, and adding slip rings, and 2 turned Mahog table legs, and a stretcher, and Beech rail, screws, Glue, Oyl, £1. 9. 0.' [Dundas patronage is discussed, *Apollo*, September 1967; Coleridge, *Thomas Chippendale*, p. 147, pl. 393]

ROYAL PALACES. 1764–73: France's first bill (£488 9s 3d) was paid in 1764, and was for stuffing the frames of armchairs, 6 new beds etc. for the King's apartments at St James's, for work at the Lodge at Richmond, and pavilions at Hampton Court.

1765: St James's, Queen's House. His Majesty's apartment, curtains, making cases for 4 large armchairs, 12 back stool chairs, 'sophas' etc., £339 2s 1d.

1766: Preparations for the Duke of Cumberland's funeral (£416 16s 5d). [1764–66, PRO, LC 9/293]

1766–68: Worked at the Prince of Wales's apartment at St James's (£546 10s 6d). [PRO, LC 9/316]

1769–70: Received £1,156 16s 11d for several works. [PRO, LC 9/317]

1770: Covering easy chairs, square stools, covers for a press bedstead etc. for St James's (£285 14s 10d); also work at Kensington and Westminster.

1771: Received £1,735 7s for several works. [1770–71, PRO, LC 9/318]

1772: Received £2,071 11s for several works. [PRO, LC 9/319]

1772: Worked further at the Queen's private apartments, St James's, the Earl of Rochford's office, the Earl of Suffolk's office, etc. (£447 18s 8d) [PRO, LC 9/320]

1773: Received £220 0s 9d.

1774: Last account 'The late William France' (£6 8s 6d). [1773–74, PRO, LC 9/321]

THE VYNE, Hants. (John Chute). 1765–67: Vile and Cobb had worked at The Vyne in 1752–53 which may account for continuation of patronage to their former journeymen. France and Bradburne's accounts, 1765–67 [Hants. RO] also relate to Chute's London house in Charles St, but the surviving furniture is at The Vyne. [*C. Life*, 25 July 1963]

SYON HOUSE, Middlx (1st Duke of Northumberland). 1767: The 1st Duke's bank account [Hoare's] includes a payment of £56 on 26 February 1767 to France.

KENWOOD HOUSE, Middlx (1st Earl of Mansfield). 1768–70: France was responsible for much of the furniture supplied during Robert Adam's commission, 1768–70. Some of it was illustrated in R. & J. Adam's *Works in Architecture*, 1773, pl. viii. Although the contents of Kenwood were dispersed by sale in 1922, much has been traced and some brought back. [Iveagh Bequest, Kenwood Catalogue, *To Enhance and Preserve*, 1975] Apart from France's accounts, the Mansfield bank account [Hoare's] lists payments. A bill for 1768 (V & A archives, copies at Kenwood) reads:

The Rt-Hon Lord Mansfield | Bought of Wm France

For three scrole-headed sopha frames for the windows carv'd and gilt in burnish'd gold, with carving all done on the same principal as the sophas £48. [undated]

The underwritten articles are what I perform'd from Mr Adam's designs:

For 2 very rich frames for your Tables with 8 legs to each richly carv'd ornaments under the rails finished in a masterly manner and mouldings also and sweep'd stretching rails glued up 4 times. £67. 12s.

For 2 frames to the plates of glass in the two Recesses to Mr Adam's drawing with upright pillars and angular do, all enriched with the most Delicate Antique ornaments and Arches of light ornaments issuing from the pillars, and with a frieze at the top of the whole and bottom ornaments supported from the Base for the centre of each plate with a Baso Relieve, and all the ornaments curiously worked and the whole gilt in burnish'd gold and plate Brass behind all the centre ornaments to keep square. £149. 8s.

8 chairs stamped with initials 'W.F.' are believed to have been made for Kenwood. [V & A archives; *Conn.*, April 1957] A table, one of a pair [E. Harris, *Adam Furniture*, p. 69] invoiced by France in March 1770 was returned to Kenwood from America. [*Antiques*, September 1981, p. 520] *GCM*, pl. 181 illustrates a reading stand (V & A Museum) 'supplied by William France to Kenwood in 1770' but some doubt now surrounds this attribution. For other members of the France family and partnerships see Edward France; William France jnr; Beckwith & France; Banting, France & Co. G.B.

France, William jnr, 31 Pall Mall, London, u (1807–40). William jnr, who may have been a son of Edward France, is first noted in the *London POD*, 1807, as 'Upholder to His Majesty', a title held with his sometime partners Samuel and William Beckwith, and latterly with William Banting and Thomas France. From the evidence of bills rendered to John, 6th Duke of Bedford [Bedford Office, London] it appears that by 1810 France had taken a son (not named, but probably Thomas) into the business which was then styled William France & Son. This continued until 1812 when William's name disappears and the firm became France & Banting. This is confirmed by directory entries which show France & Banting for the first time in 1812 [*Post Office Annual Directory*] as 'upholders to His Majesty'. In this year also, perhaps to commemorate the new partnership, William France gave a copy of Sheraton's *Drawing Book*, 1793 to William Banting (MMA, NY, inscr: 'William France, with best wishes to W. Banting, 1812').

The main work for the Duke of Bedford was the furnishing between June 1807 and April 1810 of his London houses: 15 St James's Sq., 1 Hamilton Pl., and in Stanhope St, Mayfair. For this work a bill of 1808 totalled £538 13s 6d, and one of 1810 was for £556 14s 3d. Besides a supply of furniture and bedding on hire, and the provision and cleaning of roller blinds, curtains and carpets, new furniture was provided, the main items being:

From June 1807 to May 1808

A large mahogany bidet with white Wedgwood pan, the top stuffed & covered with satin & finished with chair gimp. £3. 10. 0.

A 4ft 3in eliptic tester field-bedstead with sacking bottom, japanned white, turned feet pillars & on castors. £3. 18. 0.

A bed wagon with heater & key & extra large stand. £1. 5. 0.

A mahogany crib bedstead with framed sliding sides & feet, caned. (for Woburn) £9. 9. 0.

Two very large deal library bookcases to fit testers, with open fronts, sliding shelves with racks & pilasters Japanned white, 6ft 6 in × 8ft 1in. £32 15s each.

From January–April 1810

4 3ft 6in wide field-bedsteads with eliptic testers, turned beech pillars, japanned white. £16. 18. 6.

6 Mahogany dressing chests of drawers with solid fronts and strong handles, 3ft 9in and 3ft 6in. £67. 0. 0.

3 3ft 6in wainscot chests of drawers. £23. 10. 0.

4 mahogany Pembroke tables with drawers. £19. 0. 6.

12 deal wash hand tables with drawers, moulded edges and high washboards. £21. 18. 6.

A plain mahogany kneehole writing desk . . . for steward's room. £14. 0. 0.

For commissions after 1812 see France & Banting. G.B.

France & Banting, 31 Pall Mall, St James's, London, u (1812–40). This partnership of William France jnr and William Banting was established in 1812. They are well represented in the Royal Household accounts, 1813–19. [PRO, LC 11/15; LC 11/27] They did upholstery, repairs, cleaning, moving, alterations and fixing at various places such as Westminster Hall, Carlton House, Swinley Lodge, Brighton, etc. Their invoice for the quarter ending 5 January 1814 [PRO, LC 11/15] includes much library furniture in the Duke of Sussex's apartments at Kensington Palace, including a mahogany pedestal table supported on octagon pillars, £96 10s, mahogany book cases, £31 8s, a carved antique chair with lions heads, paws, rosettes etc., £97 18s 4d. For the Military Chapel, Whitehall, in the same quarter (January 1815) they invoiced for a handsome richly carved lion, unicorn, crown etc., stars gilt in burnished and matt gold, £36 10s.

There was no diminution in activity in succeeding years. From 1823 to June 1830 with invoices headed 'Bantings France and Banting', and (in 1831) 'Thomas Banting', they supplied men for general jobbing, cleaning work on carpets, upholstery etc. at some twenty Government offices, or Royal apartments. [PRO, LC 11/41–11/18; LC 11/59–68 are headed as 'Bantings, France and Bantings'] In latter years there is evidence that the title changed so that Banting came first, before France. See Banting, France & Co. G.B.

France & Paten, 17 James St, Haymarket, London, u (1825). [D]

Frances, William, 77 West St, Bristol, cm (1775). [D]

Francies, Jane, Cheap St, Bath, Som., upholder (1805). [D]

Francis, David, 2 Turnstile Alley, Drury Lane, London, broker and cm (1806). Took out a Sun Insurance policy on 12 August 1806 for £200 of which stock, utensils and goods in trust accounted for £180. [GL, Sun MS vol. 437, ref. 792614]

Francis, H., address unrecorded. In December 1839 he supplied to Buckingham Palace '4 new Spanish mahogany sideboards, carved & gilt' costing £150; and carried out alterations to six others for £130. He charged £62 for a further '4 fine Spanish mahogany sideboards with bold frieze & compo. mouldings: rich front, carved mahogany legs, enclosed at back for glasses, and compo. moulding, round deal loose tops to drop in — French polished — to fit up with plain mahogany carcases'. In June 1841, he provided three mahogany chests of drawers for £16 10s. [Windsor Royal Archives, RA, Box 1, item 2]

Francis, Hamilton G., Golden Sq., London, upholder (1774). [Poll bk]

Francis, Jacob, 57 Kenwyn St, Truro, Cornwall, cm (1830). [D]

Francis, Joseph, High Wycombe, Bucks., chair bottomer

(b. c. 1796–1841). Son James bapt. in 1819. Aged 45 at the time of the 1841 Census. [PR(bapt.)]

Francis, Maria, 29 Bostock St, Liverpool, u (1834). [D]

Francis, R., Lancaster, caner (1794–95). [Westminster Ref. Lib., Gillow records]

Francis, Stephen, Walworth, London, cm, u and undertaker (1826–39). Trading also as Venetian blind maker at 2 Hampton St in 1826; and listed at 52 Trafalgar St (or Sq.), 1835–39. [D]

Francis, Thomas, 2 Church St, Drypool, Hull, Yorks., cm (1838–39). [D]

Francis, Thomas, Noble St, Wem, Salop, joiner and cm (1840). [D]

Francis, William, 104 New Bond St, London, cm and u (1793–1840). For details of Francis's career in partnership with his brother-in-law see entry on Charles Elliott.

He was involved with Elliott in much work for various of the Royal palaces. He was assigned the lease of 17 Portland Pl., London in 1828 [Marylebone Lib., deed 1092], and having succeeded Elliott about this time his name is the one appearing in the Royal Household accounts. [PRO, LC 11/56–74] He occurs in trade directories between 1827 and 1839 at 104 New Bond St. The following PRO, LC entries, 1832–40, show the range of work:

ST JAMES'S PALACE [PRO, LC 11/77]
HAMPTON COURT, Stud Lodge: jobbing work [PRO, LC 11/80] 3 Spanish mahog. writing tables with drawers, on pilaster ends & claw feet 18gns
Mahogany hanging bookshelf with drawers (Best Bedroom Floor) £1. 10s.
Attic Bedrooms 8 mahog. swing frame dressing glasses, 14″ × 10″ £6. 12s.
2 × 3′ 3″ wainscot chests of 5 drawers each £9. 8s.
6 mahogany hanging dressing glasses, 10″ × 8″ £2. 8s.
24 japanned rush seat chairs £7. 4s.
Entrance Hall 2 oak gothic tables, each of 1 drawer, octagon-turned legs £8. 14s.

ST JAMES'S PALACE, Harrington House [PRO LC 11/83]
Gentlemen of the Wine Cellar
Mahogany high sloping desk on 4 upturned legs £6. 4s.

WINDSOR CASTLE [PRO, LC 11/86]
18 × 3′ 6″ mahogany chests of 5 drawers, moulded bases & turned feet £121. 10s.
10 swing dressing glasses, 18″ × 14″, in mahogany-cased pillar frames £33. 0s.
11 mahog. dressing tables, 3′ 6″, 2 drawers, rims to tops & shelf below £58. 1s.
4 mahoga. washing tables, 3′ 6″, with deep splash boards, 3 drawers in each & a shelf at bottom £22. 16s.
12 mahog. front easy chairs with sunk grooves, on turned legs & castors, each with a loose cushion covered in buttoned Morocco £110. 8s.

ST JAMES'S PALACE
4 hanging dressing glasses in mahog. frames for Servants' Rooms £1. 12s.

ST JAMES'S PALACE, Lord Chamberlain's Office [PRO, LC 11/89]
A good mahogany chest of drawers on turned feet £5. 16s.

ST JAMES'S PALACE, Footmen's Rooms [PRO, LC 11/92]
4 hanging dressing glasses in mahogany frames £1. 16s.

ST JAMES'S PALACE, Lord Chamberlain's Office [PRO, LC 11/95]
8 Feb. 1837: Japanned bamboo washhandstand, lifting top enclosed under, with a drawer, a plugged basin & fittings & tin receiver £8. 0s.

KENSINGTON PALACE, Housekeeper's Apartments
7 March 1837: Tent bedstead with mahogany sides £9. 14s.

2 single japanned French bedsteads £8. 0s.
3 japanned chests, each of 5 drawers £10. 4s.
2 mahog. Pembroke tables with turned legs, a drawer in each £6. 6s.
2 single ½-tester servant's bedsteads £7. 2s.
12 birch caned-seat runner chairs £5. 14s.
1 double japanned washhandstand with washboard, 2 drawers & shelf £3. 10s.
1 Spanish mahog. dressing table, 2 drawers, on turned legs £3. 18s.
1 swing dressing glass, 18″ × 14″, in mahogany tray frame 12. 8s.

ST JAMES'S PALACE, Sec. to the Board of Green Cloth [PRO, LC 11/98]
3′ 6″ Honduras mahogany chest of 5 drawers £5. 5s.

BUCKINGHAM PALACE [PRO, LC 11/104]
2 × 3′ 6″ Span. mahog. chests of 5 drawers, on turned feet £16. 0s.
1 × 4′ Span. mahogany chest of 6 drawers, turned feet £10. 10s.
3 × 3′ 6″ good mahog. chests of 5 drawers, on turned feet £18. 10s.

BUCKINGHAM PALACE, Prince Albert's Wardrobe [PRO, LC 11/110]
4 mahogany wardrobes with moulded cornices & mahog. pilasters £33. 0s.
Another £14. 14s.
Another, matching, to form a closet £9. 14s.

BUCKINGHAM PALACE [PRO, LC 11/100]
A bedchair stuffed and covered in Manchester stripe £2. 0s.

Francis, William Scaggs, 18 Ratcliff Highway, London, cm and u (1827–37). Polled at Malden, Essex, in 1826. [D]

Francis, Gilbert & Bonner, 43 Aldersgate St, London, cabinet warehouse (1790–93). [D]

Frangton, George, Stratford-upon-Avon, Warks., cm (1798). [D]

Frank, John, Leeds, Yorks., journeyman cm (1791). Named in the *Leeds Cabinet and Chair Makers' Book of Prices*, 1791, as a journeyman in basic sympathy with its contents.

Frank, William, Castlegate, Helmsley, Yorks., joiner and cm (1823–34). [D]

Frankland, Henry, 16 Willow Walk, Shoreditch, London, chairmaker (1808). [D]

Frankland, James, Kennington Lane, London, cm and u (1827–28). [D]

Frankland, Joseph, 38 Brick Lane, Spitalfields, London, u (1813). [D]

Frankland (or Franklin), Joseph, Preston, Lancs., chairmaker, dealer in furniture and cane-worker (1814–34). Recorded at 19 Friargate, 1814–18; Shambles in 1822; 19 Shambles in 1825; and no. 2 in 1828. [D]

Frankland, William, Egton, near Whitby, Yorks., chairmaker (1840). [D]

Frankland & Co., 37 Church St, Liverpool, carvers and gilders, artists' repository and commission rooms for sale of pictures, drawings and works of art (1824). [D]

Franklin (or Franklyn), Arthur, Paradise Row, London, cm and u (1820–37). Trading at no. 22, 1822–28; no. 11, 1835 and 1837, when he is recorded as a 'flour factor'. [D]

Franklin, Benjamin, 15 Harp Alley, Fleet Mkt, London, cm (1803). Took out a Sun Insurance policy on 26 August 1803 for £200 of which £50 accounted for utensils and stock. [GL, Sun MS vol. 426, ref. 752059]

Franklin, Frederick, Rochester Row, London, carver (1774). [Poll bk]

Franklin, J., Paradise St, Rotherhithe, London, u (1826–27). [D]

Franklin, J., 47 North St, Brighton, Sussex, cm and u (1827). [D]

Franklin, Jacob A., 1 St Ann's Pl., Manchester, barometer and looking-glass maker (1838–40). [D]

Franklin, James, 227 Shoreditch, London, cabinet manufactory owner (1825). [D]

Franklin, James, Market Sq., St Neots, Hunts., cm (1839). [D]

Franklin, Jeremiah, Oxford, master carpenter (1705–32). In 1729 he received an order from All Soul's College to provide bookcases, referred to as desks, for the ground floor of Codrington Library, at a cost of £32 14s each, excluding 'Lock, Wier work and painting'. Those on the north wall seem to have been completed by 1732 at an estimated cost of £999, those of the south wall costing £338. Franklin did not complete the job. On 5 July 1705 he took as app. Thomas Phillips, who became a leading master carpenter in London during the reigns of George I and II. [All Souls, MS, DD256]

Franklin, John, address unrecorded, u (1803). Subscribed to Sheraton's Cabinet Dictionary, 1803.

Franklin, John, 11 Tufton St, Westminster, London, u (1817–39). [D]

Franklin, Richard, Alcester, Warks., cm (1818). [Evesham poll bk]

Franklin, Thomas, address unrecorded, cm (1803). Subscribed to Sheraton's Cabinet Dictionary, 1803.

Franklin, Thomas, 5 Warden's Ct, Clerkenwell Close, London, chairmaker (1803). Took out a Sun Insurance policy on 16 May 1803 for £100 of which £20 accounted for utensils and stock 'in dwelling house of Oakley in St. Paul's Church Yard.' [GL, Sun MS vol. 426, ref. 747656]

Franklin, Thomas, 47 North St, Brighton, Sussex, cm and u (1826). [D]

Franklin, Thomas, Rochester, Kent, cm (1830). [Poll bk]

Franklin, Thomas, 10 College St, Southampton, Hants., cm and chairmaker (1839). [D]

Franklin, William, Lower St, Stroud, Glos., sworn measurer and architectural surveyor, gilder and painter (1820). [D]

Franklin, William, High St, Bedford, cm and u (1823). [D]

Franklyn, —, Folkestone, Kent, u (1807). [D]

Franklyn, Margaret, Bristol, u (1814–23). Trading at Cock & Bottle Lane in 1814; 40 Castle Green, 1819–22; and 11 St Paul's St in 1823. [D]

Franks, —, London, cm (d. 1748). Notice in General Advertiser, 14 February 1748 read: 'Yesterday one Franks, a Cabinet Maker, who has been missing for several days was found hanging in an Apartment near Carpenters' Hall, at London Wall.'

Franks, —, Sandwich, Kent, cm (1807). [D]

Franks, James, 42 Webber Row, Blackfriars, London, cm (1837). [D]

Franks, John, 62 Edgware Rd, London, bedstead maker (1839). [D]

Fraser, —, London(?), cm (1741). On 24 January 1741 he was paid £4 for 'a Glass Book-case & other Work' done for Charles Rogers, Lawrence Pountney Lane, London. [Charles Rogers' accounts, Cottonian Coll., Plymouth City Museum and Art Gallery; Apollo, December 1960, pp. 196–98]

Fraser (or Frazer), Alexander, London, cm and u (1817–39). Recorded at 28 Norfolk St, Fitzroy Sq., 1817–21; 10 Charlotte St, Rathbone Pl., 1822–28; and 6 Tottenham Ct Rd in 1839. [D] See J. & A. Fraser.

Fraser, George, Clerkenwell, London, fancy chair and sofa manufacturer (1802–13). Recorded at 36–37 Rosoman St, 1802–08; 33 Rosamond's Row, 1808–11; and no. 38 in 1813. Took out a Sun Insurance policy on 16 June 1802 for £900 of which £200 accounted for utensils and stock. [D; GL, Sun MS vol. 423, ref. 732981]

Fraser, J., 10 Rathbone Pl., London, u (1823–25). [D]

Fraser, J. & A., 28 Norfolk St, Fitzroy Sq., London, cm (1813–16). [D] See Alexander Fraser.

Fraser, John, 11 near Duke St, Portman Sq., London, upholder (1782). Insured his house for £200 in 1782. [GL, Sun MS vol. 303, p. 652]

Fraser, John, 46 Castle St, Oxford St, London, upholder (1790–93). [D]

Fraser, John, Charles St, Marylebone, London, u (1793). Subscribed to Sheraton's Drawing Book, 1793, in which year he was named in Bailey's list of bankrupts.

Fraser, John, 21 John St, Fitzroy Rd, London, cm (1829–40). Took out Sun Insurance in 1840. [D; GL, Sun MS ref. 1339644]

Fraser, Robert, 4 Newgate St, Newcastle, carver and gilder (1838). [D]

Fraser, William, 6 Stafford Pl., Richmond Row, Liverpool, upholder (1834). [D]

Fraser & Scott, 12 Francis St, Tottenham Ct Rd, London, cm (1817–19). [D]

Fray, John, Chowbent, Bolton, Lancs., joiner and cm (1818–25). [D]

Frazer, John, Liverpool, cm (b. 1783–d. 1827). Trading at 4 Ward St in 1811. Death aged 44, in Manchester but late of Liverpool, reported in Liverpool Mercury, 6 July 1827. [D]

Frazer, William, Last Lane, Dover, Kent, carver and gilder (1839). [D]

Frazier, Thomas, Aldersgate St, London, cm (1822–35). Recorded at no. 113 in 1822, and no. 71 in 1835. Took out a Sun Insurance policy on 11 September 1822 for £500 on household goods. [D; GL, Sun MS vol. 490, ref. 995676]

Freame, —, Worcester, cm, u, auctioneer and appraiser. Two early 19th-century trade cards give addresses at 11 Goose Lane and 52 High St. The first, probably slightly earlier, shows a Klismos chair, a bed with a pediment bearing a Classical urn, and a bureau bookcase. The second card is embellished with splendid draped curtains across two windows, two chairs and a Classical sofa. [Heal and Hodgkin Colls, BM] On 8 December 1823 Freame of Worcester supplied Nicholas Pearse of Loughton Hall, Essex, and Marylebone, London, with a portable bidet costing £3. [Essex RO, D/DHt A1/3] Probably Charles or T. Freame.

Freame, Charles, Goose Lane, Five Doors from the Cross, Worcester, cabinet, upholstery and fancy chair manufactory, carver and gilder, paper hangings, carpets, fringes, portable tables, sofas, chair beds etc. (1820). [D]

Freame, Charles, Worcester, cm, u and fancy chair manufacturer (1818–40). Trading in partnership with Ann Freame at 11 Grove Lane in 1822 and 11 St Swithin St, 1830–40. Admitted freeman in 1818, and named in the Worcester freemen rolls on 1 December 1835. Trade card, c. 1820, shows sofa and two side chairs displayed against elaborately draped windows, and reads: 'CHARLES FREAME, CABINET, UPHOLSTERY AND FANCY CHAIR MANU-FACTURER &c. WORCESTER, CARVER, GILDERS &c. PAPER HANGINGS, CARPETS, FRINGES &c. PORT-ABLE TABLES, SOFA'S, CHAIR BEDS &c. AUCTIONEER & APPRAISER. FUNERALS FURNISHED.' [D; D. White-head, The Book of Worcester, p. 65]

Freame, Frederick, 76 Well St, Oxford St, London, cm and chairmaker (1826–27). [D]

Freame, Henry, London, u (1828–35). Admitted freeman of Worcester in 1828, and named in the freemen rolls on 1 December 1835.

Freame, T., Goose Lane, Worcester, cm and u (1820). [D] See Freame, —, and Charles Freame.

Freare, John, Knottingley, near Ferrybridge, Yorks., cm (1822). [D]

Freckleton, Henry, Preston, Lancs., u and innkeeper (1778–82). Declared bankrupt, *Gents Mag.*, February 1778. Named in the Preston Guild record of burgesses in 1782.

Fredric, George, 10 Crown St, Soho, London, cm (1826–27). [D]

Free, Thomas, Hull, Yorks., trunk, chest and box maker and lottery agent (1790–1834). Addresses given at The Butchery, 1790–1803; 20 Queen St, 1806–17 and 1831–34; and no. 12, 1821–26. Trading as Thomas & Son, trunk and portmanteau manufacturers, in 1831. [D]

Freelove, —, address unrecorded. On 13 September 1739 he proposed providing bedding in the new wards at St Bartholomew's Royal Hospital, London. Mentioned again in connection with the Hospital on 24 July 1740, and 5 February 1741. [St Bartholomew's archives, Ha 1/11 Journal, 1734–48, pp. 203, 236 and 249]

Freelove, Richard, address unrecorded, upholder (1713–d. 1776). Son of William Freelove, yeoman of Kilburne. App. to Charles Williams on 3 June 1713, and admitted freeman of the Upholders' Co. by servitude on 15 February 1721. Named as master in 1751. Took app. named Andrew Braint, 1743–58. [GL, Upholders' Co. records]

Freelove, Richard, London, u (1726–36). Addresses given at Little Ormond Yd, Ormond St in 1726; Ormond St, 1728–32; and Queen Sq., 1734. Named in newspapers, 1728–32. [Heal] Took out Sun Insurance policies on 24 June 1726 for £500; and on 5 March 1734 for £300 on household goods, stock in trade and goods in trust in his house. Supplied furniture (largely walnut, some mahogany and some gilt wood), chimney furniture and upholstery to the value of £391 1s 6d to Temple Newsam House, Leeds, between May 1728 and July 1729; and July to December 1736. [Poll bk; GL, Sun MS vol. 23, p. 21; vol. 38, ref. 63231; *Conn.*, December 1964, p. 224; *Furn. Hist.*, 1967]

Freelove, William, Lincoln's Inn Fields, near Clare Mkt, London, upholder and broker (1726). Notice in the press, 21 April 1726 read: 'I, John Henley, clerk, teacher, or preacher to a congregation of protestants dissenting from the Church of England, scrupling infant baptism, pursuant to the statute in that case made, do hereby certify to his Majesty's justices of the peace now assembled in Quarter Sessions in Hicks Hall, that I have appointed the house now in the possession OF ONE William Freelove, upholder and broker, in Great Lincoln's Inn Fields, near Clare Market, in the parish of St. Giles-in-the-Fields, to assemble and meet in for religious worship.' [Heal; Winterthur, Delaware, Symonds papers, 75x69.29]

Freelove, William, London, u (1756). Named in the Burlington papers, Chatsworth, in December 1756 receiving £13 12s. [Abstract of tradesmen's accounts, f. 16]

Freeman, —, London(?), u (1703). Named in the personal account book of the Duke of Leeds on 19 March 1703 being paid 14s. [YAS, DD5/39]

Freeman, —, London, cm (b. 1756–d. 1803). Death, aged 47, reported in *Gents Mag.*, May 1803.

Freeman, —, London, cm (1793). Subscribed to Sheraton's *Drawing Book*, 1793.

Freeman, —, Oxford, cm and joiner (1793). Subscribed to Sheraton's *Drawing Book*, 1793.

Freeman, Ant(h)ony, London, u (1722–27). In 1722 he supplied materials for a chair and canopy of state of crimson Genoa damask trimmed with gold and silver fringe to Stephen Poyntz, 'one of His Majesty's Ambassadors Extra-ordinary'. In 1727 he provided another ambassador with a canopy of estate, cushions and stools, all covered with damask and costing £34, supplied to Kensington Palace. [Winterthur,

Delaware, Symonds papers, 75x64.14, p. 133; PRO, LC9/287, pp. 1522–153]

Freeman, Charles, Halesworth, Suffolk, cm (1824). [D]

Freeman, Edmund, Nantwich, Cheshire, u (d. 1788). Buried on 25 March 1788 as u and pauper. [Chester RO, PR]

Freeman, Edward, Bristol, u (1719). Took app. named Perkins in 1719. [S of G, app. index]

Freeman, Edward, Norwich, cm and chairmaker (1760–1803). On 19 April 1760 Edward Freeman, cm, son of Edward Freeman, carpenter was admitted a freeman of Norwich. He is recorded in the Norwich poll bk of 1768. The *Norwich Chronicle*, 11 September 1779 carried the advertisement 'Now SELLING OFF at PRIME COST, at Freeman's Cabinet and Chair Warehouse, at the back of the Inns, Norwich, All Sorts of Goods in the Cabinet and Chair Branches; consisting of Mahogany and Wainscot Dining Tables of all Sizes, Tea, Card and Dressing Tables of all Sorts, Mahogany and Wainscot Desks, Book-cases, Bureaus and Chests of Drawers of all Sorts, forty Dozen of Mahogany and other Chairs of various Patterns, Tea Chests and Tea Trays, Variety of Jamb and Dressing Glasses, neat Oval Sconces, gilt Frames of the newest Patterns, Bureau and Four-post Bedsteads, and Bedding of all Sorts, handsom Beaufets new and second-hand and many other Articles in the Cabinet and Chair Trade'.

The Rev. James Woodforde, Rector of Weston Longueville, Norfolk, noted in his diary for October 1779, that Freeman at the Back of the Inns, Norwich, supplied him with '2 sets of Chest of Drawers in Mahogany, a Chest of Drawers of Ditto and half a Dozen new Ash Chairs for my Kitchen pd in Part 1 ; 1 ; 0'. He subsequently paid Freeman £10 15s.

Chase's *Directory*, 1783 records him at no. 20 Back of the Inns but from Bailey's *British Directory*, 1784 up to his last entry in Peck's *Norwich Directory*, 1803 he is recorded at no. 16. [Norwich freemen admission reg.; *Antique Collector*, December 1953; *The Diary of James Woodforde*]   R.W.

Freeman, Elizabeth, 18 Rose & Crown Ct, Finsbury, London, u (1839). [D] See Rob. Freeman.

Freeman, Francis, 1 Little Newport St, London, tobacco seller and turner (1794). Took out a Sun Insurance policy on 7 May 1794 for £950 on his house. [GL, Sun MS vol. 401, ref. 628230]

Freeman, James, Norwich, cm (1798–1818). *The Universal British Directory*, 1798 contains the first record of James Freeman. He was enrolled as a freeman of Norwich on 24 February 1811. The Norwich poll bk of 1818 lists him in the parish of St Peter Mancroft. [Norwich freemen rolls]

Freeman, James, 2 Marlborough St, Southwark, London, cm and u (1839). [D]

Freeman, Jeremiah and successors, Norwich, carvers and gilders (1792–1850). Jeremiah Freeman, carver was admitted a freeman of Norwich on 18 June 1792. The *Universal British Directory*, 1798, Peck's *Norwich Directories*, 1801, 1803 and Holden's, 1805 list him as a carver and gilder at 2 London Lane, Norwich. This is the address on a trade card [GL] which states: 'FREEMAN, Carver and Gilder, Looking-Glass Manufacturer, and Print-Seller, No. 2, London-Lane Norwich, Makes all kinds of Furniture in Carving and Gilding; variety of Looking-glasses, Girandoles, Brackets, Gold Border for Rooms &c. &c. in the first style of elegance'. Berry's *Directory*, 1810 lists Freeman & Son, carvers and gilders at London Lane, no doubt Jeremiah and William Freeman of London Lane, whose invoices made out to Wm Foster are dated between 1814–20, that of 1814, for £17 3s 6d including a chimney glass in a gild frame at £15 15s 6d. Their label is also found on one of four torchères at Felbrigg Hall, Norfolk, headed 'Jeremiah and William Freeman, Carvers, Gilders & Looking-Glass Manufacturers,

Wholesale & Retail, No. 2, London-Lane, Norwich'. The will of Jeremiah Freeman was proved at Norwich in 1823. William Freeman is listed in the Norwich poll bk of 1818. Pigot's *Directories*, 1822 and 1830 record him as a carver, gilder and looking-glass manufacturer at 2 London Lane (altered to St by 1830). The directories from 1836–50 list him as a cm, u, carver, gilder and mahogany merchant at 2 London St and Pottergate. William Freeman also used a trade label, a copy of which is on a gilt Rococo-style table with a marble top at Blickling Hall, Norfolk. This has the address 'London & SWAN LANE, Norwich' (Swan Lane runs from London St to Bedford St, formerly part of Pottergate) with the words London and Norwich in bold type, which has caused confusion as indicating a London branch of the business. No record of this has been found and it was most probably arranged that way so that the type was balanced although giving the idea of a London connection was probably not unwelcome. William Philip Barnes Freeman, carver and gilder, son of William Freeman, carver and gilder was admitted a freeman of Norwich on 25 July 1835. [Norwich freemen reg.; invoices, Norwich Local Hist. Lib.; Nat. Trust guide to *Felbrigg Hall*; Norfolk Record Soc., index of wills; *Furn. Hist.*, 1974] R.W.

Freeman, Jeremiah, London Lane, Norwich, carver and gilder (1808). [D]

Freeman, John Norwich, cm and u (1801–12). Peck's *Norwich Directory*, 1801 and Berry's of 1810 both record John Freeman at 11 and 12 Upper Market. The last poll bk to list his name is that of 1812. He was also a subscriber to Thomas Sheraton's *Cabinet Dictionary*, 1803. In 1802 he supplied furnishings to the value of almost £2,000 to John Worth, The White House, Oakley, Norfolk. This included equipping the dining-room, drawing-room, study, bedrooms etc. Extracts from the account are liberally quoted and chairs, sideboard, tables and cabinets are illustrated by H. M. Walker, *Conn.*, LXIX (1924).

Freeman, John, Upper Market St, Norwich, cm (1808). [D]

Freeman, Jonah, Laxton's Ct, Long Acre, Southwark, London, cm (1786). Took out a Sun Insurance policy on 4 July 1786 for £56 on household goods and £130 on utensils and stock in his workshop. [GL, Sun MS vol. 339, p. 28]

Freeman, Jos., 7 Broad St, Golden Sq., London, carver and gilder (1823). [D; *Furn. Hist.*, 1974]

Freeman, Joseph, near the Turnpike, Borough Rd, London, looking-glass frame maker (1803). Took out a Sun Insurance policy on 13 June 1803 for £1,200 of which £600 accounted for utensils and stock. [GL, Sun MS vol. 426, ref. 747839]

Freeman, Joseph, 29 John St, Tottenham Ct Rd, London, carver and gilder (1829). [D]

Freeman, Matthew, Dolphin Ct, Ludgate Hill, London, cm (1778). Took out a Sun Insurance policy in 1778 for £100, £80 on utensils and stock. [GL, Sun MS vol. 271, p. 26]

Freeman, Matthew, 28 Addle Hill, Doctors Common, London, cm (1787–89). Insured household goods for £100 on 9 April 1787. [D; GL, Sun MS vol. 344, p. 393]

Freeman, Rob., Rose & Crown Ct, Moorfields, London, chair and sofa manufacturer (1823–37). Recorded at no. 17, 1823–28; and no. 18, 1829–35. [D] See Elizabeth Freeman.

Freeman, Thomas, Wood St, Stratford-upon-Avon, Warks., joiner and cm (1828–30). [D]

Freeman, W., 4 Praed St, Paddington, London, u (1826–27). [D]

Freeman, William, Chesham, Bucks., chairmaker (1725). Took app. named Rolls in 1725. [S of G, app. index]

Freeman, William, Norwich, cm (1811–39). William Freeman, cm was enrolled as a freeman of Norwich on 24 February 1811. He is recorded in the poll bk of 1812 at St Andrew's and that of 1830 in the parish of St Simon and St Jude. Robson's

Directory, 1839 lists him as a general furniture maker and broker at St Andrews. A plain mahogany two door cupboard of approximately this date has been noted with 'From Freemans/MANUFACTORY/St. ANDREWS NORWICH' stencilled on the back (Fig. 17). William Hicklenton, cm, app. of William Freeman, was admitted a freeman of Norwich on 3 May 1818. [Moss's of Baldock, *125 Years of Cabinet-making* (Exhib. cat.) July 1984; Norwich freemen reg.] R.W.

Freeman, William, Water Lane, Faversham, Kent, chairmaker (1832–34). [D]

Freer, John, George St, Tamworth, Staffs., chairmaker (1818). [D]

Freer, John, Oldbury, Tewkesbury, Glos., chairmaker (1827). [PR(bapt.)]

Freer, Matthias, York, carver and gilder (1760). Son of Matthias Freer of Gawthorpe; app. to Christopher Fairbank, carver and gilder, on 12 April 1760. [York app. reg.]

Freetum, William, Richmond, Yorks., cm (1818). [PR(bapt.)]

Freiker & Henderson, New Bond St, London, carvers and gilders (1813–18). Worked at Carlton House, preparatory to fitting up the Pagoda and Chinese Pavillion in the Orange Groves in the Gardens. They were paid £23 12s on 10 October 1813 for 'removing old Chinese ornaments, arranging ditto — & preparing & cleaning the same for the Pagoda and Pavillion. Assisting the decorators in fitting them up and the tables — and removing, repairing, cleaning and putting away after the dejeuné.' On 10 October 1818 their bill totalled £899 2s for work done in the Entrance Room at Carlton House, comprising '4 richly carved panels for door heads consisting vitruvious foliage . . . 4 rich frames surrounding pictures . . . 154 feet of 4" moulding . . . Work on mouldings in large blue velvet room and small blue velvet room.' [Royal Household accounts, PRO, LC11/15 and 18]

Frembly, John, 1 Belvidere Pl., St George's Fields, London, looking-glass frame maker (1820). [D]

French, —, address unrecorded, u (1836–39). Recorded in the account books of 3rd Lord Braybrooke of Audley End, Essex, London, and Billingbear, Berks., in April 1836 receiving £6 0s 3d; and in June 1839, £6 5s 6d. [Essex RO, D/DBy/A363]

French, C., 8 Nottingham St, Marylebone, London, cm, u etc. (1820). [D]

French, Flanders, St Neots, Hunts., chairmaker (1764). [Hunts. RO, trade index, marriage bonds]

French, George, Long St, Dursley, Glos., plumber, glazier, painter, sign writer and gilder (1820). [D]

French, J., Weaverham, Cheshire, clockcase maker. The gilt inscription 'J. French, Cabinet Maker, Weaverham, Cheshire' has been recorded on the hood-frieze of at least six long-case clocks by Richards of Weaverham.

French, J., Lancaster, caner (1800). [Westminster Ref. Lib., Gillow records]

French, John, Canterbury, Kent, cm (1741). [Canterbury freemen rolls]

French, John, 10 Queen St, Cheapside, London, u and cm (1784–94). Admitted freeman of the Upholders' Co. by redemption by order of the Court of Aldermen on 7 April 1784. Trade card, *c.* 1785, is the same in design to that of Elward & Marsh. Declared bankrupt, *Williamson's Liverpool Advertiser*, 19 January 1789. [D; GL, Upholders' Co. records; Banks Coll., BM]

French, John, 10 Holywell Row, Shoreditch, London, cabinet varnisher (1826–27). [D]

French, John, 10 Upper Fitzroy St, Fitzroy Sq., London, cm and upholder (1826–28). [D]

French, John, 2 Clipstone St, Fitzroy Sq., London, u (1839). [D]

French, Michael, Heighington, Co. Durham, joiner and/or cm (1834). [D]

French, Robert, 43 Savile St, Hull, Yorks., joiner and bedstead manufacturer (1826). [D]

French, Thomas, London(?), cm (1731). In 1731 he received £44 16s 2d for unspecified work done for James Brydges, 1st Duke of Chandos at Canons, Middlx. [Huntington Lib., California, MS ST/82, p. 81]

French, Thomas, Clayton St, Colne, Lancs., chairmaker (b. *c.* 1801–1841). Aged 40 at the time of the 1841 Census.

French, Thomas, 30 Newington Causeway, London, cm etc. (1816). [D]

French, William, London, cm, u and undertaker (1803–39). Trading at 7 Edward St, Portman Sq., 1820–39. Subscribed to Sheraton's *Cabinet Dictionary*, 1803. [D]

Frerars, Pet., 67 Quadrant, Regent St, London, carver and gilder (1835). [D]

Fretwell, Allen, Pontefract, Yorks., cm and appraiser (d. 1788). Notice in *Leeds Intelligencer*, 3 June 1788 read: 'Saturday night Allen Fretwell died — for many years a considerable appraiser & cabinet maker (in Pontefract).'

Fret(t)well, Allen, 128 (High) Holborn, London, cm and auctioneer (1789–93). Named in Bailey's list of bankrupts, 1790. [D]

Fretwell, Peter, Leeds, Yorks., journeyman cm (1791). Named in the *Leeds Cabinet and Chair Makers' Book of Prices*, 1791, amongst journeymen in basic sympathy with its contents.

Fretwell (or Fretwill), William, Cherry St, Birmingham, upholder (1800–18). [D]

Fretwill, Mary, Cherry St, Birmingham, u (1822). [D]

Fricker, Charles, Town's-end, Kingston, Surrey, u etc. (1822). [D]

Fricker, James, Kingston, Surrey, u (1826–32). Recorded at Pig Mkt in 1826, and Church St, 1832. [D]

Fricker, Thomas, New St Sq., Fetter Lane, London, glass seller (1777). *Daily Advertiser*, 4 July 1777 announced that Fricker had ceased to be in partnership with Purcell. [Wills, *Looking-Glasses*]

Fricker & Henderson, New Bond St, London, paper-hanging warehouse (*c.* 1820–23). Directories during the first decade of the 19th century record the firm at no. 161, and at no. 80, 1820–21. Executed carving and gilding at the Royal Pavilion, Brighton, *c.* 1820, including the Music Room, costing £1,321 15s 10d; the Saloon, more that £3,000; and the Banqueting Room, £7,944 8s 2d, the latter including £216 18s for the chimney glasses. [D; Wills, *Looking-Glasses*] See Henderson and Jas. Henderson.

Friend, Caril, London, upholder (1746–d. 1779/80). Son of George Friend I, upholder of London, and brother of George Friend II. Admitted freeman of the Upholders' Co. by patrimony on 5 February 1746/47, and master in 1773. Declared insolvent in 1775. Recorded in Clerkenwell in 1778. Father of George Friend III. [GL, Upholders' Co. records]

Friend, George I, London, u (1709–d. 1741). Trading near the Pump, Watling St, 1713–32. Father of George Friend II and Caril Friend; grandfather of George Friend III. Master of the Upholders' Co. in 1741. Took apps named John Wattson 1709–16/17; Andrew Milhum in 1715; Isaac Cooke, 1715–22; Thomas Stratford in 1722; William Kilpin, 1725–33/34; Samuel Whiting, 1728–35; George Friend II, 1732/33–1741; and Thomas Whitworth, 1735–44. Took out a Sun Insurance policy on 27 April 1713 on his goods; and a Hand in Hand policy on 14 August 1716 for £225 on his dwelling. Named in newspapers, 1726–32. [GL, Upholders' Co. records; GL, Sun MS vol. 3, ref. 3076; GL, Hand in Hand MS vol. 16, p. 112; Heal]

Friend, George II, London, upholder (1732–d. 1784). Recorded in Clerkenwell, 1778–81. Son of George Friend I, upholder of London, and brother of Caril Friend. App to his father on 31 January 1732/33, and admitted freeman of the Upholders' Co. by servitude on 16 December 1741. Named as master in 1769. [GL, Upholders' Co. records]

Friend, George III, London, upholder (1775–1802). Trading at St James Walk, Clerkenwell, 1794–1802. Son of Caril Friend; admitted freeman of the Upholders' Co. by patrimony on 3 May 1775. [GL, Upholders' Co. records]

Friend, James, The Parade, Tunbridge Wells, Kent, Tunbridge-ware manufacturer and fancy repository (1810–39). [D; poll bk; trade card, Johnson Coll., Bodleian Lib., Oxford; Kent RO, Speldhurst poor rate bks, P344/11/1]

Friend, Thomas, Canterbury, Kent, u (1704). [Canterbury freemen rolls]

Friend, Thomas, Canterbury, Kent, cm and furniture broker (1826–39). Addresses given at 5 Best Lane, 1826–29; 15 Orange St, 1832–34; and 75 Northgate, 1838–39. [D; poll bk]

Friend, Thomas, High St, Bishop Wearmouth, Sunderland, Co. Durham, cm (1827). [D]

Friend & Vinton, 140 High St, Ramsgate, Kent, cm, brokers and undertakers (1838–39). [D]

Frint, Charles, Norwich, chairmaker (1744–90). Son of William Frint; admitted freeman on 12 May 1744. [Poll bks; Norwich freemen rolls]

Frisby, Thomas, address unrecorded, cm (1826). His son, James of London, admitted freeman of Leicester in 1826 as a servant. [Leicester freemen rolls]

Frith, Gabriel, St James's, Westminster, London, upholder (1741–46). Took out Hand in Hand Insurance policies in 1741 for £400, £250 and again £250; assigned to John Aldridge in 1746. [GL, Hand in Hand MS vol. 62, refs 13736, 67529 and 67530]

Frith, H., address unrecorded. Impressed mark, 'H. FRITH', recorded on two pieces of mid-Regency furniture, stamped on upper edge of door; one is a marble-topped cabinet with brass inlay and glazed double doors.

Frith, William, address unrecorded, upholder (1743–52). Son of William Frith, barber of Surrey; app. to Thomas Parkes on 7 December 1743, and admitted freeman of the Upholders' Co. by servitude on 2 April 1752. [GL, Upholders' Co. records]

Frizell, George, Cornwallis Sq., South Shields, Co. Durham, cm and joiner (1828–29). [D]

Froggart (or Froggatt), Abraham, Brook St, Chorlton Row, Manchester, u (1825–36). Trading at no. 7 in 1825; no. 13, 1829–33; and no. 37 in 1836. [D]

Frogley, Arthur, Oxford, master carpenter (1664–95). Worked on the Sheldonian Theatre as master carpenter with Wren, 1664–69. Carried out the panelling in the Hall at Brasenose, and his bill survives for benches, chairs and tables made for it, 1683–84. Carried out the woodwork in the chapel of St Edmund's Hall, 1680–82; and in 1695 the scroll-work altar rails at St Mary's, Trinity College Chapel at a cost of £5 8s. [*Wren Soc.*, vol. XIX, p. 82]

Frohock, John, Silver St, Bedford, cm and u (1839). [D]

Frool, Henry, Coombe St, Exeter, Devon, cm (1836). Son Jesse bapt. at St Mary Major on 17 March 1836. [PR(bapt.)]

Froom, William, 136 Strand, London, carver and gilder, looking-glass manufacturer (1825–39). Trading as Froom & Crib(b) in 1829. [D] Handwritten bill on unheaded paper, dated 1826, lists four ornamental frames for looking-glasses and a pair of carved eagle brackets, supplied by Froom at a total cost of £110 17s. Bill notes in addition a pair of carved and gilt brackets forwarded for approval. [Cornwall RO, CCR DN CN 3445/1–18 (12)] In 1829 Froom & Cribb supplied a Louis XIV-style overmantel to Kilruddery, Co. Wicklow. [*C. Life*, 21 July 1977, p. 149]

Frost, Daniel, address unrecorded, u (1787–90). Provided furniture for Stoneleigh Abbey, Warks., between 3 April and 22 June 1787, costing £9 6s 4d. Between March and August 1788 items supplied included an inlaid fire screen stand, £1 1s; an oak chest bed and bedding, £7 19s 1d; '2 pillow & claw stands Inlaid', £2 10s; and 'A Large Mahogany Cabinett Inlaid frame sash front glaz'd', at £9 16s. From December 1789 to September 1790 Frost's bill lists four mahogany state chairs with stools, costing a total of £29; 'A Cormode chest of Drawers banded', £8 10s; '6 Japan'd chairs', £3 12s; a mahogany wardrobe, £9 9s; and 'A Black & gold frame glaz'd', 6s 6d. [Shakespeare Birthplace Trust, Leigh receipts DR 18/5]

Frost, George, Newmarket, Cambs., carpenter and cm (1776). Took out a Sun Insurance policy in 1776 for £300 of which £60 accounted for stock and workshop. [GL, Sun MS vol. 247, p. 346]

Frost, George, 2 Manor St, Clapham, London, cm and u (1839). [D]

Frost, Henry, Exeter, Devon, cm (1830–40). Recorded in Longbrook St, 1839–40. Children bapt. at St Sidwell's: Ellen Elizabeth on 24 June 1830 and Helen on 28 October 1835. [D; PR(bapt.)]

Frost, James, Norwich, cm (1771). Admitted freeman, not by apprenticeship, on 20 March 1771. [Norwich freeman reg.]

Frost, James, High St, Clapham, London, cm and u (1832–39). In 1837 he was paid £23 17s 6d by James Brogden, MP, for two new bedsteads, and repairing, renovating and re-upholstering chairs. [D; Essex RO, D/DSe 10]

Frost, Matthew, Exeter, Devon, cm (1832). [Voters list]

Frost, Richard, Broomhall, Chester, chairmaker (1741). Took app. named Whitaker in 1741. [S of G, app. index]

Frost, Richard, Cullompton, Devon, cm (1823–38). Recorded in Fore St, 1830–38. [D]

Frost, Samuel, Well St, Bury St Edmunds, Suffolk, chairmaker (1836). [Poll bk]

Frost, Sam., West St, Wiveliscombe, Som., cm (1839). [D]

Frost, Thomas, Norwich, u (1660–1710). Former app., James Thompson, admitted freeman on 23 January 1660. [Norwich freemen rolls; poll bk]

Frost, Thomas, Canterbury and Faversham, Kent, cm (1818–39). Addresses given at Jewry Lane, Canterbury in 1818; Faversham, 1830–38, in Tanner St, 1838. [D; poll bks]

Frost, Thomas, 2 Narrow Weir, Bristol, cm and undertaker (1828–31). [D]

Frost, William, Sidwell St, Exeter, Devon, chair caner (b. 1783–d. 1834). Named in *Exeter Journal*, 1827–34. Death, aged 51 'after a long illness', reported in *Exeter Flying Post*, 7 August 1834.

Frowd, Joseph, 21 Francis St, Tottenham Ct Rd, London, u and undertaker (1808). [D]

Froy, William, London, carver and gilder (1826–39). Trading at 3 Mansion House Pl., Camberwell, 1826–27, and 11 Dorville Row, Hammersmith, 1839. [D]

Fruin, William, 192 High St, Cheltenham, Glos., cm (1839). [D]

Fry, Edward, Fareham, Hants., cm and upholder (1781–84). Took out a Sun Insurance policy in 1781 for £1,000 of which utensils, stock, workshop and warehouse accounted for £450. [D; GL, Sun MS vol. 290, p. 536]

Fry, H., Albion St, Cheltenham, Glos., cabinet carver (1839). [D]

Fry, James, Magdalen St, Exeter, Devon, cm (1818). Daughters Esther and Jane bapt. at Holy Trinity Church on 21 January 1818. [PR(bapt.)]

Fry, James, Cheltenham, Glos., carver and gilder (1820–39).

Recorded at 8 St James's St in 1820, 6 Henrietta St, 1822–30, and Henrietta St, 1839. [D]

Fry, John, The Parade, Tunbridge Wells, Kent, cm, u and Tunbridge-ware manufacturer (1789–1829). Trade card, 1801, shows putti, one packing a parcel labelled 'Tunbridge Wares'. [D; Kent RO, U749/E15–9; Banks Coll., BM]

Fry, Mary, Parade, Tunbridge Wells, Kent, Tunbridge-ware maker (1772–78). In October 1778 she provided a loom, frame and broom for Gertrude, Dowager Duchess of Bedford. The bill for this is endorsed 'for Tunbridge ware', and totals £2 2s. [Bedford Office, London]

Fry, Richard, Brighton, Sussex, Tunbridge-ware manufacturer (1824–30). Addresses given at 57 Cavendish St in 1824; Nelson St in 1825; and Carlton Row in 1830. Named in the Brighton rate book, August 1824. Son Alfred bapt. in 1825 and daughter Prusilla in 1830. [D; Brighton RO, SB 351.2 BRI rate bk; E. Sussex RO, PR(bapt.)]

Fry, Samuel, 1 Lambeth Terr., London, chair and sofa maker (1839). [D]

Fry, Thomas, Blandford, Dorset, joiner and cm (1762). Took app. named Muston in 1762. [S of G, app. index]

Fry, Thomas, 16 Broad St, Bristol, carver and gilder (1801–17). Trading also at 4 Kington's Buildings, 1810–17. [D]

Fry, William, 2 New Dock St, Hull, Yorks., cm (1818). [D]

Fry, William, Constance Ct, Bridewell Lane, Bristol, cabinet carver (1832). [D]

Fryer, —, 19 Old Cavendish St, London, u (1803). See Edward Foxhall & Fryer.

Fryer, Benjamin, Broad Wear, Bristol, carpenter and cm (1805–07). [D]

Fryer, Francis, King St, Cheapside, London, wholesale u (1759–68). [D] See Robert & Ralph Fryer.

Fryer, George, Masham, Yorks., joiner and cm (1828–29). [D]

Fryer, James, 16 Sheppard St, Hanover Sq., London, upholder (1790–93). [D]

Fryer, Jonathan, West Wycombe, Bucks., chairmaker (b. c. 1806–41). Aged 35 at the time of the 1841 Census.

Fryer, Michael, York, cm (1819–23). Trading at Fossgate in 1823. His son, Ralph Page Fryer, was app. to George Stones on 29 March 1819. [D; York app. reg.]

Fryer, Ralph Page, York, cm (1819). Son of Michael Fryer, cm; app. to George Stones, cm, on 29 March 1819. [York app. reg.]

Fryer, Ralph, Barn St, Little Bolton, Lancs., cm (1840). Took out a Sun Insurance policy in 1840. [GL, Sun MS vol. 267, ref. 1332114]

Fryer, Richard, Bristol, cm (1758–75). Recorded at 21 Wilder St in 1775. Took apps named Bailly in 1758 and Flower in 1759. [D; S of G, app. index]

Fryer (or Fryar), Richard, 13 Guildford St, Leeds, Yorks., carver and gilder (1828–37). Addresses given at 16 Bond St, 1828–30, and 13 Guildford St, 1834–37. [D]

Fryer, Robert & Ralph, London, wholesale u and cm (1767–93). Trading together at 23 King St, Cheapside, 1767–68; and 23 Aldermanbury, 1769–70. Robert is recorded there alone, 1770–79; and at 24 Addle St, 1790–93. Robert and Ralph were declared bankrupt, *Gents Mag.*, August 1768; and the sale of their stock in trade was announced in the *Public Advertiser*, 25 October 1768. [D] See Francis Fryer.

Fryer, Robert, York, cm (1822). Son of Michael Fryer; app. to John Taylor, cm, on 5 March 1822. [York app. reg.]

Fryer, Thomas, Lancaster. Named in the Gillow records in 1789 working on a Guardavin. [Westminster Ref. Lib., Gillow vol. 344/95, p. 526]

Fuhrlohg, Christopher, 24 Tottenham Ct Rd, between Percy St and Hanaway Yd, 22 Gerard St, and 12 Gt Russell St, Bloomsbury, London, cm, inlayer and u (b. c. 1740–d. after

1787). Christopher Fuhrlohg came from a Swiss family which emigrated to Sweden. He was born in Stockholm in about 1740 as the 4th child of the master cm Johan Hugo Fürloh (1724–47). It is not known to whom he was app., but he set off on his travels as a journeyman with his friend Georg Haupt, who eventually became his brother-in-law, in 1762. They worked in Amsterdam and, by 1764, were both in Paris, probably employed in the workshop of Simon Oeben. There are no signed or otherwise documented works by Christopher Fuhrlohg undertaken during his employment in France. However, a piece signed by Georg Haupt and made in 1767 for the Duc de Choiseul's country seat, the Château de Chanteloup represents the newly developing, severe Neo-classical taste to which the two young Swedish cm were exposed in Paris.

Fuhrlohg came to London, either late in 1766, or very early in 1767. He was joined by Haupt in 1768, and it is thought that both were given employment by John Linnell at his workshop in Berkeley Sq. Fuhrlohg's connection with John Linnell is firmly established by the presence in the album of John Linnell's furniture drawings [V & A Print Dept, E 59–414, 1929] of a design for a marquetry commode. The commode itself, executed after this design, is signed and dated in ink on the carcase 'Christopher Fuhrlohg fecit 1767'. It was supplied to the 5th Earl of Carlisle, a client of John Linnell, probably for Castle Howard, where it still survives. [J. Hayward, 1972]

1769 was a year of change for the small group of Swedish cm, all friends and inter-related, who were to spend time in London. Georg Haupt was recalled to Sweden as Royal cm. Another cm, Carl Gustav Martin arrived and set up in Dean St, Soho with a member of his family, David Martin, described in London directories as a 'Furniture designer' who had come to London in 1765. Yet another relation, the painter Elias Martin, who had come to London with Haupt, also lived in the same house in Dean St. More important to Fuhrlohg was the arrival in 1769 of his half-brother Johann Christian Linning with whom he was to set up his own workshop at 24 Tottenham Ct Rd. The rate bks for that address do not survive before 1773 but they record Fuhrlohg's presence in that year and until 1784. It is, therefore, not possible to establish exactly in which year Fuhrlohg left the Linnell workshop to make his own way with Linning. It seems probable that it was in 1769. Fuhrlohg's first trade card [Banks Coll., BM] however, makes no mention of his half-brother. It is engraved with a picturesque scene of a ruined tomb inscribed 'Fuhrlohg Cabinet Maker in the Modern, Grecian and Chinese Taste, No. 5 between Percy Street & Hannaway Yard, Tottenham Court Road at the most reasonable prices'. The wording is couched to describe the transitional stylistic phase between the 'modern' or outgoing Rococo taste and the newly developing severity of the Parisian Grecian or 'à la Greque' manner, contrasted with the interest in Chinoiserie still prevalent in England. The reference to 'reasonable prices' also suggests that this trade card was designed for a cm anxious to establish himself and was probably printed in about 1769 or 70.

Fuhrlohg was clearly an accomplished inlayer as well as being a cm with experience of the latest Parisian fashions. A pair of elaborately inlaid commodes in the transitional style survive. One, formerly in the Knapp Coll. (Sotheby's, 11 April 1975, lot 140), is signed 'C. Fuhrlohg Fecit MDCCLXXII'. The pair to this piece is in the Lady Lever Art Gallery, Port Sunlight. Both introduce marquetry roundels after Angelica Kauffmann whose name is inscribed upon one representing Classical nymphs and also parquetry decoration. [J. Hayward, 1972] On the basis of the pair, a number of other pieces,

including a commode in the MMA, NY, two smaller commodes in the same museum, two square piano cases and a writing-table at Alnwick Castle, Northumb. have been identified. [Streeter, 1971] These pieces probably date between 1772 and 1777. The pianos were both made by Frederick Beck, one dated 1775 and the other 1777. Fuhrlohg was well-informed concerning the sources from which he could draw ideas for the marquetry roundels with Classical figures used to ornament his pieces. They included Philippe de Stosch's *Gemmae Antiquae Caelatae*, Amsterdam, 1724, *Le Pitture Antiche d'Ercolano*, Naples, 1760 and Pierre François d'Hancarville's publication of Sir William Hamilton's collection of vases, Naples 1766–67. [J. Hayward, 1977]

Such marquetry roundels could also be sold individually. Fuhrlohg's compatriot, Carl Gustav Martin was the first of the group of Swedish inlayers to exhibit his work at the Free Society of Artists in 1771. He was followed by Christopher Fuhrlohg who exhibited 'A Bacchante in Inlay' in 1773 from his address at '24, Tottenham Court Road, between Percy Street and Hanaway Yard'.

In 1774 he showed 'A Venus attired by the Graces' and 'A Flora in Inlay', while Linning exhibited 'The Muse Erato', and 'Diana, a circle' in 1774 and 1775, his address being given as 'Inlayer at Mr. Fuhrlogh's, 24 Tottenham Court Rd'. It was Linning's last year in London for he returned to Sweden in 1776. It is clear that 24 Tottenham Ct Rd (between Percy St and Hanaway Yd) was the same address as that quoted on Fuhrlohg's first trade card where 'No. 5' is mentioned but this is, nevertheless, also between Percy St and Hanaway Yd. There may have been changes in the street numbering system to account for this apparent inconsistency. His address was again given as 24 Tottenham Ct Rd in 1778 when he advertised in *Morning Post*, 13 February 'that during the summer months he has compleated several curious and elegant pieces of furniture, inlayed after the designs of the most eminent artists, and will think himself honoured by the visits of amateurs of this kind of work; and he flatters himself that his 'customers will have every reason to be satisfied with their purchases, as he is able to answer for the goodness of the work which he continues to sell at the most reasonable terms'. Fuhrlohg's second trade card reveals his appointment as cm to the Prince of Wales. It is a dignified design, headed by the Prince of Wales' feathers and inscribed 'Fuhrlohg Ebeniste to his Royal Highness the Prince of Wales 24 Tottenham Court Road'. [J. Hayward, 1972] The date of his appointment is unknown but it was before 1783. His work for the Prince is not recorded in detail. The Windsor Castle archives contain only ledger entries listing payments of £8 9s 6d in 1784 and £19 9s in 1785 for work at Carlton House undertaken under William Gaubert. Further payments are listed of £10 16s on 5 January 1786 and 5 July 1787. [Windsor RA 88620, RA 88663] He must, however, have delivered commodes and tables to his royal patron at an earlier date as the ledgers show payments to the bronze founder, Dominique Jean, as follows: By Mr. Gaubert's orders. Work done for His royal Highness the Prince of Wales.

1783 Nov. 3: Cleaning the ornaments of two commodes gilt in ormolu and 3 tables gilt'd & Gilding, several pieces deld. to Mr. furlogh   £18

Dec. 28: Gilding the ornaments of an inlaid commode delivered to furlogh   £3

2 plain Branches, 1 square iron, springs and 1 branch for three Candles silvered, delivered to Mr Furlogh

Dominique Jean evidently had a close relationship with Furlohg for whom he provided gilt cabinet mounts for furniture delivered to Lord Howard at Audley End, Essex on 9 June 1786. [V & A archives]

Until 1785, Fuhrlohg remained at 24 Tottenham Ct Rd. From this address he provided Sir John Griffin Griffin of Audley End with 'an inlaid commode' on 15 February 1779. [Essex RO, D/DBy/A37/2] In 1783 the Duke of Portland was supplied with a secretaire and had his travelling case repaired. [Nat. Reg. of Archives, no. 3, 1971, no. 2804] Fuhrlohg was also employed by the Dilettanti Society between 1780–83. [Minutes of the Dilettanti Soc.; C. Harcourt-Smith] He is regularly recorded in Kent's *London Directory* between 1776–83, and again from 1785–87 as a cm and inlayer. In 1784 he appears, instead in Bailey's *British Directory* as 'upholder'.

In 1785 Fuhrlohg moved to 22 Gerard St North where he appears in the rate bks as 'Christopher Fuhrlohg & Co.'. This property consisted of a dwelling house, coach house and stable, with loft above, which he insured with contents and stock, with the Sun Co. on 14 January 1786 for a total of £900, and on 1 February 1787 for £2,000. [GL, Sun MS vol. 335, p. 217 and vol. 343, p. 52 respectively] By this time, as Bailey's *British Directory* indicates, the range of his activity was wide. Between June 1786 and February 1787 the bills he rendered to Lord Howard at Audley End totalled £60 3s 4d for items as varied as an inlaid commode and a large dressing table, to 53 feet of mahogany, 19 ft of mahogany veneer, castors and gilt screws, lacquered brass joints and a painted flower stand on castors. [Essex RO, D/DA, 44/9, D/D By A44/11, D/D By A45/3] Just at this time he must have been extremely short of ready money for Christie's auctioned his household furniture and stock-in-trade at his Gerard St house on 21 February 1787. In the sale catalogue his stock is described as consisting of a 'Great Variety of Elegant Mahogany and Sattin-Wood articles, curiously Inlaid, several of which are on new Constructions, such as Book-Cases, Commodes, Dining Tables, Secretaires, Pembroke, Card and Pier Tables, Two Eight Day Clocks, sundry Prints and Drawings, Six pieces of Irish Linen etc. etc.'

After this sale, Fuhrlohg moved to 12 Gt Russell St from which his last trade card was issued. Again headed by the Prince of Wales' feathers, it is inscribed 'C. Fuhrlohg Cabinet-maker, Inlayer and Ebeniste to his Royal Highness the Prince of Wales No. 12 Great Russell Street, Bloomsbury, Makes and sells all kinds of Inlaid work, executes all Orders in the Upholstery Cabinet-branches in the most modern taste with punctuality and dispatch on the lowest terms.' [J. Hayward, 1972] His name does not appear in the rate bks for this last address and no reference to his name or work after 1787 has come to light. His influence as a cm in the introduction and development of the Neo-classical style and in the use of subtle marquetry decoration was vital. Only two apprenticeships to him have hitherto been noticed, that of Benjamin Gooden on 25 November 1771 for the fee of £21 and of John Pleasance on 29 July 1778 for the nominal fee of 5s. [PRO, IR1/27 and 29] The lack of apps may, perhaps be explained by Fuhrlohg's having preferred to engage his own compatriots of whom, as yet, too little is known. The painter, Elias Martin has left us a water-colour portrait of Christopher Fuhrlohg, inscribed 'Fourlow Ebenist i London', probably painted on Martin's second visit to London between 1788 and 1791. [Nordiska Museet, Stockholm (ill. J. Hayward, 1972)]

[A. Graves, *Society of Artists of Great Britain, 1761–91*, London, 1907; C. Harcourt-Smith, *The Regalia and Pictures of the Society of Dilettanti*, 1932, pl. vi; Arts Council Exhib. Cat., *Elias Martin (1737–1818)*, 1963; H. Hayward, 'The Drawings of John Linnell', *Furn. Hist.*, 1969; J. Hayward, 'Christopher Fuhrlohg, an Anglo-Swedish Cabinet-Maker', *Burlington*, CXI, 1969. pp. 648–55; C. Streeter, 'Marquetry furniture by a brilliant London Master', *Met. Museum*

Bulletin, June 1971, Part I, pp. 418–29; J. Hayward, 'A newly discovered commode signed by Christopher Fuhrlohg', *Burlington*, CXIV, 1972, pp. 704–12; J. Hayward, 'A further note on Christopher Fuhrlohg', *Burlington*, CXIX, 1977, pp. 486–93; H. Hayward and P. Kirkham, *William and John Linnell*, 1980; H. Hayward, 'A Taste of Quality', *C. Life*, June 1981, pp. 551–52.   H.H.

Fulcher, Nathaniel, King's Rd, Chelsea, London, cm and u (1823). [D]

Fuller, James, Holt, Norfolk, cm and chairmaker (1830). [D]

Fuller, James, 29 Hyde St, Bloomsbury, London, furniture japanner (1835–39). [D]

Fuller, John, Colchester, Essex, u (d. 1684). Probate will dated 1684. [*Wills at Chelmsford*]

Fuller, John, 'Three Cane Chairs', St Paul's Churchyard, London, cane chairmaker (1699). Married Jane Simms at Holy Trinity Church in 1699. [Westminster Ref. Lib., PR]

Fuller, John, Windsor, Berks., carver and gilder (1798). [D]

Fuller, John, Swaffham, Norfolk, u (d. 1824). Will proved at Norwich in 1824. [Norfolk Record Soc., index of wills]

Fuller, Robert, Canterbury, Kent and London, cm (1780–96). Admitted freeman of Canterbury in 1780. Polled at Canterbury of Southwark in 1790; and St George's, London, 1796. [Canterbury freemen rolls and poll bks]

Fuller, Thomas, 31 Camomile St, London, upholder and cm (1809). Took out a Sun Insurance policy on 7 September 1809 for £500 of which £150 accounted for stock and utensils. [GL, Sun MS vol. 443, ref. 834518]

Fuller, Thomas, Lewes, Sussex, cm (1812). [Poll bk]

Fuller, Thomas, St John St, Hereford, chairmaker and turner (1822). [D]

Fuller, William, High Wycombe, Bucks., chairmaker (1815). Son bapt. in 1815. [PR(bapt.)]

Fuller & Levet, 13 Brownlow St, Holborn, London, cm, u, portable desk, dressing case, work box and pocket book manufacturers (1835–39). Trading as Fuller & Batley in 1835. [D]

Fullerton, Francis, Lenham's Buildings, Osborne St, Hull, Yorks., cm (1838–42). [D]

Fullerton, William, Manchester, upholder (1783–88). Named in Bailey's list of bankrupts, 1783. Trading at Smithy Door in 1788. [D]

Fulluck, Edmund, 18 Lawrence St, Birmingham, chairmaker (1835). [D]

Fulwood, Charles, at 'The Eagle & Child', Castle St, Leicester Fields, St Martin's-in-the-Fields, London, cm (1723). Took out a Sun Insurance policy on 17 August 1723 for £300 on goods and merchandise in his house. [GL, Sun MS vol. 16, ref. 29672]

Fungus, John, Counterslip, Bristol, chairmaker (1814). [D]

Furber, Jonathan, 6 Court, Upper Tower St, Birmingham, cabinet case maker (1835). [D]

Furber, William, 122 Gt Portland St (or Pl.), London, cm and u (1809–c. 1840). Recorded as S. W. Furber in 1835. Trade card, c. 1840, reads: 'Cabinet manufacturer by appointment to Her Majesty'. Took out Sun Insurance policies on 23 January 1809 for £700, £450 accounting for stock, utensils and goods in trust; on 27 January 1812 for the same, with an extra £300 on his house and warehouse; on 2 February 1820 and 26 April 1821 for £1,400 on household goods, respectively at 27 and 26 Margaret St, Cavendish Sq.; on 15 November 1821 for £2,850, £2,000 on stock, utensils and goods in trust; on 14 November 1822 for £3,050, £2,000 on stock etc. and £200 on that in workshops in Little Portland St; on 30 October 1823 for £1,900; and a further policy in 1840. [D; Heal; GL, Sun MS vol. 448, ref. 825881; vol. 459, refs 867057 and 869244; vol. 483, ref. 962843; vol. 488, refs 978762 and 985443; vol. 493, ref. 997385; vol. 498, ref. 1008784; ref. 1339992]

Furguson, Thomas, London, cm (1793). Subscribed to Sheraton's *Drawing Book*, 1793.

Furguson, William, Friernhay St, Exeter, Devon, carver and gilder (1830). [D]

Furley, Samuel, 35 (New) Bond St, London, carver, gilder and printseller (1784–89). Took out a Sun Insurance policy in 1784 for £800 of which utensils, stock and goods accounted for £250. [D; GL, Sun MS vol. 324, p. 87]

Furlong, John, Powis St, Woolwich, London, cm and u (1832–39). Trading at no. 131 in 1839. [D]

Furnas, Thomas, Liverpool, cm (1770). Declared bankrupt, *Gents Mag.*, February 1770.

Furnass, Joseph, Newcastle, u (1763). App. to William Hudon; admitted freeman on 10 October 1763. [Newcastle freemen reg.]

Furneaux, John, London, cm and u (1829–39). Recorded at 44 Theobald's Rd in 1829; and 13 Duke St, Bishopsgate St in 1839. [D]

Furneaux, John, Green St, Middlx, cm (1832). Declared bankrupt, *Liverpool Mercury*, 20 April 1832.

Furner, William, Lymington, Hants., cm (1823). [D]

Furness, George, Birstal, Yorks., joiner and cm (1830–37). [D]

Furness, Martin, 377 Strand and 21 Belgrave Pl., Pimlico, London, cm and u (1827–28). [D] Probably Martin Furnis.

Furness (or Furnas), Thomas, Liverpool, cm (1766–74). Trading in Cleveland Sq. in 1772. Sale advertised in *Williamson's Liverpool Advertiser*, 11 September 1767, of stable in Argyle St, tenanted by Thomas Furness, cm. On 25 December 1772 the same paper advertised sale by George Parker, auctioneer, 'at the house of Thomas Furnas, Cabinet Maker, near the Old Dock at the Entrance in Cleveland Square, Several Pieces of very neat new made Cabinet Goods & Household Furniture.'

Furnihough, James, Church St, Leek, Staffs., joiner and cm (1818). [D]

Furnis, Martin, address unrecorded, cm (1803). Subscribed to Sheraton's *Cabinet Dictionary*, 1803. Probably Martin Furness.

Furr, Thomas, 8 Hodgson's Ct, Hunter St, Liverpool, cm (1796). [D]

Furrance, Jacob, Gt Yarmouth, Norfolk and London, chairmaker (1774–1818). App. to Samuel Bream; admitted freeman in 1774. Another Jacob, cm, son of Jacob Furrance, was admitted freeman by birth in 1796. Polled at Gt Yarmouth, 1777–1818, of London in 1795. [Gt Yarmouth freemen rolls and poll bks]

Furranie, Jacob, Jane St, St George's East, London, cm (1808). [D]

Furse (or Furze), Christopher, Exeter, Devon, carver and gilder (1796–1813). Recorded at Peter's Yd, 1796 in *Exeter Pocket Journal*; and St George's Lane, 1813. Daughter Sophia born in June 1802, and twins, Christopher and Rachel, born in September 1804, all bapt. on 29 January 1813, at St George's Church. [PR(bapt.)]

Furse, John, 39 Upper St, James's St, Brighton, Sussex, French polisher and japanner (1832–43). Advertisement in directory of 1843 gives addresses at nos 39–41; and offers thanks for 'the liberal encouragement he has received for the last fourteen years'. [D]

Fursse & Clark, 3 Shepperton Pl., New North Rd, London, cm and chairmakers (1835). [D]

Furze, Mrs, North St, Bridgwater, Som., u (1840). [D]

Fusedale, John, Dartmouth St, Westminster, London, cm (1790–1808). Recorded at no. 13, 1790–93; and as Fusedale only, at no. 14 in 1808. [D]

Fusedale, Thomas & John, High Holborn, London, upholders (1778). Declared bankrupt, *Gents Mag.*, May 1778.

Fusedale, Thomas, George St, Croydon, Surrey, cm, carver and gilder (1808). [D]

Fuss, George, Wye, Kent, u (1728). [Canterbury freemen rolls]

Fussell, John, 27 Joiners' St, Lambeth Rd, London, cm and u (1839). [D]

G

Gabbitass Elizabeth, Eastgate, Worksop, Notts., Windsor chairmaker (1839–44). Wife of John Gabbitass who died 1839. A number of chairs stamped 'E. GABBITASS WORKSOP' have been recorded. [D; *Furn. Hist.*, 1978; Christie's, 1 November 1979, lot 125]

Gabbitas(s), John, Worksop, Notts., Windsor chairmaker (1832–d. 1839). Trading at Radford, Worksop in 1832. One of a group of Windsor chairmakers operating in north Notts. from the second quarter of the 19th century. Two chairs have been recorded branded under the seat 'I GABBITASS'. His will was proved 9 January 1840. The business was carried on by his wife Elizabeth. [D; Temple Newsam Exhib., Cat., *Common Furniture*, 1982, no. 26; Notts. RO, probate records]

Gablin, Thomas, London, upholder (1710). In 1710 moved from the 'Blackamoor's Head' in Chandos St to the 'Blackamoors Head' in Bedford St, Covent Gdn. He stated that he continued 'to serve the Army & Navy with Tents, Field Beds and Sea Beds as formerly'. [Heal; *Evening Post*, 29 June 1710]

Gabriel, James, Willow St, Oswestry, Salop, cm (1835–36). [D]

Gabriel, T. & C. & Sons, 31–32 Banner St, Bunhill Row, London, (1801–11). In 1801 advertised themselves as piano and looking-glass manufacturers. In 1804 chairmaking was added to the description and by 1807 they described their business solely as chairmaking. One directory of 1809 lists the firm as mattress makers. [D]

Gabriel, William, Islington Row, Birmingham, manufacturers of bath chairs, rocking horses and childrens' carriages (1818). [D]

Gace, Nathaniel, 12 Blue Bell Entry, Wells St, Hull, Yorks., cm (1823). [D]

Gad, Thomas, Shropshire St, Market Drayton, Salop, chairmaker (1840). [D]

Gadbury, George, London, carver and gilder (1804–12). At 115 Whitechapel, 1804–08, and 7 King St, Tower Hill, 1809–12. [D]

Gadd, Richard, Bell Lane, Market Drayton, Salop, chairmaker (1822). [D]

Gadd, Thomas, Castle Precincts, Bristol, carver and gilder (1784). [Poll bk]

Gaddick, Thomas, Stourbridge, Worcs., cm (1758). In 1758 took app. named Brown. [S of G, app. index]

Gadesby, William, Northgate St, Canterbury, Kent, u and cm (1805–09). [D]

Gadsby, E., Waterloo St, London, bent timber manufactory (1829). [D]

Gadsby, William, 1 York St, Ducie Bridge, Manchester, cm and u (1838–39). [D]

Gadsly, E., 103 East St, Manchester Sq., London, carpenter and cm (1820). [D]

Gaffield, —, address unknown, cm (1754). Subscribed to Chippendale's *Director*, 1754. Probably in partnership with

John Taitt, 1770–99, this business being later carried on as Gordon & Taitt at Little Argyle St, Golden Sq., London. [D]

Gagnon, Alexander John, 51 John St, Tottenham Ct Rd, London, carver (1778). In 1778 insured his house for £200. [GL, Sun MS vol. 262, p. 606]

Gaillard, James Benjamin, London, u (1811–23). At 28 Gerrard St, Soho, 1811–19, but from 1819 the number changed to 29. A Thomas Gaillard is shown in one directory at 28 Gerrard St in 1820 only. [D]

Gaimes, E., London, cm and portable desk maker (1808–14). At 12 Edward St in 1808 when his trade was described as cm. In 1814 at 53 St Paul's Churchyard when described as a jeweller and portable letter copying machine and writing desk manufacturer. A portable desk with two different labels affixed has been recorded. The addresses listed on these labels are 54 St Paul's Churchyard, 56 Cornhill and 23 Surrey St, Blackfriars Rd. [D; *C. Life*, 9 December 1965, p. 1633]

Gainer, Benjamin, 7 Church St, Minories, London, bedstead maker (1839). [D]

Gainforth, Richard, Kirkgate, Thirsk, Yorks., cm (1840). [D]

Gainge, —, address unknown, joiner (1732–40). Recorded supplying furniture to Earl Fitzwalter for Moulsham Hall, Essex. In November 1734 he was paid £2 12s 6d for a mahogany dining table 4ft 3in. by 5ft, and in August 1738 18s for a settee for the Earl's dressing room. A garden seat and 'a framed stand for the gardener to clip the garden hedges with' were paid for in July 1740. These appear rather minor items for which a local craftsman might be employed. In 1732 however an account was submitted by Gainge, of which no details survive, for £513 17s 4d of which amount £498 5s was settled, suggesting a much larger scale of operation and the possibility that he was a London craftsman. [A. C. Edwards, *The Accounts of Benjamin Mildmay, Earl Fitzwalter*, pp. 62, 106, 108]

Gair, William, Union St, Morpeth, Northumb., joiner and cm (1827). [D]

Gairdner, George snr and jnr, London, cm (1806–39). In 1806 trading as George Gairdner & Thomas Whitby from 10 Hemmings Row. In September of that year they insured for £150 stock, utensils and goods in trust at Hemmings Row; and in November of the same year for a similar sum stock and utensils 'in workshops and lofts over stables in West St, Seven Dials.' No further mention of Whitby has been traced and in January 1809 the business was trading as a partnership of George Gairdner snr and his son George. Although insurance cover of £300 was taken out only £100 of this was in respect of stock, utensils and goods in trust. A year later however the figures had risen to £650 and £250 respectively. In January 1809 the business was trading from 3 Peters Ct, St Martin's Lane and a year later from 15 Green St, Leicester Sq. The first mention of the business in directories is in 1819 and from this date until 1827 is simply recorded as George Gairdner, though upholstery is added to the trade previously offered. From 1819–25 the address was 132 Long Acre, but from 1823 80 Tottenham Ct Rd is also listed and this was to continue after 1825 as the sole address. The insurance cover in 1823 on the Tottenham Ct Rd premises was £600 of which £390 was for utensils and stock. In 1839 the business was trading as George Gairdner & Sons, u. [D; GL, Sun MS vol. 437, refs 792972, 795687; vol. 445, ref. 825518; vol. 448, ref. 839188; vol. 498, ref. 1008772]

Gaite, David, Shepton Mallet, Som., cm (1830). [D]

Galabert, Philip, 169 Fenchurch St, London, cm (1809). [D]

Gale, Edward, opposite the Circus, St George's Fields, London, cm and broker (1791). Took out insurance cover on 24 August 1791 for £800 which included £240 for utensils and stock, £30 for an open shed and workshops and £50 for

stock kept in the workshops and yard. [GL, Sun MS ref. 587684]

Gale, George, Bampton, Devon, fancy chairmaker (1830). [D]

Gale, John, Hull, Yorks., cm (1780). [Poll bk]

Gale, John, 8 Stable St, Piccadilly, Manchester, carver (1825). [D]

Gale, Joseph, Manchester, carver and gilder, barometer, looking-glass and picture frame maker (1828–40). In 1829 at 98 Market St but from 1832–33 at no. 32. In 1839 at 16 King St and from 1836–40 the number is recorded as 46. [D; Goodison, *Barometers*]

Gale, R., 19 Philip St, Bath, Som., cm (1819–26). [D]

Gale, Thomas, Catherine St, Strand, London, u (1772–78). In 1772 described as the patentee for 'a newly invented bedstead which when shut up, presents the appearance of a bookcase or wardrobe'. In 1776 insured his house and goods for £900 and in the following year his utensils and stock for £800. Bankruptcy announced March 1778. May have been in partnership with William Gale from 1777 though he is not mentioned in connection with the bankruptcy proceedings. Although the existence of the business appears to have been relatively short it did attract influential customers. In the period 1775–77 the 2nd Earl of Shelburne was supplied with goods to the value of £556 3s for either his London house or Bowood, Wilts. Lord Mahon paid Gale £617 6s 6d in the years 1776–77 and the Rev. Mr Drake of Shardeloes, Amersham, Bucks. provided patronage in 1777. Of this latter commission we have details of the items supplied. They included '10 upright splatt back chairs japann'd white & green ornament' charged at £19, eight 'Southampton' chairs at £4, an inlaid card table at £4 4s and a mahogany Pembroke table at £2 14s 6d. [D; V & A archives; GL, Sun MS vol. 246, p. 113; vol. 258, p. 459; *Gents Mag.*, March 1778; Heal; Bowood MS; Kent RO, U590 A61/7–8; Bucks. RO, D/DR/5/105]

Gale, William, St Pancras, Chichester, Sussex, chairmaker and turner (1826–39). [D]

Gale & Seabrook, 'The Walnut Tree', Houndsditch, London, cm and u (1758). Mr Gale died in 1758. [Heal; Harris, *Old English Furniture*, p. 21]

Galer, Thomas, Back St, Hitchin, Herts., cm, u and turner (1839). [D]

Gales, Joseph William, Christchurch, Hants., cm (1839). [D]

Gallando, Peter, London, upholder (1736–47). Son of Peter Gallando of the parish of St Clement Danes, London, Gent. App. to Henry Winton on 25 March 1736 and then to John Planner, freeman of the Merchant Tailors' Co., on 4 May 1743. Free of the Upholders' Co. by servitude, 4 May 1743. [GL, Upholders' Co. records]

Gallaway, Edward, Hog Lane, London, u (1749). [Heal]

Gallaway, Robert, London, upholder (1778–80). At 15 Clements Inn in 1778 when he insured utensils, stock and goods for £300. In 1780 at 45 Duke St, Lincoln's Inn Fields where he took out insurance cover of £700 which included £390 for utensils and stock. [GL, Sun MS vol. 267, p. 273; vol. 284, p. 142]

Galletti, William & Anthony, Liverpool, carvers, gilders, print sellers and opticians (1821–39). Established their business at 10 Castle St in November 1821 after having previously lived in Glasgow. They offered to frame and glaze prints and drawings, clean and varnish paintings and re-gild picture frames. They also undertook 'Window Cornices, Gold Mouldings for Rooms, with every kind of Carving & Gilding Work done on the shortest notice'. They also made and repaired thermometers, barometers and telescopes. They continued to occupy the shop in Castle St until the termination of the business but in 1839 the number is given as

19. In 1827 their house is given as 6 Shaw's Brow and in 1835 Anthony was living at 6 Beau St, the number changing to 11 in 1839. By 1833 the partnership appears to have ended and Anthony continued the business himself. His stock also diversified and in that year he offered additionally 'a valuable & choice Collection of Ancient & Modern PAINTINGS', picture frames, artists' colours and materials, optical and mathematical instruments, spectacles, jewellery, fishing equipment and 'Ornamental Shells, Curiosities etc. Napoleon Medals in Silver & Bronze Coins etc.' [D; *Liverpool Mercury*, 23 November 1821, 13 September 1833]

Galley, Andrew, 166 Ratcliffe Highway, London, looking-glass manufacturer (1839). [D]

Galley, George, 13 Long Acre, London, u (1763–85). In 1775 insured his house for £300. This was raised to £400 in 1781 but fell to £200 in 1782. [D; GL, Sun MS vol. 242, p. 542; vol. 291, p. 62; vol. 303, p. 354; vol. 304, p. 134]

Galley, Gregory, Leeds, Yorks., cm (1826–34). In 1826 at Garden St, Meadow Lane; in 1830 at Mulberry St, Little Holbeck; and in 1834 at Garden St, Sweet St. [D]

Galley, John, 3 Spring Gdns, Manchester, print seller, weather glass and picture frame maker (1797). [D]

Galley, Thomas, Denzell St, Clare Mkt, London, cm, u and portable desk maker (1827). [D]

Galliene, R., Ratcliffe Terr., Goswell Rd, London, cm (1835). [D]

Gallienne, Abraham, 115 Goswell Rd, London, cm and u (1839). [D]

Gallier, Peter, Christchurch, Hants., chairmaker (1839). [D]

Galliers, Henry, 58 Cable St, London, cm and broker (1823–24). In February 1823 took out insurance cover of £500 which included £280 for stock, utensils and goods in trust and £70 for goods in a workshop with a loft over and in the yard behind. In the following year the cover of the stock was reduced to £175 with £50 for that in the workshop. In this year he insured additionally four houses in Welclose Pl., Cable St for £400. [GL, Sun MS vol. 490, ref. 1001524; vol. 495, ref. 1014335]

Gallimore, Robert, Ashley's Sq., Newcastle-under-Lyme, Staffs., cm (1822–37). [D; poll bks]

Gallop, George, Caroline Row, Poole, Dorset, cm and u (1840). [D]

Gallosmith, Charles, 12 Worship St, Finsbury Sq., London, painted and japanned chairmaker (1807). On 6 December 1807 took out insurance cover for £350 which included £250 in respect of stock and utensils. [GL, Sun MS vol. 446, ref. 823611]

Galloway, Edward, Hog Lane, Westminster, London, u (1749). [Poll bk]

Galloway, John, 64 New Bond St, London, u (1809–18). In 1818 his workshop was damaged by fire when it spread from Messrs Johnston's cabinet making premises in Brook St. [D; *Gents Mag.*, supplement to 1818, pt II, p. 625]

Gally, Paul & Peter, London, looking-glass and picture frame makers (1804–40). In 1804 at 7 Beauchamp St, Leather Lane but by 1809 at 8 Turnmill St, Clerkenwell though after 1815 the number was changed to 9. In 1826 moved to 50 Exmouth St. After c.1810 directories record their trade solely as looking-glass makers. One directory of 1839 records Peter Galley at 70 Parsons St, East Smithfield though the Exmouth St, Spitalfields address continued to be occupied until 1848. [D; Goodison, *Barometers*]

Gamage, Thomas, Horse Fair, Bristol, cm (1799–1813). In 1815 the business was operated by Sophia Gamage, probably his widow. [D]

Gambee, William Robert, Hawley Pl., Kentish Town, London, cm and u, carpenter (1838–39). [D]

Gambier, William, St Giles-in-the-Fields, London, picture frame carver (1733). Took as app. Thomas Thompson but in 1733 he was released because of ill treatment. Gambier was described as 'being of passionate temper' and it was stated that he had struck Thompson with a large iron poker. It was also stated that he had 'been forced to go without victuals for a considerable time.' [Winterthur, Delaware, Symonds papers]

Gamble, —, address unknown, gilder (1765). In 1765 received £6 16s for gilding an organ case (still in the Music Room) at Kedleston, Derbs., [Kedleston archives, 3.R; V & A archives]

Gamble, Edward, Melton Mowbray, Leics., cm (1796–99). In July 1796 announced that he now had drying sheds for timber. In April 1799 advertised for a journeyman and stated that new timbers had arrived from which he could produce household furniture. [*Leicester Journal*, 22 July 1796, 5 April 1799]

Gamble, John, Stamford, Lincs., u. Admitted freeman of Stamford by purchase in the late 17th century. [Stamford freemen reg.]

Gamble, John, Belgrave St (or Gate), Leicester, cm (1835). [D]

Gamble, Richard, St James' Green, Millgate, Thirsk, Yorks., cm and u, chairmaker (1828–40). [D]

Gamble, S., address unknown, u (1803). Subscribed to Sheraton's *Cabinet Dictionary*, 1803.

Gamble, William, St James' Sq., Thirsk, Yorks., cm/chairmaker (1840). Probably the successor of Richard Gamble at the same address. [D]

Gamble & Bridgen, 15 Irongate, Derby, cm and u (1809–35). In 1835 Gamble appears to have been the sole proprietor. [D]

Gambling, James, late of Whitefriars. London, cm (1761). Discharged from Debtors' Prison, September 1761. [*London Gazette*]

Game, John, 52 Bunhill Row, London, cm (1792). On 26 September 1792 took out insurance cover of £200 of which £70 was in respect of utensils and stock including that in his workshop. [GL, Sun MS vol. 388, p. 632]

Gamerson, John, Birmingham, cm, u and chairmaker (1816–39). At High St, Deritend, 1816–22, when his trade was listed solely as chairmaker. In 1828–30 at Camphill, in 1835 at 36 Digbeth, and in 1839 at New Inkleys. [D]

Gamlyn, Thomas snr, London, u (1707–14). Freeman of London. At Castle St, Leicester Fields in 1707 when he took out insurance cover of £150 on his rented house. By 1714 the cover had been reduced to £100. Took two apps in 1712. Dead by June 1714 when his widow was in possession of the house in Castle St. [GL, Hand in Hand MS vol. 13, p. 63; Sun MS vol. 2, p. 26; S of G, app. index]

Gamlyn, Thomas jnr, Bedford Ct, Covent Gdn, London, u (1725–31). In 1731 supplied furniture for the Royal Hospital, Chelsea. His son William was made free of the Upholders' Co. by patrimony in 1730. [Heal; GL, Upholders' Co. records]

Gamlyn, William, London, upholder (1720–30). Son of Thomas Gamlyn jnr, freeman upholder. App. to Richard Wood, 6 April 1720 and Thomas Gamlyn jnr, 2 October 1722. Free of the Upholders' Co. by patrimony, 7 October 1730. [GL, Upholders' Co. records]

Gammage (or Gamidge), Robert, 'The Crown', two doors above the School, St Paul's Churchyard, London, chairmaker (1710–d. by 1725). First mentioned by name on 20 December 1712 when James Logan of Philadelphia, USA, wrote to James Askew, his factor in London ordering '2 finest Virginia Walnut Chairs . . . the same wth those I had of Gamage at the Crown in Pauls Ch^h Yard with Paws at the feet'. The business was clearly in existence well before this date and *London Gazette*, 28–31 January 1709/10 advertised that Richard Lewis an app. cane chairmaker, born in Shropshire, had absconded from his master at 'The Crown' in St Paul's Churchyard. It is highly likely that Gammage was the master involved. Gammage was dead by March 1725 in which month his widow advertised that she had for disposal 'All Sorts of Chairs and Couches, Mahogenny Wood, Virginia Walnut, English Walnut, and Walnut-Tree Wood for Gun Stocks'. She indicated that she was 'designing to leave off trade'. From 1725–30 the premises were used as a tavern retaining the previous trade sign, but in the latter year they reverted once more to a chairmaking and furniture business when John Brown took them over. [Hist. Soc. of Pennsylvania, Logan papers; *Conn.*, vol. 93, p. 181; *Daily Courant*, 13 March 1725]   B.A.

Gamman, R., 11 Leather Lane, Holborn, London, picture frame maker (1835). [D]

Gamwell, A., 21 Sandhills Lane, Whitehaven, Cumb., joiner/cm (1811–34). [D]

Gandy, William, 31 Steep Hill, Lincoln, carver and gilder (1822–40). Recorded at no. 31, 1826–40. [D]

Gann, John, Oundle, Northants., cm (1840). [D]

Ganning, Timothy snr and jnr, Norwich, u (1692–1768). Timothy Ganning snr was app. to Joseph Robins and free 21 September 1692. Soon he was himself taking apps commencing with John Osborne, admitted freeman on 8 November 1700. Gasgoine Rutter followed, free on 9 October 1704. Others declared free after app. to Timothy Ganning snr were Timothy Money on 3 May 1724 and Andrew Felgate on 21 September 1735. He also took apps named Smythe in 1711 and Cushing in 1732. His son Timothy was app. to him and declared free on 3 May 1724, and was probably a partner by the early 1730s when the business was referred to as Timothy Ganning & Co. Later apps such as Cooke in 1741 and Chapman in 1742 were probably trained by Ganning jnr.

The business was located in the parish of St Peter Mancroft, but by 1768 had moved to the parish of St Gregory. [Poll bks; S of G, app. index; Norwich freemen reg.]

Ganns, Richard, North St, Oundle, Northants., cm/joiner (1823). [D]

Gantry, —, address unknown, u (1835). Paid sums of £1 2s and £3 3s in 1835 by the 3rd Lord Braybroke in connection with either Audley End, Essex, or his London house. [Essex RO, D/DBy/A363]

Garbanati, Frederick, 12 West St, Covent Gdn, London, carver and gilder (1826). [D]

Garbanati, Joseph, London, carver and gilder (1807–39). Shown in 1808 at both 22 and 89 High Holborn. The latter address is listed for a Joshua Garbanati but his different Christian name is almost certainly a directory error. From 1811–26 at 404 Strand and thereafter at 37 Southampton St, Strand. The nature of the business is indicated on Garbanati's trade card in the Landauer Coll., MMA, NY. He claimed to have in stock 'A Choice Collection of French Carved Picture, Chimney & Pier Frames, also French Carved Console & Pier Tables, Cabriole Chairs, Sofas &' and offered a service of restoring frames and mirrors. He also relined and restored paintings. Garbanati attracted influential clients. In June 1807 Sir John Geers Cottrell of Garnons, near Hereford paid him £5 13s 6d for looking-glass frames though it is not known if these were for Garnons or his London house in Hertford St. In June 1826 the Duke of Norfolk was supplied with 'a Handsome French Frame' for £6 12s. [D; Heal; Herefs. RO, Garnons W69/III/182; Arundel Castle records, A2094]

Garbanati & Sargood, 19 St Martin's Ct, London, carvers, gilder and looking-glass manufacturers (1839). [D]

Garbet, James, Wem, Salop, cm (1797–98). [D]

Garbett, Joseph, 5 Spitalfields, Liverpool, cm (1805). [D]

Garbett, Robert, Derby St, Liverpool, cm (1810). [D]

Garbett, Thomas, Adam's Mews, Hanover Sq., Westminster, London, cm (1749). [Poll bk]

Garbit, Robert, Liverpool, cm (1827–29). In 1827 at 16 Comus St but by 1829 the number had changed to 24. [D]

Garbitt, Joseph, 7 Bradshaw St, Manchester, cm (1797). [D]

Garbut, Francis, Back Cross St, Bolton, Lancs., cm and joiner (1824). [D]

Garbut, Joseph, Brighton, Sussex, cm and u (1821–32). From 1821–23 in North St but in 1823 at Prince's Pl., moving again to Regent Hill by 1829. Only recorded in directories for 1832 when he was trading from 31 Bond St. Three sons and three daughters bapt., 1821–32. [D; PR(bapt.)]

Garbut, Robert, Finkle St, Selby, Yorks., joiner and cm (1828–30). [D]

Garbutt, George, Ampleforth, Helmsley, Yorks., joiner/cm (1834). [D]

Garbutt, John, Tubwell Row, Darlington, Co. Durham, joiner and cm (1827). [D]

Garbutt, John, Wallsend, Northumb., joiner and cm (1828). [D]

Garden, William & Co., 29 West St, Brighton, Sussex, cm and u (1832). [D]

Gard(e)ner, James, 1 Bradshaw Ct, Shudehill, Manchester, cm and bedstead maker (1838). [D]

Gardener, Matthew, 17 Whitechapel, Liverpool, cm (1794). [D]

Gardener, Thomas, Bilston St, Wolverhampton, Staffs., cm (1805–08). [D]

Gardiner, —, address unknown, cm (1744). In 1744 supplied a mahogany claw table to Holkham Hall, Norfolk at a cost of 16s. [V & A archives]

Gardiner, John, Norwich and London, carver (1786–1818). App. to Benjamin Jagger and admitted freeman of Norwich on 24 February 1786. At this date living in the parish of St Andrew, but by 1790 in the parish of St Peter Mancroft. By July 1802 had moved to London and was to remain there. [Norwich freemen reg. and poll bks]

Gardiner, John, Castle St, Hereford, cm (1832). [Poll bk]

Gardiner, T., Witney, Oxon., carpenter, joiner and cm (1779). Announced in October 1779 that he had taken a house in Witney 'where he intends carrying on the Carpenters, Joiners, Mangle and Cabinet Work'. Dealt also in secondhand furniture and brushes and brooms. [*Jackson's Oxford Journal*, 23 October 1779]

Gardiner, Thomas, 27 New James St, London, cm (1779). In 1779 insured his house for £200. [GL, Sun MS vol. 274, p. 188]

Garding, J., address unknown, cm (c. 1815–20). Supplied a set of quartetto tables to Erddig, Clwyd. [V & A archives]

Gardner, Andrew, Woburn, Beds., u (1799–1830). Trading at Market Pl. in 1830, Regularly features in the Woburn Abbey accounts as an u and general handyman. Most of the furniture supplied was for the servants' quarters or for estate use. Amongst the items produced were a 4ft 6in. wide stained 4 post bed on castors 'for Judge, the keeper' at £10 9s 5½d in July 1809; six cherry tree chairs for the stables at 4s 9d each in January 1811; and twelve cherrytree wheel back stool chairs for the laundry and London Lodge in June 1816 at £5 2s. [Bedford Office, London]

Gardner, Charles, 72 Paradise St, Rotherhithe, London, u and cm (1808–20). [D]

Gardner, Christopher, Flemish Churchyard, St Catherine's, London, cm (1777). In 1777 insured some houses for £500. [GL, Sun MS vol. 254, p. 12]

Gardner, Daniel, Lancaster, u (1768). Admitted freeman, 1768–69, when stated 'of Kendal', Westmld. [Lancaster freemen rolls]

Gardner, Denny, 14 Wood St, Cheapside, London, cm and u (1829–39). [D]

Gardner, Draper, London, upholder and horse hair manufacturer (1781–1804). At 57 Gt Wild St, 1781–84. In 1781 took out insurance cover of £200 of which £90 was in respect of utensils, stock and goods. In 1784 the total was £400, £240 of this accounting for utensils, stock, goods and workshop. By 1785 had moved to 12 Vere St, Clare Mkt, where utensils etc. were insured for £230 with a further £50 for the workshop and its contents. By 1804 the number had changed to 14. [D; GL, Sun MS vol. 298, p. 108; vol. 324, p. 312; vol. 333, p. 459]

Gardner, Edward, Dorcas Buildings (or Pl.), Hammersmith, London, cm (1826–32). [D]

Gardner, Henry, London, cm etc. (1820–39). Successor to Charles Gardner. At 72 Paradise St, Rotherhithe 1820–27 but by 1839 at 30 Paradise St. In 1827 the business was described as that of auctioneer and appraiser and in 1839 as u. [D]

Gardner, J., West Smithfield, end of Long Lane, and 75–76 Long Acre, London, carver, gilder and looking-glass manufacturer. Late 18th-century trade card is in the Heal Coll., BM.

Gardner, James, Lancaster, cm (1760–68). App. to H. Baines in 1760, and admitted freeman, 1767–68. [Lancaster app. reg., freemen rolls and poll bk]

Gardner, James, Charles St and 19 Whitechapel, Liverpool, cm (1790). [D]

Gardner, James, Chester, cm and auctioneer (1790–d. 1808). App. to John Cooke and admitted freeman on 7 July 1790. Took over John Cooke's app. named Griffith in 1791, and had another app. named Evans assigned to him in 1793. In 1792 at Higher Bridge St, and at Eastgate St, 1793–95. In 1797 the address was Talbot Row. Subscribed to Sheraton's *Cabinet Dictionary*, 1803. Died on 22 September 1808 at Nantwich, Cheshire. [D; Chester freemen rolls and app. bks; *Liverpool Courier*, 5 October 1808]

Gardner, James, London, cm and furniture broker (1826–35). At 7 Cumberland Pl., Newington in 1826, and 5–7 Cumberland Pl. in 1835. In 1827 however shown at King's Row, Newington. [D]

Gardner, John, 14 Dartmouth Row, Westminster, London, upholder (1778). In 1778 insured his utensils and stock for £50 out of a total cover of £100. [GL, Sun MS vol. 267, p. 449]

Gardner, John, Chester, cm (1808–29). Free 15 October 1808. His business premises were in Eastgate St but from 1818 an alternative address in Paradise Row is sometimes shown. In 1829 the business was referred to as Gardner & Sons. A three-drawer writing table from Eaton Hall, Cheshire, is signed underneath in ink 'Gardner 1824'. [Chester freemen rolls and poll bks; *Chester Chronicle*, 1 May 1829]

Gardner, John Rayner, Northgate, Canterbury, Kent, cm (1818). [Poll bk]

Gardner, John, Aston St, Birmingham, cm (1818). [D]

Gardner, John, 20 George St, Blackfriars, London, looking-glass frame manufacturers (1820). [D]

Gardner, John, 2 Brunswick Row, Brunswick St, St George's Rd, London, carver and gilder (1822). On 3 January 1822 took out insurance cover of £200 of which £20 was in respect of stock and utensils. [GL, Sun MS vol. 489, ref. 987531]

Gardner, John, Avenham Rd, Preston, Lancs., builder, cm and joiner (1834–42). [D]

Gardner, John, 4 Canterbury St, Liverpool, u and feather dealer (1834–39). Associated with J. O'Neill & Co. [D]

Gardner, John & Henry, 2 Green Harbour Yd, London, looking-glass manufacturers (1839). [D]

Gar(d)ner, Mary & Sons, Hotel Row, Chester, cm and u (1816–28). [D] See Samuel Gardner

Gardner, Matthew, Liverpool, cm (1796–d. 1815). Son of John Gardner, pot painter. Free 25 May 1796. In 1800 at 22 Whitechapel, the number changing to 85 in 1805 and 90, 1807–11. By 1813 at 79 Mount Pleasant. Took as apps William Williams (free 1812), and John Mecomb (free 1818). Died on 6 September 1815 aged 44, after a lingering illness, and in the following month the sale of his stock was announced. This comprised 'Mahogany Clock-cases, Chairframes, Gardervins, Tea Chests, Cheese Waggons, Children's Chairs, Ladies Work Tables, Chests of Drawers etc. etc. with a valuable Assortment of Veneers, Mahogany Planks & Boards, Tool Chests & Tools, Three Benches, Grinding Stone, Sofa Frame etc.' [D; Liverpool freemen reg. and committee bk; *Liverpool Mercury*, 13 October 1815]

Gardner, Matthew, Lancaster, cm (1803–22). Free 1806–07. Named in the Gillow records, 1803–14, 1816 and 1822. [Lancaster freemen rolls; Westminster Ref. Lib., Gillow]

Gardner, Samuel, Liverpool, u (1818). App. to Mathew Gregson and admitted freeman on 23 June 1818. [Liverpool freemen reg.]

Gar(d)ner, Samuel, Hotel Row, Eastgate St, Chester, cm and u (1817–40). Admitted freeman on 1 November 1817. Several local commissions by this maker are recorded and imply a good reputation with local patrons. In 1836 furniture was supplied and work undertaken for Charles Morrall of Stanley Pl., Chester, amounting to £66 3s 11d. This commission included a pair of simulated rosewood cabinets charged at £8. Worked for the Chapter of Chester Cathedral and in 1836 supplied a writing table in the Gothic style for the Song School. An oak library bookcase at Burton Court, Herefs., originally made for the Rev. Mr Evans of Burton Court, c. 1830, has a note attached to indicate that it came from Samuel Gardner's workshops. An advertisement in an 1840 directory indicates that he also dealt in plate glass, carpets and blankets, and arranged funerals. [D; Lloyds Bank archives; *Architectural History*, vol. 14, p. 74] See Mary Gardner & Sons.

Gardner, Thomas, Rood Lane, Fenchurch St, London, upholder (1709–d. by 1762). Son of Richard Gardner of Liverpool, Gent. App. to J. Vignell on 25 July 1709 and free of the Upholders' Co. by servitude, 26 December 1720. Also freeman of Preston by patrimony. Master of the Upholders' Co., 1743. [GL, Upholders' Co. records; Preston freemen reg.; Heal]

Gard(e)ner, Thomas, Alton, Hants., cm (1823). [D]

Gardner, Thomas, London, cm and u (1835–39). At 119 London Rd, 1835–37, and 19 Rockingham Row, 1839. [D]

Gardner, William, 'The One Cane Chair', south side of St Paul's Churchyard, London, cane chairmaker (1703–12). The date 1703 appears on his trade card and is probably the date of the establishment of the business. This card is illustrated with an engraving of a cane chair of the type fashionable in the early years of the reign of William and Mary and becoming somewhat dated by 1703. It indicates that he made and sold 'Cane Chairs, Couches and Cane-Sashes'. The card was still being used in July 1712 and on the 10th of that month Gardener used one to provide a receipt for Lady Heathcote for £3 17s. [Heal; Lincoln RO, 2 ANC 12/D/6]   B.A.

Gardner, William, Worcester, carver and gilder (1820–28). Trading at Broad St in 1820 and 98 High St in 1828. [D]

Gardner, William, 1 Robert St, Blackfriars Rd, London, carver and gilder (1829). [D]

Gardner, William, 6 City Rd, London, looking-glass manufacturer (1839). [D]

Gardner, William, Downley, High Wycombe, Bucks., chairmaker (b. c. 1816–41). Aged 25 at the time of the 1841 Census.

Gardner & Gouch, 20 Featherstone St, London, chairmakers and japanners (1798). [D]

Gardom, Barnabas, Epsom, Surrey, upholder etc. (1794). [D]

Gardom, James & George, Epsom, Surrey, u (1838–39). [D]

Gardom, M. & Son, Epsom, Surrey, carpenter, builder, auctioneer, cm and agent for the Albion Fire Office (1822). [D]

Garencieres, John, Malton, Yorks., u (1790). Son of William Garencieres of Malton, u. Made freeman of York as an u, 1790. [York freemen reg.]

Garencieres, William, York and Malton, Yorks., u (1744–84). Son of Theophilus Garencieres of Scarborough, Yorks., clerk. App. to Richard Farrer of York, u, 17 July 1744. Free as an u, 1758. Recorded working in Malton from 1758. Father of John Garencieres. [York poll bks; York app. and freemen regs]

Garey, James, 8 Richmond St, St Luke's, London, cm (1809). [D]

Garfoot, Robert, 28 Cannon St, Manchester, cm (1772–73). [D]

Garland, Francis Burrall, Devonport, Devon, cm (1829–30). In November 1829 declared to be 'entitled to the benefit of the Act, and ordered to be discharged accordingly'. In 1830 established at 39 Marlborough St. [D; *Exeter Flying Post*, 12 November 1829]

Garland, Ganul, 13 Old Compton St, London, cm (1786). On 1 July 1786 took out insurance cover of £100 of which £80 was in respect of utensils etc. [GL, Sun MS vol. 337, p. 641]

Garland, John, Bridge St, Gainsborough, Lincs., cm and u (1822–35). [D]

Garlick, Thomas, 3 Lawrence Lane, London, cm and u (1839). [D]

Garndult, Samuel, 106 Leadenhall St, London, u (1775). In 1775 took out insurance cover of £400 of which a half was in respect of utensils and stock. [GL, Sun MS vol. 240, p. 611]

Garner, Charles, 51 Ironmonger Row, St Luke's, London, cm and u (1839). [D]

Garner, James, Brandon, Suffolk, cm and chairmaker (1830–39). [D]

Garner, John, Hotel Row, Chester, cm (1814). Business continued after 1818 by Mary Garner & Sons. [D]

Garner, John, Liverpool, cm (1817). Married in December 1817 at St Ann's Church Miss Anne Hammerton. [*Liverpool Mercury*, 5 December 1817]

Garner, Richard, High St, Huntingdon, u, cm and paper hanger (1830–39). [D; poll bk]

Garner, Thomas, 7 Cotter's Ct, Chapel St, Liverpool, cm (1796). [D]

Garnett, G., 8 Gt Newport St, Long Acre, London, carver and gilder. Early 19th-century trade card is in the Landauer Coll., MMA, NY. Garnett produced looking-glass and picture frames and offered 'cutting up in the white to the trade'.

Garnett, John, Lancaster, cm and broker (1801–04). App. to Isaac Greenwood, cm, on 22 February 1791, and free, 1801–02. Declared bankrupt, *Lancaster Gazette*, 7 January 1804. [Lancaster app. reg. and freemen rolls]

Garnett, Thomas, Werburgh's St (or Lane), Chester, cm (1814–28). [D]

Garnett, Robert & Sons, Warrington, Lancs., cm (1824–40). Several items of furniture by this maker of late 19th-and early 20th-century date bearing labels, plates and stamps are known. These claim that the firm was established 1824 though they are not noted in contemporary trade directories.

Garnett, Thomas, Prospect Cottage, Kirkby Lonsdale, Westmld, joiner/cm (1829–34). [D]

Garnett, Thomas, North St, Middlesborough, Yorks., joiner and cm (1840). [D]

Garnett, William, 77 Queen St, Portsea, Portsmouth, Hants., cm, u and auctioneer (1823–30). [D]

Garrard, Joseph, 25 Porter St, Long Acre, London, cm (1791). In 1791 took out insurance cover of £100. [GL, Sun MS vol. 379, p. 257]

Garrard, Thomas, East St, Chichester, Sussex, cm and u (1775). In 1775 took out insurance cover of £900. This included £400 for utensils and stock and £250 for stock in 'stockhouses' in St Martin's Lane. [GL, Sun MS vol. 253, p. 72]

Garrard, William, Brow Top, Workington, Cumb., joiner/cm (1829). [D]

Garrard, William, 101 Mary St, Hampstead Rd, London, cm (1835–37). [D]

Garratt, Dingley, Gt Southsea St, Portsea, Portsmouth, Hants., cm and u (1830). [D]

Garratt, G., Boughton, Chester, cm (1819). [Poll bk]

Garratt, Henry, London, cm (1808–29). At 32 Stanhope Lane in 1808. In 1820 he was at 1 Little Chapel St, Soho and in 1825 at no. 6. For 1829 two addresses are shown: 22 Francis St, Tottenham Ct Rd and 17 Bath Pl., New Rd, Marylebone. After 1820 his trade is recorded as dressing case and writing desk maker. [D]

Garratt, Samuel, Chester, cm (1812–40). Free 6 October 1812 and at that date at Prince's St. In 1818 at Mount Pleasant St and the following year Mount St. By 1816 he had moved to Brook St; in 1837 was at Northgate St; and in 1840 at Hotel Row, Eastgate St with a house in Handlaridge. [D; poll bks; freemen rolls]

Garrett, John, 5 Beak St, London, cm (1787). On 14 May 1787 took out insurance cover on goods for £100. [GL, Sun MS vol. 342, ref. 530394]

Garret, John, Newcastle, joiner, cm and pawnbroker (1811–24). At Bigg Mkt, 1811–24, but in 1833 at Nun's-gate. The pawnbroking part of the business is first mentioned in 1824 and in 1833 was stated to be the sole occupation. [D]

Garrett, John, 47 Circus St, Liverpool, carver and gilder (1816). [D]

Garrett, John Alexander, London, carver and gilder (1826–39). In 1826 at 6 Wardour St, Soho and from 1835 occupied both 6 and 7. A directory of 1829 however lists 2 Carburton St as his address. [D]

Garret(t), Thomas, Chester, u (1754–95). App. to Harwar Harvey, u, 1754–55 for eight years and free, 13 January 1762. At Bridge St, 1771–92, but in 1795 shown at Eastgate St. In 1775 took out insurance cover of £500 though his 'shops' were insured for £30 only. [D; freemen rolls; poll bks; GL, Sun MS vol. 240, p. 21]

Garside, W., Lawton St, Congleton, Cheshire, cm (1789). [D]

Garstone, John, St Martin's St, Hereford, cm and undertaker (1822–30). [D]

Garstone, William, Hereford, cm, u, builder, turner and chairmaker (1822–35). In 1822 at St John's Pl. By 1835 at St Martin's St where he probably took over the business of John Garstone to whom he may have been related. At this period his trade was that of chairmaker and turner. [D]

Garth, James, Serle St, Lincoln's Inn, London, u (1768–87). His earliest recorded commission was for Richard Hoare of Boreham House, Essex who in 1768 paid him 12s 6d for two looking-glasses. By the 1780s however he was obtaining substantial patronage from many important clients. Between 1781–85 he was working on furnishings for Paul Methuen at Corsham Court, Wilts., and was paid £165 on 8 March 1781, £67 on 27 February 1782 and £7 on 10 June 1785. At the same time he was working at Longford Castle, Wilts. and in this connection was paid £73 7s in 1781 and £10 7s 6d in 1787. [D; Heal; Essex RO, D/Du 649/2; V & A archives]

Garth, James, Far Fold, Mabgate, Leeds, Yorks., cm (1816–22). [D]

Garton, Samuel, London, upholder (1756–69). Son of Richard Garton of the parish of St Gregory, London. App. to William Cope on 6 May 1756 and free by servitude, 6 December 1769, as a member of the Upholders' Co. [GL, Upholders' Co. records]

Garton, William, 10 George's Ct, St John's Lane, London, cm (1809). [D]

Garway, William, Taunton, Som., cm (1721). In 1721 took app. named House. [S of G, app. index]

Garwood, John, Exeter Ct, Westminster, London, cm (1774). [Poll bk]

Gascoigne, Edward, Wolverhampton, Staffs., cm (1757). In 1757 took app. named Brown. [S of G, app. index]

Gaskell, —, Ulverston, Lancs., cm (1821). [*Liverpool Mercury*, 24 August 1821]

Gaskell, John, 2 Ravald St, Salford, Lancs., cm (1808–17). [D]

Gaskell, John, Liverpool, cm and u (1832–39). In 1832–35 at 30 Islington where in addition to the trades of cm and u he described himself as a paper hanger and spring stuffer. At this period he had only recently established his business. In 1837 he was at 38 Byrom St and in 1839 at 107 St James St. [D; *Liverpool Mercury*, 15 June 1832]

Gaskill, Thomas, Castle Donnington, Leics., chairmaker (1835). [D]

Gasley, George Alexander, London, u and furniture broker (1825–27). At 11 Gt Newport St, Soho, 1825–26; but in 1827 in another part of London for the address is simply given as Middlx. Bankruptcy announced, 10 April 1827. [D; *Liverpool Mercury*, 13 April 1827]

Gasley, Richard, London(?), u (1676). On 11 December 1676 paid by order by William 5th Earl of Bedford, 5s for two days work and £11 18s 4d for 2 cwt of goose feathers. [Bedford Office, London]

Gasson, James, Middle Ward, Tottenham, London, u (1839). [D]

Gasson, William, parish of SS Peter and Paul, Tonbridge, Kent, cm and Tunbridge-ware maker (1825–26). Sons Charles and Henry bapt. 2 March 1825 and 8 November 1826 respectively. [PR(bapt.)]

Gastard, J., 28 Gerrard St, Soho, London, u (1819–25). [D]

Gastrell, Miles, Ulverston, Lancs., chairmaker (1798). [D]

Gatcliffe, Thomas snr, Liverpool, cm (1719). In 1719 took app. named Leech. [S of G, app. index]

Gatcliffe, Thomas jnr, Liverpool, cm (1726–67). Free 6 May 1726. Trading in Pool Lane, 1766–67. [D; freemen rolls]

Gatehouse, John, 'The Golden Ball' by the Ditch-side, near Holborn Bridge, London, cm (1695). A walnut bureau cabinet, formerly at Herriard Park, Hants. (now at Temple Newsam, Leeds) bears the trade label of this maker. On this he indicated that he made and sold 'all Sorts of Cabinet Work, Chests of Drawers, Book-Cases, Cabinets, Scrutores; All Sorts of Glasses, Pier-Glasses, Chimney-Glasses and Sconces; And all Sorts of Joiners-Work; as Oval-Tables &c.' He is listed in a document of 1695 concerned with assessments of persons living in the parish of St Andrew, Holborn but appears to have continued his trade into the early years of the 18th century. [Gilbert, *Leeds Furn. Cat.*, vol. I, pp. 40–41; V & A archives]

Gatenby, William, Boroughbridge, Yorks., joiner/cm (1834). [D]

Gates, George, 26 Union St, Old Kent Rd, London, chair and sofa maker (1839). [D]

Gates, John, Ferry Boat Landing, Blyth, Northumb., cm, cartwright and undertaker (1827–34). [D]

Gates, Richard, 34 Garden Row, London Rd, London, chairmaker (1835). [D]

Gates, Stephen, London, chair, sofa and cabinet manufacturer (1829–39). At 77 Prospect Pl., Southwark in 1829, 79 St George's Rd, Southwark in 1835 and 6 Providence Buildings, Kent Rd, 1837–39. [D]

Gates, Thomas, Lewes, Sussex, cm (1816–40). At St John's St, 1816–18, but from 1826 in Spring Gdns. Up to 1837 listed as a journeyman cm thereafter merely as cm. [Poll bks]

Gates, William, St Martin's Lane, London, cm (1774–after 1800). William Gates was a cm who specialized in fine inlay and engraved woodwork. He succeeded John Bradburn as a tradesman to the Great Wardrobe, his warrant from George III being dated July 1777. Gates's first recorded commission from the Royal Household came in 1778 when he supplied 'a very neat mahogany cistern' for the dining room of the Queen's House, St James's Park, at a cost of £8 10s.

Like many English 18th-century cm Gates's life has glaring gaps through lack of information. In 1779 Gates was insured for a total of £1,000 which covered stock and goods. [GL, Sun MS vol. 275, p. 289] In March 1780 he was listed as bankrupt. [*Gents Mag.*] Gates obviously weathered this crisis for he kept his Royal Warrant and the Lord Chamberlain's Office returns for the quarter ending January 1781 list him as having supplied a 'Sattinwood writing table with a Tambour top'; this table was inlaid and engraved with the feathers of the Prince of Wales, and cost £24 19s.

Two seminal pieces in Gates's *oeuvre* are '2 very fine Sattinwood inlaid commode tables to stand under piers with semi-circular fronts'. These were supplied in 1781 to the Prince of Wales, later George IV, for his apartments in the Queen's House, St James's Park (Buckingham Palace). The cabinets cost £80 plus an extra £3 1s 6d for two leather covers. Each commode has three drawers in the frieze, two doors in the centre, which open to reveal drawers, and two doors either side enclosing cupboards. The doors are inlaid with ovals enclosing tall urns; the semi-circular tops have urns in the centre with Neo-classical floral scrolls emerging from the base. They are still in Buckingham Palace. [*Burlington*, July 1931, pp. 22–27] Gates also made other, less elaborate furniture, an example of which is the 'Clothes Press with fluted Cornice and carved Paterae' supplied for £20 to a Mr Hawkins of Kew, Surrey.

In 1738 William Gates formed a short-lived partnership with Benjamin Parran, the nephew of Benjamin Goodison. During 1784 Gates lost his Royal Warrant. This may have had a connection with the fact that George, Prince of Wales, was allowed his own household and his accounts were no longer controlled by the Lord Chamberlain's Office. It is not known why the Prince should have withdrawn his patronage but it must have had a detrimental effect on Gates's career. In 1784 he moved from the fashionable cabinet makers' street of St Martin's Lane to 30 St Albans Hill. [D] He continued in business and at least by the turn of the century was associated with Charles Elliott. The date of his death, like that of his birth, is not known.

To judge from the surviving examples of his work Gates was one of the foremost inlay workers of his day. He probably designed his own pieces but in at least one case he worked to a drawing supplied by the Prince of Wales. This was in 1780 for a pair of 'superb tripods or thermes'. Apart from cabinet making, Gates may have been involved in building speculation for in 1774 he took out a policy with the Sun Insurance Co. on a house in Owens Row, Islington. The house, no. 5, still stands and Gates insured it for £200, it being described as 'A Brick house . . . not finished'. [GL, Sun MS, vol. 235 and vol. 240, p. 360]

QUEEN'S HOUSE, St James's Park. In 1778 Gates supplied for the dining room of the Queen's house 'a very neat mahogany cistern on a pedestal, the inside lined with lead, a brass cock & cover to d°. and very neat brass mould by way of hoops neatly wrought & wrought handles to d°. (size of the whole 3 feet 2 inches high & 15½ inches wide & deep, with reel carved mouldings) £8 10s. [V & A archives]

GEORGE, PRINCE OF WALES. In 1780 Gates supplied 'an exceedingly fine Sattinwood writing table with a Tambour top neatly inlaid & engraved with various services, on the top a plume of Feathers very neatly inlaid, & the motto', £24 10s. [Lord Chamberlain's Office, Bills for the quarter ending 5 January 1781; V & A archives]

QUEEN'S HOUSE, St James's Park, London (George, Prince of Wales). In 1781 Gates supplied for the Prince of Wales's apartments in the Queen's House '2 very fine Sattinwood inlaid Commode tables to stand under piers with semi-circular fronts, 4 drawers each & 3 drawers over ditto, one drawer of each with a sliding board over d°, cover'd with green cloth to write on, the doors, drawers, and tops richly engraved with Urns, Vases, flowers and ornaments in woods of different colours, with locks and bolts to d°. Size of each, 3 feet 9 inches long, and 3 feet high. £80. (2 leather covers £3 1s 6d)'. [PRO, Lord Chamberlain's papers, no. 328]

GEORGE, PRINCE OF WALES. In 1781 Gates supplied the Prince of Wales with a 'chimney-glass in a carved frame, a very fine top to d° with clusters of flowers hanging in festoons from vases, & other ornaments, & husks down the sides of the frame all very neatly gilt in burnish'd gold, a large Plate in the middle and border to d°. (size of the frame 5 feet 7 wide & 3 feet 9 high) £63'. [V & A archives]

MR HAWKINS' HOUSE, Kew, Surrey. In 1781 Gates supplied 'a very good mahogany Clothes Press with fluted Cornice and Carved Paterae, 6 shelves with inside made in two parts with 2 long and 2 short drawers . . . £20'. [V & A archives]

GEORGE, PRINCE OF WALES. In 1781 Wm Gates charged the Prince £9 15s 'for three very fine trays curiously inlaid and engraved with different devises rims to d° & a silvered string round d° & handles'. [V & A archives]

QUEEN'S HOUSE, St James's Park (George, Prince of Wales). In 1781 Gates supplied 'two very fine card tables in a semi circular form and inlaid with different woods of different colours and neatly . . . and the top lined within with green cloth £21'. [V & A archives] T.R.

Gathereole, B. & C., 31 Trinity St, Rotherhithe, London, auctioneer and cabinet manufacturer (1820). [D]

Gatliffe, Thomas, Pool Lane, Liverpool, cm (1728–68). Took apps named Bencoft in 1728 and Nagle in 1752. Later apps were Thomas Dobb (free 1760), Isaac Wardley (free 1765) and John Molyneux (app. 1754, free 1765). In June 1768 he announced his retirement from the trade, 'being advanced in years'. His 'Stock of ready made Cabinet Goods & Looking Glasses' were sold off from his Pool Lane premises from 8 June 'the lowest Price Ticketted on each Piece of Furniture'. [S of G, app. index; Liverpool freemen's committee bk; *Williamson's Liverpool Advertiser*, 3 June 1768]

Gattie, Charles, 89 Leather Lane, Holborn, London, looking-glass manufacturer, carver and gilder (1816–22). [D; Goodison, *Barometers*]

Gattrell, John, High St, Lymington, Hants., u and cm (1839). [D]

Gattrell, Joseph, Lymington, Hants., cm and u (1823–30). Recorded at High St in 1830. [D]

Gaty, William, address unknown, cm (1765). Payment of £10 10s in 1765 listed in the abstract of tradesmen's accounts, Chatsworth, Burlington Papers.

Gaubert, Guillaume, Panton St, London, maker of ornamental furniture (1785–95). When Horace Walpole visited Carlton House in 1785 he attributed the decoration to 'Gobert'. In 1795 this maker claimed £1,133 19s 8d for work on ornaments for Carlton. [DEF]

Gaul, John, George St, Ope, Devonport, Devon, turner, carver and screw cutter (1830). [D]

Gaulton, Henry, Bere Regis, Dorset, cm (1830). [D]

Gauntlett, George, Exeter, Devon, carver (1823–39). In Coombe St in November 1823 when his son George Thomas and daughter Mary Anne were bapt. In 1825 at Paul St and in 1839 in Friar's Terr. [D; PR(bapt.), St Mary Major]

Gautby & Bell, High St, Barton-on-Humber, Lincs., joiner and cm (1835). [D]

Gavins, John, Newsome's Yd, Briggate, Leeds, Yorks., cm and joiner (1837). [D]

Gawan, Curtis, Marlborough Pl., Brighton, Sussex, cm (1823–40). Three sons, Henry, Joseph and Charles bapt., 1823–30. [PR(bapt.); poll bks]

Gawan, John, 11 Union St, Somers Town, London, cm and undertaker (c. 1806–17). Son of John Gawan of London, painter. App. to John Stephenson of Hull on 13 November 1799. By 1817 trading in London at the Union St address. [D; Hull app. reg.]

Gawler, Peter, Christchurch, Hants., turner and chairmaker (1823). [D]

Gawthorp, James, Leeds, Yorks., cm (1822–37). At Lower Templar St in 1822 but from 1828 at 5 Upperhead Row. [D]

Gawthorp, Robert, Caldicoates, Carlisle, Cumb., joiner/cm (1829). [D]

Gawthorp & Flesher, Turner St, Albion St, Leeds, Yorks., u and cm (1822). [D]

Gay, John Daniel, 91 Hoxton Old Town, London, chair and sofa maker (1839). [D]

Gay, Thomas, Rochford, Essex, cm etc. (1826). [D]

Gay, William, Rochford, Essex, cm etc. (1826). [D]

Gaylor, James, 68 Castle St, Oxford St, London, carver (1806). On 19 November 1806 took out insurance cover of £400, of which half was in respect of a house at Harmondsworth, Middlx. [GL, Sun MS vol. 437, ref. 795933]

Gaylor (or Gayler), Peter, Purewell, Christchurch, Hants., turner and chairmaker (1823–30). [D]

Gaywood, William, Lower Hillgate, Stockport, Cheshire, cm (1798–1808). [D]

Gazely, Joseph, 9 Church St, Spitalfields, London, carver and gilder (1790). [D]

Gazy, Thomas, Coleshill St, Birmingham, cm (1767). [D]

Geagan, John, address unknown, cm (1803). Subscribed to Sheraton's *Cabinet Dictionary*, 1803.

Geake, Robert & Thomas, Hendford, Yeovil, Som., cm and u (1830). [D]

Geake, Thomas, West St, Tavistock, Devon, cm (1823). [D] Possibly:

Geake, Thomas, Westgate St, Launceston, Cornwall, cm and u (1824–30). Between February 1829 and September 1830 supplied substantial quantities of furniture and furnishings to a N. Lawrence Esq. These included '8 Black Chairs with Caned Seats & Cushions' at £10, 'a Couch in Canvas' at £8 and '4 Mahogany Chairs' at £7. [D; Cornwall RO, DD. LR. 14]

Geake, Thomas, Middle St, Hendford, Yeovil, Som., cm and u (1839). [D]

Geake, Thomas, Cheap St, Sherborne, Dorset, cm and u (1840). [D]

Gear, Samuel, Nottingham, cm (1807–18). In April 1807 took app. named William Root (or Rook) of Hull, and in February 1818 app. named James Wilford, also of Hull. [Hull app. reg.]

Geare, —, Yeovil, Som., cm (1829). In May 1829 it was reported that a floor had collapsed in a factory in which this maker was involved. [*Exeter Flying Post*, 28 May 1829]

Geare, James, Weymouth, Dorset, cm (1779). Mentioned in connection with a deed. [*Dorset Nat. Hist. and Arch. Proceedings*, 1931, p. 70]

Gearing, H., address unknown. Submitted an account dated 11 April 1772 for an 'Old Japan Box & stand' charged at £22 in connection with Croome Court, Worcs. [V & A archives]

Geatenby, George, South Moulton St, Westminster, London, carver (1774–75). Declared bankrupt, *Gents Mag.*, August 1775. [Poll bk]

Geaves, George, 4 New Dock St, Hull, Yorks., cm and u (1816). [D]

Gebhard, John, London, cm, u and undertaker (1820–29). At 4 Pell St, Ratcliffe Highway, 1820–22, and 5 Princes' Pl., Commercial Rd from 1826. [D]

Geddes, Charles Alexander, address unknown, cm (1803). Subscriber to Sheraton's *Cabinet Dictionary*, 1803.

Geddes, James, 11 Crown Ct, Pulteney St, London, cm (1779). In 1779 insured a house for £100. [GL, Sun MS vol. 276, p. 79]

Gedge, Ambrose, Wensum St, Norwich, cm and u (1818–22). App. to Thomas Cutler and free 7 December 1818. Trading by 1822. [D; freemen reg.]

Gedling, Robert, Commerce St, South Shields, Co. Durham, cm (1827). [D]

Gee, Edward, King's Lynn, Norfolk, cm (1784). [Poll bk]

Gee, Edward, Mount East St, Nottingham, cm (1835). [D]

Gee, George, Mount Sorrel, Leicester, chairmaker (1840). [D]

Gee, Henry, Warwick Row, Blackfriars Rd, London, upholder (1803). Son of William Gee of Acton, Middlx, fellmonger. App. to Henry Terry on 1 December 1790 and free of the Upholders' Co. by servitude, 6 July 1803. [GL, Upholders' Co. records]

Gee, John, 32 Redcliffe St, Bristol, cm (1775). [D]

Gee, John, 70 Stamford St, Ashton-under-Lyne, Lancs., cm, u and joiner (1824–34). [D]

Gee, Martha, London, bed and mattress maker (1820–27). At Warwick Row, Blackfriars, 1820–23, and 22 Bridge House, Newington Causeway in 1827. Possibly the widow of Henry Gee. [D] Succeeded by William Charles Gee.

Gee, John, London, chairmaker and turner (1779–*c*. 1824) also listed as **Gee & Sons** (1809) and **Gee, Thomas Ayliffe** (1804–09?). In about 1779 John Gee replaced Thomas Ayliffe as partner to Benjamin Crompton, who had been Turner in Ordinary to George III since 1762. On 14 October 1787 Gee was sworn in as turner 'jointly with Thos. Ayliffe his partner', but his name, unlike Ayliffe's, does not appear in the *Court and City Register* until 1799. Ayliffe was the fourth member of his family to be a turner to the King, so Gee was probably the junior partner. In 1790 Lord Wilton bought chairs for the Music Room at Heaton Hall, Lancs. '2 June 1790 Aycliffe & Gees Bill for chairs etc. £49 8s.'. [Preston RO, DD/Eg 153/1–8] From 1799, when he is described as 'Chair-maker, 49 Wardour Street, Soho', Gee is listed in London directories. In 1803 [D] he is called 'Chairmaker & Turner to His Majesty' and this title occurs regularly in entries up to 1823; in most directories, however, this appointment is omitted. Gee is also included in the list of master cabinet makers attached to Sheraton's *Cabinet Dictionary*, 1803. The last directory listing for Gee is 1823–24. On 8 November 1804 Thomas Ayliffe Gee was appointed Turner in Ordinary to the King jointly with his father and briefly, in one directory of 1809 the firm is listed as 'Gee & Sons, Turners & chair makers'. John Gee's name is shown in the *Court and City Register* until 1831, well after his apparent retirement. Charles Holme Bridges, who succeeded Gee at 49 Wardour St in 1824 received a royal warrant in 1822 but is first entered as a turner in the 1832 *Register*. Gee's productions have been identified through stamped marks: 'J GEE', 'GEE', I GEE', 'Jn. G' and a crown, J within G, and 'GEE WARDOUR ST' have been noted. Certain chairs are stamped with initials: 'RR', 'GL', 'GH', 'IT' and 'WG' have been noted. These are probably the marks of individual chairmakers in Gee's employ. His seems to have been a substantial undertaking. The following summary list records chairs by Gee in the order of their emergence: Pride's of London, 1962, 6 chairs, painted trophies on green and brown background, stamped 'J GEE'. [*C. Life*, 1 March 1962, supplement p. 34 and *Conn.*, May–August 1962]; Bearne's Sale Rooms, 1964, settee, 2 armchairs, 7 chairs, stamped 'J GEE'; 8 chairs, brass inlay, stamped 'J GEE'. [*C. Life*, 12 March 1964, supplement p. 35]; Sotheby's, London, 19 June 1970, lot 80, 4 chairs, simulated rosewood, gilt, stamped 'GEE' and 'RR'; Sotheby's, London, 23 October 1970, lot 170, 6 chairs, simulated rosewood and brass inlay, stamped 'GEE' and 'GL' (some only); Sotheby's, London, 11 June 1971, lot 192, 2 armchairs, ebonised and gilt, stamped 'GEE'; Christie's, London, 20 January 1972, lot 64, 8 chairs, ebonised, stamped 'I GEE' and 'GH'; Bearnes & Waycotts, 1974(?), armchair, painted. [G. Wills, *Craftsmen and Cabinet-makers of Classic English Furniture*, 1974, p. 127]; Christie's, London, 31 October 1974, lot 98, 3 chairs, gilt, one branded 'Jn. G' twice with crown, the other two branded with crown, and with trade label of Copworth Bros. & Harrison, 22 Old Bond Street, Carpet & Cabinet Manufacturer to Her Majesty; Pride's of London, 1975, 6 chairs, simulated rosewood and brass inlay. [*Conn.*, May 1975]; Temple Newsam House, Leeds, 1976, 2 armchairs, ebonised and painted, stamped J within G and 'IT'. [C. Gilbert, *Leeds Furn. Cat.*, I, p. 100]; Mrs G. M. Douglas, Bath, 1978, 3 chairs, painted green, stamped 'GEE WARDOUR ST' and 'WG'. [Simon Jervis, 'John Gee of Wardour Street', *Furn. Hist.*, 1979, p. 69]; Sotheby's, London, 14 November 1979, lot 277, 2 chairs, painted with flowers, one stamped 'GEE'. [ibid.] Private House, Monmouthshire, 1985, 8 chairs, ebonised, all stamped 'GEE' and 'IT', and 2 settees, *en suite*, both stamped 'GEE' and (?) 'WP'. S.J.

Gee, Osgood, 60 Gee St, London, cm (1811). In association with William Furze insured on 22 January 1811 his dwelling house and one adjoining for £330 and two houses, 2 and 3 Willace Rd for a further £120. [GL, Sun MS vol. 449, ref. 852717]

Gee, Richard, St Martin's, Oxford, u and cm (1802–24). In partnership with Wharton, 1810–30, at Corn Mkt, 1823–30. Supplied goods and undertook work for the Leigh family at Stoneleigh Abbey, Warks., from October 1810 to January 1811. 'A neat mahogany chest of drawers with oak inside' was charged at £7 7s on 16 October 1810 and further work and materials were charged at £8 6s 6d in January of the following year. On 13 March 1824 the Radcliffe Asylum, Oxford, was charged £1 1s for a mahogany writing table, £3 3s for six yew chairs and 6s for a large rope mat. [Poll bk; Shakespeare Birthplace Trust, Leigh receipts, DR 18/5; Radcliffe Asylum archives]

Gee, Thomas, 8 Stanley St, Liverpool, cm and broker (1827–29). [D]

Gee, Thomas Ayliffe, see John Gee.

Gee, William jnr, Lombard St, Lichfield, Staffs., cm (1835). [Poll bk]

Gee, William Charles, 22 Bridge House Pl., Newington Causeway, London, u, bed and mattress maker (1837–39). Successor to Martha Gee. [D]

Geerme, T., 4 Sidney Pl., King's Rd, London, cm (1826). [D]

Geeves, Ann, Church Lane, Hampstead, London, u (1839). [D]

Gegan, James, High St, Maidstone, Kent, carver and gilder (1826–39). In 1834 had a house in Bank St. [D]

Geldard, William, Lee's Yd, Meadow Lane, Leeds, Yorks., joiner and cm (1822). [D]

Gelder, Henry, Lancaster, carver (1783–84). [Lancaster freemen rolls; poll bk]

Gelder, Robert, Beverley, Yorks., cm (1774). [Poll bk]

Gell, Richard, Hull, Yorks., carver, gilder and furniture painter (1821–40). At 12 Manor Alley in 1821, 8 New Dock St, 1822–23, and 9 Wellington Mart in 1826. After 1831 the business remained in Saville St, the number being given as 30, 1831–40 and 38 and 31 in 1835 and 1839–40. [D]

Gell, Thomas, 14 Church St, York, cm and u (1834–40). [D]

Gell, William, Wragby, Lincs., chair and wheel maker (1826–40). [D]

Gellard, John, Schoolhouse Yd, Clerkenwell, London, cm (1777). Declared bankrupt, *Gents Mag.*, January 1777.

Gellion, Samuel, Chester, cm (c. 1796–1826). App. to Charles Ridgeway of Chester, cm, 20 April 1789. Nothing further is recorded until 1818 when he was living in White Alley and elegible to vote as a freeman. He is also recorded at this address in the following year but by 1826 had moved to Bridge St. [Chester app. and poll bks]

Gendall, John, Exeter, Devon, carver and gilder (1825–38). At 270 High St, 1825–32, but in August 1832 his bankruptcy was announced. By 1834 however he was once more in business with premises in Cathedral Yd. [D; *Exeter Flying Post*, 16 August 1832]

Gennills, John, New St, Woodbridge, Suffolk, cm (1839). [D]

Gennings, William, Abingdon, Berks., cm (1790–93). [D; poll bk]

Gent, George, Cheap St, Sherborne, Dorset, cm (1830–40). [D]

Gent, John, London, clock case maker (1778–84). At 18 Fore St, Cripplegate in 1778 and 70 Wood St, Cheapside in 1784. In both years he insured his house for £100. [GL, Sun MS vol. 266, p. 645; vol. 324, p. 50]

Gent, Samuel, Warrington, Lancs., cm (1828–34). At Bridge St in 1828 and Union Ct in 1834. [D]

Geoff, John, 54 Church St, Brighton, Sussex, furniture japanner (1832). [D]

George, —, Henrietta St, Covent Gdn, London, cm (1775). On 6 January 1775 a Daniel Beaumont took out insurance cover of £100 on items 'at Mr Georges Cabinet maker in Henrietta Street'. [GL, Sun MS vol. 236, ref. 348679]

George, George, High Wycombe, Bucks., cm (b. c. 1792–1841). Three sons and two daughters bapt., 1820–31. Aged 49 at the time of the 1841 Census. [PR(bapt.)]

George, John, Berwick St, Westminster, London, cm (1784). [Poll bk]

George, Remy, Bartholomew Close, London, upholder (1704–27). App. to Thomas Dixon and free of the Upholders' Co. by servitude on 28 August 1704. Took as apps George Buckle, 1709–16; Charles Evers, 1711–18; Michael Gravelay, son of Edmund Gravelay of Halton Yorks., 1712–19; and Arthur Skelton, 1717–24. Two accounts referring to the supply of furniture to Arthur Ingram, 3rd Viscount Irwin, in February and May 1718 exist. The first account amounting to £843 3s 2½d was for furniture supplied to Barrowby Hall, near Leeds, and included a fine crimson damask bed and eight chairs *en suite* accounting for £170 alone. A set of '42 fine matted chairs mouldings about ye seat' amounting to a further £15 15s. The second was for furniture for Temple Newsam, Leeds and Hills Place, near Horsham, Sussex, amounting to £475 8s 1d. A set of '18 fine walnuttree Veneared Indian Backe chaires with Indian feet the seats covered with Blacke Spanish Leather' was charged at £27 while a set of '24 fine walnuttree chaires with turned Indian Backs &

Indian feet' accounted for a further £22. [GL, Upholders' Co. records; Heal; *Furn. Hist.*, 1967]

George, Richard, Fleet Mkt, London, u and cm (1771–93). Son of Joseph George of Ramsbury, Wilts., yeoman. Admitted freeman of the Upholders' Co. on 22 January 1771 under the terms of the 1750 Upholders' Act. At 30 Fleet Mkt in 1777 where he took out insurance cover of £200 of which £150 was in respect of utensils, stock and goods. Later in the same year a further policy for £500 including £300 for utensils, stock and goods was taken out on 59 Fleet Mkt, an address to which he had moved his business. He was to continue here until 1793 though from 1788 the address was referred to as 59 Fleet St. [D; GL, Upholders' Co. records; Sun MS vol. 256, p. 348; vol. 258, p. 49]

George, Richard, Newcastle House, Clerkenwell Green, London, cm and u (1779). Card in Banks Coll., BM.

George, Robert, 34 Chandos St, London, cm (1778–80). In 1778 took out insurance cover of £1,000 of which £550 was for utensils, stock and goods and £80 for a workshop. In the following year the total insurance was reduced to £800 of which £470 was for utensils, stock and goods. Declared bankrupt, *Gents Mag.*, April 1780. [GL, Sun MS vol. 262, p. 502; vol. 274, p. 168]

George, Samuel, Flushing, Cornwall, cm (1743). In 1743 took app. named Pinch. [S of G, app. index]

George, Thomas, Totnes, Devon, cm and u (1791–1823). In 1791 took out insurance cover of £400 of which £350 was in respect of stock and goods in trust. By 1794 the business was in financial difficulties and in February of that year he assigned his estate and effects to Samuel Curtis and Richard Cole in trust for the benefit of his creditors. A Thomas George shown trading as a cm in Totnes in 1823 may be the same man or possibly his son. [D; GL, Sun MS vol. 374, ref. 580799; *Exeter Flying Post*, 27 January 1794]

George, Thomas, 25 Greek St, Soho, London, bed and mattress maker (1822). [D]

George, Thomas, St Columb, Cornwall, cm (1823–24). [D]

George, William, Charles St, Worcester, u (1835). [Worcester freemen rolls]

Geover, John, Warrington, Lancs., cm (1759). In 1759 took app. named Lawson. [S of G, app. index]

Gepp, Thomas, 20 Clown Row, Mile End Rd, London, cm (1837). [D]

Gerard, Joseph, Liverpool, cm (1840). Son of N. Gerard, joiner. Free 28 July 1840. [Freemen reg.]

Gerardus, Henry, 9 Oxford Chapel Pl., London, carver and gilder (1809). [D]

Geronimo, Peter, 8 Old Market St, Bristol, looking-glass and picture frame maker (1826). Declared bankrupt, *Liverpool Mercury*, 11 August 1826. [D]

Gerrard, Charles, 27 Church St, Soho, London, carver and gilder (1807–08). Supplied picture frames to the Earl of Egremont for Petworth House, Sussex, 1807–08. [D; C. *Life*, 25 September 1980, p. 1032]

Gerrard, G. W., 33 Temple St, Bristol, blind maker and cm (1835). [D]

Gerrard, James, Queen St, Lymington, Hants., chairmaker etc. (1830). [D]

Gerrard, John, Beaminster, Dorset, chairmaker (1729). In 1729 took William Gerrard as app. for 7 years. The £1 10s premium was paid by the overseers of the poor. [Dorset RO, P57/DV21]

Gerrard, Thomas, Liverpool, cm (1756–61). Thomas Potter, who had been app. to Thomas Gerrard for five years, petitioned freedom in 1761. [Freemen's committee bk]

Gervas, Wells, Piccadilly, London, carver (1775). [Bailey's list of bankrupts]

Gesleth, William, 32 South Molton St, London, carver and gilder (1809). [D]

Getskell, John, Lancaster, (1785–1801). [Westminster Ref. Lib., Gillow records]

Getskell, Joseph, Lancaster, cm (1797). Named in the Gillow records working on chests in 1797. [Westminster Ref. Lib., Gillow vol. 344/97, pp. 1345, 1374]

Getskell, William, Lancaster, (1787–1801). [Westminster Ref. Lib., Gillow records]

Gettings, Oxford St, Bilston, Staffs., cm and u (1830–38). [D]

Ghrame, —, address unknown, u (1803). Subscribed to Sheraton's *Cabinet Dictionary*, 1803.

Gianinetty, Joseph, address unknown, cm (1770). In 1770 supplied a 'very fine inlaid writing desk' to Blair Castle, Tayside, Scotland. [V & A archives]

Gibb, William, Noch St, Berwick St, London, victualler and upholder (1775). In 1775 insured his stock and utensils for £100 out of a total cover of £200. [GL, Sun MS vol. 238, p. 386]

Gibb & Thomas, 23 Swan St, Manchester, chairmaker (1815). [D]

Gibbard, John, London, cm, upholder and chairmaker (1817–27). At Pell St, Ratcliffe Highway in 1817 and 9 Chapel St, Holywell Mt in 1827. [D]

Gibbins, John, 99 Edgware Rd, Tyburn Turnpike, London, undertaker and u (1817). [D]

Gibbins, William, 103 Edgware Rd, London, cm and u (1822). [D]

Gibbon, William, Kirkby Stephen, Westmld, joiner/cm (1834). [D]

Gibbons, Daniel, Liverpool, joiner and cm (1784). Free 2 April 1784. [Freemen reg.]

Gibbons, Edward, London, u, undertaker and auctioneer (1789–1825). At 3 Goldsmith St, Wood St, 1789–93, but from 1794 at 3 Bucklersbury. Subscriber to Sheraton's *Drawing Book*, 1793 and named in his list of master cabinet makers in Sheraton's *Cabinet Dictionary*, 1803. [D]

Gibbons, George, 26 Tower St, Seven Dials, London, cm and undertaker (1820–35). [D] See William Gibbons.

Gibbons, Grinling, London, carver (b. 1648–d. 1721). Son of James Gibbons who was free of the Drapers' Co., 12 September 1638. The father moved to Holland and Grinling was born in Rotterdam in 1648. James Gibbons returned to England in 1659 and his son probably travelled with him. He is said to have been employed initially as a ship carver and lived at Deptford. It was here that Evelyn claimed to have discovered him working on a copy of 'The Crucifixion' of Tintoretto in wood, which so impressed the diarist that he brought him to the attention of Charles II. Evelyn's first contact with Gibbons is recorded as 18 January 1671. An alternative version of the introduction of Gibbons to royal attention named Sir Peter Lely as the agent, the royal portrait painter having seen some carved work executed at the new playhouse in Dorset Gdns known as the Duke's House. It was certainly from the 1670s that his work was increasingly recognised by London society. He was admitted a member of the Drapers' Co. by patrimony in 1672 and later took office as Renter-Warden, 1704–05; Second Warden, 1712–13; and First Warden, 1714–15. He worked for the Crown at Windsor Castle and was subsequently appointed Master Carver in Wood to the Crown. This post he held from the reign of Charles II through to that of George I. His fame rests mainly on his work as a woodcarver and many commissions for fixed woodwork are known or attributed to him. His workshops also produced a considerable range of work in stone, particularly for Blenheim Palace, some of which is noted in Gunnis. His involvement in furniture making is less

well recorded. A walnut and limewood sidetable said to have been made by Gibbons for John Evelyn and included in an inventory of Wotton House, Surrey in 1702 was sold by Christie's in their sale of 17 March 1977. Gibbons's addresses in London are recorded as Belle Sauvage Ct, Ludgate Hill until 1677 and 'King's Arms', Bow St, Covent Gdn thereafter. [Gunnis; Heal; D. Green, *Grinling Gibbons*, 1967]

Gibbons, Israel, 19 Charles St, Hatton Gdn, London, carver and bed joiner (1778–93). Took out insurance cover of £200 in 1778 and 1786, £400 in 1791 and £300 in 1793. Of these sums utensils and stock amounted to £40 in 1778 and £60 in 1786. His address in 1778 was opposite the 'White Hart' in Lukemers Lane but after 1786 he was at 19 Charles St, Hatton Gdn. [GL, Sun MS vol. 266, p. 381; vol. 338, p. 465; vol. 375, p. 626; vol. 395, p. 620]

Gibbons, John, Hythe, Kent, carpenter, cm and ironmonger (1794). [D]

Gibbons, Joseph, London, cm (1793). Subscribed to Sheraton's *Drawing Book*, 1793.

Gibbons, Richard, Dover, Kent, cm (1830). [Poll bk]

Gibbons, William, 26 Tower St, Seven Dials, London, cm and u (1827). Note also George Gibbons working at this address at this period. [D]

Gibbs, —, London(?), cm (1744–51). Supplied Charles Rogers of Laurence Pountney Lane, London with furniture between February 1744 and June 1751. This included wainscot bookcases of which three were supplied charged at £10 2s and fifteen wainscot frames for drawings charged at £2 9s. [*Apollo*, December 1960, pp. 196–98]

Gibbs, Anthony, Cornhill, London, upholder (1712–18). Free of the Upholders' Co., 1712. Included in the registers of unclaimed dividends of Bank of England stock, 1718. [GL, Upholders' Co. records; Heal]

Gibbs, David, Whitecross Alley, Moorfields, London, chairmaker (1789). In 1789 took app. named John Walker. [Westminster Ref. Lib., MS E 2566, p. 154a]

Gibbs, John, 92 High St, Poplar, London, cm and u (1835–39). [D]

Gibbs, Robert, 86 Long Alley, Moorfields, London, cm and chairmaker (1817–20). [D]

Gibbs, Samuel, Market Sq., Aylesbury, Bucks., cm and u (1823–39). [D]

Gibbs, Thomas, Bristol, cm (1774). [Poll bk]

Gibbs, William, Poland St, London, cm (1772–74). Bankrupt June 1772. [Bailey's list of bankrupts; Westminster poll bk]

Gibbs, William, 11 George's Ct, St John's Lane, Clerkenwell, London, cm (1808–11). May also have used a workshop at 12 George's Ct next to his dwelling house, both of which were the property of Joseph Warren. In 1810 the workshop was insured for £100. [D; GL, Sun MS vol. 452, ref. 844194]

Gibbs, William, High Wycombe, Bucks., 'fallow chairmaker' (b. c. 1791–1841). Aged 50 at the date of the 1841 Census.

Gibbson, —, address unknown, upholder (1685). Entry for £1 in the accounts of Charles Blunt, upholder. [PRO, C114/164, pt 1]

Giblett & Atkins, 6 Argyle Pl., Regent St, London, u (1829). [D]

Gibson, Mr, address unknown, artist and frame maker (1702). The account book of Sir John Newton of Barr's Court, Gloucester lists under 10 February 1702 a charge of £12 'for copying my fathers & mothers pictures' and a further £3 for two frames due to Mr Gibson. [Lincoln RO, Cragg 2/17/2]

Gibson, —, Newport St, St Ann's, Soho, London, u (c. 1780). His trade card in Heal indicates that he sold 'all Sorts of Emboss'd, Chintz, Painted & Common, PAPER for ROOMS, with Variety of Papier Mâché & Ornaments for Ceilings, Halls, Stair Cases &c. NB. Paper made to imitate any Furniture, and compleatly fixed up.'

Gibson, Abraham, Huddersfield, Yorks., cm (1814–22). At Castlegate in 1814 but in High St, 1818–22. [D]

Gibson, Charles, 10 Halle Buildings, Windmill St, Manchester, cm (1817). [D]

Gibson, Christopher, 'The King's Arms', St Paul's Churchyard, London, u (1730–45). In April 1730 he received payment of £4 15s for chairs supplied to the East India Co. for East India House in Leadenhall St. A further £4 was paid by the same Co. in September 1732 for 'eight chairs'. In 1742 the business was named as Gibson & Grimstead. It is possible that Christopher Gibson may have taken over the business of Joseph Grimstead who is recorded trading at 'The King's Arms' in St Paul's Churchyard, 1707–12. The Grimstead who was his partner in 1742 was no doubt related to Joseph Grimstead. An engraver's proof for Gibson's trade card exists giving some idea of an upholsterer's premises of this period. Stock shown includes cane chairs, chairs and a stool with upholstered seats, an angel bed, a mirror, funeral hatchments and numerous bales of cloth. The engraving shows two ware-rooms overlooking a courtyard and a wide flight of steps leading up to the first floor. Gibson's business is last recorded in 1745, and by 1747 the premises at the sign of 'The King's Arms' was in the occupation of James Brown, u and cm. [D]; *Apollo*, November 1965, p. 405; Cornforth & Fowler, *English Decoration in the 18th Century*, p. 83]   B.A.

Gibson, Clement, Lancaster, carver (1792–93). [Lancaster freemen rolls]

Gibson, Edward, 33 Low St, Sunderland, Co. Durham, cm (1832). [D]

Gibson, George, York, carver and gilder (1758–75). Took as apps John Cockran, 1759; Henry Brother, 1761; and James Griffiths, 1764. In July 1774 announced that he had taken a shop in The Shambles 'joining to Crux Church'. He offered to execute 'Chimney Pieces, Picture and Glass Frames, and Mouldings for Rooms, and other Ornaments.' He stated that he had 'engaged proper Assistants, well qualified to execute all the above Branches in the most elegant Manner'. It was also indicated that he intended 'to give up the Pawn-broking Business entirely.' In 1775 he insured his house for £400. One commission for Harewood House, Yorks. is recorded. On 13 April 1776 he charged £3 4s for gilding a girandole. [App reg.; *York Courant*, 19 July 1774; GL, Sun MS vol. 244, p. 115; Leeds archives dept, Harewood MS 248]

Gibson, George, address unknown, u and chairmaker (1765–75). Supplied Sir John Griffin Griffin of Audley End, Essex with upholstery materials etc. in 1765 and six ash chairs at 2s 3d each in 1775. [Essex RO, D/DBy/A23/10]

Gibson, George, 53 Ratcliffe Highway, London, cm, undertaker and u (1774–1839). The long period of trading of this business suggests that there must have been two George Gibsons involved. George Gibson snr was the son of James Gibson of the parish of St Andrews, Holborn, Gent. He was app. to Thomas Palmer and Joseph Reed, merchant tailors, 5 January 1770. He was admitted freeman of the Upholders' Co. by servitude, 2 February 1774, and is first recorded in trade directories in 1789. His trade card [Leverhulme Coll., MMA, NY] describes the business as an 'Upholstery, Cabinet, Looking Glass and Carpet Warehouse' and stated that he also undertook the trades of appraiser, auctioneer and undertaker. Insurance records list the address as 54 Ratcliffe Highway but this may be his dwelling house. In 1775 he also used an address near 'The Dolphin', Long Alley, Moorfields insured for £200 of which £100 was for utensils, stock and goods. Cover was raised to £300 with £140 for utensils and stock in the following year and for 1779–80 were £500 and £250 respectively. Took as app. George Norris White, 1790–1802. [D; GL, Upholders' Co. records; Sun MS vol. 237, p. 210; vol. 246, p. 591; vol. 272, p. 426; vol. 187, p. 620]

Gibson, Henry, Lancaster, joiner and cm (1756–68). App. to Christopher Walker, joiner and cm, 10 June 1753 and free as a joiner, 1756–57. On 5 July 1768 took an app. and at this time described his trade as cm. [Lancaster app. reg. and freemen rolls]

Gibson, Henry, Lancaster, carver and gilder (1784–97). [Westminster Ref. Lib., Gillow records; poll bk]

Gibson, Henry, Huddersfield, Yorks., cm (1814–28). At Castlegate in 1814 and High St, 1818–28. These addresses were also used by Abraham Gibson over a similar period of time described above and the two makers must be related or associated. [D]

Gibson, James, London, upholder (1791–1805). At 3 Little Portland St in 1791, 7 Westmorland St, Marylebone, 1792–1801 and 42 Goodge St in 1805. In 1791 he insured his house only for £400 and in the following year arranged cover for £900 which included his house, utensils and six tenements. In 1801 the sum insured was £600 of which £360 was for utensils and stock. By 1805 cover had been reduced to £540 of which stock and goods in trust accounted for a mere £50. [GL, Sun MS, 5 August 1791, ref. 587259; vol. 389, ref. 602214; vol. 419, ref. 721169; vol. 434, ref. 777194]

Gibson, James & John, James St, Covent Gdn, u (1746–74). [Heal; Westminster poll bks]

Gibson, John, parish of St Paul, Covent Gdn, upholder (1748). Declared bankrupt, *Gents Mag.*, June 1748.

Gibson, John snr, 'Queen's Head', Groat Mkt, Newcastle, joiner and cm (1761). In April 1761 announced that he was terminating his business and selling off the stock by auction. This included 'chests of drawers, chairs, tables, looking-glasses and various other articles in the cabinet way'. [*Newcastle Journal*, 11–8 April 1761]

Gibson, John jnr, Newcastle, u, joiner and cm (c. 1762–1801). Took app. named Henry Reed, admitted freeman, 3 May 1769. In 1801 at Low Friar-gate. [D; freemen reg.; poll bks]

Gibson, John, Wardour St, Soho, London, cm and u (1817–37). At 39 Wardour St, 1817–21, but from 1822 the address is given as Ship Yd, Wardour St. In 1821 took out insurance cover of £1,000 on stock, utensils and goods in trust in workshops, warehouses and stables and in open yard. Cover was increased in the following year to £2,000 with a further £800 for the dwelling house. These sums suggest a substantial business. [D; GL, Sun MS vol. 488, ref. 981828; vol. 493, ref. 993875]

Gibson, John, London, cm, u and Tunbridge-ware manufacturer (1826–40). Listed in 1816–18 as a Tunbridge-ware dealer. At Ray St Pl., Clerkenwell from 1826–40, but one directory gives address at 7 Richmond Buildings, Soho in 1835. [D]

Gibson, John, Tyne St, North Shields, Northumb., carver and gilder (1827–34). Recorded at no. 32, also as a bird preserver, in 1834. [D]

Gibson, John, Penrith, Cumb., joiner and cm (1828–34). At Frier St in 1828 but by the next year had moved to Nether End. [D]

Gibson, John, Liverpool, cm (1837–39). At 25 Comus St in 1837 and 20 Clare St in 1839. [D]

Gibson, Malby, Micklegate, York, carver and gilder (1787). [D]

Gibson, Mary, 20 Gascoyne St, Liverpool, chair bottomer (1813). [D]

Gibson, Ralph, 32 Brownlow St, Long Acre, London, cm (1787). On 10 April 1787 insured his new dwelling house and goods for £300. [GL, Sun MS vol. 342, ref. 529917]

Gibson, Richard, Lancaster, cm (1764–99). App. to Gillow, 1764. Free 1779–80. Named in Gillow records, 1787–91, 1793–96 and 1799. [Westminster Ref. Lib., Gillow; Lancaster app. reg.]

Gibson, Richard, 21 Albion St, Liverpool, carver and gilder (1811). [D]

Gibson, Robert, Bristol, cm, u and undertaker (1815–40). At 11 Mercant St, 1815–21, and 3 Old King St, 1821–33. In 1826 however an address in Ellbroad St is recorded in one directory. From 1834 at 16 Horse Fair. [D]

Gibson, Thomas, Darlington, Co. Durham, cm (1793). Subscribed to Sheraton's *Drawing Book*, 1793.

Gibson, Thomas, Birmingham, cabinet and dressing case maker (1800–18). Recorded at 49 Coleshill St as cm and knife case maker in 1800, and at Prospect Row, 1816–18. [D]

Gibson, W., Lancaster, carver (1785–86). [Westminster Ref. Lib., Gillow records]

Gibson, William, Warner St, Coldbath Fields, London, carver (1763). [D]

Gibson, William, Salisbury Ct, London, cm (1779–92). In 1779, 1785 and 1792 fined for non-service at St Bride's Guildhall. [GL, MS 6561, p. 10]

Gibson, William, South Parade, Burnley, Lancs., cm and joiner (1818). [D]

Gibson, William, Liverpool, cm and beer shop (1823–39). In 1823 at 23 Ranelagh St but from 1835 at 35 Clayton St. [D]

Gidley, John, parish of St Mary Major, Exeter, Devon, cm (1803). [Militia Census]

Gidney, Christopher, 40 Castle Ditches, Norwich, cm (1802). [D]

Gidney, Samuel, Gt Yarmouth, Norfolk, cm (1777). [Poll bk]

Gibson & Grimstead, see Christopher Gibson.

Gifford, Joseph, 15 Merchant St, Bristol, Windsor and fancy-chair maker (1818–19). [D]

Gifford, Joseph, Bristol, chairmaker and French polisher (1831–40). At 17 Barton St, 1831–35 and 5 Charles St, 1836–40. [D]

Gifford & Wilding, 63 Castle St East, London, chairmakers (1835). [D]

Gilbank, Thomas, Cable St, Manchester, chairmaker (1819). [D]

Gilbanks, M., Lancaster (1837–40). [Westminster Ref. Lib., Gillow records]

Gilbert, —, address unknown, cm and u (1775). Subscribed to Thomas Malton's *Compleat Treatise on Perspective*, 1775. Possibly the John Gilbert (1742–84) below.

Gilbert, Francis, 4 William St, Blackfriars Rd, London, cm, u and undertaker (1808–09). [D]

Gilbert, Henry snr, St George's St, Stamford, Lincs., cm and u (1809–40). [D; poll bks]

Gilbert, John, St Giles, parish of St Martin-in-the-Fields, London, upholder (1727–d. 1729). Undertook work for the Royal Household and at the time of his death in 1729 was referred to as 'upholsterer to his Majesty'. Supplied and undertook work on canopies, bedding, curtains and quilts for the Crown and in 1728 repaired a bed at Hampton Court, originally supplied for the use of the Prince of Wales in 1715. May be the father of the John Gilbert trading in Gt Queen St from 1732. [Heal; GL, Sun MS vol. 26, p. 475; PRO, LC9/287; *St James's Evening Post*, 6 September 1729; *Conn.*, June 1933, p. 379]

Gilbert, John, Gt Queen St, London, upholder (1732–33). Said to have made the bed for the marriage of the Princess Royal and the Prince of Orange. [Harris, *Old English Furniture*, p. 21; Heal]

Gilbert, John, Southwell, Middlx and Mount St, Golden Sq., London, carver (1742–84). Took out insurance cover on a house at Southwell for £150 between 1742–49. In 1749 he moved to Mount St, Golden Sq. which was to be his address from this date until the termination of the business. His earliest commission was in connection with the interior design and furnishing of the new Mansion House. In 1752 he

supplied 'eight rich carved frames with glass & branches gilt with Burnish gold' for the Great Parlour for which £84 was charged and 'six Brackets richly carved' for the Vestibule which cost an additional £15. Apart from fixtures 'one large table' was supplied for the Great Parlour at £20 8s. The mirrors and brackets are still in place but other furniture no longer survives. For work at the East India House, Leadenhall St he received £86 3s in August 1756 and £86 1s in October of the same year. At this period he was also working for Sir John Hinde Cotton of Madingley Hall, Cambs. and received payments of £60 both on 3 December 1756 and 23 September 1757.

During the 1760s and 70s he worked on a number of commissions in houses whose interiors were the design responsibility of Robert Adam. From March 1767 to December 1768 he was engaged on carved work at Berkeley Sq. (Lansdowne House) for Lord Shelburne 'by order of Messrs. Adams Esq.' The total account came to £313 4s 3½d and included 'carving a table frame enriched for hall £3 13s', 'making, carving and gilding in burnished gold a large glass frame with ornaments at top and bottom £33' and 'making, carving and gilding in burnished gold a circular table frame under ditto, fully enriched £30'. At the same period he was working at Croome Court, Worcs. and Mersham-le-Hatch, Kent. At Osterley, Middlx he was engaged on carving work for Robert Child as early as 1773 and in that year received £32 15s in payment. In May of the following year he submitted an account for two pedestals for the Entrance Hall 'Inriched with Oak Leaves and Rafled Leaves &c.' charged at £17 11s. These are still in the possession of the Earl of Jersey's family. The last Osterley commission known was the carving in 1784 of four elm pineapples for the top of the corner turrets which cost £24. The only commission unconnected with Adam houses in this phase yet noted was the carving of a looking-glass frame for Charles Rogers of Laurence Poultney Lane, London at a cost of £4 8s. This was paid for on 8 June 1768. [D; poll bks; GL, Hand in Hand MS vol. 63, ref. 8674; *Conn.*, December 1952 p. 181; *DEF*; Bolton, *The Architecture of Robert and James Adam*, 2, p. 314, appendix D; Cambs. RO, S88/A33; *Apollo*, December 1960, pp. 196–98, November 1965, p. 405, June 1970, p. 445; *Met. Museum Bulletin*, November 1959; V & A archives; Tomlin, *Catalogue of Adam Period Furniture*, p. 18]

Gilbert, John, Camden Alley, Portsmouth, Hants., cm and ironmonger (1781–98). Took out insurance cover in 1781 for £1,400 of which £750 was for utensils, stock and workshops. [D; GL, Sun MS vol. 296, p. 502]

Gilbert, Robert, 19 Shaw's Brow, Liverpool, cm (1804). [D]

Gilbert, Sarah, London, u (1729–41). Probably the widow of John Gilbert of St Giles, London who died in 1729. Recorded in the Royal Household accounts, 1729–36, and in this period supplied bedding, re-upholstered chairs and carried out repairs at Hampton Court, Kensington Palace, St James's Palace and the Houses of Parliament. In 1731–32 made up a green damask four post standing bed, the frame supplied by Henry Williams, at a cost of £30 for Hampton Court. Supplied 108 turkey work chairs, 2 Russia leather folding stools for the clerks and 7 turkey carpets for the House of Peers and 48 turkey work chairs and 3 large arm chairs *en suite* for the House of Commons Committee Room during the period 1729–33. In 1733 was responsible for the decoration of the 'French Chapel' for the marriage of the Princess Royal to the Prince of Orange. From 1736–41 in partnership with William Reason, u. [PRO, LC9/288–90; Winterthur, Delaware, Symonds, 75×64.14 p. 190; *Old Furniture*, II, 1927, p. 183; *Conn.*, April 1934, p. 224]

Gilbert, Thomas, Ashby-de-la-Zouch, Leics., chairmaker

(1790–93). In partnership with William Gilbert in 1790 but both partners were trading independently by 1793. [D]

Gilbert, William, 3 doors below Fetter Lane, Fleet St, London, u (c. 1780). Trade card shown in Heal. The business was described as a 'Blanket, Carpet and Upholstery Warehouse' and the articles mentioned in the list of stock suggest retail and wholesale sale rather than manufacture. At the bottom of the card, however, is the sentence 'Upholstery Work done in yᵉ Compleatest manner'.

Gilbert, William, Ashby-de-la-Zouch, Leics., chairmaker (1790–93). In partnership with Thomas Gilbert in 1790 but both partners were trading independently by 1793. [D]

Gilbert, William, Manchester, chairmaker and broker (1813–40). At 23 New St in 1813 but from 1816 in Shudehill. From 1816–29 the number is 27; in one directory of 1832 it is 35, but directories from 1832–40 show no. 53. [D]

Gilbert, William, High St, King's Lynn, Norfolk, carver and gilder (1830–36). In 1830 the number is shown as 38 High St but in 1836 it is 39. [D]

Gilboa, John, Long Acre, London, cm (1709). [Heal]

Gilbody, Henry, Staining Lane, Wood St, London, cm (1784). [D]

Gilchrist, Andrew, 92 Wardour St, Soho, London, cm and u (1789–96). In 1789 took app. named William Stephenson. Gilchrist was imprisoned for debt in 1793 and in April of that year Stephenson petitioned for release from his apprenticeship. He complained that he had been 'taught nothing of the cabinet or upholstery business . . . only put to making deal tables.' He further stated that Gilchrist had before his arrest secretly removed the greater part of his stock. His customers were said to be mainly 'women of the town, many of whom bought his furniture in weekly instalments of a guinea or half a guinea.' When in prison Gilchrist tried to persuade his app. to smuggle tools into this building in the hope that he could, with Stephenson's assistance, continue production. This was frustrated by the app.'s successive appeals for his discharge. Directories show this business operating as late as 1796 at the Wardour St address but this may be failure on the part of the directory publisher to delete the entry. [D; GL, Middlx session bk]

Gilchrist, John, 21 Ducie St, Strangeways, Manchester, cm and u (1836–40). Shown at 21 Ducie St, 1836–40, and 2 Gt Ducie St in 1840. [D]

Gildard, William, Thomas St, Liverpool, chairmaker (1790). [D]

Gilder, John, Hull, Yorks., cm (1835–40). At 8 Upper Union St in 1835 but in 1838 the address is shown as 4 William's Sq., Upper Union St. [D]

Gilding, Benjamin, Minories, London, upholder (1719). [GL, Sun MS vol. 9, p. 164]

Gilding, Edmund, Red Cross St, London, cm and chairmaker (1739–d. 1757). Supplied furniture to Sir Richard Hoare, a partner in Hoare's Bank and Lord Mayor of London in 1745. This was for Barn Elms House. The earliest account of July 1739 was for eight chairs which with some labour charges came to £8 8s 6d. More chairs and a table amounted to £3 5s and were charged in the following year. From November 1742 to May 1744 items were supplied including dressing glasses, tables, a desk and a couch totalling £23 6s 10d. Further chairs, a tea box and repairs and alterations between August 1752 and June of the following year amounted to £32 6s 7d and in 1754 a large mahogany dining table and stools etc. were charged at £9 19s 6d. Another member of the same family to patronise this maker was Henry Hoare of Stourhead, Wilts. Between April 1753 and June 1756 he paid a number of sums for furniture. These included settlement for five Chinese chairs at £1 10s each on 11 April 1753, and the

large sum of £176 1s on 16 March 1754 for chairs and furniture. Edmund Gilding died on 12 August 1757 at his house in Red Cross St. [V & A Lib., 86. NN. 3; Wilts. RO, MS 383.6; *London Chronicle*, 16 August 1757]

Gilding, Francis, 113 Aldersgate St, London, cm and u (1759–96). Son of Edmund Gilding of Red Cross St to whose business he succeeded. The manufactory he operated was substantial. In 1759 he took out a licence to employ thirty non-freemen for six weeks, and in 1778 and 79 took out further licences to employ fifty non-freemen for periods of up to three months. Apart from the Aldersgate premises he had other workshops. On 29 May 1790 he took out insurance cover for £6,000 on premises at Newcastle House, Clerkenwell Close, £5,000 of which was in respect of stock. On 18 June 1791 warehouses and workshops in Long Lane, Smithfield, were insured for £2,000. A number of Gilding's apps are known. In 1767 he took as app. Alexander Boote, son of John Boote of Ardington Berks., Gent. and received the substantial premium of £84. James Bagley, son of William Bagley of Arton, Cheshire, was app. in the same year, paying £63. On 5 May 1772 he took as app. Francis Banner, son of John Banner, freeman plumber of London. Francis Banner lived with Gilding in his house and subsequently became his partner. The only other app. known is Thomas Handiside who was accepted on 4 December 1792 on payment of a premium of £102. Francis Gilding subscribed to Thomas Malton's *Treatise on Perspective*, 1778, and is recorded in 1790–91 as a Fellow of the Society for Arts and Manufactures. His partnership with Francis Banner is first recorded in 1786 but the last years of the business were marked by crisis. In December 1790 was reported a terrible fire at his warehouse and in 1795 he was declared bankrupt. It is significant that Francis Banner was not named in the bankrupty proceedings which may suggest that the partnership had been dissolved before these commenced.

Two of Francis Gilding's customers are known. On 5 October 1768 he charged Charles Turner, Esq. of Stretton Hall, Staffs., £2 6s for a mahogany dining table. A more significant commission was that of Lord Howard of Audley End, Essex, who received an account in August 1786 for goods supplied from 22 October of the previous year amounting to £21 10s 6d. The main items were a 'Square back Bergere Elbow Chair' charged at £3 13s 6d, 'a Solid Mahogany Eliptic Side board' at £4 4s and 'a Neat Elbow Chair' and four stools en suite which together cost £12 1s 6d. [D; GL, City Licence bks, vols 2 and 9; Sun MS ref. 570053; vol. 379, p. 134; Joiners' Co. app. bindings, vol. 7; *Gents Mag.*, December 1790; *Billinge's Liverpool Advertiser*, 1 June 1795; 27 July 1795; 14 December 1795; 7 November 1796; 26 December 1796; V & A Lib., Box II 86 KK; Essex RO, D/DBy/A44/11]

Giles, F., John St, Bath, Som., carver and gilder (1793). [D]

Giles, Henry, Newton Bushel, Newton Abbot, Devon, cm (1830–38). [D]

Giles, Isaac jnr, Atherton St, Liverpool, u (1774–81). Son of Isaac Giles snr, shoemaker of 47 Atherton St. Petitioned freedom by patrimony in 1774 and admitted freeman, 2 November 1775. He set up business at 46 Atherton St in 1774 but in 1781 was at no. 41. [D; freemen's committee bk and reg.]

Giles, James, Oxford, u and cm (1802–30). Recorded in the parish of All Saints, 1802–05, and High St, 1808–30. [D; poll bk]

Giles, James, opposite Belgrave Pl., Vauxhall, London, cm and upholder (1827). [D]

Giles, John, Quiet St, Bath, Som., carver and gilder (1787–91). [D]

Giles, N., 12 Poland St, Oxford St, London, u (1823). [D]

Giles, Samuel, Clarence St, Plymouth, Devon, cm (1836). [D]

Giles, Thomas, Cumberland St, Woodbridge, Suffolk, cm and u (1805–30). [D; *Ipswich Journal*, 30 March 1805]

Giles, William, 6 Morgan's St, Commercial Rd, London, cm and upholder (1802–17). Freeman of Maidstone. [D; Maidstone poll bks]

Giles, William, High Wycombe, Bucks., cm, undertaker and u (1823–39). Listed at Frogmore ward in 1823 and High St in 1830. In 1839 the business is listed as W. Giles & Son. [D]

Gilham, Frederick A., 9 Beer Cart Lane, Canterbury, Kent, cm (1830–39). [D; poll bk]

Gilkes, Thomas, Butcher Row, Buckingham, u (1839). [D]

Gilkes, William, Buckingham, cm and u (1823–30). Trading at Horn St in 1823 and West St in 1830. [D]

Gill, —, 24 Mint St, Southwark, London, bedstead maker (1826). [D]

Gill, Benjamin, 7 Paradise St, Liverpool, u (1813–18). In 1818 made two elaborate painted chairs used to chair the elected MPs for the borough, George Canning and General Gascoyne, after the announcement of the poll. [D; *Liverpool Mercury*, 1 January 1813, 3 July 1818]

Gill, Cornelius, Royal Hill, Greenwich, London, cm (1808). [D]

Gill, Daniel, High St, Dudley, Staffs., cm and u (1835). [D]

Gill, David, Sheffield, Yorks., cm (1821–30). At Chapel St, Bridgehouses in 1821 and 51 Nursery St in 1830. [D]

Gill, F., Lillington Lane, Leamington, Warks., u (1822). [D]

Gill, George, London, upholder (1780–1802). Admitted freeman of the Upholders' Co. by redemption by order of the Court of Aldermen, 5 July 1780. At that time living at 12 Tower Royal, but in 1794 moved to Aldersgate St, and in 1802 recorded at 89 Watling St. [GL, Upholders' Co. records]

Gill, George, 121 Upper Thames St, London, wholesale u (1782–83). Heal lists George & Maxey Gill at this address in 1783. [D] See Gill & Maxey.

Gill, George, 'The King's Head', Virginia St, Ratcliffe, London, victualler and cm (1783–85). In 1783 took out insurance cover of £300, utensils, stock and goods accounting for £100. In 1785 the cover was £100, half of this being for utensils and stock. [GL, Sun MS vol. 333, p. 329]

Gill, Henry, Liverpool, cm (1806). App. to Isaac Marsh and admitted freeman on 31 October 1806. [Freemen reg.]

Gill, Henry, Liverpool, cm (1812). App. to John Meers and admitted freeman on 12 October 1812. [Freemen reg.]

Gill, Henry, High St, Lowestoft, Suffolk, cm (1824–39). [D]

Gill, James, Whitby and Hull, Yorks., cm (1758–74). Freeman of York. Shown working at Whitby in 1758 and Hull in 1774. [York poll bks]

Gill, James, Liverpool, cm and u (b. 1790–1823). Born 14 March 1790, son of Joseph Gill, butcher. Admitted freeman by patrimony on 5 October 1812, and by 1814 trading at 8 Paradise St. In 1818 moved to 66 Whitechapel and in March of that year described the stock held at his new premises. This consisted of 'Brussels & Kidderminster Carpets, Paper Hangings, Lobby Cloths, Feather Beds, Mattresses & all kinds of Cabinet Goods'. Also in 1818 an address at 8 Virgil St is shown, but this may be his dwelling house. In 1821 the number in Whitechapel was 56 and by 1823 he had moved to Gt Howard St. In 1812 took app. named William Beckerstaffe, admitted freeman in 1820. [D; freemen's committee bk; *Liverpool Mercury*, 13 March 1818]

Gill, James, Colne, Lancs., chairmaker and turner (b. c. 1793–1841). Recorded at Market Pl., 1828–34. Took his son Henry as app., aged 16 at the time of the 1841 Census. [D]

Gill, James, 239 Tottenham Ct Rd, London, picture framer etc. (1820). [D]

Gill, James Carver, 97 Pottergate, Norwich, cm and u (1822–40). [D]

Gill, James, Sheffield, Yorks., cm (1833–37). In 1833 at 17 Castle Green and in 1837 at 29 Osborne St. [D]

Gill, John, Maddox St, Hanover Sq., London, u (1747–52). Between 1747–52 was paid £500 for fabrics and fringes supplied for Kirtlington Park, Oxon. [*Apollo*, January 1980; Westminster poll bk]

Gill, John, Clerkenwell, London, cm (1754). Took app. named Duffield in 1754. [S of G, app. index]

Gill, John, Somerton, Som., cm (1774–84). [Bristol poll bks]

Gill, John, London, cm (1784–1808). At 24 St John's Lane, Clerkenwell, 1784–89, but from 1790 the number is given as 20. [D]

Gill, John, Tiverton, Devon, cm (1798). [D]

Gill, John, 6 Gt Suffolk St, Southwark, London, carver and gilder (1812–15). [D]

Gill, John, Faulkner St, Manchester, cm (1822–34). The number in Faulkner St is shown as 21, 1822–25; 22, 1828–29; and 47, 1832–33. In 1825 his dwelling house was also listed as Back York St, Clifford St, Chorlton Row and by 1834 he appears to have given up the Faulkner St premises and was working from his house. [D]

Gill, Jonas, Birstall, Yorks., joiner/cm (1837). [D]

Gill, Joseph, Manchester Rd, Ashton-under-Lyne, Lancs., cm and joiner (1828–34). [D]

Gill, Joshua, Newcastle, cm and joiner (c. 1830–38). Initially at Nun's Field but by 1833 had moved to Fenkle St where he took over premises formerly occupied by the late Mr Cummings. [D; Landauer Coll. of trade cards, MMA, NY]

Gill, Richard, Finkle St, Thorne, Yorks., joiner, cm and u (1822–21). [D]

Gill, Richard, 20 Fontenoy St, Liverpool, u and household broker (1827). [D]

Gill, Richard, 51 Nursery St, Sheffield, Yorks., cm (1837). [D]

Gill, Robert, Liverpool, cm (1812). At Threlfalls Ct or Catherine Ct, Charter St. Free 12 October 1812. [Freemen reg.]

Gill, Thomas, Chester, joiner, turner and carver (1711–20). In 1711 took apps named Williams and in 1720, Chubb. [S of G, app. index]

Gill, Thomas, late of St George's, Hanover Sq., London, u (1761). Discharged from Debtors' Prison 16 April 1761. [*London Gazette*]

Gill, William, Market Pl., Bedale, Yorks., cm, joiner and carpenter (1823–40). [D]

Gill, William, Norwich, cm (1829). Free 23 May 1829. [Freemen rolls]

Gill, William, Brierley Hill, Staffs., u/cm (1839). [D]

Gill & Crossley, Harrington St, Liverpool, cm and japanners (1805). [D]

Gill & Maxey, London, wholesale u and cotton dealers (1783–88). At 121 Upper Thames St, 1783–84; 38 Friday St, 1786–87; and 135 Aldersgate in 1788. [D] See George Gill.

Gillach (or Gilloch), John, 38 Holywell Lane, Shoreditch, London, cm and u (1808–27). [D]

Gillam, Joseph, Bristol, upholder (1754–81). At Bedminster in 1754 but from 1774–81 in the parish of St James. [Poll bks]

Gillard, Ann, Thomas St, Bristol, u (1819–23). [D]

Gillard, Ferdinand, James St, Covent Gdn, London, u (1774–78). Declared bankrupt, *Gents Mag.*, April 1778. [Poll bk]

Gillard, Henry, Thomas St, Bristol, cm (1815–21). In 1821 shown also in Trenchard St. [D]

Gillard, John Oswald, 15 Pile St, Redcliffe, Bristol, cm (1822). [D]

Gillard, John, Lower South St, Exeter, Devon, cm (1829).

Daughter Frances Louisa Mills bapt. at St David's Church, 5 April 1829. [PR(bapt.)]

Gillard, John, 2 Church Lane, Temple St, Bristol, camp desk maker (1835–37). [D]

Gillard & Cornish, 48 Strand, London, looking-glass and picture frame makers, carvers and gilders (1829). [D]

Gillatt, George, Coulston St, Sheffield, Yorks., cm and u (1828). [D]

Gillbank, William, Cable St, Manchester, chairmaker (1813–21). Recorded at no. 22 in 1813. [D]

Gillbanks, Thomas, Manchester, chairmaker (1816–25). At Angel St in 1816 but from 1818 at 16 Cable St, Oldham Rd. [D]

Gilles, —, Oxford St, London, see Ferguson, Whiteside & Co.

Gillespie, Andrew, Manchester, cm and u (1816–25). In 1816 in partnership with D. Gillespie at 63 Oldham St but in 1818 was trading by himself at the same address. He was still there the following year but from 1824–25 was at 34 Church St, as Andrew & Co. [D]

Gillespie, Andrew, 106 Meadow Lane, Leeds, Yorks., cm (1828–30). One directory of 1828 records him at no. 100. [D]

Gillespie, Richard, Wormald's Yd, 15 Briggate, Leeds, Yorks., cm and u (1834). [D]

Gillespie, Robert, Wormald's Yd, 15 Briggate, Leeds, Yorks., cm and u (1834). [D]

Gillespie, William, 9 Manchester St, Liverpool, joiner and cm (1835). [D]

Gillespy, Daniel, 43 University St, Tottenham Ct Rd, London, carver and gilder (1839). [D]

Gillett, John, Bristol, chairmaker (1810–40). In 1810–12 and 1827–40 the address is given at Temple Backs, but from 1819–20 at Temple St, when the trade is stated as 'Windsor & Fancy Chair maker'. [D]

Gillett, John jnr, Avon St, Great Gdns, Bristol, Windsor, fancy and cane chairmaker (1833). [D]

Gillett, John, 37 Argyle St, London, u (1820). On 31 May 1820 took out insurance cover of £400 on household goods in his dwelling house. At the same time a separate policy was issued in the names of John Gillett and Robert Atkins, cm and u at the same address. This covered stock, utensils and goods to the value of £800 and china and glass for an additional £200. [GL, Sun MS vol. 483, refs 968231–32]

Gilley, Matthew, 95 Old Gravel Lane, London, cm and u (1822). [D]

Gilliam, John, London, joiner (1712–30). Provided the altar-piece, pulpit, reader's and clerk's desks at St Paul's, Deptford, for which he received £200. [*Architectural Review*, March 1950, p. 196]

Gillingtons, —, address unknown (c. 1815). Regency brass inlaid rosewood sofa table, rectangular top, and two drawers in frieze on four turned supports and sabre legs, sold at Sotheby's, 12 January 1979, lot 218, bears the stamp 'GILLINGTONS 3009'.

Gillion, Samuel, Nantwich, Cheshire, cm (1815). On 12 December 1815 his son Thomas was bapt. [PR(bapt.)]

Gillis & Taylor, Oxford St, London, (c. 1776). Included in the list of furniture makers drawn up by the Duchess of Northumberland, c. 1766. [Gilbert, *Chippendale*, p. 154]

Gillman, David, Deal and Canterbury, Kent, cm (1795–1818). Freeman of Canterbury. Recorded living at Deal, 1795–96, but in 1796 moved to Canterbury and in 1818 was living at Palace St. [Canterbury poll bks]

Gillman, James, Faversham, Kent, cm (1780–90). [Canterbury poll bks]

Gillman, John, Back of the Inns, Norwich, u, cm and chairmaker (1835–40). Son of John Gillman, linen draper and free 24 February 1835. [D; freeman reg.]

Gillman, William, Norwich, cm (1742). In 1742 took app. named Thirkettle. [S of G, app. index]

Gilloch, Mary, 38 Holywell Lane, London, cm (1835–37). [D]

Gillock, Thomas, 10 Worship St, Moorfields, London, cm and chairmaker (1793). Subscribed to Sheraton's *Drawing Book*, 1793.

Gillock, Thomas, 28 Holywell Lane, Shoreditch, London, cabinet carver (1835). [D]

Gillott, George, Sheffield, Yorks., cm and broker (1821–37). At 8 Coulston St, 1821–33, and 52 Bridge St in 1837. [D]

Gillow, Lancaster and London cm (c. 1730–after 1840). The name 'Gillow' has been firmly associated with furniture making from at least the 1730s until the present day, though the active participation of the Gillow family ceased in the early 19th century. The firm was based in Lancaster though a full London branch had been established in Oxford St in 1769. The Gillow archives have been purchased by Westminster City Council.

Robert Gillow (b. 1704–d. 1772) came to Lancaster about 1718, obtained his freedom in 1727/28, married Agnes Fell in 1730 and retired from the firm in 1769. His two sons were Richard I (b. 1734–d. 1811), elected freeman 1754/55, became a partner from 1757 to 1800 while Robert II (c. 1745–95) obtained his freedom 1766/67 and became a partner in 1769 with responsibility for managing the London branch. Richard I's three sons Robert III (b. 1765–d. 1838); George (b. 1766–d. 1822) and Richard II (b. 1772–d. 1849) all became partners in 1785, 1787 and 1796 respectively, while Robert II's son, Robert IV became a partner in 1795 until his death sometime before 1800. The vital commercial decision was to open a London branch in 1769 under Robert II's control while Richard I, who had been trained as an architect, stayed in Lancaster.

Entries for the firm appear (not necessarily accurately) in successive London Trade Directories as Gillows & Taylor, 1771–77 (there is a 'Trou Madame' games table at Abbot Hall, Kendal, Cumbria bearing their label); Robert, Thomas & Richard Gillow, 1777–83 (but also as Robert, Richard and James Gillow 1781–85). Then either as Robert Gillow & Co. or as Robert & Richard Gillow 1785–94; then George and Richard Gillow from 1802–12, thereafter simply as Gillow & Co. However a bill at Arundel Castle is headed Gillow & Ferguson. In Lancaster, Richard II succeeded his father in business in 1796 and lived at Leighton Hall, Lancs.; his son, Richard Thomas (b. 1806) was the last member of the family to be directly associated with the business. He retired in 1830 and d. 1866.

In Bentham's *Directory*, 1805 the firm was trading as 'Redmayne, Whiteside & Ferguson (late Gillow & Co.)'. Leonard Redmayne was app. to the firm in 1795 and in 1809 was described as 'book keeper' to Gillows; William James Ferguson cm, had premises adjacent to Gillows in Oxford St and Henry or Edward Whiteside had both served as cm apps with Gillows. Under Redmayne's direction the firm was generally known as 'Gillow & Co.'.

Clarke, in his *Historical and Descriptive Account of Lancaster*, 1807 stated: 'the town has long been famous for the great quantities of mahogany furniture which have been made in it for home-use and exportation ... Mr Gillow's extensive ware-rooms, stored with every article of useful and ornamental mahogany furniture are well worth the attention of strangers, as they are said to be the best stocked of any in this line out of the metropolis'. In 1800 Richard Gillow took over a patent for the Imperial Extending Dining Table which earned the firm a great reputation. The practice of punching the stamp 'GILLOWS·LANCASTER' began about 1780 (although it was used selectively) and tradesmen sometimes signed their name in ink or pencil unobtrusively on articles during the early 19th century (Figs 11–12). Relatively few pieces of furniture made by the firm prior to 1780 have been securely identified.

The Gillow's archive is the most complete to survive of any leading English furniture manufacturer, but it is the sequence of Estimate Sketch Books from the 1760s onward that indicate the range and detail of the firm's huge output. The watercolour drawings of the Travellers' pattern book of c.1770–1810 further reveal the firm's ready response to fashionable demand, indicating that much now dubbed 'Sheraton' or 'Hepplewhite' is in fact the production of the Gillows. The firm also undertook architectural joinery, such as chimneypieces, doors and doorcases and — as a Catholic family — they attracted commissions for altarpieces and tabernacles from their co-religionists. The Gillow enterprise included importing West Indian sugar and spirits, as well as exotic hardwoods, and they enjoyed a worthwhile export trade in furniture to both the West Indies and the ports of northern Europe. Lancaster being close to the Cumbrian slate mines the firm quickly developed a specialist trade in newly fashionable billiard tables. From the start the firm recognized that the potential offered by the expanding middle class market, whether in South Lancashire or in London, would also serve all but the most opulent seeking to furnish country houses. In the last quarter of the 18th century, when greater simplicity became fashionable under the influence of architects such as James Wyatt, they expanded into every range of furnishing. Wyatt by 1774 was designing furniture to be made by Gillows for Heaton Hall, Lancs. By the end of the 18th century the firm was furnishing the largest mansions and town houses completely. As well as impressing their stamp on items they sometimes, as a further advertisement, named them after fashionable patrons, e.g. 'Uxbridge', 'Cavendish', 'Manvers', 'Ashburnham', etc.

According to the earliest surviving account book of 1731, the firm maintained the joinery side from which the business had sprung and did repair-work alongside furniture-making in oak, pine, walnut, mahogany and ebony. Brass mouldings were an occasional added refinement. Pattern books were studied and sketches of London pieces sought in order to keep abreast of fashion, and trade increased sufficiently for them to set up in the West End of London on their own account in 1769. A new set of furniture designs was evolved for this purpose. To obtain further business, existing clients were asked to recommend the firm, and the travelling salesman was equipped with a handsomely drawn and coloured pattern-book. Sketches were readily sent out by post. To reduce transport costs, the Gillows dispatched furniture ready for final assembly at the destination, or would offer a discount to patrons who agreed to a group dispatch of their orders.

Both the designs, and the colour schemes of japanned furniture, were typically devised to harmonise with a client's wallpaper and/or upholstery. Turned or painted decoration was frequent, but inlay, except for contrasting crossbanding or stringing, was kept to a minimum, as was carved work. Sometimes the latter was done by specialists in London. The Gillows usually bought in all their metal work, ormolu or gilt brass being generally confined to handles, escutcheons or pierced galleries. In 1785 the Lancaster branch was extended to include upholstery services. The colourful japanned seat furniture was complemented by that of satinwood — for example, desks, smaller bookcases, bureaux and cabinets, the ground veneer inset with kingwood, purplewood or green-stained harewood. After 1800, japanning became less fashionable save for the simulation of bamboo, and new woods such as rosewood and later maple, became more popular.

There was also an increasing demand for copies of older pieces, at first simply to match existing items, but by the 1820s for 'reproduction' pieces sold as such. Hitherto the description 'Antique' had denoted the Greek or Roman Revivals; henceforth the word described virtual copies of 'Old English' furniture, the details of which were typically derived from either an amalgam of late 16th and mid to later 17th-century motifs, that is, in 'Elizabethan' style; or a closer adaptation of the Baroque designs of c.1710–30. They also made furniture in the 'Louis' style as one alternative, and from the mid 1820s they produced small numbers of pieces in a wholly convincing Chippendale 'Director' style, such as a 'Salisbury' Antique table with Gothick cluster legs and fret in 1828 or a plain tray-top commode, and a large and handsome Library Desk of 1835 similar to that they had made for Denton Park in 1778. The Gillows Gothic Revival work was less antiquarian in spirit, rather a grafting of Gothic motifs onto standard contemporary shapes. Nevertheless during the 1830s many other Gillow designs were of extreme simplicity, echoing the so-called Square Style of Sir Robert Smirke, their rectilinear character in marked contrast to the strong patterns and rich colours of the wallpapers and carpets shown in contemporary Gillows contract books.

Each generation of the Gillow family, as we have seen, took up their freedom at Lancaster, and were described as joiners or cm. In turn they took apps, some of whom long served their masters' firm. Their number was substantially supplemented by skilled craftsmen, employed as individuals in their own right. These men were thus free to accept or reject the work offered them, but as the Gillows occasionally pointed out to them the firm tried to employ them all the year round even when trade was slack. As a consequence their piecework rate might occasionally be below that offered elsewhere, a disadvantage offset by the regularity of their employment. In practice once a craftsman had proved a specific skill, the firm generally gave him that class of work, to mutual advantage. In the more difficult times of the wars, first in North America and then with Revolutionary France, the Gillows devised a 'Book of Prices' to which their craftsmen had to subscribe.

The nobility did not flock to Gillows until after 1800 when they bought lavishly from a stock of items, typically of mahogany, less often of rosewood. By then japanning, except for 'bamboo' and black and gold, was no longer in vogue. The firm, unlike its many rivals in Oxford St, did not encourage the use of gilded 'composition' when a rich effect was needed, and here they ignored fashion. From 1816, in steadily increasing quantity, Gillows manufactured more and more furniture for the firm of Ferguson, their neighbour at 177 Oxford St, until by 1840 furniture for Fergusons almost dominates the Gillows Estimate Sketch Books. The firm astutely realized the huge market possibilities offered by the middle and upper-middle class households of the later Georgian and early Victorian eras. They foresaw this demand as that for items well made out of good materials, and in a style that would remain acceptable when the immediate fashion had waned; that is, in their designs they achieved a satisfactory mean between the merely conservative and the ultra fashionable. This is one reason for their survival. No firm gained a wider geographical spread of patronage, though with a greater concentration in north western England, and in those parts better served by the steadily improving land or water carriage. The Gillows always remained aware that the lower wages payable in Lancaster had to be counterbalanced against the high transport costs of sending goods to London, and that too great a rise in either cost could be fatal to their enterprise.

Though many hundreds of patrons employed the firm, little of the outcome is either now *in situ* or traceable. This is specially true of the furniture supplied to middle-class town-houses in, for example, Liverpool or Manchester. Before the opening of the London branch in 1769, the firm was strongly local in character and supplied items piecemeal or in small groups even to new-built houses such as Lytham Hall where in 1765–66 Thomas Clifton bought tables and chairs, or Alexander Butler of Kirkland Hall had chimney pieces carved, a sideboard, glass frame, tea kettle stand, and other items made for the interior plus a hotbed frame for the garden. Mr Parker of Browsholme, also ordered items to which his successors continued to add until the early 19th century.

This pattern changed after 1769 when the fashionable and ambitious also gave their patronage. For example, the 1st and 2nd Earls of Wilton bought for Heaton Hall, Lancs. in 1771 a billiard table, in 1774–75 dining-room chairs, in 1776 bedroom furniture, in 1777–78 fire screens and clothes maids, etc., in 1780 saloon sofas, and more items in 1787, 1791, 1794, and in the 1820s the doors, book cases, library table, etc., for the new library. Workington Hall, Cumbria, was remodelled for John Christian Curwen *c.* 1788 with John Carr as architect and the Gillows as furnishers. The items supplied included several types of pier tables, commodes, curtain cornices, dining room, hall, and dressing-room chairs, sideboards, pedestals and urns, fire screens, stools, work tables and night tables, many of them shown in the Travellers' Pattern Book, and in the most elaborate Gillows style. The Workington Hall commission was probably the most important they had attracted to date and seems to have exerted a dramatically stimulating effect on the business. Some of this Curwen furniture is still at Belle Isle, Windermere. The Streatham Park furniture which Gillows supplied to Mrs Piozzi was the cause of a major dispute due to the firm's over-charging, and here they were forced to make a reduction.

At Farnley Hall, Yorks., and Trafford Hall, Lancs., their owners added handsomely to the older buildings. At Farnley, Walter Hawkesworth (later Hawkesworth-Fawkes) had long patronised the Gillows, but the main new account is for 1790–91 when the new wing was ready for furnishing. [*C. Life*, 24 June 1954] Much of the furniture remains *in situ*. The items for Trafford Hall resembled those at Workington.

A quite different group of clients were Roman Catholics; they included such families as the Cliftons of Lytham, Lancs., who were patrons of the Gillows for over sixty years, the Trappes family of Clayton Hall, the Scarisbricks of Scaris-brick, the Duke of Norfolk and the Earl of Surrey, the Constable-Maxwells of Everingham, Yorks., the Tempests of Broughton Hall, Yorks., the Stapletons of Carlton Towers, Yorks., the Blundells of Ince-Blundell, Lancs., the Towneleys of Towneley Hall, Lancs. and the Gascoignes of Parlington Hall, Yorks. (Fig. 10).

Among notable industrialists were the elder Sir Robert Peel and Peter Drinkwater, both of whom made fortunes from the Lancashire cotton trade. Among churchmen there were the Bishop of St Asaph, and in the 1830s the Archbishop of York. Perhaps the most lavish single commission before 1840 was the new furnishing, in the Gothic taste, of the rebuilt Eaton Hall, Cheshire for the Marquess (later Duke) of Westminster, while in a simpler Regency classical style and Rococo revival idiom the Gillows new-furnished Tatton Park, Cheshire for the Egerton family.

No attempt has been made here to give more than a general overview of the firm of Gillows because their business records and surviving furniture are to be the subject of Dr L. Boynton's forthcoming major monograph.

THE GILLOW ARCHIVE. The Gillow family kept meticulous records and their business archive, although incomplete, is by far the most comprehensive to have survived from any 18th-century firm of furniture makers. It would be difficult to exaggerate its importance. The papers were acquired by Westminster City Lib. Archives Dept in two accessions numbered 344 and 735; there is also a large collection of MS designs at Lancaster Museum and of course documents in various country house archives. Sarah Nichols provides a very good description of the earlier records in an appendix to her MA dissertation (see bibliography), while the Westminster archives department have compiled indexes of personal, corporate and place names and furniture from 1784–1825, The following classes of material give an idea of the scope of the collection. Journals/waste books (1729 onwards), day books, cash books, bill books, sales ledgers, salaries books, order books, estimate sketch books, drawing books, pattern book, memorandum books, stock books, accounts and letters, cost books, packing books and jobbing books (some containing samples of fabrics and wallpapers).

Bourne, S., 'Gillow at Parlington', *LAC*, no. 72 (1973), pp. 14–20

Burkett, M. and others, *A History of Gillows of Lancaster*, Lancashire County Museum Service, 1984

Coleridge, A., 'The firm of Gillow & Co. at Blair Castle', *Conn.*, 157 (1964), 88–93

Cottle, S., 'A sport of Georgian ladies — Gillows' Trou-Madam Tables', *C. Life*, 24 January 1980, pp. 220–21

Gilbert, C., *Furniture at Broughton Hall* (exhib. cat.) Temple Newsam House, Leeds, 1971

Goodison, N., 'Gillows Clock Cases', *Antiquarian Horology*, v, pt 10 (1969), 348–61

Goodison, N. and Hardy, J., 'Gillows at Tatton Park', *Furn. Hist.*, 1970, pp. 1–40

Hall, I., 'Patterns of elegance: the Gillows' furniture designs', *C. Life*, 8 June 1978, pp. 1612–15

Hall, I., 'Models with a choice of leg: the Gillows' furniture designs', *C. Life*, 15 June 1978, pp. 1740–42

Ingram, K. E., 'The West Indian trade of an English furniture firm in the 18th century', *Jamaican Historical Review*, March 1962

Nichols, S., 'Furniture made by Gillow & Company for Workington Hall', *Antiques*, June 1985, pp. 1353–59

Nichols, S., 'Gillows of Lancaster: the role of the upholsterer', *Abbot Hall Quarterly Bulletin*, January 1984, pp. 7–11

Nichols, S., 'A Journey through the Gillow Records', *Antique Collecting*, February 1986, pp. 36–39

Oswald, A., 'Leighton Hall, North Lancashire', pts 1 and 2, *C. Life*, 11 and 18 May 1951

Whitehead, M., 'The Gillows and their work in Georgian Lancaster' in *Catholic Englishmen*, ed. J. A. Hilton, 1984, pp. 21–27

Dissertations

Harrison, P., *Richard Gillow of Lancaster 1734–1811, Architect and Cabinet-Maker*, Cambs. BA dissertation [copy at Judge's Lodging Museum, Lancaster]

Nichols, S., *Gillow and Company of Lancaster, England: an eighteenth century business history*, University of Delaware MA thesis, 1982. [Copies at Winterthur Museum and Temple Newsam House, Leeds]   I.H.

Gillpatrick, Joseph, address unknown (1740). On 23 April 1740 paid £1 4s by Lord Monson for two sacking bottom bedsteads. [Lincoln RO, Monson 11/50]

Gilmore, Francis, London, carver and gilder (1821–22). On 21 June 1821 took out insurance cover of £300 on household goods in his dwelling house at 21 Duke St, Bloomsbury. On 17 July 1822 however he appears to have been living in the house of Gosland, a painter at 7 Bloomsbury Mkt at which address he took out similar insurance cover. [GL, Sun MS vol. 488, ref. 980756; vol. 493, ref. 993592]

Gilmore, William, Newgate St, Bishop Auckland, Co. Durham, joiner and cm (1827–34). [D]

Gilney, Christopher, Castle Ditches, Norwich, cm (1793–1806). First recorded in 1793 as a subscriber to Sheraton's *Drawing Book*. By May 1795 however his property was in the hands of assignees and his stock was sold off in a series of auction sales commencing on 1 June. The stock of furniture consisted of 'a great variety of mahogany, bamboo, and other very neat fancy chairs, 2 mahogany wardrobes, a pair of very beautiful inlaid card tables, several other mahogany card tables in pairs; a very handsome inlaid vase spoon case; chests of drawers; a great variety of pier and dressing glasses, caddies, firescreen stands, wash-hand stands, moveable water closets, cellarets &c. &c.' Materials held in stock consisted of 'upwards of 20,000 feet of very fine dry Spanish and other mahogany, in boards, planks and logs, satin, rose and tulip wood, a very large quantity of fine Spanish and other veneers, some fine wainscot boards, deals &c. &c. also a large quantity of fashionable brass work for furniture, locks, hair seating &c. &c.'. In November 1797 the Norwich freemen reg. lists the admission of a Christopher Gilney, admitted other than by apprenticeship, and by 1801 the business appears to have re-commenced at 40 Castle Ditches. It is possible however that this new enterprise was operated by a son of the same name. [D; poll bks; *Bury and Norwich Post*, 27 May 1795]

Gilpin, John, Bedford St, Covent Gdn, London, upholstery warehouse (1768–83). On 3 August 1770 Sir Thomas Egerton of Heaton Hall, Manchester paid Gilpin £995. [D: Preston RO, DD Eg. bank deposit and account bks]

Gilpin, John, Fairfield, near Manchester, cm etc. (1825). [D]

Gilroy, John, Westminster, London, upholder (1774–82). Worked for the Royal Household and in 1776 provided furnishings for the 'New Court in Westminster Hall, for the Tryal of Elizabeth, who stiles herself the Dutchess of Kingston, on the 15th of April'. Supplied bedding, curtains, carpeting etc. for the Crown. Heal lists the address of Gilroy as Newton Ct, 1774–83, but in 1780 insurance cover of £2,600 was taken out for an address in Lower Grosvenor St. Of this sum £1,800 was for stock, goods and utensils, suggesting a considerable scale of operation. The business was described as that of upholder and cm. The insurance cover was jointly in the names of John Gilroy and Hannah Farmborough. It is possible that John Gilroy died, 1781–82, for accounts of this period made out in his name were receipted by Lucy Gilroy and from 1782 accounts are made out in her name only. [Heal; GL, Sun MS vol. 284, p. 129; PRO, LC9/323–28]

Gilroy, Lucy, London, u (1781–83). Successor and possibly the widow of John Gilroy. Supplied bedding, cushions etc. to royal residences 1781–83. By 1783 however appears to have married a Charles Smith and receipts of this year are given in the name of Lucy Smith. [PRO, LC9/328–30] See Charles Smith of Lower Grosvenor St.

Gilson, Henry, Chelmsford, Essex, cm (1784). [D]

Gilson, Robert, Straight Bargate, Boston, Lincs., cm and u (1803–35). Subscribed to Sheraton's *Cabinet Dictionary*, 1803. Recorded at Wide Bargate in 1819, and as Gilson & Reynolds at Straight Bargate in 1835. [D]

Gilson, Thomas, Chelmsford, Essex, u (1793–d. 1811). Subscribed to Sheraton's *Cabinet Dictionary*, 1803. Died 7 November 1811. [D; *Gents Mag.*, December 1811]

Gilsthorpe, George, Warsergate, Nottingham, cm (1828). [D]

Gimber, Charles, London, carver and gilder (1808–37). At 17 Flower de Luce Ct, Fetter Lane, 1808–20; 8 Spreadeagle Ct, Finch Lane, Cornhill 1826; and 124 Fetter Lane, 1835–37. [D]

Gimber, Sophia, 124 Fetter Lane, London, carver and gilder (1829). [D]

Gimber, Thomas, 17 Fetter Lane, Fleet St, London, carver and gilder (1809). [D]

Gimson, John, Hungate St, Aylsham, Norfolk, cm (1830). [D]

Giradus, Henry, 9 Chapel Pl., Oxford St, London, carver and gilder (1809). On 27 March 1809 took out insurance cover of £1,430 which included £250 for a workshop behind his dwelling house in Chapel Pl. and £30 for stock and utensils. He also insured a house in Mansfield Pl., Kentish Town. [GL, Sun MS vol. 448, ref. 828854]

Girard (or Le Girardy or Girardi), —, address unknown, u (c. 1784). Responsible for the painted state bed at Inveraray Castle, Strathclyde. [*C. Life*, 8 June 1978, p. 1622]

Girling, —, London, cm (1793). Subscribed to Sheraton's *Drawing Book*, 1793.

Girling, James, Lakenham, Norwich, chairmaker (1796–1818). [Norwich poll bks]

Gironimi, L., Leather Lane, London, looking-glass manufacturer and picture frame maker (1829–39). At 4 Leather Lane in 1829 but the number is 93, 1835–39. [D]

Gironimo, B., London, looking-glass manufacturer (1817–37). At 4 Leather Lane, 1817–21; 27 Maiden Lane, Covent Gdn in 1825; and 93 Leather Lane 1837. [D]

Gironimo, S., 4 Leather Lane, London, looking-glass manufacturer (1825). [D]

Giscard, John, 131 High St, King's Lynn, Norfolk, cm and furniture broker (1836–40). [D]

Gites, John jnr, 70 Jubilee St, Brighton, Sussex, chairmaker (1839). [D]

Gittens, Thomas William, 112 High St, Camden Town, London, cm and u (1838–39). [D]

Gitter, John, 43 Chapel St, Liverpool, cm (1790). [D]

Gittons, William, Folkestone, Kent, cm (1826–35). [Dover poll bks]

Giusani (or Guissani), Peter, Cock St, Wolverhampton, Staffs., carver and gilder (1816–38). Listed at 42 Cock St, 1822–34, also Darlington St in 1833. Trading also as artists' repository and fancy stationer in 1834. Goodison records the business as P. Giusani & Sons in 1835 with a branch at Bilston, Staffs. Undertook work for Josiah Hinckes of Tettenhall Wood, near Woverhampton, between February 1826 and November 1827, making and gilding picture frames [D; Goodison, *Barometers*; Herefs. RO, Foxley papers B47/S40]

Gilvin, Joshua, 4 Canon St, Bristol, cm (1834). [D]

Gladwell, Thomas & Henry, 21 Gracechurch St, London, picture and looking-glass frame makers (1839). [D]

Glaister, William, Whitehaven, Cumb., cm (1834). [D]

Glanfield, John, Exeter, Devon, cm (1817–22). In the parish of St Paul in December 1817 when his son John was baptised. By September 1820 had moved to the parish of St Sidwell and in July 1822 was living at Lion's Holt. A John Glanville of the parish of St Sidwell, cm, who was reported as having absconded in August 1822 may be the same person. [PR (bapt.); *Exeter Flying Post*, 1 August 1822]

Glanvill, James, Queen St, the Mint, Southwark, upholder (1775). Admitted freeman of the Upholders' Co. by redemption, 2 August 1775. [GL, Upholders' Co. records]

Glanville, Julian, St Austell, Cornwall, cm (1839). Insolvent by January 1839. [Cornwall RO, DDSHM 937, 859]

Glanville, Thomas, address unknown, u (1729). On 20 March 1729 submitted to the Earl of Rockingham an account for £3 15s 8d, the main item being 'a couch bed yᵉ box wainscot' at £1 12s. The remaining items were repairs and alterations of a general nature. The account was settled on 26 April 1729. A further account dated 20 March 1729 also exists for £1 13s which includes 'a turnup bed' at 18s. This also was settled on 26 April. [Lincoln RO, Monson 11/61, 11/62F]

Glasgow, Abraham, Hill St, Birmingham, cm (1800). [D]

Glasgow, Robert, Hill St, Birmingham, cm (1818–22). [D]

Glass, John, 7 Old Bond St, London, carver and gilder (1812). Took app. John Stoker in 1812. [Westminster Ref. Lib., MS B1268]

Glassbrook, Edward, Hallgate, Wigan, Lancs., chairmaker (1816–18). [D] See Edward Glazebrook.

Glassbrook, John, 9 Markland Row, Bolton, Lancs., chairmaker (1818). [D]

Glave, R., 21 Draggets Ct, Finsbury Circus, Eldon St, London, cm (1835–37). [D]

Glazebrook, Edward, Wigan, Lancs., chairmaker (1798). [D] See Edward Glassbrook.

Glazebrook (or Glasbrook), Paul, 21 St Peter's St, Derby, cm and u (1822–29). [D]

Gleadow, John, Hull, Yorks., cm (before 1808). James Gleadow, son of the late John Gleadow, cm, was app. to Edward Dickson of Hull, July 1808. [Hull app. reg.]

Gleave, John jnr, 38 Bridport St, Liverpool, cm (1837). [D]

Gledhill, Ely, Bolton-le-Moors, Lancs., cabinet and wheel maker (1793). [D]

Gledhill, John, 15 King's Cross St, Halifax, Yorks., cm (1837). [D]

Gledhill, Jonathan, Liverpool, u (1831). On 30 June 1831 married Anne Kempster at St James' Church. [*Liverpool Mercury*, 22 July 1831]

Gledhill, William, Chapman St, Cannon St Rd, St George's East, London, cm (1809). [D]

Glen, A., 73 Paul St, Finsbury, London, carver and gilder (1820). [D]

Glen, Henry, 5 Junction Dock St, Hull, Yorks., cm and turner (1840). [D]

Glenister, Daniel, Tylers Green, High Wycombe, Bucks., chairmaker (b. c. 1811–41). Aged 30 at the date of the 1841 Census.

Glenister, Joseph, High Wycombe, Bucks., chairmaker (1825–40). Two daughters and a son bapt., 1825–28. Listed in directories subsequent to 1840. [D; PR (bapt.)]

Glenny, Hugh, 6 Bridges St, Covent Gdn, London, cm and broker (1783–85). In 1783 took out insurance cover for £300 of which £200 was in respect of utensils and stock. On 18 April 1785 took out cover for £500 on utensils etc., with a further £50 in respect of a workshop and sawpit. [GL, Sun MS vol. 313, p. 166; vol. 329, p. 119]

Glenston, James, Richmond, Yorks., upholder (1784). [D]

Glenwright, John, Haltwhistle, Northumb., joiner and cm (1827–28). [D]

Glossop, Daniel, Beetwell St, Chesterfield, Derbs., cm (1818–22). [D]

Glossop, John, 8 Downing St, Corn Market (Ardwick or Chorlton-upon-Medlock), Manchester, cm (1836–40). [D]

Glossop, Nathan, Sheffield, Yorks., cm (1825–37). At 68 Scotland St in 1825 and 56 Pool Pl. 1833–37. [D]

Glover, Charles, 63 Piccadilly, London, u, carpet and cabinet warehouse (1803–08). Included in the list of master cabinet makers in Sheraton's *Cabinet Dictionary*, 1803. Successor to John Glover at this address. [D]

Glover, Charles, New Inkeys, Birmingham, cm (1839). [D]

Glover, James, Warrington(?), Lancs., cm (1755). In 1755 took app. named Perpoint. [S of G, app. index]

Glover, Jane, Dog-bank, Newcastle, cm and furniture broker (1833). [D]

Glover, John & Co., Warrington, Lancs., cm (1757). In 1757 took app. named Lee. [S of G, app. index]

Glover, John, Liverpool, cm (1761). Free 5 March 1761. [Freemen reg.]

Glover, John (or Jonathan), Piccadilly, London, upholder (1774–1803). Initially operated from 12 Piccadilly, on the corner of Albemarle St but by 1792 had moved to 63. From 1792 traded as Glover & Sons and the Charles Glover who took over the business in 1803 was one of these. In 1779 utensils, stock and goods were insured for £300. A house at 10 Queen St appears to have been tenanted by John Glover in 1785, and in 1804 the number of the house is given as 15. Two of John Glover's patrons are known. On 25 April 1785 Lord Monson settled an account for £32 19s 7d and on 26 April 1790 £1 10s 6d was paid to a G. Glover. On 28 August 1787 Baron Grey de Wilson of Heaton Hall, Manchester paid £4 19s 6d to Glover for some fire screens. Charles Glover subscribed to Sheraton's *Drawing Book*, 1793. [D; poll bks; GL, Sun MS vol. 279, p. 560; vol. 329, p. 502; vol. 342, ref. 526211; vol. 431, ref. 767606; Lincoln RO, Monson 10/1/14/6; Preston RO, DD Eg. bank account and deposit bks]

Glover, Joseph, Newcastle, cm and chairmaker (1798–1838). Trading at Queen St, 1798–1834; 28 Stowell St in 1834 and St Nicholas Churchyard in 1838. [D]

Glover, Joseph, High St, Tewkesbury, Glos., cm (1814). [PR]

Glover, Joseph, Keswick, Cumb., joiner/cm (1828–34). [D]

Glover, Richard, Painter-heugh, Newcastle, cm (1824–27). [D]

Glover, Samuel, Bramley's Yd, Lowerhead Row, Leeds, Yorks., carver and gilder (1822). [D]

Glover, Samuel, London, u and cm (1826–39). The business commenced as a partnership with Parke at 10 Davies St, Grosvenor Sq. in 1826. By the next year however the partnership had broken up but Glover continued to trade at the same address until at least 1829. At 7 Woods Mews, Grosvenor Sq., 1835–39. [D]

Glover, Samuel, Pontefract, Yorks., carver and gilder (1830). [D]

Glover, Samuel, 7 Bull Green, Halifax, Yorks., carver and gilder (1837). [D]

Glover, T., 201 Piccadilly, London, u (1803). Included in the list of master cabinet makers in Sheraton's *Cabinet Dictionary*, 1803.

Glover, T., 19 Northampton Pl., Old Kent Rd, London, cm (1835). [D]

Glover, Thomas, Circus St, Liverpool, carver (1830). Son of T. Glover, shoemaker. Free 29 November 1830. [Freemen reg.]

Glover, W. J., 1 Orange Row, Kennington Rd, Newington and 1 York Pl., Kennington Rd, Lambeth, London, carver and gilder (1835). [D]

Glover, William, opposite the 'New Inn', Exeter, Devon, carver and gilder (1770). In March 1770 claimed that he was 'from London' and stated that he made and sold 'all Sorts of Carved and Gilt Looking Glass & Picture Frames, Jerondoles, Tables, Brackets, Dressing Glasses, Swingers, and all Sorts of Ornamental Work for Chimney Pieces'. He stated that he would re-frame and re-silver mirror plates and take old plates in part exchange. [*Exeter Evening Post*, 23–30 March 1770]

Glover, William, Leicester, cm (1772–89). App. to Thomas Johnson in 1772 and free 1789. [Freemen rolls]

Glover, William, Groat Mkt, Newcastle, cm/carpenter (1778). [D]

Glover, William, 14 Painter's-heugh, Newcastle, cm (1834). [D]

Glover, William, West St, Bridgwater, Som., carver and gilder (1839). [D]

Goad, George, 24 James St, Devonport, Devon, cm and u (1830). [D]

Goadby, John, Nottingham, u (1699). [Freemen rolls]

Goate, John, 6 Rose St, Soho, London, carver and gilder, cm and u (1820–29). [D]

Gobart, John, Norwich, u (1681). Son of Thomas Gobart, free 20 July 1681. [Freemen reg.]

Gobart, Thomas, Norwich, u (1681). Son of Thomas Gobart, free 20 July 1681. [Freemen reg.]

Gobbett, Daniel, Halesworth, Suffolk, furniture broker and u (1830). [D]

Goble, James, London, upholder (1700). Admitted freeman of the Upholders Co., 6 March 1699/1700. [GL, Upholders' Co. records]

Godard, Joseph Goodwin, 1 Hatchetts Ct, Little Trinity Lane, London, cm (1821). On 28 February 1821 took out insurance cover for £100 but no tools or trade materials were included. [GL, Sun MS vol. 486, ref. 978082]

Godart, Peter, 7 Wilmot St, Brunswick Sq., London, carver and gilder (1808–13). Listed in 1808 also as a tallow chandler and in 1813 as a dealer in tobacco. In 1810 both Peter Godart snr and jnr are referred to. In 1808 insurance cover on household goods was £150, stock and utensils £350 and 'stock and utensils as a carver & gilder in workshop behind' £100. In 1810 Peter Godart snr insured the stock and utensils of his trade as a carver and gilder for £150 while his son's insurance for such items amounted to £400. In 1813 stock and utensils in the dwelling house amounted to £50 with an additional £100 in the shop nearby. Total insurance in that year, including household goods in the dwelling house was £400. [GL, Sun MS vol. 442, ref. 812643; vol. 451, refs 839671–72; vol. 463, ref. 885135]

Godarth, Herbert, 51 Penton Pl., Pentonville, London, carver and gilder (1829–35). [D]

Godbold, Charles, Kingsland Rd, London, cm (1822–35). At 164 Kingsland Rd, 1822–29, and in 1835 at no. 57. In 1822 took out insurance cover of £300 of which £100 was in respect of stock and utensils kept in his dwelling house. [D; GL, Sun MS vol. 491, ref. 997485]

Godbold, Francis, Uxbridge, Middlx, cm and u (1786–93). On 23 September 1786 took out insurance cover of £700 of which £600 was in respect of utensils and stock. This would represent a fairly substantial business. By December 1793 however he was insolvent. [GL, Sun MS vol. 338, p. 474; *Williamson's Liverpool Advertiser,* 2 December 1793; *Billinge's Liverpool Advertiser,* 5 October 1795, 7 March 1796]

Godbold, Francis, 147 Tottenham Ct Rd and 38 Grafton Sq, Tottenham Ct Rd, London, cm and u (1839). [D]

Godbold, George, Market Pl., Halesworth, Suffolk, u and cm (1839). [D]

Godbold (or Godboult), John, London, cm and u (1809–13). At 8 Hatton Wall in 1809 and 59 Hatton Gdn, 1811–13. [D]

Godby, James, Berwick St, London, carver (1774). [Westminster poll bk]

Godby, James, 25 Norfolk St, Fitzroy Sq., London, carver (1808). [D]

Goddard, —, 3 Bradleys Buildings, Bath, Som., cm (1819). [D]

Goddard, Henry, 'The White Lion', corner of George Alley, Fleet Ditch, London, u (1724–33). On 16 July 1724 took out insurance cover on goods and merchandise in his dwelling house for £500. In 1733 fined for non-service at St Brides [Heal; GL, Sun MS vol. 17, ref. 32461; MS 6561, p. 57]

Goddard, Isaac, Brighton, Sussex, chairmaker and turner (1823–40). At 50 Middle St, 1823–26, but from 1832–35 the number was 52. In 1839 moved to 8 Ship St Lane. In one 1832 directory the trade of block maker is listed. [D]

Goddard, John, 45 Middle St, Brighton, Sussex, turner and chairmaker (1793–1800). A directory of 1793 describes him as a turner and patten maker. [D]

Goddard, Ralph, 113, Wardour St, Soho, London, cm (1820). [D]

Goddard, Thomas, Cornhill, London, upholder (1718–d. 1773). Son of Edmund Goddard of Marlborough, Wilts., draper. App. to William Braithwaite, 25 November 1709, and free of the Upholders' Co. by servitude, 12 November 1718. Master of the Upholders' Co., 1753. Took as app. Nathaniel Spurling, 1738–54. [GL, Upholders' Co. records; Heal]

Goddard, Thomas, 16 Milk St, St Lawrence Jewry, London, u (1734–92). On 6 November 1778 insured his household goods and stock in trade for £500 [D; GL, Sun MS vol. 26, p. 524; Heal]

Goddard, William, London, carver (1722–48). In 1722 his address was listed as Wapping and in 1741 as St Anne's, Limehouse. His insurance cover in the period 1741–48 was £450. [GL, Hand in Hand MS vol. 26, p. 341; V & A archives]

Goddard, William, London, cm and u, auctioneer and appraiser (1826–35). At 17 Cross St, Newington in 1826; Portland House, Walworth Rd, 1827–29; and 4 Walworth Rd in 1835. [D]

Goddard, William, Louth, Lincs., joiner and cm (1831–35). Recorded at Monks Dyke in 1835. [D]

Goddart, Peter, 103 Wardour St, Soho, London, carver and gilder (1790). On 20 December 1790 took out insurance cover of £100 on his house and goods. [GL, Sun MS ref. 577511]

Godden, —, Church St, Folkestone, Kent, u (1807–39). [D; Canterbury poll bk]

Godden, Edward, Whitecross St, London, cm (1762–70). Freeman of the Joiners' Co. In 1762 obtained a licence to employ three non-freemen for three months. Bankruptcy reported, *Gents Mag.,* March 1770. [GL, City Licence bks, vol. 3]

Godden, Mary, Redcross St, London, cm (1770–71). Freeman of the Joiners' Co. and described as a widow. She may well have been the wife of Edward Godden. In the period 1770–71 took out licences to employ non-freemen. [GL, City Licence bk, vol. 7]

Godden, Thomas, 21 Tottenham Ct Rd, London, cm (1808–09). [D]

Godden, William, 9 Carburton St, Fitzroy Sq., London, cm (1822). On 6 March 1822 took out insurance cover of £100, none of it for tools or trade stock. At the time he was living in the house of a tinman named Broster. [GL, Sun MS vol. 493, ref. 989353]

Goddin, Daniel, King's Lynn, Norfolk, upholder (1666–67). Free by gratuity, 1666–67. [Freemen rolls]

Goddiar, —, 'The two Green Flower-Pots', Charles St, near St James's Sq., London, u (1709). [*Daily Courant,* 1 September 1709] See Goodiar, —.

Goddin, Richard, 53 Hawley Sq., Margate, Kent, cm (1839). [D]

Godding, John, Maidstone, Kent, upholder (1761–90). In 1778 took out insurance of £900 of which £500 was for utensils, stock and goods in a warehouse. [D; poll bks; GL, Sun MS vol. 268, p. 177]

Godfrey, —, Flamsted's End, Cheshunt, Herts., japanner (1806). Fire on 14 November 1806 caused by 'overheating the stoves for drying new-invented tea-tables composed of various layers of rags & paper pounded in a method superior to Clay's of Birmingham'. [*Gents Mag.,* November 1806]

Godfrey, Edward, Westgate, Tickhill, Yorks., chairmaker (1837). [D]

Godfrey, Isaac, Bristol, carver and gilder (1823–40). At 2 Power St, Hotwells, 1823–24, and 12 Carloline Pl., Hotwells,

1825–30. In 1829–30 an additional address in Hotwells Rd was also recorded and from 1831 no. 33 was the sole address. From 1834–35 the address changed to Hope Chapel Hill and in 1836–40 he was working at Power St, Dowry Sq. [D]

Godfrey, John, Bristol, cm, chair and bedstead maker (1830–40). In 1830 at 6 Narrow Weir. The business is recorded as John & S. Godfrey in 1832 at Castle Mill St. From 1833–40 however John Godfrey is once more in sole control and working from 10 Castle Mill St. From 1832 the business is described solely as that of bedstead maker. [D]

Godfrey, Nicholas, London, cm and u (1809–37). In 1809 at 13 Compton Sq, Clerkenwell and in 1820 at 21 King St, Goswell St. By 1827 the address is recorded as 23 King St, Compton St, Clerkenwell. [D]

Godfrey, Richard, St Margaret's St, London, upholder (1784). [D]

Godfrey, Richard, London, u and cm (1762–1811). Son of Richard Godfrey of Brockall, Northants., grazier. App. to William Adams, 13 June 1755, and free by servitude, 13 June 1762. Not recorded in trade directories until 1781 when he was at New Palace Yd, Westminster. He seems to have used these premises until 1804 when on 3 October they were destroyed by fire. From 1790 however he had been using an additional address in Union St, Westminster. The fire may well have been the cause of another move and in January 1805 he was at 66 Millbank St, Westminster. Here he took out insurance cover for £1,300 of which utensils and stock amounted to £200, the main item covered being household goods valued at £1,000. He was included in the list of master cabinet makers in Sheraton's *Cabinet Dictionary*, 1803. He is probably the maker who supplied Lady Cotton of Madingley Hall, Cambs., with a camp stool costing 8s 6d in November 1802. A brass inlaid rosewood centre table is recorded signed 'RD. Godfroy'. [D; GL, Upholders' Co. records; Sun MS vol. 319, p. 227; vol. 431, ref. 772287; *Gents Mag.*, October 1804; Cambs. RO, 588/A45; *C. Life*, 18 January 1962, p. 107; Sotheby's, 3 June 1977, lot 151]

Godfrey, Richard, 16 Robert St, Grosvenor Sq., London, u (1835). [D]

Godfrey, Robert, 73 Chiswell St, Finsbury, London, cm (1820). [D]

Godfrey, Thomas, 32 Hackney Rd, London, cm and u (1839). [D]

Godfrey, William, 1 Knowle Ct, Carter Lane, London, cm (1785). On 4 May 1785 took out insurance cover of £70 on household goods. [GL, Sun MS vol. 328, p. 208]

Godfrey, William, London, cm and chairmaker (1790–1813). At 14 Gt Distaff Lane, 1790–1809, but in 1811 at 7 Basing Lane. [D]

Godfrey, William, Bristol, cm (1809–17). In 1809 at 106 Redcliffe St but thereafter in Pile St. [D]

Godier, Jonathan, address unrecorded, carver (early 18th century–1732). Did most of the joiner's work at Wentworth Castle, Yorks., 'being then servant' to William Thornton of York. [BL, Add. MS 22141, ff.102.114.129]

Godling, Robert, Sunderland, Co. Durham, cm (1803). Subscribed to Sheraton's *Cabinet Dictionary*, 1803.

Godling, Samuel, Maidstone, Kent, u (1790). [Poll bk]

Godman, John, parish of St John Timberhill, Norwich, cm (1781). In 1781 insured workshop with utensils and stock for £200. [GL, Sun MS vol. 296, p. 182]

Godman, Michael, Swaffham, Norfolk, cm (1798). [D]

Godon, Samuel, Maidstone, Kent, u (1794). [D]

Godson, Charles, Essex, chairmaker and turner (1744). In 1744 took app. named Couzens. [S of G, app. index]

Godson, George, Hull, Yorks., cm (1758–84). Freeman of York but working in Hull. [York poll bks]

Godson, Thomas, Hull, Yorks., cm (1758–84). Freeman of York but working in Hull. [York poll bks]

Godwin, George, 290 High Holborn, London, portable desk maker (1820). [D] A brass bound mahogany portable desk box of military type inscribed 'LOUISA FLEET' recorded bearing printed label: 'G. GODWIN/PORTABLE DESK, DRESSING CASE + LADIES WORK BOX/MANUFACTURER/290 HOLBORN'.

Godwin, Ian, Northernhay, Exeter, Devon, cm (1819). Son bapt. at St David's Church, 25 February 1819. [PR (bapt.)]

Godwin, James, Winchester, Hants., chair and basket maker (1770). On 2 April 1770 advertised for two journeymen basket-makers and a chairmaker in *Reading Mercury and Oxford Gazette*.

Godwin, Richard, London, upholder (1700). Free of the Upholders' Co., 1 May 1700. [GL, Upholders' Co. records]

Godwin (or Goodwin), Thomas, Winchester, Hants., cm, u, auctioneer and appraiser (1823–39). Address given as Piazza in 1823 but from 1830–39 at 121 High St. By 1839 the business was styled T. Godwin & Sons. A mahogany Pembroke table, banded with rosewood and with inlaid ebony lines bearing the trade label of Thomas Godwin, was sold by Phillips' in 1962 and again in 1963. [D; Phillips', 16 October 1962, lot 51; 26 February 1963, lot 62]

Goertz, H. L. (Heinrich Ludwig or Henry Louis), Windsor, Berks., u and cm (1814–40). Goertz apparently immigrated to England from his native Hanover between 1799 and 1802 when that city was under Napoleonic threat. Seemingly, in Royal employ at Windsor for at least a quarter of a century, he was constantly involved with routine upholstery work, repairs and jobbing, but also supplied certain major pieces to the Court and much ordinary furniture for the use of household and staff.

Sophia Davenport, daughter of Thomas Davenport, Assistant to the Queen's Page, and of Anne Davenport, Housekeeper at Lower Lodge (1812–17), was Goertz's first wife and during this period they lived in the Devil's Tower, Windsor Castle and he is known to have made several return journeys to Hanover. On 2 November 1820, he was married for a second time to Lucretia Morris at Windsor Castle — their son born 5 May 1825, was probably involved with the family firm.

Court and City Registers in Windsor for the period 1814–19 list Goertz as Upholsterer to Queen Charlotte at Frogmore House. Later he was Upholsterer in Ordinary to King George IV and Cabinet-Maker and Upholsterer in Ordinary to William IV. Bills of the year 1837 are headed H. L. Goertz & Son, and a directory of 1838 lists 'Goertz & Son, 36 High Street, Windsor', as 'Cabinet-Makers, Upholsterers & House Agents'. By 1844, Henry Goertz, 26 High St, is entered as 'Cabinet-Maker, Upholsterer & Paper-Hanger' — apparently Goertz's son who supplied goods to Queen Victoria and her mother, the Duchess of Kent, but did not hold a Royal Warrant. The firm of H. L. Goertz continued to appear in the Royal accounts until the end of the century.

The Goertz name does not figure in the Windsor Royal Archive accounts until 1826, but the 1835–40 Lord Chamberlain's accounts [Book G–H] presents a total of £573 11s 5d still due to him for the period October 1820–23 for work undertaken at the Castle, Cumberland Lodge and the Cottage. This sum seems to be in addition to bills already paid. Considerable furniture is listed in these bills but the 1823–31 accounts [PRO, LC 11/47–74] mention no furniture, only extensive jobbing, repairing and cleaning work at the King's Lodge, Cumberland Lodge, Lower Lodge, the Castle, Hampton Court and Brighton Pavilion. However, in 1824–26, certain major orders included: 'two Rosewood

Cylinder Book-Stands — each on table of 4 drawers & 4 tiers of revolving book-shelves supported by 114 sham books, Morocco-Calf backs . . .' for Carlton House, £65, and for the Pavilion: 'to a Hyacinth Stand lined with a cistern of tin . . . Japanned in imitation of Bamboo, and blue & white china with Pagoda for centre — plate glass in bamboo frames — Lacquer Basin with Shellwork — £110 3s 1d'. [Windsor RA 25403]

After the accession of William IV, Goertz's increased responsibility is shown by sizeable quarterly bills for the period from July 1830 to the end of 1832, detailing his involvement in the general upkeep of the Castle, the refurbishment of the Royal Lodges, and the furnishing of household and staff apartments. October 1830 entries mention: 'Redoing Cumberland Lodge for HRH the Duke of Sussex — marking furniture throughout, and taking Inventory of the same', and in April 1831: 'Preparing Castle for their Majesties. Fitting up the Queen's Wardrobe. Remaking a card table into a Rosewood Loo Table'. A quarterly bill 30 September 1832 lists 'Repairing & cleaning mahogany Chairs, Cheval Glasses, Writing Tables, Screens, making Rollers for Blinds, Window Laths, taking down, repairing & putting up Bedsteads, unripping and restuffing Couches, Bed Ends — and charges for 111 days of Cabinet Makers' work and 71½ days of Upholsterers' time'. [Windsor RA, accounts 1827–32] Records indicate similar work at Windsor Castle, Kew Palace St James's, Virginia Water, Hind Lodge and Harrington House during the years 1832–37. [PRO, LC 11/77–98] In June 1834, lengthy estimates were submitted for furnishing the North Star Front Chambers at Windsor. [Windsor RA, Item 17, Box 31, Estimates]

In 1837 Goertz was assisting in 'making 6 ebony chairs and 6 ebony bookcases for Buckingham Palace'. [PRO, LC 11/98] His firm may have collaborated with that of Anne McBean of Windsor as they frequently sent in similar bills beginning 'Assisting . . .'.

In March 1838 Heinrich Ludwig apparently retired from regular work for the Lord Chamberlain's Office. The account books for 1835–40 mention that he was still owed £1,622 6s 11d for the period 1829 to March 1838 — seemingly in addition to amounts already paid and not including the sum outstanding for 1820–23.

The fifth hall bk of the borough of Windsor, 1828–52 lists Goertz's appointment as Upholsterer to the Windsor Corporation in January 1837. On 3 July 1838, he was given the position of Overseer to collect the New Borough Rate, while on 7 January 1841, he is listed as Corporation Upholder. He had probably died before 1844 when his son Henry Goertz, 26 High St, Windsor, is listed in a local directory. [Joy, *English Furniture 1800–1851*, 1977]

N.N.T.

Goff, —, 41 East St, Brighton, Sussex, cm (1832). [D]

Goff, Henry, Brighton, Sussex, u (1828–37). At 31 East St in May 1828 when he described his business as an 'Upholstery, Featherbed, Matress, Carpet and Hearth Rug Warehouse'. He aimed his advertisement at 'Hotel, Tavern, Lodging house keepers and Families' and stated that his stock featured bedding, drawing, dining and sitting room chairs and sofas, carpeting and paper hangings. In the period 1832–35 he was living in Ship St and in July 1837 in Middle St. Three sons and two daughters were bapt., 1832–37. [Poll bk; *Brighton Herald*, 17 May 1828; PR (bapt.)]

Goff, James Copeland, Eccleston St, Pimlico, London, u, cm and undertaker (1835–39). [D]

Goff, William, Queen St, Westminster, London, upholder (1744–49). Son of Hugh Goff. App. to James Rowe, 4 March 1718, and admitted freeman of the Upholders' Co., 6 September 1744. [GL, Upholders' Co. records; poll bk]

Goff & Gulley, Exeter, Devon, cm (*c.* 1790). Name recorded on brass plate on a Sheraton-style satin and rosewood card table. [*C. Life*, 3 December 1981, supplement, p. 77]

Goffe, Thomas, 9 Smallbrook St, Birmingham, cm (1835). [D]

Goffin, Robert, North Quay, Gt Yarmouth, Norfolk, cm (1830–40). [D; poll bks]

Goffrey, John, address unknown, u (1803). Subscribed to Sheraton's *Cabinet Dictionary*, 1803.

Golborn (or Goiborn), John, 73 Thomas St, Manchester, cm (1825–33). [D]

Gold, James, Southampton, Hants., cm (d. 1821). Died in 1821 aged 38. [*Gents Mag.*, February 1821]

Goldby, Henry, Boar St, Abingdon, Berks., cm (1830–40). [D]

Goldby, John, nearly opposite the sign of 'The Gate', Hackney Rd, London, upholder (1787). On 3 February 1787 insured goods for £200. [GL, Sun MS vol. 343, p. 80]

Goldie, James, Liverpool, cm and victualler (1805–24). At 26 Ranelagh St in 1805 but from 1807–14 the number is shown as 27. By 1821 had moved to 10 Back Lime St and 1823–24 at 16 Grosvenor St. [D]

Golding, Abraham, Cambridge, turner, chairmaker and broker (1839–40). In 1839 at George St, Barnwell but by 1841 had moved to Newmarket Rd. [D]

Golding, George, 9 St Agnes Circus (or City Terr.), Old St Rd, London, cm and u (1820–29). [D]

Golding, James, Liverpool, cm (1761). App. to Thomas Pender and free, 9 February 1761. [Freemen reg.]

Golding, James, Wimborne, Dorset, chairmaker and turner (1823). [D]

Golding, Joseph, Bartholomew St, Newbury, Berks., upholder (1780–98). In 1780 took out insurance cover of £500 with £180 of this sum specified for utensils and stock. [D; GL, Sun MS vol. 283, p. 276]

Golding, Joseph, 8 Houndsditch, London, u and auctioneer (1808–11). [D]

Goldsborough, Richard, Hurworth, Co. Durham, cm (1828). [D]

Goldsmith, Charles, 12 Worship St, Finsbury Sq., London, painter and japanned chairmaker (1808–11). In both 1808 and 1811 took out insurance cover of £350 which included £200 for stock and utensils, and an additional £50 for similar items in a yard and open shed. [GL, Sun MS vol. 446, ref. 823611; vol. 451, ref. 856890]

Goldsmith, Charles, Curtain Rd, Shoreditch, London, mahogany and japanned desk manufacturer and sofa maker (1816–23). Shown at 75 Curtain Rd, 1816 and 19; at no. 70 in 1817 and 82 in 1820–23. [D]

Goldsmith, Francis, 19 Whitecross Pl., Wilson St, Finsbury Sq., London, chair manufactory (1808–09). [D]

Goldsmith, Joseph, West St, Horsham, Sussex, cm etc. (1832–39). [D]

Goldsmith, Thomas, at the sign of 'Cupid on a Shell Rock', Greece Ct, Old Jury, Cheapside, London, cm (1693–94). In 1693 supplied a looking-glass table and stands japanned white for Queen Mary II at Hampton Court, Middlx. [PRO, LC9/280, p. 140a]

Goldsping, John, 132 Blackfriars Rd, London, u (1835–39). Trade card in the GL, Dept of Prints, illustrates two sabre legged chairs, a sofa, a chiffonier and a chest of drawers. [D]

Goldstone, William, 19 Caroline St, Princess Rd, London, cabinet carver (1839). [D]

Goldsworthy, Robert, Thomas St, Bristol, cm (1792–94). [D]

Goldthorp, Benjamin, 63 Stamford St, Ashton-under-Lyne, Lancs., cm, joiner and furniture broker (1824–34). [D]

Gole, Cornelius, London, cm (*c.* 1689–91). Employed by Queen Mary II in the early years of her reign. She had possibly used him, or his uncle Adrian before 1689, for the latter was recorded in Amsterdam from 1683, having moved from Paris. Princess Mary's account book for this period records transactions with 'Goal, the Cabinetmaker' on several occasions. When she came to London after the Revolution he followed and commissions are listed in 1691. In August of that year is recorded 'a large table of markatree, the sides, drawer & supports carved with ornaments & flowers & finely lackred, also a pair of stands carved & Lackred suiteable'. For these £20 was charged. In the same year Queen Mary was supplied by Gole with 'a large frame for a looking glass carved richly with ornament & flowers & inlaid with wood of all sorts of colours £14'. Also made was another frame 'richly carved with cyphers & their Majestie's arms with an Imperial crowne & other ornaments'. [PRO, LC9/280, p. 27a]

Golland, Joseph, East Retford, Notts., cm (1815–d. 1824). Will dated 15 December 1815, proved 1824. [Notts. RO, probate records]

Gollion, Samuel, Gorst Stacks, Chester cm (1818). Free 18 May 1818. [Freemen rolls]

Gollop, George, Bell Lane, Poole, Dorset, joiner and cm (1789–98). In 1789 took out insurance cover on his new dwelling house and 'joiners shop adjoining' which was 'in the tenure of himself & Wm Waterhouse, joiner'. The building was of brick and tiled and insured for £150, utensils and stock kept in it for an additional £30. [D; GL, Sun MS vol. 362, p. 372]

Gollop, George, Gt Titchfield St, Fitzroy Sq., London, cm, u and undertaker (1827). [D]

Gollop, Henry, 70 Gt Titchfield St, Haymarket, London, chair and sofa maker, cm and u (1820–27). [D]

Gollop, Thomas, 19 Gower Pl., Euston Sq., London, cm and u (1835–39). [D]

Golsby, James, Calthorpe Lane, Banbury, Oxon., cm and u (1830–41). [D]

Gomersall, Thomas, Dewsbury, Yorks., cm (1830–37). At Long Causeway in 1830 but in 1837 the business was styled Thomas Gomersall & Son and at Crackenedge Lane. [D]

Gomm, Tom, London, cm (1731). Supplied Richard Hoare for Barn Elms House bottle stands, a backgammon table, a chest of drawers etc. costing £23 13s 3d in 1731–32. [V & A Lib., 86 NN. 3]

Gomm, William & Richard, London, cm and u (c. 1698–1794). William Gomm was born c. 1698 the son of Richard Gomm, a yeoman farmer of Chinnor, Oxon. In 1713 he was app. to Hugh Maskall of London, a member of the Leathersellers' Co. which Gomm also joined on the completion of his apprenticeship. In 1770 he was made free of the Upholders' Co. under the terms of the 1750 Upholders' Act. By January 1725 he had established himself as a cm at Peterborough Ct, Little Britain in the parish of St Bartholomew, Smithfield. He took out insurance cover on 14 January of that year for £500 and by July 1731 this had risen to £800. Although some of this was in respect of household goods the great majority was for stock which was kept in his dwelling house, a shed (£300) and a yard (£200). Whilst at Peterborough Ct he married in 1728 Dinah Cookman. The marriage took place at Harefield parish church in Middlx. In 1736 Gomm moved to Newcastle House, Clerkenwell Close. This building, just off Clerkenwell Sq., had been the property of the Dukes of Newcastle but as London expanded the out-of-date house, part of which was formerly a pre-Reformation nunnery, became less attractive as a residence. The last member of the family to occupy it was the Dowager Duchess of Montagu, and on her death in 1734 a decision was made to dispose of it. Gomm, seeking accommodation for his expanding business, took it over and built a double range of workshops over the surviving basement of the medieval nun's hall. For purposes of rating the property was valued at £80. Gomm's first wife died soon

after the move aged 39 and in 1737 he married Marianne de Moivre, a widow possibly of Huguenot descent. He had three sons from his first marriage of whom Richard, the eldest, was to be associated with the business. Two daughters and two further sons resulted from the second marriage.

Gomm is remembered particularly because of his association with Abraham Roentgen. In the 1730s Roentgen travelled to Paris, Rotterdam and then London to gain experience in the cabinet-making trades in those cities. Family memoirs mention working with a number of skilled furniture makers in London including one named as 'Gern', at Newcastle House, St John's Sq. This was without doubt William Gomm and the use of the Newcastle House address suggests that he was with him in the period post 1736. By 1756 William had taken his eldest son Richard into partnership and in that year Richard was paying rates on the larger western side of the premises and his father on the eastern side only. In 1763 the business was styled William Gomm & Son & Co. William Gomm was still active in the business at this period. A series of manuscript designs bearing his signature and dated July, August and November 1761 exist at the Henry Francis Du Pont Museum, Winterthur. These are Rococo in character and of varied originality. To some degree a number of them depend on the published work of Chippendale, Lock & Copland and Thomas Johnson. They show a knowledge of and an appreciation of the Chinese and Gothick tastes popular at this period. The items illustrated include looking-glasses, a girandole, a table frame, an elbow chair, a clothes press, bookcases, a bed, a sideboard table, a library table, a commode and a cabinet on stand. Four related drawings illustrate a scheme for the furnishing of a fashionable drawing room and feature seating furniture, pier glasses and tables in the Chinese taste, girandoles, an oval mirror, Rococo picture frames and festoon window curtains with elaborate pelmets. Another drawing shows the furnishing of an ante-room in similar taste. [*Antiques*, April 1971, pp. 556–59]

As early as 1747 Gomm started to purchase property in his native village of Chinnor. In that year he purchased Nethercote House for £700 and in 1758 bought the rest of the estate for £3,873. He no doubt hoped to retire there leaving the obviously prosperous business ever more under the direction of his son Richard. The failure of the business and bankruptcy proceedings in 1776 must have been a profound shock to William in his old age. It was probably as a result of this that in 1777 he sold the estate, subject to his own life interest, to Richard Paul Jodrell for £8,400. He died in 1780 aged 82.

His eldest son Richard was born c. 1729 and was never formally app. to his father's trade. He does however appear to have been associated with the business from an early date. He married at the age of seventeen. In 1754 he subscribed to Chippendale's *Director*, and two years later was paying rates on part of the Clerkenwell property. In 1763 he took as app. Joshua Bottom. It thus seems likely that by the late 1750s and early 1760s he was taking on an ever increasing degree of responsibility for the running of the business although his father's name continued to be linked with his in the trading styles adopted. Additional premises at 3 Freeman's Ct, Cornhill, were used in 1767–72. These were taken over from John Gomm, possibly Richard's brother by the first marriage. A Francis Peter Mallet is mentioned as a partner in 1765 and in 1771 the business was trading as Gomm, Son & Mallet, though other sources of the same year name it as Richard Gomm & Co. By this period the properties in the Clerkenwell area hd been numbered and Gomm's business traded from 48 (later 47), The Close. In 1776 bankruptcy occurred though it

was stated that Richard Gomm 'failed by faults not his own'. In the following year he was living at 8 Red Lion St, Clerkenwell where he insured a house for £200. He still declared his trade as cm but probably was not trading from this address. He had certainly given up the furniture making trades by October 1784 in which month he was offered and accepted the Stewardship of St Bartholomew's Hospital. He died in 1794. Richard Gomm's son William was made free of the Upholders' Co. under the terms of the 1750 Upholders' Act, 5 December 1770 but there is no evidence that he played any role in the business and subsequently became a minister of the Church of England and at the time of his father's death was Rector of West Dean, near Salisbury.
[D; *Burlington*, June 1980, pp. 395–402; GL, Upholders' Co. records; Sun MS vol. 22, p. 24; vol. 26, p. 30; vol. 32, ref. 54780; vol. 256, p. 93; *Gents Mag.*, April, July and September 1776, November 1784]

The business used its trade label to identify its products though this practice appears to have been on a very limited scale. To date only one item so marked is known. This is a mahogany Pembroke table on square section legs which are joined near the base by X form stretchers. The label used bears both the Newcastle House and Freeman's Ct address and is in the name of Richard & William Gomm. It therefore probably dates from the late 1760s or early 1770s. A manuscript endorsement on the label reads 'John Mordant Cope' probably the patron concerned who can be identified with a person of that name resident at Bramshill, Hants. [*Burlington*, June 1980, p. 402; Sotheby's, 24 February 1967, lot 145; 19 July 1968, lot 152] The table is a plain serviceable piece of furniture probably typical of much of the Gomm's output. Although patronized from time to time by members of the aristocracy and gentry the location of the business away from the most fashionable London makers was probably a disadvantage in obtaining such customers.

The earliest known commission by William Gomm was in the period 1731–33 when furniture was supplied to Richard Hoare of Barn Elms. Items supplied included a walnut framed dressing glass, two mahogany arm chairs, a 'lolling' chair, a backgammon table, a mahogany chest, two dressing tables, two other tables and a 'fine mahogany tea chest'. [*Burlington*, June 1980, pp. 395, 397] On 23 January 1756 furniture was invoiced to J. Buller of Morval, Cornwall. This consisted of a mahogany sofa 6½ ft long in canvas with two cushions and bolsters at £8 10s and a mahogany folding screen at £1 10s. On 17 January 1757 a teaboard at 3s was purchased and the account for all these items settled on the same day. Also in 1757 a mahogany desk was supplied to the new banking premises of Glyn, Halifax & Co. in Birchin Lane, London. The desk was 8 ft long and was designed to provide space for five clerks. It cost £18. [Cornwall RO, DDBU 337; R. Fulford, *Glyn's 1753–1953*, p. 8] In 1762 payment was made to the Gomm's in respect of furniture supplied to Richard Weddell for his house in Pall Mall, London. He was the father of William Weddell of Newby Hall, Yorks., a well-known collector of Classical antiquities. The items supplied included 'a fine Mahogany Compass Cutwork Tea Table on Castors' at £5 10s and a 'Mahogany Bed Chair Stuff'd & finish'd at £1 3s. A set of armchairs was supplied to Kenure Park, Co. Dublin in 1763, and in the following year Gomm was negotiating with Alexander Voronstov, the elder brother of Count Voronstov, later the Russian ambassador in London. Gomm had four mahogany armoires which had cost him £200 and a table frame and marble top which he was anxious to dispose of. Voronstov offered him £100 or £120 for the armoires. [Leeds archives dept, Newby NH 2787; *Burlington*, June 1980, p. 399; C. *Life*, 15 March 1973]

The most extensive commission known to have been carried out by this firm was for the 5th Lord Leigh at Stoneleigh Park, Warks. from 1763, the year in which Lord Leigh came of age. Much modernization took place paricularly to the bedrooms and the Gomm's were the main furniture suppliers employed, working in association with the decorators Bromwich & Leigh. The first items were supplied on 12 May 1763 and continued to be delivered until October of the following year. The account totalled to £818 9s. A total of 183 assorted chairs were included together with tables, dressing tables, clothes presses, close stools, a chest on chest, shaving table, commode dressing table and a Pembroke table and a sideboard. A number of these items survived in the house until 1981 when they were sold by auction. [Shakespeare Birthplace Trust, Leigh receipts, DR 18/5; Christie's, 15–16 October 1981]

After the collapse of the Gomm business in 1776 the enterprise was carried on by Francis Peter Mallett. B.A.

Gomme, Dinah, High Wycombe, Bucks., cm and u (1830). [D]

Gomme, James, High Wycombe, Bucks., cm (1790–1823). Previous to 1790 had been a partner with Lawrence Gomme in a similar type of business. Recorded at High St, 1823. Used a trade label which he attached to his furniture stating that the article was 'SOLD at the original Upholstery Warehouse, of *James Gomme* in High-Wycombe, where Cabinet Work is done, and Orders for Household-Furniture of every Description executed in the best, and most fashionable Manner'. An example on a three-drawer bow-fronted chest is dated 1790 and another label is known dated 1789. His trade card is in the Heal Coll., BM. In 1811 he issued a trade token with a view of the Market Hall on one side and a swan on the other. [D; Weaver, *High Wycombe Furniture*, 1929, p. 12; V & A archives]

Gomme, James Chettle, King St, Hammersmith, London, cm (1832). [D]

Gomme, Lawrence & James, High Wycombe, Bucks., carpenters and timber merchants (1784), appraisers, cm, undertakers and joiners (1790). From 1790 James Gomme traded as the sole proprietor. [D]

Gondy, John Mill, Liverpool, cm (1826). Declared bankrupt, *Liverpool Mercury*, 10 March 1826.

Gonner, Thomas, Colchester, Essex, chairmaker (1784). [Poll bk]

Gooch, James, Norwich, cm (1781). In July 1781 apprehended at Ditchingham near Bungay in Suffolk and committed to the city gaol in Norwich accused of stealing 'a large quantity of mahogany planks and boards, together with 130 wainscot boards, the property of several reputable persons in the city'. Difficulty was experienced in returning the stolen property to its owners as Gooch had planed off identification markings. [*Norwich Chronicle*, 5 May, 7 July, 4 August, 11 August 1781]

Gooch, John, London, turner and u (1808–11). At 43 Curzon St, Mayfair in 1808 and 19 Lower Brook St, Grosvenor Sq. in 1811. [D]

Gooch, Richard, 19 Lower Brook St, Grosvenor Sq., London, u (1811–13). Successor to John Gooch at this address. In 1813 in partnership with H. Gooch. [D]

Good, Edward, London, upholder (1723–31). Son of Arthur Good of Winchester. App. to John Tatnall, 2 May 1723; James Clarke, freeman draper, 2 May 1723; and Thomas Clarke, freeman draper, 1 October 1729. Free of the Upholders' Co. by servitude, 16 December 1731. [GL, Upholders' Co. records]

Good, George, 121 Fleet St, London, u (1762–79). Son of Peter Good a Glasgow excise officer. App. to Edward Webster on 15 February 1743 and Francis Say on 10 October 1745. Free of the Upholders' Co. by servitude, 4 November 1762. Fellow of the Society of Arts, 1763–65. Declared bankrupt, *Gents Mag.*, August 1779. [D; GL, Upholders' Co. records]

Good, James, London, upholder (1754). Member of the Joiners' Co. Subscribed to Chippendale's *Director*, 1754. [H. L. Phillips, *Annals of the Joiners' Co.*]

Good, John, High St, Royston, Herts., cooper and u (1826). [D]

Good, Thomas, London, cm and u (1822–39). At 3 Old St, St Luke's in 1822 and 1826–29 at no. 1. By 1835 had moved to 10 Upper King St, Bloomsbury and in 1839 was at 4 Gray's Inn Lane Terr. [D]

Goodall, David, Ouseburn, Newcastle, cm (1833). [D]

Goodall, Elizabeth, Leeds, Yorks., cm (1826–34). At Wood St, Park Lane, 1826–30, and 100 Park Lane in 1834. [D]

Goodall, Henry, Back Walls, Stafford, chairmaker (1828–35). [D]

Goodall, James, Hanley and Newcastle-under-Lyme, Staffs., cm and u (1818–39). At Totine Ct, Hanley in 1818; Penkill St, Newcastle-under-Lyme in 1828; High St, 1834–39, no. 18 in 1836 also as victualler, and no. 13 and/or 14 in 1839. [D]

Goodall, Joseph, Iron Mkt, Newcastle-under-Lyme, Staffs., cm and u (1812–30). In 1822 listed as J. & J. Goodall and it is possible that his partner was the James Goodall shown at Hanley in 1818 and Newcastle in 1828. In the 1830 election his vote was objected to on the grounds of non-residence. [D; poll bks]

Goodall, Richard, High St, Uttoxeter, Staffs., cm/clock case maker (1834–35). [D]

Goodall, Samuel, Newcastle-under-Lyme, Staffs., cm (1790–98). [D; poll bks]

Goodall, Thomas snr, Newcastle-under-Lyme, Staffs, cm (1774–98). [D; poll bks]

Goodall, Thomas jnr, Newcastle-under-Lyme, Staffs., cm (1790–1812). [D; poll bks]

Goodall, William, Newcastle-under-Lyme, Staffs., cm (1790–1812). [D; poll bks]

Goodbody, William, 17 New Inn Yd, Shoreditch, London, cm and u (1839). [D]

Goodcheap, William, Goswell St, London, cm and undertaker (1790–1808). At 144 Goswell St in 1790 but from 1791 at no. 142. On 14 August 1790 took out insurance cover of £800 which included £250 for stock in a warehouse. On 27 September 1791 took out cover for £300 on utensils in trust in Bullyard, Aldersgate St. Included in the list of master cabinet makers in Sheraton's *Cabinet Dictionary*, 1803. Heal cites a trade card of this maker with the address 115 Aldersgate St which dates it c. 1810. [D; GL, Sun MS ref. 572741; vol. 379, p. 635]

Goodchild, John, Broad St, parish of St Benedict, London, u (1727–28). Son of John Goodchild of Combes, Suffolk, Gent. App. to Samuel Conder on 13 October 1719 and free of the Upholders' Co. by servitude, 4 January 1726/27. On 3 June 1728 took out insurance cover of £500 on his household goods and dwelling. [GL, Upholders' Co. records; Sun MS vol. 26, p. 214]

Goode, Basil, Atherstone, Warks., cm (1828). [D]

Goode, John, London, cm, u and furniture broker (1820–39). At 8 Clerkenwell Green in 1820 but by 1826 the number had changed to 12. In the period 1835–39 moved to 83 Goswell Rd. [D]

Goode, John, Rugby, Warks., chairmaker, turner and furniture broker (1828–35). [D]

Goode, William, Chesterton Rd, Cambridge, turner and chairmaker (1835–40). Two children bapt., 1835–41, parish of St Clement. [D; PR (bapt.)]

Goodenough, J., 35 Regent St, Leamington, Warks., cm and u (1837). [D]

Goodeyre, John, address unknown, cm (1754). Subscribed to Chippendale's *Director*, 1754.

Goodfellow, Lall, Salisbury, Wilts., u (1770–74). Payments of £3 5s 6d in January 1770 and £4 10s 4d in 1774 are listed in the Longford Castle, Wilts. accounts. Declared bankrupt, *Gents Mag.*, September 1772. [V & A archives]

Goodhall, Henry, 8 Rathbone Pl., London, cm and u (1839). [D]

Goodhall, John, 29 Greek St, Soho, London, gilder and frame maker (1803). [D]

Goodhall, Samuel, London, upholder (1708). Free of the Upholders' Co., 7 July 1708. [GL, Upholders' Co. records]

Goodhart, George, Turner's Hill, Cheshunt, Herts., cm and u (1832). [D]

Goodheart, James, 63 Snowhill, London, portable desk, dressing case, work box and cabinet case maker (1839). [D]

Goodheart, William, 2 Charterhouse St and 12 Coppice Row, Clerkenwell, London, cm and u (1839). [D]

Goodhill, John, Yorkersgate, Malton, Yorks., cm and u (1823). [D]

Goodhind, John, Shouldhart St, Bryanston St., London, cm (1820). [D]

Goodiar, —, at the 'Two Green Flower Pots', Charles St, St James's Sq., London, u (1709). [Heal] See Goddiar, —.

Goodiham, John, Tunbridge Wells, Kent, cm and u (1832). [D]

Goodill, —, Ipswich, Suffolk, cm (1793). Subscribed to Sheraton's *Drawing Book*, 1793.

Gooding, John, 28 Baldwyn St, City Rd, London, bedstead maker (1826). [D]

Gooding, Thomas Robert, 16 Mortimer St, London, cm and u, fancy cm (1822–29). [D]

Gooding, W., 20 Wyndham St, London, carver and gilder (1835). [D]

Goodison, Benjamin, 'Golden Spread Eagle', Long Acre, London, cm (c. 1700–67). Benjamin Goodison first comes to notice on 7 September 1719 when he signed for money for 'my master' James Moore from the Duchess of Marlborough. [BL, Add. MS 61354, f.76; Ian Caldwell in *The Antique Collector*, May 1986, p. 96] Further on 1 April 1720 he signed a receipt for £6 6s for work done by 'My Master, James Moore' for the 3rd Earl of Burlington. We may assume he was born about 1700 and he may still have been app. to Moore in 1720, but there is no record of this. The name is common in South Yorks., but again there is no record of the name in the York freeman rolls. [Surtees Soc., 1896, 1899] However by 1725 Goodison had set up on his own, a fact attested by his taking an app. Thomas Barber on 16 January [PRO, IR/1/10], and details of the Saunderson commission (below). In an advertisement he inserted in *Daily Courant*, 22 August 1727, repeated 23–24 August, he asked for information about 'a large old fashioned Glass Sconce, in a Glass Frame, with Gold Flowers painted on the Glass Frame, and a Green Ground' which had been stolen from his shop at the 'Golden Spread Eagle in Long Acre'. It might have been one he had acquired from Mrs Moore, or was repairing for her. After her husband's death she advertised in *Daily Courant*, 26 July 1727, the disposal of 'all her stock'.

In the way that James Moore succeeded his (presumed) master John Gumley in royal service, so Goodison succeeded Moore in 1726–27. He first comes to notice in the 1729 accounts when he supplied a lantern to Hampton Court for the Queen's Great Staircase costing £138 [PRO, LC 9/26] His name then appears with regularity, and notably with a massive bill in 1737 [PRO, LC 5/48, pp. 16, 31, 44, 61, 76, 93, 109, 1029] when payments to Mrs Moore, as her husband's executor, cease.

It has been a temptation to attribute much that is 'Kentian' to Goodison. The argument is worth rehearsing against the possible discovery of some documentation. From the late 1730s the Great Wardrobe was under the control of Sir Thomas Robinson, as its Master, who authorized all payments to Kent and his circle, which included Goodison. The accounts submitted by Goodison are long and involved, but provide the best clues to the range of work he was able to do. Part of an account rendered in 1737 reads: 'Item: to Benjamin Goodison, Cabinetmaker, for two Chimney Glasses in Wallnuttree Frames, Two Pair of wrought brass Arm & One hanging Glass in a Walnuttree Frame, Eight Dressing Glasses in Walnuttree Frames, two smaller ditto, fifteen Side Glass Lanterns in Walnuttree Frames with fifteen brass Candlesticks and Shades to twelve of them. One Fire Screen in a Walnuttree Frame cover'd with India paper, Two Screens with four leaves Each in Ditto Frames and Cover'd Ditto. Two Mohogony Tea Kettle Stands, A New Glass to a Wallnut tree side Lantern, One very large Mohogony Chest of Drawers, One ditto and One other ditto, one round Mohogony Table on a pillar and Claw Foot, Two Mohogony Oval Dining Tables, Ten Mohogony Shelves for Book Cases, New Lacquering a pair of Double Wrought Arms, A Mohogony Stand on a pillar, and Claw Foot for Our Service at St James's . . . .'. [PRO, LC 5/48, f. 16]

In 1739 he was asked to provide 'a square Mohogony flat Table six feet long and three feet and an half wide to lay the Prince of Wales's Robes on at the Parliament House' as well as 'a looking Glass in a black Frame for the Dublin Yacht'. He was needed (in 1740) to newly gild 'a large Peer Glass Frame and repairing the Carved Work of ditto, new Gilding the Frame of another Glass, repairing the carved work, silvering and fitting the Glass and Gilding the Pillasers to Dito the whole heighth of the Room' — work he was presumably well versed in from the days of his apprenticeship. Royal preoccupations involved him in as varied provisions as a 'Mohogony Stand & Perches for a Parrot' (1741) and a 'Mohogony Library Table with Drawers on one side and Cupboards on ye other ye top covered with black leather & Castors to ye Bottom — £16.10s.' (1750). [PRO, LC 5/48, f. 45 (1739); f. 61 (1740); f. 76 (1741); LC 9/291, f. 27 (1750)]

Goodison also worked for Frederick, Prince of Wales, and his name appears in the relevant account books [e.g. Duchy of Cornwall Office, Vouchers VI (1), 1735–37, £450 7s]; for work at Hampton Court and St James's Palace [PRO, A.O. 3/1166] and as noted in commissions below.

We have noted Sir Thomas Robinson's official 'supervision' of Goodison's work. Two mahogany commodes made for Sir Thomas, c. 1740, are now in the Royal Collection. [Burlington, July 1977, pl. 14] It seems sensible to assume that he commissioned Goodison to make for him privately what he knew he was well capable of making, and that some of the superb mahogany furniture with Greek frets and gilt enrichments — such as items at Longford Castle, Wilts. (where Goodison's name is in the accounts) — should be credited to him. In 1932 it was noted that items (such as the commodes at Goodwood, C. Life, 26 November 1932) then held to be 'early Vile' might be by Goodison. The fact that Vile was still calling William Hallett I 'my Master' in 1749 [Furn. Hist., 1975] tilts certain items of furniture prior to this date in Goodison's favour. Note should be taken of similar pieces at Chatsworth which are however by John Boson. The stuff of attribution is always heady, but is strong in a circumstantial way in the Longford Castle and Sir Thomas Robinson commissions.

From about 1743 Goodison had as an assistant Edward Grifiths. He did some work for Lord Cardigan (see commissions, below), particularly at the Dover St, London,

house. He also was employed on gilding in the Drawing Room at Longford Castle in 1747 (£88 15s). He later left to set up on his own at Dean St, Soho. [Heal]

Two other significant private patrons were Sarah, Duchess of Marlborough, who employed Goodison at several houses, including her London residence in Dover St, and her heirs, the Spencers, sometimes Earls of Sunderland, at Althorp. The various fire insurance policies Goodison took out in the 1740s [GL, Hand in Hand MS vols 60, pp. 50, 252, 340 (1741); 64, ref. 140 (1743); 65, ref. 222, ref. 328 (1744) and the three apps recorded to him [PRO, IR/1/124. 13 January 1736 app. Thomas Dawson; 2 May 1741, Benjamin Parran (Goodison's nephew, cf. GCM, p. 106); 4 June 1746, John White] are but a partial indication of success. Goodison seems to have had a wide-ranging mind, and one also inclined to religion; at least his will [PRO, Prob. 11/476 f. 446] shows him to have been unusually pious. He subscribed in 1736 to Stephen Duck's Poems on Several Occasions, and in 1748 to Thomas Warton's Poems on Several Occasions. He was noted in the lists as 'Cabinet Maker to their Majesties' but appeared in the Westminster poll bk only as 'cabinet maker' in November–December 1749.

Goodison's Royal service often involved preparation for various occasions. At the start of a Royal life he was ordered in March 1740 to 'send a man to mend the Crown of Prince George's cradle and fit it on [Duchy of Cornwall, vouchers bk IX], and morbidly, in March 1751, he was required to help with the funeral arrangements after the death of Frederick, Prince of Wales, his long-time patron. The death chamber and the Henry VII Chapel in Westminster Abbey were set out with black hangings provided by the u William Reason and with eighty black sconces by Goodison. He also helped to embalm the body and lay the Prince in the lavish coffin provided by the joiner Henry Williams. [PRO, LC 9/291, ff. 46–47]

We do not know who, or when, Goodison married, but at some time in the late 1740s one of his two daughters, Sarah, married William Hinchliff, of the family of talented sculptors and carvers who became well versed in the provision of scagliola tops for table frames. [Gunnis, p. 202] He was also serving the same royal masters as his father-in-law in the 1760s. [PRO, LC 5/56, ff. 11, 115] Goodison's son, also named Benjamin, was treated well by his father. He entered Westminster School in January 1750 at the (late) age of 14, was admitted a pensioner at Trinity Hall, Cambridge in 1755, Scholar, 1756, and matriculated, 1758. He was admitted to Lincoln's Inn, and was a Bachelor of Law by 1764. [G. F. R. Baker & A. H. Stenning, The Record of Old Westminsters, I, 1928 confirmed by J. & J. A. Venn, Alumni Cantabrigiensis, Pts II, III, p. 84, 1947] At his father's death in 1767 he was left household effects and a sum of £8,000, approximately half the estate. The business was continued by Goodison snr's nephew, and erstwhile partner, Benjamin Parran, who had been app. to his uncle in 1741. [PRO, Boyd's index to IR app. reg.] For a time about 1769 he was in partnership with Goodison jnr, who in view of his legal training dealt presumably with the business side of affairs. [GCM, p. 106] Indeed they seem to have serviced the funeral of the Duke of Newcastle in November 1768. [R. A. Kelch, Newcastle, 1974, pp. 187–88]

It is not known whether he was the Benjamin Goodison who was a Fellow of the Society for Arts and Manufactures, 1760–77, and Chairman of the Committee of Correspondence and Papers, 1770–72. He may have died in 1783 when Parran went into partnership with William Gates.

The final tidy act after Goodison snr's death was to present the probate of his will to the Great Wardrobe. They noted that administration of the estate had been granted on 9 December

1767 to Benjamin Goodison (son) and William Hinchliff (son-in-law), the surviving executors. [PRO, LC 5/105, f. 72] Service to the Crown had already passed swiftly to William Vile and John Cobb, and at Vile's death in the same year as Goodison, to William France. We may for completeness conclude with a note of Benjamin Goodison snr's recorded fire insurance cover. He had a house at Mitcham, insured with the Hand in Hand Co. [GL, Hand in Hand MS vol. 94, 1760, p. 62 and vol. 105, 1766, p. 124] It had 2 storeys, garrets, 14 rooms, 8 marble chimneypieces, stables, a coach house. Insured £1600 brick, £200 timber. His London properties, 1740–43, are noted in vol. 60, pp. 50, 252, 340; 64, p. 146; 65, pp. 222, 238.

NORTH CRAY, Lincs.? (Hon Wrey and Lady Mary Saunderson; Lord Monson). 1725–51: 'May 2. Pd Mr Goodison a bill for chairs etc.' (£19 12s) includes 'For a Great Japan'd Chair with elbows' (£2 10s). [Lincoln RO, Monson 10/1/A/16] Goodison also worked for Lord Monson in 1738–39, 1741, 1747 (bill not settled until 1754). On 1 March 1738 he provided 'A Mahogany Dining Table to holde from eight to twelve people (£8 10s) and in July 1739 'Six walnut chairs with stufft seats covered with black Spanish leather and brass nails at 28s (£8 8s). In 1747 he repaired a large library table and provided '2 Wallnutt Chairs with French Elbow & Stuffed backs & Seats at 39s. ea'. The check linen cases for them cost 9s each, and sacking 7s 6d. [ibid. Monson 12] Goodison was still active for the family in 1751. [Monson 11/50]

ROYAL PALACES. 1729–68: The PRO, LC books record in great detail Goodison's activities. His first account in 1729 included tables, glasses, sconces, etc., for St James's, Kensington, Kew and Windsor Castle. The following is a brief selection. Three pages of items in 1733 alone amounted for expenditure of £2,604 15s 6d, with an equal division between use of walnut and mahogany. His accounts run almost without interruption to 1760 with huge bills in various years — for example when Prince William and Prince Henry's house in Leicester Sq. was being embellished, 1757–58. In 1735 Goodison provided a mahogany case for an organ and mechanical harpsichord to Kensington Palace [Coleridge, *Thomas Chippendale*, pl. 15] which was altered in 1763 to a cabinet by William Vile. Further to the LC Books there are extensive references to his work for the Prince of Wales at Carlton House, Leicester House, Kew, Pall Mall, Cliveden, Park Pl., etc., 1747–50, in the Windsor Royal Archives, namely:

1747: RA 54545–54553: £355 16s; incl.: carved pillar and claw screen (£3 3s), 4 carved frames for Indian glasses (20 gns each), picture frames, 1 mahog. 3-part map press (£24). Also repairs.

1748: RA 54556–54561: £730 3s 6d, incl.: carved and silvered table frame (£24), 2 carved and gilt picture frames with flowers and mosaic work (£126).

1749: RA 54863–54869: £459 13s, incl.: large mahog. library press (£46), picture frames and repairs.

March 1750: RA 55287–55293: £388 8s. 6d, incl.: cheap mahog. furn., cleaning and alterations. Also 'three long handles for garden Tools', 7s.

Windsor, Abstract of Augusta, Princess of Wales Annual Expenses 1/7/1740–1/7/1741 (55426) April 1741, £10 13s.

Items in the Royal Collection attributed to Goodison are illustrated in GCM, pls 37–43, and include a fine Japanese lacquer cabinet on stand, two tables, three looking-glasses (one for Frederick, Prince of Wales) and various pedestals or stands. These are characterized by carved fish-scale decoration (a technique also praticed by James Richards and John Boson). A carved and gilt mirror bearing the Prince of Wales's

feathers is now in the V & A. [GCM, pl. 46] A pair of George I giltwood torchères attributed to Goodison was sold Sotheby's, 8 November 1963, lot 166, and resemble those in the Royal Collection. The Robinson commodes are noted in the biographical text above. With related items they are also well illustrated by Coleridge, *Thomas Chippendale*, but understandably, in the light of earlier research, attributed to William Vile (pls 2–7).

LONGFORD CASTLE, Wilts. (1st and 2nd Viscounts Folkestone). 1737–50 The Longford accounts (at Castle) note names and payments only.

1737, 23 Dec. Mr Goodison — Cabinet-maker — a bill with some old goods exchanged	£148
1740, 21 Oct. Goodison furniture	£413
1741, 1 Dec. Goodison	£71. 11s.
1742, 21 May. Goodison	£100. –.
1743, 28 May. Goodison cabt maker	£90. —.
1743, 15 Dec. Goodison	£342. 5s.
1745, 22 Feb.	21. 3s. 6d.
Gallery at Longford	
Goodison	400.

These payments amount to £1,585 19s 6d and allow attribution of the mahogany and gilt day-beds, stools, armchairs and chairs upholstered in green damask in the Long Gallery and elsewhere, (and those in Genoa cut-velvet) to Goodison. [GCM, pls 44–45, 48] A pair of pedestals, similar to those at Hampton Court, are after a drawing by John Vardy. [P. Ward-Jackson, *English Furniture Designs of 18th Century*, pl. 41]

SARAH, DUCHESS OF MARLBOROUGH. 1739: After her daughter Isabella had been left a widow in 1739 Sarah purchased a property for her in Dover St, London. Goodison bid for it in July 1740 (£1,915). He did repairs there and provided 4 walnut elbow chairs at 18s 6d each and 9 chairs at 8s 9d each. He also provided chimney-pieces, pier-glasses and several marble tables with walnut frames. 275 yards of green damask and enough white damask for a bed were not included in Goodison's bill or that of the u Sherard Paxton. The architect in charge was Henry Flitcroft. [Earl Spencer in C. Life, 13 March 1942, p. 517]

HOLKHAM HALL, Norfolk (1st Earl of Leicester). Scrutiny of the Holkham 'Weekly Departmental Accounts' produces several payments to Goodison. The first is in 1739 (1st quarter)

for ye temple at Holkham pd Goodison for making 8 mahogany stools	8. 16. 0.
do for cases & packing	— 16. 0.
do for two wrought brass moulding frames fitting & fixing 2 Porphyry tables for the drawing room at London [Thanet House]	15. 10. –.
for repairing & fixing the seat in ye water closet at London	— 12. –.
(1739) May 5. to Mr Goodison for 8 mahogany stools with composts & seats at 22s.	8. 16. –.
for cases & packing the same	16. –.
(1740) Feb. Goodison for the hire of chandeliers at Holkham	6. 16. –
(1757–59) Jan. 1757, Mr Goodison for a Mahog. table press carved & gilt with wire doors for ye Gallery [Apollo, February 1964, p. 127, pl. 8]	14. 16. 0.
Do 2 card tables to do	12. 10. 0.
Do 4 high stands for do	11. 12. 0.
Do for 4 carvd & gilt branches for candles	12. 16. 0.
Do for a gilt frame to ye Picture of Corialanus [This painting is by Pietro da Cortona]	74. 0. 0.
Do for covers, lining, packing &c (Goodison receipted the account £131 19s on 11 June 1757)	6. 5. 0.

Apart from the abstract in the 'Weekly Departmental Accounts' there is a 4-page bill from Goodison together with a letter of 29 January 1757 to Lord Leicester apologizing for some damage in carriage, and continuing 'the table for the drawing room is in forwardness . . .'.

DITTON, Bucks. 1739: Paid three sums of £22, £245 17s and £42. [Marchant's accounts, Boughton]

MANSION HOUSE, London. 1739: In the accounts by contractors, 1728–44 [Box 1, folder 20] is a draft agreement, 20 February–5 March 1739 between the Mayor and various tradesmen including 'Benjamin Goodison of Long Acre, Cabinet maker'.

DEENE PARK, Northants. (4th Earl and Countess of Cardigan). 1739–45: The Earl engaged Goodison at Deene and at Dover House, London. His accounts (now at Deene) record him supplying (1743–44) picture frames, and doing repairs. In 1741 he supplied a 'carved and gilt dolphin table frame to match another', new glass (allowing for old glass) to a chimney frame and 'painting the frame white'. The transaction cost Goodison 'above 2 pounds a looser'. [GCM, p. 45, quoting 4th Earl's account bk; V & A archives]

BLENHEIM PALACE, Oxon. (1st Duchess of Marlborough). A note in the 1740 inventory states 'looking glasses paid for in Mr Goodison's bill by the Duchess of Marlborough'.

ALTHORP, Northants. (Earl Spencer). 1746: Goodison and the London u, Richard Freelove drew up an inventory. It would seem Goodison would not have been invited to do this unless furniture had been obtained from him. This is itemized in *Apollo*, March 1968, pp. 182–83, and includes, possibly, two white-painted tables (Ent. Hall), and the stand for the terra-cotta bust of Van Dyck by J. M. Rysbrack, 1743.

3rd EARL OF BURLINGTON. c. 1747: The Earl's quarto green vellum account bk (Chatsworth) includes minor payments, 1747–51 to Goodison, e.g. 'Goodison for a box £1. 10. 0d.'.

BEDFORD HOUSE, London (4th Duke of Bedford). 1750–51 December–January: Taking down a picture & taking to 'the painter'
A two-leaf fire screen — mahogany frame — Indian pictures to the back and colouring a map of London & putting it on the inside.
Returning picture from painter & re-hanging. [Bedford Office, London]   Total £2 6.

Goodison probably did work for the 4th Duke at Woburn Abbey as a suite at the house (4 day-beds, pair of settees, 12 stools) resembles closely the suite at Longford Castle, attributed to Goodison because of the large payments to him (see entry above). The Woburn suite illus. *Apollo*, December 1955, pp. 203–05.

2nd DUKE OF GRAFTON.

1755–57: 'Goodison Cabinett maker   £19. 6. 4.
                                            £31. 15. 0.
[Suffolk RO, Grafton MS AA105. The sums, being 'debts of his late Grace Duke of Grafton for his expence in London' are repeated in MS 10WS/23, 2 July 1761, and coupled with a payment to 'Hinchcliffe & Co. Silk Mercers']

NO DATE. Finally we may note a pair of mahogany chairs at Hardwick Hall, Derbs., covered in Genoa velvet. A velvet of identical pattern, supplied through Goodison, covers chairs at Holkham Hall. [V & A archives]   G.B.

Goodlad, John, Paradise St (or Sq.), Sheffield, Yorks., cm (1805–08). [D]

Goodman, Benjamin, Northampton, upholder (1823–30). Recorded at Market St in 1823 and Abington St, 1826–30. [D; poll bk]

Goodman, Humphrey, Fish St, Kidderminster, Worcs., cm and u (1830). [D]

Goodman, John, Lacock, Wilts., chairmaker (1777). [Wilts. RO, Archdeaconry wills, 12 August 1777]

Goodman, John, 28 King St, Golden Sq., London, cm (1791–93). On 17 August took out insurance cover of £100 for household goods and wearing apparel. He is possibly the Goodman, cm of London, who in 1793 subscribed to Sheraton's *Drawing Book*. [D; GL, Sun MS ref. 587641]

Goodman, Richard, 62 Sun St, Bishopsgate, London, cm, upholder and appraiser (1807–22). Trade card [Landauer Coll., MMA, NY] indicates that he produced 'Solid Cabinet Work for Exportation. Bedsteads and Chairs of all kinds. Funerals Performed'. [D]

Goodman, Stephen, Norwich, cm (1820). Free 16 March 1820 by servitude as app. to William Norris. [Freemen reg.]

Goodman, Fraser & Speare, 113–14 Aldersgate St, London, cm, u, appraisers and undertakers (1823–27). One of the firms of makers who endorsed P. & M.A. Nicholson's *Practical Cabinet Maker*, 1826. [D]

Goodman, J. & L. & Co., 42 Mansell St, London, looking-glass manufacturers and cm (1806–09). [D]

Goodram, John jnr, Gt Yarmouth, Norwich and London (1790–96). At Gt Yarmouth, June 1790, and Norwich, May 1795. In October 1796 however in London. [Gt Yarmouth poll bks]

Goodred, Jonas, Rochester, Kent, carver (1780). [Poll bk]

Goodrham, John, Tunbridge Wells, Kent, cm and u (1838–39). In 1838 at Bedford Terr. but in 1839 at Chapel Pl. [D]

Goodrich, William, King St, Leicester, cm (1827–28). Trading at King St in 1827 and Oxford St in 1828. [D]

Goodrich, William, 28 Old Change, Cheapside, London, cm (1826). [D]

Goodrich, William, Milton St, Nottingham, cm (1832). [D]

Goodrick, John, Newcastle, cm, carpenter and joiner (1778–1801). At Pudding-chair, 1778–90, but in 1801 at Bigg Mkt. [D]

Goodrick, John, Market Pl., Malton, Yorks., cm and u (1823–30). [D]

Goodricke, William, Crossgate, Durham, cm (1827–28). [D]

Goodsall (or Goodfail), John, 15 Steelhouse Lane, Birmingham, cm (1777–80). [D]

Goodson, William, 1 Ogle St, Upper Foley St, London, picture and looking-glass frame maker (1839). [D]

Goodwin, —, address unknown, u (1684–88). Issued an invoice on 23 June 1684 for a bedstead amounting to 19s 6d and another on 23 April 1688 for £1 13s in connection with Gorhambury House, St Albans, Herts. [Herts. RO, account bk XI 21]

Goodwin, Christopher, 2–3 Thomas St, Weymouth, Dorset, cm and u (1840). [D]

Goodwin, Edward, 28 Barons Ct, Back Turner St, Manchester, cm (1813). [D]

Goodwin, George, London, Woodbridge and Ipswich, Suffolk, clock case maker and cm (1812–39). By September 1812 at Thoro'fare, Woodbridge where he claimed to be 'from London'. This claim is also recorded on his trade labels. In 1839 at Carr St, Ipswich where he was practising as a cm. [D; *Ipswich Journal*, 26 September 1812; Robinson, *The Long Case Clock*, p. 343] See William Bezant Goodwin.

Goodwin, George, 4 Union St, Stretford New Rd, Manchester, cm (1836–40). [D]

Goodwin, Henry, 44 Church St, Little Minories, London, broker and cm (1802). On 17 April 1802 took out insurance cover of £300. [GL, Sun MS vol. 423, ref. 730478]

Goodwin, Henry, 48 Goodge St, Tottenham Ct Rd, London, chair and sofa maker (1839). [D]

Goodwin, James, Stamford, Lincs., chairmaker (1776). Son of

George Goodwin and free of Stamford by patrimony, 1776. [Freemen reg.]

Goodwin, John F., Wokingham, Berks., chairmaker and turner (1798). [D]

Goodwin, John, Fargate, Sheffield, Yorks., joiners and cm (1817). [D]

Goodwin, John, Wellow, Notts., chairmaker (1832–40). [D]

Goodwin, John, Car St, Ipswich, Suffolk, cm and u (1839). [Poll bk]

Goodwin, Jonathan, Westgate, Wakefield, Yorks., cm (1743–62). In 1743 stated that he made and sold 'all Sorts of Cabinet Works, Tables, Chairs &c &c after the newest Fashion'. He took as apps Burditt in 1745; John Brailsford, 1757; William Brailsford, 1758; Clarkson, 1759; Elemes, 1759 and Jenkinson, 1762. [York Courant, 11 October 1743; S of G, app. index]

Goodwin, Matthias, 53 Ray St, London, carver (1835). [D]

Goodwin, Noah, Stanley St, Macclesfield, Cheshire, chairmaker (1828). [D]

Goodwin, P., address unknown, carver (1721–23). Worked at Chicheley Hall, Bucks. In November 1721 he was paid 10s 6d for carving 'ye Cornishes' and in 1722 £24 12s for 'marble table and other things'. In January 1723 received a further £3 0s 6d. [Bucks. RO, D/C/2/36(iii), D/C/2/3(ii); V & A archives]

Goodwin, Robert, Manningtree, Essex, cm (1823–39). In 1839 described as a carpenter, builder and u. [D]

Goodwin, Stephen, Halesworth, Suffolk, chairmaker (1806). [Ipswich Journal, 22 March 1806]

Goodwin, William, 15 Clerkenwell Green, London, chairmaker (1824–29). In April and May 1824 took out two insurance policies providing £1,200 cover about half of which was for his workshop and its contents. [D; GL, Sun MS vol. 496, ref. 1016564; vol. 497, ref. 1017278]

Goodwin, William, 28 Old Change, London, cm and u (1827). [D]

Goodwin, William Bezant, Thoro'fare, Woodbridge, Suffolk, cm and u (1824–39). Probably took over from George Goodwin when he moved to Ipswich. [D]

Goodwyn, Daniel, King's Lynn, Norfolk, u (1681–82). Former app. John Harvey, free 1681–82. [Freemen rolls]

Goodyer, William, Bank St, St Ives, Hunts., cm (1839). [D]

Goolding, Henry, Oxford, cm (1817). Married Frances Davenport at All Saints Church, 19 October 1817. [Bodleian index of Oxf. marriage bonds]

Goolding, Mareham, Brewer St, London, upholder (1774–76). In 1776 insured his household goods for £300. [Poll bk; Sun MS vol. 246, p. 550]

Goolding, Walter, Salisbury, Wilts., chairmaker (1715–24). His son James was app. to Jonathan House, broadweaver, 26 October 1715. Walter Goolding took app. named Joseph Simms, son of John Simms, 3 August 1724. [Wilts. Apps and their Masters]

Goore, Charles, Moor St, Ormskirk, Lancs., cm (1834). [D]

Goore, James, Ormskirk, Lancs., cm (1822). [D]

Goore, Thomas, Ormskirk, Lancs., cm (1819). Married Miss Cockee, second daughter of Richard Cockee of Ormskirk, printer, December 1816. [Liverpool Mercury, 10 December 1819]

Goose, William, Churchgate St, North Walsham, Norfolk, cm (1830). [D]

Goose, William, Southend, Lowestoft, Suffolk, cm (1839). [D]

Gooseman, J., 14 Duke St, Portland Pl., London, cm and turtle shell manufacturer (1804–08). [D]

Gorden, Richard, Exeter, Devon, cm and chairmaker (1763–74). In September 1763 at the sign of the 'Mahogany-Tree', Northgate St where he made and sold 'all Sorts of Cabinet and Chair Work'. He also sold looking-glasses. He was however to move to Fore St where he established himself opposite the Corn Mkt. By early 1770 however he had decided to give up the business and take over the 'Seven Stars Inn', Exeter, which had been run for many years by his mother. As a result he announced a sale on 5 March 1770 of his entire stock consisting of a 'great Variety of Chairs, Tables, all kinds of Drawer Work, Looking-Glasses'. A further sale was held on 11 April when not only his stock in trade but also household goods and furniture, work benches and utensils were offered. Despite this change of occupation in 1770, he was still declaring his trade as cm in 1774. [Exeter Flying Post, 22 September 1763, 16 February 1770, 30 March 1770; freemen rolls]

Gordon, —, Brewer St, Golden Sq., London, u (1747). [Heal]

Gordon, George, Liverpool, cm (1787–90). In 1787 at Paradise St but by 1790 had moved to Pitt St where in that year his number is given in one directory as 73 and in another as 105. [D]

Gordon, Henry, 29 Eaton St, Pimlico, London, carver and gilder (1839). [D]

Gordon, James, 40 Brewer St, London, cm (1778–84). In 1778 insured his house for £1,000. [D; GL, Sun MS vol. 263, p. 493]

Gordon, John and **Taitt, John and Richard**, London, cm and upholders (1748–96). Although the firm of John Gordon and John Taitt received a number of important commissions in the 1770s, relatively little is known about the two partners' early careers. The origins of John Gordon have yet to be discovered, but from his will in which he leaves a bequest to his spinster sister in Stranrawor, Galloway, it might be surmised that he had come from that place. A John Gordon was working in 1725 at Hopetoun House, W. Lothian. He is mentioned on an order of wainscots amounting to £133 from William Adam [Hopetoun accounts, No. 4] but from the early date and signature it is unlikely to be the same John Gordon who in 1756 was providing furniture for the 2nd Duke of Atholl at Blair Castle, Perthshire.

John Gordon's address is first cited on two bills in the Blair Castle accounts for 30 March and 29 April 1748 as the corner of Swallow St, Argyll Buildings. Heal lists a John Gordon at this address quoting a trade card of 1748. In 1749 a John Gordon, cm of King St, Golden Sq., London is featured in the polling list for a Westminster by-election. Little Argyle St is a turning off Swallow St and probably the same address; and King St is immediately behind Swallow St. We are therefore probably dealing with a single complex of buildings throughout Gordon's career, but variously described. The type and range of furnishings supplied to the Duke of Atholl indicates that John Gordon ran a sizeable establishment, providing a variety of cabinetmaking, uphol-stery and joinery services. Two fully documented suites of seat furniture still survive at Blair Castle. The quality of these pieces, together with the descriptions of other items in the accounts indicate the work of a fashionable craftsman.

John Gordon's next recorded commission, for the Duke of Gordon, illustrates the variety of services he offered. Gordon supplied furniture and upholstery for the Duke's London houses between the years 1747 and 1753. As well as undertaking repairs, he provided a wide range of goods from a cradle to a house for two goats, a child's painted cart, and a mahogany hardboard for cutting cucumbers. For Sanston House, Gordon received a grander order which included 12 beds with bedding, numerous carpets and 2 dozen wainscot hall chairs. In 1750, however, a dispute arose between the Duke and Gordon, who had been asked to supply furniture and furnishings to the Duke's house in Upper Grosvenor St, leased from the Earl of Holderness. He had been instructed by the Duke to take possession of the house while His Grace was in Scotland and to supply some furniture together with Alexander Dingwall, cm. Gordon is alleged to have dismissed Dingwall, and to have exceeded his instructions, supplying furnishings totalling over £863 in the Duke's absence. Gordon was faced with ruin and in June 1750, the Duke paid on account £100 and a note for £600. He called in two arbitrators, tradesmen of character, who made a detailed appraisal [Scottish RO, GD44/49/20/16] and concluded he had overcharged £170 11s on a grand total of £1,226 19s 9d. [Scottish RO, GD44/49/20/3]

In 1753 John Gordon, upholder and cm in the parish of St James, Westminster, renounced all claims 'on the estate of Cosmo George, late Duke of Gordon'. [Scottish RO, GD44/51/309/4/77] The official document was dated 24 April 1753, and on that same day the Dowager Duchess, widow of the Duke, paid him £431 16s.

It may be that this dispute caused a severe financial setback and/or forced Gordon into the greater security of a partnership, but for whatever reason, there is no further record of John Gordon for the years 1756–67. He may, however, be the 'Mr. Gordon, upholder . . . to Sir William Chambers' who is listed as a subscriber to Chambers's *Treatise on Civil Architecture*, 1759. There is a possibility that at this time John Gordon was associated with the William Gordon, cm who is named as a subscriber to Chippendale's *Director*, 1754. Other than a reference in the app. reg. to a 'Jn Bencroft app. to Wm Gordom of St James Westminster, carv. £20' in 1762, there is no further clue to the identity of William Gordon.

It could also be that during these years John Gordon was in partnership with Thomas Landall, cm of Little Argyle St. A tradecard of c.1750 advertises 'Landall & Gordon Joyners, Cabinet and chairmakers at ye Griffin & Chair in Little Argyle Street by Swallow St Makes all sorts of Tables, Chairs, settee-beds, looking glasses, picture frames, window blinds and all sorts of cabinet work'. [Heal] The next certain information we have about John Gordon, however, is found in the accounts for a commission for the Earl of Coventry at Croome Court, Worcs, in 1767. Gordon was now in partnership with John Taitt whose earlier career is undocumented. The Croome Court bills were submitted in 1767 and 1769 and are signed for 'Mr. Gordon & self John Taitt'. They reveal that the firm had supplied among other items a very grand suite of carved and gilded Neo-classical furniture.

From 1767–70 Gordon and Taitt are located at King St, Golden Sq, according to London directories. By 1771 they appear to have expanded their business to premises on Swallow St. [Essex RO, A.31/3 1773] Directories list the firm at Little Argyle St from 1771–79. The size of their next two commissions, which were undertaken almost simultaneously, would seem to indicate that their trade was flourishing. For Sir Griffin Griffin at Audley End between 1771–73 they worked, under Robert Adams's direction, supplying the entire furnishings for the Great Drawing Room, the Little Drawing Room, the Great Parlour and the Library. The large suite of green and gilt furniture for the Great Drawing Room is still in place, as is the exceptional double-headed couch, one of the two original small couches and the four matching stools made for the Little Drawing Room.

The extent of Gordon and Taitt's commission in the early 1770s for the Earl Spencer is harder to determine. Stylistically a number of items of furniture now at Althorp show similarities with the furniture Gordon supplied to Blair Castle in the 1750s, and the quality of the furniture at Audley End would seem to support the argument that Gordon and Taitt

might have supplied in the 1760s some of the grand Neo-classical furniture for Spencer House, including the lion suite for which it is known they made the loose covers in 1772.

The close relationship John Gordon may have had with the Spencer household is revealed by his appointment of the Earl's steward as an executor in his will, of 1778. What is known is that the firm provided a great deal of upholstery in the 1770s for the Spencer houses, including the furnishings for an elaborate bed costing £16 5s. Of the furniture only a few minor pieces are itemized in the bills including a lunar table, a quilting frame, some low stools with cane seats, an expensive dressing table, a 'Trou-madame' table and a neat mahogany French writing table.

In addition, they carried out in 1772 a considerable amount of repair work, mending and regilding the John Vardy hall lantern at Spencer house, and making loose covers and cases for the furniture designed by James Stuart.

In 1776, the year the 1st Duchess of Northumberland included 'Gordon, London' in her list of furniture makers [C. Gilbert, *Chippendale*, p. 154] the firm of Gordon and Taitt of Swallow St insured its utensils, stock and goods for £2,200. [GL, Sun MS vol. 248, p. 590] Two years later in July 1778, John Gordon's will was proved at London. The exact date of his death, however, is not known. This will, which was drawn up in 1777, describes the bequests of 'John Gordon, cabinetmaker and upholster of the Parish of St. James within the Liberty of Westminster'. His executors were his two brothers (whom he does not name), John Taitt of Swallow St, cm, to whom he left £20, and Thomas Townsend, steward to the Earl Spencer. [PRO, Prob., 11/1044] After Gordon's death, John Taitt continued in business under his own name, trading at 75 Swallow St from 1779–85.

On a trade card c. 1780 Taitt of 75 Swallow St advertises his services as u, cm, appraiser and undertaker, carver and gilder. [BM] Taitt's documented commissions included two for earlier clients. He provided in 1781 a neat mahogany pillar and claw table to the Earl of Coventry for which he received payment in the following year. The note acknowledging receipt of payment on behalf of John Taitt was signed by William Taitt. Also in 1781 John Taitt received another valuable commission from Sir John Griffin Griffin to supply 12 cabriole carved and gilt chairs and two sofas to match for his house on Burlington St. The bill in this case was submitted by John Taitt and Richard Taitt. Despite these commissions business seems to have gone badly, and in the *Gents Mag.*, June 1786, it was announced that John Taitt had been declared bankrupt.

The sale of his household furniture, stock in trade and other effects was held by Christie's, 13–17 March 1786, at Taitt's house and warehouses in Swallow and King Streets, Hanover Sq. The extensive premises included upholstery shop, wareroom, upholder's shop, Blanket room and counting house at Swallow St with the saw pit, warehouses, cabinetmaking and carvers shops on King St. The stock in trade included a complete dining suite as well as numerous small decorative items. Among the books in the sale was a copy of Chippendale's *Director*. One of the Taitts bought in several of the lots of timber in the sale, and by 1787 John Taitt is listed in the London Directories at 254 Oxford St, with his occupation given as cm and u. He is listed at that address until 1799.

Both John and Richard Taitt appear in the Lord Chamberlain's accounts for 1793–96. Richard Taitt is described as an u and joiner and his address is given as Jermyn St between 1793 and 1795. [Fastnedge, *Sheraton Furniture*] John Taitt's death at Exeter is recorded in the *Gents Mag.*, October 1800.

BLAIR CASTLE (2nd Duke of Atholl). 1748 bill to John

Gordon, Swallow St, Argyle Buildings for bedstead, 12 cherrytree Marlbro chairs, large wainscot library table, etc., £33 8s 6d. 1753 bill for panama card table & watch case, £4 4s. 1753 bills for bedsteads, 6 mahogany chairs with lion paws, 2 settees do. etc., £36 10s. 1756–57 bills for '8 mahogany chairs carved frames in fish scales with a french foot and carved leaf on the toe, 6 mahogany 3 footed stools with a French scroll toe, 2 pillar & claw tables and 6 library stools . . . £49 12s 6d. [Blair Castle archives] The 'lion's paw' and 'fish scale' suites still survive at Blair.

CONDUIT ST, London (Duke of Gordon). 1749 detailed bill of goods supplied and services rendered by John Gordon, parish of St James Westminster, including a cradle, mahogany tea chest, childs cart and sundry repairs to furniture and the house. Total £29 4s 7d. [Scottish RO, GD44/49/20/2]

SANSTON HOUSE (Duke of Gordon). 1749 bill from John Gordon for house furnishings including 12 beds, 4 Wilton carpets (one 'Roman Pavement') wainscott hall chairs, etc. Total £285 15s. [Scottish RO, GD44/51/302/84]

UPPER GROSVENOR ST (Duke of Gordon). Undated account of stuff given by Duke of Gordon to John Gordon to be made into furniture for Gothic tester bed, etc. [Scottish RO, GD44/49/20/5] 1750 note of furniture to be returned from Duke of Gordon's house to John Gordon. Total £75 17s. 6d. [Scottish RO, GD44/49/20/4] 1750 account for joiner work, e.g. mahogany desk & bookcase, walnut chair & firescreen. Total £33 5s 6d. [Scottish RO, GD44/49/20/1] 1750 Memorandum of dispute between the Duke of Gordon and John Gordon over the dismissal of Alexander Dingwall, cabinetmaker and for exceeding instructions. [Scottish RO, GD/44/49/20/3] 1750 Appraisers called in and conclude that Duke had been overcharged £170 11s on a grand total of £1,226 16s 9d. [Scottish RO, GD44/49/20/16] 1753 sealed document renouncing all claims by John Gordon, upholder & cabinetmaker on the estate of the Duke of Gordon [Scottish RO, GD44/51/309/4/77] 1753 receipt for £431 16s paid by the Dowager Duchess. [Scottish RO, GD44/51/309/4/78]

CROOME COURT (Earl of Coventry). 1767 bill from Gordon & Taitt for fitting a marble slab upon a frame. 1768 payment received for 'Mr Gordon & self, John Taitt' for '8 large elbow chairs richly carved in the antique manner & gilt 3 large sophas to match'. Total £217 1s 11d. 1769 bill for dressing glass in japanned frame and firescreen £8 8s. 1781 bill from John Taitt, cabinetmaker & upholderer of 75 Swallow Street, for 'a neat mahogany pillar & claw table' £1 13s. 1782 'account Recd 23 May 1782 The content in full for John Taitt' signed William (?) Taitt. [Worcs. RO, Croome Court, papers]

AUDLEY END (Sir John Griffin Griffin). 1771 account sent by Gordon & Taitt for '2 sofas carved and gilt covered in damask' supplied to Sir John Griffin Griffin £52 10s; '8 cabriole elbow chairs to match' £58 16s; '4 scrold stools, carved and gilt' £25 4s; '2 large plates of glass' £200; '2 table frames under the glasses carved and gilt' £16 16s; '2 very rich inlaid tops for do' £30; 'a very large double headed couch, richly carved after the antique and gilt, covered in flowered satin' £30; '2 scrold stolls to match' £35; '4 small stools to match' £22. Total £695 11s. 3d. [Essex RO, D/DBy/A31/3] 1772 bill for large plate glass for the Little Drawing Room £73 10s. 1772 receipt for £500 signed John Gordon & Taitt. 1773 receipt for the balance. [Essex RO, D/DBy/A31/3] 1782 John Taitt of 75 Swallow St account for supplying '12 cabriole elbow chairs richly carved & gilt in burnished gold' £50. 8d. and '2 sofas do.'. Total bill £132 19s 5d. Pencil note indicates that furniture was intended for Burlington St, London. 1783 Receipt for payment in full signed by John Taitt. [Essex RO, D/DBy/A41/3]

BROCKENHURST PARK, HANTS. (Edward Morant). 1772 notebook entry 'To your bill to John Tait £92 10/–.' [MS notebook 'Edward Morant Esq. accounts & notes 1764–1777' in possession Edward Morant Roydon Manor, Hants.]

ALTHORP
1772 bills for repairing & gilding hall lantern by Vardy; repairing leather case for Stuart tripod stands; repainting 12 hall chairs and making cases (loose covers) for 2 sofas and 6 elbow chairs in Bow Room.
1773 account of locks sent from Althorp to London to be gilded by 'Ordr. Mr Gordon'.
1774 bill for furnishing a bed at Wimbledon £16 5s 0d.
1775 letter from John Taitt asking for payment of a bill and in which he mentions his brother.

QUEEN ANN ST (Lord Cork).
1775 bill from Gordon & Taitt £49 9s 6d.
1776 bill from John Tait (sic) for £327 12s. [Stanhope papers K.R.O. U590 A61/7]

CHATSWORTH
1785 Upholsterer Taitt account for 31.16.6
1787   „   „   „   for 10.3.0 and 10.0.0.
[Chiswick Account Book Vol. Chatsworth C 166, Vol. A. pp. 180 & 250]

[A. Coleridge, 'Chippendale, The Director and some Cabinetmakers at Blair Castle', Conn., December 1960; J. D. Williams, Audley End, The Restoration 1762–97 (1966), p. 61; P. J. Drury & Ian Gow, Audley End Guidebook, 1984; P. Thornton, 'A very special year', Conn., June 1978; P. Thornton and J. Hardy, 'The Spencer Furniture at Althorp', Apollo, vols LXXX, VII and LXXXVIII, 1968] See Richard Tait(t)
G.C.

Gordon, Joseph, 40 Vernon St, Liverpool, cm (1827). [D]

Gordon, Norman, Brighton, Sussex, u (1833–39). In December 1833 living in Suffolk St and in April 1835 at Russell Pl. In 1837 set up in business at 16 Cranbourn St, West St. [D; PR (bapt.)]

Gordon, Thomas, Coventry, Warks., journeyman cm (1764). Worked at Stoneleigh, Warks., for twenty-six days making two large linen presses. This item is included in Robert Keene's bill to Lord Leigh. [Shakespeare Birthplace Trust, Leigh receipts, DR 18/5]

Gordon, Thomas, 38 Vernon St, Liverpool, cm (1807). [D]

Gordon, Thomas, St Clement's, Fore St, Ipswich, Suffolk, broker and cm (d. 1819). Died 9 February 1819. [Gents Mag., March 1819]

Gordon, Thomas, Exeter, Devon, cm (1822–40). In December 1822 when his son Edwin James was bapt. at St Paul's Church, he was living in Paul St. At 2 Back Lane, 1825–27, but in Rock St, 1834–40. [D; PR (bapt.)]

Gordon, Thomas, Rossbottom St, Stalybridge, Lancs., cm and joiner (1825). [D]

Gordon, William, 25 Lamb St, Bristol, chairmaker (1775). [D]

Gordon, William, London, cm, u and joiner (1803–37). Probably the Gordon, cm, u who subscribed to Sheraton's Cabinet Dictionary, 1803. By February 1810 living at 16 Artillery St, Bishopsgate but by July had moved to 17 Kenton St, Brunswick Sq. After 1826 the number changed to 16. In February 1810 took out insurance of £500, stock and utensils accounting for £150. At the new address in Kenton St cover was reduced to £400 with only £30 for utensils and stock in the workshop behind the dwelling house. By November of the same year the total cover was raised to £500 again with £130 for stock and utensils. [D; GL, Sun MS vol. 451, ref. 841315; vol. 453, ref. 846287; vol. 453, ref. 850637]

Gordon, William, Exeter St, Tavistock, Devon, cm (1823). [D]

Gordon, William, Micklegate St, Hartlepool, Co. Durham, joiner and cm (1828–34). [D]

Gore, James, Moor St, Ormskirk, Lancs., cm (1825–28). [D]

Gore, John, Liverpool, joiner and cm (1835–39). At Gateacre, 1835–37, but in 1839 at Little Woolton. [D]

Gore, Joseph, Gateacre, Liverpool, joiner and cm (1827). Succeeded at this address by John Gore. [D]

Gore, Thomas, Clements Lane, Westminster, London, cm (1774). [Poll bk]

Goreham, Edward, Norwich, cm and u (1818–40). At Middle St, St George's, until 1839 but by 1842 had moved to Gildengate St. [D]

Gorman, Henry, 2 Owen's Ct, Harrison Ct, Liverpool, joiner and cm (1821). [D]

Gornal, John, 6 Bowran St, Preston, Lancs., cm (1825). [D]

Gornall, John, Liverpool, cm (1822). Freeman of Preston, Lancs. [Preston freemen rolls]

Gorringe, Charles, parish of SS Peter and Paul, Tunbridge, Kent, cm (1813–16). This parish not only included the town of Tonbridge but a large part of Tunbridge Wells. In June 1813 declared his trade as Tunbridge-ware maker but in October 1816 as cm. [PR (bapt.)]

Gorse, Joseph, Ashbourne Rd, Derby, chairmaker and turner (1835). [D]

Gorst, Richard, Chester, cm (1795–1827). App. to Thomas Astle of Chester, cm, and free by servitude, October 1795. At Foregate St, 1814–16 but from 1818 at 6 Watergate Row. Poll bks of 1819 however list an address in North St which was probably his dwelling house. Took as apps John Sellers, 1801; Joseph Lister, 1817; and Samuel Dale, 1827, who had to be assigned to a new master when Richard Gorst's business ceased trading [D, poll bks; freemen rolls; app. bks]

Gorstage, Henry, 22 Robert St, Liverpool, chairmaker (1811). [D]

Gorton, James, 11 Trafford Lane, Liverpool, cm and victualler (1810). [D]

Gorton, John, Liverpool, cm (1796–1815). Son of Thomas Gorton, cm and free by patrimony, 25 May 1796. At this date at 22 Cavendish St. Directories show him at Dale St in 1800 but in the same year he moved to 36 Whitechapel. He remained in this road for several years being at 33 in 1804 and 38 in 1805, in which year he moved to 131 Dale St, the number being 134 in 1807. In 1810 at 14 Derby St and in 1818 at 20 Cavendish St. He took as apps William Cummings, 1800–12 and Isaac Hadfield, 1796–1815. John Gorton was the father of William Gorton, cm, born 21 May 1797 and who petitioned freedom in 1818. [D; freemen reg. and committee bk]

Gorton, John Muir, 115 Mill St, Stanley St North, Liverpool, cm (1827). Son of John Gorton and free, 17 October 1827. [Freemen reg.]

Gorton, Joseph, Liverpool, cm (1830). Son of Thomas Gorton, cm, and free, 15 November 1830. [Freemen reg.]

Gorton, Thomas, 26 Vernon St, Liverpool, cm (b.1740–d.1792). Son of William Gorton and free 1761. Took as app. Joseph Evans 1791, free 1814. Thomas Gorton's son John petitioned freedom by patrimony in 1795. He died in June 1792 aged 52 'after a long and tedious illness'. [D; freemen's committee bk and reg.; *Williamson's Liverpool Advertiser*, 25 June 1792]

Gorton, Thomas jnr, Vernon St, Liverpool, cm and victualler (b.1775–d.1815). Free 27 May 1796 and in business at 13 Vernon St by 1811. From 1813–14 at 38 Vernon St. Took as apps John Dutton 1805 and free 1816, and Henry Yates 1807 and free 1818. Died 12 May 1815 aged 40 at his house in Vernon St. [D; freemen's committee bk; *Liverpool Mercury*, 19 May 1815]

Gorton, William, 11 Horatio St, Liverpool, cm (1818). Son of John Gorton and free 11 June 1818. [Freemen reg.]

Gorton, William, Bristol, turner and chairmaker (1793–1821). At Old King St, 1793–95; Penn St, 1799–1812; Trenchard St, 1813; and St James's Back, 1814–21. In 1793 supplied John Pinney the Bristol merchant who lived in Gt George St, with six Windsor chairs, and also painted two others. For this commission he charged £1 10s. [D; Bristol Univ. Lib., John Pinney's cash bk]

Gorton & Parker, 1 Old St, Bristol, chairmakers (1799–1806). Appear to have occupied the Old St premises vacated by William Gorton when he moved to Penn St in 1799. This suggests that the John Gorton who was one of the partners was probably the son of William Gorton. At first the partners declared their trade as turners and chairmakers but from 1805 as cabinet and chairmakers. [D]

Gosby, Edward, London, carver and gilder (1826–39). In 1826 at 2 Thornton St, Horsleydown, and in 1839 at 60 Holland St, Blackfriars. [D]

Gosby, William, 2 Thornton St, Horsleydown, London, carver and gilder (1829). Possibly the successor of Edward Gosby at this address. [D]

Gosden, John, address unknown, cm (1803). Subscriber to Sheraton's *Cabinet Dictionary*, 1803.

Gosler, John, London, bedstead maker (1794–1826). In April 1794 it was reported that Sarah Hammett had an illegitimate child by John Gosler. At this date he had been lodging with Mrs Alderson at Goss's Garden, opposite Goodge St, Tottenham Ct Rd. In 1826 Gosler was operating his own business at 2 Pitt St, Kent Rd. [D; GL, P33/MRY, 1/869/169]

Goslet, W., 32 South Molton St, Grosvenor Sq., London, carver, gilder, picture frame and glass maker (1809–35). [D]

Goslin, Byatt, Colchester, Essex cm (1812–31). [Poll bk]

Gosling, George, 90 Far-gate, Sheffield, Yorks., cm and u (1787–97). [D]

Gosling, George, High St, Colchester, Essex, cm (1808). [D]

Gosling, John, Bartholomew St, Newbury, Berks., cm (1823). [D]

Goss, Benjamin, parish of St David, Exeter, Devon, cm (1804–16). Freeman of Exeter. [Freemen reg.; poll bk]

Goss, Joseph, St Margaret's Plain, Ipswich, Suffolk, cm (1839). [D]

Goss, Miss Martha, Bristol, u (1828–35). At 3 Gloucester St, St Paul's, 1828–33, but from the next year at 87 Stoke's Croft. [D]

Gosse, —, Queen St, Westminster, London, u (1747). [Heal]

Gosset, —, nearly opposite 'The Black Bull', Kingsland Rd, London, cm (1813). On 15 April 1813 took out insurance cover of £2,100. None of this was in respect of trade goods or utensils but covered six houses and a workshop, with £250 for his household goods. [GL, Sun MS vol. 463, ref. 881338]

Gosset, Gideon, Berwick St, London, frame maker and carver (1744–d.1785). A member of the famous family of carvers of French extraction, who had fled from Normandy to Jersey at the time of the revocation of the Edict of Nantes and later settled in London. Elder brother of the better known Isaac Gosset. In 1744 supplied picture frames for Petworth, Sussex and in 1747 was paid £19 for picture frames and glasses supplied to the Grimston family. Probably the Mr Gosset referred to in a letter by William Hogarth dated 28 June 1748 when he obtained a quotation for framing the picture *Paul Before Felix* which he had painted for the hall in Lincoln's Inn. [Heal; Gunnis; poll bk; V & A archives; *C. Life*, 9 May 1985]

Gosset, Isaac, London, frame maker and modeller in wax (b.1713–d.1799). Sixth son of Jean Gosset and probably born in St Helier, Jersey. One of the best and most noted of the

18th-century wax modellers who worked for the Royal Family and a distinguished list of clients. For this aspect see Gunnis. Also active as a frame maker. Initially he may well have been associated in this aspect of his work with his elder brother Gideon, and for some of the earlier commissions it is not easy to distinguish responsibility. Until 1774 worked from the same address as his brother in Berwick St, but from this year moved to 14 Edward St, Portman Sq. In January of that year he was appointed 'Joyner to His Majesty' and from the next year the business is sometimes referred to as Gossett & Co. A number of commissions for carved woodwork are known. He may well have been the 'Gousette' who in 1758 was paid £56 by James Calthorpe for sconces in connection with alterations being carried out on his house in Pall Mall, London. In the period 1762–63 he supplied picture frames for Petworth, Sussex. The 4th Duke of Bedford paid £75 in September 1765 'for gilding ten picture frames and mending four chandeliers & gilding them and scaffolding to put them up'. The first commission known was for the 7th Lord Digby at Sherborne, Dorset where an account book of 1764 records 'Gosset for Picture Frames £51 18s'. [Sherborne papers] On 29 March 1765 he was paid £37 16s for 'a picture & frame for the use of Mr. Hoare'. The patron about whose commissions we know most was however Sir Gilbert Heathcote who regularly employed Isaac Gossett from March 1765 to April 1775. Work on gilding frames, cleaning and repairing pictures and frames in September and October 1765 totalled £77 1s 6d of which the predominant item was 'Ten rich frames for the chimneys' at £52. Gossett appears to have used papier mâché where the material seemed appropriate. The largest item in 1766 was a 'rich frame sent in the country' which was charged at £35. Only minor work was undertaken in 1768 but from 1770 important commissions were undertaken which resulted in an account for £429 8s. The major items were mirrors, 'large pier glass frame to the end of the Great Room' costing £66, and 'two large glasses', £125. Work through 1774 and to 1 January 1775 amounted to £26 3s and was in the main for maintenance and repair to frames, though 'a brackett for a cabinet' costing £4 14s 6d was included. Work in the remainder of 1775 and the two years that followed was of a similar nature amounting in total to £21 7s. This was settled on 24 January 1778. Named in the Duke of Beaufort's accounts for Badminton House, Glos., on 2 May 1768 receiving £16 5s 6d. [Heal; Gunnis; Gilbert, *Chippendale*, p. 129; *C. Life*, 25 September 1980, p. 1030; *Conn.*, June 1981, p. 144; PRO, LC3/58; Bedford Office, London; Lincoln RO, 2 ANC, 12/d/23–4, 27, 30–2, 5 ANC 6/E/1, Badminton papers, accounts bks; *C. Life*, 9 May 1985]

Gosset, Jacob, Warwick St, Golden Sq., London, carver (b.1701–d.1788). A further member of the well-known Huguenot family of carvers active in the 18th century. The Jersey connection of the family is illustrated in the taking of John Le Fousey of that island as app. in 1726. Subscribed to Leoni's edition of *Alberti* in this year. In 1733 worked for Frederick, Prince of Wales, and at this period actively engaged on work for members of the aristrocracy and gentry. The 'Gosset' who was paid £42 12s in 1732 by the Duke of Montrose for 'some picture frames & a gilded frame for the Dining Room screen' for Cley House was probably Jacob. It is also likely that he was the 'Gousset' engaged by Earl Fitzwalter to work at Moulsham Hall, Essex in the same year. On 19 April he was paid for 'a large frame of a Table and for Two frames for my wife's and my Pictures at full length' at a total cost of £19 4s 6d. In 1736 he was paid £25 for 'a carv'd & gilded frame' supplied to Frederick, Prince of Wales for a full length portrait of the Duke of Dorset (now at Easton Neston) and £35 10s for a frame for another version of the

same portrait now at Raby Castle, Co. Durham. A further £21 was paid for a frame for a portrait of Frederick with cupids, now at Buckingham Palace. [Westminster poll bk; Boyd's index to IR app. reg., 18, p. 3531; Duchy of Cornwall vouchers VI(1); Scottish RO, GD 220/6/31; p. 640; V & A archives; W. Sussex RO, Petworth II, 6613; *C. Life*, 9 May 1985]

Gosset, James, Berwick St, Soho, London, wood carver and wax modeller (1749–67). Of the famous Huguenot family of carvers. His address would suggest that he was living with and probably co-operating with Gideon Gossett. His only known commission is that for Peter Du Cane of Braxted Park, Essex, though the work was for his London house in St James's Sq. On 1 May 1749 James Gosset was paid £41 16s for new picture frames and repairs and renovation to old ones. [D; Heal; Essex RO, D/DDc A17, fl. 73]

Gosset, Joseph & Co., London, carvers and gilders (1769–70). Between May 1769 and July 1770 supplied frames and plate glass to John, 4th Duke of Bedford, at a cost of £14 14s. In September 1765 the Duke had used Isaac Gossett for similar work and there may be a close trade connection between Joseph and Isaac. [Bedford Office, London]

Gosset, Matthew, Berwick St, Soho, London, carver (b.1683–d.1744). Uncle of Isaac Gossett. Living in London by 1709 when his daughter Angelique was bapt. at the French Church of Le Carré in Berwick St. Gunnis cites a number of commissions in stone and wax but no evidence of his work in wood has yet come to light. In 1716 took out insurance cover of £300 on his dwelling in Berwick St. [Gunnis; GL, Hand in Hand MS vol. 16, p. 37; *C. Life*, 9 May 1985]

Gostling, John S., Market Pl., Thetford, Norfolk, cm (c. 1820). The text describes him as a 'Cabinet Maker, Upholsterer, Paper Hanger &c' and mentions that he stocked 'Floor Cloths & Carpeting — Chimney, Pier and Dressing Glasses &c'. [D]

Gotobed, Luke, Market Hill, Ely, Cambs., chairmaker (1824). [D]

Gouch, Henzell. Signed the top of a Regency peunwork sofa table in the V & A. [w31–1937]

Goucher, James, St Alkmund's Sq., Shrewsbury, Salop, cm (1830). [Freemen rolls]

Goud, William, 7 Old Montague St, Whitechapel, London, cm (1808). [D]

Goudy, Comus St, Liverpool, cm (1837–39). At 23 Comus St in 1837 but by 1839 the number had changed to 26. [D]

Gough, —, Bird Cage Alley, the Mint, Southwark, London, chairmaker (1787). Living in a house rented from James Bates, cm. [GL, Sun MS vol. 340, p. 496]

Gough, —, 13 Wharton's Ct, Holborn, London, toy and cm (c. 1790). Trade card states that he 'Makes Spring Guns and Pistols of various Sizes and Prices likewise all sorts of Mahogany and Kitchen furniture as Chairs, Buroes, Commodes, Bason Stands, Glasses, Chests of Drawers Etc'. [Heal]

Gough, —, 101 High St, Worcester, cm and u (1822). [D]

Gough, Abraham, Horse fair, Bristol, cm (1792–93). [D]

Gough, Benjamin, Walsall St, Wolverhampton, Staffs., chairmaker (1818). [D]

Gough, James, Piccadilly, London, carver and gilder and manufacturer of composition ornaments (1785–93). At 19 Piccadilly until 1789 but from 1790 at 219. Bankrupt 1793. Patronised by Lord Howard of Audley End, Essex, 1786–87. For the period 2 June to 5 August 1786 his purchases totalled £70 14s 10d from which a discount of £8 3s 6d was allowed. Two large picture frames cost £13 15s 7½d each, while a glass frame 'in Burnish gold & silver with inrichments containing 21 feet 2 inces at 8s' cost £8 9s 4d. The largest item was however '398 feet 6 in of Broad Hollow Mould^g in best Burnish gold' costing in total

£16 12s 1d. Accounts in the following year included 'a large sq. frame in Burnish gold & silver' at £11 17s 6d and sundry other items totally £17 13s. The business operated by James Gouch was of respectable size from the onset of trading and in 1785 he insured his stock for £500. [D; GL, Sun MS vol. 328, p. 145; Bailey's list of bankrupts; Essex RO, D/DBy/A44/10, A45/3, A45/8, A46/4]

Gough, John, Ogle St, St Marylebone, London, cm (1774–84). Freeman of Bristol. [Bristol poll bks]

Gough, Richard, Bromyard, Herefs., cm and furniture broker (1830). [D]

Gough, Thomas, Hillgate, Stockport, Cheshire, cm and joiner (1816). [D]

Gough, Thomas, Stafford St, Wolverhampton, Staffs., chairmaker (1816). [D]

Gough, Thomas, Liverpool, cm (1732). [Poll bk]

Gough, William, London, upholder (1721). Son of Thomas Gough of Salop, Gent. App. to Nathanial Derret on 6 September 1708 but 'by consent served his time with Wm. Wood Citizen & Girdler of London by Trade an Upholder'. Free of the Upholders' Co., 15 November 1721. [GL, Upholders' Co. records]

Gough, William, London, cm, u, stationer and paper hanging manufacturer (1778–90). Free of the Upholders' Co. under the terms of the 1750 Upholders' Act, 4 October 1780. He was however trading at least two years earlier from 6 Gt Bell Alley. In association with Leonard Hatton he insured a warehouse, utensils and stock for £700 in 1778. His trade at this date was stated to be cm and u. From 1787 a new address at 6 Aldgate was used but he also operated part of his business from 22 New St, Bishopsgate St which was described as warehouse and offices and together with the stock there was insured for £700. [D; GL, Sun MS vol. 268, p. 37; vol. 343, p. 405; Upholders' Co. records]

Gough, William, 69 Houndsditch, London, cabinet, upholstery and patent engine bedstead warehouse (1784–90). [D]

Gough, William, Henry St, Chester, cm (1838). Free 25 July 1838. [Freemen rolls]

Gouiett, J., 52 Foley St, Cavendish Sq., London, picture frame maker (1823–25). [D]

Goulburn, John, 6 Edge St, Manchester, cm (1817). [D]

Gould, Henry, 78 Gracechurch St, London, u (1782–95). At the same period William Gould was trading from the same address as an upholder, cm and looking-glass manufacturer. [D]

Gould, John, 'The Three Nunns', parish of St Olave, Southwark, London, u (1724). Took out insurance cover on the goods and merchandise in his dwelling house in 1724 for £500. [GL, Sun MS vol. 19, ref. 35042]

Gould, Samuel, parish of St Giles-in-the-Fields, London, chairmaker (1722–23). In 1722 took as app. John Kemp from Sherborne, Dorset for seven years at a premium of £10. In this and the following year he was employed by a committee appointed to superintend the repair and enlargement of Hicks Hall, and for them provided twelve walnut chairs costing £1 8s 8d. [Dorset RO, D204/SC62; Winterthur, Delaware, Symonds Papers, 75x69.29]

Gould, Thomas, London, upholder (1699). Free of the Upholders' Co., 5 July 1699. [GL, Upholders' Co. records]

Gould, William, 78 Gracechurch St, London, upholder, cm, glass grinder and looking-glass manufacturer (1758–1812). Son of John Gould of the parish of St Botolph, Aldgate, lighterman. App. to George Kemp on 24 June 1758 and free of the Upholders' Co. by servitude, 3 July 1765. The business was conducted after 1795 in partnership with his son William. The father was still active in the business as late as

1812. [D; GL, Upholders' Co. records, Sun MS vol. 457, ref. 875460]

Gould, William & Son, 78 Gracechurch St, London, carvers and gilders, looking-glass manufactory (1781–1840). William Gould jnr was app. to his father on 4 July 1781 and free of the Upholders' Co. by servitude, 6 August 1788. The partnership is first mentioned in directories in 1796. A pier glass in the Adam style decorated with a Wedgwood plaque and a blue and gold decorative panel and bearing the label of 'Gould & Son' is recorded. Chinoiserie chimney glass [sold Sotheby's, 26 June 1959, lot 181] bears label on back which reads: 'Gould & Son's, Looking & Coach Glass Manufactory, No. 78, 6 Church Street, London. Wholesale and for Exportation.' (illus.). The business was a substantial one and insurance cover on stock and utensils in 1812 amounted to £1,500. [D; GL, Upholders' Co. records; Sun MS vol. 457, ref. 875460; C. Life, 31 May 1962, supplement, p. 32]

Gould, William, Bristol, cm and u (1809–12). At Nelson St 1809–10, but in 1812 at 20 College Green. [D]

Gould, William, 12 Gilbert St, Clare Mkt, London, cm and u (1827). [D]

Gould, William, 31 Gloucester St, Hoxton, London, cm and u (1839). [D]

Goulden, —, 10 Queen St, Edgware Rd, London, cm (1809). [D]

Goulden, Henry, parish of St Margaret, Canterbury, Kent, cm (1818). [Poll bk]

Goulden, James, parish of St Mildred, Canterbury, Kent, cm (1830). [Poll bk]

Goulden, John, York St, Leeds, Yorks., cm (1817). [D]

Goulden, John, Howden, Yorks., joiner and cm (1823–34). At Bridgegate in 1823 but in 1834 at St John's St. [D]

Goulden, John, Canterbury, Kent, cm (1826–38). In the parish of St Mildred, June 1826, but in 1838 at Kingsbridge. [D; poll bk]

Goulden (or Gounden), Michael, Altrincham, Cheshire, cm (1781–93). [D]

Goulden, Thomas, Canterbury, Kent, u (1794–1830). At Westgate in 1796 but in July 1830 in the parish of St George. [Poll bks]

Goulden, William, Canterbury, Kent, chairmaker (1805–39). Shown at Borough, 1805–09, and the parish of St George in 1818. From 1823 at 4 St Peter's St but from 1832 took additional premises at 18 Church St. [D; poll bks]

Gouldie, James, 27 Ranelagh St, Liverpool, cm and u (1805–c. 1820). Trade card [Landauer Coll., MMA, NY] describes his trade as 'Cabinet, Grecian Couch & Chair Manufacturer' with residence at 27 Ranelagh St and manufactory at Mitchell Pl., Ranelagh St. In 1805 he signed the supplement to the *Liverpool Cabinet and Chair Prices* on behalf of the journeymen. An 1823 directory lists the firm of Gouldie & Logan at 32 Naylor St, a veneer sawmill. [D]

Goulding, J., 11 Leonard St, Shoreditch, London, upholder and chair stuffer (1817). [D]

Goulding, John, Finsbury, London, u and cm (1826–39). At 39 Paul St, 1826–29, but by 1835 had moved to 9 Wilson St. [D]

Goulding, John, 9 Holywell Row, London, cm (1829). [D]

Goulding, Richard, near Broker Row, Moorfields, London, u (1781). In 1781 took out insurance cover of £100 of which £57 was in respect of utensils, stock and goods. [GL, Sun MS vol. 293, p. 578]

Goulding, Timothy, Brompton, London, upholder (1738–98). Son of John Goulding of Swindon, Wilts., farmer. App. to William Greer on 5 April 1738 and free of the Upholders' Co. by servitude, 6 February 1755. Should have been Master of the Co. in 1787 but S. Swaine was elected as a special honour and Goulding refused a second term as Senior Warden. Took

Edward Chase as app., 1755–62. [GL, Upholders' Co. records]

Goulding, William, 8 Houndsditch, London, (1809). [D]

Goulds, William Ellis, 19 Moorgate St, London, looking-glass manufacturer (1839). [D]

Gouldthorpe, John, 5 Gt Underbank, Stockport, Cheshire, cm (1837). [D]

Gourley, John, Gt Yarmouth, Norfolk, cm (1776). In 1776 took out insurance cover of £200 of which £50 was in respect of a workshop. [GL, Sun MS vol. 246, p. 476]

Gouthier, Charles Francis, 14 Berwick St, London, carver and gilder (1777). In 1777 insured his house for £400. [GL, Sun MS vol. 256, p. 197]

Govan, James, Portsmouth, Hants., cm (d. 1767). In 1767 died intestate. [Hants. RO]

Gove, John, Exeter, Devon, cm and u (d. 1822–40). At Mary Arches St, 1822–25, and South St, 1827–30. An address at Holloway St recorded in 1828 may be his dwelling house. From 1830 the business operated at Bartholomew Yd, Bartholomew St. Three sons bapt., 1825–34. [D; PR (bapt.); freemen rolls]

Gove, John Lowton, parish of St Mary Major, Exeter, Devon, cm (1780). App. to his father Joseph Gove snr. [Freemen rolls]

Gove, Joseph snr, parish of St Mary Major, Exeter, Devon, cm (1780–1802). Had two sons who followed him in the trade, Joseph jnr and John Lowton. The former was free by patrimony 1802 and the latter app. to his father 1780. [Freemen rolls]

Gove, Joseph jnr, Exeter, Devon, cm (1802–16). In 1802–03 in the parish of Holy Trinity. Free in 1802 by patrimony. By 1816 in Magdalen St. [D; freemen rolls; Militia Census]

Gove, Robert, Exeter, Devon, cm (d. 1822). Died 1822 aged 71 'formerly a respectable cabinet maker of this city'. [*The Alfred*, 12 March 1822]

Gove, William, Magdalen St, Exeter, Devon, cm (1791–96). [D]

Gover, John, London, stringing maker (1793). Subscribed to Sheraton's *Drawing Book*, 1793.

Gover, John, Crediton, Devon, turner and chairmaker (1823). [D]

Govis, William, Lyme Regis, Dorset, cm (1840). Robson's *Directory* of 1840 shows both William Govis at Middle Row, and Govis & Son at Pound St.

Gow, Alexander, London, cm (1808–11). At 4 Holles St, Clerkenwell in 1808 and 3 Mercer St, Long Acre in 1811. [D]

Gow, John, Ipswich, Suffolk, cm (d. 1834). Will proved at Norwich 1834. [Norfolk Record Soc., index of wills]

Gower, Daniel, Hull, Yorks., cm and u (1831–40). At 2 Saville St in 1831 and 3 New Garden St, 1837–39. One directory in 1838 and another in the following year use the Christian name David. Listed as Daniel Gower at 3 New Garden St in 1840. [D]

Gower, Edward, Bridgnorth, Salop, cm (1822–40). In 1822 and 1828 at Listerly St, and in 1840 in High St. In 1840 the business is described as Gower & Powell. [D]

Gower, Thomas, 32 King St, Snowhill, London, carver and gilder (1802). [D]

Gower & Powell, High St, Bridgnorth, Salop, cm (1835). [D]

Gowing, James, 2 Cannon Row, Westminster, London, cm and u (1835–39). [D]

Gowing, Ralph, Ripon, Yorks., cm and joiner (1828–37). At King St, 1828–30, but at High Skellgate, 1834–37. [D]

Gowland, Sunderland, Co. Durham, cm (1803). Subscribed to Sheraton's *Cabinet Dictionary*, 1803.

Goy, George, London, cm (1796–1802). Married Elizabeth Pyle, former maidservant to Thomas Haig, partner in Chippendale & Co. Haig left her £100 in his will which was proved in 1803. [PRO, Prob. 11/1394, fo. 536]

Goyer, Benjamin, Newman St, Oxford St, London, carver and gilder (1808–09). In 1808 at 42 Newman St but in 1809 at no. 41. [D]

Goyer, John, 42 Duke St, St James's, London, cm and u (1809). [D]

Goyer, Philip, 21 Cumberland St, London, carver and gilder (1778). In 1778 took out insurance cover for £200 of which £80 covered utensils and stock. [GL, Sun MS vol. 266, p. 613]

Gozna, John, 16 Long Acre, London, cm (1778–93). In 1778 insured his house for £100. Subscribed to Sheraton's *Drawing Book*, 1793. [GL, Sun MS vol. 269, p. 491]

Graburn, William, Barton-on-Humber, Lincs., joiner, carpenter, wheelwright and cm (1825). In partnership with John Hall. Also made bricks and tiles and dealt in timber. [*Lincs. Archivist's Report*, no. 7, p. 29]

Grace, Henry, address unknown, gilder (1820). Worked for Charles William Vane, Marquess of Londonderry in the furnishing of Wynyard Park, Co. Durham. [Durham RO, D/LO/E 492]

Grace, James, 51 Pitt St, Liverpool, chairmaker (1781). [D]

Grace, William, Kirkgate, Wakefield, Yorks., carver and gilder (1830–37). [D]

Gracey, —, 3 Crown St, Finsbury Sq., London, looking-glass manufacturer, carver and gilder. A girandole mirror, probably late 18th-century has been noted with the trade label of this maker. He also repolished and silvered old glasses. [V & A archives]

Gracey, William, 3 St John's Ct, Cow Lane, West Smithfield, London, cm (1784). Took out insurance cover of £300 which included £100 for utensils, stock and goods. [GL, Sun MS vol. 322, p. 479]

Gradon, Thomas, address unknown, carpenter (1812). Made a bedstead for the servants' hall, Streatlam, Co. Durham. [Durham RO, D/Dt/V 352]

Gradwell, John, 75 Shaw's Brow, Liverpool, u and cm (1839). [D]

Grafer, E., 57 Kingsland Rd, London, bedstead maker (1837). [D]

Graham, Mr, St Paul's Churchyard, London, upholder and cm (1768). Report that his shop window had been 'broke open and robbed of several Pieces of Morines and check' appeared in *Public Advertiser*, 26 July 1768. Probably Joseph Graham & partners.

Graham, Christopher, address unknown, (1803). Subscribed to Sheraton's *Cabinet Dictionary*, 1803. A stool has been noted stamped 'C. GRAHAM'. [V & A archives]

Graham, F., address unknown, cm (1803). Subscribed to Sheraton's *Cabinet Dictionary*, 1803.

Graham, Frederick Henry, London, cm, u and broker (1820–32). At Red Cross St, Southwark, 1820–28. On 13 March 1822 he took out insurance cover for £1,100 which included £450 for stock, utensils and goods, £50 for a workshop adjoining the house and £20 for a shed in the yard. In the early 1830s in partnership with Samuel Harrison at Newington Causeway. It was this address that was used in connection with the notification of bankruptcy in March 1832. [D; GL, Sun MS vol. 490, ref. 989825; *Liverpool Mercury*, 9 March 1832]

Graham, J., Abbey St, Carlisle, Cumb., joiner and cm (1810). [D]

Graham, James, 3 King's Ct, Lombard St, London, u (1821–23). [D]

Graham, James, 12 Milk St, London, u (1823). [D]

Graham, James, 35 Gerrard St, Soho, London, u (1835). [D]

Graham, Jane, Liverpool, u (1835–37). At 10 Blair St, 1835–37, but in 1837 moved to 19 Blake St. [D]

Graham, John, Newcastle and London, u (1774–80). App. to

George West and free as an u, 15 October 1774. Recorded living in London, 1774–80, and may the John Graham who entered into the partnership with William Litchfield in 1781. [Newcastle freemen reg. and poll bks]

Graham, John, 72 St Martin's Lane, London, u (1809–16). Partner with William Litchfield in the firm of Graham & Litchfield which traded from this address, 1781–1809. Successor to this business, which was of a very substantial nature, with insurance in 1809 amounting to £6,000. This covered the dwelling house, warehouse, shop and sheds 'being four houses laid into one'. Stock, utensils and goods held in trust were insured for £4,000 of this total. No feather stores were maintained on the premises but a pipe stove for drying feathers was permitted in the warehouse. The business premises were situated on the corner of Long Acre. Part of the property appears to have been in Long Acre for in 1812, when the insurance was renewed, no. 1 Long Acre was specified as the dwelling house, rented from the Bedford estate, and no. 2 Long Acre was also being used. Cover on stock and utensils in 1812 had fallen to £3,000. [D; GL, Sun MS vol. 448, ref. 836351; vol. 459, refs 867098, 867099, 867254]

Graham, John snr, Abbey St, Carlisle, Cumb., joiner and cm (1810–29). [D]

Graham, John, Liverpool, cm (1827–39). At 21 Lionel St with a house at 29 Trowbridge St in 1824. For most of the remainder of the life of the business it traded from Cumberland St, the numbers being 37 in 1827, 33 in 1837 and 36 in 1839. For 1835 however, an address at 6 St James St North is shown. [D]

Graham, John, Eaglesfield St, Maryport, Cumb., joiner and cm (1828). [D]

Graham, John, Corn Market, Wigton, Cumb., joiner/cm (1829). [D]

Graham, John jnr, Bacchus Walk, Carlisle, Cumb., cm/joiner (1834). [D]

Graham, John, High Wycombe, Bucks., cm (1839). [PR (marriage)]

Graham, Joseph, Lancaster, chairmaker (1764–68). Free 1764–65. [Freemen rolls; poll bk]

Graham, Joseph & partners, London, cm and u (1767–1829). This business started by Joseph Graham involved various other members of the family in partnership. It operated from 7 St Paul's Churchyard, 1767–1814, and then the number changed to 3 for the period 1816–19. On 17 January 1820 the business opened at a new location in the West End at 5 and 6 Waterloo Pl., Pall Mall. Joseph Graham, the founder of the business, was the son of John Graham of Abingdon, Berks., an apothecary. He was app. to Charles Stanton, 10 October 1755 and was free of the Upholders' Co. by servitude, 2 June 1763. In 1797 he became Master of the Upholders' Co. He was in sole control of his furniture manufacturing business until 1798 when he took his son John into partnership and from this year the business is referred to as Graham & Son. John was app. to his father, 2 April 1788 and free of the Upholders' Co. by servitude, 6 December 1797.

By 1814 a Nathaniel Graham was involved in the business signing receipts for payments. By 1819 he was recognised as a partner and the business is listed as Joseph & Nathaniel Graham with no further mention of John. This poses the question whether there was a Joseph Graham jnr? Nathaniel stayed with the business until at least 1825, but for the years 1827–28 directories show a carpet manufacturer of this name operating from Regent St. Significantly the last directory entry for the Waterloo Place business is in the name of Joseph Graham only. The number of recorded patrons suggests that the business was of significance, though perhaps only of modest size. Only three apps of Joseph Graham are known:

William Bayley, 1771–80; Richard White, 1778–86; and his son John Graham. He did however take out licences to employ eight non-freemen for six weeks in 1776 and ten non-freemen for twelve weeks in the following year. The only insurance material located is a modest £500 cover for the house and workshop at 7 St Paul's Churchyard in 1780. In common with other members of the trade, he would buy in materials and finished articles to satisfy customer demand. In 1795 he is recorded purchasing from Kennet & Kidd, cm and u of New Bond St a 3ft field bed and bedding amounting to £7 8s. Graham subscribed to both Sheraton's *Drawing Book* 1793, and *Cabinet Dictionary*, 1803. The death of Joseph's wife is recorded in 1792. [D; *Times*, 11 January 1820; GL, Upholders' Co. records; GL, Sun MS vol. 287, p. 446; City Licence bks, vol. 9; PRO C114/181; journal 3, p. 207; *Gents Mag.*, March 1792] See Graham, —. Known patrons and commissions of this business are:

MERSHAM-LE-HATCH, Ashford, Kent, In June 1771 Sir Edward Knatchbull paid Graham £51 14s. [Kent RO, U951 A19/2]

CUSWORTH HALL, Yorks. John Battie paid £22 2s on 2 August 1771 for six library chairs, two carpets and two screens. [Leeds archives dept, Battie-Wright MS A/165]

GLOUCESTER PL., PORTMAN SQ., London or **ELMLEY CASTLE,** Worcs. In March 1813 supplied to Robert Clavering Savage a folding library ladder painted white at £2 2s. Payment was received a year later. [Worcs. RO, 4600/705:550/763/3]

GORHAMBURY, St Albans, Herts. Payments were made to Graham from July 1775 to February 1776. In 1775 £41 16s 6d was paid in March and £14 6s in July. [Herts. RO, accounts XI 63]

HEATON HALL, Manchester. Invoices cover the period August 1775 to June 1777. On 5 August 1775 four oval back chairs, 'japan'd in variegated collors grain'd seats' with other items were charged at £11 12s. These were supplied to the order of James Wyatt, the architect of Heaton, and despatched by the Manchester waggon. On 15 June 1776 the invoice totalled £24 9s, the major item being six mahogany chairs charged at £6 15s. No further invoices are known until June 1777 when £25 2s 6d was charged. The bulk of this was for a large mahogany clothes press japanned white and green which cost £13 13s. Also included was a night table and a folding top dressing stand. [Greater Manchester RO, DDEG 41(1)]

CROOME COURT, Worcs. Furniture supplied 1778–82. This included a mahogany breakfast table in March 1778 charged at £2 2s. A more significant commission followed in 1780 which included a satinwood commode dressing table charged at £18 18s, six japanned chairs at £7 6s and a bergère chair. These items were despatched from 'The Bull Inn' by Harn's Worcester waggon direct to Croome. In the following year a large mahogany bookcase was invoiced in July costing £13 13s and a 4ft chest of drawers charged at £6 16s 6d. A large gilt pier glass was the major item supplied in August 1782 on an invoice totalling £13 13s. [V & A archives]

MOCCAS COURT, Herefs. or **STANHOPE ST, LONDON.** On 30 May 1783 payment of £4 14s 6d was made by Sir George Cornewall for a dressing glass for Lady Cornewall. [Herefs. RO, Moccas J56/IV/3]

VINTNER'S HALL, London. In February 1799 repairs were executed to the frame of a pier glass in the State Room for which £2 2s was charged. [V & A archives]

CHARLECOTE PARK, Warks. In 1827 supplied an 'ebony Queen Elizabeth sofa covered in crimson damask' costing £105 out of a total for the invoice of £109 7s 6d. [V & A archives]

OTHER COMMISSIONS. On 5 May 1781 Lord Monson paid £100 on account to Graham & Co. [Lincoln RO, Monson 10/1/A/6] In April and July 1823 furniture was supplied to Lord Gwydir. In April three bamboo maple wood French bedsteads with poles were charged at £5 5s each and a French polished one at £12 12s, the invoice totalling with other items £31 5s. In July a further maple wood French bedstead was charged at £5 5s with a packing charge of 15s. [Lincoln RO, 2/ANC 6/202/18] B.A.

Graham, Joseph, Main St, Cockermouth, Cumb., cm/joiner (1834). [D]

Graham, Joseph, 35 Gerrard St, London, cm and u (1839). [D]

Graham, T. D. & T., 9–11 Grove St North, Liverpool, cm (1834). [D]

Graham, Thomas, Newgate St, Newcastle, joiner and cm (1796). In October 1796 indicated his intention 'to decline keeping a front shop' and as a consequence offered the 'large quantity of Furniture on Hand' at reduced prices. [*Newcastle Courant*, 29 October 1796]

Graham, Thomas, Liverpool, u and victualler (1804–39). In 1804 at 20 Union St, Oldhall Rd; in 1824 at 20 Shaw's Brow; in 1827 at Ironmonger Lane and 7 Pellaw St; in 1829 at 8 Garden Lane; in 1837 at 27 Tenderden St; and in 1839 at 80 Bostock St. [D]

Graham, Thomas, 37 Pavement, York, cm etc. (1840). [D]

Graham, William, 5 Chorley St, Water St, Liverpool, cm (1796). [D]

Graham, William, 48 Threadneedle St, London, cm and u (1808–22). [D]

Graham, William, Crakehall, Yorks., joiner and cm (1823). [D]

Graham, William, 1 Angel Ct, Throgmorton St, London, u (1823–27). [D]

Graham, William, Liverpool, cm (1823–39). At 47 Gt Crosshall St in 1823 where he had a shop and yard. In the period 1824–29 the number is 44; in 1835, 41–42; and in 1837, 17. Other addresses shown are 90 Byrom St in 1834 and 110 Brownlow Hill in 1839. [D]

Graham, William, 46 Foley St, London, cm and u (1827). [D]

Graham, William, Dalston, Carlisle, Cumb., joiner and cm (1828). [D]

Graham, William, Spring Garden Lane, Sunderland, Co. Durham, joiner and cm (1828). [D]

Graham, William, 22 Clipstone St, Gt Portland St, cm and u (1835–39). [D]

Graham & Boardman, 30 Fleming's Sq., Blackburn, Lancs., carvers and gilders (1824–28). [D]

Graham & Co., 294 High Holborn, London, u and cm (1835–37). [D]

Graham & Farrer, Northgate, Bradford, Yorks., cm (1828). [D]

Graham & Litchfield, See Litchfield & Graham, and John Graham.

Graham & Son, Greek St, Soho, London, carvers and gilders (1800–08). At 16 Greek St in 1800 but from 1801 at 18. [D]

Grainge, John, Butcher Row, Abingdon, Berks., cm (1823–40). Between 1830–40 moved to Boar St. [D]

Grainger, —, Snow Hill, London, u (1734). [Heal]

Grainger, George, parish of St Swithin, Worcester, cm (1747). [Poll bk]

Grainger, John, 26 Smallbrook St, Birmingham, cm and u (1830). [D]

Grainger, Thomas, Clare St, Bristol, cm and u (1793–98). Subscribed to Sheraton's *Drawing Book*, 1793. Bankrupt March 1798 and his stock sold off in April. On offer was cabinet furniture, paper hangings and carpeting. [*Exeter Flying Post*, 22 March 1798; *Farley's Bristol Journal*, 21 April 1798]

Gramlick, William, London, upholder (1774–86). Son of John Gramlick of St Margaret Moses, London, sugar refiner. App. to Robert Phipps, 4 June 1767, and free of the Upholders' Co. by servitude, 6 July 1774. In the period 1774–78 at Snow Hill but by 1780 bankrupt. In 1786 living at Castle Lane Park, Southwark. [GL, Upholders' Co. records; *Gents Mag.*, November 1780]

Gramshaw, John, London, carver (1774–84). In 1774 at Woodstock Ct and in 1784 at Blenheim St, Hanover Sq. [Westminster poll bks]

Grange, Charles, 'The Royal Bed', Snow Hill, London, u and cm (1710–63). Free of the Upholders' Co., 13 September 1710, and master in 1748. Took as apps William Horsley, 1717–29; Barry Johnson, 1732–40; James Grange, his son, 1740–49; William Hunter, 1741–49; Richard Wallin, 1747–54; John Stephens, 1750–58; James Wootton, 1754–62; William Pinckney, 1755–66; and Joseph Graham, 1755–63. This would seem to suggest that the business was at its most active in the 1740s and 50s. The only insurance record located is for 1723 and on 16 January of that year cover for goods and merchandise in his dwelling house was £500. Associated with Thomas Cooke, who in 1746 advertised his intention of going into partnership with 'Mr Nash at the Royal Bed, Holbourn-Bridge'. Thus Grange is associated with Cooke in the furnishing of the new Mansion House. Trade card [Heal Coll., BM] with a fine Rococo frame, shows that in the latter years of the business he took his son James into partnership. At this period Charles Grange & Son offered 'all Sorts of Four Post & Standing Beds ... Feather Beds, Chairs, Tables, Glasses, Bureaus, Chests of Drawers, Carpets, Quilts, Blankets, Damasks. Harrateens &c' also a 'Variety of Paper Hangings & Furniture Checks'. They also acted as undertakers. By 1767 James Grange was trading on his own account from 96 High Holborn. [D; GL, Upholders' Co. records; Sun MS vol. 16, ref. 30965; *Conn.*, December 1952, p. 181; Heal]

Grange, James, 96 High Holborn, London, u and cm (1740–83). Son of Charles Grange who operated an extensive business as an u, 1710–63, from an address in Snow Hill, James was app. to his father on 13 September 1740 and free of the Upholders' Co. by servitude, 3 August 1749; master of the Co. in 1783. He was in partnership with his father by the early 1760s and responsible for some of the apps. The following were trained by James Grange: John Mills, 1760–68; Noah Chivers, 1765–70; William Shore, 1767–69; Samuel Ford, 1768–80; and John Walsh, 1770–84. From 1773 in partnership with John Mills, the business being referred to as Grange & Mills. At this period the trade was probably on an extensive scale and in 1777 utensils, stock and goods held in trust were insured for £1,800. The partnership probably ended in 1779 and in the following year James Grange's name was the only one appearing on the insurance policy. Utensils, stock and goods in trust were now insured for only £880. [D; GL, Upholders' Co. records; Sun MS vol. 261, p. 314; vol. 286, p. 422]

Grange, M. & R., Turners Hill, Cheshunt, Herts., u (1838). [D]

Grange, Samuel, High Wycombe, Bucks., chairmaker (1798). [D]

Grange, Susanna, Boar St, Abingdon, Berks., cm and u (1840). [D]

Granger, Hugh, 'The Carved Angel', Aldermanbury, London, cm (1692–1706). In 1692 was churchwarden of St Mary's Church, Aldermanbury. Ceased trading in 1706 when he advertised that his stock 'may be bought of Cabinet Work & Glasses; the House being let to another trade & must be cleared of all the goods in as little time as possible can be. Monday 27th August the sale will begin'. Trade label depicting his shop sign and announcing that 'Fashionable

Household Goods at Reasonable rates' were made by him has been found pasted to a number of items of late 17th-and early 18th-century furniture. Two chests of drawers lavishly decorated with panels of floral marquetry, a walnut secretaire cabinet with fall front, a bureau cabinet, the doors fronted with looking-glass and the interior decorated with raised gilt scenes on a red japanned ground, a walnut writing table and a walnut bureau are amongst items so marked. [Heal; *Daily Courant*, 24 August 1706; V & A archives; Sotheby's, 15 June 1951, 6 May 1955, 5 October 1973; Wills, *English Furniture 1550–1760*, p. 190]

Granger, Thomas, Boston, Lincs., cm and chairmaker (1788). On 7 March 1788 advertised for a 'Journeyman PIN CHAIR-MAKER' and a chair bottomer. [*Lincoln, Rutland and Stamford Mercury*, 7 March 1788]

Grant, Alexander, St James's, London, cm (1770). Declared bankrupt, *Gents Mag.*, January 1770.

Grant, Ellen, 22 Bevington Bush, Liverpool, u (1837). [D]

Grant, James, Lancaster (1838–40). [Westminster Ref. Lib., Gillow records]

Grant, John, London, cm and u (1822–39). At 1 Ryders Ct, Leicester Sq., 1822–29, according to London directories. An insurance record of June 1823 however gives the number as 19 Ryders Ct in Cranbourn St. Cover for £900 was taken out of which £200 was for utensils and stock. From 1835–39 the address is given as 20 Cranbourn St. [D; GL, Sun MS vol. 498, ref. 1005758]

Grant, John & Anderson, Christopher, Hallgate (or Hall Garth), Hexham, Northumb., joiners and cm (1827–34). [D]

Grant, John W., 2–5 Castle St, Long Acre, London, cm and u (1835–39). [D]

Grant, Joseph, Bristol, cm (1774–1801). In 1775 at 23 Church St but 1799–1801 in Old Park. [D; poll bks]

Grant, Joseph, Bristol, cm undertaker, appraiser and auctioneer (1818–40). From 1818–23 at Frogmore St, though from 1822–23 also at 1 Upper Culver St. From 1834–40 at Host St. [D]

Grant, Peter, Brighton, Sussex, cm and u (1832–39). At 125 St James's St in 1832 and Old Steyne St in 1839. [D]

Grant, Robert, 30 John St, Blackfriars, London, cm, u and undertaker (1839). [D]

Grant, Thomas, Market Drayton, Salop, upholder and auctioneer (1784). [D]

Grant, W., London, cm (1793). Subscribed to Sheraton's *Drawing Book*, 1793.

Grant, W., 61 Mortimer St, Cavendish Sq., London, upholder and undertaker (1817–21). [D]

Grant, W., 20 Jermyn St, London, cm and auctioneer (1835). [D]

Grant, W., George Yd, Princes St, Soho, London, u (1835). [D]

Grant, Walter, Bristol, cm (1774). [Poll bk]

Grant, William, London, u (1761). Freeman of Canterbury. [Canterbury poll bk]

Grant, William, Norwich and Hardingham, Norfolk, cm (1784–1807). At Colney in 1784, parish of St Andrew, 1786–1802, and Hardingham, Norfolk, 1806–07. [Norwich poll bks]

Grant, William, 386 Oxford St, London, u (1806–16). [D]

Grant, William, 3 Castle St, Long Acre, London, cm (1826). [D]

Grant, William, St James's, London, cm (1832). Bankrupt 25 May 1832. [*Liverpool Mercury*, 1 June 1832]

Grant, William, 34 Brewer St, Golden Sq., London, cm, u and undertaker (1839). [D]

Grant, Zachariah, Westham, Essex, u (d. by 1712). His son was app. in 1712. Father then noted as 'deceased'. [S of G, app. index]

Grant & Hurley, 226 Piccadilly, London, u (1806–15). [D]

Grantham, George, 34 New St, Brighton, Sussex, turner, basket, chair and seive maker (1799–1800). [D]

Grantham, John, parish of St Thomas, Winchester, Hants., upholder (1701–27). On 10 June 1701 married Frances Little of Oxford. Had premises described as a dwelling house in High St, Winchester and on 30 August 1727 took out insurance cover on household goods and stock in trade for £400. [Bodleian index of Oxf. marriage bonds; GL, Sun MS vol. 25, ref. 42422]

Grantham, John, 57 Upper Moorfields, London, cm (1790–93). [D]

Grantham, John, 22 Kirby St, Hatton Gdn, London, cm (1808). [D]

Grantham, John, 1 William Walk, Old St Rd, Shoreditch, London, cm (1808–11). In 1811 took out insurance cover for £300 of which £200 was in respect of stock and utensils. [D; GL, Sun MS vol. 452, ref. 858385]

Grantham, John, Southampton St, Camberwell, London, cm and u (1826). [D]

Granville, Robert, 99 Fore St, Devonport, Devon, cm and u (1838). [D]

Grassam, John, (Gt) Driffield, Yorks., cm and broker (1818–40). In Middle St 1823–28, but from 1831–40 in Market Pl., though a directory of 1834 still records the Middle St address and it is possible that both premises were used in the early 1830s. In July 1818 took as app. Joseph Fendeman of Beverley, Yorks. [D; Hull app. reg.]

Grassey, Stephen, Wolverhampton, Staffs., carver, gilder and silversmith (1834–38). At Piper's Row in 1834 but from 1834–38 at Queen St, no. 42 in 1838. Sold looking-glasses, barometers and thermometers, traded as a jeweller and dealt in paintings. [D]

Grateford, —, the sign of 'The Castle', south side of St Paul's Churchyard, London, cane chairmaker (1714). [GL, Sun MS vol. 3, ref. 3905]

Gratrix, Robert, 18 Gregson St, Manchester, cm (1817). [D]

Graupner, Peter, London, cm (1777–93). At 12 Little Chapel St, Soho in 1777 where he took out insurance cover of £200, half of which was in respect of utensils and stock. By 1779 at 33 Greek St with the insurance cover raised to £500 of which £300 was for utensils and stock. [D; GL, Sun MS vol. 256, p. 618; vol. 276, p. 79]

Gravel, Robert, 28 Warwick St, Golden Sq., London, carver and gilder (1809–25). Trade card [Banks Coll., BM] indicates that he manufactured looking-glass and picture frames. In November 1810 paid £21 6s 6d by the 2nd Lord Braybrooke of Audley End, Essex. [D; Essex RO, D/DBy/A376]

Graveley, J. Name branded on bottom of brass-inlaid cabinet, *c.* 1735, illus. *V & A Bulletin*, January 1965, p. 15.

Graveley, Michael, Davies St, Westminster, London, u (1712–49). Son of Edmond Graveley of Halton, Yorks., grazier. App. to Remey George, 15 April 1712, and free of the Upholders' Co. by servitude, 9 September 1719. [GL, Upholders' Co. records; poll bk]

Gravell, S., 8 Jewin St, Cripplegate, London, carver and gilder (1835).

Gravell, Thomas, 61 Jewin St, Cripplegate, London, carver, gilder and looking-glass warehouse (1823–39). [D]

Gravenor, James, Derby, carver (1763–68). Known in connection with his work at Kedleston Hall, Derbs., for Sir Nathaniel Curzon. Here he carved columns, door cases and mirror frames for the Drawing Room and pier glasses with oak leafed frames and ornamental detail for an organ case for the Music Room. His greatest achievement is however the fine palm tree bed for the State Bedroom on the west front which he completed in 1768. The posts are carved to resemble the trunks of palms with gilt leaves. The same theme is repeated in a pair of palm tree candlesticks for a dressing table, some chairs and two pier glasses in the same room and a large palm tree mirror in the Dressing Room. [*Conn.*, July 1978, pp. 203–04 and 207; *C. Life*, 2 February 1978, p. 264, 9 February 1978]

Gravenor, John, London, u (1690–1730). In 1690 at 'The Bear & Ragged Staff', Cornhill, next to Stocks Mkt. Later he moved to 'The Royal Bed & Chair' in Gt Rider St, St James's where in 1730 a sale of furniture stock was advertised. [Heal]

Graves, Isaac Smith, Bishopsgate St, London, cm and u (1781–93). Son of Mark Graves of the parish of St Mary, Lambeth, London, Gent. App. to James Surridge, turner. Free of the Upholders' Co. under the terms of the 1750 Upholders' Act, 7 February 1781. Initially went into partnership with Shipman and until 1784 traded as Graves & Shipman. After this traded on his sole account. The number in Bishopsgate is initially 54 but *c.* 1790 changed to 56. Trade card [Heal Coll., BM] indicates that he also acted as an undertaker, auctioneer and appraiser. [D; GL, Upholders' Co. records]

Graves, James, 42 Red Lion St, Clerkenwell, London, cm (1804). On 11 January 1804 took out insurance cover of £100 which included £60 for his household goods in the dwelling house of Brown, carpenter, and £20 for his chest of tools kept in the house of Bonnington, cm, at 22 Red Lion Sq. [D; GL, Sun MS vol. 430, ref. 757303]

Graves, John, 53 Rathbone Pl., London, u and cm (1809–11). [D]

Graves, Joseph, Fleet Mkt, London, upholder (1775–93). Free of the Upholders' Co. under the terms of the 1750 Upholders' Act, 2 August 1775. [D; GL, Upholders' Co. records]

Graves, Lumley, Hull, Yorks., cm etc. (1835–40). At 16 Waterhouse Lane, 1835–37, but from 1838–40 at 23 Junction Dock St. [D]

Graves, Richard, Warwick St, Golden Sq., chairmaker (1749). [Westminster poll bk]

Graves, Robert, High St, March, Cambs., carpenter, joiner and cm (1830). [D]

Graves & Hull, 399 Oxford St, London, u and chairmaker (1821). [D]

Grawe, William, 386 Oxford St, London, cm and u (1808). [D]

Gray, —, address unknown, cm (1755). Received payment of £2 10s for a walnut bureau, and £3 19s for four dressing tables and a pillar table supplied to Holkham Hall, Norfolk. [Holkham Hall accounts]

Gray, Alexander, see Richard Cope & Alexander Gray.

Gray, Charles, 191 Shoreditch, London, cm (1789). [D]

Gray, Charles, West Wycombe, Bucks., chairmaker (b. *c.* 1807–41). Aged 34 at the date of the 1841 Census.

Gray, Drummond, Chichester, Sussex, carver, gilder and print seller (1823–40). At West St, 1823–26, but by 1832 had moved to East St. [D]

Gray, George, Wardour St, Soho, London, u (1725). Took out on 30 September 1725 insurance cover of £500 on goods and merchandise in his dwelling house. [GL, Sun MS vol. 21, ref. 36830]

Gray, Henry, York, cm and u (1834–40). Recorded at 102 Micklegate, 1834–37 and 8 Davygate in 1840. [D]

Gray, Henry, Booker, High Wycombe, Bucks., chairmaker (b. *c.* 1811–41). Aged 30 at the date of the 1841 Census.

Gray, J., London, u (1793). Subscribed to Sheraton's *Drawing Book*, 1793.

Gray, James & Allsop, Thomas, address unknown, cm and brokers (1785). On 10 March 1785 took out insurance cover for £180 of which £60 was in respect of utensils, stock and goods in trust. [GL, Sun MS vol. 327, p. 438]

Gray, James, 7 South Row, Somers Town, London, cm (1808). [D]

Gray, James, London, cm (1818). Free of Chester, 1 July 1818. Address given as London. [Freemen rolls]

Gray, James, Foregate St, Chester, cm (1826). [Poll bk]

Gray, James, 95 Bunhill Row, London, furniture japanner (1829). [D]

Gray, James, Skinnersgate, Darlington, Co. Durham, joiner/cm (1834). [D]

Gray, John, opposite Sidney College, Cambridge, joiner, cm and u (1762). Stocked both new and secondhand furniture. [*Cambridge Chronicle*, 20 November 1762]

Gray, John, Piccadilly, Manchester, u (1797–1805). At 24 Piccadilly in 1797 but from 1802–05 at no. 97. [D]

Gray, John, Parade, Rochdale, Lancs., u and cm (1805–08). [D]

Gray, John, 12 Brook St, New Rd, London, cm (1809). [D]

Gray, John Godfrey, Cambridge, cm and furniture broker (1820–40). In 1820 living in the parish of St Andrew the Great. At Emmanuel St in 1830 but from 1832 living in Eden Walk. [D; poll bks; PR (bapt.)]

Gray, John, Barnes and Mortlake, Surrey, cm (1826–39). At Barnes, 1826–32, but by 1838 at Mortlake. [D]

Gray, John, Hull, Yorks., cm (1826–40). In George Yd, 1826–39, the number being 9 in 1826, 12 in 1831 and 20, 1838–40. At 11 Ocean Pl. in 1840. [D]

Gray, John, Downley, High Wycombe, Bucks., chairmaker (b. *c.* 1811–41). Aged 30 at the date of the 1841 Census.

Gray, Joseph(?), Brewer St, Westminster, London, u (1784). [Poll bk]

Gray, Joseph, Norwich, cm and u (1815–39). Free of Norwich, 21 June 1815, and by 1822 trading at Dove Lane. From 1830 recorded at Dove St and in 1836 listed as having a house at Heigham Grove. Took as app. Joshua Browne who was free 27 September 1832. [D; freemen rolls and reg.]

Gray, Joseph, 12 Brook St, New Rd, London, bedstead manufacturer (1820). [D]

Gray (or Grey), Joseph, Littlehampton, Sussex, cm (*c.* 1832). [H. J. F. Thompson, *Littlehampton Story 5 — The Early 19th Century*, 1983, pp. 57–59]

Gray, Joshua, 10 Holywell Row, Shoreditch, London, cm (1837). [D]

Gray, Palmer, London, upholder (1776–82). In 1776 at 7 Butcher Hall Lane, where he insured utensils, stock and goods for £100 out of an entire insurance cover of £700. By 1782 at 4 Bencross Almshouses, Mile End where he insured a house for £300. [GL, Sun MS vol. 247, p. 209; vol. 300, p. 375]

Gray, Richard, Bixteth St, Liverpool, cm (1835–37). At 29 Bixteth St in 1835 but in 1837 the number was 33. [D]

Gray, Richard, West Wycombe, Bucks., chairmaker (b. *c.* 1784–1841). Aged 57 at the date of the 1841 Census.

Gray, Robert, Plymouth, Devon, house carpenter and picture frame maker (1798). [D]

Gray, Robert, Norwich, cm (1801–18). At 22 Wymer St, 1801–03, but from 1805–08 at Charing Cross. [D; poll bk]

Gray, Samuel, 13 Duke St, Lincoln's Inn Fields, London, auctioneer, appraiser and u (1822–23). [D]

Gray, Samuel, Lancaster, cm (1838). App. to Leonard Redmayne in 1830 and free, 14 April 1838. Named in the Gillow records, 1832. [Freemen rolls; Westminster Ref. Lib., Gillow]

Gray, Stephen, 46 Brewer St, London, upholder (1780–87). In 1780 took out insurance cover of £2,000 of which £500 was for utensils, stock and goods. In the same year supplied Sir John Griffin Griffin of Audley End, Essex, with a large mahogany dessert tray at £1 2s with a further 2s for packing. Bankrupt 1787. [D; GL, Sun MS vol. 282, p. 84; Bailey's list of bankrupts; Essex RO, D/DBy/A38/10]

Gray, Stephen, Mortlake and Barnes, Surrey, cm and u

(1808–22). At Mortlake in 1808 and Barnes in 1822. Business carried on by John Gray, 1826–39. [D]

Gray, Thomas, Union St, Liverpool, upholder and victualler (1796–1807). At 3 Union St, 1796–1800. In 1800 moved to no. 20, and from 1805–07 traded at 2 Union St. [D]

Gray, Thomas, Manchester, chairmaker (1808–25). At 4 Thomas St in 1808, 17 High St in 1813, 44 Thomas St, 1816–17, and 33 Edge St and 4 Crown St in 1825. [D]

Gray, Thomas, 102 Micklegate, York, cm and u (1838). Successor to Henry Gray at this address. [D]

Gray, William, 'The Golden Cup', Addle St, Aldermanbury, London, turner and cm (1747). Trade card [Banks Coll., BM] states that he made 'Mohogony Tables, Chairs, Glasses and all sorts of Turner & Cabinet work'. Declared bankrupt, *General Advertiser*, 4 May 1747.

Gray, William, West Wycombe, Bucks., chairmaker (1798). [Militia Census]

Gray, William, 2 Lloyd's Ct, St Giles, London, cm (1808). [D]

Gray, William Holden, Norwich, cm and u (1817–30). App. to Holden Gray and admitted freeman on 27 September 1817. At Lower Westwick St in 1822 and Charing Cross in 1830. [D; freemen reg.]

Gray, William, Earl St, Coventry, Warks., chairmaker and turner (1818–28). Recorded also at Spon St in 1822. [D]

Gray, William, Newgate St, Bishop Auckland, Co. Durham, cm and u (1827–28). [D]

Gray, William, Downley, High Wycombe, Bucks., chairmaker (b. c. 1781–1841). Aged 60 at the date of the 1841 Census.

Gray & Co., Market St, Plymouth, Devon, u (1818). In July 1818 announced the opening of ware-rooms in Plymouth after moving from London. They offered furniture and designs for every branch of interior design and indicated that they wanted good workmen for the business. [*Exeter Flying Post* (?)]

Gray & Hall, Brighton, Sussex, cm and u (1839). In 1839 shown at both North St and 25 (or 24½) Duke St. [D]

Gray & Hull, Oxford St, London, japanned chairmakers, cm and sofa makers (1808–26). At 399 Oxford St, 1808–23, but from 1825 at 4 Newman St, Oxford St. [D]

Grayburn, John, 10 Edgar St, Hull, Yorks., cm (1838–39). [D]

Grayfoot, J., Rotherhithe, London, carver (1808–25). In 1808 at Horseferry, Rotherhithe but in the following year in partnership with Overton at Pageants, Rotherhithe. The partnership which continued until 1825 described itself as carvers and ship carvers. [D]

Graygoose (or Greygoose), —, 57 Gt Queen St, London, cm (c. 1820). A Regency mahogany architect's table and a desk, are recorded bearing the stamp of 'Graygoose, 57 Gt. Queen St'. The table was sold at Christie's, 26 May 1983, lot 68.

Grayson, Henry, Lees Ct, Red Bank Manchester, chairmaker (1813). [D]

Grayson, John, Holmfirth, Yorks., joiner/cm (1834). [D]

Grayson, Joseph, Brow Top, Workington, Cumb., joiner/cm (1811–28). [D]

Grayson, Thomas, Brow Top, Workington, Cumb., joiner/cm (1811). [D]

Grayson, William, Brow Top, Cumb., joiner/cm (1834). [D]

Grayson & Moore, Priestgate, Workington, Cumb., joiner/cm (1829). [D]

Greasley, John, Nottingham, joiner and cm (1834–40). In 1834 took app. named Edward James. Trading at High Pavement in 1840 as an u only. [D; app. bk]

Greasley, Thomas, 'The Providence Inn', Francis St, Hull, Yorks., victualler and cm (1837–40). [D]

Greatbatch, Daniel, Stoke-on-Trent and Newcastle-under-Lyme, Staffs., cm and u (1835–39). Recorded at Church St, Stoke in 1835 and 19 High St, Newcastle in 1839. [D]

Greatbatch, Henry, Church St, Stoke-on-Trent, Staffs., cm and chairmaker (1834). [D]

Greathead, Joseph, Bucklersbury, London, cm (c. 1715). [Heal]

Greathead, Matthew, Newbiggin, Richmond, Yorks., joiner and cm (1827). [D]

Greathead & Haslehurst, 25 St John's Sq., London, dealers in tortoiseshell and case makers (1790). [D]

Greatole, Thomas Charles, London, carver and gilder (1837). Shown at both 1 Knightsbridge and 6 Charles St, Grosvenor Sq. [D]

Greatrix, William, Wirksworth, Derbs., cm (1798). [D]

Greaves, —, address unknown, (1785). Supplied to Chatsworth, Derbs., '4 setts of black wood Tables' at 11s each and other items costing a total of £5 16s 8d. [Chatsworth papers, no. 75/13/10/1785]

Greaves, Elizabeth, 179 Borough, London, upholstery and carpet warehouse (1801–08). Successor to John Greaves at the same address. In 1808 the business is listed as Elizabeth Greaves & Son. [D]

Greaves, George, Lancaster, cm and mariner (1772–86). App. to R. Thorney 1772 and free 1785–86. [Lancaster app. reg. and freemen rolls]

Greaves, John, 179 Borough, London, carpet warehouse and u (1781–96). In 1781 took out insurance cover of £600 of which £450 was in respect of utensils and stock. The insurance records show the number as 199 Borough but this may be an error. The business was continued after 1801 at the same address by Elizabeth Greaves. [D; GL, Sun MS vol. 296, p. 510]

Greaves & Dore, 179 Borough, London, upholders and cm (1806–09). Successor to Elizabeth Greaves at this address. [D]

Greaves, Thomas, Cambridge, joiner (1724–d. 1750). The Cambridge Corp. common day bk records that on 2 June 1724, 'Thomas Graves Joyner' paid £5 5s for his freedom. Following the death of Cornelius Austin jnr in 1729, Greaves received regular payments from St John's College, up to his own death in 1750. At this period the accounts only give the odd detail of the work undertaken. A payment in the year 1731/32 indicates that he also worked as an u: 'T. Graves bill for Damask and work about covering chairs in ye Lodge £3. 6s. 3d.' and in 1749/50, 'Greves for two mahogany tables for the Parlour', £7. 7s. The Corp. records show that Greaves was a common councillor from 1724 and later an alderman, but on 16 August 1750 'Mr. Alderman Graves . . . having been Chosen Mayor Elect . . . Signifyed to his Corporation that by Reason of Sickness and the Great Indisposition of Body he at present Labours under, he desires to pass the Said Office'. The *Cambridge Journal and Weekly Flying Post* reported on 8 September 1750 that 'On Saturday last died . . . Mr. Greaves an eminent Carpenter and Joiner of this town'. He is known to have taken at least six apps: Isaac Morton, James Harrimore, Nicholas Mason, all made free on 11 January 1737, Golding Merrill made free January 1742, Marmaduke Whitred made free 8 January 1751 and Edward Yorke made free 17 January 1755. Thomas Greaves, u of Cambridge, took app. named Corey in 1745. Possibly father of Timothy Greaves. [Cambs. RO, Cambridge Corp. archives; archives of St John's College; S of G, app. index]

R.W.

Greaves, Timothy, Cambridge, joiner and cm (1737–55). Possibly related to Thomas Greaves. Recorded in 1737 taking the lease of a house in the parish of St Andrew. Worked for Trinity College, 1744–51, but few details are given of the work involved though he did repair a table. Worked at St John's College, 1748–49, and is probably the Greaves recorded in 1751. The two apps Marmaduke Whitred (free 8 January 1751) and Edward York (free 7 January 1755) recorded in the name of Thomas Greaves, probably received some of their training under Timothy. [Cambs. RO, Corp. common day bk, p. 343]

Greaves, William, Guisborough, Yorks., cm (1834). [D]

Greaves, William, Cross Hills, Halifax, Yorks., cm (1837). [D]

Grecian, Thomas, Sunderland, Co. Durham, cm (1803). Subscribed to Sheraton's *Cabinet Dictionary*, 1803.

Greedy, William, South St, Wellington, Som., cm (1822). [D]

Green, —, Bury St, St James's, London, u (1725–27). [Heal]

Green, —, Red Cross St, London, chair caner (d. 1740). At the time of his death in August 1740 he was master of Cripplegate workhouse but was stated to have formerly been 'a chair-caner of large dealings in Red Cross Street of that parish'. [*London Evening Post*, 19 August 1740]

Green, —, address unknown, cm (1778–92). Recorded in the accounts of Longford Castle, Wilts. In 1788 he was paid £2 10s for a bed and further small payments were made in 1779, 1781, 1783, 1784, 1786, 1787 and 1792. The largest amount was £6 12s 6d in 1786. [V & A archives]

Green, —, Ipswich, Suffolk, cm (1793). Subscribed to Sheraton's *Drawing Book*, 1793.

Green, Ann, 20 Mortimer St, London, cm, u and undertaker (1803–08). The Green at this address in the list of master cabinet makers in Sheraton's *Cabinet Dictionary*, 1803, may be Ann or her predecessor (possibly her husband). [D]

Green, Charles, Cross Keys Passage, Cheltenham, Glos., chairmaker and turner (1822). [D]

Green, Charles, Carlton, Royston, near Barnsley, Yorks., cm (1837). [D]

Green, Charles, Circus Yd, Shrewsbury, Salop, cm and u (1840). [D]

Green, Denton, Newcastle, joiner and cm (1811). In May 1811 announced that he had commenced a business above the Nun-gate. By November of the same year however he had moved to Pilgrim St. [*Newcastle Courant*, 18 May and 16 November 1811]

Green, Edward, 8 Bird St, West Sq., London, cm (1808). [D]

Green, Elias, Market Pl., Wincanton, Som., cm and u (1839). [D]

Green, Ellen, 16 Gt Richmond St, Liverpool, u (1811). [D]

Green, G., 4 Cambridge Rd, Mile End, London, carver and gilder (1829). [D]

Green, George, Sheffield, Yorks., cm (1822–37). In 1822 at Kilham Island with a house at Shales Moor. By 1828 at 3 Queen St; in 1833 at 81 Spring St; and in 1837 at 10 Workhouse Croft. [D]

Green, Henry, West Bromwich, Staffs., joiner/cm (1834). [D]

Green, Henry, 3 Court, Bell Bars Rd, Birmingham, cm (1839). [D]

Green, Henry, 14 St Mary St, Weymouth, Dorset, carver and gilder (1840). [D]

Green, J., Brandon, Suffolk, cm (1824). [D]

Green, James, Bradford, Yorks., cm and joiner (1814–18). In 1814 at Market St but in 1818 in Kirkgate. [D]

Green, James, Highcross St, Leicester, cm (1828). [D]

Green, James, 34 Gt Chart St, Hoxton New Town, London, cm and u (1839). [D]

Green, John, Salisbury, Wilts., cm (1754). Took as app. Joseph Bucket on 28 December 1754 at a premium of £17 10s. [*Wilts. Apps and their Masters*]

Green, John, Leeds(?), chairmaker (1773). Twelve Windsor chairs at 5s each and a garden seat at £1 16s were purchased by Edwin Lascelles of Harewood House, Yorks., in October 1773. [*Furn. Hist.*, 1965, 1979]

Green, John, Oxford, cm (1775). On 9 January took out insurance cover for £300 of which £20 was for utensils and

stock and a further £20 for workshops in the yard. [GL, Sun MS vol. 236, ref. 348463]

Green, John, 11 Temple Lane, London, upholder (1777). Son of John Green of Temple Lane, Whitefriars, victualler. App. to Francis Hamilton, 4 April 1777 and listed as free of the Upholders' Co., 7 May 1777. [D; GL, Upholders' Co. records]

Green, John, Prince's St, Bristol, cm (1793). [D]

Green, John, address unknown, cm (1803). Subscribed to Sheraton's *Cabinet Dictionary*, 1803.

Green, John, High St, Leicester, cm (1815). [D]

Green, John, Barnsley, Yorks., cm (1822–37). At Cheapside in 1822, Church St in 1828 and Shambles St, 1834–37. [D]

Green, John, Sheep Mkt, St Ives, Hunts., cm and u (1824–39). [D; Cambs. RO (Hunts.), deed 1677/6]

Green, John, Leicester, cm (1826). [Leicester freemen reg.]

Green, John, 52 Market St, Bradford, Yorks., cm (1830). Also had house at 64 Bridge St. [D]

Green, John, Wakefield, Yorks., cm (1834). [D]

Green, John, Liverpool, u (1840). Son of Thomas Green, jailer. Free 25 July 1840. [Freemen reg.]

Green, Joseph, Charles St, Middlx Hospital, London, carver and gilder (1802–39). The number in Charles St is given as 15 until 1825 and 14 from 1826. [D]

Green, Joseph, Angel Row, Nottingham, cm and u (1814–32). [D]

Green, Joseph, High Cross St, Leicester, cm, chairmaker and u (1818–40). Took as app John Bothman, c. 1820. [D; app. reg.]

Green, Joseph, Middlegate, Penrith, Cumb., cm/joiner (1834). [D]

Green, Joseph & Joshua, 33 Carver St, Sheffield, Yorks., cm (1834–37). [D]

Green, Joshua, High Cross St, Leicester, cm and chairmaker (1822). [D]

Green, Philip, 'The Three Golden Chairs', near the Church Wall, Houndsditch, London, upholder (1717–20). Son of William Green, freeman blacksmith of London. App. to Edward Warren, 5 July 1710, and free of the Upholders' Co. by servitude, 7 August 1717. [GL, Upholders' Co. records]

Green, Philip, Devizes, Wilts., cm etc. (1793). [D]

Green, Richard, Crown Ct, Westminster, London, cm (1749). [Poll bk]

Green, Richard, Pipers Row, Wolverhampton, Staffs., u and paper hanger (1833–34). Recorded at no. 7 in 1834. [D]

Green, Richard, 5 Castle St East, London, chair and sofa maker (1839). [D]

Green, Richard, Church St, Bishops Castle, Salop, chairmaker (1840). [D]

Green, Robert, Market Sq, Chorley, Lancs., joiner and cm (1822–24). [D]

Green, Robert, Cambridge, cm, u and paper hanger (1824–40). In Trumpington St, 1824–25, but from 1839–40 at St. Sepulchre's Passage. [D; poll bk; PR (bapt.)]

Green, Robert, Eastgate, Louth, Lincs., chairmaker and turner (1819–35). [D]

Green, Samuel, Salisbury, Wilts., cm (1762). In 1762 took app. named Marshall. [S of G, app. index]

Green, Samuel, Wetherby, Yorks., joiner/cm (1837). [D]

Green, Sarah, Bristol, u (1813–30). At 11 Philadelphia St, 1813–22, and 25 College Green, 1823–30. By the following year a Mrs Clifford (late Mrs Green) was trading from this address. [D] See William Green, 11 Philadelphia St.

Green, T., Burton-on-Trent, Staffs., cm (1795). [D]

Green, Thomas, Norwich, cm (1711–17). In 1711 took app. named Barnes and in 1717, Lawes. [S of G, app. index]

Green, Thomas, address unknown, chairmaker/u (1723). In

1723 supplied a walnut dressing chair to Temple Newsam House, Leeds. [*Furn. Hist.*, 1967]

Green, Thomas, London, cm (1793–1803). Subscribed to Sheraton's *Drawing Book*, 1793 and *Cabinet Dictionary*, 1803.

Green, Thomas, Masshouse Lane, Birmingham, cm and u (1816). [D]

Green, Thomas, 3 Hollen St, Soho, London, japanner and gilder (1835–39). [D]

Green, Thomas, Todley, Keighley, Yorks., joiner/cm (1837). [D]

Green, Thomas, 37 Long Alley, Finsbury, London, cm and u (1839). [D]

Green, Truelove, Hanover Sq., London, u (1734). Declared bankrupt, *Gents Mag.*, March 1734.

Green, William, Rupert St, London, u (1749). [Westminster poll bk]

Green, William, Swine Mkt, Sheffield, Yorks., cm (1774). [D]

Green, William, Bromsgrove, Worcs., cm (1780). In 1780 took out insurance cover of £500 which included £200 for utensils, stock and workshops. [GL, Sun MS vol. 281, p. 45]

Green, William, 20 Mortimer St, Cavendish Sq., London, upholder and cm (1775–1806). Recorded in 1775 as a sworn appraiser in connection with the executorship accounts concerning the furniture at Ickworth Lodge (Hervey v Bristol). He is named in association with a Henry Bullen. First recorded in trade directories, 1790. [D; PRO, C103/174]

Green, William, Maidstone, Kent, (1790). [Poll bk]

Green, William jnr, Maidstone, Kent, u (1802). [Poll bk]

Green, William, Milk St, Bristol, cm (1793–94). [D]

Green, William, 16 Gt Portland St, London, u (1800–01). [D]

Green, William, Exeter, Devon, cm (1803–20). Included in Militia Census, 1803. Three sons bapt. at St Sidwell's Church, 1813–20. [PR (bapt.)]

Green, William, Church St, Bilston, Staffs., u (1818). [D]

Green, William, 11 Philadelphia St, Bristol, bedstead maker (1818–20). Sarah Green is shown working as an u from this address, 1813–22. [D]

Green, William, West End, Wellingborough, Northants., cm (1823). [D]

Green, William, Exeter, Devon, cm (1826–37). Eight children bapt. at St Sidwell's Church, 1826–38. In 1837 living at Red Lion Ct. [PR (bapt.)]

Green, William, Bolton, Lancs., u and cm (1814–34). At 153 Deansgate in 1818 and New Market Pl., 1824–28. [D]

Green, William, Oxford St, London, portable desk and dressing case maker (1814–37). At 170 Oxford St, 1814–20, but by 1829 the number had changed to 168. A brass inlaid rosewood box has been noted with the label of this maker from 170 Oxford St. This claims that he was 'Portable desks & Dressing Case Manufacturer to their Royal Highnesses the Dukes of Kent & Gloucester'. [D]

Green, William, Corbridge, Northumb., cm and joiner (1828–34). [D]

Green, William, Barnsley, Yorks., cm (1828–37). In Castlereagh St, 1828, but by 1837 in Pitt St. [D]

Green, William, Birmingham, cabinet case maker (1835–39). Trading at 3 Howard St in 1835 and Constitution Hill in 1839. [D]

Green, Bainer & Co., 19 Blackman St, Southwark, London, carvers and gilders (1817). [D]

Green & Co., 29 Wine St, Bristol, u (1792). [D]

Green & Elliott, Angel Row, Nottingham, u (1798–99). [D]

Green & Morton, 21 Lambert St, Sheffield, Yorks., cm (1816). [D]

Green & Parkinson, 45 Rose Pl., Liverpool, u (1821–39). [D]

Green & Walker, George Yd, Dean St, Soho, London, chair and sofa manufacturer (1829). [D]

Greenacre, James, London, cm (1837). Tried for murder 1837. [*Gents Mag.*, May 1837]

Greenacre, Thomas, Charlotte St, Gt Yarmouth, Norfolk, cm and chairmaker (1830–39). [D]

Greenacre, William, Howard St, Gt Yarmouth, Norfolk, (1839). [D]

Greenalgh, William, Henry St, Bury, Lancs., joiner and cm (1816–18). [D]

Greene, Isaac, London(?), joiner (1689). In 1689 made the pulpit for the Chapel, Petworth House, Sussex. [Nat. Trust guide to *Petworth*]

Greene, John, parish of St Mary, Chelmsford, Essex, chairmaker (1661–71). Baptisms of daughters, 24 February 1661 and 21 November 1671. [PR (bapt.)]

Greene, John, 'King's Arms', Poultry, London, glass seller (1670). Imported glass from Venice and a letter survives from Greene to Antonio Morelli in Venice dated 10 February 1670 concerning the quality and size of glasses that he required. [Wills, *Looking-Glasses*]

Greene, John, address unknown, u (1705). On 1 December 1705 invoiced 'walnut-tree elbow chairs w. corner elbows' at £4 for Drayton House, Northants. [V & A archives]

Greene, Mark, London, upholder (1704). Free on the London Upholders' Co., 6 December 1704. [GL, Upholders' Co. records]

Greene, William, 16 Portland St, London, cm (1778). In 1778 took out insurance cover for £400 of which £250 was in respect of utensils and stock. [GL, Sun MS vol. 264, p. 451]

Greener & Chiesa, Whitechapel, Liverpool, carvers and gilders (1830–39). Probably founded earlier than the first recording in 1830, for in an advertisement in *Gore's Directory*, 1837, they claimed to have been trading for sixteen years. At 34 Whitechapel, 1830–36 but then moved to premises at 39. They also owned premises in Williamson St. In 1835 their manufactory was at 17 Williamson St and in 1837 their ware-rooms were in premises adjacent to their Whitechapel address but entered from Williamson St. An 1839 directory gives the Whitechapel number as 44. They claimed to keep 'an assortment of PIER, CHIMNEY & DRESSING GLASSES in great variety' and solicited trade orders from builders, glaziers, merchants and shipowners. Imported German clocks. [D; *Liverpool Mercury*, 26 March 1830]

Greenfinch, Benjamin, Norwich, upholder (1820). Son of Benjamin Greenfinch, weaver. Free 23 February 1820. An 1830 poll bk shows a Benjamin Greenfield, upholder, in the parish of St Peter Mancroft and it is likely that this is an error of surname and is the maker here listed. [Freemen reg.]

Greenhalgh, Samuel, Manchester, u (1813–40). In 1813 at Presshouse Steps Parsonage but from 1825 at Southgate with a residence at 10 Wood St, Salford. [D]

Greening, Edward, 7 Peter St, Bishopsgate, London, looking-glass manufacturer, carver and gilder (1835–37). [D]

Greening, James, 83 Shoe Lane, Fleet St, London, cm (1781). In 1781 took out insurance cover of £100 of which half was in respect of utensils and stock. [GL, Sun MS vol. 290, p. 457]

Greening, William, London, carver and gilder, looking and coach glass maufacturer (1820–39). At 14 Wormwood St, Bishopsgate, 1820–29, but by 1835 at 79 Coleman St. [D]

Greenland, Augustus, Canterbury, Kent, cm (1782–1830). In the parish of St Alphege, 1794; Turnagain Lane, 1818; and Knott's Lane 1826. [Poll bks]

Greenleaf, Richard, St Clements, Fore St, Ipswich, Suffolk, cm and u (1830–39). [D; poll bks]

Greenough, James, 59 Bridge St, Manchester, cm and u (1836–39). [D]

Greenshield, David, York St, Nottingham, cm (1825). [D]

Greenwell, Walter, North Shields, Northumb., u (1827–34).

Trade card in Landauer Coll., MMA, NY. Trading at Tyne St in 1827 and 4 Linskill St in 1834. [D]

Greenwell, William & John, corner of Linskill St, Tyne St, North Shields, Northumb., cm and u (1827–34). [D]

Greenwood, Charles, 5 Rood Lane, Fenchurch St, London, upholder and cm (1753–d. 1783). Son of Charles Greenwood of Newgate St, London, cheesemonger, and brother to Thomas Greenwood also an upholder. App. to John Perkins of the Sadlers' Co., upholder, 2 March 1741. Admitted freeman of the Upholders Co. under the terms of the 1750 Upholders' Act, 6 September 1753. Master of the Upholders' Co., 1781. Recorded in London directories from 1765 but clearly trading before this date. Took as apps James Senols, 1757–64; Captain Hawkins, 1761–68; John Cooper, 1768–75; and James Duthoit, 1777–85. From the late 1770s probably had a business relationship with a James Senols who was living in his house in 1777 and in 1781 took out a joint insurance cover with Charles Greenwood on stock and utensils. These were insured for £900. Charles Greenwood was probably a person of some substance by this date as he took out insurance cover of £3,000 on some houses including 7 Rood Lane. His card [Banks Coll., BM] states that he made 'all sorts of Four Post and Standing Beds'. In 1780 entered a partnership with James Senols his former app. See James and Thomas Greenwood at this address. [D; GL, Upholders' Co. records; Sun MS vol. 259, p. 495; vol. 290, p. 610; vol. 291, p. 570]

Greenwood, E., 16 Westgate St, Bath, Som., cm and broker (1826). [D]

Greenwood, Erasmus, Norwich, cm (1796–1830). Freeman of Gt Yarmouth, Norfolk. [Gt Yarmouth poll bks]

Greenwood, Isaac, Lancaster, cm (1773–1818). App. to Robert Thorney, cm, 23 February 1767 and free, 1773–74. In 1805 at Cable St but in 1809 at Green St. Named in Gillow records, 1784–86, and it is possible that he was either an employee or operating on a limited basis on his own at this phase. It was not until 1791 that he appears to have taken any apps though from February of that year until May 1807 he took no fewer than twelve. Father of John Greenwood, another Lancaster cm. [D; freemen rolls; app. reg.; Westminster Ref. Lib., Gillow]

Greenwood, James, 23 Fenchurch St, London, upholstery warehouse (1784). [D] See Thomas Greenwood at this address.

Greenwood, James, Sheffield, Yorks., cm, razor strap and case maker (1814–22). At Wicker in 1814 and Nursery in 1822. [D]

Greenwood, John, Green-area, Lancaster, cm (1797–1818). Son of Isaac Greenwood of Lancaster, cm. Free 1797–98. Named in the Gillow records, 1789–98. On 2 April 1807 took an app. jointly with his father which might suggest that he was working in his business at this date. On 4 January 1815 took an app. on his sole responsibility. [D; poll bks; freemen rolls; app. reg.; Westminster Ref. Lib., Gillow]

Greenwood, John, Haworth, Yorks., cm (1822). [D]

Greenwood, John, Lower Allithwaite, Cartmel, Westmld, cm (1829). [D]

Greenwood, Jonathan, 6 Charles St, Sheffield, Yorks., cabinet case maker (1818). [D]

Greenwood, Peter, Skerton, Lancaster, cm (1768). [Poll bk]

Greenwood, Robert, Lancaster and London, joiner and cm (1766–89). Named in Gillow records from 1766–89 as a joiner, though amongst the items he was employed on was a desk. For part of this time he was an app. having been indentured to G. Blackburn, Bateman & Forren in 1766. Free 1783–84. The freemen rolls give his address as Little Russell

St, London. [App. reg.; freemen rolls; Westminster Ref. Lib., Gillow]

Greenwood, S., 3 Mill St, Lambeth, London, bent timber manufacturer (1829). [D]

Greenwood, Samuel, Lancaster, cm (1806–07). [Lancaster freemen rolls]

Greenwood, Thomas, London, upholder (1768–1811). Son of Thomas Greenwood of Wych St, St Clement Danes, staymaker. App. to Ralph Fryer, innholder, 18 May 1768 and Barnard Baker, 8 May 1772. Free of the Upholders' Co. by servitude, 16 November 1791 and then living at the house of a Mr Savil at 1 Bishopsgate St. In 1811 at Paul St, Finsbury Sq. [GL, Upholders' Co. records]

Greenwood, Thomas, London, upholder (1778–84). In 1778 at Duke St, Lincoln's Inn Fields where he took out insurance cover for £200 which included £50 for utensils and stock. In 1784 at 14 Bath St, Cold Bath Fields where the insurance cover only totalled £100 of which £20 was in repect of utensils and stock. [GL, Sun MS vol. 263, p. 483; vol. 319, p. 350]

Greenwood, Thomas, 23 Fenchurch St, London, u and cm (1787–1808). Son of Charles Greenwood, upholder of Fenchurch St whose business he continued. Freeman of the Upholders' Co. by patrimony, 5 September 1787. It is not clear when he commenced working in the family business. His father died in 1783 but since 1780 the business had been carried on by the partnership of Greenwood and Senols and this continued after Charles Greenwood's death. In 1784 a James Greenwood is shown in one directory at 23 Fenchurch St and 1788–89 the partnership of Greenwood & Sebire. From 1790 however Thomas Greenwood is shown in sole control. In 1803 subscribed to Sheraton's *Cabinet Dictionary*. The premises first occupied by his father at 7 Rood Lane were retained and in July 1792 utensils and stock here was insured for £250. Thomas Greenwood was clearly a person of some wealth and in 1790 took out insurance cover on five houses of £3,200. In January 1803 insurance cover totalled £5,350. [D; GL, Upholders' Co. records; Sun MS vol. 388, p. 240; ref. 670738; vol. 427, ref. 743700]

Greenwood, Thomas, Lancaster and Preston, Lancs., u (1817–18). Free of Lancaster, 1817–18, when stated 'of Preston', and in 1818 living at Avenham Rd, Preston. [D; Lancaster freemen rolls]

Greenwood, Thomas, Derby Rd, Nottingham, joiner and cm (1832). [D]

Greenwood, Thomas, 19 Old Market, Halifax, Yorks., u (1828–37). Recorded in one directory at no. 20 as a cm and u in 1830. [D]

Greenwood, William, Brighouse, Yorks., cm (1822–34). [D]

Greenwood, William, Dollar St, Cirencester, Glos., cm and u (1827–40). [D; PR (bapt.)]

Greenwood, William, High Ousegate, York, cm and u (1830–40). Recorded at no. 1 in 1830 and no. 32 in 1840. In April 1839 advertised that he had taken over the premises formerly occupied by John Clemesha, a hatter in High Ousegate. [D; *York Gazette*, 20 April 1839]

Greer, William, Rupert St, Westminster, London, u (1720–66). Son of Alexander Greer of Critchel More, Dorset, Gent. App. to Phineas Sale, 14 September 1720, and free of the Upholders' Co. by servitude, 6 June 1733. In 1738 took app. named Gedding. Attracted patrons of note. In April 1743 submitted a long account for work done at Gibside, Co. Durham for the Bowes family and for furniture hired for a house in Pall Mall and work undertaken at another London house in Conduit St. In total the account came to £521 7s 10½d and was settled in May 1747. A further £40 was paid in August 1746 in part settlement for goods supplied earlier in the month. In May 1755 Greer was paid for 'a picture of a landscape'. On 11 December 1766 the 1st Duke of Northumberland paid for bedsteads, lace, buckram etc. supplied by Greer. [GL, Upholders' Co. records; S of G, app. index; poll bk; Durham RO, D/St/247, D/St/V.990, D/St/V.1488–90; V & A archives]

Greetham, James, East End Old Dock, Liverpool, carver (1766). [D]

Greeves, John, High St, King's Lynn, Norfolk, u (1805–08). [D]

Greey, Frederick B., Ramsgate, Kent, cm (1832–37). Freeman of Sandwich, Kent. [Sandwich poll bks]

Gregg, Christopher, Micklegate, York, cm (1823). [D]

Grego, Antonio, 27 Leather Lane, Holborn, London, looking-glass manufacturer and picture frame maker, carver and gilder (1817–37). [D] See S. Grego & Son.

Grego, Anton, Eyre St Hill, London, carver and gilder, looking-glass manufacturer and frame maker (1835–39). In 1835 shown at 236 Eyre St Hill but this may be an error for 36, the number shown in 1837. In 1839 at 35 Eyre St Hill. [D]

Grego, Anthony Lewis, 22 Fetter Lane, London, carver and gilder (1839). [D]

Grego, S. & Son, 27 Leather Lane, London, looking-glass manufacturer (1839). Successor of Antonio Grego at this address. [D]

Grego, T. jnr, 13 Backhill, Hatton Gdn, London, looking-glass and picture frame maker (1835). [D]

Gregory, Benjamin, Wolverhampton, Staffs., cm and u (1816–22). Listed at Dudley St in 1816; and High St and/or High-green in 1822. [D]

Gregory, Benjamin, Silver St, Stockton, Co. Durham, cm (1832). [D]

Gregory, Catherine, York, u (1796). In March 1796 supplied furniture including chairs to the Retreat Quaker Asylum near York. The bills totalled £19 14s 4d. [Borthwick Inst. York, Retreat MS, H/1]

Gregory, Charles, Gt Surrey St, Blackfriars Rd, London, cm (1828). Declared bankrupt, *Chester Chronicle*, 25 July 1828.

Gregory, Edward, 1 Nassau St, London, carver and gilder (1839). [D]

Gregory, Emanuel, Exeter, Devon, carver and gilder (1836–40). Three daughters bapt., 1836–40. In 1836 at Wells Lane and in 1838 Clarence Pl. [PR (bapt.), St Sidwell's]

Gregory, J., 3 Runts Ct, Castle St, Leicester Sq., London, guncase and plate chest manufacturer (1835). [D]

Gregory, J. H., Exeter, Devon, carver (1839–40). Married Miss Vanstone in June 1839. [*Exeter Flying Post*, 20 June 1839, 4 March 1840]

Gregory, John, Piccadilly, Manchester, cm and u (1822–34). At 21 Piccadilly, 1822–29, and 47, 1832–34. House at 2 Rose Cottage, Moss Lane, Hulme, 1824–25. On 31 December 1822 supplied carpets etc. to Dunham Massey, Cheshire, amounting to £98 8s 4d. [D; Dunham Massey papers]

Gregory, John, Nelson St, Stroud, Glos., cm (1835). [PR (bapt.)]

Gregory, John, 95 Old St, London, u, undertaker and broker (1840). [GL, Sun MS vol. 574, refs 1333211]

Gregory, Joseph, 17 Castle-grubb St, Sheffield, Yorks., cm (1797). [D]

Gregory, Richard, Hill St, Richmond, Surrey, cm (1838). [D]

Gregory, Robert, Smithy Row, Nottingham, joiner and cm (1778–84). In 1778 insured some houses for £200 and in 1781 took out cover for £700 which included £90 for utensils and stock. In 1779 took app. named William Hedderley, and in 1784 advertised for craftsmen. [GL, Sun MS vol. 269, p. 431; vol. 295, p. 102; app. reg.; *Nottingham Journal*, 31 July 1784]

Gregory, William, 125 High Holborn, London, u (1824). Took out insurance cover of £500 on a house and offices at 6 Upper King St, Bloomsbury in the tenure of a mould figure-maker,

and £150 on household goods in a dwelling house and carpenter's shop, with stock and utensils accounting for a further £350. [GL, Sun MS vol. 496, refs 1019203–04]

Gregory, William, Manchester, cm and u (1825–40). At 74 King St in 1825 and bankrupt the following year. In business again in 1834 at Old Church Yd and from 1832–40 at 27 Half St. [D; *Liverpool Mercury*, 29 September 1826]

Gregson, Benjamin, Lancaster, cm (1829–30). [Lancaster freemen rolls]

Gregson, Charles, 114 Mill St, Harrington, Liverpool, carver and gilder (1839). [D]

Gregson, Joseph, Lancaster, u (1806–07). Admitted freeman, 1806–07, when stated 'of London'. [Lancaster freemen rolls] Possibly:

Gregson, Joseph, London and Liverpool, u and interior surveyor (1812–d. 1827). Son of William Gregson, block maker and nephew of Mathew Gregson of Liverpool, cm and u. Freeman of Liverpool 5 October 1812. Already by this date however he appears to have been practising as an u in London. He was at 25 Chapel St, Grosvenor Sq. in December 1808 where he took out insurance cover of £150, which included £15 for his tools. He declared his trade as upholder. By February 1812 he was trading on a more extensive scale from 2 Charles St, Grosvenor Sq. with insurance cover of £800 which included £500 in respect of stock and utensils. At this stage he appears to have changed the nature of his trade and declared himself to be an interior surveyor. He offered his services not only in London but also in his home town of Liverpool, using an address at 131 Duke St (changed in 1813 to 129). This address was also used by Ellen & J. Gregson, perfumers, gloves and tea dealers. The Miss Gregson was possibly his sister.

The nature of the services offered at this period are laid out in an advertisement of July 1812. These were the 'Arranging, Planning & Estimating the Interior DECORATIONS of HOUSES, Warming & Ventilating Rooms of all descriptions on the most safe & scientific principle & Preventing DAMP WALLS, SMOKEY CHIMNEYS & DRY ROT'. In December 1813 he was endorsing a patent smoke conductor designed to remedy smoky chimneys which had been devised by John Fisher of Oundle, Northants. These trading activities continued in both London and Liverpool for a number of years and by 1816 he had a partner, John Browne. They also acted as estate agents and in April 1819 advertised for furnished houses that their clients required. They also offered for sale household furniture which had been made to order and no longer needed by the owners. This included a 'Town made' Merlin's Chair, a mahogany secretaire bookcase, a large painted bookcase and a set of mahogany dining tables on tripod claw supports. By August of that year however the partners were bankrupt. Both the London and Liverpool addresses are cited in the bankruptcy proceedings and the partners were declared to be upholders and cm. The furniture making part of the business had certainly continued in Liverpool since the formation of the partnership. In 1821 Joseph Gregson once more appears in the Liverpool directories at 119 Duke St trading on his own account as a 'working upholsterer etc'. He died on 11 January 1827, aged 40, after a lingering illness. He was declared to have been 'many years a member of the Royal Institution & Surveyor & upholsterer in London & Liverpool'. [D; Liverpool freemen reg.; GL, Sun MS vol. 445, ref. 823769; vol. 459, ref. 867614; *Liverpool Mercury*, 31 July 1812, 24 December 1813; April 1819, 13 August 1819, 19 January 1827; Liverpool RO, GRE 920 2/25 42, 920 GRE 3/2 4] B.A.

Gregson, Mary, 29 Marylebone St, London, u (1839). [D]

Gregson, Mathew, Liverpool, u and cm (1749–1824). The son of a Thomas Gregson, block maker; app. to William Litherland, u, April 1765, in partnership with Elizabeth Urmson 1778–88 and Bullen 1800–06. Two trade cards featuring an oval mirror leaning against a tree in a landscape inscribed 'GREGSON/upholsterer/Preeson's Row /Liverpool' are in the Banks Coll., BM, and one of the same design headed GREGSON & BULLEN is in the Landauer Coll., MMA, NY. A painted satinwood urn table [V & A W.45–1935] is inscribed in ink 'M. Gregson, Liverpool, 1790' although he may not have made it. A Pembroke table, a satinwood side table and a satinwood cabinet recorded labelled 'GREGSON / Upholsterer / Preeson's Row / LIVERPOOL / Makes & Sells every Article in the / Present Taste / From the Plain and Neat to the / Most Superb / Looking Glasses / in Carved & Gilt Frames / Cabinet Goods in the / Best Construction / Designs Made for Interior /DECORA-TIONS / Goods for Exportation'.

Gregson was one of the most successful Liverpool cm of his generation and by the age of 60 had acquired three country estates, the principal one being at Overton Hall, Cheshire; he was elected an FSA following publication in 1817 of his *Fragments Relative to the History and Antiquities of the County Palatine and Duchy of Lancaster* and played a leading part in developing the public institutions of Liverpool. He was twice married and fathered eight children. At an exhibition of the Society of Artists in Liverpool in 1774 he showed designs for beds in the Chinese, Palmyrean & Gothic tastes. [*Walpole Soc.*, vol. VI, p. 74] He was sworn a Freeman of Lancaster in 1779–80, of Liverpool in 1786; and subscribed to Sheraton's *Drawing Book*, 1793 and *Cabinet Dictionary*, 1803. Richard Watt paid Gregson £788 in 1809–10 for furnishing Speke Hall, the contents of which were sold by auction in 1812. George Bullock had equipped the Great Hall in the same years.

Gregson's main premises were in Preeson's Row, Richmond Row and Paradise St. In 1801 his warehouse, workshop and saw pit in Richmond Row were insured for £800. [GL, Sun MS, vol. 43, ref. 726206] He traded as a paper, looking-glass and feather merchant, u and cm, serving clients in Liverpool, Cheshire and Wales. Sale catalogues of his stock in trade (1814) and of Speke Hall (1812) reveal he was a complete house furnisher and decorator. [Liverpool RO, 920 HOL 6 & GRE 5/22] His library included the pattern books of Chippendale, Ince & Mayhew, Hepplewhite, Sheraton and George Smith as well as volumes of French designs. He designed iron hospital beds and produced a special line of whalebone furniture; in 1804 he patented a new method of stoving feathers and in 1812 submitted a scheme for preventing damp and dry rot.

The Gregson papers [Liverpool RO, 920 GRE] contain copious records of the firm's commissions including an order book J–Z from 1807 onwards, several Journals, a catalogue of his closing down sale in 1814 and a fabric pattern book (there is evidence he designed textiles). Gregson's biography, details of his changes of address, work force, apps and business activities are fully detailed in a dossier compiled by the author and deposited in the Furniture Dept at the V & A.

J.D.

Gregson, Robert, Knutsford, Cheshire, cm/joiner (1822). [D]

Greig, Ebenezer, Farringdon St, London, cm and u (1835–39). Shown at Wheatsheaf Yd, Farringdon St, 1835–37, and 27 Farringdon St in 1839. [D]

Greig, William, City Rd, London, u, cm and carpet manufacturer (1819–27). At 11 Union Pl., City Rd in 1819 and from the next year at 32 City Rd. [D]

Grendey, Giles, London, cm (b. 1693–d. 1780). Giles Grendey was born in Wotton-under-Edge, Glos., the son of William Grendey, and his wife Anne (*neé* Hall). In 1709 he was app. to William Sherborne, a second-generation London joiner. [GL, Indenture] His seven years expired in 1716 when he became a freeman, and by 1726 he was taking apps, one of whom, Christopher Petfield, then petitioned the Middlx general sessions for his discharge from his apprenticeship to Grendey, and also for the repayment of the 'consideracon money' of £5. The order for discharge recorded that Grendey 'beat the pet.er in a very barbarous manner, sometimes with a great stick and at other times knocking him downe and then kicking him in the face and other parts and in stead of learning him his trade of Joyner sett him to sawing large timber which noe ways relates to the trade and hath likewise often theatened to be the death of the s.d peter'. In 1720 Grendey, of St Paul's, Covent Gdn, married Elizabeth Van Knyven of St Gregory, London, at St Mary Magdalen, Old Fish St. Grendey was elected to the Livery of the Joiner's Co. in 1729. [H. L. Phillips, *Annals of the Worshipful Company of Joiners*, London, 1915] and became a freeman of the City of London. Indication of Grendey's status in 1731 is provided by newspaper accounts of a fire which attacked his workshop in Aylesbury House, St John's Sq., Clerkenwell, in the early morning of August 3rd. [*Daily Courant, Daily Journal, Daily Post, Daily Advertiser*, all 4 August 1731; *Read's Weekly Journal or British Gazeteer*, 7 August 1731] The fire started on the premises of Mr Briggs, an organ maker, but Grendey, described as 'Cabinet-Maker and Chair-Maker', was the greatest loser, among the stock destroyed being 'an easy Chair of such rich and curious Workmanship, that he had refus'd 500 Guineas for it, it being intended, 'tis said, to be purchas'd by a Person of Quality who design'd it as a Present to a German Prince' and furniture to the value of £1,000, which he 'had pack'd for Exportation against the next Morning'. However the house and Grendey's stock were insured. In 1731 Grendey began again to take apps. The full list, with date, name, and sum of consideration is as follows [PRO, IR 1/12/–18, and GL, Joiners' Co. bindings]:

July 24 1731	William Dickenson	£10
Dec. 20 1731	James Ludford	£15
Apr. 15 1735	Edw. Airey	£15
Oct. 3 1737	John Tudgey	£20
Nov. 18 1737	John Holloway	£21
June 18 1741	James Tomlyn	£40
Sept. 30 1741	James Turney	£10
April 14 1747	Wm. House	£15
June 1 1747	James Simpson	£10
Dec. 5 1752	John Ashton	£43
June 11 1754	Joseph Lawed	£30

Tudgey came, like Grendey, from Wotton-under-Edge. Simpson had already served three years with Philip Box. From 1732–39 Grendey supplied furniture to Richard Hoare of Barn Elms, and in 1739 he worked for Sir Jacob de Bouverie of Longford Castle. In 1740 his wife, Elizabeth died at her house in St John's Sq., Clerkenwell; she had borne Grendey several children, Mary (bapt. 18 January 1721), buried 1 December 1722), Elizabeth (bapt. 23 October 1722); a second Mary, another daughter, Sukey, and a son, Samuel (bapt. 7 January 1723). Grendey was on the occasion of his wife's death described as 'a great Dealer in the Cabinet Way'. [*London Evening Post*, 9 August 1740] In 1743 Grendey bought a house in Middlx. [*Daily Advertiser*, 22 April 1743] From 1746–56 he supplied furniture to Henry Hoare of Stourhead. In 1747 Grendey became Upper Warden of the Joiners' Co. and advertised himself in the *Daily Advertiser* as 'cabinet maker in St John's Square Clerkenwell'. He is listed in the *London Directory* of 1755 as 'Grindey, Giles, St. John's Square' and in the same year, on 31 March, his daughter

371

Sukey married John Cobb, the great cm (Grendey was described as 'an eminent Timber Merchant', *General Evening Post*, 1 April 1755): Cobb's bank account at Drummonds records substantial payments to 'Mr Grendey' in 1759 and 1763. On 16 January 1758, Grendey 'of St John's Square Clerkenwell' insured 'his fine house only No 2 Lyon St in Clerkenwell in tenure of £1000' and on 13 April of the same year 'his household goods utensils stock in trade (glass excluded) in dwelling house & warehouse £800. Stock in yard £200. Total £1000'. [GL, Sun MS vol. 121, p. 542; vol. 122] In 1762 Grendey supplied mahogany to Kedleston Hall, Derbs. In 1757 Grendey again became Upper Warden of the Joiners' Co. and in 1766 Master, thus emulating his master, Sherborne, who had filled the same post in 1726. However Grendey, by then aged 72, seems to have neglected his duties; in June 1767, the Clerk was directed to write to him to request better attendance and that he was to be present at the next Court, or 'such methods will be taken as shall be adjudged proper, which 'tis hoped he will prevent as the same will be equally disagreeable to the Court as to himself'. In 1755 Grendey, still at Clerkenwell, made his will leaving £1,000 to each of his daughters and leaving the rest of his property to be shared equally between his two sons-in-law both described as merchants, Goodson Vines, of Bedford Row, who had married Elizabeth, and Frederick Rasch, of London, who had married Mary. The former was a son of Samuel Vines and Christiana Goodson, who had married in 1730 at Wotton-under-Edge, and thus a fellow-townsman to Grendey, whose own son, Samuel, presumably died before his father. In 1770 the premises of George Seddon, insured for £4,300, were mortgaged to Grendey. [GL, Sun MS, 1770, ref. 281763] By 1779, when he added a codicil to his will, Grendey, then described as 'gentleman', had moved to Palmer's Green, where he had 'a dwelling house, Coach House, Stable building, and ground . . . lately purchased . . . and which I have since converted into five cottages'. He died there on Friday, 3 March 1780 aged 87. [*London Evening Post*, 7–9 March 1780, *Gents Mag.*, 1780, p. 154] Grendey labelled at least some of his products, and surviving labels have allowed their identification. Two labels are known; one reads 'Giles Grendey In St John's-square, Clerkenwell, London, Makes and Sells all Sorts of Cabinet-Goods, Chairs and Glasses'; the other adds 'Tables', has different typography and lay-out, and a small variation in wording (Fig. 31). The labels have been noted on a wide variety of pieces all apparently dating from about 1735 to 1755; there is no obvious conclusion to be drawn from the type of label used. Seat furniture by Grendey is sometimes stamped with initials: 'HW', 'EA', 'GIL', 'TM', 'IT'. 'TT', 'MW', and 'ID' have been noted (Fig. 30). Such initials are likely to be those of individual chairmakers employed by Grendey. Grendey's known works are listed below in chronological order of discovery or publication: most fall into three stylistic groups: neat well-made pieces in walnut and mahogany, similar pieces lacquered in scarlet for the Spanish market, and a minority of more elaborate works with idiosyncratic carved decoration and shaped panels. Grendey seems not to have worked to any great extent for the nobility and gentry, and the portrait which emerges from the existing evidence is of a provincial immigrant to London who made good through middle-class goods for the home market, specialized goods for the export trade, and was also active as a timber merchant.

[R. W. Symonds, 'Giles Grendey (1693–1780), and the Export Trade of English Furniture to Spain', *Apollo*, 1935, pp. 337–42; R. Edwards and M. Jourdain, 'Georgian Cabinet-Makers VIII — Giles Grendey, and William Hallett', *C. Life*, 1942, pp. 176–77; R. W. Symonds, 'In Search of Giles Grendey', *C. Life*, 1951, pp. 1792–94; GCM; C. Gilbert, 'Furniture by Giles Grendey for the Spanish trade', *Antiques*, XCIX, 1971, 544–50 (see also C, 1971, 919); C. Gilbert, 'A Chest of Drawers by Giles Grendey', *LAC*, 1973; S. Jervis, 'A Great Dealer in the Cabinet Way', Giles Grendey (1693–1780), *C. Life*, 1974, pp. 1418–19]

BARN ELMS, Surrey (Richard Hoare). 1732 bill for chest of drawers, 'Burow Table'. dressing glasses, chimney glasses, 'Wrighting Disk', etc. Total £38 14s 6d; 1732 bill for wall sconces, gold frames for glasses, tables, chest, etc. Total £14 16s 6d; 1737 bill for dressing chair, cabinet with glass doors, etc. Total £21 17s; 1739 bill for alterations to furniture, glass frames, etc. Total £17 6s 6d. [V & A Lib., English manuscripts, tradesmen's bills, Sir R. Hoare, 1731–54, 86 NN3]

LONGFORD CASTLE, Wilts. (Sir Jacob de Bouverie). 1739 ledger payment: 'May 14 Greenday the chair maker a bill with an allowance of £8 8s for a sidebord table he had from Red Lyon Street' £68.

STOURHEAD, Wilts. (Henry Hoare). 1746–56 account book payments, including 29 April 1746 £64 for chairs; March 27 1751, £133 2s 9d; June 24 1752, £10 17s. [Wilts. RO, MS 383/6]

KEDLESTON HALL, Derbs. (Lord Scarsdale). 1762 bill of 13 January for '1 Fine Jamai? Mahog. Plank . . ., £21.0.0. To Sawing I Cut in Do 1s. 4d, to Carrying to the Swan Inn 1s 6d, Total £1 2 10 Receiv'd Josh. Lawes'. [Kedleston Hall archives]

LABELLED FURNITURE. Armchair and chair, mahogany, boldly carved. [P. Macquoid, *Age of Mahogany*, 1906]

Armchair, (Fig. 29) chairs, day-beds, mirrors, tables, and tripod candle-sticks, deal, oak and beech with scarlet japanning, at least 77 pieces, Duke of Infantado, Lazcano Castle, Spain, now widely scattered. [R. W. Symonds, 1935, C. Gilbert, 1971]

Wardrobe, mahogany, broken pediment, shaped panels. [R. Edwards & M. Jourdain, 1942]

Cabinet, mahogany, scrolled pediment, mirrored doors, carved apron, Colonial Williamsburg. [R. Symonds, 1951]

Mirror, in farmhouse in Southern Norway. [Joy, *Conn.*, CLXIX, 1968, 18]

Chest of drawers, mahogany. [Sotheby's, London, 15 October 1971, lot 73]

Double chest of drawers, walnut. [C. Gilbert, 1973]

Mirror, walnut, gilt eagle in roundel, private collection, Norway. [S. Jervis, 1971]

Six chairs, walnut, ladderback, Newport Church, Essex. [S. Jervis, 1974]

Table, mahogany, drop-leaf. [Sotheby's, London, 9 November 1977, lot 47]

Chest of drawers, mahogany. [Christie's, London, 30 November 1978, lot 97]

Twelve chairs, walnut, cabriole legs. [C. Gibbs Ltd, London, 1979]

Four chairs and small sofa *en suite*, mahogany, boldly carved, same pattern as Macquoid chairs. [Gunton Park, Norfolk, Sale, 25 November 1980, lot 2014]

Three chairs, and armchair, walnut, shells on legs and top rail. [Sotheby's, NY, 21 November 1981, lots 233–35]   S.J.

Grenons, James, 'The Black Lyon', Witch St, St Clement Danes, London, upholder (1720). On 9 February 1720 insured goods and merchandise in the house of John Probart, coachmaker at the sign of 'The Angel' in Little Queen St. [GL, Sun MS vol. 10, ref. 16592]

Gresley, Thomas, Hull, Yorks., cm and victualler (1834–40). In 1834 at North St, Prospect Pl. but by 1838 had taken the

'Providence Inn', Francis St and added the trade victualler to that of cm [D]

Gretton, Thomas & Lake, Richard, Dorchester, Dorset, joiners and cm (1778). In 1778 insured their utensils and stock for £100. [GL, Sun MS vol. 263, p. 599]

Grevett, John, London, upholder (1707–15). Son of Richard Grevett, freeman upholder of London. App. to Constable Wheeler, 6 August 1707, and free of the Upholders' Co. by servitude, 9 February 1714/15. [GL, Upholders' Co. records]

Grevett, Richard, London, upholder (1715). Father of John Grevett. Freeman of the Upholders' Co. [GL, Upholders' Co. records]

Greville, George, 43 Wheeler St, Spitalfields, London, chair and sofa maker (1827–35). [D]

Greville, Henry & Co., 28 Brokers Row, Moorfields, London, cm (1820). [D]

Greville, Henry, 39 Buttesland St, City Rd, London, carver and cm (1839). [D]

Grew, John, address unrecorded, carver (late 17th century). Assistant to Edward Pearce of London at Sudbury Hall, Derbs. [C. Life, 22 June 1935]

Grewer, William, 67 John St, Fitzroy Sq., London, upholder (1808). [D]

Grews & Wright, London, carpenters (1790–92). Carried out furniture repairs including a new claw for a dumb waiter and fitting drawers to a bookcase for Gertrude, Dowager Duchess of Bedford at 49 and 112 Pall Mall, London. [Bedford Office, London]

Grewny, Hugh, 181 Drury Lane, London, upholders, undertaker and auctioneer (1786). On 8 April 1786 took out insurance cover of £900 of which utensils and stock at the address above accounted for £300 and similar items in another building £400. [GL, Sun MS vol. 337, p. 178]

Grey, —, Brownlow St, Holborn, London, see Belcher & Grey.

Grey, John, Leeds, Yorks., cm (1817–30). In 1817 at Market Pl. and in 1822 recorded at Bay Horse Yd, Market Pl. where he traded until at least 1826. At 26 Albion St in 1830. From 1826 also joiner. [D]

Grey, Peter, 13 East St, Manchester Sq., London, cm (1808). [D]

Grey, T. B., Meeting St, Ramsgate, Kent, cm (1838). [D]

Grey, W., 2 Jermyn St, London, cabinet, gun case and window blind maker (1837). [D]

Grey, W. P., London, cm and u (1827–37). At 48 Wardour St, Soho from 1827–29, but in 1837 at Caromile St, Bishopsgate St where his trade was stated to be cabinet and gun case maker. [D]

Grey, William jnr, Liverpool, u (1818). Free 20 June 1818. Trade stated to be u, 'now Tailor and Breeches Maker'. [Freemen reg.]

Grice, Edward, London, upholder (1730). Son of Thomas Grice of Charlton, Middlx, Esq. App. to William Redknap, 7 August 1723, and free of the Upholders' Co. by servitude, 7 October 1730. [GL, Upholders' Co. records]

Grice, Joseph, Dedham, Essex, cm (1815). Aged 41 in this year. [Essex RO, Q/RJ1/12]

Gridley, Charles, High St, Taunton, Som., carver and gilder (1822–39). [D]

Gridley, Timothy, Norwich, cm (1783). Free 24 February 1783, not by servitude. [Freemen reg.]

Grief, J., Brandon, Suffolk, cm (1824). [D]

Grieve, Thomas, 43 Cow Cross St, London, cm (1803). On 15 July 1803 took out insurance cover of £400 of which £300 was in respect of utensils and stock. [GL, Sun MS vol. 427, ref. 750394]

Grieve, William, Morpeth, Northumb., joiner and cm (1827–28). In 1827 at Buller's Green but in 1828 at Newgate St. [D]

Grieves, Thomas, South Shields, Co. Durham, (1834). [D]

Grieveson, Valentine, Milburn Gate, Durham, cm and joiner (1828). [D]

Griffey, John, Palace St, Canterbury, Kent, carver, gilder, herald and sign painter (1823). [D]

Griffin, —, Wardour St, Soho, London, cm (d. 1731). Noted as a wealthy maker. Died at his lodgings in Lambeth Marsh, 1731. [Harris, Old English Furniture, p. 22]

Griffin, Edward, South Lane, Exeter, Devon, cm (1836). Son Edward bapt. at Holy Trinity, 16 October 1836. [PR (bapt.)]

Griffin, H., Lambeth, London, carver and gilder (1826–29). In 1826 at 27 Lower Lambeth Marsh and in 1829 at Binwall Rd. [D]

Griffin, James, Clements Lane, London, cm and carpenter (1777). In 1777 insured his utensils, stock and goods for £90 out of a total cover of £200. [GL, Sun MS vol. 257, p. 253]

Griffin, James, High St, Dudley, Worcs., cm and u (1820–40). [D]

Griffin, John, High Wycombe, Bucks., chairmaker (1832–35). Two daughters bapt., 1832–35. [PR (bapt.)]

Griffin, Richard, High St, Bewdley, Worcs., cm (1793–1831). [D; Worcs. poll bk]

Griffin, Thomas, 23 Pill St, Tottenham Ct Rd, London, carver (1777). In 1777 insured his house for £200. [GL, Sun MS vol. 254, p. 493]

Griffin, Thomas, London, sedan and invalid chairmaker, chair and sofa maker (1820–39). References earlier than 1820 exist for this maker but at this period he was probably in the employ of William Griffin & Co. of Whitcomb St, sedan chairmakers to George III. In the period 1820–29 at 28 Princes St, Leicester Sq. at which address in 1821 he took out insurance cover on utensils and stock for £1,000. By 1838 at 6 Leicester Sq. [D; GL, Sun MS vol. 488, ref. 976715]

Griffin, William, London, sedan, porters' hall and invalid chair makers (1787–1825). In Coventry St, 1787–1806, but from 1791 had additional premises in Whitcomb St which soon became the centre of the business operations. The number is shown as 1 from 1800–04, 31 in 1807 and 74 from 1808. Insurance cover in 1807 on stock and utensils was £500. From 1808 the business is listed as William Griffin & Co. Patrons included the Royal Family, the Duchess of Bedford and the Marquis of Salisbury. Much of the business appears to have been in the manufacture and maintenance of sedan chairs but Sheraton included this maker in the list of master cabinet makers in his Cabinet Dictionary, 1803. [D; GL, Sun MS vol. 440, refs 804745–46; Windsor Royal Archives, RA 25076, 25196, 88962; Hatfield House MS, bills 612/52, 630; Bedford Office, London]

Griffin, William, 18 Gt Sutton St, Clerkenwell, London, cm (1806–08). Bankruptcy announced in February 1806 but a directory entry exists for 1808 which may suggest a recommencement of the business. [D; Liverpool Chronicle, 5 February 1806]

Griffin, William, High St, Bewdley, Worcs., cm and u (1835). [D]

Griffin, William, Market St, Tring, Herts., cm and u (1839). [D]

Griffin & Row, 4 Little Bridge St, Blackfriars, London, japanned chair manufacturers (1816–25). [D]

Griffith, —, Chester, cm (1786–92). App. on 16 December 1786 to John Coake, cm, but on 7 December 1791 assigned to James Gardner, cm. Free 22 November 1792. [App. bk]

Griffith(s), Charles, Watergate St Row, Chester, cm and u (1831–40). Freeman of Chester, 27 April 1831. Bankrupt March 1838 and on 3 April his stock was offered for sale at his premises at 89 Watergate St Row. This consisted of 'four post and tent bedsteads with chintz curtains lined and fringed, hair and flock mattresses, goose feather beds, mahogany and painted chests of drawers, washing and dressing tables, looking glasses, chairs and bedroom carpets'. Despite his financial difficulties he soon recommenced business and in April 1840 advertised from his new premises at 44 Watergate St Row that he was maintaining a 'GENERAL UPHOL-STERY, Cabinet, Carpet, Rug and Paper Hanging Establishment'. He stated that 'Cabinet and Upholstery Furniture of every description manufactured on the premises from a well-seasoned stock of mahoganies, and other Fancy Woods' was available. He was agent for the British Plate Glass Co., acted as a general appraiser and offered to supply mahogany and rosewood in plank and veneer. By July 1840 however he was once more insolvent and his stock was sold off by auction. [D; freemen rolls; *Chester Courant*, 20 and 27 March 1838; 24 April, 24 July and 14 August 1840]

Griffith, Edward, Chester, cm (1818–26). Free 14 May 1818. At St Martin's Pl., 1818–19, but in 1826 at Bedward Row. [Freemen rolls; poll bks]

Griffith, H, 45 Comrel Rd, Lambeth, London, carver and gilder (1835). [D]

Griffith, Isaac, Stafford St, Market Drayton, Salop, cm (1822). [D]

Griffith, J., Red Cross St, Southwark, London, cm (1794–1803). Included in Sheraton's list of master cabinet makers in his *Cabinet Dictionary*, 1803.

Griffith, John, Chester, cm (1771–77). Son of Thomas Griffith, innholder. App. to John Johnson, cm, 13 January 1771 and free 30 January 1777. [App. bk]

Griffith, John, Chester, cm (1783). Free 24 March 1783. [App. bk]

Griffith, John, Chester, cm and carpenter (c. 1791). Took as app. Richard Kidd c. 1791. Probably either of the two cm above. [App. bk]

Griffith(s), John, 7 Lant St, Southwark, London, cm, u and undertaker (1809–39). From 1816 listed as John & William Griffith. The business was probably of a substantial size for in August 1809 out of a total insurance cover of £1,400 no less than £1,200 was for utensils and stock. By 1820 the cover for utensils and stock had risen to £1,400. [D; GL, Sun MS vol. 446, ref. 834278; vol. 485, ref. 972520]

Griffith, John, Charlotte Row, Walworth, London, carver and gilder (1826–29). [D]

Griffith, John, Lower Bridge St, Chester, spirit dealer and u (1840). [D]

Griffith, Samuel, 90 Dale End, Birmingham, upholder (1805–08). [D] Possibly Samuel Griffiths.

Griffith(s), Thomas, Market Drayton, Salop, cm (1822–35). Recorded at Shropshire St, 1822–28, and High St, 1835. [D]

Griffith, Thomas, Wishing Steps, City Walls, Chester, u (1831–40). Free 28 April 1831. [D; freemen rolls]

Griffith, William, Suffolk St, Haymarket, London, u (1698–1709). App. to Robert Roads, merchant tailor and free of the Upholders' Co., 24 October 1698. [GL, Upholders' Co. records; Heal]

Griffith, William, 5 Blossom St, Norton Falgate, London, chairmaker (1808). [D]

Griffith, William & Co., 8 Giltspur St, Smithfield, London, cabinet brass founder, cabinet furniture manufacturer and factor (1815). [D]

Griffith & Payne, 16 Long Lane, West Smithfield, London, oval turners, carvers, gilders and picture frame makers (1806–11). Trade card in Banks Coll., BM. [D]

Griffiths, Charles, 5 Fairhurst St, Cheapside, Liverpool, u (1790). [D]

Griffiths, Charles, Raven St, Shrewsbury, Salop, u (1796). [Freemen rolls]

Griffiths, Charles, Birmingham, u and paper hanger (1822–35).

Listed at Worcester St in 1822 and Ladywell Walk in 1835. [D]

Griffiths, Charles Overton, Church St, Hackney, London, carver and gilder (1826). [D]

Griffith(s), Edward, Dean St, Soho, London, u and cm (1743–59). Assistant to Benjamin Goodison and possibly his nephew. Set up his own business in Dean St which attracted influential patrons. He was employed by the 4th Earl of Cardigan at Longford Castle, Wilts. in 1747 and charged £88 15s for gilding the cornice, chair rail and other mouldings. Also worked at the Earl's London house in Dover St. Between 1746–49 he supplied for Dover House a number of tables, picture frames, screens and boxes, repaired 'a small India cabinet' and made a six-fold screen with a mahogany frame on which eighteen pictures could be mounted. In December 1750 a bill from Griffiths for £75 9s is recorded and a further one in April 1759 for £40. Also worked at Deene Park, Northants. Subscribed to Chippendale's *Director*, 1754. [Heal; *GCM*; *DEF*; *C. Life*, 26 December 1931, p. 715; Westminster poll bk]

Griffiths, G., 15 Pearl St, Spitalfields, London, cm and u (1839). [D]

Griffiths, George, 9 Waterloo Rd, London, carver and gilder, looking-glass maker (1835–39). In 1839 shown as George & John Griffiths. [D]

Griffiths, Griffith, London, cm and u (1820–39). At 125 Old St, St Luke's in 1820 and 28 King St, Regent St in 1839. [D]

Griffiths, Henry, Upper Priory, Birmingham, u (1816). [D]

Griffiths, Henry, 44 Charlotte St, Somers Town, London, cm and u (1827–35). [D]

Griffiths, Henry, 17 Commercial Rd, Lambeth, London, carver and gilder (1829–32). [D]

Griffiths, Henry, 22 Mount St, Lambeth, London, carver and gilder (1832). [D]

Griffiths, Henry, 27 Drury Lane, London, furniture dealer, carver and gilder (1835–39). [D]

Griffiths, Henry, 94 Broad Wall, London, looking-glass manufacturer (1837). [D]

Griffiths, Isaac, Market Drayton, Salop, cm and builder (1822–35). Recorded at Stafford St in 1822 and Staffordshire St, 1828–35. [D]

Griffiths, James, Liverpool, u (1827–34). In 1827 the address is given in one directory as 48 Adlington St and in another as 24 Hunter St. In 1834 at 26 Trowbridge St. [D]

Griffiths, Joel, London, carver, gilder and looking-glass maker (1802–27). At 3 Prince's St, Blackfriars Rd in 1802 when he took out insurance cover of £300 which included £100 for utensils and stock. He remained at this address until at least 1808 but in 1826 had moved to 19 Prince's St, Gt Surrey Rd. [D; GL, Sun MS vol. 424, ref. 738461]

Griffiths, John, Llanyblodwel, Salop, cm (1759). In 1759 took app. named Jones. [S of G, app. index]

Griffiths, John, Southwark, London, bedstead maker and u (1774–93). Addresses given at the Mint, Southwark, 1774–84, and Falcon Ct, 1782–93, though these may represent the same location. Took out insurance on a house or houses ranging from £150 in 1774 to £1,000 in 1793. In 1784 the policy was taken out in the names of John & Thomas Griffiths. [GL, Sun MS vol. 302, p. 130; vol. 319, p. 337; vol. 395, p. 386; Hand in Hand MS vol. 116, ref. 55418]

Griffiths, John, Bentinck St, Westminster, London, u (1784). [Poll bk]

Griffiths, John, Bristol, cm (1792–1823). Shown at Horse Fair for the full span of operations except in 1815 when an address at 29 Frogmore St was listed. [D]

Griffiths, John, 27 Little Alie St, Goodman's Fields, London, u and cm (1794–1812). From 1809 the business is listed as

Griffiths & Barrett. In the list of master cabinet makers in Sheraton's *Cabinet Dictionary*, 1803. [D; Heal]

Griffiths, John, 5 Queen Sq., Moorfields, London, chair stuffer (1808). [D]

Griffiths, John, Bolingbroke Row, Camberwell, London, looking-glass manufactory (1822). [D]

Griffiths, John, 21 Berry St, Liverpool, chairmaker (1827). [D]

Griffiths, Joseph, London, carver and gilder (1809–26). At 8 Prince's St 1809–20, and in 1826 at 19 Graval Lane, Southwark. [D]

Griffiths, Richard, Bridge St, Kington, Herefs., chairmaker and turner (1822–40). [D]

Griffiths, Richard, 17 Lower West St, Bristol, cm and cabinet carver (1829–c. 1840). [D]

Griffiths, Robert, 13 St Martin's Liverpool, joiner and cm (1835). [D]

Griffiths, Robert, Dedham, Essex, cm (1839). [D]

Griffiths, Samuel, Brewer St, Golden Sq., London, upholder (1790). [D]

Griffiths, Samuel, Bristol St, Birmingham, u (1822). [D] Possibly Samuel Griffith.

Griffiths, Samuel, Bristol, cm, chairmaker and bedstead maker (1836–40). At 46 Redcliffe St in 1836 but by the following year the number had changed to 49. By 1839 had moved to 43 Merchant St. In 1838 one directory lists the business as Stephen Griffiths. From 1837 the business declared that they sold both retail and wholesale. [D]

Griffiths, Thomas, Liverpool, cm (1761). Former app. Mathew Page, admitted freeman in 1761. [Freemen's committee bk]

Griffiths, Thomas, Pimlico, London, upholder (1784). [Westminster poll bk]

Griffiths, Thomas, Bristol, cm and u (1817–34). At 65 Broadmead, 1817–20, and 6 Lower Montague St, 1821–34. [D]

Griffiths, Thomas, Bridge St, Kington, Herefs., turner and chairmaker (1830). [D]

Griffiths, Thomas, Liverpool, cm (1835–39). In 1835 maintained a shop at 6 Brook's Alley but in 1837 the address is given as Paradise Ct, Paradise St and in 1839 as 91 Islington. [D]

Griffiths, Thomas, 107 London Rd, London, carver and gilder (1839). [D]

Griffiths, William, Chester and Wrexham, Clwyd, N. Wales, u (1732). Freeman of Chester but in 1732 living at Wrexham. [Chester poll bk]

Griffiths, William, St John St Rd, Clerkenwell, London, cm (1827). Father of an illegitimate child born to Emma Saunders of Islington. [GL, P83/MRYI/877, p. 118]

Griffiths, William, 9 Church St, Kensington, London, cm (1835). [D]

Griffiths, William, 23 Northampton St, Liverpool, cm (1837). [D]

Griffiths, William, 2 Crown St, Walworth Rd, London, cm and u (1839). [D]

Grigg, James, Bristol, cm (1781). [Poll bk]

Grigg, William, Broad-ware, Bristol, cm (1793). [D]

Grigg, William, Rayleigh, Essex, ironmonger and u (d. 1821). Probate on his will granted 1821. [*Wills at Chelmsford*]

Griggi, Joseph, 22 Parker St, Liverpool, looking-glass and picture frame maker (1829). [D]

Griggs, Isaac, Holborn, London, carver and gilder (1790–1820). At 216 Holborn, 1790–93, but from 1800 at 125. [D]

Grigson, James, London, upholder (1698). Free of the Upholders' Co., 7 December 1698. [GL, Upholders' Co. records]

Grime, George, Deansgate, Bolton, Lancs., cm (1814–18). [D]

Grime, Joseph, 115 Deansgate, Bolton, Lancs., cm and u (1814–18). [D]

Grime, Thomas, Wray, near Lancaster, joiner and cm (1828–33). On 7 November 1833 his youngest daughter Sophia married T. Walker, cm of Lancaster, at Melling. [D; *Liverpool Mercury*, 15 November 1833]

Grime & Greasdale, Bolton, Lancs., cm and wheel wrights (1793). [D]

Grimes, —, address unrecorded, cm (1793). Subscribed to Sheraton's *Drawing Book*, 1793.

Grimes, Christopher, Bethnal Green, London, cm (1808). [D]

Grimes, John, Coventry, Warks., cm (1755–56). In 1755 took app. named Taylor. Recorded working for the Hon. Mrs Leigh at Stoneleigh Abbey, Warks. in 1756. He supplied a 'neat mahogany table with a drawer' at £1 4s and a 'wallnot stool' at 5s. [S of G, app. index; Shakespeare Birthplace Trust, Leigh receipts, DR/18/5]

Grimes, John & Thomas, 69–70 Red Lion St, Camberwell, London, cm and u (1795–1823). From 1795–1800 the business is listed as Grimes, Dawes & Co. but from 1801 as John & Thomas Grimes. From 1813 the business appears to have been in the sole control of John Grimes. One of their specialist lines was the manufacture of medicine chests. [D]

Grimmer, Thomas, St Martin's, Norwich, carver (1805). [D]

Grimsdell, James, West Wycombe, Bucks., chairmaker (1798). [Militia Census]

Grimsey, Rowning, 23 Butcher Row, Ratcliffe, London, broker and cm (1821). On 1 August 1821 took out insurance cover of £200 which included £45 for utensils and stock. [GL, Sun MS vol. 486, ref. 981977]

Grimson, John, Aylsham, Norfolk, cm and joiner (1822). [D]

Grimstead, —, Aylesbury House, St John's Sq., London, cm and chairmaker (1731). [*Daily Advertiser*, 4 August 1731]

Grimstead, Joseph, 'The King's Arms', St Paul's Churchyard, London, chairmaker (1707–12). Employed at Boughton, Northants., 1707–08, and at the time of the death of the 1st Duke in 1709 was owed £27 6s. This was settled in 1712. In September 1708 supplied eighteen walnut chairs at a cost of £9 6s to the 2nd Duke of Bedford. [V & A archives; Bedford Office, London]

Grindall, Thomas Witty, 43 and 35 Waterworks St, Hull, Yorks., cm (1840). [D]

Grindley, Jeremiah, London, chairmaker (1818). Freeman of Norwich. [Norwich poll bk]

Grinling, Robert, Halesworth, Suffolk, cm (1759). In 1759 took app. named Pake. [S of G, app. index]

Grinold, William, Broad St Park, Sheffield, Yorks., chairmaker (1822). [D]

Grisbrook, William, St John Lane, London, cm (d. 1799). Death recorded, May 1799. Stated to have been 'near 40 yrs a cabinet-maker'. [*Gents Mag.*, May 1799]

Grisbrook, William, East Cross, Tenterden, Kent, looking-glass and picture frame maker, painter, plumber and paper hanger (1839). [D]

Grist, Edward, Portsea, Portsmouth, Hants., turner and chairmaker (1778–81). In 1781 insured a number of houses for £800. [GL, Sun MS vol. 269, p. 347; vol. 296, p. 560]

Grist, Samuel, Upton Scudamore, Wilts., u (1723). On 5 August 1723 his son Edward was app. to William Carpenter of Upton Scudamore, broad-weaver. [*Wilts. Apps and their Masters*]

Gritten, Henry, London, carver and gilder (1820–37). At 22 Mount St, Westminster Rd, but from 1835 trading also at Duncannon St, Charing Cross. [D]

Gritten, J., 8 Mount St, Lambeth, looking-glass manufacturer (1817). [D]

Gritton, Thomas, Dorchester, Dorset, cm (1793). [D]

Groaters, John, London, cm (1793). Subscribed to Sheraton's *Drawing Book*, 1793.

Groce, Joshua, Grape Lane, York, carver, gilder and barometer maker (1830–38). At 15 Grape Lane in 1830 but from 1837–38 the number is shown as 14. [D]

Grocock, James, Hull, Yorks., cm and u (1834). [D]

Grocock, John, Hull, Yorks., cm, u, auctioneer and broker (1831–40). At 15 Blackfriargate in 1834, 3 Junction Dock St, 1834–40 and 30 Silver St in 1838. [D]

Grocott, William, 13 Simpson St, Manchester, cm (1817). [D]

Groffman, D., 2 Cannon St Rd, London, cm and chairmaker (1837). [D] Succeeded by:

Groffman, Ebenezer, 2 Cannon St Rd, London, cm and u (1839). [D]

Grogan, Charles, address unknown, gilder (1772). On 22 December 1772 received £53 2s for gilding work at Corsham Court, Wilts. [V & A archives]

Grogan, F. M., address unknown, gilder (1768–72). Received £12 18s for gilding picture frames at Corsham Court, Wilts. Subsequent payments were made to a Grogan, gilder from June 1768 to 21 September 1772 for gilding work but these may have been made to either F. M. or Charles Grogan. The amounts total £242 6s 6d. Some of the work may have been on mirrors designed by Robert Adam. [V & A archives; *C. Life*, 5 November 1938]

Gronoufe, James, London, upholder (1707). In 1707 insured a brick house in the parish of St Clement Danes for £500. [GL, Hand in Hand MS vol. 6, ref. 15419] Probably:

Gronous, James, 'The Black Lyon', Wych St, Strand, London, upholder (1700–39). App. to Henry Heasman and free of the Upholders' Co., 7 August 1700. Master of the Upholders' Co., 1739. Took as apps Richard Brisco, 1705–24; Richard Kerrington, 1708–20; William Schouten, 1720–28; Roger Tomlin, 1720–21; and George Dale, 1720–29. In February 1707 he took out insurance cover for £100 on a house on the east side of Butcher Hall Lane in Christchurch parish and may have been living here at this date. By February 1714 however he was at 'The Black Lyon' in Wych St which he insured for £500. In 1725 a similar sum was designated as cover for goods and merchandise at this address. He had possibly ceased to trade as an upholder by the mid 1730s as a newspaper report in December 1735 referred to him as 'late an eminent upholsterer'. His only known commission is that for the 1st Duke of Portland who, for equipage, furniture and workmanship to August 1721, had provided patronage to the extent of £652 12s 3d. [GL, Upholders' Co. records; Hand in Hand MS vol. 6, ref. 15419; vol. 14, ref. 15419; vol. 21, ref. 36672; *London Daily Post*, 17 December 1735]

Groom, John, New St, Wellington, Salop, chairmaker and turner (1840). [D]

Groom, William, Trinity St, Chester, cm (1826). Free 17 June 1826. [Freemen rolls]

Groome, Edward, North End, Gt Yarmouth, Norfolk, cm, u and chairmaker (c. 1810–22). Trade card [Norwich Local Hist. Lib.] describes the business as that of a 'Cabinet & Chair Maker, Upholstery & Paper Hanging Warehouse'. The card is illustrated with engravings of patent beds, a chair, cabinet and sofa. [D]

Grose, J., 44 Newman St, Oxford St, London, cm (1829). [D]

Grossmith, William, Minster St, Reading, Berks., carver and gilder (1820–26). [Poll bks]

Grosvenor, Elizabeth, 54 Burlington Arcade, London, writing and dressing case maker (1835). [D]

Grosvenor, John, Broad St, Ludlow, Salop, cm and u (1840). [D]

Grosvenor, Richard, London, upholder (1700). App. to Thomas Ward and free of the Upholders' Co., 27 August 1700. [GL, Upholders' Co. records]

Grove, Edmund, High Wycombe, Bucks., chairmaker (b. c. 1776–1841). Son Thomas bapt., 1820 and a daughter two years later. Aged 65 at the date of the 1841 Census. [PR (bapt.)]

Grove, J., 33 Brick Lane, Old St, London, u and cm (1820). [D]

Grove, John, 46 Houndsditch, London, cm (1781–87). In 1781 insured his house for £200 and in 1787 household goods for £300. [GL, Sun MS vol. 293, p. 34; vol. 345, p. 318]

Grove, John, 18 Brownlow St, Holborn, London, upholder and auctioneer (1817). [D]

Grove, John Howton, parish of St Paul, Exeter, Devon, cm (1832). [Poll bk]

Grove, William, High Wycombe, Bucks., chairmaker (1835). Daughter bapt., 1835. [PR (bapt.)]

Grover, J., Oxford Pl., Westminster Rd, London, bent timber manufacturer (1829). [D]

Grover, James Yeall(?), Hull, Yorks., cm (1831–40). App. to John Dickon of Hull in 1812. Trading at 21 West St in 1831 but from 1834–40 at 27 Middle St. [D; Hull app reg.]

Grover, Robert, Brighton, Sussex, cm, u and undertaker (1822–40). Baptisms of five daughters and a son recorded, 1822–40. At 35 Ship St in 1822 but by the next year the number had changed to 37. By 1827 at Crown Gdns, and from 1832–35 at North Gdns. Later addresses are Norfolk Sq. in 1837 and 10 Western Rd, 1839–40. [PR (bapt.)]

Groves, Charles, London, japanner and gilder (c. 1750). Trade card [Banks Coll., BM] dates from the mid 18th century and states that he has 'Removed from Long Acre to ye Golden Head, the further End of Brownlow St. from Drury Lane'.

Groves, George, Walmgate, York, joiner/cm (1816–18). [D]

Groves, George, 22 Jamaica Row, Rotherhithe, London, cm (1821). On 4 April 1821 took out insurance cover of £100 which included £50 on his 'Chest of tools in the workshop of Hanebuth 27 Lant St. Borough'. [GL, Sun MS vol. 489, ref. 991234]

Groves, George, Cerne Abbas, Dorset, cm (1840). [D]

Groves, John, 53 Rathbone Pl., London, u (1809). [D]

Groves, John, Richmond, Yorks., cm (1816). [PR (bapt.)]

Groves, John, 8 Gun St, Bishopsgate St, London, carver and gilder (1829). [D]

Groves, John, Bury Hill End, Chesham, Bucks., chairmaker (1830). [D]

Groves, John, 6 Steward St, Spitalfields, London, carver and cm (1839). [D]

Groves, John, Prewett St, Cathay, Bristol, chairmaker (1838–40). [D]

Groves, Michael, 26 Holywell Row, Shoreditch, London, cm (1820–27). [D]

Groves, Thomas & Robert, Boroughgate, Appleby, Westmld, cm/chairmaker (1829–34). [D]

Groves, William, Worthing, Sussex, cm and u (1823–40). At Montague St, 1823–32, and from 1839 at Chapel St. [D]

Groves, William, King Sq., York, cm and u (1815–40). App. to Thomas Walls, cm of York, 14 February 1815. Took his first app. William Snow, on 15 April 1829. Subsequently he took William Crowther, 4 August 1830; Benjamin Masterman, 26 October 1831; John Hill, 11 April 1833; William Shepherd, 20 January 1834; Benjamin Linto Suggett, 1 January 1835; George Bean, 4 January 1837; William Bland, 30 January 1838; Thomas Snow, 6 March 1839; and Henry Owen, 1 June 1840. At 2 King Sq., 1830–40 but in 1838 the number was 3. [D; York app. reg.]

Grubb, Edward, 4 Edmund St, Birmingham, mason and carver (1770). [D]

Grubb, Samuel, 4 Edmund St, Birmingham, mason and carver (1770). [D]

Grubb, William, Cambridge, joiner (1673–d. 1725). William

Grubb received two payments from Trinity College in 1673 and 1679 for general joinery work. Two payments were also made to him by Christ's College, both for supplying furniture, 28 March 1690 'To W Grub for 18 chair frames, and one Elbow chair frame p bill £2.13.0.' John Lunton upholstered them in leather. The other payment in 1691 'June 3 paid Willm Grub for the exchange of ye old table and old cupboard for An oval table and two sideboard tables in ye Lodging', £1.15s. He died in the parish of St Michael, Cambridge in 1725. [Archives of Trinity and Christ's Colleges; Will AR2:35 University Lib.]   R.W.

Grube, Gotlieb, 17 Old Burlington St, London, cm and inlayer (1780). In 1780 took out insurance cover of £300 which included £200 for utensils and stock. [GL, Sun MS vol. 282, p. 572]

Grumbridge, J., 42 Poland St, London, cabinet turner (1835). [D]

Grundy, Isaac, Bolton Ct, Preston, Lancs., u and paper hanger (1834). [D]

Grundy, John, Wirlaton, Wickham, Durham, joiner and cm (1828). [D]

Grundy, John Clowes, 4 Exchange St, Manchester, carver, gilder, barometer and looking-glass maker (1832–40). In 1836 listed as Grundy & Goadsby. [D] See Fox & Grundy.

Grundy, Joseph, Nottingham, joiner and cm (1818). In 1818 took app. named Elijah Middup. [App. reg.]

Grundy, William, Woolwich, London, cm (1823–39). At William St from 1823–32 but in 1838 at 101–02 Powis St though in 1839 the number had changed to 103. [D]

Grundy, William, Parliament St, Nottingham, cm (1835). [D]

Grundy & Fox, 25 St Anne's Sq., Manchester, carvers, gilders, picture frame and looking-glass repairers (1829). [D]

Grundy & Goadsby, 4 Exchange St, Manchester, carvers and gilders (1836). [D]

Guanziroli, Guiseppe, 106 Hatton Gdn, London, looking-glass and artificial flower maker (1834–40). [Goodison, *Barometers*]

Gudd, Robert, Powis St, Woolwich, London, cm and u (1832). [D]

Gudgeon, Robert & Son, Winchester, Hants., cm, u, appraiser and auctioneer (1812–39). Recorded at Piazza in 1823 and 114 High St, 1830–39. In November 1812 announced that he had taken over the premises formerly occupied by a Mr Mercer. He claimed to have worked 'at one of the first houses in the metropolis' and stated that he was able to fit up 'Drawing-rooms, Saloons, and Boudoirs . . . in the first style of elegance and fashion'. He also indicated his need for an app. 'of respectable connections' from whom a premium would be expected. [D; *Hampshire Courier*, 30 November 1812]

Guest, —, Chancery Lane, London (1794). Advertised for journeymen cm 'accustomed to either town or country work in the Cabinet Branch'. These he promised immediate employment at good wages if they applied to his house at the sign of 'The White Hart' in Chancery Lane. [*Williamson's Liverpool Advertiser*, 15 December 1794]

Guest, John & James, London, wholesale japan warehouse (1794–1825). At 16 Staining Lane, Wood St, 1794–1808. There is then a long gap in directory entries until 1825 when the business was at 10 Gough Sq., Fleet St in addition to the Staining Lane address. [D]

Guest, John, 47 Speldhurst St, Burton Cresc., London, u and cm (1820–28). [D]

Guest, John, 73 St James's St, London, u (1823–25). [D]

Guest, Joseph, 54 Stanley St, Liverpool, carver and gilder (1839). [D]

Guest, Ralph, Bury St Edmunds, Suffolk, cm and u (1777–1804). Insured his stock for £160 in 1777 and £150 the following year. In *Ipswich Journal*, 27 October 1804 announced that he was transferring his business to W. Hunter. [D; GL, Sun MS vol. 256, p. 644; vol. 267, p. 528]

Guest, Thomas, Trish Cross, Sheffield, Yorks., chairmaker (1787). [D]

Guest, Thomas, 21 St John's Lane, Clerkenwell, London, bedstead maker (1791). On 28 January 1791 took out insurance cover of £200 of which £70 was for utensils and stock and £10 for tools at 3 Onslow St, Saffron Hill. [GL, Sun MS vol. 375, p. 315]

Guest, William, 4 Newbridge St, Exeter, Devon, cm and u (1838). [D]

Guest, Zephaniah, Dudley, Worcs., cm/u (1838–40). Trading at Stafford St in 1840. [D]

Gugeri, Andrew, London, looking-glass, thermometer and barometer maker (1829–40). At 15 Upper Union Ct, Holborn in 1829 and 16 Charles St, Hatton Gdn, 1830–40. [Goodison, *Barometers*]

Guggiari, Charles, 32 Church St, Sheffield, Yorks., carver and gilder etc. (1828–30). The case of a wheel barometer by A. Alberti, Sheffield, bears the trade label of Charles Guggiari. This indicates that he was a 'Wheel Barometer, Thermometer, Hygrometer, Looking Glass & Picture Frame Manufacturer'. [D; Temple Newsam Exhib., *Furniture made in Yorkshire*, 1974,(9)]

Guggiari, Domenico, Pelham St, Nottingham, carver, gilder, themometer, barometer and looking-glass maker (1832–40). The business also traded under the style D. & Anziani Guggiari. [D; Goodison, *Barometers*]

Guibert, —, 179 Borough, Southwark, London, (1803). [Heal]

Guibert, Philip, German St, St James's, London, upholder (1692–1739). In both 1708 and 1715 took out insurance cover of £450 on a house in German St. Late in the reign of William III he was heavily involved in royal commissions at Windsor Castle and Kensington Palace. In 1697 he supplied a walnut couch, the headboard of which was carved with the royal cypher for which £8 was charged and 'a fine black soffa in a new fashion' for £14. Apart from seating furniture he was active in the making of fine beds. In 1697 he also supplied a bed for the royal yacht *The Lady Portland* at £7 15s with an additional £8 10s for carving it and £2 15s for carved walnut work for its foot. Metalwork in connection with this bed cost £7 18s and upholstery work £22 15s. A 'great bed of Genoa damask' was supplied to Kensington Palace costing £37 17s 6d also in 1697. On 1 February 1698/99 Guibert's petition for the payment of £1,695 5s 3d due to him for work furnishing the King's bedchamber and dining room at Windsor, and his house at Hounslow and other lodgings, was forwarded to the Earl of Montagu, Master of the Great Wardrobe, for verification. On 26 May 1699 payment of £1,000 on account was made. A further payment of £350 to Guibert is recorded in 1702 after the King's death. Members of the nobility followed the King's lead and patronised this maker. In 1702 the 2nd Duchess of Bedford paid £171 14s 7d for furniture which was probably supplied to Bedford House, London. This consisted of an oak bedstead for her bedchamber complete with sky blue damask bed furniture, 2 large window and 3 matching door curtains, 2 easy chairs, 4 back chairs and 4 stools upholstered *en suite*. Ten chairs and window curtains were included for the drawing room. Another patron was the 1st Duke of Leeds, and furniture supplied to him may have been for his house at Wimbledon. It is thought that the day bed and sofa with his carved monogram, now at Temple Newsam, Leeds, may have been by this maker. Payments to Guibert by the Duke have been recorded including the sum of £73 10s on 30 June 1702 to a 'Mr Hibbert' which may have been a misunderstanding of his surname.

A notice in the *St James' Evening Post* of 6 September 1729 stating that 'Mr Gilbert, Upholsterer to His Majesty' had died that morning has been assumed to refer to this maker. This however seems unlikely. There is no evidence that Guibert worked for George II and a much more likely candidate is John Gilbert of St Giles, London. Guibert appears to have been alive in 1739 and is referred to in a letter dated 3 July concerned with the building works at Rousham House, Oxon. William White, who was Clerk of the Works at Rousham states in this letter which he wrote to General Dormer in London, that he would give it into the hands of 'Mr Guibert, the Upholsterer' by whom it would be conveyed in 'the flying coach' for London. This strongly suggests that Guibert worked at Rousham, possibly under the direction of William Kent. [GL, Hand in Hand MS vol. 6, ref. 1505; vol. 14, p. 583; *DEF*; V & A archives; Worcs. RO, 2252/705:366/6(iii); Bedford Office, London, PRO, LC5/43/245; Gilbert, *Leeds Furn. Cat.*, vol. 2, pp. 264–68; William & Glyn's Bank (Child's) — Duke of Leeds account; Heal] B.A.

Guichard, John Bruno, London, carver, gilder, u, cm and painter (1776–1802). In February 1787 at 4 Stephens St, Rathbone Pl., London where he insured household goods, stock etc. for £300. By February 1802 however he had moved to 14 Marlborough St, near Oxford St and took out insurance cover for £3,000 of which £300 was in respect of utensils and stock. Named in the list of furniture makers compiled by the 1st Duchess of Northumberland *c.*1776. [GL, Sun MS vol. 342, ref. 527533; vol. 423, ref. 727847; Gilbert, *Chippendale*, p. 154] Also named in the Broadlands papers. [*C. Life*, 5 February 1981]

Guichard, P., 22 Lisle St, Leicester Sq., London, u, carver and gilder (1810–19). A debt of £25 13s 4d is referred to in a letter dated 23 May 1810 from Sir Francis Baring to Richard, 2nd Baron Ashburton. This had been settled on the behalf of the late Dowager Lady Ashburton by the Bank. [D]

Guidot, Anthony, London, upholder (1708–27). Son of Richard Guidot of Ropley, Hants., Gent. Brother of William Guidot snr, who was his app. 1716–24, and father of William Guidot jnr, both London upholders. Anthony Guidot was app. to Thomas Ferrers on 14 July 1708 and free of the Upholders' Co. by servitude, 5 September 1716. In 1718 he was trading from an address at the sign of 'The Sun', Fleet St but by 1722 had moved to the sign of 'The Royal Bed' in Shug Lane, Marylebone St. On 20 July of that year he took out insurance cover of £500 which included £100 for goods and merchandise, £100 for a warehouse and £300 for goods in it. In 1718 he was working for the 1st Duke of Montrose at his house in Bond St, London. He charged £18 14s for making up the Crimson Mohair Room, and in addition 31 yards of blue mohair was supplied at 5s 6d per yd. A further commission of the same year for this house included the foot and head part of a bedstead, cushions, curtains, the making of a settee, chair bottoms and 14 yards of blue serge for lining a chapel pew. This bill amounted to £22 14s 5½d. Work for the Duke continued until 1725 and Guidot's bills for furnishings at Bond St and Hanover Sq. totalled £216 18s 6d. [GL, Upholders' Co. records; Sun MS vol. 14, ref. 25943; Heal; Scottish RO, GD 220/6/1192/10, 1192/36, GD 220/6/3/ P147] See Andrew Guidott.

Guidot Brettrell, William, 122 High Holborn, London, upholder and cm (1786). In October 1786 took out insurance cover of £1,500 which included £700 for utensils, stock and goods in trust and £500 more for utensils etc. in a yard. [GL, Sun MS vol. 339, p. 517]

Guidot, William snr, the sign of 'The Three Tents', near New Broad St Buildings, Moorfields, London, u (1716–24). Son of Richard Guidot of Ropley, Hants., Gent. Brother of Anthony Guidot, upholder to whom he was app. on 14 February 1716. Admitted freeman of the Upholders' Co. by servitude, 5 August 1724. Trade card [Leverhulme Coll., MMA, NY] states that he bought and sold 'all manner of Household Goods, both New & Old' and furnished funerals. [GL, Upholders' Co. records; Heal]

Guidot, William jnr, London, u (1742–62). Son of Anthony Guidot, freeman upholder of London. Free of the Upholders' Co. by patrimony, 5 May 1742. Took as apps James Cox, 1748–55; Samuel Jenkins, 1749–56; Thomas Draper 1752–59; John Proudman, 1758–61; and John Forfar, 1759–62. [GL, Upholders' Co. records]

Guidot, William, Dog Row, Bethnal Green, London, upholder (1792). [Heal]

Guidott, Andrew, London, u (1720–21). Carried out work for the 1st Duke of Montrose, 1720–21, including the supply of two 'lath coach bedsteads'. It is possible that the incorrect Christian name was stated and this is an additional commission of the maker Anthony Guidot who was working for the Duke during this period. [Scottish RO, GD 220/6/1208/10]

Guilbaud, John, 'The Crown & Looking-Glass', Long Acre, London, cm (*c.* 1700). Trade label recorded on a walnut, drop front writing cabinet states that he sold 'all manner of Cabbinet work and Japan Cabbinets, Large Tables, Small suets of all manner of Looking Glasses, Pannells of Glasse, Chimney peaces and all sorts of Glasse Sconces'. In 1703 he was paid for two overmantel mirrors supplied to Hopetoun House, South Queensferry, Scotland. [Wills, *English Furniture*, I, pp. 108–09; V & A archives] See John Guilliband.

Guildford, James, 6 Castle St and Stone St, Brighton, Sussex, cm and u (1839–40). [D]

Guilett, J. C., Silver St, Kensington Gravel Pits, London, carver and gilder (1838). [D]

Guillet, James Charles, Hollen St, Soho, London, carver and gilder (1820–39). At 5 Hollen St in 1820 but by 1829 the number had changed to 4. [D]

Guilliband, John, London, cm (1690–91). On 31 July 1690 charged £30 for two scriptors 'inlaid with flowers' supplied for Queen Mary II. In the following year 'a plain scriptoire' was made for Whitehall Palace. Possibly John Guilbaud working from 'The Crown & Looking-Glass' in Long Acre at this period. [*Conn.*, vol. 57, p. 90; Symonds, *Furniture Making in 17th and 18th Century England*, p. 108]

Guillot, James Lewis, parish of St Anne, Westminster, London, carver (1754). In 1754 took app. John Lemaitre. [Boyd's index to IR app. reg., vol. 18, p. 3540]

Guillotin, —, next 'The Black Lion', Pall Mall, near St James's, London, u (1691). [Heal]

Guischard, Peter, 21 Lisle St, Leicester Sq., London, upholder (1820). [D]

Gulielmus, Newill, Townhead, Rochdale, Lancs., cm and u (1825). [D]

Gulley, John, London Lane, Norwich, u (1805–08). [D]

Gulley, John, Limekiln Dock, Bristol, carpenter and cm (1823–25). [D]

Gullifer, James, Bristol, cm and broker (1824–27). At 32 Philadelphia St in 1824, 13 Merchant St in 1825, 18 Merchant St in 1826 and 12 Denmark St in 1827. [D]

Gulliver, John, Woodstock, Oxon., cm (1771–d. 1799). In September 1771 mentioned in an advertisement for the sale of cottages at Horley near Banbury, Oxon. In October 1780 the furniture of John Gulliver, cm, was offered for sale by John Churchill though the reason for this sale is not known.

Despite this he continued to trade in Woodstock. Probate on his will was granted on 8 May 1799. [D; *Jackson's Oxford Journal*, 7 September 1771, 17 October 1780; Bodleian Lib., Oxford, index of wills]

Gumbrell, John & Chiles, Edward, Richmond, Surrey, carpenters and u (1797). Declared bankrupt, *Billinge's Liverpool Advertiser*, 17 April 1797.

Gumbrell, William, George St, Richmond, Surrey, carpenter, upholder and ironmonger (1777). In 1777 took out insurance cover of £2,400 of which £740 was in respect of utensils and stock. [GL, Sun MS vol. 260, p. 255]

Gumley, Elizabeth, London, cm (1674–d. 1751); **Gumley, John**, cm and manufacturer of plate- and looking-glass (1691–1727). There is no lack of references in the press to the Gumley family from 1694 onwards, but many are contradictory and make it difficult to distinguish fact from fiction. In the former category are advertisements in John Houghton's *A Collection for the Improvement of Husbandry and Trade*, 6 April 1694 and in the *London Gazette*, 21 June 1694, of which the first-named announced that 'At Salisbury-Exchange in the Strand, where the Manufactory was kept, by John Gumley, Cabinet-maker, at the corner of Norfolk-street ... is a Sale of all sorts of Cabinetwork, as Japan Cabinets, Indian and English, with Looking-glasses, Tables, Stands, Chests of Drawers, Screutores, Writing-Tables, and Dressing Suits of all sorts ...'. Less credible is a series of wedding announcements in the *Gents Mag.*, 1735, pp. 559, 681 and 737, relating to a Miss Gumley and a Mr Lake. The former's surname is given correctly in the columns of the publication, as GUMBLEY in the index, and as GUMBLY in the *General Index ... 1731–86*.

John Gumley's mother, Elizabeth, would seem to have traded in partnership with her son until *c.* 1727, when it may be assumed he had died, and thenceforward she traded in company with William Turing. In that year they presented jointly a bill for three tables supplied to Hampton Court Palace (see below). According to John Gumley's will [Extracts given by R. W. Symonds in a letter to *C. Life*, 27 February 1942, pp. 406–07] Gumley and his wife, Susan, had three sons and four daughters, one of the latter, Anna Maria, marrying in 1714 William Pulteney; the political rival of Sir Robert Walpole, Pulteney was ennobled in 1742 as Earl of Bath. The mother of the Countess died at the age of 77 according to the *Gents Mag.*, 24 January 1751, p. 42, leaving 'her estate real and personal, which is considerable ... to her only son Col. Gumley'. Her late husband's will mentions his third son, Samuel, as holding a commission in the army, confirming that detail in the magazine report.

In his will Gumley stated firmly that his eldest son, George, was 'very profligate and disobedient', and was left £150 per annum so long as he did not 'obtrude himself upon or molest my wife'. His second son, John, succeeded his father as a partner in the glass manufactory of Richard Hughes & Co. of Vauxhall, and Gumley House, Isleworth was settled on him in 'strict entail'. In 1727 John stood for Parliament for Bramber, Sussex, but was defeated through Walpole influencing the handful of voters in favour of his cousin, James Hoste. [J. H. Plumb, *Sir Robert Walpole*, 1960, II, 182]

A glass manufactory was established at Lambeth by Gumley and others by 1705, Gumley himself being admitted a freeman of the Glass Sellers' Co. as a 'Looking Glass Grinder' on 22 June 1704. [GL, MS 1645] The Lambeth concern was immediately attacked by a firm in Southwark, the Bear Garden glasshouse, whose proprietors conducted a pamphlet war and then went to Parliament where their claim for a monopoly was disallowed. [*Conn.*, December 1935, pp. 315–21; Wills, *Looking-Glasses*, p. 46]

In 1714 Gumley entered into partnership with James Moore, an association that endured until Moore's death in 1726. In 1714 also, Gumley announced in Richard Steele's *The Lover*, 24 April: 'These are to give Notice. That John Gumley hath taken for a Ware-house, and furnished all the upper Part of the New Exchange in the Strand ... with the largest and finest Looking Glasses in Frames, and out of Frames ... Likewise all sorts of Coach-Glasses, Chimney-Glasses, Sconces, Dressing-Glasses, Union-Suits, Dressing-Boxes, Swinging-Glasses, Glass Schandeleres, Lanthorns, Gilt Brockets, Desks and Book-Cases, India Chests and Cabinets, Screens, Tea Tables, Card-Tables of all kinds, Strong Boxes, and the like ... Also John Gumley's House and Shop the Corner of Norfolk-street, is to be Lett ...'.

The Norfolk St property had belonged to Gumley for some years. On 13 August 1703 he had insured with the Hand in Hand Insurance Co. '... a brick house on the South side of the Strand and the East side of Norfolk street ... being his dwelling House ... for seven years, £600'.

Steele himself contributed to *The Lover*, 13 May 1715 a fulsome essay on the New Exchange showroom, which he recommended strongly to his readers. There, he wrote, 'they will certainly be well pleased, for they will have unavoidable Opportunities of seeing what they most like, in the most various and agreeable Shapes and Positions, I mean their dear selves'. The advice was taken by a young man of 24, Dudley Ryder, who was training for the Bar and who duly became Chief Justice of the Court of King's Bench and a Privy Councillor. He noted in his diary on 3 November 1715: 'Went into the glass warehouse over the New Exchange. There is indeed a noble collection of looking-glass, the finest I believe in Europe. I could not as I passed by there help observing myself, particularly my manner of walking, and that pleased me very well, for I thought I did it with a very genteel and becoming air'. [W. Matthews (ed.), *The Diary of Dudley Ryder*, 1939, p. 130]

ROYAL PALACES. 1691 'Octob 2d 1702. Received from Mr Henning [Caspar Frederick Henning, Treasurer to the Groom of the Stole and 1st Gentleman of the Bedchamber to William III] the Summe of Sixty pounds being in full for a lookeing-glass of 96 Inches by 46½ delivered for his late Majties use in the Year 1691 And in full of All Claims and demands whatsoever on acct of his sd Late Majtis privy-purse, I say, recd by me John Gumley'. [Worcs. RO, 2252/705: 366/6(iii)]

1714–15 'A large glass in a gilt frame and top'. [*GCM*]

1727 Elizabeth Gumley and William Turing for Hampton Court: 'For 3 very large walnut quadrille tables covered with green velvet £15'. [*Old Furniture*, II, 182]

1729 Elizabeth Gumley and Co. were censured by the Comptroller of the Great Wardrobe. According to the *Daily Journal*, 20 December 1729, 'upon the Comptroller inspecting the work said to be done by Mrs Elizabeth Gumley and Company, Cabinet Makers for his Majesty at St James's and Kensington, in the quarter ended at Michaelmas, 1729, he found at the last Place the much greater part of their charge not done at all, and both there and at St James's he found very little work done in the manner they charged: so that in the whole, after allowing such a price as, according to the said Comptroller's best Judgment the Nature of the Performance deserv'd, he thought there might reasonably be abated out of their bill, which amounted to £512.12s. the sum of £361.10s.6d.'. A letter to the Comptroller (Ralph, Duke of Montagu) stated that 'Mrs Gumley and Mr Turing were no longer to be employed as tradesmen for the Wardrobe on account of their notorious impositions'. [*GCM*]

In the Public Dining-room at Hampton Court Palace is a

large looking-glass, one of a pair having the central plate flanked by vertical pilasters of looking-glass. [*DEF*, II, 323, fig. 31] The pilasters are divided by narrow strips of giltwood, one of which is lettered 'GUMLEY'. [Ibid., II, 251]

THOMAS, 1st DUKE OF LEEDS. The Duke paid J. Gumley the undermentioned sums: 3 May 1700, £54; 17 May 1705, £77; 3 May 1706, £108. [1st Duke of Leeds's account with Williams and Glyn's Bank]

DUKE OF BEDFORD. In December 1702 John Gumley supplied Wriothesley, 2nd Duke of Bedford with a 'neat panel of glass with a top' for £60; 'a plain black table' for £1 10s; and 'a gilt table made to an Indian table' for £4 10s. [Bedford Office, London]

WILLIAM, 1st DUKE OF DEVONSHIRE. 1702: 'Pd the Smith for 18 stayes for the Looking glasses at 4d a pair 6/–; 21 hooks for Looking glasses 3/6. [Chatsworth account bk, p. 77] 1703: 'Paid Mr Gumley for 2 large Looking Glasses £200. Paid Mr Chadwick for going to Chatsworth with ye glasses £16'. [*DEF*, II, 252] One of the pair bears the scratched inscription 'John Gumley 1703'. [*GCM*] 1703: 'Pd Gilbert Ball Carriage for 2 large Looking glasses & frames 2 other large Cases with furniture chair frames £6.10s'. [Chatsworth account bk, p. 82] 1705: July 'for 280 squares of [plate] glass for West front £280'. [Chatsworth account bk, vol. VII]

JAMES 1st DUKE OF MONTROSE (The Duke of Montrose's Lodging in the Drygate, Glasgow). 1714: Receipted account for a walnut Desk and Bookcase £11. [Scottish RO, GD220/6/1162/84] 1717: 18 June 'Bought of John Gumley a neat walnut tree chimney glass £5.10.0' plus 5/s for a packing case. [GD220/6/1170/35] 1718: For the Duke's London house in Bond St: 'Hanging glass' £5 10s; 'Glass lanthern' £3; 'Walnut tree Desk' £8; '3 Dressing glasses' £5. Total £21 10s. [GD/220/6/1192/35] For the same residence also in 1718 payment of £56 8s to 'John Gumley, Cabinet Maker, London' for goods supplied. [GD220/6/28/p. 84] 1722: 28 February 'Rec. from His Grace the Duke of Montrose by the hands of Mr Andrew Gardner [Montrose's secretary] £2 10s. sterling for a dessert table received by me for my Mrs [mistress] Elizabeth Gumley, John Draper'. [GD220/6/1213/27] 1723: Receipted account for 'a neat Virginia Walnut tree clothes chest £5. A small square mahogany table bordered with manchineel, £1,10.0.'. [GD220/6/1238/13]

PAUL FOLEY (The Temple and Little Ormond St, London; Newport House, Almeley, Herefs.). 1720: 'Bought of John Gumley/March 26th A dutch Table 12s./A packing Matt and Cord for Ditto 1/6d./Aprill 9th A neet Swinging Glass in a blue Japand frame £1.4s./One Ditto in a black Japand frame £1./A packing for the glasses 2/6d./A neet hand tea Table done in Jerran 15s./July ye 1st A large Wallnuttree Burow Table £6./A packing Case for Ditto 9s.' Total £10.4s. Receipt dated 5 July 1720 and signed by 'Eliz Gumley'. [Herefs. RO, F/AIII/55] 1730: 'Bought of Elzath. Gumley/June 1st Two New Glasses and a New Door to a Lantern Agreed at 12s.' Receipt dated 2 June 1730, signed on behalf of Mrs Gumley by Wm Flack, witnessed by Cha: Parkes. [F/AIII/55]

JOHN MELLER (Erddig Park, Wales). 1724: 'Bought of Elizabeth Gumley December 3 A Sconce in a Carv'd and Gilt Frame £4.5s. Rec'd at the same time the full contents of the above and all Accompts — pd: me Eliz Gumley'. [Clwyd RO, D/E/484]

JOHN MORGAN (Tredegar Park, Monmouthshire). 1726: 'June 1 Mrs Gumley for a walnut tree Quadrille table £3.10s.' [Nat. Lib. Wales, Tredegar papers, MS 315–45]   G.W.

Gumley, Peter, 'The Cabinet', Strand, London, cm and china dealer (1674–1702). Peter Gumley is recorded as a cm in 1674, with premises named *The Cabinet*, near St Clement's Church in the Strand. Two purchases, one certain and the

other 'possible' from him are noted by John Hervey, later 1st Earl of Bristol. Both transactions took place in 1702: 'April 30. Paid Gumley for my bureau & some china ware, £11.10s.'; and 'Dec. 16. Paid Peter Gumley for China & Japan ware, £29'. [*Diary of John Hervey*, Wells, 1894, pp. 146–47] As John Gumley is not known to have dealt in chinaware, it might be assumed that the first of the payments was made to the same man as the second.

It may also be thought that he is the Peter Gumley, son of John and Mary Gumley, christened at St Martin's, Ludgate, on 26 February 1642. Finally, a brief obituary in the *Gents Mag.*, 1735, p. 387 may be pertinent: '5 July. Mrs Gumley, aged 92, who kept the great China-Warehouse in Exeter Change, about 15 years ago'.   G.W.

Gummery, Thomas, Church St, Warwick, cm (1831). [Poll bk]

Gunby, Day, see George and Thomas Seddon.

Gundall, James, The Paved Ct, St James's, London, cm (1749). [Westminster poll bk]

Gundy, William, Steep Hill, Lincoln, carver and gilder (1835). [D]

Gunnel, Ralph, Barking, Essex, upholder (1808). [D]

Gunnell, William, 55 Rosoman St, Clerkenwell, London, carver and gilder (1820). [D]

Gunnis, —, address unknown (1791–92). Received £6 4s 6d on 5 September 1791 for 'bed furniture repairs' and £6 17s 10d for bed hangings. [Lincoln RO, MM 9110]

Gunns, Edward, address unknown, cm (1803). Subscribed to Sheraton's *Cabinet Dictionary*, 1803.

Gunson, Anthony, Baggraw, Wigton, Cumb., joiner/cm (1829). [D]

Gunson, Joshua, Lancaster (1827–31). [Westminster Ref. Lib., Gillow records]

Gunter, —, Holborn, London, u (d. 1746). Stated at the time of his death in 1746 to be 'an eminent upholsterer'. [Heal]

Gunter, Barbary, Holborn, London, upholder (1754–60). [D]

Gunter, Joseph, Manchester House, 1 Regent Pl., Cheltenham, Glos., cm and u (1820). [D]

Gunton, James, 4 Timberhill St, Norwich, cm and chairmaker (1796–1823). One directory of 1805–08 gives the address as Hoghill. His son Edward, grocer, was admitted freeman, 27 September 1823. [D; poll bks; freemen reg.]

Gurbett, John, Broseley, Salop, cm (1822–28). [D]

Gurden, John, High Wycombe, Bucks., chairmaker (1814). Daughter bapt., 1814. [PR (bapt.)]

Gurnell, Thomas, Lancaster, cm (1787–1795). App. to Gillow and named in the Gillow records, 1787, 1790 and 1792–95. [Westminster Ref. Lib., Gillow vol. 344/96, p. 955; Lancaster app. reg.]

Gurney, Samuel, parish of St Stephen, Norwich, cm (1830). [Poll bk]

Gurney, Thomas, 110 Aldersgate St, St Martin's-le-Grand, London, cm and wholesale cabinet warehouse (1806–23). [D]

Gurney, William, West Stockwell St, Colchester, Essex, cm and u (1832). [D]

Gurry, Ebenezer, St Neots, Hunts., chairmaker (1823–24). [D]

Gurry, Samuel, Market Sq., St Neots, Hunts., chairmaker and turner (1830). [D]

Gustar, John, High St, Poole, Dorset, cm and u (1840). [D]

Guthrie, Claud, 4 Walles Pl., Lambeth Rd, London, cm and u (1827). [D]

Guthrie, J., Forth St, Newcastle, joiner, cm, sofa and clock case maker (1824–28). [D]

Gutteridge, John, Kingsmead St, Walcot, Bath, Som., cm (1746–52). In 1746 took app. named Bowen. The house he occupied was rented from Elizabeth, Dowager Countess of Hyndford of Bath and in 1752 was insured for £300. [S of G, app. index; GL, Sun MS vol. 98, ref. 132831]

Gutteridge, Benjamin, High Wycombe, Bucks., chairmaker (1798). [Militia Census]

Guy, —, Brownlow Hill, Liverpool, upholder and cm (1818). In May 1818 married Miss Williams, eldest daughter of a glover trading in Lord St, at St Anne's Church. [*Liverpool Mercury*, 15 May 1818]

Guy, Henry, Little Albion St, Hull, Yorks., cm (1838–39). [D]

Guy, Henry Remington, 13 Junction Dock St, Hull, Yorks., cm (1837–40). In 1840 stated to be also a furniture broker and to have been keeping the 'Tally-ho Inn', Bond St. [D]

Guy, James, Hull, Yorks., cm (1837–40). In 1837 at Leadenhall Sq., and from 1839 at Manor St. In 1840 his trade was listed as shop-keeper and in 1842 as a furniture broker. [D]

Guy, John, 41 St John St, Rd, London, jewellery case maker (1839). [D]

Guy, Richard, St Thomas's Buildings, Dale St, Liverpool, cm (1796–1803). Son of Richard Guy, bricklayer. Free 25 May 1796. In 1800 at 11 St Thomas's Buildings, Dale St but in 1803 at no. 35, in 1805 at no. 18. [D]

Guy, Thomas, Liverpool, cm (1805–19). Signed a supplement to the *Liverpool Cabinet and Chair Prices*, 1805, on behalf of the journeymen. Trading at Langhorne Ct, Clayton St, 1813–14, and at 17 Fleet St in 1818. Partnership with Hodgson as Hodgson & Guy was dissolved in December 1819. [D; *Liverpool Mercury*, 3 December 1819]

Guy, Thomas, 10 Junction Dock St, Hull, Yorks., cm (1838–40). In 1839–40 shown as furniture broker. [D]

Guy, William, 2 Humber St, Hull, Yorks., joiner and cm (1822–39). In December 1822 took app. Marmaduke Sturdy. First recorded in directories 1838. One directory of this date lists him as a furniture broker. [D; Hull app. reg.]

Guy, William jnr, Liverpool, u (1818–35). Free 20 June 1818 when his trade was listed as u, now breeches maker. At this date at 27 Williamson St and Aigburth St. In 1818 at 6 Brownlow Hill, 1829 at 1 Rice St and in 1835 at 3 Pilgrim St. [D; freemen reg.]

Guyer, Thomas, parish of St Michael, Bristol, upholder (1774–84). [Poll bks]

Guyon, John, London, chairmaker (1780–1812). Freeman of Colchester, Essex. [Colchester poll bks]

Guzziari, Dominico, Pelham St, Nottingham, carver, gilder and looking-glass maker (1834–35). [D]

Gwennap, John, Falmouth, Cornwall, u etc. (1783–d. 1794). Died 2 October 1794. [D; *Exeter Flying Post*]

Gwilliam & Barnard, Fleet Mkt, London (c. 1800). Label recorded on a Sheraton mahogany wardrobe with satinwood inlay. [Phillips, 1 July 1968 (Sandways Pl., Kent), lot 26]

Gwillym, Thomas, St Owen St, Hereford, cm, u and joiner (1822). Former app. Samuel Davies, admitted freeman in 1822. [D; freemen reg.]

Gwinnell, William, 'The Looking-Glass', south side of St Paul's Churchyard, London, cm and glass grinder (1729–41). In 1729 insured his household goods and stock in trade for £1,000. Trade card in the Heal Coll., BM, states that he sold 'all sorts of Looking Glasses, Sconces, Coach Glasses and all sorts of Cabinet and Japan'd work; likewise all sorts of the Best & most Fashionable Chairs either matted or Can'd, Blinds for Windows made and Curiously Painted on Canvas Silk or Wire'. On 4 January 1736 invoiced to St John's College, Cambridge, for the Common Room '20 walnut chairs covered with leather at 14s 6d'. These were made to a pattern supplied by the College and 2s 6d was charged on the bill for carrying the pattern chair. [GL, Sun MS vol. 29, ref. 48261; St John's College, Common Rm file]

Gwyn, Peter, London, u (1718–49). In 1718 his address was 'against the Crown Tavern in Catherine St in the Strand in the parish of St Mary le Savoy'. By 1747 in St James's, Haymarket. [GL, Sun MS vol. 8, refs 12217–18; Heal; Westminster poll bk]

Gwynn, —, Somerset Ct, Bath, Som., chairmaker (1819). [D]

Gyer, John, Hird's Buildings, Skipton, Yorks., joiner/cm (1837). [D]

Gynne, George snr and jnr, 17 Red Lion Lane, Norwich, upholders (1775–84). George Gynne jnr was admitted a freeman of Norwich by patrimony 19 June 1775. In the following year both father and son are recorded trading in partnership. Insurance cover of £1,500 was taken out in this year of which £500 was in respect of utensils and stock. The father was not recorded in the 1781 city poll and was probably dead by this date. [D; GL, Sun MS vol. 249, p. 344; poll bk]

H

Habbot, James, Chester, joiner and cm (1752–55). App. to Joseph Wilkinson, joiner and cm, 13 January 1752 to 1 May 1755. [Chester app. bks]

Habever, Martin, 4 Horseferry Rd, London, buhl manufacturer (1827–28). [D]

Habever, Martin, 17 Seymour Pl., Bryanston Sq., London, cm, u and chairmaker (1827–28). [D]

Habgood, Henry, Wimborne, Dorset, u and cm (1840). [D]

Habgood, William, London, carver, gilder and frame maker (1783–1808). Declared bankrupt, in partnership with Edward Stephens at Gt Portland St, *Gents Mag.*, May 1783; and alone, at Dufour's Pl., St James's, Westminster, *Billinge's Liverpool Advertiser*, 14 November 1796. Probably the Habgood, or Hopgood, carver, gilder and frame maker, named in the Longford Castle, Wilts. accounts in 1799 being paid £15 10s 6d; in 1800, £14 18s; in 1803, £9 15s; in 1804, £10 10s 'for frames'; and in 1808, £39 1s 6d. [V&A archives]

Hacche, John, South St, South Molton, Devon, u and cm (1838). [D]

Hack, R, 17 South Audley St, London, cm and u (1839). [D]

Hack, William, Baxtergate, Loughborough, Leics., joiner/cm (1822). [D]

Hacker, —, address unrecorded, cm (c.1775). Supplied furniture to Denton Park, Yorks., c.1775, totalling £9. [*Furn. Hist.*, 1968]

Hacket, —, address unrecorded. Named in the Holkham Hall, Norfolk accounts in 1743, receiving £18 for making two beds. [V&A archives]

Hackett, John, Gt Bridge, West Bromwich, Staffs., cm and u (1830). [D]

Hackett, Joshua, Attleborough, Warks., chairmaker and turner (1835). [D]

Hackett, Thomas, Sleaford, Lincs., joiner and cm (1798). [D]

Hackett, William, 62 Shude Hill, Manchester, cm (1825). [D]

Hackford, John, Bawtry, Yorks., joiner and/or cm (1834). [D]

Hacking, William, Liverpool, cm (1813–21). Trading at 48 Lace Lane, 1813–14; no. 49 in 1816; no. 19 in 1818; and 47 Standick St in 1821, when he is also recorded as a butcher. [D]

Hackitt, John, Dudley, Worcs., cm (1839). [D]

Hackwaite, —, address unrecorded. In 1746 received £3 9s for a settee, a stand for a basin and mending a table at Holkham Hall, Norfolk. [V&A archives]

Hacon, Henry, George St, Gt Yarmouth, Norfolk, cm and u (1839). [D]

Had, Robert, Bridgnorth, Salop, cm (1797–98). [D]

Hadden, William, 7 Crescent, Cambridge, carver and gilder (1830). [D]

Haddock, Benjamin, Bristol, u (1721–22). [Poll bk]

Haddock, Elka (Elkanah or Elkunah), London, joiner and cm (1732–43). Recorded as Elkanah in Denmark St, St Giles-in-the-Fields, in 1732; as Elkunah in Greek St, 1737; and Elkanah, late of Dean St, Soho, in 1743. Took out a Sun Insurance policy on 20 September 1732 for £400, including £100 on goods and utensils. [GL, Sun MS vol. 37, ref. 58684] On 13 December 1735 he was paid the large sum of £220 9s 1d for work at Wilton House, Wilts. [*Apollo*, July 1964, p.4a; *GCM*] In 1737 Elka Haddock rendered a bill, totalling £8 1s to 'the Honble. Genl. Dormer' of Rousham, Oxon., in which he charged £1 10s for 'a Neat Mahog. Night table wth a tray on top'; and £6 6s for 'a Neat large Mahog. Easy Chair wth brass Castors, ye back seat and elboes Stuffd Cov.^d with red Morocco leather Naild with brass Nailes.' Bill receipted on 13 October 1737. There is also an item 'to cleaning the ambina [amboyna] Table and polishing do. 5s.' [Rousham archives] Elkunah Haddock of Greek St, cm, is named in the accounts of Earl Fitzwalter for Moulsham Hall, Essex on 30 April 1737, supplying 'a Library Table cover'd with green Cloth and with nine Drawers', costing £15. [A. C. Edwards, *The Accounts of Benjamin Mildmay, Earl Fitzwalter*, p. 107] On 4 March 1739 Elka Haddock was commissioned to make the 'sella curulis' chair for the Society of Dilettanti 'for the use and dignity of the Presid^t.' On 5 May 1739, Sir Brownlow Sherrard, Bart, paid Haddock £4 10s for the chair, described as 'a mahogany compass seat Elboe Chair', covered with crimson velvet, with a mahogany pedestal and castors. [Lionel Cust, *History of the Society of Dilettanti*, p. 27] A notice regarding the payment of creditors of Elkanah Haddock, late of Dean St, Soho, cm, appeared in *Daily Advertiser*, 31 August 1743. [DEF; Harris, *Old English Furniture*]

Haddon, late Graham, 72 St Martin's Lane, London, cabinet and chair manufacturer, upholder and undertaker (*c.*1800). [Trade card in GL Coll.] See John Haddon at this address.

Haddon, George, 40 Carr Lane, Hull, Yorks., chairmaker (1823). [D]

Haddon, John, Hull, Yorks., chairmaker (1804). App. to George Spenceley of Hull in 1804. [Hull app. reg.]

Haddon (or Hadden), John, Long Alley, Worship St, London, cm, u and chairmaker (1802–28). Addresses given at no. 3 in 1802; no. 67, 1817–23; and no. 1, 1817–28. Took out a Sun Insurance policy on 30 November 1802 for £500, of which £300 accounted for utensils and stock. Subscribed to Sheraton's *Cabinet Dictionary*, 1803. [D; GL, Sun MS vol. 427, ref. 740491]

Haddon, John, 72 St Martin's Lane, London, u and cm (1819–27). [D]

Haddon, Joseph, Nuneaton, Warks., chairmaker and turner (1828–35). [D]

Haddon, Joseph, Market Pl., Buckingham, cm and furniture broker (1823). [D]

Haddon, William, Hinckley, Leics., turner (1790–1829). [D]

Haddon, William, 67 Sawney Pope St, Liverpool, cm (1839). [D]

Haddrick, —, Hercules Buildings, Lambeth, London, carver and gilder (1809–11). [D]

Haddrick, Thomas, Pudding Lane, Maidstone, Kent, cm (1838). [Poll bk]

Haden, William, Deritend, Birmingham, picture frame maker (1800). [D]

Hadfield, Isaac, Liverpool, cm (1796–1815). App. to John Gorton in 1796. Petitioned freedom on servitude in 1815, paying 6s 8d. Admitted freeman on 24 August 1815. [Liverpool freemen's committee bk and reg.]

Hadfield, Robert, Stalybridge, Lancs., cm and joiner (1834). [D]

Hadkinson, Henry, Williamson Sq., Liverpool, cm (1768). Announcement in *Williamson's Liverpool Advertiser*, 17 June 1768 that Hadkinson had been taken as a partner by Thomas Dobb in June 1768, having previously served as his foreman.

Hadley, Thomas, 91 Smallbrook St, Birmingham, cm and u (1828). [D]

Hadnutt, William, Aldersgate St, London, cm (1779). Took out a Sun Insurance policy in 1779 for £200, of which £10 accounted for utensils. [GL, Sun MS vol. 274, p. 515]

Haffen, George, Little Newport St, Covent Gdn, London, carver (1749). [Poll bk]

Hagg, Thomas, Skipton, Yorks., cm (1837). [Holy Trinity PR]

Hagger, Thomas, Market Pl., Potton, Beds., cm, u and auctioneer (1830). [D]

Hagley, John, Harrogate, Yorks., joiner and cm (1834). [D]

Hagley, William, Weymouth, Dorset, cm (1823–30). Addresses given at New St in 1823 and 24 St Mary St in 1830. [D]

Hague, John, Newcastle, cm (1750). Took app. named Gair in 1750. [S of G, app. index]

Hague, Josiah, West St, Bristol, cm, chair and bedstead maker (1836–40). [D]

Hague, Mary, Manchester, u (1808–11). Trading at 12 Windmill St in 1808 and 31 Bridge St, 1811. [D]

Hague, Richard, Lancaster, cm (1823–27). Admitted freeman, 1823–24, and named in the Gillow records, 1825–27. [Lancaster freemen rolls; Westminster Ref. Lib., Gillow]

Hague, Robert, Lancaster, cm (1823–24). [Lancaster freemen rolls]

Hague, Thomas, 39 Wood St, Manchester, u (1817). [D]

Hague, Thomas, Clarkson's Passage, Walmgate, York, cm (1823). [D]

Hagyard, Thomas, Market Pl., Pocklington, Yorks., cm (1840). [D]

Haiden, William, Birchole St, Deritend, Birmingham, picture frame maker (1803). [D]

Haig, Andrew, 13 Gt May's Buildings, St Martin's Lane, Covent Gdn, London, cm, chairmaker and u (1817–28). [D]

Haig, Andrew, 17 Bedford Ct, Bedford St, Covent Gdn, London, cm and u (1823). Took out a Sun Insurance policy on 9 October 1823 for £1,000. [D; GL, Sun MS vol. 498, ref. 1008478]

Haig, John, St Martin-in-the-Fields, London, cm (1796–1803). He was left £500 by his cousin, Thomas Haig (of Chippendale & Co.) whose will was made in 1796, codicil in 1802, and proved in 1803. John subscribed to Sheraton's *Cabinet Dictionary*, 1803. [PRO, Prob. 11/1394, fo. 536]

Haig, John snr and jnr, & Thomas, Gt Newport St, London, cm (1806). Took out a Sun Insurance policy on 7 October 1806 for £300 including £275 on household goods of a brass founder, and £25 on a chest of tools in workshop of Smith, cm, in Grosvenor Mews. [GL, Sun MS vol. 437, ref. 795161]

Haig, John, 14 Castle St, Leicester Sq., London, cm (1808). [D]

Haig, Thomas, St Martin's Lane, London, cm (1754–d. 1803). A Scot, who was book-keeper to Thomas Chippendale's first partner James Rannie and remained with the firm after his master's death in 1766. He emerges from the records as a competent administrator who generally remained in London to deal with clerical work and settle accounts, leaving Chippendale free to supervise the worshops, collaborate with architects, prepare designs and travel into the country to oversee commissions and meet clients. Chippendale jnr was trained up to assist his father with artistic and craft matters. In 1771, to save the firm from bankruptcy, Haig borrowed £2,000 from Rannie's widow and purchased a one-third share in the business which was thereafter styled 'Chippendale,

Haig & Co.'. He subscribed to George Richardson's *Book of Ceilings*, 1776. After Thomas Chippendale snr died in 1779 Haig became the senior partner, the firm trading as 'Haig & Chippendale' until his retirement in 1796. He died a bachelor in 1803 aged 76 and expressed a wish to be buried 'near to the body of my late revered and venerable master Mr Rannie' in the vault of St Martin's Church. He is described in his will [PRO, Prob. 11/1394 c 7021] as 'Gentleman' and disposed of an estate worth over £10,000. [C. Gilbert, *Chippendale*]
C.G.G.

Haig(h), Thomas, How(e) End, Kirbymoorside, Yorks., cm and/or joiner (1828–40). [D]

Haigh, Francis, Scarborough, Yorks., cm and u (1831–40). Trading at Newborough St in 1831 and 45 Cross St, 1834–40. [D]

Haigh, George, 11 Charlotte Terr., New Ct, London, u (1820). [D]

Haigh, John, Manchester, chairmaker (1813–33). Addresses given at 13 John St, Gt Ancoats St in 1813, and 41 Thomas St, 1832–33. [D]

Haigh, John, Liverpool, u (1827). App. to Bartholomew Tyrer in 1827. [Liverpool app. enrolment bk]

Haigh, Thomas, Dukinfield, Lancs., cm and joiner (1824–34). Trading at New Rd, 1828–34. [D]

Hail, John, High Wycombe, Bucks., chairmaker (1828–39). Sons bapt. in 1828 and 1831, daughters in 1837 and 1839. [PR (bapt.)]

Hail, William, Mill Bridge, Skipton, Yorks., joiner and/or cm (1837). [D]

Haines, George, 229 High St, Cheltenham, Glos., cm and u (1820). [D]

Haines, George, Grosvenor Row, Chelsea (Pimlico), London, cm, u, auctioneer, appraiser and undertaker (1835–39). Recorded at no. 6 in 1835 and no. 9 in 1839. [D]

Haines, John, Kempsey, Worcs., upholder (1747). [Worcester poll bk]

Haines, John, Belgrave Gate, Leicester, cm (1827). [D]

Haines, Richard, 7 Drake St, Red Lion Sq., London, carver and gilder (1835–39). [D]

Haines, William, St Martin-in-the-Fields, London, cm (1766–67). Acted as witness to the will, dated 1767, of William Hallett jnr.

Hains, —, Buckingham, carver (1746). Received a letter in 1746 which read: 'I have orders from my mother to acquaint you she will not have any frame at all round the Diall Plate of ye Clock...'. [G. Eland, ed., *The Purefoy Letters*, p. 122]

Hainsworth, James, Shipley, Yorks., cm (1822–30). [D]

Hainsworth, Jonathan, Ling Cross Lane, Halifax, Yorks., chair and cm (1788). Announced in *Leeds Intelligencer*, 10 June 1788 that he 'wishes to extend his business in Cabinet Lane', and has a 'Large assortment of cabinet goods in his warehouse, bottom of Ling Cross Lane. Chests of drawers, tables, wardrobes, desks, 2 bookcases, various new patterns of mahogany chairs, sofas etc.'.

Hair, William, 225 Kent St, London, chairmaker (1809–11). [D]

Hake, John, near 'The Sun Tavern', Upper Shadwell, London, u (1734). Took out a Sun Insurance policy on 31 January 1734 for £400, stock in trade accounting for £300. [GL, Sun MS vol. 38, ref. 62990]

Hakes, John, 'Queen's Head', Upper Shadwell, London, u (1724). Took out a Sun Insurance policy on 2 June 1724 for £500 on goods and merchandise in his house. [GL, Sun MS vol. 17, ref. 32075]

Hakes, Joseph & Edward, 'Queen's Head', Upper Shadwell, London, u (1725). Took out a Sun Insurance policy on 10 September 1725 for £500 on goods and merchandise in their house. [GL, Sun MS vol. 21, ref. 36651]

Hakewell, John, London, furniture painter (1769). In April 1769 he was paid £2 8s 'for Painting 8 Cabriole Chairs Crimson and White' at Shelburne House, Berkeley Sq., London. [Bowood MS]

Halbert, —, London, carver (1793). Subscribed to Sheraton's *Drawing Book*, 1793.

Halden (or Haldon), William, Alston, Cumb, joiner and/or cm (1828–34). [D]

Hale, John, Chepping Wycombe Borough, High Wycombe, Bucks., chairmaker (1798). [Militia Census]

Hale, John, High Wycombe, Bucks., chairmaker (b. c. 1805–41). Aged 36 at the time of the 1841 Census.

Hale, Richard, 12 St Anne's Ct, Soho, London, chair and sofa maker (1809–11). [D]

Hale, William, 5 Warren St, London, cm (1792). Took out a Sun Insurance policy on 19 November 1792 for £100. [GL, Sun MS vol. 389, ref. 607303]

Hale, William, 13 Lumber St, Tythebarn St, Liverpool, chairmaker (1800). [D]

Hale, William, Church St, Spitalfields, London, u and cm (1821–25). Trading at no. 21, 1821–23; and as Hale & Co. at no. 22 in 1825. Took out a Sun Insurance policy on 4 October 1821 for £1,000, of which stock and utensils accounted for £800. [D; GL, Sun MS vol. 484, ref. 983748]

Hale, William, 6 Osborn Pl., Brick Lane, Whitechapel, London, u and cm (1825–27). [D]

Hales, —, address unrecorded, cm (1739). Supplied '6 low back'd Windsor chairs', costing £5 19s 6d to Holkham Hall, Norfolk, in 1739. [V&A archives]

Hales, —, 1 Bolt Ct, Fleet St, London, u (1803). Named in Sheraton's list of master cabinet makers, 1803. Probably either Charles or R. Hales.

Hales, Charles, 1 Bolt Ct, Fleet St, London, cm, u, appraiser, auctioneer and undertaker (1802–23). Took out a Sun Insurance policy on 2 October 1802 for £1,900, of which £1,400 accounted for utensils and stock. [D; GL, Sun MS vol. 424, ref. 738047] See R. Hales.

Hales, Frederick, 36 Marylebone St, Golden Sq., Piccadilly, London, u and cm (1820–25). [D]

Hales, James, St Gregory's Churchyard, Norwich, cm (1839). [D]

Hales, John, High St, Rochester, Kent, u (1730). Took out a Sun Insurance policy on 10 December 1730 for £500, £350 on household goods and stock in trade, £100 on stock in the house adjoining his own; and £50 on that in the house of John Dickeson, hatter. [GL, Sun MS vol. 33, ref. 52597]

Hales, John, Wem, Salop, cm and joiner (1822). [D]

Hales, Jonathan, High St, King's Lynn, Norfolk, u and cm (1784). [D]

Hales, R., 1 Bolt Ct, Fleet St, London, u (1804–11). [D] See Charles Hales.

Hales, Samuel, 165 Gt Hampton St, Birmingham, cabinet case manufacturer (1835). [D]

Hales, T., 24 Little St Thomas Apostle, London, cm and chair manufacturer (1837). [D]

Hales, Thomas, Widnes, Lancs., upholder (1744). Took app. named Urmston in 1744. [S of G, app. index]

Hale(s), Thomas, Liverpool, u (1734–59). Admitted freeman on 16 October 1734. Thomas Hale took app. named Samuel Bird in 1737. Former app., Edward Roberts, petitioned freedom in 1759. Co-valuer with George Parker, cm, of John Harrison's goods on 6 February 1746. [Liverpool app. enrolment bk, freemen reg. and committee bk; Liverpool RO, 920 GRE 3/1, 5]

Hales, Thomas, 6 New Ct, Bow Lane, and 96 Charlotte St, Fitzroy Sq., London, cm and u (1839). [D]

Hales, William, Wem, Salop, cm (1822–30). Trading at High St in 1828. Declared bankrupt, *London Gazette*, 28 December 1830. [D]

Hales, William, Bakehouse Lane, Lutterworth, Leics., turner (1840). [D]

Haley, Henry, Rose & Crown Ct, Cheltenham, Glos., cabinet turner (1839). [D]

Haley, John, Hull, Yorks., carver (1781). [D]

Haley, John, Thurlstone, near Penistone, Yorks., joiner and cm (1822). [D]

Haley, Philip, Plymouth Dock, Devon, cm (1812). Declared bankrupt, *Exeter Flying Post*, 16 July 1812.

Haley, Robert, Trove St, Plymouth Dock, Devon, joiner and cm (1777–86). Took out a Sun Insurance policy in 1777 for £700 of which stock and workshop accounted for £300; and on 7 October 1786 for £200 on his house. [GL, Sun MS vol. 258, p. 266; vol. 338, p. 545]

Haley, William, 8 Bermondsey New Rd, London, cm (1829). [D]

Halfe, James, Oxford, upholder (1798). [D]

Halfe, Thomas, Oxford, cm (1802). [Poll bk]

Halfehide, Thomas, Fleet St, London, cm (1715–23). Recorded in Bride Lane, 1715–21; and Salisbury Ct, Fleet St, 1717–23. Fined for non-service at St Bride's in 1715, 1716 and 1721, and served as Questman in 1717. Took out a Sun Insurance policy on 5 October 1717 on goods and merchandise in his house. Advertised sale of goods on 'leaving off trade', in *Daily Post*, 18 March 1723. Stock included 'Several fine scarlet and gold desks and book-cases, several blue and gold, and black and gold, fine cabinets, chests of drawers, desks, and bowfets of all sorts; large lacquere'd trunks, chests and screens ... fine lacquer'd tea-tables, several chimney-glasses, peer-glasses, and sconces in gold frames; and several union suits.' [GL, MS 6561, p. 3; GL, Sun MS vol. 7]

Halford, —, address unrecorded (1779–84). Submitted bills in 1784 for a fire screen provided for the Court Room, Vintners' Hall, London, costing £9 9s 6d; and in 1779–80 for repairing 'Great Room skreens £10.10 –'. [V&A archives]

Halford, Edward, Sleaford, Lincs. Oak dressing table, *c*.1740, recorded, bearing label which reads: 'EDWARD HALFORD, In Sleaford, Lincolnshire. Where you may be furnished with all sorts of Cabinets and Joyners Work, and Looking-Glasses; all sorts of Maps, English, French and Dutch Prints; all sorts of fine Earthen Ware, English and Delf; all sorts of the Best Flint-Glass, and several sorts of fine Toys at the lowest prizes.' Table has cabriole legs, and one drawer with the remains of one cotter-pin brass back plate; a shaped apron at the front with applied beading.

Halford, F. W., 6 Baynes Row, Cold Bath Sq., London, Tunbridge-ware manufacturer (1811–25). Recorded, presumably wrongly, as J.W. in 1817–18. [D]

Halford, John, address unrecorded, upholder (1699). Admitted freeman of the Upholders' Co. on 9 May 1699. [GL, Upholders' Co. records]

Halford, John, Gloucester, cm (1821–30). Trading at Mitre St in 1830 as cm and u. Children bapt. at St Aldgate in 1821, 1826 and 1827. [PR (bapt.)]

Halford, Robert, St Michael Royall, London, cm (1689). His app., John Evans, died in 1689, whilst in his service. [PCC Wills, Index Lib., vol. 11, p. 93]

Halford, Robert, 13 St Paul's Churchyard, London, gilt leather and screen manufacturer (1770–94). [D]

Halford, Samuel, London, upholder (1734–35). His daughter, Sarah Halford, admitted freeman of the Upholders' Co., 1734–35. [GL, Upholders' Co. records]

Halford, Sarah, London, upholder (1734–35). Daughter of Samuel Halford, upholder of London; admitted freeman of

the Upholders' Co. by patrimony on 5 March 1734/35. [GL, Upholders' Co. records]

Halford, Thomas, 12½ Cowper St, Finsbury, London, cm and u (1839). [D]

Halford, William Henry, address unrecorded, upholder (1737–45). Son of William Henry Halford, Gent., of St Martin-in-the-Fields, London; app. to Henry Weedon on 3 August 1737, and admitted freeman of the Upholders' Co. by servitude on 7 February 1744/45. [GL, Upholders' Co. records]

Halfpenny, E., 70 Paul St, Finsbury, London, u (1826–35). [D] See William Halfpenny.

Halfpenny, John, Earl St, Radford (Retford?), Notts., turner and fancy chairmaker (1832). [D]

Halfpenny, John, New Lenton, Nottingham, chairmaker (1835). [D]

Halfpenny, Joseph, Little Blake St, York, cm (1787–93). Subscribed to Sheraton's *Drawing Book*, 1793. [D]

Halfpenny, Joseph, Belgrave Gate, Leicester, chairmaker (1822–28). [D]

Halfpenny, Joseph, Nottingham, chairmaker (1832–40). Addresses given at Canal St in 1832, Prospect Pl., Lenton in 1834 and Butcher St in 1840. [D]

Halfpenny, Thomas, Liverpool, cm (1813–16). Trading at 7 Williamson St, 1813–14, and 17 Tarleton St, 1816. [D]

Halfpenny, William, York, u (1778–98). Trading in Little Blake St in 1798. Son of Thomas Halfpenny, gardener, of Market Weighton; app. to Matthew Browne, u, on 3 April 1778. Admitted freeman in 1789. [D; York app. reg. and freemen rolls]

Halfpenny, William, London, u (1820). Son of William Halfpenny, u, of London; admitted freeman of York in 1820. [York freemen rolls]

Halfpenny, William, 70 Paul St, Finsbury, London, u (1839). [D] See E. Halfpenny.

Halfred, J., London, cm (1793). Subscribed to Sheraton's *Drawing Book*, 1793.

Halhead, Hannah, Market Pl., Kendal, Westmld, cm and looking-glass silverer (1834). The manager of the business was Thomas P. Dillon. [D]

Halhead, James, Market Pl., Kendal, Westmld, cm and u (1828–29). [D] See James Hallhead.

Halhead, John, Market Pl., Kendal, Westmld, cm and u (1784–1829). Polled at Lancaster in 1784. [D] See John Hallhead.

Hall, —, Houndsditch, London, undertaker and u (1741). Referred to in *London Morning Advertiser*, 11 November 1741, as 'wealthy undertaker & upholsterer. One of the Common Councilmen of Portspoken Ward.'

Hall, Benjamin, address unrecorded, cm (1796). Submitted a bill for cabinet work done at the Court Room, Vintners' Hall, London, costing £10 12s, on 16 February and 17 September 1796. [V&A archives]

Hall, Benthan, Newcastle, carver and gilder (1813–38). Recorded at Newgate St in 1813, and 75 Pilgrim St, 1824–38. Trade card of Benthan Hall reads 'Carver & Gilder, Picture Frame Manufacturer, Dealer in Looking Glasses &c. 75 Pilgrim Street, Newcastle. NB. Old Plates repolished and silvered, and Old Paintings carefully cleaned.' Trade card of B. Hall & Son gives the same information. Advertised in *Newcastle Chronicle*, 15 May 1813. [D; Landauer Coll., MMA, NY]

Hall, Charles, Loft St, Grimsby, Lincs., joiner and cm (1835). [D]

Hall, Christopher, 193 Piccadilly, London, u (1837–39). [D]

Hall, Collinson, London, cm and upholder (1801–12). Addresses given at 3 Bennett St, Rathbone Pl. in 1801, and 85 Charlotte St, Fitzroy Sq., 1806–12. Took out a Sun Insurance policy on 15 July 1801 for £500 of which £280 accounted for utensils and stock. [D; GL, Sun MS vol. 419, ref. 721414]

Hall, Cornelius, Market Pl., Hexham, Northumb., joiner and cm (1827–34). Recorded also at Old Church, 1828–29. [D]

Hall, David, 11 Charles St, City Rd, London, cm and u, cabinet inlayer (1839). [D]

Hall, Edward, Coventry Ct, London, u (1749). [Poll bk]

Hall, Edward, Durham Rd, London, upholder (1749). [Poll bk]

Hall, Edward, Mill St, Gt Driffield, Yorks., cm (1823). [D]

Hall, Edward, Dog Bank, Newcastle, carver and gilder (1834). [D]

Hall, Elking^n, at 'The Royal Bed', Holborn Bridge, London, u (1722–49). Partner in Nash, Hall & Whitehorne. [Poll bks; Heal]

Hall, Francis, 10 Craven Buildings, City Rd, London, carver and gilder (1826–37). [D]

Hall, Francis, Applegate St, Leicester, cm (1840). [D]

Hall, George, Preston, Lancs., cm (1782). App. to Michael Emett of Preston, cm, in 1782. [Preston Guild record of burgesses]

Hall, George, King St, Woolwich, Kent, u (1838–39). [D]

Hall, George, Bristol, painter and fancy chairmaker (1838–40). Addresses given at 14 All Saints' St, 1838–39, and 4 St James's Churchyard in 1840. [D]

Hall, George, 12 Edmund St, Birmingham, u and paper hanger (1839). [D]

Hall, George Thomas, 63 George St, Hastings, Sussex, cm and u (1839). [D]

Hall, George, Cave Lane, Malton, Yorks., joiner and cm (1840). [D]

Hall, Henry, London, upholder and sworn appraiser (1746–d.1796). Rococo trade cards give addresses at 'The Three Crowns & Dove', corner of Old Bedlam, Moorfields, c.1760; and later at 'The Three Crowns', Old Bedlam, c.1770. Directories and Upholders' Co. records give 1 Moorfields, 1767–72; Moorfields in 1778; Staining Lane, 1781; and Guildhall in 1794. Son of Richard Hall, yeoman of Hertford; app. to Jonathan Fair, draper and upholder, on 16 September 1746. Admitted freeman of the Upholders' Co. on 24 May 1756, and master in 1784. Took apps named Benjamin Harper, 1760–67; Mark Dawes until 1773; Samuel Holden, 1767–72; and John Rogers Harper until 1793. [D; Banks Coll., BM; GL, Upholders' Co. records]

Hall, Henry, Low Town, Bridgnorth, Salop, cm (1822–35). Trading at Mill St in 1835. [D]

Hall, Henry, Frankwell, Shrewsbury, Salop, cm and carver (1828). [D]

Hall, Henry, St Mary Gate, Chesterfield, Derbs., cm (1835). [D]

Hall, Isaac, Cirencester, Glos., cm (1815–24). Children born in 1815, 1816, 1820, 1822 and 1824. [PR]

Hall, James, Bishop Auckland, Co. Durham, joiner (1665). Made ceilings and presses for Bishop Cosin's chapel at Auckland Castle, Bishop Auckland in 1665. [C. Life, 3 February 1972, p. 267]

Hall, James, Worcester, chairmaker (1747). [Poll bk]

Hall, James, Nottingham, joiner and cm (1791). Son of Thomas Hall, framework knitter of Nottingham; app. to Samuel Dodd in 1791. [Nottingham app. list]

Hall, James, address unrecorded, cm (1803). Subscribed to Sheraton's *Cabinet Dictionary*, 1803.

Hall, James, Chester, cm (1808). Admitted freeman on 28 January 1808. [Chester freemen rolls]

Hall, James, Spilsby, Lincs., joiner and cm (1822–35). [D]

Hall, James, Durtwick St, North Shields, Northumb., cm and joiner (1827–34). Recorded also at Mount Pleasant in 1834. [D]

Hall, Jesse, Bristol, carver (1734). [Poll bk]

Hall, John, Nottingham, u (d. 1678/79). Probate will dated 1 March 1678/79. [Notts. RO, probate records]

Hall, John, Chester, carver (1708). Son of William Hall of Mostyn, Co. Flint; app. to John Tilston, carver, and admitted freeman of Chester on 10 April 1708. [Chester freemen rolls]

Hall, John, St James's, Westminster, London, upholder (1709). Declared bankrupt, *London Gazette*, 20 December 1709.

Hall, John, Sheffield, Yorks., u (1723). Took app. named Smithys in 1723. [S of G, app. index]

Hall, John, Canterbury, Kent, chairmaker (1734). [Canterbury freemen rolls]

Hall, John, Chester, cm (1774–76). App. to George Fothergill, cm, 15 January 1774 to 20 November 1776. [Chester app. bks]

Hall, John, Chester, joiner and cm (1787). Son of William Hall; app. to John Walker, joiner and cm, 17 April to 21 August 1787. [Chester app. bks]

Hall, John, Tenterden, Kent, chairmaker (1790). [Canterbury poll bk]

Hall, John, Stockton-on-Tees, Co. Durham, cm (1793–98). Subscribed to Sheraton's *Drawing Book*, 1793. [D]

Hall, John, London, chairmaker (1799). [Norwich poll bk]

Hall, John, Butcher Lane, Bury, Lancs., joiner and cm (1816–18). [D]

Hall, John, Liverpool, cm (1807–39). Addresses given at 9 Cooper St in 1807; 4 Upper Hanington in 1811; and Tarleton St, 1837–39. [D]

Hall, John, 122 Old St, London, bed pillar, bedstead, chair and sofa manufacturer (1817–27). Trade card, showing engravings of two Regency chairs and turned and carved bedposts, reads: 'J. Hall, BED PILLOW, Chair, & Music Stool Manufacturer, No. 122, Old Street, London. Turning in General.' [D; London Borough of Hackney, archives dept, 332 TDE/14] See Hall & Barfoot.

Hall, John, Barton-upon-Humber, Lincs., joiner, carpenter, wheelwright and cm (1825). Trading in partnership with William Graburn, also making bricks, tiles and dealing in timber. [D]

Hall, John, Darn Crook, Newcastle, u (1828). [D]

Hall, John, Mount Pleasant, Skipton, Yorks., joiner and cm (1830). [D]

Hall, John Henry, Worcester, cm (1834). App. to Daniel Cowell; admitted freeman on 17 November 1834. [Worcester freemen rolls]

Hall, John, 3 Tottenham Ct Rd, London, iron bedstead maker (1839). [D]

Hall, John, address unrecorded (c.1765). Assisted James Gravenor as a carver in the execution of the Palm tree mirror in the dressing room at Kedleston, Derbs. [C. Life, 9 February 1979, p. 323] Possibly Joseph Hall

Hall, Jonathan jnr, Lancaster, cm (1787–99). Named in the Gillow records, 1787–88. App. to William Blackburn in 1792, and admitted freeman, 1798–99. [Lancaster app. reg. and freemen rolls; Westminster Ref. Lib., Gillow] Possibly two craftsmen are concerned here.

Hall, Joseph, Hull, Yorks., cm, carpenter and joiner (1740–54). Son of Joseph Hall, joiner; admitted burgess in 1740. In 1749 his app. William Lodge appealed successfully to the Magistrates for release from his apprenticeship on grounds of ill-treatment. Polled at Hull in 1754. Trade card, c.1745–55, shows an early-Georgian pedimented mirror, kneehole desk with dressing glass, two tripod tables, one bearing a kettle, a side table with elaborate cabriole leg and festoons, an unusual chest of drawers topped by a bookcase(?), and a Classical pavilion with columns showing stock inside: a coffee grinder, cruet, saucepan and violin. Card reads: 'Joseph Hall, Blackfrier Gate, Hull. Makes & Sells all Sort of Cabinett

Work; Viz. Chest of Drawers of all Sorts, Desks, and Bookcases, Bueros, Desks, Card Dining Breakfast & Dressing Tables (in Mahogany, Walnut tree & Wainscott). Chairs of all sorts, Settee, Buero & Standing Bedsteads, Sconces, peir, Chimney and Dressing Glasses, Tea Chests, Tea Boards, China Trayes, Fire Screens, Dumb Waiters, Picture Frames Stained Carved & Gilt &c. Likewise all Sorts of Carpenters and Joiner's Work Performed all at very Reasonable Rates.' [Heal Coll., BM; *Antique Collector*, March–April 1946, p. 59, and March 1966; *C. Life*, 3 October 1974; *Furniture Made in Yorkshire*, Temple Newsam Exhib. Cat., p. iv]

Hall, Joseph, address unrecorded, carver (c.1758–70). Received £2,501 3s 4½d, c.1758–70, for work done at Kedleston Hall, Derbs., including in 1765 carving the mirrors for the State Bedroom. [V&A archives; *Conn.*, July 1978, p. 206]

Hall, Joseph, 6 Wallbrook, London, u (1808–15). [D]

Hall, Joseph, 12 Gt Dover St, St George's, Southwark, London, u (1816–27). [D]

Hall, Joseph Mayor, 35 Broad St, Bristol, cm (1816–32). [D]

Hall, Joseph, 19 Thomas St, Bristol, chairmaker (1825–26). [D]

Hall, Joseph, 1 John St, Marylebone, London, u (1826–27). [D]

Hall, Joseph, Denton's Green, St Helens, Lancs., joiner and cm (1828). [D]

Hall, Joseph, Castle Foregate, Shrewsbury, Salop, cm (1830). [Shrewsbury burgess roll] See Thomas Hall, his brother.

Hall, Mark, London, cm (1784). [York poll bk]

Hall, Matthew, 30 Newgate St, Newcastle, cm (1834). [D]

Hall, Peter, London, cm and u (1761). Arrival from London to USA announced in *South Carolina Gazette*, 19 December 1761.

Hall, Pierce (or Pearce), at 'The Chair', in St John's St, near Hicks Hall, London, cm and chairmaker (1754–c.1760). Rococo trade card, c.1755–60, shows Chippendale-style chair in an elaborately shaped surround. Subscribed to Chippendale's *Director*, 1754. [Banks Coll., BM]

Hall, R., London, cm (1793). Subscribed to Sheraton's *Drawing Book*, 1793.

Hall, Richard, Lancaster, cm (1767–68). Admitted freeman, 1767–68, when stated of Halifax, Yorks. [Lancaster freemen rolls]

Hall, Richard, Skerton, Lancaster, chairmaker (1811–34). Admitted freeman, 1811–12. [D; Lancaster freemen rolls]

Hall, Richard, South Shields, Co. Durham, cm and/or joiner (1834). [D]

Hall, Robert, 'The Angel', Hounsditch, St Botolph's, Aldgate, London, u (1714). Took out a Sun Insurance policy on 14 August 1714 on goods and merchandise in his house. [GL, Sun MS vol. 4, ref. 4405]

Hall, Robert, Gt St Helen's, within Bishopsgate, London, u (1713–26). Took apps on 15 June and 30 December 1713. Named in directories and newspapers, 1717–26. [PRO, app. reg.; Heal]

Hall, Robert, 16 Albion St, Rotherhithe, London, wood and cabinet carver (1839). [D]

Hall, Samuel, Poland St, London, u (1784). [Poll bk]

Hall, Samuel, St James's Mkt, London, cm (1784). [D]

Hall, Samuel, 4 Little Hampton St, Birmingham, cabinet case maker (1835). [D]

Hall, Thomas, Lancaster, cm (1770–80). App. to Thomas Lister, 1770, and admitted freeman, 1779–80. [Lancaster app. reg. and freemen rolls]

Hall, Thomas, 20 (Gt) Garden Row, London Rd, London, cm, u and joiner (1808–28). Trading as Hall & Son, 1820–28. [D]

Hall, Thomas, Snig-brook, Blackburn, Lancs., cm and joiner (1814–18). [D]

Hall, Thomas, Newcastle, cm and u (1815). Advertised for workmen in *Newcastle Chronicle*, 16 September 1815.

Hall, Thomas, Bowling Green, Rainford, Lancs., victualler, joiner and cm (1825). [D]

Hall, Thomas, Leeds, Yorks., cm and joiner (1826–34). Trading at 26 Wellington Yd, 1826, and 18 Harper St, 1830. [D]

Hall, Thomas, Howard St, North Shields, Northumb., cm, joiner and u (1827–29). [D]

Hall, Thomas, 2 Tyne St, North Shields, Northumb., u (1834). [D]

Hall, Thomas, Hospital St, Nantwich, Cheshire, u (1828–29). [D]

Hall, Thomas, Back St, Brampton, Carlisle, Cumb., joiner and/or cm (1829). [D]

Hall, Thomas, Chester, weaver and u (1831). Admitted freeman on 25 April 1831. [Chester freemen rolls]

Hall, Thomas, Castle Foregate, Shrewsbury, Salop, cm (1835). [Shrewsbury burgess roll] See Joseph Hall, his brother.

Hall, Thomas, High St, Hereford, cm and u (1835). [D]

Hall, Thomas, Bridge St, Kington, Herefs., turner and chairmaker (1835–40). [D]

Hall, Thomas, 3 East St, Finsbury Mkt, London, cm and u (1839). [D]

Hall, William jnr, Derby, carver (1741). [Poll bk]

Hall, William, Sheffield, Yorks., cm (1748). Took app. named Barnes in 1748. [S of G, app. index]

Hall, William, 2 Broker Row, Moorfields, London, cm (1792–1811). Trading in partnership with Hersant, 1803–11, and succeeded by Hunter & Hersant. Hall & Hersant are named in Sheraton's list of master cabinet makers, 1803, and their trade card is recorded. [D; Heal]

Hall, William, Lancaster, chairmaker (1810–12). Took app. on 15 November 1810. His son Richard was admitted freeman as a chairmaker in 1811–12. [Lancaster app. reg. and freemen rolls]

Hall, William, Hull, Yorks., cm (1812). App. to Edward Dicken in March 1812. [Hull app. reg.]

Hall, William, 49–50 Windmill St, Haymarket, London, u and undertaker (1816–19). [D]

Hall, William, Norwich, cm (1818–30). [Poll bk]

Hall, William, 2 Newman St, Oxford St, London, cm and chair manufacturer (1820). [D]

Hall, William, 21 Church St, Spitalfields, London, cm and u (1822). [D]

Hall, William, Kingsland Rd, London, cm (1823). [D]

Hall, William, Skerton, Lancaster, chair and bedstead maker (1822–25). [D]

Hall, William, 17 High St, St Giles, Bloomsbury, London, cm and u (1826–28). [D]

Hall, William, High Row, Darlington, Co. Durham, cm (1827–29). [D]

Hall, William, Rothbury, Northumb., cm and/or joiner (1828–34). [D]

Hall, William, Gomersal, Birstall, Yorks., cm and joiner (1828–29). [D]

Hall, William, Carlisle, Cumb., joiner and/or cm (1829–34). Addresses given at Elliotts Lane, Scotch St, and Back St, Brampton in 1829; and Union Ct, Scotch St in 1834. [D]

Hall & Barfoot, 122 Old St, St Lukes, London, cm (1829). [D] See John Hall.

Hall & Rostill (or Rostilt), Hill St, Birmingham, 'manufacturers of leather, tortoiseshell & ivory snuff boxes, sugar, etui bottle &c cases, caddies, chests & ladies workboxes' (1808–18). [D]

Hall & Tildesley, South Molton St, London, cm and u (1826–37). Trading at no. 45, 1826–28, and no. 43 in 1837. [D]

Halla, William, London, cm (1793). Subscribed to Sheraton's *Drawing Book*, 1793.

Halladay, —, Bath, Som., cm (1819–26). Listed at 5 Trim St in 1819 and 4 Parsonage Lane in 1826. [D]

Halladay, Stephen, Canterbury, Kent, cm (1790–96). Recorded at Burgate in 1790 and St Andrew in 1796. Took out an undated Sun Insurance policy for £300 on his house in Burgate St; and a further policy for £400 including two houses under one roof in Sun St. [Poll bks; GL, Sun MS vols 370 and 388, p. 560]

Hallam, E., Houndsgate, Nottingham, cm (1774–d.1796). Recorded at Angel Row in 1774. [Poll bk; Notts. RO, probate records] See Hallam & Green and Hallam & Pid(l)ock.

Hallam, Edward, Lenton, Nottingham, cm (1812). [Poll bk]

Hallam, Edward, Warsop, Notts., joiner and cm (1832). [D]

Hallam, James, Dudley, Worcs., chairmaker (1839). [D]

Hallam, John, address unrecorded, joiner (1700). Named in the Chatsworth account book 6 in June 1700, 'For makeing 24 yards of deal wainscot in a Press to hang his Graces Clothes in at 6d a yard', costing £1 12s; and 'Making a Cupboard in ye passage to ye Stewards parlour', 3s. Hallam also carried out general joinery duties such as taking down and putting up furniture.

Hallam, John, St Peter'sgate, Nottingham, joiner and cm (1832–34). Listed at Chandler's Lane in 1834. Declared bankrupt, *London Gazette*, 22 April 1834. [D] See Joseph and Thomas Hallam.

Hallam, Joseph, Nottingham, cm (1832–40). Recorded at St Peter'sgate, also as a joiner, in 1832; at Petergate and Warsergate, also as a u, in 1834; and at Petergate and Houndsgate in 1840. [D]

Hallam, Richard, Leeming St, Mansfield, Notts., cm (1819). [D]

Hallam, Samuel, Dudley, Worcs., cm and u (1838–40). Advertised in *Bentley's Directory of Dudley*, 1838, as 'S. HALLAM, chair Manufacturers, Dudley. All kinds of fancy & Windsor Chairs in the most modern style of workmanship. India Canework in all its Branches, Rosewood Graining etc.'. Trading at High St in 1840. [D]

Hallam, Thomas, Rotherham, Yorks., cm (1802). App. to John Chapman of Hull on 2 May 1802. [Hull app. reg.]

Hallam, Thomas, St Peter'sgate, Nottingham, joiner and cm (1832). [D] See John and Joseph Hallam.

Hallam & Green, Angel Row, Nottingham, cm, joiners and u (1805–08). [D] See Edward Hallam.

Hallam & Pid(l)ock, Nottingham, cm, joiners and carpenters (1784–91). Advertised with other tradesmen in *Nottingham Journal*, 31 July 1784, wanting cabinet-makers, joiners and carpenters immediately. Signed the *Nottingham Cabinet and Chair Makers' Book of Prices*, 1791, on behalf of the masters. See Hallum & Pidcock.

Hallert, John, Nottingham. Signed the *Nottingham Cabinet and Chair Makers' Book of Prices*, 1791, on behalf of the masters. Probably John Hallet(t).

Hallet, J. M., Chapel Bar, Nottingham, cm (1803). [Poll bk]

Hallet(t), John, Nottingham, joiner and cm (1798–99). Recorded as Hallet at Toll House Hill in 1799. [D] Probably John Hallert.

Hallett, Charles, 53 Dorset St, Portman Sq., London, u (1839). [D]

Hallett, J. B., Berkeley, Glos., cm (1839–40). [D]

Hallett, William snr, Gt Newport St, Long Acre, London, cm (b. *c*.1707–d.1781), **Hallett, William jnr**, cm (*c*.1730–d. 1767). In 1938 the late R. W. Symonds published an article on Hallett, Vile and Cobb [*Conn.*, April 1938, pp. 183–91] in which he stated that William Hallett was born in July 1707 and died in December 1781. Despite a very extensive search it has not proved possible to establish the source for the July 1707 date. However we know Hallett died on 17 December 1781, and was buried at St Lawrence, Whitchurch on 28 December. [PR; *Furn. Hist.*, 1985] He was 74 years old which seems a credible span for his life. Hallett was

born, seemingly, at Crewkerne, Som., to William and his wife. Her maiden name is unknown. William had brothers, George, and (Sir) James, who died in 1733. It was Sir James's son, also James (d. 1723 in France) who was the father of Lettice (or Letitia) who married William Hallett, the cm, as his second wife, in 1756. In other words William married his cousin. However the reader should be spared the full intricacies of an involved story; it is set out, with pedigrees in *Furn. Hist.*, 1985.

What is interesting however about the Crewkerne origin for Hallett is that he could have encountered William Vile — whom he was later to support financially — at an early age. Vile was born somewhere in Somerset about 1700–05. An aid to being more precise is denied through the destruction of the many Hallett and Vile wills (Taunton Archdeaconry) in Second World War raids on Exeter. [Listed E. A, Fry (ed.), *Taunton Wills, 1537–1799*, British Record Soc., 1912] There is no reason to assume he was the app. of this name put to John Baxter of Sarum, Wilts. in 1728. [S of G, app. index] Indeed, Hallet snr had set up as a cm by 1730, when he took his first app., Ralph Sharrington, for £15, a fee which was slightly lower than the average fee for the period. This 1730 expansion is further support for the presumed year of his birth. Apprenticeship at age 14 in say, 1721, with service of seven years would bring the date to 1728–29. Furthermore as William Hallet jnr was born by 1730 his father's marriage to Anne ——, had taken place about the time he ended his years of training. William set up in London at Great Newport St, Long Acre, and his first recorded commission from that address was in 1735. We know of another ten over the same number of years.

By 1747 William, using whatever money his father had left, and the success of his business, bought items at the demolition sale of the 1st Duke of Chandos's great house of Cannons at Edgeware, and then built himself a house on the old centre foundations. He is shown holding a plan of his new house in a conversation-piece by Francis Hayman, RA, *c.* 1750 (frontispiece, *GCM*; Hughes–Hallett Coll.). The dates of marriages and births however do not allow us to be certain who the seven figures depicted in the painting are, but they are held to be Hallett's wife, his son, daughter-in-law, grand-daughter, and his father and mother-in-law by his (first) marriage. William Hallet jnr, born about 1730, married in December 1753 his first wife, Hannah Hopkins, the heiress of the successful financier and South Sea stock speculator, John 'Vulture' Hopkins of Brittons, Essex. [*Gents Mag.*, 23, 1753/ 54, 590; *London Evening Post*, 15–18 December 1753] William snr's second marriage to Lettice Hallett had brought over her considerable dowry. From the early 1750s therefore he seems to have been drawn more and more to his property interests, allowing his son to continue his business, however casually, and supporting, albeit as a sleeping partner, the new partnership (1751–52) of William Vile and John Cobb. Vile was still calling Hallett 'my Master' in 1749 [*Furn. Hist.*, 1975] and was probably his journeyman at this time.

For this theory to be credible it is necessary to assume that William Hallett I made no furniture after the mid 1750s, or in any case after his second marriage in 1756. The theory holds in the evidences accumulated for this *Dictionary*, and is confirmed, if we can read a little into a letter from Hallett to James Whittle of April 1755. In asking consent for his nephew Samuel Norman to visit Ann Whittle with a view to marriage, Hallett implied that he desisted before in encouragement because Norman was of the same business 'but as things are now Surcomstanc'd that Objection is removed with regard to myself'. [PRO, C112/194, pt 2] The state of the complex arguments may be summarized as follows: (a) William Hallett snr made furniture from about 1730 — with work for Lord

Irwin as the first recorded commission (1735) — until the early 1750s. (b) He allowed his son, William jnr to carry on running some sort of furniture-making business after he had more or less retired in the early 1750s as the squire of Cannons. The son, due to his wealth, pursued the business with casual inattention. (See also Reynolds, Commissions 1750 below.) (c) William snr (and to a certain extent his son) acted as 'sleeping partners' in the firm of Vile & Cobb. This is attested by payments and receipts in the Hallett, Vile and Cobb bank accounts. [Drummonds Branch, Royal Bank of Scotland] William jnr predeceased his father in 1767 [will PRO, Prob. 11/928, f.180], and Cannons was left in his father's will [PRO, Prob. 11/1086, f.25] to the grandson, William (1764–1842). (d) It is William III, with his first wife Elizabeth Lettice Stephen who are the subjects in Thomas Gainsborough's *The Morning Walk* (National Gallery, London) 1786. He is not known to have had any furniture-making connections. (e) Most of the family are buried at St Lawrence, Whitchurch but it has not been established where William snr was married or where his son William jnr was baptized. (f) Confusion with a William Hallot, cm has occurred.

It is important to pursue genealogical probems in order to see what is probable. It is my belief that certain items of furniture with foliate ovals which can be dated to c.1750 are more likely to be by William Hallett snr than his journeyman William Vile, and that Vile continued the 'style' in later years (e.g. the bookcase c.1762, for Queen Charlotte. [*Burlington*, July 1977, p.485, pls 17–18]

Some of the transfer of style may have been done in workshop terms through Samuel Reynolds, and in 1753 Hallett had moved his business from Newport St to St Martin's Lane. He took premises next to Vile & Cobb's. Two years later his name is crossed through in the rate bks [Westminster Ref. Lib.] and Cobb's is inserted. Reynolds had signed for money on Hallett's behalf in 1750, but a year or two later he did so on behalf of Vile & Cobb. I have noted this 'transfer' as early as 1753 (Commissions, below, Canons Ashby).

Within their business the Halletts were also served for a time by Edward Edwards who later established himself as a painter and was appointed a Royal Academician. [H. Walpole, *Anecdotes of Painters*, 1798] The business took apps from 1730 (Ralph Sharrington); 1732 (Philip Davis); 1733 (Chris. Bingham); 1736 (Joseph Beale); 1742 (James Cole); 1756 (James Stewart). The app. recorded in 1765 was to William Hallot. At some point Hallett snr was in 'partnership' with the successful painter-stainer, Thomas Bromwich. This was about 1745, but as late as 1756 Richard Cambridge coupled their names in his *Elegy Written in an Empty Assembley Room* '. . . In scenes where *Hallet's* genius has combin'd with *Bromwich* to amuse and cheer the mind . . .'. They both worked at Holkham and Uppark [*Furn. Hist.*, 1965] and both were mentioned by the inveterate letter-writer, Horace Walpole, who had some Gothic furniture by Hallett, and wrote also of his 'mongrel Chinese' furniture.

Finally we must dismiss, I hope with certainty, the reported event of Hallett's bankruptcy in 1769. I have advanced good reasons [*Furn. Hist.*, 1985] to show that this has been an orthographical confusion with the separate cm, William Hallot. The bankruptcy record and Hallot's signature (compared to that of the two Halletts) establishes a separate person, whose work has been, alas, credited to the squire of Cannons. The entry in 1769 for Hallot [*Gents Mag.*, 39, 1769] confirmed as 'Hallot' by title, and signature [*London Gazette*, 22–25 April 1769; PRO, B/6. A 11, p.55, and Bailey's list of bankrupts, 1773, p.35] was mistaken as

Hallett in *Furn. Hist.*, 1966. The fortunes left by Hallett and his son, and the fact that Hallett jnr at least had predeceased the alleged bankruptcy pushes it further to the name of William Hallot. However, mystery persists, with the West-minster rate bks showing an otherwise unknown Samuel Hallett living in Long Acre in 1753 (when Hallett snr was in St Martin's Lane). He stayed there until at least 1762 — the books for 1763–64 are missing and there are no Hallett entries for 1765–71. Could he be another son of William snr? Research continues, but is unlikely to upset the pattern established above for Hallett snr's removal from active cabinet-making in the early 1750s.

ARTHUR INGRAM, 7th VISCOUNT IRWIN. 1735: August, 18 carved walnut tree chairs at 23s, 22 other chairs. September, 12 matted chairs, 2 tables, 6 common chairs. February 1736, three tables, dressing glass, two voyders etc. Received £45 13s 6d from Viscountess Irwin, an executrix of her husband, but not until 28 years later in 1763. The furniture was made for the London house, and sent in 1736 to Temple Newsam House, Leeds. [*Conn.*, December 1964, pp.224–25 advert. John Keil Ltd; Sotheby's, 24 June 1966, lot 127; ibid., lot 200, January 1978]

OKEOVER HALL, Staffs. (Leake Okeover). 1736–38: 2 mahogany chests, 'a Handsome glass in a Carved and gilt frame in Burnish gold, £19. 10s.'. [*C. Life*, 30 January 1964, p.288, fig.15]

ROUSHAM HOUSE, Oxon. (General James Dormer). 1737: 'For a Large Wainscot press for Books, £7.10.0. For a Lybrary stool on Castors. 0.15.0.'. [Rousham MS at house]

HOLKHAM HALL, Norfolk (1st Earl of Leicester). 1737–52: 18 March 1737, 'Mr Hallett for a pattern chair for Holkham £3. 5s.' (This may be the chair illus. *Apollo*, February 1964, p.128, and *Furn. Hist.*, 1965, p.15, but surely the payment is too low?) 15 April 1738, for a pattern chair £3 5s — 'in exchange for a pattern chair which he received £3. 5s. for on the 18th of March last. £2. 5s.' 1747: 'For a canvas screen, altering a glass frame & polishing.' 1748: '2 mahogany trays for long dishes £2.3.0. do. for glasses £1.4.0. 2 mahogany stands £2.10.0. 2 canvas screens 1.18.0. 2 night tables 1.8.0. mahogany dumb waiter (London) 1.11.0. 43 yds of check linnen for chair covers £3.3.—.' 1749: trays, screens, stands, etc. 1751: '2 night tables £1.4.6. 2 chess tables £3.3.—. Mending a voider £—.9.6.'. 1752: '2 night tables & a case £1.15.0.'. [Holkham, Weekly Departmental Accounts, transcript in V&A archives; *C. Life*, 11 February 1980, pp.427–31]

GIBSIDE, Co. Durham. 1739–45: 'For a good mahog. couch', £12 17s. 30 April 1745: 'Paid Hallett ye Cabinet-maker his bill in full of accounts. £89.13s.6d.'. [Mrs Bowes's cash accounts, Durham RO, D/St/326; V.1325]

AUGUSTA, Princess of Wales. 1740–41: Abstract of expenses, 1 July 1740–1 July 1741. 4 April 1741. Received £38 7s. [Windsor Royal Archives, 55426]

BADMINTON, Glos. (4th Duke of Beaufort). 24 June 1740: Paid £100. 24 April 1742: Received £16.13s. Possibly for Kentian style seat furniture, or library table, North Hall. [Badminton papers, 308.101.2, Hoare's Bank vouchers]

CANNON HALL, Yorks. (John Spencer). 1741 May 15: Card Table £2 2s; Dining Table £2 2s; Mahogany Writing Table £5. 5s; Straining Frame £1. 4s; Total £10. 13s. '4 Chairs, £3; 8 Do, £8. 8. 0; 1 Do, £2. 10; 1 Do, £1. 8; Total £15. 6. 0. Book Case Gilding and Locks, all Deal £9. 19. 0. 2 Sconces & Frames £8. 15. 0. Gilding –. 8. –. 3 India Pictures £1. 2. 6. To June 2, 1741. £46. 3. 6.'. Hallett also provided a bed and its bedclothes and dressed it with green Harateen. This amounted to a further £18. 9s 1d making a final total of

£64 12s 7d, with carriage charges, in November 1741, of £3 14s 9d. [Sheffield City Lib., archives dept, JS 60685–87]
DITCHLEY PARK, Oxon. (2nd Earl of Lichfield). 1742: 'For tables, stands and screen'. [Oxford RO, Dillon I/p/3/b1]
DUCHESS OF MONTROSE. 1742: '2 Chimney glasses in carved mahogany frames £6.8.0. & £4.0.0.; a sconce in a carved mahogany frame £10.10.0.; 13 black frames with gilt edges for pictures £2.9.6.', receipted account, 1742. [Scottish RO, GD220/6/899/63]
WILTON HOUSE. Wilts. (7th Earl of Pembroke). 1742: 7 April. 'To Hallett, 3 pair of candlestands, silvered nozzles, £5.8s. od.' [Apollo, July 1964, p. 4]
DEENE PARK, Northants. 1745: Unspecified work. [GCM]
REDBRAES CASTLE, Berwicks., Scotland. 1745: Hallett & Bromwich, Cabinet-maker and paper-hanger. Received £184 15s. [Scottish RO, GD. I/651/19]
MOULSHAM HALL, Essex (Earl Fitzwalter). 1745–48: 6 March 1745: 'Pd Mr Halett of Newport Street for Ten black leather bottom'd chairs for my dining room in town £17. 10s.' (i.e. Schomberg House). 12 March 1746: 'Pd Mr Hallett, upholster, his bill in full' £9 19s. 1 April 1747: 'Pd Mr Hallett for a little firescreen' £1. 1s. 17 May 1748: Pd Mr Wm Hallett for a light fire screen £1. 1s. [A. C. Edwards, The Accounts of Benjamin Mildmay, Earl Fitzwalter, pp. 110–12]
ST GILES'S, Dorset (4th Earl of Shaftesbury). 1745: 2 February, 'Paid as pr Bill to Mr Hallet for carved chairs. £167'. As Hallett's chairs for Lord Irwin (above) cost 23s each many of the chairs formerly at the house may be Hallett's (listed Christie's, 26 June 1980, p. 8). 1746: 26 April, 'Paid as pr Bill to Mr Hallet for making and putting up ye bed (This refers to a blue damask bed for which 45 yds of blue damask was provided at a cost of £22 1s on 15 April 1746). The bed does not survive. 1746: 3 June, 'Paid as pr Bill to Mr Hallet. £17. 10s. od' 1752: 20 August, 'Paid Mr Hallet as pr Bill for Mahogany Cisterns £5. 15s. 0.' [Archives at house: copies, V & A archives; see also Christie's, 26 June 1980, account illus. as catalogue endpapers; see this sale, lots 91–96, and Sotheby's, 18 November 1983, lot 54] A mahogany commode which may have been by Hallett (rather than Vile) was sold Christie's, 27 March 1952, lot 75, and another, Christie's, 3 July 1953, lot 283. There is a similar example at the Toledo Museum (GCM, pl. 56), and a number are illustrated by Coleridge, Thomas Chippendale (e.g. pls 9–10). Caution is necessary however as documentation is lacking in all cases.
KIRTLINGTON PARK, Oxon. (Sir James Dashwood). 1747–52: Payments of 2 November 1747 (£425), 12 March 1750 (£42), 22 February 1752 (£31) in 'General Account of money expended on my new house and the outworks about it begun 12 Sept. 1741'. [Apollo, January 1980]
SIR WM BEAUCHAMP PROCTOR. 1748: 2 May–9 August, furniture including '3 large Mahog. Dining Tables to join to Dine from £15. 5; Carved & Gilt Picture Frames £9. 10s. Received £64. 13s. 4d. less £5 Recd by 2 tea tables much broke'. Intended for Langley House, Norfolk, or a London house in Bruton St. [Norfolk RO, BEA 305/41]
ALSCOT, Warks. (James West). 4 August 1748: mahogany knife tray, brass corners (14s); two mahogany pails on frames, brass hoops and handles (£4); mahogany tray to carry dishes (12s); mahogany chest of drawers with a sliding board (£4); mahogany bottle tray on castors (£1 5s); glass case in a redwood frame & ebony mouldings (£16). Received £26 18s 6d on 13 January 1749. On 29 February 1752 William Hallett jnr receipted a bill for a 'Globe Lanthorn, etc. in the sum of £7 8s 'for my Father Willm Hallett'. This was for work of 20 July 1750. [Alscot MS at house]
1748: At a sale of the **EARL of CHOLMONDELEY'S** estate, Richmond, Surrey, the Catalogue and plans could be

inspected at 'Mr Hallett's Gt. Newport Street, Long Acre'. [General Advertiser, 30 March 1748]
LONDON, St James's Sq. (Peter Du Cane). 1749:

	£	s	d
July 3. For Securing the Gold of a Sett of Dressing boxes		12	
Jany. 19. For puting a Draw in a bookcase With a Loose Standish to take out		14	
For Nailing Some Gilt Leather Round Som Doors		1	
29. For Mending 2 Chest of Draws at your house		5	
For 10 Rings & Roses 5 Scutchens & 2 Corner Plates of brass & 8 Screws		5	6
For Neat Mahogany China Dishstands	1	2	

[Essex RO, D/DC A12, f. 73; A 80. Du Cane's seat was at Great Braxted, Essex, hence these bills at Essex RO]
3rd EARL of BURLINGTON. 1750: f. 22 (1750) 'Paid Mr William Hallett, cabinet maker (for Chiswick) £21. 8. 0. f. 98 (5 Aug. 1751) Paid Mr Willm Hallett by Saml Reynolds the sum of £8 5. 0 for a Machine Chair'. (Signed by Reynolds for Hallett. This is interesting further confirmation of Hallett's involvement with Vile and Cobb, as Reynolds was later in their employ after Hallett had, as suggested, 'retired'.) [Chatsworth, Ledger, 'An Account current with . . . the Earl of Burlington commencing 11 Ap. 1750 by John Ferrett']
UPPARK, Sussex (Sir Matthew Featherstonhaugh). 1754: 27 March, 'Pd Mr Hallett for a cabinet £43. 5. 6d'. This may refer to a glazed mahogany cabinet of architectural design on a stand at Uppark. [Conn., November 1967, pp. 158–59, fig. 1]
STRAWBERRY HILL, Middlx (Horace Walpole). 1755: 20 September, Sofas, chairs, pier glass in Gothic style for the Great Parlour or Refectory. 4 chairs are in the W. S. Lewis Coll., Farmington, USA. One chair is at V & A Museum (W29–1979), and the Glass is Coll. Lord Walpole. [Paget Toynbee (ed.), Strawberry Hill Accounts, 1927, pp. 6, 82–85; Horace Walpole and Strawberry Hill, Orleans House, Twickenham (1980) Nos 84–85] Walpole in a letter to Richard Bentley, 5 July 1755, writes of Hallett's 'mongrel Chinese' (furniture). [Yale edn H. Walpole's Correspondence]
LORD ANSON. 1756: 24 November, £220 credited to Hallett's bank account from Lord Anson. [Drummonds Branch, Royal Bank of Scotland] 1763: A pencil inscription 'William Hallet(t), 1763 Long Acre' appears on the carcase of the base of a cabinet, formerly colls Lord Wharton; Colonel Norman Colville (Christie's, 1 December 1977, lot 124, Sotheby's, 19 March 1982, lot 45). For views on this see Furn. Hist., 1965 and ibid., 1985. A related cabinet was sold Christie's, 21 May 1984, lot 374, bought P. Hewat-Jaboor. The cabinets are likely to date to the 1750s with the inscription being added for some reason in later years. The inscription was first published by A. Coleridge in Furn. Hist., 1965, p. 11.
HATFIELD PRIORY, Essex (John Wright). 1769: 'William Hallet £75'. This late entry would be after William Hallett jnr's death, 1767, and was rendered presumably as a late debt to his father. [Hoare's Bank, London, vol. 79, f. 160] G.B.

Halley, Edmund, 24 Bourne St, Hull, Yorks., chairmaker and Hackney gig owner (1826). Recorded as grocer and flour dealer at 14 Worship St and Bourne St, 1831–34. [D]
Halley, George, Stoke Damarell, Devon, cm (1759). Took app. named Angrove in 1759. [S of G, app. index]
Halley, George snr and jnr, Shifnal, Salop, cm and auctioneer (1797–98). [D]
Halley, George Henry, Wakefield, Yorks., cm and u (1803–05). Trading at Northgate in 1805. Subscribed to Sheraton's Cabinet Dictionary, 1803. [D]

Halley, Thomas, Hull, Yorks., coach and furniture painter (1823). Took app. named William Clark of York in April 1823. [Hull app. reg.]

Hallhead, James, Lancaster, u (1811–12). Admitted freeman, 1811–12, when stated 'of Kendal'. [Lancaster freemen rolls] See James Halhead.

Hallhead, John, Lancaster, cm and carver (1771–80). App. to J. Neill in 1771, and admitted freeman, 1779–80, when stated 'of Kendal'. [Lancaster app. reg. and freemen rolls] See John Halhead.

Halliday, Andrew, 47 Fleet St and 4 Lettman Pl., Bolton St, Liverpool, cm (1824). [D]

Halliday, Henry, York, cm (1826). Son of John Halliday; app. to Thomas Walls, cm and u, of York, on 18 December 1826. [York app. reg.]

Halliday, Henry, 30 Lower Edmund St, King's Cross, London, veneer cutter (1835). [D]

Halliday, John, Parsonage St, Dursley, Glos., u and cm (1816–23). Children born in 1816 and 1820. [D; PR]

Halliday, Thomas, Bedfordbury, St Martin-in-the-Fields, London, cm (1774). [Poll bk]

Halliday, Thomas, Old Round Ct, Strand, London, cm (1784). [D]

Hallier, Charles, London, upholder (1780–1802). Trading at 24 Watling St in 1788, and Sewers Office, Guildhall, in 1802. Son of William Hallier, tin plate worker of Bread St; app. to Edward Shipman on 1 March 1780, and admitted freeman of the Upholders' Co. by servitude on 5 March 1788. [GL, Upholders' Co. records]

Halling, William, Gloucester, cm (1828–32). Children bapt. at St John Baptist Church between 1828–32. [PR (bapt.)]

Hallock, John, Hautboys, Norfolk, cm (1839). [D]

Hallot, William, Long Acre, London, cm, u, dealer and chapman (1762–73). It might well be thought that 'William Hallot' is a mistake for 'William Hallett'. However a letter written by Hallot, the question of the dates of his activity, comparison of the handwriting and signatures of William Hallett, his son, and William Hallot do seem to point to a separate personality, albeit one who went bankrupt in 1769. This discreditable act was levelled at William Hallett snr (*Furn. Hist.*, XI, 1975, p. 114) on the assumption that unconventional orthography in writing 'William Hallot' — [*Gents Mag.*, April 1769, vol. 39, p. 216; repeated as Hallot in *The Universal Magazine*, April 1769, vol. 44, p. 223] — was a mistake for Hallett.

Hallot's only known bill and letter relate to furniture supplied in July 1762 to James Leigh of Stoneleigh, Warks., (Shakespeare Birthplace Trust, Leigh MS, DR 18/8/5, Household Accounts, Box 2, Bundle 2). His letter sent to Leigh from London on 2 August 1763 has many differences to the hand of either William Hallett snr, or his son. I have published the three relevant signatures [*Furn. Hist.*, XXI, 1985] and have been able to look at some twenty examples of the Hallett hand which stays consistent throughout, and consistent in its differences to that of Hallot.

In the case of the bankruptcy we would, by its date (1769), have in any case to exclude confusion with William Hallett jnr (who died in 1767). His father William Hallett snr's bank account [Drummonds Branch, Royal Bank of Scotland] shows a good balance for 1768 — the A–H ledger for 1769 is not extant. Also Hallett's daughter married in 1779 with a dowry of £70,000 [*Gents Mag.*, 1779, p. 566] Hardly the background of a bankrupt father and impecunious daughter. I believe therefore we must accept William Hallot. He is recorded in that name as taking an app. William Wightwize(?) in 1765, noted as 'William Hallot Upholder, St Martin's, Westminster', for a premium of £50. To confuse us however the name is not in the rate bks covering Long Acre. The

London Gazette, 22–25 April 1769, noted 'Commission of Bankruptcy is awarded against William Hallot of Long Acre ... Upholder, Cabinet-Maker, Dealer and Chapman'. Only the bankruptcy certificates survive for 1769 [PRO, B/6–A.11, 1769–71, p. 55] and not a fuller record, but a 'Hallot' bankruptcy is further noted in Bailey's *List of Bankruptcies*, 1773, p. 35 [GL] The quest continues for his will, and for more commissions, as enough evidence seems to be available to sketch in an identity separate from the 'squire' of Cannons.

G.B.

Hallowell, Edw., Coronation St, Bishop Wearmouth, Sunderland, Co. Durham, furniture broker and cm (1827). [D]

Hallowes, James, Foregate St, Chester, cm (1824). Admitted freeman on 19 October 1824. [Chester freemen rolls]

Hallowes, Thomas, Chester, cm and u (1831). Admitted freeman on 20 April 1831. [Chester freemen rolls]

Hallows, John, at 'The Crown & Scepter', Moorfields, London, u and sworn appraiser (c.1760). Trade card with Rococo embellishment states that he 'Makes & Sells all Sorts of Standing Beds & Bedsteads. Feather Beds, Blankets, Quilts, Glasses, Chairs, Cabinet Work, Brasiery & Iron Work, & all other Sorts of Household Goods, both New & Old, at yᵉ Cheapest Rates. NB. Goods Bought or Sold by Commission.' [Leverhulme Coll., MMA, NY]

Hallows, John, Chester, cm and beer house (1811–40). Addresses given at 1 Foregate St, 1812, 1819 and 1840; and Claremont Walk, 1818, 1819 and 1826. A John Hallows was admitted freeman on 7 August 1811. [D; poll bks; Chester freemen rolls]

Hall(s)pike, Christopher, London, cm and u (c.1780–1827). Trading at 13 Wilderness Row, Goswell St, 1807–08; 10 Little Queen St, Holborn in 1822; and 25 St John Sq., 1826–27. Took out Sun Insurance policies on 5 November 1807 for £300; and on 12 March 1822 for £300, of which £30 accounted for a chest of tools at Seddons in Aldersgate St. Mahogany sideboard, said to have been made for John Barrow, c.1780, bears manuscript label inside drawer inscribed: 'Chris Hallpike No 862'. [D; GL, Sun MS vol. 441, ref. 809717; vol. 490, ref. 989822; *Conn.*, LXVIII (1924), p. 35]

Hallpike, V., Settle, Yorks., cm (1798–1837). Two mahogany hall chairs, c.1800, at Skipton Museum are of circular back pattern and impressed under seat rail 'V. HALLPIKE'. [D]

Halls, Edward, address unrecorded, cm (c.1770). App. to Edward John Elwick of Wakefield, Yorks., c.1770. [*Furn. Hist.*, 1976]

Halls (or Halse), Richard, Ashburton, Devon, cm and auctioneer (1826–30). Trading at North St in 1830. Notices in *The Alfred*, 13 June 1826, and *Exeter Flying Post*, 13 July 1826, concerned his wife, Sarah's, appeal for and entitlement to benefit through the Act of Relief of Insolvent Debtors. [D]

Halls, William jnr, Norwich, cm (d. 1830). Will proved in 1830. [Norfolk Record Soc., index of wills]

Hallsall, Charles, 78 Stanley St, Liverpool, cm and broker (1821–23). [D]

Hallso, William, 11 Eaton St, Liverpool, cm (1821–27). [D]

Hallum & Pidcock, Nottingham, cm (1793). Subscribed to Sheraton's *Drawing Book*, 1793. See Hallam & Pid(l)ock.

Halmarack, Richard, Castle St, Stone, Staffs., chairmaker (1822). [D]

Halmshaw, John, Upperthong, near Huddersfield, Yorks., joiner and cm (1822). [D]

Halmshaw, Joseph, Westgate, Dewsbury, Yorks., cm (1830). [D]

Halsall, Anthony, 'Vest Bromedge' (West Bromwich, Staffs. ?), carver (1774). [Bristol poll bk]

Halsall, Richard, Moorflat, St Helens, Lancs., joiner and cm (1828). [D]

Halsall, William, 5 Eaton St, Liverpool, cm (1839). [D]

Halse, James, High St, Oxford, u and cm (1808). A mahogany clothes press, c.1800 bearing a label inscribed: 'Halse's UPHOLSTERY & CABINET MANUFACTORY High Street, Oxford. Appraiser & Auctioneer' was sold at Christie's, 29 June 1978, lot 75. [D]

Halse, William, Truro, Cornwall, cm (1752–57). Took app. named Thomas Woolcock in 1752 for £12, and other apps in 1757 including William Bromley. Subscribed to Chippendale's *Director*, 1754. [S of G, app. index]

Halsey, John, St Giles-in-the-Fields, London, carver (1745–61). Took app. named John Walker in 1745 for £5. Subscribed to Chippendale's *Director*, 1754. Discharge from Debtors' Prison announced in *London Gazette*, 1761. [S of G, app. index]

Halsey, Thomas William, 11 Orange St, Canterbury, Kent, cm and u (1838). [D]

Halson, Charles jnr, address unrecorded, cm (1823). Took out a Sun Insurance policy on 24 September 1823 for £400, of which £340 accounted for household goods in the warehouse of Messrs Goodman & Co., cm, 113 Aldersgate St, and £60 on musical instruments, prints and pictures, china and glass. [GL, Sun MS vol. 496, ref. 1008571]

Halstaff, John, 47 Museum St, Holborn, London, writing desk and dressing case maker (1829). [D]

Halstaff, William, 68 Margaret St, Cavendish Sq., London, dressing case manufacturer (1835–37). [D]

Halton, Richard, 35 Woodstock St, Liverpool, cm (1834). [D]

Ham, Archibald, address unrecorded, cm (1803). Subscribed to Sheraton's *Cabinet Dictionary*, 1803.

Ham, Elias, Exeter, Devon, u (1728). Took app. named Glanvill in 1728. [S of G, app. index]

Ham, John, Fore St, Marazion, Cornwall, cm (1824). [D]

Ham, John, Fore St, Padstow, Cornwall, cm (1824–30). [D]

Ham, Nicholas, address unrecorded, upholder (1722–29). Son of Richard Ham, tailor, of St Mary-le-Grand, Middlx. App. to John Underwood on 1 August 1722, and admitted freeman of the Upholders' Co. by servitude on 6 August 1829. [GL, Upholders' Co. records]

Hambidge & Halliday, High St, Stroud, Glos., cm and paper hanger (1830). [D]

Hambleton, —, at 'The Talbot', Long Lane, near West Smithfield, London, u (1724–30). Recorded in newspapers in partnership with John Howard, 1724–30. [Heal] See Howard & Hambleton and Joseph Hamilton.

Hambleton, —, see John Sherrott snr.

Hambleton & Son, Edward, Penzance, Cornwall, cm (1824–30). Trading at West St in 1823–24, and North Parade in 1830. [D]

Hambleton, Joseph, Kirkgate, Thirsk, Yorks., cm (1823). [D]

Hambley, Peter, London, u (?) (1715). Named in Lady Grisell Baillie's accounts at Mellerstain, Berwickshire, supplying '3 pices yellow Damask for window curtains', costing £18; and '6 pices of Green Damask for hangins, chairs, & window curtains', £36. [MS accounts, f. 367]

Hame, Edward, London, cm (1818). [Norwich poll bk]

Hamer, John, Coal St, Lime St, Liverpool, cm (1829). [D]

Hamersham, Thomas, 245 Borough, London, u (1800). [D]

Hames, Henry, 40 Barbican, London, broker and cm (1802). Took out a Sun Insurance policy on 21 April 1802 for £500, utensils and stock accounting for £350. [GL, Sun MS vol. 424, ref. 730902]

Hamford, James, London, cm (1705/06). Supplied items to Samuel Tufnell of Middle Temple, London, receiving £16 10s on 27 November 1705 for 'A Desk & foulding tables & teay

table for My Masters use'; and £22 on 1 February 1705/06, for '2 peer Glass & 2 Chimney Glass for my Master use'. Both bills were receipted by John Etherington. [Essex RO, D/DTu, 276]

Hamilton, —, Whitechapel, London, u (1747). Named in newspapers in 1747. [Heal] Possibly William Hamilton.

Hamilton, David, 3 Burleigh SN [*sic*], Strand, London, cm (1808). [D]

Hamilton, Francis, London, upholder (1746–86). Recorded at 20 Smithfield, 1767–83, in partnership with Kirkham, 1773–83; and at West Smithfield, 1778–86. Son of Joseph Hamilton, draper of London. App. to his father on 26 March 1746, and admitted freeman of the Upholders' Co. by redemption on 7 May 1761. Took apps named John Milsom, 1761–68; John Kirkham until 1772; and John Green in 1777. [D; GL, Upholders' Co. records]

Hamilton, George, address unrecorded, carver and gilder (1774). Announced in *The Virginia Gazette*, 28 July 1774 that he was 'just from Britain', and advertised his business from the Edward Dickinson shop, Williamsburg.

Hamilton, Jacobus, Preston, Lancs., u (1722) [Preston Guild record of burgesses] Father of Willus Hamilton, u.

Hamilton, John, Lancaster, chairmaker (1823–24). [Lancaster freemen rolls]

Hamilton, John, High Wycombe, Bucks., u (b. c. 1801–41). Daughters bapt. in 1823 and 1829. Aged 40 at the time of the 1841 Census. [PR (bapt.)]

Hamilton, Joseph, Long Lane, West Smithfield, London, upholder (1742). Announced in *Daily Advertiser*, 2 November 1742, that he was selling catalogues for the sale of stock in trade and household goods of John Howard, who had run a carpet and upholstery warehouse in the same street.

Hamilton, R. T., 2 Cullum St, Fenchurch St, London, cm and u (1809–19). [D]

Hamilton, R., London, u (1820–37). Trading at 126 Fenchurch St, 1820–25, and 127 Houndsditch in 1837. [D]

Hamilton, Robert, Brewer St, London, cm (1774). [Poll bk]

Hamilton, Thomas, New Bond St, London, upholder (1736). Declared bankrupt, *Gents Mag.*, October 1736.

Hamilton, Thomas, 7 Lower Marsh, Lambeth, London, cm etc. (1820). [D]

Hamilton, W., 76 Wardour St, London, upholder (1794). Named in newspapers in 1794. [Heal]

Hamilton, William, 54 Whitechapel, London, upholder and undertaker (1759–1811). Recorded also at no. 55 in 1808. Trading as William & Son, 1760–72; and as Hamilton & Cruffall (or Creessall), 1782–83. William alone is named in newspapers in 1790, and in Sheraton's list of master cabinet makers, 1803. [D; Heal]

Hamilton, William, High St, Berwick-upon-Tweed, Northumb., u and cm (1827–34). [D]

Hamilton, Willus, Preston, Lancs., u (1722). Son of Jacobus Hamilton, u. [Preston Guild record of burgesses]

Hamilton & Mogany, High St, Lambeth, London, cm (1825). [D]

Hamlin, John, London, carver and gilder (1839). [D]

Hamlin, Thomas, Cuckfield, Sussex, cooper, turner and chairmaker (1823). [D]

Hamm, Henry, Norwich, cm (1797–99). [D; poll bks]

Hammersley, G., 22 Walcot St, Bath, Som., cm (1826). [D]

Hammersley, Joseph T., 78 Bishopsgate Without, London, cm (1808–11). [D]

Hammersley, Joseph, 55 Chamber St, Leman St, London, cm and u (1839). [D]

Hammersley, William, Laurence Lane, Boston, Lincs., chairmaker and turner (1835). [D]

Hammerton, George, Brighouse, Yorks., cm (1830). [D]

Hammeth, Robert, Fore St, Kingsbridge, Devon, cm (1830). [D]

Hammett, James, West Ham, London, cm (1809–11). [D]

Hammond, —, address unrecorded, frame maker (1732). Received £3 15s 6d from Sir Richard Hoare on 8 November 1732. [Hoare's Bank, Fleet St, private accounts] Probably:

Hammond, Christopher, Phoenix Ct, Long Acre, London, frame maker and gilder (1732). Trade card recorded. [Heal]

Hammond, David Henry, 2 Jane St, Commercial Rd East, London, cm and u (1839). [D]

Hammond, Edward, 18 Christopher Sq., Long Alley, Moorfields, London, chair and sofa maker (1824–28). Took out a Sun Insurance policy on 3 May 1824 for £500 of which £150 accounted for utensils and stock. [D; GL, Sun MS vol. 497, ref. 1016753]

Hammond, George, London and Canterbury, Kent, u (1790–1807). Recorded at Oxford St, London in 1790, Butter Mkt, Canterbury in 1794, and Burgate St, Canterbury, 1805–07. [D; poll bks]

Hammond, George, 7 Broad St, Golden Sq., London, cm etc. (1820). [D]

Hammond, H., 1 Gt Warner St, Clerkenwell, London, firescreen maker (1816–19). [D]

Hammond, H., 139 High St, Ramsgate, Kent, cm (1838). [D]

Hammond, Henry, 5 Cranbourn Alley, Margate, Kent, cm (1826–34). [D]

Hammond, Henry, Liverpool, ship-carver (1831). Notice in *Liverpool Mercury*, 26 August 1831, that he was one of the survivors from the wreck of the steamer *Rothsay Castle*, and had been 'employed in executing some ornaments in the vessel, & worked during the voyage to save time.' See John & Henry and Joseph Hammond.

Hammond, John, at 'The Cabinet & Crown', Broker's Row, Lower Moorfields, London, broker and upholder (1779). Bill head dated 28 September 1779 continues: 'Buys and Sells all Sorts of HOUSEHOLD GOODS, both Second hand and New.' [A. Scott Coll., Basingstoke]

Hammond, John, Liverpool, carver (1810–29). Addresses given at 24 Stanhope St in 1810 and 90 Lime Kiln Lane in 1829. [D]

Hammond, John & Henry, 47 Trentham St, Liverpool, ship-carvers and gilders (1837). [D] See Henry Hammond.

Hammond, Joseph, 17 Trentham St, Liverpool, ship-carver and gilder (1835). [D]

Hammond, Mary, 24 Worcester St, Birmingham, cm (1835). [D]

Hammond, Richard, Ashby-de-la-Zouch, Leics., cm (1791). [D]

Hammon(d), Richard, Ashford, Kent, cm and u (1793–1824). Polled at Canterbury in 1796. [D]

Hammond, Richard, 4 Blacklion Yd, Whitechapel, London, cm and u (1839). [D]

Hammond, William, Nottingham, u (1779). [Nottingham burgess list]

Hammond, William, 63 or 73 North St, Brighton, Sussex, cm (1822–23). [D]

Hammond, William, Bury St Edmunds, Suffolk, cm and u (1830–39). Trading at 41 Guildhall St in 1830 and St Andrew St in 1839. [D]

Hammond, William, 25 Worcester St, Birmingham, cm, u, chairmaker and broker (1828–30). [D]

Hammond, William, 141 High St, Camden Town, London, cm and u (1839). [D]

Hamnett, Thomas, East Ham, London, cm (1808). [D]

Hampshaw, & Thomas, Skelmanthorpe, Yorks., joiners and cm (1834). [D]

Hampshire, George, Deptford, London, cm (1791–93). [D]

Hampshire, James, Lady Bridge, Leeds, Yorks., cm (1822). [D]

Hampshire, Jonas & Brother, Holmfirth, Yorks., joiner and/or cm (1834). [D]

Hampson, Henry, Clayton St, Liverpool, cm (1811–14). Recorded at no. 24 in 1811 and no. 34, 1813–14. [D]

Hampson, James, Manchester, cm (1788–1825). Trading at 14 Back Red Bank, 1788–1813, and Johnson St, Ducie Bridge in 1825. [D] See Hampson & Heaton.

Hampson, Thomas, Back Red Bank, Manchester, cm (1794–1811). Trading at no. 30 in 1794; no. 5 in 1804; and no. 14 in 1811. [D]

Hampson & Heaton, Johns(t)on St, Ducie Bridge (or Cheetham), Manchester, cm (1828–40). Recorded at no. 28, 1829–33. [D] See James Hampson.

Hampton, John, address unrecorded, cm (1803). Subscribed to Sheraton's *Cabinet Dictionary*, 1803.

Hampton, John, Cirencester, Glos., cm (1831–38). Children born in 1831, 1834 and 1838. [PR]

Hampton, John, 6 Hanover Pl., Regent's Park, London, carver and gilder (1835–39). [D]

Hampton, William, 18 Mount St, Lambeth, London, carver and gilder (1839). [D]

Hamshaw, William, Market Harborough, Leics., cm (1791). [D]

Hamson, James, Macclesfield, Cheshire, cm (1790–1808). [D]

Hanbury, John, London, u (1757). Trade card recorded. [Heal]

Hancock, —, Weymouth, Dorset, u (1820). Advertised catalogues for sale of Gloucester Lodge, in *Exeter Flying Post*, 6 July 1820. Possibly Anthony or J. & W. B. Hancock.

Hancock, —, Bury St Edmunds, Suffolk, amateur cm (1826). In July 1826 'Mr. Hancock received unsolicited payment of £105 for a beautiful cabinet of his own manufacture intended as a present to His Majesty and delivered to Carlton House.' [George IV's accounts, Windsor Royal Archives, RA 25414]

Hancock, Anthony, 30 St Mary St, Weymouth, Dorset, cm and u (1823). John Hancock is listed at the same address as an auctioneer. [D] See Hancock, —, Hancock & Son and J. & W. B. Hancock.

Hancock, Colebron, Hedge Lane, Charing Cross (later called Whitcomb St), London, glass cutter (1775). J. T. Smith in *Nollekens and His Times* noted that the premises of William Wilton were later occupied by a glass manufacturer of the name of Hancock, 'for whom Doctor Johnson wrote a handbill'. He was a cutter of glass other than looking-glass, and is perhaps the Col. Hancock who supplied '2 pr. curious girandoles for holding two lights each', costing £31 10s, to Croome Court, Worcs. on 13 March 1775. [Wills, *Looking-Glasses*; V&A archives]

Hancock, David, 33 Willow St, Finsbury Sq., London, chairmaker (1808). [D]

Hancock, J., 2 New St, Cloth Fair, London, upholder and blind maker (1808). [D]

Hancock, J. & W. B., 62 St Thomas St, Weymouth, Dorset, cm and u (1840). [D] See Hancock, —, Anthony Hancock and Hancock & Son.

Hancock, James, Marlborough, Wilts., cm and u (1779–98). Took out Sun Insurance policies in 1779 for £200, utensils and stock accounting for £155; and in 1791 for £400 on three tenements and a brewhouse. [D; GL, Sun MS vol. 273, p. 39; vol. 376, p. 243]

Hancock, James, 1 Christopher's Ct, London, cm (1784). [Poll bk]

Hancock, James, 9 Princess St, Bradshawgate, Bolton, Lancs., cm (1818). [D]

Hancock, John, Bristol, carver (1784–1800). Recorded in Eugean St, 1795–1800. [D; poll bk]

Hancock, John, 29 Longworth St, Manchester, cm (1808–09). [D]

Hancock, John, Boutport St, Barnstaple, Devon cm and u (1823–38). [D]

Hancock, John, 9 Bradford St, Birmingham, cabinet, dressing case and portable desk makers (1830). [D]

Hancock, T., Cumberland St, Plymouth Dock, Devon, carver and gilder (1814). [D]

Hancock, Thomas, Tetbury, Glos., upholder (1778–98). Insured his house for £300 in 1778. [D; GL, Sun MS vol. 264, p. 285]

Hancock, Thomas, 4 Back Irwell St, Manchester, cm (1808–09). [D]

Hancock, Thomas, Gloster St, Cirencester, Glos., carver and gilder (1839). [D]

Hancock & Co., London, glass and chandelier manufacturers (1820–35). Supplied items to Chatsworth, Derbs., between 1820 and 1835, totalling £913 10s 5d. Named in the Chiswick household accounts receiving £483 4s 6d for 'Branches for Grace's apartments'. [Chatsworth furnishing accounts; Chiswick accounts, cl66, vol. A]

Hancock & Rixon, address unrecorded, lamp lustre makers (1832–38). By 31 March 1838 trading as Hancock, Rixon & Dant. Loaned items to Stud House, Hampton Court, including lamps, ormolu girandoles, pedestals, blue glass girandoles and candlesticks. On 29 June 1833 supplied 'One 4-light gold coloured antique lamp', costing £12, to St James's. On 31 December 1835 the firm was paid £998 18s 9d, including £640 11s 8d for '4 large chandeliers for the Grand Reception Rms — Windsor'; for 'fitting & fixing metalwork ... & Gold Colouring the Same'; and £92 7s 1d for 'New Glass Work cutting etc.'. On 30 June 1840 Hancock, Rixon & Dant received £5 17s for '2 very thick handsome Maplewood Stands French Polished & covered w. silk velvet'. [PRO, LC11/77; 11/80; Royal Windsor account bks G–H]

Hancock & Son, 34 St Mary St, Weymouth, Dorset, cm and u (1830). [D] See Anthony, and J. & W. B. Hancock.

Hancock & Thomas, Gloster St, Cirencester, Glos., carvers and gilders (1839–40). [D]

Hancox, James, Ashted Row, Birmingham, cm, u and broker (1828–30). [D]

Hancox, James, Henley St, Stratford-upon-Avon, Warks., cm (1835). [D]

Hancox, Nicholas, Belton St, opposite Brownlow St, Long Acre, London, glass grinder (1783–90). 'Hancox & Co, looking-glass men' were owed the sum of £2,337 13s 2d for work at, and goods supplied to, Carlton House for the Prince of Wales between 1783–86. By 1790 he was recorded as being in business at Castle St, Long Acre. [Wills, *Looking-Glasses*] See Hancox & Co.

Hancox & Ashlin, London, looking-glass makers. On 26 December 1785 supplied to Chatsworth, Derbs., '2 plates best British Manufacture' at £76 5 4s; '2 top plates', £33 5s 4d; and blankets 'to pack the large plates that broke'. [Chatsworth papers, 81] Possibly:

Hancox & Co., Belton St, Long Acre, London, glass-grinders and carvers (1783–87). [D] See Nicholas Hancox.

Hand, —, address unrecorded, u (1822–24). Received payments for unspecified work at Dunham Massey, Cheshire, on 31 December 1822 for £242 0s 10d; and on 9 February 1824 for £75. [John Rylands Lib., Manchester Univ., Dunham Massey papers]

Hand, Charles, 47 Queen St, Manchester, cm (1822). [D]

Hand, Daniel, Crispin St, Northampton, cm (1830). [D]

Hand, John, Manchester, cm (1800–17). Addresses given at New Jerusalem Pl. in 1800, 55 Tickle St in 1813, and 13 Byrom St in 1817. [D]

Hand, John, Liverpool, u and cm (1805–39). Recorded at 11 New Scotland Rd in 1805; 20 Davies St in 1807; 46 Church St in 1810; 47 Church St in 1811; no. 50, 1813–14;

no. 47 in 1818; no. 53, 1821–23; 89 Bold St, 1824–27; no. 93 in 1829; no. 109 in 1834; no. 97 in 1835; no. 105 in 1837; no. 32 and also 27 Lord Nelson St in 1839. Trading as John & Son from 1834–39. Carried out work at Liverpool Town Hall, receiving £443 15s 9d on 30 June 1819; £260 7s on 7 February 1820; and £60 7s on 14 June 1823. [D; *Furn. Hist.*, 1970]

Hand, Joseph, 68 Bridge St, Manchester, cm (1836–40). [D]

Hand, Stephen, 35 Stafford St, Liverpool, u and cm (1839). [D]

Hand, Thomas, Oakham, Rutland, joiner and turner (1721–39). App. to Thomas Thickpenny of Leicester in 1721, and admitted freeman in 1731. Took app. named Thomas Tipler in 1739. [Leicester freemen rolls]

Hand, Thomas, Manchester, cm (1817–36). Trading at 49 Quay St in 1817; no. 47, 1818–19; and 12 Back St (or South) Parade in 1836. [D]

Hand, Uriah, 31 Ironmarket, Newcastle-under-Lyme, Staffs., chairmaker (1836–39). [D]

Hand, Uriel, Newcastle-under-Lyme, Staffs., chairmaker (1818–39). Recorded at Shoreditch in 1818 and 11 Bath St, 1839. [D]

Hand, William, Iron Mkt, Newcastle-under-Lyme, Staffs., chairmaker (1822). [D]

Handcock, George, address unrecorded, cm (1803). Subscribed to Sheraton's *Cabinet Dictionary*, 1803.

Handcock, James, Borough Walls, Bath, Som., cm (1793). [D]

Handford, James, Swallow St, St James's, London, cm (1784). [Bristol poll bk]

Handford, James, 7 Strand, London, manufacturer of writing desks, dressing cases etc. (1837). [D] See Thomas Handford.

Handford, John, Exeter, Devon, cm (1824–38). Recorded at South St in 1824; St Thomas in 1828; and Stepcote Hill in 1838. Daughter Elizabeth bapt. at St Mary Major on 15 February 1824, and son James at St George on 7 October 1838. Notice in *Exeter Flying Post*, 11 September 1828 stated that John Handford had been treated at the Devon and Exeter Hospital for a viper bite. The three-foot long viper was killed between Christow and Canonteign, where Handford had been gathering blackberries. [PR (bapt.)]

Handford, Samuel, Manchester, cm (1825–40). Addresses given at 1 Bakehouse Ct, Tickle St in 1825; Thomas St in 1834; 274 Deansgate, 1836–38; and 15 Thomas (or Tonman) St in 1840. [D]

Handford, T., 84 St James St, London, writing desk manufacturer (c.1800). Trade card reads: 'Manufacturer of Copying Machines, Writing Desks and all kinds of Ladies and Gentleman's PORTABLE CASES'. [Westminster Ref. Lib., Gardener Coll.] Probably:

Handford, T., 94 Strand, London, writing desk manufacturer (1804–c.1840). Recorded as Handford & Co. in 1804. Brass bound portable mahogany writing desk, c.1830–40, recorded, bearing trade label inside which reads: 'Handford's Improved Writing Desks. T. HANDFORD, No. 94 Strand, MANUFACTURER of Copying Machines, Writing Desks and all kinds of Ladies & Gentleman's PORTABLE CASES for every purpose Completed & adapted for travelling in any part of the World ... Old Desks are repaired or taken in Exchange. Orders for the East or West Indies punctually executed and Country Dealers supplied on the most reasonable terms.' Label also found inside fine quality lap desk, c.1810, veneered in partridge wood crossbanded in kingwood with brass lines.

Handford, Thomas, Strand, London, patent cork trunk maker and patentee of the waterproof travelling trunk edged with brass (1820–37). Recorded at no. 7 in 1820, and no. 6 in 1837. [D]

Handford, William, London, cm (1835). [D]

Handisyde, Henry, 14 Johns Mews, Little James St, Bedford Row, London, cm (1839–40). Took out a Sun Insurance policy in 1840. [D; GL, Sun MS vol. 574, ref. 1331484]

Handisyde (or Handasyde, Handesyde, Handalyde or Handyside), Thomas, London, u, cm, appraiser and undertaker (1803–53). Addresses given at 10 (Upper) King St, Bloomsbury Sq., 1807–21; and 55 Lambs Conduit St, Holborn, 1823–53. Trading as Handasyde & Mayo in 1809; and as Thomas Handyside & Son, 1809–53. [D] Trade card gives King St address. [Landauer Coll., MMA, NY] Subscribed to Sheraton's *Cabinet Dictionary*, 1803. Took out Sun Insurance policies on 17 August 1807 for £850 of which £400 accounted for utensils and stock; on 27 July 1808 for £1,800, £500 on stock and utensils; and another policy in 1840. [GL, Sun MS vol. 441, ref. 806413; vol. 444, ref. 819597; ref. 5141331483] Ledgers of Thomas & Son for 1809–34 and 1842–53 survive. [GL, MS 4597 (Bn. 36:F); 10883/1; 18882/2]

Handley, Henry snr, Willan's Yd, Leeds, Yorks., cm and u (1814–40). Trading also at Swin(e)gate, 1814–18, and Mill Hill in 1817–28. [D]

Handley, Henry jnr, Willan's Yd, Mill Hill, Leeds, Yorks., cm (1822). [D]

Handley, John, Leeds, Yorks., cm and u (1822–40). Addresses given at 15 Hope St in 1822; Harrison St in 1826; 18 North St, 1828–37; and 16 Hope St in 1839. [D] See William Handley.

Handley, Thomas, Conisbrough, Yorks., joiner and cm (1834). [D]

Handley, William, Hope St, Leeds, Yorks., cm and u (1814–37). Recorded at no. 2, 1814–20; then either nos 70 or 71. [D] See John Handley.

Hands, Benjamin, Bridewell Lane, Bristol, cabinet carver (1831). [D]

Hands, Humphrey, Warwick, joiner (1723–43). Took out a Sun Insurance policy on 31 December 1723 for £300, £200 accounting for goods in his house. Probably the craftsman who supplied furniture to Lord Leigh of Stoneleigh, Warks., between 1740–43, comprising several mahogany tables, and in February 1741 'frames with 2 Glasses for prints one for the Master of the Roles and one for Mr. Smith Gilt edges', costing 6s; and 'One Gilt frame for Adm. Vernon and a frame for port[rait] a bell', 6s. [GL, Sun MS vol. 15, p. 349; Shakespeare Birthplace Trust, Leigh receipts, DR 18/5]

Hands, Jonathan, Bristol, cm (1805–26). Trading at 2 Nelson St in 1805; as Hands & Barnard in Nelson St, 1806; as J.H. in 1810; at Greville St, 1812–17; and Harford St, 1819–26. [D]

Hands, Thomas, Micklegate, York, cm, u, appraiser, auctioneer and undertaker (1828–38). Trading at no. 14, 1828–30; and no. 85, 1834–38. Son of Richard Hands, combmaker; admitted freeman in 1819. Submitted bill totalling £12 13s 9d to the trustees of St Saviour's Chapel in August 1834 for 'extending Gallery across the Chapel, laying an inclined floor in large Pew below, making Benches for Gallery and Pew, widening the seats around the alter Table and covering with matting.' [D; York freemen rolls]

Hands & Jenkins, 34 Loveday St, Birmingham, manufacturer of commode handles, picture frames and looking-glasses (1803). [D]

Handscombe, Isaac, Dunstable St, Ampthill, Beds., u (1839). [D]

Handsen, John, address unrecorded, cm (1803). Subscribed to Sheraton's *Cabinet Dictionary*, 1803.

Handsombody, E. & L., Bristol, u (1836–40). Trading at Brandon Hill Steep, 1836–37, and 15 College St, 1838–40. [D] See J. & L. Handsombody.

Handsombody, Frederick, Bristol, cm (1829–40). Trading at

5 Lower Berkeley Pl., 1829–37, and 10 Upper Portland Pl., Clifton, 1838–40. [D]

Handsombody, J. & L., Brandon Hill Steep, Bristol, u (1835). [D] See E. & L. Handsombody.

Handy, William, Worcester, cm and auctioneer (1788–1812). Recorded at 'The George', Tything in 1788 also as an innkeeper, and at 13 Foregate St in 1794. Former app., John Nayers, admitted freeman on 13 October 1812. [D; Worcester freemen rolls]

Hanebuth, Frederick & Co., 27 Lamb St, Southwark, London, cm and u (1820–29). [D] Possibly Frederick Haniebuth.

Hanford, Francis, Ludgate Hill, Fleet Ditch, London, turner (1703–17). Took out Hand in Hand Insurance policies on 26 April 1703 and 5 June 1717 for £250 on his house. [GL, Hand in Hand MS vol. 2, p. 458; vol. 17, p. 138]

Hanford, James, London, cm (1710–11). Trading at the 'Blew Boar', Cornhill in 1710. Submitted bills to Sir Gilbert Heathcote on 4 May 1710 for 'one no. 12 put in a Frame & Two New Screens', costing 7s; and on 17 May for 'One Combox made up & a Powder Box Mended', 12s. The bill was receipted on 19 September 1810 by Richard Nixon. On 22 November 1710 Hanford supplied eight glass sconces for a total of £4 15s, received on 30 November by Nixon. On 7 July 1711 his bill listed two japan frames, 'One combox japand', mending a frame, and 'rounding ye wainscot table edg.' Bill was receipted on 1 August 1711. [Lincoln RO, 2 ANC 12/D/5]

Haniebuth, Frederick, court on the east side of Old George St, Gt Suffolk St, Southwark, London, cm (1806). Took out a Sun Insurance policy on 4 November 1806 for £400 of which £345 accounted for stock, utensils and goods in trust in workshop and yard. [GL, Sun MS vol. 438, ref. 795784] Possibly Frederick Hanebuth.

Hanion, Henry, Norwich, cm (1796). [Poll bk]

Hankens, James, Liverpool, upholder (1747). [Chester poll bk]

Hankey, Peter, Eastgate St, Chester, u (1820). Admitted freeman on 18 April 1820. [Chester freemen rolls]

Hankey, Robert, Chester, cm (1750–84). Address given in Foregate St, 1784. Son of Sarah Hankey, widow of Chester; app. to Thomas Astle, cm, for seven years on 2 February 1750. Admitted freeman on 3 April 1784. [Chester app. indentures, freemen rolls and poll bk]

Hankin, Thomas, at 'The Cannon', Long Lane, Aldgate, London, u (1715). Insured goods and merchandise in his house on 22 January 1715. [GL, Sun MS vol. 4, p. 156]

Hankins, William, Worcester, upholder (1771). App. to Richard Meredith, upholder; admitted freeman on 11 November 1771. [Worcester freemen rolls]

Hankins, William, 33 Brewer St, Golden Sq., London, undertaker and upholder (1817). [D]

Hankinson, V. J., London (?). In 1773 supplied Sir John Griffin Griffin of Audley End, Essex, with 'one Field Bedstead & check furniture', costing £2 15s; and 'one feather bed bolster & pillow', £3 5s. [Essex RO, D/DBy/A31/2]

Hanks, John, Bristol, upholder (1784). [Poll bk]

Hanley, John, 41 Preston St, Liverpool, wood and ivory turner (1835). [D]

Hanley, Peter, Friar St, Worcester, cm, u and register office for hiring servants (1828). [D]

Hanley, Stinsil, 21 Bolton St, Copperas Hill, Liverpool, cm (1835). [D]

Han(n), Elias, Exeter, Devon, u (1715–23). Admitted freeman in 1715. Took app. named Bamfield in 1721. Took out a Sun Insurance policy on 10 May 1723 for goods and merchandise in his house. [Exeter freemen rolls; S of G, app. index; GL, Sun MS vol. 15, ref. 26231]

Hann, Henry, London, cm (1830). [Norwich poll bk]

Hann, Peter, St Giles-in-the-Fields, London, cm (1712/13). Took app. on 4 March 1712/13. [PRO, app. reg.]

Hannaford, W. F., Kingsbridge, Devon, cm and u (1807–d.1815). Advertised in *Exeter Flying Post*, 30 April 1807, for two or three journeymen, stating 'piece work given if required'; and on 19 July 1810 for an app. and a journeyman. Death by consumption reported on 23 March 1815.

Hannah, George, Manor St, Clapham, London, u (1839). [D]

Hannah, John, Tuxford, Notts., joiner and cm (1822–32). Trading at Eldon St in 1832. [D]

Hannah, William, 35 Dance St, Liverpool, cm (1839). [D]

Hanne, J., 5 Walks, Bath, Som., auctioneer, upholder and appraiser (1819). [D]

Hannibal, John, Lancaster (1818–21). Named in the Gillow records in 1818 and 1821. [Westminster Ref. Lib.]

Hanns, George, Scotland Rd, Liverpool, cm (1837–39). Recorded at no. 203 in 1837 and 200 in 1839. [D]

Hannys, John, Liverpool, cm (1757). Admitted freeman on 17 October 1757. [Liverpool freemen reg.]

Hansan, George, address unrecorded. In 1772 supplied nine picture frames costing £24 2s 2d to Mersham-le-Hatch, Kent. [Kent RO, Mersham accounts]

Hanser, John, 19 Williamson St, Church St, Liverpool, u (1804). [D]

Hansford, John, St Cuthbert St, Wells, Som., cm and u (1839). [D]

Hansford, William, George St, Ryde, Isle of Wight, cm and u (1839). [D]

Hanshaw, Samuel, Nohill St, London, chairmaker (1774). [Poll bk]

Hansom, Henry, Tanners Row, York, joiner, funeral furnisher, carpenter, housebuilder and cm (1823). [D]

Hansom, Richard, 36 Micklegate, York, joiner and cm (1830). [D]

Hanson, —, 19 Bowling Green Lane, Clerkenwell, London, carver and gilder (1809–11). [D]

Hanson, —, John St, London. Named in Loudon's *Encyclopaedia*, 1833 (pp. 1039 and 1101) as specialising in making from old fragments 'curious specimens' of antiquarian oak furniture.

Hanson, Abram, Liverpool, cm and victualler (1813–24). Addresses given at 2 New Bird St with cabinet warehouse at no. 5 in 1813, and 2 Brown Pl., Copperas Hill, in 1824. [D]

Hanson, Christopher, Bingley, Yorks., cm and u (1822–37). Trading at Main St in 1837. [D]

Hanson, Herbert, 24 Hanover St, Manchester, cm (1836). [D]

Hanson, John, Cable St, Liverpool, cm (d.1767). Death reported in *Williamson's Liverpool Advertiser*, 27 March 1767.

Hanson, John, Huddersfield, Yorks., cm (1803–34). Trading at Castle St in 1814; New St, 1818–20; High St, 1822; and New St, 1828–29. Subscribed to Sheraton's *Cabinet Dictionary*, 1803. [D]

Hanson, John jnr, 34 New St, Huddersfield, Yorks., cm, u and paper hanger (1830–37). [D]

Hanson, John, Slisbridge Lane, Bradford, Yorks., cm (1837). [D]

Hanson, Samuel, 16 John St, Oxford St, London, cm and u (1827–39). In 1833 he charged £34 16s to Thomas Whitmore of Apley Park, Salop, for 'a Mahogany Stand for Parrot Cage', 'two carved Pier Tables', a washstand, and packing and carriage to Paddington. [D; Essex RO, D/DWt A3]

Hanson, Samuel, 33 Prince's St, Leicester Sq., Soho, London, cm and u (1822–27). Took out Sun Insurance policies on 7 February 1822 for £300 on household goods in warehouses; on 5 February 1823 for £1,400, £1,050 on utensils and stock; and on 12 February 1824 for £1,550, £1,200 on

stock and utensils in his house, workshops communicating and workshop in George Yd nearby. [D; GL, Sun MS vol. 493, ref. 989021; vol. 498, ref. 1001049; vol. 499, ref. 1012916]

Hanson, William, address unrecorded, carpenter (1759). Put together the gilded State Bed designed by Borra for Stowe, Bucks., and now in the Lady Lever Art Gallery, Liverpool. [V&A archives]

Hanson & Parsons, Broad Weir, Bristol, cm (1799–1800). [D]

Hanway & Co., address unrecorded. Provided furniture and mantlepiece for the Board Room of the Marine Society, London, c.1775. [Huntington Lib., California, Stowe MS, T3/LL/3/2]

Hanwell, John, Oxford, cm (1768). [Poll bk; *Survey of Oxford*]

Happerton, —, address unrecorded, cm (1803). Subscribed to Sheraton's *Cabinet Dictionary*, 1803.

Happ(e)y, William, 32 Canning St, Hull, Yorks., cm (1838–39). [D]

Haradge, —, address unrecorded, frame maker (1709). Named in the accounts for Felbrigg, Norfolk, in January 1709 receiving £6; in July, £4 18s; and in August, £6 12s. [Norfolk RO, Felbrigg papers, WKC 6/23, index of payments]

Harald, James, Coventry, Warks., joiner and cm (1720). Took app. named More in 1720. [S of G, app. index]

Harbidge, Ann, 18 Finch Lane, Cornhill, London, chest maker and undertaker (1801). [D]

Harbidge (or Harbridge), John, 18 Finch Lane, Cornhill, London, chest maker and undertaker (1788–1804). [D]

Harbron, James, Houghton-le-Spring, Co. Durham, joiner and cm (1827–29). [D]

Harbron, John, 8 Junction Dock Walls (or St), Hull, Yorks., cm and broker (1837–40). [D]

Hardcastle, Aaron, Fewston, Harrogate, Yorks., cm and joiner (b.1724–d.1755). His tombstone in St Lawrence's Parish Church, Fewston, bears the inscription: 'Here Lyeth the body of Aaron, son of Aaron Hardcastle of Fewston, cabinet maker and joyner, who departed this life April ye 22nd 1755 in full hope of a happy resurrection, aged 31 years...'.

Hardcastle, John, York, cm (1814). Son of Knottingly Hardcastle; app. to Hugh Rusby, cm, on 31 December 1814. [York app. reg.]

Hardcastle, Robert, 'on the sunny side of Westminster Bridge', London, carver in wood (1763). [D]

Hardcastle, Thomas, 15 Seahook Pl., White Lion St, Pentonville, London, clock case maker (1821). Took out a Sun Insurance policy on 22 March 1821 for £125 of which £25 accounted for his tools and tool chest in a workshop behind 58 Red Lion St, Clerkenwell. [GL, Sun MS vol. 485, ref. 978549]

Hardcastle, William, Boroughbridge, Yorks., joiner and cm (1828–34). [D]

Harden, —, address unrecorded, cm (1803). Subscribed to Sheraton's *Cabinet Dictionary*, 1803.

Harden, Benjamin, 36 Coppice Row, London, cm and u (1839). [D]

Harden, C., 14 Little St Thomas Apostle and 33 Bread St, London, japan dressing case manufacturer (1819–25). [D]

Harden, G. B., Queen St and/or St Ann's, Manchester, u and cm (1810–11). Submitted bill to Sir John Leicester of Tabley House, Cheshire, on 12 November 1810, totalling £23 8s 6d and paid on 9 May 1811. Bill listed '2 Bamboo bedsteps covered in Brussels Carpet', a hearth rug, mahogany table, looking-glass and three bamboo wash tables. [Chester RO, Tabley House vouchers]

Harden, John, Drury Lane, St Martin-in-the-Fields, London, cm (1727). Insured goods and stock in trade in his house for £400 on 29 December 1727. [GL, Sun MS vol. 25, p. 440]

Harden, John, Duck (or Dark) Lane, Bilston, Staffs., cm (1818–22). [D]

Hardern, James, Liverpool, chairmaker (1766–81). Addresses given at 150 Dale St, 1766–69, 1 Temple St in 1772, and recorded as 'Gent.' at 3 Richmond St in 1781. [D]

Hardet, Andrew, address unrecorded, cm (1803). Subscribed to Sheraton's *Cabinet Dictionary*, 1803.

Hardie, John, 48 Market Pl., Whitehaven, Cumb., joiner and/or cm (1828–34). [D]

Hardie, Robert, Moore St, London, gilder (1784). [Poll bk]

Hardie, Thomas, address unrecorded, cm (1803). Subscribed to Sheraton's *Cabinet Dictionary*, 1803.

Harding, Abraham, 46 Marsham St, Westminster, London, carver and gilder (1809–11). [D]

Harding, C., 1 Long Lane, Smithfield, London, japan dressing case manufacturers (1802). [D]

Harding, Charles, 2 Wardour St, Soho, London, chair and sofa manufacturer (1826–35). [D]

Harding, Charles, Exeter, Devon, cm (1836–40). Recorded in *Exeter Pocket Journal* at Palace St, 1836–38, and South St, 1839–40.

Harding, George, Bilston, Staffs., cm and u (1828–38). Recorded at Temple St, Newtown in 1828 and Oxford St, 1833–38. [D]

Harding, J., London, cm (1793). Subscribed to Sheraton's *Drawing Book*, 1793.

Harding, J. M., Cross St, Barnstaple, Devon, carver and gilder (1838). [D] See John Harding.

Harding, James, Mill St, Loughborough, Leics., cm (1835–40). [D]

Harding, John, Haymarket, London, upholder (1747–49). Polled at Westminster in 1747 and named in newspapers in 1749. [Heal]

Harding, John, Pipewellgate, Gateshead, Co. Durham, joiner and cm (1811). [D]

Harding, John, Cross St, Barnstaple, Devon, carver and gilder (1823–24). [D] See J. M. Harding.

Harding, John, Duck Lane, Bilston, Staffs., cm (1833). [D]

Harding, Jonathan, Redcliff Ct, St Luke's, London, cm (1784). [Bristol poll bk]

Hardin(g), Joseph, West Wycombe, Bucks, chairmaker (b. c. 1796–1841). Aged 45 at the time of the 1841 Census. [D]

Harding, Richard, Broad St, Carnaby Mkt, London, carver (1775). Took out a Sun Insurance policy in 1775 for £400 of which £20 accounted for utensils and stock. [GL, Sun MS vol. 239, p. 313]

Harding, Richard, Berwick St, Soho, London, carver and gilder to the King (1789–93). Trade card, 1791, gives address at no. 7, and reads 'Carver and Gilder to Her Majesty'. [D; Heal]

Harding, Richard, 24 Little Moorfields, London, carver and picture frame maker (1824). Insured his household goods for £100 on 21 January 1824. [GL, Sun MS vol. 495, ref. 1012765]

Harding, Robert, address unrecorded. On 13 August 1784 received £3 2s 6d for a picture frame and case, possibly for a Gainsborough portrait, supplied to Hon. H. Fane. [Lincoln RO, Fane 7/1]

Harding, Samuel, 20 Noble St, Falcon Sq., London, carver and gilder (1817–25). [D]

Harding, Thomas, 13 Cranbourne St, Brighton, Sussex, cm and u (1832). [D]

Harding, William, Lee's Yd, Spear St, Manchester, cm (1817). [D]

Harding, William & Son, High Wycombe, Bucks., chairmaker and shopkeeper (1827–38). Daughters bapt. in 1827, 1831, 1833 and 1828; son in 1835. [PR (bapt.)]

Harding & Son, 70 Fore St, Cripplegate, London, cm and u (1839). [D]

Hardingham, Nicholas, Norwich and London, chairmaker and cm (1783–1830). App. to James Parot, chairmaker; admitted freeman of Norwich on 21 September 1783. Polled at Norwich, of London, 1786–1807; and of Norwich in 1830. [Norwich freemen reg. and poll bks]

Hardisty, John, Albion St, Halifax, Yorks., cm (1822–30). Recorded also at Carrier St in 1830. [D]

Hardman, —, address unrecorded. Between 1737 and 1744 supplied items to Holkham Hall, Norfolk: in 1737 a coffee table, six chairs and three looking-glasses, costing £5 11s; in 1742 four bed ticks, bolsters, two quilts and six blankets, £7 19s; in 1742–43, check chair cases; in 1743 three bed ticks, bolsters and quilts, £4 19s; and in 1744 a dressing glass, £1 1s. [V&A archives] Possibly John Hardman.

Hardman, —, Lancaster. Named in the Gillow records in 1818 working on a bookcase and a wardrobe. [Westminster Ref. Lib., Gillow vol. 344/100, pp. 2082 and 2094]

Hardman, Benjamin, 14 Wood St, Salford, Lancs., joiner and cm (1804–08). [D]

Hardman, Benjamin, Swan Ct, Manchester, carver and gilder (1836). [D]

Hardman, John, Drury Lane, London, upholder (1749–54). Polled at Westminster in 1749. Subscribed to Chippendale's *Director*, 1754. [Poll bks]

Hardman, Richard, Liverpool, cm (1827–39). Addresses given at 2 Roscoe St in 1827; 79 Lime St in 1829; 15 Harford St in 1835; and 34 Renshaw St in 1839. [D]

Hardman, Robert, Liverpool, cm (1830–34). Trading at 35 Peter St in 1830, when admitted freeman on 15 November as son of James Hardman, shipwright. Marriage to Miss Mary Edge of Liverpool on 29 September 1834 at St Oswald's reported in *Chester Courant and Advertiser for North Wales*, 30 September. [Liverpool freemen reg. and committee bk]

Hardman, Samuel, 123 Rasbottom St, Stalybridge, Lancs., joiner and cm (1834). [D]

Hardman, Thomas, Liverpool, carver and gilder (1826–34). Recorded at 82 Gloucester St in 1834. App. to William Cashin in 1826. [Liverpool app. enrolment bk]

Hardman, William, 17 Union St, Manchester, cm (1840). [D]

Hards, Thomas, Lichfield St, Tamworth, Staffs., cm and u (1835). [D]

Hardwick, Asty, King's Lynn, Norfolk, u (1755). Took app. named Chadwick in 1755. [S of G, app. index] See Asty Harwick.

Hardwick, Richard, 16 Upper Newington, Liverpool, cm (1837). [D]

Hardwick, Robert, Liverpool, cm and joiner (1780–96). Addresses given at 33 Thomas St in 1781; 11 Ranelagh St and 1 Cases St, 1790–94; with cabinet shop at 12 Ranelagh St in 1794. Admitted freeman by birth as son of Joseph Hardwick in September 1780. Former app., John Kendall, petitioned freedom in 1796. [D; Liverpool freemen's committee bk]

Hardwick, Thomas, Leeds, Yorks., u (1772–78). 'Hardwick' submitted a bill to Harewood House, Yorks. on 8 January 1772 for upholstery costing £7 8s 8d; and Thomas Hardwick of Leeds, on 24 December 1778 for canvas and curled hair. [Leeds archives dept, Harewood MS 491, folios 103 and 181]

Hardwick, William, Well St, London, cm (1790). [Lincoln poll bk]

Hardwick & Waddy, 30 Park Row, Leeds, Yorks., cm and u (1837). [D]

Hardy, C., Lancaster. Named in the Gillow records, 1827–32. [Westminster Ref. Lib., Gillow vol. 344/103, p. 3917]

Hardy, Charles, York, turner, fancy case maker and cm (1824–40). Trading at 6 Coney St, 1838–40. Son of John Hardy, turner and cm; app. to his father on 7 December 1824. [D; York app. reg.]

Hardy, David, Pocklington, Yorks., cm (1828–34). Trading at Silver St, 1828–30, and Waterloo Buildings, 1831–34. [D]

Hardy, Edmund, Russell Ct, London, cm (1749). [Poll bk]

Hardy, Edward, St Martin-in-the-Fields, London, cm (1749). [Poll bk]

Hardy, George, Lincoln, cm (1790). [Poll bk]

Hardy, George, Duck Lane, Bilston, Staffs., cm and u (1830). [D]

Hardy, James, address unrecorded. Supplied a marble table to Temple Newsam House, Leeds in 1720. [*Furn. Hist.*, 1967]

Hardy, James, address unrecorded, cm (1770). Advertised in *York Courant*, 27 February 1770. [*Furn. Hist.*, 1971]

Hardy, James, Union St, North Shields, Northumb., carver and gilder (1827). [D]

Hardy, James, Aglionby, Carlisle, Cumb., joiner and/or cm (1829). [D]

Hardy, James jnr, 60–61 Blackett St, Newcastle, carver and gilder (1833–38). [D] Trade card of J. Hardy, Newcastle, reads: 'Carver & Gilder, Picture, Looking Glass, Frame and Cornice Manufacturer, Dealer in Oil Paintings. Near the Grainger St. Grey Column.' [Landauer Coll., MMA, NY] Announced in *Durham Advertiser*, 22 November 1833, the opening of a shop in Saddler St, Durham, with S. Jacobson jnr, where they were to sell Continental oil paintings. See Robert Sandley Scott at this address in 1834.

Hardy, John jnr, Norwich and London, u (1779–1830). Recorded in Norwich, 1779–1818; London in 1799; and Lakenham in 1830. App. to John Marks, and admitted freeman of Norwich on 3 May 1779. [Norwich freemen reg. and poll bks]

Hardy, John, Coney St, York, turner and cm (1824–43). Announced that he was taking over the business of Martha Marshall (or Doughty) in *Yorkshire Gazette*, 8 May 1824. Made spinning wheels (one in the Castle Museum, York, bearing the stamp of 'Hardy York') until c.1832, when his advertisement in the *Yorkshire Gazette* made no mention of this branch of his business. Notice of business closure appeared in the same paper, 30 September 1843. See Charles Hardy.

Hardy, John, Ferrybridge, Yorks., joiner and/or cm (1834). [D]

Hardy, John, 26 New Dock Walls, Hull, Yorks., cm (1835). [D]

Hardy, R., Pilgrim St, Newcastle, carver and gilder (1801). [D]

Hardy, Robert, High Friar St, Newcastle, carver and gilder (1827–38). Trading at no. 1, 1833–38. [D]

Hardy, S. C., 12 Hooper St, Clerkenwell, London, cm (1835). [D]

Hardy, Seth, York, carver (1726). Took William Hardy, carver, possibly his son, as app. in 1726 for eight years. [York app. reg.]

Hardy, William, 5 Old Montague St, Buck Lane, London, cm and chairmaker (1814). Took out a Sun Insurance policy on 23 November 1814 for £200, £100 accounting for stock and utensils. [GL, Sun MS vol. 463, ref. 899738]

Hardy, William, Lancaster. Named in the Gillow records, 1826–32. [Westminster Ref. Lib.]

Hardy, William, High St, Maidenhead, Berks., cm and u (1840–42). [D]

Hare, —, 25 Church Row, Newington, London, chair manufacturer (1809–11). [D]

Hare, Catherine, 16 James St, Devonport, Devon, chairmaker (1838). [D] See Richard Hare.

Hare, George, York, cm (1770). Son of John Hare, yeoman of Brandsby; app. to John Wright, cm, on 24 October 1770. [York app. reg.]

Hare, George, 92 Seymour Pl., London, u (1829). [D]

Hare, James, Market St, Tamworth, Staffs., cm (1835). [D]

Hare, Moses, Exeter, Devon, cm (1803–08). Addresses given at 13 Magdalen St in 1806 and 246 High St in 1807. Named in the Militia Census in 1803. Advertised sale of timber and veneer in *Exeter Flying Post*, 10 April 1806. On 21 May 1807 announced his removal to 246 High St, and advertised sale of mahogany and 'a quantity of elegant cabinet furniture, e.g. drawing room sets of tables highly varnished in mahogany & satin wood etc.'; he also required a 'good workman'. Advertised again on 30 July 1807 when stock included 'new & second-hand mahogany & painted chairs, sets of dining, card & other tables; drawers, wardrobe, press & other bedsteads.' Declared bankrupt, 12 November 1807 and 29 September 1808. Notice on 14 January 1808 concerned his app. John Isaac, 19 years old, who had run away.

Hare, Patrick, 19 Jackson's Pl., North St, Prospect St, Hull, Yorks., cm (1838–39). [D]

Hare, Richard, James St, Devonport, Devon, chair and sofa maker (1822–30). Trading at nos 15–16 in 1826, and 16–17 in 1830. Advertisement in *Exeter Flying Post*, 10 April 1828, reads: 'West of England Fancy Chair and Sofa Manufactory, 15 and 16 James Street, Devonport. Wholesale, Retail, and for Exportation, RICHARD HARE, respectfully solicits the attention of the Public to his Work and Warerooms, situate as above, for the display and manufacture of Fancy Chairs, Sofas etc. which articles he can guarantee to be equal in every respect to those made in London; and his terms more advantageous to purchasers. And, in earnestly requesting the inspection of the Trade, and the Public generally, to his extensive Stock, he can assure them that every article of it has been made under his immediate inspection, by expert workmen, and from the best materials...'. [D]

Hare, Robert, Norwich, u (1833). App. to Benjamin Hambling Roe; admitted freeman on 3 May 1833. [Norwich freemen reg.]

Hare, Thomas, 24 Lambeth Rd, St George's Fields, London, fancy japanned chair and sofa maker (1808–27). Took out a Sun Insurance policy on 12 February 1823 for £300, £200 accounting for house and workshops, £50 on stock, utensils and goods in trust. [D; GL, Sun MS vol. 489, ref. 1001478]

Hare, Thomas, Stamford, Lincs., picture frame maker. Established firm, c.1830, at St George's Sq., and was succeeded by his son and grandsons. [*Stamford with Oakham and Uppingham*, 1911]

Hare, Valentine, formerly of Dog-and-Bear Yd, Southwark, late of Dock-head, Southwark, London, chairmaker (1761). Discharge from Debtors' Prison announced in *London Gazette*, 20 June 1761.

Hare, William, 12 Union St, Plymouth, Devon, chairmaker (1836–38). [D]

Harefinch, Peter, Chester, u (1695). App. to Samuel Kirkes of Chester, and admitted freeman on 16 November 1695. [Chester freemen rolls]

Harely, John, York, carver and gilder (1756). Took app. named Barker in 1756. [S of G, app. index]

Harewood, J., Hoddlesden, Darwen, Lancs, joiner and cm (1825). [D]

Harford, Benjamin, Liverpool, carver and gilder (1818–24). Addresses given at 18 Haymarket in 1818; 24 Copperas Hill in 1821; and Thomas Ct, New Scotland Rd in 1824. [D]

Harford, Charles, Liverpool, carver and gilder (1781–96). Trading at Ranelagh St in 1781; 107 Park Lane in 1783; Church St in 1790, no. 40 in 1794. Advertisement in *Williamson's Liverpool Advertiser*, 23 October 1783 reads: 'CHARLES HARFORD, CARVER, GILDER, GLASS-GRINDER, OVAL-TURNER, PICTURE-FRAME MAKER, No. 107 PARK-LANE, LIVERPOOL. WHERE he hopes every thing in his business will be made to please those who favour him with their commands — Old frames gilt or cleaned. N.B. An apprentice wanted.' [D]

Harford, J., London, cm (1793). Subscribed to Sheraton's *Drawing Book*, 1793.

Harger, Robert, Settle, Yorks., joiner and/or cm (1834–37). [D]

Hargitt, Richard, York, cm (1759). Son of Richard Hargitt of St Michael-le-Belfrey parish; app. to Henry Anderson, cm, on 3 September 1759. [York app. reg.]

Hargrave, —, Hull, Yorks. Mahogany serpentine side table, c.1780, recorded, bearing label. Designed in the French taste, and made of finely figured wood with crossbanded angles to its four cabriole legs; one drawer and gilded handles above a shaped apron. [Spinks, 1979] Probably Jeremiah or Joseph Hargrave.

Hargrave, Henry, 3 Somerset St, Portman Sq., London, u and cm (1835). [D]

Hargrave (or Hargrove), Jeremiah, Hull, Yorks., carver in stone and wood, architect and furniture maker (c.1726–86). Took app. named Foster in 1753. [S of G, app. index] Addresses given at Scale Lane, 1773–80, and listed as Jeremiah & Son, Joseph, at Saville St until 1802. Supplied items to Burton Constable, Yorks., including in 1768–69 carved and gilt Neo-classical side tables, wine cisterns, girandoles and statuary plinths. Some furniture was made to designs of James Wyatt. Between 1771–80 Hargrave provided various picture frames, one for 'Barratt painting of House' in 1773; carved 'a large trophy of war for west front', and in 1774 'the Crest & Ornament in Pediment'. In 1778 he supplied carved and gilt girandoles, and in 1780 carved 'the ornament & mouldings for 3 Chimneypieces.' Jeremiah and Joseph carried out further carving of picture frames and chimney pieces, and silvering glass in August 1784. [Humberside RO, Burton Constable vouchers, DDCC; *C. Life*, 3 June 1976, p. 1476; 6 and 13 May 1982, pp. 1359–60; I. and E. Hall, *Historic Beverley*, p. 47] See Joseph Hargrave.

Hargrave, John, Colne, Lancs., cm (1797). [D] Possibly John Hargreave.

Hargrave, Joseph, Hull, Yorks., carver in stone and wood, gilder, architect and furniture maker (1766–1802). Trading at Back Ropery Lane in 1784; Scale Lane before 1790; and with his father, Jeremiah, at Saville St, Dockside, 1790–1802. Insured his house for £300 in 1777 with the Sun Co. Imprisoned for debt in 1794. Supplied items to Burton Constable, Yorks, with his father, in 1784. [D; GL, Sun MS vol. 261, p. 494; I. and E. Hall, *Historic Beverley*, p. 47] See Jeremiah Hargrave.

Hargrave (or Hargreave(s)), Josephus, Leeds, Yorks., cm and u (1828–41). Addresses given at 17 St James St, 1828–37; and 25 or 35 Woodhouse Lane, 1834–41. [D]

Hargrave, William, Newport St, Long Alley, London, u (1749–52). Polled at Westminster in 1749. Named in newspapers in 1752. [Heal]

Hargrave, William, York, cm (1781). Son of Elizabeth Hargrave; app. to Christopher Seller, cm, on 20 August 1781. [York app. reg.]

Hargraves, —, Cloth Hall, Leeds, Yorks., cm (1793). Subscribed to Sheraton's *Drawing Book*, 1793.

Hargraves (or Hargreaves), William, Burnley, Lancs., cm and joiner (1814–28). Trading at Bridge End in 1814; Whitehouse Croft in 1818; 5 Fountain St in 1824; King St, 1824–25; and Nile St in 1828. [D]

Hargreave & Co., Park Row, Leeds, Yorks., joiners and cm (1790). [D]

Hargreaves, Francis & Co., Bold St, Liverpool, carvers and gilders (1834–39). Recorded as Hargreaves & Co. at no. 65 in

1834; Francis & Co. at no. 63, 1835–37; and no. 88 in 1839. [D]

Hargreaves, J., Royal Oak Yd, Leeds, Yorks., cm and u (1817). [D]

Hargreaves, John, Colne Lane, Colne, Lancs., timber merchant, joiner and cm (1814–34). [D] Possibly John Hargrave.

Hargreaves, John, Burnley, Lancs., cm (1824–34). Addresses given at Thomas (or Thorn) Inn Yd in 1824; Market St and Yorkshire St in 1828; and South Parade in 1834. [D]

Hargreaves, Thomas, Lancaster, cm (1785–1834). Named in the Gillow records, 1785–1834, and admitted freeman, 1831–32. [Westminster Ref. Lib., Gillow; Lancaster freemen rolls] Probably two craftsmen are concerned here.

Hargreaves, Thomas, Burnley, Lancs., timber merchant and cm (1792–d. by 1819). Dead by 1819 when referred to concerning bankruptcy proceedings against him in *Liverpool Mercury*, 18 June. Mahogany long-case clock, c.1788–1800, recorded, with scroll pediment, arched dial, boxwood stringing, door with pointed arch, and inlaid panels in the Neo-classical style. [D]

Hargreaves, Thomas, Scotland Rd, Liverpool, u (1804). [D]

Hargreaves, William & John, Mill Hill, Leeds, Yorks., cm and builders (1791). Took out a Sun Insurance policy on 21 January 1791 for £1,500. [GL, Sun MS vol. 374, ref. 578936]

Harker, Anthony, London, cm (1793). Subscribed to Sheraton's *Drawing Book*, 1793.

Harker, Anthony, 22 Harp Alley, Shoe Lane, London, chair and sofa maker (1827–28). [D]

Harker, Jonathan, Lancaster. Named in the Gillow records, 1789–96. [Westminster Ref. Lib.]

Harker, Jonathan, Kendal, Westmld, on 10 June 1825 supplied to Rydal Hall a new sedan chair costing £26. [V&A archives]

Harker, Ralph, 67 Long Mill Gate, Manchester, cm (1802). [D]

Harker, Richard, Hawes, Yorks., joiner and cm (1840). [D]

Harker, Thomas, Stanley St, Bury, Lancs., joiner and cm (1816–18). [D]

Harker, William, 12 Four Yards, Manchester, cm (1832–40). Recorded also at no. 12, 1836–40. [D]

Harkness, Joseph, High Holborn, London, cm (1782–84). Recorded at no. 316, 1782–83, and no. 96 in 1784. Took out Sun Insurance policies in 1782 for £500 on his house and warehouse; and in 1783 with Thomas Browne, for £2,000 of which £1,350 accounted for utensils, stock and goods. [D; GL, Sun MS vol. 300, p. 439; vol. 313, p. 36]

Harland, James, 30 Red Cross St, Cripplegate, London, cm (1826–27). [D]

Harland, John snr, Low Fold, North St, Leeds, Yorks., cm (1817–40). [D]

Harland, John jnr, Leeds, Yorks., cm and clock-case manufacturer (1821–37). Trading at Bramley's Yd, Lowerhead Row, 1821–34, and Mabgate Green, 1834–37. [D]

Harland, John & William, 44 Meadow Lane, Leeds, Yorks., cm (1834–37). [D]

Harland, Joseph, Leeds, Yorks., cm (1826–30). Trading at 12 Crown St in 1826 and 10 Swinegate in 1830. [D]

Harland, Thomas, York, cm (1824). Son of Thomas Harland, labourer of Clifton; app. to Joseph Marsh, cm, on 26 July 1824. [York app. reg.]

Harland, William, 65 Meadow Lane, Leeds, Yorks., cm (1839). [D] See John & William Harland.

Harle, William, at 'The Nag's Head', Pilgrim St, Newcastle, cm (?) (1754–55). Sale of furniture on closure of wareroom advertised in *Newcastle Courant*, 17 August 1754 and 12 April 1755, consisting of a variety of cabinet work including 'bason stands' and 'voiders'.

Harles, Henry, address unrecorded. Carried out numerous repairs and alterations to furniture and woodwork between

12 March 1756 and 12 March 1757 for James Leigh of Stoneleigh, Warks., totalling £1 11s 4d, and paid on 24 March 1757. [Shakespeare Birthplace Trust, Leigh receipts, DR 18/5]

Harley, Alexander, 40 Berwick St, Soho, London, cm and chairmaker (1823). Took out a Sun Insurance policy on 27 November 1823 for £300 of which £200 accounted for utensils and stock. [GL, Sun MS vol. 498, ref. 101382]

Harley, Alexander, 82 Margaret St, London, chair and sofa manufacturer (1829). [D]

Harley, Cornelius, Gt Yarmouth, Norfolk, u (d. by 1759). His son Robert, u, admitted freeman in 1759. [Gt Yarmouth freemen's calendar]

Harley, David, 38 Hunslet Lane, Leeds, Yorks., cm and u (1817). [D]

Harley, H. S., 75 Albany St, Regent's Park, London, cm (1835). [D]

Harley, Henry, 1 Clarence St, Regent's Park, London, cm, u and chairmaker (1839). [D]

Harley, James, Sun St, Barnwell, Cambridge, turner and chairmaker (1830). [D]

Harley, John, 8 Robert St, Blackfriars Rd, London, cm, ornamental stringing inlayer and wood dyer (1808–39). [D]

Harley, Robert, Gt Yarmouth, Norfolk, u (1759–87). Son of Cornelius Harley, u, deceased; admitted freeman by birth in 1759. Former app. of Harley and William Seaman, named John Kemp, u, admitted freeman by apprenticeship in 1787. Harley insured his household goods for £800 in 1776 with the Sun Co. [Gt Yarmouth freemen's calendar and poll bk; GL, Sun MS vol. 247, p. 284]

Harling, John, Liverpool, cm (1774–77). Petitioned freedom by birth as son of Joseph Harling, cm, in 1774. Admitted freeman on 8 September 1777. [Liverpool freemen reg. and committee bk]

Harling, Joseph, Liverpool, cm and timber merchant (1751–81). Trading at Moore St in 1769; 26 James St, 1772–81; as cm and glass grinder in 1774; as Joseph Harling & jnr, timber merchants in 1781; and in partnership with Nicholas Cross, then his son John Cross, timber merchants, with timber yards in Park Lane and Redcross St in 1780. Joseph Harling was admitted freeman on 16 April 1751, and his son, John, petitioned freedom by birth in 1774. Notices in *Williamson's Liverpool Advertiser*, 19 and 30 August 1765 read: 'Wanted in Warrington, two or three compleat hands Cabinet Makers who may be constantly employed all the winter...'. Another notice on 18 February 1780 concerned the ending of the partnership between Harling and Nicholas Cross, on the latter's death, and the starting of a new one with his son, John Cross, a timber merchant. Sale of stock and utensils of the late Nicholas Cross, with or without shop and warehouse, also advertised. [D; Liverpool freemen reg.]

Harman, —, address unrecorded, u (1664–68). Samuel Pepys visited 'Mr. Harman the upholsterer' on seven occasions. The earliest entry, on 23 August 1664, reads: 'called at Harman's and there bespoke some chairs.' In 1666 he went to the shop three times during August and September when he was choosing a bed and hangings for 'my new closet'. Finally on 19 October 1668 he set out from home 'by coach with my wife and Deb. and Mr. Harman, the upholster, and carried them to take measure of Mr. Wren's bed at St. James's, I being resolved to have just such another made me.' [*Diary of Samuel Pepys (1659–69)*]

Harman, George, High Wycombe, Bucks., chairmaker (b. c.1820–41). Aged 21 at the time of the 1841 Census.

Harman, James, 1 Bathwick Pl., Bath, Som., cm (1826). [D]

Harman, Joseph, High St, Taunton, Som., cm (1778–98). Took

out a Sun Insurance policy in 1778 for £300, £200 accounting for utensils and stock. [D; GL, Sun MS vol. 267, p. 118]

Harman, Thomas, Baldwins Gdns, London, cm (1784). Insured houses for £200 in 1784. [GL, Sun MS vol. 322, p. 196]

Harman, William & Son, 1 John St, Oxford St, London, invalid chair maker (1829). [D]

Harmer, B., address unrecorded. Early 19th-century library reading chair recorded bearing the stamp of 'B. HARMER'. [Christchurch Mansion, Ipswich, Ipswich Museums and Art Galleries, L.1941–125] Stamp also found on set of hall chairs with lunette crestings at Petworth House, Sussex; also on set of six mahogany shield-back chairs, c.1790, each with five curved splats headed by sprays of leaves, with nailed leather seats and chamfered legs; and on a mahogany piano stool with stuffed circular legs [Sotheby's, 26 October 1962, lot 158; 11 October 1974, lot 146]; also on a suite of Regency ebonised and parcel gilt dining chairs. [Christie's, 29 November 1984, lot 32 (illus.)]

Harmer, Wodehouse, Norwich, u (1741–53). Son of Samuel Harmer, cutler; admitted freeman on 29 January 1741. Former app. of Harmer and Paul Colombine, named Isaac Hoyle, u, admitted freeman on 3 May 1753. [Norwich freemen reg.]

Harness, William, Liverpool, cm (1834–39). Trading at 3 Albion Pl., Pembroke Gdns in 1834, and 5 Springfield St in 1839. [D]

Harold, John, Norwich, u (1692–1712). Son of William Harold, u; admitted freeman on 22 June 1692. Former app., Thomas Harold, admitted freeman on 4 February 1712. [Norwich freemen reg.]

Harold, Thomas, Norwich, u (1712–18). App. to John Harold, and admitted freeman on 24 February 1712. Took app. named Morse in 1718. [Norwich freemen reg.; S of G, app. index]

Harold, William, Norwich, u (1692). His son, John Harold, admitted freeman on 22 June 1692. [Norwich freemen reg.]

Harpe, Thomas, 18 Lawrence St, Liverpool, u (1834). [D]

Harper, Anthony, Birchall St, Birmingham, cm, u and broker (1828–30). [D]

Harper, Benjamin, address unrecorded, upholder (1760–67). Son of Benjamin Harper, blacksmith of Barnwell, Cambs., and father of John Rogers Harper, upholder. App. to Henry Hall on 12 January 1760, and admitted freeman of the Upholders' Co. by servitude on 25 March 1767. [GL, Upholders' Co. records]

Harper, George, Liverpool, cm (1774–80). Petitioned freedom on servitude to Thomas Bailey in 1774, paying 6s 8d, when his indentures were produced and certified. Admitted freeman on 9 September 1780. [Liverpool freemen reg. and committee bk]

Harper, George, Hull, Yorks., joiner and cm (1812). Took app. named George Fish of Paull in Holderness in April 1812. [Hull app. reg.]

Harper, George, Shropshire St, Market Drayton, Salop, cm and joiner (1840). [D]

Harper, John, King St, Covent Gdn, London, carver (1774). [Bristol poll bk]

Harper, John Rogers, 17 John St, Minories, London, upholder (1793). Son of Benjamin Harper, upholder; admitted freeman of the Upholders' Co. by patrimony on 7 February 1793. [GL, Upholders' Co. records]

Harper, John, 23 Kent St, Southwark, London, chair and sofa maker (1826–28). [D]

Harper, Joseph, Norwich, cm (1818). App. to Joseph Pigg; admitted freeman on 24 February 1818. [Norwich freemen reg.]

Harper(s), Joseph & Samuel, Broad St, Ludlow, Salop, cm and u

(1822–35). Trading with John Harper in 1822. Trade card of J. J. & S. Harpers [Heal Coll., BM] gives trade as bed, window cornice and pier glass makers and shows elaborately draped curtains, Regency chair, folding bed, secrétaire and a classical sofa with drapery hanging over the ends. [D]

Harper, Richard, Coventry St, St James's, Haymarket, London, upholstery warehouseman (1765–75). Trading as Harper & Shipton, 1768–74. [D]

Harper, Robert, Dam St, Lichfield, Staffs., chairmaker and turner (1834). [D]

Harper, Thomas, Liverpool, u (b.1788–1839). Addresses given at 5 Gt Oxford St North, Low Hill in 1827; 20 Burlington St, 1827–29; 9 Gill St, 1829; and 18 Low Hill, 1835–39. Born on 5 April 1788, and admitted freeman on 5 October 1812. [D; Liverpool freemen reg.]

Harpham, Ishmael, Gracious St, Whittlesey, Cambs., cm (1830). [D]

Harpham, Miles, 14 Rahere St, City Rd, London, cm and u (1839). [D]

Harpley, Richard, Guisborough, Yorks., joiner, carpenter and/or cm (1828–34). [D]

Harpley, William jnr, Guisborough, Yorks., joiner and/or cm (1823). [D]

Harradin, Richard, 85 on the Terrace, Tottenham Ct Rd, London, carver and gilder (1779). Insured his house for £100 in 1779. [GL, Sun MS vol. 274, p. 531]

Harradan (or Harraden), Richard, 83 St Martin's Lane, London, carver, gilder and printseller (1790–93). [D]

Harraden, —, London, carver, gilder and printseller (1792–94). Addresses given on trade cards at 78 Wells St, Oxford St in 1792, and 16 Little Newport St, Leicester Sq., 1793–94. Identical Neo-classical cards show female figure in classical dress bearing a lamp, and about to stab a man sleeping in a Klismos chair. [Banks Coll., BM] Possibly the Harrader of London who subscribed to Sheraton's *Drawing Book*, 1793.

Harraden (or Harredon), —, address unrecorded, carver and gilder (1806–29). In 1806 received £23 for cleaning a picture and gilding frames at Madingley Hall, Cambs. Carried out work at Trinity College, Cambridge, between 1808–29, in 1808 supplying a plate glass for King Henry VIII's Room at the lodge, costing £52 10s; and 'Enriching the Kings Arms over Do.', costing £2 10s. [Cambs. RO, Madingley Hall archives, S88 A33; Trinity College archives]

Harraden, Jabez Richards (or Richard Jabez), St Mary St, Cambridge, cm and u (1824–30). Declared bankrupt, *London Gazette*, 13 April 1830. [D]

Harratt, Thomas, 3 Broad St, Soho, London, cm, u and undertaker (1839). [D]

Harrington, John snr, 311 High Holborn, London, plate case maker (1801). [D]

Harriot, Archibald & John, Library Stairs, North Shields, Northumb., carvers and gilders (1834). [D]

Harriot, James, Edgbaston St, Birmingham, cm (1767). [D]

Harriot, William, Vine St, London, cm (1774). [Poll bk]

Harris, —, Meeting-House Yd, near Barber Surgeon's Hall, London, cm (1742). Report in *London Evening Post*, 21–24 August 1742, of a fire on his premises 'which consumed great Part of the said House.'

Harris, —, at 'The Golden Anchor', no. 8, near Bedlam Walk, between New Broad St and Old Bedlam, Moorfields, London, upholder, cm and sworn broker (1771). Invoice for a large glass in a carved frame, costing £6 6s is dated 11 February 1771, and receipted by Thomas Harris. Reverse of invoice bears trade label which states that he 'MAKES, buys, sells, and appraises, all Manner of Household Furniture &c. Note, Funerals Furnished.' [GL, print dept]

Harris, —, Ottery St Mary, Devon, chairmaker (1797–98). [D] Probably William Harris.

Harris, —, Church St, Lambeth, London, chairmaker (1803). Subscribed to Sheraton's *Cabinet Dictionary*, and named in his list of master cabinet makers, 1803.

Harris, —, address unrecorded. In February 1828 was paid 'for taking back Patent Bed', by 3rd Lord Braybrooke of Audley End, Essex, London, and Billingbear, Berks. [Essex RO, D/DBy/A361]

Harris, —, Foregate St, Chester, picture frame maker (1840). Death of his wife on 17 October 1840 reported in *Chester Chronicle, Cheshire and North Wales Advertiser*, 23 October.

Harris (or Harries), Arthur, Shrewsbury, Salop and London, u (1721–47). Named in the Shrewsbury burgess roll, of London, in 1721. Of Shrewsbury, took app. named Hulse in 1747. [S of G, app. index]

Harris, Benjamin, Toft, Cambs., chairmaker (d.1724). [Cambridge Univ. Lib., will WR 12:30]

Harris, Benjamin, Norwell Pl., Bethnall Green Rd, London, bedstead maker (1839). [D]

Harris, C. R., 18 Poland St, London, carver and gilder (1835). [D]

Harris, Caleb, West Wycombe, Bucks., chairmaker (b. c.1811–41). Aged 30 at the time of the 1841 Census. [D]

Harris, Charles, 7 Percy St, Tottenham Ct Rd, London, carver and gilder (1839). [D]

Harris, Christopher, 1 Artillery Lane, Bishopsgate St, London, cm (1820). [D]

Harris, D., 73 George St, Portman Sq., London, u (1835). [D]

Harris, E., 7 Church St, Southwark, London, bedstead and cm (1820). [D]

Harris, Edmond, West Wycombe, Bucks., chairmaker (b. c.1791–1841). Aged 50 at the time of the 1841 Census.

Harris, Edward, 275 Kent St, Southwark, London, bedstead and cornice maker (1820). [D]

Harris, Edward, 9 Bridge St, Southwark, London, cm and u (1825–29). [D]

Harris, Edward, 8 Little Charles St, York St, Regent's Park, London, chairmaker (1835). [D]

Harris, Edward, 14 New Rd, Fitzroy Sq., London, chair and sofa maker (1839). [D]

Harris, Francis, 7 Stoney Hill, Bristol, carver (1775). [D]

Harris, Francis, High St, Godalming, Surrey, cm and u (1839). [D]

Harris, George, 136 Union St, Southwark, London, bedstead maker (1826). [D]

Harris, Henry, St James, Bristol, upholder (1739–54). [Poll bks]

Harris, Henry snr (?), West Wycombe, Bucks., chairmaker (1790–1830). [D; Militia Census, 1798]

Harris, Henry jnr (?), West Wycombe, Bucks., chairmaker (b. c.1786–1841). Aged 55 at the time of the 1841 Census.

Harris, Isaac, Compton St, Westminster, London, cm (1715–20). Took out a Hand in Hand Insurance policy on 12 April 1715 on his house and workshop. Insured goods and merchandise in his house on 25 April 1715 and 15 March 1720 with the Sun Co. [GL, Hand in Hand MS vol. 14, p. 225; GL, Sun MS vol. 4, p. 236; vol. 11, p. 38]

Harris, J., address unrecorded. Name stamped on a painted Sheraton-style chair, c.1800, at Burghley House, Lincs.

Harris, J., 16 Ladymead, Bath, Som., cm and broker (1819). [D]

Harris, J., Plymouth, Devon, joiner and carver (1826). Declared bankrupt, *Liverpool Mercury*, 6 October 1826.

Harris, Jabez, South St, Greenwich, London, cm and u (1832–38). [D]

Harris, James, 45 St Andrew's St, London, carver (1806). Took out a Sun Insurance policy on 27 October 1806 for £100 of which £30 accounted for stock and utensils. [GL, Sun MS vol. 437, ref. 795645]

Harris, James, Ilfracombe, Devon, cm (1823–30). Birth of his son announced in *The Alfred*, 18 April 1826. [D]

Harris, James, Worcester, carver and gilder (1828–37). Recorded at 26 High St, 1828–30; 10 Copenhagen St in 1835; and Greenhill Terr., 1837. [D]

Harris, James, Exeter, Devon, cm (1833–37). Recorded at Paul St, 1833–35, and Paris St in 1837. Son John bapt. at St Paul's on 31 January 1833; daughter Jane on 30 August 1835; and daughter Ellen at St Sidwell's on 31 August 1837. [PR (bapt.)]

Harris, John, address unrecorded, upholder (1712). Admitted freeman of the Upholders' Co. on 26 August 1712. [GL, Upholders' Co. records]

Harris, John, address unrecorded, upholder (1712–44). Son of John Harris, yeoman of Preston-upon-Wye, Herefs.; app. to William Scrimshire, in trust for George Cure, on 19 February 1712. Admitted freeman of the Upholders' Co. by servitude on 13 June 1744. [GL, Upholders' Co. records]

Harris, John, St Martin-in-the-Fields, London, carver (d.1736). Death reported in *Gents Mag.*, November 1736.

Harris, John, Vinegar Yd, London, picture frame maker (1749). [Poll bk]

Harris, John, Leadenhall St, London, joiner and cm (1758–59). Rococo trade card of John Harris and Richard Moseley gives address 'opposite the East India House, Leadenhall St., London,' and states: 'Makes & Sells all Sorts of Cabinet Chair & Looking Glass Goods at the most Reasonable Rates. N.B. For Exportation.' [BM] In 1758 John Harris employed three non-freemen for six weeks, then six months. In his will, made in February 1759, and witnessed by Richard Moseley and Henry Bagshaw, he left all to his wife, Sarah. Probate dated October 1759. [D; GL, City Licence bks, vol. 2; Will PRO, Prob. 11 328; Harris, *Old English Furniture*, p. 22]

Harris, John, Thaxted, Essex, cm (b.1735–d.1814). Took app. named Moore in 1760. Named in the Essex freeholders' bk for Dunmow Hundred in 1768. Took out a Sun Insurance policy in 1784 for £200, utensils and stock accounting for £100. Paper label recorded on inside of the secret drawer of a mahogany bureau, which reads: 'John Harris, Thaxted in Essex, Fecit. Practising the Trade of a Cabinetmaker above 62 years, During which Period made and sold upwards of 500 Bureaus, made this in the 78th Year of his Age, May 22, Anno Dom. 1813.' [D; S of G, app. index; Essex RO, Q/RJ1 3; GL, Sun MS vol. 322, p. 11; *C. Life*, 5 July 1979; *Wills at Chelmsford*]

Harris, John, Horksley, Essex, upholder (1768). [Colchester poll bk]

Harris, John, 43 Moor St, Birmingham, cm (1767–70). [D]

Harris, John, Bury St Edmunds, Suffolk, upholder (1780). [Colchester poll bk]

Harris, John, 120 Blackman St, London, cm (1789). [D]

Harris, John, 39 Wilson St, Finsbury Sq., London, cm (1802–08). Took out Sun Insurance policies on 20 October 1802 for £800; on 11 April 1803 for £1,500; and on 17 October 1808 for £1,500, of which stock, utensils and goods in trust accounted for £200, and timber £1,200. [GL, Sun MS vol. 423, ref. 738715; vol. 427, ref. 745858; vol. 444, ref. 821754]

Harris, John, Conduit St, Hanover Sq., London, carver, gilder and frame maker (1807–28). Recorded at no. 30, 1806–09; no. 31, 1809–28; no. 34 in 1826; and as Harris & Pearse from 1815–28. Trade card of Harris, carver and gilder, gives address at 31 Conduit St. Harris & Pearse charged £2 4s to Lord Crewe of Crewe Hall in 1828 for '1 Rich Frame Gilt in Old Gold & Varnishing the Picture.' [D; Banks Coll., BM; Chester RO, Crewe Hall papers, DCR/47/Box 4]

Harris, John, 28 Gerrard St, Soho, London, carver and gilder (1808). [D]

Harris, John, 14 Frith St, Soho, London, cm and u (1809). [D]

Harris, John, 40 Crawford St, London, upholder and undertaker (1817–21). Presumably the u of 40 Crawford St whose lease and stock were sold on 17 July 1821 by Edward Foster of 14 Greek St. The catalogue 'of the fashionable & Well-Manufactured stock of Upholstery & Cabinet Work' included four-post bedsteads and 'Chintz Furnitures', French canopy bedsteads and bedding; rosewood and mahogany chests of drawers, loo, card and sofa tables; drawing room and library chairs, Grecian couches and sofas, carpets and 'Satin Hair Cloth'. [D; V&A archives]

Harris, John, Bristol, u, undertaker, house and estate agent (1818–25). Addresses given at 8 Prichard St in 1818; 13 Wilson St in 1820; no. 10, 1821–23; and 7 St John St, 1824–25. [D]

Harris, John, Bristol, cabinet carver and furniture broker (1836–40). Addresses given at 11 Philadelphia St, 1836–37; 34 Broad Mead in 1838; and 3 Merchant St, 1839–40. [D]

Harris, John, Saville House, Leicester Sq., London, upholder and carpet warehouseman (1820). Took out a Sun Insurance policy on 11 September 1820 for £1,300 of which £250 accounted for household goods in his house at 7 Edward St, Kensington; and £500 on a house in High St, Hampstead. [GL, Sun MS vol. 483, ref. 970600] Possibly:

Harris, John, High St, Kensington, London, u (1823). [D]

Harris, John, 7 Gt Earl St, Seven Dials, London, cm and u (1827–29). [D]

Harris, John, 231 Tottenham Ct Rd, London, u (1826–39). [D]

Harris, John, 28 Union St, Middlx Hospital, London, cm and u (1827–28). [D]

Harris, John, 2 Court, Milk St, Birmingham, cm and u (1830). [D]

Harris, John, 15 Gt Adam St, Manchester Sq., London, u and undertaker (1835). [D]

Harris, John, 45 Hampden St, Somerstown, London, cm and u (1839). [D]

Harris, John, Market St, Lane End, Staffs., cm and u (1834–35). [D]

Harris, John, 16 Essex St, Toxteth Park, Liverpool, joiner and cm (1837). [D]

Harris, Jonah, 3 Talbot Ct, Gracechurch St, London, upholder and carpet warehouseman (1783). [D] See Josiah Harris at this address.

Harris, Jonathan, near Fleet Bridge, London, 'an eminent upholder' (d.1748). Death at his house near Fleet Bridge reported in *General Advertiser*, 1748. He died 'universally lamented', a widower who 'hath left an only Daughter bewailing...'.

Harris, Jos., Leadenhall St, London, turner (1780). Declared bankrupt, *Gents Mag.*, October 1780.

Harris, Jos., 2 Norfolk St, Middlx Hospital, London, cm and u (1827–28). [D]

Harris, Joseph, address unrecorded, upholder (1713/14). Son of Gamaliol Harris, Gent. of Kinlingbury, Northton [Northampton?]; app. to Richard Camfield, and admitted freeman of the Upholders' Co. on 3 February 1713/14. [GL, Upholders' Co. records]

Harris, Josiah, Ipswich, Suffolk, cm (1775–d. 1784). Took out Sun Insurance policies on houses in 1775 for £900; in 1779 for £400; and in 1780 for £400 on houses and office. Will proved at Norwich in 1784. [GL, Sun MS vol. 236, p. 626; vol. 276, p. 619; vol. 280, p. 78; Norfolk Record Soc., index of wills]

Harris, Josiah, Aldersgate St, London, u (1779). Took out a Sun Insurance policy in 1779 for £100 of which £30 accounted for utensils and stock. [GL, Sun MS vol. 276, p. 185]

Harris, Josiah, 3 Talbot Ct, Gracechurch St, London, upholder and carpet warehouseman (1781–91). Took out Sun Insurance policies in 1781 and 1784 for £2,100 and £1,500 respectively, utensils, stock and goods accounting for £1,000 and £500. Took app. named William Hutchins in February 1791 for £20, £5 of which was charity money from Christ's Hospital. [D; GL, Sun MS vol. 295, p. 552; vol. 324, p. 196; GL, Joiners' Co. records, vol. 7, p. 230] See Jonah Harris at this address.

Harris, Jubas, West Wycombe, Bucks., chairmaker (b. c. 1806–41). Aged 35 at the time of the 1841 Census.

Harris, Katherine, address unrecorded, upholder (1708/09). Admitted freeman of the Upholders' Co. on 2 February 1708/09. [GL, Upholders' Co. records]

Harris, Mary, address unrecorded, upholder (1721/22). Daughter of John Harris, upholder; admitted freeman of the Upholders' Co. on 15 February 1721/22. [GL, Upholders' Co. records]

Harris, Michael, High Wycombe, Bucks., chairmaker (1823–37). Four sons and four daughters bapt. between 1823 and 1837. [PR (bapt.)]

Harris, Maurice, Bristol, carver (1751). Took app. named Evans in 1751. [S of G, app. index]

Harris, Ralph, Mountsorrel, Leics., turner and carpenter (1784). [Leicester freemen rolls]

Harris, Ralph, 43 or 48 Mary-le-Bone Lane, London, carver and gilder (1809–11). [D]

Harris, Ralph, High St, Maidenhead, Berks., cm (1823–30). [D]

Harris, Ratcliff, Boar St, Lichfield, Staffs., cm (1835). [Poll bk]

Harris, Richard, Witch St, St Mary-le-Savoy, London, u (1692). In June 1692 fined as a Papist for refusing Oath of Fidelity. [Westminster Ref. Lib., Middlx session bk, 498, p. 76–79]

Harris, Richard, Northampton, cm (1820–40). Trading at Sheep St, 1820–23 and College St, 1826–40. [D; poll bks]

Harris, Richard, Breadmarket St, Lichfield, Staffs., cm and auctioneer (1822–35). Addresses given at Market St in 1822 and Breadmarket St, 1828–35. [D]

Harris, Robert, St Mary Tower, Ipswich, Suffolk, cm (1782–84). Named in the calendar of marriage licence bonds on 21 November 1782. Recorded in Tavern St in 1784. [D; Suffolk RO, FAA: 50/2/105]

Harris, Robert, 6 King St, Bloomsbury, London, upholder (1783–1823). Recorded as R. & Co., bed and mattress makers, 6 Upper King St, 1822–23. Took out Sun Insurance policies on 29 September 1783 and 29 September 1809 for £1,700 of which £700 accounted for stock, utensils and goods in trust; and on 1 September 1808 for £700 on his house. [D; GL, Sun MS vol. 448, ref. 804645; vol. 445, ref. 819970; vol. 448, ref. 834644]

Harris, Robert, 125 High Holborn, London, bedstead and bedding manufacturer (1822–39). Trading as Harris & Co., 1822–28. [D]

Harris, Robert, 23 Old St, St Luke's, London, chair and sofa maker, cm (1835–39). [D]

Harris, Robert, 4 Haworth St, Everton, Liverpool, cm (1839). [D]

Harris, Robert, Stalbridge, Dorset, joiner and cm (1840). [D]

Harris, S., Little Brook St, Hanover Sq., London, carver and gilder (1826–27). [D]

Harris, Samuel, Manchester, upholder (1754–88). Trading at 18 Hanging Ditch, 1772–88. Took app. named Bancroft in 1754. [D; S of G, app. index]

Harris, Samuel, St Edmund's, Exeter, Devon, cm (1803). [Militia Census]

Harris, Samuel, Booker, High Wycombe, Bucks., chairmaker (b. c. 1811–41). Aged 30 at the time of the 1841 Census.

Harris, Shepherd, Bristol, cm (1754–81). Recorded in Castle Precincts, 1754–74, and Temple parish, 1781. [Poll bks]

Harris, Simeon, Broad St, Bloomsbury, London, cm (1809–11). [D]

Harris, Thomas, Lancaster, cm (1781–1811). App. to Thomas Bagot in 1781, and admitted freeman, 1801–02. Named in the Gillow records in 1788, 1799 and 1811. [Lancaster app. reg. and freemen rolls; Westminster Ref. Lib., Gillow]

Harris, Thomas, 2 Frontier Ct, St Martin's Lane, London, cm (1786). Took out a Sun Insurance policy on 31 July 1786 for £100, £20 accounting for utensils. [GL, Sun MS vol. 338, p. 231]

Harris, Thomas, West Wycombe, Bucks., chairmaker (1790–98). [D; Militia Census]

Harris, Thomas, West Wycombe, Bucks., chairmaker (b. c. 1791–1841). Listed in a directory of 1830. Aged 50 at the time of the 1841 Census.

Harris, Thomas, 406 Oxford St, London, u, bed and bedding manufacturer (1803–25). [D]

Harris, Thomas, 1 Warwick Row, Blackfriars Rd, London, u (1808). [D]

Harris, Thomas, Liverpool, cm (1804–27). Trading at Brownlow Hill in 1804 and 16 McKee St in 1827. [D]

Harris, Thomas, Ellbroad St, Bristol, turner and chairmaker (1806–17). Trading at no. 1, 1809–17. [D]

Harris, Thomas, 30 Penn St, Bristol, timber merchant and cm (1831–40). [D]

Harris, Thomas jnr, Homes's Ct, adjoining 41 Castle St, Bristol, turner and bedstead manufacturer (1832–40). Trading also as cm from 1839. [D]

Harris, Thomas, 1 Bishops Ct, Old Bailey, London, mahogany case manufacturer (1820). [D]

Harris, Thomas, 40 Crawford St, Montague Sq., London, u (1820). [D]

Harris, Thomas, 56 Greek St, Soho, London, u and bedstead warehouseman (1820). [D]

Harris, Thomas, 37 White St, Southwark, London, cm and u (1827–28). [D]

Harris, Thomas, Henley St, Stratford-upon-Avon, Warks., chairmaker (1830). [D]

Harris, Thomas, 9 New St and 19 New Summer St, Birmingham, u, furnishing draper, carpet dealer and paper hanger (1829–35). Submitted bill to Mr Lloyd, 1829–30, totalling £1 14s 8d for 'Gothic Chintz'. Bill head gives address at 9 New St, and lists stock of 'Brussels, Kidderminster, Scotch and Venetian Carpets, EARTH RUGS, DRUGGETS, DOOR & CARRIAGE — MATS, INDIA & IMPERIAL MATTING, Floor Cloths … Table Linens … Counterpanes, Quilts, Blankets, Bed Ticks, Moreens, Chintz & Dimity Furniture, Curtain Muslins, Coloured Furniture Linings, Window Hollands … Tassels, Fringes, Bed Laces &c. Bedsteads fitted up in a Superior Manner …'. [D; Herefs. RO, F60/295)

Harris, Thomas, Luke St, Islington, Birmingham, cm (1835). [D]

Harris, Thomas, Tamworth, Staffs., cm and u (1818–34). Recorded at Bolebridge St, 1818–22, and Lichfield St, 1828–34. [D]

Harris, Thomas, Dudley, Worcs., picture frame maker (1839). [D]

Harris, W. & Son, Bread Market St, Lichfield, Staffs., cm and u (1818). [D]

Harris, William, at 'The Golden Head', St Alban St, St James's, London, upholder (1718–25). Named in newspapers, 1718–25. Insured goods and merchandise in his house on 3 December 1719. [Heal; GL, Sun MS vol. 9, p. 31]

Harris, William, address unrecorded, upholder (1719). Son of James Harris, yeoman of Long Rugby, Northton; app. to

Richard Campfield, and admitted freeman of the Upholders' Co. on 7 October 1719 by servitude. [GL, Upholders' Co. records]

Harris, William, St Martin-in-the-Fields, London, cm (1749). [Poll bk]

Harris, William, Barnstaple, Devon, joiner, cm and chapman (1750). Declared bankrupt, *General Advertiser*, 8 August 1750.

Harris, William, Ottery St Mary, Devon, cm (1760). Took app. named Hake in 1760. [S of G, app. index] See Harris, —.

Harris, William, Cob's Ct, Blackfriars, London, chairmaker (1808). [D]

Harris, William, 'Tunbridge', Kent, chairmaker (1816). Son Thomas bapt. on 1 December 1816, in parish of SS Peter and Paul. [PR (bapt.)]

Harris, William, Norton St, London, bedstead maker (1820). Took out a Sun Insurance policy on 16 November 1820 with Thomas Wildey of 25 Berwick St for £800 on Wildey's house and workshop behind. [GL, Sun MS vol. 483, ref. 972684]

Harris, William, 7 Peter St, Bath, Som., cm (1826). [D]

Harris, William, 42 Curtain Rd, Shoreditch, London, u and cm (1826–28). [D]

Harris, William, 24 Wilson St, Soho, London, u (1829). [D]

Harris, William, 136 Union St, Southwark, London, bedstead maker (1829). [D]

Harris, William, Gloucester, cm and chairmaker (1820–30). Trading in Southgate St in 1820; as carver and gilder at Lower Northgate St, 1822–23, and Glo'ster Pl., London Rd in 1830. Children bapt. at St John Baptist, 1821, 1825 and 1827. [D; PR (bapt.)]

Harris, William, Towns End, Dover, Kent., cm (1826–39). [D; poll bks]

Harris, William, Younder St, Ottery St Mary, Devon, chairmaker (1830). [D] See Harris, —.

Harris, William, Marsh St, Hanley, Staffs., joiner, builder and cm (1834). [D]

Harris, William, Greenhill Terr., Worcester, carver and gilder (1835). [D]

Harris, William, Mount Pleasant, Brixton Hill, Brixton, London, u and cm (1838). [D]

Harris, William, 11 Lower Castle St, Bristol, turner, hat and bonnet block, pressing machine and bedstead manufacturer (1838–40). [D]

Harris, William, South St and Cold Bath Row, Greenwich, London, cm and u (1839). [D]

Harris & Catton, West Wycombe, Bucks., chairmakers (1830). [D]

Harris & Chapman, 8 Denmark St, St Giles, London, invalid chair makers (1829). [D]

Harris & King, London (?). In 1772 received payment for furniture supplied to Sir John Griffin Griffin of Audley End, Essex. [Essex RO, D/DBy/A203]

Harrison, Mrs, London, upholder and supplier of Oriental goods (1695). Mrs Harrison supplied a 'Japan Cabinet & a black carved fraime' costing £52 for Petworth House, Sussex, in 1695. [Nat Trust guide to *Petworth*, p. 15]

Harrison, —, at the 'Cross Keys', Fleet Ditch, London, u (1748). Named in newspapers in 1748. [Heal] Possibly Jonathan Harrison.

Harrison, —, address unrecorded, u (1775–76). Named in the private accounts of Richard Hoare of Boreham House, Essex, on 1 November 1775 receiving £1 2s 9d; and on 12 April 1776, 5s 6d. [Essex RO, D/Du 649/2]

Harrison, —, London, cm (1793). Subscribed to Sheraton's *Drawing Book*, 1793.

Harrison, —, Norwich, cm (1793). Subscribed to Sheraton's *Drawing Book*, 1793.

Harrison, Andrew, Sussex St, Sunderland, Co. Durham, joiner and cm (1828–29). [D]

Harrison, Benjamin, Gowthorpe, near Selby, Yorks., joiner and cm (1834–37). [D]

Harrison, Cleave, address unrecorded, upholder (1719–27). Son of Stephen Harrison, confectioner of Cambridge; app. to Thomas Dawson on 20 August 1719, and admitted freeman of the Upholders' Co. by servitude on 5 July 1727. [GL, Upholders' Co. records]

Harrison, Edward, Windmill St, Tottenham Ct Rd, London, u (c.1802–09). Lent to James Belcher Ball, cordwainer of Kensington, deceased, £280 towards £560 penal sum on bond. [PRO, C13 118/16, bill 1809]

Harrison, Edward, English St, Carlisle, Cumb., cm and/or joiner (1834). [D]

Harrison, George, Liverpool, u (b.1817–40). Admitted freeman on 27 July 1840. [Liverpool freemen rolls]

Harrison, George, Temple Sowerby, Westmld, joiner and/or cm (1829–34). [D]

Harrison, George, 28 Middle St, Newcastle cm and furniture broker (1834). [D]

Harrison, George, Market Pl., Pontefract, Yorks., cm (1834–37). [D]

Harrison, George, Wycliffe, Yorks., joiner and cm (1840). [D]

Harrison, Henry, Liverpool, cm (1825). App. to William Atkinson in 1825. [Liverpool app. enrolment bk]

Harrison, Henry Wood, Liverpool, u (1827). Admitted freeman on 18 October 1827. [Liverpool freemen reg.]

Harrison, Herbert, St Sepulchregate, Doncaster, Yorks., carver and gilder (1837). [D]

Harrison, Isaac, 14 Brown St, Granville St, Liverpool, and 2 Cornwallis St, joiner and cm (1824). [D]

Harrison, J., Carlisle Pl., Lambeth, London, chairmaker (1809–11). [D]

Harrison, James, Norwich, u (1717–60). Recorded in both St Andrew's and St Peter Mancroft parishes in Norwich poll of 1734, possibly implying two craftsmen of the same name. James (Jacob) Harrison, son of William Harrison, admitted freeman on 13 November 1717. His app., William Notley, upholder, was assigned to Paul Colombine, u, and admitted freeman on 3 May 1760. Harrison took app. named Durrant in 1720. [Poll bk; Norwich freemen reg.; S of G, app. index]

Harrison, James, Bakehouse Lane, Leicester, cm and joiner (1767–80). App. to William Jennings and admitted freeman in 1767. Advertised sale of stock in trade in *Leicester Journal*, 29 January 1780. [Leicester freemen rolls]

Harrison, James, 44 Upper Rathbone Pl., London, cane worker (1808). [D]

Harrison, James, 1 Back Hill, Hatton Gdn, London, bedstead maker (1809–11). [D]

Harrison, James, 21 Lawton St, Liverpool, cm (1821). Admitted freeman on 20 October 1821. [Liverpool freemen reg.]

Harrison, James, Golborne St, Warrington, Lancs., chairmaker (1822). [D]

Harrison, James, 1 Howard St, Sheffield, Yorks., joiner and cm (1822). [D]

Harrison, James, Bridge St, Belper, Derbs., joiner and cm (1835). [D]

Harrison, John, Canterbury, Kent, u (1742). Declared bankrupt, *Gents Mag.*, June 1742.

Harrison, John, Newcastle, u (1774). Son William admitted freeman by patrimony on 2 July 1774. [Newcastle freemen reg.]

Harrison, John, 6 North side of Church St, St Ann's, London, cm (1777). Took out a Sun Insurance policy in 1777 for £300, £160 accounting for utensils, stock and goods. [GL, Sun MS vol. 258, p. 51]

Harrison, John, Liverpool, joiner and cm (1777–d.1790). Trading at 2 Tarleton St in 1777; 23 Argyle St in 1781; Rainford's Gdns, 1787–90, no. 5 in 1787. Death reported in *Williamson's Liverpool Advertiser*, 15 February 1790. [D]

Harrison, John, Bury St Edmunds, Suffolk, u (1784). [Colchester poll bk]

Harrison, John, Lancaster. Named in the Gillow records between 1791–1824, including work on a fishing stool. [Westminster Ref. Lib., Gillow vol. 344/96, p. 889]

Harrison, John, 5 Smithy Door, Manchester, cm (1794). [D]

Harrison, John, Corn Mkt, Shrewsbury, Salop, cm (1796). [Shrewsbury burgess roll]

Harrison, John, address unrecorded, cm (1803). Subscribed to Sheraton's *Cabinet Dictionary*, 1803.

Harrison, John, 6 North St, Pentonville, London, chair caner (1808). [D]

Harrison, John, 6 Newton St, High Holborn, London, caner, chair and sofa maker (1808–28). [D]

Harrison, John, 22 Crown Ct, Princes St, Soho, London, cm (1809–11). [D]

Harrison, John, Golborne (or Colborne) St, Warrington, Lancs., chairmaker (1816–25). [D]

Harrison, John, 19 Marklands Row, Bolton, Lancs., chairmaker (1818). [D]

Harrison, John, Gisburn, near Skipton, Yorks., joiner and cm (1822). [D]

Harrison, John, Nottingham, joiner and cm (1823). Son of William Harrison, maltster of Spondon, Derbs.; taken as app. in 1823. [Nottingham app. list]

Harrison, John, Market Pl., Otley, Yorks., joiner and cm (1828–30). [D]

Harrison, John, King St, Thorne, Yorks., joiner and cm (1828–34). [D]

Harrison, John, Church St, Mansfield, Notts., chairmaker (1828–35). [D]

Harrison, John, Meeting House Lane, Chatham, Kent, cm and u (1832–34). [D]

Harrison, John, Bridge St, Belper, Derbs., joiner and cm (1835). [D]

Harrison, John, New St, Walsall, Staffs., cm and u 1834–35). [D]

Harrison, John, Manor-chare, Newcastle, carver and gilder (1838). [D]

Harrison, Jonathan, St Bride's, London, upholder (1719–34). Recorded at 'Cross Keys', Fleet Ditch in 1719; and Ditch Side, 1725–34. Took out a Sun Insurance policy on 12 October 1719. Fined for non-service at St Bride's in 1725 and 1734. Served as a Questman in 1727. [GL, Sun MS vol. 10, ref. 15416; GL, MS 6561, p. 42] See Harrison, —, at the 'Cross Keys'.

Harrison, Jonathan, Whitehaven, Cumb., cm (1798–1829). Trading at 77 George St, 1811–29. [D]

Harrison, Jonathan, address unrecorded, turner (1816). Submitted bill to Earl of Strathmore of Gibside and Streatlam, Co. Durham, on 31 August 1816 totalling 18s for 'turning 2 bed pillars', '8 paterness circular' and '8 paterness oval'. On 14 September he charged 5s for 'Turning 5 large vases for bed'. [Durham RO, Strathmore MS, D/St/Box 198]

Harrison, Joseph, New Town, Bilston, Staffs., cm (1818). [D]

Harrison, Joseph, 29 Harper St, Toxteth Park, Liverpool, with shop at 41 Mulberry St, joiner and cm (1839). [D]

Harrison, Matthew, Ripon, Yorks., cm (1798). [D]

Harrison, Matthew, Union St, Wisbech, Cambs., cm, auctioneer and appraiser (1839). [D]

Harrison, Michael, Drypool, near Hull, Yorks., cm (1818). App. to Robert Waugh in October 1818. [Hull app. reg.]

Harrison, Ralph, 26 Church St, Sunderland, Co. Durham, joiner and cm (1827–29). [D]

Harrison, Richard, Liverpool, cm (1760–61). Petitioned freedom on birthright as son of Samuel S. G. Harrison, blacksmith, paying 3s 4d in 1760. A Richard Harrison was admitted freeman on 28 January 1761, and another on 28 May. [Liverpool freemen's committee bk and reg.]

Harrison, Richard, address unrecorded. In 1776 supplied a tent bed costing £21 2s 4d to Joseph Harrington, steward of the 6th Duke of Bedford's Bloomsbury Estate, who lived in Gt Russell St, London. [J. Harrington's cash bk, Colin Frost, bookseller, 1983]

Harrison, Robert, Poulton, Lancs., spinning-wheel maker (1797–98). [D]

Harrison, Robert, Richmond, Yorks., cm (1820). [PR (bapt.)]

Harrison, Robert, Thorner, near Leeds, Yorks., cm (1822). [D]

Harrison, Robert, Wisbech, Cambs., cm and u (1824–30). Trading at Artillery St in 1824 and Norfolk St West in 1830. [D]

Harrison, Robert, Penny St, Lancaster, chair and bedstead maker (1825). [D]

Harrison, Robert, 78 Norton St, Fitzroy Sq., London, cm (1835). [D]

Harrison, Samuel, Chester, joiner and carver (1720). Took app. named Catherall in 1720. [S of G, app. index]

Harrison, Samuel, Fleet St, St Bride's, London, cm (1767). Took out a Hand in Hand Insurance policy in July 1767 for £200 on property in Falcon Ct, and £600 on a house in Fleet St. [GL, Hand in Hand MS vol. 106, p. 68]

Harrison, Samuel, 14 Alfred Pl., Newington, London, chair, sofa and stool manufacturer (1820–32). Declared bankrupt in association with Frederick Graham, *London Gazette*, 2 March 1832. [D]

Harrison, Samuel, Mill St, Leek, Staffs., chairmaker and turner (1834).

Harrison, Samuel, 1 Sussex Pl., Southwark and 84 St George's Rd, London, chair manufacturer (1835). [D]

Harrison, T., Harrington, Workington, Cumb., joiner and/or cm (1811–34). [D]

Harrison, Theophilas, Canterbury, Kent, cm and u (1800–38). Trading at Iron Bar Lane in 1818; St Margaret's, 1823–34; and Longport, 1838. Admitted freeman in 1800. [D; poll bk; Canterbury freemen rolls]

Harrison, Thomas, late of Maidstone, Kent, u (d. by 1713?). His son was app. to a baker in 1713. [S of G, app. index]

Harrison, Thomas, Middleham, Yorks., cm (1740). Advertised in *York Courant*, 21 October 1740 'That he makes and sells all Sorts of Cabinet Work, as Chairs, Tables &c either in Mahogany, or otherwise, after the best Italian, French, Dutch or English Fashions at the lowest Rates. N.B. He likewise Carves upon Tables, Chairs &c in the neatest Manner.'

Harrison, Thomas, Church Gate, Loughborough, Leics., cm (1791–95). Advertised auction of furniture and stock in trade, consisting of chairs, tables, beds, clock cases etc., in *Leicester Journal*, 3 March 1795.

Harrison, Thomas, 3 Bridport St, Liverpool, carver and gilder (1837). [D]

Harrison, W., 1 Hanover Pl., Old Kent Rd, London, u (1835). [D]

Harrison, W. H., 3 Bride Lane, Fleet St, London, carver and gilder (1835). [D]

Harrison, W. H., Bow St, Covent Gdn, London, carver and gilder (1837). [D]

Harrison, Watson, Keswick, Cumb., joiner and cm (1828–29). [D] Probably William Watson Harrison.

Harrison, William, St Peter Mancroft, Norwich, u (1692–1717). App. to Jacob Tompson, and admitted freeman on 24 February 1692. His son, James Harrison, admitted freeman on 13 November 1717. [Poll bks; Norwich freemen reg.]

Harrison, William, Oxford Rd, London, cm (1749). [Poll bk]

Harrison, William, Ropemakers Alley, Moorfields, London, billiard table maker (1756). Advertised in *Public Advertiser*, 27 April 1756.

Harrison, William, London, u (1793). Subscribed to Sheraton's *Drawing Book*, 1793.

Harrison, William, Liverpool, cm (b.1780–d.1824). Addresses given at 3 Clayton Sq. Yd, 42 Wood St in 1827; and 3 Clayton Sq. Yd, 12 Wood St in 1829. Petitioned freedom on birthright as son of Daniel Harrison, cordwainer, in 1806, paying 3s 4d. Admitted freeman on 5 November 1806. Took app. named Samuel Thompson in 1821. Death reported in *Liverpool Mercury*, 20 February 1824. [D; Liverpool freemen's committee bk. and reg.; app. enrolment bk]

Harrison, William, Diss, Norfolk, cm and u (1812–39). Trading at Crown St, 1830–39. Polled at Colchester, Essex, in 1812, 1820 and 1831. [D]

Harrison, William, Wigan, Lancs., cm (1814–34). Recorded at Queen St, 1814–22, and Wallgate, 1828–34. [D]

Harrison, William, Market St, Chorley, Lancs., cm (1822). [D]

Harrison, William, Bridge St, Warrington, Lancs., cm (1822). [D]

Harrison, William, Egremont, Cleator, Cumb., joiner and cm (1828–29). [D]

Harrison, William, Keswick, Cumb., cm and/or joiner (1829–32). Recorded as William Watson Harrison at the Forge in 1832. [D] Probably Watson Harrison.

Harrison, William, Tradesmen's Mart, Nottingham, cm and u (1832–35). Recorded at 'The Mart' in 1835. [D]

Harrison, William, 88 High St, Ramsgate, Kent, cm (1832–34). [D]

Harrison, William, Fleet St, Bury, Lancs., cm (1834). [D]

Harrison, William, 26 Peach St, Liverpool, cm (1839). [D]

Harrison, William, High St, Bridlington, Yorks., cm (1840). [D]

Harrison, William, Hamilton Pl., Chester, cm, chairmaker and u (1840). [D]

Harrison & Jiggs, Bridge St, Horncastle, Lincs., joiners, cm and builders (1819–22). [D]

Harrison, Jonathon & Hill, London, u (1732). Trade card recorded. [Heal]

Harrock, John, address unrecorded, cm (1803). Subscribed to Sheraton's *Cabinet Dictionary*, 1803.

Harrocks (or Horrocks), John, Liverpool, cm and joiner (1780–1813). Addresses given at 17 Edmund St in 1787 and 1794; no. 46, 1790–96, with timber yard at 31 Tithebarn St in 1790; at 45 Edmund St, Old Hall St in 1800; no. 17, 1803–04; and 17 Plumb(e) St, 1805–13. Admitted freeman on 11 September 1780. Marriage to Mrs Nelsa at St Nicholas's Church on 19 December 1789 reported in *Liverpool Advertiser*, 28 December. [D; Liverpool freemen reg.]

Harrold, Edward, Bath St, Frome, Som., cm (1830). [D]

Harron, C., London, cm (1793). Subscribed to Sheraton's *Drawing Book*, 1793.

Harrop, Philip snr, Worcester, cm and u (1828–30). Listed at Union St in 1828 and Friar St, 1830. [D]

Harrop, Philip jnr, Worcester, cm and u (1822–40). Recorded at Friar St, 1822–30, no. 9 in 1822; 46 Copenhagen St in 1828; and 21 Mealcheapen St, 1830–40. Admitted freeman in 1826 and named in the Worcester freemen rolls on 1 December 1835. [D] See William Harrop.

Harrop, Sarah, 6 Upper Cleveland St, Fitzroy Sq., London, cm and u (1827–28). [D]

Harrop, William, 6 Upper Cleveland St, Fitzroy Sq., London, cm and appraiser (1826–27). [D]

Harrop, William, Friar St, Worcester, cm (1826–35). Admitted freeman in 1826, and named in the Worcester freemen rolls on 1 December 1835. See Philip Harrop.

Harroway, John, Greenwich, London, carver and gilder (1791). [D]

Harrowell, William, Rugby, Warks., u and paper hanger (1835). [D]

Harsant, M., 9 Sherborne Lane, Lombard St, London, cm and undertaker (1817). [D]

Harsant, M., 4 Bush Lane, Cannon St, London, carpenter and cm (1820). [D]

Harsant, William, 53 Tower St, Tower Hill, London, undertaker and upholder (1817). [D]

Harstead, John, 10 Lower Coleman St, Bunhill Row, London, cm (1786). Took out a Sun Insurance policy on 16 March 1786 for £500 of which utensils etc. accounted for £300. [GL, Sun MS vol. 336, p. 5]

Harston, Standish, St Peter Mancroft, Norwich, u (1710). [Poll bk]

Harston, William, Newark, Notts., cm and u (1828–d.1836). Trading at Appletongate, 1828–35, in 1835 also as a paper hanger. Died in 1836 and will proved on 1 July. [D; Notts. RO, probate records]

Hart, A. H., London, cm and u (1829–39). Recorded at 376 Strand in 1829; 350 Oxford St in 1835; 356 Oxford St in 1837; and 3 Dean St in 1839. [D] See Aaron Henry Hart, Aaron Hyam Hart, and Henry Hart.

Hart, Aaron Henry, London, cm, upholder and broker (1804–07). Addresses given at 37 St Martin's Lane, 1804–05; and 331 corner of Argyle St, Oxford St in 1807. Took out Sun Insurance policies on 14 August 1804 for £700 on utensils and stock in his house, where no cabinet work was done; on 8 February 1805 for £800, £650 on utensils and stock at 4 Greek St, Soho, where no cabinet work was done; and on 28 October 1807 for £1,800, £1,500 on utensils and stock. [GL, Sun MS vol. 431, refs 764399 and 772607; vol. 441, ref. 809412] See Henry and Hyam Hart. Possibly:

Hart, Aaron Hyam, 58 Greek St, Soho, London, u (1807). Took out a Sun Insurance policy on 11 August 1807 for £1,000 of which £850 accounted for household goods at 20 Callum St. [GL, Sun MS vol. 442, ref. 806348]

Hart, Balguy jnr, late of Latonstone, Essex, u (1761). Discharge from Debtors' Prison announced in *London Gazette*, 22 August 1761. See Thomas Hart, upholder.

Hart, Charles, 28 Pool Lane, Liverpool, u (1767–75). In 1775 subscribed £1 1s to Mayor's fund for the relief of soldiers and dependents in the American War. [D; *Liverpool Advertiser*, 17 November 1775]

Hart, Charles, Hull, Yorks., cm and u (1803). App. to John and George Chapman of Hull on 20 June 1803. [Hull app. reg.]

Hart, George, George St, Gt Yarmouth, Norfolk, u (1838). [Poll bk]

Hart, Henry, Liverpool, cm (1816–23). Addresses given at 5 Fore St in 1816; 37 Milton St in 1821; and 7 All Saints Lane, Rose Pl. in 1823. [D]

Hart, Henry, 376 Strand, London, u (1826–27). [D] Probably Aaron Henry Hart.

Hart, Hyam, 37 St Martin's Lane, London, u and cm (1808). [D] Probably Aaron Hyam Hart.

Hart, John, Langport, Som., house carpenter, joiner and cm (1809). Advertised for a workman in *Sherborne Mercury*, 24 July 1809.

Hart, John, Guildford St, Southwark, London, turner and chairmaker (1807–11). Addresses given at 12 in the Grove, Gt Guildford St, 1807–11; and 11 Little Guildford St in 1810.

Took out Sun Insurance policies on 10 August 1807 for £400 of which £150 accounted for utensils and stock; and on 1 January 1810 for £400, £200 on stock and utensils. [D; GL, Sun MS vol. 440, ref. 806204; vol. 447, ref. 839213]

Hart, Joseph, 1 Brandon St, Bristol, fancy chair, cornice and glass enameller (1817). [D]

Hart, Joseph, Edgbaston St, Birmingham, cm (1818). [D]

Hart, Mary, Missenden, Bucks., chair manufacturer (1830). [D]

Hart, Peter, 47 Hurst St, Liverpool, cm (1781). [D]

Hart, Peter, 56 Union St, Salford, Lancs., cm (1804–08). [D]

Hart, Richard, Holborn, London, turner (1707). Insured his house for £200 on 19 December 1707. [GL, Hand in Hand MS vol. 5, ref. 1433]

Hart, Robert jnr, Wimborne, Dorset, coach and cm (1782). Took out a Sun Insurance policy in 1782 for £400 of which £220 accounted for utensils, stock and workshop. [GL, Sun MS vol. 303, p. 119]

Hart, Stephen, Silver St, Cirencester, Glos., cm (1820). [D]

Hart, Thomas, address unrecorded, upholder (1723–30). Son of Baulghy Hart, victualler of Leyton, Essex; app. to James Wolfe on 24 April 1723, and admitted freeman of the Upholders' Co. by servitude on 6 May 1730. [GL, Upholders' Co. records] See Balguy Hart snr.

Hart, Thomas, 2 Broughton St, Salford, Lancs., cm (1817). [D]

Hart, Thomas, Gainford, near Darlington, Co. Durham, joiner, cm and cooper (1827–28). [D]

Hart, Thomas, Appleby, Leics., u (1835). [D]

Hart, Thomas, Barton St, Tewkesbury, Glos., chairmaker (1839). [D]

Hart, William, London, carver (1774–81). Trading at Swallow St, Piccadilly in 1774 and Poland St, St James's, Westminster in 1781. [Bristol poll bks]

Hart, William, Southampton, Hants., cm (d.1790). [Will at Hants. RO]

Hart, William, 15 Hogg Hill, Norwich, cm and chairmaker (1789–1818). Recorded also at 1 Orford St, 1801–02. Admitted freeman, not by apprenticeship, on 13 June 1804. Parson J. Woodforde mentioned him in his diary on 13 November 1789: 'Bought this day of Will.ᵐ Hart, Cabinet Maker on Hog Hill, Norwich 2 large second hand double-flapped Mahogany Tables, also one second hand Mahogany dressing Table with Drawers, also one new Mahogany Washing-Stand, for all which paid £4.14.6., that is for the 2 Tables 2.12.6. Dressing Table 1.11.6. Mahogany Wash-Stand 0.10.6. I think the whole of it to be very cheap.' [D; poll bks; Norwich freemen reg.; *Diary of a Country Parson, 1758–1802*, ed. J. Beresford]

Hart, William & John, Market Pl. (or Row), Gt Yarmouth, Norfolk, u (1805–07). [D]

Hart, William, 11 Bolsover St, Oxford St, London, carver and gilder (1808). [D]

Hart, William, Tewkesbury, Glos., chairmaker (1818–37). Trading at High St in 1818; Smith's Lane in 1822 as William Shakespeare Hart; Barton St in 1830; and Church St in 1837 when children's births registered. [D; PR]

Hart, William, Gt Yarmouth, Norfolk, cm and u (1822–39). Trading at George St, 1822–36; Howard St in 1838; and Gaol St, 1839. [D; poll bk]

Hart, William, Wormgate, Boston, Lincs., cm and joiner (1826). [D]

Hart, William, Stockton-upon-Tees, Co. Durham, joiner and cm (1827–32). Recorded at High St in 1827 and Dovecot St in 1832. [D]

Hart, William, High Wycombe, Bucks., chairmaker (b. c.1811–41). Daughter bapt. in 1835, son in 1837. Aged 30 at the time of the 1841 Census. [PR (bapt.)]

Hart & Son, 121 Digbeth, Birmingham, joiners, cm and chairmakers (1805). [D]

Hartdrig, William, 29 Gt Pearl St, Spitalfields, London, cm and u (1839). [D]

Harte, George, Shakespeare's House, Stratford-upon-Avon, Warks., turner and chairmaker. Grandfather of John Harte, chairmaker. See John Harte.

Harte, Jane, Leamington, Warks., chairmaker. Grand-daughter of George Harte. See John Harte.

Harte, John, Cirencester, Glos., chairmaker (1817). Information about him and his ancestors George and Jane, also chairmakers by trade, published in *Chester Guardian and Cambrian Intelligence*, 13 December 1817.

Harterton, William, 79 Christian St, Liverpool, cm (1834). [D]

Hartery, George, 29 Peter St, Bath, Som., cm (1826). [D]

Hartforth, John, Low Rd, Sunderland, Co. Durham, cm and joiner (1828–29). [D]

Hartland, Richard, at 'The King's Head', St Paul's Churchyard, London, cane chairmaker (1717). Insured 'Warehouse only in Labour in rain yard on Lambeth Hill' on 10 December 1717. [GL, Sun MS vol. 7]

Hartland, William snr, 7 Lower Maudlin St, Bristol, carpenter and cm (1805–06). Trading as William & Son in 1806. [D]

Hartland, William jnr, 7 Lower Maudlin St, Bristol, carpenter and cm (1806–09). Trading with his father in 1806. [D]

Hartley, Bernard, Pontefract, Yorks., joiner and cm (1778–96). Took out a Sun Insurance policy in 1778 for £300, £250 accounting for utensils and stock. [GL, Sun MS vol. 266, p. 255] Submitted bill for beds and mahogany furniture totalling £200 8s 6d supplied between December 1794 and August 1796 to G. Wentworth of Woolley Hall, Yorks. [YAS, Wentworth papers, MD 272/2]

Hartley, Christopher, formerly of Whitehaven, Cumb., now of Kingston, Jamaica, cm (1828). Death of his wife Hannah 'at Kingston, Jamaica, a few weeks after her arrival in the Island from London', reported in *Liverpool Mercury*, 13 February 1828.

Hartley, David, Leeds, Yorks., journeyman cm (1791). Named in the *Leeds Cabinet and Chair Makers' Book of Prices*, 1791, amongst other journeymen in basic sympathy with its contents. [*Furn. Hist.*, 1974] Probably:

Hartley, David, 38 Hunslet Lane, Leeds, Yorks., cm and u (1816–26). [D]

Hartley, Edward, Oxford, cm (1798). [D]

Hartley, Edward, Hull, Yorks., wood and ivory turner and bed post carver (1823–26). Trading as a turner in Parade Row, 1823; and at 15 New John St in 1826. [D]

Hartley, George, Bramley's Yd, Lowerhead Row, Leeds, Yorks., cm (1818). [D]

Hartley, George, Broughton-in-Furness, Lancs., chairmaker (1824–28). [D]

Hartley, James, Lancaster, cm (1791–1807). App. to J. Addison in 1791, and admitted freeman, 1806–07, when stated 'of London'. [Lancaster app. reg. and freemen rolls]

Hartley, James, Crown St, Leeds, Yorks., cm (1834–40). [D]

Hartley, John, Lewes, Sussex, cm and chairmaker (1762–80). Advertised in *Sussex Weekly Advertiser*, 3 May 1762 his business 'At the Shop late Mr. William Kelter's in Lewes, MAKES and sells all Sorts of Desk and Book Cases, Bureaus, Chests of Drawers, Cloath Presses, Dining, Dressing and Tea Tables, Tea Trays, Tea Boards, and Tea Chests, Shaving and Bason Stands, Clock Cases &c. &c. Likewise Looking Glasses of all Sorts, and Variey of Chairs and Cabinet Furniture in the genteelest Manner, and at the most reasonable Rates. N.B. Looking Glasses fram'd and Silver'd.' Advertised again on 18 March 1771; and on 5 June 1780 a notice regarding bankruptcy proceedings appeared. [Poll bks]

Hartley, John, 23 Paradise St, Finsbury Sq., London, cm, looking-glass frame maker and undertaker (1808). [D]

Hartley, John, Leeds, Yorks., cm (1822–34). Addresses given at back of Brook St in 1822; 92 Kirkgate, 1826; 2 East Row, 1830; and the Calls, 1834. [D]

Hartley, John jnr, 16 Orange St, Halifax, Yorks., cm (1837). [D]

Hartley, John, Chipping Campden, Glos., cm and u (1839). [D]

Hartley, Lawrence, 3 Spencer Buildings, Hunter St, Liverpool, chairmaker (1829). [D]

Hartley, Richard, Manchester, carver and gilder (1834–40). Recorded at 7 Fountain St in 1834, 17 Abraham's Ct, 1836, and 11 Cooper St, 1840. [D]

Hartley, Richard, 3 Ramsden St, Huddersfield, Yorks., carver (1837). [D]

Hartley, Robert, Leeds, Yorks., cm and joiner (1822–26). Trading at Leylands in 1822 and 8 Little Bridge St, 1826. [D]

Hartley, Robert, 14 Kirkus' Buildings, Hull, Yorks., carver and gilder (1838–39). [D]

Hartley, Thomas, Newgate St, London, freeman merchant tailor, carver and gilder (1767–94). Trading at no. 108, 1777–94; with house at 29 Paradise Row, Islington in 1785. Neo-classical trade card shows chimney-piece and oval frame above with husk chains, and reads: 'Hartley, Carver and Gilder, in Newgate Street, No. 108. Performs all manner of house & furniture Carving, &c. Looking Glasses & frames for Exportation. Prints and Paintings, framed, Cleaned & Lined.' In 1767 employed four non-freemen for six weeks. Took out Sun Insurance policies on 23 November 1785 for £200 on his house at 29 Paradise Row, Islington; in 1777 for £100 on utensils and stock; and in 1793 for £400 on a house at 6 Warwick Lane in tenure of a coney salesman. [D; Banks Coll., BM; GL, City Licence bks, vol. 5; GL, Sun MS vol. 333, p. 500; vol. 261; p. 395; vol. 392, p. 362] See William Hartley, and Hartley & Son.

Hartley, Thomas, Manchester, chairmaker (1813–39). Addresses given at 177 Gt Newton St in 1813; 177 Oldham Rd in 1817; no. 249 in 1825; and 35 Portland St, 1839. [D]

Hartley, Thomas, Wilsden, Yorks., joiner and/or cm (1837). [D]

Hartley, William, 74 Queen St, Lincoln's Inn Fields, London, gilder (1775). Insured his house for £150 in 1775. [GL, Sun MS vol. 238, p. 313]

Hartley, William, Newgate St, London, case and cm, undertaker (1778–83). Addresses given at no. 80, 1778–79; no. 45, 1779–82; and no. 78 in 1783. Neo-classical trade card gives address at no. 80 and trade as knife-case maker. [BM] Admitted freeman of the Upholders' Co. on 2 August 1780. Took out Sun Insurance policies in 1779 for £600 on his house; and in 1781 for £600, £500 accounting for utensils and stock. Named in Bailey's list of bankrupts, 1783. [D; GL, Upholders' Co. records; GL, Sun MS vol. 278, p. 516; vol. 289, p. 410] See Thomas Hartley, and Hartley & Son.

Hartley, William, 23 St James St, Burnley, Lancs., cm and u (1824–25). [D]

Hartley, William, 200 Gt Ancoats St, Manchester, chairmaker (1828). [D]

Hartley, William, Wigton, Cumb., joiner and cm (1828–34). Trading in High St, 1828–29, and West St, 1834. [D]

Hartley, William, Smith St, Warwick, cm and u (1835). [D]

Hartley & Littlewood, Upperhead Row, Leeds, Yorks., cm and u (1817). Possibly the Thomas Littlewood trading alone at Barley Bar in 1818. [D]

Hartley & Son, 108 Newgate St, London, looking-glass and frame makers (1796). [D] See Thomas and William Hartley.

Hartly, Thomas, 6 Bedford Sq., London, carver (1783). Carried out work for Alexander Wedderburn in 1783, receiving payments of £21 10s and £8 8s 'For Mitcham'. [Scottish RO, A. Wedderburn cash bks, GD164/Box 20/177/2–3]

Hartnall, Andrew, Bridgewater, Som., cm (1759–61). Took app named Hutchens in 1759 and Shanock in 1761. [S of G, app. index]

Hartridge, John, Maidstone, Kent, upholder (1734). [Poll bk]

Hartridge, W., Woodbridge, Suffolk, cm (1809). Notice in *Ipswich Journal*, 3 June 1809.

Hartshorn, J., High St, Shrewsbury, Salop, cm (1786–98). [D]

Hartshorn, Michael, 40 Campo Lane, Sheffield, Yorks., cm and u (1828–33). [D]

Hartshorne, George, Broseley, Salop, cm (1822–35). Recorded as George jnr, 1822–28. [D]

Hartstongue, Robert, Norwich, u (1710). His son, Standish, admitted freeman on 6 September 1710. [Norwich freemen reg.]

Hartstongue, Standish, St Peter Mancroft, Norwich, u (1710–d. 1717). Son of Robert Hartstongue; admitted freeman on 6 September 1710. Will proved in 1717. [Norwich freemen reg. and poll bk; Norfolk Record Soc., index of wills]

Harvey, —, address unrecorded. Received payments for furniture from 2nd Viscount Palmerston at Broadlands, Hants. [*C. Life*, 29 January 1981, p. 290]

Harvey, Benjamin, Canterbury, Kent, cm (1796–1830). Trading in Broad St, 1818 and 1830, and St Paul's, 1826. Listed as freeman in 1796. [Poll bks; Canterbury freemen rolls]

Harvey, C., Worthington's Lane, Dover, Kent, cm (1831). [D]

Harvey, Charles, London, freeman u (1714–20). Trading at 'The Cross Keys', Ludgate Hill, 1714–17; moved to Salisbury Sq. on 15 April 1719; and Hind Ct, Fleet St on 22 August 1720. Insured goods and merchandise in his house on 22 July 1714 with the Sun Co. Fined for non-service at St Bride's in 1717, in which year he was named in newspapers. [GL, Sun MS vol. 4, ref. 4239; GL, MS 6561, p. 21; Heal]

Harvey, Charles, Colchester, Essex, cm (1830–31). [Poll bks]

Harvey, Christopher, Colchester, Essex, cm (1806). [Poll bk]

Harvey, Christopher jnr, Colchester, Essex, cm (1812–20). [Poll bks]

Harvey, Edward, Chester, upholder (1747). [Poll bk]

Harvey, George, Frodsham, Cheshire, chairmaker (1822–34). [D]

Harvey, George, 647 Steep Hill, Lincoln, cm, u and furniture broker (1841). [D]

Harvey (or Harvie), Harwar, or Harwar, Harvey, Chester, u (1736–59). Son of Lucretia Harvie, widow; app. to Abner Scoles, u, and admitted freeman on 9 October 1736. Polled in 1747. Took apps named John Stringer in 1749, Thomas Garratt in 1754 and Brown in 1759. [Chester freemen rolls and app. bks; S of G, app. index]

Harvey, Henry, Marylebone, London, upholder (1792). [Bailey's list of bankrupts]

Harvey, Henry, Falmouth, Cornwall, cm (1809). Purchased property in the parish of Stithians. [Cornwall RO, DD WH 3182] See Harvey & Son.

Harvey, Henry, 25 Holywell Lane, London, chair and sofa maker (1822–28). [D]

Harvey, Henry, Oaten Hill, Canterbury, Kent, cm (1830). [Poll bk]

Harvey, Henry, 11 Artillery St, Bishopsgate, London, chair and sofa maker (1839). [D]

Harvey, James & Edward, Church St, Penzance, Cornwall, cm etc. (1823–30). Recorded also in North St, 1824. [D]

Harvey, John, King's Lynn, Norfolk, u (1681–82). App. to Daniel Goodwyn, u, and admitted freeman, 1681–82. [King's Lynn freemen's calendar]

Harvey, John, Helston, Cornwall, cm (1793). Named with others regarding lease of property in Perran Sands, dated 27 and 28 December 1793. [Cornwall RO, DD SHM 435/1–2]

Harvey, John, 12 Brunswick St, Liverpool, cm (1827). [D]

Harvey, Richard, Hull, Yorks., cm, paper hanger and broker (1814–26). Trading at 7 New Dock St in 1814; 18 Postern Gate, 1817–23, and no. 17 in 1826. [D]

Harvey, Richard, High Gate, Hawkhurst, Kent, cm and carpenter (1838). [D]

Harvey, Robert, King St, London, carver (1784). [Poll bk]

Harvey, Robert, Witham, Essex, cm and upholder (1784). [D]

Harvey, Robert, Aylsham, Norfolk, carver and gilder (1822–d. 1842). Trading in Hungate St, 1830. Will proved at Norwich in 1842. [D; Norfolk Record Soc., index of wills]

Harvey, Samuel, 10 George St, Derby, cm and u (1835). [D]

Harvey, Thomas, King's Lynn, Norfolk, cm (1776–77). App. to James Lyther, cm; admitted freeman, 1776–77. [King's Lynn freemen's calendar]

Harvey, Thomas, 56 Ratcliff Highway, London, u (1829). [D]

Harvey, William, Liverpool, cm and u (1794–1827). Addresses given at Tempest Hey in 1794; 23 Haymarket in 1805; no. 22, 1807–11; 16 Brunswick Pl. with shop at 3 Spitalfields, 1813–14; 10 Brunswick Pl., 1818; no. 12, 1821–33; 13–14 Brunswick St in 1824; 58 London Rd. and 16 Brunswick Rd in 1827. Marriage to Miss Donnelly at St Nicholas's Church on 2 March 1794 reported in *Williamson's Liverpool Advertiser*, 3 March. Petitioned freedom as son of Joseph Harvey, baker, in 1796, paying 3s 4d. Admitted freeman on 27 May 1796. Took apps named George Peers and Thomas Howard in 1803, petitioned freedom in 1812; John Allen in 1804 and Joseph Robinson in 1805, both petitioned freedom in 1812; William Brown in 1808, petitioned freedom in 1816; Robert Summers in 1810, petitioned in 1818; George Brown and Daniel Keating in 1811, petitioned in 1818; Thomas Kneen in 1815, petitioned in 1822; John McMay in 1816, petitioned in 1823; and Henry Davies in 1817, petitioned in 1824. Took apps named Richard Smith in 1818; Henry Seddon in 1820; John Evans in 1822; Thomas Davies in 1823; and Richard Seddon in 1824. [D; Liverpool freemen's committee bk and app. enrolment bk] Possibly two tradesmen of the same name are concerned here.

Harvey, William Henry, 1 Portland Row, Morice Town, Devonport, Devon, cm and u (1830). [D]

Harvey, William, Damgate St, Wymondham, Norfolk, cm and chairmaker (1830–39). [D]

Harvey, William, on the Mount, Ipswich, Suffolk, cm and u (1839). [Poll bk]

Harvey & Son, Falmouth, Cornwall, cm (1805). [D] See Henry Harvey.

Harvy, John, Liverpool, cm (1757). Petitioned freedom on servitude to Josiah Baxendale in 1757, paying 6s 8d. [Liverpool freemen's committee bk]

Harwell, Thomas jnr, Bristol, cm and sworn measurer (1805–21). Trading at 8 Newfoundland St in 1805; 3 Grove, 1809–13; 4 King St in 1814; and 3 Grove, 1815–21. [D]

Harwick, Asty, King's Lynn, Norfolk, u (1743–60). App. to Thomas Preston, u; admitted freeman, 1743–44. Former apps admitted freemen: Robinson Crusoe, 1754–55, and John Chadwick jnr, 1759–60. [King's Lynn freemen's calendar] See Asty Hardwick.

Harwick, Thomas, King's Lynn, Norfolk, u (1689–99). Admitted freeman by apprenticeship, 1698–99. [King's Lynn freemen's calendar]

Harwin, Robert, Swaffham, Norfolk, cm (1795–98). [D; poll bk]

Harwood, Abraham, 16 Wenrose Sq., London, u (1789). [D]

Harwood, J., 49 Rosoman St, Clerkenwell, London, cm etc. (1835). [D]

Harwood, James, 20 Stanley St, Liverpool, cm and furniture broker (1837). [D]

Harwood, John, 51 Spring Gdns, Bolton, Lancs., joiner and cm (1818). [D]

Harwood, John, Liverpool, cm (1827–39). Trading at 10 Poplar Lane in 1827; 18 Stanley St, 1829–37; and no. 35 in 1839. [D]

Harwood, John Philip snr, Shrewsbury, Salop, cm (1796). Father of John Philip Harwood jnr, cm. [Shrewsbury burgess roll]

Harwood, John Philip jnr, Frankwell, Shrewsbury, Salop, cm (1830). Son of John Philip Harwood snr, cm. [Shrewsbury burgess roll]

Harwood, Richard, 23 Hanway St, London, broker, carver and gilder (1775). Took out a Sun Insurance policy in 1775 for £500 of which utensils, stock and goods accounted for £300. [GL, Sun MS vol. 243, p. 348]

Harwood, Samuel, 79 Leman St, Goodman's Fields, London, u (1809–11). [D] See Harwood & Allen.

Harwood, Thomas, St Peter Mancroft, Norwich, u (1729–61). Son of Thomas Harwood, Esq., admitted freeman on 26 April 1729. [Norwich freemen rolls and poll bks]

Harwood, Thomas, 125 Bishopsgate St Without, London, upholder and cm (1781–83). Son of William Harwood, upholder of Brick Lane, Spitalfields; app. to his father on 5 February 1772, and admitted freeman of the Upholders' Co. by servitude on 4 April 1781. Took out a Sun Insurance policy in 1781 for £1,000 of which £800 accounted for utensils and stock. Declared bankrupt, *Liverpool Advertiser*, 10 and 29 April 1783. [GL, Upholders' Co. records; GL, Sun MS vol. 290, p. 635] See William Harwood.

Harwood, William, Brick Lane, Spitalfields, London, u (1771–84). Admitted freeman of the Upholders' Co. on 3 April 1771. Took his son, Thomas, as app., 1772–81, when admitted freeman. Insured house with Robert Woodgate, Esq., for £500 in 1775. Took out Sun Insurance policies with Thomas Harwood in 1780 for £1,500, £1,000 on utensils and stock; and in 1783 Ann Hayden at William Harwood's, upholder, 55 Brick Lane, insured houses for £1,600. [D; GL, Upholders' Co. records; GL, Sun MS vol. 240, p. 610; vol. 281, p. 99; vol. 317, p. 515] See Harwood & Allen.

Harwood, William, 18 Conduit St, London, carver and gilder (1794). On 10 April 1794 receipted bill of Mary Cowper for pottery supplied to Sir John Nelthorpe. [Lincoln RO, NEL VIII/13]

Harwood & Allen, Wellclose Sq., London, cm (1790–93). May be related to Samuel and William Harwood in the nearby Goodman's Fields and Spitalfields. [D]

Harwood & Haines, 9 Grosvenor Rd, Chelsea, London, u (1826–27). [D]

Haselden, —, Lancaster, cm (1795). Death of his wife on 25 April reported in *Billinge's Liverpool Advertiser*, 27 April 1795.

Haselden, William, Soup St, Ashton-under-Lyne, Lancs., painter and gilder (1824). [D]

Haselton, William, Cheltenham, Glos., cm (1777). Took out a Sun Insurance policy in 1777 for £200, utensils, stock and goods accounting for £50. [GL, Sun MS vol. 261, p. 583]

Hasert, Peter, London, cm and looking-glass maker (1692–1746); Hasert, Peter, cm and looking-glass maker (1746–51). In June 1692 Hasert, sometimes called Hazard, was fined as a Papist for refusing the oath of fidelity. [Westminster Ref. Lib., Middlx session bk 498, pp. 76–79] He was then working as a cabinet-maker in Long Acre. He is next noted in 1720 as working for Robert Harley, first Earl of Oxford (1661–1724), when his address was 'at the Hen & Chickens in Great Queen Street', premises occupied by a cm named Davis in 1710. [Heal] Hasert worked for Harley at his London library in Dover St and at Wimpole Hall, Cambs., and continued to work for Edward Harley, second Earl of

Oxford (1689–1741) until at least 1725. In early 1720 Robert Harley employed a cm named Bridgewater, whom Hasert may have succeeded. Hasert's work, as recorded by Harley's librarian, Humfrey Wanley, involved maintenance, the making of pedestals for statues, book-presses, drawers for coins, and the packing of books for transport. Wanley also reveals that in 1724 Hasert gave as an excuse for delay that 'one of his Men is gone beyond the seas'. In July 1722 Wanley received the upholsterer Humfrey Skelton, who wished to inspect the disposition of the presses at Dover St on behalf of Robert Myddleton of Chirk Castle, who was planning to build a library there, and in April 1723 he was visited by Ellis Roberts, the joiner, who came to inspect some of the book presses, having been commissioned to make some more for the Earl of Oxford; on both occasions works by Hasert may have served as potential models. On 31 August 1724 Hasert, described as cabinet and looking-glass maker (Wanley also hints at the latter activity), insured his goods and merchandize for £200 and on 31 October his goods, merchandize and dwelling house for £800. [GL, Sun MS vol. 13] In 1722 and 1725 Hasert worked for Rebecca Tufnell of Langleys; in 1726 he was a supplier to Tredegar House, Mons.; in 1727–29 he worked for Sir William Monson and Lord Monson; and in 1735 for Lady Fortescue, born a Huddleston and therefore a recusant. The next reference [Heal] is to Hasert's involvement, with other tradesmen, in an elaborate hoax played on Hulton the printseller in Pall Mall in 1744. This may, however, refer to his future successor of the same name, as Hasert must have been old for jokes by then, and died in early July 1746 in Paris 'on his intended journey for Italy': he was then described as 'a very eminent Cabinet Maker near Lincoln's Inn Fields'. [*General Advertiser*, 16 July 1746] This absence abroad so soon after 1745 raises the suspicion that Hasert may have been not only a Papist, but also a Jacobite. His business came to an end in 1751 when the following announcement appeared in the *London Evening Post*, 13–16 April: 'To be sold by Hand, at the Hen & Chickens in Great Queen Street, near Lincoln's Inn Fields, on Thursday the 18th instant, and the following Days, The general Stock in Trade of Mr Peter Hasert, Cabinet and Looking Glass Maker; also the Materials for grinding and silvering Looking Glass, and the Benches and Tools for Cabinet-makers. All will be sold cheap, he leaving off Trade. The Household Goods will also be sold.'
DOVER ST, London and WIMPOLE HALL, Cambs. (Robert Harley, 1st Earl of Oxford, and Edward Harley, 2nd Earl of Oxford). 1720–25: Sixty mentions in the diary of Humfrey Wanley, librarian to the first and second Earls of Oxford. [C. E. Wright and R. C. Wright (ed.), *The Diary of Humfrey Wanley 1715–1726*, 1966, I, 70–71, 109, 128, 130, 183; II, 213, 220, 249, 260–61, 266, 285, 291–92, 301–02, 304, 312, 314–16, 318–24, 327, 344–45, 351, 353, 356–58, 363]
LANGLEYS, Essex (Rebecca Tufnell). 1722 and 1725: account book entries, the first 19s for 'Mounting a Screen', the second is for 'Japaning a Tea Table Black'. [Essex RO, D/D Tu278]
TREDEGAR HOUSE, Mons. (Sir William Morgan). 1726: Payment 'Cabinet Maker £79.0.0, Mr Hasert the cabinet maker £4.14.6'. [Nat. Lib. Wales, Tredegar papers, MS 315–45]
BURTON HALL, Lincs. (Sir William Monson, Bt, and John, 1st Baron Monson). 1727–29: Bills. One bill dated 24 July 1727, headed 'Work done for the Honble. Sr Willm Monson', who died in 1726/27, for 'Makeing a dineing table of your own mahogany', etc., £1 18s 6d, receipted 1728. One bill dated 1729 to Lord Monson 'For a mahogany table on a pillow & claw the top 24 inches overturned £1.10.0'. [Lincoln RO, Monson 11/50]
SAWSTON HALL, Cambs. (Lady Fortescue). 1735-36 Bill to 'the Honble Lady Fortescue' (Mary, daughter of Richard

Huddleston', total £13 6s, including (February 1735/36) a mahogany corner table, a large mahogany voyder, a dressing glass in a walnut frame, and (May 1736) 'A Sconce in a tabernacle frame carv'd and guilt . . . with a pair of brass branches'. [Cambs. RO, Sawston Hall accounts]   S.J.

Haskens, Joseph, Bristol, u (1713). Took app. named Crump in 1713. [S of G, app. index].

Hasker, Ann, 11 Marshall St, Carnaby Mkt, London, u (1784). Took out a Sun Insurance policy in 1784 for £100, utensils, and stock accounting for £50. [GL, Sun MS vol. 322, p. 641]

Haskins, Edward, Bristol, u (1734). [Poll bk]

Haskins, James, Bristol, cm (1754). [Poll bk]

Haslegrave, Benjamin, Heath, near Wakefield, Yorks., cm (1822). [D]

Haslehurst (or Hazehurst, Hazelhurst or Hazlehurst), Samuel, Liverpool, chairmaker (1769–1834). Addresses given at 21 Paradise St, 1769–87; no. 24 in 1790; as S. Hazehurst, stained chair warehouse, Manesty's Lane, 1781–90; 43 Paradise St, 1813–14; and 14 Wellington St, 1829–34. Took out a Sun Insurance policy in 1776 for £300, workshop, utensils and stock accounting for £150. Sale of land fronting Manesty's Lane, 'now used as a yard by Samuel Haslehurst, chairmaker', announced in *Williamson's Liverpool Advertiser*, 1 August 1782. Declared bankrupt, *Derby Mercury*, 13 February 1794. [D; GL, Sun MS vol. 247, p. 129] Probably two tradesmen of the same name are concerned here.

Haslep, Peter, Foundry Lane, Warrington, Lancs., cm (1828). [D]

Hasler, Thomas, 6 East St, Finsbury Mkt, London, japan furniture maker (1829–39). [D]

Haslet, David, 15 St James's St, Liverpool, cm (1807). [D]

Haslewood, Henry, Bridgnorth, Salop, cm (1751). Took app. named Cartwright in 1751. [S of G, app. index]

Haslop, Isaac, Radford, Worksop, Notts., cm (1835). [D]

Hason(?), Thomas, address unrecorded. On 26 April 1783 received £10 10s for a set of dining tables supplied to Sir John Nelthorpe. [Lincoln RO, NEL 9/5/15]

Hassall, Charles, formerly of Whitehaven, Cumb., joiner and cm (1831). His eldest daughter's marriage on 17 July 1831 to Ross McIntyre at St Martin-in-the-Fields reported in *Liverpool Mercury*, 22 July 1831.

Hassall (or Hassell), Samuel, 23 Bull Green, Halifax, Yorks., carver and gilder (1834–47). Three carved mirrors recorded as by Hassall, two in the Rococo revival style, c.1830–40, bearing label. Undated trade card also known. [Christie's NY, 30 June 1979, lot 90, illus.; *Conn.*, August 1963, p. xii; *C. Life*, 3 October 1974, pp. 932–33]

Hassall, Thomas, address unrecorded, upholder (1706). Admitted freeman of the Upholders' Co. on 7 August 1706. [GL, Upholders' Co. records]

Hassall (or Hassell), William, 13 Greengate St, Salford, Lancs., carver and gilder (1832–33). Recorded as William jnr in 1833. [D]

Hassan, George, London, carver (1749–74). Recorded at Little Newport St in 1749 and Thatched House in 1774. Provided picture frames for Sir Edward Knatchbull of Mersham-Le-Hatch, Kent, in 1772: seven costing £38 11s 9d, and nine, £24 2s 2d. [Westminster poll bks; Kent RO, U.951, A.18/68–69]

Hassocks, Nathaniel, 31 Brighton Pl., Brighton, Sussex, carver and gilder (1823). [D]

Hastings, John, Oxford, cm (1729). Took app. named Smith in 1729. [S of G, app. index]

Hastings, John, Spilsby, Lincs., joiner and cm (1826–35). [D]

Hastrick, John, 16 Rolls Buildings, Fetter Lane, London, cm (1829). [D]

Haswell, William, Bowser's Yd, Market Pl., Morpeth, Northumb., joiner and cm (1827–29). [D]

Hatch, Edward, 442 High St, Cheltenham, Glos., cm, u and carpet manufacturer (1820). [D]

Hatch, John, High Holborn, London, cm (1763). [D]

Hatch, Joseph, Robert St, Bedford Row, London, cm (1802). Notice regarding bankruptcy proceedings in *Billinge's Liverpool Advertiser*, 21 June 1802.

Hatch, William, Norwich, cm (1793–98). Subscribed to Sheraton's *Drawing Book*, 1793. [D]

Hatch, William Proctor, Norwich, cm (1808–30). App. to William De Caux, cm; admitted freeman on 24 September 1808. [Norwich freemen reg.; poll bk]

Hatcher, Charles, Tarrant St, Arundel, Sussex, chairmaker (1839). [D]

Hatcher, Robert, Southampton, Hants., cm (1823–39). Trading at 108 High St, 1823–24, and Behind the Walls, 1836–39. [D]

Hatchwell, Robert, East St, Newton Abbott, Devon, cm (1823–38). [D]

Hathaway, John Hankin, address unrecorded, upholder (1756). Son of Thomas Hathaway, freeman upholder of London. Admitted freeman of the Upholders' Co. by patrimony on 3 Jun 1756. [GL, Upholders' Co. records]

Hathaway, Thomas, address unrecorded, upholder (1726–d. by 1756). Son of John Hathaway, freeman barber-surgeon of London; app. to John Howard jnr and admitted freeman of the Upholders' Co. on 6 July 1726. Took apps named John Hodges, 1727–30, and Thomas Denham, 1735–41. [GL, Upholders' Co. records]

Hathwell, —, London, frame maker (1781). Charles Towneley of Towneley Hall, Lancs., paid Hathwell £10 10s for frames for two 'Views' by da Costa on 3 March 1781. [Towneley's account bk, private ownership]

Hathwell, J., facing the Dial Slip, Broad Quay, Bristol, frame maker (c.1800). Printed label recorded on back of small rectangular gilt frame with bead moulding, c.1800, in the V&A Museum. Label reads 'Gold enamelling on glass ... frames for glasses, pictures & drawings mounted ... black frames in a new style...'. [V&A archives]

Hathwell, John, King St, Westminster, London, carver and gilder (1767–68). Declared bankrupt, *Gents Mag.*, October 1767, and notice regarding bankruptcy proceedings in *Williamson's Liverpool Advertiser*, 1 January 1768.

Hathwell (or Hatherwell), Thomas, 17 High St, Bloomsbury, London, japan chair and sofa maker (1820–28). Recorded alone and also as Hathwell & Pastor. [D]

Hatley, Thomas, London, upholder (1706–23). Recorded in the Drury Lane area, 1722. Admitted freeman of the Upholders' Co. on 2 October 1706. Took app. named John Fox, 1708–23. Took out a Hand in Hand Insurance policy in 1722 for £475 on three houses, let. [GL, Upholders' Co. records; GL, Hand in Hand MS vol. 26, p. 318]

Hat(t)ley, William, Belford, Northumb., joiner and cm (1827–34). [D]

Hatley & Purves, High St, Berwick, Northumb., cm and u (1828–29). [D]

Hatt, John, Aldersgate St, London, cm, chairmaker and glass grinder (1759–79). Trading at no. 23, 1767–73; and no. 142, 1774–79. Rococo trade card, 1759, gives address at 'The Blue Ball & Artichoke', Aldersgate St, and states that Hatt is successor to John Arrowsmith, and 'Makes & Sells all Sorts of Comodes & Book Cases, Desk & Book Cases, Library Cases, Chests of Drawers, Cloaths Presses, Bedsteads, Comodes, Dressing & Tea Tables & all manner of Chairs & Cabinet work. Likewise does Upholstery work in the neatest manner. Also Blinds for Windows & Spring Curtains, Looking Glasses of all Sorts, Coach Glasses & Lanthorns. Variety of Gothic &

Chinese work in Chairs & Cabinet furniture made up and Sold Wholesale and Retail at very reasonable Rates, & for Exportation. NB. Funerals Furnishd.' [D; Heal]

Hattlebarrow, Samuel, 39 Little Lever St, Manchester, chairmaker (1825). [D]

Hatton, Edward, 5 Kirkman Pl., Tottenham Ct Rd, London, carver (1792). Took out a Sun Insurance policy on 17 November 1792 for £100. [GL, Sun MS vol. 379, ref. 607302]

Hatton, John, Lancaster, u (1811–12). [Lancaster freemen rolls]

Hatton, John, Liverpool, cm (1825). App. to William Atkinson in 1825. [Liverpool app. enrolment bk]

Hatton, Leonard, Broker's Row, Moorfields, London, cm and u (1778–93). Recorded at no. 13, 1790–93. Took out a Sun Insurance policy in 1778 with William Gough for £700 on warehouse, utensils and stock. [D; GL, Sun MS vol. 268, p. 37]

Hatton, Thomas, Lancaster. Named in the Gillow records, 1790–91 and 1802, including work on a table. [Westminster Ref. Lib., Gillow vol. 344/98, p. 1713]

Haugh, John, Carlisle, Cumb., u (1793–1810). Trading in Market Pl., 1810. [D]

Haughton, George, London, later Philadelphia, USA, u (before 1775). Advertised in *Penn'a Packet*, 30 January 1775 that he was 'Lately from London' and 'has taken a house in Second-street ... where he proposes to follow the Upholstery business in all its various branches. As he has had the advantage of serving a regular apprenticeship to that trade in one of the most capital shops in London, and of working in most of the others, and has done the principal work some time in this city for Mr. Webster, he does not doubt of giving satisfaction to those Ladies and Gentlemen that will please to employ him in any part of the business ... He makes the new fashion'd French corner chairs, conversation stools, sofas, Venetion window blinds, and bedsteads of all sorts; Fringe line Tossels made to any pattern or quality, on the shortest notice.' Repeated the advertisement in *Penn'a Gazette*, 22 March 1775, adding 'rooms neatly papered, and ship cabins fitted up in the neatest manner, chairs, sofas, &c. stuffed on very low terms for Cabinet-makers, in exchange for cabinet goods ... Any Merchant that has a quantity of paper hangings may meet with a purchaser, by applying as above.' Advertised for an app. in *Penn'a Evening Post*, 18 May 1776, and announced that he had moved to premises in Front St 'where he makes and sells every article in the upholstery business. Likewise makes and sells drums, colours, tent bedsteads, chairs, stools, tables, mattresses, markees, and every other article necessary for the military...'. Advertised again in the same paper on 14 October 1777 as 'formerly a workman to Mr. Trotter in London'; and in *Penn'a Packet*, 16 April 1782 that he 'has again entered into his former business' in Front St, presumably after a break. He again described his trade, adding 'he has followed the Upholstery Business for some years, in this city, very extensively and with general applause, both for his workmanship and low charges...'. [*Walpole Soc.*, 1929]

Haughton, Thomas, Stamford, Lincs., u (1735). Admitted freeman in 1735 on payment of £15. [Stamford freemen rolls]

Haughton & Cranburn, Oxford St, London, upholders and cm (1765). [D]

Haupt, Georg, resident in London 1767 or 1768–69, cm (b.1741–d.1784). Georg Haupt was born in Stockholm on 10 August 1741. His father, Elias Haupt, was a master cm whose position in the Cabinet-Makers' Guild appears to have entitled his son to preferential treatment. The young man was app. at thirteen, some nine months before he was eligible, to a leading Swedish cm, Johan Conrad Eckstein. His apprenticeship lasted for five years only, from 1754–59 after which he was given temporary work with Eckstein's uncle, Friedrich Eckstein, Master of the Cabinet-Makers' Guild.

The significant years of his career, in so far as his work in London is concerned, were those he spent as a journeyman. His first visit was to Germany in 1760. Then, together with his future brother-in-law, Christopher Fuhrlohg he set off in 1762 to Amsterdam, moving on in 1764 to Paris. It is not known for whom the two young men worked in Amsterdam but evidence suggests that they were employed in Paris in the workshop of Simon Oeben, brother of Jean-François. The basis for this suggestion is the existence of a *bureau plat*, signed by Haupt. [Institut Géographique National, Paris] The inscription on the piece in red chalk reads: 'George Haupt Suedois a fait cet bureau a Chanteloup 1767.' The desk bears the inventory mark of the Château de Chanteloup, country seat of the Duc de Choiseul, Simon Oeben's foremost patron. It is of solid mahogany and, for such an early date, severely Neo-classical in style. A writing desk and filing cabinet [Musée des Beaux-Arts, Tours] also bears the inventory marks of the Château de Chanteloup. These pieces, decorated with marquetry in a geometrical design, have been attributed to Simon Oeben. Svend Eriksen has expressed the view, however, that their quality is not such as to justify an attribution to the French master and that they may, more probably, have been made by the young journeyman, Georg Haupt, while he was working at Chateloup in 1766–67. A study of the signed bureau plat and the writing desk and filing cabinet [illus. Svend Eriksen, op. cit., below] throws light on the experience of the newly emerging Neo-classical style that Haupt had gained in Paris.

Meanwhile, in the Summer of 1766, Haupt's nephew, the painter Elias Martin, had arrived in Paris to join his two compatriots. Christopher Fuhrlohg was the first to move on to London. Elias Martin and Haupt followed either at the end of 1767 or early in 1768. It may have been in Paris or after their arrival in London that Martin painted a portrait of his uncle, now in the possession of the Nodiska Museet, Stockholm. It shows the young man, in lace cravat and blue silk waistcoat, seated casually at a carved and gilt table with an open book and a pair of compasses in his hands. [illus. Lagerquist, op. cit.]

There were two points of contact of which Haupt made use on his arrival in London. The first was the Swedish Church where the young cm received communion, according to the church records, on 7 February 1768. The second was the architect, William Chambers, who had been born in Sweden and is known to have kept closely in touch with Swedish immigrants and visitors to England. He was also on good terms with the Swedish Court and subsequently, in 1772, was awarded a Knighthood in the Order of the Polar Star. Haupt's relationship with Chambers is documented by the only piece of furniture (now in the V & A) definitely known to have been made by him while he was in England. This is a small square satinwood table with one drawer, inlaid with laurel festoons, the top consisting of nine specimen plaques of coloured marbles. It is inscribed beneath in ink 'Cette table a été Commandé et Dessiné par Mr. Chambers Premier Architect de Sa Majesté Britannique et execute par son très humble Serviteur George Haupt Suedois, Londres le 4 Fevrier 1769'. [illus. Hayward and Kirkham]

Haupt may have set up his own workshop in London but there is no evidence to support this view. There is, however, evidence that Christopher Fuhrlohg was employed for a limited period by John Linnell at his Berkeley Sq. workshop until he eventually set up on his own at 24 Tottenham Ct Rd. There are grounds for suggesting that Haupt may have joined

his friend in working for John Linnell for the short time which he spent in England. Fuhrlohg's connection with John Linnell is established elsewhere. This connection very probably originated through William Chambers since Chambers and the Linnell firm had both been employed by the Child family at Osterley Park, Middlx. When Fuhrlohg, and then Haupt, arrived in England, John Linnell was engaged upon furnishing the Library at Osterley Park. Of the pieces provided and still in the Library, the two *bureaux plats* are essentially French in character. The large pedestal desk is richly inlaid with laurel wreaths, heavy oak-leaf swags and urns with stiff, angular handles. All these motifs can be paralleled in Haupt's work executed in Sweden after his return to his own country. [Lagerquist, op. cit.] They were certainly not then part of the repertoire of marquetry ornament used by John Linnell. One further piece supplied to Osterley at the same time is even more relevant in pointing to Haupt's authorship: the fall-front medal cabinet made for Robert Child and still in the possession of Lord Jersey, descendant of the family. [illus. Hayward and Kirkham] This is inlaid with motifs such as diaper patterns, medallions with heavy swags looped and suspended into heart-shaped surrounds and urns set on pedestals with high, angular handles. These features occur in Haupt's work and, in particular, on a writing-table and filing cabinet made by Haupt for the King of Sweden in 1770. [The Royal Palace, Stockholm, illus. Hayward and Kirkham] There are hardly such telling parallels between the Osterley pieces and the known pieces made subsequently by Fuhrlohg in England although both Swedish cm may have been involved. Their shared experiences came to an end when Haupt was informed by the Swedish envoy, Gustav Adam von Nolcken on 1 August 1769 of his appointment in Sweden as *Ébeniste du Roi*. His work in England must have been outstanding to warrant such an appointment. The Osterley pieces are certainly of the highest quality and if, indeed, they were his work, they would surely have demonstrated his skill. [M. Lagerquist et M. Jarry, 'Note sur une table d'ébeniste George Haupt découverte en France', *Revue de l'Art Français*, 1953, pp. 239–40; G. de Bellaigue, 'English Marquetry's debt to France', *C. Life*, 13 June 1968; J. Hayward, 'Christopher Fürlohg, an Anglo-Swedish Cabinet-Maker', *Burlington*, CXI, 1969, 648–55; J. Harris, *Sir William Chambers, Knight of the Polar Star*, London, 1970; C. Streeter, 'Marquetry furniture by a brilliant London Master', *Met. Museum Bulletin*, June 1971, pt 1, pp. 418–29; J. Hayward, 'A newly discovered commode signed by Christopher Fürlohg', *Burlington*, CXIV, 1972, 704–12; E. Andrén, *Snickare Schatullmakare och Ebenister i Stockholm*, Nordiska Museet, Stockholm, 1973; S. Eriksen, *Early Neo-Classicism in France*, London, 1974; J. Hayward, 'A further note on Christopher Fürlohg', *Burlington*, CXIX, 1977, 486–93; H. Lagerquist, *Georg Haupt Ebéniste du Roi*, Nordiska Museet, Stockholm, 1979; H. Hayward and P. Kirkham, *William and John Linnell*, 1980] H.H.

Hauxwell, —, Coppergate, York, cm (1773). Advertised in *York Courant*, 23 November 1773. [*Furn. Hist.*, 1971] Possibly William Hawkswell (or Hawxwell).

Havard, James, 48 John St, Fitzroy Sq., London, carpenter, joiner and cm (1808). [D]

Have, Thomas, 24 Lambeth Rd, London, chair and sofa maker (1827–28). [D]

Haven, Edward, Liverpool, u (1761–1802). Admitted freeman in 1761. His son, Edward Haven, mariner, born 1763, petitioned freedom on birthright in 1802. [Liverpool freemen's committee bk]

Haven, Margaret, 32 Chorley St, Liverpool, u (1790). [D]

Havre, John, address unrecorded, picture frame maker (1741).

A Hugenot, he supplied frames for Petworth House, Sussex, in 1741. [*C. Life*, 25 September 1980, p. 1030]

Haw, William, address unrecorded, carpenter (1812). He repaired and adapted kitchen furniture at a total cost of £101 15s for the 6th Duke of Bedford at the time of the latter's move from Stanhope St to Hamilton Pl., London, on about 10 March 1812. [Bedford Office, London]

Haward (or Hayward), William, London, chairmaker (1812–31). [Colchester poll bks]

Hawes, Edmund, High Wycombe, Bucks., chair caner (1827–32). Sons bapt. in 1827, 1829, 1830 and 1832. [PR (bapt.)]

Hawes, James, West Wycombe, Bucks., chairmaker (1798). [Militia Census]

Hawes, M., 2 Eldon Pl., Islington, London, cm (1826–27). [D]

Hawes, Mary, 2 Lower St, Islington, London, cm and u (1827–28). [D]

Hawes, Samuel, address unrecorded, cm (1803). Subscribed to Sheraton's *Cabinet Dictionary*, 1803.

Hawes, Thomas, 184 Holiwell St, London, u (1784). [D]

Hawes, William, High Wycombe, Bucks., chairmaker (1798–1839). Listed in the Militia Census, 1798. Sons bapt. in 1835 and 1839. [PR (bapt.)]

Hawey, —, St Columb, Cornwall, cm (1798). [D]

Hawford, James, at 'The Blue Boar', Cornhill, London, cm (1710–18). Submitted bill, dated 22 November 1710, to Sir Gilbert Heathcote for five glass sconces at 10s, and three at 15s. Took out Sun Insurance policies on 18 October 1717 for his house; and on 6 November 1718 for goods and merchandise in his house at Enfield, Middlx. [Lincoln RO, 2 ANC 12.d.5; GL, Sun MS vol. 7; vol. 8, ref. 12516]

Hawitt, William, Newton-upon-Ouse, Yorks., cm (1774). Son of William Hawitt, baker; admitted freeman of York in 1774. [York freemen rolls and poll bk]

Hawke, Richard, St Day, Cornwall, chairmaker (1830). [D]

Hawker, George, Bristol, upholder (1774–1817). Trading at 9 Norfolk St, 1809–12, and no. 21, 1813–17. [D; poll bks]

Hawker, John, 5 Old St, London, cm (1808). [D]

Hawkes, Henry, London, cm (1818). [Norwich poll bk]

Hawkes, Thomas, Cross Lane, Long Acre, London, carver (1779). Took out a Sun Insurance policy in 1779 for £200 of which £50 accounted for utensils, stock and goods. [GL, Sun MS vol. 278, p. 490]

Hawkesford, William, 30 Whittal St, Birmingham, cm (1839). [D]

Hawkesworth, William, 32 Newman St, Oxford St, London, appraiser and u (1817–19). [D]

Hawking, Abraham, 114 Whitechapel Rd, London, bedstead and cm (1809–11). [D]

Hawkings, —, 6 Lisson Grove North, London, u (1835). [D] Probably John Hawkins.

Hawkins, —, at 'The Royal Bed', New Bond St, Hanover Sq., London, upholder, cm and sworn appraiser (d. by 1767). Rococo trade card continues: 'Makes & Sells all sorts of Upholstery Goods &c. And furnishes Funerals Public or Private at Reasonable Rates.' Bill on back of card dated 23 November 1767 from Elizabeth Hawkins, perhaps the tradesman's widow. [Heal] Possibly John Hawkins.

Hawkins, —, Norwich, cm (1793). Subscribed to Sheraton's *Drawing Book*, 1793. Possibly Parker or Robert Hawkins.

Hawkins, —, 89 Gt Titchfield St, Oxford Mkt, London, cm etc. (1820). [D]

Hawkins, Alexander, Norfolk St, King's Lynn, Norfolk, working u (1836–39). Recorded at no. 113 in 1836 and no. 103 in 1839. [D]

Hawkins, Benjamin, Chelsea, London, cm (1793). [D]

Hawkins, Captain, address unrecorded, upholder (1761–68).

Son of John Hawkins, victualler of Warminster, Wilts.; app. to Charles Greenwood on 1 October 1761, and admitted freeman of the Upholders' Co. by servitude on 1 December 1768. [GL, Upholders' Co. records]

Hawkins, Charles, Silver St, Golden Sq., London, carver (1774). [Poll bk]

Hawkins, Charles, 1 Hatfield Pl., Westminster Rd, London, chair and sofa maker (1839). [D]

Hawkins, David, Liverpool, cm (1827–40). App. to William John Roberts in 1827 and admitted freeman on 30 July 1840. [Liverpool app. enrolment bk and freemen reg.]

Hawkins, E., House of Industry, Chester, upholder (1819). [Election for Sheriff]

Hawkins, Edward, Chester, u (1727–47). Admitted freeman on 8 July 1727. [Chester freemen rolls and poll bks]

Hawkins, Edward, Eastgate, Chester, u (1784). Son of James Hawkins, u of Chester; admitted freeman on 1 April 1784. [Chester freemen rolls and poll bk]

Hawkins, Edward, Prince's St, Westminster, London, upholder (1784). [D]

Hawkins, Edward, 35 New Compton St, Soho, London, chair manufacturer etc. (1820–23). [D]

Hawkins, Elizabeth, at 'The Royal Bed', New Bond St, Hanover Sq., London, cm and u (1767). Possibly the widow of (John?) Hawkins, whose trade card bears a bill on the back dated 23 November 1767, which reads: 'Bought of Eliz. Hawkins'. [Heal] See Hawkins, —, and John Hawkins.

Hawkins, Frederick, 47 Cirencester Pl., London, carver and gilder (1835–39). [D]

Hawkins, George, 36 Broad St, Bath, Som., u, auctioneer and broker (1833). [D]

Hawkins, H., Compton St, Soho, London, looking-glass and frame maker (c.1760). [Heal]

Hawkins, Henry, Chester, cm (1785). App. to Richard Hawkins, cm, 10–14 November 1785. [Chester app. bks]

Hawkins, Henry, High Wycombe, Bucks., chairmaker (1818–33). Four daughters and three sons bapt. between 1818 and 1833. [PR (bapt.)]

Hawkins, J. D., Cavern House, Blackheath Hill, London, cm (1808). [D]

Hawkins, James, Liverpool, u (1747). [Chester poll bk]

Hawkins, James snr, Chester, u (1747–84). Recorded in Eastgate St, 1781–84. Son of Edward Hawkins of Chester, u; admitted freeman on 23 July 1747. Took his son, James Hawkins as app. in November 1775. [D; Chester freemen rolls, app. bks and poll bk]

Hawkins, James jnr, Chester, u (1784–1826). Addresses given in Eastgate St, 1784–89; Princess St, 1812; George St, 1818; William St, 1819; and Frodsham St, 1826. Son of James Hawkins, u of Chester; admitted freeman on 1 April 1784. [D; Chester freemen rolls; poll bks and election of Sheriff, 1819]

Hawkins, James, Dorchester, Dorset, ironmonger and u (1784–99). Took out a Sun Insurance policy in 1794 for £800 of which utensils and stock accounted for £30. Will dated 1799. [GL, Sun MS vol. 322, p. 436; Dorset RO, DA/W/1799/20]

Hawkins, James, 12 Clerkenwell Close, London, mahogany merchant, cabinet and looking-glass manufacturer, toyman and u (1808–09). In association with Thomas Gisborne Molineux and Francis Molineux took out Sun Insurance policies for warehouse, stock, utensils and looking-glass plates on 7 April 1808 for £3,000; and on 25 May 1809 for £3,500. [GL, Sun MS vol. 443, ref. 814884; vol. 446, ref. 830948]

Hawkins, John, Bath, Som., cm (1732). Took app. named Harvey in 1732. [S of G, app. index]

Hawkins, John, Bond St, London, u (1749). [Poll bk] Possibly Hawkins, —, husband of Elizabeth Hawkins, at 'The Royal Bed'.

Hawkins, John, 86 Ratcliff Highway, London, cm and broker (1793). Insured his house, utensils and stock for £200 on 28 March 1793. [GL, Sun MS vol. 392, ref. 613028]

Hawkins, John, 9 Broad St, Bloomsbury, London, cm (1802–03). Named in Sheraton's list of master cabinet makers, 1803. [D]

Hawkins, John, Mill St, Hull, Yorks., cm and u (1806). [D]

Hawkins, John, London, cm (1806–18). Recorded in Greenwich, 1806. [Norwich poll bks]

Hawkins, John, Woodford, Essex, cm (1823–24). [D]

Hawkins, John, 53 Seymour Pl., Bryanston Sq., London, u (1826–27). [D]

Hawkins, John, West St, Warwick, cm (1831). [Warwick poll bk]

Hawkins, John, 6 Lisson Grove North, London, u (1839). [D] See Hawkings, —.

Hawkins, John, Broadway, Stratford, Essex, cm and u (1839). [D]

Hawkins, Joseph, St Paul's Churchyard, London, cm (1750–53). Polled as a Liveryman of the Joiners' Co. in 1750. Sale of entire stock in trade, consisting of 'all sorts of cabinet work in a neat & modern taste', announced in *Daily Advertiser*, 16 June 1753. [GL, Joiners' Co. Livery records]

Hawkins, Joseph, 5 Cock Gates, Manchester, cm (1797). [D]

Hawkins, Matthew, Oldham St, Manchester, upholder (1788). [D]

Hawkins, Parker, Norwich and London, upholder (1794–1802). Recorded in Norwich, 1794–98, and London in 1802. [D; Norwich poll bks]

Hawkins, Peter, 15 St Martin's Lane, London, cm (1793). [D]

Hawkins, Richard, Chester, cm (1767–89). Trading at Common Hall Lane in 1784. Son of Edward Hawkins, u; admitted freeman on 15 December 1767. Took apps named Henry Hawkins in 1785 and Charles Boulton in 1789. [Chester freemen rolls, poll bks and app. bks]

Hawkins, Richard, London, turner, cm and looking-glass manufacturer (1790–1800). Recorded alone, 1792–93; as Hawkins & Dillin(g), 1790–94; and Hawkins & Rhodes, 1796, at 41 Snow Hill; alone at 13 Clerkenwell Close in 1799; as Hawkins & Rhodes there, 1797–1800. [D]

Hawkins, Richard, Sherborne, Dorset, carver and gilder (1823–30). Trading in Long St, 1823–24, and Cheap St, 1830. [D]

Hawkins, Richard, 40 Fore St, London, u (1839). [D]

Hawkins, Robert, Norwich, chairmaker (1762). Took app. named Winslow in 1762. [S of G, app. index]

Hawkins, Robert, Norwich, upholder and cm (1782). Son of John Hawkins, baker; admitted freeman on 4 May 1782. [Norwich freemen reg.]

Hawkins, Robert, Hull, Yorks., cm and u (1803–06). Trading at Whitefriargate in 1803 and Hope St, 1806. [D]

Hawkins, Samuel, King's Lynn, Norfolk, cm (1784–85). Trading in High St, 1784. Took out a Sun Insurance policy on 10 February 1785 for £350 on utensils and stock in his shop and warehouse. [D; GL, Sun MS vol. 327, p. 304]

Hawkins, Samuel, 1 King's Rd, Chelsea, London, u, cm and undertaker (1808). [D]

Hawkins, William, London, upholder (1773–83). Trading at 62 New Bond St, 1773–75, and Wigmore St, 1781–83. Polled at Westminster of Bond St in 1774. [D]

Hawkin(s), William, Micklegate, York, cm (1774–1811). Took app. named William Thorp on 8 July 1775. Former app., Thomas Melrose, admitted freeman in 1779. Assigned from John Wright app. named Robert Hernage, admitted freeman cm in 1802. Took apps named William Carrick on 10 October 1772; Robert Kidd on 22 July 1782; William Boddy on 16 February 1784; Benjamin Ellis on 8 February 1789; and Thomas Fisher on 17 April 1804. Subscribed to Sheraton's *Drawing Book*, 1793. Took inventory of Newby Park in 1794. [D; poll bks; York app. reg. and freemen rolls; Leeds archives dept, Newby papers, NH 2802]

Hawkins, William, 6 Queen St, Soho, London, chairmaker (1809–11). [D]

Hawkins, William, Dorchester, Dorset, cm, u and auctioneer (1823–40). Addresses given at High St, 1823–24, and High East St in 1830. [D]

Hawkins, William, High (or Castle) St, Berkhamsted, Herts., carpenter, joiner and cm (1828–39). [D]

Hawksey, Andrew, Market St, St Helens, Lancs., joiner, cm and u (1834). [D]

Hawksley, Francis, Nottingham, u (1722). [Notts. RO, index of burgesses]

Hawkswell (or Hawxwell), William, York, cm, furnisher of funerals, appraiser and salesman (1771–87). Recorded in Peter Lane, 1771, and High Ousegate, 1784–87. Submitted bill on 19 April 1771 for a total of £4 13s 10d including eleven chairs at 4s 6d each; one glass, two tables, a dresser, and several items of ironmongery. [D; poll bk; Castle Museum, York] See Hauxwell, —.

Hawksworth, George, York, cm (1833). Son of George Hawksworth, labourer; app. to Thomas Walls, cm, on 1 September 1833. [York app. reg.]

Hawksworth, Hannah, 3 Shales Moor, Sheffield, Yorks., u (1822). [D]

Hawksworth, John, South Parade, Thorne, Yorks., joiner and cm (1830). [D]

Hawkyard, Henry, Elland, near Halifax, Yorks., cm (1822). [D]

Hawley, —, 9 Milk St, Bristol, cm (1775). [D]

Hawley, William, Parliament St, Nottingham, cm and u (1834–40). Recorded at no. 36 in 1835. [D]

Haworth, Henry, 8 Denmark St, London, carver (1760–d.1781). Took over work from his father, Samuel, at Carron, Stirlingshire, 1779–81. See Samuel Haworth.

Haworth, Henry, 20 Barter St, Duke's Dock, Liverpool, cm (1804). [D]

Haworth (or Howarth), John, Wigan, Lancs., cm and u (1814–18). Trading in Standishgate, 1814, and Wallgate, 1816–18. [D]

Haworth (or Hayworth), Samuel, London, carver and gilder (1749–79). Recorded at Rose St, Covent Gdn in 1749; Denmark St, 1763, no. 8 by 1779. [D; poll bk] Subscribed to Chippendale's *Director*, 1754. In 1763 worked at Egremont House, London. [W. Sussex RO, Petworth II, 6615] In 1764 submitted two designs to the governors of Middlx Hopital for a frame for the portrait by R. E. Pine of the Duke of Northumberland. He supplied it at a cost of £19 19s 6d. In 1766 he was involved in a matter of arbitration between Sir Lawrence Dundas and the upholder, Samuel Norman, over the latter's charges for gilding the gallery at Moor Park. [Gilbert, *Chippendale*, pp. 158–59] In 1773 Haworth was commissioned to carve portraits of the King and Queen to ornament hobgrates to commemorate the granting of a Royal Charter of Incorporation from King George III to the Carron Co., Scotland. Samuel's son, Henry, worked at Carron from 1779 until his death in 1781, when son William took over, remaining for fifty-six years. [*Conn.*, May–August 1963, pp. 21–24; R. Lister, *Decorative Cast Ironwork in Great Britain*] See Henry and William Haworth.

Haworth, Thomas, near 'The Angel', High St, Doncaster, Yorks., u and cm (1766). Advertised in *Cambridge Chronicle and Journal*, 28 June 1766, as 'Some years foreman to Mr.

Saunders, late of Soho Square, now of Great Queen Street, London ... He furnisheth all sorts of Upholstery and Cabinet Work in the Newest Taste and on the most reasonable Terms, having laid in a fresh Assortment of Goods of the Best Qualities and Newest Fashions. Great Choice of Paper Hangings, Entire New Patterns; Turkey, Wilton, Persia, and Scotch Carpets; Papier Machee, Ornaments, Frames, Girandoles, Borders &c. Journeymen Cabinet or Chair Makers that are Good Hands may be sure of Constant Employ. Also Wanted a Person as Foreman in the Cabinet Branch. One Qualified for such an undertaking May Depend on Encouragement equal to Merit.'

Haworth, Thomas, shop at 2 Gay St, Liverpool, cm (1821–23). [D]

Haworth, William, 8 Denmark St, London, carver (1759–1838). Took over work from his father Samuel, and brother Henry at Carron, Stirlingshire, from 1781–1837. Many of his original carvings are preserved at Falkirk Museum. See Samuel Haworth.

Haws, Isaac, Downley, High Wycombe, Bucks., chairmaker (b. c. 1806–41). Aged 35 at the time of the 1841 Census.

Hawson, —, John St, London, u (1833). Recorded in *Loudon's Encyclopaedia*, 1833, p. 1039, as a dealer in ancient and curious furniture.

Hawson, John jnr, Strait, Lincoln, cm and u (1822). [D]

Hawthornthwaite, John, Lancaster, cm (1762–77). App. to Robert Gardner, cm, on 9 April 1762, and admitted freeman, 1768–69. Took app. cm on 21 January 1777. [Lancaster app. reg. and freemen rolls] Possibly:

Hawthornthwaite, John, Shields, Co. Durham or Northumb., cm (1784). [Lancaster poll bk]

Hawtridge, William, Woodbridge, Suffolk, cm (1824). [D]

Hawtyn, William, address unrecorded, upholder (1718–25). Son of Samuel Hawtyn, maltster of London; app. to Philip Green on 3 September 1718, and admitted freeman of the Upholders' Co. by servitude on 3 November 1725. [GL, Upholders' Co. records]

Hay, Alexander, 26 Red Lion St, Holborn, London, cm and u (1808–39). Recorded also at 3 Prince's St, Red Lion Sq., 1827–28. [D]

Hay, John, 38 Drury Lane, London, cm (1809–17). [D]

Hay, Peter, shop at 3 South End, Dry Dock, Liverpool, carver (1807). [D]

Hay, Samuel, 73 Long Acre, London, cm (1802–03). Hay of this address named in Sheraton's list of master cabinet makers, 1803. [D]

Hay, Tempest, Long Acre, London. Sent and receipted a bill of Philip le Caron submitted to Corsham Court, Wilts. [V&A archives]

Hay, Thomas, London, cm (1793). Subscribed to Sheraton's *Drawing Book*, 1793.

Hayden, William Isaac, Fair St, Horsleydown, London, cm and undertaker (1777). Took out a Sun Insurance policy in 1777 for £400 of which utensils and stock accounted for £200. [GL, Sun MS vol. 257, p. 209]

Haydon, W. H., 48 Pearson St, Kingsland Rd, London, carver and gilder (1839). [D]

Hayes, —, at 'The White Swan', on the South Side of St Paul's Churchyard, London, u (1694). He was followed at this address by John Coxed. [Hilton Price, *Signs of Old London*]

Hayes, George, High St, Tewkesbury, Glos., cm and chairmaker (1839). [D]

Hayes, Henry, Market St, Alton, Hants., cm and u (1830). [D]

Hayes, J., Liverpool, cm (1817). Marriage to Elizabeth, eldest daughter of Mr H. Crowther, Crosshall St, on 16 June 1817, reported in *Liverpool Mercury*, 27 June.

Hayes, James, 20 Norfolk St, Liverpool, cm (1790). [D]

Hayes, James, 10 Cumberland St, near Middlx Hospital, Oxford, chairmaker (1802). [Poll bk]

Hayes, James, 5 Woodward's Pl., Horatio St, Liverpool, cm (1834). [D]

Hay(e)s, Jeffrey, Stoke-on-Trent, Staffs., chairmaker (1834). As Hays recorded in High St. [D]

Hayes, John, St Mary's Kalendar, Hants., cm (1761). Took app. named Muspratt in 1761. [S of G, app. index]

Hayes, John, Bristol, cm (1774–84). Recorded in St James's parish in 1774 and 1784, and St Thomas's in 1781. [Poll bks]

Hayes, John, Liverpool, cm (1796–1835). Addresses given at 11 Derby St in 1818; 78 Crosshall St with shop at 28 Tarleton St in 1821; 77 Crosshall St with shop at 3 Brooks Alley, 1823–24; 77 or 78 Crosshall St with shop at 26 Richmond Row, 1827–29; 4 Thomas St and 10 Shaw's Brow in 1827; and 77 Crosshall St with shop at 29 Tarleton St, 1834–35. Admitted freeman on 27 May 1796. [D; Liverpool freemen reg.]. Possibly more than one tradesman of the same name is concerned here.

Hayes, John, 34 Windmill St, Tottenham Ct Rd, London, cm (1802). [Oxford poll bk]

Hayes, John, Manchester, cm and u (1814–40). Addresses given at 58–59 Bridge St, 1814–21; no. 63 in 1824; no. 65, 1822–29; no. 24, 1832–38; and 47 Liverpool Rd in 1840. [D]

Hayes, John, Haymarket, Sheffield, Yorks., cm and u (1828–29). [D]

Hayes, R. N., 26 New Bond St and 10 Mount St, Berkeley St. London, camp equipage maker and u etc. (1835). [D]

Hayes, Robert, near the Dial, Long Alley, Moorfields, London, u (1777). Took out a Sun Insurance policy in 1777 for £300 of which utensils, stock and goods accounted for £120. [GL, Sun MS vol. 258, p. 233]

Hayes, Shepherd, Bristol, cm (1781). [Poll bk]

Hayes, Thomas, 1 Thomas St, Liverpool, cm (1790). [D]

Hayes, William, address unrecorded, upholder (1713). Took app. on 3 July 1713. [PRO, app. reg.] Probably William Hays.

Hayes, William, Winchester, Hants., cm (1768–d.1779). Notice in *Oxford Gazette and Reading Mercury*, 25 April 1768 read: 'WINCHESTER, Lately Arrived, a large Quantity of MAHOGANY of different sorts, the Property of WILLIAM HAYES, Cabinet-Maker, which he is determined to sell to the Trade as cheap as any Market in England: likewise a Choice of very fine Phinears and Dining-Table wood of a fine Quality. Coach Pannelling cut on very reasonable terms.' Died intestate in 1779. [Hants. RO; C. *Life*, 11 June 1953, p. 1892]

Hayes, William, 31 Goode St, London, upholder (1777). Took out a Sun Insurance policy in 1777 for £300 of which utensils, stock and goods accounted for £50. [GL, Sun MS vol. 256, p. 190]

Hayes, William, Greece St, London, chairmaker (1802). [Oxford poll bk]

Hayes, William, Millgate, Wigan, Lancs., cm (1825). [D]

Hayes, William, Liverpool, u (1830). App. to William Bickerstaff in 1830. [Liverpool app. enrolment bk]

Haygarth, James, 39 Upper John St, Tottenham Ct Rd, London, u (1816). [D]

Hayhurst, Richard, Liverpool, cm (1757–65). Admitted freeman on 9 June 1757. Took apps named William Ren and William Fairclough in 1765. [Liverpool app. and freemen reg.] Possibly:

Hayhurst, Richard, Liverpool, cm (d.c.1765). Notice in *Williamson's Liverpool Advertiser*, 14 June 1765, requested that 'All Persons who have any Demands on the Estate of ... Mr. Richard Hayhurst, Cabinet maker, deceased, are desired to render in their Accounts to James France, Cable-street, that they may be settled & paid ... And all Persons indebted to the said Estates, are desired to pay their respective Debts forthwith … otherwise they will be sued without further Notice.' Son of Richard Hayhurst, Thomas, merchant, petitioned freedom on birthright in 1784. [Liverpool freemen's committee bk]

Hayhurst, Richard, Mount Pleasant, Liverpool, u and flour dealer (1813–18). Trading at no. 85, 1813–14, and no. 86 in 1818. [D]

Hayley, John, Hull, Yorks., carver (1781). [D]

Hayley, John, 4 Oxford Mkt, London, cm (1829). [D]

Hayley, William, 5 Little George St, Westminster, London, cm and undertaker (1808). [D]

Hayley & Co., 140 Long Acre, London, u (1807). Submitted bill dated 6 March 1807 for fringe for furniture in the Drawing Room at Gorhambury, St Albans, Herts., costing £18 2s. [Herts. RO, Gorhambury accounts, no. XI, 77]

Hayling, Thomas, Gosport, Hants., cm and upholder (1781). Took out a Sun Insurance policy in 1781 for £400 of which utensils and stock accounted for £250. [GL, Sun MS vol. 295, p. 473]

Hayman, Christopher, 6 Grafton St, Soho, London, organ and cm (1792). Took out a Sun Insurance policy on 26 April 1792 for £350. [GL, Sun MS vol. 382, ref. 599636]

Hayman, Ester, 36 Gt St Andrew St, London, u (1808). [D]

Hayman, Richard, Deal, Kent, joiner, cm and u (1782-1807). Took out a Sun Insurance policy in 1782 for £800 of which workshop accounted for £150. [D; GL, Sun MS vol. 306, p. 302]

Hayman, William, Beach St, Deal, Kent, cm and u (1823–34). [D]

Hayne, J., 120 High Holborn, London, dressing case manufacturer (1835). [D]

Haynes, A., 99 Paul St, Finsbury Sq., London, chair stuffer and cm (1817). [D]

Haynes, Edward, St Albans, Herts., cm and u (1832–39). Recorded at Market Pl. in 1832 and St Peter's St, 1838–39. [D]

Haynes, Henry, London, carver and gilder (1826–39). Addresses given at 21 Seymour Pl., Camden Town in 1826; 52 George St, Euston Sq. (or Hampstead Rd), 1835–39; and 16 Gt Windmill St, 1839. [D]

Haynes, John, 29 Dartmouth St, St Margaret's, London, gilder (1835). Took app. in 1835. [Westminster Ref. Lib., E 3559, Grinsell's charity app. indentures]

Haynes, John, King St, Gt Yarmouth, Norfolk, cm and u (1836). [D]

Haynes, John, 23 Theobalds Rd, London, cm and u (1839). [D]

Haynes, Joseph, 36 East St, Red Lion Sq. (or Lamb's Conduit St), London, cm, u and undertaker (1835–39). [D]

Haynes, Joshua, Chapel Paved Way, Gt Yarmouth, Norfolk, cm and chairmaker (1830). [D]

Hayne(s), Matthew, Bloomsbury, London, portable desk manufacturer, cm and u (1814–39). Addresses given at 1 Hyde St in 1814; 13 Peter St, 1817; no. 63, 1819; 54 Museum St, 1820–39; also 1 Hyde St in 1820 and 1827–28; 5½ Museum St in 1823. Hyde St may be the back street behind Museum St. [D]

Haynes, Richard, Coventry St, Stourbridge, Worcs., cm and u (1828–35). [D]

Haynes, Robert, 38 Wilson St, Finsbury Sq., London, upholder (1808). [D]

Hayne(r)s, Roger, Sheffield, Yorks., joiner and cm (1828–37). Addresses given at 39 South St, 1828–29, and 3 Cumberland St, 1833–37. [D]

Haynes, Samuel, address unrecorded, upholder (1714–28). Son of Richard Haynes, merchant of London; app. to John Crouch on 2 February 1714/15, and admitted freeman of the

Upholders' Co. by servitude on 12 December 1728. [GL, Upholders' Co. records]

Haynes, Thomas, Shrewsbury, Salop, joiner and cm (1776). Took out a Sun Insurance policy in 1776 for £300 of which utensils and stock accounted for £200. [GL, Sun MS vol. 246, p. 32]

Haynes, Thomas, King St, Gt Yarmouth, Norfolk, cm (1822–41). Declared bankrupt, *Liverpool Mercury*, 13 April 1832. [D; poll bks]

Haynes, William, Park, Bristol, cm (1794). [D]

Haynes, William, South St, Exeter, Devon, cm (1833). Daughter Eliza bapt. at St Mary Major on 14 September 1833. [PR (bapt.)]

Haynes, William Carter, North Quay, Gt Yarmouth, Norfolk, cm (1838–41). [Poll bks]

Hays, —, London, chairmaker (1793). Subscribed to Sheraton's *Drawing Book*, 1793.

Hays, John, 11 John St, Gt Ancoats St, Manchester, chair bottomer (1808–09). [D]

Hays, Thomas, address unrecorded, cm (1803). Subscribed to Sheraton's *Cabinet Dictionary*, 1803.

Hays, William, London, upholder (1827–34). Addresses given at St George's Church, Southwark, 1827–34, and Blackman St, parish of St George the Martyr, 1829. Took out a Sun Insurance policy on 16 May 1829 for £400, £100 on a house in Duke St in tenure of a lace weaver; £100 on a house in Lombard St in tenure of a chandler; and £200 on a house in Suffolk St in tenure of a victualler and hatter. [Poll bks; GL, Sun MS vol. 29, ref. 47712] Probably William Hayes.

Hayson, James, Harrington Harbour, Workington, Cumb., cm and joiner (1834). [D]

Hayter, George, address unrecorded, picture frame maker (1825). Named in the Chatsworth furnishing accounts in 1825 receiving £47 5s.

Hayter, John, 21 Cavendish St, London, carver (1778). Insured his house for £300 in 1778. [GL, Sun MS vol. 264, p. 373]

Hayter, Thomas, 6 George Buildings, Old St, London, bedstead maker (1839). [D]

Hayton, Joseph, 11 Back Lane, Manchester, cm (1797). [D]

Hayward, —, Ipswich, Suffolk, u (c.1765–70). [E. D. H. Tollemache, *The Tollemaches of Helmingham and Ham*, p. 103)

Hayward, —, address unrecorded. On 12 January 1779 received £10 7s as part of his bill for furniture supplied to Sir George Cornewall of Moccas Court, near Hereford, and Stanhope St, London. [Herefs. RO, Moccas papers, J56/IV/3]

Hayward, Charles, Bedford St, Covent Gdn, London, u (1809–29). Recorded at no. 23, 1809, and no. 33, 1811–29. [D]

Hayward, Ebenezer, High St, Croydon, Surrey, cm, u, turner and chairmaker (1809–26). [D]

Hayward, Edward, Sidney St, Liverpool, cm (1827–29). Trading at no. 11 in 1827, and no. 17, 1829. [D]

Hayward, Henry, Grey Coat Pl., Horseferry Rd, London, carver and gilder (1839). [D]

Hayward, J., 6 London Rd, London, u and cm (1835): [D]

Hayward, J., Fore St, Topsham, Devon, upholstress (1838). [D]

Hayward, James, 147 High St, Poplar, London, cm and u (1827–28). [D]

Hayward, James, Camberwell Grove, Camberwell, London, cm and u (1839). [D]

Hayward, John, St Paul's, Covent Gdn, London, cm (1744–45). App. to James Smith, 1744–45, 'by the Sons of the Clergy'. [Heal]

Hayward, John, Poole, Dorset, cm (1756–84). Took app. named Gutheridge in 1756. Insured house and offices for £200 in 1780 with the Sun Co. [D; S of G, app. index; GL, Sun MS vol. 283, p. 113]

Hayward, John, 12 Stephen St, Tottenham Ct Rd, London, picture frame maker (1835). [D]

Hayward, Miles, New St, Woodbridge, Suffolk, cm and u (1839). [D] See Robert Hayward and Hayward & Son.

Hayward (or Hayword), Richard, Henley-on-Thames, Oxon., upholder and apraiser (1758–69). In 1758 purchased two houses and malt house in Hart St for £250, paying a deposit of £2 2s. [Oxford RO, MISC. Berks., VI/V/6] Advertised sales of bankrupts' or deceaseds' effects in *Jackson's Oxford Journal*, 29 July 1759, 20 April 1761 and in 1765, 1766, and 1768; and sale of house in Hart St, 24 January 1760. Announcement on 17 December 1768 that the auctioneer, Hayward, was retiring, and on 28 January 1769 that his business was being taken over by John Byles, draper, mercer and u, and Hayward's house in Hart St was to let.

Hayward, Richard, Wimborne, Dorset, cm and joiner (1784) [D]

Hayward, Robert, Liverpool, chairmaker (1811–16). Shop address given at 10 Cases St in 1811; and recorded at 54 Copperas Hill in 1813, and 21 Stanley St in 1816. [D]

Hayward, Robert, Woodbridge, Suffolk, turner and chairmaker, cm (1824–30). Trading at Market Hill in 1830. [D] See Miles Hayward and Hayward & Son.

Hayward, Thomas, 23 Bedford St, Covent Gdn, London, u (1809–11). [D]

Hayward, Thomas, 22 Hatton Gdn, London, u and house agent (1835). [D]

Hayward, Thomas, 18 High Holborn, London, u (1835–37). [D]

Hayward & Son, Market Hill, Woodbridge, Suffolk, cm (1839). [D] See Miles and Robert Hayward.

Haywood, James, Witham, Hull, Yorks., cm (1826–46). [D]

Haywood, Thomas, Manchester, u and dealer in household furniture (1833). Declared bankrupt, *Liverpool Mercury*, 4 October 1833.

Haywood (or Hayward), William, Nantwich, Cheshire, chairmaker (1833–38). Married Elizabeth Wilson on 8 June 1833. Son John bapt. on 25 April 1834; daughter Sarah on 10 December 1836; and son Henry on 18 June 1838. [Chester RO, PR (bapt.)]

Hayzen, James, 24 Sidney Pl., Commercial Rd, London, u (1839). [D]

Hayzen & Co., 9 St Ann's Pl., Commercial Rd, Limehouse, London, bed and bedding manufacturer (1835). [D]

Hazard, Mary, South St, Dorchester, Dorset, cm and u (1830). [D] See Thomas Hazard.

Hazard, Peter, see Peter Hasert.

Hazard, Thomas, Nottingham, joiner and cm (1786–d. 1799). Trading at High Pavement in 1799. Took an app. in 1786 and one named Samuel Sharp in 1798. Probate will dated 30 December 1799. [D; Nottingham app. list; Notts. RO, probate records]

Hazard, Thomas, Cornhill, Dorchester, Dorset, cm, u and auctioneer (1823–24). [D] See Mary Hazard.

Hazel, Sampson, Bolt Lane, Gloucester, chairmaker (1802). [D]

Hazelhurst, John, Paradise St, Liverpool, cm (1769). [D]

Hazelrigg, Medcalf, Newcastle, u (1733). Admitted freeman on 8 October 1733. [Newcastle freemen reg.]

Hazelwood, Moses, Baxtergate, Whitby, Yorks., cm/chairmaker (1840). [D]

Hazlehurst (or Haslehurst), Ann, 56 Stanley St, Liverpool, chairmaker (1823–35). [D]

Hazlehurst, Hannah, 56 Stanley St, Liverpool, chairmaker (1827). [D]

Hazlehurst, John, Stanley St, Liverpool, chairmaker (b.1774–d.1822). Recorded at no. 15 in 1811; no. 16, 1813–

14; and no. 36 in 1821. Death on 12 November 1822, aged 48, reported in *Liverpool Mercury*, 22 November. [D]

Hazlewood, Thomas, Cambridge, turner and chairmaker (1824–32). Trading at Trumpington St in 1824; Redhart Yd, 1830; and Hyde Park Corner in 1832. [D; poll bk]

Head, —, Gt George St, Liverpool, cm (1824). The *Liverpool Mercury*, 31 December 1824, contained a story about an imposter who stole two tea caddies from C. Jones, fancy cm in Trowbridge St, under the pretence of having been sent to collect them by Mr Head, cm, of Gt George St, and claimed he would bring the payment in a few days. When asked, however, Mr Head said that 'he had never sent for any such articles as those above mentioned.' Possibly Jonathon Head.

Head, Henry, 5 Junction Dock St, Hull, Yorks., cm (1837–39). [D]

Head, Jeremiah, Liverpool, cm (1790–1800). Addresses given at 26 and 32 King St in 1790; 17 Paradise St in 1794; no. 8 in 1796; and no. 7 in 1800. [D]

Head, Jonathan, Liverpool, joiner and cm (1805–35). Addresses given at 15 Milk St in 1807; 58 St James St in 1810; no. 52 in 1811; no. 2 in 1816; no. 15 Leander St in 1827, with shop at 28 Wood St, 1827–34; 27 Leander St in 1829; no. 28 in 1834; and no. 29 in 1835. Signed the supplement to the *Liverpool Cabinet and Chair Prices*, 1805, on behalf of the masters. [D]

Head, Jonathon, Gt George St, Liverpool, cm (1813). Sale of his stock in trade 'by order of the assignees', by Trother & Magill, cm and auctioneers, advertised in *Liverpool Mercury*, 9 April 1813. Stock consisted of 'an excellent Billiard Table, Balls, Mace & Cues, handsome Mahogany Secretaire & Bookcase, Chest of Drawers, Rosewood Bookcase, Shower Bath, a set of Bedsteads & other effects belonging to the estate of Mr. Jonathon Head, Cabinet Maker. The Stock in Trade consists of Mahogany, Oak, Ash, Birch & Deal Planks & Boards & a small quantity of Brass work, excellent Benches, Iron Stove & Pipe etc. . . .'. See Head, —.

Head, Joseph, Liverpool, cm (b.1760–d.1829). Addresses given at Toxteth Park, 1796–1805; High Park, 1807–10; Hood St, Harrington, with shop at 2 St James Pl., 1813–14; and 9 Dexter St in 1827. Death aged 69 on 4 February 1829 reported in *Liverpool Mercury*, 13 February. [D]

Head, Samuel, New St, Woodbridge, Suffolk, u and cm (1839). [D]

Head, Thomas, Leeds, Yorks., journeyman cm (1791). Named in the *Leeds Cabinet and Chair Makers' Book of Prices*, 1791, amongst other journeymen in basic sympathy with its contents.

Head, Thomas, 1 Vine St, Clare Mkt, London, cm (1787). Insured goods for £400 on 8 June 1787. [GL, Sun MS vol. 342, ref. 531412]

Head, William, London, cm (1793–94). Subscribed to Sheraton's *Drawing Book*, 1793. Commissioned by Lady Northampton to supply furniture for the Mansion House at Leighton. On 10 April 1794 he was paid £2 2s for a 'Mahogany card table with green cloth for the Hon. Miss Leigh'; and on 30 May 1794, £1 1s for 'making a set of full sized furniture'. [Shakespeare Birthplace Trust, Leigh receipts, DR 18/5]

Head & Lissel, 1 Hill St, Liverpool, joiners and cm (1807). [D]

Headdon, Benjamin, 148 Queen St, Portsea, Portsmouth, Hants., u and chairmaker (1839). [D]

Headley, Robert, Church St, Gainsborough, Lincs., chairmaker and carver (1831). [D]

Headley (or Heady), Thomas, 8 Union St, East Pl., Lambeth, London, chairmaker (1796–1811). In 1796–97 submitted a bill to Mr Devenish for '6 Black Round Seats' for £1 16s. [Heal Coll., BM] Took out a Sun Insurance policy on

26 January 1801 for £300 of which £60 accounted for stock and utensils. [D; GL, Sun MS vol. 419, ref. 712764]

Heaford, Thomas, New St, Wellington, Salop, chairmaker and wood turner (1840). [D]

Heal(e), Fanny & Son, 203 Tottenham Ct Rd, London, feather bed and mattress maker (1818–40). [D; Heal]

Heal, John Harris, London, feather bed and mattress maker (1810–28). Addresses given at 33 Rathbone Pl., 1810–18, and 203 Tottenham Ct Rd, 1822–28. [D; London rate bks] See Heal & Son and Fanny Heal(e) & Son.

Heal, Joseph, Westgate Quarters, Exeter, Devon, cm (1834). Son Joseph bapt. at St Mary Steps on 3 August 1834. [PR (bapt.)]

Heal & Son, 196 Tottenham Ct Rd, London, bedding and cm, feather dressers and French mattress makers (1840–41). Advertised in *Morning Chronicle*, 24 April 1841 offering mattresses as made in Paris, workmen to any part of the country, and remaking of old mattresses and bedding. [Heal]

Heald, Daniel, 21 George St, Brighton, Sussex, cm and u (1832). [D]

Heald, John, Witton St, Northwich, Cheshire, chairmaker (1822–34). [D]

Heald, John, Milton St, Nottingham, cm (1835). [D]

Heald, William, Lower Bridge St, Chester, chairmaker (1793–97). [D]

Heald, William, Ormskirk, Lancs., chairmaker (1798). [D]

Heald, William, Liverpool, chairmaker (1804–05). Trading at 37 Park Lane in 1804, and at the Painted Chair warehouse, 42 Park Lane in 1805. [D]

Healey, Benjamin, Daw Green, Dewsbury, Yorks., cm (1828–34). Trading in partnership with David Healey in 1830. [D]

Healey, David, Daw Green, Dewsbury, Yorks., cm (1828–34). [D]

Healey, John, 9 Taylor's Buildings, Woolwich, London, cm and u (1839). [D]

Heall, Joseph, 12 East Cheap, Hull, Yorks., cm (1838–42). [D]

Hea(r)n, William, London, cm, u, chair and sofa manufacturer, undertaker and appraiser (1819–39). Addresses given at 12 Little Wild St, Long Acre, 1819–35; 11 Wild St, 1835; and 30 Russell St, Bloomsbury, 1837–39. Paper label recorded inside drawer of simple mahogany Pembroke table.

Heap, George, Liverpool, joiner and cm (1834–39). Addresses given at 23 Fox St, 1834–35, and 159 Richmond Row, Richmond Fair in 1839. [D]

Heap, Robert, New Brentford, Middlx, u, cm and chairmaker (1839). [D]

Heap, Samuel, Liverpool, cm and woollen draper (1823–29). Recorded at 16 Gt Richmond St with shop at 11 and 14 Woollen Hall, Richmond Row in 1823; 7 and 9 Gt Richmond St in 1827; and 13 Fox St with shop at 17 Fox St and Woollen Hall, 1829. [D]

Heap, William, Wharf St, Ashton-under-Lyne, Lancs., joiner and cm (1834). [D]

Heard, —, Moretonhampstead, Devon, cm (1808). Marriage to Mrs Pinn, widow of Exeter, reported in *Exeter Flying Post*, 15 December 1808.

Heard, Amos, Exeter, Devon, cm (1830–33). Recorded at Idol Lane in 1830; and St Mary Arches St in 1833. Son Henry George bapt. at St George's on 21 November 1830; and daughter Elizabeth Ann on 28 April 1833. [PR (bapt.)]

Heard, Charles, Dartmouth, Devon cm and u (1804). Advertised sale of stock in trade in *Exeter Flying Post*, 1 November 1804, having 'carried on business in both branches successfully but is obliged to quit owing to recent family misfortune.'

Heard, John, Portland Buildings, Nottingham, joiner and cm (1799). [D]

Heard, Richard, High St, Bideford, Devon, cm and builder (1830). [D]

Heard, William, Lower Bridge St, Chester, chairmaker (1792). [D]

Hearder, Cath., Lower Broad St, Plymouth, Devon, broker and cm (1822). [D]

Hearder, Gilbert, Torquay, Devon, cm, upholder, dealer and chapman (1816–24). Trading at Old Quay, 1823–24. Notice in *Exeter Flying Post*, 11 January 1816. Declared bankrupt, *Western Luminary*, 23 January 1816, and sale of stock in trade announced on 30 January 1816. [D]

Hearder, Jonathan, address unrecorded, cm (1803). Subscribed to Sheraton's *Cabinet Dictionary*, 1803.

Hearder, Sarah, Torwood St, Torquay, Devon, cm (1830). [D] Possibly the Mrs Hearder, u, of Torquay, who advertised in *Exeter Flying Post*, 4 June 1829 as supplier of catalogues for sale by auction at Messrs Hearder's of Newton Abbot on 11 June 1829.

Heardson, —, London, u (1728). Named in the SPCK subscription ledger and cash book on 30 July 1728 receiving £1 12s for upholsterer's work. [SPCK, Holy Trinity, Marylebone Rd, London, FT9/2]

Hearne, Edward snr, Potton, Beds., upholder (1752–69). His sons admitted freemen of the Upholders' Co.: Edward jnr in 1752, Richard in 1756, and John in 1769. [GL, Upholders' Co. records]

Hearne, Edward jnr, London, upholder (1752–d.1795). Recorded at Little New St, Shoe Lane, 1778–86, and Holborn in 1794. Son of Edward Hearne, u of Potton, Beds., and brother of John and Richard Hearne. Admitted freeman of the Upholders' Co. by redemption on 2 April 1752; and beadle from 1770. [GL, Upholders' Co. records]

Hearne, J., 8 Seymour Pl., Camden Town, London, cm and u (1826–35). [D]

Hearne, James, 11 Shorts Gdns, Drury Lane, London, upholder (1792). Son of John Hearne, upholder; admitted freeman of the Upholders' Co. by patrimony on 2 May 1792. [GL, Upholders' Co. records]

Hearn(e), James, 6 Ryder's Ct, Cranbourn St, Leicester Sq., London, cm, u, portable desk manufacturer and undertaker (1804–28). Took out Sun Insurance policies on 14 May 1804 and 14 April 1809 for £800 on his house, also belonging to Daniel Woodward. [D; GL, Sun MS vol. 431, ref. 762285; vol. 448, ref. 830623]

Hearne, John, London, upholder (1762–69). Recorded at corner of Brook St, Holborn in 1768, and 75 Holborn in 1769. Son of Edward Hearne snr, upholder of Potton, Beds., and brother of Edward and Richard Hearne. App. to his brother Richard on 5 February 1762, and admitted freeman of the Upholders' Co. by servitude on 12 May 1769. Marriage to Miss Hamilton of Stamford at St Andrew's, Holborn, reported in *Cambridge Chronicle and Journal*, 28 May 1768. [GL, Upholders' Co. records]

Hearne, Richard, Holborn, London and Potton, Beds., upholder and cm (1748–81). Addresses given at Brook St, Holborn, 1763–68; 143 and 45 Holborn, 1767–75; nos 35 and 45 in 1775; as Richard & Co., 1769–70; as Richard & John in 1770; and in Potton, Beds., 1778–81. Son of Edward Hearne snr, upholder of Potton, Beds., and brother of Edward and John Hearne. App. to William Chesson, haberdasher, on 7 April 1748, and admitted freeman of the Upholders' Co. on 3 June 1756. Took app. named George Bowditch, 1759–62, John Hearne, his brother, 1762–69, and Charles Richards until 1771. Advertised auction of furniture at Mansion House, Gamlingay Park, in *Cambridge Chronicle*, 17 September 1763. In 1767 employed one non-freeman for six weeks.

[D; GL, Upholders' Co. records; GL, City Licence bks, vol. 5] See William Hearne.

Hearne, Richard, address unrecorded, upholder (1784). App. to Thomas Waldron, upholder, on 17 April 1784, paying £40. [PRO, IRI/32]

Hearne, Thomas, address unrecorded, upholder (1707). Admitted freeman of the Upholders' Co. on 3 September 1707. [GL, Upholders' Co. records]

Hearne, William, 45 Holborn, London, upholder (1790–93). [D] See Richard and John Hearne.

Hearsman, John, see Bartholomew Bearman.

Hearson, Charles, High St, Barnstaple, Devon, rocking-horse, fancy chairs and brushwood manufacturer (1823–24). [D]

Hearson, George, Barnstaple, Devon, rocking-horse, fancy chairs and brushwood manufacturer (1823–38). Addresses given at High St, 1823–24; Pilton, 1830; and Litchdon St, 1838. [D]

Hearsy, John, address unrecorded. Supplied items to Lady Leigh of Stoneleigh, Warks., totalling £3 14s 2d, paid on 13 May 1682. Hearsy's bill included '3 fationable Cane Chayes Carved & varnished', and '4 Elbo Chayers of ye same'. [Shakespeare Birthplace Trust, Leigh receipts, DR 18/5/664; Christie's, 15–16 October 1981, Stoneleigh sale cat., lot 99]

Heasman, Henry snr and jnr, London, freemen upholders (1687–1750). Heasman snr traded in the Great Piazza, Covent Gdn, 1712–50. Took apps named James Gronous until 1700; Robert Cox, 1708–19; his son, Henry Heasman jnr 5 March 1710 to his freedom by servitude, 3 April 1728; and William Light in 1718. Took out a Sun Insurance policy on 7 August 1712 for his goods; and Hand in Hand policies on 12 June 1712 for £700 on his house; on 30 October 1714 and 18 November 1721 for £300 on his house. [Poll bks; GL, Upholders' Co. records and Livery lists; GL, Sun MS vol. 2, p. 84; GL, Hand in Hand MS vol. 10, ref. 23163; vol. 14, p. 38; vol. 24, p. 239] A newspaper of 1712 read: 'In the Great Piazza in Covent Garden is to be let part of the house Sir Godfrey Kneller lived in: a back house, coach house and stables in parts or together. Inquire of Mr Heasman, upholsterer, who lives in the house.' [Heal] Between 1687–90 carried out upholsterer's work totalling £300 at the Royal Hospital, Chelsea. [*Wren Soc.*, vol. XIX, p. 85] Between 1715–30 Henry Heasman snr and/or jnr supplied upholstery items to the Hon. Wrey and Lady Mary Saunderson. A bill of 11 June 1715, totalling £104 15s 8½ and receipted on 10 December 1716, included 'a Bedsted with a Rissing Testor, a Carved Scroll & Cornors, a Carved Head-Board, a Sett of Large Cornishes, Carv'd off all Ends', and many yards of lace, including 77 of 'Willo Green Ffine Ffigured Broad Lace' for 'the Bed & Chaires, Windo Curtains, Vallans, Cornishes & Windo Cushins, with Valliance'. On 17 December Heasman was paid £102 3s; and on 3 June 1730, £14 14s 11d for re-upholstering two window seats with curled hair and green and gold coverings; and two large settees, recovered with green silk 'Flowerd with Gold' and trimmed with lace. Heasman submitted another large bill for goods sold and work done for Lady Mary Saunderson between 27 January 1729 and 10 April 1730, totalling £43 6s 11½, received on 6 June 1730. Work included re-upholstering japanned chairs and stools, recovering with 'Blew Mohair', making cases for them of 'Fine Blew Cheny Water'd . . . lin'd with Paper, & lapt Round'; and transporting the furniture from and to Grosvenor Sq. [Lincoln RO, Monson, 10, 1/A/16; 12] The account book of the Earl of Rockingham records payment of £6 15s to Mr Heasman, u, on 30 May 1717. [Lincoln RO, Monson 10 A/1] Henry Heasman jnr was recorded as a member of the Livery of the Upholders' Co. in 1750. [GL, Upholders' Co. records]

Heasman, Henry jnr, address unrecorded, upholder (1710–28). Son of Henry Heasman snr, freeman upholder of London; app. to his father on 5 March 1710, and admitted freeman of the Upholders' Co. by servitude on 3 April 1728. [GL, Upholders' Co. records]

Heath, —, Farnham, Surrey, cm (1811). [D]

Heath, A., 15 Berwick St, London, cm (1780). Trade card recorded. [Heal]

Heath, Abraham, 51 Broad St, Carnaby Mkt, London, furniture warehouseman (1784). [D]

Heath, Charles, Bristol, carver and gilder (1817–40). Addresses given at 4 Broadmead, 1817–18; 17 Broad St, 1819–20; no. 26, 1821–39; and nos 26–27 in 1840. [D]

Heath, Charles, Wolverhampton, Staffs., cm (1838). [D]

Heath, E., 9 Caroline Buildings, Bath, Som., cm (1833). [D]

Heath, George, address unrecorded, upholder (1725–33). Son of Herman Heath, potter of Lambeth, London; app. to Daniel Chappell on 18 September 1725, and admitted freeman of the Upholders' Co. by servitude on 2 May 1733. [GL, Upholders' Co. records]

Heath, James, London, upholder and cm (1776–86). Recorded at 35 Wood St, Cheapside, 1775–76; Crutched Friars, 1776–81; no. 27 in 1776; and Cripplegate, 1778 and 1786. Admitted freeman of the Upholders' Co. on 3 January 1776. Took out Sun Insurance policies in 1775 for £300, £200 on utensils and stock; and in 1776 for £200 on utensils and stock; and another policy for £600, £400 on utensils and stock. [GL, Upholders' Co. records; GL, Sun MS vol. 240, p. 411; vol. 249, pp. 146 and 487]

Heath, James, Walthamstow, Essex, u (1781). Took out a Sun Insurance policy in 1781 for £400 of which £270 accounted for utensils and stock. [GL, Sun MS vol. 297, p. 378]

Heath, John, address unrecorded, upholder (1706–30). Son of Robert Heath, mason of Thame, Oxon., and father of Robert Heath, upholder. App. to Thomas Cooke on 24 March 1706, and admitted freeman of the Upholders' Co. by servitude in 1717. Took app. named Barton Shuttleworth, 1717–1729/30. [GL, Upholders' Co. records]

Heath, John, at 'The Rising Sun', Wych St, London, upholder (1718–34). Took out a Sun Insurance policy in association with James Bostock on 22 January 1718 on goods and merchandise; and alone on 11 January 1727 for £400 of which household goods and stock in trade accounted for £360. [Poll bks; GL, Sun MS vol. 7; vol. 25, ref. 43538]

Heath, John, London, u (1721). [Shrewsbury burgess roll]

Heath, John, Pillory St, Nantwich, Cheshire, cm (1834–40). [D]

Heath, P., Brewer St, Golden Sq., London, cm and u (1793). [D] See Thomas Heath.

Heath, Randle, Welsh (or Welch) Row, Nantwich, Cheshire, cm (1813–29). Daughter Mary bapt. on 22 February 1813; son William on 14 October 1814; and daughter Martha on 29 November 1818. [D; PR (bapt.)]

Heath, Richard, 13 Snowhill, Birmingham, chair and gun rod maker (1777–80). [D]

Heath, Richard, High St, Burton-on-Trent, Staffs., cm (1818). [D]

Heath, Robert, address unrecorded, upholder (1748). Son of John Heath, upholder; admitted freeman of the Upholders' Co. by patrimony on 27 October 1748. [GL, Upholders' Co. records]

Heath, Robert, Broad Ct, London, upholder (1748–49). Robert Heath, upholder and auctioneer of Broad Ct, Bow St, Covent Gdn, advertised sale of household furniture at the 'Bull-head and Three Tuns Tavern, facing Bow Church' in *General Advertiser*, 1 November 1748. Of Broad Ct, Drury Lane, polled in 1749.

Heath, Robert, St Martin-in-the-Fields, London, upholder (1758). Declared bankrupt, *Gents Mag.*, December 1758.

Heath, Robert, 34 Brush Lane, Cannon St, London, Tunbridge-ware manufacturer (1826–28). [D]

Heath, Thomas, London, upholder and cm (1771–1821). Trading at 40 Brewer St, 1784–93; no. 42, 1787–1808; and 4 Lower James St, Golden Sq. in 1809. Trading as appraiser and house agent in 1820. Son of Thomas Heath; app. to Peter and John Deschamps, and admitted freeman of the Upholders' Co. by servitude on 5 June 1771. Took out Sun Insurance policies on 3 August 1786 for £500 on his house; and on 9 January 1787 for £400 on goods and utensils. [D; poll bks; GL, Upholders' Co. records; GL, Sun MS vol. 338, p. 567; vol. 342, ref. 526282] See P. Heath.

Heath, Thomas, York St, Shelton (or Hanley), Staffs., cm and u (1834–35). [D]

Heath, William, Nantwich, Cheshire, cm (1832). Married on 18 October 1832. [Chester RO, PR]

Heath Abbott, Hannah, 7 Cornhill, London, carver and gilder (1790). Insured her stock and goods for £2,400 in 1790. [GL, Sun MS vol. 370]

Heathcote, John, Prussia St, Oldham St, Liverpool, cm (1800–03). Trading at no. 32 in 1800 and no. 18 in 1803. [D]

Heathcote, Thomas, Market Pl., Rotherham, Yorks., cm (1822–29). [D]

Heathcott, I., Webb Sq., Shoreditch, London, cm (1820). [D]

Heather, William, 111 St John's St, West Smithfield, London, cm and chairmaker (1817–20). [D]

Heaton, James, King St, Bolton, Lancs., chairmaker (1814–34). Trading also as a glass dealer in 1818. [D] See Thomas Heaton.

Heaton, John, Manchester, cm (1817–40). Addresses given at 11 Back Red-Bank in 1817; Johnson St, Ducie Bridge in 1824–25; and no. 6 in 1840. [D]

Heaton, Thomas, Liverpool, cm (1761–d. by 1817). Admitted freeman on 29 January 1761. [Liverpool freemen reg.]

Heaton, Thomas, 60 Deansgate, Bolton, Lancs., chairmaker (1814–18). [D] See James Heaton.

Heaven, John, at 'The Floorcloth', Bedford St, facing Bedford Row, London, joiner and turner (c.1760). Trade card recorded. [Heal]

Heaviside, John, Stockton-upon-Tees, Co. Durham, joiner and cm (1827–32). Trading at Blue Post Yd, 1827–29, and Ramsgate, Stockton, in 1832. [D]

Heavyse(d)ge, Thomas, Swan Yd, Kirkgate, Huddersfield, Yorks., cm and/or u (1830–37). [D]

Heavyside, Thomas, Swan Yd, Huddersfield, Yorks., cm and u (1830). [D]

Hebbard & Rockwood, 46 Gt Ormond Yd, London, cm and u (1839). [D]

Hebbirt, John, Buxton, Derbs., cm (1822). [D]

Hebblethwaite, James, Halifax, Yorks., cm (1814–37). Addresses given at King's Cross Lane, 1814–20; Bull Green in 1822; and Little Lane in 1837. [D]

Hebden, William, Shelf, Rishworth, Yorks., joiner and cm (1837). [D]

Hebdersley, T., 11 Little Chapel St, Soho, London, cm and chairturner (1817). [D]

Hebdish, Charles, Sherborne, Dorset, cm (1798). [D]

Hebditch, Charles, 2 Black Horse Ct, Aldersgate St, London, cm (1792). Took out a Sun Insurance policy in 1792 for £200 on his house, goods, stock and utensils, stock accounting for £60. [GL, Sun MS vol. 391, p. 622]

Hedderley, Thomas, Nottingham, joiner and cm (1773). [Nottingham burgess list]

Hedderley, William, Nottingham, joiner and cm (1779). Son of Thomas Hedderley, bellfounder of Nottingham; taken as app. in 1779. [Nottingham app. list]

Hedge, John, address unrecorded, cm (1803). Subscribed to Sheraton's *Cabinet Dictionary*, 1803. Probably John Hedges.

Hedge(s), William, Tithebarn St, Liverpool, cm and u (1827–34). Trading at no. 71, 1827–29, and no. 62 in 1834. [D]

Hedger (or Hedges), John, 136 Whitechapel Rd, London, cm and broker (1807–20). Took out Sun Insurance policies on 19 October 1807 for £600 of which stock and utensils accounted for £300, plus £100 on those in workshop; and on 16 November 1808 for £600, £300 on stock and utensils in his house, and £100 on those in warehouse. [D; GL, Sun MS vol. 442, ref. 809218; vol. 443, ref. 823364]

Hedges, John, Soho, London, looking-glass manufacturer (1817–29). Recorded at 31 Dean St and 53 Old Compton St in 1817; 14 Old Compton St in 1820; and 46–47 Dean St in 1829. Trade label found on rectangular gilt wood pier glass with pannelled surround, applied ribbon-ties, flower-heads and acorns; frieze with gadrooned urn with birds and entwined vine chaplets at the corners. Lable reads: 'J. Hedges, Looking Glass Manufacturer &c. Corner of Dean and Compton Streets, Soho.' [D; Sotheby's, 21 June 1968, lot 143; 3 July 1970, lot 85] See K. Hedges.

Hedges, John, 7 Gee St, Euston Sq., Somerton, London, cm and u (1835–39). [D]

Hedges, K., corner of Dean and Old Compton St, Soho, London, looking-glass manufacturer (1811–20). Recorded at 14 Old Compton St in 1819. Advertised in the *Times*, 2 April 1811, his 'LOOKING-GLASS MANUFACTORY … Having every convenience within his premises of making and gilding frames of every description …'. He also offered to supply plate glass. [D] See John Hedges at this address.

Hedgland, John, Cowick St, Exeter, Devon, cm (1823–28). Daughter Fanny Sarah bapt. at St Thomas's Church on 14 December 1823, and son George on 23 November 1828. [PR (bapt.)]

Hedgman, Cornelius, 13 Little New St, Shoe Lane, London, water gilder (1808–16). [D]

Hedley, James, 1 Gloucester Pl., Chelsea, London, cm and u (1823). [D]

Heensley, Peter, Wednesday Mkt, Beverley, Yorks., cm and u (1818). [D]

Heffer, Edmund, 57 Chalton St, London, carver and gilder (1839). [D]

Heffer, Edward, 30 Brewer St, Somerstown, London, carver and gilder (1839). [D]

Heffer, John, Stanfield, Suffolk (?), gilder (1729). [S of G, app. index]

Heffer, Samuel, St Olave, Exeter, Devon, cm (1830–35). Recorded at Frierhay St in 1833. Children bapt. at St Olave's Church: son James Perry on 25 July 1830; daughter Matilda Maria on 25 November 1833; and son Samuel Thomas on 6 September 1835. [PR (bapt.)]

Hegan, Samuel Van, 66 Paradise St, Liverpool, carver (1790). [D]

Heitman, Detloffe, St Martin-in-the-Fields, London, cm (d.1678). [PCC, Wills, Index Lib., vol. 10, p. 165]

Helderbrant, Charles, 26 Coleman St, Lothbury, London, carver and gilder (1817). [D]

Hele, I. (J.), address unrecorded. 'I.HELE' recorded stamped under rail of early 19th-century armchair with stuffed back and seat on sabre legs.

Hele, John, at the sign of 'The Looking Glass', in King St, near Prince's St, St Ann's, Soho, London, cm (d.1746). Death reported in newspapers in 1746. [Heal]

Hele, John, Lowe's Bank, Newcastle-under-Lyme, Staffs., joiner and cm (1818). [D]

Hele, John, Lower North St, Exeter, Devon, cm (1823). Daughter Eliza Caroline bapt. at St David's Church on 20 December 1823. [PR (bapt.)]

Heley, John, Penkahall St, Newcastle-under-Lyme, Staffs., cm and u (1835). [D]

Hellings, William, Queen St, London, cm (1784). [Poll bk]

Helm, Robert, 13 Lawley St, Birmingham, cm (1816). [D]

Helm, Robert, Helmet Row, Old St, London, cm, u, chairmaker and appraiser (1827–28). [D]

Helme, Charles, London, carver and gilder (1835–39). Addresses given at 41 Fenchurch St, 1835, and 32 Gt Sutton St, Clerkenwell, 1839. [D] Probably the C. Helme in partnership with T. Helme, 1826–27. See Thomas Helme.

Helme, T. & C., 15 Tabernacle Sq., Finsbury, London, carvers and gilders (1826–27). [D]

Helme, Thomas, London, carver and gilder (1835–39). Trading at 15 Tabernacle Sq., Finsbury, 1835–39, and at 81 Paul St, Finsbury in 1839, also as looking-glass frame maker. [D]

Helme, William, Lancaster, cm (1759). Took app. named Gardiner in 1759. [S of G, app. index]

Helme, William, Lancaster and Preston, Lancs., cm (1783–1801). Admitted freeman of Lancaster, 1783–84, when stated 'of Preston'. Polled at Lancaster of Preston in 1784. Named in the Gillow records, 1799–1801. [Lancaster freemen rolls; Westminster Ref. Lib., Gillow]

Helme, William, Liverpool, cm (1796–1814). Addresses given at 18 Baptist Lane, back of Gerrard St, 1796, and 12 Addison St, 1813–14. [D]

Helme, William, Garstang, Lancs., joiner and cm (1834). [D]

Helmes, Robert, Norwich and London, chairmaker (1777–96). Polled at Gt Yarmouth of Norwich in 1777, and of London in 1796.

Helsby, George, 101 Portland St, Liverpool, cm (1839). [D]

Helsdon, —, address unrecorded. Mahogany chest of drawers recorded bearing maker's label. [C. Life, 21 February 1980, p. 547] Probably J. J. Helston.

Helsdon, James, 12 Castle Ct, Strand, London, u (1829). [D]

Helsdon, Langley, Norwich, chairmaker (1829). Son of Henry Helsdon, tin-plate worker; admitted freeman of Norwich on 26 August 1829. [Norwich freemen reg.]

Helsman, Charles, Preston St, Exeter, Devon, cm (1838). Daughter Louisa bapt. at St Mary Major on 16 September 1838. [PR (bapt.)]

Helston, J. J., 36 Gt Queen St, Lincoln's Inn Fields, London, furniture broker, appraiser and undertaker (late 18th century). Mahogany breakfront bookcase recorded, the upper part with arcaded cornice and Gothic barred glazed doors, the lower part with fitted secretaire drawer flanked by drawers above cupboards with oval-panelled doors; supported on a solid plinth. One small drawer with label. [Sotheby's, 26 January 1968, lot 41]

Helyer, Charles, 18 Noel St, Wardour St, London, u (1839). [D]

Hembrough, Peter, address unrecorded, cm (1803). Subscribed to Sheraton's *Cabinet Dictionary*, 1803.

Heming, George & Co., London. In 1772 submitted bill to Sir Edward Knatchbull of Mersham-le-Hatch, Kent, for furnishings, metalwork, carvings etc., shipped to Kent, costing a total of £196 15s. [Kent RO, U951 A18/70]

Hemingway, Samuel, London, cm (1775). Bound as app. to Ince & Mayhew in 1775 for £210. [*Furn. Hist.*, 1974]

Heminway, T., Cawthorne, Yorks., cm (1837). [D]

Hemmel, John, 3 Brewer St, London, broker, cm and upholder (1800). Took out a Sun Insurance policy on 14 October 1800 for £1,000 of which £400 accounted for utensils and stock. [GL, Sun MS vol. 419, ref. 709301]

Hempson, John, 20 Neptune St, Hull, Yorks., cm (1838–39). [D]

Hemsley, Joseph, 16 Carthusian St, London, cm and u (1839). [D]

Hemsley, William, Nottingham, joiner and cm (1791). Son of John Hemsley of Gedling; taken as app. in 1791. [Nottingham app. list]

Hemstead, Henry, 89 Old St, London, cm and u (1839). [D]

Henden (or Hender), Robert, at 'The Cock', Knave's Acre, St James's, Westminster, London, u (1725–26). Took out a Sun Insurance policy on 18 March 1725 for £500 on goods and merchandise in his house in Pall Mall in occupation of Mr Thorp, u. Took out insurance in 1726. [GL, Sun MS vol. 21, ref. 38186; Heal]

Henderson, Alexander, Castle St, Leicester Fields, Westminster, London, cm (1749). [Poll bk]

Henderson, Alexander, Livery St, Birmingham, u (1816–18). [D]

Henderson, Andrew, 17 Moseley St, Newcastle, cm and u (1827–29). Recorded also at 13 Blackett St, probably his house, in 1827. [D]

Henderson, Christopher, Newcastle, joiner and cm (1787–95). Recorded at West end Denton-chair, 1787–90, and Side, 1795. Subscribed to Sheraton's *Drawing Book*, 1793. [D]

Henderson, David, 6 Broad St, Golden Sq., London, u (1808). [D]

Henderson, E., address unrecorded, carver and gilder (1839). Named in the Lord Chamberlain's accounts, Windsor Royal Archives, on 31 December 1839 receiving £45 2s 10d, including £17 2s 4d for 'preparing the hop & ribbon moulding for glass frames to design, the ornaments boosted [?] and carved (in part)'.

Henderson, James, Gt Russell St, Bloomsbury, London, upholder (1780s–1800). Trading as Henderson & Co. at no. 115, 1796–1800. Nephew and successor in business to Daniel Sands. Involved in legal case between Kennett and Kidd in the 1780s. [D; PRO, C12 680/34; 259/18]

Henderson, James, New Bond St, London, carver and gilder (1823–37). Recorded at no. 80, 1823–25. Carried out repairs and jobbing work at St James's Palace, 1832–37. [D; PRO, LC11/80; 95–98; Joy, *English Furniture, 1800–1851*, p. 187]

Henderson, John, Chester, cm (1774–77). Son of William Henderson; app. to John Johnson, cm, 10 April 1774–30 January 1777. [Chester app. bks]

Henderson, John, Winchester, Hants., cm (b.1762–1797). Recorded in the St Mary Kalendar Book of Examinations of the Poor, 5 June 1797, as 'Born Arleymarkey, county Fife, Scotland. Aged 35. Rented 8 years ago [1791] house of Surgeon Ford, in St. Botolph, Aldersgate Street, London at £16 p.a. for over 3 years. Married Ann 3 yrs. ago [1794] at St. Maur and has one child Olive 17 mos. About 10 years ago married Jane [1787] at St. James, Westminster, who has been dead 7 years and had 3 children by her, but only one living.' [S of G, Winchester settlement papers]

Henderson, John Burdett, 2 Davies St, Liverpool, cm (1790). [D]

Henderson, John, London, cm, chair and sofa maker, u and appraiser (1809–39). Address given at 58 Newman St, Oxford St, 1809–11; 42 Windmill St, Tottenham Ct Rd, 1820–28 and 1835–39; and 152 Tottenham Ct Rd, 1827–28. [D] More than one tradesman may be concerned here.

Henderson, John, Kirkby Fleetham, Yorks., joiner and cm (1823). [D]

Henderson, John, Rotherhithe, London, carver and ship carver (1835–37). Trading at 15 Rotherhithe, 1835, and 6 Paradise Pl., 1837. [D]

Henderson, Robert, Maidenhead, Berks., carpenter and upholder (1783). Took out a Sun Insurance policy in 1783 for £700 of which £200 accounted for workshop, utensils and stock. [GL, Sun MS vol. 314, p. 94]

Henderson, Robert, 51 Rupert St, Haymarket, London, cm, upholder and undertaker (1808–28). [D]

Henderson, Robert, 7 St George's St, Sheffield, Yorks., carver and gilder (1822–30). [D]

Henderson, William, Newcastle, upholder (1709–41). App. to Thomas Webster, and admitted freeman on 12 December 1709. Took apps named Richardson in 1712, Lambert in 1720, and Watson in 1728. Took out Sun Insurance policies for £500 on 24 June 1722 for goods and merchandise in his house; and on 22 October 1726 for £500. Possibly the William Henderson who supplied William Ramsay jnr, of Park House, Gateshead, c.1711–15, with a dozen walnut chairs at 8s 3d, two armchairs at 11s 9d, 66½, yards of 'blew print', and '1,000 gullets with nails and thread'. He also charged 5s for 'hanging the room', and 9s 'for making three pair of window vallance and curtains'. [Poll bks; Newcastle freemen reg.; S of G, app. index; GL, Sun MS vol. 14, ref. 21202; vol. 22, p. 425; E. Hughes, *North Country Life in the 18th Century, the North-East, 1700–50*, 1952, p. 49]

Henderson, William, London. One of Chippendale's employees who receipted the Duke of Atholl's account, dated 1758, on behalf of the firm. [Blair Castle papers]

Henderson, William, Chester, cm (1754–93). Addresses given at Nicholas St in 1789, and Lower Bridge St in 1792. Admitted freeman on 21 October 1779. Subscribed to Chippendale's *Director*, 1754, and Sheraton's *Drawing Book*, 1793. Took apps named Robert Clubb in 1787; Thomas Roberts and Coleclough in 1790; Litler in 1791; and George Todd, c.1793. [D; poll bk; Chester freemen rolls and app. bks]

Henderson, William James, 19 Northumberland St, Marylebone, London, cm and u (1835–39). [D]

Henderson & Rich, 424 Strand, London, u (1794). [D]

Hendrich, John, Bridge St, Warrington, Lancs., u (1778). Insured utensils, stock and goods for £250 out of a total of £300 in 1778. [GL, Sun MS vol. 268, p. 571]

Hendy, —, Newton Bushel, Devon, cm (1797–98). [D]

Heneage (or Hernage), Robert, York (1777–1802). Of Butterwick, app. to John Wright, cm, on 10 December 1777. Assigned to William Hawkins, and admitted freeman in 1802. [York app. reg. and freemen rolls]

Hen(n)ekin, George, London, carver and gilder (1784–1809). Addresses given at 9 Marylebone St, 1784, and 7 Charles St, Berners St, 1804–09. Neo-classical trade card with female figure and gryphon reads: 'GEO. HENNEKIN, Carver & Gilder in General, N.° 9 Marylebone Street, GOLDEN SQUARE. Pictures & Prints, Framed & Glaz'd...'. Heal dates card to 1809. [D; poll bk; Banks Coll., BM] Possibly George Henniken.

Hen(n)ekin (Heneken or Henniken), Simon, London, carver and gilder (1749–76). Addresses given at Wardour St in 1749, and Edward St, opposite Broad St, Soho, 1763–76. Trade card with classical female figure, and putto sculpting a term reads: 'CARVING and GILDING Either in the Building, Ship, Superior Furniture Way — Executed with the utmost expedition at Reasonable Prices ... NB. Frames of all sorts made in the neatest taste.' Described as 'Eminent for making laymen for painters etc.'. Compiled an *Album of Original Drawings*, of upwards of 400 coats of arms, dated 1776. [D; poll bk; Heal]

Heness, Richard, Bristol, carver and gilder (1799–1838). Addresses given at St James's Churchyard, 1799–1801; 7 St Michael's Hill, 1807–09; St Michael's Hill, 1810–12; St John's St, 1813; 1 Queen St, St Michael's, 1819; and Callowhill St in 1838. [D]

Heness, Thomas, 15 Palace Row, New Rd, London, carver and gilder (1839). [D]

Henessy, John, 12 King St, Toxteth Park, Liverpool, cm (1837–39). [D]

Henley, —, Newton Abbot, Devon, cm (1793–1809). Subscribed to Sheraton's *Drawing Book*, 1793. Sale of dwelling house advertised in *Exeter Flying Post*, 20 July 1809.

Henley, John, 8 Robert St, London, wood carver, cm and bedpillar carver (1832–34). [D]

Henling (or Henlins), Peter, 1 Hunts Ct, St Martin's Lane, London, cm (1786). Took out a Sun Insurance policy on 4 April 1786 for £200, of which utensils etc. accounted for £100. [GL, Sun MS vol. 336, p. 114]

Henman, John, 7 Charles St, City Rd, London, bed and mattress maker (1822–28). [D]

Hennen, John, 16 Cow Cross St, London, cm (1823). Took out a Sun Insurance policy on 1 December 1823 for £150 on household goods in house of an umbrella maker, where no cabinet work was done; and £30 for a chest of tools in workshop of Blackman, cm, 7 Green St, Leicester Sq. [GL, Sun MS vol. 499, ref. 1010727]

Hennesy & Pelly, 105 Wardour St, Oxford St, London, u and dealers in second-hand furniture. George III mahogany 'bonheur du jour' recorded: the concave-fronted superstructure with four small drawers flanked by cupboards; and the lower part with two drawers, one fitted with a rising leather panel and compartments; raised on square tapering legs. The writing table bears label which gives address and trade, and reads: 'Furniture Repaired, warehoused and packed. Funerals Conducted.' [Sotheby's, 10 December 1971, lot 97]

Henniken, George, 1 Wethey Ct, White Cross St, London, cm (1775). Insured his house for £300 in 1775. [GL, Sun MS vol. 243, p. 521] Possibly George Hen(n)ekin.

Henniker, Sir John, Bart, 31 Litchfield St, Soho, London, chair and cm (1790–93). [D] See John Henning.

Henning, David, London, upholder (1782–1823). Recorded in partnership with Samuel Parke in Piccadilly before August 1782, when declared bankrupt, *Gents Mag.*; 23 Leicester Sq., 1794–1821; and 66 St James St, 1822–23. Named in Sheraton's list of master cabinet makers, 1803; and in the Windsor Royal Archives, on 10 January 1817 receiving £3 for 'Taking down cleaning replacing furniture at the Opera Box.' [D; RA 35509]

Henning, George, 112 Wardour St, Soho, London, chair and sofa maker (1820–28). Trading with Thomas Henning in 1820; and with Sawyer in 1823. [D]

Henning(s), George, 10 Broad St, Golden Sq., London, cm and chairmaker (1829–35). [D]

Henning, John, 31 Litchfield St, Soho, London, chair and cm (1790–93). Subscribed to Sheraton's *Drawing Book*, 1793. [D] See Sir John Henniker.

Henningham, J. & G., 3 New Compton St, Soho, London, japanners and cabinet varnishers, ornamental painters of musical instruments (1812–19). [D]

Henry, G., address unrecorded, gilder (1792–95). Named in the account book, 1792–95 of Kennet & Kidd, cm and u, New Bond St, London. [PRO, C114/181, journal no. 3]

Henry, Girardus, 11 Union St, Oxford St, London, carver and gilder (1775–95). Took out a Sun Insurance policy in 1775 for £200, £50 on utensils and stock. On 12 October 1795 took app. named William Lipper for £32 6s. [GL, Sun MS vol. 242, p. 75; PRO, IRI/36]

Henry, John, 45 Little Bartholomew Close, London, cm (1824). Took out Sun Insurance for £400 on 8 January 1824. [GL, Sun MS vol. 497, ref. 1012464]

Hensell, Charles, 5 David St, Marylebone, London, cm and u (1827–28). [D]

Henshaw, George, 3 North St, Fitzroy Sq., London, cm and u (1839). [D]

Henshaw, James, London, carver and gilder (1808–39). Addresses given at 1 Mason Pl., Somerstown in 1808; 53 Chapel St, Pentonville in 1835; and 61 Chapel St, 1837–39. [D]

Henshaw, John, Chester, cm (1789). Son of Mary Henshaw, widow; app. to Robert Adams, cm, 20 August to 3 December 1789. [Chester app. bks]

Henshaw, John, Nottingham, joiner and cm (1796–1808). Son of James Henshaw, fish-hook maker of Nottingham; taken as app. in 1796. Took apps named Sam. Littlewood in 1807 and John Shelton in 1808. [Nottingham app. list]

Henshaw, William, 'The Cabinet & Chair', South side of St Paul's Churchyard, London, cm (1754–73). A member of the Joiners' Co. His trade card indicates that he made and sold 'all Sorts of Glass, Chair and Cabinet Work'. The card is framed in the Rococo manner with figures of Chinamen and engravings of a chair and cabinet on stand in the Chippendale style. Patronage was invited from 'Gentlemen, Merchants and Others'. In 1754 Henshaw subscribed to Chippendale's *Director.* Henshaw took out licences to employ non-freemen in 1757–58 and 1770–72. These licences covered the employment of three or four men only on a short-term basis. He took as app. in 1759 Richard Brocas at a premium of £31 10s and William Goldsmith at £10 10s. In 1761 John White was also taken as app. at a premium of £40. By 1763 his premises in St Paul's Churchyard had been numbered 18 and by 1770 he had taken a partner, Henry Kettle, who was to continue the business alone after c. 1773. [D; Heal; GL, City Licence bks, vols 1, 3 and 7] B.A.

Henshaw, William, address unrecorded. In August 1667 supplied inlaid cabinet, table and stands to the Duke of Richmond. [Charles Stuart, Duke of Richmond papers, vol. 4, bills 1661–73: notes from Symonds papers, Winterthur, Delaware in V&A archives]

Henshaw, William, St Matthew's St, Ipswich, Suffolk, carver and gilder (1824). [D]

Hensman, Thomas, New St, Birmingham, cm and u (1809–35). Recorded at no.15, 1814–22, and no.18 in 1830–35. Submitted bill to Mrs Leigh of Stoneleigh, Warks. on 26 April 1814 totalling £29 7s 2d, and including 'A Mahog. Loo Table on a Grecian Claw Stand, best Castors', £12 12s; 'A fine green Cloth cover to D°. made up with silk binding', £1 2s; Kidderminster carpeting costing £21 3s 6d, cut and fitted over Brussels carpeting; and a hearth rug. The bill head gave address of manufactory and warerooms at 15 New St, which contained 'a general Assortment of elegant Furniture'. Trade card, c.1800–15, recorded. [D; Shakespeare Birthplace Trust, Leigh receipts, DR 18/5; Landauer Coll., MMA, NY]

Hensman, W. D., High St, Thrapston, Northants., cm/joiner (1823). [D]

Henzell, Gabriel, Newcastle, joiner, cm and house carpenter (1783–1824). Recorded at Flesh Mkt, 1783–1809; and Bigg Mkt in 1824 as G. Henzell jnr. In 1783 advertised in *Newcastle Courant,* 24 May, 'that his Mother having declined the Joiner and Cabinet business ... he intends carrying on the Business, in all its branches, at his Shops in the Flesh-market ... Apprentice wanted.' 'Mrs. Henzell, inkeeper' recorded in Flesh Mkt in 1801. In *Newcastle Courant,* 22 April 1809, Gabriel Henzell announced that he had commenced business as appraiser and auctioneer. [D]

Henzell, William, Newcastle, joiner and cm (1775–87). Addresses given at St Nicholas's Churchyard in 1778, and Bigg Mkt, 1787. Named in *Newcastle Courant,* 2 December

1775 as cosignator of letter supporting Britain in American War. [D]

Hepbourne, Francis, Annapolis, USA, late of London, cm and chairmaker (1769). Advertised in *Maryland Gazette,* 22 June 1769.

Heppel(l(), John, 53 Wigmore St, Cavendish Sq., London, upholder (1793–1816). Named in Sheraton's list of master cabinet makers, 1803. [D]

Hepple, Tristram, Blyth, Northumb., joiner and/or cm (1834). [D]

Hepplewhite, Alice & Co., see George Hepplewhite.

Hepplewhite, George, Redcross St, Cripplegate, London, cm (d. 1786). A very elusive figure recorded in only one trade directory [Lowndes, 1786] as Kepplewhite & Son (*sic*), cm of 48 Redcross St. At Christmas 1785 George Applewhite (*sic*) snr and jnr took out a Sun Insurance policy on the premises of which 'utensils and stock' accounted for £500. [GL, Sun MS vol. 327, p. 32] Another son John living at the same address subscribed to George Richardson's *Treatise on the Five Orders of Architecture,* 1787. [Liverpool RO, 920 GKE/2/20] The father died intestate and administration was granted on 27 June 1786 to his widow, Alice; accounts were passed in December and again in June 1787 showing that his estate was worth less than £600. [PRO, Prob. 6/162, p. 300] A notice in the *Public Ledger,* 10 October 1786 announced that 'the valuable stock in trade and household furniture of Mr Hepplewhite, cabinet manufacturer deceased' were to be sold by auction. Two years after his death I. & J. Taylor published a folio volume of furniture designs, *The Cabinet-maker and Upholsterer's Guide,* from drawings by 'A Hepplewhite & Co., Cabinet-Maker', suggesting that his widow continued the business. Advertisements for this book in the *Lincoln, Rutland and Stamford Mercury,* 18 January 1788 and *Williamson's Liverpool Advertiser,* 18 February 1788 show that it cost £2 2s and was promoted by subscription. The *Guide* was reprinted with one additional plate and minor alterations in 1789, while a third 'improved' edition appeared in 1794 containing an extra plate and a free revision of the designs for chairs. Six engravings in *The Cabinet-Makers' London Book of Prices,* 1793, are signed 'Hepplewhite' or 'Heppelwhite'.

The note to plate X states that a hall chair 'has been executed with good effect for His Royal Highness the Prince of Wales', but no bills for furniture supplied by the firm have ever been traced. Accordingly, Hepplewhite's fame rests entirely on the pattern book issued by his widow; none of the plates are signed so even his authorship of the designs is open to doubt. However, the *Guide* provides a valuable record of respectable household furniture dating from the mid 1780s which, in the words of the preface seeks 'to unite elegance and utility, and blend the useful with the agreeable'; the writer further states 'we designedly followed the latest and most prevailing fashions'. In 1791 Sheraton criticized Hepplewhite's designs, particularly the chairs, observing they have 'already caught the decline', a jibe which explains the revisions to the 1794 edition. There is no evidence for the tradition that Hepplewhite was app. to Gillows, apart from the rather striking resemblance of some plates in the *Guide* to certain drawings in their Estimate Sketch Books; indeed they informed a customer on 27 March 1801 'We have not Hebblethwaite's Publication and are at a loss to know the form of the Brackets you approve of . . .'. [Westminster Ref. Lib., Gillow records] C.G.G.

Heptinstall, Joseph, Edmund St, Birmingham, cm, u and broker (1830). [D]

Heptinstall, William, address unrecorded, u (1803). Subscribed to Sheraton's *Cabinet Dictionary,* 1803.

Hepworth, J., 12 Little St Martin's Lane, Long Acre, London, cm, u and undertaker (1795–1806). Named in Sheraton's list of master cabinet makers, 1803. [D]

Hepworth, James, Raistrick, Yorks., joiner and/or cm (1834). [D]

Hepworth, John, Brighouse, Halifax, Yorks., cm, u and joiner (1828–34). Trading as John Hepworth & Son, 1830–34, at Hipperholme-cum-Brighouse in 1830. [D]

Hepworth, Joseph, Brighouse, Halifax, Yorks., joiner and/or cm (1834). [D]

Hepworth, Thomas, Snaith, near Selby, Yorks., cm and house carpenter (1822–26). [D]

Hepworth, William, 33 Bond St, Golden Sq., London, cm and upholder (1816–29). [D]

Hepworth, William, 53 Market St, Bradford, Yorks., cm (1834). [D]

Herbert, Charles, 5 Punderson Pl., Bethnal Green Rd, London, cm and u (1839). [D]

Herbert, Edward Geoffrey, Lancaster, joiner and cm (1811–12). [Lancaster freemen rolls]

Herbert, John, Lancaster, 'glazier and maker' (1796–1840). [Westminster Ref. Lib., Gillow records]

Herbert, John, Lancaster, cm (1820–29). App. to L. Redmayne in 1820, and admitted freeman, 1828–29. [Lancaster app. reg. and freemen rolls]

Herbert, Peter, Exeter, Devon, cm (1816). [Poll bk]

Herbert, Peter, St Michael's parish, Bristol, cm (1781–84). [D]

Herbert, Thomas, Marske, Yorks., joiner, cm and/or cartwright (1834). [D]

Herford, —, King St, Soho, London, cm (1745). Notice in *London Evening Post*, 5–7 February 1745, read: 'On Saturday Night as one Mr. Herford, a Cabinet Maker in King Street, Soho, was passing by the Seven Dials, he was attack'd by Three Ruffians who robb'd him of Eighteen Shillings and some Half Pence, and got off with their Booty.'

Herley, James, 5 Whitmore St, Hoxton, London, desk, writing box and cm (1839). [D]

Herman, Julius David, 16 Soho Sq., London, carver and gilder (1837–39). [D]

Hermann, Louis, 4 Greek St, Soho, London, carver and gilder (1835). [D]

Hermow & Son, Richard, 22 King St, St James's London. Named in the Windsor Royal Archives, Lord Chamberlain's accounts on 19 January 1838, receiving £2 for '2 Wine Coolers Lined with Lead.'

Hernage, Robert, 11 Vaughan's Buildings, Old Haymarket, London, cm (1835–37). [D]

Herne, Richard, Brook St, Holborn, London, u (1765). [D]

Herod, Edward, 6 Castle St, Long Acre, London, broker and u (1808). [D]

Heron, J. & T., Manchester, cm (1826). Declared bankrupt, *Liverpool Mercury*, 10 March 1826. Probably John and Thomas.

Heron, John, New Bailey St, Manchester, cm and chairmaker (1811–29). Trading at no. 8, 1811–22; and no. 6, 1824–29. [D] See Thomas Heron.

Heron, John & Son, Jones St, Salford, Lancs., cm (1828). [D]

Heron, Thomas, 6 New Bailey St, Manchester, cm (1828). [D]

Herrin, William, Millburngate, Durham, upholder (1757). Took app. named Smith in 1757. [S of G, app. index]

Herring, Ann, 17 Trinity St, Bristol, house-upholsterer (1775). [D]

Herring, George, High St, Newington Butts, London, cm (1804–28). Trading at 2 Fredericks Pl., High St in 1804; 20 High St, 1809 and 1822–28; and no. 14 in 1817. Took out Sun Insurance policies on 7 May 1804 for £200, £80 accounting for stock and utensils; and on 23 October 1809

for £450, £150 on stock and utensils. [D; GL, Sun MS vol. 430, ref. 762344; vol. 443, ref. 836174] See Joseph Herring.

Herring, Henry, 13 Lad Lane, London, cm and wholesale upholder (1735–68). Herring, Smith & Slack, successors to Henry Herring, were trading at this address, 1763–68. [D; Heal]

Herring, Henry, London, u and warehouseman (1743–71). Recorded in St Lawrence Jewry, on 11 January 1743/44 when admitted freeman of the Upholders' Co. by redemption. Took apps named John Smith, 1743–57, and George Humphries, 1763–71. [GL, Upholders' Co. records]

Herring, James, address unrecorded, upholder (1787–94). Son of James Herring of Devizes, Wilts.; app. to John Phillips on 22 March 1787, and admitted freeman of the Upholders' Co. by servitude on 2 April 1794. [GL, Upholders' Co. records]

Herring, James, address unrecorded. Submitted bill to G. Wentworth of Woolley Hall, Yorks., for furniture and upholstery supplied between January and March 1795, totalling £39 3s. [YAS, Wentworth papers, MD 272/2]

Herring, John, 11 Queen St, Hoxton, London, chair and sofa maker (1839). [D]

Herring, John, 9 Thomas St, Whitechapel, London, wood carver and cm (1839). [D]

Herring, Joseph, 20 High St, Newington, London, blind and cm (1820). [D] See George Herring.

Herring, Robert, Fleet St, London, upholder, cm, appraiser, auctioneer and undertaker (1769–1839). Presumably two tradesmen, snr and jnr, the latter being called Robert William Herring. Recorded at 96 Fleet St, 1771–83; and no. 109, 1784–1839. Trade card showing draped four-post bedstead gives address at 109 Fleet St. [Banks Coll., BM] Admitted Freeman of the Upholders' Co. by redemption on 1 November 1769. Took apps named Joseph Clowes, 1776–83, and William Chivers, 1785–94. Fined for non-service at St Bride's, 1779, 1821 and 1827; and served as Collector for the Poor in 1789. [GL, MS 6561, p. 110] Took out Sun Insurance policies in 1780 for £1,000, of which £500 accounted for utensils and stock; and on 28 December 1807 for £1,800, of which stock and utensils accounted for £1,050. Subscribed to Sheraton's *Cabinet Dictionary*, and named in his list of master cabinet makers, 1803. [D; GL, Upholders' Co. records; GL, Sun MS vol. 281, p. 100; vol. 442, ref. 812191]

Herring, William, Castlegate, Penrith, Cumb., joiner and cm (1828–34). [D]

Herring & Co., 112 Wardour St, Soho, London, chair manufacturers (1816). [D]

Herrington, H., High St, Wandsworth, London, cm (1838). [D]

Herrol, John, Strangeways, Manchester, cm (1804). [D]

Hersant, Charles, 25 Old Bethlem, London, cm, u and auctioneer (1822–23). [D]

Hersant (or Horsant), John, 2 Brokers Row, Moorfields, London, cm, u and undertaker (1820–21). [D]

Hersant, W., 2 Brokers Row, Moorfields, London, cm and u (1823–25). [D]

Hertoch, Jacob, address unrecorded, frame maker (1702). Enlarged two Italian pictures of architectural subjects for overdoors in the 2nd Duchess of Bedford's drawing room, probably at Bedford House, London. [Bedford Office, London]

Hervé, François, Johns (or John) St, London, cm and chairmaker (1781–96). While François Hervé is known to have worked for the most fashionable and fastidious patrons, such as the Prince of Wales, the Duke of Devonshire and Earl Spencer, he still remains a shadowy figure. His name is virtually absent from the London directories, but two entries of 1790 and 1793 record that an 'F. Herve chairmaker' worked at 32

Johns St, off Tottenham Ct Rd. He had earlier been in partnership with John Meschain of the same address. Both names appear on a brass tablet found upon a folding library table-cum-steps, of their invention (Fig. 43). Meschain is recorded from at least 1769 as a cabriole chairmaker, and in 1770 he took app. named Gabriel Laurent La Porte, presumably also of French extraction. [Boyd's index to IR app. reg., 4, p. 682] In January 1769 he supplied '18 French Cabriolets' at £1 7s each to Shelburne House, Berkeley Sq., London. [Bowood MS] In 1777 'John Meschain, cabinet and chairmaker' took out an insurance policy for £600 on premises at 32 St John St, his utensils and stock being covered for £350. In 1781 Meschain was rated upon a £30 rental — a higher figure than for most others in the street, but was superseded there by Hervé from 1781 until at least 1791. He had moved to 64 John St by 1796, presumably in larger premises across the street (now the middle part of Whitfield St) and was well placed in a still fashionably developing part of London. Whether Francis Hervé fell on harder times is uncertain, but that name is recorded in Holden's 1808 directory as a turner and brushmaker in Kingsgate St, Theobald Rd. In 1782 the John St premises were insured by Catherine Mortel, spinster, with £200 attributable to the workshop and £500 to Hervé's utensils and stock. [GL, Sun MS vol. 298, p. 385]

Hervé's style is now best represented by the documented pieces at Chatsworth where it can be seen as a light, elegant and adroit mixture of English and French detail. Thus the back legs of his chairs are splayed in the English manner, while some of his carved detail, for example the interlocked C-scrolls or the undulating shaping of his chair backs is wholly French, and a very conservative survival of the Rococo motifs of the 1750s. Most extant Hervé pieces were either painted to harmonize with the soft furnishings elsewhere in the rooms concerned or were gilded. In directory entries Hervé described himself as 'a cabriole chairmaker'. Many of his chairs have caned backs or seats, and, to reduce costs, he sometimes employed 'composition' ornaments in substitution for hand-carving. His output included beside seat furniture, pier tables, state beds and chandeliers. Hervé worked in conjunction with well-known architects such as John Carr at Chatsworth (for the Duke of Devonshire), and perhaps at Welbeck (for Devonshire's brother-in-law, the Duke of Portland) with James Wyatt; at Heveningham (for either Sir Gerard Vanneck, or his brother, later created the 1st Lord Huntingfield) and with Henry Holland at Althorp for Earl Spencer; and at Carlton House for George, Prince of Wales. There is no firm evidence that Hervé was dependent upon any of those architects for furniture designs though the proportions of several of his larger pieces were determined by the spaces allotted for them within those architects' designs. Hervé was also linked with his fellow Frenchmen, such as Guillaume Gaubert at both Chatsworth and Carlton House. The style of his documented pieces embodies certain distinctive features, among them the stepping down of the seat rails at their junction with the legs, a sensible constructional device that retained the slender elegance of the seat rails while providing a stronger joint at the leg junctions. The top-most part of the leg is frequently a quadrant in plan, sometimes overlaid with a patera or a half patera of radiating petals or foliage. The leg below the seat frame often has a turned necking band deeper than that found upon wholly English chairs, and the flutes of the legs are sometimes further enriched with reeding or with the carved chandelles that are also French in inspiration.

CHATSWORTH, Derbs. (5th Duke of Devonshire). 1782–85: Supplied numerous suites of upholstered and caned seat furniture, many of which can still be identified at the house. [I. Hall, 'A neoclassical episode at Chatsworth', *Burlington*, June 1980, pp. 400–14]

CARLTON HOUSE, London (Prince of Wales). 1783–94: Supplied considerable amounts of furniture for interiors, notably the Chinese Drawing Room. [*Burlington*, September 1967, pp. 518–28; *Conn.*, June 1977, pp. 116–25]

WINDSOR CASTLE (George III). 1789–92: Received payments on account 10 October 1789, £100 and 8 August 1792, £150. [Windsor RA 88736 and 88812]

ALTHORP, Northants. (Lady Spencer). 1791: A bill dated 25 January 1791 invoices '6 Cabriole Backstools' at £2 0s 6d each and '2 Tete a Tete to match' at £3 13s each 'by order of Messrs Holland and Daguire'. [*Apollo*, June 1968, pp. 271–72]

WOBURN ABBEY, Beds. (5th Duke of Bedford). 1791: Paid £45 7s 7d in December 1791 for unspecified work by order of Henry Holland. [Bedford Office, London]

BROADLANDS, Hants. (2nd Viscount Palmerston): A furniture design is inscribed 'Herve'. [*C. Life*, 5 Feburary 1981, p. 346]

LIBRARY STEPS (with label). Sets of library steps that fold down to form a table have been recorded with the inscription on a wood tablet 'Herve Fecit No. 32 John Street/Tottenham Court Road'; an example is at the V & A (W.7–1932). Other sets bear brass labels engraved 'Invented & SOLD BY MESCHAIN & HERVÉ, No. 32 in Johns Street TOTTENHAM Court ROAD' (Sotheby's, 7 July 1967, lot 167). There is a signed set at Heveningham Hall, Suffolk.   I.H.

Heselden (or Heseldon), John, Lancaster, cm (1784–d.1811). Death reported in *Lancaster Gazette*, 21 January 1811. [Poll bk]

Hesketh, Thomas, Chester, cm (1818–26). Addresses given at Common-Hall St in 1818 and Northgate St, 1819–26. Admitted freeman in 1818. [Chester freemen rolls and poll bks]

Heskin, Sidney, Liverpool, u (1827). App. to William Bickerstaff in 1827. [Liverpool app. enrolment bk]

Hescox & Cooper, 105 Aldersgate St, London, cm and joiner (1808). [D]

Heslop, George, Westgate, Ripon, Yorks., cm and joiner (1822–29). [D]

Heslop, Thomas, Richmond, Yorks., u (1823–40). Addresses given at Rosemary Lane, 1823; Finkle St in 1827; and Maison Dieu, 1840. [D]

Hesp, John, Eastgate, Pickering, Yorks., joiner and cm (1840). [D]

Hesseldon, Isaac, Lancaster. Named in the Gillow records, 1787–1800. [Westminster Ref. Lib.]

Hesseldon, Isaac jnr, Lancaster, caner (1800). [Westminster Ref. Lib., Gillow records, vol. 344/98, p. 1598]

Hesseldon, John, London, cm (1784). [Lancaster poll bk]

Hesseldon, John, Lancaster. Named in the Gillow records, 1785–1807. [Westminster Ref. Lib.]

Hestlow, Joseph, 13 New St, Cloth Fair, London, cm (1809–11). [D]

Hetherington, Francis, 15 Gt Newton St, Manchester, cm (1794). [D]

Hetherington, George, Front St, Brampton, Carlisle, Cumb., joiner and/or cm (1829). [D]

Hetherington, Jonathan, Kirkgate, Cockermouth, Cumb., cm and joiner (1828–29). [D]

Hetherington, Michael, Strand St, Whitehaven, Cumb., looking-glass manufacturer (1811). [D]

Hetl(e)y, Thomas, Witch St, London, upholder (1709–16). Took out Hand in Hand Insurance policies on 29 April 1709 and April 1716 for £225 on his house; and a Sun policy on

7 July 1716 on goods and merchandise in his house. [GL, Hand in Hand MS vol. 7, ref. 2676; vol. 15, p. 621; GL, Sun MS vol. 5, ref. 6964] Possibly the Thomas Hetley, u, who supplied upholstery and furniture to Hatfield House, Herts., 1710–11. In June 1710 he was paid £233 18s including £21 3s for a wainscot bedstead; £20 for a woodwork tester; and £5 for six walnut framed chairs and two square stools. In December 1710 he received £100 in part for upholstery; and in May 1711, £267 for general supply of materials. [Hatfield House, MS bills 473] Named in the Felbrigg, Norfolk papers on 5 March 1710 receiving £50; and in February 1711, £40. [Norfolk RO, Felgrigg papers, WKC 6/23]

Hetley & Purvis, High St, Berwick-upon-Tweed, Northumb., cm and u (1827). [D]

Heward, John, Brampton, Cumb., joiner and cm (1828–29). [D]

Hewatt, C., Lancaster. Named in the Gillow records in 1813 working on a screen, and in 1814 on a press. [Westminster Ref. Lib., Gillow vol. 344/99, pp. 1943 and 1967]

Hewell, William, Barnstaple, Devon, cm (1745–53). Took apps named Price in 1745 and Dark in 1753. [S of G, app. index]

Hewetson, George, 19 Noel St, London, cm (1808). [D]

Hewetson, John, 36 Lower Marsh, Lambeth, London, cm and buhl manufacturer (1822–28). [D]

Hewetson, John, Basin, Pimlico, London, cm (1829). [D]

Hewetson, Thomas, 59 Portplace Lane, London, carver and fret cutter (1835). [D]

Hewetson, Thomas, 8 Robert St, Bedford Row, London, wood carver and cm (1839). [D]

Hewetson, Thomas, William & John, 204 Tottenham Ct Rd, London, cm, u and dealer in carpets (1839–40). Took out a Sun Insurance policy in 1840. [D; GL, Sun MS vol. 574, ref. 1328756]

Hewetson Brothers, 185 Oxford St, London, u (1839). [D]

Hewett, —, Shrewsbury, Salop, u (1798). [D] Probably Thomas Hewett.

Hewett, G., Deacon Ct, Southampton, Hants., cm (1836). [D]

Hewett, James, St Peter St, Tiverton, Devon, cm (1830–38). [D]

Hewett (or Hewitt), James, West St, Farnham, Surrey, turner and chairmaker (1832–38). [D]

Hewett, John, Liverpool, cm (d.1811). Death of this 'eminent cabinet maker' in Liverpool on 7 August 1811 reported in *Liverpool Mercury*, 16 August. See John and Thomas Hewit(t) of Liverpool.

Hewett, Mary, Fuller St, Church Row, Church St, Bethnal Green, London, chairmaker (1814). Took out a Sun Insurance policy on 20 July 1814 for £450, £150 accounting for stock, utensils and workshop. [GL, Sun MS vol. 461, ref. 895716] See Richard and William Hewett.

Hewett, Richard, 23 Fuller St, Bethnal Green, London, chair and sofa maker (1839). [D] See Mary and William Hewett.

Hewett, William, Castleford, Yorks., cm (1822). [D]

Hewett, William, Fuller St, Bethnal Green, London, Windsor chair and sofa maker (1829–39). Recorded as W. & R. Hewett at no. 29, 1827–29, and alone at no. 31, 1835–39. [D] See Richard Hewett.

Hewett & Jefferson, Sunderland, Co. Durham, cm (1793). Subscribed to Sheraton's *Drawing Book*, 1793. Possibly John F. Hewitt.

Hewick, Charles, Clayton St, Colne, Lancs., u (b. c. 1796–1841). Recorded in the 1841 Census as not of local origin.

Hewison, Richard, Louth, Lincs., cm and joiner (1826–28). Recorded at Westgate in 1826 and Upgate in 1828. [D]

Hewit, Charles Daniel, 3 New North St, Finsbury, London, cm and u (1839). [D]

Hewit, John snr, West Cowes, Isle of Wight, Hants., cm (1780).

Insured his house for £100 in 1780. [GL, Sun MS vol. 288, p. 160]

Hewit(t), John, Liverpool, cm (1769–1803). Addresses given at School Lane, 1769–73; 19 Tarleton St, 1774; no. 23 in 1781 and 1794; no. 24 in 1790; no. 26 in 1796; as Hewit & Son at no. 23 in 1800 and no. 26, 1800–03. Took out a Sun Insurance policy on 21 July 1792 for £400, including £100 on workshops and utensils in yard. Marriage of John Hewitt jnr, cm of Tarleton St to Miss Smith, daughter of Captain Smith of Hunter St, at St Ann's Church, reported in *Billinge's Liverpool Advertiser*, 11 February 1799. [D; GL, Sun MS vol. 388, p. 331] Presumably two related tradesmen are concerned here. See George Hewitt.

Hewit, John, 4 Fleet St, Hanover St, Liverpool, cm (1800). [D]

Hewit, Nathaniel, address unrecorded, upholder (1740–47). Son of Samuel Hewit, Gent. of St Saviour's, Southwark; app. to Ambrose Pearman on 4 June 1740, and admitted freeman of the Upholders' Co. by servitude on 2 July 1747. [GL, Upholders' Co. records] Possibly Nathaniel Hewitt.

Hewit(t), Thomas, Shrewsbury, Salop, u (1780–86). Trading in Market Pl., 1786. [D; Shrewsbury burgess roll] See Hewett, —.

Hewit & Tyrer, 30 Sparling St, Liverpool, cm (1805–07). [D]

Hewitt, —, Lancaster. Named in the Gillow records, 1794 and 1815. [Westminster Ref. Lib.]

Hewitt, Catherine, Wolverhampton, Staffs., chair bottom rusher (1838). [D]

Hewitt, George, Liverpool, u (1817–39). Addresses given at 28 Tarleton St, 1835–37, and 26 Virgil St, 1839. App. to George Philander Lyon in 1817, and admitted freeman, as George Wood Hewitt, on 2 November 1826. [D; Liverpool app. enrolment bk and freemen reg.]

Hewitt, Henry, Knotty Ash, West Derby, Lancs., joiner and cm (1834). [D]

Hewitt, John, London, upholder, dealer and chapman (1760–86). Recorded in Gt George St, Hanover Sq., 1769–72, and George St, 1774–86. Son of Edward Hewitt, tallow chandler of St George's; app. to Thomas Dobyns on 3 July 1760, and admitted freeman of the Upholders' Co. by servitude on 1 October 1767. Named in Bailey's List of bankrupts, January 1774; and as bankrupt in *Williamson's Liverpool Advertiser*, 8 June 1774. [GL, Upholders' Co. records]

Hewitt, John, London (?). In 1771 supplied furniture to Charles Long of Saxmundham, Suffolk, totalling £8 0s 6d: on 12 March a 'Mahogany Shirt horse'; on 23 May 'A Mahogany Box with a good lock and Key'; and on 24 May, two pairs of Wilton bedside carpets and a pair of Scotch carpets. [Suffolk RO, 18/EC/6]

Hewitt, John, cm (1777). See John Tilleard.

Hewitt, John, London, cm (1793). Subscribed to Sheraton's *Drawing Book*, 1793.

Hewitt, John F., Sunderland, Co. Durham, cm (1798–1827). Trading at Coronation St, Bishop Wearmouth in 1827. [D] Possibly of Hewett & Jefferson.

Hewitt, John & William, 131 and 160 Goswell St, London, kitchen furniture and lamps, wholesale dealer in lanthorn leaves (1819–37). [D]

Hewitt, John, Downley, High Wycombe, Bucks., chairmaker (b. c. 1791–1841). Aged 50 at the time of the 1841 Census.

Hewitt, (or Hewett), Nathaniel, at 'The Crown & Cushion', near St Thomas's Gate, Southwark (42 Borough), London, u, appraiser and undertaker (1768–77). Rococo trade card reads: 'Makes & Sells all Sorts of fashionable Standing Beds, Feather Beds, Blankets, Quilts, Ruggs, Coverlets, Flanders and English Ticking; Also Leather, Cane and Matted Bottom Chairs at reasonable Rates, Wholesale or Retail. N.B. All

Sorts of Cabinet Work at the lowest Price.' [D; Heal] Possibly Nathaniel Hewit.

Hewitt, Phillip, Chapel St, Stockwell, London, u (1839). [D]

Hewitt (or Hewett), Richard, Upton-cum-Chalvey, Slough, Bucks., chairmaker and wheeler (d.1777). Windsor chair of elm, fruitwood, ash, beech and stained red recorded, bearing fragments of paper label on the bottom of the seat, reading 'RICHARD HEWETT / CHAIR-MAKER, / At Slough, in the ...ar Windsor, / MAKES and sells ... Forest Chairs / and all sorts ...'. Described at his burial, 7 September 1777 as a wheeler, or wheelwright. [Coll. of T. Crispin; *Furn. Hist.*, 1978, pl. 53B; 1979, pl. 84; Exhib. Cat., *Common Furniture*, Temple Newsam House, Leeds, 1982]

Hewitt, Robert, Stanwix, Carlisle, Cumb., joiner and cm (1828–29). [D]

Hewitt, Thomas, 14 Ann St, Pentonville, London, upholder (1793). Son of John Hewitt, upholder; admitted freeman of the Upholders' Co. on 7 August 1793. [GL, Upholders' Co. records]

Hewit(t), Thomas, Tarleton St, Church St, Liverpool, cm (1800–d.1816). Trading at no. 23, 1800–04; no. 26 with shop at 8 Church Alley, St Peter's, 1805–07; no. 25, 1813–14, with shop at 8 Church Alley in 1814; and 24 Tarleton St, 1816. Signed supplement to the *Liverpool Cabinet and Chair Prices*, 1805, on behalf of the masters. Death reported in *Liverpool Mercury*, 6 December 1816. Notice from Hewitt's widow in the same paper on 20 March 1818 read: 'TO CABINET-MAKERS & OTHERS, TO BE LET, And may be entered upon immediately THAT old established Concern in the Cabinet Making Business, belonging to the late Mr. Thomas Hewitt, in Tarleton-street, Liverpool, where it has been carried on with reputation & advantage for the last forty years...'. [D] See John Hewit(t) and George Hewitt.

Hewitt, Thomas, 45 Richmond St, Manchester, cm (1817). [D]

Hewitt, Thomas, 3 Market St, Leeds, Yorks., cm (1839). [D]

Hewitt, William, North Walsham, Norfolk, cm (1830–39). Trading at Queen St in 1839. [D]

Hewitt, William, William IV Yd, Stockton-on-Tees, Co. Durham, cm (1832). [D]

Hewitt, William, Pontefract, Yorks., joiner and/or cm (1834). [D]

Hewkins, Henry, 8 Tarr's Ct, Manchester, cm (1804). [D]

Hewlett, Charles, Royal Colonnade, New Rd, Brighton, Sussex, u, paper hanger and undertaker (1822–27). Recorded at Marine St in 1822, 2 New Rd, 1824, and 2 Royal Colonnade, 1826. Son Frederick Charles, by wife Martha Hewlett, bapt. on 20 March 1822, and son Frederick on 22 March 1826. [D; E. Sussex RO, PR (bapt.)]

Hewlett, Charles, Castle Gates, Shrewsbury, Salop, cm (1830). [Shrewsbury burgess roll] See William Hewlitt.

Hewlett, George, Wenlock, Salop, cm (1822). [D]

Hewlett, John, Bristol, cm, u and undertaker (1805–13). Addresses given at 7 Bath St, 1805, no. 15, 1806–12; and 10 Bridge St and 51 Redcliff Hill in 1813. [D]

Hewlett, John, Eastgate St, Gloucester, cm, u, auctioneer, appraiser and chairmaker (1820–23). Possibly the J. Hewlett, cm and chairmaker at Bell Lane, c.1822. [D] See Hewlett & Warner.

Hewlett, Robert, Wimborne Minster, Dorset, chairmaker (1761). Took app. named Whitcher in 1761. [S of G, app. index]

Hewlett, Robert, Poole, Dorset, chairmaker (1823–40). Trading at Fish St, 1823–30, and Langland St, 1840. [D]

Hewlett, Stephen, Langland St, Poole, Dorset, chairmaker (1840). [D]

Hewlett, William, Castle St (or Foregate), Shrewsbury, Salop, cm and u (1822–35). [D]

Hewlett & Warner, Eastgate St, Gloucester, cm and u (1830). [D] See John Hewlett.

Hewlings, Samuel, Reading, Berks., upholder (1777). [Poll bk]

Hewlins, P., 15 St Martin's Lane, Charing Cross, London, cm etc. (1792–94). [D]

Hewlin(s), Peter, Strand, London, cm and u, Tunbridge manufacturer (1802–14). Trading at no. 2, 1802–03, and no. 164, 1807–14. Named in Sheraton's list of master cabinet makers, 1803. [D]

Hewlitt, William, Castle Gates, Shrewsbury, Salop, cm and u (1822–28). [D] See Charles Hewlett.

Hewson, J. Bothomley, Wollaton, Notts., cm (1832). [D]

Hewson, Thomas, 8 Yardley St, Spitalfields, London, cm and u (1839). [D]

Hey, James, Eldon St, Finsbury Circus, London, cm (1826–35). Trading at no. 19, 1826–27, and no. 5, 1829–35. [D]

Hey, John, Liversedge, Yorks., joiner and cm (1830). [D]

Hey, William, Church St, Whitby, Yorks., cm/chairmaker (1840). [D]

Heyes, Ann, 28 Marlborough St, Liverpool, u (1835). [D] See Ann Heywood.

Heyes, J., Liverpool, cm (1824). Sale of stock by Stewart & Benton advertised in *Liverpool Mercury*, 12 November 1824. Notice read: 'HOUSEHOLD FURNITURE of a very superior description, the property of Mr. J. HEYES, Cabinet maker (who is removing from the premises he at present occupies in consequence of their being sold) consisting of Mahogany Pembroke, Card & Sofa Tables, Trafalgar Chairs, Sets of Drawers, Mahogany Circular Loo Table, Secretaires, Bookcases & wardrobes, a handsome & complete Gentleman's Writing Table & Secretaire, Ladies' Mahogany & Rosewood Work Tables, on a new plan, a complete set of superb Drawing-room Tables, in Rosewood, richly inlaid, & of exquisite workmanship & beauty...'.

Heyes, John, 59 Bridge St, Manchester, u (1811). [D]

Heyland, Charles, Liverpool, cm (1819). App. to Richard Holliwell in 1819. [Liverpool app. enrolment bk]

Heyley, William, Milford St, Salisbury, Wilts., cm and u (1830). [D]

Heys, Henry, Marsden Sq., Haslingden, Lancs., joiner and cm (1834). [D]

Heywood, Ann, 28 Marlborough St, Liverpool, u (1835). [D] See Ann Heyes.

Heywood, Edward, 27 London Rd, Liverpool, chairmaker (1807). [D]

Heywood, John, 49 Gravel Lane, Salford, Lancs., cm (1797–1804). [D]

Heywood, John, 53 London Rd, Manchester, cm (1813). [D]

Heywood, John, Manor St, Bolton, Lancs., cm and u (1816–18). [D]

Heywood, Martin, Halstead, Essex, u (b.1699–1759). Named in the Essex freeholders book for Hinekford Hundred in 1759 as owning estate in Colne Engaine when aged 60. [Essex RO, Q/RJ1/2]

Hezlewood, Moses, Whitby, Yorks., cm and u (1823–40). Addresses given in Flowergate, 1823, Golden Lion Bk (?), 1828–29, and Baxtergate, 1840. [D]

Hiam, Edward Somerset, 12 Bull & Mouth St, London, u (1780). Insured his house for £200 in 1780. [GL, Sun MS vol. 286, p. 192]

Hiam, J., London, carver and gilder (1835–37). Recorded at 14 Pantechnicon Area, Belgrave Sq., 1835, and 6 Pantechnicon Arcade, 1835–37. Late Regency carved and gilt box recorded inscribed 'HIAM from London, Carver & gilder, etc.' [D; V&A archives]

Hiatt, William, 16 Milk St, Bristol, furniture and ornamental painter, house and sign painter (1838–40). [D]

Hibbeart, John, Hull, Yorks., cm (1780). [Poll bk] Probably John Hibbert.

Hibberd, William, Blandford St Mary, Blandford Forum, Dorset, cm, u and builder (1830). [D]

Hibberdine, John, address unrecorded, upholder (1712–44). Son of William Hibberdine of Woodstock, Oxon.; app. to Thomas Dawson on 19 February 1712. Admitted freeman of the Upholders' Co. by servitude on 25 January 1722/23. Took apps named Peter Fleuriot, 1726–33, and Samuel Hibberdine, 1742–44. [GL, Upholders' Co. records] Possibly:

Hibberdine, John, Philpot Lane, London, upholder (1744). Declared bankrupt, *Gents Mag.*, October 1744.

Hibberdine, Samuel, address unrecorded, upholder (1742–d.1776). Son of William Hibberdine, surgeon of Swerford, Oxon.; app. to John Hibberdine on 29 July 1742, and Samuel Walker, draper, on 16 November 1744. Admitted freeman of the Upholders' Co. by servitude on 2 August 1759. Took apps named William Hill, 1749–58, John Fisher, 1757–65, and Richard Mayow, 1760–67. [GL, Upholders' Co. records]

Hibberdine, William, Crutched Friars, London, upholder (1792–1802). Trading at no. 27 in 1792. Son of Samuel Hibberdine, freeman upholder of London. Admitted freeman of the Upholders' Co. by patrimony on 3 October 1792. [GL, Upholders' Co. records]

Hibbert, Charles, Back Wallgate, Macclesfield, Cheshire, cm (1816). [D]

Hibbert, John, London, u (1668–d.1717). Trading in Bartholomew Close by 1717, when he died and was succeeded at this address by his partner, Philip Bodham. [Heal] The *Weekly Journal or Saturday Post*, 18 May 1717, reported that at his death Hibbert was 'estimated to be worth £100,000'. Clearly a notable tradesman receiving Royal patronage, several of his commissions are documented. In 1668–69 he hired goods to the Lord Chamberlain's Office and is presumably the Mr Hibbert, u of London named in the accounts of C. Blunt, u, for work done in the Royal Household in 1686–87, being paid £17 15s 7d; and in 1687–88, £32 3s 7d. In 1697 Hibbert requested payment by the Lord Chamberlain 'for a Wainscott bedstead Angell fashion with black japaned posts & a set of Rods & Ironwork to the ceiling'. [Lord Chamberlain's Office, PRO, LC9/279; C114/164, pt 1; V&A archives] Between 1685–87 John Hibbert supplied the 5th Earl of Bedford with upholstery, cane chairs, walnut chairs, dressing-tables etc. for Bedford House, including 'a suite of fine landscape tapestry lined with canvas'. Further items were supplied between 1690–91, among them 'a fine horse bone black japanned chair frame for a chair of state and a foot stool upholstered in rich green velvet with a fine green silk fringe', for £12 5s 6d. The total bill amounted to £289 8s 4d and was presented to the 5th Earl by John Hibbert and Thomas Dixon, the receipt being signed by John Hibbert 'for self and partner' in March 1690–91. All previous and one subsequent bill dated September 1691 were in the name of John Hibbert alone. [Bedford Office, London] John Hibbert & Co. receipted a bill in the Annandale accounts, 1701, for '2 rich pieces of fine Japanese tapestry' costing £69. [Hopetoun NRA(S) 888/637] In 1702 the Duke of Leeds paid 'Mr. Hibbert £73.10.0.'. [Child's Bank (Williams & Glyn's)]. In 1711 Nicholas Carey, Esq. of London bought of John Hibbert fabric, window cornices, a walnut wood chair frame, wainscot frame to a bed, bedding etc., costing £216 7s 1d. [Berks, RO, BRO D/ELI 26]

Hibbert, John, Hull, Yorks., cm (1784). [Poll bk] Probably John Hibbeart.

Hick, —, Briggate, Leeds, Yorks., carver, gilder, picture frame maker and looking-glass manufacturer (1815). Advertised in *Leeds Intelligencer*, 30 January 1715. Possibly Joseph Hick.

Hick, Ben., 24 Broad St, Bloomsbury, London, bedstead maker and turner (1817). [D]

Hick, George, 62 Mill St, Hull, Yorks., cm (1826). [D]

Hick(s), John, Blackfriargate, Hull, Yorks., cm, furniture broker and joiner (1803–63). Trading at no. 30, 1803–34, and no. 31, 1838–63. Subscribed to Sheraton's *Cabinet Dictionary*, 1803. [D]

Hick(s), Joseph, Hull, Yorks, cm and chairmaker (1804–31). Addresses given at 10 Wells St, 1817–23, and 21 Osborne St, 1826–31. App. to George Spenceley of Hull in January 1804. Took apps named Richard Carrall and Stephen Newton of Hull in January and July 1817; William Dunning of York in November 1818; and Thomas Whiting in June 1819. [D; Hull app. reg.]

Hick, Joseph, Leeds, Yorks., carver and gilder, varnish maker, furniture japanner, sign and ornamental painter (1817–37). Recorded at 56 Mill Hill in 1817; 9 West Bar, 1828–34 and 12 Westbar in 1837. Trade card gives Mill Hill address and reads: 'Imitations of Wood & Marble. Old Bed & Window Cornices, Wash Stands, Dressing Tables, Chairs &c repainted to any Colour & Varnished to look equal to new. Sofas, Chaise &c Stained in Imitation of Rosewood. India Cabinets repaired & imitated. Bronzing &c. Ladies Work Boxes & Screens neatly Varnished & Polished.' [D; Landauer Coll., MMA, NY] Possibly Hick, —.

Hickes, James, New St, Worcester, cm and u (1828). [D]

Hickey, —, 57 Foregate St, Worcester, carver and gilder (1797–98). [D]

Hickin, James, Dudley St, Birmingham, cm (1818). [D]

Hickin, James, High St, Leominster, Herefs., cm (1835). [D]

Hickin, William, Birmingham, cm, u and chairmaker (1796–1830). Recorded at 112 Dale End in 1828 and 16 Ct, Dale End in 1830. Named in the Shrewsbury burgess roll, 1796. [D]

Hicklenton, William, parish of St Martin at Palace, Norwich, cm (1818–30). App. to William Freeman, and admitted freeman on 3 May 1818. [Norwich freemen reg. and poll bk]

Hicklin, William, 33 Newhall St, Birmingham, cm and u (1835). [D]

Hickman, —, Houndsditch, London, cm (d.1741). Notice in *Daily Post*, Tuesday 28 July 1741 read: 'On Sunday died Mr. Hickman, a wealthy Cabinet-maker in Houndsditch.'

Hickman, Richard, Temple St, Bilston, Staffs., cm (1818–22). Listed also at Newtown in 1818. [D]

Hicks, Frederick, Mount Pleasant Rd, Tunbridge Wells, Kent, cm and u (1839). [D]

Hicks, J., Lower Pembroke St, London. Mahogany easel toilet mirror recorded with rectangular plate and pierced swan-neck pediment, the frame stamped 'J. Hicks, Pembroke Street'. The stamp of 'J. Hicks, 5 Lr. Pembroke St.' also found on pair of marquetry corner cupboards, the tops with radiating panels of sycamore inlaid with satinwood anthemions and rosettes, with ribbon borders in green stained wood; the front with similar motifs and shelves enclosed by doors inlaid with satinwood medallions and urns on a hardwood ground. [Sotheby's, 10 February 1967, lot 90; 19 June 1959, lot 50]

Hicks, James, address unrecorded. Giltwood Neo-classical table recorded as by James Hicks, with top inlaid by Pietro Bossi. [*C. Life*, 11 November 1976, pp. 1358–59]

Hicks, James, 26 Wigmore St, Cavendish Sq., London, manufacturer of portable writing desks, dressing cases, work boxes, tea chests etc. (1809–37). Domed top rosewood work and banded with amaranth, enclosing fitted interior with two mahogany and satinwood caddies and glass mixing bowl. [D; Heal; Christie's, 11 November 1982, lot 18]

Hicks, James, 2 Chapel St, Lamb's Conduit St and Bedford Row, London, cm and u (1835–39). [D]

Hicks, John, St George's parish, Stamford, Lincs., u (1830–32). [Poll bks]

Hicks, John jnr, Sandwich, Kent, cm (1832–39). Shared business with Donne at Margaret St in 1839. [D; poll bks]

Hicks, Joseph, Briggate, Leeds, Yorks. carver and gilder (1816). [D]

Hicks, Leonard, Norwich, cm and u (1818–30). Recorded in St Stephen's, 1822, and St Michael at Thorn, 1830. App. to John Norris, and admitted freeman on 24 February 1818. [D; poll bk and freemen reg.]

Hicks, Peter, Bristol, cm (1781). [Poll bk]

Hicks, Thomas, Bell Lane, Gloucester, cm, carver, gilder, house &c. painter (1822–23). [D]

Hicks, William, at 'The Peacock', Houndsditch, Aldgate, London, u (1714). Insured goods and merchandise in his house on 26 June 1714. [GL, Sun MS vol. 4, ref. 4072]

Hickson, Henry, 27 Hart St, Liverpool, carver and gilder (1835). [D]

Hickson, Mathew jnr, Lincoln, cm (1806). [Lincoln freemen rolls]

Hide — See also Hyde.

Hide, Benjamin (or Beal), Bloomsbury, London, bedstead and cabinet manufactory, turner (1816–37). Trading at 24 Broad St in 1816, and 22 High St, 1820–27. Declared bankrupt, *Brighton Gazette*, 18 November 1824. [D]

Hide (or Hyde), Daniel, Dorking, Surrey, upholder (1792–93). Insured utensils and stock in his house and shop for £300 on 10 June 1792. [D; GL, Sun MS vol. 388, p. 55]

Hide, Edward, 13 High St, Worthing, Sussex, cm, u, builder and undertaker (1823–32). [D] See Hide & Patching.

Hide, John, Beverley, Yorks., cm (1807). App. to John Stephenson of Beverley in June 1807. [Hull app. reg.]

Hide, Ralph, Stockwell St, Leek, Staffs., joiner and cm (1818). [D]

Hide & Patching, High St, Worthing, Sussex, cm and undertakers (1839). [D] See Edward Hide.

Hidrid, Thomas, Tattershall, Lincs., chair turner (1822). [D]

Hiers, Joshua, Fairles St, South Shields, Co. Durham, cm (1827–29). [D]

Hiett, William, Mount St, Taunton, Som., cm and u (1839). [D]

Hiffer, Edmund, 57 Charlotte St, Somerstown, London, picture frame maker (1835). [D]

Higby, David, St Andrew's, Holborn, London, upholder (1718–35). Insured goods and merchandise at 'The Sun', Fleet Ditch, on 11 July 1718 with the Sun Co. Named on lease for a messuage in Stadhampton, Bucks. dated 1735. [GL, Sun MS vol. 8, ref. 11478; Oxford RO, Fa V/10]

Higgens, James, Sherborne, Dorset, u (1738). App. to Thomas Thorne, u of Sherborne, in 1738. [Dorset app. indentures]

Higgin, Samuel, Liverpool, cabinet trunk maker (1796–1803). Addresses given at Lord St, 1796, no. 7 in 1800, and Whitechapel in 1803. [D]

Higginbottom, James, Market St, Lane End, Staffs., cm (1834). [D]

Higginbottom, John, Market St, Lane End, Staffs., cm and u (1835). [D]

Higgins, Charles, Wood St, Ashby-de-la-Zouch, Leics., turner (1829). [D]

Higgins, George, Holmfirth, Yorks., joiner and/or cm (1834). [D]

Higgins, Henry, Norwich, cm (1825). Former app., James Manthorpe, cm, admitted freeman on 3 May 1825. [Norwich freemen reg.]

Higgins, John, Chandos St, near Old Round Ct, St Paul's, Covent Gdn, London, turner (1709). Insured his goods on 25 March 1709. [GL, Sun MS vol. 3, ref. 2935] Possibly John Higgons.

Higgins, John, St Mary Magdalene, Oxford, cm (1768). [Poll bk]

Higgins, John, London, u (1809–23). Addresses given at 25 Cork St, Burlington Gdns, 1809–11; 30 Brewer St, Golden Sq., 1811; 16 Saffron St, Holborn, 1817; and 3 Saffron Row, Saffron Lane, 1822–23. [D]

Higgins, Maria, St Andrew's Broad St, Norwich, working u (1836). [D]

Higgins, Michael, 34 New Rd, St George's East, London, carver and gilder (1808–11). [D]

Higgins, Samuel, Bridgwater, Som., cm (1780). [Poll bk]

Higgins, Samuel, Shorts Gdn(s), Drury Lane, London, picture frame maker (1810). Took out a Sun Insurance policy on 5 February 1810 for £100 of which £75 accounted for stock, utensils and goods in trust. [GL, Sun MS vol. 453, ref. 841223]

Higgins, Samuel Cook, Gloucester, u (1826–28). Declared bankrupt, *London Gazette*, 1 December 1826. Bankruptcy superseded, same paper, 5 August 1828.

Higgins, Thomas, Liverpool, carver and gilder (1834–37). Trading at 71 Bold St, 1834, and 1 Newsham St, 1835–37. [D]

Higginson, Francis, Eastbourne, Sussex, cm (1762). Took app. named Williams in 1762. [S of G, app. index]

Higginson, Francis, Midhurst, Sussex, upholder, auctioneer, cm and u (1784–94). [D] See Francis Higinson.

Higginson, Henry, Liverpool, cm (1809–34). Addresses given at 23 Batchelor St in 1811; no. 26, 1813–14; 11 Dance St, 1816; 34 High St, Edge Hill in 1823; 10 Norman St in 1827; 8 Mansfield Ct in 1829; 10 Rose St with shop in Mill Lane, 1834–35; no. 24 Mill Lane, Shaw's Brow in 1835; and 9 Rose St with shop at 33 Mill Lane in 1839. Probably the H. Higginson, cm of Liverpool, whose marriage to Miss Mary Burgess on 17 August at Trinity Church was reported in *Liverpool Courier*, 13 September 1809. [D]

Higginson, Nathaniel, Middlewich, Cheshire, cm (1762). Took app. named Whitlow in 1762. [S of G, app. index]

Higgons, —, near Gray's Inn, London, cm (1699). Named in newspapers in 1699. [Heal]

Higgons, John, St Paul's, Covent Gdn, London, turner (1742). Declared bankrupt, *Gents Mag.*, May 1742. Possibly John Higgins.

Higgs, —, London, cm (1793). Subscribed to Sheraton's *Drawing Book*, 1793.

Higgs, — jnr, Market Pl., Reading, Berks., cm (1791). Insured utensils and stock for £1,000 on 24 June 1791. [GL, Sun MS vol. 377, p. 609] See Benson Higgs, Holland Thomas Higgs, and Thomas Higgs; also Higgs & Ford.

Higgs, Benjamin, Castle Alley, between Long Acre and Castle St, St Martin-in-the-Fields, London, cm (1712). Insured his house for £50 on 18 August 1712. [GL, Hand in Hand MS vol. 10, ref. 8756]

Higgs, Benson, Reading, Berks., upholder (1780–82). [Poll bks]

Higgs, Edward, Baker's Row, Whitechapel, London, bedstead maker (1820). [D]

Higgs, Holland Thomas, Reading, Berks., upholder and cm (1745–83). Married Mary Harvard of Nuffield on 29 July 1745, and as a widower, Anne Benwell on 17 April 1763. Took app. named Line in 1750 and Higgs in 1761. Insured his house for £2,000 in 1776 with the Sun Co. Named in 1793 as 3rd party in a lease of property in Goring. [Poll bks; Bodleian index of Oxf. marriage bonds; S of G, app. index; GL, Sun MS vol. 248, p. 450; Oxford RO, FIX/138–39] See Higgs jnr, —, Thomas Higgs, Higgs & Ford, and Thomas Holland.

Higgs, Holland Thomas, Market Pl., Reading, Berks., u (1820). [Poll bk] See T. Holland Higgs.

Higgs, Joseph, St Margaret, Westminster, London, joiner (1792). Patented a 'new invented bedstead' on 11 February 1792. [Patent Office]

Higgs, Samuel, Westminster, London, cm (1802). [Oxford poll bk]

Higgs, T. Holland, Market Pl., Reading, Berks., cm (1823). [D] See Holland Thomas Higgs and Thomas Holland.

Higgs, Thomas, Reading, Berks., u (1754). Took app. named Knight in 1754. [S of G, app. index]

Higgs, Thomas, 5 Upper Marylebone St, London, cm (1794). Insured his house, workshop and utensils for £400 on 14 June 1794. [GL, Sun MS vol. 401, ref. 628570]

Higgs, Thomas, 248 Whitechapel Rd, London, cm, u and broker in household goods (1802–39). Recorded at no. 245 in 1802. Trade label shows draped four-post bedstead, Hepplewhite-style writing desk, Regency chairs, chest of drawers and pier table; window blind and drapes. Card reads: 'Cabinet, Bedstead, Venetian Blind & Chair Manufactory, Upholsterer, Appraiser & Auctioneer, No. 246 Roadside Whitechapel, London. Funerals Performed.' [Heal] Took out Sun Insurance policies on 29 September 1802; on 29 October 1807 for £1,000; and on 4 November 1818 for £1,600 on household goods in his new house and adjoining shops, on four houses at 12–15 Thomas St, Whitechapel, and two houses in Bethnal Green. [D; GL, Sun MS vol. 424, ref. 738027; vol. 441, ref. 809473; vol. 480, ref. 946764]

Higgs, Thomas, 5 Upper Marylebone St, London, bedstead and cm (1808). [D]

Higgs, Thomas, Gloucester, cm (1813). Child bapt., at St John Baptist in 1813. [PR (bapt.)]

Higgs, William, Aylesbury Rd, Tring, Herts., cm and u (1839). [D]

Higgs & Ford, Reading, Berks., cm and u (1798–1813). Trading as Higgs, Son & Ford in 1798; as Higgs & Co. and Higgs & Ford, 1809–13; and in Market Pl., 1809. Carried out work for 2nd Lord Braybrooke at Audley End, Essex, Billingbear, Berks., or his London house, receiving payment of £3 10s in December 1802. Specifically for work at Billingbear, the firm was paid £65 1s 5d in December 1809; £41 8s 6d in December 1810; £47 6s 6d in December 1811; £59 0s 9d in December 1812; and £7 18s in December 1813. [Essex RO, D/DBy/A357; A376] The Gents Mag., June 1809 reported the death, aged 74, of an employee of Higgs & Ford, William Line, journeyman cm of Reading, employed for sixty years in the firm, during which time he never lost a day's work, had a holiday, or 'been once disguised in liquor'. [D]

High, William, Lancaster. Named in the Gillow records, 1818–36. [Westminster Ref. Lib.]

Higham, Thomas, Marton, near Hull, Yorks., estate joiner (1748–d. 1793). Received payment of £2 9s 4d for '8 Calves skins for Chairs' supplied in 1748. Will proved in 1793. Highams, estate joiners, made furniture for Burton Constable, Yorks., during the mid 18th century. [C. Life, 3 June 1976, p. 1476]

Highfield, George, Liverpool, cm (1784). Petitioned freedom on servitude to Edward Lowe, and admitted freeman on 1 April 1784. [Liverpool freemen reg.]

Highfield, John, Liverpool, cm (1761–d.1811). Addresses given at Atherton St, 1766–67; 87 Park Lane, 1787; 64 Shaw's Brow, 1794; no. 56 in 1796; 12 Church St in 1790; 60 Shaw's Brow in 1800; no. 48 in 1803; no. 51 in 1810; and no. 54 in 1811. Petitioned freedom on servitude part of time to George Pachon and John Suddorth, and admitted freeman on 28 January 1761. Death of wife reported in Billinge's Liverpool Advertiser, 27 January 1800; own death on 9

November 1811, in Liverpool Mercury, 22 November. [D; Liverpool freemen reg.]

Highman, George, High St, Shaftesbury, Dorset, cm (1823–30). [D]

Highton, William, Ormskirk, Lancs., cm (1822–34). Trading at Moor St in 1834. [D]

Higinson, Francis, Midhurst, Sussex, u, carpenter and joiner (1776). Insured utensils, stock, goods and workshop for £700 in 1776. [GL, Sun MS vol. 246, p. 131] See Francis Higginson.

Hignet, Thomas, Liverpool, cm (1797–1806). App. to Samuel Chubbard in 1797, and admitted freeman on 31 October 1806. [Liverpool freemen reg.]

Higson, William, Liverpool, cm (1761). Admitted freeman on 2 April 1761. [Liverpool freemen reg.]

Hildebrand, —, temporarily in London, 'Proprietor and Maker of the most Magnificent Cabinet in the World'. A notice, c.1780, advertised the spectacle of his extraordinary cabinet at 'Mr. Jerom Johnson's, Cut-Glass Warehouse, opposite the "Black-Bear, Piccadilly"', one shilling admittance. The cabinet, 'properly adapted for the Dressing-Room of a Princess', was inlaid with 'many hundred thousand Pieces of Wood of various Colours' representing 'Landscapes, Huntings, Ruins of "Roman" Temples, intermix'd with the Figures of various Animals ... The Outside represents a Bureau of an half oval Form of Walnut-tree, adorned with gilt Borders and other Ornaments, inlaid with different Sorts of Metal, Mother of Pearl, Ivory, and Wood of various Colours, in a Manner which surpasses the Imagination, representing whole Hunting-matches, Men, Animals, Flowers, Perspectives, Prospects, &c. so like and lively as Nature itself ...'. The cabinet contained a total of one hundred and six drawers of different sizes, some of which 'come out as if it were by playing on a Harpsichord'; and many doors which opened onto various secret moving compartments achieving novel effects, such as the disappearance and re-appearance of objects placed within. The cabinet, claimed Mr Hildebrand, was acknowledged to be 'the most exquisite Piece of Art ever Seen' by 'The Greatest Connoisseurs who have travelled throughout Europe ...'. [GL, trade card coll.]

Hildebrant, Charles, 10 Gilbert Buildings, Westminster Rd, London, carver and gilder (1826). [D]

Hildebrant, William, London, cm (1793). Subscribed to Sheraton's Drawing Book, 1793.

Hilder, Edward, 1–2 High St, Rye, Sussex, u (1839). [D]

Hilder, James, 20 Old Compton St, Soho, London, carver and gilder (1840). Took out a Sun Insurance policy in 1840. [GL, Sun MS ref. 1341311]

Hildersley, Francis, Soho, London, chairmaker (1808–27). Trading at 48 Wardour St in 1808 and 18 Hollen St, 1826–27. [D]

Hildersley, William & Martha, Soho, London, carvers and gilders (1829–39). Trading at 18 Hollen St in 1829 and 49 Upper John St, Fitzroy Sq., 1829–35. Martha is recorded alone in 1837, and William alone in 1839. [D]

Hilditch, Eliza, 50 Downing St, Chorlton-on-Medlock, Manchester, u (1840). [D]

Hildor, William, Gt Tower St, London, turner (1717). Insured his house for £250 on 15 January 1717. [GL, Hand in Hand MS vol. 18, p. 128]

Hilker, Anthony, Husband St, Gravel Pits, near St Ann's, London, cm, carver and gilder (1747–75). Simple, unembellished trade card reads: 'Cabinet Work, Carv'd & Gilt Frames, Ornaments, Prints Framed & Glaz'd, Maps fitted up in a new Taste, Packing carefully done and Cases made — All kinds of Goods Appraised, Funerals performed in the decentest manner, at Reasonable Rates.' [BM] Took app.

named Richard Bastallas in 1748 for £10. [V&A archives] Polled at Westminster in 1749. Subscribed to Chippendale's *Director*, 1754. Probably the Anthony Hilker, picture frame maker, late of Child St, Strand, whose discharge from Debtors' Prison was announced in *London Gazette*, 12 September 1761. Anthony Hilker submitted a bill to Sir Richard Hoare on 30 October 1747 'for pear tree frames carved & gilt', costing £1 18s 1d supplied for Barn Elms House. He is presumably the Mr Hilker, frame maker, who charged Sir Richard £35 18s between 25 August 1747 and 22 June 1753, including payment for framing maps and a plan of London. [V&A Lib., English Manuscripts, tradesmen's bills; Sir Richard Hoare's private account, Hoare's Bank, Fleet St] On 7 July 1775 Nathaniel Ryder, 1st Lord Harrowby of Sandon Hall, Staffs., paid 'Hilker Cabinet maker', £1 4s. [Harrowby MS Trust, Notebooks] Possibly Anthony Hilkes.

Hilker, Stephen, next to Clements Inn, Clement Lane, London, picture frame maker and gilder (1775). Took out a Sun Insurance policy in 1775 for £400 of which £200 accounted for utensils, stock and goods. [GL, Sun MS vol. 237, p. 130]

Hilkss, Anthony, London, cm (1760). [Canterbury freemen rolls] Possibly Anthony Hilker.

Hill, —, Long Lane, near West Smithfield, London, clock-case maker (d.1743). [Harris, *Old English Furniture*, p. 23]

Hill, —, address unrecorded, cm (1756). On 19 November 1756 Hill charged £3 3s to Henry Hoare of Stourhead, 'to my Tools in full'. [Wilts. RO, MS 383/6]

Hill, —, London (?), u (1760–74). Payments recorded in Paul Methuen's day book, (1760–74), for upholstery work done at Corhsam Court, Wilts. Between 20 June 1760 and 17 December 1774, Hill received a total of £1,057 14s 6d. [Wilts. RO]

Hill, —, Marlborough, Wilts., u and coachmaker (1768). Mentioned in the diaries of Henry Knight of Tythegston, Glam. in 1768. [*C. Life*, 5 October 1978, p. 1024] Possibly Henry Hill.

Hill, —, Piccadilly, near St James's Church, London, u (1798). Fire on Thurs. 5 April reported in *Gents Mag.*, April 1798. Possibly Peter Hill, or Hill & Woolley.

Hill, Ambrose, 13 Dansie St and Minshull St, Edge Hill, Liverpool, joiner and cm (1830). Admitted freeman on 13 November 1830. [Liverpool freemen reg.]

Hill, Arthur, New Windsor, Berks., cm (1794–1804). [Poll bks]

Hill, Benjamin, Churchgate, Retford, Notts., cm and u (1822). [D]

Hill, Benjamin, Rotherham, Yorks., cm (1834). [D]

Hill, Charles, Litton, near Kettlewell, Yorks., cm (1822). [D]

Hill, Charles, Hockley, Nottingham, u and paper hanger (1834–40). [D]

Hill, David, Wickham Mkt, Suffolk, cm (1830–39). [D]

Hill, Edward, Brighton, Sussex, upholder and cm (1793–1824). Addresses given at 8 Middle St in 1799; West Cliff in 1817; and 2 Grand Parade, 1824. Daughter Elizabeth, by Sarah Hill, bapt. at St Nicholas's Church on 26 February 1817. [D; PR (bapt.)]

Hill, Edward, Thurlow St, Liverpool, carver and gilder (1827–34). Recorded at no. 20, 1827–29. Sudden death of his wife, Margaret, aged 32, on 8 August, and of his son, Edward, aged 4, on 13 August, reported in *Chester Courant and Advertiser for North Wales*, 19 August 1834. [D]

Hill, George, Mayfair, London, carver (1749). [Poll bk]

Hill, Harry, Penkhull (or Penkhill) St, Newcastle-under-Lyme, Staffs., joiner, u and cm (1798–1828). [D] See Thomas Hill.

Hill, Henry, Marlborough, Wilts., cm (1741–77). Took app. named Joseph Lideard, son of Elizabeth, on 12 January 1741/42, by common indenture and counterpart, for £12; Thomas Smith on 10 March 1752 by indenture, for £30; and

William Neat on 1 January 1753 by indenture, for £35. Took out a Sun Insurance policy for £3,000 in 1777, of which £1,125 accounted for utensils, stock and goods; £100 for his office; and £100 for timber. [*Wilts. Apps and their Masters*; GL, Sun MS vol. 262, p. 45]

Hill, Henry, High Wycombe, Bucks., chairmaker (b. *c*. 1791–1841). Sons bapt. in 1814, 1817, 1824, 1829, 1833 and 1836. Daughter Mary born in 1819, and daughters bapt. in 1822 and 1827. Acted as witness at marriage of his daughter in 1839. Aged 50 at the time of the 1841 Census. [PR (bapt.)]

Hill, Henry, 14 Portland St, Manchester, cm (1834–40). Recorded at no. 51 in 1840. [D]

Hill, Henry William, London, cm (1835–39). Trading at 47 Pennyfields, Poplar in 1835; and 22 Mary Pl, High St and 27 Pennyfields, Poplar in 1839. [D]

Hill, I., Fieldterrace, Bagniggewells, London, u (1820). [D]

Hill, Isaac, Ipswich, Suffolk, cm (1816–39). Recorded in St Mary Keys parish in 1816; St Margaret's, 1832–35; and Cox Lane, 1839. Named in the calendar of marriage licence bonds on 1 April 1816. [Poll bks; Suffolk RO, FAA: 50/2/118, pp. 119–20]

Hill, J., London, u (1793–1803). Subscribed to Sheraton's *Drawing Book*, 1793, and *Cabinet Dictionary*, 1803.

Hill, J., Chester, u (1829). Listed amongst tradesmen subscribing to a gold cup of 100 gs value, for the Chester Races of 1829, he having contributed 10s. [*Chester Chronicle and North Wales Advertiser*, 1 May 1829] Possibly John Hill of Chester

Hill, Jacob, 16 Holborn London, bed and mattress maker (1822–28). [D]

Hill, James, Bromley, Staffs., chairmaker and turner (1793). [D]

Hill, James, Merchant St, Bristol, cm (1801). [D]

Hill, James, Hull, Yorks., cm (1813–39). Recorded at 2 Trafalgar Sq., Lower Union St, 1838–39. App. to George Chapman of Hull in July 1813, and assigned to Robert Waugh in March 1818. [D; Hull app. reg.]

Hill, James, 15 Brunswick Pl., Liverpool, carver (1821). [D]

Hill, James, 16 East St, Manchester Sq., London, cm and u (1827–28). [D]

Hill, James, Longtown, Carlisle, Cumb., joiner and/or cm (1828–29). [D]

Hill, James, 3 Court, Old Inkleys, Birmingham, cm, u and bedstead maker (1830). [D]

Hill, James, Abbots Bromley, Staffs., chairmaker (1834). [D]

Hill, John, Fleet Bridge, St Bride's, London, upholder (1734–39). Fined for non-service, and served as Questman and Collector for the Poor at St Bride's in 1734. Served as a Sidesman in 1739. [GL, MS 6561, p. 58]

Hill, John, Windsor, Berks., chairmaker and cm (1740). Admitted freeman of the Borough of Windsor on 30 April 1740. [Second hall book of the borough of New Windsor]

Hill, John, Worcester, chairmaker (1747–61). Polled in 1747 of St Helen's parish. Former app., Thomas Hill, admitted freeman on 19 March 1761. [Worcester freemen rolls]

Hill, John, address unrecorded, upholder (1766–73). Son of Nathaniel Hill, brazier of Barbican, London. App. to William Gould on 11 July 1766, and admitted freeman of the Upholders' Co. by servitude on 6 October 1773. [GL, Upholders' Co. records]

Hill, John, Little Wild St, London (?), u (1775). Declared bankrupt, *Gents Mag.*, October 1775.

Hill, John, High Wycombe, Bucks., chairmaker (1798–1821). Named in the Militia Census, 1798. Daughter Sarah bapt. in 1819, another in 1821. [PR (bapt.)]

Hill, John, Liverpool, carver and gilder (1804–13). Trading at 5

Shaw's Brow in 1804; no. 7 in 1805; no. 8, 1807–11; and 15 Brunswick Pl. in 1813. [D]

Hill, John, Liverpool, cm (1827–39). Trading at 23 Pinnington St in 1827 and 8 Cypress St, 1839. [D]

Hill, John, 3 Crescent Pl., St George's Fields, London, painter and gilder (1808). [D]

Hill, John, Sheffield, Yorks., carver and gilder (1814–22). Addresses given at York St, 1814, George St, 1817, 30 High St, 1821, and no. 31 in 1822. [D]

Hill, John, Castle St, Chester, u (1824–37). Admitted freeman on 20 October 1824. [D; poll bk; Chester freemen rolls] See J. Hill of Chester.

Hill, John, Malton, Yorks., cm (1828–40). Recorded at Greengate, 1828–29. [D]

Hill, John, Bromsgrove St, Birmingham, cm, u and broker (1828–30). Recorded at 4 Court in 1828. [D]

Hill, John, Budby, Edwinstowe, Notts., joiner and cm (1832). [D]

Hill, John, York, cm (1833). Son of William Hill, waggoner; app. to William Groves, cm, on 11 April 1833. [York app. reg.]

Hill, John, Whiting St, Bury St Edmunds, Suffolk, cm (1836). [Poll bk]

Hill, Jonas, Little Horton, near Bradford, Yorks., cm (1814–22). [D]

Hill, Jonas, Chapel Lane, Bradford, Yorks., joiner and cm (1818). [D]

Hill, Jonathan, Philadelphia St, Bristol, timber dealer and cm (1831–40). Trading also as a tea dealer at 34 Castle St, 1831–35, and 10 Milk St, 1835–40. [D]

Hill, Joseph, George St, Sheffield, Yorks., cm (1818). [D]

Hill, Josiah (or Joshua) William, Newcastle-under-Lyme, Staffs., u and cm (1823–39). Recorded at Iron Mkt, 1828–39, no. 72 in 1839 also as a victualer. [D; poll bks]

Hill, Josias, York, u (1779). A Blue Coat boy, app. to James Marshall, u and cm, on 9 October 1779. [York app. reg.]

Hill, Josias William (or I.W.), London, cm, u and undertaker (1808–39). Addresses given at 11 Leather Lane, Holborn, 1808–19, and 101–02 Hatton Gdn, 1820–39. [D]

Hill, Mary, Portland (?) St, Leeds, Yorks., working u (1834). [D]

Hill, Peter, 190 Piccadilly, London, u (1799–1801). [D] See Hill & Woolley and Hill, — of Piccadilly.

Hill, Richard, High Wycombe, Bucks., chairmaker (b. c.1781–1841). Named in the Militia Census, 1798. Daughters bapt. in 1815; 1817; Silena in 1820, another in 1824; son Remus in 1822, another in 1828. Aged 60 at the time of the 1841 Census. [PR (bapt.)]

Hill, Richard, High St, Lewes, Sussex, u (1816–39). Recorded at no. 77, 1823–24, and no. 2 in 1839. [D; poll bks]

Hill, Richard, 55 Oakley St, London, bed and mattress maker (1835). [D]

Hill, S., Middlx, upholder (1826). Declared bankrupt, *London Gazette*, 30 June 1826.

Hill, Samuel, Doncaster, Yorks., cm (1733). Took app. named Briley in 1733. [S of G, app. index]

Hill, Samuel, 36 Gt Russell St, Bloomsbury, London, u etc. (1826–27). [D]

Hill, Samuel, 24 Hockley Hill, Birmingham, cm (1835). [D]

Hill, Thomas, address unrecorded, u (1715). Provided the Prince of Wales with a bed, now at Hampton Court. [*Conn.*, June 1977, p. 141]

Hill, Thomas snr, King's Lynn, Norfolk, cm (1730–58). Took out a Sun Insurance policy on 18 January 1730 for £400, household goods, stock, utensils and workshop accounting for £230. Former app., Thomas Hill jnr, admitted freeman, 1735–36, and James Lyther, 1757–58. Took app. named

Glasscock in 1743. [GL, Sun MS vol. 32, ref. 53057; King's Lynn freemen's calendar; S of G, app. index]

Hill, Thomas jnr, King's Lynn, Norfolk, joiner and cm (1835–36). App. to Thomas Hill snr, and admitted freeman, 1735–36. [King's Lynn freemen's calendar]

Hill, Thomas, Worcester, chairmaker (1761). App. to John Hill, chairmaker, and admitted freeman on 19 March 1761. [Worcester freemen rolls]

Hill, Thomas, St Clement Danes, London, cm (c.1780). His son, Isaac, entered St Paul's School in 1785, and for 36 years he was headmaster of The Mercers' School, 1804–40. [Heal]

Hill, Thomas, London, cm (1793). Subscribed to Sheraton's *Drawing Book*, 1793.

Hill, Thomas, Brighton, Sussex, cm and u (1814–32). Addresses given in Ship St, 1814; West St, 1816–18; and 11 Grenville Pl., 1832. Daughter, Sarah Ann by Dianah Hill, bapt. at St Nicholas's Church on 11 March 1814; son Benjamin on 19 May 1816; and daughter Rebecca on 12 April 1818. [D; PR (bapt.)]

Hill, Thomas, parish of SS Peter and Paul, Tunbridge, Kent, chairmaker (1816–20). Daughter Hannah, by wife Hannah, bapt. on 10 November 1815, and son Thomas on 17 December 1820. [PR (bapt.)]

Hill, Thomas, Church gate, Loughborough, Leics., joiner/cm (1822). [D]

Hill, Thomas, Skate Lane, Whitby, Yorks., cm (1823). [D]

Hill, Thomas, Newcastle-under-Lyme, Staffs., cm and builder (1823–37). Trading in Penkhull St, 1832–39, no. 81, 1836–39. [D; poll bks] See Harry Hill.

Hill, Thomas, St Julian's Friars, Shrewsbury, Salop, cm (1830). [Shrewsbury burgess roll]

Hill, Thomas, 1 and 14 North St Mews, Fitzroy Sq., London, bedstead maker and japanner (1839). [D]

Hill, Walter, Church St, Kidderminster, Worcs., cm and u (1828–35). [D]

Hill, Warwick, 142 Kingsland Rd, London, cm (1835). [D]

Hill, William, at 'The Sign of the Star', Little St Martin's Lane, London, turner (c.1730). Trade card continues: 'Where all Sorts of Turners Work for Cabinet Makers and Joyners is done in general'. [Westminster Ref. Lib., Gardener Box 63, No. 40D]

Hill, William, Stratford, London, upholder (1749–72). Son of Samuel Hill, freeman merchant tailor; app. to Samuel Hibberdine on 7 December 1749. Admitted freeman of the Upholders' Co. by servitude on 2 March 1758. [GL, Upholders' Co. records]

Hill, William, parish of St Giles, London, bed joiner (1771). Took app. named Benjamin Baker in 1771. [Westminster Ref. Lib., St Martin-in-the-Fields PR]

Hill, William, Lancaster, joiner and cm (b. c.1772–d.1848). Son of William, late of Lancaster, twinespinner; admitted freeman, 1806–07. Named in the Gillow records, 1825–27. Between 24 December 1829 and 17 August 1839 took four apps. Died on 31 December 1848, aged 60, and buried in Lancaster Priory Churchyard. [Lancaster freemen rolls and app. reg.; Westminster Ref. Lib., Gillow]

Hill, William C., Bristol, carver and gilder (1809–40). Trading at John St, 1809–17; Marlborough Hill, 1813–16; and 12 Clare St, 1819–40; also as a tea dealer, 1819–27; and picture dealer from 1828. [D]

Hill, William, address unrecorded, u (1812). Received payment on 15 March 1812 for items supplied to Edward Turner, steward at Welbeck Abbey, 1811–13. [Notts. RO, Welbeck Abbey accounts]

Hill, William, Bridge St, Newcastle-under-Lyme, Staffs., cm, joiner and u (1828–39). Listed at no. 31, 1836–39. [D]

Hill, William, Coton Hill, Shrewsbury, Salop, cm (1835). [Shrewsbury burgess roll]

Hill, William, 4 Ironmonger's Row, St Luke's, London, carver and gilder (1839). [D]

Hill, William, 120 London Rd, Brighton, Sussex, cm, u and furniture broker (1839). [D]

Hill & Hewitt, Shrewsbury, Salop, upholders and auctioneers (1784). [D]

Hill & Perkins, 2 Common Land (or Hard) or 2 Commercial Hard, Portsea, Portsmouth, Hants., cm, u, auctioneer and chairmaker (1823–39). [D]

Hill & Woolley, 109 Piccadilly, London, u (1797). [D] See Peter Hill.

Hillary, Thomas, Newington Causeway, Newington Butts, London, cm, broker and auctioneer (1803–28). Recorded at no. 62 in 1803; no. 5, 1809–25; and no. 4, 1827–28. Took out a Sun Insurance policy on 26 April 1803 for £800 of which £550 accounted for utensils and stock. [D; GL, Sun MS vol. 246, ref. 747308]

Hiller, Edward, address unrecorded, upholder (1710–29). Son of Robert Hiller, freeman upholder of London; app. to his father on 2 August 1710, and admitted freeman of the Upholders' Co. by servitude on 1 March 1720/21. Took app. named John Blackwell, 1727–29. [GL, Upholders' Co. records]

Hiller (or Hillier), Frederick John, 183 Snargate St, Dover, Kent, cm, u, gilder, agent and broker (1823–39). Declared bankrupt, Liverpool Mercury, 8 June 1827. [D]

Hiller, Robert, address unrecorded, upholder (1710–21). Admitted freeman of the Upholders' Co. on 2 August 1710. Took his son, Edward Hiller, as app., 1710–20/21. [GL, Upholders' Co. records] Possibly:

Hiller, Robert, St Olave's, Southwark, London, freeman upholder (1716–20). Recorded in St Olave's St, 1716–17, when he insured his house on 2 January with the Sun Co. Took out Hand in Hand policies on 19 May 1720 for £50 on a house in Walnuttree Alley, and for £100 on a house in St Olave's St. [GL, Sun MS vol. 6, ref. 7721; GL, Hand in Hand MS vol. 22, p. 42]

Hilliam, John, High St, Stamford, Lincs., cm and u (1828–41). [D; poll bks]

Hilliard, Edward, London, turner (1712–18). Recorded in Bishopsgate St, at 'The Sign of the Cross Keys', St Peter Cornhill, in 1712, when he insured his house for £250 on 20 September. On 29 March 1718, insured his house on the east side of the Old Change, Old Fish St, St Mary Magdalene, for £125; also four other houses. [GL, Hand in Hand MS vol. 10, ref. 23755; vol. 18, p. 243]

Hillier, Ann, Bristol, upholsteress (1830–40). Trading at 9 Lower Wells St in 1830; 9 Wells St, 1832–35; and 19 Thomas St, 1837–40. [D]

Hillier, Charles, 13 Ogle St, St Marylebone, London, cm (1802). [Oxford poll bk]

Hillier, J., Leicester Sq., London, carver and gilder (1809). Declared bankrupt, Ackermann's Repository of Arts, July 1809.

Hillier, John, 64 High St, Bloomsbury, London, carver and gilder (1815–27). [D]

Hillier, Joseph, London, carver and gilder (1806–11). Trading at 33 Rathbone Pl., 1806 and 1809–11; at 24 Castle St, Oxford Mkt in 1808; and in partnership with James Hillier in 1809. Took out a Sun Insurance policy on 6 September 1806 for £1,000, of which £500 accounted for his house and workshop behind, and £200 on stock, utensils and goods in trust. [D; GL, Sun MS vol. 437, ref. 792903]

Hillier, Mary, wife of Robert, St Tooly's, Southwark, London,

upholder (1712). Took app. on 5 December 1712. [PRO, app reg.]

Hilliker, Samuel, Marlborough, Wilts., cm and upholder (1781). Took out a Sun Insurance policy in 1781 for £700, of which utensils, stock and goods accounted for £495. [GL, Sun MS vol. 295, p. 629]

Hillingham, John, Stamford, Lincs., cm and u (1840). [D]

Hillman, Edmund, 27 Sloane Sq., London, carver and gilder (1839). [D]

Hillman, Edwin, 55 Parliament St, Westminster, London, carver and gilder (1835–37). [D]

Hills, Henry, Bath, Som., u (d. by 1778). Supplied furniture to Penrice Castle, Glam., including wheel-back chairs at 35s each. [C. Life, 25 September 1975, pp. 754–56, illus.]

Hills, Joseph, Bridge St, Cambridge, cm, u and paper hanger (1839). [D] See Robert Hills.

Hills, Newman, 8 Berkeley Ct, Berkeley St, Clerkenwell, London, cm (1823–29). Took out Sun Insurance on 20 October 1823 for £300, £200 accounting for stock and utensils. [D; GL, Sun MS vol. 495, ref. 1008912]

Hills, Robert, Cambridge, paper hanger and cm (1813–50). Trading in St Clement's parish when named in the Corp. common day book in 1813; and between 1815–30 when five children were baptised. Recorded in Bridge St, 1831–50. Employed for twenty years in the firm of Elliot Smith until the closure of the cabinet side of this business in 1831, when Hills advertised as a paper hanger in Cambridge Chronicle and Journal, 14 October. [D; poll bk; Cambs. RO, PR (bapt.)] See Joseph Hills.

Hills, William, Cambridge, chairmaker (d.1710). [Will at Cambridge Univ. Lib., W1710]

Hills, William, Newcastle, u (1721). Son Matthew admitted freeman by patrimony on 9 October 1721. [Newcastle freemen reg.]

Hills, William, St James's, Westminster, London, cm (1830). [Canterbury poll bk]

Hillyard, James, address unrecorded, upholder (1710/11). Admitted freeman of the Upholders' Co. on 7 March 1710/11. [GL, Upholders' Co. records]

Hillyard, Maria, 14 High St, King's Lynn, Norfolk, carver and gilder (1830–39). [D]

Hillyard, S., High St, King's Lynn, Norfolk, carver, gilder and painter (1822). [D]

Hilps, George, Stallards Lane, Trowbridge, Wilts., cm (1839). [D]

Hilstrip, William, York, cm (1822). Son of Thomas Hilstrip, joiner; app. to John Lockey, cm, on 30 September 1822. [York reg.]

Hilton, George, Preston, Lancs., cm (1742). Named as son of Thomas Hilton of Preston, shoemaker, in the Preston Guild record of burgesses, 1742.

Hilton, Henry, London, cm (1790–1808). Trading in Seething Lane, 1790–93, and 14 Moor St, Soho, 1808. [D]

Hilton, Henry, Southampton St, Covent Gdn, London, u (1792). Declared bankrupt, Derby Mercury, 21 June 1792.

Hilton, James, 6 Pleasant St, Liverpool, cm (1839). [D]

Hilton, Richard, Cambridge, cm (1760). Took app. named Smith in 1760. [S of G, app. index]

Hilton, Richard, Leeds, Yorks., journeyman cm (1791). Named in the Leeds Cabinet and Chair Makers' Book of Prices, 1791, amongst other journeymen in basic sympathy with its contents.

Hilton, Thomas, Tottenham Ct Rd, London, chairmaker (1775). Declared bankrupt, Gents Mag., May 1775.

Hilton, William, Edgbaston St, Birmingham, cm (1816–22). [D]

Hinchcliff, James, 150–51 Whitechapel Rd, Aldgate, London, cm (1813–39). [D]

Hinchcliffe, John, Birstall, Yorks., joiner and cm (1830). [D]

Hinchcliffe, John, Thorne, Yorks., joiner and cm (1834). [D]

Hinchcliffe, John, Hatfield, near Doncaster, Yorks., joiner and cm (1834). [D]

Hind, John, Liverpool, cm (1780). Petitioned freedom on servitude to Lee (Leigh?) Sutton in 1780, paying 6s 8d. [Liverpool freemen's committee bk] Possibly John Hinds.

Hind, John jnr, Gainsborough, Lincs., cm and upholder (1792–1828). Recorded in Lord St, 1819–28. Subscribed to Sheraton's *Drawing Book*, 1793. [D] See William Hind.

Hind, Richard, Bawtry, York, cm (1787). Insured his goods for £500 on 5 March 1787. [GL, Sun MS vol. 343, p. 214]

Hind, Thomas, Goldsmith Row, Hackney Rd, London, cm, u and undertaker (1827–28). [D]

Hind, W., Market Harborough, Leics., turner (1822). [D]

Hind, William, Hull, Yorks., cm and u (1826–31). Recorded at 2 New Dock St in 1826 and 5 Ann's Pl., Collier St, 1831. William Hind, beer retailer, traded in Collier St in 1834. [D]

Hind, William, Lord St, Gainsborough, Lincs., cm and u (1831–41). [D] See John Hind.

Hind, William, High St, Stamford, Lincs., cm and u (1835–41). [D]

Hinde, James, Lancaster, cm (1733–34). [Lancaster freemen rolls]

Hinde, Robert, Maryport, Cumb., cm and joiner (1834). [D]

Hinde, Thomas, 1 Hulme St, Manchester, chairmaker (1824). [D]

Hinde, Thomas, 14 Bond St, Manchester, u and paper hanger (1825). [D]

Hinde, Thomas, 1 Hulme St, Manchester, u (1825). [D]

Hinder, Robert, Crown Ct, Poultney St, Westminster, London, upholder (1719). Insured goods and merchandise in his house on 20 February 1719. [GL, Sun MS vol. 9, p. 109]

Hindersley, John & William, 18 Hollen St, London, chair and sofa maker (1839). [D]

Hindes, James, address unrecorded, cm (1764). Named in the Earl of Egremont's accounts in 1764 receiving £12 3s 9d for work done at Petworth House, Sussex, including carpet work, wainscotting, and providing a mahogany Pembroke table. [V&A archives]

Hindes, William, Gt Charles St, Birmingham, cabinet case maker (1839). [D]

Hindes, William, 9 Parade, Birmingham, dressing case and writing desk manufacturer (1839). [D]

Hindle, Charles, 86 Gerrard St, Liverpool, joiner and cm (1835). [D]

Hindle, James, Darlington, Co. Durham, cm (1827–34). Trading at High Row in 1827 and Bondgate, 1834. Joseph Hindle was at Bondgate, 1828–34. [D] See John Hindle.

Hindle, John, 62 Shoreditch, London, upholder (1782–83). [D]

Hindle, John, Hardwick's Yd, Leeds, Yorks., cm (1817). [D]

Hindle, John, Bondgate, Darlington, Co. Durham, cm and joiner (1828–34). [D]

Hindle, Patrick, 10 Timble Bridge, Leeds, Yorks., cm and joiner (1834–53). [D]

Hindley, Mrs, 2 Water St, Salford, Lancs., cm (1808). [D] See John Hindley.

Hindley, C. & Son(s), 154 Oxford St, London, cm (c.1820–30). Mark recorded on Regency kidney-shaped desk, veneered in yew and panelled with boxwood and ebony inlay, ornamented with finely-chased mounts and beadings, c.1830. [*Conn.*, November 1978; V&A archives] Mark also found on rosewood writing table, c.1820, with centre drawer and turned legs [*Antiques*, March 1982, p. 669]; also on a William IV mahogany writing table with two drawers in the frieze faced with walnut, and raised on fluted tapering legs. [Sotheby's, 24 July 1964, lot 93]

Hindley, John, Salford, Lancs., cm (1788–1804). Addresses given at 43 Chapel St, 1788; 3 Water St, 1800 and 1804; and no. 2 in 1802. [D] See Mrs Hindley.

Hindley, John, 4 Gt Ancoats St, Manchester, cm (1822–25). [D]

Hindley, Thomas, Liverpool, cm (1812). Petitioned freedom on servitude to Edward Myers and John Ward Turner, and admitted freeman on 7 October 1812. [Liverpool freemen reg.]

Hindley, Thomas, Bondgate Green, Ripon, Yorks., joiner and cm (1834). [D]

Hindley, William, Webster's Entry, High St, Hull, Yorks., joiner and cm (1840). [D]

Hindley & Sons, Oxford St and Berners St, London, cm (1766–1895). Incorporated Miles & Edwards, and Benjamin Nias. [Day and cash bks, letter bk, accounts and correspondence, Marylebone Lib., MS 494]

Hindmarsh, Matthew, Silver St, Newcastle, (1786). Advertised sale of mahogany, including 'fourteen hundred feet of Jamaica Mahogany in Logs and Planks', in *Newcastle Courant*, 16 September 1786.

Hindmarsh, Thomas, Berwick-upon-Tweed, Northumb., cm (1793). [D]

Hinds, Frederick, Ryders Ct, Leicester Fields, London (1740–76). See Frederick Hints (or Hintz).

Hinds, George, Leicester St, London, cm (1784). [Poll bk]

Hinds, George, Effingham Pl., Ramsgate, Kent, cm and undertaker (1823–29). [D]

Hinds, J., Bristol, cm (1837–40). Trading at Charles St, 1837–38, and Duke St, 1839–40. [D]

Hinds, John, Liverpool, cm later shipwright (1780). Admitted freeman on 11 September 1780. [Liverpool freemen reg.] Possibly John Hind.

Hinds, Peter, Witham, Hull, Yorks., cm (1790–99). [D]

Hinds, T. W., 65 White Lion St, Pentonville, London, cm (1835). [D]

Hinds, William, 19 Ann St, Birmingham, cabinet case maker (1835). [D]

Hindson, Joseph, Townhead, Penrith, Cumb., joiner and cm (1828–29). [D]

Hine, Robert, High St, Highgate, London, carver, gilder and paper hanger (1839). [D]

Hingston, James, North St, Bristol, carpenter, cm and upholder (1791–1826). Recorded at no. 7 in 1795; as Hingston & Richardson at no. 6, 1805–06; nos 6–7 in 1816; and 7, 1817–25. In 1791 he was paid £42 10s for work done for John Pinney of Gt George St, Bristol, now the Georgian House Museum. [D; Bristol Univ. Lib., J. Pinney's account bk] See Thomas Hingston.

Hingston, John, 41 Cirencester Pl., Fitzroy Sq., London, cm. Regency rosewood 'Musicatheca' recorded bearing inscription: 'John Hingston invenit et fecit' and address. Hinged top raised with an easel support and a milled border. There is a frieze drawer and an open compartment with shaped dividers, and further drawer in base. [Sotheby's, 29 March 1968, lot 250]

Hingston, Thomas, Bristol, cm, u, appraiser and undertaker (1826–40). Trading at 7 North St, 1826–35, as Hingston, Brice & Co. in 1832; at 6 North St, 1836–37; and 10 Park St, with manufactory at 10 St James's Sq., 1838–40. [D] See James Hingston.

Hinksman, Thomas, Bromyard, near Hereford, cm (1830–35). [D]

Hinley, Daniel, High Wycombe, Bucks., cm (1825). Son bapt. in 1825. [PR (bapt.)]

Hinsley, George, res. at Hinsley's Ct, Wellington St, Hull, Yorks., cm (1838–39). Recorded also as a joiner in Finkle St, Hull, with res. in Hinsley's Ct, 1838. [D]

Hinsley, John, Hull, Yorks., cm (1808–42). Addresses given in New Dock St, 1818–20; Paradise Row, 1823; 20 Sewer Lane, 1838; and 1 Keelin's Entry, Mytongate, 1842. App. to John Dickon of Hull in April 1808. Took apps named Joseph Knight of Hull in June 1817; John Hunter of Hull in July 1819; and James Whyte jnr, of Hull in June 1821. In September 1823 assigned his apprenticeship of John Hunter to William Silbon. [D; Hull app. reg.]

Hinton, —, address unrecorded. Stamp found on elm joint stool with rectangular top on turned columnar legs and H-shaped stretcher. [Christie's, 12 June 1980, lot 128]

Hinton, John, London (?), turner (1750). Submitted bill for 18s 6d to the Countess of Oxford on 25 September 1750. [Notts. RO, DD5P. 14/1 Ledger house bk]

Hinton, William, Cheltenham, Glos., u and cm (1822–40). Addresses given at 132 High St in 1822, 12 St George's Pl. in 1830 and North St in 1839. [D]

Hints (or Hintz), Frederick, at 'The Porcupine', Newport St, near Leicester Fields, London, cm (1738). Advertised in *Daily Post*, 22 May 1738, the sale of 'a choice Parcel of Desks and Book cases of mahogany, tea tables, tea chests, tea-boards etc. all curiously made and inlaid with fine figures of Brass and mother-of-pearl. They will be sold at a very reasonable rate, the maker Frederick Hintz, designing soon to go abroad.' An alternative spelling of his name — Hintz — indicates that he was of German origin. The labels of a Frederick Hinds of Ryders Ct, Leicester Fields, presumably the same maker, or a relative, have been found on some stringed instruments dating between 1740 and 1776. [GCM; *C. Life*, 9 March 1945 and 2 May 1957; Harris, *Old English Furniture*, p. 23; V&A *Bulletin*, January 1965, p. 13]

Hipkins, Russell, 34 New Rd, St George's East, London, carver and gilder (1817–20). [D]

Hipkins, S., Dudley, Worcs., chairmaker (1829). [D]

Hippisley, Edward & Britten, Stephen, Bristol, carpenters and furniture makers (1733–37). Between 1733–37 carried out work in St John's Church, Bristol, charging a total of £713 15s 1d, including £249 1s 8d for panelling, £150 for altarpiece; £45 for pulpit; £47 10s for communion rails, and £2 12s for table. The bill was disputed, legal action taken and assessors appointed who found the work 'good, Substantial, Artificial & Workmanlike'. Their work was destroyed in 19th-century restorations. [*Furn. Hist.*, 1976, pl. 22A]

Hipston, William, Dover St, Hanover Sq., London, upholder (1778). Declared bankrupt, *Gents Mag.*, July 1778.

Hipwood, Joseph & Benjamin, London, cm and u (1820–29). Trading at 24 Cannon St Rd, St George's East, 1820–28; nos 23–24 in 1823; and also 12 Wellclose Sq., 1827–28. Joseph was recorded alone in 1826–27 and 1829. Together they took out Sun Insurance policies on 2 October 1823 for £400 on 23–24 Cannon St Rd; £250 on stock and utensils in houses; £100 on workshop in yard behind; £100 on stock utensils and goods in trust or on commission; and £150 on those in open yard and under workshop. Joseph alone insured household goods at 24 Cannon St Rd for £300; and with Benjamin insured nos 23–24 for £500. [D; GL, Sun MS vol. 496, refs 100857–58; 1008587–90]

Hircombe, Thomas, Speenhamland, Newbury, Berks., cm (1823). [D]

Hird, George, Boroughbridge, Yorks., joiner and cm (1830). [D]

Hird, John, Boroughbridge, York., joiner and cm (1822–34). [D]

Hird, William, address unrecorded. On 4 March 1750 submitted a bill to Lady Monson for 'A Large Japan Tea Water', costing £1 5s, and two small ones, £1 15s. Bill paid on 9 March 1750. [Lincoln RO, Monson 12]

Hirst, Edward, 15 Marshall St, Carnaby Mkt, London, u (1784). [D; poll bk]

Hirst, James, Garden St, Wakefield, Yorks., joiner and cm (1830). [D]

Hirst, John, top of Green, Huddersfield, Yorks., cm (1814–18). [D]

Hirst, John, Liversedge, Yorks., joiner and cm (1830). [D]

Hirst, John, Holmfirth, Yorks., joiner and/or cm (1834). [D]

Hirst, Jonathan, Clayton, near Bradford, Yorks., cm (1822–30). [D]

Hirst, Joseph, Church St, Woodhouse Moor, Leeds, Yorks., cm (1830–37). [D]

Hirst, Robert, Whitby, Yorks., cm and u (1834). [D]

Hiscock, Jos., Shaftesbury, Dorset, joiner and cm (1798). [D]

Hiscox, John, 133 Thomas St, Bristol, cm (1817–19). [D]

Hitch, James, Star Lane, Ware, Herts., cm and u (1832–39). [D]

Hitcham, Richard, Totteridge, High Wycombe, Bucks., chairmaker (b. c. 1771–1841). Aged 70 at the time of the 1841 Census.

Hitchcock, Abraham, 2 New Mkt Passage, Broad St, Bristol, cm (1775). [D]

Hitchcock, James, 36 Hackney Rd, London, chair, sofa and bath chair maker (1822–23). [D]

Hitchcock, Joseph, address unrecorded, upholder (1697–d.1744). Son of Joseph Hitchcock of Ebisham, Surrey, yeoman, deceased. App. to John Staples on 5 May 1697, and William Giffard on 26 February 1701. Admitted freeman of the Upholders' Co. by servitude on 16 May 1729, and beadle of the Co., 1740–44. [GL, Upholders' Co. records]

Hitchcock, Joseph, London. On 22 October 1729 signed a receipt for £6 5s received on behalf of his master John Howard, upholder, of the 'Talbot', Long Lane, West Smithfield, London. [Herefs. RO, Foley papers, F/AIII/55]

Hitchcock, Peter, Liverpool, cm (1819). App. to John O'Neill in 1819. [Liverpool app. enrolment bk]

Hitchcock, Robert, Woolwich, London, cm and u (1832–39). Trading at Wellington St, 1832–34, and 35 Green's End, 1838–39. [D]

Hitchcock, Samuel, 14 Widegate St, Bishopsgate St, London, carver and gilder (1808). [D]

Hitchcock, Thomas, Mint Lane, Exeter, Devon, cm (1821). Son John Lendon bapt. at St Olave's on 5 September 1821. [PR (bapt.)]

Hitchcock, Thomas, St Michael's Sq., Southampton, Hants., cm (1839). [D]

Hitchcock, William, St Giles-in-the-Fields, London, u (1726). Declared bankrupt, *British Journal*, 7 May 1726.

Hitchens, —, Upper West St, Gloucester, chairmaker (1802). [D]

Hitchin, Charles, at 'The White Hart', East end of St Paul's, London, cm (1709). Named in newspapers in 1709. [Heal]

Hitchin, William, 21 Bridgewater Gdns, Barbican, London, tea caddy, snuff box and card case maker etc. (1835–39). [D]

Hitchings, Daniel, Horsley, Glos., chairmaker (1800). Took out a Sun Insurance policy on 27 December 1800 for £300, of which £180 accounted for his new house and shop; £50 on stock and utensils, and £20 on his stable. [GL, Sun MS vol. 37, ref. 73191]

Hitchings, John, Gloucester, cm (1818). Child bapt. at St Catherine's Church in 1818. [PR (bapt.)] Probably John Hitchins.

Hitchings, John, Barton St, Bristol, fancy chair maker (1819–40). Recorded at no. 12 in 1819 and no. 4, 1820–23, 1826–40 [D]

Hitchings, William & Co., North St, Bedminster, Bristol, chairmakers (1805–22). Recorded at the 'Star Inn', North St, 1814–30. [D]

Hitchins, —, 46 Ship St, Brighton, Sussex, chair bottomer (1832). [D]

Hitchins, John, Gloucester, chairmaker (1813). Child bapt. at St Michael's Church in 1813. [PR (bapt.)] Probably John Hitchings.

Hitcombe, Thomas, Union Rd, Clapham, London, cm and u (1832). [D]

Hitterley, William, address unrecorded, upholder (1708–24). Son of William Hitterley, freeman haberdasher of London; app. to Thomas Coulton on 5 May 1708, and admitted freeman of the Upholders' Co. by servitude on 5 February 1723/24. [GL, Upholders' Co. records]

Hixon, Thomas, London, u (1793). Subscribed to Sheraton's *Drawing Book*, 1793.

Hixon, Thomas, 8 John St West, Blackfriars Rd, London, u (1829). [D]

Hoale, Amos, New St, Ross, Herefs., cm (1830). [D]

Hoale, Moses, New St, Ross, Herefs., cm (1835). [D]

Hoar, Richard, Petersfield, Hants., cm (1839). [D]

Hoare, E. W., address unknown. Satinwood sewing table, c.1800, recorded bearing stamp of 'E W HOARE CVII'. Table has two drawers, a bag drawer, and fine turned legs.

Hoare, James, Hull, Yorks., cm (1814). App. to Robert Waugh in May 1814. [Hull app. reg.]

Hoare, Richard, 18 Gracechurch St, London, carver and gilder, looking-glass and frame maker, printseller and glazier (1804–39). Took out Sun Insurance policies on 11 October 1803 for £500 on house at 30 Brooke St, Holborn, in tenure of a turner and chinaman; on 28 June 1804 for £1,000, including £500 on stock and utensils; and on 8 November 1820 for £1,000, £400 on stock, utensils and goods in trust, prints and paintings; and £65 on stock of glass. Rococo-style giltwood mirror recorded bearing label. [D; GL, Sun MS vol. 430, ref. 527233; vol. 430, ref. 762911; vol. 487, ref. 972854; Christie's NY, 20 June 1979, lot 106, illus.]

Hoare, Thomas, London. Tradesman employed by Morel & Seddon who signed the frame of a dining chair supplied to Windsor Castle in 1828. [Gilbert, *Leeds Furn. Cat.*, vol. 1, pp. 101–02]

Hoare, Thomas, 5 Wardour St, Soho, London, u and cm (1835–39). [D]

Hoarsy, John, address unrecorded. Possibly the maker of a Charles II walnut open armchair from Stoneleigh Abbey, Warks. Chair has narrow cane-panelled splat edged with scrolls, crown and putto cresting. A surviving account from John Hoarsy, receipted 13 May 1682, totalling £3 14s 2d includes £1 4s 'for fashionable cand chayers carved & varnished at 8s', and £2 4s 'for Elbo Chayers of ye same at 11s.' [Christie's, 15 October 1981, lot 99; Shakespeare Birthplace Trust, Leigh receipts, ref. 664]

Hobbird, Martin, 16 Noble St, Falcon Sq., London, upholder and undertaker (1817). [D]

Hobbs, —, 3 Leather Lane, Hampstead Yd, Holborn, London, cm (1808). Rented workshops and sawpits at above address from John Brook, carpenter, of 27 Castle St, Holborn, who took out insurance on 7 April 1808. [GL, Sun MS vol. 443, ref. 814880]

Hobbs, George, London, cm (1764). Mahogany kneehole writing table recorded with label inside drawer stating: 'London 27 June 1764. Mr. Field. My sisters receipt shall be a discharge from me to you whenever you shall please to pay her. George Hobbs.' 'July 13 1764. Received of Mr. Field of Campton the sum of Ten Pounds eleven shillings and sixpence in full for a library Table bought of my brother Geo. Hobbs and all demands by me. Ann Hobbs. Witness Wm. Aspin.'. Table has three drawers at the top, with three graduated drawers at each side; original pierced back-plate handles,

leather top, and dummy drawers on reverse. [*Conn.*, June 1953, p. 35]

Hobbs, George, Windsor, Berks., cm (1806). Named in rate bks, but did not poll, in 1806.

Hobbs, George, Mary St, Bridgwater, Som., cm (1840). [D]

Hobbs, James, High St, Abingdon, Berks., brazier, tinman, smith and upholder (1784). Took out a Sun Insurance policy in 1784 for £600, of which utensils and stock accounted for £500. [GL, Sun MS vol. 321, p. 523]

Hobbs, John, London, cm and u (1827–39). Recorded at 13 Charlotte St, Old St Rd in 1827; 9 Exmouth St, Spitalfields in 1829; 7 Yardley St, Spitalfields in 1835; and 27 King's Rd, Chelsea in 1839. [D]

Hobbs, John, Ebrington St, Plymouth, Devon, cm (1836). [D]

Hobbs, John, Marsh Lane, Southampton, Hants., cm (1839). [D]

Hobbs, Joshua, London, cm (1808–28). Addresses given at 41 Eagle St, Red Lion Sq., 1808; 59 Leather Lane, Holborn in 1813; no. 45 in 1816; 20 Wilson St, Finsbury in 1820; 23 Old Bethlem in 1822; and 2 Liverpool St, Finsbury Circus, 1826–29. [D]

Hobbs, Nic., corner of Long Acre and St Martin's Lane, London, cm and u (1753). Notice in *Public Advertiser*, 9 June 1753, read: 'Lost on Wednesday the 7th inst. a Parcel cont a red letter Portfolio, with Drawings & other Papers, three or four Pieces of Flock Paper, & two mahogany legs for chairs tied tog in a White Linnen wrapper. Whoever brings the said things to Mr. Nic. Hobbs' Cabinet & Upholstery Warehouse, the corner of Long Acre & St. Martin's Lane, shall have half a guinea reward, they being of no use but to the Owner.'

Hobbs, Nicholas, West Exe, Tiverton, Devon, cm (1830–38). [D]

Hobbs, Samuel, 24 Lower Maudlin Lane, Bristol, cm (1775). [D]

Hobbs, William, High Wycombe, Bucks., chairmaker (1790). [D]

Hobcraft, Edward jnr, Gravesend, Kent, cm (1824). [D] See John and John Edward Hobcraft of Gravesend.

Hobcraft, John, London (?), joiner, carpenter and builder (1768–84). Submitted long bills for work done for Sir John Griffin Griffin of Audley End, Essex, between 1768–84. Between 1 June and 9 September 1768 he carried out designs for a Gothic chapel, including details of the interior, and furnishings such as 'seats and Desks for the side Isles and makeing a modle for Each of Ditto; 'Drawing and Estimating the Parson's Desk & Chair and Steps'; designing the altar rail and niches above; the iron gate for the cummunion rail, and 'makeing a modle for Parsons Chair & Desk & Steps'. On 9 September Hobcraft also charged for '8 Journeys to Audley End to give Directions & measure the Work'. The designs for the chapel were generally sent to 'Wheeler', perhaps the architect. From October 1769 to 15 August 1770 Hobcraft's bill included £37 2s for '212 Days Works of Joiners makeing Gothic Chair & Desk', £16 for 'Alkins Bill for Carving', and materials for making the steps on castors. His work for the chapel totalled £32 12s 3½d. Other work which he carried out for Sir John Griffin Griffin included, on 1 May 1770 'makeing a Straining frame for a Picture' and a peruke stand. On 18 December he charged for 'Mahogany from Messrs. Park & Reed'; and £4 1s for 'a Gothick Pattern Chair & Drawing for Do.', and packing case. The full bill was paid by 20 November 1772. Hobcraft submitted a further bill to Sir John on 24 May 1775, charging £10 10s 'To 5 Temple seats or Chairs'; £5 5s 'To a Pedestal Table for Temple'; and £6 3s 'To Carving Ditto by Mr. Alkin'. He also provided 'Strong Dovetaild packing Cases for Marble pedestale from Nollekins' and for a harpsichord; and 'A Cart from Berkley Square and New Burlington Street to ye Waggon at Mr. Nollekins'. The bill totalled £29 13s 2d and was paid on 29 March 1776. As Lord Howard de Walden, Sir John Griffin Griffin paid Hobcraft £16 19s 10d in 1784, including payment for '6 Garden seats at £2.8s.' [Essex RO, D/DBy/A30/11; A34/3; ALL3/6] He is probably the John Hobcraft of Titchfield St, London, who carved the wooden fireplace in the Green Room at Broadlands and worked at Croome Court and Bowood. [*C. Life*, 11 December 1980, p. 2250] He was possibly also the supplier of the Gothic furniture at Tissington Hall, Derbs. [*C. Life*, 22 July 1976, p. 216]

Hobcraft, John, Gravesend, Kent, cm (1824–29). Trading in High St, 1829. [D] See Edward Hobcraft.

Hobcraft, John Edward, Windmill St, Gravesend, Kent, cm (1832–34). [D] See Edward and John Hobcraft.

Hobday, William, Borough Longport, near Canterbury, Kent, cm (1780). Took out a Sun Insurance policy in 1780 for £200 of which utensils and stock accounted for £50. [GL, Sun MS vol. 284, p. 209]

Hobson, G., London, cm (1793). Subscribed to Sheraton's *Drawing Book*, 1793.

Hobson, George, Bean Ing, Leeds, Yorks., cm (1822). [D]

Hobson, Henry, Frodsham, Cheshire, u (1839). Admitted freeman of Chester on 3 June 1839. [Chester freemen rolls]

Hobson, James, Newcastle, cm (1740). Declared bankrupt, *York Courant*, 18 January 1740.

Hobson, John, Boyne's Yd, near White Cloth Hall, Leeds, Yorks., cm (1822). [D]

Hobson, Jonath., Thames St, London, upholder (1753). Declared bankrupt, *Gents. Mag.*, December 1753.

Hobson, Joseph, 39 Cooper St, Sheffield, Yorks., cm (1793–97). Subscribed to Sheraton's *Drawing Book*, 1793. [D]

Hobson, Joseph, West Wycombe, Bucks., chairmaker (b. *c*.1776–1841). Aged 65 at the time of the 1841 Census.

Hobson, Michael, 27 Bottle-bank, Gateshead, Co. Durham, cm and joiner (1838). [D]

Hobson, Nathaniel, Coventry, Warks., cm (1731–54). Took app. named Dan. Mason in 1731 for £20. [S of G, app. index]

Hobson, Nathaniel, London, cm (1754). Subscribed to Chippendale's *Directory*, 1754, and in the same year was bound app. to Chippendale for a consideration of £20. [PRO, IR 1/19]

Hobson, Samuel, London, carver and gilder (1808–37). Trading at 15 Castle St, Long Acre in 1808 and 17 Phoenix St, Soho, 1835–37. [D]

Hobson, Thomas, 9 Gresse St, Rathbone Pl., London, cm and undertaker (1827–28). [D]

Hobson, William, Darlington, Co. Durham, joiner and cm (1827–34). Trading at Market Pl., 1827, and Tubwell Row, 1828–34. [D]

Hoby, —, address unrecorded, u (1831). In September 1831 charged 13s 7d to 3rd Lord Braybrooke for work done at Audley End, Essex, Billingbear, Berks., or his London house. [Essex RO, D/DBy/A358]

Hoby, James, Skinner St, Snowhill, London, u, trimming manufacturer and warehouseman (1823–39). Trading at no. 17 in 1823, and as Hoby, Robson & Knowles at no. 22, 1835–39. [D]

Hockey, Thos., 10 Kingsmead Sq., Bath, Som., cm (1833). [D]

Hocking, John jnr, 4 James St, Plymouth, Devon, u (1823–24). [D]

Hocking, William, 4 Cornwall St, Devonport, Devon, cm and u (1830). [D]

Hockmill, Daniel, King St, Westminster, London, cm and broker (1779–83). Took out Sun Insurance policies in 1779 for £100, £80 accounting for utensils, stock and goods; and in 1783 for £300, £240 on utensils, stock and goods. [GL, Sun MS vol. 277, p. 263; vol. 317, p. 84] See H. Hocknill.

Hockney, John, 11 St Anne's St, Manchester, u and paper hanging manufacturer (1825). [D]

Hocknill, H., King's St, Westminster, London, upholder and auctioneer (1784). [D] See Daniel Hockmill.

Hodder, Benjamin, South St, Dorchester, Dorset, cm (1840). [D]

Hodder, Charles, Southwark, London, cm and upholder (1755–87). Recorded at 'The Mahogany Desk & Bookcase', corner of Union Yd, no. 100 Tooley St, 1776–87. Took app. named Gilbert in 1755. On 7 March 1766, Charles Hodder, cm and widower of St Olave's, Southwark, and Sarah Osman, widow of St John's, Southwark, were named in the Surrey allegations of marriage. Trade card recorded. [D; S of G, app. index; Heal]

Hodder, John, address unrecorded, turner (1740). Son of William Hodder of Som.; app. to Nathaniel Trimbey, turner, of Marden, Wilts., on 23 June 1740 by common indenture and counterpart, for £3. [*Wilts. Apps and their Masters*]

Hodder, John, Belvedere Rd, Lambeth, London, cm and u (1839). [D]

Hodder, Richard, Market St, Croydon, Surrey, cm (b.*c*.1770–d.1845). Recorded in Croydon at the time of the 1811 Census.

Hodder & Son, Portsea, Portsmouth, Hants., cm, brokers and auctioneers (1792–98). [D]

Hoddinet, —, Sherborne, Dorset, cm (1763). Supplied a 'Norway Oak Bureau' to the Rev. James Woodforde of Ansford, Som., on 3 October 1763, costing £3 3s. On 15 October 1763 valued the contents of a house at Wells belonging to James Woodforde's uncle. [*The Ansford Diary of the Rev. James Woodforde*, ed. R. L. Winstanley, vol. 1, p. 73; vol. 2, p. 74] Either John Hoddinet or James Hoddinot(t)(s).

Hoddinett, John, Sherborne, Dorset, cm (1763–d. by 1768). Took app. named Allen in 1736. [S of G, app. index] Succeeded by:

Hoddinot(t)(s), James, Sherborne, Dorset, cm, u and sworn appraiser (1768–74). Announced that he was taking over the business of his late brother, John, in *Western Flying Post or Sherborne and Yeovil Mercury and General Advertiser*, 30 May 1768. His notice read: 'Gentlemen and Ladies may be assured of having their work done in the most elegant Manner, and on as reasonable Terms as in London. N.B. He has a large and genteel Assortment of the newest Patterns of Paper-Hangings, which he sells and puts up in the best Manner.' J. Hoddinott, u, late of Sherborne, declared bankrupt, *Gents Mag.*, December 1770. James took out a Sun Insurance policy in 1774 for £200, £100 accounting for utensils and stock. [GL, Sun MS vol. 324, p. 375]

Hodge, James, Liverpool, cm (1792). Found guilty, with James Basnett, turner, of stealing a case bottle and rum, the property of J. Lee, at the General Quarter Sessions in Liverpool, and 'committed to the house of Correction for two months'. [*Williamson's Liverpool Advertiser*, 17 December 1792]

Hodge, James, Plymouth, Devon, cm (1798–1814). Address given at Southside St in 1814. [D]

Hodge, John, 13 Rose St, Covent Gdn, London, cm (1782–85). Took out Sun Insurance policies in 1782 for £100, £50 accounting for utensils, stock and goods; and on 26 September 1785 for £100 on utensils, stock and goods in trust, and £80 on household goods. [GL, Sun MS vol. 304, p. 319; vol. 331, p. 630]

Hodge, John, 20 Charlotte St, Fitzroy Sq., London, u, appraiser and undertaker (1809–11). [D]

Hodge, John, 69 Old St, St Luke's, London, cm (1837). [D]

Hodge, Robert, address unrecorded. Mahogany armchair, *c*.1780 or later, recorded with small stamp of raised letters on seat rail, 'ROBT HODGE'. Chair has upholstered oval back, arm pads, stuffed-over seat, and straight front legs.

Hodge, Samuel, James St, Devonport (or Plymouth) Dock, Devon, cm (1814–38). Recorded at no. 82, 1823–38. [D]

Hodge(s), William, 9 Ratcliff(e), Highway, London, cm and broker (1780–93). Took out a Sun Insurance policy in 1780 for £300, £100 accounting for utensils and stock. [D; GL, Sun MS vol. 287, p. 528]

Hodges, George, Mardol, Shrewsbury, Salop, u (1796). [Shrewsbury burgess roll]

Hodges, Henry, London, cm (1793). Subscribed to Sheraton's *Drawing Book*, 1793.

Hodges, Jesse, Weymouth, Dorset, joiner and cm (1798). [D]

Hodges, John, address unrecorded, upholder (1727–34). Son of Thomas Hodges, freeman painter stainer of London. App. to Thomas Hathaway on 7 June 1727 and Richard Righton on 7 August 1730. Admitted freeman of the Upholders' Co. by servitude on 2 October 1734. [GL, Upholders' Co. records]

Hodges, John, Shrewsbury, Salop, u (1777–80). Recorded at Shoplatch when took out a Sun Insurance policy in 1777 for £500 of which £400 accounted for utensils and stock. Named in the Shrewsbury burgess roll in 1780. [GL, Sun MS vol. 262, p. 66]

Hodges, John, 9 Mercer St, London (?), upholder (1781). Insured houses for £300 in 1781. [GL, Sun MS vol. 295, p. 373]

Hodges, John, 1 Aldgate Within, London, u, bed and mattress warehouseman (1829–35). [D]

Hodges, John, 10 Hoxton Mkt, London, cm and beer engine maker (1835). [D]

Hodges, Joseph, parish of St Mary Redcliffe, Bristol, cm (1774). [Poll bk]

Hodges, Richard, Wyle Cop, Shrewsbury, Salop, cm (1796). [D; Shrewsbury burgess roll]

Hodges, Richard, Tewkesbury, Glos., cm (1814). [PR (bapt.)]

Hodges, Richard, Hereford, cm (1818). [Poll bk]

Hodges, Richard, Homend, Ledbury, Herefs., turner and chairmker (1830–35). [D]

Hodges, Richard, Ordnance Wharf, Pedlar's Acre, London, Tunbridge-ware manufacturer (1826–28). [D]

Hodges, Richard, 54 Gravel Lane, Southwark, London, cm, u and undertaker (1835–39). [D] See Thomas Hodges.

Hodges, Thomas, Bristol, upholder (1739). [Poll bk]

Hodges, Thomas, Liverpool, carver and gilder (1805–11). Addresses given at 54 Paradise St in 1805, 61 Church St in 1810, and no. 64 in 1811. [D]

Hodges, Thomas, 15 Edward St, Blackfriars Rd, London, chairmaker (1808). [D]

Hodges, Thomas, 28 Gravel Lane, Southwark, London, cm (1809–29). Trading as Thomas & Son in 1820. [D] See Richard Hodges.

Hodges, Thomas, 101 Dale End, Birmingham, cm and upholder (1816–18). [D]

Hodges, Thomas, Chester, carver and gilder (1816–37). Recorded at Bridge St Row, 1816–18, and City Walls, 1834. [D]

Hodges, Thomas, Tunbridge Wells, Kent, u (1832–36). Son William by Frances Hodges bapt. on 6 June 1832; and son Frank on 7 September 1836. [PR (bapt.)]

Hodges, Thomas, Manchester, carver and gilder (1833). His son, James Edward's death aged 20 on 22 August 1833 at Manchester reported in *Chester Courant and Advertiser for North Wales*, 3 September.

Hodges, W. J., 16 Bouverie St, London, writing desk and dressing case maker (1829–35). [D]

Hodges, William, Sawclose, Bath, Som., cm (1819–26). [D]

Hodges & Lawrence, Pride Hill, Shrewsbury, Salop, u (1786–98). [D]

Hodges & Pratt, 15 Gower Pl., Euston Sq., London, carver and gilder (1835). [D]

Hodgkins, Charles, 26 Colmore Row, Birmingham, cm (1770–80). Insured his house for £300 in 1776. [D; GL, Sun MS vol. 253, p. 519]

Hodgkins, Timothy, Chipping Campden, Oxon., cm, u, undertaker and auctioneer (1823–30). Trading at High St in 1830. [D]

Hodgkins, William, Birmingham, cm and u (c.1753–1801). Addresses given at Bull St, 1767; 9 The Square, 1770–80, no. 81 in 1773; and Long Entry, Colmore Row, 1800–01. Probably two generations are concerned here. Received payment for furniture supplied to Matthew Boulton and to his warehouse, 1753–63, including £15 15s 'for making my desk & wood & brasswork'. Took app. named Stokes in 1762. [D; City of Birmingham Lib., Boulton MS early accounts, 161–66; notebook 1, p. 43; S of G, app. index]

Hodgkins & Son, Chipping Norton, Oxon., cm, u and builders (1823–53). Trade card reads: 'Carpets & Hearth Rugs, Bedds, Ironmongery, Paper Hanging, Coffin Furniture, Glasses Framed & Silvered, General Assortment of Household Furniture, Barometers, Umbrellas, Desks, Tea Chests & Caddies...'. [D; Johnson Coll., Bodleian Lib., Oxford; *Furn. Hist.*, 1974, pl. 45]

Hodgkinson, Francis, Liverpool, chairmaker (1807–14). Addresses given at 16 Cunliffe St, 1807–11, with shop at 34 Park Lane, 1811, and no. 42, 1813–14. [D]

Hodgkinson, Francis, Salford and Blackburn, Lancs., chairmaker (1828). [D]

Hodgkinson, Isaac, Nottingham, cm (c.1800–60). One of a family of cm and chairmakers of the name of Hodgkinson or Hodgkison. The family lived in the Amersham, High Wycombe and Thame districts between 1770–80. One of them, another Isaac Hodgkinson, chairmaker, emigrated to Australia and formed a business with Henry Corlass of Yorkshire, cm. Other members of the Hodgkinson family spread to other parts of England, including John Hodgkinson, chairmaker, to Carlisle, and Isaac, cm, to Nottingham. The family chairmaking firm is still in existence in High Wycombe, the family having moved there from either Derbyshire, or Lancashire, possibly the Preston area, long associated with chairmaking.

Hodgkinson, James, West Wycombe, Bucks., chairmaker (b. c.1811–41). Aged 30 at the time of the 1841 Census.

Hodgkinson, John, Carlisle, Cumb., chairmaker, see Isaac Hodgkinson.

Hodgkinson, Richard, Grove St, Retford, Notts., u (1832). [D]

Hodgkinson, Samuel, Snidullgate, Dean parish, Westhoughton, near Bolton, Lancs., chairmaker (1825). [D]

Hodgkinson, Thomas & Co., 91 New Bond St, London, furniture printers, carpet manufacturers and general u (1837). [D]

Hodgson, —, Newington, London, cm and upholder (1808). [D]

Hodgson, Charles, Aiskew, near Bedale, Yorks., cm (1840). [D]

Hodgson, Christopher, Lancaster, cm (1789–90). Lancaster freemen rolls state 'of Liverpool'.

Hodgson, Daniel, Newcastle, u (1723–41). Admitted freeman by apprenticeship on 22 July 1723. [Newcastle freemen reg. and poll bk]

Hodgson, David, Lancaster. Named in the Gillow Records, 1784–97. [Westminster Ref. Lib.]

Hodgson, Elizabeth, Suffolk St, Liverpool, u (1835–39). Trading at no. 6, 1835–37, and no. 11 in 1838. [D]

Hodgson, Francis, Wych St, London, cm and u (1787–93). Recorded at no. 49 in 1787; no. 47 in 1789; and no. 49 in

1793. Insured goods to the value of £300 on 8 June 1787. [D; GL, Sun MS vol. 342, ref. 531409]

Hodgson, George, Brook St, Holborn, near 'The Sun Tavern', London, u and cm (1745). [Harris, *Old English Furniture*, p. 23]

Hodgson, George, York, cm (1775). Son of Michael Hodgson, deceased, of Scarborough; app. to John Sanderson, cm, on 9 November 1775. [York app. reg.]

Hodgson, Henry, Oxford Rd, High Wycombe, Bucks., carver (1839). [D]

Hodgson, Isaac, 21 Hanover St, Liverpool, with shop in College Lane, cm (1818). [D]

Hodg(e)son, James, Lancaster, joiner and cm (1769–89). App. to Bateman & Forrest in 1769, and admitted freeman, 1779–80. Named in the Gillow records, 1786–89. [Lancaster app. reg. and freemen rolls; Westminster Ref. Lib., Gillow]

Hodgson, James, Eastgate, Pickering, Yorks., cm and chairmaker (1830–40). [D]

Hodgson, John, Lancaster, cm (1767–68). [Lancaster freemen rolls]

Hodgson, John, Caton, Lancs., cm (1784). [Lancaster poll bk]

Hodgson, John, Lancaster, cm (1788–1826). Two contemporary tradesmen of the same name are recorded, one app. to R. Mashiter in 1785, the other to J. Neill in 1787. One was admitted freeman, 1789–90, the other, 1801–02. One was named in the Gillow records, 1788–1804. One was trading at Friargate in 1811 when he announced in the *Lancaster Gazette*, 1 June that 'he intends to decline the undertaking of funerals'. John Hodgson, cm, traded in Moor Lane, 1816–22; and of Moor Lane and Friar St he advertised in the same paper on 13 May 1826 'that he has taken into partnership, his Foreman, John Battersby, who has been many years in his service; and Robert Battersby, late of the firm of Lodge & Battersby of this town; and it is their intention to carry on the business upon a more extensive scale, under the firm Hodgson & Battersbys at the same shop and premises in Friar Street and Moor Lane...'. A notice in *Lancaster Gazette*, 13 May 1826 read: 'Turner & Hodgson, upholsterers, return their thanks to their numerous friends and the public, for all favours conferred upon them in the above business and respectfully solicit a continuance of their support.' [D; Lancaster app. reg. and freemen rolls; Westminster Ref. Lib., Gillow]

Hodgson, John, Hull, Yorks., cm (1803–06). Trading at 16 Robinson Row in 1803 and Witham in 1806. [D]

Hodgson, John, Liverpool, cm (1811–34). Recorded at 24 Limekiln Lane in 1811; no. 32 in 1813–14; Bloomsbury Buildings, Milton St in 1816; and 48 Milton St in 1834. [D] See John Hodson of Liverpool.

Hodgson, John, St Ann's Staith, Whitby, Yorks., carver and gilder (1823). [D]

Hodgson, John, Back St, Brampton, Carlisle, Cumb., joiner and/or cm (1829–34). [D]

Hodgson, John, Maldon, Essex, cm (1832–39). [D]

Hodgson, Joseph, Liverpool, cm and u (1818–19). Trading at 2 Limekiln Lane in 1818. Marriage to Miss Mary Ann Alderson, lamp and oil merchant, on Tuesday 13 April 1819, reported in *Liverpool Mercury*, 23 April. [D]

Hodgson, Joseph, Workington, Cumb., cm and joiner (1834). [D]

Hodgson, Leonard, Staindrop, near Barnard Castle, Co. Durham, cm (1815–17). Daughters bapt. on 11 May 1815 and 30 November 1817. [PR (bapt.)]

Hodgson, Leonard, Liverpool, cm (1816–19). Recorded at 18 White Hill St in 1816, and in partnership with Thomas Guy at 36 Wood St in 1818. Dissolution of this partnership announced in *Liverpool Mercury*, 3 December 1819. [D]

Hodgson, Mrs, 59 Sir Thomas Building, Liverpool, u (1813–14). [D]

Hodgson, Mary, 14 Manesty's Lane, Liverpool, u (1818). [D]

Hodgson, Philip, Newcastle, u (1777). [Poll bk]

Hodgson, Ralph, York, cm (1831). Son of Ralph Hodgson of Holgate, York; app. to John Taylor, cm, on 26 April 1831. [York app. reg.]

Hodgson, Richard, Liverpool, joiner and cm (1761). Former app., Richard Jolly, petitioned freedom in 1761. [Liverpool freemen's committee bk]

Hodgson, Richard, Wolsingham, Co. Durham, spinning wheel maker (1827). [D]

Hodgson, Richard, Camberwell, London, cm and u (1826–29). Trading at High St in 1826. Declared bankrupt, *London Gazette*, 16 January 1829.

Hodgson, Robert, Preston, Lancs., cm (1702–22). Named in the Preston Guild record of burgesses in 1702 being admitted on payment of a fine of £3; and named again in 1722.

Hodgson, S., 7 Swan Ct, Gt Dover St, London, cm (1835). [D]

Hodgson, Septimus, Walcot Pl., Lambeth, London, u (1826–35). [D]

Hodgson, Thomas, Lancaster, cm (1773–80). App. to H. Baines in 1773, and admitted freeman, 1779–80. [Lancaster app. reg. and freemen rolls]

Hodgson, Thomas, 12 Tufton St, Westminster, London, cm (1787). Took out a Sun Insurance policy on 14 February 1787 for £300 on household goods, and stock in a timber workshop in the yard. [GL, Sun MS vol. 342, ref. 527583]

Hodgson, Thomas, London, u (1808–12). Trading at 40 Blackman St, Southwark, 1808–11; in parnership with James Hodgson, 1809–11; and at 24 Westminster Rd in 1812. Declared bankrupt, Ackermann's *Repository of Arts*, July 1809. [D]

Hodgson, Thomas, Thomas, York, cm (1812–34). Addresses given at Stamford Bridge in 1820; and 41 Walmgate in 1830. Son of Richard Hodgson, yeoman of Acomb, York; app. to John Taylor, cm, on 2 March 1812, and admitted freeman in 1820. [D; York app. reg. and freemen rolls]

Hodgson, Thomas, High St, Camberwell, London, cm and u (1822). [D]

Hodgson, Thomas, 15 Middle Row, Reading, Berks., u and cm (1826–40). [D]

Hodgson, Thomas, Church St, Brighton, Sussex, cm and u (1832). [D]

Hodgson, William, Gt Queen St, Lincoln's Inn Fields, London, u and cm (1777–1811). Addresses given at no. 39 in 1777, no. 70, 1783–1803, and no. 50, dates unspecified. Took out Sun Insurance policies in 1777 for £1,000 of which utensils, stock and goods accounted for £720; and on 9 May 1801 for £500. Named in Sheraton's list of master cabinet makers, 1803. [D; GL, Sun MS vol. 260, p. 591; vol. 419, ref. 718347]

Hodgson, William, 10 Lord St, Chorlton Row, Manchester, cm (1825). [D]

Hodgson, William, Wigton, Cumb., joiner and cm (1828–34). Addresses given at West St in 1828–29; Union St in 1829; and Water St in 1834. [D]

Hodgson, William, Gt Dockray, Penrith, Cumb., chairmaker (1834). [D]

Hodkin, Christopher, Holywell St, Chesterfield, Derbs., cm (1818–22). [D]

Hodkin, Daniel, Holywell St, Chesterfield, Derbs., cm (1818–22). [D]

Hodsden, John, address unrecorded, upholder (1686–1717). Son of Richard Hodsden, freeman plumber of London; app. to James Sargeant on 2 April 1686, and admitted freeman of the Upholders' Co. by servitude on 18 June 1717. [GL, Upholders' Co. records]

Hodskins, William, Birmingham, cm (1751). Took app. named Rock in 1751. [S of G, app. index]

Hodson, —, address unrecorded. In March 1725 supplied Sir John Chester with 'Chairs & Stooles for ye Gt. Parlour', costing £34, for Chicheley Hall, Bucks. [Bucks. RO, ref. D/C/3/ii)]

Hodson, —, address unrecorded, cm (1733–42). Named in the accounts for Holkham Hall, Norfolk in 1733 providing a table costing £1 8s; in 1734, a 'neat two leaf screen on turn'd pillars, mahogany frame and covered with French prints', £1 16s, and a 'new pillar to a round mahogany table', £1; and in 1742, a 'beditt', costing £5 15s. [V&A archives] Probably John Hodson of London.

Hodson, —, 16 Titchfield St, London. In 1782 supplied pier glasses, Carlo Maratta picture frames, a chimney glass, and '3 tops to glasses' for Blickling Hall, Norfolk. [Norfolk RO, 19180]

Hodson, Benjamin, address unrecorded, upholder (1709–30). Son of Benjamin Hodson, clerk of Broughton, Hunts.; app. to Thomas Ferrers on 8 February 1709, and admitted freeman of the Upholders' Co. by servitude on 6 May 1730. [GL, Upholders' Co. records]

Hodson, Charles, West Wycombe, Bucks., chairmaker (b. c. 1811–41). Aged 30 at the time of the 1841 Census.

Hodson, John, London, upholder and cm (1709–86). Son of Thomas Hodson, innholder of Lincoln. App. to Thomas Arne jnr on 23 February 1709, and admitted freeman of the Upholders' Co. by servitude on 3 December 1718. Took app. named Lawrence Rudyard, 1733–45. [GL, Upholders' Co. records] Appears to have succeeded Robert Hodson, and acted as head of the firm of Hodson's, looking-glass and cabinet warehouse in Frith St, Soho, from 1723 until as late as 1786. An earlier address for John Hodson, in Bedford St, St Paul's, Covent Gdn, is given in 1718, when he insured goods and merchandise on 4 November with the Sun Co. A note added to the policy on 12 October 1723 stated that he had moved to 'The Fleece', Frith St, St Ann's. John Hodson took out another policy on 12 December 1730 for £1,400 on household goods and stock in trade in workshops adjoining the 'Slade House', next to his own house. [GL, Sun MS vol. 8, ref. 12498; vol. 33, ref. 52401] The firm appears to have been headed firstly by Robert Hodson, who wrote to the Earl of Radnor in September 1725 concerning a 'compting bureau' supplied to Longford Castle. [V&A archives] Later bills from Hodsons were generally submitted by John, and from 1730–86 often have the same heading which shows furniture in the style of the 1730s–40s: elaborately carved pier and dressing tables, an elbow chair, tripod reading desk, japanned cabinet on stand, kettle table, and looking-glass with carved masks and flanking candle holders. The heading bears the inscription: 'At Hodsons Looking Glass and Cabinet Warehouse in Frith Street, Soho, is ready made great variety of all sorts of Furniture in the neatest and most Fashionable manner, by choice and experienced Workmen employ'd in his own house. By which means Customers may better depend on the goodness of ye materials and duration of the Work: There are also many well contriv'd Machines for weak and Sickly people, all perform'd at moderate prizes, and in the utmost perfection. NB. Coach, Chair, and Sash Glasses are sold, at the very lowest prizes.' [Banks Coll., BM; C. Life, 9 June 1966, p. 1462; 26 January 1967, p. 184] The earliest known bill with this heading was submitted to Robert Packer, Lord of Shellingford Manor, on 18 March 1730, and was for a pillar and claw table, dressing glass, walnut corner cupboard, and sconces. [Berks. RO, Hartley Russell MS D/EHy A2/4 and 36] In April 1732 John Hodson charged a Mr Stannix £4 12s for a table and various repairs. [Chetham Lib., Manchester,

Halliwell-Phillipps Coll. of Broadsides, no. 1242] In 1736 he supplied mahogany tables costing £44 to Holkham Hall, Norfolk. [V&A archives] He sent two accounts to Lord Monson dated 1735 and 1741 [Lincoln RO, Monson papers]; and one to the Duke of Atholl of Blair Castle, Tayside, dated January 1738, amounting to £150 1s 6d. Items he supplied include a tripod table, mahogany claw table with galleried top, a fine carved and painted side table and a wine cooler. It may be possible to identify furniture from this commission with that still at Blair Castle. [Conn., April 1963, pp. 223–30; G. Bernard Hughes, 'Mahogany Claw Tables', C. Life, 17 March 1955, illus.; 18 November 1949; Heal] The usual heading occurred on a bill sent by Hodsons to Sir Herbert Pakington of Westwood Park, Worcs., dated 2 May 1733, for 'a Large Oblong mohogeney dining Table with 2 flapps to hold 12 people', costing £3 13s. [Worcs. RO, 2309–705: 380–17] A bill headed as before was submitted to Coll. Kennedy for items supplied to Dalquharran, 1735–36, costing a total of £14 6s. This included £3 18s for '6 Virginia walnutt Chairs' on 3 October 1735; and £2 12s 6d for 'a mohogoney Armd Chair on brass Castor' on 18 September 1736, all with 'seats Stuft and covered with black Leather'. On 24 December 1736 Hodsons charged for transporting looking-glasses from Chelsea to London; and on 14 February 1736–37, for packing furniture including a pillar and claw table, a 'mahogeney Elbow Chair', '6 Yoak back chairs', and '18 Walnut Chairs', and transporting them from Frith St to Scotland Yd, '& Expences it being parliament time', and paying a man for 'going to put the Goods on board the ship'. Hodson also cleaned and repaired furniture, beds, bedding and window curtains. [V&A archives] Another extant bill with the usual Hodson heading was sent to William Clayton in December 1744, totalling £17 8s, including £4 4s for a 'neat wainscott Cloaths Press'; £10 10s for '10 Neat mohog. Chairs Stuft and covered with black Spanish leather studed with brass nails'; and two elbow chairs with quilted leather cushions. The bill to Clayton was receipted by P. Smagget for 'Hodson & Self'. [Heal Coll., BM] Bills with the usual heading were sent from Hodson & Co. to the Duke of Gordon in 1745. The first, dated 28 March 1745 is for '2 Neat Redwood Standishes with Drawers & Covers', for £1 6s. Another, dated and receipted by P. Smagget on 3 May 1745, was for '2 Neat Saxogotha Standishes with Drawers & Covers', costing the same. On 1 June 1745 two further standishes were bought, one of 'neat alliganxant', with silver handle and hinges; and both with cut glass bottles mounted with silver, totalling £5 10s. [Scottish RO, GD 44/51/202/2/23 and 33; GD 44/51/300/1/62] See Hodson & Rudyard.   A.E.

Hodson, John, at the 'Sherpherdess', Myton St, Hull, Yorks., as victualler, and Trundle St as cm and u (1823). [D]

Hodson (or Hodgson), John, 51 Milton St, Liverpool, cm (1827–29). [D] See John Hodgson of Liverpool.

Hodson, Richard & Corney, William, 4 Broad St, Carnaby Mkt, London, brokers and cm (1791). Took out a Sun Insurance policy on 23 August 1791 for £1,800 on their household goods, house, workshop, and house at 14 Bentinck St. Policy included £1,250 on utensils, stock and goods in trust, and £150 on workshop. [GL, Sun MS ref. 587677]

Hodson, Robert, at 'The Cabinet', Frith St, Soho, London, cm (1712–24). Took out a Sun Insurance policy on 25 March 1712 on his goods; and a Hand in Hand policy for £250 on his house on 11 July 1716. On 27 May 1719 insured goods and merchandise in his house with the Sun Co. A note added to this policy on 31 August 1723 stated that these had been removed to Mr Smith's, apothecary, a few doors away. Insured goods and merchandise for £1,000 on 9 November 1723 with the Sun Co. [GL, Sun MS vol. 2, p. 3; vol. 9, p. 271;

vol. 16, ref. 30360; GL, Hand in Hand MS vol. 16, p. 67] Appears to have been the predecessor of John Hodson who headed the firm of Hodson's in Frith St during the 18th century. In 1718 he supplied chairs and stools for the Duke of Montrose's London house in Bond St; and a bill for '10 Walnut chairs with Matted Seats', costing £10, receipted in 1724, was probably also for the Duke of Montrose. [Scottish RO, GD 220/6/1192/38; 1250/30] On 19 June 1724 he provided 'a Neat Mahogeny Tea Table' at £1 15s to Temple Newsam House, Leeds. [*Furn. Hist.*, 1967] Robert Hodson wrote to the Earl of Radnor in September 1725 concerning a 'compting bureau' supplied to Longford Castle. [V&A archives]

Hodson, Samuel, 11 Back Queen St, Manchester, gilder (1800). [D]

Hodson, Thomas, East Retford, Notts., chairmaker (1759). Will dated 2 June 1759. [Notts. RO, probate records]

Hodson, Thomas, Liverpool, cm (1761). Admitted freeman on 29 November 1761. [Liverpool freemen reg.]

Hodson, William & Co., 18 Booth St, Tib Lane, Manchester, gilders and embossers (1813). [D]

Hodson & Rudyard, St Ann's, Soho, London, u (1748). Declared bankrupt in 1748. [Heal; Harris, *Old English Furniture*, p. 23] Possibly John or Robert Hodson of Frith St.

Hogarth, John, Corbridge, Northumb., joiner and cm (1828–29). [D]

Hogben, John, 19 Vine Ct, Spitalfields, London, cm (1820–24). Took out Sun Insurance policies on 5 November 1821 for £250 of which £230 accounted for stock and utensils; and on 1 January 1824 for £350, £205 on stock and utensils. [D; GL, Sun MS vol. 487, ref. 985261; vol. 496, ref. 1012289]

Hogben, Robert, Canterbury, Kent, u (1705). [Canterbury freeemen rolls]

Hogg, —, address unrecorded, cm (1757). Named in the accounts for Felbrigg, Norfolk, on 17 May 1757 receiving 10s for glasses. [Norfolk RO, Felbrigg papers, WKC 6/454, index to payments]

Hogg, —, Brandons Row, Newington, London, bedstead maker (1820). [D]

Hogg, George, Skinnergate, Darlington, Co. Durham, joiner and cm (1827). [D]

Hogg, George, Middleham, Yorks., joiner and cm (1834). [D]

Hogg, George, 11 Castle Lane, Pimlico, London, cm and u (1839). [D]

Hogg, James F., Sunderland, Co. Durham, cm (1798–1827). Recorded at High St, Bishop Wearmouth in 1827. [D]

Hogg, John, Howard St, Gt Yarmouth, Norfolk, carver and gilder (1822). [D]

Hogg, John, St Stephen St, Norwich, carver and gilder (1830). [D; poll bk]

Hogg, John, Keswick, Cumb., cm and joiner (1834). [D]

Hogg, Robert, London, cm (1793). Subscribed to Sheraton's *Drawing Book*, 1793.

Hogg, Thomas, Sheep St, Skipton, Yorks., joiner and/or cm (1837). [D]

Hogg, William, Newcastle, cm, joiner and carpenter (1778–82). Recorded at Castle Yd in 1778 and High Bridge in 1782. [D]

Hogg, William, 50 Close, Newcastle, u (1824–38). [D]

Hogg, William Johnson, Lowestoft, Suffolk and Bungay, Norfolk, cm (1818–30). Polled at Norwich of Lowestoft in 1818; and of there, named in the calendar of marriage licence bonds in 1819. Polled at Norwich of Bungay in 1830. [Suffolk RO, FAA: 50/2/118, p. 61]

Hogg & Co., Stephen St, Tottenham Ct Rd, London, chairmakers (1793). Subscribed to Sheraton's *Drawing Book*, 1793.

Hoggart, Barton John, Lancaster, cm (1789–90). Admitted freeman, 1789–90, when stated of Moorfields, London. [Lancaster freemen rolls]

Hoggart, John, Lancaster, cm (1768–80). App. to J. Wright in 1768, and admitted freeman, 1779–80. [Lancaster app. reg. and freemen rolls]

Hoggat, William, Lancaster, cm (1806–07). Admitted freeman, 1806–07, when stated 'of London'. [Lancaster freemen rolls]

Hogget, John, Tadcaster, Yorks., joiner and/or cm (1834). [D]

Hoghton, James, London, cm (1742). Named in the Preston Guild record of burgesses in 1742 as brother of Thomas Hoghton of Preston, tinman.

Hoil, Thomas, Mint, Rye, Sussex, chairmaker and turner (1826–39). [D; Dover poll bks]

Hoit, William, 70 Oldham St, Manchester, cm (1819). [D]

Hoitwell, Samuel, 3 Barnet St, Hackney Rd, London, cm and u (1839). [D]

Holbart, Thomas, Berwick St, Westminster, London, u (1749). [Poll bk]

Holbeach, —, Bristol, u (1707). Notice in *London Gazette*, 27 November 1707 concerned a 'Box of Writings' which was to have been 'left with Mr. Holbeach, an Upholsterer, upon the Bridge in Bristol', and was delivered to 'The Swan' on Holborn Bridge, London, on 19 July, but is now missing. A reward was offered to the finder.

Holbird, Isaac, 13 Catherine St, Strand, London, u and cabinet manufacturer (1816–17). [D]

Holbird, James, 19 White Lion Row, Islington, London, u (1779). Took out a Sun Insurance policy in 1779 for £700, £190 accounting for utensils, stock and goods. [GL, Sun MS vol. 279, p. 429]

Holbird (or Holberd), James, 16 Noble St, Cheapside, London, upholder, appraiser and undertaker (1789–1803). Notices regarding bankruptcy in *Billinge's Liverpool Advertiser*, 17 October and 19 December 1796. Named in Sheraton's list of master cabinet makers, 1803. [D]

Holbird (or Holberd), M., 16 Noble St, Foster Lane, London, u (1802–23). [D]

Holbrook, George, 24 Trenchard St, Bristol, chairmaker and turner (1827–28). [D]

Holbrook, James, 4 Merchants Passage, Bath, Som., cm and u (1826). [D]

Holbrook, Richard, Bristol, cm (1774–81). Recorded at 35 Old Mkt in 1775. [D; poll bks]

Holbrook, William, Bristol, cm (1774–75). Recorded in St Mary's parish, Redcliffe, 1774, and 49 Redcliffe St in 1775. [D; poll bk]

Holbrow, Daniel, address unrecorded, upholder (1755–65). Son of Thomas Holbrow, Gent. of Bagspear, Glos. App. to Thomas Humphreys on 6 February 1755, and admitted freeman of the Upholders' Co. by servitude on 4 March 1762. Took app. named Robert Brooke, 1764–65. [GL, Upholders' Co. records]

Holcroft, Richard, Salford, Lancs., cm (1808–17). Trading at Shaw Brows in 1808 and 32 Spinning Field in 1817. [D]

Holden, Andrew, Kent Rd, London, u and auctioneer (1809–11). [D]

Holden, Henry, Dearden Gate, Haslingden, Lancs., joiner and cm (1834). [D]

Holden, James, Cheetham Hill, Manchester, cm (1832–40). Recorded as J. & James, 1832–39; James & Son in 1834; and alone, 1836–40. [D]

Holden, John, Millgate, Wigan, Lancs., cm and chairmaker (1818–34). [D]

Holden, John, Belgrave Gate, Leicester, u (1828). [D]

Holden, John, Liverpool, cm (1835–37). Trading at 7 Codrington St in 1835 and 32 Prescot St, 1837. [D]

Holden, Samuel, London, upholder, cm, undertaker, appraiser and auctioneer (1767–94). Addresses given at 9 Aldersgate St, 1775–81; Whitecross St in 1786; 37 Charles St, Westminster in 1792; and near the Horse Guards in 1794. Son of Robert Holden, freeman mercer of London. App. to Henry Hall on 28 September 1767, and Samuel Martin on 1 April 1772. Admitted freeman of the Upholders' Co. by servitude on 5 October 1774. Took out Sun Insurance policies in 1778 for £3,700 of which £2,000 accounted for utensils, stock and goods; and in 1779 with Josiah Phipp, for £2,000, £800 on utensils, stock and goods. Declared bankrupt with Josiah Phipps, *Gents Mag.*, October 1781. Rococo trade card of Holden, 9 Aldersgate St is in the BM. [D; GL, Upholders' Co. records; GL, Sun MS vol. 264, p. 131; vol. 275, p. 142]

Holden, Stephen, North St, Lewes, Sussex, chairmaker and turner (1832–39). Recorded in North St, Greenwall, 1837, and Green Wall, 1839. [D; poll bk]

Holden, Thomas, at 'The Sign of the Chair', Hanover St, near Castle St, Long Acre, London, cm, appraiser and undertaker (c.1750). Trade card shows Rococo cartouche framing an elbow chair with compass seat, cabriole legs with scroll feet, back and front, and a tall shaped upholstered back. Card states that Holden 'Makes & sells all sorts of Cabinet Makers Work in the newest and compleatest Manner at the most reasonable Rates: ALSO Buys & Sells Second hand House-hold Furniture of all Sorts.' [Heal; *C. Life*, 7 July 1966, p. 48; Humberside RO, DDCC/150/114, Chichester Constable MS]

Holden, Thomas, Barnsley, Yorks., cm and joiner (1793). [D]

Holden, Thomas, 18 Highfield St, Liverpool, chairmaker (1794). [D]

Holden, Thomas, 13 Clayton St, Liverpool, chairmaker (1835–39). [D]

Holden, Thomas Patrick, Liverpool, u (b.1815–1836). Son of Thomas Holden gunsmith; admitted freeman on 9 July 1836. [Liverpool freemen reg. and committee bk]

Holden, William, Upper Union St, Hull, Yorks., cm and u (1823). [D]

Holden, William, 13 George St, Halifax, Yorks., cm (1834–37). [D]

Holden (or Holder), Willoughby, Knutsford, Cheshire, u (1822–30). Trading at Silk Mill Yd in 1822. Death of his wife reported in *Chester Courant and Anglo-Welsh Gazette*, 12 October 1830. [D]

Holder, George, Union St, North Shields, Northumb., cm and u (1827). [D]

Holder, Nathan, 29 Trenchard St, Bristol, cabinet turner in general (1835–37). [D]

Holder, Samuel, St James's, Bristol, picture frame maker (1739–54). [Poll bk]

Holder, W., 29 Scale Lane, Hull, Yorks., carver and gilder (1840). [D]

Holder, William, St Giles, Oxford, cm (d.1766). Probate will granted on 30 May 1766. [Bodleian Lib., Oxford, index of wills]

Holder (or Holdon), William, Hull, Yorks., cm (1813–18). App. to George Spencely of Hull in June 1813, and assigned to Robert Waugh in November 1818. [Hull app. reg.]

Holdford (or Holdforth), Joseph, Leeds, Yorks., u (1782–1801). Trading in Kirkgate in 1798. Took out Sun Insurance policies in 1782 for £600, £475 on utensils and stock; and on 16 August 1786 for £200 on household goods, and £300 on utensils and stock. On 17 January 1801 bought 'a plot of land with Building abutting on the south of the Coloured Cloth Hall at a place called Green Hill', from Samuel Smith of Leeds (who held a sixty-year lease on the property) for £840 'for the remainder of the term'. [D; GL, Sun MS vol. 304, p. 346; vol. 338, p. 305; Leeds archives dept, DB 32/31]

Holding, Charles, Wigan, Lancs., chairmaker (1798–1822). Trading at Millgate, 1816–17, and Scholes, 1822. [D] See John Holding.

Holding, George, Scholes, near Wigan, Lancs., chairmaker (1828). [D]

Holding, Henry & Son, 32 Princess St, Manchester, carver and gilder (1836–40). [D] See Thomas Eccles.

Holding, J., 7 Grafton St, Soho, London, cm (1820). [D]

Holding, John, Millgate, Wigan, Lancs., chairmaker (1814–25). [D] See Charles Holding.

Holding, W., 5 Grays Buildings, Bath, Som., cm (1819). [D]

Holdsworth, Samuel, Hull, Yorks., cm (1784). (Poll bk)

Holdsworth (or Houldsworth), William, Liverpool, u (1809–34). Addresses given at 30 Mount Pleasant in 1816; South Myrtle St in 1818; 4 Vine St in 1827; and 18 South Myrtle St, 1834. Indenture dated 1809. Petitioned freedom on servitude to George Philander Lyon in 1818, paying 6s 8d. Admitted freeman on 15 June 1818. [D; Liverpool freemen's committee bk and reg.]

Hole, Amos, Park St, Frogmore St, Bristol, cm (1818–19). Trading as Hole & Norris in 1818. [D]

Hole, Amos, Ross-on-Wye, Herefs., cm (1822). [D]

Hole, John, Dunster, Som., cm, u and appraiser (1840). [D]

Holey, Thomas, Leeds, Yorks., cm and u (1834–56). Addresses given at 18A Call (or Castle) Lane, 1834; Lambert's Yd, Briggate, 1837, and no. 9 in 1839. [D]

Holford, —, address unrecorded, chairmaker (1739). On 9 August 1739 provided Earl Fitzwalter with 'a Windsor Chair for 3 people' costing £1, for Moulsham Hall. [A. C. Edwards, *The Accounts of Benjamin Mildmay, Earl Fitzwalter*, p. 108]

Holford, J., 30 Mint St, Southwark, London, upholder and cm (1817). [D]

Holhead, John, Market Pl., Kendal, Westmld, cm (1808). [D]

Holiday, George, 15 Dooley St, Toxteth Park, Liverpool, cm (1837). [D]

Holinshade, —, 15 Dooley St, Toxteth Park, Liverpool, cm (1837). [D]

Holinshade, —, King St, Drury Lane, London, cradle maker (1803). Named in Sheraton's list of master cabinet makers. Possibly William & Joseph Hollinshed.

Holl, Richard, 11–12 King St, Holborn, London, upholder and cm (1823–27). Took out a Sun Insurance policy on 24 September 1823 for £3,500 of which £850 accounted for utensils and stock. [D; GL, Sun MS vol. 498, refs 1008169–71]

Holl, Samuel, Bethel St, Norwich, cm (1839). [D]

Holladay, William, Canterbury, Kent, cm (1791). [Canterbury freemen rolls]

Holland, —, near Red Lion St, London, cm (1765). Marriage to Miss Alice Peck of Histon, Cambs., reported in *Cambridge Chronicle*, 26 January 1765. Possibly Philip Holland.

Holland, —, Frankfort St, Plymouth, Devon, cm (1812). [D]

Holland, —, Devonport, Devon (1825). Death of infant son reported in *The Alfred*, 1 March 1825.

Holland, —, Plymouth, Devon, cm (1828). Notice in *Exeter Flying Post*, 21 February 1828 reads 'A cocoa nut in a perfect state, was discovered on February 14, 1828, in a log of mahogany belonging to Mr. Holland, Cabinet Maker, Plymouth, by the sawyers who were emplyed in cutting it…'. Possibly John Holland of Plymouth.

Holland, Alice, Liverpool, upholsteress (1774–1803). Addresses given at 42 School Lane, 1774–77; no. 39 in 1790; and 1 Murray St in 1796. [D]

Holland, Charles, at 'The Golden Key', Drury Lane, London, upholder (1719). Took out a Sun Insurance policy on 10 April

1719 for goods and merchandise in his house. [GL, Sun MS vol. 9, p. 181]

Holland, Charles, St Martin-in-the-Fields, London, cm (1766). Taken as app. on 3 March 1766 for £26 10s. [PRO, IRI/24]

Holland, George, Chester, cm and timber dealer (1814–22). Trading at Northgate St, 1814–15; and Lower Bridge St, 1816–22, nos 45–46 in 1821. Admitted freeman on 26 October 1814. Advertised in *Chester Guardian and Cambrian Intelligence*, 15 February 1821, 'that having declined keeping a sale shop in the Cabinet line he will in future attend to orders only and particularly to the Timber Trade which he means to extend. AND in consequence of the above arrangement the whole of his STOCK OF CABINET GOODS, which is considerable and manufactured of the best and finest mahogonies etc. will be SOLD BY AUCTION without the least reserve on the Premises, No. 45 and 46 Lower Bridge St. Chester on Thursday the 22nd February inst. By MR. S. NICKSON . . .'. [D; poll bks; Chester freemen rolls]

Holland, J., Old Town St, Plymouth, Devon, cm (1814). [D]

Holland, James, Hereford, upholder, cm and joiner (1761–77). Took app. named Smallman in 1761. Advertised in *Pugh's Hereford Journal*, 23 January 1777 refuting the report that 'hath for some time past been propagated (and with seeming industry circulated)' that he 'intended soon to leave off and retire from the trade'. He announced that 'he had no such intention', and 'intends to carry on his trade as usual . . . NB, He has now ready for sale variety of Mahogany chairs and other Cabinet Work of the newest fashion and best workmanship, and sundry other articles of Furniture in the Upholstery way, at the most reasonable rates.' [S of G, app. index]

Holland, James, 31 Shudehill, Manchester, cm and broker (1813). [D]

Holland, John, address unrecorded, upholder (1750–57). Son of John Holland, weaver of Norwich; app. to Nicholas Pennington on 19 July 1750, and admitted freeman of the Upholders' Co. by servitude on 8 September 1757. [GL, Upholders' Co. records]

Holland, John, Totnes, Devon, cm and u (1782–85). Taken as app. in 1782. Took out a Sun Insurance policy on 22 January 1785 for £50 on household goods, and £150 on utensils and stock in his house and adjoining workshop. [D; app. indentures, Totnes Museum; GL, Sun MS vol. 237, p. 202]

Holland, John, Plymouth, Devon, u and cm (1822–38). Addresses given at Whimple St in 1822; no. 8, 1823–24; no. 32 in 1830; and 45 Union Pl. in 1838. [D] See Holland, —, of Plymouth.

Holland, John, London, u (1835–39). Addresses given at 75 Castle St, Oxford St in 1835; and 3 Summers Ct, Bishopsgate Within, 12 West St, Seven Dials and 16 Lower St, Islington in 1839. [D]

Holland, John & Sons, Humberstone Gate, Leicester, cm (1840). [D]

Holland, Joseph, Hereford, cm (1826–40). Trading at The Close in 1835 and in St Nicholas Sq., 1837–40. [D; poll bks]

Holland, Matthew, Chester, cm (1819–26). Recorded in Boughton in 1819, and Watergate St, Chester, in 1826. [Poll bks]

Holland, Matthias, Chester, cm (1793–1801). Son of Matthias Holland, painter; admitted freeman in March 1793. Took app. named James Roberts in 1797, assigned to William Faulkner in 1801 with three years left to serve. [Chester freemen rolls and app. bks]

Holland, Philip, 4 Chapel St, Red Lion Sq., London, cm (1779). Took out a Sun Insurance policy in 1779 for £500 of which £40 accounted for utensils, stock and goods. [GL, Sun MS vol. 277, p. 144] Possibly Holland, —, near Red Lion St.

Holland, R., 1 Lower Union Ct, Lower Union St, Hull, Yorks., cm (1838–39). [D]

Holland, Robert, Ardleigh, near Colchester, Essex, chairmaker (1747). Supplied six kitchen chairs costing 9s to Peter Creffeild of Ardleigh in July 1747. [Essex RO, D/DRc F29]

Holland, Robert, West St, Poole, Dorset, cm and u (1840). [D]

Holland, Robert, Market Pl., Bridlington, Yorks., cm (1840). [D]

Holland, Samuel, London, joiner and cm (1768). Petitioned freedom on servitude to Richard Copeland in 1768, paying 6s 8d. [Liverpool freemen's committee bk]

Holland, Thomas, address unrecorded. From June to October 1740 he made, cleaned, varnished and repaired frames for a total of £2 6s 2d for Sir R. Hoare at Barn Elms House. [V&A Lib., English Manuscripts, tradesmen's bills]

Holland, Thomas, Liverpool, cm (1784–1812). App. to John Horocks in 1784. Petitioned freedom on servitude in 1812, but petition postponed. [Liverpool freemen's committee bk]

Holland, Thomas, Market Pl., St Lawrence's parish, Reading, Berks., cm and u (1785–91). Took out Sun Insurance policies on 21 June 1785 with Higgs for £2,800, including £420 on house, shops and warehouses, all adjoining, and £990 on utensils and stock; and on 24 June 1791 for £1,000, all on utensils and stock. [GL, Sun MS vol. 329, p. 480; vol. 377, p. 609] See Holland Thomas Higgs.

Holland, Thomas, Chepping Wycombe Borough, High Wycombe, Bucks., chairmaker (1798). [Militia Census]

Holland, Thomas, Tarporley, Cheshire, cm (1828). [D]

Holland, Thomas, 49 King St, Southwark, London, cm (1835–39). [D]

Holland, William, Hull, Yorks., cm (1780–1810). Recorded in Wincolmlee, 1790–99, and Mill St, 1803–10. [D; poll bks]

Holland, William, Fore St Hill, Exeter, Devon, cm (1791–96). [D]

Holland, William, address unrecorded. App. to Edward Binns, cm, of St George's Hanover Sq., London, for £20, 1794–1801. [PRO, IRI/36]

Holland, William, address unrecorded, cm (1803). Subscribed to Sheraton's *Cabinet Dictionary*, 1803.

Holland, Williamson, Whalley parish, Padiham, Lancs., joiner and cm (1825). [D]

Holland & Roberts, 6 Post Office Pl., Liverpool, cm (1837). [D]

Holland & Sons. Their Victorian activities are beyond the scope of this work (see Taprell & Holland for work to 1843) but the enquirer should consult the late Edward T. Joy's typescript on the firm. [V&A archives]

Hollandish, Andrew, 11 Bridewell Lane, Bristol, cm (1830). [D]

Hollandish, John, 7 Narrow Wine St, Bristol, coach and cabinet carver (1821). [D]

Hollands, Thomas, 2 Castle St, Clerkenwell, London, cm (1808). Took out a Sun Insurance policy on 23 April 1808 for £300 of which £200 accounted for stock and utensils. [GL, Sun MS vol. 446, ref. 816325]

Hollaway, Richard, 34 King St, St Ann's, London, cm, milliner and haberdasher (1786). Took out a Sun Insurance policy on 27 July 1786 for £200, £70 on utensils, stock and goods in trust. [GL, Sun MS vol. 339, p. 180]

Holleday, —, London, joiner or carver (1694). On 26 June 1694, as a member of the 'Company of Joyners Carvers of London', he signed a petition presented by that Company to the City of London. [*Furn. Hist.*, 1974]

Holler, William, St John St, Lewes, Sussex, journeyman cm (1818). [Poll bk]

Holliday, Henry Spence, 73 Leather Lane, London, cm (1790). Took out a Sun Insurance policy on 27 July 1790 for £500 of which £200 accounted for utensils and stock in workshop and yard. [GL, Sun MS p. 375, ref. 572209]

Holliday, Matthew, Easingwold, Yorks., joiner and cm (1834). [D]

Holliday, Robert, Epsom, Surrey, cm (1838). [D]

Holliday, Thomas, High Wycombe, Bucks. chairmaker (1834–38). Daughters bapt. in 1834 and 1838, son in 1836. [PR (bapt.)]

Holliday, William, London, cm (1803–31). Subscribed to Sheraton's *Cabinet Dictionary*, 1803. [Colchester poll bks]

Hollingberry, William, Canterbury, Kent, cm (1791). [Canterbury freemen rolls]

Hollingsworth, Francis, King's Ct, High St, Hull, Yorks., cm (1838–39). [D]

Hollingsworth, John, 9 Brokers Alley, Drury Lane, London, upholder and cm (1820–23). Took out a Sun Insurance policy on 27 March 1823 for £400, of which £300 accounted for utensils and stock. [D; Sun MS vol. 498, ref. 1001928] Susannah Hollingsworth was trading as a furniture broker at 3 Brokers Alley, 1835–39. [D]

Hollingsworth, Samuel, 6 Bedford St, Bedford Row, London, cm and u (1813–27). Recorded also as S. & J. Hollingsworth, 1813–27. Took out a Sun Insurance policy alone on 30 July 1823 for £1,000, £900 on stock and utensils. [D; GL, Sun MS vol. 496, ref. 1006454]

Hollingsworth, Thomas, Liverpool, cm (1807–23). Addresses given at 81 Hanover St in 1807, with timber yd at 18 Mason St, 1807–11; 11 Williamson St, 1810–16; 2 Hood St, 1818; 4 and 16 Lime St in 1821; and nos 4, 3 and 16 in 1823. [D]

Hollingsworth, Thomas, 15 Robinson Row, Hull, Yorks., carver and gilder (1837–46). Trading as a ship and general carver in 1842, and ornamental carver in 1846. [D]

Hollingsworth, William, Hull, Yorks., carver, gilder, looking-glass manufacturer (1826–34). Trading at 2 Queen St, 1826–31, and 27 Silver St in 1834. [D]

Hollingworth, James, Meltham, Huddersfield, Yorks., joiner and/or cm (1834). [D]

Hollingworth, John, Meltham, Huddersfield, Yorks., cm (1822–34). [D]

Hollingworth, William, Leicester, cm (1744). App. to Thomas Hand of Oakham, cm, and admitted freeman in 1744. [Leicester freemen rolls]

Hollingworth, William, address unrecorded. Subscribed to Chippendale's *Director*, 1754.

Hollingworth, William, Baxtergate, Gt Grimsby, Lincs., joiner cm and u (1819–35). [D]

Hollinrake, James, Hebden Bridge, Yorks., cm (1822). [D]

Hollins, George, Stafford Row, Hanley, Staffs., chairmaker (1818–23). [D]

Hollins, George, York, carver and gilder (1821). Son of John Hollins, tailor; app. to William Fawcett Dodgson, carver and gilder on 7 July 1821. [York app. reg.]

Hollins, John, Newcastle-under-Lyme, Staffs., cm (1802–18). [D; poll bk]

Hollins, William, address unrecorded, cm (1803). Subscribed to Sheraton's *Cabinet Dictionary*, 1803.

Hollinshed, Daniel, Chestergate, Macclesfield, Cheshire, cm (1816). [D]

Hollinshed, Thomas, corner of Gt Queen St, Drury Lane, London, turner (1755). Rococo trade card states that he 'Makes & Sells all Sorts of Turnery Goods, in Mahogany, Wallnuttreee &c. Viz. Dumb Waiters, Claw Tables, fire Screens, Tea kettle Stands, Candle Stands, Shades & Screens, Trays & Tea Boards, in the newest fashion; also Mops, Brushes, Brooms, Baskets & Matts. NB. Turning Work done for Cabinet Makers, House & Bed Joyners, Ornaments for Carvers, Models for Chasers, Sculpt. &c. Temples, Vases, Flower Pots &c. for Shell Work.' [Heal; *C. Life*, 2 May 1957, pp. 865–66]

Hollinshed (or Hollinshead), Thomas, 21 High St, St Giles, London, turner and cm (1804–08). Took out a Sun Insurance policy on 1 September 1804 for £600 of which £150 accounted for utensils and stock, and £250 on goods in trust in workshop and open yards. [D; GL, Sun MS vol. 431, ref. 764776]

Hollinshed (or Hollingshead), William & Joseph, King St, Seven Dials, London, bedstead makers and u (1808–39). Trading at no. 60, 1808–20, and no. 56, 1825–39. [D] Possibly Holinshade, —.

Hollin(s)worth, William, address unrecorded, u (1758–61). The 4th Duke of Bedford ordered 'a neat French commode' from William Hollinsworth for £16 16s in June 1758, probably for Woburn Abbey. In the following October he paid W. Hollin(s)worth & Co. £109 16s for the spectacular carved and gilt chandelier with eighteen branches which still hangs in the Saloon at Woburn. Another of the same design was sold Christie's, 29 November 1984, lot 43. [Bedford Office, London; *Apollo*, March 1956, p. 79, fig. XXIII; G. Scott Thomson, *Family Background*, 1949, p. 70]. Trade card of W. Hollingworth, u, 1761, recorded. [Heal]

Hollis, John, 101 Dale-end, Birmingham, cm (1822). [D]

Hollis, Robert, Fish St and Little London St, Whittlesey, Cambs., cm (1839). [D]

Hollister, John, Bristol, cm (1650– beyond 1696). Son of John Hollister, mason; app. to Thomas Fry, joiner, on 16 August 1650. Made a burgess of Bristol on 1 October 1657. He and his wife Edith took several apps, and appear in a rate assessment list for 1696. [Manchester City Art Gallery archives] A chest of drawers, c.1690, veneered in laburnum oyster wood at Wythenshawe Hall, Manchester, bears label which reads: 'Bought of John Hollister, At the Stair in Horstreet In Bristol'. Similar chests of drawers are recorded, one of oyster laburnum, decorated with floral marquetry of various woods on a walnut ground, the sides with oval panels inlaid with grotesque masks in profile; inscribed in top drawer: 'Bought of John Hollister in horsestreet ye Sine of ye Star in Bristoll'. [*C. Life*, 6 March 1975, supplement, p. 47] Another, or the same, veneered chest of drawers is recorded bearing the inscription: 'Bought of John Hollister in Hogestreet at ye Sine of ye Star in Bristoll'. [V&A archives]

Holliwell, John, Shepton-Mallet, Som., cm (1798). [D]

Holliwell, Richard, Liverpool, cm (1806–35). Recorded at Warren Ct, Heath St and 2 Park Lane in 1816. Petitioned freedom on servitude to John Ward Turner in 1806. Admitted freeman on 16 June 1816. Took apps named Charles Heyland in 1819 and Thomas Moreton in 1822. [Liverpool freemen reg. and committee bk]

Holliwood, —, Fleet Ditch, near Black-Fryers, London, bedstead maker (1734). Named in newspapers in 1734. [Heal]

Holloway, —, address unrecorded, upholder (1779–83). Named in the Longford Castle, Wilts. accounts in 1779 receiving £80; in 1781, £20 2s; and in 1783, £7 7s 6d. [V&A archives] Possibly Richard Holloway of St Martin's Churchyard.

Holloway, —, Banbury, Oxon., cm and u (1834–39). Trading at Catherine Wheel Yd, 1834–37, and Calthorpe Lane, 1839. [D]

Holloway, Charles, Tamworth, Staffs., chairmaker and turner (1828–35). Addresses given at Lichfield St in 1828, Church St in 1834 and George St in 1835. [D]

Holloway, George, Christchurch, Hants., glazier and furniture maker (1823–24). [D]

Holloway, George, Castle St, Christchurch, Hants., u (1830). [D]

Holloway, J., Worcester St, Stourbridge, Worcs., cm (1820). [D]

Holloway, Jeremiah, 231 Whitechapel Rd, London, chair and sofa maker (1839). [D]

Holloway, John, 101 Gt Saffron Hill, London, cm and u. Trade card recorded. [Heal]

Holloway, John William, Hart St, parish of St Olave, London, cm (1783). Took app. named William Smith in 1783. [Westminster Ref. Lib., MS E2566, p. 105, register of St Margaret and St John]

Holloway, John, North St, Wolverhampton, Staffs., carver and gilder (1827–38). [D]

Holloway, John, Bromsgrove, Worcs., cm (1820–31). Trading at Worcester St in 1820. [D; poll bk]

Holloway, John, Chester, u, cm and furniture broker (1838–40). Trading in Watergate St in 1838, when admitted freeman on 25 July. Recorded in 1840 as late of Cook St, previously of Watergate St Row, when declared bankrupt, *Chester Chronicle, Cheshire and North Wales Chronicle*, 12 April. [Chester freemen rolls]

Holloway, Richard, Oxford, u (1761–84). Recorded in High St in 1766. Took app. named Smith in 1761. [D; poll bk; S of G, app. index] Made regular announcements in *Jackson's Oxford Journal* between 1763 and 1780. Election as bailiff reported on 19 September 1763. On 17 November 1764 announced that he had decided to remain in Oxford rather than go to a shop in London, where he served his apprenticeship. Notice of 20 February 1766 read that William Smith, app., had run away from Holloway, and was suspected of thefts. Holloway advertised a large number of sales between 1766 and 1780. A notice from him of 20 October 1770 denied a charge of embezzling land tax collected for 1765, declared in an anonymous paper on St Mary's Church door; the Vestry testified in his favour. On 17 February 1773 he advertised sale of 30–40 tons of lead; and on 10 March 1775 offered a reward for the return of two spoons missing from the Judges' Lodgings. Election as City Assistant, replacing Ralph Kirby who resigned, announced on 6 November 1775; and election and swearing-in as Mayor on 15 September and 30 September 1777. Acted as agent in bankruptcy case reported on 25 April 1778.

Holloway, Richard, St Martin's Church Yard, London, 'Cabinet & Chair Maker, Upholder &c. Funerals Furnished' (1777). Rococo trade card reads as above, and shows Chippendale-style chair and bureau bookcase. [Banks Coll., BM] Took out a Sun Insurance policy in 1777 for £400, of which £300 accounted for utensils, stock and goods. [GL, Sun MS vol. 261, p. 433] See Robert Holloway, and Holloway, —.

Holloway, Richard, 34 Rathbone Pl., London, u and undertaker (1800–08). Named in Sheraton's list of master cabinet makers, 1803. [D]

Holloway, Robert, Church-yard, St Martin's Lane, London, cm (1784). [D] See Richard Holloway.

Holloway, Thomas, address unrecorded, u (1712). Took app. on 9 October 1712. [PRO, app. reg.]

Holloway, William, Christchurch, Hants., turner and chairmaker (1747–93). In 1747 took app. named Ayles, possibly Benjamin Ayles, to whom he was appointed Guardian in 1749 for the administration of the estate of James Ayles. Took app. named Gutheridge in 1753. [S of G, app. index and Winchester Guardianships] Took out a Sun Insurance policy in 1778 for £200, utensils and stock accounting for £34. [D; GL, Sun MS vol. 264, p. 586]

Holloway, William, Market Harborough, Leics., cm (1822–28). Recorded at Sheep Mkt in 1828. [D]

Hollowell, Mrs, Church Lane, Banbury, Oxon., cm, u and joiner (1833–37). [D]

Hollowell, Charles, Church Lane, Banbury, Oxon., cm, u and joiner (1830–32). [D]

Holly, T., 3 Sheffield St, London, carver and gilder (1820). [D]

Hollyday, Mary, address unrecorded, upholder (1716). Daughter of John Cooper; admitted freeman of the Upholders' Co. on 5 December 1716 'by her father's copy'. [GL, Upholders' Co. records]

Hollyer, Matilda, 31 Burlington Arcade, Piccadilly, London, Tunbridge-ware manufacturer (1835). [D]

Hollyoak, Roach, 55 Weamon St, Birmingham, u (1830). [D]

Holman, —, 10 Bartholomew Sq., London, cm (1835). [D] See Nathaniel and William Holman.

Holman, Edward, Cranbrook, Kent, cm (1826–29). [D]

Holman, James, formerly of the parish of SS Philip and Jacob, Bristol, late of St Giles-in-the-Fields, Holborn, London, joiner and cm (1757). Declared a 'Fugitive for Debt' in *London Gazette*, 14–17 June 1757.

Holman, James, 97 Broadwall, Blackfriars Rd, London, u (1839). [D]

Holman, John, Merchant St, Bristol, cm (1795). [D]

Holman, John, Magdalen St, Exeter, Devon, cm (1835). Son Robert bapt. at Holy Trinity Church on 12 July 1835. [PR (bapt.)]

Holman, Nathaniel, 13 Bartholomew Sq., London, cm and u (1839). [D] See Holman, —.

Holman, William, London, carpenter, cm and u (1808–39). Addresses given at 1 Brick Lane, Old St in 1808; 23 Ironmonger(s) Row, Old St in 1822; no. 93, 1827–28; and 12 Bartholomew Sq. in 1839. Took out a Sun Insurance policy on 25 February 1822 for £300, of which stock and utensils accounted for £200. [D; GL, Sun MS vol. 491, ref. 989493] See Holman, —.

Holme, Henry, Lancaster, cm (d.1791). Death on 1 September 1791 reported in *Williamson's Liverpool Advertiser*, 5 September.

Holme(s), James, Liverpool, cm (1760–61). Petitioned freedom on servitude to Thomas Rigby in 1760, and admitted freeman on 29 November 1761. [Liverpool freemen's committee bk and reg.]

Holme(s), James, Turk's Head Ct, Preston, Lancs., joiner and cm (1814–18). [D]

Holme(s), John, Turk's Head Ct, Preston, Lancs., joiner and cm (1816). [D]

Holme(s), Robert, Lancaster, cm (1823–32). App. to L. Redmayne in 1823, and admitted freeman, 1830–31. Named in the Gillow records in 1826 and 1832. [Lancaster app. reg. and freemen rolls; Westminster Ref. Lib., Gillow]

Holme, Thomas, Lancaster, cm (1767–68). [Lancaster freemen rolls]

Holmes, —, address unrecorded, chairmaker (1789). Recorded in the account book of Sir George Cornewall of Moccas Court, near Hereford, and Stanhope St, London, on 13 May 1789 receiving £6 11s 6d. [Herefs. RO, Moccas papers, J56/IV/4]

Holmes, —, London, cm (1793). Subscribed to Sheraton's *Drawing Book*, 1793.

Holmes, Alexander, 15 Brokers Row, Moorfields, London, cm, broker, appraiser and undertaker (1790–1811). Trade card gives address at 'The Unicorn', 15 Brokers Row. Recorded at 15 Moorfields, 1809–11. [D; BM]

Holmes, Charles, 15 Blackfriargate, Hull, Yorks., cm and u (1814–26). [D] See Joseph Holmes.

Holmes, Edward, Nottingham, cm (d. 1806). Probate will dated 3 May 1806. [Notts. RO, probate records]

Holmes, George & Griffin, William Morley, Whitcomb St, Leicester Fields, London, sedan chairmakers (1778–99). Recorded also at Coventry St, St James's, 1780–88, so presumably their business was at the corner of Coventry St and Whitcomb St. Took out Sun Insurance policies in 1780 for £300 on utensils and stock; in 1782 for £1,400, £1,000 on utensils and stock; in 1784 for £400 on premises at 22 Warwick St, Golden Sq.; and on 5 July 1791 for £900 on utensils, stock and goods in trust in their house. [D; GL, Sun MS vol. 286, p. 532; vol. 301, p. 638; vol. 324, p. 621; ref. 586102] A bill in the Monson archives, dated 24 July 1777 is for making sedan chairs costing £130 13s. [Lincoln RO, Mon/II/9] In 1784 Holmes & Griffin submitted a bill to Alexander Wedderburn for £28. 8s. [Scottish RO, GD 164/120 Box/A7/2 and B] On 21 March 1786 the firm was paid £1 10s 6d by Baron Grey de Wilton (formerly Sir Thomas Egerton, Bart., later 1st Earl of Wilton) for items supplied to Heaton Hall, Manchester. [Preston RO, Bank deposit and account bks, DDEg] Holmes & Griffin, chairmakers, are named in the Royal Household accounts on 5 April 1788 receiving £7 8s; and on 5 April 1794, £17 11s 6d. [Windsor Royal Archives] See W. & T. Griffin.

Holmes, George, Rosemary Lane, Fisher St, Carlisle, Cumb., joiner and/or cm (1811). [D]

Holmes, George, Long Causeway, Peterborough, Northants., carver and gilder (1822–23). [D]

Holmes, Henry, Lancaster. Named in the Gillow records, 1805–34. [Westminster Ref. Lib.]

Holmes, Henry, Corn St, Leominster, Herefs., cm (1840). [D]

Holmes, J. H., 13 Fish St, Hull, Yorks., cm (1828–29). [D]

Holmes, James, St George Colgate, Norwich, cm (1761–80). [Poll bks]

Holmes, James, Uppingham, Leics., cm (1791–98). [D]

Holmes, James, Bridge St, Belper, Derbs., joiner and cm (1835). [D]

Holmes, James Biggs, 43 Basinghall St, London, portable desk, dressing case, work box and cabinet case maker (1839). [D]

Holmes, John, address unrecorded, upholder (1727–38). Son of John Holmes, carpenter of Southwark, London. App. to Isaac Cooke on 3 May 1727, and admitted freeman of the Upholders' Co. by servitude on 3 May 1738. [GL, Upholders' Co. records]

Holmes, John, London, upholder (1752). Notice in *Gents Mag.*, June 1752, reads: 'The Lord Mayor nominated for sheriffs ... John Holmes, upholder ... He paid a fine to avoid duty'.

Holmes, John, late of Wood St, St Alphege, London, cm (1761). Discharge from Debtors' Prison reported in *London Gazette*, 25 August 1761.

Holmes, John, Aldersgate St, London, freeman clothworker, cm (1773). Employed one non-freeman for six weeks in 1773. [GL, City Licence bks, vol. 8]

Holmes, John, 2 Red Cross Sq., Jewen St, London, carver (1775). Insured house for £100 in 1775. [GL, Sun MS vol. 243, p. 202]

Holmes, John jnr, 4 London Rd, St George's Fields, London, carver and gilder (1803). Took out a Sun Insurance policy on 2 February 1803 for £150. [GL, Sun MS vol. 426, ref. 745411]

Holmes, John, London, carver and gilder, looking-glass and frame maker (1808–23). Addresses given at 16 George's Ct, Clerkenwell in 1808, and 57 Red Lion St, Clerkenwell, 1809–23. [D]

Holmes, John, 10 Bridge Rd, Lambeth, London, looking-glass and frame maker (1820) and u (1823–29). [D]

Holmes, John, Norwich, cm (1818). App. to William Norris; admitted freeman on 24 February 1818. [Norwich freemen reg.]

Holmes, John, 2 Commercial St, Leeds, Yorks., floor cloth warehouseman and cm (1826). [D]

Holmes, John, Sidmouth, Devon, cm (b.1803–d.1826). Notice in *Exeter Flying Post*, 30 March 1826, read: 'An inquest was held yesterday, at the Yorkminster Arms, Foley-street, Mary

la bonne, on the body of John Holmes, aged 23, who shot himself. The deceased was a cabinet-maker, and resided in Ogle Mews. He was a native of Sidmouth, in Devon, where he became enamoured of a dairy-maid, who however did not return his love, but preferred the society of a more favoured swain. The deceased provided himself with a pistol and challenged his rival, who declined the invitation. Finding all attempts to gain the fair one ineffectual, came to London, and brooding over his misfortunes, he became phrenzied, and shot himself. The jury returned a verdict of Insanity.'

Holmes, Jonathan, Gt Pulteney St, London, carver (1784). [Poll bk]

Holmes, Joseph, Jon & Robert, London, u (1722–23). Trading at 'The Bell Inn', Aldersgate, in 1722, when they insured goods and merchandise in warehouse there for £500 on 17 January. A memo of 17 December 1723 adds that they removed to a warehouse opposite the gate in the 'Spread Eagle Inn', Gracechurch St. [GL, Sun MS vol. 15, ref. 27417]

Holmes, Joseph, Graham Pl., Fontenoy St, and 96 Fontenoy St, Liverpool, cm (1804–12). App. to Edward Lowe in 1804. Admitted freeman on 5 October 1812. [Liverpool freemen reg. and committee bk]

Holmes, Joseph, Wokingham, Berks., cm (1823). [D]

Holmes, Joseph, Hull, Yorks., cm, u and furniture broker (1823–34). Addresses given at 32 Blackfriargate in 1823; no. 15, 1826–31; and 21 Humber Dock St in 1834. [D] See Charles Holmes.

Holmes, Mathew, Hinckley, Leics., cm (1791). [D]

Holmes, Norman, York, carver and gilder (1821). Son of William Holmes of Christ parish, carver and gilder; app. to his father on 16 August 1821. [York app. reg.]

Holmes, Richard, Barbican, London, freeman carpenter, cm, looking-glass manufacturer and glass grinder (1755–86). Recorded at no. 55, 1777–78; no. 22, 1778–86; and as Richard Holmes & Son, 1781–86. Rococo trade card, *c*.1781, shows Chippendale-style chair, tea table with deep fretwork rims, and tea chest, and reads: 'Rich.d Holmes, Cabinet Maker & Glass Grinder at the Tea Chest in Barbican, LONDON. Makes all Sorts of Looking Glasses in Carved and Mahogany Frames. Likewise all Sorts of Cutt Trays, Scollop & Round Tea Boards. Tea Chests for Exportation. NB. Old Glasses New Framed & Silvered.' In 1755 he employed one non-freeman for three months; in 1771, seven for twelve weeks; and in 1780, fifteen for six weeks. Took out Sun Insurance policies in 1778 for £1,800, of which £800 accounted for utensils and stock; and in 1781 for £2,800, £1,500 on utensils and stock. [D; Heal; *C. Life*, 9 December 1971, p. 1666, 2 May 1983, pp. 865–66, and vol. CXXX, no. 3350, p. 91; GL, City Licence bks, vols 1, 7 and 10; GL, Sun MS vol. 266, p. 101; vol. 294, p. 61] See Thomas Holmes of Barbican.

Holmes, Richard, Ingleton, near Settle, Yorks., cm (1822). [D]

Holmes, Robert, Clement's Lane, London, u (1742–45). Trading as Robert & Co. in 1742. [D] See Holmes, Wheatley & Holmes.

Holmes, Rob., Nottingham. Signed the *Nottingham Cabinet and Chair Makers' Book of Prices*, 1791, on behalf of the masters.

Holmes, Robert, Gomersal, Yorks., cm and joiner (1828–37). [D]

Holmes, Robert, 2 Broad St, Pendleton, Lancs., cm and u (1836–40). [D]

Holmes, Robert, 8 Margaret St, Hackney Fields, London, cm and u (1839). [D]

Holmes, Thomas, Liverpool, cm (1762). Petitioned freedom on servitude to Nicholas Cross, who appeared in person to certify servitude, in 1762. [Liverpool freemen's committee bk]

Holmes, Thomas, address unrecorded, cm and glass grinder (1786). Took out a Sun Insurance policy on 10 July 1786 for £1,500, £100 on utensils and stock; £500 on those in silvering rooms and workshop; and £100 on glass in trust therein. [GL, Sun MS vol. 339, p. 53] Possibly:

Holmes, Thomas, 22 Barbican, London, cabinet and looking-glass manufacturer (1786). [D] See Richard Holmes of Barbican.

Holmes, Thomas, Northampton St, Clerkenwell, London, cm (1796). Notices regarding bankruptcy appeared in *Billinge's Liverpool Advertiser*, 12 September and 28 November 1796.

Holmes, Thomas, High St, Burton-on-Trent, Staffs., cm and u (1818–34). [D]

Holmes, Thomas, Northampton St, Leicester, chairmaker (1835). [D]

Holmes, Thomas, 111 Gt Titchfield St, London, u and cm (1835–37). [D]

Holmes, Thomas, 112 London Rd, St George's East, London, u, cm and undertaker (1835–39). [D]

Holmes, W., Tonbridge, Kent, u (1826–30). [D]

Holmes, William, Liverpool, cm (1800–39). Addresses given at 21 Mersey St, 1800–03; no. 22 with shop at no. 32 in 1805; 60 Hurst St in 1807; 32 Gilbert St in 1823; and 1 Spencer Buildings, Hunter St, 1829–39. [D]

Holmes, William, York, carver and gilder (1806–23). Recorded in Christ parish in 1821; and Hay Market in 1823. Son of Joseph Holmes, baker; admitted freeman in 1806. Took his son William as app. on 16 August 1821. [D; York app. reg. and freemen rolls]

Holmes, William, Morrow & Parry, William, 194 Oxford St, London, u, cm, auctioneers and appraisers (1814–21). Holmes & Parry alone took out Sun Insurance policies on 22 November 1820 for £1,500 on their house and workshops; and on 22 February 1821 for £1,000, £500 on house and workshops, £500 on stock and utensils therein. [D; GL, Sun MS vol. 483, ref. 972908; vol. 488, ref. 976498]

Holmes, William, 21 Duke St, Bloomsbury, London, cm and u (1821). Took out a Sun Insurance policy on 7 May 1821 for £1,500, of which £500 accounted for stock and utensils. [GL, Sun MS vol. 488, ref. 980751]

Holmes, William, 48 Albemarle St, Piccadilly, London, cm and u (1821–29). Took out a Sun Insurance policy on 1 November 1821 for £1,500, £500 accounting for stock and utensils. [D; GL, Sun MS vol. 488, ref. 985157]

Holmes, William, 69 Church St, Whitehaven, Cumb., cm (1829). [D]

Holmes, William, 21 Camelford St, Brighton, Sussex, carver and gilder (1832–40). [D]

Holmes, William, 12 St John's St, Leeds, Yorks., cm and u (1834–57). Recorded sometimes also at nos 6 and 11. [D]

Holmes & Guichenet(t), Threadneedle St, London, upholders (1742–55). [D]

Holmes, Wheatley & Holmes, Clement's Lane, London, u (1753–55). [D] See Robert Holmes at this address.

Holroyd, John, Honley, near Huddersfield, Yorks., cm (1830–37). [D]

Holroyd, John, Holme, Yorks., joiner and/or cm (1837). [D]

Holroyd, Squire, Goodman's End, Bradford, Yorks., cm (1822). [D]

Holroyd, Tym, Hull, Yorks., cm (1753). Took app. named Travis in 1753. [S of G, app. index]

Holsgrove, George, Cambridge St, Golden Sq., London, upholder (1790–93). [D]

Holson, Joseph, West Wycombe, Bucks., chairmaker (1798–1830). Named in the Militia Census in 1798, and directories in 1830.

Holston, William, 294–95 High Holborn, London, cm and u (1840). [GL, Sun MS ref. 1333645]

Holt, Edward, Berry St, Liverpool, cm etc. (1827–39). Addresses given at no. 24 in 1827, no. 28, 1827–29, no. 41, 1835–37, and no. 29 in 1839. [D]

Holt, George, North St, Guildford, Surrey, cm (1831–37). [Poll bks]

Holt, James, Langfield, Todmorden, Yorks., cm (1822–37). Trading at York St in 1837. [D]

Holt, James, Blackburn, Lancs., cm, joiner and house-builder (1824–34). Trading at Redlam Brow, 1824–28, and Witton, near Blackburn, in 1834. [D]

Holt, John, High St, Lewes, Sussex, turner and chairmaker (1794–1839). Recorded at no. 16, 1795–1832, and no. 17 in 1839. [D; poll bks]

Holt, Rachel, 34 Ben Jonson St, Liverpool, u (1824). [D]

Holt, Richard, 30 Berwick St, Soho, London, cm (1826–28). [D]

Holt, Richard, 12 King St, High Holborn, London, cm and upholder (1827–28). [D]

Holt, William, London, cm (1793). Subscribed to Sheraton's *Drawing Book*, 1793.

Holt, William, 70 Oldham St, Manchester, cm (1808–18). [D]

Holt & Morris, Liverpool, u etc. (1834–39). Trading at 2 Webster St, Everton, 1834–37, and 2 Bute St, Fox St in 1839. [D]

Holworthy, —, 3 Onslow St, Hatton Gdn, London, cm and u (c.1800). Trade card framed by Neo-classical drapery swags centring on an urn shows Sheraton-style writing or artist's desk, and bookcase. Card gives address and reads: 'Estm.d Holworthy, UPHOLSTERER, Cabinet Chair Maker and Undertaker … BEDSTEAD MANUFACTORY, NB. variety of Paper Hangings.' [BM]

Holyoak & Dixon, 158 Fenchurch St, London, turners (1799). [D]

Holyoake(s), William, Cirencester, Glos., carver and gilder (1820–40). Trading at Gosditch St, 1820–22 and Castle St, 1839–40. [D]

Homan, John, 136 Fenchurch St, London, u (1813). [D]

Homer, Benjamin, Wednesfield, Staffs., joiner and/or cm (1834). [D]

Homer, Benjmain, Willenhall, Staffs., joiner and/or cm (1834). [D]

Homer, Thomas, address unrecorded. George I pier glass recorded, in carved wood and gesso frame with foliate mouldings; arched cresting carved with eagles' heads centred by winged cherubs' heads and overlapping foliage; the back inscribed in ink: 'The Maker Thomas Homer'. [Sotheby's, 9 March 1951, lot 143]

Homer, William, Weaman St, Birmingham, gilder (1818). [D]

Homer, William, St Peter's, Norwich, cm and u (1822). [D]

Homersham, Thomas, Southwark, London, upholder and cm (1781–1816). Addresses given at 238 St Margaret's Hill in 1781; 238 Borough High St, 1784–96; and no. 245, 1786–1816. Took out Sun Insurance policies on 22 March 1786 for £500 of which utensils and stock accounted for £250; on 23 April 1807 for £800 on his house where no cabinet work or carpentry was done; and on 2 April 1818 for £1,000 on his house. Named in Sheraton's list of master cabinet makers, 1803. [D; GL, Sun MS vol. 337, p. 9; vol. 438, ref. 802367; vol. 449, ref. 841782]

Hone, John, Leather Lane, Holborn, London, cm (1775). Took out a Sun Insurance policy in 1775 for £1,000 of which utensils and stock accounted for £800. [GL, Sun MS vol. 242, p. 319]

Hones, Richard, Liverpool, cm (1780). Former app., William Rea petitioned freedom in 1780. [Liverpool freemen's committee bk]

Honey, —, 6 Golden Lion Ct, Aldersgate St, London, cm (1829). [D]

Honey, H. & W., Plymouth, Devon, cm (1814). Dissolving of partnership announced in *Western Luminary*, 22 February 1814. H. Honey recorded alone at Frankfort St in 1814. [D]

Honey, R., Frankfort St, Plymouth, Devon, cm (1814). [D]

Honeycroft, —, Brown St, Salisbury, Wilts., chairmaker (1839). [D]

Honeywell, John, Fordingbridge, Hants., chairmaker (1792–1824). [D]

Honeywell, John, The Quay, Weymouth, Dorset, chairmaker (1840). [D]

Honeywell, Richard, Downton, Wilts., chairmaker (1742–76). Took app. named Jacob Taunton, 1742–43. Took out a Sun Insurance policy in 1776 for £100, £80 accounting for stock. [*Wilts. Apps and their Masters*; GL, Sun MS vol. 249, ref. 369454]

Honiss, William & Edward, York House Hastings, and 43 Marina, St Leonards, Sussex, cm, u, painters and glaziers (1831–40). Trading as plumbers and auctioneers at Priory and 43 Marina St in 1832. Trading only in St Leonards in 1833 and 1840. Honais, plumber and painter, traded in Hastings in 1833. [D]

Honiss, William Henry, York St (or Buildings), Hastings, and 43 Marina, St Leonards, Sussex, u (1837–39). Advertised in *Sussex Agricultural Express*, 10 June 1837, offering thanks for fifteen years of liberal patronage, and stating that he has 'an extensive assortment of Furniture which is is enabled to offer at very low prices, for ready money consisting of loo, dining, Pembroke and other tables; chiffonirs, sideboards, elegant mahogany and other chairs, wardrobes, chests of drawers, mahogany, stained and painted bedsteads, beds, matresses, wash-hand-stands, dressing tables, chimney, pier, and swing glasses, floor cloths, painted baizes &c.' He also offered invalid furniture for hire or purchase to visitors; wallpaper fitting service; and hire of furniture, plate and cutlery. He also offered his services as auctioneer, appraiser, house and estate agent; and gave his address at York House, Priory, Hastings. Advertised sale of 'Patent Imperial Cottage Piano Forte' in *Sussex Agricultural Express*, 23 September 1837; and an auction on 31 March 1838. [D]

Honor, George, Brueton's Walk, Birmingham, chairmaker and cm (1835). [D]

Honshaw, Samuel, Noel St, London, chairmaker (1784). [Poll bk]

Honton, James, New Market Pl., Bradford, Yorks., cm and u (1834). [D]

Hood, David, 4 Crescent St, London, painter and gilder (1808). [D]

Hood, James, Tweedmouth, Northumb., joiner and cm (1834). [D]

Hood, John, Wyle Cop, Shrewsbury, Salop, chairmaker (1747). [Poll bk]

Hood, Robert, Southwark, London, then Tower Hill, and died at Enfield, cm and naval carpenter (b.1696–d.1795). Member of the Livery of the Joiners' Co. in 1750. Report of his death in *Gents Mag.*, February 1795 stated that he was born on 15 August 1696 at Lower Deeping, Lincs., and 'made the wooden model for Westminster Bridge, and fitted-up, at considerable expence, Lord Rodney's first cabin; and then retired'. [GL, Joiners' Co. records, list of Liverymen]

Hood, Thomas, address unrecorded, upholder (1705–15). Son of Thomas Hood, freeman joiner of London; app. to Samuel Halford, in trust for R. Farmer, clothworker, on 9 January 1705/06. Admitted freeman of the Upholders' Co. by servitude on 9 March 1714/15. [GL, Upholders' Co. records]

Hood, Thomas, Bristol, cm (1774). [Poll bk]

Hood, Thomas Frederick, Islington, London, carver and gilder (1818–26). Admitted freeman of Hereford in 1818, and polled there in 1826. [Hereford freemen rolls] Possibly:

Hood, Thomas, 27 Meredith St, Clerkenwell, London, carver and gilder (1835–39). [D]

Hook, John, Newham, Glos., cm (1839). [D]

Hook, Richard, St Martin's Lane, Lewes, Sussex, journeyman cm (1818). [Poll bk]

Hook, William, Windmill Hill, Hampstead, London, cm (1809–11). [D]

Hooker, John, Greenwich, London, cm and u (1824–38). Trading at Blackheath Hill, 1824–26 and Greenwich Rd in 1838. [D]

Hooker, Robert, Chester, cm (1757). App. to Philip Presbury on 18 April 1757. [Chester app. bks]

Hookey (or Hockey), George Goldfwyre/er, Southampton, Hants., carver (1774–81). [Bristol and Southampton poll bks]

Hookey, George, High St, Southampton, Hants., upholder and auctioneer (1805–11). [D; Southampton reg.]

Hooks, Robert, Thornton, Norfolk, cm (1836). [D]

Hoole, John, London, u (1690–1710). Announced in *London Gazette*, 1 May 1690, that he had 'removed from the Rose in Cornhill, to the Rose in Bishopsgate Street near Cornhill; who hath new fashioned Silk and Stuff Beds ready standing Glasses, Tables and Chests of Drawers, to be sold at reasonable Prices.' Advertised in *Athenian Mercury*, 18 March 1693; and a notice in *Daily Courant*, 17 October 1709 read: 'John Hoole, Upholsterer, at the Rose in Bishopsgate-street over against Thread-needle-street, leaving off his Trade, selleth his Goods very cheap: The House and Shop to be Lett, having 4 Rooms and Closets on a Floor.' [Heal; Hilton Price, *Signs of Old London*; Harris, *Old English Furniture*, p. 23]

Hooper, —, Sittingbourne, Kent, cm (1803). [D]

Hooper, —, 19 Upper Boro' Walls, Bath, Som., u (1815). [D]

Hooper, Ann, 'The Blue Boar', Cornhill, London, cm (1744). See John Hooper.

Hooper, Frederick William, Leamington, Warks., carver and gilder, looking-glass and picture frame manufacturer (1831–37). Recorded at Leamington Priors, 1831–34, and 47 Bath St, 1835–37. Declared bankrupt, *Liverpool Mercury*, 24 June 1831, and *Chester Courant and Advertiser for North Wales*, 8 July 1834. Carried out work for Charlecote Park, Warks., in 1833, receiving a total of £40, including £22 10s for carving and gilding a cheval glass. [D; Warwick RO, L6/1118] See M. Hooper.

Hooper, George, corner of Love Lane, Ramsgate, Kent, u and cm (1762–86). Took app. named Taylor in 1762. Took out Sun Insurance policies in 1780 for £800, £400 accounting for utensils and stock; and in 1786 for £200 on two houses. [S of G, app. index; GL, Sun MS vol. 280, p. 331; vol 337, p. 276]

Hooper, H., Bristol, upholsteress (1824–39). Addresses given at 11 St Paul St, 1824–27; 32 Milk St in 1834; and 17 Newfoundland St, 1835–39. [D]

Hooper, Henry, Frome, Som., cm (1817–22). Declared bankrupt, *Exeter Flying Post*, 12 June 1817, but trading again by 1822 as cm and u at North Parade. [D]

Hooper, John, Honiton, Devon, cm (1730). Took app. named Lowman in 1730. [S of G, app. index]

Ho(o)per, John, at 'The Blue Boar', Cornhill, London, cm (1730–44). After his death in 1744 the business was carried on by his widow, Ann Hooper. [Hilton Price, *Signs of Old London*] See John Hoper.

Hooper, M., Bath St, Leamington, Warks., carver and gilder (1830). [D] See Frederick William Hooper.

Hooper, Richard, High St, Tewkesbury, Glos., cm (1814–32). Six children bapt. between 1814–32. [PR (bapt.)]

Hooper, Thomas, 146 Blackfriars Rd, London, cm (1835). [D]

Hooper, William, Bristol, cm and undertaker (1836–39). Addresses given at 1 Sim's Alley, 1836–37; St James's Back in 1838; and 20 Canon St in 1839. [D]

Hooth, John, St Peter Mancroft, Norwich, u (1778). Took out a Sun Insurance policy in 1778 for £300, £250 accounting for stock. [GL, Sun MS vol. 266, p. 455]

Hooton, John, Gainsborough, Lincs., cm and furniture broker (1826–35). Trading in Church Lane, 1826, and Beastmarket, 1831–35. [D]

Hootton, Charles, High Wycombe, Bucks., chairmaker (1824–31). Son bapt. in 1824, daughter in 1831. [PR (bapt.)]

Hop, John, address unrecorded. Signed and dated, 1721, a side table japanned in vermillion and yellow. [Conn., July 1970, advert., J. Kingel, Paris]

Hope, Edward, 88 and 89 North St, Leeds, Yorks., chairmaker, carver and gilder (1828–35). Trade label recorded on looking-glass in simple rectangular frame with split-baluster moulding, topped by a plain architrave. Label reads: 'Edward Hope Carver & Gilder Wholesale & Retail Looking Glass Manufacturer 88 & 89 North Street, Leeds. The trade supplied with leaf Gold.' [D; Bonham's Sale Room, London, 17 January 1985] See Hope & Foster.

Hope, Frances, 88 North St, Leeds, Yorks., carver and gilder (1837). [D] See Hope & Foster.

Hope, John, Bristol, cm (1778). [Bailey's list of bankrupts]

Hope, John, Dalton, Lancs., cm (1797–98). [D]

Hope, John, 24 Howell Croft, Bolton, Lancs., cm (1818). [D]

Hope, Robert, London Rd, Liverpool, joiner and cm (1824–27). Trading at no. 49 in 1824 and no. 84 in 1827. [D]

Hope, Samuel, Paradise Row, Birmingham, cm (1767). [D]

Hope, Samuel, 26 North St, Dale St, Liverpool, chairmaker (1796). [D]

Hope, William, 15 Fenchurch St, London upholder (1768). [D]

Hope, William, 36 Rathbone Pl., Oxford St, London, auctioneer, u, cm and 'Licensed & Sworn Appraiser' (1805–39). Trade card shows classical female figure beside inscribed pedestal. Took out Sun Insurance policies on 25 May 1820 and 20 September 1821 for £2,000, of which stock, uttensils and goods in trust and workshops accounted for £1,700. Named in contemporary newspapers. [D; Heal; GL, Sun MS vol. 483, ref. 966989; vol. 488, ref. 983081]

Hope & Foster, Leeds, Yorks., carvers, gilders, looking-glass and picture frame manufacturers (1816–22). Trading at 2 North Parade, 1816–1822, and North Town End in 1818. Advertised in Leeds Mercury, 6 and 13 April 1816 that they intended 'Carrying on the above Business in all its Branches, and from their experience of the same having always been at the first shop in London...'. Advertised again in Leeds Intelligencer, 10 February 1817, and in the four consecutive issues; and in Leeds Mercury, 15 February 1817, and the five consecutive issues, returning thanks 'for the very liberal Encouragement they have experienced ... they trust by their unlimited exertions to produce a Superiority of Workmanship at the lowest charges ... they now polish and silver old Plates without sending them to London...'. Announced in Leeds Mercury, no. 2761, that 'Mr. Hope has just returned from London, where he has made large purchases from the first Houses of every Article in the Fancy line ... NB. The Trade supplied with leaf gold of superior quality at reduced prices.' The firm seems very quickly to have become mainly purveyors of goods from London. [D] Probably Edward or Frances Hope.

Hoper, John, address unrecorded, cm (1721–22). Submitted a bill to 'Mad.ᵐ Heathcoat' on 22 July 1721 for £3 10s for 'a Neat Wallnt Chest', a leather cover and a mat. Receipted on 6 January 1721/22. [Lincoln RO, 2 ANC 12/D)11]

Hopewell, George, Hucknall-Torkard, Notts., chairmaker (1784). [BM, trade card coll.]

Hopewell, John, Cherry Orchard, Nottingham, joiner and cm (1799–d. 1812). Will dated 21 January 1802, proved, 26 August 1812. [D; Notts. RO, probate records]

Hopkin, William, Vale St, Birmingham, cm (1777). Insured his house for £100 in 1777. [GL, Sun MS vol. 263, p. 59]

Hopkins, David, Hart St, Westminster, London, cm (1749–54). Subscribed to Chippendale's Director, 1754. [Poll bk]

Hopkins, David, Westbury on Trym, Glos., cm (1774–84). [Bristol poll bks]

Hopkins, E., Staines, Middlx, cm (1798). [D]

Hopkins, Edward & Richard, 46 Goodge St, Tottenham Ct Rd, London, chair and sofa maker (1820–28). [D]

Hopkins, Henry, Rotherhithe, London, carver and ship carver (1780–1819). Addresses given at Prince's Stairs, 1780–81 and 1819; 45 Rotherhithe in 1788; and 61 Paradise St in 1801. Took out Sun Insurance policies in 1780 for £400, utensils and stock accounting for £50; and in 1781 for £400 on his house. [D; GL, Sun MS vol. 285, p. 552; vol. 296, p. 80]

Hopkins, J., 10 Bedford St, Bath, Som., cm (1819–26). [D]

Hopkins, James, 15 Prince's St, Bedford Row, London, u (1826–27). [D]

Hopkins, James, 4 Southampton Row, Russell Sq., Bloomsbury, London, u (1829–40). Took out a Sun Insurance policy in 1840. [D; GL, Sun MS vol. 577, ref. 1333797]

Hopkins, John, 22 Peter St, Cow Cross, London, cm (1777). Took out a Sun Insurance policy in 1777 for £200 of which utensils and stock accounted for £100. [GL, Sun MS vol. 258, p. 83] See Samuel Hopkins.

Hopkins, John, Counterslip, Bristol, chair painter (1812). [D]

Hopkins, Richard, 4 Broadmead, Bristol, cm (1824–26). Declared bankrupt, Exeter Flying Post, 27 April 1826. [D]

Hopkins, Richard, 21 Leece St, Liverpool, cm and u (1839). [D]

Hopkins, Samuel, Peter St, Bloomsbury, London, carver and cm (1777–84). Took out a Sun Insurance policy in 1777 for £200 of which tools accounted for £20. Polled at Bristol in 1784. [GL, Sun MS vol. 254, p. 329] See John Hopkins.

Hopkins, Thomas, Salford and Manchester, carver and gilder (1813–25). Addresses given at Green Bank, Salford, 1813–14; no. 5 in 1815; 58 Bridge St, Manchester, 1816–18; Broughton Rd, 1821–22; no. 6 in 1824; and 50 Dale St, Manchester in 1825. [D]

Hopkins, William, at the corner of Rood Lane, 15 Fenchurch St, London, freeman joiner, upholder, cm and sworn appraiser (1746–74). Rococo trade card states that he 'Makes & Sells all sorts of Cabinet Goods, Chairs & Looking Glasses, likewise all sorts of Bedsteads with damask Moreen, Harateen, Chinese Prints, Hollon Check & Linen Furniture, Ticking for Beds & Goose Feathers, with all sorts of Carpets, Wholesale & Retail. NB. Funerals Furnished and Goods Appraised.' [Banks Coll., BM] Named as a member of the Livery of the Joiners' Co. in 1750. Notice in the Daily Advertiser, 20 July 1752 reads: 'On Saturday morning was found dead in her Bed, Mrs. Hopkins, wife of Mr. Hopkins, an eminent Cabinet Maker in Fenchurch Street. She went to bed the night before in good health.' In 1762, 1763 and 1764 Hopkins employed six non-freemen for three months each year. [D; GL, Joiners' Co. records, list of Liverymen; GL, City Licence bks, vols 3 and 4]

Hopkins, William, London (?), cm (1751). A magnificent full-size billiard table on carved lion-paw cabriole legs from Parham Park, Sussex, is signed on part of the original bed 'William Hopkins maker 1751'. [Conn., vol. 143, 1959, pp. 26–28, fig. 2]

Hopkins, William, parish of St James West, Middlx, carpenter, joiner, journeyman and cm (1755). Notices regarding bankruptcy appeared in *Public Advertiser*, 6 March and 26 June 1755.

Hopkins, William, Dublin, Eire, carver (1752). A notice in *General Advertiser*, 13 August 1752, reads that on 4 August in Dublin William Hopkins, an English carver, flung himself out of a window.

Hopkins, William, Cambridge, cm (1755). Declared bankrupt, *Gents Mag.*, January 1755.

Hopkins, William, Shoreditch, London, carver and gilder (1789–93). Recorded at no. 18 in 1789 and no. 184 in 1793. [D]

Hopkins, William Frederick, Christopher Alley, Shoreditch, London, carver and gilder (1787). Took app. in 1787. [Westminster Ref. Lib., St Martin-in-the-Fields, app. indentures]

Hopkins, William, Greek St, Soho, London. On 12 November 1802 supplied the Prince of Wales with a 'very neat Etruscan Japand Chinese Lanthorn', with imitation bamboo canes and canopy top with twelve brass bells. Costing £9 9s, it was intended for the Princess of Wales at Blackheath, and made to match a 'Water Gold Lanthorn' at Carlton House. [Windsor Royal Archives, 25117]

Hopkins, William, St George's St, Leeds, Yorks., cm (1817–22). [D]

Hopkinson, Cunliffe, Newchurch, Haslingden, near Burnley, Lancs., cm (b. c. 1806–1841). Aged 35 at the time of the 1841 Census.

Hopkinson, Francis snr, Carolgate, Retford, Notts., cm and u (1819–22). [D]

Hopkinson, Francis jnr, Carolgate, Retford, Notts., cm and u (1822). [D]

Hopkinson, Henry, Birstall, Yorks., joiner and/or cm (1837). [D]

Hopley, William, near 'The Four Swans', Bishopsgate St, London, upholder (1732–49). Named in contemporary newspapers. [Heal].

Hopper, Edmund, Old Elvet, Durham, cm and joiner (1828–20). [D]

Hopper, Edward, Sittingbourne, Kent, cm (1824). [D]

Hopper, H., London (1812–25). Signed and dated 1 January 1812, an elaborate giltwood chandelier with eight foliate arms supporting gilt-metal fittings with moulded opaque glass 'flame' shades, and centred by a plinth supporting a plaster group of man, woman and cherub flying above; the whole hung by four chains from a giltwood corona topped with stars. [Sotheby's, 8 April 1982, lot 121] H. Hopper signed and dated 2 March 1818 an ebonised bracket, formed of a rectangular moulded shelf on corbel support carved with gadrooning. [Sotheby's, 9 February 1968, lot 151] Another painted plaster wall bracket is recorded by H. Hopper, signed and dated 20 February 1825, and consists of a moulded shelf supported on a female head wreathed in oak leaves and framed by a goatskin. [Sotheby's, 31 July 1970, lot 79]

Hopper, Mary, 23 Cook St, Liverpool, upholder (1796). [D]

Hopper, Michael, Witton-le-Wear, Durham, joiner and cm (1828–29). [D]

Hopper, Richard Mandeville, Newcastle, cm (1827–34). Addresses given at Yd 48, Groat Mkt and 8 Percy Ct in 1827; and 46 Leazes Cresc., 1833–34. [D]

Hopper, Thomas, address unrecorded, cm (1754). Subscribed to Chippendale's *Director*, 1754, for two copies.

Hopperton, Edward, Liverpool, u (1820). Declared bankrupt, *Liverpool Mercury*, 26 May 1820.

Hoppeston, William, address unrecorded, cm (1803). Subscribed to Sheraton's *Cabinet Dictionary*, 1803.

Hoppey, James, 17 Barbican, London, turner (1780–83). [D]

Hopton, Shadrach, Gloucester, cm and chairmaker (1815–40). Trading at Barton St in 1820, and Longsmith St in 1839. Child bapt. at St John Baptist's Church in 1815. [D; PR (bapt.)]

Horden, William, Broad Bridge St, Peterborough, Northants., cm and u (1830). [D]

Horlton, William, the Old Ropery, Stockton, Co. Durham, cm (1832). [D]

Horman, John, Essex St, Strand, London, cm and upholder (1765–97). Recorded as John & Son at no. 49, 1784–97, and no. 48, 1794–96. Took out a Hand in Hand Insurance policy in February 1765 for £275. Probably the John Horman who submitted a bill to Rev. Mr Brooks on 26 May 1767 for £10 8s 6d, paid on 15 June. [D; GL, Hand in Hand MS vol. 102, ref. 63799; Heal Coll., BM]

Horn, Andrew, London, cm (1793). Subscribed to Sheraton's *Drawing Book*, 1793.

Horn, Benjamin, Northampton, cm (1820–30). Recorded at Bridge St in 1820 and Newland in 1826. [Poll bks]

Horn, Edward, Norwich and London, cm (1781–1812). Son of Edward Horn, weaver; admitted freeman of Norwich on 2 June 1781. Polled at Norwich of London, 1784–1812. [Norwich freemen reg. and poll bks]

Horn, John, Short's Gdn, London, cm (1768). [Oxford poll bk]

Hornblow, William, Fetter Lane, London, freeman joiner (1762–65) and carver and gilder (1766–70). Employed non-freemen for several months: in 1762 and 1764, eight non-freemen; in 1765, six; in 1766 and 1767, fourteen; and in 1770, eighteen. [GL, City Licence bks, vols 3–7]

Hornblow, William, New Park St, Southwark, London, mahogany looking-glass frame maker (1835). [D]

Hornblower, Jesse, Chacewater, Cornwall, cm (1793). [D]

Hornby, James, Wellgate, Clitheroe, Lancs., joiner, cm, housebuilder etc. (1822–24). [D]

Hornby, William, Swan's Pl., Hessle New Rd, Hull, Yorks., cm (1838–39). [D]

Horne, Abial(l) & Son, Wellclose Sq., London, cm and glass grinders (1765–83). Recorded at no. 19, 1768–83. Rococo trade card states that he 'Sells all Sorts of Looking Glasses, Cabinet & Upholstery Goods at the Lowest Prices. NB. For Exportation.' Notice in *Leicester Journal*, 1778, reads that he had sold out on his premises in December 1777, and it was now being resold by an auctioneer in Leicester in January 1778. Recorded in Directories up to 1783, however. [D; Heal]

Horne, Abraham & Son, Wellclose Sq., London, cm (1768). [D]

Horne, Charles, address unrecorded, upholder (1715). Son of John Horne, freeman upholder of London; admitted freeman of the Upholders' Co. 'by his father's Copy' on 7 September 1715. [GL, Upholders' Co. records]

Horne, Enoch, London St, Swaffham, Norfolk, cm (1830–39). [D]

Horne, James, 5 Chenies St, Bedford Sq., London, u (1829). [D]

Horne, James, High St, Hythe, Kent, cm and u (1838–39). [D]

Horne, James, 49 Foley St, Foley Pl., London, u (1839). [D]

Horne, John, London, upholder (1708–30). Took app. named John Horne, 1708–29/30. His son, Charles Horne, admitted freeman of the Upholders' Co. in 1715. [GL, Upholders' Co. records]

Horne, John, address unrecorded, upholder (1708–30). Son of William Horne, Gent. of South Normanton, Derby. App. to John Horne, upholder of London, on 1 September 1708. Admitted freeman of the Upholders' Co. by servitude on 4 February 1729/30. [GL, Upholders' Co. records]

Horne, John, Brewer St, St James's, London, upholder (1712–27). Took app. on 23 December 1712. Named in contemporary newspapers. [PRO, app. reg.; Heal]

Horne, John, Nottingham, u (1720). [Nottingham burgess list]

Horne, S. & Co., Manchester, u, chairmakers and warehouse-men (1819–21). Addresses given at 17 St Anne's St in 1819 and 44 Piccadilly in 1821. [D]

Horne, Samuel, 85 Church St, Manchester, u (1840). [D]

Horne, Thomas, address unrecorded, u (1712). Took app. on 16 August 1712. [PRO, app. reg.]

Horne, William, Britwell, Oxon., chairmaker (1824). Participant in a conveyance for a property in South Weston to be converted into a chapel or meeting house for the Society of Methodists. [Oxford RO, Bi II/i/9]

Horne, William, 34 New Montague St, Spitalfields, London, cm and u (1827–28). [D]

Horner, —, Queen St, Westminster, London, u (1712). Named in contemporary newspapers. [Heal] Possibly George Horner.

Horner, —, at the west end of St Ann's, Soho, London, u (1720). Named in contemporary newspapers. [Heal]

Horner, Benjamin, Harrogate, Yorks., cm (1822–34). [D]

Horner, Charles, 10 Chapel St, Shoreditch, London, cm and u (1839). [D]

Horner, Christopher, 72 Broad St, Radcliffe Highway, London, cm (1789–93). [D]

Horner, George, corner of Little Queen St, Westminster, London, u (1712). Insured his goods on 31 July 1712. [GL, Sun MS vol. 2, p. 82] See Horner, —, of Queen St.

Horner, George, Coleshill St, Birmingham, chairmaker (1839). [D]

Horner, Hannah, 75 Thomas St, Manchester, cm (1836–40). Recorded also at no. 77 in 1836. [D]

Horner, J., address unrecorded, u (1808–09). Submitted a bill to Lord Monson in 1808 for £103 12s, including payment for paper hanging and upholstery; 7s 6d for '3 Glasses Framing' on 2 January; and 2s for a glass frame on 15 November. Receipted on 16 January 1809. [Lincoln RO, Monson 11/50]

Horner, James, address unrecorded, cm (d.1757). Notice of his death on 24 September 1757 in *London Chronicle*, 27 September [*Apollo*, February 1960, p. 36]

Horner, James Beck, High St, Lincoln, u and cm (1805–26). [D]

Horner, James, 27 Mill Hill, Manchester, cm (1817). [D]

Horner, James Horner, Norwich, cm (d. 1818). Will proved at Norwich in 1818. [Norfolk Record Soc., index of wills]

Horner, James, High Harrogate, Yorks., cm (1830). [D]

Horner, John, Manchester, cm, u and furniture broker (1813–34). Addresses given at 2 Hanbrian's Ct in 1813; home at 13 Thomas St 1816–28; also Lever St, 1824–33; no. 17 in 1825–29 and no. 33 or 35, 1832–33. Recorded also at 14 Thomas St in 1828 and 31 Thomas St, probably wrongly, in 1834. [D] See Mary Horner.

Horner, John, Court 51, Micklegate, York, cm etc. (1840). [D]

Horner, Jonathan, Bewerley, near Pateley Bridge, Yorks., cm (1822). [D]

Horner, Jos., High St, Harrogate, Yorks., cm (1828–34). [D]

Horner, M., High St, St Benedict's Lincoln, cm (1828). [D]

Horner, Malachi, Bishops Waltham, Hants., upholder (1719). Insured his house on 17 September 1719. [GL, Sun MS vol. 10]

Horner, Mary, 13 Thomas St, Manchester, cm (1819). [D] See John Horner.

Horner, Peter, formerly of Ashley Lane, and late of Red-bank and Pump Yd, Cock-gates, Manchester, cm (1829). Notice regarding his case in the Court of Relief of Insolvent Debtors appeared in *Liverpool Mercury*, 25 October 1829.

Horner, Samuel, Castle Hill, Lincoln, cm and u (1822–35). Addresses given at Bail in 1822, Castle Hill, 1826–28, and Steep Hill, 1835. [D]

Horner, Thomas, London, upholder (1774–94). Recorded at Cross St, Rathbone Pl., 'at Mr. Parker's' in 1781; and Aldersgate St, 1786–94. Son of Christopher Horner, mariner

of Shadwell. App. to John Phillips on 5 October 1774, and admitted freeman of the Upholders' Co. by servitude on 7 November 1781. [GL, Upholders' Co. records]

Horner, William, Tothill St, Westminster, London, u (1749). [Poll bk]

Horniman, Richard, address unrecorded, upholder (1758–65). Son of Robert Horniman, butcher of Abingdon, Berks. App. to Samuel Walker, draper, on 6 September 1758, and admitted freeman of the Upholders' Co. on 5 December 1765. [GL, Upholders' Co. records]

Horniman, Richard, Windsor, Berks., u (1794–98). [D; poll bk]

Horniman, William, 80 Peascod St, Windsor, Berks., cm and u (1830). [D]

Horning, James, 43 Store St, Bedford Sq., London, carver and gilder (1839). [D]

Hornsby, Nicholas, Church Yd, Penrith, Cumb., joiner and/or cm (1829–34). [D]

Hornsby, Thomas, Fenkle St, Newcastle, joiner and cm (1833–38). [D]

Hornzee, George, 2 Church Lane, Whitechapel, London, cm and u (1839). [D]

Horoson, James, New St, London, u (1784). [Poll bk]

Horrell, George, Exeter, Devon, cm (1822–40). Addresses given at 2 Back Lane, 1822–23; Bampfylde House, 1831–33; and Magdalen St, 1838–40. Sons George Thomas and Frederick John bapt. at St Mary Major on 8 January 1822. [D; *Exeter Pocket Journal*; PR (bapt.)]

Horrell, W., Exeter, Devon, cm (1826). Report that his app. had been imprisoned for disorderly conduct appeared in *The Alfred*, 14 March 1826.

Horrill, Thomas, North St, Exeter, Devon, cm and joiner (1792). Took out a Sun Insurance policy on 4 April 1792 for £600, including £300 on house, workshop and offices in North St, and £200 on utensils and stock. [GL, Sun MS vol. 386, p. 246]

Horris, (?), —, address unrecorded, u (1768). Payment to 'upholdstoror Horris' on Lady Day 1768 recorded amongst half-yearly bills listed by John Bragge of Sadborow, Thorncombe, Dorset. [Dorset RO, D104/F4]

Horrocks, —, Lancaster. Named in the Gillow records, 1794–1801. [Westminster Ref. Lib.]

Horrocks, Alexander, address unrecorded, upholder (1699–d. by 1731). Admitted freeman of the Upholders' Co. by redemption on 1 September 1699. Took his son, Christopher Horrocks, as app. on 1 July 1719. His son, John Horrocks, admitted freeman in 1731. [GL, Upholders' Co. records]

Horrocks, Alexander, at 'The White Bear', against Gray's Inn Gate, Holborn, London, upholder and undertaker (1724–32). Trade card and contemporary press notice recorded. [Heal]

Horrocks, Barnard E., Sheffield, Yorks., wood turner and chairmaker (1821–22). Recorded at St James St in 1821; and 80 Fargate in 1822. [D] See Joseph Horrocks.

Horrocks, Christopher, address unrecorded. App. to his father, Alexander Horrocks, on 1 July 1719, but apparently not admitted freeman of the Upholders' Co. Brother to John Horrocks. [GL, Upholders' Co. records]

Horrocks, John, address unrecorded, upholder (1731). Son of Alexander Horrocks, freeman upholder of London. Admitted freeman of the Upholders' Co. by patrimony on 1 December 1731. [GL, Upholders' Co. records]

Horrocks, John, Liverpool, cm (1780–85). Admitted freeman on 11 September 1780. Took apps named Thomas Holland in 1784 and James Woodward in 1785. [Liverpool freemen reg.]

Horrocks (or Horrox), Joseph, 81 Fargate, Sheffield, Yorks., chairmaker (1814–18). [D] See Barnard E. Horrocks.

Horrod, James, 3 Little Chapel, Westminster, London, gilder (1809). Took out a Sun Insurance policy on 6 March 1809 for £300 on goods in his house. [GL, Sun MS vol. 448, ref. 828545]

Horrox, Hammond, 84 English St, Hull, Yorks., cm and furniture broker (1840). [D]

Horsey, Joseph, Portsea Common, Portsmouth, Hants., chairmaker and turner (1783). Took out a Sun Insurance policy in 1783 for £900 of which utensils, stock and workshop accounted for £230. [GL, Sun MS vol. 314, p. 574]

Horsfall, James, Todmorden, Yorks., cm and joiner (1822–37). Trading with Samuel Horsfall at Church Gates, Todmorden Chapelry, in 1837. [D]

Horsley, —, 1 Worship St, Finsbury, London, chairmaker (1803). Named in Sheraton's list of master cabinet makers, 1803. Probably John Horsley.

Horsley, Edward, Caldew Bridges, Carlisle, Cumb., joiner and/or cm (1829). [D]

Horsley, James, 1 Worship St, Moorfields, London, chairmaker (1792). Took out a Sun Insurance policy on 28 September 1792 for £300, £40 on utensils and stock, £60 on two warehouses. [GL, Sun MS vol. 388, p. 645]

Horsley, James, 4 Austin St, Shoreditch, London, cm and u (1827–28). [D]

Horsley, John, Marsh St, Bristol, cm (1792–93). [D]

Horsley, John, 1 Worship St, Moorfields, London, japanned chairmaker (1801–02). [D] See Mary Horsley.

Hors(e)ley, John, Steelhouse Lane, Birmingham, cm, u, broker and builder (1822–35). Recorded at no. 15, 1828–35. [D]

Horsley, Luke, Newcastle, u (1753). Notice in *Newcastle Courant*, 29 December 'that persons indebted to Mr. Luke Horsley, Upholsterer in Newcastle should pay their debts to . . . Jas. BELL . . .'.

Horsley, Mary, 1 Worship St, Moorfields, London, japanned chairmaker (1803). [D] See John Horsley.

Horsley, Matthew, 25 Sloane Sq., Chelsea, London, cm (1826–39). [D]

Hors(e)ley, Richard, Bristol, cm (1752–94). Recorded in St Stephen's parish, 1754–74; 69 Lewin's Mead, 1775; and St Maryport's parish in 1781. Took app. named Andrews in 1752. [D; poll bks; S of G, app. index]

Horsley, William, address unrecorded, upholder (1717–29). Son of James Horsley, freeman joiner of London. App. to Charles Grange on 5 February 1717, and admitted freeman of the Upholders' Co. by servitude on 3 September 1729. [GL, Upholders' Co. records]

Horsley, William, 4 James St, Green Sq., London, cm (1784). [D; poll bk]

Horsley, William, St Augustine St, Norwich, cm (1830–42). [D]

Horsmaill (or Horsnail), Thomas, High St, Strood, Kent, cm and u (1807–39). Polled at Rochester in 1830. [D]

Horsmaill (or Horsnaill), William, 11 Snargate St, Dover, cm and u (1824–39). Trading as Horsmaill & Son, 1826–29. [D]

Hort, Peter, 56 Union St, Salford, Lancs., cm (1800–02). [D]

Horth, John, Norwich, upholder (1783–1818). Addresses given at White Lion Lane, 1784–1808; no. 18 in 1784, no. 17, 1801–02; and Swan Lane in 1810. Former app., William David, admitted freeman on 21 September 1804; and David Elliot on 21 September 1805. [D; poll bks; Norwich freemen reg.]

Hortley, Thomas, address unrecorded, freeman u (1713). Took app. on 13 June 1713. [PRO, app. reg.]

Horton, Daniel, address unrecorded, cm (1803). Subscribed to Sheraton's *Cabinet Dictionary*, 1803.

Horton, Daniel, 27 Mortimer St, Cavendish Sq., London, cm, u and buhl inlayer (1820–28). Took out a Sun Insurance policy on 14 January 1822 for £600, of which £250 accounted for

stock, utensils and goods in trust, workshop and yard. [D; GL, Sun MS vol. 490, ref. 987640]

Horton, David, address unrecorded, cm (c.1829–41). Named in the accounts of Charles William Vane, Marquess of Londonderry for furnishing carried out at Wynyard Park, Co. Durham. [Durham RO, Londonderry papers, D/LO/E484, vol. 1]

Horton, George, Piccadilly, London, upholder (1761). The will of Lt Gen. Huske included £500 to Horton. [*Gents Mag.*, January 1761]

Horton, George, Bolebridge St, Tamworth, Staffs., cm (1834). [D]

Horton, Henry, Walcot St, Bath, Som., cm and broker (1826–40). Trading at no. 36 in 1826 and no. 37 in 1840 when he took out insurance. [D; Sun MS vol. 268, ref. 1343850]

Horton, John, Charles St, Birmingham, cm and joiner (1767). [D]

Horton, John, Leeds, Yorks., cm (1822–37). Trading at Kirk Ings Wharf in 1822, and 3 Groves, Kirkgate, 1834. Recorded as Jonathan at 3 Cookson's Yd, Kirkgate in 1837. [D]

Horton, John, High St, Chippenham, Wilts., cm (1830–39). [D]

Horton, Joseph, Panton St, London, u (1709). [Rate bks]

Horton, Joseph, 123 Moor St, Birmingham, cm (1770). [D]

Horton, Joseph, Bridge St, Lane End, Staffs., chairmaker (1834–35). [D]

Horton, Joshua, Ader St, Manchester Sq., London, buhl manufacturer (1837). [D]

Horton, Luke, Postor (?) St, London, cm (1784). [Poll bk]

Horton, Richard, Newport, Salop, cm (1797–98). [D]

Horton, Walter, 87 London Rd, Liverpool, cm and u (1832). Advertised sale of 'a considerable quantity of ready-made Furniture' in *Liverpool Mercury*, 2 March 1832, offering thanks 'for the liberal encouragement he has received in the CABINET & UPHOLSTERY BUSINESS'. Stock comprised 'Mahogany Four-post & Tent Bedsteads, set of Mahogany French Bedsteads, hung with Moreen, two sets of Mahogany Trafalgar Chairs, two Mahogany Sofas, Mahogany & Painted Pembroke & other Tables, & a great variety of useful Cabinet Furniture.'

Horton, William, 19 Mt Pleasant, Gray's Inn Lane, London, cm, u and furniture broker (1827–35). [D]

Horton, William, Ramsgate, Kent, cm (1830). [Dover poll bk]

Horvard, William, 19 Mercer St, London, carver (1785). Took out a Sun Insurance policy on 16 December 1785 for £100 on household goods and clothes. [GL, Sun MS vol. 333, p. 602]

Horwell, William, 24 Gt Queen St, Lincoln's Inn Fields, London, miniature frame maker (1835). [D]

Hose, John, Compton St, Westminster, London, freeman upholder (1712–14). Insured his house for £100 on 18 August 1712, and again in 1714. [GL, Hand in Hand MS vol. 10, ref. 8783; vol. 13, p. 282]

Hosken, William, Seal St, St Day, Cornwall, cm (1830). [D]

Hosken, William Veal, Lower St, Penryn, Cornwall, cm and u (1830). [D]

Hoskins, Charles, 16 Trenchard St, Bristol, cm and u (1805–24). Trading with George Hoskins as chairmakers and painters in general, 1805–10. [D] See Rachel Hoskins.

Hoskins, Mary, Bristol, u (1733). Declared bankrupt, *Gents Mag.*, March 1733.

Hoskins, Mrs Rachel, Trenchard St, Bristol, cm and u (1825). [D] See Charles Hoskins.

Hosted, Samuel, Mill Lane, Oundle, Northants., chair turner (1823–30). [D]

Hother, William, St John's parish, Lewes, Sussex, cm (1812). [Poll bk]

Hotton, John, Market St, Falmouth, Cornwall, cm and u (1830). [D]

Hough, Edward Fletcher, Liverpool, cm (1796–1826). Petitioned freedom as son of Robert Hough, joiner, and admitted freeman on 25 January 1796. His son, Edward Fletcher Hough, tailor, born on 7 March 1802, petitioned freedom on birthright in 1826. [Liverpool freemen reg. and committee bk]

Hough, James, Lewin St, Middlewich, Cheshire, cm (1828). [D]

Hough, Robert, Liverpool, cm (1761). Former app., Edward Bevan, petitioned freedom in 1761. [Liverpool freemen's committee bk]

Hough, Thomas, 14 Paradise St, Liverpool, cm (1839). [D]

Hougham, White, London, cm (1790–96). Recorded in Carnaby Mkt, 1790, and Queen St, Soho, 1796. [Canterbury poll bks]

Houghton, —, 96 Holborn, London, cm (1793). Subscribed to Sheraton's *Drawing Book*, 1793. See A. and Michael Houghton, and Houghton & Son.

Houghton, A., 96 High Holborn, London, carpet and cabinet warehouseman (1811–19). [D] See Michael Houghton, and Houghton & Son.

Houghton, Edward, Haverhill, Suffolk, cm (1824). [D]

Houghton, George, 186 Queen St, Portsea, Portsmouth, Hants., cm and u (1830). [D]

Houghton, George, 65 Gt Dover St, London, u (1837). [D]

Houghton, Henry, High St, Southwark, London, u (1829–35). Trading at no. 103 in 1829 and 2 Adams Pl., High St in 1835. [D]

Houghton, Henry, 65 Gt Dover St, London, u (1839). [D]

Houghton, Isaac & Samuel, Parr Sq., Prescot, Lancs., joiners and cm (1828). [D]

Houghton, James, 54 Duckinfield St, Liverpool, u (1837). [D]

Houghton, John, Liverpool, cm (1780–1818). Addresses given at 24 Cumberland St, 1790–96; 11 Fontenoy St in 1796; 4 Rainfords Gdns, 1800–03; 42 Brownlow Hill in 1804, with shop in Lord St, 1804–14; no. 67, 1813–14; 71 Brownlow Hill in 1805; 58 Mt Pleasant St in 1807; no. 38 in 1810; no. 57 in 1811; 3 Bold Pl., 1813; no. 2 in 1814; 2 Mt Pleasant in 1816; and no. 68 in 1818. Petitioned freedom on servitude to George Parker, and admitted freeman on 15 September 1780. John Houghton jnr, book-keeper, petitioned freedom on servitude to John Houghton snr, cm, in 1796. Sale of stock on dissolution of partnership with Edward Lowe at Lord St, Castle Yd, advertised in *Liverpool Courier*, 24 May 1809. [D; Liverpool freemen reg. and committee bk] Two tradesmen may be concerned here. See Lowe & Houghton.

Houghton, John, Liverpool, u (1816–d. by 1820). Admitted freeman on 10 June 1816. [Liverpool freemen reg.]

Houghton, John Christian, Liverpool, u (1836–39). John Houghton was trading at 15 Flint St in 1839. John Christian Houghton was admitted freeman on 29 July 1836. [D; Liverpool freemen reg.]

Houghton, Michael, 96 High Holborn, London, u and cm (1808–17). [D] See A. Houghton, and Houghton & Son.

Houghton, Richard, Norwich, cm (1818). App. to Launcelot Howlett, and admitted freeman on 24 February 1818. [Norwich freemen rolls]

Houghton, William, address unrecorded, u (1803). Subscribed to Sheraton's *Cabinet Dictionary*, 1803.

Houghton, William, 161 New Bond St, London, portable desk, dressing case, work box and cabinet case maker (1839). [D]

Houghton & Son, 96 High Holborn, London, u, cm, appraisers and undertakers. 19th-century trade card continues: 'Carpeting and Bedding. Dealers in Brussels & other Carpets, Hearth Rugs, Druggets & Oil Clothes. The Trade Supplied.' [Landauer Coll., MMA, NY] See A. and Michael Houghton.

Houlden, John, Leicester, cm and u (1818–35). Addresses given at Belgrave Gate, 1818–22, and Granby St in 1835 also as a house agent. Advertisement showing elegant Regency premises at Belgrave Gate appeared in Leicester trade directory of 1822. [D]

Houl(d)gate, Thomas, York, cm (1812–30). Resident in Petergate in 1823 and St Michael le Belfrey parish in 1830. App. to John Taylor, cm, and admitted freeman in 1812. His son, William, app. to Richard Carter on 19 May 1830. [D; York app. reg. and freemen rolls] See William Houlgate.

Houldon, William, 17 Western Rd, Brighton, Sussex, cm and u (1839). [D]

Houlds, John, Hounsditch, London, freeman joiner, cm (1780). Employed ten non-freemen for six weeks in 1780. [GL, City Licence bks, vol. 10]

Houlgate, Robert, York, cm (1833). Son of William Houlgate, butcher; app. to John Taylor, cm, on 23 January 1833. [York app. reg.]

Houlgate, William, York, cm (1830). Son of Thomas Houlgate, cm of St Michael le Belfrey parish, York; app. to Richard Carter, cm and u of Bishophill Senior parish, on 19 May 1830. [York app. reg.] See Thomas Houldgate.

Houlker, William, 5 Church St, Blackburn, Lancs., cm, u, paper hanger, looking-glass manufacturer and carpet warehouseman (1818–34). Recorded at 4 Church St in 1828. Traded at 72 St James St, Burnley on Mondays. Advertised sale of stock in *Liverpool Mercury*, 14 December 1827: 'To be DISPOSED of immediately, the STOCK in TRADE of an UPHOLSTERER, who is declining business; Comprising a new & well assorted stock of Carpet, Paper Hangings, Oil Cloths, Hair Seating, & all other articles necessary for carrying on the above business respectably. The premises are eligibly situated in the Centre of the town of Blackburn, & may be had for a term of years, if required, at a reasonable rent. The above Concern presents an advantageous opportunity for any person wishing to embark in the above Trade as the Stock is quite modern, & the Connexions most respectable.' Houlker may have acted as the agent in the sale of another tradesmen's stock, since he is named in trade directories in 1834, still at 5 Church St, Blackburn. [D]

Houlton, Gracious, Bristol, cm (1781–1801). Trading in Wilder St, 1792–1801. [D; poll bks]

Houlton, James, Manchester, cm (1794–97). Trading at Prussia St in 1794, and 'The White Lion', 7 Thomas St in 1797. [D]

Houlton, Matthew, address unrecorded, upholder (1704). Admitted freeman of the Upholders' Co. on 6 September 1704. [GL, Upholders' Co. records]

Hounsworth, Jesse, Low Church Alley, Hull, Yorks., chairmaker etc. (1814). [D] See Jesse Ounsworth.

House, —, London, m (1793). Subscribed to Sheraton's *Drawing Book*, 1793.

House, George, 36 Devonshire Pl., Brighton, Sussex, cm (1839). [D]

House, Ralph, 5 French Yd, Bowling Green Lane, Clerkenwell, London, carver (1808). [D]

Household, Robert, 16 New Rd, Back Lane, Ratcliff, London, bedstead and cm (1781–89). Took out a Sun Insurance policy in 1781 for £200, of which utensils and stock accounted for £130. [D; GL, Sun MS vol. 298, p. 159]

Household, Thomas, London, bedstead manufacturer, u and cm (1820–39). Trading at 72 St George's Pl. in 1820; 27 New Rd, St George's East in 1822; and 14 Crombie's Row, Commercial Rd in 1839. [D]

Houseman, John, address unrecorded, upholder (1711–25). Admitted freeman of the Upholders' Co. on 6 June 1711. Took apps named Francis Kellow, 1712–21; and Thomas Roby, 1715–25. [GL, Upholders' Co. records] Probably John Housman.

Housley, Peter, Nottingham, joiner and cm (1770–80). Son of

Sam Housley of Arnold; taken as app. in 1770. Took app. named William Bird in 1780. [Nottingham app. list]

Housman, John, St Bartholomew Close, London, freeman upholder (1712). Took out a Hand in Hand Insurance policy on 23 December 1712 for £250 on his house and workshop. [GL, Hand in Hand MS vol. 11, p. 73] Probably John Houseman.

Houston, James, North Birkenhead, Cheshire, u and feather dealer (1834–39). Trading at 3 Portland Pl. in 1834; 8 Portland St in 1835; 10 Gt George Pl. in 1737; and 44 Bridge St in 1839. Recorded in association with O'Neill & Co. in 1834. [D]

Hovell, Richard, Liverpool, cm (1811–16). Addresses given at 4 Hodson St in 1811; 17 Gt Crosshall St in 1813; and no. 37 in 1816. [D]

How(e), —, Chelmsford, Essex, u (1737–40). Named in Earl Fitzwalter's accounts on 19 July 1737, 'pulling down & setting up beds & furniture' for £15 19s 8d; and on 15 August 1738 'for stuffing a base of Blew' for a settee made by Gainge, joiner. On 24 September 1740 How was paid £30 in part payment of a bill for £104 16s 3½d. [A. C. Edwards, *The Accounts of Benjamin Mildmay, Earl Fitzwalter*, pp. 107–09] Possibly Samuel How.

How, Bennett, Westgate St, Newcastle, cm and carpenter (1790). [D] See Bennet Howe.

How, Charles, Newcastle, cm, carpenter and joiner (1778–87). Trading at Flesh Mkt in 1778 and Silver St in 1787. [D]

How, J., Tiverton, Devon, cm (1829). Marriage to 'Miss Reed of the Prince Blucher, Westexe' at St Peter's Church, reported in *Exeter Flying Post*, 10 December 1829.

How, John, address unrecorded, carver (1731–36). Worked at Kew Palace and the Wren City Churches as partner of John Benson (fl. 1727–43). [*Conn.*, June 1981, p. 144] Carried out work for Sir Richard Hoare between 1731–36, receiving £23 12s 6d on 21 December 1731; and £24 11s 11d in November 1732 for work on a chimney and glass frames, cornice and wainscotting; and carving and gilding two pedestals for candles supplied to Barn Elms House. In March 1736 How charged Sir Richard £3 14s for carving and gilding picture frames. [Private accounts, Hoare's Bank, Fleet St; V&A Lib., English Manuscripts, tradesmen's bills]

How, Robert, Germain St, London, upholder (1726–d.1758). Polled at Westminster of 'German' St and Duke St in 1749. Named in contemporary newspapers. Death at his home in Jermyn St reported in *London Chronicle*, 22 April 1758. [Heal]

How, Samuel, Chelmsford, Essex, upholder (1707–34). Son of Philip How, milliner of Chelmsford; app. to Arthur Osborne on 2 September 1707, and admitted freeman of the Upholders' Co. by servitude on 4 March 1723/24. Took app. named Robert Phipps, 1723–31. Named in the Essex Freeholders' book in 1734. [GL, Upholders' Co. records; Essex RO, Q/RJ 1/1] See How(e), —.

How, Thomas, Jarman St, corner of Duke St, Westminster, London, u (1710–33). Took out separate insurance policies in 1714–15 on his goods and a house in Brompton, parish of Kensington. [GL, Sun MS vol 3, ref. 3753 and GL, Hand in Hand MS vol. 14, p. 397] In 1710–11 he provided furnishings to the value of £830 to the 5th Earl of Salisbury at Hatfield House, Herts., the State bed alone costing £289. He also supplied richly upholstered seat furniture for the waiting room, the green damask room, the dining room and the red room at Hatfield, as well as two more beds. [Hatfield House MS no. 467; *C. Life*, 22 December 1983, p. 1853] The Monson papers include a bill dated 1733 from Thomas How to Lady Sonds for bedding, upholstery materials, cushions, etc., amounting to £13 6s 6½d; it is receipted 'pr Tho How by

ye hands of Mr John Delacourt'. [Lincoln RO, Monson papers, no. 12] The name 'Thomas How of Westminster, gentleman, upholsterer' occurs on an inscribed lead plaque found at Sutton Scarsdale, Derbs. recording the names of the architect and fifteen master tradesmen responsible for building, decorating and equipping the hall. The tablet, which bears two dates 1724 and 1728 is described in *C. Life*, 15 February 1919, p. 171. The survivors from a walnut suite formerly at Sutton Scarsdale, embellished with *verre-eglomisée* armorial panels and gilt lead mounts (now divided between the MMA, NY, the Frick Coll., the Cooper Hewitt Museum and Temple Newsam, Leeds) are likely to be from How's workshop.   C.G.G.

How, Thomas, Downton, Wilts., cm (1756). Took app. named James Field in 1756. [*Wilts. Apps and their Masters*]

Howard, —, Newport St, St Ann's, London, picture frame maker (1746). Announcement in *London Evening Post*, 4–6 September 1746, that Mr Howard, formerly a picture frame maker, by which he made a handsome fortune, had given up this trade in order to become Master Joiner to the Palace of St James, a post he had resigned some time before to one of his sons. Possibly Gerrard or John Howard, carvers and gilders.

Howard, —, address unrecorded, cm (*c*.1775). Submitted a bill totalling £8 for furniture supplied to Denton Park, Yorks. [*Furn. Hist.*, 1968]

Howard, Ann, 25 Gerrard St, London, paper stainer and upholder (1783). Took out a Sun Insurance policy in 1783 for £600 of which utensils, stock and goods accounted for £350. [GL, Sun MS vol. 313, p. 328] See Thomas Howard of Gerrard St.

Howard, Charles, Lancaster, cm (1752–68). App. to Christopher Walker in 1752, and admitted freeman, 1767–68, when stated of London. [Lancaster app. reg. and freemen rolls]

Howard, Charles, Bawtry, Yorks., joiner and/or cm (1834). [D]

Howard, Charlotte, 16 Russell St, Plymouth, Devon, working u (1830). [D]

Howard, Edward, Liverpool, cm and household broker (1790–1824). Addresses given at 129 Dale St in 1790; 42 Derby St in 1794; 36 Stanley St in 1805; no. 39, 1807–11; no. 45 in 1813; and various numbers between 1816–24. [D] See Thomas Howard of Liverpool.

Howard, Edward, Liverpool, cm (1838). App. to William John Roberts in 1838. [Liverpool app. enrolment bk]

Howard, George, Preston, Lancs., joiner and cm (1816–18). Trading at Grimshaw St, 1816–18, and 27 Shambles in 1818. [D]

Howard, George, Fore St, Cullompton, Devon, carver and gilder (1830–38). [D]

Howard, Gerrard, address unrecorded, Carver and Gilder to the Royal Family (1727–41). Supplied a number of carved and gilt frames for the Royal Palaces from 1727–41. In 1734–35 he submitted an account 'for very large carved 9:4 frame' costing £54 3s, for the great staircase at Hampton Court. [PRO, LC, 3/20] Receipted a bill from John Howard in 1727. Named in the accounts of Earl Fitzwalter for frames supplied to Moulsham Hall, Chelmsford, or Schomberg House, Pall Mall, London. On 6 March and 12 October 1731 he was paid a total of £25 5s 6d for a stretching frame, and cleaning a portrait of the Duke of Schomberg by Kneller. On 21 October 1740 he received £10 1s for a frame 'for a Naked Picture of Beluchis, now at Moulsham, £6, and for a Frame for a Picture of Ulrick done by Vandermayne £3.3s.'. [A. C. Edwards, *The Accounts of Benjamin Mildmay, Earl Fitzwater*, pp. 188–91; *DEF*] Possibly Howard, —, of Newport St, London.

Howard, Henry, Philip Lane, near Aldermanbury, London, cm

(1725). Insured goods and merchandise in his house for £500 on 25 December 1725. [GL, Sun MS vol. 20, ref. 37609]

Howard, Henry snr, Liverpool, cm (1767–84). Admitted freeman on 15 October 1767. Former app., Henry Howard jnr, admitted on 13 December 1784. [Liverpool freemen reg. and committee bk]

Howard, Henry jnr, Liverpool, cm (1784–d. by 1820). Addresses given at 19 Barter St in 1790; no. 21 in 1796; no. 47 in 1800; and no. 20, 1800–10. Petitioned freedom on servitude to Henry Howard snr, and admitted freeman on 13 December 1784. [D; Liverpool freemen reg.] Possibly Henry Howards.

Howard, Henry, High St, Strood, Kent, cm (1830–38). [D]

Howard, J., Chesham, Bucks., cm (1839). [D]

Howard, J., 7 Friary Pl., Guildford, Surrey, cm, carver and turner (1839–40. [D]

Howard, John, at 'The Talbot', Long Lane, near West Smithfield, London, upholder, appraiser and dealer in tapestries and Oriental carpets (1710–d.1742). Admitted freeman of the Upholders' Co. on 3 August 1710, and master in 1734. Took apps named Thomas Hathaway until 1726; Thomas Roberts, 1716–27; James Smith, 1721–29; and Thomas Denham, 1741–42. Took out a Hand in Hand Insurance policy on 20 March 1713, renewed on 3 April 1721, for £400 on his house. [D; GL, Upholders' Co. records; GL, Hand in Hand MS vol. 12, p. 534] Newspapers record him in partnership with Hambleton, 1724–30. [Heal] Submitted a bill to Gilbert Heathcote on 22 November 1728 for 'a fine Carpet', costing £3 5s. Accompanying trade card states that Howard 'Makes and Sells all manner of Household Furniture, viz. Damask, Mohair, Workt and Stuff Beds, & Bedding, with Chairs & Glasses, all sorts of Silk Worsted Damask Camblets & Water'd Cheneys, &c. by Wholesale or Retale. Where are also sold all Sorts of Persia Muskat and Turkey Carpets, fine and ordinary Tapestry Hangings, at reasonable Rates. NB. Fine Tapestry and Carpets are clean'd after the best manner.' [Lincoln RO, 2 ANC 12/D/18] On 22 October 1729 Howard sent a bill to Paul Foley of the Temple and Little Ormond St, London, and Newport House, Almeley, Herefs., for a 'Fine Large Turke Carp!' at £3 5s, and one at £3, receipted by Joseph Hitchcock for his master. A similar bill to Foley is dated 1 January 1730. [Herefs. RO, Foley papers, F/A III/55] Howard provided carpets costing £12 5s to Sir Richard Hoare on 3 November 1732. [Private accounts, Hoare's Bank, Fleet St; Heal Coll., BM] John Howard's death on 9 September 1742 was reported in *Gents Mag.* He left handsome fortunes to his son and daughter. The sale of his stock and household furniture was announced in the *Daily Advertiser*, 2 November 1742; catalogues to be had from Jos. Hamilton, upholder of Long Lane. Howard's son, John, born at Enfield and bred a Presbyterian Dissenter (b.c.1724–d.1790) achieved fame as a philanthropist and prison reformer. His obituary in *Gents Mag.*, March 1790, noted that his father was allied to the families of Tatnall, Cholmley, Bernardiston, and Samuel Whitbread, Esq., MP for Bedford. [*DNB*; Harris, *Old English Furniture*, p. 23]

Howard, John, London, joiner, carver and gilder, picture frame maker (1721–29). In 1721 he provided 'a frame carv'd & gilt with gold' for 'yo.! Hon.ble Picture over the Chimney' for Walpole at Chelsea. [*C. Life*, 22 January 1921] On 31 January 1727 John Howard, 'joyner of the Privy Chamber' supplied 'carved & gilded frames for his Majesty's pictures', costing £141 19s 2d. [Lord Chamberlain's Office 5/18] Supplied carved and gilt picture frames to the Duke of Montrose, receiving a total of £22 18s in 1722. One frame, costing £6 6s was for a portrait of the Duke, another, for the Duke of Roxburghe's portrait. In 1727 Howard was paid for

picture frames supplied in 1723, one for a portrait of Montrose's great grandfather, James, 2nd Marquis, Lord Northesk. Mr De Mar (?), gilder, was paid for mounting the pictures. [Scottish RO, GD 220/6/1230/2; GD220/5/858/16] Sent two picture frames to William Aikman in 1727, one of black and gold for a picture of 'Secretary Johnson'; the bill was receipted by Gerrard Howard. [Scottish RO, GD220/6/1356/20] Bill from John Howard recorded for 2 ¾ frames carved & gilt with gold the Italian Moulding', at £3, dated 1729. [Scottish RO, GD220/6/1381/12] Possibly Howard, —, 87 Newport St.

Howard, John, St Ann's Ct, Covent Gdn, London, chairmaker (1749). [Poll bk]

Howard, John, 3 Parker St, Manchester, cm (1797). [D]

Howard, John, 26 Skelhorne Pl., Liverpool, u (1811). [D]

Howard, John, Goodman's Fields, London, cm and u (1820–39) Trading at 24 Leman St in 1820, and 34 Little Alie St in 1835. [D] Trade card reads; 'JOHN HOWARD, Cabinet Manufacturer, Upholster, Appraiser & Undertaker, CARPET & FEATHER WAREHOUSE, 34 Alie Street, Goodman's Fields. Plain & Ornamental Paper Hanging. Furniture for Exportation.' [GL] See Samuel Howard of 79 Leman St.

Howard, John & Co., 122 Forest St, Cripplegate, London, looking-glass manufacturer (1839). [D]

Howard, Joseph, 3 Abrahams Ct, Bath, Som., cm (1826). [D]

Howard, Joseph jnr, Walmer Rd, Sandwich, Kent, cm (1832). [Poll bk]

Howard, Maria, George St, Gt Yarmouth, Norfolk, cm and upholder (1839). [D]

Howard, Nathaniel, Plymouth, Devon, chairmaker (1758). Took app. named Buckingham in 1758. [S of G, app. index]

Howard, Peter, Liverpool, cm (1831). Declared bankrupt, *Liverpool Mercury*, 9 September 1831.

Howard, Richard, Liverpool, cm (1812–37). Admitted freeman on 5 October 1812. Recorded at 8 Mansfield St in 1835 and 3 Sidney St East in 1837. [D; Liverpool freemen reg.]

Howard, Richard, London, u and appraiser (1820–39). Trading at 16 Old St in 1820 and 27 Goswell St in 1837. [D]

Howard, Robert, address unrecorded. On 24 October 1787 he was paid 19s 10d for painting seven chairs at Dunham Massey, Cheshire. [John Rylands Lib., Manchester Univ., George Cooke's accounts]

Howard, Robert, Rock St, Redvales, Bury, Lancs., cm and chairmaker (1816–18). [D]

Howard, Samuel, 10 Gt Queen St, London, organ builder, cm and broker (1781). Took out a Sun Insurance policy in 1781 for £200 of which £150 accounted for utensils, stock and goods. [GL, Sun MS vol. 296, p. 570] See Thomas Howard at this address.

Howard, Samuel, 79 Leman St, Goodman's Fields, London, cm (1808). [D] See John Howard of Goodman's Fields.

Howard, Thomas, Gerrard St, Soho, London, upholder (1775–76). Named in Bailey's list of bankrupts in 1776. [D] See Ann Howard.

Howard, Thomas, 3 Foster St, Half Moon Alley, Bishopsgate St, London, joiner and carver (1778). Insured his house for £100 in 1778. [GL, Sun MS vol. 271, p. 229]

Howard, Thomas, 10 Gt Queen St, Lincoln's Inn Fields, London, carver (1782). Insured his house for £200 in 1782. [GL, Sun MS vol. 302, p. 624] See Samuel Howard at this address.

Howard, Thomas, 8 Gt Andrews St, London, carver (1791). Took out a Sun Insurance policy on 28 March 1791 for £300 including £50 on the workshop behind his house. [GL, Sun MS ref. 581357]

Howard, Thomas, Liverpool, cm (1803–39). Recorded at 32 Stanley St, 1829–37, and nos 63 and 65 in 1839. App. to

William Harvey in 1803, and admitted freeman on 9 October 1812. [D; Liverpool freemen reg. and committee bk] See Edward Howard.

Howard, Thomas, 8 North St Mews, London, cm and u (1839). [D]

Howard, Timothy Thomas, High Wycombe, Bucks., chairmaker (1840). [PR (marriage)]

Howard, W. H., 16 Clarence St, Cheltenham, Glos., cm and u (1839–40). [D]

Howard, alias Howitt, William, Hungate, York, cm (1784). [Poll bk]

Howard, William, 15 Baptist St, Liverpool, cm (1821). [D]

Howard, William, Wye, Kent, chairmaker (1826–34). [D]

Howard, William, London, manufacturer of pocket books, work boxes, dressing cases, backgammon boards etc. (1831–63). Trading at 68 Aldersgate, 1831–35; no. 63, 1835–37; 62 Barbican, 1838–39; and nos 62 and 63 thereafter. Trade card in Heal Coll., BM. [D]

Howard, William, East St, Ipswich, Suffolk, cm and u (1839). [D]

Howard & Hambleton, at 'The Talbot', Long Lane, near West Smithfield, London, u (1724–30). Named in contemporary newspapers. [Heal] See John Howard at this address.

Howard & Whitehead, 10 Alport St, Manchester, carvers, gilders and looking-glass manufacturers (1794). [D]

Howards, Henry, Liverpool, cm (1804). Marriage to Miss Elizabeth Hooton of Barton's Lane, Oldhall St, 'after a TEDIOUS courtship of SIX DAYS', at St Nicholas's Church, reported in *Liverpool Chronicle*, 3 October 1804. Possibly Henry Howard

Howarth, Jeremiah, Halifax, Yorks., cm (1793–1837). Trading at 35 Swine Mkt in 1837. Subscribed to Sheraton's *Drawing Book*, 1793. [D]

Howarth, John, Wallgate, Wigan, Lancs., u (1818–22). [D]

Howarth, John, Dockray Sq., Colne, Lancs., joiner and cm (1824). [D]

Howarth, John, Brotherton's Buildings, Wigan, Lancs., u (1825). [D]

Howarth, John, Lancaster, cm (1826–38). App. to Henry Walker in 1826, and admitted freeman, 1827–28. [Lancaster app. reg. and freemen rolls]

Howarth, Joseph, 18 Lambert St, Liverpool, cm (1835). [D]

Howcraft, Thomas, at 'The Looking-Glass', Cornhill, and 'The India Cabinet', Long Acre, London, joiner, cm and glass seller (1711). In partnership with Richard Robinson, supplied looking-glasses to the 1st Earl of Nottingham at Burley-on-the-Hill, Rutland in 1711. One of them cost £82 1s 6d which included patterned and scalloped glass borders and a cut coat of arms in the shaped top panel. Earlier in 1711 Thomas Howcraft, joiner, of St Martin-in-the-Fields parish was declared bankrupt, *London Gazette*, July, and 11 and 14 August 1711. Overmantel recorded in the V&A archives. [Wills, *Looking-Glasses*, p. 21; Pearl Finch, *History of Burley-on-the-Hill*; C. *Life*, 15 February 1930; *Antique Collector*, November–December 1947; Harris, *Old English Furniture*, p. 23]

Howcraft, Thomas, Liverpool, cm (1834). App. to William John Roberts in 1834. [Liverpool app. enrolment bk]

Howdell, William, London, chairmaker (1754–60). Subscribed to Chippendale's *Director*, 1754. Took app. named Richard Moreley for £20 in 1760, when recorded in St James's, Westminster. [S of G, app. index]

Howe, —, Strand, London, cm (1793). Subscribed to Sheraton's *Drawing Book*, 1793.

Howe, Bennet, Cowpen Horton, Northumb., joiner and cm (1828). [D] See Bennett How.

Howe, David, West Auckland, Co. Durham, joiner and cm (1827–29). [D]

Howe, George, Church St, Crewkerne, Som., carver and gilder (1840). [D]

Howe, James, Church St, Salisbury, Wilts., carver and gilder (1839). [D]

Howe, Joseph, Ellis St, Exeter Row, Birmingham, interior decorator, cm and u (1828–35). Recorded at no. 41 in 1835. [D]

Howe, Thomas, 49 Duke St, Liverpool, carver and gilder (1839). [D]

Howel, William, 46 Long Alley, Moorfields, London, cm (1808). [D]

Howell, —, near Orange Ct, Swallow St, London, cm (1763). Mentioned in a Sun Insurance policy of 5 March 1763 of John Adams, Gent., at 'Mr. Howells'. [GL, Sun MS ref. 197283]

Howell, —, Red Cross St, London, chairmaker (1803). Subscribed to Sheraton's *Cabinet Dictionary*, 1803.

Howell, Charles, Upper King St, Bloomsbury, London, upholder (1776). Insured his house and goods for £500 in 1776. [GL, Sun MS vol. 246, p. 542]

Howell, David, address unrecorded, cm (1803). Subscribed to Sheraton's *Cabinet Dictionary*, 1803.

Howell, Edward, 69 Weaman's St, Birmingham, chairmaker (1835). [D]

Howell, George, Bricklin St, Birmingham, chairmaker (1830). [D]

Howell, Henry, 35 Barrack St, Devonport, Devon, cm (1838). [D]

Howe(l), James, Bristol, upholder (1754–57). Recorded in St Nicholas's parish in 1754. Took apps named Stiffe in 1754, Mayo in 1755, and Bennet in 1757. [Poll bk; S of G, app. index]

Howell, James, Norwich, cm (1826). App. to Joseph Pigg, and admitted freeman on 3 May 1826. [Norwich freemen rolls]

Howell, John, Liverpool, cm (1761–69). Trading in Derby St, 1767–69. Admitted freeman in March 1761 on servitude to James Robinson. [D; Liverpool freemen reg. and committee bk]

Howell, John, Brownlaw St, near the hospital, London, cm (1777). Took out a Sun Insurance policy in 1777 for £300 of which £150 accounted for utensils, stock and goods. [GL, Sun MS vol. 254, p. 334]

Howell, John, Redcliffe St, Bristol, cm and u (1784–94). [D; poll bk]

Howell, Mary, Bristol, upholder (1761). Took apps named Thorn and Rise in 1761. [S of G, app. index]

Howell, Mathew, Wickwar, Glos., upholder (1784). [Bristol poll bk]

Howell, P., Goldsmith St, Exeter, Devon, cm (1816–d.1823). Death on 13 May 1823 reported in *Exeter Flying Post*, 15 May. [D; *Exeter Pocket Journal*] Possibly:

Howell, Philip, SS Paul and Bradninch, Exeter, Devon, cm (1803). [Militia Census]

Howell, Robert, 39 Kew Pl., Church St, Brighton, Sussex, cm (1822). [D]

Howell, William, address unrecorded, upholder (1712–19). Son of Andrew Howell, yeoman of St James Weston; app. to John Horn on 6 August 1712, and admitted freeman of the Upholders' Co. by servitude on 2 November 1719. [GL, Upholders' Co. records]

Howell, William, against St Ann's Church, Princes St, Westminster, London, upholder (1722). Insured goods and merchandise in his house for £500 on 17 July 1722. [GL, Sun MS vol. 14, ref. 25920]

Howell, William, North St, Ripon, Yorks, cm (1822–37). [D]

Howell & Jones, 9 Regent St, formerly 89 Pall Mall, London, late Ryder & Scribe. In January 1828 supplied items totalling £36 18s 6d to Burton Constable, Yorks., including a buhl inkstand, four Eau de Cologne standishes, and a mother-of-pearl candlestand. [Burton Constable, voucher bundles, Humberside RO, DDCC]

Howell & Son, 15 Bridge St, Bristol, u (1775). [D]

Howes, —, address unrecorded. The impressed mark 'HOWES' is recorded on two Windsor chairs, the style and construction of which resemble chairs known to have come from the Thames Valley. [Bowes Museum, Barnard Castle, Co. Durham; *Furn. Hist.*, 1978, pl. 55a]

Howes, George, Leicester, cm (1826). App. to his father, possibly Joshua Howes of Leicester (1789–1815, D); and admitted freeman in 1826, of Birmingham. [Leicester freemen rolls]

Howes, Simon, St Gregory's Churchyard, Norwich, cm (1836). [D]

Howes, William, Wymondham, Norfolk, cm and chairmaker (1822). [D]

Howett, John, Shelford, Notts., joiner and cm (1832). [D]

Howey, Joseph, Portsea, Portsmouth, Hants., turner, chair and pattern maker (1792–98). [D]

Howin, John, 22 Clerkenwell Green, London, bedstead maker (1809–11). [D]

Howis, Edward, Piccadilly, London, upholder (1811). Took out a Sun Insurance policy on 30 December 1811 with John Turner, upholder, on a house at 12 Berwick St in the latter's tenure, for £500. [GL, Sun MS vol. 459, ref. 864461]

Howland, Frederick, High Wycombe, Bucks., chairmaker (b. c. 1816–41). Sons bapt. in 1835 and 1837. Aged 25 at the time of the 1841 Census. [PR (bapt.)]

Howland, Russen, High Wycombe, Bucks., chairmaker (1830). [D]

Howles, G., 17 North Audley St, London, u (1825). [D]

Howlett, Charles, Norwich, cm (1818). Son of Launcelot Howlett, cm; admitted freeman on 4 April 1818. [Norwich freemen reg.]

Howlett, Elija (or Elisha), Hull, Yorks., carver, gilder and glass silverer (1831–40). Addresses given at Parker's Gal., 14 Trippett in 1831; 22 Savile St in 1834; no. 24 in 1835; and no. 40, 1838–40. [D] See William Howlett.

Howlett, Heasman Thomas, Norwich, cm (1812). Son of Launcelot Howlett, cm; admitted freeman on 15 February 1812. [Norwich freemen reg.] Possibly Thomas Howlett.

Howlett, Henry, Norwich and London, cm (1807–18). Son of Launcelot Howlett, cm; admitted freeman of Norwich on 31 October 1807. Polled at Norwich of London in 1818. [Norwich freemen reg.]

Howlett, James, London, chairmaker (1812). [Norwich poll bk]

Howlett, James, 6 Saville Pl., Mile End, London, cm and u (1839). [D]

Howlett, Launcelot, Norwich, Norfolk, Yarm, Yorks.; and Ipswich, Suffolk, cm and chairmaker (1780–1818). Polled at Norwich of St John Sepulchre's parish in 1780; of Yarm, Yorks. in 1784; of St John Timberhill, Norwich, in 1786; of Ipswich in 1806; and of St Swithin's parish, Norwich, in 1818. His sons, Henry Howlett, Heasman Thomas Howlett, and Charles Howlett, all cm, admitted freemen of Norwich on 31 October 1807, 15 February 1812, and 4 April 1818 respectively. Former app., Richard Houghton, admitted freeman on 24 February 1818. [Norwich poll bks and freemen reg.]

Howlett, Stephen, St Andrew's, Norwich, chairmaker (1734–56). Former app., Thomas Durrant, chairmaker, admitted freeman on 24 February 1756. [Norwich poll bks and freemen reg.]

Howlett, Thomas, London, cm (1786). [Norwich poll bk]

Howlett, Thomas, Norwich, chairmaker (1818–30). Recorded

in the parishes of St John Maddermarket in 1818 and St Benedict, 1830. [Poll bks] Possibly Heasman Thomas Howlett.

Howlett, William, 19 Trippett, Hull, Yorks., furniture painter etc. (1840). Trading as a painter only, before 1840; and as a house and ship painter after 1840. [D] See Elija Howlett.

Howorth, John, Birchen Lane, Manchester, cm (1788). [D]

Howson, Charles, 15 Bradshaw St, Manchester, carver and gilder (1822–33). Trading also at 64 Hanover St, 1824–29. [D]

Howson, James, Blackwell Row, Darlington, Co. Durham, cm and joiner (1828–34). [D]

Howson, Robert, Bank, Barnard Castle, Co. Durham, joiner and cm (1827–29). [D]

Howson, Robert, Bondgate, Darlington, Co. Durham, joiner and cm (1827–34). [D]

Howton, Benjamin, Ludlow, Salop, u (1720). Took app. named Penny in 1720. [S of G, app. index]

Howton, Thomas, Worcester, upholder (1785). Former app., Abraham Fluck (or Fluke) admitted freeman on 17 January 1785. [Worcester freemen rolls]

Hoy, Thomas, 74 Old St Rd, London, bedstead maker (1808). [D]

Hoy, Thomas Daniel, London, cm, chair manufacturer and u (1820–27). Trading at 8 Hare St, Spitalfields in 1820 and 2 Devonshire Pl., Commercial Rd, 1826–27. [D]

Hoy, W., London, furniture broker, cabinet and bedstead manufacturer (1835–39). Trading at 3 Pleasant Row, King's Cross in 1835 and 9 Lower St, Islington in 1839. [D]

Hoy, William, 5 New Inn Yd, Shoreditch, London, cabinet manufacturer and u (1820–35). [D]

Hoyle, Henry, Rochdale, Lancs., cm (1825–34). Home address given at High St in 1825. Recorded at Cheetham St in 1834. [D] See John Hoyle.

Hoyle, Isaac, Norwich, u (1753–68). Recorded at St Peter Mancroft parish in 1768. App. to Woodhouse Harmer and Paul Colombine, and admitted freeman on 3 May 1753. Took apps named Bentle in 1756; Crisp in 1757; and Driver in 1759. Subscribed to Chippendale's *Director*, 1754. [Norwich poll bk, freemen and app. reg.]

Hoyle, James, 46 Kennedy St, Manchester, carver and gilder (1836–40). [D]

Hoyle, John, Rochdale, Yorks., cm (1816–28). Trading at Cheetham St, 1816–25, and High St in 1828. [D] See Henry Hoyle.

Hoyle, John, Manchester, carver and gilder (1834–40). Trading at 19 Cooper St in 1834 and 46 Kennedy St, 1838–40. [D]

Hoyle, William, 14 Princes St, Bristol, cm (1813–25). [D]

Hubart, Adam, Wapping, London, picture frame maker (1716). Took app. named Dod in 1716. [S of G, app. index]

Hubbard, —, Wymer St, Norwich, cm (1810). [D]

Hubbard, —, Teignmouth, Devon, u (1814–29). Advertised as agent in sales of property in *Exeter Flying Post*, 16 June 1814; 24 July 1817 of the house of the Right Hon. Lord Clifford at Shaldon, near Teignmouth; on 12 March 1829; and 23 July 1829. Probably John Peters Hubbard.

Hubbard, —, 19 Rose & Crown Ct, Southwark, London, cm (1835). [D]

Hubbard, J. P., address unrecorded. On 23 August 1818 received £4 14s 6d by William Baldwin in full payment for a marble table he provided for Endsleigh House, near Tavistock, Devon. [Bedford Office, London] Probably John Peters Hubbard.

Hubbard, James, address unrecorded. In December 1679 he was paid £5 by the 5th Earl of Bedford (later 1st Duke) for thirteen cane walnut chairs. [Bedford Office, London]

Hubbard, James, Norwich, cm, u and chairmaker (1801–22).

Trading at 12 St Andrews, Bridge St, 1801–1803, and Gun Lane in 1822. [D]

Hubbard, James, Powis St, Woolwich, London, cm (1823–38). [D]

Hubbard, James, 22 Booth St, Spitalfields, London, cm and u (1827–28). [D]

Hubbard, John, Queen St, Bloomsbury, London, carver (1755). Notice in *Public Advertiser*, 13 September 1755 concerning his app., Joseph Goulding who had absented himself from his master's service, warned 'all Persons not to harbour or employ him, for they shall be prosecuted according to law . . .'.

Hubbard, John, 21 Middle Moorfields, London, cm and chairmaker (1787). Insured his utensils and stock for £600 on 19 February 1787. [GL, Sun MS vol. 344, p. 129]

Hubbard, John Peters, Teignmouth, Devon, cm and u (1805–40). Trading in the Strand, 1823–24, and Regent Pl., 1830. Advertised in *Exeter Flying Post* for a cabinet maker on 23 May 1805; for workmen on 5 February 1807 and 3 March 1808; and as agent in the sale of a house in Teignmouth on 30 November 1809. Declared bankrupt on 28 May 1840. [D] See Hubbard, —, and J. P. Hubbard.

Hubbard, John, 21 Wilson St, Finsbury Sq., London, u, cm and furniture warehouseman (1807–14). [D]

Hubbard, John, 14 Grubb St, Cripplegate, London, cm and broker (1810). Took out a Sun Insurance policy on 7 or 9 June 1810 for £300, of which stock and utensils accounted for £210. [GL, Sun MS vol. 449, ref. 846041]

Hubbard, John, address unrecorded, cm (1810). Submitted a bill to the Duke of Northumberland in 1810 for a 'mahogany eliptic breakfast table' costing £2 10s; two square ones at £3 3s; a backgammon box, £1 4s; and a tea tray. [V&A archives]

Hubbard, John, Louth, Lincs., cm and joiner (1819–41). Trading at Eastgate, 1819–35, and Bridge St in 1841. [D]

Hubbard, John, address unrecorded, cm and u (1830). Sent a bill to J. S. Russell, Esq., for work done and goods supplied to Russell's yacht in 1830, totalling £16 16s. Items included, on 15 June 'Hire of Mahogany Biddett, small Bedst.ᵈ & fuste and hair matting for Dᵒ to the 6th Sept. 12 W'ks. at 2/6'; on 17 June, a painted floor cloth costing £2 7s 6d; on 18, a tea caddy at 13s. and a 'stout Brussel Carpet', £3 16s 3d and fitting it; on 19 June 'Two Setts Mahogany Bookshelves with 4 brass plates and 4 brass Rods for Do.', £1 1s; and on 22 June a 'Corner Shelf for Mrs. Russell's Cabinet', 5s 6d. J. S. Russell later changed his name to Pakington on inheriting Westwood Park, Worcs. He became 1st Lord of the Admiralty and 1st Lord Hampton. [Worcs. RO, 2309/705: 380/55 (i)]

Hubbard, John, Granby Yd, Grantham, Lincs., chairmaker and wheelwright (1841). Named in the 1841 Census. Windsor chair recorded bearing stamp of 'HUBBARD GRANTHAM'. [*Furn. Hist.*, 1978, pl. 49A and B]

Hubbard, William, Norwich, cm, Windsor and fancy chairmaker and dealer in Dutch rushes (1801–42). Recorded at 12 Broad St, St Giles in 1801; 12 St Giles's, c.1803; Fisher's Lane in 1810; and Bethel St from 1822. Admitted freeman on 3 May 1803, not by apprenticeship. Former app., Edmund Drury, chair turner, admitted freeman on 24 February 1828. [D; Norwich freemen reg. and poll bks]

Hubbard, William, Watton, Norfolk, turner and chairmaker (1822–30). [D]

Hubbard, Zechariah, Hampstead, London, cm (1770). Took out a Hand in Hand Insurance policy in 1770 for £150 on brick, and £50 on timber. [GL, Hand in Hand MS, vol. 110, ref. 81851]

Hubbeck, Katherine, address unrecorded, upholder (1712). Admitted freeman of the Upholders' Co. on 1 October 1712. [GL, Upholders' Co. records]

Hubbersley, William, Preston, Lancs., chairmaker (1822–42). Named in the Preston Guild records in 1822 and 1842 as son of Thomas Butcher, deceased. Probably of Hubbersley & Kelley, chairmakers, Skye St, Preston, 1842. [D]

Hubbert, Thomas, address unrecorded, cm (1803). Subscribed to Sheraton's *Cabinet Dictionary*, 1803.

Hubberts, Messrs, Westgate St, Bath, Som., cm (1812). Destruction of premises by fire on 26 December 1812 reported in *Gents Mag.*

Hubbock, William, Cragg, Whitby, Yorks., cm (1823). [D]

Hubie, John, Ogleforth, York, cm, joiner, carpenter and house-builder (1823). [D]

Hubie, William, 3 Ogleforth, York, joiner and cm (1830). [D]

Huby, Henry, Lower Westwick St, Norwich, furniture broker and cm (1836). [D]

Huby, Richard, Lower Westwick St, Norwich, furniture broker and cm (1817–42). Son of Simon Huby, barber; admitted freeman on 22 November 1817. [D; Norwich freemen reg. and poll bk]

Huby, William, Norwich, cm (1818–30). Recorded in St Lawrence's parish in 1818, and St Margaret's in 1830. [Poll bks]

Huck, John, Lancaster and London, cm (1756–68). App. to G. Rawes in 1756, and admitted freeman of Lancaster, 1767–68, when stated of London. Polled at Lancaster of London in 1768. [Lancaster app. reg. and freemen rolls]

Hucks, Phil., Harwich, Essex, cm (1785). Probate will dated 1785. [*Wills at Chelmsford*].

Hucks, William, Harwich, Essex, cm (1823–24). [D]

Hucks, William, 18 Punderson Pl., Bethnal Green Rd, London, cm and u (1827–28). [D]

Huddesford, John, address unrecorded. Submitted a bill to Lord Leigh dated 1747–48, for 'A Large neat Tea Board' costing £2 2s; 'A large Waiter', 8s 6d, and a small one at 10s. Bill receipted by Huddesford's nephew, Richard Steane. [Shakespeare Birthplace Trust, Leigh receipts, DR 18/5]

Huddleston, Edward, Liverpool, cm (1780–1818). Addresses given at Pilkington's Ct, Leeds St in 1780, and 7 Vauxhall Rd in 1818. Petitioned freedom on servitude to John Walker, and admitted freeman on 11 September 1780. Father of John Huddleston, cm, who petitioned freedom in 1812. Took app. named William Osborne in 1810, who petitioned freedom in 1818. [D; Liverpool freemen reg. and committee bk]

Huddleston, Edward John, 24 Vernon St, Liverpool, cm (1818). Admitted freeman on 11 June 1818. [Liverpool freemen reg.]

Huddleston, George, 6 Nassau St, Middlx Hospital, London, cm, u and chairmaker (1826–28). Trading in partnership with James Huddleston. [D]

Huddleston, George, 80 High Holborn, London, chair and sofa manufacturer (1829). [D]

Huddleston, George, Manchester Row, Holloway Rd, Holloway, London, cm, chair and sofa manufacturer (1838). [D]

Huddleston, James, 6 Nassau St, Middlx Hospital, London, cm, u and chairmaker (1826–39). Trading in partnership with George Huddleston, 1826–28. [D]

Huddleston, William, Leeds, Yorks., cm (1828–30). Trading at 26 Park Lane, 1828–29, and 1 Meadow Lane in 1830 also as an u. [D]

Huddlestone, John, Liverpool, cm (1811–12). Trading at 18 and 19 Smithfield St in 1811. Petitioned freedom as son of Edward Huddleston, cm, and admitted freeman on 5 October 1812. [D; Liverpool freemen reg.]

Huddon, Alexander, Headon St, London, cm (1784). [Poll bk]

Hude, Robert, address unrecorded, cm (1803). Subscribed to Sheraton's *Cabinet Dictionary*, 1803.

Hudgebout, James, at 'The Looking Glass', Cornhill, London, glass grinder and cabinet seller (1704). Advertised in the press in 1704 that he was 'selling off stock as he is leaving off trade'. [Heal] See John Burrough at the same address until *c*.1690.

Hudleston, —, Whitehall, London. Named in the Royal Wardrobe accounts in 1676 receiving £1 16s 'for a chaire with Elbowes and Iron worke in them and a table to it moveable with Iron worke.' [*Conn.*, vol. 108, 1941, p. 168]

Hudleston, Mrs, Whitehaven, Cumb., u (d.1832). Death on 5 July 1832 'after only two days illness' reported in *Liverpool Mercury*, 13 July.

Hudson, —, address unrecorded. On 29 July 1718 he was paid £4 3s for a japan card table supplied to the Hon. Wrey and Lady Saunderson. [Lincoln RO, Monson 10, 1/A/16]

Hudson, —, St James's St, London, u (d.1735). Death reported in contemporary newspapers. [Heal]

Hudson, —, Marylebone Way, London, carver and gilder (1771). Mentioned in a memorandum at the end of the 1771 diary of Edward Morant of Brokenhurst Park, Hants. [Owned by E. Morant, Royden Manor, Hants.]

Hudson, Mrs, Durtwick St, North Shields, Northumb., cm and joiner (1827). Widow of Andrew Hudson. [D] See John Hudson at this address.

Hudson, David, St Nicholas's parish, Bristol, u (1715–22). [Poll bks]

Hudson, Edward, Lancaster, cm (1802–05). Announced in *Lancaster Gazette*, 20 November 1802, that 'he intends, in a few days, to commence carrying on the above business, in all its branches, at the shop on the Green Area, Lancaster, lately occupied by Mr. Jeremiah Sowerby; and hopes, by employing the best workmen, and charging the lowest prices, to merit a share of the patronage of the public. E. Hudston has to let, and may be entered upon immediately, the house late in the possession of the said Mr. Sowerby, on the Green Area.' Declared bankrupt by 27 April 1805, when the sale of his household and stock furniture was advertised in *Lancaster Gazette*. Stock consisted of 'feather beds, bedsteads and hangings; mahogany card tables, chairs and corner cupboards, writing desks, chests of drawers, swing and pier looking glasses, carpets, and a variety of other house and kitchen furniture. Also a large quantity of New Furniture; consisting of wardrobes, toilets, liquor cases, tea caddies, clocks and cases, looking glasses, dining tables, card tables, and a variety of other new goods'; as well as mahogany and other timber, benches, tools and brasswork.

Hudson, Edward, High Wycombe, Bucks., caner (b. *c*.1816–41). Aged 25 at the time of the 1841 Census.

Hudson, Elizabeth, 7 Richmond St, Salford, Lancs., u (1836). [D]

Hudson, Ellin, address unrecorded, joiner and/or chairmaker (1691). Provided a chest of drawers, two armed cane chairs and twelve other chairs, costing a total of £8 2s 6d to Temple Newsam House, Leeds. [*Furn. Hist.*, 1967]

Hudson, Francis, York, joiner (1709–33). Trading in Stonegate in 1729. Son of Francis Hudson, whitesmith; admitted freeman by patrimony in 1709. Took apps named John Busfield on 4 April 1716; Anthony Busfield on 5 October 1719; John Hagues on 11 February 1723; Watt Myers on 7 September 1730; and William Varley on 29 September 1733. Advertised sale in *York Courant*, 5 August 1729, at his premises 'at the sign of the Buroe, Coffin and Chair, in Stonegate, nigh the Minster-Gates, York, Cabinets of all Kinds, Cane Chairs, Bass-bottom'd Chairs, Leather-bottom'd Chairs, and Wood-bottome'd Chairs, Dutch Tables, Card Tables &c. Corner Cupboards, Desks and Book-Cases, and all other Sorts of Joiner Work: Likewise all sorts of Baskets, and Basket Work.' [*Surtees Soc.*, vol. 102, p. 197; York app. reg.]

Hudson, George, address unrecorded. Supplied Charles II with

two looking-glasses twenty-five inches in length, described at the time as 'large'. [Wills, *Looking-Glasses*]

Hudson, James, Tickhill, Yorks., cm (1731–54). Took app. named Jos. Wood of Milton in 1731 for £6 6s. Possibly the James Hudson who subscribed to Chippendale's *Director*, 1754. [S of G, app. index]

Hudson, James, Newcastle, upholder (1734). [Poll bk]

Hudson, James, 170 Pilgrim St and 50 Carliol St, Newcastle, joiner and cm (1827–29). [D]

Hudson, John, St Anne's Westminster, London, cm and u (1747–58). Declared bankrupt with his partner, Lawrence Rudy(e)ard, *Gents Mag.*, August 1747; and *Williamson's Liverpool Advertiser*, 1 December 1758, when they are described as 'late of Thrift Street [Frith St, Soho], in the parish of St. Ann'.

Hudson, John, Salisbury, Wilts., cm (1755). App. to John and Thomas Snow, cm, of Salisbury, on 27 August 1755, by indenture for £31 10s. [*Wilts. Apps and their Masters*]

Hudson, John, Green St, Leicester Fields, London, carver and gilder (1777). Insured his house for £100 in 1777. [GL, Sun MS vol. 254, p. 497]

Hudson, John, Newcastle, u (1777–92). Former apps admitted freemen: Ralph Wightman on 25 February 1777, and Lancelot Bourne on 12 July 1792. [Newcastle freemen reg.]

Hudson, John, Durtwick St, North Shields, Northumb., cm (1828–34). Recorded at no. 34 in 1834. [D] See Mrs Hudson.

Hudson, John, 7 Nelson Pl., Old Kent Rd, London, cm (1835–37). [D]

Hudson, John, 13 Humber St, Hull, Yorks., chairmaker (1835). John F. Hudson was trading at no. 12 as a furrier in 1838. [D]

Hudson, Joseph snr, London, freeman upholder (1715–d. by 1732/33). Took app. named Thomas Doughty, 1715–33. His son, Joseph Hudson jnr, admitted freeman of the Upholders' Co., 1732–33. [GL, Upholders' Co. records]

Hudson, Joseph jnr, address unrecorded, upholder (1732–33). Son of Joseph Hudson, upholder of London; admitted freeman of the Upholders' Co. by patrimony on 7 March 1732/33. [GL, Upholders' Co. records] Possibly:

Hudson, Joseph, next door to 'The Fountain Tavern', Southwark, London, u (1733). Insured household goods and stock in trade in his house only for £1,000 on 25 July 1753. [GL, Sun MS vol. 38, ref. 61462]

Hudson, Joseph, 39 Wardour St, London, cm and upholder (1785). Took out a Sun Insurance policy on 3 May 1785 for £50 on household goods, and £150 on utensils, stock and goods in trust. [GL, Sun MS vol. 328, p. 205]

Hudson, Joseph, 21 St Paul's Churchyard, London, cm and u (1785–d.1788). Took out a Sun Insurance policy on 31 December 1785 for £800, utensils, stock and goods in trust accounting for £500. Death reported in *Gents Mag.*, July 1788. [D; GL, Sun MS vol. 335, p. 127]

Hudson, Joseph, Newcastle, joiner and cm (1811–24). Trading at Ouseburn in 1811 and Pilgrim St in 1824. [D]

Hudson, Joseph, 4 St Ann's Terr., Liverpool, cm (1835). [D]

Hudson, Joseph, Henry & Henry, 257 Whitechapel Rd, London, cm and u (1839). [D]

Hudson, Joseph, High Wycombe, Bucks., caner (b. *c*.1816–41). Aged 25 at the time of the 1841 Census.

Hudson, Richard, address unrecorded, upholder (1736–44). Son of Edward Hudson, yeoman of Haverford West, Pembroke, S. Wales; app. to Daniel Demee on 26 January 1736. Admitted freeman of the Upholders' Co. by servitude on 1 February 1743/44. [GL, Upholders' Co. records]

Hudson, Richard, 4 High St, Marylebone, London, cm (1785–86). Took out Sun Insurance policies on 2 May 1785 for £50 on household goods; and on 14 July 1786 for £200 on house and shed in Hanover Rd. [GL, Sun MS vol. 328, p. 204; vol. 331, p. 267]

Hudson, Robert, Westminster, London, cm (1713). Took app. named John Maunders, son of John, late of Southwark, surgeon, for £10. [V&A archives]

Hudson, Robert, address unrecorded, cm (1754). Subscribed to Chippendale's *Director*, 1754.

Hudson, Solomon, house and manufactory at 16 Gt Titchfield St, Cavendish Sq., London, carver and gilder, cm and upholder (1780–93). [D] Clearly a skilful and highly-esteemed craftsman, he received prestigious patronage, and carried out work according to Robert Adam's designs. Simple trade card, c.1791, with anthemion border is in the Heal Coll., BM. Of 16 Litchfield St, he took out a Sun Insurance policy on 10 April 1787 for £1,700 on household goods, utensils and stock in workshops behind his house. [GL, Sun MS vol. 342, ref. 529400] He subscribed to George Richardson's *Treatise on the Five Orders of Architecture*, 1787.

WEST WYCOMBE PARK, BUCKS. Hudson supplied looking-glass frames for which he was paid £42 on 25 November 1780. [James Lees-Milne, *West Wycombe Park, Bucks*.]

NEW BURLINGTON ST, LONDON. Carried out much clearly sumptuous work for Sir John Griffin Griffin of Audley End, Essex, carving and gilding picture frames and architectural features at his London house. In 1781 he was paid £160 for two pier glasses and frames; and on 27 May 1783 he receipted a long bill for £107 10s 4d. This included, on 23 December 1782, '4 Oval straining frames for Mr. Rebecca's pictures', costing 10s, and sent to Audley End; on 28 December regilding the ogee moulding in the Drawing Room at New Burlington St; on 31 December 'Carving of 4 rich Garandoles from Mr. Adam's designs, Gilt in Burnish Gold, with 2 branches to Each Compleat', costing £31 4s; and 'Carving 4 Rich Ornaments with 4 Oval frames Gilt in Burnish Gold Compleat' and fixing, £32 3s. In 1783 Hudson charged £16 for 'Carving a Large Oval Carlomoral picture frame for Lady Griffins portrait Gilt in Burnish Gold wood-work and Turning Compleat'; and 'Carving a Large Ornament of Drapery festoons with other enrichments Gilt in Burnish Gold from Mr. Adam Design', for £6 16s 6d. On 18 February 1783 he charged 11s for 'One Man's time & Materials making good the Gilding of all the Chairs & Sophas in Drawing Room'; and on 17 May, for 'Carving of two large Circular picture frames, Gilt in Burnish Gold, Turning & Wood work Comp.'. [Essex RO, D/DBy/A 39/4; A41/5; A212] Hudson is also recorded as having supplied a 'rich picture frame 4 ins broad to a pattern gilt in burnish gold wood and complete for the View of Audley End House', costing £5 10s 6d in 1789. [J. D. Williams, *Audley End, the Restoration of 1762–1797*, p. 40] As Lord Howard, Sir John Griffin Griffin continued to patronise Solomon Hudson, commissioning three carved and gilt picture frames from him for his London House in New Burlington St in 1790, totalling £15 13s 3d. [Essex RO, D/DBy/A50/4]

BLICKLING HALL, NORFOLK. Solomon Hudson is recorded as having supplied the Earl of Buckinghamshire with large gilt pier and chimney glasses, frames for tapestry and two full-length portraits of George III and Queen Charlotte in June 1782. His bill totalled £409 6s 6d. [Nat. Trust Guide to *Blickling Hall*, p. 38; Wills, *Looking-Glasses*; Heal]

In 1793 Hudson retired from trade, and his remaining stock in trade was sold by Mr Christie at 16 Gt Titchfield St on 12 and 13 June. The catalogue listed his stock, which included 'Pictures, fine prints by Hogarth, framed and glazed, loose drawings, prints, books, and a variety of valuable effects … large glasses of distinguished magnitude, superb girandoles

and candelabras; beautiful inlaid pier tables, writing desks, teaboards, chests, caddies, excellent mahogany tables of various denominations; dressing stands, glasses, escritoires, and a profusion of neat articles in the cabinet, carving and gilding branches, finished in a stile of superior workmanship, from the most approved designs of the principal nobility. Also a large quantity of old picture frames, carved ornaments, work benches, old iron, lead &c….'. [Christie's archives, 8 King St, London; *C. Life*, 6 October 1950, p. 1090] He is perhaps the Hudson, carver of London named in the account book of Rev. Robert Thelwall of Redbourne Hall, Lincs., on 22 November 1772, receiving £95. [Lincoln RO, RED 3/1/4/6/2] He is also perhaps the 'S.H., carver', who published *Twelve New Designs for Frames for Looking-Glasses, Pictures &c.*, on 3 February 1779. He has been recorded, apparently erroneously, as Stephen Hudson.

Hudson, T., York, cm (1826). Declared bankrupt, *London Gazette*, 18 March 1826.

Hudson, Thomas, Sunderland, Co. Durham, cm (1803). Subscribed to Sheraton's *Cabinet Dictionary*, 1803.

Hudson, Thomas, 13 Shorely St, Burnley, Lancs., cm (1824). [D]

Hudson, Thomas, 21 Little Wild St, London, chair and sofa maker (1839). [D]

Hudson, Timothy Smithson, Hull, Yorks., painter and gilder (1838–42). Trading at 3 Fenkle St, 1838–39, and 9 Sewer Lane in 1840. [D]

Hudson, William, Newcastle, u (1740–80). Admitted freeman in 1740. Former apps admitted freemen: Joseph Furnass on 10 October 1763; Thomas Crosby on 24 August 1765; Gilbert Liddell on 8 October 1774; and John Eltringham on 12 September 1780. His sons William and Edward admitted freemen by patrimony on 10 October 1774 and 25 February 1777 respectively. Advertised in *Newcastle Courant*, 16 June 1770, that he 'sells all kinds of Cabinet work & chairs & he has taken a convenient room in Alnwick where attendance will be given every Saturday for sale of the same — Newton on the Moor, near Alnwick.' [Newcastle freemen reg. and poll bks]

Hudson, William, Rochdale Rd, Bacup, Lancs., cm (1825–28). [D]

Hudson, William, Louth, Lincs., cm and joiner (1819–28). Recorded at Eastgate, 1819–22, and Maiden Row, 1826–28. [D]

Hudson, William, Oldham Lane, Oldham, Lancs., cm (1834). [D]

Hudson, William, Wetherby, Yorks., joiner and/or cm, auctioneer (1837). [D]

Hudson & Co., London, cm (1746). Named with Messrs Campbell-Bruce in the London account of the Rt Hon. Earl of Stear, receiving payments. [Scottish RO, GD135/Box 55/31]

Hudson & Corney, 4 and 13 Broad St, Soho, London, upholders and cm (1790–1811). [D] Late George III satinwood secrétaire-cabinet recorded, with three-quarter galleried top and two narrow glazed cupboard doors backed by pleated silk above the panelled fall-flap enclosing short drawers, the base with a drawer on square tapering legs joined by a concave-fronted platform shelf, bearing the trade label of 'Hudson and Corney, CABINET MAKERS, Upholsterers, UNDERTAKERS &c. At their Manufactories and Ware Rooms, N°. 4 and N°. 13 Broad Street, Soho. NB. Rout Chairs &c. let on hire.' Inscription is inside oval Neo-classical frame, illustrated by two simple ladder and splat-back chairs. [Christie's, 29 November 1979, lot 59 and 11 June 1981, lot 103] Subscribed to Sheraton's *Drawing Book*, 1793, and *Cabinet Dictionary*, 1803. Named in his list of master cabinet makers, 1803. Hudson, cm of Broad St, took out a Sun Insurance policy on 14 May 1804 for £100 on a warehouse belonging to John Bayford. [GL, Sun MS vol. 431, ref. 762292]

Hudspeth, George, 17 Pilgrim St, Gateshead, cm and furniture broker (1824–38). [D]

Hudspeth, George, John & William, Dog Bank, Gateshead, cm and furniture brokers (1827). [D]

Hudspeth, John, Dog Bank, and 34 High St, Gateshead, cm and furniture broker (1824–34). [D]

Hudspeth, John & Thomas, Newcastle, cm and furniture brokers (1834). [D]

Hudspeth, Rachel, Dog Bank, Gateshead, cm and furniture broker (1824–33). [D]

Hudspeth, Robert, 179 High St, Gateshead, Co. Durham, cm (1833). [D]

Hudspeth, Thomas, Dog Bank, Gateshead, Co. Durham, cm and furniture broker (1833–34). Trading at no. 10 in 1834. [D]

Hudspeth, William, Roddam's Ct, Gateshead, Co. Durham, cm (1828–29). [D]

Hües, Michel, address unrecorded, gilder (1703). Rendered an account for £56 3s 10d to the 2nd Duke of Bedford for making and gilding armchairs, chairs, stools and walnut mouldings. [Bedford Office, London] Possibly:

Huet, Michael, address unrecorded, dealer in lacquer (1695). Supplied picture frames to Petworth House, Sussex. [C. Life, 4 September 1980, p. 800; Apollo, May 1977, p. 361]

Hufton, William, address unrecorded, u (1803). Subscribed to Sheraton's Cabinet Dictionary, 1803.

Hugall, Thomas, William St, Bishop Wearmouth, Sunderland, Co. Durham, cm (1823–27). Notice in Durham County Advertiser, 30 August 1823, that the partnership between Thomas Hugall and Thomas Armstrong, joiners and cm, had been dissolved. 'The businesses will in future be carried on by each partner individually'. [D]

Huges, John, address unrecorded, u (1803). Subscribed to Sheraton's Cabinet Dictionary, 1803.

Huggett, John, address unrecorded, upholder (1725–60). Son of John Huggett, blacksmith of Brockham, Surrey. App. to Benjamin Robinson on 20 January 1725, and admitted freeman of the Upholders' Co. by servitude on 3 May 1736. Took app. named James Buggs, 1750–60. [GL, Upholders' Co. records]

Huggett, John, London, chairmaker (1803–11). Recorded at Borough Rd, 1803–04; Bow Rd in 1808; and as Huggert in 1811. Named in Sheraton's list of master cabinet makers, 1803. [D; PRO, IRI/37]

Huggett, John, 11 Charlotte St, Old St Rd, London, chair and sofa manufacturer (1827–28). [D]

Huggins, Henry, Norwich, cm, u and chairmaker (1794–1836). Trading at Middle Westwick, opposite 'The Duke of York' in 1810; Upper Westwick St, 1822 and 1836; and St Benedict St, 1830. Former apps admitted freemen cm: James Rackham on 3 May 1826; Francis Ryder on 24 February 1828; and Paul Springall Cubbitt on 24 February 1830. [D; Norwich freemen reg. and poll bks]

Huggins, John, Coombe St, Exeter, Devon, cm (1838). Daughter Ann Lovering bapt. at St Mary Major on 1 April 1838. [PR (bapt.)]

Huggins, Miss Maria, Norwich, u (1839–42). Trading at St Andrew's, Broad St, St John's Maddermarket in 1839, and 10 St Andrew's St in 1842. [D]

Huggins, Richard, Bristol, upholder (1801–24). Recorded at St Augustine's Back in 1801; no. 13, 1805–12; and 21 Orchard St in 1824. Declared bankrupt, Exeter Flying Post, 11 October 1804. [D]

Hughes, —, address unrecorded, cm (1767). Supplied bed and furniture for Audley End, Essex, costing £52 on 30 May 1767. [V&A archives]

Hughes, —, London (?). The household expenses of the Digby family included payment in 1774 of £13 6s to 'Mr. Hughes … For Furniture sent to Sherborne last year'. [Sherbourne Castle papers]

Hughes, —, London, u (1793). Subscribed to Sheraton's Drawing Book, 1793.

Hughes, —, New St, Devonport, Devon, cm (1814). [D]

Hughes, —, address unrecorded. In 1838 supplied 'new furniture' for Stafford House, London, costing £64. [Staffs. RO, D593/R/1/26/8]

Hughes, Alice, Mill Lane, Liverpool, u (1834–39). Recorded at no. 5, 1804–05, no. 7 in 1837, and no. 12 in 1839. [D]

Hughes, Benjamin, Busby St, near Church Row, Church St, Bethnal Green, London, broker of household goods and cm (1812). Took out a Sun Insurance policy on 28 December 1812 for £400 of which £20 accounted for stock and utensils in workshop, and £120 for a house in Brick Lane, Spitalfields. [GL, Sun MS vol. 455, ref. 877383]

Hughes, Daniel, Wheelock St, Middlewich, Cheshire, cm (1828–34). [D]

Hughes, Edward, 14 Stamford St, Ashton-under-Lyne, Lancs., joiner and cm (1828–34). [D]

Hughes, Edward, Summer Row, Handsworth, Birmingham, cm and chairmaker (1828–35). Recorded at no. 2, 1828–30. [D]

Hughes, George, Whitchurch, Salop, cm and chairmaker (1828–40). Recorded at Claypit St, 1828–35. Named in a list of shareholders of the Whitchurch and Ellesmere Banking Co. in Chester Chronicle and North Wales Advertiser, 14 August 1840. [D]

Hughes, Henry, Little Berrington St, Hereford, chairmaker and turner (1830). [D]

Hughes, Howell, London, upholder (1772–79). Son of Thomas Hughes, Gent. of Glasbury, Radnor. App. to Herbert Pyefinch, spectacle maker, on 9 March 1772, and John Phillips on 14 December 1775. Discharged by judgement of the Chamberlain, and admitted freeman of the Upholders' Co. on 2 July 1779, in which year his address is given at 20 Fleet St, Salesbury Ct. [GL, Upholders' Co. records]

Hughes, Hugh, address unrecorded, upholder (1722–30). Son of Hugh Hughes, yeoman of Brombo, Denbigh. App. to Michael Bradshaw on 18 October 1722, and admitted freeman of the Upholders' Co. by servitude on 7 October 1730. [GL, Upholders' Co. records]

Hughes, Hugh, Witton St, Northwich, Cheshire, cm (1822). [D]

Hughes, James, London, cm (1793). Subscribed to Sheraton's Drawing Book, 1793.

Hughes, James, Liverpool, u (b.1778–d.1801). Notice in Billinge's Liverpool Advertiser, 25 September 1801 reads: 'DIED On Thursday se'nnight Mr. James Hughes, upholsterer, aged 23, son of Mrs. Sarah Ryan, widow, Tarleton-street, & on Friday last Mr. John Hughes, Ornament Painter, aged 26, brother to the above. Their faithful service to their masters & sobriety of manners, rendered them truly exemplary, & their loss is regretted by all who knew them & severely felt by their disconsolate mother.'

Hughes, James, Gt Brook St, Birmingham, gilder (1818). [D]

Hughes, James, 27 Oldham Rd, Manchester, chairmaker (1828). [D]

Hughes, James, Park St, Chester, cm (1833). Son of the late James Hughes, gardener, his death on 3 April 1833 'after a protracted illness' was reported in Chester Courant and Advertiser for North Wales, 6 April.

Hughes, Job, Derby, cm (1800–22). Took app. named William Bakewell in 1800. [Leicester freemen rolls] Recorded at King St, 1818–22. [D]

Hughes, John, Bristol, u (1715). [Poll bk]

Hughes, John, Bath, Som., upholder (1774). [Bristol poll bk]

Hughes, John, Brewer St, London, cm (1774). [Bristol poll bk]

Hughes, John, parish of St James, Bristol, upholder (1781–84). [Poll bks]

Hughes, John, Liverpool, chairmaker (1790–1829). Addresses given at back of 10 Fontenoy St in 1790; 5 behind Haymarket, with manufactory at 19–21 Haymarket, 1807–13; 13 Haymarket, 1813–14; nos 21–25, 1814–16; 18 Trowbridge St in 1821; and 21–23 Clayton St, 1827–29. [D]

Hughes, John, Market Harborough, Leics., u and broker (1810). [D]

Hughes, John & Outhwaite, 23 St Paul's Churchyard, London, u (1813–16). [D]

Hughes, John, Liverpool, cm (1816). Petitioned freedom on servitude to John Ward Turner, and admitted freeman on 7 June 1816. [Liverpool freemen reg.]

Hughes, John, Stamford St, Ashton-under-Lyne, Lancs., joiner and cm (1828). [D]

Hughes, John, 20 King St, Derby, cm and u (1828–35). [D]

Hughes, John F., 138 Westgate St, Gloucester, cm and u (1839–40). [D]

Hughes, Joseph, Eaton St, Liverpool, cm (1818–29). Trading at no. 22 in 1818; no. 8 in 1823; and 61 in 1829. [D] See Thomas Hughes.

Hughes, Joseph, Goswell St Rd, London, upholder and undertaker (1820–35). Trading at no. 11 in 1820; no. 26 in 1821; no. 43 in 1825; and 11 Goswell Rd in 1835. [D]

Hughes, Joseph, London, cm (1826). [Hereford poll bk]

Hughes, Patrick, 'opposite ye Royal Hospital in ye Market Place, Greenwich', London, cm, u etc. (1778–c.1780). Trade card, c.1780, shows Chippendale-style furniture, elaborate bed, break-front bookcase, serpentine cabinet, chest of drawers and two chairs. Declared bankrupt, Gents Mag., 1778. [Heal Coll., BM]

Hughes, Peter, 19 Rose St, Preston, Lancs., cm (1825). [D]

Hughes, Richard, St Peter, Bristol, cm (1754). [Poll bk]

Hughes, Richard, Mardol, Shrewsbury, cm (1796). Named in the Shrewsbury burgess roll as brother of Thomas Hughes in 1796.

Hughes, Richard, Willow St, Oswestry, Salop, cm and joiner (1828). [D]

Hughes, Robert, see Nicholas Morel & Robert Hughes.

Hughes, Robert, Liverpool, cm (1804–39). Addresses given at 76 Stanley St, Dale St in 1804; 6 Casey St in 1813; 31 Bispham St in 1835; and 10 Grenville St North in 1839. [D]

Hughes, Robert, 115 Piccadilly, opposite Green Park, London, undertaker, u and cm to their Royal Highnesses the Duke and Duchess of Cambridge (1827–39). Submitted a bill to the Rt Hon. Lord Gwydir, receipted on 5 June 1827. Bill totalled £17 14s and included 'a Mahogany Boot and Shoe Horse with a Low Shelf and Brass Handle, including a Brown Holland Curtain to Hang over the Top to keep Dust from Shoes', costing £1 6s on 20 March; 'a Large Handsome Mahogany Bergere with High Scroll Back ... Damaged ... the Seat and Stuft Elbows Covered in Green Morocco finished with Silk Tufts' on 14 April; and '6 Small Light Chairs with Carved Tops and Twisted Spindles in the Back, Stained and Polished, Pink and White Willow Seats', costing £6 12s on 11 May. A further bill to Lord Gwydir listed 'a French Circular Table de Nuit in Fine Mahogany Highly Polished & Marble Slab', costing £3 3s on 15 December 1827; two cushions for Lord Gwydir's easy chair, covered with green leather, on 20 December; and a 'Tripod Flower Stand with Plinth Frieze & Feet in Fine Mahogany Highly Polished Supported by 3 Brass Columns Statuary Marble Slab Green Pan & Wire

Work', ornamented 'with 6 Ormolu Patras', costing £8 4s on 3 June 1828. [D; Lincoln RO, 2 ANC 6/202/65 and 78]

Hughes, Robert, 24 Long Alley, Finsbury, London, cm (1835–39). [D]

Hughes, Samuel, 8 St John's Pl., Liverpool, chairmaker (1811). [D]

Hughes, Samuel, Liverpool, u (1819). App. to Bartholomew Tyrer in 1819. [Liverpool app. enrolment bk]

Hughes, Samuel, 18 Bryam St, Liverpool, chair and bedstead manufactory (1823). [D]

Hughes, T., Cheltenham, Glos., cm (1839–40). [D] See Thomas Hughes.

Hughes, Thomas, Mardol, Shrewsbury, cm (1796). Named in the Shrewsbury burgess roll as brother of Richard Hughes in 1796.

Hughes, Thomas, Birmingham, cm (1800–35). Addresses given at 27 Moor St in 1800 and Gt Hampton St, 1816–35, no. 52 in 1835. [D]

Hughes, Thomas, Liverpool, cm (1818–34). Trading at Eaton St, 1818–23, and 4 Rose Sq., Rose Hill in 1834. [D] See Joseph Hughes.

Hughes, Thomas, Gloucester, cm and chairmaker (1820). [D]

Hughes, Thomas, Liverpool, rosewood stainer and painter (b.1799–d.1830). Death aged 31, 'much respected', reported in Liverpool Mercury, 15 October 1830.

Hughes, Thomas, 18 Clarence St, Cheltenham, Glos., cm and u (1839). [D]

Hughes, Timothy, 27 Devon St, Liverpool, cm (1839). [D]

Hughes, Walter, College Green, Bristol, cm, paper hanging warehouseman and house agent (1835–40). Trading at no. 35, 1835–36; nos 35–36, 1837–39; and as Walter Hughes & Co. at no. 34 in 1840. [D] See William Hughes.

Hughes, William, Liverpool, cm (1786–96). App. to Robert Copeland in 1786, and admitted freeman on 25 May 1796. [Liverpool freemen reg.]

Hughes, William, Liverpool, cm (1816–d. by 1835). App. to John Mears, and admitted freeman on 7 June 1816. [Liverpool freemen reg.]

Hughes, William, Willow St, Oswestry, Salop, cm (1822–28). [D]

Hughes, William, Bristol, cm (1834–40). Trading at 35 College Green in 1834, and 33 King St, Queen Sq., 1839–40. [D] See Walter Hughes.

Hughes, William, Doctor's-fields, Maidstone, Kent, cm (1837–38). [Poll bks]

Hughes, William & Richard, Hatton Gdn, Liverpool, timber merchants, joiners and cm (1837–39). Trading at no. 4, and also 41 Stanley St in 1837; and 7 Hatton Gdns in 1839. [D]

Hughes & Son, Hackney Rd, London, cm (1826–27). [D]

Hughgill, John, Wibsey, Bradford, Yorks., cm (1822). [D]

Hulbeart, Thomas, at 'The Ship & Anchor', over against Gun Yard, Houndsditch, London, u and cm (1689–90). Advertised his business in contemporary newspapers: 'Where you may be furnished with several sorts of lin'd beds as Velvet, Damask, Mohair and Camblet ... already standing up with silk quilts suitable. Likewise Screwtores, Tables, Stands, Looking-glasses of Japan or other work as also Tapestry-Hangings of several sorts.' [Heal]

Hulbert, Edwin, Bristol, cm (1831–35). Addresses given at 2 St James's Terr., St James's Sq. in 1831; 27 Milk St, 1832–34; and 19 Broadmead in 1835. [D]

Hulbert, Messrs, Bath, Som., u and cm (1819–26). Addresses given at 24 Westgate St and 8 Kingsmead St in 1819 and 8 Quiet St in 1826. [D]

Hulett, Peter, Little Bartholomew Close, London, frame maker gilder (c.1760). His trade card features a Mannerist strapwork cartouche flanked by terms and centring on masks, framing inscription. [Heal]

Hull, —, Radcliff Highway, with house at Peckham, London, 'Eminent cabinet-maker and glass seller' (d.1743). [Harris, *Old English Furniture*, p. 24]

Hull, Charles, 2 Newman St, Oxford St, London, u and cm (1820). [D]

Hull, Christopher, Embsay, near Skipton, Yorks., cm (1822). [D]

Hull, Edwin, Devonshire Sq., Loughborough, Leics., cm (1840). [D]

Hull, Henry & Son, High St, Newmarket, Suffolk, u and cm (1839). [D]

Hull, James, address unrecorded, cm (1737). Submitted a bill dated 28 September 1737 to Temple Newsam House, Leeds, for two mahogany tables costing £3 2s 6d, one dining table for £2 4s, and 'One Frame for a Large Cabinet', £1 15s 6d. [*Furn. Hist.*, 1967]

Hulland, Samuel, Quay St, Worcester, cm (1835). Admitted freeman on 1 December 1835. [Worcester freemen rolls]

Hullard, Thomas, Stoke-on-Trent, Staffs., cm (1834). [D]

Hullard, Thomas, Hanford Bridge, Burton-on-Trent, Staffs., cm and chairmaker (1834). [D]

Hulley, James, St Mark's Lane, Newark, Notts., carver and gilder (1828). [D]

Hully, Christopher, Lancaster. Named in the Gillow records in 1808 working on a mangle. [Westminster Ref. Lib., Gillow vol. 344/99, p. 1850]

Hulme, Joseph, 25 Whitecross Bank, Manchester, u (1825). [D]

Hulme, Joseph Hilton, Salford and Manchester, cm and u (1828–40). Trading at 136 Chapel St, Salford, 1829–33; no. 138, 1836–39; and 34 Moseley St, Manchester in 1840. [D]

Hulme, Thomas, 23 Market Pl., Manchester, carver and gilder (1838–40). [D]

Hulme, William, 43 Thomas St, Manchester, cm (1829). [D]

Hulms, John, Nantwich, Cheshire, timber merchant and cm (1781). [D]

Hulse, Charles, Tunstall, Staffs., joiner, chairmaker and cm (1818–35). Recorded at Market Pl. as cm and u, 1828–35. [D]

Hulse, Henry, St Martin's St, Birmingham, u (1830–35). Trading at no. 3 in 1830 and no. 5 in 1835, also as a paper hanger. [D]

Hulston, John, Worcester St, Birmingham, cm (1835–39). Listed at no. 35 in 1835 and no. 34 in 1839. [D]

Hulton, Abraham, Walsall, Staffs., cm (1834). [D]

Hulton, Joseph, address unrecorded, upholder (1706–18). Admitted freeman of the Upholders' Co. on 31 July 1706. Took app. named Samuel Siddall, 1711–18. [GL, Upholders' Co. records]

Hulton, Robert, facing the Hay Market, Pall Mall, Westminster, London, picture framer (1720). Insured goods and merchandise in his house on 23 July 1720. [GL, Sun MS vol. 12, ref. 191999] Possibly:

Hulton, Robert, address unrecorded. On 21 October 1743 receipted a bill submitted to Lord Monson for £1 15s for cleaning and mending pictures and providing 'A Peartree Frame with a Gilt Sang'. [Lincoln RO, Monson 12]

Humberston, J., Baldock, Herts., cm, u and undertaker. Trade card, *c.*1820–30, is illustrated with elaborately-draped curtains, tip-up breakfast table, pole firescreen, sofa, chair and armchair. [Heal Coll., BM]

Humberstone, James, Milk St, Bristol, coach and cabinet carver (1818–40). Trading at no. 53, 1818–19, and no. 52, 1820–40. [D]

Humberstone, L., 15 Dighton St, Bristol, cabinet carver (1820). [D]

Humberstone, Matthew, Bristol, carpenter, cm and undertaker (1829–40). Trading at Hope Chapel Hill, near Dowry Sq., 1829–35; 6 Dowry Sq., 1826–28; and Green St, 1839–40. [D]

Humberstone, Thomas Garland, Bristol, cabinet carver (1815–19). Trading at Moon St, Black Fields in 1818; 15 Upper Maudlin St, 1816–17; and 15 Dighton St in 1819. [D]

Humble, Messrs., Newcastle, cm (1833–37). Supplied £1,650 worth of furniture and fittings for Lilburn Tower, Northumb., between 1833–37, made according to the designs of the architect. [*C. Life*, 8 November 1973, p. 1443]

Humble, H. G., Blackett St, Newcastle, carver and gilder (1838). [D]

Humble, John, address unrecorded. In 1828 supplied a set of heavily carved elm dining room furniture, consisting of a table, ten chairs, two armchairs and a cellaret, to Nunnykirk House, Northumb. The cellaret is of sarcophagus form, carved with gadrooning and acanthus decoration, and supported on lion-paw feet. The chairs have backs formed of two attenuated acanthus scrolls connecting a central palmette splat with plain top rail and acanthus cresting. The front legs take the form of consoles. A letter from Humble requesting payment mentions also drawing room furniture. [Bowes Museum, Barnard Castle, Co. Durham, photographic archive]

Humble, Thomas & Henderson, Jonathan, Strand, London, cm and u (1788–95). Trading at no. 424 in 1788. Notices regarding bankruptcy appeared in *Williamson's Liverpool Advertiser*, 3 November 1794, and *Billinge's Liverpool Advertiser*, 27 April 1795. [D]

Humble & Hartshorn, 20 Knightsbridge, London, cm (1835). [D]

Hume, —, address unrecorded. Provided furniture to Belvoir Castle, Lincs., early in the 19th century according to Wyatt's letters. [C. Hussey, *English Country Houses: Late Georgian*, p. 138]

Hume, James, 38 High St, Wapping, London, cm (1835). [D]

Hume, John, Wellingborough, Northants., cm (1823–30). Listed at Market Pl. in 1823 and Broad Green in 1830. [D]

Hume, John, Wooler, Northumb., joiner and cm (1827). [D]

Hume, Joseph, 43 Thomas St, Manchester, cm (1832–33). [D]

Hume, Robert, London, carver, gilder and cm (1808–40). Addresses given at 11 Crown St, St Giles's in 1808; 34 Gt Titchfield St, Cavendish Sq., 1809–11; 4 Gt Portland St, 1817; 4 Little Portland St in 1820; and 65 Berners St in 1837. Possibly the Robert Hume who is recorded in 1828 as furniture maker and agent to William Beckford. Possibly of Robert Hume & Son, carvers and gilders, who supplied pictures and carried out repairs and gilding, and carved and gilt frames at Charlecote Park, Warks., in 1829–32 for £100; and in 1836 for £126 16s 6d. Their bill was receipted in 1840. [D; *Burlington*, December 1980, p. 822; Warwick RO, L6/1118] Possibly of:

Hume & Son, London, carvers and gilders, cm (1820–35). Trading at 53 Wigmore St in 1820 and 56 Berners St in 1829. [D]

Hume, William, Manchester, timber merchant and cm (1831). Declared bankrupt, *Liverpool Mercury*, 30 September 1831.

Hummel, John Philip, 5 Brewer St, Golden Sq., London, cm (1808). Took out a Sun Insurance policy on 31 March 1808 for £800 on his house. [D; GL, Sun MS vol. 445, ref. 814917]

Humphery, John, Charing, Kent, u and barber (1776). Insured his house for £200 in 1776. [GL, Sun MS vol. 253, p. 532]

Humpherys, William, Audley St, London, carver (1749). [Poll bk]

Humphrey, C., 63 North St, Brighton, Sussex, cm and u (1827). [D]

Humphrey, George, 63 North St, Brighton, Sussex, cm and u (1826). [D] See George Humphreys.

Humphrey, George, 2 Edward Terr., Kensington, London, cm and u (1839). [D]

Humphrey, Henry, Honiton, Devon, cm and u (1808). Advertised sale by auction on leaving the district in *Sherborne Mercury*, 22 August 1808.

Humphrey, J. N., Brixton, London, u and cm (1838). [D]

Humphrey, John, 4 Elder St, London, cm and chairmaker (1784). [D]

Humphrey, Joseph, Woodall Pl., North Brixton, London, cm (1835). [D]

Humphrey, Mary, High Wycombe, Bucks., chairmaker (b. *c.* 1786–1841). Aged 55 at the time of the 1841 Census.

Humphrey, Robert, Charing, Kent, u (1793). [D]

Humphrey(s), William, address unrecorded, upholder (1711–13). Took app. named John Bristow of London on 7 November 1711 for £35 15s; Edward Slatford of Oxford on 2 July 1712 for £53 15s; and Anthony Brown of Hereford on 7 October 1713. [PRO, app. reg., IRI/1 and 2] Possibly:

Humphrey, William, Fetter Lane, London, u (1732). Declared bankrupt, *Gents Mag.*, May 1732. See William Humphreys and William Humphry.

Humphrey, William, Brighton Pl., Brighton, Sussex, cm and u (1831–43). Recorded at no. 10 in 1839 and no. 15, date unspecified. Children by wife Sarah bapt.: William on 10 March 1831; Sarah Elizabeth on 17 August 1832; Cornelius on 9 February 1834; George on 9 April 1835; Benjamin on 20 November 1836; and Harriet on 15 April 1838. [D; poll bks; PR (bapt.)]

Humphreys, Arthur, Bridge St, Kington, Herefs., cm and u (1840). [D]

Humphreys, Charles, Castle St, the Potteries, Staffs., cm (1818). [D]

Humphreys, Charles, 1 Bear Lane, Blackfriar's Rd, London, carver (1827–29). [D]

Humphreys, George, Worcester, joiner and cm (1761). App. to Robert Bele (?), joiner and cm; admitted freeman on 12 January 1761. [Worcester freemen rolls]

Humphreys, George, Lewes, Sussex, journeyman cm (1826–41). Recorded in North St, date unspecified, and Spring Gdns in 1837. [Poll bks]

Humphreys, George, 114 North St, Brighton, Sussex, cm and u (1839). [D] See George Humphrey.

Humphreys, Gwynn, Church St, Kington, Herefs., cm and u (1840). [D]

Humphreys, J., St Paul's Churchyard, London, u (1748–49). Appears to have acted as auctioneer in sale of stock of Radford, retiring toyman. [*General Advertiser*, 30 November 1748, 10 January 1749]

Humphreys, John, White Lion St, London, cm and chairmaker (1776–88). Trading at no. 4 in 1788. Took out a Sun Insurance policy in 1776 for £700 of which £510 accounted for utensils, stock, sawpit and shed. [D; GL, Sun MS vol. 253, p. 389]

Humphreys, John, parish of St Nicholas, Hereford, joiner and cm (1820). Admitted freeman on 17 July 1820. [Hereford freemen reg.]

Humphreys, John jnr, parish of All Saints, Hereford, joiner and cm (1832). App. to John Humphreys, joiner and cm of Hereford. Admitted freeman on 13 July 1832. [Hereford freemen reg.]

Humphreys, John, Church Lane, Walthamstow, London, cm and u (1832). [D]

Humphreys, Leonard, Birmingham, cm (1719–23). Took apps named Clare in 1719 and Green in 1723. [S of G, app. index]

Humphreys, Robert, address unrecorded, upholder (1732). Son of William Humphreys, upholder of London. Admitted freeman of the Upholders' Co. by patrimony on 3 May 1732. [GL, Upholders' Co. records]

Humphr(e)ys, Robert, Knightsbridge Terr., London, cm and upholder (1820–35). Trading at no. 4 in 1820; nos 4 and 6 in 1826 also as carpet warehouseman; and no. 6 in 1835. Took out Sun Insurance policies on 10 February 1820 for £1,450 of which stock and utensils accounted for £1,250; and on 7 February 1822 for £2,000, stock and utensils accounting for £1,800. [D; GL, Sun MS vol. 483, ref. 962857; vol. 493, ref. 989022]

Humphreys, Thomas, London, u and auctioneer (1731–d. 1766). Son of Thomas Humphreys of Winchcomb, Glos. 'Clerk'. App. to Arthur Osborn on 7 April 1731 and then to William Kilpin, 11 November 1735. Free of the Upholders' Co. by servitude, 3 February 1742. In 1747 trading in Newgate St but by 1756 had moved to St Paul's Churchyard. It was in June of this year that he auctioned the furniture and stock in trade of Stephen Theodore Janssen at the enamel works in York Pl., Battersea. Sale catalogues were obtainable from Humphreys or from William Chesson, a fellow upholsterer. Took as apps William Pinckney, 1749–55, Daniel Holbrow, 1755–62, and Noah Chivers, 1762–65. In 1762 he was elected a Fellow of the Society of Arts but four years later his death was announced. He appears to have owned eleven houses in Green Dragon Ct, Cow Lane, Snow Hill and after his death these were insured by Mary Jones and continued to be so insured until 1774. On 1 August 1753 Humphreys was paid £28 11s by the Earl of Dumfries. [GL, Upholders Co. records; Hand in Hand MS vol. 105, pp. 42, 192; Heal; *General Evening Post*, 29 May 1756; Dumfries papers DH 17]   B.A.

Humphreys, William, Fleet St, London, freeman upholder (1715–17). Took out a Hand in Hand Insurance policy on 29 April 1715 for £700 on his house. In 1716 and 1717 fined for non-service at St Bride's. [GL, Hand in Hand MS vol. 14, p. 285; GL, MS 6561, p. 9]

Humphreys, William, address unrecorded, freeman upholder (1732). His son, Robert Humphreys, admitted freeman of the Upholders' Co. by patrimony in 1732. [GL, Upholders' Co. records]

Humphreys, William, 13 Gt Earl St, London, cm and broker (1782). Took out a Sun Insurance policy in 1782 for £200 of which utensils and stock accounted for £80. [GL, Sun MS vol. 301, p. 369]

Humphreys, William, 78 Tottenham Ct Rd, London, cm (1791–93). Took out a Sun Insurance policy on 9 April 1791 for £300, £200 accounting for utensils, stock and goods in trust. [D; GL, Sun MS ref. 581992]

Humphreys & Atkinson, 177 Sloane St, Chelsea, London, cm and u (1823). [D]

Humphries, (or Humphrys), Thomas, London, upholder (1707). Free of the Upholders' Co., 6 August 1707. [GL, Upholders' Co. records]

Humphries, William, 4 Chapel St, Holywell Mount, London, chair and sofa manufacturer (1829). [D]

Humphris, Mrs, Parson's Lane, Banbury, Oxon., cm and u (1834). [D]

Humphris, Richard, Parson's Lane, Banbury, Oxon., cm and u (1833). [D]

Humphry, William, Fetter Lane, London, upholder (1724–27). Named in contemporary newspapers. [Heal] See William Humphrey.

Hundey, Thomas, 330 High St, Cheltenham, Glos., cm and u (1820). [D]

Hundrey, John, Plymouth, Devon, cm (1752). Took app. named Thomas in 1752. [S of G, app. index]

Hunsley, John, York, carver and gilder (1787–95). Son of John Hunsley, excise supervisor; app. to Robert Blakesley, carver and gilder, on 12 November 1787. Assigned to Robert Tomlinson, carver and gilder. Admitted freeman in 1795. [York app. reg. and freemen rolls]

Hunsley, Peter, Beverley, Yorks., cm (1777–1814). Trading at Market Pl. in 1814. Took out Sun Insurance policies in 1777 for £500, £200 accounting for his house and shops, £100 on stock; and on 24 February 1786 for £40 on his house, and £260 on thirteen houses adjoining. [D; poll bks; GL, Sun MS vol. 257, p. 392; vol. 334, p. 572]

Hunstan, Thomas, Boston, Lincs., cm (1784). [D]

Hunt, —, Castle St, near Cross Lane, Long Acre, London, u, broker, auctioneer and sworn appraiser (c.1780–84). Trade card shows two mirrors, two dining chairs, a tallboy, chest, Pembroke table, stand-up desk and grate, none distinguished. [Banks Coll., BM; Heal] See James Hunt of 1 Castle St.

Hunt, Anthony, 28 Bridge St, Bristol, cm (1794). [D]

Hunt, Benjamin, Brighton, Sussex, cm and u (1805–d.1824). Owned workshop and premises at top of Dorset Gdns, Edward St, 1805–07; recorded in St James's St, 1805–24, no. 27 in 1822, and no. 31, 1823–24. Edward St and St James's St run parallel with each other and are connected by Dorset Gdns. Children by Sarah Hunt bapt. at St Nicholas's: Lusha on 20 August 1815; Sarah Jane on 19 January 1817; Benjamin on 29 November 1820; and Frederick Joseph on 12 January 1825, by which time Benjamin had died. Sale of stock on bankruptcy advertised in *Brighton Herald*, 31 January 1807, 'at the Workshop and Premises, top of Dorset Gardens in Edward Street' on 21 February 1807: 'THE STOCK IN TRADE and HOUSEHOLD PROPERTY of Mr. Benjamin Hunt, a bankrupt; consisting of Mahogany Logs, Planks, Boards and Veneers, Oak Planks, Clamp Boards, Deals, Timber &c. A Press Bedstead and a variety of other Materials'. Sale also included freehold workshop, three freehold houses, and the lease of a large house facing Dorset Gdns. Auction of household furniture of Benjamin Hunt and lease of 7 St James's St advertised on 19 February 1807. Death reported in *Brighton Gazette*, 29 July 1824. Marriage of Louisa Sarah Hunt of 11 Grafton St, daughter of Benjamin Hunt, u, to George Marchant took place on 25 January 1840. Hunt & Marchant, cm and u, were trading at 31 St James's St in 1839. [D; PR (bapt. and marriage)] See Sarah Hunt.

Hunt, Charles, Cambridge, cm (1835–d.1840). Trading at Northampton St in 1835. Death reported in *Cambridge Chronicle and Journal*, 11 April 1840. [Poll bk]

Hunt, Charles B., George St, Gt Yarmouth, Norfolk, carver and gilder (1839). [D]

Hunt, Charles, 21 Cork St, Bond St, London, billiard table maker (1839). [D]

Hunt, George, Park Lane, Arundel, Sussex, cm and u (1832). [D]

Hunt, Henry, 12 Host St, Bristol, cm (1831). [D]

Hunt, Henry, 107 Regent's Quadrant, London, billiard table maker (1839). [D]

Hunt, J., 8 New Richmond, Pendleton, Salford, Lancs., cm and u (1829). [D] Possibly James Hunt of Pendleton.

Hunt, James, 1 Castle St, Long Acre, London, u (1813–19). [D] See Hunt, —.

Hunt, James, Cambridge, cm and u (1814–32). Recorded in Gt St Mary's parish in 1820, and Market Hill, 1832. Advertised in *Cambridge Chronicle and Journal*, 3 February 1832 as having been employed for eighteen years by Elliot Smith, who was now giving up the cabinet side of his business, whilst Hunt was running a cabinet and upholstery warehouse on Market Hill. Sale advertised on 28 September on Hunt's declining business and leaving Cambridge. Named in the calendar of marriage licence bonds on 19 September 1820. [Suffolk RO, FAA:50/2/119, p. 76]

Hunt, James, Pendleton, Salford, Lancs. u (1822–33). Listed near Leaf Sq., 1824–25, and at 8 New Richmond, 1829–33. [D]

Hunt, John, Salisbury Ct, Fleet St, London, u (1723). Took out a Sun Insurance policy on 3 August 1723 for £300 of which £250 accounted for his house where Thomas Gilmore of Faversham, Kent, lived; and £50 on warehouses. [GL, Sun MS vol. 15, ref. 29534]

Hunt, John, Wootton under-Edge, Glos., cm and u (1810–30). Trading at Long St in 1820–30, and Haw St, 1822–23. Took app. named William Clark in 1810. [D; Glos. RO, app. indentures]

Hunt, John, Marsh St, Newcastle-under-Lyme, Staffs., joiner and cm (1818). [D]

Hunt, John, Nottingham, chairmaker (1827). Son of John Hunt, tailor of Nottingham; taken as app. in 1827. [Nottingham app. list]

Hunt, John, South Molton, Devon, cm (1832–38). Marriage on 13 February 1832 to Mary, daughter of Mr A. Kingdon, wool-stapler of South Molton, reported in *Exeter Flying Post*, 23 February 1832.

Hunt, John Greaves, Cambridge, cm (1832–45). Trading in Bridge St in 1832, and East Rd, 1835–45. [Poll bks]

Hunt, John, High St, Burton-on-Trent, Staffs., cm and u (1828–35). [D]

Hunt, Joseph, 6 Edmund St, Liverpool, gilder (1794). [D]

Hunt, Joseph, High Wycombe, Bucks., chairmaker (1813–23). Daughters bapt. in 1813, 1816 and 1823; sons in 1819 and 1821. [PR (bapt.)]

Hunt, Joseph, Worcester, carver and gilder (1826–40). Admitted freeman in 1826, and named in the Worcester freemen rolls on 1 December 1835, when trading at Factory Row. Trading at New St, 1835–40. [D]

Hunt, Nicholas, Stepcote Hill, Exeter, Devon, cm (1821). Son Henry bapt. at St George's Church on 18 March 1821. [PR (bapt.)]

Hunt, Philip, 'the Looking Glass & Cabinet', East end St Paul's Churchyard, London, u and cm, (c.1690). His trade card takes an unusual form. It illustrates a marquetry looking-glass of late 17th-century date bearing the interlaced cypher of William III and Mary II supported by a lion and unicorn in the arched cresting. The square wooden cushion moulded frame is decorated with floral marquetry. The mirror plate reflects a marquetry cabinet on stand with twist turned legs of similar date. The text beneath indicates the nature of Philip Hunt's trade at this period. He offers 'Cabenetts, Looking Glasses, Tables and stanns, Seretor^s, Chests of Drawers, And Curious inlaid Figures for any works'. This maker has also been identified with the Mr Hurt or Hunt who in 1720 was involved in the production of the elaborate state bed for John Mellor for his recently acquired house, Erddig, North Wales. Philip Hunt was however clearly a cm and it was an u who was involved in this bed. The long period of about thirty years that separate this commission and the trade card throw further doubt on this attribution. A much more likely craftsman is John Hutt, an u trading in St Paul's Churchyard 1710–29. [Heal, *GCM*; Nat. Trust guide to *Erddig*]   B.A.

Hunt, Rachael, 34 Ben Jonson St, Liverpool, u (1823). [D]

Hunt, Richard, 3 Hunts Ct, St Martin's Lane, London, carver and gilder (1780). Insured his house for £200 in 1780. [GL, Sun MS vol. 280, p. 625]

Hunt, Richard, 1 Nelson St, Bristol, u and furniture broker (1828–40). Trading as furniture broker only from 1837. [D]

Hunt, Robert, address unrecorded, upholder (1723–31). Son of Robert Hunt, draper of High Wycombe, Bucks. App. to Edward Warren on 3 September 1723, and admitted freeman of the Upholders' Co. by servitude on 2 June 1731. [GL, Upholders' Co. records]

Hunt, Samuel, Exeter, 'Change, Strand, London, billiard table maker (1820). [D]

Hunt, Samuel William, 11 Catherine St, Strand, London, billiard table and backgammon board maker (1832). [D]

Hunt, Sarah, 31 St James's St, Brighton, Sussex, u and auctioneer (1824–43). Trading also at no. 39 in 1832. Advertised in *Brighton Gazette*, 26 August 1824, offering thanks 'for all Favours conferred on her late husband', Benjamin Hunt, and requesting 'Future patronage to enable her to support a large Family. S.H. will have the assistance of an experienced elderly man in the upholstery line, as well as that of her son (now nearly of age) who has been employed by one of the first houses in London.' [D] See Benjamin Hunt and Hunt & Marchant.

Hunt, Thomas, address unrecorded, upholder (1754). App. to Richard Smith, upholder of Salisbury, Wilts., on 21 December 1754, by indenture for £30. [*Wilts. Apps and their Masters*]

Hunt, Thomas, Newcastle, u (1768–84). Former apps admitted freeman: William Spence on 13 October 1768; Jacob Barclay on 7 October 1774; Michael Lamb on 6 March 1777; and George Carr on 15 April 1784. [Newcastle freemen reg. and poll bk]

Hunt, William, Boutport St, Barnstaple, Devon, cm and u (1823–30). [D]

Hunt, William, Cambridge, u and cm (1830–35). Trading in Sidney St, 1830–32, and Market Hill, 1834–35. Child bapt. at All Saints parish in 1832. [D; poll bks; PR (bapt.)]

Hunt & Marchant, 31 St James's St, Brighton, Sussex, cm and u (1839). [D] See Benjamin and Sarah Hunt.

Huntback, John, Worcester, upholder (1771). App. to William Ward snr, upholder. Admitted freeman on 21 January 1771. [Worcester freemen rolls]

Hunter, —, Bridgnorth, Salop, carver and gilder (1828). Took legal action against Reynolds, a customs and excise worker, for seducing and abducting his daughter, Ann Hunter, who bore him a child which her father had to support. Hunter was awarded £70 damages. [*Chester Chronicle and North Wales Advertiser*, 28 March 1828]

Hunter, Andrew, Bury St Edmunds, Suffolk, cm (1793). [D]

Hunter, E. & C., address unrecorded. In 1834 supplied '1 large burnished gold frame' costing £4 10s to Erddig, Clwyd. [V&A archives] Probably:

Hunter, Elizabeth & Catherine, Chester, carvers and gilders (1828–34). Trading at Northgate St in 1828 and Eastgate St Row in 1834. [D] Probably successors to James Hunter.

Hunter, Henry, 23 Bondgate, Alnwick, Northumb., cm, joiner and u (1834). [D]

Hunter, Hugh, 1 Charles St, Westminster Rd, London, chair and sofa maker (1827–28). [D]

Hunter, James, address unrecorded, upholder (1769–77). Son of William Hunter, upholder of 465 Strand. App. to his father on 15 November 1769, and admitted freeman of the Upholders' Co. by servitude on 2 April 1777. [GL, Upholders' Co. records]

Hunter, James, 432 Oxford St, London, cm (1784–86). Took out a Sun Insurance policy on 25 July 1786 for £200 of which utensils, stock and goods in trust and in workshop accounted for £120. [D; poll bk; GL, Sun MS vol. 339, p. 175]

Hunter, James, King St, Golden Sq., London, cm and u (1791).

Declared bankrupt, *Williamson's Liverpool Advertiser*, 16 May 1791.

Hunter, James, Chester, cm (1812–22). Trading at Northgate St in 1812, when admitted freeman on 13 October and still there in 1816 as a carver and gilder. [D; poll bk; Chester freemen rolls]

Hunter, James, Market St, Bradford, Yorks., joiner and cm (1818). [D]

Hunter, James, Liverpool, cm (1821–23). Trading at 10 Portland Pl. in 1821 and 33 New Scotland Rd in 1823. [D]

Hunter, James, Ebenezer Pl., Commercial Rd, London, cm and u (1839). [D]

Hunter, John, 44 corner of Swallow St, Piccadilly, London, carver and gilder, glass grinder (1779–93). Took out Sun Insurance policies in 1779 for £400 on his house; in 1781 for £700 of which £300 accounted for utensils and stock; and on 14 October 1790 for £2,000 on warehouse, glass and stock at 153 Swallow St. Polled at Westminster as Jonathan Hunter in 1784. [D; GL, Sun MS vol. 277, p. 121; vol. 295, p. 370; ref. 575121] Possibly:

Hunter, John, address unrecorded, carver and gilder, frame maker (1788–96). Recorded in Lord Monson's accounts on 2 June 1788 receiving £2 7s for two gold picture frames; on 1 June 1789, £4 8s; and between 10 May 1795 and 25 January 1796, a total of £31 3s 5d for picture frames, including on 10 May one of 'Burnished Gold, 10 feet at 2/6d the foot'; and on 8 January 1796, 'Enamelled Glass and Letters, at £1 2s. [Lincoln RO, Monson 10/1/A/6; 11/50] Sent a bill to Sir John Nelthorpe in April 1790 totalling £1 19s 6d for 'Framing Drawing in Burnish Gold Containing 8 ft. of Moulding at 2s 6d per foot', glazing and mounting. [Lincoln RO, NEL 9/12/29]

Hunter, John, Richmond, Surrey, cm (1798). [D]

Hunter, John, Hull, Yorks., cm (1819–23). App. to John Hinsley in July 1819, and assigned to William Silbon in September 1823. [Hull app. reg.]

Hunter, John, 7 Finsbury Pl. South, London, u (1823–25). [D]

Hunter, John, Bury St Edmunds, Suffolk, cm and u (1784–1836). Trading in Cook Row, 1784, and 24 Abbeygate St, 1824–30. [D; poll bk]

Hunter, John, Kirkgate, Cockermouth, Cumb., joiner and/or cm (1828–34). [D]

Hunter, John, 3 Low Ousegate, York, cm etc. (1840). [D]

Hunter, Matthew, St Oswald's parish, Durham, spinning-wheel maker (d.1719). Buried on 15 November 1719. [PR]

Hunter, T., 14 Chancery Lane, London, cm (1809–11). [D]

Hunter, Thomas, Lancaster. Named in the Gillow records in 1818 working on a table. [Westminster Ref. Lib., Gillow vol. 344/100, p. 2080]

Hunter, Thomas, 10 New Richmond, Manchester, cm (1825–40). [D]

Hunter, Thomas, Williams St, Dale St, Liverpool, cm (1790–1803). Recorded at no. 17 in 1790 and no. 2, 1796–1803, also as a victualler in 1796. Marriage to Miss Margaret Wilson at St Ann's Church reported in *Liverpool Advertiser*, 24 September 1789. [D]

Hunter, W., 17 Broker's Row, Moorfields, London, furniture warehouseman (1819). [D]

Hunter, W., Lancaster. Named in the Gillow records in 1839. [Westminster Ref. Lib.]

Hunter, William, Beverley, Yorks., joiner and cm (1720). Took app. named Bradley in 1720. [S of G, app. index]

Hunter, William, London, upholder (1741–d.1802 or 03). Addresses given at 465 Strand in 1769; Bond St in 1786; Lewisham in 1794; and Margate, Kent in 1802. Son of William Hunter, mariner of St John's, Wapping; app. to Charles Grange on November 1741. Admitted freeman of the

Upholders' Co. by servitude on 3 August 1749, master in 1780. Took his son, James Hunter, as app., 1769–77. [GL, Upholders' Co. records] Possibly:

Hunter, William, in Token House Yard, near the Royal Exchange, London, upholder and appraiser (1755–c.1760). Rococo trade card, c.1760, states that he 'Makes after the Newest Fashion all sorts of Four Post & Standing Beds. Likewise Sells all sorts of Upholstery & Cabinet Goods ... Feather Beds, Chairs, Tables, Glasses, Bureaus, Chests of Drawers, Turkey, Persia & Wilton Carpets, Quilts, Blankets, Damasks, Harrateens &c. Also Variety of Paper Hangings, Furniture, Checks, Flannells, Swanskins & Bayes. NB. Funerals Furnish'd Publick or Private.' [Heal] A William Hunter subscribed to Chippendale's *Director*, 1754.

Hunter, William, Stamford, Lincs., cm and u (1800–28). Recorded in St Mary's St, 1819–28. Admitted freeman in 1800 on payment of £12. [D; Stamford freemen rolls]

Hunter, William, Bury St Edmunds, Suffolk, u (1804). Announced in *Ipswich Journal*, 27 October 1804 that he had taken over the business of R. Guest.

Hunter, William Luddington, Hull, Yorks., cm (1818). App. to John Dickon in March 1818. [Hull app. reg.]

Hunter, William, Liverpool, cm (1805–37). Addresses given at 30 North St in 1805; 64 Stanley St in 1813; no. 56 in 1816; no. 22 in 1818; no. 62, 1821–34; and no. 63 in 1837. [D]

Hunter, William, 13 and 14 Moorfields, London, auctioneer, cm and u (1817–25). [D]

Hunter, William, Moorfields, London, u (1826). [Maldon, Essex, poll bk]

Hunter, William, London, u, cm, appraiser, auctioneer and undertaker (1823–39). Trading at 7 Finsbury Pl. South, c.1823; 30 Moorgate St in 1839; and as Hunter & Son in 1835, Hunter & Sons in 1837. Trade card gives address at 7 Finsbury Pl. South. [D; Landauer Coll., MMA, NY]

Hunter, William, East Rainton, Houghton-le-Spring, Durham, cm and/or joiner (1834). [D]

Hunter, William, Leeds, Yorks., cm (1826–37). Addresses given at Turkington's Yd, St Peter's Sq. in 1826; Cornhill in 1830 or 1834; and High St in 1837. [D]

Hunter & Hersant, 2 Broker Row, Finsbury, London, cm (1808–15). Trade card gives address at 2 Lower Moorfields, opposite the Middle Walk. Late Hall & Hersant. [D; Heal]

Hunter & Son, 24 Abbeygate St, Bury St Edmunds, Suffolk, u, cm and auctioneer (1839). [D]

Hunter & Wyles, Bellargate, Nottingham, joiner and cm (1832). [D]

Hunting, William, 34 St James's St, Manchester, picture frame maker (1794). [D]

Huntingdon, E., address unrecorded, u (1803). Subscribed to Sheraton's *Cabinet Dictionary*, 1803.

Hunton, Christopher, Stockton-upon-Tees, Co. Durham, joiner and cm (1827–32). Trading in the Square, 1827, and Stockton Green in 1832. [D]

Hunton, James, Bradford, Yorks., cm and u (1822–37). Recorded at 124 Westgate in 1822 and Newmarket Bazaar in 1830. [D]

Hunton, John, York, cm (1830). Son of John Hunton, shoemaker; app. to Thomas Walls, cm, on 27 September 1830. [York app. reg.]

Huntsman, W., address unrecorded. Mahogany chair, c.1760–70, recorded bearing stamp with name in rectangle below a crown. [Colonial Williamsburg Coll., 1930/232] Similar stamp found on a set of six George III mahogany dining chairs, including a pair of armchairs, the backs with curved top-rails and pierced vase-shaped splats with stuffed serpentine seats and raised on moulded chamfered legs. [Sotheby's, 4 December 1970, lot 161] Possibly the Hunts-

man, chairmaker of London, who subscribed to Sheraton's *Drawing Book*, 1793.

Hurdacre, Joseph, Huntspill, Som., joiner (1739). A cupboard, originally one of a pair built-in on either side of the fireplace in a cottage near Bristol, is inscribed on the lining of the left-hand drawer 'Mr. John Howarde this Woorke was done in ye year of our Lord 1739 by Joseph Hurdacre Joyner of ye parish of Huntspill Somersett Shire.' (Fig. 7). John Howard was tenant of three cottages on the Ashton Court estate. [Som. and Bristol RO; *Furn. Hist.*, 1976, pl. 39]

Hurdle, —, Budleigh Salterton, Devon, u (1828–30). Advertised house sale in *Exeter Flying Post*, 12 June 1828. [D]

Hurdle, John, Exeter, Devon, cm (1816). [Poll bk]

Hurle, James, 66 Bartholomew Close, London, carver and gilder (1809–25). [D]

Hurley, Richard, 61 Conduit St, Hanover Sq., London, u and undertaker (1816–39). Trading as Hurley & Collinson in 1839. In 1828 acted as counterpart of a lease to William Shakespear for a messuage on the south side of Ranelagh St. [D; Marylebone Lib., deed 72/122]

Hurll, William, High St, Winchester, Hants., cm (1823–24). [D]

Hurscroft, William, High St, Tadcaster, Yorks., cm (1818). [D]

Hurst, E., 3 Norman St, St Luke's, London, u (1835). [D]

Hurst, Edward, Marshall St, London, cm (1774). [Poll bk]

Hurst, Francis, address unrecorded, upholder (1733–34). Son of Thomas Hurst of Little Gunnerby, Lincoln, app. to Robert Milner on 10 January 1733, and admitted freeman of the Upholders' Co. by servitude on 2 December 1741. [GL, Upholders' Co. records]

Hurst, George, Little Compton St, St Ann's, Soho, London, carver and gilder (c.1780). Trade card recorded. [Heal]

Hurst, Henry, Warrington, Lancs., u (1798). [D]

Hurst, Joseph jnr, Mark St, Leeds, Yorks., cm (1839–40). [D]

Hurst, Nicholas, over against the Rose Tavern in Russell St, Covent Garden, London, u (1666). Named in contemporary newspapers as one 'who fled from the Plague'. [Heal]

Hurst, William, King St, Ramsgate, Kent, cm and u (1823–38). [D]

Hurst, William, 48 North St, Prospect St, Hull, Yorks., cm (1831). [D]

Hurtley, Barnard, Pontefract, Yorks., cm (1797–98). [D]

Hurtridge, John, Maidstone, Kent, upholder (1730). Took app. named Hodges in 1730. [S of G, app. index]

Hurwood, John, Rufull St, Rotherhithe, London, carver (1779). Took out a Sun Insurance policy with Thomas Saweard in 1779 for £200, utensils and stock accounting for £100. [GL, Sun MS vol. 278, p. 392]

Hurwood, William, 15 Church St, St Ann's, London, carver and mantuamaker (1780). Took out a Sun Insurance policy in 1780 for £400, utensils, stock and goods accounting for £150. [GL, Sun MS vol. 280, p. 180]

Hurwood, William, 18 Conduit St, London, carver and gilder (1792). Took out a Sun Insurance policy on 13 November 1792 for £550. [GL, Sun MS vol. 389, ref. 606487]

Husband, Christopher, Blossomgate, Ripon, Yorks., cm (1822–37). [D]

Husband, D., 9 Gt Pulteney St, Golden Sq., London, cm (1825). [D] See John Husband.

Husband, J., 53 Marshall St, Golden Sq., London, cm, chair and sofa maker (1826–28). [D]

Husband, J., Middlx, cm and u (1826). Declared bankrupt, *Liverpool Mercury*, 17 March 1826.

Husband, John, 19 Gt Pulteney St, Golden Sq., London, cm and u (1823–28). Took out a Sun Insurance policy on 1 December 1823 for £350 on household goods, and £200 on stock and utensils in house and yard. [D; GL, Sun MS vol. 499, ref. 1010730] See D. Husband.

Husband, John, Centre Lane, Tadcaster, Yorks., joiner and/or cm (1837). [D]

Husband, John, 33½ Upper Guildford St, London, cm and u (1839). [D]

Husband, Philip, Yealmpton, near Plymouth, Devon, chairmaker (1837). [Exeter RO, PR; *Furn. Hist.*, 1976, pl. 38A and B]

Husband, Thomas, 8·Ellis St, Sleeve St, London, cm and u (1829–39). [D]

Huscroft, William, High St, Tadcaster, Yorks., cm (1822). [D]

Huskisson, Matthew, 4 Ship St Gdns, Brighton, Sussex, cm and u (1837–39). [D; poll bk]

Huskisson & Co. (or Huskisson & Walker), 10 Ship St, Brighton, Sussex, cm (1832). [D]

Hussey, Edmund, Wincanton, Som., cm (1793). [D] Probably the 'Mr. Hussey of Wincanton Cabinet-Maker &c.' who is recorded as having 'spent the Morning or most part of it at Cole', in James Woodforde's *Diary of a Country Parson*, ed. John Beresford, 1921, vol. 4, p. 50.

Husson, Edward, North St, Ashburton, Devon, cm (1838). [D]

Husson, Stephen Lawrence, address unrecorded, upholder (1736–44). Son of Paul Stephen Husson, Gent. of St Leonard's parish, Shoreditch. App. to Edward Webster on 5 January 1736, and admitted freeman of the Upholders' Co. by servitude on 11 January 1743/44. [GL, Upholders' Co. records]

Hustcroft, Samuel, Low-Jubbergate, York, cm (1787). [D]

Hustwick, Francis, Hull, Yorks., coach and furniture painter (1820). Took app. named John Wheatley in May 1820. [Hull app. reg.]

Hutchings, Edward, 4 Grosvenor St, Brighton, Sussex, cm (1840). Son of John Hutchings, cm; married Elisabeth Thorp on 16 August 1840. [PR]

Hutchings, Jn, address unrecorded, cm (1754). App. to Henry Watson of St James's, London in 1754 for £210. [V&A archives]

Hutchings, John, Peascod St, Windsor, Berks., cm (1824). [D]

Hutchings, John, Queen St, Hammersmith, London, cm (1826). [D]

Hutchings, John, Canal Walk, Southampton, Hants., cm (1836). [D]

Hutchings, William, Lower Marsh, High Wycombe, Bucks., chairmaker (b. c. 1806–41). Daughters bapt. in 1828 and 1831. Aged 35 at the time of the 1841 Census. [PR (bapt.)]

Hutchins, —, King St, Covent Gdn, London, upholder (d.1746). [Harris, *Old English Furniture*]

Hutchins, —, London, cm (1747). Notice in *General Advertiser*, 18 September 1747 read: 'Wednesday Night, about Eleven o'clock, Mr. Hutchins, a Cabinet Maker, was robb'd near Little Turnstile in Holborn, by Two Ruffians, who searched all his Pockets, took from him Two Guineas and made off without the least Molestation from the Watch.'

Hutchins, Abraham, address unrecorded, u (1753–60). He was employed regularly by the 4th Duke of Bedford at Bedford House, London, and at Woburn Abbey, Beds., supplying curtains and bed furniture, cleaning and scouring textiles, upholstering chairs and making covers for the Duchess's and her daughter's dressing-tables. In 1753 he also supplied '14 beach chairs covered in Spanish leather'. From 1757 he worked with Abigail Hutchins, who was probably his mother. The latter was succeeded by Hassall Hutchins. [Bedford Office, London]

Hutchins, Abigail, address unrecorded, u and cm (1757–70). She worked with Abraham Hutchins for the 4th Duke of Bedford between 1757–60. After 1760 Abigail continued on her own, regularly supplying, cleaning and repairing bed furniture, curtains, damask wall hangings and upholstery for the Duke at Bedford House, London, Woburn Abbey, Beds., and the family house at Streatham. In August 1769 she provided, perhaps for Woburn Abbey, crimson silk and worsted line 'to hang the pictures in the room that was hung with Tapestry according to Mr. Chambers' plan'. Some furniture was supplied to the Duke, mainly for the servants' rooms, but including, in 1764, six walnut back stools for Woburn Abbey, 'the frames in dead white and gilt in burnished gold', for £28 7s. Hassall Hutchins, probably her son, joined her in or before October 1769. [Bedford Office, London]

Hutchins, Ann, Exeter, Devon, u (1725). Advertised in *Brice's Weekly Journal*, 10 September 1725: 'Any Person, having occasion to imploy an Upholsterer, may be faithfully serv'd by Ann Hutchins, who performs all sorts of work in that business and will work at any Gentleman's or other's house in city or country for 2d. per day; or will take in any sort of such work, to be performed at her own house, on very moderate terms. She may be enquired for at Mrs. Condly's or the King's Arms in St. Sidwell's, Exon.'

Hutchins, George, Wincanton, Som., chairmaker (1798). [D]

Hutchin(s), Hassall (or Hassil), London, upholder, cm and auctioneer (1769–90). Recorded at King St, Covent Gdn, 1773–83; and no. 41, 1783–90. In 1777 Hassett Hutchins of Hart St, Covent Gdn, insured a house at 115 Strand, near Somerset House, for £60. [D; GL, Sun MS vol. 258, p. 438] He joined Abigail Hutchins, probably his mother, in or before October 1769, and together they served the Duke of Bedford as regular upholsterers, supplying, cleaning and repairing textiles at Bedford House, London, and Woburn Abbey, Beds. From 1771–81, Hassall Hutchins continued on his own to supply the 4th Duke and subsequently the 5th Duke and the Dowager Duchess. Some furniture was supplied over this period, mainly for the servants' rooms, but also for the family bed-chambers. Funerals for the household servants were also arrayed by Hassall Hutchins who charged £10 5s 8d in September 1777 for funeral expences for Gaspard Schuman, including a coffin lined with crepe, covered with black baize and fitted with an inscription plate and flowered handles. For this occasion he hired out a velvet pall, crepe armbands, gloves, cloaks for men and hoods and scarves for the ladies. [Bedford Office, London]

Hutchins, John, Chepping Wycombe Borough, High Wycombe, Bucks., chairmaker (1798). [Militia Census]

Hutchins, John, Wardour St, London, chair and sofa manufacturer (1815–23). Recorded at no. 7 in 1815 and 1820, and no. 8 in 1817. Trade card gives address at no. 7. [D; Johnson Coll., Bodleian Lib., Oxford; *Furn. Hist.*, 1974, p. 43]

Hutchins, John, Brighton, Sussex, cm and chairmaker (1822–40). Addresses given at 126 North St, 1822–24, also no. 47 in 1822, and 15 Poplar Pl. in 1826. His daughter, Caroline Hutchings of 12 Sussex St married on 8 July 1838. His son, Edward Hutchings, cm of 4 Grosvenor St married Elizabeth Thorp on 16 August 1840. [D; E. Sussex RO, PR]

Hutchins, John, 101 Gt Titchfield St, London, cm and u (1827–39). [D]

Hutchins, John, 54 Foley St, Foley Pl., London, cm, u, chair and sofa maker (1839). [D]

Hutchin(g)s, Jonathan, High Wycombe, Bucks., chairmaker (1822–30). Daughters bapt. in 1822 and 1829, son in 1830. [PR (bapt.)]

Hutchins, Richard, 56 Newman St, Oxford St, London, chair and sofa maker (1822–39). [D]

Hutchins, Robert, New Round Ct, Strand, London, cm (1780). Insured his house for £100 in 1780. [GL, Sun MS vol. 286, p. 541]

Hutchinson, —, Saffron Walden, Essex, cm (1771). Advertised in *Cambridge Chronicle and Journal*, 5 January 1771. Possibly John Hutchinson.

Hutchinson, Anthony, Boar Lane, Leeds, Yorks., carver, gilder and music seller (1828). [D]

Hutchinson, Edmund, High Wycombe, Bucks., chairmaker (b.1801–41). Daughters bapt. in 1820, 1822 and 1824, son in 1826. Aged 40 at the time of the 1841 Census. [PR (bapt.)]

Hutchinson, George, Nottingham, chairmaker (1744). Married, aged 28, on 26 December 1774. [Notts. RO, marriage licence index lib., vol. 2]

Hutchinson, George, address unrecorded, cm (1803). Subscribed to Sheraton's *Cabinet Dictionary*, 1803.

Hutchinson, George, 7 Riding House Lane, London, cm (1835). [D]

Hutchinson, George, 8 Chapel Pl., Oxford St, London, carver and gilder (1839). [D]

Hutchinson, George, 12 Huntley St, Bedford Sq., London, cm (1840). [GL, Sun MS ref. 1339678]

Hutchinson, Henry, Lombard St, Newark, Notts., cm and u (1822). [D]

Hutchinson, James, Pontefract, Yorks., cm (1785). Referred to in *Leeds Mercury*, 30 August 1785.

Hutchinson, John, address unrecorded, u (1762–67). Submitted bill to Sir John Griffin Griffin of Audley End, Saffron Walden, Essex, in 1762 for fixing curtains and moving a field bed for 16s 6d; and in 1771 for two dressing glasses and a painted frame at a total of 11s 10d. [Essex RO, D/DBy/A15; A29/9] Possibly Hutchinson, —.

Hutchinson, John, Kirkby Stephen, Westmld, joiner and cm (1828–29). [D]

Hutchinson, John, Queen St, Barnard Castle, Co. Durham, cm and/or joiner (1834). [D]

Hutchinson, Peter, Lees, near Ashton-under-Lyne, Lancs., joiner and cm (1825). [D]

Hutchinson, Peter, Staindrop, Co. Durham, joiner and cm (1827). [D]

Hutchinson, Richard, Church St, Hackney, London, upholder and cm (1808–11). [D]

Hutchinson, Robert, address unrecorded, cm (1803). Subscribed to Sheraton's *Cabinet Dictionary*, 1803.

Hutchinson, Stephen, address unrecorded, cm (1803). Subscribed to Sheraton's *Cabinet Dictionary*, 1803.

Hutchinson, Thomas, Nottingham, joiner and cm (1769). Son of William Hutchinson, farrier of Kirkby Bogg; taken as app. in 1769. [Nottingham app. list]

Hutchinson, Thomas, Iron Market, Newcastle-under-Lyme, Staffs., cm (1818–22). [D]

Hutchinson, Thomas, Beaumond St, Newark, Notts., cm (1835). [D]

Hutchinson, William, Durham, cm (1783–93). Daughter bapt. at St Mary-le-Bow, Durham, on 18 August 1783. [D; PR (bapt.)]

Hutchinson, William, St Mary's Chare, Hexham, Northumb., joiner and cm (1827). [D]

Hutchinson & Co., London, carvers and gilders (1824). Submitted a bill in 1824 to Thomas Whitmore, MP, of Apley Hall, Salop, for 'a Rich Carved Frame for Looking Glass', costing £22, charged by Baldock; 'Silver'd Plate for ditto', £22 17s 1d; and 'Gilding Frame in burnish.d Gold', for £15. [Essex RO, D/DWt A3]

Hutchon, John, Liverpool, carver (1733–d. by 1780). Admitted freeman on 31 December 1733. [Liverpool freemen reg.]

Hutchon, Richard, Liverpool, carver (1720). Admitted freeman on 4 August 1720. [Liverpool freemen reg.]

Huton, Thomas, 44 Rathbone Pl., London, cm and chairmaker (1792). Took out a Sun Insurance policy on 4 December 1792 for £200. [GL, Sun MS vol. 389, ref. 607385]

Hutt, Elizabeth & Son, at 'The Blew Curtain', St Paul's Church Yard, London, upholders (1741–49). Submitted a bill, dated 1741 and made out to 'Mr. Howard', to the Duke of Norfolk, for 'a Dressing Table and Glass £6.6s.0d.'. [Banks Coll., BM] In 1749 Elizabeth Hutt provided the Duke of Gordon with 'A large Wilton; carpet 29 yards @ 6/6 — £9.8.6.'. Bill head states that she made and sold 'all sorts of glass, Cabinet & Chairwork'. She was succeeded by John Iliffe. [Heal; Scottish RO, GD44/51/380]

Hutt, John, London, upholder (1710–d.1729). Recorded at 'The Three Pillows', over against the South Gate, St Paul's Church Yard, 1712–21. John Hutt, u, was paid by St John's College, Cambridge, in 1710–11, for supplying a bed and coverings, chairs, curtains, walnut table, looking-glass, carpet and quilt; and 'Mr. Huts Upholsterer on the South side of St. Paul's' is named on 9 September 1719 in the records at King's College Library, Cambridge. [KCL, Coll. I, f58] John Hutt of 'The Three Pillars' insured his house, goods and merchandise on 17 November 1719. [GL, Sun MS vol. 10, ref. 15779] Shortly before 1821 John Hutt and William Langmore, upholder in Cornhill, took an inventory of the goods of Sir John Blunt of Birchin Lane and Stratford, West Ham, a Director of the South Sea Co., and supplied him with goods to the value of £370. He charged £66 6s 'for chimney glasses and sconces at Stratford'. Hutt charged Sir Robert Chaplin, Bart of Castle St, St Martin-in-the-Fields, and Camringham, Lincoln, £100; and Robert Chester of Briggens Park, Herts., £209 13s; in both cases for unspecified items. John Hutt was probably the Mr Hurt or Hunt, who in 1720 was involved in the production of the elaborate state bed for John Mellor for his recently acquired house, Erddig, Clwyd, N. Wales. Simon Yorke, his nephew, wrote from London on 17 April 1720 regarding this bed. He had attempted to call on 'Hunt' but found him absent and had to be content with the assurances of his wife that the bed would be sent on Monday next. The delay was blamed on the wait for the gilding and carving to be completed. This had been sub-contracted possibly to John Belchier whose workshop was near at hand and had supplied much other furniture to Erddig. It has been suggested previously that the craftsman involved was Philip Hunt of 'The Looking Glass & Cabinet', East end St Paul's Churchyard, but he appears to have been a cm, not an u, and there is no evidence that he was trading as late as 1720. [Nat. Trust guide to *Erddig*] John was succeeded in St Paul's Churchyard by Richard Hutt. Named in contemporary newspapers. [Heal; Hilton Price, *Signs of Old London*; GCM]

Hutt, Joseph, 24 Rosoman St, Clerkenwell, London, cm and u (1827–28). [D]

Hutt, Richard, St Paul's Churchyard, London, u and cm (1745–48). Successor to John Hutt. Notice in *Daily Advertiser*, 2 January 1745 read: 'On Friday, as Mr. Hutt, an eminent Cabinet Maker in St. Paul's Churchyard, and his Wife, were travelling the Essex Road in a Chaise, they were overturned, by which Accident she had the Misfortune to break her Leg, in so terrible a Manner, that her Life is despair'd of.' Her death on 3 January 1745 was reported in the same paper on 9 January. Richard Hutt was declared bankrupt in *Penny London Post*, 10 June 1748. [Harris, *Old English Furniture*]

Hutton, —, address unrecorded, carver (1744). Supplied picture frames for Petworth, Sussex, in 1744. [*C. Life*, 25 September 1980, p. 1030]

Hutton, —, Lancaster, japanner and furniture painter (1790–1838). [Westminster Ref. Lib., Gillow records]

Hutton, Alexander, 16 Heddon St, London, cm (1808). Took out a Sun Insurance policy on 16 April 1808 for £1,000, of which £400 accounted for a private house at 17 Heddon St. [GL, Sun MS vol. 445, ref. 816401]

Hutton, George, Lancaster, furniture painter (1799–1815). [Westminster Ref. Lib., Gillow records]

Hutton, Henry F., Colchester, Essex, cm etc. (1793). [D]

Hutton, James, Lancaster, furniture painter and japanner (1794–1808). [Westminster Ref. Lib., Gillow records]

Hutton, James, Britwell, Oxon, chairmaker (1824). Participant in a conveyance for a property in South Weston to be converted into a chapel or meeting house for the Society of Methodists. [Oxford RO, Bi II/i/9]

Hutton, James, Leeds, Yorks., cm and u (1830–1840). Trading at Holbeck Lane, 1830–34, and 102 Wellington St in 1837. [D]

Hutton, James, Woolpack Yd, Bradford, Yorks., cm (1837). [D]

Hutton, John, London, worker in gilt leather (1728–37). Recorded at St Paul's Churchyard in 1735 On 22 November 1728 he provided Sir Gilbert Heathcote with 'A Six Leave Gilt Leather Screen Eight Feet High Painted Bleu and Gold Alt', costing £6 6s. [Lincoln RO, 2 ANC 12/D/18] On 10 February 1735, John Hutton of Paul's Church Yard was paid £22 by Earl Fitzwalter for 'a set of gilt leather hangings, blue and gold, with a damask figure & mosaic border, for the room next the street at the head of the great stairs in the house in Pall Mall.' [A. C. Edwards, *The Accounts of Benjamin Mildmay, Earl Fitzwalter*, p. 73] The Duke of Gordon bought 'Two Gilt Leather Fire Screens with Figures & Landscapes and Mahogany Frames', costing £2 10s on 30 November 1737. [Scottish RO, GD44/51/465/3/41]

Hutton, John, Gainsborough, Lincs., cm (1784). [Hull poll bk]

Hutton, John, Lancaster, furniture painter (1804–10). [Westminster Ref. Lib., Gillow records]

Hutton, John, Thursby, Wigton, Cumb., joiner and cm (1828–29). [D]

Hutton, Jonathan, 26 Mortimer St, Cavendish Sq., London, cm (1817). [D]

Hutton, Richard, Lancaster, furniture painter (1825–29). [Westminster Ref. Lib., Gillow records]

Hutton, Richard, 36 Crawford St, London, u (1839). [D]

Hutton, Robert, Norwich, u (d. 1733). Will proved in 1733. [Norfolk Record Soc., index of wills]

Hutton, Robert, Haddenham, Cambs., cm (d.1764). Sale of stock in trade on death advertised in *Cambridge Chronicle and Journal*, 8 September 1764.

Hutton, Samuel, 40 Gun St, Manchester, cm (1813). [D]

Hutton, Thomas, Nottingham, joiner and cm (1775–1813). Son of Sam Hutton, whipmaker of Nottingham; taken as app. in 1775. Took apps named William Bonner Bilby in 1791, Richard Russel and George Newberry in 1792, Isaac Newton in 1787, and Thomas Hutton in 1813. Signed the *Nottingham Cabinet and Chair Makers' Book of Prices*, 1791, on behalf of the masters. Declared bankrupt, *Williamson's Liverpool Advertiser*, 16 December 1793. [D; Nottingham app. list]

Hutton, William, Barnstaple, Devon, cm, u and auctioneer (1828–36). Addresses given at 93 High St, c.1815–20, and no. 102 in 1829. Advertised in *North Devon Journal*, 8 October 1829 stating 'that he is removed from his late residence to No. 102, the House late-occupied by Mr. R. GRIBBLE, in High Street, where he solicits a continuance of that distinguished patronage with which he has been honoured since his establishment in business.' Marriage to Elizabeth Moon at Ilfracombe reported in *The Alfred*, 22 July 1828. Label giving address of W. Hutton's cabinet and upholstery warerooms at 93 High St, recorded on small toilet mirror of solid mahogany, and softwood veneered with mahogany and oak, c.1815–20. Label of William Hutton of Barnstaple found on mahogany commode chest of well-

figured wood, with a rising top and the front with four simulated drawers. [Sotheby's, 24 July 1963, lot 292] Sale of his 'well-established Business' on his retirement advertised in *Exeter Flying Post*, 16 June 1836. The business comprised the lease of a house in 'the centre and most eligible part of the High-street, in Barnstaple, and is in every way adapted for carrying on an extensive Manufacturing Business in the above Line, having been fitted up expressly for the business with Saw Pit, Timber Yard, Drying Sheds, and Workshops, in which fifteen hands are now employed, and all on goods ordered; a large and valuable assortment of Seasoned Wood in Plank and Veneers, part of which has been cut upward of eight years, and comprise about 7,000 feet of Mahogany, 2,000 feet of Birch and Beech, about four tons of Rose, Zebra and Satin Woods, about 4,000 feet of Veneer; with a general assortment of other Woods, Ironmongery and Upholstery: And a Modern Assortment of Manufactured Goods. Any assistance for six or twelve months, in the conducting of the Business may be had by application to W. HUTTON, who is about to reside about one mile from the town . . .'.

Hutton, William, Britwell, Oxon, chairmaker (1824). Participant in a conveyance for a property in South Weston to be converted into a chapel or meeting house for the Society of Methodists. [Oxford RO, Bi II/i/9]

Huttons, —, Lancaster, japanners and furniture painters (1804–37). [Westminster Ref. Lib., Gillow records]

Huwood, Thomas, Norwich, u (1750). Took app. named Humphrey in 1750. [S of G, app. index]

Huxley, Charles, 16 John St, Oxford St, London, u (1826–27). [D]

Huxley, Joseph, Chester, u (1824–37). Addresses given at Newgate St in 1824, Weaver St in 1826, and Princess St in 1837. Admitted freeman on 19 October 1824. [Chester freemen rolls and poll bks]

Huxley, Thomas, Foregate St, Chester, u (1812). [Poll bk]

Huxley, Thomas Croft, Liverpool, cm (1812–39). Addresses given at 52 Park Lane in 1812; 28 St James St with shop at 50 Park Lane in 1823; 52 Park Lane and 70 Sparling St in 1827; 52 Park Lane and 77 Sparling St, 1827–29; 46–47 Park Lane in 1837; and nos 97–99 in 1839. Admitted freeman on 14 October 1812, when stated 'sailmaker now cabinet maker'. Took apps named William Latham Huxley in 1822; Henry Pidger Cohen in 1824; Samuel Major in 1828; Robert Peppitt and Thomas Walker Shepherd in 1822, admitted freemen in 1830; and James Shillito in 1831, freeman in 1840. [D; Liverpool freemen reg. and committee bk]

Huxley, Thomas, 38, shop 39, Fox St, Liverpool, cm (1837). [D]

Huxley, William Latham, Liverpool, cm (1822). App. to Thomas Croft Huxley in 1822. [Liverpool app. enrolment bk]

Huyton, William, Moor St, Ormskirk, Lancs., cm (1825). [D]

Hweitson, Isaac, 68 Wardour St, London, chairmaker (1808). [D]

Hyatt, John, Sherborne, Dorset, u and cm (1755–98). App. to Thomas Thorne of Sherborne, u, for seven years in 1755. [D; Dorset app. indentures]

Hyatt, Thomas, Linehall St, Chester, u (1826). Admitted freeman on 12 June 1826. [Chester freemen rolls and poll bk]

Hyatt, Thomas, Friar St, Warwick, cm (1831). [Poll bk]

Hyatt, William, 53 Dorset St, Portman Sq., London, u, cm and chair and sofa maker (1820–25). Declared bankrupt, *Brighton Gazette*, 25 November 1824. [D]

Hyde, Daniel, Liverpool, joiner and cm (1772–84). Trading in King St, 1772–73. Notices regarding bankruptcy appeared in *Williamson's Liverpool Advertiser*, 25 March and 27 May 1784. [D]

Hyde, G. B., 29 Thomas St, Manchester, carver and gilder (1832–33). [D]

Hyde, Hannah, 31 Gerrard St, Soho, London, cm and u (1839). [D]

Hyde, James, late of 34 Lord St, Liverpool, cm (1832). Sale of remaining stock advertised in *Liverpool Mercury*, 9 March 1832, consisting 'of a general assortment of Ladies Rosewood & Mahogany Work Boxes, Dressing Cases, Portable Writing Desks, Tea Chests, Backgammon Boards & Chess Men, Card Cases, Tablets, a great variety of Toys, Jewellery, & Silver Articles, Cutlery etc.'

Hyde, John, 15 Newton St, Chorlton Range (or Row), Manchester, cm (1832–34). [D]

Hyde, Jonathan, 20 Stanley St, Liverpool, cm (1777). [D]

Hyde, Richard, Park St, Worksop, Notts., cm, builder, surveyor and appraiser (1832). [D]

Hyde, Robert, Worksop, Notts., table maker (1786). Mahogany kneehole desk recorded, with three graduated drawers each side of the arch, a pair of simulated cupboard doors on the reverse, and supported on short turned legs with leaf-cast sockets to castors. Inscription under the top reads: 'Robe. Hyde. Table Maker ye Worksop Nottinghamshire 12 August 1786'. [*Conn.*, September 1973, Jeremy Ltd, London] Possibly:

Hyde, Robert, Worksop, Notts., cm, u and builder (1819–35). Recorded at Forest Lane in 1819, Park St in 1828 and Coney St in 1835. [D] Possibly:

Hyde, Robert, Worksop, Notts., joiner (1816–d.c.1834). Carried out joinery work for the Earl of Surrey at Worksop Manor in 1816, repairing furniture and supplying minor furniture such as bidets, butlers' trays, wood-bottomed chairs, swing-glass frames and bed steps. In 1817 he provided a mahogany high chair. [Arundel Castle records, MD662; 1308–09] Will dated 7 April 1829, proved in 1834. [Notts. RO, probate records]

Hyde, Robert, address unrecorded, cm (1803). Subscribed to Sheraton's *Cabinet Dictionary*, 1803.

Hyde, Robert, address unrecorded, cm and u (1812). Recorded in the Welbeck Abbey accounts of Edward Turner, steward, being paid £119 10s 5d on 13 May, and £51 16s 11d on 31 December 1812. [Notts. RO]

Hyde, Thomas, Bath, Som., cm (1826–33). Addresses given at 15 Broad St in 1826 and 1 Charles St in 1833. [D]

Hyde, W., 1 Charles St, Bath, Som., fancy cm (1819–26). [D]

Hyde, William Wilson, Hull, Yorks., cm and broker (1803–21). Trading in Blackfriargate, 1803–06, no. 20 in 1805; as Hyde & Dunlin, auctioneers, cabinet makers and brokers at Silver St in 1810; alone as appraiser, auctioneer and commission man at 29 Silver St in 1814; and auctioneer at 1 Princess Row, Dock St, 1817–21. [D]

Hyfield, —, 35 Old Compton St, Soho, and 7 London Rd, St George's Fields, London, looking-glass manufacturer, carver and gilder. Trade card states that he 'Carves and Gilds All sorts of glass and picture frames . . . Oval and pier glasses on the lowest terms. New frames Old glass to the present fashion. Merchants, Captains and Country Dealers served on the shortest notice . . . resonable Rates Old glasses new silvered.'

Hyland, James, 21 Croydon St, St Marylebone, London, bedstead maker (1833). Took app. in 1833. [Marylebone Lib., Paddington Charities app. indentures]

Hyland, William, 21 Croydon St, Bryanston Sq., London, bedstead maker (1839). [D]

Hylt, John, 16 High St, Lewes, Sussex, chair manufacturer (1839). [D]

Hynes, Thomas, address unrecorded. Signed a Sheraton-period sideboard in the Neo-classical style. [*Collector's Guide*, September 1952, Frank Caira, London]

Hynmers Taylor, —, near St James's Church, Piccadilly, London, upholstery, cabinet and carpet warehouseman (1767–68). Supplied Lady Ann Connorly with a carpet costing £21 2s 6d in January 1767, for Stretton Hall, Staffs. [V&A Lib., English Manuscripts] On 9 April 1768 Mrs Long of Saxmundham, Suffolk, paid Hynmers Taylor £1 8s 6d for a night table and waiter, and on 15 April, £1 12s for a basin stand and wash table. [Suffolk RO, HA18/EC/4]

I

Ibberson, William Covey, Petty Cury, Cambridge, u and cm (1839–40). [D; poll bk]

Ibbe(r)tson, James Mortimer, 29 Bromsgrove St, Birmingham, carver and gilder (1828–30). [D]

Ibbetson, Christopher, 122 Gt Portland St, London, upholder, appraiser etc. (1784–1802). [D]

Ibbotson, J. M., Friar's Wynd, Richmond, Yorks., carver and gilder (1823). [D]

Ibbotson, Thomas, Hartshead, Sheffield, Yorks., cabinet case maker and flour dealer (1821). [D]

Ibbot, Francis, Somersham, Hunts., joiner, carpenter and cm (1830). [D]

Ibetson, Jno., 238 High Holborn, London, carver and chair manufacturer (1835). [D]

Ibetson, John, 19 Lamb's Conduit Passage, London, carver and gilder (1839). [D]

Ibitt, William, London, upholder (1700). Free of the Upholder's Co. in 1700. [GL, Upholders' Co. records]

Iden, Henry, London, cm and looking-glass seller (1687–88). From 1687–88 traded at the sign of the 'Looking-Glass' in Ludgate St. On 16 February 1688 announced that he was leaving off trade; and on 14 June when he advertised 'All sorts of Cabinet Work to be sold as Cabinets, Secretores, Chest of Drawers, Tables, Stands and Looking Glasses to be sold' he gave his address as 'lately at the Sign of the Looking Glass, Ludgate Street'. The address he moved to was Bell Yd, Carter Lane. [Heal; *London Gazette*, 16 February, 14 June 1688]

Ideson, Francis, Marsden Hall, Nelson, Lancs., cm and joiner (b. c.1811–1841). Recorded in 1841 Census.

Ifield, E. C., Bristol, bedstead, chair and plane maker (1820–30). At Jacob St, 1820–21, and 73 Old Market St, 1822–24. In 1824 also at 17 West St, and this is given as the sole address from 1825–26. At 31 Milk St, 1829–30 where the trade is given as furniture broker. [D]

Ikin, Abel, against the 'King's Arms', Briggate, Leeds, Yorks., u (1729–32). In April 1729 stated that he stocked 'Bedding viz. Quilts, Rugs, Blankets, Coverlids, Harateens, Chayneys, printed Stuffs, Flordys and English Bed-Ticks of all sorts, Lincolnshire Feathers, choice of new fashioned Paper for hanging Rooms, Bed Buckram, Bed and Saddle Laces, oyl'd Cloth for Floors, Mattin of all sorts . . .'. In 1732 took app. named Batt. Scattered payments to this maker occur in the Temple Newsam, Leeds, accounts. [*Leeds Mercury*, 15–22 April 1729; S of G, app. index]

Ikin, William, Mill St, Nantwich, Cheshire, cm/joiner (1822). [D]

Ikin & Biass, 430 Oxford St, London, cm and u (1839). [D]

Iles, William, 35 Bell Yd, Temple Bar, London, cm, window blind maker and undertaker (1822–27). [D]

Iley, Mary, 77 Marylebone High St, London, broker and cm (1821). On 12 March 1821 took out insurance cover for £2,000 which included £1,100 for utensils and stock. Warerooms and a workshop were maintained at this address. [GL, Sun MS vol. 488, ref. 978110] Successor to:

Iley, William, 77 Marylebone High St, London, u, cm and broker (1802–20). The growth of this business is well recorded in the insurance cover taken out. In January 1802 the total cover was £900 of which £550 was in respect of utensils and stock. The corresponding figures for December 1812 are £1,850 and £1,000; and for January 1810, £2,000 and £1,100. [D; GL, Sun MS vol. 424, ref. 725834; vol. 434, ref. 779931; vol. 453, ref. 839437]

Iley, William, Church St, Whitby, Yorks., cm (1840). [D]

Iliffe, John, London and Kettering, Northants., upholder (1753–94). Son of William Iliffe of Desborough, Northants., farmer. App. to Elizabeth Hutt of London, upholder, and also to Thomas Burnet. Made free of the Upholders' Co. under the terms of the 1750 Upholders' Act on 6 December 1753. Soon after this date he took over the business of Elizabeth Hutt at the sign of 'The Blue Curtain', St Paul's Churchyard. During the period that he operated his business from this address it was numbered 5 St Paul's Churchyard. He took as app. William Shore from 1751–67 and Henry Broughton from 1759–63. His trade card [Leverhulme Coll., MMA, NY] states that he made and sold 'all sorts of Beds and Beding, Mohair, Silk, worstead, and mix'd Damasks … Great Choice of English, French & Turkey Carpets; Screens of every kind, Rich Carved Sconces, Tables & Picture Frames. Brass Lanthorns and Arms with All manner of Glass, Cabinet & Chair Work'. He also undertook funerals and acted as an appraiser. There are no further entries in London directories after 1768, and by 1778 he appears to have left London and returned to his home county. He is shown living in Kettering, 1778–94. [D; GL, Upholders Co. records]

Illidge, Thomas, Wolverhampton, Staffs., papier-mâché maker (c. 1810–20). Trays stamped 'ILLIDGE' exist. [*Conn.*, August 1967, p. 251]

Illing, Susannah, Hillgrove St, Bristol, upholder (1794–1805). [D]

Illingworth, James, Ingrow Bridge, Keighley, Yorks., joiner/cm (1837). [D]

Illingworth, John, Thornton, Bradford, Yorks., cm (1837). [D]

Illingworth, Richard, Hebden Bridge, Yorks., joiner/cm (1834). [D]

Illison, —, address unknown, carver (1721). Assisted on carving of the staircase at Chicheley Hall, Bucks. [*Records of Bucks.*, 1961, XVII, pt. 1]

Illsley, Charles, 10 St Mary's Butts, Reading Berks., cm (1820–26). [D; poll bks]

Image, —, address unknown. In 1738 he was paid £13 for supplying '2 glass arms' and repairing 'lanthorns & tables' at Holkham Hall, Norfolk. [V & A archives]

Imber, Edward, 92 Hatton Gdn, London, u and auctioneer (1814). On 23 November 1814 took out insurance cover of £1,550 on the contents of his house which included £1,000 for utensils and stock. The house itself was separately insured for £950. [GL, Sun MS vol. 463, refs 899704–05]

Imeson, Joseph, 2 Union St, Berkeley Sq., London, u and cm (1820). [D]

Impey, William, address unknown, u, cm and brazier (1762–63). In 1762 supplied to Sir John Griffin Griffin at Audley End, Essex, a mahogany silk frame at 14s, a mahogany stand at 15s and a fire screen at 16s 10d. In the following year carried out a number of small repairs. [Essex RO, D/DBy/A15]

Imray, George, 12 Red Lion Close, Spitalfields, London, cm and u (1827). [D]

Imray, J., 84 Curtain Rd, London, cm (1835). [D]

Ince, —, 23 Holles St, Cavendish Sq., London, cm (1803). Included in the list of master cabinet makers in Sheraton's *Cabinet Dictionary*, 1803.

Ince, John, 'the Upper End of Bow-street, Covent Garden', London, glass grinder (d. 1748). Sale on his death of his goods and effects at 'his late Dwelling house' above, on 6 and 7 April advertised in *General Advertiser*, 31 March 1748.

Ince, William, see John Mayhew & William Ince.

Inch, John, Little Thomas Lane, Redcliffe St, Bristol, japanner (1822–40). In 1837 the business became John Inch & Son, japanners and painters. [D]

Inchley, Claypole George, Wellington St, Leicester, cm and u (1840). [D]

Inchley, George, Ashwell St, Leicester, cm and paper hanger (1835). [D]

Indermaur, Frederick, Southwark, London, cm (1822–39). Initially at 27 Lant St where on 4 April 1822 he took out insurance cover of £100. This included £50 to cover utensils and stock in the workshop of Hannebuth behind his house in Lant St. By 1835 in partnership with Jacob Indermaur and working from 40 and 27 Lant St. One directory of 1835 records Frederick Indermaur at 71 Union St. [D; GL, Sun MS vol. 489, ref. 991224]

Indermaur, John, 8 New St, Carnaby Mkt, London, cm (1781). In 1781 insured his house for £100. [GL, Sun MS vol. 295, p. 405]

Indge, John, Newington Causeway, London, Windsor chair manufacturer (1820). [D]

Indson, Charles, 27 Little Alie St, Goodman's Yd, London, cm and upholder (1820). [D]

Ingham, John, Church St, Colne, Lancs., Windsor chairmaker (1824–34). The 1834 directory entry states Church Yd. [D]

Ingham, John, Chester and Dublin, cm (1732). Stated to be son of the late William Ingham of Chester, cm, at the time of his freedom on 12 October 1732. In the same year living in Dublin. [Chester freemen reg.; poll bk]

Ingham, John, Todmorden, Yorks., cm (1834–37). In 1834 at Gate Bottom. The 1837 directory entry is for a John Ingham jnr, who may be the son. He was living at Newton Grove, Stansfield, Todmorden, and his trade was given as joiner/cm. [D]

Ingham, Joseph, Jubbergate, York, cm and maker of sky and fan lights (1823). [D]

Ingham, Peter, Cross St, Sheffield, Yorks., cm (1821). [D]

Ingham, Robert, Chester and Dublin, cm (1732). Free 10 October 1732. Son of the late William Ingham of Chester, cm. In 1732 living in Dublin. [Chester freemen rolls; Chester poll bk]

Ingham, Thomas, Liverpool, cm (1812–37). Admitted freeman on 5 October 1812 on servitude to Edward Lowe. By 1818 trading at 84 Gerard St, and from 1821–29 at 2 and 4 Back Pickup St. From 1834–37 working at 6 Ben Johnson St. [D; freemen reg.]

Ingham, William, Chester, cm (1690–1700). Free 24 September 1690. Took as apps Thomas Comerbach in 1696 and Edward Twanbrook before 1700. Father of John and Robert Ingham who were free of Chester as cm in October 1732. Their father was dead by this date. [Freemen rolls; app. bk]

Ingle, Joseph, 20–22 Timble Bridge, Leeds, Yorks., (1826–40). [D]

Ingle, Joseph, Eccleshill, Yorks., joiner and cm (1837). [D]

Inglesant, William, Long Row, Nottingham. joiner and cm (1783–1803). Son of John Inglesant of Nottingham, Gent. App. in 1777 and free, 1783. [D; app. reg.; freemen rolls; poll bk]

Ingleton, Joseph S., London and Macclesfield, Cheshire, carver and gilder (1808–27). Addresses used are 16 Drury Lane, 11 Charing Cross, George Yd, Macclesfield and 27 Frith St, Soho. [D]

Inglis, William, 38 Whitechapel Rd, London, bed and mattress maker (1822). [D]

Inglish, M., 27 Long Alley, Moorfields, London, u etc. (1820–26). [D]

Inglish, Richard, 5 Little Cheapside, Sun St, Finsbury Sq., London, chair stuffer (1808). [D]

Ingmire, B., 50 Leather Lane, Holborn, London, cm (1809). [D]

Ingold, Robert, Hotel St, Bolton, Lancs., cm (1824). [D]

Ingold, Robert, Clough St, Bury, Lancs., cm (1834). [D]

Ingoldby, James, Maiden Row, Louth, Lincs., chairmaker and turner (1822–40). [D]

Ingram, Benjamin, London, bedstead and cabinet maker (1801–29), At 17 Old Bethlem but later the address changed to 51 Old St, St Luke's. Between 1802–08 the business was listed as J. & B. Ingram, 17 Old Bethlem. [D]

Ingram, Benjamin, 23 and 24 Broker Row, Moorfields, London, cm (1822–25). In 1825 the address is given as 23–24 Eldon St, Finsbury Cresc. [D]

Ingram, Benjamin jnr, 58 Crown St, Finsbury, London, cm and u (1837–39). A maker of the same name and trade is also recorded for this period at 38 Beech St, Barbican. [D]

Ingram, George, New Bedminster Bridge, Bristol, chairmaker (1822–23). [D]

Ingram, George, West St, Wilton, Wilts., cm (1839). [D]

Ingram, John, London, japan and Windsor chair manufacturer (1803–39). At 1 Worship St in 1803 but from 1804 at 29 City Rd, Finsbury Sq. A substantial maker who specialised in fancy and rustic chairs. Stock in 1803 was valued at £1,100 and in 1804 one insurance policy was effected on 20 January which provided cover of £1,000 of which stock and utensils accounted for £700, and a further policy was effected on 28 July for £300 which covered a workshop and store in Tabernacle Row nearby, a japanning shop and their contents. By November 1806 the cover had increased to the impressive sum of £5,500 all but £300 of which was in respect of utensils and stock in various warehouses and workshops. In 1812 the business was termed a 'RUSTIC MUSEUM, and cheap Japan and Windsor Chair Manufactory'. In July Ingram informed the public of the success of a twelve day public auction which had cleared his warehouses of their old stock. They were now filled with the very latest goods which included 'every description of fancy japanned Windsor, mahogany and dyed chairs, sofas, couches, bedsteads, cornices, flower-stands, garden and rustic seats, bridges, alcoves, summer-houses &c.' He was offering a similar range in 1820. His trade card [Johnson Coll., Bodleian Lib., Oxford] lists similar wares and informs the public that he undertook funerals. From 1829 the business traded as John Ingram & Son. [D; GL, Sun MS vol. 426, ref. 745088; vol. 430, refs 764524, 757653; vol. 438, ref. 798035; Times, 9 July 1812, 7 April 1820]

Ingram, John, Clapham, London, upholder (1808–26). Recorded at High St in 1826. [D]

Ingram, Joseph, Gt Yarmouth and Hickling, Norfolk and London, cm (1818–31). Freeman of Gt Yarmouth and living in that town in 1818. In March 1820 at Hickling and in April 1831 in London. [Gt Yarmouth poll bks]

Ingram, Stephen, Bristol, carpenter, joiner and u (1817–27). At Smith's Cottage, Hotwell Rd in 1817 but from then until 1822 had additional premises at Clifton. From 1823 the address changes to Lodge House, Hotwell Rd but this may be just an alteration of house name. The Clifton premises, now given as Clifton Pl., became the sole address in 1827. [D]

Ingram, T., 16 Tavistock St, Covent Gdn, London, carver and gilder (1835). [D]

Ingram, Thomas, 1 Church St, Camberwell, London, u (1835). [D]

Ingram, William, 11 City Rd, Finsbury, London, upholder and auctioneer (1817). [D]

Ingram, William, Parsonage House, Coney St, York, house, sign, furniture and coach painter (1823). [D]

Inkpen, Joshua, 42 St Thomas St, Weymouth, Dorset, cm and u (1840). [D]

Inman, James, Liverpool, joiner and cm (1823–24). In 1823 at 10 Frederick St, St James' but in 1824 at 26 St James' St. [D]

Inman, Joseph, 30 Manor St, Liverpool, joiner and cm (1827). [D]

Inman, S., Tonbridge, Kent, cm (1803). Possibly the Inman who subscribed to Sheraton's Cabinet Dictionary, 1803. [D]

Innebe, Thomas, King's Lynn, Norfolk, u (1786). Freeman of Norwich. [Norwich poll bk]

Innes, James, Croydon, Surrey, cm, broker and u (1793). [D]

Innes, John, address unknown (1765). In 1765 supplied a tea chest to Blair Castle, Perthshire. [V & A archives]

Inns, William, High St, Towcester, Northants., cm/joiner (1823). [D]

Insull, Henry, New St, Worcester, cm (1812–40). App. to John Timmings of Worcester, cm and u, and free 5 October 1812. In 1830 may have been employed by Anderson & Perry of 59 Foregate St, as an Insull appears in an account sent to J. S. Russell of Powick Court, near Worcester. Insull and Jno. Perry appear to have fixed hooks for lamps in the drawing and dining rooms at High Park, Salwarpe on 6 April and Insull alone was responsible for fixing a hook in the dining room ceiling at Powick. [Freemen rolls; poll bk; Worcs. RO, 2309/705:380/18(i)]

Insull, William, Worcester, cm and u (1820–30). At 17 Foregate St in 1820, no. 18 in 1822; High St in 1828 and New St in 1830. [D]

Introvino, Antonio, Liverpool, carver, gilder, looking-glass and picture frame maker (c. 1817–24). Set up on his own account after the breakup of the partnership with Gaspar Introvino. In October 1818 he announced his move from Old Hall St, Lord St to 128 Duke St. He claimed to manufacture 'all sorts of Mirrors, Looking Glasses, Barometers, Thermometers & Hygrometers' He offered a framing service, the re-gilding of old frames and the re-silvering of mirror plates. Old looking-glasses and pictures would be taken in part exchange. He also stocked 'Prints, Medallions, Gold Borders & Ornaments. Gold, Fancy & Drawing Paper, Colours, Brushes & Pencils, Drawing Books etc.'. By 1821 at 138 Duke St and by 1823 this number had changed to 140. In an advertisement of December 1823 he admitted that he had been forced into bankruptcy in 1820 because of bad debts, and rumours of his financial difficulties which caused his creditors to press for payment. Afterwards, with the support of 'gentlemen who wished well to him', he re-established his business. In addition to the range of goods that he had on offer he also informed the public that he would teach the Italian language to those who wished to learn, As a native of that country he felt himself well qualified to undertake such work. [D; Liverpool Mercury, 9 October 1818, 19 December 1823]

Introvino, Antonio & Gaspar, Manchester, barometer and looking-glass makers (1814–16). At 49 Thomas St in 1814 but in 1816 shown at both 43 Thomas St and 39 Bridge St. A. Introvino was trading at 30 Bridge St in 1815 as carver, gilder and printseller. [D]

Introvino, Gaspar, 43 Thomas St, Manchester, carver, gilder, barometer, mirror and picture frame maker (c. 1817–40). When the partnership with Antonio Introvino broke up he took over the premises in Thomas St that they had previously used. [D]

Inwood, Benjamin, St Giles St, Northampton, chair turner (1826). [Poll bk]

Inwood, John, High St, Leighton Buzzard, Beds., cm and u (1830–39). [D]

Inwood, Jno., Market Pl., Stoney Stratford, Bucks., cm (1839). [D]

Ion, Christopher Appleby snr, London, upholder (1741). Son of Thomas Ion of Paulet, Som., clerk. App. to Benjamin Baron on 21 April 1732 and free of the Upholders' Co. by servitude on 6 May 1741. [GL, Upholders' Co. records]

Ion, Christopher Appleby jnr, London, upholder (1768). Son of Christopher Appleby Ion snr. Admitted freeman of the Upholders' Co. by patrimony, 2 March 1768. In 1771 either father or son was living at Coal Harbour, Upper Thames St. [GL, Upholders' Co. records]

Ireland, —, Prince's House, Leicester Fields, London, u (d. 1726). Died in 1726 and said to be 'Upholsterer to their Royal Highnesses'. [Heal]

Ireland, Benson Harrison, Lancaster, cm (1823–30). App. to L. Redmayne in 1823 and free, 1829–30. [Lancaster app. reg. and freemen rolls]

Ireland, E. & Hollier, C. W., London (1793). Supplied Gertrude, Dowager Duchess of Bedford of 112 Pall Mall with 'a neat inlaid case with a bottle & place for sugar & tea spoon' (a tea caddy). [Bedford Office, London]

Ireland, Edward, St John's Hill, Shrewsbury, Salop, cm (1796). [Freemen rolls]

Ireland, Hugh, 25 and 5 Dean St, Soho, London, u (1815–16). [D]

Ireland, John, Bow St, London, upholder (1779). [Bailey's list of bankrupts]

Ireland, John, London, upholstery warehouse (1783–99). At 3 Friday St and 26 Watling St, 1783–88, and then at 29 Compton St. In 1786 took out insurance cover of £2,000 of which £1,500 was for utensils, stock and goods in trust. [D; GL, Sun MS vol. 339, p. 217]

Ireland, John, Horsham Sussex, ironmonger and cm (1811). [D]

Ireland, John, Duck Lane, Bilston, Staffs, cm (1835). [D]

Ireland, Richard, Bow St, Covent Gdn, London, u (1769–84). Fellow of the Society of Arts, 1770–74. Bankrupt 1779. Attracted a number of influencial patrons. He is probably the 'Ireland', u, mentioned in the letters of Edward Gibbon as the supplier of white and gold bookcases for his house at 7 Bentwick St in 1772. He supplied furniture and undertook work on a regular basis for Richard Hoare of Boreham House, Essex between 1769–76, possibly for his London house. In total the patronage amounted to £157 13s, the largest sum being £59 5s paid on 8 November 1774. [D; poll bk; Heal; *Leicester Journal*, 19 June 1779; Essex RO, D/Du 649/2]

Ireland, Richard, Norwich, upholder (1771–86). Son of Daniel Ireland, weaver, admitted freeman on 31 August 1771. [Freemen rolls; poll bk]

Ireland, Richard, London, cm (1807–11). In 1807 at 18 Richmond St, Old St where he took out insurance cover of £400, half of which was for utensils and stock. By March 1811 he had moved to 24 Gt Mitchell St, Brick Lane, Old St. Here the insurance cover was £700 of which £400 was for stock and utensils. [GL, Sun MS vol. 438, ref. 800308; vol. 449, ref. 854905]

Ireland, Richard, 19 Blackman St, Southwark, London, carver and gilder, upholstery and looking-glass warehouse (1821–25). In 1821 and 1823 took out insurance cover of £500 though some of this was for household goods. He had warerooms, a gilding shop and a glass room and three stores. [D; GL, Sun MS vol. 484, ref. 978358; vol. 490, ref. 1001514]

Ireland, William, North St, Ripon, Yorks., joiner/cm (1837). [D]

Iremonger, Thomas, 'The Three Chairs', Drury Lane, London, cm (1727). His dwelling house was at the corner of Middlx Ct, Drury Lane. On 13 January 1727 he took out insurance cover of £300 on household goods and stock in trade kept there. [GL, Sun MS vol. 25, ref. 43544]

Irish, John, 36 Windmill St, Tottenham Ct Rd, London, cm and u (1839). [D]

Irlam, Jane, Manchester, u (1817–39). In 1817 at 17 Sandywell Lane, Salford. No further directory entries are recorded until 1838–39, when she was at 3 Buxton St, Manchester. [D]

Irlam, John, Sandywell, Salford, Lancs., u (1808). [D]

Irlam, Mary, Salford, Lancs., u (1813–25). At 12 Barlows Croft in 1813 and 3 Irwell St in 1825. [D]

Iron, John, Clifford St, Westminster, London, upholder (1749). [Poll bk]

Iron, John, Leicester, u (1798). Son of Nathaniel Iron of Ipswich, u. In 1789 app. to Mark Oliver, possibly Mark Oliver Iron of Ipswich, u. Free 1789. [Leicester freemen rolls]

Iron, Mark Oliver, Old Butter-market, Ipswich, Suffolk, cm and u (1809–39). Married in 1809 at the Church of St Lawrence, Ipswich. Probably the son of Nathaniel Iron of Ipswich, u. His business from 1805–09 was described as Nathaniel Iron & Son. Mark Oliver Iron is first recorded trading on his own behalf in 1817. [D; Suffolk RO, FAA: 50/2/114, pp. 77–78, 50/19/3.5; poll bks]

Iron, Nathaniel, Butter-market, Ipswich, Suffolk, u (1759–1809). Married on 1 January 1759 and trading in the Buttermarket as early as 1784. Subscribed to Sheraton's *Drawing Book*, 1793. After 1805 the business is listed as Nathaniel Iron & Son. [D; *Ipswich Journal*, 8 September 1804, 3 June 1809, Suffolk RO, FAA 50/2/89–93]

Ironmonger, William, Sittingbourne, Kent, cm (1839). [D]

Irvin, —, Wigan, Lancs., cm (1798). [D]

Irvin, George, Newbeddin, (Newbiggin) Richmond, Yorks., joiner and cm (1813–40). [D; PR (bapt.)]

Irvin, Richard, Lancaster, (1818–40). Named in the Gillow records, 1818–19, 1821–40. [Westminster Ref. Lib., Gillow]

Irvin, Thomas, Garden Ct, Roscoe St, Liverpool, cm (1827). [D]

Irving, Edward, Wigton, Cumb., jointer/cm (1828–34). At Black Swan Lane, 1828 but from 1829 at Water St. [D]

Irving, John, Rickersgate, Carlisle, Cumb., joiner/cm (1829). [D]

Irwin & Potter, 5 Paradise St, Liverpool, cm (1790). [D]

Isaac, A., address unknown, chairmaker (*c.* 1840). A high back Windsor chair at Temple Newsam House, Leeds, is stamped 'A ISAAC'.

Isaac, Isaac, Precinct of Bedford, Exeter, Devon, cm (1803). [Militia Census]

Isaac, John, Liverpool, cm (1739). In 1739 took app. named Harrison. [S of G, app. index]

Isaac, John, Exeter, Devon, cm (1813–40). Living at Excise Passage, 1813–14, when his daughter Ann and son John were bapt. In 1817 at Gandy St and from 1831 at 24 Holloway St. [D; poll bk; PR (bapt.)]

Isaac, William, London, upholder (1767). Son of Abraham Isaac of St Luke's, London, purse maker. App. to J. Chapman of the Armourers' & Braziers' Co. on 8 May 1760. Free of the Upholders' Co. on 4 June 1767 under the terms of the 1750 Upholders' Act. [GL, Upholders' Co. records]

Isaac, William, Market St, Weymouth, Dorset, cm (1779–98). Insurance cover on utensils and stock rose from £100 in 1779 to £200 in 1785. By the latter year he had a warehouse and workshop which were insured for an additional £100. In 1789 his dwelling house and shop and trade goods kept there were insured for £200 and a further £400 was taken out on a warehouse, outhouse and workshop and their contents. He also owned in this year a house in St Thomas's St tenanted by a T. Smith, linen draper. In 1789 his business was described as an u, cutler and cm and in 1798 as a joiner, cm and auctioneer.

In 1789 he was described as William Isaac jnr. [D; GL, Sun MS vol. 276, p. 204; vol. 330, p. 96; vol. 362, p. 601; vol. 386, p. 165]

Isaack, Jonathan, London, upholder (1718–29). His father was William Isaack Esq., a native of Devon. App. to Randolph Baron on 16 January 1718/19, and free of the Upholders' Co. by servitude on 5 March 1728/29. [GL, Upholders' Co. records]

Isaacs, Henry, 6 Colonnade, Salford, Lancs., cm and joiner (1828). [D]

Isaacs, Matthew, Excise Passage, Exeter, Devon, carver (1832). His son Matthew bapt. at All Hallows, Goldsmith St on 17 February 1832. [PR (bapt.)]

Isaacson, Philip, Cambridge, cm, u, auctioneer and appraiser (1796–1803). An advertisement appeared in the *Cambridge Chronicle and Journal* for 3 September 1796, from Philip Isaacson, 'Upholsterer and Cabinetmaker in the Petty Cury, Cambridge' wanting a journeyman cm. He again advertised on the 1 April 1797 that he was taking up the business's of auctioneer and appraiser. The Corporation day bk records on 14 November 1797: 'Ordered that the Treasurer pay to Mr Isaacson his bill of £20 9. 6. this day delivered for chairs for the Aldermans Parlour' and for 9 January 1798 'Ordered that the Mayor pay to Mr. Philip Isaacson the sum of Twenty pounds in full for his bill this day delivered for Furniture for the Aldermans Parlour'. The newspaper for 15 December 1803 advertised the sale by auction of 'All the stock in Trade, Household Furniture and other effects of Philip Isaacson, Upholsterer and Cabinet Maker in Petty Cury, Cambridge' with details of the furniture and materials to be sold. [Cambs. RO, Corp. day bks]　　　　　　　　　　R.W.

Isherwood, —, London(?) (1773–74). In the Digby papers for 1774 is a list headed 'For Furniture sent to Sherborne last year'. This includes a sum of £52 against 'Isherwood'. [Sherborne MS]

Isherwood, I. F., 20 Lamb's Conduit St, London, painter, paperhanger, carver and gilder (1835–37). In 1837 also at 6 New Bond St. [D]

Isherwood, John, 6 New Bond St, London, decorator and u (1840). [Heal]

Isherwood, Nicholas & Son, 35 Ludgate Hill, London, house painters, carvers and gilders, looking-glass makers and paper hangers to Their Majesties (1835–39). [D]

Isherwood & Bradley, 'The Golden Lyon', 35 Ludgate Hill, London, u, decorators and paper stainers (1787–92). Their trade card [Heal Coll., BM] states that they were partners with Thomas Bromwich. The business was described as a 'Paper-Hanging, Carving, Gilding, Looking-Glass and Screen Warehouse'. [D; Heal; *Conn.*, vol. 130, p. 108]

Isherwood & Smith, 7 Gt Eastcheap, London, wholesale u and cotton merchants (1769–74). In 1772 an address at 129 Upper Thames St is given in one directory. [D]

Isle, Sussana, Vollan's Row, Hunslet Lane, Leeds, Yorks., working u (1830). [D]

Ismay, Joseph, Whitehaven, Cumb., joiner/cm (1829–34). In 1829 at 145 Queen St and in 1834 at 8 Duke St. [D]

Issard, John, Half Moon Alley, Bishopsgate St, London, cm (1765). [Heal]

Issit(t), Mary, Belvoir St, Leicester, working u and paper hanger (1828–35). [D]

Issott, Joseph, Butcher Row, Beverley, Yorks., gilder and painter (1831–40). [D]

Ives, Edmund, 124 High Holborn, London, cm and u (1835–39). [D]

Ives, John, London, upholder (1713–23). Son of William Ives of Wickham, Hants., Gent. App. to Benjamin Powell on 10 December 1713 and free of the Upholders' Co. by

servitude on 4 December 1723. [GL, Upholders' Co. records]

Ives, William, Byland(?), Exeter, Devon, carver and gilder (1834). Daughter Sarah bapt. at St David's on 3 July 1834. [PR (bapt.)]

Ives, Dialls & Co., 6 Long Acre, London, varnish and japan manufacturers (1801–07). Trade card [Banks Coll., BM] states 'Late Wall's, Japanners to their Majesties and the Prince of Wales'. [D]

Ivey, J., 32 Temple St, Bristol, plasterer, painter, glazier, plumber, Windsor and fancy chairmaker (1836–37). [D]

Ivison, James, Keswick, Cumb., joiner/cm (1828–34). [D]

Ivory, John, Cambridge, carver and gilder (1668–70). In 1668 paid by Trinity College for gilding 'ye noblemans table in ye Buttery' and for putting names on it. In 1670 he was paid £3 10s by St John's College for making a new table of Benefactors and Masters of the College and framing a picture.

Ivory, Richard, St Clement's, Oxford, cm (1802–08). [D; poll bk]

Ivory, Robert, St Leonard, Shoreditch, London, carver (1761). [GL, P91/LEN]

Ivory, Thomas, St Martin's at Oak, Norwich, joiner and cm (1744). On 26 May 1744 advertised his ability to carry out joinery or cabinet work in mahogany and offered to supply the trade with mahogany at London prices plus the cost of carriage to Norwich. In June of the same year he offered furniture to the public in walnut or mahogany such as chairs and settees and table frames. He claimed that his standards of workmanship and prices were equal to those of London makers. [*Ipswich Journal*, 26 May 1744, 16 June 1744]

Ivory, William, address unknown, cm (1784–96). Supplied furniture to Audley End, Essex for Lord Howard, 1784–96. Probably a local Essex craftsman. In 1784 and 1786 an assortment of furniture made of fruitwood, mahogany, oak and olivewood was supplied. In 1794 a one leaf dining table of deal was charged at 18s. This was for the Steward's Room but a wainscott chest of drawers supplied at the same time and costing £3 10s was for Lord Howard's Dressing Room. In 1795–96 a mahogany dressing table with ten drawers was charged at £3 3s, a deal 'closett chest' with folding doors and six drawers at £3 5s and one with four drawers at £2 16s. Essex RO, D/DBy/A52/6, D/DBy/A54/1]

Izard, John, 18 St James St, Brighton, Sussex, Tunbridge-ware manufacturer and fancy repository (1822–40). [D; poll bk; rate bks]

Izon, John Parnell & Sons, Dale End, Birmingham, cm and u (1822–28). Recorded at no. 33 in 1822 and no. 32 in 1828. [D]

Izon, John, George & Thomas, Dale End, Birmingham, cm, paper hangers and u (1829–30). Shown at 33 Dale End in 1829 but by 1830 at no. 32. [D]

Izott, Joseph, Kirkgate, Wakefield, Yorks., cm (1814–20). [D]

J

Jack, Richard, Charles Ct, Westminster, London, u (1749). [Poll bk]

Jackman, James, North St, Ripon, Yorks., joiner/cm (1828–37). [D]

Jackman, Paul, over against Magdalen College, Oxford, cm (c. 1740). His trade card [Landauer Coll., MMA, NY] indicates that he made and sold 'all sorts of Cabinet Work, as Desks, Buroes, Scrutores, Book Cases, Chests of Drawers,

Corner Cupboards, Tea Boards, Tables & Chests, Dressing & Dining Tables, Chairs Matted, or Leather & Glasses in new fashioned Frames from London'. Other items mentioned were 'Bellows, Cloaths & Hearth Brushes' and 'Hard Wares'.

Jackman, Richard, 67 Old Gravel Lane, London, carpenter, cm, broker and undertaker (1803). In July 1803 took out insurance cover of £300 of which £80 was in respect of utensils and stock. [GL, Sun MS vol. 426, ref. 750469]

Jackman, William, Gt Yarmouth, Norfolk, cm (1831–40). From 1832 shown as William Jackman jnr. [Poll bks]

Jackson, —, Tottenham Ct Rd, London, turner of oval frames (1763). [Heal]

Jackson, —, Marlborough St, London, cm (1795). Birth of 21st child recorded in *Gents Mag.*, August 1795.

Jackson, —, Baliffgate, Alnwick, Northumb., cm and joiner (1834). [D]

Jackson, Benjamin, 2 Dukes Ct, Bow St, London, cm (1776). In 1776 took out insurance cover of £200 of which £80 was in respect of utensils, stock and goods in trust. [GL, Sun MS vol. 246, p. 549]

Jackson, Benjamin, New Compton St, Soho, London, upholder, cm and appraiser (c. 1790). Trade card [Heal Coll., BM] states that he also undertook carving and gilding and acted as an undertaker.

Jackson, C., 60 West St, Brighton, Sussex, cm (1839). [D]

Jackson, Charles, 12 Cranbourn St, Brighton, Sussex, cm and u (1839–40). [D]

Jackson, Daniel & Peter, Manchester, carvers, gilders, looking-glass and picture frame makers (1816–38). At 1 Spring Gdns, 1816–25, but by 1828 had moved to 83 Market St. Their bankruptcy was announced in December 1830 and subsequently Peter recommenced trading on his own behalf. He is recorded at Wolstenholmes Ct in 1832 and from 1834 in New Common St, where the number was 35 in 1834 and 29 from 1836. The business probably developed a reputation locally and he supplied items to Lord de Tabley, Tabley Hall, Cheshire. Frames were invoiced on 18 March, 20 April and 17 May 1823 at a total cost of £35, and in October of the same year hearth rugs are listed, at £49 13s. An annual account submitted in January of the following year totalled £130 16s 7d, and included a handsome mahogany cabinet with drawers at £5 and paper hangings. [D; *Chester Courant*, 14 December 1830; Chester RO, Tabley Hall vouchers DLT]

Jackson, Edward, Fennil St, Manchester, cm and joiner (1772–73). [D]

Jackson, Edward, Church St, Totnes, Devon, cm and u (1838). [D]

Jackson, Edwin, 33 Charles St, City Rd, London, cm and u (1839). [D]

Jackson, Ephraim, Charles Ct, Westminster, London, cm (1749). [Poll bk]

Jackson, Frances, Buckingham Rd, Aylesbury, Bucks., u and cm (1839). [D]

Jackson, George, King's Lynn, Norfolk, cm (1774–75). App. to James Lyther, cm, and free by servitude, 1774–75. [Freemen rolls]

Jackson, George, Wisbech, Cambs. and Sutton St Mary, Lincs. cm (1784–1822). Freeman of King's Lynn, Norfolk and possibly the George Jackson who was free, 1774–75. In 1784 at Wisbech and in 1822 at Sutton St Mary. [King's Lynn poll bks]

Jackson, George, Aylesbury, Bucks., cm and broker (1793). [D]

Jackson, George, Lancaster, cm (1802–07). App. to W. Blackburn in 1802 and free, 1806–07. Appears to have moved to London. [Lancaster app. reg. and freemen rolls]

Jackson, George, Hospital St, Nantwich, Cheshire, cm/joiner (1817–34). Married on 21 January 1817. In 1822 listed also as a joiner. See Joseph Jackson, chairmaker at this address, 1822–28. [D]

Jackson, George, Church St, Berwick-on-Tweed, Northumb., joiner and cm (1834). [D]

Jackson, George, Upper Duke St, Liverpool, carver and gilder (1835–39). At 12 Upper Duke St, 1835–37, but in 1839 at no. 4. [D]

Jackson, George, Fore St, Hertford, auctioneer, cm and u (1823–39). Probably the supplier of two 'splat back Windsor chairs' and 'two best Windsor chairs' for Panshanger, Herts. in 1836. These chairs were charged at 5s 6d each. [D: Herts. RO, Panshanger box 56]

Jackson, George, 20 Greengate, Salford, Lancs., carver and gilder (1840). [D]

Jackson, George, 49–50 Rathbone Pl., Oxford St, London, picture frame maker (1756–1840). Established his firm in 1780 using his large stock of boxwood moulds to press out Adam-style composition ornament. He is mentioned in Loudon's *Encyclopaedia*, 1833, as a maker of looking-glass frames using composition. By 1840 trading as George Jackson & Sons and supplying the Royal household. In March 1840 four 'large glass frame heads with composition enrichments' were supplied for the Small Drawing Room, Buckingham Palace at a cost of £39. Also for the same room were six 'large glass frames richly ornamented with composition husk & acorn with festoons of fruit & flowers, brass foliage, bases & ornament laid on glass with carved initial V.R. to design'. With other frames for pictures the total of the goods invoiced in March came to £188. [GL, Sun MS vol. 576, ref. 1339385; Windsor Royal Archives, box 1]

Jackson, Henry, Morpeth, Northumb., cm (1784). [D]

Jackson, Henry, Broughton, Lancs., cm (1784). [D]

Jackson, Henry, London, u and cm (1822–39). At 33 Rathbone Pl., 1822–28, and from 1835 at 76 Gt Queen St. [D]

Jackson, Henry, Bishop St, Coventry, Warks., cm and u (1835). [D]

Jackson, James, Newcastle, u (1730–31). Free by servitude on 27 January 1730/31. [Freemen reg.]

Jackson, James, 2 Husband St, London, broker and cm (1779–1809). In 1779 took out insurance cover of £200, half of which was for utensils and stock. Probably the James Jackson who subscribed to Sheraton's *Drawing Book*, 1793. [D; GL, Sun MS vol. 271, p. 361]

Jackson, James, Leadenhall Sq., Hull, Yorks., cm (1790–99). [D]

Jackson, James, Leeds, Yorks., cm (1834–40). At Mabgate Green in 1834 but from 1837 at Millwright St. [D]

Jackson, James, Laycock, Keighley, Yorks., joiner/cm (1837). [D]

Jackson, James & John, Kearsley, Bolton, Lancs., cm (1834). [D]

Jackson, Jasper, Buckingham Rd, Aylesbury, Bucks., cm and u (1823–30). [D]

Jackson, John snr, London, upholder (before 1706). Dead by 1706 when his son John was app. [GL, Upholders' Co. records]

Jackson, John, London(?), carver (1695–1709). Recorded as a carver in the Monson archive from 1695–1702. Submitted an account to Wriothesley, 2nd Duke of Bedford, totalling £15 9s 9d, for work carried out between September 1708 and June 1709. This was for 'peartree framing'. [Lincoln RO, Monson 28B/6/1; Bedford Office, London]

Jackson, John jnr, London, upholder (c. 1715–51). Son of John Jackson snr, freeman upholder of London. App. to Sarah Jackson, widow of John Jackson snr on 28 October 1706 but not free of the Upholders' Co. until 2 June 1742. Took as app. Samuel Mann, 1742–1750/51. [GL, Upholders' Co. records]

Jackson, John, London, upholder (1747). Son of Stephen Jackson, freeman upholder of London. App. to his father on 5 March 1739 and free of the Upholders' Co. by servitude on 5 February 1746/47. [GL, Upholders' Co. records]

Jackson, John, Drury Lane, London, cm and upholder (1773–93). At 43 Drury Lane in 1773, in Broad Ct, Drury Lane in 1774, at no. 24 in 1784, 26 in 1789 and 25, 1790–93. In 1773 shown as cm but from 1784 as an upholder. A Mary Loben is associated with Jackson in 1791 in the insurance of two houses at the corners of Marshall and Silver St, one of which was occupied by Ram, cm. [D; GL, Sun MS ref. 581988, 9 April 1791]

Jackson, John, 9 Aldersgate St, London, upholder and cm (1782–93). A fairly substantial business which insured its stock and utensils in 1782 for £550 and in 1785 for £1,000. Probably the John Jackson who supplied furnishing fabrics and eight chairs in 1786 to Lord Howard de Walden of Audley End, Essex, at a cost of £10 10s. [D; GL, Sun MS vol. 229, p. 364; vol. 328, p. 551; Essex RO, D/DBy/A44/6]

Jackson, John, Pendleton, Lancs., joiner and cm (1787). On 5 March 1787 took out insurance cover of £200 on goods. [GL, Sun MS vol. 343, p. 209]

Jackson, John, Knutsford, Cheshire, joiner and cm (1790). [D]

Jackson, John, Hull, Yorks., cm (1790–1810). At Saville St, 1790–99 and from 1803 at Bond St. [D]

Jackson, John, Nottingham, cm (1791–98). In 1791 signed the *Nottingham Cabinet and Chair Makers' Book of Prices* on behalf of the masters. [D]

Jackson, John, Highgate, Kendal, Westmld, cm/u (1805–34). [D]

Jackson, John, 7 Gt Earl St, Seven Dials, London, carver, gilder and picture frame maker (1816–25). His trade card [Landauer Coll., MMA, NY] states 'Frames Regilt, Gilt Border Mouldings for Rooms'. [D]

Jackson, John, Castle St, Chester, cm (1812–19). Shown in poll bks as early as 1812 but not sworn a freeman until 18 May 1818. [Poll bks; freemen rolls]

Jackson, John, 109 Gt Portland St, London, u and cm (1820–23). [D]

Jackson, John, Sheffield, Yorks., cm and joiner (1822–33). At Hick's Lane in 1822 and 1 Portobello St, in 1833. [D]

Jackson, John, Tweedmouth, Berwick-upon-Tweed, Northumb., cm (1827). [D]

Jackson, John, Whitby, Yorks., cm (1828–30). In 1828 at St John's Staith but in 1830 at St Ann's Staith. [D]

Jackson, John, Tirril, Stockbridge, Barton, Westmld, chairmaker (1829–34). [D]

Jackson, John, Holmfirth, Yorks., joiner/cm (1834). [D]

Jackson, John, Old Malton Gate, Malton, Yorks., joiner and cm (1840). [D]

Jackson, John, High St, Uppingham, Rutland, chairmaker and turner (1835–40). [D]

Jackson, John L., Stockgill, Ambleside, Westmld, cm (1829). [D]

Jackson, John Matthew, Brighton, Sussex, cm and u (1799–1837). At 2 Middle St Lane, although one directory of 1832 lists 1 Ship St Lane. This may however refer to the same locality. In January 1828 advertised 'Patent elastic beds, pillows, easy chairs, sofas, carriage seats, invalid beds &c' and stated that he was the sole agent for the sale of 'PRATT'S Patent Elastic Couches, Ottomans . . . Beds, Bolsters, Pillows, Carriage-Seats, small chair seats'. These patent articles were offered at 'the Manufacturers' Prices, or by a card of reference to the Inventor's Warehouse, Bond-street, London'. In addition to these items, aimed at those living in, or staying at the spa, for reasons of health, he also stocked a range of conventional furniture such as 'chairs, couches, French beds and cabinet furniture' of his manufacture. He also offered 'brass carriers and cornice rods, stair rods, dry oil cloth, paper hangings, seasoned feathers' and offered to furnish funerals. Bankrupt October 1830, but recorded in directories as late as 1832 and still living in the town in 1837. [D; poll bk; *Brighton Gazette*, 22 January 1824; *Brighton Herald*, 19 January 1828; *London Gazette*, 5 October 1830]

Jackson, Joseph, London, cm (1754–d. 1799). At 5 Bull Head Ct, Jewin St in 1754 but from the early 1790s this address was renamed 5 The Crescent, Jewin St. By 1794 the number had changed to 9. His father may have been Joseph Jackson, joiner of Cockermouth, Cumb. who took app. between 1720–36. Subscribed to Chippendale's *Director*, 1754. In the period 1755–87 took out licences to be renewed quarterly to employ non-freemen, and in the period 1764–87 the number licenced was never less that sixteen. This would suggest a substantial business and confirmation is given from insurance records. In 1777 total insurance amounted to £3,700 of which £2,800 covered utensils, stock and goods in trust. By 1791 it was £6,600 with £3,000 for trade stock. Joseph Jackson died early in 1799 and his stock was offered by auction. This included 'case furniture, chair frames, glasses also timber, veneers, benches, tools etc.' It was also stated that his business premises were to let. They consisted of 'spacious warerooms, work-shops, yards and sheds, with a communication into Red Cross-street and two dwellings in front'. [D: GL, City Licence bks, 1–10; Sun MS vol. 254, p. 54; vol. 287, p. 145; vol. 370, 1791; vol. 397, p. 400; *Times*, 16 March 1799]

Jackson, Joseph, Carnaby St, London, cm (1781–82). In both 1781 and 1782 took out insurance cover of £300 of which £100 was for utensils and stock. [GL, Sun MS vol. 290, p. 581; vol. 302, p. 497]

Jackson, Joseph, Aylesbury, Bucks., cm and u (1793–1823). Trading at Buckingham Rd in 1823. A George Jackson was also trading as a cm and broker in the town in 1793. [D]

Jackson, Joseph, Hospital St, Nantwich, Cheshire, chairmaker (1822–29). A George Jackson, cm, was also trading from this address, 1817–34. [D]

Jackson, Joseph, Hepworth, Yorks., cm (1837). [D]

Jackson, Joseph & William, 1 and 4 Maze Pond, Southwark, London, cm and chairmakers (1813–39). Directories show Joseph & William Jackson until 1837 but other directories show Joseph Dickenson Jackson at this location from 1823. [D]

Jackson, L., Ambleside, Westmld, cm and joiner (1828). [D]

Jackson, Mary, London, u (1685–92). Supplied mats, hangings, cushions, quilts, chairs etc. for St James's and Whitehall Palaces, 1685–86, 1688–89 and 1692. In February 1685/86 provided furnishings for the mourning of Mary of Modena, (wife of James II) at the death of Charles II. [PRO, LC9/278–80]

Jackson, Peter, 1 and 2 Harp Alley, Shoe Lane, Fleet St, London, u and furniture broker (1803–39). His billhead in the GL, Dept of Prints lists his trade as 'Brokers, Upholders, Appraisers and Auctioneers'. At this early stage of the business it was a partnership trading as Jackson & Hind. Hind had probably left the business by 1810 however. Peter Jackson was obviously a person of some substance for in December 1810 he took out insurance cover of £1,000 on two houses that he owned. [D; GL, Sun MS vol. 452, ref. 852033]

Jackson, Peter, Bailiffgate Sq., Alnwick, Northumb., joiner and cm (1827–34). [D]

Jackson, Peter, Manchester, carver, gilder, looking-glass and picture frame maker (1832–38). Recorded at Wolstenholme's Ct, 1832–33, and 29 New Cannon St, 1836–38. [D] See Daniel & Peter Jackson.

Jackson, Ralph, 15 Mill Hill, Manchester, cm (1813). Possibly the Ralph Jackson who was app. to Thomas Astle, cm, on 30 December 1784. [D; app. bk]

Jackson, Richard, Friar St, Reading, Berks., carver and gilder (1820). [Poll bk]

Jackson, Robert, London, upholder and cm (1774–93). At Rupert St in 1774 but from 1789 shown at 16 Berwick St. His trade card [Banks Coll., BM] shows a Sheraton-style cabinet and bed and incorporates the Prince of Wales' feathers, but no further claim is made on the card to Royal patronage. [D; Heal; Westminster poll bk]

Jackson, Robert, Lancaster (1798). Named in the Gillow records in 1798 in connection with making a door. [Westminster Ref. Lib., Gillow vol. 344/97, p. 1427]

Jackson, Robert, 25 Gt Pulteney St, Golden Sq., London, cm and u (1808). [D]

Jackson, Stephen, London, upholder (1708–47). Free of the Upholders' Co. on 7 July 1708. His son John was his app., 1739–1746/47, and free by servitude on 5 February 1746/47. [GL, Upholders' Co. records]

Jackson, Thomas, 13 Queen's Row, Hoxton, London, cm (1801–09). On 25 November 1801 took out insurance cover of £300 and of this £120 was in respect of stock. [D; GL, Sun MS vol. 423, ref. 725295]

Jackson, Thomas, Lancaster, cm (1811–12). [Lancaster freemen rolls]

Jackson, Thomas, Lancaster, cm (1817–18). Admitted freeman, 1817–18, when stated 'of Preston'. [Lancaster freemen rolls]

Jackson, Thomas, 39 Wood St, London, cm and u (1822). [D]

Jackson, Thomas, Selby, Yorks., cm (1822–37). At Ship Yard Row in 1822 but at Ousegate, 1834–37. [D]

Jackson, Thomas, 61 Leonard St, Shoreditch, London, cm (1826). [D]

Jackson, Thomas, Kearsley, Bolton, Lancs., joiner and cm (1828). [D]

Jackson, Thomas, Lancaster, carver (1814–34). Named in the Gillow records, 1814–34. [Westminster Ref. Lib., Gillow]

Jackson, Thomas, Lancaster, cm (1826–34). Free 1829–30 when stated 'of Ulverstone', Lancs. Named in the Gillow records 1826–27, 1829 and 1834. [Lancaster freemen rolls; Westminster Ref. Lib., Gillow]

Jackson, Thomas, 25 Northgate, Bradford, Yorks., cm (1830). [D]

Jackson, William, London(?), joiner and chairmaker (1677–85). On 26 February 1677 his app. Richard Blanchard was paid on his behalf £3 6s for seven cane chairs by William, 5th Earl of Bedford. On 23 March 1685/86 Lady Leigh paid a William Jackson £3 for a walnut table bed. It is possible that this maker may be the William Jackson who in 1702 and 1707 took out insurance on property in the parish of St Giles-in-the-Fields, London. [Bedford Office, London; Shakespeare Birthplace Trust, Leigh receipts, DE 18/5/872; GL, Hand in Hand MS vol. 2, ref. 2601–02; vol. 5, ref. 836]

Jackson, William, Severn Stoke, Worcs., cm (1747). [Worcester poll bk]

Jackson, William, 14 Brownlow St, Holborn, London, cm (1807–11). Traded in partnership with Whitehead as Jackson & Whitehead. [D]

Jackson, William, 111 Newgate St, London, carver and gilder (1809). [D]

Jackson, William, Lancaster, cm (1809–18). App. to Thomas Lister in 1809 and free, 1817–18 when stated 'of Middleton near Manchester'. [Lancaster app. reg. and freemen rolls]

Jackson, William, Sheffield, Yorks., cm (1822–33). at 4 Potter's Yd, Eyre Lane in 1822, 9 Pinstone St in 1828 and Fitzwilliam St in 1833. [D]

Jackson, William, Potter St, Bedford, cm and u (1823). [D]

Jackson, William, High Wycombe, Bucks., chairmaker (b. c. 1823–41). Aged 18 at the time of the 1841 Census.

Jackson & Graham, 37 and 38 Oxford St, London, cm and u (1836–40). One of the leading furniture makers of the Victorian period but in business at 37 Oxford St by June 1836. An invoice dated 14 June 1836 in the Museum of London is for a French polished rosewood sofa at £19 and other items. A trade card of this early period, giving the address as 37 and 38 Oxford St shows an engraving of the exterior of their premises and states their trade as 'Upholsterers, Carpet Manufacturers, Furniture Printers and Interior Decorators'. [D; Museum of London, Z1704/190; Westminster Ref. Lib., Gardener Box 63 10A]

Jackson & Jervis, 30 Rathbone Pl., Oxford St, London, u and auctioneers (1820–25). [D]

Jackson & Stalvies, Marsh St, Newcastle-under-Lyme, Staffs., cm and u (1836). [D]

Jackson & Wood, Leeds, Yorks., carver (1833). Dissolution of partnership announced in *Chester Courant*, 26 November 1833.

Jacob, Edward, St Lawrence, Reading, Berks., cm (1754–68). In 1754 took app. named Higgs. [S of G, app. index; poll bks]

Jacob, Jacob & Co., Market St, Falmouth, Cornwall, cm and u (1823–24). [D]

Jacob, John, parish of St Mary, Reading, Berks., u and cm (1718–40). Took apps named Pether in 1719, Whitehouse in 1722, Berry in 1727, and Howell in 1740. [S of G, app. index; GL, Sun MS vol. 7, 21 February 1718]

Jacob, John, Marylebone St, Golden Sq., London, carver and gilder (1772–79). In 1772 supplied Sir John Griffin Griffin of Audley End, Essex with a 'Glass Girandole Stand' costing 8s and in 1779 for the same patron repaired a girandole. [Essex RO, D/DBy/A30/2, D/DBy/A37/3]

Jacobs, —, Lancaster (1820). [Westminster Ref. Lib., Gillow records]

Jacobs, Benjamin, 30 Minories, London u (1829). [D]

Jacobs, F., 64 Northgate St, Canterbury, Kent, u (1838). [D]

Jacobs, Jacob, 74 Northgate St, Canterbury, Kent, cm and furniture broker (1832–38). In 1838 at 65 Northgate St, the same address as F. Jacobs, u. [D]

Jacobs, John, Newbury, Berks., cm (1756). In 1756 took app. named Parce. [S of G, app. index]

Jacobs, Michael, 4 Theatre Ct, Finkle St, Hull, Yorks., cm (1838–39). [D]

Jacques, Catherine, 12 Brownlow Hill, Liverpool, u (1821). [D]

Jacques, John, Holborn, London, carver and gilder (1783–1808). The address is usually given as 'The King's Arms', 14 Holborn but in 1808 it was 14 High Holborn and Heal lists an earlier address of 301 Holborn. From the 1790s their work was mostly in composition ornament and the production of chimney pieces. By 1801 Jacques was claiming a Royal appointment. In 1783 Alexander Wedderburn paid this maker £8 7s 9d, probably for picture frames. [D; Heal; Banks Coll., BM; Scottish RO, GD 164/Box 20/177/2–3]

Jacques, John, 102 Hatton Gdn, London, portable desk, dressing case, work box and cabinet case maker (1839–40). [D] Partner and successor to:

Jacques, Thomas, London, turner and Tunbridge-ware manufacturer (c. 1790–1839). The main base of trade was 65 Leather Lane, Holborn, but from 1817–23 used in addition an address at 22 Baldwin Gdns, Leather Lane. Initially specialised in ivory turning, with billiard balls an important product. Hardwoods and bone were also turned and ivory, tortoiseshell and hardwoods dealt in. Tunbridge-ware was also manufactured at an early stage, though there is no indication whether this was purely of turnery items or if cabinet wares were made. Certainly cabinet wares were being made by the mid 1830s and were to form the main part of the business of the firm for the future. In c. 1817 Thomas Jacques took John Jacques as his partner and the business traded under the style Thomas & John Jacques until c. 1839 when it moved to 102 Hatton Gdn and continued under the sole direction of John Jacques. [D; Heal]

Jacques & Hartill, 148 Old St, London, cm and u (1839). [D]

Jafensen, —, address unknown, cm (1679). Paid £1 10s, by Sir Richard Temple of Stowe, Bucks. [Huntington Lib., California, MS ST 155, p. 8]

Jaffrey, Charles, Hanover St, London, u (c. 1772–76). In 1767 'Thomas Chippendale, upholsterer' received a premium of £20 for taking on Charles Jaffrey as an app. for four years. Declared bankrupt, *Gents Mag.*, December 1773, but may have recommenced business and is possibly the 'Jaffray' who was reponsible for the funeral of the 1st Duchess of Northumberland in 1776 at a cost of £523 2s 2d. [PRO, 1/R1/25; Alnwick MS V.1.53(1)]

Jagger, Benjamin, Norwich, carver, gilder, picture frame maker and printseller (1762–1810). In 1768 recorded in the parish of St Andrew but from 1783 the address is given as 30 London Lane. Freeman of Norwich on 21 September 1762 as a carver but had not served his apprenticeship in the city. Took as apps Samuel Cushion (free 21 September 1770), Jno. Gardiner (free 24 February 1786) and on 13 January 1810 his own son Matthew Anderson Jagger described as 'Gent' was also made free. [D; poll bk; freemen reg.; *Norfolk Chronicle*, 24 April 1784]

Jakeman, —, London(?), cm. Death by drowning reported in *Gents Mag.*, July 1731

Jakeman, John, Hull, Yorks., cm (1823–29). At Church St, Drypool in 1823 and Cent per Cent St in 1829. [D] Possibly:

Jakeman, John, Market Pl., Beverley, Yorks., cm and u (1826). [D]

Jalland, John, Nottingham and London, cm (1737–54). Son of John Jalland, frame work knitter, and app. in 1725 as a cm. Free 1737 and by 1754 resident in London. [Nottingham app. reg., freemen rolls and poll bk]

Jamar, Jervais, 37 Gerrard St, Soho, London, French cm (1820). [D]

Jamar, S., London and Liverpool, cm (1818–26). In 1818 at 29 Wardour St, Soho. In February of that year he advertised his range of furniture in the French manner which he manufactured in London. He claimed that it was 'equal to any made in Paris, and at a rate that upon calculation will be admitted considerably advantageous than importing from abroad, also without incurring the risk of being damaged on the journey'. He also offered to repair old furniture, bronzes and gilt work. His nationality is not known but in 1819 he claimed to be cm to the King of Holland. He had also changed his address to 37 Gerard St, Soho. From this year he appears to have taken an interest in selling his wares and establishing a trade connection with Liverpool. In September 1819 he advertised in the *Liverpool Mercury* that he was displaying a range of 'Superb French Cabinet Furniture from his Manufactory' in Samuel Smith's Large Room in Lord St. Amongst the items on display were 'a beautiful Secretaire representing the French coffee house in Paris with 1000 columns; elegant & superb Bedsteads, modelled from one in the possession of the Empress of France; handsome Tables, in rosewood, mahogany & marble; superb antique & musical Clocks, richly ornamented with Sundry Cabinet Furniture'. This furniture was to be sold by auction on 29 September 1819, though the sale appears to have been postponed until 1 October when Samuel Smith conducted it. At the same time that he was promoting his elegant furniture to the affluent citizens of South Lancs. he was also seeking business partners

for a venture to utilise two machines for timber conversion. One machine, it was claimed, would 'cut Six Veneers or more, in the Inch, in Mahogany or any other Wood'. The other was able to 'saw Sixty Boards at once, of any thickness not less than a quarter of an inch'. This latter machine was claimed to do the work of 120 men. He indicated that he was prepared to lay out his part of the capital before requiring his partners to do so. He was also looking for partners in a venture to manufacture furniture of a similar type to that he was producing in London. Nothing more is recorded about his machines and he does not appear to have set up manufacturing facilities at Liverpool. Perhaps local capital was not forthcoming. He did not however entirely forget his ambitions to serve the Liverpool area and in March 1826 announced that he was opening a repository at 1 Gt Charlotte St. Here he put on a display of furniture 'which for taste in design & elegance in execution . . . can find no parallel', and an admittance fee of a shilling was charged to view it. It is possible that the exhibition may have been of a temporary nature, however, rather than a permanent feature.

A number of pieces of furniture stamped 'S. JAMAR' are known. These include a rosewood writing table with gilt mounts (Parke–Bernet NY, 1 April 1967, lot 66), a rosewood table with burr-elm veneered drawers on a turned yew column with four splayed legs (Christie's, 21 July 1966, lot 42), a rosewood cheval mirror (Sotheby's, 8 December 1978, lot 242), a rosewood fall front secretaire (Christie's, 19 November 1970, lot 46) and a similar item in the Egyptian taste inscribed on the lockplate 'Jamar Cabinetmaker 37 Gerard Street Soho' (Parke–Bernet NY, 8 March 1968, lot 71). [*Morning Chronicle*, 16 February 1818; *Liverpool Mercury*, 24 September 1819, 1 October 1819, 10 March 1826] B.A.

Jamar, William, London, French cm (1817–20). Shown at 29 Wardour St in 1817, an address known to have been used by S. Jamar by February of the following year. In 1820 shown at 37 Wardour St. By this date S. Jamar was at 37 Gerard St and it is possible that this entry may be a directory error. It suggests a close relationship between the two makers. A writing table stamped on the edges of the drawers with this maker's name was sold at Sotheby's, 26 October 1962, lot 168. [D]

James, —, address unknown, turner (1788). In July 1788 he was paid £24 3s for an inlaid table in July 1788 supplied for the Royal Household. [Windsor Royal Archives, 88695]

James, Andrew, 5 Sutton St, Soho Sq., London, timber bender (1829). [D]

James, Charles, Norwich and London, cm (1812–30). In the parish of St Saviour, Norwich, 1812–18 but by July 1830 living at Islington, London. [Norwich poll bk]

James, Edmund, East Walls, Carlisle, Cumb., chairmaker (1793–1810). The death of one of his workmen, John Brown was reported in *Gents Mag.*, March 1807. [D]

James, Edward, High St, Tewkesbury, Glos., chairmaker (1813–30). [PR (bapt.)]

James, Geoffrey, 96 James St and Francis Alley, Devonport, Devon, cm, u and dealer in marine stores (1822–23). In 1823 the business was trading as Geoffrey James & Son. [D]

James, George, Oxford, cm (b. c. 1711–d. by 1778). His address is recorded in 1744 at St Clement's, Bladon, Oxford and later at Bridgesett, St Clement's. At the time of his marriage to Anna Maria Southby of Oxford at St Giles on 28 April 1744 he was aged 33. In the same year he took app. named Badcock and was subsequently to take Simms in 1746, Smith in 1751 and Seabright in 1762. By June 1778 he was dead and in this month the goods in his house 'at the foot of new bridge, St. Clement's' were sold. In October of the following year

Gabriel Slatter, cm from London, announced that he had taken the shop of the late Mr James 'at the foot of Magd. Bridge, St. Clements'. James is recorded in connection with furniture for Christ Church Library. On 11 July 1764 he was paid £40 for five mahogany desks and on 26 September 1765, £18 18s for a set of library steps. The latter incorporate a carved floral medallion which also featured in a set of twelve stools supplied by Thomas Chippendale for the Library in the previous year. This furniture is still in use in the Library. [Bodleian index of Oxf. marriage bonds; S of G, app. index; poll bk; *Jackson's Oxford Journal*, 14 July 1764, 16 June 1778, 2 October 1779; *C. Life*, 5 January 1945, p. 29]

James, George, Tiverton, Devon, cm (1778). In 1778 took out insurance cover of £200 of which £50 was in respect of utensils and stock. [GL, Sun MS vol. 266, p. 270]

James, George, Plymouth, Devon, u and cm (1801). In November 1801 his stock was sold for the benefit of his creditors. Items offered included 'mahogany wardrobes, chests etc., circular end & square dining tables, octagon, oval, card & pembroke tables, claw tables, chairs with red, green & black Morocco seats, reeded pillar bedsteads etc'. [*Exeter Flying Post*, 12 November 1801]

James, George, 13 Dover St, Blackfriars Rd, London, cm and undertaker (1808). [D]

James, Hugh, Carlisle, Cumb., chairmaker (1829–34). At St Alban's Row in 1829 and 25 East Tower St in 1834. Possibly the successor of Edmund James. [D]

James, James, Plymouth, Devon cm (1798). [D]

James, John, King's Arms Yd, Holborn, London, carver (1761). On 22 August 1761 his release from Debtors' Prison was announced. He was stated to be 'formerly of the Old Bailey, late of King's-arms-yard, Holborn, St. Sepulchre'. [*London Gazette*, 22 August 1761]

James, John, Old Compton St, Soho, London, joiner and u (1808–20). Shown at 33 Old Compton St in 1808 when his trade was listed as joiner. In 1820 at no. 30 with his trade as u. [D]

James, John, 27 Atherton St, Liverpool, cm (1816–d. 22). App. to Isaac Marsh in 1807 and John Ward Turner in 1810. Petitioned freedom in 1816 but this was at first rejected, as the representatives of I. Marsh refused to take out letters of Administration, and no assignment of his indenture could be obtained. This difficulty does not appear to have deterred him, however, and he set up in business in this year. He was eventually shown free 24 June 1818. [D; freemen's committee bk and reg.]

James, John, 80 Pilgrim St, Newcastle, u, cm and paper hanger (1814–38). Commenced his business in Pilgrim St in June 1814 and before this had been employed by J. C. Ford. In 1833–34 referred to as John & Charles James, at 78 Pilgrim St in 1834. [D; *Newcastle Chronicle*, 18 June 1814]

James, John & William, 9 Cumberland Row, Newington, London, cm (1826–27). [D]

James, Jordan, St Botolph Without, Bishopsgate, London, carver (1761). Discharged from Debtors' Prison, September 1761. Said to be late of St Botolph Without, Bishopsgate. [*London Gazette*, 26 September 1761]

James, Joseph, Bristol, cm and chairmaker (1801–13). In 1801 at Bedminster Causeway as a chairmaker, but from 1805–13 at 58 Castle St, and from 1810 also indicated as a cm. [D]

James, Joseph, Nicholas Steps with factory at Back St, Bristol, basket and chairmaker, fancy brushes and toys (1839–40). [D]

James, Martin, High Wycombe, Bucks., chair turner (1840). [PR (marriage)]

James, Mathew, Rennington, Newcastle, cm (1759). In 1759 took app. named Hood. [S of G, app. index]

James, P., Retreat Pl., Cheltenham, Glos., cm (1839). [D]

James, Philip, 63 Holywell St, Shoreditch, London, u and undertaker (1769–1811). A business of modest size. In 1770 warehouses and workshops were insured for £500 but later figures suggest a decline in cover for trade stock. In 1777 the warehouses and workshops were only covered for £200 and in 1782 a similar figure was thought sufficient for the utensils and stock. Total insurance cover in 1777 was £900, falling to £800 in 1791 and rising again to £1,200 in 1802. Of this latter total however only £60 appears to have been for utensils and stock. The business is included in the list of master cabinet makers in Sheraton's *Cabinet Dictionary*, 1803. [D; GL, Hand in Hand MS vol. 110, ref. 68982; Sun MS vol. 255, p. 176; vol. 304, p. 70; vol. 377, p. 615; vol. 423, ref. 732368; vol. 424, ref. 738097]

James, Richard, Bristol, cm and victualler (1754–75). Living in the parish of St Peter in 1754 but soon after moved to the parish of St James and then to Bedminster. He was imprisoned for debt and released in June 1761. In 1774 he was living in Bedminster but in the following year his address was given as 38 Horse St, Bristol. [D; poll bks; *London Gazette*, 20 June 1761]

James, Richard, Bristol, carver and gilder (1824–32). At 20 North St from 1824–26, 12 Lower Arcade, 1827–28 and 2 Park St, 1829–32. [D]

James, Richard, Emscote, Warwick, cm and u (1835). [D]

James, Robert, Bristol, cm and u (1784–1831). Recorded living in the parish of St Augustine, 1784. In Terill St, 1793–95 and St Michael's Hill, 1799–1801. After 1805 the firm traded from 35 Broadmead and is recorded as Robert James & Co., 1805–06; James, Fry & Co., 1807–13; and once more reverted to Robert James & Co., 1814–15. From 1816 reverted to the pre-1805 style of Robert James. In 1818 he was declared bankrupt, but despite this the business quickly recovered and was probably at its height of achievement in the 1820s. In 1821 he advertised himself as the 'Manufacturer of the Beautiful Polyanthus Wood'. In the following year he received a Royal patent and thereafter described himself as 'Manufacturer in British Woods to his Majesty'. Clearly at this stage he was using woods with a wide range of colour variation and intricate grain patterns. He stated in an advertisement that 'his present manufactured stock of POLYANTHUS AND OTHER BRITISH WOODS ... will be found to excel any other yet offered, for beauty of Colours, and variety to the imagination, exhibiting on its highly polished surface, Woods, Landscapes, and in some instances, Animals, Fish &c are represented, which has a grand and pleasing effect'. The Duke of York also appears to have patronised James in 1826. In the 1820s he labelled some of his products, and a number of examples are known. These include a secretaire bookcase [*C. Life*, 11 June 1953, p. 1882], a yew-wood table [*Furn. Hist.*, 1966], a sofa table, yew-wood cross-banded with burr wood [Sotheby's, 20 May 1955, lot 157] and a large pedestal table veneered in burr oak and elm, and a tea caddy veneered in rosewood and burr yew, in the BM Coll. [D; poll bk; *Exeter Flying Post*, 26 February 1818; *Furn. Hist.*, 1976; V & A archives]

James, Robert, Exeter, Devon, carver and gilder (1815–34). Known through the baptisms of his six children at St Sidwell's Church, 1815–34. The eldest son, Robert was bapt. on 26 December 1815; but as this name was given to another child in 1829, it is likely that the previous one did not survive childhood. In 1824 at Bartholomew St and in 1834 at Well Lane. [PR (bapt.)]

James, Robert, Front St, Brampton, Cumb., joiner/cm (1828–29). [D] Possibly:

James, Robert, Rowcliff Lane, Penrith, Cumb., cm/joiner (1834). [D]

James, Stephen, 14 Albemarle St, St John's Sq., Clerkenwell, London, cm (1778). In 1778 insured his house for £200. [GL, Sun MS vol. 268, p. 124]

James, T. & G., Castle St, Bristol, cm and chairmaker (1814–35). In 1814 listed as T. & E. James but this may be an error. At 51 Castle St, 1814–15, but thereafter at 58. In 1822 Thomas James is recorded trading on his own behalf, and he continued on this basis until 1835. [D]

James, Theodore, New Bridge St, Exeter, Devon, cm and u (1838–40). [D]

James, Thomas, Nottingham, joiner and cm (1752–74). Took as apps Robert Moore in 1752, Thomas German in 1754 and Hezekiah Holmes in 1758. In 1774 living at Hockley, Nottingham. [Nottingham app. and poll bks]

James, Thomas, Redcross St, Southwark, London, chairmaker (1808). [D]

James, Thomas, Cathay, Bristol, chairmaker (1809–36). In 1816 listed as fancy chairmaker, and from 1821 as ship's mast and chairmaker. In 1835–36 at Prewett St, Cathay. [D]

James, Thomas, Bristol, looking-glass maker (1810–26). At 1 Ellbroad St, 1810–15, but in 1815 shown in addition at Barton Alley. Between 1816–19 4 Barton Alley is the only address shown; but from 1820–22 James traded at St Augustine's Back; from 1823–24 at 17 St John's St and from 1825–26 at Bridewell Lane. [D]

James, Thomas, Castle St, Bristol (1814–35), see T. & G. James.

James, Thomas, James St, Devonport, Devon, cm (1814). [D]

James, William, Halesowen, Staffs., cm (1752). In 1752 took app. named Lane. [S of G, app. index].

James, William, Gt Russell St, Covent Gdn, London, u (1755). Bankruptcy announced in *Gents Mag.*, May 1755.

James, William, 26 Baron's Buildings, Blackfriars Rd, London, cm (1809). [D]

James, William, 1 St John's Bridge, Bristol, cm, u and appraiser (1817–18). [D]

James, William, High St, Tewkesbury, Glos., chairmaker (1820–22). [D]

James, William, Charles St, Truro, Cornwall, cm and joiner (1830). [D]

James, William, Carter's Lane, Poole, Dorset, cm (1830). [D]

James, William, Widemarsh St, Hereford, carver and gilder (1835). [D]

James, William, 17 Paget Pl., Waterloo Rd, London, cm and u (1839). [D]

James, Wilson, Dam Side, Morpeth, Northumb., cm (1828). [D]

James & Co., Charlotte St, Russell Sq., London, cm (1825). [D]

James & Penberthy, Helston, Cornwall, builders, cm and u (1810–24). In 1810 advertised for two cm and six joiners 'who will meet with constant employ'. In April of this year debtors and creditors of the late firm of Penberthy & James, builders of Helston were asked to settle to, or send their accounts to, James & Penberthy. In 1824 they were in Church St and still advertising themselves as builders, as well as cm and u. [D]

James & Playfair, 14 New Bond St, London, trunk and plate case makers (1797–1817). Claimed to be suppliers to 'Their Majesties, the Prince of Wales and the Duke of York', and were successors to 'Mr. Broomfield'. From 1797–1804 patronised by the 5th and 6th Dukes of Bedford for whom they made and supplied knife trays at £1 16s each, and plate buckets at the same price. John James and Thomas Playfair appear to have parted company *c*. 1810, and in 1813 Playfair was trading from 17 New Bond St, probably the same address, as both are said to be 'corner of Clifford St'. In 1813 he supplied the 6th Duke for Endsleigh Cottage, Devon, 'two

field bedsteads complete with mattresses, pillows, bolsters, blankets, counterpanes, carpets, furniture, boxes and valises &c. matting &c.' at £43 12s 6d. For the same property he provided in 1817 'two best folding bedsteads' which with bedding, curtains, carpets and other items came to £44 10s 10d. An oak box covered with tan leather has been recorded with the trade label of 'James, Military Trunk Canteen and Plate Chest Maker to His Majesty' giving an address at 25 Coventry St opposite Lanton Sq., London. [Bedford Office, London]

James & Wise, 5 Frederick Pl., Southwark, London, chair and sofa makers (1839). [D]

Jameson, Daniel, Newbro' St, Scarborough, Yorks., cm and u (1823–30). [D]

Jameson, Daniel, Bridge St, Newark, Notts., cm and u (1832–35). [D]

Jameson, James, 63 Tythbarn St, Liverpool, joiner and cm (1774–77). [D]

Jameson, James, Bristol, cm (1792–1806). At Frog Lane, 1792–95, but from 1799 shown at Frogmore St. [D]

Jameson, John, York, cm, turner and toyman (1780–1806). Noted for the production of spinning wheels for drawing room use. One of his wheels (Pitt–Rivers Museum, Oxford) has 'John Jameson' carved on the inside rim of the drawer, and another (Castle Museum, York) has a trade label pasted in the drawer. This gives his address as Carlisle Buildings, Little Alice Lane, and stated that at his toy and turnery manufactory work was carried out in wood, ivory, brass and pewter. He was using this address as early as August 1788 when he invited 'ingenious mechanics to expose their work in his showroom' and indicated his intention of employing the industrious poor in his manufactory. His address is also recorded as College St. Advertisements regarding the sale of his stock in trade were issued in August 1802 and November 1806. In the latter case the sale was to be by auction. [*Furn. Hist.*, 1978]

Jameson, Peter, Chester, cm (1819–37). In 1819 at Foregate St and in 1837 at Peter Churchyard. [Poll bks]

Jameson, Richard, North Bar St Without, Beverley, Yorks., cm and u (1799–1840). Recorded in a poll bk in 1799, but not in directories until 1814. He was however active between these dates and in 1807–08 supplied furniture for the Sessions House in Beverley. A set of twenty mahogany chairs was made costing £33 and four elbow chairs at £9 10s extra. These still survive at the Sessions House and incorporate some inlay. Other items supplied in October 1807 were three mahogany Pembroke tables at £10 4s, two gilt framed pier glasses at £4 6s a large mahogany dining table at £4 19s 6d and a mahogany frame at £2 16s. Other items supplied in January 1808 included fourteen mahogany arm chairs. The total account for this furnishing scheme came to £109 5s 6d. Richard Jameson was also involved in the supply of furnishings for Grimston Garth, Yorks., and correspondence of 1812 exists, regarding two chaise longues. From 1826 the firm traded as Richard Jameson & Son. [D; E. Yorks. Quarter Sessions accounts and vouchers; V & A archives; poll bk]

Jameson & Smith, Whitehorse Yd, Hull, Yorks., joiners and cm (1803). [D]

Jamison, —, address unknown, u (1803). Subscribed to Sheraton's *Cabinet Dictionary*, 1803.

Jane, John, 146 Aldersgate St, London, cm (1821). On 3 January 1821 took out insurance cover of £100 but none of this was for tools or stock. [GL, Sun MS vol. 486, ref. 974947]

Jaques, John, Parade Row, Hull, Yorks., chairmaker and ship joiner (1823). [D]

Jaques, Thomas, Hull, Yorks., japanner, furniture painter and fancy chairmaker (1806–35). At Parade Row in 1806; 16 St

John's St, 1810–22; 7 Wellington Mart, 1820; 59 Humber St, 1831; and 9 Junction St, 1835. [D]

Jaquin, Henry, 10 Richmond St, St James's, London, carver and gilder (1835–57). [D]

Jarman, —, York St, Covent Gdn, London, cm (1736). In April 1736 Earl Fitzwalter paid for furniture supplied by Jarman, for Moulsham Hall, Essex. This consisted of a mahogany chest of drawers at £4 16s and a mahogany table to seat ten at £2 2s. [A. C. Edwards, *The Accounts of Benjamin Mildmay, Earl Fitzwalter,* p. 106]

Jarman, —, address unknown, frame maker (1825). He was paid £257 15s 10d at the desire of Sir William Knighton for work carried out for the Royal Household. [Windsor Royal Archives, 35593]

Jarman, Ann, London, frame maker (1747–50). In March 1747 supplied two frames for Felbrigg, Norfolk at a cost of £2 14s. In 1749 supplied frames for Peter Du Cane of Braxted Park, Essex for his London house in St James's Sq. Three frames supplied in January 1749 were charged at £13 10s and the account paid in March 1750. [Norfolk RO, Felbrigg WKC 7/156; Essex RO, D/Dc A80, D/DDc A 12 folio 73]

Jarman, James, Castle Hedingham, Essex, cm (1832). [D]

Jarman, Joseph, London, cm and u (1803–28). At 10 Broad St, Carnaby Mkt, 1803–08, but in 1809 at 8 William St, Manchester Sq. No further directory entries are recorded until 1820–21, when a Josh. Jarmain is listed at 14 Bulstrode St, Manchester Sq. In 1826–28 this maker is shown at 27 Wyndham St, Bryanston Sq. [D]

Jarman, Thomas, London, cm (1803–20). Freeman of Nottingam but resident in London. In 1820 at Smithfield. [Nottingham poll bks]

Jarrett, John, Bristol, cm (1792–95). At Earls Mead in 1792 but Old King St, 1793–95. [D]

Jarrett, John, Evesham, Worcs., cm (1820–28). Addresses given at Bridge St in 1820 and High St in 1828. [D]

Jarrett, Thomas, Bengworth, Evesham, Worcs., cm (1835). [D]

Jarrit, Henry, parish of St James, Bristol, cm (1754). [Poll bk]

Jarrot, Thomas, Evesham, Worcs., cm, joiner and shopkeeper (1778–84). In 1778 insured his house for £100 but in 1779 took out cover for £500 which included £130 for utensils and stock. In 1784 the total insurance was £300 and stock and utensils accounted for £120 of this. [GL, Sun MS vol. 268, p. 44; vol. 278, p. 189; vol. 324, p. 243]

Jarry, William, London, chairmaker (1802–06). Freeman of Norwich but resident in London. [Norwich poll bks]

Jarves, John Jackson, London, cm, chairmaker and clock case maker (before 1787–d. 1823). In 1787 at 76 Newbury St, Boston, Mass., USA. On his trade card [Boston Museum of Fine Arts] he claimed to be from London.

Jarvis, A., address unknown, frame maker (1769). In January 1769 supplied John, 4th Duke of Bedford with four peartree frames at 9s each and one other, the total account being £2. [Bedford Office, London]

Jarvis, Alfred, Brighton, Sussex, cm and u (1839). Shown at Little Preston St in one directory but 60 Preston St in another. [D]

Jarvis, Benjamin, 4 Love Lane, Hull, Yorks., cm (1831). [D]

Jarvis, Francis, Cambridge, cm (1816–31). At Sidney St in 1816 and the parish of St Clement, 1831. [PR (bapt.)]

Jarvis, George, Church St, Market Drayton, Salop, cm and builder (1822). [D]

Jarvis, Henry, 171 Tottenham Ct Rd, London, bedstead and cornice manufacturer (1811–20). A William J. Jarvis engaged in the same trade is shown at this address in 1829. [D]

Jarvis, Henry, Norwich, upholder (1829). Admitted freeman 5 December 1829. [Freemen rolls]

Jarvis, John, 54 Goswell Rd, London, (1826). [D]

Jarvis, Robert, Parsons Lane, Banbury, Oxon., cm and u (1830–35). [D]

Jarvis, Samuel, Snow Hill, London turner and looking-glass manufacturer (1740–86). Heal records a hardwood turner of this name at 'The Rose and Crown and Fowler' in Snow Hill and quotes from an invoice of 1740 for the supplying of '6 small lignum vitae dishes' at 6s. The property was numbered 41 Snow Hill and this was in use as early as 1775 when the business was trading as Jarvis & Sharp, looking glass-manufacturers. From 1781 traded as Samuel Jarvis & Co., and both turnery and looking-glass manufacture appear to have been carried on. [D; Heal]

Jarvis, Thomas, Wilsford, Wilts., cm (1753). In 1753 took app. named William Proviss. [*Wilts. Apps and their Masters*]

Jarvis, Thomas, Norwich, u and paper hanger (1768–1834). In the parish of St Peter Mancroft, 1768; St Michael at Thorn, 1799–1802; St Gregory, 1807 and 1830; and St Andrew 1812. Shown at Pottersgate St, 1822. Had two sons Thomas jnr, and Henry, both u and admitted freemen 5 December 1829. Another son, Edward Gibson Jarvis, a plane maker, was made free on 30 April 1834. [D; poll bks; freemen reg.]

Jarvis, Thomas, 12 St James' St, Portsea, Portsmouth, Hants., cm and u (1830) [D]

Jarvis, William, 41 Turvile St, Bethnal Green, London, bedstead maker (1829). [D]

Jarvis, William, 10 Etham Pl., Old Kent Rd, London, cm and u (1835–39). Address also shown at Kent St, Southwark. [D]

Jarvis, William J., 171 Tottenham Ct Rd, London, bedstead and cornice manufacturer (1829). See Henry Jarvis at this address, 1811–20. [D]

Jary, Roger, Norwich, chairmaker (1802). Son of Robert Jary, wool comber. Free 18 September 1802. [Freemen reg.]

Jay, Benjamin, Salisbury, Wilts., upholder. (1709). Bankrupt November 1709, but he had possibly already absconded, as a newspaper advertisement required him to surrender to the Bankruptcy Commissioners on 12 and 19 December. [*London Gazette,* 30 November 1709]

Jay, George, 73 Oxford St, London, u (1826). Freeman of Maldon, Essex. [Maldon poll bk]

Jay, James, London, u (1826–34). Freeman of Maldon, Essex. At 13 Broad St, Golden Sq., 1826–30; but in August 1830 declared bankrupt. He appears to have re-established his business in Welbeck St but was again declared bankrupt in February 1834. [D; Maldon poll bk; *London Gazette,* 24 August 1830; PRO, C13 942/6; *Liverpool Mercury,* 21 February 1834]

Jay, Jane, Church St, Hackney, London, u (1823). [D] See Jay and Son.

Jay, Joseph, Church St, Hackney, London, u (1835–39). [D]

Jay, Thomas, 6 Hare Ct, Aldersgate St, London, cm (1775). In 1775 insured his house for £100. [GL, Sun MS vol. 237, p. 339]

Jay, William, Colchester, Essex, chairmaker (1723). In 1723 took app. named Mays. [S of G, app. index]

Jay, William, address unknown (1803). Subscribed to Sheraton's *Cabinet Dictionary,* 1803.

Jay, William, London, u and cm (1812–28). At 15 Poland St, Oxford Sq. and then moved to 13 Broad St, Golden Sq. From 1817 the business traded as William & James Jay. [D]

Jay, William, 53 Charlotte St, London, u (1826). Freeman of Maldon, Essex. [Maldon poll bk]

Jay, William, High St, Stroud, Glos., cm and u (1839). [D]

Jay & Son, Hackney, London, u (1826). [D] See Jane Jay.

Jayne, John, Bristol, cm (1754). [Poll bk]

Jaynes, John, Bristol, cm (1793–1801). Shown at Park, 1793–95, and Old Park, 1799–1801. [D]

Jeacock, Caleb, London, cm (1754–83). Subscribed to

Chippendale's *Director*, 1754. In Oxford St opposite Poland St, 1769–70, and from 1771 the number is listed as 76. On 7 November 1775 paid £100 by Sir Thomas Egerton of Heaton Hall, Manchester 'for the Green Bed etc'. [D; Preston RO, DD.Eg., bank deposit and account bk]

Jean, Peter Dominique, near Windmill St, Tottenham Ct Rd, London, ormolu maker (1764–1807). As Jean Dominique, he is recorded in the Royal Household accounts and Jourdain, *Regency Furniture* trading at Marshall St as a gilder and founder, 1783/95. An important supplier of fine mounts to the leading London furniture makers of his day. On 20 October 1764 he married Marie Françoise, daughter of the cabinet maker Pierre Langlois, and probably thereafter supplied mounts for his father-in-law. He also took Pierre Langlois's son, Daniel, as app. in 1771. It is not only with Langlois that there are clear connections. Amongst the items supplied by Jean in the last months of 1783 were mounts for furniture and chimney pieces, some of which were for delivery to the cm Christopher Fuhrlohg. A further connection with Fuhrlohg is found in the accounts for Audley End, Essex. In 1786 Lord Howard paid Jean for gilding ornaments for two commodes, gilding five sets of locks and 'gilding and finishing 5 rings for a Cabinet delivered to Mr. Fuhrlohg'. A sum of £27 was paid in November 1786 in settlement. It also seems likely that the mounts on the library desk at Osterley, Middlx came from Jean, and this in turn might point to John Linnell as one of his customers.

Apart from items supplied for the embellishment of furniture and passing through the hands of various cm, Jean supplied ormolu directly to clients. Between October 1783 and midsummer 1786 he provided furnishings for Carlton House to the order of the Prince of Wales amounting to £1,409 16s. Only one detailed invoice survives, and is for the period October to 2 December 1783. The major item in this was a pair of five branch chandeliers with figures and trophies, for which £320 was charged. At Carlton House Jean worked for Gaubert and Holland, gilding 'the ornaments of an inlaid commode delivered to M. Furlogh', and supplying mouldings to 'Mr Walker' (Wacker?), 'Mr Furlogh', and M. 'Prussurot'. For this work, Jean's bill totalled £480. [RA, Windsor, 34953–54, 25050; Essex RO, D/DBy/A44/7–8; Goodison, *Ormolu*, pp. 21–22, 173]

Jeanes, Charles, West St, Bristol, cm (1813). [D]

Jeanes, Charles, London cm, u and appraiser (1820–39). At 109 Bermondsey St in 1820 and 4 George Row, Bermondsey in 1839. [D]

Jeanes, Richard, 16 Pithay, Bristol, cm and furniture broker (1838–40). [D]

Jeary A. H. & Co., High St, Salisbury, Wilts., u (1839). [D]

Jebb, John, St Agnes St, Tabernacle Sq., London, carver and gilder (1808). [D]

Jebb, Joshua, Nottingham, joiner and cm (1722–36). Took as apps Joseph Coultart in 1723; Thomas Revell in 1725; Joseph Conway and John Salter in 1726; Thomas Orme in 1728; Joseph Tims and Timothy Chambers in 1730; John Stephenson in 1734 and George Mycroft in 1736. [App. bk]

Jebb, Richard, 3 Church St, Gt Surrey St, London, carver and gilder (1826). [D]

Jebson, Thomas, Liverpool, cm (1812). App. to Thomas Dutton and free, 5 October 1812. [Freemen reg.]

Jee, Edward, Cannon St, Birmingham, picture frame maker (1800–05). Recorded at no. 30 in 1800, also as a printseller. [D]

Jee, Samuel, Mount Sorrel, Leicester, turner and chairmaker (1787). In October 1787 advertised for a journeyman chairmaker to make turned chairs. [*Leicester Journal*, 13 October 1787]

Jeeves, Jeremiah, 11 and 12 King St, Bloomsbury, London, cm and u (1808–28). In 1808 trading as Jeeves & Holt but from 1809–11 as Jeeves & Co. Thereafter Jeeves & Holt is used for most years but one directory in 1820 and 1827 list Jeeves & Hall. The business was probably substantial and in 1823 insurance cover of £3,500 was taken out of which £850 was for utensils and stock. [D; GL, Sun MS vol. 498, refs 1008169–71]

Jefferies, Benjamin, Maldon, Essex, chairmaker (1760–1812). Freeman of Colchester, Essex. In 1760 took app. named Howard. [Colchester poll bks; S of G, app. index]

Jefferies, J., Francis St, Westminster Rd, London, cm (1835). [D]

Jefferies, James W., 76 Old Market St, Bristol, sign and furniture painter and glazier (1827–32). [D]

Jefferies, William, Bristol, upholder (1774). [Poll bk]

Jefferies, William, 12 East Rd, City Rd, London, cm and u (1839).[D]

Jefferis, Richard, 14 Kingsmead St, Bath, Som., joiner, picture framer and cm (1833). [D]

Jefferis, Robert, 26 Well St, Oxford St, London, cm (1809). [D]

Jefferson, G., Lancaster, turner (1805). Named in the Gillow records in connection with making a firescreen. [Westminster Ref. Lib., Gillow vol. 344/98]

Jefferson, Henry, 13 Fish St, Hull, Yorks., cm and shopkeeper (1826). Shown in directories up to 1834 but only as a shopkeeper. [D]

Jefferson, John, Wheelgate, Malton, Yorks., cm and u (1823–34). [D]

Jefferson, M., Whitehaven, Cumb., cm (1798). [D]

Jefferson, Robert, Court 12, Church St, Sunderland, Co. Durham, cm (1827). [D]

Jefferson, William, 6 Cleveland St, Fitzroy Sq., London, cm and u (1839). [D]

Jeffery, Benjamin, 12 Meard's Ct, Dean St, Soho, London, glass and picture frame maker (1820–22). In November 1821 took out insurance cover of £300 of which £200 was in respect of utensils and stock. A year later however he insured his dwelling house for £700 with a further £700 for a house in the tenure of Cooke. [D; GL, Sun MS vol. 488, ref. 985474; vol. 493, ref. 997751]

Jeffery, John, Stephen's Lane, Ipswich, Suffolk, cm and u (1830). [D]

Jeffery, John, 3 Foundling Terr., Gray's Inn Rd, London, cm (1835–39). [D]

Jeffery, Joseph, Queen St, Ipswich, Suffolk, cm, u and chairmaker (1824–39). [D]

Jeffery, Richard, 6 Mulberry Sq., Brighton, Sussex, cm and u (1839). [D]

Jeffery, Samuel, Sherborne, Dorset, cm (1768). [*Dorset Nat. Hist. and Arch. Proceedings*, LIII, 1931]

Jeffery, William, East Bergholt, Suffolk, chairmaker (1768–84). Freeman of Colchester. [Colchester poll bks]

Jefferyes, George, Durham, cm (1760). In 1760 took app. named Whitefield. [S of G, app. index]

Jefferys, Charles, Brittox, Devizes, Wilts., u and cm (1839). [D]

Jefferys, James, 44 Mytongate, Hull, Yorks., cm (1828). [D]

Jefferys, John & Co., 66 Lowgate, Hull, Yorks., with residence at Anne St, Osborne St, auctioneers, appraisers and cm (1831). [D]

Jefferys, John S., 17 Coldbath Sq., London, cm and u (1839). [D]

Jefferys, Nathaniel, address unknown, cm (1756). Referred to in the tradesmens' accounts of the Bowes estate, Co. Durham, receiving £1 13s in June 1756 for a tea board. [Durham RO, D/St/239]

Jefferys, Peter, 33 Gee St, Goswell St, London, cm (1808). [D]

Jeffier, —, address unknown, cm (1754). Subscribed to Chippendale's *Director*, 1754.

Jeffrey, Charles, Hanover St, London, upholder (1773). Bankrupt December 1773. [Bailey's list of bankrupts]

Jeffrey, Emanuel, Clayton Pl., Kennington, London, bed and mattress maker (1827–35). Also listed at 14 Kennington in 1827 which may be the same address. [D]

Jeffrey, James, London(?), looking-glass maker (1826–27). In March 1826 supplied Lord Gwydir with a glass 52″ by 42″ 'with a large mahogany and gold beaded circular top frame' and also 'the stained glass round the same'. Subsequently he prepared 'stained glass, silvered, which was sent to Mr. Dowbiggin who was preparing a glass & frame to match'. The cost of this commission was £52 12s and it was settled in May 1827. [Lincoln RO, 2 ANC 6/202/56]

Jeffrey, James, Calverley-cum-Farsley, Yorks., cm (1837). [D]

Jeffrey, James, 35 Union St, Middlx Hospital, London, carver and gilder (1837). [D]

Jeffrey, John, Alnwick, Northumb., cm (1767). In March 1767 he announced that he had devised 'a New Method of Destroying BUGS, entirely unknown to any person or persons whatsoever but himself . . . He will undertake to kill them either in Beds or in any other Kind of Household Furniture wherein they may be lodged, and will uphold the same to stand for the Term of Seven Years'. [*Newcastle Courant*, 21 March 1767]

Jeffreys, James jnr, Waterhouse Lane, Hull, Yorks., cm (1828). [D]

Jeffreys, Richard, Liverpool, carver and gilder (1811–39). Shown at 23 Byrom St in 1811 and 34 Lime St in 1813. No further directory entries are noted until 1839 when the address was 42 Brownlow St. [D]

Jeffries, Edward, Hurst St, Birmingham, cm (1818). [D]

Jeffries, Henry, 2 St George's Rd, Brighton, Sussex, carver and gilder (1839–40). [D]

Jeffries, John, address unknown, upholder (1754). Subscribed to Chippendale's *Director*, 1754.

Jeffries, Thomas, Chester, u (1812–d. 1828). Free 9 October 1812. At Castle St, 1812–18, and thereafter at St Werburgh St. Died on 6 May 1828, a coroner's inquest concluding that he had 'died in consequence of being suffocated through intoxication'. [D; poll bks; freemen rolls; *Chester Chronicle*, 9 and 16 May 1828]

Jeffrys, Thomas, Nantwich, Cheshire, chairmaker (1780). Son Francis bapt. 25 June 1780. [PR (bapt.)]

Jeffs, James, Westgate St, Gloucester, carver and gilder (1839). [D]

Jeffs, John, High St, Towcester, Northants., cm (1823–30). [D]

Jeffs, Thomas, 29 Upper Titchfield St, Fitzroy Sq., London, carver and gilder (1808). [D]

Jeffs, Thomas, High St, Towcester, Northants., cm/joiner (1823). [D]

Jelfe, Peter, King St, Westminster, London, glass frame maker, carpenter and victualler (1770). Bankruptcy announced in *Gents Mag.*, February 1770.

Jelley, Richard, Granby St, Leicester, u and cm (1833–40). Free 1833. His billhead survives (Dept of Prints, V & A). [D; freemen reg.]

Jellicoe, Richard, 62 London Wall, London, upholder (1792). Son of William Jellicoe, upholder and member of the Skinners' Co. Grandson of Thomas Jellicoe, also a member of the Skinners' Co. Free of the Upholders' Co. by patrimony on 14 November 1792. [GL, Upholders' Co. records]

Jellicoe, William, Fleet St, London, u (1760–81). Member of the Skinners' Co. Traded initially at the sign of the 'Chair & Anchor' in Fleet St. He claimed to be the successor to 'the Widow Smith' and stated that he made and sold 'all Sorts of Upholstery Goods. Cabinets, Chairs, Glasses &c in the newest Fashion'. Two copies of his trade card survive and

feature a Rococo Chinoiserie frame. [Heal Coll., BM; Leverhulme Coll., MMA, NY] When Fleet St was numbered, his premises became no. 88, but after 1773 no. 135 was used. Betwen 1773–75 the business traded as Jellicoe & Wheeler but by 1781 had reverted once more to William Jellicoe's sole charge. From the late 1760s he held a number of parish offices in St Bride's, Fleet St, being Collector for the Poor in 1766 and then Sidesman and Questman between 1767–70 and finally Church-warden in 1780–81. His son Richard was made free of the Upholders' Co. by patrimony in 1792. [D; GL, Upholders' Co. records; MS 6561, p. 97; Heal]

Jellings, Thomas, address unknown, cm (1754). Subscribed to Chippendale's *Director*, 1754.

Jelly, Richard, Hotel St, Derby, u and paper hanger (1835). [D]

Jeneper, Samuel, Bury St Edmunds, Suffolk, upholder (1733–44). Elected Common Councillor on 16 October 1733. In 1744 took app. named Judd. [Suffolk RO (Bury), index of Corp. Members; S of G, app. index]

Jenkins, Alexander, Peascod St, Windsor, Berks., cm (1824). [D]

Jenkins, C. & Co., 45 Brewer St, Golden Sq., London, upholstery warehousemen (1816–25). [D]

Jenkins, Edward, 123 Aldersgate St, London, cm and upholder (1825–27). [D]

Jenkins, Edward, Cross St, Ellesmere, Salop, cm and auctioneer (1828–35). Recorded at Cross St in 1828 and Willow St in 1835. [D]

Jenkins, Francis, Bristol and London, carver and gilder (1761). In August 1761 discharged from Debtors' Prison. Stated to be formerly of Bristol and late of Cockpit Alley, Drury Lane, London. [*London Gazette*, 12 August 1761]

Jenkins, James, Bristol, cm (1801–10). In 1801 at Charles's St and John's Bridge, but from 1805 at 12 Charles's St only. [D]

Jenkins, James, 48 Strand, London, carver and gilder (1807–37). From 1823–25 one directory lists Martha Jenkins at this address in the same trade. [D]

Jenkins, James, 18 Philadelphia St, Bristol, cm (1820). [D]

Jenkins, James, Axbridge, Som., cm (1830–40). Trading at The Square in 1840. [D]

Jenkins, John, 75 Long Acre, London, upholder and cm (1794–1808). From 1777 the business traded as Jenkins & Strickland but after 1794 came under the sole control of John Jenkins. Subscribed to Sheraton's *Drawing Book*, 1793, and *Cabinet Dictionary*, 1803, and included in the list of master cabinet makers in the latter. The business was on a fairly substantial scale and in 1800 insurance cover came to £2,350 of which utensils and stock accounted for £600. Undertook work for the 2nd Duke of Northumberland at Northumberland House, London and Syon, Middlx for which he was paid £268 on 30 June 1795. One directory of 1808 lists John Jenkins, cm, u and undertaker at 18 Fulwood's Rents, London. [D; GL, Sun MS vol. 419, ref. 709392; V & A archives] See Strickland & Jenkins.

Jenkins, John, Goodman's Fields, London, u and cm (1820–39). In 1820 at 6 Leman St, Goodman's Fields but from 1825 at 61 Gt Prescott St, Goodman's Fields. Recorded as Jno. & J. Jenkins, 1835–39. [D]

Jenkins, John, London, carver and gilder (1820–39). In 1820 at 31 Commercial Rd, Whitechapel, but by November 1822 at 14 Hertford Pl., Commercial Rd. He remained at this address until 1835 but subsequently is recorded at 2 Lucas Pl., Commercial Rd. The business was modest in size, the total insurance in 1822 being £300 of which £80 was for utensils and stock, and the corresponding figures for 1823 are £400 and £150. [D; GL, Sun MS vol. 489, ref. 997664; vol. 490, ref. 999964]

Jenkins, John, Exeter, Devon, cm and u (1825–32). In December 1825 announced his removal from his residence in Goldsmith

St to a shop previously occupied by 'Mr. Pillbrow's Grand Musical Repository' at 150 Fore St opposite St John's Church. Stock advertised included 'Carpetings, Floor Cloths, Moreen and Chintz Furniture, Paper Hangings &c' and 'stoved goose feathers'. The business traded as a 'Cabinet, Chair and Upholstery Warehouse'. In June 1828 the property was put up for sale and described as 'brick-built'. It had a cellar, a shop, parlour and kitchen on the ground floor, a drawing room, 22ft square, and three lodging rooms on the first floor, five lodging rooms on the second floor and an equal number on the third. The third floor was at this time being used by Jenkins for workshops. Despite this notice of sale the property appears to have remained in the occupation of John Jenkins. [D; *Exeter Flying Post*, 22 December 1825, 12 June 1828]

Jenkins, John, 9 Broad Weir, Bristol, cm, u and undertaker (1833–40). From 1835 featured the manufacture of Venetian blinds. [D]

Jenkins, John, Lower Union St, Torquay, Devon, cm and u (1838). It is possible that this is the same John Jenkins who was trading in Exeter, 1825–32. [D]

Jenkins, John, 2 Lucas Pl., Commercial Rd, London, cm and u (1839). [D]

Jenkins, Joseph, Lostwithiel, Cornwall, cm (1830–32). Declared bankrupt, *Exeter Flying Post*, 29 March 1832. [D]

Jenkins, Martha, 48 Strand, London, carver and gilder (1823–35). See James Jenkins of the same trade, at this address, 1807–37. [D]

Jenkins, Mary, St Mary's St, Newport, Salop, cm and u (b. 1813–35). Daughter of and successor to Thomas Jenkins who traded at this address as a cm, 1814–28. [D]

Jenkins, Matthew, Liverpool, cm (1790–1803). In 1790 at 21 Vernon St but in 1796 at 77 Tithebarn St and from 1800–03 at no. 81. In 1796 also shown as an earthenware dealer. [D]

Jenkins, R., 18 Fullwood Rents, London, u (1835). John Jenkins, cm, u and undertaker is shown at this address in 1808, and Rd. Jenkinson, cm and u, in 1827. [D]

Jenkins, Richard, 18 Beaufort Sq., Bath, Som., cm (1833). [D]

Jenkins, Samuel, London, upholder (1756). Son of John Jenkins of St Dunstans-in-the-East, mariner. App. to William Guidott on 6 July 1749 and free of the Upholders' Co. by servitude on 18 November 1756. [GL, Upholders' Co. records]

Jenkins, Thomas, 21 Gerrard St, Liverpool, cm (1796). [D]

Jenkins, Thomas, 20 Chambers St, Goodman's Fields, London, u (1811). Bankrupt February 1811. Still listed in one directory in 1812 but this may have been an oversight. The bankruptcy proceedings give the address as Prescot St, Goodman's Fields. [D; *Sussex Weekly Advertiser*, 25 February 1811]

Jenkins, Thomas, St Mary St, Newport, Salop, cm and u (1814–28). Succeeded at this address by his daughter Mary. [D; PR (bapt.)]

Jenkins, Thomas, Gloucester Mews, Clifton, Bristol, paper hanger and u (1836–40). [D]

Jenkins, Uriah, Russell St, Exeter, Devon, carver and joiner (1835). Daughter Mary Jane bapt. at St Sidwell's Church, 27 September 1835. [PR (bapt.)]

Jenkins, William, 16½ Moon Pl., Vauxhall Rd, London, carver and gilder (1839). [D]

Jenkins & Brock, 7 Horfield Rd, Bristol, cm (1825). [D]

Jenkins & Speed, Rownham Pl., Hotwells, Bristol, cm and u (1836–40). [D]

Jenkins & Strickland, see John Jenkins of Long Acre, London, and Strickland & Jenkins.

Jenkins & Watson, 25 Maiden Lane, Covent Gdn, London, carvers, gilders etc. (1803–08). [D]

Jenkinson, John, 23 Paradise Sq., Sheffield, Yorks., joiner, cm and u (1777–98). Insurance records indicate a small scale of business in 1777. Total cover was £200 of which £70 was in respect of utensils and stock. Subscribed to Sheraton's *Drawing Book*, 1793. [D; GL, Sun MS vol. 256, p. 582]

Jenkinson, John, 6 Featherstone St, City Rd, London, cm (1820–29). [D]

Jenkinson, John, Gt Charles St, Birmingham, cm, u and broker (1828–30). Recorded at no. 95 in 1828. [D]

Jenkinson, John, Cockermouth, Cumb., joiner/cm (1828–34). At Gallowberry in 1828, Sand Lane in 1829 and Main St in 1834. [D]

Jenkinson, John, 4 Ironmonger Row, Old St, London, cm (1808). Thomas Jenkinson is shown at this address in 1809. [D]

Jenkinson, Joseph, Reuben Terr., Little London, Leeds, Yorks., cm and joiner (1837). [D]

Jenkinson, Nehemia, Pinchbeck, Lincs., chairmaker (1716). [Lincoln RO, LCC, ADM. 1716/12]

Jenkinson, Rd., 18 Fullwood Rents, London, cm and u (1827). R. Jenkins, u is shown at this address in 1835 and John Jenkins, cm, u and undertaker in 1808. [D]

Jenkinson, Thomas, 4 Ironmonger Row, Old St, London, cm (1809). A John Jenkinson is shown at this address in 1808. [D]

Jenkinson, William, 19 Cow Green, Halifax, Yorks., u (1837). [D]

Jenks, Robert, Ware, Herts., cm and u (1777). In 1777 took out insurance cover of £200, his utensils and stock for £150. [GL, Sun MS vol. 257, p. 382]

Jenks, Robert, London, cm and mahogany merchant (1785–96). In 1785 at Bull Stairs, Upper Ground, Southwark, his premises being described as 'the Mahogany Yard' but his trade as cm. Insurance taken out in this year valued his utensils and stock at £20. He is shown in directories of 1790–96 as a mahogany merchant at New Jamaica Wharf, Upper Ground, Christchurch, Surrey. [D; GL, Sun MS vol. 328, p. 271]

Jenks, Robert, London, looking-glass manufacturer (1794–1839). From 1794–1807 he traded from an address at 21 Surrey St, Blackfriars. From 1815–25 the business is referred to as Robert Jenks & Son, the address given being either 81 or 82 Fleet St. In 1829 R. J. Jenks, possibly the son, was trading from 16 Gt Distaff Lane and from 1835–39 an address at 55 Bread St, Cheapside was used by Robert Isaac Jenks, probably the same maker. [D]

Jenks, Thomas, Fleet St, London, looking-glass manufacturer, cm and u (1819–37). In 1819 fined for declining office in the parish of St Bride, Fleet St, but in 1824 acted as Overseer. Initially at 81 Fleet St in partnership with J. M. Jenks, 1822–28. The use of this address from 1822–29 suggests a relationship with Robert Jenks. In the 1830s at 90 Fleet St, and a trade card of this period survives [Landauer Coll., MMA, NY] which lists his trade as 'Carver, Gilder, Looking Glass & cabinet Manufacturer'. [D]

Jennens, C., 42 Poland St, London, carver and ormolu worker (date unknown). [Heal]

Jennens & Bettridge, Birmingham and London, papier-mâché ware manufacturers (1816–40). In 1816 took over the Birmingham works of Henry Clay, and by 1837 had opened up London showrooms at 3 Halkin St West, Belgrave Sq. In 1825 they took out a patent for 'ornamenting papier-mâché with pearl shell' and this technique together with painted decoration and gilding provided a brilliant effect because of the iridescent quality of the mother-of-pearl. The quality of their work was quickly recognised and by 1825 they could claim to be 'Japanners in Ordinary to His Majesty'. They were patronised not only by George IV, but also by William IV, and Queen Victoria. Initially the bulk of their production was trays and other small wares. By 1839 however they were producing larger items, and in that year supplied Buckingham Palace with two folding screens. One which had a cream ground was decorated with birds and flowers and cost £24 5s; the other was charged at £26 5s. Apart from new items of this nature they were employed on repair of furniture in the Royal collection. The business reached its zenith in the early 1850s with its exhibits at the Great Exhibition, and the opening of branches in New York and Paris. [D; Windsor Royal Archives, box 1, item 2, account bks, 1833–41; PRO, LC11/104; Toller, *Papier-mâché*, pp. 29–32]

Jennens & Co., 316 Oxford St, London, button, military ornament, patent royal footstool and swing chair manufacturers (1820). [D]

Jenner, James, 39 Duke St, Grosvenor Sq., London, u and cm (1819–29). [D]

Jenner, Thomas, 93 Peascod St, Windsor, Berks., carpenter and joiner (1784–1840). First recorded in 1784 as Jenner & Son. By 1824 Thomas Jenner was describing himself as 'Joiner to His Majesty'. He is recorded in the Royal accounts on numerous occasions from 1827 and from time to time supplied simple furniture. In July 1831 an estimate was received from Jenner for thirty deal dining table tops and six wainscot coat stands. The table tops were to be japanned and they were estimated at £86 out of a total of £110 10s 3d. They were for use in St George's Hall, Windsor, as were also sixty-six trestles estimated at £65 in September 1832 and six strong, one-flap deal tables with two drawers estimated at £21 in March 1833. [D; Windsor Royal Archives, account bks, box 1, item 17; PRO, LC11/77]

Jenner, Walter, 14 Gerrard St, London, cm and u (1839). [D]

Jenner, William, 42 Foley St, Portman Sq., London, undertaker and u (1817–20). [D]

Jennings, —, address unknown, cm (1803). Subscribed to Sheraton's *Cabinet Dictionary*, 1803.

Jennings, Charles, West St, Hackney, London, cm and u (1839). [D]

Jennings, David (or William), Manchester, u (1779). Bankruptcy announced in *Gents Mag.*, November 1779.

Jennings, Henry Kickweed, 17 Bartholomew St, St Luke's, Pimlico, London, cm (b.c. 1807–40). Son of Withers Jennings, farmer, bapt. 14 April 1807 at Great Wakering, Essex. Moved to London and married Sarah Smith. Eldest of their four children bapt. on 8 January 1837. [PR (bapt.)]

Jennings, James, 10 Chapel St, Tottenham Ct Rd, London, carver and gilder (1839). [D]

Jennings, John, Newgate St, London, u and cm (1764–1800). Son of John Jennings snr, freeman and member of the Joiners' Co. John Jennings jnr, was made free of the upholders' Co. by patrimony under the terms of the 1750 Upholders' Act on 2 August 1764. Took an app. Josiah Roberts, 1776–84. In 1776–79 he was at 41 Newgate St. A house was insured for £300 in 1776 and houses for £600 in 1779. His business is shown trading from 15 Newgate St, 1786–1800. [D]

Jennings, John, 46 New Compton St, Soho, London, carver and gilder (1817). Thomas Jennings of the same trade is shown at this address in 1808 and 1820. [D]

Jennings, John, 24 Cliff, Lewes, Sussex, cm and u (1823–26). [D]

Jennings, John, Meneage St, Helston, Cornwall, cm, carpenter and joiner (1830). [D]

Jennings, John, Spring Gdns, Nantwich, Cheshire, chairmaker (1838–40). Daughter Mary Ann bapt. on 5 September 1838. [D; PR (bapt.)]

Jennings, John, New St, Woodbridge, Suffolk, cm and u (1839). [D]

Jennings, Leonard, St Martin-in-the-Fields, London, cm (1753–57). Subscribed to Chippendale's *Director*, 1754.

Took one app. in 1753 and another named David Lewis in 1757 at a premium of £31 10s. [S of G app. reg.]

Jennings, M. A., 79 Berwick St, London, carver and gilder (1835–37). [D]

Jennings, Robert, Watling St, London, upholder (1760). Son of John Jennings of Norton Falgate, Middlx, yeoman. App. to Samuel Whiting on 3 September 1747, and free of the Upholders' Co. by servitude on 2 October 1760. [GL, Upholders' Co. records]

Jennings, Robert, Love Lane, Nantwich, Cheshire, chairmaker (1840). Married on 30 December 1840. [PR (marriage)]

Jennings, Samuel, 5 Goswell St, London, carver and gilder (1824–40). Trade label recorded with address at Duke St, Manchester Sq., Oxford St, claiming to be carver, gilder and printseller to the Queen and the Royal Family. This would appear to be post-1840. [D]

Jennings, Thomas, Skeldergate, York, cm (1758). [Poll bk]

Jennings, Thomas, 46 New Compton St, Soho, London, carver and gilder (1804–20). A John Jennings following the same trade is recorded at this address in 1817. In 1804 insurance was taken out by Thomas Jennings on the house he rented in New Compton St for £300. [D; GL, Sun MS vol. 431, ref. 767618]

Jennings, Thomas, Tacket St, Ipswich, Suffolk, carver, gilder and barometer maker (1830–39). [D; poll bks]

Jennings, William, Ock St, Abingdon, Berks., cm (1775–1830). In 1775 took out insurance of £200 of which only £30 was cover for utensils, stock and workshop. Listed in directories, 1823 and 1830, but the long span of time between these two sources might suggest that the directory entries refer to a son. [D; GL, Sun MS vol. 244, p. 110]

Jennings, William, Nantwich, Cheshire, Chairmaker (1821). Daughter Ann bapt. on 5 October 1821. [PR (bapt.)]

Jennings & Walkington, the Vine, Long Acre, London, upholders and cm (1754–c. 1770). In 1754 a watch was stolen from the premises and a reward offered. [*Public Advertiser*, 22 February 1754; Heal]

Jenny, Winslow Thomas, Norwich, cm (1769). Son of Thomas Jenny, Gent. Free 11 January 1769. [Freemen reg.]

Jensen, Gerrit, St Martin's Lane, London, cm (1680–d. 1715). Gerrit Jensen, whose name occurs in the Lord Chamberlain's accounts spelt in fourteen different ways (sometimes anglicized as plain Garrard Johnson), has been called 'the English Boulle'. The leading London cm in the reigns of William and Mary and Queen Anne, he is also the only one known to have produced furniture employing inlaid metals, and ironically more pieces in this technique can now be attributed to him than to his great French counterpart.

Nothing is known of Jensen's origins, and even the assumption that he was Flemish or Dutch by birth is open to question: one Garrett Johnson, a 'carver in stone' who could well have been his ancestor, is found in the records of the Dutch Church living in Southwark as early as 1582–83 [*Furn. Hist.*, 1971, p. 115] and Jensen could thus have been a 3rd or even 4th generation immigrant. His name first occurs in the Royal accounts in 1680 as making a set of furniture which Charles II presented to the Emperor of Morocco. But he may be the 'Garrett Johnson' who purchased his freedom of the City in 1667, and the 'Gerrard Johnson' who became a liveryman of the Joiners' Co. in 1685 — steps up the ladder of the London guild system which would not normally have been open to a foreigner.

The patent renewing his appointment as 'Cabinet Maker in ordinary' to William and Mary, drawn up in 1689, which exists in the PRO, describes him as 'Cabinet maker and Glasse seller . . . for the makeing provideing and Selling of all Sorts of Cabbinets Boxes Looking Glasses Tables and Stands

Ebony Frames, and for the furnishing provideing and Selling of all Sorts of Glasse plates as well plained and polished as not plained and pollished', an indication of the wide range of Jensen's activities. The Royal Household accounts show that he held a monopoly in supplying overmantel and pier glasses to the palaces during the reign, while at Chatsworth in the same period he supplied the bevelled glass sash panes for the east and south fronts, and the large mirror panels for the doorcase in the State Dining Room, reflecting the enfilade of state rooms beyond. Mirrors such as these were extremely expensive: four measuring 62 inches by 36 inches in the 'Painted Gardain Roome' at Hampton Court cost £320 in 1701, while 'two Glasses each 81 inches long and 45 broad with guilt wooden frames rich & carv'd' were supplied for Queen Anne's 'new Drawing roome' at St James's for £450 in 1703. By contrast his pieces of carcase furniture, either japanned, or of marquetry, inlaid with walnut, olivewood, prince-wood, ebony, brass, pewter and even silver, seem relatively inexpensive. The personal interest that William and Mary took in Jensen's work is implied by his provision of 'two modells of a deske and table' supplied for £6 in 1696, and in the inventory of goods made the following year of 'her late Maj's Lodgings of Blessed Memory' at Kensington, which mentions metal-inlaid tables, looking-glasses and stands which were 'bespoke by the Queen and came in after her death from Mr. Johnson'.

The Westminster City rate bks show that Jensen occupied premises in St Martin's Lane from 1693 onwards, paying an annual rate ranging from £1 6s 8d to £2 8s. According to his will, drawn up on 15 August 1715, and proved the following February, the property consisted of two houses and a warehouse (presumably his workshop) held on lease from the Earl of Salisbury. One of these houses 'situate on the north side of St. Martin's Church between St. Martin's Lane and Castle Street' was insured for £50 in 1713, while the other 'on the west side of St. Martin's Lane' (presumably including the workshops) was insured for £300. [GL, MS 8674, vol. 12, refs 1250, 1251] Besides these he owned a country house with 1 acre and 3 roods of land at Brook Green, Hammersmith, and also had houses and land at Great and Little Harefield in the parish of Selling, Kent, leased from Corpus Christi College, Oxford. These affluent circumstances are confirmed by his bequests of plate and jewels, as well as portraits painted of himself, his two wives and eldest son. His son by his first wife must have predeceased him, for a daughter-in-law, Anne Jensen, and a grand-daughter Winifred, are mentioned as beneficiaries. His second wife Hellen seems to have borne him four children, Francis, Hellen, Isaac and Katherine, all of whom were under the age of 21 at the time the will was made. The parish registers of St Martin-in-the-Fields record the death of 'Mr. Garret Johnston' on 2 December 1715, but unfortunately without revealing his age; but comparison of his signatures on receipts of the 1690s compared with an increasingly shaky hand on later documents seems to suggest that he lived to a comparatively old age. These signatures seem invariably to use the spelling 'Gerrit Jensen', which is the form used here.

In style Jensen's furniture is consistently French in form, and particularly close to the work of Pierre Golle, Boulle's famous predecessor. Golle's will mentions a sum of money owed to Jensen for glue, suggesting that close contact existed between the two masters. The catalyst here may well have been Golle's brother-in-law, Daniel Marot, the Huguenot designer and engraver trained under Bérain, who left France before the Revocation of the Edict of Nantes, entering the service of William and Mary first in Holland and then in England. Marot's engraved furniture designs show remark-able similarities with Jensen's documented pieces in the Royal Collection, and others attributed to him at Boughton, Drayton and elsewhere. It is possible that Jensen had French craftsmen working for him: for instance one Peter Berew, who signs a receipt on his behalf at Drayton in 1693. French terms, barely anglicized, occur constantly in the accounts, and indeed the 'beuro' or 'scrutore' (escritoire) with 'drawers to stand on the top' (otherwise known as the 'caddinet') may be a form which Jensen introduced to this country from France, together with the narrow gateleg table with a folding top. If seaweed marquetry pieces, and other types of carcase furniture dating from the Baroque period, are now more readily associated with Gerrit Jensen's name than is justified by documentary evidence, his output is of such high quality that it deserves, like that of Thomas Chippendale, to stand for the work of a whole generation of English cabinet makers. [DEF; GCM; Conn., vol. 95, 1935, pp. 263–74; Conn., vol. 96, 1935, pp. 188–92; C. Life, 22 May 1942; Conn., January 1963, pp. 31–34]

GOODWOOD, Sussex (1st Duke of Richmond). Supplied a table and stands and a strong box for £10. [BM, Charles Stuart, Duke of Richmond papers, vol. IV — bills 1661–73]

LEVENS HALL, Cumbria. A travelling desk by Jensen is said to survive at the house, together with associated correspondence.

DRAYTON HOUSE, Northants. (2nd Earl of Peterborough and his daughter the Duchess of Norfolk). 1675–1705: Jensen received £50 for furniture supplied for the Earl's embassy to France in 1675 and 'Mr Johnson Cabinet Maker's Bill' for 1679–88 includes '12 Arm'd chairs', 'a folding bed-wallnut', 'guilding the mother of pearle cabinet frame', and 'a large press of wallnut'. His name also occurs in the accounts of the Earl's daughter, the Duchess of Norfolk up to 1705, and he must undoubtedly have supplied the table and candlestands, inlaid with pewter, brass and ebony, now in the State Bedchamber, as well as other pieces still in the house.

ROYAL PALACES. 1680–1714: Regular bills in the Lord Chamberlain's accounts [PRO] for furniture supplied to all the royal palaces including Whitehall, St James, Somerset House, Kensington, Windsor Castle and Hampton Court, the royal residence at Newmarket, the yachts *Fubbs* and *Isabella*, and the House of Commons. Among those pieces still in the Royal Collection that can be firmly attributed to Jensen are a marquetry writing table (probably the 'Folding writeing table fine Markatree with a Crowne & Cypher' supplied for £22 10s on 30 October 1690), a glazed cabinet ('a glass case of fine markatree upon a Cabonett with doors' costing £30 on 24 July 1693) — both of these supplied 'for her ma^ts use at Kensington' — and a 'fine writing desk table inlaid wth mettall' made for the King in 1694–95 at a cost of £70, and also intended for Kensington. A pier glass at Hampton Court with the royal cypher and crown in blue glass must be the 'pannel of glass 13 feet long with a glass in it of 52 inches with a Crown and cypher and other ornaments', described in a bill of 1699. A marquetry mirror frame at Windsor may well be from an earlier set of furniture supplied to James II in May, 1686 — 'att Windsor Castle Queenes Side / In ye Gallery / For a Table, Stands a glasse Inlayd in wallnuttree the glasse 39 inches £40'. The last of Jensen's bills for the Royal Household is dated 10 August 1714, five days before his will was drawn up.

BURGHLEY HOUSE, Lincs. (5th Earl of Exeter). Jensen was paid a total of £534 and a writing table inlaid with pewter (similar to one at Drayton) can be attributed to him. [Child's bank ledgers; Exeter MS]

CHATSWORTH, Derbs. (4th Earl, later 1st Duke of Devonshire). 1688–98: Bills for providing glass on south front 1688, for 'glass for the door of the great chamber [now the State Dining Room] and for japanning the closet' in 1692. [*DEF*, II, 271] The latter, described by Celia Fiennes as 'wainscoted with hollow burnt Japan' (i.e. coromandel, or incised lacquer), was dismantled in 1700, when the panels were re-used on furniture including two chests on stands now in the State Drawing Room. In 1691, Jensen was also paid £160 'for glasses tables and stands for Chatsworth'.

ARUNDEL CASTLE, Sussex (Lord Thomas Howard). 1689: payment 'to Garrat Johnson in full £143.10s.' in Lord Thomas Howard's account bk. [Arundel Castle Records A117]

HAMILTON PALACE, Lanarkshire (1st Duke of Hamilton). *c.* 1690: A small dressing table, now at Lennoxlove, with a top formed of four sliding panels, all inlaid in brass and pewter on ebony, can be firmly attributed to Jensen on stylistic grounds and may well have been acquired by the Duke in the 1690s, when he is known to have patronized other leading London cm.

KNOLE, Kent (6th Earl of Dorset). 1680–1690: On 5 June 1680 Jensen presented his bill amounting to £407 5s for the famous suite of silver furniture consisting of a dressing table, looking glass and pair of candlestands. [U269 A185/2] Among other pieces mentioned in a bill of 21 December 1690 are 'Table Stands and Glass Japan'. The table and candle-stands are thought to be those now in the Spangled Bedchamber; the pier glass is now missing; the set was supplied at a cost of £18. [Kent RO, A192/10]

BOUGHTON HOUSE, Northants. (1st Duke of Montagu). *c.* 1690–1700: Jensen is listed as one of the Duke's creditors after his death in 1712, for work carried out in the 1690s, totalling £412 13s 6d and including for instance 'making up two large bookcases upon cabinets with doors of Indian skreen with Glasses in the Door Silver'd' costing £40. Among the pieces of furniture at the house which can be firmly attributed to him are a magnificent pair of metal-inlaid cabinets, each with nine drawers, and very similar to a documented example at Windsor Castle. These cabinets, in *premiere* and *contre-partie*, have a pair of mirrors *en suite*, one with the monogram of Ralph Montagu under an earl's coronet in the cresting (dating them to between 1689 and 1705), the other with a heart pierced by arrows, perhaps symbolizing his second marriage.

Another pier glass veneered with coromandel and with the same monogram in silver in the cresting, may also be by Jensen, along with its matching table which has a coromandel top and japanned frame. Several other pieces of elaborate marquetry furniture, including a number of caryatid candle-stands which are close in style to the engravings of Daniel Marot, could equally have come from Jensen's workshop, though it is tantalizing that the original accounts have not survived.

PETWORTH HOUSE, Sussex (6th Duke of Somerset). *c.* 1695: Several pieces of furniture including a magnificent pair of *verre eglomisée* pier glasses in the private dining room, and a seaweed marquetry table top with hinged flaps bearing the Duchess of Somerset's monogram, can be attributed to Jensen on grounds of style.

A bill for £119 15s paid in two parts in 1692 and receipted by Jensen includes: '*Duchess of Somerset*', 'Apr. 19, 1690 for Glass in a black Japan frame and a Table to fall Like a Bewro and Stands £16.' 'Jan. 22 1691 for a fine Markatree Bewro and Guilt pillars, a pare of Stands and Glass of the same £30' and 'for 2 large Cabinets with Dores on the top and Drawers under, for the cornars of the Dressing roome £24'. [W. Sussex RO, Petworth papers, PHA/652]

WELBECK ABBEY, Notts. (1st Earl of Portland). *c.* 1695–98:

An account bk kept by Caspar Frederick Henning, treasurer to the Earl of Portland, Groom of the Stole and First Gentleman of the Bedchamber to William III, records payments to Jensen in both the Earl's official and personal capacities between 1695 and 1698 totalling £608. [Worcs. RO, 2252/705; 366/1]

CASTLE BROMWICH HALL, Warks. (Lady Bridgeman). 1697–98: bills for 'chimney glasses' and other mirrors, including some with frames of 'Ceader pheneare', total of £9 5s. [Staffs. RO, D 1287, 18/4/1]

ICKWORTH, Suffolk (1st Earl of Bristol). 1696: Recorded as being paid on 25 May, 'ye black set of Glass, table and stands and for ye glasses etc. over ye chimneys & elsewhere in my dear wife's apartment £70' in the 1st Earl's *Diary*, published in 1874, p. 443.

KENSINGTON, Earl of Albemarle's Lodgings. *c.* 1699–1703: payments for items including 'a pair of chimney sconces wrought blue glass & a pair of branches double guilded £4 15s.' [PRO, LC 9/281]

HATFIELD HOUSE, Herts. (5th Earl of Salisbury). 1710–14: Supplied a *verre eglomisée* mirror ('a large looking glass, the frame drawn with scarlet and silver, the mouldings gilt'), another in a japanned frame 'with a folding table underneath which is also japan', a 'walnut writing desk, the top for books and patons and glass in the doors asked', and many other pieces listed in a detailed bill of June 1710–October 1711 totalling £427; together with another bill of 1714 itemizing 'gilt tables', etc. [Hatfield F.P.S. MS 3/179, bills 475, 476]

G.J.-S.

Jepps, Samuel, Southwark, London, bedstead maker (1826–35). At Redcross St in 1826 and 2 Gt Guildford St in 1835. Samuel Jepps, furniture broker, is recorded at 5 York Pl., Kensington in 1839 and may be the same person. [D]

Jepps, William Henry, London St, Uxbridge, Middlx, cm and u (1826). [D]

Jepps, William Henry, Reigate, Surrey, cm and u (1832). [D]

Jepson, Charles, 27 Basnett St, Liverpool, cm (1827). [D]

Jepson, Joseph, Conisbrough, Yorks., joiner and cm (1834). [D]

Jeram, Francis, Stokesley, Yorks., cm (1757). In 1757 took app. named Potter. [S of G, app. index]

Jerard, I., address unknown (*c.* 1805). Name stamped on tea boxes in an early Regency mahogany rectangular tea caddy.

Jeremy, Thomas & Bragg, William, 28 Southampton St, Covent Gdn, London, u and cm (1824–29). In 1824 took out insurance cover of £4,000, all but £300 of which was for stock, utensils and goods in trust. The trade of the partners was stated to be 'upholsterers & furniture warehousemen'. In 1829 Thomas Jeremy is recorded trading on his own behalf from this address an an u. [D; GL, Sun MS vol. 499, ref. 1016381; Heal]

Jermain, —, 10 Broad St, Golden Sq., London, cm (1803). Included in the list of master cabinet makers in Sheraton's *Cabinet Dictionary*, 1803.

Jermyn, Edmund & John, Harwich, Essex, cm and auctioneers (*c.* 1790–1830). Edmund Jermyn was Capital Burgess and Chamberlain of the Borough.

Jerome, Jas., New Town, Southport, Portsea, Portsmouth, Hants., carver and gilder (1830). [D]

Jerome, Josh., New Town, Southport, Portsea, Portsmouth, Hants., carver and gilder (1823). [D]

Jerrett, Henry, Bridgwater, Som., cm (1780). [Poll bk]

Jerritt, James, 108 Temple St, Bristol, cm (1804–05). Declared bankrupt, *Exeter Flying Post*, 12 July 1804, though still listed in a directory 1805.

Jerritt, James, Well St, Barnstaple, Devon, cm and u (1823–26). Thomas Smith, an app. aged 16, was committed to the borough gaol in August 1826 for assaulting Jerritt's seven year old daughter. [D; *Exeter Flying Post*, 17 August 1826]

Jerritt, John, Old King St, Bristol, cm (1794). [D]

Jervis, Frederick, 13 Rathbone Pl., Oxford St, London, u (1826–35). [D]

Jervis, Henry, Stafford St, Market Drayton, Salop, cm (1835–36). [D]

Jervis, John, Romsey, Hants., cm (1784). [D]

Jervis & Holl, 11 King St, Holborn, London, cabinet manufacturers (1817). [D]

Jess, George, Liverpool, cm (1807–27). At 9 Hodson St in 1807 and 72 Tithebarn St in 1827. [D]

Jessett, Mrs, 67 Chatham St, Reading, Berks., u (1837). [D]

Jessop, Mrs Ann, Fargate, Sheffield, Yorks., cm and u (1833–40). At 95 Fargate, 1833–37. She succeeded James Jessop at this address and was probably his widow. About 1839 moved to 26 Fargate and used labels to identify furniture supplied. These are known bearing the 26 Fargate address on a Windsor chair, and on another item. The business was described on the label as a 'Cabinet, Upholstery, Picture Frame, and Looking Glass manufactory'. [D]

Jessop, Benjamin, Uttoxeter, Staffs., cm (1798–1818). Recorded at Market Pl. as cm and u in 1818. [D]

Jessop, James, 95 Fargate, Sheffield, Yorks., cm (1830). By 1833 Mrs Ann Jessop, probably his widow, had taken over the business at this address. [D]

Jessop, John, Uttoxeter, Staffs., cm and u (1822–34). Recorded at Market Pl. in 1828. Executors of John Jessop listed in 1834. [D]

Jessop, Thomas, Sheffield, Yorks., cm (1821–22). In 1821 at South St and in 1822 in Little Sheffield. [D]

Jessop, Thomas, Higher Brook St, Tavistock, Devon, cm (1823). [D]

Jeves, William, Poplar, London, cm, u and undertaker (1827–39). Initially at 64 Pennyfields but later moved to 1 High St. [D]

Jewell, S. & H., 29–31 Little Queen St, Holborn, London, cm (1830–40). A billhead at Standen, East Grinstead, Sussex for furniture supplied to the house on 1 May 1894 by this firm states that it was founded in 1830. No pre-1840 directory entries have been traced.

Jewell, William, The Square, Barnstaple, Devon, carver and gilder (1830). [D]

Jewell, William, London, carver and gilder (1802–37). The business is first recorded as a partnership trading as Jewell & Black at 26 Coventry St from 1802–11. Thereafter William Jewell traded on his own behalf. He is shown in directories at the Coventry St address in 1812 but by 27 April of that year was at his new address of 27 Henrietta St, Covent Gdn. This property he insured for £1,200. He remained here until at least 1820 but by 1823 was at 55 Sloane St (or Sq.), Chelsea. He was to remain at this address until 1837. [D; GL, Sun MS vol. 459, ref. 869700]

Jewster, Mary, 2 Angel Ct, Leadenhall St, London, backgammon table maker (1802). Took out insurance in 1802 for £200 of which £100 was for utensils and stock. [GL, Sun MS vol. 423, ref. 732301]

Jeynes, Joseph, Hereford, cm and u (1830–40). At St Owen St in 1830 and Church St, 1835–40. Patronised by Capt. N. L. Pateshall of Hereford between 1830–36, but over this entire period the accounts only amount to £23 19s 9½ and are concerned with repairs and sundries only. [D; Herefs. RO, FO/212, 229, 274, 618]

Joacham, James, parish of St Augustine, Bristol, joiner and cm (1722–57). In November 1756 married Mrs Chalinder. At this date his address was Horse St. In January 1757 advertised that he was selling up and leaving off the cabinet business. A

walnut bookcase with gilt markings by this maker is recorded. [Poll bks; *Farley's Bristol Journal*, 20 November 1756, 15 January 1757; *C. Life*, 17 November 1983, supplement, p. 32]

Joachim, John, London, upholder (1786–94). Son of Joseph Joachim of Faversham, Kent, grocer. App. to Thomas Joachim on 2 June 1779 and free of the Upholders' Co. by servitude, 5 July 1786. In 1786 at Howard St, Strand, and in 1794 at St Mary at Hill. [GL, Upholders' Co. records]

Joachim, Thomas, London, upholder (1774–94). Free of the Upholders' Co. by redemption, 10 August 1774. Stated to be a tea dealer. Took as app. John Joachim, 1779–86. His addresses are Cannon St in 1774, Upper Thames St in 1778, Cannon St again in 1781, Thames St in 1786 and St Mary at Hill in 1794. The latter address is also that given by John Joachim in 1794. [GL, Upholders' Co. records]

Joad, John, Ramsgate, Kent, upholder (1767–80). Son of Gibb Joad of Ramsgate, mariner. Trained in London and app. to George Kemp, 27 October 1767, and John Button, 6 December 1771. Free of the London Upholders' Co. by servitude, 23 December 1779–5 January 1780. Probably never worked in London subsequent to this, as his address is given as Ramsgate. [GL, Upholders' Co. records]

Job, Robert, Hull, Yorks., cm (1774–1805). In 1805 took as app. Henry Fox of Rotherhithe, London. [Poll bk; Hull app. reg.]

Jobson, Robert, Alnmouth, Alnwick, Northumb., cm (1828–34). Listed as cm and joiner at Alnmouth in 1834. [D]

Joel, George, 23 Acorn St, Bishopsgate, London, looking-glass manufacturer (1839). [D]

Joel, M., 14 Crown St, Finsbury, London, (1835). [D]

Joel, Thomas, London, u (1724–38). In 1724–27 recorded at the 'Angel & Crown' in Barbican. In 1738 in Houndsditch. In December of this year some 'rich Linnens of the Chints Pattern for Bed-Quilts' was stolen from his premises, and Patrick Casey was committed for trial in this connection. [Heal; *Daily Post*, 19 December 1738]

Joggett, William, Taunton, Som., carver and gilder (1787). Suicide reported in *Exeter Flying Post*, 3 May 1787.

John, Samuel, London, cm (1785–92). In 1785 at 6 Faulconberg Ct, Sutton St where he took out insurance cover of £137 for household goods. In 1792 shown at 'The King's Head', Old Jury with a house at 11 Milk Alley, Dean St, Soho. He took out insurance cover of £200 of which £84 was in respect of his house. [GL, Sun MS vol. 329, p. 274; vol. 389, ref. 602605]

John, William, address unknown, chairmaker and carpenter (1778). A simple elm and oak chair is known, inscribed beneath the seat 'William John, Carpenter fecit/ October 28 1778'. [*Furn. Hist.*, 1976]

Johns, Francis, Killigrew St, Falmouth, Cornwall, cm and u (1830). [D]

Johns, George, Chelmsford, Essex, upholder and cm (1784–93). [D]

Johns, Samuel, Wendron St, Helston, Cornwall, cm, carpenter and joiner (1830). [D]

Johnson, —, address unknown, u (1721). Paid £2 19s 6d by Lady Bowes for 'hanging the parlour'. Probably a local craftsman from the Darlington area of Co. Durham. [Durham RO, Strathmore MS, D/St/Box 352/2, 30 November 1721]

Johnson, —, Broadgate, Lincoln, cm (1763). In December 1763 his entire stock in trade was offered for sale. This consisted of 'Desks, Chests of Drawers, Dining and Tea Tables, China Tables, Chairs, Glasses, Tea Chests, Tea Boards and also a large quantity of fine English walnut-tree, well seasoned in blocks, planks and veneers'. [*Cambridge Chronicle*, 21 December 1763]

Johnson, —, 69 Dean St, London, upholder and cm (1794).

Living at the house of a Mr Smith. Took out insurance cover of £300. [GL, Sun MS vol. 401, ref. 628211]

Johnson, —, Preston. See Winder & Johnson.

Johnson, —, Newcastle, cm (1803). Subscribed to Sheraton's *Cabinet Dictionary*, 1803.

Johnson, —, Hurst St, Birmingham, u (1828). [D]

Johnson, A. E., Fletcher Gate, Nottingham, u and paper hanger (1835). [D] See Edwin Johnson.

Johnson, Archibald, 11 Tarleton St, with shop at 1 Williamson Sq., Liverpool, cm and mattress maker (1827). [D]

Johnson, B. J., 79 Houndsditch and 10 Kingsland Rd, London, cm and u (1822–25). [D]

Johnson, Barry, London, upholder (1740–d. 1778). Son of Thomas Johnson of Leicester, grocer. App. to Charles Grange, 7 February 1732, and free of the London Upholders' Co. by servitude, 3 December 1740. [GL, Upholders' Co. records]

Johnson, Benjamin, Fetter Lane, London, knifecase maker (1785). In 1785 took as app. George Johnson. [Westminster Ref. Lib., MS B 1266]

Johnson, Benjamin, 16 Duke St, Lambeth, London, cm and undertaker (1827). [D]

Johnson, Charles Edward, 57 High St, Gravesend, Kent, cm and undertaker (1832–39). See Thomas & Charles Johnson in High St, Gravesend (1823–29). [D]

Johnson, E., 8 Gt Newport St, Long Acre, London, cm (1829). [D]

Johnson, E., 10 Eldon St, Finsbury Circus, London, cm (1829). [D]

Johnson, Edmund, London, cm (1780). Freeman of Hull. [Hull poll bk]

Johnson, Edmund, Moorfields, London, bedstead and cm (1820–37). At 28 Long Alley initially, though subsequently the number was changed to 29. Probably the same maker who was shown in June 1824 at 10 Moorfields, and who insured his stock and utensils in his dwelling house for £300. [D; GL, Sun MS vol. 495, ref. 1017522]

Johnson, Edmund, Liverpool, u (1807). Free 6 May 1807. [Freemen reg.]

Johnson, Edward, Newcastle u (1717). Married at the Church of St Nicholas, 28 November 1717. [PR (marriage)]

Johnson, Edward & Bailey, Edmund, 11 Gt Queen St, Lincoln's Inn Fields, London, brokers and cm (1782). In 1782 took out insurance cover of £200 of which £180 was in respect of utensils and stock. [GL, Sun MS vol. 304, p. 531]

Johnson, Edward, 14 Catherine St, Strand, London, upholder and cm (1784). Took out insurance cover of £600 in 1784 and of this £400 was in respect of utensils, stock and goods. [GL, Sun MS vol. 322, p. 466]

Johnson, Edward, London, cm (1790). Freeman of Beverley, Yorks. [Beverley poll bk]

Johnson, Edward & Sons, Barton-upon-Humber, Lincs., carpenters, builders, cm and raft merchants (1793). [D]

Johnson, Edward, Spencer St, Hull, Yorks., cm (1803–06). [D]

Johnson, Edward, 155 Leadenhall St, London, camp, travelling and cabin furniture maker (1839). Advertised in *Pigot's Directory*, 1839 as late Merriman, makers by appointment to the East India Co. Featured their 'Newly Invented Metallic Folding Bedstead' which they claimed was particularly suited for military personnel, emigrants or those who might require to accommodate additional guests. These beds when folded up were said to 'form an elegant piece of drawing-room furniture' and to take up 'less than one-twelfth part of the room occupied by the common French Bedstead'. They also offered swing cots, spring mattresses, portable chests of drawers, wardrobes, bookcases, wash hand stands, camp and cabin chairs and bedding. They offered to fit up at short notice cabins for those about to set off on sea voyages.

Johnson, Edwin, Fletcher Gate, Nottingham, u (1834). [D]

Johnson, Ellen, Market Pl., Wigan, Lancs., u (1805–08). [D]

Johnson, Emanuel, Leicester, cm and joiner (1796). Third son of Emanuel Johnson, deceased. App. to John Brothers, cm, and free by servitude in 1796. [Freemen rolls]

Johnson, Emanuel, Market Pl., Wokingham, Berks., cm (1830). [D]

Johnson, Francis, Long Acre, London, cm (1692). In June 1692 fined as a Papist for refusing the Oath of Fidelity. [Westminster Ref. Lib., Middlx session bk, 498, pp. 76–79]

Johnson, Frederick, 6 Foundling Mews, Gray's Inn Rd, London, cm and u (1835–39). [D]

Johnson, G. & T., 34 Cary St, London, cabinet manufacturers (1802). [D]

Johnson, George, Northgate St, Chester, cm (1765–84). Son of Thomas Johnson, carpenter. Free 16 June 1765. In 1768 took app. named Thomas Cross. Later apps were John Baker (free 1778), and John Norbury (free 1784). [Freemen rolls; app. bk; poll bk]

Johnson, George, New Cut, Lambeth Marsh, London, cm (1809). [D]

Johnson, George, 6 Clarence Pl., Hackney Rd, London, cm and u (1827). [D]

Johnson, George, Liverpool, cm (1828–35). App. to John Chesters in 1828 and free, 1835. [Freemen's committee bk]

Johnson, George, 25 Curtain Rd, London cm (1835). [D]

Johnson, George, Ripon, Yorks., joiner/cm (1834–37). At Duckhill Bank in 1834 and North St in 1837. [D]

Johnson, H., Goodramgate, York, cm, u and undertaker (c. 1815–20). Trade card [Banks Coll., BM] shows a chair, sofa, dressing table and a length of wallpaper displaying Regency taste.

Johnson, Henry, Grantham, Lincs., joiner (1770). In March 1770 advertised for two journeymen joiners: 'better if they can work in the cabinet way'. [*Cambridge Chronicle*, 31 March 1770]

Johnson, Henry, 11 Bedford Pl., Commercial Rd, London, cm, u and undertaker (1835–39). [D]

Johnson, Henry William, Belgrave Gate, Leicester, cm (1827–40). [D]

Johnson, Isaac, Rea St, Birmingham, cm, u and broker (1830). [D]

Johnson, J. & M., Clipstone St, Fitzroy Sq., London, cm and u (1822–27). In 1822 at 23 Clipstone St but from 1826–27 the number was 22. [D]

Johnson, J., 13 Eldon St, Finsbury Circus, London, u (1829). [D]

Johnson, J., 41 Edgcumbe St, Stonehouse, Plymouth, Devon, cm (1830). [D]

Johnson, J., London St, Southwark, London, chairmaker (1835). [D]

Johnson, James, 'The Golden Lion', The Side, Newcastle, cm (1754–55). Appears to have ceased trading in 1754, since on 28 December his stock in trade was offered including 'goods in the cabinet-making way together with pier-glasses &c' and 'unwrought timber'. The residue was again offered on 8 February 1755 and the shop together 'with a convenient shade and several workshops' offered for rental. [*Newcastle Courant*, 28 December 1754, 8 February 1755]

Johnson, James, Preston, Lancs., joiner and cm (1814–18). At 21 Lord St but one directory of 1818 shows Avenham St. [D]

Johnson, James, 10 City Rd, London, cm (1825). [D]

Johnson, James, 16 Paddington St, Marylebone, London, cm and u (1826–27). [D]

Johnson, James, Stockton, Co. Durham, joiner and cm (1827–32). In 1827 at Park Row and in 1832 at Quayside. [D]

Johnson, James, Helmsley, Yorks., tailor and u (1840). [D]

Johnson, Jeremiah, Church Lane, Strand, London, cm (1784). [D]

Johnson, Jeremiah, Hobson St, Cambridge, turner and chairmaker (1823–40). [D; poll bks]

Johnson, Jeremiah, South End, Alford, Lincs., chair turner and joiner (1835). [D]

Johnson, Job, Charlotte St, Gt Yarmouth, Norfolk, cm (1812–22). Listed as cm and joiner in 1822. [D; poll bks]

Johnson, Job jnr, London, carver (1831). Freeman of Gt Yarmouth but resident in London. [Gt Yarmouth poll bk]

Johnson, John, 'The Kings Arms', Long Acre London, cm (before 1695). In February 1695 the widow of John Johnson announced that she was leaving off the trade and was offering at reasonable rates 'all sorts of Cabinet-makers Goods, both Indian and English'. [London Gazette, 10–13 February 1695]

Johnson, John, address unrecorded, upholder (1764). Son of John Johnson of Surrey, yeoman. App. to Robert Thorpe and Edward Wright, draper, 5 May 1757. Free of the Upholders' Co. under the terms of the 1750 Upholders' Act, 2 August 1764 [GL, Upholders' Co. records]

Johnson, John, Chester, cm (1771–84). It would seem likely that there were two cm of this name in Chester from the 1770s. One was accepting app. from 1771 whereas the other was not free until 28 October 1772. The first of these took as apps John Griffith (1771), Charles Cans (1774), John Henderson (1774), James Phoenix (1776) and George Thorpe. The latter was assigned to him in 1777 presumably having started his apprenticeship elsewhere. The second John Johnson was the son of Charles Johnson, dyer. Subsequently one of these two cm had a business in Lower Bridge St, and in December 1783 he announced the sale of all his household goods and furniture at this address. By October of the following year one of the John Johnsons announced the opening of 'Wine and Spirituous Liquor Vaults at the premises formerly occupied by Mr. Davison in Higher Bridge St'. He evidently continued with the cabinet side of the business however, for at the same time he advertised for several journeymen cm. On 24 June of this year one of the John Johnson's was paid 5s 6d for bottoming two rush-bottom chairs at Dunham Massey, Cheshire. [App. bks; freemen rolls; Chester Chronicle, 19 December 1783, 22 October 1784; John Rylands Lib., Manchester Univ., George Cooke's accounts]

Johnson, John, Leicester, cm (1787). Son of Joseph Johnson, cm, and free in 1787. [Freemen rolls]

Johnson, John, Buxton, Derbs., cm (1793). [D]

Johnson, John, Knight St, Berry St, Liverpool, cm (1800–10). At 25 Knight St in 1800 but from 1803–10 at 29. [D]

Johnson, John, Pleasant St, Preston, Lancs., joiner and cm (1818). [D]

Johnson, John, 'King's Head', Piccadilly, Shelton, Staffs., victualler, joiner and cm (1818–22). [D]

Johnson, John, Market St, Hanley, Staffs., cm and u (1828). [D]

Johnson, John, Leicester, cm (1826–32). Eldest son of Joseph Johnson, joiner and cm of Leicester. Free 1826 or 1832. [Furn. Hist., 1976; freemen rolls]

Johnson, John, 71 Old St, London, cm and u (1839). [D]

Johnson, John, 51 Long Alley, Finsbury, London, bedstead maker (1839). [D]

Johnson, John, Magdalene St, Cambridge, cm, u and paper hanger (1839). [D]

Johnson, John, West-end, Kirkbymoorside, Yorks., cm and joiner (1840). [D]

Johnson, Jonathan, Wigan, Lancs., upholder (1792–98). On 20 July 1792 married Miss Markland of Wigan at Hindley Chapel. Trading in Wigan in 1798. [D; Williamson's Liverpool Advertiser, 13 August 1792]

Johnson, Joseph, Leicester, cm (1758–99). Eldest son of William Johnson, joiner and cm, and free on 9 March 1758–60. Took as apps Thomas Johnson his brother (1760–67), John Dugler (Douglas?) (1761–90), John Onely (1764–79) and John Lewin (1767–79). Traded in 1759 from an address in the High St but in 1761 moved to Northgate. A sale of his contents was announced in 1773. It is possible that he gave up the business because of illness, for in December 1799 his wife appealed in the Leicester Journal for information, as he was missing, and was said to be 'mentally deranged'. [Furn. Hist., 1976; freemen rolls; Leicester Journal, 1759, 1761, 1773, 6 December 1799]

Johnson, Joseph, 7 George's Row, St Luke's, London, bedstead maker and carpenter (1808). [D]

Johnson, Joseph, Liverpool, u (b. 1779–d. by 1840). In Caxton Buildings, 1813–16, and at 1 Lawson Ct, Hodson St, in 1821. Aged 43 in 1822 and dead before 1840. [D; Liverpool RO, 352/CON 5/1 A–J]

Johnson, Josiah jnr, Royston, Herts., u and basket maker (1798). [D]

Johnson, Joshua, 99 Row, Gt Yarmouth, Norfolk, cm (1836–39). [D]

Johnson, Moses, Cauk St, Leicester, cm (1835). [D]

Johnson, Moses, Cank St, Derby, cm (1835). [D]

Johnson, Nathaniel, Ipswich, Suffolk, cm and joiner (1757–61). In 1757 took app. named Smith and in 1761, Ribbons. [S of G, app. index]

Johnson, Nicholas, 14 York Pl., Brighton, Sussex, cm (1817–23). In December 1817 when his son Ebenezer was bapt. he was living in Steyne Gdns. The York Pl. address is shown in directories, 1822–23. [D; PR (bapt.)]

Johnson, Peter, 65 Old Sneet Rd, London, cm (1808). [D]

Johnson, R., 84 Crawford St, Montague Sq., London, carver, gilder etc. (1820). [D]

Johnson, Richard, Derby, u (1793). [D]

Johnson, Richard, Berkhampstead, Herts., cm (1793). [D]

Johnson, Robert, Liverpool, carver (1722). Free 26 March 1722. [Freemen reg.]

Johnson, Robert, Newcastle, u (1722). Free by servitude, 12 March 1721/22. [Freemen reg.]

Johnson, Robert, Cambridge, cm (before 1740). Voted for the pewing of Gt St Mary's Church, Cambridge. [BL, Add MS 5833 (William Cole, vol. 32), f. 120]

Johnson, Robert, London, carver and gilder (1745–49). In 1746 shown at St James, Westminster but otherwise at 'The Golden Head', Frith St, Soho. In 1746 took app. named Joshua Chenn. His trade card [Heal Coll., BM] states that he made 'all Sorts of Carv'd frames for Marble Tables & Chimney pieces, Picture frames, and Glass Sconce frames, Prints and Drawings fram'd & Glaz'd, Pictures Clean'd Lin'd & Mended with all other Carv'd & Gilt Ornaments'. Supplied picture frames for Petworth House, Sussex. [Westminster poll bk; Boyd's index to IR app. reg., VI; Heal; C. Life, 25 September 1980, p. 1030]

Johnson, Robert, 3 Talbot Ct, Gracechurch St, London, upholder (1765–75). Son of Richard Johnson of Staines, Middlx, fellmonger. App. to Jacob Grant, freeman of London and a member of the Wheelwright's Co., on 16 June 1752. Free of the Upholders' Co. under the terms of the 1750 Upholders' Act 1750 on 25 June 1765. His trade card survives (Leverhulme Coll., MMA, NY). The business is described as Robert Johnson & Co. (Late Grant's), Blanket, Carpet and Upholstery Warehouse. Apart from stocking carpets, 'Cotton, Check, Moreen' etc. he offered to undertake upholstery work. [D; Heal; GL, Upholders' Co. records]

Johnson, Robert, Westgate St, Newcastle, carver and gilder (1801–27). In August 1825 he announced a move of premises in Westgate St 'to one nearly opposite, a little below the end of Collingwood-street. This new address was numbered 10 in 1827. [D; *Durham County Advertiser*, 27 August 1825]

Johnson, Robert, 1 Cross St Row, Apollo Rd, London, cm (1808). On 6 September 1808 took out insurance cover of £300. This included £70 for 'workshops with rooms joined in one building behind' and £110 for stock and utensils in them. [GL, Sun MS vol. 443, ref. 821024]

Johnson, Rob., 29 Widegate St, Bishopsgate, London, cm (1809). [D]

Johnson, Rob., 85 Fleet Mkt, London, cm (1809). [D]

Johnson, Robert, Liverpool, cm (1812). App. to John Kendall, cm, in 1801, but when he petitioned freedom on servitude in 1812 he declared his trade to be book keeper. [Freemen's committee bk]

Johnson, Robert, Liverpool, u (1820–23). In both 1820 and 1823 shown at Clayton St but a directory of 1821 lists 33 Tarleton St with a shop at 21 Church St. Free 10 March 1820 and in this year he married Miss Elizabeth Dawson at St Anne's Church. Their infant son Julius died in June 1823 aged 22 months. [D; freemen reg., *Liverpool Mercury*, 14 June 1820, 6 June 1823]

Johnson, Robert, Pickering, Yorks., cm (1834–40). [D]

Johnson, Robert, Epworth, Lincs., cm (1835). [D]

Johnson, Robert, Lancaster, u (1829–37). App. to L. Redmayne, 1829, and free, 1836–37. [Lancaster app. reg. and freemen rolls]

Johnson, Robert, 86 Old St, London, cm and u (1839). [D]

Johnson, Samuel, Chester, cm (1775). Free 4 November 1775. [Freemen rolls]

Johnson, Samuel, 40 Skinner St, Bishopsgate, London, cm (1820–22). [D]

Johnson, Samuel, 13 Old St, London, cm (1826). [D]

Johnson, Samuel W. H, 20 Edgecumbe St, East Stonehouse, Plymouth, Devon, cm and u (1838). [D]

Johnson, Thomas, various addresses in and around Soho, London, carver, gilder and designer (b. 1714–c. 1778). Thomas Johnson, son of Thomas and Mary Johnson, was bapt. at the church of St Giles-in-the-Fields, London on 13 January 1714. Nothing is known of his apprenticeship nor of his work as a young man. He made his name as a designer of carvers' pieces, issuing in September 1755 his first recorded set entitled *Twelve Gerandoles* from Queen St, Seven Dials, Soho. This property had been rented in the name of his widowed mother in 1747 although she ceased to be the ratepayer in 1748 and her son's name does not appear in the rate bks. However, Thomas evidently retained a connection with Queen St, from which *Twelve Gerandoles*, engraved by William Austin on four sheets at 2s each, was issued. Very few designs for girandoles in the Rococo style had hitherto been published. Johnson's contribution on this occasion introduced rustic themes often inspired by Francis Barlow's illustrations to Aesop's *Fables* (1687), and executed in a lively, staccato Rococo style. Their success led to a new venture announced in a broadsheet dated 1755. This document is headed by an illustration of a romantic landscape designed and drawn by Thomas Johnson himself and engraved by William Austin. It advertises the forthcoming publication of designs for 'Glass, Picture, and Table Frames; Chimney Pieces, Gerandoles, Candle-stands, Clock-cases, Brackets, and other Ornaments in the Chinese, Gothick, and Rural Taste', to be obtained by subscription from 'Thomas Johnson, Carver, at the Corner of Queen-street, near the Seven Dials, London'. [BM, 1872, 6–8–543; MMA, NY, Print Room, no. 32.61] The designs, on fifty-two sheets,

appeared in four parts in 1756 and 1757. They were engraved by James Kirk and B. Clowes. A collected edition then appeared in 1758 but issued from a new address, Grafton St, Soho, to which Johnson had moved early in 1757. This was without title. Public demand for these animated Rococo designs must have been considerable for yet another edition, this time with a dedication to Lord Blakeney, President of the Antigallican Association and with a formal title *One Hundred and Fifty New Designs*, containing one additional plate, making a total of fifty-three, was published in 1761. Preparatory drawings for two console tables survive. [V&A, D731–1906] The style of these designs follows the vigorous, picturesque manner already introduced in the earlier proposals for girandoles. In composing his themes, Johnson constantly studied the work of earlier designers, introducing motifs taken from engraved ornament by Jean Bérain, Daniel Marot, William de la Cour, J. B. Toro and Francis Barlow.

The name of Johnson's workshop in Grafton St was 'The Golden Boy'. While the two collected editions mentioned above bear witness to Johnson's success as a designer, two further sets of designs published from this address in 1760 reveal another aspect of his involvement in the field of publishing. The first set appeared on 16 December and probably consisted of four sheets, each illustrating a girandole emblematic of the Elements. Only one sheet survives, representing Earth. It is etched in a crayon manner by Thomas Johnson himself and inscribed 'T. Johnson inv: delin & Sculpt; Published by Act of Parlimt, . . . by ye Proprietor at the Golden Boy in Grafton Street St. Anne's Soho London where this & all other Ornaments are Carv'd & Gilt'. [BM, 1862, 11–8–219] The second set consisted of a title page inscribed 'A New Book of Ornaments by Thos. Johnson . . . T. J. fecit' and seven plates. These two sets show Johnson experimenting with etchings in imitation of ink and wash drawings. They are close in manner to the aquatinted plates in his book *A Brief History of Free Masons*, the second edition of which was published in 1784. [BM, Print Room] Johnson was Clerk of the Charlotte St Chapel and Janitor to several other Masonic Lodges. Evidently the method of etching his designs appealed to Johnson and a further set, titled *A New Book of Ornaments* 'Designe'd for Tablets and Frizes for Chimney-Pieces Useful for Youth to draw after' appeared in August 1762. The title suggests that Johnson was concerned with teaching drawing and indeed, he was described in Mortimer's *Universal Director*, 1763 as a 'Carver, Teacher of Drawing and Modelling and Author of a Book of Designs for Chimney-pieces and other ornaments and of several other pieces'. He even designed a trade card for himself, now preserved in the Heal Coll., BM, inscribed 'Thos. Johnson Drawing Master at ye Golden Boy in Charlotte Street Bloomsbury London'. It is a drawing showing a pupil working at a table.

While the 1762 designs are still in the Rococo style, one surviving sheet, dated August 1775, from a lost set shows three mirrors or sconces in the Neo-classical taste. [MMA, NY, Print Room 56.586.8]

As a carver, Johnson's achievements are as yet undocumented but a number of pieces directly after his designs are recorded, such as: one pair of mirrors supplied to Paul Methuen of Corsham Court, Wilts. between 1761–63, possibly through George Cole of Golden Sq.; a pair of mirrors ordered for Newburgh Priory, Yorks. and now on loan to Temple Newsam House, Leeds; four candlestands from Hagley Hall, Worcs. two now being at the Philadelphia Museum, one in the V&A and one at Temple Newsam House, Leeds; an overmantel at Fairlawne, Kent; and a chimney piece at Fonmon Castle, Glam.; a number of girandoles and mirrors after published designs have appeared on the art market over the years. While such pieces may well have been carved and gilt in Thomas Johnson's workshop the lack of any supporting documentary evidence makes firm attributions impossible. There are a number of pieces featuring decorative motifs used by Johnson such as a pair of girandoles at Corsham Court and four pier glasses and three console tables supplied to the 2nd Duke of Atholl's Scottish seats, Dunkeld House and Blair Castle between 1761–63 by George Cole. Evidence suggests that Cole may, indeed, have supplied items by Thomas Johnson both to Paul Methuen and to the Duke of Atholl but there are no surviving accounts.

As a carver, Thomas Johnson remains a shadowy figure. A carver of that name, resident in Store St, Tottenham Ct Rd in the parish of St Giles-in-the-Fields, was declared bankrupt, *London Gazette*, 11–15 September 1764. This may be the author of the designs with whom we are concerned, for after May 1763 he is no longer recorded in the rate bks for Grafton St. If that is so, he continued to live at Store St until 1778, after which his name no longer appears in the rate bks. [A. Coleridge, *Chippendale Furniture, 1968*; C. Gilbert, *Leeds Furn. Cat.*, nos 268, 272, 355, 1978; H. Hayward, *Thomas Johnson and English Rococo*, 1964; H. Hayward, 'Thomas Johnson and Rococo Carving', *The Conn. Year Bk*, 1965, pp. 94–100; H. Hayward, 'Newly-discovered designs by Thomas Johnson, *Furn. Hist.*, 1975, pp. 40–42; M. Heckscher, 'Gideon Saint, an Eighteenth Century Carver and his Scrapbook', *Met. Museum Bulletin*, February 1969, pp. 299–310; *Rococo Art and Design in Hogarth's England* (Exhib. Cat.) V&A, 1984, nos C23, D29, E22, G47, 48, L19, 20, 43–48, 62, 72, M15, 18, 21, 25, 29, O36 45, S48; P. Ward-Jackson, *Furniture Designs of the 18th Century*, 1958.   H.H.

Johnson, Thomas, Liverpool, carver (1755). In 1755 took app. named Atwood. [S of G, app. index]

Johnson, Thomas, Boston, Lincs., cm (1756). In 1756 took app. named Winpenny. [S of G, app. index]

Johnson, Thomas, Lincoln, joiner and cm (1761–64). Son of William Johnson of Lincoln, cm and joiner. On 14 March 1761 took over the mastership of his father's app. because of his death. Probably the craftsman who supplied Lord Monson with a chest of drawers at a cost of £2 5s in 1764. [App. bk; Lincoln RO, Monson 10/1/A/5, 11/62/S]

Johnson, Thomas, Leicester, joiner and cm (1767). Brother of Joseph Johnson to whom he was app. on 29 September 1759. Free, 20 August 1767. [Freemen rolls; *Furn. Hist.*, 1976]

Johnson, Thomas, Nine Houses, Chester, cm (1767–71). App. to John Croughton and free by servitude, 11 December 1767. [Freemen rolls; poll bk]

Johnson, Thomas jnr, Gravesend, Kent, cm and carpenter (1777). In 1777 insured his workshop, storeroom, utensils and stock for £100 out of a total cover of £500. [GL, Sun MS vol. 260, p. 272]

Johnson, Thomas snr, Union St, Cambridge, carver and gilder (1801–35). Recorded working at Trinity College, 1801–33. In 1801 he was paid for gilding organ pipes but the usual work was supplying and gilding frames. At St John's College payments for similar work were made in 1818, 1825, 1829 and 1830. Thomas Johnson jnr, almost certainly his son, is also recorded in Union St, 1832–35. [D; Trinity College, Junior Bursar's accounts; St John's College accounts; poll bks]

Johnson, Thomas & George, 34 Carey St, Lincoln's Inn Fields, London, cm (1802). [Heal]

Johnson, Thomas, Fleet Mkt, London, cm (1805–09). Bankruptcy announced, September 1805. In 1808 at 85 Fleet Mkt where he insured his stock and utensils for £150. By 1809 at 5 Fleet Mkt and of the £400 insurance taken out £120 was for

stock and utensils and £200 for similar items in a warehouse. [D; *Leeds Intelligencer*, 2 September 1805; GL, Sun MS vol. 442, ref. 814074; vol. 444, ref. 825733]

Johnson, Thomas, 21 Gt Sutton St, Clerkenwell, London, japanned chairmaker (1808–28). [D]

Johnson, Thomas, 44 Gloucester St, Queen's Sq., London, carver and gilder (1816–37). [D]

Johnson, Thomas, Church St, Guisborough, Yorks., joiner and cm (1823). [D]

Johnson, Thomas, Stockwell St, Leek, Staffs., cm (1818–34). [D]

Johnson, Thomas, Belper, Derbs, cm and u (1822). [D]

Johnson, Thomas & Edward, High St, Gravesend, Kent, cm (1824–29). See Charles Edward Johnson at 57 High St, 1832–39. [D]

Johnson, Thomas, Brook St, Chester, u (1826). Free 12 June 1826. [Freemen rolls; poll bk]

Johnson, Thomas jnr, Union St, Cambridge, carver and gilder (1832–40). [Poll bks]

Johnson, W., Gt Hampton St, Birmingham, cm, u and broker (1830). [D]

Johnson, William, Nottingham, carver (1707). [Freemen rolls]

Johnson, William, Lincoln, joiner and cm (1773–d. 1761). Undertook work for Lord Monson in 1733 and 1741–42 at Burton. Most of the work undertaken was general carpentry and repairs but included some simple furniture such as a night table at 18s invoiced on 7 September 1742 and two large walnut arm chairs on 11 September at 16s each. William Johnson took apps named Eubulus Thorold Darwin in 1757, and John Portwood probably earlier. Died in 1761 and his son Thomas, also a cm and joiner, took over his app., probably Darwin. [Lincoln RO, Monson 12, vouchers; app. bk]

Johnson, William, Newtown Linford, Leics., joiner and cm (1750–60). His eldest son Joseph was app. in 1750 and sworn a freeman of Leicester, 9 March 1758–60. Another son Thomas was app. to his brother in 1760. [Leicester freemen rolls]

Johnson, William, address unknown (1765–66). Employed at Kedleston, Derbs. in 1765 lengthening pedestals for silver cisterns and vases, making drawers in the library etc. In 1766 he worked on the organ case for 158 days, including the carving of 62 feet of moulding for it. [Kedleston Hall archives, 3R no. 12; V&A archives]

Johnson, William, 10 Hanover St, Long Acre, London, cm (1791). Took out insurance cover of £200 in May 1791 which included £50 for utensils, stock and goods in trust and £30 for stock and goods in trust in the workshop of Cook, cm in Russeter's Building, Holborn. Also insured a house at Mortlake, Surrey for £60. [GL, Sun MS 25 May 1791, ref. 583759]

Johnson, William, Liverpool, chairmaker (1794–1821). At Derby St in 1794; 17 John St with a shop in Stanley St, 1800–03; 11 Poplar Lane, Cumberland St, 1807 and 1821; and 5 Poplar Lane, 1811–18. [D]

Johnson, William, 2 Chariot St, Hull, Yorks., cm (1817). [D]

Johnson, William, Commercial Rd, London, cm u and appraiser (1820–39). At 3 Devonshire Pl., Commercial Rd. in 1820 but from the following year it appears to have been renamed 3 Collet Pl. and is sometimes referred to as just 3 Commercial Rd. On 7 June 1821 took out two insurance policies amounting to £1,450 and £400 respectively. The first of these included £450 for stock and utensils with a further £100 for a warehouse in the yard behind and £100 in addition for stock and utensils kept there. The second policy was for a house and factory at the corner of Albion St and Commercial Rd in the tennure of a tallow chandler and oilman. [D; GL, Sun MS vol. 487, refs 980978–79]

Johnson, William, 2 Castle St, Long Acre, London, broker, and cm (1822–26). On 30 January 1822 took out insurance cover of £600 of which £500 was in respect of stock, utensils and goods in trust. [D; GL, Sun MS vol. 493, ref. 987881]

Johnson, William, 12 Foley St, London, cm and chairmaker (1822–29). On 14 November 1822 took out insurance cover of £300 of which £70 was for workshops behind his dwelling and £130 for stock and utensils in it. [D; GL, Sun MS vol. 493, refs 997705–06]

Johnson, William, 14 York Pl., Brighton, Sussex, cm (1822). Nicholas Johnson is also shown in directories at this address in 1822–23. [D]

Johnson, William, Tuxford, Notts., cm and joiner (1822). [D]

Johnson, William & Son, Wokingham, Berks., cm (1823). [D]

Johnson, William, Holbeach, Lincs., chairmaker (1822–26). One of the subscribers to Sheraton's *Drawing Book*, 1793 was a Johnson of Lincolnshire. [D]

Johnson, William, Padehole, Louth, Lincs., cm and joiner (1826). [D]

Johnson, William, Leicester, framesmith (1826). Son of Joseph Johnson of Leicester, joiner and cm. [*Furn. Hist.*, 1976]

Johnson, William, Belgrave Gate, Leicester, cm (1828–35). [D]

Johnson, William, Orchard St, Newcastle, trunk maker and u (1827). [D]

Johnson, William, Stockton, Co. Durham, joiner and cm (1827–32). In Dovecot St, 1827; Brunswick St, 1828; and William St, 1832. [D]

Johnson, William, Bildeston, Suffolk, cm and joiner (1830–39). [D]

Johnson, William, 34 Fargate, Sheffield, Yorks., cm (1834–40). [D; GL, Sun MS vol. 269, ref. 1343141]

Johnson, William, Harlow Pl., Mile End Rd, London, cm (1835–39). Bankruptcy announced in *Sussex Agricultural Express*, 20 April 1839. [D]

Johnson, William, Leathley Lane, Leeds, Yorks., cm and joiner (1837–40). [D]

Johnson, William, 24 Platt Terr., Kings Cross, London, cm and u (1839). [D]

Johnson & Garbutt, Brighton, Sussex, cm (1822–23). At 10 Prince's Pl. in 1822 and 135 North St, 1823. [D]

Johnson & Smith, Stockton, Co. Durham, builders and cm (1818). In October 1818 advertised that they had added auctioneering and appraising to their activities. They also stated that they could supply 'architectural designs for Plans, Elevations and Sections'. [*Durham County Advertiser*, 31 October 1818]

Johnson & Son, Gravesend, Kent, cm (1811). [D]

Johnston, —, London, cm (1793). Subscribed to Sheraton's *Drawing Book*, 1793. This entry is in addition to that of William Johnston of London, another subscriber.

Johnston, Archibald, Liverpool, u and broker (1823–34). At 23 Hatton Gdn in 1823 and 3 Williamson Sq. in 1834. [D]

Johnston, D., Bristol, u (1820–30). At 1 All Saints St in 1820, then in Nelson St. The number in Nelson St was 2 from 1821–24, 3 from 1826–29 and 4 in 1830. In 1830 he declared himself to be a feather merchant and manufacturer of beds, hair, wool, millpuff and straw mattresses in addition to an u. [D]

Johnston, Ellen, Williamson Sq., Liverpool, upholder and furniture broker. Successor to Archibald Johnston and probably his widow. At 3 Williamson Sq., 1835–37 but in 1839 the number was 5. [D]

Johnston, James, 1 Algar's St, Everton, Liverpool, carver and gilder (1839). [D]

Johnston, Robert, Albion St, Halifax, Yorks., cm (1822). [D]

Johnston, Stanley J., 34 Berry St, Liverpool, carver and gilder (1835). [D]

Johnston, Thomas, Liverpool, carver and gilder (1813–d. 1834). In 1813–14 shown at 29 Tarleton St. In 1821–24 the number was 33, in 1827 it was 2 and in 1829 it was 9. Dead by March 1834 when his son William announced his intention of carrying on the business. [D]

Johnston, William, London, cm (1793). Subscribed to Sheraton's *Drawing Book*, 1793. Another Johnston of London, cm, was also a subscriber.

Johnston, William S., 2 Tarleton St, Liverpool, carver and gilder (1834). Son of Thomas Johnston, carver and gilder. Took over his father's business on his death which was probably early in 1834. [D; *Liverpool Mercury*, 28 March 1834]

Johnstone, James, Chester, cm (1829). Came from Scotland. Had 8s stolen by a female pick-pocket in 1829. [*Chester Chronicle*, 11 December 1829]

Johnstone, William, Longtown, Carlisle, Cumb., joiner and cm (1828–29). In 1828 the business was listed as Wm Johnstone & Son. [D]

Joinson, Thomas, Stockwell St, Leek, Staffs., joiner and cm (1818–34). [D]

Jole, William, London, upholder (1736–51). Son of Robert Jole of Chiswell St, London, brazier. App. to Thomas Jole, stationer, 1 February 1736 and to Samuel Sleigh in 1740. Free of the Upholders' Co. under the terms of the 1750 Upholders' Act, 3 January 1750/51. [GL, Upholders' Co. records]

Joliffe, James, 64 Shaw's Brow, Liverpool, mattress and bedstead maker (1827). [D]

Jolit, Francis, 6 Old Broad St, Royal Exchange, London, cm (1802–39). Heal lists the Christian name as Frederick but this would appear to be an error. After 1829 the business traded as Francis Jolit & Son. [D]

Jolley, Richard, Liverpool, cm (1762). In the Preston freemen rolls said to be 'grandson of John of Hutton'.

Jollie & Sons, Market Pl., Carlisle, Cumb., booksellers and u (1810). [D]

Jolliffe, Paul, Buckingham(?), joiner, carpenter and carver (1660). Reward offered for his apprehension on a charge of murder. [*Mercurius Politicus*, 16–23 February 1660]

Jolly, Edward, Warrington, Lancs., cm (1759). In 1759 took app. named Lea. [S of G, app. index]

Jolly, Henry, Haverhill, Suffolk, u (1839). [D]

Jolly, James, Goulborne St, Warrington, Lancs., chairmaker (1798–1814). [D]

Jolly, John, 12 Stephen St, Tottenham Ct Rd, London, chair and sofa maker (1839). [D]

Jolly, Richard, Liverpool, joiner and cm (1761). Petitioned freedom on servitude to Richard Jolly. [Freemen's committee bk]

Jones, —, St James's St, two doors above St James's Palace, London, u (1717). [Heal]

Jones, —, London, cm (1793). In addition to John Jones and Thomas Jones, the list of subscribers to Sheraton's *Drawing Book*, 1793 contains two entries merely indicated as Jones, London, cm.

Jones, Aaron, Castle St, Westminster, London, carver (1749). [Poll bk]

Jones, Aaron, Bristol, carver and gilder (1757–84). At Tower Lane (or Tower Hill) until 1774 when he moved to 10 Clare St. In 1757 he provided a wooden chandelier to the Moravian Chapel in Bristol. In 1758 took app. named Horner. In February 1772 he advertised that he had in his warehouse 'a large Stock of LOOKING-GLASSES and GERONDOLES, in carv'd and burnish'd Gold Frames' which he offered for sale both retail and wholesale. He listed ten sizes of square plates that he had available ranging from 12″ × 20″ up to 28″ × 41″. He also offered most sizes in mahogany frames, parcel gilt. He claimed to be the manufacturer of these items and offered to re-polish and re-silver old plates. In 1774 he described himself as a glass grinder. As he was a manufacturer he was anxious to sell to retailers and merchants and ship's captains for export. He particularly featured his range of 'Swinging and small Dressing-glasses' as suitable for trade and export purchase. In 1774 after his move to Clare St he described his stock as consisting of 'a Large Assortment of Oval and Square Glasses, in Burnish Gold Frames, in the newest Taste; Toilet Glasses, in Japan and Burnish Gold; Gerondoles, with double or single Branches; Mahogany Sconces, plain and ornamented; Dressing Glasses of all Sizes'. [D; S of G, app. index; *Bristol Journal*, 29 February 1772, 27 February 1773, 20 August 1774; B. Little, *City and County of Bristol*, 1954, p. 221]

Jones, Alexander, Preston, Lancs., cm (1818). Shown at 57 High St in one directory and Shepherd St in another. [D]

Jones, Ann, Bristol, carver and gilder (1759). In 1759 took app. named Taylor. [S of G, app. index]

Jones, Ann, 4 Lawrence Pl., Lawrence St, Liverpool, u (1834–37). [D]

Jones, Benjamin, Windsor, Berks., cm (1757). [Poll bk]

Jones, Benjamin, parish of St James, Bath, Som., cm (1784). Freeman of Bristol. [Bristol poll bk]

Jones, C., Gt George St, Liverpool, fancy cm (1824). In December 1824 he announced the theft of two tea caddies. One was described as 'a handsome black rose-wood tea chest, banded with tulip wood hollow round the top, with two canisters & a basin-place in the middle' valued at £2 14s. The other was 'a mahogany double tea caddie with bevelled top' valued at 16s. [*Liverpool Mercury*, 31 December 1824]

Jones, C., Norwich, cm (1826). On 3 May 1826 William Quilley, cm, app to C. Jones and Jno. Kerry, was admitted a freeman of Norwich. [Freemen reg.]

Jones, C. H., 98 High St, Guildford, Surrey, carver and gilder (1840). Announced that he had recently 'commenced in the above Business in all its Branches'. He offered 'every description and pattern of Maple, Rose-wood and Oak Frames'. He also offered 'Gold Bordering for Rooms' and the re-gilding of old frames and the re-silvering and re-polishing of old mirror plates. [*Russell's Guildford Almanack*]

Jones, Cad., 4 John St, Curtain Rd, London, cm (1809). [D]

Jones, Charles, London, upholder (1709–24). Free of the Upholders' Co., 5 August 1709. Took as apps Joseph Richard Lee (1709) and Paul Mombray (1713 and free 1723–24). [GL, Upholders' Co. records]

Jones, Charles, parish of St Leonard, Shoreditch, London, cm (1758). Thomas Jones, son of Charles Jones, cm, admitted freeman of the Upholders' Co., 1758. [GL, Upholders' Co. records]

Jones, Charles, 57 Castle St East, Oxford Mkt, London, carver and gilder (1817). [D]

Jones, Charles Edward, Windy Bank, Colne, Lancs., joiner and cm (1824). [D]

Jones, Charles, Gloucester, cm (1836). Child bapt., church of St John the Baptist. [PR (bapt.)]

Jones, Daniel, Liverpool, cm (1803–35). In 1803 subscribed to Sheraton's *Cabinet Dictionary*. At Addison St in 1810, 8 Freeman's Row in 1818, and 39 Banastre St in 1835. [D]

Jones, David William, Oxford, carver and gilder (1782–98). On 5 October 1782 married Ann Benwell of Oxford at St John's Church. At the time he was aged 24 and declared his trade as japanner. In 1793 living in the parish of St Mary when he took out insurance cover of £700. This included £100 for utensils and tools. In conjunction with William Folker he furnished the rooms at Christ Church, Oxford for Lord William Russell when he was an undergraduate there (1784–87). In April he received £6 15s in connection with this work. In January 1786 a burnished gold mirror was supplied to the same patron at a cost of 10s 6d. [D; Bodleian index of Oxf. marriage bonds; GL, Sun MS vol. 395, p. 609; Bedford Office, London]

Jones, David, 15 Castle St, Long Acre, London, broker and cm (1795–1812). In 1795 took app. named David Francis. On 16 November 1812 took out insurance cover of £400 of which stock and utensils accounted for £360. [GL, Sun MS vol. 459, ref. 875671; Westminster Ref. Lib., MS 4309]

Jones, David, Liverpool, cm (b. 1799–1829). Born 2 April 1799, son of Thomas Jones, cm. Free by patrimony, 16 October 1827. Shown at Richmond Fair and Norris St, but a directory of 1829 lists his trade address as 12 Gladstone St. [D; freemen's committee bk]

Jones, Dodo, St Leonard's Churchyard, Bridgnorth, Salop, cm (1829–35). [D]

Jones, Dorothy & Ashworth, T., York, cm (1825). Bankrupt 11 June 1825. [*Liverpool Mercury*, 17 June 1825]

Jones, Edward, London, upholder (1706). Free of the Upholders' Co. on 8 November 1706. [GL, Upholders' Co. records]

Jones, Edward, King's Head Ct, St Martin-le-Grand, London, cm (1736). Offered reward for the apprehension of the person who stole several items of value from him. [*Daily Post*, 6 October 1736]

Jones, Edward, London, cm (1750). Member of the Joiners' Co. [GL, Joiners' Co. records, Livery lists]

Jones, Edward, Frodsham, Cheshire, cm and victualler (1790). [D]

Jones, Edward, Liverpool, cm (1797–1806). App. to Samuel Chubbard in 1797 and free, 1806. [Freemen's committee bk]

Jones, Edward, Manchester, cm (1828–29). At 67 Post St in 1828 but 71 Hart St in 1829. [D]

Jones, Edward, Bromsgrove St, Birmingham, cm, u and broker (1830). [D]

Jones, Edward, 53 Dudley St, Birmingham, cm (1835). [D]

Jones, Edward, Bennett's Hill, Birmingham, carver, gilder and toilet looking-glass manufacturer (1835). [D]

Jones, Edward, Beastmarket Hill, Nottingham, cm and u, paper hanger (1825–40). Trading at Chapel Bar in 1825; Market Pl., 1828–35; and Beastmarket Hill, 1834–40. In 1834 took app. named James Hopkinson, whose memoirs were published in 1968 under the title *Memoirs of a Victorian Cabinet Maker* (ed. J. B. Goodman).

Jones, Edward, Tamworth, Staffs., cm and u (1818–35). Addresses given at Silver St in 1818, George St in 1822, and Colehill, 1828–25. [D]

Jones, Elizabeth, Farquhar, John & Crumin Michael (also recorded as **Jones, Elizabeth & Maccrumin, John Farquhar**), Bridge St, Westminster, London, u (1792). Bankrupt June 1792. [Bailey's list of bankrupts; *Derby Mercury*, 21 June 1792]

Jones, Ellis, Oswestry, Salop, cm (1797–98). [D]

Jones, Francis, Bloomsbury, London, upholder (1719). [Heal]

Jones, Francis, Bishop Stortford, Herts., upholder etc. (1745). In 1745 took app. named Berry. [S of G, app. index]

Jones, Francis, Ann St, Birmingham, cm u and broker (1828–30). Recorded at no. 29 in 1828. [D]

Jones, Garnett, Market St, Tring, Herts., cm and u (1839). [D]

Jones, George, Rownham Wharf, Bristol, cm and joiner (1805–06). [D]

Jones, George, Tempest-hey, Liverpool, carver (1833). [*Liverpool Mercury*, 12 April 1833]

Jones, George, Liverpool, furniture carver (1834–39). At 50 Lime St in 1834; Whiteheads' Buildings, 1 Mill Lane, Shaws Brow in 1837; and 17 Mill Lane with a shop at 66 Lime St in 1839. [D]

Jones, George, High Wycombe, Bucks., chair turner (1838). [PR (marriage)]

Jones, Henry, Hackney, London, upholder (1702–10). In 1702 and 1710 insured two houses on Ludgate Hill, London for £300. [GL, Hand in Hand MS vol. 8, refs 3300–01]

Jones, Henry, 40 Kirby St, Hatton Gdn, London, carver and gilder (1817). [D]

Jones, Henry, 32 Plat Terr., Islington, London, cm and u (1827). [D]

Jones, Henry, 9 Gloucester Terr., London, carver, gilder and looking-glass maker (1839). [D]

Jones, Henry, Wednesbury, Staffs., u (1839). [D]

Jones, Hugh, Peter St, Westminster, London, upholder (1727). [Heal]

Jones, Hugh, Liverpool, cm (1806–34). App. to Samuel Chubbard and free on 2 November 1806. Took app. named William Cubbins in 1819. At Nelson Ct, Gt Nelson St East initially, but by 1818 had moved to 1 Naylor St and in 1834 was at 21 Islington. [D; freemen reg.; app. bk]

Jones, Isaac, Salford, Lancs., chairmaker (1811–13). In 1811 at 11 Cooke St and in 1813 at 14 Chapel St. [D]

Jones, Isaac, 37 Duke St, Aldgate, London, cm and u (1839). [D]

Jones, J., Cross St, Oswestry, Salop, cm and joiner (1828). [D]

Jones, J., Bridge St, Sheffield, Yorks., cm and u (1828). [D]

Jones, J., 12 Denmark St, Soho, London, looking-glass frame maker (1835). [D]

Jones, J., 2 Church St, Spitalfields, London, fancy cm (1837). [D]

Jones, James, parish of St Nicholas, Bristol, carver (1784). [Poll bk]

Jones, James, 147 Old Gravel Lane, London, carver and gilder (1790–93). [D]

Jones, James, 49 Anchor & Hopeall, Wapping, London, carver and gilder (1808). [D]

Jones, James, 6 Catherine St, Strand, u (1816). [D]

Jones, James, 4 Holme St, Blackburn, Lancs., carver and gilder (1824–34). [D]

Jones, James, West St, Warwick, chair manufacturer (1830–35). [D]

Jones, James, Liverpool, cm (d. 1819). Death on 14 April 1819 reported in *Liverpool Mercury*, 23 April 1819.

Jones, James, Hanley St and Wood St, Liverpool, carver and gilder (1834–39). In 1834 at 6 Hanley St and 10 Wood St; in the following year at 6 Hanley St and 6 Wood St; in 1837 at 7 Hanley Ct and 63 Wood St; and in 1839 at 8 Hanley Ct and 25 Wood St. [D]

Jones, James, 3 Cumberland Pl., Newington Butts, London, cm (1835). [D]

Jones, James, Worcester, cm (1835). Free 1 December 1835. [Freemen rolls]

Jones, James, Handbridge, Chester, cm (1838). Free 28 July 1838. [Freemen reg.]

Jones, James, Market Pl., Wantage, Oxon., cm and u (1840). [D]

Jones, John, 'The Angel', Minories, London, u (1708). Household and trade goods sold by auction March 1708. His stock included 'Standing-Beds, Suits of Curtains, Quilts, Blankets etc'. [*Daily Courant*, 1 March 1708]

Jones, John, London, upholder (1711–25). Son of John Jones of Oxford, tobacconist. App. to Arthur Osborn on 18 October 1711, but not free of the Upholders' Co. until 3 April 1723. Took as app. John Brown, 1718–25. [GL, Upholders' Co. records]

Jones, John, Liverpool, cm (1761–77). Free 4 February 1761. Took as app. Edward Bostock (free 1777). In 1774 in Cleveland Sq., and in 1777 at 14 Prussia St. His son John was born in 1777; and in 1804, when he petitioned for freedom, was a master mariner. [D; freemen reg.]

Jones, John, 1 Pitchey Ct, Bell Alley, Coleman St, London, carver (1775). In 1775 took out insurance cover for £300 of which £100 was in respect of utensils and stock. [GL, Sun MS vol. 240, p. 398]

Jones, John, 44 Ludgate Yd, Half Moon Alley, Bishopsgate St Without, London, carver and gilder (1775). In 1775 insured his house for £200 and household goods for a similar sum. [GL, Sun MS vol. 236, p. 52]

Jones, John, 3 Meards Ct, Dean St, Soho, London, cm (1779–84). In 1779 insured his house for £100. [GL, Sun MS vol. 270, p. 489; poll bk]

Jones, John, Cambridge St, Golden Sq., London, cm (1790–93). Possibly the person who subscribed to Sheraton's *Drawing Book*, 1793. [D]

Jones, John, London, u etc. (1808–11). In 1808 at 112 Wardour St, Soho and in 1811 at 38 Davies St, Berkley Sq. [D]

Jones, John, 2 Bream's Building, Chancery Lane, London, carver and gilder (1808–19). In 1809 listed as carver and gilder to HRH the Princess of Wales. [D]

Jones, John, Stanley St, Liverpool, chairmaker and household broker (1811–21). At 11 Stanley St in 1811, but from 1813–21 at 12. [D]

Jones, John, Peas Market Hill, Cambridge, cm, builder, acutioneer and appraiser (1816–21). In 1816 advertised for an app. in the cm and building trade. In March 1818 stated that he had taken up auctioneering and appraising. Three children bapt. at the Church of St Edward, 1817–21. [PR (bapt.); *Cambridge Chronicle*, 6 September 1816, 27 March 1818]

Jones, John, Liverpool, cm (1818). Married on 29 June 1818 Miss Mary Harrison at Walton Church. [*Liverpool Mercury*, 10 July 1818]

Jones, John, Berwick St, Soho, London, tea chest and cabinet inlayer (1819–29). At 41 Berwick St, 1819–23, but in 1826 the number was 35 and in 1829 it was 8. [D]

Jones, John, Liverpool, u (1821–37). Had a shop at 12 Derby St in 1821, but from 1827–29 in Wilde St. The number is shown as 12 in one directory of 1827 and 8 in another. It was 8 in 1829. By 1835 he had moved to 6 Hart St and in 1837 was at 3. [D]

Jones, John, Liverpool, cm (1823). On 8 September 1823 married Miss Margaret Wilcock of Liverpool. [*Liverpool Mercury*, 3 October 1823]

Jones, John, Lime St, Liverpool, cm (1823–32). At 22 Lime St from 1823–27 but shown at 25 in 1829 and 23 in 1832. In May 1832 he advertised that he was declining the business 'through indisposition' and that the enterprise would be carried on by his son at 1 Commutation Row. [D; *Liverpool Mercury*, 25 May 1832]

Jones, John, Congellers, Wolverhampton, Staffs., joiner and cm (1827). [D]

Jones, John, Marylebone Lane, London, cm and u (1827–35). In 1827 at 18 Marylebone Lane but in 1835 at 17. [D]

Jones, John, Mellbecks, Kirkby Stephen, Westmld, cm (1828–34). [D]

Jones, John, Cross St, Oswestry, Salop, cm (1828–35). [D]

Jones, John, Portsea, Portsmouth, Hants., cm, u and chairmaker (1830–39). Trading at 21 St James' St in 1830 and Hanover St in 1839. [D]

Jones, John, 5 Adam's Ct, Stoke's Croft, Bristol, cm (1832–34). [D]

Jones, John, Summer Gdns, Kirkdale, Liverpool, cm (1834). [D]

Jones, John, Chester, cm and furniture broker (1834–40). At Foregate St in 1834; Princess St in 1838, and Francis St in 1840. [D]

Jones, John, 12 Dean St, Soho, London, carver, gilder, looking-glass maker (1835–37). In 1835 trade stated to be 'wholesale fancy cabinet & dressing glass manufacturer'. [D]

Jones, John, High Wycombe, Bucks., chairmaker (b. c. 1811–41). Son bapt. in 1839. Aged 30 at the date of the 1841 Census. [PR (bapt.)]

Jones, John, Liverpool, cm (1840). Free 28 July 1840 on servitude to John Atkinson. [Freemen reg.]

Jones, Jonathan, Duke St, Grosvenor Sq., London, upholder (1803–29). Most directories list either 28 or 29 Duke St although there are a few entries which state 23. A Joseph Jones, upholder, is shown at 29 Duke St in 1817 in one directory but this is probably an error. [D]

Jones, Joseph, King St, Twickenham, Middlx, cm and u (1823–39). Recorded at London Rd, 1823, and King St, 1826–39. [D]

Jones, Lewis, George's Yd, Grosvenor Sq., London, cm and u (1827). [D]

Jones, M., 38 Crucifix Lane, Bermondsey, London, u (1820). [D]

Jones, M., Liverpool, chairmaker (1822). His son William was aged 15 in 1822. [Liverpool RO, 352/CON 5/1 A–J]

Jones, M., 30 Old Compton St, London, u and haberdasher (1820–29). [D]

Jones, Margaret, Pitt St, Liverpool, u (1810–18). At 10 Pitt St in 1810 but in 1818 at no. 14. [D]

Jones, Mary, High St, Folkestone, Kent, cm (1838). [D]

Jones, Matthew, London, upholder (1742). Son of Matthew Jones of Whitefriars, London, victualler. App. to Richard Evatt on 6 August 1735 and free of the Upholders' Co. by servitude, 1 September 1742. [GL, Upholders' Co. records]

Jones, Morgan, London, upholder (1715–30). Son of Samuel Jones of Cheriton, Hants., yeoman. App. to Richard Wood on 5 December 1715 and free of the Upholders' Co. by servitude, 4 February 1729/30. [GL, Upholders' Co. records]

Jones, Nicholas, Barnstaple, Devon, cm (1830–38). On the Quay in 1830 but in 1838 in Boutport St. [D]

Jones, Owen, address unknown, cm (1754). Subscribed to Chippendale's *Director*, 1754.

Jones, Owen, 18 Fazakerley St, Liverpool, cm (1818). The *DEF* has an illustration of a work table of Regency date which bears an engraved brass plaque inscribed 'OWEN JONES FECIT' which may refer to this maker. [D]

Jones, Peter, within two doors of Durham Yard, Strand, London, upholder and cm (d. 1744). [Heal]

Jones, Pilcher, High St, Folkestone, Kent, furniture broker and cm etc. (1823–32). [D]

Jones, Rice, near Princes St, Swallow St, London, cm (1774–76). In 1776 insured his utensils, stock and goods for £200. [Westminster poll bk; GL, Sun MS vol. 248, p. 419]

Jones, Richard, Clifton, Bristol, cm (1719). In 1719 took app. named Daniel. [S of G, app. index]

Jones, Richard, near King Edward's Stairs, Wapping, London, cm (1720). [Heal]

Jones, Richard, parish of St James, Bristol, cm (1754). [Poll bk]

Jones, Richard, London, upholder (1774–1802). Free by redemption as a member of the Upholders' Co., 6 April 1774. His trade was stated to be warehouseman. At Princes St near the Mansion House, 1774–81; St Mildred's Ct, Poultry in 1786; and yet again at Princes St in 1802. He took as app. Thomas Wakeman (free 1798). [GL, Upholders' Co. records]

Jones, Richard, St Ann's Ct, Dean St, Soho, London, cm (1776). In 1776 insured his utensils, stock and goods for £180 out of a total insurance cover of £200. [GL, Sun MS vol. 244, p. 585]

Jones, Richard, address unknown, u. Given a cash allowance when he worked at Audley End, Essex. Payments were made to Jones from the 1760s–90s. [Williams, *Audley End*, p. 22]

Jones, Richard, Mardol, Shrewsbury, Salop, u (1796). [Freemen rolls]

Jones, Richard, Liverpool, cm (1810–29). At 5 Brownlow Hill in 1810–11 and at no. 6, 1813–14. Shown at 6 Turnbock St in 1816; 8 Stanley St, 1823–24, 77 Stanley St in 1827; and 51 Shaws Brow in 1829. [D]

Jones, Richard, 41 Princes St, Soho, London, cm and u (1822). [D]

Jones, Richard, 1 Leicester Pl., Camberwell New Rd, London, cm and u (1835). [D]

Jones, Robert, 15 School Lane, Paradise St, Liverpool, cm (1804). [D]

Jones, Robert, Liverpool, cm (1816–37). Free 10 June 1816. At 7 Stanley St, 1827–29 and at 1 Grove Pl., Kirkdale, 1834–37. [D; freemen reg.]

Jones, Robert, London, designer (1817–23). A designer employed by Frederick Crace at the Royal Pavilion, Brighton, 1817–23. Undertook a wide range of design work including furniture. A set of nine light chairs with stuffed seats and backs, the frames carved and gilt, were supplied for the Prince Regent to Jones' design at a cost of £697. [Musgrave, *Royal Pavilion*, 1951, p. 89; *C. Life*, 28 November 1963, p. 1399]

Jones, S., 5 Cumberland Row, Bath, Som., cm (1819). [D]

Jones, S., 11 Vere St, Clare Mkt, London, portable desk maker (1820). [D]

Jones, Samuel, 'The Woolpack & Crown', Strand, London, upholder (1729). [Heal]

Jones, Samuel, 'The Three Chairs', facing the south gate, St Paul's Churchyard, London, chair and cabinet maker (1728–40). A Jones appears in the Holkham Hall, Norfolk, accounts, 1728–42, and may be this maker. The frequency of the surname, however, coupled with the fact that some of the entries refer to an u, may mean that some under this name refer to another craftsman. In 1728 £37 8s was paid, and in the fourth quarter of 1732 the amount was £63. In 1734 two amounts totalling £41 were paid; and in 1737, £63 was expended on furniture for the London house. Sixteen chairs and a couch were supplied for the dining room. A further account of 1737 was for £11 1s and concerned the supply of three sconces and two glasses, credit being given on an old glass taken in part exchange. The last entry of 1742 was for a chest of drawers charged at only 14s 2d. This latter item is unlikely to have been supplied by Samuel Jones for his business appears to have terminated in May 1740 when his stock was sold by auction. It consisted of a 'variety of Chairs, Cabinet Work, Sconces etc.'. Jones also supplied the Royal Household, an account for £68 11s 6d surviving for furniture supplied to Windsor, St James's, Hampton Court, Kew and Richmond. [Heal; V & A archives; *GCM*; *Daily Post*, 29 April 1740]

Jones, Samuel, 33 Lamb St, Bristol, victualler and cm (1775). [D]

Jones, Samuel, Gloucester, cm (1817–39). Five children bapt., parish of St Michael, 1817–31. [D; PR (bapt.)]

Jones, Samuel, North St, Colchester, Essex, carver and gilder (1823). [D]

Jones, Samuel, Bolt Ct, Eastgate St, town unspecified, cm and u (1830). [D]

Jones, Sandys, Pall Mall, London, upholder (1706–63). Son of William Jones of Cricklade, Wilts., Gent. App. to Christopher Broughton, 3 July 1706, and free of the Upholders' Co. by servitude, 14 November 1722. The reason for the considerable lapse of time between the commencement of his apprenticeship and his freedom is not clear, but as early as 1719 he was referring to himself as upholder living at Durham Yd, Strand, where he took out insurance on goods and merchandise. Attracted influential patronage and in 1728 was supplying the household of Frederick, Prince of Wales. He supplied a feather bed and bolster, a bedstead, tacking and bedding costing £35. Employed by Benjamin Mildmay, Earl Fitzwalter of Moulsham Hall, Chelmsford mainly in connection with his London home, Schomberg House, Pall Mall. Accounts for this patron commence in 1736 and continue until 1746. In February 1737 he submitted an account for work done at the London house 'hanging the yellow drawing room below-stairs. Putting up the Blew Mohair Bed and hanging the bed-chamber . . . and putting the blew-mohair bed and hanging my Lord Holdernesses Bed Chamber'. The cost was £64 17s 6d. On 29 December of this year £13 13s was paid on account in connection with a bill of £43 10s 6d for goods 'sent to Hampton Court'. A payment of £89 17s 3d was made in May 1740 but thereafter the sums are smaller though they continued until July 1746. In 1738 paid £16 9s by the Duke of Montrose for a Chinese bed for his house at Cley in Norfolk. Took as app. Jeremiah Bullock, 1743–63. [GL, Upholders' Co. records; Duchy of Cornwall household accounts; A. C. Edwards, *The Account Books of Benjamin Mildmay, Earl Fitzwalter*, pp. 99–111; Scottish RO, GD 220/6/32/P728]

Jones, Stephen, 50 London Wall, London, carver and gilder (1789—93). [D]

Jones, Thomas, 'The Seven Stars', St Paul's Churchyard, London, cm and looking-glass seller (1724–25). In 1725 announced that he was 'leaving off shop-keeping and moving to his marble manufactory at Craven House in Wych St. [Heal; Wills, *Looking-Glasses*; *Daily Post*, 29 November 1725]

Jones, Thomas Cason, London, upholder (1733). Son of Charles Jones of Battersea, London, Gent. App. to John Watson, 18 November 1725, and free of the Upholders' Co. by servitude, 1 August 1733. [GL, Upholders' Co. records]

Jones, Thomas, 'The Golden Plow', corner of Little Moorgate and London Wall, London, upholder (1758–d. 1769). Son of Charles Jones of the parish of St Leonard, Shoreditch, cm. App. to Samuel Phene, member of the Stationers' Co., 7 August 1750, and free of the Upholders' Co. under the terms of the 1750 Upholders' Act, 1 June 1758. Went into partnership with Samuel Phene at 'The Golden Plow' and this arrangement continued until his death on 8 October 1769. Recorded employing non-freemen, 1762–69 on a continuous basis. From 1764 the licences covered eight and occasionally ten workmen. [GL, Upholders' Co. records; City Licence bks, vols 3–6; *Gents Mag.*, October 1769]

Jones, Thomas, London, u (1758). Freeman of Canterbury. [Canterbury poll bk]

Jones, Thomas, Liverpool, cm (1784–1811). Free 2 April 1784. At back of 33 Mersey St, 1790; 48 Frederick St, 1796; 30 Upper Frederick St in 1804; 21 Scotland Rd in 1805; 5 Wood St in 1810 and 6 Wood St in 1811. His three sons, Thomas Jones jnr, carver and gilder, Owen, musician and David, cm, all petitioned freedom by patrimony. [D; freemen reg. and committee bk]

Jones, Thomas, Liverpool, u (1787–93). In 1787 at Tarleton St and in 1790 at 7 Church Alley, St Peters. Bankrupt by November 1793. [D; *Williamson's Liverpool Advertiser*, 4 November 1793]

Jones, Thomas, 104 High Holborn, London, carver and gilder (1789–1825). In 1789 listed also as a glass grinder. A medium size business reflected in the £700 insurance cover taken out on utensils, stock, plate and workshop on 3 July 1792. [D; GL, Sun MS vol. 389, ref. 602288]

Jones, Thomas, London, cm (1793). Subscribed to Sheraton's *Drawing Book*, 1793.

Jones, Thomas, Liverpool, chairmaker, japanner and broker (1810–35). At 10 Stanley St in 1810; 5 Webster St in 1818; 8 Highfield St, 1821–24 and 5 Stanley St in 1835. In 1824 he lived at 83 Highfield St. Chairmaking is only mentioned in 1810 and from 1818–24 the trade is described as 'japanner & varnish maker', with 'tin plate worker' added only in 1824. [D]

Jones, Thomas, 64 Stoke's Croft, Bristol, cm (1814). [D]

Jones, Thomas jnr, Garden Ct, Comus St, Liverpool, carver and gilder (1816). Son of Thomas Jones, cm. Free by patrimony, 10 June 1816. [Freemen reg.]

Jones, Thomas, Birmingham, carver, gilder, looking-glass and picture frame maker (1818–35). At Alcester St and Bradford St in 1818; 8 Moat Row in 1830; and 47 Dudderston Row in 1835. [D]

Jones, Thomas, 3 Plant's Ct, Preston, Lancs. cm (1825). [D]

Jones, Thomas, 8 Gt Sutton St, Clerkenwell, London, u and undertaker (1826). [D]

Jones, Thomas, 56 Seymour St, Euston Sq., London, cm and u (1827). [D]

Jones, Thomas, Barnstaple, Devon, cm (1828). Married Elizabeth Sloly of Barnstaple. [*The Alfred*, 1 January 1828]

Jones, Thomas, Exeter, Devon, cm (1829–34). At Spiller's Lane, 1829–32, but in 1834 at Cheke Lane. Five children bapt., 1829–34. [PR (bapt.)]

Jones, Thomas, Portland St, Leamington, Warks., cm (1830). [D]

Jones, Thomas, Commutation Row, Liverpool, cm and u (b. 1809–39). Born 27 May 1809 and free by patrimony in 1831. His father was John Jones, cooper. In 1834 had also a shop at 2 Back Commutation St. [D; freemen's committee bk]

Jones, Thomas, Liverpool, cm (1840). Free 23 July 1840. [Freemen reg.]

Jones, W., 6 Porter St, Newport Mkt, London, carver and gilder (1820). [D]

Jones, W. G., 56 Ratcliffe Highway, London, bedstead, chair and cabinet maker (1820). [D]

Jones, William snr, Tower Hill, London, upholder (1712–50). Father of William Jones jnr, also an upholder. Free of the Upholders' Co., 6 August 1712 and master in 1745. Took as apps Ambrose Pearman, 1713–23; Ebenezer Braithwaite, 1717–26; Joseph Nicholson, 1721–29 and William Pryce, 1729–35. On 4 April 1717 took out insurance of £300 on a house on Little Tower Hill described as being of timber construction. Although this address was to feature throughout his career he also took out insurance cover on rented property in Mary Gold Alley, Strand in 1718 and the Griffon, Cloth Fair in 1728. These may have been dwelling houses. In 1728 described as a draper in partnership with Oliver Edwards, u. In this year they insured six bales of silk valued at £1,000 jointly. Subscribed to the *Gentleman's and Builders' Companion*, 1739. On 3 April supplied to St Bartholomew's Hospital bedding and curtains. The only other patron known is Lord Monson, to whom a four-leaf fire screen was supplied, for which £2 4s was paid in February 1744. [GL, Upholders' Co. records; Hand in Hand MS vol. 17, p. 53; vol. 18, p. 293; vol. 18, p. 328; Sun. MS vol. 27, ref. 45533; Heal; St Barts Hospital *Journal*, Ha 1/11; Lincoln RO, Monson 12, vouchers 1731–43]

Jones, William jnr, London, upholder (1748–59). Son of William Jones snr. Free of the Upholders' Co. by patrimony, 4 February 1748. Took as apps William Bellingham, 1749–56; George Bowditch, 1754–59; John Boulton, 1752–57. [GL, Upholders' Co. records]

Jones, William, 54 Horse fair, Bristol, victualler and cm (1775). [D]

Jones, William, 8 Canterbury Row, Newington, London, upholder (1788–1802). Son of William Jones of Mold Mountain, Flintshire, North Wales, Gent. Free of the Upholders' Co. by redemption, 23 January 1788. [GL, Upholders' Co. records]

Jones, William, Price St, Birmingham, picture framer and gilder (1803). [D]

Jones, William, Horse fair, Bristol, cm (1805–07). [D]

Jones, William, 39 Dartmouth St, Westminster, London, cm (1809). [D]

Jones, William, 31 Old Compton St, Soho, London, u and haberdasher (1812–19). In 1813 the business was listed as William Jones & Co. In 1819 trading at 30 Old Compton St. [D]

Jones, William, Liverpool, cm (1821–39). At 2 Downe St with a shop at 1 Swan Corner, Feather St in 1821–23 but in 1824 at 2 Bridport St with a house at 60 Renishaw St. After 1827 in Circus St, the number being 17 from 1827–35, 18 in 1837 and 35 in 1839. One directory of 1829 gives an address at 10 Shaw's Brow. [D]

Jones, William Lewis, 5 Lower Castle St, Bristol, cm (1822). [D]

Jones, William David, Market Pl., Cambridge, carver and gilder (1824–30). In 1830 the address is recorded as Market Hill. Paid in 1827 for new picture frames by Trinity College. [D]

Jones, William, Liverpool, cm (1834–35). At 15 Dryden St in 1834 and 3 Prescott St in 1835. [D]

Jones, William, Cirencester, Glos., carver and gilder (1827–29). Children bapt. in 1827 and 1829. [PR (bapt.)]

Jones, William, Liverpool, carver (1828–39). Born 14 May 1807, son of Hugh Jones, cm. Free by patrimony in 1828. Took app. named Alexander Wells, 1829–39. [Freemen's committee bk]

Jones, William, Bristol, turner, bedstead maker and cm (1829–36). In Mark Lane, 1829–35, but in 1836 at St John's steps. Turning appears to have been his main occupation and cabinet making is not mentioned until 1836. [D]

Jones, William, Liverpool, carver and gilder (1830–39). Free 17 November 1830 at which date he was at 30 Duncan St. From 1835 in Russell St, the number being 40 from 1835–37 and 4 in 1839. [D; freemen reg.]

Jones, William, Finsbury, London, cm and u (1835–39). At 61 St Paul St in 1835 and 23 Tabernacle Walk in 1839. [D]

Jones, William, Tipton, Staffs., cm/u (1838). [D]

Jones, William, Ipswich, Suffolk, carver and gilder (1839). Shown in one directory at St Margaret's Green and in another at Soame St. [D]

Jones, William, 22 Rahere St, Goswell Sq., London, cm and u (1839). [D]

Jones, William, High St, Folkestone, Kent, cm (1839). [D]

Jones, William, 67 and 68 Broadmead, Bristol, cm and u (1840). [D]

Jones, William, Beastmarket Hill, Nottingham, cm (1840). [D]

Jones & Barker, 16 Lichfield St, Birmingham, makers of brass cabinet furniture (1793–1803). An oval brass repoussé picture frame is known with their trade label affixed. This states that they were 'manufacturers of brass furniture, for cabinet makers & upholsterer's use'. Their products included locks, knobs, coffin furniture, oval and square picture frames and looking-glass frames, 'ornaments and borders for rooms, in stampt, burnish'd & gilt metal, composition carved ornaments, chimney pieces etc'. [D]

Jones & Cowen (or Cowan), London Rd, Manchester, cm, furniture brokers and chairmakes (1838–40). At 5 London Rd in 1838 and 20 in 1840. [D]

Jones & Farquhar, see Elizabeth Jones, John Farquhar and Michael Crumin.

Jones & Macrumin, see Elizabeth Jones, John Farquhar and Michael Crumin.

Jones & McLauchlan, London, carvers, gilders and u (1819–23). Shown at 9 Cooke's Ct, Carey St as carvers and gilders in 1819, and 17 Mount St, Grosvenor Sq. as u in 1823. From 1819–25 Jones & Sheldon, u, are also shown in the same directory at 17 Mount St. [D]

Jones & Parry, 2 Williamson Sq., Liverpool, u (1790). [D]

Jones & Perkins, 3 Walker's Pl., Hatton Gdns, Liverpool, cm (1823–27). [D]

Jones & Sheldon, 17 Mount St, Grosvenor Sq., London, u (1819–25). See Jones & McLauchlan, u, at this address in 1823. [D]

Jones & Son, Bath, Som., cm (1819–26). Listed at 52 Walcot St in 1819 and 4 Abbey St in 1826. [D]

Jones & Weller, London, upholsterer's warehouse (1820–25). In 1820 shown in one directory at 7 New Rd, Somers Town and in another at 8 Charles St, Middlx Hospital. After 1820 all directories list the Charles St address. [D]

Jonstones, —, Barton, Lincs., cm (1793). Subscribed to Sheraton's *Drawing Book*, 1793.

Joplie, James, address unknown, u (1803). Subscribed to Sheraton's *Cabinet Dictionary*, 1803.

Jopling, John, Chester-le-Street, Co. Durham, joiner and cm (1793). [D]

Jopling, Joseph & Thomas, Chester-le-Street, Co. Durham, cm and joiner (1828–34). In 1834 Joseph Jopling is shown trading on his sole behalf. [D]

Jopling, William, Newcastle, u (1774). App. to Edward Coates and free, 11 October 1774. [Freemen reg.]

Jordan, David, Tubwell Row, Darlington, Co. Durham, cm/joiner (1834). [D]

Jordan, George, Newcastle, joiner, cm and broker (1811–34). At Dog-bank, 1811–16, but in July 1816 announced his move to 'a large house adjoining the old Bird-in-Bush Inn, Pilgrim St.'. In 1827 an address at Fountain Yd, Pipewell St is shown in one directory but the Pilgrim St premises appear to have been retained and in 1833–34 were numbered 189. In this year he was also using 43 Carliol St. He kept a stock of new and secondhand furniture and claimed to manufacture new goods. His stock consisted of 'double, dressing, straight & circular fronted lobby chests of drawers, new & second-hand; sets of dining tables, single large & small ditto, turnover pembroke & wainscot ditto; mahogany chairs, beech, black, rush & cane bottomed ditto; sofas; night tables; wash stands; dressing tables; mahogany four-post bed steads; birch & beech ditto, camp ditto, with or without hangings; mahogany circular & straight-fronted lobby beds, wainscot ditto; mahogany wardrobe beds & other ditto; secretaires & bookcases; feathers & feather beds; new and secondhand carpets, carpeting etc. best hangings in different-kinds. KITCHEN FURNITURE OF ALL KINDS'. He stated that he bought, sold and exchanged all sorts of furniture and supplied goods on advantageous terms to country dealers. [D; *Durham County Advertiser*, 13 July 1816, 25 October and 7 June 1817, 16 May 1818]

Jordan, Henry, London, carver and gilder (1835). The 1835 edition of *Robson's Directory* has two entries under this name, one at 29 Lower Eaton St, Pimlico and the other at 34 Broad St, Golden Sq. Both worked in the same trade.

Jordan, J., 39 Fort St, Spitalfields, London, cm (1803). [D]

Jordan, J. L., Edde Cross St, Ross, Herefs., cm (1840). [D]

Jordan, James, London, cm (1793). Subscribed to Sheraton's *Drawing Book*, 1793.

Jordan, James, Leighton Lane, Leeds, Yorks., cm (1834–40). Initially at 4 Leighton Lane but later the number was changed to 7. [D]

Jordan, James, South Pl., Finsbury, London, u (1839). [D]

Jordan, John, 15 Artillery St, London, cm and chairmaker (1789–1804). Included in the list of master cabinet makers in Sheraton's *Cabinet Dictionary*, 1803. William James Jordan is shown at 16 Artillery St, 1808–13, and Thomas Jordan in 1813. [D]

Jordan, John, 7 Norton Falgate, near 39 Stewart St, Spitalfields, London, chair and cabinet maker (1793–1816). In 1803 took out two insurance policies, one for £300 and the other for £650 of which £350 was for utensils and stock. [D; GL, Sun MS vol. 426, ref. 745760; vol. 427, ref. 747780]

Jordan, John Nathaniel (or Nathaniel John), 18 Silver St, Golden Sq., London, carver and gilder (1801–20). In 1801 took out insurance cover of £300 of which £100 was for utensils and stock. In 1820 the cover was £400 of which 'household goods in dwelling house and workshops' accounted for £230. William Evans also traded from this address, in partnership, 1808–11. [D; GL, Sun MS vol. 419, ref. 712742; vol. 483, ref. 962590]

Jordan, Joseph, Alton, Hants., cm and auctioneer (1784–d. 1818). [D; Hants. RO, will]

Jordan, Joseph jnr, High St, Alton, Hants., cm and auctioneer (1823–39). Probably succeeded his father in 1818 when he died but there are no directory entries until 1823. [D]

Jordan, Thomas, adjoining 'The Rose & Crown', Snow Hill, London, turner and cm (1703–35). Insurance policies taken out between 1703–18 list his trade solely as a turner. He appears to have been a substantial property owner and in 1712 insured 27 other properties in addition to his own house. Although many of these buildings were insured for as little as £50 each, one house in 1703 was covered for £250 alone. His stock in trade was sold off in March 1735 and on the cabinet side included 'fine Mahogany, walnut-tree & other Bookcases, Buroes, Chest-tables, Pier & chimney glasses, sconces etc'. [Heal; GL, Hand in Hand MS vol. 2, refs 4405–11; vol. 4, 22 October 1705, ref. 11508; vol. 10, ref. 11508; vol. 19, ref. 36883; *General Evening Post*, 13–15 March 1735]

Jordan, Thomas, Duke St, Chester, u (1808–40). Free 21 January 1808. [D; poll bks; freemen rolls]

Jordan, Thomas, 16 Artillery St, Spitalfields, London, chairmaker (1809–11). John Jordan traded from 15 Artillery St, 1789–1804, as a cm and chairmaker, and William James Jordan traded from 16 Artillery St, 1808–13. [D]

Jordan, Thomas, Leicester, u and paperhanger (1828–35). Trading at Churchgate in 1828 and Colston St in 1835. [D]

Jordan, William, Milton, near Sittingbourne, Kent, upholder and ironmonger (1794). [D]

Jordan, William James, 16 Artillery St, Bishopgate, London, chair and cm (1808–13). In 1808 took out insurance cover of £300 of which £120 was in respect of utensils and stock. The corresponding figures for January 1810 were £500 and £150. By November 1810 he had moved his residence to 10 Wormwood St and increased his insurance cover to £600. Stock and utensils at the new address were insured at £150 while those at Artillery St were valued at £100. Directory entries continue to use the Artillery St address. John Jordan was trading at 15 Artillery St in the same trade, 1789–1804; and Thomas Jordan, chairmaker, at 16 Artillery St in 1813. [D; GL Sun MS vol. 443, ref. 823331; vol. 451, rev. 841315; vol. 452, ref. 850356]

Jordan, William Jones, Bordesley St, Birmingham, chairmaker and cm (1822–30). [D]

Jordan, & Evans, 18 Silver St, Golden Sq. See John Nathaniel Jordan.

Jordan, John, Truro, Cornwall, upholder (1757). In 1757 took app. named Prisk. [S of G, app. index]

Jorden, John, Dean House, Holme, Yorks., joiner/cm (1837). [D]

Joscelyne, Benjamin, High St, Braintree, Essex, cm and u, furnishing undertakers (1823–40). From 1832–39 the business was styled Benjamin Joscelyne & Son. Probate was granted on the father's will 1840. [D; *Wills at Chelmsford*]

Joscelyne, Benjamin jnr, High St, Chelmsford, Essex, cm and u (1832). [D]

Joscelyne, John, Stowmarket, Suffolk, cm (1824). [D]

Joscelyne, Samuel, Market Hill, Sudbury, Suffolk, cm (1830–39). [D]

Joseph, B, 113 Wardour St, Soho, London, cm (1829–33). In June 1833 the 3rd Lord Braybrooke of Audley End, Essex paid Joseph for a commode and slab costing £10. It is uncertain for which of Lord Braybrooke's houses this piece of furniture was intended. [D; Essex RO, D/DBy A358, A363]

Joseph, Benjamin, Mint St, Southwark, London, cm (1808). [D]

Joseph, Sarah, 42 Dudley St, Birmingham, cm and u (1830). A Sarah Josephs, cm was trading at 57 Edgbaston St, date unspecified. [D]

Joseph, William, Suffolk Pl., Southwark, London, cm (1761). Discharged from Debtors Prison, August 1761, and said to be late of Suffolk Pl., Southwark. [*London Gazette*, 12 August 1761]

Joseph, William, 21 Grange Rd, Bermondsey, London, cm (1826). [D]

Joubert, A., 8 Maddox St, Regent St, London, u (1839). [D]

Jourd, William Handel, 13 Kingsgate St, Winchester, Hants., cm and u (1830). [D]

Jouret, Henry, London, carver, gilder and frame maker (1755–75). Initially at 'The Architectural Frame', Grafton St, Soho, but subsequently moved to 'The Gold Frame', Maiden Lane, Covent Gdn. His trade card [Heal Coll., BM], displays a fine Rococo frame, and was engraved for him by Matthias Lock. In addition to making frames in 'Black and Gold' for 'Paintings, Prints and Glasses', he undertook carved ornaments, gilding and the sale of prints. Lord Monson paid him for a pear-tree looking-glass frame in June 1755. Records of payments also exist, of 10s 6d for a gilt frame; and of £5 5s for a frame and Packing Case Dº Wright Picture' on 27 January 1775. This latter was paid by a 'Mr. Crosse'. [Heal; Lincoln RO, Monson 12; V & A 86R12]

Joy, George, London(?), cm (1796). Thomas Haig in 1796 bequeathed £110 to 'my late maid servant Elizabeth Pyle now the wife of George Joy, cabinet maker'.

Joy, Heronles(?), Bristol, carver (1760). In 1760 took app. named Radford. [S of G, app. index]

Joyce, George, Basingstoke, Hants., turner, chair and basket maker (1823–30). Listed at Church St in 1830. [D]

Joynson, Richard, see Caleb Welch.

Joyner, John, address unknown, u (1664). Recorded in the Royal Household accounts in 1664 supplying feather beds, bolsters etc. to a value of £63. [PRO, LC5/39]

Joyner, Thomas, Smith St, Warwick, cooper and chairmaker (1831). [Poll bk]

Joynes, John, Hoole, Cheshire, upholder (1747). Son of Mary Joynes and app. to John Kirkes of Chester, u. Free 13 July 1747 and shown at Hoole in the Chester poll bk of that year. [Freemen rolls]

Joynson, —, Lancaster, japanner (1788–89). [Westminster Ref. Lib., Gillow records]

Joynson, Richard, 119 Fleet St, London, horse hair weaver and cm (1791). In 1791 took out insurance cover of £2,200 of which £2,000 was in respect of utensils and stock. [GL, Sun MS vol. 379, p. 547]

Joys, Richard, Baxtergate, Grimsby, Lincs., joiner, cm, furniture broker and builder (1831–40). Recorded also at Loft St in 1835. [D]

Joys, Robert, Fluttergate, Grimsby, Lincs., joiner, cm, builder and timber merchant (1826–31). In 1831 also a surveyor. [D]

Jubb, William, Crofts, Rotherham, Yorks., cm (1830). [D]

Juckes, Edward, 111 Newgate St, Cheapside, London, carver and gilder (1817). William Juckes operated from this address in the same trade, 1807–35, and Elizabeth Juckes in 1820. [D]

Juckes, Elizabeth, 111 Newgate St, London, carver and gilder

(1820). William Juckes operated from this address in the same trade, 1807–35, and Edward Juckes in 1817. [D]

Juckes, Robert, Southend St, Ledbury, Herefs., cm (1830–40). [D]

Juckes, William, London, carver and gilder (1802–35). In 1802 at 12 Giltspur St. On 24 July insurance cover of £500 was taken out of which £300 was in respect of utensils and stock. In October of the same year these figures were both revised upwards by £50. At 111 Newgate St from 1807, and also operating from this address in the same trade were Edward Juckes in 1817 and Elizabeth Juckes in 1820. There is a trade card, c. 1800 [Museum of London] of 'JUCKES', carver and gilder, with an address at 93 Fenchurch St. He described himself as 'Carver, Gilder, Glass Grinder & Picture Frame Maker'. [D; GL Sun MS vol. 423, ref. 730147; vol. 424, ref. 735190]

Judd, John, 42 London Rd, London, cm and u (1839). [D]

Judd, Robert, 145 Powis St, Woolwich, London, cm (1823–39). Freeman of Rochester, Kent. [D; Rochester poll bk]

Judge, Joseph, 3 Wellington St, Goswell St, London, cm, picture and looking-glass frame maker (1835–39). [D]

Judson, Charles, 27 Little Alie St, Goodman's Fields, London, cm and u (1820–28). From 1823 the business styled itself Judson, Cook & Judson, or Judson & Cook. [D]

Judson, Charles, North St, Ripon, Yorks., cm and u (1822–37). Bankruptcy announced of Charles Judson jnr, 25 December 1829. [D; *Liverpool Mercury*, 1 January 1830]

Judson, John, Bogthorn, Keighley, Yorks., joiner/cm (1837). [D]

Judson, Jonas, Horton, Gisburn, near Colne, Lancs., cm (1822). [D]

Judson, Robert, Regent St, Pocklington, Yorks., cm (1828–40). [D]

Judson, Thomas snr, Nantwich, Cheshire, chairmaker (1807–21). Five sons and one daughter bapt., 1807–21. [PR (bapt.)]

Judson, Thomas jnr, Nantwich, Cheshire, chairmaker (1830–38). Son of Thomas Judson, bapt. on 14 December 1809. Married on 28 December 1830, and two sons and two daughters bapt., 1832–38. [PR (marriage and bapt.)]

Judson, William, Cherry Villa, Pocklington, Yorks., cm (1831). [D]

Jump, Edward Tyror, New Rd, Prescot, Lancs., joiner and cm (1816–34). [D]

Jump, Richard, Harrington St, Liverpool, cm (1772–73). [D]

Junipee, Thomas, King's Lynn, Norfolk, u (1780–84). Freeman of Norwich. (Norwich poll bks]

Juniper, —, 16 Cranbourn St, West St, Brighton, Sussex, cm (1837). Tenant of a shop and dwelling house. In 1837 the property was taken over by Mr Gordon, cm. [Brighton Ref. Lib., particulars of sale]

Jupe, Henry, Quay St, Newport, Isle of Wight, Hants., cm and u (1823). [D]

Jupe, Robert, 47 Welbeck St, Cavendish Sq., London, u (1839–40). [D]

Jupp, Elizabeth & Thomas, 5 Eagle St, Red Lion St, London, frame makers and gilders (1790–93). [Heal]

Jupp, John, St Giles, London, upholder (1792). [Bailey's list of bankrupts]

Jupp, Stephen, High Holborn, London, cm (1714). His app. Edward Anderson, aged 'about 15 years' absconded, 31 March 1714. [*London Gazette*, 12 April 1714]

Jupp & Batchelor, 5 Palace Row, New Rd, London, cm, u and undertaker (1839). [D]

Jury, Edward, Maidstone, Kent, cm (1830–38). In St Faith St, 1832–38, but in 1837 shown in High St. [Poll bks]

K

Kain, Henry, Brook St, Chester, cm (1840). Free 30 August 1840. [Freemen rolls]

Kamp, Jacob, 68 Margaret St, Cavendish Sq., London, cm (1782–86). In 1782 took out insurance cover of £400 of which £300 was in respect of utensils and tools. In 1786 utensils and stock, including that kept in a workshop, were covered for £280. [GL, Sun MS vol. 302, p. 127; vol. 339, p. 151]

Kampf, Frederick, address unknown, cm (1805). In 1805 supplied to the Princess of Wales an 'Antique circular table with Sphinx Egyptian Feet with inlaid brass and brass fret gallery' at £52 10s. Also in the same year provided '12 Handsome Gothic Chairs in Bronze & Gold, cain'd seats' at £66. This maker went bankrupt and payment was made to assignees John Gostling and John Appletree. [RA, 25192]

Karby, George, 2 Chambers St, Goodman's Yd, London, looking-glass frame maker (1820). [D]

Kashiere, Joseph, Compton St, Covent Gdn, London, cm (1749). [Westminster poll bk]

Kay, A. & Co., Cranberry Fold, Darwen (Over), Blackburn parish, Lancs., joiners, cm and machine makers (1825). [D]

Kay, George, 17 Hart St, Manchester, cm (1836). [D]

Kay, James, Bury, Lancs., u and cm (1787–95). Bankrupt November 1787. [*Gents Mag.*, November 1787; *Billinge's Liverpool Advertiser*, 15 June 1795]

Kay, James, Liverpool, cm (1802). Free 5 July 1802. [Freemen reg.]

Kay, James, Newton Sq., Leigh, Lancs., chairmaker etc. (1825). [D]

Kay, John, Preston and Liverpool, chairmaker (1782–1802). Freeman of Preston, 1782. Described as grandson of 'John the Baker'. In 1802 his son, Joseph, chairmaker was made free of Preston. At the time both Joseph and his father were working in Liverpool. John Kay snr had two other sons, James and John. [Preston freemen rolls]

Kay, John, Manchester, cm and u (1804–34). In 1804 at 72 Market St, but from 1814–18 the number is 74. By 1828 had moved to Fountain St, where the number was 86, but had changed to 38 by 1834. [D] See John and William Kaye.

Kay, John, Kirkburton, near Huddersfield, Yorks., joiner/cm (1834). [D]

Kay, Joseph, Preston and Liverpool, chairmaker (1802). Son of John Kay of Preston, working in Liverpool, 1802. Joseph Kay was free of Preston in 1802, but like his father working in Liverpool. He has two brothers, James and John jnr. [Preston freemen rolls]

Kay, Joseph, Kirkburton, near Huddersfield, Yorks., joiner/cm (1834). [D]

Kay, Joshua, Davies Mews, Oxford St, London, cm and u (1827). [D]

Kay, Peter, Liverpool, cm (1802). Free 5 July 1802. [Freemen reg.]

Kay, Quintin, 14 Ludgate Hill, London, u (1754–d. 1807). Son of John Kay of Doncaster, Yorks., Gent. Free of the London Upholders' Co. by redemption under the terms of the 1750 Upholders' Act, 16 November 1763. It is probable however that he already had an interest in the furniture trade before this date as his name is recorded in the list of subscribers to Chippendale's *Director*, 1754. In 1763 he entered into partnership with Frances Say and carried on the business after Say's death in 1778. Kay was probably in effective charge well before this as his name appears on documents dating from 1775 and Say died at 'Hadley' (Hadleigh, Suffolk?). He is recorded in 1778–79 obtaining a licence to employ one non-freeman. The business was already by this date of a substantial size and in 1775 the insurance cover on utensils and stock amounted to £3,200. This had increased substantially by January 1787 when utensils, stock, a warehouse and a workshop in Peacock Ct, Bridge St, Blackfriars were insured for £5,100. This workshop was to remain the main centre of production for the business throughout its entire existence and in 1804 stock there accounted for £3,300 out of an entire insurance cover of £11,050. In that year his dwelling house, shops and warehouse in Ludgate Hill accounted for £4,100, the remaining cover being for five houses in tenure to others. In 1792–93 a house at 25 Hatton Gdn was insured and was being used either for manufacturing or displaying and storing goods. Included in the list of master cabinet makers in Sheraton's *Cabinet Dictionary*, 1803. Kay died in July 1807 after 'more than half a century a respectable upholder'. Directory entries continue to 1811.

As the size of the business suggests that Quintin Kay was one of the largest of the London upholders at this period one would expect his patronage to be extensive and substantial. He is recorded in the Longford Castle, Wilts. accounts, 1780–81 and 1790. No details are known of the items supplied or work undertaken, but in 1780 he was paid £100; in 1781, £31 11s 6d; and in 1790, £29 3s. In the period 1792–94 he supplied furniture to a value of £1,550 to Penrice Castle, Glam. which included pier glasses, a satinwood table and a fire screen. Between May and December 1798 he supplied goods and undertook work for Sir Thomas Baring of the Manor House, Lewisham, Kent. The main item was a cylinder writing desk which was charged at £16 16s but a pair of blankets and the repair of two boxes brought the total to £19 11s 6d. In the year of his death, 1807, he supplied furniture to Petworth House, Sussex. [D; GL, Sun MS vol. 240, p. 421; vol. 340, p. 537; vol. 386, p. 553; vol. 392, p. 6; vol. 395, p. 381; vol. 430, ref. 757673; City Licence bks, vol. 9; Upholders' Co. records; *Gents Mag.*, July 1807; *C. Life*, 25 September 1975, pp. 755–56; *Apollo*, May 1977, p. 366; V & A archives; Heal] B.A.

Kay, Samuel, Nantwich, Cheshire, u (1815). On 21 February 1815 married Elizabeth Hesketh. Daughter Mary bapt. on 15 November of same year. [PR (bapt.)]

Kay, Samuel, Liverpool, cm (1840). Free 28 July 1840. A Samuel Kay was app. to Bartholomew Tyrer, u of Liverpool in 1828 and may be the same man. [App. bk; freemen reg.]

Kay, William, Fountain St, Manchester, carpenter, joiner and cm (1788). [D]

Kay, William, Salford, Lancs., cm and chairmaker (1804–40). In 1804 at 11 Brown's Cross St and from 1817–25 at 6 Johnson St. The latter address was his dwelling house and in 1825 he also had premises at 5 Kay's Ct. From 1832 in New Bailey St, the number being 5 or 6, 1832–33 and 8 from 1836–40. [D]

Kaye, Henry, Goodramgate, York, cm (1765–88). Son of Thomas Kaye, coppersmith. Free as cm in 1765. He offered timber for sale, 5 April 1774. His son Joseph was app. to William Ford, cm, on 7 September 1773, and another son, Robert was free as a cm in 1788. [D; poll bk; freemen rolls; *York Courant*, 5 April 1774]

Kaye, James, Liverpool, chairmaker (b. 1807–30). Born 30 October 1807, son of Thomas Kaye, freeman of Liverpool. Petitioned freedom by patrimony in 1828. Free 1830. [Freemen's committee bk]

Kaye, John, back of Crosshall St, Liverpool, chairmaker (1790–96). In 1790 at back of 75 Crosshall St but in 1796 at back of 36. [D]

Kaye, John, Manchester, cm and u (1803–40). Probably the John Kaye of Manchester who subscribed to Sheraton's

Cabinet Dictionary, 1803. By 1811 at 74 Market St and remained at this address until c. 1825. In this year he is shown with a house at Green Heys, Charlton Row. About 1825 moved to 38 Fountain St where he stayed until at least 1829. From 1832–40 at 86 Fountain St as an u, and also recorded at no 16 in 1832–33 as a cm. In 1825 supplied to Lord Leicester (later Lord de Tabley), at Tabley Hall, Knutsford, Cheshire, a Brussels carpet at a cost of £34 5s. The billhead gives an address at 1 Market St and indicates that apart from his work as a cm and u he maintained a carpet, paper and feather warehouse. [D; Chester RO, Tabley Hall vouchers]

Kaye, Joseph, Moorfields, Liverpool, cm (1796–1810). At 29 Moorfields in 1796 but in 1805 the number was 41 and from 1807–10 it was 39. [D]

Kaye, Richard, 40 Fazackerley St, Liverpool, cm (1796). [D]

Kaye, Robert, York, cm (1788). Son of Henry Kaye of Goodramgate, York, cm. Free 1788 as a cm. [Freemen rolls]

Kaye, Robert, London, cm (1793). Subscribed to Sheraton's *Drawing Book*, 1793.

Kaye, William, Liverpool, carver and gilder (1818–39). At 15 Skelhorne St in 1818 but thereafter in Lime St. Here he was at 55 in 1821–24, both 57 and 53 in 1827, 63 in 1829–35, 51 in 1837 and 48 in 1839. [D]

Kaye, William, 86 Fountain St, Manchester, cm and u (1836). The same address was occupied by John Kay(e) in 1836. [D]

Kayes, Michael snr, Long Row, Nottingham, joiner, cm and u (1756–d. 79). Took as apps James Bond (1756), John Shelton (1758, John Heydon (1759), George William Cartwright (1768), Joseph Kyte (1774) and Morgan Leeson (1775). [App. bks; Notts. RO, probate records; poll bk]

Kayes, Michael jnr, Long Row, Nottingham, joiner, cm and u (1779–83). Carried on his father's business after his death. Took as apps William Wylde (1781) and Lancelot Machin (1783). [App. bks; poll bk; *Leicester Journal*, 6 February 1779]

Kaygill, Daniel Mandevil, London, carver, gilder and looking-glass manufacturer (1791–1801). At 11 King St, Holborn in 1791, where he took out insurance cover of £300 which included £100 for utensils and stock. In 1800–01 at 494 Strand. [D; GL, Sun MS 22 August 1791, ref. 687665]

Kaygill, William, address unrecorded, cm (1754). Suscribed to Chippendale's *Director*, 1754.

Kayns, Ayliff(e), High St, Malmesbury, Wilts., cm, u and appraiser (1830–39). [D]

Kean, John, address unknown (c. 1796). Supplied furniture for Woburn Abbey, Beds. [*C. Life*, 8 July 1965, p. 102]

Kearney, James, Narrowgate, Alnwick, Northumb., carver and gilder (1827). [D]

Kearsley, James, King St, Wigan, Lancs., cm (1816). [D]

Kearsley, James, Manchester, carver and gilder (1822–29). At 1 China Lane in 1822, 12 Back Piccadilly in 1825 and 68 Port St in 1829. [D]

Kearsley, John, Millgate, Wigan, Lancs., cm (1818–25). [D]

Kearsley, John, Westgate, Ripon, Yorks., joiner/cm (1834–37). [D]

Kearsley, William, King St, Wigan, Lancs., cm (1814). Business continued by James Kearsley at this address. [D]

Kearsley, William, Salford and Manchester, Lancs., furniture broker and cm (1819–34). At Old Bridge, Salford in 1819; but in 1824–25 at Tib St, Stable St in one directory, and Stevenson Sq., Manchester with his house at 3 Bennet St in another. The address in Bennet St, Oldham (or Lever) St was used from 1825–29, but in 1832–33 an address at 32 Spear St is listed, and in 1834 Stevenson's Sq., Lever St. [D]

Keary, Daniel, Wells, Som., chairmaker (1798). [D]

Keasley, Ann, High St, Reigate, Surrey, u etc. (1838–39). [D]

Keasley, John, Reigate, Surrey, cm (1826–32). [D]

Keates, Joseph, Hartshead, Sheffield, Yorks., turner and chairmaker (1822). [D]

Keating, —, Grosvenor Mews, Grosvenor Sq., London, cm (1832–34). [D] See Ball & Keating at this address.

Keating, Daniel, 13 Prices St, Liverpool, cm (1823–d. 1828). Recorded at Prices St, 1823–24. Died 27 February 1828 in New York. [D; *Liverpool Mercury*, 2 May 1828]

Keating, David, Liverpool, cm (1818). Free 15 June 1818. [Freemen reg.]

Keating, William, 4 Portland St, Wardour St, Soho, London, cm and u (1821–39). In both 1821 and 1822 took out insurance cover of £750. Of this £500 was for the dwelling house but there were workshops behind, one of which was occupied by Bowman, cm. In 1822 the insurance policy was taken out in conjunction with William Harris. Keating does not appear in London directories until 1835. [D; GL, Sun MS vol. 488, ref. 985449; vol. 493, ref. 993073]

Keating, William, Liverpool, cm (1835–39). In 1835 at 3 Dickson St, Hartington and in 1839 had a shop at 55 St James St. [D]

Keats, John, North St, Dorchester, Dorset, cm (1823–30). [D]

Keats, Joseph, 10 Hartshead, Sheffield, Yorks., chairmaker (1830). [D]

Kebbell, —, Beauvoirtown, Dalston, London, cm (1826). [D]

Kebblewhite, Thomas, Lidard Millicent, Wilts., turner and chairmaker (1782). Took out insurance cover of £100 of which half was in respect of utensils and stock in trade. [GL, Sun MS vol. 298, p. 436]

Kebe, —, address unknown, cm (1803). Subscribed to Sheraton's *Cabinet Dictionary*, 1803.

Keck (or Keek), John, Moreton-in-Marsh, Glos., joiner, cm and mortgager (1782–84). Insured his house for £300. [D; GL, Sun MS vol. 299, p. 598]

Keeble, Elizabeth, Nicholas St, Colchester, Essex, cm and u (1839). [D]

Keeble, Robert, Robert, Crow St, Stowmarket, Suffolk, cm (1830). [D]

Keeble, Samuel, 11 Old Change, Cheapside, London, joiner and carver (1781–1823). Mentioned in the app. records of the Goldsmiths' Co., 2 May 1781. [D; PRO, C132/35]

Keegan, John, Paradise St, Rotherhithe, London, u (1826). [D]

Keel, William, parish of St Mary Magdalene, Oxford, cm (1768). [Poll bk]

Keele, Arthur, Oxford, cm (1745–d. 1771). In 1745 took app. named Ford. Dead by March 1771 when his stock of new furniture was sold off. [S of G, app. index; *Jackson's Oxford Journal*, 5 March 1771]

Keeler, Jabez, 1 Picton St, Bristol, cm (1833–35). [D]

Keeler, John, parish of St Alphage, Canterbury, Kent, cm (1795–96). Free 1795. [Freemen rolls; poll bk]

Keeler, Philip & Butler, Philip, opposite 'The King's Head Tavern', Middle Row, Holborn, London, cm (1752). Both partners were dead by 1752 when their stock was sold by auction. [*General Advertiser*, 11 May 1752]

Keeling, Ambrose, 39 Guildford Pl., Ken Lane, London, cm and u (1827). [D]

Keeling, Benjamin, Stafford, cm, u and maker of fancy chairs (1818–35). Trading at Salter St in 1818 and Goalgate St, 1822–35. [D]

Keeling, William, Chester, cm (1812–26). Free 6 October 1812. Shown in Princess St, 1812 and 1826, but in 1819 at George St. [Freemen rolls; poll bks]

Keen, D., 25 Hedge Row, Islington, London, cm etc. (1820). [D]

Keen, John, 59 Fleet Mkt, London, chairmaker, cm and broker (1775). Took out insurance of £1,000. Only £30 of this was in respect of utensils and stock kept at Fleet Mkt, but he had a manufactory at 29 Rosamund Row, Clerkenwell and utensils and stock here was valued at £225 with a similar sum in addition for stock in the yard. [GL, Sun MS vol. 244, p. 129]

Keen, John, 10 Northampton Row, Spitalfields, Clerkenwell, London, cm (1790). Took out insurance cover of £500 in 1790. Of this £300 was in respect of workshops, a wareroom, a counting house and a shed. [GL, Sun MS 22 June 1790, ref. 570731]

Keen, Joseph, West Wycombe, Bucks., chairmaker (b. c. 1805–41). Aged 36 at the time of the 1841 Census.

Keen, S., London, cm and upholder (1806–25). At 4 Upper North Pl., Gray's Inn Rd, 1806–16. In 1816 an address at 181 Piccadilly is also shown. By 1820 the number of the Upper North Pl. address was shown as 20. The S. Keen, cm at 6 Doughty St, Mecklenburg Sq. in 1825 is probably the same maker. [D]

Keen, Samuel, 5 Upper Marylebone St, London, cm, u and bedstead maker (1811–27). The business commenced as a partnership known as Keen & Durley. This lasted until 1823 when Samuel Keen commenced trading on his own behalf. [D]

Keenan, Nicholas, Horse Mkt, Warrington, Lancs., chairmaker (1814–34). [D]

Keene, David, 10 Gt Warner St, Cold Bath Fields, London, cm (1813). [D]

Keene, John, Oxford St, London, cm (c. 1820). Label recorded on a Regency rosewood breakfast table with brass inlay banding, supported on a circular pillar with a concave three sided base.

Keene, R., London, u (1793). Subscribed to Sheraton's *Drawing Book*, 1793.

Keene, Robert, Coventry, Warks., cm (1757–78). Supplied furniture to the Leigh family for Stoneleigh Abbey, Warks. In 1757 two pearwood frames 'gilt & frosted' were charged at £4. On 14 March 1764 two large linen presses were invoiced at £24 9s 6¼. These were of oak and the main craftsman employed in their making was Thomas Gordon who worked on them for twenty-six days. He was assisted in erecting them by two other employees, Samuel Phillips and John Binney. A further invoice was concerned with the supply of two mahogany knife boxes, four large mahogany dish trays, three mahogany glass trays, a mahogany cistern and stand and two mahogany pails. The total cost of these items was £15 6s 6d. The two accounts were settled on 12 October 1764 with a payment of £39 16s and a warning on the account against attempts to bribe servants in Lord Leigh's employment. The oak presses were in the Stoneleigh Abbey sale (Christie's, 15 October 1981, lots 155–56). Robert Keene was bankrupt, May 1778, but the notice of bankruptcy lists him as Robert Keene the Younger and it is possible that both father and son were involved in the business. [Shakespeare Birthplace Trust, Leigh receipts, DR/5; *Gents Mag.*, May 1778]

Keene, Samuel, 356 Oxford St, London, cm, u and appraiser (1819–29). His premises were near the Pantheon. In 1821 he stated he made 'card, dining and sofa tables on the most improved principles' and 'also ladies work tables, dressing cases, desks, tea chests'. [D; PRO, B3/1354]

Keep, Richard, Richmond, Surrey, cm (1798). [D]

Keep, Thomas, Harpsden, Oxon., u (1763). On 8 August 1763 married Mary Knight of Shiplake, Oxon. at Shiplake. [Bodleian index of Oxf. marriage bonds]

Keeton, John, Cuckney, Notts., cm and joiner (1832). [D]

Keighley, John, Birstal, Yorks., joiner and cm (1828–37). [D]

Keir, John, Milk Ct, Westminster, London, cm (1774). [Poll bk]

Keith, George, 16 Wardour St, Soho, London, upholder (1788). [D]

Keith, William, 11 Phipps St, Shoreditch, London, chairmaker (1808). [D]

Keith, William, 54 Burlington Arcade, London, portable desk, dressing case, work box and cabinet case maker (1839). [D]

Kelham, John, 5 Berwick St, Soho, London, cm (1823). Took out insurance cover of £300 on 7 May 1823. Of this £130 was for utensils and stock. [GL, Sun MS vol. 498, ref. 1005001]

Kelk, William, Portland St, Newark, Notts., cm and u (1819–28). [D]

Kellam, Richard, 1 Brazenose St, Manchester, chairmaker (1808). [D]

Keller, Phillip, address unknown, looking-glass maker (1708–09). Supplied a number of small looking-glasses in walnut or olive wood frames to the 2nd Duke of Bedford at a total cost of £3 19s 6d. [Bedford Office, London]

Kellett, John, 32 Chancery Lane, Higher Ardwick, Manchester, builder, joiner and cm (1825). [D]

Kellett, John Patrick, 14 Dean St, Soho, London, bedstead maker and u (1829–39). [D]

Kelley, William, Catherine-wheel Alley, London, cm (1793). Subscribed to Sheraton's *Drawing Book*, 1793.

Kelley, William, 21 Cleveland St, Marylebone, London, carver (1829). [D]

Kellow, Francis, London, upholder (1721–24). Son of William Kellow, member of the Skinners' Co. of London. App. to John Houseman, 17 September 1712, and free of the Upholders' Co. by servitude, 5 July 1721. Recorded working at Chicheley, Bucks., 1722–24. In 1722 he was paid £6 7s for a gilt 'chair bed'; in December 1723, £6 0s 7d for a chair, quilt, blankets etc.; and in January 1724, £2 13s for a featherbed. [GL, Upholders' Co. records; Bucks. RO, D/C/2/3(ii); V & A archives]

Kelly, —, address unknown, picture frame maker (1781). On 12 December 1781 charged £4 14s 6d for a picture frame supplied to Sir George Cornewall of Moccas Court, near Hereford, and Stanhope St, London. [Herefs. RO, Moccas papers J56/IV/3]

Kelly, Charles, 12 Cambridge St, Golden Sq., London, cm (1816–29). [D]

Kelly, Charles, 51 Fontenoy St, Liverpool, cm (1827). [D]

Kelly, Henry, Chester, cm (1831–40). Free 21 April 1831 and on 8 September of the same year married at St Peter's Church, Liverpool. At Lower Bridge St, Chester in 1834 but in 1840 at Russell St. [D; freemen rolls; *Chester Courant*, 13 September 1831]

Kelly, James, Chester, cm (1818–19). In 1818 at Mill St but in 1819 at Thomas Buildings. [Poll bks]

Kelly, James, Newport, Salop, u (1833). [PR (bapt.)]

Kelly, John, 27 Dartmouth St, London, cm and case maker (1801). In February 1801 took out insurance cover of £500 of which £300 was for utensils and stock. [GL, Sun MS vol. 419, ref. 715218]

Kelly, John, Mortimer St, London, chair and sofa maker (1822–27). At 10 Mortimer St in 1822 but by 1827 the number had changed to 59. [D]

Kelly, Martin, Liverpool, furniture painter (1824–37). At 2 Derby St, Whitechapel in 1824, 3 Brooker's Alley, Stanley St in 1835 and 3 Stanley Ct, Stanley St in 1837. [D]

Kelly, Matthew, London, chairmaker (1808–20). In 1808 at 18 Stephen St, Tottenham Ct Rd, but in 1820 the business is listed as Matthew Kelly & Son at 60 Mortimer St, Cavendish Sq. [D]

Kelly, Richard, Catherine Wheel Alley, Whitechapel, London, cm (1783). In 1783 insured his utensils and stock in trade for £500. [GL, Sun MS vol. 306, p. 515]

Kelly, Richard, East St, South Molton, Devon, cm (1823–30). [D]

Kelly, Robert, Rainsford's Gdns, Liverpool, chairmaker (1818–39). Shown at 16 Rainsford's Gdns in 1818 and 1834, 23 and 24 in 1821–24, 16 in 1834, 8 in 1835, 9 in 1837 and 12 and 14 in 1839. Additional addresses shown are 13 Bostock St in 1837 and 74 Stanley St in 1839. [D]

Kelly, Mrs Sarah, Bridge St, Chester, cm, u and furniture broker (1837–40). Address shown as Lower Bridge St in 1834 and Bridge St Row in 1840. [D]

Kelly, Thomas, 25 Thayer St, Manchester Sq., London, upholder 1808. [D]

Kelly, William, Newman St, Oxford St, London, carver and gilder (1817). [D]

Kelly, William, 15 Berners Mews, Castle St East, London, wood and cabinet carver (1839). [D]

Kelly & Co., 23 Wells St, Oxford St, London, cm (1823). [D]

Kelsall, Edward, 1 King St, Hulme, Manchester, cm (1834). [D]

Kelsall, Thomas, London, upholder (1710–36). Free of the Upholders' Co., 1710. Recorded at St Mary Axe, 1724–34, and in St Lawrence Lane, 1736. Bankrupt August 1736. [GL, Upholders' Co. records; Heal; *Gents Mag.*, August 1736]

Kelsey, James, Lancaster, cm (1817–18). [Lancaster freemen rolls]

Kelsey, James snr, Hull, Yorks., cm, u and broker, (1814–31). At 13 Blackfriargate in 1823 but by 1826 at no. 28. In 1831 at 49 Dock St. [D]

Kelsey, James jnr, Blackfriargate, Hull, Yorks., cm, u and broker (1831–40). At 28 Blackfriargate in 1831 but from 1834–40 at no. 9. [D]

Kelsey, John, London, cm (1729–46). In May 1729 living in Leicester St, parish of St Ann, Westminster. He appears to have kept part of his stock here which together with household goods was valued at £150. The bulk of his stock valued at £250 was however kept in a shop that was next door to the 'Red Lion' in King St. In 1746 his address was 'over against the Bull and Gate in Holborn', and it is probable that he was at this address two years earlier when in June 1744 he was attacked in Holborn. He is said to have stopped trading in 1746. Between April and September 1738 he supplied to Sir Richard Hoare for Barn Elms House a mahogany bed table, a screen on pillars and claws, a fine mahogany bed enriched with carving and a table etc. for which £17s 15s 4d was charged. [GL, Sun MS vol. 29; Heal; *General Advertiser*, 16 June 1744; Harris, *Old English Furniture*, p. 24; V & A, 86 NN. 3]

Kelsey, John & Co., Paradise St, Liverpool, upholders (1787). [D]

Kelsey, John, 7 Grotto Sq., Mason St, Hull, Yorks., cm and shopkeeper (1817–34). In 1835–38 at the same address but shown only as a shopkeeper. In 1839 the trade is listed as grocer. [D]

Kelsey, John, Walker Sq., Hull, Yorks., joiner and cm (1823–40). In 1823 the address is listed as Walker Sq., Paragon Pl.; in 1826–35 as Walker Sq., Sykes Pl. (or Sykes St); and from 1838 as 7 Walker's Sq. [D]

Kelsey, Thomas, London, cm (1831). Freeman of Sandwich, Kent. [Sandwich poll bk]

Kelshaw, J., Lancaster (1789–92). [Westminster Ref. Lib., Gillow records]

Kelshaw, James, Liverpool, cm (1753). In 1753 took app. named Bolton. [S of G, app. index]

Kelshaw, Jos., 5 Blackmoor St, Clare Mkt, London, carver and gilder (1809). [D]

Kelson, Chas., 10 Caroline Buildings, Bath, Som., cm (1826). [D]

Kelter, William, Lewes, Sussex, cm (before 1762). In 1762 or before, his shop was taken over by John Harley, cm. [*Sussex Weekly Advertiser*, 3 May 1762]

Kemble, Samuel, 11 Old Change, London, carver and gilder (1784). [D]

Kemm, William, Castle St, Salisbury, Wilts., carver and gilder (1839). [D]

Kemp, Ebenezer, London, upholder (1816). Son of Matthew Kemp, upholder. Admitted freeman of the Upholders' Co., 6 March 1816. [GL, Upholders' Co. records]

Kemp, George, Cornhill London, upholder, cm and glass grinder (1755–97). Son of George Kemp of Ramsgate, Kent, mariner. Father of Matthew Kemp and George Kemp jnr, both members of the Upholders' Co. George Kemp snr was made free of the Upholders' Co. by redemption under the terms of the 1750 Upholders' Act on 28 August 1755. In 1788 he was master of the Co. He was already trading by 1757 and for the next ten years is recorded taking out licences to employ non-freemen. In 1765 and 1767 licences were granted for ten men for three months. He took as apps John Southeram, who was free 1765; John Joad from 1767–71; and his own son George, 1788–95. Early addresses are given as either Ball Ct, Cornhill, or the sign of the 'Golden Ball', Cornhill. His business premises were however later numbered 64 Cornhill. A trade card with a fine Rococo frame [Heal Coll., BM] describes the nature of his business. He made 'all Sorts of Cabinets, Chairs, Upholstery, Glasses, Chests of Drawers, Desks, Book-cases, Bureau furnitures, Cabinet, Commode, Dressing, Dining, Pembroke & Breakfast TABLES; easy French Settee & Bed-Chairs, SOPHA'S, Camp, Tent, Field & Down Beds & Blankets of all Sorts. Floor Carpets made to Rooms of any Size. Sconce, Pier, Chimney, Swinging and Dressing Glasses in yᵉ genteelest Taste'. He took out insurance cover for considerable sums but this was in the main on property in various parts of London. His utensils and stock were however valued at £400 in 1777 and a warehouse similarly valued in 1781. It is possible that he manufactured at other locations to that in Cornhill, since in November 1765 a fire in Bishopsgate St was said to have damaged the premises of many tradesmen including Kemp & Co., cm. This may well have been a correct designation for the business at this period, for directories in 1769–70 list the business as Kemp & Gould. George Kemp was a Fellow of the Society of Arts, 1762.

About 1785 he took his son Matthew into the business and it is from this date listed as George Kemp & Son. In the mid 1780s insurance cover amounted to £500 for utensils and stock and a further £500 specifically for glass. This reflected a growing interest in mirror production. In April 1794 George and Matthew Kemp petitioned the House of Commons regarding the Plate Glass Co. of Ravenhead. In 1790 this company had agreed to supply the Kemps with equipment to build a mill to polish and grind plate glass and to instruct them in their processes. In return the Kemps were to share their experience in plate glass polishing and grinding. A mirror of c. 1760 in style but later in date, is known with a trade label inscribed 'George Kemp & Son, GLASS-GRINDERS, London'. [D; GL, Upholders' Co. records; Sun MS vol. 259, p. 520; vol. 260, p. 29; vol. 261, p. 627; vol. 296, p. 27; vol. 299, p. 216; vol. 321, p. 586; vol. 334, p. 167; Hand in Hand MS vol. 105, p. 73; City Licence bks, vols 2–5 *Gents Mag.*, November 1765, p. 535; Heal; Wills, *Looking-Glasses*, pp. 50, 154; *Antiques*, May 1968, p. 647] B.A.

Kemp, George jnr, 64 Cornhill, London, upholder (1795). Son of George Kemp snr and brother of Matthew Kemp. App. to George Kemp snr on 6 August 1788 and free of the Upholders' Co. by servitude, 2 September 1795. [GL, Upholders' Co. records]

Kemp, James, parish of St Stephen, Norwich, cm (1826–30). Son of Isaac Kemp, cordwainer. Admitted freeman, 16 December 1826. [Freemen reg.; poll bk]

Kemp, John, Gt Yarmouth, Norfolk, u (1787–98). App. to Robert Harley and William Seaman and free 1787. Trading at Gt Yarmouth in 1798. [D; freemen rolls; poll bks]

Kemp, John, 77 Mark Lane, London, upholder (1800). Son of Richard Kemp of Moorfields, Shoreditch, hosier. App. to Joseph Taylor on 4 June 1783 and Henry Blaxland on 2 February 1785. Free of the Upholders' Co. by servitude, 2 July 1800. [GL, Upholders' Co. records]

Kemp, Matthew, 64 Cornhill, London, cm and glass grinder (c. 1798–1816). Son of George Kemp snr and brother of George Kemp jnr. Father of Ebenezer Kemp. Free of the Upholders' Co. by patrimony, 1 May 1782. Partner with his father in the business of George Kemp & Son, c. 1785–97. He then took over the business, though one directory still shows M. & G. Kemp as late as 1802. It is possible that as Matthew's initial is listed first that this might be George jnr rather than his father. In 1803 listed in Sheraton's *Cabinet Dictionary* as a master cm. [D; GL, Upholders' Co. records]

Kemp, Matt., Mead Pl., Lambeth, London, cm and chairmaker (1827). [D]

Kemp, Richard, Richmond, Surrey, cm (1798). [D]

Kemp, Thomas, Norwich and London, cm (1789–1806). Son of David Kemp, weaver. Admitted freeman, 28 November 1789. A Thomas Kemp cm, working in London from 1799–1806, is probably the same craftsman. [Norwich freemen reg; poll bks]

Kemp, William, London, upholder (1711–47). Son of William Kemp of the parish of St Giles, Middlx., baker. App. to Ezra Doughty on 11 July 1711, and free of the Upholders' Co. by servitude, 1 July 1724. Took as apps James Robinson, free 1739, and Thomas Bennett, 1726–1746/47. [GL, Upholders' Co. records]

Kempster, Samuel, 'against the General Post Office, Broad St, London', upholder (1713). Freeman of London. [GL, Sun MS vol. 3, p. 78]

Kendal, John, Lancaster (1823). Named in Gillow records in connection with making a dressing table. [Westminster Ref. Lib., Gillow vol. 344/101, p. 3247]

Kendal, John, Langwathby, Penrith, Cumb., joiner/cm (1829). [D]

Kendall, George Knipe, Lancaster, u (1837). App. to James Kendall of Lancaster, u and cm in 1830, and free, 1837–38. [Lancaster app. reg and freemen rolls]

Kendall, James, Bondgate, Otley, Yorks., cm (1798–1822). May be related to and associated in business with William Kendall of Otley, fl. 1798. [D]

Kendall, James, Lancaster, u and cm (1821–38). Recorded at Cheapside, 1834. [D] App. to H. T. Smith, u, in 1821, and free as an u, 1827–28. Between 1830–35 took three apps, one of whom was George Knipe Kendall, free 1837–38. Three further apps were taken, 1836–38. [Lancaster app. reg. and freemen rolls]

Kendall, John, 'the Chest of Drawers and Sconce, near the Red Lyon', Colchester, Essex, joiner and cm (1726–30). His trade card [Colchester Museum] states that 'All Sorts of Joiners and cabinet maker's goods . . . all sorts of glasses . . . canes, maps and prints, all sorts of womens and childrens shoes, cloggs, pattens etc.' were stocked. The card shows a tallboy and a sconce. In 1730 took app. named Trumble. [S of G, app. index]

Kendall, John, Union St, York, joiner and cm (1791). On 8 February 1791 took out insurance cover of £900. [GL, Sun MS vol. 374, ref. 579972]

Kendall, John, Marshall St, Liverpool, u (1794). [D]

Kendall, John, Liverpool, cm (1796–1807). App. to Robert Hardwick and free, 25 May 1796. In that year took app. named Robert Johnson, who may not have completed his apprenticeship, since in 1812, when he petitioned for freedom he was a book-keeper. John Kendall is shown trading at 5 Trueman St, Dale St in 1800 and 11 Crofton Ct in 1807. [D; freemen's committee bk]

Kendall, John, Bondgate, Otley, Yorks., cm, joiner and builder (1828). [D]

Kendall, Joseph, Ratcliffe Highway, London, carver and gilder (1776). In 1776 took out insurance cover for £200 of which £50 was for utensils and stock. [GL, Sun MS vol. 249, ref. 369961]

Kendall, Joseph, Market Rasen, Lincs., joiner and cm (1780). Insured his house for £100 in 1780. [GL, Sun MS vol. 284, p. 109]

Kendall, Nathaniel, Otley, Yorks., joiner and cm (1759). In 1759 took app. named Strickland. [S of G, app. index]

Kendall, O., Salisbury St, Blandford Forum, Dorset, cm (1823). [D]

Kendall, Robert jnr, Colchester, Essex, upholder, hosier and draper (1775–84). In 1775 insured his stock for £1,900 out of a total cover of £2,000. [GL, Sun MS vol. 236, p. 605; poll bk]

Kendall, Robert, Harwich, Essex, cm (1781). Freeman of Colchester. [Colchester poll bk]

Kendall, Robert, Norwich, cm (1784). Freeman of Colchester. [Colchester poll bk]

Kendall, Robert, Harford St, Liverpool, cm (1818). On 1 February 1818 married Mary Parkinson at St Anne's Church. [D; *Liverpool Mercury*, 20 February 1818]

Kendall, Robert, 2 or 3 Back Falkner St, Manchester, cm and chairmaker (1834–40). [D]

Kendall, Thomas, parish of St Nicholas, Colchester, Essex, joiner and cm (1716–22). Took out insurance cover in 1716 and 1722. In October 1722 both Thomas Kendall snr and jnr are referred to. The dwelling house of the the latter was insured for £300. [GL, Sun MS vol. 5, ref. 6533; vol. 14, p. 388]

Kendall, William, Colchester, Essex, cm (1755–56). Peter Du Cane of Braxted Park, Essex paid Kendall £19 7s 6d on 18 November 1755 and £6 7s 6d on 16 October 1756. No details of the goods and work involved are listed. [Essex RO, D/DDC A13 folio 59]

Kendall, William, Norwich, cm (1757). In 1757 took app. named Lewis. [S of G, app. index]

Kendall, William, Otley, Yorks., cm (1798). May be related to or associated with James Kendall of Otley. [D]

Kendall, William, 117 Westgate, Bradford, Yorks., cm (1830–37). [D]

Kendall & Son(s), New St and Lombard St, Birmingham, cabinet, dressing case and portable desk makers (1830–35). Recorded at 17 New St with manufactory in 49 Lombard St in 1835. [D]

Kendall & Son, 447 West Strand and 1 Adelaide St, London, and 63 Wire St, Bristol, perfumers, jewellers, cabinet case makers and importers of foreign fancy merchandise to the Royal Family (1836–37). In 1838 succeeded by G. B. Worboys. [D]

Kendel, Thomas, Bowman Lane, Leeds, Yorks., cm (1814–16). [D]

Kendell, John, Leeds, Yorks., cm (1783–1840). An important Leeds maker whose business was eventually taken over in 1863 by the equally well known firm of Marsh & Jones. The earliest known reference occurs in 1783 when insurance cover of £700 was taken out of which £600 was for utensils, stock and sheds. By 8 March 1791, when the address was listed as Vicar Lane, the insurance cover had risen to £1,000 and in the following year to £1,400. The 1792 cover included a workshop and warehouse valued at £150, utensils and stock in a yard valued at £350 and three houses and three workshops in Vicar Lane 'all under one roof' valued at £150. In 1783 the business had been described as that of a

'carpenter, cabinetmaker & merchant', in 1791 as a 'cabinet maker & joiner' and in 1792 as a 'timber merchant and cabinet maker'. In 1793 he subscribed to Sheraton's *Drawing Book*. Subsequent addresses for the firm are Mill Hill in 1798 and West Bar, Mill Hill from 1811. The number in West Bar was 44 in 1811, 55 in 1816, 7 in 1826–34 and 10 in 1837. Listed also at 55 Mill Hill in 1816–17. The premises taken over in 1811 were formerly occupied by Samuel Stead and were near the 'Coloured Cloth Hall'. From 1816 the words '& Co.' were added to the trading style, while in 1822 the increasing interest in seating furniture is reflected by the adoption of the words 'hair seating & curled hair manufacturers' to their trade description.

A number of patrons of the firm are known. Between 1818–22 they were employed by the Earl of Harewood at Harewood House, near Leeds. The amounts are fairly modest, that in 1818 amounting to £39 for instance. A much more substantial volume of work was carried out between 1827–30 for a Miss Currer totalling £1,000. Kendell also worked at Farnley Hall, Otley, Yorks., and for the period 1833–34 £620s 10d was paid to the firm. Kendell & Co. probably from the 1830s started to adopt a policy of labelling their furniture. The labels provided spaces for a serial number and the name of the craftsmen employed on the project. The lowest serial number so far noted is 66000 on a writing table sold as 'William IV' from the Rudding Park, Yorks. sale (Christie's 14 October 1972). A further pair of mahogany writing tables from the same sale bore the number 69295. Two library tables whose appearance suggests a date of *c.* 1830–40 bearing the numbers 67383 and 69294 were sold by Lawrence's of Crewkerne in March 1983. A rosewood portfolio stand described as 'Regency' was sold at Christie's (25 November 1976) but was numbered 85809 suggesting a later date than the other items mentioned. In the absence of the business records of the firm, dating can only be assessed by the style of the piece, but if the numbers run consecutively, as one would expect, they do provide a valuable relative dating guide between pieces so numbered. [D; GL, Sun MS vol. 317, p. 488; vol. 375, p. 553; vol. 386, p. 83; *Leeds Intelligencer*, 28 October 1811; *Furn. Hist.*, 1967; Joy, *English Furniture 1800–1851*, p. 235] B.A.

Kendell, Thomas, Quebec, Leeds, Yorks., cm (1765–93). By tradition the business was established *c.* 1760 and Thomas Kendell was an ex-employee of Gillows of Lancaster. For this assertion there is no documentary evidence. The business was however in existence by 1765 when it is mentioned in the Harewood House archives for work carried out at Gawthorp. On 3 April 1788 Thomas 'Kendall' leased a site 'opposite Quebec in Leeds' for 60 years at £10 per annum to erect a dwelling house. His former address is not known. In 1791 he signed the dedication of *The Leeds Cabinet and Chair Makers' Book of Prices* on behalf of the master cabinet makers of Leeds, an indication of his status in the trade. On 15 June 1793 he took out insurance cover of £600 of which only £150 in respect of utensils and tools. By this date he was elderly; the enterprise of John Kendell had been trading for a number of years and it is probable that he was running down his own business. [D; Leeds RO, Harewood MS and Leases; GL, Sun MS vol. 395, p. 300; *Furn. Hist.*, 1967]

Kendrick, Edward, parish of St Michael, Bristol, carver (1734–54). [Poll bks]

Kendrick, James, Liverpool, cm (1822). Married Miss Betsy Smith at St Paul's Church on 7 April 1822. [*Liverpool Mercury*, 19 April 1822]

Kendrick, John, Sankey St, Warrington, Lancs., u (1781–87). [D]

Kendrick, Peter, Warrington, Lancs., u (1798). [D]

Kengall, Charles, 5 David St, Marylebone, London, cm and u (1822). [D]

Keningale, Robert, Old Butter Mkt, Ipswich, Suffolk, u and appraiser (1806–39). Married in 1806 at the church of St Lawrence, Ipswich. Not recorded in directories until 1830 however. [D; Suffolk RO, FAA: 50/2/113, p. 34; poll bks]

Keninmore, John, 22 Featherstone St, near City Rd, London, cm (1820–29). His trade card [archives dept, Hackney Libraries] describes him as a 'Fire Screen and Cabinet Maker'. He claimed to make and sell 'Fire Screens, Ladies Work, Loo & Card Tables of Rose Wood, Mahogany Dining Tables of different descriptions ready made of fine wood'. He dealt in 'Fine Veneers, Dining Table Wood' and stated 'Ladies Needle Work & Paintings Framed & Glazed for Fire Screens' and 'Dressing Glasses made to any size'. The card is illustrated with engravings of a cabinet, pole screen, games table and a four-fold screen. [D]

Kenna, James, Chester, u (1732). [Poll bk]

Kenneday, Anthony, Bedfordbury, London, chairmaker (1749). [Westminster poll bk]

Kennedy, Daniel, London, carver and gilder (1811–16). At New Lisle St, Leicester Fields in 1811 but from 1814–16 at 51 Rathbone Pl., Oxford St. In January 1816 advertised 'Pier, Chimney and Dressing Glasses ... manufactured on premises' and 'frames for artists, glasses re-silvered, old work re-gilt'. [D; *Times*, 4 January 1816]

Kennedy, James, 32 Earl St West, Lisson Grove, London, carver and gilder (1835). [D]

Kennedy, John, Windsor, Berks., chairmaker (1720). In 1720 eight 'forrest chairs' were supplied to Temple Newsam House, Leeds at a cost of 6s each. Carriage was charged in addition from Windsor. [*Furn. Hist.*, 1967]

Kennedy, John, Bolton Yd, Tyne St, North Shields, Northumb., cm (1828–34). [D]

Kennedy, Josiah, Liverpool, joiner and cm (1824–39). In 1824 at 76 Hanover St; in 1837 at 6 Kent St; and in 1839 at 12 Kent St. [D]

Kennedy, Thomas, 19 Church Way, North Shields, Northumb., cm (1834). [D]

Kennedy, William, Liverpool, cm (1802–d. 1813). App. to Isaac Marsh 1802 but experienced some difficulty in being sworn free as his master died about a year before his term of servitude expired. He was however made free on 11 October 1812, but his active life as a trained cm was short, for he died on 7 February 1813. [Freemen's committee bk and reg.]

Kennell, Hugh, 21 Gilbert St, Liverpool, cm (1821). [D]

Kennett, Robert & Kidd, William, London, u (1766–95). Amongst the Chancery Masters' Exhibits in the PRO is an account book of a furniture-making firm for 1792–95. [PRO, C114/81] It is one of the few known ledgers of an 18th-century furniture-making firm and reveals an extensive trade. The firm was Robert Kennett & Co., later Kennett & Kidd. Kennett was almost certainly the person who was bound app. to the famous firm of Ince & Mayhew in 1766 for the extremely high sum of £157 10s. [PRO, IR 25/23] The Mr Kennett who supplied furniture to Lady Isabella Finch in 1759 and to the 4th Earl of Holderness in 1763 may have been his father or brother. Robert Kennett finished his apprenticeship in 1773 and by 1776 was in partnership with Thomas Vernon, working from premises near Air St, Piccadilly. In 1776 they insured their stock, utensils and goods for £1,000 [GL, Sun MS ref. 365936] and when Kennett set up on his own at 67 New Bond St in the following year he insured similar items for the same sum. [Ref. 391441] The new premises came into his possession after the death of his eldest brother, John, but the new venture ran into some financial difficulties. In 1783 he was taken to court by William

Crawford, an auctioneer of Holborn, and John King of Soho, with whom he had been involved in some complicated financial dealings, and in 1785 was declared bankrupt. [PRO, B 4/22]

His business recovered and he supplied furniture to Lord Howard of Audley End, 1789–90. In 1791 the firm designed and made the carved and gilt Grand Master's Throne for the Prince of Wales who became Master of the Grand Lodge of the Free Masons in 1790. Kennett won an open competition for the throne and two warden's chairs which are in the French Louis Seize style admired by the Prince. [*Conn.*, July 1965, figs 8 and 9] The account book of 1792–95 includes work for the 'Grand Committee of Free Masons', mainly for cleaning and preparing the furniture ready for meetings and putting on protective cases afterwards.

It may have been the success of this prestigious commission which encouraged Kennett to borrow £3,000 and buy a £4,000 property in Essex in 1791. He was also in debt to his clerk, William Kidd, who had worked for him since 1787 and with whom he entered an unofficial partnership in 1792. [PRO, C12 259/18, 680/34 and 1736/2] They agreed to divide the business and profits on a 4:1 ratio with Kennett retaining the major share. This arrangement was formalized in 1794 when Kennett and Kidd signed a seven-year partnership agreement dating back to 1792. The partnership reflected the former concerns of the two men: Kidd looked after the book keeping and administrative side while Kennett supervised manufacture. The firms of Kennett & Co. (1792–94) and Kennet & Kidd (1794–95) were referred to in directories as 'Upholsterers' but carried out a wide range of activities including cabinet making, chair making and paper hanging as well as services such as arranging funerals. House furnishings and letting was one of their specialities. During the partnership Kennett bought or took leases on several houses and the partners furnished them and let them at 'considerably advanced rents'. They also acted as estate agents, letting houses, taking inventories and seeing to repairs, etc., for clients who were out of London. They also furnished entire houses or the principal rooms in a number of houses, mainly in Dublin and London, for which the owners became indebted to them for 'considerable amounts of money'. These sums can be seen in the account book which reveals an extensive array of wealthy and titled customers.

The firm appears to have been a favourite with members of the Anglo-Irish aristocracy in the 1790s. The largest order in the book is that for the Earl of Ormonde, for his town house in Dublin and Kilkenny Castle, which totalled £7,096 12s 10d. Other large orders came from the Earl of Westmeath (£2,059 14s 9d); Lord Viscount Dillon (£1,837 19s 2d); — Dickinson Esq. (£1,455 10s 5d); George Templar of Somerset, who later acted as lawyer on behalf of the beneficiaries of Kennett's late father-in-law [PRO, C13 160133] (£1,049 3s 6d) and Edward Wheeler (£1,020 8s 3d). Those who placed orders over £500 were: J. H. Casamajor; Dr Morton; Charles Floyer; Mr Davis; Augustus Floyer; Colonel Bridges; John Parlby; Mr Spencer (plasterer); Culling Smith; Lt John Charlton; William Anderson; Sir John Dalling; Christopher Hodgson; Thomas Carter; William Gill; Baron de Robech; Mrs Horne; Mr Davies; Major Lewis; Madam Herbert; W. Earle Welby; Earl of Montreath; David Digges La Touche jnr; Joseph Dimelo (carpenter); Montgomery Crothers (Dublin); Devall (stone mason); Charles Stanley; J. Rawlins; Thomas Oakes; Charles Knatchbull; George Stodart; Patrick Bride (Dublin); Hon. Hugh Howard (Dublin); Colonel Bridges; Lord Viscount Hawarden; Executors late Mrs Mary Clavell; Thomas Mann; Zachary Burton; Mrs Crofton; Rev. Mr Lowry; John Lyons; James Smart;

Obadiah Standert; John Dechever; Robert Brent; Robert Brown and Henry Methol.

It is not possible to detail all the accounts, nor even that of the Earl of Ormonde, whose Dublin account of 1794–95 alone came to £6,321 12s 8d. It included wages and expenses for a cm who travelled from London and spent nine weeks in Dublin fixing up furniture with the assistance of a local cm. The furniture was mainly of satinwood and mahogany and a great deal was painted, japanned and inlaid. It was designed in the French style although the accounts simply refer to items as 'French' whether they were designed and made in France (as presumably was the case with three French clocks, one costing £84 and two £52 10s, and 'a large French plate glass in white and gold with a beautiful painting of figures in a panel', £90) or whether they were designed and made in London. The overall colour scheme was white and gold as was that of the elegant main drawing room at the Duke of Leinster's imposing home, Leinster House, which was already furnished in 1794 and which Ormonde may have been trying to emulate. There is a small order for Leinster House in the Kennett & Kidd account book but there is no evidence to suggest that they furnished Leinster House.

The main furniture supplied to Ormonde included three carved white and gold cornices with bronzed eagles in the centre, £56 14s (for the main drawing room); two small 'French' sofas, richly carved in gold and white with 'very handsome' painted tablets in the backs, £40; two magnificent tripods 'beautifully designed and executed in the very first style of manufacture, richly carved and gilt in white and gold and elegantly ornamented . . . cut glass saucers with cut drops and gilt tassells for lights', £189 and a 'French' cabinet richly inlaid and ornamented with flowers, with a marble top and brass galleries, £63. The Kilkenny Castle account totalled £774 11s 2d, of which £525 was spent on one item which Kennett and Kidd rather boastfully described as 'A very Super Glass in Compartments to fill the whole end of Gallery at Kilkenny Castle with very magnificent ornaments, including your Coat of Arms . . . a beautiful painting of figures in Relief embroidered in a Tablet in the Centre . . . the whole forming the most Complete thing ever executed'. Many splendid Irish Georgian houses are now empty or bereft of their original furniture, as are large and small houses of the 1790s in England, and it has not yet proved possible to trace any of the furniture detailed in the account book, although research continues.

The partnership of Kennett and Kidd was not a happy one and was dissolved in October 1795. The entire stock and goods in trade were sold at a sale which lasted for seven days and raised over £3,850 while money and bills were received to the tune of £7,904. There were, however, outstanding debts, including one of £2,000 to Thomas Parlby, Kennett's father-in-law. The effects of the partnership were assigned to Trustees but, when no agreement was reached as to how to settle the partnership accounts, matters were referred to James Henderson, Upholsterer, Joseph Brown, Gentleman, and James Davidson, Accountant. When they finally decided that Kidd owed Kennett over £400, matters went to litigation. [PRO, C12 259/, 680/34 and 1736/2]

Although Kennett & Co. were listed in directories until 1799, the firm was dissolved in 1795, and there is no known work from Kennett after that date. He is listed in Holden's *Triennial Directory*, 1802–04 as an u at 4 Ranelagh Green, Chelsea, but in 1804 was referred to as a former u who was by then a tooth-ache curer! [*London Gazette*, 21–24 January 1804] He was declared bankrupt in 1804, with debts of over £3,000, mostly from when he worked as a furniture maker. His creditors were so convinced that he would not attempt to pay off his debts that in 1809 they threatened further litigation. Robert Kennett is last heard of in that year in litigation involving his son Henry, who had received money from the sale of his father's property but had not paid his creditors. Henry ended up in prison but refused to reveal his father's whereabouts lest he too be arrested.

The records of Kennett's bankruptcy case of 1803 indicate that he was indebted to persons who either worked for him or supplied him with goods for his trade. They included G. E. Woodhouse, Oxford St, linen draper; William Moore & Benjamin Millward, Oxford St, undertakers; Richard Ovey, Tavistock St, furniture printer; Cruis(?) Waring, Margaret St, carver and gilder; William Walker, Covent Gdn, cm; Alexander Cleland, Middlx Hospital, cm; Thomas Wakeman & Richard Jones, St Mildred's Ct, carpet manufacturers and Richard Dyer, Witney, Oxon., blanket weaver. [PRO, B3 2811A]

When William Kidd died in 1812 he was not in such dire circumstances as his former partner. One major creditor, namely Kennett's father-in-law, had refrained from harrassing Kidd during his lifetime in recognition of the part played by Kennett in his downfall. Kidd bought items from the partnership sale and continued to work as a furniture maker. He is listed in directories at 62 New Bond St until his death in 1812. He worked for Richard Griffin, 2nd Lord Braybrooke, at Audley End, Essex in 1801–02, and in 1803, the year in which he appeared in Sheraton's list of master cabinet makers, supplied a large amount of furniture to Castle Coole, Co. Fermanagh for the 1st Earl Belmore. He worked in partnership with his brother Joseph from about 1803–08 but by the latter date was in partnership with John Johnstone, whom he referred to as a partner when he made his will in 1808. After Kidd's death in 1812 [PRO, C13 160/33] Johnstone operated not from 62 New Bond St but from number 67, the former premises of Kennett & Kidd. [Chancery cases relating to Kennett & Kidd C114/18, C12 259/18, C12 680/34, C12 925/3, C12 1736/2, C12 160/33 and bankruptcy cases B3 522, B3 2811 A & B, B4/22]

BADMINTON HOUSE(?), Glos. (5th Duchess of Beaufort). 1781–82: Robert Kennett charged a total of £24 8s 9½d for 2 mahogany carved cabriole-leg chairs, 6 mahogany hall chairs with oval backs and crest and cypher, upholstery, etc. [Badminton archives, bills and receipts; the Duchess of Beaufort's red leather account bk]

AUDLEY END, Essex (Lord Howard de Walden). 1789–90: Robert Kennett's account for white and gold carved pole stands and frames totalled £10 5s. [Essex RO, D/DBy/A48/2]

GRAND LODGE OF FREEMASONS. 1791: Robert Kennett made the throne for the Prince of Wales and two Warden's Chairs at Freemasons Hall. [*Conn.*, July 1965]

CLIENTS of Kennet & Co. who spent more than £500, see text. [1792–95 Account Book, PRO, C114/18]

AUDLEY END, Essex (2nd Lord Braybrooke) 1801–11: Kidd and Kidd & Co. are named in the account bks for bills for furniture, etc.: in 1801 (£28 2s 8d); 1802 (£26 15s 8d); 1802 (£270 1s 10d); 1810 (£28 2s 8d) and 1811 (£175 8s. 8d). [Essex RO, D/DBy/A357 and A375]   P.K.

Kenning, W., James St, Devonport, Devon, cm (1814). [D]

Kenningham, Henry, Hull, Yorks., cm and u (1807–40). App. to William Robinson of Hull, cm, 1807. First listed in directories in 1826 at Dock Office Row with a residence at Graham's Row, Drypool. Drypool was the address given on the app. indenture records. His business premises at Dock Office Row were occupied through to 1840, the number being listed as 2, 1834–40. One directory of 1831 however lists an address of Witham. [D; Hull app. reg.]

Kennington, William, Bridge St, Brigg, Lincs., u and cm (1826–28). [D]

Kensell, Charles, 5 David St, Portman Sq., London, cm (1829). [D]

Kensett, E., 25 Nassau St, Soho, London, chair and sofa manufacturer (1822). [D]

Kensett, George, 102 Wardour St, London, chairmaker (1821). On 7 June 1821 took out insurance cover of £300, half of which covered stock and utensils in a workshop which contained a stove for drying feathers. [GL, Sun MS vol. 488]

Kensett, John, 25 Nassau St, Soho, London, chair and sofa manufacturer (1820). Succeeded by E. Kensett at this address. [D]

Kensett, T., 66 Mortimer St, Cavendish Sq., London, cm (1814). Succeeded by William Kensett at this address. [D]

Kensett, William, 66 Mortimer St, Cavendish Sq., London, chairmaker (1815–39). Later directory entries refer to him as a fancy chairmaker and in 1833 J.C. Loudon in his *Encyclopaedia* records him as having 'some curious specimens both of Elizabethan and more ancient furniture'. In addition to the sale of these 'antiques' he made a 'correct facsimilie of a chair taken from Tintern Abbey, and now in Troy House, Monmouthshire; and two other chairs from Glastonbury; one of which, called the abbot's chair, is of very elaborate workmanship'. He also maintained in Mortimer St a room fitted up with 'Elizabethan fragments' for client's inspection. [D]

Kent, Mrs, near the Conduit, Fore St, Exeter, Devon, cm and u (1766–80). Described as 'widow Kent' and probably the wife of Thomas Kent snr. Already trading by October 1766 when she was included in a list of persons from whom goods had been obtained by false pretences. Her stock in trade was sold by auction on 19 January 1780 and consisted of 'Four-post Bedsteads, with Moreen and other furniture. Mahogany tables, chairs, chests of drawers, wardrobes, bureaus etc.' [*Exeter Flying Post*, 17 October 1766, 12 December 1779]

Kent, Abbot, the Carpenters' Hall, 65 and 67 London Wall, London, u and cm (1769–c. 1810). Son of William Kent of Braintree, Essex, peruke maker. He was the brother of John Kent and the father of William Kent, both London upholsterers. Abbot Kent was app. to William Kent on 3 July 1760 and to Samuel Luck, shipwright on 4 September 1762. He was made free of the Upholders' Co. by servitude on 5 April 1769. In 1778 his address was given as Whitechapel but from 1781 at London Wall. From 1779 the business was conducted as a partnership with Samuel Luck, the son of the man he was apprenticed to. This partnership traded as Kent & Luck. He took as app. his son William, 1788–96, and by 1810 he had also joined the partnership. Alternative trading styles noted in this period are Kent, Luck & Kent, Kent & Co. and Kent & Sons. They claimed to be sole agents for the sale of Axminster Carpets and carpet manufacturers to Her Royal Highness the Princess of Wales and to the Duke of Kent. They undertook funerals and conducted appraisements. William Kent was recorded as a subscriber to Sheraton's *Drawing Book* in 1793, and the *Cabinet Dictionary* 1803, and Kent & Luck are included in the list of master cabinet makers in the latter publication. The firm was employed under the direction of Sir John Soane to make furniture for the Bank of England, and supplied Sir Thomas Baring with six hearthrugs on 20 December 1798 at a cost of £7 7s. Lady Ann Connolly was a customer in 1810. The exact date when Abbot Kent relinquished his interest in the firm is unknown but from c.1810 William Kent was probably the most active member of the family engaged in its affairs. [D; GL, Upholders' Co. records; Museum of London A22547; Heal; R.A. Woods, *English Furniture in the Bank of England*, p. 1]

Kent, Bartholomew, Side, Newcastle, u (b. 1727–d. 1803). App. to William Smith of Newcastle whose daughter he later married. After receiving his freedom traded in London and Bath, Som. for seven years. In 1755 returned to Newcastle to take over the business of William Smith, his father-in-law, on his death. He used his experience of the London trade to buy stock in the capital for his business. In June 1757 he advertised that he had returned from London with an assortment of paper hangings and in 1760 in addition to fresh supplies of these he had 'morines, harateens, cheneys, Turkey, Wilton and Scotch carpets, quilts, blankets'. By 1801 John Kent his nephew had joined him as a partner in the business but the arrangement was probably unsatisfactory as it was terminated by July of that year. Kent died in January 1803 aged 75 and the business was continued by his niece Elizabeth Willcox who was later partnered by her son, Bartholomew Kent Willcox. Bartholomew Kent took app. named Watson in 1761. Kent's name is recorded in the Strathmore papers, 1759–71, but the amounts paid out are very small, with the exception of an account for £9 3s in 1759. [D; *Newcastle Courant*, 7 June 1755, 18 June 1757, 25 July 1801, 29 January 1803; *Newcastle Journal*, 16–23 August 1760; Durham RO, D/ST/277, D/ST/v1510, D/ST/v995; S of G, app. index]

Kent, Edward, Gt Yarmouth, Norfolk, cm (1830). [Poll bk]

Kent, Gabriel, Exeter, Devon, cm (1760–61). In 1760 took apps named Bryant and King. In the following year took app. named Call. [S of G, app. index]

Kent, Jacob, Damgate St, Wymondham, Norfolk, cm and chairmaker (1830). [D]

Kent, John, Stoney Stratford, Bucks., chairmaker (1742). In 1742 took app. named Stephens. [S of G, app. index]

Kent, John, London, cm (1761–1802). Son of William Kent of Braintree, Essex, peruke maker. Brother of Abbot Kent. Free of the Upholders' Co., 1 October 1761 by redemption under the terms of the 1750 Upholders' Act. He appears to have followed the trade of cm however and from 1764–68 took out a series of licences to employ non-freemen. During this period the licences are continuous and involve permission for up to eight men. His address was given as Hounsditch, but in 1772 it was Whitechapel; from 1778–86 High St, Aldgate; in 1794 Freemans Ct, Cornhill and in 1802 Princess Sq. Took as apps George Brand, 1764–71, and Thomas Wilson, 1771–79. [GL, Upholders' Co. records; City Licence bks, vols 4–6]

Kent, Richard, Knutsford, Cheshire, u and paper hanger (1782–91). Employed by the 5th Earl of Warrington at Dunham Massey, Cheshire, 1784–91. On 5 November 1784 he was paid £75 3s for goods and work; and payments of £15 9s 6d on 23 September 1785, £39 8s 11d on 21 October 1787, £17 3s 8d on 18 December 1789 and £45 7s on 16 September 1791 followed. [D; *Apollo*, July 1978, p. 22]

Kent, Richard, St Bartholomew St, Newbury, Berks., chairmaker (1840). [D]

Kent, Robert, Drypool Sq., Mason St, Hull, Yorks., cm (1823–40). [D]

Kent, Samuel, 59 Westgate St, Newcastle, u, cm and furniture broker (1833–34). [D]

Kent, T., Knutsford, Cheshire, upholder (1782–84). [D]

Kent, Thomas snr, Exeter, Devon, cm (1716–66). In 1716 took app. named Laskey. Dead by 1766 when his widow was carrying on the business. [S of G, app. index; *Exeter Flying Post*, 17 October 1766] See Mrs Kent.

Kent, Thomas jnr, Fore St, Exeter, Devon, cm and u (1779–97). Kent had a substantial business, for as early as 1779 utensils and stock were insured for £850 and in December 1792 he was advertising for staff, requiring 'sawyers in the cabinet and chair line'. In July 1796 he was obliged to move from the premises that he was occupying in Fore St and as a consequence offered his stock in trade at reduced prices. This consisted of 'pier, swing glasses, mahogany dining, card & Pembroke tables, satinwood, mahogany and other chairs, inlaid sideboard tables'. He soon however re-established himself in Fore St and in September 1796 was advertising new and secondhand furniture. He, in common with others, always had secondhand goods available, and in June 1794 advertised a Kirkman harpsichord. The business was bankrupt by May 1797. [D; GL, Sun MS vol. 273, p. 521; *Exeter Flying Post*, 27 December 1792, 19 June 1794, 14 July 1796, 29 September 1796, 4 May 1797]

Kent, Thomas, Dudley St, Wolverhampton, Staffs., u (1770). [D]

Kent, Thomas, 10 Albemarle St, Clerkenwell, London, looking-glass manufacturer (1820). [D]

Kent, Thomas, 28 Charles St, Middlx Hospital, London, cm, u and broker (1826–35). [D]

Kent, Thomas, Newcastle, u and cm (1824–27). In June 1824 announced that he had commenced trading from 'the commodious WARE ROOMS lately occupied by MR. JOSEPH FELL, AUCTIONEER, FOOT OF DEAN STREET'. His stock consisted of 'Brussels & Kidderminster Carpeting, Hearth Rugs, Oil Cloths, Moreen & Chintz Hangings, Fringes, Feathers, Bed Ticks & Paper Hangings; also a large variety of Cabinet Goods, of excellent patterns & workmanship, consisting of Sideboards, Sofas, Dining, Card & Loo Tables, Chests of Drawers, Pole & Camp Bedsteads, Chimney & Dressing Glasses etc.' In 1834 shown at 89 Side with a house at Spital Tongue. [D; *Durham County Advertiser*, 19 June 1824]

Kent, William, Exeter, Devon, cm (b. 1704–d. 1785). Died in November 1785 aged 81. He had recently retired from the trade and was said to have been in business 'more than fifty years'. The size of the business is difficult to ascertain but already in the late 1740s William Kent owned property in the city including houses tenanted to others. [*Exeter Flying Post*, 1 December 1785; GL, Sun MS vol. 76, ref. 105246; vol. 85, ref. 115855]

Kent, William, 'The Black Lion & Tent', opposite the Church wall in Hounsditch, London, upholder and cm (1760–61). Son of William Kent of Sussex, yeoman. App. to William Marston on 31 January 1752 and then to Thomas Ridgeway, a member of the Skinners' Co., 6 January 1756. Free of the Upholders' Co. by servitude, 3 January 1760. Recorded in the next year employing a non-freeman for six months under licence. His trade card [Leverhulme Coll., MMA, NY] states that he made and sold 'Four Post & other Bedsteads, with Damask Morine, Harrateen, and Washing Furnitures, Feather Beds, Blankets, Quilts & Counterpains, fine Turkey & English Carpets, Variety of Mohogany and Wallnut-Tree Chests of Drawers, Book Cases, Chairs, Tables and Looking Glasses &c'. He also acted as an undertaker, appraiser and estate agent. [GL, Upholders' Co. records; City Licence bk, vol. 2]

Kent, William, Hull, Yorks., cm (1768–84). [Poll bks]

Kent, William, Carpenter's Hall, 67 London Wall, London, u and cm (c. 1810–21). Son of Abbot Kent and app. to him on 1 October 1788. Free of the Upholders' Co. by servitude, 6 July 1796 and probably entered the service of Kent & Luck immediately after. He was recognised as a partner by 1810 and from about this date took over his father's responsibilities in the firm. By 1820 however he is shown trading on his own behalf from the London Wall address in directories. An advertisement placed by William Kent in the *Times* in July 1821 however shows that this is misleading. He was in fact still in partnership with Samuel Luck, and also another brother who was probably Samuel. William Kent appears to have been responsible for the cabinet making and upholstery side of the business while Samuel Luck and Samuel Kent were responsible for the carpet warehouse which had always been an important feature of the firm's trade. In July 1821 William Kent made a decision to retire and as a consequence the stock of 'mahogany and rosewood furniture, four post bedsteads with chintz and other hangings, best seasoned goose feathers &c.' was sold off at reduced prices. The carpet warehouse was continued from the London Wall address and appears in subsequent directories. Despite the announcement of William Kent's retirement from the business the insurance effected on 5 November 1821 to cover stock valued at £1,400 was in the name of William Kent of Clapton, upholder. Associated with him in the policy was Samuel Luck described as of 'Carpenters Hall' and William Pearson of London Wall. No commissions of importance are recorded for this period though Kent & Luck are listed amongst the creditors of Zachariah Button Esq. deceased of Belmont Castle, Essex. The invoice in question was dated 1 November 1815 and was for £5 1s for carpets. [D; GL, Upholders' Co. records; *Times*, 6 July 1821; PRO, C13 283/34]

Kent, Tomkins & Williams, 67 London Wall, London, carpet, upholstery and cabinet warehouse (1812–17). Listed by Heal. Would appear to have a connection with the partnership of William Kent and Samuel Luck who traded from this address between the same dates.

Kenton, John, Guys Ct, Westminster, London, chairmaker (1749). [Poll bk]

Kenwood, James, Gentle St, Frome, Som., cm (1830–39). [D]

Kenwood, John, Frome, Som., cm and u (1822–40). Trading at Bath St in 1822 and Gentle St in 1840. [D]

Kenwood, William, Silver St, Ottery St Mary, Devon, cm (1830). [D]

Kenworthy, J. B., 13 Dale St, Manchester, carver and gilder (1818). [D]

Kenworthy, Joseph Brook, Ellis St, Birmingham, carver and gilder (1828–30). Recorded at no. 22 in 1828. [D]

Kenyon, John, Liverpool, cm (1768). App. to Joseph Brown and petitioned freedom in 1768. [Freemen's committee bk]

Kenyon, William, Liverpool, carver and gilder (1827). App. to William Cashen and free 18 September 1827. Recorded at Rose Pl. and St George's Pl., Leece St. [Freemen reg.]

Kerbs, Christian, address unknown, cm (1803). Subscribed to Sheraton's *Cabinet Dictionary*, 1803.

Kerby, —, 55 New Oxford St, London (early 19th century). Late Georgian simulated rosewood writing table stamped 'Kerby 55 New Oxford St.' included in Christie's sale, 24 November 1977, lot 51.

Kerby, Richard, Sackville St, London, cm and u (1756–66). In 1763 the lease for the building in Sackville St was taken jointly by Kerby and John Swale who may have been a partner at this date. Kerby supplied furniture to a number of influential patrons. In January 1756 he supplied Wilton carpeting and a mahogany night table to Dumfries House, Scotland, which, together with other items, came to £15 8s 6d. In the years 1758–59 he supplied an oval mahogany cistern, a black inkstand and undertook some gilding at Temple Newsam House, Leeds. A small sum of £1 16s 2d is recorded as being paid to this maker in August 1766 for mahogany used on work at Burlington House for the Duke of Portland. [D; Lincoln RO, NEL X 6/1; *Furn. Hist.*, 1967; Notts. RO, DDSP 3/1]

Kerfoot, Daniel, Liverpool, cm (1761). Free 9 February 1761. [Freemen reg.]

Kerfoot, John, Chorley, Lancs., joiner and cm (1793). [D]

Kerfoot, Richard, Chorley, Lancs., joiner and cm (1793). [D]

Kerfoot, Richard, Liverpool, cm (1804–39). In 1804 shown at 9 Thurlow St, Richmond Row, and in the next year at 4 Shaw's Brow. He then moved to Shelhorne St where he was at no. 4 in 1807 and no. 8, 1810–11. In 1821 the address was 1 Duncan Pl., Duncan St East, and in 1824 2 Duncan Pl. is shown to be his house. He also had a shop at 8 Albion St, 1823–24. After 1827 all addresses given are in Christian St, the numbers being 61 in 1827, 67 in 1829, 65 in 1834–35 and 48 in 1839. [D]

Kerr, Benjamin, 28 Clifton St North, Finsbury, London, u (1835–39). [D]

Kerr, George, 14 Brownlow Hill, Liverpool, cm (1839). [D]

Kerr, J., Orford St, Norwich, cm, u and chairmaker (1822). [D]

Kerr, J., address unknown, cm (1803). Subscribed to Sheraton's *Cabinet Dictionary*, 1803.

Kerr, James, Norwich, cm and u (1822–36). In St Giles in 1822 and Distillery St in 1836. [D]

Kerr, James, 20½ Clipstone St, Fitzroy Sq., London, chair and sofa manufacturer, glass and emery paper maker (1835). [D]

Kerr, John, 31 Pall Mall, London, cm and u (1790–1808). A subscriber to Sheraton's *Drawing Book*, 1793 and *Cabinet Dictionary*, 1803. A number of substantial commissions undertaken by this maker are known. On 5 April 1790 he was paid £400 on account for furniture supplied to the Royal Household, and a balance of £172 5s 3d on 5 July. On 10 October 1791 a further sum of £178 5s 3d was paid and this appears to have been for furniture supplied 1789–90. This consisted of a mahogany writing table with fifteen drawers and two cupboards charged at £22 1s and a satinwood one at £16 9s. A large mahogany table and a dining table were invoiced at £7 17s 6d each, and an elegant satinwood wardrobe added a further £25. Also included in this payment appears to have been a bill for £72 11s 6d for furniture supplied to Mrs Fitzherbert which Henry Holland, the Prince of Wales's architect, had an interest in. The Henry Holland connection is also represented in the furniture supplied to Woburn Abbey, Beds., and Oakley House for Francis, 5th Duke of Bedford between 1791–95. The furniture supplied to Woburn in the first two months of 1791 cost £83 8s and included five mahogany shaving tables, five night tables and a mahogany writing table of fifteen drawers and two cupboards possibly similar to that supplied in 1789 to the Royal Household. Between December 1791 and September 1792 two fire screens, two dining tables and six shaving tables went to Woburn and chairs, tables and curtains to Oakley. Payment passed through Holland for this commission was £148. In 1795 an extra large set of mahogany dining tables were delivered to Woburn at a cost of £52. Sir John Nelthorpe purchased a large mahogany table from Kerr in 1796 for £7 7s and in the next year a dining table at £10 10s, his existing one being taken in part exchange. Petworth House, Sussex was supplied with a set of dining chairs covered in red morocco leather in 1801 and these are now displayed in the Square Dining Room. [D; Windsor Royal Archives, RA 88751, 88756, 88798, 25091; Bedford Office, London; Lincoln RO, NEL 9/19/57,58, NEL 9/18/38; Nat. Trust Guide to *Petworth*] B.A.

Kerridge, John, Exeter, Devon, cm and u (1838–40). His trade address was North Bridge St but he had a residence at St David's Hill. His son John Webber was bapt. on 27 December 1838 and his daughter Elizabeth Frances on 27 October 1839. [D; PR(bapt.)]

Kerrington, Richard, London, upholder (1708–20). Son of Richard Kerrington of Glensford, Suffolk, clerk. Brother to Robert Kerrington, also a London upholder. Richard Kerrington was app. to James Gronous on 14 February 1708 and free of the Upholders' Co. by servitude, 3 August 1720. A maker by this surname working at 'The Boar's Head' within Aldgate in 1731 may be either Richard or Robert. [GL, Upholders' Co. records; Heal]

Kerrington, Robert, London, upholder (1706–14). Son of Richard Kerrington of Suffolk and brother to Richard Kerrington, another London upholder. App. to Thomas S[?]holl, in trust for Samuel Parkes, draper on 21 June 1706 and free of the Upholders' Co. by servitude, 6 October 1714. A maker with the same surname working at 'The Boar's Head' within Aldgate in 1731 may be either Richard or Robert. [GL, Upholders' Co. records; Heal]

Kerrison, Peter, 184 Wapping, London, cm (1781). In 1781 took out insurance cover of £500 of which £300 was in respect of utensils and stock. [GL, Sun MS vol. 192, p. 528]

Kerry, —, Evesham, Worcs., chairmaker (early 19th century). A chair impressed 'KERRY EVESHAM 1808' has been recorded and another ladder back chair, [Temple Newsam House, Leeds] is impressed 'KERRY'. Possibly:

Kerry, John, High St, Evesham, Worcs., cm, u and broker (1840). [D]

Kerry, John, Norwich, cm and chairmaker (1819–40). Free 1819 and in 1822 trading at Fishgate St. In 1830 the address was St Edmund St and from 1836 Lower Westwick St. On 20 June 1831 his app. cm, John Bailey jnr, was made free and on 3 May 1826 William Quilley, another app. cm who had served both C. Jones and John Kerry was made free. [D; freemen reg.]

Kershaw, Charles, Market Pl., Northampton, u (1830). [D]

Kershaw, Thomas, Egerton St, Hulme, Manchester, chairmaker (1817). [D]

Kerwmock, Alexander, address unknown, cm (1803). Subscribed to Sheraton's *Cabinet Dictionary*, 1803.

Keston, William, Lewes, Sussex, cm (1758). Took app. in 1758 named Miles. [S of G, app. index]

Kett, Jacob, Damgate St, Wymondham, Norfolk, cm (1822–39). [D]

Ketterich, Thomas, Corner of Fleetbridge, parish of St Bride, London, u (1714). [GL, Sun MS vol. 3, ref. 3705]

Kettle, Henry, St Paul's Churchyard, London, cm, upholder and undertaker (c. 1773–97). A member of the Brewers' Co. though there is no evidence that he practiced this trade. Partner with William Henshaw from c. 1770 and subsequently his successor trading at 18 St Paul's Churchyard. In 1774 took over the business of Philip Bell at 23 St Paul's Churchyard and thereafter appears to have centred his business at this address. Took out licences to employ non-freemen 1778–81. In 1793 subscribed to Sheraton's *Drawing Book*.

Used his trade label to identify productions. The collection at Saltram House, Devon contains two items so marked. One is a mahogany secretaire bookcase with three long drawers beneath the secretaire drawer. Carved paterae and swags are featured on the frieze of the bookcase section. The other item is a fine Pembroke table in satinwood inlaid with kingwood and incorporating panels of mahogany. A further Pembroke table without a label also appears to be Kettle's work. The label in the drawer of the first Pembroke table gives the address at 18 St Paul's Churchyard and was probably produced in the early years of Kettle's sole control of the business. The bills of 1796–97 at Saltram are headed 'Oakley & Kettle' suggesting a short-lived partnership with George Oakley at this period. Other pieces of furniture noted with labels include a bureau bookcase, chests of drawers including ones with shaped fronts, a wardrobe, tables with drawers beneath, Pembroke tables and dwarf bookcase. These are mostly in mahogany, some with boxwood stringing and crossbanded but the use of satinwood was also a feature of some of his furniture.

Apart from the items at Saltram which were probably purchased new by the Parker family, other commissions for country landowners are known. The notebook of Edward Knight of Wolverley House, Worcs. records the payment of £3 13s 6d to Kettle on 6 July 1780 for a writing desk. On 18 July 1781 a bookcase was invoiced for Burton Constable, Yorks. costing £11 11s, while Ralph Leake of Longford Hall, Salop patronized the firm in 1793. [D; Heal; V & A archives; GL, City Licence bks, vols 9, 10; Nat. Trust, *The Saltram Collection*, p. 51; *Furn. Hist.*, 1966; *C. Life*, 16 August 1962, p. 351; 7 November 1974, p. 163; *Conn.*, April 1968; January 1976, pp. 25, 29; Christie's S. Kensington, 14 October 1982; Kidderminster Lib., Knight MS; Burton Constable vouchers]   B.A.

Kettle, James, parish of St Julian, Norwich, cm (1806). [Poll bk]

Kettle, John, Chester, joiner, carver and turner (1660). [Freemen rolls]

Kew, George, 'Royal Oak', Catton, Norfolk, cm and victualler (1834–36). App. to Joseph Bexfield of Norwich and free, 3 May 1834. [D; freemen reg.]

Kew, John, Spring Gdns, Northampton, cm (1830). [D]

Kewley, John, Suffolk St, Liverpool, cm (1837–39). At 8 Suffolk St in 1837 and 15 in 1839. In the latter year he also had a shop at 11 Forest St. [D]

Kewley, John, 8 or 6 Angel St, St George's Rd, Manchester, cm (1840). [D]

Key, Benjamin, London, upholder (1725–36). Son of William Key of Hackney, London, mason. App. to Joseph Welsh 7 July 1725 and free of the Upholders' Co. by servitude, 3 November 1736. [GL, Upholders' Co. records]

Key, George, 74 Lower Grosvenor St, London, u etc. (1808–35). [D]

Key, James, address unknown, cm (1788). On 30 October 1788 George Cooke paid £15 19s to Key for writing desks supplied to Dunham Massey, Cheshire. In November of the same year payment of £21 8s 6d was made for 'materials & work in Lord Greys appartment'. [John Rylands Lib., Manchester Univ., George Cooke's accounts]

Key, John, Chester, cm (1784). App. to John Croughton of Chester, cm and free 31 March 1784. [Freemen rolls]

Key, John, Lincoln, cm (d. 1799). Death announced, *Gents Mag.*, September 1799. Said to have died 'in the prime of life'.

Key, Joseph, 18 Lower Brook St, London, upholder and house agent (1825–39). [D]

Key, Thomas, Eynesbury, St Neots, Hunts., cm (1830). [D]

Key, William, 77 Marylebone High St, London, broker and cm (1810). On 9 January 1810 took out insurance cover for £2,000 of which £750 was for his dwelling house with work room and workshop and £1,100 for stock, utensils and goods in trust. [GL, Sun MS vol. 453]

Keybold, Edward, address unknown, chairmaker (1725). In 1725 he was paid £1 7s for chairs supplied to Stowe, Bucks. [Huntington Lib., California, Stowe MS ST 82 p. 184]

Keylock, John, 11 Hatton St, London, looking-glass manufacturer (1780–89). In 1780 insured a house for £300. [GL, Sun MS vol. 285, p. 126]

Keymer, Samuel, London, upholder (1706). Free of the Upholders' Co., 15 October 1706. [GL, Upholders' Co. records]

Keynes, William, Salisbury, Wilts., cm and u (1822–39). Recorded at Castle St in 1822, St John St in 1830 and in 1839 as Keynes & Son. [D]

Keys, James, Chelmsford, Essex, u (1765). Bankruptcy announced in *Gents Mag.*, May 1765.

Keys, John, Chelmsford, Essex, upholder (1768). [Essex RO, Q/SMg 20]

Keys, Michael, Long Row, Nottingham, u, cm and joiner (1781). In 1781 took out insurance cover of £1,300 of which £800 was in respect of utensils and stock. [GL, Sun MS vol. 299, p. 41]

Keys, Philip, 'The Golden Key', opposite Berwick St, Oxford St, London, upholders and cm (1752–54). In both 1752 and 1754 took out insurance cover of £1,000. He had a timber store, warehouse and two workshops behind his dwelling house and also used the house immediately to the east of his dwelling house for stock which was said to be mainly 'Grocery & chandlery goods'. Most of the sum insured was for premises and stock used in his business. [GL, Sun MS vol. 95, ref. 129900; vol. 105, ref. 140289]

Keys, Richard, Hampstead, London, u (1724). Took out insurance cover of £500 on his dwelling house. [GL, Sun MS vol. 19, ref. 34143]

Ketye, John, Kidderminster, Worcs., builder and u (1802). Insolvent and dividend declared, *Billinge's Liverpool Advertiser*, 31 May 1802.

Keyte, Richard, Windsor St, Uxbridge, Middlx, Windsor chairmaker (1826). [D]

Keyte, William, Rugeley, Staffs., cm and u (1828–35). Recorded at Market St in 1834 and Market Pl. in 1835. [D]

Kibble, John, Liverpool, u (1785–d. 1794). In June 1785 announced the opening of his shop at 57 Castle St. He claimed to have been employed for many years by the leading shops in London and had worked at Carlton House and for the 'Duke of Grafton, Duke of Queensborough and the Marquis of Lonsdale' at this period. The business was probably of modest size, the utensils and stock being insured for £400 in June 1791. He died in 1794 and at that time was trading from Marshall St and 49 Lord St. Attempts were made to sell his stock as a whole in May 1794 but this was only partially successful and the residue was offered without reserve to the public for two weeks in August 1794. [D; GL, Sun MS vol. 376, p. 638; *Williamson's Liverpool Advertiser*, 16 June 1785, 5 March 1794, 12 May 1794, 18 August 1794]

Kibblewhite, James, Goodramgate, York, cm (1779–84). Son of John Kibblewhite, cm, and free 1779. [Freemen rolls; poll bk]

Kibblewhite, John, York, cm (c. 1770). Father of James Kibblewhite who was free as a cm in 1779. [Freemen rolls]

Kiberd, George, 36 Skinner St, Bishopsgate, London, cm and chairmaker (1820). In May 1830 took out insurance cover of £350 which included £200 for stock and utensils. [GL, Sun MS vol. 484, ref. 968152]

Kibler, William, Castle St, Warwick, cm (1828–31). [D; poll bk]

Kidd, David, Mastyard (or Mart Yd), Gainsborough, Lincs., cm and u (1822). [D]

Kidd, Joseph, Newcastle, u (1765). App. to George West and free 7 October 1765. [Freemen reg.]

Kidd, William & Co., see Robert Kennett.

Kidder, Thomas, Canterbury, Kent, cm (1765). [Freemen rolls]

Kiddle, Charles, North Walsham, Norfolk, cm and u (1822). [D]

Kiddle, George, Market Pl., North Walsham, Norfolk, cm and u (1830). [D]

Kiddle, George, Castle Acre St, Swaffham, Norfolk, cm and u (1836–39). [D]

Kiddle, John, Puddletown, Dorset, cm (1820). His will dated 1820 left everything to his children John and Jane. John Kiddle snr may perhaps be identified with the person of that name who was app. to James Begbie, cm of Salisbury on 2 February 1757 for six years at a premium of £26 5s. [Dorset, RO, DA/W/1820/49; *Wilts. Apps and their Masters*]

Kidson, John, 47 Baldwin St, Bristol, cm (1774–81). At Baldwin St in 1775 and in 1781 in the parish of St James. [D; poll bks]

Kidson, John, Lamb St, Bristol, cm (*c.* 1760). The following label recorded on a longcase clock of about 1760 (the movement by Bilbie of Axbridge):

JOHN KIDSON,
CABINETMAKER
LIVING IN LAMB STREET,
at the sign of the
CLOCK-CASE & STAR, near THE WHITE HART,
WITHOUT LAWFORD'S GATE BRISTOL
makes and sells all sorts of
CABINET GOODS CHEAP.
FOR THE SAKE OF READY MONEY
There are none shall exceed me
For cheapness and Goodness of Goods.
Likewise
I will always keep them in order for any family, except any
Damage happen thro' careless or wilful Abuse.
Any
Gentlemen, Merchants, Captains, Mates or Boat-
swains, or any other Persons, that have any
MAHOGANY or VIRGINIA WALNUT,
May have it made into any sort of Goods
To their advantage, or Exchanged for Goods.
☞ I will endeavour to give them such Satisfaction, that they will not have any Reason to say, it is Cheaper to buy out of the shops

Kidston, Charles, 5 Leadenhall St, London, u (1811–25). Thomas Kidson, u, is shown at this address in 1809 and one directory lists William Kidson in 1812. [D]

Kidston, James, 1 Slater St, Bethnal Green, London, cm (1804–09). In November 1807 an address at 77 Brick Lane is shown in use. Insurance cover taken out was £700 in 1804 and 1807 but it was increased to £800 in the following year. A large proportion of this was in respect of property in Slater St and Brick Lane mostly in tenure. Cover for utensils and stock in trade was modest being £100 in 1807 and £150 in the following year. [D; GL Sun MS vol. 430, ref. 757654; vol. 442, ref. 809856; vol. 446, ref. 823668]

Kidston, James, Sidney St, Mile End, London, cm and u (1839). [D]

Kidston, T., 77 Brick Lane, Spitalfields, London, cm (1808). This address appears to have been in use by James Kidston in the same period for he took out insurance on the property on 20 November 1807. [D; GL, Sun MS vol. 442, ref. 809856]

Kidston, Thomas, 5 Leadenhall St, London, upholder, appraiser and cm (1809–35). One directory shows Charles Kidston at this address, 1811–25. [D]

Kidston, William, 5 Leadenhall St, London, u (1812–15). Charles Kidston and Thomas Kidston are also shown at this address in some London directories during this period. [D]

Kidwell, Cole, High St, Rochester, Kent, cm (1811–26). Robert Kidwell was at the same address in 1826. [D]

Kidwell, J., Rochester, Kent, cm (1807). A Rochester poll bk for August 1830 shows a John Kidwell, u, living in London. [Poll bk]

Kidwell, John, 88 Wimpole St, Cavendish Sq., London, upholder and cm (1778–92). In 1778 insured his house for £500 but no cover taken out for trade stock. His trade card [Banks Coll., BM, dated 1792, and Leverhulme Coll., MMA, NY], states that he made 'Four Post Bedsteads, with Drapery & other Furniture, Desks & Book Cases, Chairs, Soffas, Tables, Glasses, Venetian & Spring Blinds &c.'. Household goods were bought, sold, appraised and exchanged, funerals undertaken and paper hangings stocked. [GL, Sun MS vol. 262, p. 482]

Kidwell, John, 427 Oxford St, London, cm, u and undertaker (1817–27). Shown using 428 Oxford St in addition in a directory of 1817. May be the John Kidwell, freeman of Rochester Kent, who is shown in that town in 1807 but by August 1830 was living in London. [D; Rochester poll bk]

Kidwell, Robert, Rochester, Kent, cm and furniture maker (1823–39). In 1823 at Free School Lane but from 1826 most directories list him in High St. One of 1832 however gives the address as Eastgate. [D]

Kier, John, St Giles Fields, London, cm (1754–60). Subscribed to Chippendale's *Director*, 1754. In 1756 took app. named Aaron Cross at a premium of £18 18s when his address was listed as Brownlow St. Took another app. in 1760. [S of G, app. index]

Kilberd, George, 82 Curtain Rd, London, chair and sofa maker (1827). [D]

Kilbourn, John, Sheep Mkt, Market Harborough, Leics., cm and u (1835). [D]

Kilburn, John, Kettinging Rd, Market Harborough, Leics., cm (1835). [D]

Kilburn, Thomas, 186 St John's St, Clerkenwell, London, cm and u (1763–89). On 7 December 1774 insured his dwelling house and business premises for £800. These were said to be 'two houses laid into one & warehouse communicating'. [D; Heal; GL, Sun MS vol. 235, ref. 347213]

Kilgour, James, 13 Gt St Mary's Buildings, St Martin's Lane, London, u (1809). [D]

Kilham, Thomas, 4 Exeter St, London, carver (1784). In 1784 insured his house for £100. [GL, Sun MS vol. 322, p. 294]

Killeck, William, Guildford, Surrey, u, joiner and cm (1784–94). [D]

Killick, John, 32 King St, Smithfield, London, carver (1790). [D]

Killick, William, Dorking, Surrey, u (1811). [D]

Killingley, Edward, Nottingham, joiner and cm (1826). [Nottinham freemen rolls]

Killingley, James, 237 High Holborn, London, upholder and broker (1784). In 1784 took out insurance cover of £500 of which stock and goods in trust accounted for £400. [GL, Sun MS vol. 322, p. 453]

Killingley, Joseph, Nottingham, cm (1781–1803). Son of John W. Killingley, cordwainer of Castle Donnington, Leics. Taken as app. in 1781. Shown as a freeman of Nottingham in 1803. [Nottingham app. bk and freemen rolls]

Killingley, Thomas, parish of St Mary-le-Strand, London, upholder (1771). Son of Thomas Killingley of the parish of St Sepulchre, London, oilman. App. to Thomas Burnett of the Merchant Tailors' Co. and admitted to the Upholders' Co. by servitude, 3 July 1771. [GL, Upholders' Co. records]

Killingworth, J., address unknown, cm (1803). Subscribed to Sheraton's *Cabinet Dictionary*, 1803.

Kilminster, Matthew, Union Pl., Brighton, Sussex, cm (1839). [D]

Kilmister, Matthew, 3 Upper Maudlin St, Bristol, cm and Venetian blind maker (1832). [D]

Kilner, J. jnr, Lancaster, carver (1809–13). Named in Gillow records. The library bookcases at Tatton Park, Cheshire, were carved by Kilner. [Westminster Ref. Lib., Gillow, vol. 344/99, pp. 1866, 1933]

Kilner, John, Lancaster (1786–1825). Named in the Gillow records 1786–89, 1791–92, 1794, 1797–1805, 1812 and 1825. [Westminster Ref. Lib., Gillow]

Kilner, John, Preston, Lancs., cm (1828–34). At Paul St in 1828 and 121 Church St in 1834. [D] See William Kilner.

Kilner, Thomas, 11 Minsprit Wiend, Preston, Lancs., chair-maker (1818). [D]

Kilner, Thomas Earl, Lancaster, cm and carver (1818–27). App. to L. Redmayne in 1818 and free, 1824–25. Named in the Gillow records as a carver 1825 and 1827. [App. reg.; freemen reg.; Westminster Ref. Lib., Gillow]

Kilner, W., 27 North Audley St, Grosvenor Sq., London, u (1835). [D]

Kilner, William, St John's St, Preston, Lancs., chairmaker (1816–34). At 13 St John's St, 1816–28, but in 1834 the number had changed to 15. Trading in partnership with John Kilner in 1822. [D]

Kiloh, —, 18 Air St, Golden Sq., London, cm (1793). Subscribed to Sheraton's *Drawing Book*, 1793.

Kilpin, Joseph, High St, St Mary's, Bedford, u, cm, appraiser and paper hanger (1823–30). Between 1823–28 submitted seven accounts to John Gibbard Esq., of Sharnbrook near Bedford for work undertaken, and goods supplied. Repairs to furniture and the supply of upholstery materials constitute the main items but some new furniture was supplied, such as on 5 October 1824 'mahogany music stool covered with leather and French-stuffed' at £2 12s. [D; Beds. RO, GA66]

Kilpin, William, Mark Lane, London, upholder (1725–d. 1762). Son of Charles Kilpin of Hardingstone, Northants., yeoman. App. to George Friend on 5 May 1725 and free of the Upholders' Co. by servitude, 6 March 1733/34. In 1754 undertook upholstery work for Lord Folkestone's Gallery, Longford Castle, Wilts. for which £125 was charged. Insolvent by November 1759 and died in 1762. [GL, Upholders' Co. records; Heal; *Williamson's Liverpool Advertiser*, 2 November 1759]

Kilpin, William, Bedford, u and broker (1784–85). [D]

Kilrington, —, address unknown, cm (1803). Subscribed to Sheraton's *Cabinet Dictionary*, 1803.

Kilshaw, James, Liverpool, cm (1749). Free 2 March 1749. [Freemen reg.]

Kilvington, Israel, 9 Newman Mews, Castle St East, Oxford Mkt and 102 Norton St, Marylebone, London, cm (1820). On 9 March 1820 took out insurance cover of £500 on utensils, stock and goods in trust in workshops at Newman's Mews. A new policy taken out in May raised this cover to £1,000 with an additional £100 cover for such items at his dwelling house in Norton St. Household goods at Norton St were insured for a mere £200. [GL, Sun MS vol. 483, refs 964084, 966658]

Kilvington, John & Sons, 102 Norton St, Portland Pl., London, cm (1820–39). Successors to Israel Kilvington at the same address. [D]

Kimberley, Jesse, Birmingham, cm, u and chairmaker (1828–39). Trading at 24 Worcester St in 1828 and 15 Hurst St, 1835–39. [D]

Kimberley, Joseph, Church St, Bilston, Staffs., cm and u (1830). [D]

Kimberley, William, Windsor, Berks., upholder, appraiser and auctioneer (1807). In 1810 indebted to Catherine Tidersley, widow, of Vine St, Westminster, for the proceeds of some furniture disposed of on her behalf in 1807. Said to be late of Windsor. [PRO, C13/122/31]

Kimmins, Thomas, 61 Pembroke St, Devonport, Devon, cm (1830). Successor to William Kimmins at this address. [D]

Kimmins, William, Devonport, Devon, cm (1822–30). Shown at Pembroke St in 1822 and at 62 Pembroke St in 1830, but one directory of 1823 gives his address as 19 George St. This may be a failure to correct an address following a move. Succeeded by Thomas Kimmins in 1830. [D]

Kimpton, Daniel, address unknown, cm (1803). Subscribed to Sheraton's *Cabinet Dictionary*, 1803.

Kimpton, John Hanyan & Son, Fore St, Hertford, cm and u (1823–39). Trading at Fore St, 1826–39, in 1838 also as auctioneers and surveyors. [D]

Kimpton, William, Hertford(?), chairmaker (1792). In 1792 supplied two wood bottom chairs at 16s and twelve leather bottom chairs at £3 6s to Panshanger, Herts. [Herts. RO, Panshanger accounts, box 44 D/EP]

Kimpton, William, 41 London Rd, St George's Fields, London, cm (1817). [D]

Kinaston, —, Shrewsbury, Salop, carver (1798). [D]

Kincey, T., 42 Bishopsgate Within and 213 Whitechapel Rd, London, couch manufacturer etc. (1825). [D]

Kindell, John, Liverpool, cm (1787–1805). Traded at Marshall St, 1787–95, the number being given as 2 in 1790. In 1790 one directory gives an alternative address in Cable St. By June 1795 the business was insolvent and on 11 June a meeting of the creditors was called at the 'Star and Garter Tavern' in Paradise St. This resulted in a formal declaration of bankruptcy in November of the same year. By 1800 however he was back in business as a cm and victualler at Cooper's Row, Old Dock, the number being given as 3 in 1804. Kindell may have attained some status as spokesman for the Liverpool furniture makers, for in March 1805 he advertised in *Liverpool Chronicle* denouncing the demands of the journeymen of the city. They had not only produced a new *Chair Book of Prices*, but also wanted the adoption of a supplement to the cabinet prices. The employers estimated the advance in rates to be about 10% and these they rejected as being higher than those currently on offer in London. Kindell indicated that the employers were prepared to advance some rates to London levels, but rejected the demand as a whole. Public support for the employers' stand was asked and Kindell indicated that 'Men wanting employment will meet every encouragement at the above prices the Masters have offered, by application' to himself. [D; *Billinge's Liverpool Advertiser*, 8 June 1795, 30 November 1795, 2 July 1798; *Liverpool Chronicle*, 27 March 1805]

Kindley, William, London, trunk, cabinet, case and portable desk maker (1776–1825). In 1776 at 30 Green Arbor Ct, Little Old Bailey where he took out insurance cover of £300 of which £200 was in respect of utensils and stock. By December 1785 he was at 78 Watling St and insurance cover had increased to £700 of which £500 was for utensils, stock and goods in trust. He was declared bankrupt in 1789 at which date he was at 28 Bridge Row, Cannon St. He was however soon back in business and in 1790 is shown at 3 Gt Carter Lane. From 1806 15 Horseshoe Ct, Ludgate Hill became the address of this maker, and in this year business is listed as William Kindley & Son. In the period 1809–11 the style Kinley & Slades was adopted. From 1819 the trade is simply given as cm. [D; GL, Sun MS vol. 249, ref. 370491; vol. 335, p. 67; Bailey's list of bankrupts]

Kindon, G. & Co., Thomas St, Bristol, cm (1805–06). [D]

Kindon, Henry, Bristol, basket and chairmaker (1825–30). At 12 Redcliffe St in 1825 and 25 Peter St in 1830. [D]

Kindon, James, Market St, Leicester, u, appraiser and auctioneer (1775). In 1775 announced the opening of the business in Market St. [*Leicester Journal*, 8 April 1775]

Kindred, Phineas, Halesworth, Suffolk, cm (1794). Married in 1794. [Suffolk RO, FAA: 50/2/109]

King, —, 'The Black Lyon', Cambridge St, by Broad St, St James's, London, u (1727). [Heal]

King, —, 'The King & Queen', Bicester, Oxon., chair frame maker (1736). On 14 July 1736 Elizabeth Purefoy wrote to a Mr King of Bicester, 'As I understand you make chairs of wallnut tree frames with 4 legs without Barrs for Mr. Vaux of Caversfield, if you do such I desire you will come over here in a week's time any morning but Wednesday. I shall want about 20 chairs'. [Eland, *Purefoy Letters*, vol. 1, no. 165]

King, —, Chapel St, Mayfair, London, cm (1793). Subscribed to Sheraton's *Drawing Book*, 1793.

King, —, Norwich, cm (1793). Subscribed to Sheraton's *Drawing Book*, 1793.

King, —, Camomile St, Bishopsgate St, London, u (1838). Fire on his premises reported, *Times*, 16 August 1838.

King, Benjamin, address unknown, u (1755–61). Supplied textiles to Woburn Abbey, Beds. for the furnishing of some of the new rooms after the rebuilding. The materials were of the simpler kinds and included Scotch and Irish cloth, cotton cloth, chintz, green and white check cloth, blankets and ticking. The total cost was £80 6s 10d. [Bedford Office, London]

King, Benjamin, Warwick, carver and gilder (1756). Had an extensive business in the Midlands, working at Radway Grange, Arbury Hall, Packington Hall, Newnham Paddox, Warwick Castle, etc. He supplied picture frames and carved ornament to Edward Pytts of Kyre Park, Worcs. The total came to £28 15s 11d and was paid on 27 December 1756. King often worked to the supervision of the architect William Smith (1705–47). [Beard, *Craftsmen and Interior Decoration*, p. 267; Gunnis; Worcs. RO, 4958/899:432/6]

King, Benjamin, Old Market, Bristol, cm (1793–95). [D]

King, Charles, address unknown, cm and carver (1705–16). An English cm working from 1705–16 in Germany. Little is known about his life and work. Some good panelling by him exists at the Schloss Charlottenburg in a post-Gibbons tradition. Only one craftsman with the same name is recorded with an address in England at this period and he was a joiner with a house and workshop in Carter Lane, parish of St Gregory, by St Paul's, London. He took out insurance cover on his house of £100 on 16 April 1718. [V & A archives; *Furn. Hist.*, 1973; GL, Hand in Hand MS vol. 18, p. 270]

King, Charles, Bristol, cm (1806–19). In 1806 at Old Park but in the following year at 61 College St. From 1809–19 at 49 King St and in 1809 shown with additional premises at 13 Clarence Pl. Bankrupt 1812. [D; *Exeter Flying Post*, 17 December 1812]

King, Charles, High St, Shifnal, Salop, cm and u (1822–35). [D]

King, Charles, London, chair and sofa maker (1835–39). At Union St, Borough Rd in 1835 and 48 Belvedere Pl., Borough Rd in 1839. Also used 3 Broad Pl., New Inn Yd, Shoreditch. [D]

King, Daniel, Loughborough, Leics., turner and chairmaker (1791). [D]

King, Daniel, Ivegate, Bradford, Yorks., joiner and cm (1814–18). [D]

King, Edward, High Wycombe Bucks., chairmaker (b. c. 1776–1841). Aged 65 at the date of the 1841 Census.

King, Edward, 47 Lant St, Southwark, London, picture frame maker (1835–37). [D]

King, Elizabeth H., St Augustine St, Norwich, working u (1836). [D]

King, Francis, Jury St, Warwick, cm and u (1822–35). Declared bankrupt 28 February 1824 but by 1828 once more in business. [D; *Liverpool Mercury*, 5 March 1824; poll bk]

King, George, Frome, Som., cm (1801). Declared bankrupt, *Exeter Flying Post*, 12 November 1801.

King, H., Austin St, King's Lynn, Norfolk, u and paper hanger (1822). [D]

King, James snr, York, upholder (1777–87). Free 1777. In 1784 at Petergate and in 1787 Feasgate. [D; freemen rolls; poll bk]

King, James jnr, York, u (1800–03). Son of James King snr and free 1800. Subscribed to Sheraton's *Cabinet Dictionary*, 1803. [Freemen rolls]

King, James, Court 9, Norfolk St, King's Lynn, Norfolk, cm and u (1818–36). [D; poll bks]

King, James, Southgate, Gloucester, u (1822). [D]

King, James, Newcastle, carver and gilder (1834–38). Recorded at High Friar St in 1834 and 22 Newgate St in 1838. [D]

King, James, 18 Beer Lane, Tower St, London, cm (1835–39). [D]

King, John, St Paul's Churchyard, London, chairmaker. Dead before April 1703. [*The Postman*, 22–24 April 1703]

King, John, Sherborne, Dorset, cm (1722–38). Took app. named Martin in 1722 and another of the same name in 1723. Later apps were Gorst (1725), Bound (1731) and Lester (1738). In 1729 insured his house stock and building for £300. [S of G, app. index; GL, Sun MS vol. 28]

King, John, Castle St, Long Acre, London, u and cm (1772–94). Attracted important clients and considerable patronage. For Audley End, Essex he supplied goods to the value of £241 9s 1d in 1772 and in 1787 further items were delivered amounting to £272 7s 3d. Active at Althorp, Northants. 1790–91, and possibly earlier. At this period Henry Holland was undertaking a scheme of redecoration in the house. In May 1790 King submitted an account for upholstery and cabinet work amounting to £1,029 5s 9d. This included a large mahogany sideboard for the dining room, and two angle sideboards which together cost £53. These are still in the house. Further sums of £200 on 12 April 1791 and £100 on 12 July 1791 are recorded. One of the items supplied in May of this year was a large set of mahogany library steps for which £45 was charged. Another commission in which he was associated with Henry Holland was the furnishing of the Drury Lane Theatre. He submitted estimates for sofas, chairs, canopies and curtains, and appears in the 1794 building accounts with a payment of £100. He also supplied furniture to Broadlands, Hants., another house where Henry Holland was working. In 1791 and the following year King supplied two portfolios in mahogany to Sir John Nelthorpe at a cost of £2 10s. In 1793 he subscribed to Sheraton's *Drawing Book*. [D; Heal; V & A archives; *Apollo*, October 1968, pp. 272, 277; Stroud, *Henry Holland*, pp. 101, 122; Booker, *Face of Banking*, 1979; C. *Life*, 29 January 1981, p. 290; Lincoln RO, NEL 9/13/49, NEL 9/14/16]

King, John, Shepherd St, Shepherd Mkt, Mayfair, London, u and cm (1784–1811). For a time in the 1780s in partnership with a Peter Debharms but this was dissolved in May 1787. A further partnership was formed by 1804 and endured till 1811 with a tradesman named Smith. In 1801 insurance cover of £2,000 was taken out, but of this only £100 appears to have been in respect of utensils and stock. [D; poll bk; *Williamson's Liverpool Advertiser*, 2 July 1787; GL, Sun MS vol. 419, ref. 715573]

King, John, Hull, Yorks., cm and broker (1803–26). At Blackfriargate in 1803, Queen St in 1806, Posterngate Walls in 1810, 14 New Dock St, 1814–23 and in 1826 at 16 New Dock St. [D]

King, John, 3 Little Essex St, Strand, London, cm (1808). [D]

King, John, York, u (1810–18). Son of Richard King, coal dealer, and app. to William Smith, u, 21 May 1810. Free 1818. [Freemen rolls]

King, John, 30 Sidney Pl., Commercial Rd, London, u (1829). [D]

King, John, Northgate, Bradford, Yorks., cm (1830). [D]

King, John & William, Friar Hill, Sudbury, Suffolk, cm (1830). [D]

King, John, Brook St, Ipswich, Suffolk, cm and u (1839). [Poll bk]

King, Joseph, parish of St Mary Keys, Ipswich, Suffolk, cm (1823). Married in 1823. [Suffolk RO, FAA: 50/2/120, p. 114]

King, Joseph, South St, Bishops Stortford, Herts., cm (1826). [D]

King, Peter, St Marylebone, London, cm (1783). In 1783 took app. named Francis Bower. [Westminster Ref. Lib., MS E3559]

King, Peter, parish of St James, Bristol, bed joiner (1784). [Poll bk]

King, Richard, 3 Prospect Pl., Kingsland Rd, London, chair and sofa maker (1839). [D]

King, Robert, Northgate, Bradford, Yorks., joiner and cm (1814–18). Successor of William King at this address. [D]

King, Susan, 2 Lant St, Southwark, London, u (1839). [D]

King, Thomas, Hereford, u (1697). Free August 1697. [Herefs. RO, Common Council Minutes, p. 50]

King, Thomas, Long Acre, London, cm and gilder (1742). In October 1742 his stock in trade was sold by auction. The items included 'Crimson Velvet and Crimson and Blue Mohair Beds, Chairs, Setees and Couches; . . . Marble Sideboard Tables, a curious India Wood Chest, Mahogany Buroes and Booke cases, Walnut-Tree and Mahogany Chairs, Matted and Black Leather Chairs, Writing and Card Tables, fine Turkey and French Carpets, Mahogany, Oblong, Oval and Claw Tables'. The Long Acre address was said to be his 'late Dwelling-House'. [*Daily Advertiser*, 13 October 1742]

King, Thomas, Swinegate, York, u (1806–16). Son of James King, u. Free 1806. [D; freemen rolls]

King, Thomas, 17 Gate St, Lincoln's Inn Fields, London, u and designer (1829–39). In the mid 1830s claimed to have had forty-five years experience with leading London makers. Between 1829–39 produced some fifteen furniture pattern books. [Joy, *English Furniture 1800–1851*, p. 149; Jervis *Dictionary of Design*, pp. 270–71]

King, Thomas William & Co., 12 Turn-again Lane, Snowhill, London, cabinet, knife-case and backgammon table maker (1790–93). [D] See William Henry King.

King, William, address unknown, picture frame maker (1727). In 1727 was paid £2 9s by John Henry, 1st Earl of Bristol, for a frame. [V & A archives]

King, William, St Paul's Churchyard, London, upholder (1766–74). Son of William King of St Albans, Herts., distiller. App. to Phillip Bell, upholder, 3 September 1766. Bell had his business in St Paul's Churchyard and was a freeman and member of the Vintners' Co. King was made free of the Upholders' Co. by servitude, 6 April 1774. [GL, Upholders' Co. records]

King, William, 1 Clarkes Buildings, Snow Hill, London, cm (1774). On 17 October 1774 insured goods for £100. [GL, Sun MS vol. 235]

King, William, Worcester, cm (1776). App. to Ely Crump and free 1776. [Freemen rolls]

King, William, Lancaster, joiner and cm (1788–90). Free 1789–90. Named in the Gillow records, 1788–90. [App. reg.; Westminster Ref. Lib., Gillow]

King, William, Loughborough, Leics., turner and chairmaker (1791). [D]

King, William, Whitehaven, Cumb., cm and looking-glass maker (1793–1834). King, cm of Whitehaven, was a subscriber to Sheraton's *Drawing Book*, 1793. It was probably either William or Michael King, who were in partnership at King St, 1805–08 as cm and looking-glass manufacturers. William King was trading on his own behalf from an address in Lowther St in 1811 and by 1829 had moved to 13 Tangier St. In 1834 William Alkin King was trading from this address as a cm, carver, gilder and looking-glass manufacturer. [D]

King, William, Wardour St, London, u (1802). Freeman of Oxford. [Oxford poll bk]

King, William Henry, London, cm (1808–39). At 15 Fleet St, 1808–12, 40 Shoe Lane, 1820–26, but from 1829 at 48 Fetter Lane. In 1835, 55 Fetter Lane is also shown. Heal lists a maker

of the same name at 12 Turn-again Lane, Snow Hill and 2 Bartlett's Buildings, Holborn, 1790–1827. See Thomas William King & Co. [D; Heal]

King, William, Northgate, Bradford, Yorks., joiner and cm (1814). Succeeded by Robert King at this address. [D]

King, William, Duke St, Bermondsey, London, u and paper hanger (1814–39). At 26 Duke St, 1814–25, but after 1829 at 31. [D]

King, William, 72 Ratcliffe Highway, East Smithfield, London, cm and appraiser (1817). [D]

King, William, 5 Rathbone Pl., Oxford St, London, u and cm (1820–21). [D]

King, William, London, cm and chairmaker (1820–39). At 25 Holywell Row, Chapel St, Shoreditch, 1820–26. On 4 December 1820 took out insurance cover of £800. Of this £300 was for his dwelling house and manufactory, £300 for the house adjoining and £100 for utensils, stock and goods in trust. In 1839 at 1 New North St, Finsbury, where he declared his trade to be chair and sofa maker. [D; GL, Sun MS vol. 486, ref. 974270]

King, William Henry, London, cm (1820–39). At 40 Shoe Lane, 1820–26, but from 1829 at Fetter Lane. In 1835 55 Fetter Lane is also shown. [D]

King, William, Northumberland Rd, Commercial Rd, London, cm and u (1822–23). [D]

King, William, 41 Blackfriargate, Hull, Yorks., cm and broker (1826). [D]

King, William, Norwich, cm (1829). Son of Jeremy King, weaver. Free 16 May 1829. [Freemen rolls]

King, William, New St, Barnsley, Yorks., cm and u (1829–37). [D]

King, William, Ipswich St, Stowmarket, Suffolk, cm (1830–39). [D]

King, William, New St, Doncaster, Yorks., cm and u (1837). [D]

King, William, 8 Woodstock St, Oxford St, London, cm and u (1839). [D]

King & Co., 11 Somers Pl. West, New Rd, Pancras, London, u (1829). [D]

King & Debharms, see John King, Shepherd Mkt.

King & Lidbitter, Union St, Southwark, London, Windsor chairmakers (1829). [D]

King & Smith, Shepherd Mkt, London, see John King.

King & Smith, Friar St, Sudbury, Suffolk, u (1839). [D]

Kingdom, John, Bristol, cm (1802). Declared bankrupt, *Exeter Flying Post*, 11 March 1802.

Kingdon, Jane & Son, Fore St, Exeter, Devon, paper stainers and u (1832–38). Successors to T. M. Kingdon & Co. Manufactured wall hangings and maintained carpet and upholstery warerooms. Their billhead claimed 'ROOMS decorated in a superior manner by the first Artists after the most tasteful designs. Fancy Painting in all the branches'. Their custom may not have been purely local for J. S. Pakington of Westwood, near Droitwich, Worcs. received goods from them in December 1832 and paid the sum of £4 5s 2½d which was due, on 8 March 1833. [D; Worcs. RO, 2309/705:380/56/v]

Kingdon, T. M. & Co., 180 Fore St, Exeter, Devon, paper stainers and u (1822–32). From 1832 the business continued as Jane Kingdon & Son. [D]

Kingham, —, Long Acre, London, frame maker (1763). Heal states that he was frame maker to George III.

Kingham, Thomas, 2 Long Acre, London, painter and gilder (1804–25). From 1809 the business is described as Thomas Kingham & Son. Framed the Raphael cartoons at Hampton Court for George IV at a cost of £500. In 1804 employed at Hatfield House, Herts., repairing and gilding fifty picture frames, mirror frames, the ornament to 'Queen Elizabeth's frame' and two large window cornices. This, with other items, totalled £155 10s 4d. [D; *C. Life*, 6 October 1950; Hatfield House MS Bills 613]

Kingley, Gabriel, Shrewsbury, Salop, u (1721). In 1721 took app. named Lloyd. [S of G, app. index]

Kingsbury, —(widow), New St Hand Alley, 'The Three Crowns' without Bishopsgate, London, u. Mid 18th-century trade card [Leverhulme Coll., MMA, NY] states that she sold 'Upholders Goods, Feather Beds, Blankets and Quilts, Chairs, Tables, Glasses &c' and also undertook the appraising of goods and the conduct of funerals.

Kingsford, Edmund, Folkestone, Kent, chairmaker (1794). [D]

Kingsman, Thomas, Bear St, Leicester Fields, London, upholder (1708–14). Insurance cover on his own house for £500 was taken out in 1708 and 1714 and in the latter year other houses in New St off St Martin's Lane were insured in addition for £425. [Heal; GL, Hand in Hand MS vol. 14, p. 304; vol. 13, p. 578]

Kingsman, Thomas, the sign of 'The Red Lamp', Broad St, Golden Sq., London, upholder (1715–d. 1718). Free of the Upholders' Co., 9 February 1714/15. [Heal; GL, Upholders' Co. records]

Kingsmill, Comfort, Middle St, Deal, Kent, cm and u (1803–29). [D]

Kingsnorth, John, 57 Friday St, London, upholder (1754–83). In 1754–67 the business was a partnership trading as Kingsnorth & Rowley. From 1759 however John Kingsnorth was trading on his own account from the same address. [D]

Kingston, James, Wellington St and Pocklington Walk, Leicester, cm and u (1822–40). [D]

Kingston, John, Scarborough, Yorks., cm (1798). [D]

Kingston, John, 41 Cirencester Pl., Fitzroy Sq., London, (c. 1840). Plaque on a music stand, dated as 'William IV'. [Sotheby's, 21 April 1972, lot 93]

Kingston, Samuel, Spalding, Lincs., cm and u (1819–35). Recorded at Bridge St, 1819–22, and Church St in 1835. [D]

Kingston, Thomas, Durston, Som., cm (1744). In 1744 took app. named Hartnall. [S of G, app. index]

Kingston, Thomas, Bristol, cm (1834). Bankrupt September 1834. [*Chester Courant*, 7 October 1834]

Kingston, William, Clifton, Bristol, cm. (1816–26). At 9 Wellington Pl., 1816–17 and 14 Wellington Pl., 1818–21. By 1823–25 had moved to Royal York Cresc., and in 1826 to Meridian Pl. From 1823 listed as cm, u, undertaker, carpenter and builder. [D]

Kingwill, Joseph, Southampton, Hants., cm and u (1823–39). At 14 Upper East St, 1823–24, where apart from his work as an u and cm he offered to hang paper and sold china and class. At 124 High St in 1830 and from 1836–39 at 28 High St. [D; *Southampton Herald*, 26 April 1824]

Kinlock, James & William, London, cm (1777–1808). In 1777 the address was given as near Brewer St in Warwick St, Golden Sq. and in 1781 as yard behind 4 Warwick St. These are almost certainly the same property. In 1777 utensils and stock were insured for £400, but in 1781 when James Kinlock was solely responsible for the cover it was reduced to £200. The business continued in Warwick St until 1793 but the last mention of the partnership was in 1784 and after this date only James is named. William however probably set up on his own and in 1808 is recorded at 31 Swallow St, Picadilly. [D; GL, Sun MS vol. 256, p. 616; vol. 296, p. 594]

Kinnebrook, David, Norwich, cm (1761–68). In 1761 in the parish of St Mary but in 1768 in both the parish of St Stephen and St Benedict. [Poll bks]

Kinnebrook, William, parish of St Peter Mancroft, Norwich, cm (1766–1818). Son of David Kinnebrook, joiner. Free 26 April 1766. [Freemen reg.; poll bk]

Kinsey, Matthew, 315 Oxford St, London, furniture printer and upholsterer's warehouseman (1825). [D]

Kinsman, Thomas, St Mary Arches St, Exeter, Devon, cm (1830–32). His son James Chapple was bapt. on 16 May 1830 at St Mary Arches. [PR (bapt.); poll bk]

Kippax, George, Carolgate, Retford, Notts., carver and gilder (1832). [D]

Kippin, William, London(?), cm (1752–53). Employed in the furnishing of the Mansion House, London, 1752–53. [*Conn.*, December 1952, p. 181]

Kipping, J., Symondsbury, Bridport, Dorset, cm (1840). [D]

Kipps, Henry, Blisset St, Greenwich, London, cm etc. (1824–26). [D]

Kipps, Thomas, Sevenoaks, Kent, u (1776). Insured houses for £300 in 1776. [GL, Sun MS vol. 253, p. 403]

Kirby, —, address unknown, carpenter (1799–1806). On 31 August 1799 charged £2 8s for enlarging a dining table at Gorhambury House, St Albans, Herts. A more substantial commission for this house was invoiced on 11 December 1805, when a library table and cornice were charged at £30 2s. [Herts. RO, accounts bk XI 77]

Kirby, Edward, London, upholder (1773–1802). Free of the Upholders' Co. by redemption by order of the Town Clerk, 7 July 1773. At Little Britain, 1773–94, but in 1802 at Portsmouth St. In 1773 may have been trading as a stationer. [GL, Upholders' Co. records]

Kirby, George, Market Pl., Pickering, Yorks., cm (1828–40). [D]

Kirby, Henry, Liverpool, chairmaker (1820). Married in June 1820 at Trinity Church. [*Liverpool Mercury*, 30 June 1820]

Kirby, James Harrison, 44 Leadenhall St, London, upholder (1787). Son of John Kirby of Nottingham, soap boiler. App. to Thomas Cathrow on 1 July 1778 and then to Mary Cathrow on 7 June 1782. Free of the Upholders' Co. by servitude, 14 November 1787. [GL, Upholders' Co. records]

Kirby, Joseph, Bedminster, Bristol, basket and chairmaker (1805–23). [D]

Kirby, Richard, Drury Lane, London, cm (1749–67). His nephew Joseph was app. to him in 1767. [Westminster poll bk; GL, P83/MRY1/867/90]

Kirby, Richard, address unknown, cm (1803). Subscribed to Sheraton's *Cabinet Dictionary*, 1803.

Kirby, Robert, Backside, Beverley, Yorks., cm (1784–91). [D; poll bks]

Kirby, Thomas, Market Pl., Pickering, Yorks., joiner and cm (1823). [D]

Kirby, W., 29 Hart St, Bloomsbury, London, carver and gilder (1826). [D]

Kirby, W., 23 York St, Westminster, London, furniture broker and u (1835–39). [D]

Kirby, William, 5 Cannon St Rd, London, carver and gilder (1820–39). [D]

Kirby, William Henry, Finkle St, Stockton, Co. Durham, cm (1832). [D]

Kirk, —, Holborn, London, chairmaker (1743). [Heal]

Kirk, David, address unknown, cm (1803). Subscribed to Sheraton's *Cabinet Dictionary*, 1803.

Kirk, Edward, 35 Black Church Lane, London, bedstead maker (1839). [D]

Kirk, J., Cambridge, cm and u (1824–26). In 1824 at Pembroke St but in 1826 shown in Trumpington St. [D; PR (bapt.)]

Kirk, John, London, u (1813–39). At Charles St, Middlx Hospital, 1813–20, though a directory of 1819 gives the number as 28. From 1826–27 at 119 Cromer St, Brunswick Sq. and in 1838–39 at Old Brentford, Middlx. [D]

Kirk, John, 27 Club Rd, Shoreditch, London, bedstead maker (1839). [D]

Kirk, Joseph Bustle, Northgate St, Gloucester, cm and u (1830). [D]

Kirk, Mary, Salisbury, Wilts., cm (1762). In 1762 took app. named Wilkie. [S of G, app. index]

Kirk, Nathaniel, 3 Sherrard St, Golden Sq., London, cm, blindmaker, auctioneer and undertaker (1808). [D]

Kirk, Paul, Bracebridge, Lincoln, chairmaker (1684–96(?)). [Lincoln RO, LCC, ADM 1684/96]

Kirk, Samuel, Woodhouse Lane, Leeds, Yorks., cm (1837). [D]

Kirk, Thomas, 48 Brewer St, London, cm (1791). See Thomas Fletcher.

Kirk, Thomas, King St, Derby, joiner, cm, appraiser, maltster and 'plate licens'd auctioneer' (1792). In March 1792 announced his move to King St 'to the Premises of the late Thomas Lowe, deceased'. He also stated that he required 'a good workman in the CABINET Branch'. [*Derby Mercury*, 15 March 1792]

Kirk, Thomas, 8 Rose St, London, cm (1793). Subscribed to Sheraton's *Drawing Book*, 1793.

Kirk, Thomas, 17 Greek St, Soho, London, cm (1794). [D]

Kirk, Thomas, Ward's End, Loughborough, Leics., joiner/cm (1822). [D]

Kirk, William, corner of Salisbury St and the Strand, London (1749). His trade card [Heal Coll., BM] states that he made and sold 'all sorts of Cabinet Work, Chests of Drawers, Desks, Bookcases, Buroe Dining Card & Tea Tables, Sconces, Pier and Chimney Glasses &c. Feather Beds Blankets and Quilts &c. Blinds for Windows'. He also appraised goods and undertook funerals in 'any Part of England'. [Heal]

Kirk, William, 78 Strand, London, cm (1749). [Poll bk]

Kirkbride, Isaac, King St, Whitehaven, Cumb., joiner/cm (1811). [D]

Kirkbride, J., Nether End, Penrith, Cumb., cm (1811). [D]

Kirkbride, John, Lancaster, (1790–92). [Westminster Ref. Lib., Gillow records]

Kirkbride, John, Monkwearmouth, Sunderland, Co. Durham, joiner and cm (1828). [D]

Kirkbride & Baty, Fisher St, Carlisle, Cumb., cm (1829). [D]

Kirkby, George, Car(r)olgate, Retford, Notts., joiner and cm (1819–22). [D]

Kirkby, Robert, Beverley, Yorks., cm (1793). [D]

Kirkby, Thomas, Maryport, Cumb., cm and joiner (1834). [D]

Kirkes, Hamnett, Chester, u (1678). [Freemen rolls]

Kirkes, Hamnett, Chester, u (1714–d. by 1747). Son of Samuel Kirkes of Chester, u, and free 7 January 1714. [Freemen rolls]

Kirkes, John, Chester, u (1731–47). Son of Samuel Kirkes of Chester, u, and free 30 April 1731. Took as apps John Joynes and James Leigh, both free 1747. [Freemen rolls; poll bk]

Kirkes, Samuel snr, Chester, u (1671–95). Free 26 December 1671. Took as apps his son Samuel and Peter Harefinch, both free 16 November 1695. [Freemen rolls]

Kirkes, Samuel jnr, Chester, u (1695). Son of Samuel Kirkes snr of Chester, u, and free 16 November 1695. [Freemen rolls]

Kirkes, Samuel, Chester, u (1732). Son of Samuel Kirkes jnr of Chester, u, and free 18 September 1732. [Freemen rolls; poll bk]

Kirkes, Samuel, Chester, u (1747). Son of Hamnett Kirkes of Chester, u, who was dead by the time his son was sworn free on 21 July 1747. [Freemen rolls]

Kirkes, Samuel, 64 Old Hall St, Liverpool, upholstery warehouse (1781–84). [D] This shop was being used 1792–94 by Robert Smith in the same trade.

Kirkham, John, Blackheath, London, upholder (1772–1802). Son of Thomas Kirkham and app. to Francis Hamilton. Free of the Upholders' Co. by servitude on 3 June 1772 and from 1794 living at Blackheath. [GL, Upholders' Co. records]

Kirkham, John, West Smithfield, London, upholder (1793–1811). Son of Charles Kirkham of Clerkenwell, London, sawyer. App. to Milicent Walker on 9 March 1793 and free of the Upholders' Co. by servitude, 7 April 1802. Shown at 1 Cow Lane at this date but by 3 July was at 29 Long Lane, an address which he was to occupy until 1811. In 1802 took out insurance cover of £300 of which £130 was in respect of utensils and stock but in the following year the total was £500 with £330 for stock and utensils. [D; GL, Upholders' Co. records; Sun MS vol. 423, ref. 732654; vol. 426, ref. 750478]

Kirkham, Jno., 4 Crown St, Finsbury, London, cm (1835). [D]

Kirkham, Thomas, Liverpool, u (b. 1792–d. 1834). Free 5 October 1812. At 25 Byrom St in 1818, 4 New Scotland Rd in 1821 and 44 Gerrard St, 1827–29. Died in April 1834 aged 42. [D; freemen reg.; *Liverpool Mercury*, 18 April 1834]

Kirkham, Thomas, 4 Wood St, Chorlton Row, Manchester, u (1825). [D]

Kirkham, William, Cow Lane, Nottingham, u (1780–1806). Son of Richard Kirkham of Nottingham, labourer. Free 1780. [D; freemen rolls; poll bks]

Kirkland, George, Pittville St, Cheltenham, Glos., carver and gilder (1839). [D]

Kirkland, William snr, Spondon, near Derby, cm and u (1828–29). [D]

Kirkland, William jnr, Spondon, near Derby, cm and u (1828–29). [D]

Kirkman, Thomas, 'King's Head', Aldermanbury, London, cm (1745). On 11 October 1745 took out insurance cover of £200 on his household goods and stock in trade. [GL, Sun MS vol. 74, ref. 103601]

Kirkpatrick, James, 24 Fleet St, Liverpool, cm (1827). [D]

Kirks, Samuel, Liverpool, u (1731–d. 1785). App. to Charles Aven in 1731. Also had a Chester connection for he is shown in the 1747 poll bk of that city even though he was at this date resident in Liverpool. Took as apps John Charleton (free 1767) and Thomas Ellison (free 1774). Established at 63 Old Hall St in 1766 and he was to remain in this street until his death in November 1785, though the number is given as 64 in 1781 and his upholstery warehouse as 2 in 1783. In November 1775 he subscribed £1 1s to the Mayor of Liverpool's fund for the relief of soldiers and their dependants in the 'American war'. Took as app. Thomas Moncas, free 1790. His death occasioned the need to sell off his stock in February 1786. This consisted of 'Damasks, Morines, Cheneys, Bed Tickings of various qualities, with variety of Carpets, Paper Hangings, Looking Glasses of all sizes'. [D; app. bk; freemen's committee bk; Chester poll bk; *Williamson's Liverpool Advertiser*, 17 November 1775, 28 November 1785, 6 February 1786]

Kirkup, John, Church St, Monkwearmouth, Sunderland, Co. Durham, cm (1827). [D]

Kirkup, Simpson, Bishop St, Stockton, Co. Durham, cm and joiner (1828). [D]

Kirton, John, Lincoln, chair turner (1819–35). Recorded at Water Side, 1819–22, and Cornhill, 1835. [D]

Kirkwood, John, Heddon St, Westminster, London, cm (1749). [Poll bk]

Kirkwood, William, cm (1803). Subscribed to Sheraton's *Cabinet Dictionary*, 1803.

Kirlew, Thomas, Stonegate, York, cm (1779–84). App. to John Sanderson, cm, and free in 1779. At Stonegate in 1784. [App. bk; poll bk]

Kirshaw, Charles, Swan Yd, Northampton, upholder (1826). [Poll bk]

Kirtland, John, parish of St Peter in the East, Oxford, cm (1802). [Poll bk]

Kirton, George, Post House Weind, Darlington, Co. Durham, turner, chairmaker and carver (1827–28). [D]

Kirton, James, address unknown, cm (1727). Supplied a card table costing £4 5s to Temple Newsam House, Leeds. [*Furn. Hist.*, 1967]

Kirton, John, St Michael, Lincoln, chairmaker (1783–d. 1807). Employed by Lord Monson to repair chairs and possibly other work, 1783–90. The sums involved are small, the largest being £3 12s 6d in December 1785. Death reported in March 1807. [Poll bk; Lincoln RO, Monson 10/1/A/6, pp. 29, 59, 68, 80, 87, 101, 112; *Gents Mag.*, March 1807]

Kirton, John, Waterside, Lincoln, chairmaker (1826). [D]

Kirton, John, Silver St, Stockton, Co. Durham, cm (1832). [D]

Kirton, Joseph, 4 Little Portland St, Cavendish Sq., London, cm (1780). In 1780 insured his house for £100. [GL, Sun MS vol. 287, p. 50]

Kishere, Joseph, 'The Four Coffins', Compton St, Westminster, London, cm and u (1749). On 20 October 1749 took out insurance cover of £400. [GL, Sun MS vol. 87, ref. 118192]

Kisling, Christian, London, u and cm (1803–19). Subscribed to Sheraton's *Cabinet Dictionary*, 1803. At 43 Wigmore St, 1812–14, and 32 Dorset St, Portman Sq., 1817–19. [D]

Kitchen, David, Leeds, Yorks., chairmaker (1837–40). In 1837 at 12 York St, and in 1839 at 20 York Tavern Yd. [D]

Kitchen, George, Doncaster, Yorks., cm (1717). In 1717 took app. named Richardson. [S of G, app. index]

Kitchen, George, 22 Chester Rd, Hulme, Manchester, builder, joiner and cm (1825). [D]

Kitchen, Henry, Nantwich, Cheshire, cm (1798). [D]

Kitchen, James, Cable St, Lancaster, cm (1818–25). Shown in the Gillow records, 1818–24, but in 1825 trading on his own account at Cable St. [D; Westminster Ref. Lib., Gillow]

Kitchen, Jonathan, Thorne, Yorks., joiner and cm (1826–31). At Stonegate, 1826–30, but in 1831 at Poorhouse Lane. [D]

Kitchen, Joseph, Liverpool, cm (1834–37). Maintained a shop at 7 St Ann's, Liverpool, 1834–37, but also shown at Richmond Row in 1834, 11 Beresford St, Everton in 1835 and 10 Beresford St in 1837. [D]

Kitchen, Joseph, Tinsley, Rotherham parish, Yorks., cm (1837). [D]

Kitchen, Kelita, Wetherby, Yorks., joiner/cm (1837). [D]

Kitchen, Richard, Nantwich, Cheshire, cm (1798). [D]

Kitchen, Robert, Tythbarn St, Liverpool, cm (1769–81). In 1777 the address is given as 12 Temple St and the trade auctioneer. [D]

Kitchen, William, Whitehaven, Cumb., cm (1798). [D]

Kitching, Mordecai J., Hull, Yorks., cm and u (1826–38). At Blanket Row, 1826 and 1834, but in 1831 shown at 13 Queen St. By 1838 at 21 Bridge St and in the next year at Humber Dock Walls. [D]

Kite, Ralph, address unknown, carver (*c*.1730). Worked at Houghton, Norfolk for James Richards. [*Conn.*, June 1981, p. 144]

Kite, Thomas, Hull, Yorks., cm (d. 1794). Death reported, *Hull Packet*, 10 November 1794.

Kitson, Joshua, Haslingden, Lancs., cm, u, joiner and house builder (1822–24). Trading at Higher Lane in 1824. [D]

Kitson, Thomas, 96 High St, Hoxton, London, cm and u (1839). [D]

Kitson, William, 29 Montague St, London, cm (1826). Freeman of Maldon, Essex. [Maldon poll bk]

Kitten, John, Norwich, cm (1806). Son of Robert Kitten, grocer. Free 12 November 1806. [Freemen reg.]

Kittle, James, King St, St Anne's Lane, Norwich, cm and mahogany merchant (1802–12). [D; poll bks]

Kitty, Robert, Marlborough Mews, Westminster, London, chairmaker (1749). [Poll bk]

Knaggs, 15 Moor Lane, Fore St, London, cm and chairmaker (1790–93). [D; Heal]

Knapp, Alexander, Strand, London, cm (1774). [Westminster poll bk]

Knapp, F. A., 21 Lower Grosvenor St, London, u (1835). By 1837 succeeded by John & Henry Knapp at the same address. [D]

Knapp, George, 55 Hanover St, Portsea, Portsmouth, Hants., cm and u (1823). [D]

Knapp, James William, 21 Lower Grosvenor St, bedstead maker and u (1839). Successor to John & Henry Knapp at this address. [D]

Knapp, John, Guildford St, Chertsey, Surrey, cm (1822). [D]

Knapp, John, Portsea, Portsmouth, Hants., cm, u, and chairmaker (1830–39). Recorded at 174 Queen St in 1830 and 83 Queen St in 1839. [D]

Knapp, John & Henry, 40 Cirencester Pl., 54 Toley St, 21 Lower Grosvenor St, Cirencester Wharf, Regent's Canal, Augustor St, London, builders, statuaries, cm, u, house agents, general decorators, hydrostatic waterbed manufacturers (1837). F. A. Knapp occupied 21 Lower Grosvenor St in 1835 and James William Knapp the same address in 1839. [D]

Knapp, Thomas, Brighton, Sussex, cm and builder (1784–92). [D]

Knapton, Samuel, Gt Queen St, St Giles, London, looking-glass seller (b. 1673–d. 1720). Master of the Glass Sellers' Co., 1712. Died on 12 December 1720 aged 47. [Wills, *Looking-Glasses*]

Knebworth, James, 7 Hanover St, Manchester, cm (1825). [D]

Knee, William, Round Stone St, Trowbridge, Wilts., cm (1839). [D]

Kneen, Ellen, 10 Stanley St, Liverpool, cm (1827). [D]

Kneen, Thomas, Stanley St, Liverpool, cm (1815–27). App. in 1815 and in 1822 petitioned freedom on servitude to William Harvey. Sworn free, 17 October 1827. At this date living at 9 Stanley St, but a directory of the same year gives 63 Stanley St. [D; freemen reg.]

Knibb, —, Oxford, upholder (d. by 1754). Dead before August 1754. Referred to as Alderman Knibb. [*Jackson's Oxford Journal*, 14 September 1754]

Knibb, George, Newport Pagnell, Bucks., joiner and cm (1780–98). In 1780 took out insurance cover of £400 of which £140 was for utensils and stock. [D; GL, Sun MS vol. 284, p. 267]

Knibbey, John, Peter St, Westminster, London, chairmaker (1749). [Poll bk]

Knife, John, London, upholder (1783–1802). Son of John Knife of St Luke's, handkerchief printer. App. to John Evans, cook, on 22 February 1776 and admitted freeman of the Upholders' Co. by servitude, 2 July 1783. In 1783 Skinner St, but in 1802 Harp Alley, Fleet Mkt. [GL, Upholders' Co. records]

Knight, —, London, u (1689–90). In 1789–90 paid £1 5s by the church wardens of St Michael's, Crooked Lane. [*Wren Soc.*, vol. XIX, p. 44]

Knight, —, address unknown, upholder (1768–73). Payments to 'Upholder Knight' recorded from Michaelmas 1768 by John Bragge of Sadborow, Thorncombe, Dorset. [Dorset RO, D104/F4]

Knight, —, Honiton, Devon, cm (1813). On 5 October 1813 Married at Honiton to Miss Crabb of Churchstanton. [*Western Luminary*, 1813–15]

Knight, C., London, u (1826–39). At 3 Portland St, Soho in 1826 but at 4 Gt Titchfield St, 1829–39. [D]

Knight, Charles John, London, cabinet inlayer (1813–25). At 2 Clerkenwell Green, 1813–15, when insurance cover of £400 was taken out of which £150 was in respect of utensils and stock. In 1822 shown at 12 Clerkenwell Green and the trade was listed as buhl manufacturer. He was soon however to move to Bleeding Hart Yd, Saffron Hill, Hatton Gdn. [D; GL, Sun MS vol. 462, 26 June 1813; vol. 462, ref. 901705; GL, P83/MRYI/876/167]

Knight, Charles, Hill St, Poole, Dorset, cm and u (1840). [D]

Knight, Edward, 150 High St, Southampton, Hants., cm and u (1839). Advertised himself also as auctioneer, appraiser, house and estate agent and undertaker. Offered to fit up yachts and indicated that he held stocks of 'Cabinet Household Furniture, Bedding, Floor Cloths, Paper-Hangings &c'. Undertook funerals. [D]

Knight, Elizabeth, Cornhill, Bridgwater, Som., cm and u (1830). [D]

Knight, Elizabeth, Nottingham, u and paper hanger (1834–40). Addresses given at Byard Lane in 1834–35 and Pepper St, 1840. [D]

Knight, F., 5 Charles St, Covent Gdn, London, looking-glass and picture maker (1829). [D]

Knight, Francis, 39 Booth St, Spitalfields, London, cm, u and chair japanner (1827). [D]

Knight, George, Back St, Petworth, Sussex, cm and victualler (b. c. 1773–1841). Born at Angmering, Sussex, c. 1773, and trading in Petworth by 1819 and possibly 1815. Apart from the cm side of his business he was the landlord of the 'White Hart Inn' in Back St. [1841 Census]

Knight, George, Upton, near Tewkesbury, Glos., cm (1813–26). [PR (bapt.)]

Knight, George, High St, Tewkesbury, Glos., cm, u, builder and chairmaker (1820–39). [D]

Knight, George, Cheap Side, Derby, cm and brooker (1823). [D]

Knight, George, Liverpool, carver (1835–39). At Richardson Pl., 14 Lambert St in 1835, 21 Lambert St in 1837 and 59 Peter St in 1839. In 1837 also maintained a beer shop. [D]

Knight, George, 11 Page's Walk, Bermondsey, London, picture and looking glass frame maker (1839). [D]

Knight, James, Long Acre, London, cm (1709). [Heal]

Knight, James, Queenhithe, London, u (1727). [Heal]

Knight, James, Shaftesbury, Dorset, cm (1782). In his will, dated 1782 he left everything to his wife. [Dorset RO, DA/W/1782/58]

Knight, James, London, (1791–1808). A James Knight undertook repairs and alterations for Gertrude, Dowager Duchess of Bedford, 1791–92, amounting to £5 17s 1d. At this period she was living at 112 Pall Mall. This cm is probably the Knight cm who subscribed to Sheraton's *Drawing Book*, 1793. There was also a James Knight recorded in a directory at 49 Welbeck St, Cavendish Sq. in 1808 who may well be the same person. [D; Bedford Office, London]

Knight, James, East St, Chichester, Sussex, cm, u and undertaker (1823–32). [D]

Knight, James, Hight St, Bridgwater, Som., cm and u (1830). [D]

Knight, James Thomas, Brittox, Devizes, Wilts., cm and u (1830). [D]

Knight, John, Hastings, Sussex, cm and carpenter (1794). [D]

Knight, John & James, Brittox, Devizes, Wilts., cm etc. (1822). [D]

Knight, John, London, bed and mattress maker (1822–35). At 40 Carnaby St in 1822 and 13 Little Compton St, Soho in 1835. [D]

Knight, John, Coombe St, Lyme Regis, Dorset, cm and builder (1823). [D]

Knight, John, 1 Lower College St, Bristol, cm (1825–28). [D]

Knight, John, Altrincham, Cheshire, cm (1828). [D]

Knight, John, 56 Poland St, London, u (1829). [D]

Knight, John, Market Pl., Ely, Cambs., turner and chairmaker (1830–39). [D]

Knight, John, 19 Wellington Mart, Hull, Yorks., turner and bed pole carver (1831–39). From 1834 listed merely as wood turner and in 1839 the address is given as 'Summergang'. [D]

Knight, John, Nottingham, joiner and cm (1837). [Freemen rolls]

Knight, Joseph, London, upholder (1759). Son of Joseph Knight of St George's, Hanover Sq., vintner. App. to Thomas Dobyns on 2 November 1752 and free of the Upholders' Co. by servitude, 6 December 1759. [GL, Upholders' Co. records]

Knight, Joseph, Tunbridge Wells, Kent, Tunbridge-ware manufacturer (1786–94). Label recording him as 'Tunbridge-Ware Maker to Her Majesty' known on oval harewood tea caddy with marquetry of flowers and leaves. Knight is recorded paying poor rate in Tunbridge parish, 1786–94.

Knight, Joseph, 34 Alport Lane, Manchester, cm (1808). [D]

Knight, Philip, Bristol, u (1715–34). In 1719 took app. named Stokes. Living in the parish of St Peter in 1721 and Christchurch parish in 1734. [S of G, app. index; poll bks]

Knight, Philip, parish of St Philip and St Jacob, Bristol, u (1774). [Poll bk]

Knight, Richard, Devizes, Wilts., u and auctioneer (1793). [D]

Knight, Richard, Midhurst, Sussex, cm and clothes salesman (1823–39). [D]

Knight, Robert, Harwich, Essex, cm and auctioneer (1793). [D]

Knight, Samuel, 'The Crown', Noble St, London, u (1714). [GL, Sun MS vol. 4, 15 July 1714]

Knight, Samuel, 3 Sweetings Alley, Cornhill, London, print seller and frame maker (1821). On 22 February 1821 took out insurance cover of £800 of which £200 was for his shop and £300 for stock and utensils. [GL, Sun MS vol. 486, ref. 978037]

Knight, T. W., Speenhamland, Newbury, Berks., carver and gilder (1840). [D]

Knight, Thomas, London, upholder (1700–07). Free of the Upholders' Co., 6 November 1700. [GL, Upholders' Co. records]

Knight, Thomas, Bread St, London, upholder (1747). [Heal]

Knight, Thomas, London, glass seller (c. 1772). He was paid £115 'for looking glasses' in connection with the furnishing of The Pantheon (built 1769–72). [*Survey of London*, vol. 31, p. 271n]

Knight, Thomas, Lancaster, furniture painter and japanner (1787–90). Named in the Gillow records, 1787 and 1789–90. [Westminster Ref. Lib., Gillow]

Knight, Thomas, 22 Bentick St, Cavendish Sq., London, u (1808). [D]

Knight, Thomas, 15 Broad St, Bath, Som., cm, u, auctioneer and appraiser (1826). [D]

Knight, Thomas, Doldory (or Doldy), Worcester, cm and u (1822–30). [D]

Knight, Thomas, Jamaica Row, Birmingham, cabinet case etc. maker (1839). [D]

Knight, William, 'The Crown', Leadenhall St, London, u (1722–25). In 1722–23 supplied two pier glasses for the Great Dining Room at Hicks Hall, London for which he charged £20, though an abatement of £1 was later made. On 29 December 1725 took out insurance cover of £1,000 which included £450 on goods and merchandise in his dwelling house, £100 on 'a back house' and £50 on goods kept there. [Winterthur, Delaware, Symonds papers, 75x69.29; GL, Sun MS vol. 15, ref. 29060; vol. 20, ref. 37637]

Knight, William, London, upholder (1765). Son of Edward Knight of Essolt, Northants., baker. App. to Carill Pitt of the Fishmongers' Co., 7 September 1758. Free of the Upholders' Co. under the terms of the 1750 Upholders' Act, 5 December 1765. [GL, Upholders' Co. records]

Knight, William, High St, Salisbury, Wilts., cm and u (1830). [D]

Knight, William, Cathedral Yd, Canterbury, Kent, carver and gilder (1832). [D]

Knight, William Jeffries, Cornhill, Bridgwater, Som., cm and u (1822–40). [D]

Knighton, George, Sutton-in-Ashfield, Notts., chairmaker (1828–35). Trading at High St in 1828. [D]

Knighton, William, Clumber St, Nottingham, fancy chairmaker (1814). [D]

Knights, Nathaniel, London, chairmaker (1818). Freeman of Norwich. [Norwich poll bk]

Knights, Samuel, 7 Cornhill, London, upholder (1803). Son of Thomas Knights of Pedlars Acre, London. App. to John Walker, 4 July 1792, and free of the Upholders' Co. by servitude, 2 February 1803. [GL, Upholders' Co. records]

Knipe, John, Lancaster (1792). Named in the Gillow records in connection with making a table. [Westminster Ref. Lib., Gillow vol. 96, p. 843]

Knipe, William Garnet, Salford, Lancs., carver and gilder (1808–40). At 8 Palmer St in 1808 and 1 Palmer St in 1813. Thereafter the addresses are in Greengate, the number being 14 in 1814–21, 15 in 1824–29 and 16, 1832–36. Also recorded at no. 16 in 1822. [D]

Knipe & Mower, 208 Oxford St, London, upholder and cm (1803). [D]

Knott, Thomas, Wadsley, Sheffield, Yorks., cm (1834–37). In 1837 at the 'Star Inn', Wadsley. [D]

Knott, W., Lancaster (1809). Named in the Gillow records in connection with making a bookshelf. [Westminster Ref. Lib., Gillow vol. 344/99, p. 1870]

Knowles, Alexander, address unknown, cm (1803). Subscribed to Sheraton's *Cabinet Dictionary*, 1803.

Knowles, Daniel, Canterbury, Kent, chairmaker (1793). [D]

Knowles, Edward, 'The India Cabinet', Fryar St, Reading, Berks., upholder. His mid 18th-century trade card [Leverhulme Coll., MMA, NY] indicates that he undertook both upholstery and cabinet making, bought, sold and appraised household goods and did work 'by Designs and Designs given'.

Knowles, Mrs Elizabeth, Rotherhithe, London, upholder (1740). A widow. Took out insurance cover of £200. [GL, Sun MS vol. 54, p. 462]

Knowles, Henry Sidney, 107 Wardour St, Soho, London, u (1835–39). [D]

Knowles, James Spencer, Southwark, London, u and cm (1821–29). At 29 High St in 1821 but from the following year at 291. In both 1822 and 1823 took out insurance cover of £1,100 but only £300 of this was in respect of stock, utensils and goods in trust. [D; GL, Sun MS vol. 490, ref. 989206; vol. 492, ref. 1003146]

Knowles, John, 'The Cabinet and Four Coffins', Tooley St, Southwark, London, joiner, cm, appraiser and undertaker (1729–47). On 16 October 1729 took out insurance cover amounting to £500 much of which was connected with his stock in trade. Apart from his dwelling house, in which some stock was kept, a timber warehouse is mentioned. His trade label has been recorded in a walnut chest of drawers of early 18th-century date. [Heal; GL, Sun MS vol. 29]

Knowles, John, Horsleydown, Southwark, London, cm (1750). Member of the Joiners' Co. [GL, Joiners' Co. records, Livery lists]

Knowles, John, King St, Leigh, Lancs., joiner and cm (1825–34). From 1828 the business traded as John & William Knowles. [D]

Knowles, John, High St, St Martin's, Lincoln, cm and u (1826–28). [D]

Knowles, Richard, London, cm (1783–93). In 1783 at 8 Gt Earl St, Seven Dials where he took out insurance cover for £400 of

which half was for utensils and stock. From 1789 at 27 Tottenham Ct Rd. [D; GL, Sun MS vol. 317, p. 82]

Knowles, Richard, High St, St Peter's, Lincoln, cm and u (1819–28). [D]

Knowles, Robert, Liverpool, carver (1804–23). At 29 Brownlow Hill in 1804 and 63 Brownlow Hill in 1807. In 1810 at 14 Stanhope St and in the following year at 3 Gloucester St. By 1818 the address had changed to 5 Craven St and in 1821–23 it was 11 Bridport St. [D]

Knowles, Thomas, 51 Featherstone St, City Rd, London, chair and sofa maker (1839). [D]

Knowles, Thomas, Sittingbourne, Kent, carver, gilder, plumber and painter (1839). [D]

Knowles, William, Sun St, Canterbury, Kent, u (1805–09). [D]

Knowles, William, Liverpool, cm (1827). Son of R. Knowles, watchmaker. On 25 December 1827 married Miss Williams at St Anne's Church. [*Liverpool Mercury*, 4 January 1828]

Knowles, William Maddock, Liverpool, cm (1819–40). App. in 1819 to William John Roberts and free in 1840. [Freemen's committee bk]

Knox, James, Liverpool, carver and gilder (1805–24). In 1807 recorded in one directory at 6 Mount St, Elliott Hill but all others give addresses in Duncan St until 1818 and after that at Copperas Hill. In 1805 and 1810 8 Duncan St is listed, and in 1811 a shop at 4 Duncan St is also shown. In 1813 the number is 15, in 1816, 16, and in 1818, 21. The numbers in Copperas Hill are 65 in 1821, 82 in 1823 and 83 in the following year. [D]

Knox, John, 84 Fore St, Devonport, Devon, cm (1812–23). [D]

Knox, Michael, 11 Bedford Pl., Old Kent Rd, London, cm and u (1839). [D]

Knox, William, London, carver and gilder (1808–20). In 1808 at 29 Joiner's Pl., St George's Fields, and in 1820 at 15 High St, Newington Butts. [D]

Knox, William Perry, 107 Jermyn St, St James's, London, cm and upholder (1839–40). [D; GL, Sun MS ref. 1339660]

Kowin, William, address unknown, carver and gilder (1776). He was paid £6 6s in August 1776 for 'a very rich picture frame in burnish gold with a coronet & other enrichments of laurell leaves etc.' This item which was invoiced a month earlier, was said to be for 'Percy's portrait' and for the 'New Guild Hall'. [V & A archives]

Krampf, —, address unknown, upholder (1806–08). He was paid £117 2s 9d in 1806 and £43 9s in 1808 in connection with Longford Castle, Wilts. [V & A archives]

Kreyer, —, address unknown, u (*c.* 1757). Undertook work on upholstery and chair stuffing at Holkham Hall, Norfolk [*C. Life*, 14 February 1980, p. 427]

Kriege, Frederick, 11 Ormond Row, Chelsea, London, cm and u (1808–20). [D]

Kripe & Mower, Upper Oxford Rd, London, cm (1803). [Heal]

Kune, David, 11 Gt Warner St, Clerkenwell, London, cm etc. (1811–13). [D]

L

Labbett, H., address unknown, frame maker (1829). Recorded working at Moor Hall Park, Essex in 1829. He supplied twelve 'new frames for Drawings, with sanded flutes and Composition stars on mitres' gilded, at £18 and five other rich gilt frames at £21 10s. [Essex RO, D/DEs T50]

Laburn (or Laben), Thomas, The Morledge (or Morlidge), Derby, chairmaker and turner (1818–29). [D]

Laccohee, William M., 10 Bartholomew Sq., St Luke's, London, picture and looking-glass frame maker and cm (1839). [D]

Lace, Henry, 8 Church St, Liverpool, cm and u (b. 1796–1824). Born on 28 February 1796, son of William Lace, master mariner. Free by patrimony, 12 June 1818. In February 1822 announced the opening of his business as cm and u at 8 Church St. He claimed to have 'lately returned from London' where he had acquainted himself 'with the newest & most tasteful Fashions & has selected & manufactured his Stock agreeably to the best Patterns'. Although he did not describe his stock in any detail he felt it necessary to emphasise that he did not stock 'Yorkshire Carpets'. In 1824 he is shown both at the Church St address and at 12 Wolstenholme Sq. [D; freemen's committee bk; *Liverpool Mercury*, 15 February 1822]

Lacey, James, 10 Well Yd, Little Britain, London, u (1809). A Lacey of London subscribed to Sheraton's *Drawing Book*, 1793, and may be this James Lacey. [D]

Lacey, John, Cheap St, Frome, Som., cm and chairmaker (1762). In 1762 took app. named Ayres. His trade card [Heal Coll., BM] states that he made all sorts of cabinet goods and 'sells common, round and quartered Ash and Elder Chairs, white or coloured, from eight to forty shillings per Dozen'. [S of G, app. index]

Lacey, John, Market Pl., North Walsham, Norfolk, cm and u (1822–30). [D]

Lacey, Richard Culley, Market Pl., North Walsham, Norfolk, u and cm (1839). Successor to John Lacey at this Address. [D]

Lacey, T., Market Pl., Shrewsbury, Salop, cm (c. 1796). [D]

Lacey, William, London, cm (1806–10). Maintained workshops above five tenements in the Hole in the Wall Passage, Baldwins Gdns. The address on an insurance policy issued in 1806 was however stated as 'William Beasleys Timber Yard, West St, West Smithfield' and in 1808 and 1810 as 11 Brooks Mkt. In 1806 insurance cover amounted to £1,300 of which £240 was in respect of utensils and stock in Baldwins Gdns. The value of his untensils and stock declined to £150 in 1808 and was £200 in 1810. [GL, Sun MS vol. 438, ref. 798423; vol. 441, ref. 812518; vol. 451, ref. 836699]

Lack, James, Dorking, Surrey, cm (1839). [D]

Lackenby, William, Nottingham, u (1822–32). Recorded at Friar Lane in 1822 and Granby St in 1832. [D]

Lacy, Tenant, Market St, Shrewsbury, Salop, cm (1786–98). Freeman of Shrewsbury. [D; freemen rolls]

Lad, Richard, 19 Burr St, East Smithfield, London, upholder and auctioneer (1789–93). [D]

Ladbrooke, Robert, White Lion St, St Peter Mancroft, Norwich, carver and gilder (1830–39). [D; poll bk]

Ladd, Richard, St Mary's Yd, Exeter, Devon, u (1835–40). Four sons bapt. at St Mary Major, 1835–40. [PR (bapt.)]

Laddell, Robert Stephen, Norwich, carver and gilder (1826). Free 3 May 1826. [Freemen reg.]

Ladderdale, John, Thorngate, Barnard Castle, Co. Durham, joiner and cm (1827–34). [D]

Ladkin, William, Rugby, Warks., cm (1835). [D]

Ladson, James, London, cm, writing desk and dressing case maker (1808–40). Initially at 9 Crown St, Hoxton but then moved to 25 Primrose St, Bishopsgate. [D; GL, Sun MS vol. 574, ref. 1341665]

Ladson, James, 5 King St, Ramsgate, Kent, carver and gilder (1838–39). [D]

Ladson, Joseph, Canterbury, Kent, carver and gilder (1801–39). Initially in St Margaret's St but from 1824 at 5 Guildhall St. In 1801 took out insurance cover of £300 of which £100 was in respect of utensils and tools. [D; GL, Sun MS vol. 40, ref. 719381; Canterbury and Dover poll bks]

Ladson, L., Guildhall St, Canterbury, Kent, carver and gilder

(1838). Same address as Joseph Ladson, so this may be a directory error. [D]

Ladson, W. B., 8 Queen St, Margate, Kent, carver (1838). [D]

Ladyman, George, 'Queen's Head', Hawkshead, Lancs., joiner, builder, cm and victualler (1824–34). [D]

Ladyman, Henry, 51 Fleet Mkt, London, upholder (1771–1804). Son of Henry Ladyman of Ickenham near Uxbridge, Middlx, Gent. Free of the Upholders' Co. under the terms of the 1750 Upholders' Act, 2 January 1771. Took as app. Samuel Search until 1774, in which year he obtained a licence to employ six non-freemen for six months. In 1804 the business traded as Ladyman & Doolan. [D; GL, Upholders' Co. records; City Licence bks, vol. 8]

Ladyman, Thomas, Theatre St, Preston, Lancs., joiner, builder and cm (1828–42). [D]

Ladyman, Thomas, Keswick, Cumb., joiner/cm (1828–34). [D]

La Feuillade, George, Farningham, Kent, cm (1838). [D]

Laggett, , James, Canterbury, Kent, u (1705). [Freemen rolls]

Laggett, Thomas, Canterbury, Kent, u (1683). [Freemen rolls]

Laidley, William, Wavertree, Liverpool, joiner and cm (1823). [D]

Lain, James, High St, Stockport, Cheshire, cm (1828). [D]

Laing, —, 3 Lee St, Manchester, cm (1800). [D]

Laing, Charles, 20 George St, Adelphi, London, cm (1809). [D]

Laing, James, Westage, Guisborough, Yorks., joiner/cm (1840). [D]

Lake, Cockell, Attleborough, Norfolk, cm, chairmaker and joiner (1822). [D]

Lake, Joseph, 15 Coburg Pl., Borough Rd, London, cm, u and bedstead maker (1835–39). In 1835 listed as a furniture broker. [D]

Lake, Nathaniel, Exeter, Devon, u (1688). [Freemen rolls]

Lake, Richard, see Thomas Gretton.

Lake, Thomas, Maidstone, Kent, upholder (1719–34). In 1719 took app. named Pett. [S of G, app. index; poll bk]

Lake, Thomas, Stoke-on-Trent, Staffs., cm and u (1818–35). In 1822 at New Rd; in 1834 at Glebe St; and in 1835 at Church St. [D]

Lake, Thomas Constable, Norwich, cm (1830–40). Freeman of Gt Yarmouth, Norfolk. [Gt Yarmouth poll bks]

Lake, William, Norwich, u (1704). Free 9 October 1704, not by apprenticeship. [Freemen reg.]

Lake, William, Exeter, Devon, cm (b. 1799–d. 1837). Married on 4 January 1827 at the Church of St Mary Major, Exeter but his wife Charlotte died on 12 February 1829 aged 30. At this period resident at Pancras Buildings but later at Catherine St where he is shown as late as 1838 in directories. This may be a case of the same name or a directory error, since his death in 1837 aged 38 was reported in *Exeter Flying Post*, 18 May 1837. [D; *The Alfred*, 9 January 1827]

Lakeman, William, Artillery St, Spitalfields, London, bed and window cornice maker (1809). [D]

Laker, William, 'Tunbridge', Kent, cm (1819). Daughter bapt. on 4 April 1819. Living in the parish of Tunbridge which not only included the town of Tonbridge but considerable parts of Tunbridge Wells. [PR (bapt.)]

Lakin, Benjamin & Son(s), High St, Whitchurch, Salop, cm (1822–28). Trading as Lakin & Sons in 1822 and Lakin & Son 1828. [D]

Lakin, Thomas, Angel Row, Nottingham, cm and u (1825–40). A small mahogany Regency Pembroke table with the name 'T. LARKIN' impressed on the drawer edge has been recorded. [D]

Lakin, William, Market Pl., Burton-on-Trent, Staffs., turner and chairmaker (1828). [D]

Lakin, William & Abraham, High St, Whitchurch, Salop, cm (1835). [D]

Laking, Charles, Diglake, Stafford, cm (1818–22). [D]

Laking, Thomas, Mount St, Nottingham, chairmaker (1828). [D]

Lamb, Charles, 12 Snargate St, Dover, Kent, chairmaker and u (1826–39). Possibly the son of Elizabeth Lamb. Recorded in directories trading on his own behalf, 1826–29. From 1833–39 the business is listed as Lamb & Son. [D; poll bks]

Lamb, Daniel, 29 Cumberland St, Manchester, cm (1825). [D]

Lamb, Elizabeth & Son, Snargate St, Dover, cm and u (1824). The son was probably Charles. [D]

Lamb, George snr, London, upholder (d. by 1727). Freeman and member of the Upholders' Co. Father of George jnr and Samuel Lamb, both upholders. [GL, Upholders' Co. records]

Lamb, George jnr, London, upholder (1727). Son of George Lamb snr, freeman and upholder of London. Brother of Samuel Lamb, upholder. Free of the Upholders' Co. by patrimony, 3 May 1727. [GL, Upholders' Co. records]

Lamb, Henry, Feathers Ct, Westminster, London, carver (1738–49). In September 1738 submitted an account to Richard Hoare for a set of mahogany vases, bracket tables etc. amounting to £13 19s 6d which was settled in October. [V & A, 86 NN 3; Hoare's Bank, private accounts; poll bk]

Lamb, Henry, Hadleigh, Suffolk, cm (1824). [D]

Lamb, James, Dover, Kent, upholder (1705). Freeman of Canterbury. [Canterbury freemen rolls]

Lamb, James, Dover, Kent, u and auctioneer (1790–96). Freeman of Canterbury. [D; Canterbury poll bks]

Lamb, John, Lincoln, chairmaker (1765). In March 1765 advertised for a 'spindle or a varnish chair maker and likewise a chair bottomer: both shall have constant employment'. In October 1762 Lord Monson settled an account with a John Lamb amounting to £1 37s 4d for a 'seeing glass', a japanned tea tray and two mahogany trays. These may have been supplied by this craftsman whose business may have extended beyond chairmaking. The sum of £2 12s paid by the executors of the 2nd Duke of Ancaster in 1742 to a Mr Lamb, upholsterer, probably also refers to a local craftsman in the Lincoln area. [*Cambridge Chronicle*, 16 March 1765; Lincoln RO, Monson 12, 5 ANC 8/2/5]

Lamb, John, Boston, Lincs., cm (1805–08). Recorded in High St, 1808. [D]

Lamb, Joseph, Newcastle, u (1781). App. to Edward Coates and free, 15 January 1781. [Freemen reg.]

Lamb, Michael, Newcastle, u (1777). App. to Thomas Hunt and free, 6 March 1777. [Freemen reg.; poll bk]

Lamb, Nathaniel, Denton-chare, Newcastle, joiner, cm and fruiterer (1790–1811). The trade of fruiterer is first recorded in a directory of 1801. In an 1824 directory he is listed solely as a fruiterer. [D]

Lamb, Ralph, Bigg-market, Newcastle, joiner and cm (1811). [D]

Lamb, Samuel, London, upholder (1729). Son of George Lamb snr, freeman of the Upholders' Co., and brother of George Lamb jnr, also a member of the Upholders' Co. Free of the Upholders' Co. himself, by patrimony, 2 July 1729. [GL, Upholders' Co. records]

Lamb, Thomas, 102 James St, Devonport, Devon, carver and gilder (1838). [D]

Lamb, William, Snargate St, Dover, upholder (1784–1803). In 1803 the business was trading as Lamb & Son. For successors see Elizabeth Lamb and Charles Lamb. [D]

Lamb, William, 9 and 10 Jewin St, Aldgate, London, cm and u (1798–1811). Son of John Lamb of Scarborough, Yorks., vintner, and free of the London Upholders' Co. by redemption, 7 March 1798. Shown in directories from 1801 and in 1803 included in the list of master cabinet makers in

Sheraton's *Cabinet Dictionary*. [D; GL, Upholders' Co. records]

Lamb, William Henry, High St, Hadleigh, Suffolk, u and cm (1830–39). Probably the successor of Henry Lamb. [D]

Lamb, Woolhouse, St James's, Westminster, London, upholder (1742). Executor of the will of James Brown, upholder, Covent Gdn. [PRO, C108/367]

Lamb & Wells, 44 New Bond St and 34 Cockspur St, London, pocket book and desk makers (1820–35). In 1835 described as writing and dressing case makers. [D]

Lambden, Edward, Reading, Berks., u (1722–48). In 1722 took app. named Blanch. Named in 1748 as the recipient of the sum of £6 6s from the executor of the will of a member of the Neville family of Bilingbear, Berks. [S of G, app. index; Essex RO, D/DBy/A379]

Lambden, James, Henley-on-Thames, Oxon., upholder (1740). In 1740 took app. named Hayward. [S of G, app. index]

Lambden, John, West Wycombe, Bucks., chairmaker (1798). [Militia Census]

Lambdon, Charles, Reading, Berks., upholder (1748). Took out insurance cover of £600 in 1748. [GL, Sun MS vol. 83, ref. 111840]

Lambe, John, Cockspur St, London, dressing case maker (1837–39). On 11 August 1837 appointed dressing case maker to the Lord Chamberlain's Offices on the recommendation of the Duchess of Northumberland. The drowning of Lambe jnr is recorded in July 1839. [PRO, LC5/243, p. 41; *Gents Mag.*, July 1839]

Lambe, Richard, 24 High St, Cliffe, Lewes, Sussex, u and cm (1805–40). In 1810 he was paid £2 9s for the use of 94 chairs, two tables and two glasses at the Shire Hall, Lewes. Further payments were made from 1810–11 for upholstery materials and furniture amounting to £58 19s 2d and on 15 February 1812 a further £63 10s for furniture. This patronage was in connection with the furnishing of the new County Hall in Lewes. After 1832 the business traded as Richard & William Lamb. In May 1838 they advertised for an app. in the upholstery and paper hanging side of their business who would 'be treated as one of the family' though a premium was expected. An oak library table in a Jacobean revival style bearing a lead plaque underneath inscribed 'Rd. Wm. Lambe, cabinet makers, Lewes 1838' was included in Christie's sale of 7 February 1980, lot 79. [D; poll bks; E. Sussex RO, QAH/1/ES(264), QAH/1/7/E2, no. 259; *Sussex Agricultural Express*, 19 May 1838]

Lambe, Richard, 96 Gracechurch St, London, carver, gilder, frame maker and printseller (1821–39). In 1821 took out insurance cover of £1,000 of which £600 was for untensils, stock and goods in trust and £100 for glass. This was a substantial amount for this trade. In 1839 the business is recorded as Richard Lambe & Son. [D; GL, Sun MS vol. 486, ref. 985037]

Lambe, William, Lewes, see Richard Lamb.

Lambert, —, Hull, Yorks., cm (1793). Subscribed to Sheraton's *Drawing Book*, 1793.

Lambert, —, 37 Regent St, corner of Piccadilly, London, upholder, undertaker, auctioneer and appraiser (c. 1820). Trade card in Banks Coll., BM

Lambert, Benjamin & Jane, 'New Church', u (1728). In 1728 took app. named Hayter. [S of G, app. index]

Lambert, Charles, London, cm and u (1835–39). At 184 High St, Wapping in 1835 and 177 Old Gravel Lane, Ratcliffe in 1839. [D]

Lambert, Christopher, 177 New Market St, Old Gravel Lane, London, cm (1822–24). In 1822 took out insurance cover for £300 of which £30 was in respect of a 'chest of tools in Ferguson & Co. manufacturing in Providence Court, North

Audley St.' The New Market St address was occupied by Charles Lambert in 1839. [GL, Sun MS vol. 491, ref. 991555; vol. 497, ref. 1016724]

Lambert, Cornelius, Carolgate, Retford, Notts., cm (1832–40). [D]

Lambert, George, 'The Rose & Dolphin', London Wall, over against Little Moorgate, London (1727). Advertised tapestries for sale in 1727. [Heal]

Lambert, George, York and Doncaster, Yorks., u (1739–58). Son of Stephen Lambert, butcher. Free of York as an u in 1739 and in 1741 living in Spurriergate. By 1756 had moved to Doncaster and in that year took app. named Ellis. Still living in Doncaster in 1758. [Freemen rolls; York poll bks; S of G, app. index]

Lambert, Henry, Moorgate, Retford, Notts., cm (1830–35). [D]

Lambert, James, Godalming, Surrey, cm and u (1822–26). [D]

Lambert, James, 1 Lambeth Pl., Clapham Rd, London, u (1835). [D]

Lambert, John, Newcastle, u (1728–d. by 1753). Free on 8 January 1727/28 by servitude. In 1745 took app. named Reed. By February 1753 he was dead and in that month his warehouse and shop goods and also his household goods were sold by auction. His son John was free by patrimony, 7 April 1766. [Freemen reg.; S of G, app. index; *Newcastle Courant*, 17 February 1753]

Lambert, John, address unknown, joiner and cm (1739–59). Undertook work for Lord Monson in 1739, 1746–47 and 1758–59. Only one indication is given of where the work was undertaken. In 1758 the carpentry was for Charles Monson's dwelling house in Spring Gdns. Two carved tabernacle frames were supplied in 1746 at £1 16s, and in 1759 a walnut library table, part of which appears to have been delivered in January and part in March. For this £16 was charged. [Lincoln RO, Monson 12, Monson 11/27]

Lambert, John, Lancaster, cm (1789–1802). App. to R. Mashiter in 1789 and free, 1801–02. [Lancaster app. reg. and freemen rolls]

Lambert, John, Leeds, Yorks., cm (1791). A journeyman cm named in the list of workmen in sympathy with the *Leeds Cabinet and Chair Makers Book of Prices*, 1791, which was printed at the end of the book.

Lambert, John, 20 Berwick St, London, cm (1792–94). On 9 April 1792 took out insurance cover of £200 on utensils, stock and goods in trust 'in his timber workshop behind 42 and 43 Wardour St.' In 1794 described as a broker and cm when he insured his new dwelling house for £200. [GL, Sun MS vol. 382, ref. 598475; vol. 401, ref. 626900]

Lambert, John, Stoney Stratford, Bucks., u (1798). [D]

Lambert, , John, Primrose Hill, Liverpool, cm (1818–21). In 1818 at 1 Primrose Hill and in 1821 at 21. [D]

Lambert, John, 11 Earl St, London, carver and gilder (1839). [D]

Lambert, John, 8 Upper Clapton St, Finsbury, London, wood carver and cm (1839). [D]

Lambert, John, 12 Broad St, Soho, London, cm and u (1839). [D]

Lambert, Joseph, Lancaster (1797–99). Named in the Gillow records, 1797–99, in connection with an altarpiece. [Westminster Ref. Lib., Gillow vol. 344/98, p. 1488]

Lambert, Joseph, 11 Lower St, Islington, London, carver and gilder (1808). [D]

Lambert, Philip, London, cm (1793). Subscribed to Sheraton's *Drawing Book*, 1793.

Lambert, Pierre, address unknown, cm (1701). Undertook minor work in 1701 for Lord Monson, the largest item being the supply of '15 square glasses' at 15s. A fine lock costing 5s was provided for 'ye book case'. [Lincoln RO, Monson 12]

Lambert, Robert, London, upholder, cm, appraiser and undertaker (1767–93). A partner with Robert Chipchase in the business of Chipchase & Lambert, 1767–88. In 1774 Robert Lambert was shown living at New St and in 1784 at Beak St. When the partnership was dissolved in 1788 Robert Chipchase moved to 39 Dover St, leaving Robert Lambert in possession of the former business premises in Warwick St, Golden Sq. and Beak St. He traded on his own account until 1790 when he went into partnership, trading as Lambert & Turner. The business was carried on in a substantial manner and of the £2,700 insurance cover taken out in January 1791, £1,600 covered 'the shops, warehouse, counting house & shop and yard nearby' used by the business. The remainder was cover for Robert Lambert's dwelling house. The business continued to trade until 1793. A number of the customers of Chipchase & Lambert transferred their patronage to Robert Lambert. In 1788 the Earl of Stair paid £63 13s 1d for work undertaken and goods supplied. Lord Howard of Audley End, Essex patronised Lambert in connection with his London house in New Burlington St, 1789–91. Much of the work was of a minor nature but on 20 January 1791 an account for £23 10s 6d was submitted for alterations and new hangings for a bed. Lambert's billhead shows a crown on a cushion supported by three feathers, but no commissions for the Royal Household have come to light. [D; poll bks; GL, Sun MS vol. 373, ref. 579443; Scottish RO, GD 135/Box 52/6/24–25X; Essex RO, D/DBy/A47/3, A49/2, A49/5, A50/2]

Lambert, Robert, Lower Edmonton, London, u (1809). [D]

Lambert, Robert, 6 All Saint's Pl., 12 Grosvenor St, Liverpool, cm (1839). [D]

Lambert, Thomas, 1 Naval Row, East India Docks, London, cm and u (1827). [D]

Lambert, Thomas, 154 New Bond St, London, u (1829). [D]

Lambert, Thomas, Brough, Westmld, joiner and cm (1834). [D]

Lambert, William, High St, Knaresborough, Yorks., cm and u (1822–28). [D]

Lambert, William Henry, South Parade, Bawtry, Yorks., cm and joiner (1834–37). [D]

Lambert & Turner, see Robert Lambert, London.

Lambley, Abraham, Birmingham, cabinet travelling and dressing case maker (1800–18). At Moseley St, Deritend, 1800–05, Bordesley and Deritend, Birmingham in 1809 and Birchole St, 1816–18. Recorded as Abraham Lambley & Co., 1816–18. [D]

Lambley, James William, Birchole St, Birmingham, case maker (1793). [D]

Lambley, James, 33 Deritend St, Birmingham, 'manufacturer of all forms of small cabinet articles for travelling &c.' (1800). [D]

Lambley, James & William, Birmingham, writing desk and dressing case makers (1818–21). Their advertisement in *Wrightson's Directory of Birmingham*, 1818, declares them to be successors to Abraham Lambley & Co. They manufactured 'Writing Desks, Work Boxes, Liquer Bottle Cases, Stands, Tea Chests, Caddees, Shaving Cases, Toilet Cases, Medicene Chests, Card Boxes, Knife Cases etc.'. Copying machines for office use were also manufactured. Initially the business was in Moseley St, but by 1821 had transferred to 10 New St. By this year James Lambley was also selling pianofortes and church and chamber organs. [D]

Lambley, William & Abraham & Co., 86 Caroline St, Birmingham, writing desk and cabinet case manufacturers (1822–23). In 1823 the business was taken over by Wagner & Cottrell. [D]

Lambourn, John, Bell St, Henley-on-Thames, Oxon., chair-maker (1830). [D]

Lamdin, Charles, 30 Northbrook St, Newbury, Berks., cm and u (1840). Successor to Joseph Lamdin. [D]

Lamdin, Joseph, Northbrook St, Newbury, Berks. cm and u (1830). By 1840 the business was in the hands of Charles Lamdin, probably a son. [D]

Lamerton, Julia, Guinea St, Exeter, Devon, u (1830–38). [D]

Laming, John, St Peter, Canterbury, Kent, cm (1826–30). [Poll bks]

Lammas, Edmund, Moulton, Norfolk, cm (d. 1717). Will proved at Norwich, 1717. [Norfolk Record Soc., index of wills]

Lamson, Thomas, Stamford, Lincs., cm (1809). A Thomas Lambson appears in the Stamford poll bks, 1830–34. [Poll bk]

Lancaster, Benjamin, London, upholder (1709–d. by 1737). Father of Thomas and Jane Lancaster. Benjamin was free of the Upholders' Co., 1 June 1709. [GL, Upholders' Co. records]

Lancaster, George, Narrow Weir, Bristol, cabinet and bedstead maker and size maker (1818–29). At 4 Narrow Weir, 1818–21, but after this the number was 6. From 1820 listed as furniture broker and size maker. [D]

Lancaster, H., 2 Winkworth Buildings, City Rd, London, cm (1829). [D]

Lancaster, Henry, 8 Edgar Terr., Tunbridge Wells, Kent, cm (1831–39). Daughter bapt. on 23 November 1831. Bankruptcy announced, *London Gazette*, 14 February 1834, but despite this resumed business. [D; PR (bapt.)]

Lancaster, James, Upper Westwick St, Norwich, chair and cabinet maker (1824–39). App. to James Ringer and free, 24 February 1824. [D; freemen rolls; admission reg.]

Lancaster, Jane, London, upholder (1748). Daughter of Benjamin Lancaster, freeman of the Upholders' Co. and sister to Thomas Lancaster. Free of the Upholders' Co. by patrimony, 4 May 1748. [GL, Upholders' Co. records]

Lancaster, John, 135 Wapping, London, carpenter, undertaker and cm (1823). Took out insurance cover for £1,000 in November 1823. Of this £400 was in respect of utensils, stock and a workshop with loft over. A saw pit was located under the workshop. [GL, Sun MS vol. 496, ref. 1010182]

Lancaster, John, Heighington, Co. Durham, joiner/cm (1834). [D]

Lancaster, Joseph, Wycombe Marsh, High Wycombe, Bucks., chairmaker (1816–22). Two sons bapt., 1816–22. [PR (bapt.)]

Lancaster, R., 5 Rose St, Covent Gdn, London, chairmaker (1826). [D]

Lancaster, Richard, 122 St Martin's Lane, London, cane worker (1808). [D]

Lancaster, Thomas, London, upholder (1737). Son of Benjamin Lancaster, member of the Upholders' Co. Brother of Jane Lancaster. Free of the Upholders' Co. by patrimony, 12 October 1737. [GL, Upholders' Co. records]

Lancaster, William, Liverpool, cane worker (1797–1814). At 2 Preeson's Row in 1797, but from 1800–03 the number was 4, and in 1806, 10. At 34 Paradise St, 1807–09, and in 1814 at London Rd. Employed by Mathew Gregson, cm and u, and in 1809 in a letter to Sir John Sinclair, Gregson indicated that Lancaster had worked for him for the last twelve years. William Lancaster was brother of the celebrated educationalist, Joseph Lancaster, and in 1814 was the contact through whom tickets could be obtained for a lecture on the 'Royal Lancastrian System of Education' which was to be given by his brother. Co-operated with Mathew Gregson in his experiment to manufacture furniture from whalebone. [D; Liverpool RO, GRE 920 2/23, 920 GRE 2/23/2; *Liverpool Mercury*, 8 July 1814]

Lance, George, 37 Castle St East, Oxford Mkt, London, cm and chairmaker (1817–29). In 1827 listed as a buhl maker and in 1829 as a buhl manufacturer and cm.]D]

Lanceley, Thomas, Chester, cm (b. 1771–d. 1834). At Gorst stacks in 1812, Brook St in 1818 and George St, 1819–26. Died on 17 Feburary 1834 aged 63 after a protracted illness. [Poll bks; *Chester Courant*, 25 February 1834)

Land, Benjamin Cole, Woodbridge, Suffolk, cm (1803). Married in 1803. [Suffolk RO, FAA: 50/2/112 A, p. 5]

Land, John, 8 Wild Ct, Wild St, London, upholder (1775). In 1775 insured his house for £100. [GL, Sun MS vol. 236, p. 406]

Land, Samuel, Bampton St, Tiverton, Devon, cm (1803–38). In September 1803 married Mary Chapple, linen draper. [D; *Exeter Flying Post*, 15 September 1803]

Land, Titus, 30 Seward St, Goswell Rd, London, dyed chair manufacturer (1793–1808). [D]

Landall, Thomas, Little Argyle St, Westminster, London, cm and upholder (1724–c. 1756). In 1749 took as app. William Lenden, the premium of £20 being met from a fund for apprenticing the sons of poor clergymen. In the 1750s trading as Landall & Gordon under the sign of the 'Griffin & Chair', Little Argyle St. They made 'all sorts of Tables, Chairs, Setee-Beds, Looking-Glasses, Picture-frames, Window-Blinds & all sorts of Cabinet work'. Their trade card is embellished with engravings of an elaborate splat back chair and a tea chest. [Heal; poll bks; *General Advertiser*, 17 April 1749]

Landcastle, John, Bristol, turner, cm and undertaker (1825–29). In 1825–27 at 26 Clare St, but in 1828 at Nicholas St and Brislington, and in 1829 under the Bank and Brislington. Carried on a varied trade which included the sale of jewellery, perfumery, wooden toys, carpentry and building. A drawing [Bristol Art Gallery] shows his workshop at Brislington. In 1829 he supplied stools for Brislington Church. [D; Bristol Art Gallery, K4826; Brislington Churchwarden's accounts]

Landells, George, Church St, Whitehaven, Cumb., tool and cabinet maker (1811). [D]

Landen, Joyce, next 'The Cross Keys', Beton St, London, upholder (1777). In 1777 living in the house of W. Luthys, carver. Took out insurance cover of £100 of which £40 was in respect of utensils, stock and goods. [GL, Sun MS vol. 258, p. 545]

Lander, Francis, Gt Brook St, Birmingham, coffin maker, cm and u (1828–30). [D]

Lander, John, London, upholder (1730). Son of Thomas Lander of London, a freeman of the Upholders' Co. His son John was free of the Company by patrimony, 1 September 1730. [GL, Upholders' Co. records]

Lander, Paul, Norwich, u (1777). Will proved at Norwich 1777. [Norfolk Record Soc., index of wills]

Lander, Thomas, London, upholder (1730). Member of the Upholders' Co. His son John was free by patrimony, 1 September 1730. [GL, Upholders' Co. records]

Lander & Co., 1½ Frances Pl., Westminster Rd, London, cm (1829). [D]

Landers, James, 87 and 93 South St, Sheffield Moor, Sheffield, Yorks., cm (1814–37). [D]

Landor, G, Clemens St, Leamington, Warks., cm and u (1837). [D]

Lands, David, 12 Gt Russell St, Bloomsbury, London, upholder and cm (1785). Took out insurance cover of £400 on his utensils, stock and goods in trust. His house was insured for £600 more. [GL, Sun MS vol. 334, p. 7]

Landsall, Matthew, 4 Water St, Manchester, cm (1825). [D]

Lane, Charles, High Wycombe, Bucks., chairmaker (b. c. 1816–41). Son bapt. in 1840. Aged 25 at the time of the 1841 Census. [PR (bapt.)]

Lane, Edward, London and Basingstoke, Hants., upholder

(1733–80). Son of Edward Lane of Basingstoke, grocer. App. to Robert North snr of London on 22 December 1733 and free of the Upholders' Co. by servitude, 3 August 1749. Living with his brother in Bartholomew Lane in 1750 but by 1778–80 had returned to Basingstoke, Hants. [GL, Upholders' Co. records, Livery lists, 1750]

Lane, Henry, 1 Litchfield St, Soho, London, upholder and undertaker (1837). [D]

Lane, Israel, parish of St Martin-at-Palace, Norwich, cm (1825–30). Son of Robert Lane. Free 5 February 1825. [Freemen rolls and admission reg.; poll bk]

Lane, Jacob, parish of St Clement, Cambridge, cm (1818). Child bapt. at St Clement's Church in 1818. [PR (bapt.)]

Lane, James, Beccles, Suffolk, cm (1797–98). [D]

Lane, James, 51 Vine St, Westminster, London, u (1835). [D]

Lane, John, Little Britain, London, cm (1790–93). The nearness of this address to St Martin-le-Grand makes it possible, that despite Sheraton's emphasis on the separation of the trades of cm and knife case maker, this maker was the John Lane recorded in his *Drawing Book*, 1793. [D]

Lane, John, 44 St Martin-le-Grand, London, knife case maker (1791–93). Subscribed to Sheraton's *Drawing Book*, 1793, in which he is mentioned as an eminent knife case maker. Sheraton emphasised that this was a separate trade from that of cabinet maker.

Lane, John, 1 Brick Lane, Old St, London, cm (1809). [D]

Lane, John, 47 Sloane St, London, carver and gilder (*c.* 1820). A giltwood convex mirror with inner ebonised border and deep surround set with balls was included in the Sotheby's sale of 29 September 1978, lot 124. This item had Lane's trade label affixed, as did also two carved and gilt brackets, with a label inscribed 'John Lane of Knightsbridge', sold at Sotheby's, 30 November 1962, lot 214.

Lane, John, Tavistock Lane, Devonport, Devon, turner, carver and chairmaker (1822). [D]

Lane, John & Co., Bristol, cm (1829–34). At 5 and 6 All Saints St in 1829, 6 All Saints St and 43 Wire St in the following year and John Lane, 6 All Saints St and Narrow Wire St, 1831–32. From 1833–34 traded in addition at 26 Union St. [D]

Lane, Joseph, 49 Millbank St, Westminster, London, u (1839). [D]

Lane, Richard, parish of St Giles, Norwich, chairmaker (1800–06). Son of Thomas Lane, weaver and free, 15 February 1800. [Freemen admission reg.; poll bks]

Lane, Robert, Norwich, cm and u (1805–d. 1837). At St Lawrence, 1805–22, but in 1830 at Heigham. Will proved at Norwhich in 1837. His son Israel was admitted free on 5 February 1825. [D; poll bks; freemen admission reg.; Norfolk Record Soc., index of wills]

Lane, Samuel, St Martin's parish, Westminster, London, cm (1749). [Poll bk]

Lane, Samuel, 38 Tything, Worcester, u (1822). [D]

Lane, T., Ambrose St, Cheltenham, Glos., cm (1839). [D]

Lane, Thomas, Exeter, Devon, cm (1819–27). At Cowick St, St Thomas in 1819 when his son Charles Thomas was bapt., and Gandy St in 1827 when his son Henry was bapt. [PR (bapt.)]

Lane, Thomas, 7 James St, Plymouth, Devon, cm (1822–38). [D]

Lane, Timothy, London, u, auctioneer and undertaker (1816–20). At 3 North Audley St in 1816 and 5 Vernon Pl., Bloomsbury Sq. in 1820. [D]

Lane, William, Cricklade St, Cirencester, Glos., chairmaker (1839). [D]

Lane & Billing, London, writing desk and dressing case makers at 60 and 74 St Paul's Churchyard initially, then 86 Strand and finally at 22 Coventry St, Haymarket. [D]

Lang, George, 8 Brooks St, Liverpool, cm (1804–12). Petitioned

freedom on servitude to John Mears in 1804 but not sworn free until 5 October 1812. [Freemen's committee bk; freemen reg.]

Lang, M., London, cm (1793). Subscribed to Sheraton's *Drawing Book*, 1793.

Langdale, John, Yarm, Yorks., joiner and cm (1827). [D]

Langdale, John, Tanner's Hill, Deptford, London, cm (1839). [D]

Langdon, —, London, u (1793). Subscribed to Sheraton's *Drawing Book*, 1793.

Langdon, Edward, 15 Old St Rd, London, look-glass manufacturer (1789). [D]

Langdon, John, London, upholder, cm, auctioneer, appraiser and undertaker (1795–1830). At 5 Old Bailey, 1795–96 and 3 Pilgrim St, 1797–99. At this period he listed his trade as cm and auctioneer. From 1799–1830 at 3 Broadway, Blackfriars. His trade card of 1830 lists in addition an address at Blackheath Hill. Declared bankrupt, *Chester Courant*, 25 May 1830. [D; PRO, B3/3111]

Langdon, John, High St, Barnstaple, Devon, cm, chairmaker and u (1808–d. by 1812). In 1808 advertised for a journeyman cm. By May 1812 he was dead and his business, utensils and stock were put up for sale. [*Exeter Flying Post*, 5 May 1808, 28 May 1812]

Langdon, William, Cottles Lane, Bath, Som., cm (1833). [D]

Lange, Charles, 54 Crown St, Finsbury, London, cm (1840). [D]

Langford, J. L., Chester, cm (1833). One of the creditors of William Thomas & Henry Hesketh, bankers. [*Liverpool Mercury*, 20 September 1833]

Langford, John, Yeovil, Som., cm (1784). Freeman of Bristol. [Bristol poll bk]

Langford, John, address unknown, cm (1803). Subscribed to Sheraton's *Cabinet Dictionary*, 1803.

Langford, John, Birmingham, chairmaker (1830–35). Recorded at 233 Bradford St in 1830 and 22 Court, Bradford St in 1835. [D]

Langford, John, 89 East St, Lambeth, London, chair and sofa maker (1839). [D]

Langford, Joseph, Bristol, cm (1774–84). In Bedminster, 1774–81, but in 1784 at Worle, Som. [Bristol poll bks]

Langford, R., Church St, Worcester, chairmaker (1820). [D]

Langford, Richard, Dudley, Worcs., cm (1783). In 1783 insured his house for £140. [GL, Sun MS vol. 314, p. 130]

Langford, Richard, 26 and 27 Broker Row, Moorfields, London, u (1789–1802). In the period 1789–93 only 27 Broker Row used. In 1790 the business was referred to as a 'cabinet warehouse'. [D]

Langford, Richard, Church St, Worcester, chairmaker (1820). [D]

Langford, Richard, St George's Mkt, London Rd, London, chair and sofa maker (1839). [D]

Langford, Robert, Hatton Gdn, London, cm (1774). Freeman of Bristol. [Bristol poll bk]

Langford, Thomas, Hart St, Covent Gdn, London, cm (1749). [Westminster poll bk]

Langford, Thomas Stringer, Upper Bridge St, Chester, u (1792–1802). Despite the fact that he was in business as early as 1792 he is not shown as free until 15 April 1797 after servitude to J. Stringer of Chester, u. It would seem unlikely that two persons with exactly the same names would be present in Chester at this period. Declared bankrupt, *Liverpool Advertiser*, 5 July 1802. [D; freemen rolls]

Langford, William, 13 New Compton St, London, upholder (1802). Freeman of Oxford. [Oxford poll bk]

Langford, William G., Leonard St, Finsbury, London, cm and u (1826–39). At 88 Leonard St in 1826 and at 15 in 1839. [D]

Langford, William, Hitchin, Herts., cm and u (1823–39).

Trading at Sun St, 1826–39, and as Langford & Son, cm, u, appraisers and ironmongers, 1838–39. [D]

Langford, William, High St, Witney, Oxon., cm and u (1830). [D]

Langham, George, Harwich, Essex, cm (1784–88). Probate granted on will, 1788. [D; *Wills at Chelmsford*]

Langham, Henry, Lothbury, London, u (1764). [Heal]

Langham, Peter, London, upholder and cm (1775–79). At 23 Wardour St in 1775 when he took out insurance cover for £400 of which half was to cover utensils, stock and goods. In the period 1777–79 at the corner of Upper James St, Golden Sq. Here the insurance cover was much more substantial indicating a considerable extension of the scale of the business. In 1777 it was £2,400 with £1,000 for utensils and stock, and in 1779 the corresponding figures are £1,500 and £1,000. Bankrupt in 1779. [GL, Sun MS vol. 239, p. 327; vol. 260, p. 581; vol. 271, p. 579; Bailey's list of bankrupts]

Langland, William, Bromley, Kent, cm (1823). [D]

Langlands, James, 34 White Hart Yd, London, grocer and cm (1775). In 1775 insured his utensils and stock for £100 out of a total insurance cover of £200. [GL, Sun MS vol. 239, p. 630]

Langlands, John, Epsom, Surrey cm (1838). [D]

Langlands, Robert, Bedlington, Northumb., joiner and cm (1827). [D]

Langlers, Edward, Church Lane, St Martin's, London, carver and gilder (1780). In 1780 insured his house for £200. [GL, Sun MS vol. 282, p. 625]

Langles, John, West Wycombe, Bucks., chairmaker (b. c. 1801–41). Aged 40 at the time of the 1841 Census.

Langley, —, London, cm (1769). In April 1769 submitted an account for French pattern chairs etc. amounting to £25 13s 6d, supplied to Shelburne House, Berkeley Sq., London. [Bowood MS]

Langley, George, 29 Broad-chare, Newcastle, cm (1833). [D]

Langley, James, 1 Blakey St, Blackburn, Lancs., cm, joiner and house builder (1824). [D]

Langley, John, High Wycombe, Bucks., chairmaker (1814). Son bapt. in 1814. [PR (bapt.)]

Langley, John, 'Tunbridge', Kent, cm (1837). Son James bapt. on 3 September 1837 in Tunbridge parish, which included not only the town of Tonbridge but also large parts of Tunbridge Wells. [PR (bapt.)]

Langley, Jos., 50 Foley St, London, carver (1835). [D]

Langley, Richard, Frome, Som., carver (1722–39). Freeman of Bristol. [Bristol poll bks]

Langley, Richard, Salisbury, Wilts., carver (1759). Took app. named William Elderton in 1759. [*Wilts. Apps and their Masters*]

Langley, Stephen, house on north side of Hart St and west side of Southampton Sq., parish of St Giles-in-the-Fields, London, upholder (1712–d. by 1735). In 1712 insured two houses that he owned, but not his own dwelling, for £550. Dead by 1735 when his account for 'two saffoy frames with carved feet, elbows and other ornaments richly gilt in gold, made suitable to the chairs' at £11 15s was submitted to the 3rd Countess of Burlington. [GL, Hand in Hand MS vol. 10, ref. 4394; V & A archives]

Langley, Thomas, London, upholder (1667–82). Name included in the records of the parish of St Mary, Woolchurch, Hawe. [Heal]

Langley, Thomas, Melton Mowbray, Leics., cm (1762). In 1762 took app. named Hides. [S of G, app. index]

Langley, Thomas, Downley, High Wycombe, Bucks., chairmaker (b. c. 1806–41). Aged 35 at the time of the 1841 Census.

Langley, William, Uppingham, Rutland, cm (1822). [D]

Langley & Cross, London, u (1700). In September 1700 paid by the executors of the 1st Duke of Bedford for 'putting pulpit etc in Covent Garden Church into mourning'. [Bedford Office, London]

Langley & Denne, 166 Lower St, Deal, Kent, cm (1839). [D]

Langlois, Daniel, London, cm and ormolu maker (c. 1778). Probably the son of Pierre Langlois. App. to Dominique Jean in 1771, and after training probably carried on Pierre's business, or worked in it. A fine inlaid commode in the collection of the Fitzwilliam Museum, Cambridge has the signature of Daniel Langlois on the carcase. [Goodison, *Ormolu*, p. 21]

Langlois, Pierre, 39 Tottenham Ct Rd, London, cm (1759–81). Pierre Langlois was one of the leading cm in London in the 1760s and 1770s. He produced a wide range of furniture in the French manner, specializing in commodes in the Louis XV and Louis XVI styles decorated with floral marquetry and gilt-bronze mounts. His trade card [Heal Coll. BM] advertised cabinets and commodes, secretaries, corner cabinets and clock cases 'Inscrutez de fleurs en Bois et Marqueteries garnies de Bronzes, doreez.' It is illus. by Heal, but the text, in English (and French) reads: Peter Langlois|CABINET-MAKER|In Tottenham Court Road near Windmill Str.| Makes all Sorts of Fine Cabinets and|Commodes made & inlaid in the Politest manner|with Brass & Tortoiseshell & Likewise all rich Orna-|mental Clock Cases, and Inlaid work mended|with great Care. Branch Chandelier & Lanthorns|in Brass, at the Lowest Prices.|Pierre Langlois Ebeniste|dans Tottenham Court Road Proche Windmill St|Fait touttes sortes de Commodes . . .'. [Text follows in French the English text above]

In the *Universal Director*, 1763, Thomas Mortimer noted that Langlois made 'all sorts of curious inlaid work, particularly commodes in the foreign taste, inlaid with tortoiseshell, brass, etc.'. His early marquetry was closely related to that of the Parisian ébéniste, Jean-François Oeben, in whose workshop he may have trained. He was probably well established in London by 1759, when he began to provide furniture for the Duke of Bedford at Woburn Abbey. He continued to pay rates at his shop at 39 Tottenham Ct Rd, which he shared with the bronze caster and gilder Dominique Jean, through to 1781. It was Jean who probably made the elaborate mounts for his furniture. Langlois had a fashionable clientele, including, in addition to the Duke of Bedford, Lady Louisa Conolly at Castletown, the Duchess of Northumberland at Alnwick, Horace Walpole at Strawberry Hill and the Earl of Coventry at Croome Ct. Surprisingly few bills and references to his work are known but two securely documented pieces of furniture survive: a commode at Woburn (1760) and a commode from Croome Court, now in the MMA, NY (1764). P. Thornton and W. Rieder published a series of five articles on Langlois in 1971–72 in which all the bills and documents are quoted and a body of furniture is attributed to him. They divided the furniture into twelve stylistic groups, based on repeated patterns of marquetry, gilt-bronze mounts, general shape and constructional features. Subsequently the name has been applied rather too generously in the auction rooms, and in the trade, to many pieces of English furniture in the French taste that were more likely executed by several different, still anonymous cabinet-makers. [A. Coleridge, 'Pierre Langlois, His Oeuvre and Some Recent Discoveries', *Gazette des Beaux Arts*, September 1967; R. Fastnedge, 'An Unpublished Commode Attributed to Pierre Langlois', *Furn. Hist.*, 1967; N. Goodison, 'Langlois and Dominique', *Furn. Hist.*, 1968; T. Dell, 'A Langlois Commode', *V & A Bulletin*, April 1968; P. Thornton and W. Rieder, 'Pierre Langlois, Ébéniste', pts 1–5,

Conn., December 1971, February–May 1972; W. Rieder, 'More on Pierre Langlois', *Conn.*, September 1974]

WOBURN ABBEY, Beds. (4th Duke of Bedford). 1759–60: 1759: 13 Apr: A japan'd fire screen £2.20. 19 May. Une table de vide poche incrusté de fleur de bois violette des indes enjolivée de ornement de bronze dorée du prix de neuf quinée £9.9.0.
1760: 10 Dec. A large inlay'd commode table. £78.8.0. [now Yellow Drawing Room at Woburn] 'Received Decm 18th 1760 of his Grace the Duke of Bedford by Richd Branson, Seventy Eight pounds Eight Shillings in full for a large Inlay'd Commode Table £78:8:0. Witness, P. Beaumont [Signed] Pierre Langlois'. 17 Dec. Madame la Duchesse de Bettefort pour une caisse pour emballer la grande commode incrustée (sent to Woburn Abbey) £1.10.0. 18 Dec. An Inlay'd writing desk £41.12.0.' This last piece may have been made for Francis Marquess of Tavistock. Langlois did make furniture for him, for after the Marquess's death in 1767 the list of payments made to his creditors includes one to 'Veuve Langlois for two comode tables of inlaid wood — £14.0.0.'. This perhaps refers to the pair of rectangular commodes now in the so-called Sporting Room at Woburn. It is of interest that at the same time as the widow Langlois was paid, Sir William Chambers was paid 10 guineas for work unspecified: could he have been involved with their design? [Bedford Office, London]

CROOME COURT, Worcs. (6th Earl of Coventry). 1764. Illus. Thornton & Rieder, pt 3, figs 1–2, p. 176.
Juliette Le 20 1764. Aux tres Honnorable Mon Segner Le Conte De Coventry. Pour une Grande Commode Pour Mettre Des Abit incrustée de fleur du bois Natturelle des hinde et ornée de bronze Dorée du prix de £55–0–0
Plus pour La Caisse de bois de Pouce £1–5–0
pour deux botte de paille ficele et papier £0–4–4
Le Totale £56–9–4
Le meme jour recu Le Contens de ce billiet en plen et toutte Demende par moy. [Signed] Petter Langlois
SHERBORNE, Dorset (7th Lord Digby). 1762: 21 May. To Peter L'Anglois £12.12s. [Hoare's Bank, Digby account] 1764: 23 June. 'Money paid in London — L'Anglois £23'. [Sherborne Castle MS, Burnet's accounts. Possibly for the 'ostrich' tables in the Red Drawing Room] W.R.

Langman, George, St Pancras, London, cm (1818). On 4 April 1818 married Hannah Giles of Littlemore, Oxon., at the Church of St Mary the Virgin, Oxford. [Bodleian index of Oxf. marriage bonds]

Langman, John, High St, Downham Market, Norfolk, u and cm (1822–39). [D]

Langmead, William, High St, Hampstead, London, carver and gilder (1838–39). [D]

Langmore, William & Co., corner of King St, Guildhall Yd, London, upholders (1726–27). A large business if insurance records provide a true picture. In 1726 insured their stock for £1,000 which was increased in the following year to £2,000. [GL, Sun MS vol. 23, p. 121; vol. 25, ref. 43059]

Langrich, John, Arundel, Sussex, upholder (1772). [Bailey's List of bankrupts]

Langridge, John, London, chairmaker (1808–20). In 1808 at Holywell Row, Shoreditch and in 1820 at 48 Halfmoon Alley, Bishopsgate. [D]

Langshaw, William, Bristol, cm (1793–1806). At Milk St, 1793–95, but by 1801 had moved to Stokes Croft. The number in Stokes Croft was 53 in 1805–06. In 1793 subscribed to Sheraton's *Drawing Book*. [D]

Langslow, Edward, 13 Peter St, Bloomsbury, London, u (1789–93). [D]

Langstaff, Francis, Richmond, Yorks. u (1823–40). At Market Pl., 1823–27, but in 1840 in Frenchgate. [D]

Langstaffe, Joseph, Newcastle, upholder (1734). [Poll bk]

Langthorn, Mr, near Corner of Coventry Ct, Haymarket, London, glass grinder and glass seller (1768). Sale of entire stock in trade and household furniture on his retirement, at his house above, announced in *Public Advertiser*, 15 March 1768.

Langthorn, Henry, parish of St Martin-in-the-Fields, London, frame maker (1706–16). In addition to his own house he possessed at least two other houses that he rented out. One was in the parish of St Martin-in-the-Fields and was insured for £125 in 1706, and the other in Portugal St was valued at £175 in 1716. Supplied frames for Felbrigg, Norfolk in 1708 to a value of £3 4s 6d. [GL, Hand in Hand MS vol. 4, ref. 10729; vol. 16, ref. 31439; Norfolk RO, Felbrigg WKC 6/23]

Langton, David, 10 Queen St, Cheapside, London, upholder (1737–d. 1795). Son of William Langton of Southwark, tanner. App. to William Rose, 7 August 1723 and free of the Upholders' Co. by servitude, 5 October 1737. Master of the Upholders' Co., 1772. Took as apps Samuel Stephens (1739–47), Edward Polhill (1747–56), William Meade (1755–62), Powell Buckler (1769–76), William Chinnery (1771–73) and Joseph Stephens (free 1778). At a date between 1778 and 1781 he took a partner named Buckler probably his former app., and the partnership continued until c. 1783 when David Langton retired. In 1786 he was living at Silver St, Edmonton, London and his death was recorded in November 1795. [D; GL, Upholders' Co. records; *Gents Mag.*, November 1795]

Langton, Robert, St Mary's Gate, Grimsby, Lincs., joiner and cm (1826). [D]

Langton, Robert, Epworth, Lincs., cm and joiner (1835). [D]

Langton, William, Epworth, Lincs., cm and joiner (1835). [D]

Lankford, Joseph, parish of St Mary Redcliffe, Bristol, cm (1754). [Poll Bk]

Lankford, Robert, Bristol, cm (1754). [Poll Bk]

Lannder, Paul, Norwich, u (1743). Free 20 June 1743 but not by apprenticeship. [Freemen rolls]

Lanning, —, 9 Kirby St, Hatton Gdn, London, carver and gilder (1835). [D]

Lanning, Thomas, 43 Theobalds Rd, London, cm and u (1835–39). [D]

Lano, W., 40 Greek St, Soho, London, white wood box maker (1835). [D]

Lansdale, Matthew, Manchester, cm (1808–17). In 1808 at Both St, but from 1813 at 4 Water St, Bridge St. Recorded at 22 Back King St in 1815. [D]

Lansdell, George, Mays Buildings, Kings Rd, Brighton, Sussex, cm and u (1820–24). Two daughter bapt. in 1820 and 1824. [PR (bapt.)]

Lansdell, James, 48 Union Pl., Brighton, Sussex, carver and gilder (1826–27). [D]

Lansdell, John, Brighton Pl., Brighton, Sussex, cm, u, carver and gilder (1805–24). One directory of 1822 lists the number in Brighton Pl. as 5 and another as 6. In 1824 it was 6. Some directories list the trade as cm or cm and u and others as carver and gilder. [D]

Lansdell, Stephen, Brighton, Sussex, carver, gilder and looking-glass manufacturer (1832–40). In 1832 shown by one directory at 55 Meeting House Lane and another at 54 Union Pl. The latter address was in use in 1833. In 1839 at 50 East St where the manufacture of looking-glasses is mentioned for the first time. May have been a partnership as some directories refer to Messrs Lansdell. [D]

Lansdell, Stephen, 31 South St, Worthing, Sussex, carver and gilder (1839). Possibly a branch of the Brighton maker. [D]

Lansdell & Moppett, 6 East St, Brighton, Sussex, cm and u (1799–1800). [D]

Lantheon, J., address unknown, cm (1803). Subscribed to Sheraton's *Cabinet Dictionary*, 1803.

Lapierre, Francis, Pall Mall, London, u (1688–d. 1717). An important Huguenot u who was employed on an extensive scale by the Crown and on major furnishing schemes in the last years of the 17th and the first two decades of the 18th century. His French nationality led him to be prosecuted in 1697 as an alien enemy.

The earliest commissions of this maker occur in the year of the Revolution in 1688 which placed William III and Mary II on the throne. He had worked for the Crown before the overthrow of James II, however, for commissions in connection with the furnishing of the Royal Hospital, Chelsea commence in the early months of that year. They carried on until 1692 and involved the supply of beds, chairs, cushions and other upholsterer's work costing £1,361 7s 6d. Immediately following the Revolution Lapierre supplied on loan for the Duke of Schomberg's appartment at St James's an ornate bed of crimson Genoese velvet, six walnut chairs and a large Turkey carpet. These were retained until August 1690, and for the 20 months hire a charge of £230 was made. In the period 1693–94 fifteen 'French frames' were provided for Hampton Court at a cost of £26 5s. The upholstery materials provided at the same time as the chair frames was however more significant from the point of view of cost and the whole account totalled £337 13s 4d. For Kensington Palace a large Persian carpet was supplied in 1691 for the Queen's Gallery at a cost of £64 10s.

This patronage by the Royal Household was matched by that of the aristocracy and nobility. For Chatsworth, Derbs. extensive furnishings were provided. In 1694 Lapierre was paid £5 for his expenses in travelling to Chatworth and in the years that followed rich furniture was produced in his workshops for this house. A bed supplied in 1697 cost £470 and arrangement was made to pay for this at £6 per week. The first seventeen payments amounting to £102 were made at Michaelmas of that year. A further £70 was incurred in altering another bed. The canopy and back of Lapierre's bed survive in the Long Gallery at Hardwick Hall, Derbs., another Cavendish property. Payments to Lapierre at Chatsworth continue to March 1700 when 22 yds of velvet were charged at £29 5s and some gold brocade at £15 13s 6d. At Drayton House, Northants. commissions are recorded as early as 1689 and again beds were involved. An account of the Earl of Peterborough's debts drawn up in May 1702 included a sum of £50 due to Lapierre. For Boughton House, Northants. considerable work was undertaken with balances reaching as much as £1,432 4s in 1704. Supplying mending and cleaning tapestries and hangings alone for the period 1695–1705 came to £448 5s. This account was settled in February 1712. The renowned designer Daniel Marot, a fellow Huguenot, is associated with this work at Boughton. At Knole, Kent, gilt chairs and stools were supplied and these are now in the ballroom. The name 'Lapierr 1695' has also been found on a marble fireplace in one of the main bedrooms. He also worked for the 5th Earl of Exeter at Burghley House, Northants. [*Wren Soc*, vol. XIX, p. 85; V & A archives; *DEF*; Nat. Trust guide to *Hardwick*, p. 28; PRO, LC5/43, LC9/125, pp. 34–35, LC9/126, p. 30, LC9/280, LC9/128, p. 17; *Apollo*, April 1975; *C. Life*, 9 June 1977, p. 1620; *Conn.*, April 1981, p. 282; Glyn Mills Bank (Child's), Exeter account] B.A.

Lapierre, Jean, address unknown, u(?) 1707. This name is recorded in the accounts for Dalkeith House, near Edinburgh,

On 9 May 1707 £15 was paid to him 'for helping yᵉ Groom of yᵉ Chamber' furnish the house.

Lapley, James, 'The Three Cocks', upper end of Cheapside, London, goldsmith. On 21 February 1688/89 offered for sale a silver table, stands and looking-glasses with andirons, sconces and several pieces of plate. [*London Gazette*, 21 February 1688/89]

Lappington, Thomas, Piccadilly, London, upholder (1709). In November 1709 insured his house and workshop ajoining for £250. In 1720 a Mrs Lappington was carrying on the business, suggesting that Thomas was by this date dead. [GL, Hand in Hand MS vol. 7, ref. 19266; Heal]

Larche, Peter, 29 Gresse St, Rathbone Pl., London, carver (1806). In 1806 took out insurance cover of £100 on household goods 'in the house of Linney a cabinet maker'. [GL, Sun MS vol. 437, ref. 795193]

Large, James, 226 Piccadilly, London, see Eyre & Large.

Large, James, 19 Old Cavendish St, London, upholder (1825–37). [D]

Large, Thomas, Church St, Wellington, Salop, cm (1822). [D]

Large, W., address unknown, cm (1793). Subscribed to Sheraton's *Drawing Book*, 1793.

Larkin, Philip, Queen St, Chelsea, London, bedstead maker (1837). [D]

Larking, Thomas, Mount St, Nottingham, cm, u and paper hanger (1835). [D]

Larner, William, Church St, Chelsea, London, cm and u (1823). [D]

Laroche, William, Bridgwater, Som., draper and u (1754). [Poll bk]

Larrance, Samuel, Norwich and London, cm, chairmaker and u (1777–1812). In 1777 trading from an address in Dove Lane, when he took out insurance cover of £250 on his utensils, stock and goods and £50 on his warehouse. He was made a freeman of Norwich on 6 November 1778 but had not been app. in the City. By March 1780 he had come to a decision to leave Norwich and advertised his stock in trade for sale by auction. Later in this year he commenced trading from 42 Carnaby St, London as a cm. He took out insurance cover of £300 of which half covered his utensils and stock. His stay in London was however brief and by 1786 he was back in Norwich and living the parish of St John Maddermarket. From 1801 his business address was 1 St Andrew's Plain. [D; poll bks; freemen admission reg.; *Norfolk Chronicle*, 18 March 1780; GL, Sun MS vol. 255, p. 325; vol. 282, p. 443]

Larson, William, parish of St Martin-in-the-Fields, London, carver (d. 1661). 'Died abroad or at sea'. [*PCC Wills*, 1935, p. 148]

Larter, Thomas, St Gregory's Churchyard, Norwich, cm and u (1829–40). On 24 February 1829 his app. Robert Riches jnr was admitted a freeman, which suggests that his business was active well before the first directory entry in 1830. [D; poll bk]

Larter, William, Colegate St, Norwich, cm (1836). [D]

Lary, Joseph, 6 Oxford St, Commercial Rd East, London, cm and u (1839). [D]

Lasbury, F, 2 Bruton St, Bath, Som., u (1819). [D]

Lascelles, Robert, Exeter, Devon, carver and gilder (1824–40). Four sons and three daughters bapt. at St Sidwell's Church, 1824–40. From 1834–36 at Well Lane, but in 1840 at Summer Lane. [PR (bapt.)]

Lascelles, William, Lancaster, cm (1767–68). [Freemen rolls]

Lascells, Edmund, Exeter, Devon, carver (b. 1758–d. 1839). At New Bridge St in 1791 and St Sidwell St, 1825–28. Died 12 December 1839 aged 81. [D; *Exeter Flying Post*, 26 December 1839]

Lashmar, Charles, Brighton, Sussex, cm (1793). [D]

Laskey, John, Exeter, Devon, cm (1727). Free 1727 and in the same year took app. named Waye. [Freemen rolls; S of G, app. index]

Laskey, John, Exeter, Devon, cm and chairmaker (1791–1811). In 1791 also a linen draper. In this year he insured his utensils, stock and goods for £300. In a Militia Census of 1803 his address is recorded as St Paul and Bradninch. In February 1811 announced a change of address from North St to Goldsmith St. [GL, Sun MS vol. 376, p. 362; *Exeter Flying Post*, 21 February 1811]

Laskey, Robert, Exeter, Devon, cm (1796–1816). At North St in 1796 and Goldmith St in 1816. These addresses suggest some relationship to John Laskey. [D]

Laskey, Samuel, London, cm and u (1827–39). At 1 Francis St, Gray's Inn Rd in 1827, 11 Sidmouth St in 1829, 31 Judd Pl., New Rd in 1835 and 4 Wakefield St, Brunswick Sq. in 1839. [D]

Lassell, Thomas, Liverpool, joiner and cum (1811–24). At 1 Sefton St in 1811, 1 Hill St, 1813–14, 10 Park Lane, 1823 and 1 Park Lane in 1824. [D]

Latchford, Thomas, Liverpool, cm (1761). When in September 1761 he was released from Debtors' Prison, he was said to be 'late of Liverpool'. A person of the same name and trade became a freeman of Chester in 1770 and established a business in that city. [*London Gazette*, 13 September 1761]

Latchford, Thomas snr, Northgate St, Chester, cm (1770–84). Free 23 June 1770. His son Thomas Latchford jnr was his app. and free in 1784. A craftsman of the same name described as 'late of Liverpool' was discharged from Debtors' Prison in 1761. [Freemen rolls; poll bk]

Latchford, Thomas jnr, Chester cm (1784). Son and pupil of his father Thomas Latchford snr. Assigned to John Cooke of Chester and free, 6 April 1784. [Freemen rolls]

Lates, John James Benjamin, High St, Walsall, Staffs., cm and u (1830). [D]

Lates, John, 16 Tonk St, Birmingham, u (1839). [D]

Latham, Edmund, Bradford St, Birmingham, u (1828). [D]

Latham, Henry, Dole Lane, Chorley, Lancs., cm and joiner (1818–22). [D]

Latham, James, Gt Wild St, Lincoln's Inn Fields, London, cm (1820–22). In 1820 at 60 Gt Wild St and in 1822 at 50. [D]

Latham, James, St Helens, Lancs., cm (1818–34). In Parr St 1818–25 and also in 1834, but one directory of 1828 shows the address as Church St. [D]

Latham, James, Liverpool, cm (1829–39). At 86 Norfolk St in 1829 but from 1834 in St James St. The number here is 43 in 1834, 40 in 1835, 57 in 1837 and 83 in 1839. [D]

Latham, Joseph, Gray's Inn Rd, London, cm and u (1825–29). At 6 Terrace, Gray's Inn Rd in 1825 but subsequently at 4 Upper North Pl. In 1825 declared his trade to be wholesale cm. [D]

Latham, Joseph, Welsh (or Welch) Row, Nantwich, Cheshire, cm (1828). Associated with Samuel Latham at this address. [D]

Latham, Peter, Chapel Lane, Wigan, Lancs., cm (1822–25). [D]

Latham, Peter, Chapel Lane, Salford, Lancs., cm (1828–34). [D]

Latham, Samuel, Welsh (or Welch) Row, Nantwich, Cheshire, cm (1822–28). Associated with Joseph Latham who followed the same trade at this address in 1828. [D]

Latham, Thomas, Cross Lane, London, carver (1749). [Westminster poll bk]

Latham, William, Tickle St, Manchester, cm (1800–04). At 23 Tickle St in 1800 and 24 in 1804. [D]

Latham, William, Sheffield, Yorks., cm (1821–28). At Whitehouse Lane in 1821 and 32 Fargate in 1828. [D]

Latimar, D., Brampton, Cumb., cm (1811). See also James Lattimer trading as a joiner and cm in Brampton in 1828. [D]

Latleff, John, 30 Bacon St, Spitalfields, London, chair and sofa maker (1839). [D]

Latta, Robert, address unknown, cm (1803). Subscribed to Sheraton's *Cabinet Dictionary*, 1803.

Latten, James, London, u (1799–30). Freeman of Norwich. [Norwich poll bks]

Latter, James, Culverden Gate, Tunbridge Wells, Kent, Tunbridge-ware maker (c. 1795). Trade card in the Sprange Coll., Tunbridge Wells Museum.

Lattimer, James, Brampton, Cumb., joiner and cm (1828). Probably related to the D. Latimar trading in Brampton as a cm in 1811. [D]

Lattimore, —, Lane End, Staffs., joiner and cm (d. 1807). [*Staffordshire Advertiser*, 22 August 1807]

Latton, James, Norwich, upholder (1786). Son of James Latton, pattern maker. Free 28 October 1786. [Freemen admission reg.]

Latus, William, 3 Bridge St, Preston, Lancs., chairmaker (1818). [D]

Lauder, David, New St, Soho, London, cm (1774). [Westminster poll bk]

Lauder, John, London, cm and upholder (1774–86). In 1774 at 48 Chandos St. His trade card [Heal Coll., BM] displays fashionable Rococo furniture and announces that he also conducted funerals. In 1786 at 20 King St, St Ann's. Here he took out insurance cover for £400 but only £90 of this was in respect of utensils, stock and goods in trust. [Westminster poll bk; GL, Sun MS vol. 338, p. 580]

Lauder, John, Rotton Row, Derby, cm and u (1835). [D]

Laughton, Henry, King St, St Ann's Soho, London, carver, gilder and frame maker (1759–64). In August 1759 supplied to John, 4th Duke of Bedford 'a rich carved pier frame & gilt in burnished gold' for which £11 11s was charged. This was probably for Woburn Abbey, Beds. which had recently been rebuilt by Henry Flitcroft. In 1764 frames were supplied by this maker to Sir Lawrence Dundas for his London house, 19 Arlington St. [Bedford Office, London; N. Yorks. RO, ZNK X1/7/74]

Laughton, Henry, Nottingham, chairmaker (1834). [Freemen rolls]

Laughton, Saunders, Stamford, Lincs., cm and joiner (1743). In 1743 took L. Rayner as app. [Stamford Town Hall bk 2A/1/3]

Launder, William, Groombridge, Kent, turner and chairmaker (1761). In February 1761 advertised for four journeymen, a chairmaker, a pail maker, a shovelmaker and a hollow turner. [*Sussex Weekly Advertiser*, 16 February 1761]

Laurance, Thomas, Dunholme, Lincs., cm (1760). In 1760 took app. named Priestley. [S of G, app. index]

Laurence, Alexander, Macclesfield, Cheshire, chairmaker (1761). In 1761 took app. named Allen. [S of G, app. index]

Laurence, Samuel, 'The Crown & Coffee Mill', Fenchurch St, London, turner (1730). In July 1730 supplied Sir Gilbert Heathcote with a large pair of backgammon tables and dice boxes at £1 3s. [Lincoln RO, 2 ANC 12/0/12]

Laurikens(?), Mark Anthony, 37 Greenhill Rents, Smithfield, London, shagreen case maker (1810). Insured his household goods for £300 in December 1810. [GL, Sun MS vol. 449, ref. 852162]

Lavallin, John, Goldsmith's St, Exeter, Devon, cm and u (1770). In May 1770 announced the establishment of his shop in Goldsmith's St where he traded as a 'working' cm. He sold mahogany 'solid Chests of Drawers, with or without Sliding Desks; Commode Chests of Drawers, Tables, Desks, Book-Cases, and Wardrobes; Writing Tables of all Sorts, with Spring Tops; Mahogany Chairs of the newest Patterns, &c. &c. all which he sells at Fifteen per Cent. cheaper than the usual Prices for Ready Money'. He also undertook upholstery work and featured in his advertisement 'BED and WINDOW CURTAINS, In the True Festoon Manner'. He stocked pier glasses. The advertisement ended with an appeal for workmen in the cabinet and chair branches to assist in the business. [*Exeter Evening Post*, 18–25 May 1770]

Lavallin, Michael, High St, Colchester, Essex, cm and u (1805–08). [D]

Lave, Edward, 5 Bedford St, Commercial Rd, London, u (1839). [D]

Lavender, James, Portsmouth, Hants., cm (1717). In 1717 took app. named Knight. [S of G, app. index]

Lavender, William, 15 Old Cavendish St, Cavendish Sq., London, japanner, chair and cabinet maker (1807–11). In 1808–09 the trade was listed as japanner and chairmaker but from 1809–11 it was japanner and cm. [D]

Laverock, James, London, cm and u (1826–29). At 53 Paddington St, Marylebone, 1826–27, but in 1829 at Bedford St, Bedford Row. [D]

Law, John, 10 Derby St, Liverpool, cm (1796). [D]

Law, Joseph, Sedgeley, Staffs., cm (1761). In 1761 took app. named Taylor. [S of G, app. index]

Law, Magnus, Duke's Ct, St Martin's Lane, London, cm (1790–93). [D]

Law, Robert, Wooler, Northumb., cm, u and joiner (1827–34). [D]

Law, Stephen, London, cm and u (1809–39). At 66 Gt Titchfield St, Cavendish Sq. in 1809 and 102 Gt Portland St, 1812–39. [D]

Law, William, Sedgeley, Staffs., cm (1759–61). In 1759 took app. named Clark and in 1761, Bowyer. Law's address in 1761 was stated to be 'Tedby', Staffs. [S of G, app. index]

Law, William, 28 Upper King St, Bloomsbury, London, cm and u (1827). [D]

Law, William, Ulverston, Lancs., cm and u (1828–34). In 1828 in Market St; in 1829 in King St; and in 1834 in Brook St. [D]

Law, William Henry, London, cm and u (1822–39). In October 1822 at 38 King St, Holborn. He took out insurance cover for £650 of which £500 was for utensils, stock and goods in trust. His workshop was in Upper King St over a cowhouse and he appears to have been living at this date in the house of a man called Holland, a coachmaker. By February 1824 he had moved to 48 Devonshire St, Queen Sq. which he was to occupy until 1839. In February 1824 his insurance cover was increased to £750. He still retained the workshop in Upper King St, but this was now rented out to a maker of pianos and was covered for £250. His main place of work was now Devonshire St which had a warehouse behind valued at £100. Utensils and goods were valued at £175 with an additional £30 for glass plates and smaller sums for prints and pictures, china and glass. [D; GL, Sun MS vol. 489, ref. 997188; vol. 495, ref. 1014388]

Lawcock, John, Pontefract, Yorks., cm (1754). In 1754 took app. named Reynold. [S of G, app. index]

Lawder, Andrew, London, u (1807–39). Shown at 3 James St, Grosvenor Sq. in an 1808 directory, with the number changed to 4 in the following year. Insurance records however show him at 4 Grosvenor St as early as 20 November 1807 when he took out cover for £600. At 3 King St, Portman Sq. in 1835 and two years later the business changed its style to Andrew Lawder & Son. A further move was made to 105 High St, Marylebone. [D]

Lawdor, David, New St, London, cm (1784). [Westminster poll bk]

Lawes, Samuel, St Clement's, Norwich, cm (1786). [Poll bk]

Lawes, (or Laws), William, Dover, Kent, cm (1826–28). [Poll bks]

Lawford, William, 13 Marchmont St, Brunswick Sq., London, u (1839). [D]

Lawkland, Thomas, Lancaster, cm (1779–84). Free 1779–80 when stated 'of London'. Almost certainly the cm with the same name at 126 Wardour St, London in 1781. In this year he took out insurance cover for £100. He is included in the 1784 Lancaster poll bk when his address is listed as London. [GL, Sun MS vol. 297, p. 114; Lancaster freemen rolls]

Lawledge, Mathias, London, cm and u (1820–39). Probably the son of Thomas Lawlidge who was trading from 76 Harley St, Cavendish Sq. as an upholder and appraiser in 1817. Mathias Lawledge traded from this address 1820–35 and from 26 Weymouth St, Portland Sq., 1837–39. [D]

Lawler, William, Cirencester, Glos., cm (1828–29). [PR (bapt.)]

Lawless, J., Henrietta Pl., Bath, Som., cm (1833). [D]

Lawley, John, 18 Redlion Ct, Spitalfields, London, bedstead maker (1839). [D]

Lawley, Thomas jnr, Sandford St, Lichfield, Staffs., cm (1830–35). [Poll bks]

Lawlidge, Thomas, 76 Harley St, Cavendish Sq., London, upholder and appraiser (1817). Succeeded at this address in 1820 by Mathias Lawledge. [D]

Lawrance, Samuel, St Andrew's Pl., Norwich, cm and appraiser (1808). [D]

Lawrance, William, Boar Lane, Leeds, Yorks., joiner and cm (1798–1807). In 1807 he sold his business and advertised his intention of trading as an 'Architect & Valuer of Buildings' and also carried on the business of a 'Raff-Merchant'. [*Furn. Hist.*, 1974]

Lawrence, —, Wyle Cop, Shrewsbury, Salop, u (1796). [Freemen rolls]

Lawrence, Ann, 258 Tottenham Ct Rd, London, cm and u (1827). Probably the widow of Charles Lawrence who traded from this address up to 1826 in the same trade. [D]

Lawrence, Charles, 258 Tottenham Ct Rd, St Giles, London, cm, u and undertaker (1817–26). Succeeded by Ann Lawrence in 1827. [D]

Lawrence, Christopher, Barker Lane, York, cm (1778–84). Son of Thomas Lawrence, glover, and free 1778. [Freemen rolls; poll bk]

Lawrence, D. W., 9 Upper Castle St, Leicester Sq., London, carver and gilder (1813–16). [D]

Lawrence, David, 13 New St, Cloth Fair, London, cm (1802). Freeman of Oxford. [Oxford poll bk]

Lawrence, George, 9 New Bond St, pocket book, dressing case and desk maker (1822–39). Nephew and successor to Mrs Elvey. Claimed to be maker to the Royal Family, the King of Prussia and the Prince of Orange. In 1822 supplied an inlaid kingwood writing desk to George IV at a cost of £3 13s 6d. The account was not settled until May 1826. Other patronage came from the Rt Hon. Lord G. Hervey, an invoice existing in the Suffolk RO at Bury St Edmunds. Lawrence is also recorded carrying out repairs from 1833–34 amounting to £13 6s for the Earl of Hopetoun at Hopetoun House, Lothian, Scotland. [D; Windsor Royal Archives, RA25415, 35604; Suffolk RO, 941/73/16; Scottish RO, Hopetoun, bundle 250]

Lawrence, George, Union St, Tottenham Ct Rd, St Pancras, London, chairmaker (1823–24). On 16 October 1823 took app. named James Wood, but the apprenticeship was cancelled from 18 August 1824 by the magistrate at the Marylebone St Office on the grounds of ill treatment. [GL, P83/MRY1/876/152]

Lawrence, James, Fossgate, York, cm (1780–1816). Son of Thomas Lawrence, cm and free 1780. In April 1801 took his son Thomas as app. Thomas and his brother Edward were sworn free as cm in 1812, and a further son Christopher was free as a cm 1816. [Poll bk; freemen rolls]

Lawrence, James, Gloucester Pl., Southwark, London, bedstead maker (1826). [D]

Lawrence, James, Arches St, Newport, Isle of Wight, Hants., u (1839). [D]

Lawrence, John, Bloomsbury, London, carver (1761). In 1761 discharged from Debtors' Prison. His address was stated to be formerly of Bloomsbury, St Giles, Middlx. [*London Gazette*, 22 August 1761]

Lawrence, John, 150 Bishopsgate St Without, London, u (1765–73). His trade card [Heal Coll., BM] indicates that he was also an undertaker and appraiser. He also sold cabinet goods, and a tallboy, a bureau and two tables are illustrated on his trade card. [D]

Lawrence, John, 29 Litchfield St, Soho, London, carver and gilder (1820). [D]

Lawrence, John, Commercial Rd, Cheltenham, Glos., cm and u (1830). [D]

Lawrence, Joseph, Shrewsbury, Salop, u (1776). In 1776 insured his shop, utensils and stock for £600. In 1796 a Lawrence, u, was trading at an address in Wyle Cop. [GL, Sun MS vol. 247, p. 285]

Lawrence, Joseph, Market Pl., Henley-on-Thames, Oxon., cm and u (1823). [D] See Lawrence & Owthwaite

Lawrence, Matthew, London, carver and gilder (1835–39). In 1835 at 77 Whitelion St, Pentonville and in 1839 at 7 Well St, Oxford St. [D]

Lawrence, R. Thomas, 31 Hercules Buildings, Lambeth, London, carver and gilder (1826–27). [D]

Lawrence, Richard, Chester and Bristol, u (1732). Son of Richard Lawrence of Chester, tailor. Freeman of Chester, 12 October 1732. [Freemen rolls]

Lawrence, Richard, address unknown, carver (1732–37). In connection with Cley, the Duke of Montrose's house in Norfolk, he is recorded supplying marble tables '& glasses for the tabernacles' at a cost of £71. These were paid for in 1732. [Scottish RO, GD 220/6/31, p. 640] Lawrence also worked with James Richards, Master Sculptor and Carver to the Crown, in 1737 on the Queen's Library, St James's Palace. [H. M. Colvin, ed., *History of the King's Works*, vol. 5 p. 243, fn.1]

Lawrence, Richard, Wardour St, Soho, London, carver (1732–95). App. to Sefferin Alken in 1746, and presumably son of Richard Lawrence above. Working for the Crown by 1760 at Windsor, where he was given care of Grinling Gibbons's carved woodwork, much to the disgust of George Murray (d. 1761), who had been appointed Master Sculptor and Carver to the Crown in February 1760. Lawrence undertook a considerable amount of carving in stone at Greenwich Hospital, including the restoration of the Chapel following the fire of 1779. Worked at Somerset House, Strand, 1777–91, in both stone and wood. Also worked at Strawberry Hill, Westminster Hall, Milton Manor, Berks., Inveraray Castle, the Duke of Buckingham's London house in Pall Mall, and Shardeloes, Bucks. [D; Beard, *Craftsmen and Interior Decoration*, 1981; Gunnis; Bucks. RO, Tyrwhitt Drake MS 5/27]

Lawrence, Thomas, Chester, upholder (1747). [Poll bk]

Lawrence, Thomas, Leeds and York, cm (1758–84). Freeman of York. In Leeds in December 1758 but by 1774 had returned to York and lived in Walmgate, 1774–84. His son James was free as a cm in 1780. [York poll bks; freemen rolls]

Lawrence, Thomas, Wyle Cop, Shrewsbury, Salop, cm (1796). An u named Lawrence is also shown in this street in the same year. [Freemen rolls]

Lawrence, Thomas, York cm (1801–12). Son of James Lawrence, cm of York, and app. to him on 13 April 1801. Free 1812. [Freemen rolls]

Lawrence, Thomas, Bristol, carver and gilder (1817–20). At 3 Barra St, 1817–18, and 6 Syms's Alley, 1819–20. [D]

Lawrence, William, Bristol, cabinet and chair carver (1826–35). At 3 Maudlin Buildings, Upper Maudlin St in 1826, and 12 Horse Fair, 1828–35. [D]

Lawrence, William, Deal, Kent, u (1826). Freeman of Canterbury. [Canterbury poll bk]

Lawrence, William, 10 Gt Quebec St, London, cm and u (1839). [D]

Lawrence & Owthwaite, Market Pl., Henley-on-Thames, Oxon., cm and u (1830). [D] See Joseph Lawrence.

Lawrenson, John, Ormskirk St, St Helens, Lancs., joiner and cm (1834). [D]

Lawson, —, Listergate, Nottingham, fancy chairmaker (1814). Elizabeth Lawson, chairmaker, was at this address in 1832. See James Lawson and Matthew Lawson. [D]

Lawson, Benjamin, 29 New St, Cloth Fair, London, chairmaker (1808). [D]

Lawson, Charles, London, cm and u (1809–27). At 12 Maiden lane, Covent Gdn in 1809 and 4 Wild Passage, Drury Lane in 1827. [D]

Lawson, Elizabeth, Listergate, Nottingham, chairmaker (1822–32). A person named Lawson was working in Listergate as a fancy chairmaker in 1814. [D] See James Lawson and Matthew Lawson

Lawson, George, Coppergate, York, cm (1774–84). [Poll bks]

Lawson, George, Marlborough St, Liverpool, chairmaker (1827–39). The number in Marlborough St is given as 23 in 1827 and 1837, 24 in 1829, 43 in 1834 and 45 in 1839. [D]

Lawson, Gilbert, London, victualler and cm (1777–84). In 1777 at the Chequers, Abingdon St, Westminster where he took out insurance cover of £500 of which £300 was for utensils and stock. In 1784 in Park St, Westminster. [GL, Sun MS vol. 254, p. 331; poll bk]

Lawson, J., 33 Wilks St, Spitalfields, London, chairmaker (1820). [D]

Lawson, James, 4 Chandos St, Covent Gdn, London, cm (1763–78). In the period 1763–65 recorded in directories as James & Peter Lawson but after 1767 solely as James Lawson. Carried out extensive commissions for Sir Lawrence Dundas for Moor Park, Herts., Aske Hall, Yorks. and his London house at 19 Arlington St. Between June 1763 and April 1764 goods to the value of £399 6s 9½d were supplied and from April 1764 to October of the same year bills from this maker totalled £359 9s 7½d. After this amounts became less, and from December 1764, to September 1765 only £68 18s 3d was due. A document of c. 1770 exists, in which Sir Lawrence totalled the sums paid to craftsmen in connection with his houses in England and against Lawson's name the sum is listed as 'about £1,100'. Detailed invoices survive for the furniture supplied in 1763 and 1764. A great quantity of Lawson's furniture for Sir Lawrence was useful rather than highly decorative, for this patron was also emloying Samuel Norman, France & Bradburn, Thomas Chippendale and Fell & Turton to provide furniture for him at this time. He did however buy from Lawson one expensive suite of giltwood furniture. A hall chair, one of a set of five originally supplied, a pair of mahogany serving tables and a mahogany clothes press, all now at Aske Hall have been identified as items supplied on these invoices in 1764. Another house in which Lawson's name is recorded in the accounts is Burton Constable, Yorks. Here an account survives for a mahogany writing table 'with a top to rise' which was invoiced on 10 August 1771 at £7 10s. In 1778 he was paid £11 8s by Sir Edward Knatchbull of Mersham-le-Hatch, Kent for 'putting up, cleaning the walls & for brown paper'. [D; *Apollo*,

September 1967; N. Yorks. RO, ZNK X 1/7/26–30, 72; Kent RO, U951 A19/2]

Lawson, James, London, cm and chairmaker (1801–08). Bankruptcy announced, *Liverpool Advertiser*, 7 December 1801. Subscribed to Sheraton's *Cabinet Dictionary*, 1803, and in 1808 trading from 17 Montague St, Spitalfields. [D]

Lawson, James, Keswick, Cumb., joiner/cm (1811). [D]

Lawson, James jnr, 21 Princes Sq., Ratcliffe Highway, London, chair and sofa maker (1820–37). [D]

Lawson, James, Stratford, Essex, cm (1823). [D]

Lawson, James, Burscough St, Ormskirk, Lancs., chairmaker (1825). [D]

Lawson, James, Nottingham, chairmaker (1825–35). Recorded at Listergate, 1825–28, and Leen Side in 1835. [D] See Lawson, —, Elizabeth Lawson and Matthew Lawson.

Lawson, James, Lancaster, turner (1827–28). Named in the Gillow records in connection with chair manufacture. [Westminster Ref. Lib., Gillow vol. 344/102, p. 3647]

Lawson, James, 16 Worship St, Finsbury, London, cm (1835). [D]

Lawson, John, Pall Mall, London, upholder (1718–22). The location in Pall Mall is given as 'Against Pall Mall Court' in 1720, 'next door to the Royal Oak' in 1721 and on the north side in 1722. His dwelling house here was insured for £300 in 1722. Recorded working for Judith, Countess of Jersey, 1718–20. The largest amount paid was £21 1s for chairs and window curtains. A number of picture frames were made, a picture cleaned, a bed set up, a large glass sconce, a 'pair of stairs' and some 'walnut drawers for a bureau to stand on' supplied. [Heal; GL, Sun MS vol. 10, ref. 16461; vol. 26, p. 351; PRO, C111/54]

Lawson, John, Cambridge, cm, u and joiner (1763–66). John Lawson is first recorded when on 4 June 1763 he advertised in the *Cambridge Chronicle*, saying that 'he has taken a SHOP next Door to the Black-Bear in Bridge-Street'. On 24 September of the same year he advertised that he would have a Booth 'with a very great Choice of Goods' at the annual Sturbridge Fair, held just outside Cambridge. He advertised again on 7 April 1764, when moving to a shop on the corner of Shoemaker Row, Cambridge, describing himself as an 'Upholsterer and Cabinet Maker from London'. On 7 June 1766 a two-day auction was advertised of all 'the Shop Goods of John Lawson, Upholsterer and Cabinet maker . . . leaving off those Branches of Business except bespoke Goods . . . The Carpenters and Joiners Work carried on . . . as before'.
R.W.

Lawson, John, Lancaster (1789–1840). Named in the Gillow records in 1789, 1814, 1819–20, 1822–26, 1830, 1833, 1840. [Westminster Ref. Lib., Gillow]

Lawson, John, Lancaster, cm (1803–12). App. to William Blackburn 1803 and free 1811–12. [App. Reg.]

Lawson, John, Blaydon, Co. Durham, joiner/carpenter/cm (1834). [D]

Lawson, Joshua, Main St, Cockermouth, Cumb., chairmaker (1829). [D]

Lawson, Matthew, Listergate, Nottingham, chairmaker (1835–40). [D] See Lawson, —, Elizabeth Lawson and James Lawson.

Lawson, Richard, Coppergate, York, cm (1774). [Poll bk]

Lawson, Richard, London, cm (before 1785). In July 1785 working in the state of Maryland in the USA and had been resident there for a time. He claimed to have been employed for thirteen years in 'Mr Seddon's warehouse, in London'. [*Maryland Journal*, 29 July 1785]

Lawson, Robert, Lancaster, cm (1805–33). App. to J. Hodgson 1805 and free, 1811–12. Named in the Gillow records 1818,

1820–27, 1830 and 1832–33. [App. reg.; Westminster Ref. Lib., Gillow]

Lawson, Stephen, Rotherhithe, London, carver (1780–86). Operated 1780–83 as Lawson & Hopkins from near Prince's Stairs but in 1786 Stephen Lawson was declared bankrupt. Trading once more on his own account from 36 Rotherhithe in 1788. Most of his emloyment appears to have been ship carving. [D; *Gents Mag.*, June 1786]

Lawson, Thomas, Huntriss Row, Scarborough, Yorks., cm (1823). [D]

Lawson, Thomas, Red St, Nottingham, chairmaker (1825). [D]

Lawson, William, Holme, Notts., chairmaker and turner (1719). In 1719 took app. named Pratt. [S of G, app. index]

Lawson, William, High St, Oldham, Lancs., cm (1834). [D]

Lawson, William, Parliament St, York, cm etc. (1840). [D]

Lawther, Matthew, 16 Bride Lane, Bridge St, London, cm (1823). In January 1823 took out insurance cover of £150 which included £30 for a chest of tools in William Baynes's workshop in Wheatsheaf Yd, Fleet Mkt. [GL, Sun MS vol. 489, ref. 999880]

Lawton, John, Manchester, cm (1772–81). In 1772 at Long Millgate, in 1773 at Deansgate and in 1781 at High St. [D]

Lawton, John, 35 Cow Lane, West Smithfield, London, glass grinder and plated frame maker (1811). In March 1811 took out insurance cover of £2,800. His premises included a workshop and a warehouse and his utensils and stock were covered for £1,600 and his stock of glass for £800. [GL, Sun MS vol. 449, ref. 854956]

Lawton, John, 75 Oldham St, Manchester, cm and u (1819). [D]

Lawton, Joseph, Drighlington, near Bradford, Yorks., cm (1822). [D]

Lawton, Joseph, Warrington, Lancs., cm (1825–28). At 1 Church St in 1825 and Sandy Lane in 1828. [D]

Lawton, Samuel, Deansgate, Manchester, cm (1755–72). In 1755 took app. named Boardman. In 1773 a John Lawton, cm was trading in this street and may have been his successor. [D; S of G, app. index]

Lawton, William, Hart St, Manchester, cm (1794). [D]

Lay, E., 39 Dean St, Soho, London, carver, gilder and print seller (1790–93). [D]

Lay, Henry, Dean St, Soho, London, carver, gilder (1772–80). A bill of *c.* 1772 exists for goods supplied by Henry Lay to a club in Arlington St run by Cullen, a former furniture maker. This was for £77. Bankruptcy announced June 1778, but re-established his business in Dean St, near St Ann's Church, and in 1780 took out insurance cover for £700, which included £530 for his workshop. The Eleanor Lay trading at 38 Dean St in 1790 was probably his wife. She gilded 5 circular frames for the Navy Board Room at Somerset House in 1789, charging £2 5s 0d each. [*Gents Mag.*, June 1778; GL, Sun MS vol. 281, p. 290; PRO, C104/146, pt 1; RIBA Library, Somerset House accounts, 3]

Lay, William, Norwich, cm (1774). Son of William Lay. Free 19 February 1774. [Freemen admission reg.]

Laycock, Daniel, Burnley, Lancs., cm (b. 1785–41). At Yorkshire St in 1818 but by 1841 had moved to Hargreaves St. [D; census]

Laycock, G. H., 17 St James's Churchyard, Bristol, chair carver and grainer (1822–40). From 1831 advertised himself as a cane worker and dealer in rattan cane. [D]

Laycock, John, York St, Covent Gdn, London, leather box maker (1783). Declared bankrupt, *Gents Mag.*, February 1783.

Laycock, Thomas, parish of St Ann, Blackfriars, London, cm (1691). [Heal]

Laycock, William, Silsden, near Keighley, Yorks., chairmaker (1822–37). [D]

Laydeman, T., Keswick, Cumb., joiner/cm (1811). [D]

Layfield, Richard, 24 Gt Pulteney St, Golden Sq., London, cm (1829–39). [D]

Layfield, Robert, Darlington, Co. Durham, joiner and cm (1827–34). At Dun Cow Yd, High Row in 1827, Post Office Wynd in 1828 and Skinnergate in 1834. [D]

Layton, Edward, High St, Poole, Dorset, u and paper hanger (1823). [D]

Layton, Frederick, Sunbury, Middlx, u (1838). [D]

Layton, Samuel, Putney, London, upholder (1808). [D]

Layton, Thomas, 37 Bury St, St James's, London, u (1826). [D]

Layton, Thomas, 3 Ogleforth, York, cm (1838). [D]

Layton, William, 52 Cheapside, Dale St, Liverpool, chairmaker (1796). [D]

Layton, William, High St, Staines, Middlx, cm (1823–26). [D]

Lazenby, Thomas, London, carver, gilder, frame maker and print seller (1780–93). In 1780 at 227 Strand where he took out insurance cover of £300 but only £80 of this was in respect of utensils, stock and goods. Bankrupt in 1789, but from 1790–93 in business again at Gt Surrey St, Blackfriars. [D; GL, Sun MS vol. 284, p. 462; Bailey's list of bankrupts]

Lea, J., 19 Poppins Ct, Fleet St, London, case maker (1826). [D]

Lea, James, 417 Oxford St, St Giles, London, upholder and undertaker (1817–19). [D]

Lea, John, address unknown, cm (1803). Subscribed to Sheraton's *Cabinet Dictionary*, 1803.

Lea, Thomas, 1 Northumberland St, Strand, London, cm and upholder (1820–28). [D]

Lea, William, Kidderminster, Worcs., cm (1760). In 1760 took app. named Weston. [S of G, app. index]

Leace, Catherine, Liverpool, u (1827–29). At 32 Wood St in 1827 and 14 Grafton St, Harrington in 1829. [D]

Leach, Charles, Oxford, carpenter, joiner and cm (1798). [D]

Leach, George, Lambeth, London, cm (1830). Freeman of Canterbury. [Canterbury poll bk]

Leach, George, 102 High St, Southampton, Hants., cm, u and chairmaker (1839). [D]

Leach, Henry jnr, 63 Falkner St, Manchester, cm (1829). [D]

Leach, James, Lancaster (1831–33). [Westminster Ref. Lib., Gillow records]

Leach, Martha, Bristol, chairmaker (1821–30). At Redcliffe back, 1821–26 and 1828–30 when the number was 4. In 1827 however shown at 44 Mardyke, Hotwell Rd. [D]

Leach, Robert, Canterbury, Kent, u (1830–38). In the parish of St George in June 1830 but in 1838 at 16 Palace St. [D; poll bk]

Leach, William, Liverpool, cm (1730). In 1730 took app. named Bevins. [S of G, app. index]

Leach, William, Plymouth, Devon, upholder and cm (1784–98). [D]

Leadbeater, John, 14 Piccadilly, Manchester, cm and u (1824–32). In partnership with a J. Barlow in September 1832 when their bankruptcy was announced in *Chester Courant*, 4 September 1832. [D]

Leadbeater, Thomas, 8 Cobourg Pl., Borough Rd, London, chairmaker (1835–39). [D]

Leadbeater, William, Chapelgate, Retford, Notts., cm (1832). [D]

Leadbeater & Barlow, 31 King St, Manchester, cm and u (1832–33). [D]

Leadbetter, Thomas, Liverpool, u (1767–d. by 1772). Free 24 November 1767 but did not trade for long. In December 1772 an auction sale of the remaining stock of the late Thomas Leadbetter was announced. This consisted of 'Morines, Chineys & Checks for Bed Furniture; Counterpanes, coverlets, quilts, Wilton & Scotch carpeting; hair cloth for chair seats, royal matting; great variety of papers for hanging rooms; buckram, bed laces, fringe, tassels, line, curtain rings etc: Together with several Bedsteads & Hangings, good Feather Beds, Chests of Drawers, Mahogany Chairs & Tables, Looking Glasses, some China etc.'. [*Williamson's Liverpool Advertiser*, 25 December 1772; freemen reg.]

Leadbitter, Jno., 32 Marshall St, Golden Sq., London, cm and u (1826–29). [D]

Leader, George, Oxford St, London, carver and gilder (1784–1819). From 1792 advertised himself as Carver to His Majesty. Also made moulds for cooks and confectioners and from c. 1809 dealt in turnery and toys both wholesale and retail. Shown at 218 Oxford St in 1784, but from 1792 the number was 188. His trade card survives. [Banks Coll., BM] In November 1796 charged £10 18s for carving and gilding a Royal coat of arms for Totterridge Church, Herts. He also carved a coat of arms and other figures for John, 6th Duke of Bedford in March 1806 for which £3 12s was charged. [D; Hatfield House bills 597; Bedford Office, London]

Leader, George, Bridge St, Nottingham, carver and gilder, mould and block maker (1832). [D]

Leadman, John, Stepney, London, carver (d. 1685). [PCC Wills, vol. X]

Leak, George, 5 Upper Union St, Hull, Yorks., u and cm (1834–39). Shown as a working u, 1834–35, and as a cm, 1837–38. [D]

Leak, William, Eastgate, Louth, Lincs., cm and joiner (1826–35). Recorded as William T. in 1835. In 1841 an Edward Leak was trading as a cm and joiner in this street. [D]

Leake, A., 59 Greek St, Soho, London, chairmaker (1826). [D]

Leake, Eileen, Wyle Cop, Shrewsbury, Salop, cm (1786). A person by the name of Leake is also shown in a directory of 1798 and may be Eileen or her successor. [D]

Leake, Eslem, Wyle Cop, Shrewsbury, Salop, cm (c. 1796). [D]

Leake, George Edward, Wyle Cop, Shrewsbury, Salop, u (1835). [Freemen rolls]

Leake, James, Wyle Cop, Shrewsbury, Salop, cm (1839). [Freemen rolls]

Leake, William, Parliament St, Nottingham, cm (1814). [D]

Leake, William, Trenchard St, Bristol, cabinet, coach and ivory turner (1837–40). At 16 Trenchard St, 1837, but from the following year the number was 29. [D]

Leaman, Samuel, Ixworth, Suffolk, cm and auctioneer (1839). [D]

Lean, —, address unknown, cm (1803). Subscribed to Sheraton's *Cabinet Dictionary*, 1803.

Leaper, Daniel, East St, Coggeshall, Essex, cm (1823–39). [D]

Lear, Henry, Arundel, Sussex, cm and auctioneer (1784–93). [D]

Lear, James, High St, Arundel, Sussex, cm and u (1811–40). After 1832 the business is styled Lear & Sons though in 1839 Lear & Co. and James Lear & Son are both used. In 1845 the business was being run by Henry Lear who was probably one of James's sons. The Earl of Surrey's Littlehampton account book records a payment of 10s to James Lear in January 1830. [D; Arundel Castle records, A 2077]

Learner, Henry, London, cm (1835–37). In 1835 at 59 Gt Titchfield St and in 1837 at 59 Wells St, Oxford St. [D]

Leath, Isaac, 9 Commercial Rd, London, broker and cm (1821). In February 1821 took out insurance cover of £400 of which £300 was for utensils, stock and goods in trust. [GL, Sun MS vol. 485, ref. 976984]

Leath, Samuel, Norwich and London, cm (1799–1830). Son of Simon Leath, worsted weaver and free 14 September 1799. Still working in Norwich, July 1802, but by November 1806 was in London where he was to stay. In 1806 and 1818 declared his trade as chairmaker but in 1830 as cm. [Norwich poll bks]

Leatham, S., 12 Cow Cross St, London, carver and gilder (1809). [D]

Leathead, William, Alnwick, Northumb., cm and house carpenter (1793). [D]

Leather, John, Johnson St, Liverpool, joiner and cm (1790). [D]

Leather, W. U., 30 Curtain Rd, London, cm (1829–32). [D; Shoreditch archives, Rose Lipman Lib., MS M3545, p. 39]

Leatherbarrow, William, Liverpool, cm (1751–59). Free 4 July 1751. His app. Thomas Lyon petitioned freedom in 1759. [Freemen reg.; committee bk]

Leavers, James, 13 Newington Causeway, London, u and auctioneer (1800–09). [D]

Lecand, Benjamin Louis, London, carver and gilder (1809–39). At 38 Gt Prescot St, Goodman's Fields, 1809–25, and then after a gap at 246 Tottenham Ct Rd, 1835–39. A number of Regency convex mirrors with eagle surmounts are known bearing the trade label of this maker. A pair of these mirrors are in the collection of the Norsk Folkemuseum, Oslo, Norway, and other examples are known there, suggesting a flourishing export business. His trade embraced picture frame manufacture, the restoration of paintings, the sale of stationery and the hanging of wall paper. His insurance in 1820 totalled £1,000. This covered his house in Prescot St, and a workshop with dwelling rooms over in the yard behind. Stock, including pictures and glass, was valued at £300 with an additional £200 for his stock as a stationer and paper hanger. In 1824 the cover had fallen in £750 of which stock and utensils accounted for £325. Items covered included a silvering table. [D; *Apollo*, May 1955, p. 144; *Conn. Year Book*, 1959; *Conn.*, September 1968, p. 18; Wills, *Looking-Glasses*; GL, Sun MS vol. 484, ref. 968797; vol. 487, ref. 983615; vol. 497, ref. 1012424]

Le Caron, Philip, Long Acre, London, u (1716–28). Supplied furniture to the Methuen family at Corsham Court, Wilts. On 8 March 1716/17 an invoice was issued for six servant's bedsteads with curtains and half testers at £2 12s each. These with other items totalled £37. Four further beds were supplied in 1720 at a cost of £14. The last recorded transaction was on 20 November 1728 when a receipt was issued for the sum of £9 paid by Sir Paul Methuen. [V & A archives]

Le Cerf, James, Canterbury, Kent, and London, cm (1767–96). Freeman of Canterbury in 1767 but by January 1790 was living at 'Western-park' London. In 1796 his address in London was given as Drury Lane. [Freemen rolls; Canterbury poll bks]

Le Clercq, John Francis, 10 Mary Bone St, Haymarket, London, billiard table maker (1785). [GL, Sun MS vol. 329, p. 505]

Lecount, Richard, 12 Lambeth Walk, London, cm and Tunbridge-ware maker (1812). On 14 December 1812 took out insurance cover of £300, half of which was in respect of utensils and stock. [GL, Sun MS vol. 455, ref. 877337]

Ledger, Richard, Moorfields, London, cm (1783). [Bailey's list of bankrupts]

Ledger, Richard, Liverpool, u and cm (1818–39). In the period 1818–21 at 40 and 42 Circus St, but by 1823 had moved to Byrom St. The number in this street was 46 from 1823–29. In December 1829 however a fire broke out which destroyed his workshops and part of his house. While re-building was taking place he moved to 24 Byrom St. The number 48 appears in directories in 1827 and 1835; 17 in 1834 and 1837; and 97 in 1839. In November 1832 the death of his second son Richard at the age of 11 was announced. [D; *Liverpool Mercury*, 18 December 1829, 23 November 1832]

Ledger, Richard, Kirkby South, near Barnsley, Yorks., cm etc. (1822). [D]

Ledgerwood, —, 'Greenlaw', cm (1793). Subscribed to Sheraton's *Drawing Book*, 1793.

Lediard, Thomas, Macclesfield, Cheshire, cm (1759). In 1759 took app. named Bowman. [S of G, app. index]

Ledsham, John, Gorst Stacks, Chester, cm (1812–37). Free 6 October 1812. [Freemen rolls; poll bks]

Ledsham, Richard, Chester, joiner and cm (1751). Shown as master to Charles Thompson in 1751. A Richard Ledsham was Sheriff, 1753–54 and 1774–75, but his occupation is not known. [App. bks]

Lee, —, address unknown, cm(?) (1690). In July 1690 provided locks and keys to a cabinet and its drawers for Mrs Elizabeth Howland of the Manor House, Streatham, London. At the same time supplied two black japanned stands at £2 10s. The total invoice was £9 5s 6d. [Bedford Office, London]

Lee, —, address unknown, u (1743). In 1743 supplied to Holkham Hall, Norfolk 24 yds of 'dimithy for glasses', £2 8s, and 'For 4 looking glasses', 17s. [V & A archives]

Lee, —, Sunderland, Co. Durham, u (1771). Mentioned in an advertisement for James Davenport's paper hanging manufactory. [*Newcastle Courant*, 18 May 1771]

Lee, — jnr, Shrewsbury, Salop, carver and gilder (1798). [D]

Lee, Abraham, 2 Court, Little Hampton St, Birmingham, cm (1835). [D]

Lee, Charles, 23 Fleet St, London, carver and gilder (1822). In May 1822 took out insurance cover of £450 but stock and utensils amounted to a mere £40. [GL, Sun MS vol. 491, ref. 993166]

Lee, David K., Hyde Hill, Berwick-upon-Tweed, Northumb., cm (1827). [D]

Lee, George, St Martin-le-Grand, London, frame maker, carver and gilder (1792–1825). The number was 49 in 1792, 39 1807–19 and 59 in 1825. Listed as George Lee & Co. at 49 Little Britain in 1820. [D]

Lee, George, Marylebone, London, chairmaker (1822). [Suffolk RO, FAA: 50/2/120, p. 98]

Lee, George, Castle St, Shrewsbury, Salop, cm and u (1828–35). [D]

Lee, Giles, address unknown, cm (1803). Subscribed to Sheraton's *Cabinet Dictionary*, 1803.

Lee, Harman, York, cm and joiner (1830). Shown in one directory of this year at 47 Tanner Row and in another at 27 St Andrewgate. [D]

Lee, Henry, 29 Castle St East, Oxford Mkt and Ogle Mews, London, chair and sofa maker and undertaker (1827). [D]

Lee, Henry, Back St, Exeter, Devon, cm (1839). Daughter bapt. at the Church of St Mary Major, 2 June 1839. [PR(bapt.)]

Lee, Isaac, Allendale, Northumb., joiner/cm (1834). [D]

Lee, J., Frodsham, Cheshire, cm and u (1822–34). [D]

Lee, J., South St, Torrington, Devon, cm and u (1838). [D]

Lee, James William, Crossall St, Liverpool, u (1790–94). In 1790 at no. 5, and in 1794 at no. 6. [D]

Lee, James, Nottingham, joiner and cm (1819–22). In 1819 took William Asling as app. and in 1822, Sam Booth Ireland. [Notts. RO, app. list]

Lee, James, 33 Sims Croft, Sheffield, Yorks., carver and gilder (1822). [D]

Lee, James, 9 Coldbath Sq., Clerkenwell, London, cm and buhl manufacturer (1829). [D]

Lee, James, Scarborough, Yorks., cm (1828–40). At Long Westgate 1828 but at 13 St Sepulchre St, 1831–40. [D]

Lee, James, 40 New Church St, Birmingham, cabinet case maker (1835). [D]

Lee, James, Broad St, Lyme Regis, Dorset, cm (1840). [D]

Lee, James, 13 St Sepulchre St, Scarborough, Yorks., cm (1840). [D]

Lee, John, 6 Poplar Lane, Stanley St, Liverpool, cm (1790). [D]

Lee, **John**, Westminster, London, cm and u (1790–94). At 1 Bridge St, 1790–93 and 30 Parliament St in 1794. [D]

Lee, **John**, opposite 'The Crown', St George's St, Southwark, London, cm (1792). Took out insurance cover of £300 on his dwelling house in November 1792. [GL, Sun MS vol. 391, p. 486]

Lee, **John**, 36 Castle St, Oxford St, London, chairmaker (1809). [D]

Lee, **John**, Werburgh's Lane, Chester, cm (1814). [D]

Lee, **Jno.**, 23 Circus St, New Rd, London, cm and u (1827). [D]

Lee, **John**, Edgar Ct, Edgar St, Liverpool, chairmaker (1830). Free 15 November 1830. [Freemen reg.]

Lee, **John jnr**, Manchester, cm u and furniture broker (1814–40). At 9 Thomas St and 61 King St, 1814–28. One directory of 1816 adds also 248 Deansgate. Recorded at 61 King St, 1821–29 and no. 24, 1832–33. From 1825 also had premises in Brazenose St and these are in 1836 coupled with 11 Ridgefield, in 1838 with no. 12, and in 1839 with 12 Bridge St. In 1840 at 27 Brazenose St and 31 King St. The business was a substantial one, and in April 1825, apart from advertising for journeymen, he also sought a foreman to manage his workshops in King St. Here he claimed 20 or 30 benches were employed. [D; *Liverpool Mercury*, 8 April 1825]

Lee, **John**, Malton, Yorks., cm and u (1823–40). At Greengate in 1823 but in Wheelgate, 1828–40. [D]

Lee, **John**, Frodsham, Cheshire, cm/joiner (1828). [D]

Lee, **John**, High St, Bideford, Devon, cm and u (1830–38). On 28 March 1838 married at Torrington, Devon, Mrs Randle, the daughter of Mr Bartlett of Bideford, ironmonger. [D; *Exeter Flying Post*, 5 April 1838]

Lee, **John**, New St, Wem, Salop, joiner and cm (1840). [D]

Lee, **John**, High Wycombe, Bucks., chairmaker (b. c. 1821–41). Married 1840. Age 20 at the time of the 1841 Census. [PR (marriage)]

Lee, **Joseph Richard**, London, upholder (1729). Son of Samuel Lee of Westminster, Gent. App. to Charles Jones in August 1709 and free of the Upholders' Co. by servitude, 6 November 1729. [GL, Upholders' Co. records]

Lee, **Nathaniel**, Silver St, Uttoxeter, Staffs., cm (1828). [D]

Lee, **Nicholson**, Liverpool, cm (1767–77). At Poplary Wient 1767 and 1772–77 but in 1769 shown at 11 Cumberland St. In 1777 his trade was listed as planemaker and cm. [D]

Lee, **Richard**, Chester, u (1720). Free 12 October 1720. [Freemen rolls]

Lee, **Richard**, 39 St Martin-le-Grand, London, carver and gilder (1808). This address was also occupied by George Lee following the same trade between 1807 and 1819. [D]

Lee, **Robert**, Wakefield, Yorks., joiner and cm (1798). [D]

Lee, **Robert**, St Mary St, Weymouth, Dorset, cm, u and auctioneer (1803–40). At 76 St Mary St, 1823–30, but in 1840 the number was 79. In 1803 subscribed to Sheraton's *Cabinet Dictionary*. [D]

Lee, **Samuel**, Mill St, Bideford, Devon, cm (1830). [D]

Lee, **Samuel**, Bridgwater, Som., cm and u (1830–40). Addresses given at High St in 1830, Cattlemarket in 1839 and Mary St in 1840. [D]

Lee, **Thomas**, Hull, Yorks., cm (1768). [Poll bk]

Lee, **Thomas**, Ipswich, Suffolk, cm and chairmaker (1776–77). Married on 22 July 1776. In 1777 insured a house in Eastgate St, Bury St Edmunds for £100. [Suffolk RO, FAA: 50/2/94–104; GL, Sun MS vol. 255, p. 249]

Lee, **Thomas**, Lymington, Hants., chairmaker (1792–93). [D]

Lee, **Thomas**, 42 Upper Rathbone Pl., London, chairmaker (1809). [D]

Lee, **Thomas**, 8 Aytoun St, Manchester, cm (1829). [D]

Lee, **Timothy**, Heckmondwike, near Dewsbury, Yorks., cm (1822–30). [D]

Lee, **William**, Fargate, Sheffield, Yorks., chairmaker (1814). [D]

Lee, **William**, 31 Prince's St, Soho, London, cm and u (1822). [D]

Lee, **William**, Wheelgate, Malton, Yorks., cm and u (1823). [D]

Lee, **William**, Bearward St, Northampton, cm (1826–30). [Poll bk]

Lee, **William**, 62 Cable St, Wellclose Sq., London, cm and appraiser (1827). [D]

Lee, **William**, 10 Cleveland St, Fitzroy Sq., London, cm and furniture broker (1835–39). [D]

Lee, **William**, Princess St, Shrewsbury, Salop, cm and u (1840). [D]

Leech, **James**, Oxford Rd, Newtown, Bilston, Staffs., cm and u (1828–38). [D]

Leech, **John**, Bristol, cm (1825–27). At 15 Lower Castle St, 1825–26, and 4 Broadmead 1827. [D]

Leech, **Joseph**, Tipton, Staffs., joiner/cm (1818). [D]

Leech, **Robert**, 13 Schoolhouse Yd, St James Walk, Clerkenwell, London, cm (1781). In 1781 insured his utensils and stock for £400. [GL, Sun MS vol. 290, p. 450]

Leech, **William**, Liverpool, cm (d. by 1759). Took as apps Thomas Bouvrier (free 1759) and Thomas Lloyd and Jonathan Brownhill (free 1761). William Leech had however died before 1759 when Bouvrier petitioned for his freedom. [Freemen's committee bk]

Leech, **William W.**, Castle St, Framlingham, Suffolk, cm and u (1839). [D]

Leedel, **John**, Duke St, Doncaster, Yorks., turner and chairmaker (1837). [D]

Leedel, **William**, Wisbech, Cambs., turner and chairmaker (1798). [D]

Leeder, **Besome** (or **Begoni**), Market Pl., Fakenham, Norfolk, cm (1822–39). [D]

Leeds, **Levi**, Marylebone St, London, upholder (1749–53). Declared bankrupt, *Gents Mag.*, May 1753. [Westminster poll bk]

Leek, **William**, Waterworks St, Hull, Yorks., cm (1803–10). [D]

Leemin, **Robert**, London, cm (1740–d. 1750). In April 1740 at 'The Golden Chair' in St Martin's Lane where he took out insurance cover for £700. In May of the following year however his bankruptcy was announced. The business was established once more and at the time of his death in 1750 he was trading from his dwelling house at Lee St, Red Lion Sq., Holborn. Here in July his stock in trade and household effects were sold by auction. On offer were 'several Sets of Chairs, Tables, Buroes, Cameras, a Japan Chest of Drawers . . . a Travelling Coach, a curious inlaid Cabinet, an Ebony and Ivory Desk and Bookcase, and a Silvering Stone and Frame'. [GL, Sun MS vol. 54, p. 518; *Daily Post*, 6 May 1741; *General Advertiser*, 2 July 1750]

Leeming, **John**, Lancaster, cm (1817–30). Free 1817–18. Named in the Gillow records, 1821, 1825–26 and 1829–30. [Freemen rolls; Westminster Ref. Lib., Gillow]

Leeming, **Richard**, Lancaster (1793–99). Named in the Gillow records 1793–95 and 1797–99. [Westminster Ref. Lib., Gillow]

Leeming, **Robert**, Windy Bank, Colne, Lancs., cm/joiner (1814–34). [D]

Leeming, **Thomas**, Preston, Lancs., cm (1799–1802). Named in the *Preston Cabinet Makers' and Chair Makers' Book of Prices* in the editions of 1799 and 1802 as one of the masters assenting.

Leeming, **William**, Lancaster (1790–1829). App. to Gillows of Lancaster 1786 and named in the Gillow records in

1790–1803, 1807, 1809, 1813–16, 1818–27 and 1829. [Westminster Ref. Lib., Gillow]

Leeming, William jnr, Lancaster, cm (1799–1809). Free 1799–1800. In 1799 recorded in a directory as a letter case maker. Bankrupt by January 1809 at which time his trade was stated to be cm. [D; freemen rolls: *Lancaster Gazette*, 14 January 1809] Possibly:

Leeming, William jnr, Lancaster (1821–28). Named in the Gillow records 1821–22 and 1825–28. [Westminster Ref. Lib., Gillow]

Leeremans, James, Fleet Mkt, London, u and cm (before 1761). Discharged from Debtors' Prison, April 1761. He was stated to be 'late of Fleet Market, London'. [*London Gazette*, 2 April 1761]

Lees, —, address unknown, cm (1803). Subscribed to Sheraton's *Cabinet Dictionary*, 1803.

Lees, Benjamin, Rye Mkt, Stourbridge, Worcs., cm and u (1835). [D]

Lees, George, Nottingham, joiner, builder and cm (1831–33). In 1831 took app. named Henry Barrows Smith and in 1833 another named Charles Wright. [App. reg.]

Lees, James snr, Nottingham, cm, carpenter and joiner (1778–d. 1788). In 1778 insured his house for £500. His will dated 29 March 1787 was proved 4 October 1788. [GL, Sun MS vol. 262, p. 418; Notts. RO, probate records]

Lees, James jnr, Nottingham, joiner and cm (1798–1832). Signed the *Nottingham Cabinet and Chair Makers' Book of Prices* 1791 on the behalf of the masters. His will dated 12 November 1808 was proved, 20 August 1832. [D; Notts. RO, probate records]

Lees, James, Worcester Rd, Stourbridge, Worcs., cm and u (1828–35). [D]

Lees, John, Birmingham, inlayer and gilder (1717). In 1717 took app. named Cave. [S of G, app. index]

Lees, John, Nottingham, cm (1791–99). In 1791 signed the *Nottingham Cabinet and Chair Makers' Book of Prices* on the behalf of the masters. [D]

Lees, John, Union Buildings, The Potteries, Staffs., cm (1818). [D]

Lees, John, 6 Lord St, Preston, Lancs., cm (1825). [D]

Lees, John, Nottingham, joiner, cm and u (1828–41). Listed at Glasshouse St in 1828; Newcastle St, 1832–40, and by 1841 had moved to St Peter's Sq. Recorded in partnership with James Lees in 1835. [D]

Lees, Joseph, 127 Gt Portland St, London, cm (1812). In January 1812 was associated with Israel Kilvington in taking £500 insurance cover on their stock, utensils and goods in trust. In the policy was specified a stove for drying feathers. [GL, Sun MS vol. 459, ref. 864768]

Lees, Philip, Nottingham, joiner and cm (1791–99). Signed the *Nottingham Cabinet and Chair Makers' Book of Prices*, 1791. [D]

Lees, Robert, 9 Kirkham Pl., Tottenham Ct Rd, London, cm (1798). In 1798 took app. named Mary Gould. [Westminster Ref. Lib., MS B1267]

Lees, Robert, , Nicholas St, Chester, cm (1816–28). [D]

Lees, Thomas, 5 Green St, Gartside St, Manchester, chairmaker (1828). [D]

Lees, Thomas Taylor, Willenhall, Staffs., joiner/cm (1834). [D]

Lees, Thomas Taylor, Wednesfield, Staffs., joiner/cm (1834). [D]

Lees, Thomas, Mount St, Nottingham, cm (1835). [D]

Lees & Redgate, Clumber St, Nottingham, carvers and gilders (1835). [D]

Leese, Richard, 35 Paul St, Finsbury, London, picture and looking-glass frame maker (1839). [D]

Leeson, William, Leicester, cm (1788–d. 1811). In May 1788 advertised for a cm and chairmaker. In 1790 moved from Town Hall Lane to High St. His trade card is in the Heal Coll., BM. Died on 20 January 1811. [D; *Leicester Journal*, 24 May 1788; *Gents Mag.*, January 1811]

Leftwich, Thomas, Manchester, u and cm (1784–1825). In 1794 at 7 Ann's Sq.; in 1816–18 at 47 King St; and in 1825 at 26 Union Pl. [D]

Le Gaigneur, Louis Constantin, buhl manufactory, 19 Queen St, Edgware Rd, London, cm (1815–1816). Very little is known about Le Gaigneur, a Frenchman who apparently transferred his workshop to London. On 14 November 1815 he received £500 advance payment for two library tables for Carlton House [RA 25351] and also supplied some inkstands. The writing tables are now at Windsor Castle, one being inscribed 'Le Gaigneur / IXX Queen St. / Fecit', the other 'Le Gaigneur'. There is a similar table in the Wallace collection [Cat. No. F.4791] signed twice. A Boulle desk recently acquired for Brighton Pavilion is incised 'L. L. Gag' (No. 340–322] and a handsome mahogany cylinder desk and cabinet sold by Jeremy, Ltd in 1986 is inscribed 'Le Gaigneur No 19 Queen St., Edgware Road, London, 1816'. Unsigned Boulle furniture of closely similar design is recorded. [G. F. Laking, *The Furniture of Windsor Castle*, 1905, p. 114, *repr.*: *Burlington*, June 1980, p. 416; Jourdain & Rose, *English Furniture: the Georgian Period, 1750–1830*, p. 150]

Legg, Robert, 'The Leg', near Southampton St, Holborn, London, upholder and undertaker (c. 1760). Son of the late Robert Legg. His mother Elizabeth Legg traded from the same address as a haberdasher and undertaker in 1723. [Heal]

Legg, Samuel, London, u (1776–1819). Son of John Legg of Reading, carpenter. App. to Samuel Walker, draper, 28 September 1768 and then to Thomas Savill, draper and u of Aldgate, 27 March 1771. Free of the Upholders' Co. by servitude, 4 September 1776. From 1776–78 in Fleet St, but by 1781 had moved to 51 Snow Hill where he set up business. In both 1781 and 1782 his total insurance cover was £700 but in 1781 utensils and stock were covered for £350 and this was increased to £500 in 1782. From 1790–93 shown at Johnson's Ct, Fleet St, and from 1794 at 71 Fleet St. From 1812 the business is referred to as Legg & Son. Included in the list of master cabinet makers in Sheraton's *Cabinet Dictionary*, 1803. [D; GL, Upholders' Co. records; Sun MS vol. 295, p. 134; vol. 304, p. 270]

Legg, Thomas, 37 Windmill St, Tottenham Ct Rd, carver and gilder (1820–37). [D]

Legg, William, Bristol, cm (1774–81). In 1774 living in the parish of SS Philip and Jacob and in 1781 in the parish of St Nicholas. [Poll bks]

Leggat, Andrew, Little Edward St, Seven Dials, London, chair and sofa maker (1839). [D]

Leggat, James, Mercery Lane, Canterbury, Kent, u (1713–34). In 1713 took app. named Parker. Leggat's insurance cover in 1726 amounted to £500. A James Leggat is shown sworn as a freeman 1734 and this might be a son. [S of G, app. index; GL, Sun MS vol. 23, p. 156; freemen rolls]

Leggat, Alexander, Windsor, Berks., u (1806). [Poll bk]

Legge, Samuel, St Paul's, Canterbury, Kent, cm (1839). [D]

Legge, Thomas, Cambridge, cm (1822–41). App. to Thomas and John Chandler, turners in Cambridge, 4 February 1822 and free 16 August 1829. In 1832 at Union St, 1834 in St Peter St, 1835 Mount Pleasant and in 1837 in White Hart Yd. In 1841 Thomas Legge was trading from King St, James Legge from New Sq., and Samuel Legge from Bridge St. On 1 April 1834 took John Evans as app. [App. bk; freemen rolls; poll bks]

Legget, D., 35 Tavistock St, Covent Gdn, London, cm (1835). [D]

Legget, David, 16 King St, Covent Gdn, London, cm and furniture broker (1835–39). [D]

Leggett, John, Bungay, Suffolk, cm and u (1824). [D]

Leggett, Josiah, Canterbury, Kent, u (1734–40). Free 1734. In 1740 took app. named Watson. [Freemen rolls; S of G, app. index]

Leggett, Samuel, Bridewell Alley, Norwich, upholder, cm, carpenter and appraiser (1783–84). A mahogany chair on turned reeded legs and with a padded back at Felbrigg Hall, Norfolk is stamped 'Leggett', twice, and may be by this maker. [D; poll bk]

Leggott (or Leggitt), David, Butchery, Brigg, Lincs., cm and u (1819–35). [D]

Leggott (or Legget), Thomas, Scot(t) Lane, Doncaster, Yorks., cm (1818–37). [D]

Le (or La) Grange, —, London, u (1674–75). Upholsterer to the Royal Household in the reign of Charles II. In 1674 supplied for Windsor Castle a bed of 'crimson ffringed velvet for the Queenes Bedchamber.' He also delivered in this year six folding stools, two elbow chairs and a couch frame. On 18 December 1674 he charged £1 for 'a Folding stoole of Walnuttre twisted, with fine feathers', 15s for matching footstool' and £1 for 'a little Chaire'. He also charged for travelling to Windsor to set up the bed and furniture for the Queen's Chapel. Further commissions included 'crimson Taffety hangings' for the Queen's Oratory at the Whitehall Palace and ornaments for the Somerset House Chapel. On 5 June 1675 charged £299 18s 8d for a yellow damask bed for the Queen's Bedchamber at Whitehall Palace. [PRO, LC9/261; LC9/274/224–29; *Conn.*, 1934, p. 86]

Legrant, Peter, London, joiner (1709–22). Member of the French Church in London. In July 1722 paid 19s by the Earl of Rockingham for an oak box. [Lincoln RO, Monson 10A/1]

Le Gros, Thomas, 'The Cross Keys', corner of Harp Alley in Shoe Lane, London, upholder (1713–14). In 1714 insured his house for £200. [GL, Sun MS vol. 2, p. 199; Hand in Hand MS vol. 13, p. 369]

Legune, Thomas, High St, Southampton, Hants., cm and u (1783–84). [D]

Leicester, Charles, Macclesfield, Cheshire, chairmaker (1810–40). Recorded at Chestergate, 1816–28, no. 18 in 1816 and no. 120 in 1828. On 17 October 1810 supplied twelve chairs for Sir John Fleming for Tabley House, Cheshire. The chairs cost 7s each and the bill for £4 4s was settled on 9 November. Stamped a number of his chairs and three exist at Temple Newsam House, Leeds, marked 'C. LEICESTER'. This maker produced a distinctive type of rush seated ladder-back chair with a turned top rail and barrel terminals. Other chairs are known with impressed marks 'LEICESTER' 'MACCLESFIELD' and 'W LEICESTER'. [D; Chester RO, Tabley House vouchers DLT; *Antique Collecting*, October 1976, pp. 4–5]

Leicester, John, Peterborough, Northants., cm (1762). In 1762 took app. named Black. [S of G, app. index]

Leicester, Thomas, Lancaster, cm (1768). [Poll bk]

Leicester, William, Raven St, Shrewsbury, Salop, carver (c. 1796). [D]

Leicester, William, 42 Baldwin's Gdns, Gray's Inn Rd, London, cm and carpenter (1808). [D]

Leigh, Alexander, 2 Maxwell St, Canal, Liverpool, u (1796). [D]

Leigh, James, Chester, u (1747). Son of John Leigh and app. to John Kirkes of Chester, u. Free 14 July 1747. [Freemen rolls; poll bk]

Leigh, James, Chester, cm (1820–37). Free 17 April 1820. At Watergate St, 1818–26, and St Anne's St, 1837. [Freemen rolls; poll bks]

Leigh, John, Shrewsbury, Salop, upholder (1744). In 1744 took app. named Longford. [S of G, app. index]

Leigh, John, Deansgate, Bolton, Lancs., chairmaker (1814–18). [D]

Leigh, Ralph, Water St, Salford, Lancs., chairmaker (1794). [D]

Leigh, Richard, 159 Deansgate, Bolton, Lancs., chairmaker, baker and flour dealer (1818–28). [D]

Leigh, Robert, Bedford St, Covent Gdn, London, cm (1726–27). On 13 May 1727 the 1st Earl of Bristol recorded in his diary that he had paid this maker for 'putting in new glasses to ye silver sconces, & India cutt jappan frame & for a dumb waiter £10 10s'. [Heal; Wills, *Looking-Glasses*; *Apollo*, LXII, p. 137; *Conn.*, December 1946, pp. 71–78]

Leigh, Thomas, Warrington, Lancs., cm (1816–22). In 1816 at Bewsey St and from 1818–22 at Riding St. [D]

Leigh, Thomas, 17 Cooke St, Chorlton Row, Manchester, cm and shopkeeper (1825). [D]

Leigh, Thomas, Duke's Alley, Bolton, Lancs., chairmaker (1834). [D]

Leigh, William, Bolton, Lancs., chairmaker and cm (1814–34). At 33 Deansgate but in 1834 shown at both Oxford St and Knowsley St. In 1828 his trade was listed as chairmaker but from this date also cm. [D]

Leighton, —, Lancaster, carver (1818–22). [Westminster Ref. Lib., Gillow records]

Leighton, Alexander, Liverpool, u (1766–1805). In 1766 at Water St; in 1781–84 at 55 Whitechapel; in 1787 at Gibraltar St, Canal; in 1796 at 2 Maxwell St, Canal; but from 1803 at Gibraltar Rd, Gt Howard St. The number here was 7 in 1803 and 2 from 1804. [D]

Leighton, Thomas, Gt Yarmouth, Norfolk, cm (1818–40). [Poll bks]

Leike, Thomas, Windsor, Berks., u (1784). [D]

Leinaje, Charles, 26 Robert St, Hoxton, London, chair and sofa maker (1827). [D]

Leister, Robert, Lancaster (1826). [Westminster Ref. Lib., Gillow records]

Leitch, William, 2 Hatfields Pl., Apollo Rd, London, carpenter, cm and broker (1821). Took out insurance cover for £1,000 in November 1821. This covered his own house and one adjoining. [GL, Sun MS vol. 486, ref. 972790]

Leith, Isaac, 9 King's Pl., Commercial Rd, London, cm and u (1820–29). [D]

Leith, James, London, carver and gilder (1809–37). At 8 Gt Chapel St, Soho, 1809–20; 40 Upper Thornaugh St in 1826; and 33 Judd St, Brunswick Sq., 1835–37. [D]

Leith, James, 9 Commercial Rd, Whitechapel, London, cm and u (1822). [D]

Leith, John, St Margaret's Bank, Rochester, Kent, u and cm (1784–1801). In 1784 took out insurance cover of £1,500 of which £660 was for utensils, stock and his workshop. A directory of the same year gives his address as Chatham. [D; GL, Sun MS vol. 324, p. 184; Rochester poll bk]

Leith, John, 13 Crescent St, Euston Sq., London, carver and gilder (1839). [D]

Leithhead, William jnr, Narrowgate, Alnwick, Northumb., joiner, cm and u (1804–34). Advertised vacancies for cabinet and chair makers in *Newcastle Courant*, 18 August 1804. [D]

Leivers, William, address unknown, u (1755). Submitted an account for fitting up the South-west end rooms in the Alcove appartment at Wimpole, Cambs., for the 2nd Countess of Oxford. The bill totalled £73 1s 11d. [Notts. RO, DD.5P. 14/2]

Lejeune, Edward, East St, Southampton, Hants., joiner and cm (1744–74). In 1744 took app. named Ray. [S of G, app. index; Southamtpon Corp. leases, SC4/4/471; poll bk]

Lejeune, Thomas, Romsey, Hants., cm (1756–62). In 1756 took app. named Filldew and in 1762 another named Rawlins. [S of G, app. index]

Lejeune, Thomas, Southampton, Hants., cm (1774–81). In 1781 insured a house in York for £400. [Poll bk; GL, Sun MS vol. 294, p. 101]

Leler, Philip, Holborn, London, cm (d. 1749). [*London Evening Post*, 14 October 1749]

Lellan, William M., near the Market Pl., Mansfield, Notts., joiner, upholder, cm and undertaker (1780). In 1780 took out insurance cover of £400 and of this £120 was in respect of utensils, stock and goods. [GL, Sun MS vol. 280, p. 208]

Lemage, Charles Samuel, 45 Exmouth St, Spa Fields, London, cm (1823). In 1823 took out insurance cover of £400 of which half was for utensils and stock. [GL, Sun MS vol. 497, ref. 1008076]

Lemaigne, Peter, Mercers St, Long Acre, London, cm (1749). [Westminster poll bk]

Le Nain, Ivon, London, cm (1776–93). Initially at 2 Swedeland Ct, Bishopsgate St Without but later the address became Widegate St, Bishopsgate St Without and from 1787, 154 Bishopsgate St. In both 1776 and 1778 took out insurance cover for £400, but in 1776 only half of this sum was specified for utensils and stock, whereas in 1778 the full sum was used to cover these items in a shop in Bell Lane, Whites Row, Spitalfields. Total insurance cover in 1781 rose to £1,200 falling to £500 in 1783 and rising again to £1,500 in 1787. Of these totals the amount of cover in respect of utensils and stock was £850 and £250 respectively in 1781 and 1783, while in 1787 the total covered both household goods and trade goods in his workshop. [D; GL, Sun MS vol. 245, p. 257; vol. 273, p. 387; vol. 289, p. 308; vol. 313, p. 527; vol. 346, p. 289]

Lenard, James, Monday, Market St, Devizes, Wilts., cm (1839). [D]

Lenden, William, London, cm and upholder (1749). App. to Thomas Landall, cm and upholder of St James's, Westminster, under the Sons of the Clergy scheme, in 1749. [*General Advertiser*, 17 April 1749]

Leng, Robert, Hull, Yorks., cm (1754). [Poll bk]

Lenham, Thomas, Hull, Yorks., turner and carver (1831–40). At 46 Blackfriargate with a residence at 6 Chapel St in 1831 and thereafter from 1834 at Old Dock. From 1834 listed only as an ivory and wood turner. [D]

Lenn, Andrew, Gt Marlborough St, corner of Poland St, St James's, London, upholder (1717–24). Freeman of the Upholders' Co. Father of John Lenn free, 3 February 1724. [GL, Sun MS vol. 6, p. 148, 4 February 1717; Upholders' Co. records]

Lenn, John, 'The Crown & Cushion', Conduit St, London, u (1724). Son of Andrew Lenn, freeman and upholder of London. John Lenn was free of the Upholders' Co by patrimony, 3 February 1724. On 25 March of the same year he took out insurance cover of £500 on goods and merchandise in his dwelling house. [GL, Upholders' Co. records; Sun MS vol. 16, ref. 31424)]

Lennard, —, 17 Wilde St, Liverpool, cm (1837). [D]

Lennard, Elizabeth, Little Russell Ct, Drury Lane, London, upholder (1778). In 1778 took out insurance cover of £100 of which £20 was in respect of utensils, stocks and goods. [GL, Sun MS vol. 264, p. 383]

Lenoir, Peter, Northampton, looking-glass maker (1688). In January 1688 supplied two coach glasses, one of 21" and the other of 27". The smaller cost £1 5s and the larger £1 15. The patron was Lord Leigh of Stoneleigh Abbey, Warks. [Shakespeare Birthplace Trust, Leigh receipts, DR 18/5/930]

Lenols, James, 5 Rood Lane, Fenchurch St, London, u (1777–81). Associated with Charles Greenwood at this address. In 1777 and 1781 took out insurance cover jointly. In 1781 the stock was valued at £900. In 1777 Lenols insured on his own behalf a house valued at £1,000 and in 1779 the cover was raised to £1,500. [GL, Sun MS vol. 259, p. 256; vol. 260, p. 289; vol. 277, p. 638; vol. 290, p. 610] Probably James Senols

Lensel, George, 138 Old St, London, cm (1808). [D]

Lent, George, Bridgegate, Rotherham, Yorks., turner and Windsor chairmaker (1833–37). [D]

Lenthall, Francis, Wigan, Lancs., u (1781–84). [D]

Lenthall, James, Wigan, Lancs., u (1798). [D]

Lenton, John, Horncastle, Lincs., chairmaker (1819–22). Trading at St Lawrence Lane in 1819 and Market Pl. in 1822. [D]

Lenton, John, Brighouse, Yorks., cm (1822). [D]

Lenton, John, 8 Mansfield St, Liverpool, cm (1834). [D]

Leonard, Peter, London, upholder (1706–19). App. to William Meakins and free of the Upholders' Co. by servitude, 3 May 1706. Took as app. Thomas Sutton, 1706–19. [GL, Upholders' Co. records]

Lepine, Charles jnr, Canterbury, Kent, u and cm (1790–1811). Shown living in the parish of All Saints, 1790–96 when his trade was u. From 1805–09 in St Peter's St with the trade stated as cm. [D; poll bks]

Lepine, John, Best Lane, Canterbury, Kent, cm (1818). [Poll bk]

Lepine, Stephen, High St, Canterbury, Kent, cm (1818). [Poll bk]

Lepsay, William, 21 Aldborough St, Hull, Yorks., chairmaker (1838–39). [D]

Lervis, William, Gt Newport St, London, carver and gilder (1785). In 1785 took out insurance cover of £600 of which £350 was in respect of utensils and stock. [GL, Sun MS vol. 328, p. 597]

Le Sage, John, St James's, London carver (1685–1706). A craftsman probably of Huguenot extraction, who attracted Royal and aristocratic patronage. In 1699 he was working on the decoration of the Presence Chamber at Hampton Court. His account for £70 11s 7½d included £28 for 'carving 2 pieces of Limetree on the sides of the picture frame over the Chimney being 9 ft long 17 inches wide with flowers & Fruit'. Earlier, in 1690, he had worked at Kensington Palace. In 1685 he had supplied picture frames for Sir Giles Isham of Lamport, Northants. In February 1690 Le Sage was paid by the 1st Earl of Bristol for two carved and gilt frames for half lengths £8 15s and bought four small pictures in gilt frames additionally for £11 15s. By 1706 however Le Sage was bankrupt. A Huguenot silversmith, John le Sage, registered his mark at London, 1708. [H. Hayward, *Huguenot Silver in Engand*, 1959, p. 10; V & A archives; *London Gazette*, 14 November 1706; *Wren Soc.*, vol. IV, p. 60]

Lesley, William. 4 Peter St, London, carver and gilder (1839). [D]

Leslie, John. Church St, Wells, Norfolk, cm (1822–39). [D]

Leslie, R.. 194 Mile End Rd, London, u and cm (c. 1820). His trade card [Landauer Coll., MMA, NY] declares his trade to be 'Cabinet, Chair, Sofa & Bedstead Manufacturer'.

Leslie, Robert, 8 Church Lane, Commercial Rd, London, bedstead, mattress and cornice maker (1817–28). From 1822 listed as a cm and u. In 1827 in addition to the Church Lane address he is also recorded at Devonshire Pl. [D]

Leslie, Robert, London, cm (1820–35). At 12 Northumberland St, Commercial Rd, 1820–29, but in 1835 at 194 Whitechapel Rd. [D]

Lessley, James, Wells, Norfolk, joiner and cm (1798). [D]

Lester, George, 16 Clarendon Sq., London, cm (1826). [D]

Lester, John, St Paul & Bradninch, Exeter, Devon, carver (1803). [Militia Census]

Lester, John, Leeming St, Mansfield, Notts., chairmaker (1832). [D]

Lester, Joseph, 6 Crosbie St, Liverpool, cm (1839). [D]

Lester, Thomas, Bispham St, Liverpool, chair manufacturer (1811–14). At 13 Bispham St in 1811 but at 14 in 1813–14. [D]

Letchemond, Francis, St Martin's Lane, York, cm (1828). [D]

Letchworth, Joseph, London, carver (1784). Freeman of Colchester, Essex. [Colchester poll bk]

Leuchars, Lucy, 38 Piccadilly, London, writing desk and dressing case maker (1829–37). [D]

Leuty, Charles Emanuel, 44 Garden St, Hull, Yorks., cm (1826). In 1831–34 listed as a victualler at the Juno Tavern, 33 Church Lane. [D]

Levell, John, Debenham, Suffolk, cooper and chairmaker (1724). In 1724 took app. named Hunt. [S of G, app. index]

Levens, John, West St, Warwick, chairmaker (1831–35). Polled of West St in 1831 and listed and Brook St in 1835. [D; poll bk]

Lever, —, Charles St, Westminster, London, cm (1741). On 7 August 1741 a fire broke out at his house but it was extinguished by firemen who prevented it from spreading. [Daily Post, 7 August 1741]

Lever, Mary, Davenport Ct, 125 Deansgate, Manchester, u (1808). [D]

Leverett, Henry, Westgate St, Ipswich, Suffolk, cm and u (1824–39). [D]

Leverett, J., Elm St on the Mount, Ipswich, Suffolk, cabinet and chairmaker (1839). [D]

Leverett, Robert, St Matthew's St, Ipswich, Suffolk, cm (1830–39). [D]

Leverett, William, Market St, Saffron Walden, Essex, cm and u (1823). [D]

Leverett, William, Harwich, Essex, cm (1826–32). Recorded at Church St in 1832. [D]

Leveridge, Samuel, London, upholder (1799). Son of William Leveridge of Pall Mall, London, auctioneer. Free of the Upholders' Co. by redemption, 6 September 1799. [GL, Upholders' Co. records]

Leveridge, William, 234 Shoreditch, London, broker and cm (1802–04). In 1802 took out insurance cover of £600 of which £400 was for utensils and stock. In the following year the corresponding figures were £850 and £650, but in 1804 these were reduced to £300 and £150. In 1804 reference was made to stock in open yards and open sheds in Worship St. [GL, Sun MS vol. 436, ref. 735244; vol. 426, ref. 743220; vol. 430, ref. 764868]

Leversage, Thomas, Nantwich, Cheshire, u (1724–d. 1731). In 1725 took app. named Scheviz. Bapt. of six children recorded, 1724–30. Thomas Leversage died in 1731, and was buried on 18 March. [S of G, app. index; PR (bapt. and burial)]

Leverton, John, 13 Jubilee St, Plymouth, Devon, carver and gilder (1836–38). [D]

Levet, Joseph, Churchgate St, Soham, Cambs., cm and u (1839). [D]

Levett, George Alms, 2 Bishop St, Portsea, Portsmouth, Hants., cm and u (1830). [D]

Levett, John, Hull, Yorks., cm (1793–1831). At Hodgson St in 1818 and 2 Garden Sq., Princess St in 1831. Subscribed to Sheraton's Drawing Book, 1793. In 1817 took over the apprenticeship of William Gibson from John Clark, cm of Witham to whom he had been indentured in 1815. In October 1828 the Duke of St Albans paid £3,849 5s 5d for the furnishing of Bradbourne Hall to a Hull craftsman named Levitt who was described as a u. This may have been John Levett or William Day Levitt, both of Hull. [D; Hull app. reg.; Lincoln RO, 2 RED 4/4/14]

Levett, Mathew, 62 Edgar St, Hull, Yorks., cm (1823). [D] See M. Levitt.

Levett, Robert, London and Hull, Yorks., cm and u (1793–1805). Employed in London for seven years. At 53 Lowgate in Hull 1793 but by 1803 had moved to 42 Whitefriargate. [D; Hull Packet, 1793]

Levett, William Day, Junction Dock Rd, Hull, Yorks., cm and u (1828–40). In 1828 the address is given as Old Dock End but this may be the same location as Junction Dock Rd. The number in this road was 16 in 1831–34 and 14 after this date. [D] See William Levitt.

Levi, Emanuel, Wells, Norfolk, cm and furniture broker (1822). [D]

Levi, Moses, Westgate Without, Canterbury, Kent, cm and broker (1824). [D]

Levi, Samuel, 4 Back Russell St, Liverpool, cm (1837–39). [D]

Levien, J. M., 10 Davies St, Grosvenor Sq., London, cm (c. 1790). [Heal]

Levin, Jno. Thomas, 6 Albion Pl., Kennington Lane, London, cm and u (1839). [D]

Levington, Henry, 54 Greek St, Soho, London, carver and gilder (1817). [D]

Levis, William, 5 Gt Newport St, London, carver and gilder, dealer in prints and pictures (1805). In 1805 took out insurance cover of £700 of which £600 was for his dwelling house and only £50 for utensils, stock and goods in trust. [GL, Sun MS vol. 434, ref. 777199]

Levison, William, 2 Carburton St, London, carver and gilder (1826). [D]

Levitt (or Levett), John, Belvoirgate, Nottingham, cm (1828). [D]

Levitt, M., 7 Aldborough St, Hull, Yorks., chairmaker (1838–39). [D] See Mathew Levett.

Levitt, Richard, Hull, Yorks., cm (1831–40). At 4 Agnes Pl., Myton in 1831 and 11 Ann St, Osborne St, 1839–40. [D]

Levitt (or Levett), Thomas, Junction Dock Rd, Hull, Yorks., cm (1831–40). In 1834 listed as a cm and u. The number in Junction Dock Rd is given as 7 in 1831, 8, 9 and 11 in 1834 and 7 and 11 in 1835. Recorded as Levett at nos 7 and 11 in 1840. [D]

Levitt, William, 12 Chapel St, Hull, Yorks., cm (1840). [D] See William Day Levett.

Levy, Joseph, 7 Lower College St, Bristol, cm (1835). [D]

Levy, Joseph, 286 High Holborn, London, glass and cabinet warehouse (1835). [D]

Lewell, William, High St, Loughborough, Leics., joiner/cm (1822). [D]

Lewes, Edward Tyler, Norwich, cm (1768–84). In 1780 was living in Cocket Lane but in 1784 at Magdalen St. [D; poll bks; Norfolk Chronicle, 3 June 1790]

Lewes & Co., 213 Tottenham Ct Rd, London, cm (1825). [D]

Lewin, John, Leicester, joiner and cm (1779). App. to Joseph Johnson, 11 February 1768, a premium of £10 10s being paid. Free 20 April 1779. [Furn. Hist., 1976]

Lewin, John Field, Watford, Herts., cm (1832). [D]

Lewin, John Thomas, 117 Curtain Rd, Shoreditch, London, u (1826–35). In 1826 listed as Thomas Lewin jnr. In 1827 also cm. [D]

Lewis, Adam, 35 Walcot St, Bath, Som., cm (1833). [D]

Lewis, Benjamin, Salisbury, Wilts., cm and u (1777–80). In 1777 took out insurance cover for £300 of which £250 was for stock in a warehouse. In 1780 the total insurance had risen to £1,200 of which £665 was in respect of utensils and stock. [GL, Sun MS vol. 258, p. 602; vol. 290, p. 516]

Lewis, C., 64 High Holborn, London, work box etc. manufacturer (1820). [D]

Lewis, George, Castle Hill, Lincoln, u (1770–73). Opened his shop in Castle Hill in February 1770. He claimed to be from

London. The business was however short-lived for by March 1773 he was bankrupt. [*Cambridge Chronicle*, 24 February 1770; *Williamson's Liverpool Advertiser*, 12 March 1773, 12 August 1774]

Lewis, George, 13 Jewin St, Cripplegate, London, cm and u (1827). [D]

Lewis, Isaac, St James, Bristol, carver (1754). [Poll bk]

Lewis, Israel, 151 Fleet St, London, cm and u (1769–83). Son of Israel Lewis of Maidstone, clerk. App. to William Marston, 5 August 1762 and free of the London Upholders' Co. by servitude, 6 December 1769. In 1771 took out patent 1142 and in the following year patent 1162 for window curtains. In addition to the Fleet St premises he owned at least from 1776 a house at Hampstead which he insured in that year for £700 out of a total cover of £1,300. There are no further directory entries after 1783 and the records of the Upholders' Co. from this date show him at Hampstead. He may thus have retired from the trade. He continued his interest however and in 1793 subscribed to Sheraton's *Drawing Book*. Shown at Hampstead until 1802 which may be the year of his death. An entry in the accounts of the Dunne family of Gatley Park near Leominster, Herefs. of a payment to 'MR LEWIS, Upholsterer' dated 8 March 1783 may refer to this maker. [D; GL, Upholders' Co. records; Sun MS vol. 249, p. 126; Herefs. RO, Gatley F76/III/40]

Lewis, J. A., 4 St Vincent Row, City Rd, London, carver and gilder (1808). [D]

Lewis, James, London, chairmaker (1818). Freeman of Hereford. [Hereford poll bk]

Lewis, John, Fleet St, London, upholder (1763). [D]

Lewis, John, Bristol, carver (1774–84). Living in the parishes of St Nicholas, 1774, St James, 1781, and St Michael, 1784. [Poll bks]

Lewis, John, 43 Baldwin St, Bristol, bed joiner (1775). [D]

Lewis, John, 4 Little Distaff Lane, London, carver and gilder (1779). In 1779 took out insurance cover for £200 of which £50 was for utensils and stock. [GL, Sun MS vol. 273, p. 531]

Lewis, John, Horse Fair, Bristol, cm and broker (1799–1801). [D]

Lewis, John, Bridge St Row, Chester, cm (1816–18). [D]

Lewis, John, London, carver, gilder and frame maker (1817–26). At 19 Bridgewater Sq., Barbican in 1817, but from 1823–26 at 20 Charterhouse Sq. In 1823 took out insurance cover of £500 of which £230 was in respect of utensils and stock. A workshop in a yard valued at £20 was referred to. [D; GL, Sun MS vol. 495, ref. 1006857]

Lewis, John, Hereford or London, chairmaker (before 1818). In 1818 Joseph Lewis of London, eldest son of John Lewis, chairmaker, deceased, was admitted a freeman of Hereford by patrimony. [Freemen rolls]

Lewis, John, Church St, Calne, Wilts., cm and u (1822–30). [D]

Lewis, John, St James St, Manchester with residence at 43 Bloom St, cm (1825–39). In 1825 at 66 St James St but from 1836–39 the number was 2. [D]

Lewis, Jno., 4 Denmark St, Soho, London, chair and sofa maker (1835). [D]

Lewis, John, address unknown, u (1839). In 1839 insured a house in Broad St, Ludlow, Salop in the tenure of Ceasar Cole, surgeon apothecary, for £600. [GL, Sun MS vol. 376, p. 114]

Lewis, John, 44 Newman St, Oxford St, London, chair and sofa maker (1839). [D]

Lewis, Joseph, 5 Hollen St, Wardour St, London, cm (1818–26). Son of John Lewis, chairmaker who was already dead by 1818 when Joseph was declared a freeman of Hereford by patrimony. [Hereford freemen rolls; Hereford poll bk]

Lewis, Jos. Ekins jnr, Union St, Northampton, cm (1826). [Poll bk]

Lewis, Joshua, 'The Three Tents', by Fleet Ditch (later Fleet St), London, u (1724–63). Trading as early as March 1724 when insurance cover of £500 was taken out on goods and merchandise in his house. He also acted as an auctioneer and in October 1740 advertised (following her death) the furniture of Mrs Chichley, widow of Dr Chichley, Secretary to the late Archbishop of Canterbury. Her house in Gt Marlborough St contained such rich items as 'Genoa and other Silk Damask Furniture in Beds and Window Curtains', Turkey carpets and 'Antique Cabinets embellished with silver'. Joshua Lewis was Questman and Collector for the Poor for the parish of St Bride in 1732 and a Sidesman in 1737. The business traded as Joshua Lewis & Son from 1753–63. Took Thomas Morrison as app. in 1749 under the Sons of the Clergy Scheme at a premium of £20. [*General Advertiser*, 17 April 1749] Joshua Lewis was patronised by the Hoare family, 1751–62. The earliest payment known was in June 1751 and amounted to £32 12s. In February of the following year funeral expenses were met costing £37 14s, but this was small compared with Lewis's account for the funeral of Lady Hoare also in 1752, which came to £152. Other amounts settled in 1753 came to £315 19s. After this however the amounts are less. Another customer was J. Buller of Morval, Cornwall who in January 1759 was invoiced for a mahogany 'Beauroe Bedstead' at £4. [D; GL, Sun MS vol. 19, ref. 34973; MS 6561, p. 52; *London Daily Post*, 31 October 1740; *Daily Advertiser*, 28 May 1748; V & A archives, Hoare's Bank, private accounts; Cornwall RO, DDBU 337]

Lewis, Josiah, the corner of Barnaby St, Tooley St, Southwark, London and later at Smarden, Kent, upholder (1772). [Heal]

Lewis, Newton, parish of St Nicholas, Bristol, bed joiner (1774). [Poll bk]

Lewis, Obadiah, parish of St Lawrence, Ipswich, Suffolk, cm (1823). Married 1823. [Suffolk RO, FAA: 50/2/120, p. 102]

Lewis, Richard, London, cane chairmaker (1710). Born in Shropshire. App. to a maker at 'The Crown' in St Paul's Churchyard. May not have completed his apprenticeship before he joined the First Regiment of Foot-Guards. By January 1710 he had deserted, and an advertisement was placed seeking his apprehension. At that time he was 21 years of age. [*London Gazette*, 25–31 January 1709–10]

Lewis, Richard, Brentford, Middlx, upholder and cm (1789). Party to an assignment concerning a property in Goring, Oxon. [Oxford RO, F IX/258]

Lewis, Richard, Bromley-St-Leonards, London, upholder (1791). Son of Benjamin Lewis of Bromley, millwright and engineer. App. to John Mears, 5 July 1780, and free of the Upholders' Co. by servitude, 4 May 1791. [GL Upholders' Co. records]

Lewis, Robert, Charles Ct, Charles St, St James's, London, cm and broker (1794). In 1794 took out insurance cover of £200 on his house, goods and utensils. [GL, Sun MS vol. 401, ref. 628558]

Lewis, Robert, King St, Soho, London, cornice and chair manufacturer (1817–22). At 54 King St in 1817 and no. 56, 1820–22. [D]

Lewis,, Samuel, Abingdon, Berks., brazier and upholder (1734). [Poll bk]

Lewis, Samuel, Fleet St, London, upholder (1758). In 1758 fined for declining parochial office, parish of St Bride. [GL, MS 6561, p. 94]

Lewis, Samuel George, 87 Drury Lane, London, cabinet inlayer (1808–39). In 1808 one directory described him as a manufacturer of ornamental stringing. [D]

Lewis, Samuel, Bell Lane, Ludlow, Salop, cm and u (1822–28). [D]

Lewis, Thomas, Sidbury, Worcester, chairmaker (1788). [D]

Lewis, Thomas, 14 New St, Dock Head, London, upholder (1795–1802). Son of Samuel Lewis of New St, Dock Head, pipe maker. App. to Isaac Vizard, 1 July 1795, and subsequently to his widow. Free of the Upholders' Co. by servitude, 4 August 1802. [GL, Upholders' Co. records]

Lewis, Thomas, Vauxhall, London, japanned chair manufacturer (1808). [D]

Lewis, Thomas, Horfield Rd, Bristol, carver and gilder (1818–21). At 26 Horfield Rd in 1818 and 20 in 1819–21. [D]

Lewis, Thomas, 10 Warren St, Fitzroy Sq., London, u (1819). [D]

Lewis, Thomas, Soutergate, Ulverston, Lancs., cm (1828). [D]

Lewis, Thomas, Liverpool, cm (1835–39). At 23 St Vincent St, St James', 1835–37, and 1 Hardy St in 1839. [D]

Lewis, William, London, carver and gilder (1778–93). At 15 Gt Newport St, Long Acre, 1778–89 and then 81 Newport St, Long Acre 1790–93. In 1778 took out insurance cover of £400 of which £150 was for utensils and stock. [D; GL, Sun MS vol. 264, p. 629]

Lewis, William, 25 Gt Ormond St, London, japanned chair manufacturer (1808–13). [D]

Lewis, William, Southampton Row, Bloomsbury, London, u and cm (1813). In 1813 took out insurance cover of £3,000. Of this very substantial sum £1,800 was in respect of his dwelling house, £200 for a workshop and £800 for stock and utensils in the dwelling house. [GL, Sun MS vol. 461, ref. 885459]

Lewis, William, 31 Gloucester St, Queen Sq., London, u (1816). [D]

Lewis, William, Shoplatch, Shrewsbury, Salop, carver and gilder (1822–28). [D]

Lewis, William, Shaw's Brow, Kendal, Westmld, chairmaker/turner (1829). [D]

Lewis, William, Highworth, Wilts., u and cm (1839). [D]

Lewtas, Edward, Breck St, Poulton-le-Fylde, Lancs., joiner and cm (1828–34). [D]

Lewtas, John, Manchester u (1817–18). At 7 Ancoat's Pl. in 1817 and 75 Oldham St in 1818. [D]

Ley, George, 52 High St, Birmingham, upholder (1777–80). [D]

Ley, Sarah, High St, Birmingham, u (1767). [D]

Leycock, Thomas, near 'The Black Bull', New Gravel Lane, Wapping, London, carpenter and cm (1775). In 1775 took out insurance cover of £300 of which £110 was in respect of utensils and stock. [GL, Sun MS vol. 236, p. 544]

Leyland, Samuel, Fazakerley St, Preston, Lancs., joiner and cm (1834). [D]

Libbey, Henry, 67 Sawney Pope St, Liverpool, cm (1823). [D]

Libbey, John, 3 Sawney Pope St, Liverpool, cm (1827). [D]

Libbey, Richard, Barrs St, Bristol, cm (1792–94). [D]

Libbey, Richard, Liverpool, cm (b. 1788–d. 1827). In 1816 had a shop at 18 Richmond St but in 1824 shown as Richard Libbey & Son with a shop at 67 Sawney Pope St and a house at 22 Stockdale St. As a Henry Libbey is also shown at the Sawney Pope St in a directory of 1823 this man is probably Richard's son. Richard Libbey died on 25 February 1827 'after a long and severe illness', at the age of 39. [D; Liverpool Mercury, 16 March 1827]

Libbis, George, 5 Quickset Row, New Rd, London, cm and u (1839). [D]

Liddell, Gilbert, Newcastle, u (1774). App. to William Hudson and free, 8 October 1774. [Freemen reg.]

Liddiard, Thomas, Macclesfield, Cheshire, cm (1755). In 1755 took app. named Wilkson. [S of G, app. index]

Liddle, George, Haltwhistle, Northumb., joiner and cm (1827–28). [D]

Liddle, Matthew, Cart Yd, Drury Lane, London, cm (1775). In 1775 insured his house for £100. [GL, Sun MS vol. 243, p. 578]

Lidgett, Elizabeth, 9 Myton Sq., Hull, Yorks., u (1831). [D]

Lidgett, Miss Esther, Hull, Yorks., u (1834–39). At 8 Upper Union St, 1834–35, and Adelaide St, 1838–39. In 1835 the trade is named as 'bedmaker'. [D]

Lidgier, Henry, 'King's Arms', near Symonde Lane, Chancery Lane, London, cm and upholder (1780). In 1780 took out insurance cover of £2,500 of which utensils, stock and goods were £1,400. [GL Sun MS vol. 285, p. 21]

Light, David, London, cm (1803–09). In 1803, when he took an app., he was trading at North Green, Shoreditch, but in 1808–09 he was listed at Paul St, Finsbury Sq. [D; Rose Lipman Lib., Shoreditch archives, MS M3494]

Light, John, Worship St, Moorfields, London, cm (1779). Bankruptcy announced, Gents Mag., November 1779 and Bailey's list of bankrupts.

Light, Thomas, Salisbury St, Mere, Wilts., cm (1839). [D]

Light, William, London, upholder (1725). Son of John Light of Goudhurst, Kent, timber merchant. App. to Henry Heasman, 21 August 1718, and free of the Upholders' Co. by servitude, 6 October 1725. [GL, Upholders' Co. records]

Lightfoot, —, 24 Lant St, Southwark, London, cm (1826). [D]

Lightfoot, Joshua, Exeter, Devon, cm and u (1823–30). In 1823–25 at 73 South St. In an advertisement of 1823 he directed the public to 'his designs for CHAIRS, COUCHES etc which he flatters himself are not surpassed, if equalled by any in the West of England'. On 11 December 1827 an auction of his stock in trade was advertised. Amongst the items offered were 'Mahogany & other four-post bedsteads & furniture; dining, pembroke & other tables; dining & drawing room chairs; handsome pedestal sideboard; bed steps; wash stands; dressing glasses, butlers' trays; tea caddies; ladies' work boxes; mahogany sofas'. Despite this announcement he advertised only thirteen days later that he intended to continue his business at 74 Bell Hill, South St. He also stated that he had 'several dozen of handsome Drawing-room chairs at a great reduction in price'. The Bell Hill address features in directories, 1827–28, but in 1830 South St is recorded as the address. [D; The Alfred, 15 April 1823, 11 December 1827, 24 December 1827]

Lightfoot, Luke, Mile End and Southwark, London, carver (b. c. 1722–d. 1789). A man whose career embraced the trades of wood and stone carver, cm, architect and surveyor and victualler. Son of Theophilus Lightfoot of the parish of St Giles-in-the-Fields, Gent., Luke Lightfoot was free of the Drapers' Co. by patrimony, 16 November 1743 and was described as a carver of Mile End, Old Town. Took as apps Abraham Jennings (1749), William Lovell (1754), Theophilus Williams (1757), John Birdseye (1760), James Lewis Pajon and T. Finch (1766), and Richard Matthews (1767). From 1757 extensively employed by Ralph, 2nd Earl Verney at Claydon, Bucks. not only as a mason and carver but also as a master builder, surveyor and architect to this, and other properties. This involved work at Verney's London house in Mayfair, and on property and building sites in London bought as speculations. Most of Luke Lightfoot's efforts were however expended on a grandiose extension and re-decoration of Claydon House from 1757–69. The exceptional Rococo carved woodwork of this house, some in the prevailing Gothick and Chinese taste, together with the inlaid staircase, are major achievements and show well the quality of the work that was produced under his direction. Relations with his patron deteriorated, especially after the appointment of Sir Thomas Robinson as architect in 1767. Lightfoot was accused of falsely accounting for money advanced by Verney and misappropriation of materials. The dispute ended with an action brought in the court of chancery in 1771 by Verney. During the period that work at Claydon was progressing Lightfoot had his works in Gravel Lane, Southwark, and in 1766 was living in Blackman St in the same part of London. In 1769 however he moved to Denmark Hall near Dulwich and here set up as a victualler. He died on 1 March 1789. [*Furn. Hist.*, 1966; V & A Museum, *Rococo* exhib. cat. 1984, refs cited]

Lightfoot, Robert, Bawtry, Yorks., cm (1753–d. 1788). In 1753 took app. named Senior. Probate given September 1788. Still listed in a directory of 1793 which raises the possibility of a son of the same name continuing the business. [D; S of G, app. index; Notts. RO, probate records]

Lightfoot, William, Gilesgate, Durham, cm (1828–34). [D]

Like, Thomas & Turner, Henry, 47 Frith St, Soho, London cm, u, auctioneers and appraisers (1777–87). Henry Turner was the foreman of John Cobb, the noted u, and this partnership appears to have been established a year before Cobb's death. From the commencement the partnership was a business of substantial proportions. In 1778 total insurance cover amounted to £3,100 with utensils and stock valued at £2,030. Thomas Like was additionally operating a business in Thames St, Windsor, Berks., 1779–84, and in 1779 an insurance cover of £700 including £600 for utensils and stock, was maintained on this part of the business in addition. Like was a freeman of Windsor and probably maintained a house there. The business there is recorded in his name only, but the insurance cover is in the name of the partnership. In 1785 the partners also took out insurance cover on a house at 45 Queen Anne St. They may have ceased trading soon after 1787, as that is the last year they are recorded in trade directories. An invoice for a mahogany sofa supplied to Lord Howard of Audley End, Essex at a cost of £7 12s 6d including carriage in 1787 is issued in the name of Thomas Like only. In the following year Like is shown in a Westminster poll bk at St James' St, but in 1798 he was at Soho Sq., In 1780–81 he appears to have morgaged the Frith St premises to a William Allam, a watchmaker of Bond St. Allam's widow entered an action in the court of chancery against Little but it was not heard until her death in 1798 when it was pressed by the executors. They claimed £1,400 and interest. [D; *Apollo*, February 1960, p. 35; GL Sun MS vol. 260, p. 525; vol. 265, p. 171; vol. 271, p. 524; vol. 277, p. 479; vol. 331, p. 195; poll bk; Essex RO, D/DBy/AU5/9; PRO, C13/447]

Liley, Joseph, Maltby's Yd, Mill St, Leeds, Yorks., cm and joiner (1837–40). [D]

Liller, John, Churchgate, Retford, Notts., cm, joiner and appraiser (1822–40). The business is listed as Liller & Marshall in 1822 and Liller & Son in 1841. [D]

Lilley, William, Doncaster, Yorks., cm (1793–1806). Supplied furniture to Doncaster Mansion House, 1802–06. This consisted of a set of mahogany dining chairs, of which twenty-six survive *in situ*, supplied in 1802. These chairs have the impressed mark 'W LILLEY' on the back rails, and have also been crudely stamped with the date 1802. Payment was made for these on 21 November 1804, the amount being £66 14s. Payments were made for window blinds on 21 August 1801, and on 7 October 1806 for three sideboard tables made at a cost of £49 8s 6d. These tables are also still in the Mansion House. [D; Doncaster Borough archives, ledger]

Lillie, George & Tucker, Thomas, 315 High Holborn, London, u and cm (1789–94). A substantial business which took out insurance cover on their house and warehouses in 1789 and 1791 of £1,000. In 1791 £750 of this sum was in respect of utensils and stock. [D; GL, Sun MS vol. 362, p. 336; vol. 374, ref. 578565]

Lillie & Copeman, address unknown, cm and joiners

(1739–57). Known only in connection with work undertaken and furniture supplied to Holkham Hall, Norfolk. In 1739 and 1741 work at the 'old house' consisting of furniture repairs and joinery was paid for. At the same period furniture was being supplied for the new house. In 1739 this consisted of two bed heads, three chairs, a settee, a table and a chest of drawers. These were charged in total at £19 2s 9d. In 1741 tables and picture frames were charged at £12 5s 5d, tables and a chest of drawers at £15 5s and picture frames at £9 11s. After 1743 work was on a less regular basis with a payment in 1747 for two oval frames and four palm branches for the dining room, and in 1752 £9 6s 6d for 'setting up scaffold for the painter'. A later account of 1757 was submitted in the name of Lillie only. This was for framing three small looking glasses, four walnut chairs and a sofa for the Saloon and picture frames, the total cost being £17 6s 6d. [V & A archives; *C. Life*, 14 February 1980, p. 427]

Lilly, John, Falmouth, Cornwall, cm, carpenter and joiner (1754–77). In 1754, took app. named Gellard. Insurance cover in 1777 amounted to £700 of which £260 was in respect of utensils and stock. [S of G, app. index; GL, Sun MS vol. 258, p. 3]

Lilly, Richard, London, cm (1807–20). In 1807 at King John Ct, Holywell Lane, Shoreditch. At this address he took out insurance cover for £350 of which £150 was specified for stock and utensils. By 1818 the address had changed to 6 Batemans Row, Shoreditch which was specified as being 'his new workshop and dwelling house'. Total insurance cover at this adddress was £300. [D; GL, Sun MS vol. 441, ref. 812232; vol. 480, ref. 948920]

Lilly, Robert, 'The George', Market Pl., Hoxton, London, victualler and cm (1775). In 1775 took out insurance cover of £500 of which £350 was specified as utensils, stock and goods. [GL, Sun MS vol. 238, p. 484]

Lily, John, 6 Crown St, Hoxton, London, cm (1808). [D]

Limpus, John, Bishops Waltham, Hants., cm and auctioneer (1792–93). [D]

Lincett, Ash, Malton, Yorks., cm (1793). Subscribed to Sheraton's *Drawing Book*, 1793.

Lincoln, Robert, parish of St John Sepulchre, Norwich, cm (1801–02). Free 24 January 1801. [Poll bk; freemen reg.]

Linderbusch, H., Marylebone, London, cm (1787). [Bailey's list of bankrupts]

Lindley, William, 4 Beer St, Leicester Sq., London, cm and u (1839). [D]

Lindon, Joseph, High St, Bilston, Staffs., chairmaker (1828). [D]

Lindon, Malachi, London and Worcester, carver (1749–79). At Dufour's Ct, London in 1749 but declared bankrupt, *Gents Mag.*, December 1750. In 1779 living in Worcester, and in that year insured some tenements there for £300. [Westminster poll bk; GL, Sun MS vol. 279, p. 161]

Lindop, Richard, Liverpool, cm (1809–27). In 1809 married in Liverpool Miss Alice Appleton of that town. Not listed in directories until 1821 when he was living at Rawlinson Ct, Craven St with a shop at 2 Feather St. By 1824 his house was numbered 5 Craven St, and in 1827 it was listed as Craven Ct, Craven St. [D; *Liverpool Courier*, 20 September 1809]

Lindsay, Benjamin & Sons, 4 and 16 Broker Row, Finsbury, London, u (1806–11). One directory of 1808 gives the address as 4 and 16 Lower Moorfields. [D]

Lindsay, Benjamin, 48 Shoreditch, London, u (1819–26). [D]

Lindsay, George, Chester, cm (1768). In 1768 took as app. Thomas Newns. [App. bk]

Lindsay, J., Bridge St, Sunderland, Co. Durham, carver and gilder (*c.* 1820–30). His trade card [Landauer Coll., MMA, NY] indicates that he made picture and looking-glass frames, and offered 'Gold & other Bordering for Rooms & Bed &

Window Cornices'. Pictures could also be cleaned and re-varnished. It is highly likely that this craftsman was either James or John Lindsay, both of whom were active in the trade in Sunderland at this period.

Lindsay, James, Nile St, Bishop Wearmouth, Sunderland, Co. Durham, carver, gilder and ship's carver (1827). [D]

Lindsay, John, London, cm and chairmaker (before 1785). In December 1785 at Norfolk, Virginia, USA. He advertised that he had 'just arrived from London'. [*Maryland Journal and Baltimore Advertiser*, 6 December 1785]

Lindsay, John, Back High St, Bishop Wearmouth, Sunderland, Co. Durham, carver and gilder (1820–27). Worked at Wynyard Park, Co. Durham, for the Marquess of Londonderry in 1820. [D; Durham RO, D/LO/E 484, vol. 1829–41]

Lindsay, John, West Wycombe, Bucks., chairmaker (b. c.1790–1841). Aged 51 at the time of the 1841 Census.

Lindsay, Joseph, Lancaster, joiner (1784–88). [Westminster Ref. Lib. Gillow records, vol. 344/94, p. 459]

Lindsay, Thomas, Lancaster (1784–87). [Westminster Ref. Lib., Gillow records]

Lindsay, William, Elm Hill, Norwich, u and paper hanger (1830). [D]

Lindsey, John, 82 Paul St, Finsbury, London, cabinet and feather warehouse (1814). [D]

Lindsey, Robert, 25 Cateaton St, London, upholder (1773). [D]

Lindsey, Robert, Couiscliffe, Darlington, Co. Durham, cm/joiner (1834). [D]

Lindsey, Robert, Battle Hill, Hexham, Northumb., joiner and cm (1834). [D]

Lindsey, Sarah, Elm Hill, Norwich, working u (1836). Probably the successor and widow of William Lindsay. [D]

Lindsley, John, Mabgate, Leeds, Yorks., cm (1817). [D]

Line, William, Market Pl., Reading, Berks., journeyman cm (b. 1735–d. 1809). At the time of his death in 1809 aged 74 he was said to have been employed in the business of Higgs & Ford of Market Pl., Reading for sixty years. He had never in this time lost a day's work, had a holiday or 'been disguised in liquor'. [*Gents Mag.*, June 1809]

Line, William jnr, High St, Taunton, Som., cm and u (1822). [D]

Line, William, Coventry, Warks., cm and u (1828–35). Trading in High St, 1828 and Earl St in 1835. [D]

Line & Johnson, High St, Coventry, Warks., cm (1818–28). [D]

Line, William, Wilden St, Amersham, Bucks., chairmaker (1830). [D]

Liney, —, 29 Gresse St, Rathbone Pl., London, u, appraiser and undertaker (1808). [D]

Linfey, William, 59 Frederick St, Liverpool, cm (1781). [D]

Linfoot, Mark, 17 St Andrewgate, York, cm (1838). [D]

Linfoot, Ralph, Strenshall, near York, joiner and cm (1823). [D]

Linfoot, Thomas, London, u and cm (1754–71). Subscribed to Chippendale's *Director*, 1754, and subsequently undertook work for Thomas Chippendale. In 1771 he was paid 10s 6d by Chippendale for repairing a folding iron bedstead which he had earlier supplied to the Earl of Shelburne, (later 1st Marquess of Lansdowne). It is in connection with the furnishing of the Earl of Shelburne's properties that Linfoot's name is known. In February and June 1767 he supplied bedding for Bowood House, Wilts. and from November 1767 to September 1768 was responsible for furnishings including tables, chairs and bedsteads for Lansdowne House, London, costing £178 10s 7d. Work continued here and at other properties until 1771 and a total of £508 was paid to Linfoot by the Earl. [Bolton, *Architecture of Robert and James Adam*, 2, p. 314; Bowood MS, Bundle 11 B.3.7]

Linford, William, West Wycombe, Bucks., chairmaker (1798). [Militia Census]

Ling, Mrs Elizabeth, Bridewell, Alley, Norwich, cm and u (1830–40). [D]

Ling, John T., Bridewell Alley, Norwich, cm and u (1818–36). Took as app. Thomas Bennett, free as an u, 30 May 1819, and John Chapman, free as a cm, 21 September 1829. His trade card in the Norwich Local Hist. Lib. indicates that he also carried on the business of appraiser and auctioneer. Undertook carpentry and paper hanging and offered to supply the trade with mahogany and upholstery goods. [D; freemen admission reg.] Trade card of J. Ling, Bridewell Alley, states: 'Manufacturer of Improved Cabinet & Upholstery Furniture ... Appraiser & Auctioneer.' [Grosvenor House Antiques Fair, 1985]

Ling & Son, Bridewell Alley and Petergate, St Andrews, Norwich, u, cm, carpet and paper warehouse (1839). [D]

Lingard, I., York St, Commercial Rd, Whitechapel, London, bedstead maker (1835). [D]

Lingard, John, 32 Queen St, Manchester, chair bottomer (1817). [D]

Linger, James, Rampant Horse St, Norwich, cm and u (1830). [D]

Lingon, Henry, Worcester, u (1719–27). In 1719 took as app. Harry Nash who was free, 24 August 1727. [S of G, app. index; freemen rolls]

Lingwood, George, Diss, Norfolk, cm (1784–d. 1816). In 1785 took out insurance cover on a dwelling house for £130. Will proved at Norwich, 1816. [D; GL, Sun MS vol. 333, p. 567; Norfolk Record Soc., index of wills]

Lingwood, Isaac, St Botolph St, Colchester, Essex, carver and gilder (1832–39). Recorded also as a picture dealer in 1832. [D]

Lining, Thomas, London, cm, chairmaker, carpenter and joiner (before 1748). In May 1748 in South Carolina, USA. He stated that he had 'lately arrived from London'. [*South Carolina Gazette*, 11 May 1748]

Linnell, J., 34 Hart St, Bloomsbury, London, carver and gilder (1835). [D]

Linnell, James, St Martin's Lane, London, wood carver (1720). [Heal]

Linnell, James, London, carver, gilder, picture frame maker and print seller (1790–93). At 14 Craven Buildings in 1790 and also recorded at 2 Streatham St, Bloomsbury. Father of John Linnell, the artist. A looking-glass of Neo-classical design in a carved and gilt frame at 10 Downing St, London bears a hand-written label with the Bloomsbury address. [Wills, *Looking-Glasses*]

Linnell, John, London, cm, u and carver (1729–d. 1796). John Linnell was the eldest son of William Linnell and his wife, Mary Butler. He was probably trained as a furniture maker in his father's workshop although he was not formally app. to his father nor has any record of his apprenticeship come to light. However, he became free of the Joiners' Co. by patrimony in 1758 and entered the Livery in 1781 where the records describe him as a carver.

As a young boy John Linnell's talent as an artist must have been evident to his father who sent him to study at St Martin's Lane Academy, founded by William Hogarth in 1735. There he found himself among an international group of students and teachers and in studying Rococo design, particularly by French exponents of the style, he was able to equip himself to become the firm's designer both of interiors and furniture and to enjoy painting in water-colour for his own pleasure. By 1749 he was already helping his father in running the firm. The business was rapidly growing and after a short period at 8 Long Acre, to which the family moved in the year after John joined his father, an important step was taken in 1754 in transferring the business to the West End and establishing a new and larger workshop, with a dwelling house, at 28 Berkeley Sq. Father and son worked here together for nine years, building up a distinguished clientèle and covering a wide range of activities as carvers, furniture makers and upholsterers. At William's death in 1763 John found himself in sole charge of a firm employing some forty or fifty people of which the stock-in-trade had been valued at £1,052 19s 8d. Many of the firm's clients continued to patronise John Linnell, including William Drake of Shardeloes, Bucks., Lord Scarsdale and Francis Child, all of whom also employed Robert Adam. The preservation in the V&A of a large number of original designs drawn by John Linnell and his draughtsmen for the firm's clients are of the utmost importance in tracing the development of his style, in understanding the range of his work and in identifying some of his customers. [Print Room, E.59–414 1929] Many are in pen and ink and colour wash, providing the customer with an attractively presented design, sometimes offering alternative proposals from which he could make his choice. Those executed between about 1750 and 1760 reveal John Linnell's mastery of Rococo, using idioms adapted from contemporary French engraved designs. Some introduce Chinoiserie and Gothick features. It was during this period of his life that he found time to issue a set of engraved designs for silver. A small publication consisting of a title-page and four sheets with ten designs for coffee-pots, vases, jugs and sugar castors appeared in 1760. He probably also intended to issue a set of engraved designs for carved girandoles in 1761 as a drawing for a draft title page survives. [V&A, E. 217 1929] But this plan, if it existed, does not apear to have materialized. It was a time of varied opportunities. With his uncle, Samuel Butler, a well-known coach builder, he prepared a design for a new State coach for the coronation of George III. Although this was not accepted, an engraving of his design was published in 1761, dedicated to his patron, Lord Scarsdale. This proved to be an appropriate dedication for in that same year Lord Scarsdale was considering the furnishing of his state drawing-room at Kedleston Hall, Derbs. He commissioned two pairs of sofas of exceptional size and magnificence which were intended to be the only items of seat furniture in the room and were to take up the entire wall space with the exception of the window wall. These were duly designed by John Linnell and made by the firm, the main decorative features consisting of carved and gilt merfolk and dolphins based upon ideas which he had already expressed in his design for the coronation coach. The sofas survive at Kedleston. Gradually, between 1760–65, Linnell's creative ideas were adapting themselves to the growing interest in antiquity. William Kent seems to have been a source of inspiration and he may have come across 'Athenian' Stuart's abortive designs for Kedleston. By 1765 he had certainly mastered Neo-classical form and ornament, partly on account of his familiarity with French designs, such as those by Delafosse, and partly as a result of his contact with Robert Adam. His links with another Neo-classical architect, Sir William Chambers, may also have been instrumental in promoting his understanding and adoption of forms and decorative features inspired by the work of French Neo-classical cm. Some drawings of about 1765 and also items of furniture, such as a pair of marquetry card-tables delivered in that year to Kedleston Hall, Derbs. for Lord Scarsdale, owe much to French example. An even closer connection with contemporary French taste arose with the arrival in London and the probable employment at 28 Berkeley Sq. in 1767–68 of two Swedish cm, Georg Haupt and Christopher Fuhrlohg who had both been working in France. A drawing for a commode in the French taste, perhaps by Fuhrlohg himself is among those by John Linnell in the V&A [E 292 1929] while

the piece, executed after the design for the 5th Earl of Carlisle and still at Castle Howard, Yorks., is signed by Christopher Fuhrlohg on the carcase in pencil. It would seem very likely that the two Swedes were still working with John Linnell when the library furniture for Robert Child at Osterley Park was provided. The pedestal desk, two library tables and set of eight chairs which survive in the library at Osterley all came from the Berkeley Sq. workshop and include decorative features previously used by John Linnell as well as Franco-Swedish characteristics.

While business seems to have been going well in the 1760s, John Linnell's friendship with a group of artists involved him in business affairs which almost drove him to bankruptcy in the early 1770s. In addition to these problems he was taken to Court by Lord Conyngham on a charge of fraudulency in which Linnell's mistress was involved and the affair was not settled until the end of 1771. While commissions continued to come to the firm from as far afield as Inveraray Castle in Scotland and Castle Howard, Yorks., lack of money on account of his unfortunate business adventures was a constant cause of worry. Nevertheless, he continued to search for new outlets and in 1773 took steps to sell furniture to the Empress of Russia and her Court through his friend Pierre Etienne Falconet. A late commission brought him into contact with the architect, John Vardy the Younger, when he was designing interior features for the 1st Earl of Uxbridge at Uxbridge House, Burlington Gdns, London. Subsequently, between 1791–94 he was preparing designs for the decoration of the boxes at the Theatre Royal, Drury Lane, under the direction of Henry Holland. He appears to have stopped working in the furniture trade shortly after 1793. His health was not good and to alleviate his gout he rented a house in Bath in 1794. He died in 1796 without issue although he appears to have married in the last years of his life. The firm then came to an end. Thomas Tatham, younger brother of the architect, Charles Heathcote Tatham, who was the son of one of John Linnell's cousins and had been trained by John Linnell at Berkeley Sq., took on the burden of sorting out his kinsman's estate, and a few years later is known to have founded his own firm, Tatham & Bailey at 13–14 Mount St, London. [G. Eland, (ed.), *Shardeloes Papers of the 17th and 18th Centuries*, 1947; J. Hardy and H. Hayward, 'Kedleston Hall, Derbyshire', *C. Life*, 26 January, 2 and 9 Febuary 1978; H. Hayward, 'Some English Rococo Designs for Silversmiths', *Proceedings of the Society of Silver Collectors*, 1969–70, pp. 60–62; H. Hayward, 'The Drawings of John Linnell in the Victoria & Albert Museum', *Furn. Hist.*, 1969; H. Hayward, 'Ordered from Berkeley Square, Inveraray and the furniture of John Linnell', *C. Life*, 5 June 1975, pp. 1485–88; H. Hayward, 'A Pair of Mirrors and Consoles by John Linnell', *Conn.*, January 1976, pp. 12–13; H. Hayward, 'A Fine Pair of Commodes by John Linnell', *Catalogue, Summer Exhibition, 1985*, Partridge Fine Arts Ltd, London; J. F. Hayward, 'A Newly discovered commode signed by Christopher Furlohg', *Burlington*, CXIV, 1972, 704–12; H. Hayward, and P. Kirkham, *William and John Linnell Eighteenth Century London Furniture Makers*, London, 1980. (Reproduces all bills, correspondence and the Inventory of the Berkeley Sq. workshop, 1763); C. Hussey, 'Ammerdown House, Somerset — I', *C. Life*, 16 February 1929, pp. 226–36; P. Kirkham, 'The careers of William and John Linnell', *Furn. Hist.*, 1967, pp. 29–40; G.W.W., 'A set of Cornishes by J. Linnell', *The Antique Collector*, October 1959, pp. 42–43]

SHARDELOES, Bucks. (William Drake). 1749–75: William Linnell had been employed by Drake to work at his London house. Between 1765–68 John Linnell appears to have been in sole charge of furnishing Shardeloes and his bills, totalling over £1,000 reveal the details and comprehensive nature of the commission. [Bucks. RO]

KEDLESTON HALL, Derbs. (1st Baron Scarsdale). 1758–96: William Linnell was patronized by Nathaniel Curzon before his client was ennobled. John Linnell continued to be employed at Kedleston and worked side by side with the architect, Robert Adam. Ledgers recording expenditure on the building and on the furnishings of the house show that regular payments were made to the Linnell firm between 1759 (before William's death) and 1796 (when John Linnell died) totalling nearly £3,000. No details are given of the furniture supplied. However, John Linnell's designs for the two pairs of sofas for the state drawing-room survive in the V & A Museum. [Print Dept, E131, 138, 140, 1929] while the executed pieces remain at Kedleston. Marquetry card-tables for this room were delivered in 1765 and are also still in the house. Twelve carved gilt and painted stools were provided by John Linnell for the Great Hall shortly after 1775 and there are two further sets of seat furniture preserved at Kedleston which can be attributed to the firm on stylistic grounds. [Kedleston Hall, Scarsdale archives]

OSTERLEY PARK, Middlx (Robert Child). c. 1760–84: Robert Child's brother, Francis Child, who had inherited Osterley Park, died in the same year as William Linnell, who he had employed. Robert, on taking over the house in 1763, continued to use the Linnell firm where John was to work side by side with Robert Adam. Adam's design for the sideboard and accompanying pair of pedestals and urns for the dining-room were executed by the Berkeley Sq. workshop in 1767. A design for the chimney piece and overmantel for Mrs Child's dressing room by John Linnell is among the drawings in the V & A Museum. [Print Room, E281 1929] The chimney piece after this design survives in the house, as, indeed, does much of the original furniture, including the seat furniture for the drawing-room provided after Linnell's design. [V & A, E93 1929] Other sets of seat furniture can be attributed to Linnell on stylistic grounds including eight armchairs *en suite* with a pedestal desk and two library tables made for the library in 1768 or 1769. Later commissions of 1779–82 probably included the execution of a bed, designed by Adam, with accompanying furniture, for the 'yellow taffaty bed chamber' at Osterley. Robert Child died in 1782 but his widow continued to employ John Linnell. The only bill which has been traced describing work carried out over all the years in which the firm was employed dates from 1783 (receipted 1784) and covered cleaning and repair work at Mrs Child's London house in Berkeley Sq.

SYON PARK, Middlx and **ALNWICK CASTLE**, Northumb. (18th Earl of Northumberland, created 1st Duke in 1766). 1762–72: Among the names of outstanding debtors to William Linnell at his death was that of the Earl of Northumberland and it may be that carving work at Syon Park, where Robert Adam was working on the reconstruction of the house, had already been commissioned from the Linnell firm. John Linnell was employed after his father's death and payments to the firm amounted to over £1,000 between 1763–72. [Northumberland account, Ledger C, folio 122, 1763, folio 326, 1765, ledger D, folio 194, 1966, ledger E, folio 164, 1771, folio 397, 1772. Hoare's Bank, Fleet St, London] No details are given but the regular nature of some of the early payments suggest that they were for carving work in the house. At Alnwick, Adam was providing designs for 'Gothick' interiors after the Northumberlands began to convert the castle into a residence in about 1755. The Duchess commissioned a set of fourteen carved and gilt armchairs from John Linnell for her saloon of the same design as those

provided for the drawing room at Osterley. Thirteen survive at Alnwick although they no longer have their original Gobelins upholstery. Two card-tables and two Pembroke tables still preserved at Alnwick can also be attributed to Linnell on stylistic grounds. The ledger entries quoting payments in 1771 and 1772 referred to above, amounting to a total of £250 probably relate to these furnishings for Alnwick. The Duchess died in 1776.

BOWOOD HOUSE, Wilts. and **LANDSDOWNE HOUSE**, Berkeley Sq., London. (2nd Earl of Shelburne, created 1st Marquis of Lansdowne 1784). 1763–96: The 2nd Earl of Shelburne succeeded to the title and to Bowood House, as yet unfinished, in 1761. He employed Robert Adam to alter the interior and finish the house. William Linnell seems to have carried out work for Lady Shelburne before he died and may have been recommended by Adam. John Linnell was commissioned in 1763 to carry out major carving work at Bowood and payments made to him between 1763–66 totalled £1,013 9s 5d. [Building accounts, Henry Holland, Lansdowne archives, Bowood] The house was being furnished between 1763–68 and Linnell provided a set of hall stools after Adam's design, probably at the end of 1768. A bill survives at Bowood containing an item dated 28 July 1768 'To making and carving 5 hall stools like them at Bowood and painting the same £21.5.0.'. In the following November '3 hall stools to match the above' were provided. All these pieces were ordered for the new London property Shelburne House, Berkeley Sq. later to become Lansdowne House, but the wording of the bill makes it clear that Linnell had previously supplied identical stools to Bowood. The stools from the London House were sold in 1806 but those at Bowood remain there. The furnishing of Shelburne House was proceeding in 1768–69 and on 4 February 1769 John Linnell charged £19 for 'making and carving a large sideboard table after Mr. Adam's design and painting the same with large brass handles complete'. [Tradesmen's accounts, Lansdowne archives, Bowood] The dining room is now in the MMA, NY. The sideboard has not been traced.

INVERARAY CASTLE, Argyll (5th Duke of Argyll). 1773–81: The 5th Duke of Argyll was buying furniture in London for his castle in Scotland in 1773 and subsequent years. Payments were made to John Linnell totalling nearly £900 between 1774–81. [5th Duke's bank account, The Royal Bank of Scotland, Charing Cross, London] No details are given. Six carved and gilt armchairs and two confidantes can be attributed to the firm as they closely follow a Linnell drawing in the V & A. [Print Room. E.22 1929] Other items surviving at Inveraray Castle which also probably came from the Linnell workshop include a further set of carved and gilt oval-backed chairs and three marquetry tables.

SANDON HALL, Staffs. (Nathaniel Ryder, created 1st Lord Harrowby in 1776). 1762–77: Nathaniel Ryder had employed William Linnell in 1762–63. After his father's death, John Linnell was employed as a cm for which payments were made to him annually from 1764–67, 1770–71, 1773–75. These payments do not give details but they were probably for furniture needed for a London house since Sandon Hall was not acquired by Lord Harrowby until 1777. Two sums of £400 each were paid to Linnell on account in August 1777 and these payments could well be part settlements for furniture ordered for Sandon. [Harrowby MS Trust, Notebooks, Sandon Hall, vols 330, 334, 337, 338]

HILLS PLACE, near Horsham, Sussex (9th Viscount Irwin). 1772–73: A bill totalling £55 9s 7d for eight cabriole elbow chairs, carved and painted white and green and two French elbow chairs *en suite* and also a sideboard is dated 26 August

1772. Another of May–July 1773 amounting to £43 7s 2d lists further sets of seat furniture and tables.

HEATON HALL, Manchester (Sir Thomas Egerton, Bt, created 1st Earl of Wilton in 1801). 1775–77: John Linnell was employed by Sir Thomas Egerton in the furnishing of Heaton Hall. A total payment of £57 for furniture is recorded in Sir Thomas's bank account book for 6 November 1775. In addition, an invoice for £37 0s 4d, for items delivered between 24 August 1776 and 18 June 1777 refers to 'A neat Dressing table made of Sattin Wood with a Glass and bottles . . . a neat wash hand stand made of Sattin Wood the top king'd to lift up, 2 Glass cups, 2 cut Glassbottles, 2 Water bottles and Tumblers and a Spring lock to Do. The front with Foulding doors Compleat' and 'a neat Cloaths press made of Sattin Wood and Cross banded with rose wood and the bottom with foulding doors and sliding shelves lined with marble paper and green baize falls and 2 Drawers at top handles locks and key Compleat . . .'. [Egerton documents, Preston RO, DD Eg 41 (1)]

WOODHOUSE, Salop (William Mostyn Owen). 1774: A workshop drawing in the V & A Museum [Print Room E.3495 1911] is inscribed with the name of 'Mr. Mostyn Owen' and dated March 1774. The mirror survives in the house.

UXBRIDGE HOUSE, Burlington Gdns, London (1st Earl of Uxbridge). 1789–93: Designs for an organ [V & A, E.391, 392, 1929] and for chimney-pieces [V & A, E.319, 382, 1929] document Linnell's employment by the Earl of Uxbridge while his patron's bank account records payments to John Linnell of nearly £6,000 up to June 1793. [Drummonds, Royal Bank of Scotland, Charing Cross, London]

AMMERDOWN HOUSE, near Frome, Som. (Thomas Samuel Joliffe). 1795: Three unpublished bills of 1795 refer to '2 large frames with ornaments in therm'd legs and gollosses in the rails gilt in burnished gold . . . for your slabs £18.18.0', '8 satinwood tablet back'd elbow chairs with mouldings gilt in burnished gold round the painted tablets, the elbow carved, the legs turned . . . £44.0.0.', '2 large sofas to match' and 'A pair of satin wood fire screens, the ovals covered with green silk'. These pieces survive at Ammerdown House. [Accounts, Lord Hylton, Ammerdown House]

UNSPECIFIED WORK.— The names of many clients of John Linnell are known although no details of the commissions are recorded. [See Kirkham (1967), Hayward (1969) and Hayward and Kirkham (1980)]   H.H.

Linnell, William, London, carver, cm and u (b. c. 1703–d. 1763). William Linnell was the son of a yeoman, John Linnell of Hemel Hempstead, Herts. He went to London in 1717 to serve his apprenticeship with Michael Savage, a member of the Joiners' Co. In 1719 he was turned over to John Townshend with whom he completed his apprenticeship in 1724. A few years later he set up his own carving workshop in Long Acre and, in 1729, became free of the Joiners' Co. After only four years he was already a member of the Livery. In the meantime he had married Mary Butler, daughter of a leading coachmaker, Samuel Butler. Their first son, John, was born in July 1729. There were five further children of the marriage. A second son, Richard, was app. to an artist but died as a young man. Of a third son, William, nothing is known. Mary, the elder of three daughters, married one of her father's apps, William Bond, by whom she had a son, John Linnell Bond, named after her own brother who was the child's godfather. William Linnell Bond grew up to be a successful architect.

No records survive of the clients who employed William Linnell in the first ten years of the life of his workshop but he evidently concentrated upon carving. His early documented commissions, the first dating from 1739, refer mainly to the provision of architectural elements and mouldings and items such as picture- and mirror-frames, consoles, pedestals and cornices. An unpublished bill dated January 1749 rendered to the 4th Duke of Bedford for work at Woburn Abbey refers to 'Carving the cupola eight large trusses and eight key stones . . . £17.10.0.', 'Carving two stone pediments by model . . . £80.0.0.' and 'Carving one Ditto with your arms by model . . . £4.16.0.'. [Bedford Office, London] Other, previously published accounts rendered to the Duke are for carving mouldings, cornices, chimney-pieces and frames at Woburn Abbey under the direction of Henry Flitcroft. Tables and seat furniture, however, the latter stuffed and upholstered, also figure in the early surviving bills, notably those rendered to Richard Hoare of Barn Elms between 1739–54. Over this period the workshop was flourishing and growing and, far from being confined to carving, William Linnell was increasing his range and is referred to in Richard Hoare's bank account of 1747 as 'carver and cabinet-maker'. A splendid mahogany card-table, carved with lion masks at the knees and a bacchanalian mask festooned with grapes on the rail was supplied to Richard Hoare in October 1740 for £11 11s and survives at Stourhead, Wilts. along with a mahogany sofa and ten armchairs. William was joined by his son as early as 1749. This is documented by the presence of two hitherto unpublished vouchers for carver's work at Woburn Abbey receipted in October and November 1749 by John Linnell. [Bedford Office, London] Father and son then worked together until William Linnell's death.

In 1750 the family moved to a larger establishment at 8 Long Acre. It was shortly after this move that William Linnell received a commission from the 4th Duke of Beaufort to provide a suite of Chinoiserie furniture for a bedroom in the Chinese taste at Badminton House, Glos. Many pieces from this famous commission survive, notably the bed, japanned commode and shelves in the V & A Museum and another set of shelves in the Lady Lever Art Gallery, Port Sunlight. Increased business led to a further move in 1754 to 28 Berkeley Sq. in the fashionable West End of London where there was spacious family living accommodation and a large workshop, complete with ware room or show room. A full inventory of the contents of the dwelling house and of the stock-in-trade in the workshops at Berkeley Sq., taken at William Linnell's death in 1763, survives and has been published, revealing that the firm employed at that time some forty to fifty people and had a stock-in-trade worth £1,052 19s 8d. The workshops themselves consisted of a yard with saw-pit, a joiners' shop, a cabinet shop, a chair room, a carving shop, a gilding shop, three upholstery shops and a feather garret, a glass room, a store room and a packing and transport room. There were also two ware-rooms for display. At the time of his death, William Linnell had built up an important business and had demonstrated his sense of enterprise in moving to the West End. His clients included William Drake of Shardeloes, the 6th Earl of Coventry; Nathaniel Curzon, later 1st Earl of Scarsdale; the bankers, Francis and his brother Robert Child; and Hugh Smithson, 18th Earl and subsequently 1st Duke of Northumberland. All these patrons also employed Robert Adam as their architect. The way was open for William's son, John Linnell, on taking over the firm, to exploit the opportunities created by his father's good management and to benefit from collaboration with one of the greatest Neo-classical architects of the late 18th century. [Beard, *Georgian Craftsmen*; GCM; H. Hayward and P. Kirkham, *William and John Linnell, 18th Century London Furniture Makers*, 1980 (reproduces bills and correspondence); P. Kirkham, 'The careers of William and John Linnell', *Furn. Hist.*, 1967]

BARN ELMS, Surrey and London (Richard Hoare Esq., Knighted after 1745). 1739–54: Various bills for carving and providing tables and seat furniture (a carved whist table, a sofa and ten chairs survive at Stourhead), upholstery and repair work. [V & A Lib., 86.N.N.3]

RADCLIFFE CAMERA, Oxford (Trustees of the Radcliffe Camera). 1745–48: Accounts, describing the carving work carried out by William Linnell, published by Stanley George Gillam, 'The Building Accounts of the Radcliffe Camera', *Oxford Hist. Soc.*, new series, xiii, 1958.

THE FOUNDLING HOSPITAL, London (Trustees of the Foundling Hospital). 1747–52: Description of the decision to commission William Linnell to provide a frame for the chapel altar picture published in *The Foundling Hospital General Committee Minutes*, vols i–iv, 1739–55, Thomas Coram Foundation for Children, 40 Brunswick Sq., London.

WILLIAM DRAKE'S LONDON HOUSE. 1749–75: Eight bills rendered between 1749–62 refer to furniture and repair and cleaning work carried out at Drake's London houses. Linnell appears to have been in sole charge of every aspect of furnishing and maintenance. From 1763 bills were rendered to John Linnell and from 1765 these refer to work at Shardeloes. [Bucks. RO, Drake archive]

WOBURN ABBEY, Beds. and London (4th Duke of Bedford). 1749–51: Bill amounting to £133 for carving at Woburn, including the carving of models for the pediment designed by Flitcroft in July and November 1749. Between January–April 1751, £324 15s 3d was paid to Linnell for carving chimney-pieces in the Duke's Dressing room, the Venetian room, the Duchess's Dressing room and three other rooms on the ground floor. Work also included the carving of door architraves, window architraves and the mouldings on shutters and doors. Two vouchers for carving work (unspecified) were receipted in October and November 1749 by John Linnell. There is also correspondence in 1749–50 between Henry Flitcroft and the Duke's agent concerning the appointment of William Linnell as the Duke's carver at Woburn. [Bedford Office, London]

ALSCOT PARK, Warks. (James West Esq.). 1750–51: Bill of 1750 for £19 11s 9d, including 'To a six-legged table by a design of Kents with a mahogany top ... the frame gilt in parts and painted of a wainscot colour' and another for £33 11s 9d of 1751 which includes an item for the repair and restoration of a 17th-century Flemish cabinet with *verre eglomisé* panels which survives in the house. [Alscot Park MS, West papers]

CROOME COURT, Worcs. and London (6th Earl of Coventry). 1751–61: The first account dating from August 1751, is of small importance. It includes a clothes-press and was probably for the London house at 29 Piccadilly. The re-building of Croome Court under 'Capability' Brown necessitated carving work on a considerable scale for which William Linnell was partly responsible together with James Lovell. Three bills of 1758–59 list carving work, including 'carving a chimney-frame very handsome by drawing and gilt in burnished gold for Lady Coventry's Dressing Room'. A further bill of 1761 for £52 16s 9d refers to the provision and making of curtains and carpets for Croome. [Croome Estate Trust, High Green, Severn Stoke, Worcs., Coventry papers]

BADMINTON HOUSE, Glos. (4th Duke of Beaufort). 1752–55: Payments made to William Linnell between October 1751 and December 1755 amounting to a total of £800 are recorded in the 4th Duke of Beaufort's bank account (Ledger N, folios 329, 448, Ledger X, folios 142, 143, Ledger Y, folio 133, Hoare's Bank, Fleet St, London] These payments were very probably for the furniture made for the Chinese bedroom at Badminton known to have been completed by

1754 when Dr Richard Pococke visited the house. No inventory exists for the room but the furniture provided included a bed, eight armchairs, a dressing-commode and two pairs of standing shelves. The bed and dressing-commode are now in the V & A Museum while one pair of shelves belongs to the Lady Lever Art Gallery, Port Sunlight, Cheshire (one of this pair being at present on loan to the V & A) and a second pair is in the MMA, MY. A pen and ink and water-colour design for the chairs by John Linnell is in the V & A Museum (E.71 1929).

HILL ST, Mayfair, London (Mrs Elizabeth Montagu). 1752: A letter from Mrs Montagu to Gilbert West, 16 November 1752, contains complaints over William Linnell's high prices. (*Elizabeth Montagu, Her Correspondence from 1720–61*, ed. Emily V. Climenson, II, 1906, 17] A japanned secretaire commode and cabinet-on-stand believed to have been made for Hill St are in the possession of Mrs Montagu's descendants at Came House, Dorset.

KEDLESTON HALL, Derbs. and London (Sir Nathaniel Curzon, Bt, created 1st Baron Scarsdale, April 1761). 1758–96: Lord Scarsdale employed the Linnell firm for nearly forty years. Household ledgers record payments for unspecified items, made regularly from 1759–96. [Scarsdale archives, Kedleston Hall] There is also one bill, dated 27 March 1759 for items supplied to the London house in Audley Sq. including 'six neat gothick chairs covered with Spanish leather, two large sofas with stuffed backs and seats' and a 'four post bedstead'. [Scarsdale archives] These items have not been identified. It is probable that the sum of £49 16s 2d paid to William Linnell in 1761, as recorded in the ledgers, was for the provision of a bookcase, designed by Robert Adam, for Lady Scarsdale's Dressing-room. This piece survives in the house. It was delivered in 1761. In that same year Lord Scarsdale was considering the provision of seat furniture for Kedleston and a chair design by John Linnell inscribed with his patron's name survives in the V & A Museum (E.81 1929). It does not appear to have been executed. On the other hand three finished drawings by John Linnell for two pairs of sofas for the drawing-room, prepared in 1761–62 were used as a basis for the two pairs made by the firm and delivered in 1765 after William Linnell's death. [V & A, E.131, 138, 140, 1929] For subsequent deliveries to Kedleston, see John Linnell.

OSTERLEY PARK, Middlx (Francis Child, d. 1763 and Robert Child). c. 1760–84: The name 'Mr. Child' occurs among the debtors to William Linnell at his death. [See P. Kirkham, op. cit. 1967] It is not known to what this refers. Only one late bill survives and evidence concerning the furnishing of Osterley Park by Robert Child after his brother's death and after the death of William Linnell rests largely on stylistic judgement. (See John Linnell.)

STOWE, Bucks. (Lord Temple). 1760: Bill 14 January 1760 'To 6 mahogany french elbow chairs on castors stuffed and covered with your own morrino and brass nailed all complete £15.15.0, To 12 open backed mahogany chairs carved and covered with Spanish leather welted and quilted and the best princes metal nails all complete at 1–10–0. . . . £18.0.0., To 2 mahogany french elbow chairs on castors covered with Spanish leather welted and quilted all complete £7.0.0.' This bill, for a total of £40 15s was receipted on behalf of his father on 30 May 1760 by John Linnell. It is unclear whether the items were purchased by Lord Temple for Stowe or for his London house in Pall Mall. [Huntingdon Lib., California, Stowe Coll., Grenville accounts, household accounts; Stowe 1749–62. STG Accounts Box 144 (in bundle marked '1760')]

NATHANIEL RYDER, created 1st Lord Harrowby in 1776. 1762–77: Payments are recorded to the firm (all but one unspecified) over the period 1762–77. Two of these payments were made during William Linnell's lifetime: (1) 29 July 1762 'for a mahogany bottle stand and dumb waiter £4.0.0.' and (2) unspecified, 22 July 1763 £1 13s 6d. It is not known for which house the items purchased were intended as Nathaniel Ryder only bought Sandon Hall in 1777 at which date he purchased furniture for the house from John Linnell. [Harrowby MS Trust, Notebooks, vols 330, 334, 337, 338] UNSPECIFIED. At the death of William Linnell, the list of the debtors to his estate included three hundred and eighty-four names many of whom must have been his clients but no details about their various commissions are known. [See P. Kirkham, op. cit., 1967] H.H.

Linney, George, Chester, cm (1763). App. to Richard Cottingham cm of Chester and free, 5 November 1763. [Freemen rolls]

Linney, John, Chester, cm (1764). App. to Philip Presbury cm of Chester and free, 18 February 1764. [Freemen rolls]

Linney, John, Market St Lane, Manchester, cm (1772–88). [D]

Linney, John Peter, Chester, cm and u (1840). Free 30 July 1840. [Freemen rolls]

Linney, Joseph, Half Moon Ct, Westminster, London, cm (1774). [Poll bk]

Linney, Roger, London, upholder (1709). Free of the Upholders' Co., 7 December 1709. [GL, Upholders' Co. records]

Linning, Johan Christian, Tottenham Ct Rd, London, inlayer (1769–76). A Swede who worked as an inlayer in London for his half-brother, the cm Christopher Fuhrlohg, 1769–76. He exhibited panels of marquetry at the Exhibition of the Free Society of Artists of Great Britain, 1775–76. Sold marquetry panels to furniture makers and musical instrument makers. [Burlington, July 1977, June 1980]

Linscott, John, parish of St Sidwell, Exeter, Devon, cm (1824–29). Married Miss Mary Harris, November 1824. Two sons bapt., 1826 and 1829. [PR (bapt.); Exeter Flying Post, 18 November 1824]

Linsell, George, Oxford and London, cm (1779–1802). In October 1779 announced that he had taken over the shop in High St, Oxford near All Saints Church, which had previously been maintained by a person named Edmonds, joiner, cm and chairmaker. The business must have been of a modest nature for in the following year cover of only £100 was maintained on utensils and stock. In 1802 was living at St Luke's, Old St, London. [GL, Sun MS vol. 281, p. 149; Oxford poll bk]

Linsell, William, 1 Clerkenwell Green, London, japanner and gilder (1812–19). [D]

Linsey, B. & Son, 54 Paul St, Finsbury, London, cabinet and feather warehouse (1808–11). [D]

Linsey, William, 59 Frederick St, Liverpool, cm (1784). [D]

Linsley, William, 55 Mill St, Hull, Yorks., cm and u (1823–31). Listed as cm in 1823 but from 1826 as u. [D]

Lintel, —, 'The Cabinet', Stonecutter St, near Fleet Ditch, London, cm (1727). [Heal]

Linter, R., Teignmouth, Devon, cm (1815). In March 1815 married Miss Paddock of Teignmouth. [Western Luminary, 21 March 1815]

Linton, Arthur, East Reach, Taunton, Som., cm (1830). [D]

Linton, Arthur, North Curry, Som., cm (1840). [D]

Linton, John, Bullring, Horncastle, Lincs., chairmaker (1826). [D]

Linton, Richard, New Riverside, Limehouse, London, cm (1809). [D]

Linton, Robert, Upper High St, Taunton, Som., cm and u (1839). [D]

Linwood, Matthew, Birmingham, fancy box maker (c. 1813). Tea caddy so marked. [Sotheby's, 15 January 1971, lot 99]

Liot, G., 17 York St, Bryanston Sq., London, u (1835). [D]

Lipskin, Joseph, West Wycombe, Bucks., chairmaker (1798). [Militia Census]

Liret, —, address unknown (1832). Named in the accounts of Sir Charles Blois of Cockfield Hall, Yoxford, Suffolk as the supplier of furniture to the value of £185 18s. [Suffolk RO, HA30: 312/418]

Lisle, Devergy snr, Newcastle, cm and u (1778–1808). First recorded in directories in 1778 at Manors. In January 1780 advertised his business which was then at the 'Commode and Cabriole' at the foot of Pilgrim St. He offered his services to the customers of his former master George Lowes who had retired from the trade. He remained at this address until April 1786 when he announced a move to 'a large and commodious Ware-house behind the New Buildings in Mosley St. His business was initially that of a joiner and cm but he now expanded the range of items produced and sold. In February 1788 he indicated that he had recently entered the glass-grinding business and was able to offer looking- and coach-glasses. From 1803 he added an upholstery branch. He was a subscriber to Sheraton's Drawing Book, 1793. His only known patron was Cuthbert Ellison of Hebburn Hall, Gateshead, Co. Durham. The invoice [Ellison papers, Gateshead Ref. Lib.] dated 1808, is for £9. One interesting feature of the invoice is the terms of trade which were six months credit, or a 3% discount for payment within a month. [D; Newcastle Courant, 8 January 1780, 22 April 1786, 9 February 1788, 16 February 1788, 1 March 1788, 7 May 1803; Furn. Hist., 1976]

Lisle, Devergy jnr, Newcastle, u and cm (1808–17). Son of Devergy Lisle snr. On 16 January 1808 advertised that he had commenced business on his own behalf from an address at 4 Mosley St where he maintained upholstery ware rooms. He seems to have taken over at least some of his father's former customers and in 1808 and 1812 supplied Cuthbert Ellison of Hebburn Hall. He obtained supplies of materials from London and both in April 1808 and May 1809 advertised his recent return with goods 'from the First houses in London'. By 1811 he had moved the location of his business to 15 Pilgrim St where he maintained upholstery and cabinet ware rooms. By October 1815 however he was in financial difficulties and an auction sale of his remaining stock was advertised. Only a month later however he was once more back in business declaring that 'the indulgence of his creditors having enable him to surmount his late difficulties by granting him a certificate under his bankruptcy, he has resumed the business of an upholsterer'. His new premises were also in Pilgrim St 'a little above his late situation'. Here he claimed to have an entirely new stock. A notice in Durham County Advertiser, 14 June 1817 advised debtors of Devergy Lisle to pay their accounts to Amor Spoor, cm of Newcastle. [D; Newcastle Courant, 16 January 1808, 2 April 1808, 6 May 1809, 30 May 1812; Newcastle Chronicle, 6 June 1812, 7 October 1815; Durham County Advertiser, 11 November 1815]

Lisle, John, Newcastle, joiner and cm (1778–79). At Flesh-market in 1778 but in September 1779 announced his move to Postern. [D; Newcastle Courant, 4 September 1779]

Lisle, John, Close, Newcastle, joiner and cm (1824). [D]

Lisle, William, 55 Gee St, Goswell St, London, chairmaker (1809). [D]

Lisney, James, High Wycombe, Bucks., u (1790–93). In 1791 insurance cover was £400 and in 1793, £700. [D; GL, Sun MS vol. 375, p. 521; vol. 395, p. 250]

List, —, Ipswich, Suffolk, cm (1793). Subscribed to Sheraton's Drawing Book, 1793.

Lister, George, Hebden Bridge, Yorks., timber merchant and cm (1830–34). [D]

Lister, Jacob, Newcastle, u (1738). [Freemen reg.]

Lister, John, Lancaster, cm (1793–1807). Named in the Gillow records, 1793–1807. Free of Lancaster, 1806–07, when stated 'of London'. [Westminster Ref. Lib., Gillow; Lancaster freemen rolls]

Lister, John, Sheffield, Yorks., cm (1834). [D]

Lister, John, Halifax, Yorks. cm (1834). [D]

Lister, John, Brick House, Keighley, Yorks., joiner/cm (1837). [D]

Lister, Joseph, John St, Chester, cm (1817–26). Son of Joseph Lister of Chester, coachmaker. App. to Richard Gorst, cm, 23 September 1817 and free by servitude, 20 October 1824. [App. indenture; freemen rolls; poll bks]

Lister, Robert, Lancaster, cm (1768–1806). Son of Thomas Lister and app. to him in 1768. Free, 1779–80. Named in the Gillow records 1793–94, 1796–97, 1801–02, 1806. [Westminster Ref. Lib., Gillow; poll bk; app. reg.; freemen rolls]

Lister, Robert, Skipton, Yorks., cm (1828). [PR (bapt.)]

Lister, Thomas, Lancaster, cm (1754–1812). Two apps with this name were indentured to Richard Gillow, one in 1754 and the other in 1761. The 1754 app. was free, 1763–64 and subsequently took thirteen apps between February 1768 and August 1812. The Gillow records show a Thomas Lister employed c. 1785 and 1787–96. [App. reg.; freemen reg.; Westminster Ref. Lib., Gillow]

Lister, Thomas jnr, Lancaster (1797). Named in the Gillow records in connection with making a table. [Westminster Ref. Lib., vol. 344/97, p. 1394]

Lister, William, Church Lane, Gainsborough, Lincs., cm and u (1822). [D]

Lister, William, High Bridge, Knaresborough, Yorks., joiner, cm and builder (1828–37). [D]

Lister, William, Workhouse Croft, 18 Union St, Sheffield, Yorks., cm and broker (1828–37). [D]

Lister, William, Dewsbury, Yorks., cm (1830–37). In 1830 at Daw Green and in 1837 at Webster Hill. [D]

Litchfield, Jonathan, 4 Grindle St, Manchester, cm (1817). [D]

Litchfield, William, parish of St Peter, Oxford, cm (1768). [Poll bk; Frowde, *Survey of Oxford*, 1912]

Litchfield, William, 12 Barretts Ct, Henrietta St, Cavendish Sq., London, cm (1776). In 1776 took out insurance cover of £200 but only £20 of this was for utensils and stock. [GL, Sun MS vol. 248, p. 408]

Litchfield & Graham, 72 St Martin's Lane, London, u and cm (1779–1808). The premises occupied by this partnership were on the corner of St Martin's Lane and Long Acre and the address is sometimes given as 1 Long Acre. Some directories also state 1 St Martin's Lane, but this would appear to be a misunderstanding based on the Long Acre number. From its commencement the partnership was of a substantial nature. They claimed to be successors to the renowned u, John Cobb, who died in 1778, and they undoubtedly took over many of his wealthy and influential patrons as well as his former business premises. In 1779 their insurance cover was £5,000 with £4,200 allocated to utensils and stock. By 1783 these figures had fallen to £4,000 and £3,000 respectively but even at these levels indicated that this was amongst the largest enterprises in this field in London.

A number of their clients are known. For the 6th Earl of Coventry at Croome Court, Worcs., substantial amounts of furniture were supplied in the period 1779–95. Much appears to have been bedroom furniture. In February 1785, £76 17s 5d was paid for a four-post bed, bedding, dressing tables, a wine cistern and curtains, and in August of that year a further substantial bill for £68 1s 2d covered a further bedstead and bedding, a night table, firescreen, curtains, and carving a pier glass frame. The largest single amount paid, for goods supplied in the year from June 1793, amounted to £137 19s 4d and was for similar items. The Hon. Mrs Leigh of Stoneleigh Abbey, Warks. was in December 1781 invoiced for a satinwood tea caddy and workbox costing £4 9s, while in the following year William Constable of Burton Constable, Yorks., was supplied with a mahogany wheel chair costing £7 10s which is still in the house. Constable also bought from Litchfield & Graham a set of six japanned chairs with a pair of matching arms chairs and caned stools. Alexander Wedderburn paid the partners £26 16s 6d in 1784 and Baron de Grey of Heaton Hall, Manchester £7 in 1786 for a writing table. The accounts of Lord Monson show payments to the firm of £300 in June 1785, £200 in April 1787 and £133 12s in May 1789, while the 2nd Lord Palmerston used their services in connection with the furnishing of Broadlands, Hants.

From 1809 the business was carried on solely by John Graham. A payment to Litchfield, Morel & Co. is stated to exist for 1798 in the Southill, Beds. accounts. Nothing further is however recorded under this trading style and the subsequent patronage of Graham in 1808 might suggest an error in the household accounts at Southill, rather than an intriguing connection between Nicholas Morel and the house of Litchfield & Graham. [D; GL, Sun MS vol. 276, p. 650; vol. 306, p. 613; V & A archives; Shakespeare Birthplace Trust, Leigh receipts, DR 18/5; Scottish RO, GD 164/Box 20/177/2–3; Preston, RO, DD Eg. bank deposit and account bk; Lincoln RO, Monson 10/1/A/6; *C. Life*, 29 January 1981, p. 290]

Litherland, William, Liverpool, u (b. 1735–d. 1807). App. to Robinson Cooke and free by servitude, 13 March 1761. By July of the following year he was trading from a 'warehouse joining Mrs Fleetwood's in Tythebarn-Street'. He offered to sell on both retail and wholesale terms a selection of blankets and indicated that he also stocked mattresses and 'sea beds'. By 1765 he had a shop near the Old Shambles in the High St which he was to occupy for a number of years. Here he kept an assortment of 'all Sorts of Upholstery Goods'. He also advertised for an app. The app. that he took was Matthew Gregson who trained under him, 1765–72, and was later to establish an important business himself. He also acted as executor at the time of Litherland's death in 1807. Earlier, Litherland had taken another app. named Hart in 1762, soon after the commencement of his business. At the time of his death Litherland was aged 72. [D; freemen's committee bk; freemen reg.; S of G, app. index; Liverpool RO, 920 GRE 3/1 45; *Williamson's Liverpool Advertiser*, 16 July 1762, 22 March 1765; *Liverpool Chronicle*, 8 April 1807]

Lithgo, Robert, Market Pl., Darlington, Co. Durham, cm/joiner (1834). [D]

Littell, Thomas, 39 Baelzephon St, Bermondsey, London, carver and gilder (1835–39). [D]

Litten, James, Highworth, Wilts., cm (1830). [D]

Little, George, Parton, Whitehaven, Cumb., cm/joiner (1834). [D]

Little, James, 47 Mortimer St, Cavendish Sq., London, u, cm and paper hanger (1802–39). Included in the list of master cabinet makers in Sheraton's *Cabinet Dictionary*, 1803. Initially Little appears to have had a workshop at 126 Gt Portland St in addition to the Mortimer St address. In November 1806 this workshop was valued for insurance at £200 and an additional £500 of cover was taken on utensils, stock and goods in trust. In 1810 the cover was raised to £300 and £700 respectively, but by January 1812 this workshop, now numbered 127, was in the tenure of Joseph Lees, cm, and Little was only paying for insurance cover on the building. His trade appears to have been conducted from the Mortimer St address and at some time before 1821 he appears to have taken his son into partnership and the trading style is sometimes listed as James

Little & Son. The business being undertaken was substantial and insurance on utensils, stock and goods was £1,000 in January 1821. James Little also appears to have owned a house, stables, coach houses and offices at 35 Wimpole St which were in the tenure of Robert Hibbert in December 1804 and insured for £3,000. His only known commission was for J. J. C. Bullock of Faulkbourne Hall near Witham, Essex, and Harley St, London. Upholstery work to the value of £7 13s was undertaken for him, 1829–30. [D; GL, Sun MS vol. 431, ref. 769170; vol. 437, ref. 795959; vol. 453, ref. 839442; vol. 459, ref. 864776; vol. 488, ref. 976045; vol. 498, ref. 1005324; Essex RO, D/DVv 46]

Little, John, Bridgegate, Howden, Yorks., joiner and cm (1834). [D]

Little, Joseph, Front St, Brampton, Cumb., joiner etc. (1834). [D]

Little, Robert, Back St, Brampton, Cumb., joiner/cm (1829–34). [D]

Little, Thomas, address unknown, cm (1803). Subscribed to Sheraton's *Cabinet Dictionary*, 1803.

Little, Thomas, Liverpool, u (1810–39). App. to Bartholomew Tyrer in 1810 and free, 11 June 1818. In 1821 at 4 Stockdale St; in 1824 at Rainsford Gdns and 1 Mercer Pl., Sawney Pope St; in 1827 at 44 Sawney Pope St; in 1829 at 49 Sawney Pope St; and in 1834 at 33 Combermere St. From 1835 the addresses are in Park St, Toxteth Park and the numbers were 36 in 1835, 47 in 1837 and 51 in 1839. In 1829 took app. named John Connell. [D; freemen's committee bk; app. bk]

Little, Thomas, Lowther St, Carlisle, Cumb., chairmaker (1829–34). [D]

Little, Thomas, Askrigg, Wensleydale, Yorks., joiner and cm (1840). [D]

Little, William, Lowther St, Carlisle, Cumb., joiner/cm (1829). [D]

Littledale, Joseph, Whitehaven, Cumb., u (1826). The only evidence regarding this maker is a bill submitted in 1826 for furniture supplied and work undertaken in connection with Rydal Hall for Lady Le Fleming. The furnishing scheme seems a very ambitious one for a local craftsman. In total the bill came to £349 4s 10d and included such items as 'A Suit of Crimson Silk Damask Bed Curtains with Draperies Silk Fringe &c. &c.' for which £119 was charged, and 'three Crimson Damask Silk Window Curtains with pole, Cornices, Ornaments etc' which cost £59 10s. Most of the account was for fabrics but a 'Mahogany Couch in Linen' was also supplied at £7 7s. [V & A archives]

Littledale, Mary, Whitehaven, Cumb., cm and u (1834). Probably successor to Joseph Littledale. [D]

Littleton, John, Liskeard, Cornwall, cm (1778). Advertised in 1778 for 'a couple of experienced journeymen cabinet-makers'. [*Exeter Flying Post*, 25 September 1778]

Littlewood, Joseph, 170 Briggate, Leeds, Yorks., cm (1837). [D]

Littlewood, Thomas, see Hartley & Littlewood

Littlewood, Thomas, York St, Kirkgate, Leeds, Yorks., cm (1822). [D]

Littlewood & Smith, 22 Boar Lane, Leeds, Yorks., cm and u (1828–30). [D]

Litton, Richard, Northgate, Canterbury, Kent, chairmaker (1826). [Poll bk]

Liverelt, Jno., 26 John St, Fitzroy Sq., London, cm and u (1827). [D]

Livermore & Son, 23 Little Carter Lane, St Paul's, London, bed and mattress manufacturer (1820–22). [D]

Liversedge, Richard, Honley, near Huddersfield, Yorks., cm (1822–34). [D]

Livesay, John, Church Row, Limehouse, London, cm, u and undertaker (1803). In January 1803 took out insurance cover for £1,400 of which £305 was for utensils and stock. [GL, Sun MS vol. 427, ref. 743360]

Livesay, Samuel, Walsall, Staffs., cm (1773). Bankruptcy announced, *Gents Mag.*, January 1773.

Livesey, John, 69 Friargate, Preston, Lancs., cm (1825). [D]

Livesey, William, 154 Friargate, Preston, Lancs., cm (1818). [D]

Livett, Richard, 3 High St, Marylebone, London, u and house agent (1819). [D]

Living, George & Charles, 2 Gt Union St, Borough Rd, London, chair and sofa maker (1839). [D]

Livingston, John, Manchester, cm and u (1828–40). In 1828 at 5 Little Bennett St, Lever St; in 1829 at 229 Gt Ancoats St; in 1834 at no. 60 and from 1836–38 at no. 68. In 1840 at 35 Portland St. [D]

Livingstone, James, by Pulteney St, Westminster, London, carver (1749). [Poll bk]

Livingstone, James, 38 Gt Pulteney St, London, cm and u (1754–79). An enterprise of modest size with an insurance cover of £900 in 1779 of which £630 was for utensils and stock. In 1754 it was reported that a dovetail saw had been stolen from his workshop bearing the maker's name 'W. Squires'. In July 1761 supplied furniture to Robert Dundas, Lord Arniston for Arniston House, Midlothian, Scotland. This included four chairs, a four post bedstead, cornices and festoon window curtains and amounted in cost to £51 9s 4½d. An additional £1 17s was asked in September 1765 for 'patterns in water colours for Embroiderer'. [Poll bks; GL, Sun MS vol. 274, p. 238; *Public Advertiser*, 16 November 1754; Arniston House accounts]

Livsey, George, High St, Knaresborough, Yorks., joiner/cm (1828–34). [D]

Llewellyn, William, 38 Cornwall Buildings, Bath, Som., cm and broker (1833). [D]

Lloyd, David, Bartholomew St, Exeter, Devon, cm (1820–40). Two sons and three daughters bapt., 1820–30 at St Mary Arches. [D; PR (bapt.)]

Lloyd, Edward, Manchester, u (1822–40). At 5 Tib Lane, 1822–29, but from 1832–34 the number was 15. In 1836 at 28 Pool St and 1838–40 at 79 Piccadilly. [D]

Lloyd, George, Shipyard, London, carver (1774). [Westminster poll bk]

Lloyd, George, Chester cm (1797). Free 15 July 1797. Son of G. Lloyd, victualler of Chester, deceased. [Freemen rolls]

Lloyd, George, 51 Featherstone St, City Rd, London, cm, chair and sofa manufacturer (1826–29). [D]

Lloyd, Henry, Clifton Pl., Bristol, carpenter, builder, under-taker, cm and u (1831). [D]

Lloyd, James, 116 London Rd, Brighton, Sussex, cm and u (1839–40). [D]

Lloyd, John, Dean's Pl., Westminster, London, cm (1749). [Poll bk]

Lloyd, John, New St, St James's, London, u (1768). Bankruptcy announced *Gents Mag.*, March 1768; and granting of certificate given in *General Advertiser*, 27 June 1768.

Lloyd, John, Lumley Ct, Strand, London, firescreen maker (1776). In 1776 took John Ferguson as app. [Westminster Ref. Lib., MS F 4309 p. 22]

Lloyd, John & William, Atherstone, Warks., cm (1835). [D]

Lloyd, John, Ironbridge, Salop, cm (1835–36). [D]

Lloyd, Joseph William, Market St, Hinckley, Leics., cm (1840). [D]

Lloyd, Luke, London, upholder (1739–49). Son of Luke Lloyd of St Katherine's near the Tower, butcher. App. to James Robinson on 2 February 1739 and William Garnham, freeman haberdasher, 31 July 1746. Free of the Upholders' Co. by servitude, 8 December 1749. [GL, Upholders' Co. records]

Lloyd, Richard, 129 Strand, London, upholder (1779). In 1779 took out insurance cover of £200 of which £50 was in respect of utensils, goods and stock. [GL, Sun MS vol. 278, p. 332]

Lloyd, Samuel, Ebenezer Pl., Commercial Rd, Limehouse, London, carver and gilder (1835–39). [D]

Lloyd, Thomas, 2 Queen St, Liverpool, cm and joiner (1761–1802). App. to William Leech and free 1761. Took as app. John Ward Turner in 1789 and he petitioned freedom in 1802. [D; freemen's committee bk]

Lloyd, Thomas, Stratford, Essex, cm, u and auctioneer (1791–1808). In 1791 took out insurance cover of £400 of which £290 was in respect of utensils and stock. [D; GL, Sun MS vol. 379, p. 433]

Lloyd, Thomas, 74 Islington Rd, Birmingham, cm (1835). [D]

Lloyd, Thomas, 8 White Mill St, with shop at 13 Vincent St, Liverpool, carver (1837). [D]

Lloyd, William, High St, Shrewsbury, Salop, cm and u (1808–35). Listed in the Shrewsbury freemen rolls in 1808. [D]

Lloyd, William, 2 Foregate St, Chester, cm and chairmaker (1814–40). In 1827 was employing a Thomas Turner at his works. A summons against him for assult on a Joseph McCluskey was dismissed. [D; *Chester Chronicle*, 8 June 1827]

Lloyd, William, 16 Pitt St, Fitzroy Sq., London, u (1822–23). In 1822 insured houses 9 and 10 James St, Camden Town, London, that he was renting out for £500. [GL, Sun MS vol. 493, ref. 995058; vol. 498, ref. 1006300]

Lloyd, William, 18 Bedford Pl., Commercial Rd, London, cm (1826–28). [D]

Lloyd, William, Okehampton St, Exeter, Devon, cm (1832–36). [D; poll bk]

Lloyd, William, High St, Shrewsbury, Salop, u (1835). [D]

Lloyd, William, Sidney St, Mile End Rd, London, cm and u (1839). [D]

Loader, Edward snr & jun, London, cm (1790–1823). At 5 Broker's Row, Moorfields, 1790–1806. Edward Loader jnr is first mentioned in 1803 when, like his father, he was listed in Sheraton's *Cabinet Dictionary* in the directory of master cabinet makers. The son's address was however given as 14 Broker's Row and in a directory of 1806 this division between Edward snr, at 5 and jnr at 14 is also given. After 1806 however all entries are for Edward jnr, and the address at 14 Broker's Row used. In 1821 the business moved to 55 Crown St, Finsbury Sq. but from the following year the number is given as 65. Although in most cases the trade is given as cm, in 1802 one directory describes the business as a upholstery warehouse. [D; Heal]

Loader, Edward, 64 Tabernacle Walk, Finsbury, London, cm, u and looking-glass manufacturer (1820–29). In 1820 referred to as a cabinet and looking-glass manufacturer and wholesale u. [D]

Loader, George, 41 High St, Mile End Rd, chair and sofa maker (1839). [D]

Loader, John, London and Richmond, Surrey, upholder (1774–1802). Son of Thomas Loader of Richmond, Surrey, brewer. App. to Francis Pyner, 4 May 1774 and free of the Upholders' Co. by servitude, 5 December 1781. In 1782 foreman to Francis Pyner whose address was 37 Lombard St. By 1794 at Richmond Surrey and so recorded in a directory of 1798. Still in this town in 1802. [D; GL, Upholders' Co. records]

Loader, Obadiah, parish of St Swithin, Norwich, cm (1830). [Poll bk]

Loader, Richard, 14 Broker Row, Finsbury, London, u (1815). This is the same address as that occupied by Edward Loader jnr, 1803–23. [D]

Loader, Richard, London, cm, u and looking-glass manufac-turer (1822–35). At 27 Noble St, Cheapside, 1822–28, but from 1826 also occupied 28. The business is named as Richard Loader & Son in 1827. From 1829–35 at 85 Newgate St. Also advertised themselves as appraisers and undertakers in 1823. Initially the business was small with insurance cover in January 1822 being only £450 of which £130 was for stock and utensils. By July 1822 however these figures were raised to £650 and £330 respectively. [D; GL, Sun MS vol. 490, ref. 987620; vol. 489, ref. 993964]

Loader, Richard, 23 Finsbury Pavement, London, cm, chair-maker and looking-glass manufacturer (1837–40). At a later date manufactured papier mâché furniture. A table in this material on end supports, painted with bouquets of flowers and gilt detail was sold by Sotheby's Belgravia, 5 August 1981. It was stamped 'R Loader Manufacturer 23 & 24 Pavement Finsbury London'. [D; *Antiques Trade Gazette*, 19 September 1981]

Loader & Atkinson, 39 Ludgate Hill, London, cm, u, appraisers and auctioneers (1816–20). In April 1816 the partners advertised the opening of their 'extensive premises' on Ludgate Hill and stated that they had there a 'display of elegant and fashionable furniture of every description manufactured by superior workmen under their own supervision'. The quality of their work can be judged for they appear to have applied trade labels to the items that they manufactured. A dining chair, card table and a pedestal table are recorded bearing the labels of this firm. Their trade card [Landauer Coll., MMA, NY] indicates that they also acted as undertakers as well as paper hangers and decorators. From 1820–24 the business was continued by Thomas Atkinson using both 38 and 39 Ludgate Hill. [D; *Times*, 2 April 1816; *Furn. Hist.*, 1978]

Lobb, Henry, London, joiner (1689–91). Possibly brother of Joel Lobb (below). Employed at Kensington Palace. Apart from working on wall panelling and other joiner's work, he manufactured in partnership with Alexander Fort picture frames, shelves, presses, tables, forms etc. A further Henry Lobb, son of Joel (below), was app. to Wm Hickman, carver, in 1714. [Winterthur, Delaware, Symonds papers 75x69.27; GL, MS 8052, 4, p. 41]

Lobb, Joel, White Lion St, St Giles-in-the-Fields, London, carver (1688–1715). Had an extensive patronage, including, in 1688–89 working at Hampton Court where he was paid £19 3s 6d for carving a very rich chimney-piece. He also worked at Chatsworth, and Castle Howard. At White Lion St, 1707–15. [*Wren Soc.*, XX, refs cited; Hand in Hand MS vol. 5, ref. 597; vol. 15, p. 11 F. Thompson, *History of Chatsworth*, pp. 36–37; *Survey of London*, XXIX. p. 36]

Loben, Mary, see John Jackson, Drury Lane, London.

Lock, Daniel, Aldersgate St, London, carver (1765). Freeman of London and member of the Joiners' Co. In 1765 licenced to employ three non-freemen for three months. [GL, City Licence bk, vol. 4]

Lock, George, Mill St, Bideford, Devon, cm (1823–38). [D]

Lock, George, Ringwood, Hants., cm (1839). [D]

Lock, James, London, upholder (1700). Free of the Upholders' Co. on 18 July 1700. [GL, Upholders' Co. records]

Lock, James, High St, Maidenhead, Berks., cm and u (1823–40). [D]

Lock, Joseph, 24 King St, Covent Gdn, London, u (1825–39). [D]

Lock, Matthias, Castle St, Long Acre, London, carver (b. c. 1710–d. 1765). Matthias Lock was the first Englishman to publish designs in the fully-developed Rococo style. He is one of a number of joiners or carvers, spanning three or more generations, of the same name. In 1724 he is recorded, variously, as having been app. to his father Matthias, a joiner in the parish of St Paul's, Shadwell [GL, Joiners' Co. app. bindings, vol. 4, p. 141] and to Richard Goldsaddle, carver in the parish of St Martin-in-the-Fields. [GL, MS 8052 (3), p. 87] Among the elder Lock's other apps were his sons Edward (1701), James (1722), and John (1729), and a James Cavitt (1717). [Ibid., pp. 41, 44, 141, 145] Since apprenticeships customarily began at age fourteen and ran for seven years, Lock must have been born about 1710 and became a journeyman carver about 1731. In July 1734 he married Mary Lee at St Paul's, Covent Gdn. We know nothing of Lock's professional life during this decade, but in the 1740s he emerged as a masterful designer and carver of the French Rococo. The first indication of his activities are some memoranda of charges for minor carving commissions between 1742–44, included in the collection of drawings that descended in the Lock family until acquired by the V & A. In the same collection are seven small sheets with rough sketches of carved furniture. Next to each sketch are recorded the names of the artisans (Messrs Lock, Lomar, Mill, Wood, and Loo) who made the piece and the number of days spent on it. In each case Lock's name leads the list. These pieces were made for the 2nd Earl Poulett of Hinton House, Hinton St George, Somerset, probably shortly after he succeeded to the title in 1734. A pier glass and pier table (now at the V & A) and two stands, all furnishings for the Hinton House 'Tapestry Room', survive; they are of superlative quality and stylistically combine Rococo decoration with Baroque scale.

At about the same time Lock undertook an ambitious programme to publish carvers' ornament in the new French taste. The first dated suite of plates, *Six Sconces*, appeared in 1744. It was followed two years later by *Six Tables*, a large cartouche on a single sheet, and Lock's own trade card. On the latter two pieces his address is given as 'Nottingham Court, Castle Street, near Long Acre'. He lived at 9 Nottingham Court until 1750. *A Book of Ornaments* (later reissued as *A Book of Shields*) appeared in 1747. Although the illustrations of 1744 have a certain massive quality not found in the later ones, all the designs exhibit a consistent and fully developed Rococo style. Even more distinctive is the style of engraving. Lock, who did his own, used etching almost exclusively, enabling him to produce informal, sketch-like prints. Two other suites, *A New Drawing Book of Ornaments, Shields, Compartments, Masks, &c.*, and *The Principles of Ornament, or the Youth's Guide to Drawing of Foliage*, although undated, are stylistically similar to his work of 1746/47. In 1752, in collaboration with H. Copland, Lock published *A New Book of Ornaments* with his address given as 'near ye Swan Tottenham Court Road'. Comprising twelve leaves, each with multiple motifs, it was the most ambitious book of Rococo ornament prior to Chippendale's *Director*. Of a similar style is Lock's *A New Book of Ornaments for Looking Glass Frames, Chimney Pieces &c in the Chinese Taste*.

Meanwhile, Lock continued to work with wood. The second state of his trade card, bearing his later address, described him as 'Carver'. And in the Lock Collection at the V & A, on sheets of paper from a 1752 diary, are his notations about furniture carved for Lord Holderness, Lord (presumably the 2nd Earl, and later 1st Duke of) Northumberland, and a Mr Bradshaw. Also in that collection is the drawing for an armchair *c.* 1755 which is now in the V & A. The chair was acquired by the painter Richard Cosway for use in his studio. The existence of drawings by Chippendale in the Lock Collection suggests a working relationship: Lock probably did piece-work carving for him. Lock is conspicuously absent from the list of master craftsmen in *Mortimer's Universal Directory*, 1763. By that time, presumably, he had left the trade. He died in 1765 and was buried at St Paul's, Covent Gdn, on 22 December.

Almost all of Lock's engravings were re-issued posthumously in 1768 by the publisher Roger Sayer, at which time he was described as 'the famous Mr Matt Lock recently deceased who was reputed the best Draftsman in that way that had ever been in England'. In 1769 a Matthias Lock executed *A New Book of Foliage for the Instruction of Young Artists* and *A New Book of Pier Frame's, Oval's, Gerandole's, Table's &c*, two suites of Neo-classic carvers' ornament; and between 1788–97 a carver of the same name is recorded at Clerkenwell Green. This Matthias Lock must be a son; and it would be his descendent George Lock from whom the V & A purchased the Lock collection in 1862–63: 78 loose sheets of drawings (Nos 2547–2624), and 168 drawings in a folio scrapbook entitled *Original Designs by Matts. Lock Carver 1740–1765* (Nos 2848/1–168). [F. Kimball and E. Donnell, 'The Creators of the Chippendale Style', *Met. Museum Studies*, I, Pt II, 1929, 115–54; P. Ward-Jackson, *English Furniture Designs of the 18th century*, 1958, pp. 38–40; J.F. Hayward, 'Furniture designed and carved by Matthias Lock for Hinton House, Somerset', *Conn.*, January 1961, pp. 284–86; G. Wills, *English Furniture 1550–1760*, pp. 241–53; H. Hayward, 'A Unique Rococo Chair by Matthias Lock', *Apollo*, October 1973, pp. 268–71; M. Heckscher, 'Lock and Copland: A Catalogue of the Engraved Ornament', *Furn. Hist.*, 1979, pp. 1–23; pls 1–67; *Rococo: Art and Design in Hogarth's England*, V & A (exhib. cat.), 1984, nos L4, 10–14, 17]

M.H.H.

Lock, Philip, 33 Lambert St, Goodman's Fields, London, chair and cabinet maker (1808). [D]

Lock, Robert, 32 Brownlow St, Long Acre, London, carver (1781). Took out insurance cover of £100 on his house in 1781. [GL, Sun MS vol. 293, p. 254]

Lock, Robert, 27 Cirencester Rd, Tottenham Ct Rd, London, carver and gilder (1825–39). [D]

Lock, S., 215 Oxford St, London, u (1813–14). An invoice for chair covers and cushions and upholstery to a value of £2 13s 3d dated 4 August 1813 was made out to Robert Clavering Savage of Gloucester Pl., Portman Sq., London and Elmley Castle, Worcs. This was receipted on 18 January 1814 by James Lock. [Worcs. RO, 4600/705:550/763/3]

Lock, Thomas, North St, Portsea, Portsmouth, Hants., cm and u (1823). [D]

Lock, William Cook, Angel Row, Nottingham, cm, furniture broker and u (1832–40). [D]

Lock & Richards, 3 Silver St, Clerkenwell, London, japanners and varnish makers (1790–93). [D]

Locke, William, Forest Pl., Radford, Notts., cm (1832). [D]

Locker, Joseph, London, upholder (1754). Son of Joseph Locker freeman and member of the Merchants Tailors' Co. App. to Samuel Luck, freeman shipwright, 3 June 1749, and free of the Upholders' Co. under the terms of the 1750 Upholders' Act, 3 October 1754. [GL, Upholders' Co. records]

Locker, William, Leicester, cm and u (1828–40). At Wharf St, 1828–35, but by 1842 had moved to Brook St. [D]

Locket(t), John, Mill St, Congleton, Cheshire, u and cm (1816–22). [D]

Lockett, John, Horninglow St, Burton-on-Trent, Staffs., cm (1818). [D]

Lockey, John, York, u (1818). Son of William Lockey, coachman. App. to William Smith u and cm, 21 October 1811, and free as a cm, 1818. [Freemen rolls]

Lockhart, Andrew, 7 Wood St, Liverpool, u (1834). [D]

Lockhart, James, 125 Fetter Lane, London, billiard table and backgammon board maker (1822). [D]

Lockier, James, 45 Wine St, Bristol, u (1775–93). Shown in 1781 living in Christ Church parish and in 1784 in the parish of St James. In 1791 supplied a leather cover for the altar at Christ Church. Bankrupt 1793. [D; poll bks; *Furn. Hist.*, 1976; Bailey's list of bankrupts]

Locking, William, St Swithin's, Lincoln, cm (1790). [Poll bk]

Lockley, F. R. & W., Goat St, Wolverhampton, Staffs., carvers and gilders (1816). [D]

Lockley, Francis, Wolverhampton, Staffs., frame maker (1818–27). Trading at North St as a carver and gilder in 1822. In 1820 advertised himself as a 'Manufacturer of Looking Glass, Picture & Miniature Frames'. He offered to regild old frames, and manufacture gilt cornices, mouldings and borders. Engravings were bleached, paintings cleaned and varnished and mahogany dressing and swing glasses sold. [D] See T. Lockley & Co, and William Lockley.

Lockley, George, 14 Fossgate, York, joiner and cm (1816–34). The surname is recorded in some directories as Lockey. [D]

Lockley, Richard, Newcastle, carver and gilder (1761–90). In 1778 at Nungate but from 1782 at Postern. On 2 April 1761 paid 14s 9d for gilding fifteen small picture frames for Gibside, Co. Durham. [D; Durham RO, D/St/V.994]

Lockley, T. & Co., North St, Wolverhampton, Staffs., carver and gilder (1818). [D] See Francis Lockley

Lockley, William, North St, Wolverhampton, Staffs., carver and gilder (1828). [D]

Lockley & Cartwright, North St, Wolverhampton, Staffs., carvers and gilders (1835). [D]

Lockly, Benjamin, 10 North St, Fitzroy Sq., London, carver and gilder (1808). [D]

Lockwood, J., 8 Stephen St, Tottenham Ct Rd, London, cm and chairmaker (1817–25). [D]

Lockwood, John, Hull, Yorks., cm and joiner (1741–74). Freeman of York. Cm in 1741 and 1774 but joiner in 1758. [York poll bks]

Lockwood, John, Streatham, London, cm and u (1832–39). In 1839 his address was given as Streatham Spa, Streatham. [D]

Lockwood, John, Denby near Penistone, Yorks., joiner/cm (1834). [D]

Lockwood, John, Rowley, Kirkburton, near Huddersfield, Yorks., joiner/cm (1834). [D]

Lockwood, Samuel, next door to 'The Rose Inn', parish of St Peter, Ipswich, Suffolk, u and joiner (1739). Bankruptcy declared June 1739 when the sale of his stock was advertised. The items offered included 'Standing Beds of divers Sorts . . . Mahogany and Walnut-tree Screen Tables, Oval Tables, Looking-Glasses, Corner Cupboards, with great Variety of Chairs'. Some stock that still remained was advertised for sale in Sempteber of the same year. [*Ipswich Journal*, 30 June 1739, 15 September 1739]

Lockwood, Stephen, 8 Stephen St, Tottenham Ct Rd, London, cm and chairmaker (1817). See also J. Lockwood at this address, 1817–25. [Heal]

Lockwood, William, Ipswich, Suffolk, cm (1725). In June 1725 insured his house, brewhouse and outhouse for £500. [GL, Sun MS vol. 21, ref. 36116]

Lockyer, —, address unknown, carver and gilder (1732). On 17 October 1732 paid £1 10s for a gilt picture frame by John Dutton of Sherborne House, Glos. [Glos. RO, Sherborne D 678 accounts 1790]

Lockyer, Joseph, London, u (1754). Free of the Upholders' Co. in 1754, in which year he subscribed to Chippendale's *Director*.

Lockyer & Reynold, Bedford St, Exeter, Devon, cm etc. (1839). [D]

Locock, W. R., Bristol, cm (1823–32). At foot of Durdham Down 1823–25, Sedan Chair Passage, Quay, 1826–31, and Love St, Hotwells in 1832. Also listed as a grocer 1823–25. [D]

Loder, E., Wilson St, Finsbury Sq., London, u (1824). Bankruptcy announced, *Brighton Gazette*, 12 February 1824.

Loder, Thomas, Dorchester, Dorset, u(?) (1734). Free 1734. [Mayo & Gould, *Municipal Records*, 1908, p. 431]

Lodge, Edward, Stone Well, Lancaster, cm, u and paper hanger (1795–1831). Initially may have worked in London for at the time that his son James was made free in 1823–24, Edward was described as 'late of Bateman's Buildings, Soho, London'. In May 1795 Edward Lodge married Miss Lawley, a Lancaster milliner. Between July 1802 and January 1831 took five app. cm and five app. u. Some of these apps were taken jointly with Robert Battersby who from c. 1820 to May 1826 was his partner. By 1831 his son James was active in the business and in January took an app. jointly with his father. [D; app. reg.; freemen rolls; *Billinge's Liverpool Advertiser*, 25 May 1795; *Lancaster Gazette*, 13 May 1826, 20 May 1826]

Lodge, Edward, Lancaster, u (1808–18). Addresses given at George St in 1808 and Gt John St, 1816–18. [D]

Lodge, Henry, London and Colchester, Essex, u (1731–84). Son of William Lodge snr, of Colchester, sadler. App. in London to Roger Tomlyn, 16 November 1724 and free of the Upholders' Co. by servitude, 1 December 1731. His stay in London was probably short for by 1738 he had returned to Colchester and in that year supplied Peter Creffield of Ardleigh with furniture. This included 'a bedstead with a double sacking and castors a set of cornishes a moulding teaster a frame headcloth carvd headboard and base moulding' for which £2 5s was charged and 'for making the green bed and three pairs of window curtains and fixing them up complete' £1 14s. He took app. named Halburn in 1743 and another named Barlow in 1755. In 1779 he took out insurance cover of £700 but of this only £150 was in respect of utensils and stock. His business premises in 1784 were in the High St. [D; poll bk; GL, Upholders' Co. records; Sun MS vol. 277, p. 390; vol. 319, p. 189; S of G, app. index; Essex RO, D/DRc F 33]

Lodge, James, Lancaster u (1823–34). Son of Edward Lodge in whose business he worked. Free 1823–24 and in January 1831 took an app. jointly with his father. [Freemen rolls; app. reg.] Listed as a chairmaker at St Nicholas St in 1834. [D]

Lodge, John, Lancaster, u (1817–30). Son of Edward Lodge. Free 1817–18, and in August 1826 took an app. Married Miss Jane Proctor of Lancaster on 27 June 1830. [Freemen rolls; app. reg.; *Liverpool Mercury*, 9 July 1830]

Lodge, Robert, 26 Kirkgate, Leeds, Yorks., cm and joiner (1837–40). [D]

Lodge & Battersby, Penny St, Lancaster, cm (1818–22). [D]

Lodge & Bittlestone, 128 Strand, London, u (1825). [D]

Lodsley, Nottingham, see Weston & Lodsley

Lodwick, Jeremiah, 'The White Lyon', Houndsditch, London, u (d. 1731). [Heal]

Loerhuick, Anthony, address unknown, carver (late 17th century). Carried out carving at the Chapel Royal, Whitehall. [*Wren Soc.*, VII, p. 131]

Loft, Matthew, 'The Golden Spectacles', the Backside of the Royal Exchange, London, cm (early 18th century). [Winterthur, Delaware, Symonds papers]

Loft, William, Toll Gavel, Beverley, Yorks., cm (1840). [D]

Lofthouse, George, 4 New Bayley St, Manchester, painter, gilder and japanner (1808–09). [D]

Lofthouse, William, Lancaster, cm (1837). App. to John Battersby and free, 1837–38. [App. reg.]

Logan, Hugh, Liverpool, carver and gilder (1835–37). In 1835 at East Side, Queen's Dock as a carver and gilder. In 1837 listed as a ship's carver at 31 Rathbone St in a directory which also lists in a similar trade Logan & Venn at 2 Eastside, Queen's Dock. [D]

Logan, James, Grosvenor St, Liverpool, veneer sawyer (1824). [D]

Loggin, Robert, Hull, Yorks., working u (1826–35). At 3 Old Post Office Entry in 1826 and 123 High St in 1835. [D]

Lohr, John, 1 Fountain Ct, Strand, London, carver and gilder (1808–17). [D]

Lolli, John, Ormskirk, Lancs., cm (1822–34). Recorded as a cm and timber merchant in 1822, and trading at Church St, 1825–34. [D]

Lollie, William, King St, Liverpool, cm (1774–90). At 14 King St, 1774–81, but in 1790 at 17. In 1790 his trade was stated to be chairmaker. [D]

Lomas, —, Derby, joiner and cm (1790). Daughter married October 1790. [*Derby Mercury,* 14 October 1790]

Lomas, Jos., Bellargate, Nottingham, cm (1791–99). Signed the *Nottingham Cabinet and Chair Makers' Book of Prices* on behalf of the masters. [D]

Lomas, William, Manchester, u (1813–22). Recorded at 2 Back of Queen St in 1813 and 8 King St, 1821–22. [D]

Lomax, Francis, Mardol, Shrewsbury, Salop, cm and u (c. 1730–c. 1750). App. to Joseph Thomas of Shrewsbury, cm and joiner 1723. His son George, later to follow his father's trade, was born 10 July 1733. A George II walnut dressing glass is known bearing his trade label which is probably the earliest usage of this method of publicity in the provincial cabinet trade. The label states that he sold 'all maner of Cabinet Work and fine Compass Seat Chairs with Upholster'd Seats both in Mohogany and fine Walnut after the newest and best fashion, all sorts of *India* Back Chairs either with Upholster'd Seats or fine Dutch or matted Bottoms, Cane Chairs and Dutch Chairs both Course and fine, all manner of wood-Work for Beds, Easy Chairs Dressing Chairs and Writing Chairs, Settee Beds, Card, Backgamen and Writing Tables, Buroe Tables, Mohogany work of all Sorts, the best Dineing Tables Dressing Tables Drinking Tables and Handboards both Scollopt and round, Salvers Corner Cupboards and Clock cases both arch'd and plain, Dumb waiters, walnut Bellows with Brushes, the best Dutch Tables, Looking Glasses of all Sizes Sconces both Gilt in Gold and walnut Frames, Chimney Glasses Dressing Glasses Piere Glasses Dressing Glasses with union Sutes, Coach Glasses of all sizes, all manner of Gilt and Stain'd Frames to Pictures, Gilt Balls for Clock Cases with friezes, all sort of Varnish and all other Goods in the Cabinet-makers and Joyners way at Reasonable Rates. N.B. Old Looking Glasses, New Silvered Fram'd Cabinet-work and Glass work Neatly mended and made fashionable'. [*Furn. Hist.,* 1973]

Lomax, Frederick, 5 Circus St, Marylebone, London, u (1835–39). [D]

Lomax, George, Dog Lane, Shrewsbury, Salop, cm (b. 1733–98). Son of Francis Lomax of Shrewsbury, cm and u and born 10 July 1733. Free 1771. In 1780 took out insurance cover of £1,000 but of this only £100 was in respect of utensils and stock. [D; PR (bapt.); freemen rolls; GL, Sun MS vol. 286, p. 224]

Lomax, William, Bolton-le-Moors, Lancs., cm and auctioneer (1793). [D]

Lomax (or Lomas), William, New St, Birmingham, cabinet, case and portable desk maker (1830–39). Recorded at nos 43 and 44 in 1830, and nos 33 and 34 in 1835. [D]

Lomax & Nightingale, 11 St Ann's St, Manchester, u (1818–19). [D]

Lombardini, John, Market Pl., Huddersfield, Yorks., carver and gilder (1830–37). Trading at no. 2 in 1830. [D]

Lombardini, S., 3 Lower Castle St, Bristol, looking-glass and picture frame maker (1833–40). [D]

London, C. P., 15 Wardour St., Soho, London, u and cm (1825–39). His trade card [Landauer Coll., MMA, NY] indicates that he also was responsible for interior decoration, paper hanging and funeral arrangements. Trading on his own behalf in 1825 but 1826–29 in partnership, trading as London & Craymer. In June 1827 the partners invoiced to Lord Gwydir 'a mahogany French bedstead' for £15 and an 'ornamental table with purple band etc' at £5. By 1839 London was once more trading on his own behalf. [D; Lincoln RO, 2 ANC 6/202/71]

London, James, Bristol, cm and u (1827–40). In Upper Maudlin St, 1827–39, the number being 23 in the period 1830–39. In 1840 shown at 81 Stoke's Croft. [D]

London, William, Worcester, u and cm (1802). App. to John Timmings and free 21 June 1802. [Freemen reg.]

Loney, James, 5 Blake St with a shop at 2 Newington, Liverpool, cm (1837). [D]

Long, —, address unknown, u (c. 1775). Supplied Brockenhurst Park, Hants. c. 1775. [*Antique Collector,* vol. 25, p. 134]

Long, Charles, London, upholder (1762–70). Son of Thomas Long of Malden, Essex. Thomas Long was by trade a surgeon but was already dead at the time of his son's apprenticeship. Charles Long was app. to John Baron, 15 April 1755, and then to James Woodroffe, tiler and bricklayer, 6 May 1757. He was free of the Upholders' Co. by servitude, 6 May 1762. Charles Long took as app. Charles Elliott but in 1770 he was transferred to Paul Saunders. [GL, Upholders' Co. records; *Furn. Hist.,* 1973]

Long, Charles, The Close, Salisbury, Wilts., cm (1792–98). In 1792 renting a house and workshop form a Henry Edwards of The Close, Salisbury. [D; GL, Sun MS vol. 391, p. 316]

Long, George, 13 Gt Newport St, London, u, cm, auctioneer and undertaker (1800–23). Subscribed to Sheraton's *Cabinet Dictionary,* 1803. An invoice dated 9 April 1805 amounting to £3 10s covered furniture supplied to Mr Colfax of Bridport, Dorset. [D; Dorset RO, D43/F4]

Long, George, Liverpool, cm (1817). In 1817 married Miss Jane Soloman of Liverpool. [*Liverpool Mercury,* 2 May 1817]

Long, John, 7 Little Compton St, Soho, London, cm, turner and dealer in glass and ceramics (1779–86). In 1779 took out insurance cover of £400 of which £130 was in respect of utensils and stock. Probably the John Long, living in London, recorded in Norwich poll bks, 1784–86. [GL, Sun MS vol. 274, p. 191; Norwich poll bks]

Long, John, Beaufort Pl., Chelsea, London, cm and u (1823). [D]

Long, Peter, Host St, Bristol, cm (1795). [D]

Long, Sarah, Foregate St, Chester, cm (1834). [D]

Long, Sarah, West St, Bridgwater, Som., u (1840). [D]

Long, Thomas, address unknown, cm (1803). Subscribed to Sheraton's *Cabinet Dictionary,* 1803.

Long, Thomas, London, cm (1826–37). At 44 Goodge St, Tottenham Ct Rd, 1826–27, 17 Blenheim St in 1835 and 49 Castle St East, Oxford Mkt in 1837. [D]

Long, William, London, carver (1748–63). In 1748 took app. named Gettings. Long's address at this period was recorded as the parish of St Giles-in-the-Fields. In 1763 in Long Acre. Undertook work for Norman & Whittle. [D; S of G, app. index; *Burlington,* August 1969]

Long, William, Long Acre, London, upholder (1774). [Westminster poll bk]

Long, William, London, cm and carver (before 1785). From 1785 trading at an address in Union St, Philadelphia, USA. Claimed to be 'Late of London'. Specialised in invalid chairs one of which was said to have been approved of by the Royal Society in London. [*Penn'a Packet,* 10 September 1785]

Longbotham, —, address unknown, frame maker (1701). Paid £1 15s on 31 July 1701 by Sir John Newton of Barr's Court, Gloucester, for some frames. [Lincoln RO, Cragg 2/17/2]

Longbotham, Henry, Snow Fields, London, carver and gilder (1790–93). [D]

Longbottom, J., 23 St George's St, Leeds, Yorks., cm (1817). [D]

Longden, Thomas, 24 Rawstone St, Goswell St, London, cm and u (1839). [D]

Longdon, T., 44 Upper St, Islington, London, u (1820). [D]

Longford, John, Northgate, Bridgnorth, Salop, chairmaker (1840). [D]

Longhurst, —, address unknown, cm (1758). In March 1758 supplied three library bookcases at a cost of £8 7s 8d for Chevening, Kent. [Kent RO, U1590 A61/5]

Longlands, Joseph, Sutton Bridge, Long Sutton, Lincs., cm and builder (1835). [D]

Longley, Edward, 4 Dorvill Row, Hammersmith, London, furniture broker and bedstead maker (1839). [D]

Longley & Sutton, King St, Hammersmith, London, Windsor, rustic and garden chairmakers (1832–38). [D]

Longmore, Thomas, St Mary's Row, Birmingham, brass founder and picture frame maker (1812). [D]

Longshaw, John, 1 Thurlo St, Liverpool, cm (1837). [D]

Longworth, John, Whitefield, near Prestwich, Lancs., cm (1834). [D]

Longworth, Richard, Liverpool, cm (1754). Free 12 April 1754. [Freemen reg.]

Lonie, Douglas, 83 High St, Sunderland, Co. Durham, cm (1832). [D]

Lonrie, William, 6 Elizabeth Pl., St George's Field, London, cm (1794). In May 1794 insured four houses for £1,000. [GL, Sun MS vol. 401, ref. 628292]

Lonsdale, Edward, 12 Princes St, Cavendish Sq., London, cm (1784–93). [D]

Lonsdale, Joseph, Richmond, Yorks., cm, joiner and carpenter (1752–d. by 1794). In 1752 took app. named Arundale. Joseph Lonsdale was dead by October 1794 when his premises were offered for rent. They consisted of a 'modern-built sashed dwelling-house . . . a saw-house and ware-house . . . large convenient work-shop and a small room for goods over the Saw-house and ware-house, and proper Out-offices'. [S of G, app. index; *Newcastle Courant*, 4 October 1794]

Lonsdale, Matthew, Salford and Manchester, cm (1800–33). In 1800 at Catcliffe St, Salford, Lancs. and in 1832–33 at 11 Water St, Manchester. [D]

Lonsdale, Robert, Coney St, York, carpenter, joiner and cm (1787–91). In November 1791 took out insurance cover of £800. [D; GL, Sun MS vol. 381, p. 606]

Lonsdale, Thomas, Lancaster, (1792–1800). Named in the Gillow records 1792, 1794, 1796–97, 1799–1800. [Westminster Ref. Lib., Gillow]

Lonsdale, William, Hull and Bridlington, Yorks., cm (1784–90). Freeman of Beverley, Yorks. In Hull in 1784 and Bridlington in 1790. [Beverley poll bks]

Lonsdale, William, 7 Bread St, Soho, London, cm and upholder (1795–1815). Subscribed to Sheraton's *Drawing Book*, 1793, and included in the list of master cabinet makers in his *Cabinet Dictionary*, 1803. In June 1807 took out insurance cover of £1,000 of which £850 was for utensils and stock. [D; GL, Sun MS vol. 440, ref. 804265]

Looker, Francis, 163 Union St, Southwark, London, chair and sofa manufacturer (1829). Successor to John Looker at this address. [D]

Looker, John, 163 Union St, Southwark, London, chair and sofa maker (1826). Succeeded by Francis Looker at this address by 1829. [D]

Lord, Aaron, St John's Madder Market, Norwich, cm and u (1830–40). [D]

Lord, Ann, St Ann's Terr., St Ann's, Liverpool, u (1835–37). In 1835 the number in St Ann's Terr. is given variously as 18 or 16 and in 1837 as 17. [D]

Lord, Isaac, Birstall, Yorks., joiner and cm (1830). [D]

Lord, James, Adwalton, near Morley, Birstall, Yorks., cm (1822). [D]

Lord, John, London, carver and gilder (before 1766 and after 1775). By 1766 had established himself in South Carolina in the trade. He claimed to have received his training and skills 'from the best shops in London' and to have been employed 'doing all the different parts of his Business at the Shop of Mr. Norman, Carver and Gilder to her Majesty' — a reference to the important furniture maker, Samuel Norman. In May 1767 he announced the importation by the ship *London* of a 'large assortment of Looking Glasses'. He left to return to London in March 1775. [*South Carolina Gazette*, 17 June 1766, 12 May 1767]

Lord, Jonathan, Leeds, Yorks., cm and joiner (1817–40). In 1817 at White-Cloth-Hall St, in 1830 at 4 East Row; and in 1834 at 20 Cheapside. [D]

Lord, Samuel, Market St, Bradford, Yorks., joiner and cm (1814–22). [D]

Lord, William, opposite 'Ben Johnson's Head', Shoe Lane, London, u (1783). In 1783 insured his house for £100. [GL, Sun MS vol. 314, p. 228]

Lord, William, Church St, Whitby, Yorks., cm and u (1823–34). [D]

Lord, William & Son, 28 Newbro' St, Scarborough, Yorks., cm (1840). [D]

Lorrimer, William, London, carver and gilder (1778). In 1778 insured a house jointly with John Cobham of Ware, Herts., malt factor. [GL, Sun MS vol. 265, p. 446]

Lorthwick, Samuel, Manchester, carver (1759). In 1759 took app. named Radcliff. [S of G, app. index]

Lortin, Thomas, Marybone, Liverpool, u (1796). [D]

Lotchfield, William, London, u (1802). Freeman of Oxford. [Oxford poll bk]

Lott, Ann, 18 Edgecumbe St, East Stonehouse, Plymouth, Devon, cm and u (1838). [D]

Lott, Timothy, Devizes, Wilts., chair and basket maker (1774). In November 1774 took out insurance cover on his two houses which adjoined one other for £150 and an additional £50 for stock kept in them. [GL, Sun MS vol. 235, ref. 346918]

Lott, Timothy, Newcastle-under-Lyme, Staffs., chairmaker (1798). [D]

Lough, Francis, Tweedmouth, Northumb., joiner and cm (1834). [D]

Lough, Robert, 66 Berwick St, Soho, London, cm (1821–22). In February 1821 took out insurance cover of £300 on household goods in his dwelling house and rooms behind. [GL, Sun MS vol. 488, ref. 9760093]

Lough, William, Percy St, Alnwick, Northumb., cm and joiner (1834). [D]

Louth, Daniel, London, upholder (1734). Son of Robert Louth of the parish of St Mary-le-Strand, London, Gent. App. to William Dunton, 11 May 1727, and free of the Upholders' Co. by servitude in 1734. [GL, Upholders' Co. records]

Louth, Henry, London, upholder (1713). Freeman of London. On 17 October 1713 took an app. [S of G, app. index]

Lovat, Samuel, 43 Sadlergate, Derby, cm and u (1829). [D]

Lovat(t), James, Sad(d)lergate, Derby, u and cm, carver and gilder (1822–23). [D]

Lovatt, Robert, Kilwarby St, Ashby-de-la-Zouch, Leics., cm, builder and tea dealer (1822). [D]

Love, John, High St, Newport, Isle of Wight, cm and u (1802–30). Trading at High St, 1802 and 1830 and in Quay St, 1823. Took out insurance cover in 1802 for £999. This included stock and utensils in his dwelling house valued at £150, an upholsterer's workshop and feather store with stock at £80 and a cabinetmaker's workshop with stock and utensils at £200. [D; GL, Sun MS vol. 43, ref. 728427]

Love, John Alger, Beccles, Suffolk, cm and u (1824–39). At Northgate St in 1824 and one directory of 1839, and Saltgate St, 1830–39. [D]

Love, Knelm(?), 2 Seething Lane, London, chairmaker (1808). In August 1808 took out insurance cover of £100 of which £70 was in respect of household goods. [GL, Sun MS vol. 447, ref. 819858]

Love, Kelah, 14 Duke's Row, New Rd, St Pancras, London, chair and sofa maker (1829). Still trading from this address in 1835 but trade then stated to be furniture broker. [D]

Love, Peter, London, carver and gilder (1784). Freeman of Colchester, Essex. [Colchester poll bk]

Lovegrave, James, 5 Kennington Green, London, chair and sofa maker (1839). Stated that the Gothic style was his speciality. [D]

Lovegrove, —, 9 Assembly Row, Mile End Rd, London, chair and sofa manufacturer (1829). [D]

Lovegrove, Henry, Slough, Bucks., chairmaker (1798). [D]

Lovegrove, Henry jnr, Slough, Bucks., Windsor and garden chairmaker (1823). [D]

Lovegrove, Richard, Egham, Surrey, Windsor, fancy and garden chairmaker (1822–39). Also furniture broker in 1822. [D]

Lovegrove, William, Prospect Pl., Kent Rd, London, chair and sofa maker (1826). [D]

Lovejoy, Peter, 3 St John St Rd, London, bedstead maker and broker (1804). In July 1804 took out insurance cover of £400 of which £300 was for his dwelling house, shop and warehouse. No stove for drying feathers was on the premises. [GL, Sun MS vol. 430, ref. 764503]

Lovel, Thomas, parish of St Sidwell, Exeter, Devon, cm (1818). In February 1818 convicted at Exeter of 'wilfully and maliciously cutting down several young trees from the hedge of a field in the parish'. He was ordered to pay compensation of £5. [Exeter Flying Post, 19 February 1818]

Lovelace, —, address unknown, cm (1803). Subscribed to Sheraton's Cabinet Dictionary, 1803.

Lovelady, Edward, Liverpool, joiner and cm (1827–29). In 1827 at Paradise Ct, Paradise St but in 1829 in addition to this address which was said to be a shop, one at 25 Manesty Lane was given. In 1829 he was listed only as a cm. [D]

Lovelady, Edward, Liverpool, carver (1827–39). In 1827 at 31 Sir Thomas' Buildings but in 1834 at St John's Pl., Old Haymarket. From 1835 in Derby St, the number being 9 in 1835, 8 in 1837 and 14 in 1839. [D]

Lovelady, Lawrence, Liverpool, carver (1810–24). At 15 Love Lane in 1810 and 5 Love Lane, 1811–18. In 1824 at 2 Dixon Ct, Lace St. [D]

Lovelady, Thomas, Liverpool, chairmaker (1796–1827). At back 20 Atherton St in 1796. From 1800 at the Old Ropery, Fenwick St, the number being 6, 1803–10, with the exception of 1807 when it was 10. In 1813 at Haughton's Pl., Water St and in 1827 at Brunswick St. [D]

Loveland, James, Ditch Side, St Bride's, London, upholder (1741–69). In 1741 fined for declining parish office, parish of St Bride, Fleet St. In 1756 was Collector for the Poor, in 1757 Sidesman and in 1769 Scavenger. [GL, MS 6561, p. 70]

Loveland, Richard, London, upholder (1717–33). Son of John Loveland of the parish of St Sepulchre, London. App. to Samuel Abbott 4 September 1717 and free of the Upholders'

Co. by servitude, 3 October 1733. [GL, Upholders' Co. records]

Lovell, Abraham, Plymouth, Devon, u (1776). Bankruptcy announced, Exeter Flying Post, 15 march 1776.

Lovell, George, Wells, Som., upholder (1784). Freeman of Bristol. [Bristol poll bk]

Lovell, George, High St, Towcester, Northants., cm/joiner (1823). [D]

Lovell, James, St Marylebone, London, carver (c. 1775). Insolvent, and dividend declared, Leicester Journal, 13 December 1777.

Lovell, James, 8 Margaret St, Cavendish Sq., London, carver and gilder (1809–19). [D]

Lovell, Michael, Gracechurch St, London, upholder (1712–31). On 13 June 1712 took out insurance cover of £200 jointly with a Samuel Arnolde on a house on the south side of Crown Court, Gracechurch St. The house was said to be rented. This may have been Lovell's house and business premises at this date as subsequently from 1724 Gracechurch St is always quoted as his address. Seven days earlier however he had taken out a policy for £200 in his own name only for a house of timber construction in Bishopsgate St Within, and it may have been here that he was living in 1712. On 5 March 1712/13 he took an app. named Lovell who was a freeman of London and a member of the Upholders' Co. In 1731 his son William was declared free of this company by patrimony. [GL, Hand in Hand MS vol. 10, refs 7420, 8201; Upholders' Co. records; S of G, app. index; Daily Journal, 20 March 1724, 30 October 1727]

Lovell, Richard, London, broker and cm (1715–d. by 1742). In October 1715 took out insurance cover of £100 on a house in Hosier Lane, parish of St Sepulchre. He was stated to be a freeman joiner. By August 1723 he was living next to 'The Boar's Head' in the Barbican where he took out cover for £300. This insured goods and merchandise in his house for £100, similar items in the Carpenters' Hall, London Wall for £100 and the same sum for timber in a yard near his house. He was living in Aldermanbury in 1725 when a claim was paid to him by the Union Fire Office. He was already dead by November 1742 when his stock was put up for auction. He was then living in Brooke St, Holborn. The stock consisted of 'all Sorts of Bedding, Chairs, Cabinets, Desks, and Bookcases, Chests of Drawers, Dressing Tables, Dining Tables, Mahogany Claw Tables.' [GL, Hand in Hand MS vol. 15, p. 314; Sun MS vol. 16, ref. 29609; V & A archives; Daily Advertiser, 11 November 1742]

Lovell, Samuel, London, cane chairmaker (1718–20). In 1718 his address was given as Ditch Side, parish of St Bridget. But by 1 October 1720 had moved to 'The Double Chair', corner of Stone Cutters St, near the Ditch Side. [GL, Sun MS vol. 8, ref. 11234]

Lovell, Thomas, Catherine St, Exeter, Devon, cm (1818–23). Daughter bapt. at St Sidwell's Church 23 August, 1818. In 1822 in partnership with Sugg as Lovell & Sugg. [D; PR (bapt.)]

Lovell, Thomas, High St, Towcester, Northants., cm/joiner (1823). [D]

Lovell, William, London, upholder (1731). Son of Michael Lovell, freeman and members of the Upholders' Co. William was free of the Upholders' Co. by patrimony, 4 March 1730/31. [GL, Upholders' Co. records]

Lovelock, Henry, 3 Kingsland Rd, London, cm and u (1820–39). [D]

Lovelock, Henry, 20 Crescent Pl., Margate, Kent, cm and u (1839). Successor to J. Lovelock at this address. [D]

Lovelock, J., 20 Crecent Pl., Margate, Kent, u (1838). Succeeded in 1839 by Henry Lovelock at this address. [D]

Loveridge, James, West St, Bridport, Dorset, cm (1839). Bankrupt 1839 but despite this still shown in a directory of 1840. [D; *Exeter Flying Post*, 4 July 1839]

Loves, William, Gt Yarmouth and Barney, Norfolk cm (1812–20). Freeman of Gt Yarmouth and in the town October 1812. At Barney, 1818–20. [Gt Yarmouth poll bks]

Lovett, Edward, 65 St James' St, Liverpool, cm and u (1835). [D]

Lovett, James, Liverpool, cm and broker (1827–39). In 1827 shown in one directory at 1 St Vincent St, and in another at 26 St James' St. After 1827 all addresses are in St James' St, the number being 23 in 1829, 68 in 1834, 69 in 1835, 67 in 1837 and 131 in 1839. In 1839 shown additionally at 4 Uphill St, Toxteth Pk. [D]

Lovett, Richard, Worcester, upholder (1780–88). Listed at Broad St, also as an auctionner in 1788. App. to Richard Meredith, upholder, and free by servitude, 7 February 1780. In the following year he took out insurance cover of £400 of which £300 was in respect of utensils and stock. [D; freemen admission reg.; GL, Sun MS vol. 290, p. 340]

Lovett, Samuel, 43 Sadlergate, Derby, cm and u (1828). [D]

Lovett, William, Castle St, Oxford Mkt, London, buhl and cabinet maker (1820s). [*Burlington*, June 1980, p. 416]

Lovewell, T. S., St Michael's Coslany, Norwich, cm and u (1822). [D]

Lovick, Samuel, Walsingham, Norfolk, cm (1807). Freeman of Norwich. [Norwich poll bk]

Loving, Thomas, London, cabinet and chairmaker (1803–23). In 1803 subscribed to Sheraton's *Cabinet Dictionary*. At 23 Well St, Oxford St, 1809, but by 1816 had moved to 102 Wardour St, Soho. In July 1823 he took out insurance cover on this address for £1,000 of which £300 was in respect of utensils and stock. [D; GL, Sun MS vol. 498, ref. 1006314]

Loving, Thomas, 10 Basnett St, Liverpool, cm and u (1834). [D]

Lovitt, John, 57 Whitefriargate, Hull, Yorks., cm and u (1826–31). Shown with residence at 10 Parliament St from 1831–40. From 1834 the business was carried on in partnership with Thomas Lovitt. In October 1828 supplied furniture on a substantial scale to the Carter-Thewall family of Redbourne Hall, Lincs. The total furnishing bill came to £3,849 5s 5d. [D; Lincoln RO, 2 RED 4/4/14] Thomas Lovitt was living at 4 Baker St from 1835. [D]

Low, John, Richmond, Surrey, cm (1759). In 1759 took app. named Jackson. [S of G, app. index]

Low, Stephen, 102 Gt Portland St, St Marylebone, London, cm (1817). [D]

Lowcock, John, Skipton, Yorks., cm (1834). [PR]

Lowcock, Mary, Pontefract, Yorks., cm (1754). In 1754 took app. named Barbar. A business recorded as Lowcock & Wing cm was trading in this town in 1751. [S of G, app. index]

Lowcock, William, Mill Bridge, Skipton, Yorks., joiner/cm (1837).

Lowcock & Wing, Pontefract, Yorks., cm (1751). Also house joiners. Offered for sale 'all Sorts of Tables, Chairs, Chests of Drawers, Bed-work, and all Kinds of Cabinet-work'. A Mary Locock was trading as a cm in this town in 1754. [*York Courant*, 4 June 1751]

Lowdell, —, 108 Blackman St, Southwark, London, cm (c. 1780). [Heal]

Lowe, Charles, 40 Queen St, Birmingham, cabinet and bedstead maker (1830). [D]

Lowe, Edward snr, Liverpool, cm (b. 1737–d. 1807). App. to Josiah Baxendale and free by servitude, 14 March 1761. At Pool Lane, 1766–67, 4 Red Cross St, 1769–90 and Suffolk St in 1796. The number of apps taken suggests a business of some importance. These were Thomas Basnett and John Alexander (free 1780), George Highfield (free 1784), Thomas Robinson and Edward Lowe jnr (free 1790), William Atkinson and Thomas Maddocks (1784–96), and John Chesters (1794–1806). Died in 1807 at the age of 70. [D; freemen reg.; freemen's committee bk]

Lowe, Edward jnr, Liverpool, cm (1790–1829). Son of Edward Lowe snr and app. to him. Free by servitude, 20 June 1790. At 5 Riley's Gdns, Tempest Hey, 1790–1803, and in 1796 shown additionally with a shop at 17 Cable St. In 1800 living in a new house at 1 Slater St, Duke St which he continued to occupy until at least 1805. This property was clearly of some value and in January 1801 was insured together with its household contents for £1,200. Although no manufacturing was carried on here it is the address given in several directories of this period. From 1804 he was in partnership with a person named Croft, probably Joseph Croft. Initially the business was in Feather St, Richmond Row, but from 1807 at Downes St, Richmond Row, a property leased from Mathew Gregson, u and cm. The partners undertook work for Gregson and in 1807 were paid £657 3s 1d, and in the following year £677 19s 4d. No further references are made to the partnership after December 1808, but Edward Lowe jnr carried out further work for Gregson, 1811–14. In some cases for this later work the amounts due were settled in the form of goods or work carried out in return. Lowe was using 39 Old Scotland Rd in 1810 and 6 Old Bush Rd in the following year. From 1813 addresses are in Bevington Bush, the number being 17 in 1813–14, 21 in 1818, 41 in 1821–23 and 33 in 1829. Additionally he appears to have retained the shop in Feather St, now numbered 1. Like his father he took a large number of apps. These were Thomas Lowe (1797–1806), Thomas Wilding (1800–12), Thomas Ingham and Joseph Holmes (1804–12), John Robbs (1797–1812), Samuel Whittaker (1802–12), Edward Lowe (1799–1812), Richard Williams (1801–12) and Robert Jones (1807–16). [D; freemen reg.; freemen's committee bk; GL, Sun MS vol. 37, ref. 714302; vol. 43, ref. 726845; Liverpool RO, 920 GRE 1/27]

Lowe, Edward, Liverpool, cm (1799–1812). The relationship of this Edward Lowe to to the other two cm of this name working in Liverpool is uncertain. He was app. to Edward Lowe jnr in 1799, only nine years after the latter had received his own freedom which would suggest that he was not the son of Edward jnr. After serving Edward Lowe jnr for seven years he petitioned for his freedom in 1806. This was however refused as the indenture had been lost and the application was postponed. It is possible that at this stage he left Liverpool and went to work in Shrewsbury. This is based on the assumption that he is the Lowe who was married in 1809 to a Miss Margaret Keen at St Peter's Church, Liverpool. He eventually became a freeman of Liverpool on 5 October 1812. [Freemen reg.; freemen's committee bk; *Liverpool Courier*, 1 February 1809]

Lowe, George, Newcastle-under-Lyme, Staffs., cm and u (1818–28). In 1818 and 1828 shown at Ireland in the town and in 1822 at Deane Gate. [D]

Lowe, Isaac, 35 Beswick Row, Manchester cm (1836). [D]

Lowe, James, Taunton, Som., cm (1798). [D]

Lowe, James, 5 Craven St, Liverpool, cm (1839). [D]

Lowe, John, Sadlergate, Derby, chairmaker/turner (1829). [D]

Lowe, Jno., 52 Berwick St, Soho, London, cm and u (1835–39). [D]

Lowe, John, Leeds Rd, Bradford, Yorks., u (1837). [D]

Lowe, Musgrave, Wardour St, Soho, London, cm (1767). [Heal]

Lowe, Peter, Castle St, Long Acre, London, u and cm (1790–93). Successor to Richard Lowe at this address. [D]

Lowe, Richard, Castle St, Long Acre, London, bedstead maker (1784). Succeeded by Peter Lowe at this address by 1790. [D]

Lowe, Richard, Merry Vale, Worcester, chairmaker (1788). [D]

Lowe, Richard, 74 Turnmill St, Clerkenwell, London, buhl manufacturer (1829). [D]

Lowe, Robert, 39 Newman St, Oxford St, London, bedstead maker (1829–37). [D]

Lowe, Thomas, address unknown, carver (late 17th century). Carried out carving in three London City Wren churches. [*Wren Soc.*, x, p. 124, pls 58, 60]

Lowe, Thomas, Stamford, Lincs., cm (1776). In 1776 took as app. William Lee for seven years at a premium of £20. [Stamford Town Hall bk, 2A/1/4]

Lowe, Thomas, Liverpool, cm (1806–21). App. to Edward Lowe jnr and free, 31 October 1806. He was probably the Mr Lowe, cm who was on 1 July 1811 married to Miss Brotherton of Liverpool. At 10 Gildart Gdn, 1813–14 and 55 Gerard St in 1821. In 1821 listed as a joiner and victualler. [D; freemen reg.; *Liverpool Mercury*, 12 July 1811]

Lowe, Thurston, Gainsborough, Lincs., cm (1803). Freeman of Nottingham. [Nottingham poll bk]

Lowe, William, Corn Market, Stamford, Lincs., cm and u (1753–70). In 1753 a William Lowe of Stamford, cm, took app. named Nodes. A marriage of a person of the same trade and name is recorded at Stamford in March 1769, but there is the possibility that this may be a son of the former one. In 1770 trading at Corn Mkt as a cm and u. [S of G, app. index; *Cambridge Chronicle*, 18 March 1769, 24 March 1770]

Lowe, William, 7 Bucklersbury, London, u and cm (1776–77). In 1776 took out insurance cover of £1,000 of which £600 was in respect of utensils and stock. Free of the Upholders' Co. by redemption, 3 September 1777. [GL, Sun MS vol. 253, p. 613; Upholders' Co. records]

Lowe, William, Liverpool, cm (1780–1835). Free 11 September 1780. Subscribed to Sheraton's *Drawing Book*, 1793. In 1790 at 46 Peter St; in 1804 at 29 Cheapside, Dale St; but then moved to Lionel St. The number in Lionel St was 14 in 1805 and 16 in 1807–10. By 1818 he was at 34 Sawney Pope St; in 1823 at 8 Old Hall St; and in 1835 at 22 Richmond Fair. The length of the period of trading might suggest that there were a father and son of the same name involved. [D; freemen reg.]

Lowe, William, 25 Drury Lane, London, cm and broker (1808–09). [D]

Lowe, William, 13 Bridge Rd, Lambeth, London, looking-glass maker (1826). [D]

Lowe & Croft, see Edward Lowe jnr

Lowe & Houghton, Lord St, Liverpool, cm (1805–09). At Barrack Yd in 1805 and Castle Yd in 1809. In May 1809 the partnership was dissolved and the stock sold off. Manufactured stock included 'an elegant Sideboard, Wardrobes, set Dining Tables, Night Chairs, Pembroke Tables, Ladies' Work Tables, Chairs, Bedsteads etc.' Timber included 'Mahogany in Logs, Boards & Veneers, Dry Oak & Deal Boards, Maple' while 'Brasswork, Hair Seatings, Benches, Utensils etc.' were also on offer. [D; *Liverpool Courier*, 24 May 1809]

Lowe & Parry, Paradise St, Liverpool, cm (1800–03). The number in Paradise St was 10 in 1800 and 14 in 1803. [D]

Lowell, Robert, near 'The Kings Head', Mile End Rd, London, cm (1779). In 1779 took out insurance cover of £700 of which only £100 was in respect of utensils and stock. [GL, Sun MS vol. 278, p. 634]

Lowen, John, 280 Whitechapel Rd, London, u (1829–39). One directory of 1835 lists Lowen & Son at 290 Whitechapel Rd. [D]

Lower & Sons, 79 St James's St, Brighton, Sussex, cm, u and paperhanger (1826). [D]

Lowes, George, the sign of 'Robin Hood', Pilgrim St, Newcastle, cm (1756–80). In 1756 took app. named Adear. Apart from his cabinetmaking business he also may have acted on occasions as agent for the disposal of property, and in 1776 is recorded advertising a number of freehold messuages for sale. By 1778 he had closed his business and in March of that year offered his stock for sale. An 'elegant eight day clock with chimes' was mentioned and trade stock included supplies of mahogany and 'a number of Joiner and Cabinet-maker's benches, and several new attick sashes and other Windows'. He may possibly have recommenced business or failed to dispose of his stock, for a further advertisement in January 1780 once more announced that he had declined business. Devergy Lisle snr, a fellow cm, was concerned with the disposal of stock and announced that he was able to offer his services to Lowes' customers. In the same month that this advertisement appeared he was trading from 'The Commode and Cabriole' in Pilgrim St, and may have taken over Lowes' premises. Lowes had been his former master. Devergy Lisle sought tenders for Lowes' stock which consisted of 'Cabinet Goods, 350 feet of fine Veneer, 2419 feet and upwards of Mahogany in planks and boards, Wainscot ditto &c.' Failing receipt of satisfactory offers for the entire stock, he indicated that he would lot the materials for sale in March. [D; S of G, app. index; *Newcastle Courant*, 15 June 1776, 11 March 1778, 8 January 1780]

Lowes, Richard, Newcastle, u (1741). [Freemen reg.]

Lowick, W., 36 Satchwell St, Leamington, Warks., cm and u (1837). [D]

Lowle, Peter, High St, above St Giles' Church, London, broker and cm (1752). In March 1752 his stock in trade was offered for disposal as he was 'going into another way of Business'. [*Daily Advertiser*, 18 March 1752]

Lowman, Philip, Honiton, Devon, cm (1752). In 1752 took app. named Bennet. [S of G, app. index]

Lowndes, J. & W., 18 Haymarket, London, military and camp equipage warehouse (1827). Trade card in Banks Coll., BM. Offered 'Marquees, tents & all Sorts of Camp Furniture . . . Camp Bedsteads . . . Mahogany Writing Cases, Dressing do.' [D]

Lowndes, James, 9 St John's St, Manchester, cm (1832–33). [D]

Lowndes, Joseph, 9 Cavendish St, Liverpool, cm (1810). [D]

Lowndes, William, 48 Oxford St, Manchester, furniture broker and cm (1839–40). [D]

Lowrie, Hugh, 9 Leicester St, Swallow St, London, cm (1786). In August 1786 insured household goods for £100. [GL, Sun MS vol. 338, p. 560]

Lowry, Henry & Anne, 7 Phoenix St, London, cm (1780). In 1780 insured their house for £500. [GL, Sun MS vol. 280, p. 314]

Lowry, Henry, 8 Gravel Lane, Southwark, London, cm and undertaker (1808). [D]

Lowry, John, Hull, Yorks., cm (1765–68). App. to Highams. Worked for William Constable at Burton Constable, Yorks. and London. In 1765 he supplied a library table and also '2 Large Dining Tables to fix together' and for the latter £7 was charged. In 1767 four mahogany elbow chairs were made costing £10 10s and in the following year fourteen single chairs 'with Backs & Front Carv'd Commode Seats Ship'd and Covered with Leather & Brass Nails for which £28 was charged. He also produced frames for scagliola tables. [Humberside RO, Burton Constable vouchers; *C. Life*, 3 June 1976]

Lowry, Sarah, London, u (1759–44). Associated with William Reason, u, in the supply of furniture. In 1739 they supplied two leather folding stools, twelve 'pincushion seats for chairs' and a Turkey carpet for the Lord Great Chamberlain's Room in the 'House of Peers'. Supplied furnishings for various royal residences, 1742–44. [Winterthur, Delaware, Symonds papers, 75×69–15, p. 73; PRO, LC 9/290]

Lowth, Charles, London, upholder (1728–29). Son of Henry

Lowth and brother of William Lowth. His father was already dead by 5 March 1728/29 when Charles was admitted a member of the Upholders' Co. by patrimony. His father had formerly been a freeman of the Company. [GL, Upholders' Co. records]

Lowth, Henry, Little Alley leading from Cherry Tree Alley, parish of St Giles Without Cripplegate, London, upholder (1713–23). In both 1716 and 1723 took out insurance cover on his house, which was rented, of £50 only. He did however also insure six further properties. He took as app. John Locke, 1713–20. He was dead by 5 March 1728/29 when his son Charles was made free of the Upholders' Co. by patrimony. A younger son William was also made free by patrimony, 16 December 1731. [GL, Hand in Hand vol. 16, p. 198; vol. 27, p. 322; Upholders' Co. records]

Lowth, William, London, upholder (1731). Son of Henry Lowth, freeman and Upholder of London. William was free of the Upholders' Co. by patrimony, 16 December 1731. His father Henry had died several years earlier. [GL, Upholders' Co. records]

Lowther, Henry, York, cm (1756–74). Son of Luke Lowther, innkeeper. Free as a cm, 1756, and two years later living in Lendal. In 1774 in Monkgate. [Freemen rolls; poll bks]

Lowther, Isaac, Bird St, Westminster, London, carver (1749). [Poll bk]

Lowther, John, Lancaster, joiner and cm (1739–49). Free as a joiner, 1739–40. Took an app. joiner in March 1742 and app. joiners and cm in January 1746, January 1748 and March 1749. A mahogany fall-front bureau of good quality exists [Judges' Lodging Museum, Lancaster] which bears the label of this maker, on the inside of the centre cupboard door in the interior. [Freemen rolls; app. reg.]

Lowther, John, Liverpool, cm (1761). In 1761 took app. named Dodgson. [S of G, app. index]

Lowther, John, Crosbie St, Maryport, Cumb., joiner/cm (1811). [D]

Lowther, John, 3 Smeaton St, Hull, Yorks., cm (1837–40). [D]

Lowther, Thomas, 58 Red Lion St, Clerkenwell, London, clock case and cabinet makers (1820–40). In 1839 the business was listed as Lowther & Son. In 1839–40 clock case maker only. [D]

Lowthian, John, 41 Adam St West, Portman Sq., London, cm and u (1809). In 1809 took out insurance cover of £200. This included £50 in respect of a chest of tools in Gillow & Co.'s store in George St, Oxford St. [GL, Sun MS vol. 448, ref. 836807]

Lowthian, Richard, Lancaster, cm (1805–35). Named in the Gillow records 1805–07, 1809, 1811, 1814–15, 1822–23, 1832 and 1834–35. In 1823 named in connection with making a bookcase. [Westminster Ref. Lib., Gillow vol. 344/101, p. 3303]

Lowthian, Thomas, Lancaster, cm (1817–23). App. to J. Hodgson and free, 1817–18. Named in the Gillow records, 1821–23, including the making of a table in 1821. [App. reg.; Westminster Ref. Lib., Gillow vol. 344/100, p. 3117]

Loxham, Edward, Liverpool, u (1761–80). Son of Edward Loxham, mariner and petitioned freedom by patrimony in 1761. By 1767 trading from an address in Castle St, and from 1769–77 at 9 Cleveland St. Took as app. John Williams, but in May 1767 he absconded and Loxham advertised his description in the hope that he might be apprehended. The business was probably small, for in 1777 he was combining his trade with the post of Overseer of the Poor. In 1773 he had been described as an u, dealer and chapman. Probably the business was not particularly profitable. He was declared bankrupt in 1772 and was again insolvent by 1780. [D; freemen's committee bk; Bailey's list of bankrupts; William-

son's *Liverpool Advertiser*, 8 May 1767, 17 December 1773, 25 May 180]

Lucas, —, Bath, Som., carver (d. 1806). [*Gents Mag.*, February 1806]

Lucas, Mrs, 58 Campo Lane, Sheffield, Yorks., looking-glass manufacturer (1825). Probably successor to John Lucas. [D]

Lucas, Edmund, address unknown, (1769). On 11 April 1769 invoiced a japanned dressing-table and frame for the Dowager Princess of Wales at a cost of £15 15s. [RA 55582]

Lucas, Henry, London, u and paper hanger (1820–35). At 33 Newman St, Oxford St, 1820–25. In 1820 took out insurance cover for £400 of which £100 was in respect of utensils and stock. In 1821 the figures were raised to £500 and £200 and for 1822 were £350 and £250 respectively. His trade tools and stock were in his dwelling house but in 1822 for the first time a workshop is mentioned which contained stock and tools valued at £50 compared with those in the house at £200. By 1824 cover had reached £1,000 which included £500 for stock and utensils in his dwelling house though it was stated that no cabinet work was carried out there. Lucas also insured another dwelling house at 5 Seymour Row, Little Chelsea valued at £100. From 1821–24 he described himself additionally as a cm. In 1826 he was at 127 Long Acre and the same year saw him also at 1 Crown St, Walworth trading as a bedstead maker. He remained at this latter address until at least 1829, but in 1835 was at 7 Charles St, Hampstead Rd. [D; GL, Sun MS vol. 483, ref. 962879; vol. 488, ref. 976409; vol. 493, ref. 995716; vol. 499, ref. 1014243]

Lucas, James, Hitchin Herts., u (1726). In October 1726 took out insurance cover of £600. [GL, Sun MS vol. 22, p. 374]

Lucas, James, London, u (1789–93). At 8 Warwick Ct, Newgate St in 1789 but by the following year was at 66 Chiswell St, where he was trading as an undertaker, cm and u. [D; Heal]

Lucas, John, 67 Campo Lane, Sheffield, Yorks., looking-glass manufacturer (1821). In 1825 the business was at 58 Campo Lane and under the direction of a Mrs Lucas. [D]

Lucas, Jno., 25 Thayer St, Manchester Sq., u (1826). [D]

Lucas, Richard, London, cm (1793). Subscribed to Sheraton's *Drawing Book*, 1793.

Lucas, Richard, Chorley, Lancs., joiner and cm (1822–24). Trading at Bolton St in 1822 and 3 Market St in 1824. [D]

Lucas, William, London, u (1741). Freeman of Canterbury. [Canterbury poll bk]

Lucas, William, 'Liesforme', Som., chairmaker (1744). In 1744 took app. named Pointing. [S of G, app. index]

Lucas, William, 83 Bull St, Birmingham, cm (1777–80). [D]

Lucas, William & Beaumont, William, Middle Yd, Gt Queen St, London, cm (1788–89). Bankruptcy announced, January 1788, though not recorded in the *Gents Mag.* until May of the following year. [*Williamson's Liverpool Advertiser*, 21 January 1788]

Lucas, William, Pipemaker's Lane, Boston, Lincs., cm and joiner (1826). [D]

Lucas, William, Dudley St, Walsall, Staffs., cm and u (1828–30). [D]

Lucas, William, 1 Cambridge Rd, London, carver and gilder (1839).

Lucas & Beaumont, See William Lucas & William Beaumont.

Lucas & Leggett, 35 South Audley St, London, u (1839). [D]

Luccock, John, Garden St, Hull, Yorks., cm (1806). [D]

Luccock, Marmaduke, Hull, Yorks., cm (1784). [Poll bk]

Luccock, William, Hull, Yorks., cm (1774–1806). At Southend, High St, 1790–99, and Humber St, 1803–06. On 7 June 1774 supplied a wainscot Pembroke table to Burton Constable, Yorks. [D; poll bk; Humberside RO, Burton Constable vouchers]

Lucera, Anthony, address unknown, (1742). On 26 December 1742 paid £4 10s 6d for 'a Chest of Florence' purchased by Benjamin Mildmay, Earl Fitzwalter, for Moulsham Hall, Essex. [A. C. Edwards, *The Accounts of Benjamin Mildmay, Earl Fitzwalter,* p. 109]

Lucini, P. & F., Leather Lane, Holborn, London, carvers and gilders (1835–39). In 1835 at 16 Leather Lane, but by 1839 the business was in the sole hands of Paovino Lucini at 91 Leather Lane. He declared his trade to be a picture and looking-glass frame maker. [D]

Luck, Joseph, London, u (1779–1802). Son of Samuel Luck, freeman shipwright of London. Free of the Upholders' Co. by patrimony on 7 July 1779. At Bread St, Cheapside, 1779–81, but in 1781 moved to Carpenters' Hall, 65 London Wall where he entered into partnership with a man called Kent, probably Abbot Kent who had been app. to Samuel Luck from 4 September 1762 and free of the Upholders' Co. by servitude, 5 April 1769. In both 1781 and 1783 the business was described as that of u and carpet warehouse. The business was carried on under various trading styles such as Luck & Kent, Kent, Luck & Kent, Kent & Co. and Kent & Sons. The number in London Wall was also listed as 67 and 68 at various dates. Joseph Luck's name is not listed in the records of the Upholders' Co. after 1802 and this may be the year of his death. The business relationship between the two families was however to survive and in 1839 the firm of Luck, Kent & Cumming was still trading from addresses at 4 Regent St and London Wall. [D; Heal; GL, Upholders' Co. records]

Luck, Samuel, Carpenters' Hall, 67 London Wall, London, upholder (1750–*c.* 1779). Freeman of London and members of the Shipwrights' Co. On 4 September 1762 took as app. Abbot Kent who was made free of the Upholders' Co. by servitude, 5 April 1769. His business is described as a carpet, upholstery and cabinet warehouse on a billhead dated 30 July 1761. [MMA, NY] The father of Joseph Luck who took over the business in 1779. [Heal]

Luck, William, Beavoir Town, Dalston, London, cm (1826). [D]

Luck, William, King St, Hammersmith, London, carver and gilder (1839). [D] See Luck & Co.

Luck, William, High St, Stoke Newington, London, carver and gilder (1839). [D]

Luck & Co., King St, Hammersmith, London, carver and gilder (1838). [D] See William Luck

Luck, Kent & Cumming, 4 Regent St and London Wall, London, u (1839). See Joseph Luck. [D]

Lucker, Joseph, London, u (1761). When he was discharged from Debtors' Prison in November 1761 his address was given as 'formerly of Howford Court, Fenchurch Street, London, late a lodger in Lagett's Passage, Devonshire Square'. [*London Gazette,* 14 November 1761]

Luckett, William, George St, Richmond, Surrey, carver and gilder (1838–39). [D]

Lucking, William, 128 Jermyn St, London, carpenter and cm (1785). In August 1785 took out insurance cover which included £100 for his dwelling house and £50 for utensils and stock. [GL, Sun MS vol. 330, p. 453]

Lucraft, Benjamin, High St, Taunton, Som., cm (1830). [D]

Ludgater, Benjamin, address unknown, joiner, carver and chairmaker (1744–46). Recorded working for Robert & Ann Nugent at Gosfield Hall, Essex, and at their London house in Dover St. The earliest account was in June 1744 and included 'an ovolo Intablature carved to ye Chimney Piece £3. 10s'. In August 1745, carving carried out in the Dressing Room and Great Antiroom came to £19 9s 3½d. The major amount of work appears to have been carried out at Gosfield in 1746 and the carpenters' and joiners' work undertaken amounted to well over £200. This involved the new Dressing Room, the Little and Great Antichambers, and the Bowling Green Parlour. Most of the payment was for carving and general joinery work, but also included the supply of twelve chairs at 10s each. [Essex RO, D/Du 502/2, pp. 149, 196, 241]

Ludgates, —, London, carver (1766–68). In September 1766 and February 1768 submitted accounts for carving picture frames, chimney-pieces etc. at Bowood, Wilts. [Bowood MS]

Ludlow, Thomas, Newcastle-under-Lyme, Staffs., u (1777). In 1777 insured his house for £400. [GL, Sun MS vol. 259, p. 235]

Luff, —, London, u (1793). Subscribed to Sheraton's *Drawing Book,* 1793.

Luff, Charles, 96 Curtain Rd, Shoreditch, London, carver and gilder (1826). [D]

Luff, John, Marlborough, Wilts., cm (1779). Insured a house for £100 in 1779. [GL, Sun MS vol. 272, p. 492]

Luff, Joseph, 25 Coppice Row, Cold Bath Fields, London, upholder (1784). In 1784 insured a house for £100. [GL, Sun MS vol. 324, p. 651]

Luff & M'kewan, 11 Ordnance Row, Portsea, Portsmouth, Hants., carver and gilder (1830). [D]

Lugg, Francis, Market Jew St, Penzance, Cornwall, cm etc. (1830). [D]

Luke, David, Barbican, London, jewel case maker (1801–29). At 3 Beech St in 1801, 59 Red Cross St in 1820 and 12 Beech St in 1829. [D]

Luke, Thomas, Glebe St, Stoke-on-Trent, Staffs., cm and chairmaker (1834). [D]

Luke & Turner, 47 Frith St, Soho, London, upholders and tent makers (1785). [D]

Lukes, Joseph, Gravesend, Kent, cm (1794). [D]

Lulham, R., 28 Charles St, City Rd, London, cm and u (1827–35). In 1835 the trade was listed as writing desk manufacturers. [D]

Lulham, Thomas, Brighton, Sussex, u (1760). In 1760 took app. named Farnes. [S of G, app. index]

Lumb, William & Thomas, Leeds, Yorks., joiners and cm (1804–12). In 1804 announced that they had moved from their premises at the bottom of Albion St to those formerly occupied by Johnson & Cullingworth at the back of Park Row. In 1809 they described their trade as builders and cm and stated that they had taken out a licence to practise as auctioneers and appraisers. A sale of several thousand feet of Honduras mahogany in planks and boards and a large quantity of 'Norwegian deals' was advertised in 1812. The sale took place in the yard of the late William Cookson in the Calls. [*Leeds Mercury,* nos 2006–07 2273–78, 2445]

Lumber, Charles, Chester, u (1790). Son of Charles Lumber, barber. Free 6 November 1790. [Freeman rolls]

Lumbley, John, 17 Scale Lane, Hull, Yorks., cm (1828). [D]

Lumbly, John, London, cm (1793). Subscribed to Sheraton's *Drawing Book,* 1793.

Lumby, John, Stanningley, Leeds, Yorks., cm and joiner (1830). [D]

Lumby, Thomas, address unknown, u (1756). In September 1756 charged Lord Monson £6 6s 11d for making four mattresses 'for the nursery'. [Lincoln RO, Monson 12]

Lumley, J. T., 13 Lower Chapman St, St George's, London, cm, u and undertakers (1839). [D]

Lumley, John, North Bar St Without, Beverley, Yorks, cm and u (1790–1826). First recorded as an u as well as cm in 1826. [D]

Lumsden, George, Lisle St, Newcastle, cm (1790–95). [D]

Lumsdon, James, 14 Groat Mkt, Newcastle, cm, furniture broker and flour dealer (1827–34). [D]

Lumsdon, John, Hedworth St, Monkwearmouth, Sunderland, chairmaker (1827). [D]

Lund, John, 10 Marybone St, Golden Sq., London, u,

warehousemen, haberdashers and manufacturers (1807–39). [D]

Lund, Richard, London (1744). In 1744 paid £125 7s for furniture by the Earl of Stair. [Scottish RO, 9D 135/Box 51/2/1–2]

Lund, Thomas, 56 and 57 Cornhill, London, portable desk manufacturer, cutler and dressing case maker (1819–39). In 1819 declared himself to be a 'cutler, manufacturer of portable desks, pens & quills, importer of filtering stones'. Two tortoise-shell tea caddies are known marked with this maker's stamp. One with a domed rectangular lid and ivory feet is marked 'Lund, Maker, 57 Cornhill London' and the other, an octagonal one, is stamped on the inside ivory rim 'LUND CORNHILL ST'. [D]

Lund, Thomas, Whitby, Yorks., cm (1823–29). In Church St, 1823, but at St Ann's Staith in 1829. [D]

Lund, William, 24 Fleet St, London, dressing case maker and cutler (1835). A tobacco box is known with an inlaid brass strip stamped 'LUND 24 Fleet St. LONDON'. [D]

Lundie, William, Minster Moor Gate, Beverley, Yorks., cm (1831–40). [D]

Lunn, Thomas, St Sepulchre St, Scarborough, Yorks., cm (1823). [D]

Lunsdale, —, Newcastle, cm (1793). Subscribed to Sheraton's *Drawing Book*, 1793.

Lunson, George, 33 Devonshire St, Queen Sq., London, fancy cm (1835). [D]

Lunt, Luke, 9 Phythian St, Liverpool, cm (1812–14). Son of Luke Lunt, mason. Free by patrimony, 5 October 1812. [D; freemen reg.]

Lunton, John, Cambridge, u(?) (1690). In the records of Christ's College for 1690 there is a payment to W. Grub [William Grub] for eighteen chairs. After this entry is recorded 'to Lunton for making £2 14s 4d' and 'for leather £2 17s'.

Luny, William, Lancaster, cm (1801–07). Named in the Gillow records in connection with the making of a blind frame in 1801 and a stand in 1802. Free 1806–07. [Westminster Ref. Lib., Gillow vol. 344/98, pp. 1650, 1688; freemen rolls]

Lupton, —, address unknown, u (1768). Recorded as an u in the Massingberd account book with a payment of £2 19s. [Lincoln RO, MM 9/9]

Lupton, —, Lancaster, (1765–1817). App. to Gillows in 1765. Named in the Gillow records in 1788, 1806 and 1810–17. [App. reg; Westminster Ref. Lib., Gillow]

Lupton, Charles, Lancaster, (1794–1800). [Westminster Ref. Lib., Gillow records]

Lupton, James, Killinghall, near Harrogate, Yorks., (1822). [D]

Lupton, John, Lancaster, glazier (1801–16). Named in the Gillow records, 1801–02, 1811 and 1816. [Westminster Ref. Lib., Gillow]

Lupton, John, Jubbergate, York, cm and u (1816–23). [D]

Lupton, Thomas, Manor St, Chelsea, London, cm (1808–09). In 1808 at 13 Manor St and in the following year at 4. [D]

Lupton, Thomas, Avenham St, Preston, Lancs., cm (1828). [D]

Lupton, William, London, cm and chairmaker (before 1743). By September 1743 trading in South Carolina, USA, but stated that he was from London. [*South Carolina Gazette*, 26 September 1743]

Lupton, William, Lancaster (c. 1768–1807). App. to Richard Gillow, 1760–61, and named in the Gillow records in 1784–88, 1792, 1796–99 and 1807. [App. reg.; S of G, app. index; Westminster Ref. Lib., Gillow]

Lupton, William, Lytham, Lancs., joiner and cm (1825). [D]

Lurton, Joseph, Liverpool, u (1827). In March 1827 married Miss Frances Stephenson at St Nicholas's Church, Liverpool. [*Liverpool Mercury*, 30 March 1827]

Lurton, Thomas, 6 Queen's Head Ct, Gt Windmill St, London, upholder (1791). On 31 May 1791 insured his house for £150. [GL, Sun MS ref. 583788]

Lurton, Thomas, Liverpool, u (1803–11). Commenced business in Church St at number 33 but this was changed to 40 by 1805. This first venture was not a success and in October 1805 Lurton was obliged to assign all his property to meeting his debts. It is possible that the expense and disruption of a move to Whitechapel in this year may have occasioned this financial crisis. The sale by auction of his stock commenced from 11 November 1805 and consisted of 'about 12 Pieces of Sattin Ground & Coloured Paper Hanging, with Rich Flock & Coloured Borders. Brussells & Kid/minster Carpets half ell & half yard Venetian ditto, Patent Lobby Cloths, Morine yard ell wide Furniture, Cottons, Hair Seating & Girth Webb, Pier & Dressing Glasses, handsome mirrors in rich Bronzed & Gilt Frames, Hair Mattresses, Bedticks, Fringes, Lines, Tassels, Carpet Binding etc'. As a result of this sale and other measures a first dividend of 7s 6d in the £ was declared on 20 November. By 1807 Lurton had recommenced trading from 115 Whitechapel, and from 1810–11 was at 20 Ranelagh St. [D; *Liverpool Chronicle*, 30 October 1805, 6 November 1805, 20 November 1805]

Lush, George, High St, Castle Carey, Som., cm (1840). [D]

Lush, William, 46 Ratcliffe Highway, London, cm (1825). [D]

Lusley, James, 24 Little Windmill St, Golden Sq., London, cm (1808). [D]

Luson, William, Queen St, Southwark, London, carver and gilder (1808). [D]

Lutherborough, William, Hull, Yorks., cm (1768–80). [Poll bks]

Luttich von, ('Merlin'), Hanover Sq., London, inventor and patentee (1811). His best-known piece of furniture was a mechanical chair which was illustrated and described in Ackermann's *Repository of the Arts*, October 1811. His portrait, and an example of this form of chair are at Kenwood House, Hampstead, London.

Lutz, T., address unknown, cm (c. 1830). The name is recorded as stamped under the top of a rosewood worktable.

Luvate, Dominic, Friargate, Preston, Lancs., optician and looking-glass maker (1828–34). In 1828 at 43 Friargate and in 1834 at 27. [D]

Luxham, Edward, Liverpool, u (1779). By 1778 in financial difficulties and in January of the following year a dividend was paid to creditors. [*Leicester Journal*, 30 January 1779]

Luxmore, John, 20 Princess St, Devonport, Devon, cm (1838). [D]

Lyall, Charles, 17 Princes St, Red Lion Sq., London, carver and gilder (1820). An M. Lyall is recorded at this address in 1817 in the same trade. [D]

Lyall, George, London, cm (1803–23). In 1803 at 243 Holborn and subscribed to Sheraton's *Cabinet Dictionary*. In 1820–23 took out insurance cover at 7 Museum St. Although the cover was substantial reaching £1,100 in 1823, £800 of this was in respect of the dwelling house and in 1823 only £90 covered stock utensils and goods in trust. See also James Lyall. [Heal; GL, Sun MS vol. 483, ref. 966229; vol. 495, ref. 1003320]

Lyall, James, London, cm (1793–1835). In 1793 subscribed to Sheraton's *Drawing Book*, In the period 1825–35 trading from 7 Museum St, an address occupied from 1820–23 by George Lyall, cm. James's trade was declared to be an u, cm and cabinet founder. [D]

Lyall, M., 17 Princes St, Red Lion Sq., London, carver and gilder (1817). In 1820 Charles Lyall was trading from this address. [D]

Lyall, Walter, 19 Wall St, Jewin St, London, cm (1793). In January 1793 took out insurance cover of £200 of which £20 was in respect of utensils in 'Mr Seddon's Workshops adjoining in Aldersgate Street'. [GL, Sun MS vol. 392, p. 250]

Lyall, William, 34 Chiswell St, London, u and cm (1800–11). Named in the list of master cabinet makers in Sheraton's *Cabinet Dictionary*, 1803. [D]

Lycett, Joseph, John St, Golden Sq., London, cm and u (1746–54). In 1754 was paid £11 14s by Trinity College, Cambridge for '2 large mahogany Tables in the Lodge'. A large drop leaf, club foot mahogany table still survives in the Lodge and may be one of these. [Heal; Westminster poll bk; V & A archives]

Lycett, Sampson, Aldermanbury, London, cm (before 1761). Dischared from Debtors' Prison, September 1761 and said to be 'late of Aldermanbury'. [*London Gazette*, 29 September 1761]

Lyde, John, 3 Lower Northampton St, Clerkenwell, London, cm (1804). In November 1804 took out insurance cover of £180 but only £40 of this was in respect of stock and utensils in his workshop. [GL, Sun MS vol. 430, ref. 760620]

Lyden, John, 44 Sawney Pope St, Liverpool, trunk and chairmaker (1839). [D]

Lyel, Joseph, Schonswar's Sq., Dagger Lane, Hull, Yorks., cm (1806). [D]

Lyel, Miles, Hull, Yorks., cm (1831–40). At Red Lane with a residence at 2 Sykes St in 1831, but in 1834 at 3 Bridge St. From 1835 used the Sykes St address, but also recorded at 21 Bridge St in 1840. [D]

Lymont, John Francis, London(?), cm (before 1741). In 1742 his app. George Winterbottom was discharged 'as his master (Lymont) had been in goal for nearly two years'. [GL, Middlx session bk 990, p. 57]

Lymposs, William, 8 Spital St, Guildford, Surrey, cm (1814–40). Described as a cm and broker, 1839–40. [D; Surrey RO (Guildford), BRT/T/982/5, BR/T/982/8]

Lyne, Francis, London, u and cm (1800–17). At 13 Vere St, Oxford St, 1800–04. Subscribed to Sheraton's *Cabinet Dictionary*, 1803, and included in the list of master cabinet makers in it. In 1806 at 150 New Bond St, but from 1809 the number is shown as 158. [D]

Lyne, John, London, cm and chairmaker (1802–08). In 1802 at 34 Fashion St, Spitalfields where in July he took out insurance cover of £300, half of which was in respect of utensils and stock. By 1808 at 15 Tower St, St George's Fields. [D: GL, Sun MS vol. 423, ref. 735230]

Lyne, Joseph, Westgate, Grantham, Lincs., joiner, cm and ironmonger (1787). In January 1787 took out insurance cover of £600 on his house, warehouse, workshop and one other house and brewhouse. [GL, Sun MS vol. 341, p. 472]

Lynham, James, Berwick St, Westminster, London, frame maker (1749). [Poll bk]

Lynn, Andrew, Gt Marlborough St, London, u (1708). In June 1708 advertised a reward of a guinea for information about an app. Francis Proctor who had absconded. [*Daily Courant*, 28 June 1708]

Lyon, Alexander, Silver St, Westminster, London, cm (1784). [Poll bk]

Lyon, D., 17 Duke St, Manchester Sq., London, u (1802–08). [D]

Lyon, George, Duke St, Manchester Sq., London, u (1803). Subscribed to Sheraton's *Cabinet Dictionary* and included in the list of master cabinet makers in it. Must be associated with the D. Lyon shown at 17 Duke St in directories, 1802–08.

Lyon, George, 1 Williamson Sq., Liverpool, u and cm (1805–07). [D]

Lyon, George Philander, Tarleton St, Liverpool, u (1806–39). Son of George Lyon, book-keeper. Free by patrimony on 7 November 1806. Took as apps William Holdsworth (1809–18), Berkett Edmundson (1810–18), George Blink-

horn (1811–20), Moreton Thomas (1815–22); and George Hewitt (app. 1817), William Taylor (app. 1820), Richard Lewtas (app. 1824), Joseph Suddlow (app. 1827), John Houghton Christian (app. 1829) and Thomas Blamer (app. 1834). Shown at 17–18 Tarleton St in 1835 but in 1837 the number was 16–17 and in 1839 it was 32. [D; freemen reg.; freemen's committee bk; app. enrolment bk]

Lyon, George jnr, Tarleton St, Liverpool, u and cm (1810–34). The number in Tarleton St is given as 15, 1810–24; 16 and 17 in 1817–18; and 17 and 18 in 1834. [D]

Lyon, George Frederick, Liverpool, u (1837–39). At 7 Bold St in 1837 but in 1839 in addition to his shop which was now numbered 13 Bold St, an address at 43 Russell St is recorded. [D]

Lyon, George, St Peter's Pl., Canterbury, Kent, cm and u (1838). [D]

Lyon, George, High St, Godalming, Surrey, cm and u (1839). [D]

Lyon, James, 99 Duke St, Whitehaven, Cumb., cm (1811–34). [D]

Lyon, James, Liverpool, u (1816–39). At 21 Fontenoy St, 1816–18; 43 Christian St and 29 Edmund St in 1827; 8 Commucation Row in 1829; 3 Ranelegh Pl. in 1835; 6 Adelaide Buildings, Ranelegh Pl. in 1837; and 7 Adelaide Buildings in 1839. [D]

Lyon, John, the sign of 'The Angel', Old Change, parish of St Mary Magdalen, Old Fish St, London, cm (1727). In June 1727 took out insurance cover on household goods and stock in trade in his dwelling house amounting to £300. [GL, Sun MS vol. 25, ref. 41983]

Lyon, John, Liverpool, carver (1806–d. 1812). Son of George Lyon, book-keeper and brother of George Philander Lyon. Free by patrimony, 5 November 1806. Died on 10 September 1812. [Freemen reg.]

Lyon, John, Manchester, cm (1816–25). At 12 Dyche St in 1816, Oak St in 1819 and 18 George Leigh St and 4 Silk St in 1825. [D]

Lyon, Joseph, Myton Walls, Hull, Yorks., cm (1803–06). [D]

Lyon, Robert, 294–95 High Holborn, London, see Lyon, Hotson & Co.

Lyon, Thomas, Union St, Liverpool, cm (1761–96). App. to William Leatherbarrow and free by servitude, 27 February 1761. At Union St, 1766–73. Died February 1796. [D; freemen reg.]

Lyon, Hotson & Co., High Holborn, London, u and cm (1839–40). At 293 High Holborn in 1839 and described as u. In 1840 a Robert Lyon took out insurance cover on 294–95 High Holborn declaring his trade as cm. [D; GL Sun MS ref. 1333645]

Lyons, —, Wardour St, Soho, London, cm (1803). A fire occurred at his workshop on 24 July 1803. [*Gents Mag.*, July 1803]

Lyons, Charles, Bold St, Liverpool, cm (1823–39). In 1833 claimed to have been trading for ten years, though not recorded in Liverpool directories until 1829, when he is shown at 72 and 73 Bold St. These numbers were probably out of date at the time of the publication of the directory, for in October 1829 Lyons advertised that he had moved from 82 to 70 Bold St. He also indicated that he had a warehouse and manufactory in Fleet St 'opposite Messrs. Salters' Saw Mills'. He was still at 70 Bold St in September 1830 when he advertised an auction of surplus stock by Messrs. Taylor & Hime at 28 Bold St. On offer were 'elegant Pedetal sideboards, Sets of Dining Tables on Telescope Frames, Loo, Card, Pembroke Sofa, Breakfast & Work Tables, Sets of Chairs, Sliding Fire Screens, Wardrobes, Chests of Drawers, Chiffoniers, Sofas, Lounging Chair, Sarcophagus Garduoines,

Music Stands etc: a Superb Drawing-room Suite of REAL SOLID ROSEWOOD, consisting of a Couch, twelve Chairs, Fire-screen, Loo, Sofa, Card & Work Tables, Chiffonier, & other valuable articles'. In June 1838 a similar type of sale was advertised, this time conducted by Winstanley & Sons, and Lyons may have held these on a regular basis to dispose of slow moving stock. A similar range of goods was included to those advertised in 1830 but also included were 'sets of antique shaped and Trafalgar chairs, couches and sofas, Easy chairs with spring stuffed seats, Knee hole toilet tables and washstands and a variety of small articles'. Lyons was active in promoting sales by advertisement and in December 1833 was claiming that because of advantageous purchases of 'the best Spanish Mahogany, also Rosewood of the finest growth' he was able to offer a discount of 15% for cash sales. He claimed to stock furniture not only in the two timbers named but also in 'Zebrawood, Oak, Painted, Stained & Japanned.' He occupied 78 Bold St from 1835–38, though an 1837 directory shows 84 and one of 1839 shows 74. He also had showrooms at Newington Bridge the number being shown as 19 in 1835 and 23 in 1837. [D; *Liverpool Mercury*, 31 October 1828, 24 September 1830, 15 December 1833; *Chester Courant*, 12 June 1838]

Lyons, John, Bath, Som., u (1840). [GL, Sun MS ref. 1327511]

Lyons, Samuel, 82 Bold St with shop at 14 Wood St, Liverpool, silversmith and cm (1827). [D]

Lyth, George, Colliergate, York, cm (1758). [Freemen rolls; poll bk]

Lyth, John, Hull, Yorks., cm (1826–34). In 1826 at Fountain's Buildings, Leadenhall Sq. with a residence at Charles Sq., Wincolmlee, but in 1834 shown at Guildhall Passage. [D]

Lythe, George, Yorks., cm (1747–48). App. to John Busfield, cm of York, at a premium of £20 in 1747 under the Sons of the Clergy scheme. [*General Advertiser*, 29 April 1748]

Lythe, Robert, Hull, Yorks., cm (1780). [Poll bk]

Lyther, James, King's Lynn, Norfolk joiner and cm (1757–84). App. to Thomas Hill, joiner and cm, and free, 1757–58. Lyther took as apps George Jackson (free 1774–75), Thomas Harvey (free 1776–77) and Thomas Bouch (free 1777–78). By April 1784 living at Newmarket, Suffolk. [Freemen reg.; poll bk]

Lytholl, John, London, upholder (1706–23). Son of John Lytholl of Little Paxton, Hunts., tailor, deceased. John Lytholl was app. to Thomas Bowyer, 24 May 1706, and free of the Upholders' Co. by servitude, 3 November 1714. He took as app. Richard Smith, 1716–23. [GL, Upholders' Co. records]

Lyus, John, 10 Tabernacle Walk, Finsbury, London, cm and undertaker (1820–37). In 1837 his trade was described as 'coffin maker & furnishing undertaker'. [D]

Lyus, William, 14 Moor Lane, London, cm (1811–13). In May 1811 took out insurance cover of £800 on utensils and stock, £500 of which was in a workshop and lofts over and £300 in an open yard. Similar cover was renewed in May 1813. [GL, Sun MS vol. 452, ref. 858056; vol. 462; ref. 881889]

M

Note: **Mac** — **M'**, **Mc**, **Mac**, are all treated as 'Mac', and the next letter in the name determines the position. Names such as 'Mace' and 'Mack' are included with the above.

Mabrey, John, Felicity Pl., Oldham St, Liverpool, cm (1827). [D]

Maby, Thomas, St James's Churchyard, Bristol, cm (1813–17). [D]

Maby, William, Bristol, cm (1819–28). Recorded at 'The Queen's Head', St James's Churchyard, St James's Barton, 1819–26; and at 'The Queen's Head & Arcade' tavern, 1827–28. [D]

McAlister, John, Liverpool, u and cm (1837–39). Trading at 23 Ranelagh St in 1837 and 25 Bold St in 1839. [D]

McAllester, John, shop at 9 Bittern St, Liverpool, u (1834–35). Recorded also at no. 13 in 1835. [D]

McAlley, John, Portland Pl., Borough Rd, London, bed and mattress maker (1837). [D]

M'Allister & Gibson, Manor Chare, Newcastle, joiners and cm (1827). [D]

Macalpine, Hugh B., Liverpool, carver and gilder (1837–39). Addresses given at 116 Richmond Row in 1837 and 35 Seymour St with shop at 88 Richmond Row in 1839. [D]

McAndrew, James, Darling Pl., Dog Row, Bethnal Green, London, cm (1820). [D]

Macay, John, address unrecorded, cm (1803). Subscribed to Sheraton's *Cabinet Dictionary*, 1803.

McBean, Anne, Castle Hill, Windsor, Berks., cm and u (1820–41). Anne McBean was regularly employed at Windsor Castle and other royal residences in the Great Park over a period of twenty years in a manner which exemplifies the use of competent, but less expensive, local craftsmen by the Lord Chamberlain's Office. Between 1820–40 her name appears in the Household account bks [Windsor RA] of 1829–31 (with references to unpaid bills, 1820–22), estimate accounts and 1835–40 Household accounts [Windsor RA], as well as the PRO accounts from 1823–40. [PRO, LC 11/41–92]

Much work was of a routine nature, typical of an u in regular employ, and involved cleaning, repairing, altering and jobbing in the Castle and also in the King's Closet at St George's Chapel, for which she appears to have been generally responsible. At different periods she was engaged in refurbishing and refitting Adelaide Lodge, Lower Lodge, Cumberland Lodge, Royal Cottage, the Mews and apartments and rooms for Household members of staff in various areas of the Castle precinct. Lengthy bills for the repair of cabinet work and upholstery include specific items, often of a backstairs nature: '8 black-stained & rush seat chairs' as well as more important items: 'Library table — Royal Lodge' — £11 8s, October 1823. [LC 11/41] Commissions for refitting included important work at Windsor Library in 1836: 'Repairing & altering old mahogany library tables & Chairs, staining the same as ebony, inlaying ivory buhl ornaments — covering the tops with scarlet morocco leather . . .'. [Windsor RA, 1835–40 accounts]

Occasionally, general jobbing work was done at St James's Palace and Brighton Pavilion, and Anne McBean would assist in supplying a piece of furniture: '31 Dec., 1833 — Brighton Pavilion — Assisting in making a mahogany Sideboard with Bamboo ornaments', £8 15s 6d. Her firm may well have been assisting that of H. L. Goertz as they often estimated for the same work and identical accounts frequently appear. Anne McBean was almost certainly related to James and Thomas McBean of Windsor (see below). [Joy, *English Furniture, 1800–1851*]   N.N.T.

McBean, J., 1 Duke St, Grosvenor Sq., London, u (1802). [D]

McBean, James, Windsor, Berks., cm and u (1793–1806). A McBean of Windsor subscribed to Sheraton's *Drawing Book*, 1783, and James McBean is listed in the Windsor poll bk in 1794, 1802, 1804, and 1806 in which year his name stood on the rate bk but he did not poll. Listed as upholsterer. This is probably the same McBean listed as Upholsterer to Princess Elizabeth in 1801 and 1805. [D; PRO, C13 661/29]

McBean, Thomas, 9 Castle St, Windsor, Berks., cm and u (1830–34). Thomas McBean is listed in Pigot's *Directory*, 1830 at above address, and in the fifth hall bk of the borough of New Windsor, 1828–52 as follows: 'Lease of Two Tenements and Premises in St. Alban's Street renewed to Representatives of Mr. Tho. McBean, deceased.'

McBeth, Alexander, Liverpool, carver and gilder (1822). App. to Harry Wilson in 1822. [Liverpool app. enrolment bk]

Macblane, —, address unrecorded. On 30 May 1774 he was paid £1 'for mending a Tea Table etc.' for Sir Richard Hoare of Boreham House, Essex. [Essex RO, D/Du 649/2]

McBride, George, Liverpool, cm (1839). Admitted freeman on 25 July 1839. [Liverpool freemen reg.]

McCabe, Thomas, Chester, cm (1828). Son of Hannah McCabe, widow; app. to William Morgan, cm, on 6 May 1828 for seven years. [Chester app. indentures]

McCann, Andrew, 12 Brook St, London Rd, Manchester, chairmaker (1825). [D]

McCann, James, 34 Drury Lane, London, cm (1803). Took out a Sun Insurance policy on 1 February 1803 for £500. [GL, Sun MS vol. 427, ref. 743923]

McCann, William, Salford, Lancs., chairmaker (1808–25). Addresses given at 21 Spain St in 1808, 3 Wright's Ct in 1813, and 153 Chapel St, 1822–25. [D]

McCan(n)s, Charles, Chester, cm (1768–84). Trading at Newgate St, 1771–84. App. to William Venables, joiner, and admitted freeman on 18 December 1768. [Chester freemen rolls and poll bks]

McCarthy, George Packer, St Stephen's parish, Bristol, cm (1774–81). [Poll bks]

M'Carthy, John, Bristol, cm (1827–39). Addresses given at 44 Redcliff Hill, 1827–30; 30 Guinea St, 1831–32; 26 Redcliff St, 1833–34; and 9 Somerset Sq., 1835–39. [D]

McCathey, Charles, 26 Blackman St, Southwark, London, bed and mattress maker (1822–28). [D]

McCathy, Dennis, 13 Trafalgar St, Walworth, London, bedstead maker (1839). [D]

McCauley, William John, Hull, Yorks., joiner and cm (1808). App. to George Spenceley of Hull in October 1808. [Hull app. reg.]

McClay, Hugh, 9 Well St, London, cm (1777). Took out a Sun Insurance policy in 1777 for £300 of which utensils, stock and goods accounted for £200. [GL, Sun MS vol. 261, p. 449]

McClay, Hugh, Swan Stable Yd, Wardour St, London, cm (1780). Took out a Sun Insurance policy in 1780 for £300, of which utensils, stock and goods accounted for £180. [GL, Sun MS vol. 287, p. 446]

McClellan, James, London, then South Carolina, USA, cm (before 1732). Advertised in the *South Carolina Gazette*, 27 January 1732, that he was '…from London, living next door to Mr. Joseph Massey, in Church-Street, Makes and sells all sorts of Cabinet Ware, viz: Cabinets, Desks and Book Cases, Buroes, Tables of all sorts, Chairs, Tea-boxes, and New-fashioned Chests, etc. where may be had Looking Glasses, and Joiners Tools.'

McClennan & Flint, 114 Gt Russell St, Bloomsbury, London, cm (1808). [D] See Robert McLellan.

McCliesh, Andrew, Meards Ct, Dean St, Soho, London, cm (1778). Insured his house for £100 in 1778. [GL, Sun MS vol. 271, p. 216]

M'Closkey, J., Little Whitelion St, London, cm and u (1839). [D]

M'Cloud, Henry, 18 Warren St, Fitzroy Sq., London, cm and u (1839). [D]

M'Cloud (or McCloud), John, Bolton St, Chorley, Lancs., joiner and cm (1824–34). Trading at no. 91 in 1824. [D]

McComb, John, Liverpool, cm (1809–18). App. in 1809 to Mathew Gardner, who assigned him to William Turner in

1815. Petitioned freedom on servitude in 1818, paying 6s 8d. [Liverpool freemen's committee bk]

McConnell, John, 5 Circus St, Liverpool, cm (1816–18). [D]

McConvill, Peter, Liverpool, cm (1821–27). Trading at 4 Norris St in 1821 and 46 Pitt St in 1827. [D]

McCoomb, John, Windermere Pl., Wellington St North, Liverpool, cm (1818). Admitted freeman on 11 June 1818. [Liverpool freemen reg.]

McCormick, Charles Hinten, Liverpool, cm (1812). Admitted freeman on 5 October 1812 on servitude to John Parry. [Liverpool freemen reg.]

McCourt, Thomas, Liverpool, cm (1823). App. to John Armstrong in 1823. [Liverpool app. enrolment bk]

McCraken, James, 41 Berners St, Oxford St, London, u (1839). [D]

M'Cready (or M'Credie), John, Claremont Hill, Shrewsbury, Salop, cm and u (1822–28). [D]

McCreary (or McCreery), Isabella, Liverpool, u (1827–39). Addresses given at 2 Frederick St, 1827–29; 2 Newton St in 1835; no. 8, 1837–39 with workshop at 27 South John St, 1835–37 and no. 34 in 1839. [D]

M'Culloch, William, 46 Wardour St, London, cm and u (1839). [D]

McDaniel, John, Liverpool, cm (1811–23). Trading at 4 Bolton St in 1811 and 33 Circus St in 1823. [D]

McDonald, A., Rose St, Soho, London, cm (1803). Subscribed to Sheraton's *Cabinet Dictionary*, 1803.

Macdonald, Alexander, 10 Stafford St, Lisson Grove, London, carver and gilder (1839). [D]

McDonald, Archibald, Cumberland St, Dale St, Liverpool, cm (1804). [D]

McDonald, Archibald, 27 Wood St, Manchester, cm (1811). [D]

McDonald, D., address unrecorded, u (c.1829). Mentioned in the accounts for the erection and furnishing of Wynyard Park, Co. Durham, by Charles William Vane, Marquess of Londonderry, 1820–40. [Durham RO, Londonderry papers, D/LO/E484, vol. 1829–41]

McDonald, Donald, 3 Somerset St, Portman Sq., London, u and cm (1820). [D]

M'Donald, Donald, High St, Stockton-upon-Tees, Co. Durham, u and furniture warehouseman (1827). [D]

M'Donald, G. F., Limekiln Lane, Bristol, cm (1826–27). [D]

McDonald, Hugh, Guiana Ct, 11 Parr St, Liverpool, cm (1835). [D]

McDonald, John, 3 Castle St, Holborn, London, water gilder (1809–11). [D]

McDonald, John, 3 Bolton St, Copperas Hill, Liverpool, cm (1818). [D]

McDonald, John, St Andrew St, Liverpool, cm (1825). Death of his wife, aged 64, reported in *Liverpool Mercury*, 29 April 1825.

McDonald, William, London, cm (1793). Subscribed to Sheraton's *Drawing Book*, 1793.

McDonald, William, 1 Upper Montague St, London, u (1839). [D]

McDonough, J., 20 Little Wild St, Lincoln's Inn Fields, London, water gilder (1808). [D]

McDonough, John, 11 Cursitor St, Chancery Lane, London, water gilder (1785). Took out a Sun Insurance policy on 7 March 1785 for £300, utensils, stock and goods in trust accounting for £150. [GL, Sun MS vol. 327, p. 415]

McDouall, James, at 'The Royal-Bed', Strand, near Durham Yd, London, cm, u and appraiser (1766–70). Trade card of 1766, among the accounts of Sir John Griffin Griffin of Audley End, Essex, states that he 'MAKES and SELLS all Sorts of Cabinet and Upholstery Work; as Desks and Book-Cases, Buroes and Double-Chests of Drawers; Dressing-Chests and Tables;

Three Drawer Dressing-Tables; Breakfast, Dining, Card, Turn-Over and Tea-Tables; Tea Boards and Tea-Chests: Chairs in Mahogany, Walnut-Tree, Beach, &c. Looking, Chimney and Sconce-Glasses, in French, Carved, Pediment and Gilt, Mahogany and Walnut Tree Frames; Dressing, Swinging and Hanging-Glasses, in Mahogany and Walnut-Tree Frames: Damask, Moreen, Harrateen, Chiney, Linseis and Checks, of all Colours, in Whole and Half-Teasters: Feather-Beds of all Sorts, with Blankets, Quilts, Coverlids and Rugs: Settee, Buroe, Chest of Draws, Four-Posts and Turn-Up Bedsteads: Scotch and other Carpets and Floor-Cloths; with all other Sorts of Furniture, for Exportation: Brass and Steel-Stoves, Shovels, Tongs, Pokers, &c. and Kitchen Furniture. Any Gentleman in Town or Country, who are pleased to Favour me with their Commands, may depend upon being punctually served on reasonable Terms. N.B. FUNERALS PERFORMED.' [Essex RO, D/DBy/A24/11] Declared bankrupt, *Gents Mag.*, December 1770.

Macdougall, Alexander, 37 Long Acre, London, carver and glass grinder (1789). [D]

Macdowel, Alexander, Windsor, Berks., cm (1806). [Poll bk]

M'Dowell, —, Tottenham St, Tottenham Ct Rd, London, chairmaker (1803). Named in Sheraton's list of master cabinet makers, 1803.

McDowell, James, Poynton St, Liverpool, cm (1835–37). Trading at no. 14 in 1835, and no. 13 in 1837. [D]

McDowell, John, 3 Cumberland St, Middlx Hospital, London, chairmaker (1809–20). [D]

McDowell, Joseph, Strand, London, cm (1774). [Poll bk]

M'Dowell, R., William's Mews, Hampstead Rd, London, cm and u (1839). [D]

McDowell, Robert, address unrecorded, chairmaker (?) (1803). Subscribed to Sheraton's *Cabinet Dictionary*, 1803.

Macdowell, William, Bury St Edmunds, Suffolk, cm (1753). Took app. named Prigg in 1753. [S of G, app. index]

McDowell, William, Market St (or Strand), Falmouth, Cornwall, cm and u (1816–30). [D]

McDuff, Archibald, Husband St, Carnaby Mkt, London, cm (1774). [Poll bk]

Mace, Charles, 69 Church St, Berwick-on-Tweed, Northumb., cm and joiner (1834). [D]

Mace, John, address unrecorded, upholder (1711). Admitted freeman of the Upholders' Co. on 5 September 1711. [GL, Upholders' Co. records]

Mace, John, North Walsham, Norfolk, cm, u and joiner (1822). [D]

Mace, John, Bedale, Yorks., joiner and cm (1840). [D]

Mace, Joseph, North Walsham, Norfolk, cm (1830–39). Recorded at Market Pl. in 1830 and Church Plain in 1839. [D]

Macefield, Robert, 13 New St, Birmingham, cm and upholder (1767–70). [D]

M'Entire, James, 3 Chapel St, Hull, Yorks., chair manufacturer (1838–39). [D] See John M'Intire.

McEwen, Alexander, London, cm (1793). Subscribed to Sheraton's *Drawing Book*, 1793.

M'Ewen, John, Queen St, Southwark, London, looking-glass warehouseman (c.1790). [Wills, *Looking-Glasses*]

McEwen, Jonah, Castle St, Oxford Mkt, London, cm (1793–97). Trading at no. 13 in 1793, when he subscribed to Sheraton's *Drawing Book*. Notices regarding his bankruptcy appeared in *Billinge's Liverpool Advertiser*, 23 May 1796 and 23 January 1797. Probably Jonah McGwan.

Macy, Uriah, 28 Foley St, Foley Pl., London, upholsterer's warehouseman (1839). [D]

McFarlane, —, London, cm (1793). Subscribed to Sheraton's *Drawing Book*, 1793.

McGill, Ralph, 18 Shaw's Brow, Liverpool, cm (1805–07). [D]

McGoulrick, George, Slater St, Liverpool, master cm (b. c.1795–d.1823). Death aged 28 reported in *Liverpool Mercury*, 10 January 1823.

McGowen, Alexander, 6 America St, Southwark, London, cm (1808). [D]

McGrath, Richard, London, then South Carolina, USA, cm and u (1771). Advertised in the *South Carolina Gazette*, 8 August 1771 that he was 'lately from London and 'intends to remove up the Path, a little way within the Town Gate; where the Cabinet-Makers and Upholsterer's Business will be carried on in a more extensive Manner than it has since his arrival in Charles Town…'.

McGwan, Jonah, 13 Little Castle St, London, cm (1787). Insured household goods, utensils, stock, goods in yard and stock in workshop for £400 on 20 January 1787. [GL, Sun MS vol. 342, ref. 526790] Probably Jonah McEwen.

Machan, Allison, Castlegate, Huddersfield, Yorks., cm (1814–20). Trading at Rosemary Lane, 1818–20. [D]

Machan, Matthew, Wakefield, Yorks., cm (1798). [D]

Machan, William, Lofthouse Gate, Wakefield, Yorks., joiner and cm (1804). [PRO, C13 55/17]

Machell, James, Lancaster, cm (1827–28). [Lancaster freemen rolls]

Machell, William, Lancaster, cm (1804–07). App. to J. Wakefield in 1804 and admitted freeman, 1806–07. [Lancaster app. reg. and freemen rolls]

Machen, Lancelot, Nottingham, cm (1783). Son of Bakewell Machen, farmer of Summercotes, Alfreton, Derbs.; taken as app. in 1783. [Nottingham app. list]

Machin, Edward, 54 Snowhill, Birmingham, u (1835–39). [D]

Machin, George, Prees, near Wem, Salop, joiner and cm (1840). [D]

Machin, Thomas, 12 Gt Hampton St, Birmingham, cabinet case maker (1835). [D]

McIlraith, John, London, cm (1826–39). Trading at 96 Gt Portland St, 1826–28, and 77 High St, Marylebone in 1835. [D]

M'Intire, John, Hull, Yorks., chair spindle maker, chairmaker and wood turner (1823–39). Trading at 5 Waterhouse Lane, 1823–26; 20 Wells St in 1831; Well's Entry, Waterworks St in 1835; as McIntrye & Battle, fancy chairmakers in Well's Yd, Waterworks St in 1837; and as M'Entire & Battle of Waterworks St in 1838–39; and as McIntyre & Battle, Wells St in 1840. [D] See James M'Entire.

M'Intosh, John, address unrecorded, cm (1803). Subscribed to Sheraton's *Cabinet Dictionary*, 1803.

McIntosh, John, 5 Little Titchfield St, London, cm (1835). [D]

McIntosh, William, 17 Peters St, Berwick St, London, cm (1778). Insured his house for £100 in 1778. [GL, Sun MS vol. 270, p. 115]

McIntosh, William, 11 Crown Ct, Pulteney St, London, cm (1790). Took out a Sun Insurance policy on 8 December 1790 for £100 on household goods in a house, not his own. [GL, Sun MS ref. 576737]

Mac(k)intyre, George, 23 Portland St, Wardour St, London, cm, upholder and undertaker (1817–20). [D]

McJay, Barnard, North St, Keighley, Yorks., cm and u (1830). [D]

Mack, Bernard, 41 Kirby St, Hatton Gdn, London, carver and gilder (1819). [D] See Bernardi Mack(i)e.

Mack, William, 17 London Rd, Southwark, London, furniture broker, u and cm (1835–37). [D]

Mack, William, 24 Little Marylebone St, London, u (1839). [D]

Mackarall, James, Lancaster, joiner and cm (1829–30). [Lancaster freemen rolls]

Mackay, —, address unrecorded, u (1775). Subscribed to Thomas Malton's *Compleat Treatise on Perspective*, 1775.

Mackey, —, address unrecorded. On 8 June 1774 he was paid £17 9s 'for Chairs etc. to 22nd May 1774' supplied to the Earl of Ancaster. [Lincoln RO, 2 ANC 6/16]

McKay, —, London, cm (1783). In 1783 he was paid £13 19s by Alexander Wedderburn. [Scottish RO, GD/64/Box 20/177/2 and 3]

Mackay, Charles, 171 Piccadilly, London, u (1784). [D] See James Mackay at this address.

Mackay, George, London, cm (1793). Subscribed to Sheraton's *Drawing Book*, 1793.

Mackay, James, 171 Piccadilly, London, u (1761–84). [D; poll bk] Probably James Mackey.

McKay, James, Manor-chare, Newcastle, carver and gilder (1811). [D]

McKay, John C., Handbridge, Chester, cm (1819–26). Admitted freeman on 21 October 1819. [Chester freemen rolls and poll bks]

Mackay & Durno, address unrecorded, u (1756). Recorded in Henry Hoare's account book of 1749–70, receiving £18 6s on 3 December 1756. [Wilts. RO, MS 383/6]

Mack(i)e, Bernardi (or Benjamin), 7 Greville St and 41 Kirby St, Hatton Gdn, London, carver, gilder and picture frame maker (1809–20). [D] See Bernard Mack.

Macke, Francis Joseph, Thayne St, Manchester Sq., London, u (1795). Declared bankrupt, *Billinge's Liverpool Advertiser*, 1 June 1795.

Mackenzie, —, address unrecorded, cm (1803). Subscribed to Sheraton's *Cabinet Dictionary*, 1803.

Mackenzie, Alexander, Newcastle, u (1777). [Poll bk]

Mackenzie, Alezander, 4 James St, Golden Lane, London, cm (1781). Took out a Sun Insurance policy in 1781 for £300, £220 accounting for utensils, stock and goods. [GL, Sun MS vol. 290, p. 286]

Mackenzie, Alexander & Blissatt (or Blisset(t)), Marylebone St, Golden Sq., London, cm and upholders (1784–1815). Mackenzie was recorded alone at no. 34 in 1784, and with Blissatt there between 1786 and 1811. The firm's address was given as no. 37 in 1790, 1808–09 and 1812–15; and no. 36 in 1801 and 1803. The same premises were probably renumbered throughout the period. The firm took out a Sun Insurance policy on 29 March 1786 for £1,200, of which utensils etc. accounted for £840. Subscribed to Sheraton's *Drawing Book*, 1793, and *Cabinet Dictionary*, 1803. Succeeded in 1816 by Mackenzie & Wakeling. [D; GL, Sun MS vol. 336, p. 91]

McKenzie, Daniel, Preston, Lancs., cm (1802–22). [Preston Guild record of burgesses]

McKenzie, Daniel, 10 Turnstile Alley, Drury Lane, London, cm (1807). Took out a Sun Insurance policy on 20 January 1807 for £500 of which £300 accounted for stock, utensils and goods in trust. [GL, Sun MS vol. 437, ref. 798783]

Mackenzie, Ebenizer, Huntingdon, cm (1831). Taken as app. on 30 May 1831. [Hunts. RO, app. indentures]

Mackenzie, George, 25 Gt George St, Liverpool, cm (1839). [D]

Mackenzie, P., Sheffield, Yorks., u (1824). Declared bankrupt, *Brighton Gazette*, 25 March 1824. See W. Mackenzie.

McKenzie, Thomas, 3 Derby St, Whitechapel, Liverpool, cm (1823). Advertised sale of remaining stock on declining business, in *Liverpool Mercury*, 28 February 1823, to take place on 6 March. Stock consisted of clocks, 'Mahogany & Painted Articles, Pier & Dressing Glasses, Gentleman's capital knee-hole Desk with seventeen drawers, Cabinet-maker's Tool Chest, large Kitchen Range, with hot hearths, a few Mahogany Ends, in planks, boards etc. suitable for Cabinet & Chairmakers, Iron-founder's Blowing-machine, a large stove, & other useful Articles.'

Mackenzie, W., Sheffield, Yorks., u (1824). Declared bankrupt, *Brighton Gazette*, 25 March 1824. See P. Mackenzie.

Mackenzie, William, 11 Market Pl., Sheffield, Yorks., silversmith, broker, u and music seller (1817–22). Trading as Mackenzie & Son in 1817. [D]

M'Kenzie, William, 32 Blackfriargate, Hull, Yorks., u and broker (1826). [D]

M'Kenzie, William, St Ives, Hunts., chairmaker and cm (1830–39). Trading at Crown St in 1830 and Merry land in 1839. [D]

Mackenzie & Son, Bishop Wearmouth, Sunderland, Co. Durham, cm (1832). [D]

Mackenzie, Steains & Pryer, 30 Brydge's St, Strand, London, u (1811–25). [D] See Pryer, Steains & Mackenzie.

Mackenzie & Wakeling, 37 Marylebone St, Golden Sq. and 36 Gerrard St, Soho, London, u (1816–20). [D] Successors to Mackenzie & Blisset.

Mackereth, S., Lancaster, furniture painter (1788–91). [Westminster Ref. Lib., Gillow records]

Mackery, George & Speare, James, 6 Princes St, Drury Lane, London, carvers (1775). Took out a Sun Insurance policy in 1775 for £300, £120 accounting for utensils, stock and goods. [GL, Sun MS vol. 236, p. 233]

Mackery, George, 12 Brownlow St, Long Acre, London, cm (1783). Took out a Sun Insurance policy in 1783 for £200, £100 on utensils and stock. [GL, Sun MS vol. 313, p. 77]

Macket & Co., 186 Sloane St, London, u (1837). [D]

Mackett, —, 26 Sloane St, London, cm (1832–34). [D] See Atkinson & Mackett.

Mackewen, Thomas, 28 Gt Charlotte St, Blackfriars Rd, London, looking-glass manufacturer (1813–29). [D]

Mackey, James, Piccadilly, London, upholder (1774). [Poll bk] Probably James Mackay.

Mackey, James, London, cm (1793). Subscribed to Sheraton's *Drawing Book*, 1793.

Mackie, George, address unrecorded, cm (1803). Subscribed to Sheraton's *Cabinet Dictionary*, 1803.

Mackie, Robert, 106 Wardour St, Soho, London, cm, u and undertaker (1803–35). Subscribed to Sheraton's *Cabinet Dictionary*, 1803. [D]

Mackie, Thomas, 96 Curtain Rd, London, carver and gilder (1835). [D]

Mackinder, George, King St, Golden Sq., London, carpenter and cm (1739–44). Provided the Duke of Gordon with items for his London house in 1739, totalling £3 13s 6d and including 'A Fine Mahogany pillar & claw table'. His bill of 26 April 1739 included 'A Fine Mahog. Teabox wth an inside Spring Drawer', 'A Fine Wood Voider', a tray, a small inlaid salver and '2 Bottle Dishes', totalling £2 12s 6d. [Scottish RO, GD 44/51/465 and 465/4/28] Declared bankrupt, *London Daily Post and General Advertiser*, 5 March 1744. Sale of household goods, furniture, 'Pictures by many eminent Masters, and all his Stock in Trade, consisting of fine Mahogany and Walnut-Tree Planks and Veneers, Cherry-Tree, Beech, etc....', announced in *Daily Advertiser*, 19 March 1744. Notice regarding payment of debts to Mackinder appeared in the same paper on 28 April 1744.

McKinley, Thomas, Cable St, Oldham Rd, Manchester, carver and gilder (1836–39). Recorded at no. 26, 1836–38, and no. 35 in 1839. [D]

McKinnon, —, 79 Tottenham Ct Rd, London, cm (1804). Took out a Sun Insurance policy on 5 July 1804 for £400 on a house at the corner of Turnstile in Lincoln's Inn Fields in tenure of a stationer. [GL, Sun MS vol. 431, ref. 762888] Probably John McKinnon.

McKinnon, Angus, corner of Holborn Row, Lincoln's Inn Fields, London, cm (1783–d. by 1792). Took out Sun

Insurance policies in 1783 for £500, of which £300 accounted for utensils, stock and goods, and a further policy for £600 on his house; on 16 July 1785 for £200 on utensils, stock and goods; and on 13 January 1787 for £600 on seven houses. [D; GL, Sun MS vol. 313, p. 157; vol. 314, p. 471; vol. 331, p. 282; vol. 342, ref. 526749] Probably father of:

McKinnon, John, London, cm (1791–92). Recorded at 9 Little Rider St, St James's on 26 August 1791 when he took out a Sun Insurance policy for £800 on an empty house at 15 Sackville St. On 12 July 1792 he insured this house for £500, and also a house at the corner of Turnstile in Lincoln's Inn Fields in tenure of McKinnon, widow, for £200. [GL, Sun MS ref. 587700; vol. 389, ref. 602680] Probably McKinnon, —, of 79 Tottenham Ct Rd.

Macklecan, John, Southwark, London, chairmaker (1746). Took app. named Lay in 1746. [S of G, app. index]

Mackleton, —, Leadenhall St, London, cm (d.1750). Notice in *General Advertiser*, 19 November 1750 read: 'On Thursday morning died at his House at Woodford Mr. Mackleton formerly an eminent Cabinet Maker in Leadenhall St.'

Mackley, John, 3 Bridge Ct, Westminster Bridge, London, cm and u (1827–35). [D]

Mackley, William, Southgate, Market Weighton, Yorks., cm (1840). [D]

Macklin, R., 22 High St, Bloomsbury, London, bedstead maker (1829). [D]

Macklin, Thomas, Bateman's Buildings, Soho Sq., London, carver and gilder (1775). Took out a Sun Insurance policy in 1775 for £300, utensils, stock and goods accounting for £100. [GL, Sun MS vol. 236, p. 508]

Macklin, Thomas, 39 Fleet St, London, printseller, carver and gilder (1780–89). Took out a Sun Insurance policy in 1780 for £1,000 of which £750 accounted for utensils and stock. Trade card recorded. [D; GL, Sun MS vol. 284, p. 6; Heal]

Macknam, Thomas, High Wycombe, Bucks., chairmaker (b. c. 1791–1841). Aged 50 at the time of the 1841 Census.

Macknecan, John, London, cm (1761). [Maidstone poll bk]

McKnight, Alexander, 21 Scotch St, Whitehaven, Cumb., joiner and cm (1829). [D]

McKnight, Robert & Sons, Queen St, Whitehaven, Cumb., joiners and cm (1811). [D]

McKrobie, William, 2 Colvile Ct, Rathbone Pl., London, cm (1809–11). [D]

McLachlan, James, 41 Duckinfield St, Liverpool, cm (1837). [D]

Maclagan, Alexander, 158 Regent St, London, u and cm (1835). [D]

Maclaren, Daniel, 8 Hamilton Row, Battlebridge, London, cm (1826–27). [D]

McLauchlan, Andrew, 53 Commercial Rd, Lambeth, London, carver and gilder (1826–37). [D]

McLauchlan (or McLaughlan), David, 3 Printing House Sq., Blackfriars, London, carver and gilder, looking-glass and picture frame manufacturer (1800–37). Parcel-gilt mahogany pier table recorded, with marble top above a pierced frieze carved with scrolling leaves on two large cabriole legs carved with 'C' scrolls, on a rectangular base; bearing label of 'D. J. McLauchlan' of the above address and trade. [D; Sotheby's, 19 June 1981, lot 147]

McLaughlin, David, 1 Naked Boy Ct, Ludgate Hill, London, carver and gilder (1779). Took out a Sun Insurance policy in 1779 for £500 of which £200 accounted for utensils, stock and goods. [GL, Sun MS vol. 271, p. 475]

McLaughlin, James, 2 Crosbie St, Liverpool, chairmaker (1835). [D]

McLean, Charles, 25 Portland St, Oxford St, London, u (1829–39). [D]

M'Lean, Charles, 181 Fleet St, London, looking-glass and picture frame maker (1839). [D]

McLean, Charles, 1 Wellington St, Southwark, London, carver and gilder 1839). [D]

M'Lean, George, address unrecorded, cm (1803). Subscribed to Sheraton's *Cabinet Dictionary*, 1803.

McLean, John & Son, London, cm, upholders (1770–1825). The origins of this firm may possibly be found on the south side of Little Newport St, Leicester Sq., where in June 1770 a 'Jⁿ Mc Lane' became the tenant of a 'Ho & workshops' at a rent of £36 pa. In 1774 'Jno M'Clean cabinet maker' is listed in the same street [poll bk] and he remained at this address until 1783. His decorative trade card issued from this address features a dressing table and is inscribed: 'Jno Macklane | Cabinet, Chair Maker and | UPHOLDER | in Little Newport Street | near Leicester Square | London | NB. Funerals Perform'd'. [Heal, p. 106] His address between 1783 and 1790 is not known, but in the second half of that year he became tenant of 55 Upper Marylebone St [rate bks] and the firm remained here until its demise in 1825. [D] There is no documentary proof linking these two McLeans although they are probably one and the same person. The firm is also recorded as having premises at two other addresses at the turn of the century: these were Pancras St, Tottenham Ct Rd, and Upper Terr., Tottenham Ct Rd. They occupied the former building c. 1799–1805 and vacated the latter in the same year. [D; rate bks] After John died c. 1815 and his son William took over, the business declined. Until 1816 the rates were promptly paid, the value of the rent having risen in this year to £100. However in 1819 goods were distrained for rent, there were arrears in 1820, and in 1821 William McLean was in receipt of Poor Relief and the clerk noted 'In Prison — Landlord has taken all the goods'. In 1822 McLean was 'a Bankrupt in Prison'. The final entry in 1825 states 'Died so poor that his body was sent in a box by waggon into the country to relations'.

Two fire insurance policies have been traced, in 1806 the household goods were covered for £100, stock and utensils in the warehouse were valued at £500, the workshop behind (stoves therein) £200, in the open yard £200. Total sum insured £1,000. In 1810 the figure was unchanged. [GL, Sun MS vol 437, ref. 792347; vol. 453, ref. 850499]

The firm used two different trade labels which have been found on a dozen or so pieces of furniture. The version employed c. 1799–1805 reads 'Manufactured and Sold by | J. M'LANE & SON | Pancrass Street, Tottenham Court | Road, and | 58, Upper-Mary-le-bone-street | Portland Place'. [V & A–W.10–1944] The wording on labels employed c. 1805–15 is as follows: 'Manufactured and Sold by | JOHN McLEAN and SON, | 58, Upper Mary-le-bone-Street, | The end of Howland Street, Portland-Place'. [*Furn. Hist.*, 1978, pls 31B and 31C] Two pictorial trade cards are known, one inscribed 'Upholstery & Cabinet | Manufactory | Upper Marylebone Street, | Portland 58 Place' with an elaborately styled Gothic shop front below displaying the sign board 'Ino MACLEAN & SON'. [Heal Coll., BM] The other portrays a fashionably furnished drawing room with the word 'Elegant | PARISIAN FURNITURE | WAREROOMS | John McClean & Son | CABINET MAKERS & UPHOLDERS' followed by their address. [Banks Coll., BM]

Several notices were placed in *The Times*: on 31 January 1806 the firm announced 'they have re-opened their Warerooms with a new and elegant assemblage of Parisian Furniture'; and advertised on 11 February 1811 'JOHN M'CLEAN and SON beg leave to acquaint the Nobility, Gentry and Public in general, they have in their Ware rooms a new and elegant assortment of every article of useful and ornamental furniture, upon the most approved principle, for furnishing houses, complete, which being the production of their own manufactory, they are enabled to offer on terms most advantageous: bedding of every description: pier and chimney glasses, carpeting, &c'. Further advertisements appeared in the *Times* on 4 January 1812, 2 October 1812 and 6 March 1817.

McLean subscribed to Sheraton's *Cabinet Dictionary*, 1803 and his name also appears in the list of master cabinet makers appended to that volume. In the text Sheraton illustrates a pouch work table, p. 292 commenting 'The design . . . was taken from one executed by Mr M'Lean in Mary-le-bone street, near Tottenham court road, who finishes these small articles in the neatest manner'.

The group of labelled furniture displays such a distinctive artistic personality that many similar unlabelled items can be confidently attributed to their workshops. The pieces owe much to French influence, not only in their design but in their lavish use of delicate gilt brass mounts. They favoured dark rosewood, sometimes combined with boxwood strings and satinwood crossbanding, but in later work the technique of brass inlay in the manner of Boulle is found, together with brass strips engraved with paterae and fronds. Sometimes a sparing use of water-gilt enrichment is present. The cabinet work is of a consistently high order and the gilt mounts are finely chased. The firm's furniture displays little stylistic development, although there is a discernible movement from lightness and delicacy, inspired by French prototypes, towards heavier forms with a certain weakening and coarsening in the decoration. This decline seems to have occurred after William inherited the business from his father about 1815. Another distinctive feature of their house-style was the use of a unique repertoire of cast and chased brass mounts, not encountered on other furniture of the period and therefore a valuable aid to attribution. The firm was clearly of some size and importance and their work is of particular interest because it betrays no debt to fashionable Regency pattern books of the day.

A labelled games table survives at Saltram, Devon, another of the same pattern is recorded from Grimsthorpe Castle, Lincs., and there are unlabelled pieces at Harewood, Yorks., but only one country house commission has so far been documented. This account for general furnishings supplied to the 5th Earl of Jersey's seat Middleton Park, Oxon. and his town house in Berkeley Sq. covers the period July 1806 to April 1807 and totals £4,793 11s. None of the items have been identified. [S. Redburn, 'John McLean and Son', *Furn. Hist.*, 1978, pp. 31–37; *Furn. Hist.*, 1966, pp. 37–39; GCM; Jourdain and Rose, *English Furniture: the Georgian Period*, figs 70, 71; *C. Life*, 28 May 1964, p. 1337; 16 July, p. 110 and 3 September, p. 430, 1943; 12 June 1969; 20 January 1983, p. 139; *Conn.*, March 1974; March 1976; vol. 132 (1953), p. 187; C. Musgrave, *Regency Furniture*, pl. 76; G. Wills, *English Furniture 1760–1900*, p. 183; Sotheby's, 12 November 1982, lot 84; V & A archives]   S.R.

Maclean, John, Whitehall, London, u (1749). [Poll bk]

McLean, William, York, u (1812–20). Son of John McLean, cordwainer; app. to Hugh Rusby and Francis Ellis, u and cm, on 24 November 1812. Assigned to Arthur Shores and Edward Steward. Admitted freeman in 1820. [York app. reg. and freemen rolls]

M'Leland (or McClelland), John William, Kensington, London, cm and u (1823–39). Listed at High St in 1823 and Gravel Pits, 1826–39. [D]

M'Lellan, Elizabeth & Son, Market Pl., Mansfield, Notts., cm (1819). [D]

McLellan, John, Dragon Ct, Mansfield, Notts., joiner and cm (1832). [D]

McLellan, Robert, Gt Russell St, Bloomsbury, London, u (1809–39). Recorded at no. 114, 1809–21; no. 106, 1823–35; and no. 107, 1837–39. Took out a Sun Insurance policy on 4 August 1824 for £3,600. [D; GL, Sun MS vol. 497, refs 1019497–98] See McClennan & Flint.

Maclellan, Thomas, Falmouth, Cornwall, u (1768–83). Advertised for an app. in *Sherborne Mercury*, 4 January 1768. Document dated 5 October 1779 records the sale of his house in Falmouth. Insured his house for £600 in 1781 with the Sun Co. [D; Cornwall RO, BRA 846/18; GL, Sun MS vol. 292, p. 158]

McLellan, William, Mansfield, Notts., joiner, cm and u (1819–35). Addresses given at Stockwellgate in 1819, Church St, 1828–32, and Toothill Lane in 1835. [D]

M'Lellan & Sons, Mansfield, Notts. Subscribed to Sheraton's *Cabinet Dictionary*, 1803.

McMay, John, Liverpool, cm (1816–27). App. to William Harvey in 1816. Petitioned freedom on servitude in 1823 paying 6s 8d, and admitted freeman in 1827. [Liverpool freemen's committee bk]

McMillan, Alexander, 17 Mortimer St, London, cm (1794). Took out a Sun Insurance policy on 7 July 1794 for £100 on goods and utensils in his workshop. [GL, Sun MS vol. 401, ref. 630147]

McMillan, John, Liverpool, furniture painter etc. (1811–18). Trading at Pownall St, 1811–14; no. 6, 1811–13; and 5 Upper Milk St, 1816–18. [D]

McMillan, Theodore, 2 Dorrington St, Coldbath Fields, London, u (?) (1813). [D]

McMullin, Robert, 6 Highfield St, Liverpool, cm (1835). [D]

McNab, Neil, Liverpool, cm (1822). App. to Cattrall & Whittingham in 1822. [Liverpool app. enrolment bk]

McNabb, Archibald, 5 White St, Liverpool, cm (1821–23). [D]

McNay, John, Priest Ct, St Andrew St, Liverpool, cm (1827). Admitted freeman on 10 October 1827. Probably the John M'Nay, cm, whose marriage to Miss Elizabeth Dawson at St Nicholas's Church was reported in *Liverpool Mercury*, 22 June 1827. [Liverpool freemen reg.]

McNeill, J. & Co., 6 Cable St, Liverpool, u (1835). [D]

McNevin, Anthony, London, u, cm and appraiser (1826–28). Addresses given at 92 Dorset St, Salisbury Sq., 1826–27; and 86 Dorset St and 85 Crown Ct, Blackfriars, 1827–28. Trade card recorded. Successor to Mr Hill. [D; Heal]

McNicol, Alexander & Lewis, Liverpool, cm and u (1834–39). Trading at 32 St James St in 1834; 22 St Vincent St, St James's, 1835–37; and 61 St James St in 1839. [D]

Macom, Alexander, 3 Ebenezer Ct, McGuire St, Liverpool, cm (1803). [D]

Macom, James, Manchester, cm (1731). Took app. named Worthington in 1731. [S of G, app. index]

M'Phearson, J., 44 Lime St, Liverpool, architectural and furniture carver, plain and ornamental gilder (1827). Advertised in *Liverpool Mercury*, 18 May 1827, that he was from London, and had just commenced business at the above address, and 'flatters himself that from the practical knowledge he has already acquired in the profession with the promptitude displayed in the execution of the orders of his Friends & those who may honour him with their Commands, will alone ensure him that share of the patronage of a Liverpool public, which it will ever be his anxious study to merit. AN APPRENTICE WANTED.'

Macpherson, J., English St, Carlisle, Cumb., carver and gilder (1810). [D]

Macquistin, George, address unrecorded, upholder (1742–49). Son of Bryce Macquistin, linen draper of St Mary-le-Grand;

app. to Samuel Whiting on 29 July 1742, and admitted freeman of the Upholders' Co. by servitude on 31 August 1749. [GL, Upholders' Co. records]

M'Shane, Manasses, 32 Foley Pl., Portman Sq., London, upholder and undertaker (1817–39). [D]

Mactaggart, Alexander, Liverpool, cm (1837–39). Trading at 6 Leece St in 1837 and 39 Warren St in 1839. [D] See Robert Carson & Alexander Mactaggart.

M'Taggart, John, 16 Clayton Sq. and 12 Ranelagh St, Liverpool, u and paper manufacturer (1823). Notice in *Liverpool Mercury*, 25 July 1823 concerned the assignment of his estates to creditors, presumably on his bankruptcy. Announcement in the same paper on 29 August 1823 read: 'JOHN M'TAGGART & CO. late JOHN M'TAGGART, Nº. 16 Clayton Square, beg leave to acquaint their friends & the Public that they continue their Paper Hanging Manufactory, at Nº. 12 Ranelagh Street, where they have on hand a large quantity both of Papers & Borders of all descriptions at very low prices . . .'.

Mactaggart, Robert Carson & Alexander, 6 Leece St and 27 Benson St, Liverpool, u, cm and paper hanging manufacturers (1839). [D] See Alexander Mactaggart.

Mactavish, John, 81 Gt Titchfield St, London, u (1829). [D]

McTier, John, 17 Tash St, Gray's Inn Lane, London, wood and cabinet carver (1839). [D]

M'Vay, Bernard, North St, Keighley, Yorks., cm and u (1828–29). [D]

M'Williams, Alexander, address unrecorded, cm (1803). Subscribed to Sheraton's *Cabinet Dictionary*, 1803.

Maddams & Son, William, Hackney Rd, 68 Theobalds Rd, London, cm and u (1827–35). [D]

Madden, John, Walcott, Som., cm (1759). Took app. named Neal, 1759. [S of G, app. index]

Madden (or Maddan), Thomas, London, carver and gilder (1781–84). Of 10 Glasshouse St, took out a Sun Insurance policy in 1781 for £300 of which £70 accounted for utensils, stock and goods. Recorded at Meards Ct, Dean St, 1783–84, as Maddan at no. 13 in 1783 when he took out another policy for £300, utensils, stock and goods accounting for £70. [GL, Sun MS vol. 294, p. 510; vol. 313, p. 364; poll bk]

Maddern, John, Bristol, cm (1781). [Poll bk]

Maddison, Charles, Broadway, Stratford, Essex, cm and u (1823–39). Named in the Essex Jurers' Book for Becontree Hundred in 1838. [D; Essex RO, Q/RJ/2/1]

Maddison, Francis, Huntingdon, cm, u, auctioneer and appraiser (1817–32). Recorded at Princess St in 1830. Advertised in *Cambridge Chronicle and Journal*, 24 January 1817. [D; poll bk]

Maddison, John, High St, Huntingdon, auctioneer, appraiser, u and cm (1819–39). Eldest son of Mr Maddison, cm and u, his marriage to Miss Sale of Huntingdon was reported in *Cambridge Chronicle and Journal*, 16 April 1819. [D; poll bk]

Maddison, John, Court 48, Groat Mkt, Newcastle, working u (1827–38). Recorded at Court 48, Groat Mkt, 1827–33, and 2 Spital in 1838. [D]

Maddison, Michael, 31 Bigg-Mkt, Newcastle, joiner, cm and green grocer (1833). [D]

Maddison, Philip, Bishop Wearmouth, Sunderland, Co. Durham, cm and u (1832). [D]

Maddison, Samuel, Gt Yarmouth, Norfolk, cm (1826–41). Trading at 85 Row, with house at no. 87 in 1836. [D; poll bks]

Maddison, William, Gt Yarmouth, Norfolk, cm (1818–41). [Poll bks]

Maddock, Edward, Chester, u (1830). Son of Hugh Maddock, butcher of Chester; app. to William Podmore, u, on 17 July 1830, for seven years. [Chester app. indentures]

Maddock, Elias, 24 Milk St, Bristol, cm and chairmaker (1799–1800). [D]

Maddock, James, Nantwich, Cheshire, upholder (1724). Took app. named Smith in 1724. [S of G, app. index]

Maddock, John, East St, Ashburton, Devon, cm (1838). [D]

Maddock, Samuel, Chester, u (1697–98). Son of Mary Madcock, widow; app. to Abner Scoles, u, 10 February–3 March 1697/98 for eight years. [Chester app. bks]

Maddock, Samuel, 127 Gt Ancoats St, Manchester, chairmaker (1825). [D]

Maddock, Samuel, 39 Pellow St, Liverpool, chairmaker (1829). [D]

Maddocks, Thomas, Liverpool, cm (1796). Admitted freeman on servitude to Edward Lowe on 25 May 1796. [Liverpool freemen reg.]

Maddox, —, address unrecorded. Gilder employed in the mid 1770s at Chatsworth, Derbs. [*Burlington*, June 1980, p. 413]

Maddox, Charles, Greenhill, Lichfield, Staffs., cm (1830–35). [Poll bks]

Maddox, George, 21 Baker St W., and 20–21 Blandford Mews, London, manufacturer. A set of six Regency mahogany dining chairs recorded, of Classical form, the seats in horsehair on reeded scimitar legs; bearing trade labels. [Phillips', 21 November 1967, lot 80]

Maddox, John, Castle St, London, carver (1749). [Poll bk]

Maddox, John, Walcot, Bath, Som., cm (1753). Took app. named Ring in 1753. [S of G, app. index]

Maddox, John, 18 Scotland Pl., Liverpool, furniture painter (1816–18). [D]

Maddox, Joseph, Liverpool, cm (1823–24). Trading at 15 Leeds St in 1823 and Gt Oxford St North in 1824. [D]

Maddox, Ralph, 14 Gt Russell St, Bloomsbury, London, carver and gilder, cm (1777–1817). Took out Sun Insurance policies in 1777 for £400 of which £100 accounted for utensils and goods; and in 1779 for £1,000, £50 on utensils, stock and goods. [D; GL, Sun MS vol. 257, p. 353; vol. 276, p. 32]

Maddox, Ralph Henry, 25 Welbeck St, London, u and cm (1835–39). Trade card recorded. [D; Heal]

Maddox, Richard, Oswestry, Salop, cm (1797–98). [D]

Maddox, Robert, High St, Marlow, Bucks., cm, joiner and builder (1823). [D]

Maddox, Samuel, 7 Bridgewater Pl., Bridgewater, Liverpool, cm (1837). [D]

Madge, Mat(t)hew, Plymouth, Devon, cm and u (1814–38). Probably the Madge listed at Higher Broad St in 1814. Recorded in Lower Broad St in 1822; 27 Buckwell St in 1830; and Duckwell St in 1838. Named in the list of creditors of Thomas Smith, cm of Plymouth, in *Exeter Flying Post*, 2 March 1815. [D]

Madgwick, John, address unrecorded, upholder (1722). Son of Edward Madgwick of Bodenham, Wilts.; app. to James Parker, upholder of Salisbury, Wilts., on 21 June 1722 by common indenture and counterpart for £10. [*Wilts. Apps and their Masters*]

Madin, Mathew, Pitt, Wilts., cm (1724). Took app. named Davis in 1724. [S of G, app. index].

Madoin (or Madgin), John, Silver St, Durham, cm (d. 1816). Sale of business and stock on his death advertised in *Durham County Advertiser*, 21 December 1816. Stock consisted of 'a variety of ready made Furniture and Cabinet-Work, with a quantity of well-seasoned Mahogany in logs & planks, Elm, Beach, Sycamore, & wood of every description of the best quality. Possession of the sale & workshops situate in Silver Street may be had immediately, and further particulars upon application to Mrs. Anne Madgin, Framwellgate Bridge, who begs leave to return her grateful acknowledgement for the liberal encouragement experienced by her late Son while in business, & respectfully to solicit the payment of all debts unsettled at the time of his decease: & also that those who have demands against him will send her an account of their claims, in order that they may be speedily discharged.'

Maggs, G., 6 Queen St, Bath, Som., cm (1819). [D]

Maggs, J., Bath, Som., cm and chairmaker (1819–26). Listed at 3 Nelson Pl. in 1819 and 14 Beaufort Sq. in 1826. [D] His trade card is in Bath Ref. Lib.

Maggs, J., Harp Alley, Fleet Mkt, London, japanner and gilder (1820). [D]

Maggs, John, Bath, Som., chairmaker (1831). Declared bankrupt, *Liverpool Mercury*, 16 December 1831.

Maggs, Joseph, 44 Upper East Smithfield, London, backmaker (1779). Insured his house for £100 in 1779. [GL, Sun MS vol. 273, p. 369]

Magill, Ralph, Liverpool, cm (1796–1839). Addresses given at 56 Christian St in 1796; 18 Shaw's Brow, 1800–11; no. 19 in 1810; no. 20, 1813–14; no. 18 in 1818; no. 6, 1821–24; no. 7, 1827–29; 56 Christian St, 1834; no. 36 in 1835; no. 63 and also 65 Vergil St in 1837; and 22 Vergil St in 1839. Admitted freeman on servitude to Edward Myers on 25 May 1796. Took app. named William Catterall in 1806, petitioned freedom in 1818. [D; Liverpool freemen reg. and committee bk]

Magnus, —, London. Billiard table with trade label at Hopetoun House, West Lothian, mentioned in the 1800 inventory.

Magnus, Richard, Wells, Norfolk, cm and joiner (1822). [D]

Magor, H., 8 Church St, Greenwich, London, u (1838). [D] See John Taylor Major.

Maguire, C., 14 Windmill St, Tottenham Ct Rd, London, carver and gilder (1820). [D]

Maguire, Richard, Liverpool, cm (1813–30). App. to Nathan Newell in 1813, and admitted freeman in 1830. [Liverpool freemen's committee bk]

Mahanah, John, Tarporley, Cheshire, chairmaker (1798). [D]

Maidstone, Nathaniel, St Lawrence Pountney's Lane, London, chairmaker (1718). [D]

Mailane, John, Newport St, London, cm (1780). Insured a house in Adam St, Portman Sq. for £400 in 1780. [GL, Sun MS vol. 289, p. 67]

Maile, William, George St, Hampstead Rd, London, u (1818). [Marylebone Lib., deed 495]

Maile, William, 3 New Millman St, London, cm and u (1839). [D]

Maile, William, 6 Park St, Dorset Sq., London, u (1839). [D]

Mailler, James, 3 Cross Keys Ct, Little Britain, London, cm (1809–11). [D]

Main, —, address unrecorded. Named in Paul Methuen's Day Book for Corsham Court, Wilts., on 10 May 1790, supplying 'a Bird Organ & Inlaid Work Box' costing £5 5s. [V&A archives]

Mainlove, —, address unrecorded, u (1754). Subscribed to Chippendale's *Director*, 1754. Probably Richard Manlove.

Mainwaring, William, Sedgley, Staffs., cm (1834). [D]

Mairis, A., 282 High Holborn, London, u and cm (1796). [D]

Mairis, Robert, address unrecorded, furniture warehouseman (1794). Sent a bill to Mr Turner in 1794. [V&A archives]

Mais, —, address unrecorded. Named in the Massingberd account books in May 1785 receiving 12s 6d for repairing a drawing board; and on 9 July 1782, £2 19s for picture frames and glass supplied in Bath. [Lincoln RO, MM 9/10] Probably:

Mais, Henry, Bath, Som., carver, gilder and builder (1791–92). Notices regarding bankruptcy appeared in *Williamson's Liverpool Advertiser*, 26 September 1791 and 6 August 1792. Described as 'late of Bath' in 1792.

Maitland, Robert, address unrecorded, cm (1793–1803). Subscribed to Sheraton's *Drawing Book*, 1793, and *Cabinet Dictionary*, 1803.

Major, John Taylor, Church St, Greenwich, London, cm, u, carpenter and joiner (1808–34). [D] See H. Magor.

Major, John W., 90 Fore St, Exeter, Devon, formerly of London, upholstery, chair and cabinet warehouseman (1822–24). Advertised commencement of business in *The Alfred*, 30 July 1822, and sale of cabinet goods 'of the best workmanship & well-seasoned wood', at very low prices, on 22 July 1823. Marriage to Miss Tout at South Molton reported on 28 October 1823. Sale of stock and effects 'under an Execution from the Sheriff' advertised in *Exeter Flying Post*, 17 June 1824. [D]

Major, John Taylor & Samuel, Poole, Dorset, u (1837). Declared bankrupt, *Sussex Agricultural Express*, 24 June 1837. See Samuel Major.

Major, Samuel, Liverpool, cm (1828). App. to Thomas Croft Huxley in 1828. [Liverpool app. enrolment bk]

Major, Samuel, Colyton, Devon, cm (1830). [D]

Major, Samuel, High St, Poole, Dorset, cm and u (1837–40). [D] See John Taylor Major.

Makepeace, Joseph, foot of Westgate St, Newcastle, u, sworn auctioneer and appraiser (1783). Advertised in *Newcastle Courant*, 25 October 1783, his 'large assortment of paper hangings of the newest pattern from London, fringe for beds, &c., lace, window line, tassels and cloak pins…'.

Makepeace, Mark, Tyne St, North Shields, Northumb., u (1827). [D]

Makepeace, Mary, 17 Upper Ashley St, Northampton Sq., London, carver and gilder (1826–27). [D]

Makin, John, Alford, Lincs., u (1793). Subscribed to Sheraton's *Drawing Book*, 1793.

Makin, John, Chapel St, Salford, Lancs., u (1794–1813). Recorded at no. 149 in 1794; no. 193 in 1804; no. 192 in 1811; and no. 203 in 1813. [D]

Makins, Benjamin, Gainsborough, Lincs., cm (1805–08). [D]

Makins, Thomas, Gainsborough, Lincs., cm (1809–11). [D]

Makins, Thomas, 14 Wellington Terr., Waterloo Rd, London, cm (1835). [D]

Makinson, I., Manchester, looking-glass manufacturer. Label recorded on early 19th-century wall mirror with bands of satinwood. [Sotheby's, 26 March 1954, lot 122]

Maklin, Thomas, Bateman's Buildings, St Martin-in-the-Fields, London, gilder (1775). Took two apps in 1775. [Westminster Ref. Lib., MS 6048]

Malbone, John, address unrecorded, upholder (1739–50). Son of Joseph Malbone, brewer of Spitalfields, London. App. to Thomas Perrot on 5 September 1739, and admitted freeman of the Upholders' Co. by servitude on 7 August 1750. [GL, Upholders' Co. records]

Malcher, John, St Bride's, London, u (1723–24). Named as son and heir of John Malcher, late of Long Coombe, Oxon., Gent., deceased, concerning the lease and release of a messuage in New Woodstock. [Oxford RO, Misc., Has. II/8]

Malcolm, George, address unrecorded, cm (1803). Subscribed to Sheraton's *Cabinet Dictionary*, 1803.

Malcolm, Michael, Panton St, London, cm (1745–56). [D] Possibly:

Malcolm, Michael, St Martin-in-the-Fields, London, cm (1753). Declared bankrupt, *Gents Mag.*, May 1753. Possibly:

Malcome, Mitchell, St Martin-in-the-Fields, London, cm (1749). [Westminster poll bk]

Male, Charles, Market Pl., Crewkerne, Som., cm (1822–30). [D]

Male, James, Yeovil, Som., cm (1798). [D]

Male, Joseph, Borough, Yeovil, Som., cm (1822). [D]

Male, Robert, Hotwells, Bristol, cm, u and undertaker

(1825–35). Trading at 9 Caroline Pl. in 1825; 11 Dowry Sq., 1826–35; and as a Venetian and Indian blindmaker from 1827. [D]

Malim, Thomas, Doncaster, Yorks., upholder (1760). Took app. named Armitage in 1760. [S of G, app. index]

Malin, Edward, London, cm (1750). [GL, Joiners' Co. records, list of liverymen] Probably Edward Maylin.

Malin (or Malyn), Thomas, London, cm (1661–63). The earliest reference to a cm in the Royal Accounts appears to be that of Thomas Malin, dated 1661–62 regarding the purchase of 'Two pairs of stands and two tables of Marble Speckled wood for Hampton Court', costing £18; 'Two Tables and Two pairs of stands of Jamaica Wood', probably mahogany, at £18; 'A very larg Table of marble wood inlaid', £15; '2 Marble colour'd tables of Violett wood for the Queenes closett at Whitehall', £11; and 'one large looking glass with an ebony frame for our Groome of the Stoole', for £25. The account totalled £87. At Michaelmas 1663 Malin supplied 'one faire looking glasse of Venice glasse wth an Ebbony frame', costing £20. [PRO, LC5/39; *Conn.*, vol. 105, 1940, p. 201; R. W. Symonds, *Furniture Making in 17th and 18th Century England*, pp. 105 and 116] Possibly:

Malin(e), Thomas, address unrecorded, cm (1699). He rendered two bills to the 5th Earl of Bedford (later 1st Duke) for furniture ordered, very probably, for Bedford House, London. The first, dated 30 June 1699, for £8 10s, lists a mirror cresting of French walnut carved with 'a crown etc.', and a pair of stands 'with ureated pillars'. The second, dated 31 August 1699 for £4 9s, accounts for the remainder of the 'triad' suite: a walnut table 'on twisted pillars', and a walnut frame 'for my Lord's great looking-glass'. Both bills are endorsed 'Thos. Malin'; the name suggests that he was a French Huguenot. [Bedford Office, London]

Mal(l)ins, William Hill, Birmingham, cabinet case maker (1830–39). Addresses given at 16 Court, Charles St in 1803; 16 Little Charles St in 1835 and Gt Charles St in 1839. [D]

Malkin, Thomas, Hawke St, Liverpool, cm (1816–21). [D]

Mallam, C. R., Banbury, Oxon., cm and u (1832–41). Listed at Parsons Lane, 1832–35; Parsons St in 1837 and High St, 1839–41. [D]

Mallam, Charles Richard, 30 Broad St, Worcester, cm and u (1828). [D]

Mallam, Robert & Charles, St Aldate's, Oxford, cm and u (1830). [D]

Mallard, Edward, Castle Foregate, Shrewsbury, Salop, u (1840). [Shrewsbury burgess roll]

Mallender, Paul, Brighton, Sussex, cm (1822–24). Recorded at 22 Portland St in 1822 and Devonshire Pl. in 1824. Daughter Emma and son Paul by Hannah Mallender bapt. on 21 April 1822 and 27 June 1824 respectively. [D; E. Sussex RO, PR (bapt.)]

Mallet, Francis Peter, 48 Clerkenwell Close, Clerkenwell Green, London, cm and u (b. 1729–d. 1799). First noted in 1765 by which year he had become a partner with William and Richard Gomm in the business which operated from the former Newcastle House, the Close, Clerkenwell. In 1771 the business was named as Gomm, Son & Mallet and on 6 February of that year Mallet was made free of the Upholders' Co. under the terms of the 1750 Upholders' Act. His address was recorded as 'of Clerkenwell'. Directories of 1774–75 list Mallet and give his address as Clerkenwell Green or Garraway's Coffee House, Exchange Alley. Mallet may have ceased his partnership by this date, possibly because of the anticipated financial difficulties of the business for, when bankruptcy occurred in 1776 only William and Richard Gomm are named in the proceedings. Mallet was further conveniently on hand to take over the business. Insurance

cover taken out in that year was in his name and indicates the extensive size of the manufactory. Newcastle House was said to have six warehouses and workshops and shed and a sawpit which were covered by insurance of £9,100 of which £6,000 was for goods and stock. Insurance was also taken out earlier in this year on 8 Red Lion Sq. for £5,000 which included £3,200 for utensils and stock. Following on his bankruptcy Richard Gomm was living at this address in 1777 taking out insurance cover of £200 on the house only. The scale of production under Mallet's ownership was probably smaller and in 1782 insurance cover was a mere £600 including £100 for utensils and stock. Soon after 1790 Mallet probably retired and in 1794 he was recorded at Buckingham. He died in November 1799 at Islington Spa aged about 70 and was said at that time to be resident at Edmonton. He was described in his obituary notice in the *Gents Mag.* as 'an eminent cabinetmaker and successor to Mr. Gomm'. An invoice from Mallet is in the Heal Coll., BM. It is made out to a — Peck Esq., dated 24 December 1783, and concerns the supply of a large mahogany secretaire bookcase costing £21 15s. This bookcase on a cupboard base survives. [D; GL, Upholders' Co. records; Sun MS vol. 245, p. 580; vol. 248, p. 305; vol. 301, p. 305; V & A archives]   B.A.

Mallett, Henry, Market Gates, Gt Yarmouth, Norfolk, chairmaker (1839). [D]

Mallett, Robert, Gt Yarmouth, Norfolk, chairmaker (1830–36). Trading at George St in 1830 and Market Gates in 1836. [D]

Mallett, William, Bath, Som., cm (b. 1707–d. 1791). Fashionable craftsman working during the reign of George II and the early years of George III. His name was continued after his death by his son, and the family was in business at The Octagon, Bath, until the early years of this century, when W. E. Mallett wrote *An Introduction to Old English Furniture.* Wing chair recorded with the name 'Mallett of Bath' and the date 1785 carved on the underside of the seat. [*Collector's Guide*, September 1949]

Mallett, William, 5 Chariot St, Hull, Yorks., chairmaker (1831). [D]

Malley, John, Lancaster. Named in the Gillow records, 1784–1833. [Westminster Ref. Lib.]

Malley, Peter, Lancaster. Named in the Gillow records, 1816–22, including work on a bedstead in 1822. [Westminster Ref. Lib., vol. 344/100, p. 3167]

Malley, William, Lancaster. Named in the Gillow records in 1808 working on a chair. [Westminster Ref. Lib., vol. 344/99, p. 1850]

Mallinson, John, Penrith, Cumb., chairmaker (1811–34). Trading at Town Head in 1811 and Burrowgate in 1834. [D]

Malorie, Thomas, Lady Lane, Leeds, Yorks., u, joiner and cm (1805–08). [D]

Mally, B. J., Lancaster. Named in the Gillow Records in 1790. [Westminster Ref. Lib.]

Malone, Thomas, 27 Portland St, Manchester, cm and u (1836–40). [D]

Maltby, Francis, Hull, Yorks., cm (1768). [Poll bk]

Maltby, William, Nottingham, cm (1798). [D]

Maltman, James, London, cm (1793). Subscribed to Sheraton's *Drawing Book*, 1793.

Malton, Perry, address unrecorded, carver (1689–90). Provided picture frames for Hampton Court, Kensington Palace and Petworth House, Sussex. [*C. Life*, 4 September 1980, p. 799]

Malton, Thomas, Hull, Yorks., cm (1768). [Poll bk]

Malton, Thomas, the Strand, London, cm (b. 1726–d. 1801). Known principally as an architectural draughtsman, teacher of geometry and perspective. A former pupil, William Hickey, recorded in his memoirs (1772) that 'Mr Malton had been for several years a cabinet maker, having a large shop in the Strand, but as nature had blessed him with an extraordinary mechanical genius he was constantly engaged in experiments upon different subjects therein ... So powerfully did this inclination operate as his knowledge increased that he at length relinquished his trade . . . he left off business with only about £2000, having a wife and six children'. He is mentioned in a footnote to part two of Thomas Sheraton's *Drawing Book* and is recorded as binding an app. in 1761 for a fee of £10. The first edition of Malton's *Compleat Treatise on Perspective*, 1775 contains one plate and the third edition, 1779, a second featuring in all eleven items of fashionable furniture. The second edition of his *Royal Road to Geometry*, 1793 included a criticism of Sheraton's *Drawing Book*. [*Furn. Hist.*, 1975; A. Spencer (ed.), *Memoirs of William Hickey*, 1948, I, 281]

Malton, Thomas, Nottingham, cm (1754–55). Subscribed to Chippendale's *Director*, 1754 and in 1755 took app. named John Flannell for a consideration of £20. [S of G, app. index]

Maltster (or Malster), Robert, Norwich, cm (1818–30). Recorded in the parish of St Martin-at-Palace in 1818, and St Gregory, 1830. [Poll bks]

Malvern, Charles, Worcester, cm (1831–35). Admitted freeman in 1831, and named in the Worcester freemen rolls on 1 December 1835.

Malvern, Charles, Leamington, Warks., cm and u (1835–37). Listed at 14 Warwick St in 1835 and 5 Windsor St in 1837. [D]

Mames, William, address unrecorded, cm (1803). Subscribed to Sheraton's *Cabinet Dictionary*, 1803.

Manarin, —, 'from London', enameller and gilder. Late 18th-century trade card recorded. [Banks Coll., BM]

Manasses & M'Shane, 32 Foley Pl., Cavendish Sq., London, u (1819–25). [D]

Manby, George, High St, Leeds, Yorks., cm (1817). [D]

Manby, William, Hull, Yorks. and Louth, Lincs., cm (1780–84). Polled at Hull of Hull in 1780, of Louth in 1784.

Mancer, William, 27 Wardour St, London, chairmaker and painter (1820). Took out a Sun Insurance policy on 27 July 1820 for £800 of which £500 accounted for stock and utensils in workshops behind his house. [GL, Sun MS vol. 483, ref. 970075]

Manchee, John, 10 New Inn Sq., Bateman's Lane, Shoreditch, London, carver (1823). Took out a Sun Insurance policy on 14 May 1823 for £200. [GL, Sun MS vol. 497, ref. 1005270]

Manchester, John, Nantwich, Cheshire, cm (1771–75). Son Henry bapt. on 17 March 1771, William on 5 September 1773, and James on 17 September 1775. [Chester RO, PR (bapt.)]

Manchip, John, West St, Bridgwater, Som., cm and u (1830–40). [D]

Mander, Benjamin & Son, Wolverhampton, Staffs., papier-mâché maker (c.1792–after 1812). Trays stamped 'MANDER' recorded. [*Conn.*, August 1967, p. 251]

Mander, John, 5 Upper East Smithfield, London, cm, bedstead maker and undertaker (1808–28). [D]

Mander, Joseph, address unrecorded, upholder (1719/20). Son of John Mander, freeman butcher of London, deceased. App. to William Shepard and admitted freeman of the Upholders' Co. by servitude on 13 January 1719/20. [GL, Upholders' Co. records]

Mangenot, N., Lancaster, engraver (1801). [Westminster Ref. Lib., Gillow records]

Mankin, Arthur, Market St, Falmouth, Cornwall, cm and u (1823–24). [D]

Manklelow, Edmund, Battle, Sussex, cm and u (1832–39). [D]

Manklin, Benjamin, Hull, Yorks., cm (1747–58). Son of

Benjamin Manklin, furrier; admitted freeman of York in 1750. Polled at Hull in 1747 and 1754, and at York in 1758. [York freemen rolls]

Manknell, William, Holywell St, Chesterfield, Derbs., cm (1818–22). [D]

Manley, R., 8 Albion Pl., Bath, Som., chair and couch maker (1826). [D]

Manley, Samuel & Son, Bradford, Barnstaple, Devon, cm (1838). [D]

Manlove, Richard, address unrecorded, upholder (1723–42). Son of Thomas Manlove of Lappington, Salop, Gent., deceased. App. to Thomas Gardner on 30 July 1723, and admitted freeman of the Upholders' Co. by servitude on 7 July 1731. Took app. named John Phipps, 1734–42. [GL, Upholders' Co. records]

Manlove, Richard, near St Antholin's Church, Watling St, London, upholder (c.1770). Trade card recorded. [Heal]

Manlove, Rowland, Market Pl., Uttoxeter, Staffs., cm and clockcase maker (1835). [D]

Mann, Benjamin, London, wholesale u and cm (1801–20). Addresses given at 28 Rood Lane, 1801–06; 117 Bishopsgate St in 1807; as Mann & Jordan there, 1811–12; and alone at 47 Somerset St, Aldersgate in 1820. Named in Sheraton's list of master cabinet makers, 1803. [D]

Mann, Charles, Gt Magdalen St, Thetford, Norfolk, cm, chairmaker and joiner (1822). [D]

Mann, H., High St, Lincoln, cm (1805–07). [D]

Mann, James, Framwellgate, Durham, joiner and cm (1831–34). Notice in *Durham Advertiser*, 13 May 1831 stated that 'JAMES MANN, of the late firm of SHAW and MANN, JOINERS AND CABINET-MAKERS', would be carrying on the business alone since the death of his partner, John Shaw; including 'Printers' Joiner Work, as heretofore, executed with the greatest accuracy & on the most reasonable terms, viz: Cases, Frames, Gutters, Side & Foot Sticks, Shutting Sticks, Riglets, Quoins & everything connected with the business...'. [D]

Mann, John, Liverpool, joiner and cm (1790–1803). Recorded in Whitechapel in 1790; Mann St, off Harrington St, with shop at Sir Thomas Buildings in 1796; and Mann St, Stanhope St in 1803. [D]

Mann, John, 127 Fore St Hill, Exeter, Devon, cm (1823–34). Advertised in *The Alfred*, 25 November 1823, 'a large assortment of mahogany & other CHAIRS, & mahogany & rosewood SOFAS, manufactured with the best materials & offered at unprecedented low prices. American wood CHAIRS with hair seats, made at half the price of mahogany. Graining in exect imitation of Rosewood, Done or taught.' [D; voters list]

Mann, John P., Stamford, Lincs., cm and u (1832–41). Recorded in St George's parish in 1832, and at St Mary's St, 1835–41. [D; poll bk]

Mann, John, Broad St, Nottingham, cm (1835). [D]

Mann, Richard, 13 Paradise Row, Chelsea, London, cm and u (1823). [D]

Man(n), Robert, Little Queen St, Holborn, London, u and cm (1789–93). Recorded at no. 31 in 1789. [D]

Mann, Samuel, address unrecorded, upholder (1742–51). Son of Robert Mann, school master of London; app. to John Jackson on 7 July 1742, and admitted freeman of the Upholders' Co. by servitude on 12 January 1750/51. [GL, Upholders' Co. records]

Mann, Thomas, York, cm (1740–58). Recorded as 'lately in possession of a house next the Church in Spurriergate', in *York Courant*, 12 February 1740. Took app. named John Tate in 1743. Living in Feasegate at the York poll of 1758. [York app. reg.]

Mann, W. R., 1 Pollard Row, Bethnal Green, London, cm (1829). [D]

Mann, William, Hull, Yorks., cm (1803–05). Recorded at Adelpher Yd in 1803 and 24 Lowgate in 1805. [D]

Mannall, John, Colechester, Essex, cm and joiner (1781–82). Insured his house for £1,000 in 1781 and £600 in 1782. [GL, Sun MS vol. 289, p. 278; vol. 299, p. 132]

Manners, John, Morpeth, Northumb., joiner and cm (1827–34). Addresses given at Hair's Yd, Oldgate in 1827 and Old Gate, 1828–34. [D]

Manners, Matthew, Vine Lane, Newcastle, cm (1838). [D]

Manners, Robert, Brunswick St, Stockton-upon-Tees, Co. Durham, joiner and cm (1827). [D]

Manners, William, address unrecorded. Rosewood teapoy recorded bearing paper label: 'Made by Wᵐ Manners Cabinet Maker June 17 1834'.

Manning, James, St Clement's, Ipswich, Suffolk, cm (1818). Named in the calendar of marriage licence bonds in 1818. [Suffolk RO, FAA: 50/2/118, p. 53]

Manning, John, Cirencester, Glos., u (1817). [PR (bapt.)]

Manning, William, Holbeach, Lincs., joiner and cm (1826). [D]

Manning, William, Ipswich, Suffolk, carver and gilder (1830–35). Trading at Tower St in 1830 and Butter Mkt in 1835. [D; poll bks]

Mans, Joseph, Leicester, cm (1749). App. to John Elliott, and admitted freeman in 1749. [Leicester freemen rolls]

Mansel, Row. Dawkin, Jermyn St, London, upholder (1774). [Poll bk]

Mansell, E., High St, Chippenham, Wilts., cm etc. (1839). [D]

Mansell, Joseph, Bromsgrove Rd, Birmingham, cm (1822). [D]

Mansell, William, Penryn, Cornwall, joiner and cm (1792). Insured a house in Falmouth for £200 on 29 February 1792. [GL, Sun MS vol. 386, p. 42]

Mansell & Son, Princess St, Shrewsbury, Salop, cm and u (1840). [D]

Manser, Thomas, 8 Carpenter St, London, cm (1827). Children John and Charlotte by his wife Charlotte, bapt. on 30 October 1827 at the Methodist Westminster Chapel. [PRO, Non-Conf. Reg. RG4/4313]

Manser, William, London, furniture japanner, carver and gilder, chairmaker, broker and antique furniture and china dealer (b.1779–d.1862). Trading at 27 Wardour St, 1819–44. Son of William and Elizabeth Manser, bapt. at St James's, Clerkenwell on 7 July 1779. He married Ann Ashley at St Saviour's, Southwark, on 15 April 1801. During the 1830s and 1840s Manser invested in property, and acquired long leases of many of the houses in Myddelton Sq., Clerkenwell. He died on 29 July 1862 at 17 Myddelton Sq., and was buried in the Abney Park Cemetery. [D]

Mansergh, John, Lancaster, cm (1770–84). App. to R. Bateman and W. Forrest in 1770, and admitted freeman, 1779–80. [Lancaster app. reg., freemen rolls and poll bk]

Mansfield, H., 9 Corn St, Bath, Som., cm (1833). [D]

Mansfield, Thomas, Bethlem, Gt Grimsby, Lincs., joiner and cm (1831). [D]

Mansfield, Thomas jnr, Salisbury St, Shaftesbury, Dorset, cm, u and paper hanger (1840). [D]

Mansford, Daniel, 45 Leather Lane, Holborn, London, cm and furniture broker (1817–20). [D]

Mansford, David, Baker St, Spa Fields, London, cm and barometer case maker (1824). Took out Sun Insurance policies on 15 March 1824 for £300, of which £200 accounted for stock, utensils and goods in trust; and on 24 June 1824 for £500. [GL, Sun MS vol. 495, ref. 1014807; vol. 497, ref. 1017827]

Mansford, David, 6 Baker St, Bagnigge Wells, London, cm (1826–39). [D]

Mansford, John, Town St, Shepton Mallet, Som., cm (1839). [D]

Mant, John, Chichester, Sussex, cm (1782). Insured his house for £200 in 1782. [GL, Sun MS vol. 301, p. 570]

Mant, John, Winchester, Hants., cm and auctioneer (1792–1808). Recorded in High St, 1805–08. [D] Clothes press recorded, with four drawers in the base, surmounted by a cupboard with two doors with oval panels of mahogany veneer; the top surmounted by four urn finials. It bears a printed label with Neo-classical cartouche framing inscription which reads: 'Mant, UPHOLDER & CABINET MAKER, High Street, WINCHESTER, NB. Goods Appraised & Sold by Auction on the most reasonable Terms.' [Hotspur Ltd., London, c.1981; Heal Coll., BM; Apollo, February 1954] Identical label recorded on a roll-top desk with metal gallery, drawer and tapering legs with castors. [V&A archives]

Manthorpe, James, Norwich, cm (1825–30). Recorded in St Lawrence's parish in 1830. App. to Henry Higgins, and admitted freeman on 3 May 1825. [Norwich freemen reg. and poll bk]

Mantica, Charles, 6 Coppice Row, Clerkenwell, London, looking-glass manufacturer (1839). [D]

Mantle, James, Mile Town, Sheerness, Kent, cm (1838–39). Trading in High St, 1838. [D]

Mantle, T., 26 Upper York St, Bryanston Sq., London, cm (1835). [D]

Mantle, Thomas, Market Pl., Dover, Kent, cm and u (1793–1830). Took out a Sun Insurance policy on 19 July 1792 for £100, including £50 for workshop and storerooms in the yard near his house in Market Pl., plus £50 for utensils and stock. Polled at Dover, 1826–30. [D; GL, Sun MS vol. 387, p. 342]

Mantle, Thomas, 16 Marylebone Lane, London, cm (1826–28). [D]

Mantle, Thomas, 4 Shouldham St, London, cm and u (1839). [D]

Manton, Edward, Coventry Rd, Warwick, cm (1831). [Poll bk]

Manton, George, 29 Essex St, Birmingham, cm (1835). [D]

Manwaring, Robert, Haymarket, London, cm (1760–66). The author of two modest furniture pattern books *The Cabinet and Chair-Maker's Real Friend and Companion*, 1765 and *The Chair-Maker's Guide*, 1766, he also contributed some fifty designs to *Genteel Houshold Furniture in the Present Taste* sponsored by a Society of Upholsterers and Cabinet-makers in 1760. Available information about Manwaring, including the fact that he was a cm with premises in the Hay-Market, London, is derived from his own publications. His designs — all for stylish seat furniture — are much less fluent than the work of Chippendale or Ince & Mayhew; Sheraton described them as 'worthless', but the best parlour chairs displaying bold interlaced splats, his elaborately fretted Chinese and Gothic specimens and highly picturesque rural examples express an individual artistic personality. Manwaring claimed 'they are actually Originals, and not pirated or copied', adding 'there are very few designs advanced, but what he has either executed himself, or seen completely finished by others'. C.G.G.

Manzies, Robert, Orange St, Leicester Fields, London, cm (1780). Took out a Sun Insurance policy in 1780 for £500, utensils, stock and goods accounting for £100. [GL, Sun MS vol. 281, p. 401]

Manzochi, Girolano, 22 Brook St, Hull, Yorks., looking-glass maker (1838). [Goodison, *Barometers*]

Mapey (or Masey), Abram, address unrecorded. Named in the account book of Edward Monnington of Sarnesfield Court, near Kington, Herefs., on 29 June 1728, receiving £10 10s for a bureau. [Herefs. RO, P94/6] Possibly Abraham Massey.

Maplebeck, John, Wirksworth, Derbs., chairmaker (1822). [D]

Mapleson, Charles, Stoney Hill, Bristol, cm (1793–94). [D]

Maplestone, Charles jnr, Blyburgate St, Beccles, Suffolk, surveyor, builder cm, u and carpenter (1824–39). [D]

Maram, Philip, Church Lane, Strand, London, u (1709). [Rate bks]

March, Edward, 49 Queen St, Birmingham, cm (1830). [D]

March, George, Gainsborough, Lincs., cm (1805–07). [D]

Marchant, John, Cross Corner, Carnaby Mkt, London, upholder (1774). [Poll bk]

Marchant, John, London, cm, u and bedstead manufacturer (1814–29). Recorded at 1 corner of Church St, Shoreditch, 1816–19; 64 Shoreditch in 1820. 1 Cloak Lane, Shoreditch, 1827; and 1 Old Cock Lane, Bethnal Green in 1829. Heal rcords trade card. [D] See Sabourin & Marchant, also John Merchant.

Marchant, Peter, at 'The Royal Bed & Star', near Fleet Bridge, London, u and appraiser (c.1760). Trade card shows Daniel Marot type 'Lit d'Ange', with the Royal Arms in auricular-style cartouche. Card states that he 'Makes & Sells all sorts of Upholsters & Cabinet-Makers Goods. Funerals Perform'd to any part of Great Britain.' [Banks Coll., BM] See Peter Merchant.

Marchant, S., 51 Tooley St, Southwark, London, looking-glass frame maker (1820). [D]

Marchant, Samuel, 4 St George's Rd, Southwark, London, carver and gilder (1839). [D]

Marchant, William, 48 Church St, Bethnal Green, London, cm (1808). [D]

Marchese, Lewis, 1 Richmond St, Liverpool, carver and gilder (1818). [D]

Marchese & Co., 20 Haymarket, Liverpool, carvers and gilders (1816). [D]

Marcroft, John, Providence Pl., Leeds, Yorks., cm (1822). [D]

Marcuccis, Charles, 6 Barlow St, Marylebone, London, carver and gilder (1785). Took out a Sun Insurance policy on 24 May 1785 for £200 on his house, and £30 on utensils, stock and goods in trust therein. [GL, Sun MS vol. 329, p. 281]

Mardn, Samuel, 32 Walbrook, London, upholder (1777). [D]

Maren, Stephen, New Compton St, London, carver and gilder (1749). [D] See Stephen Marin.

Mares, John, Deritend, Birmingham, chair and gun case maker (1818). [D]

Mare(s), John, Banbury Rd, Birmingham, cm and chairmaker (1822). [D]

Mares, William & J., Pimlico, London, cm and u (1827–39). Addresses given at 12 Upper Ranelagh St, 1827–28; 91 Lower Belgrave St in 1835; and no. 21 in 1839. [D]

Marganis, —, St Anne's, London, cm (1730). Report that he had been stabbed appeared in *Daily Journal*, 5 August 1730.

Margarom, Robert William, Norwich, cm and chairmaker (1822–d.1825). Trading at Castle Ditches in 1822. Will proved at Norwich in 1825. [D; Norfolk Record Soc., index of wills]

Margerson, Joseph, Elbow Lane, Dale St, Liverpool, chair bottomer (1804). [D]

Margrie, George, Lyme Regis, Dorset, cm and u (1830–40). Addresses given at Broad St in 1830 and Church St in 1840. [D]

Margrie, Jacob, Bridport, Dorset, cm and auctioneer (1823–40). [D]

Marin, Stephen, 71 Long Acre, London, carver (1775). Took out a Sun Insurance policy in 1775 for £400, £100 accounting for utensils and stock. [GL, Sun MS vol. 242, p. 512]

Marin, Stephen, 66 New Compton St, Soho, London, carver, gilder and oval turner (1797–1819). Trading in partnership with Baughan in 1819. Elegant Neo-classical trade card also bears inscription in French. [D; Banks Coll., BM]

Mariner, William, York, cm (1783–90). Son of Henry Mariner; app. to John Sanderson, cm, on 30 January 1783. Admitted freeman of the Liberty of St Peter in 1790. [York app. reg. and freemen rolls]

Maris, Samuel, address unrecorded, upholder (1741–48). Son of Richard Maris, Gent. of Worcester. App. to Jonathan Fawconer on 5 August 1741, and admitted freeman of the Upholders' Co. by servitude on 1 September 1748. [GL, Upholders' Co. records]

Mark, Mark, Thornton St, Dockhead, London, carver and gilder (1832–34). [D]

Marker, John, Newbridge, Exeter, Devon, cm (1831). Son William bapt. on 8 January 1831 at St Edmund's Church. [PR (bapt.)]

Markey, Cornelius, at the third door from Tooley St in Southwark, London, u and cm (1752). Named in contemporary newspapers. [Heal]

Markey, John, Blackheath Hill, Greenwich, London, cm and u (1823–39). [D]

Markham, George, at 'The Windmill', Houndsditch, Aldgate, London, cane chairmaker (1720). Insured goods and merchandise in his house on 8 January 1720. [GL, Sun MS vol. 10, ref. 16199] See John le George Markham.

Markham, Gregory, Little Moorfields, London, u (d.1666). [*Richard Smyth's Obituary*, 1849]

Markham, John le George (?), at 'The Golden Chair', Houndsditch, Aldgate, London, cane chairmaker (1719). Took out a Sun Insurance policy on 2 November 1719. [GL, Sun MS vol. 10, ref. 15632] See George Markham and Lawrence Markham.

Markham, John, Bridge St, Worksop, Notts., cm and u (1822). [D]

Markham, Lawrence, at 'The Golden Chair', near Gravel Lane, Houndsditch, Aldgate, London, chairmaker (1729). Took out a Sun Insurance policy on 12 April 1729 for £300, including £100 on household goods and stock in trade in his house; and £200 on stock in his warehouse and sheds in adjoining yard. [GL, Sun MS vol. 29, ref. 47414] See John le George Markham.

Markham, Thomas, Gainsborough, Lincs., cm and u (1828–35). Listed at Gt Church Lane in 1828 and Church St in 1835. [D]

Markland, Ralph, Bull St, Birmingham, cm (1793). [D]

Marks, Henry, Cirencester, Glos., cm (1834–39). [PR (bapt.)]

Marks, James, Cirencester, Glos., cm (1828–32). [PR (bapt.)]

Marks, John, Norwich, u (1762–97). Trading at 12 Market Pl. in 1780, and no. 28 in 1783. Son of John Marks, plumber and glazier; admitted freeman on 11 September 1762. Former app., John Hardy, admitted freeman on 3 May 1779; and John Reynolds, u, on 17 March 1792. Announced in *Norfolk Chronicle*, 24 June 1780, that Mr Notley had left their co-partnership of Notley & Marks, as he was declining business, and Marks would trade on his own account. Trade card, c.1790, reads: 'MARKS, Upholsterer & Appraiser, Makes & Sells on the lowest Terms, All Sorts of Upholstery Furniture, In the newest, and most approv'd Taste, AT No. 12 MARKET PLACE, NORWICH.'. [D; poll bks; Norwich freemen reg.; Norwich Local Hist. Lib.]

Marks, John, 8 Batchelor Row, Battle Bridge, London, cm (1826–28). [D]

Marks, John, Cock St, Hitchin, Herts., cm and u (1823–39). Listed also as auctioneer and builder in 1838. [D]

Marks, M., 93 Blackman St, Southwark, London, carver and gilder (1835–39). [D]

Marks, M., Old St, London, cabinet manufacturer (1835–39). Trading at no. 51 in 1835 and no. 72 in 1839. [D]

Marks, Sterry, London, upholder (1771–79). Recorded 'at his fathers Nº 19 St. Thomas's, Southwark' in 1779. Son of Job. Marks; app. to John Boulton on 2 October 1771, and Benjamin Soundy on 9 August 1774. Admitted freeman of the Upholders' Co. by servitude on 3 February 1779. [GL, Upholders' Co. records]

Marks, William, address unrecorded, cm (1803). Subscribed to Sheraton's *Cabinet Dictionary*, 1803.

Marks, William, College Yd, Worcester, carver and gilder (1820–40). Recorded at no. 6 in 1822 and no. 7 in 1830. [D]

Marks, William, South St, Manchester Sq., London, u and furniture broker (1829–39). [D]

Marks, Osborn & Co., 5 Albion Pl., St Pancras, London, auctioneers, appraisers, u and undertakers (1835–39). [D]

Marks Harding, John, Barnstaple, Devon, carver and gilder (1826). Birth of daughter announced in *The Alfred*, 8 August 1826.

Marland, John, Manchester, chairmaker and cm (1818–40). Recorded in partnership with James Marland at 23 Thomas St, 1818–25, and also at no. 74 in 1824 and 1828–29, no. 72 in 1825; Redfern St, 1828–29 and 10 Thomas St, 1833–34. Listed alone at 10 Thomas St in 1832 and at 1 Blukely (or Blakeley) St, Miller St in 1840. Recorded as Marland & Farron, cm and chairmakers at 21 Thomas St in 1836 and no. 23, 1836–40. [D]

Marlen (or Marlin), Francis Thomas, West St, Faversham, Kent, cm (1832–39). [D]

Marlen, William, Last Lane, Dover, Kent, cm, u and chairmaker (1839). [D]

Marley, John, Workington, Cumb., joiner and/or cm (1811–34). Trading at Griffin St in 1811 and Priestgate, 1828–29. [D]

Marleys, Robert, address unrecorded. On 27 February 1734 he was paid 16s 2d for 'a Mahogone Tea Table', bought in 1733 for Gibside, Co. Durham. [Durham RO, Strathmore MS, D/St/v. 987]

Marlow, James, Hill St, Stoke-on-Trent, Staffs., cm and u (1828–35). [D]

Marlow, Thomas, Steelhouse Lane, Birmingham, cm (1830–35). Recorded at 15½ Court in 1830 and 92 Steelhouse Lane in 1835. [D]

Marlowe, Richard, Watling St, near St Antholin's Church, London, upholder, undertaker and appraiser. Rococo trade card recorded. [Banks Coll., BM]

Marlton, John, Cock St, Wolverhampton, Staffs., joiner and cm (1780). [D]

Marples, William Edward, Barker's Pool, Sheffield, Yorks., carver and gilder (1828–30). [D]

Marples, William, Chapel Yd, Tuxford, Notts., joiner and cm (1832). [D]

Marples & Hibbert, 72 Fargate, Sheffield, Yorks., carvers and gilders (1837). Advertised in White's *Directory of the West Riding of Yorkshire*, 1837, as: 'Carvers, Gilders, – Print-Sellers and Artists' Repository, — Manufacturers of Picture Frames, Looking Glasses, Cornices, Pier Tables, Brackets and every description of Gilt and Ornamental Fancy Furniture. —Ornamental Models in Wood, Wax, Clay or Plaster; Composition Ornaments for Architectural or other purposes, to any design. Old Glasses Re-silvered, Oil Paintings, Prints, Drawings and Maps cleaned, lined, repaired and varnished. Gentlemen's Houses attended to repair or re-gild any article in the above line. Cabinet-Makers' and Upholsterers' orders well and promptly executed. Materials for Painting in Oil or Water-Colours.'

Marr, Henry, Newcastle, u (1774). App. to Edward Coates, and admitted freeman on 17 June 1774. [Newcastle freemen reg.]

Marr, James, Byker Buildings, Newcastle, cm (1827). [D]

Marr, Samuel, 72 Old St Rd, London, broker and chairmaker (1802–11). Took out a Sun Insurance policy on 10 March 1802 for £300, including £60 on utensils and stock. [GL, Sun MS vol. 424, ref. 730083]

Marr, Thomas, above White-cross, Newcastle, cm and carpenter (1778). [D]

Marr, Thomas, Southergate, Ulverston, Lancs., cm (1822). [D]

Marr, William, Nottingham, joiner and cm (1814). Took app. named Joseph Wright in 1814. [Nottingham app. list]

Marr, William, 33 Bread St, Cheapside, London, japan dressing case maker (1829–35). [D]

Marrable, John, 6 High St, Chatham, Kent, carver and gilder (1826–34). [D]

Marrable, John, High St and St Margaret's Bank, Rochester, Kent, carver, gilder, paper hanger, undertaker etc. (1838). [D]

Marrack, Alex, Falmouth, Cornwall, cm (d. 1835). Report in *Exeter Flying Post*, 31 December 1835, that he had been found drowned.

Marrack, John, Market Strand, Falmouth, Cornwall, cm and u (1830). [D]

Marrell, Joseph, address unrecorded, u (1803). Subscribed to Sheraton's *Cabinet Dictionary*, 1803.

Marrian, Thomas, 29 St James's St, St Margaret, Westminster, London, water gilder (1818). Took app. named Jos. William Ball in 1818. [Westminster Ref. Lib., MS B1268, St Clement Danes reg.]

Marriat, Samuel, Thames St, London, upholder (1734). [Poll bk]

Marriner, Christopher, 3 Edgar Ct, Liverpool, cm (1821). [D]

Marriner, George, Liverpool, carver and gilder (1813–16). Addresses given at Hill St, Copperas Hill in 1813; 1 Hill St in 1814; and 13 Renshaw St in 1816. [D]

Marriott, Mrs, Swann's Yd, Long Row, Nottingham, u (1840). [D]

Marriott, John & Thomas, Westgate, Dewsbury, Yorks., cm (1822). [D]

Marriott, Luke, Earls Heaton, near Dewsbury, Yorks., cm (1822). [D]

Marriot(t), Samuel, London, upholder (1703–17). Address given in Thames St, 'St Mary Somersett' in 1717. Son of William Marriot, victualler of London. App. to William Braman on 27 May 1703, and admitted freeman of the Upholders' Co. by servitude on 4 May 1715. Took out a Hand in Hand Insurance policy on 18 December 1717 for £750 on his own house in Thames St, and for £750 on a rented house. [GL, Upholders' Co. records; GL, Hand in Hand MS vol. 18, p. 91]

Marriot(t), Thomas, Leeds, Yorks., cm and joiner (1791). Advertised in *Leeds Intelligencer*, 6 September 1791, giving address at 'Mr. Butler's Yard opposite the Crown, Kirkgate', where '... he continues to Make and Sell the Portable Patent Machines for Washing Linen, Invented by Thomas Todd ...'. Advertised again in *Leeds Mercury*, 13 September 1791, and *Leeds Intelligencer*, 4 October 1791, giving notice that 'he has entered upon the Premises at the top of the Leylands, lately occupied by Mr. Hawkswell ...'. Re-advertised in the same paper that he 'continues to make Todd's celebrated washing machines, now universally used — it is unnecessary to mention the savings both in soap & labour as it is to dwell upon their other excellencies.'

Marriott, Thomas, 4 Camomile St, London, u (1810–16). Took out Sun Insurance policies on 6 June 1810 for £500, of which £300 accounted for stock and utensils; and on 27 January 1814 for £700, £300 on stock, utensils and store. [D; GL, Sun MS vol. 449, ref. 846020; vol. 461, ref. 889827]

Marriott, William, Fotheringay, Northants., gilder (1741). Took app. named Wright in 1741. [S of G, app. index]

Marriott, William, Northampton, cm (1784–96). Addresses

given at 'Drapery' in 1784; St Mary's St in 1796; and Bridge St in 1790. [Poll bks]

Marris, Thomas, 1 Foster's Entry, Humber St, Hull, Yorks., joiner and cm (1838–39). [D]

Marsden, Elizabeth, Deansgate, Bolton, Lancs., cm and u (1814–18). [D]

Marsden, George B., Manchester, u and cm (1800–22). Recorded at 6 North Parade, St Mary's in 1800; 18 Queen St, St Ann's in 1804; Queen St in 1808; and 22 St Ann's St, 1813–22. [D] See Mary Marsden.

Marsden, Henry, Eastgate St, Chester, cm (1824). Admitted freeman on 9 October 1824. [Chester freemen rolls]

Marsden, James, address unrecorded, carver (1739–42). Named in the accounts for Holkham Hall, Norfolk, in 1739 receiving £58 5s for carving two table frames, two glass frames, and a large chimney frame; in 1740 for carved work totalling £136, including thirteen friezes for doors costing £4 9s; chimney frames at £7 16s and £10 6s; and two large glass frames '& ornaments prepar'd' at £6 2s 6d. In 1742 he supplied two large pier glasses for the dressing room costing £73. [V&A archives]

Marsden, James, Hipperholme, Yorks., joiner and cm (1830). [D]

Marsden, James, Raistrick, Yorks., joiner and/or cm (1834). [D]

Marsden, John, Wigan, Lancs., u, chairmaker and cm (1811–25). Trading in Millgate, 1814–17, and Wallgate, 1818–22. Announcement of marriage to Miss Moorfield of Wigan on 2 July 1811 in *Liverpool Mercury*, 12 July. [D]

Marsden, John, Westgate, Wakefield, Yorks., cm and u (1828–34). [D]

Marsden, John, Head St, Colchester, Essex, fancy cm (1832). [D]

Marsden, Mary, 22 St Ann's St, Manchester, cm and u (1824–29). Trading in partnership with G. Mather in 1829. [D] See George B. Marsden

Marsden, R., 51 St John's St, London, cm and u (1808). [D]

Marsden, Reuben, Colchester, Essex, cm and broker (1791–93). Recorded at Market Cross, when he took out a Sun Insurance policy on 4 January 1791 for £600, of which £350 accounted for utensils and stock. [D; GL, Sun MS vol. 375, p. 120]

Marsden, Robert, Hallgate, Wigan, Lancs., u and cm (1814–22). [D]

Marsden, Thomas, Sheffield, Yorks., cm (1816–21). Addresses given at 42 Burgess St in 1816 and Alsop's Row, Little Sheffield, in 1821. [D]

Marsden, Thomas Barton & Bather, Thomas, Manchester, u (1830). Declared bankrupt, *Chester Courant and Anglo-Welsh Gazette*, 31 August 1830.

Marsden, Thomas, Gt Bull Yd, Wakefield, Yorks., cm and/or u (1837). [D]

Marsden, William, Bakehouse Lane, Stanley St, Liverpool, cm (1796–1818). Recorded at no. 8 in 1796 and no. 12, 1803–04. [D]

Marsden, William, Westgate, Wakefield, Yorks., cm, u and paper hanger (1824–37). [D] Former foreman of John Robinson, cm of Wakefield, entered into partnership with Thomas Powell in 1824. [*Furn. Hist.*, 1976, p. 42]

Marsh, —, address unrecorded, cm (1740). Received payment of 6s in April 1740 by Augusta, Princess of Wales. [Windsor Royal Archives, RA 55425]

Marsh, —, address unrecorded, upholder (1778–1801). Named in the accounts for Gorhambury, St Albans, Herts. in January 1778 receiving payment of £16 0s 4d; on 27 February 1788, £2 4s 'For Fitting up two Drawers to hold Medals'; on 5 June 1788 for supplying a dressing table costing £11 12s; and on 13 May 1801, receiving £10 4s 6d. [Herts. RO, Gorhambury account bk XI, 63, 71 and 74]

Marsh, —, Margate, Kent, cm (1803–07). [D]

Marsh, Cornelius, Longfleet, Poole, Dorset, cm and u (1840). [D]

Marsh, Edward, Birmingham, cm, u and broker (1828–35). Addresses given at 49 Queen St in 1828, Queen St in 1830 and 45 Colemore St in 1835. [D]

Marsh, George Moses, Chester, u (1716). Son of Moses Marsh, u, late of Chester. Admitted freeman on 12 January 1716. [Chester freemen rolls]

Marsh, George, address unrecorded, cm (1754–76). Subscribed to Chippendale's *Director*, 1754; and probably the Mr Marsh, cm and u, who subscribed to Thomas Malton's *Treatise on Perspective*, 1776.

Marsh, George, Gainsborough, Lincs., cm (1805–08). [D]

Marsh, Henry, Clement's Inn Passage, Clare Mkt, London (1739/40). Advertised in *London Daily Post and General Advertiser*, 5, 6, 7 and 10 March 1739/40, as the 'inventor of The Chamber Horse which is also known by the alternative names of Excercise Chair & Dandy Horse'. [*C. Life*, 20 October 1955, pp. 846–47; *Furn. Hist.*, 1981]

Marsh, Henry, 23 Orchard St, Bristol, carver (1775). [D]

Marsh, Isaac, Liverpool, cm (b.1737–d.1809). Addresses given at Water St in 1767; Pool Lane, 1767–69; 35 Atherton St in 1774; no. 53 in 1777; no. 48 in 1781; 7 King St in 1787; no. 9 in 1790; 8 King St, Pool Lane, 1796–1804; no. 9 in 1805; and no. 10 in 1807. Petitioned freedom as freeborn son of Richard Marsh, 'musicioner', in 1759, and admitted freeman in 1761. Former app., Edward Myers, petitioned freedom in 1780; and Thomas Jones in 1784. Took apps named Charles Pemberton in 1788, petitioned freedom in 1796; Mathew Massey in 1792, petitioned in 1802; Robert Corrin in 1795, Henry Gill in 1798, and John Swaine in 1799, all three petitioning freedom in 1806; William Kennedy in 1802, petitioned freedom in 1812; and John James in 1807 who was app. to John Ward Turner in 1810 after Marsh's death, and petitioned freedom in 1816. Marsh advertised that he 'makes & sells all kinds of CABINET GOODS on the most reasonable terms' and had rooms in Pool Lane to let, in *Williamson's Liverpool Advertiser*, 24 July 1767. Notice of his death, aged 72, on 15 November 1809, as 'a man of the strictest integrity & uprightness', reported in *Liverpool Courier*, 29 November. [D; Liverpool freemen's committee bk]

Marsh, James, address unrecorded, cm (1803). Subscribed to Sheraton's *Cabinet Dictionary*, 1803.

Marsh, James, 16 College St, Bristol, cm (1775). He also ran lodgings and boarding premises. [D]

Marsh, James, Liverpool, cm (1776–1800). Addresses given at 77 Whitechapel, 1790–96; no. 81 in 1800. His son and former app., Peter Marsh, petitioned freedom in 1776. [D; Liverpool freemen's committee bk]

Marsh, James, 21 Field St, Everton, Liverpool, cm (1837). [D]

Marsh, John, address unrecorded, upholder (1721–29). Son of John Marsh, wire drawer of London. App. to George Robinson on 15 November 1721, and Samuel Tilbe, freeman draper, on 3 March 1724. Admitted freeman of the Upholders' Co. by servitude on 27 August 1729. [GL, Upholders' Co. records]

Marsh, John, Manchester, chairmaker (1794–1813). Addresses given at 30 Gt Newton St in 1794; no. 19 in 1804; 62 Shudehill in 1811; and no. 64 in 1813. [D]

Marsh, John, Cheapside, Dale St, Liverpool, chairmaker (1796–1805). Trading at no. 49 in 1796 and no. 45 in 1805. [D]

Marsh, John, 70 Newington Causeway, London, upholder (1835). [D]

Marsh, Joseph, 26 Feasgate, York, cm and u (1818–37). Trading as Joseph & Son, 1837–40. [D]

Marsh, Joseph, Park St, Grosvenor Sq., London, upholder and cm (1820–29). [D]

Marsh, Moses, Chester, u (1680). [Chester freemen rolls]

Marsh, Moses jnr, Chester, u (1701). Son of Moses Marsh, u of Chester. Admitted freeman on 5 January 1701. [Chester freemen rolls]

Marsh, Moses, Chester, glazier (1703). Supplied items to Nicholas Blundell of Crosby Hall, Lancs., on 18 December 1703, receiving payment for coach glass; and for silvering and polishing a looking-glass, providing a 'black frame and head', two further glasses and four black frames, at a total cost of £4 15s 6d. [F. Tyrer, *The Great Diurnal of Nicholas Blundell*, vol. 1; Nicholas Blundell's Disbursement Book, 1702–36, at Crosby Hall]

Marsh, Peter, Liverpool, cm (1776–1823). Addresses given at 62 Peter St, Whitechapel in 1790; nos 70 and 83 in 1796; and no. 70, with flour shop at 83 Whitechapel, 1800–03; 9 and 10 Byrom St in 1805; and 131 New Scotland Rd in 1823. Admitted freeman on servitude to his father, James Marsh, on 3 October 1776. [D; Liverpool freemen reg.]

Marsh, Samuel, Blandford, Dorset, u (1747–54). Mentioned in the will of Perrias Spearing, u of Blandford, who had no issue and left everything to Samuel Marsh in 1747. Took app. named Percy in 1754. [Dorset RO, DA/W/1747/5; S of G, app. index]

Marsh, Thomas, Winchester, Hants. joiner (1723). Provided tables and stools for the Duke of Montrose's house at Shawford, Hants., receiving £6 9s in 1723. [Scottish RO, GD 220/6/1236/9]

Marsh, Thomas, Southgate, Sleaford, Lincs., chairmaker (1822–42). Several Windsor chairs of the second quarter of 19th century recorded, each bearing stamp on the back of the dished seat, reading: 'MARSH' or 'MARSH/SLEAFORD'. Local directories and the Census returns show there were two families named Marsh working as chair-turners in Sleaford, Lincs., during the second quarter of the 19th century. [D; Exhib. Cat., *Common Furniture*, Temple Newsam House, Leeds, 1982, no. 54]

Marsh, William, see George Elward & William Marsh.

Marsh, William, South St, London, upholder (1784). [Poll bk]

Marsh, William, St David's, Exeter, Devon, cm (1803–38). Named in the Exeter Militia List, 1803. Recorded at St David's Hill, 1814–38. Sons bapt. at St David's Church: Edward on 20 March 1814; Daniel on 2 February 1817; William on 11 March 1829; William Charles on 5 September 1832; and Edward on 14 November 1838. [PR (bapt.)]

Marsh, William, Wiskersley, near Rotherham, Yorks., cm (1822). [D]

Marsh, William, 7 St Margaret's Ct, Southwark, London, chair and sofa maker (1839). [D]

Marsh & Tatham, see George Elward & William Marsh.

Marsh & Johnson, York, cm and u (1834). [D]

Marshall, —, address unrecorded, upholder (1797). Worked at Panshanger, Herts., receiving payments on 17 May 1797 for £509 and £127 5s. [Herts. RO, account bk D/EP A2]

Marshall, —, address unrecorded, cm (1803). Subscribed to Sheraton's *Cabinet Dictionary*, 1803.

Marshall, Mrs, Russell St, Plymouth, Devon, u (1836). [D] See John Marshall at this address.

Marshall, Alexander, Holborn, London, carver and gilder (1785–1839). Addresses given at 17 Brownlow St in 1785; 2 (Back of) Middle Row, 1789–93; 2 Holborn Bars, 1802–27; and 2 Middle Row, 1835–39. Took out a Sun Insurance policy on 5 August 1785 for £15 on utensils, stock and goods in trust; and £60 on his house. [D; GL, Sun MS vol. 331, p. 361]

Marshall, Benjamin, Horsefair, Pontefract, Yorks., cm (1837). [D]

Marshall, Charles, York, cm (1757). Son of Elizabeth Marshall, widow; app. to Thomas Calvert, cm and joiner, on 31 January 1757. [York app. reg.]

Marshall, Charles, Monmouth St, London, cm (1782). Took out a Sun Insurance policy in 1782 for £200, of which £20 accounted for utensils and stock. [GL, Sun MS vol. 299, p. 627]

Marshall, Charles, Knaresborough, Yorks., cm (1784). [York poll bk]

Marshall, Charles, Dartford, Kent, cm (1793). [D]

Marshall, D., 40 East St, Brighton, Sussex, u (1827). [D]

Marshall, Dorothy, Pontefract, Yorks., cm (1834). [D]

Marshall, Edward, Liverpool, u (1818). Admitted freeman on servitude to Benjamin Tyrer on 11 July 1818. [Liverpool freemen reg.]

Marshall, Elizabeth, London, bed warehouseman (1819–28). Trading at 35 Tooley St in 1819 and 16 Eltham Pl. Kent Rd, 1827–28. [D] See Mary Ann Marshall.

Marshall, G., Mount St, London, cm (1793). Subscribed to Sheraton's *Drawing Book*, 1793.

Marshall, George, York, u (1764–84). Son of James Marshall, cm; admitted freeman in 1764. Polled at York of London in 1784. [York freemen rolls]

Marshall, George, York, u (1764–98). Established a business in Coney St in 1764; and recorded in High Petergate in 1798. [D; *Furn. Hist.*, vol. 1]

Marshall, George Sugar, York, cm and u (1785–1840). Recorded at Goodramgate in 1814, with glass and china warehouse there in 1823; and 92 Goodramgate in 1828. Son of Thomas Marshall, cm; admitted freeman in 1785. Took apps named Thomas Skelton, admitted freeman in 1812; and Francis Robinson, admitted in 1817. [D; York app. reg. and freemen rolls]

Marshall, George, address unrecorded. Signed one 'Gothick' chair of six: 'GEO. MARSHALL, April 7th, 1772'. [*Antique Collector*, May–June 1949]

Marshall, George, 9 Upper Edward St, Brighton, Sussex, cm (1839). [D]

Marshall, J. H., 5 Honduras St, St Luke's, London, cabinet turner in general (1826–27). [D]

Marshall, James, Bristol, carver (1754). Took app. named Prichard in 1754. [S of G, app. index]

Marshall, James snr, York, joiner and cm (1741–d.1768). Trading in Colliergate, 1741–58. On his death in 1768, debts were made payable to James Marshall, u in Petergate, probably his son. [Poll bk; *Furn. Hist.*, 1965]

Marshall, James jnr, York and Leeds, cm, upholder and appraiser (1755–d.1796). Appears to have run businesses either simultaneously or firstly in Leeds, c.1755–66, then in York from 1768 until his death in 1796. Son of James Marshall snr, joiner of York; admitted freeman of York in 1758, in which year he polled there, but of Leeds. He was recorded in Leeds in 1755, when he took app. named Lambert. In 1761 James Marshall of 'The Naked Boy in Briggate', Leeds, supplied to Temple Newsam House, various materials and equipment for 'Making & Fixing one Drop Curt'n' costing £1 6s 10d. In 1766 James Marshall jnr advertised in *York Courant* that he had moved his cabinet and upholstery business to Leeds (presumably from York); and had also 'lately opened shop in Pontefract', and needed journeymen in the 'cabinet & chair branches'. Rococo trade card of James Marshall of Leeds is in the Banks Coll., BM, and shows putto displaying wallpaper. The card lists mainly bed and upholstery materials, including 'Rabbit down', but also chairs, tables and other furniture. There is another example at

Bradford Central Library [Spencer-Stanhope MS: 2317/21/121] inscribed on the reverse 'Received 27th Nov. 1760 of John Stanhope Esq. £18 1s in full etc. Jas Marshall.' Addresses in York are given from 1768 until James Marshall's death in 1796. In 1768 James Marshall snr died, and debts were made payable to his son, James Marshall jnr, u of Petergate, York. He polled at York 'of Petergate' in 1774 and 1784. Advertised in *York Chronicle*, 1775, that he had returned to Petergate, York, from London with an assortment of household furniture, and had built new workshops. In 1778 James Marshall of High Petergate submitted an account to 'Mr. Cholmney' for minor items. In 1779 the firm became James Marshall & Son, and opened a shop in Briggate, Leeds. They advertised in *Leeds Mercury*, giving address 'Opposite the Old King's Arms, Briggate', 'where the business will be carried forward in its full extent, and the Nobility, Gentry and Others … may depend upon their Furniture well-finished in Taste and at the most reasonable prices …'. The firm appears to have continued or re-established trading in York, being recorded there in Directories in Petergate, 1781–87. Trade card from Cusworth Hall, Yorks., used to cover a bundle of letters dated 1781–94, gives addresses in High Petergate. Another, probably later, address for James Marshall, 'near Bootham Bar', York, is given on a label (Fig. 13) recorded on a mahogany secretaire bookcase, *c*.1780–90, with dentil cornice above fluted frieze, glazed upper doors; desk drawer and panelled doors in the lower stage. [Florian Papp Coll., NY; G. Tarn Bainbridge & Son, Darlington, 7 August 1979, lot 559, illus.] Probably the 'Mr. Marshall, Upholsterer' who submitted a bill for £8 to Harewood House in 1760. [D; poll bks; S of G, app. index; York freemen rolls; *Furn. Hist.*, 1965 and 1967; *C. Life*, 3 October 1974, pp. 932–33] A Thomas Marshall had a warehouse in Briggate, 1763.

Marshall, James, London, upholder and cm (1772–79). Trading at Houndsditch, 1772–74; no. 127 in 1773; and 189 Oxford St in 1779. Son of William Marshall, upholder; admitted freeman of the Upholders' Co. by redemption on 3 June 1772. Took app. named David Brown, 1772–79. Employed twelve non-freemen for eighteen weeks, and fourteen for twelve weeks in 1772; between twelve and fourteen freemen in 1773; and eight for six weeks in 1774. Declared bankrupt, *Gents Mag.*, June 1774. [D; GL, Upholders' Co. records; GL, City Licence bks, vols 7 and 8]

Marshall, James, Carnaby Mkt, London, cm (1784). [Poll bk]

Marshall, James, 1 Duke St, Grosvenor Sq., London, cm (1825). [D]

Marshall, James, 40 East St, Brighton, Sussex, cm and u (1826–32). Trading also at no. 42 in 1832. [D]

Marshall, James, Darlington, Co. Durham, u and cm (1827–34). Trading at High Row in 1827 and Cudworth Yd, 1828–29. [D] See Marshall & Dodds.

Marshall, James, Drapery, Northampton, carver, gilder and bird and beast stuffer (1830). [D]

Marshall, James, Exe Island, Exeter, Devon, chairmaker (1831–40). [D; *Exeter Pocket Journal*]

Marshall, Jo., address unrecorded, upholder (1731). Named in the accounts for Stowe, Bucks., in 1731 receiving £6 13s 4d. [Huntington Lib., California, Stowe MS ST82, p. 35]

Marshall, John, London, joiner (1714–18). The Montrose accounts record payment to John Marshall of £2 5s in 1714 for a large chest with iron work, and a wainscot table. In 1718 he supplied to the Duke's London house in Bond St '2 oak Steallions for the Beer Cellar'; a '6 Leaf Horse for Drying the Linen'; A 'Furm Pr. of Steps, Stool & A Long Spout for the Wash House, Racks, Cupboard & Shutter', costing a total of £11 18s 5d. [Scottish RO, GD 220/6/1159/41; 1192/11]

Marshall, John, near St James's Church, London, u (1721). Named in contemporary newspapers. [Heal]

Marshall, John, Framlingham, Suffolk, 'Maker from London' (1728). Advertisement in *Ipswich Journal*, 11 May 1728 read: 'At Framlingham, in Suffolk, is to be Made and Sold Cabinets, Desks and Book-Cases, Desks, Chest of Drawers of all Sorts, Card-Tables, Gammen-Tables, Chairs of all Sorts, Dressing-Tables, Close-Stools, Ovel-Tables at Reasonable Rates, by John Marshall, Maker from London.'

Marshall, John, Walker's Ct, Knave's Acre, Golden Sq., London, cm and upholder (1749). [Poll bk]

Marshall, John, London, upholder (1771–78). Recorded at Eagle St in 1778. Son of John Marshall; app. to William Palliser on 7 July 1771, and admitted freeman of the Upholders' Co. by servitude on 5 August 1778. [GL, Upholders' Co. records]

Marshall, John, St Martin's Lane, Charing Cross, London, upholder (1772–77). Recorded at no. 2, 1774–77. Admitted freeman of the Upholders' Co. by redemption on 1 September 1773. [D; poll bk; GL, Upholders' Co. records]

Marshall, John, 6 Leigh St, Red Lion Sq., London, cm (1775–76). Took out Sun Insurance policies in 1775 with Joseph Bunny for £200 on utensils and stock; and in 1776 alone for £400 of which £250 accounted for utensils, stock and goods. Tambour writing table at Cannon Hall, near Barnsley, Yorks., bears his label. [GL, Sun MS vol. 244, p. 60; vol. 253, p. 454]

Marshall, John, opposite Mays Buildings, Bedford Ct, Bedford St, London, cm (1777). Took out a Sun Insurance policy in 1777 for £300 of which utensils, stock and goods accounted for £100. [GL, Sun MS vol. 258, p. 550]

Marshall, John, Berwick St, London, u (1784). [Poll bk]

Marshall, John, London, cm, u, joiner and chairmaker (1793–1840). Addresses given at 21 Gerrard St, Soho, 1794–1808; and 31 Soho Sq., 1811–40. Subscribed to Sheraton's *Drawing Book*, 1793; and named in his list of master cabinet makers in his *Cabinet Dictionary*, 1803, to which he also subscribed. Took out a Sun Insurance policy on 27 May 1807 for £1,000, all on utensils and stock. [D; GL, Sun MS vol. 440, ref. 802938] Placed similar advertisements in the *Times* on 7 January 1801, 7 January 1804, 1 April 1805, 29 January, 28 February and 14 March 1806. His advertisement of 29 January 1806 read: 'JOHN MARSHALL'S New Invented Patent DINING-TABLES made to any size, and far preferable to any heretofore made, which when turned up at the end or side of a room, not only take up a great space, but deform the appearance of the apartment, whereas these Tables possess every advantage without either of the foregoing inconveniences, and will, on trial, be found superior in point of utility and elegance to those now in use. Also Antique Chair-Sofas, Couches, Cabinets and Window-curtains, made in a particular manner, which for elegance, are not yet equalled; and every other article in the Cabinet and Upholstery branches, from the plain and useful, to the superb and ornamental; on reasonable terms — Manufactured by John Marshall, No. 21 Gerrard-street, Soho, three doors from Princes-street, Leicester square.' Carried out work for James Leigh of Stoneleigh, Warks. His bill dated 14 February and 11 March 1818 was for two clothes presses, one for Stoneleigh, the other for Leigh's London house in Portman Sq., and fixing them, at a total cost of £100 11s 2d. The first was described in the bill as 'a Capital Mahogany Ladys Winged Clothes Press of fine wood the Centre fitted up in the top part with doors inclosing 5 trays of Cedar the lower part with draws the End one with Pegs for hanging dresses the other with loose shelves as pr. Order Inclosed by Pannelld doors supported on turned stump feet the top with rich moulded Mahogany Cornice and carved Scroll Piedmount top the whole finished in a Superior Style of workmanship, as pr. Agreement', costing £46. [Shakespeare Birthplace Trust, Leigh receipts, DR/18/5] John Marshall carried out much jobbing work at St James's Palace, 1837–40; and also at Buckingham Palace in September 1837, his bill totalling £192 16s 5d. His supplied striped awnings and sunshades; re-upholstered beds; provided bedsteads; deal 'trussels for Ironing Boards' for the Queen's Wardrobe Room; two music tables 'with a bevil top on a frame with square legs, made portable, the whole painted over stone colour', costing £13 9s 8d; twelve birch chairs with cane seats for £4 19s; 'Stout Bedroom Chairs with Black frames & Rush Seats', £7 4s; and '3 Pedestals made of very strong wood for supporting marble figures, finished in the best Manner, the whole grained in Sienna in a very superior style'. [Windsor Royal Archives, RA Box 1, item 2; PRO, LC 11/95 and 110] On the sale of the house and furniture of Robert Heathcote in Hill St, Berkeley Sq., held at Phillips' on 20 March 1805 it was reported in *Gents Mag.* that Heathcote had paid Marshall & Co. £6,020 for furnishings, £1,500 for looking-glasses, and £482 for chandeliers. Regency oak pedestal table recorded, with circular tip-up top inlaid with geometric and cube-pattern parquetry in various woods including maple, tulipwood, ash, ebony and rosewood; on foliate shaft, concave-sided triangular base and paw feet; bearing label inscribed: 'Notice this article to be used with great care; and not exposed to too much sun, fire or damp J. Marshall Maker'. Pair of gilt-wood settees with gryphon arm supports, now owned by Brighton Pavilion, bear label which reads: 'Marshall, Soho 24 September 1810.' [Christie's, 12 February 1981, lot 38, illus.; 14 May 1981, lot 46; *Antiques*, February 1969, p. 190.]

Marshall, John, 22 Upper King St, Bloomsbury, London, cm and u (1781–1811). Took out Sun Insurance policies in 1781 for £700, utensils, stock and goods accounting for £470; on 23 September 1800 for £1,200, £400 on utensils and stock; on 26 February 1803 for £1,300; and on 7 June 1810 for £1,000, including £500 on a house at 37 Rosoman St, Clerkenwell, in tenure of a chairmaker; and £500 on house and workshop at no. 18 in the same tenure. [D; GL, Sun MS vol. 295, p. 240; vol. 419, ref. 706510; vol. 427, ref. 745264; vol. 449, ref. 846051]

Marshall, John, 48 Church St, Bethnal Green, London, cm (1808). [D]

Marshall, John, New John St, Hull, Yorks., cm (1823). [D]

Marshall, John, Claypath, Durham, cm (1827). [D]

Marshall, John, York, cm (1827). Son of George Marshall of Fulford, York; app. to John Taylor, cm, on 27 August 1827. [York app. reg.]

Marshall, John, Lichfield St, Tamworth, Staffs., chairmaker and turner (1828–35). [D]

Marshall, John, Bishop Wearmouth, Sunderland, Co. Durham, cm (1832). [D]

Marshall, John, 105 High St, Leeds, Yorks., cm and joiner (1837). [D]

Marshall, John, Russell St, Plymouth, Devon, cm and u (1838). [D] See Mrs Marshall.

Marshall, L., 19 Radnor St, St Luke's, London, fancy cm (1835). [D]

Marshall, Martha, Coney St, York, toy, Tunbridge-ware and cm (1802–24). Traded as Martha Doughty until 1814. Early 19th-century spinning wheel recorded, on tripod stand set with ivory tablets, incribed: 'MARSHALL late DOUGHTY York.' [D; *Furn. Hist.*, 1978] See Marshall & Doughty.

Marshall, Mary Ann, Eltham Pl., Kent St, Southwark, London, bed and mattress manufacturer (1820–23). Trading at

nos 6 and 16 in 1820, and at no. 16, 1822–23. [D] See Elizabeth Marshall.

Marshall, Matthew Chitty, York, u (1784). Son of James Marshall, u of Leeds; admitted freeman of York in 1784. [York app. reg.; *Furn. Hist.*, 1965]

Marshall, Matthew, 1 Duke St, Grosvenor Sq., London, cm and u (1827–28). [D]

Marshall, Matthew, 2 Richmond Buildings, Soho, London, fancy cm, portable desk, dressing case, writing box and cabinet case maker (1835–39). [D]

Marshall, Michael, Castle St, Salisbury, Wilts., cm and u (1839). [D]

Marshall, Richard, St Martin's Lane, near Long Acre, London, u (1778). Declared bankrupt, *Gents Mag.*, June 1778.

Marshall, Richard, Low St, Malton, Yorks., u (1823–40). [D]

Marshall, Richard, Best Lane, Canterbury, Kent, cm (1830). [Poll bk]

Marshall, Robert, address unrecorded, cm (1793–1803). Subscribed to Sheraton's *Drawing Book*, 1793, and *Cabinet Dictionary*, 1803.

Marshall, Robert, East St, Horncastle, Lincs., joiner and cm (1835). [D]

Marshall, Thomas, address unrecorded. Between 1687/88 and 1690 he supplied twelve dozen cane chairs to the Royal Hospital, Chelsea, at a cost of £39 12s. [*Wren Soc.*, vol. XIX, p. 85]

Marshall, Thomas, Leeds, Yorks., cm (1756–63). Recorded in Kirkgate, with warehouse in Briggate, 1763. Took app. named Smith in 1756. Son of James Marshall cm; admitted freeman of York in 1757, and polled but of Leeds, in 1758. Advertisement in *Leeds Intelligencer*, nos 465–66, 1763 read: 'A Cabinet Maker in full business wants one or two apprentices, — apply to Mr. Thomas Marshall, Cabinet Maker in Kirkgate, Leeds, at whose warehouse in Briggate may be had all sorts of Cabinet and Chair work made in the newest and most genteel Taste, and at reasonable prices.' [S of G, app. index; York freemen rolls] James Marshall jnr of York and Leeds traded in Briggate, Leeds in 1761.

Marshall, Thomas, York, cm (1774–85). Recorded in St Saviourgate at the 1774 poll, and Walmgate in 1784. Took app. named William Chambers on 4 April 1775. His son George Sugar Marshall, admitted freeman in 1785. [York poll bks, app. reg. and freemen rolls]

Marshall, Thomas, St Luke Old St, 4 Checker Alley, Whitecross St, London, looking-glass frame maker (1787). Took app. named William Fitzpatrick in 1787. [Westminster Ref. Lib., MS B1266, St Clement Danes reg.]

Marshall, Thomas, Hull, Yorks., u and paper hanger (1807–23). Trading at 14 Trundle St, 1817–22. App. to George and John Chapman of Hull in January 1807. [D; Hull app. reg.]

Marshall, Thomas, 1 Charles St, Brighton, Sussex, carver and gilder (1839). [D]

Marshall, William, Chapel St, Tadcaster, Yorks., cm (1822). [D]

Marshall, William, Gillygate, Pontefract, Yorks., cm (1837). [D]

Marshall, William, Adelphi Ct, George Yd, Hull, Yorks., cm (1838–39). [D]

Marshall, William, Coombe St, Exeter, Devon, cm (1815–18). Daughter Mary Anne bapt. at St Mary Major on 10 December 1815; and son William on 19 June 1818. [PR (bapt.)]

Marshall, William Henry, St George's Lane, Exeter, Devon, cm (1823–30). Sons bapt. at St George's Church: William Henry on 26 October 1823; William Henry on 1 October 1826; and George Uglar on 26 December 1830. [PR (bapt.)]

Marshall & Dodds, High Row, Darlington, Co. Durham, cm and/or joiner (1834). [D] See James Marshall.

Marshall & Doughty, Coney St, York, toy, turnery, umbrella and cabinet manufacturers (1795). Joseph Doughty and a partner named Marshall advertised their 'toy, Tunbridge & spinning wheel manufactory' in *York Herald*, 14 February 1795. See Martha Marshall.

Marshall & Newman, Blyth, Northumb., joiner and/or cm (1834). [D]

Marsham, William, 71 Fleet St, London, upholder (1777). [D] See William Marston.

Marsland, James, Grove St, Salford, Lancs., cm (1800–02). [D]

Marsom, John, High St, Epping, Essex, chairmaker (1823–24). [D]

Marston, John, Cock St, Wolverhampton, Staffs., joiner and cm (1780). [D]

Marston, William, London, upholder, cm and rent collector (1751–d.1795). Recorded at St Bride's in 1751; Fleet St, 1753–94; no. 71, 1753–87. Admitted freeman of the Upholders' Co. by redemption in 1751, and master in 1782. Took apps named William Kent, 1752–56; Israel Lewis in 1762; and Timothy Ridge until 1791. Fined for non-service at St Bride's in 1753; served as Scavenger there in 1757; Collector for the Poor in 1761; and Questman and Sidesman, 1762–63. Probably the Marstow, upholder of Fleet St who advertised in *Gazetteer and London Daily Advertiser*, 18 November 1756. Death reported, *Gents Mag.*, July 1795, when he was described as 'an eminent upholsterer' who 'had lately retired from business'. [D; GL, Upholders' Co. records; GL, MS 6561, p. 88]

Marston, William jnr, 71 Fleet St, London, upholder (1792). [D]

Marston & Legg, 71 Fleet St, London, upholders (1788–93). [D] See Samuel Legg.

Marston, William, Bristol, cm (1784–95). Recorded at Temple in 1784 and Island Ct in 1795. [D; poll bk]

Martain, John, address unrecorded, looking-glass maker (1718–20). Supplied looking-glasses to the Duke of Northumberland in 1718 costing £73 10s, and in 1720, £348. [V&A archives]

Marten, John, Lewes, Sussex, u (1802). [Poll bk] See Marten & Adams

Marten, William, Last Lane, Dover, Kent, cm (1838). [D]

Marten, William jnr, High Wycombe, Bucks., chairmaker (b. c.1820–41). Aged 21 at the time of the 1841 Census.

Marten & Adams, High St, Lewes, Sussex, u (1805). [D] See John Marten.

Martens, Peter, 8 Nassau St, Goodge St, London, cm and u (1839). [D]

Martin, —, Norwich, cm (1803). Subscribed to Sheraton's *Cabinet Dictionary*, 1803.

Martin, Alexander, Hedge Lane (now Coventry St), London, cm and upholder (1774–93). [D; poll bks]

Martin, Alexander, Whitcomb St, Leicester Sq., London, cm and u (1790–93). [D] Possibly connected with Thomas & Alexander Martin of 15 Panton St, Leicester Sq., an address close to Whitcomb St.

Martin, Ann, Merry Vale, Worcester, chair bottomer (1788). [D]

Martin, Benjamin, St Martin-in-the-Fields, London, cm (1709–28). Recorded in the St Martin's poor rate bk in 1709 at Oxindon St. Took app. named Joseph, son of Ken Woore joiner of Herefs., on 1 March 1714 for £10. Address given at Openden St, St Martin's, when he took out a Sun Insurance policy on 20 August 1728 for £200 on his house, glass in trade, and wearing apparel. [PRO, app. reg.; GL, Sun MS vol. 27, ref. 45480]

Martin, C., Boston, Lincs., cm and builder (d.1807). Recent death reported in *Gents Mag.*, July 1807.

Martin, Carl Gustav, address unrecorded, cm and furniture designer (1769). Came to London from Stockholm in 1769,

and remained in England for the rest of his life. A nephew of George Haupt and brother of the painter Elias Martin. Sold marquetry roundels to furniture makers and musical instrument case makers. [*Burlington*, 1972, p. 711; June 1980, p. 416]

Martin, Charles, 97 St John St, West Smithfield, London, cm and inlayer (1789–93). Declared bankrupt, *Derby Mercury*, 5 February 1789. [D]

Martin, Charles, Ipswich, Suffolk, upholder (1790). [Norwich poll bk]

Martin, Charles, Norwich, u (1801–18). Addresses given at 26 Hungate St, 1801–02, and 26 Elm Hill, c.1803–10. Trading also as an auctioneer in 1808. Former app. of Charles Martin and Benjamin Row, named George Arnold, upholder, admitted freeman on 27 September 1817. Former app. of Martin alone, named Edmund Henry Sheen, upholder, admitted freeman on 20 June 1818. [D; Norwich freemen reg. and poll bks]

Martin, Christopher, St Bride's, London, cm and bedstead maker (1747–69). Trade card gives address at 'The Star', by Fleet Mkt, near Fleet St, and states that he 'Makes & Sells all Sorts of Bedsteads, tables, Chests of Drawers, Desks, & all other Sorts of Joyners Goods in Mahogany, Walnut Tree & Wainscott, at Reasonable Rates.' Recorded at Ditch Side in 1747 and 1749 when he was fined for non-service at St Bride's; and in 1754 when he served as Scavenger, and in 1755 as Sidesman. Named in the Livery of the Joiners' Co. in 1750. His son, George Martin, was admitted freeman of the Upholders' Co. in 1769. Named in newspapers in 1747. [Heal; GL, Upholders' and Joiners' Co. records; GL, MS 6561, p. 80]

Martin, Cornelius, Dover, St, London, cm (1763). [Heal citing registers of unclaimed dividends of bank stock]

Martin, E. J., Northgate, Darlington, Co. Durham, carver and gilder (c.1835). Label in ornamental frame recorded on a gilt dolphin console table of late Regency date in the Fogg Art Museum, Harvard, Massachusetts. [Acc. No. 1943, 1482]

Martin, Edward, address unrecorded, upholder (1699). Admitted freeman of the Upholders' Co. on 15 August 1699. [GL, Upholders' Co. records]

Martin, Edward, at 'The Looking Glass', Cannon St, London, cm (1751). Sale of stock in trade by Mr Ashley announced in *General Advertiser*, 7 September 1751. Stock consisted of a 'great variety of Mahogany and Walnut-Tree Desks, and Bookcases with brass ornaments, sundry Mahogany Tables, a large parcel of Looking Glasses, an Indian Japan Cloaths Chest, India screens, some work Benches and sundry effects in the Cabinet Way. A Month Clock by Quare, in a Grenoble wood case.'

Martin, Edward, 41 Rupert St, London, u (1808). [D]

Martin, Edward, 28 Michael's Pl., Brompton, London, cm and u (1839). [D]

Martin, Frederick, Stratford, London, cm and u (1823–39). Recorded at Stratford Grove, 1835–39, and as Marten at Grove Common in 1838 when named in the Essex Jurors' Book for Becontree Hundred. [D; Essex RO, Q/RJ/2/1]

Martin, G., Union Pl., 93 North St, Exeter, Devon, cm (1832). [D] Probably George Martin.

Martin, George, Tenter Alley, Little Moorfields, London, cane chairmaker (1726). Took out a Sun Insurance policy on 6 April 1726 for £300, £200 accounting for utensils, stock and a shed. [GL, Sun MS vol. 21, ref. 38393]

Martin, George, Ipswich, Suffolk, chairmaker (1757). Named in the calendar of marriage licence bonds on 24 September 1757. [Suffolk RO, FAA: 50/2/89–93]

Martin, George, address unrecorded, upholder (1762–69). Son of Christopher Martin, bedstead maker of St Bride's, London;

app. to Richard Walker on 3 April 1762, and admitted freeman of the Upholders' Co. by servitude on 3 May 1769. [GL, Upholders' Co. records]

Martin, George, 11 Little Moorfields, London, u and cm (1789–93). [D]

Martin, George, Exeter, Devon, cm and chair manufacturer (1818–22). Trading in St Sidwell's parish in 1818; and at Lower North St in 1819. Marriage to Miss Jane Halls, eldest daughter of Mr Halls, supervisor of excise in Exeter, at St John's Church, reported on 10 December 1818 in an Exeter newspaper. Daughter Ann bapt. at St David's Church on 13 October 1819. [*Exeter Pocket Journal*, 1822; PR (bapt.)]

Martin, George, Neptune Pl., Trippett, Hull, Yorks., cm (1838–39). [D]

Martin, Hugh, Liverpool, cm (1833). App. to William John Roberts in 1833. [Liverpool app. enrolment bk]

Martin, J., 5 Middle New St, Shoe Lane, London, cm (1835). [D]

Martin, James, Drury Lane, London, u (1720–30). Recorded at 'The Golden Key & Crown', corner of White Hart Yd on 19 April 1720 when he took out a Sun Insurance policy on goods and merchandise in his house, and at 'The Crown & Key' in 1730 in newspapers. [GL, Sun MS vol. 11, p. 143; Heal]

Martin, James, Ipswich, Suffolk, cm (1751). Took app. named Tye in 1751. [S of G, app. index]

Martin, James, Bristol, cm (1823–37). Addresses given at 'The Swan with two Necks', Little Ann St in 1823; 13 Redcliff St in 1824; 4 Merchants Parade, Hotwells, 1828–29; and the 'White Lion', Gloucester Lane, 1836–37. [D]

Martin, James, 52 Campo Lane, Sheffield, Yorks., cm and u (1833). [D]

Martin, James, Whitehaven, Cumb., cm (1834). [D]

Martin, John, Ormskirk, Lancs., cm (1787–98). [D]

Martin, John, Market Harborough, Leics., cm (1791). [D]

Martin, John, 7 Pitfield St, Hoxton, London, cm (1820–28). [D]

Martin, John, 14 Greetham St, Liverpool, joiner and cm (1821–23). [D]

Martin, John, Doncaster, Yorks., cm (1822–37). Addresses given at Spring Gdns in 1822; Wood St, 1828–29; and Baxter Gate in 1837. [D]

Martin, John, 41 Bow Lane, Cheapside, London, cm (1826–27). [D]

Martin, John, Queen St, Bishop Wearmouth, Sunderland, Co. Durham, u (1827). [D]

Martin, John, Maidstone, Kent, cm (1831–39). Recorded as freeman in Romney Pl. in the 1834 register of electors. Trading there in 1838. [D; poll bks]

Martin, John, 63 Curtain Rd, London, cabinet turner (1835). [D]

Martin, John, 113 Union St, East Stonehouse, Plymouth, Devon, cm and u (1838). [D]

Martin, John, 64 Greenland St, Liverpool, joiner and cm (1839). [D]

Martin, Joshua, London, cm (1826–30). [Dover poll bks]

Martin, Minton, Bethnal Green Rd, London, carver and gilder (1831). [PRO, C13 322/19]

Martin, Richard, at 'The White Horse', Little Brickell [Little Brickhill], Bucks., upholder (1719). Took out a Sun Insurance policy on 11 April 1719 for goods and merchandise in his house only. [GL, Sun MS vol. 9, p. 184]

Martin, Richard, White Cross St, London, chairmaker (1741). Took out a Hand in Hand Insurance policy on 20 February 1741 for £100. [GL, Hand in Hand MS vol. 62, ref. 67465]

Martin, Richard, High Burgess St, Grimsby, Lincs., joiner and cm (1835). [D]

Martin, Rob., Bury St Edmund's, Suffolk, cm (1752–93). Took

apps named Blake in 1752 and Wood in 1756. [D; S of G, app. index]

Martin, Robert, Harts Row, Exeter, Devon, cm (1830). [*Exeter Pocket Journal*]

Martin, Robert, 48 Hurst St with shop at 31 Cornwallis St, Liverpool, joiner and cm (1837). [D]

Martin, Samuel, London, upholder (1754–86). Addresses given at Bucklersbury, 1771–75, no. 19, 1773–75; Walbrook, 1776–78; no. 32, 1776–77; and Snow Hill in 1786. Son of Harwood Martin, malt distiller of Bromley, Middlx; app. to Samuel Sleigh and Nicholas Vipond on 7 August 1754. Admitted freeman of the Upholders' Co. by servitude on 6 May 1762. Took apps named Samuel Ferris, 1771–78, and Samuel Holden, 1772–74. Declared bankrupt, *Gents Mag.*, November 1775. Recorded concerning a partnership in 1778–79. [D; GL, Upholders' Co. records; PRO, C13/2366/32]

Martin, Samuel, Norwich, cm, u and chairmaker (1799–1830). Addresses given at 2 Surrey St, c.1803; Surrey St in 1808; and St Stephen's, at some date between 1806–30. Admitted freeman on 21 September 1799, not by apprenticeship. Former app., Charles Fabb, cm, admitted on 24 February 1817; and Robert Riches, cm, on 3 May 1826. [D; Norwich freemen reg. and poll bks] See Martin & Perry.

Martin, Solomon, Union Rd, Plymouth, Devon, cm (1836). [D]

Martin, T., Lancaster. Named in the Gillow records in 1799 working on a chest. [Westminster Ref. Lib., vol. 344/98, p. 1543]

Martin, Thomas, address unrecorded, cm (1662). Supplied the Royal Household with a large table of inlaid wood in 1662. [PRO, LC 5/39, p. 171]

Martin, Thomas, Sunderland, Co. Durham, u (1784–98). Trading at Church St in 1784. [D]

Martin, Thomas, 11 Westmorland Buildings, Aldersgate St, London, cm (1808–12). [D]

Martin, Thomas & Alexander, 15 Panton St, Leicester Sq., London, cm (1808–27). [D]

Martin, Thomas, Norwich, cm (1818–d. 1845). Polled in 1818 of the parish of St Michael at Thorn. Will proved at Norwich in 1845. [Norfolk Record Soc., index of wills]

Martin, Thomas, High St, Worthing, Sussex, chairmaker (1823–39). [D] See Martin & Bennett.

Martin, Thomas, Bristol, cm, u and undertaker (1824–32). Addresses given at 24 Montague St in 1824; 8 Lower Montague St, 1825–26; Horse Fair, 1827–31; and 33 Redcliff Hill in 1832. [D]

Martin, Thomas, Ormskirk, Lancs., cm (1822–34). Trading at Moor St, 1825–34. [D]

Martin, Thomas, Newton Abbot and Newton Bushel, Devon cm (1838). [D]

Martin, W., Chester, cm (1812–19). Trading at Gorst Stacks in 1812 and Bridge St, 1818–19. [Poll bks]

Martin, William, Cambridge, u (1706). Notice in *London Gazette*, 6 March 1706 concerned the dividends of his estate on bankruptcy.

Martin, William, London, then Philadelphia, USA, upholder (before 1770). Advertisement in *Penn'a Chronicle*, 8 October 1770 read: 'WILLIAM MARTIN, Upholder, (Who served his apprenticeship to Mr. Palmer of London) Has opened shop in Front street, next door to the City Vendue House, where he intends to sell all sorts of chairs, sofas, couches, deception beds, and every thing in the upholders way. He being a young beginner in the business, hopes for encouragement from the gentry and public in general ...'.

Martin, William, Mount St, Hanover Sq., London, upholder (1781). Notice in *Leicester Journal*, 3 March 1781, concerned the dividends of his estate on bankruptcy.

Martin, William, address unrecorded, cm (1803). Subscribed to Sheraton's *Cabinet Dictionary*, 1803.

Martin, William, Bristol, cm, u and undertaker (1805–37). Addresses given at 22 Wilder St, 1805–07; Milk St in 1809; Barton Alley, 1810–12; 11 North St in 1813; 12 North St, 1814–33; and 15 Stoke's Croft, 1834–37. [D]

Martin, William, 77 Shudehill, Manchester, cm and chairmaker (1814–15). [D]

Martin, William, Liverpool, cm (1827–39). Addresses given at 58 Renshaw St in 1827; no. 28 in 1829; 16 Upper Newington with shop at 17 Renshaw St in 1835; 63 Park Lane with shop at 79 Blundell St in 1837; and 33 Lime St in 1839. [D]

Martin, William, 45 Southampton Row, Russell Sq., London, u (1829–39). [D]

Martin, William, 19 Charlotte St, Southport, Portsea, Portsmouth, Hants., cm and u (1830). [D]

Martin, William, 74 Worcester St, Birmingham, u (1830–35). Trading also at 59 Worcester St in 1830. [D]

Martin, William, Christchurch, Hants., u (1839). [D]

Martin & Bennett, North St, Worthing, Sussex, turner and chairmaker (1839). [D] See Thomas Martin.

Martin & Parry, address unrecorded. On 8 January 1832 supplied Sir Charles Blois of Cockfield Hall, Yoxford, Suffolk, with three hall chairs costing £7 8s. [Suffolk RO, HA30: 312/418] Probably:

Martin & Perry, Norwich, cm and u (1830–c.1840). Recorded at St Stephen's St in 1830. Trade card, c.1840, gives address at 1 and 2 Surry St and reads: 'Funerals Performed — The Trade Supplied — MARTIN & PERRY, Upholsterers and Cabinet Makers … Goods taken in exchange.' Card shows two coats of arms. [D; Norwich Local Hist. Lib] See Samuel Martin.

Martin & Smith, Norwich. Regency telescopic dining table recorded with backplates inscribed: 'New Invented dining tables by Martin & Smith, Norwich.' The end sections have broad rectangular tops with rounded corners, reeded edges and panelled friezes; each supported on four fluted legs, the outer two of sabre form, and joined by curved platform stretchers with brass lion-paw feet. [Sotheby's, 31 January 1964, lot 231]

Martindale, —, address unrecorded, u (1770). Named in the accounts of Lady Caroline Fleming Leicester of Tabley Hall, Cheshire, receiving £4 14s 3d in February 1770. [Chester RO, DLT/D46/2]

Martindale, Hector, High St, Grantham, Lincs., cm and u (1835). [D]

Martindale, John, 14 Brewer St, Golden Lane, London, upholder and cm (1784). [D]

Martindale, John, Stockton, Co. Durham, cm (1793). Subscribed to Sheraton's *Drawing Book*, 1793.

Martindale, Nathan, Whitcomb Ct, Hedge Lane (now Coventry St), London, cm (1755–74). Subscribed to Chippendale's *Director*, 1755. [Poll bk]

Martindale, Robert, address unrecorded, upholder (1760–84). Received regular payments for work, mostly unspecified, carried out for Lord Monson between 1760 and 1784; and ranging from £1 2s on 23 February 1761 to £63 13s on 22 January 1765. Items specified were a water clock, costing £1 2s on 23 February 1761; and a chair at £2 2s on 11 April. Between 1779–81 he carried out repairs, supplied carpets and curtains, and provided 'a Mah. Childs Chair Brass Plates Iron Fastenings to Foot Board etc.' This bill, dated 28 March 1781, totalled £31 14s 8d. He is probably the Martindale who supplied inner and outer elm coffins for the funeral of the Hon. Harriet Ann Monson. [Lincoln RO, Monson 10/1/A/3, 5 and 6; 11/27; 11/62/S]

Martindale, Robert, 14 Brewer St, Golden Sq., London, upholder and cm (1774–85). [D; poll bk]

Martindale, Thomas, Lancaster. Named in the Gillow records, 1818–27. [Westminster Ref. Lib.]

Martindale (or Mattindale), Thomas, 71 King St, Whitehaven, Cumb., joiner and cm (1828–34). [D]

Martinelli, Lewis, 82 Leather Lane, London, carver, gilder, printseller, barometer and thermometer manufacturer (1803–11). Trade card shows classical female figure, weeping widow and two barometers. [D; Goodison, *Barometers*; Banks Coll., BM]

Martinelli, Lewis & Son, 62 King St, Southwark, London, looking-glass, barometer and thermometer makers, optician (1838–46). [Goodison, *Barometers*]

Martinelli, Peter, 33 New Inn Yd, Shoreditch, London, looking-glass manufacturer (1839). [D]

Martinet, André, London, cm or 'menuisier' (1681). Named in the Threadneedle St Relief records on 28 March 1681 as having 'Arrived from Paris 15 days ago with a wife & 4 children', and being given £2 5s since he 'wanteth some tools'. [*Hogarth Soc.*, 1949, p. 138]

Martlew, Richard, Moor St, Ormskirk, Lancs., cm (1825–34). [D]

Martlew, William, 2 Mary Ann St, Brownlow Hill, Liverpool, chairmaker (1835). [D]

Martley, Richard, Ormskirk, Lancs., cm (1822). [D]

Marton, Ellis, Church Gate, Leicester, cm (1828). [D]

Martyn, Thomas, London, cm (1774). Supplied an inlaid commode costing £12 to Burton Constable House on 13 October 1774. [Humberside RO, Burton Constable vouchers]

Marvin, Edward, Camden Alley, Portsea, Portsmouth, Hants., cm, u and chairmaker (1823–39). Recorded at no. 5 in 1830 and no. 6 in 1839. [D]

Marvin, Edward, Union St, Ryde, Isle of Wight, Hants., cm and u (1830–39). [D]

Marvin, George, Point, Cowes, Isle of Wight, Hants., cm (1830–39). [D]

Marvin, R., 34 Queen St, Portsea, Portsmouth, Hants., cm and u (1839). [D]

Marvin, Robert & Thomas, Walkergate, Alnwick, Northumb., cm and joiner (1834). [D]

Marwick, John, corner of Heathlock Ct, Strand, London, carver (1775). Took out a Sun Insurance policy in 1775 for £100 of which utensils, stock and goods accounted for £10. [GL, Sun MS vol. 243, p. 356]

Marwood, John, Exeter, Devon, cm (1813–38). Recorded at Fore St Hill in 1813 when his daughter Eliza was bapt. at St Mary Steps on 10 June. [D; PR (bapt.)]

Mascitti, P., 5 Commercial Rd, Whitechapel, London, looking-glass frame maker (1835). [D]

Mase(lon), Phillip, West Wycombe, Bucks., chairmaker (b.c.1791–1841). Aged 50 at the time of the 1841 Census.

Masey, William, address unrecorded, upholder (1707). Admitted freeman of the Upholders' Co. on 18 June 1707. [GL, Upholders' Co. records]

Mash, —, Wardour St, Soho, London, cm (d.1749). His obituary in *General Advertiser*, Monday 4 September 1749 read: 'Thursday last died at his House at Chelsea Mr. Mash formerly an eminent Cabinet Maker in Wardour Street, Soho, having acquired a handsome fortune, had retir'd from Business.'

Mash, Thomas, 102 Wardour St, Soho, London, u and furniture broker (1829–39). [D] Late 18th- or early 19th-century mahogany secretaire-bookcase recorded, the glazed panelled doors in the upper part with arched astragals; the centre with deep drawer forming a secretaire; and a cupboard below with beaded borders to the panels; stamped: 'Thomas Mash, 102 Wardour Street'. His stamp is also found on a Regency mahogany breakfast table, crossbanded and inlaid with brass stringing; on turned baluster stem and splayed four-leg base. [Christie's, 27 November 1969, lot 145; 7 April 1983, lot 73]

Mashiter, Gardner, Lancaster, cm (1799–1800). [Lancaster freemen rolls]

Mashiter, George, Lancaster, cm (1799–1802). Admitted freeman, 1799–1800. Named in the Gillow records, 1801–02. [Lancaster freemen rolls; Westminster Ref. Lib., Gillow records]

Mashiter, George, Liverpool, cm (1823–27). Addresses given at 22 Bedford St in 1823; and 9 and 18 Park Pl. in 1827. [D]

Mashiter, John, Liverpool, u (1816–23). Described as 'late of Lancaster', when his marriage to Miss Catherine Swift of Liverpool at St Peter's Church was reported in *Liverpool Mercury*, 6 September 1816. Recorded at 1 Pepper St in 1821 and 9 Springfield St in 1823. [D]

Mashiter, Richard, Lancaster, cm (b. *c*.1754–d.1806). Admitted freeman, 1771–72. A Richard Mashiter of Lancaster is recorded as having taken eighteen app. cm between 6 January 1785 and 6 April 1807. Described as 'Gentleman' when he acted as executor of John Caton's will on 24 September 1805. Died on 16 January 1806, aged 52, and buried in Lancaster Priory Churchyard. [Lancaster app. reg., freemen rolls and poll bk; Lancaster Ref. Lib.] Possibly two tradesmen of the same name are concerned here.

Maskens (or Maskins), Adrian (or Adrianus), Soho, London, carver, gilder and picture frame maker (1780–1807). Addresses given at 46 Compton St in 1780; 42 Greek St, 1789–1802; and 27 Little Newport St in 1807. Took out Sun Insurance policies in 1779 for £1,000, utensils, stock and goods accounting for £550, plus £300 on his workshop; in 1780 for £400 on his house; in 1784 for £1,700 of which utensils, stock and goods accounted for £450, workshop, £300; on 22 April 1801 for £900, utensils and stock accounting for £600; and on 26 March 1807 for £800, £150 on utensils and stock. Trade card recorded, stating: 'Three Quarters Kit-Cats and Half-lengths may be had in a Minute's Notice for Ready Money.' [D; GL, Sun MS vol. 276, p. 75; vol. 277, p. 149; vol. 284, p. 389; vol. 322, p. 293; vol. 419, ref. 718195; vol. 440, ref. 800677; Heal]

Maskens, John, 42 Greek St, Soho, London, carver and gilder (1803–08). [D]

Maskill, Boyce, Beccles, Suffolk, u (1797–98). Declared bankrupt, *Liverpool Advertiser*, 9 April 1798. [D]

Maskins, Ernest, Compton St, Soho, London, carver and gilder (1784). [D]

Maslin, Thomas, 4 Goldsmiths Row, East Harding St, Fetter Lane, London, gilder (1779). Insured his house for £100 in 1779. [GL, Sun MS vol. 273, p. 206]

Maslin, Thomas, 25 John St, Holland St, Blackfriars Rd, London, carver and gilder (1808). [D]

Mason, —, address unrecorded, gilder (1732). Named in the accounts of Benjamin Mildmay, Earl Fitzwalter, on 7 April 1732 receiving £3 12s for 'gilding the two chimney pieces in the N.E. rooms' chief apartment'; on 29 April £1 7s 'for gilding the frame of the table in the Picture Room and the medal and in full for gilding to this day'; and on 25 September, £2 12s 5d 'for gilding the chimney piece in the drawing room & in full of all accounts for gilding to this day.' [A. C. Edwards, *The Accounts of Benjamin Mildmay, Earl Fitzwalter*, pp. 46 and 48]

Mason, —, address unrecorded (1810). On 4 December 1810 he was paid £60 for picture frames supplied to Sir John Geers Cotterell, Bart, of Garnons, near Hereford, and Hertford St, London. [Herefs. RO, Garnons papers, W69/III/182] On 24 April 1815 he was paid 11s for a table, and 9s for mending a clothes press for Mr Dunne of Gatley Park, near Leominster,

Herefs. [Herefs. RO, Gatley papers, F76/III/40] Possibly John Mason of High Town, Hereford.

Mason, —, Derby, u (1822). Named in the Chatsworth furnishing accounts receiving £24 4s in 1822.

Mason, Alice, 66 Vauxhall Rd, Liverpool, u (1811). [D]

Mason, Allan, Low Ackworth, Yorks., joiner and cm (1837). [D]

Mason, Ann, Southgate, Sleaford, Lincs., chairmaker and woodturner (1826). [D]

Mason, Charles, Thames St, London, cm (1705). Notice in *The Post Man*, 15 December 1705 read: 'Lost or mislaid, since the 3rd of December, a Bank Note, No. 135, dated November 26th, 1705, for £45 payable to Mr. Will. Stuart Bearer. Whoever hath taken it up, and will bring it to Mr. Ch. Mason, Cabinet-maker, by the Still-yard in Thames-street, shall have a Guinea Reward, it being of no use to any but to the Owner, payment being stopt at the Bank.'

Mason, Christopher, Charles Ct, London, carver and gilder (1749). [Poll bk]

Mason, Christopher, Andover, Hants., cm (1792–93). [D]

Mason, Daniel, London, cm and u (1749–74). Recorded at the 'Golden Ball', corner of Newport St, Long Acre in 1756, and King St, Covent Gdn, 1749–74. Polled at Westminster in 1749. Subscribed to Chippendale's *Director*, 1754. Bill from Mason in the BM is to the Earl of Winterton, dated 14 June 1756, for mahogany and oak furniture, including a dressing glass in a mahogany frame, at 16s 6d; a 'Mohog.ʸ fier Screen', £1 5s; 'a Large Mahog.ʸ Butlers Trea with Brass Corners', 12s; 'a Mahog.ʸ Knife Trea Brass Handel & Corners', 8s 6d; and two wainscott bureaus at £2 16s each. Bill heading is embellished with Mason's shop sign, a ball hanging from a Rococo bracket. On 27 May 1762 the Earl of Ancaster paid Dan. Mason £3 13s 6d for a 'Wallnutt Tree Table'. [Poll bks; *C. Life*, 2 May 1957, pp. 865–66; *Conn.*, 1923, p. 208; Lincoln RO, 2 ANC 6/8, p. 102]

Mason, Edward, St Martin's, Stamford Baron, Lincs., chairmaker (1722). Advertisement in *Stamford Mercury*, 23 August 1722 read: 'These are to give Notice to all Persons that have Occasion for fine Chairs of the newest Fashion; crooked Backs with French or Claw-Feet, or of any stain upon the polished Work, that they may be furnished by Edward Mason, Chair-Maker in St Martin's, Stamford Baron, as cheap as in London, and the work as good.'

Mason, Edward, Edward St, London, cm (1749). [Poll bk]

Mason, Edward, 23 Eaton St, Liverpool, cm (1823). [D]

Mason, Elizabeth, College Hill, St Michael's Royal, London, cm (1723–24). Took out a Sun Insurance policy on 5 September 1723 for £500 on goods and merchandise in her house. A memo dated 15 January 1724 read 'Elizabeth Mason daughter administratrix'. [GL, Sun MS vol. 16, ref. 29806]

Mason, George, Lancaster, cm (1827–28). [Lancaster freemen rolls]

Mason, George, Heigham Fields, Norwich, cm and u (1839). [D]

Mason, Henry, Beverley, Yorks., cm (1759). Took app. named Bird in 1759. [S of G, app. index]

Mason, Henry John, Norwich, upholder (1828–30). Polled in 1830 of the parish of St Stephen. Son of Henry Mason, printer; dates for admission as freeman given on 16 and 23 August 1828. [Norwich freemen reg. and rolls]

Mason, Henry R., 29 Coldbath Sq., Clerkenwell, London, fancy cm and u (1835–39). Trading also at 18 Coppice Row in 1835. [D]

Mason, Isaac & Haygarth, James, Depford-Bridge, Greenwich, London, cm, broker and upholder (1791–1802). Declared bankrupt in *Williamson's Liverpool Advertiser*, 1 April 1793. Notices concerning dividends appeared in *Billinge's*

Liverpool Advertiser, 12 December 1796 and 1 May 1797. Mason alone was declared bankrupt in *Billinge's Liverpool Advertiser*, 20 December 1802. [D]

Mason, James, Carey St, Lincoln's Inn, London, upholder (1765). [D]

Mason, James, Lancaster, cm (1779–87). Admitted freeman, 1779–80. Named in the Gillow records in 1787. [Lancaster freemen rolls; Westminster Ref. Lib., Gillow]

Mason, James, High St, Guildford, Surrey, chairmaker (1796). [Poll bk]

Mason, James, Wem, Salop, cm (1797). [D]

Mason, James, Broad St, Worcester, cm, u and paper hanger (1822–40). Recorded at no. 48 in 1828, no. 49 in 1830, no. 44 in 1835, no. 45, 1830–37, and College St in 1840. Admitted freeman in 1822, and named in the Worcester freemen rolls in December 1835. Former app., George Loudon Chandler, admitted freeman in 1835. [D]

Mason, John, Bedford Ct, London, cm (1749). [Poll bk]

Mason, John, Godalming, Surrey, chairmaker (1761). Discharge from Debtors' Prison reported in *London Gazette*, 15 September 1761.

Mason, John, New St, Carnaby Mkt, London, u (1774). [Poll bk]

Mason, John, Basingstoke, Hants., upholder and auctioneer (1784). [D]

Mason, John, 21 Montague St, Spitalfields, London, chairmaker (1790–93). [D]

Mason, John, 21 Pelham St, Spitalfields, London, chandler, chairmaker and dealer in coals (1791). Took out a Sun Insurance policy on 3 September 1791 for £650 of which utensils and stock accounted for £250. [GL, Sun MS vol. 379, p. 487]

Mason, John, Wem, Salop, cm (1797–98). [D]

Mason, John, St John's Sq., Clerkenwell, London, cabinet japanner (1808–17). Recorded at no. 32, 1808–16, and no. 13 in 1817. [D]

Mason, John, 13 Hunt St, Mile End, New Town, London, chairmaker (1809–11). [D]

Mason, John, 17 Lambeth Marsh, London, cm and chairmaker (1813). [D]

Mason, John, 44 Charlotte St, Gt Surrey St, London, cm (1829). [D] See Mason & Co.

Mason, John, High Town, Hereford, cm and u (1822). [D] See Mason, —.

Mason, John, Lancaster (1817–40). Admitted freeman, 1817–18. Named in the Gillow records, 1827–40. [Lancaster freemen rolls; Westminster Ref. Lib., Gillow]

Mason, John, London, cm (1830). [Maidstone poll bk]

Mason, John, Horse Shoe Corner, Lancaster, cm (1834). [D]

Mason, John jnr, Lancaster. Named in the Gillow records in 1838. [Westminster Ref. Lib.]

Mason, Jos., address unrecorded. In 1767 carried out furniture repairs for Sir John Griffin Griffin at Audley End, Essex. [Essex RO, D/DBy/A25]

Mason, Joseph, Bean Ing, Leeds, Yorks., cm (1822). [D]

Mason, Jos., Sandgate, Penrith, Cumb., joiner and/or cm (1829). [D]

Mason, Richard, address unrecorded, carver and gilder (1765–66). Submitted bill to the Earl of Winterton for a number of household jobs including making a 'frame in burnish'd gold' for a 'large Carlo Moratt picture', at a cost of £13 4s; and re-gilding another frame for £1 4s. He also whitened some ceilings. [Heal Coll., BM]

Mason, Richard, London. On 28 May 1774 Edward Knight of Wolverley House, Worcs., paid 'Mason for a Tortoiseshell inlaid commode £17.10.0.' [Kidderminster Lib., Knight MS]

Mason, Richard, Frederick Pl., Tottenham Ct Rd, London,

carver and gilder (1810). Took out a Sun Insurance policy on 14 April 1810 for £1,200 of which £100 accounted for household goods and store in a house at 34 Norfolk St, Middlx Hospital, in his own tenure, and £200 on stock, utensils and glass therein. [GL, Sun MS vol. 453, ref. 844603] Late 18th- or early 19th-century trade card of R. Mason gives address at 34 Norfolk St, Middlx Hospital, and trade as carver and gilder to HRH the Prince of Wales. [Banks Coll., BM]

Mason, Richard, 34 Newman St, Oxford St, London, carver and gilder (1813). [D]

Mason, Richard, 5 Union St, South Audley St, London, cm and u (1839). [D]

Mason, Robert Crump, Birmingham, cm, u and broker (1822–30). Trading at Snow Hill in 1822, and 53 Snow hill and 136 Gt Hampton St, 1828–30. [D]

Mason, S., Weaverham, Cheshire, cm. Mahogany long-case clock, c.1800, recorded bearing inscription on hood: 'S. MASON CABINET MAKER WEAVERHAM'.

Mason, Sophia, 26 School Lane, Liverpool, u (1829). [D]

Mason, Theophilus, Newcastle-under-Lyme, Staffs., cm (1823–37). Recorded at Lower St in 1832. [Poll bks]

Mason, Thomas, Leicester, cm (1723). App. to John Brothers, cm, in 1723. [Leicester freemen rolls]

Mason, Thomas, London, u and/or cm (1783). On 22 December 1783 Charles Towneley paid Mason £2 2s for a medal case; and on 23 December £6 6s for 'a Sopha value 4.4- for a Sopha covered wᵗʰ blue Morocco'. [Charles Towneley's account bk in private ownership]

Mason, Thomas, Back 22 North St, Dale St, Liverpool, cm (1796). [D]

Mason, Thomas, High St, Guildford, Surrey, chairmaker (1796–1818). Recorded 'in the yard at the back of his son's house in High St.' in 1818. [Poll bks]

Mason, Thomas, Worcester, cm (1802–30). Trading at Friar St, 1828–30, also as an u and broker. App. to Richard Crump; admitted freeman on 1 February 1802. [D; Worcester freemen rolls]

Mason, Thomas, 22 Milton St, Liverpool, cm (1818). Admitted freeman on 11 June 1818. [Liverpool freemen reg.]

Mason, Thomas, 59 Princes St, Leicester Sq., London, cm, u, auctioneer and appraiser (1822–39). Trade card recorded. [D; Heal]

Mason, Thomas, Ripley, Yorks., cm (1830). [D]

Mason, Thomas, Cambridge, cm (1832–41). Recorded at Bradwell's Yd, St Andrew's St in 1832, and Orchard St, 1835–37. [Poll bks]

Mason William, Norwich, u (1677). Former app., Sam Reeve, admitted freeman on 11 July 1677. [Norwich freemen reg.]

Mason, William, Hawes, Yorks., joiner and cm (1823). [D]

Mason, William, London, cm (1826). [Maidstone poll bk]

Mason, William, 1 Ship St, Brighton, Sussex, carver and gilder (1832–40). [D]

Mason, William, Lanchester, Durham, joiner and cm (1828–29). [D]

Mason, William, 185 Sloane St, Chelsea, London, cm (1839). Took app. named William Andrews in 1839. [D; Westminster Ref. Lib., MS E3559, Grinsell's Charity app. indentures]

Mason, William, St Mary's Passage, Cambridge, carver and gilder (1839). [D]

Mason & Co., 44 Charlotte St, Blackfriars, London, cm (1826–27). [D] See John Mason.

Mason & More, 110 Paul St, Finsbury, London, wholesale cabinet, chair and sofa manufacturers and dealers in mahogany (1837–39). [D]

Mason & Norris, Charing Cross, St John's Madder Mkt, Norwich, u (1839). [D]

Maspoli, Augustus, Hull, Yorks., looking-glass, picture frame, weather-glass, barometer and thermometer manufacturer, jeweller and silversmith (1826–51). Addresses given at 49 Salthouse Lane, 1826–31; in partnership with James Maspoli, 1831–35; and at 79 Lowgate, 1835–51. Also sold telescopes and spectacles. [D; Goodison, *Barometers*]

Maspoli, James, Hull, Yorks., looking-glass, picture frame and barometer maker, optician and jeweller (1831–59). Addresses given at 49 Salthouse Lane in 1831; 79 Lowgate in 1835; and 17 Robinson Row, 1839–48. In partnership with Augustus Maspoli, possibly his father, 1831–35. [Goodison, *Barometers*]

Massa, William, at 'The Golden Head', near New Inn, Wych St, Drury Lane, London, carver and gilder (c.1780). Trade card recorded. [Heal]

Massey, —, address unrecorded, cm. In 1737 he was named in 'An account of all workmen's bills paid by the Duke of Norfolk for repairing & altering, furnishing his Grace's house in St. James' Street for ye reception of His Royal Highness ye Prince of Wales & his Family'. Mr Massey, cm, was paid £13 3s. [Duchy of Cornwall Office, Household accounts of Frederick, Prince of Wales, vol. 7, p. 186]

Massey (or Massay), Abraham, London, japanner and cm (1713–d.1746). Recorded at 'The Two White Posts', Gt Queen St, St Giles-in-the-Fields, on 18 September 1728, when he took out a Sun Insurance policy for £800 of which £100 accounted for utensils and stock. Took app. on 22 June 1736. Obituary in *General Advertiser*, 18 January 1746 read: 'A few days ago died, at his House in Great Queen Street, Mr. Abraham Massay, said to be the most eminent Japanner in England'. [GL, Sun MS vol. 27, ref. 45486; PRO, app. reg.]

Massey, John, 1 Johnson's Yd, High St, Liverpool, chairman (1790). [D]

Massey, Jonathan, Broad St, Ludlow, Salop, cm (1782). Took out a Sun Insurance policy in 1782 for £800, of which £350 accounted for utensils and stock. [GL, Sun MS vol. 301, p. 580]

Massey, Mathew, Liverpool, cm (1792–1802). App. to Isaac Marsh in 1792, and petitioned freedom on servitude in 1802, paying 6s 8d. [Liverpool freemen's committee bk]

Massey, Robert, Liverpool, cm (1809). Admitted freeman as son of George Massey, cooper, on 28 August 1809, paying 3s 4d. [Liverpool freemen's committee bk]

Massey (or Masey), Thomas, 124 Blackman St, Southwark, London, cm (1789–1811). [D]

Massey, Thomas, Blackfriar's Rd, Southwark, London, cm (1811). His wife, Sarah (late Sarah Jenner) is recorded as having workshops in Robin's Ct, Blackman St. [PRO, C13 661/12]

Massey, Thomas, Chester, cm (1830). Marriage to Miss Mary Bell of Chester at St Oswald's Church on 7 February reported in *Chester Courant and Anglo-Welsh Gazette*, 9 February 1830.

Massey, William, Glover's Yd, Market Pl., Leeds, Yorks., joiner and cm (1815–16). Advertised in *Leeds Mercury*, 1816, that he had taken over the premises of his late brother-in-law, Thomas Weare, and 'hopes, by a strict attention to Business, to merit the continued Favours of Mr. Weare's friends, as well as a share of Public Patronage.' Placed a similar notice in *Leeds Intelligencer*, 6 March 1815.

Massey, William, Altrincham, Cheshire, cm (1822). [D]

Masson, J., 53 Dorset St, Manchester Sq., London, u (1835). [D]

Masson, John, 11 Henrietta St, Cavendish Sq., London, u (1820). [D]

Masson, John, 29 Orchard St, Portman Sq., London, u (1825–28). [D]

Masterman, Benjamin, York, cm (1831). Son of Benjamin Masterman, farmer of Nun Monkton; app. to William Groves, cm, on 26 October 1831. [York app. reg.]

Masterman, John, Queen St, Park, Southwark, London, Windsor, dyed and garden chairmaker (1790–96). [D]

Masters, Charles, at 'The Eagle & Child', at the ditch near Holborn Bridge, London, u (1725). Took out a Sun Insurance policy on 8 July 1725 for £500 on goods and merchandise in his house. [GL, Sun MS vol. 20, ref. 36275]

Masters, David, Tenterden, Kent, cm and auctioneer etc. (1824–38). [D]

Masters, James, 2 Castle St, Bristol, cm (1792–94). [D]

Masters, James, High St, Tenterden, Kent, cm (1839). [D]

Masters, John, 40 East St, Weymouth, Dorset, cm and u (1840). [D]

Masters, John, St Alban's Row, Weymouth, Dorset, cm and u (1840). [D]

Masters, Joseph, 45 Hill St, Birmingham, cm (1818). [D]

Masters, M., Romsey, Hants., chair and basket maker (1823–24). [D]

Masters, Richard, Reading, Berks., cm (1784). [Bristol poll bk]

Masters, Stephen, 23 and 24 High St, Hastings, Sussex, cm and u (1826). [D]

Masters, William, at 'The Golden Fleece', Coventry St, Piccadilly, London, cm, upholder, appraiser and undertaker (c.1740–61). Ran a flourishing business, although his only recorded productions are at Blair Castle, Perthshire, supplied to the 2nd Duke of Atholl between c.1747–60. Twenty bills with the heading of a fleece in a Rococo cartouche are preserved at Blair Castle, totalling about £4,700. He was largely responsible for refurbishing the State Rooms, and pieces identified by his bills are dumb waiters, supplied in 1749; a 'Large mahogany frame for a slab with shaped feet & a leaf on the Knees' on 10 May 1749; a set of twelve oak hall chairs in 1751; a large mahogany sideboard table 'in one piece of fine Wood, Keywork round the frame & Gothick brackets', on 10 February 1753; a mahogany tripod table with an octagonal top supplied in 1751 or 55; a set of chairs in the blue bedroom in 1756; a four-poster bed with clustered Gothic shafts and a cresting decorated with 'fleur-de-lys' and Rococo ornament, hung with the original crimson damask, in 1756; a tea-table with a gallery top, and a set of chairs and stools in the small drawing room, 1756; and on 20 February 1756 '2 Mahogany candlestands with openwork tops and fluted pillars ribb'd … £3.' [DEF; GCM, pls 220–21; C. *Life*, 11 and 18 November 1949; *Conn.*, vol. 154, 1963, pp. 77–83; A. Coleridge, *Thomas Chippendale*, pp. 156–57, pls 395–402]

Masters, William, Princes St, Wardour St, London, u (1749). [Poll bk]

Mastin, Charles & Son, Market Pl., Boston, Lincs., upholders (1805). [D]

Maston, J., 81 Hatton Gdn, London, u (1820). [D]

Matheon, Robert, London, cm (1793). Subscribed to Sheraton's *Drawing Book*, 1793.

Mather, Mrs, Cheapside, Nottingham, u (1799–1822). Recorded as Mrs Mather & Son in 1822. [D] See H. Mather & Son, John Mather and Mather & Son.

Mather, D., 20 Seymour St, Portman Sq., London, cm (1835). [D]

Mather, H. & Son, Cheapside, Nottingham, u (1818). [D]

Mather, John (snr?), Nottingham, u (1759–d. 1779). Named in the Nottingham burgess list in 1759. Took apps named James Trubshaw in 1765 and William Kirkham in 1772. Probate will dated 24 April 1779. [Notts. RO, probate records; app. list] Possible confusion with:

Mather, John (jnr?), Nottingham, cm and u (1774–1825). Recorded at Rotten Row in 1774, and Cheapside, 1806–25.

Named in the Nottingham burgess list in 1794. [D; poll bks] See Mather & Son.

Mather, John, Broad Ct, Long Acre, London, cm (1775). Insured houses in Lambeth for £500. [GL, Sun MS vol. 245, p. 81]

Mather, John, Red Lion Ct, Drury Lane, London, cm (1778). Insured his house for £200 in 1778. [GL, Sun MS vol. 267, p. 299]

Mather, Robert, Hall's Ct, Newgate St, Newcastle, u (1833). [D]

Mather, William, address unrecorded, upholder (1732–44). Son of John Mather, Doctor of Divinity at Oxford University; app. to John Fox on 16 July 1737, and admitted freeman of the Upholders' Co. by servitude on 4 October 1744. [GL, Upholders' Co. records]

Mather, William, 29 Redcross St, Liverpool, chairmaker (1774–77). [D]

Mather & Son, Cheapside, Nottingham, u (1805). [D] See Mrs Mather, H. Mather & Son and John Mather.

Mathew, Mathew, 14 Plumber's St, City Rd, London, cm (1808). [D]

Mathews, —, address unrecorded, u (1721). Named in the accounts for Erddig, Clwyd, on 10 November 1721 receiving payment for three days work of 4s 6d; and on 29 November for a shaving-glass costing 15s. [V&A archives]

Mathews, —, London, u (1766). Named in the Duke of Portland's account book kept by his steward John Hutchinson, on 1 November 1766 receiving £20 19s for work carried out at Burlington House. [Notts. RO, DD5P 3/1]

Mathews, Charles, 1 Powells Pl., City Rd, London, u (1826–27). [D]

Mathews, George, 30 Gutter Lane, Cheapside, London, turner and polisher of silver (1808). [D]

Mathews, George & Thomas, 100 Norton St, Portland Pl., London, carvers and gilders (1826–39). Thomas was trading from 1826–35 and 1839, George in 1837. [D]

Mathews, H., 16 Budge Row, London, u (1829). [D]

Mathews, J. F., Market Pl., Leighton Buzzard, Beds., cm (1839). [D] See Matthews, —.

Mathews, Jane, 441 Strand, London, carver and gilder (1779). [D] See also John Matthews at this address, possibly Jane's father. J. Mathews was trading in 1800–01, and is probably the daughter continuing her father's business.

Mathews, John, Worksop, Notts. (?), u (1765–66). Carried out work at Welbeck Abbey, 1765–66, receiving payment of £20 19s 1d. [Notts. RO, DD5P, 3/4]

Mathew(s), Samuel, Thames Ditton, Surrey, u and builder (1838–39). Trading as Samuel & Son, u and cm, in 1839. [D]

Mathews, Thomas, High St, Leighton Buzzard, Beds., cm (1839). [D] See Matthews, —.

Mathews, William, 24 John St, Marylebone, London, cm (1835). [D]

Mathews, William, Liverpool, cm (1836). App. to William John Roberts in 1836. [Liverpool app. enrolment bk]

Mathews, William, High St, Wincanton, Som., cm and u (1839). [D]

Mat(t)hias, Lewis, London, cm (1810–20). Addresses given at 88 Upper East Smithfield, 1810–20; and also 6 and 7 King St, Tower Hill in 1813. Took out Sun Insurance policies on 28 March 1810, 3 May and 1 July 1813 each for £300, stock and utensils accounting for £100. [D; GL, Sun MS vol. 449, ref. 841708; vol. 462, ref. 881832; vol. 463, ref. 883543]

Mathieson (or Matheson), Robert, Jervis St, Liverpool, cm (1835–39). Recorded at no. 4, 1835–37, and no. 7 in 1839. [D]

Mathison, Joseph, address unrecorded, cm (1754). Subscribed to Chippendale's *Director*, 1754.

Mathison, Richard, Southwark, London, cm (1770). The *Cambridge Chronicle and Journal*, September 1770, reported that he sold his goods at the annual Stirbitch Fair held in September just outside Cambridge. [*Furn. Hist.*, 1978]

Mathson, Robert, 4 Randles Pl., Christian St, Liverpool, cm (1829). [D]

Mathue(?), Samuel, Norwich, cm (1817). Former app., Percy St Quintin, cm, admitted freeman on 3 May 1817. [Norwich freemen reg.]

Mathyson, Mr, Maiden Lane, Covent Gdn, London, picture frame maker (1747). A Mr Salmon gave lectures on geography at his rooms on Mathyson's premises. [*General Advertiser*, 19 July 1747]

Mathyson, Charles, London, picture frame maker (1749–c.1770). Rococo trade card, c.1770, states that he had '…Removed from Grafton Street to Maiden Lane facing Bedford Street, Covent Garden' and that he 'Makes and Sells all Sorts of Frames for Paintings, Glasses and Prints in Black or Gold and all other Ornaments, Carv'd and Gilt at the Lowest Prices. N.B. Paintings & Prints carefully Clean'd, Lin'd and Mended in the best Manner.' Polled at Westminster in 1749. [Heal]

Maton, Thomas, Hereford, cm and u (1830–37). Recorded at Broad St in 1835 and St Owen St in 1837. Supplied 'A Mahogany Consul Table' costing £6 16s 6d to Captain N. L. Pateshall, of Hereford, on 1 October 1830. [D; poll bk; Herefs. RO, F60/228]

Matron, John, Skipton, Yorks., cm (1831). [Holy Trinity PR]

Matson, Benjamin, Sculcoates, Hull, Yorks, cm (1808). App. to Thomas Robinson of Hull in June 1808. [Hull app. reg.]

Matson, Charles, Canterbury, Kent, u (1780–96). Trading in Wincheap, 1790–94, and Northgate in 1796. Named as a freeman of Canterbury in 1780. [Canterbury freemen rolls and poll bks]

Matthew, John, parish of St Leonard, Bristol, upholder (1784). [Poll bk]

Matthew, Samuel, 27 Tabernacle Walk, Finsbury Sq., London, cm and u (1808–27). [D]

Mat(t)hewman, George, Wakefield, Yorks., cm and u (1828–37). Recorded at Kirkgate, 1828–29, and Westgate, 1830–37. [D]

Matthews, —, Leighton Buzzard, Beds., cm and u (c.1840). Mahogany chest of drawers, c.1840, recorded bearing printed paper label which reads: 'MATTHEWS CABINET AND UPHOLSTERY WAREHOUSE LEIGHTON BUZZARD.' See J. F. Mathews, and Thomas Mathews.

Matthews, Edward John, Bury St Edmunds, Suffolk, u, cm, paper hanger, carver and gilder (1836–39). Trading at College St in 1836 and 27 Angel Hill in 1839. [D; poll bk] See William Matthews.

Matthews, Henry, South Parade, Penzance, Cornwall, cm etc. (1830). [D]

Mat(t)hews, James, 191 White Cross St, Cripplegate, London, cm and u (1790–1811). Took out a Sun Insurance policy on 3 September 1790 for £300, including £20 on utensils and stock in his workshop only. [D; GL, Sun MS ref. 573208, p. 542]

Matthews, James, 110 Fenchurch St, London, appraiser, upholder etc. (1809–19). Filed a Chancery suit together with William Tuck, wine merchant of Tower St, in 1811. Matthews was trading as Matthews & Co. in 1817, and as Mathews & Taylor in 1819. [D; PRO, C13 661/7]

Matthews, John, address unrecorded, upholder (1760). Son of Amos Matthews, merchant of Tiverton, Devon. Admitted freeman of the Upholders' Co. by redemption on 2 October 1760. [GL, Upholders' Co. records]

Matthews, John, 420 Strand, London, carver, gilder and printseller (1782). Took out a Sun Insurance policy in 1782 for £500 of which utensils, stock and goods accounted for £200. [GL, Sun MS vol. 298, p. 312]

Mat(t)hews, John, 441 Strand, London, carver and gilder (1789–97). Jane Mathews is recorded at this address in 1799, and J. Mathews, 1800–01, presumably Jane succeeding her father. [D]

Matthews, John, Precinct of Bedford, Exeter, Devon, cm (1803). [Militia Census]

Matthews, John, Barton St, Bristol, u (1805–39). Trading at no. 8, 1805–16, and no. 9, 1817–39. [D]

Matthews, John, 15 Chapel St, Grosvenor Pl., Knightsbridge, London, cm, carpenter and undertaker (1808). [D]

Matthews, John, 33 Gray St, Blackfriars, London, carver and gilder (1809–11). [D]

Mat(t)hews, John, 15 Northside of Broker Row, Spitalfields/Moorfields, London, upholder and cm (1810). Took out a Sun Insurance policy on 5 December 1810 for £800 of which £785 accounted for stock and utensils in his house, where no cabinet work was done, and £15 on stock and utensils in his shed in yard nearby. [GL, Sun MS vol. 452, ref. 852094]

Matthews, John, New St, Ledbury, Herefs., builder, cm and u (1830–40). [D]

Matthews, John Felix, Market Pl., Leighton Buzzard, Beds., cm and u (1839). [D]

Matthews, John R., Torquay, Devon, cm and u (1838–40). Recorded at Market St in 1838. Marriage to Miss Killegrew of Livermead House at Cockington Church reported in *Exeter Flying Post*, 17 December 1840. [D]

Matthews, Jonathan, near the Hermitage in Artichoke Lane (London ?), cm and carpenter (1775). Took out a Sun Insurance policy in 1775 for £1,200 of which £150 accounted for utensils and stock. [GL, Sun MS vol. 237, p. 35]

Matthews, Luke, St Martin's Lane, London, upholder (1709). [Rate bks]

Matthews, Nicholas, parish of St Sepulchre, Cambridge, chairmaker (d.1713). [Univ. Lib., Will AR 2:3]

Matthews, Sampson, address unrecorded, cm (1803). Subscribed to Sheraton's *Cabinet Dictionary*, 1803.

Matthews, Thomas, Bristol, u (1818–29). Addresses given at Clifton Pl. in 1818; Montague St, 1819–21; 19 Charles St, 1825–26; 9 Charles St in 1827; and Leek Lane, 1828–29. [D]

Matthews, Thomas, 50 Spitalfields, Leeds, Yorks., chairmaker (1837). [D]

Matthews, Thomas, High St, Leighton Buzzard, Beds., cm and u (1839). [D]

Matthews, Timothy, St Bride's, London, u (1729–65). Recorded at Ditch Side, 1729–43, and Fleet St, 1754–65. Trade card or bill head of 1748 shows him in partnership with Erasmus Delafield at 'Ye Royal Bed & Rising Sun', near Salisbury Ct, Fleet St. Dissolution of partnership announced, *General Advertiser*, 19 July, 1747 when leaving Matthews to trade alone at the same shop. Matthews was fined for non-service at St Bride's in 1729 and 1743; served as Questman in 1733; and as Collector, excused as Scavenger, in 1737. [D; Heal; GL, MS 6561, p. 50] See Delafield & Matthews.

Matthews, William, 46 Rupert St, London, carver and gilder (1784–93). [D; poll bk]

Matthew(s), William, 27 Angel Hill, Bury St Edmunds, Suffolk, cm, carver and gilder (1824–30). [D] See Edward John Matthews.

Matthews, William, 14 Nicholas Lane, London, carver and gilder (1835). [D]

Matthews, William, 4 Bevington Bush, Liverpool, u (1835). [D]

Matthews, William, High St, Stratford, London, furniture japanner (1839). [D]

Matthews & Taylor, 110 Fenchurch St, London, u and cm (1819). [D] See James Matthews at this address.

Matthewson, David, address unrecorded, cm (1803). Subscribed to Sheraton's *Cabinet Dictionary*, 1803.

Matthewson, John Jaques, 9 Junction St, Hull, Yorks., ornamental painter and fancy chairmaker (1838–40). [D]

Matthie, John, 10 John's Hill, Ratcliffe Highway, London, cm (1808). [D]

Matthurs (?), Patrick, Gt Pulteney St, London, cm (1784). [Poll bk]

Mattinson, James, South Shields, Co. Durham, cm and/or joiner (1834). [D]

Matti(n)son, John, 14 Port St, Manchester, cm (1836–40). [D]

Mattinson, Thomas, 10 Henrietta St, Covent Gdn, London, uholder (1784). [D]

Mattison, Charles, address unrecorded, picture frame maker (1739). Announcement in *Gents Mag.*, December 1739, read: 'Promotions — Charles Mattison, Esq. — Picture-Frame-Maker to the Royal Palaces.'

Mattison, Quincey, High St, Boston, Lincs., cm and u (1819–22). [D]

Mattison, Thomas, Rothbury, Northumb., cm and joiner (1834). [D]

Mattock, Charles, address unrecorded, upholder (1713). Admitted freeman of the Upholders' Co. on 3 June 1713. [GL, Upholders' Co. records]

Mattocks, Alexander, Frome, Som., cm and u (1839–40). Recorded at Bath St in 1839 and Behind Town in 1840. [D]

Mattocks, R., New Bond St, Bath, Som., cm (1819). [D]

Maudsley, Henry, Nottingham, cm (1771). Will dated 30 October 1771. [Notts. RO, probate records]

Maudlsey, Henry, Brompton, Kent, cm and scavenger to the barracks at Chatham (d.1780). Death reported in *Gents Mag.*, December 1780.

Maugham, Thomas, St George's parish, Stamford, Lincs., cm and u (1809–35). Listed at St George's St, 1828–35. [D; poll bks]

Maugham, William, West Halton, Lincs., joiner and cm (1815). App. to William Rollett of Gainsborough, Lincs. in March 1815. [Hull app. reg.]

Maul, William, address unrecorded, upholder (1710). Admitted freeman of the Upholders' Co. on 6 September 1710. [GL, Upholders' Co. records]

Maulden, James, address unrecorded, upholder (1715–38). Son of John Maulden, joiner of St Saviour's, Southwark, London. App. to Thomas Dawson on 8 April 1715, and admitted freeman of the Upholders' Co. by servitude on 25 January 1722. Took apps named Samuel Bowler, 1723–31; John Blackwell, 1729–35; and Samuel Trevett, 1731–38. [GL, Upholders' Co. records] Probably:

Maulden, James, at 'The King's Arms', St Saviour's Dockhead, St Olave's parish, Southwark, London, u (1723). Took out a Sun Insurance policy on 11 June 1723 for £500 on goods and merchandise in his house only. [GL, Sun MS vol. 15, p. 441]

Maulden, James, Tooley St, Southwark, London. Named in contemporary newspapers in 1746. [Heal]

Maule, William, Sheep St, Wellingborough, Northants., cm (1830). [D]

Maulin, Hurmee, Bewdley, Worcs., cm (1758). Took app. named Wooley in 1758. [S of G, app. index]

Maullin, Shernice, Bewdley, Worcs., cm (1762). Took app. named Farmer in 1762. [S of G, app. index]

Maund, John, Broad St, Hereford, cm and u (1830–35). [D]

Maunder, —, London, cm (1793). Subscribed to Sheraton's *Drawing Book*, 1793.

Maunder, Thomas, Romsey, Hants., cm (1798). [D]

Maurice, Charles, address unrecorded, cm (1803). Subscribed to Sheraton's *Cabinet Dictionary*, 1803.

Mavin, Robert, Glanton, near Alnwick, Northumb., cm and joiner (1828–29). [D]

Mavin, Robert & Thomas, Alnwick, Northumb., cm (1834). [D]

Mavin, William, Glanton, near Alnwick, Northumb., cm and/or joiner (1834). [D]

Maw, George, 1 Drake's Buildings, Short St, Hull, Yorks., carver and gilder (1838–42). [D]

Maw, Marmaduke, York, cm (1826). Son of James Maw, flaxdresser; app. to John Bellerby, cm and u, in 1826. [York app. reg.]

Maw, S., London. Impressed mark recorded on the base of a small 19th-century mahogany wall cabinet with two plain glazed doors. Possibly a Victorian piece.

Mawbey, Charles Edward, 5 New St, Clothfair, London, cm and u (1839). [D]

Mawer & Smith, London, cm and u (1827–28). Addresses given at 29 and 29½ Orchard St, Portman Sq., and 208 Oxford St. [D]

Mawer, H. & Stephenson, London. Stamp recorded on various pieces: a George III mahogany partner's desk with rectangular leather-lined top with nine drawers surrounding a central kneehole [Christie's, 22 January 1981, lot 131]; a small mahogany drum table [Chelsea Antiques Fair, March 1983]; a mahogany tambour-fronted writing desk with a pull-out writing slide, the interior with pigeon-holes and drawers, with two drawers in the frieze, raised on tapering legs [Sotheby's, 27 January 1967, lot 142]; on an early 19th-century mahogany pedestal table, with fall flaps and two shallow drawers, on tapered triangular formed pedestal and triform base with bobbin supports; also on a mahogany bow-fronted hall table, c.1800, with single drawer, on four tapered legs, and with box-wood stringing; also on a bow-fronted marquetry rosewood sideboard, with three drawers, two cupboards and gilt handles; and on an ebonised sideboard with oval inlay in top, central drawer flanked by two deeper drawers on each side, applied fretwork to centre drawer; top of centre inscribed: 'H. Mawer & Stephenson London'. Label underneath reads: 'J. & B. Blower, Shrewsbury'. This firm may have been furniture brokers rather than makers.

Mawn, Benjamin Hardman, Swan Ct, Manchester, carver and gilder (1836). [D]

Mawrice, Joseph, Bayleyfield, Sheffield, Yorks., cm (1814). [D]

Mawson, J., Keswick, Cumb., joiner and/or cm (1811). [D]

Mawson, J., Nether-End, Penrith, Cumb., cm (1811). [D]

Mawson, John, address unrecorded, u (1785). On 21 October 1785 he provided 'Cotton Furniture' to George Cooke at Dunham Massey, Cheshire, costing £1 16s. [John Rylands Lib., Manchester Univ., George Cooke's accounts]

Mawson, John, Leeds, Yorks., journeyman cm (1791–93). Named in the *Leeds Cabinet and Chair Makers' Book of Prices*, 1791, with other journeymen in basic sympathy with its contents. Probably the John Mauson of Leeds who subscribed to Sheraton's *Drawing Book*, 1793.

Mawson, Joseph F., Penrith, Cumb., cm (1798). [D]

Mawson, Thomas, Knaresborough, Yorks., cm (1774–84). Son of John Mawson bricklayer; admitted freeman of York in 1774, and polled at York in 1784 as a cm in Knaresborough. [York freemen rolls]

Mawson, William, Ellerby Lane, Leeds, Yorks., cm (1822). [D]

Mawton, Richard, 14 King St, Truro, Cornwall, cm (1830). [D]

Maxey, —, 121 Upper Thames St, London, u (1783). [D] See Gill, George & Maxey.

Maxey, Charles, Wallingford, Berks., cm (1768). [Oxford poll bk]

Maxey, George, Wallingford, Berks., cm (1798). [D]

Maxey, Henry, 4 Worship St, Finsbury, London, buhl manufacturer (1829). [D]

Maxey, Samuel, London, wholesale u and cotton dealer (1782–1804). Addresses given at 12 Tower Royal in 1782; Friday St in 1787; and 60 Aldersgate St, 1792–1804. Son of John Maxey, freeman cooper of London; admitted freeman of the Upholders' Co. on 3 July 1782. Named in Sheraton's list of master cabinet makers, 1803. [D; GL, Upholders' Co. records]

Maxey, Thomas, Watlington, Oxon., cm (b.1741–84). Aged 39, he married Mary Taylor of Watlington on 12 October 1780. [D; Bodleian index of Oxf. marriage bonds]

Maxwell, Benjamin, Liverpool, cm (1821–34). Addresses given at 7 Starbeck St, 1821–23; 175 Dale St and 21 Hatton Gdn in 1827; and 13 Silkhouse Lane, 1829–34. [D]

Maxwell, Charles, at 'The Lion & Lamb', corner of New Broad Ct, Drury Lane, London, u and appraiser (1749). Trade card states that he 'Buys & Sells & Appraises all Sorts of Household Goods, also Useful & Ornamental Old China. Funerals Decently Performed. Sackings for Beds of all Sorts & Sizes, Wholesale & Retail.' [Poll bk; Leverhulme Coll., MMA, NY]

Maxwell, James, London, u and cm (before 1774). Announced in *Hibernian Journal*, 23 May 1774, that he 'has commenced Business in College Green [Dublin] … where he intends carrying on the Upholsterers and Cabinet Business in all its Branches, & as he has had several years experience in London at Messrs. France, Chippendale & Linnells … some of the most Capital in that Metropolis he hopes that will be a means to recommend him to the Public.'

Maxwell, Joseph, 26 Church St, Whitehaven, Cumb., joiner and/or cm (1828–29). [D]

Maxwell, L., 62 Berwick St, Soho, London, looking-glass manufacturer (1839). [D]

Maxwell, Robert, parish of St James, Westminster, London, upholder (1710–11). Took out Hand in Hand Insurance policies on 8 May 1710 for £300 on a house in Manchester Ct, St Margaret's; and on 4 August 1711 for £200 on houses in Eagle St. [GL, Hand in Hand MS vol. 7, ref. 20078; vol. 9, p. 187]

Maxwell, Robert, Stone Bridge Fields, St Martin-in-the-Fields, London, upholder (1716). Insured an empty house on a 'new intended street in Stone Bridge Fields' for £500 on 22 September 1716. [GL, Hand in Hand MS vol. 16, p. 315]

Maxwell, Robert, Gt Pulteney St, near Golden Sq., London, cm, u and undertaker (c.1760). Fine Chinoiserie card recorded showing sofa with canopy and chinamen in Rococo arches. [Heal Coll., BM]

Maxwell, William, at the 'Black Lyon', corner of Compton St, Westminster, London, upholder (1720). Took out a Sun Insurance policy on 3 April 1720 on goods and merchandise in his house only. [GL, Sun MS vol. 11, p. 107]

Maxwell, William, Paul St, Finsbury Sq., London, bedstead maker (1808). [D]

Maxwell, William, Blyth, Northumb., joiner and/or cm (1834). [D]

May, —, Plymouth, Devon. Subscribed to Sheraton's *Drawing Book*, 1793.

May, Mrs, Plymouth, Devon, cm (1798). [D]

May, —, Mint St, Southwark, London, chairmaker (1826). Fire at his premises reported in the *Times* in 1826.

May, Charles, address unrecorded, u (1706). Carried out repairs at St Michael's, Queenhythe, London in 1706, for which he charged £11 5s. [*Wren Soc.*, vol. XIX, p. 43]

May, Charles, Ditch Side, St Bride's, London, later Oxford, upholders (1713–28). Recorded at 'The Ship' in 1713, when he took out a Sun Insurance policy on 15 October. Fined for non-service in three offices at St Bride's in 1715; served as Church Warden in 1719; Sidesman in 1720 and 1728, when he left the parish and went to Oxford. [GL, Sun MS vol. 3, ref. 3290; GL, MS 6561, p. 3]

May, Edward, Bethel St, Norwich, cm and u (1830). [D]

May, J. & S. W., 39 Sparling St, Liverpool, chairmakers (1834). [D] Probably John and Solomon William May.

May, James, Liverpool, cm (1802–d. by 1820). Admitted freeman on 8 July 1802. [Liverpool freemen reg.]

May, James, 6 Queen St, Grosvenor Sq., London, carver and gilder (1808). [D]

May, John, Beverley, Yorks., cm (1804). App. to John Stephenson of Beverley in March 1804. [Hull app. reg.]

May, John, 18 Redburn St, Southwark, London, chair manufacturer (1826–27). [D]

May, John & William, 75 Sparling St, Liverpool, chairmakers (1827). [D] Probably the J. & W. May, chairmakers of Liverpool, who announced the dissolution of their partnership in *Chester Courant and Advertiser for North Wales*, 18 March 1838. See J. & S. W. May

May, John, Liverpool, chairmaker (1834–39). Trading at 11 Mason St in 1834; in partnership with Solomon William May at 61 Park Lane, 1835–37; and alone at 129 Park Lane with shop at 76 Upper Frederick St in 1839. [D]

May, Joseph, Plymouth, Devon, u (1759). Took apps named Williams and Hewett in 1759. [S of G, app. index]

May, Joseph Ball, Plymouth, Devon, u and cm (1777–86). Declared bankrupt, *Sussex Weekly Advertiser*, 29 April 1777. Auction of estate and effects advertised in *Exeter Flying Post*, 2 May 1777. Declared bankrupt again and dividends announced in the latter paper on 3 August 1786.

May, Richard, Preston, Lancs., u (1822). [Preston Guild record of burgesses].

May, Robert, Spalding, Lincs., chairmaker (1744–97). Took app. named Button in 1744. [D; S of G, app. index]

May, Robert, Red Lion Mkt, Whitechapel, London, bed and mattress maker (1822–23). [D]

May, Solomon William, Liverpool, chairmaker (1834–37). Trading at 39 Sparling St in 1834; and in partnership with John May at 61 Park Lane, 1835–37. [D]

May, William, Sharp, Peter & Wilson, Isabella, Liverpool, u, dealers and chapmen, cm and modellers (1817). Declared bankrupt, and sale of stock and effects advertised in *Liverpool Mercury*, 10 January 1817. Sale advertised again on 17 January of 'THE entire STOCK in TRADE of Messrs. May & Sharp, UPHOLSTERERS, CABINET MAKERS and MODELLERS, consisting of a large assortment of modern Paper Hangings with rich flock borders, London Chintz Furnitures, Trimmings, Brussels & Kidderminster Carpets, Oil Cloths, several sets of Drawing-room Chairs, Couches, Cabinets, Sofa, Card & Pembroke Tables, in a variety of fancy woods, excellent Mahogany articles, in a set of Patent Dining Tables, wardrobes, Drawers, Secretaire & Chairs, Looking Glasses, Bronzed & Gilt Busts, Lamps & various ornaments etc. etc. Also the manufactured Stock Consisting of Choice Mahogany in Veneers, Boards & Planks, Tulip & Rosewood, a large assortment of modern Brass Work, Plate Glass, Lathe, Benches etc....'. Sale re-advertised on 21 February 1817 at the firm's premises in Bold St, 'consisting of a large sized Four-post Bedstead, the feet posts & cornice richly carved & brilliantly ornamented in burnished gold, several sets Four-post Bedsteads, with mahogany feet-posts, handsome Sofa, Work, Chess & Card Tables in fancy woods, Cabinets, Secretaire & Book case, Couches, Brussels & Kidderminster Carpets, Paper Hangings, Feather Beds etc....'.

May, William Morris, New St, Torrington, Devon, cm (1823–30). [D]

May, William, 34 Norfolk St, Liverpool, chairmaker (1829). [D]

May & Loftus, Market Pl., Beverley, Yorks., cm (1840). [D]

Maybin, Samuel, 39 Little Queen St, Holborn, London, bedstead maker and u (1835–39). [D]

Maybin, William, 47 Webber St, New Cut, London, bedstead maker (1829). [D]

Maybrick, John, Liverpool, cm (1840). Admitted freeman on servitude to William Catterall and Thomas Whittingham on 25 July 1840. [Liverpool freemen reg.]

Maybury, William, Manchester, chairmaker (1834–40). Addresses given at 140 Long Millgate in 1834; Steele's Yd, Ashley Lane in 1836; 6 Long Millgate in 1838 and Holme's Yd, Long Millgate in 1840. [D]

Maychell, —, Lancaster. Named in the Gillow records, 1800–33. [Westminster Ref. Lib.]

Maychell, James, Lancaster. Named in the Gillow records, 1827–33. [Westminster Ref. Lib.]

Maychell, William, Lancaster. Named in the Gillow records, 1806–31. [Westminster Ref. Lib.]

Mayer, —, address unrecorded, cm (1803). Subscribed to Sheraton's *Cabinet Dictionary*, 1803.

Mayer, Edward, North Walsham, Norfolk, upholder (1798). [D]

Mayer, George, Gt Homer Pl., Collingwood, Liverpool, cm (1835). [D]

Mayer, Hayman, 97 Drury Lane, London, chair painter (1824). Took out a Sun Insurance policy on 11 March 1824 for £100, including £20 on stock and utensils. [GL, Sun MS vol. 499, ref. 1014622]

Mayer (or Mears), John, Liverpool, cm (1761–d.1800). Admitted freeman on 9 July 1761. Died in November 1800. [Liverpool freemen reg.]

Mayer, Lewis, 9 Coleman St, London, tortoiseshell carver and water gilder (1808). [D]

Mayer & Larzo, address unrecorded (1833). Named as chair repairers in the accounts of Anna McBean for work done for the Royal Household between April and September 1833, being paid 3s 3d for re-caning a 'Trafalgar Chair'. [V&A archives]

Mayers, Henry, 66 Leadenhall St, London, carver, gilder, picture frame and looking-glass maker (1837–39). [D] See Morris Mayers.

Mayers, Jacob, 15 York Pl., Asylum, London, upholder and undertaker (1817). [D]

Mayers, Morris, All Saints' St, Bristol and London, looking-glass manufacturer (1839–40). Trading also at 66 Leadenhall St, London in 1839. [D] See Henry Mayers.

Mayes, Edward, St Matthew's St, Ipswich, Suffolk, cm (1839). [D]

Mayfieldstone, Charles jnr, Hungate St, Beccles, Suffolk, cm and u (1839). [D]

Maygill, John, 80 Meadow Lane, Leeds, Yorks., chairmaker (1814). [D]

Maygor, —, Lower Brook St, Tavistock, Devon, cm (1838). [D]

Mayhew, Edward, Upper Olland St, Bungay, Suffolk, cm and u (1839). [D]

Mayhew, John, 45 Wigmore St, Cavendish Sq., London, cm, u and house agent (1801–08). Dividends on bankruptcy announced in *Liverpool Chronicle*, 5 February 1806. [D]

Mayhew, Thomas Eaton, Coggeshall, Essex, cm (1812). [Colchester poll bk]

Mayhew, Thomas, London, cm (1820). [Colchester poll bk]

Mayhew, John (1736–d.1811) and **Ince, William** (d. 1804), London, cm. The partnership of John Mayhew and William Ince (1758/59–1804) was one of the most significant, probably the longest lived but, as far as identified furniture is concerned, the least well-documented of any of the major

London cm of the 18th century. A biographical note by Pat Kirkham [*Furn. Hist.*, 1974, pp. 56–59] summarized the available facts and this, with the addition of some more recently discovered information, forms the basis for the following account.

Mayhew was app. to Bradshaw (probably William Bradshaw, u of Soho Sq.). Ince was app. to John West of Covent Gdn from 1752 until West's death in 1758. In November of that year West's premises were taken over by Samuel Norman, James Whittle and Mayhew. However, by 25 December 1758 yet another new partnership — this time between Mayhew and Ince — was in existence, advertising for business in January 1759 from the address in Broad St, Carnaby Mkt of Charles Smith, whose premises and stock they had purchased. The partnership was intended to run from 1759 to 1780 but continued under the original articles to 1799 when a new agreement was signed. Full details of the partnership articles (methods of accounting, sharing of profits, etc.) are given in Kirkham, op. cit.

The firm's business style in the London directories from the beginning until 1812 was 'Mayhew and Ince', in which form they also generally appear on bill headings though 'Ince and Mayhew' is occasionally used and both forms occur in the *Universal System* (see below). From about 1794 'Mayhew, Ince & Sons' occasionally appears on bills, probably indicating the advent of William Ince's son Charles and one (possibly more) of Mayhew's relations: Bartholomew Mayhew (not, apparently, a son; perhaps a nephew) is recorded at Marshall St from 1790 [*UBD*] and John Mayhew the younger (one of the elder John's four sons) worked independently in Wigmore St from about 1804–08 and from 1808 at Marshall St.

The activities of the firm advertised in directories and on bills varied over the years: in 1763 for instance they are described as 'cabinet-makers, carvers and upholders'. [*Mortimer's Directory*] In 1778 'Manufacturers of plate glass' appears on a bill heading [*Croome Bills*, No. 80] and by 1799 'dealers in plate glass' [*Kent's Directory*] has replaced 'carvers'. On one occasion only 'Auctioneers' is added to the list [Bedford Office, 5th Duke's Bills, 1788, no. 17]: no information about this branch of the business survives. From the 1780s the categories of 'cabinet-maker' and 'upholsterer' predominate. These revisions no doubt reflect the change in taste from carved to veneered and inlaid furniture characteristic of the period 1760–80 and the increasingly predominant role of upholstery in the furnishing of interiors from the 1790s. As for other cm, the supply of fine mirror glass formed a most important part of their trade. The firm's links in this branch of the business were significant: Ince's father and brother were glass grinders; and in 1782 the firm lent £100 to the Plate Glass Company. [Kirkham, op. cit]

The signing of a new agreement between the partners in 1799 coincided with a serious crisis in the firm's finances and in the period 1800–04 steps were taken to dissolve the partnership. After Ince's death early in 1804 (6 January), an acrimonious legal battle commenced between Ince's executors (led by his widow Ann) and Mayhew which was still unresolved at the time of Mayhew's death in May 1811. Mayhew's will dated 21 January 1811 refers to 'the suit now pending in Chancery'. [PRO, Prob. 11/1522] As a direct result of this action in the Court of Chancery, much fuller information survives about the daily workings and finance of the 45-year partnership than for any other 18th-century cabinet-making firm. [Kirkham, op. cit. and PRO, C13 623/44]

The partners originally shared the same house, where the business was also located, at the upper (West) end of Broad

(now Broadwick) St, Soho. On 20 February 1762 they married two sisters, Ann and Isabella Stephenson in St George's Hanover Sq. and continued to live at the same address until Mayhew's wife died in 1763. About a year later, Mayhew moved into an adjacent house, divided from the Ince's by the furniture warehouse. The Inces' house had four storeys and fourteen rooms: Mayhew's was probably much the same. The clerks and porters of the firm were divided between the two houses until 1781 when Mayhew (who subsequently re-married and fathered four sons and two daughters) took them all. As the business expanded additional premises were purchased: 20 Marshall St (the adjacent street) by 1780 (recorded until 1804) and 47 Marshall St by 1790 (recorded until 1812). There is no record of the numbers of employees at any given time though an advertisement in the *Public Advertiser*, 5 July 1768, reveals something of the scale of operations: the partners were then appealing for 'upwards of 100 Men, Cabinet-makers, Chair-makers, and some very good Joyners who will be immediately employed on the best Work' and for 'Some Men who can do inlaid Work in Woods &c and engrave and work in Brass'. Four bindings of apps. are recorded, at the highest premiums of any West End firms: William Dewey at £63 in 1760, John Watts at £105 in 1764, Robert Kennett at £157 in 1766 and Samuel Hemingway at £210 in 1775. [Kirkham, op. cit.] William Moore was also employed by the firm for an unknown length of time during which he gained 'long experience' before setting up in Dublin in 1782. He was presumably trained as a marqueteur as his advertisement recommends 'every article in the inlaid way' and stresses his use of 'remarkable fine coloured woods'. [*GCM*] Mayhew's will records the names of five employees who in 1811 had been with the firm 'for very many years': Higham and Parker 'cabinet-makers', Pasmore and Hall 'workwomen' and George Reynolds, clerk. Other workmen's names noted in bills include Jones, Elwood and Bolton; and Joseph Phelps, Molineaux and S. Habberton receipted a few of the extant bills. The firm's only known bank account [Drummonds, in Mayhew's name, 1764–65] lists a certain number of employees names (including Parker) and is signed by the then clerk, George Dixon.

At some later stage the partners also bought themselves country properties: Mayhew a house at Hornsey and about 25 acres; Ince a house at Crouch End; and by 1804 they owned seven houses in the neighbourhood of Broad St (three with shops and yards) probably connected with the cabinet-making business and six others in streets immediately North of Piccadilly which were let out furnished. Mayhew also owned on his own account two houses in Queen St, Cheapside, both of which were let at the time of his death. [Mayhew's will]

The decision to dissolve the partnership, mooted in 1799, was announced in the newspapers in April 1800; the same announcement also stated that Charles Ince would continue the business at the Broad St address. However the proposed dissolution proved complicated. The first sale to raise the £7,000 needed to meet the partnership debts was of 'The Valuable Capital, and Extensive Stock . . . of Messrs Mayhew and Ince dissolving partnership', [Christie's, on the premises, 'the Upper End of Broad Street, Soho', 11 May 1801 and three days ff.] This was not a great success: over a third of the 370 lots remained unsold and only £1,086 10s was raised. A second attempt [Christie's, 18–19 April 1804] 'to settle all the Partnership Concerns with the Executors' — Ince had died three months before — was slightly better with only 41 of the 207 lots unsold. Many of the lots in this sale were re-offered items from the 1801 sale. Ince's own household furnishings were sold for the Executors by Christie's on the premises in

Broad St on 9–10 March 1807 though the proceeds from this sale presumably remained with the Ince family.

The fluctuating state of the partnership's finances which eventually precipitated these sales is highlighted in the Chancery documents referred to above. Between 1768 and 1770 for example the firm's turnover was in excess of £52,000, though outgoings always seem to have been high: in the early 1760s they were running at nearly £1,000 per month. Mayhew, who was responsible for the majority of the book-keeping (but did not adhere to the formula devised at the outset of the partnership for drawing up regular accounts) complained that they were often 'inconvenienced for ready cash' — a frequent worry of 18th-century cm — and that he had over the years, being a man of private means unlike Ince, put about £9,000 of his own money into the business. By 1802 Mayhew claimed £31,270 11s 7d owing to him and only £6,093 6s 8d to Ince, figures that were strenuously disputed by Ann Ince. The final solution of this long drawn-out wrangle may be inferred from Mayhew's will: in the third codicil dated 9 February 1811, three months before his death when the matter was evidently preying on his mind, he urged his executors to consider settling the suit pending with Ince's executors 'out of Court and without waiting the ultimate decision of Chancery' on 'just, reasonable and expedient' terms.

Mayhew's memorial in St James's Church, Piccadilly (the wording and design of which he specified in his will) records his residence in the parish above 50 years and that he was Churchwarden in 1804. The deliberate omission of his profession confirms the clear impression in the Chancery papers that Mayhew (whose rôle in the business was agreed to be chiefly managerial) regarded himself as the more polished and cultivated partner, the possessor of a collection of 'choice and pleasing cabinet pictures' [Mayhew's sale, Christie's, 22 May 1812], and the one with whom the more important clients liked on the whole to deal, even if Ince retained certain major clients (e.g. Palmerston). Although Mayhew contributed eleven plates to the *Universal System* and owned a grangerized copy of Batty Langley's *Treasury of Designs*, 1740 [*Furn. Hist.*, 1974] Ince was undoubtedly the firm's designer and draughtsman and as a trained cm superintended that side of the business having given up trying to keep the accounts very early on in the partnership. He did, however, continue to receipt bills into the 1790s (e.g. Coventry). His interest in design (apart from his contribution of the majority of the plates in the *Universal System* extended to subscriptions to the following: Chippendale's *Director*, 1754; George Richardson's *A Book of Ceilings*, 1776, *Iconology*, 1779 and *Treatise on the Five Orders of Architecture*, 1787; and Thomas Malton's *Compleat Treatise on Perspective*, 1775. Ince also owned a copy of Isaac Ware's *Designs of Inigo Jones*.

Hitherto, in the striking absence of much documented furniture, the firm's chief claim to attention has been the ambitious publication in 1762 of *The Universal System of Household Furniture*, a handsome volume of eighty-nine numbered folio plates and six leaves with pairs of smaller plates, dedicated to the 4th Duke of Marlborough. Originally issued in serial form between July 1759 and August 1760, it was intended to run to 160 plates, modelled very closely (as the pre-publication advertisement makes clear) on the example of 'the very ingenious artificer' Thomas Chippendale whose *Director* had first appeared in 1754. [The exact progress of the publication has been elucidated by M. Heckscher in *Furn. Hist.*, 1974] Lack of money and experience, together with the appearance of another edition of the *Director* (also now in serial form) between 1759 and 1762 frustrated the original plan; further delays may have been caused by the partners' contribution of about twenty plates to another book of designs entitled *Houshold Furniture in Genteel Taste for the year 1760*.

The dependence of the *Universal System* on both the idea and the content of the *Director* has never been in doubt. However the inclusion of a small number of distinctive and original furniture types, notably tripod or 'Claw' tables, goes some way to relieving the charge of plagiarism as does the accomplished re-interpretation of certain forms popularized by Chippendale. The most idiosyncratic and individual feature of the designs is the repeated use of a variety of symmetrically formed half-Gothic half-Chinoiserie lattice-work panels, either pierced or applied to a solid ground. The dry linearity of this motif, suggestive of cut-card decoration on early 18th-century silver, also characterizes the much used lambrequin border ornament and contrasts strongly with the florid and highly charged Rococo detail of the designs for mirrors and girandoles.

The relative lack of success of the *Universal System* as a design manual (there were no further editions) and the paucity of documented furniture in the style of the publication (despite the claims that a number of engraved pieces had been executed) are no doubt connected. By 1762 the Rococo style was passing its zenith and taste in furniture was shifting from exuberance to relative sobriety. Chippendale's third edition of the *Director*, 1759–62, included a sprinkling of Neo-classical details noticeably absent from the *Universal System*. In practice, the firm was quick to take advantage of the change, the majority of their known work even in the early 1760s being broadly Neo-classical in character.

In addition to the primary business of making and selling furniture, the firm's activities extended (in common with most other leading cm) in several other more or less closely related directions. Importing of French furniture from Paris 'for immediate Sale, very much under the original Cost' was advertised [Heal]; two large mirrors for Lord Exeter were imported from Paris in 1768 [Burghley archives, Ex90/51]; and an attempt at attracting a continental clientèle is suggested by the inclusion of a French text in the *Universal System*. Certainly the firm established strong links among the francophile patrons of Henry Holland and with the expatriate French (e.g. Daguerre and Gaubert) who also worked in that circle.

House-agency played a significant if not especially lucrative part in the business. Letting out of furnished houses was generally on their own account: they owned two houses in Albemarle St, one in Sackville St, and three in Grafton St, including no. 9 for which the Earl of Stair paid £168 for ten weeks rent in 1788. [Breadalbane papers, Scottish RO] The firm also rented property for sub-letting: a house in Charles St from the 4th Duke of Marlborough (1789–90) and another at 72 Lower Grosvenor St from George Stovell (1794–1807); others are known. For clients of particular standing, the partners were prepared to go to great lengths: for the Dowager Duchess of Bedford they advertised for and eventually found a new house (112 Pall Mall), arranged the new lease with the outgoing tenant (Earl Cowper), listed the existing contents and put the house into good internal order (1786–87); for her younger son Lord John Russell they found and fitted up 49 Pall Mall (1787); and in June 1789 Mayhew went to look over Micheldever and Stratton Park, Hants., to plan the furnishings for Lord John and his wife, having sent a man down in April to attend the sale and buy the fixtures at Stratton and another to Micheldever to examine the inventory and place the furniture in order. [Bedford Office, 5th Duke's accounts 1789] Undertaking (as noted on many of their bill headings) also formed part of the complete service that the firm offered, ranging from a simple funeral for the Dowager Duchess of Bedford's cook at one extreme (£11 6s 1d) to the magnificent affair for the third Earl of Darnley at the other (£962 18s). For fashionable clients like the Bedfords and the Coventrys with London houses, the firm regularly hired out furniture for entertainments; and especially where they were the only or principal firm involved in a commission, the range and detail of their work, painstakingly charted in the bills, indicates a service of the most exacting quality: from the supply of the most expensive cabinet-work to the humblest towel-rail, from paperhanging to carpet laying, from cleaning beds with 'bug wash' to everyday maintenance and repair of furniture. A striking feature of many of the commissions, presumably reflecting a high level of satisfaction on the part of clients, is their great longevity — more than twenty years is not unusual and in one instance (Darnley) the accounts run for 42 years.

With London houses such an all-embracing service was relatively easily accomplished; for farther flung commissions such as that for Lord Caledon in Co. Tyrone, distance greatly magnified the difficulties and much of the supervision necessarily took the form of written instructions. By the same token, remoteness from London also gave provincial cm the opportunity to supplement a Mayhew & Ince commission with supplies and services at a lower rate (Kirchhoffer of Dublin at Caledon, Brailsford of Sheffield at Chatsworth and Routledge of Romsey at Broadlands).

In general the firm seems to have enjoyed more or less 'exclusive' relationships with their most influential clients (e.g. the Bedford family) though occasionally they seem just to have been one of a number of cm on a fashionable 'shopping list' (e.g. the Duchess of Northumberland). Where another (or several other) London firms were already ensconced (e.g. Vile and Cobb with Lord Coventry) they seem to have been content to work alongside (which they did from 1764–73), though they assumed the dominant rôle in this commission from the mid 1760s and more or less exclusive status from 1773–94. Once established in a lucrative commission they were extremely tenacious, supplying more than one generation of the same family if possible (e.g. Darnley and Bedford). Evidently some introductions to new clients arose through contacts with architects (especially Adam) though no doubt word of mouth and kinship between clients (e.g. Marlborough and Bedford, Derby and Coventry) as well as perhaps political connections among the Whigs played a part. Professional contacts gave rise to the Westminster Fire Office commission (1792/93) — both Ince and Mayhew were Directors; and James Mayhew (John's second son) became surveyor there in 1798. [Colvin, p. 545] Old partnership links no doubt ensured that Mayhew was involved (with Chippendale and Bradshaw) in the arbitration between Sir Lawrence Dundas and Samuel Norman in 1766 [Gilbert, *Chippendale*, pp. 158–59] and something similar may have given Ince the job of joint appraiser at Hartlebury Castle and The Palace, Worcester, in 1781. [*Worcester Hist. Soc. Miscellany*, 1, 1960, 60–91] An East India Company connection may also be surmised (Caledon, Hastings, etc.).

The firm's relationship with architects ranged from close to perfunctory in the same way that commissions from clients varied from casual purchases to the wholesale equipping of new (or newly altered) houses. In either case, the partners (Mayhew especially) seem to have gone out of their way to try and maintain a direct relationship with the client, parallel (and not necessarily subservient) to the architect. Sir William Chambers (as in his dealings with Chippendale) automatically assumed the dominant position when major 'architectural'

furniture was in question (e.g. the Blenheim State Bed), though the firm's connection with the dedicatee of the *Universal System* was to outlast Chambers's involvement by some twenty years. A more fruitful and substantial link seems to have been forged with Lancelot Brown and later with his son-in-law Henry Holland. Both architects, particularly the latter, worked extensively for the francophile Whig aristocracy centred on the Prince of Wales, and the frequent involvement of Mayhew and Ince in these circles (e.g. Burghley in the 1760s, Broadlands, Woburn and Carlton House in the 1780s) suggest a substantive professional relationship. Predictably, it would appear that Holland's hand was most strongly felt in the design of such architectural items as pier glasses and tables and considerably less so elsewhere; however in certain circumstances the influence of Dominique Daguerre, Holland's collaborator on several commissions, extended to vetting the firm's supply (and perhaps design) of furniture (e.g. Woburn, 1791).

From the early 1760s to the early 1780s, in which period the firm evolved one of its most characteristic and influential styles, the dominant architectural relationship — as in the case of Thomas Chippendale — was undoubtedly with Robert Adam. The firm's earliest collaboration with Adam seems to have been at Coventry House, Piccadilly and Croome Court for the 6th Earl of Coventry (from 1764), followed by work at Sherborne Castle, Audley End, Shelburne House, Northumberland House, Kimbolton and Derby House. From the surviving documentation it is clear that from time to time the firm was content to reproduce Adam's designs virtually to the letter (e.g. the Derby House commode); equally, the vast majority of the firm's accounts for an extensive commission such as Croome indicate that within limits they had a more or less free hand and even for some major pieces (e.g. the Tapestry Room chairs) apparently supplied their own designs. [Croome Bills, No. 58] Certainly Adam's choice of Mayhew and Ince to execute some of his most celebrated creations (and to supply the furnishings for some of his most fashionable interiors) indicates a close partnership, closer, probably, than that with Chippendale whose artistic independence has been noted. [Gilbert, p. 121] Other architects working for clients at the same time as Mayhew and Ince were supplying furniture (and mostly on more than one occasion) include Carr of York, George Shakespear, James Wyatt, S. P. Cockerell and James Paine though with none of these is there yet enough evidence available to point up either the working relationship or the stylistic cross-currents (if any).

While the *Universal System* may have become quickly outdated, the firm's ability to produce very early on furniture in the most startlingly advanced Neo-classical taste is beyond doubt and, as in the case of their work for Lord Coventry (from 1764 onwards), certainly owed much to their early collaboration with the country's leading Neo-classical architects. However, there is a variability in the style, construction and quality of the firm's output at any given date which precludes characterization of a single easily recognizable Mayhew and Ince 'house style' and has contributed greatly to the difficulty of making even tentative attributions of undocumented pieces. It seems that the firm was capable of working simultaneously in a number of distinct styles (in some instances on the same commission, e.g. Burghley in 1767–68), all to some extent overlapping and related but essentially self-contained. In terms of form (as opposed to decoration) this variety is encompassed by a French-inspired fully developed Rococo at one extreme (generally confined to carved giltwood) and a refined and sober Neo-classicism at the other. Running through the latter there is a deliberate streak of antiquarianism in design, particularly in evidence when supplying furniture to 'old' houses (e.g. Burghley). Neo-classical forms predominated from the later 1760s and the firms's vocabulary in this idiom was greatly strengthened and enlarged by their association first with Sir William Chambers (Blenheim, Woburn, etc.) and then with Robert Adam with whom originated one of the firm's most enduring furniture types, the semi-circular commode (e.g. Derby House).

Adam may also have inspired another characteristic form in which the firm specialized, the severely rectilinear box-like commode (Coventry House, Burghley, etc.), often made with side-opening doors and designed principally for the display of marquetry. Alongside this relatively advanced Neo-classicism a restrained conservative French influence persisted in the continued use of — for example — the 'Transitional' commode with undulating or serpentine front of a type popularized by John Linnell and Pierre Langlois, and in the retention of a slightly retardatory 'Louis XV' style of chair with cabriole legs and curved back (e.g. Broadlands, Cobham).

A common link in the production of this diverse range of forms may be found in the firm's highly proficient and adventurous use of marquetry, distinguished by a variety of techniques and pointing to a significant number of specialist marqueteurs in the firm's employ (or within its ambit). This constitutes the firm's single most original contribution to furniture decoration in the 1770s and '80s. The Coventry House commodes of 1764 — the earliest documented marquetry so far discovered — already incorporate three of the features of the Mayhew and Ince marquetry style which, with variations, recur in the firm's work for more than 30 years: the use of large-scale 'Antique' motifs (habitually urns or tripods) derived from engravings, simply coloured and boldly inlaid on a contrasting ground; extensive and delicate surface engraving to achieve the illusion of depth; and subtle inlaying (usually of foliage designs), differentiated from the ground wood only by the natural colour and figure of the inlay. This last technique is comparable to the end-cut marquetry of B.V.R.B. and is sometimes found in conjunction with yew-wood, the only wholly idiosyncratic veneer wood the firm used and possibly unique to Mayhew and Ince among London cm of this date. As a variation (especially in the 1760s) yew-wood was inlaid with simple foliate scrolls or clasps of light wood engraved in a manner reminiscent of the *Universal System*, pl. 2. In either case, moulded borders of commodes, tables and chests, especially when free of ormolu mounts, were often strengthened by ebonizing, a highly unusual device perhaps unique to the firm (e.g. Goodnestone, 1764, etc.). Other characteristics of the firm's marquetry repertoire include the sympathetic modernization and re-use of good examples of late 17th-century floral panels, the most notable examples of which are found at Burghley (1767), a house where the owner's antiquarian desire to harmonize furnishings with venerable interiors seems to have been paramount. Late 17th-century marquetry techniques, where vivid pictorial effects are created by the inlaying of delicately coloured and scorched woods (with far less engraving), seem to have influenced another variation of the firm's style, seen at its best preserved on a pair of pier tables at Chirk (1782) and on a pair of Pembroke tables at Chatsworth (1785). This technique is sometimes seen (especially on commodes) in combination with painted medallions (e.g. Derby House, 1775).

Much of the firm's most expensive cabinet-work was enriched with ormolu mounts and as they are known to have had a fruitful business relationship with Boulton and Fothergill, e.g. over the Duchess of Manchester's cabinet [*Furn. Hist.*, 1966] — and were apparently the only cabinet-making firm to do so — it seems likely that many (and certainly the best) of their mounts came from Soho. However, the variety both in quality and design on documented pieces suggests the existence of more than one source; and some may well have been imported.

HILLSBOROUGH HOUSE, C. Down, Ireland or (?) **DOWNSHIRE HOUSE, 20 HANOVER SQ.**, London (1st Earl of Hillsborough, later 1st Marquess of Downshire). 1761–63: Three payments in Drummond's Bank ledgers. Total £186 2s 2d.

COBHAM HALL, Kent (3rd and 4th Earls of Darnley). 1761–1803: No bills but payments in personal account books (with Coutts). Total £3,978 18s 4d (3rd Earl) and £3,605 9s 3d (4th Earl), excluding account (bill extant) for extraordinarily elaborate funeral of 3rd Earl. Total £962 18s. [Kent RO, Darnley papers, U565] Some attributable furniture survives (part *in situ*) including: blue and white painted four-post bed; pair of painted and gilded sofas and four window seats (for Gilt Hall); suite of eight giltwood armchairs and pair of sofas; suite of seven blue and white painted armchairs and one sofa; mahogany library desk and (?) pair of silver-bordered satinwood commodes. [*C. Life*, 24 February, 3 and 9 March 1983]

LADY FLUDYER. Plate LXV of the *Universal System*, 1762 showing the 'side section of the Dressing Room' — a fully developed Rococo interior with a 'Turkish Soffa' in an alcove flanked by girandoles and a pair of chairs — is dedicated to 'the Honble. Lady Fludyer', presumably Caroline, daughter of Hon. James Brudenell, wife of Sir Samuel Fludyer, 1st Bt, of Lee Place, Kent, Lord Mayor of London in 1761. [*Burke's Peerage*, 1863] Though apparently executed, this interior is not known to survive.

(?) **SANDWELL PARK**, Staffs. (2nd Earl of Dartmouth). 1762–68: Payments in Hoare's Bank ledgers. Total £83 15s 10d (including three payments (£46 18s 10d) to 'Peter Ince', (?) Ince's brother the glass grinder).

SHERBORNE CASTLE, Dorset and **14 DOVER ST**, London (7th Baron Digby). 1763–85: No bills but payments in personal account books [Sherborne muniment room] (repeated with substantial additions in Hoare's Bank ledgers). Total (including one specified payment of £67 6s for London) £2,192 0s 6d. Attributable surviving furniture at Sherborne includes yew-wood table with re-used 17th-century marquetry top and ebonized borders, pair of inlaid and engraved serpentine commodes and part set of painted chairs in French style. 7th Baron's copy of *Universal System* survives in Library.

GOODNESTONE PARK, Kent (Sir Brook Bridges, 3rd Bt). 1764: No bills but payment in personal account book (with Hoare's Bank). Total £100. [Kent RO, Bridges papers U373–A2] Earlier payment in account at Hoare's Bank to Peter Ince, June 1763, £24 2s 6d (cf. Lord Dartmouth). Surviving attributable furniture at Goodnestone includes a pair of yew-wood commodes (cf. Alscot 1766) and a pair of yew-wood card tables with ebonized borders inlaid with engraved flowersprays. [*Treasures from Kent Houses*, Royal Museum, Canterbury (exhib. cat.) 1984, nos 56, 63 and pl. 17]

CROOME COURT, Worcs. and **29 PICCADILLY**, London (6th Earl of Coventry). 1764–94: Twenty-three receipted bills (not always specifying for which house) covering a major part of the furnishings of Robert Adam's newly finished interiors. Total £1,359 15s 8d discounted to £1,345 11s 9d. [Worcs. RO, numbered bills] Significant identifiable surviving items include: a pair of inlaid satinwood commodes of advanced Neo-classical form (1764, £40); a redwood tripod stand for

Sèvres ewer and basin (1767, £14 7s); six giltwood chairs and two sofas covered in Gobelins tapestry (1769, £133 18s excluding covers, etc., but including patterns), now in the MMA, NY (*Kress Collection Catalogue*, 1964); and a satinwood 'Cabinet for Curiosities' (1781, £31 10s). Other disbursements cover moving, cleaning, altering and repair of furniture; upholstery; joinery; paper and tapestry hanging; designs for needlework; and the hire of furniture for entertainment. Contents now widely dispersed. [Sotheby's, 25 June 1948; Bentley Hobbs & Mytton on the Premises, 7–10 December 1948; Christie's, 30 November 1978]

ALSCOT PARK, Warks. (James West). 1766: Receipted bill includes 'a neat French commode . . .' (£12 12s) of yew-wood bordered with rosewood and a chest of drawers 'stain'd & polish'd Black, the top to fold . . .' (£5 5s) both of which survive at Alscot. Total £30 18s 2d. [Alscot Park papers; Gilbert, *Chippendale*, pp. 150–51]

(?) **THE GROVE**, Watford, Herts. (1st Baron Hyde of Hindon, later 1st Earl of Clarendon). 1766–75: Two payments in Hoare's Bank ledgers. Total £48. An armchair with Clarendon provenance related to Plate LX of *Universal System* sold Christie's London, 11 April 1985 lot 127.

HOUGHTON HOUSE, Beds. (Francis, Marquess of Tavistock). 1767: Executor's account for Lord Tavistock (d. 1767) 'for Tables & Chairs'. Total £24 8s. [Bedford Office, London]

(?) **COMPTON VERNEY**, Warks. (14th Baron Willoughby de Broke). 1767: Payment in Hoare's Bank ledgers. Total £28 15s 6d. Possibly coinciding with R. Adam's re-modelling of c.1761–67.

18 GROSVENOR SQ., London (8th Earl of Thanet). 1767–68: Payments in Hoare's Bank ledgers. Total £1,671 10s.

BURGHLEY HOUSE, Lincs. and **LOWER GROSVENOR ST**, London (9th Earl of Exeter). 1767–79: Bill (1767–68) and payments in Daybook (1770–79) for major re-furnishing mainly of private apartments of Burghley (and a small repair in London). Total £1,922 6s 11½d. [Burghley archives, EX 90151 and Estate Bks, 1770–1800] Notable surviving 'antiquarian' pieces include four-post bedstead in Blue and Silver Bedroom hung with flowered tabby (1768, £186 19s 7½d); cleaning and repairing the 17th-century tapestries in the same room (1767, £12 2s); and pair of ormolu-mounted commodes and corner cupboards with re-used 17th-century marquetry (1767, £237 15s). Rococo style represented by florid giltwood overmantel in Red Drawing Room (1767, £110) and four 'richly carved and gilt' tripods 'for the Hall' (1768, £120). [*Rococo Exhibition*, V & A, 1984, L69] Advanced Neo-classical taste seen in pair of illusionistically inlaid box-like commodes for piers of Library (1767, £57) and pair of giltwood mirrors with French plates above (£348). Daybook payments probably cover *inter alia* mahogany four-post bed with crimson velvet hangings [P. Macquoid, *Age of Mahogany*, 1906, pl. VI], pair of mahogany sideboard pedestals [ibid., *Age of Satinwood*, 1908, fig. 60] and several other attributable pieces including an inlaid yew-wood bureau and two chests of drawers with ebonized borders. [*C. Life*, 7 June 1973, pp. 1604–07]

AUDLEY END, Essex or **10 NEW BURLINGTON ST**, London (Sir John Griffin Griffin Bt). 1767–80: Six bills coinciding with Robert Adam's redecoration (1762 onwards). Total £41 16s 1½d. [Essex RO D/DBy/A25/12, A26/11, A27/5, A32/2, A32/10, A38/9] Includes 'a table for the Saloon sanderswood Top border'd with Rosewood, Carv'd & painted frame' (1767, £4 10s). '6 Stools Carv'd & Enrich't to Match the Table & 4 Dorick Stools in Taste and painted' (£12 12s), 6 Dressing Glasses in Mahogany Frames (1768, £3 3s), 6 neat French Cabriolets painted green and white (1773, £6 6s) and a 'neat Morroco Backgammon Table &

Leather Boxes' (1774, £2). Not identified. Sir John (later 4th Lord Howard de Walden and 1st Lord Braybrooke) also purchased 'a superb pier table, comprized of the choicest woods curiously inlaid . . .' (£12 12s) from the sale of the Earl of Kerry (q.v.) [Christie's, 29 March 1778, Room XXX (Large Dining Parlour), lot 13], probably supplied by Mayhew & Ince.

CRICHEL HOUSE, Dorset (Humphrey Sturt). 1767–80: Payments in Hoare's Bank ledgers coinciding with James Wyatt's re-modelling. Total £340. Some attributable furniture survives *in situ*. [*Journal of Soc. of Architectural Historians*, 1984, pp. 268–69]

BEDFORD HOUSE, London (4th Duke and Duchess of Bedford, 5th Duke of Bedford). 1767–97: Extensive series of bills (mainly for 5th Duke during and after Holland's remodelling). Total in excess of £1,100 (work for Bedford House, Woburn, Oakley and Clarges St not always clearly separated). [Bedford Office, 4th and 5th Duke's bills] One major bill missing (1786, £402 19s 6d) possibly relating to Library and Dining Room furniture. Majority of remainder record payments for new and repaired upholstery (especially bed hangings and curtains), frequent repairs, moving, cleaning and polishing (some joinery work and dusting of ceilings), hire of furniture for entertainment, etc. Notable items (not now identifiable) included '2 mahogany Horizontal Tables' for Dining room piers 'the frame carved legs to match the Sideboards' (1788, £21) and a yellow leather upholstered mahogany bathing couch with tinned copper 'reservoir' and adjustable head and feet (1790, £42 16s including alterations).

SHELBURNE (later **LANSDOWNE**) **HOUSE**, Berkeley Sq., London (2nd Earl of Shelburne, later 1st Marquess of Lansdowne, and Countess of Shelburne). 1768–75: Lady Shelburne records (1768) a visit to 'Mayhew and Inch [sic] where is some beautiful Cabinet work, and two pretty cases for one of the rooms in my apartment, and which, though they are only deal, and to be painted white, he charges £50 for'. [A. Bolton, *The Architecture of Robert and James Adam*, p. 312] Her aunt Lady Louisa Fermor wrote (5 March 1766) to report an earlier visit to see 'a famous table at Mayhew's in which I was disappointed'. [Fitzmaurice-Villars, *Earl of Shelburne*, 1912, vol. 1, p. 273] Miscellaneous expenditure in Lansdowne House account book. [Bowood MS] Total £73 8s 6d. Includes '2 Cabinets to Shelburne House' (1768–69, £28 1s 6d), 2 fire screens, 2 bell ropes, etc. (1767–68, £5 6s 6d).

ADDERBURY HOUSE, Glos. or **20 GROSVENOR SQ.**, London (3rd Duke of Buccleuch). 1769: Payment in accounts [*C. Life*, 3 May 1984, p. 1232] Total £117 13s 6d. Coincides with Chambers's work at both houses c. 1767–68.

PORTMAN SQ., London (3rd Earl of Kerry). 1769–72: Payment in Bank of England ledgers (1769). Total £1,000. Luxurious furniture supplied for house on East side of square. Firm's supervision extended to purchases of ormolu for Lord Kerry (chimney ornaments, girandoles, tripods, etd.) from Boulton & Fothergill 1771–72. [Goodison, *Ormolu*, p. 228, etc.] Contents dispersed in Sale of 'Magnificent Furniture' etc. [Christie's on the premises, 25 February and 8 days following, 1778, postponed to March 23–31] Many lots purchased by clients of the firm (e.g. Lady Derby, Lord Monson, Sir John Griffin Griffin) and 12 lots bought back by Mayhew. Items identified from this sale include: ormolu-mounted yew-wood sideboard and pair of pedestals ;7th day, Dining Parlour, lots 16–18 £55. 13s) now in Lady Lever Art Gallery [P. Macquoid, *Catalogue*, nos 81 and 84] and (possibly) mahogany secretaire-cabinet. [Christie's London, 11 April 1985, lot 162]

BOREHAM HOUSE, Essex (Richard Hoare). 1770: Payment in private accounts. Total 3s. [Essex RO, D/DU 649/2]

TYTHEGSTON COURT, Glamorgan (Henry Knight). 1770: Payment recorded in diary. Total £14 4s. [*C. Life*, 5 October 1978, p. 1026]

COMBE ABBEY, Warks. or BENHAM PARK, Berks. (6th Baron Craven). *c.* 1770–75: Goodison, *Ormolu*, p. 133, credits the firm with work at Combe. No payments found in Craven papers. [Bodleian Lib., Oxford; Berks RO] Attributable pieces include: marquetry cabinet inlaid with views after Buck, Clérisseau, etc., and a satinwood chest of drawers. [Christie's, 28 June 1979, lots 111 and 112]

SOHO MANUFACTORY (Boulton & Fothergill). 1771–84: 24 letters from Boulton & Fothergill to the firm survive indicating a friendly business relationship. [*Furn. Hist.*, 1966] Most are concerned with orders for Lord Kerry and the Duchess of Manchester. In 1771 Boulton & Fothergill ordered 'Several Cabinets made to the enclosed sketches to hold our Vases & Ornamental Goods'. [Ibid., p. 28]

NORTHUMBERLAND HOUSE and (?) SYON HOUSE (1st Duke and Duchess of Northumberland). *c.* 1772–73: First mention in Duchess's notebook dated 'Sion 1766' comparing prices of rival makers; again on list probably of *c.* 1771 and on another of *c.* 1776. [Gilbert, *Chippendale*, pp. 153–54] Rough notebook of 1772 [Alnwick MS, 121/43] probably referring to Northumberland House records '12 chairs for . . . Blue Room 2 Arms Mayhew & Ince large size' . . . 'My AntiRoom . . . 12 Chairs 2 with Arms are bespoke of Mayhew & Ince come home but 6 have arms' . . . 'To send to Mayhew & Ince for Chairs for my Anti-Room'. Not identified. Possible attributable items include marquetry breakfront commode and pair of satinwood commodes with ebonized borders in Long Gallery, Syon.

BLENHEIM PALACE, Oxon. and (?) MARLBOROUGH HOUSE, London (?) EALING GROVE, Middlx (?) LANGLEY PARK, Bucks. (?) WHITEKNIGHTS, Berks. (4th Duke of Marlborough). Before 1773–*c.* 1793: Dedication of *Universal System*, 1762, work for Duchess's family (Bedford) and (presumably) influence of Chambers (who worked for Duke from 1766) advanced the firm to this prestigious commission. No bills but steward's daybook of 'Furniture sent from Blenheim' and 'Furniture that came to Blenheim' 1772–1800 [Blenheim MS] records continuous activity to and from 'Mr Mayhew's' including tapestry cleaning, alteration and repair of furniture, new upholstery (especially curtains, wallhangings and carpets) gilt room borders, cornices, wallpaper and mahogany doors and large quantity of new furniture for Chambers's remodelled private apartments including: 12 gilt Cabriolet chairs and a settee for the Winter drawing room covered with white silk damask, 12 mahogany chairs covered with red leather (1774), picture frames (1775), 10 gilt chairs covered in crimson Genoa Damask for the Grand Cabinet (1777), a canopy bed for Duke's dressing room (1779), a large mahogany library table, 8 gilt mahogany chairs covered in needlework for the Grand Cabinet (1780), a commode (1782), 24 walnut chairs covered with red leather (1783), a pair of mahogany steps for the Observatory (1785), a secretary for Duke's dressing room (1787), a mahogany bookcase with mirror doors, 20 mahogany chairs for the Great Hall (1789), 12 crested mahogany chairs for Saloon (1792), etc. The firm also made to Chambers's design (and under his supervision) the state bed, *c.* 1772–73 [BM, Add. MS 41133; Chambers folios 104r, 105r, 107r] and (probably) several large pier glasses. [*C. Life*, 23 January 1975] Chambers's decorations now largely dismantled and furniture dispersed. Additional attributable pieces with Marlborough provenance include: satinwood and marquetry com-

mode [*Catalogue of coll. of Sir G. Cooper, Bt*, Hursley Park, privately printed, 1912, p. 62] and a pair of sabicu and marquetry commodes from Whiteknights. [Christie's, 25 May 1972, lot 89 (wrongly given as 90 in catalogue)] Abstracts of 4th Duke's expenditure 1789–93 record payments from the firm for rent of 26 Charles St. [Blenheim MS, Estate papers, Box 3; and Marylebone Lib., 72/38]

BUCKINGHAM HOUSE, London (The Royal Nursery). 1773: Payment in Queen Charlotte's Treasurer's accounts for 1761–77 [BM Add. MS 17870, f.84] unspecified work 'for the Royal Nursery' attested by Lady Charlotte Finch 'Governess to Their Royal Highnesses the Younger Princes and Princesses'. Total £7 7s.

(?) BLYTH HALL, Notts. or ALBEMARLE ST, London (Charles Mellish). 1773: Payment in Goslings Bank ledgers. Total £9 12s.

BADMINTON HOUSE, Glos. (5th Duke of Beaufort). 1773: Payment in personal account book [Badminton papers] for 2 frames. Total £15 10s. A pair of stools (one painted, one stripped) at Badminton conform closely to a 'Lady's Dressing Stool' (Pl. XXXIV, bottom right) in the *Universal System*.

KIMBOLTON CASTLE, Hunts. (4th Duke and Duchess of Manchester). *c.* 1774–75: Celebrated marquetry cabinet [now in V&A] mounted with 11 Florentine pietra dura plaques dated 1709. No bill. Preliminary designs by R. Adam [Soane Museum, vol. 17, no. 218 and vol. 27, no. 51] dated (one) 1771. Ormolu mounts made by Boulton & Fothergill 1774–75. Total £73 11s. [*Furn. Hist.*, 1966, pp. 23–36 and Goodison, *Ormolu*, pp. 133–35, etc. and pls 55–58, 61–62]

(?) WARWICK CASTLE, Warks. (2nd Earl of Warwick). 1774–77: Payments in Hoare's Bank ledgers. Total £180. Nothing identified but cabinet with re-used 17th-century French marquetry now in Bowes Museum possibly attributable. [Christie's, 30 May 1968, lot 85]

GEORGE AUGUSTUS SELWYN. 1775: Bill for 'Crib Bedstead'. Total approx £14 18s. Receipted in 1789. [Castle Howard archives, S — papers of G. A. Selwyn]

23 GROSVENOR SQ., London (12th Earl of Derby). 1775: Bill for '2 Tripod Pedestals' (£120) and a 'circular Commode of fine and curious Woods very finely inlaid with Etruscan Ornaments . . . from a Design of Messrs. Adams' (£88). Total £205 6s. [Knowsley archive, unsorted papers] Major Neoclassical commode made to Robert Adam's design [Soane Museum, vol. 17, nos 24 and 25] for Lady Derby's Dressing Room. Tripods not extant; house demolished. [*Burlington*, May 1985, pp. 275–82] Reference on Croome bill [1777, no. 80] implies further work for Derby; and Lady Derby was a buyer at the Kerry sale. Attributable furniture with Derby provenance includes inlaid satinwood folio case on stand. [Coll. the late Sir Albert Richardson]

CHEVENING HOUSE, Kent or (?) 2 STRATFORD PLACE, London (2nd Earl Stanhope). 1775: Payment in Lady Stanhope's 'Scribble Book' for 'black bordered Commode London'. Total £10 10s. [Kent RO, U1590 A61/5] probably to be identified with one now at Chevening [*Treasures from Kent Houses* (Exhib. cat.) Royal Museum, Canterbury, 1984, no. 63] Undocumented inlaid and engraved yew-wood secretaire with ebonized borders at Chevening attributable on stylistic grounds.

WYNNSTAY, Denbighshire or 20 ST JAMES'S SQ., London (Sir Watkin Williams Wynn, 4th Bt). 1775–76: Payment in account books for a small tea waiter and a mahogany child's stool. Total 13s. [Nat. Lib. Wales, Wynnstay MS, Box 115/7; Clwyd RO (Ruthin), DDWY 5516]

BERNERS ST, London (James Alexander, later 1st Earl of Caledon). 1775–77: Bill for miscellaneous repairs, cleaning, hire and storage; supply of some minor pieces of furniture.

Total £42 9s 1d. [PRO, (N. Ireland) D2433/A/2/3/2] Includes 'a neat Cribb Bedstead' (1777 £2 10s), 'a Walnuttree double Slope field Bedstead (1776 £10), etc. Also 'Porterage with an inlaid Commode ... from Mr Dupre's Portman Place' (presumably his brother-in-law Josias Dupre, Governor of Madras of Wilton Park, Bucks.), repairing and cleaning it and transporting it to Hungerford (?eventually to Ireland — see Caledon Castle, Co. Tyrone below.)

APPULDURCOMBE HOUSE, Isle of Wight, Hants. (Sir Richard Worsley, Bt). 1776: Payment in Hoare's Bank ledgers. Total £12 2s. [Gilbert, *Chippendale*, pp. 280–82]

HEATON HALL, Manchester (Sir Thomas Egerton, 7th Bt, later 1st Earl of Wilton). 1776: No bills but payment in cash account books. Total £25. [Preston RO, DDEg — uncalendared, vol. 2]

ADELPHI, London (Henry Hoare). 1776–77: Bill for furniture. Total £413 10s 1d [Hoare's Bank, family archive] Includes a press bed (£21), '5 Cabriole Elbow Chairs ... painted pink and white' (£15 15s), '2 large French Birjair Chair Frames painted pink and white' (£10 10s), '2 Tripods ornamented with carv'd Swags of Husks &c. & painted Etruscan' (£10 10s), 'Cartridge Paper glu'd to the Size of a large Glass and fixing it up for your Approbation' (2s 8d), 'A large extra siz'd Plate of French Glass silver'd Compt. agreed at £210', 'A Frame richly carv'd with Beads water leaves Honeysuckles and other Ornaments with an ornamental Top of an Altar, a Sphinx on each Side ... richly gilt [and] A circular Table Frame richly carv'd and gilt ... to go under the Glass' (together £75 16s) and miscellaneous repairs and upholstery etc.

GIDEA HALL, Essex (Richard Benyon). 1777–78: Payments in personal account book. Total £49 5s 6d. [Berks. RO, Benyon MS A3 and C. *Life*, 26 Feburary, 5 and 12 March 1981] (See also ENGLEFIELD HOUSE below)

DENTON PARK, Yorks. (Sir James Ibbetson, 2nd Bt). c. 1778: Payment on document belonging to Chippendale Soc. Total £18. [Gilbert, *Chippendale*, p. 286]

STOKE GIFFORD HOUSE, Glos. and **BERKELEY SQ.**, London (4th Duchess of Beaufort). 1778–98: Six bills for furnishing both houses. [Badminton papers] Total £302 1s 3d (£185 14s 3d for Stoke; £116 7s for London). Further payments in personal account books (with Hoare's) [Badminton papers], in part duplicating bills, bring total to £1,542 18s 6d. Stoke bills include curtains carpets and upholstery; bedroom furniture (e.g. a mahogany lady's dressing table (1778, £7 17s 6d); picture frames; a surviving pair of refined Neo-classical pier tables, originally painted grey and white (1778, £30) with inlaid marble tops made up to the firm's order by John Devall (1779, £23); a surviving satinwood and marquetry Pembroke table (1785, £10); 14 mahogany bannister back chairs with green leather seats (1790, £33); 6 'cottage pattern' chairs with feather ornament backs, japanned green and white (1790, £3 12s); 6 crested mahogany hall chairs (1790, £9 9s) (to correspond with 6 supplied for Berkeley Sq. by Robert Kennett (a former app.) at £10 4s in 1782). London bills mainly for interior decorating, alterations and repairs and hire of furniture.

ENGLEFIELD HOUSE, Berks. (Executors of Paulet Wrighte). 1780–82: Payments in account book of Rev. Peter Beauvoir and Richard Benyon (of Gidea, q.v.) as executors of Paulet Wrighte (d. 1779). Total £1,422 12s 11d. [Berks. RO, Benyon MS A5] Some attributable furniture remains. [C. *Life*, 26 February, 5 and 12 March 1981] Also 5 letters from Mayhew to R. Benyon (6 November 1779–28 April 1781) re disposal of Wrighte's lease on 12 Upper Harley St. (in competition with G. S. Bradshaw) and payment of Wrighte's outstanding account. [Benyon MS, C1–3]

CHILLINGHAM CASTLE, Northumb. (4th Earl of Tanker-ville). 1780–83: 3 Payments in Hoare's Bank ledgers. Total £400. Attributable secretaire of yew-wood and marquetry sold Sotheby's, 20 May 1955, lot 168, now in Fitzwilliam Museum, Cambridge. [M6–1957]

BROADLANDS, Hants., and **22 HANOVER Sq.**, London (2nd Viscount Palmerston). Before 1782–97: No bills but payments in personal account book (1785–98). Total £1,959 9s 0d. [Hants RO, Broadlands archive, 27 M 60 Box CXLIX] Several related letters mentioning Ince (e.g. 11 November 1796) [B. Connell, *Portrait of a Whig Peer*, 1957, pp. 346–49]; and Lady Palmerston's inventory (1797) mentions 'Secretary made by Ince' (1782). [C. *Life*, 29 January and 5 February 1981] Furnishing at Broadlands continuous but in two main phases: first coincides with Brown's remodelling of 1765–74, e.g. pair of giltwood pier glasses and marble-topped tables in Drawing room, painted hall chairs, marble-topped painted side tables in Dining room and dome bed in Green bedroom; second with Holland's work of 1788–92, e.g. pair of painted pier tables in Wedgwood room (and at Hanover Sq., 1792–97). Furniture largely *in situ* (with possible additions from London and Sheen).

CHIRK CASTLE, Denbighshire (Richard Myddelton). c. 1782–83: No bills but 2 letters from Ince, 3 October 1782 and 11 September 1783 [Nat. Lib. Wales, Chirk MS E5126–7], first asking Myddelton 'to see what subjects the paintings in the Cieling of the Saloon' are so that 'the compartments over the Glasses in the piers might be correspondant with them'; second refers to 'Mr Meyrick' and 'Putney Lodge' (re letting?) and 'repairs'. In addition to the pair of pier glasses, the firm also supplied for the Saloon a pair of semi-elliptical giltwood tables with characteristically inlaid tops; presumably also four giltwood torchères and suite of fourteen armchairs and two sofas (originally green and white japanned and upholstered in green 'tabory'). [Nat. Lib. Wales, Chirk MS, 1795 Inventory]

CALEDON CASTLE, Co. Tyrone, Ireland (James Alexander, later 1st Earl of Caledon). 1783–96: Four bills, one estimate and sixteen letters (one from client, rest from Mayhew) covering this lucrative commission for furnishing the newly-built Caledon. Total approximately £2,555. [PRO, N. Ireland D2433/A/2/3/1–21 and A/2/4/2] Correspondence mainly concerns payment and detailed answers to complaints of excessive charging — 'you was most particularly desirous that all your Furniture might be done in the *best manner*' (29 November 1785); arrangements for shipping (to Newry); caution as to unpacking of goods — 'for ... they are very careless in that Business on your side the Water' (17 August 1785) and instructions about the hanging of curtains, etc.; and recommendations for room decorations. (Apparently Mayhew never visited Caledon.) First phase (1785) includes principal furnishings for major groundfloor rooms (Oval drawing room, large Dining Parlour, Library, Common Parlour, Hall and Staircase): 12 Cabriolet chairs (£50 8s); 2 pier glasses in frames carved with dolphins (£264 14s); 2 inlaid pier tables on silver wood frames (£70); 20 mahogany banister back chairs (£64 10s); dining table (£50); sideboard (£22 15s); cistern (£8 17s); 8 crested hall chairs (£14 8s); octagonal lantern (£20 15s); 2 painted therms with vase lamps (£9 8s). Second phase (1791–95) includes three mirrors for Drawing room (£120), Dining Parlour (£140) and Common Parlour (£116); 2 gilt girandoles (£57 10s); mahogany cylinder desk (£16 16s); 2 painted satinwood octagonal tables (£12 12s); 12 japanned elbow chairs (£42); three large mirrors in carved frames (£336 10s) as well as carpets and curtains (the letter sent with an assembly drawing). Most of foregoing high quality pieces survive at Caledon. In addition two undocumented commodes: marquetry one (possibly from Josias Dupre: see Berners St above), of scaled-down Derby House type; the other serpentine, inlaid with urns.

BURTON HALL, Lincs. (3rd Lord Monson). 1785–92: 4 payments in personal accounts and one bill for hire of card tables and chairs. Total £19. [Lincoln RO, Monson archive 10/1/A/6 and 11/55]

CHATSWORTH, Derbs. and **DEVONSHIRE HOUSE**, London (5th Duke of Devonshire). 1785–86: Bill for furniture. Total £111 17s 3d. [Chatsworth papers, Household bills, voucher no. 20] Includes 'bringing a large Secretaire from Devonshire House to our WareRooms (5s) and (for Chatsworth) '2 very large oval Sattinwood Pembroke tables . . . inlaid with Trophies of Musical instruments . . .' (£43 10s) which survive as does 1 of the 4 satinwood music desks (£52 8s) but not the music stool (£10 10s). [*Burlington*, June 1980] Additional attributable furniture now at Chatsworth (some from other houses, e.g. Compton Place, Devonshire House, Burlington House, etc.) include three pairs of ormolu-mounted marquetry corner cupboards [*Treasures from Chatsworth*, 1979–80, no. 183], pair of satinwood flower-inlaid bedside cupboards, a marquetry kneehole writing table, etc. Dispersed items include a pair of marquetry box-like commodes [Christie's, 11 December 1930, lot 45] and pair of semi-elliptical marquetry commodes. [Christie's, 11 July 1929, lot 39]

KINGSTON LACY, Dorset (Henry Bankes). 1786: Single bill for 'A Large Mahogany Semi Oval Sideboard Curiously Inlaid . . . the whole richly Engrav'd'. Total (including oil cloth cover and packing) £29 18s 3d. [Dorset RO, Bankes Papers D/BKL] Table survives *in situ* [*C. Life*, 24 April 1986]

112 PALL MALL, London (Gertrude, Duchess of Bedford). 1786–92: Series of 10 bills and three related documents. Total £810 7s 5d. [Bedford Office, Dowager Duchess bills] Starts with '8 Advertizments in front of Paper, for a House . . .' (1786, £2 4s); negotiating new lease (£336 for 7 months) with out-going tenant (Earl Cowper) and proprietor (Mrs Kendall); witnessing inventory of contents (purchased outright in 1790) with J. Taitt for Lord Cowper (£2 2s); supplying additional furniture (mainly for servants rooms); moving, cleaning and altering furniture from Bedford House; joinery (1786–88); funeral of cook Nicholas Bertholdt (1787, £11 6s 1d). Major refurbishing (1789–90) mainly upholstery, e.g. '176 Yards Rich Silk blue & white Taboret (made on purpose)' (£57 4s) and '80 Yards best Wilton Carpet & Border' (£24); decoration, e.g. '575 Yards Stampt Elephant Paper' (£7 4s) and 708 feet of gilt moulding (£44 5s); and jobbing repairs, alterations, etc.

49 PALL MALL, London (Lord John Russell). 1787: Bill for furnishing (paid by Dowager Duchess). Total £407 6s 5d [Bedford Office, Dowager Duchess bills] includes: mahogany shaving table with canted corners and Queen's Ware fittings (£7 17s 6d) for Dressing Room; mahogany sofa covered 'with your Crimson silk Damask' (£10 10s) for Drawing Room; mahogany bed with japanned corners (£56 19s 6d including bedding) and mahogany dressing commode (£12 12s) for Bedchamber; 12 mahogany 'Parlour chairs with shaped fan backs' (£19 19s) for Dining room; alterations, repairs, etc.

HEYTESBURY HOUSE, Wilts. (Sir William Pierce Ashe A'Court, 1st Bt). 1787: Payment in Hoare's Bank ledgers. Total £440. Contents dispersed. Reference in *C. Life*, 27 July 1929, p. lxii to 'a receipted bill from the firm (1782–87) with a drawing of a commode formerly in the possession of Mr W. P. A'Court'.

CLARGES ST, London (5th Duke of Bedford). 1787–90: 4

bills. Total £43 2s 9d. [Bedford Office, 5th Duke's bills] Thorough spring cleaning of rooms, including cleaning upholstery and curtains with sand and bread, beating and relaying carpets, minor alterations to furniture; 'lengthening Mrs Hills' Bedstead' (1788 £1 11s 6d); minor joinery and redecoration.

DAYLESFORD HOUSE, Glos. (Warren Hastings). 1787–92: No bills but five payments in Goslings Bank ledgers. Total £2,176. Also receipt (from Cockerell) for plate glass. Total £236 19s 7d. [BM, Add MS 29 227–29, 231] Major commission to furnish S.P. Cockerell's newly-built house. Large attributable group of fine quality satinwood (now at Sandon Park) includes marquetry pedestal desk; adjustable reading table; pair of fall-front secretaires; two semi-elliptical commodes (one with painted ovals). Painted group includes 4 plume back chairs and suite of bedroom furniture decorated with peacock feathers. [*Burlington*, August 1970, 508–20] Attributable furniture elsewhere with Daylesford provenance: pair inlaid satinwood secretaires (Dalmeny House).

WOBURN ABBEY, Beds. (5th Duke of Bedford). 1787–93: Extensive series of bills coinciding with Holland's remodelling. Total in excess of £1,750. [Bedford Office, 5th Duke's Bills] Majority of work in bedrooms on demolished East front (Lord Maynard's Apartments, etc.). Apart from curtains, carpets and painted floor cloths notable payments are for chairs: 12 'very large' mahogany elbow chairs (1790, £42); an 'extra large sized' sofa (1790, £43 16s); 4 mahogany round back large dressing chairs (1793, £23 2s); beds: mahogany 4 post bed (1790, £105 17s 6d), with bedding; two white japanned double-headed couch beds (1792, £68 16s and £55 19s 2d) and bedroom cabinets, chests and tables; a mahogany 'circular commode' and two 'Coigns' [corner cupboards] with circular fronts (1791, £16 16s and £12 12s); a 'Machine mahogany step ladder to form a table (1791, £16 16s); 'Very neat Mahogany Secretary' (1791, £31 10s); Range of mahogany presses (1792, £45 6s); mahogany commode dressing table (1790, £22 5s). Curiosities include: a mahogany cupboard in four divisions for four pots (1790, £6 16s 6d) and 2 ormolu-mounted mahogany Billiards markers with silvered dials (1792, £12 12s). One bill [Beds. RO, R394, undated but 1791/92] is endorsed by D. Daguerre and Daguerre's bill [Beds. RO, R394] (1791) includes £29 10s for 'Commission on the Tradesman's bills for the furniture of the East Apartment' (including Mayhew & Ince's bill and probably those of Breteuil upholsterer and Boileau painter).

5th EARL OF STAIR. 1788: Rented 9 Grafton St for 10 weeks. Total £168. [Scottish RO, Breadalbane papers, GD135, Box 45/5/9]

CARLTON HOUSE, London (The Prince of Wales). 1788–89: Two bills for furniture. Total £37 6s 6d. [PRO, HO.73/21] Includes two bedside tables and three round Loo tables (£5, £9 and £9 9s), the most expensive with central mahogany pool, five counterwells and three branch adjustable light. Part of the less elaborate furnishings for Holland's remodelling of 1783–96. A large bill from Daguerre for Carlton House was referred to the firm 'to report on the upholstery articles'. [*GCM*]

OAKLEY PARK, Beds. (5th Duke of Bedford). 1791–94: 4 Bills, coinciding with Holland's re-modelling of 1789–92. Total £442 16s 11d. [Bedford Office, 5th Duke's bills] Includes mahogany four post bed with japanned cornices (1791, £76 6s 11d including bedding): 2 window cornices to match (£2 16s); 2 japanned elbow chairs for the Drawing Room (1793, £6 10s); another mahogany and japanned 4 post bed, with chintz hangings (1794, £84 10s including bedding); a single-headed Couch bed (1794, £8 18s); four japanned elbow chairs with tablet splats (1794, £6); a mahogany

'angular Bason stand' with Wedgwood fittings (1794, £2 6s 6d); a mahogany secretaire with sliding desk (1794, £12 12s), etc.; moving furniture round between Woburn, Oakley and London, including some 'to Lady Eliz. Forster's Room'.
WESTMINSTER FIRE OFFICE, London. 1792–93: Directors minutes record (7 June 1792) order to Ince for 18 single chairs and 1 armchair and 'desks'. 12 June 1793 bill queried. 20 June bill paid. Total £102 9s. Five matching chairs supplied 1813. Backs embody portcullis badge of Fire Office. Both partners served several 2-year periods as Directors of Fire Office. James Mayhew (son) and Charles (grandson) became Surveyors to Fire Office. [C. Life, 21 December 1951, p. 2090; GCM; Colvin, p. 545]
MADINGLEY HALL, Cambs. (Lady Cotton). 1800: Payment in personal account book. Total £9. [Cambs. RO, 588/A45]
BRYNBELLA, Denbighshire (Mrs Hester Piozzi). 1802: Letter mentions 'furniture expected from Mayhew and Inch, to decorate pretty Brynbella'. [The Intimate Letters of Hester Piozzi and Penelope Pennington 1778–1821, 1914]

H.R. and C.C.

Mayle, William, London. In 1723 he supplied the Duke of Montrose with a 'Table bedstead' or field bed. [Scottish RO, GD220/6/1239/50 and 56]

Maylin, Edward, Cannon St, London, freeman joiner and cm (1714–33). Took app. named Alexander Parratt in 1714. Notice in London Gazette, 2 March 1733 read: 'This is to give notice to Mr. Alexander Parratt, formerly apprentice to Mr. Maylin, Cabinetmaker in Cannon Street, that if he applies to Captain Joseph Willoughby in Abchurch Lane, Lombard Street, he may be informed of something to his advantage.' [S of G, app. index] Probably Edward Malin.

Maynard, —, address unrecorded (1750). Named in the accounts for Holkham Hall, Norfolk, in 1750, supplying a leather chair costing £9 9s, with packing case at 10s. [V&A archives]

Maynard, Braddick, parish of St Augustine, Bristol, cm (1784). [Poll bk]

Maynard, Charles, London, upholder (1737–d.1781). Son of Charles Maynard, farrier of Coleman St; app. to John Carr on 16 April 1737. Admitted freeman of the Upholders' Co. by servitude on 6 September 1744, master in 1778. [GL, Upholders' Co. records]

Maynard, Edward, South St and Seahouses, Eastbourne, Sussex, carpenter, cm, u and builder (1832–39). [D] See L. Maynard & Sons.

Maynard, Elizabeth, Shepherd St, Hanover Sq., London, upholder (1780–81). Took out Sun Insurance policies in 1780 for £500, utensils and stock accounting for £150; and in 1781 with John Cartwright Maynard and James Bunch for £700, of which utensils and stock accounted for £250. [GL, Sun MS vol. 282, p. 93; vol. 289, p. 571]

Maynard, James, 16 Northumberland Pl., Bath, Som., cm (1833). [D]

Maynard, John, Poland St, London, u (1749). [Poll bk]

Maynard, John Cartwright, see Elizabeth Maynard.

Maynard, John, Shepherd St, Hanover Sq., London, u (1784). [Poll bk] See Maynard & Dunch.

Maynard, John E., Sheep St, Bicester, Oxon., cm and u (1830). [D]

Maynard, Joseph, Bristol, cm (1792–1801). Addresses given at Narrow Plain 1792; St Philip's Plain, 1793–94; and Castle St, 1799–1801. [D]

Maynard, Joseph, Wells, Som., cm (1811). Declared bankrupt, Exeter Flying Post, 14 March 1811.

Maynard, L. & Sons, South St, Eastbourne, Sussex, builders, carpenters, joiners, furniture makers and undertakers (1837).

Advertised in Sussex Agricultural Express, 6 May 1837. See Edward Maynard.

Maynard & Dunch, Shepherd St, Bond St, London, upholder (1782–93). [D] See John Maynard.

Mayne, George, High St, Winslow, Bucks., cm and builder (1823). [D]

Mayne, Goldsworth, Buckingham St, Aylesbury, Bucks., cm and u (1823). [D]

Mayne, Richard, 16 Rider Ct, Leicester Fields, London, upholder (1781). Admitted freeman of the Upholders' Co. on 4 April 1781. [GL, Upholders' Co. records]

Mayo, James, High Wycombe, Bucks., chairmaker (1826). Daughter bapt. in 1826. [PR (bapt.)]

Mayo, William Hayward, 4 Shoe Lane, London, u and cm (1808–11). Took out a Sun Insurance policy on 14 January 1808 for £400, including £300 on utensils and stock. In 1810 he was fined for non-service at St Bride's. [D; GL, Sun MS vol. 441, ref. 812549]

Mayo, William, 15 Goodge St, London, chair and sofa manufacturer (1829). [D]

Mayor, —, address unrecorded, u (1803). Subscribed to Sheraton's Cabinet Dictionary, 1803.

Mayow, Richard, London, upholder and cm (1760–74). Trading at 46 Crutched Friars, 1770–74. Son of Richard Mayow, shoemaker of Oxford. App. to Samuel Hibberdine on 10 April 1760, and admitted freeman of the Upholders' Co. by servitude on 16 April 1767. [D; GL, Upholders' Co. records]

Mayson, Joseph, Sandgate Head, Penrith, Cumb., cm and/or joiner (1828–34). [D]

Meacock, Robert, Chester, u (1662). Admitted freeman on 6 October 1662. [Chester freemen rolls].

Mead, J., St Andrew's Terr., Bath, Som., u (1819). [D]

Mead, James, 14 Pollen St, Maddox St, London, u (1839). [D]

Mead, James, Booker, High Wycombe, Bucks., chairmaker (b. c. 1801–41). Aged 40 at the time of the 1841 Census.

Mead, John, 8 Castle St, Long Acre, London, u and undertaker (1820). [D]

Mead, John, High Wycombe, Bucks., chairmaker (b. c. 1801–41). Aged 40 at the time of the 1841 Census.

Mead, Samuel, West Wycombe, Bucks., chairmaker (b. c. 1806–41). Aged 35 at the time of the 1841 Census.

Mead, Thomas, address unrecorded, upholder (1719–29). Son of Thomas Mead, poulterer of Stepney, London. App. to Thomas Sutton on 3 June 1719, and admitted freeman of the Upholders' Co. by servitude on 3 December 1729. [GL, Upholders' Co. records]

Mead, Thomas, Leck (or Leek) St, Leighton Buzzard, Beds., cm and u (1839). [D]

Mead, Thomas, West Wycombe, Bucks., chairmaker (b. c. 1784–1841). Aged 57 at the time of the 1841 Census.

Mead, William, address unrecorded, cm (1794). Lady Northampton, the Hon. Mrs Leigh, ordered furniture from Mead for the Mansion House at Leighton. On 30 May 1794 he was paid for 'Making a full sized bed compleat', an elbow chair, three stools and two seats; and in August 1794 he charged the Hon. Miss Leigh £2 2s for a 'Mahogany card table with green cloth.' Amongst the Leigh receipts is a bill for furniture supplied to John Stone, including '1 paire Mahogany bed post', costing £1 11s 6d; '2 sets of oak sliders', 3s; a 'New taister rail', 2s 6d; and 'puting up 2 beds', for 4s. [Shakespeare Birthplace Trust, Leigh receipts, DR 18/5]

Meade, Abraham, West Wycombe, Bucks., wheelwright and chairmaker (1790–1844). [D]

Meade, William, address unrecorded, upholder (1755–62). Son of Thomas Meade, linen draper of Princes Risborough, Bucks. App. to David Langton on 13 May 1755, and admitted freeman of the Upholders' Co. by servitude on 7 October 1762. [GL, Upholders' Co. records]

Meader, John, at the 'White Lyon over against the Church in Aldermanbury', London, cm and joiner (1707–21). Trade card states that he 'maketh and selleth all sorts of Cabinets and Joyners Work, viz. Cabinets, Scrutores, Chests of Drawers, Book-Cases, and Desks; and all sorts of Japan-Work, as Indian Cabinets, Tea-Tables, and Folding-Tables; and all sorts of Looking-Glasses, Peere-Glasses, Chimney-Glasses, Sconces, &c. at reasonable Rates.' [Landauer Coll., MMA, NY] As a joiner, he took out Hand in Hand Insurance policies on 16 October 1707 for £200 on his house; on 3 July 1714 for £300 on his house and £200 on the house adjoining; on 7 March 1721 for £300 on a house in St Paul's Alley, St Gregory's parish, and £300 on a house abutting north of Page St; and on 29 July 1721 for £300 on his house. [GL, Hand in Hand MS vol. 5, ref. 14576; vol. 13, p. 243; vol. 23, p. 151; vol. 24, p. 57]

Meader, William, Shaftesbury, Dorset, cm (1798). [D]

Meadley, Richard, Beverley and Hull, Yorks., cm and chairmaker (1799–1831). Polled at Beverley in 1799. Recorded in Sculcoates, Hull in November 1806 when he took app. of Hull named John Strateon; in February 1810, Thomas Feetam; and in July 1811, Daniel Clark. Trading at 52 Roper St, Hull, 1828–31. [D; Hull app. reg.]

Meadley, William, York, cm (1771). Son of Henry Meadley, deceased, of Grimston; app. to Joseph Swale, cm, on 14 November 1771. [York app. reg.]

Meadows, John, Applegate St, Leicester, chairmaker (1827–28). [D]

Meadows, John, 15 Hill's Yd, Meadow Lane, Leeds, Yorks., chairmaker (1837–40). [D]

Meadows, John, 71 Princes St, Leicester Sq., London, carver and gilder (1839). [D]

Meadows, Samuel, Nottingham, fancy and Windsor chairmaker (1818–40). Listed at Mount St, 1818–35, and Leen Side in 1840. [D]

Meakin, James, Manchester, cm (1744). Took app. named Low in 1744. [S of G, app. index]

Meal, William, Hall Lane, East Dereham, Norfolk, cm (1836). [D]

Mealing, Edward, High St, Marlow, Bucks., cm and u (1830–39). [D]

Mealing, Henry, High Wycombe, Bucks., chairmaker (b. c. 1788–1841). Son bapt. in 1826. Recorded as having married in 1837. Aged 53 at the time of the 1841 Census. [PR]

Mealing, John, High Wycombe, Bucks., chairmaker (1814–38). Daughters bapt. in 1814, 1816 and 1821. Acted as a witness at his son's wedding in 1838. [PR (bapt.)]

Mealing, Joseph, High Wycombe, Bucks., chair (French) polisher (b. c. 1811–41). Son bapt. in 1830. Aged 30 at the time of the 1841 Census.

Mealing, Thomas, High Wycombe, Bucks., chairmaker and chair caner (b. c. 1805–41). Son bapt. in 1828; daughters in 1835, 1837 and 1840. Aged 36 at the time of the 1841 Census. [PR (bapt.)]

Mealing, William, High Wycombe, Bucks., chairmaker (b. c. 1811–41). Listed as cm and u at High St in 1823 and as chairmaker at New Lands in 1839. Daughters bapt. in 1835 and 1839, son in 1836. Aged 30 at the time of the 1841 Census. William Mealing & Son, u and chairmakers, worked for the Royal Household from 1838–41. In March 1838 they supplied to Brighton Pavillion two carved and gilt music chairs, one covered in 'His Majesty's silk', and the other, of maple, in green morocco leather. They also provided six further carved and gilt maple chairs to Windsor Castle and Buckingham Palace, and '12 maple fly chairs' at 36s each. On

31 December 1838 they charged £8 17s 6d for twenty-four cane-seated stools supplied to Windsor; and on 30 June 1839, £16 16s for forty-eight beechwood caned stools for the Music Room at Buckingham Palace, at 7s each. The accounts of 31 December 1840 record '3 Easy Framed Chairs with Rosewood Rails, Carved Legs, & Brass Socket Castors', costing £12 9s, bought for Windsor; and on 30 June 1841, a further twenty-four caned beech stools for Windsor, and one chair for Buckingham Palace. [D; PR (bapt.); Windsor Royal Archives, Item 2, Box 1; PRO, LC 11/99, 101 and 110] Possibly two tradesmen of the same name are concerned here.

Mealyard, Martin, Bryanstone, Dorset, carver (1760). Took app. named Hancock in 1760. [S of G, app. index]

Meane, John, 54 Friday St, London, chestmaker (1784). [D]

Mear, John, Peter St, Bath, Som., cm (1793). [D]

Meares, George, 8 Sawney Pope St, Liverpool, cm (1827). [D]

Mearing, John, 98 Gt Portland St, London, u and cm (1837–39). [D]

Mearns, Alexander, address unrecorded, cm (1803). Subscribed to Sheraton's *Cabinet Dictionary*, 1803.

Mears, George, Walker Pl., 2 Hatton Gdn, Liverpool, picture frame manufacturer (1823–24). [D]

Mears, Henry, 17 Ratcliffe Highway, Upper East Smithfield, London, carver and gilder (1817). [D]

Mears, John, Leadenhall St, London, upholder and cm (1779–98). Addresses also given at 98 Leadenhall St, 1779–81; 220 Borough High St, 1782–86; and no. 218 in 1784. Son of William Mears, freeman butcher of London; admitted freeman of the Upholders' Co. by patrimony on 2 July 1779. Took app. named Richard Lewis in 1780. Took out Sun Insurance policies in 1779 for £400, including £275 on utensils, stock and goods; in 1782 for £1,000, £680 on stock and goods; and in 1784 for £1,000, £620 on utensils, stock and goods. Named in Bailey's list of bankrupts in 1787. [D; GL, Upholders' Co. records; GL, Sun MS vol. 276, p. 93; vol. 300, p. 118; vol. 319, p. 535]

Mears, John, London, then Philadelphia, USA, u, cm, chair and Venetian blind maker (before 1788). Advertised in *Penn'a Packet*, 31 May 1788, that he was from London, and now trading on the south side of Market St between Seventh and Eighth Streets, Philadelphia. He 'Makes and sells cabriole and plain sophas and chairs, bed furniture and window curtains, carpets, sea bedding, mattresses, &c. &c. in the genteelest taste, and on very moderate terms, for ready money only. N.B. Venetian blinds repaired, new painted and mounted. Genteel Boarding and Lodging for Gentlemen.'

Mears, John, Liverpool, cm (1761–96). Admitted freeman in 1761. Former app., John Rycroft, petitioned freedom in 1780. His sons, Richard, John and Thomas Mears, cm, petitioned freedom on birthright in 1796, each paying 3s 4d. [Liverpool freemen's committee bk] Possible confusion with:

Mears, John, Liverpool, cm (1790–1822). Addresses given at 12 Queen St, Oldham St, 1790–96; 4 Upper Milk St with shop at 37 Smithfield St, 1807–14; 5 New Milk St in 1815; 6 Upper Milk St in 1816; 77 Stanley St in 1818; and 26 Gt Crosshall St in 1821. In 1796 he petitioned freedom on birthright as son of John Mears, cm, paying 3s 4d. Admitted freeman on 25 May 1796. Took apps named William Rimmer in 1801, Robert Gill in 1803, George Lang in 1804, and Henry Gill in 1805, all admitted freemen in 1812. Took apps, John Waring in 1806, William Hughes, and John Armstrong in 1808, all three admitted freemen in 1816; Samuel Moffett in 1813, admitted freeman in 1822; William Tute in 1813, admitted in 1830; and William Hughes jnr, app. in 1808. Sale of John Mears's household furniture and stock in trade 'for the Benefit of the Creditors', presumably on bankruptcy, advertised in *Liverpool Mercury*, 21 July 1815. Furniture for sale comprised 'Camp Bedsteads & Hangings, Feather Beds & Bedding, mahogany Chairs, Sofa, Chest of Drawers, Pembroke, Snap & Dining Tables, some Kitchen Requisites etc. The Stock in Trade will consist of Mahogany Plank Boards & Veneers, Birch, Maple, Oak & Deal Boards & Planks, Bedwood, Benches, a few Tools, & quantity of Slates, old Timber etc.' [D; Liverpool freemen reg. and committee bk]

Mears, John, Duddeston St, Birmingham, cm (1818). [D]

Mear(s), Richard & Catherine, Duke St, St James's, Westminster, London, upholders (1749–51). [Poll bk; Children apprenticed by the Sons of the Clergy cited in Heal]

Mears, Richard, Liverpool, cm (1796–1818). Son of John Mears, cm; admitted freeman on 26 May 1796. His son, William Dobson Mears, book-keeper, was born on 9 August 1796, and petitioned freedom on birthright in 1818. [Liverpool freemen reg. and committee bk]

Mears, Thomas, Liverpool, cm (1796). Son of John Mears, cm; admitted freeman on 26 May 1796. [Liverpool freemen reg.]

Measam, F., address unrecorded. Chairs, c.1795, recorded bearing the stamp of 'F. MEASAM' on the back. [V&A archives]

Measam, Francis, 19 Primrose St, Bishopsgate St Without, London, cm and chairmaker (1791). Took out a Sun Insurance policy on 27 September 1791 for £200. [GL, Sun MS vol. 379, p. 646]

Mease, Thomas, parish of St Leonard, Bristol, upholder (1774). [Poll bk]

Measom, Daniel, Gales Row, Greenwich, London, carver and gilder (1826). [D]

Measures, John, Leicester, cm and u (1803–35). Recorded at Humberstone Gate, 1815–22, and Gallowtree Gate in 1827–35. App. to Joseph Spencer, u, and admitted freeman in 1803. [D; Leicester freemen rolls]

Measures, William John, Belgrave Gate, Leicester, u (1805). [D]

Meatvard, William, 78 Mount St, Grosvenor Sq., London, u and paper hanger (1820). [D]

Mecey, John, 150 High St, Southampton, Hants., u and cm (1823–24). Advertised in *Southampton Herald*, 2 October 1823. [D]

Mecham, Joseph, London, cm (1820–29). Addresses given at Dog Row, Bethnal Green, 1820–28, and 32 Cambridge Rd, Whitechapel in 1829. [D]

Mechi, J. J., 130 Leadenhall St, London, writing desk and dressing case maker (1829). [D]

Medcalfe, —, address unrecorded, chairmaker (1756). Received payment of £4 4s from the Duke of Beaufort for work done at Badminton House, Glos. [Badminton papers: account bks]

Medcalfe, Hesilrigg, Newcastle, u (1741). [Poll bk]

Medd, William, Skinner Lane, Whitby, Yorks., cm (1823–34). [D]

Meddom (or Meddons), William, Lime St, London, u (1730–44). Named in newspapers in 1730. The *Daily Advertiser*, 14 May 1744 announced sale of furniture and plate of Thomas Blechynden, deceased; catalogues to be had from 'Mr. William Meddons, Lime Street; Mr. Thomas Cardnor, Pood Lane, Upholsterers...'. [Heal]

Medforth, Flinton, Hull, Yorks., cm (1765). Named in the Burton Constable papers in 1765, supplying a bedstead costing £18 18s. Medforth continued the business of his mother, 'Mrs. Whitfield'. [Humberside RO]

Medhurst, —, 153 St John's St, West Smithfield, London, cm, upholder and undertaker (1793). Subscribed to Sheraton's *Drawing Book*, 1793. Trade card shows Empire-style couch bed, shield-back arm chair and dressing table; and states that Medhurst supplied 'Fire Screens & Portable Desks', 'Dispensary and Medicine Chests'. [BM] Bow-fronted mahogany

chest of drawers, c.1790, recorded, cross-banded in satinwood, bearing label in top drawer. [Private Coll.] Probably:

Medhurst, David, St John's Lane, West Smithfield, London, cm (1796). Declared bankrupt, *Billinge's Liverpool Advertiser*, 27 June 1796.

Medhurst, George, High St, St Ann's, Lewes, Sussex, Tunbridge-ware manufacturer (1832–41). [D; poll bks]

Medlicott, Thomas, Church St, Bishops Castle, Salop, chairmaker (1836). [D]

Medowes, Arthur, Colchester, Essex, chairmaker (1670). Probate dated 1670. [*Wills at Chelmsford*]

Mee, Benjamin, 9 Kennington Row, London, cm and u (1839). [D]

Meek (or Meck), H., 11 Forster St, Bishopsgate, London, bedstead and chair manufacturer (1802–04). Meek of this address subscribed to Sheraton's *Cabinet Dictionary*, 1803. Possibly Hannah Meek, trading in Moorfields, 1808. [D] See William Meek.

Meek, Samuel, Market Pl., Bridlington, Yorks., cm (1830). [D]

Meek, William, Moorfields, London, freeman upholder, bedstead and chairmaker (1777–89). Addresses given at Long Alley, 1777–82, and 11 Forster St, Half Moon Alley, Bishopsgate St Without, 1783–89. Took out Sun Insurance policies in 1777 for £200, utensils and stock accounting for £100; in 1781 for £400, £300 on utensils and stock; in 1782 for £500, £400 on utensils and stock; and in 1789 for £100 on utensils and stock in his warehouse 'nearly opposite his dwelling house in Forster Street'. Admitted freeman of the Upholders' Co. by redemption on 3 December 1783. Between 1783 and 1785 he employed twenty non-freemen for three months each year. [GL, Sun MS vol. 261, p. 549; vol. 288, p. 433; vol. 299, p. 266; vol. 362, p. 659; GL, Upholders' Co. records; GL, City Licence bks, vol. 10] See H. Meek.

Meeke, George, London, cm (1793). Subscribed to Sheraton's *Drawing Book*, 1793.

Meek(e), George, Duke St, Manchester Sq., London, cm (1802–06). Recorded at no. 9 on 1 December 1802 when he took out a Sun Insurance policy for £850. Named as one of the orators and creditor of John Wrangham, late of Tunbridge Wells, Kent, deceased, in the case between Mann and Hulme. [GL, Sun MS vol. 427, ref. 740496; PRO, C13, 360]

Meeks, John, Warwick and Leamington, Warks., cm and u (1828–37). Trading in partnership with Thomas Gummery (or Gommery) as cm, u, carvers and turners at Lower Church St, Warwick, 1822–29; St Nicholas's Church St, Warwick, and Regent St, Leamington, 1828–30. Recorded alone at Church St, Warwick in 1831 and 35 Regent St, Leamington, 1835–37. Meeks and Gummery were declared bankrupt in *London Gazette*, 2 December 1831. [D; poll bk]

Meens, John, parish of St Andrew, Norwich, cm (1812). [Poll bk]

Meens, William, Doncaster, Yorks., cm (1834). [D]

Meere, Richard, late of Vine St, St James's, Westminster, London, u (1766). [PRO, C12 1522/18]

Meeres, John N., St Mary's Gate, Great Grimsby, Lincs., joiner, cm and builder (1826–35). Recorded at Baxter-gate in 1835. [D]

Meers, John, High St, Bridgnorth, Salop, cm (1840). [D]

Meggitt, Thomas, Hull, Yorks., carver and gilder (1826–39). Carried out much work at Burton Constable, including gilding and silvering furnishings in the Chinese Room in 1826, japanning chairs in 1834, and providing '— Cabinet stands Jap^g elegantly Gold Bronze Black etc.', for £21. In 1839 he supplied four rosewood thermometers and a barometer obtained from Maspoli of 79 Lowgate, Hull. [Humberside RO, Burton Constable papers]

Meggitt, William, 16 Fish St, Hull, Yorks., cm and u (1818–20). [D]

Meggs, John, Tottenham Ct Rd, St Pancras, London, broker and upholder (1785–87). Named in Bailey's list of bankrupts, 1785. Described as late of Tottenham Ct Rd when the dividends on bankruptcy were announced in *Williamson's Liverpool Advertiser,* 9 July 1787.

Megson, John, Hull, Yorks., cm (1818–39). Addresses given at 23 Carr Lane in 1823; 15 New Dock St in 1826; 14 Junction Dock St, 1826–31; 12 Wells St with res. at Little Albion St, 1837–38; and 12 Wells Yd, Waterwork St in 1839. Took apps of Hull named Thomas Wardale in January 1818; James England Stockdale in January 1822; and Henry Newsham in April 1823. [D; Hull app. reg.]

Mehanna, John, Tarporley, Cheshire, chairmaker (1748–91). Had children bapt. at Tarporley in 1748 and 1751. Described as a pauper in 1791. [PR (bapt.)]

Mein, James, London, cm (1793). Subscribed to Sheraton's *Drawing Book,* 1793.

Meineke (or Meincke), John, Liverpool, cm (1829–39). App. to William John Roberts in 1829, and admitted freeman on servitude on 31 July 1839. [Liverpool freemen reg.]

Melbourn, —, 26 Gresse St, Rathbone Pl., London, cm (1808). [D]

Melhuish, Edwin, Back St, Exeter, Devon, carver and turner (1836). Son Edwin John Murch bapt. on 6 March 1836 at St Mary Major. [PR (bapt.)]

Meller (or Mellor), John, Liverpool, upholder (1774–84). Trading at 60 Park Lane, 1781–84. In 1774 he petitioned freedom as son of Thomas Mellor, blockmaker, freeborn. Admitted freeman on 12 September 1780. Marriage at Waverham, Cheshire, to Miss Lea of Liverpool reported in *Williamson's Liverpool Advertiser,* 12 May 1775. [D; Liverpool freemen reg. and committee bk]

Meller, John, Common, Worksop, Notts., cm and u (1835). [D]

Meller, Richard, Nottingham, cm (d. 1819). Probate will dated 16 November 1819. [Notts. RO, probate records]

Mellet(t), John, Knave's Acre, Westminster, London, cm (1749). [Poll bk]

Mellin, Thomas, Halifax, Yorks., cm (1784–90). Advertised in *Leeds Intelligencer,* 7 December 1790. [D; *Furn. Hist.,* 1971]

Mellineaux, George, Liverpool, cm (1747). [Chester poll bk]

Melling, George, Liverpool, carver (1803–04). Recorded at Dale St in 1803 and 4 Davies's St, Dale St in 1804. [D]

Melling, John, address unrecorded, cm (1762). Named in the Preston Guild record of burgesses in 1762 as son of Nicholas Melling, flaxdresser of Lancaster.

Melling, John, 9 Greenhill Rents, St John St, London, carver (1779). Took out a Sun Insurance policy in 1779 for £100 of which utensils and stock accounted for £15. [GL, Sun MS vol. 274, p. 273]

Mellish, John, 2 Air St, Piccadilly, London, cm, u, writing desk and dressing-case maker (1826–29). [D]

Mello, —, South Audley St, London, carver (1771). Mentioned in a letter from Thomas Robinson, 2nd Lord Grantham, to Lord Fitzwilliam regarding the proposed furniture for Milton, Northants. [*C. Life,* vol. cxxix, no. 3352, pp. 1272–73]

Mellor, Hugh, Mill St, Macclesfield, Cheshire, cm (1816). [D]

Mellor, Hugh, Etchells St, Stockport, Cheshire, cm (1834). [D]

Mellor, James, Barum Top, Halifax, Yorks., cm and u (1830). [D]

Mellor, James, 19 Mill Lane, Ashton-under-Lyne, Lancs., joiner and cm (1834). [D]

Mellor, John, 50 Old St, Ashton-under-Lyne, Lancs., joiner and cm (1834). [D]

Mellor, John, Shudehill, Manchester, cm, chairmaker and furniture broker (1828–40). Trading as broker only at no. 81 in 1828, and also as cm and chairmaker at no. 48, 1832–40. [D]

Mellor, John, Church St, Dunstable, Beds., cm and u (1839). [D]

Mellor, William, Oswestry, Salop, cm (1822–36). Recorded at Willow St in 1822 and Cross St, 1835–36. [D]

Mellowes, John, 88 Old St, St Luke's, London, cm and u (1839). [D]

Melmoth, John, Priests Row, Wells, Som., carver and gilder (1839). [D]

Melmouth, John, Chamberlain St, Wells, Som., cm (1830). [D]

Melnoth, John, High St, Wells, Som., cm and u (1822). [D]

Melrose, Thomas, Halifax and York, cm (1784–98). Polled at York of Halifax in 1784. Trading at Bishophill, York, in 1798. [D]

Melsam (Melsom or Milsom), John, Bristol, carver (1712–34). Recorded in St Stephen's parish, 1721–34. Took app. named John Felto in 1712. [Poll bks; *Wilts. Apps and their Masters*]

Melsham, Joseph, St Clement's parish, Oxford, cm (1768). [Poll bk; Frowde, *Survey of Oxford*]

Melson, —, address unrecorded. In January 1770 he was paid £1 18s 6d for 'Chairs Bottom.ᵈ'. [Lincoln RO, MM9/9]

Melton, John, Liverpool, u (1780). Admitted freeman on 12 September 1780. [Liverpool freemen reg.]

Melvill, Robert, address unrecorded, cm (1754). Subscribed to Chippendale's *Director,* 1754.

Melvin, J., Bond St, Newcastle, joiner and cm (1824). [D]

Menardeau, Pierre, London, cm or 'menuisier' (1681). On 4 December 1681 he arrived from La Forest-sur-Seiurs, his wife dying in childbirth shortly afterwards. He was granted £2 15s 6d Threadneedle St Relief, and a further 10s on 28 March 1682 to go to Ireland. [*Hogarth Soc.,* 1949, p. 140]

Mendall, J., Mount Beacon, Bath, Som., cm (1819). [D]

Menday, James, High Wycombe, Bucks., chairmaker (1814–16). Son bapt. in 1814, daughter in 1816. [PR (bapt.)]

Menday, James, Snowsfields, Bermondsey, London, chair and sofa manufacturer (1826–39). Recorded at no. 13, 1826–29, and no. 58 in 1839. [D]

Mendez, —, Strand, opposite Southampton St, London, 'Repository for all sorts of new and second hand furniture' (1763). [D]

Mendham, Richard, 10 Park Pl., Locksfields, London, chair and sofa maker (1839). [D]

Mendinhall, G., 13 Gibbs Ct, Bath, Som., chair and sofa maker (1826). [D]

Mendus, Thomas, 3 Little Carter Lane, St Paul's, London, bedstead maker (1820). [D]

Menty, John, Christchurch, Hants., cm (1839). [D]

Menzies, Archibald, London, cm (1772–74). Recorded at Orange Ct, St Martin-in-the-Fields in 1772, when he took app. named Hannah Newbury. Polled at Westminster of Orange St in 1774. [Westminster Ref. Lib., St Martin's PR, MS F4309, p. 12]

Menzie(r)s, John, Berwick-upon-Tweed, Northumb., u (1778). Declared bankrupt, *Gents Mag.,* September 1778.

Mercer, — jnr, Newark, Notts., carver, gilder and painter (1790–98). [D; poll bk]

Mercer, George, near Cavendish Sq., London, carver (1740–80). According to Gunnis, *Dictionary of British Sculptors,* p. 258, he was a subscriber to Kent's *Designs of Inigo Jones,* and was employed at Longford Castle in 1740. In 1757 he supplied four console tables to the Earl of Dumfries, for Dumfries House, Scotland. Mercer executed the tables according to directions from John Adam, who noted in a memorandum on 3 November 1755: 'Between the Windows there should be fine Marble tables with handsome frames. From the floor to the underpart of the belt or surbase moulding that goes round the room is 2 feet 8 ins and to the top of it is 3 feet which dimentions will regulate the height of these frames and tables, and their length must not exceed

4 feet 2 ins. Under these Tables Jarrs or Pieces of China are very propper parts of Ornamental furniture.' The tables were invoiced on 6 August 1757 as '2 Sienna Marble and 2 Jasper Marble Tables with Carved & Gilt frames, the whole agreed at £88.' Two chimney pieces were also mentioned, one for the Drawing Room, costing £130, and one for the Dining Room at £95. The bill was followed by a letter explaining that the tables had been 'ship'd on Board the St. Andrew ... Bound for Leith', and asking for an error in costing to be taken into account when the bill was settled: 'One thing I beg leave to lay before your Lordship, that is when I made the Estimate of the Table Frames I only thought of painting but nothing of Gilding which cost Twelve guineas. Therefore Humbly submit it to your Lordship to make me such an allowance as you shall think proper. I shall by this post write to Messrs Adams to take care of them untill your Lo'p shall send Carriages for them. I have let Mr. Smith of Compston Street know that your Lo'p had a long time expected to hear from him, so suppose he will write soon, he call'd here once about the Table frames, & I told him they were done, he seem'd a little surprized, I suppose your Lo'p had forgot that you had agreed with me for them & had wrote to him about them.' [*Burlington*, November 1969, p. 664] George Mercer, carver of London, worked at Inveraray Castle, Argyll. [*C. Life*, 5 June 1975, p. 1488]

Mercer, Henry, address unrecorded, upholder (1722–d. by 1748). Son of John Mercer, freeman upholder of London. App. to his father on 2 May 1722, and admitted freeman of the Upholders' Co. by servitude on 6 August 1729. [GL, Upholders' Co. records]

Mercer, J., Chester, cm (1812–19). Trading at Duke St in 1812 and Park St in 1819. [Poll bks] Possibly John Mercer.

Mercer, John, address unrecorded, upholder (1707–37). Admitted freeman of the Upholders' Co. on 1 October 1707. Took apps named James Wolfe, 1714–23; Samuel Fenn, 1719–26/27; his son, Henry Mercer, 1722–29; and Isaac Watlington, 1730–37. [GL, Upholders' Co. records]

Mercer, John, Lothbury, London, upholder (1713–18). Recorded at Drapers Ct, Princess St on 31 October 1713; and at 'The Blue Ball' on 12 April 1718 when he took out Sun Insurance policies on goods and merchandise. [GL, Sun MS vol. 3, p. 73; vol. 8, ref. 10814]

Mercer, John, Hull, Yorks., cm (1780–84). [Poll bks]

Mercer, John, Liverpool, cm (1811–39). Addresses given at 6 Oldham St, Oldham Ct in 1829; 6 Oldham Ct, Oldham St in 1835; and 3 Templar Terr., 11 Gt George St in 1839. App. to John Chesters in 1811, and petitioned freedom on servitude in 1818, paying 6s 8d. [D; Liverpool freemen's committee bk]

Mercer, John, City Walls, Chester, cm (1834). [D] Possibly J. Mercer.

Mercer, Joseph, Warrington, Lancs., chairmaker (1816–34). Trading at Winwick St, 1816–18, and Sankey St in 1834. [D]

Mercer, Samuel, Liverpool, carver (1750). Took app. named Chubbard in 1750. [S of G, app. index]

Mercer, Samuel, Chester, cm (1775–1828). Addresses given at Nine Houses in 1784; City Walls, 1789–97; Park Lane in 1816; and Park St, 1819–28. Son of Ralph Mercer, cm; admitted freeman on 30 November 1775. Took apps named John Roberts in 1784 and Samuel Gellion in 1790. Former app., Joseph Turner, admitted freeman in 1794. Subscribed to Sheraton's *Drawing Book*, 1793. [D; Chester freemen rolls, app. bks and poll bk]

Mercer, Thomas, Liverpool, joiner and cm (1777–90). Addresses given at 9 Pownall St with joiner and cabinet warehouse at 38 Park Lane in 1777; no. 39, with shop and timber yard at no. 40 in 1781; no. 79 in 1784; and nos 44 and 46 in 1790. [D]

Mercer, William, Liverpool, carver (1747–61). Took apps

named Mercer in 1747, Lindsay and Prescott in 1750. Former app., John Folds, petitioned freedom in 1759; and Michael Wareing in 1761. [S of G, app. index; Liverpool freemen's committee bk]

Mercer, William, 11 Whitechapel, Liverpool, cm (1781). [D]

Mercer, William, Midhurst, Sussex, cm and carpenter (1823–26). [D]

Mercers, Long & Sutton, King St, Hammersmith, London, rustic and garden chairmakers (1826). [D]

Merchant, John, Wine Office Ct, St Bride's, London, cm (1728). Fined for non-service at St Bride's in 1728. [GL, MS 6561, p. 49]

Merchant, John, 1 Old Cock Lane, Shoreditch, London, cm and u (1827–28). [D] See John Marchant.

Merchant, John, Benedict St, Glastonbury, Som., cm (1839). [D]

Merchant, Peter, Ditch Side, St Bride's London, upholder (1754). Served as Constable at St Bride's in 1754. [GL, MS 6561, p. 90] See Peter Marchant.

Meredith, Charles, address unrecorded, upholder (1742–55). Son of Thomas Meredith, joiner of Coldbath Fields, London, App. to Charles Master, freeman bricklayer, on 31 March 1742. Admitted freeman of the Upholders' Co. on 1 May 1755. [GL, Upholders' Co. records]

Meredith, John, Maid Lane, Southwark, London, cm (1739). Declared bankrupt, *Daily Post*, 7 May 1739.

Meredith, John, Chester, u (1820–40). Trading in Princess St, 1837–40. Admitted freeman on 17 April 1820. [D; Chester freemen rolls and poll bk]

Meredith, Richard, Worcester, upholder (1754–94). Recorded at Cross in 1788 and no. 27 in 1794. App. to Samuel Bolus, and admitted freeman on 2 September 1754. Former apps admitted freemen: Samuel Bardin in 1764; William Hankins in 1771; William Curtis in 1775; and Richard Lovett in 1780. Trading also as auctioneer, 1780–94. [Worcester freemen rolls]

Meredith, William, Stafford St, Bilston, Staffs., carpenter, joiner and cm (1827–35). [D]

Merle, John, 36 Leadenhall St, London, carver and gilder (1812–27). Fire at his premises reported in *Gents Mag.*, October 1812. [D] Probably the son of:

Merle, Thomas, at 'The Golden Key', 36 Leadenhall St, London, picture frame maker, carver and gilder, printseller (1783–1826). Trading as T. Merle & Son in 1826. [D] 18th-century oval giltwood mirror recorded, with pierced cresting centred by a curling leaf flanked by scrollwork and carved with husks, all gathered into an arched band of flames and flanked by flame mouldings overlaid with boldly-scrolling acanthus leaves; the lower part of the frame formed of palm branches overlaid with flowers and springing from the heart-shaped apron-piece carved with oak leaves. Trade label on the back reads: 'Thomas Merle (Successor to the late Mr. [J.] Overlove) Picture Frame Maker, Carver, Gilder and Print-seller, at the Golden Key, no. 36 Leadenhall Street, London. Makes and Sells all sorts of Picture Frames, Carves and Gilds Lookinglass Frames and Girandoles in the newest taste and at the Most Reasonable Prices. Landscapes and Seascapes Neatly Painted. Pictures carefully Cleaned, Lined and Mended. Old Frames New Gilt on the Shortest Notice. Mouldings of Different Patterns and Lengths for the Conveniency of exportation.' [Sotheby's, 4 December 1959, lot 140, illus.; *C. Life*, 14 January 1960, p. 71] Label also recorded on a convex early Regency looking glass.

Merlin, John Joseph, London (b.1735–d.1803). A very versatile 'ingenious mechanic', born in Belgium, who came to England in 1760. He specialised as a mathematical instrument maker but also enjoyed a reputation for horology and took out patents for musical instruments and furniture. His life and work are the subject of a major exhibition catalogue [Kenwood, London, 1985] which contains much biographical information and many details of his inventions. He is best remembered by furniture historians for his invalid or 'gouty' chair, a version of which was illustrated in Ackermann's *Repository of Arts*, 1811, pp. 225–26. The Iveagh Bequest, Kenwood owns an example as well as a portrait of Merlin. On 18 September 1788 Merlin wrote to Lord Howard of Audley End, Essex about a mechanical bedstead he had supplied costing £13 4s [Essex RO, D/DBY/A 46/10] On 30 April 1794 he supplied 'a mechanical Gouty-chair with a foot and leg board complete' costing £18 to Croome Court and on 13 March 1795 he provided 'Gouty Chairs' costing £42 10s 6d to the Duke of Northumberland. [V&A archives]

Merone, Joseph, Market St, Manchester, barometer, looking-glass and picture frame maker, carver and gilder (1800–41). Recorded at no. 93, 1814–16; no. 98, 1815–24; no. 28, 1822–41; and also no. 100, 1828–29. Recorded also with house called Cheetham Cottage in 1815; and at 130 Market St in 1829. [D; Goodison, *Barometers*]

Merredith, John, Swan Lane, Stroud, Glos., cm (1830). [D]

Merrett, Joseph, Painswick, Glos., chairmaker (1820–30). [D]

Merrett, Thomas, Newent, Glos., carver, gilder etc. (1822). [D] See Robert Merritt.

Merrick, George, London, carver and gilder (1823–39). Addresses given at 1 Orange Row, Kennington in 1823; 12 Tonbridge Pl., Lambeth, 1832–34; 12 Bridge Rd, Lambeth in 1835; and no. 89 in 1839. Took out a Sun Insurance policy on 2 October 1823 for £150. [D; GL, Sun MS vol. 498, ref. 1008442]

Merrick, Joseph, St Nicholas's parish, Bristol, cane chairmaker (1739–54). [Poll bks]

Merrick, Phillip, Newbury, Berks., cm (1802). [Oxford poll bk]

Merrick, William, St Peter in the East, Oxford, cm (b.1751–1774). Married Mary Warr of Watlington at Watlington on 7 April 1774. [Bodleian index of Oxf. marriage bonds]

Merrick, William, St Nicholas's parish, Bristol, chairmaker (1754). [Poll bk]

Merrick, William, Newbury, Berks., cm (1802). [Oxford poll bk]

Merrick, William, Clerkenwell, London, Tunbridge-ware manufacturer (1809–45). Trading at 3 Coppice Rd, 1809–11; and 6 St John's Sq., 1817–45, from 1826 as a portable desk and dressing case maker. [D]

Merriman, A. H., 155 Leadenhall St, London, camp and travelling furniture, trunk and travelling equipage manufacturer (1835). [D]

Merritt, Robert, Newent, Glos., cm (1839). [D] See Thomas Merrett.

Merryfield (or Merrifield), William, at 'The Three Chairs & Crown', Fleet Ditch (or Side or Mkt), London, upholder (1722–60). Took out a Sun Insurance policy on 20 July 1722 for £500 on goods and merchandise in his house. Served as Constable at St Bride's in 1726; Collector for the Poor in 1736; Scavenger in 1741; Questman in 1743; and Churchwarden in 1746. [D; GL, Sun MS vol. 14, ref. 25944; GL, MS 6561, p. 46]

Merryfield, William jnr, Ditch Side, St Bride's, London, upholder (1755). Fined for non-service at St Bride's in 1755. [GL, MS 6561, p. 91]

Merryman, Joseph, London, upholder and cm (1758–78). Addresses given at Hounsditch in 1759; the Minories, 1763–65; as Joseph & Co., cm, u and auctioneers at Heydon Sq., Minories, 1767–72; no. 42, 1773–77; and Fenchurch Buildings in 1778. Son of William Merryman, freeman joiner of London. Admitted freeman of the Upholders' Co. by patrimony on 2 February 1758. Took apps named Henry

Chapman, 1761–71; Henry Terry, 1765–73; George Adams, 1769–77; and John West, 1773–77. In 1759 he employed one non-freeman for three months and six weeks; in 1763, one for six weeks; and in 1765, two for three months. J. Merryman, cm of the Minories, was declared bankrupt in *Gents Mag.*, November 1763. [D; GL, Upholders' Co. records; GL, City Licence bks, vols 2–4]

Merryweather, Francis, 71 Gt Prescott St, London, desk, dressing and writing case manufacturer (1839). [D]

Meschain, John, see François Hervé.

Messenger, Charles, Oxford, cm (1823–30). Trading at High St in 1823 and Broad St in 1830. Declared bankrupt, *Brighton Gazette*, 4 March 1824. [D]

Messenger, Michael, London, cm (1784–93). Recorded as Messenger & Son at 2 Newman St in 1784, and alone at Upper Ground Southwark in 1790. [D]

Messinger, John snr & jnr, 7 Holland St, Soho, London, cm (1779). Took out a Sun Insurance policy in 1779 for £500 of which £300 accounted for utensils, stock and goods. [GL, Sun MS vol. 279, p. 574]

Metcalf(e), —, Primrose St, Bishopsgate, London, cm (1804). Fire at his premises reported in *Gents Mag.*, September 1804. It took place on 28 August 1804, and 'the whole of the stock of timber, mahogany, finished goods etc. ... were destroyed ... The tools, benches etc. belonging to 15 working men, were all wholly consumed.'

Metcalf, Anthony, Liverpool, carver and gilder (1815). Marriage to Miss Sarah Gatley of Manchester at the Collegiate Church, Manchester, reported in *Liverpool Mercury*, 22 September 1815.

Metcalf (or Medcalf), Christopher, Wardour St, London, cm (1775–84). Trading at no. 6, 1775–79. Took out Sun Insurance policies in 1775 for £500, £365 accounting for utensils, stock and goods; in 1777 for £1,500, £100 on his workshop; in 1778 for £300 on a house in New Norfolk St, Grosvenor Sq.; and in 1779 for £500 on his house and warehouse. [GL, Sun MS vol. 239, p. 506; vol. 255, p. 133; vol. 265, p. 10; vol. 273, p. 252; poll bk]

Metcalf, Cuthbert, 64 Peter St, Whitechapel, Liverpool, cm (1804).

Metcalf, Foster, London, cm (1793). Subscribed to Sheraton's *Drawing Book*, 1793.

Metcalf, George, Knottingley, Yorks., joiner and/or cm (1834). [D]

Metcalf, Henry & Son, London, upholders and cm (1803–11). Recorded at 20–21 Broker's Row, Moorfields in 1803; nos 12 and 13 and also 20–21 New Broad St in 1808; and 9 Broker's Row, 1809–11. [D]

Metcalf, John E., 3 Junction St, Hull, Yorks., cm (1838–39). [D]

Metcalf, John, Stockton-upon-Tees, Co. Durham, cm (1793). Subscribed to Sheraton's *Drawing Book*, 1793.

Metcalf, Joseph, address unrecorded. Submitted a bill, dated 9 May 1752 and totalling £964 5s for minor articles of furniture, jobbing work, paper hanging, mending and altering furniture either at Pembroke House, Whitehall, or Wilton House, Wilts. [Pembroke papers, Wilton Estate Office] Possibly Joseph Metcalfe who worked at Norfolk House in 1752.

Metcalf, Richard, 41 Renshaw St, Liverpool, u and paper hanger (1837). [D]

Metcalf(e), Robert, Newcastle, u (1741). [Newcastle freemen reg. and poll bk]

Metcalf, Robert, London, upholder (1787–1802). Recorded at 7 Lower Moorfields in 1795, and Moorfields in 1802. Son of Henry Metcalf, victualler of Limehouse, Middlx. App. to Benjamin Wilson on 5 September 1787, and admitted freeman of the Upholders' Co. by servitude on 3 June 1795. [GL, Upholders' Co. records]

Metcalf, Thomas, 6 George St, Whitehaven, Cumb., cm and joiner (1834). [D]

Metcalf, Warren, Hawes, Yorks., joiner and cm (1823). [D]

Metcalfe, —, at 'The Helmet', Fleet St, London, u (1692–97). [D; Hilton Price, *Signs of Old London*]

Metcalfe, Charles, Wardour St, Soho, London, cm (1784). [D]

Metcalfe, James, Cambridge, cm, u and undertaker (1809–39). An advertisement appeared in the *Cambridge Chronicle and Journal*, 8 July 1809 to announce that the partnership between John Bedells and James Metcalfe joiners and cm was to be dissolved. Pigot's directories of 1823–24, 1830 and a poll bk of 1832 record Metcalfe in business in Trumpington St. An advertisement in the newspaper of 28 October 1831 announced that James Metcalfe had taken his son into the business, which was to be known as Metcalfe and Son, adding that 'they are enabled to manufacture Furniture, with taste, elegance and durability'. Poll bks from 1834 list James Metcalfe in Sidney St, and from 1835 the name Thomas Metcalfe, presumably the son, is also included. Pigot's directory of 1839 lists Metcalfe and Son in Bridge St. R.W.

Metcalfe, James, Masham, near Ripon, Yorks., joiner and cm (1823–40). Trading in partnership with John Metcalfe in 1840. [D]

Metcalfe, James, West Field, Richmond, Yorks., joiner and cm (1827). [D]

Metcalf(e), John, Ripon, Yorks., cm (1803–37). Recorded at All Hallowgate, 1822–37. Subscribed to Sheraton's *Cabinet Dictionary*, 1803. [D]

Metcalfe, John, Hawes, Yorks., joiner and cm (1840). [D]

Metcalfe, Joseph, York, u (1730). Son of Thomas Metcalfe, haberdasher; app. to Barnaby Bawtry, u, on 25 March 1730. [York app. reg.]

Metcalfe, Joseph, London, u (1752). Presented a large bill to the Duke of Norfolk for work done at Norfolk House, dated 9 May 1752. Items supplied include bedsteads with bed furnishings, furniture covers, curtains, upholstered chairs and stools, furniture repairs and 'India damask wallpaper'. The bill totalled £1,078 2s 4½d. [Arundel Castle records, MD18, pt 2] Possibly Joseph Metcalf. See also Medcalfe, —.

Metcalfe, Lascels, Gracechurch St, London, u (1740). Named in contemporary newspapers. [Heal]

Metcalfe, Richard, Newcastle, upholder (1734). [Poll bk]

Metcalfe, Robert, St Clement's parish, Cambridge, cm (1815–d.1831). Five children bapt. between 1815 and 1823. Will dated 1831. [Cambridge RO, PR (bapt.); Univ. Lib., AR3:182]

Metcalfe, Thomas, Hull, Yorks., cm (1814–39). Address given at 2 Providence St, 1826–39. Son of Thomas Metcalfe, cm; app. to Edward Dickon in April 1814. [D; Hull app. reg.]

Metcalfe, Thomas, Sidney St, Cambridge, u (1834–41). [Poll bks] Presumably the son of James Metcalfe. See Metcalfe & Son.

Metcalfe, Thomas, Hawes, Yorks., joiner and cm (1840). [D]

Metcalfe & Son, Bridge St, Cambridge, cm, u and undertakers (1831–39). [D] Succeeded the business of James Metcalfe in 1831. See James and Thomas Metcalfe.

Metherill, Thomas, East St, Ashburton, Devon, cm (1830). [D]

Metzner, W. M., Greenwich, London, carver and gilder (1839). Recorded as W.M. jnr at Stockwell St in 1839. [D] Frame recorded bearing trade label, c.1840, which reads: 'FANCY, GILT & LOOKING-GLASS FRAME MAKER, HOUSE AND ORNAMENTAL PAINTER, &c. 14, ROYAL HILL, GREENWICH ... WORK AND EMBROIDERY TASTE-FULLY MOUNTED IN STOOLS, SCREENS, & ...'.

Mew, Richard, High St, Newport, Isle of Wight, Hants., cm and u (1823–30). [D]

Mewkill, Josiah, address unrecorded. His bill, dated 24 August to 22 December 1807, sent to the Earl of Jersey for 'sundries' for Middleton, Bicester, is preserved amongst the Osterley Park bills. Items Mewkill supplied included a set of fire irons, six black chairs, two elbow chairs, a bed and bolster, wood chairs, tables, curtain rings, a glass bread basket, a lantern, a bureau and thirteen 'matts'. [V&A archives]

Mewton, —, James St, Plymouth, Devon, cm (1821). Death of his wife reported in *The Alfred*, 13 January 1821.

Mewton, R., James St, Devonport, Plymouth, Devon, cm and u (1822). [D]

Mewton, William, James St, Devonport, Plymouth, Devon, cm and u (1814–38). Recorded at no. 89, 1823–24, and no. 80 in 1830. [D]

Meyer, Elias, Goulston Sq., Whitechapel, London, cm and dealer in glass (1786). Took out a Sun Insurance policy on 12 May 1786 for £300, of which £50 accounted for utensils and stock. [GL, Sun MS vol. 336, p. 420]

Meyer, Henry, Hull, Yorks., cm and u (1826–39). Addresses given at 8 Bowl Alley in 1826, and Castle St, 1838–39. [D]

Meyer & Berkenn, 44 Whitall St, St Mary's Sq, 16, 17 and 18 Sand St, Birmingham, 'Articles of Foreign Furniture of every Description ... Able & Experienced Decorators, as Designers, Gilders & Carvers, either English, German or French, sent to any part of the Country ...'. [Trade card at Grosvenor House Antiques Fair, 1985]

Meyers, —, address unrecorded. In May 1823 he was paid £50 for a billiard table supplied to Nicholas Pearse of Loughton, Essex, and Marylebone, London. [Essex RO, D/DHt A1/3]

Meymott, Thomas, 3 Lower Moorfields, near Old Bethlem, London, cm, upholder, appraiser and auctioneer (1799–1814). Shield-shaped trade card bears the Prince of Wales Feathers. [Banks Coll., BM; Heal]

Meynell, George, York, cm (1814). Son of Robert Meynell, barber of Petergate, York. App. to George Beal, cm, on 17 October 1814. [York app. reg.]

Miall, William, Daniel St, Portsea, Portsmouth, Hants., cm, u and auctioneer (1823–39). Addresses also given at 28 Cross St in 1823 and 37 Daniel St in 1830. [D]

Michael, William, Worcester, cm and u, broker (1797–1820). Trading as 'Carpet Manufacturers to their Majesties' in 1797–98 at 15 Bridge St; and at 100 High St in 1820 as cm and u. On 5 October 1812 William Michael jnr, first born son of William Michael snr, cm and u, was admitted freeman. [D; Worcester freemen rolls]

Michaux, Thomas, 7 Buckingham St, Strand, London, gilder (1820–27). [D]

Michelin, Charles, 22 George St, Portland St, carver and gilder (1839). [D]

Michelin, Nicholas, 26 Wardour St, Soho, London, carver and gilder (1789–90). Took out a Sun Insurance policy on 20 December 1790 for £100 on his house. [D; GL, Sun MS ref. 577512]

Michell, J. S. (?), address unrecorded. On 24 March 1823 he received £2 10s for a sofa table supplied to Nicholas Pearse of Loughton, Essex, and London. [Essex RO, D/DHt A1/4]

Michie, J., 23 Duke St, Grosvenor Sq., London, carver and gilder (1835). [D]

Michon, Peter & Nicholas, Piccadilly, London. Supplied furniture to Queen Mary in 1691. [DEF]

Middlebrook, Robert, 29 Tabernacle Walk, Finsbury Sq., London, cm and window blind manufacturer (1808). [D]

Middlebrooke, Richard, Thorne, Yorks., joiner and cm (1828–34). Addresses given at Ellison St, 1828–29 and Silver St in 1834. [D]

Middleditch, William, 7 Houghton St, Clare Mkt, London, upholder (1787). Insured goods to the value of £100 on 7 July 1787. [GL, Sun MS vol. 342, ref. 532945]

Middlefell, Richard, Lancaster. Named in the Gillow records, 1818–23. [Westminster Ref. Lib.]

Middleton, —, Upper St Martin's Lane, London, chairmaker (1710–11). Named in the accounts for Felbrigg, Norfolk, on 26 April 1710 receiving £6 2s; and on 31 March 1711, £6 8s. [Norfolk RO, Felbrigg papers, WKc 6/23]

Middleton, Charles, Tottenham Ct Rd, near Windmill St, London, papier-mâché manufacturer (1763). [D]

Middleton, Christopher, East Grinstead, Sussex, cm (1795). [D]

Middleton, Erasmus, Horncastle, Lincs., cm (1768). Advertised for an app. and a journeyman cm in *Cambridge Chronicle and Journal*, 10 December 1768.

Middleton, George, Eastgate, Louth, Lincs., cm, joiner and u (1826–41). [D]

Middleton, H. M., address unrecorded. Mahogany child's feeding chair recorded, with rectangular caned back, sides and seat, panelled frieze, tapering, square fluted legs joined by stretchers, the arms fitted with a sliding tray; stamped on bottom: 'H.M.M.', with a label which reads: 'H.M. Middleton, from … Lodge.' [Sotheby's, 21 November 1969, lot 163] Possibly outside our time frame.

Middleton, James, London, writing desk, dressing case and pencil maker (1829–39). Trading at 48 Lombard St, 1829–35; no. 46 in 1835; and 7 King William St, 1837–39. [D] The label of Middleton, 48 Lombard St is recorded on a writing box. [V&A archives]

Middleton, James & Henry, Sevenoaks, Kent, upholders (1830). Declared bankrupt, *Chester Courant and Anglo-Welsh Gazette*, 28 December 1830.

Middleton, John, Lancaster, u (1798–1824). Named in the Gillow records, 1798–1824. Admitted freeman, 1817–18. [Westminster Ref. Lib., Gillow; Lancaster freemen rolls]

Middleton, John, York, cm (1807–09). Took apps named Edward Agar on 8 December 1807, and John Briggs on 1 May 1809. [York app. reg.]

Middleton, John, Kirkgate, Wakefield, Yorks. cm (1814). [D]

Middleton, Nicholas, 162 Strand, London, pocket book and pencil maker, cm and dealer in cutlery and hardware (1801–10). Took out Sun Insurance policies on 5 October 1804 for £1,000, of which £820 accounted for utensils and stock; and on 29 December 1806 for £2,500. [GL, Sun MS vol. 431, ref. 767264; vol. 437, ref. 798272] In July 1801, N. Middleton supplied the Royal Household with 'a Case for Box seat to the Nabob', costing £1 16s; and on 27 December 1810, a writing box costing £5 4s 10d, recorded in the accounts on 22 January 1812. [Windsor Royal Archives, 88916, 89031] Regency brass-bound mahogany portable desk recorded, hinged to reveal two baise-lined sloping flaps enclosing fitted and open wells, a glass sander and secret drawers; bearing trade label which reads: 'N. Middleton, 162 Strand, Manufacturary of … writing and dressing desks…'. [Sotheby's, 14 November 1969, lot 78; 13 February 1970, lot 130] A good quality brass-bound writing box is recorded, bearing label with Royal Arms, which reads: 'N. MIDDLETON, 162 STRAND, OPPOSITE NEWCASTLE STREET, THE CORNER OF STRAND LANE, POCKET BOOK & PENCIL MAKER TO THE KING & PRINCE OF WALES, MANUFACTURER OF COPYING MACHINES, WRITING & DRESSING DESKS & ALL KINDS OF PORTABLE CASES FOR TRAVELLING, STATIONARY OF ALL KINDS, COPPER PLATE ENGRAVING & PRINTING, IMPROVED CRAYON PENCILS FOR DRAWING IN COLOURS. WARRENTED RAZORS & ALL KINDS OF FINE CUTLERY.' [Bonham's,

10 June 1982, lot 14] Label also recorded on a small satinwood desk.

Middleton, R., Rochester, Kent, cm (1802). [Poll bk]

Middleton, Robert, Kirkgate, Wakefield, Yorks., cm and furniture broker (1830). [D]

Middleton, Thomas, King St, London, cm (1784). [Poll bk]

Middleton, Thomas, High St, Lambeth, London, chairmaker (1808). [D]

Middleton, Thomas, Vauxhall Bridge Rd, London, cm and u (1836–39). Trading at 3 Windsor Terr. as Thomas & Co. in 1839. Son Charles by his wife Maria bapt. at Westminster Methodist Chapel on 20 March 1836. [D; PRO, Non-Conf. Reg., RG/4/4313]

Middleton, Warren, Union Pl., Stourbridge, Worcs., cm and u (1835). [D]

Middleton, William, address unrecorded, cm (1803). Subscribed to Sheraton's *Cabinet Dictionary*, 1803.

Middleton, William, 29 Thomas St, Manchester, chairmaker (1825–29). [D]

Middleton, William, White Swan Yd, Wakefield, Yorks., cm (1830). [D]

Middleton & Co., 4 Upper North St, Brighton, Sussex, cm and u (1832). [D]

Midgley, John, Bramley, Yorks., cm (1830). [D]

Midgley, John, Keighley, Yorks., joiner and/or cm (1837). [D]

Midgley, Joseph, Keighley, Yorks., joiner and cm (1837). [D]

Midgley, Robert, Broad Stones, Bradford, Yorks., joiner and cm (1814). [D]

Midgley, T., 2 Lambeth Rd, London, cm (1820). [D]

Midgley, Thomas, 9 Dorrington St, Clerkenwell, London, cm (1827–28). [D]

Midlane, Henry, Havant, Hants., cm, builder and upholder (1780–84). Trading in partnership with George Midlane in 1784. Took out a Sun Insurance policy in 1780 for £800 including £320 on utensils, stock, storehouses and workshops. [D; GL, Sun MS vol. 281, p. 35]

Midleton, —, Stonehouse, Plymouth, Devon cm (1792). Marriage to Miss Mary Curtis in Stonehouse Chapel reported in *Exeter Flying Post*, 8 November 1792.

Mien, Robert, Norwich, u (1751). Admitted freeman on 21 September 1751, not by apprenticeship. [Norwich freemen reg.]

Miers, William, 111 Strand, London, ormolu worker and miniature frame maker, by Appointment to the Queen (1802–39). Trade card recorded. [D; Heal]

Miggs, John, West Wycombe, Bucks., chairmaker (b. c.1816–41). Aged 25 at the time of the 1841 Census.

Milam, William, near Ratcliffe St in Ratcliffe Highway, London, cm and broker (1755). Took out a Sun Insurance policy on 4 January 1755 for £400, incuding £250 on household goods, utensils and stock in trade; £30 on utensils and stock in wareroom and workshop behind his house; and £20 on timber. [GL, Sun MS vol. 108, ref. 144339]

Milborne (Mil(l)bourne or Milburn), James, Strand, London, carver and gilder, picture frame and looking-glass maker, glass grinder (1774–1817). Recorded at no. 221 in 1784 and 1790; no. 121, 1789–93; and no. 347, 1793–1800. Polled at Westminster in 1774. Trading in partnership with Robert Milbourne from 1812–16, and succeeded by James Milbourne jnr. Took out a Sun Insurance policy on 15 January 1793 for £1,300 on his house, utensils, stock, goods and wearing apparel. [D; GL, Sun MS vol. 389, ref. 610825]

Milbourn, William, Armthwaite, u (1780). [Newcastle poll bk]

Milbourne, James jnr, Strand, London, carver, gilder, glass grinder and looking-glass manufacturer (1819–39). Trading at no. 347, 1820–29, and no. 195 in 1839. [D]

Milbourne, Robert, London, carver and gilder (1826–34).

Trading at 8 Nelson Pl., Old Kent Rd in 1826; and 9 Winters Lambeth Walk in 1832. [D]

Milbourne (or Milburn), Thomas, Newcastle, upholder (1726–34). Admitted freeman on 13 October 1726. [Newcastle freemen reg. and poll bk]

Milburn, John, Newgate St, Newcastle, carver and gilder (1827–38). Recorded at no. 5 in 1827 and no. 52 in 1838. [D]

Milburn, Joseph, Newcastle, cm (1801–11). Trading in Cowgate in 1801, also as a publican; and in Pilgrim St in 1811, also as a joiner. [D]

Milburn, Robert, Newcastle, u (1755–81). Admitted freeman in 1755. Son William admitted freeman by patrimony on 7 September 1780, and Henry on 23 April 1781. [Newcastle freemen reg.]

Milburn, Thomas, Corby Hill, Carlisle, Cumb., chairmaker (1834). [D]

Miles, —, at 'The White Swan', Wych St, London, u (1688). Named in newspapers in 1688. [Heal]

Miles, —, address unrecorded, frame maker (1774–75). Referred to in the private accounts of Richard Hoare of Boreham House, Essex, on 13 July 1774 receiving £3 12s 6d; and on 14 February 1775, £1 3s. [Essex RO, D/DU 649/2]

Miles, —, Woodbridge, Suffolk, u (1801). Named in *Ipswich Journal*, 31 January 1801. See Edmund, Francis and Richard Miles.

Miles, Charles, New St, Wellington, Salop, chairmaker and wood turner (1840). [D]

Miles, Edmund, Woodbridge, Suffolk, cm (1820). Named in the calendar of marriage licence bonds in 1820. [Suffolk RO, FAA: 50/2/119, p. 88] See Miles, —, of Woodbridge.

Miles, Edward, Liverpool, cm (1780–1829). Addresses given at 6 Old Church Yd, 1800–14; 15 Chapel St in 1818; and 25 Ormond St in 1829. Admitted freeman on servitude to John Sharp on 11 September 1780. [D; Liverpool freemen reg.]

Miles, Francis, Woodbridge, Suffolk, cm, u and dealer in bricks and tiles (1784–98). Subscribed to Sheraton's *Drawing Book*, 1793. [D] See Miles, —, of Woodbridge.

Miles, Frederick, 16 Christophers Alley, Moorfields, London, cm (1785). Took out a Sun Insurance policy on 13 November 1785 for £30 on his house, and £35 on utensils and stock. [GL, Sun MS vol. 333, p. 385]

Miles, Henry & Edwards, John, 134 Oxford St, London, furniture printers, u and cm (1822–44). Henry Miles, 'dealer in Moreens and Printed Furniture' at this address, took out a Sun Insurance policy on 26 February 1823 for £1,800, of which £1,500 accounted for utensils and stock. [GL, Sun MS vol. 498, ref. 1001630] The firm of Miles & Edwards flourished from 1822–44, and appeared in directories in 1823 and 1835–39. The firm had many prestigious patrons including, in 1830, the British Ambassador in Paris and the Empress of Russia; and in 1834 the Turkish Ambassador, to whom the firm was introduced by Lord Palmerston. In 1844 Miles & Edwards were taken over by Charles Hindley & Sons. Edwards, probably the junior partner, may later have been connected with the firm of Edwards & Roberts, recorded in a London directory of 1854 as makers of reproduction furniture and restorers of antique furniture. Several account books, journals, stock lists and letter books of Miles & Edwards survive, dating from 1825–44. The letter books record correspondence with patrons, such as D. Burton, Esq., to whom Miles & Edwards wrote on 16 August 1837: 'Messrs. Miles & Edwards beg to return to Mr. Burton the sketch for the Sideboard made according to his instructions, for Mr. Briscoe & have marked the size upon it as desired.' The sideboard had a plate glass back. [Westminster Ref. Lib., archives dept; *Furn. Hist.*, 1970; Joy, *English Furniture,*

1800–1851, p. 261] A number of the firm's commissions are documented:

AUDLEY END, Essex, **BILLINGBEAR**, Berks. or 3rd Lord Braybrooke's London house. The firm received payments in June 1831 of £119 and £21 1s 6d; in December 1834, £7 9s 4d; in December 1836, £46 5s 10d; in June 1837, £2 10s 6d; and in December 1839, £27 13s ½d. [Essex RO, D/DBy/A358; A361; A363]

BURTON CONSTABLE, Yorks. Miles & Edwards received a commission totalling £183 9s 3d. Furniture supplied included, in 1834, '2 handsome Gilded Cheval Screens carved in style of Louis Quatorze … Backs covered with India Silk Damask at 13 gns. £27.6.0.'; and an oval glass in a gilt frame, costing £2 2s. On 26 November 1834 the firm provided 'Conversation Chairs richly carved & gilded with Foliage Ornaments stuffed seats etc.', costing £15 15s; and on 29 February 1835, a 'Vis a Vis Sofa with Gilded legs', at £12 15s. [Humberside RO, Burton Constable papers; *Furn. Hist.*, 1972]

HAMPTON COURT, Leominster, Herefs. Miles & Edwards submitted a bill to John Arkwright on 10 August 1842 for £21 14s 10d. [Herefs. RO, A63/161]

HOPETOUN HOUSE, Lothian, Scotland. In 1834 the firm supplied a 'Vis a Vis in blue Twell', costing £8 8s; 'A Rosewood Spanish Easy Chair', £5 15s; 'A Mahogany Fr. Bedstead w. Sideboard', £12 12s; and 'A Shaped Back Nelson Chaise Longue', £4 10s. In 1838 they provided a 'supply of chintz paper & of striped chintz', costing £21 16s ½d; and in 1840 a 'supply of silk striped tabouret', at £45 0s 6d. [V&A archives]

PANSHANGER, Herts. On 20 June 1833 Miles & Edwards, 'Designers & Manufacturers of Superior Furniture', supplied a 'Marqueterie stand' costing £1 18s; and '2 Mahogany tables with drawers', £3 8s; and in 1835, '2 Genoa Chairs/Barbary seating', £2 10s; '2 Sweep back Genoa Chairs', £2 10s; and a mahogany book rest, 16s 6d. [Herts. RO, Panshanger, Box 56]

STAFFORD HOUSE, London. In 1838 Miles & Edwards submitted a bill for £126 12s 11d. [Staffs. RO, D593/R/1/26/8]

WYNYARD PARK, Co. Durham. Charles William Vane, Marquess of Londonderry, commissioned Miles & Edwards to supply furnishings, c.1829–41. [Durham RO, Londonderry papers, D/LO/E 484, vol. 1829–41] Many pieces of furniture survive bearing the stamp of Miles & Edwards, including a pair of rosewood chiffoniers, c.1830, with pierced brass three-quarter-galleried shelf supported on turned columns; the lower parts with a central set of open adjustable shelves with a cupboard door on either side, faced with gilt-metal trellis-work and divided by ring-turned pilasters; stamped with the numbers 4586 and 4587. [Sotheby's, 21 April 1972, lot 92; *Furn. Hist.*, 1970, pls 34–37] A set of six rosewood buckle-back pattern chairs at Broughton Hall, Yorks. are impressed with the firm's name and address, and the number 8232. Four Rococo revival gilt chairs from Hitchin Priory, now in private ownership in Yorks., bear the firm's stamp, the number 12130, and the initials 'I.G.'. A Regency bookcase, c.1820, also bears the stamp of Miles & Edwards; also a small Victorian chair, numbered 31821; also a fretwork armchair *prie dieu*, c.1830, with oval in the back painted with a scene of the 'Temerère', and 'Trafalgar', on a scroll; all three pieces are in private ownership. A set of rosewood chairs also bear the stamp of Miles & Edwards. [V&A archives] A.E.

Miles, Henry, Westgate, Canterbury, Kent, chairmaker (1830). [Poll bk]

Miles, Henry, Richmond, Surrey, cm and u (1832–39). Trading at Marsh Gate, 1832–38, and King St in 1839. [D]

Miles, J., 5 Charles St, London, cm and undertaker (1817–21). [D]

Miles, James, London, cm (1793). Subscribed to Sheraton's *Drawing Book*, 1793.

Miles, James, London, carver and gilder (1800–13). Recorded alone at 18 Princes St, Red Lion St in 1800; 11 Orange St, 1808–11; in partnership with Thomas Abbey as carvers, gilders and joiners there from 1808–13; and also at 15 Cooks Row, St Pancras in 1808. Miles alone took out Sun Insurance policies on 27 August 1800 for £200 including £50 on utensils and stock; and on 17 October 1808 for £500, including £300 on stock, glass and utensils in his house, and £200 on household goods, stock and utensils at 15 Cooks Row. Miles and Abbey took out Sun Insurance policies on 29 December 1808 and 25 January 1810 for £600, £300 on stock, utensils and glass in their house; and £300 on household goods, stock and utensils at a house in their tenure, 15 Cooks Row; and on 12 February 1812 for £800, including £100 on Abbey's household goods, £400 on stock, utensils and glass, and £300 on James Miles's household goods in a house at Foulmin, Cambs. [D; GL, Sun MS vol. 419, ref. 706226; vol. 447, ref. 821498; vol. 443, ref. 825053; vol. 451, ref. 839652; vol. 457, ref. 867716]

Miles, John, London, upholder (1783–1802). Recorded at Bishopsgate St, 1794–1802. Admitted freeman of the Upholders' Co. by redemption in 1783. [GL, Upholders' Co. records] See Richard Miles, and William, Richard & John Miles.

Miles, John, address unrecorded, u (1803). Subscribed to Sheraton's *Cabinet Dictionary*, 1803.

Miles, John & Co., London, wholesale u and furniture warehouseman (1812–16). Addresses given at 1 College Hill in 1812; 238 Tottenham Ct Rd in 1813; and 282 High Holborn, 1814–16. Trading as a furniture printer in 1815. Took out a Sun Insurance policy on 4 May 1814 for £3,000 on stock, utensils and goods in trust. [D; GL, Sun MS vol. 462]

Miles, John, 11 Beauchamp St, London, cm (1835). [D]

Miles, John, 91 Leather Lane, London, cm (1839). [D]

Miles, Joseph, address unrecorded, upholder (1739). Son of Robert Miles, freeman upholder of London, and brother of Robert Miles jnr. Admitted freeman of the Upholders' Co. by patrimony on 4 July 1739. [GL, Upholders' Co. records]

Miles, Joseph, Castle Meadow, Norwich, u (1836). [D]

Miles, Richard, Bishopsgate St Within, London, upholder (1783–93). Recorded at no. 93 in 1783; no. 92 in 1788; and 93 in 1789. Admitted freeman of the Upholders' Co. by redemption on 2 July 1783. Trading in partnership with John Miles as upholstery warehousemen and wool dealers, 1788–93. [D; GL, Upholders' Co. records] See John Miles and William, Richard & John Miles.

Miles, Richard, Woodbridge, Suffolk, u, cm and paper hanger (1814–39). Trading in the Thorofare, 1824–39. Named in the calendar of marriage licence bonds on 12 October 1814. [D; Suffolk RO, FAA: 50/2/117, pp. 132–33] See Miles, —, of Woodbridge.

Miles, Robert snr, London, freeman upholder (1738–39). His son, Robert, admitted freeman of the Upholders' Co. in 1738, and Joseph in 1739. [GL, Upholders' Co. records]

Miles, Robert jnr, London, upholder (1738). Son of Robert Miles, freeman upholder of London, and brother of Joseph Miles. Admitted freeman of the Upholders' Co. by patrimony on 7 December 1738. [GL, Upholders' Co. records]

Miles, Thomas, 136 Broad St, Birmingham, cm (1839). [D]

Miles, W., Lewes, Sussex, cm (1774). [Poll bk]

Miles, W., London. In 1818–19 he supplied bed furniture costing £21 3s 6d to the Duke of Montrose for Buchanan House, West Stirlingshire. [Scottish RO, GD220/6/52]

Miles, William, Richard & John, 93 Bishopsgate Within, London, wholesale upholders (1784–93). [D] See John and Richard Miles.

Miles, William, 33 Oxford St, London, furniture printer, cm and u (1811–28). Trading in partnership with John Miles in 1811. [D]

Miles, William, Baldertongate, Newark, Notts., chairmaker and turner (1819–41). [D]

Miles, William, Regent St, London, u (1826–28). Recorded at no. 235, 1826–27. Declared bankrupt, *Chester Chronicle and North Wales Advertiser*, 30 May 1828. [D]

Miles, William, Sandwich, Kent, cm (1831). [Poll bk]

Miles, Duffil, Cromar & Co., 32 Charing Cross, London, carpet manufacturers and u (1835). [D]

Milhum, Andrew, address unrecorded, upholder (1715–24). Son of Andrew Milhum, Gent. of St Martin-in-the-Fields, London. App. to George Friend on 14 March 1715, and turned over to Overbury Hale, draper. Admitted freeman of the Upholders' Co. by servitude on 7 October 1724. [GL, Upholders' Co. records]

Mill, —, Greek St, Soho, London, cm and u (1778). Fine Neo-classical trade card recorded, showing urn supported by gryphons, with an anthemion border. [Banks Coll., BM] Almost certainly:

Mill, John, address unrecorded, cm (c.1772). Complained about furniture smuggling to the Commissioners of Customs, c.1772. [*Apollo*, August 1965]

Mill, Michael, 12 Ebury Sq., Pimlico, London, cm (1839). [D]

Mill, Thomas, Compasshill, Tetbury, Glos., cm (1822–23). [D]

Millar, —, Newcastle, cm (1803). Subscribed to Sheraton's *Cabinet Dictionary*, 1803. Possibly James Miller or Miller's of Pilgrim St.

Millar, Henry, Nantwich, Cheshire, cm (1779). Married on 25 December 1779. [Chester RO, PR (marriage)]

Millar (or Miller), James, London, cm (1808–23). Trading at 22 Charterhouse Lane in 1808 and 9 Clerkenwell Green in 1813. [D]

Millard, Mrs, St James St, Cheltenham, Glos., chair and sofa manufacturer (1839). [D]

Millard, J., 8 Cumberland St, Curtain Rd, London, chair manufacturer (1837). [D]

Millard, Jabez, 1 Lambeth Hill, Upper Thames St, London, cm and u (1839). [D]

Millard, James, Littlehampton, Sussex. In May 1831 he carried out repairs to and re-bottomed chairs for the Earl of Surrey at Surrey House, Littlehampton, at a cost of £1 3s. [Arundel Castle records, A1960]

Millard, John & Edward, Albion St, Cheltenham, Glos., cm, chair and sofa manufacturer (1839). [D]

Millard, W., 9 Skinner St, Snowhill, London, trunk, chest and case maker (1835). [D]

Millard, William, Bristol, cm (1792–1829). Addresses given at 44 Marlborough St in 1792; Maryport St, 1793–94; Marlborough St in 1795; Earl St, 1801–05; at the 'Ship' in Earl St in 1828; and Lower Maudlin St in 1829. [D]

Millard, William, 30 Chapel St, Curtain Rd, London, cm (1835–39). [D]

Millard & Son, 3 Greek St, Soho, London, painters and gilders (1817–25). [D]

Milldew, —, address unrecorded, cm (1754). Subscribed to Chippendale's *Director*, 1754.

Milledge, John, St Mary St, Weymouth, Dorset, cm and u (1830–40). Trading at no. 95 in 1830 and no. 105 in 1840. [D]

Miller, Mr, Tower St, near Seven Dials, London, cm (1768). Fire at his premises reported in *Public Advertiser*, 16 April 1768: 'by timely Assistance it was happily extinguished.'

Miller, —, Old George St, Southwark, London, cm (1787). He rented a house owned by James Bates, cm, insured in 1787. [GL, Sun MS vol. 340, p. 496]

Miller, —, address unrecorded, cm (1803). Subscribed to Sheraton's *Cabinet Dictionary*, 1803.

Miller, Alexander, London, carver, gilder and looking-glass maker (1802–39). Addresses given at 13 High St, Marylebone, 1802–11; and 35 Thayer St, Manchester Sq., 1817–39. Took out Sun Insurance policies on 23 July 1802 for £350, £50 accounting for utensils and stock; and on 1 November 1810 for £600, of which £100 accounted for utensils, stock and goods in trust and workshop. [D; GL, Sun MS vol. 423, ref. 735531; vol. 453, ref. 850155]

Miller, David, Black Swan Ct, Bath, Som., u (1826). [D]

Miller, Devereux, Vicar Lane, Louth, Lincs., chairmaker and turner (1826–41). Trading in partnership with William Miller in 1841. [D]

Miller, E., 4 Leonard Sq., Shoreditch, London, u (1826–27). [D]

Miller, G., 18 Bridgehouse Pl., London, cm, u, chair and bedstead maker (1835–39). [D]

Miller, George, address unrecorded, upholder (1747–54). Son of Samuel Miller, sailmaker of Southampton. App. to Robert Phipps on 5 November 1747, and admitted freeman of the Upholders' Co. by servitude on 14 November 1754. [GL, Upholders' Co. records]

Miller (or Millar), George, St George's, Hanover Sq., London, u (1779). Declared bankrupt, *Gents Mag.*, May 1779, and Bailey's list of bankrupts.

Miller, George, 17 Blackmoor St, Clare Mkt, London, cm (1808). [D]

Miller, George, Hale St, Liverpool, carver (1810–11). Recorded at no. 9 in 1810, and no. 8 in 1811. [D]

Miller, Henry, Lancaster, cm (1779–80). Admitted freeman, 1779–80, when stated of Newcastle. [Lancaster freemen rolls]

Miller, Henry, 10 Leonard Sq., Shoreditch, London, u (1808). [D]

Miller, Humphry, London, cm (1793). Subscribed to Sheraton's *Drawing Book*, 1793.

Miller, Isaac, King St, Canterbury, Kent, cm (1830). [Poll bk]

Miller, J., 17 Gt Charlotte St, Gt Surrey St, London, u (1835). [D]

Miller, Js. (or J.S.), 4 Marchmont St, London, cm and u (1827–28). [D]

Miller, James, Holkham Hall, Norfolk, and London, carver and gilder (1755–75). His only recorded work is that carried out at Holkham Hall, Norfolk. In 1755 he charged £2 8s for a card table and two breakfast tables; and in 1759 he was paid £117 15s 6d for a mirror frame, a picture frame and gilding two sofas and eight chairs. In 1760, after the death of the 1st Lord Leicester, Miller was retained at Holkham in the service of Lady Leicester, at a salary of £50 a year. An inventory drawn up in that year shows that the State Rooms were at that time unfurnished, and Miller carved the frames for the chairs and tables in the East Drawing-room and Green State Bedchamber, also the window cornices in these rooms and the Chapel pillars. [C. W. James, *Chief Justice Coke*, p. 280] The set in the State Bedroom consists of a settee, armchairs and stools. They are upholstered in cut Genoa velvet already supplied by Benjamin Goodison, and the frames, gilt and carved with acanthus and scaling, are in an earlier style. [*GCM*; *DEF*; *C. Life*, 11 or 14 February 1980, pp. 427–31; V&A archives] He is probably the James Miller, carver, who in 1764 leased land bounded by Berners St and Wells St Mews, London; and 26 Charles St 'et alia' to John Maudell. In

1765 he is recorded regarding the counterpart lease of 30 Charles St to Stackhouse; and in 1775, the assignment to Miller of the lease of house and ground facing east on Berners St. [Marylebone Lib., deeds 1140; 1542; 1507; 2499] James Miller, carver of Marylebone, was declared bankrupt in *Gents Mag.*, May 1767.

Miller, James, Lancaster, u (1779–80 or 1789–90). [Lancaster freemen rolls]

Miller, James, Chepping Wycombe Borough, High Wycombe, Bucks., chairmaker (1798). [Militia Census]

Miller, James, 16 Newington Causeway, London, u and cm (1809–16). [D]

Miller, James, 26 School Lane, Liverpool, cm (1818). [D]

Miller, James jnr, 19 Mint St, Southwark, London, u (1820–29). [D] See Miller & Woodward.

Miller, James, St Alphege, Canterbury, Kent, cm (1826). [Poll bk]

Miller, James, Hurst, near Ashton-under-Lyne, Lancs., joiner and cm (1828). [D]

Miller, James, Denton Chare, Newcastle, cm (1834). [D] Possibly Millar, —; or Miller's of Pilgrim St.

Miller, James, 13 Blackman St, Southwark, London, cm and u (1835–40). Recorded also at no. 21, 1835–37. Took out a Sun Insurance policy in 1840. [D; GL, Sun MS vol. 576, ref. 1331574]

Miller, John, Lancaster, cm (1757–68). Admitted freeman, 1757–58. Polled in 1768 as the son of Henry Miller. [Lancaster freemen rolls]

Miller, John, Drury Lane, London, cm (1763–76). Recorded opposite Gt Queen St in 1763. In 1776 he insured a house in Ealing for £400. [D; GL, Sun MS vol. 248, ref. 369867] Possibly of Miller & Eddiesson.

Miller (or Millar), John, Fleet Lane, London, cm (1775). Declared bankrupt, *Gents Mag.*, September 1775, and named as Millar in Bailey's list of bankrupts.

Miller, John, 36 Wells St, London, upholder (1775). Took out a Sun Insurance policy in 1775 for £400, of which £35 accounted for utensils, stock and goods. [GL, Sun MS vol. 239, p. 274]

Miller, John, Liverpool, u (1810–11). Trading at 8 Bridport St in 1810 and 2 Harford St in 1811. [D]

Miller, John, Worksop, Notts., cm, u, builder, joiner and carpenter (1816–35). Trading at Common, 1822–28, Low Town and Bridge Pl. in 1832, and Bridge Pl. in 1835. Carried out general joinery work and made looking-glass and picture frames for Worksop Manor, 1816–18; and in 1818–19 he supplied press and camp bedsteads, a tablecloth press, dressing tables and a chest of drawers. In 1834 regular payments are recorded to John Miller, carpenter, in the Duke of Norfolk's Worksop accounts, some of which may well have been for cabinet maker's work. [D; Arundel Castle records, MD662, MD1309, MD1310, A2073]

Miller, John, Windsor, Berks., u (1818). Sudden death of his wife, aged 34, reported in *Liverpool Mercury*, 10 April 1818.

Miller (or Millar), John, Lancaster (1815–36). App. to L. Redmayne in 1815, and admitted freeman, 1823–24. Named as Millar in the Gillow records, 1821–25; as Miller, 1826–36. [Lancaster app. reg. and freemen rolls; Westminster Ref. Lib., Gillow]

Miller, John, Mount St, Lambeth, London, u (1829–39). Trading at no. 26, 1829–35; and as a furniture broker only at no. 30 in 1839. [D]

Miller, John, 1 Pithay, Bristol, bedstead and chairmaker (1831–34). [D]

Miller, John, Hurst Brook, near Ashton-under-Lyne, Lancs., cm and joiner (1834). [D]

Miller, John, High Wycombe, Bucks., cm (1836). Son bapt. in 1836. [PR [bapt.)]

Miller, Joseph, Liverpool, carver (1818–24). Addresses given at 19 Leigh St in 1818; 3 Houghton St in 1823; and 2 Houghton St and 4 Newington Bridge in 1824. Joseph Miller, carver and gilder of 28 Basnett St was paid £40 on 12 February 1820 and £7 12s on 7 April 1820 for carving chairs and the pillar of a dining table at Liverpool Town Hall. Recorded incorrectly as James Miller in C. *Life*, 23 July 1927, pp. 120–31. [D; *Furn. Hist.*, 1970]

Miller, Joseph, Bristol, cm and u (1827–40). Trading at Rownham Pl., Hotwells, 1827–32, also 6 Ashton Pl., Hotwells in 1828; as cm, u, carpet and paper hanging warehouseman, 1831–32; at Princes Buildings in 1839, and Prince's Pl., Clifton in 1840. [D]

Miller, Joseph, Chester, cm (1828–40). Addresses given at 9 Watergate St Row in 1828 and Watergate Row in 1840. [D]

Miller, Joseph, 27 St Anne's Ct, Soho, London, cm and u (1839). [D]

Miller, Matthew, address unrecorded, cm (1803). Subscribed to Sheraton's *Cabinet Dictionary*, 1803.

Miller, Nathan, King St, Cambridge, u and furniture broker (1830). [D]

Miller, Nathan, London Rd, Kingston, Surrey, u (1832). [D]

Miller, Peter, 'in the Savoy', St Mary-le-Savoy, London, cm (1723–24). Took out a Sun Insurance policy on 17 April 1723 for £500 on goods and merchandise in his house only. Superb walnut bookcase recorded in Barcelona in 1982, inscribed 'Peter Miller 23 June Anno 1724 ... in the Savoy'. [GL, Sun MS vol. 15, ref. 28208; V&A archives]

Miller, Peter, Wardour St, London, cm and inlayer (1776). Took out a Sun Insurance policy in 1776 for £200, including £150 on utensils, stock and goods. [GL, Sun MS vol. 249, p. 579]

Miller, Peter, Newington Causeway, Newington Butts, London, cm (1791). Took out a Sun Insurance policy on 30 March 1791 for £400 including utensils, stock and goods in trust. [GL, Sun MS ref. 581383]

Miller, Ruth, St Michael-at-Plea, Norwich, cm (1839). [D]

Miller, Simeon, Riding House Lane, Gt Portland St, London, cm (1829). [D]

Miller, Thomas, Lancaster, cm (1779–80). [Lancaster freemen rolls]

Miller, Thomas, Plymouth, Devon, cm (1798). [D]

Miller, Thomas, Lancaster, cm (1817–18). [Lancaster freemen rolls]

Miller, Thomas, London, cm (1830–31). [Colchester poll bks]

Miller, Thomas & Son, 70 Scotland St and West St, Sheffield, Yorks., cm (1837). [D]

Miller, W., Christchurch, Hants., joiner and cm (1793). [D]

Miller, William, London, cm (1754–76). Recorded at Oxford St in 1774; and as upholder in St James's, Westminster in 1776. A William Miller, cm, subscribed to Chippendale's *Director*, 1754; and received payment from Adam in 1760. [GL, MS 3070 (S1 21–6)] Polled at Westminster in 1774. On 5 November 1775 the account books of Sir Thomas Egerton, Bart. (later 1st Earl of Wilton) for Heaton Hall, Manchester, record 'Millars Bill for Chairs etc. for the South East Bedchamber £38-4-0.' [Manchester RO, DDEg] Declared bankrupt, *Gents Mag.*, February and March 1776.

Miller, William, Chepping Wycombe Borough, High Wycombe, Bucks., chairmaker (1798). [Militia Census]

Miller, William, Dorset St, Manchester Sq., London, carver and gilder (1824–27). Trading at no. 53, 1825–27. Declared bankrupt as W. P. Miller in *Brighton Gazette*, 30 December 1824. [D]

Miller, William, High St, Newport Pagnell, Bucks., cm and u (1830–39). [D]

Miller, William, address unrecorded, joiner (1831). Named in the Royal Household Accounts for work done at Windsor Castle and Brighton Pavillion. On 30 September 1831 he was paid £4 5s for 'Repairing & regilding candelabras & sundry chairs' and 'A Maplewood frame'; and £8 17s 6d for '13 Picture frames repaired & regilded'. His bill totalled £37 11s 9d. [Windsor Royal Archives]

Miller, William, Dorking, Surrey, cm, upholder, surveyor and undertaker (1832–39). [D]

Miller, William, Sheffield, Yorks., cm (1834). [D]

Miller & Eddiesson (or Miller & Eddleston), 40 Drury Lane, London, u (1784). [D] Possibly John Miller.

Miller & Woodward, 9 Mint St, Southwark, London, cm and chair manufacturers (1820). [D] Possibly James Miller jnr.

Miller's, Pilgrim St, Newcastle. Probably early 19th-century wine cooler recorded, bearing label which reads: 'FROM MILLER'S GOTHIC WAREHOUSE OF FASHIONABLE CABINET FURNITURE PILGRIM STREET NEWCASTLE-UPON-TYNE.' Possibly Millar, —; or James Miller.

Millett, Stephen, parish of SS Philip & Jacob, Bristol, carver (1784). [Poll bk]

Millican, Edward, Gt Yarmouth, Norfolk, cm (1830–41). [Poll bks]

Millican, John, Senhouse St, Maryport, Cumb., joiner, cm and ironmonger (1811). [D]

Milligan, Thomas, Nottingham, joiner and cm (1778). App. to William Calar in 1778. [Nottingham app. list]

Milligan, Thomas, Chester, cm (1824–26). Recorded at Thomas St in 1824, when admitted freeman on 9 October 1824. [Chester freemen rolls and poll bk]

Milliker, —, address unrecorded, upholder (1781–82). Recorded as being paid £50 13s in 1781; and £60 17s in 1782. [V&A archives]

Millikin, Halley Benson, address unrecorded, upholder (1771–95). Son of James Millikin, freeman apothecary of London. Admitted freeman of the Upholders' Co. by redemption on 2 October 1771, and translated to the Grocers' Co. in 1795. [GL, Upholders' Co. records]

Millington, James, Halifax, Yorks., carver, gilder and manufacturer. Trade card recorded showing Rococo revival pier table. [V&A archives]

Millington, Matthew, Broad St, Nottingham, cm (1835). [D]

Millington, Robert, Chester, joiner, carver and turner (1680). [Chester freemen rolls]

Millium, Andrew, Fleet St, London, upholder (1734). Named in contemporary newspapers. [Heal]

Millman, William, Yealmpton, near Plymouth, Devon, chairmaker (1812). [Exeter RO, PR; *Furn. Hist.*, 1976, pl. 38A and B]

Mil(l)ne, George, Liverpool, carver (1813–30). App. to John Summer in 1813; petitioned freedom on servitude in 1822, paying 6s 8d, and admitted freeman on 17 November 1830. [Liverpool freemen's committee bk and reg.]

Millne, George, 10 Rigby St, Salford, Lancs., carver (1825). [D]

Mill(e)s, —, London (?), upholder (1684–85). He bought goods costing £9 5s 10d from Charles Blunt, upholder, in 1684–85. At a later date Mr Miles of Grevile St paid Blunt 9s and £10 3s 10d. [PRO, C114/164, pt 1]

Mills, —, address unrecorded, u (1803–04). Named in Sir Gilbert Heathcote's account book for Normanton Hall, Rutland, on 20 November 1803 receiving £21 1s; and in November 1804, £53 'for Sundries'. [Lincoln RO, 3 ANC 6/25, 6/380]

Mills, Abraham, London, carver (1739). [Bristol poll bk]

Mills, Ambrose, York, cm (1745). Listed on 11 October 1745 under Papists recognizances. [York City archives, quarter sessions bk, 1744–56]

Mills, C. E., High St, Stamford, Lincs., cm, u, auctioneer, appraiser and undertaker (1815–22). Billhead recorded. [D; Stamford Town Hall, ref. T22, binder 1]

Mills, C., 102 Mount St, Grosvenor Sq., London, u etc. (1835). [D] See Mills & Co.

Mills, Charles, 192 Church St, Shoreditch, London, bedstead and cabinet manufacturer (1820). [D]

Mills, Charles, 77 High St, Marylebone, London, u (1823–28). Recorded at no. 7, 1826–27. [D] See William Mills at this address.

Mills, Charles, 21 Everett St, Coram St, London, invalid and recumbent chair and sofa maker (1839). [D]

Mills, Daniel, at 'The Japan Cabinet & Cistern', Vine St, Hatton Gdn, London, japanner and cm (1765–78). Recorded at Vine House, Hatton St in 1775; and in partnership with Joseph Mills, 1767–77. Rococo trade card, c.1760, shows a japanned cabinet on a simple stand, and states that Daniel Mills 'Japans and Sells all sorts of Japan, Cabinet and other Wares for Exportation, Wholesale or Retail. ALSO Japans upon all Sorts of Goods made of Copper, Brass, Tin, Lead, &c. to ye utmost perfection. N.B. All Sorts of Materials sold for JAPANNERS.' [D; Heal]

Mills, David, Norwich, chairmaker and cm (1768–86). Recorded in St Andrew's parish in 1768; St Gregory's in 1780; St Laurence's, 1784; and St Martin-at-Oak, 1786. [Poll bks]

Mills, George, address unrecorded, cm (1803). Subscribed to Sheraton's *Cabinet Dictionary*, 1803.

Mills, George, Paradise Sq., Sheffield, Yorks., cm (1814). [D]

Mills, James, Castle St, Oxford St, London, cm and upholder (1775–1808). Recorded at no. 13 in partnership with William Caldwell, 1775–85; alone at no. 68 in 1778; and no. 19, 1792–1808. Took out Sun Insurance policies with Caldwell in 1775 for £700, £380 on utensils and stock; and on 16 December 1785 for £200 on household goods only. Mills took out policies alone in 1778 for £400, including £280 on utensils and stock; on 25 February 1792 for £500 on household goods at his private house, 63 Harley St; and on 13 January 1808 for £650, £480 accounting for utensils and stock. [D; GL, Sun MS vol. 240, p. 363; vol. 333, p. 609; vol. 270, p. 40; vol. 382, ref. 597063; vol. 440, ref. 812906]

Mills, James Henry, 12 High St, Brighton, Sussex, u and furniture broker (1832–39). [D]

Mills, James, Gt Surrey St, Blackfriars Rd, London, bedstead maker (1837). [D]

Mills, John, Ipswich, Suffolk, cm (1756). Took app. named Higgin in 1756. [S of G, app. index]

Mills, John, Loughborough, Leics., cm and u (1778). Auction of his stock in trade by Mr Drake announced in *Leicester Journal*, 27 June 1778.

Mills, John, Holborn, London, cm and upholder (1760–1813). Addresses given 'opposite the Bull & Gate' in 1777; at 96 High Holborn in 1778; no. 41, 1780–93; Bedford Row, Brownlow St, 1794–1809; South End of Bedford Row, 1794; 15 South End in 1799; Bedford St, Bedford Row, 1794–1808; and 13 Brownlow St, 1804–12. Trade card gives address at Bedford Row, Brownlow St. [BM] Address also given at 17 Walcot Pl. in 1813. App. to James Grange on 6 March 1760, and admitted freeman of the Upholders' Co. by servitude on 6 April 1768. Took out a Sun Insurance policy in 1777 in association with James Grange. Took out policies alone in 1780 for £800, £600 on utensils and stock; in 1781 for £1,300, £1,000 on utensils and stock; on 29 September 1802 and 18 February 1803 for £500; and on 14 or 19 January 1804 for £300 on his three houses at 1, 2 and 3 Meeting House Ct, Miles Lane, Carmon St. Took out a further Sun Insurance policy on 1 March 1813 for £2,000, including £150

on his dwelling house at 17 Walcot Pl., £350 on household goods at Wellington House, Hackney Rd, £250 on house and counting house at 15 Bedford St, Bedford Row, £250 on a house at 12 Brownlow St in tenure; £250 on house and counting house at no. 13; and £400 on stock and utensils. Subscribed to Sheraton's *Cabinet Dictionary*, and named in his list of master cabinet makers, 1803. Probably the J. Mills whose stamp is recorded on a pair of George III satinwood open armchairs, the rectangular backs with beaded borders and recessed upper corners, capped by leaf finials; the padded arms on fluted supports, the caned seats with fluted rails carved with paterae; on turned fluted legs; the back, arms and seat cushions covered in sage green velvet. [D; GL, Upholders' Co. records; GL, Sun MS vol. 280, p. 457; vol. 296, p. 610; vol. 424, ref. 738018; vol. 426, ref. 745093; vol. 430, ref. 757633; vol. 457, ref. 879759; Christie's, 25 February 1971, lot 175, illus.]

Mills, John, Allens Ct, London, chairmaker (1784). [Westminster poll bk]

Mills, John, Park St, Cirencester, Glos., cm and u (1813–40). Nine children bapt. between 1813–30. [D; PR (bapt.)]

Mills, John, 5 Charles St, Middlx Hospital, London, cm (1820). [D]

Mills, John, Gee-Cross, Hyde, near Stockport, Lancs., wood turner (1825). [D]

Mills, John, St John St, Wolverhampton, Staffs., chairmaker (1827–28). [D]

Mills, John, 27 Harcourt St, Marylebone, London, furniture japanner (1829). [D]

Mills, John, 7 Dorrington St, Coldbath Fields, London, u (1839). [D]

Mills, Joseph, London, cm and japanner (1775–1825). Recorded at Gt Earl St, Seven Dials, 1775–93; and as a japanner only at no. 11 in 1808; and 40 Gt Russell St, Bloomsbury, 1812–25. [D]

Mills, Joseph, Norwich, u (1822–39). Recorded at St Gregory's Churchyard in 1822 and Castle Ditches in 1839. [D]

Mills, Joseph, Henley St, Stratford-upon-Avon, Warks., cm (1828). [D]

Mills, Mary, 24 Peter St, Half Moon Alley, Bishopsgate St, London, upholder (1823–24). Took out a Sun Insurance policy on 19 November 1823 for £550, including £100 on household goods in dwelling house, where no cabinet or carpenter's work was done; £300 on stock and utensils; and £150 on a house at 3 Gloucester St, Hackney Rd in private tenure. Took out a further policy on 1 April 1824 for £800 of which £400 accounted for utensils and stock. [GL, Sun MS vol. 495, ref. 1010564; vol. 497, ref. 1016173]

Mills, Richard, 26 Walbrook, London, upholder (1804). Took out a Sun Insurance policy on 2 April 1804 for £100 including £50 on stock and utensils. [GL, Sun MS vol. 430, ref. 760611]

Mills, Robert, workshop at Lord St, Liverpool, cm (1800–03). Addresses also given at 2 Rainford Gdns, Harrington St in 1800, and Byrom St in 1803. [D]

Mills, Robert, Eden St, Cambridge, cm (1840–41). [Poll bks]

Mills, Rowland, 37 Goswell St, London, Venetian blind and bedstead maker, undertaker (1808). [D]

Mills, Samuel, Stamford, Lincs., cm and u (1801–d. by 1835). Took app. named Francis Whitehead, u, on 19 November 1801. Admitted freeman in 1802 as son of William Mills, freeman burgess of Stamford. [Stamford app. reg. and freemen rolls]

Mills, Thomas D., Bartholomew Pl., West Smithfield, London, morocco case maker, portable desk, dressing case, work box and cabinet case maker (1829–39). Trading at no. 2 in 1829; no. 1 in 1835; and 3 Bartholomew Terr., City Rd in 1839. [D]

Mills, Thomas, High St, Stourbridge, Worcs., chairmaker (1828–30). [D]

Mills, Thomas, Smallbrook St, Birmingham, cm and u (1828–35). Addresses given at no. 68, 1828–30, and no. 71 in 1835. [D]

Mills, Thomas, 61 Market St, Bradford, Yorks., u and paper hanger (1837). [D] Rosewood stool, c.1840, recorded, with X-frame supports joined by a pole stretcher; the top upholstered with remnants of continental *gros point* wool-work; the underside bearing traces of the label of 'Thomas Mills, Upholsterer & Paper Hanger, Market St., Bradford.' [Sotheby's, 22 July 1983, lot 31]

Mills, W., opposite Slaughter's Coffee House, St Martin's Lane, London, cm (1775). See Charles Evans, regarding Sun Insurance policy.

Mills, William, Exeter, Devon, cm (1777). Took out a Sun Insurance policy in 1777 for £500 of which £180 accounted for utensils and stock. [GL, Sun MS vol. 259, p. 38]

Mills, William, Lancaster, cm (1791–1807). App. to William Blackburn in 1791, and admitted freeman, 1806–07, when stated 'of Milnthrop' (Milnthorpe). [Lancaster app. reg. and freemen rolls]

Mills, William, Monument Yd, London, u (1801–09). Recorded also at 'The Swan', Norwich, 1801–02. Took out a Sun Insurance policy on 30 March 1809 for £3,000 on a warehouse and counting house in Coleman St Buildings. [D; GL, Sun MS vol. 447, ref. 828737]

Mills, William, address unrecorded, cm (1803). Subscribed to Sheraton's *Cabinet Dictionary*, 1803.

Mills, William, Loman's St, Southwark, London, carver and gilder (1817–26). Recorded at no. 14, 1817–20. [D]

Mills, William, Lavenham, Suffolk, cm (1824–30). [D]

Mills, William, 77 High St, Marylebone, London, u (1825). [D] See Charles Mills at this address.

Mills, William, Liverpool, cm (1832–40). App. to William John Roberts in 1832, and admitted freeman on 25 July 1840. [Liverpool app. enrolment bk and freemen reg.].

Mills & Co., 102 Mount St, Grove [Grosvenor] Sq., London, u (1835). [D] See C. Mills.

Millsham, Joseph, St Clement's, Oxford, carver (1778). Insured his house for £200 in 1778. [GL, Sun MS vol. 262, p. 544] See Thomas Milsham.

Millward, Edward, 24 Upper Clifton St, Finsbury, London, bedstead maker (1835–39). [D]

Mil(l)ward, George, London, cm and bedstead maker (1808–39). Trading at 54 Gt Sutton St, Clerkenwell, 1808–11; no. 51 in 1820; and 9 Queen St, Finsbury in 1839. [D]

Millward, James, Shropshire St, Market Drayton, Salop, chairmaker (1828). [D]

Millway, Thomas, address unrecorded, upholder (1699). Admitted freeman of the Upholders' Co. on 6 December 1699. [GL, Upholders' Co. records]

Milne, David, 120 Wardour St, Soho, London, cm (1808). [D]

Milne, John, Ipswich, Suffolk, joiner and cm (1760). Took app. named Baker in 1760. [S of G, app. index]

Milner, Francis jnr, Beverley, Yorks., cm (1784). [Poll bk]

Milner, Henry, Kington, Herefs., carpenter, joiner, cm and u (1830–40). Trading at Bridge St, 1830–35, and Mill St in 1840. [D]

Milner, James, King St, near Guildhall, London, u (1690). Named in contemporary newspapers. [Heal]

Milner, James, at the sign of 'The Mortar & Pestle', Milk St, London, upholder (1718). Took out a Hand in Hand Insurance policy on 20 August 1718 for £300 on a rented house at the above address. [GL, Hand in Hand MS vol. 19, p. 120] Possibly master of Robert Milner below.

Milner, James, 24 Oxford St, Liverpool, u (1829). [D]

Milner, John, York, cm and u (1816–38). Recorded at 47 Goodramgate, 1830–38. Son of Thomas Milner of New Malton; app. to William Smith, u, on 23 July 1816. [D; York app. reg.] See Milner & Harland.

Milner, John, Thornhill, near Dewsbury, Yorks., carpenter and cm (1822). [D]

Milner, John, Holmfirth, Huddersfield, Yorks., joiner and cm (1834). [D]

Milner, Josiah, 8 Milner's Sq., Hull, Yorks., turner and carver (1831). [D]

Milner, Mark, 39 Cheapside, London, cutler, desk and dressing case manufacturer (1835–39). Trading as portable desk, dressing case, work box and cabinet case maker in 1839. [D]

Milner, Michael, 34 Litchfield St, Soho, London, cm (1790–1808). Trading in partnership with Richard Milner, 1790–93. [D]

Milner, Michael, Ryegate, Helmsley, Yorks., joiner and cm (1823–40). [D]

Milner, Robert, London, upholder (1707–45). Recorded in 1727 poll bk at Wood St. Son of Robert Milner, apothecary of Worcester. App. to James Milner on 1 August 1707, and admitted freeman of the Upholders' Co. by servitude on 4 January 1715. Took apps named Walter Savage, 1723–32/33; and Francis Hurst, 1733–41. Notice in *Gents Mag.*, 24 June 1745, concerning the office of Sheriff of London read: 'Robert Milner, Esq., upholder and Henry Flitcroft, Esq., joyner, have not paid their fines to be excused from serving the said office.' [GL, Upholders' Co. records]

Milner, Robert, High Wycombe, Bucks., cm (1834–38). Sons bapt. in 1834, 1836, and 1838. [PR (bapt.)]

Milner, Samuel, Upper High St, Leeds, Yorks., cm (1822). [D]

Milner, William, Nottingham, cm (d. 1798). Probate will dated 7 March 1798. [Notts. RO, probate records]

Milner & Harland, 47 Goodramgate, York, cm etc. (1840). [D] See John Milner.

Milnes, Edward, Kirkgate, Wakefield, Yorks., cm and u (1818–37). [D]

Milnes, Enoch, 75 Bridge St, Bradford, Yorks., cm and joiner (1830–34). [D]

Miln(e)s, Henry, Bowling Lane, Bradford, Yorks., cm (1828–34). Trading also at Hope St in 1830. [D]

Milns, Edward, London, carver and gilder (1829–39). Trading at 1 Sarah Pl., Coburg St, Clerkenwell in 1829, and 15 Rosoman St in 1835. [D]

Milsham, Thomas, St Clement's, Oxford, cm (1802). [Poll bk] See Joseph Millsham.

Milsom, Arthur, Preston, Lancs., u and paper hanger (1802–18). Trading at 22 Fishergate, 1805–18, in partnership with Greenwood in 1818. Named in the Preston Guild record of burgesses in 1802. [D]

Milsom, John, London, upholder (1761–73). Trading at 50 Gracechurch St in 1773. Son of Adam Milsom, Blue maker of St Leonard, East Cheap. App. to Francis Hamilton on 1 October 1761, and admitted freeman of the Upholders' Co. by servitude on 2 November 1768. [D; GL, Upholders' Co. records]

Milsom, John, Groves (Lime St to Stoneferry), Hull, Yorks., cm (1817). [D]

Milson & Walker, 71 Fleet Mkt, London, upholders (1790–93). [D]

Milton, Charles, 50 High St, Mile End, London, cm and u (1839). [D]

Milton, John, 26 Willow Walk, Shoreditch, London, cm (1808). [D]

Milward, Benjamin, see Edward Walbank, concerning Sun Insurance policy taken out in 1782.

Milward, Stephen, Newport, Salop, chairmaker (1797–98). [D]

Milward, William, address unrecorded, upholder (1722–48). Son of Thomas Milward, yeoman of Bottle Clayton, Bucks.; app. to George Tarry on 5 September 1722, and admitted freeman of the Upholders' Co. by servitude on 5 August 1730. Took app. named Joseph Sandwell, 1746–48. [GL, Upholders' Co. records]

Mimpriss, R., 32 Gt Windmill St, Haymarket, London, carried out painting, glazing, gilding and japanning (1807). Trade card recorded showing female figure holding glass which reflects the colours of a rainbow on to a palette. [Banks Coll., BM]

Mincky, John, near 'The Mitre', Goswell St, London, carver and gilder (1777). Took out a Sun Insurance policy in 1777 for £300 of which utensils and stock accounted for £100. [GL, Sun MS vol. 254, p. 613]

Mind, William, 7 Valentine Row, Blackfriars Rd, London, cm (1809–12). [D]

Mindham, John, Wells, Norfolk, cm and joiner (1822–30). Trading at High St in 1830. [D]

Mindham, Robert, Wells, Norfolk, cm and ironmonger (1784–98). [D]

Mindham & Son, Holt, Norfolk, cm and organ builder (1839). [D]

Minett, William, 3 Mount Row, Lambeth, London, u (1826–27). [D]

Mingay, John, Bridge St, Norwich, cm and u (1830). [D]

Miniken, Thomas, 64 Berwick St, Soho, London, cm and u (1827–29). Recorded as Thomas & Son in 1829. [D]

Minikin, James, Lancaster. Named in the Gillow records in 1799 working on a cupboard. [Westminster Ref. Lib., Gillow vol. 344/95, p. 1498]

Minikin, Thomas, Lancaster. Named in the Gillow records, 1798–99, making two tables. [Westminster Ref. Lib.]

Minikin, Thomas, address unrecorded, cm (1803). Subscribed to Sheraton's *Cabinet Dictionary*, 1803.

Minikin, Thomas, address unrecorded. Tea caddy in the V&A Museum recorded as made by Thomas Minikin in 1804. [V&A archives]

Minks, J., Middleborough, Colchester, Essex, chairmaker (1823–27). [D]

Minks, Robert, Stanwell St, Colchester, Essex, chairmaker (1832). [D]

Minky, John, Little Wild St, London, carver (1788). [Bailey's list of bankrupts] Probably John Mincky.

Minn (Minne or Mynne(s)), Thomas snr & jnr, address unrecorded, joiners (1682–83). Received payment for a case of drawers for the 'Repository', the Old Ashmolean Museum, Oxford, 1682–83. [Vice Chancellor's account payment]

Minnet, William, 100 London Rd, London, cm and u (1827–28). [D] See William Minett.

Minnez, —, Ha[r]t St, Covent Gdn, London, cm (1758). Notice in *London Chronicle*, 3–5 January 1758, referred to the curing of his two blind daughters.

Minnican, John, 14 New Cavendish St, London, u (1839). [D]

Minnis, James, Little St, Brixham, Devon, cm (1823–24). [D]

Minns, James jnr, Norwich, cm and chairmaker (1812–39). Recorded in the parish of St John Sepulchre, 1812–18; Lakenham in 1830; and Lakenham Hall Rd in 1839. [D; poll bks]

Minns, William, London, cm (1818). [Norwich poll bk]

Minns, William, East Dereham, Norfolk, carver (1830). [Poll bk]

Minshall, John, London, carver and gilder (1769–75). Settled in Dock St in 1769, establishing a large business in carved frames for mirrors. In 1775 Minshall's looking-glass store in Hanover Sq., opposite to Mr Goelet's sign of 'The Golden Key', advertised 'an elegant assortment of looking glasses, in

oval and square ornamental frames; ditto mahogany. Any Lady or Gentleman who has glass in old-fashioned frames may have these cut into ovals or any pattern desired. The above frames may be finished in white, or green and white, purple, or any other colour that suits the furniture of the room, or gilt in oil or burnished gold.' This reference to the process of oil gilding is interesting at a time when most mirrors were 'water gilt'. The accounts for the decoration of Lord Mansfield's house at Kenwood include a bill dated 1769 for carving executed for Robert Adam and bears his covering signature. Minshall executed library bookcases and shelves, and much of the carved work in the room, at a total cost of £200 0s 5½. He also charged £5 12s 7d for 'flowers on end of staircase steps', at 1s 6d each. Advertisements in the *New York Journal* cause confusion since they might be interpreted to mean that Minshall emigrated to or spent some time in New York. A notice of 7 December 1769 read: 'Minshall, carver and gilder, from London, lives in Dock-Street' and makes 'carved frames for glasses, picture frames, tables, chairs, girandoles, chimney pieces, brackets, candle stands, clock and watch cases, bed and window cornicing; he makes proper ornaments for ceilings and stair cases, in the present mode.' In advertisements in the same paper of 1771–72 he mentioned that he taught drawing. In 1775 he advertised in the same paper 'Minshall's Looking-Glass Store in Hanover Square, opposite to Mr. Goelet's the sign of the Golden Key...'. Minshall's link with America might suggest that he was one of the most influential transmitters of Neo-classicism to the American Colonies, where it is usually associated with the 'Federal' style of the 1780s and later. Trade card of 1769 recorded. [*DEF*; *GCM*; Wills, *Looking-Glasses*; V&A archives; Harris, *Old English Furniture*, p. 15; R. S. Gottesman, *The Arts and Crafts in New York*, 1954; Heal]

Minshull, —, Lancaster. Named in the Gillow records in 1808 working on a box cover. [Westminster Ref. Lib., Gillow vol. 344/99, p. 1847]

Minshull, George & Sons, Lombard St, Birmingham, cm, fancy box, case and caddy maker (1816–35). Listed at no. 90 in 1835. [D]

Minter, George, Margate, Kent, cm (1794). [D]

Minter, George, London, cm, u, bath and wheel chairmaker (1829–54). Addresses given at 26 Princes St, Haymarket, 1829–31; 33 Gerrard St, Soho, 1835–50; also 51 Frith St, Soho, 1850–54. Trading as 'Patentee of the self-acting chair' in 1839; and filed a patent in 1845 together with Jonathan Badger, carpenter and builder of Walworth, London, for improvements in the construction of easy chairs. [D; Patent no. 10, 918] Several chairs by Minter survive. A large carved arm chair, with a pull-out foot rest, reputed to have belonged to Darwin, has carved on one leg: 'George Minter, Gerrard Street, Soho'. [Darwin Museum] Armchair, *c*.1800, recorded, with Hepplewhite-style 'camel back', heavy cabriole front legs with acanthus carving and lion paw feet. The chair has vestiges of a ratchet mechanism which probably enabled the seat to slide forward and the back to move lower. The rear legs are impressed: 'G. MINTER, 23 PRINCES STREET SOHO WR Pat 383'. Gouty chair also recorded bearing stamp of 'MINTER WR 39 GERRARD ST. LONDON PATENT 672'. [V&A archives] A mahogany reading chair noted with adjustable back, leg rest (now missing) and swivel reading stand (also missing), is stamped on one leg: 'G. MINTER 33 GERRARD STREET WR PATENT Nº 1638'. Stamp also recorded on a carved mahogany-framed gout chair in black leather with reclining buttoned wing back, scroll arm supports and stuffed-over seat, fitted with sliding adjustable foot rest on foliate decorated tapered legs and brass capped castors. Stamp reads: G. MINTER 55 GERRARD ST. SOHO

WILLIAM IV PATENT NO. 1734'. [Phillips', 11 January 1983, lot 50] See John Minter.

Minter, Henry, Faversham, Kent, cm (1780–1811). Took out Sun Insurance policies in 1780 for £300 on his house; and in 1781 for £400, £60 on utensils and stock. [D; poll bk; GL, Sun MS vol. 283, p. 602; vol. 295, p. 214]

Minter, John, Canterbury, Kent, cm (1793–96). Admitted freeman in 1793. Polled in 1796 of King St. [Canterbury freemen rolls]

Minter, John, Princes St, Soho, London, u, cm and chair manufacturer (1830). Patented 'Minter's reclining chair' in 1830. [Patent no. 6034] See George Minter. John may be an error.

Minter, Thomas, West St, Faversham, Kent, cm (1823–39). [D]

Minter, William, Faversham, Kent, cm (1796). [Canterbury poll bk]

Mirfin, Thomas, May Day Green, Barnsley, Yorks., cm (1828–37). [D]

Misson, John, Nottingham, joiner and cm (1802). App. to Samuel Dodd in 1802. [Nottingham app. list]

Mitcham, Joseph, Dog Row, Bethnal Green, London, cm and chairmaker (1817). [D]

Mitchamore, Samuel, Ewings Lane, Exeter, Devon, cm (1836). Son Samuel Adam bapt. at St Mary Steps on 31 July 1836. [PR (bapt.)]

Mitchel, John, Kendal, Westmld, joiner and cm (1770). Tiny trade card recorded illustrated with printer's stock decorations. [Heal Coll., BM] Printed label, dated in ink '25 Dec. 1770', found on a plain oak chest of drawers. [Poll bk]

Mitchel, William, Beverley, Yorks., cm (1799).

Mitchell, —, address unrecorded. In 1759 he supplied a mahogany writing table with pigeon hole to Chevening, Kent, at a cost of £5 5s. [Kent RO, Stanhope papers, U/590 A61/5]

Mitchell, —, Lancaster, carver and/or gilder (1790). [Westminster Ref. Lib., Gillow records]

Mitchell, Alexander, London, cm (1778–1825). Recorded at 12 Princes St, Drury Lane, London, in 1778; as cm, tobacconist and dealer in rushes at 91 Upper East Smithfield in 1786; as cm and ship joiner at 17 St Catherine St in 1808; at 17 St Catherine's, Tower, or Tower Hill, 1811–25; and as cm, ship joiner and dealer in bull rushes at 17 New St, Catherine's Bridge in 1812. Took out Sun Insurance policies on 6 February 1808 for £1,650; on 27 April 1809, due in 1810, in association with Andrew Blythe for £1,650 of which £500 on a house at Highbury Terr., Islington; and £1,150 on houses at 60, 65, 66, 69 and 70 Sun St, Bishopsgate St; and on 4 February 1812 for £2,400, including £1,000 on house and workshop, £500 on workshop and warehouse in Pillory Lane, and £300 on stock, utensils and goods in trust. Acted as executor of the will of George Young, painter and glazier, late of Gt Hermitage St, St George. [D; GL, Sun MS vol. 266, p. 640; vol. 336, p. 613; vol. 441, ref. 814238; vol. 447, ref. 830380; vol. 455, ref. 867455; PRO, C13, 524, Richardson v Baxter]

Mitchel(l), Aylmer, Gt Warner St, Clerkenwell, London, candle and fire screen maker (1823–29). Recorded at no. 1, 1826–29. [D]

Mitchell, Edward, 1 Radnor St, City Rd, London, wood and cabinet carver (1839). [D]

Mitchell, Francis, Bristol, cm and chairmaker (1817–29). Trading at Temple St, 1817–20; 25 Somerset St, Redcliff in 1825; 18 Hillgrove St, 1826–27; Newfoundland Lane in 1828; and at Temple St in 1829, also as a grocer. [D]

Mitchell, George, John St, Golden Sq., London, upholder (1774–84). [Poll bks]

Mitchell, George, Newcastle, cm (1803). Subscribed to Sheraton's *Cabinet Dictionary*, 1803.

Mitchell, George, 190 Church St, Bethnal Green, London, auctioneer, u etc. (1809–11). [D]

Mitchell, George, London, cm, broker of household goods and auctioneer (1811–19). Recorded at the corner of Crown St, Finsbury, on 22 January 1811; corner of Craven St, Wilson St on 20 May 1811; Wilson St, Finsbury Sq., 1813–19; and 28 Wilson St, Moorfields in 1817. Took out Sun Insurance policies on 22 January 1811 for £1,750 of which stock and utensils accounted for £1,500; and on 20 May 1811 for £1,100, £100 on houses and offices, £1,000 on stock and utensils. [D; GL, Sun MS vol. 452, ref. 852600; vol. 451, ref. 858565]

Mitchell, George, Ashton-under-Lyne, Lancs., cm and joiner (1816–34). Addresses given at Stylebarn, 1816–24; Park Parade in 1828; and 264 Manchester Rd in 1834. Trade Directories of 1816–18 add 'and Loom'. [D]

Mitchell, George, 7 Broadway, Blackfriars/Ludgate Hill, London, u (1820–25). Trading as Mitchell & Co., 1820–21. [D]

Mitchell, George, 7 Norton Falgate, London, auctioneer and u (1825). [D]

Mitchell, George, Brighton, Sussex, cm, u and furniture broker (1826–39). Addresses given at Poplar Pl., 1826–27; 15 New Rd in 1832; and 2 Meeting House Lane and Union Lane, 1839. His daughter, Mary Ann Mitchell of 42 Russell Sq. married on 7 March 1838. [D; East Sussex RO, PR] See J. Mitchell.

Mitchell, J., Garner's Hill, Nottingham, fancy chairmaker (1812–14). Took app. named James Barwick in 1812. [D; Nottingham app. list]

Mitchell, J., 2 Meeting House Lane, Brighton, Sussex, cm and u (1827). [D] See George Mitchell at this address.

Mitchell, James, Newcastle, u (1767). App. to William Charnley, and admitted freeman on 12 October 1767. [Newcastle freemen reg.]

Mitchell, James, Lymington, Hants., chairmaker (1781). Took out a Sun Insurance policy in 1781 for £200, of which £150 accounted for utensils and stock. [GL, Sun MS vol. 297, p. 594]

Mitchell, James, Hunslet, Leeds, Yorks., cm (1793). Placed notice in *Leeds Intelligencer*, 1793, which read: 'Whereas I, James Mitchell of Hunslet in the Borough of Leeds, in the County of York, Cabinet Maker, did leave the work of Robert Brown of Hunslet aforesaid, Cabinet Maker, in an unfinished state, for which he obtained a warrant against me, and that after such a warrant was obtained, I did violently assault and ill-treat the said Robert Brown; now, I the said James Mitchell do ask pardon to said Robert Brown for so doing, and thank him for the lenity towards me, and promise never to be guilty of the like in future; and request that this may be published in the Leeds Intelligencer at my expence. As witness my hand this 22nd of November, 1793, James Mitchell.'

Mitchell, James, York, cm (1799–1806). Trading in Minster Yard, 1806. Son of Samuel Mitchell, aledraper of Minster Yard. App. to Peter Davies, cm, on 1 January 1799, and admitted freeman in 1806. [York app. reg. and freemen rolls]

Mitchell, James, 1 Radnor St, St Luke's, London, wood carver (1835). [D]

Mitchell, John, Barnes, Surrey, carpenter and u (1795–97). Notices regarding bankruptcy, certificate and dividends appeared in *Billinge's Liverpool Advertiser*, 25 May and 1 August 1795; and 6 February 1797, when described as late of Barnes.

Mitchell, John, Garner(s) Hill, Nottingham, chairmaker (1818–28). [D]

Mitchel(l), John, Abbey Pl., Plymouth, Devon cm and u (1830–38). [D]

Mitchell, John, Watford, Herts., cm (1832–39). [D]

Mitchell, Joseph, 28 Tower St, Seven Dials, London, cm (1808). [D]

Mitchell, Joseph, Liverpool, cm (1823–39). Trading at 10 Back Rathbone St in 1839. App. to Cattrall & Whittingham in 1823. [D; Liverpool app. enrolment bk]

Mitchell, Martha, Prince's St, Westminster, London, u (1784). [D]

Mitchell, Matthew, 78 Friargate, Preston, Lancs., cm (1818). [D]

Mitchell, Patrick, Silver St, Newcastle, looking-glass manufacturer (1777). Advertised in *Newcastle Courant*, 29 March 1777 that he '…has just arrived from London, a neat & elegant assortment of carved burnished gold, and blue & white frames, which he fits up on terms as reasonable as in London. N.B. Old plates new polished, silvered, and framed in the best manner; and plate glasses of all sizes, wholesale & retail.'

Mitchell, Richard, High St, Burslem, Staffs., chairmaker (1834). [D]

Mitchell, Robert, Dog & Duck Lane, Beverley, Yorks., cm (1814). [D]

Mitchell, Robert, Liverpool, carver and gilder (1834–39). Addresses given at 5 Back Seel St in 1834; 6 Seel St in 1837; and 7 Plaistow Buildings, 6 Seel St, with shop at 9 Seel St in 1839. [D]

Mitchel(l), Thomas, 85 Charlotte St, Rathbone Pl., London, cm (1797–1801). [D]

Mitchell, Thomas, Baseter (or Baxter) Gate, Loughborough, Leics., cm (1798). Announced in *Leicester Journal*, 19 January 1798 that he was handing the business over to his son, Thomas.

Mitchell, Thomas, Kirkburton, near Huddersfield, Yorks., cm (1822). [D]

Mitchell, Thomas, King St, Hammersmith, Middlx, cm and u (1839). [D]

Mitchell, W. T., West Pl., St George's Fields, London, chair japanner (1808). [D]

Mitchell, William, address unrecorded, upholder (1714). Son of Nicholas Mitchell, Gent. of Oxford. App. to Thomas Goodhard, weaver, and admitted freeman of the Upholders' Co. by servitude on 17 March 1713/14. [GL, Upholders' Co. records]

Mitchell, William, Princes Ct, Princes St, Westminster, London, cm and upholder (1776–79). Took out Sun Insurance policies in 1776 for £300, £200 accounting for utensils and stock; and in 1779 for £600, £350 on utensils, stock and goods. [GL, Sun MS vol. 247, p. 94; vol. 275, p. 116]

Mitchell(s), William, Frith St, Soho, London, cm (1779–84). As Mitchells, took out a Sun Insurance policy in 1779 for £200 on utensils and stock. Polled at Westminster as Mitchell in 1784. [GL, Sun MS vol. 276, p. 289]

Mitchell, William, Portsea, Portsmouth, Hants., chairmaker (1792–98). [D]

Mitchell, William, 79 St Martin's Lane, London, cm (1823). Took out a Sun Insurance policy on 28 May 1823 for £100. [GL, Sun MS vol. 498, ref. 1005357]

Mitchell, William, 12 Gee St, Goswell St, London, cm (1826–27). [D]

Mitchell, William, 52 Featherstone St, London, cm and u (1827–28). [D]

Mitchell, William, 7 Pump Row, Old St Rd, London, cm (1835). [D]

Mitchell, William, 5 Upper Rupert St, Soho, London, cm (1835). [D]

Mitchell, William, 228 Kent St, Southwark, London, bed and mattress maker (1837). [D] See Mitchell & Son.

Mitchell & Binns, Damside, Keighley, Yorks., joiners and/or cm (1837).

Mitchell & Son, 45 Newman St, Oxford St, London, u (1825). [D]

Mitchelson, J., 45 Newman St, Oxford St, London, u etc. (1820). [D]

Mitchelson, John, 57 Upper John St, Fitzroy Sq., London, u etc. (1826–27). [D]

Mitchi(n)son, Jacob, High St, Gateshead, Co. Durham, cm and furniture broker (1827–33). Trading at no. 97 in 1833. [D]

Mitchinson, John, Oulton, near Wigton, Cumb., cm and/or joiner (1834). [D]

Mitford, Humphrey, address unrecorded, upholder (1714–22). Son of William Mitford, clerk of Elsden, Northumb. App. to William Humphreys on 26 August 1714, and admitted freeman of the Upholders' Co. by servitude on 8 February 1721/22. [GL, Upholders' Co. records]

Mitford, James, Blaydon, Co. Durham, joiner, carpenter and/or cm (1828–32). [D]

Mitley, Charles George, Featherstone, Yorks., carver (1705–d. 1758). App. in 1720 to Daniel Harvey (Hervé) who had worked at Castle Howard and Wentworth Castle. Mitley's commissions included the carving on a Gothic pulpit to William Kent's design for York Minster; and work, with Fisher, for William Aislabie at Studley Royal, near Ripon. Died 26 August 1758, buried in St Cuthbert's, York. [C. *Life Annual*, 1965, Beard, *Craftsmen and Interior Decoration in England*, p. 271]

Mitten, William, 34 High St, Brighton, Sussex, cm (1821–24). Mary Anne, daughter of William and Mary Anne Mitton, High St, bapt. on 12 August 1821. [D; PR (bapt.)]

Mittens, T., Penn St, Bristol, cm (1813). [D]

Mitton, Edward, Haslar St, Gosport, Hants., u and undertaker (1839). [D]

Mitton, John, Bristol, cm (1813–40). Recorded at St Michael's Hill, 1813–17; no. 9, 1819–26; 19 Montague St, 1827–28; and no. 3, 1829–40. Working as cm, u and undertaker from 1824. [D]

Mitton, John, Sheep St, Wellingborough, Northants., chairmaker (1823). [D]

Mitton, Thomas, Charles St, Bristol, cabinet, chair and ornamental carver (1835–40). [D]

Mivart, John, George St, Richmond, Surrey, u (1838–39). [D]

Moakes, J. K., Benniworth, Lincs. (late of Louth), cm (1830). Death of his wife, Elizabeth, aged 27, after a painful illness, reported in *Drakard's Stamford News and General Advertiser*, 12 March 1830. Possibly:

Moakes, James, Eastgate, Louth, Lincs., cm, joiner and u (1826). [D]

Moate, William, Mill Lane, Folkestone, Kent, cm and furniture broker (1832–39). [D]

Moates & Hincks, 32 Gt Corter Lane, London, cm and u (1839). [D]

Mockeridge, Henry, North Town, Taunton, Som., cm (1781–82). Took out Sun Insurance policies in 1781 for £400, £50 accounting for utensils and stock; and in 1782 for £200, £30 on utensils and stock. [GL, Sun MS vol. 293, p. 616; vol. 303, p. 374]

Moestley, Richard, Leadenhall St, London, cm (1759?). Partner of John Harris, to whose will he acted as witness. [Harris, *Old English Furniture*, p. 22]

Moffat (or Moffett), Henry, London, cm (1780–93). As Moffett of 6 Orange Ct, Swallow St, insured his house for £100 with the Sun Co. in 1780. As Moffat of London, subscribed to Sheraton's *Drawing Book*, 1793. [GL, Sun MS vol. 282, p. 100]

Moffatt (Moffett or Moffitt), Samuel, Liverpool, cm (1813–27).

Recorded as Moffatt, 6 College Lane in 1824; and Moffitt at 5 Smithfield St and Ormes Pl., Milk St in 1827. As Moffett, app. to John Mears in 1813, and petitioned freedom on servitude in 1822, paying 6s 8d. As Moffitt, admitted freeman on 19 October 1827. [D; Liverpool freemen's committee bk and reg.]

Moffett, James, Bristol, carver and gilder (1781). [Poll bk]

Mogford, Robert, 27 Drury Lane, London, cm and u (1827–28). [D]

Mogford, Samuel, 14 Turk's Row, Chelsea, London, cm and u (1823). [D]

Mogridge, Thomas, Ashburton, Devon, cm (1825–30). Trading in North St, 1830. Marriage at Bovey Tracey to Miss Letitia Wills of Gale Farm, Bickington, reported in *The Alfred*, 1 March 1825. [D]

Mogridge, William, Bristol, sign and furniture painter (1828–32). Addresses given at Ellbroad St, 1828–29; 6 Mitchell Lane, St Thomas St, 1830–31; and 10 Ellbroad St in 1832. [D]

Moir, William, 7 Bowling St, Marylebone, London, carver and gilder (1835–39). [D]

Moisant (Moysant), Jacques, London, cm ('menuisier') (b.1653–1681). Named in the Threadneedle St Relief records on 26 August 1681 as having 'arrived from Paris last week with wife and two sisters aged 28 & 26. £1.' [*Hogarth Soc.*, 1949]

Moizer, Richard, Lancaster, cm (1839). [Lancaster freemen rolls]

Mold, Thomas, Commercial St, Northampton, cm (1830). [D]

Mold, William, East Hill, Wandsworth, London, cm (1838). [D]

Molden, Edward, Norwich, cm and joiner (1729–52). Recorded in St Andrew's parish in 1733. Took app. named Baldwin in 1729; and Edward Molden & Co. took app. named Leake in 1752. Took out a Sun Insurance policy on 21 April 1733 for £200 on household goods and stock in trade in his house. [S of G, app. index; GL, Sun MS vol. 36, ref. 60541]

Molden, Nathaniel, Norwich, cm (1761). Took app. named Bacon in 1761. [S of G, app. index].

Molesworth, Thomas, Birmingham, cm and u (1785–1818). Recorded at 29 Dale End, 1800–18; and supplying 'Barometers on an improved principle' in 1809. Took out a Sun Insurance policy on 22 December 1785 for £150 on utensils and stock in his warehouse in High St, £100 on those in his workshop, and £50 on those in his feather warehouse 'at top of yard'. Probably the Molesworth, cm of Birmingham whose marriage was reported in *Gents Mag.*, February 1796. [D; GL, Sun MS vol. 334, p. 81]

Molinare, James, 2 West St, Smithfield, London, looking-glass frame maker (1820). [D] Possibly J. Molinari.

Molinari, Andrew, 13 Leather Lane, Holborn, London, looking-glass maker (1835–39). [D]

Molinari, J., West St, West Smithfield, London, looking-glass manufacturer (1815–25). Recorded at no. 22, 1815–20; and no. 58 in 1825. [D] Possibly James Molinare.

Moline, —, address unrecorded. On 22 January 1753 he was paid £1 3s for 'a round mahog. claw-table' supplied to Moulsham Hall, Chelmsford. [Essex RO, Moulsham Hall archives]

Moline, Robert, address unrecorded. In 1749 supplied items to Lady Monson: on 14 April 'A 19 inch Silver Fashion Tea Board', costing 8s 6d; '2 Moho^g Salvers', 4s 6d; '3 Bottel Dishes Line'd', 3s; and on 22 April 'A Moho^y Tea Kettle Stand', 10s 6d; 'A Large Moho^y Knife Tray', 5s; and 'A Large Wans^t Tray', 6s. The bill totalled £1 17s 6d, and was receipted on 4 May 1749. [Lincoln RO, Monson 12]

Moline, Robert, Charing Cross, London, cm (1760–66). Named as a Fellow of the Society for Arts & Manufactures, 1760–66;

and in registers of unclaimed dividends of bank stock in 1761. [Heal]

Moline, William, London, u (1710). Son of Anthony Moline, late of the parish of St Giles-in-the-Fields, u, he 'put himself apprentice to William Meakins Jun. cllr. and upholder of London for seven years from the date 7th February 1710.' [GL]

Molineux, Francis & Molineux, Thomas Gisborn(e) & Hawkins, James, 12 Clerkenwell Close, London, mahogany merchants, cabinet and looking-glass makers, toymen and u (1808–15). Trading as Francis & Co. in 1815. Took out Sun Insurance policies on 7 April 1808 for £3,000 including £800 on warehouse, £1,100 on stock and utensils, £600 on looking-glass plates, and £500 on stock and utensils in open yard, stable and loft; on 25 or 31 May 1809 for £3,500, including £1,000 on warehouse, £2,500 on stock, utensils and glass; and on 11 November 1813 for £3,500 including £1,000 on warehouse, £200 on stove house, stable and loft, and £2,300 on stock, utensils and livestock in buildings and open yard. [D; GL, Sun MS vol. 443, ref. 814884; vol. 446, ref. 830948; vol. 461, ref. 887648]

Molineux, John, Whitechapel, Liverpool, upholder (1800). [D]

Molineux, Joseph, Newcastle-under-Lyme, Staffs., cm (1823–37). Recorded at Marsh Parade in 1832. [Poll bks]

Molineux, Michael, Hertford, cm and u (1831). Declared bankrupt, *Liverpool Mercury*, 13 December 1831.

Molineux, William, Michael St, Andrew St, Hertford, cm and u (1832). [D]

Mollineaux, George, Liverpool, cm (1747). [Chester poll bk]

Mollineux, John, Liverpool, cm (1767). Admitted freeman on 24 November 1767. [Liverpool freemen reg.] See John Molyneux.

Molteni, Alexander, 13 Baldwin's Gdns, Leather Lane, London, looking-glass, barometer and thermometer maker (1829–34). [D] See Battistessa, Molteni & Guanziroli.

Molteni, Innocent & Co., 28 Spear St, Manchester, carver and gilder, picture frame maker (1825). [D]

Molton, Charles Edward, picture frame maker (1827). In September 1827 he made and supplied five picture frames to the Duke of Norfolk at a cost of £14 14s including carriage. [Arundel Castle records, A2105]

Molton, & Son, 44 King St, Soho, London, carvers and gilders (1839). [D]

Molyneux, Henry, Liverpool, cm (1828). App. to William John Roberts in 1828. [Liverpool app. enrolment bk]

Molyneux, John, Liverpool, cm (1765–67). Petitioned freedom on servitude to Thomas Gatliff, paying 6s 8d in 1765. Admitted freeman on 12 November 1767. [Liverpool freemen's committee bk and reg.] See John Mollineux.

Molyneux, John, Back 32 Henry St, Liverpool, upholder (1796). [D]

Mombelli, John Comolli, London, carver and gilder (1835–39). Addresses given at 22 Vine St, Hatton Gdn 1835 and 1839; and 23 Brookhill, Clerkenwell in 1837. [D]

Mombray (Mombrey or Mowbray), Paul, London, u (1713–49). Recorded at Albemarle St, St George's, Hanover Sq., 1726–49. Son of Abraham Mombray, peruke maker of St Paul's, Covent Gdn. App. to Charles Jones on 3 February 1713, and admitted freeman of the Upholders' Co. by servitude on 5 February 1723/24. Took out a Sun Insurance policy on 3 November 1726 for £500. Named in newspapers in 1728, and polled at Westminster in 1749. [GL, Upholders' Co. records; GL, Sun MS vol. 23, p. 151; Heal]

Mombrim, —, 40 Windmill St, Rathbone Pl., London, cm (1803). Subscribed to Sheraton's *Cabinet Dictionary*, 1803.

Monaghan, John, Manchester, cm and u (1834–40). Marriage on 16 June 1834 at St Werburgh's Church to Miss Jane Lloyd of Foregate St reported in *Chester Courant and Advertiser for North Wales*, 24 June. Listed at 2 David St in 1840. [D]

Monat, John, 1 Trafalgar St, Walworth, London, cm and u (1827–28). [D]

Moncas, Thomas, Liverpool, u (1790–d.1793). Petitioned freedom on servitude to Samuel Kirks (or Kirke) in 1790. Death reported in *Williamson's Liverpool Advertiser*, 1 July 1793. [Liverpool freemen's committee bk]

Moncaster, John, Liverpool, cm (1761–d. by 1780). Admitted freeman on servitude to James Barton on 12 March 1761. [Liverpool freemen reg.]

Moncuer (or Moncur), James, Coventry Ct, Haymarket, London, cm (1749). [Poll bk]

Monday, Richard, 106 High St, Southampton, Hants., cm, u and chairmaker (1836–39). [D]

Monday, William, Ashburton, Devon, cm and u (1793–1830). Trading at West St in 1830. Monday, cm of Ashburton, advertised in *Exeter Flying Post*, 1 October 1829, that he was to be applied to for viewing a property on sale. [D]

Monet (Manet, or Momet), Francis Peter, 48 Clerkenwell Close, London, upholder and cm (1785). [D]

Money, T., 16 Cheltenham Pl., Westminster Rd, London, chairmaker (1835). [D]

Money, Thomas, address unrecorded, upholder (1707–36). Son of Thomas Money, Gent. of Kempstone, Beds. App. to Daniel Woodroffe on 10 May 1707, and admitted freeman of the Upholders' Co. by servitude on 3 July 1723. Took app. named John Price, 1726–35/36. [GL, Upholders' Co. records]

Money, Thomas, Preston, Lancs., cm (1742–62). [Preston Guild record of burgesses]

Money, Timothy, Norwich, later Gt Yarmouth, Norfolk, u (1724–59). Recorded in Norwich, 1724–42, in the parish of St Peter Mancroft, 1734–35 at the Norwich poll; and at Gt Yarmouth, 1751–59. App. to Timothy Ganning, and admitted freeman of Norwich on 3 May 1724. His son, Timothy Money, admitted on 14 August 1734. Former app., Francis Brooke, admitted on 24 February 1745. Of Norwich, took apps named Cobb (presumably John Cobb) in 1729, and Smith in 1742; of Gt Yarmouth, Harley in 1751, and Jackson in 1759. [Norwich freemen rolls; S of G, app. index]

Moneyment, Matthew, Swaffham, Norfolk, cm and u (1827–30). Declared bankrupt, *Chester Courant and North Wales Advertiser*, 20 July 1827, but trading again at Castle Acre St in 1830. [D] Trade card of M. Moneyment recorded giving trades of cm, u, paper hanger, appraiser and auctioneer, and address at Castle Acre St. It states: '... Houses fitted up in the first style & on the shortest notice. Floor cloths for Halls & passages, Chintz, Dimity & Moreen Furnitures, Looking Glasses etc.' [Grosvenor House Antiques Fair, 1985]

Moneyment, Matthew, Newtown, Bexleyheath, Kent, cm and u (1838–39). [D]

Moneypenny, G. snr, Derby, carver (1793). [D]

Monk, Charles Thomas, St Ann St, Chester, cm (b.1814–d.1838). Death on 10 April 1838 aged 24 reported in *Chester Courant and Advertiser for North Wales*, 17 April.

Monk, John, St Andrew's, Norwich, cm (1790). [Poll bk]

Monk, Samuel, at 'The Unicorn', Peter St, Mint, Southwark, London, cm and appraiser. 18th-century trade card states that he 'Makes and sells all sorts of Cabinet, Chair & Upholsterers Work, in the Neatest Manner & on the lowest terms. Likewise buys and sells Second-hand Goods, &c.' [Landauer Coll., MMA, NY]

Monk, Samuel, Church St, Hackney, London, cm and u (1826–39). [D]

Monk, Thomas, 12 and 13 Paradise St, Marylebone, London, cm (1826–27). [D]

Monk, William, Reading, Berks., upholder (1777). [Poll bk]

Monkfield, J., 2 Ironmonger St, St Luke's, London, bedstead maker (1829). [D]

Monkhouse, George, Bloomsbury, London, cm and u (1820–29). Addresses given at 15 Bury St, 1820–23; 18 Gilbert St in 1823; and 50 Gt Wild St, Lincoln's Inn Fields in 1829. Took out Sun Insurance policies on 22 March 1821 for £1,100, including £850 on stock, utensils and goods in trust in open yard and in workshops at 17 Gilbert St; and on 7 August 1823 for £800, £600 on utensils and stock. [D; GL, Sun MS vol. 488, ref. 978180; vol. 498, ref. 1006355]

Monkhouse, J., Brough, Westmld, spinning wheel maker (1793). [D]

Monkman, William, Old Malton Gate, Malton, Yorks., cm and u (1823). [D]

Monro, William, 24 Graval Lane, Salford, Lancs., cm (1836–38). [D]

Monroe, David, Chandos St, London, cm (1749). [Poll bk] See David Munro, and Mure & Monro.

Monsear, Robert, Princes St, Norwich, cm (1836). [D]

Montague, Henry, 15 Wyndham St, Portman Sq., London, u (1839). [D]

Montague, John, parish of SS Philip and Jacob, Bristol, cm (1774–81). [Poll bks]

Montague, John, Bradford-upon-Avon, Wilts., cm (1784). [Bristol poll bk]

Montellier, Joseph, Castle St, Oxford St, London, cm (1784–93). Trading at Little Castle St in 1784 and 58 Castle St, 1790–93. [D]

Montfort, John, address unrecorded, upholder (1704). Admitted freeman of the Upholders' Co. on 3 May 1704. [GL, Upholders' Co. records]

Monthorpe, James, Norwich, cm (1825). Admitted freeman on 3 May 1825. [Norwich freemen rolls]

Montravers, John Samuel, Cherry Gdn St, Rotherhithe, London, cm (1782). Took out a Sun Insurance policy in 1782 for £200, of which utensils and stock accounted for £50. [GL, Sun MS vol. 301, p. 237]

Mood, —, Nun-gate, Newcastle, cm and joiner (1801). [D]

Moody, David, Corporation Row, 16 Leese St, Liverpool, cm (1835). [D]

Moody, Edmund, 10 Brunswick St, Bath, Som., cm (1833). [D]

Moody, John, parish of St Peter-le-Poer, London, upholder (1755). As Gent., admitted freeman of the Upholders' Co. by redemption on 25 April 1755. [GL, Upholders' Co. records]

Moody, John, St Ives, Huntingdon, u (1798). [D]

Moody, John & James, Basingstoke, Hants., cm and u (1823–39). Recorded at Market Pl., 1830–39. [D]

Moody, Joseph, Bristol, Bath, later London, carver and picture frame maker (1739–74). Recorded in St James's parish, Bristol in 1739; Bath in 1754; and Purpool Lane, Gray's Inn Lane, London in 1774. [Poll bks]

Moody, Moses, Cheltenham, Glos., cm and u (1793–1840). Listed at 63 High St in 1820. [D]

Moody, Thomas, Louth, Lincs., cm (d.1796). Will dated 1796. Died in Lincoln Castle. [British Record Soc., *Calendar of Wills and Administrations*, vol. 4, p. 325]

Moody, Thomas, 101 Mabgate, Leeds, Yorks., cm and joiner (1837). [D]

Moody, Thomas, Dicking's Buildings, Ann St, Osborne St, Hull, Yorks., cm (1838–39). [D]

Moon, James, Sheep St, Northampton, cm (1820–23). [D; poll bk]

Moon, James Carter, Lancaster, cm (1817–beyond 1840). App. to Leonard Redmayne of Lancaster for seven years on 14 August 1817. Named as James Moon in the Gillow records, 1821–22. Described as 'Book-keeper of Lancaster' in the will of his aunt, Mary Carter, 1846. Recorded as having two sons, James and George, both cm in London, in the will, dated 1847, of his wife, Ellen's aunt, Margaret Turner. [Lancaster app. reg.; Preston RO, DDX 112; Westminster Ref. Lib., Gillow records]

Moon, Joseph, Leeds, Yorks., journeyman cm (1791). Named in the *Leeds Cabinet and Chair Makers' Book of Prices*, 1791, amongst journeymen in basic sympathy with its contents.

Moon, Joseph, Hull, Yorks., cane worker, fancy chair manufacturer (1826–39). Trading at 23 English St, 1826–31, and 28 Finkle St, 1838–39. [D]

Moon, Philip, Charlotte St, Gt Yarmouth, Norfolk, cm and u (1822–41). [D; poll bks]

Moon, Thomas, Lancaster, cm (1824–40). App. to L. Redmayne in 1824. Named in the Gillow records, 1826–29, 1833–34, and 1838–40. [Lancaster app. reg.; Westminster Ref. Lib., Gillow records]

Moon, William, London, chairmaker (1775–94). Recorded at 7 White Hart Ct, Long Acre, West Smithfield in 1775; Long Lane, 1777, and 141 St John's St, 1779–94. Took out Sun Insurance policies in 1775 for £200 of which stock accounted for £28; and in 1779, as chairmaker, broker and undertaker, for £300, £100 accounting for utensils, stock and goods. In 1777, as 'Citizen & Fruiterer, by trade a chairmaker', he employed twelve non-freemen for three months and six weeks. Trade card reads: 'William Moon, Coffin and Chair-Maker, Broker, and Sworn Appraiser, At his Manufactory, No. 141 St. John Street, near Smithfield. Where the Public may be supplied with all sorts of Mahogany, Walnut-tree, Cherry-tree and Beach Chairs, on the lowest Terms of any Man whatsoever who doth Justice to his Customers. The most Money given for any Parcel or House of Goods. All things necessary for Funerals at an Hour's Notice in Town or Country.' [D; GL, Sun MS vol. 239, p. 225; vol. 275, p. 551; GL, City Licence bks, vol. 9; Landauer Coll., MMA, NY]

Moon, William, address unrecorded, upholder (1797). [D]

Moon, William, Blackburn, Lancs., u (1798). [D]

Moon, William, Lancaster. App. to Gillow of Lancaster and Oxford St, London, on 7 April 1827. [Lancaster app. reg.]

Mooney, Elizabeth, Liverpool, u (1834–39). Recorded at Linacre Marsh, with shop at 220 Scotland Rd, 1834–37; in partnership with Ellen Mooney at 231 Scotland Rd in 1837; and alone at 134 Richmond Row in 1839. [D]

Mooney, Ellen, New Scotland Rd, Liverpool, upholder (1827–37). Trading at nos 188 and 125 in 1827; and in partnership with Elizabeth Mooney at 231 Scotland Rd in 1837. [D]

Mooney, James & Co., Salford, Lancs., carvers, gilders, looking-glass and picture frame makers (1828–40). Addresses given at 1 Pleasant St, Broughton Rd, 1828–29; 26 Cross St, King St, 1832–33; 28 Cross St, 1834–36; and 22 Bridge St, 1838–40. [D]

Mooney, John, Huntingdon, cm (1831). App. to Ebenizer Mackenzie of Huntingdon on 30 May 1831. [Huntingdon app. reg.]

Moor, —, Fuller's Rents, Holborn, London, cm (1760). Named in contemporary newspapers. [Heal]

Moor, Dennis, Bristol, cm (1715). [Poll bk] Probably Demus Moore.

Moor, George, Lancaster, cm (1779–80 or 1789–90). [Lancaster freemen rolls]

Moor, George, 19 Collingwood St, Newcastle, cm and u (1838). Trade card [Landauer Coll., MMA, NY] gives nos 19 and 20 and reads 'Fashionable Upholstery and Cabinet furniture Warerooms'. [D]

Moor, John, Paternoster Row, London, u (d.1721). Named in contemporary newspapers as having 'hanged himself'. [Heal]

Moor(e), Joseph, Orchard Lane, Southampton, Hants., chairmaker (1830–39). [D]

Moor, Richard, 11 Upper Ashby St, Goswell St, London, carver (1820). [D]

Moor, Thomas, St Martin-in-the-Fields, London, cm (d.1737). Notice in *London Evening Post*, 5–7 May 1737 read: 'All persons indebted to the Estate of Mr. Thomas Moor, late of St. Martin-in-the-Fields, in the County of Middlesex, Cabinet-Maker, deceased are required forthwith to pay their respective Debts to Mr. John Tovey of Lancaster Court in the Strand.' Possibly Thomas Moore of St Martin's Lane recorded as having died in 1738.

Moor, William, 19 Monmouth St, London, cm (1787). Took out a Sun Insurance policy on 28 February 1787 for £200 on household goods, utensils and stock. [GL, Sun MS vol. 342, ref. 528001]

Moor(e)croft, James, Ormskirk, Lancs., cm (1787–98). Edition of J. Marmaduke's *The Evening-Office of the Church according to the Roman Breviary*, 1778, recorded with bookplate of 'J. Moorcroft cabinet maker Ormskirk'. [D]

Moore, —, London, joiner or carver (1694). On 26 June 1694, as a member of the 'Company of Joyners Carvers of London', he signed a petition presented by that Company to the City of London. [*Furn. Hist.*, 1974]

Moore, —, Bearward Lane, Nottingham, joiner and cm (1788–99). Son of Thomas Moore, joiner of Nottingham; taken as app. in 1788. [D; Nottingham app. list]

Moore, —, Priestgate, Workington, Cumb., joiner and/or cm (1829). [D] See Grayson & Moore.

Moore, A. W., 40 Hackney Rd, London, cm and u (1820–35). [D]

Moore, Abraham, London, cm (1809–39). Trading at Coppice Row, Clerkenwell, 1809–11; no. 4, 1820–29; and 4 Back Hill, Leather Lane in 1839. [D]

Moore, Alexander, 4 Coppice Row, Clerkenwell, London, cm etc. (1816–19). [D]

Moore, Benjamin, Court St and Market Pl., Trowbridge, Wilts., cm (1839). [D]

Moore, Charles, 11 Guildford St, East Spa Fields, London, picture frame and looking-glass maker (1824). Took out a Sun Insurance policy on 4 February 1824 for £300. [GL, Sun MS vol. 497, ref. 1014083]

Moore, Charles, Clerkenwell, London, carver and gilder (1835–39). Trading at 9 Coburg St, 1835–37, and 29 St John's St in 1839. [D]

Moore, Charles, West Wycombe, Bucks., chairmaker (1841). [Census]

Moore, Christina, 43 Stonegate, York, billiard table maker (1838). [D]

Moore, Daniel, Fore or High St, Exeter, Devon, cm and joiner (1776–1812). Named in *Exeter Pocket Journal*, 1791 and 1796. Recorded in St Lawrence's parish in Exeter Militia list, 1803. Recorded at 226 High St before March 1812, and no. 42 afterwards. Took out Sun Insurance policies in 1776 for £150 on house and workshop, £450 on utensils and stock; on 18 July 1785 for £400 on utensils and stock in workshop; and on 19 June 1790 for £700, including £300 on utensils and stock. Advertised house for sale in *Exeter Flying Post*, 28 June 1792; for sawyers in the cabinet and chair line on 27 December 1792; and his removal from no. 226 to no. 42 High St on 12 March 1812. Marriage of Daniel Moore to Mrs Elizabeth Bassett reported on 5 November 1812. [GL, Sun MS vol. 249, p. 228; vol. 331, p. 146; ref. 569790, p. 27] Possible confusion with:

Moore, Daniel, Magdalen St, Exeter, Devon, cm and u (1813–d.1826). Named in *Exeter Pocket Journal*, 1816, 1822 and 1825. Advertised his removal to 21 Magdalen St, 'formerly of

London', in *Western Luminary*, 21 December 1813. The marriage of Daniel Moore's daughter, Jane Grace, to Mr J. I. Ladd of Kensington, reported in *The Alfred*, 2 May 1825. Daniel Moore's death, aged 50, reported in the same paper on 25 April 1826. [D]

Moore, Daniel, Gomersal, Yorks., cm and joiner (1828–29). [D]

Moore, Demus, parish of St Thomas, Bristol, cm (1721–22). [Poll bk] Probably Dennis Moor.

Moore, E., Bengeworth, Evesham, Worcs., cm (1820). [D]

Moore, Elizabeth, New St, Wellington, Salop, chairmaker (1835–36). [D]

Moore, Francis, Chesterfield, Derbs., cm (1793). [D]

Moore, George, Sherborne, Dorset, cm (1786). Took app. named Henry Wittridge for seven years in 1786 for 45s. [Dorset app. indentures]

Moore, George, High St, Horncastle, Lincs., joiner/cm (1822). [D]

Moore, George B., High St, Uxbridge, Middlx, cm and u (1826–39). Recorded at Greenfield, High St in 1826, also as paper hanger; and at Binfield, High St in 1832. [D]

Moore, H., 19 Ratcliffe Highway, London, chairmaker (1809–11). [D]

Moore, Henry, Tamworth, Staffs, chairmaker (1740). Took app. named Allen in 1740. [S of G, app. index]

Moore, Henry & Benjamin, Tamworth, Staffs., chairmakers and turners (1798). [D]

Moore, Henry, George St, Tamworth, Staffs., chairmaker (1818–22). [D]

Moore, Isaac, Workington, Cumb., cm and joiner (1834). [D]

Moore, James snr, Nottingham Ct, Short's Gdns, St Giles-in-the-Fields, London, cm (c. 1670–d. 1726). Moore may be the 'James Moore' born to James and Mary Moore, and christened on 10 December 1670 at St Dunstan's, Stepney. [PR] However when Moore gave evidence against Henry Joynes, Comptroller of the works at Blenheim Palace (Sarah, Duchess of Marlborough having gone to law against many of the Blenheim craftsmen in 1724–25) he stated his age to be fifty-four. [D. Green, *Blenheim Palace*, 1951, p. 217] We can assume therefore that he was born c. 1670, and that his presence on jobs in an app. capacity came about 1685–90. There is no note of his apprenticeship among the records of either the Joiners' or Glass Sellers' Companies [GL], but it seems sensible to assume an early connection with the Gumleys. In 1708 he subscribed to a book by the architect John James — his translation of Claude Perrault's *A Treatise of the Five Orders of Columns in Architecture*. From 1714 he was in partnership with John Gumley for royal commissions [PRO, LC 5/45; 5/46; 5/57] but he was of course able to deal also with private work, and seems to have been able to undertake commissions from about 1700.

The trade he had learned under Gumley included familiarizing himself with the creation of carved and gilded mirrors (on two of which Gumley's name has been noted) and with all the problems inherent in the moulding and working of japan and gesso. There is a small group of gesso-covered tables and stands in the Royal Collection, or at houses such as Boughton. One stand [*Burlington*, July 1977, pl. 11] in the Royal Collection bears the crowned cipher of George I, and is incised 'MOORE' on the top rim. Others are in a style reliably enough his to warrant firm attribution. These items have been illustrated [*GCM*, pls 18–26], together with an incised chest formerly belonging to the 1st Duke of Marlborough. [*Burlington*, July 1977, pl. 13] They are similar to examples in the Royal Collection by John Pelletier, and by those (relying on French influence) made at Augsburg by Aberell and Eichler, but of course inlaid with silver and tortoiseshell.

In 1716 Sarah, Duchess of Marlborough dismissed Sir John Vanbrugh from supervising the building of Blenheim Palace. She turned then to James Moore, who became known as her 'Oracle' and who became as much involved with building work and the supervision of fitting out apartments as with cabinet-making. [Sarah, Duchess of Marlborough, *Letters from Madresfield Court*, ed. 1875, p. 107; Green, op. cit.] By this time Moore had set up separately from Gumley at Short's Gdns in the London parish of St Giles-in-the-Fields. Insurance he took out on 4 June 1712 'for his goods' (no sums stated) was 'over against the Golden Bottle in Shorts Gardens' [GL, Sun MS vol. 2, p. 35] and may imply the firm date of his setting up business there. He insured further in 1714 — dwelling house £100, household goods and stock in trade, £100, stock in trade in shed, £200, glass in shed £100, stock in hand in 3 sheds, and yard £200. Total £700. [Sun MS vol. 27] From this address Moore had married his first wife, Rebecca Moss, and by her had eight children. [PR; Ian Caldwell in *The Antique Collector*, May 1986, p. 94]

It is necessary to set the record straight on Moore's alleged (but incorrect) association with the Meller family of Erddig, N. Wales. In 1944 Edwards and Jourdain illustrated a gesso side-table at Erdigg which they attributed to James Moore. [*GCM*, p. 93, citing A. Cust, *Chronicles of Erthig*, 1914, p. 236] However when the relevant archives were re-examined [Clwyd RO, Hawarden] the frequent use of the phrase 'received more' to denote cash payments was noted as being the likely cause of earlier attributions of furniture to James Moore (especially the State Bed, by John Belchier and John Hutt, 1720–21, cf. John Hardy, Shield Landi and others, *The State Bed from Erthig*, V & A, 1975).

Whilst the Blenheim Comptroller, Henry Joynes and his assistant Jefferson, against whom Moore had given evidence, may have been biased in their opinion Jefferson recorded that Tilleman Bobart, another of the Blenheim Comptrollers and James Moore were rogues: 'Its hard to tell which is the Biggest for Bobart has as bad a name in the country as the other has in London'. [*DEF*, II, 369–70] In 1720 Moore's business was at a level where he had, as journeyman, a maker who became one of the most important in the reigns of George I and II, Benjamin Goodison. His own son James Moore jnr was also involved with the family business. James Moore snr died in October 1726: 'one day last week died Mr Moore, the King's cabinet-maker of a wound on his head, Fell when walking in the Street'. [*Weekly Journal, or British Gazetteer*, 22 October 1726] He was buried at St Giles-in-the-Fields on 18 October 1726 (church register entry). His will [PRO, Prob. 11/611 f. 207] had as its executors John Goudge and the plasterer David Audsley, and mentions, in addition to his second wife Elizabeth and son, James, two daughters. Everything was put to one quarter shares, and included 'all my estate in Kingston on Thames and all my household goods and plate and jewells together with the . . . dwelling house in Shorts Gardens'. Moore's entire stock was advertised to be sold in *Daily Post*, 1 July 1728, a seemingly surprising event in view of his son being a cm. [*Burlington*, July 1977] Some light is however thrown on this by Moore's will in which he leaves his son 'my Materialls of Trade, namely Woods and Tooles' but if his wife Elizabeth were to follow the trade she was to pay her son £100.

DALKEITH PALACE, Scotland. 1700–01: 'Worke done for her Grace ye Dutches of Bucclough by James Moore.' Moore supplied 'pedestals for china, black and gold corner slabs; poles to carry them; 2 Pedistalls for the Jarrs under the Cabinetts; a speckled Cabinett & frame with black & Gold hinges & Locks; a Buro made of Japan & Locks; 3 black & Gold frames for the Glas Painting; 4 guilt Pedistalls for Bottles; 2 flowerd Japan Cabinetts & frames with Locks &

Hinges'. [Scottish RO, MS 9D 224/25/15 vouchers 12–13; 224/29; 924/45–46]

BLENHEIM PALACE, Oxon. (1st Duke of Marlborough). c. 1705–20: In view of Moore's association with building work at the Palace after Vanbrugh's dismissal it would be not unusual to find references to furniture provided. A gesso chest (ex coll. 1st Duke) was illus. *Burlington*, July 1977, pl. 11, and is similar to one at Boughton (*GCM*, pl. 23). The 1740 inventory of Blenheim stated 'Long Cabinet, a black lacquired table of Mr Moores'; Little Round Room before the Three-Cornered Room 'a folding black lacquer table of Mr Moore's'. Some was noted in the *C. Life* article (below). [V & A archives, xerox of inventory; *C. Life*, 20 April 1951]

ROYAL PALACES. 1707–26: With John Gumley he provided pier-glasses, hanging glasses, bureaus, tables and did repairs. [PRO, LC 5/45, pp. 319, 344; 5/46, p. 5; 5/47, pp. 14, 28, 53, 62, 69, 78, 89, 100, 107, 114. See also LC 9/286 and 9/287, various pages] I have assumed that work for William Kent at Kensington Palace 1722/23 had more to do with the Palladian enthusiasms of Moore's son, James (below). Two carved and gilt stands were provided for Kensington Palace in 1707. [BL, Add. MS 61354, f. 76; Ian Caldwell in *The Antique Collector*, May 1986, p. 96] There is a gesso side-table with the crowned cipher of George I, incised 'Moore', c. 1715 [*GCM*, pl. 19], and a second, again carved with the crowned cipher of George I on the apron. This cipher also appears on the top, and is incised 'Moore'. [*GCM*, pls 24–25] Various stands are also incised 'Moore' or attributed to him on stylistic evidence. [*GCM*, pls 26–30] A walnut side table, one of four made for Kensington Palace, was attributed to Gumley and Moore by R. W. Symonds, *C. Life*, 14 March 1947, p. 473, but he noted that in their accounts there 'appears no item that from its description would allow it to be identified as relating to them'. See however Ian Caldwell, *The Antique Collector*, October 1985, pp. 79–80, for a further comment on these tables.

GCM, pls 18–26 gives a good idea of Moore's gesso furniture but the attribution of furniture to him at Erddig (pls 31, 35–36) is not substantiated, being as noted in the foregoing biographical account, a misreading of accounts, 'more' meaning money.

RALPH, 1st Duke of Montagu. 1708: *DEF*, II, 369 notes that reference to Moore occurs in the domestic expenses of the Duke's household. It has not proved possible to trace the text, but a chest and table at Boughton in his style is some indication of a possible service by Moore. [*GCM*, pls 23, 33]

NORTH CRAY, Lincs. (Hon. Wrey and Lady Mary Saunderson). 1708–15, 1716–17, 1722: June 15, 1708. 'Pd Mr Moore's Bill. £18. 10s.' June 16. 'Pd Mr Moore for adding more gilding in my cabinet and for mending a mitre coap & giving to his man. £10.'

Further payments appear in each year 1709–15 (with further items in 1716, 1717 and 1722) for japan dishes, glass and stands, gilding a cabinet frame, putting up pictures, including 'Indian Pictures . . . in blew & gold frames' and '4 Black & Gold frames'; 'altering a scriptor', '4 Dutch Fasheon Chaires', 'a sweet meate presse'. Moore charged on 15 September 1715 for 'a day my selfe and horse, £1. 5s.' and '2 dayes for a man. 0s. 10d.'. It is idle to speculate if this 'man' may have been Benjamin Goodison who was calling Moore 'my master' as late as 1720. [Lincoln RO, Monson 10/1/A/16, Saunderson House Book, 1699–1727]

MARLBOROUGH HOUSE, London (1st Duchess of Marlborough). 1709–11: Provided furniture and also some supervision during building. [BL, Add. MS 61357, ff. 99, 103; 61659; Caldwell, *op. cit.*, (May 1986), pp. 97–98]

UNSPECIFIED LOCATION. 1720: 24 December. £20 paid. [Alnwick MS, U I 36]

BURLINGTON HOUSE, Piccadilly (3rd Earl of Burlington). 1720: 1 April, Sconces and Branches £6. 6s. 'received for the use of my Master, Mr James Moore by me Benjamin Goodison'. [Chatsworth MS Graham & Collier, Joint Accounts, date cited]

HARCOURT HOUSE, Cavendish Sq., London (1st Viscount Harcourt). 1724: Unspecified work. [Harcourt papers, I, 84]

G.B.

Moore, James jnr, London, cm and u (c. 1690–d. by 1734). We have no record of James Moore's birth, but as his father, James snr was born c. 1670 it might be assumed as c. 1690. He was presumably app. to his father, but again there is no confirmation.

In his active years, from the early 1720s until his early death in 1734, he was associated with William Kent and the team of craftsmen surrounding him. He and/or his father helped Kent with the furnishing of Kensington Palace, 1722/23. He provided 'four large sphinx stands for tables' and two 'fine sphinx table frames'. Some of these can be seen in the illustrations to W. H. Pyne's *Royal Residences*, 1819.

It may therefore be possible to attribute firmly some other Kentian tables to Moore. Reference should be made to the table frames noted in the Sherborne accounts, below, which were carved by James Richards, Carver to the Crown after Grinling Gibbons [*Burlington*, October 1985], who was one of the finest craftsmen of his day, and associated with Kent from c. 1720 to 1748. A fine sphinx table formerly at Ditchley [Sotheby's, 26 May 1933, now at Ramsbury] may also be by Moore jnr, carved by Richards.

In 1732 Moore was appointed cabinet and chairmaker to Frederick, Prince of Wales. [*C. Life*, 27 February 1942, p. 407] However he comes to notice in the Prince's accounts only twice: 1732/33, £861 12s 6½d, and 1733/34, £401 6s. [Duchy of Cornwall Office, LXIV, 1732–33] He worked to Kent's design once more at Sherborne House (below), but by 1734 was dead. [*C. Life*, op. cit.]

SHERBORNE HOUSE, Glos. (Sir John Dutton). 1731: 2 November. Packing Cases 'for ye best Damask Bed'; 9 carved mahogany chairs 'for my Hall' (£5 10s each); 12 walnut chairs with stuffed backs and seats 'for my best Bed-chamber' (18s each); 12 walnut chair frames with bainster backs 'for my Drawing Room up Stairs' (28s each). The bill has three further significant entries: 'To making 2 Table Frames for ye carver for 2 marble Tables at ye Lodge' (£5 10s) and 'To Mr Richards Carving ye two Table Frames above' (13s 10d), and 'To Mr Moore for 2 Mohoggony Settees for ye Dining Room at ye Lodge Carved' (£30) and 'To Ditto for 4 Stools . . .' (£20). The pair of settees were made according to William Kent's design and are illustrated in John Vardy's *Some Designs of Mr Inigo Jones and Mr William Kent*, 1744, pl. 42. They are now at Temple Newsam House, Leeds, and were described and illus. by C. Gilbert, *Burlington*, March 1969, pp. 148–49, figs 51–54, together with one stool and a hall chair. Gilbert, *Leeds Furn. Cat.*, p. 269 notes other hall settees related to the same design.

DAVENPORT HOUSE, Salop (Sharington Davenport). 1732: February. 'Paid Mr Moore ye Upholsterer. £29'. (A pair of pier-glasses with carved and gilt cresting at Davenport could be associated with Moore, cf. *C. Life*, 11 July 1952, p. 116.)

G.B.

Moore, James, London, cm, upholder and undertaker (1782–1803). Recorded at 267 opposite Red Lion St, High Holborn, 1782–84; and Leopard's Ct, Baldwin's Gdns, 1790–1803. Trade card reads: 'James Moore, Upholder, Cabinet Maker & Undertaker, at No. 267, opposite Red Lyon St, Holborn, London. NB. Goods Bought & Sold.'

Named in Sheraton's list of master cabinet makers, 1803. [D; Landauer Coll., MMA, NY]

Moore, James, 24 Red Lion Sq., London, carpenter and cm (1802–08). Took out a Sun Insurance policy on 10 July 1802 for £1,300 of which £600 accounted for utensils and stock. Recorded in partnership with Paul Moor as u and cm in 1808. [D; GL, Sun MS vol. 424, ref. 732767]

Moore, James, 119 Old St, St Luke's, London, cm and u (1839). [D]

Moore, James, Pippett St, Bradford-upon-Avon, Wilts., cm (1839). [D]

Moore, John, St Martin-in-the-Fields, London, upholder (1720). Notice in *London Gazette*, 30 August 1720 states that John Moore, upholder, late of St Martin's in the Fields was 'a prisoner in the Marshalsea'.

Moore, John, Stockport, Lancs., carver (1734–35). Received payments for work at Lyme Park, Cheshire, 1834–35, on the staircase, executed in a rather old-fashioned manner; and the heavy Doric doorcases in the Bright Gallery. [Nat. Trust guide to *Lyme Park*]

Moore, John, Thringston, Leics., frame maker (1759). Took app. named Roe in 1759. [S of G, app. index]

Moore, John, Whitechapel, London, cm and upholder, freeman musician (1768–77). Recorded at no. 127, 1773–83; and near 'The Angel & Crown', Whitechapel in 1775. Took his son, Thomas Moore, as app., 1768–75, when he was admitted freeman. Took out Sun Insurance policies in 1775 for £3,300, including £2,650 on utensils, stock and goods; in 1776 for £500 on a house in Gt Alice St; in 1777 for £900, including £400 on workshops, warehouses, sheds and timber; and a further policy in 1777 for £800, £400 on warehouse and workshop. [D; GL, Upholders' Co. records; GL, Sun MS vol. 237, p. 383; vol. 249, p. 628; vol. 260] See Thomas Moore. Possibly:

Moore, John, Stratford, London, cm and upholder (1775–86). Recorded 'next the George', 1775–80, when he took out Sun Insurance policies in 1775 for £400 on his house; in 1776 for £200 on his warehouse; in 1778 for £2,000, including £1,350 on utensils and stock, and £200 on his warehouse; in 1780 for £2,880 including £750 on utensils and stock in workshops and warehouses; and a further policy in 1780 for £1,800, including £400 on his house, workshop and warehouses, and £1,160 on utensils, stock and goods. Named in Bailey's list of bankrupts in 1786. [GL, Sun MS vol. 242, p. 499; vol. 249, ref. 369998; vol. 270, p. 236; vol. 280, p. 119; vol. 287, p. 195]

Moore, John Lawrence, Bristol, carver and gilder (1812–40). Addresses given at St Michael's Buildings in 1812; 56 Stoke's Croft, in 1814; 14 Clare St in 1816; 56 Stoke's Croft, 1817–18; Picton St in 1819; 14 Clare St, 1821–30, also 52 Stoke's Croft, 1822–28, and no. 62, 1829–30; 7 Under the Bank in 1831; 8 St Augustine's Back in 1832; and 30 Trenchard St in 1840. [D]

Moore, John jnr, Bristol, carver and gilder (1834–40). Recorded at 9 St Michael's Hill, 1834–37, and 4 St Michael's Cresc., 1839–40. [D]

Moore, John, 1 West St, Seven Dials, Soho, London, carver and gilder, looking-glass and picture frame maker (1825–39). [D]

Moore, John Ayres, 11 Holywell Row, London, cm and u (1826–29). [D]

Moore, John, High St, Whitchurch, Salop, cm (1835). [D]

Moore, Joseph Wright, 43 Stonegate, York, carver and gilder (1840). [D]

Moore, Marmaduke, Lancaster, cm (1781). Took app. on 23 July 1781. [Lancaster app. reg.]

Moore, Mary, Goat Lane, St Gregory, Norwich, u (1839). [D]

Moore, Napthali, Rushatt St, Walsall, Staffs., cm (1778–80).

Insured houses for £200 in 1778; and house and shop for £200 in 1779. [D; GL, Sun MS vol. 266, p. 168; vol. 272, p. 223]

Moore, Norris, Fleet Mkt, London, widower, freeman, paper stainer, carver, gilder and picture frame maker (1760–67). Employed three non-freemen for six weeks in 1760; four for six weeks and three for three months and six weeks in 1762; three for six months in 1763; six for three months in 1764; one for three months and two for six weeks in 1765; one throughout the year in 1766; and one for nine months in 1767. [GL, City Licence bks, vols 2–5]

Moore, Paul, 16 Ashby St, Northampton Sq., London, cm (1826–27). [D]

Moor(e), Richard, London, cm (1716–20). Recorded at 'The Two Twisted Posts', St Martin's Lane when he insured goods and merchandise with the Sun Co. in July 1718. The policy is endorsed: 'Mem.ᵐ the Interest of this Policy is become the side property of Daniel Bell in Right of his wife Relict and Executrix of the within mentioned Richd. Moore Deceased, Ent.ᵈ Nov. 25th 1721'. [GL, Sun MS vol. 8, ref. 11553] Listed at St Martin's Lane in 1720, when he took out a Sun Insurance policy on 12 July for goods and merchandise in his workshop adjoining his house. [GL, Sun MS vol. 12, ref. 8945] In 1716 Richard Moore '& Partner' sent from London 'walnut chairs & stools' to the Duke of Montrose's lodging in Glasgow. Richard Moor and Partners received payment of £30 14s for chairs supplied, probably for the Duke's house in Hanover Sq., London, in the same year. From 1718–20 Richard Moor(e) is again mentioned in the Duke of Montrose's furnishing account for his house in Bond St, London. In 1718 Moore provided furniture costing £169 17s, including '18 Walnut Tree Chairs with low backs, stuffed seats & covered with Spanish leather'; '8 Walnut tree Chairs with Ribbed backs & stuffed seats covered with blue Mohair'; 'Walnut Tree writing table'; 'Redwood Oval table in Walnut tree frame'; 'A Walnut tree Marble slab frame'; 'A neat Japanned couch frame'; 'Walnut tree table with Claw foot'; dressing chairs and stools; he also charged for 'Cutting a door, Making New Mouldings'. In 1720 Moore supplied the Duke with 'A Neat walnut tree couch covered with Montrose's own Damask with the loose case', costing £11 10s; and 'A Neat walnut tree hoop petticoat chair with a cushion seat Covered with blue Mohair', £4 5s. In 1720 Richard Moore, chairmaker, was paid £17 for a couch hoop petticoat chair costing £17. [Scottish RO, GD 220/6/1168/21–24; 220/6/28/pp. 50 and 85; 220/6/1192/12; 220/6/1196/16; 220/6/21/p. 65] He is probably the Richard Moore, cm, who supplied furniture for Temple Newsam House, Leeds, 1718–20. [*Furn. Hist.*, 1967] See Thomas Moore, partner of Daniel Bell.

Moore, Richard, New St, Wellington, Salop, chairmaker (1822–28). [D]

Moore, Richard, 162 Deansgate, Manchester, chairmaker (1825). [D]

Moore, Robert, Swan St, Kidderminster, Worcs., cm and u (1818–22). [D]

Moore, Sam., Castle St, Exeter, Devon, u and cm (1803). Advertised sale of mahogany etc., 'being about to decline the cabinet business', in *Exeter Flying Post*, 26 May 1803; and sale of stock of furniture on 14 July 1803.

Moore, Sam(p)son (or Simpson), Liverpool, cm (1818–35). Addresses given at 45 Pitt St in 1818; 101 Brownlow Hill, 1821–23; nos 101 and 114 in 1827; no. 122 in 1829; no. 152 in 1834; and no. 157 in 1835. Notice in *Liverpool Mercury*, 2 November 1821 concerned the sale 'By order of the Trustee' of land and warehouse on the south side of Brownlow Hill, opposite to Hawke St, 'containing in front 23 feet 6 inches, & extending backwards to Buckley-Court, on the east side 27 feet ... together with a small Piece of Ground, & the Building thereon, near the said warehouse at the back, in Buckley-court ... in front of the said Court 3 feet 5 inches, & in depth 6 feet 4 inches ... now in the occupation of Simpson Moore, Cabinet-maker ... The above Property is held by Lease under the Corporation of Liverpool for two Lives & twenty one years after the decease of the Survivor.' [D]

Moore, Samuel, Tewkesbury, Glos., cm (1823–33). Recorded at Church St in 1823. Children bapt. in 1823, 1826, 1830 and 1833. [PR (bapt.)]

Moore, Stephen, Norwich, cm (1799). Admitted freeman, not by apprenticeship, on 3 May 1799. [Norwich freemen reg.]

Moore, Stephen, Wimborne, Dorset, u and cm (1840). [D]

Moore, Thomas, address unrecorded, upholder (1697–1715). Son of Thomas Moore, Gent. of Bridgwater, Som. App. to Charles Williams on 28 February 1697/98, and admitted freeman of the Upholders' Co. by servitude on 20 January 1714/15. [GL, Upholders' Co. records]

Moore, Thomas, London, cm (1734–d.1738). Heal records him at St Martin's Lane, and mentions a trade card, references in contemporary newspapers in 1734, and death in 1738. In partnership with Daniel Bell, Moore supplied 'The Honourable Counsellor Rider' with a quantity of furniture in May and June 1734. These bills are receipted: 'Daniel Bell and Self, Thos. Moore'; but the bills for further consignments from 31 October to 18 December of that year are receipted by Moore only. Included in these later bills are ten 'handsome walnut-tree chairs broad banister backs cutt in a shape with scrole tops, finished very good wood, loose compass seats stuft in white Hessing with rich carved fore feet with Lyons faces on ye knees and Lyons Paws and O.Ge back feet with scroles and carved shells to ye fore rails.' Furniture Moore supplied totalled a cost of £108 6s. There was another similar set, and some of these chairs are still at Sandon Hall, Staffs. The younger James Moore, son of the Royal cm, died in 1734, and it seems probable that Thomas was a member of the family who at that date or earlier had entered into partnership with Daniel Bell. Moore & Bell supplied furniture to Earl Fitzwalter at Moulsham Hall. [DEF; Old Furniture, vol. 4, 1928, pp. 48–53, fig. 1] See Bell & Moore, and Richard Moore at the 'Two Twisted Posts'. Probably Thomas Moor.

Moore, Thomas, at the 'Bishop Blaze', 77 Chiswell St, Finsbury, London, carpet weaver and hosier (1756–78). Fine trade card shows mitred figure holding wool-comb and book, with Rococo decoration surrounding sheep, cushions and a loom. Card reads, 'Thomas Moore, Hosier and Manufacturer — At the Bishop Blaze Chiswell Street, LONDON, Makes and Sells both for Foreign Trade and Home Consumption all sorts of Silk Cotton Thread & Worsted Hose. Frame-knit Pieces for Waistcoats and Breeches of every kind, with Cotton, Thread, Silk and Worsted-Caps. Thread, Cotton, Worsted and Silk Mitts and Gloves, Silk Purses &c. Also any Sort of Unwrought Materials for making the Said Goods. NB. He being THE FIRST in England engaged in making THE ROYAL VELVET TAPESTRY, after the manner of the Persians: has now with many Improvements brought the 'manufactury of CARPETS, SCREENS, SEATS of CHAIRS &c. to the greatest perfection — Both for Beauty, and Cheapness.' [Heal; DEF] Possibly the Thomas Moore of London who submitted a bill dated 12 February 1759 for eight tapestry seats costing £4, and four large ones costing £2 12s supplied to Dumfries House, Scotland, although the character of the panels resembles the work of Peter Parisot. [V&A archives] Thomas Moore supplied carpets to Horace Walpole and Lord Coventry; and a carpet with his name woven in was made for Syon House, dated 1769. More carpets are known, including those in the Drawing Room and Tapestry Room at Osterley Park,

Middlx. [Heal; guide book to Osterley] Moore submitted a bill totalling £115 5s 10d to Sir Thomas Egerton, Bart (later 1st Earl of Wilton) at Heaton House, Manchester. On 17 May 1776 he charged £84 for 'a very fine Persian carpet Circular of 24 feet in diameter made from Mr. Wyatts design', being James Wyatt, the architect of Heaton House. This carpet, now sold and untraced, was intended for the circular domed room in the Etruscan taste, known as the Dowager Lady Egerton's Dressing Room. At the same time, Moore supplied 'a yard wide Green Baize Cover for Containing 73 yards', at £6 13s 10d; and charged £3 3s for 'painting the pattern at large'. On 13 July he charged £20 18s 6d for '93 Yards of ¾ inde Green Stair Case Carpettry'. [Manchester RO, DDEg 41 (1); Burlington, December 1977, pp. 840–48]

Moore, Thomas, Hackney, London, upholder (1766–94). Recorded at St Thomas Sq., Mare St in 1778. Son of Thomas Moore; app. to Samuel Swaine on 1 May 1766, and admitted freeman of the Upholders' Co. by servitude on 7 October 1778. [GL, Upholders' Co. records]

Moor(e), Thomas, Whitechapel, London, upholder, cm and broker (1768–86). Recorded 'near the Old Angel & Crown Tavern in Whitechapel', 1775–81; 5 Whitechapel in 1781; and no. 136, 1781–86. Son of John Moore, freeman musician and cm of Whitechapel. App. to his father on 3 August 1768, and admitted freeman of the Upholders' Co. by servitude on 6 September 1775. Trade card reads: 'Thomas Moore, Upholder & Cabinet Maker, Opposite White Chapel Church, London. Makes up in ye Newest & Genteelest Taste Four Post Bedsteads w Drapery & other Furniture. Desk and Book Cases, Chairs, Soffas, Tables, Glasses, Venetian & Spring Blinds &c. Household Goods Bought sold & Appraised. Variety of Paper Hangings. Funerals Equipt.' [Landauer Coll., MMA, NY] Took out Sun Insurance policies in 1775 for £300 on his house; in 1777 for £2,300 including £1,530 on utensils, stock and goods, and £300 on warehouse and workshop; in 1780 for £1,800, including £1,400 on utensils and stock in warehouse and workshop; in 1781 for £300 on his warehouse, and a further policy for £1,000 including £750 on utensils, stock and goods. In 1782 he insured houses for £600, £300 and £200. On 11 April 1785 he insured utensils and goods in trust for £200, and household goods for £100; and on 12 December 1786, two houses in Little Stanhope St, St Clare Mkt, for £600. [D; GL, Upholders' Co. records; GL, Sun MS vol. 242, p. 450; vol. 261, p. 631; vol. 280, p. 102; vol. 290, pp. 233 and 246; vol. 300, pp. 32 and 391; vol. 328, p. 40; vol. 34, p. 341]

Moore, Thomas, Stratford, London, cm and u (1782–92). Recorded 'Next The George' in 1792. Took out Sun Insurance policies on 14 March 1786 for £150 on house and warehouse, and £500 on utensils, stock and goods in trust; and on 18 May 1792 for £1,200, including £450 on utensils and stock, and £100 on warehouse at the bottom of the garden. [GL, Sun MS vol. 335, p. 613; vol. 386, p. 570]

Moore, Thomas, 5 Barbican, London, picture frame maker (1793). [D]

Moore, Thomas, Wolverhampton, Staffs., chairmaker (1802–20). Recorded at 47 St John St in 1802; John St in 1808; and St John St, 1816–18. [D]

Moore, Thomas, 13 Sidney St, Liverpool, cm (1820). [D]

Moore, Thomas, 97 High St, Sunderland, Co. Durham, cm (1828–29). [D]

Moore, Thomas, Richard St, Woolwich, London, cm (1838–39). [D]

Moore, Thomas, 90 St Martin's Lane, London, cm (1839). [D]

Moore, William Lacey, Romford, Essex, cm and upholder (1780). Took out a Sun Insurance policy in 1780 for £900, of which £600 accounted for utensils, stock and goods. [GL, Sun MS vol. 286, p. 409]

Moore, William, London, then Dublin, cm (c.1782–1815). Worked for a considerable period with Ince & Mayhew before setting up business in Dublin, c.1782. Moore's first address, 1785–90, was Abbey St, and in 1791 he removed to 'a better address, in Capel Street'. A commode at Welbeck Abbey was made by Moore in 1782 for the third Duke of Portland, who was sent to Ireland as Viceroy in April 1782. In an advertisement in the *Dublin Evening Post*, May 1782, 'William Moore most respectfully acknowledges the encouragement he has received, begs leave to inform those who may want Inlaid work, that by his close attention to business and instructions to his men, he has brought the manufacture to such perfection, to be able to sell for almost one half his original prices; as the greatest demand is for Pier-Tables, he has just finished in the newest taste a great variety of patterns, sizes and prices, from three guineas to twenty; Card tables on a new construction (both ornamented and plain) which appear like small Pier Tables, with every article in the inlaid Way, executed on shortest notice, and hopes from his long experience at Messrs. Mayhew and Ince, London, his remarkable fine coloured woods, and elegant finished work, to meet the approbation of all who shall please to honour him with their commands.' An inlaid harewood commode in the V&A Museum has been attributed to Moore on stylistic grounds, and also a side table, formerly at Lismore Castle, Co. Waterford. [*DEF*; *C. Life*, 3 May and 18 October 1946, p. 725; Wills, *English Furniture, 1760–1900*, p. 124]

Moore, William, Lancaster. Named in the Gillow records in 1792 making 'the frame bottom back' of a bookcase, the rest made by another craftsman 'at the shop'. [Westminster Ref. Lib., vol. 344/96, p. 883]

Moore, William, John St, Wolverhampton, Staffs., chairmaker (1798–1809). [D]

Moore, William, 77 Chapel St, Salford, Lancs., chairmaker (1804). [D]

Moore, William, Belgrave Gate, Leicester, chairmaker (1815–28). Recorded also at Yeoman St, 1822–27. [D]

Moore, William, Knottingley, near Ferrybridge, Yorks., cm (1822–34). [D]

Moore, William, Wimborne, Dorset, chairmaker and turner (1823–24). [D]

Moore, William, White Horse Yd and Ct 51, Groat Mkt, Newcastle cm (1824–34). [D]

Moore, William, Newcastle, cm and joiner (1834–38). Listed at Nun-field in 1834 and Westmorland St in 1838. [D]

Moore, William Henry, Northampton, cm (1826–30). Recorded at St Mary's Pl. in 1826 and St Andrew's Gdns in 1830. [Poll bks]

Moore, William, New St, Wellington, Salop, chairmaker (1828–35). [D]

Moore, William, Norwich, u (d. 1837). Will proved in 1837. [Norfolk Record Soc., index of wills].

Moore & Gumley, see James Moore.

Moore & Townley, Lancaster, cm and furniture brokers (1789–1834). Listed in the Lancaster freemen rolls 1789–90. Trading at Sun St as cm and u in 1834. [D]

Moorecroft, Joseph, West Wycombe, Bucks., chairmaker (b. c.1801–41). Aged 40 at the time of the 1841 Census.

Moorehead, —, 30 Effingham Pl., Ramsgate, Kent, carver and gilder (1826–27). [D]

Moores, John, parish of St James, Bristol, cm (1784). [Poll bk]

Moores, John, Pepper Alley, Whitchurch, Salop, cm and chairmaker (1828). [D]

Moores, Robert, Chester, cm (1753). Son of Thomas Moores

cordwainer of Chester, deceased. Admitted freeman on 11 October 1733. [Chester freemen rolls]

Moorhouse, Benjamin, Henley-upon-Thames, Oxon., cm, u, appraiser and furniture dealer (1769–75). Recorded at Bell St in 1774. Advertised in *Jackson's Oxford Journal* as conducting sales on 27 September 1769; 18 June 1771; 1 July and 6 December 1773; 14, 23 and 29 September and 14 October 1774; and 18 January 1775. Named regarding lease and release of property in 1769; and as counterpart of a sixty-year lease of property in North St in 1776. [Oxford RO, Mercer III/i/3–5]

Moorhouse, John, Settle, Yorks., joiner, cm and u (1834). [D]

Moorhouse, William, Westgate, Buxton Rd, Huddersfield, Yorks., cm and u (1828–34). [D]

Moors, Joseph, Newton Lane, Manchester, cm (1794). [D]

Moortin, John, 7 Pitfield St, Hoxton, London, cm (1820). [D]

Morwood, Thomas, 6 Pitt St, Fitzroy Sq., London, cm and u (1827–28). [D]

Morwood, Thomas, 31 Charles St, Middlx Hospital, London, fancy cm (1835). [D]

Moran, James, Birkenhead, Cheshire, cm (1827). [D]

Moran, Thomas, Liverpool, cm (1818–39). Addresses given at 22 Milton St and 28 Summer Seat in 1818; 25 Milton St in 1829; 23 Hilton St in 1834; 39 Summer Seat in 1835; no. 40 in 1837; and no. 12 in 1839. Admitted freeman on servitude to Thomas Dutton on 11 June 1818. [D; Liverpool freemen reg.]

Morant, G., address unrecorded, picture frame maker (1825–28). Named in the Windsor Royal Archives on 7 October 1826 receiving £249 1s for items supplied in 1825; and on 17 July 1827, £100 3s for items supplied in 1826. Submitted bills dated April 1827 and 20 November 1828 for four matching frames supplied for portraits owned by George IV at Windsor Castle. [RA 35610; RA 35622; *Furn. Hist.*, 1972] Probably:

Morant, George, London, interior decorator, cm, carver and gilder (1790–1839). In 1790 he founded a well-known firm of decorators and cm. His earliest bill-heads appear to date from the beginning of George IV's reign, when he described himself as 'Ornamental Painter and Paper-hanging Manufacturer to their Royal Highnesses the Dukes of Sussex and Cambridge, No. 88 New Bond Street, London. House Painting and every article in the Gilding Line.' The firm's Bond St shop front was designed by John Buonarotti Papworth, 1817–19, and the business was styled George Morant & Son, 1825–39. Messrs George Morant applied successfully for Royal Appointment at the beginning of Queen Victoria's reign, on the recommendation of the Duchess of Gloucester. Morant took out a Sun Insurance policy on 15 March 1824 for £5,200 including £1,000 on household goods in house, workshops and warehouse communicating with house in tenure of a tailor, and with a house and store at 4 Wood St; and £4,200 on drawings, engravings and pictures. [D; Colvin; PRO, LC3/60; GL, Sun MS vol. 495, ref. 1014866] Between 1820–22 Morant decorated Farnborough Hill and a small house adjacent to it at Farnborough, called the Pavilion for Mrs Luke Foreman, widow of a wealthy merchant. His bills for paper hanging survive, and he appears to have supplied much of the furniture. [*DEF*] G. Morant & Sons, u, supplied furnishings for Wynyard Park, Co. Durham, for Charles William Vane, Marquess of Londonderry, c.1823–34. [Durham RO, Londonderry papers, D/LO/E 492] In 1833 the firm submitted a bill to the Duke of Sutherland for 'papering & colouring' at Bridgewater House, costing £584 2s 11d. In 1837 they charged £1,766 and £280 for work at Stafford House; and in 1838, £450 for furniture supplied there. [Staffs. RO, D/593/R/2/13/20; R/1/26/26] Payments are recorded to

Morant by the 6th Earl of Cardigan for Deene Park, Northants. [*C. Life*, 1 April 1976, p. 811] The stamp of Morant's is recorded on Boulle pieces at Mamhead, Devon, to which the firm supplied the state bed for Queen Adelaide's visit in 1838. [*C. Life*, 2 June 1955; *Conn.*, June 1977, pp. 144–45] The firm also supplied furniture to Melford Hall, Suffolk, for Sir William Parker. [*Nat. Trust Studies*, 1981, p. 72] See Morrant & Son.

Morcar, William, Liverpool, carver and painter (1731). Admitted freeman on 15 November 1731. [Liverpool freemen reg.]

Morchird, James, address unrecorded, cm (1793). Subscribed to Sheraton's *Drawing Book*, 1793.

Morcomb, John, St Columb, Cornwall, cm (1830). [D]

Morcombe, D., 73 Duke St, Devonport, Plymouth, Devon, cm (1830). [D]

Morcombe, Thomas, 73 Duke St, Devonport, Devon, cm (1838). [D]

Morcombe, William, Duke St, Devonport, Plymouth, Devon, cm and u (1822). [D]

Morden, James, London, u (1830–31). [Colchester poll bks]

Mordue, John, Ryton, Co. Durham, joiner, carpenter and/or cm (1828–34). [D]

More (or Mure), Hutchenson, address unrecorded, cm (1745). [Harris, *Old English Furniture*, p. 25]

More, John, address unrecorded, cm (1803). Subscribed to Sheraton's *Cabinet Dictionary*, 1803.

Morecock, Michael, at 'The White Hart', Fleet Ditch Side, Holborn, London, u (1716). Took out a Sun Insurance policy on 12 December 1716 for goods and merchandise in his house only. [GL, Sun MS vol. 6, p. 83]

Morecock, Thomas, at 'The Chest of Drawers', in Harp Lane by Fleet Ditch, London, joiner (shop sign suggests also cm) (1718). Took out a Sun Insurance policy on 3 July 1718 for goods and merchandise. [GL, Sun MS vol. 8, ref. 11373]

Morefly, Henry, Ormskirk, Lancs., cm (1784). [D]

Morehead, James, 16 Gerrard St, Soho, London, u and cm (1806–39). [D]

Morehen, Henry, Burleigh St, Cambridge, cm (1834–35). [Poll bks]

Morehen, John, Cambridge, cm (1828). [Univ. Lib., Will, WR 19:193]

Morehouse, —, address unrecorded, cm (1766–77). Named in the accounts of Nathaniel Ryder, 1st Lord Harrowby, for Sandon Hall, Staffs., receiving payments totalling £69 7s 2d. On 21 December 1766 he was paid £2 9s 4d; on 27 July 1770, £8 19s 10d; on 19 January 1771, £8 4s 6d; on 31 July 1771, £2 5s 3d; on 11 April 1773, £10 12s 6d; on 31 July 1773, £6 2s 7d; on 31 January 1774, 14s 5d; on 1 August 1774, £9 1s 7d; on 14 January 1775, £3 16s 9d; on 26 January 1776, £11 11s 9d; and on 10 January 1777, £5 8s 8d. [Harrowby MS Trust, Notebooks]

Morehouse (or Moorehous), James Blisset, High St, Wells, Som., cm and u (1822–30). Declared bankrupt, *Exeter Flying Post*, 13 February 1823. [D]

Moreing, John, St Paul's, Covent Gdn, London, cm (1762–71). Recorded at Maiden Lane 1762–68. Took out a Sun Insurance policy in 1762 for £400. A letter dated 1768 in the Heal Coll., BM, mentions 'John Moreing, cabinet-maker, Maiden Lane, Covent Garden 1768', with regard to a 'fine cabinet ornamented with ebony and tortoiseshell'. Moreing was declared bankrupt, *London Chronicle*, 13 March 1771. [GL, Sun MS ref. 187097] Also recorded as S. Moreing.

Moreing, Joseph, 6 Bedford St, Bedford Row, London, u (1776). Insured his house for £600 in 1776. [GL, Sun MS vol. 246, p. 364]

Moreing, Joseph, Maiden Lane, London, cm (1784). [Poll bk]

Moreing, S., Maiden Lane, Covent Gdn, London, cm (1768). Recorded in a letter dated 1768, concerning 'a fine cabinet, ornamented with ebony and tortoiseshell, thorough'ly repair'd and new gilt', which cost a Mr Grimston thirteen guineas. [M. E. Ingram, *Leaves from a Family Tree*, p. 63] Also recorded as John Moreing.

Morel, Nicholas and **Morel & Hughes, Robert**, London, cm and u (1790–1830). Although no firm evidence has been discovered Nicholas Morel may have been of French extraction and seems to have been associated with the group of Anglo-French craftsmen who worked for Henry Holland and Dominique Daguerre, particularly at Carlton House. Daguerre's will in 1796 was in fact witnessed by a Nicholas Morel who may have been the same individual. The earliest mention of Morel so far discovered is in the accounts of the Prince of Wales, patron of Holland and Daguerre, when he was paid £5 19s 4d on account of a bill of £251 9s 4d. The payment of some part of a bill on account was a common occurrence for debtors of the Prince of Wales and sizeable arrears continuing for a number of years were also common. Morel, described as a cm and u of Tenterden St, Hanover Sq. submitted a bill for £192 for work at Carlton House in the accounts optimistically drawn up by the Commissioners for the Prince of Wales's debts on his marriage in 1795. In the same year the Prince took a lease for twelve years of The Grange, Hants., a hunting box owned by the Drummond family, although he only used it for a year. Morel supplied a number of furnishings for it but the payments are recorded in arrears 1800–01.

Morel's standing as a fashionable cm and u, patronized by the Prince of Wales and his circle, is further illustrated by his involvement at Southill, Beds. where Holland designed interiors and probably some furniture for Samuel Whitbread II. Morel was amongst a group of prominent cm including William March, who were paid a total of £2,167 4s 3d in 1798 and £1,580 7s 5d in 1800, while further small payments were made during the period 1804–07. Whilst it is not possible to identify Morel's work, since no detailed accounts have survived, the strongly Francophile flavour of the splendid furniture remaining at Southill must owe something to his workshop.

From 1802 Morel is listed [D] at 13 Gt Marlborough St where he was joined soon after 1805 by Robert Hughes, probably because increased business required sharing the financial responsibility. The premises by 1821 included a dwelling house, warehouse, workshops and a warm air stove in the cabinet making shop. The stock and tools were insured for £5,000, indicating a fairly large business. It is not clear exactly when the partnership ended since some directories continued to list both Morel and Hughes at no. 13 until 1828, while the *POD* gives both in 1826, and only Morel in 1827. Because of evidence suggesting that both partners were involved in their own projects in 1826 it is likely that this is the year when the partnership ended.

Nicholas Morel continued to supply the Prince of Wales with furniture and furnishings, particularly for Carlton House, and typical payments include one in 1803 for £53 6s for cleaning and repairs, £332 10s for gilt bronze candelabra and inkstands, and in 1804 £239 16s 8d for a bed and its upholstery. In 1804 he also provided four pedestals for some of the Prince's statues costing £11 11s and was paid two years' interest of £30 on a total of £302 10s outstanding for a Parisian inkstand, bronze Egyptian figures and ormolu girandoles. These were typical of the lavish objects, many of them French, with which Carlton House and Brighton Pavilion were furnished. In 1810 Morel and Hughes provided a mahogany sideboard with bronzed mounts and griffin supports for £182 16s for the New Dining Room at Carlton House, presumably the room created on the lower floor overlooking the garden by James Wyatt in 1804. They also made various repairs and new covers for furniture at Carlton House, including the Prince's large polonaise bed and furniture in the Throne Room at a total cost of nearly £900. Other interesting pieces supplied by the firm for the Prince at Carlton House which cannot now be positively identified include six bergère chairs with carved chimeras supplied in 1812 for £951 12s.

Presumably Morel and Hughes continued to supply furniture for the Prince until the 1820s when Morel and George Seddon formed a partnership in 1827 to provide furniture and furnishings for Windsor Castle. Morel was granted a warrant as Upholsterer in Ordinary to George IV on 11 July 1828, presumably for the Windsor Castle commission, and this suggests that his partnership with Hughes was terminated in that year. [*Furn. Hist.*, 1972]

Morel and Hughes also worked for a number of aristocratic patrons, one of the earliest being the 1st Earl of Bradford (2nd creation) at Weston Park, Staffs., 1802–03 and 1805–06. The second commission is itemized in an account among the family papers [Staffs. RO]; the total cost was £4,714 16s 4d. The firm provided new decorations and upholstery for the Drawing Room, Library, Dining Room, Study and Billard Room, new furniture for the Library and Drawing Room and new curtains, blinds, carpets, bed hangings and upholstery for the bedrooms and dressing rooms. Chintzes and calicoes were ordered separately by Lord Bradford from Richard Ovey, Furniture Printer to the Prince of Wales and the Duke of York, and made up by Morel and Hughes, who supplied all other materials.

The account emphasizes the fashionable aspects of the designs with frequent mention of new patterns; for example, the curtains of the Dining Room were 'of an entire new form ... of crimson unwatered morine bound, ornamented, & fringed with silk vandyke lace made to flow over Antique Bows ... richly carved & highly finished as rosewood & gold.' Although the curtains have perished, the bows survive in their original setting, now the Library, repainted and fixed as cornices above the present curtains. A good deal of furniture supplied by the firm survives in the house including a handsome set of gilded chairs for the Drawing Room with carved ram's heads on the arms. There is also a fascinating example of early functional design in two library chairs 'with pivots to turn round' on a central support with four feet, a forerunner of the revolving desk chairs popular in the later 19th century.

This important commission relatively early in the partnership was followed by others for similar patrons, unfortunately without similar documentation. The firm are listed in the Earl of Mansfield's account book for work at Kenwood in 1808, the sum paid being £20 17s; provided furnishings at Grosvenor Pl. House for Lord Whitworth 1808–10; worked at Harewood House, Hanover Sq. for Edward, Lord Lascelles in March 1809 for £68 16s; and provided materials for the 6th Duke of Bedford 1807–08. They also made repairs and alterations to a tortoiseshell cabinet for the Duke which included new inlay of tortoiseshell and ivory and a new stand on 'large carved antique feet' in April 1808. In 1813 Morel and Hughes were paid £1,242 for work at 75 South Audley St for the Duke of Buccleuch, a very sizeable sum suggesting a major scheme of refurnishing. They also worked in 1813 for the 2nd Marquess of Bath. [Longleat archives, Cage 6, Box A, item 12] Although these patrons are only a proportion of the number who must have commissioned furniture and fur-

nishings from Morel and Hughes they do indicate the fashionable aspect of the firm's work.

Some idea of the cost of individual items of furniture supplied by Morel and Hughes may be seen in a bill in 1813 for work for James Henry Leigh. [Shakespeare Birthplace Trust, Leigh receipts] A pair of 'neat Pole Fire Screens of wood as ebony relieved with brass ornaments, the mounts covered with blue silk pleated' cost £5 12s while a 'handsome Mahogany Parisian Secretary the fall covered with purple morocco and gilt lines round it the whole resting on bronzed lions claws the top finished with a dove marble slab' cost £31 10s. The description of the secretaire emphasizes the French influence associated with much of Morel's work and would of course have been very fashionable.

Perhaps the most important commission of the later period of the firm's existence was their work at Northumberland House, Strand, London. The 3rd Duke of Northumberland had commissioned Thomas Cundy to make alterations to the south wing about 1820 which included changes to Robert Adam's interior decorations in the Glass Drawing Room. Shortly afterwards Morel and Hughes refitted all the rooms in the south wing and their bill in 1823 for the Glass Drawing Room was £1,898 15s 10d and for the entire project £34,111 9s 7d.

The new furniture supplied for the Glass Drawing Room included a pair of gilt fire screens, a pair of gilt footstools, a Turkish divan or woolsack and an oblong aburra and canary wood sofa table with stuffed foot rail which cost £221 16s. Repairs were carried out to furniture supplied by Adam, including strengthening a carved side table with iron plates and adding two new legs and a back rail, new carving by Mr Ponsonby, for £9 18s, and 'thoroughly repairing and strengthening' the frames of two semi-circular pier tables with marble tops inlaid with scagliola, again with new carving by Mr Ponsonby, for £7 14s. These tables, which stood on the window wall in the Glass Drawing Room are now in the Red Drawing Room at Syon Park, Middlx. Morel and Hughes also provided new curtains and draperies for the room besides repairing the frames and renewing the upholstery of the sofas, confidantes and twelve cabriole chairs, and covering them with 'green ground rosette silk' and matching silk and gimp. New squabs and pillows were also provided for the sofas and confidantes.

Among other rooms in the south wing Morel and Hughes furnished the Ante Room to the Crimson Drawing Room, on the first floor at the top of the Grand Staircase. The suite of furniture supplied included four ottomans, two bergères, eight light chairs, eight stools, two cheval screens, an ebony cabinet inlaid with ivory and a flower stand, while wall hangings, window draperies, cornices and carpets were also replaced. Four of the chairs, and the stools, now forming four tables, survive at Syon Park and Alnwick Castle, while four chairs and two bergères were sold at Wateringbury, Christie's, 1 June 1978, lots 522, 523.

The bergères, one of which is now in the V & A, were originally described by Morel and Hughes as 'from the antique of your Grace's aburra wood, highly polished and richly carved and gilt with ornamental trusses, foliage leaves, scroll sides and tablets back seats stuffed with the best horse hair in canvas, standing on brass socket castors' at a cost of £225 16s for the pair. The mention of aburra wood, similar to rosewood and native to Nigeria, is interesting since it was apparently supplied by the Duke, and family tradition suggests that he had been presented with it by the King of Portugal. Upholstery of grey striped silk with rosettes finished with silk gimps and cord cost £5 18s for the pair. The light chairs, two of which are now at Towneley Hall Museum and

Art Gallery, Burnley, were also made of aburra wood supplied by the Duke, and cost £189 12s for the set of eight.

Reference was made to the furniture supplied by Morel and Hughes for Northumberland House by Rudolf Ackermann in *The Repository of Arts*, March 1825, pl. 17, where a carved and gilded armchair with sphinxes supporting the arms was illustrated. This apparently 'reminds the spectator of the splendid furniture lately executed for the Duke of Northumberland by Messrs. Morell and Hughes'. Robert Hughes in fact continued to supply furniture for the Duke and apparently worked at Syon in 1826 and 1829 after his association with Morel had ended. In 1829 Hughes supplied two long sofas for the Red Drawing Room at Syon, their design reflecting that of the Neo-classical suite of seat furniture designed for the room by Robert Adam in the late 1760s, but with Rococo ornament on the arms which was highly fashionable in the late 1820s. The sofas, which cost £587 12s and were upholstered in a Spitalfields copy of the original wall hangings, are now in the V & A.

Nicholas Morel's working life spans a very interesting period in the development of Regency furniture from the Anglo-French late Neo-classical style of the 1790s through to the rich and opulent pieces produced by him and Robert Hughes in the 1820s. Until more documented pieces of furniture by the partnership or by Morel himself are found it is necessary to speculate about the range of pieces produced, but the surviving examples, although few in number, are evidence of an important cabinet maker and of an interesting partnership. F.C.

Morel & Seddon, see George Seddon.

Moreland, John, 'against the Horn & Horses Tavern in Chancery Lane in the Liberty of the Roles', London (?), cm (1714). Took out a Sun Insurance policy on 16 March 1714 for his goods. [GL, Sun MS vol. 3, ref. 3655]

Moreland, John, Lancaster, u (1767–68). [Lancaster freemen rolls]

Moreland, Robert, address unrecorded. In 1750 he submitted a bill for £11 11s to Peter Du Cane snr, of Braxted Park, Essex, either for alterations to, or furniture for a house in St James's Sq., London. [Essex RO, D/DDc A12, folio 72]

Moreley, Richard, London, chairmaker (1760). App. to William Howdell, chairmaker of St James's, Westminster, in 1760 for £20. [V&A archives]

Moresly, Henry, Ormskirk, Lancs., cm (1784). [D]

Moreton, Thomas, Liverpool, u (1815–22). Indenture as app. to George Philander Lyon dated 1815. Moreton petitioned freedom on servitude in 1822, but his application was rejected, his indentures being antedated. [Liverpool freemen's committee bk]

Moreton, Thomas, Liverpool, cm (1822–30). Recorded at 7 Norris St and 4 Craven St in 1830. App. to Richard Holliwell in 1822, and admitted freeman on 13 November 1830. [Liverpool app. enrolment bk. and freemen reg.]

Moretti, J. C., 7 Norfolk St, King's Lynn, Norfolk, carver, gilder and barometer maker (1839). [D]

Morgan, —, address unrecorded. Provided four 'India wood chests' costing £10 19s to Holkham Hall, Norfolk, in 1742–43. [V&A archives]

Morgan, —, address unrecorded, u (1809). Submitted a bill dated 24 May 1809 for upholstery work costing £19 19s carried out at Gorhambury, St Albans, Herts. [Herts. RO, account bk 11, 81]

Morgan, Charles, London, upholder (1767–74). Recorded at Bishopsgate St, St Botolph's in 1774. Son of James Morgan, freeman grocer of London. App. to Joshua Cooke on 2 April 1767, and admitted freeman of the Upholders' Co. by servitude on 3 August 1774. [GL, Upholders' Co. records]

Morgan, Charles, Exeter, Devon, cm (1803–32). Recorded at St Mary Major in the 1802 Militia Census, and St Mary Arches St, 1816–22. Sons bapt. at St Olave's: Samuel on 11 May 1816, and Charles on 2 June 1822. Recorded as chairmaker in the 1832 voters list. [PR (bapt.)]

Morgan, Daniel, Mixbury, Oxon., cm (b.1724–1747). He married Ann Walton of Mixbury on 18 December 1747. [Bodleian index of Oxf. marriage bonds]

Morgan, Daniel, address unrecorded, cm (1803). Subscribed to Sheraton's *Cabinet Dictionary*, 1803.

Morgan, David, 13 Terrace, Kensington, London, cm and u (1839). [D]

Morgan, Edward, Liverpool, cm, u and furniture broker (1824–37). Addresses given at 30 Bispham St in 1824; 10 Derby St in 1835; and no. 9 in 1837. [D]

Morgan, H., address unrecorded, cm (1803). Subscribed to Sheraton's *Cabinet Dictionary*, 1803.

Morgan, Henry, parish of SS Peter and Paul, Tunbridge, Kent, cm (1816). Son Mathew Thomas by wife Jane bapt. on 24 November 1816. [PR (bapt.)]

Morgan, Isaac, London, cm (1774–84). Recorded at Bishopsgate St in 1774; Mile End in 1781; and Castle St, Southwark in 1784. [Bristol poll bks]

Morgan, James, 27 Skinner St, Bishopsgate, London, cm and u (1826–28). [D]

Morgan, James, 19 Worship St, London, cm and u (1839). [D]

Morgan, John, parish of St Augustine, Bristol, cm (1781–84). [Poll bks]

Morgan, John, Warminster, Wilts., coach and cm (1798). [D]

Morgan, John, parish of SS Peter and Paul, 'Tunbridge', Kent, cm (1819–21). Daughter Eliza by wife Hannah bapt. on 9 July 1819; son Zechariah on 25 July 1821. [PR (bapt.)]

Morgan, John, Church St, Ross-on-Wye, Herefs., cm (1822–30). [D]

Morgan, John, Dry Bridge Hill, Woodbridge, Suffolk, cm (1839). [D]

Morgan, Josiah, Little Titchfield St, London, carpenter and picture frame maker (1822). Took out a Sun Insurance policy on 4 July 1822 for £400 on stock and utensils in his house. [GL, Sun MS vol. 493, ref. 993529]

Morgan, Miles, Bristol, upholder (1774–81). Recorded in St Stephen's parish in 1774, and St Peter's in 1781. [Poll bks]

Morgan, Philip, Brook St, St Dunstan, Stepney, London, cm (1769). Recorded concerning a deed dated 22 August 1769. [Sussex RO, (G) Deed 65/13/6]

Morgan, Philip, London, upholder and cm (1773–81). Recorded at Fore St, Cripplegate in 1773; no. 129 in 1774; and Fleet Mkt, 1778–81. Son of Philip Morgan; admitted freeman of the Upholders' Co. on 3 March 1773. Took out a Sun Insurance policy on 16 November 1774 for £400 on several properties in tenure of others; and in 1775 insured houses for £700. Declared bankrupt, *Leicester Journal*, July 1776. [GL, Upholders' Co. records; GL, Sun MS vol. 235, ref. 346455; vol. 243, p. 323]

Morgan, Richard, Cirencester, Glos., cm (1830). [PR (bapt.)]

Morgan, Thomas, see Morgan & Sanders.

Morgan, Thomas, 41 Farmer St, Shadwell, London, cm (1801). Took out a Sun Insurance policy on 22 December 1801 for £200 of which £70 accounted for utensils and stock. [GL, Sun MS vol. 423, ref. 725581]

Morgan, Thomas, address unrecorded, cm (1803). Subscribed to Sheraton's *Cabinet Dictionary*, 1803.

Morgan, Thomas, 17 Upper Thornhaugh St, Bedford Sq., London, u and cm (1808). [D]

Morgan, William, address unrecorded, carver (late 17th century). Worked at the Royal Hospital, Chelsea. He also worked in Scotland at Holyrood House and Hamilton Palace. Some of his carving is now at the Boston Museum of Fine Arts. [C. *Life*, vol. CLXXII, p. 1583; Beard, *Craftsmen and Interior Decoration in England*, p. 272]

Morgan, William, Bristol, bedstead maker and cm (1792–94). Addresses given at Narrow Wine St, 1792–94, and Broad Ware in 1794. [D]

Morgan, William, London, upholder (1793–1802). Recorded at 134 Fenchurch St, 1800–02. Son of Charles Morgan, Gent. of Glasbury, Radnor. App. to John Phillips on 6 July 1793, and admitted freeman of the Upholders' Co. by servitude on 2 August 1800. [GL, Upholders' Co. records]

Morgan, William, Chester, cm (1818–d.1838). Recorded at Northgate St and Queen St in 1818; and George St in 1826. Admitted freeman in 1818. Took app. named Thomas McCabe in 1828. Death on 25 August 1838 reported in *Chester Courant and Advertiser*, 28 August. [Chester freemen rolls, app. bks and poll bks]

Morgan, William, parish of SS Peter and Paul, Tunbridge, Kent, cm (1821–23). Son Alfred by wife Elizabeth bapt. on 9 March 1821; daughter Matilda Ann on 9 March 1823. [PR (bapt.)]

Morgan, William, Watergate St, Whitchurch, Salop, chairmaker and cm (1822–35). [D]

Morgan, William, 12 Barton St, Bristol, cm (1827). [D]

Morgan, William, 14 Curtain Rd, London, chairmaker (1835). [D]

Morgan, William, 30 Mansionhouse St, Kennington, London, fancy cabinet and portable desk maker etc. (1835–39). [D]

Morgan, William, Bear Lane, Blackfriars, London, looking-glass frame maker (1835–39). Recorded at no. 37, 1835–37, and no. 27 in 1839. [D]

Morgan & Sanders, 16 and 17 Catherine St, Strand, London, cm and u (1801–20). A partnership of Thomas Morgan and Joseph Sanders, both former employees of Thomas Butler of 13 and 14 Catherine St. Before joining Butler, Thomas Morgan had traded as a linen draper in Newgate St and later in Newport St. He was employed by Butler as an under-clerk in his counting house. Joseph Sanders was employed for a time by Elward & Marsh, the Royal cm, at 13 Mount St, and had altogether four years' experience before joining Butler. He was well regarded and for eight years prior to setting up in business with Morgan had superintended the manufacturing side of Butler's enterprise. He claimed to have been in sole management for the last three years and to have made a number of improvements to the sofa beds, chair beds and four post bedsteads that featured in Butler's range. He also claimed to be the inventor of the Imperial Dining Table.

In 1800 Butler decided to retire and Morgan and Sanders expressed an interest in purchasing the business. Butler however sold it to Thomas Oxenham, a patent mangle and napkin-press maker of 354 Oxford St. Infuriated by this double-dealing Morgan and Sanders set up business at 16 and 17 Catherine St and claimed to be the true successors to Thomas Butler. Oxenham may not have been happy with this situation of hostility and fierce and immediate competition, and by early April 1802 had moved the production of the ranges of patent furniture to the Oxford St premises where he made items to the Butler specifications using some of Butler's former staff. With Oxenham's move Thomas Butler re-commenced the business at 13 and 14 Catherine St and all the ill will was revived and openly expressed in advertisements and advertising broadsheets.

Much is known about the business of Morgan & Sanders because of their involvement with Rudolph Ackermann, print seller, art dealer and publisher of the Strand. For his monthly periodical *The Repository of Arts* they supplied a succession of furniture designs which were published between 1809 and 1815 and they also took advertising space. In August 1809 a coloured illustration of their upstairs warerooms was published in the *Repository* with accompanying letterpress no doubt provided by the partners. They had by this date named their premises 'Trafalgar House' to capitalize on the death of the naval hero Lord Nelson for whom they were providing furniture for his house at Merton, Surrey in 1805. Amongst the furniture shown in the plate is a wardrobe, pole scren, lyre-back chairs, a cheval glass, pier and convex glasses, a globe writing table, or work table, a Gothic bookcase and a fine bed embellished with naval motifs. Butler finally retired from the trade in September 1814 and by April 1816 Morgan & Sanders were advertising that they had 'taken a considerable part of Mr Butler's late Ware-rooms in Catherine-street adjoining their own and communicated the same'. Sanders appears to have died in 1818 and although the business continued to trade as Morgan & Co. until 1820 it was early in that year sold to John Durham, Thomas Morgan's foreman.

Morgan & Sanders aggressively promoted the ranges of patent furniture that they produced. This was done by advertising not only in London newspapers but also a wide selection of the provincial press. They also produced elaborate broadsheets illustrating the ranges of patent furniture that they were able to offer. They also claimed royal patronage but on rather flimsy grounds. The only entry for this firm in the Lord Chamberlain's records was in the quarter to 5 April 1814 when they supplied '2 whole length figures of his Majesty in Brass finely chased' at £52 10s. In the *Repository* of February 1810 the partners did however claim to have supplied their Pitt's Globe Writing Table to the Royal family and the illustration used by Ackermann was said to be based on one ordered by the Princess Augusta. Thomas Morgan also claimed that whilst in Butler's employ he had visited Buckingham House and showed a model of his Imperial Dining Table to the King, Queen and other members of the Royal Family.

The partner's claim to have supplied furniture to Nelson is supported by a payment of £549 in 1810 to Morgan & Co, from money provided by the Marquess of Queensbury to clear part of the debts of Lady Hamilton who had inherited Nelson's house at Merton. One of the items that Morgan & Sanders claimed to have received an order for from Nelson was a patent sideboard, so constructed that the dining table and leaves when not in use could be stored underneath. The partners emphasized the suitability of their furniture for army and naval officers and it is likely that Nelson bought such items for his use at sea. Several items of furniture at the National Maritime Museum and the Royal Naval Museum, Portsmouth are said to have belonged to Nelson but none can with certainty be attributed to Morgan & Sanders.

A number of other patrons have been identified. In July 1811 two large mahogany armchairs were supplied for the new County Hall at Lewes, Sussex. They were charged at £21 each and two footstools at £2 2s each. The remainder of the account amounting to £71 10s was for upholstery materials. An unexecuted design for a chair in connection with this commission survives. For H. H. Leigh of Stoneleigh, Warks., a set of Imperial Dining Tables were provided on 4 May 1819 at £29 8s and earlier on 3 November 1817 Mrs Leigh was invoiced with a patent folding chair bed and cushions at £11 11s. It is possible that Sir Joseph Banks bought from the firm as one of Morgan & Sanders's broadsheets is addressed to him. Another client may have been the Marquess of Winchester.

Not all the furniture provided was of the type loosely known as 'Patent', but it was these items which featured in their advertising. Expanding tables, portable bedsteads, chairs converting into beds were extensively featured. The Metamorphic Library Chair which performed equally as a set of library steps or as an armchair was featured in Ackermann's *Repository* in July 1811 and Pitt's Cabinet Globe Writing Table in February 1810. Morgan & Sanders were also interested in invalid furniture and in September 1801 were offering William Pocock's 'patent Boethema or rising matress' and in October 1811 supplied Ackermann with the illustration of 'Merlin's Mechanical Chair' published in that month. A number of tables, beds and library steps have been found with brass plates affixed indicating that they were of Morgan & Sander's manufacture. [D; Banks Coll., BM; *Antique Collecting*, February 1979; *C. Life*, 2 January 1958; *Conn.*, November 1974, pp. 180–91; *Exeter Flying Post*, 15 December 1814; *Cambridge Chronicle*, 11 August 1817; *Durham County Advertiser*, 31 January 1818; Phillips', 17 May 1966, lot 89; Sotheby's, 31 July 1970, lot 124, 23 October 1970, lot 160, 5 November 1982, lot 98; Christie's, 1 August 1974, lot 154]   B.A.

Morice, John, at 'The Half Moon', over against Foster Lane, Cheapside, London, cm (1685). [Hilton Price, *Signs of Old London*, 1903–08] See Captain Morrice.

Morin, —, London, carver and gilder (1700–48). On 16 December 1700 he married Frances Platel. Newspapers record him at Old Belton St, facing Brownlow St, St Giles, in 1748. [GL, MS 10.091; Heal]

Morland, John, address unrecorded, u (1768–69). A long bill in the Kendal RO from John Morland to Thomas Morland is dated July 1768, totals £55 6s 9¼d, and was receipted in full on 5 June 1769. A substantial part of the bill lists materials for making beds, including two pairs of 'turned Beach Feet Pillars of a Bedstead Stained mahog? Colour — on Castors'; '41¼ Yds. of Saxon Blue Morine'; '79 yds. Silk covrd Lacd'; 'a set of Teaster laths & a set of Base Slips'; a 'Neat Cut Cornish'; and various fabrics including 'Buckram', 'Tammy', 'Irish Cloth for Head & Teaster Cloths & Inside Valls'; '88 yd of the Best white washing lace'; and 'Scotch Cloth to back line Outside Vallans'. Morland also charged for 'Making up your Green Damask furn lin'd with Irish & covering the Cornishes Compleat'; and making six 'festoon W Curtains', using 'Corded Dimity', 'tossells', 'Yellow Harrateen', 'Best Crimson Worsted Damask', silk covered lace, and 'Deep Knotted fringe'. He also supplied 'A Japand Shaped Dressing Glass', '2 Mahog? Marlbro ElbChairs stuffd in fine Linnen & on Casters', £1 16s each; '8 Mahog? Backstools to Match the ElbChairs', 21s each, with cases of crimson worsted check. The bill also lists materials and men's time in packing. [V&A archives]

Morland, John, Prince's St, Leicester Sq., London, upholder and cm (1783–1800). Recorded in partnership with John Rava(u)ld at no. 29 in 1789, and probably wrongly as John Morgan & Ravald in Prince's St at the same date. In 1783 Morland took out a Sun Insurance policy in association with Ravauld. Morland & Co. of 13 Princess St are referred to in the Windsor Royal Archives on 10 October 1788, receiving £9 9s. [D; GL, Sun MS; RA 88703] See Margaret Morland.

Morland, John, Poland St, London, u (1784). [Poll bk]

Morland, John, 10 Thomas St, Manchester, chairmaker (1832). [D]

Morland, Margaret, Prince's St, Leicester Sq., London, upholder and cm (1801). [D] Probably the widow or daughter of John Morland at this address.

Morland (or Mouland), William, Ringwood, Hants., chairmaker (1823–39). [D]

Morley, David, Upper Brook St, Ipswich, Suffolk, carver and gilder (1830). [D]

Morley, Henry, Shrewsbury, Salop, cm and u (1822–28). Recorded at Baker St in 1822 and Claremont Hill in 1828. [D]

Morley, Henry, 17 York St, Westminster, London, carver and gilder (1839). [D]

Morley, James, 2 Whitehorse Pl., Mile End Rd, London, cm (1829). [D]

Morley, John, Hayle, Cornwall, cm and u (1830). [D]

Morley, John, Conisbrough, Yorks., joiner and cm (1834). [D]

Morley, Joshua, Rothwell, Yorks., joiner and cm (1822). [D]

Morley, Thomas, High St, Uttoxeter, Staffs., cm (1818). [D]

Morley, William, New St, Westminster, London, cm (1749). [Poll bk]

Morley, William, Oxford Rd, opposite Poland St, London, cm and broker (1770). Sale of remaining stock in trade at his house on quitting business conducted by Mr Christie on 8 June 1770. Catalogue states that stock consisted of a 'Variety of Mahogany and other Furniture in Book-Cases, Cloaths-Presses, Bureaus, Chests of Drawers, Dining and other Tables, Pier, Chimney, and other Glasses, and other Effects…'. [Christie's archives, London]

Morley & Co., 70 Fargate, Sheffield, Yorks., cm and wholesale general furnishing warehouse (1837). [D]

Mornbray, Paul, Albemarle St, London, u (1750). Named as a member of the livery of the Upholders' Co. in 1750. [GL, Upholders' Co. records, Livery lists]

Morrall, Benjamin, Dudley, Worcs., cm and u (1835–40). Listed at Stafford St in 1835 and New St in 1840. [D]

Morrall (or Morrell), William, Dudley, Worcs., cm and u (1830–40). Recorded as Morrell at Castle St in 1830; as Morrall in High St, 1835; and High St and Queen St in 1840. [D]

Morrant & Son, London, furniture makers (1828). Named in the Chatsworth furnishing account in 1828 receiving £35 9s. Probably George Morant.

Morrell, R., 48 Belvedere Pl., Borough Rd, London, cm (1835). [D] Set of four dining chairs recorded impressed 'R. MORRELL'.

Morrey, John, Holmfirth, Huddersfield, Yorks., joiner and/or cm (1834). [D]

Morrice, Captain, address unrecorded, but possibly as John Morice above, u (1660–61). His name occurs three times in Samuel Pepys's Diary, 1660–61, twice as 'Captain Morrice' and, on 22 June 1660, as 'Mr. Morrice the Upholsterer, came himself to day to take notice what furniture we lack for our lodgings at Whitehall.'

Morrice, George, Upper Clapton, London, cm and u (1838–39). [D]

Morris, —, Frith St, Soho, London, u (1722). Named in contemporary newspapers in 1722. [Heal]

Morris, —, Week St, Maidstone, Kent, cm (1823–24). [D] Of the firm Carter & Morris. See Henry and Samuel Morris.

Morris, Abraham, 26–28 Richmond Pl., Brighton, Sussex, Tunbridge-ware, fancy cabinet, desk, dressing case, work box and tea chest manufacturer (1836–48). May have commenced business in 1835 on the death of John Witten (or Sargeant Witten) Morris. Alfred Morris, probably an error, is recorded at this address, 1838–39. [D] Morris is recorded in the Windsor Royal Archives on 30 September 183–(?), receiving £9 2s 6d for '6 Day & 1 Cap Stands', and in March 1841, £6 for '4 doz. Cap Stands'. See Edward, and John Witten Morris.

Morris, Alexander, Windsor, Berks., cm (1806). Named in rate bk, but did not poll, in 1806.

Morris, Ann, 21 Small St, Bristol, 'curious cabinet seller' (1813). [D]

Morris, Corner, London, upholder (1750–84). Recorded at Fenchurch St in 1772; and as C. Morris, upholder and undertaker at no. 121 in 1784. Son of John Morris, coffeeman of St Swithin's Alley. App. to William Kilpin on 16 September 1750, and admitted freeman of the Upholders' Co. by servitude on 2 February 1758. [D; GL, Upholders' Co. records]

Morris, Edward, 4 Richmond Gdns, Brighton, Sussex, Tunbridge-ware manufacturer (1839–47). [D; poll bk] The relationship of this business to that of the main Morris showrooms and manufactory nearby in Richmond Pl. is unknown. See Abraham, and John Witten Morris.

Morris, Francis, St Owen St, Hereford, builder, cm and u (1840). [D]

Morris, George, Newport, Salop, cm (1816). [St Mary's PR (bapt.)]

Morris, George, 8 Harrow Rd, Edgware Rd, London, cm (1835). [D]

Morris, George, 10 Bell St, Westminster, London, cm (1837). Children Eliza and George by wife Susan bapt. at Westminster Methodist Chapel in July 1837. [PRO, Non-Conf. reg.]

Morris, Griffith, Salop Rd, Oswestry, Salop, cm and joiner (1822). [D]

Morris, Henry, Week St, Maidstone, Kent, u (1834–35). [Poll bk and reg. of elect.] See Morris, —; and Samuel Morris.

Morris, James, Chester, u and cm (1829). Notice in *Chester Chronicle and North Wales Advertiser*, 28 August 1829 read: 'JAMES MORRIS Begs leave to respectfully announce to his friends, and the public in general, that he has become a partner with Mr. WILLIAM PODMORE of the late firm of PODMORE and POWELLS, Upholsters and Cabinet Makers; and hopes from his experience in the business, added to a strict attention in the execution of such orders as they may be favoured with, to merit a share of public patronage and support.'

Morris, James, Hereford, cm and u (1830–32). Addresses given at Bewell St in 1830 and Eign St in 1832. [D; poll bk]

Morris, James, Lancaster. Named in the Gillow records in 1837. [Westminster Ref. Lib.]

Morris, John, address unrecorded, upholder (1709). Admitted freeman of the Upholders' Co. on 4 May 1709. [GL, Upholders' Co. records]

Morris, John, at 'The Lion & Crown', Fleet Ditch, London, u (1717–18). Provided the Duke of Montrose's Bond St House with '4 Mounted beds: 1 green mohair lined with Green Satin. 1 light green complet lined with a striped Satin. 1 Red stuft bed & 1 blue' totalling a cost of £42. He also charged £85 5s 1d for feather beds, bolsters, pillows, bedsteads, curtains and vallances. [Scottish RO, GD 220/6/1192/34 and 41; GD 220/6/28/p. 84]

Morris, John, Kirby St, Hatton Gdn, London, upholder (1719–27). Polled in 1719, and named in newspapers in 1727. [Heal]

Morris, John, Norwich, carver (1762). Included in James Paine's papers relating to work for the Duke of Norfolk at Norwich in 1762. [Arundel Castle records, MD18, pt 1]

Morris, John, 2 Foster St, Halfmoon Alley, Bishopsgate St, London, cm (1782). Took out a Sun Insurance policy in 1782 for £100 of which utensils and stock accounted for £50. [GL, Sun MS vol. 300, p. 95]

Morris, John, at 'The Three Brushes and Coffee-Mill', New Bond St, London, turner. 18th-century advertisement lists stock including Windsor chairs, close stools, tea boards, tea chests, 'Four Wheel Chaises for Children', and 'Chamber Horses'. [Leverhulme Coll., MMA, NY] See Morris, —.

Morris, John, 36 Brick Lane, Spitalfields, London, cm and chairmaker (1809–11). [D]

Morris, John, 24 Fort St, Spitalfields, London, cm (1810). Took out a Sun Insurance policy on 12 July 1810 for £300 of which stock, utensils and timber in workshop accounted for £120,

pictures, prints, frames and glass, £20. Took out a further policy on 24 July for £300 including £20 on stock and utensils. [GL, Sun MS vol. 452, ref. 846465; vol. 449, ref. 846669]

Morris, John, Liverpool, u (1811–27). Addresses given at 9 Sidney St in 1811; 16 Orange St in 1818; and 4 Fontenoy St in 1827. [D]

Morris, John, Mount Gate, Frankwell, Shrewsbury, Salop, u (1814). [Shrewsbury burgess roll]

Morris, John Witten (or Sargeant Witten), Brighton, Sussex, Tunbridge-ware manufacturer (1814–d.1835). Recorded at Trafalgar Pl. in 1814, the address also found on his trade card in the Banks Coll., BM; and 26 and 27 Richmond Pl., 1821–35. His son, Sargeant Witten, by wife Elizabeth, was bapt. on 10 July 1814; and Frederick William on 28 Febuary 1821. In 1835 rate was collected from the executors of S. W. Morris, presumably after his death. Heading on an undated bill for £14 3s in the Monson archive shows elegant shop-front of 'MORRIS'S ROYAL REPOSITORY', 'opposite the New Church' of 1828, and reads: 'Jewellery, Stationery, Perfumery, and every Article In the Fancy Line. Work Boxes & Other Articles Revarnished (equal to new). Old Jewellery Taken in Exchange'. [D; E. Sussex RO, PR (bapt.); rate bk Lincoln RO, Monson 11/51]

Morris, John, 76 Union St, Southwark, London, cm and broker (1819–20). [D]

Morris, John, 6 Gower Pl., New Rd/Bedford Row or Sq./Euston Sq., London, cm and u (1827–39). [D]

Morris, John, Carey's Ct, High St, Maidstone, Kent, turner and chairmaker (1839). [D]

Morris, Joseph, St Ann's, Westminster, London, upholder (1723). Took out a Hand in Hand Insurance policy on 11 July 1723 for £300 on 'a house with a dancing bear adjoining on the south side of Queen St. and east side of Frith St in the parish aforesaid'. [GL, Hand in Hand MS vol. 27, p. 210]

Morris, Joseph, address unrecorded. In 1725 he charged £10 10s for 'tapestry and all demands', and £2 2s for a chair supplied to Stowe, Bucks. [Huntington Lib., California, Stowe MS ST82, p. 185] Probably Joshua Morris

Morris, Joseph, 7 New John St, Liverpool, cm (1811). [D]

Morris, Joseph, Sheffield, Yorks., cm (1816–37). Addresses given at 23 Bailey St, 1816–20; Townehead St in 1821; no. 22, 1822–29; 66 Hollis Croft, 1833–34; and no. 65 in 1837. [D]

Morris, Joseph, London, cm and u (1827–39). Trading at 10 Susannah Row, Curtain Rd, 1827–28; and 4 Bateman's Row, Shoreditch in 1839. [D]

Morris, Joshua, at 'The Golden Ball', Pall Mall, London, tapestry worker and u (1720–29). Involved in a lawsuit in 1727 with William Hogarth for attempting to repudiate a commission for a design for tapestry representing 'The Element of Earth'. The case was decided in Hogarth's favour. Morris was well known as a supplier of Arabesque tapestries from his Soho workshop in Frith St, 1720–28. In 1729 he was declared bankrupt, and his premises were taken over by William Bradshaw. [*Survey of London*, 34, 1966, pp. 515–20, 542–43; *The Treasure Houses of Britain*, Washington, 1985–86, cat. no. 137; *DNB*]

Morris, Marmaduke William, 16 John St, Oxford Mkt, London, cm (1786). Took out a Sun Insurance policy on 28 March 1786 for £400, including £210 on utensils etc. [GL, Sun MS vol. 336, p. 86]

Morris, Peter, Aighton Bailey and Chaigley, in the parish of Mitton, Lancs., chairmaker and bobbin turner (1815). Witness to the petition made to Quarter Sessions by Mark Chippindale concerning the loss he sustained in fire on 19 September 1815. [Preston RO, Cat. no. QSP, 1813; *Furn. Hist.*, 1981] Possibly:

Morris, Peter, Brown St, Bolton, Lancs., chairmaker (1818–34). [D]

Morris, R., Chapel St, King's Lynn, Norfolk, bedstead manufacturer (1822). [D]

Morris, R., Berkeley Sq., Gloucester, u (1839–40). [D]

Morris, Richard, 28 St James's St, Cheltenham, Glos., cm, u and paper hanger (1820). [D]

Morris, Robert, at 'The Golden Lyon', Cornhill, London, 'Royal Upholsterer Extraordinary' (1660–70). Appointed u to Charles II after the Restoration, but in 1661 was forced, as several other Royal u were, to humbly petition the King for settlement of his account. He wrote that he had always been ready 'to manifest his duty to your Mat.ie, since your happy Restauration, by supplying your Wardrobe with all such provisions, as ye Lord Gen.l Montague and others the officers thereof, have, from time to time, desired amountinge unto nine thousand Eight hundred & odd pounds, and never yet received any more than Six hundred pounds thereof (w.ch was about fourteen months Since), though your Pet.er can Safely affirme, that noe man hath Supplied your Mat.ies occasions with more cheerefullnesse, and cheaper goods, or Shall for the future, if your Pet.er might be reasonably enabled, by payment of what is already due, without which, he is in most apparent danger to loose his Credit, and thereby to bring inevitable ruine on his family ...'. Charles 'taking notice of the great debt due to the Peticoner', 'Captaine' Morris, ordered the Earl of Sandwich, Master of the Great Wardrobe, to take steps for its discharge, the order being dated 20 January 1661. Morris had supplied chairs, couches, bedsteads, cushions, blankets, curtains and carpets to the Crown; also seventy-five turkeywork chairs to the House of Commons. For the Queen Mother's Lodging, and Princess Henrietta's Lodging at Whitehall, Morris provided ten French tables, twenty-five chairs and stools 'of cloth', 'six high Turkey Work Chairs & 36 Turkey Work Chairs'. Morris also hired out beds, tapestries, turkeywork and leather chairs to the Prince of Lygny, Ambassador Extraordinary from the King of Spain at Campden House, on 29 September and 13 October 1660. [PRO, LC5/39–40; *DEF*; *Conn.*, vol. III, 1943, p. 116 and January 1934, p. 18; *Burlington*, September 1942, p. 218; *C. Life*, 11 February 1960, p. 275; Winterthur, Delaware, Symonds papers, 75×69.18, p. 8]

Morris, Robert, Liverpool, cm (1754). Took app. named Mosson in 1754. [S of G, app. index]

Morris, Robert, Newark, Notts., u (1805–08). Listed at Millgate in 1805 and Kirkgate in 1808. [D]

Morris, Robert, Norfolk St East, Wisbech, Cambs., cm, u and paper hanger (1830). [D]

Morris, Robert, King's Lynn, Norfolk, cm (1830–39). Trading at Austin St in 1830 and 103 Norfolk St, 1836–39. [D]

Morris, Robert & John, St Werburgh St, Chester, painters, carvers and gilders (1840). [D]

Morris, Rowland, 3 Lower Thurlow St, Liverpool, cm (1823). [D]

Morris, Samuel, 110 Week St, Maidstone, Kent, cm and u (1832–39). [D; poll bks; reg. of elect.] See Morris, —; and Henry Morris.

Morris, Thomas, London, freeman wheelwright, cm, chairmaker and u (1768–1832). Recorded at Budge Row, 1768–71, no. 3 in 1775; St Paul's Churchyard, 1777–78; no. 15, 1780–90; and no. 26, 1790–1828. Recorded in partnership with William Morris, 1784–1827, and as Morris & Son in 1828. Trading as Thomas Morris & Son, cm and u, 345 Strand, 1829–32, by which time clearly a second or third generation was in business. Thomas Morris employed three non-freemen for three months in 1768; four for six weeks and five for three months in 1769; six for three months and eight for nine months in 1770; eight throughout 1771; forty for three months in 1777; and forty for six weeks in 1778. Subscribed to Sheraton's *Drawing Book*, 1793, and *Cabinet Dictionary*, 1803, when named in the list of master cabinet makers. [D; GL, City Licence bks, vols 6, 7 and 9; Fastnedge, *English Furniture Styles, 1500–1830*, p. 305] See William Morris, and Morris & Cupiss.

Morris, Thomas, 55 near Gt Turnstile, Holborn, London, upholder and warehouseman (1776). Took out a Sun Insurance policy in 1776 for £2,000 including £1,380 on utensils, stock and goods. [GL, Sun MS vol. 246, p. 151]

Morris, Thomas, Liverpool, cm (b.1785–1818). Born on 21 December 1785, he petitioned freedom on birthright as son of Edward Morris, boat builder, in 1816, paying 3s 4d. Admitted freeman in 1818. [Liverpool freemen's committee bk]

Morris, Whalkin, Downley, High Wycombe, Bucks., chairmaker (b. c.1816–41). Aged 25 at the time of the 1841 Census.

Morris, William, St Paul's Churchyard, London, upholder and cm (1781–1833). Recorded at no. 15, 1781–1802; no. 26, 1790–1809; and at 345 Strand in 1833. Trading in partnership with Thomas Morris, 1784–1827. Son of Thomas Morris, shoemaker of Derby. Admitted freeman of the Upholders' Co. by redemption on 1 August 1781. Probably the William Morris, u, who subscribed to Sheraton's *Cabinet Dictionary*, 1803. [D; GL, Upholders' Co. records] See Thomas Morris, and Morris & Cupiss.

Morris, William, parish of St Peter Mancroft, Norwich, cm (1806). [Poll bk]

Morris, William, Liverpool, u (1812–39). Addresses given at 6 Clayton St, 1813–14; 3 Atkinson St in 1816; 57 Gerrard St in 1821; 146 Scotland Rd in 1839. Admitted freeman on servitude to Gregson & Bullen on 16 October 1812. [D; Liverpool freemen reg.]

Morris, William, 8 Barrs St, Bristol, cm (1832–34). [D]

Morris, William, 76 Union St, Southwark, London, cm and chairmaker (1817). [D]

Morris & Cupis(s), 15 St Paul's Churchyard, with manufactory at 10 St Bennet's Hill, Doctors Commons, London, cabinet and chair manufacturers, upholders, appraisers and auctioneers (1789). Trade card, c.1780, bears inscription within carved and draped bedstead, and shows Venetian blind, shield-back armchair, Hepplewhite-style writing desk, and looking-glass embellished with palm leaves or feathers, surmounted by a tied ribbon. [D; Heal] See Thomas Morris and William Morris.

Morris & Son, John St, Oxford St, London, cm (1799). [D] See Marmaduke William Morris.

Morrison, Alexander, address unrecorded, cm (1793). Subscribed to Sheraton's *Drawing Book*, 1793.

Morrison, D., 1 Bevendon St, Hoxton, London, cm (1835). [D]

Morrison, James, New St, Broad St, London, cm (1774). [Poll bk]

Morrison, James, 13 Duke's Ct, Bow St, Covent Gdn, London, cm (1808–10). Took out a Sun Insurance policy on 13 February 1810 for £100 on household goods and wearing apparel in his house, where no work was done. [D; GL, Sun MS vol. 453, ref. 841263]

Morrison, Robert, Liverpool, cm (1816–d.1829). App. to John Ward Turner, and admitted freeman on 7 June 1816. Referred to as 'abroad, Roberts. Corrobable', 1818–20, and 'drowned coming from South America' in 1829. [Liverpool freemen reg.]

Morrison, Thomas, corner of Chancery Lane, Fleet St, London, upholder (1748–63). Named in directories and app. records. [Heal]

Morrison, Thomas, London, u (1749). App. to Joshua Lewis, u of Fleet St, at a premium of £20 under the Sons of the Clergy scheme. [*General Advertiser*, 17 April 1749]

Morrison, Thomas, London, cm and undertaker (1820–28). Trading at 63 Upper King St, Bloomsbury, 1820–23; and 9 Leigh St, Red Lion Sq., 1824–28. Took out a Sun Insurance policy on 8 January 1824 for £200 on household goods etc. in his new dwelling house. [D; GL, Sun MS vol. 499, ref. 1012092]

Morritt, John, York, cm (1825). Son of William Morritt; app. to John Taylor, cm, on 11 May 1825. [York app. reg.]

Morrod, Joseph, Hull and York, cm (1774). [Hull poll bk]

Morrow, John, near the Church, Limehouse, London, cm (1778). Insured utensils, stock and goods for £200 in 1778. [GL, Sun MS vol. 265, p. 87]

Morrow, Richard, Peter St, Bristol, cm (1792–94). Trading at no. 16 in 1792. [D]

Morrow, William, 25 Wilson St, Finsbury Sq., London, water gilder (1801–27). [D]

Morse, Henry, London, cm, u and undertaker (1803–20). Trading at 18 Charlotte St, Rathbone Pl., 1813–17, and no. 10, 1819–20. Declared bankrupt, *London Gazette*, 8 November 1817. Probably the Henry Morse, cm, who subscribed to Sheraton's *Cabinet Dictionary*, 1803. [D]

Morsely, —, Doncaster, Yorks., cm (1793). Subscribed to Sheraton's *Drawing Book*, 1793.

Mor(e)ten, Henry, Hillingdon End, Uxbridge, London, cm and u, paper hanger and undertaker (1838–39). [D]

Morten, Thomas & Charles, London St, Uxbridge, Middlx, cm and u (1826). [D]

Morth, John & Son, Horsham, Sussex, cm and organ builders (1811). [D]

Morthost, Paul, 1 Little Tower Hill, London, cm (1784–93). [D]

Mortimer, F. J., 80 Pitt St (town not given), picture frame manufacturer. George III mahogany easel toilet mirror recorded, with oval plate raised on shaped trestle supports, bearing label on back. [Sotheby's, 9 November 1973, lot 51]

Mortimer, Francis, 41 Well St, Oxford St, London, cm (1835). [D]

Mortimer, John E., 47 Old Compton St, London, cm and u (1839). [D]

Mortimer, William, Bristol St, Birmingham, cm (1835–39). Listed at no. 201 in 1839. [D]

Mortimore, John, 11 Cumberland St, Devonport, Devon, u and cm (1838). [D]

Mortimore, Jos. Pollyblank, Devonport, Devon, cm and u (1830–38). Recorded at 19 Ker St in 1830. J. P. Mortimore, cm and u, was declared bankrupt, *Exeter Flying Post*, 7 May 1835, and 29 November 1838. [D]

Mortlock, Charles, Clare, Suffolk, cm (1839). [D]

Mortlock, J., Hingham, Norfolk, cm and chairmaker (1822). [D]

Morton, Alexander, 14 Bulstrode St, London, cm and u (1839). [D]

Morton, Andrew, parish of St Oswald, Durham, spinning-wheel maker (1716). His wife's burial was recorded on 19 November 1716. [PR]

Morton, Andrew, 269 High St, Poplar, London, cm (1826–28). [D]

Morton, Eli, Holmfirth, Huddersfield, Yorks., joiner and/or cm (1834). [D]

Morton, Ellis, Church Gate, Leicester, cm (1827). [D]

Morton, F. T., address unrecorded. Stamp found on mahogany bachelor's chest. [*Antique Collecting*, July 1968, p. 30]

Morton, Henry, London, fancy cm and miscellaneous dealer (1835–39). Trading at 28 Holywell St, Strand and 13 Colville St, Fitzroy Sq. in 1835; and Colville Ct, Tottenham Ct Rd in 1839. [D]

Morton, J., Broad St, Worcester, cm and u (1820). [D]

Morton, James, 33 Paddington St, Marylebone, London, carpenter and upholder (1801). Took out a Sun Insurance policy on 27 May 1801 for £350. [GL, Sun MS vol. 419, ref. 718400]

Morton, James, Worcester, cm (1806). App. to his father, Richard Morton, cm and admitted freeman on 16 June 1806. [Worcester freemen rolls]

Morton, James, 107 Swallow St, London, cm (1809–11). [D] See Thomas Morton at this address.

Morton, James, 1 Waterloo Rd, London, chair and sofa maker (1839). [D]

Morton, John, Gainsborough, Lincs., cm (1792–94). [D]

Morton, John, London, cm (1793). Subscribed to Sheraton's *Drawing Book*, 1793.

Morton, John, 36 Gun St, Spitalfields, London, cm (1808). [D]

Morton, John, Worcester, cm (1806–22). App. to his father, Richard Morton, cm, and admitted freeman on 16 June 1806. [Worcester freemen rolls] Supplied items to Croome Court, Worcs., being paid £6 14s from 7–13 October 1815 for two mahogany chairs and recovering and repairing two oval firescreens; £7 6s 9d from 7 August to 19 October 1816 for a further two mahogany chairs, and recutting old glass; and £11 10s 6d from 1–4 November 1817 for a rug, swing-glass and dressing table. [V&A archives] Recorded at 21 Broad St, Worcester, 1820–22. [D]

Morton, Richard, Worcester, cm, u and undertaker (1768–1817). Recorded at Mealcheapen St in 1788 and 21 Broad St, 1794–98. Listed as Surveyor to the County, 1794. App. to William Reding, joiner, carpenter and cm, and admitted freeman on 20 June 1768. Former apps admitted freemen: James Barrett and Edward Redding in 1780; and his own sons, William, John and James in 1806. Took out a Sun Insurance policy on 5 May 1791 for £1,600, including farmhouse, brewhouse, dairy and millhouse. Trade card, *c.*1800, in the Heal Coll., BM, shows Regency woman mourning by a tomb. Morton supplied items to Croome Court, Worcs., receiving £7 15s between 1 June and 10 August 1811 for 'a pair of handrawn Imperial bedside carpets … silvered glass plate and cutting do. to pattern. 2 mahogany BIDETS with turned legs, tops stuffed with best horsehair and covered with black satin, hair and brass nailed'. In 1815 Richard and John Morton supplied two mahogany chairs costing £6 14s; in 1816 charged for two further mahogany chairs and for repairing and cleaning a tea chest at £7 16s 9d; and in 1817 for a carpet and mahogany dressing table, costing £11 10s 6d. [D; Worcester freemen rolls; GL, Sun MS vol. 376, p. 392; V&A archives]

Morton, T., Gt Swan Alley, Coleman St, London, bedstead maker (1829). [D]

Morton, Thomas, London, carver and gilder, frame maker to HRH the Duke of Gloucester (1817–27). Trading at 107 Swallow St, Piccadilly, 1817–20; 18 Maddox St in 1825; and no. 19, 1826–27. Trade card recorded. [D; Heal] See James Morton at Swallow St.

Morton, Thomas, Sheffield, Yorks., cm (1834). [D]

Morton, Thomas, Liverpool, u (1835–39). Trading at 41 Rose Pl. in 1835; 2 Seacombe Lane, Belle St in 1837; and no. 3 in 1839. [D]

Morton, Thomas, High Wycombe, Bucks., chairmaker (b. *c.*1781–1841). Aged 60 at the time of the 1841 Census.

Morton, William, Worcester, cm (1806). App. to his father, Richard Morton, cm, and admitted freeman on 16 June 1806. [Worcester freemen rolls] See James, John and Richard Morton.

Morton, William, Allerton Bywater, Castleford, Yorks., joiner and cm (1837). [D]

Morver, Isaac William, 208 Oxford St with workshop at 30–31 Orchard St, Portman Sq., London, upholder and cm (1805–22). Took out Sun Insurance policies on 9 January 1805 for £1,700, including £1,000 on utensils, stock and goods in trust, and £400 on those in sawpit and workshop at 31 Orchard St; on 29 April 1806 for £1,400, including £400 on sawpits and workshop at 31 Orchard St; on 18 July 1809 for £1,400, including £800 on stock, utensils and goods in trust, £400 on those in sawpits and warehouse; and on 2 August 1820 for £500 on a private house at 35 Edgware Rd, Paddington. On 6 November 1822, in partnership with Thomas Smith as cm and u, Morver took out insurance for £3,000, including £800 on stock, utensils and goods in trust; £500 on those in old and new workshops, open sheds and saw pits at 30 Orchard St; and £500 on the new workshop building. [GL, Sun MS vol. 431, ref. 769967; vol. 437, ref. 787879; vol. 448, ref. 834117; vol. 483, ref. 970321; vol. 493, ref. 997360]

Morwood, Thomas, 6 Pitt St, Fitzroy Sq., London, writing desk and dressing case maker (1829). [D]

Mose, Henry, London. In 1688–89 he supplied the Queen with 'Japan Mirror, table and Stands', costing £74. [PRO, LC9, 123, p. 58]

Mosedale, Edward, Wolverhampton, Staffs., joiner and cm (1838). [D]

Moseley, Charles, 44 Lichfield St, Birmingham, cm and chairmaker (1830). [D]

Moseley, Elizabeth, 5 Commercial St, Leeds, Yorks., carver, gilder and printseller (1804–22) At no. 3 in 1816. Advertised in *Leeds Intelligencer*, 25 November 1816 offering her 'most grateful thanks … for the numerous favours conferred upon her since her late father's decease', probably Robert Moseley. In *Leeds Mercury*, nos 2641–42, 1816, she announced 'that with the Assistance of a Foreman who has been employed for the last twelve years by Mr. Robert Moseley of Derby … every care and attention will be paid to executing their orders in a workmanlike manner and punctually.' A later advertisement in *Leeds Mercury*, nos 2682–83, 1816, suggests the business was concentrating more on dealing than making. [D] See Robert and Thomas Moseley.

Moseley, J. R., Hemel St, Old St, London, looking-glass and picture frame maker (1829). [D]

Mos(e)ley, John, Market St, Huddersfield, Yorks., cm, u and joiner (1818–30). [D]

Moseley, John, Hampstead, London, working u (1823–39). Recorded as u and paper hanger in 1823 and listed at Heath St, 1838–39. [D]

Moseley, Joshua & James, King St, Huddersfield, Yorks., cm, u and joiners (1830–34). [D]

Moseley, Richard, London, freeman joiner and cm (1762–92). Recorded at Leadenhall St, 1763–70; 119 Aldersgate St, 1767–75; and Cheapside in 1792. Rococo trade card reads: 'Moseley, Cabinet Maker, At his Warehouse opposite ye East India House Leadenhall Street — London, Makes & Sells all sorts of Cabinet Chair & Look^g Glass Goods at the most Reasonable Rates. NB. for Exportation.' [GL, trade card coll.] Named as a Fellow of the Society for Arts and Manufactures, 1761–67. In 1762 he employed six non-freemen for three months; in 1763, two for three months; and in 1764, six for six weeks. [D; GL, City Licence bks, vols 3 and 4] See Moseley & Harris.

Moseley, Richard, address unrecorded, carver and gilder (1820–31). Recorded in the Chatsworth furnishing account in 1820 receiving £24 2s 5d; in 1821, £32 8s 6d; in 1822, £59 9s; in 1824, £142 7s 6d; in 1825, £142 7s 6d; in 1826,

£105 6s; in 1827, £154 17s 6d; in 1829, £95 12s 6d; in 1830, £213 13s 3d; and in 1831, £33 13s 11d. Possibly Robert Moseley of Cornmarket, the name Richard being an error.

Moseley, Robert, Leeds, Yorks., carver and gilder (1805–15). Trading at Briggate in 1805, and Commercial St in 1811. Advertised for an app., offering 'moderate terms', in *Leeds Mercury*, 1805; and announced his removal from Briggate to Commercial St in 1809. Advertised later in 1809 that he had changed his address in Commercial St, and emphasized that work was actually done in his workshops, particularly framing for mirrors, 'got up equal to any in London, and on much more moderate terms …'. In 1813 he advertised for two apps, stating that 'none need apply but from very respectable Parents'; and in 1814 for a journeyman gilder: 'none need apply but a good steady workman. Likewise an apprentice … a youth of a respectable family in Leeds will be treated with.' Moseley appears to have died in 1815, to be succeeded by his daughter Elizabeth and son Thomas.

Moseley, Robert, Cornmarket, Derby, carver and gilder (1823–36). Trading at no. 36, 1828–35. [D] Recorded also as a jeweller in 1822. He was the publisher of S. Rayner's *The History and Antiquities of Haddon Hall*, 1836, and his label inside the book reads: 'By APPOINTMENT — R. MOSELEY — Carver and Gilder to the King — JEWELLER, SILVERSMITH. Agent to the British Plate Glass Company — PICTURE GALLERY & FANCY REPOSITORY — CORNMARKET DERBY — Copper Plate Engraving, Printing & Seal Engraving — FREE ADMITTANCE TO THE GALLERY … SPA & MARBLE MUSEUM … VASES, OBELISKS &c….'. See Elizabeth Moseley, and Moseley & Tunnicliff. Possibly it was an earlier Robert Moseley for whom Elizabeth Moseley worked. Possibly Richard Moseley recorded as working at Chatsworth, 1820–31.

Moseley, Thomas, 1 Trinity Lane, Leeds, Yorks., carver and gilder, picture frame maker (1816–17). Son of Robert Moseley of Leeds, and took over the business on the death of his father, c.1815. Advertisement in *Leeds Mercury*, 1816, read: 'Thomas Moseley, Son and Foreman of the late Robert Moseley … begs leave most respectfully to return his grateful thanks to the Nobility, Gentry and other Friends of his late Father for the many favours conferred on him in his life-time; and to inform them that he has removed from his Father's late shop to the more commodious one, lately occupied by Mr. Lumb, as an auction room, No. 1 Trinity-Lane, where he proposes continuing the business in all its various branches. Having been engaged several years in the First House in the Trade in London, and ever since Foreman to his Father, where the Principal Part of the Business has been done either by himself or under his immediate Inspection, he is encouraged to hope it will be in his power to give the same satisfaction … NB. An apprentice wanted.'

Moseley, William, Stafford, cm and u (1834–35). Listed at Foregate in 1834 and Goal Sq. in 1835. [D]

Mosel(e)y & Harris, John, Leadenhall St, London, cm (1759–60). [D; Harris, *Old English Furniture*] See Richard Moseley, and Harris & Mosely.

Moseley & Tunnicliff, Corn Mkt, Derby, carvers and gilders (1818). [D] See Robert Moseley.

Mosely, Henry, address unrecorded, u (1670–92). Named in the Royal Household Accounts in 1670 and 1692. [PRO, LC9/280, LC5/40]

Moser, John, London, u and cm (1835–39). Trading at 143 Oxford St and 3 Winsley St in 1835; and 63 Mortimer St in 1839. [D]

Moses, Robert, Wolsingham, Durham, joiner and cm (1828–29). [D]

Moses, Samuel, 23 Norton St, St Mary-le-Bone, London, cm, u and buhl manufacturer (1817–23). [D]

Moses, Thomas Metcalfe, High St, Stockton-upon-Tees, Co. Durham, joiner and cm (1827–32). [D]

Mosley, Benjamin, Tanner Row, York, cm (1823). [D]

Mosley, Charles, Church St, Manchester, cm (1781). [D]

Mosley, Henry, Woolpack St, Nottingham, cm (1828). [D]

Mosley, Joseph, Cawthorne, Yorks., cm (1837). [D]

Mosley, Robert, 24 Penston Lane, Sheffield, Yorks., carver and gilder (1797). [D]

Mosley, Samuel, address unrecorded. In 1794–95 submitted a bill to Godfrey Wentworth of Woolley Hall, Yorks., for household furniture costing a total of £58 17s. [YAS, Wentworth papers, MD272/2] Possibly Samuel Mozley.

Mosley, Thomas, 16 Back Gdn, Manchester, cm (1808–09). [D]

Moss, Barnett, 54 Leman St, Goodmanfields, London, carver and gilder, looking-glass manufacturer (1835–39). [D]

Moss, George, Lincoln, cm (1806). Named in the Lincoln freemen rolls in November 1806.

Moss, George, 21 Westbar Green, Sheffield, Yorks., chairmaker (1837). [D]

Moss, George, Brook St, Chester, cm (1838). Admitted freeman on 1 October 1838. [Chester freemen rolls]

Moss, Henry, Ripon, Yorks., joiner and/or cm (1834–37). Trading at Kirkgate in 1834 and Duck Hill in 1837. [D]

Moss, John, Nottingham, u (1773). Son of John Moss of Nottingham, staymaker; taken as app. in 1773. [Nottingham app. list]

Moss, John, Derby, u (1794). Notice in *Derby Mercury*, 25 September 1794 requested that his debtors pay their respective debts to Henry Browne or William Wright of Derby, presumably on Moss's bankruptcy or death.

Moss, John, Chester, cm (1794–1850). Recorded at Brook St in 1837. App. to Philip Presbury, cm, and admitted freeman in July 1794. Took app. named George Clubbe in 1818. [D; Chester freemen rolls, app. bks and poll bk]

Moss, Joseph, 36 Lloyd St, Manchester, looking-glass and picture frame maker (1834). [D]

Moss, Mathew, St Sepulchre Gate, Doncaster, Yorks., cm and/or u (1837). [D]

Moss, Moses, 32 Gouldston St, Whitechapel, London, looking-glass and picture frame maker (1839). [D]

Moss, Richard, at 'The Three Pillows', upper end of Broad St, behind the Royal Exchange, London, u (1725–49). Named in contemporary newspapers. [Heal]

Moss, Robert snr, Liverpool, cm (1759–d.1795). Recorded at 19 Cleveland Sq., 1766–87, no. 10 in 1784. R. Moss & Son were trading at 72 Hanover St in 1787, and as cm and glass-grinders at 55 Hanover St with cabinet shop at back of 27 Frederick St in 1790. Took apps named Leadbitter in 1759 and Thompson in 1761. Death reported in *Liverpool Advertiser*, 16 February 1795. [D; S of G, app. index]

Moss, Robert jnr, Liverpool, cm (b.1782–d.1824). Death aged 42 on 15 May 1824 reported in *Liverpool Mercury*, 24 June.

Moss, Samuel, Church St, Ashton-under-Lyne, Lancs., cm and joiner (1828). [D]

Moss, Thomas, 41 Fontenoy St, Liverpool, cm (1837). [D]

Moss, Thomas, 3 Terrace, High St, Kensington, London, cm and u (1838–39). [D]

Moss, William, Liverpool, joiner and cm (b.1758–d.1799). Recorded at 33 and 63 Pitt St in 1790; 66 Hanover St and 9 Ropewalk, Whitechapel and 12 Bolten St, Copperas Hill in 1796; and Hanover St in 1799. Death aged 41 reported in *Billinge's Liverpool Advertiser*, 6 May 1799. W. Moss, cm, possibly related, is recorded in the account of lives in leases granted by the Corp. of Liverpool, in 1721 when his daughter Eileen was aged 35. [D]

Moss, William, Liverpool, chairmaker and undertaker (b.1776–d.1817). Trading at 3 West Gate, St John's Church, 1805–11; and Haymarket when he died, aged 41, on 27 May 1817. [D; *Liverpool Mercury*, 6 June 1817]

Moss, William, Liverpool, chairmaker (1816–18). Recorded at 3 Seymour St in 1816 and 21 Orange St in 1818. [D]

Moss, William, Liverpool, cm (1829–39). Addresses given at 29 Marlborough St in 1829; 17 Stanley St in 1834; nos 17 and 25 1835; no. 25 in 1837; and no. 49 in 1839. [D]

Moss & Alsop, Potter St, Worksop, Notts., chairmakers and turners (1832). [D]

Mossley, James & Co., 1 Pleasant St, Manchester, carver and gilder (1829). [D]

Mote, Edward, Southwark, London, cm (1835–39). Trading at 74 Union St in 1835 and 12 Frederick Pl., Borough Rd in 1839. [D]

Moth, William, Basingstoke, Hants., u (1720). Took out a Sun Insurance policy on 12 January 1720 in association with John Spencer jnr, u. [GL, Sun MS vol. 10]

Moth, William, High St, Cowes, Isle of Wight, Hants., cm (1830). [D]

Motherhaw, Thomas, Derby, u (1760). Took app. named Pecarpoint in 1760. [S of G, app. index]

Motley, Daniel, Leeds, Yorks., journeyman cm (1791). Named in the *Leeds Cabinet and Chair Makers' Book of Prices*, 1791, with other journeymen in basic sympathy with its contents.

Mott, John, Cranbrook, Kent, upholder (1793). [D]

Motteram, William, Frodsham, Cheshire, cm/joiner (1822–37). [D]

Mottershaw, Thomas, Derby, u and cm (1757–d. by 1790). In 1757 he announced in *Derby Mercury* his removal to Irongate, near 'The Bull's Head', All Saints' parish. Recorded in All Saints in 1785, and at Irongate in 1786. Married Sarah of All Saints, and had three children: Sarah, born in 1761, and Thomas, born in 1762, who both died within the year of their birth; and another, Thomas, born in 1764, who survived. Took out a Sun Insurance policy on 27 December 1786 for £2,500 on his house, brewhouse, workshop, warehouse, stabling, and twenty-three other houses and workshops tenanted by others. Announced in *Leicester Chronicle*, 1777, that his app., John King, had absconded. Mottershaw seems to have been subcontracted by Joseph Pickford, probably for interior decorative woodwork, at Etruria Hall, Staffs., for Josiah Wedgwood. Mottersham wrote to Wedgwood in October 1770 concerning unspecified chimney pieces. In 1785 Mottershaw was left a legacy in the will, dated 28 July, of William Key, cork cutter, late of Little East Cheap, London. Mottershaw is referred to later in the 1780s concerning this legacy as deceased. It is possible that his son, Thomas, continued the business, and that he could be the Thomas Mottershaw mentioned as a Derby cm and u after 1784. [D; PR; Derby Lib., bound MS 9237, p. 3, no. 97; GL, Sun MS vol. 341, p. 402; Wedgwood Museum (Etruria) archive, 31141–1; PRO, C13 14/10]

Mottershead, Henrietta, 15 Hilton St, Manchester, u (1813). [D]

Motteux, Pierre Antoine, London, cm (1707–11). In 1707 he provided the Duke of Montrose with '1 fine Japan tea table', 'A dressing suite', and 'A framed glass'. Named in newspapers in 1711. [Scottish RO, GD 220/6/4/20; Heal]

Mottram, Joseph, High St, Uttoxeter, Staffs., cm (1818–28). [D]

Mottram, William, Liverpool, cm (1809). Marriage on 26 April 1809 at St Nicholas's Church to Miss Ann Lastley of Liverpool, reported in *Liverpool Courier*, 8 March 1809.

Mouat, John, Walworth, London, cm (1822–35). Trading at Queen's Row in 1822 and 1 Trafalgar St in 1835. [D]

Moucar, James, Coventry Ct, Westminster, London, cm (1749). [Poll bk]

Mould, Benjamin, Market St, Winchester, Hants., cm (1839). [D]

Mould, E., 11 New Inn Yd, Shoreditch, London, chairmaker (1835). [D]

Mould, Henry, The Square, Winchester, Hants., cm and u (1823–30). [D]

Mould, Thomas, Red Lion Lane, Buckingham, cm (1839). [D]

Mould, William, Stock-bridge, Northumb., joiner and cm (1824). [D]

Moulder, Thomas, Cambridge, u (1687–1729). The accounts of Christ's College note on 1 June 1687 that a bill of Thomas Peters 'the upholsterer' was 'recov^d by his Apprentice Tho Moulder'. Payments to Thomas Moulder, u, are recorded in the accounts of St John's College from 1692–1710 and 1726–29. The early ones recording quite detailed payments; 1695 'for 15 gilded leather skins nails and work about ye screen in ye Masters Lodge £5.10.6.', 1697 'for 65 yds of Matting for a room in ye Masters Lodge ye bill £1.1.8.', 1706 'for a new stool covered with Blew Bays 7s. 6d.', 1710 'for a Damask bed bolster and six cane chairs c matts a work in the Masters Lodging £26.1.2.'. Two payments between 1696–98 are recorded in the accounts of Trinity College. [Archives of Christ's, St John's and Trinity Colleges] R.W.

Moule, John, London. In 1787 he supplied the Duke of Montrose with mahogany tables, costing £7 1s. [Scottish RO, GD 220/6/1585/10]

Moule, Thomas, 13 Upper North Pl., Gray's Inn Rd, London, writing desk and dressing case maker (1829). [D]

Moullin, Sternec, Bewdley, Worcs., cm (1752–54). Took apps named Windle in 1752 and Haydock in 1754. [S of G, app. index]

Moulson, —, 21 College Lane, Liverpool, cm (1837). [D]

Moulton, Ann, Liverpool, forewoman (b.1747–d.1814). Worked as forewoman to Mathew Gregson, cm and u, who traded at 38 Castle St as Urmson & Gregson, 1778–81; at Preeson's Row in 1787; alone at 5 Preeson's Row in 1790; no. 2 in 1796; no. 4, 1800–03; no. 10 in 1806; and 34 Paradise St, 1807–12. Ann Moulton retired in 1812, having worked with Gregson for '38 years & upwards', and left legacies to various charities, and houses to some of her 'shop mates'. Her retirement and death, aged 67, were reported in *Gents Mag.*, 1814. [D]

Moulton, Francis, 36 Low Sloane St, Chelsea, London, cm and u (1823). [D]

Mouncey, William, 5 Old Bridge St, Salford, Lancs., sacking manufacturer and cm (1825–28). [D]

Mounsear, Robert, Norwich, u (1810–42). Trading at Hungate St in 1810; Princes(s) St, St Peter Hungate in 1839; and as u and paper hanger at Prince's St, Tombland in 1842. [D; poll bks]

Mounsey, Joseph, Hull, Yorks., cm (1774). [Poll bk]

Mount, J., 2 Trafalgar St, Walworth, London, cm (1835). [D]

Mount, John, Queen's Row, Walworth, London, cm (1823). [D]

Mountain, Francis, 1 Grape Lane, York, cm and u (1837–40). [D]

Mountain, John, Boston and Thorpe Arch, Yorks., cm (1837). [D]

Mountain, John, Bondgate, Otley, Yorks., joiner and/or cm (1837). [D]

Mountain, Joseph, 13 Howarth's-gates, Manchester, cm (1808). [D]

Mountain, Peter snr & jnr, Kirkgate, Leeds, Yorks., cm (1798–1805). Recorded in directories, 1798–1805, but terminated business soon afterwards. They advertised the sale of their business and stock in *Leeds Mercury*, 19 January 1805,

stating: 'To Cabinet-Makers and Private families, to be sold by Private Contract: A quantity of Elegant Furniture, entirely New-made of beautiful, well-seasoned wood, and in a fashionable style, consisting of Mahogany Book-Cases, Ward-robes, chests of drawers, single and double; a variety of Pier Glasses, side-boards, sofas, dressing tables, dining tables, and several other pieces of handsome furniture ... A Cabinet-Maker has now an excellent Opportunity of fixing himself comfortably in Business, as the Stock consists altogether of marketable Articles, to which is united an established business, and Premises suitable for conducting it with Advantage. The Premises are situated in a central Part of Leeds, and consists of a good DWELLING-HOUSE with a Front Shop, adjoining to which is a Work Shop, of Fourty Feet in Length, a good Wood Yard, Saw Pits, Sheds and every other Convenience. The Rent is very reasonable.' [D; *Furn. Hist.*, 1974]

Mountain, Richard, Leeds, Yorks., cm and u (1790–1800). Recorded in Kirkgate, 1790–98, and signed the *Leeds Cabinet and Chair Makers' Book of Prices*, 1791. Trade card in Leeds City Lib., local history dept., shows shield-back chair with Prince of Wales feathers, canopied bedstead, and dressing glass. Richard Mountain had either retired or died by 1800, and appears to have been succeeded by Peter Mountain, snr and jnr.

Mountain, Richard, York, cm (1825). Son of Francis Mountain, groom; app. to John Hardy, cm, on 20 April 1825. [York app. reg.]

Mountain, William, 11 Middle Row, Bloomsbury, London, cm (1799–1808). [D]

Mountford, Henry, Worcester, cm (1802). App. to Samuel Redding, cm, and admitted freeman on 12 July 1802. [Worcester freemen rolls]

Mountford, Joseph, Severn Side, Bewdley, Worcs., cm (1830). [D]

Mo(u)ntford, (Mountfort or Mountfield), Thomas, St Mary's St, Market Drayton, Salop, cm (1828–40). Recorded also at Church St, 1828–35; New St in 1835 as cabinet case maker and jeweller; and 17, 21 and 61 New St in 1839 as perfumer, cabinet case maker and importer of foreign merchandise to the Royal Family. [D]

Mountier, Thomas, address unrecorded, upholder (1721–29). Son of Thomas Mountier, cook of Cheveley, Cambs.; app. to Robert Thorpe on 11 November 1721, and admitted freeman of the Upholders' Co. by servitude on 5 March 1828/29. [GL, Upholders' Co. records]

Mouseley, John, Colehill, Tamworth, Staffs., cm (1834). [D]

Mouston, James, West Wycombe, Bucks., chairmaker (b.c.1791–1841). Aged 50 at the time of the 1841 Census.

Mowain (?), William, Norwich, cm (1811). Former app., Barber William Tooke, cm, admitted freeman on 5 June 1811. [Norwich freemen reg.]

Mowat, Robert, 30 Henry St, Hampstead Rd, London, cm and u (1839). [D]

Mowatt, William, London, wood and cabinet carver (1829–39). Addresses given at 3 Chapel St, Tottenham Ct Rd in 1829; 31 Castle St East, Oxford Mkt in 1835; and 7 Noel St, Soho, in 1839. [D]

Mowatt & Co., Prince's St, Leicester Sq., London, upholders, (1784). [D]

Mo(w)bray, Christopher, London, cm and upholder (1766–93). Recorded opposite Rose St, near St Martin's Lane, Long Acre in 1766; Long Acre in 1774; and Porter St, Newport Mkt, 1784–93, no. 4 in 1784 as Mowbray & Co. Submitted a bill to Charles Long of Saxmundham, Suffolk, in 1766 for 'a mohogany Shaving table with a Glass etc. Compleat', costing £3 3s on 7 June; 'a Large Mohogany Shaving Table with 3

Couberts & a Drawer to Do. & folding tops & Brass Casters', costing £4 4s, on 10 June. The bill totalled £7 8s 6d and was receipted in full on 14 June. The heading shows an armchair with upholstered seat and back, and frame carved with heavy Rococo acanthus leaves; card gives address opposite Rose St, and states that he 'Makes and Sells all Sorts of Upholstery, Cabinet and Chair Work in the neatest Fashion. N:B: Funerals Perform'd at the most Reasonable Rates.' Mowbray took out a Sun Insurance policy in 1781 for £600 of which £380 accounted for utensils, stock and goods. [D; poll bks; Suffolk RO, HA18/EC/3/35; GL, Sun MS vol. 295, p. 398]

Mowbray, Robert, Boston, Lincs., cm, u and joiner (1819–35). Recorded at Wide Bargate, 1819–22, West Bargate in 1826, and Strait Bargate in 1835. [D]

Mowbray, William, house at 10 Coppergate, York, cm (1837). [D]

Mowbray & Wilson, 10 Coppergate, York, cm etc. (1840). [D]

Mowbray's, Albemarle St, London, u (1728). [Harris, *Old English Furniture*, p. 25]

Mower, J. William, London, cm (1793). Subscribed to Sheraton's *Drawing Book*, 1793. Possibly William Mower.

Mower, John, London, cm and u (1813–23). Addresses given at 18 New Inn Yd, Shoreditch, 1813–20, and 9 Holywell Row, 1821/23. Took out Sun Insurance policies on 12 May 1813 and/or 1814 for £550 of which £400 accounted for stock and utensils in workshop and open yard. [D; GL, Sun MS vol. 462, ref. 893772]

Mower, William, 48 Brewer St, London, cm (1791). Took out a Sun Insurance policy on 18 March 1791 in association with James Fletcher. [GL, Sun MS ref. 580689] See J. William Mower.

Mower, William, 208 Oxford St, London, u and cm (1803–39). Mowyer & Co. at this address are named in Sheraton's list of master cabinet makers, 1803. Mower & Smith were trading there, 1826–27; and Mower & Tasker in 1839, as well as at 27 Duke St, Grosvenor Sq. [D]

Mowett, Peter, 25 Lawton St, Liverpool, cm (1818). [D]

Mowles (or Moules), William, South Brink, Wisbech, Cambs., cm and u (1839). [D]

Mowsend, John, Holborn, London, dressing-case manufacturer (1832). Declared bankrupt, *Liverpool Mercury*, 2 March 1832.

Moxey, James, Coombe St, Exeter, Devon, carver and gilder (1819). Son James bapt. at St Mary Major on 17 June 1819. [PR (bapt.)]

Moxley, Thomas, 29 Duke St, Lincoln's Inn Fields, London, cm and u (1826–28). [D]

Moxon, Hewley, York, u (1712–41). Trading at Walmgate in 1741. Son of John Moxon; admitted freeman in 1712. [York poll bk and freemen rolls]

Moxon, John, Leeds, Yorks., carver (1798–1808). Listed at Sheepscar Rd, 1798–1805; and Sheepscar St in 1808. [D]

Moxon, William, 33 Drury Lane, London, cm (1789). [D]

Moxon, William, 4 Waingate, Sheffield, Yorks., u (1822). [D]

Moyle, Hugh Mason, East St, Penzance, Cornwall, cm and u (1823–24). [D]

Moyse, Charles, St Sidwell's Terr., Exeter, Devon, carver and gilder (1834). Son Charles bapt. at St Sidwell's on 9 March 1834. [PR (bapt.)]

Moyses, John, Elm St, Wisbech, Cambs., cm and u (1822–24). [D]

Moze, James, Greenwich, London, cm and u (1808–26). Trading at Park Pl., 1808–09, and Maze Hill, 1823–26. [D]

Mozley, Samuel, Doncaster, Yorks., cm (1793). [D] Possibly Samuel Mosley.

Muddell, Thomas, 2 Little Russell St, Bloomsbury, London, u (1824). Took out a Sun Insurance policy on 15 April 1824 for £300 on household goods, and £100 on stock and utensils. [GL, Sun MS vol. 499, ref. 1016348]

Muddell, William, London, u, cm, wine and beer merchant (1826–40). Addresses given at 10 Bow Lane, Cheapside, 1826–39; also 6 Little Thomas Apostle, 1835–40; and Worcester Pl., Upper Thames St in 1840. Took out a Sun Insurance policy in 1840. [D; GL, Sun MS vol. 574, ref. 1331411]

Mudge, W., 32 Boscawen St, Truro, Cornwall, cm (1811–13). Advertised in *Royal Cornwall Gazette*, 2 March 1811 that he was selling 'Goods at very reduced & half price', and had 'a large choice of cabinet goods made at his manufactory in Lemon St: with handsome, well-seasoned wood & by the best workmen that can be procured. viz: Dining & Pembroke tables, Card & Sofa Tables, Secretaires & Book cases, Bed Pillars, Sideboards, wash-stands & receptacles. Mahogany chests of drawers. Mahogany & Drawing room chairs — together with a great variety of Broadwood...'. On 9 April 1813 he advertised sale of 'ELEGANT CABINET FURNI-TURE', listing examples of his 'extensive assortment of many types of furniture manufactured under his own inspection, of the best materials & of excellent workmanship'. Stock included 'a considerable assortment of Convex Mirrors, Pier & Chimney Glasses. Paper hanging in the newest patterns. Parish Register Chests. N.B. Goods to the amount of ten pounds upwards forwarded to any part of the Country — Carriage free.'

Muff, William, Bradford, Yorks., cm and joiner (1793–1820). Recorded in Skinner Lane, 1818–20. A William Muff jnr, who was trading in Westgate, 1818–20, may be the same or another tradesman. [D]

Muggeridge, Frederick, Dorking, Surrey, cm and architect (1832). [D]

Muggleston, Isaac, Toll House Hill, Nottingham, joiner and cm (1799). [D]

Muggleworth, Henry, parish of St Werburgh, Bristol, upholder (1734–39). [Poll bks]

Mugg(e)ridge, Robert, London, cm (1826–35). Addresses given at 8 High St, Newington Butts, 1826–29; and Albion Pl., Walworth Rd in 1835. [D]

Muir, David, address unrecorded, cm (1793). Subscribed to Sheraton's *Drawing Book*, 1793.

Muir, James, 40 Union St, Middlx Hospital, London, cm (1785). Took out a Sun Insurance policy on 16 September 1785 for £40 on utensils and stock. [GL, Sun MS vol. 331, p. 577]

Muir, Nathan, 12 Peter St, Liverpool, cm and shopkeeper (1818). [D]

Mulford, Henry, Pye St, London, chairmaker (1794). [Poll bk] Possibly Henry Mumford.

Mullet, Thomas, High Wycombe, Bucks., chairmaker (1815–25). Sons bapt. in 1815 and 1825. [PR (bapt.)] Possibly Thomas Mullett.

Mullet, William, Chepping Wycombe Borough, High Wycombe, Bucks., chairmaker (1798). [Militia Census]

Mullett, James, Chepping Wycombe Borough, High Wycombe, Bucks., chairmaker (1798). [Militia Census]

Mullett, James, Moorfields, London, u (1819–35). Addresses given at 10 Broker Row, 1819–25; 9, 10 and 11 Bloomfield St, Finsbury Circus, 1826–27; 10 Blomfield St, Moorfields, 1827–28; and 1 and 2 Eldon St, Finsbury in 1835. [D] See Paul Mullett, possibly James's father.

Mullett, James & Co., 375 Strand, London, u and cabinet manufacturers (1835). [D]

Mullett, John, High Wycombe, Bucks., chairmaker (1798). [Militia Census]

Mullett, John, High Wycombe, Bucks., chairmaker

(b. *c.* 1791–1841). Sons bapt. in 1813, 1818 and 1823. Aged 50 at the time of the 1841 Census. [PR (bapt.)].

Mullett, Paul, Moorfields, London, u and furniture warehouse-man (1804–37). Various but probably synonymous addresses given at South Pl., Finsbury, as Mullet & Son, 1804–11; 1 Wilson St, Broker Row in 1808; 1 Moorfields, 1809–11; corner of Wilson (or Wilton) St, Finsbury, 1811–14; Finsbury House, South Pl., Finsbury Sq., 1820–27; 4 and 5 Bloomfield St, Finsbury Cresc. in 1825; and Eldon St, Finsbury Circus in 1837. Took out a Sun Insurance policy on 1 January 1824 for £2,500, including £1,300 on a house in the 'Spur Inn' Yd, Southwark Mkt, lodging rooms and stables; and £1,200 on stables, offices, warehouse, coach, counting and dwelling houses. [D; GL, Sun MS vol. 496, ref. 1012292] See James Mullett, possibly Paul's son.

Mullett, Samuel, Chepping Wycombe Borough, High Wycombe, Bucks., chairmaker (1798). [Militia Census]

Mullett, Thomas, Chepping Wycombe Borough, High Wycombe, Bucks., chairmaker (1798). [Militia Census] Possibly Thomas Mullet.

Mullett, Thomas, High Wycombe, Bucks., chairmaker (b. *c.* 1818–41). Aged 23 at the time of the 1841 Census.

Mullett, William, High Wycombe, Bucks., chairmaker (b. *c.* 1813–41). Daughter bapt. in 1835. Aged 28 at the time of the 1841 Census.

Mulley, John, Ipswich, Suffolk, u and cm (1830–39). Recorded in partnership with Benjamin Mulley at Northgate St in 1830; and both are listed as freemen burgesses in the Ipswich poll of 1832. John is recorded alone at Tavern St in 1839. [D; poll bks]

Mulligan, Robert, Mint St, near St George's Church, South-wark, London, sworn appraiser, bedstead maker and undertaker (*c.*1790). Trade card shows tea chest, bureau-bookcase with scroll pediment, drop-leaf table, dressing-glass and chair with pierced vase back splat. Card states that Mulligan '... Makes Cabinet & Upholstery work in General. Furnishes Houses on easy terms. Sells by Auction Household Goods, Estates & Merchandise of every kind ... N.B. serves Brokers & Upholsterers with Bedsteads ...'. [Heal]

Mullinder, John, Abbey St, Carlisle, Cumb., joiner and/or cm (1811–34). [D]

Mullings, Samuel, 19 Grafton St East, Tottenham Ct Rd, London, carver (1826–27). [D]

Mullins, Benoni, Northgate St, Devizes, Wilts., u and cm (1839). [D]

Mullins, James, New Park St, Devizes, Wilts, chairmaker (1839). [D]

Mullins, Thomas Owen, North St, Exeter, Devon, cm (1839). Son John Horn bapt. at St Mary Major on 31 March 1839. [PR (bapt.)]

Mumford, Charles, 5 Bedford Pl., Commercial Rd, London, u (1829). [D]

Mumford, F. jnr, 27 Bathwick St, Bath, Som., upholder (1819). [D]

Mumford, Francis, Bath, Som., u (1840). [GL, Sun MS vol. 267, ref. 1327511]

Mumford, Henry, Pye St, Westminster, London, chairmaker (1749). [Poll bk] Possibly Henry Mulford.

Mumford, Joseph, Old Kent Rd, Camberwell, London, cm and u (1822–28). Trading at Eden Pl. in 1822 and 8 Canal Pl., 1827–28. [D]

Mumford, Joseph, Severn Side, Bewdley, Worcs. cm and u (1835). [D]

Mumford, William, Norwich, cm (1812–30). Recorded in St Gregory's parish, 1812–18, and St Lawrence's, 1830. [Poll bks]

Mumford & Bailey, 2 Burton St, Bath, Som., u, cm and auctioneers (1826). [D]

Mummery, Stephen, London, cm and u (1818–39). Trading at Drury Lane in 1818, and 36 Brill Row, Somerstown in 1838. Polled at Canterbury in 1818 and 1830. [D]

Muncur, James, St Martin-in-the-Fields, London, cm (1749). [Poll bk]

Munday, James, Snow Fields, Bermondsey, London, chair-maker (1822). Took out a Sun Insurance policy on 15 May 1822 for £100 of which £50 accounted for stock and utensils. [GL, Sun MS vol. 490, ref. 991987]

Munday, Thomas, Oxford, upholder (1725–d. by 1772). Recorded in St Mary's parish in 1725, and St Aldates in 1772. As Thomas Monday, took out a Sun Insurance policy on 10 December 1725 for £500 on goods and merchandise in his house in St Mary's parish. On 3 December 1742 supplied St John's College with a mahogany dumb waiter costing £1 11s 6d, and an armchair for the Bursar's table, £2 5s. Appointment as Councillor reported in *Jackson's Oxford Journal*, 30 September 1769. On 11 November 1772 a probate was granted to his widow, Dame Sarah. [GL, Sun MS vol. 21, p. 316; Oxford consistory wills index] Possible relation to and confusion with:

Munday, Thomas, Oxford, upholder (1773–1802). Appoint-ment as Chamberlain reported in *Jackson's Oxford Journal*, 30 September, 1773. Recorded at High St in 1778 when an itinerant portrait painter from London advertised as lodging there in *Jackson's Oxford Journal*, 21 March. Named in the accounts for Worcester College on 10 March 1789, being paid 12s for 'Covering a card table with Green Cloath'. His youngest daughter, Mary's, marriage to Rev. Morgan Davis of Worcester College on 19 August 1790, reported in *Gents Mag*. Polled in 1802. [D; Worcester College archives.]

Munday, Thomas, London, u (1758). Named as heir of Thomas Munday of Pangbourne, Berks. regarding the lease and release of property in Whitchurch, Hants. [Oxford RO, FVI/10]

Munday, Thomas, High St, St Albans, Herts., cm/chairmaker (1826). [D]

Munday, William, 5 Lordship Pl., Chelsea, London, cm and u (1823). [D]

Munden, Stephen, Dover, Kent, cm (1826–35). Recorded at Market Pl. in 1832. [Poll bks]

Mundin, John, 2 Onslow St, Saffron Hill, London, chairmaker (1782–86). Took out Sun Insurance policies in 1782 for £300, £200 accounting for stock, stock and goods; and on 20 September 1786 for £100 on utensils etc. in shop and yard. [GL, Sun MS vol. 299, p. 652; vol. 338, p. 456]

Mundin, William & Mary, Round Ct, Onslow St, Saffron Hill, London, chairmakers (1792). Took out a Sun Insurance policy on 13 July 1792 for £150, including £130 on utensils and stock in workshops and open yard. [GL, Sun MS vol. 388, p. 268]

Munfort, Peter, East Dereham, Norfolk, cm (1743). Took app. named Drew in 1743. [S of G, app. index]

Munn, Joseph, Bunhill Row, London, cm (1820). Named as an orator in a court case concerning houses and mortgages in 1820. [PRO, C13 266/5]

Munns, Richard, Oxford St, London, furniture warehouseman, u, cm and furniture printer (1827–40). [D] Recorded as Munns & Co., late Miles, in 1827, 1832–39; and as R. Munns & Son at nos 33 and 34 in 1840. As Munn, named as party in a courtcase against Pittman in 1827. [PRO, C13 1476] Submitted a bill to John Arkwright of Hampton Court, Leominster, Herefs., dated 21 December 1832, for a mahogany sideboard costing £26. In his covering letter, Munns wrote: 'We should feel much obliged by the favour of the amount & soliciting your further esteemed commands which shall at all times have our best & immediate attention.' [Herefs. RO, A63/161] R. Munns & Son advertised in *Morning Chronicle*, 16 October 1840, their immense stock of cabinet furniture, offered a little more than half the price usually asked by the trade in London. Stock included dining tables and sideboards of every size, a hundred dozen parlour chairs, two hundred and twenty rosewood chairs; every article being manufactured 'by first rate workmen of best seasoned materials'. Goods would be exchanged if not approved in twelve months. On 17 October 1840 the firm advertised sale of upholstery materials, including 'splendid & superior drawing room curtains ... unequalled novelties of drawing, dining room & boudoir curtains'; and stock of Lyons and Spitalfields silk damask, 'satin stiped tabarets', mohair, 'merino damasks', 'arabesque tournays', cashmeres, 'town printed chintzes', 'velours d'Utrecht', embroidered cloths, gilt cornices and rich fringes. As manufacturers and importers, they claimed their rates were 25% cheaper, through not using a middle-man.

Munns, Thomas, Cambridge, chairmaker (1710). Described as a 'poor chairmaker' in Cooper's *Annals of Cambridge*, 1852, p. 92.

Munro, David, near Covent Gdn, London, cm (1753). Marriage to Miss Freebairn reported in *Public Advertiser*, 20 October 1753. See David Monroe, and Mure & Monro.

Munro, John, Chandos St, London, cm (1749). [Poll bk]

Munro, R., 33 Oxford St, London, printer, u and cm (1825). [D] See R. Munns at this address.

Munro, Thomas, Dunning St, Sunderland, Co. Durham, joiner and cm (1828–29). [D]

Munro, Thomas, 50 Howland St, London, cm and u (1835–39). [D]

Munro, William, Manchester and Salford, Lancs., builder, joiner and cm (1825–40). Recorded at 140 Long Millgate, Manchester in 1825; no. 148 in 1832–33; 24 Gravel Lane, 1834–40; as Monro in 1834; and 61 Gravel Lane in 1840. [D]

Munt, George, 85 Blackman St, London, upholder (1782). [D]

Murch, W., 1 Oxenden St, Coventry St, London, carver etc. (1826–27). [D]

Murcott, William, Gloucester, cm (1777). Insured his house for £300 in 1777. [GL, Sun MS vol. 259, p. 119]

Murdoch (or Murdock), John, Blackmoor (or Blackman) St, Clare Mkt, London, cm and u (1774–93). Insured his house for £300 in 1774. [D; poll bk; GL, Sun MS vol. 272, p. 474]

Murdock, W., 56 Warren St, Fitzroy Sq., London, carver and gilder (1809–11). [D]

Mure, H. & Monro, David, at 'The Chair', Wardour St, St Anne's, London, cm (1785). Trade card recorded. [Heal] See David Monroe and David Munro.

Murgatroyd, A., 2 Knightsbridge, London, portable desk maker (1820). [D]

Murgatroyd, A., 18 Stafford Row, near the New Palace, Pimlico, London, military trunk and solid leather portmanteau maker, undertaker (1837–39). Named in the Royal Household Accounts on 24 August 1837 supplying 'four Square Boxes for Bonnets', costing £6 8s; and on 30 June 1839, '9 strong Wainscot Chests' and '3 Chests 3' 2" long', totalling £69 15s. [Windsor Royal Archives]

Murie, Mary, 39 Frederick St, St James's, Liverpool, u (1837). [D]

Murphy, John, Liverpool, cm (1819). App. to Thomas Dutton in 1819. [Liverpool app. enrolment bk]

Murray, Alexander, London, glass grinder, probably carver and gilder (1773–80). Recorded at White Lyon St, St Giles, in 1780 when he acted as assignee of commission in the bankruptcy case against William Gates, cm to the Lord

Chancellor's Office, on 3 March. [PRO, LC5/106, p. 40] In 1773 Murray supplied furniture to the Morant family of Brokenhurst Park, Hants. An entry in Edward Morant's notebook, dated 10 July 1773 refers 'To your bill to Alexander Murray pr. glasses £316.', provided for Morant's London house at 17 Park Lane. They can be identified as the pair of large gilt mirrors in the Adam taste, with wide frames pierced with ovals and surmounted by a design of braziers and pairs of winged gryphons. Once at Brokenhurst, the mirrors are now at Basildon Park, Berks. Murray's receipt for them is in the MMA, NY. Murray also supplied to Morant's Park Lane house two semi-circular tables with caryatid supports. A gilt settee in the French taste from a suite of furniture from Brokenhurst Park has been attributed to Murray, as the carved detail agrees closely with that of his looking-glasses. [*Antique Collector*, August 1954, pp. 132–40; *Conn.*, March 1974; *C. Life*, 12 May 1977, p. 1230; V&A archives]

Murray, Archibald, St Martin-in-the-Fields, London, u and cm (1754–62). Took app. named Thomas Pallant for £31 10s in 1754, when an Archibald Murray subscribed to Chippendale's *Director*. Of St Martin's Lane he took out Sun Insurance policies on 21 May 1761; and on 23 August 1762 for £900, including £150 on utensils and stock in a brick workshop in yard. [GL, Sun MS refs 182760 and 191993]

Murray, Charles & Son, High St, Uxbridge, Middlx, cm and u (1826). [D]

Murray, David, address unrecorded, cm (1803). Subscribed to Sheraton's *Cabinet Dictionary*, 1803.

Murray, George, London, cm, carver and picture frame maker (1744–52). Master Sculptor and Carver to the Crown, and earlier assistant to James Richards. [*Conn.*, June 1981, p. 144] Polled at Westminster of Pall Mall in 1749. Named in part of Edward Godfrey's account to Augusta, Princess of Wales, submitting a bill in January 1744/45 for £7 17s 6d. [Windsor Royal Archives, RA 55435] Carried out work at Moulsham Hall, Essex, for Earl Fitzwalter, receiving £20 of his bill for £48 17s 6d on 18 February 1747; and £28 11s on 17 July, as well as a further payment of £95 11s 6d. On 17 December 1748 his bill for £5 17s 6d was paid in full. [A. C. Edwards, *The Accounts of Benjamin Mildmay, Earl Fitzwalter*, pp. 111–12] In 1752 Murray carved the Great Room chimney frame at Mr Pelham's house in Arlington St, London. [RIBA Lib., MS 728.3 (42.13A)]

Murray, George, Tweedmouth, Northumb., cm, u and carpet manufacturer (1757–d.1768). Took apps named Oliver in 1757 and Cowen in 1758. [S of G, app. index] Advertised in *Newcastle Courant*, 13 June 1767 that he 'has just imported from Sussex, a large quantity of Field Turnip Seed ... which he proposes to sell...'. Dead by 13 February 1768, when notice of the sale on 14 March of his household furniture and stock in trade appeared in *Newcastle Chronicle*. Stock included 'a very large Assortment of Mahogany and other Tables, Bureaus, Chests of Drawers, Glasses, a great variety of Paper Hangings, Wilton and Scotch Carpets, many webs of Carpeting, a great Quantity of wool, Longwood, Madder, Cochineal, and other Dyes used in dying the Yarn for carpets &c. Also all the Looms, and Cabinet-Maker's tools, and many other Articles too tedious to particularize. After the sale of the above-mentioned Goods, about 6,000 feet of Mahogany and a large Quantity of Beech, Walnut Tree, Wainscot and other wood will be put up to sale in small lots of about 100 feet each Lot...'. A similar advertisement appeared in *Newcastle Chronicle*, 7 May 1768.

Murray, James, 1 King St, Golden Sq., London, cm (1808). [D]

Murray, John, 42 Clipstone St, Marylebone, London, cm (1809–11). [D]

Murray, Martin, Drake St, Rochdale, Lancs., cm and chair-maker (1825). [D]

Murray, Richard, Wyle Cop, Shrewsbury, Salop, u (1796). [Shrewsbury burgess roll]

Murray, Richard, Wolverhampton, Staffs., u (1818–22). Trading at King St in 1822. [D]

Murray, Richard, Digbeth, Walsall, Staffs., cm and u (1834–35). [D]

Murray, Thomas Slater, Liverpool, cm (b.1811–d.1833). Death aged 22 reported in *Liverpool Mercury*, 2 August 1833.

Murray, Thomas, Adelaide Pl., Exeter, Devon, cm (1834). Son Thomas bapt. at St Sidwell's on 13 April 1834. [PR (bapt.)]

Murray, William, The Broadway, Westminster, London, cm (1774). [Poll bk]

Murray, William, Stamford, Lincs., cm (1791–98). [D]

Murray & Jeacocke, 28 Charles St, Tottenham Ct Rd, London, cm and u (1839). [D]

Murrell(s), Ambrose, Sepulchre St, Sudbury, Suffolk, cm (1839). [D]

Murrell, Charles, Chelmsford, Essex, cm (1826). [Maldon poll bk]

Murrell, James, Lindfield, Sussex, chairmaker (1832). [D]

Murrell, John, 14 Gibson St, Lambeth, London, cm, u and undertaker (1839). [D]

Muscroft, John, Tadcaster, Yorks., joiner and/or cm (1834). [D]

Muse, John, Haydon Bridge, Hexham, Northumb., joiner and cm (1828–29). [D]

Musgrave, George, Kirkby Malzeard, near Masham, Yorks., cm (1822). [D]

Musgrave, Thomas, 14 Spring St, Paddington, London, carver and gilder (1826–27). [D]

Musgraves, George, Garden St, Wakefield, Yorks., cm (1814). [D]

Musgrove, Edwin Duckworth, Liverpool, u and cm (1837–39). Trading at 48 Gt Orford St in 1837 and 9 Commutation Row in 1839. [D]

Mush, Frederick, York, cm (1809). Son of William Mush, gardener of Fulford, York; app. to Thomas Walls, cm, on 2 January 1809. [York app. reg.] Possibly Frederick Musham.

Mush, John, 47 King St, Manchester, u and paper hanging manufacturer (1825). [D]

Musham, Frederick, York, cm and upholder (1821–40). Recorded at Blake St in 1823, no. 6, 1828–37; and 100 Micklegate in 1840. Took apps named Leonard Lumley on 13 February 1821, George Scott on 18 June 1832, and Thomas Scott on 25 February 1835. [D; York app. reg.] Possibly Frederick Mush.

Musker, Robert, Liverpool, cm (1823). App. to John Chesters in 1823. [Liverpool app. enrolment bk]

Muskett, Joseph, West St, London, picture frame maker and gilder (1776–77). Took out Sun Insurance policies in 1776 for £100 of which utensils, stock and goods accounted for £40; and in 1777 for £200, utensils, stock and goods accounting for £100. [GL, Sun MS vol. 246, p. 535; vol. 257, p. 284]

Muspratt, Thomas, Colebrook St, Winchester, Hants., cm (1823–24). [D]

Muspratt, Thomas, Southampton, Hants., cm and u (1823–30). Recorded at Colebrook St in 1823 and 11 Bedford Terr. in 1830. [D]

Musto, Charles, Back St, Horslydown, (London?), cm (1777–84). Took out Sun Insurance policies in 1777 for £500, £380 accounting for utensils and stock; and in 1780 for £200, £70 on utensils and stock. [D; GL, Sun MS vol. 256, p. 150; vol. 283, p. 175]

Musto, Charles, 104 Barnaby St, London, cm (1780). Took out a Sun Insurance policy in 1780 for £200, £100 on utensils and stock. [GL, Sun MS vol. 285, p. 114]

Muston, James, Hatton Gdn, London, wholesale u (1806–39). Recorded at no. 80, 1806–19; no. 81, 1820–39; and at 27 Leather Lane in 1825. This may be the back entrance to Muston's Hatton Gdn premises. [D]

Mutch, John, 101 Finch St, Liverpool, u (1829). [D]

Mutton, Henry, All Saints' Passage, Cambridge, carver, gilder and printseller (1839–41). Trade card gives address at no. 4, and reads: 'Rose, Maple, Satin & other woods in great Variety. Arms, Crest, Visiting, Compliment & Address cards, Engraving & Copper Plate Printing.' [D; poll bks; Johnson Coll., Bodleian Lib., Oxford; *Furn. Hist.*, 1974]

Mutton, William, Huntingdon, carver and gilder (1821–32). Recorded at High St, 1830–32. Possibly the 'Mutton carver & gilder' who was paid £4 10s 6d for work at Brampton House, for Lady O. B. Sparrow, 1821–23. [D; poll bk; Hunts. RO, DDM 16/5]

Mutton, William, Trinity St, Cambridge, carver and gilder (1839–41). [D; poll bks]

Myatt, William, Piccadilly, Hanley (or Shelton), Staffs., cm and u (1818–35). [D]

Mycroft, John, Newark, Notts., cm (1793–98). [D]

Myers, Christopher, address unrecorded, upholder (1709). Admitted freeman of the Upholders' Co. on 2 November 1709. [GL, Upholders' Co. records]

Myers, Christopher, Whitehaven, Cumb., cm (1748). Took app. named Wilson in 1748. [S of G, app. index]

Myers, Edward, Liverpool, cm (1780–1810). Addresses given at 44 Ranelagh St, 1787–90; no. 41 in 1794; no. 42, 1800–07; also no. 40 in 1800 and 1804; 28 Clarence St in 1805; and Bridport St in 1810. Admitted freeman on servitude to Isaac Marsh on 11 September 1780. Took apps named Robert Roberts in 1787, petitioned freedom in 1802; Ralph Magill in 1788, petitioned in 1796; and Thomas Hindley in 1804, assigned to John Ward Turner in 1809, and petitioned freedom in 1812. George Bibby was assigned by Edward Myers in 1795, and petitioned freedom in 1802. His son, William Myers, cm, petitioned freedom on birthright in 1802. [D; Liverpool freemen reg. and committee bk]

Myers, Emanuel, 28 High St, Whitechapel, London, looking-glass manufacturer (1839). [D]

Myers, Michael, 21 Blackman St, Southwark, London, cm (1829). [D]

Myers, Richard, High St, Edgehill, Liverpool, cm (1827–35). Recorded at no. 50 in 1827 and 1834; no. 51 in 1829; and no. 52 in 1835. [D]

Myers, Thomas, Lancaster, joiner and cm (1760–80). App. to J. Wright in 1760, and admitted freeman, 1779–80, when stated of Wrexham, Wales. [Lancaster app. reg. and freemen rolls]

Myers, Thomas, Lancaster. Named in the Gillow records, 1807–40. [Westminster Ref. Lib.] Two dressing tables made by Gillows for Parlington Hall, Yorks., were signed in pencil on the drawer bottom 'Thos Myers'. [Gilbert, *Leeds Furn. Cat.*, no. 500]

Myers, Thomas, Masham, Yorks., joiner and cm (1828–29). [D]

Myers, William, Liverpool, cm (1806). Admitted freeman on 5 November 1806 as son of Edward Myers, cm. [Liverpool freemen reg.]

Myers, William, Meltham, Huddersfield, Yorks., joiner and/or cm (1834). [D]

Myers, Wolfe, High St, Chelmsford, Essex, cm, u and furniture broker (1832–39). [D]

Myerscough, Richard, Lancaster, cm (1829). Marriage on 20 January 1829 to Miss Elizabeth Bates of Liverpool reported in *Liverpool Mercury*, 6 February 1829.

Myles Custance, John, 74 Long Acre, London, cm, u and undertaker (1785). Took out a Sun Insurance policy on 1 June

1785 for £150 on household goods, and £300 on utensils and stock. [GL, Sun MS vol. 328, p. 412]

Mynett, George, Stroud, Glos., cm (1824). [PR (bapt.)]

Myres, Watt, Low Jubbergate, York, cm (1745). Recorded in *York Courant*, 15 January 1745.

Mysell, Charles, 18 Barbican, London, clock-case maker (1810). Took out a Sun Insurance policy on 15 November 1810 for £1,300, including £500 on two houses and offices at 11 and 12 Barbican, £300 on warehouse and rooms over sawpits in the yard behind; and £500 on stock and utensils. [GL, Sun MS vol. 449, ref. 850600]

N

Nadby, George, 18 Queen St, Seven Dials, London, cm (1794). In July 1794 took out insurance cover of £400 on his house, its contents and stock in a shop. [GL, Sun MS vol. 401, ref. 630384]

Nailor, Robert, York, u (1713). In 1713 his son Francis was made a freeman of York. [Freemen rolls]

Nailor, Thomas, Wath, Yorks., joiner and cm (1798). [D]

Nairn, Thomas, 15 Rupert St, Liverpool, carver and gilder (1827–32). His trade card [Landauer Coll., MMA, NY] states that he cleaned and repaired old paintings, 'Branches for Lights, Paintings, Looking Glasses Prints & Needle Work Framed. Figures, Bronzes, Old Work Cleaned, Gilt Borders for Rooms. Transparencies Painted. Ornamental & Fancy work in General Executed'. In February 1832 his wife Ann died aged 63. [*Liverpool Mercury*, 2 March 1832]

Nairne, Charles, Ramsgate and Sandwich, Kent, cm (1831–39). Freeman of Sandwich. Living in Ramsgate 1831–32 but shown at Sandwich in July 1837. Trading in Ramsgate in 1839. [D; Sandwich poll bks]

Naisbett, John, Holywell St, Westminster, London, cm (1774). [Poll bk]

Naish, Catherine, St Mary-le-Strand, London, u and chairmaker (1759–72). A noted supplier of furniture to the Royal family. The earliest known commission was a set of eight mahogany backstools with compass fronts and tops at 15s each for Prince William's House in Leicester Sq. These were supplied in 1759 the year in which she succeeded her father Henry Williams to the business. She became chairmaker to George III in the following year and provided in that year a large state cradle with a canopy top. This had 'carved ornaments to clip each corner and round the bottom and top, and up the front of the head with a crown and plume of feathers for the top and Lions heads at each end of the rockers and gilt in burnished gold & two pairs of neat chased handles'. For the Great Drawing Room, St James's Palace a 'large four-post mahogany State Bedstead with carved headboard, being a scroll supporting a crown and other elaborate decorations, for the Queen to sit up in' was supplied at a cost of £205. For Buckingham House in 1767 a set of 'Twelve very neat Mahogany Hall chairs with Hollow Seats and open Backs and cross stretchers' were provided for the hall at £2 5s each. A number of these chairs survive. Other commissions (noted in PRO, LC accounts) included a walnut settee the feet carved with Lions' paws and leaves on the Knees to Match some chairs', supplied in 1765 at a cost of £4 10s, and a mahogany sofa on castors with four straight legs in 1772 costing £3 10s. Split wicker cradles for the royal children were also invoiced at £13 2s each. The only other known commissions are to be noted in the Strathmore papers in respect of Gibside, Co. Durham. In 1761 a 'Mr Nance' was paid through the bankers Child & Co. for 'two Moulding Desert Frames, Water Gilding ditto, two Silver'd Glasses for ditto, bought in London June last'. Despite the error in the name this commission was probably executed by Catherine Naish. She died early in 1772 or possibly the year before, for a receipt given in 1772 was in the name of her executors. [PRO, LC5/105, LC9/292–94; *C. Life* 10 November 1960, p. 1108, 21 December 1961, p. 1577; V&A Archives; H. Clifford Smith, *Buckingham Palace*, pp. 72, 79; *DEF*, III, p. 1; *CGM*; Durham RO, Strathmore MS, D/St/V 994]

Nancolas, William, Langley St, Long Acre, London, cm (1774). [Westminster poll bk]

Naniant, Francis, 'The Golden Hand', Little Newport St, Leicester Fields, London, varnish maker, frame maker and gilder (1763). [D]

Nappi, P., 7 Charles St, Middlx Hospital, London, mosaic painter (1830). On 26 June 1830 invoiced to the Lord Chamberlain's Dept 'a Malechite coffer with cameos mosaics and very richly ornamented with ormolu, size 20 in by 11, standing on a table with antique black marble top and sides, supported by curved gilt legs three feet high'. For this £241 10s was charged. [PRO, LC11/68]

Nash, Mrs, 20 Philadelphia St, Bristol, u (1827–40). [D]

Nash, Goodwin, Bristol, cm (1793–1800). Shown in directories at Lodge St, 1793–94, and Corn St in 1795. Bankrupt in February 1798 but from 1799–1800 shown trading at 14 Clarence Pl. [D; *Billinge's Liverpool Advertiser*, 19 February 1798]

Nash, Harry, Worcester, u (1727). App. to Henry Lingon and free by servitude, 24 August 1727. [Freemen rolls]

Nash, Henry, Downshire Hill, Hampstead, London, cm and u (1839). [D]

Nash, James, 16 Wapping Wall, London, cm (1776–83). In both 1776 and 1782 took out insurance cover for £400. Of this £200 covered stock and utensils in 1776 and £250 in 1782. He owned a number of houses which were valued in 1783 at £300. [GL, Sun MS vol. 247, p. 271; vol. 279, p. 606; vol. 300, p. 380; vol. 319, p. 160]

Nash, James, West St, Leominster, Herefs., turner and chairmaker (1830–35). [D]

Nash, John, London, cm, u and undertaker (1784–95). At 22 Vine St, Piccadilly, 1784–87; but from 1789 at 46 Brewer St, Golden Sq. His two trade cards dated 1787 and 1791 [Banks Coll., BM] show engravings of chairs and mirrors in the style of the 1750s and 60s. Subscribed to Sheraton's *Drawing Book*, 1793. Bankrupt June 1795. [D; *Liverpool Advertiser*, 8 June 1795]

Nash, John Downley, High Wycombe, Bucks., chairmaker (1830). [D]

Nash, Robert, address unknown (1759–65). Recorded repairing japan cabinets at Temple Newsam House, Leeds in January 1759 and cleaning and repairing an 'India Pearl Screen, a Lacquered Screen and a Tonquin Trunk' for St John Griffin Griffin at Audley End, Essex in 1765. [*Furn. Hist.*, 1967; Essex RO, D/DBy/A23/12]

Nash, Thomas, St Clement Danes, London, cm (1692). His app. was discharged as Nash had ill-treated him. [GL, Middlx session bk 494, p. 66]

Nash, Thomas, 'The Royal Bed', Holborn Bridge, London, u (1714–d. 1748). Took out a Sun Insurance policy on 16 July 1714 on goods and merchandise in his house. Advertised in November 1722 that he had a stock of calico quilts and pointed out that these would not be available so readily after Christmas when a new Act of Parliament would impose £20 fines to protect the British textile industries. In partnership with a John Hill by April 1724 and although the Holborn

Bridge premises continued to be the base of operations goods and merchandise were also kept at a new house at 'The Golden Ball', New Buildings, Fleet Ditch. Later the business traded as a partnership between Thomas Nash, Elkington Hall and Richard Whitehorne and they issued an elaborate trade card showing as fine state bed in a fashionable interior. The partners indicated that they made and sold 'Fashionable Silk & Stuff Beds, with all other sorts of Upholsterers Goods. And large Sconces, Pier & Chimney Glasses, Dressing glasses, Chest of Draw's, Buroes, Desk & Book-cases, Mahogany tables, Card tables, Chairs & Settees, and all other Sorts of Cabinet Work'. They offered their services as appraisers. Thomas Nash was clearly a person of some status and in March 1733 was nominated for Governor of St Bartholomew's Hospital. At the time of his death on 23 October 1748 he was described as an 'eminent upholsterer' and a Common Councillor for the ward of Faringdon Without; 'a person of good Character and esteem'd by all his Acquaintances'. At this point only one of the partners was still active in the business, and on 3 March 1749, due to pressure by the executors, part of the stock was sold off by auction.

Few of Nash's patrons are known, but one of them was Joseph Banks jnr who wrote to Joseph Banks of Revesby, Lincs. on 9 May 1716 complaining that 'upon examining the bed Mr. Nash of Fleet Ditch has sent me I find it the most scurvy thing that ever was imposed on any body'. Richard Hoare who supported 'Nash & Son' in May 1740 was probably more satisfied with the two mahogany bookcases and other work carried out for which £19 4s 6d was charged. He made a payment to Nash on 13 November 1741 of £17 16s 6d which was probably for other work. [GL, Sun MS vol. 4, ref. 4186; vol. 10, 11 August 1719; vol. 10, ref. 4843; vol. 16, ref. 31730; *The Post Boy*, 15 November 1722; *London Evening Post*, 11–13 November 1740, 22–25 October 1748; *Daily Advertiser*, 11 February 1749; 3 March 1749; *General Advertiser*, 25 October 1748; Heal; St Bartholomew's Hospital archives; Hill, *Letters . . . of the Banks Family . . .*, p. 21; V & A Lib., 86 NN. 3; Hoare's Bank archives]

Nash, Thomas, 14 Charles St, Cavendish Sq., London, cm (1778–79). A fairly substantial business with an insurance cover of £600 on its utensils and stock in 1778. Thomas Nash was however bankrupt by November of the following year. [GL, Sun MS vol. 264, p. 11; *Gents Mag.*, November 1779]

Nash, Thomas, High St, Stourbridge, Worcs., cm and u (1835). [D]

Nash, Timothy, Charles St, Bristol, cm (1828–32). At 19 Charles St, 1828–29, but from the following year the number was 10. [D]

Nash, William, 5 Queen St, Seven Dials, London, carver (1776). In 1776 insured his house for £100. [GL, Sun MS vol. 253, p. 441]

Nash, William, London, chairmaker (1820–39). At 24 Commercial Rd, Lambeth in 1820, 4 Robert St, Blackfriars in 1826 but in 1829 the number had changed to 8. At 14 Gibson St, Lambeth in 1835 but by 1839 the number had changed to 45. [D]

Nason, Charles William, Abington St, Northampton, cm (1830). [D; poll bk]

Nation, Robert, 175 High St, Deritend, Birmingham, cm and u (1830). [D]

Nation, Samuel, London, chairmaker (1808–39). In 1808–18 at 146 New Gravel Lane, Shadwell but 1821–35 at 87 Old Gravel Lane. In 1839 the number was 88. In December 1821 took out insurance cover of £400 of which £300 was in respect of stock and utensils in a workshop behind his house

and in an open yard. [D; GL, Sun MS vol. 480; ref. 948315; vol. 491, ref. 987276]

Natt, Joseph, 34 Back Hope St, Leeds, Yorks., carver and gilder (1822). [D]

Natt, Joseph, 10 Osmaston (or Osmarton) St, Derby, carver, gilder, looking-glass and picture frame manufacturer (1823–35). [D]

Natt, Thomas, Manchester, carver and gilder (1800–94). At 55 Hart St in 1800 and 9 Market St Lane in 1804. [D]

Natt, Thomas, 9 Market St Lane, Birmingham, carver and gilder (1805). [D]

Navin, Thomas, 16 Rupert St, Liverpool with shop at 10 Wood St, carver and gilder (1829). [D]

Nayers, John, Worcester, cm (1812). App. to William Handy and free by servitude, 13 October 1812. [Freemen rolls]

Naylor, Henry, Host St, Bristol, painter and furniture japanner (1799–1807). In 1806–07 the business is listed as Naylor & Barrett. [D]

Naylor, James, Lancaster, cm (1789–1822). Free 1813–14. Named in the Gillow records 1789, 1791, 1820, 1822. In 1820 named in the making of a commode. [Westminster Ref. Lib., Gillow vol. 344/100, p. 3042]

Naylor, James, Liverpool, cm and u (1823–31). In 1823 at 29 Soho St with a shop at 33 Woollen Hall but in the following year at 28 Soho St and 34 Richmond Fair. After 1827 at 30 Islington. It was from this address in 1829 that he advertised for sale 'a large & elegant Assortment of Household Furniture' which included 'an elegant Rosewood Cabinet Piano-forte'. By October 1831 however the business was insolvent. [D; *Liverpool Mercury*, 26 June 1829, 14 October 1831]

Naylor, James, Rawdon, Yorks, cm (1830). [D]

Naylor, John, Salford Cresc., Salford, Lancs., cm (1781). [D]

Naylor, John, 14 Mint St, Southward, London, bedstead maker and cm (1808–20). [D]

Naylor, John, Leeds, Yorks., cm (1822–34). In 1822 at Hunslet and in 1830 at Hunslet Moor Side. By 1834 had moved to 3 Bethel St, Jack Lane. [D]

Naylor, Robert H., Darlington, Co. Durham, cm (1827–34). In 1827 at Deanery, in 1829 at Thompson's Yd and in 1834 at Horsemarket. [D]

Naylor, Thomas, Liverpool, u (1803–24). At Byrom St where the number was 14 in 1804, 33 in 1805 and 29 in 1807. He was probably the Naylor, u who subscribed to Sheraton's *Cabinet Dictionary*, 1803. By 1808 however he was bankrupt and in August his stock and household furniture was sold by auction to help meet his debts. His stock at this time consisted of 'a great variety of Brussels, Kidderminster & Venetian Carpeting; Imperial Hearth Rugs; Blankets; Counterpanes; A large & Fashionable Assortment Oil Cloths (in various widths); about Thirteen Hundred Pieces Modern Paper Hanging & Flock Borders; fine Bed Ticks; Fringes; Bed Laces; Tasells; Lines; Hair Seatings; Brass Work; half a ton Flocks etc.' In July of the following year a dividend of 10s in the £ was announced for his creditors. Business must have re-commenced soon after for in 1810–11 he is shown trading at 29 and 30 Byrom St moving in 1813 to 3 Circus St. From 1816–18 he was at 3 Gerard St and in 1824 at Baptist Lane. [D; *Liverpool Courier*, 10 August 1808, 5 July 1809, 19 July 1809]

Naylor, William, Lancaster, cm (1784–1800). App. to William Blackburn 1775 and free by servitude, 1781–82. Named in the Gillow records, c. 1784 and 1786–1800. [App. reg.; poll bk; Westminster Ref. Lib., Gillow]

Neal, John, Liverpool, cm (1816). Free 6 June 1816. [Freeman reg.]

Neal, William, Clapham Common, London, upholder, joiner

and cm (1803–08). In 1808 shown as upholder at Clapham Common. The Neal of Clapham, joiner and cm who subscribed to Sheraton's *Cabinet Dictionary*, 1803, is probably the same person. [D]

Neal, William, 13 Regent St, Piccadilly, London, u (1825). [D]

Neale, Charles, Cornhill, Ipswich, Suffolk, cm and u (1830–35). [D]

Neale, James, London, u and cm and chairmaker (1826–39). At 47 Liquerpond St, Hatton Gdn, 1826–28, and 288 High Holborn, 1835–39. [D]

Neale, John, London, carver and gilder (1750–60). Supplied gilded frames and mirror surrounds to Henry Pelham's house, 22 Arlington St, London, 1750. In 1756–60 he was the gilder and painter in the State Rooms at Holkham, Norfolk. [RIBA, MS 728.3 (42.13A); Holkham MSS, Country Accts, 8]

Neale, Philip, 10 Mint St, Southwark, bedstead maker (1826). [D]

Nealey, Matthew, Workington, Cumb., joiner and cm (1828–34). At Ballast Hill in 1828, the Quay in 1829 and Henry St in 1834. [D]

Nealms, Richard, 13 Hatton Wall, London, cm and broker (1781). In 1781 took out insurance cover of £200 of which half was in respect of utensils and stock. [GL, Sun MS, vol. 299, p. 96]

Neat, John, Brook Rent near the Turnpike, Tottenham Ct Rd, London, cm (1778). In 1778 insured a house for £100. [GL, Sun MS vol. 262, p. 580]

Neate, John, Charles Ct, Hungerford Mkt, Westminster, London, cm (1774). [Poll bk]

Neate, John, 2 Brill Row, Somers Town, London, cm (1808). [D]

Neave, John, 101 High Holborn, London, cm (1767–82). [D]

Neck, John, Launceston, Cornwall, cm u and shopkeeper (1777–83). In 1777 took out insurance cover of £500 of which £400 was in respect of stock and utensils. [D: GL, Sun MS vol. 263, p. 132]

Nedby, William, 75 Lambs Conduit St, London, cm (1817). [D]

Needham, Richard, Hanley St, Liverpool, cm (1835–39). At 19 Handley St in 1835 but by 1839 the number was 8. [D]

Needle, Thomas, 26 Hurst St, Birmingham, chairmaker (1828–35). Listed at Herst St in 1828, 26 Hurst St in 1830 and no. 13 in 1835. [D]

Needs, Elizabeth, South St, Exeter, Devon, u (1816–33). [D]

Neilson, Lawrence, 7 Frith St, Soho, London, cm (1777). In 1777 took out insurance cover of £500 of which £100 was in respect of utensils and stock. [GL, Sun MS vol. 260, p. 70]

Neilson, Lawrence, 78 Margaret St, Cavendish Sq., London, u (1786). [D]

Neilson, William, 7 Bolsover St, Oxford St, London, cm (1808). [D]

Nellteton, Thomas, Pontefract, Yorks., joiner/cm (1834). [D]

Nelme, Anthony, address unknown, looking-glass maker (1714). [*C. Life*, 7 January 1960, p. 14] He may be connected with the English silversmith of that name who worked in the Huguenot manner.

Nelmes, George, Malmsbury, Wilts., u (1723). In October 1723 took out insurance cover of £300 on his dwelling house, stable and goods. [GL, Sun MS vol. 17, ref. 30092]

Nelmes, Richard, 12 Hatton Wall, London, broker and cm (1789–1809). [D]

Nelson, —, Shrewsbury, Salop, architect, carver and gilder (1798). Possibly the John Nelson (1726–1812) recorded in Gunnis. [D]

Nelson, David, Marylebone, London, cm (1770). Bankruptcy announced, *Gents Mag.*, September 1770.

Nelson, Henry, 14 New North St, Red Lion Sq., London, carver and gilder (1820). [D]

Nelson, Henry, South St, Greenwich, London, carver and gilder (1839). [D]

Nelson, Jeffrey, address unknown, carver (1794). Undertook carving at 15 St James's Sq., London. [Staffs. RO, Anson papers D615, E(H)(59)]

Nelson, John, Market Pl., Malton, Yorks., cm and appraiser (1834–40). Successor to Richard Nelson at this address. [D]

Nelson, Joseph, Liverpool, cm (1840). Free 27 July 1840. [Freemen reg.]

Nelson, Richard, Market Pl., Malton, Yorks., cm (1830). Succeeded at this address in 1834 by John Nelson. [D]

Nelson, Robert, Liverpool, chairmaker (1821–34). At 111 London Rd in 1821, 23 Lime St, 1823–24 and 11 Bottom St, Edgehill in 1834. [D]

Nelson, Robert, Market Pl., Bishop Auckland, Co. Durham, joiner and cm (1827–28). [D]

Nelson, Samuel, Liverpool, cm (1802–12). App. to John Eden and free by servitude, 5 July 1802. Shown in directories at Castle Ditch, Henington St in 1804 and 2 Union Ct, Duckworth St, 1813–14. The Liverpool freemen reg. however indicates that he died in 1812. [D; freemen reg.]

Nelson, Sefferin (sometimes 'Saffron'), Marshall St, Golden Sq., London, carver and gilder (1769–c.1796). An important craftsman employed on many of the major building projects of this period for carved work in wood. He had associations with the leading architects of the period such as Robert Adam and Henry Holland under whose general supervision he worked. He is often mentioned in Adam's bank account (Drummonds). The usual address quoted in connection with his work is that in Marshall St, probably his dwelling house. One directory of 1784 however also lists an address at 4 Carnaby Mkt. His trade card [Dept of Prints, V&A] displays the shape of a mirror frame with swags, lion masks and surmounted by a crest incorporating a lion and unicorn. The text indicates that he was carver and frame maker to 'their Royal Highnesses the Prince of Wales, the Duke of Cumberland'. The exact date of death is not known but a payment of 1797 was made to his executors. His known commissions include:

SHELBURNE HOUSE, London. Worked here under the supervision of Robert Adam, 1769.

KENWOOD, Highgate, London. Amongst the Adam drawings in the Soane Museum is one for 'a term for the great staircase at Kenwood'. This drawing includes a note that 'Mr Nelson to make one complete, if that is liked he is to do three more'.

HOME HOUSE, 20 Portman Square, London. Worked here under the supervision of Robert Adam, 1775.

DERBY HOUSE, London. An account exists dated 30 April 1776 for furniture including 'Four Girandoles on the Collumns in the Great Drawing Room from a design of Messrs Adams'. The items supplied cost £109 2s 6d.

CROOME COURT, Worcs. 1781. Capitals to columns and 2 pilasters.

CHATSWORTH, Derbs. Recorded working in the house in 1782 and 1784. In 1782 the work involved the Music Room, the Drawing Room and the Library. Major items included carving and gilding eight candelabras for the Music Room at a cost of £109 3s, supplying two glass frames for the Drawing Room at £76 12s, two tables at £58 and three curtain cornices at £67 10s. Three hundred feet of border were supplied for this room at £45 7s and gilding the cornice round the bookcases in the Library cost £37 3s. A further account of 1784 involved carved window draperies and other ornaments in the Music Room. Included in this account were two tables 'as per design of Mr Carr' which together with the carving and gilding cost £36. Eight bergère chairs and six back chairs were gilded, the former costing £4 3s each and the latter £3 12s each.

CARLTON HOUSE, LONDON. In 1786 Nelson's bills were amongst those examined by Henry Wood and in 1789 Nelson submitted an estimate of £6,500 for work required at Carlton House. In 1791 gilded a set of Chinese chairs and mirror frames.

ASHTON CLINTON. On 5 January 1786, £85 was paid to Nelson for work carried out. [RA 88619]

AUDLEY END, Essex. First recorded in 1787 at his house for gilding a dressing room and bedroom, and making a design for Arms and a Crest for which £15 was charged. Also in this year gilding of architectural details was charged at £35 14s 6d. In the period 1788–89 Nelson was carving and gilding a Gothick organ case in the Chapel, and parts of the ceiling in the same room were also gilded. This work was charged at £23 13s. In 1789 a small oval frame was supplied for Lord Howard's London house in New Burlington St and two carved frames made for views of the Elysian gardens. In 1791 he was working on the Temple of Concord at Audley End, designed by Robert Brettingham. As late as 1797 picture frames were being purchased from Nelson by the family.

ALTHORP, Northants. On 15 January 1791 charged £45 for carving and gilding the tops of the chimney and pier glasses in the Red Drawing Room on the instructions of Henry Holland. Later in the same month six cabriole backstools and two tête à tête were made to match a Canopy Bedstead. These were produced 'by order of Messrs Holland & Daguire'. Further seating furniture was made for a Dressing Room and invoiced in the same month. Payments of £100 on 30 July 1791 and £50 on 14 February 1792 are recorded.

WOBURN ABBEY, Beds. Carver's work was carried out under the direction of Henry Holland for the 5th Duke of Bedford in 1793 for which £1,376 2s was paid.

DRURY LANE THEATRE, LONDON. The building accounts of 1794 include a sum of £823 13s to Nelson.

[D; *DEF*; *GCM*; Knowsley Hall papers, Preston RO; *Burlington*, September 1967, p. 520, June 1980, p. 143; Bedford Office, London; Booker, *Face of Banking*, 1979; V & A archives; Essex RO, D/DBy/A45/9, D/DBy/A47, D/DBy/A47/5, D/DBy/A55/6; Stroud, *Henry Holland*, p. 72; H. Clifford Smith, *Buckingham Palace*, p. 104; M. D. Whinney, *Home House*, pp. 19–20. B.A.

Nelson, Thomas, Oldham St and Hilton St, Manchester, furniture broker, cm and u (1817–40). At 34 Hilton St, 1817–24; and also at 24 Oldham St, 1819–33. Also listed at 23 Oldham St, 1821–22 and nos 22 and 23 in 1824. From 1828–33 at 23–25 Oldham St and also 35 Hilton St, 1828–29. In 1836 at 45 Oldham St, and from 1838–40 at nos 45, 47 and 49. [D]

Nelson, Thomas, Lancaster, furniture painter (1789–96). Named in the Gillow records, 1789–90 and 1793–96. [Westminster Ref. Lib., Gillow]

Nelson, Thomas jnr, Norwich, cm (1830). App. to John Blomfield and free by servitude, 21 September 1830. [Freeman reg.]

Nelson, Thomas, Lancaster, cm (1834–35). [Lancaster freemen rolls]

Nelson, William, London(?), cm (1772). Signatory to *The Real State of the Complaints of the Cabinet Makers*, 1772. [*Gents Mag.*, June 1772, p. 275]

Nelson, William, Allonby, Maryport, Cumb., joiner and cm (1828). [D]

Nelson, William, Nelson's Sq., Carlisle, Cumb., cm/joiner (1834). [D]

Nelson, William, 3 Hilton St, Manchester, cm (1834–40). [D]

Nelthorpe, Thomas, Westminster, London, u (1737). Declared bankrupt, *Gents Mag.*, January 1737.

Neptune, —, Little Queen St, London, looking-glass seller (1702). [*The Post Man*, 26 May 1702]

Nervell, John, 36 St John St Rd, London, u (1821). On 18 July 1821 took out insurance cover of £1,000 of which £900 was for stock and utensils in his dwelling house. [GL, Sun MS vol. 484, ref. 981609]

Nesbit, John, Cumberland St, Bishop Wearmouth, Sunderland, Co. Durham, cm (1827). [D]

Nesbitt, Cornelius, Wool Mkt, Berwick-on-Tweed, Northumb., joiner and cm (1834). [D]

Nesbitt, William, St Peter's, Canterbury, Kent, cm (1794–96). [Poll bks]

Nesbitt, William, 73 Old St, London, cm and Tunbridge-ware manufacturer (1818–39). In November 1818 took out insurance cover of £300 on household goods 'in his new dwelling house'. In 1835 recorded as a dressing case maker and clearly had an interest in other years in small decorative cabinet goods. In 1839 also u and undertaker. [D; GL, Sun MS vol. 480, ref. 946757]

Nettlefold, Abram, 27 Lower High St, Bromley, Kent, cm (1800–40). [D: Baxter, *Itinerary of Bromley*, p. 10]

Nettlefold, John, , Bromley, Kent, u and cm (1838–39). [D]

Nettleton, Thomas, Northgate, Pontefract, Yorks., cm (1837). [D]

Nevell, John, Debenham, Suffolk, cm (1804). [*Ipswich Journal*, 9 June 1804]

Nevett & Hewitt, 113½ Bishopsgate St Without, London, cm (1835). [D]

Nevett, Samuel, Liverpool, cm (1766–87). At 122 Dale St, 1766–77, but in 1787 at Richmond St. Took as app. Robert Fairclough who petitioned for freedom in 1780. [D; freemen's committee bk]

Nevill, Samuel, Bermondsey New Rd, London, cm and u (1839). [D]

Nevill, William, 66 Green Lane, Sheffield, Yorks., joiner and cm (1822). [D]

Nevison, John, Sunderland St, Houghton-le-Spring, Co. Durham, joiner and cm (1807–34). [D]

Nevton, John, Lancaster, cm (1746–68). App. to Thomas Walker in 1746 and free by servitude, 1767–68. [App. reg. and freemen rolls]

Nevton, John, Lancaster, cm (1772–73). [Lancaster freemen rolls]

New, Harvey, 57 Robin Hood Lane, Poplar, London, cm and u (1839). [D]

New, John, 8 Aldgate High St, London, carver and gilder (1820–39). Recorded as John New in 1820 but by 1839 the business was trading as John , Edward & Frederick New. [D]

New, Thomas, Andover, Hants., cm and u (1792–99)). Patronized between 1792–99 by Richard Cox of Quarley, Hants., a banker of Pall Mall, London. Payments are recorded in his household account book. [D; Lloyds Bank archives, Cox accounts]

New, Thomas, Westbar, Sheffield, Yorks., cm and u (1828). A Thomas Newton traded at 33 Westbar as a cm and u 1833–37. [D]

Newall, John, Bristol, cm (1775–1813). At 1 Cock & Bottle Lane, in 1775; Castle St in 1792; and once more recorded in Cock & Bottle Lane, 1793–1813. [D]

Newall, John jnr, Hotwells, Bristol, cm (1810). [D]

Newall, Mathew, Liverpool, cm (1784–96). Free 1784 and in 1796 took app. named James Browless, who was however assigned to John Parry in 1797 and petitioned freedom in 1812. [Freemen's committee bk]

Newark, Henry, George St, Gt Yarmouth, Norfolk, chairmaker (1830–36). [D]

Newark, John, New Buildings, Coventry, Warks., chairmaker (1822–28). [D]

Newberry, Henry, address unknown, cm (1803). Subscribed to Sheraton's *Cabinet Dictionary*, 1803.

Newbery, David, Bristol, cabinet carver (1828–32). At 10 Charles St in 1828, 19 Castle St in 1829, 11 Lower West St, 1830–31, and 2 Clarence Rd in 1832. In 1829 also a wholesale egg warehouse. [D]

Newbery, Francis, London, upholder (1710–17). Son of Francis Newbery, freeman and member of the Wheelwrights' Co. of London. Francis jnr was app. to George Smith on 18 January 1710 and free by servitude, 5 February 1717. [GL, Upholders' Co. records]

Newbery, John, Upper Marylebone St, London, leather gilder and table cover maker (1794–1825). At 28 Upper Marylebone St in 1794 but by 1807 the number was 54. In 1808 also a morine printer and in 1825 the business was listed as an 'Upholsterer's warehouseman, Painted Baize and Leather Cover Maker'. In 1807 took out insurance cover of £800 which included £250 for utensils and stock and an additional £100 for similar items in a workshop in Ogle St. [D; GL, Sun MS vol. 440, ref. 802449]

Newbery (or Newbury), Matthew, Bristol, cabinet maker (1820–38). In 1820–21 at 12 St James's Parade, churchyard; in 1822 at Maryport St; in 1824 at 7 Dolphin St; in 1827–35 at 31 Lower Arcade and in 1838 at 17 Barton. In 1824 described as a coach and cabinet carver, in 1830 as a cm and carver and in 1838 as a cm and u. [D]

Newblatt (Newbett or Newbott), William, Grantham, Lincs., cm, u and paperhanger (1822–40). In Vine St, 1822–26; and Swinegate, 1828–40. [D]

Newborn, Mary & Matilda, Barnaby Gate, Newark, Notts., u (1835). [D]

Newbott, James, Westgate, Grantham, Lincs., cm and u (1835). [D]

Newbrook, John, Birmingham, joiner and cm (1800–30). In 1800 at 14 Steelhouse Lane; in 1805 at Lich St; in 1818 at Bath St; and in 1830 at Steelhouse Lane. [D]

Newbury, Francis, 'The Blue Boar', Moorfields, London, u (1724–30). In December 1730 insured his house for £300 and his household goods and stock for an additional £200. [GL, Sun MS vol. 32, ref. 52780; Heal]

Newby, Christopher, Lancaster (1784–87). [Westminster Ref. Lib., Gillow records]

Newby, Miss Elizabeth, at Mr Pykes, Bear St, Leicester Fields, London, upholder (1727). In October 1727 insured for £300 'her house and barn and 2 stables situate in the parish of St Margaret near the bridge in Marlborough in the county of Wiltshire in occupation of a victualler'. [GL, Sun MS vol. 25, p. 285]

Newby, John, 37 Old Compton St, Soho, London, portable desk and dressing case manufacturer (1835–37). [D]

Newcomb, —, 16 Beak St, London (1803). Subscribed to Sheraton's *Cabinet Dictionary*, 1803.

Newcomb, Alexander, 3 Albion Pl., Walworth, London, cm and u (1839). [D]

Newcomb, Oliver, Cavendish Sq., London, u (1806–20). At 23 Hollis St, Cavendish Sq., 1806–12 but in 1820 at 11 Margaret St, Cavendish Sq. His trade card [Leverhulme Coll., MMA, NY] describes his business as 'upholstery & cabinet warerooms' with house agency, appraising and undertaking as other elements in the enterprise. [D]

Newcombe, John, 32 Rathbone Pl., London, u (1829). [D]

Newdigate, Christopher, Norwich, cm (d. 1764). Will proved at Norwich 1764. [Norfolk Record Soc., index of wills]

Newell, James, Baker St, Nottingham, chairmaker (1822). [D]

Newell, John, Oxford, upholder (1756). Aged 31 in 1756 when he married Avis Drewett at the church of St John the Baptist, Oxford. [Bodleian index of Oxf. marriage bonds]

Newell, John, 36 Islington Rd, London, broker and u (1813–25). [D]

Newell, John jnr, 6 Eliza Pl., New River Rd, London, u and cm (1824–27). In July 1824 took out insurance cover of £300 of which £250 was in respect of utensils and stock kept at his dwelling house. [D; GL, Sun MS vol. 496, ref. 1019216]

Newell, John, St John St Rd, Clerkenwell, London, u (1826–39). At 39 St John St Rd, 1826–35 and by 1837 at 40. In 1837 trading as u, undertaker, etc. [D]

Newell, John, Halifax Rd, Bradford, Yorks., cm (1837). [D]

Newell, Nathan, Liverpool, joiner and cm (1784–1827). Son of Henry Newell and brother of Zachariah Newell, shipwright. Free 1 April 1784 by patrimony. Trading at Sir Thomas Ct, Dale St, 1790–96 but by 1803 in Cheapside. The number in Cheapside was 52 in 1803; 50 in 1804; 37 in 1805–07; 4 in 1810; and 40 in 1813–14. At 12 Peter St, 1824–27. Took as apps Robert Williams, 1806–18; Richard Maguire, 1813–30; and James Tunstall, app. in 1822. [D; freemen's committee bk; app. enrolment bk]

Newell, William, London, cm, carver and cm (1786–1829). Freeman of London and member of the Clockmakers' Co. In 1786 at 100 Newgate St as a chair carver where he took out insurance cover for £100 of which £25 was in respect of utensils and stock. By 1789 he had moved to 69 Wood St and also from 1791 maintained a shop at 32 White Cross St, Cripplegate Without, at which his business was conducted throughout the remainder of its long life. At times he employed non-freemen and in 1791 took out a licence to employ twelve for six weeks and in 1810 eighteen for six weeks. In 1791 the utensils, stock and other items at his shop were insured for only £200. From 1808 his son was active in the business and from 1815 the title is uniformly Newell & Son. [D: GL, Sun MS vol. 338, p. 382; vol. 376, p. 683; City Licence bk, vol. 10]

Newell & Son, 36 St John St, Clerkenwell, London, u (1820). This enterprise appears to be unconnected with a similarly named firm operating from 32 White Cross St. [D]

Newey, E. & R., 266 Newtown Row, Birmingham, desk and dressing case makers (1839). [D]

Newey, Richard, Birmingham, cabinet case maker (1828–35). Trading at 39 Cardine St, 1828–30, and 52 Water St, Ludgate Hill in 1835. [D]

Newham, Robert jnr, Stockton-upon-Tees, Co. Durham, cm (1793–98). Subscribed to Sheraton's *Drawing Book*, 1793. [D]

Newhill, James, Bowling, Bradford, Yorks., cm (1822). [D]

Newhouse, Thomas, Coltishall, Suffolk, cm (1793). [D]

Newhouse, William, London, cm (1787–1820). At 28 Charles St, Hatton St, 1787–90. Even at this early stage the business was of substantial size and an insurance cover of £1,800 was maintained on the 'house, workshops, rooms and shed all communicating behind' and the utensils and stock kept in them. By June 1792 the business had moved to 4 Kirby St, Hatton Gdn at which it was to remain for the remainder of its extended business life. Again the insurance cover was substantial amounting to £2,100 of which only £150 referred to the house itself. Workshops, sheds and a warehouse were covered for £300 and utensils and stock for £850. The old premises in Charles St, now numbered 20 and leased for Leaver Pocket, a bookmaker, were insured for £300. [D; GL, Sun MS vol. 340, p. 470; vol. 370, p. 281]

Newill, Gulielmus, Yorkshire St, Rochdale, Lancs., cm (1822–34). Listed at 'top Yorkshire St' in 1822. [D]

Newill & Horsfield, Union St, Halifax, Yorks., cm (1822). [D]

Newitt, Samuel, Liverpool, cm (1761). Free 9 February 1761. [freemen reg.]

Newland & Walker, address unknown, u (1772). Supplied a bedstead and chairs costing £4 2s 6d to Harewood House, Yorks. on 14 November and 30 December 1772. [Leeds RO, Harewood H.P. 491, f. 30]

Newman, Mr, address unrecorded, chairmaker and cm (1741–43). Listed in the Vintners' Hall archive [V&A, 1968] as a chairmaker, 1741–42, receiving £54; and as a cm in 1743 receiving £26 for tables. Possibly identified with Edward Newman of St Paul's Churchyard, London.

Newman, Aaron, Castle Hedingham, Essex, u (1838). Recorded in Jurors' Bk for Hinekford Hundred. [Essex RO, Q/RJ/2/1]

Newman, Charles, Southampton, Hants, cm (1798). Declared bankrupt, *Liverpool Advertiser*, 24 September 1798. [D]

Newman, Charles, Edward St, Portland Pl., London, cm (1802). Freeman of Oxford. [Oxford Poll Bk]

Newman, Edward, St Paul's Churchyard, cm and chairmaker (1692?–d. 1758). In January 1738 'Mr Edward Newman of St Paul Churchyard' was voted on to the Court of Livery of the Joiners Co. [GL, MS 8046/7] He was Deputy Renter Warden in May 1740 and was sworn in as Master on 24 August 1749 [GL, MS 8046/8] In July 1746 he was paid for '2 spring curtains' and in May 1748 for providing two double and four single Windsor chairs, all for Earl Fitzwalter at Moulsham Hall. [A. C. Edwards, *The Accounts of Benjamin Mildmay, Earl Fitzwalter*] A 'proper Handsome Master's Chair' for the Court Parlour of the Joiners Co. was ordered by the then Master, Mr William Smith, on 1 October 1754. Edward Newman was paid £27 6s in May 1755 for this 'large Mahogany carved chair', which is now in the V&A Museum. [GL, MS 8046/9] He died in February 1758 leaving two sons, Isaac and Richard. [PRO, Prob. 11/835, ref. 48]

There is no proof, but it is likely, in view of the name given to his son, that he can be identified with Edward Newman, son of 'Isaac Newman of Mash Gibborne in the County of Bucks, Yeoman deceased', who was app. to Edward Newman 'citizen and Joyner of London' for seven years from 4 June 1706 [GL, MS 8052] and was admitted to the freedom of the Joiners' Co. on 7 September 1714. [GL, MS 8051/3] J.G.

Newman, Edward, 'At a White House the North Side of Golden Square', London, chairmaker? (1733). Recorded as supplying 12 Walnut Chairs for Temple Newsam House, Leeds in January 1733. [*Furn. Hist.*, 1967]

Newman, Edward, St Paul's Churchyard, London, chairmaker (d. 1748). Death on 18 March 1748 'at his House at Marsh Gibbon, Bucks.' reported in *General Advertiser*, 23 March. He was described as 'formerly an eminent Chair-maker in St. Paul's Churchyard, where he acquired a plentiful Fortune with a fair Character'. See Mr Newman.

Newman, Edward, 18 Charles St, Manchester Sq., London, u and undertaker (1814–25). [D]

Newman, G., 10 Bedford Pl., Southampton, Hants., cm (1836). [D]

Newman, Gilbert, Chester, u (1726). [Chester freemen rolls]

Newman, Isaac, St Paul's Churchyard, London, cm (1750–54). Freeman of the Joiners' Co. Subscribed to Chippendale's *Director*, 1754. [GL, Joiners' Co. records, list of Liverymen]

Newman, J., 36 St John St Rd, Islington, London, u (1820). [D]

Newman, James, 47 Redcliffe St, Bristol, cm (1815–40). Also undertaker from 1833. [D]

Newman, James, East St, Chichester, cm and u (1826). [D]

Newman, John, 'The Feathers and Ball', the South Side of St Paul's Churchyard, London, chair and cabinet maker (1752–56). On his trade card [Banks Coll., BM] the text of which is framed by an elegant Rococo composition, he claimed to

make and sell 'all sorts of Chairs & Cabinet Work, Looking Glasses, Coach Glasses, Spring Curtains, Window Blinds & all other Goods in the Cabinet Makers way'. Subscribed to Chippendale's *Director*, 1754. At the time of his marriage in August 1752 described as an 'eminent cabinet maker'. His wife, Rebecca Beal, appears to have been well connected. She was stated at the time of the marriage to have a fortune of £1,500 and the wedding festivities were celebrated not only at 'The Sun Tavern' near Ludgate St but also at her uncle Mr Penney's house at Carshalton, Surrey. She was the niece to the late Captain Beal of St Paul's Churchyard. John Newman took as app. Thomas Cooper in 1756. His trade was then described as joiner. [*General Advertiser*, 21 August 1752; V&A archives]

Newman, John, Oxford and London, cm (b. 1753–1802). Aged 20 in 1773 when he married Dorothy Compton of Oxford at the Church of St Mary Magdalene, Oxford. By 1802 living in London. [Bodleian index of Oxf. marriage bonds; Oxford poll bk]

Newman, John, 13 St Catherine's St, London, u (1796–1808). Included in the list of master cabinet makers in Sheraton's *Cabinet Dictionary*, 1803. In 1808 described as a ship joiner and cm. [D]

Newman, John, Gt Peter St, Westminster, London, chairmaker (1808–29). The number in Gt Peter St was 87 in 1808, 8 in 1809 and 94 in 1829. [D]

Newman, John, Salisbury St, Blandford, Dorset, cm (1823–30). [D]

Newman, John Peter, 18 George St, Portman Sq., London, u (1826–27). [D]

Newman, John, 53 Suffolk St, Birmingham, chairmaker (1830). [D]

Newman, R., London, cm (1793). Signed a spectacular organ-case, bureau, dressing table and jewel casket which was produced to a design by Sir William Chambers by Seddon Sons & Shackleton for King Charles IV of Spain. This piece of furniture has been broken up. [F. Robinson, *English Furniture* (frontispiece); *Conn.*, vol. XLVI, pp. 188–90]

Newman, Ralph, St Peter's-in-the-East, Oxford, cm and wire worker (1777–98). In December 1777 announced that he had opened a shop in St Peter's-in-the-East. [D; *Jackson's Oxford Journal*, 6 December 1777]

Newman, Robert, St Mary Magdalene, Oxford, cm (1768). [Poll bk]

Newman, Samuel, 22 Lower Radleigh St, Pimlico, London, cm and u (1839). [D]

Newman, Thomas, next to the Great Rooms, Ship Lane, Oxford, cm (1768–77). In April 1777 advertised the display of a female dwarf aged 19 in his showrooms. By June 1777 Thomas Nelson was dead and his wife Sarah gave notice to her late husband's debtors to pay her, or Maycock, Jesus College Lane. [Poll bk; *Jackson's Oxford Journal*, 21 April 1777, 28 June 1777]

Newman, Thomas, East Peascod St, Windsor, Berks., cm and u (1830–39). [D; Fifth Hall Book 1828–52, p. 75]

Newman, Thomas, Charlton Kings, Cheltenham, Glos., rustic chairmaker (1839).[D]

Newman, William, London(?), carver (1676–94). Worked in several London City Churches as a carver, but also supplied the altar table, rails and altar-piece at St Stephen, Coleman St, 1676. [*Wren Soc.*, x, pls 28, 31–32; XIX; pp. 43–44]

Newman, William, Elmington, Worcs., cm (1759). [S of G, app. index]

Newman, William, Tuesday Market Pl., King's Lynn, Norfolk, cm (1760–84). In 1760 took app. named Fisher. Advertised in October 1767 that he had moved to Tuesday Market Pl. where he made and sold 'all sorts of Cabinet and Chair

Makers goods'. He also stated that he wanted two journeymen cabinet or chairmakers. In the 1770s the business was of substantial size for a provincial concern. In 1777 insurance cover amounted to £1,400 of which half was in respect of his workshop and stock. In 1783 the total insurance was £1,000 but only £260 was cover for sheds, utensils and stock. [D; S of G, app. index; *Cambridge Chronicle*, 5 January 1770; GL, Sun MS vol. 255, p. 60; vol. 319, p. 10]

Newman, William, parish of St James, Bristol, carver and gilder (1774–81). [Poll bks]

Newman, William, St Martin's, Marlborough, Wilts., chairmaker and turner (1830). [D]

Newman, William, High St, Newmarket, Suffolk, u, cm and paper hanger (1830–39). [D]

Newnham, Samuel, London, cm and upholder (1775–77). At 156 St John St, Clerkenwell in 1775 when cover for utensils and stock was £330 out of a total insurance cover of £600. By 1777 at 1 Albemarle St, Clerkenwell with insurance on utensils and stock only £100 out of a total cover of £300. [GL, Sun MS vol. 243, p. 299; vol. 260, p. 251]

Newns, Richard, Wem, Salop, cm (1779). In 1779 insured some houses for £400. [GL, Sun MS vol. 267, p. 283]

Newsham, Edward, London Rd, King's Lynn, Norfolk, u and mattress maker (1836–39). [D]

Newsome, John, Petter's Hill, Pickering, Yorks., cm (1828) [D]

Newson, George, 90 Old St, St Luke's, London, cm (1826–29). [D]

Newson, George William, 9 Windmill St, Finsbury, London, cm, chair and sofa maker (1835–39). [D]

Newson, James, 17 Vine St, Hatton Wall, London, bedstead maker (1829). [D]

Newson, John, Norwich, cm (1830–39). At St Matthew St in 1830, Westgate St in 1835 and Dogs Head Lane in 1839. [D]

Newstead, William, Chesterfield, Derbs., cm (1792). In July 1793 advertised a range of items of interest to hosiers, trimmers and dyers. [*Derby Mercury*, 4 July 1793]

Newton, Ann, Westbar, Sheffield, Yorks., case maker for knives, razors, etc. (1787). [D]

Newton, Edward, Dowgate Hill, London, upholder (1726). [Heal]

Newton, Edward, London, upholder (1760–94). Son of John Newton, freeman of London and a member of the Upholders' Co. Brother of Thomas Newton. Free of the Upholders' Co. by patrimony 3 April 1760. Living in 1778 at Whitechapel; 1781 at Green St, Stepney; and 1786–94 at The Grove, Mile End. [GL, Upholders' Co. records]

Newton, Edward, 74 Shudehill, Manchester, cm (1797–1818). [D]

Newton, G. W., 7 Church St, Minories, London, auctioneer, appraiser and u, etc. (1820–21). [D]

Newton, Gabriel, Birmingham, u and cm (1826). Bankrupt by July 1826. The fact that the Commissioners appointed to examine him were to meet in Liverpool may suggest that many of his suppliers of materials were located in that area. [*Liverpool Mercury*, 14 July 1826]

Newton, Gabriel, 52 Oxford St, Manchester, u (1834). [D]

Newton, George, Nantwich, Cheshire, cm (1788). Son James bapt. on 21 September 1788. [PR (bapt.)]

Newton, Henry, 'The Three Tents', Lime St, near Leandenhall Mkt, London, u (c.1760). Also offered 'Chairs, Cabinet-Work & Glasses with all Sorts of Tecks, Feathers, Quilts, Blankets, Coverlids & Ruggs'. Indicated that he bought and sold household furniture and acted as an appraiser & undertaker. [Heal]

Newton, J., 6 Smeaton St, Hull, Yorks., cm (1838–39). [D]

Newton, J., Stallards Lane, Trowbridge, Wilts., cm (1839). [D] See Thomas Newton.

Newton, James, London, cm (1738–49). At Gt Turnstile, Holborn in 1738 when his bankruptcy was announced. His trade was described as cm, milliner and chapman. Once more bankrupt in 1746 when his address was given as 'St. Giles-in-the-Fields'. In 1749 at Red Lion Ct. [*Read's Weekly Journal*, 1 July 1738; *Gents Mag.*, April 1746; Westminster poll bk]

Newton, James, 63 Wardour St, London, u and cm (1773–1821). Initially in partnership with Lawrence Fell, a former partner of Fell & Turton. James Newton is first recorded in Compton St at no. 37 in 1780 and 31 in 1781–83. In 1780 he was described as an upholder and insured a house for £200, but the Wardour St address was being used in 1781. In that year it was described as a house, and insurance cover of £300 was taken out on the property. The actual business is first recorded in trade directories in 1789, and by 1808 64 Wardour St was being used in addition to 63. By 1809 the trading style had changed to James Newton & Son, and after 1822 as Robert & James Newton. James Newton was a subscriber to Thomas Malton's *Compleat Treatise on Perspective*, 1775 and was listed in the names of master cabinet makers included in Sheraton's *Cabinet Dictionary*, 1803.

A number of Newton's commissions are known and indicate that his business was held in high regard. He was a regular supplier of furnishings for Burghley House, Northants., and between 1773 and 1804 was in receipt of payments totalling nearly £8,000. One of the finest items, which is still in the house, was a state bed supplied in 1797 in connection with a visit by the Prince of Wales. The Heathcote family purchased items in 1797–98, and in June 1803 expended £55 18s 6d. Matthew Boulton of Soho, Birmingham was supplied with furniture from June 1798 to November 1799. At Osterley House bills survive dated 1800, 1804 and 1805 for work at houses in Cumberland Pl. and Charles St for which furniture was supplied. Lord Villiers expended £437 3s with Newton in 1804. Large quantities of fine furniture were supplied to the Earl of Breadalbane, 1809–12. In 1809 two accounts alone for beds, bedding and commodes came to £2,635 1s 2d. In the following year £3,393 7s 4d is shown for furniture for Taymouth Castle, Perths., which included no fewer than eight French commodes with brasswork, two tulipwood coffee tables, a rosewood claw table, and beds, one with a large dome. This year also saw furnishings for the Earl's London property in Park Lane and Wigmore St. An elaborately carved four poster bed was sent to Taymouth Castle in 1812.

Newton appears to have adopted a policy of labelling some of his furniture. A mahogany lady's writing table and cabinet is known with the label 'James Newton. Wardour Street, 1793'. A pair of elbow chairs based on a design in Thomas Hope's *Household Furniture*, 1807 (plate 22) but bearing an inscription indicating that they were made in October 1806 are on display at the Royal Pavilion, Brighton. One of these bears a Newton label. [D; GL, Sun MS vol. 289, p. 170; vol. 296, p. 580; *C. Life*, 29 August 1974, pp. 562–64; Lincoln RO, Heathcote, 3 ANC 6/380; ANC 7/14/13; Birmingham Lib., Boulton MS, box N; Scottish RO, GD 112/20/Box 1/33/1–8, GD 112/20/4/12/2–3X; *Conn.*, June 1959, supplement, p. 63]

Newton, James & Son, Barton near Manchester, Lancs. (1803). Subscribers to Sheratons' *Cabinet Dictionary*, 1803.

Newton, James, Patricroft and Barton, Lancs., joiner and cm (1825–34). At Barton, Eccles parish 1825 when his trade was listed as cm. In 1834 at Patricroft and Barton as a cm and joiner. [D]

Newton, James, 59 Margaret St, London, u (1829). [D]

Newton, John, London, upholder (1702–26). Son of Edward

Newton of Wethersfield, Essex, Gent. Probably father of Edward & Thomas Newton. App. to Nicholas Patrick on 1 May 1702 but served his time with Thomas Collinson of King St, Westminster. Free of the Upholders' Co. by servitude, 3 March 1713/14. Appears to have taken as apps John Carrier and John Dennison in 1726. [GL, Upholders' Co. records]

Newton, John, Fleshmarket, Newcastle, cm and carpenter (1778). [D]

Newton, John, Lancaster, cm (1789–90). Free 1789–90, when Stated 'of Liverpool'. [Freemen rolls]

Newton, John, back of 21 Cropper St, Liverpool, cm (1790–97). [D]

Newton, John, Barton-on-Humber, Lincs., joiner and cm (1819–35). Listed at Market Lane in 1835.[D]

Newton, John, Newgate St, Bishop Auckland, Co. Durham, joiner and cm (1827–34). [D]

Newton, John, Liverpool, joiner and cm (1829–39). At 11 Warren St with a shop at 11 Gill St in 1829 but from 1835 in Copperas Hill where the number was 69 in 1835, 70 in 1837 and 126 in 1839. [D]

Newton, Nathaniel, 3 John St, Bath, Som., cm (1833). [D]

Newton, Robert, Lancaster and Knutsford, Cheshire cm (1764–84). App. to J. Wright in 1764 and free, 1783–84. Living in Knutsford by April 1784. [App. reg.; Lancaster poll bk]

Newton, Robert & James, Wardour St, Soho, London, upholders and cm (1822–40). A continuation of the business established by James Newton and previously trading as Newton & Son from the Wardour St address. The numbers in Wardour St are 63 and 64 until 1835; and 64 and 65 in 1839. In 1824 supplied goods and services to the Royal Household amounting to £172 10s. [D; Windsor Royal Archives, RA 35580]

Newton, Thomas, Westminster, London, upholder (1760–86). Son of John Newton, freeman and member of the Upholders' Co. Brother to Edward Newton. Free of the Upholders' Co by patrimony on 6 March 1760. Living in Down St, 1778, and Dacre St, 1781–86. [GL, Upholders' Co. records]

Newton, Thomas, 43 Grafton St East, Tottenham Ct Rd, London, cm (1816–20). A set of Regency mahogany chairs is known with ormolu feet stamped 'TN'. These initials may refer to Thomas Newton. The chairs are additionally marked 'H.F. Webster Aug. 1816'. [D; *Antique Dealer's and Collector's Guide*, June 1974, p. 28]

Newton, Thomas, Stallard's Lane, Trowbridge, Wilts., cm (1830). [D] See J. Newton.

Newton, Thomas, 33 Westbar, Sheffield, Yorks., cm and u (1833–37). A Thomas New is shown in Westbar in 1828 in one directory. [D]

Newton, William, London, cm (1793). Subscribed to Sheraton's *Drawing Book*, 1793.

Newton, William, Mount St, Nottingham, joiner and cm (1832). [D]

Newton & Draper, 4 Cleveland St, Fitzroy Sq., London, cm and u (1839). [D]

Newton & Norman, 24 Cannon St, St George's East, London, cm and u (1826–27). In 1826 listed as cabinet and bedstead makers. [D]

Nias, Benjamin Merriman, London, u (1811–33). Initially at 4 Charles St, corner of Norfolk St, Middlx Hospital as an upholder and importer of Turkey carpets. Also able to supply 'Dantzic Feathers'. By 1811 was trading as Nias & Co. There appears to have been a Benjamin Merriman jnr and this may be the date he entered the business. From 1819 an address at 32 Berners St was used as carpet and furniture warerooms in addition to the Charles St premises which were then numbered 34. From 1822 had financial connections with

Count de Rhins, from whom he took a bill for £1,000. [D; PRO, C13 283/28/29 November 1822, C13 5561]

Nible, Henry, Oldbury, Tewkesbury, Glos., chairmaker (1826). Child bapt. at Tewkesbury in 1826. [PR (bapt.)]

Niblett, Edwin, Gloucester, cm (1839). Child bapt. at St Michael's Church in 1839. [PR (bapt.)]

Niccolls, Thomas, Old Soho, Covent Gdn, London, carver (1749). [Westminster poll bk]

Nice (or Nies), Mary, Thomas St, Liverpool, u (1818–29). At 52 Thomas St in 1818 and 55, 1824–29. [D]

Nicheles, J., Essex Buildings, Stratford, London, cm (1835). [D]

Nichol, James, St Margaret's, Westminster, London, cm (1786). In 1786 his son was app. to a mason, with assistance from Grinsell's Charity. [Westminster Ref. Lib., MS E3559]

Nicholas, Edward, Edstaston Wharf, Wem, Salop, joiner and cm (1840). [D]

Nicholas, George, 52 Parliament St, London, upholder and cm (1825–27). [D]

Nicholas, Henry, Fretton, Norfolk, chairmaker (1734). Freeman of Norwich. [Norwich poll bk]

Nicholas, John, 82 High St, Worcester, cm and u (1840). [D]

Nicholas, William, 6 Smallbrook St, Birmingham, cm, clock and clock dial maker (1816–22). [D]

Nicholas, William, Barrow St, Wenlock, Salop, cm (1840). [D]

Nicholettes, —, London, cm (1750). Robbed by two footpads on Constitution Hill. [*General Advertiser*, 27 September 1750]

Nicholl, Charles, 5 Cox's Ct, Aldersgate St, London, cm (1785). In May 1785 insured his utensils and stock for £60. [GL, Sun MS vol. 329, p. 259]

Nicholl, Charles, 14 George's Ct, Red Lion St, Clerkenwell, London, cm (1792). On June 1792 took out insurance cover of £200 of which £150 covered utensils and stock. [GL, Sun MS vol. 387, p. 158]

Nicholl, John, John St, Oxford Mkt, London, carver (1763). [D]

Nicholl, Thomas, 17 Duke St, West Smithfield, London, upholder and undertaker (1724). [Heal]

Nicholl, Thomas, St Paul's Churchyard, London, upholder (1724–47). [Heal]

Nicholl, Thomas, Marylebone, London, carver (1768). [Lincoln RO, Monson, 22B/6/3]

Nicholl, Thomas, London, carver and gilder (1835–39). In 1835 the business was styled Nicholl & Brown and was trading from 21½ Foley St. By 1837 the partnership had broken up and Nicholl traded from this address on his own behalf. By 1839 he had moved to 31 Gt Titchfield St. [D]

Nicholls, Benjamin, Redruth, Cornwall, cm (1830). [D]

Nicholls, Charles, Little Church St, Wisbech, Cambs., cm, u and paper hanger (1822–30). [D]

Nicholls, Daniel, 19 Vine St, Hatton Wall, London, bedstead maker (1829). In 1839 a person of the same name was trading at 12 Brook Hill, Clerkenwell as a furniture broker. [D]

Nicholls, Humphrey, Canterbury, Kent, u (1678). [Canterbury freemen rolls]

Nicholls, J., 6 Red Lion St, Clerkenwell, London, clock and dial case maker (1812). [D]

Nicholls, Jacob, Wells, Som., cm (1774). Freeman of Bristol. [Bristol poll bk]

Nicholls, James, St Albans, Herts., cm (1829). Bankruptcy announced, *Chester Chronicle*, 31 July 1829.

Nicholls, John, Eld Lane, Colchester, Essex, cm and u (1823–26). [D]

Nicholls, John snr, Exeter, Devon, cm and u (1812–26). In partnership with his son John Nicholls jnr until 1826, and in the 1820s trading from the General Commission Rooms, Newbridge. In 1812 supplied William Wade with furniture, utensils and linen which included a mahogany post bedstead at £18 18s, a secretary and bookcase at £15 and twelve single and two arm chairs at £16 16s. William Wade probably lived in the Tintagel area of Cornwall. [Cornwall RO, DDX 139.9; *The Alfred*, 14 February 1826]

Nicholls, John jnr, Exeter, Devon, cm and u (1823–40). At the General Commission Rooms, Newbridge, 1813–16, in partnership with his father, John Nicholls snr. In 1923 they announced that they had purchased the stock of a Mr Burt of Fore St, another cm. Amongst the stock they had on offer were musical instruments such as organs and pianos which were to be sold at reduced prices. They also offered to repair and tune musical instruments. In February 1826 the partnership was dissolved. Subsequent addresses for John Nicholls jnr are Bridge St in 1830; 14 Improvements in 1834; 9 Bartholomew St, 1836–38; New Bridge St, 1838; and 146 Fore St, 1838–40. [D; *The Alfred*, 8 April 1823, 14 February 1826]

Nicholls, John, 8 Boundary Row, Blackfriars Rd, London, bedstead maker (1825–39). [D]

Nicholls, John, 82 High St, Worcester, cm and u (1828). [D]

Nicholls, Matthew, the corner of Bromley St in Drury Lane, London, frame maker (1723). Insured goods and merchandise in his dwelling house for £300 in August 1723. [GL, Sun MS vol. 16, ref. 29673]

Nicholls, Richard, Truro, Cornwall, cm (1759). In 1759 took app. named Gray. [S of G, app. index]

Nicholls, Richard, Castle St, Shrewsbury, Salop, chairmaker (1828). [D]

Nicholls, Robert, Chester, cm (1733). Son of John Nicholls of Chester, butcher. Free 7 July 1733. [Freeman rolls]

Nicholls, Thomas, 'The Three Golden Keys', west side of Houndsditch, parish of St Botolph without Aldgate, London, upholder (1708). Insured his timber house for £100 in November 1708. [GL, Hand in Hand MS vol. 6, ref. 2611]

Nicholls, Thomas, Wardour St, Soho, Westminster, London, carver (1749). [Poll bk]

Nicholls, William, 93 Long Acre, London, carver and gilder (1770–76). Employed by Horace Walpole at Strawberry Hill, Twickenham, Middlx in 1773 and 1776. [D; Heal]

Nicholls, William, 3 Meard's Ct, Dean St, Soho, London, cm u and undertaker (1809–22). [D]

Nichols, Mr, London, cm (1746). Taken ill suddenly in the Broadway, Westminster and died almost immediately. [*General Advertiser*, 28 January 1746]

Nichols, Eugene, 11 Gt Titchfield St, London, carver and gilder (1839). [D]

Nichols, Henry, parish of St Peter Mancroft, Norwich, chairmaker (1722–53). Son of Henry Nichols snr. Free 22 August 1722. Took apps named Hubard in 1724 and Barrett in 1729. Another of his apps, James Barroth was declared free on 3 May 1753. [Freeman reg.; S of G, app. index; poll bk]

Nichols, J., Teignmouth, Devon, cm (1813). In February 1813 the sale of the stock in trade and household furniture 'of the lodging house of J. Nichols' was announced. [*Exeter Flying Post*, 11 February 1813]

Nichols, James, Liverpool, cm (1761–c.1815). Free 3 April 1761 and died between 1812 and 1817. [Freemen reg.]

Nichols, James, Gt Yarmouth/London, cm (1807–30). Living in London, 1818–30. [Gt Yarmouth poll bks]

Nichols, John, Worcester, cm and u (1828–30). Listed at New St in 1828, also as a broker; and at 82 High St in 1830. [D]

Nichols, Paul, 3 Masons Row, Liverpool, picture frame maker (1827). [D]

Nichols, Richard, 20 York Terr., Borough Rd, London, bedstead maker (1835–37). [D]

Nichols, Samuel, near the Bridge, Bradford, Wilts., cm and u (1822–30). [D]

Nichols & Relph, 75 Wells St, Oxford St, London, cm (1803–20). In 1803 the firm of Oswald & Nichols is recorded trading from this address but Sheraton, in the list of master cabinet makers he included in the *Cabinet Dictionary*, 1803, listed Nichols J. & Relph. In 1813–16 traded as Nichols, Relph & Birch but by 1817 had reverted to Nichols & Relph who were listed as cm and chairmakers in 1820. [D; Heal]

Nicholson, Charles, 15 Northampton St, Clerkenwell, London, clock case maker (1839). [D]

Nicholson, Christopher, 12 King St, Liverpool, joiner and cm (1777). The King St premises were referred to as a warehouse. [D]

Nicholson, Dawson, St Mary's Chare, Hexham, Northumb., joiner and cm (1827–34). Recorded also at Back St in 1834. [D]

Nicholson, E. & W., High St, Fareham, Hants, cm and builder (1823). A mahogany reading and writing table is known bearing the label 'Nicholson, Cabinet Manufacturer, upholsterer, paper-hanger etc., High Street, Fareham'. [D; Sotheby's, 4 July 1969, lot 133]

Nicholson, Edward, Union St, Doncaster, Yorks., u (1818). [D]

Nicholson, Edward, West St, Fareham, Hants, cm and u (1830). [D]

Nicholson, Edward, Johnson's Entry, High St, Hull, Yorks., cm (1834). [D]

Nicholson, Francis, 30 St John St Rd, London, u (1826). [D]

Nicholson, George, Rockley, Notts., chairmaker (b. c.1801–41). Children bapt. at Rockley Methodist Church, 1831–36. Aged 40 at the date of the 1841 Census and had a resident app. named William Smith aged 15. Over twenty chairs of the Windsor type are known with the impressed mark 'NICHOLSON/ROCKLEY'. [*Furn. Hist.*, 1978; *Antique Collecting*, February 1974; *Antique Dealer's and Collector's Guide*, May 1978, p. 3]

Nicholson, H., Kirkby St, Maryport, Cumb., joiner/cm (1811). [D]

Nicholson, Henry, Workington, Cumb., joiner/cm (1828–29). In Key St, 1828 and Quay, 1829. [D]

Nicholson, Isaac, Cropper St, Manchester, cm (1800). [D]

Nicholson, Isaac, St Helen St, Cockermouth, Cumb., joiner/cm and wheelwright (1829). [D]

Nicholson, James, Southwell, Notts., joiner and cm (1832). [D]

Nicholson, Joash. W., Leeds, Yorks., cm and u (1826–40). At 12 West St in 1826; 70 Meadow Lane in 1828, no. 68, 1830–34; and 98 Kirkgate 1837–39. [D]

Nicholson, John, west side of Warwick St, Golden Sq., London, u (1763–d. by 1773). Son of Benjamin Nicholson, freeman and innholder of London. App. to Thomas Brown a member of the Merchant Tailors Co., 4 May 1763. Free of the Upholders' Co. under the terms of the 1750 Upholders' Act on 1 August 1770. His period of trading was probably short, for by December 1773 he was dead and his stock and household furniture was sold by auction by Mr Christie. The items in the sale included much cabinet furniture but this may have been household furniture rather than trade stock in some cases. Amongst a small number of books was one of drawings by Ince and Mayhew which was sold for £1 4s. [GL, Upholders' Co. records; Christie's, 9 December 1773]

Nicholson, John, Cannon St, London, see Nicholson & Brown.

Nicholson, John, 35 Bishopsgate Within, London, upholder (c. 1790). [Heal]

Nicholson, John, Church St, Blackburn, Lancs., u and paper hanger (1814–24). In March 1821 announced his intention of retiring and offered his stock at valuation. As an inducement he stated that 'the principal part, if required, may remain at interest, on satisfactory security'. His business was declared to be 'in one of the principal streets of Blackburn, & the business of an upholsterer hath been carried on therein for the last 30 years'. He may not have been successful in disposing of the stock for he was still trading in 1824. At this date his address was New Inn Yd, Church St, and 31 John St. One directory of 1824 lists the business as Nicholson & Boardman. [D; *Liverpool Mercury*, 2 March 1821]

Nicholson, John, Market Pl., Burnley, Lancs., u (1818). [D]

Nicholson, John, Winlaton, Co. Durham, joiner and cm (1824–34). [D]

Nicholson, Jonah Walker, 98 Kirkgate, Leeds, Yorks., cm, u and furniture broker (1837). [D]

Nicholson, Joseph, Wood St, Maryport, Cumb., joiner/cm (1811). [D]

Nicholson, Jos., Wolsingham, Co. Durham, joiner and cm (1828). [D]

Nicholson, Neile, 6 Baptist St, Liverpool, cm (1829). [D]

Nicholson, Patrick, 15 Mercer St, Long Acre, London, carver (1826–29). [D]

Nicholson, Relph, Whickham, Co. Durham, joiner/carpenter(cm (1834). [D]

Nicholson, Richard, Union Lane, Sunderland, Co. Durham, u (1776). In May 1776 Ann Davenport advertised that paper hangings produced in her manufactory might be inspected at Richard Nicholson's premises. [*Newcastle Courant*, 18 May 1776]

Nicholson, Robert, Doncaster, u (1793–1837). In 1837 at Cleveland St. [D]

Nicholson, Thomas, South Collingham, Notts., chairmaker. Probate granted on will 3 July 1785. [Notts. RO, probate records]

Nicholson, Thomas, address unknown, cm (1803). Subscribed to Sheraton's *Cabinet Dictionary*, 1803.

Nicholson, Thomas, Bridge Lane, Penrith, Cumb., joiner and cm (1828). [D]

Nicholson, Thomas, Pocklington, Yorks., cm (1831–40). At Swine Market in 1831 and 1840 but in 1834 listed at Waterloo Buildings. [D]

Nicholson, William, Carlisle, Cumb., joiner and cm (1810–11). At Abbey St in 1810 and Paternoster Row in 1811. [D]

Nicholson, William, Manchester, cm, u, feather dealer and furniture broker (1817–29). At 2 Hilton St in 1817 but from 1819 at 26 Oldham St. [D]

Nicholson, William, Skinner's Burn, Hexham, Northumb., joiner and cm (1827–28). [D]

Nicholson, William, Felling Shore, Jarrow, Co. Durham, joiner and cm (1828). [D]

Nicholson, William, Westgate, Bradford, Yorks., cm (1830). [D]

Nicholson, William, Barn St, Little Bolton, Lancs., cm (1834). [D]

Nicholson, William, 15 Platt Terr., St Pancras Rd, London, cm (1835). [D]

Nicholson & Brown, 41 Cannon St, London, u (1775–77). A partnership of John Nicholson and William Brown. Both partners were declared bankrupt in October 1777. [D; *Gents Mag.*, October 1777]

Nicholson & Graham, Castle St, Carlisle, Cumb., joiners and cm (1805–08). [D]

Nicholson & Walker, Windsor St, Putney, London, cm and u (1838). Nicholson was one of the partners. [D]

Nickalls, Thomas, London, upholder (1734–d. 1776). Son of Daniel Nickalls of Canterbury, draper. App. to William Scrimshire on 9 February 1714 and Charles Harvey of the Merchant Tailors' Co. on 3 March 1714. Free of the Upholders' Co by servitude, 3 July 1734. Took as apps Richard Wear, 1737–54; Joseph Bradshaw, 1754–61; and Thomas Bradshaw, 1761–66. In 1750 Nickalls's address was

given as St Paul's Churchyard. [GL, Upholders' Co. records, Livery list, 1750]

Nickells, James, 6 Bateman's Row, Shoreditch, London, cm and u (1820–23). [D]

Nickells, John, 37 Haymarket, London, trunk and plate case maker (1789–1819). The Longford Castle, Wilts. accounts list the payment of £1 5s to a Nickells, case maker in 1792. [D; V&A archives]

Nickels, J., 27 Henrietta St, Brunswick Sq., London, cm and chairmaker (1825). [D]

Nickels, James, Stratford, London, cm, u and auctioneer (1832). [D]

Nickels, John Pells, Colchester, Essex, cm (d. 1828). Probate granted on his will 1828. [*Wills at Chelmsford*, III, p. 236]

Nickels, William & Benjamin, 132 St John St, Clerkenwell, London, cm and u (1826–27). [D]

Nicklin, Thomas, Corbridge, Burslem (The Potteries), Staffs., cm, u and pianoforte maker (1828–35). [D]

Nicklin, Thomas, 72 Gt Guildford St, Southwark, London, chair and sofa maker (1839). [D]

Nicklin, William, Dudley, Worcs., cm (1809). [D]

Nickolds, Samuel, Norwich and Lakenham, Norfolk, cm (1817–30). App. to Elden Earl and free of Norwich by servitude, 16 June 1817. In the parish of St John Sepulchre, Norwich in June 1818 but by July 1830 at Lakenham. [Freemen reg.; poll bks]

Nickols, Thomas, London, u (1739). [Canterbury freemen rolls]

Nicks, —, 5 Dean's Row, Walworth, London, carver and gilder (1809). [D]

Nicks, J., Castle St, Warwick, builder and cm (1830). [D]

Nickson, —, Chesham, Bucks., cm (1793). [D]

Nickson, George, Tunstall, Staffs., joiner and cm (1798). [D]

Nickson, Samuel, Bridge St Row, Chester, cm and u (1802–27). Listed also at Commercial Buildings in 1816. Free 3 July 1802. Subscribed to Sheraton's *Cabinet Dictionary*, 1803. Developed an extensive business and in 1815 claimed to be employing workmen from Gillows, and Tatham & Co., London. In that year he had additional premises at County Buildings, although in 1814 the address of these was stated to be Commercial Buildings. Took apps George Langshaw in 1814 and John Simecock in 1819, although in the following year he was transferred to another master. In June 1818 however he advertised the sale by auction of his entire stock as he was retiring from business. On offer was a very extensive and elegant stock consisting of '50 elegant four post, Chinese, tent and sofa bedsteads with rich china and other furniture, mattresses, prime goose feather beds, blankets, counterpanes, Marseilles quilts, handsome wardrobes, chests of drawers, ladies dressing chests, night tables, bidets, airing maids, gentlemen's dressing tables and plain ditto, angular and square bason stands, boot racks, secretaires and bookcases, bureaus, superb sideboards with cellarets and gardivines, handsome sets of dining tables, card, sofa, loo and Pembroke tables richly inlaid and ornamented with brass and or-molu, 36 Grecian and square sofas with 20 Grecian couches, lounging, tub, easy and bed chairs, finished in satin, hair and other coverings, 24 dozen of Trafalgar, Grecian and plain mahogany dining room chairs and hall ditto, elegant rosewood and japanned drawing room chairs, neat stained and painted chairs, ditto extensive assortment of rich pier and chimney glasses, mirrors and dressing glasses, hall lamps, music stools, supper, butlers, cheese and knife trays, dining and drawing room firescreens, bed steps, portable writing desks, ladies work tables and boxes, tea chests, caddies and backgammon tables, handsome dials and eight day clocks in rich cases, two thousand pieces of paper hangings with gold, flock and common borders of the most fashionable London patterns, elegant carpets in Brussels and Turkey, hearth rugs and coach ditto'. A wide range of upholstery stock was described in addition.

The sale commenced on 29 June but the stock that was unsold was offered again by auction on 8 and 9 July. Another sale of residual stock was held on 15 July and the two days following. At the time that these sales were progressing materials still in stock were being made up into furniture which was offered with the residue of the previous sales from 5 October of the same year. That which the public did not purchase at this occasion was again auctioned on 21 and 22 October. Having failed, despite all these efforts, to dispose of all the stock it was then displayed in the auction mart labelled with the lowest price that was acceptable. Nickson claimed that these prices were 25% below those of his competitors, a claim that produced an advertisement refuting this by the other Chester furniture makers. Attempts to dispose of stock continued through December 1818. The reason for these sales became obvious for in November 1819 Nickson was declared bankrupt. Despite this experience he recommenced business and the firm of Samuel Nickson & Son at Bridge St Row is shown in an 1822 directory. In July 1827 however he took a decision to discontinue the furniture making side of his business which he had carried on for 'upwards of twenty years'. Henceforth he acted solely as an auctioneer and appraiser, and in September 1827 he opened auction rooms in Eastgate which proved a successful venture over many years. [D; freemen rolls; app. bks; *Chester Chronicle*, 2 June 1815, *Chester Guardian*, 20 June 1717, 27 June 1818, 4, 11 and 18 July 1818, 26 September 1818, 5 and 17 October 1818, 5 November 1818, 12, 18 and 31 December 1818, 25 November 1819; 3 July 1827; *Liverpool Mercury*, 26 November 1819]

Nickson, Thomas, 18 Cropper St, Liverpool, cm (1811). [D]

Nicol, Alexander, 21 St Vincent St, St James's, Liverpool, cm (1835). [D]

Nicol & Lewis, St James's St, Liverpool, cm and u (1835–37). At 29 St James's St in 1835 and 31 in 1837. [D]

Nicoll, Thomas, Printing House, Swan Alley, London, upholder (1717). In September 1717 took out insurance cover on two houses in the possession of T. Nicholl & Co. amounting to £300. [GL, Hand in Hand MS vol. 17, p. 252]

Nicols, J., Wells St, London, cm (1803). Subscribed to Sheraton's *Cabinet Dictionary*, 1803.

Nicolson, Joseph, London, upholder (1729). Son of James Nicholson of Fetter Lane, London, apothecary. App. to William Jones on 2 August 1721 and free of the Upholders' Co. by servitude, 7 May 1729. [GL, Upholders' Co. records]

Nielson, Lawrence, London, cm (1782–84). In 1782 at 44 Frith St, Soho where he took out insurance cover of £400 on his house. In 1784 at 78 Margaret St, Cavendish Sq. where he took out insurance cover of £1,000, half of which was in respect of utensils and stock. [GL, Sun MS vol. 304, p. 292; vol. 322, p. 300]

Nightingale, George, 143 Leadenhall St, London, carver, gilder and print seller (1802–35). Bankrupt by October 1802 but recommenced business by the following year. On 4 June 1815 his workshop was destroyed by fire but this does not appear to have seriously disrupted the business which continued at the same address. [D; *Gents Mag.*, June 1815; *Billinge's Liverpool Advertiser*, 4 October 1802, 29 November 1802; PRO, C13/2649, C13/14761]

Nightingale, James, Stockport, Cheshire, cm (1825–40). At Throstle Grove in 1825 but from 1828 at Heaton Lane. [D]

Nightingale, John, Liverpool, cm (1766–d. 1782). At Pool Lane, 1766–69; 2 Hanover St, 1772–74; 44 Whitechapel in 1777 and 51 Whitechapel thereafter. His bankruptcy was announced in October 1773, and in February 1774 his stock was sold by auction. Included in the sale were 'Neat Mahogany Chairs, Dining, Dressing & Pier Tables, Double Chests Drawers, neat Mahogany Desks, Dressing Chests & Commodes; a neat Mahogany Wardrobe & other Cabinet Goods'. A 'rich Crimson Silk Damask Bed with Mahogany Bedstead' and a 'Variety of Pier & Dressing Glasses' were also specified. Died 1782, though one directory still lists him at 51 Whitechapel in 1784. [D; *Gents Mag.*, October 1773; *Williamson's Liverpool Advertiser*, February 1774, 28 March 1782]

Nightingale, John, Lancaster, turner and chairmaker (1797). On 6 December 1797 took an app. [App. reg.]

Nightingale, John, 5 Heatley St, Preston, Lancs., chairmaker (1818). [D]

Nightingale, John, Bloom St, Manchester, u (1825–40). At 10 Bloom St in 1825 and 23, 1838–40. [D]

Nightingale, Thomas, London, upholder (1777). Son of John Nightingale of the Liberty of Norton Falgate, Middlx 'hare merchant'. App. to William Gould 13 May 1769 and free of the Upholders' Co. by servitude 2 July 1777. At this date he was living at 56 Bishopsgate St. [GL, Upholders' Co. records]

Nightingale, William, Goosegate, Nottingham, joiner and cm (1832–35). Recorded also at Glasshouse St in 1832. [D]

Niles, Edward, 8 Duke St, Devonport, Devon, carver and gilder (1838). [D]

Nind, Thomas, 19 Crown St, Bishopsgate, London, upholder and paper hanger (1817). [D]

Nisbett, William, 156 Oxford St, London, u, appraiser and house agent (1835). [D]

Niven, James, London, chair carver (1808–20). At 2 Old North St, Red Lion Sq., 1808–09, but in 1820 at 6 Gloucester St, Queen's Sq. [D]

Niven, S., London, carver (1826–29). At 4 Southampton Ct, Queen's Sq. in 1826 but in 1829 at 22 Gt Ormond St, Queen's Sq. [D]

Nix, Mr, London(?), glass maker and cm (1748). Notice in *General Advertiser*, 14 May 1748 announced the auction sale by Aaron Lambe of 'Furniture . . . and Effects of SAMUEL WINDER, Esq. Jun. at Roehampton, one Mile and a Half from Putney Bridge . . . Screens, Escrutores, Desks, Bookcases, Chests of Drawers in Mahogany and Walnut-tree, and curious Rose Woods; the Cabinet Work being made in the neatest and best manner, by Mr. Nix; glasses . . .'. Probably:

Nix, George, London, cm and joiner (1716–d. 1743) and

Nix, George, London, cm (1744–51). Information about George Nix is somewhat sparse. In 1716 he is described as 'citizen and joiner' and recorded taking app. named Edward, son of Edward Halfhide, citizen and joiner, on 15 August for a payment of £15. On 24 April 1718 he took Theo Martinoff, a Russian, as app. for a premium of £100 and was then described as a cm of St Paul's Covent Gdn. [PRO, IR 1/5 and 1/6] On 22 February 1739/40 he is referred to as 'Mr Nix ye Cabinet maker in King Street Covent Garden'. [PRO, C.109/25, Part 1, Daybooks and Ledgers of Thomas Wagg 1727–48, Chancery Masters Exhibits, vol. 8] In the *Memoirs* of Sir William Jones, Lord Teignmouth (1806, vol. 1, p. 10) he is described as a London cabinet maker who 'although of low extraction . . . raised himself to eminence in his profession and from the honest and pleasant frankness of his conversation was admitted to the tables of the great, and to the intimacy of Lord Macclesfield'.

In 1729 and 1730 Nix supplied a table, chair, close stool and corner cupboard to Moulsham Hall, Essex. [A. C. Edwards, *The Accounts of Benjamin Mildmay, Earl Fitzwalter*, pp. 100–04] Also in 1729 he charged the Duchess of Montrose for a 4 leaf screen covered with 'India paper'

[Scottish RO, GD 220/6/1383/11], while in 1732 the Duke of Montrose made a payment of £37 3s to a Mr Nix for his house at Cley, Norfolk. [Scottish RO, GD 220/6/31, p. 640] Nix supplied some mahogany tables to a Lord Monson in 1740 [Lincoln RO, Monson 12] and in the following year charged for a kettle stand supplied for Holkham Hall. [Holkham Hall accounts]

For Ham House he charged for a large range of items and repairs for the 4th Earl of Dysart over the period June 1729 to April 1734 at a cost of £430 13s 6d and his bill is the best source of information about the kind of goods he produced. [Lauderdale papers, Buckminster Estate Office, Grantham, Lincs.] The list of furniture supplied, from which several items can be identified, includes tables and chairs of all kinds, chests-of-drawers, close-stools, a bookcase, a reading desk, a firescreen, a dumb waiter (an early example of this type of furniture) and a chimneyboard, itemized as 'white ... grounded for Japaning'. He also charged for repairs to a number of dressing- and strong-boxes, to a crystal chandelier, a billiard table, the well-known 'blackamore' candlestands and other items. This bill also refers to 'taking down the Great Book Case in Bond Street & Setting it up again in Arlington Street' in December 1732 and in the following March to 'taking the Great Bookcases to peices & carrying it to Grosvenor Square & fixing it up in the Hind Room'.

George Nix is said to have died in 1743. [Harris, *Old English Furniture*, 1935] The business was still being carried on in 1751 under the same name, however, presumably by his son. There is a reference in 1744 (in connection with a lost dog) to 'Mr Nix, Cabinet Maker, in Exeter Street, in the Strand'. [*Daily Advertiser*, 1 May 1744] In the Westminster poll bk, 1749 he is listed as George Nix, cm of King St, near St Martin's Lane. In the Westminster rate bk, 1751 his address is given as Long Acre.

MOULSHAM HALL, Essex (Earl Fitzwalter). 1728–32: Bills for 3 tables, an easy chair, 8 chairs 'for Chinese Room', a close stool and a corner cupboard. Total £26 11s. [A. C. Edwards, *The Accounts of Benjamin Mildmay, Earl Fitzwalter*]

CLEY, Norfolk (Duke of Montrose). 1729: Receipted account to the Duchess of Montrose referring to repairs to an old screen and supplying a 4-leaf screen, covered with 'India paper'. Total £3 16s. [Scottish RO, GD 229/6/1383/11] 1732: Payment to — Nix for chairs. Total £37 3s. [Scottish RO, GD 220/6/31]

BURTON HALL, Lincs. (Lord Monson). 1740: Bills for a mahogany tea board and two mahogany dining-tables. Total £5 3s [Lincoln RO, Monson 12]

HOLKHAM HALL, Norfolk (Earl of Leicester). 1741: Bill for a tea kettle stand £2 2s. [Holkham Hall accounts]

HAM HOUSE, Surrey (Earl of Dysart). 1729–34: Bill for some 150 items totalling £430 13s 6d, from which the following can still be identified at the house. 1729: 'For a Carved and Gilt Pictor frame £1.10.0. For two Peer Glasses £12.0.0.' The pier glasses, in gilded Kentian frames with broken scroll pediments, and the little gilded Kentian picture frame, which encloses a fan painting, all have the unusual decorative motif of an anthemion attached to acanthus leaves at the corners. 1730: 'For mending and pollishing a Rosewood Dressing Box, and a New Lock Ketch and key 12.0. For a Rosewood frame for the Box £1.5.0.' These items probably refer to the strong box referred to in 1683 as a 'box wth. an extraordinary Lock', of which the stand shows signs of renewal. 1730: 'For mending and Pollishing a plainer box and a New key', 10s. This is probably the box kept by the Duke of Lauderdale in his dressing room. 1730: 'For 18 Hall Chairs painted and Varnished', £18. These oak chairs, of sgabello type, are painted on the backs with the arms of the Tollemache family,

surmounted by an earl's coronet. 1730: 'For Sawing the top of an India Cabinett, and putting on a Deale top, and Japaning the top, and New Pollishing the Cabinett and Lackering all the brass work £3.10.0. For altering the Cabinett frame and New Gilding it £4.10.0. For makeing a Table of the top of a Cabinett and a Neat Japand frame for the Table £2.15.0. For a Leather Cover for the Table lined with flanell', 6s. The Japanese lacquer cabinet and the table made from its top, with the addition of straight legs and frieze, both survive but the protective cover does not. 1730: 'For a black frame Japand, for an India Tea Table and Gilding and mending the Table, where it was broak', £1 5s. This seems to refer to the 17th-century Javanese lacquer table for which an underframing with twist-turned legs was made in order to bring it to a more convenient height. 1730: 'For New Gilding and Japaning two fine India figures', £4. This refers to the restoration of the well-known pair of 'blackamore stands'. 1731: 'For two Elbow Chairs on Casters', £3 10s. These are probably the pair of wide armchairs (later to be called 'love-seats'), covered with red and green cut velvet. No bill exists for the sofa and 18 chairs belonging to the same suite but they may also have been supplied by Nix. 1731: 'For mending an old Cabinett with Silver Corners, and other ornaments, and mending the frame, and four new black Balls, and lining the Inside with Cloth', £1 10s. These are repairs to the Duke of Lauderdale's scriptor, which Nix fitted with four new feet and a new baize writing surface. 1731: 'For New pollishing & Silvering a Glass and Cleaning & boyling the Silver, & new Silvering Ring hinges and Nayles, to Nayl the Silver on the frame', £1 10s. This is a dressing glass with embossed silver mounts. 1732: 'For a large Wallnuttree Horse frame and fixing on the Needle work on the Inner frame & India paper on the back side', £2 15s. This cheval screen has a panel of gros- and petit-point needlework on one side and Chinese painted paper on the other. [V & A archives]   M.T.

Nixers, Theophilus, London, cm and u (1741). In January 1741 the stock of Theophilus Nixers was advertised for sale. The goods had been 'taken for Execution near Long-Acre' and consisted of 'Four-Post Bedsteads, Green and Red Worsted Damask Curtains, Settee-Bedsteads, Buroes, Bedsteads, Goose-Feather Beds ... Chest-upon-Chest, Walnut-Tree Chairs, Leather Seats: Sconces, Desk and Bookcases, Glass Doors: two very good Clocks, and other sorts of goods'. [Burney Coll. newspapers, 1735–55 (BM) 3536]

Nixon, Allan, Leek, Staffs., cm (1814). [D]

Nixon, D., 21 Little Eastcheap, London, cm and u (1822). Succeeded by F. Nixon at the same address by 1823. [D]

Nixon, E., 40 Charlotte St, Blackfriars Rd, London, u, etc. (1835). [D]

Nixon, F., 21 Little Eastcheap, London, cm and u (1823–25). Successor to D. Nixon at this address and succeeded by Thomas Nixon. [D]

Nixon, Francis, Frodsham, Cheshire, cm/joiner (1828). [D]

Nixon, George, Strand, London, carver (1774). [Westminster poll bk]

Nixon, Isaac, Manchester, cm (1797–1804). At Newton Lane in 1797 and 129 Gt Newton St in 1804. [D]

Nixon, J., 21 Little Eastcheap, London, cm (1829). Successor to Thomas Nixon at this address. [D]

Nixon, James, 123 Gt Portland St, Oxford St, London, cm and u (1816–39). From 1835 trading as James Nixon & Son and by this date the nature of the business had changed. A directory of 1835 states their trade to be that of an 'importer of foreign marbles and ancient furniture'. Loudon in his *Encyclopaedia*, 1833, noted that some London upholsterers were collecting both at home and overseas 'curious and ancient furniture, including fragments ... and rearrange these curious specimens and adapt them to modern uses.' One of the firms specializing in this trade mentioned by Loudon was Nixon of Great Portland St. A Rococo marquetry table embellished with ormolu mounts of *c*. 1840 at Castle Ashby, Northants. bears a Nixon label. [D; V&A archives; Loudon, *Encyclopaedia*, pp. 1039, 1101]

Nixon, John, near the turnpike in New Rd, Back Lane, London, pawnbroker and cm (1776). In 1776 took out insurance cover of £100 which included £30 for utensils and stock. [GL, Sun MS vol. 245, p. 230]

Nixon, John, 34 Cable St, Well Close Sq., London, cm and Venetian blind maker (1790–93). [D]

Nixon, Simpson, High St, Wigton, Cumb., joiner/cm (1829). [D]

Nixon, Thomas, 3 Mercers Ct, Tower St, London, upholder (1784–91). Son of James Nixon of Richmond, Yorks., stuff manufacturer. App. to John Allen on 7 April 1784 and free of the Upholders' Co. by servitude, 4 May 1791. [GL, Upholders' Co. records]

Nixon, Thomas, 21 Little Eastcheap, London, cm (1826). Successor to F. Nixon and succeeded by J. Nixon at this address. [D]

Nixon, William, Manchester, cm (1797–1825). At 15 Beswick's Row in 1797 but from 1817 in Oldham Rd. The number in Oldham Rd was 80 in 1817 and 115 in 1825. [D]

Nixon, William, Newcastle, joiner, cm and house carpenter (1811–24). At Northumberland St in 1811 and Percy Pl. in 1824. [D]

Nixon, William, Frodsham Cheshire, cm/joiner (1828). [D]

Nixon, William, Navigation St, Birmingham, carver and gilder (1830–35). Recorded at no,. 5 in 1835. [D]

Noake, Isaac, 4 Thomas St, Bristol, cm and broker (1801–36). In 1801 took out insurance cover of £600. Shown additionally at Bedminster Causeway in 1810. [D; GL, Sun MS vol. 40, ref. 717356]

Noakes, Robert, 52 Blackman St, Southwark, London, cm and u (1822–26). In one directory of 1825 the business is listed as Noakes & Co. [D]

Noakes, Robert, 5 Cecil Sq., Margate, Kent, u (1838–39). [D]

Noar, E., Lancaster (1835–39). Named in the Gillow records 1835, 1837 and 1839. [Westminster Ref. Lib.]

Noar, John, Lancaster, cm (1766–74). App. to J. Wakefield and H. Birkett 1766 and free by servitude 1773–74. [App. reg. and freemen rolls]

Nobbs, William, 6 Crucifix Lane, Bermondsey, London, cm and u (1839). [D]

Noble, Barnard, 6 Long Acre, London, u and cm (1773–83). [D]

Noble, Bernard., 25 Castle St, Leicester Fields, London, upholder (1777). In 1777 took out insurance cover of £800 of which £300 was in respect of utensils and stock. [GL, Sun MS vol. 257, p. 443]

Noble, Henry, 4 William St, Liverpool, cm (1834–37). [D]

Noble, James, Sandgate Head, Penrith, Cumb., cm/joiner (1834). [D]

Noble, John, Northgate, Wakefield, Yorks., u, cm and coach maker (1757–98). At Northgate in March 1757 but in May 1788 announced a move to the top of this road. In this year offered a choice selection of paper hangings. Also made coach harness. Bankrupt in 1793 but still trading in 1798. [D; *Leeds Intelligencer*, 13 March 1757, 6 May 1788, 13 May 1788, 15 September 1789, 10 November 1789, 7 June 1791; 6 August 1794; *York Courant*, 27 April 1784; Bailey's list of bankrupts]

Noble, John, Cold Bath Fields, London, bedstead maker and cm (1787–88). In July 1787 insured his house, goods, plate, etc. for £700 but was made bankrupt in the following year. [GL, Sun MS vol. 345, p. 462; Bailey's list of bankrupts]

Noble, Mary, 80 Devon St, Liverpool, u (1839). [D]

Noble, Nathaniel, 'Hogsdon', Middlx, u (1727). [Oxford RO, Hwy VIII/viii/3]

Noble, Thomas, 35 Gt St Andrew's St, London, upholder (1777). In 1777 insured his house for £300. [GL, Sun MS vol. 260, p. 34]

Noble, Thomas, St James's St, London, u (1784). [Westminster poll bk]

Noble, Thomas, 82 Park St, Grosvenor Sq., London, cm and u (1808). [D]

Noble, Thomas, 23 Francis St, Tottenham Ct Rd, London, carver and gilder (1835–39). An oval convex mirror or girandole in a gilt frame of Regency character is known, the label of which describes the business as 'Cheap Window Cornice & Picture Frame Manufacturer'. It offered a wide range of frames, gilt, rosewood and maple, and stated that the business restored pictures and re-silvered mirrors. [D; *Antiques*, May 1968]

Noble, Thomas, Foundation St, Ipswich, Suffolk, carver and gilder (1839). [D]

Noble, William, Manchester Lane, Morpeth, Northumb., joiner and cm (1827). [D]

Nock, Edward, Rushall St, Walsall, Staffs., joiner and cm (1813). Successor to Thomas Nock. [D]

Nock, Thomas, Rushall St, Walsall, Staffs., cm (1780). Succeeded by Edward Noble at this address. [D]

Nock, Thomas, High St, Stourbridge, Worcs., cm and u (1830). [D]

Nodding, Michael, 33 Banner St, Bunhill Row, London, cm (1829–39). In 1839 listed as cm and u. [D]

Noden, William, Sheep Mkt, Market Drayton, Salop, cm (1840). [D]

Nodes, John, London, upholder (1706) Free of the Upholders' Co., 2 October 1706. [GL, Upholders' Co. records]

Nodes, Joseph, near the Market Pl., Huntingdon, cm, auctioneer and appraiser (1765–d. 1769). In December 1768 an app. Thomas Withnee absconded. In April of the following year Nodes announced that he had moved his premises from near the Market Pl. to the same side of the street opposite 'The Queen's Head'. His death was noted in August 1769 and in April of the following year his shop was taken over by John Box, formerly of St Ives, Hunts. [*Cambridge Chronicle*, 26 October 1765, 12 September 1767, 14 November 1767, 3 December 1768, 15 April 1769, 12 August 1769, 5 April 1770]

Nodes, William, 'The Crown', Fleet Ditch, London (1696). On 5 November 1696 the 1st Earl of Bristol paid Nodes £6 for two looking-glasses. [Wills, *Looking-Glasses*]

Nodin, John, London, trunk and chest maker, cm and undertaker (1776–95). Initially the business traded as Nodin & Houlds (1777–83) with the main address at 1 Leadenhall St but with additional premises at Lower Thames St, 1776–77 and 20 Haymarket, St James's from 1779. The Haymarket premises in turn became the main trading address and remained so until 1793 after which only the Leadenhall St address was used. In this terminal period from 1789–95 the trade is listed as cm and upholder only. Samuel Nodin was associated with John in 1787. The insurance cover maintained by this business indicates that it was of substantial size. The Leadenhall St premises was the manufacturing base and the property connected with 126, later 127 Houndsditch, which was also in use as workshops in 1779–87. An additional house, used as a workshop and warehouse, near Aldgate St was referred to in 1779. The Haymarket property was described as a house and stables. This was covered for £2,200 in 1779 while in that year two substantial policies were taken out on the other properties and the utensils and stock used in the business, one for £5,700 and the other for

£3,900. [D; GL, Sun vol. 274, pp. 387, 616; vol. 275, pp. 274–75; vol. 299, p. 383; vol. 306, p. 504; vol. 346, pp. 45, 494]

Noel, John, 225 High St, Hoxton, London, carver and gilder (1839). [D]

Noke, Thomas, Droitwich, Worcs., cm (1828). [D]

Nolden, Thomas, address unknown, u (c. 1730?). Name recorded on a chair in the Birmingham City Art Gallery Collection which bears a label inscribed 'Thomas Nolden did this chair'. [V&A archives]

Noldret, —, Duke St, Lincoln's Inn Fields, London, u (?) (1756). Maintained a warehouse in Duke St. [*Public Advertiser*, 21 December 1756]

Noller, —, address unknown, u (1762). Paid £20 11s in connection with the supply of 'Mr Cary's bed' in the Chevening, Kent accounts. [Kent RO, Stanhope MS, U590 A61/5]

Nook, Isaac, Dorchester, Dorset, joiner and cm (1760). In 1760 took app. named Bryer. [S of G, app. index]

Noon, —, London, u (1744). Lived in Enfield, Middlx. In January 1744 attacked between Stamford Hill and the Cross at Tottenham, London. [*London Evening Post*, 24–26 January 1744]

Noon, John, London, u (1793). Subscribed to Sheraton's *Drawing Book*, 1793.

Noon, Lancaster, Chelmsford, Essex, u (1730–55). Also had a son named Lancaster bapt. at Chelmsford, 27 March 1732. Took app. named Thwaites in 1730. Undertook work for Benjamin Mildmay, Earl Fitzwalter at Moulsham Hall, Chelmsford 1731–34. The total cost of work undertaken in this period was £77 13s 9d. On 4 December 1755 paid by Peter Du Cane of Braxted Park, Essex £3 7s 'for papering my rooms'. [PR (bapt.); S of G, app. index; Essex RO, D/DDC A13, folio 59; A. C. Edwards, *The Accounts of Benjamin Mildmay, Earl Fitzwalter*, pp. 102–06]

Noon, William, Anderstaff Lane, Burton-on-Trent, Staffs., turner and chairmaker (1828–35). [D]

Noone, John, 54 Bunhill Rd, London, u (1808). [D]

Norborns, —, 153 High Holborn, London, carver and gilder (1802). His trade card [Banks Coll., BM] indicates that the business was a 'General Repository', and 'Carving and gilding in the greatest taste' was offered.

Norbury, John, Chester, cm (1784–1837). App. to George Johnson of Chester, cm, and free by servitude on 6 April 1784. At Newgate St, 1784–1812; St Werburgh St, 1818–19; and Crewe St, 1837. [Freemen rolls; poll bks]

Norbury, Richard, Chester, furniture broker and cm (1818–19). Free 18 May 1818 and living at St Werburgh St but in the following year at Northgate St. [Freemen rolls; poll bks]

Norcott, —, 17 Drury Ct, by the New Church in the Strand, carver and gilder (1802–27). [Heal]

Norcross, Thomas, Lancaster and Blackburn, Lancs., cm (1779–84). App. to J. Wright and free by servitude, 1779–80. Moved immediately to Blackburn. [Freemen rolls; app. reg.; Lancaster poll bk]

Nordin, Edward, 11 Roll's Building, Fetter Lane, London, cm (1808). [D]

Nordon, Jacob, 5 Little Charlotte St, Blackfriars, London, bedstead maker (1839). [D]

Norfor, James, Timber Hill, Norwich, cm and u (1822). [D]

Norman, Albert, Barnsley, Yorks., cm/u (1822–37). Probably born in Hull for his name appears in the app. register of that town when in January 1822 he was app. to William Rollett of Gainsborough, Lincs. In 1837 in Cock Yd, Barnsley. [D]

Norman, Charles, address unknown, cm (1803). Subscribed to Sheraton's *Cabinet Dictionary*, 1803.

Norman, Ebenzer, 1 Little Turner St, Commercial Rd, London, cm, broker and mattress maker (1821–39). In May 1821 took out insurance cover of £300 of which £180 was in respect of utensils and stock. [D; GL, Sun MS vol. 487, ref. 980389]

Norman, George William, London, carver and gilder (1820–39). At 7 Stephen St, Tottenham Ct Rd in 1820; 21 Windmill St, Tottenham Ct Rd in 1826; and 22 Charlotte St, Fitzroy Sq. in 1839. A gilt torchère stand with a circular tray top on a baluster stem in a Queen Anne Style with a label from the 22 Charlotte St address has been noted. [D; Sotheby's, 13 July 1956, lot 204]

Norman, George, Market Pl., Richmond, Yorks., u (1840). [D]

Norman, Gordon, 16 Cranbourn St, Brighton, Sussex, cm and u (1839–40). [D]

Norman, Henry, 9 Ilford St, Liverpool, cm (1839). [D]

Norman, J., 7 Rathbone Pl., London, carver and gilder (1825). [D]

Norman, J., 12 Cannon St East, London, bedstead maker (1835). [D]

Norman, J., South Front, Kingsland Pl., Southampton, Hants, cm and chairmaker (1839). [D]

Norman, James, Frenchgate, Richmond, Yorks., cm and u (1823–40). In 1823 the business was trading as James Norman & Son but by 1827 as James Norman. The father had probably died or retired from the business between these two dates. In 1840 trading as Norman & Metcalfe, cm at Finkle St. [D]

Norman, James, Market Pl., Ripon, Yorks, joiner/cm and u (1837). [D]

Norman, John, 35 High St, Deritend, Birmingham, cm and u (1830). [D]

Norman, Joseph, London, carver and gilder (1802–08). In 1803–04 at 441 Strand but in 1808 at 14 Change Ct, Exeter Change. Edward Lascelles paid him £21 18s on 16 February 1802 for making frames for Harewood House, Hanover Sq. On 14 January 1805 a further £21 10s 6d was paid and £35 17s 9d followed on 21 June of this year 'for frames, drawings etc.'. [D; Leeds archives dept, Harewood MS 190, 192]

Norman, Joseph, 13 Berkeley St, Clerkenwell, London, cm (1809). [D]

Norman, Matthew, Richmond, Yorks, cm (1814–40). At Market Pl. in 1823; Millgate, 1827 and 1840; and Castle Walk from 1828–34. Six mahogany side tables with fluted term legs and Greek key fret friezes at Aske Hall, Richmond, Yorks. bear the trade label of 'M. Norman & Son, Cabinet Makers, RICHMOND'. [D]

Norman, Paul, St Owen St, Hereford, cm and u (1818–40). [D; poll bks]

Norman, Samuel, London, carver and gilder (1746–67). Samuel Norman was app. to Thomas Woodin, carver and gilder, from 1746–53 for a premium of £15 15s. [PRO, IR 1/17] He set up his own business shortly after the end of his apprenticeship. Working from King St, Soho, he took an app., John Haynes, in July 1754 for a premium of £30. [PRO, IR 1/20] There were conflicting opinions as to the health of his business in 1755 when he went into partnership with James Whittle; Norman claimed that he had stock and effects of 'very Considerable Amount or Value' whereas John Becuda, an executor of Whittle's estate, claimed that Norman 'was engaged in some small Trade or Business as a Carver and Gilder upon a Slender Capital which he had borrowed . . . of one William Hallett his Uncle'. [Kirkham, 1969] Hallett, one of the leading furniture makers of the day, took a close interest in the welfare and career of his nephew. When the only son of his old friend James Whittle died in March 1755 Hallett wrote to ask permission for Norman to call on Whittle's daughter Ann with a view to marriage. Whilst Whittle and his son were engaged in the same business as Norman, Hallett had hesitated to suggest that the young couple might court but felt free to do so when Whittle was left without a partner and with his business in a state of 'fateage'. Hallett told Whittle that he had 'a great pleasure in his [Norman's] well doing' and believed that Norman's character would 'bare the thickest inquiry, which at this time a day is one great step towards makeing a married state Hapy.' With regard to business, Hallett told Whittle that Norman was 'capeable of taking great part of the burden from you and therby prolong your days.' [PRO, C 112/194 Pt 11]

Ann Whittle and Samuel Norman were married on 24 April 1755, with Whittle borrowing Norman's £700 marriage token from Hallett. [Kirkham, 1969] At the same time Whittle and Norman became full partners. Their articles of co-partnership reflected the family links; Norman was guaranteed half of the stock and goods-in-trade of his father-in-law and a clause was inserted into the agreement whereby, if Norman's wife should have any child living at her father's death, then one half of Whittle's estate should pass to Samuel Norman. Thus, only two years after completing his apprenticeship, Samuel Norman was a full partner in an established carving and gilding firm. The work of the partnership, which ended only with Whittle's death on 10 January 1759, is detailed under Whittle & Norman.

Only thirteen days after Whittle died Norman's house, workshops, stock and records were destroyed by a fire from which Norman and his wife were fortunate to escape with their lives. [PRO, C12 1299/11] Norman set up in a large room over Exeter Exchange from whence he carried on business as best he could. In January 1760 he only insured his household goods and stock-in-trade at £350, plus £50 for plate and glass. [GL, Sun MS 1760, ref. 173411] In June 1760, however, he took over Paul Saunders's Royal Tapestry Manufactory in Sutton St, Soho, and increased his insurance on household goods and stock-in-trade to £1,100, plus £500 for china, plate and glass and £800 for stock in a yard. [GL, Sun MS 1760, ref. 176419] Norman bought Saunders's unwrought stock-in-trade valued at £1,270 19s 10d. He also came to an arrangement with Saunders whereby for one year Saunders was to have use of the tapestry room but all orders taken by him for furniture should be executed by Norman who would receive the profits less five per cent. Norman was allowed to use Saunders's stock and materials and in return supplied Saunders with goods at trade prices. Orders for funerals were to be executed by both men for one year and the profits divided equally. [See Kirkham, 1969, pp. 506–10 for schedules of stock in trade belonging to Saunders taken over by Norman, and PRO, C12 2060/2]

The business association with Saunders helped Norman through a difficult time. He set to work fulfilling orders which came from Saunders's former clients who now became his. Theresa Cornelys was one of them. In 1761 Norman built a concert room at her famous public assembly rooms, Carlisle House in Soho Sq. and Mme Cornelys hired furniture made by Norman to the value of £1,209 5s 6½d to adorn it and other rooms. [Kirkham, 1969]

The continued patronage of the Duke of Bedford, the Earl of Egremont and the Earl of Holderness helped Norman to recover after the fire. Norman rendered a bill for work done at Woburn Abbey in 1759, before Whittle's death, which included an 'exceedingly large and grand oval frame with eagles' at £97 10s and a 'grand state bed' which cost £52 13s for the frame and £123 9s 7d for the blue silk furnishings. In 1760 Norman supplied two large glass frames in burnished gold at £229, together with one plate glass measuring 76 × 44 ins for the Blue Drawing Room where they hang today. Two

years later he supplied a frame for a portrait of the Duchess and in 1763 a frame for a portrait of the Duke. Goods and services were also supplied to Bedford House, London, in 1760–61 including a magnificent set of fourteen parcel-gilt Virginia walnut chairs, with two elbow chairs, an easy chair and a 'Grand Sofa French shaped' to match in silk damask at a total cost of £122 13s 7d. [Bedford Office, London]

In 1760 Paul Saunders and Thomas Woodin appraised the two large gilt frames and the plate glass, agreeing Norman's overall charge of £142 5s which included carriage and insurance. In the following year Charles Smith and Robert Hyde examined work done by Norman 'consisting chiefly of some rich Fringes for the State Bed and Drapery Window Curtains' and a large oval glass in a gilt frame. Smith informed the Duke and his fellow valuer that he found the materials and workmanship to be of the very best quality and the prices charged to be fair. Smith, however, discovered 'an early, determined (and I'm sorry to say partial) resolution to take off £20 from the bill' to which he reluctantly agreed on the basis that if he did not then somebody else would. Consequently the bill was reduced by £20 to £358 5s. [Bedford Office, London and Scott Thomson] Norman continued to sub-contract work out to William Long who had worked for Whittle and Norman. In 1760 Long charged £23 to carve and gild an oval glass frame which may have been one of those commissioned by the Duke of Bedford. [PRO, C 12 1287/20]

Norman's prices were undoubtedly high. Sir William Chambers commented that the cornice of one room alone at Buckingham House cost nearly £200 in the 1760s. [Beard, *Georgian Craftsmen*, p. 92] Sir Lawrence Dundas queried Norman's total bill of £2,700 for work at Moor Park, Aske Hall and Arlington St from 1763–66. The Assessors (Thomas Chippendale, George Bradshaw and William Mayhew for the furniture, and Richard Brown, Samuel Haworth and William Almond the carving and gilding) made a detailed schedule of the work and reduced the sum to £2,410 1s. [N. Yorks RO, ZNK X 1/7/15–16] Norman was paid by Adam in 1764 for gilding of the gallery at Moor Park. In 1763 Mrs James Harris informed her son, the 1st Earl of Malmesbury, that she had spent the whole morning with Norman, 'partly at Whitehall and partly at his warehouse' and gave what, for her family, were large orders though, as she pointed out, 'not so great as those of Sir Lawrence Dundas'. [*Letters of Earl of Malmesbury*; GCM]

The Earl of Holderness made payments to Norman in 1760, 1763 and 1764 of £150, £231 10s and £17 17s respectively but it was not until 1768 that he paid the principal sum and interest on a bond for £250 given to Whittle ten years earlier. Although Norman held the bond, the Earl had refused to pay, claiming that the debt was due to Whittle alone. Norman, however, was a full partner in Whittle's firm at that date and, as such, entitled to his share of the profits. [BM, Egerton MS 3497] Norman also experienced difficulty in getting Sir Herbert Pakington to pay £500 on a draft which Norman had passed to Matthew Boulton who encashed it. [Birmingham City Ref. Lib., Boulton papers, Z, Walker Senior, Box 1–1, 10 December 1765]

In 1762 Norman was favoured with a royal appointment as 'Master Carver in Wood' to the office of Works and in 1763 was described as 'Sculptor and Carver to their Majesties; and surveyor of the curious carvings in Windsor Castle. [PRO, LC5/105, and Mortimer's *Universal Director*, 1763, resp.] The Windsor Castle archives note a 'Mr Norman' paid £82 7s for a pair of gilt frames in 1764, and £75 17s for a pair in the following year. It is clear from this appointment and other commissions undertaken, that Norman's business had expanded considerably from the small beginnings after the

1759 fire. His insurance policies reflect this expansion. By March 1764 he insured household goods, utensils and wrought stock for £2,250, china and glass for £2,400 and utensils and unwrought stock for £200. [GL, Sun MS ref. 207192] At the same time he also insured a number of houses and shops, together with goods therein, which he rented out. [GL, Sun MS ref. 207374] Such evidence suggests that he was poised for a long and fruitful career. However, there is no known major work by him after 1766, and he went bankrupt in 1767. [PRO, B1/46]

Although he had managed to build up his firm after the 1759 fire, Norman did not come to any satisfactory agreement with those representing the interests of James Whittle's grandson and consequently became involved in lengthy legal wrangles . He also found himself in court with representatives of Paul Saunders, with the sub-contractor William Long, with Theresa Cornelys and probably also Lord Dundas. None of these disputes were settled when he went bankrupt. [Kirkham, 1969]

A magnificent bed made by Norman was bought by James Cullen at a sale sometime in 1767 or early 1768. Cullen informed the Earl of Hopetoun, for whom the bed had been purchased, that the woodwork of the bedstead had cost Norman about £80 and apologized because the bed had 'suffered much by the curious examiners at the Sale'. The sale was probably one disposing of the bankrupt Norman's effects. Norman does not appear to have worked in any major way after his bankruptcy. [Kirkham, 1969] [GCM; Heal; DEF; Matthew Brettingham, The Plans, Elevations and Sections of Holkham House in Norfolk, 1761, p. 3; Hugh Phillips, Mid-Georgian London, 1964, p. 280; James Howard Harris (ed.), Letters of the First Earl of Malmesbury, 1745–1820, 1870, vol. 1, pp. 94–95; Rococo Art and Design in Hogarth's England (exhib. cat.) 1984, V&A, L49, L50, L51, M21; G. Scott Thomson, Family Background, 1949; The Survey of London, Soho III, The Parish of St Anne, Soho, 1966, p. 75; Geoffrey Beard, 'William Kent and the Cabinet Makers', Burlington, December 1975, p. 871; Geoffrey Beard, Georgian Craftsmen, 1966; Apollo, September 1967, pp. 191–97; Conn., November 1966, pp. 154–60; Apollo, February 1964, pp. 122–28; C. Life, February 1980, pp. 427–31; Apollo, May 1977, pp. 361–62; C. Life, 25 September 1980, pp. 1031–32; C. Life, 14 June 1984, pp. 1698–1700; Pat Kirkham, 'Samuel Norman: a study of an eighteenth century craftsman', Burlington, August 1969, pp. 503–13]

1760–61. For patrons who ordered work from Paul Saunders which was handed over to Samuel Norman see Kirkham, 1969, Appendix II. They include Lord Sondes, Sir Orlando Bridgeman, the Duke of Cumberland, Lord Irwin, Lord Scarbrough, Lord Lyttelton, George Pitt Esq., and Sir John Delaval.

CARLISLE HOUSE, London (Theresa Cornelys). 1760–61: Norman executed work she had ordered from Saunders. 1761: Norman supplied furniture including a papier mâché pier frame with a glass (36" × 21") and another with a glass 35" × 21½". He also supplied girandoles — one with a richly carved bird, one with 'Boys heads', a small one with birds and a large one 'with Sheep in China Taste'. [Kirkham, 1969]
WOBURN ABBEY, Beds. (Duke of Bedford). 1760–63: (the work is detailed in bills at the Bedford Office, London, see also G. Scott-Thomson.)
MOOR PARK, Herts., **ASKE HALL,** Yorks., **19 ARLINGTON ST,** London (Sir Lawrence Dundas). 1763–66: detailed schedule of work. [N. Yorks. RO, ZNK x 1/7/15–16] A chest of drawers from Aske Hall is in the Lady Lever Coll. [C. Life, 24 January 1980, p. 258] 1763: Mrs Harris ordered furniture

from Norman. [Malmesbury Letters and C. Life, 24 September 1921] 1760–64: (Earl of Holderness) furniture supplied. Payments until 1768. [BM, Egerton MS 3497]
WINDSOR CASTLE, Berks. (Royal Household). 1762: appointed 'Master Carver in Wood'. 1764–65: frames supplied for Windsor Castle.
BUCKINGHAM HOUSE (Royal Household), n.d. Gilding for cornice (Sir William Chambers). October 1771. reference to work done earlier by Norman. [Beard, Georgian Craftsmen, p. 92 and J. Harris, Sir William Chambers, pp. 217–18]
CHEVENING, Kent (Earl of Stanhope). 1764: 2 gilt frames with glasses — 5 gns 'for my two childrens crayon pictures'. [Stanhope papers, Kent RO, U1590 A61/5]
WESTWOOD, Worcs. (Sir Herbert Pakington), n.d. Norman passed draft given him by Pakington to Boulton. [Boulton papers, Birmingham City Ref. Lib., archive dept, Z Walker Senior, Box 1–1, 10 December 1765]
1775 (James Cullen). Painting and gilding work for Cullen at house in Arlington St, Piccadilly, London. £26–16s–10½d. [Kirkham, 1969, p. 504] See James Whittle. P.K.

Norman, Simon, Charlotte St, Gt Yarmouth, Norfolk, cm and u (1830–40). [D; poll bks]

Norman, Thomas, Burnham Market, Norfolk, cm (1822–39). In 1822 described as a 'cabinet & chair maker, joiner, machine maker' and in 1839 as a 'cabinet-maker & bell hanger'. [D]

Norman, Thomas, Blackfriars St, Carlisle, Cumb., joiner/cm (1828–29).

Norman, Thomas, Little Turner St, Commercial Rd, London, cm (1835). [D]

Norman, William, London, upholder (1708). Free of the Upholders' Co., 5 May 1708. [GL, Upholders' Co. records]

Norman, William, London, cm (1760). Probably a partner and relative of Samuel Norman. An invoice for two large frames for glasses for Woburn Abbey, Beds. was issued in 1760 by William Norman, but the receipt was signed by Samuel Norman. [DEF; C. Life, 14 February 1980]

Norman, William, London, chair and cabinet maker (1812–22). At 63 St John's St, 1812–13, but at 15 Ratcliffe Pl., City Rd, 1814–22. [D]

Norman, William, Market St, Burnham Market, Norfolk, cm (1839).

Normansell, James, 135 Deansgate, Manchester, u (1829). [D]

Normansell, Robert, 154 Long Mill, Manchester, cm, auctioneer and appraiser (1797–1802). [D]

Normansell & Wilson, 46 High St, Manchester, cm (1794). [D]

Norns (possibly Norris), Edward, London, cm (1778). Journeyman cm working for Mr Seddon in Aldersgate St. [GL, P83/MRY1/868/45]

Norris, —, 23 Tottenham St, Mddlx Hospital, cm, chairmaker and u (1781). His trade card [Banks Coll., BM] shows engravings of chairs, a demi-lune table, and a secretaire.

Norris, Edward, Manchester, cm, u and appraiser (1794–1802). In 1794 at 56 Market St Lane but from 1897–1802 at Back of 26 Market St Lane. Bankruptcy announced May 1794. [D; Williamson's Liverpool Advertiser, 19 May 1794, 27 February 1797]

Norris, Elizabeth, 8 Wilmot Sq., Bethnal Green, London, cm and u (1839). [D]

Norris, Frederick Augustus, Peterborough, Northants., cm and chairmaker (1801). In May 1801 took out insurance cover of £400. [GL, Sun MS vol. 40, ref. 717981]

Norris, George, St Mary, Blandford, Dorset, chairmaker (1840). [D]

Norris, Henry, 55 High Holborn, London, u (1820). See John Norris at this address, 1802–35. [D]

Norris, J., address unknown, cm (1793). Subscribed to Sheraton's *Drawing Book*, 1793.

Norris, James, parish of St Peter Hungate, Norwich, cm (1826–30). Son of John Norris, cm. Free 3 June 1826. [Freemen reg.]

Norris, John, Long Acre, London, joiner and frame maker (1669–1702). Samuel Pepys in his diary records a visit to Norris at Long Acre 'who showed me several forms of frames to choose by; which was pretty'. Supplied two picture frames for Hatfield House, Herts. in 1687 at a cost of £7 10s. On 16 April 1689 appointed Joiner to the Privy Council and thereafter worked on a number of commissions for the Crown. In the period 1693–95 supplied several ebony and pearwood frames to the Royal Household and early in 1696 a gilt frame for 'Her Majesty's picture at length'. In 1702 paid £428 10s in respect of work undertaken and goods supplied to household of the late King, William III. [Heal; Hatfield House MS, 145/4; V&A archives; Worcs. RO, 2252/705: 366/2, 2252/705: 366/6(iii)]

Norris, John, parish of St Peter Hungate, Norwich, cm (1761–67). Father of James Norris, cm who was made free 25 May 1771. [Poll bk; freemen reg.]

Norris, John, 20 Market St Lane, Manchester, cm (1772–88). Supplied furniture to George Cooke at Dunham Massey, Cheshire, 1773–88. On 27 October 1773 £14 14s was paid for mahogany furniture and on 19 June 1775 £5 15s 6d for two chests of drawers. A close stool paid for on 11 February 1786 cost £1 4s and a bureau was paid for on 8 July 1788 costing £5 18s. [D; John Rylands Lib., Manchester Univ., George Cooke's accounts]

Norris, John snr, Norwich, cm (1793–d. 1840). Son of Thomas Norris, cm, and free 7 December 1793. At All Saints Green in 1810 and Elm Hill from 1830. His five sons were all made freemen of Norwich between 1815–33. Four of these, Samuel (free 26 October 1815), John jnr (free 20 June 1818), Thomas (free 20 June 1818) and James (free 3 June 1826) were cm, the remaining son William (free 22 June 1833) being a tailor. Took as apps Leonard Hicks (free 24 February 1818) and Samuel Scott (free 24 February 1828). John Norris snr's will was proved at Norwich in 1840. [D; poll bks; freemen reg.; Norfolk Record Soc., index of wills]

Norris, John, Fakenham, Norfolk, cm (1796). Freeman of Norwich. [Norwich poll bk]

Norris, John, Richmond, Surrey, japanner and chairmaker (1798). [D]

Norris, John, 55 High Holborn, London, upholder (1794–1835). Son of Thomas Norris, freeman and member of the London Upholders' Co. Brother to Thomas Heaton Norris. App. to his father on 2 July 1794 and free by servitude 7 July 1802. Listed by Sheraton in his *Cabinet Dictionary*, 1803 as a master cm. From 1806 shown in partnership with his father and trading as Thomas & John Norris. From 1812 in sole control. In the period 1812 to 1825 the business was described as a carpet and upholstery warehouse but from 1826 the trade was stated as u. The enterprise was conducted on a considerable scale and in June 1820 insurance cover amounted to £3,350. This was all in respect of stock with the exception of a small amount for household goods. One warehouse alone contained goods valued at £2,000 and several properties were involved, including one at 26 Lambs Conduit St. A Henry Norris is shown in 1820 in one directory at the Holborn address. [D; Heal; GL, Upholders' Co. records; Sun MS vol. 487, ref. 968664]

Norris, John, 66 Mortimer St, Cavendish Sq., London, cm and chairmaker (1803–12). [D]

Norris, John, 36 Brick Lane, Spitalfields, London, cm and broker of household goods (1804). In May 1804 took out insurance cover of £1,000 which included £400 for his dwelling house and warehouse and £379 for utensils and stock. [GL, Sun MS vol. 430, ref. 762610]

Norris, John Frederick, George St, Richmond, Surrey, cm and u (1808–32). [D]

Norris, John jnr, Norwich and London, cm (1818). Son of John Norris snr and free, 20 June 1818. Appears to have settled in London in this year. [Freemen reg.; poll bk]

Norris, Joseph, Gloucester, cm (1821–26). Children bapt. at St Aldgate's Church in 1821 and 1826. [PR (bapt.)]

Norris, Marmaduke William, 14 John St, Oxford Mkt, London, cm (1790). On 31 December 1790 took out insurance cover of £300 of which half was in respect of utensils and stock. [GL, Sun MS ref. 578318]

Norris, Paul, parish of St Peter Hungate, Norwich, cm (1784). [Poll bk]

Norris, Richard, 9 Back St, Horslydown, London, cm (1808). [D]

Norris, Robert, Liverpool, cm (1745–60). Free 2 August 1745. Took apps named Brockbank in 1751, Howard in 1754, Patrick in 1756 and Hunter in 1760. Dead by 1780. [Freemen reg.; S of G, app. index]

Norris, Robert, 6 Red Lion Ct, Fetter Lane, London, cm (1808) [D]

Norris, Robert, 30 Chandos St, Covent Gdn, London, cm and u (1827). [D]

Norris, Samuel, parish of St Clement, Norwich, cm and chairmaker (1771–1806). Son of John Norris, cm and free 25 May 1771. [D; freemen reg.; poll bks]

Norris, Samuel, Norwich, cm (1815–30). Eldest son of John Norris snr. Free 26 October 1815. Initially lived in the parish of St Peter Hungate but in July 1830 was in the parish of St George, Tombland. [Freemen reg.; poll bks]

Norris, Thomas snr, Norwich, cm (1763–1906). Son of John Norris, joiner and free 26 November 1763. Had three sons, Thomas jnr (free 29 July 1786), Samuel Taylor (free 22 November 1788) and John (free 7 December 1793). In 1768 in the parish of All Saints but moved and was living in St Ethelred, 1780–84; St Julian in 1786; St Peter per Mounterbank 1794; and St Ethelred again from 1802. [Freemen reg.; poll bks]

Norris, Thomas jnr, Norwich, King's Lynn, Norfolk and London, cm (1786–1830). Eldest son of Thomas Norris snr and free 29 July 1786. In the parish of St Peter per Mounterbank 1794 and from 1802 was living in the parish of St Ethelred. Took as app. Edward Wood who was made free 21 September 1807. By 1818 had moved to King's Lynn and by July 1830 was in London. [Freemen reg.; Norwich poll bks]

Norris, Thomas, 55 High Holborn, London, upholder (1770–1811). Son of Robert Norris of Heaton Norris, Lancs., Gent. Father of Thomas Heaton Norris and John Norris both of whom were upholders. Thomas Norris was admitted a freeman of the Upholders' Co. under the terms of the 1750 Upholders' Act, 5 December 1770. He immediately set up business at 55 High Holborn as a 'Bedding, Carpet & Upholstery Warehouse' no doubt aiming at an extensive demand from the middle class for ready-made goods. He probably had manufacturing facilities for he took as apps William Shuffrey, 1779–83, and his sons Thomas Heaton Norris, 1793–1802, and John Norris, 1794–1802. John Norris played an active role in the business after 1802 and by 1806 it was trading as Thomas & John Norris and from 1812 he appears to have been in sole control. Of Thomas Heaton nothing is known after 1802. The business of Thomas Norris was conducted on an extensive scale from its commencement. Already by 1779 utensils and stock were valued for insurance at £1,000 and this was to increase to £6,000 by 1791. As the firm was not seeking to produce individually designed items for the wealthy, little information about individual patrons is known. On 21 May 1787 however Lord Monson paid £36 10s 6d for a 25 ft by 18 ft 3 in Turkey carpet. [D: GL, Upholders' Co. records; Sun MS vol. 276, p. 547; vol. 377, p. 47; Lincoln RO, Monson 10/1/A/6]

Norris, Thomas Heaton, 55 High Holborn, London, upholder (1793–1802). Eldest son of Thomas Norris and brother to John Norris. App. to his father on 3 July 1793 and free of the Upholders' Co. by servitude, 7 July 1802. There is no evidence however that he took an active part in his father's business and it was his younger brother John who became a partner with his father and later took over the enterprise. [GL, Upholders' Co. Records]

Norris, Thomas, 71 Pitt St, Liverpool, cm (1790). [D]

Norris, Thomas, 1 Merritts Building, Bishopsgate Without, London, bed cornice and Venetian blind manufacturer (1808). [D]

Norris, Thomas, Norwich, cm (1818). Son of John Norris snr, cm and free 20 June 1818. [Freemen reg.]

Norris, Thomas, Liverpool, cm (1818–d. 1829). Free 11 June 1818 and died on 21 October 1829. [Freeman reg.]

Norris, Thompson, address unknown, frame maker (c. 1691). About 1691 the sum of £5 5s was paid to Norris by the executors of the estate of Sir Peter Lely to whom he had supplied gilt and ebony frames. Norris also supplied the Beales with frames. [*Burlington*, November 1978, pp. 748–49]

Norris, W., Southwark, London, cm (1806–07). Freeman of Rochester, Kent. [Rochester poll bks]

Norris, William, 4 Coventry St, London, upholstery warehouse (1783). [Heal]

Norris, William, 16 John St, Oxford Mkt, London, upholder (1790–93). On 26 April 1792 he was paid 11s 6d for a deal table and lamp supplied for use at Harewood House, Hanover Sq., the London home of Edward, 1st Earl of Harewood. [D; Leeds archives dept, Harewood MS 212]

Norris, William, Norwich, cm and chairmaker (1807–40). At St Andrews, 1807–22, Orford Hill in 1830 and Maddermarket 1839. Took as apps Nathaniel Partridge (free 7 December 1818), John Holmes (free 24 February 1818) and Stephen Goodman (free 16 March 1820). His sons William Norris jnr a cm, and Samuel Gurbey Norris, a tailor, were free 14 July 1824 and 25 August 1832 respectively. [D; poll bks; freemen reg.]

Norris, William, 66 Princes St, Leicester Sq., London, bed and mattress maker (1827). [D]

Norsworthy, William, Shaldon, Devon, cm and u (1830). [D]

North, Francis, Hull and Louth, Lincs., cm (1747–84). Freeman of Hull but had already left and was living in Louth by 1747 and was to continue to live there. In 1754 took app. named Arlis. [Hull poll bks; S of G, app. index]

North, James, 10 Marsden's Ct, Manchester, chairmaker (1814–16). [D]

North, James, East St, Southampton, Hants, cm (1823). [D]

North, John, Thorganby-cum-Cottingworth, Yorks., cm (1823). [D]

North, Joseph, Manchester, chairmaker (1813–25). At 82 Shudehill in 1813 and 414 St George's Rd in 1825. [D]

North, Robert snr, London, upholder (1710–d. 1748). Free of the Upholders' Co., 4 October 1710. Father of Robert North jnr who he took as app., 1723–24. Also took as apps John Fitchett (1710–18), William Fitchett (app. in 1713), John Deare (1716–24), Philip Box (1720–30) and Edward Lane (1733–49(?)). In 1724 trading from Bartholomew Close, but from 1735–48 at Red Lion St, Holborn. Undertook commissions for Paul Foley of the Temple and Little Ormond

St, London, and Newport House, Almeley, Herefs., 1726–33. Over this period a total of £91 9s 11d was expended mainly on upholstery materials, bedding and labour charges for repairs and alterations. Another patron was Alderman Richard Hoare who employed North, 1733–48, for the supply of beds, bedding, upholstery materials and other work at his house at Barn Elms, Barnes, London. A total of well over £300 was expended during this period. The 'North' who was paid £21 for two japan cabinets supplied to Holkham Hall, Norfolk in 1741 may have been this maker. A Robert North was listed as bankrupt in February 1745, his address being given as 'St. James's, Westminster', and may be this maker. Died in 1748 when an account of Richard Hoare settled in that year was receipted on behalf of Robert North's executors. [GL, Upholders' Co. records; Heal: Herefs. RO, Foley MS F/A III/55; V&A Lib., 86.NN.3; *Gents Mag.*, February 1745; V&A archives]

North, Robert jnr, London, upholder (1731–48). Son of Robert North snr and app. to his father 14 June 1723. He was however transferred to John Spicer 19 June 1724 and made free of the Upholders' Co. by servitude 2 June 1731. On completion of his apprenticeship he appears to have joined his father's business and on 21 July 1731 signed a receipt on the behalf of 'my Father & self'. No further reference to him after this date, has however been located, and his role in the business is therefore unclear. [GL, Upholders' Co. records; Herefs. RO, Foley MS F/A III/55]

North, William, 18 Bow St, Sheffield, Yorks., cm (1837). [D]

Northcote, Ann, 4 Bridge St, Bristol, cm and u (1834–40). Successor to Richard Northcote at this address. [D]

Northcote, John, Castle St, Long Acre, London, upholder (1718). [GL, Sun MS vol. 7, 17 January 1718]

Northcote, Richard, 4 Bridge St, Bristol, cm and u (1828–33). Succeeded by Ann Northcote at this address. [D]

Northcote, William, Dartmouth, Devon, cm, u and innkeeper (1786). In November 1786 announced that he had opened 'The Globe Inn', Dartmouth but intended to continue with his business as a cm and u. [*Exeter Flying Post*, 9 November 1786]

Northend, John, Northowram, near Halifax, Yorks., joiner and cm (1822). [D]

Northend, Joseph, Stone Chair, Shelf, Rishworth, Yorks., joiner and cm (1837). [D]

Northern, J., St Martin's at Palace, Norwich, cm and u (1822). [D]

Northouse, Joseph, York and Leeds, upholder (1755–69). Son of John Northouse, flaxdresser of Leeds. App. to George Reynoldson of York, u, on 5 November 1755. Returned to Leeds after training and set up in business. The stock in trade of this enterprise was sold by auction in 1769. Amongst the items offered were a 'Variety of Paper-hangings, upwards of forty Feather-beds, great choice of Carpets, etc.'. He also sought to sell 'the utensils for grinding, polishing and silvering glass' and several hundred mirror frames, some being in papier mâché. [York app. reg.; *Leeds Mercury*, no. 148]

Norton, Alexander, 14 Bulstrode St, Manchester Sq., London, u and cm (1822–37). Insurance records suggest that the business was of substantial dimensions. In 1822, out of a total cover of £1,200, workshops were insured for £300 and stock and utensils here and in his house were covered for £700. By the following year this latter figure had been raised to £1,000. [D; GL, Sun MS vol. 493, refs 991156, 995077; vol. 498, ref. 1010032; vol. 499, ref. 1010791]

Norton, Ann, 11 Carnaby St, Golden Sq., London, chair and sofa maker (1835–39). W. Norton was trading from this address in the same trade in 1826. [D]

Norton, Benjamin, 4 Back Hill, Hatton Gdn, London, cm (1808). [D]

Norton, Charles, Salisbury, Wilts., cm and u (1801–39). Recorded at Catherine St in January 1801 when he took out insurance cover of £400 which included £300 on stock and utensils in his new dwelling house and shop which communicated with it and £50 on such items in a workshop. Listed at Market Pl. in 1822 and New St in 1839. Trading also as an auctioneer in 1808. [D; GL Sun MS vol. 37, ref. 713396]

Norton, Daniel & Godbold, Francis, Uxbridge, Middlx, u and cm (1777). In 1777 insured their utensils and stock for £300. [GL, Sun MS vol. 258, p. 378]

Norton, Edmund, Earl's (or Early) Ct, Drury Lane, London, upholder (1708–12). Mentioned in November 1709 as a contact for enquiries about a house belonging to the Duchess of Cleveland at Chiswick, London, which was advertised for rental. [The Post Man, 8 November 1709, GL, Sun MS vol. 2, p. 9]

Norton, Edmund, London, upholder (1716). App. to Thomas Turner a member of the Bricklayer & Tiler's Co., c. 1690, and admitted a freeman of the Upholders' Co. by servitude, 7 November 1716. [GL, Upholders' Co. records]

Norton, George, Digbeth, Birmingham, chairmaker (1818). [D]

Norton, George, top of Mill Hill, Leeds, Yorks., cm (1822). [D]

Norton, H., High St, Wisbech, Cambs., cm and u (b. 1774–d. 1814). In April 1807 announced that he was taking over the shop of S. Clayton, auctioneer. Died in August 1814 aged 40. [Cambridge Chronicle, 25 April 1807, 2 September 1814]

Norton, Hugh, King's Lynn, Norfolk, cm (1806). Freeman of Lincoln but living in King's Lynn, November 1806. [Lincoln poll bk]

Norton, J., 10 Workhouse Croft, Sheffield, Yorks., cm (1833).

Norton, John, parish of St Michael at Thorn, Norwich, cm (1830). [Poll bk]

Norton, John, Hatfield, near Doncaster, Yorks., joiner and cm (1834). [D]

Norton, John, Thorne, Yorks., joiner/cm (1834). [D]

Norton, John, Addington Pl., Ramsgate, Kent, cm (1838). [D]

Norton, Matthew, Norwich Rd, East Dereham, Norfolk, cm (1839). [D]

Norton, Richard, 'The Golden Anchor', corner of Stonecutter St, Fleet Ditch, London, u (1727). Insured household goods and stock in his dwelling house for £500 in April 1727. [GL, Sun MS vol. 24, ref. 41519]

Norton, Robert, Norwich, cm (1815). Free 3 May 1815. [Freemen rolls]

Norton, W., 11 Carnaby St, Carnaby Mkt, London, chairmaker (1826). Ann Norton was trading from this address in the same trade in 1835–39. [D]

Norton, William, 'The Lyon & Lamb', by Fleet Ditch, London, u (1712–27). Names in a newspaper of 1712. In 1716 fined for refusing to take parochial office, parish of St Bride's, Fleet St but in 1722 was Questman. In October 1727 insured his household goods and stock in his dwelling house for £500. Recorded in the Chicheley Hall, Bucks. accounts in 1722 in connection with 'making a blue bed'. [Heal; GL, MS 6561, p. 8; Sun MS vol. 25, ref. 42681; V&A archives]

Norton, William, Fleet Mkt, London, u (1753). [D]

Norton, William, 4 Coventry St, Piccadilly, London, upholder (1777–82). In 1777 in partnership with a Philip Abbott. The enterprise was of some size at this date, for out of a total insurance cover of £1,000, utensils and stock accounted for £900. By 1780 however Norton appears to have been trading on his own account, and in November 1782 his bankruptcy was announced. [D; GL, Sun MS vol. 261, p. 207; Sussex Weekly Advertiser, 11 November 1782]

Norton & Shuttleworth, Mill Hill, Leeds, Yorks., cm (1817–18). The address of this partnership would suggest a relationship with George Norton who was trading in this street in 1822. [D]

Norvell, John, Bristol, cm (1781). [Poll bk]

Nosotti, Charles Andrea, 2 Dean St, Soho, London, carver and gilder, u and cm (1835–40). [D]

Nosotti, Francis, 298 Oxford St, London, looking-glass and picture frame maker (1829). [D]

Nosworthy, William, Somerset Pl., Teignmouth, Devon, cm and u (1838). [D]

Notbone, —, 20 Queen's Row, Hoxton, London, cm (1809). [D]

Notley, William, Norwich, u (1760–79). App. to James Harrison but subsequently assigned to Paul Columbine. Free by servitude, 3 May 1760. In 1768 living in the parish of St Peter Mancroft, and as in 1779 his address was Market Pl. he may well have conducted his business from the same premises or at least in the same district throughout. In 1760 took app. named Carter and in 1761, Goddard. Announced his retirement from the trade in October 1779, and offered his stock of 'Paper-Hangings of the newest Patterns, Carpets of all Sorts, and all other Kind of Upholstery Goods' at low prices. [Freemen reg.; poll bk; S of G, app. index; Norfolk Chronicle, 2 October 1779]

Nott, James, 1 Phoenix St, Soho, London, painter and japanner (1826). [D]

Nott, Robert, London, u(?) (1688–89). The Royal Wardrobe accounts for 1688 record a payment of £11 3s 4d for tapestry repairs to a hanging of Diana & Actaeon. In the following year £35 was paid for Coronation robes. [PRO, LC9/123, p. 67]

Nottingham, John, London, joiner (1743–54). App. to John Ravenhill of the Joiners' Co. in 1742 and free of this company by servitude, 6 February 1749. Subscribed to Chippendale's Director, 1754, suggesting an interest in furniture making. [GL, Joiners' Co. records, freemen reg.]

Nottingham, John, Redcliffe Hill, Bristol, carver and gilder (1821–29). At 10 Redcliffe Hill, 1821–24 and at 43, 1827–29. [D]

Nottingham, John, 11 Colonnade, Cheltenham, Glos., carver and gilder (1839). [D]

Nowell, John, parish of St James, Bristol, cm (1784). [Poll bk]

Nowell, John, Lowergate, Clitheroe, Lancs., joiner, cm and house builder, etc. (1824). [D]

Nowland, Martin, 78 Dale St, Liverpool, feather bed manufacturer (1827). [D]

Nowland, Mrs Mary Anne, 25 Basnett St and Dale St, Liverpool, feather dresser and feather bed maker (1826–30). In April 1826 announced that in addition to her existing business premises in Basnett St she had opened a branch in Dale St. An advertisement of March 1827 fails to mention the Dale St establishment and it had probably closed after a short period. Her stock consisted of an assortment of 'feather beds, hair, silk, wool & cotton mattresses, sea beds, church chair & sofa cushions, pallases etc.'. Her bankruptcy was announced in July 1830. [D; Liverpool Mercury, 14 April 1826, 2 March 1827, 16 July 1830]

Nowle, Peter, London, cm and broker (1753). In May 1753 the sale by auction was announced of 'the remaining part of the Goods left undeclared' of Peter Nowle. The sale was conducted by S. Guilliford at the 'Two Blue Posts' in Holborn near Gray's Inn. [Public Advertiser, 26 May 1753]

Nowtier, Isaac, London, upholder (1712). Free of the Upholders' Co., 3 December 1812. [GL, Upholders' Co. records]

Noyes, Benjamin, Shire Lane, London, u (1749). [Westminster poll bk]

Noyes, Edward, London, upholder (1723). Son of Edward Noyes of Marlborough, Wilts. a chirurgeon. App. to William Brathwaite on 2 December 1713 and free of the Upholders' Co. by servitude, 15 January 1722/23. [GL, Upholders' Co. records]

Noyes, Edward, snr & jnr, Chester, carvers and gilders (1814–40). At City Walls, Eastgate in 1814 and Northgate St Row in 1816, also as picture dealer; but by 1818 had moved to Bridge St and in 1822 listed again at Northgate St Row. Employed at Erddig, Clwyd, N. Wales, 1818–20, repairing frames and cleaning and varnishing paintings, for which £24 was charged. In 1828 the business changed to a partnership trading as Dawes & Noyes from premises near the Feathers Inn in Bridge St Row. The wife of Edward Noyes snr died on 12 April 1829. His son Edward was free 1831 but on 29 September of the year previously had married at St Michael's Church Mary Kelly whose father was a marble mason. By February 1831 Edward Noyes jnr appears to have been in control of the business which was trading under the style E. Noyes jnr & Co. The address used was that previously recorded for Dawes & Noyes. Edward Noyes jnr claimed to manufacture 'all kinds of Modern and Antique PORTRAIT FRAMES, CHIMNEY AND PIER GLASSES made to order in the most fashionable style'. He also offered 'Antique and Modern Carving, Gold Mouldings for bordering rooms' and 'a large assortment of Portrait Frames, Chimney, Pier Mahogany, Cheval and Box Dressing Glasses'. Pictures were cleaned and upholsterers supplied. The business was still in Bridge St Row in 1840. [D; V&A archives; freemen rolls; *Chester Chronicle,* 17 April 1829, 28 August 1829, 1 May 1840; *Chester Courant,* 5 October 1830, 8 February 1831, 1 October 1833]

Noyes, Henry, Calverley Rd, Tunbridge Wells, Kent, cm and u (1832–39). [D]

Noyes, William, Cannon St, London, upholder (1761–1808). Son of John Noyes a Hampshire farmer. App. to Richard Farmer on 1 November 1753 and also on the same date to two members of the Drapers' Co., Edward Wright and Thomas Brown. Free of the Upholders' Co. by servitude on 2 July 1761 and by 1763 trading from Nicholas Lane, Cannon St. In 1772 living in Gt East Cheap. By 1782 at 61 Cannon St, an address which he continued to use until 1808. Included by Thomas Sheraton in the list of master cabinet makers in the *Cabinet Dictionary,* 1803. [D; Heal; GL, Upholders' Co. records]

Nuckridge, William, Hosier Lane, West Smithfield, London, carver and sign maker. His 18th-century trade card [Landauer Coll., MMA, NY] states that he made 'all Sorts of Signs, in Elm or Mahogany, Plain or Carved, Likewise Bacchus's Bunches of Grapes & all Manner of Carv'd Work'.

Nugent, J., 7 Corporation Row, Clerkenwell, London, cm (1808). [D]

Nunn, Samuel, Bridge St, Homerton, London, cm, u and undertaker (1839). [D]

Nunn, William, Church St, Hackney, London, picture frame and looking-glass maker (1838). [D]

Nurse, Henry, 10 Old Cavendish St, London, carver and gilder (1835–37). [D]

Nurse, Robert, Old Post Office Yd, Gentleman's Walk, Norwich, carver and gilder (1836–40). [D]

Nutcher, John, Arundel, Sussex, cm (1760). Surety for the marriage of John Ford of Arundel, clockmaker, on 26 August 1760.

Nutsford, George, Queen St, Whitehaven, Cumb., joiner/cm (1811–34). [D]

Nutsford & Ismay, Duke St, Whitehaven, Cumb., joiners/cm (1811). [D]

Nutt, Thomas, Victoria St, Bridgwater, Som., cm (1840). [D]

Nuttall, James, Bury, Lancs., cm, joiner and u (1793–1828). At 37 Union Sq. and Millgate in 1824 but earlier directory references indicate a Union Sq. address only. Trading as James Nuttall & Sons, 1824–28 and by 1828 at Fleet St. [D]

Nuttall, James, Manchester (1797–1817). At 31 Wood St in 1797 but by 1804 the number had changed to 35. In 1808 at 13 Back Irwell St; in 1813 at 36 Wood St; and in 1817 at 28 Back Bridge St. [D]

Nuttall, James, Blackwater St, Rochdale, Lancs., cm and joiner (1814–22). [D]

Nuttall, John, Cannon St, Manchester, cm (1781). [D]

Nuttall, Richard, Cock Gates, Manchester, cm and u (1838–39). [D]

Nuttall, Thomas, Ormskirk, Lancs., cm (1822–34). Listed at Burscough St, 1825–34. A chest with a handwritten label 'THOMAS NUTTALL Cabinet-maker Ormskirk' is known. [D]

Nutter, Joseph, Bradford, Yorks., cm (1820–40). Born at Pellon near Halifax, Yorks. in 1799 and said to have been app. to his relative Matthew Nutter whose workshop was in Westgate, Bradford. Established his own business in the town *c.*1820 and is shown at 37 Darley St in 1830 and 3 North Parade, 1828–40. In 1830 took Christopher Pratt as app. Nutter used labels to mark his furniture, and a set of rosewood quartetto tables, one of which has a chess board, and another a reading stand which folds inside the top, is known. [D; Temple Newsam House, Leeds, Exhib. Cat., *Victorian and Edwardian Furniture by Pratts of Bradford,* 1970; *Furn. Hist.,* 1971]

Nutter, Matthew, Westgate, Bradford, Yorks., joiner and cm (1818–30). In 1830 the number in Westgate was 10. [D]

Nutter, Thomas, Pound Hill, Cambridge, chairmaker (1763–d. 1765). First recorded on 19 April 1763 when it was agreed by the Corporation that Nutter could sink a saw pit on the Pound Hill. He had probably been in business in the town well before this however for when he died in August 1765 he was described as 'an eminent and wealthy chairmaker of this town' and was aged 79. In November 1764 advertised for two journeymen chairmakers. [Cambs. RO, Corp. day bk; *Cambridge Chronicle,* 17 November 1764, 13 August 1765]

Nutting, William, 5 Hoxton Fields, London, cm (1820). [D]

Nye, —, Ship St, Brighton, Sussex, u (1805). [D]

Nye, Carter, Maidstone, Kent, cm (1796). Freeman of Canterbury. [Canterbury poll bk]

Nye, Edmund, The Parade, Tunbridge Wells, Tunbridge-ware manufacturer (1818–40). Son of James Nye and partner to William Fenner 1810–17. Then traded independently from premises on the Parade (the Pantiles). An additional address nearby in the Market Pl. was added in 1823. His reputation was such that in 1826 he was one of the manufacturers selected to ballot for the honour of producing a work and writing table for presentation to the Princess Victoria by the inhabitants of Tunbridge Wells. Patronized by the Duchess of Kent in 1826. Used prints to decorate his early wares and one of the Parade is known dated 1827. Maintained a retail outlet at 10 Castle St, Hastings, Sussex 1826–35 and a Hastings print is known with a Nye imprint. A number of different types of printed label were used by Nye to identify his productions but all appear to be used post 1840. About 1836 Edmund Nye took into his employ Thomas Barton who later became his foreman, chief designer and successor. [D; Kent RO, U785/T10] B.A.

Nye, George, Gabriel's Hill, Maidstone, Kent, cm (1834–39). [D]

Nye, Henry, Grosvenor Rd, Tunbridge Wells, Kent, Tunbridge-ware manufacturer and fancy repository (1839–40). [D]

Nye, Isaac, Brighton, Sussex, cm and u (1826–40). At Ship St Ct in 1826; Upper Bedford St in 1828; Silwood St, 1833–36; and Rock St, 1838–40. Five daughters and two sons bapt., 1828–40. [D; PR (bapt.)]

Nye, John, Tonbridge, Kent, Tunbridge-ware manufacturer (1803–34). [D]

Nye, Robert, Ashford, Kent, cm (1790–96). Freeman of Canterbury. [Canterbury poll bks]

Nye, William, 112 High St, St Ann's, Lewes, Sussex, carver and gilder (1823–40). [D]

Nyles, William, Shipwright St, St Mary Rotherhithe, London, carver (1725). In August 1725 insured goods and merchandise in his dwelling house for £200. [GL, Sun MS vol. 30, ref. 36555]

O

Oaker, William, 3 Hart St, Covent Gdn, London, carver (1778–85). In 1778 insured his house for £200; and in 1785 household goods for £70 and let tenements for £400. [GL, Sun MS vol. 268, p. 461; vol. 333, p. 627]

Oakes, Richard, 86 Snow Hill, Holborn Bridge, London, case and cabinet maker (1775–79). In 1775 described in one directory as a 'cabinet & plate case maker'. In 1778 took out insurance cover of £2,000 on his house, wareroom and workshops. Bankrupt, *Gents Mag.*, February 1779. [D; GL, Sun MS vol. 267, p. 256]

Oakey, —, Liverpool, cm (1819). On 10 December 1819 Messrs Taylor & Pinnington advertised the coming sale of Oakey's utensils and stock 'on the Premises 25 Tarleton-street Church-street'. This consisted of 'lofty Four-post Bedsteads with carved, reeded, twisted & pannelled Feet-posts, Sideboards, Wardrobes, Chests of Drawers, set of Patent Dining-tables, Sets of Trafalgar & other Chairs, Loo, Library, Sofa, Card, Pembroke, Bagatelle, Work, Reading & Dressing-tables, Gardevines, Portable Desks, Hall Chairs, Sofa covered with Hair-cloth, Washstands, Gentlemen's enclosed ditto, Canterburys, Music-stools, Draught-boards, Tea caddies etc: Chimney & large-sized Dressing-glasses, handsome Brussels, Venetian & Kidderminster Carpets, Hearth-rugs, about 20 pairs of Blankets, a quantity of fashionable Room Paper etc: also a quantity of Tools, Benches'. [*Liverpool Mercury*, 10 December 1819]

Oakey, Caleb, Fishergate, Preston, Lancs., u and paper hanger (1825–42). At 34 Fishergate in 1825 but from 1828–42 the number was 24. [D]

Oakley, George (& various partners), London, cm and u (1773–1840). The firm of George Oakley produced stylish furniture in the Grecian taste during the decades spanning the turn of the 19th century, and was one of the pioneers of 'Buhl' inlay, a form of decoration that regained popularity during the early years of the Regency. Fashionable materials such as rosewood, mahogany and calamander were often used in Oakley's furniture, combined with inlays of satinwood and ebony, and brass stars and bands of metalwork. The high-class furniture made by George Oakley earned him a royal appointment and a contemporary reputation for fine craftsmanship.

George Oakley was the son of Richard Oakley (skinner) of Weobley, Herefs., and he was app. in 1773 to William Elliot of 2 Clements Lane, Lombard St. He was admitted freeman of the Upholders' Co. by servitude in 1782 [GL, Upholders' Co. records] and from this year until 1789 is listed in London directories as an upholder, under his own name, at 2 Clement's Lane, although in the meanwhile he had acquired other premises. His trade card [Heal and Banks Colls, BM] dated 1 March 1786 — a swagged shield surmounted by a plume of three feathers — describes him as 'Upholder, | (No. 22) | The South Side of | St. Paul's Church Yard | London | Goods Appraised | and Funerals Furnishd'. A large assortment of finished furniture was also kept at their ware rooms and manufactory in the City, which were retained until at least 1811 [D], but in the meanwhile, by 1799, new premises had been opened at 35 St Paul's Churchyard, where orders could be placed, and where a stock of fabric patterns in great variety was kept in order to accommodate the 'Wholesale Houses and their Customers in the City'. The 'Elegant Printed Furniture Warehouse at No. 67 New Bond Street, next Phillips's Auction Rooms' appears to have been devoted exclusively to the sale of fabrics of every description, also 'the most fashionable Paper Hangings and Borders' in a variety of widths. [*Morning Chronicle*, 23 February, 2, 3, 11 and 13 July] (Between 1802–05 Oakley, Dudding & Co., Furniture Printers, 67 Old Bond St are listed in trade directories since Oakley had acquired the printed textile business of Dudding & Co.) The *POD* for 1811 and 1812 also gives 35 Piccadilly as an address. Business must have been flourishing, because an entry in *The Times*, October 1812 refers to the 'late extensive additions' to his manufactory 'in which the first artists and mechanics are employed', and an advertisement mentions warerooms at 16 Old Bond St. In 1822 he became master of the Upholders' Co. and insurance records for 1823 show him still to be at 8 Old Bond St, as u and cm. An entry in the Upholders' Co. records dated 1825 gives his address as 8 Baker St, Portman Sq., and by 1838 he was at 43 Cirencester Pl., Titchfield St. He is known to have died by 1841.

George Oakley's name appears on bill-headings somewhat indiscriminately either on its own or in conjunction with other cm. His first partner was Henry Kettle, whose trade label appears on several pieces at Saltram, Devon, and the bills of 1796–97 are headed Oakley & Kettle. In 1798 George Oakley acquired new premises and a new partner, Thomas Shackleton, an upholder and cm [GL, Upholders' Co. records] who had previously worked at 115 Long Acre (1781–93) and then at 150 Aldersgate St (1793–1800) where he worked in partnership with his father-in-law, George Seddon. The style Oakley & Shackleton appears on a bill dated 1798, and two years later the firm was joined by another partner, John Evans, a water gilder, and the three names of Oakley, Shackleton and Evans appear together on bill-headings in 1800 and 1805, and are still together in 1809. After Shackleton had left the firm, Oakley and Evans remained in partnership, and are listed together in 1819 [POD] still trading from two addresses, the manufactory at 22 St Paul's Churchyard and the Magazine at 8 Old Bond St.

Visits by the royal family to Oakley's Bond St Showrooms are recorded in the *Morning Chronicle* of 1799. In May 'the ROYAL FAMILY, with the PRINCE and PRINCESS of ORANGE did Mr. OAKLEY the honour of viewing his Printed Furniture Warehouse in New Bond Street; when her MAJESTY, the Duke and Duckess of YORK, and the PRINCESSES, &c., highly approved of the splendid variety which has justly attracted the notice of the fashionable world.' Two weeks later, 'Notwithstanding the fatigues which the Royal Family underwent [at the King's Birthday Parade], the Queen and Princesses, accompanied by the Duke and Duchess of York made a tour of the most elegant shops and manufactories in the different lines of the useful Arts. We saw them at Oakley and Shackleton's magazine of furniture in Old Bond Street . . . and thus Their Majesties, in the prevailing taste for magnificence in every article of decoration, give the most flattering encouragement to the arts by their countenance and protection'. On the evening of the celebrations in honour of the King's Birthday, 'the illuminations were mostly confined to the gaming houses and the tradesmen. OAKLEY's furniture magazine was the most tasteful and novel in its design'. [*Morning Chronicle*, 23 May, 5, 6 and 17 June]

The accolade of Royal Appointment followed shortly after this tribute to royal patronage, and on 2 July an entry in the *Morning Chronicle* advertising the wide stock of fabrics available at 67 New Bond St is headed 'GEO. OAKLEY and Co. FURNITURE PRINTERS to her MAJESTY'. The lion and unicorn flanking the crowned garter on a bill-heading of 1802 [Windsor RA 25115] is corroborated by his trade card of the same year: here the premises at 8 Old Bond St are described as a 'Magazine of General and Superb Cabinet Furniture', and below the address and royal cypher, the firm of Oakley & Co., Furniture Printers to Her Majesty, 'respectfully acquaints those Ladies and Gentlemen | who do him the honor to inspect his Rooms, that the greatest Care | is taken in the manufacturing of his Articles and in the choice of | fine and well-season'd Materials. In this Magazine will be | found a constant supply of every kind of fashionable Furniture | compleat & ready for immediate delivery. The number of Artists | and Mechanics, as well as the large Capital necessarily employ'd in | this Concern, together with the extensive Stock kept for ye Accommodation | of the Public are obvious reasons which render it impossible to conduct | it by giving Credit.' Whether any of these Mechanics were employed in the manufacture of brass inlay is not known, but Sheraton's *Cabinet Dictionary*, 1803, to which George Oakley subscribed, implies that this aspect of decoration was executed by the cm rather than by specialist 'Buhl' workers — who did not set up manufactories until 1815. The jointly-addressed letter heading on George Oakley's bills gives the impression that the furniture was displayed and bought in the Magazine at 8 Old Bond St and constructed in the manufactory at 22 St Paul's Churchyard, but it would be wrong to assume the total separation of workshops and showrooms. Insurance records of 1809 confirm that a flourishing set-up of considerable size and value existed at 8 Old Bond St, consisting of a saw-pit, stables, open sheds and yard, showroom, womens' workroom, veneer room and drying lofts. Little is known of the craftsmen employed by Oakley, but his concern to satisfy clients with an up-to-the-minute taste in furnishings is witnessed by his employment of a designer, John Taylor, who later contributed four designs to Ackermann's *Repository* between 1821 and 1824. A newspaper article published in Weimar in 1804 stated that 'all people with taste buy their furniture at Oakley's' and this fashionable reputation abroad is confirmed in 1807 by another German writer who refers to the firm as being 'famous for goods of the latest fashion', and lists Oakley alongside Gillows and Charles Elliott as being the chief makers and sellers of furniture and upholstery in London. [Joy, *English Furniture, 1800–1851*]

The scope and quality of Oakley's stock was constantly advertised in glowing terms, and entries in the *Morning Chronicle* show that the firm's output was geared to a discerning and fashion-conscious clientèle. On 4 July 1788 'OAKLEY and SHACKLETON beg permission to present to the Nobility and Public a selection of Articles for their approbation, which, for their superior elegance, novelty and execution, will be found unequalled by any other House in

London. Their patent Chairs for Drawing and Eating Rooms, French and Polonese Beds, with elegant draperies, and Beds of all other kinds: Window Curtains, and every other article of elegance, of the newest invention and most tasteful design, are adapted both to the superb mansion and the cottage ornée. The Magazine, which has been honoured with the inspection and countenance of Her Majesty, accompanied by other illustrious members of the Royal Family, as well as by many of the highest Nobility, is now submitted to the public eye. The extensive stock always kept ready for delivery enables them to completely furnish capital Houses in a few days. Ladies and Gentlemen may have designs made of every article, and Rooms of Furniture to their own taste, wherein it will be the study of the Proprietors to unite elegance and convenience with economy, which has hitherto given them a decided preference, and for which they beg to return their grateful acknowledgements'.

Surviving bills show that George Oakley was patronized by many discriminating private clients as well as by public bodies and royalty. In 1788–89 he carried out an extensive commission to the order of Thomas Baring, for the Manor House at Lee (Lewisham), Kent, supplying carpets, curtains and upholstery fabrics as well as furniture throughout the house. Items listed include a bedstead 'Spanish mahogany pillars, richly japanned cornice, tester with flounced valence', a mahogany dressing table and a 'neat mahogany commode' both 'fitted up with a variety of conveniences' a 'pair of eliptic card tables of fine mahogany, satinwood border neatly inlaid' and a Pembroke table *en suite*: a large quantity of seat furniture included a 'panelled back sofa with broad tablet, caned seat on socket castors and '12 broad tablet back chairs with elbows, caned seats, Etruscan ground japanned and gilt trellis ornaments': also '16 mahogany broad tablet back chairs (with stuffed seats covered with satin covering) and finished with Princes metal nails' to go with 'a set of fine mahogany dining tables consisting of 5 pieces on fashionable shaped legs, shifting hinges and brass fastenings'. The bill totals over £170. [Private archive] A small bill to James Brogden amounting to £15 has been traced. [Essex RO, D/D5 e 8]

In 1800–02 a bill totalling £30 12s 6d for tables and for 106 yards of 'Furniture Linen' appears in the account book of Lady Cotton of Madingley Hall, Cambridge [Cambs. RO, 588/A45] and in 1801 and 1809 he supplied furniture to Edward Lord Lascelles for Harewood House, Hanover Sq., London. [Leeds archives dept, Harewood MS, 191–92] In 1800 he carried out the refurnishing of the chief bedroom at Williamstrip Park, Glos., the bill totalling £208. He supplied a 'handsome commode chest of drawers, fine wood, neatly inlaid, pillastry impannell'd with Sattin wood', a 'neat mahogany folding top Lady's dressing Table, fitted up with a variety of useful conveniences', a 'fine mahogany Lady's Writing Table neatly inlaid and a cabinet above, with drawers', also a 'fine mahogany oval pillar and claw worktable in suite'. The chief item was a 'superb lath bottom double screwed Dome Bedstead, sides and posts japanned, slate ground and enriched with ornaments, Gothic ribs supporting a square lath terminated by shorter ribs, supporting an Ovalo Dome, head and foot frames, japanned in suite, french stuffed in fine linen . . . a sett of sweep cornices to fix at the lower extremity of the tester and a set of straight do. to the upper tester, japanned, a slate ground . . . and trellis friezes with tablets of flowers in greens and whites, the mouldings relieved in pinks . . .'. All the fabrics used for furnishing this bed are minutely listed as to colour and quantity: 'pink net calico . . . and roof quilted of entire slate calico, elegant draping reversed and head vallens of the chintz bound with green Geranium Garment border, panelled with broad and narrow green trellis borders trimmed with Etruscan ornamented fringe, ditto tassels, plaitted line, light cases for the head and foot boards of slate and chintz in suite . . .'. The colour scheme was carried through to the 5 sets of French window curtains, 'pink nett chintz lined with slate ditto, with elegant draperies finished in suite with Bed and handsome japanned cornices . . .' and every item that went into the making of these is again minutely recorded in fascinating detail.

Furnishings of this sort, and general upkeep formed a substantial part of an upholder's business. In 1804 Colonel Rebow of King St, Cheltenham, was invoiced by the firm of Oakley, Shackleton & Evans for several small maintenance jobs to do with repairing, fitting and fixing a number of rollerblinds, supplying new curtains to a 4-poster bed, making dimity cases for easy chairs, carpet-laying, and replacing door-handles and sash-lines. [Private archive]

An early mention of the Boulle revival comes in an invoice dated 1810 [Windsor RA 25318] for supplying the Prince Regent with a 'capital mahogany pedestal library table, inlaid with Bhull bordering, fitted with drawers on both sides . . . the top covered with black leather and raised on brass castors'. At about the same time a sideboard was bought from George Oakley as part of the refurnishing programme at the Bank of England. [C. Life, 3 October 1947] There is also a mahogany sideboard and sidetable attributed to him in the Ballroom of the Mansion House (closely related to one at Papworth Hall, Cambs.) which is described as a 'capital mahogany sideboard supported on a stand, reeded legs and carved and bronzed paw feet, with antique bronze heads'.

Papworth Hall, Cambs. is widely quoted as George Oakley's major commission — partly, perhaps, for lack, hitherto of other documentation on his career. Built in 1809 for Charles Madryll Cheere, Papworth Hall was furnished by Oakley the following year. The furniture is now scattered, but many documented pieces survive. Two sets of chairs were designed in a modified Klysmos style: the hall chairs had sabre legs and a painted crest, and the sabre-legged dining chairs had turned arm supports and a horizontal backrest super-imposed upon and overlapping the uprights; and in the same room the sideboard was flanked by pedestals to match. Oakley also supplied a winged library bookcase of architectural design, the mahogany veneer decorated with vertical bands of palmleaf ornament and ebony dots; the pedimented cornice is enriched with ormolu scroll-work above recessed open shelves, and the doors of the projecting sidewings are filled with brass trellis backed with pleated silk. [Christie's, 1 December 1977, lot 150] Other identifiable pieces from Papworth include a toilet mirror and mahogany dressing table with central arched kneehole, the mahogany veneer outlined with ebony inlays; a pedestalled loo table of calamander wood inlaid with ebony; [both illus. DEF] a set of quartetto tables in mahogany, the top edged by broad banding inlaid with brass stars; an elegant satinwood winged wardrobe fitted with drawers and clothes shelves and elaborately inlaid with ebony. Documented evidence of this sort shows how Oakley furniture was used throughout the house to create a fashionable contemporary decor to match the newly-built mansion. So far, no comparable set of later bills has yet come to light, and the last twenty years of George Oakley's life are still wrapped in mystery, since no bills as yet post-date 1819, although George Smith in his Cabinet-Maker's Guide, 1826, refers to furniture supplied by Oakley & Evans for Alexander Copeland's house in Gt George St, Westminster.

The last evidence of George Oakley's career is found in bills invoiced to J. H. Leigh of Stoneleigh Abbey, Warks.

[Shakespeare Birthplace Trust, Leigh receipts, DR18/5] In 1813 George Oakley supplied 'an ebonized Chaise Longue with Bolster end and squab stuffed with the best hair' complete with 'a tight case of Chintz lined with white Calico and finished with Silk and Cord with Tassel to Bolster', also '12 Grecian Ebonized Chairs with brass Ornaments and Cane Seats' complete with bordered hair seat cushions. His last known bill [DR 18/5] is dated 3 July 1819, when J. H. Leigh bought of George Oakley 'an imitation rosewood sofa with seat Cushion and Bolsters stuffed with best hair . . . finished silk Gimp, Cord and Tassels' and also 'an elegant Rosewood Commode with Chiffonier top and plate glass at the back', two central wire trellis doors flanked by slightly recessed open shelves, divided by fluted pilasters, the frieze inlaid with brass foliage.

Identifiable pieces by George Oakley are typified by the architectural quality of design, the high standard of craftsmanship, and the smart Regency aspect of decoration which characterize the output of this fashionable cabinet maker, throughout the whole of his known career. [DEF; GCM; C. Life, 3 October 1947; Conn. Year Bk, 1960; adverts in The Times, 8 and 11 July 1811, 1 and 10 October 1812; Burlington, June 1980, p. 416; Joy, English Furniture, 1800–1851; F. Collard, Regency Furniture, 1985; GL, Sun MS vol. 447, ref. 823899; vol. 443, refs 836711–13; vol. 459, ref. 875079; vol. 498, ref. 1001094]   M.S.

Oakley, J. & H., Waterloo Terr., Southampton, Hants., cm and u (1834–39). [D]

Oakley, James, High St, Halstead, Essex, cm (1823–32). [D]

Oakley, James, Greenwich Rd, Greenwich, London, bedstead maker (1832–38). See John Oakley, u at this address, 1826–32. [D]

Oakley, John, Greenwich Rd, Greenwich, London, u (1826–32). James Oakley, bedstead maker traded from this address 1832–38. [D]

Oakley, John & Benjamin, Southampton, Hants., cm and u (1830–39). Listed at Bedford Pl. in 1830 and Waterloo Terr. in 1839. [D]

Oakley, Richard, Halstead, Essex, cm (1787–d. 1798). In 1787 insured his dwelling house for £300. Probate on his will granted 1798. [GL, Sun MS vol. 345, p. 78; Wills at Chelmsford, III, p. 239]

Oakley, Thomas, Hatter St, Bury St Edmunds, Suffolk, cm (early 19th century). Licensed to set apart a room in his house for the meeting of protestant dissenters. Possibly the Thomas Watts Oakley born in Halstead, Essex who moved to Bury St Edmunds and married Elizabeth Holland and was later 'called to the Baptist Ministry'. [V.B. Redstone, Records of Protestant Dissenters in Suffolk, 1912, p. 45]

Oakley, Thomas, Southend St, Ledbury, Herefs., cm and brush manufacturer (1840). [D]

Oakley & Dudding, see George Oakley.

Oakley & Kettle, see George Oakley.

Oakley & Shackleton, see George Oakley.

Oakman, Thomas, Castle St, Long Acre, London, carpenter and bedstead maker (1806–10). At 16–17 Castle St in 1806, 16 only, 1807–09, and 14 in 1810. Stock and utensils in both houses that he was using in 1806 only amounted to £100 in value but in 1808 this had been raised to £300 and in 1810 to £400. [GL, Sun MS vol. 437, ref. 795660; vol. 440, ref. 806679; vol. 445, ref. 814465; vol. 453, ref. 844475]

Oakman, William, Belton St, London, cm and bedstead maker (1780–1808). In 1780 on the corner of Shorts Gdns, but by 1804 at 11 Belton St. Total insurance cover was £400 in 1780 and £600 in 1804. [D; GL, Sun MS vol. 282, ref. 428763; vol. 431, ref. 762100]

Oaksford, James, 26 Pitt St, Old Kent Rd, London, chair and sofa maker (1839). [D]

Oates, Bartholomew, 17 and 18 Blackfriargate, Hull, Yorks., cm and broker (1821–31). In 1826 shown as u and from 1834 the business appears to have changed its nature becoming a pawnbroker and dealer in plate and by 1840 'auctioneer, sheriff's officer & pawnbroker'. [D]

Oates, John, 34 Gt Sutton St, Clerkenwell, London, cm (1808). [D]

Oates, Joseph, Leeds, Yorks., cm (1826–40). At 13 York St in 1826 and no. 26, 1828–30. By 1834 had moved to 8 Moxon's Yd, Kirkgate and in 1839 was at 12 Saville St. [D]

Oates, Mark, High St, Falmouth, Cornwall, cm and u (1830). [D]

Oates, Reuben, 16 Noble St, Goswell, London, chairmaker (1787). In June 1787 insured his goods and utensils for £100. [GL, Sun MS vol. 345, p. 215]

Oates, Richard, 11 Robinhood Ct, Shoe Lane, London, cm (1784). In 1784 insured his utensils and stock for £60 out of a total cover of £100. [GL, Sun MS vol. 322, p. 588]

Oats, Joseph, 187 Drury Lane, London, cm and u (1817–30). Freeman of Canterbury. In 1817 trading as Oats & Son but by 1820 under his own name only, suggesting that in 1817 he was in partnership with his father, who was probably Richard Oats. In 1823 was taking out insurance of £700 of which £500 was for utensils and stock. [D; Canterbury poll bk; GL, Sun MS vol. 498, ref. 1001056]

Oats, Richard, 187 Drury Lane, London, cm (1804–08). Probably the father of Joseph Oats and if this is the case trading in partnership with him at this address in 1817. Between 1804 and 1808 maintained insurance cover of £100 on utensils and goods in his dwelling house with an additional £400 cover on those items in a workshop behind. In 1804 also covered a house for insurance at 20 Judd Pl., West Somers Town valued at £400. [GL, Sun MS vol. 431, ref. 767835; vol. 434, ref. 781424; vol. 445, ref. 823239]

Oborne, W. & I., High St, Shaftesbury, Dorset, cm and u (1840). [D]

Ockford, John, Bartholomew St, Exeter, Devon, cm (1822). Son, Samuel Thomas, bapt. at St Olave's Church on 9 June 1822. [PR (bapt.)]

Ockford, Samuel, Southgate St, Gloucester, cm and chairmaker (1820). [D]

Ockleford, G., 17 Kingsland Pl. North, and 1 Brewhouse Lane, Southampton, Hants., cm (1792–1839). [D]

Odams, David, Derby, cm (1826). App. to John Shipley of Leicester, cm, and free by servitude in 1826. [Leicester freemen rolls]

Oddie, Henry, London, and Ipswich, Suffolk, u (1740). In April 1740 announced his move from London to Ipswich where he had taken premises opposite 'The Griffin' near Cornhill. He offered 'all Sorts of Upholsters Goods after the newest and best Manner or Fashion' and in addition 'Looking-Glasses and Mahogany Ware, also Trunks and Portmanteaus'. [*Ipswich Journal*, 5 April 1740]

Oddy, William, Drake St, Rochdale, Lancs., cm and u (1825–28). [D]

Odell, Mr, address unknown, u (1710–25). Supplier of furniture to Chicheley Hall, Bucks. His first commission, which involved silvering and framing glasses, was paid for in February 1710 and cost only £2. No further work is recorded until the 1720s when the sums are much more substantial. In April 1722 two sconces in burnished gilt frames were paid for at a cost of £10 and in August of this year £132 was paid for glasses, gilt frames and carpets. In January 1724 gilt tables, frames and glass was paid for amounting to £24 12s and Mr Odell was concerned in the making of a coach which cost

£105 in the following year. [Bucks. RO, D/C/3(ii), D/C/36(iii); *C. Life*, 27 February 1975, p. 500]

Odge, —, Uphill, Malmsbury, Wilts., cm and u (1793). Subscribed to Sheraton's *Drawing Book*, 1793.

Ody, John, 'The Castle', St Paul's Churchyard, London, cm and u (1723–27). Member of the Joiners' Co. In May 1727 was working on a commission which involved the supply of two pier and two chimney glasses to Thomas Foley of Stoke Edith, Herefs. Included in a letter that he forwarded to his patron on 11 May 1727 was a sketch and a discussion of alternative ways of framing and finishing the glasses. [Heal; Herefs. RO, Foley MS 12/7673] See William Old.

Offer, Robert, Gainsborough, Lincs., joiner, cm and chairmaker (1761). In 1761 took app. named Beeley. [S of G, app. index]

Officer, James, York, carver and gilder (1771–84). Son of Thomas Officer of Leeds, hatter. App. to George Gibson, carver and gilder, on 1 August 1764. Free by servitude in 1771 and living at Coney St in 1774 and North St in 1784. [Freemen rolls; poll bks]

Offord, James, 9 Lower Castle St, Bristol, chairmaker (1820). [D]

Offord, James, Brighton, Sussex, chairmaker (1830–37). At Spring St, 1830–32; Jubilee St, 1835; and 1 Mulberry Sq. in 1837. Two daughters bapt., 1830–35, and a son James married in 1837. [D; PR (bapt. and marriage)]

Ogborn, Samuel, 5 Cathay, Bristol, cm (1793–94). [D]

Ogborn, William, 19 Old George St, Southwark, London, chair and sofa manufacturer (1820). [D]

Ogden, Joseph, Mytholmroyd, Halifax, Yorks., joiner and cm (1830). [D]

Ogden, Nathan, Oxnop, near Keighley, Yorks., cm (1822). [D]

Ogden, Samuel, Birmingham, cm and u (1816–22). Listed at 7 Ann St in 1816 and 16 Church St in 1822. [D]

Ogden, Thomas, Manchester, chairmaker (1752). In 1752 took app. named Baley. [S of G, app. index]

Ogden, William, Upper Mill, Saddleworth, near Rochdale, Yorks., cm and u (1822). [D]

Ogg(s), Charles Morris (or Marris), 47 London Rd, Manchester, cm (1822–40). One directory of 1834–40 shows 103 London Rd. [D]

Ogilvie, Edward Johnson, Welton, Yorks., cm (1823). [D]

Ogilvie, James, 35 Blackfriargate, Hull, Yorks., cm and broker (1831). [D]

Ogilvy, Thomas, Peter St, Westminster, London, chairmaker (1749). [Poll bk]

Oglethorpe, Joseph, Lancaster (1805–25). Named in the Gillow records 1805, 1810, 1813, 1815 and 1819. Shown at Penny St, 1822–34 and Nicholas St in 1825. [D; Westminster Ref. Lib., Gillow]

O'Hara, T., 33 Suffolk St, Charing Cross, London, u (1820). [D]

O'Hara, Thomas, 20 Gravel Lane, Manchester, chairmaker (1825). [D]

O'Hara, Thomas, 95–96 Richmond Row, Liverpool, tailor, draper and u (1837). [D]

Okely, John, London, cm (b.1752–c.1772). Born at Bedford in 1752 and app. to Abraham and David Roentgen at Neuweid, near Cologne, in 1766. He remained with the German cm at Neuwied near Cologne until 1772. Heal records him as Oakley at 13 Dean St, Soho, c.1775–93. It has been suggested that the Okely who subscribed to Sheraton's *Drawing Book* in 1793 and was at St Paul's Churchyard may be the same person. Sheraton's subscriber may however have been George Oakley. [*DEF*; H. Huth, *Roentgen Furniture*, 1974, p. 10]

Okleford (or Okelford), George, Gloucester Sq., Southampton, Hants., cm (1805–08). [D]

Okell, George, Liverpool, painter and carver (1736). Free 7 October 1736. Dead by 1780. [Freemen reg.]

Okey, Caleb, 13 Griffin Lane, Bristol, u (1817–18). [D]

Okey, Thomas, Kensington Gore, London, upholder (1794). Son of Henry Lucas Okey of St Helens, Lancs., Gent. App. to William Yateman on 6 September 1786 and free of the Upholders' Co. by servitude, 2 April 1794. [GL, Upholders' Co. records]

Old, Thomas, London, upholder (1754–64). Son of Thomas Old of St John, Wapping, London, shopkeeper. App. to Thomas Booden on 7 September 1754 and then transferred to William Harwood, clothworker, 4 August 1756. Free of the Upholders' Co. by servitude, 1 March 1764. [GL, Upholders' Co. records]

Old, Thomas, 14 Fish St Hill, London, upholder (1778–84). Made free of the Upholders' Co. under the terms of the 1750 Upholders' Act, 7 March 1781. He appears to have been trading as an upholder and cm as early as 1778 however and in this year took out insurance cover of £600 of which £400 was in respect of utensils and tools. [D; GL, Upholders' Co. records; Sun MS vol. 264, p. 415]

Old, William, 'The Castle', St Paul's Churchyard, London, turner and chairmaker (1703–21). A payment of £1 14s to this maker by the 1st Duke of Leeds is recorded in 1703. Insurance records describe him as a wood turner. Later became a partner with John Ody at the St Paul's Churchyard address. [Heal; YAS, DDS/39]

Old, William & Ody, John, 'The Castle', St Paul's Churchyard, London, cm and chairmakers (c.1723–38). John Ody was free of the Joiners' Co. in 1723 and this may well mark the beginning of the partnership. A policy was adopted of marking their case-furniture by affixing their trade label to it. This informs us that the partners made and sold 'all sorts of Cane & Dutch Chairs, Chair Frames for Stuffing and Cane-sashes. And also all sorts of the best Looking-Glass & Cabinet-work in Japan Walnut Tree & Wainscot'. A walnut bureau cabinet with a single glazed door, flanked by pilasters and with a broken shaped pediment is recorded with this label. A walnut cabinet, the inner drawers enclosed by two doors on a chest of four long drawers is so marked, as is also a chest of drawers. William Old was dead by 1738 when his stock of cabinet goods and chairs was offered for disposal by his widow from the St Paul's Churchyard address. [DEF; Wills, *English Furniture 1550–1760*, p. 182; Christie's, 28 June 1973, lot 48; *Conn.*, May 1935, p. xxix]

Oldaker, —, address unknown, cm (1824). On 29 December 1824 paid £2 'in part for a Table' made from the wood of the Farlop Oak, a large and well-known tree in Epping Forest. The patron was Nicholas Pearse of Loughton in Essex who also had a London house. [Essex RO, D/DHt A1/4]

Oldfield, John, Milford Lane, Westminster, London, u (1774). [Poll bk]

Oldfield, Jonathan, 7 Blake St, York, billiard table maker (1838). [D]

Oldfield, William, 2 St James St, Clerkenwell, London, chairmaker (1803). In May 1803 took out insurance cover of £100 of which £20 was in respect of utensils and stock in the dwelling house of Oakley a cm in St Paul's Churchyard (George Oakley). [GL, Sun MS vol. 426, ref. 747655]

Oldfield & Farn (or Tarn), 167 Aldersgate St, London, cm (1779–94). Thomas Oldfield was a member of the Ironmongers' Co. and as early as 1779 was established in Aldersgate St as a cm and in that year took out a licence to employ two non-freemen for three months. The business is shown as Oldfield & Farn, 1782–84 but then in most years until 1791 as Oldfield & Tarn. After this date in most years listed under Thomas Oldfield's name only but in 1794 in one directory as Oldfield & Co. [D; GL, City Licence bk, vol. 9]

Oldham, —, address unrecorded, u (1756). Named in the Duke of Beaufort's accounts for Badminton House, Glos., receiving £16 13s 10d in 1756. [Badminton papers; account bks] Possibly Thomas Oldham of Tetbury, Glos.

Oldham, Anthony, Carpenters' Lane, Tib St, Manchester, carver and gilder (1840). [D]

Oldham, Daniel, 37 or 40 Clayton St, Liverpool, cm (1830). Son of James Oldham, joiner and free 15 November 1830. [Freeman reg.]

Oldham, G. & J., 40 Lower Brook St, Grosvenor Sq., London, u (1819–20). [D]

Oldham, John, 16 Davies St, Berkeley Sq., London, u etc. (1823–25). [D]

Oldham, Thomas, Tetbury, Glos., upholder (1739–54). Freeman of Bristol. [Bristol poll bks] Possibly Oldham, —.

Oldham, Thomas, Scotland, Ashton-under-Lyne, Lancs., cm and joiner (1816–24). [D]

Olding, Ebenezer, London, u etc. (1816–39). At 270 Strand, 1816–19, but by 1821 at 71 Fleet St, an address that he continued to occupy until 1839. In 1828 fined for declining parochial office in the parish of St Brides. [D; GL, MS 6561]

Oldman, John, Thetford, Norfolk, u and cm (1836–39). At Well St in 1836 and King St in 1839. [D]

Oldmeadow, Charles, Tower St, King's Lynn, Norfolk, cm (1836–39). The number in Tower St is shown as 14 in 1836 and 16 in 1839. [D]

Oldmeadow(s), James, High St, King's Lynn, Norfolk, upholder and cm (1778–1826). App. to Robinson Crusoe, upholder and cm of High St, King's Lynn, and free, 1778–79. It is possible that he took over his business. Oldmeadow took as apps Thomas Cooper and Samuel Pearson (free 1810–11), Henry Young (free 1813–14) and Daniel Coates (free 1817–18). In 1791 took out insurance cover for £500 of which £400 was for utensils and stock. Poll bks in 1824 and 1826 give his address as Gaywood. [D; poll bks; freemen rolls; GL, Sun MS vol. 381, p. 531]

Oldmeadow, W., 11 Bridge St, Westminster, London, carver and gilder (1804). [D]

Oldner (or Older), George, Bankside, Southwark, London, upholder (1703–27). Father of George Oldner. App. to William Meakins and free of the Upholders' Co. by servitude, 29 October 1703. In 1727 at Bankside. [GL, Upholders' Co. records; Heal]

Olford, Gunston, Exeter, Devon, cm (1756–58). In 1756 took app. named Sherry and in 1758 another named Clark. [S of G, app. index]

Olford, William, East St, Southampton, Hants., carver and gilder (1811). [D]

Oliffe, Robert, London, cm (1769–70). Paid £44 9s 6d for goods supplied to Sylas Neville of Scratby Hall near Gt Yarmouth, Norfolk on 7 June, 7 July and 4 August 1769. The items included a table and elbow chair. On 28 November 1769 he wrote to the same patron indicating that a claw table, an elbow chair and four cushions had been despatched to Gt Yarmouth and on 4 July 1770 sent him a sketch for a cabinet of drawers on a stand. [Norfolk RO, MC7/78–165 395X5]

Oliphant, T., London, u (1793). Subscribed to Sheraton's *Drawing Book*, 1793.

Olivant, Edward, Wakefield, Yorks., cm, u and chairmaker (1814–30). At Northgate, 1814–22, but by 1830 at Gt Bull Yd. [D]

Olive, George, London, cm (1777–80). At Silver St in 1777 but at Redcross St, 1779–80. Member of the Joiners' Co. Took out licences to employ three non-freemen in 1777 and 1779 and four non-freemen in 1780. [GL, City Licence bks, vols 9 and 10]

Olive, John Daniel, 24 Noel St, Soho, London, carver and gilder (1823). In December 1823 took out insurance cover of £200 which included £50 for stock and utensils. [GL, Sun MS vol. 499, ref. 1012039]

Olive, Nicholas, Mote Rd, Maidstone, Kent, cm (1838). [Poll bk]

Olive, William, 7 Parson's Yd, Shoreditch, London, u (1791–1816). Not shown in trade directories until 1811–16 when the address is given as 7 near The Church, Shoreditch, which may be the same address as 7 Parsons Yd. In 1791 took out insurance cover of £200 of which half was in respect of utensils and stock. [D; GL, Sun MS vol. 375, p. 184]

Olive, William, Chirwell St, London, see John Luck Baker & William Olive.

Olive, William, 5 King John's Ct, Holywell Lane, London, u (1818). In September 1818 insured household goods for £100. [GL, Sun MS vol. 480, ref. 946155]

Olive & Elkins, Charterhouse Sq., London, cm (1788–93). In 1789 the number in Charterhouse Sq. was shown as 12. See Oliver & Rayner. [D]

Oliver, —, London, u (1793). Subscribed to Sheraton's *Drawing Book*, 1793.

Oliver, Charles, Spalding, Lincs., clock-case maker (c.1820–30). Labelled clock case recorded. [A. Smith, *The Guinness Book of Clocks*, 1984, p. 104]

Oliver, Christopher James, Leeds, Yorks., cm (1826–40). Recorded at West St in 1826, no. 1 in 1830; 1 Saville Row, 1828–30; 19 Kirkgate, 1834–37, also as an u. [D]

Oliver, Daniel, Fairview St, Cheltenham, Glos., chair and sofa maker (1839). [D]

Oliver, George, Silver St, Enfield, Middlx, cm (1826). [D]

Oliver, George, High St, Sunderland, Co. Durham, joiner and cm (1828). [D]

Oliver, Iron, Humberstone Gate, Leicester, u (1797). On 5 May 1797 advertised the arrival of new materials. [*Leicester Journal*, 5 May 1797]

Oliver, Isaac, Bury St Edmunds, Suffolk, u (1722–28). In 1722 took app. named Oliver. Elected a Common Councillor for Bury St Edmunds, 21 August 1728. [S of G, app. index]

Oliver, James, 31 Castle St East, Oxford Mkt, London, cm and u (1826–27). [D]

Oliver, James, 25 Princes St, Cavendish Sq., London, cm (1837–39). [D]

Oliver, John, address unknown, u (1760). Working at Raby Castle, Co. Durham, 1760. [V&A archives]

Oliver, John, Gt Market Pl., Bury St Edmunds, Suffolk, u (1766–c.1786). Elected Common Councillor, 19 August 1771. In April 1785 insured his household goods for £200 and his utensils and stock for £400. By 1784 the business appears to have been trading as John Oliver & Son. Died c.1786. [D; Suffolk RO(Bury), 847a Acc2314; GL, Sun MS vol. 327, p. 609]

Oliver, John, Sudbury, Suffolk, u (1779–84). In 1779 took out insurance cover of £700 but only £50 of this was in respect of utensils and stock. [D; GL, Sun MS vol. 274, p. 120]

Oliver, John, Castle Foregate, Shrewsbury, Salop, cm (1796). Freeman of Shrewsbury. [Freemen rolls]

Oliver, John, Staindrop, Co. Durham, cm (1815). Son bapt. on 13 July 1815. [PR (bapt.)]

Oliver, John, 29 Houndsditch, London, u and cm (1826–29). Shown additionally at no. 30 in 1827–29. [D]

Oliver, John, Whickham, Co. Durham, joiner/carpenter/cm (1834). [D]

Oliver, Jonathan, Plymouth, Devon, cm (1759). Took app. in 1759 named George. [S of G, app. index]

Oliver, Joseph, Gould's Ct, Deansgate, Manchester, builder, joiner and cm (1825). [D]

Oliver, Joseph & Co., Sudbury, Suffolk, upholder (1784–85). Bankruptcy announced, *Gents Mag.*, October 1785. [D]

Oliver, Joseph snr, High St, St Neots, Hunts., cm and u (1839–40). Described in one directory of 1839 as a draper and u and in another as cm and furniture broker. [D]

Oliver, Laver, Andrews St, Bury St Edmunds, Suffolk, u and cm (c.1779–d.1817). First mentioned in 1779 when he insured his house in Bury St Edmunds for £300. Became a Common Councillor on 21 August 1781, Alderman, 1801–02 and Chief Burgess on 20 August 1810. On 3 August 1803 he took out a patent (no. 2727) for 'Dining, card, pembroke and other tables upon an improved construction'. Furniture was made in accordance with this patent and to this he affixed brass plates. A D-shaped card table c.1810 now at 8 Angel Hill (Nat. Trust) and a pedestal card table are known with plates inscribed 'OLIVER'S PATENT/BURY ST EDMUNDS'. A two pedestal dining table is also recorded with a plate: 'OLIVER'S PATENT No 25/ BURY ST EDMUNDS'. Paid rates on a warehouse, workshops and stables at Andrews St, 1805–11. [GL, Sun MS vol. 272, p. 616; Suffolk RO(Bury), 3847a Acc No. 2314]

Oliver, Mark, parish of St Lawrence, Ipswich, Suffolk, u (1752–58). Married 1752. Bankruptcy announced in *Gents Mag.*, November 1758. [Suffolk RO, FAA: 50/2/89–93];

Oliver, Mark, Leicester, u (1779–95). At Cole Hill in 1779 and Humberstone Gate, 1794. In December 1779 advertised for an app. and in October 1794 for a journeyman u. Took William Jennings as app. in December 1795. [D; *Leicester Journal*, 11 December 1779, 24 October 1794; app. reg.]

Oliver, Robert, London, cm (1793). Subscribed to Sheraton's *Drawing Book*, 1793.

Oliver, Thomas, Crewkerne, Som., chairmaker (1738). In 1738 took app. named Saint. [S of G, app. index]

Oliver, Thomas, Yeovil, Som., chairmaker (1744). In 1744 took app. named Bartlett. [S of G, app. index]

Oliver, Thomas, 34 South St, Manchester Sq., London, u (1826). [D]

Oliver, Thomas, 7 Braddons Row, Torquay, Devon, cm and u (1838). [D]

Oliver, Walter, 89 Week St, Maidstone, Kent, u (1838–39). [D; poll bk]

Oliver, William, Cambridge, upholder (d.1715). [Cambridge Univ. Lib., Will AR 2:9]

Oliver, William, Sudbury, Suffolk, u (1798–1802). [D; *Ipswich Journal*, 4 January 1800, 2 January 1802]

Oliver, William, Hadleigh, Suffolk and Halstead, Essex, cm and u (1800). [*Ipswich Journal*, 30 August 1800]

Oliver, William, 13 Spear St, Manchester, builder, joiner and cm (1825). [D]

Oliver, William, Back Lane, Gainsborough, Lincs., cm (1828). [D]

Oliver & Rayner, Rutland Ct, Charterhouse Sq., London, cabinet chairmakers (1784). See Olive & Elkins. [D]

Olley, Thomas, 21 Buckingham Pl., Fitzroy Sq., London, cm and u (1839). [D]

Olley, William, London, cm and undertaker (1785–1808). In 1785 insured his utensils and stock at 190 High Holborn for £50 and his household goods for £30. By 1793 however the total cover had risen to £300 of which £200 was in respect of utensils and stock. In 1808 at 23 Swan Yd, Drury Lane. [D; GL, Sun MS vol. 333, p. 670; vol. 392, p. 98]

Ollis, Thomas, 25 Berry St, Liverpool, cm (1835). [D]

Ollive, —, Aldersgate St, London, cm (1793). Subscribed to Sheraton's *Drawing Book*, 1793.

Olton, Thomas, 25 Buckingham St, York Buildings, London, chairmaker (1801). Took out insurance cover of £100. [GL, Sun MS vol. 419, ref. 715230]

Olvius, John, 1 Round Ct, London, ornamental clockcase maker (1777). In 1777 took out insurance of £600 of which £600 covered his utensils and stock. [GL, Sun MS vol. 261, p. 452]

Olyett, Robert, Deptford Green, Deptford, London, cm etc. (1839). [D]

Omans, William, St George, Queen Sq., London, upholder (1766). In 1766 insured a house at Twickenham, Middlx for £150. [GL, Hand in Hand MS vol. 105, p. 120]

Ombler, Thomas, 20 Mount Pl., Coldbath Sq., London, cm (1829). [D]

Omer, I., 18 Howland St, Fitzroy Sq., London, carver and gilder (1837–39). Trade card in the Landauer Coll., MMA, NY. [D]

O'Neal, Francis, Liverpool, u (1804). Traded from Brownlow St, Brownlow Hill with a feather and paper warehouse at 3 Cable St, Pool Lane. See James & Alan Francis O'Neill. [D]

O'Neil & Smith, White St, Southwark, London, japanned chairmakers (1793). [D]

O'Neill, Charles, 4 Eldon St, Liverpool, cm (1821). App. to John Ward Turner and free by servitude, 20 October 1821. [Freemen reg.]

O'Neill, James & Alan Francis, 3 Cable St, Liverpool, u feather merchants and paper hangers (1812–27). Before 1812 in partnership with their father who was probably Francis O'Neal. Kept in stock, feathers, paper hangings, carpets, blankets, counterpanes 'and every article in the Upholstery Business'. Claimed to have workmen 'in the Paper Hanging and Upholstery branches'. From 1827 traded as Jane O'Neill & Co. [D; *Liverpool Mercury*, 28 August 1812]

O'Neill, Jane & Co., Cable St, Liverpool, u and feather merchant (1827–39). The number in Cable St was 3 in 1827, 6 from 1834–37 and 9 in 1839. [D]

O'Neill, John, Lancaster, cm and carver (1753–87). App. to Christopher Walker, joiner and cm in 1753 and free by servitude, 1767–68. Between 1769 and 1787 took seven apps. [App. reg.; freemen rolls; poll bk]

O'Neill, John, Liverpool, cm (1816–39). App. to Thomas Dutton and free by servitude, 6 June 1816. Married on 27 September of the same year at St Peter's Church. His address at this date was Gt Crosshall St. Trading at 40 Standish St in 1818, 34 Cable St, 1821–37 and 67 Cable St in 1839. Took as apps Peter Hitchcock in 1819, William Foley in 1821, William Durante in 1823, Daniel Birchall in 1824, Colin Mackenzie Lewes in 1827, Joseph Thomas Clarke in 1828, William Welsh in 1829, Samuel Pope in 1830, Jacob Williams and Peter Erlam in 1831, Edward John Owens in 1832 and William Sharp Lyons and James Griffiths in 1834. Bankrupt by June 1826 though recommenced business from the same address. In 1834 he announced that he had in stock 'Wardrobes, Chests of Drawers, Chairs, Loo & Card Tables & various other Articles', which he claimed had been made under 'his own immediate inspection'. [D; freemen reg.; *Liverpool Mercury*, 27 September 1816, 30 June 1826, 4 April 1834; app. reg.]

O'Neill, Mary, 23 Chatham St, Liverpool, u (1835). [D]

Onely, John, Leicester and London, cm (1764–91). Son of Samuel Onely of Lutterworth, Leics. App. to Joseph Johnson of Leicester on 5 July 1764, a premium of £20 being paid. Free 7 June 1779. By 1791 at West Smithfield, London, and in this year took as app. his son John jnr. [Freemen reg.]

Onion, Edward, Temple parish, Bristol, cm (1774). [Poll bk]

Onions, George, 37 Constitution Hill, Birmingham, cm and u (1830–39). Listed at 37 Constitution Hill in 1830 and 66 Livery St in 1839. [D]

Onions, James, Worcester St, Birmingham, chairmaker (1818–22). Listed also as a broker in 1818. [D]

Onwin, Richard, 26 St James St, Pall Mall, London, cm and u (1827). [D]

Onwin, Richard, Fitzroy Sq., London, cm and u (1827–29). At

4 Howland Mews, Fitzroy Sq. in 1827 and 10 Charlotte St, Fitzroy Sq. in 1829. [D]

Oppenheim, Henry, London, looking-glass manufacturer (1817–39). At King St, Commercial Rd in 1817 when the business was listed as H. Oppenheim & Co. In 1829 at 17 Mansell St, Goodman's Fields and in 1839 at this address and also 1 King St, Commercial Rd East. [D]

Oppenheim, Michael, 27 Mansell St, Goodman's Fields, London, looking-glass and cabinet warehouse (1809–11). Succeeded by Henry Oppenheim by 1817. [D]

Opra, Richmond, 33 King St, Whitehaven, Cumb., cm (1834). [D]

Opton, Charles, Lower Northgate St, Gloucester, cm and chairmaker (1820). [D]

Oram, William, South Moulton, Devon, cm (1823–30). At Market Pl. in 1823 and Broad St in 1830. [D]

Oram, Skidmore & Co., Westbar, Sheffield, Yorks., cabinet case and razor strop manufacturers (1817). [D]

Orange, George, 23 Shoe Lane, London, cm and dealer in bird cages (1787–93). In July 1787 took out insurance cover of £500 on his household goods etc. In 1793 subscribed to Sheraton's *Drawing Book*. [GL, Sun MS vol. 345, p. 468]

Orange, Joseph, 56 Hanover St, Portsea, Portsmouth, Hants., cm and u (1830). [D]

Orange, Joseph, 7 Yardley St, Clerkenwell, London, cm and u (1839). [D]

Orange, Mary & Rebecca, Turner's Hill, Cheshunt, Herts., cm and u (1839). [D]

Orange, Samuel, Turner's Hill, Cheshunt, Herts., cm, u and appraiser (1826–32). [D]

Orchard, James, 28 King St, Soho, London, upholder, cm and undertaker (1805–33). The 28 King St address appears to have been used throughout the life of this business but in 1821 and 1823 one directory lists the number as 30. Another directory in 1826 lists George Yd, Crown St, Soho. The business was fairly substantial in size and insurance cover in April 1805 was £1,000 and in April 1806, £1,250. Of these sums £770 and about £1,000 respectively concern utensils and stock in trade. A workshop was maintained behind the dwelling house. The business had a number of important clients. In 1820 it was patronised by the 4th Marquess of Londonderry in connection with the furnishing of Wynyard Park, Co. Durham and entries are recorded in the Chatsworth, Derbs. accounts for every year from 1822 to 1833. [D; GL, Sun MS vol. 434, ref. 775612; vol. 437, ref. 787828; Durham RO, D/LO/E 492]

Orchard, Robert, Ashby-de-la-Zouch, Leics., cm (1829–40). At Church St, 1829–35, in partnership with John Orchard in 1835; but by 1842 had moved to Market Pl. [D]

Orchard, William, 40 Wellington St and Cathay, Bristol, chairmaker (1829). [D]

Orchard & Son, 46 Margarets Buildings, Bath, Som., u (1819–24). [D]

Ord, John, Bridge End, Morpeth, Northumb., joiner and cm (1827–34). Recorded also at Water Lane in 1834. [D]

Ord, Robert, London, upholder (1761). Son of Christopher Ord of Chelmsford, Essex, peruke maker. Free of the Upholders' Co. by redemption under the terms of the 1750 Upholders' Act, 7 January 1761. [GL, Upholders' Co. records]

Ordas, William, Wainfleet, Lincs., cm (1806). Freeman of Lincoln. [Lincoln poll bk]

Ore, William, Cogdell's Yd, Silver St, Westminster, London, cm (1741). [Poll bk]

Orford, John, Manchester, cm (1794–1817). At 11 Hanging Ditch in 1794 and 7 Back Baloon St in 1817. [D]

Organ, John, London, cm, u and chair and bedstead maker

(1835–39). At 50 Hoxton Sq. in 1835 and 3 Featherstone St, City Rd in 1839. [D]

Orley, Robert, East St, Bridport, Dorset, cm (1840). [D]

Ormandy, John, Lancaster (1790). [Westminster Ref. Lib., Gillow records]

Ormandy, John, Portland Sq., Workington, Cumb., joiner/cm/ironmonger (1811). [D]

Ormandy, Richard, New St, Whitehaven, Cumb., joiner/cm (1793–1811). [D]

Ormandy, William, Lancaster (1819–20). [Westminster Ref. Lib., Gillow records]

Orme, John, Liverpool, cm (1765–77). App. to Charles Charles and free by servitude, 4 May 1765. In 1769 at King St and from 1772 at 9 Ranelagh St. His son John Orme jnr, a merchant, petitioned for freedom by patrimony in 1796. [D; freemen reg.]

Orme, Thomas, opposite Meards Ct, Dean St, Soho, London, cm (d. by 1753). On 13 February 1753 the sale of his stock in trade and utensils was advertised following his death. On offer at the auction were bookcases, bureaus, tables and chairs 'amongst which are several curious pieces made by his late Master, Thomas Turner, deceased'. His stocks of timber, specified as mahogany, including some fine veneers and his work benches and tools were in the sale. [*Public Advertiser*, 13 February 1753]

Orme, Thomas, 2 Back Irwell St, Manchester, cm (1838–39). [D]

Orme, William, Bridge St, Derby, cm and u (1835). [D]

Ormes, John, Chester and London, cm (1747). Son of Richard Ormes of Chester, pipemaker, who was dead by 21 July 1747 when his son was declared free. Immediately following this date he moved to London. [Freemen rolls; Chester poll bk]

Ormes, William, Bromboren, Chester, cm (1747). [Poll bk]

Ormo, Joseph, 36 Rupert St, London, portable desk, dressing case, work box and cabinet case maker (1839). [D]

Ormrod, John, Salford, Lancs. and Manchester, chairmaker and cm (1808–34). At 21 Spaw St, Salford as a chairmaker, 1808–25, but in 1834 at 6 Bond St, Manchester as a cm. [D]

Ormrod, Richard, 168 Chapel St, Salford, Lancs., chairmaker (1813–17). [D]

Ornsby, William, Dockwray Sq. Bank, North Shields, Northumb., cm and joiner (1827). [D]

Orphin, S., 11 Monmouth St, Seven Dials, London, chair japanner (1826). [D]

Orpwood, John, 12 Hewitt's Ct, Strand, London, cm (1792–93). In December 1792 took out insurance cover of £100. Subscribed to Sheraton's *Drawing Book*, 1793. [GL, Sun MS vol. 389, ref. 609023]

Orpwood & Fetherston, 7 Church St, Minories, London, cm (1823). [D]

Orrell, —, Lombard St, Liverpool, cm (1766). In *Williamson's Liverpool Advertiser*, 31 October 1766, the auction was announced of 'all that Messuage with Appertenances in Lombard Street, now in the possession of Mr. Orrell, Cabinet Maker'.

Orrell, John, Liverpool, cm (1781–90). At 6 Edmund St, 1781 and 36 Ormond St, 1790. [D]

Orrell, Stephen, Malden, Essex, cm (1826–39). [D; poll bk]

Orrell, Thomas, Liverpool, cm (1797). Marriage to Miss Ann Tasker of Ormskirk, Lancs. announced in *Billinge's Liverpool Advertiser*, 5 June 1797.

Orridge, John, Leeds, Yorks., journeyman cm (1791–93). Included in the list of journeymen cm in basic sympathy with the *Leeds Cabinet and Chair Makers Book of Prices*, 1791. Subscribed to Sheraton's *Drawing Book*, 1793.

Orrin, Christopher, Black Boy Lane, Colchester, Essex,

chairmaker (1826–d. 1829). Probate granted on his will 1829. [D; *Wills at Chelmsford*, III, p. 241]

Orrin, William, East Hill, Colchester, Essex, chairmaker (1823). [D]

Orson, John, London and Oxford, carver and gilder (1767–68). In October 1767 at 'The Golden Eagle', High St, Oxford and advertised his arrival from London. By April of the following year he was the tenant of a house opposite 'The Two-Faced Pump' in the High St, a property which was in this month advertised for sale. [*Jackson's Oxford Journal*, 24 October 1767, 9 April 1768]

Orson (or Orsor), John, Melton Mowbray, Leics., cm and u (1822). [D]

Ortelli, Peter, 3 Leather Lane, London, looking-glass, barometer and thermometer manufacturer (1835–40). [D; Goodison, *Barometers*]

Orton, Joseph, Moseley St, Birmingham, cabinet, dressing case and portable desk maker (1828–30). [D]

Orton, Mark & Co., Last Lane, Dover, Kent, cm and u (1839). [D]

Orton, William, Hinckley, Leics., cm (1788–98). In May 1788 advertised for a partner. His son William was declared free in 1798. [D; freemen rolls; *Leicester Journal*, 24 May 1788]

Orven, Samuel, 54 Bread St, London, upholder and cm (1779). Took out insurance cover in 1779 for £300 of which £140 was in respect of utensils and stock. [GL, Sun MS vol. 274, p. 574]

Osborn, Arthur, 'The Three Chairs', Paternoster Row, London, u (1704–36). In 1704 contracted to supply a hundred beds and bedding for Greenwich Hospital to a pattern supplied. The beds were to cost £1 18s each. The beds supplied may not have been particularly comfortable, for the Clerk of Works was instructed to 'make the battens thinner so that they give somewhat'. In 1716–17 supplied six chairs for the Library at St Paul's Cathedral, London, and undertook some repairs. In 1717 made and put up four curtains for which £3 7s 6d was paid. Shown taking an app. in 1711. His insurance cover in 1726 came to £500. [Heal; *Wren Soc.*, VI, pp. 31, 49; XV, pp. 221–22; S of G, app. index; GL, Sun MS vol. 23, p. 164]

Osborn, George, 135 and 139 Tottenham Ct Rd, London furniture warehouse (1804–26). In 1804–07 shown at 135 and 139 Tottenham Ct Rd, but from 1808–14 139 alone is usually indicated, and from 1816 it is 135 alone. Described as u in 1809, 1812 and 1814–19 but as furniture broker in 1826. [D]

Osborn, George, 48 Roper St, Whitehaven Cumb., joiner and cm (1828). John Osborne was trading at this address in 1829. [D]

Osborn, James, London, u (1830–31). Freeman of Colchester, Essex. [Colchester poll bks]

Osborn, John, 9 Whiskin St, Clerkenwell, London, cm and u (1839). [D]

Osborn, Joseph, Nottingham, joiner and cm (1798). [D]

Osborn, Matthew, 179 Drury Lane, London, cm (1791). In December 1791 took out insurance cover of £400 which included £200 for utensils and stock. [GL, Sun MS vol. 382, ref. 593686]

Osborn, N., address unknown, cm (1803). Subscribed to Sheraton's *Cabinet Dictionary*, 1803.

Osborn, Robert, Norwich, u (1724). On 3 May 1724 his app. Gregory Cook was made free. [Norwich freemen reg.]

Osborn, Watkin, Sidbury, Worcester, cm (1797–98). [D]

Osborn, William, Liverpool, cm (1810–18). App. to Edward Huddleston in 1810 and in 1818 free by servitude. [Freemen's committee bk]

Osborn, William Arthur, Littlehampton, Sussex, cm and u (1834–39). Undertook work for the Earl of Surrey at

Littlehampton 1834–39. Some small pieces of furniture were supplied such as a chest of drawers charged at £2 15s and a mahogany towel horse at 4s 6d in 1838. A chair was on hire for 1s per week in 1834 but most of the work was involved in the repair and removal of furniture, curtains and upholstery, blinds and other minor items. The totals involved were – £34 8s 6d in 1834, £326 14s 4d in 1836–37 and £31 5s 9d in 1839. [D; Arundel Castle papers, A2002, A2006, A2112]

Osborne, —, London (?), chairmaker (1751). In 1751 paid £21 for chairs to an earlier design by Sir Christopher Wren, by All Souls College, Oxford. Carriage was charged additionally at 17s 6d. [MS DD, All Souls College, c.257]

Osborne, —, 5 Black Swan Ct, Bath, Som., u (1819). [D]

Osborne, Christopher, London, upholder (1712–22). Son of Thomas Osborne of Newtimber, Sussex, Gent. App. to John Osborne on 3 September 1712 and free of the Upholders' Co. by servitude, 5 December 1722. [GL, Upholders' Co. records]

Osborne, James, 1 Gwynne's Pl., Hackney Rd, London, chair and sofa manufacturer (1829). [D]

Osborne, John, parish of St Peter Mancroft, Norwich, u (1700–14). App. to Timothy Ganning and free, 8 November 1700. [Freemen rolls; poll bks]

Osborne, John, 'The Crown', corner of Crown Ct, Old Change, London, u (1710–36). Free of the Upholders' Co., 5 April 1710. Took as apps Christopher Osborne (1712–22), Benjamin Baron (1720–28) and Thomas Elmes (1727–36). In September 1723 took out insurance cover of £400 on goods and merchandise in his dwelling house. [Heal; GL, Upholders' Co. records; Sun MS vol. 16, ref. 29841]

Osborne, John, Whitehaven, Cumb., joiner/cm (1811–29). At Scotch St in 1811 and at 48 Roper St in 1829. This latter address was used by a George Osborn, joiner and cm, in 1828. [D]

Osborne, John Benjamin, London, cm (1820–21). At 6 West St, Soho in November 1820 when he took out insurance cover of £150. This included £10 in respect of a chest of tools in the workshop of Blackman, cm at 7 Green St, Leicester Sq. A year later when he had moved to 5 York Pl., Carlisle Pl., Lambeth, insurance cover had risen to £200 and the value of his tool chest at Blackman's to £20. [GL, Sun MS vol. 483, ref. 972677; vol. 488, ref. 985415]

Osborne, Joseph, Parliament St, Nottingham, joiner and cm (1786–99). In 1786 took app. named John Williamson. [D; app. bk]

Osborne, Robert, Southwold, Suffolk, u (1813). Married on 20 July 1813. [Suffolk RO, FAA: 50/2/116, pp. 96–97]

Osborne, Thomas, London, u (1812–31). Freeman of Colchester, Essex. [Colchester poll bks]

Osborne, Thomas, 29 Curtain Rd, London, cm etc. (1820). [D]

Osborne, William, 102 Wardour St, London, chair and sofa maker (1807–15). In December 1808 took out insurance cover of £1,000 which included £600 for stock and utensils and £200 cover for the tool chests of his workmen. Although directories show the Wardour St address until 1815, insurance records suggest that by June 1812 he was living at 30 Queen Sq., Bloomsbury. Here a workshop existed behind the dwelling house and stock and utensils kept here were covered for £600 out of a total of £800. [D; GL, Sun MS vol. 445, ref. 814196; vol. 459, ref. 871428]

Osborne, William, Shaw St, Lively Pl., Liverpool, cm (1810–18). App. to Edward Huddestone in 1810 and free by servitude on 11 June 1818. [Freemen reg.]

Osborne, William, London, chairmaker (1812–31). Freeman of Colchester, Essex. [Colchester poll bks]

Osborne, William, Woodbridge, Suffolk, cm (d. 1825). Will proved at Norwich 1825. [Norfolk Record Soc., index of wills]

Osborne, William, 232 Whitechapel Rd, London, cm and u (1827–39). [D]

Osbourne, Joseph, Brow Top, Workington, Cumb., joiner/cm (1811). [D]

Osbourne, William, Pow St, Workington, Cumb., joiner/cm (1811). [D]

Osburn, William, 7 Fan St, Goswell St, London, cm and u (1822–35). In 1827 listed as a firescreen and chairmaker. [D]

Osman, Mary, 57 Ratcliffe Highway, London, cm (1790–93). [D]

Osman, Robert, 47 Chiswell St, London, cm and desk maker (1822). In December 1822 took out insurance cover of £600, half this sum being for utensils and stock. He also owned a house at 19 Red Lion St, Kingsland Rd valued at £100. [GL, Sun MS vol. 489, ref. 9999289]

Osment, Edward, Paris St, Exeter, Devon, cm (1821–40). Four sons and six daughters bapt. at St Sidwell's Church, 1821–37. In 1828 an address at Marsh's Pl. is given but this may have been merely a dwelling house and the business appears to have remained in Paris St. Appears to have also acted as an agent for the sale of houses. [D; PR (bapt.); *Exeter Flying Post*, 7 May 1835]

Osmond, George, 60 London St, Fitzroy Sq., London, cm and u (1839). [D]

Osmond, J., 23 Upper Cleveland St, London, u (1835). [D]

Osmond, Joseph, London, cm (1820–31). Freeman of Colchester, Essex. [Colchester poll bk]

Osmond, S., 21 High St, Shadwell, London, cm etc. (1820). [D]

Osmond, William, 58 Minster St, Reading, Berks., cm and u (1820–40). [D; poll bks]

Ostler, Henry George, Hull, Yorks., cm (1835–40). At 51 Savile St in 1835 and 3 Castle St in 1840. [D]

Oswald & Lumley, 75 Well St, Oxford St, London, cm (1800–11). This business traded as Oswald & Lumley, 1800–01 but as Oswald & Nicols, 1803–11. It is this latter partnership which is given in the list of subscribers to Sheraton's *Cabinet Dictionary*, 1803, where they are referred to as cm and chairmakers. A man by the name of Oswald was purchasing 'Irish' cloth from Kennet & Kidd in 1794 and may be the Oswald involved in both of these partnerships. [D; PRO, C114/181, journal 3, p. 333]

Oswald & Nicols, see Oswald & Lumley.

Oswell, Andrew, Rose St, Westminster, London, cm (1784). [Poll bk]

Otewell, James, Knutsford, Cheshire, joiner and cm (1782). [D]

Othen, William, High St, Godalming, Surrey, cm and u (1832–39). [D]

Ottley, John, 32 Upper Milk St, Liverpool, cm (1839). [D]

Otton, Mr, Exeter, Devon, turner and carver (1818–23). In January 1818 married a Miss Hancock at St Edmunds Church. By April 1822 trading from an address in Cathedral Yd and advertising for an app. 'to the turning & carving business'. By the following year trading from Gandy St. [D; *Exeter Flying Post*, 22 January 1818; *The Alfred*, 16 April 1822]

Ottoway, Samuel, address unknown, u (1688). [PRO, C114/164, pt. I]

Ottway, J., 35 St Martin's Lane, London, dressing and writing case maker (1819–20). [D]

Otty, John, Upper Milk St, Liverpool, cm (1827–37). Son of William Otty, cooper. Free, 17 October 1827. At this date at Standish Ct, 40 Upper Milk St but in 1835 the number in Upper Milk St was 41, reverting to 40 in 1837. Took as apps John Ellis in 1827 and Richard Ellis in 1828. [D; freemen reg.; app. bk]

Otty, Samuel, Liverpool, cm (1816–18). At 21 Johnson Ct in 1816 and 10 Christian St in 1818. [D]

Oughton, Clement, Newington Butts, London, chair and sofa maker (1826–35). At Parsonage Walk in 1826 and 4 Providence Walk in 1835. [D]

Oughton, J., Bridge Stairs, Lambeth, London, chairmaker (1808). [D]

Oughton, John, 37 Union Row, New Kent Rd, London, cm and u (1827). [D]

Oughton, Levi, 22 Bridge Rd, Lambeth, London, chairmaker (1809–39). Trade listed as japanned chairmaker, 1813–20; chair, sofa and couch manufacturer, 1820–25; and Windsor chairmaker in 1829. [D]

Oughton, Mary, Botley, Hants., chairmaker (1830). [D]

Oughton, Samuel, 14 Grosier St, Lambeth, London, u (1835). [D]

Oughton, Thomas, 3 Bridge St, Lambeth, London, u (1826). [D]

Ould, Joseph, address unknown, cm (1803). Subscribed to Sheraton's *Cabinet Dictionary*, 1803.

Oulton, James, London, upholder (1736). Free of the Upholders' Co., 3 March 1735/36 'by order of the Court of Aldermen'. [GL, Upholders' Co. records]

Oulton, Thomas Clownes (or Clowes), King St, Knutsford, Cheshire, cm (1828–40). [D]

Ounsworth, Benjamin, Edgar St, Hull, Yorks., cm (1835–40). At 3 Edgar St in 1835 but shown as Ounsworth Ct, Edgar St, 1838–39. [D]

Ounsworth, Jesse, Hull, Yorks., u and chairmaker (1803–39). At Low Church Alley, Lowgate and Chapel Lane 1803–10; Salthouse Lane, 1821–22; Cent per Cent St, 1826; St James St in 1831; and 19 St James St, 1835–38. [D]

Ounsworth, John, Low Church Alley, Lowgate and Chapel Lane, Hull, Yorks., cm (1803–10). Between these dates Jesse Ounsworth, u and chairmaker operated from these addresses also. [D]

Ounsworth, Samuel, Hull, Yorks., cm (1774–80). [Poll bks]

Ousey, George, Staylybridge, Lancs., cm (1825–34). At 79 Rossbottom St, 1825–28, and 14 Old St in 1834. [D]

Ousey, H., Staylybridge, Ashton-under-Lyne, Lancs., cm (1825). Bankruptcy announced, *Brighton Gazette*, 10 March 1825.

Outram, John, Kingsley, near Frodsham, Cheshire, cm and joiner (1834). [D]

Outram, Richard, Sheffield, Yorks., cm (1814–28). At 26 Trippet Lane but by 1825 at 38 Portobello St. Thomas Outram, cm was trading from 30 Trippet Lane in 1821. [D]

Outram, Thomas, Sheffield, Yorks., cm (1821–33). At 30 Trippet Lane in 1821, Carver St in 1828 and 105 Rockingham St in 1833. Richard Outram, cm, was at 26 Trippet Lane from 1814. [D]

Outram, William, Sheffield, Yorks., cm (1814–34). At Wainegate 1814–16; 52 High St, 1818–28; and 20 Market Pl., 1833–34. A Regency Trafalgar type chair is known with the impressed mark 'W. OUTRAM/MAKER/SHEFFIELD'. [D]

Outrem, William, 'The Cock', Catherine St, Strand, London, u (1722–25). His name appears in a report from a committee appointed in February 1722/23 and July 1723 to superintend the repair and enlargement of Hicks Hall and the provision of furniture for it. In May 1725 took out insurance cover of £500 on his goods and merchandise. [Winterthur, Delaware, Symonds 75x69.29; Heal; GL, Sun MS vol. 20, ref. 35710]

Ouvry, James, Against Half Moon Alley, Bishopsgate Without, London, upholder (1718). [GL, Sun MS vol. 8, ref. 11455]

Ovenston, John, 72 Gt Titchfield St, Oxford St, London, cm and u (1826–39). Shown as cm 1826–35 and thereafter as u. Made a chair from the timbers of Old London Bridge in 1832 for the Hall of the Fishmongers' Co. Took over this address from John Barker, u who in 1825 or 1826 moved to 54 Dorset St, Manchester Sq. [D; Heal]

Over, James, Market Harborough, Leics., cm and u (1810–40). From 1835–40 his address was Cheapside. [D]

Overall, William, High St, Chelmsford, Essex, cm and u (1832–39). [D]

Overend, Brian, Lancaster (1793–1803). Named in the Gillow records 1793–94, 1796–98 and 1802–03. [Westminster Ref. Lib., Gillow]

Overend, Joseph, Lancaster, carver (1828–29). [Lancaster freemen rolls]

Overend, Joseph, 72 York St, Leeds, Yorks., cm and joiner (1837). [D]

Overend, William, Cheapside, Liverpool, joiner and cm (1821–39). The number in Cheapside was 66 in 1821–29; 53 in 1835–37; and 14 in 1839. [D]

Overley, William, at the sign of 'The East India House', Leadenhall St, London, joiner and cm (*c*.1710–32). Prior to 1711 Overley conducted his business from a small shop which stood at the entrance to East India House. When obliged to move he transferred four or five doors from his old place of business but retained the trade sign that he had used previously. His trade card [Heal Coll., BM] states that he made all sorts of Sea Chests in Deal or Wainscot, Ruff or Smooth Packing Chests or Cases and Cases of Bottles & Boxes of all Sizes, Presses in Deal in Wainscot & Bedstids, Tables, Desks, Book Cases, Burows & Writing-Desks, Letter holes, &c.' [Heal]

Overlove, John, 'The Golden Key', 36 Leadenhall St, London, frame maker and gilder (1775–82). Advertised on his trade card [GL] that he was 'From y[e] late Mr Evendon's in Leadenhall Street'. He stated that he made 'all Manner of Frames for Paintings, Glasses, or Prints, Fits up Indian Pictures for Stair Cases, Lines, Cleans & Repairs Pictures, new Gilds old Frames & also Makes Window Blinds, after y[e] newest fashion'. J. B. Pursseveill who had set up in business at 5 Lime St, Leadenhall St by the early 1780s claimed to have been his app. as did also William Wade. Overlove was succeeded at this address by John Merle. [D; Heal]

Overton, —, Dean St, Soho, London, upholder (1705). [Heal]

Overton, James, 180 Bristol St, Birmingham, cm and chairmaker (1830). [D]

Overton, Philip, address unknown, frame maker (1734). On 12 November 1734 submitted his invoice for 10s 6d for making a black picture frame with gold carved edge to Paul Foley. Foley had addresses in Little Ormond St and the Temple, London, and Newport House, Almeley, Herefs. [Herefs. RO, Foley F/AIII/55]

Overton, Richard, 127 Rotherhithe St, London, carver (1826). [D]

Overton, Richard, London Rd, Swaffham, Norfolk, cm and u (1830). [D]

Owen, —, 42 Little Sutton St, Clerkenwell, London, cm (1829). [D]

Owen, Catherine, 41 Duke St, Liverpool, u (1824). [D]

Owen, Francis, 35 The Quay, Bristol, cm (1755–75). In 1755 took app. named Weare. At 35 The Quay in 1775. [D; S of G, app. index; poll bks]

Owen, Francis, Wem, Salop, u (1822). [D]

Owen, J., 30 Copperas Hill, Liverpool, cm (1827). [D]

Owen, James, Hereford, chairmaker (1822–35). At Bye St, 1822, and Built's Buildings, 1830–35. [D]

Owen, John, parish of St Nicholas, Bristol, upholder (1754–59). In 1756 took app. named Ledgingham and in 1759 another named Elsley. [Poll bk; S of G, app. index]

Owen, John, Pool Lane, Liverpool, u (1761–67). App. to Charles Aven for five years and Ambrose Evans for a further two. Free by servitude, 11 February 1761. By 1766 had set up in business at Pool Lane where he had a house and shop with a cellar under. The business was not successful and in August 1767 his bankruptcy was announced. His stock, consisting of 'very good Bedsteads, with Morine & Check Furnitures, Feather Beds, Blankets, Mahogany Chairs, Tables etc.' together with his household goods had already been put up for sale in April though tenders for the whole, and enquiries about the letting of the shop and house were invited. [D; freemen reg.; freemen's committee bk; *Gents Mag.*, August 1767; *Williamson's Liverpool Advertiser*, 20 March 1767, 31 March 1767, 11 November 1767]

Owen, John, Manchester (1772–81). At 27 Market St Lane, 1772–73 and Old Church Yd, 1781. [D]

Owen, John, Liverpool, u (1790–d.1830). At 12 St Peter St, 1790–96 and 1813–14; but from 1804–11 the number was 41. In 1813–14 at 32 Standish St, and from 1816–21 at Gloucester St. By 1823 had a shop at 2 Hood St, and in 1824 the addresses are given as 5 Hood St and 5 Gloucester St. The addresses had changed to 1 Jervis St and 53 Copperas Hill by 1827–30. Probably trained in Shrewsbury but by 1790 in Liverpool where in November he was married at the Church of St Thomas to Mrs Jane Boardman. In 1805 signed the supplement to the *Liverpool Cabinet and Chairmakers' Book of Prices* on behalf of the masters. His wife died on 28 March 1821 at Clayton Sq., presumably John Clayton's dwelling house at this date. She was aged 78. Almost two years later on 18 April 1823 the death of the wife of John Owen aged 70 at Gloucester St was announced. Either John Owen re-married after the death of his first wife or there are two makers of roughly the same age and in the same trade in Liverpool at this period. John Owen of Copperas Hill died on 30 November 1830 and his stock was put up for sale in March 1831 on the instructions of his executors. The manufactured stock consisted of 'Mahogany, Zebra & Rosewood, Pembroke, Library, Loo, Card & Sofa Tables; Chests of Drawers, Parlour & Hall Chairs, Sofa, Hatstand, Music Seat, Portable Desks, long Port & Camp Bedsteads, Imitation Rosewood Chairs & various other Articles'. In addition there was a stock of materials which included 'Mahogany, Rosewood, Cedar, Oak, Ash, Birth & Pine Planks & Boards, Mahogany, Rosewood & other Veneers; Tool Chests & Tools, Work Benches, Cramps, large Iron Vice, Stoves, Brass Work etc.'. [D; *Williamson's Liverpool Advertiser*, 22 November 1790; *Liverpool Mercury*, 13 April 1821, 18 April 1823, 17 December 1830, 4 March 1831]

Owen, John Edward, Nantwich, Cheshire, u (d.1812). Buried on 17 March 1812. [PR (burial)]

Owen, John, City Rd, Finsbury, London, upholder and undertaker (1817–35). At 8 City Rd in 1817 but in 1835 the number was 1. [D]

Owen, John, Nottingham, u (1818–22). Listed at Castlegate in 1818 and Clumber St in 1822. [D]

Owen, John, 71 Leadenhall St, London, u (1821). Described as an 'Upholstery Warehouse, Mattress and Feather-bed Manu-factory, and Agency House to the Cabinet-makers' Society'. [D]

Owen, John, Old St, St Luke's, London, cm (1826–39). At 2 Old St in 1826 but in 1839 at 92. [D]

Owen, John, corner of Providence Rd and Finsbury Sq., London, cm etc. (1837). [D]

Owen, John, Knight St, Liverpool, u (1837–39). At 35 Knight St in 1837 but by 1839 the number was 10. [D]

Owen, Michael, Lyme Regis, Dorset, cm (1778). In 1778 took out insurance cover for £300 of which £50 was in respect of utensils and stock. [GL, Sun MS vol. 269, p. 370]

Owen, Owen, 2 Bannister St, Vauxhall Rd, Liverpool, u (1804). [D]

Owen, R., 23 Hackney Rd, London, chairmaker (1826). [D]

Owen, Richard, Nantwich, Cheshire, u (1808–14). Three daughters and a son bapt., 1808–14. [PR (bapt.)]

Owen, Richard, 5 and 6 Curtain Rd, Shoreditch, London, cm and furniture warehouse (1809–16). Described as cm in 1809 and furniture warehouse 1816. [D]

Owen, Robert, 17 Townwell Fold, Wolverhampton, Staffs., cm (1802). [Rate bk]

Owen, Samuel, 54 Broad St, Carnaby Mkt, Soho, London, u and cm (1781–1809). In most years trade directories described him as upholder or u, occasionally with cm added. In 1797 only the business is listed as Owen & Cox. Included in the list of master cabinet makers in Sheraton's *Cabinet Dictionary*, 1803. In 1781 took out insurance cover of £600 of which £420 was in respect of utensils and stock. In 1805 utensils and stock were valued at £850 for insurance purposes. Samuel Owen also insured in 1805 two houses near the 'King's Arms' at Acton Bottom for £900 and in the following year a house at 45 Wigmore St rented to a sadler at £400. [D; GL, Sun MS vol. 292, ref. 4444914; vol. 434, refs 777111, 777302; vol. 437, ref. 787040; vol. 440, ref. 802420]

Owen, Samuel Middleton, Bristol, cm (1784–94). At Castle Precincts 1784 and Castle Ditch 1794. [D; poll bk]

Owen, Sarah, 17 York St, Whitechapel, London, u (1839). [D]

Owen, Thomas, near Moorfields, London, cm and glass grinder (1736). [Heal]

Owen, Thomas, 17 Tarleton St, Liverpool, cm (1818). [D]

Owen, Thomas, 59 Skinner St, Snowhill, London, u (1829). [D]

Owen, William, Liverpool, cm (1796–1839). At 12 Vernon St, Dale St, 1796–1804. By 1807–14 at 31 Cable St, but in 1818 the number was 30 and in 1821–24, 28. In the period 1835–37 had a shop in Cable St and also at 3 Seymour St. [D]

Owen, William, address unknown, cm and u (1812). On 13 September 1812 supplied to Erddig, Clwyd, N. Wales a pair of dressing glasses at £1 11s. Also supplied a mahogany table costing £9 10s. [V&A archives]

Owen, William, High St, Wem, Salop. cm (1828). [D]

Owen & Cox, see Samuel Owen, 54 Broad St, London.

Owen & King, 63 Berners St, Oxford St, London, cm, u and undertakers (1835–39). [D]

Owens, Joseph, 1 Jervis St, Liverpool, cm (1827). [D]

Owens, Owen, 43 London Wall, London, victualler and cm (1785). In April 1785 insured his utensils and stock for £180. [GL, Sun MS vol. 329, p. 63]

Owens, Thomas, 27 Rose Pl., Liverpool, cm (1834). [D]

Owens, Thomas, Gt Square, Braintree, Essex, cm and u (1839). [D]

Owsley, Samuel, Kingsbury, Som., cm (1719). In 1719 took app. named Meade. [S of G, app. index]

Oxendale, Thomas, Tubwell Row, Darlington, Co. Durham, joiner and cm (1827). [D]

Oxendale, William, Preston, Lancs., joiner and cm (1816–18). In 1816 near Roe St with a house at 3 Walton St and in 1818 at Shepherd St. [D]

Oxenham, Henry, Exeter, Devon, cm (d.1823). Death on 29 October 1823 reported in *Exeter Flying Post*, 30 October.

Oxenham, Mark, Poland St, Oxford Rd, London, cm (1749). [Westminster Poll Bk]

Oxenham, Samuel, see Thomas Oxenham.

Oxenham, Thomas, London, patent mangle and napkin-press maker, cm and u (1795–1832). At 354 Oxford St in 1795 as a mangle and napkin-press maker, and claimed to be maker to 'their Majesties, Prince of Wales and Royal Family'. He was friendly with Thomas Butler of Catherine St, Strand, an important cm and u and associated with the manufacture of patent furniture. When late in 1800 Butler took a decision to dispose of the business and Joseph Sanders and Thomas Morgan, two of his employees stated an interest in taking over, Thomas Oxenham was called in to value the stock. To the outrage of Morgan and Sanders, Butler sold the business to Oxenham who subsequently stated that he had purchased from Butler 'his sole Patent-right for making the said much admired Bedsteads . . . together with all his Stock in Trade, Engines, Tools &c.'. Oxenham was in possession of Butler's Catherine St premises by June 1801 and in July insured 13 and 14 for £1,200 of which £750 was for utensils and stock. He offered to the public similar items to those formerly featured by Butler which included patent four post bedsteads, Imperial Dining Tables, 'Curious new invented Folding Chair Beds, Double and Single Sofa Beds . . . Couch Beds on various constructions; Sofa Beds for Merchant's ships and travelling in general, elegant Card and Pembroke Sofa Tables'. By April of the following year the premises in Catherine St were vacated and the trade transferred to Thomas Oxenham's Oxford St address. From here he offered his ranges of furniture 'from 10 to 20 per Cent cheaper than the boasted Manufactories in Catherine Street'. A Samuel Oxenham, using the 354 Oxford St address subscribed to Sheraton's *Cabinet Dictionary*, 1803. There is also a trade card [Banks Coll., BM] dated 1803 in the name of Samuel Oxenham & Co. Samuel was probably involved in the business as a partner and it traded as Oxenham & Co. 1806–08 and as Thomas Oxenham & Son 1809–12.

The only known patron of Thomas Oxenham for furniture was Sir George Sitwell of Renishaw, Derbs. who in 1808 purchased furniture to the value of £835. The most significant items were two 'superb sofas' the arms and front legs formed of carved lion's heads and legs, the woodwork bronzed and parcel gilt. These alone cost £120 12s 8d.

Oxenham continued to trade as a mangle manufacturer until 1832 when he retired to Welwyn, Herts. where since 1792 he had been a prominent member of the Bethel Chapel and an ardent supporter of the Duchess of Huntingdon's connection. His success in business had by this date made him a man of some means. [D; GL, Sun MS vol. 419, ref. 718891; *C. Life*, 26 November 1938, p. xc; *Conn.*, November 1974, pp. 180–81; W. Brand, *Welwyn Briefly*] B.A.

Oxerby, Geo., Barnsley, Yorks., cm (1814–16). [D]

Oxlade, James, Downley, High Wycombe, Bucks., chairmaker (b. c. 1816–41). Aged 25 at the date of the 1841 Census.

Oxland, William, Hinchingdon, High Wycombe, Bucks., chairmaker (b. c. 1816–41). Aged 25 at the date of the 1841 Census.

Oxley, Daniel, Doncaster, Yorks., cm (1782–84). In 1782 took out insurance cover for £600 of which £100 was in respect of utensils and stock. A William Oxley, cm traded in this town, 1818–22. [D; GL, Sun MS vol. 306, p. 418]

Oxley, Thomas, Plough Yd, Banbury, Oxon, chairmaker (1830–41). [D]

Oxley, William, High St, Doncaster, Yorks., cm (1818–22). See Daniel Oxley in this town as a cm, 1782–84. [D]

Oxton, Thomas, 49 Gt George St, Liverpool, cm (1823–24). [D]

P

Pace, James, Angel Ct, Strand, London, cm (1777). In 1777 took out insurance cover for £200 but only £10 of this was in respect of utensils and stock. [GL, Sun MS vol. 259, p. 348]

Packer, J. O., Southgate St, Gloucester, cm and u (1839). [D]

Packer, John, Southgate St, Gloucester, cm and u (1830). [D]

Packer, Thomas, address unknown, chairmaker (1729–30). On 20 December 1729 invoiced to Edward Monnington of Sarnesfield Court, near Kington, Herefs. '12 Handsome Chairs Compass backs & seats wᵗʰ fine Cain £18' with two matching elbow chairs and another elbow chair 'for a Close stool Chair the seat Cov'rd wᵗʰ red morrocco Leather'. The cost of the commission totalled £25 2s. [Herefs. RO, P 94/26]

Pachon, George, Liverpool, cm (1760). In 1760 his app. John Highfield petitioned freedom. [Freemen's committee bk]

Padbury, Jon., address unknown, chairmaker (1723). On 26 July 1723 receipted an account paid by Paul Foley of Little Ormond St and the Temple, London, and Newport House, Almeley, Herefs. The items supplied included a chair. [Herefs. RO, Foley MS, F/AIII/55]

Padbury, William, Gloucester St, Cirencester, Glos., cm and u (1830–39). [D]

Paddon, Cornelius, Stepcote Hill, Exeter, Devon cm (1818–20). A daughter bapt. 1818 and a son 1820 at St George's Church. [PR (bapt.)]

Paddon, George, Gate St, Lincoln's Inn Fields, London, cm (1808). [D]

Paddon, Robert, London, looking-glass manufacturer (1819–29). At 243 Whitechapel Rd, 1819–25, but in 1829 the business was listed as Paddon & Son at 4 Cambridge Rd, Mile End Rd. [D]

Paddon, Simon, 51 Charles St, Drury Lane, London, cm (1806–07). In May 1806 took out insurance cover of £200 on his household goods and £80 on utensils and stock 'behind'. By July 1807 the address was shown as 51 Lewkness Lane and the cover was £300. [GL, Sun MS vol. 437, ref. 790735; vol. 440, ref. 804775]

Paddy, Thomas, 64 Granby St, Devonport, Devon, cm and u (1830). [D]

Padget, George, address unknown, cm (1803). Subscribed to Sheraton's *Cabinet Dictionary*, 1803.

Padget, John, Lancaster, cm (1759–68). App. to John Lowther joiner and cm in 1746 and free by servitude, 1759–60. Took apps in 1761, 1765, 1767 and 1768. [Freemen rolls; app. reg.; poll bk]

Padget, Richard, Lancaster, cm (1761–68). App. to John Padget in 1761 and free by servitude, 1767–68. [App. reg. and freemen rolls]

Padget, William, Highgate, Beverley, Yorks., cm and joiner (1799–1834). [D; poll bk]

Padle, John, 1 Midford Pl., Tottenham Ct Rd, London, bedstead and cornice maker (1820–26). In 1826 described as a furniture broker. [D]

Padman, John, parish of St Oswald, Durham, u (1730). Son buried 19 December 1730. [PR (burial)]

Page, —, address unknown, upholder and carpenter (1796). Payment of £16 10s 6d in the Longford Castle, Wilts. accounts. [V&A archives]

Page, —, 62 Tabernacle Walk, Finsbury, London, cm (1826). [D]

Page, Francis, New St, Wellington, Salop, chairmaker and wood turner (1840). [D]

Page, George, Old Bridge, Exeter, Devon, cm (1815). Two daughters bapt. at St Edmund's Church on 2 February 1815. [PR (bapt.)]

Page, Henry, Silver St, Gainsborough, Lincs., cm and u (1819–22). [D]

Page, John, 1 Doughty St, Foundling Hospital, London, picture frame maker (1820). [D]

Page, John, Brighton, Sussex, cm (1832–37). At 53 Kings St in 1832 and North Lane in 1837. [D; poll bk]

Page, Joseph, Nantwich, Cheshire, u (1801). A son and a daughter bapt. 18 January 1801. [PR (bapt.)]

Page, Mathew, Liverpool, cm (1761). App. to Thomas Griffiths and free by servitude on 14 March 1761. [Freemen reg.]

Page, Nathanial Ingate, Gt Yarmouth, Norfolk, cm (1818–38). [Poll bks]

Page, Thomas, parish of St Andrew's, Norwich, u (1732–68). App. to John Pennington and free by servitude on 24 February 1732. [Freemen rolls; poll bks]

Page, Thomas Osborn, parish of St George, Bloomsbury, London, cm (1796). Leased 'The Bell' public house at Kedington, Essex for a year from 5 December 1796. [Suffolk RO(Bury), 464/4, 464/5]

Page, Thomas, London, cabinet and knifecase manufacturer (1808–20). At 63 St John's St in 1808 and 5 Prince's St, Barbican, 1816–20. In 1820 described as a 'cabinet & plate chest maker and portable desk manufacturer'. [D]

Page, Thomas, Church St, Hackney, London, carver, gilder and paper hanger (1823–26). [D]

Page, Thomas, 4 Norfolk St, Prospect Pl., Southwark, London, bedstead maker (1826–29). [D]

Page, William, Chapel Pl., Kentish Town, London, cm and undertaker (1808). [D]

Page, William, 15 Short's Building, Clerkenwell, London, carver and gilder (1808). [D]

Page, William, East Rudham, Norfolk, cm (1836). [D]

Paget, William, 1 Clerkenwell Green, London, furniture japanner (1829). [D]

Pagett, Thomas, Sheep St Lane, Cirencester, Glos., cm (1820). [D]

Paice, George & William, Winchester St, Basingstoke, Hants., cm and u (1830). [D]

Paice, William, Basingstoke, Hants., cm and u (1823–39). Listed at Winchester St, 1839. [D]

Pailey, —, address unknown, carver (1812). Employed by Edward, Lord Lascelles probably at Harewood House, Hanover Sq., London and paid on 27 January 1812 £8 7s. [Leeds archives dept, Harewood MS 192]

Paillet, George, Bishopgate St, London upholder (1766–73). Son of Clement Paillet of Deptford, malt distiller. Brother of Melchior Paillet. Free of the Upholders' Co. by redemption under the terms of the 1750 Upholders' Act, 3 April 1766. [GL, Upholders' Co. records]

Paillet, Jaques, parish of St Giles-in-the-Fields, London, cm (c.1706–d.1765). Son of Daniel Paillet of the province of Saintonge, France. Entered the French Protestant Hospital, London, 1758–59, as he had lost the use of his hands and could not work. Died there, 13 April 1765, aged 59. [*Huguenot Soc.*, vol. LIII (1977)]

Paillet, Melchior, London, and Market Harborough, Leics., upholder (1766–81). Son of Clement Paillet of Deptford, malt distiller. Brother of George Paillet. Free of the Upholders' Co. by redemption under the terms of the 1750 Upholders' Act on 3 April 1766, the same day as his brother. At Bishopsgate St in 1773 but from 1788–81 at Shewell, near Market Harborough, Leics. [GL, Upholders' Co. records]

Pailthorpe, G., 29 Long Lane, Smithfield, London, mattress and bedding manufacturer (1813). [D]

Pailthorp(e), William, Baxtergate, Grimsby, Lincs., joiner, cm and builder (1826–40). [D]

Pain, J., 14 Little Chapel St, Soho, London, carver (1829). [D]

Pain, James, address unknown, chair carver (c.1788). Married the sister of Francis Place, the reformer. Described in Place's autobiography as 'a journeyman, a good workman and remarkably swift, he could earn full four pounds a week all the year round, and never need have wanted work, chairs and other small articles of furniture which were to be carved were sent to his own workshop, and he always had much more than he could do.' [BM, Add MS 35,142]

Pain, James, Green St, Milton, Kent, cm (1838–39). [D]

Pain, John, 'The Star', Lombard St, London, cm (d.1714). [Heal]

Pain, John, Banbury, Oxon., timber merchant, builder and cm (1783). In 1783 insured his warehouse, workshop and their stock for £210 out of a total cover of £700. [GL, Sun MS vol. 313, p. 229]

Pain, John H., Clare, Suffolk, cm (1830–39). [D]

Pain, William, 7 Hickman's Folly, Dockhead, London, cm (1809). [D]

Paine, Abel, Westgate St, Gloucester, auctioneer, appraiser, u and cm (1815–30). Children bapt. in 1815, 1817, 1818 at St Michael's Church. [D; PR (bapt.)]

Paine, John, Bristol, u (1713–54). In 1713 took app. named Stringer; in 1718, Anneley; and in 1721 Watkins. Both Stringer and Watkins were taken jointly by John Paine and his wife Elizabeth. Living in the parish of St Augustine, 1722–34, the parish of St Nicholas in 1739 and the parish of St James, 1739–54. [S of G, app. index; poll bks]

Paine, John, Gloucester St, Cirencester, Glos., cm (1820–38). [D]

Paine, Joseph, Russell Ct, Westminster, London, upholder (1774). [Poll bk]

Paine, Joseph, Catherine St, Strand, London, cm and upholder (1776–84). In 1776 took out insurance cover of £1,000 of which £760 was in respect of utensils and stock. Bankruptcy announced, *Gents Mag.*, May 1784. [GL, Sun MS vol. 247, p. 74]

Paine, Joseph, 17 New St, Birmingham, upholder (1800). [D]

Paine, Joseph, Newport, Salop, chairmaker (1831). [D]

Paine, Peter, St Ann's-in-Liberty, London, cm (1712). In 1712 took an app. [S of G, app. index]

Paine, Sampson, Camberwell, London, joiner/carver and gilder (1718–d.1731). In 1718 his trade was listed as a joiner and he occupied a house with associated brew house and stables 'on the East side of the road leading from Kent St to New Cross, Camberwell'. In this year he took out insurance cover on his dwelling house for £400 and for another rented house £200. At the time of his death in 1731 he was said to be a carver and gilder and 'dwelling in the halfway house in the road to Deptford'. [GL, Hand in Hand MS vol. 19, p. 148; Harris, *Old English Furniture*, p. 26]

Paine, Thomas, Birmingham, cm and upholder (1767–1800). At 15 Steelhouse Lane, 1767–70; 14 New St, 1777–93; and 15 New St in 1800. [D]

Painter, Daniel, Bristol, cm etc. (1810–26). At Gloucester St, 1810–14, but by 1815 in 'Back'. The number here was 7 in 1816, 9 in 1817–19 and 22 in 1820–23. From 1825–26 at King St, St Nicholas. [D]

Painter, Francis & Co., 32 Finsbury Pl. South, London, cm and u (1839). Included in the Banks' Coll., BM is the trade card of Painter & Co., Finsbury Sq., London which would appear to be the same concern. The card is illustrated with an engraving of an early 19th-century shop front inscribed 'late Lackington's' and 'Established upwards of a century'. [D]

Painter, George & Co., 67 London Wall, London, cm (1835). [D]

Painter, Isaac, Bristol, upholder (1774–95). In the parish of St Augustine in 1774, and in the following year at 9 Stoney Hill. From 1784 in St Augustine's Back, the number being 13 in 1792–93. From 1793 to 1795 the business traded as Painter & Huggins. [D; poll bks]

Painter, J., Hoxton Town, London, cm and chairmaker (1789–93). [D]

Painter, John, Liverpool, cm (1757). In 1757 took app. named Painter. [S of G, app. index]

Painter, Thomas, parish of St James, Bristol, cm (1784). [Poll bk]

Painter, William, Bristol, cm (1774–1809). At 23 Bridewell St in 1775 but from 1792–1809 at 'Back'. [D; poll bk]

Paish, Charles, Gloucester St, Cirencester, Glos., cm (1820). [D]

Paiten, —, address unknown, u (1717). On 22 December 1717 Admiral Edward Russell, Earl of Orford of Chippenham, Cambs. paid Paiten £49. [Cambs. RO, R74/43]

Paley, John, 63 Mortimer St, Cavendish Sq., London, carver and gilder (1835–37). [D]

Paley, Thomas, 19 Gt Castle St, Oxford Mkt, London, carver and gilder (1817). [D]

Paley, William, 42 Margaret St, Cavendish Sq., London, carver and gilder (1820). [D]

Palfreman, Thomas, Powis St, Woolwich, London, cm, u and furniture broker (1832–39). [D]

Palfrey, Richard, Chapel Hill, Exmouth, Devon, cm, chairmaker, u and undertaker (1830–38). An Ellen Palfrey was trading from this address in the same trades by 1844. [D]

Palfrey, Robert, 'The North Country Sailor Inn', Exmouth, Devon, cm and innholder (1823–d.1827). Also acted as an agent for the sale of properties. His death was announced early in January 1827. [D; *The Alfred*, 23 August 1825, 2 January 1827]

Palfryman, John, Thursday Mkt, York, cm (1767–74). Son of John Palfryman, chandler. Free as a cm in 1767. [Freemen rolls; poll bk]

Palk, William, Swings Lane, Exeter, Devon, cm (1829). Daughter bapt. on 25 October 1829 at the Church of St Mary Steps. [PR (bapt.)]

Pallant, James, St James's Walk, Clerkenwell, London, cm (1790–1809). [D]

Palleday, William, 'The Crown', Aldermanbury, London, cm (1713). A number of walnut and oak bureaus by this maker are known with trade labels pasted on drawer interiors. These all have characteristics which would date them to the Queen Anne period. The only documented commission known, however, is one for Lady Heathcote for which payment of £1 14s 6d was received on 15 December 1713. A 13-inch glass in a walnut frame, and a square 'falling' table were supplied and repairs carried out to a chest of drawers. [V&A archives; Sotheby's, 5 October 1945, lot 82; 1 March 1974, lot 38A; Lincoln RO, 2 ANC 12/D/7]

Pallentine, W., 66 Gt Queen St, Lincoln's Inn Fields, London, carver and gilder (1837). [D]

Pallett & Smith, 13 Little Pancras St, Tottenham Ct Rd, London, chair and sofa makers (1839). [D]

Pallin, Elias, Bristol, cm (1795). In 1795 at Peter St. From 1799–1801 shown at 'The Rose & Crown', Narrow plain, but there is no indication that he carried on his trade as cm from there. [D]

Pallin, Elias, Merchant St, Bristol, cm, u, appraiser and furniture broker (1818–31). At 6 Merchant St, 1818–19, and nos 5 and 6 from 1820–31. [D]

Pallin, Elizabeth, Merchant St, Bristol, cm and broker (1801). [D]

Pallin (Palling or Pallings), Henry, Bristol, cm (1793–1800). In 1793–94 at Newgate St, but does not feature again in the directories until 1799–1800 when he was in Merchant St. In the following year the directories show Elizabeth Pallin at this address in the same trade. [D]

Palliser, Joseph, address unknown, cm and joiner (1741). Paid 16s 3d for making a clothes press for 'Mr. Leaton', the entry in the cash book of the Gibside estate, Co. Durham being dated 1 August 1741. Several generations of the Palliser family were estate joiners at Gibside and estate records frequently mention furniture repairs and the occasional making of new furniture by them. [Durham RO, Strathmore MS, D/St/V988]

Palliser, William, Long Lane, Moorfields, London, upholder and cm (1771–81). Son of George Paliser, vintner. Free of the Upholders' Co. by order of the Court of Aldermen, 3 July 1771. Went into partnership with James Paul and the partners were declared bankrupt in 1781. [GL, Upholders' Co. records; Bailey's list of bankrupts]

Pallison, Joseph, St Botolph, Aldersgate, London, upholder (1767). Took out insurance cover of £50 in December 1767. [GL, Hand in Hand MS vol. 106, p. 329]

Pal(l)ister & Barkas, 16 High Friar St, Newcastle, cm (1834). [D]

Palmer, Mr, Masham St, Westminster, London, cm (d.1746). Death reported, *General Advertiser*, 10 June 1746.

Palmer, Mr, Queen St, Cheapside, London, upholder (1748). Supplied catalogues for Robert Heath, auctioneer. [*General Advertiser*, 1 November 1748] Possibly John Palmer of Queen St.

Palmer, B. & Son, Piccadilly, London, cm and u (1822–29). At 25 Piccadilly in 1822 but from the next year the number changed to 175. [D]

Palmer, Benjamin, parish of St Swithin, Norwich, cm (1796). [Poll bk]

Palmer, Edward, Hertford St, Coventry, Warks., u (1828). [D]

Palmer, Edward, Old Bond St, Leicester, cm (1835). Described as the only surviving son of William Palmer, cm, who was the second son of Thomas Palmer, cm. [D; freemen reg.]

Palmer, Francis, 23 St John's Lane, Clerkenwell, London, cm (1780). In 1780 insured his house for £100. [GL, Sun MS vol. 280, p. 33]

Palmer, George, 1 St James's St, Piccadilly, London, writing desk and dressing case maker (1829–35). By 1834 advertising himself as 'Cutler & Dressing Case Manufacturer to His Majesty & the Royal Family'. His billhead shows that he sold 'Razors & fine Cutlery, Dressing Cases, Shaving Pouches, Writing Desks'. [D; Arundel Castle records, A2111]

Palmer, Gilbert, Exeter, Devon, carver and gilder (1833). In 1833 at Bartholomew St and in 1836 at Mary Arches' St. Daughter bapt. on 24 March 1833 and a son on 31 July 1836 at St Olave's Church. [PR (bapt.)]

Palmer, J., 2 Philip St, Bath, Som., cm (1819–24). [D]

Palmer, James, Leicester, cm (1767). Third son of Thomas Palmer, joiner and turner. Free 1767. [Freemen rolls]

Palmer, James, Portsea, Portsmouth, Hants., cm (1792–98). [D]

Palmer, John, near 'The Feathers Tavern', Queen St, Cheapside, London, upholder (1719–53). In 1719 his house in Queen St was said to be let to a T. Carter of Witney, Oxon. [D; GL, Sun MS vol. 9, p. 315; Heal] Possibly Mr Palmer of Queen St.

Palmer, John, 'The Cabinet & Star', facing Lawrence Pountney Lane, Cannon St, London, cm and u (1765). His trade card [GL] was used as a receipt dated 18 April 1765. The card is embellished with an engraving of a cabinet on stand surrounded by an elaborate Rococo frame. The text states that he made and sold 'all sorts of Cabinet & Upholstery Goods, Chairs Tables and Looking Glasses in Carv'd Gilt or Painted Frames'. He dealt both retail and wholesale, appraised goods and arranged funerals.

Palmer, John, Canterbury, Kent, u (1796–1818). At St Mary Bredin in 1796 and Dover Lane, 1818. [Poll bks]

Palmer, John, Sheldon, Newcastle-under-Lyme, Staffs., cm and ironmonger (1798). [D]

Palmer, John, 3 Staining Lane, Wood St and 9 Little Knightrider St, London, u (1809–16). [D]

Palmer, John, Bristol, carver and gilder (1819–31). At Somerset St, Redcliffe in 1819; 3 St James's Barton (or 3 Barton Alley) 1823–25; 23 Upper Arcade 1826–30; and near 'The Black Swan', Stapleton Rd, 1831. [D]

Palmer, John, Market St, Lane End, Staffs., u and cm (1818–22). [D]

Palmer, Jno., 5 Warwick Ct, Holborn, London, carver and gilder (1835). [D]

Palmer, Matt., parish of St Giles-in-the-Fields, London, u (1711–12). Took an app., 1711–12. [S of G, app. index]

Palmer, Matthew, High Holborn, London, u (1708). In November 1708 declared bankrupt and ordered to surrender himself to the Commissioners in Bankruptcy. [*London Gazette,* 29 November 1708]

Palmer, Michael, London, upholder (1784–1808). At Duke St, Grosvenor Sq., 1784–93. In 1808 at 227 Oxford St and auctioneer in addition to upholder. [D; Westminster poll bk]

Palmer, R. O., 54 Gloucester St, Red Lion Sq., London, u (1829). [D]

Palmer, Robert, Fleshmarket, Newcastle, auctioneer and cm (1801–04). On 17 May 1803 supplied to the order of the Earl of Strathmore a four post bedstead for his gardener at a cost of £1 10s. The account was paid 21 May 1804. [D; Durham RO, Strathmore MS, D/St/Box 206]

Palmer, T., 22 Warwick St, Golden Sq., London, cabinet buhl and ormolu manufacturer (1819–25). [D]

Palmer, William, 'The Cabinet', Fenchurch St, London, cm (1730–50). On 24 December 1730 took out insurance cover of £500 and of this £300 was for trade stock and £200 for a stock of glass. Palmer was a member of the Joiners' Co. in 1750. From 1768 another William Palmer was trading from 50 Fenchurch St as a cm and u and is probably related. [GL, Sun MS vol. 32, ref. 52781; GL, Joiners' Co. records, Livery lists]

Palmer, William, Leicester, cm (1767). Second son of Thomas Palmer, turner and joiner. Free 1767. [Freemen rolls]

Palmer, William, 50 Fenchurch St, London, cm and u (1768–81). Probably related to the William Palmer, cm, who was trading at 'The Cabinet', Fenchurch St, 1730–50. [D]

Palmer, William, Strand, London, carver, gilder and printseller (1780–90). At 159 Strand ('Facing the New Church') 1780–88, but from 1789 the number was 163. In 1780 took out insurance cover of £300 of which £200 was in respect of utensils and stock. In partnership with Thomas Fielding, an engraver, c.1788, and possibly the successor to William Wynne Ryland, the celebrated engraver and printseller who was executed for forgery. In 1790 advertised himself as 'printseller to Her Majesty'. Palmer's trade label has been recorded on the back of a pair of stipple engravings, after Angelica Kauffmann. [D; Sun MS vol. 280, p. 296; Christie's, S. Kensington, 5 December 1983, lot 84]

Palmer, William, St John's Lane, Newcastle, cm, carpenter and auctioneer (1790–95). [D]

Palmer, William, 43 Wardour St, Soho, London, japan chair etc. manufacturer (1806). [D]

Palmer, William, 4 Chapel Ct, Bath, Som., cm (1826). [D]

Palmer, William, Canterbury, Kent, chairmaker (1826–30). At King St, 1826–29, but in 1830 at Mill Lane. [D; poll bks]

Palmer, William, parish of St Gregory, Norwich, cm (1830). [Poll bk]

Palmer, William, 125 Crawford St, Portman Sq., London, carver and gilder (1839). [D]

Palmer, William, Cheap St, Newbury, Berks., chairmaker (1840). [D]

Panner, —, Knave's Acre, Golden Sq., Westminster, London, u (1749). [Poll bk]

Pannett, Marmaduke, Tadcaster, Yorks., joiner/cm (1834–37). At Chapel St in 1837. [D]

Panting, —, 6 Charlotte St, Rathbone Pl., London, cabinet and upholstery manufacturer (1820). [D]

Panting, Thomas, Liverpool, cm and u (1827–35). At 21 Renshaw St, 1827–29, but in 1835 at 6 Fletcher St, Toxteth Park with a shop at 6 Leese St. [D]

Panton, John, London, turner (1768–70). Supplied goods to Shelburne House, Berkeley Sq. between April 1768 and 29 September 1770 costing £94 12s 7d. Amongst the items supplied were 'Common Chairs & Tables'. [Bowood MS]

Pape, Isaac, 181 Walmgate, York, cm and u (1828–34). [D]

Pape, J., 8 Helmet Row, Old St, London, cm (1820). [D] See William Pape.

Pape, James, Market Hill, Wigton, Cumb., joiner/cm (1811). [D]

Pape, William, 12 Helmet Row, Old St, London, clock-case maker (1840). [D] See J. Pape.

Parbery, Thomas, Abingdon St, Northampton, u (1784–98). [D; poll bks]

Pardoe, John, London, cm and u (1717–48). His trade card of c.1720 indicates that he was originally established 'against St. Clements Church' but had recently moved to 'The Cabinet & Chair', next Temple Bar, Strand. He made and sold 'all sorts of Looking Glasses, Coach Glasses, Cabinet Work & Chairs, Beds & Bedding wth all other sorts of Goods in the Cabinet & Upholstere^{rs} way'. He also sought export orders. The trade card is illustrated with engravings of a cabinet with carved cresting on a stand decorated with a Baroque mask and a cabriole legged chair with a central vertical splat and curvilinear back (Fig. 24). In 1745 he was fined for declining parochial office in the parish of St Bride's, Fleet St. The business appears to have traded successfully until March 1748 when he advertised that he had 'left off trade' and offered his stock for disposal. [Heal; GL, MS 6561, p. 78; *Daily Advertiser,* 12 March 1749]

John Pardoe attracted wealthy and influential patrons. He was employed in the furnishing of Erddig, Clwyd, N. Wales 1717–23 mainly for the supply of mirrors and sconces. He is referred to in the Erddig accounts as 'Mr Pardors ye Glassman'. On 20 March 1716/17 Pardoe invoiced a large walnut 'writing desk & bookcase with looking glass doors' at £9 and in September and October 1720 supplied a number of looking-glasses and carried out restoration work on others. A pair of 'large looking glass sconces in carved and gold frame with double glass branches' were charged at £12 10s. These are still in the house. [V&A archives; *C. Life,* 13 April 1978, pp. 971–72; *Apollo,* July 1978, pp. 49–54] For Lord Leigh of Stoneleigh, Warks. items were provided in 1738. These included 'a neat carv'd & gild chimney glass' charged at £4 4s, a 'large mahogany Dining Table' which cost £2 12s 6d, and a 'mahogany voider ornamented & inlaid in brass' which was £2. [Shakespeare's Birthplace Trust, Leigh receipts, DR18/5] Another patron was Alderman Hoare who for his house at Barn Elms, Barnes, London purchased in June 1740 a mahogany desk and tea board for which the bill totalled £3 14s. [V&A, 86 NN 3] In common with a number of other London makers of this period Pardoe affixed his trade bill to drawer interiors of pieces of furniture he supplied. A number of examples have been noted including a mahogany chest of drawers with brushing slide, a walnut kneehole writing table, a mahogany dressing chest with slide and four graduated long drawers and a mahogany bureau. In the case of the bureau the label had written on it the date of supply, 3 March 1743, and the cost £3 13s 6d. [*C. Life,* 10 June 1965, p. 1421; Sotheby's, 23 May 1980, lots 129, 154] B.A.

Pardoes, William, New St, Worcester, cm, u, springbeds &c. (1840). [D]

Pardon, James, St Peter's St, Canterbury, Kent, carver and gilder (1823–29). [D]

Pardon, John, 'The Looking Glass', the corner of Gerrard St, London, cm (1718). On 24 February 1718 insured his goods and merchandise. It is possible that this is the well-known maker John Pardoe. [GL, Sun MS vol. 2]

Pare, John, Birmingham, cm and upholder (1816–22). Listed at 2 Steelhouse Lane in 1816; Dale End and Colmore Row in 1818; and 1 Colmore Row in 1822. [D]

Parfit, Owen, Bristol, cm (1774–75). Shown at Castle Precincts in 1774 and 53 Castle St, 1775. [D; poll bk]

Parfitt, Thomas, Wells, Som., joiner and cm (1719). In 1719 took app. named Notley. A person of the same surname trading in Wells as a cm in 1762, who appraised the goods of the late Samuel Woodforde, Canon Residentiary and Treasurer of the Cathedral on 27 April, was probably related. [S of G, app. index; R. L. Winstanley (ed.), *The Ansford Diary of James Woodforde*, I, p. 29]

Parfitt, Thomas, Bristol, cm (1781–1816). Probably related to Owen Parfit. Shown at Castle Precincts, 1781–84, and from 1792–1801, at Redcliffe Hill. Subsequent addresses are 7 Wine St in 1805, Redcliffe Hill, 1806–07 and 74 Redcliffe Hill in 1809, 24 Bath St, 1810–12, and 59 Baldwin St, 1813–16. [D; poll bk]

Parfitt, Thomas, Bristol, cm and u (1820–32). At 56 Castle St, 1820–22, and in 1822 referred to as a salt refiner. The number changed to 54 in the period 1825–28 and the trade is shown as cm and mahogany dealer. In 1829–30 at 57 Broadmead and from 1831–32 at 5 Redcross St where in addition to trading as a cm and u he also made Venetian blinds. His bankruptcy was announced, *Brighton Gazette*, 26 May 1825, but this does not appear to have seriously dislocated his business activities. [D]

Pargiter, George, London, chair and sofa manufacturer (1826–39). At 4 Bacon St, Spitalfields in 1826 and 16 Storship St, Finsbury in 1839. [D]

Paris, Robert, Peterborough Ct, Fleet St, London, cm and u (1839). [D]

Parisels, Marie, London(?), u(?) (1709). The account books of Boughton, Northants. include the following entry for 24 March 1709: 'Billet de Marie Parisels pour ouvrage jaite par de My Lord Duc de Montagu le 24 Mars 1709. Mt Lord Duc ayant commede et facit le marche pour l'ouvrage de douze chaises a la maniere de la chine a six guinnees per chaise desquelles six ont etc livres et la ditte Marie Parisel a Recu de Monsr Anthony la somme de £30 sur £38.14s Reste diu … 08:14:00. Pour avoir faite du changement a un Ecrand et pour y avoir facit une bordure de broderie sur da sattin blanc pour le quel le Duc de Montague fit marche de payer 1:5:0'. [Boughton, account bk 2]

Parish, Charles, Gloucester St, Cirencester, Glos., cm (1820). [D]

Parish, John, Little Chapel St, Westminster, London, upholder (1774). [Poll bk]

Parish, Joseph, High St, Braintree, Essex, cm ad u (1832). [D]

Park, —, Halifax, Yorks., cm (1793). Subscribed to Sheraton's *Drawing Book*, 1793.

Park, Edward, Coronation St, Sunderland, Co. Durham, joiner and cm (1828). [D]

Park, James, Longtown, Cumb., joiner/cm (1811–29). [D]

Park, John, Bird-in-Hand, Princes St, Warminster, Wilts., cm (1728). In August 1728 took out insurance cover of £500 on his dwelling house, household goods and trade stock. [GL, Sun MS vol. 26, p. 373]

Park, John, 9 Kennington Lane, London, cm (1820). [D]

Park, Mark, Salisbury St, Blandford, Dorset, auctioneer, cm and u (1830). [D]

Park, Thomas, Back St, Maryport, Cumb., joiner/cm (1811). [D]

Park, Walter Archibald, 13 Old Park, Bristol, cm (1834). [D]

Park, William, 13 Old Park, Bristol, cm (1833). [D]

Parke, James, London(?), u (1694). [YAS, Duke of Leeds papers, DDS Box XIII, No. 23]

Parke, James, Pitt St, Tottenham Ct Rd, London, cm (1772–82).

At 16 Pitt St in 1775 when he was referred to as a carver. In 1782 at 18 Pitt St. He was a signatory in 1772 to 'The Real State of the Complaints of the CABINET MAKERS, as published & signed by their Committee'. Insured his house for £100 in 1775 and in 1782 took out cover of £250 on his utensils and stock. [*Gents Mag.*, June 1772; GL, Sun MS vol. 236, p. 415; vol. 300, p. 311]

Parke, John, 32 Edward St, Liverpool, cm and victualler (1800–03). [D]

Parke, Jonathan, 75 Market St, Manchester, carver and gilder (1794–1802). [D]

Parke, Joseph, Liverpool, cm (1780). His app. John Blackley petitioned for freedom in 1780. [Freemen's committee bk]

Parke, Luke, 9 Little Cockey Lane, Norwich, carver and gilder (1801–08). [D]

Parke, Reuben, London, upholder (1710–20). At Arundel St, Strand, 1710–17, and in both 1710 and 1717 this property was insured for £1,000. In January 1717 moved to Richbald Ct, Red Lion Sq. next to 'The Hoop & Flask Tavern', and in December 1718 moved once again to Hind Ct, Fleet St. The reason for this last move appears to have been the termination of his trading activities as an upholder. [Heal; GL, Hand in Hand MS vol. 7, ref. 4002; vol. 17, ref. 4002; Sun MS vol. 4, ref. 4727]

Parke, Richard, 108 Richmond Row, Liverpool, carver and gilder (1834). [D]

Parke, Samuel, 20 Piccadilly, London, cm and u (1774–84). Bankruptcy announced, *Gents Mag.*, 1782. Recorded from 1781–82 trading in partnership under the style Parke & Henning. [D; Heal]

Parke, Thomas, Castlegate, Pickering, Yorks., joiner and cm (1840). [D]

Parker, Mrs, the Lines, Wigmore St, Hereford (1728). Account dated 15 June 1728 sent to Edward Monnington of Sarnesfield Court, near Kington, Herefs. for £1 1s for 'a ovell table … made of Dutch oak'. [Herefs. RO, P94/25]

Parker, Arthur, Chester, u (1747). Son of Richard Parker, innholder. Free 13 July 1747. [Freemen rolls; poll bk]

Parker, Arthur, Brick Lane, Spitalfields, London, cm and chairmaker (1800–09). At 25 Fashion St, Brick Lane 1800 and John St, Osborne Pl., Brick Lane in 1807. Total insurance cover on his house, contents and stock only came to £200 in April 1800, but by April 1807 this had risen to £1,650 of which £350 was for a workshop behind his house and £400 for stock and utensils there, in an open yard and in a sawpit. [D; Sun MS vol. 418, ref. 702400; vol. 438, ref. 802738]

Parker, Charles, High Holborn, London, upholder and carpet and upholstery warehouse (1776–93). At 124 High Holborn until 1778, but from 1781 at 123. Married in January 1783. A bill dated 11 June 1785 made out to a Mr Thomas Lucas for a number of items of bedding exists in the V&A Library. [D; *Gents Mag.*, January 1783; V&A Box II, 86 22 No. 15]

Parker, Charles, 19 Exmouth St, London, cm and u (1839). [D]

Parker, Edmund, 7 Duke St, Liverpool, u (1811–13). [D]

Parker, Edward, Liverpool, u (1814–39). First recorded at 7 Duke St in 1814. In 1821 the number was 8. By 1839 at 12 Seel St. [D] See Edmund and Edwin Parker.

Parker, Edward, Newcastle, chairmaker (1824–38). At Old Butcher Mkt in 1824 and 14 Cloth Mkt, 1833–38, with a house at Dean Ct in 1833. [D]

Parker, Edwin, Seel St, Liverpool, cm and victualler (1835–37). At 71 Seel St in 1835 when the trade was indicated as cm and beer shop. In 1837 the number was 74. [D] See Edward Parker of Liverpool.

Parker, Francis, St Martin-in-the-Fields(?), London, carver (d. *c.*1744). App. to his uncle, Mr Stone of Cook's Alley,

Bedfordbury, St Martin-in-the-Fields, until Stone's death. [Westminster Ref. Lib., F/5037/]

Parker, George, 44 Castle St, Liverpool, cm, auctioneer and toymaker (1740–81). At the Castle St address as early as 1764 and continued to trade there until at least 1781. Father of Thomas Parker, cm who was app. to his father and free 1761. Also took apps named Pellin in 1740 and Moss in 1753. Other apps who petitioned freedom were Thomas Clarke in 1764, James Clegg in 1777, Charles Rigby in 1780 and John Houghton who was app. 1762 but did not petition until 1780. As early as 1746 Parker worked with Thomas Hales as a valuer of the goods of George Harrison. He also regularly auctioned goods and in April 1766 was responsible for the sale of the household goods 'of the Rt. Hon. Richard, the late Lord Viscount Molyneux and the R. Hon. the Viscountess Molyneux'. The exact date of his death is not known but was between 1781, when he is last recorded trading, and May 1794 when his widow died. [D; S of G, app. index; freemen's committee bk; Liverpool RO, 920 GRE 3/1 5; *Manchester Mercury*, 15 April 1766; *Williamson's Liverpool Advertiser*, 16 November 1764, 6 November 1767, 12 May 1794]

Parker, George, Holywell St, Chesterfield, Derbs., cm (1818–22). [D]

Parker, George Wall, London, cm (1818–30). In June 1818 at Piccadilly and in July 1830 at Marlborough St. He was a freeman of Canterbury. [Canterbury poll bks]

Parker, H. A., 22 Pall Mall, London, cm (b. *c.* 1801–d. 1833). Foreman to France, Banting & Co., upholders, Pall Mall. Died aged 32 on 31 January 1833. [*Liverpool Mercury*, 8 February 1833]

Parker, Henry, Canterbury, Kent, u (1720). [Freemen rolls]

Parker, Henry, London, cm (1830). Freemen of Norwich. [Poll bk]

Parker, Henry, Hull, Yorks., cm (1834–35). At Charlotte St Mews in 1834 and 24 Worship St in 1835. [D]

Parker, Henry, 15 New Inn Yd, Shoreditch, London, carver, cm etc. (1839). [D]

Parker, James, Salisbury, Wilts., upholder (1722). On 21 June 1722 took as app. John Madgwick, son of Edward Madgwick of Bodenham, Wilts. at a premium of £10. [*Wilts. Apps and their Masters*]

Parker, James, Bristol, carver and gilder (1799–1810). At Barrs St, 1799–1800, Broad St in 1801 and Dove St, 1805–10. [D]

Parker, James, Bristol, carver and gilder (1817–28). From 1824 also glass polisher. At Eugene St, 1817–18, 18 Upper Maudlin St, 1821–22, 3 Upper Maudlin St, 1823, 8 St James's Churchyard 1824–26 and once again in Upper Maudlin St, 1828. [D]

Parker, James, Eton, Bucks., turner (1836–40). In June 1836 supplied paterae, knobs, chair rails, table feet and legs for furniture for use in the Royal Household. [Windsor Royal Archives, account bk P]

Parker, James, 97 Sparling St, Liverpool, cm (1837). Possibly the James Parker who was in partnership with John Parker as cm at Green Lane, Pleasant St in 1827. [D]

Parker, James, 2 Earl St, London Rd, Southwark, London, chair and sofa maker (1839). [D]

Parker, James, 52 Bromsgrove St, Birmingham, chairmaker (1839). [D]

Parker, Jane, Butcher's Row, Lichfield, Staffs., working u (1834). [D]

Parker, John, 'The Crown & Key', corner of White Hart Lane, Drury Lane, London, u (1716). On 4 December 1716 took out insurance cover on the goods and merchandise in his dwelling house. [GL, Sun MS vol. 6, p. 69]

Parker, John, Chesterfield, Derbs., cm (1753). In 1753 took app. named Parker, probably Thomas Parker. [S of G, app. index]

Parker, John, Shackleton, Yorks., upholder (1763). Bankruptcy announced, *Gents Mag.*, December 1763.

Parker, John, parish of St James, Bristol, cm (1781–84). [Poll bks]

Parker, John, Bristol, cm and chairmaker (1799–1840). From 1799–1813 described as 'Windsor & Fancy Chair Maker'. At Old King St, 1799–1837, the number being 1 in 1807–09. In the period 1838–40 at 23 Upper Maudlin St. [D]

Parker, John, Liverpool, cm and victualler (1796–1824). At 6 Edmund St in 1796 but from 1821–24 at 14 Derby St, Whitechapel. [D]

Parker, John, Lower St, Deal, Kent, cm and u (1800–29). Freeman of Canterbury. In Deal by 1800, and in 1803 subscribed to Sheraton's *Cabinet Dictionary*. [D; Canterbury poll bks]

Parker, John, Bond St, Hull, Yorks., u (1803). Another directory issued in this year describes his trade as paper stainer. [D]

Parker, John, parish of St John the Baptist Hereford, joiner and cm (1806). App. to William Parker, joiner and cm of the parish of St John the Baptist, Hereford, and free 31 July 1806. [Freemen rolls]

Parker, John, Back Lane, Brampton, Cumb, cm (1811–34). [D]

Parker, John, Low St, St Peter's, Leeds, Yorks., cm (1824). [D]

Parker, John, 8 Hodgsons Yd with a house at 20 Fox St, Preston, Lancs., cm (1825). [D]

Parker, John & James, Green Lane, Pleasant St, Liverpool, cm (1827). A James Parker, possibly the same man, was trading as a cm from 97 Sparling St in 1837. [D]

Parker, John, Thompson's Entry, 14 Cloth Mkt, Newcastle, chairmaker (1834). [D]

Parker, John, Cock St, Diss, Norfolk, cm and u (1836–39). [D]

Parker, John, 163 Piccadilly, opposite Bond St, London, carpet and floor cloth manufacturer and furnishing u etc. (1837). [D]

Parker, John & Co., 261 Oxford St, London, u (1839). [D]

Parker, Jonathan, Swan Lane, Bawtry, Yorks., cm (1822). [D]

Parker, Joseph, Chester, u (1712–30). Son of John Parker of Barton, Cheshire and app. to Randall Bingley of Chester, u. Free 23 May 1712. Took apps named Lee in 1713 and Joseph in 1719. Another app. was Griffiths Williams, free in 1730. [Freemen rolls; S of G, app. index]

Parker, Joseph, Gt Wire St, Colchester, Essex, chairmaker (1805–08). [D]

Parker, Joseph, Scawby St, Brigg, Lincs., cm and u (1835). [D]

Parker, Philip Joseph, Hereford and London, chairmaker (1826). In the 1826 poll bk for Hereford shown in London as a chairmaker and also in Hereford as a rustic chairmaker. [Hereford poll bk]

Parker, Reuben, London, upholder (1698–1714). App. to Andrew Dandy and free of the Upholders' Co. by servitude 23 August 1698. Took as app. James Warren, 1705–14. [GL, Upholders' Co. records]

Parker, Richard, Bromsgrove, Worcs., wood turner and chairmaker (1793). [D]

Parker, Richard & Thomas, Beauty Bank, Stourbridge, Worcs., chairmakers (1828–30). [D]

Parker, Richard, 112 Richmond Row, Liverpool, carver and gilder (1835). [D]

Parker, Robert, London, carver (1754–82). In 1754 in the parish of St Martin-in-the-Fields and in 1756 shown at King St, Soho. His address in 1760 was given as St James's, Westminster and in 1780 he was at 19 Tottenham St, Tottenham Ct Rd. In 1754 subscribed to Chippendale's *Director* and also took as app. James Burnett. In 1780 took out insurance cover of £200 but only £60 of this was for utensils and stock. Said to have worked on a Neo-classical commode for the print room at Woodhall House, Herts. in 1782. [GL, Sun MS vol. 287, p. 565; *C. Life*, 31 January

1925, pp. 202–03; C. Musgrave, *Adam and Hepplewhite Furniture*, p. 129]

Parker, Robinson, Wapping New Stairs, London, u and cm (1767–68). [D]

Parker, Thomas, Hemmings Row, St Martin's Lane, London, carver and cm (1748–54). Free of the Joiners' Co., 6 September 1748 by patrimony. His father was Edward Parker. In 1754 subscribed to Chippendale's *Director*. [GL, Joiners' Co. records; Westminster poll bk]

Parker, Thomas, 32 Cheapside, Dale St, Liverpool, cm (1761–96). App. to his father George Parker and free by servitude in 1761. Not recorded in any directory until 1796, probably an indication that he was employed in his fathers' business for some considerable time between these dates. [D; freemen's committee bk]

Parker, Thomas, Chesterfield, Derbs., cm and victualler (1793). [D]

Parker, Thomas, Broad St, Canterbury, Kent, cm (1796). [Poll bk]

Parker, Thomas, London, cm and buhl manufacturer (1805–30). At 19 Air St, Piccadilly from 1808–17 but by 1820 in Warwick St, Golden Sq., where the number was 22 to 1827 but 32 in 1829–30. The business attracted Royal patronage at an early stage and from 1805–09 was supplying Princess Elizabeth. By 1817, however, the firm numbered the Prince Regent amongst its customers and proudly advertised themselves as 'Cabinet & Buhl Manufacturer to H.R.H. the Prince Regent & Royal Family'. They included in their stock 'Ink Stands, Portfolios, Work Boxes, Chess & Backgammon Men & Boards' and offered to clean and repair 'India Japan, Or Molu, Bronzes &c'.

In 1817 the Prince Regent was supplied with 'A pair of Buhl coffers with stands richly ornamented with chased brass mouldings' which cost £210, and 'two round buhl tables with Boys chased heads Mouldings with drawer £210' and 'A pair of rich Buhl stands to hold light with carved & gilt ornaments £105'. Another patron was the 6th Duke of Bedford who in October 1815 purchased two buhl inkstands for £16 and in 1821 '2 black Pedestals with gilt ornaments' for £29 and further inkstands, some in ebony with brass mouldings. The Hon. Mrs Leigh for her London house made purchases between 1817–30. No less than £160 10s was spent in 1817 mostly on a pair of black ebony cabinets and a circular inlaid table both ornamented with ormolu. In August 1821 two further cabinets were invoiced utilising lacquer panels and costing together with two papier mâché trays £93 14s 1d. Her last known patronage was in 1830 when the main item was a satinwood miniature cabinet, mounted with ormolu which with some other minor items cost £20 11s 6d. [D; PRO, C13/661/29; *Burlington*, June 1980, p. 416; V&A archives; Bedford Office, London; V&A, GG65 E128–9 1943; Shakespeare's Birthplace Trust, Leigh receipts, DR 18/5]

Parker, Thomas, Judd St, Brunswick Sq., London, upholder, cm and undertaker (1817–27). At 22 Judd St in 1817 but from 1820–27 at no. 41. In some years listed as Parker & Turpin. [D]

Parker, Thomas, Newcastle, cm (1827–34). Had a house at 4 New Pandon St in 1827 but in 1833 trading at 187 Pilgrim St and in 1834 at no. 188. [D] See Parker & Amry.

Parker, William, Little St Andrew's St, London, clock case maker (d.1752). [Heal]

Parker, William, Hereford, joiner and cm (1771–96). On 20 June 1771 informed the public that he had 'taken over the house, Stock, and Timber-Yard, late in the Possession of Mr. Moore, in the King's Ditch'. From here he intended to carry on the trade of joiner and cm and offered to supply 'Building Timber, either squared or scantled'. He indicated that he had available for immediate offer oak, ash and elm floor-boarding. On 11 February 1779 he advertised his move from King's Ditch to premises opposite 'The New Inn' in Widemarsh St. On 11 April 1796, however, his bankruptcy was announced. His son John Parker was app. to him and declared free in 1806. [*Pugh's Hereford Journal*, 20 June 1771, 11 February 1779; *Billinge's Liverpool Advertiser*, 11 April 1796, 4 July 1796; freemen rolls]

Parker, William, parish of St Peter in the East, Oxford, upholder (1793). Married on 17 September 1793 at St Peter's Church to Ann Smith of the same parish. [Bodleian index of Oxf. marriage bonds]

Parker, William, Lancaster (1799–1823). Named in the Gillow records in 1799–1801, 1808, 1810, 1819, 1821 and 1823. [Westminster Ref. Lib.]

Parker, William, Manchester, joiner and cm (1804–13). At 3 Clowes St, 1804–08 and 20 Faulkner St, 1811–13. See Parker & Wragg at 20 Falkner St in 1808. [D]

Parker, William, 5 Seymour St with a shop at Shaw's Brow, Liverpool, turner and cm (1823–34). [D]

Parker, William, London, backgammon and billiard table maker (1825–39). In 1825 at 14 Hooper St, Goswell St but by 1826 had moved to 3 Marlins Pl., Spa Fields, Islington. In 1832 at 76 Hoxton Old Town and in 1839 at 10 Wilmot Sq., Bethnal Green where he traded as a billiard table maker only. [D]

Parker, William, 5 Queen St, Finsbury, London, cm and u (1839). [D]

Parker & Amry, Dog Bank and 187 Pilgrim St, Newcastle, cm (1827). The Parker was probably Thomas Parker who had a house at Pandon St in 1827 and by 1833 was trading on his own account from 187 Pilgrim St. [D]

Parker & Cluley, Sheffield, Yorks., makers of patent bedsteads (1811). Their Liverpool agent was Chew & Sons, Lord St. [*Liverpool Mercury*, 22 November 1811]

Parker, & Harris, opposite the New Church, Strand, London and Bond St, Bath, Som., carvers (1776). Advertised their ability to supply statues, bas-reliefs and busts. Their trade card [Heal Coll., BM] was used as an invoice to the Earl of Winterton for busts of Virgil and Dryden for which £1 12s was charged.

Parker & Turpin, see Thomas Parker, Judd St, London.

Parker & Wragg, 20 Falkner St, Manchester, joiners and cm (1808). One of the partners was William Parker who is recorded trading on his own behalf from 3 Clowes St, 1804–08 and also from 20 Falkner St, 1811–13. [D]

Parkes, Edwin, Bromsgrove St, Birmingham, carver and gilder (1835–39). Recorded at no. 16 in 1835 and no. 13 in 1839. [D]

Parkes, John snr and jnr, Welsh Row, Nantwich, Cheshire, cm (1799–1834). John Parkes snr is recorded as early as 1799 when his daughter Elizabeth was bapt. His son John was married to Mary Latham on 22 July 1828. She was described as the eldest daughter of Samuel Latham of 'The Swan Inn', Nantwich. [D; PR (bapt., marriage); *Chester Chronicle*, 1 August 1828] See William Parkes at this address.

Parkes, Joseph & Wells, Thomas, 19 Pierpont Row, Islington, London, u (1824). Took out insurance cover of £150 in February 1824 but of this only £90 covered utensils and stock. [GL, Sun MS vol. 495, ref. 1014381]

Parkes, Nicholas, Paternoster Row, London, u (1726–31). [Heal].

Parkes, Nicholas, 27 Ivey Lane, Newgate St, London, u (1767–72). [D]

Parkes, Samuel, 'The Golden Spread Eagle', Paternoster Row, London, u (1701–28). Between 26 July 1721 and 28 April 1722 Parkes undertook work, including cleaning beds, for Sir

Gilbert Heathcote. The bill for his services came to £35 6s 2d. A Nicholas Parkes was trading from an address in Paternoster Row as an u, 1726–31. [Heal; Lincoln RO, 2 ANC 12.D.12]

Parkes, Thomas, 'The Golden Lion', Fleet Ditch, London, upholder (1716–d.1757). Son of Thomas Parkes of Holborn, blacksmith. App. to Thomas Ward 21 September 1703 and free of the Upholders' Co. by servitude 6 February 1716. By 1722 trading from the address in Fleet Ditch and the business was already of a substantial size with £1,000 insurance cover being maintained on trade goods and household property. In 1724 fined for declining parochial office in the parish of St Bride, Fleet St, but in 1728 served as Collector for the Poor and in 1737 as Questman and Scavenger. Took as app. William Frith, 1743–52, and in 1752 was made master of the Upholders' Co. [Upholders' Co. records; MS 6561 p. 40; Sun MS vol. 14, ref. 25549; vol. 24, ref. 42908]

Parkes, William, Welsh Row, Nantwich, Cheshire, cm (1828–d.1835). Buried 9 November 1835. [D; PR (burial)]. See John Parkes snr and jnr at this address.

Parkey, Arthur, 8 Ropemaker St, Lower Moorfields, London, chairmaker (1820). [D]

Parkin, George, Richmond, Yorks., cm (1840). [PR (bapt.)]

Parkin, James, Hull, Yorks., joiner and cm (1826–40). At 18 Princess St with a residence at 24 Sykes St in 1826. All subsequent addresses are in Sykes St where the number was 12 in 1828 and 1834, 28 in 1831, 13 in 1835 and 42, 1838–40. In 1838 listed in one directory as a grocer and flour dealer. [D]

Parkin, John, 8 Bow St, Bloomsbury, London, upholder and auctioneer (1817). [D]

Parkin, Joseph, 25 Addington St, Manchester, cabinet turner (1825). [D]

Parkin, William, 440 West Strand, London, cutler and dressing case maker (1835). In 1835 claimed to be Cutler and Dressing Case Maker to the King and the Royal Family. [D]

Parkinson, Charles, Humber Bank, Hull, Yorks., cm and u (1840). [D]

Parkinson, James, Lancaster, u (1765–80). App. to J. Roberts 1765 and free by servitude 1779–80. Then moved to Liverpool. [App. reg.; freemen rolls]

Parkinson, James, Liverpool, upholder (1790–1818). Possibly the James Parkinson who became a freeman of Lancaster 1779–80. At 12 Edmund St, 1790–94, and subsequently in Harford St until 1811. The number in Harford St, Mount Pleasant St was 7 in 1796–1804, 11 in 1805–10 and 10 in 1811. In 1818 at 2 Walker St. [D]

Parkinson, John, Church St, Blackburn, Lancs., cm (1828–34). [D]

Parkinson, John, Bury, Lancs., cm (1828–34). At Bolton St and Union Sq., in 1828 but in 1834 at Bolton St only. [D].

Parkinson, Joshua, New Rd, Newcastle, cm and joiner (1838). [D]

Parkinson, Nathaniel, Stonegate, York, coach, house, sign and furniture painter (1823). Also dealer in oils, paints and colours. [D]

Parkinson, Richard, Lancaster, cm (1817–18). [Freemen rolls]

Parkinson, Richard, 45 Bold St, with shop at 20 Lime St, Liverpool, cm (1818–20). Bankruptcy announced, April 1820. [D; *Liverpool Mercury*, 21 April 1820]

Parkinson, Robert jnr, Scorton, near Lancaster, joiner and cm (1834). [D]

Parkinson, Stanfield, Little Pulteney St, Westminster, London, cm (1774). [Poll bk]

Parkinson, T. & R., Ratcliffe St, Preston, Lancs., joiners and cm (1814). [D]

Parkinson, Thomas & John, 59 Queen St, Cheapside, London, wholesale u (1773–83). [D]

Parkinson, Thomas, 27 Ray St, Clerkenwell, London, bed and mattress maker (1822–27). [D]

Parkinson, Thomas, Richmond, Yorks., cm (1824–40). In Castle Hill in 1828 and Newbiggin in 1840. [D; PR (bapt.)]

Parkinson, Thomas, Liverpool, cm and turner (1828–39). On 26 October 1828 married at St Nicholas's Church to Mary Ann, eldest daughter of Robert Wood, cm of Douglas, Isle of Man. At 2 Spenser Buildings, Hunter St in 1829, 21 Mount St in 1835, 43 Islington in 1837 and 283 Scotland Rd, in 1839. [D; *Liverpool Mercury*, 7 November 1828]

Parkinson, William, Liverpool, cm (1804–27). At 102 Dale St in 1804 but by 1814 the number had changed to 104. In 1821 at 5 Seymour St, in 1824 at 14 Shaw's Brow and in 1827 at Moore Pl. [D]

Parkinson, William, 54 Greek St, Soho, London, looking-glass and picture frame manufacturer (1825–26). [D]

Parkinson, William jnr, Liverpool, cm (1825–39). Married May 1825 at St Phillip's Church to Mary only daughter of John Grimshaw, Sir Thomas Buildings. In 1827 at 22 Shaw's Brow and in 1829 at 5 Seymour St with a shop at 15 Shaw's Brow. The shop at 15 Shaw's Brow was still in use 1834–35 but in 1834 5 Shaw's Brow was also used and in 1835 the number was 23. By 1837 the addresses were 4 Seymour St with a shop at 13 Shaw's Brow and in 1839 both 47 and 31 Shaw's Brow are shown. This William Parkinson was probably related and is possibly the son of the William Parkinson who was trading in Liverpool 1804–27. [D; *Liverpool Mercury*, 18 May 1825]

Parkinson, William, Newcastle, cm and furniture broker (1827–34). At 30 Middle St with a house at High Bridge in 1827. In 1828 at Great Mkt, and in 1833–34 at New Rd. [D]

Parkinson, William, Humber Dock St, Hull, Yorks., cm and furniture broker (1831–40). The number in Humber Dock St was 19 from 1831–34 but from 1835 it was 22. [D]

Parks, James, Sea Houses, Eastbourne, Sussex, turner and chair and basket maker (1832–40). [D]

Parks, James & Co., 1 Temple Pl., Blackfriars Rd, London, cm and brokers (1820). [D]

Parks, Thomas, 2 High St, Maidstone, Kent, turner and chairmaker (1839). [D]

Parlby, —, London, cm (1793). Subscribed to Sheraton's *Drawing Book*, 1793.

Parlior, Thomas, Liverpool, cm (1761). Free 13 March 1761. [Freemen reg.]

Parman, Charles, London, carver and gilder (1789–1837). At 2 Bedford St, Bedford Sq. in 1789 but by 1790 had moved to 21 Bedford Row, Bloomsbury at which address he continued trading until 1837. Also a print seller and a dealer in looking-glasses. In 1808 took out insurance cover of £500 of which £150 was in respect of utensils and stock. [D; GL, Sun MS vol. 441, ref. 814249]

Parman, James, 66 Old St, St Luke's, London, cm (1835). Another James Parman is shown as a furniture broker at 1 Martin St, City Rd in 1835 and 68 Old St in 1839. [D]

Parman, William, London, Windsor chairmaker (1813–39). At 88 Old St, 1813–26, but in 1829 shown at this address and also 61 Paul St, Finsbury. In 1835 at 67 Old St and in 1839 at 18 Featherstone Rd, City Rd. [D]

Parmee, Jno., 78 Lisson Grove North, Paddington, London, japanner and gilder (1826). [D]

Parmer, William, 16 Cranbourn St, Brighton, Sussex, cm and u (1832). [D]

Parnell, Jane, see T. & J. Parnell.

Parnell, John, St George's St, Canterbury, Kent, u (1785–1805). Free 1785. [D; poll bks]

Parnell, John, High St, Marylebone, London, see T. & J. Parnell.

Parnell, Joseph, The Close, Norwich, cm (1784–90). [Poll bks]

Parnell, T. & J., 39 High St, Marylebone, London, cm and u

(1816–39). In 1823 the business is shown as John Parnell and in 1839 as Jane Parnell. A Regency rosewood 'duet' music stand inlaid with brass by T. Parnell has been recorded. [D; *C. Life*, 23 April 1981 supplement, p. 53]

Parnell, Thomas, High St, Canterbury, Kent, upholder (1784). [Poll bk]

Parot, James, Norwich, chairmaker (1783). His app. Nicholas Hardingham free by servitude, 21 September 1783. [Freemen reg.]

Parr, Henry, Preston, Lancs., chairmaker (1802). [Freemen rolls]

Parr, Jonathan, Southwell, Notts., joiner and cm (1832). [D]

Parr, Mary, 52 Pall Mall, London, print seller and frame maker (1796–1812). Shown as M. Parr, 1796–1801, and Mary Parr in 1812. [D]

Parr, Richard, Bath St, Newcastle-under-Lyme, Staffs., joiner and cm (1818). [D] Possibly related to:

Parr, Thomas, Newcastle-under-Lyme, Staffs., cm (1774–1822). In 1822 at Bath St. [D]

Parr, William, 13 Shaw's Brow, Liverpool, cm (1823). [D]

Parr, William, Blackpool, Lancs., joiner and cm (1828–34). [D]

Parran, Benjamin, at the 'Golden Spread Eagle in Long Acre, London', cm and u (1741–84). In 1741 Benjamin Parran was app. to his uncle, Benjamin Goodison, of St Martin-in-the-Fields. [PRO, 16/49] He was among the subscribers to Chippendale's *Director*, 1754. At the death of his uncle in 1767 Parran continued the business and began to supply the Royal Household. A 1769 account [BM] for furniture supplied to the Duke of Newcastle by Messrs Goodison and Parran indicates that he was for a time in partnership with Benjamin Goodison jnr. The 1774 Westminster poll bk registers Parran at Long Acre. He was evidently bankrupt in 1776 when his Royal Household payments were received by a John Dubourg, assignee in a commission of bankruptcy. [PRO, LC 9/322–23] The Sun Insurance Co. insured his household utensils, goods and stock at 81 Long Acre for £200 in 1778 and at 133 Drury Lane for £400 in 1780. [GL, Sun MS vol. 264, p. 650 and vol. 284, p. 388] Royal Household accounts show an association with William Gates in 1783, and John Russell in 1784.

Parran is recorded in the Royal Household accounts from 1757–84. He continued the Goodison tradition of providing pier glasses (which Goodison had 'inherited' from his master James Moore), supplying in 1768 an 'oval pier glass in an elegant carved frame and high festoon ornaments, painted three times in flake white' for the Whitehall office of the Earl of Hillsborough, Secretary of State for American Affairs. However, much of his work for the apartments and offices at St James's, Hampton Court and the Houses of Commons and of Peers was inexpensive tables and bookcases, in addition to repairs and cleaning. In 1784 Parran and John Russell sent in bills together for a 'wainscot basinstand' supplied for the King's House at Newmarket, and for a writing table ordered for the Council Office, Whitehall.   L.K.

Parratt, Eustace Phillip, High St, Boston, Lincs., cm and u (1826–35). Recorded also at Market Pl. in 1835. [D]

Parrey, Jacob, Berwick St, Westminster, London, cm (1749). [Poll bk]

Parritt, William, London, bedstead maker (1829–39). At 3 Henrietta St, Manchester Sq. in 1829 and 17 Castle St, St Martin's Lane in 1839. [D]

Parrock, John, Oxford St, London, upholder (1779). [Bailey's list of bankrupts]

Parrot, Nathan, 24 Parkers Row, Bermondsey, London, chair and sofa maker (1826). [D]

Parrott, John, St Peter's St, Derby, u (1838). [D]

Parrott, Richard, 3 Charles St, St George's, London, chair and sofa maker (1839). [D]

Parrott, Thomas, 32 Eagle St, Spitalfields, London, chair and sofa maker (1839). [D]

Parry, Ann, Lower Church St, Ross-on-Wye, Herefs., u (1830). [D]

Parry, Charles, 194 Oxford St, London, see William Parry.

Parry, E., Victoria Pl., Cheltenham, Glos., cabinet turner (1839). [D]

Parry, George, South St, Westminster, London, carver (1774). [Poll bk]

Parry, George, 15 Prescot St, Goodman's Fields, London, carver (1782). In 1782 took out insurance cover of £200 but only £20 of this was in respect of utensils and stock. [GL, Sun MS vol. 300, p. 377]

Parry, Henry, Brackby St, Golden Lane, London, cm (1779). In 1779 took out insurance cover of £100 of which £20 was for utensils and stock. [GL, Sun MS vol. 276, p. 213]

Parry, Henry, Liverpool, cm (1790–96). At Queen's Ct, Dale St in 1790 and 9 Byrom St in 1796. [D]

Parry, Henry, Liverpool, cm (1840). Free 27 July 1840. John Parry of Liverpool, cm was free on the same day. [Freemen reg.]

Parry, J., Crane St, Chester, cm (1819). [Poll bk]

Parry, James, Liverpool, cm (1802). Free 5 July 1802. [Freemen reg.]

Parry, John, address unknown, frame maker (1769). In 1769 received payment of £3 10s for a picture frame for a full length portrait. [Lincoln RO, Monson 10/1/A/3]

Parry, John, Liverpool, cm (1780–1835). App. to Thomas Dobb and free by servitude, 11 September 1780. At 8 Church Alley, St Peters in 1790 but by 1794 had moved to 23 Atherton St, 48 Lord St in 1803, 14 Basnett St with a shop at 2 Benn's Garden in 1805, 12 Trueman St in 1818 and 9 Tenterden St in 1835. His apps were Richard Seddon Tate, 1787–96; William Brown, 1792–1802; James Browless, 1797–1812; and Charles Hinton McCormack, 1805–12. [D; freemen reg.; freemen's committee bks]

Parry, John, Bailey St, Oswestry, Salop. (1828). [D] See Joseph Parry of Bailey St.

Parry, John, Liverpool, cm (1840). Free 27 July 1840. Henry Parry of Liverpool, cm was also free on the same day. [Freemen reg.]

Parry, Joseph, Chester, cm (1812–34). In 1812 in Northgate St, but from 1818 trading in Foregate St where he is shown as a cm, except in 1837 when his trade was furniture broker. In October 1829 he advertised requesting his debtors to pay the sums due immediately, and for his creditors to submit details of the amounts that he owed. The reason for this is not known. [D; poll bks; *Chester Chronicle*, 2 October 1829]

Parry, Joseph, Bailey St, Oswestry, Salop, cm and joiner (1828). [D] See John Parry of Bailey St.

Parry, Matthew, 'The Three Pillows', Watling St, London, u (1725–28). In January 1725 took out insurance cover of £500 on goods and merchandise in his dwelling house. Bankruptcy announced, *London Gazette*, 6–9 July 1728. [GL, Sun MS vol. 20, ref. 376690]

Parry, Samuel, Liverpool, cm (1778–1834). App. in 1778, but on 5 July 1802 when his freedom was granted it was by patrimony as the son of Samuel Parry, shipwright. At Atherton St in 1802, the number being 18 from 1813–14 and 1821–29, but shown as 19 in 1816. At 30 Tenterden St in 1834. His wife Hannah died on 6 August 1833. [D; freemen reg. and committe bk; *Liverpool Mercury*, 23 August 1833]

Parry, Thomas, 1 Broad St, Soho, London, u and broker (1789–93). [D]

Parry, Thomas, 2 Eldon Pl., Liverpool, cm (1829). [D]

Parry, William, 194 Oxford St, London, u, auctioneer and house agent (1821–27). In February 1821 took out insurance cover for £600 of which £500 covered household goods in his dwelling and workshop. By 1824 the cover had been raised to £1,700 with £800 for utensils and stock. One directory of 1825 shows a Charles Parry at this address but this is probably an error. [D; GL, Sun MS vol. 488, ref. 976499; vol. 499, ref. 1012650]

Parry, William, London, cm and u (1826–37). At 11 Northampton St, Clerkenwell 1826–27, 108 Goswell St in 1829 and 127 Goswell St, 1835–37. In 1837 shown as a cm and bedstead maker. [D]

Parslow, Henry, Gray's Inn Passage, Holborn, London, upholder (1698–1709). Free of the Upholders' Co., 17 August 1698. In February 1709 took out insurance cover of £150 on his house in Gray's Inn Passage. [GL, Upholders' Co. records, Hand in Hand MS vol. 6, ref. 17888]

Parson, William, Postern, Newcastle, cm (1834). [D]

Parsonage, Joseph, London, furniture broker and u (1826–39). At 14 Queen St, Bryanston Sq., 1826–35 as a furniture broker, but at 8 Davies St, Oxford St as an u in 1839. [D]

Parsons, —, 4 St George's Pl., Bath, Som., cm (1833). [D]

Parsons, John, 10 Henry St, Pentonville, London, cm and u (1822). [D]

Parsons, John, Chelsea, London, u (1828). Bankruptcy announced May 1828. [*Chester Chronicle*, 9 May 1828] Probably:

Parsons, John, Fulham Rd, London, u (1826–31). Recorded as cm and u at Pond Pl., Fulham Rd in 1826. Bankrutpcy announced July 1831. [*Chester Chronicle*, 2 August 1831]

Parsons, Samuel jnr, London, upholder and cm (1782–87). At 9 Shug Lane, 1782–84. In 1782 took out insurance cover of £400 of which half was in respect of utensils and stock. In 1784 insured a house for £300. Bankruptcy announced, *Williamson's Liverpool Advertiser*, 24 September 1787 at which date he was living in Whitcomb St. [GL, Sun MS vol. 304, p. 550; vol. 324, p. 591]

Parsons, Sophia, King St, Plymouth, Devon, u (1836). [D]

Parsons, Thomas, Old Town, Wotton-under-Edge, Glos., cm, u and undertaker (1820–39). [D]

Parsons, Thomas, Wokingham, Berks., cm and u (1823–40). At Market St and Peach St in 1840. [D]

Parsons, Thomas, Steyning, Sussex, chairmaker and turner (1823–40). [D]

Parsons, W., London, slate billiard table maker (1835–39). At 358 Strand in 1835 and Tavistock St, Covent Gdn in 1839. [D]

Parsons, William, Hackney, London, cm (1830). Freeman of Rochester, Kent. W. Parsons jnr is shown in the May 1807 poll bk, but his location is not indicated. [Rochester poll bks]

Parsons, William, Fleet Ditch, London, upholder (1740–49). Fined in 1740 for declining parochial office in the parish of St Bride, Fleet St. In 1743, however, he served as Questman, in 1745 as Collector for the Poor, in 1746 as Sidesman and in 1749 as Scavenger. [GL, MS 6561]

Parth, John, Kennington Lane, London, cm (1820). [D]

Partington, John, 107 Market St Lane, Manchester, cm (1778–84). His trade card [Johnson Coll., Bodleian Lib., Oxford] indicates that looking-glasses were included in his stock. In 1778 he insured his utensils and stock for £300. [D; GL, Sun MS vol. 269, p. 423]

Partington, Joseph, Altrincham, Cheshire, cm (1786–93). In November 1786 was paid £3 14s for two small mahogany tables supplied to Dunham Massey House, Cheshire. On 16 May of the following year a further £1 1s was paid for altering a dressing table. [D; John Rylands Lib., Manchester Univ., George Cooke's accounts]

Partington, Robert, Millgate, Stockport, Cheshire, cm (1816–22). Recorded as R. & T. Partington in 1822. [D]

Partington, Thomas, Little Underbank, Stockport, Cheshire, cm (1784–98). [D]

Parton, Daniel, Shelton or Hanley, Staffs., chairmaker (1818–35). Listed at Miles Bank, 1818–34, and Stafford Row in 1835. [D]

Parton, David, Stafford Row, Shelton, Staffs., chairmaker (1828). [D]

Partridge, F., 11 Sussex St, Bedford Sq., London, cm (1835). [D]

Partridge, Francis, 21 King St, Upper Bloomsbury, London, upholder (1817–29). Described also as an appraiser in 1817 and cm in 1823 and 1827. One directory records the number in 1826 as 19. [D] In February 1823 took out insurance cover of £1,200 on his house and workshop and £600 on their contents, including utensils and trade stock. [D; GL, Sun MS vol. 492, refs 1001240–41]

Partridge, John, 49 New Bond St, London, camp furniture, trunk and plate case maker (1780–82). [D]

Partridge, John, London, cm (1792–1827). In 1792 at Davies St, Oxford St but by 1803 at 9 Rupert St, Haymarket. He subscribed to Sheraton's *Drawing Book*, 1793, and *Cabinet Dictionary*, 1803. At the Rupert St address until 1820, but by April 1821 this was being used by a William Partridge. From 1823–27 at 10 Charlotte Terr., Gt Charlotte St, St George's Rd as a cm and broker. In October 1823 took out insurance cover of £500; utensils and stock accounting for £420 of this. [D; Heal; GL, Sun MS vol. 498, ref. 1008449]

Partridge, Nathaniel, Norwich, cm (1818). App. to William Norris and free by servitude, 7 December 1818. [Freemen reg.]

Partridge, Thomas, 25 Stoke's Croft, Bristol, cm (1825). [D]

Partridge, William, Banbury, Oxon., cm (1754–71). In July 1754 announced the opening of a shop near 'The White Lion' where he offered 'the most fashionable furniture in the cabinet way: as chairs, drawers, Tables, bureau's, glasses, stands, waiters &c.' He also offered his services as a carpenter, joiner and carver and stated that he could produce 'brackets, umbrella, temples, pavilions, pallisadoes, fences, garden seats, windsor and forrest chairs and stools in the modern gothic and chinese taste, and all other things made in wood that are not to be had in this part of the country of any person but himself'. At this date he also had a house in Adderbury. In April 1760 he advertised for information about his app. John Rimill who had absconded and later in this year moved to Bodicote. A further move of address occurred between this date and 1771 when in October a 'New house ... in Oxford Bar late occupied by William Partridge cabinetmaker deceased' was put up for sale. [*Jackson's Oxford Journal*, 13 July 1754, 1 April 1760, 9 August 1760, 5 October 1771]

Partridge, William, London, carver and gilder (1804–15). At 15 The Cloisters, West Smithfield 1804–09 though in 1809 had additional premises at 12 City Rd. From 1811 only the City Rd address was featured. In August 1804 took out insurance cover of £400, stock accounting for £150 of this. By November 1808 total cover had been increased to £500 of which half was utensils and stock. [D; GL, Sun MS vol. 430, ref. 764577; vol. 441, ref. 823579] See Partridge & Co.

Partridge, William, 9 Rupert St, Haymarket, London, cm (1821–23). A John Partridge was trading from this address as a cm, 1803–20. In 1821 William Partridge took out insurance cover of £1,000 on a house and a workshop behind. Utensils and stock came in total to a further £800. By 1823 these figures had been adjusted to £1,200 and £500 respectively. [GL, Sun MS vol. 488, refs 978793, 981138; vol. 498, refs 1003442, 1008434]

Partridge, William, Teignmouth, Devon, cm (1823–38). At 2

Northumberland Pl. in 1823 and 6 Wellington Row in 1838. [D]

Partridge & Co., 11 Orange St, Red Lion Sq., London, carvers and gilders (1817–20). In 1820 stated to be a looking-glass manufacturer. May be the successor or associated with a William Partridge who traded as a carver and gilder from addresses at 15 The Cloisters, West Smithfield and 12 City Rd, 1804–15. [D]

Pascall, James & Ann, at 'The Golden Head', Long Acre, London, carvers, gilders and picture frame makers (1733–54). A payment of £10 10s to 'James Pascal, Frame maker' is recorded under 7 April 1733 in Sir Richard Hoare's private account at Hoare's bank, while the Stourhead papers provide an entry on 24 June 1743 'Mr Pascall the carver and gilder in full £30'. James Pascall died in 1746–47 and his widow Ann carried on the business, being paid small amounts by the Hoare family for picture framing and gilding between June 1747 and February 1754. The firm's only major documented commission concerns furnishing the newly-decorated gallery at Temple Newsam, Yorks. for Henry 7th Viscount Irwin in 1745–47. Pascall supplied a carved and gilt suite of 20 chairs, 4 sofas and a daybed, 8 candlestands, a pair of girandoles, a pair of console tables, a pair of side tables and a firescreen for a total cost of £376 17s 9d. All this furniture survives, mostly in its original setting and is generally regarded as the finest ensemble of early Rococo furniture in any English country house. The two bills are accompanied by a letter which states that everything was made in Pascall's own workshop. An advertisement in the *Daily Post*, 21 February 1738 announced the publication of 'Gribelin's Engravings of Raphael Cartoons, Ceiling of the Banqueting House, etc. A Book of Ornament of Twelve Leaves, invented and engrav'd by him: useful to all Learners and Lovers of Drawings. Mr Pascall, Picture Frame-maker, at the Golden Head, over against Hanover Street in Long Acre'. The Bedford Estate papers include a survey of the Long Acre estate [GL, E/BER/ CG/L/104] which show James Pascall, carver, to have occupied two houses in Long Acre and Bow St. The survey includes a diagram of one of these houses showing Pascall's workshop in the centre, with an open yard underneath.

About 1750 Joshua Ross, who set up as a frame carver and gilder in Bath, stated in a trade notice that he was 'From Mr Pascall's in Long Acre, London'. [Bath Ref. Lib.; *Furn. Hist.*1981; *The Quiet Conquest: The Huguenots 1685–1985* (exhib. cat.), Museum of London, 1985 (289–90)] C.G.G.

Pasco, Edward, Chichester, upholder and auctioneer (1789–93). Bankruptcy announced *Gents Mag.*, April 1789, but still trading in 1793. [D]

Pasco, Thomas, 194 High St, Chatham, Kent, cm and u (1832). [D]

Pasco, William, Brighton, Sussex, cm, u and paper hanger (1818–25). At John St in April 1818 but from March 1821 at 17 Richmond Hill. A daughter and two sons bapt., 1818–25. [D; PR (bapt)]

Pascoe, William, Chapel St, Penzance, Cornwall, joiner and cm (d. 1819). Probate granted on his will dated 23 March 1819. [Cornwall RO, DD CF 4245]

Pascoe, William, 10 Cornwall St, Plymouth, Devon, carver and gilder (1830). [D]

Paskell, John, Mistley, Essex, cm (1839). [D]

Pass, William, 18 Swan St, Minories, London, carver, gilder and preserver of birds &c. (1820–26). [D]

Passavant, Claude, address unknown, upholder (1761). Supplied John, 4th Duke of Bedford with a bed carpet 'in fine Chaillot' and six seats, backs and elbows for chairs in the same material. His bill dated October 1761 was for £128 2s. [Bedford Office, London]

Passley, Wm, North St, Martock, Som., cm (1840). [D]

Pastor, James, High St, Bloomsbury, London, chair and sofa manufacturer (1826–29). [D]

Patch, Jno., Budleigh, Devon, cm (1838). [D]

Patch, William, 2 Finsbury St, London, cm etc. (1820). [D]

Patch, Wm, West St, Ilminster, Som., cm and agent to the County Fire Office (1839–40). [D]

Patches, Thomas, 112 Bishopgate Without, London, carver and gilder (1808). [D]

Patching, Henry, 65 West St, Brighton, Sussex, u (1822). [D]

Patching, James, Brighton, Sussex, cm and u (1815–40). At Church St, 1815–17, 1819 and 1821 but in October 1817 and March 1820 shown in Duke St. By 1822 trading at 65 West St but later in this year went into partnership as Patching & Wood, and the business moved to 12 Ship St and 3 Nile St. It was probably at this point that Henry Patching took over the business premises in West St. By 1826 only the Ship St address is recorded and by 1839 the number had been changed to 11. A directory of 1837 lists James Patching once more as sole proprietor but others of 1839 and 1843 still lists the partnership. Baptisms of four sons and four daughters recorded, 1817–27, and in 1840 a daughter Sarah married Francis Fort an u of 33 Cambridge St, and a son Edward Patching was listed as a paper-hanger living at 44 Wood St. [D; PR (bapt. and marriage)]

Pate, John, St Werbergh's Lane, Chester, u (1784). App. to Thomas Powell of Chester, u and free by servitude 5 April 1784. [Freemen rolls; poll bk]

Pate, Thomas, Commonhall St, Chester, cm (1812–18). Free 6 October 1812 and living in Commonhall St by 1818. [Freemen rolls; poll bk]

Pate, William, Black Brook St, Chester, cm (1824). Free on 12 October 1824. [Freemen rolls]

Patefield, Jonathan, Lancaster, cm (1789). App. to M. Moore 1781 and free by servitude, 1789–90. Moved at this time to Manchester. [App. reg.; freemen rolls]

Patefield, Lydia, Hurdsfield, Macclesfield, Cheshire, joiner and cm (1828). [D]

Patent Wood Carving Co., See H. Wood & Co.

Pater, George, Bristol, u and cm (1799–1807). At 77 Quay, 1799–1806, but in 1807 at 13 Broad Wear as a wholesale u. [D]

Pater, Henry jnr, Bristol, upholder (1793–95). In 1793–94 at Wine St and 4 Bath St, but one directory of 1794 shows Temple St. In 1795 at Corn St. [D]

Paternoster, Jonathan, Bancroft St, Bucklesbury, Hitchin, Herts., cm and u (1823–39). [D]

Paterson, James, 15 Rupert St, Haymarket, London, cm and u (1835–39). [D]

Paterson, John, address unknown, cm (1754). Subscribed to Chippendale's *Director*, 1754.

Pates, W. A., 32 Gloucester St, Red Lion Sq., London, carver (1829). [D]

Paton, Alexander, 28 King St, Liverpool, cm (1805). [D]

Patrick, —, address unknown, frame maker (1765). In an inventory of Okeover Hall, Staffs. is listed a frame to a pier glass by 'Patrick'. [PRO, C110–163]

Patrick, John, Ship Ct, Old Bailey, London, barometer maker (1704–10). One of the earliest makers of the Diagonal Yard Arm or Signpost type of barometer which had been invented in 1670 by Sir Samuel Morland. Incorporated barometers of this type and thermometers in mirrors and in 1704 Patrick claimed that 'Ladies and gentlemen at the same time they dress may accommodate their habit to the weather — an invention not only curious but also profitable and pleasant'. [Wills, *Looking-Glasses*]

Patrick, John, South St, North Shields, Northumb., cm and joiner (1827–28). [D]

Patrick, Nicholas, Greek St, Soho, London, upholder (1715). In April 1715 insured a house for £200. [GL, Hand in Hand MS vol. 14, p. 246]

Patten, George, 4 Upper Rathbone Pl., London, chairmaker (1803–09). In 1803 subscribed to Sheraton's *Cabinet Dictionary*. [D]

Patten, John, parish of St Martin-in-the-Fields, London, cm (1745). In September 1745 took out insurance of £400 of which £250 covered his dwelling house, and wareroom and stock. The trade stock was valued at £100. [GL, Sun MS vol. 74, ref. 103299]

Patten, Robert, 26 Oxenden St, Haymarket, London, cm and u (1820–22). [D]

Patten, William, Liverpool, cm (1803–10). At 21 Marsh St, Queen St, 1803–04; 22 Prussia St in 1805; 21 Prussia St in 1807 and 25 Highfield St in 1810. [D]

Patten, William, Farnworth, Widnes, Lancs., joiner/cm (1825). [D]

Pattenden, Jeremiah, Lambeth and Brixton, London, chairmaker (1801–32). At 3 Union St, Lambeth 1801–12, and in May 1801 took out insurance cover of £300 on this address. From 1807 also at 19 Oxford St, London which was presumably used to display and sell the fashionable japanned chairs which were by this date being produced. From this year Pattenden was in partnership as Pattenden & Brown, trading under this style until at least 1812. The Oxford St premises were last mentioned in 1809 and probably closed in this year. After 1812 not recorded again until 1832 when a Jeremiah Pattenden was trading from Foxley Lane, Brixton. [D; GL, Sun MS vol. 419, ref. 718398]

Patterson, —, address unknown, chairmaker (1722–24). In 1722 paid £2 11s for six Dutch chairs supplied to Chicheley Hall, Bucks. A similar sum was paid in January 1724 for a further six chairs of the same description. [V&A archives; Bucks. RO, D/C/2/3(ii)]

Patterson, —, corner of Spring Gdn, Charing Cross, London, cm (1766). [Heal]

Patterson, Alexander, High St, Berwick-on-Tweed, Northumb., cm (1806). [D]

Patterson, Alexander, 1 Gt Hermitage St, London, cm (1808). James Patterson, cm is shown at this address, 1791–1803. [D]

Patterson, Amy, 7 Little Queen St, Lincoln's Inn Fields, London, upholder (1821). In June 1821 took out insurance cover of £150 of which only £45 was in respect of utensils and stock. [GL, Sun MS vol. 484, ref. 981083]

Patterson, Andrew, Air St, London, upholder (1779). In 1779 took out insurance cover of £500 of which £200 was for utensils and stock. [GL, Sun MS vol. 279, p. 578]

Patterson (or Pattison), Edmund, 11 Bull Ring, Birmingham, u (1770–80). Recorded as 'Edmund Wace Patterson' in 1770. [D]

Patterson, Edward, 11 Bull Ring, Birmingham, upholder (1767). [D]

Patterson, James, parish of St George the Martyr, London, turner, dealer and chapman (1747–64). Bankruptcy announced, *London Gazette*, 18–25 September 1764. He was probably the James Patterson who supplied goods to Gibside, Co. Durham, and the London house of the Bowes family. The furniture items included a 'fine Nursing Chair' on 1 March 1748 at 6s 6d; a 'neat fine Square Cradle' on 6 March 1748 at £1 11s 6d; and 'three matted chairs' at 10s 6d, 'a Peruke block and stand' at 5s and '4 chairs' at 16s in 1755–56. [Durham RO, D/St/239, D/St/V. 1488–90, D/St/326/a, D/St/339/5]

Patterson, James, London, cm (1787–1803). In 1787 at 4 Worship Ct, Worship St with workshops at Sampson's Gdns, Hermitage St and together with James Camper Harris took out insurance cover on utensils, stock and household goods of £400. No further mention of Harris is recorded and by January 1791 Patterson was at 1 Gt Hermitage St but retaining the Sampson's Gdn workshops. He took out insurance cover for £500 of which £175 was for stock in his workshops and £175 for items in an open yard and sawpit. By January 1803 the total cover had been raised to £950 and the workshops had moved to Princes St, Ratcliffe Highway and stock and utensils here were covered for £400. [GL, Sun MS vol. 345, ref. 530971; vol. 374; ref. 578060; vol. 427, ref. 743361] See Alexander Patterson at 1 Gt Hermitage St.

Patterson, James, 145 High Holborn, London, upholder and cm (1808). In December 1808 took out insurance cover of £1,550 which included £400 for utensils and stock in a workshop behind his house. [GL, Sun MS vol. 445, ref. 823759]

Patterson, James, London, u (1808–14). At 49 Red Lion Sq., Holborn in 1808 and 45 Hart St, Bloomsbury in 1814. [D] See James & William Patterson.

Patterson, James, 10 Vernon Pl., Bloomsbury Sq., London, upholder, undertaker, cm and appraiser (1817–23). In October 1822 took out insurance cover of £450 which included £196 for utensils and stock. [D; GL, Sun MS vol. 489, ref. 997187]

Patterson, James & William, London, upholders and cm (1794–1804). At 9 Little Wild St in 1794 and 49 Red Lion St, Holborn in 1804. In 1794 the total insurance cover came to only £400 of which £140 covered the workshop, sawpit and yard. By 1804, however, the cover was much more extensive suggesting a considerable increase in business. Utensils and stock in their dwelling house were covered for £400, similar items in the workshop behind for £1,000 while further sums of £280 and £50 covered buildings in which their trade was conducted. By 1808 the partnership had ended and James Patterson was carrying on the business alone from the Red Lion St address. W. T. Patterson operating from 7 Little Queen St, Holborn in 1820 may be his ex-partner. [D; GL, Sun MS vol. 401, ref. 628048; vol. 431, ref. 762007]

Patterson, Joseph, 'The Crown', New Bond St, London, turner (c.1730). His trade card [Heal Coll., BM] indicates that he sold mahogany tables, 'round Tea boards', 'Dutch Matted & Wooden Chairs' and cradles. [Heal]

Patterson, Samuel, High St, Manchester, cm (1788). [D]

Patterson, W. T., 7 Little Queen St, Holborn, London, cm and u (1820). [D] Possibly of James & William Patterson.

Pattinson, Hugh, Alston, Cumb., joiner and cm (1834). [D]

Pattinson, John, Botchergate, Carlisle, Cumb., joiner/cm (1811). [D]

Pattinson, Thomas, Hetton-le-Hole, Co. Durham, cm and joiner (1828). [D]

Pattison, —, Vine St, London, cm (1774). [Heal]

Pattison, James, Gt Newport St, St Ann's, Westminster, u (1715–23). In July 1723 insured goods and merchandise in his dwelling house for £500. [GL, Sun MS vol. 4, ref. 5039; vol. 15, ref. 29194]

Pattison, James, Bread St, Westminster, London, upholder (1749). On 25 October 1749 paid £12 2s 2½ in connection with goods and work for Felbrigg, Norfolk. [Poll bk; Norfolk RO, Felbrigg papers, WKC 6/23]

Pattison, John, 64 Close, Newcastle, cm (1833). [D]

Pattison, Joseph, Hatton Gdn, near Holborn, London, cm (1756). [Heal]

Pattison, Joseph, at Mr Foster's, Grocer, Aldersgate Bars, London, u (1767–72). [D]

Pattison, Robert, Old Flesh-market, Newcastle, joiner and cm (1801–11). [D]

Pattison, Thomas, North Shore, Newcastle, house and ship joiner and cm (1824). [D]

Pattison, Thomas, Clarence St, Newcastle, cm and joiner (1838). [D]

Pattison, William Henry, 24 Bowling St, College St, Westminster, London, carver and gilder (1840). [GL, Sun MS ref. 1339941]

Pattison & Hesp, 60 Walmgate, York, joiners and cm (1830). [D]

Pattisson, I. K. B., Maldon, Essex, cm (1826). [Poll bk]

Patty, Paul, Silver St, Westminster, London, carver (1749). [Poll bk]

Paty, James, Bristol, carver and gilder (1775–1806). In 1775 shown at 32 Broad St. By 1792 the address is given as Broadmead, and he remained here until 1806. [D]

Paty, Thomas, parish of St Augustine, Bristol, carver and architect (b.1713–d.1789). A member of the noted Bristol family of sculptors which also included James Paty the Elder (fl.1721–46) and James Paty the Younger (b. c.1746). Thomas Paty was noted for his work in stone and also as an architect. There is, however, also information about the commissions that he carried out for carved woodwork. Between 1741–43 he undertook woodcarvings for the Redland Chapel, Bristol and in 1743 was working on the new Royal Exchange building which had been designed by John Wood the Elder of Bath. His reputation was such that in 1755 he was described by John Cossins, the patron and builder of the Redland Chapel as 'generally esteemed one of the best carvers in England, either in wood or stone, by whom all the rest of ye ornaments in the Chapel were designed and carved'. A payment of £106 8s was made to him in 1743 for 'the ornaments of the chancel and pulpit in limetree' for this Chapel, 'the standard of workmanship of which is in every way equal to that of the best London craftsmen'. He took apps named Stringer in 1752, Walter in 1759 and Stephens in 1761. His son William, who was active in his father's business from the late 1770s and took over after his death, was also concerned with wood carving. [Poll bk; S of G, app. index; V&A archives; Gunnis]

Paty, William, Bristol, carver and architect (b.1758–d.1800). Son of Thomas Paty and active in his business from the late 1770s. Took over the business on the death of his father in 1789. He entered the Royal Academy Architectural Schools in 1775, and was subsequently responsible for an impressive output of sculptural work, which is listed in Gunnis. In the 1790s he undertook work at Christ Church, Bristol and was paid £105 for a new altar piece 'including Carpenter Work Painting & Carving the ornaments & gilding'. [Gunnis; Furn. Hist., 1976]

Paudevin, John, Pall Mall, London, upholder (1677–88). Upholder to Charles II and James II. Of French extraction and his surname is variously spelt Bodovine, Potvin, Popevine, Podvine, Potevine, Poictevine and Vaudvine by English clerks and officials. On 22 December 1677 supplied a sleeping chair for the Queen's Bedchamber 'neatly carved and the irons all gilt' for which £6 was charged. It has been suggested that the sleeping chairs at Ham House, Surrey were also by Paudevin in view of the close connection with the Royal court and government of the 1st Earl of Lauderdale. Very substantial commissions were given to Paudevin by his Royal patrons in the 1680s for beds, chairs of estate, turkey work chairs, Barbary and Portugal mats and curtains. The King's residences at Whitehall, Windsor and Newmarket all received new furnishings. The total for furnishings from this maker for the year 1677 came to £785 19s 9d, in 1678 to £1,371 8s 1d, in 1679 to £557 13s 1d, in 1680 to £487 5s 3d, in 1681 to £206 6s, in 1682 to £847 19s 2d and by the year 1686–87 had reached £2,461 12s.

In addition to supplying furniture for sale Paudevin also hired fine furnishings when special requirements arose. A crimson damask bed, bedding and six caned chairs were provided for six months for the lodgings of the ambassador of Savoy, and for this £36 was paid. He was also employed in 1687 for the funeral of the Duchess of Modena, and submitted a bill for £303 6s for this service. For the year 1681–82 a 'Nicholas Baudovin' upholsterer is recorded in the Royal accounts engaged to finish 'a bed of crimson velvet begun by the Aforesaid John Poctovin'. The rich furnishings provided for the Crown set the style to be followed by those in Court circles who employed the same craftsmen when available. It is thus not surprising to find Paudevin's name connected with commissions for the nobility. In 1688 he supplied the 1st Duke of Hamilton for Hamilton Palace, Scotland with a crimson mohair bed and suites of chairs and seating furniture which cost in excess of £326. He is also recorded in connection with furnishings at Petworth House, Sussex and Boughton House, Northants. [PRO, LC2/12, LC5/41, LC9/121–22, 275–76; Conn., vol. 93, pp. 225–26; vol. 127, p. 84; Rosalind K. Marshall, *The Days of Duchess Anne*, 1973, pp. 156–57; *Apollo*, May 1977, p. 360; *Furn. Hist.*, 1978]

Paudevin, Nicholas, see John Paudevin.

Paul, Charles & Reuben, London, cm and u (1812–19). At Castle Yd, Castle St, Holborn in February 1812 when they took out insurance cover of £200, utensils and stock accounting for £150 of this. By 1817 at 48 Upper Marylebone St, Gt Portland St. The partnership was dissolved in 1819 with Reuben retaining the Upper Marylebone address and Charles moving to 44 Newman St and 37 Duke St. [D; GL, Sun MS vol. 459, ref. 867289]

Paul, Charles, London, cm and u (1819–25). Directories show Charles Paul at 44 Newman St, Oxford St and 37 Duke St, Manchester Sq. from 1819 when the partnership with Reuben Paul was dissolved until 1825. In February 1820, however, he took out insurance cover of £400 on utensils and stock at a workshop in Edwards Mews, Edward St, Cavendish Sq. and his own address was shown as 141 Oxford St. From April 1822 insurance records show the Duke St address but in addition record workshops elsewhere. In April 1822 a workshop behind 44 Newman St is mentioned but it was rented to a cm named Souton. Charles Paul covered his own utensils and stock at Duke St for £850 out of a total cover of £1,100. In 1823 only £500 cover was paid for, half being for utensils and stock but in the following year cover on trade stock and tools had risen to £700 and his workshops were at 8 Blandford Mews, Blandford St, Manchester Sq. [D; GL, Sun MS vol. 483, ref. 962812; vol. 493, ref. 989766; vol. 498, ref. 1003716; vol. 499, ref. 1012309]

Paul, George, Exeter, Devon, cm (1810–16). In 1810 at New Bridge St and in March of that year he advertised for sale 2,000 ft of prime mahogany in planks, boards and veneers. By 1813 he had moved to Fore St Hill and he was still at this address in 1816. A daughter was bapt. at the church of St Mary Steps on 10 January 1813. [D; *Exeter Flying Post*, 8 March 1810; PR (bapt.)]

Paul, George, London, cm, u and chairmaker (1822–39). Initially at 4 Berners St, Rathbone Pl. but subsequently moved to 1 Charles St, Middlx Hospital and finally to 5 Upper Rathbone Pl. [D]

Paul, James, Swallow St, London, cm and u (1775). In February 1775 in partnership with Harry Sanderson. The partners took out insurance cover for £580, of which £390 was in respect of utensils and stock in the house and ware room communicating with it. [GL, Sun MS vol. 236, ref. 349489]

Paul, James, 27 King St, Soho, London, upholder (1784–93). [Westminster poll bks]

Paul, James Edward, Exeter St, Sloane Sq., London, cm (1817–26). At 23 Exeter St, 1817–20, but in 1826 at 3. [D]

Paul, John, Strand, London, cm (1771). [Heal]

Paul, John, Liverpool, cm (1802). Free 6 July 1802. [Freemen reg.]

Paul, John, 3 Cleveland St, Fitzroy Sq., London, cm and u (1839). [D]

Paul, Nicholas, address unknown, cm (1803). Subscribed to Sheraton's *Cabinet Dictionary*, 1803.

Paul, Peter, 4 Silver St, London, cm (1793). Subscribed to Sheraton's *Drawing Book*, 1793.

Paul, Reuben, 48 Upper Marylebone St, Gt Portland St, London, cm (1820–35). Formerly in partnership with Charles Paul at Castle St in 1812 and at 48 Upper Marylebone St, 1817–19. [D]

Paul, Robert, Market Pl., Saffron Walden, Essex, cm, u and ironmonger (1805–39). The nearness to Audley End house, Essex resulted in patronage by the 2nd and 3rd Lords Braybrooke. The first instance of this was in 1805. Paul's billhead stated his trade as 'Ironmonger, Brazier, Tin-Plate Worker & Upholsterer'. Small sums were paid by Lord Braybrooke for upholstery work of a modest character. [D; Essex RO, D/DBy/A63/10, A361, A376]

Paul, Thomas, 71 St John St, Clerkenwell, London, cm and u (1839). [D]

Paul, Thomas & Co., 10 Mansion House St, London, cm and u (1837–40). [D]

Paul, William, Hull, Yorks., cm (1747–54). [Poll bks]

Paul, William, North Walsham, Norfolk, upholder (1798). [D]

Paul, William, Bath, Som., cm (c.1801–40). Married at Bath Abbey on 26 September 1805. [PR (marriage)]

Paul, William, 4 Oldham St, Manchester, u and paper hanging manufacturer (1814–25). Trading as cm and u in 1815. [D]

Paul, William, parish of St Peter Mancroft, Norwich, upholder (1818). [Poll bk]

Paul & Co., address unknown (1823–24). Supplied furniture to the 3rd Marquess of Londonderry for Wynyard Park, Co. Durham, then being built by Philip Wm Wyatt (Colvin). [Durham RO, D/LO/E 492]

Paul & Sanderson, see James Paul, Swallow St, London.

Paulin, —, near Gray's Inn Gate, Holborn, London, u (1747). [Heal]

Paulins & Coates, address unknown, u (1773). Supplier of a lace 'toilette' to Burton Constable, Yorks. [Burton Constable, Exhibition, Ferens Art Gallery, Hull, 1970]

Pavie, Jacob, Berwick St, Soho, London, cm (1749). [Westminster poll bk]

Pavie, Peter, London, cm (1690–1727). Probably of French Huguenot extraction and one of a number of such craftsmen supplying furnishings to the Royal Household in the last years of the 17th and the early decades of the 18th century. In 1690–91 supplied furniture to Queen Mary which included 'a fine cabonett, a looking glass frame, a Table & Stands Suitable' for which £38 was charged on 21 August 1690. In 1696 he was paid £1 17s for 'making and gilding 4 drawers in his Graces Cabinet to put bookes in and some other work'. This commission was for the Duke of Northumberland for Northumberland House in the Strand, London, but Pavie was also employed at Petworth House, Sussex another of the Earl's properties. A 'Monsieur Passie' shown in the Chatsworth, Derbs. records as the supplier of a clock case in March 1695 is probably this maker. In 1712 he took as app. Thomas Turner, the son of the late rector of Claypole, Lincs. and

received the substantial premium of £75, indicating his status in the furniture trades. A Pavie, cm, is recorded at Compton St, Soho in 1727 and may be this maker. [Symonds, *Furniture Making in 17th and 18th Century England*, p. 108; John Bowen's disbursements, Petworth 174; Chatsworth, account bk V; S of G, app. index; Heal; *Apollo*, May 1977, p. 361]

Paviour, John, parish of St Aldates, Oxford, chairmaker (1768). [Frowde, *Survey of Oxford in 1768*]

Pawsey & Smith, Magdalen St, Norwich, cm and u (1830). [D]

Pawson, Thomas jnr, Cranbrook, Kent, u (1811). [D]

Paxon, George, High St, Hampstead, London, upholder, auctioneer and undertaker (1808–14). In 1814 claimed to be the inventor of 'the Patent Bed Frame or Bedstead for the Relief of the Bed-Ridden'. [D]

Paxton, Joseph, High St, St Neots, Hunts., cm and gunmaker (1839). [D]

Payle, —, Berwick St, Soho, London, cm (1743). The house in which he was living in July 1743 was advertised for sale 'cheap'. [*Daily Advertiser*, 4 July 1743]

Payler, Thornton, 13 Drydens Entry, 14 Salt House Lane, Hull, Yorks., joiner and cm (1823–26). In 1826 shown as joiner only. [D]

Payne, —, 'The Crown and Cushion', near Hatton Gdn, Holborn, u (1747). [Heal]

Payne, Bartholomew, London, upholder (1772–92). Son of Bartholomew Payne snr, and app. to Francis Pyner. Free of the Upholders' Co. by servitude, 7 October 1772. From 1774–81 in Southwark where his address is given as either Gravel Lane or opposite the church in St George's Rd, Blackfriars Bridge. In 1777 he insured a shop and a shed for £100 and two years later utensils and stock for £300. By 1786, however, he was trading from Tottenham Ct Rd and was still there in 1792. He took as app. James Waddilove, 1776–86. [GL, Upholders' Co. records; Sun MS vol. 261, p. 33; vol. 272, p. 44; Heal]

Payne, Benjamin, Leicester, cm, u, auctioneer and appraiser (1827–28). At Granby St in 1827 but his trade card and directories of 1828 record Gallowtree Gate, London Rd. The trade card shows that Payne was able to supply plate glass, paper hangings, carpets and feather beds. He acted as agent for the sale of estates and also canal and gas company shares. He indicated that he was in attendance at Lutterworth, Leics. every Thursday from 10 a.m. to 3 p.m. [D]

Payne, Francis, Coventry St, Stourbridge, Worcs., chairmaker (1828–30). [D]

Payne, George, Ipswich, Suffolk, cm (1820). Freeman of Colchester, Essex. [Poll bk]

Payne, Isaac, parish of St Michael, Bristol, cm (1817). Baptism of a child recorded in the parish register of Wotton-under-Edge, Glos.

Payne, James, Butter Mkt, Stowmarket, Suffolk, cm (1839). [D]

Payne, John, 3 Smarts Buildings, Holborn, London, cm (1784). Insured his house for £100. [GL, Sun MS vol. 321, p. 260]

Payne, John, All Saints, Oxford, cm (1798–1803). Possibly the John Payne, cm who subscribed to Sheraton's *Cabinet Dictionary*, 1803 [D; poll bk] See Mary Payne.

Payne, John, Southgate, Sleaford, Lincs., joiner builder and cm (1826). [D]

Payne, John, Seahouse St, Maryport, Cumb., joiner and cm (1828). [D]

Payne, Joseph, Birmingham, u (1802). Bankrutpcy announced, *Billinge's Liverpool Advertiser*, 29 November 1802, and described as 'now, or late of Birmingham'.

Payne, Joseph, Market Pl., King's Lynn, Norfolk, cm (1805–08). [D]

Payne, Mary, High St, Oxford, u and cm (1805–08). A John Payne was trading at All Saints, Oxford 1798–1803. [D]

Payne, Simon, Tavern St, Ipswich, Suffolk, cm, u and auctioneer (1805–32). [D]

Payne, Thomas, 15 Steelhouse Lane, Birmingham, cm and upholder (1770). [D]

Payne, Thomas, Coventry St, Stourbridge, Worcs., chairmaker (1820). [D]

Payne, William, Nuneaton, Warks., chairmaker and turner (1822–35). [D]

Payne, William, Sleaford, Lincs., joiner, cm and u (1822). [D]

Payne, William, High St, Oxford, u and cm (1823–30). His trade card, c.1820, survives. [Leverhulme Coll., MMA, NY] He also acted as auctioneer and appraiser. [D]

Payne, William, 10 Holywell Lane, Shoreditch, London, cm and u (1839). [D]

Payten, William, 3 Addle St, Wood St, London, cm and clock case maker (1789). [D]

Payton, Edmund, 6 Merchant St, Bristol, cm and broker (1831–32). [D]

Payton, James, High St, Stourbridge, Worcs., cm and u (1828–30). [D]

Payton, Joseph, Dudley, Worcs., carver and gilder (1809–40). Shown in High St, 1818–30, and Market Pl., 1840. [D]

Payton, Nathaniel, Bewdley, Worcs., cm (1793–1822). Listed at High St in 1822. [D]

Payton, Thomas, 55 Broad Quay, Bristol, cm and u (1799–1829). From 1822 also listed as undertaker and appraiser. [D]

Peace, Thomas, Bristol, cm (1752). In 1752 took app. named Willway. [S of G, app. index]

Peace, Thomas, Castle Green, Bristol, cm (1799–1800). [D]

Peacey, Thomas, Cock Lane, London, cm (1749). [Heal]

Peach, —, Lower North St, Gloucester, cm (1802). [D]

Peach, John, address unknown, cm (1803). Subscribed to Sheraton's *Cabinet Dictionary*, 1803.

Peach, William, 40 Wood St, Manchester, cm (1808). [D]

Peachey, Thomas, Charterhouse St, Long Lane, Smithfield, London, upholder (1764–78). Son of John Peachey of the parish of St Bartholomew-the-less, London, yeoman. App. to Joseph Hamilton, draper, 11 December 1753 and made free of the Upholders' Co. under the terms of the 1750 Upholders' Act on 14 December 1764. In 1778 at Charterhouse St. [GL, Upholders' Co. records]

Peacock, —, Sittingbourne, Kent, cm (1793). In May married Miss Mary Watts. [*Gents Mag.*, May 1793]

Peacock, Edmund, Sidney Pl., Cambridge, cm (1840). [Poll bk]

Peacock, Francis, Bridge End, Stockton, Co. Durham, joiner and cm (1827). [D]

Peacock, Henry, Tipton, Staffs., cm/u (1838). [D]

Peacock, James, 148 High St, Winchester, Hants., cm and u (1830). [D]

Peacock, James, Commercial St, Skipton, Yorks., joiner/cm (1837). [D] See John Peacock of Skipton.

Peacock, John, Godalming, Surrey, u and cm (1781–98). In 1781 took out insurance cover of £600 of which £240 was in respect of utensils and stock. By 1791 these figures had risen to £1,200 and £300 respectively. [D; GL, Sun MS vol. 289, p. 619; vol. 381, p. 220]

Peacock, John, London, cm and u (1827–39). At 2 Naval Row, East India Docks in 1827 and 212 High St, Poplar in 1839. [D]

Peacock, John, Skipton, Yorks., joiner/cm (1830–37). In Keighley Rd in 1830 and Commercial St in 1837. [D] See James Peacock of Skipton.

Peacock, Joseph, Burnt Yates, near Harrogate, Yorks., joiner (1771). On 31 December 1771 the Trustees of Admiral Long's School at Burnt Yates paid Joseph Peacock, joiner and tenant farmer, £15 12s for making a large pedimented oak

book cupboard in two stages enclosed by panelled doors. This piece of furniture is still at the School. [Temple Newsam House, Leeds, Exhib. Cat., *Town and Country Furniture*, frontispiece]

Peacock, Josiah, London, upholder (1772–1802). Son of Josiah Peacock snr of Taunton, Som., linen draper. Free of the Upholders' Co. by redemption, 3 June 1772. In 1773 in Gutter Lane and in the following year he took Joseph Stacey app. (free 1790). At Princes St, Lothbury, 1778–86; London Wall in 1792; Islington in 1794 and Paddington in 1802. [GL, Upholders' Co. records; Heal]

Peacock, Robert, Strand, London, cabinet and upholstery warehouse (1763–76). Established in the Strand by 1763 and in that year his premises suffered damage from a fire. This forced him to move to 150 Strand which was to remain in his hands until at least 1776. The new shop was a few yards to the east of his former premises. In 1764 he took over also 147 Strand but this was given up about 1768. Although declared bankrupt, *Gents Mag.*, October 1772, he continued to trade from 150 Strand. He is recorded supplying a backgammon table to the 3rd Earl of Albemarle in 1769 at a cost of £1 12s. This commission is recorded in the Bagshot Park accounts. The notebook of Edward Knight of Wolverley House, Worcs. records under 7 May 1774 the supply of a 'Commode Dr. Table' at £21 1s 6d. [D; H. Phillips, *Mid-Georgian London*, pp. 173–74; Suffolk RO (Ipswich), HA67: 461/443; Kidderminster Lib., Knight MS]

Peacock, Robert & Parlby, George, Sittingbourne, Kent, u and cm (1795). Bankruptcy declared, *Billinge's Liverpool Advertiser*, 31 August 1795.

Peacock, Robert, Lamb Inn Yd, Broadmead, Bristol, cm, upholder and sworn appraiser (1799–1800). [D]

Peacock, Robert, French St, Southampton, Hants., cm, upholder etc. (1805–08). [D]

Peacock, Robert & Co., Waterworks St, Hull, Yorks., cm and furniture warehouse (1806). [D]

Peacock, Thomas, 11 Grove, Bath, Som., u (1826). [D]

Peacock, Thomas, 16 Chariot St, Hull, Yorks., cm (1835–40). [D]

Peacock, William, Market Pl., Thirsk, Yorks., cm (1823–40). Recorded as cm/chairmaker in 1840. [D]

Peacock, William, Bedale, Yorks., cm, joiner and carpenter (1823–28). [D]

Peacock, William, Hessle, near Hull, Yorks., cm (1840). [D]

Peadle, John, London, furniture broker and bedstead maker (1823–39). At 1 Midford Pl., Tottenham Ct Rd, 1823–35, and 28 Upper Cleveland St, 1837–39. In July 1823 took out insurance cover of £200. [D; GL, Sun MS vol. 497, ref. 1006501]

Peak, Edward, 85 Goswell St, London, carver and gilder (1835–39). [D]

Peak, Robert, 4 City Rd, London, carver and gilder (1839). [D]

Peake, Henry, Dover, Kent, u (1823–37). At Fisherman's Row in 1832, Snargate St in 1835 and Seven Star St, 1837. [D; poll bks]

Peake, John, Kingston, cm (1745). In 1745 took app. named Rayley. [S of G, app. index]

Peake, Thomas, 2 Windsor Ct, Monkwell St, London, cm and plate case maker (1802–39). In March 1802 took out insurance cover of £300 of which £100 was for utensils and stock. [D; GL, Sun MS vol. 424, ref. 730018]

Peapal, Thomas, High Wycombe, Bucks., chair caner (1838–40). Sons bapt. in 1838 and 1840. [PR (bapt.)]

Pearce, —, Ludgate St, London, u (1793). Subscribed to Sheraton's *Drawing Book*, 1793.

Pearce, —, Redruth, Cornwall, cm (1798). [D]

Pearce, Abraham, London, cm and carver (before 1768). By

March 1768 in Charleston, South Carolina, USA. Claimed that he had arrived from London. [*South Carolina Gazette*, 14 March 1768]

Pearce, B., 39 West Smithfield, London, u (1797). [D]

Pearce, Earl, 18 Kirby St, Hatten St, London, u (1777). In 1777 took out insurance cover of £300 of which £100 was for utensils and stock [GL Sun MS vol. 258, p. 234]

Pearce, Edward, Shrewsbury, Salop, cm (1713–30). Free 1713. In 1730 took app. named Stephens. [Freemen rolls; S of G, app. index]

Pearce, Edward, Arundel St, Strand, London, carver (c.1665–95). Son of Edward Pearce snr, painter-stainer (fl.1630–58). Possibly app. to Edward Bird, an artist, but unlike his father he does not appear to have followed this trade to any extent. His fame rests upon his work as a sculptor but he also undertook commissions as a wood carver. He is known to have worked for George Vernon at Sudbury, Derbs. (staircase carving, doors, etc., *C. Life*, 22 June 1935) and for Sir Charles Wolseley at Wolseley Hall, Staffs. In 1686 his work in the new dining-room at Wolseley was described by Robert Plot, *Natural History of Staffordshire*, as being inferior to none in the county. He undertook woodwork in Wren churches including that of St Lawrence Jewry and received £4 for 'carving a wooden dragon for yᵉ model for yᵉ vane of copper of St. Mary-le-Bow'. He was also employed at Emmanuel College, Cambridge and by a number of City companies. He carved a wooden statue of Sir William Walworth for the Fishmonger's Company Hall. Buried at St Clement Danes, 1695. For full details of his life, and other commissions, see *Wren Soc.*, vol. xx; Gunnis; Beard, *Craftsmen and Interior Decoration in England*, p. 274.

Pearce, Francis, Long Acre, London, upholder (1709). Free 7 September 1709. [GL, Upholders' Co. records; Heal]

Pearce, George, High St, Ryde, Isle of Wight, Hants., cm and u (1839). [D]

Pearce, James, Newark, Notts., cm (1741–d. 1747). In 1741 took app. named Jellis. Probate granted on will, 12 November 1747. [S of G, app. index; Notts. RO, probate records]

Pearce, John, near St Alkmund's Church, Derby, cm (c.1740). A newspaper cutting (whose source has not been identified), stated that his stock in trade and tools were to be sold off. The stock consisted of 'Mahogany Boards, and Finears, Walnut Plank, and Finears, Pear-Tree Plank and Finears, Wainscot Boards, and several other Ware, Looking Glasses, and Frames, Brass Furniture, and Locks for Cabinet Work, all Materials for Silvering Glasses, and several other Things.'

Pearce, Joseph G., 9 Leek Lane, Bristol, house, sign and furniture painter and glazier (1830). [D]

Pearce, Michael, Penzance, Cornwall, cm (1737–61). In 1737 took app. named Milldram; in 1754, Row; and in 1761, Lake. [S of G, app. index]

Pearce, Thomas, Bristol, cm (1806–10). At 64 Old Market St, 1806–07 and Lower Castle St, 1809–10. [D]

Pearce, Thomas, 3 Adam St, Rotherhithe, London, cm (1809). [D]

Pearce, Walter, 112 Bunhill Row, Chiswell St, London, cabinet manufacturer (1820). [D]

Pearce, William, London, cm (1772). Stated that he saw 36 cases of smuggled furniture at 'Mr Cullens' (James Cullen) in Greek St. [*Apollo*, August 1965, p. 114]

Pearce, William, Lobster Lane, Norwich, cm and u (1818–22). App. to W. E. Earle of Norwich and free, 7 December 1818. At Lobster Lane in 1822. [D; freemen regs.]

Pearcey, —, parish of St Mary Magdalene, Taunton, Som., cm (c.1730). Father of Thomas Pearcey whom he took as app. [Dorset RO, P155/DV3]

Pearcey, John, Crewkerne, Som., cm (1750). Took as app. for three years Thomas Percey of Taunton who had previous to this been trained by his father. [Dorset RO, P155/DV3]

Pearcey, Thomas, Taunton, Bristol, London, Crewkerne, Som. and Sherborne, Dorset, cm (c.1730–98). Born in Taunton, in the parish of St Mary Magdalene, and trained under his father who was a cm. He then worked as a journeyman in Bristol and London; and in 1749 when he polled in the Westminster by-election, he was living in Cook Lane. About 1750 he came to Crewkerne and was bound app. for three years to John Percey, cm, probably a relative. By 1758 he had moved to Sherborne, Dorset and married. A person of this name is listed in Sherborne as a cm in a directory of 1798 [D; Westminster poll bk; Dorset RO, P155/DV3]

Pearkes, Edward, 118 Edgware Rd, London, u (1835). [D]

Pearl, James Robert, Petty Cury, Cambridge, u (1835). [Poll bk]

Pearman, Ambrose, Southwark, London, upholder (1713–d.c.1742). Son of Nicholas Pearman, husbandman of the county of Staffs. App. to William Jones, 5 April 1713 and free of the Upholders' Co. by servitude, 4 December 1723. Took as apps Thomas Coleman, 1725–33; John Venables, 1732–70; William Witton, 1734–41; and Nathaniel Hewitt 1740–47. Pearman probably died c.1742 and in that year was described as 'late the most considerable Man of that Business in the whole Borough of Southwark'. His widow married 'Mr. Whitton, a reputable upholsterer, St. Margarets Hill' and this may well have been his former app. William Witton, free 1741. [GL, Upholders' Co. records; *Daily Post*, 6 September 1742]

Pearman, Thomas, Coventry, Warks., cm (1828). Bankruptcy announced *Liverpool Mercury*, 1 February 1828.

Pears, Richard, 25 Holywell Lane, Shoreditch, London, cm and u (1839). [D]

Pears, Thomas, parish of St Mary, Stamford, Lincs., cm (1832). [Poll bk]

Pearse, Samuel, 31 Conduit St, Bond St, London, carver and gilder (1832–37). Initially traded in partnership as Harris & Pearse but by March 1832 trading on his own account. He offered to clean, line and repair pictures. On 12 March 1832 he invoiced to J. S. Pakington (later 1st Lord Hampton) of Westwood, near Droitwich, Worcs. a gilt frame which together with packing and carriage came to £3 4s 6d. By 1835 he had formed another partnership and until at least 1837 traded as Pearse & Biggs. [D; Worcs. RO, 2309/705; 380/57/ii]

Pearse & Child, 37 Ludgate St, London, cm (1792–96). [D]

Pearsey, John snr, 8 Hawkworth's Yd, High St, Sheffield, Yorks., u (1822). [D]

Pearson, —, Pitfield St, Hoxton, London, manufacturer of feather beds (1807). A fire was reported on 6 August 1807. His stock at this date was valued at £3,000. [*Gents Mag.*, August 1807]

Pearson, Archer, Red Lion St, Boston, Lincs., cm (1835). [D]

Pearson, Benjamin, 96 Dale End, Birmingham, cm (1770–93). Listed at no. 93 in 1780. [D]

Pearson, Benjamin, Shrewsbury, Salop, u (1828–35). At Abbey Foregate in 1828 but in 1830 at Claremont Hill. At Princes St in 1835. [D] See J. Pearson of Claremont Hill.

Pearson, Christopher, 10 Rutland St, Chorlton Row, Manchester, cm (1825). [D]

Pearson, David, parish of St Martin at Palace, Norwich, chairmaker (1830). [Poll bk]

Pearson, Edward, 34 York St, Westminster, London, upholder and appraiser (1817). [D]

Pearson, Edward, Leeds, Yorks., carver and gilder (1827–37). Listed at 74 North St, 1828–34, and 6 Market St in 1837. [D]

Pearson, Hewland, Without the Bar, Scarborough, Yorks., cm (1834–40). [D]

Pearson, J., Claremont Hill, Shrewsbury, Salop, u (1828). [D] See Benjamin Pearson at this address.

Pearson, J., Lowe's Lane, Wigton, Cumb., joiner/cm (1811). [D]

Pearson, James, Gargrave, near Skipton, Yorks., cm (1822). [D]

Pearson, James, Liverpool, cm (1840). Free 20 July 1840. [Freemen reg.]

Pearson, Job, 14 Coleman St, London, cm (1779). In 1779 insured his house for £200. [GL, Sun MS vol. 270, p. 628]

Pearson, John, Bramham, Yorks., cm (1774–84). App. to John Herbert of York, cm, and free by servitude in 1774. In 1784 at Bramham. [York freemen rolls and poll bk]

Pearson, John, Lancaster, joiner (1786–1800). Named in the Gillow records as a joiner. [Westminster Ref. Lib., Gillow vol. 344/94, p. 429]

Pearson, John, Whitehaven, Cumb., cm (1800). [Cumbria RO, death duty reg. relating to wills 7.1.1808]

Pearson, John, Lincoln, cm (1806). [Poll bk]

Pearson, John, Clement's Lane, London, u (1803–08). Listed in Sheraton's *Cabinet Dictionary*, 1803 as a master cm. The address was given as 25 Clement's Lane but in 1808 the number was 26. See Thomas Pearson in Clements Lane. [D]

Pearson, John, 30 Clerkenwell Green, London, cm and u (1808). [D]

Pearson, John, corner of King and Old St, Shoreditch, London, cm and chairmaker (1818–24). Signed a 21 year lease on his property in 1818 but in 1824 signed another 21 year lease for property in Old St Rd. [Shoreditch archives, Rose Lipman Lib., MS 2836, 2842]

Pearson, John, 27 Rathbone Pl., Oxford St, London, cm and u (1820–27). [D]

Pearson, John, 20 Old St Rd, London, u (1820–39). Recorded in some directories as an u and chair stuffer and in others as a chair and sofa manufacturer. [D]

Pearson, John, Boston, Lincs., cm and u (1822–35). At Bargate in 1822, Strait Bargate in 1826 and Market Pl. in 1835. [D]

Pearson, John, Great Broughton, Cockermouth, Cumb., joiner/cm (1829). [D]

Pearson, John, London, upholder (1830). Freeman of Norwich [Norwich poll bk]

Pearson, Joseph, Whitehaven, Cumb., cm (d. 1807). Probate granted on will, 4 May 1807.

Pearson, Joseph, Keswick, Cumb., joiner/cm (1828–29). [D]

Pearson, Oswald, Far Bondgate, Bishop Auckland, Co. Durham, joiner and cm (1827–34). [D]

Pearson, Peter, Stanley St, Liverpool, cm and furniture broker (1834–39). At 57 Stanley St, 1834–37, but in 1839 at 48. [D]

Pearson, Samuel, King's Lynn, Norfolk, cm (1810–26). App. to James Oldmeadow and free by servitude, 1810–11. [Freemen rolls; poll bks]

Pearson, Samuel, 48 Worcester St, Birmingham, cm and carpenter (1818–30). Trading at no. 48, 1828–30. Bankruptcy announced, February 1829, but two directories of 1830 show him trading in Worcester St. [D; *Chester Chronicle*, 13 February 1829]

Pearson, Samuel, Jamaica Row, Birmingham, cm (1822). [D]

Pearson, Samuel, High St, Bilston, Staffs., cm (1835). [D]

Pearson, Samuel, Walsall, Staffs., cm (1839). [D]

Pearson, Thomas, Berwick-upon-Tweed, Northumb., cm (1784–93). [D]

Pearson, Thomas, London, wholesale u (1788–1819). At 25 Clement's Lane, Lombard St, 1788–1803, but from 1806 at Haberdasher's House, Hoxton. In 1793 subscribed to Sheraton's *Drawing Book*, and in 1803 included in the list of master cabinet makers in his *Cabinet Dictionary*. A John Pearson was listed at this address in 1808. [D; Heal]

Pearson, Thurston, New St, Boston, Lincs., cm (1819). [D]

Pearson, William, London, chairmaker (1720). In 1720 supplied 24 walnut chairs with Indian backs and matted seats to Temple Newsam House, Leeds, at a cost of £24. [*Furn. Hist.*, 1967]

Pearson, William, Carpenters' Hall, 67 London Wall and 343 Strand, London, cabinet, upholstery and patent seasoned bedding etc. manufacturer (1821–27). Successor to Kent & Luck at the London Wall address. An insurance policy effected on 5 November 1821 covering stock valued at £1,400 was jointly in the names of William Kent, Samuel Luck and William Pearson. By 1823, however, William Pearson was clearly trading on his own behalf. An amboyna work table with a circular top, crossbanded with rosewood, with this maker's label in the drawer, is recorded. This indicates that he was also an auctioneer and appraiser. [D; Christie's, 11 November 1982, lot 104]

Pearson, William, Liverpool, u (1821–30). App. to Bartholomew Tyrer in 1821 and petitioned for freedom in 1828. Free 1830. [Freemen's committee bk]

Pearson, William, Newcastle, cm (1834). [D]

Pearson, William, 42 Kennedy St, Manchester, cm and u (1836–39). [D]

Pearson & Metcalfe, Bridge St, Little Bolton, Lancs., cm and u (1834). [D]

Pearson & Son, New St, Boston, Lincs., cm (1822–26). [D]

Peart, John, London, upholder (1742–d.1797) Son of Henry Peart of Islington, London, Gent. App. to John Clarke, freeman and scrivener of London, 6 October 1742, and free of the Upholders' Co. under the terms of the 1750 Upholders' Act, 6 September 1750. In 1752 married at St Paul's Cathedral Betsy Savage, the daughter of an eminent woollen draper of Bishopsgate. Traded from 21 Queen St, Cheapside, 1773–83, but in 1778 shown living at the south side of Blackfriars Bridge, and in 1781 at Chapel St, Bedford Row. In 1786 in Fleet St. Master of the Upholders' Co. in 1777. Heal suggests that the Peareth associated with the younger Thomas Chippendale in the rate books at 60 St Martin's Lane for 1795–96, is John Peart. [D; GL, Upholders' Co. records; Heal] See John Peareth.

Peartshire, Richard, 2 Nicholas Croft, Manchester, u (1814–15). [D]

Pease, John, Pontefract, Yorks., joiner/cm (1834). [D]

Pease, Midgley, Pontefract, Yorks., joiner/cm (1834). [D]

Pease, William, Ropergate, Pontefract, Yorks., cm (1837). [D]

Peason, William, Skipton, Yorks., cm (1838). [PR]

Peat, George, Midhurst, Sussex, cm, auctioneer and u (1823–40). By 1845 the firm is listed as George Peat & Son. [D]

Peat, Joseph, Long St, Thirsk, Yorks., cm (1823). [D]

Peat, Richard, North St, Chichester, Sussex, cm (1839–40). A Samuel Peat, cm and u traded in North St until 1823. [D]

Peat, Samuel, North St, Chichester, Sussex, cm, upholder and auctioneer (1793–1823). In 1804–05 shown as Peat & Son. Succeeded by William, Henry & Richard Peat by 1826. [D]

Peat, William, Henry & Richard, North St, Chichester, Sussex, cm and u (1826–39). In 1826 shown as W. H. & J. & R. Peat, in 1832 as Peat & Co. and in 1839 as William & Henry Peat. In 1845 only Henry is recorded. Richard Peat is shown trading on his own behalf in North St in 1839. [D]

Peaty, Charles, 64 High St, Southampton, Hants., cm, u, auctioneer and undertaker (1823–39). [D; *Southampton Herald*, 27 October 1823]

Peareth, John, London (1774–96). A senior journeyman employed by Thomas Chippendale snr and jnr in their business. Receipted bills on behalf of the firm survive, in connection with a Temple Newsam House, Leeds commission in 1774, and items supplied to Sir John Nelthorpe in 1781. The rate bk for 60 St Martin's Lane is endorsed for the year

1795–96 in the names of Thomas Chippendale and John Peareth, suggesting that the latter might have become the partner of Thomas Chippendale jnr following the retirement of Thomas Haig in 1795. Heal suggests that John Peareth is the same person as the John Peart who traded in London as a u, 1750–97. [Gilbert, *Chippendale*, p. 268; Heal]

Peck, John, Plymouth, Devon, joiner and cm (1782). In 1782 insured a house for £200. [GL, Sun MS vol. 299, p. 551]

Peck, John, Holbeach, Lincs., cm and chairmaker (1822). [D]

Peck, John, 23 Blackfriargate, Hull, Yorks., cm and broker (1831–40). Thomas Peck below is recorded at this address in the same trade 1810–26. [D]

Peck, Thomas, Hull, Yorks., cm, u, broker, auctioneer and appraiser (1793–1840). At 30 Blanket Row in 1793 where he took over the business formerly operated by Thomas Thornham. By 1803 had moved to 7 Butchery, and in this year subscribed to Sheraton's *Cabinet Dictionary*. His trade card [Landauer Coll., MMA, NY] also dates from this period. On it he advertised 'Mahogany in Plank Board and Veneer, Feather Beds, Blankets, Carpeting &c.' and offered to take old furniture in part exchange. By 1806 he had moved to Queen St and addresses in this road were to be maintained for many years. At 23 Blackfriargate by 1810, and this address continued to be used until 1826 after which a John Peck, working in the same trade, took it over. In 1823 and 1826 addresses at both 12 Queen St and 23 Blackfriargate were used, but in 1831 only the Queen St premises were listed. By this date the business was being listed as Thomas Peck & Son and Thomas Peck snr had a residence at 50 Prospect Hill. By 1835 the number in Queen St had changed to 24. From 1838 however the position is complicated by the appearance of another business established by a Thomas Peck, almost certainly the son. From 1838–40 there is therefore Thomas Peck & Son at 24 Queen St with additional premises at 62 (in 1840 at 61) Queen St; a residence for Thomas snr at 29 Kingston St, as well as the business of Thomas Peck jnr at 14 Kingston St. [D] A Pembroke table has been recorded stamped 'T. PECK QUEEN ST HULL'.

Peck, William, London, cm (1793). Subscribed to Sheraton's *Drawing Book*, 1793.

Peck, William, Laurence St, Boston, Lincs., cm (1835). [D]

Peck & Palmer, Straight Bargate, Boston, Lincs., cm and u (1835). [D]

Pecquer, Louis & Son, 9 Paddington St, Marylebone, London, u (1826–39). Bankruptcy announced, March 1830. Patronised by the 3rd Lord Braybrooke of Audley End, Essex who also had properties in London and Billingbear, Berks. He paid them £22 13s in September 1833 and £3 10s in May 1837. [D; *London Gazette*, 23 March 1830; Essex RO, D/DBy/A363]

Pedder, Richard, Kirby (Kirkby, Westmld?), u (1750). In 1750 took app. named Cowell. [S of G, app. index]

Pedder, Richard, Kendal, Westmld, u (1759). In 1759 took app. named Starkie. [S of G, app. index]

Pedder, Richard, Kendal, Westmld, upholder (1782). Son of Philip Pedder of Kendal. Became a freeman of Preston, Lancs. 1782 and returned to Kendal. By this date his father was dead. [Preston freemen rolls]

Pedder, Thomas, Lancaster, cm (1817–25). Free 1817–18. Named in the Gillow records, 1825. [Freemen rolls; Westminster Ref. Lib., Gillow]

Peddieson, —, London, cm (1793). Subscribed to Sheraton's *Drawing Book*, 1793.

Peddieson, William, London, u etc. (1807–29). At 46 Brewer St, 1807–13; St James's Pl., 1814–15; 5 George St, Adelphi in 1817 and 7 Arundel St, Strand 1826–29. [D]

Pedley, John, Southwark, London, cm, upholder and furniture broker (1827–35). At 38 London Rd in 1827 and 6 Broker Row in 1835. [D]

Pedretti, Peter, London, looking-glass and picture frame maker (1829–40). In 1829 at 15 Gt Warner St, Clerkenwell but from 1834 at 26 Bath St. Also barometer, thermometer and looking glass maker. [D; Goodison, *Barometers*]

Ped(d)uzzi, Anthony, Manchester, carver, gilder, barometer, looking-glass and picture frame maker (1815–40). At 20 Tib St in 1815; 19 Tib St in 1817, 31 Oldham St, 1818–25 and 33 Piccadilly 1832–40. [D]

Peduzzi, James, Manchester, carver, gilder, picture frame, barometer and looking-glass maker (1824–40). Addresses given at 13 Oak St in 1824; 49 Oldham St, 1829–33; and 97 Oldham St, 1836–40. [D]

Peebles, Charles, Kingston, Surrey, u and cm (1838–39). In 1838 at London Rd. By 1839 the business was trading as Peebles & Barnett from an address in Church St. [D]

Peel, Jeremiah, London, upholder (1712–46). Free of the Upholders' Co., 12 March 1711/12. Took as apps Charles Collins, 1715–25, and Elias Taylor, 1725–46. [GL, Upholders' Co. records]

Peele, T., foot of Elvet Bridge, Durham, cm, gilder and picture frame maker (1840). Advertised the commencement of his business in March 1840, and stated that he required an app. [*Durham Advertiser*, 27 March 1840]

Peeling, Henry, 32 Lord St, Liverpool, carver and gilder (1805). [D]

Peell, Walter, Bromyard, Herefs., builder, surveyor and cm (1830). [D]

Peerce, Edward, 11 Portland St, Manchester, cm (1840). [D]

Peerman, Ambrose, St Margaret's Hill, Southwark, London, upholder (1734). [Heal]

Peers, George snr, Liverpool, cm (1812–35). App. to William Harvey and free by servitude, 5 October 1812. Trading at Mathew St, 1811–14 and 31 Preston St, 1834–35. [D; freemen reg.]

Peers, George jnr, Liverpool, cm (1839). Son of George Peers snr. Free 31 July 1839 by patrimony. [Freemen reg.]

Peers, James, Handbridge, Chester, cm (1784–91). Son of James Peers of Chester. Free 5 April 1784. His son John was indentured to his father as an app. in 1791 at which date he was living in St Michael's parish and stated to be a 'poor boy'. [Freemen rolls; poll bk]

Peers, John, Foregate St, Chester, cm (1771). [Poll bk]

Peers, Thomas, Newcastle, carver and gilder (1787–95). At Gallowgate where he had a house in 1787. From 1790–95 at Fleshmarket. [D]

Peet, John, Bancroft Lane, Mansfield, Notts., joiner and cm (1832). [D]

Peet, William, Stanley St, Dale St, Liverpool, cm and broker (1794–1803). At 9 Stanley St in 1794, 21 in 1796 and 20 in 1800 and 1803, but another directory of 1800 shows no. 19. [D]

Peete, Richard, parish of St Andrew, Norwich, cm and chairmaker (1733–75). Free 21 September 1733 but not by apprenticeship. Listed as a chairmaker, 1733–59, but in 1768 as a cm in the parish of St Andrew. In 1753 took app. named Smith, in 1754 Fleming, and in 1759 Stone. [Freemen rolls; poll bk; S of G, app. index]

Peete, Robert, Norwich, chairmaker and cm (1761–84). In 1761 shown in the Cathedral Close, but in June 1776 trading from near the Red Well. In addition to his chair and cabinet goods he offered 'many curious Articles, in Inlaying and Engraving, in ornamental and useful Pieces of Furniture, never before seen in Norwich, with various diversified Foreign and English Woods, in the present Taste in London'. He also stated that he had a stock of 'elegant Looking-Glasses' which as he was over-stocked with these he was offering at cost. He also required an app. By 1784 he was living at Diss, Norfolk. [Poll bks; *Norfolk Chronicle*, 8 June 1776]

Pegg, James, New Rookery, Mansfield, Notts., joiner and cm (1832). [D]

Pegg, John, Castle Donington, Leics., chairmaker (1835). [D]

Pegg, William, Mill St, Loughborough, Leics., turner and chairmaker (1835). A Joseph Pegg, turner was at Church Gate, Loughborough in 1835. [D]

Pegg, William, Castle Donington, Leics., chairmaker (1840). Possibly the craftsman who was at Loughborough in 1835. See John Pegg at Castle Donington. [D]

Pegram, James, Lancaster, cm (1749–68). App. to H. Baines in 1749 and free by servitude, 1762–63. [App. reg.; poll bk]

Peirce, Edward, London, carver and gilder (1804–35). At 5 Denmark Ct, Exeter St, Strand in October 1804 when he took out insurance cover of £300 which included £120 for utensils and stock. By April 1814 at 41 Fenchurch St which he was to continue to occupy until at least 1826. By 1835, however, the number had changed to 52. At 41 Fenchurch St total insurance cover was £800 in 1813 and 1814, falling to £700 by 1822 and £550 by 1824. The amount covering stock and utensils rose, however, from £200 in 1813–14 to £250 in 1822–24. [D; GL, Sun MS vol. 431, ref. 767845; vol. 462, ref. 893032; vol. 462, 4 April 1814; vol. 490, ref. 991315; vol. 494, ref. 1017443]

Peirce, John Warwick, Castle Hill, Northampton, cm (1820). [Poll bk] See William Warwick Peirce.

Peirce, Joseph, 3 Gt St Andrews St, Seven Dials, London, cm (1787). Took on insurance cover on household goods, stock etc. for £200. [GL, Sun MS vol. 342, ref. 529313]

Peirce, Joseph, Northampton, inlayer, cm (1798). [D]

Peirce, William Warwick, Abington St, Northampton, cm (1820–26). [Poll bk] See John Warwick Peirce.

Peircey, Gabriel, Ship St, Brighton, Sussex, cm (1778–84). In November 1778 advertised for an app. u and cm. In 1792 listed in a directory as 'Gent'. [D; *Sussex Weekly Advertiser*, 30 November 1778]

Peirson, John, Coppergate, York, cm (1774). [Poll bk]

Peirson, Martha, London, cm and u (1826–35). At 14 Cullum St, Fenchurch St, 1826–27. At this date Thomas Peirson was also conducting a similar business from this address, and the two were obviously related. Not recorded again until 1835, when Martha was at 1 Mitre Ct, Aldgate. [D]

Peirson, Samuel, 3 South St, Hammersmith, London, cm (1832). [D]

Peirson, Thomas, London, u and cm (1778–1835). Son of Robert Peirson of Kingston, Surrey, butcher. App. to John Constable on 5 August 1778 and free of the Upholders' Co. by servitude, 3 December 1794. In this year he was at 14 Cullum St, Fenchurch St and traded from this address until at least 1829. He was included in the list of master cabinet makers in Sheraton's *Cabinet Dictionary*, 1803. In 1826–27 a Martha Peirson is also shown trading at this address as a cm and u. Thomas Peirson had moved to 3 Jury St, Aldgate by 1835. [D; GL, Upholders' Co. records; Heal]

Peirt (or Perit), Richard, 74 Shudehill, Manchester, u (1824–25). [D]

Pelham, 13 Stacey St, St Giles, London, u (1808). [D]

Pell, George, Walkergate, Louth, Lincs., cm/joiner (1822). [D]

Pell, Thomas, Wells Yd, Nottingham, joiner and cm (1799). [D]

Pelle, Jeremiah, London, upholder (1712). In 1712 took an app. [S of G, app. index]

Pelletier, John, London, carver and gilder (1690–1710). A craftsman of French extraction who carried out many commissions for the Crown in the reign of William III and Mary II. He is recorded working at Kensington Palace as early as February 1690, when he charged for gilding a frame for the chimney in the Queen's Closet and another in her Chambers at £6 each. In May of the following year he gilded a large frame to hang over the door of the Queen's Closet and a looking glass frame for the same room. For his work in 1690–91 he was paid £47. In 1699 a payment of £88 was made for gilding two tables, two pairs of stands and two looking glass frames for the bedrooms of William III and his late wife at Kensington Palace. His most ambitious commission was, however, at Hampton Court, Middlx. In 1699 he was paid £431 10s for frames, stands etc. for the Drawing Room, Privy Chamber and Gallery, and in 1701 a further £143 10s for further furniture for the Gallery. Two sets of stands at Hampton Court can be identified with items invoiced in the period, 1699–1701. One set of six pairs of stands was charged at £180, while the other for two pairs of large stands cost £70. These reflect the fashionable court taste of Louis XIV, with which Pelletier was clearly familiar. Fire screens with similar scrolled feet to the stands can also be attributed to Pelletier on stylistic grounds. Part of the work carried out 1698–99 was for the King's Privy Chamber at Windsor Castle, and this consisted of gilding a pair of stands, and a large frame for a marble table top.

He also worked at Montagu House for Ralph, 1st Duke of Montagu between 1701 and 1703. On 22 August 1701 he provided twelve ebony frames 'for the small heads of Vandyke' and supplied other frames, cornices and undertook gilding work. He probably also worked at Boughton House, Northants., another Montagu property at which Renée and Thomas Pelletier were employed between 1692 and 1708. [GCM; DEF; PRO, LC9/125, p. 46; LC9/280, pp. 27a, 44, 167a; LC11/5; V&A archives; *Conn.*, LVII (1920), p. 89]

Pelletier, Renée, parish of St Martin-in-the-Fields, London, engraver (c.1692–1708). Probably the mother of John and Thomas Pelletier. Associated with Thomas Pelletier in the work at Boughton House, Northants. for Ralph, 1st Duke of Montagu, 1692–1708. [Beard, *Craftsmen and Interior Decoration in England*, p. 275]

Pelletier, Thomas, London, carver and gilder (1692–1723). Probably brother to John Pelletier. In August 1711 he was living in a house on the south side of Covent Gdn which he insured for £450. He also owned a house in Maiden Lane which was insured for £250. This latter property was still being insured in July 1723, but his own address was then being given as the parish of St Giles-in-the-Fields. Employed at Boughton House, Northants., 1692–1708, and at the time of the 1st Duke of Montagu's death £2,382 12s 6d was owed to the Pelletiers' for work undertaken. This was claimed by Thomas as executrix for his mother in 1709, but not paid until 1712. One of the Pelletier family was active as late as 1727 when payment was received by a Mrs Pellitier, probably the wife of Thomas or John, for work undertaken for the Duke of Chandos at Cannons, Edgware, Middlx. The payment of £26 5s was for setting up a cartoon. Apart from his work as a carver and gilder Pelletier also supplied ordinary household furniture to Boughton including a pair of walnut elbow chairs at £1 10s, a walnut bureau and a folding table at £8 and a glass with a japanned frame at 16s. There is no evidence, however, to confirm that he made such items. [V&A archives; Beard, *Craftsmen and Interior Decoration in England*, p. 275; GL, Hand in Hand MS vol. 9, p. 224; vol. 27, p. 206]

Pelliseur, Leon, address unknown (1792). Worked under the direction of Henry Holland at Woburn Abbey, Beds. for the 5th Duke of Bedford. On 24 December 1792 he was paid £27 5s 2d for 'two benches at each end of the terrace South front'. [Bedford Office, London]

Pelvin, J., Shambles, Bradford-upon-Avon, Wilts., u and cm (1839). [D]

Pember, Joseph snr, Worcester, u (1741–66). App. to William Stone, u and free by servitude, 18 May 1741. Working at Shobdon Court, Leominster, Herefs., 1747–48 for the Bateman family. On 3 July 1747 Richard Bateman wrote to his agent, 'I hope that the paperman has finished my Lds. bed Chamber and that Mr Pember has done his bed'. On 16 February 1748 Richard Bateman again wrote requesting his agent to forward Pember's design 'for altering the velvet bed — a friend of mine Ld. Ilchester being very desirous of seeing it'. Joseph Pember's son, also named Joseph, was made free of Worcester 10 February 1766. [Freemen rolls; Herefs. RO, Bateman letters, G39/III/E/156, 208]

Pember, Joseph jnr, Worcester, u (1766). Eldest son of Joseph Pember snr and free 10 February 1766. [Freemen rolls]

Pember, Joseph, Newport, Salop, cm (1840). [PR (bapt.)]

Pemberton, Charles, Liverpool, cm (1796–1829). App. to Isaac Marsh and free by servitude 31 May 1796. At New Bird St, 1800–05, and 1807–10 occupied this address and additionally 27 Duncan St. At 9–11 London Rd, 1811–14, 29 Pellow St, 1816 and Brownlow Hill, 1827–29. Took as app. John Smith, 1811–21. His son David was born on 3 December 1815 and became a wood turner. He was free 1840. A Charles Pemberton signed the supplement to the *Liverpool Cabinet and Chair Prices*, 1805 on behalf of the journeymen. [D; freemen reg.]

Pemberton, John, Church St, Preston, Lancs., joiner and cm (1818). [D]

Pemberton, John, Liverpool, u (1827–39). Son of Peter Pemberton, cooper. Free 19 October 1827 and trading at 74 Upper Frederick St in that year. At White St, 1829–37 and 61 Cornwallis St in 1839. Took as apps William Ellis in 1827 and James Bell in 1831. A set of dining chairs and a table, thought to be of Liverpool origin, are known marked 'J. Pemberton, Maker, 1835'. [D; freemen reg.; app. enrolment bk; V&A archives]

Pemberton, Richard, 16 Plants Ct, Preston, Lancs., carver (1825). [D]

Pembrook (or Pembroke), Christopher, London, upholder (1705–31). In 1705 at 'The Bull', near Half Moon St, Strand but in 1731 advertised that he had moved from 'The Lyon & Bull', against the New Exchange, Strand to York Buildings, Buckingham St. [Heal]

Penberthy, William, Church St, Helston, Cornwall, cm, carpenter, joiner and builder (1830). [D]

Pender, Charles, Blackheath Hill, Greenwich, London, cm etc. (1824). [D]

Pendered, Joseph, Square, Wellingborough, Northants., cm (1830). [D]

Pendleberry, John, 1 Fox Ct, Cow Lane, London, cm (1791). In March 1791 took out insurance cover of £100 for 'utensils in workshops adjoining of Mr. Seddon, a cabinet maker in Aldersgate St.'. [GL, Sun MS vol. 375, p. 577]

Pendlebury, Collins, Liverpool, cm (1732). [Poll bk]

Pendlebury, Collins, Liverpool, cm (1734). Free 16 April 1734. [Freemen reg.]

Pendleton, John, Lancaster, cm (1767–68). App. to R. Thorney(?) 1757 and free by servitude, 1767–68. [App. reg.; poll bk]

Pendrill, Charles, 23 Knightsbridge, London, chair and sofa maker (1826). [D]

Pendrill, Richard, London, cm (1793). Subscribed to Sheraton's *Drawing Book*, 1793.

Penfold, George, London, upholder (1773). Son of Edward Penfold. App. to Richard Walker and free by servitude, 3 February 1773. [GL, Upholders' Co. records]

Penfold, George, Sun St, Lewes, Sussex, journeyman cm (1826–30). [Poll bks]

Penfold, Noah, Cuckfield, Sussex, chairmaker and turner (1832–39). [D]

Peninston, Joseph, Wellgate, Rotherham, Yorks., cm (1837). [D]

Penison, Robert, London, cm (1802). Freeman of Oxford. [Oxford poll bk]

Penketh, John, St Helens, Lancs., cm (1818–34). At Market St in 1818 and Tontine St, 1828–34. [D]

Penketh, Thomas, 25 Fontenoy St, Liverpool, cm (1837). [D]

Penley, William, 33 Rathbone Pl., Oxford St, London, u and appraiser (1820–25). [D]

Penman, Jos., London, cm and u (1826–39). At 23 Widegate St, Bishopsgate, 1826–27 but in 1839 at 7 Oxford Pl., Hackney Rd. [D]

Penman, Robert, Lambeth Marsh, Lambeth, London, cm (1795). In 1795 took as app. Thomas Skeel. [Westminster Ref. Lib., MS F4309]

Penman, Sutton, 1 Old George St, London, cm (1808). In March 1808 took out insurance cover of £200, half of this being for utensils and stock. [GL, Sun MS vol. 442, ref. 816689]

Penman, William, Kent St, Southwark, London, cm and u (1810–39). At 166 Kent Rd in 1810 but no. 177 from 1820–39. Insurance records show that the business was only a small one with cover of £300 in 1810, half of which was for utensils and stock. [D; GL, Sun MS vol. 449, ref. 846033]

Penman, William, 7 Queen's Sq., Scott's Sq., Humber St, Hull, Yorks., u (1838–39). [D]

Penn, John, Folkestone, Kent, cm (1818). Freeman of Canterbury. [Canterbury poll bk]

Penn, John, Canterbury, Kent, cm (1818–39). In 1818 shown at Burgate, and in 1838 Burgate St. By the following year the address was Iron Bar Lane. [D; poll bks]

Penn, John, Biggin St, Dover, Kent, cm (1830–39). [D; poll bks]

Penn, Joseph, Castle St, Warwick, u (1822). [D]

Penn, Joseph, Catherine St, Maryport, Cumb., joiner/cm (1829). [D]

Penn, Joseph, 38 Lawrence St, Liverpool, u (1839). [D]

Penn, Thomas, 7 Nile St, Brighton, Sussex, cm (1822–27). Living at West St in April 1826. [D; PR (bapt.); *Brighton Gazette*, 9 June 1825]

Penn, William, Burgate, Canterbury, Kent, cm (1826–39). [D; poll bk]

Pennack, Joshua, Holborn, London, picture frame maker (1760). In 1760 received a licence to employ a non-freeman for six weeks, and three non-freemen for three months. [GL, City Licence bks, vol. 2]

Pennell, Thomas, 36 Newington Causeway, London, dressing case maker (1800). [D]

Penner, John, Carfax, Horsham, Sussex, u (1839). [D]

Penney, Samuel, 23 Apple St, Leeds, Yorks., cabinet and clock case maker (1837). [D]

Penning, J., Blandford, Dorset, cm (1809–12). First recorded in 1809, when in partnership with a person called Charmbury he took over the business of Daniel Charmbury who had given up his trade in that year because of ill-health and soon after had died. The new business traded as Penning & Charmbury, builders, cm and u. By December 1812 when Penning was declared bankrupt he was trading on his own behalf. [*Sherborne Mercury*, 24 July 1809; *Exeter Flying Post*, 3 December 1812]

Penning, John, Eye, Suffolk, cooper (d.1781). Died in 1781 and the sale of his stock was advertised to take place on 3 and 4 December. This consisted of 'every Article in the Coopering, Dishturning, and Chairmaking Branches, likewise Ash

Timber, Oak Planks, Slabs, and other Boards of different Scantling'. [*Norfolk Chronicle*, 1 December 1781]

Penning, John, 6 Holles St, Cavendish Sq., London, cm and u (1818–30). Before setting up his business he was 'late managing clerk at Messrs. Gillow & Co's'. Already established, with his own business, by June 1818, when he advertised that he could offer a wide range of furniture including that produced from 'oak and other English woods'. He offered to take furniture in part exchange. By March 1820 the business was of a substantial size with insurance cover of £3,000 rising by May 1821 to £3,300. In 1821 a workshop was maintained at 22 North Harley Mews, but by the following year one behind 135 Oxford St was being used instead. Stock and utensils in Holles St were valued at £1,700 in both of these years, and similar items at the workshops at £500 in 1820 and £800 in 1822. His bankruptcy was announced in May 1830. [D; GL, Sun MS vol. 483, ref. 964395; vol. 488, ref. 980410; *Morning Chronicle*, 4 June 1818; *Chester Courant*, 18 May 1830]

Penning, John, Briggate, Knaresborough, Yorks., joiner, cm and builder (1828). [D]

Penning, Robert, Eye, Suffolk, cm (1759). In 1759 took app. named Grey. [S of G, app. index]

Pennington, — jnr, 20 Plumstand Lane, Whitehaven, Cumb., cm/joiner (1834). [D]

Pennington, Christopher & Son, 10 Shaw's Brow, Liverpool, furniture painter and japanner (1805–10). [D]

Pennington, Edward James, Chester, u (1821). Free 22 September 1821. [Freemen rolls]

Pennington, Fras., Fartown, Huddersfield, Yorks., cm (1830). [D]

Pennington, Garnett, 9 Paradise St, Preston, Lancs., cm (1818). [D]

Pennington, John, Norwich, u (1732). Took as app. Thomas Page who was free by servitude on 24 February 1732. [Freemen rolls]

Pennington, John, address unknown, cm (1750). In July 1750 living at Annapolis, Maryland, USA, but advertised that he was 'designing soon to leave this Province, and return to his native Country, England'. [*Maryland Gazette*, 18 July 1750]

Pennington, John, Lancaster, u (1789–90). Free 1789–90. The death of his son William in Trinidad at the age of 24 occurred on 13 April 1833. [Freemen rolls; *Liverpool Mercury*, 28 June 1833]

Pennington, John, Lancaster, u (1826–33). Free 1826–27. [Freemen rolls]

Pennington, John, Knaresborough, Yorks., joiner/cm (1834). [D]

Pennington, Joseph, Kendal, Westmld, cm/u (1829). [D]

Pennington, Lawrence, 4 Williamson Sq., Liverpool, furniture painter (1807). [D]

Pennington, Matthew, New Town, Huddersfield, cm (1830). Also had a house at Greenside. [D]

Pennington, Miles, Lancaster, u (1754–96). In 1754 app. to J. Helme and J. Fowler, u. Free by servitude, 1761–62, and himself took apps in 1770, 1775, 1780 and 1796. [D; freemen rolls; app. reg.]

Pennington, Miles, Lancaster, u (1817–18). [Freemen rolls]

Pennington, R. G., 42 Warren St, Fitzroy Sq., London, u (1829). [D]

Pennington, Seth, Everton, Liverpool, furniture painter (1807). [D]

Pennington, Thomas, Huddersfield, Yorks., cm and u (1818–37). At Goss Church St in 1818, Longroyd Bridge in 1828, and Longroyd Lane in 1830. Between 1834–37 the trading style of the business changed to Thomas Pennington & Sons and in 1837 they were at 21 Buxton Rd. [D]

Pennington, Thomas Matthew, Everton Terr., Liverpool, cm (1830). Son of John Pennington, artist. Free 20 November 1830. [Freemen rolls]

Pennington, William, Lancaster, u (1789–90). [Freemen rolls]

Pennington, William, Richmond, Surrey, cm (1798). [D]

Penniston, Thomas, Steander(?), Leeds, Yorks., cm (1817). [D]

Pennistone, —, Oakham, Rutland, cm (1791–98). [D]

Pennock, James, London, carver (1784). Freeman of Colchester, Essex. [Colchester poll bk]

Pennock, Joshua, White Lion St, Goodman's Fields, Whitechapel, London, cm (1790–93). [D]

Pennock, Josiah, address unknown, carver (1754). Subscribed to Chippendale's *Director*, 1754.

Penny, Philip, Banbury, Oxon., u (1716). In 1716 took app. named Whitefoot. [S of G, app. index]

Penny, Samuel, 10 Half Moon St, Bishopsgate Without, London, looking-glass maker (1804). In January 1804 took out insurance cover of £400 of which £300 was for utensils and stock. [GL, Sun MS vol. 430, ref. 757691]

Penny, Samuel, 23 Apple St, York Rd, Leeds, Yorks., cm, clock case maker and joiner (1837–40). [D]

Penny, Thomas, 48 Berkeley St West, London, carver and gilder (1839). [D]

Penny, William, 56 Long Acre, London, japanner and varnish maker (1812). [D]

Penny, William, 21 Tavistock St, Covent Gdn, London, upholder and cm (1820). In March 1820 took out insurance cover on a house of £1,200 but the cover for its contents was only £300, half of this being for utensils and stock. [GL, Sun MS vol. 483, ref. 964066]

Penny, William, Brentford End, Isleworth, Middlx, chairmaker (1839). [D]

Pennyfeather, Charles, Irish Lane, Leytonstone, London, cm (1808–39). [D]

Penrhyn, Thomas, Roushill, Shrewsbury, Salop, cm (1806). [Freemen rolls]

Penrith, John snr, East end of Sunderland, Co. Durham, cm (d.1786). Died in 1786 and business continued as a partnership of his son John with Richard Simpson. [*Newcastle Courant*, 9 December 1786]

Penrith, John jnr, East end of Sunderland, Co. Durham, cm (1786–98). On the death of his father John Penrith snr took over his business in partnership with Richard Simpson of Sunderland, who was described as a joiner and cm. They advertised themselves as joiners, cm and house carpenters. Amongst the stock taken over from the late John Penrith snr were tables, chairs, glasses, bedsteads and bureaus. [*Newcastle Courant*, 9 December 1786]

Penson, Stephen, 'The Phoenix', Leicester Fields, London, upholder (1704–13). Worked at Drayton House, Northants., and on 28 April 1704 was paid £10 'in part for upholders work'. On 30 November of the same year he charged £77 for additions to two pieces of hangings 'contains 44 ells of worke weaved by me'. Also concerned with the funeral arrangements of the 8th Duchess of Norfolk. [Heal; Harris, *Old English Furniture*, p. 26; V&A archives]

Pensotti, Joseph, High St, Dudley, Staffs., carver and gilder (1818–22). [D]

Pentin, Charles, 29 Norfolk St, Goodge St, London, chair and sofa maker (1839). [D]

Pentith, Francis, 6 Paradise Pl., Hull, Yorks., cm (1839). [D]

Pentith, William, 78 Petergate, York, cm etc. (1840). [D]

Peote, James, Mr Damant's St, Strait-bargate, Boston, Lincs., looking-glass, barometer and scientific instrument maker (1792). In October 1792 announced that he had recently arrived in the town from London and had opened shop. He offered barometers, thermometers, telescopes, 'Electrifying

Machines, Camera Obscura's and Magic Lanthorns'. He claimed to make and sell all sorts and sizes of looking-glasses and to be able to grind and polish glass plates. He stocked gilt frames for mirrors and prints, 'Tea Caddies, Gentlemen's Dressing Boxes, and Portable Desks'. He offered to supply ornamental work for builders, had a method of preventing rust in gun barrels, and made and sold fireworks. [*Lincoln, Rutland and Stamford Mercury*, 5 October 1792]

Pepall, Thomas, High Wycombe, Bucks., chairmaker and caner (1821–36). Five sons and three daughters bapt. between 1821–36. [PR (bapt.)]

Pepall, William, High Wycombe, Bucks., chair caner (b. c. 1801–41). A son bapt. in 1836 and a daughter in 1838. Aged 40 at the time of the 1841 Census. [PR (bapt.)]

Pepper, Joseph, Royal Hill, Greenwich, London, cm and u (1832–39). [D]

Pepper, William, King St, Thorne, Yorks., joiner and cm (1828–34). [D]

Pepper, William, Brighton, Sussex, carver and gilder (1834–40). At John St, 1834–36 when a son and daughter were bapt. Trading at West St in August 1839 and in 1843 the number was listed as 38. He advertised himself as a 'Practical Ornamental Carver on WOOD AND STONE, AND GILDER, PICTURE AND GLASS FRAME MANUFACTURER'. [D; PR (bapt.)]

Peppitt, Robert, 28 Bixteth St, Liverpool, (1830). App. to Thomas Croft Huxley and free 15 November 1830. [Freemen rolls]

Percival, Bosworth, Castle Donington, Leics., cm (1829). [D]

Percival, N., 2 New Bridge St, Newcastle, carver and gilder (1838). [D]

Percy, E., Blandford, Dorset, u, cm etc. (c.1770–1809). In August 1809 advertised that for u and cm a 'Desirable situation' was on offer if they would like to contact him. He further stated that his business had been carried on for forty years. He appears to have been advertising for a successor who was prepared to purchase the business on his retirement. [*Sherborne Mercury*, 31 August 1809]

Percy, Joseph, Town's End, Sherborne, Dorset, cm (1823). [D]

Percy, Robert, 4 North Terr., Scarborough, Yorks., cm (1840). [D]

Percy, William Carter Stafford, Liverpool, cm (1830). Free 22 November 1830. [Freemen rolls]

Percy, William, Witton St, Northwich, Cheshire, cm/chairmaker (1834). [D]

Peream, Andrew, Axminster, Devon, cm (1743). His will dated 22 April 1743 stated that his working tools were to be distributed to his sons Andrew and Leonard.

Pereira, Richard, London, cm and u (1808–28). At 4 Hatton Wall, Hatton Gdn, 1808–20 and this address is also used in a directory of 1827. Other directories show 26 and 70 Burlington Arcade from 1820. It is unlikely that any manufacturing could have been carried on at this latter address and the Hatton Wall premises may have been retained. [D]

Perfetti, Joseph, St Marylebone, London, carver and gilder (1760–78). In 1760 took app. named Thomas Ledieu. Two years later employed at Lansdowne House, Berkeley Sq., gilding and painting stucco work. Employed by John Parker at Saltram, Devon 1771–78. On 29 January 1771 he was paid £41 1s 'for table frames for the Great Room' and on 31 March of the following year £41 for table frames for the Velvet Room. These were executed to a design by Robert Adam, and are still in the house. A payment of £8 17s for frames made on 5 February 1778 was to Mrs Perfetti. He was also patronised by Henry Knight of Tythegston Court, Glam., S. Wales. [Boyd's index to IR app. reg., vol. 4, p. 692; A. T. Bolton,

Adam, 1922, II, p. 12; Musgrave, *Adam Furniture*, p. 124; E. Harris, *Furniture of Robert Adam*, p. 69, pls 21, 22; V&A archives; C. *Life*, 5 October 1978, p. 1024]

Periera, John, Gt Sutton St, Clerkenwell, London, knifecase maker (1785). In 1785 took app. named Samuel Cuningham. [Westminster Ref. Lib., MS F 4309]

Perinot, —, address unknown, cm (1740). An entry for £8 7s dated April 1740 is contained in the account for the expenses of Augusta, Princess of Wales at Windsor. [Windsor Royal Archives]

Perkins, —, address unknown, u (1769–78). Recorded in the accounts of Paul Methuen for Corsham Court, Wilts. An entry of 1769 is in the name of Cole jnr (George Cole?) and Perkins u, and was for £52 4s. Subsequent payments were in Perkins name only and he received £14 13s 6d on 7 January 1771, £7 2s on 11 February 1778 and £9 12s on 30 March 1778. [V&A archives]

Perkins, Mrs, Fourth St, Exeter, Devon upholder (1796). [D]

Perkins, Mr, South St, Exeter, Devon, cm (1816). In October 1816 a fire broke out at a building in South St, 'the lower part of the premises occupied by Mr. Perkins, cabinet-maker'. It was extinguished by firemen for the West of England office before any great amount of damage had occurred. A William Parker, upholder, was at South St in 1791. [*Exeter Flying Post(?)*, 17 October 1816]

Perkins, Charles, Ann St, Worthing, Sussex, cm (1832). [D]

Perkins, Christopher, Stockton, Co. Durham, joiner and cm (1778–84). In 1778 insured his workshop and stock for £400. [D; GL, Sun MS vol. 264, p. 158]

Perkins, Francis, address unknown, chairmaker (1735). On 23 August 1735 submitted a bill to Paul Foley of the Temple, Little Ormond St, London, and Newport House, Almeley, Herefs. for £3 13s 10d. It was for two walnut stools and for making their covers. [Herefs. RO, Foley MS, F/AIII/55]

Perkins, John, Fenchurch St, London, u (1755). Bankruptcy announced, *Gents Mag.*, December 1755.

Perkins, Joseph, Church Gate and Gallowtree Gate, Leicester, cm and u (1835–40). Recorded also at Rulland St as cm, u and paper hanger in 1835. [D]

Perkins, Lewes (or Lewis), 6 Groat Mkt, Newcastle, cm and furniture broker (1834). [D]

Perkins, R., 5 Old Fish St, London, fancy cm (1837–39). [D]

Perkins, Richard, Hereford, chairmaker (1754). In 1754 Edward Jones was made free. His qualification was stated to be his marriage to Elizabeth, only daughter of Richard Perkins, a freeman and chairmaker. [Freemen rolls]

Perkins, Richard H., High St, Southampton, Hants., cm and u (1823–39). At 61 High St in 1823; no. 60 in 1830; and 59, 1834–39. Advertisement in *Southampton Directory*, 1839, gives trade as u, cm, auctioneer and estate agent; also paper hanging, interior decoration, undertaker and agent for the Phoenix Fire Office and Palladium Life Co. [D]

Perkins, Richard, 21 Lambeth Hill, Doctors' Commons, London, desk and dressing case maker (1835). [D]

Perkins, Richard, Islington, London, cm and u (1835–39). At 3 High St, Islington in 1835 but in 1839 at 85 Upper St. [D]

Perkins, Thomas, London, upholder (1708–50). Son of Thomas Perkins of Kilby, Leics., Gent. App. to William Brown on 1 May 1708 and free of the Upholders' Co. by servitude, 1 August 1722. By 1 October 1722 he had set up business at 'The Key' in Trinity, Minories where he took out insurance cover of £500 on goods and merchandise in his dwelling house. In 1737 he was living in Fenchurch St and was married in this year. His wife was the sister to a Mr Stillard, a druggist. In June 1739 her death was announced in childbirth and her husband was described as being a 'wealthy upholsterer'. In 1750 his address was given as Little Minories. [GL,

Upholders' Co. records and Livery list, 1750; Sun MS vol. 14, ref. 26528; Heal; *Read's Weekly Journal*, 2 June 1739]

Perkins, Thomas, Bristol, upholder (1754). [Poll bk]

Perkins, Thomas, Castle St, Long Acre, London, upholder (1790–93). [D]

Perkins, Thomas, Hughes Ct, Johnson St, with a shop at Wacker Pl., Hatton Gdn, Liverpool, cm (1821–29). [D]

Perkins, Thomas, Manchester, looking-glass and picture frame maker (1825–40). At 61 Shudehill in 1825, 2 Jib St in 1828, 26 Cumberland St in 1829 and 22 Kennedy St in 1840. [D]

Perkins, Thomas, Bethnal Green, London, cm (1830). Freeman of Canterbury. [Canterbury poll bk]

Perkins, William, South St, Exeter, Devon, upholder (1791). Possibly the Mr Perkins, cm at South St in October 1816 when a fire broke out at his premises. [D]

Perkins, William, London, u (1808–25). At 12 Little Charlotte St, Rathbone St in 1808 and 36, Corner of Charlotte St, Tottenham Ct Rd, 1820–25. [D]

Perkins, William, 74 High St, King's Lynn, Norfolk, u (1830–39). [D]

Perkinson, John, Halifax, Yorks., cm (1793). [Subscribed to Sheraton's *Drawing Book*, 1793]

Perks, George, Madeley, Salop, cm and u (1822–35). [D]

Perks, John, Paradise St, Birmingham, cm (1777–80). In 1777 he took out insurance jointly with Elizabeth Mills, a widow, on a house. It was covered for £400. [D; GL, Sun MS vol. 254, p. 282]

Perks, Thomas, Roland St, Birmingham, cm and u (1828–30). [D]

Perrey, —, against the Playhouse, Drury Lane, London, cm and u (1744). Advertised for sale in May 1744 'Mahogany Bedsteads, curiously contriv'd, in the form of Buroes, Chests of Drawers, etc, fit for any Hall, Room or Chamber, also Mezzotinto Prints, Bed Furniture, and Window-Curtains, with other Goods in the Cabinet Way'. [*Daily Advertiser*, 12 May 1744]

Perrin, Henry, London, cm and upholder (1724–37). At 'The Japan'd Cabinet and Clock', Fleet Ditch 1724–32. His trade card [Banks Coll., BM] shows his trade sign, with representations of a long case clock and japanned cabinet on an elaborate stand. It indicated that he bought, sold and appraised 'all Sorts of Household Goods'. In 1729 and 1732 fined for declining parochial office in the parish of St Bride, Fleet St. In 1734 supplied twelve 'leather bottomed chairs for the Steward's Room' at Holkham, Norfolk at a cost of £3 5s. By 1737 he had moved to 'The Great Mahogany Warehouse; Next the stone cutters near the Duke of Newcastle's, Lincoln's Inn Fields'. From this address he supplied to Blickling Hall, Norfolk twelve walnut chairs covered in Spanish leather which with sundries came to £7 13s. The bill dated 6 May 1737 made out to Messrs Townshend & Drury, London, has at its head an engraving of a low lacquer chest on stand surmounted by a large bracket clock. Despite the change in the name of his business premises, to accord with changing taste he appears to have stuck to his old trade sign. A further account of 1737 made out to Thomas Drury Esq. totalled £285 10s 10d, the main items being four Virginian walnut compass chairs at £16 16s, three bedsteads with blue 'Cherry Furn.' at £14 5s, 'a curious Library case, sash Doores' at £10 10s, two pairs of large mahogany chests of drawers at £10 10s and a fine mahogany frame at £14 14s. [Heal; V&A archives; Norfolk RO, NRS 21089 72 x 1]

Perrin, John, 16 Redcross St, Southwark, London, u (1826). [D]

Perrin, William, parish of St James, Bristol, cm (1781–84). [Poll bks]

Perrin, William, 6 Lower Castle St, Bristol, cm and broker (1822). [D]

Perring, George, 6 Garden Row, Old St Rd, London, upholder (1789–1803). Son of Henry Perring of Shepherds Bush, London, gardener. App. to John Robins on 28 January 1789 and free of the Upholders' Co. by servitude, 5 January 1803. [D; GL, Upholders' Co. records]

Perrott, Thomas, London, upholder (1730–50). Son of Thomas Perrott of Bell Hall, Worcs. Esquire. App. to John Underwood 4 November 1730 and free of the Upholders' Co. by servitude 1 March 1737/38. He took as app. John Malbone, 1739–50. [GL, Upholders' Co. records]

Perrott, Thomas, 12 Smiths Buildings, City Rd, London, Windsor chairmaker (1826). [D]

Perrott, Thomas, Old Brentford, Middlx, chairmaker (1823–39). Trading as a Windsor chairmaker in 1826 and fancy chairmaker in 1838. [D]

Perry, Mrs, Bristol, u (1833–40). At 59 Milk St, 1833–35 and 48 Milk St, 1838–40. In 1836, however, she is shown at 1 Hiran Pl., Alfred Hill. [D]

Perry, A., 5 Brewer St, Golden Sq., London, u (1825). [D]

Perry, Alexander, Great White House, King St, Bloomsbury, London, cm (1733). In March 1733 his stock in trade was offered for sale. This included 'fine walnut-tree and mahogany chairs cover'd in the newest fashion, cover'd or uncover'd with Spanish Leather, Damask or Mohair; with other Chairs, from two shillings apiece to Forty; several fine Dressing Chairs, Shaving Chairs, Close-stool Chairs and Easy Chairs'. [*Daily Post*, 15 March 1733]

Perry, Charles, 35 Kingsmead St, Bath, Som., cm (1826). [D]

Perry, Edward, Exeter, Devon, cm (1823–26). At Exeter Barracks in 1823 when his daughter Ann was bapt. at St David's Church, and at Theatre Lane in 1826 when another daughter Catherine was bapt. at St Pancras Church. [PR (bapt.)]

Perry, Henry, Derby St, Liverpool, cm (1821–27). At 2 Derby St in 1821 but at 7 in 1823–24 and 8 in 1827. These addresses were shops, and in 1824 his house is listed as 40 Cumberland St. In 1827 the business was trading as Henry Perry & Son. [D]

Perry, Henry, Church St, Crewkerne, Som., cm (1840). [D]

Perry, James, Som., cm (1753). In 1753 took app. named Deverell. [S of G, app. index]

Perry, James, 10 Pipe Lane, Bristol, cm (1839–40). [D]

Perry, John, at the Harrow near the gate in Houndsditch, London, u (1714). [GL, Hand in Hand MS vol. 4, ref. 4458]

Perry, John, at Mrs Lowe's, Basnett St, Liverpool, cm (c.1786–d.1806). Died in October 1806 at the age of 60. Said to have boarded with Mrs Lowe 'upwards of 20 years'. [*Liverpool Chronicle*, 22 October 1806]

Perry, John, London Wall, London, u (1826–39). At 16 London Wall East in 1826 and 61 London Wall, 1835–39. [D]

Perry, John Robert, 37 Church St, Mile End, London, chair and sofa maker (1825). [D]

Perry, Jonathan, High St, Shrewsbury, Salop, u (1796). [D; freemen rolls]

Perry, Joshua, 'The Royal Bed, and Star', Bishopsgate Without, London, u (1727). In May 1727 took out insurance cover of £250 on his house and a similar cover on his household goods and stock in trade. [GL, Sun MS vol. 24, ref. 41635]

Perry, Joshua, 17 Bishopsgate Without, London, upholder and undertaker (1777–83). Heal states that a comparison of maps indicates that this address is identical with that of the Joshua Perry (above) who traded at the sign of 'The Royal Bed and Star'. [D; Heal]

Perry, M. & I., Laurence St, Chelsea, London, cm and u (1823). [D]

Perry, Richard, 18 Gt Hermitage, London, cm (1808). [D]

Perry, Robert, 4 North Terr., Scarborough, Yorks., cm (1840). [D]

Perry, T., Bath, Som., cm, auctioneer and undertaker (1819–26). Listed at 14 Union St in 1819 and 10 Quiet St in 1826. [D]

Perry, William, Worship St, Moorfields, London, cm (1774). Freeman of Bristol. [Bristol poll bk]

Perry, William, 34 Beech Rd, Chiswell St, London, cm and u (1789–93). Subscribed to Sheraton's *Drawing Book*, 1793. His trade card [Heal Coll., BM] is embellished with engravings of a fire grate, bed, Pembroke table, shield-back chair and cylinder desk and bookcase. He sold both new and secondhand furniture and undertook funerals. [D; Heal]

Perry, William, Paul St, Taunton, Som., carver and gilder (1839). [D]

Perry & Phillips, Back Castle St, Bridgnorth, Salop, cm (1840). [D]

Perryman, Francis, London, carver and gilder (1804–39). At 53 St Martin's Lane, 1804–08. In both 1804 and 1807 he took out insurance cover for £300 of which only £50 was for utensils and stock. In addition to his trade as a carver and gilder he dealt in oysters. After 1808 there is a long gap until 1835 when he was at 52 Berwick St, Soho where he traded until at least 1839. [D; GL, Sun MS vol. 431, ref. 769504; vol. 440, ref. 802958]

Peters, Charles, Northgate, Canterbury, Kent, cm (1830). [Poll bk]

Peters, George, London, cm (1793). Subscribed to Sheraton's *Drawing Book*, 1793.

Peters, George, High Wycombe, Bucks., chairmaker and cane worker (b. c. 1796–1841). Daughter bapt. in 1823 and a son in 1826. Aged 45 at the time of the 1841 census. [PR (bapt.)]

Peters, Thomas, Cambridge, u (1682–88). Worked for Christ's College, 1682–88. He was paid for covering forms with leather and for upholstering the eighteen chairs supplied by William Billups. In 1687 had an app. named Thomas Moulder. St John's College paid Peters for upholstery work in 1688. [College records]

Peters, William, London, carver (1764–68). At Bishopsgate St in 1764 and Houndsditch in 1765–68. Member of the Joiners' Co. Took out licences to employ two non-freemen, 1764–66, and one non-freeman in 1768. [GL, City licence bks, vols 4–6]

Pether, Robert, 170 Brick Lane, Spitalfields, London, bedstead maker (1829). [D]

Pether, Thomas, Berwick St, Soho, London, carver (1773). Thomas Pether published *A Book of Ornaments, Suitable for Beginners*, on 6 January 1773 consisting of a frontispiece and five plates. The title page records that he was a carver who owned a print shop in Berwick St, Soho. A catalogue issued by Taylor's Architectural Library, c. 1780 lists 'A Book of Tablets done to full size commonly used for chimney-pieces, Designed and etched by T. Pether on six plates'. No copy is known. [*Furn. Hist.*, 1975]

Pether, Thomas, Dean St, Newcastle, carver, gilder and ornamental manufacturer (1801). [D]

Pether, Thomas, 20/21 Ben Jonson St, Liverpool, carver, gilder and teacher of drawing (1810–13). [D; Gunnis]

Pethybridge, Joseph, College St, Bristol, coach and cabinet carver (1832–40). At Lamb St, College St, 1832–38 and 19 College St, 1839–40. [D]

Petman, John, 31 Thomas St, Brick Lane, London, cm and u (1839). [D]

Petrie, Andrew, Prussian Island, London, cm (1790–93). [D]

Petrie, James, Salford, Lancs., u (1804–17). At 7 Harding's Buildings in 1804, 3 Thompson St in 1813 and 5 Thompson St in 1817. [D]

Petrie, William, 23 Drury Lane, London, cm (1780). Took out insurance cover of £100 of which £60 was for utensils and stock. [GL, Sun MS vol. 282, p. 647]

Petrie & Walker, St Anne's St, Manchester, u (1818–21). Listed at no. 12, 1818–19, and no. 15 in 1821. [D]

Pett, —, Sevenoaks, Kent, chairmaker etc. (1803). [D]

Pett, Thomas, Maidstone, Kent, upholder (1734). [Poll bk]

Pettefor (or Pettefer or Pettif(e)ar), Robert, Wilson St, Newark, Notts., u (1822–35). Listed as R. Pettifear & Co. in 1822. [D]

Pettet, George Edward, Greenwich, London, cm etc. (1824–39). At Church St, 1824–26, and Lewisham Lane 1839. [D]

Pettfield, Christopher, 102 High St, Southampton, Hants., cm (1811). [Poll bk]

Pettifer, Edward, 8 Adam St West, Portman Sq., London, upholder (1808). [D]

Pettinger, Isaac Lyth, Leeds, Yorks., journeyman cm (1784–99). Freeman of Beverley, Yorks. In 1791 named in the list printed at the end of the *Leeds Cabinet and Chair Makers' Book of Prices* of journeymen as in support of its contents. [Beverley poll bks]

Pettit, Joseph, Cock St, Wolverhampton, Staffs., cm and u (1818). [D]

Pettit, Paul, London, carver and gilder (1724–57). Living in the parish of St Giles-in-the-Fields in 1724, but by 1743 in the parish of St James, Westminster. In 1749 his address was given as Silver St. Took apps named Salter in 1724, Lidiard in 1743, Morgan in 1746 and Franquet in 1757. Carried out extensive work for Frederick, Prince of Wales. In 1732 he was paid £259 10s for double gilding and painting the carving on the Royal barge, designed by William Kent for the Prince. Regular commissions for the Prince continued from 1733–50 and in some years the amounts paid were very substantial. In 1739 £160 was expended and in the following year £137 8s 6d. The total for 1743 was £301 6s, while 1749 was to see expenditure reaching £739 16s 4d. Many of these payments appear to have been for picture frames of great elaboration. One supplied in 1749 was described as 'richly carved with an eagle and septer at top, supporters with standards in their hands, trophies of war...'. Much of this work was for Cliveden, Bucks. which the Prince leased from Anne, Countess of Orkney from 1739 until his death in 1751. Smaller payments are recorded in the accounts of Augusta, Princess of Wales in April 1740 and January 1741. Pettit was also employed from 1732–33 at the London house of the Duke of Newcastle. He undertook work in the Best Parlour at a cost of £9 14s and on a gilt table frame which was charged at £6 6s. [Westminster poll bk; S of G, app. index; Duchy of Cornwall household accounts, vols II–XVII; *Burlington*, August 1970; Windsor Royal Archives, RA 54961–62, 55229, 55425, 55428; BM, Add MS 33161 10 April 1732, 20 April 1733]

Pettit & Oliver, London, u (1819–25). At 12 Broker Row, Moorfields in 1819 but by the following year the number was 9. This address is also recorded as 9 Lower Moorfields. By 1822 had moved to 152 Houndsditch and by 1825 the number here was 30. [D]

Pettitt, George, Brewer St, Golden Sq., London, u and cm (1789–1839). Son of John Pettitt of Paddington, London, u. App. to Daniel Weale on 4 December 1782 and free of the Upholders' Co. by servitude, 11 October 1790. He married in 1788 and is recorded in London directories as early as 1789 at 47 Brewer St. After 1826 the number was changed to 48. He subscribed to Sheraton's *Drawing Book*, 1793, and *Cabinet Dictionary*, 1803. Three of his trade cards survive [Banks Coll., BM]; those dated 1808–09 record that he was 'Upholsterer to Her Majesty and the Princess Elizabeth'. The long duration of his business would suggest that it was directed in its later years by another hand, possibly his son. [D; GL, Upholders' Co. records; *Gents Mag.*, 1788, p. 1124]

Pettitt, John, Paddington, London, u (1790). Father of George Pettit who traded at Brewer St, 1789–1839. [GL, Upholders' Co. records]

Petto, John, parish of St Augustine, Bristol, carver (1734). [Poll bk]

Petty, Ashley, Canal Terr., Southampton, Hants., cm and chairmaker (1839). [D]

Petty, Charwell, London, upholder (1698). Free of the Upholders' Co., 19 June 1698. [GL, Upholders' Co. records]

Petty, Henry, 49 Greenfield St, Whitechapel, London, cm and upholder (1827). [D]

Pew, Benjamin, London, cm and chairmaker (1739). When his household goods and stock in trade were put up for sale in May 1739 he was described as 'the ingenious Mr. Benjamin Pew'. His stock consisted of 'large Glass Sconces in carv'd and Gilt Frames, a large Quantity of Walnut-Tree, Mahogany and other work, as fine Desks and Bookcases with Glass Doors, Mahogany and Walnut-Tree Double Chests, with a Desk in them, or without: fine Dressing-Tables, as Walnut-Tree Mahogany and Quadrille Tables, Spring-Tables, Dining, Box Night, Corner, square and other Tables: a large Quantity of Mahogany and Walnut-Tree Chairs, cover'd or uncover'd ... Easy Chairs, etc...'. [*London Daily Post*, 25 May 1739]

Pew, John, Cirencester, Glos., cm and chairmaker (1820–28). At Thomas St in 1820; Dollar St, 1822–23, and Thomas St, in 1824. Children bapt. in 1824 and 1828. [D; PR (bapt.)]

Pewlas, Robert, Myton St, Hull, Yorks., chairmaker (1806). [D]

Pewtner, Joseph, parish of St George-in-the-Fields, London, joiner and cm (1826). Eldest son of William Pewtner also of the same parish, carpenter. He was a freemen of Hereford and his son Joseph was also made free by patrimony 18 June 1826. [Hereford freemen rolls and poll bk]

Pexton, Alfred, 37 King St, Maidstone, Kent, carver and gilder (1832–39). [D]

Pexton, James, Gabriel's Hill, Maidstone, Kent, carver and gilder (1805–29). [D]

Pexton, William, Hull, Yorks, chairmaker and woodturner (1826–40). At Blackfriargate from 1826–34 and by the following year had moved to 6 Blanket Row. In 1840 described as 'Cane & Windsor Chairmaker'. [D]

Peyrard, Jean, London, upholder (1671). Submitted his bill dated 18 December 1671 to the 5th Earl (later 1st Duke) of Bedford for 'a green damask gold coloured bed (vizt) curtains & valence & counterpain with six chairs £75'. The commission was probably for Bedford House, London. [Bedford Office, London]

Peyton, Bladwell, 'The Black Lyon', Wytch St, parish of St Clement Danes, London, upholder (1713–33). Free of the Upholders' Co., 6 May 1713, and by August of the following year in Wytch St. Took as apps John Cremer, 1714–1726/27 and Charles Whalley, 1726–33. [GL, Upholders' Co. records; Sun MS vol. 4, ref. 4366]

Phelps, George, 19 Greek St, Soho, London, carver and gilder (1790–93). [D]

Phelps, Isaac, 3 Bristol back, Bristol, cm (1775). [D]

Phelps, Thomas, Yeovil, Som., cm (1733). [Poll bk]

Phelps, William, London, cm (1793). Subscribed to Sheraton's *Drawing Book*, 1793.

Phene, Nicholas, London, upholder and auctioneer (1775–1821). Probably the son of Samuel Phene, as the trading addresses are common, and both used the sign of 'The Golden Plough' on their trade cards. At 17 Broker's Row, Moorfields, 1775–79, but from 1780 at 18 and 19 Broker's Row. In 1789 took over also 80 London Wall close at hand, which he used in conjunction with the earlier premises by this

time usually referred to as 18 and 19 Little Moorgate. By 1817 the business was trading as Phene & Son and in this year an address at 12 Broker Row is recorded in one directory. From 1819 the business is known as Phene & Sons. By 1821 new premises were being used at 20, 21, 22, New Broad St but the manufactory at London Wall was retained. Their trade card refers to the business as a carpet, cabinet and bedding warehouse. Utensils and stock were insured in 1781 for £300. After 1821 the business was continued as Phene & Williamson. [D; GL, Sun MS vol. 292, p. 333]

Phene, Samuel, London, u and cm (1750–75). Member of the Stationers' Co. Traded at the sign of 'The Golden Plow', Little Moorgate but c.1767 this address was given the new designation of 17 Broker's Row, Moorfields. On 7 August 1750 took as app. Thomas Jones who was declared free of the Upholders' Co., on 1 June 1758, under the terms of the 1750 Upholders' Act. By January 1761 Jones was in partnership with Phene, and their trade card indicated that stock included 'Standing Beds and Bedding, Chests of Drawers, Desks & Book Cases, Buroe desks, Card, Dining, Breakfast & Dressing Tables (in Mohogany Walnut-tree or Wainscot) Chairs of all Sorts, Settee and Buroe Bedsteads, Sconces, Pier Chimney and Dressing Glasses with all manner of Upholstery Cabinet & Brasiery Goods; new and old'. They also acted as appraisers and undertakers. Jones died on 8 October 1769, and Phene continued to trade until c.1775 when Nicholas Phene, probably his son, took over the business. Jones played a very active part in the business up to the time of his death. Two receipts are known signed by him and he was the person who took out licences to employ non-freemen, 1762–69. Phene himself took out a licence in 1762 to employ four non-freemen for six weeks, but he took out no further ones until 1770. [D; GL, trade card coll.; City Licence bks, vols 3, 6–9]

Phene jnr & Rickett, 20, 21, 22 New Broad St and 20 Broker's Row, Moorfields, London, u (1807–14). The Phene involved was almost certainly the son of Nicholas Phene. This appears to have been a separate business from that of Phene's father through the close proximity of the Broker's Row premises suggests co-operation. Phene appears to have re-entered his father's business some time between 1814 and 1817, from which date they traded as Phene & Son, and in 1819 Phene & Sons. The New Broad St premises were being used by Nicholas Phene in 1821. The trade card of Phene & Rickett [Landauer Coll., MMA, NY] indicates that like most upholsterers they also acted as undertakers and appraisers. [D]

Phene & Williamson, 80 London Wall and 20, 21, 22 New Broad St, London, cm, u and auctioneers (1822–40). A continuation of the business operated by Nicholas Phene and from 1821 referred to as Phene & Sons. Their billhead [GL] indicates that they were also appraisers and undertakers, 'sold Cabinet work for Exportation' and stocked Turkey carpets and iron safes. They also described themselves as carpet manufacturers. They appear at times to have used their trade label to identify their manufactures, and a mahogany writing table (having a leather covered top and two drawers on either side, on ring turned legs), is known, bearing their label. The Phene business built up over many years was probably on an extensive scale as insurance cover taken out in January 1822 by Phene & Williamson on a dwelling house and offices at Brokers Row was for £4,000. [D; Christie's, 11 May 1978, lot 76; GL, Sun MS vol. 489, ref. 987568]

Phenix, James, Chester, cm (1776–84). App. to John Johnson, cm, 8 April 1776 and 30 January 1777. Free by servitude, 1 April 1784. [App. bk; freemen rolls] Possibly:

Phenix, James, Alport St, Manchester, cm (1794–97). At 2

Alport St in 1794 but by 1797 the number was 1. [D] Probably father of:

Phenix, James, Liverpool, cm (1819–20). In 1819 he married Miss Eliza Williams of Liverpool at St Anne's Church, but his wife died aged 22 on 26 May 1820 'after a protracted illness'. [*Chester Guardian*, 1 April 1819, 1 June 1820]

Philcox, George, the Cliffe, Lewes, Sussex, cm and u (1770–1805). Claimed to be from London and was established in Lewes by December 1770 when he advertised that he had in stock 'all sorts of Cabinet Furniture; also Looking Glasses, and Venetian Shades &c. &c.' He appears to have been a person of some enterprise, and realising the growing prosperity of the rising sea-bathing resort of Brighton, he advertised in May 1773 that he had established a warehouse there stocked with his furniture and under the care of Thomas Philcox. He advertised also for an app. and a journeyman cm. In 1777 he took out insurance cover for £700, but of this only £240 was in respect of utensils and stock suggesting that the business was still of modest size. His trade card [Heal Coll., BM] dates from soon after the establishment of his business but still features furniture in the Chippendale style. [D; *Sussex Weekly Advertiser*, 24 December 1770, 10 May 1773, 26 December 1774; GL, Sun MS vol. 260, p. 617]

Philcox, Thomas, Brighton, see George Philcox, Lewes.

Philip, Richard, 3 George Ct, Bennetts Hill, Doctors Commons, London, cm (1777). In 1777 insured a house for £200. [GL, Sun MS vol. 257, p. 315]

Philip, Richard, London, cm, upholder, undertaker etc. (1778–1810). At 26 Bishopsgate St Within, 1778–94. In 1778 he took out insurance cover of £400 at this address but only half was for utensils and stock. The corresponding figures for 1779 were £500 and £300. From 1795 at 12 Gt Helen's St. Included in the list of master cabinet makers in Sheraton's *Cabinet Dictionary*, 1803. Associated in an insurance policy with a Matthew Randall in 1781, and in 1808 the business was listed as Richard Philip & Son. In November 1810 when the bankruptcy of the enterprise was announced, the order was issued in the names of Richard Philip jnr and William Gosling. [D; GL, Sun MS vol. 264, p. 176; vol. 274, p. 33; *Sussex Weekly Advertiser*, 12 November 1810]

Philip, Richard & Son, Horsham, Sussex, upholders (1811). Appear to have also traded at Brighton. [D]

Philip, Ward, Kirkgate, Bradford, Yorks., cm (1822). [D]

Philips, Charles, Worthing, Sussex, cm (1832–40). At High St in 1832 and in November 1839 at Park House, Warwick St. By 1845 had moved to 12 Bedford Row. [D]

Philips, J., Foulsham, Norfolk, cm (1796). Freeman of Norwich. [Norwich poll bk]

Philips, John, Bristol, cm (1781). [Poll bk]

Philips, John jnr, Norwich, cm (1794–1818). Living in the parish of St John Maddermarket in 1794, St Giles 1807 and 1818, and St Augustine, 1812. [Poll bks]

Philips, T. (or J.), 15 St John's Lane, London, carver and gilder (1808). [D]

Philips, William Philip, Doddington, Whitchurch, Salop, cm, u, auctioneer and appraiser (1833–36). Recorded as William Philip Phipps in 1835. His wife Maria died on 31 March 1833 at the age of 25 and his infant daughter Mary Ann Maria on 13 January of the following year. This double tragedy must have occurred at a time when he was planning to establish himself in the shop and premises at Doddington, the opening of which he announced in May 1834. He stated that he had just returned from London 'with a choice assortment of carpeting and upholstery' and intended setting aside a room 'as a repository for the sale of Furniture etc.'. [D; *Chester Courant*, 6 April 1833, 21 January 1834, 13 May 1834]

Philipson, Elizabeth, Hull, Yorks., working u (1826–35). At 14 Leadenhall Sq. in 1826 and 28 King's St, Sculcoates in 1835 when her trade was listed as 'Bed maker'. Still at this address in 1838 but no trade recorded. [D]

Philipson, Nicholas & Small, James, 190 Piccadilly, London, cm and upholders (1782). Insured their utensils, stock and goods for £800 in 1782. [GL, Sun MS vol. 306, p. 251] Probably:

Philipson, Nicholas, London, upholder (1786–87). In June 1786 he insured goods at a house in Arlington St in the tenure of Lord Herbert for £300. In June 1787 took out insurance cover on goods and property at 132 New Bond St for £1,000. [GL, Sun MS vol. 337, p. 520; vol. 342, ref. 531481]

Philipson, Thomas, 28 Gt Castle St, Oxford St, London, carver and gilder (1784). His trade card survives. [D; Banks Coll., BM]

Phill, Thomas, 'The Three Golden Chairs', Strand, London, u (1700–d.1728). Free of the Upholders' Co., 23 September 1700. Took as app. Thomas Collins of St Ives, Hunts. 2 June 1709 and he was made free, 4 November 1719. In partnership with Jeremiah Fletcher, 1713–18. Died in 1728, and on 24 May an auction sale of his household goods and stock in trade was announced at 'The Fountain Tavern', near the Exeter Exchange, Strand. Phill was described as 'upholsterer to Her late Majesty Queen Anne, to His late Majesty George I and to his present Majesty'. His extensive involvement as a supplier to the Crown is confirmed from archival sources. In 1713–14 he provided cases and case curtains for furniture and a state bed at Windsor Castle, and in 1716 upholstered and provided bedding for a large state bed made by Richard Roberts, also for Windsor Castle. For the House of Lords Phill supplied 90 Turkey work chairs, four table carpets and two leather folding stools in 1718 and in the same year for the House of Commons 48 Turkey work chairs. Such extensive commissions resulted in large payments which in one quarter of 1719 peaked at £1,233. Further furniture of a similar nature was supplied to the Houses of Parliament in 1722. In 1727 he made a cushion for the Coronation Chair in Westminster Abbey and upholstered the footstool in preparation for the Coronation of George II. In 1724 he is recorded in connection with the furnishing of the Church of St Mary-le-Strand, one of the projects promoted by the Commissioners for Building Fifty New Churches in London and Westminster. His only known commission away from the London region was at Canons Ashby, Northants. Between June 1711 and February 1714 he was employed here by Edward Dryden. The only new furniture was supplied on 22 January and 12 February 1714 and consisted of a 'walnuttree Arm'd Chair frame . . . cover'd with black Spanish Leather and Garnished with laqued pillor nailes' and '6 wallnuttree back chaires frames of ye newest fashion stufft up in Lynnen & ye seats coverd a 2nd time'. The 'Arm'd Chaire' was charged at £2 15s and the 'back chaires' at £7 10s with an additional charge for fitting them with needlework covers. This upholstery suite which was sold in the 1930s to meet death duties has now been reacquired by the National Trust and restored to the house. [GL, Upholders' Co. records; PRO, LC9/286–87; Harris, *Old English Furniture*, p. 26; *Old Furniture*, vol. 2 (1927), pp. 80, 83; *Conn.*, June 1933, pp. 377–78, vol. 133 (1954), p. 81; *C. Life*, 11 February 1960; Winterthur, Delaware, Symonds 75 × 64.14, p. 115, 75 × 64.155.18.6, p. 54; Lambeth Palace Lib., MS 2691, f. 264, item 10; Canons Ashby MS D(CA)129]

Phillip, H. T., The Shambles, Worcester, cm and u (1820). [D]

Phillip, James, 63 Shoreditch, London, u (1793). [D]

Phillips, —, 16 Dean St, Westminster, London, upholder (1808): [D]

Phillips, Mrs, 17 Cumberland St, Bristol, u (1837–38). [D]

Phillips, Benjamin, Bristol, cm (1754–84). In the parish of St

Augustine, 1754, but the parish of St James, 1774–84. The address in 1779 was given as 4 North St. [D; poll bks]

Phillips, Benjamin, Bristol, cm and u (1809–33). At 17 Peter St, 1809–17. Declared bankrupt, November 1810. By 1833 at Clifton Hill, near Berkeley Pl. [D; *Exeter Flying Post*, 8 November 1810]

Phillips, Benjamin, Millgate, Aylsham, Norfolk, chairmaker (1830). [D]

Phillips, Cornelius, 5 Angel Pl., Pentonville, London, cm and u (1839). [D]

Phillips, David, 8 Noad St and 6 Cambridge St, Golden Sq., London, u and cm (1808–09). [D]

Phillips, Edmund John, Thomas St, Bristol, cm and u (1826–35). At 127 Thomas St, 1826–31, but used additionally 24 in 1828–29 and 32 in 1830–31. The number changed to 126 in 1832–34 and 125 in 1835. [D]

Phillips, Edward, parish of St Mary, Whitechapel, London, looking-glass maker (1714–15). Freeman of London. In 1714 took out insurance cover of £25 on a house in Castle St and in June of the following year £100 cover on a house 'with Shovell board room' on Ratcliffe Highway. [GL, Hand in Hand MS vol. 13, p. 101; vol. 14, p. 464]

Phillips, Edward, Narrow Bridge St, Peterborough, Northants., cm (1822). [D]

Phillips, Edward, Berkeley Pl., Bristol, u (1823). [D]

Phillips, George, parish of St James, Bristol, cm (1784). [Poll bk]

Phillips, George, 8 Freeman St, Birmingham, cabinet case and portable desk maker (1828–30). Listed at no. 3 in 1828 as a cm, and at no. 8 in 1830. [D]

Phillips, George Edward, 208 Tooley St, London, cm, u, auctioneer and appraiser (1822–27). [D]

Phillips, H. N., London, jewel case maker (1829–37). At 13 King St, Soho in 1829 and 29 Newman St, Oxford St in 1835–37. [D]

Phillips, Henry, London(?), carver (1662–93). Master carver to the Crown during the reign of Charles II. In 1663 provided a pair of stands which came with other items to £19. Also for the Crown employed at Whitehall in 1664 where for the Queen's Closet he provided a picture frame above the chimney piece. Worked in association with Grinling Gibbons at Windsor Castle. [Beard, *Georgian Craftsmen*, p. 180; PRO, E 351/3276; LC5/39; V&A archives; H. Colvin, ed. *History of King's Works*, v, 1976 refs cited]

Phillips, Henry, South Shields, Co. Durham, cm/joiner (1834). [D]

Phillips, J. W., Bristol, timber merchant and cabinet manufactory (1814–15). Shown at 3 Alfred Hill where he is described as a timber merchant, Lewin's Mead which is described as a timber yard and 56 Broadmead, a cabinet manufactory. [D]

Phillips, James, parish of Christchurch, Bristol, cm (1784). [Poll bk]

Phillips, James, 33 Little Earl St, London, cm (1787). In July 1787 insured goods to the value of £200. [GL, Sun MS vol. 342, ref. 532909]

Phillips, James, Leominster, Herefs., cm (1820). [Poll bk]

Phillips, James, 2 Court, Cox St, Birmingham, cm (1835). [D]

Phillips, John, London (1725–62). In May 1725 at 'the corner of St Paul's Chain in St Paul's Churchyard' where he took out insurance cover of £1,000 on goods and merchandise in his dwelling house. He traded at the sign of 'The Cabinet' and when in February 1732 he moved to premises against St Peter's church in Cornhill he used this sign at the new location also. Worked at Badminton House, Glos. for the 3rd Duke of Beaufort, 1728–33, and received £444 9s 6d. Part of the bill for two frames 'richly carv'd & Guilt in Burnish'd Gold' is endorsed 'The R. Hon. the Lady Scudamore's Bill'. A narrow walnut bureau bookcase is

known with a small circular label giving the St Paul's Churchyard address. He is also recorded as being a looking glass supplier. [Heal; GL, Sun MS vol. 20, ref. 35903; *Daily Post*, 3 February 1732; Wills, *Looking-Glasses*; Glos. RO, Badminton MS 304.11.1]

Phillips, John, London, upholder (1774–1812). His father who was a farmer lived at Glaesbury, Radnor, Wales. John Phillips was app. to Philip Morgan, spectacle maker, 13 February 1767 and was declared free of the Upholders' Co. by servitude, 5 October 1774. He was established at 55 Fenchurch St by 1776 when he took out insurance cover of £800 of which £700 was for utensils and stock. By the following year the total cover had risen to £1,000 and utensils and stock to £850, a substantial sum for a business still in its early years. From 1781 he used for trading purposes an address at 134 Fenchurch St but appears to have retained no. 55 at which he was shown living as late as 1802. Addresses at Cross St, Rathbone Pl. in 1781 and Sunday St, Bishopsgate St in 1783 are recorded but these may have been dwelling houses occupied on a short time basis. Took as apps Thomas Horner 1774–81, Hughes Howell 1775–79, George Redshaw 1776–83, James Flower 1778 and James Herring 1787–94. The business was described on his trade card [Heal Coll. BM] as a 'Carpet, Upholstery, Cabinet and Paper Hanging Warehouse', and items held in stock included 'all sorts of Furniture, Bedsteads, Bedding &c., Turkey, Persia, Wilton, Kidderminster & Scotch Carpets'. He stated that he was also an 'Exchange Broker, Appraiser and Auctioneer'. In 1802 he was involved in a Chancery action concerning land in Brecknockshire, South Wales.

Phillips described himself as 'Upholder to the Hon[ble] City of London' and in 1780 provided a fine carved and gilt arm chair of state incorporating the City arms for the Lord Mayor at a cost of £80. In that year the Lord Mayor was Sir Watkin Lewes. [D; GL, Upholders' Co. records; Sun MS vol. 249, p. 404; vol. 259, p. 196; PRO, C13 360; *Conn.*, December 1952, p. 181]

Phillips, John, York, cm (1799–1840). Recorded at 36 Fetter Lane, 1830–40. Took as apps Richard Carlton Phillips snr, 17 September 1799; Joseph Laycock, 14 January 1822; William Lawson, 8 November 1824; Richard Carlton Phillips jnr, 8 November 1824 and Charles Walker, 18 May 1831. At 36 Fetter Lane, 1823–38. [D; app. reg.]

Phillips, John, Bristol, cm and u (1809–33). At Beaufort Ct, 1809–19, the number being 7 from 1809–10 and 3 in 1816–19. From 1820 to 1827 shown at Beaufort, Pl., Montague St and from 1828–33 at 5 Bridewell Lane. In 1825–27 described as sofa and mattress maker. [D]

Phillips, John, High Wycombe, Bucks., chairmaker (1813). Son bapt. 1813. [PR (bapt.)]

Phillips, John, 96 James St, Devonport, Devon, chairmaker (1830). [D]

Phillips, John, Silent St, Ipswich, Suffolk, cm (1839). [D]

Phillips, Joseph, Bristol, u (1816–21). At 3 Berkeley Pl. in 1816 and Clifton Wood in 1821. [D]

Phillips, Joseph Jackson, Northgate, St, Chester, cm (1819–25). Free 21 October 1819. Took as app. his brother Frederick, 27 July 1825. [Freemen rolls; app. reg.]

Phillips, Margaret, 1 Pomona St, Liverpool, u (1829). [D]

Phillips, Matthew, St Peter's in the East, Oxford, u (1802). [Poll bk]

Phillips, Nancy, Warrington, Lancs., chairmaker (1798). [D]

Phil(l)ips, Peter, Warrington, Lancs., chairmaker (1814–34). At Bridge St, 1814–28 but in 1822 and 1834 at Ship Yd, Bridge St. A Nancy Phillips, chairmaker was trading in Warrington in 1798. [D]

Phillips, Richard, Westbury-on-Trym, Glos., carver and gilder (1784). Freeman of Bristol. [Bristol poll bk]

Phillips, Richard, London, cm and gilder (1807–12). In January 1807 at 142 St John St, West Smithfield and took out insurance cover of £1,000. Of this £200 was for china and glass and £270 for stock and utensils. He also owned property at 5 and 6 St James Walk Clerkenwell. By 1809 he was using 6 (now renumbered 4) St James Walk and was to remain here until at least May 1812. In 1811–12 he was also using a workshop over a stable and coach house in Pear Tree Ct. Insurance cover in 1811 was £1,050 including £470 for utensils and stock and in 1812 the corresponding figures were £1,150 and £470. [D; GL, Sun MS vol. 438, ref. 798815; vol. 449, ref. 854933; vol. 455, ref. 871280]

Phillips, Richard, 5 Marylebone St, London, cm and u (1839). [D]

Phillips, Robert, Peterborough, Northants., cm (1806). [Poll bk]

Phillips, S., 11 Dighton St, Bristol, u (1839–40). [D]

Phillips, Somerset, Fenchurch St, Aldermanbury, London, cm (1767–74). Insured houses. [GL, MS 8674/106, p. 142]

Phillips, Thaddeus, 12 Upper Arcade, Bristol, carver and gilder (1838–40). [D]

Phillips, Thomas, Worcester, cm and upholder (1777). App. to Ely Crump and free by servitude, 23 June 1777. [Freemen rolls]

Phillips, Thomas, Shambles, Worcester, cm and u (1822). [D]

Phillips, Thomas, 37 Aylesbury St, Clerkenwell, London, carver and gilder (1820–26). [D]

Phillips, Thomas, 18 Finsbury Pl., South, London, cm and u (1837–39). An account dated 1839 survives for fixed bookcases of rosewood with brass trellis and lined with blue silk supplied for the Living Room at Sheringham Hall, Norfolk. The name of the supplier was T. Philips and it is possible that it was this maker. [D; C. Life, 7 February 1957, p. 239]

Phillips, William, Chester, carver (1718–25). Son of Robert Phillips of Chester, shoemaker. App. to John Tilston, carver and joiner on 25 March 1718 and free by servitude, 3 April 1725. [App. bk; freemen rolls]

Phillips, William, High St, Lambeth, London, cm, broker, milliner and haberdasher (1778). In 1778 took out insurance cover of £400 of which £300 was for utensils and stock. [GL, Sun MS vol. 266, p. 380]

Phillips, William, Bourne, Lincs., u and tailor (1797). [D]

Phillips & Co., 3 Newgate St, London, looking-glass manufactory (c.1790). [Wills, Looking-Glasses]

Phillips & Elder, 34 Titchfield St, Fitzroy Sq., London, chairmakers (1803–08). [D]

Phillips & Small, Piccadilly, London, u (1773–86). [D] Phillips may be a mis-spelling of:

Phillipson, Nicholas, London, cm and u (1771–93). In 1775 subscribed to Thomas Malton's Treatise on Perspective. Trading in partnership with James Small, 1782–85. By 1784 living in Piccadilly but from 1788–93 at 132 New Bond St. In September 1771 supplied the Earl of Ancaster with a mahogany chest of drawers for £4 and in 1780 supplied a fly table to Lord Mahon, the son of the Earl of Stanhope, in Harley St which cost 12s. [D; Westminster poll bk; Lincoln RO, 2 ANC 6/15; Kent RO, U590 A61/8]

Phillmore, John, address unknown, joiner (1734–38). Undertook work for Paul Foley of the Temple, Little Ormond St, London and Newport House, Almeley, Herefs. 1734–38. This was mainly joinery work but did include the repair of furniture. On 17 July 1736 he supplied a large chest at £2 14s 2d. [Herefs. RO, Foley MS, F/AIII/55]

Philp, Richard, see Richard Philip.

Philpot, William, Wardour St, London, carver (1749). [Westminster poll bk]

Philpott, Stephen, Canterbury, Kent, u (1797). [Freemen rolls]

Phinn, Edward Thomas, London, cm (1807–31). Freeman of Gt Yarmouth, Norfolk. Living in London from May 1807 and in 1830 his address was given as Camberwell, London. [Poll bks]

Phipp, Josiah, see Samuel Holden.

Phipps, Edward, Narrow Bridge St, Peterborough, Northants., cm and u (1823–30). [D]

Phipps, James, Broadway, Westminster, London, upholder (1784). [D]

Phipps, John, Petty France, Westminster, London, u (1742–49). Son of John Phipps of Neston, Cheshire Gent. App. to Richard Manlove 3 July 1734 and free of the Upholders' Co. by servitude 3 February 1741/42. At Petty France in 1749. [GL, Upholders' Co. records; poll bk]

Phipps, John, Stratford-on-Avon, Warks., cm and u (1828–35). Recorded at John St in 1828 and Sheep St in 1835. [D]

Phipps, John, King St, Southwell, Notts., cm (1835). [D]

Phipps, Joshua, London, upholder (1765). Son of Robert Phipps, upholder. Free of the Upholders' Co. by patrimony under the terms of the 1750 Upholders' Act, 18 July 1765. [GL, Upholders' Co. records]

Phipps, Josiah, London, upholder (1775–1802). Son of Abraham Phipps, freeman and Weaver of London. Free of the Upholders' Co. by patrimony, 3 May 1775 at which date he was living in Whitechapel. Took as app. Timothy Ridge in 1780. Living at Copthall Ct, 1794–1802. [GL, Upholders' Co. records]

Phipps, Robert, 69 Leadenhall St, London, upholder (1723–75). Son of Robert Phipps, freeman and 'Plaisterer' of London. App. to Samuel How, 4 March 1723 and free of the Upholders' Co. by servitude, 7 July 1731. Took as apps George Miller, 1747–54; Richard Butterfield, 1752–60; John Austin, 1762–73; William Gramlick, 1767–74; and Anthony Batger, free 1775. Master of the Upholders' Co. in 1759 and by this year already at the Leadenhall St address. His son Joshua was free of the Upholders' Co. by patrimony on 18 July 1765, and by 1767 the business was trading as Robert Phipps & Son. They advertised for business in the Cambridge Chronicle, 19 January 1771. From 1773 traded as Phipps & Shepherd. In 1764–65 Robert Phipps insured a property in Broad St, St George's, and in 1767 properties in Holborn and Dyers Ct. [D; GL, Upholders' Co. records; Hand in Hand MS vol. 102, p. 159; vol. 106, p. 249]

Phipps, Thomas, 81 Leadenhall St, London, u, cm and auctioneer (1757–84). Free of the Joiners' Co. From the Leadenhall St address took out licences to employ non-freemen in 1757, 1766 and 1767. William Chenery is also recorded trading at this address in 1781 and may have been his successor. A table bearing his trade label has been recorded in the collection of the National Museum, Warsaw. [D; GL, City Licence bks, vols 1 and 5; V&A archives]

Pic, Nicolas, London (1690–93). Associated with Peter Michon in the supply of four lanterns to Queen Mary for Kensington Palace, 1690–91, for which £48 12s was charged. In 1692–93 associated with James Catignou in connection with a much larger commission for Kensington Palace. This order included four pairs of glass lanterns, four pairs of gilt double candlesticks and three large glass lanterns and a bill for £512 8s was submitted. [PRO, LC9/127]

Pichford, Josiah, Linen Lane, Warwick, cm (1830). [D] See John Pickford at this address.

Pick, William, West Ham, London, cm (1777). Bankruptcy announced, Chester Chronicle, 21 November 1777.

Pick, William, Rebel Row, parish of St George, London, cm

(1787). In 1787 took app. named Robert Penman. [Westminster Ref. Lib., MS F4309, p. 56]

Pickard, Charles, Hull, Yorks., cm (1780). [Poll bk]

Picard, Esther, Leeds, Yorks., u (1830–37). Addresses given at 4 Sandford St in 1830; 17 Albion Sq. as a 'working' u in 1834; and Court 5, Albion St in 1837. [D]

Pickard, Thomas, Holywell St, Chesterfield, Derbs., cm (1829). [D]

Pickard, Thomas, Leeds, Yorks., cm (1837–39). At Little Woodhouse in 1837 and 15 St James St, 1839. [D]

Pickard, William, Elliott St, Manchester, joiner and cm (1794). [D]

Pickeret (Piqueret), Charles, London, cm (1681–82). Arrived from Paris with his son Isaac late in July 1681. Both were allowed to settle in England and were so informed, 8 March 1681/82. [*Huguenot Soc.*, 1949, p. 155]

Pickering, —, London, cm (1793). Subscribed to Sheraton's *Drawing Book*, 1793.

Pickering, Benjamin, 1 Southampton St, Pentonville, London, chairmaker (1808). [D]

Pickering, Henry & Pollard, William, 72 Hanover St, Liverpool, elastic bedding and easy chair manufacturers (1831). Bankrupt in September 1831 when their trade was described as u and cm. [*Liverpool Mercury*, 25 February 1831, 9 September 1831]

Pickering, Henry, 21 Bridge St, Lambeth, carver and gilder (1832–35). [D]

Pickering, James, New Brentford, Middlx, cm etc. (1826). [D]

Pickering, John, London, upholder (1778). Son of Richard Pickering and app. to Thomas Atkinson, joiner. Free of the Upholders' Co. under the terms of the 1750 Upholders' Act, 7 January 1778. [GL, Upholders' Co. records]

Pickering, Joseph, 77 Chester St, Birkenhead, Cheshire, cm (1837). [D]

Pickering, Joseph, St Mary St, Bedford, cm and u (1839). [D]

Pickering, Thomas, Bolebridge St, Tamworth, Staffs., chairmaker and turner (1822–35). [D]

Pickering, William, Red Lion Ct, Spitalfields, London, cm and u (1839). [D]

Pickett, Jesse, Wiston and Horsham, Sussex, chairmaker and turner (1832–40). At Wiston in 1832 when he was described as a chair and pattern maker. At West St, Horhsam in 1839–40 as a chairmaker and turner. [D]

Pickford, Adam, Shudehill, Manchester, cm and chairmaker (1824–40). At 26 Shudehill, 1824–25 but by 1832 at 51 and by 1840 the number had changed again to 18. An address at 18 Thomas St is also given in 1840. John, Thomas and Esther Pickford all used 26 Shudehill as a business address. [D]

Pickford, Esther, 26 Shudehill, Manchester, chairmaker (1821–29). [D]

Pickford, Hubert, 65 Myddleton St, Clerkenwell, London, cm and u (1839). [D]

Pickford, John, Shudehill, Manchester, cm and chairmaker (1804–18). Also referred to as a 'Fancy Chair Warehouseman'. At 86 Shudehill in 1804 but in 1811 at 62, in 1813 at 26 and in 1815–18 at 82. Adam, Esther and Thomas Pickford all traded from 26 Shudehill at various dates and are almost certainly related. [D]

Pickford, John, Linen St, Warwick, cm (1831). [Poll bk] See Josiah Pichford at this address.

Pickford, John, back of the Crescent, Clifton, Bristol, cm and undertaker (1840). [D]

Pickford, Josiah, Swan Lane, Warwick, cm (1822). [D]

Pickford, Thomas, 26 Shudehill, Manchester, chairmaker (1814–19). [D] See John Pickford, Adam Pickford and Esther Pickford at this address.

Pickles, William, Hebden Bridge, Yorks., joiner/cm (1834). [D]

Pickles, William, Haworth, Yorks., cm (1837). [D]

Pickop, Drage, London, upholder (1750–60). Son of Joseph Pickop of Clerkenwell Green, London, cheesemonger. App. to John King on 27 February 1750 and free of the Upholders' Co. under the terms of the 1750 Upholders' Act, 1 May 1760. [GL, Upholders' Co. records]

Pickstone, Thomas, London, u (1777–1811). Son of Thomas Pickstone of Reigate, Surrey, stationer. App. to Barnard Baker on 7 May 1777 and free of the Upholders' Co. by servitude, 4 August 1784. In 1784 he was living at 29 Ludgate Hill but by 1789 was trading at 38 King St, Covent Gdn at which address he remained until 1794. At 7 Newcastle St, Strand 1794–1808, but by April 1809 the number was 11. Directories continue to show him at this address until 1811 but insurance cover was taken out in April 1810 at an address at 15 Craven Buildings, Drury Lane. In 1809 insurance cover totalled £800 of which £700 was for utensils and stock. The figures for 1810 are lower at £600 and £450 respectively. Pickstone was included in the list of master cabinet makers in Sheraton's *Cabinet Dictionary*, 1803. [D; GL, Upholders' Co. records; Sun MS vol. 448, ref. 830454; vol. 453, ref. 844478]

Pickthall, William, Broughton, Lancaster, cm (1824). Bankruptcy announced, *Brighton Gazette*, 5 August 1824.

Pickthall, William, Liverpool, cm (1821–35). Used a shop at 6 Brook's Alley, 1821–27, but also had a house at 12 Sidney St in 1824 and in 1827 had another address in Wood St which is given variously in the directories of that year as 8 or 7. In 1829 at 15 Sidney St, London Rd and 2 Livesley Pl., Shaw's Brow, and in 1835 as Hanover Pl., 22 Finch St. [D]

Pickup, James, Blackfriars St, Carlisle, Cumb., cm (1828–29). [D]

Pickup, John, Edenfield, Lancs., joiner and cm (1828). [D]

Pickup, Thomas, Northgate, Blackburn, Lancs., cm (1818). [D]

Pickworth, John, London, bookbinder and cabinet gilder (1821–26). At 116 Gray's Inn Lane in January 1821 when he took out insurance cover of £200 of which £140 was for utensils and stock. In 1826 at 43 Kirby St. [D; GL, Sun MS vol. 486, ref. 976525]

Picquet, Charles, Hull, Yorks., cm (1784). [Poll bk]

Pidcock, William, Wheeling (or Wheeler Gate), Nottingham, cm and joiner (1770–89). Took as apps John Wright in 1770, William Inglesant in 1777, John Wright in 1780 and Richard Canham in 1789. [App. reg.; poll bks]

Piddell, Mrs S., Littlehampton, Sussex, u (1834). In October 1834 he was paid 3s 9d for upholstery work carried out at Surrey House, Littlehampton, for the Earl of Surrey. [Arundel Castle records A2001]

Pidding, James, 57 Hackney Rd, London, cm (1829). [D]

Pidding & Co., 1 Cornhill, London, writing desk and dressing case maker (1829). [D]

Piddison, William, 46 Brewer St, Golden Sq., London, u (1808). [D]

Piddock, Henry, Canterbury, Kent, c (1794–1809). At St Margaret's 1794–96, but in King St, 1805–09. [D; poll bks]

Piddock, John, St Paul's, Canterbury, Kent (1769–96). Free 1769. In 1781 he was paid by Sir Edward Knatchbull of Mersham-le-Hatch, Kent, £18 16s for 'a new sett of Chairs for ye Bow Parlour'. [Freemen rolls; poll bks; Kent RO, U 951 A 19/2]

Pickover, Richard, St Martin's Ct, London, cm (1739–49). On five occasions between March 1739 and February 1745 he was paid small sums by Earl Fitzwalter of Moulsham Hall, Essex for the supply of new card tables or the repair of others. [A. C. Edwards, *The Accounts of Benjamin Mildmay, Earl Fitzwalter*, pp. 108–10; Westminster poll bk]

Pidgeon, S., Friars, Merchant St, Bristol, coach and cabinet caner (1836–40). [D]

Pidler, C., 53 Marylebone St, Cavendish Sq., London, upholder and undertaker (1817). [D]

Pidock, —, see Hallam & Pidock.

Pierce, —, Greenwich, London, u (1791). [D]

Pierce, James, Dychurch Lane, Northampton, cm (1830). [Poll bk]

Pierce, Joseph, Northampton, cm (1790–1820). In 1790 at South Quarter and in 1796, Bridge St. [Poll bks]

Pierce, Joseph, High Wycombe, Bucks., chairmaker (b. c.1791–1841). Four sons and four daughters bapt. between 1815–35. Witness at son's marriage in 1837. Aged 50 at the time of the 1841 Census. [PR (bapt. and marriage)]

Pierce, Richard, High St, Stoney Stratford, Bucks., cm and u (1830–39). [D]

Pierce, Wm, Warwick, Abington St, Northampton, cm (1823–30). [D]

Piercy, Edward, London, picture dealer, carver and gilder (1808–37). At 5 Denmark St, Strand 1808, 17 Titchborne St, Piccadilly 1820–33, 3 Arthur St, Monument in 1835 and 39 Warwick St, 1837. Trade card [Banks Coll., BM] of Rococo design gives as address at 17 Titchborne St, Golden Sq. Another trade card of Neo-classical character [Landauer Coll., MMA, NY] lists an address at 2 Sherrard St, Golden Sq. Bankrupt February 1833. Edward Piercy was the successor to John Piercy at the Titchborne St address and may have been his son. One directory lists at this address John Piercy & Son still trading in 1825. [D; *Liverpool Mercury*, 1 March 1833]

Piercy, Gabriel, Brighton, Sussex, cm (1778–86). In 1778 took out insurance cover of £400 but only £100 was for utensils and stock. By July 1786 the cover had increased to £1,000 but utensils and stock were only £200. [GL, Sun MS vol. 265, p. 648; vol. 339, p. 73]

Piercy, John, 17 Titchborne St, Piccadilly, London, carver, gilder and picture frame maker (1804–25). In 1825 the business is listed as John Piercy & Son and the son was probably Edward Piercy who is shown trading independently at 5 Denmark St, Strand in 1808 and is recorded in directories 1820–33 at the Titchborne St address. John Piercy is almost certainly the 'Percy' recorded in the account books of Edward, Viscount Lascelles and who supplied goods to Harewood House, Hanover Sq., London. He is described as a frame maker and was paid £20 12s 6d on 5 July 1804 and £6 6s 6d on 18 February 1806. [D; Leeds archives dept, Harewood MS 190, 192]

Piercy, Thomas, Little St Martin's Lane, Westminster, London, cm (1751). Took out insurance cover of £200 on his stock. [GL, Sun MS vol. 95, p. 310]

Pierpoint, J., Lindfield, Sussex, carpenter and chairmaker (1838). Offered his large workshop, yard and cottage to let in November 1830. Stated that the trades of carpenter and chairmaker had been conducted there. [*Sussex Agricultural Express*, 17 November 1838]

Pierson, William, Ingworth, Norfolk, cm (1790). Freeman of Norwich. [Norwich poll bk]

Pigg, Cuthbert, Groat-market, Newcastle, cm, carpenter and surveyor (1790–1801). In 1790 listed his trade as cm and carpenter but in 1795 and 1801 as surveyor. [D]

Pigg, John, 20 Wapping Wall, London, brush and cabinet maker (1807–15). In 1809 the business was trading as Thomas & John Pigg. John Pigg took out insurance cover of £300 in January 1807 of which utensils and stock accounted for £250. A workshop was maintained behind the dwelling house. [D; GL, Sun MS vol. 438, ref. 798894]

Pigg, Joseph, Norwich, cm, u and mahogany merchant (1812–31). In 1812 living in the parish of St Paul but 1822–30 shown trading at Bridge St, St George's. His apps were Joseph Harper

(free 24 February 1818) James Howell (free 3 May 1826) and John Rudd (free 21 June 1831). [D; poll bk; freemen reg.]

Piggott, —, 34 John St, Fitzroy Sq., London, portable billiard table maker (1819). [D]

Piggott, Ed., Guildford, Surrey, cm and u (1818–33). At North St in 1818 and Park St, 1830–32. [D; Surrey RO (Guildford), BR/PAR/2/4–7c]

Piggott, Frederick, George St, Richmond, Surrey, cm, u and estate agent (1839). [D]

Piggott, James, Hill St, Richmond, Surrey, u (1798–1832). [D] See James Pigott snr. Succeeded by:

Pigott, James jnr, Richmond, Surrey, cm and u (1832–39). At Hill St, 1832–38 and 2 Castle Terr. in 1839. [D]

Pigott, John, 46 Judd St, Brunswick Sq., London, upholder etc. (1820). [D]

Piggott, William, 99 High St, Guildford, Surrey, cm and u (1839). [D]

Pigott, James snr, George St, Richmond, Surrey, u (1838). [D]

Pigott, Thomas, 12 Peter St, Manchester, u (1839–40). [D]

Pigou, Mark Anthony, London, upholder (1700–05). On 2 December 1700 married Hannah Casbeard, possibly the daughter of or related to John Casbert an upholder of French extraction working for the Crown 1660–76. Pigou was made free of the Upholders' Co. by redemption, 18 October 1703. [GL, MS 10,091; Upholders' Co. records]

Piguinett (or Piggunett), James, Portsmouth, Hants., upholder (1774–81). Freeman of Bristol. [Bristol poll bks]

Pike, John, 'The Three Tents & Lamb', corner of Bear St, Leicester Fields, London, u (1723–49). In August 1723 took out insurance cover of £500 on goods and merchandise in his dwelling house. [GL, Sun MS vol. 16, ref. 29623, vol. 26, p. 473; Westminster poll bk]

Pike, John, Stoke's Croft, Bristol, cm (1795). [D]

Pike, John & Clark, James, 20 Frith St, Soho Sq., London, cm and u (1829). Their trade card [Landauer Coll., MMA, NY] indicates that they were previously with the firm of Jeremy & Bragg who traded from an address at 28 Southampton St, Covent Garden, 1824–29. Pike & Clark stated that they were trading as 'Damask Manufacturers, Furniture Printers, Cabinet Makers & Upholsterers' and also undertook funerals. The business was probably short-lived, and the bankruptcy of the partners was announced, *Liverpool Mercury*, 12 June 1829.

Pike, Robert, 23 Mary St, Hampstead, London, cm and u (1839). [D]

Pilbrow, J., 112 Stone St, Maidstone, Kent, cm, u, furniture broker and undertaker (1838–39). [D]

Pilcher, Thomas, High St, Hythe, Kent, cm and u (1839).[D]

Pilditch, Philip, 20 George St, East Stonehouse, Plymouth, Devon, cm (1838). [D]

Pile, James, 4 New St, Cloth Fair, London, cm and u (1839). [D]

Pile, John Trevanion, Queen Elizabeth Sq., Dover, Kent, cm (1826–37). [Poll bks]

Pile, Michael, Sidmouth, Devon, u (1806–23). Probably acted also as an estate agent for he advertised property to let or for sale at Sidmouth and Budleigh Salterton, 1814–23. Bankruptcy announced, December 1822. [D; *Exeter Flying Post*, 17 March 1806, 17 March 1814, 17 October 1822, 19 December 1822, 13 March 1823]

Pile, Moses, near the New Cutt in Narrow St, Limehouse, London, cm and carpenter (1782). Took out insurance cover in 1782 for £400 but of this only £100 covered utensils, stock and a warehouse. [GL, Sun MS vol. 299, p. 335]

Pile, Robert, London, cm (1775–75). In 1775 at 1 Wethey Ct, White Cross St where he insured a house for £100, and in 1777 near St Agnes-le-Clare in Tabernacle Walk, Moorfields where a house was insured for £200. [GL, Sun MS vol. 243, p. 379; vol. 255, p. 264]

Pilgrem, J., Christchurch, Hants., joiner and cm (1792–93). [D]

Pilgrim, Thomas, Christchurch, Hants., joiner and cm (1777). In 1777 took out insurance cover of £200 of which £120 was for utensils and stock. [GL, Sun MS vol. 255, p. 453]

Pilgrim, William, 58 Old St, London, cm and u (1839). [D]

Pilltory, Thomas, address unknown, cm (1793). On 7 June 1793 received from Sir John Nelthorpe the sum of £6 6s for a large mahogany library table. [Lincoln RO, NEL 9/15/45]

Pilkell, —, George Ct, Adelphi, Strand, London, u (1808). [D]

Pilkington, —, London, u (1793). Subscribed to Sheraton's *Drawing Book*, 1793.

Pilkington, Aston, Liverpool, u (1835–39). At 9 Fletcher St, Toxteth Park in 1835 and 4 Mount Pleasant in 1839. [D]

Pilkington, Charles, Liverpool, chairmaker (1784). Free 2 April 1784. [Freemen reg.]

Pilkington, Charles, Liverpool, chairmaker (1790). Free 24 June 1790. Son of Charles Pilkington, wheelwright. [Freemen reg.]

Pilkington, Henry, Derby, cm (1790–1805). In October 1790 advertised that he had taken over the business of Mottershaw & Son. Pilkington had been employed previous to this for several years in the business of Seddon, Sons & Shackleton in London. In February 1791 he took out insurance cover of £1,400 of which £650 was for stock and utensils mainly in his house but also some in a yard and shed. In 1793 he subscribed to Sheraton's *Drawing Book*. In 1805–06 the firm of Pilkington & Co. were trading as u and cm from an address in Iron Gate, Derby, and Henry Pilkington was probably the principal of this business. [D; *Derby Mercury*, 21 October 1790; GL, Sun MS vol. 374, ref. 579543]

Pilkington, Henry, 9 Bedford St, Liverpool, u (1834). [D]

Pilkington, John, Bristol, carver and gilder (1822–40). At David St, St Philip's in 1822 but from 1823–29 shown at 3 David St, St Philip's. By 1830 had moved to 5 Parson Ct, Ellbroad St and remained here until 1837. From 1838 shown at Paron's Ct, Redcross Lane. [D]

Pilkington, Richard, 25 Darwen St, Blackburn, Lancs., cm, joiner and housebuilder (1824). [D]

Pill, Benjamin, Gloucester, cm (1826). Child bapt. at St Aldgate's Church in 1826. [PR (bapt.)]

Pilling, John, Booth Fold, near Haslingden, Whalley, Lancs., cm (1825). [D]

Pills, John, 5 Hunts Ct, Castle St, London, plate case and cabinet maker (1810). In November 1810 took out insurance cover for £500 of which £200 was for utensils and stock. [GL, Sun MS vol. 453, ref. 850680]

Pilton, Thomas, Piccadilly, London, cm (1777–97). No address is recorded prior to 1789, although commissions are known from 1777. Between 1789–97 the address is variously given as either 213 or 214 Piccadilly. In 1777 supplied a writing table at a cost of £1 13s 6d to Edward Knight of Wolverley House, Worcs. and in 1785 supplied to Croome Court, Worcs. a mahogany folding table at £2 16s and a 'Trou Madame' table and stand for £3 7s. [D; Kidderminster Lib., Knight MS, notebook of Edward Knight, 13 June 1777; V&A archives]

Pilton, William, Piccadilly, London, see John Bullock.

Pim, Joseph & Co., 23 Brook St, Holborn, London, carver and gilder (1839). [D]

Pimm, William, 22 High St, Guildford, Surrey, cm and u (1837–40). From 1838 trading as Pimm & Holt. [D; Surrey RO (Guildford), BR/PAR/2/9b, 10a]

Pincent, Thomas, Exeter, Devon, cm (1723). In 1723 took app. named Fort. [S of G, app. index]

Pinckard, Bridget, 'The Sun', Hounsditch, London, u (1714). On 31 July 1714 insured goods in her 'Back Warehouse near her Dwelling House'. Possibly the wife of Giles Pinckard. [GL, Sun MS vol. 4, ref. 4338]

Pinckhard, Giles Bly, Hounsditch, London, upholder (1707–24). Son of John Pinckhard a freeman and upholder. App. to his father, on 16 October 1707 and free of the Upholders' Co. by servitude, 9 February 1714/15. Took as app. Thomas Chewter, 1716/17–1724. In April 1720 insured his house and warehouse in Hounsditch for £200 and in March 1721 another house 'North from Devonshire St.' in the same parish for £300. [GL, Upholders' Co. records; Hand in Hand MS vol. 22, p. 9; vol. 23, p. 175]

Pinckhard, John, London, upholder (1707–15). Father of Giles Bly Pinckhard who was free of the Upholders' Co., 9 February 1714/15 on the completion of an apprenticeship under his father. [GL, Upholders' Co. records]

Pinckney, William, London, u (1749–94). Son of Charles Pinckney of Gt Marlow, Bucks., Gent. App. to Thomas Humphrys, 7 December 1749 and then Charles Grange, 9 January 1755. Free of the Upholders' Co. by servitude, 2 October 1766. At 30 St Paul's Churchyard in 1770 but declared bankrupt in 1772. His business was operating from an address in King St, Golden Sq. in 1792 and by 1794 he was living in Dover St. [D; GL, Upholders' Co. records; Bailey's list of bankrupts; Heal]

Pincombe, Abraham, 64 Cumberland St, Devonport, Devon, carver, gilder and ornithologist (1830). [D]

Pindar, John, Margate, Kent, cm (1794). [D]

Pindar, William Thornton, 33 Carr Lane, Hull, Yorks., cm (1834–35). In 1835 described as a shopkeeper. [D]

Pinder (or Pindar), James, Westgate, Louth, Lincs., cm and joiner (1826–35). [D]

Pinder, John, Lancaster, cm (1784–95). App. to T. Lister in 1784 and named in the Gillow records, 1788–90 and 1792–95. [Westminster Ref. Lib., Gillow]

Pinder, Robert, Hunslet, Leeds, Yorks., cm (1817). [D]

Pinder, Thomas, Liverpool, cm (1760). His app. James Golding was declared free in 1760. [Freemen committee bk]

Pindergate, Daniel, 25 Bow St, Covent Gdn, London, upholder and cm (1790–93). [D]

Pine, Thomas, George St, Devonport, Devon, carver and gilder (1814). [D]

Pineh, John, 3 Holywell Lane, Shoreditch, chair and sofa maker (1839). [D]

Pingstone, John, Bristol, basket and chairmaker (1822–39). At Nicholas St, 1822–26, King St, Queen Sq. in 1827 and Back St near Crow Lane, 1828–39. [D]

Pinhorne, Charles, Shaftesbury, Dorset, upholder and cm (1740). In March 1740 took out insurance cover of £500. [GL, Sun MS vol. 54, p. 399]

Pini, Joseph, London, carver, gilder, looking glass and barometer maker (1835–40). At 1 Princes St, Bedford Row in 1835 but by the following year the number had changed to 3. In 1837 at Leather Lane, Holborn and from 1838 at 23 Brook St, Holborn. In 1839 listed as Joseph Pini & Co. [D; Goodison, *Barometers*]

Pink, Joseph, East St, Southampton, Hants., chairmaker and japanner (1811). [D]

Pinkard, R., Cambridge, u (1731). Paid by St John's College in 1731 for material and work on new curtains for the Lodge.

Pinkerd, John, Ratcliffe Cross, London, u (1729). In May 1729 insured a house and other buildings. [GL, Sun MS vol. 28, 8 May 1729]

Pinkey, Joseph, Middleton-in-Teesdale, Co. Durham, cm and joiner (1828). [D]

Pinks, William, 7 Cobham Row, Clerkenwell, London, carver and gilder (1835–39). [D]

Pinman, George, Braughin, Herts., cm (1839). [D]

Pinnagar, —, 1 Edgware Rd, London, japanner (1809). [D]

Pinner, Robert, Louth, Lincs., cm and u (1788–94). Advertised in May 1789 for two journeymen cm and a joiner, and similar advertisements also appeared in March 1790 and May 1791. His name appears in the Massingberd account bk for 9 April 1788 when he was paid £3 16s 6d for mattresses and children's stools. His bankruptcy was announced, *Derby Mercury*, 13 February 1794. [*Lincoln, Rutland and Stamford Mercury*, 8 May 1789, 12 March 1790, 13 May 1791; Lincoln RO, MM 9110]

Pinnock, John, Devizes, Wilts., cm, upholder, carver and gilder (1786). His trade card [Heal Coll., BM] is illustrated with engravings of a chair, an oval mirror and a serpentine-fronted chest of drawers. His bankruptcy was announced, *Gents Mag.*, January 1786.

Pinnock, John, High St, Watford, Herts., cm and u (1838–39). [D]

Pinsent, Henry, 22 Guildford St, Russell Sq., London, carpenter and u (1820). [D]

Piotti, James, Hull, Yorks., carver, gilder and looking-glass maker (1806–23). At Queen St in 1806 and from 1814 the number is shown as 2. A directory of 1810, however gives an address at Myton Gate. Employed at Burton Constable, Yorks. as a carver. [D; *C. Life*, 17 June 1976, pp. 1622–24]

Pipe, Edward, Loddon, Norfolk, turner and chairmaker (1839). [D]

Pipe, John, Bingay, Suffolk, cm (1824). [D]

Piper, Christopher, 26 High St, Marylebone, London, cm (1829). [D]

Piper, James, High St, Bewdley, Worcs., cm (1820). [D]

Piper, Philip, Hailsham, Sussex, cm (1839). [D]

Pippin, John, High Wycombe, Bucks., chairmaker (1836). Daughter bapt. in 1836. [PR (bapt.)]

Pirkin, Thomas, Liverpool, cm (1807). Married at St Ann's Church Miss Elizabeth Harrison. [*Liverpool Chronicle*, 4 November 1807] A Thomas Perkins was trading in Liverpool as a cm, 1821–29.

Pishot, John, 13 Upper Eaton Sq., Pimlico. London, carver and gilder (1808). [D]

Pistell, William, High St, Winchester, Hants., carver and gilder (1770). Advertised that he was from London. He claimed to be able to carve 'in Wood or Stone all Sorts of Monuments, Tombs, Head-Stones and Chimney Pieces; and other Ornaments viz., Frames for Looking-Glasses, Pictures, Tables and Chairs; Brackets for Candlesticks, Girandoles etc. in the newest & most modern Taste'. [*Reading Mercury*, 9 July 1770]

Pistor, Thomas, 'The Cabinet', Ludgate Hill, London, joiner and cm (1694–d. by 1711). A member of the Joiners' Co. and a signatory of a petition presented by that Company to the City of London in 1694. Insured property in Bell Ct, Moorfields on lease to various persons 1702–09. Dead by March 1711 when his stock in the Ludgate Hill premises was sold off. This consisted of 'Three fine japan'd and walnut cabinetts, five walnut, one India scrutore, one wainscott Desk and Bookcase on Drawers, one japan'd Tortoiseshell and black plate case, and three fine Princewood strong Boxes India japan'd glass table ... one japan'd chimney glass, some japan'd swing glasses'. A kingwood fall-front cabinet formerly in the collection of the Hon. Basil Ionides is inscribed in the interior 'Mr. Thomas Pistor, Ludgate Hill, London'. [*Furn. Hist*, 1974; GL, Hand in Hand MS vol. 2, refs 2995, 2995, 2996; *Spectator*, 21 March 1711; *GCM*]

Pitcher, Amos, Lime St, Axminster, Devon, cm (1830). [D]

Pitches, Thomas, London, carver and gilder (1800–35). At 112 Bishopsgate Without 1800–09, 208 Shoreditch 1811–25, 16 High St, Shoreditch 1829 and 10 Norton Folgate 1835. In 1820 and 1829 listed as looking-glass manufacturer. [D]

Pitchford, John, Shrewsbury, Salop, cm (1676). [Freemen rolls]

Pite, Thomas, parish of St Peter, Ipswich, Suffolk, cm (1820). Later parish of St Nicholas (?). Married on 19 September 1820. [Suffolk RO, FAA: 50/2/119]

Pitkins, Roger, Little Shear Lane, near Temple Bar, London, u (1702–19). Also owned another property in Little Shear Lane in 1702 and one in Bishopsgate Without in 1719. Both properties were leased out to others. [GL, Hand in Hand MS vol. 2, ref. 2952; vol. 10, ref. 15881]

Pitman, Cuthbert, London, upholder (1728). Son of Robert Pitman, freemen and poulterer of London. Brother of Robert Pitman, upholder. Cuthbert Pitman was made free of the Upholders' Co. by redemption 5 June 1728. [GL, Upholders' Co. records]

Pitman, John, Sherborne, Dorset, cm (1722). In 1722 took app. named Bonnall. [S of G, app. index]

Pitman, Robert, London, upholder (1705–14). Son of Robert Pitman, freeman and poulterer of London. Brother of Cuthbert Pitman. App. to Thomas Nicoll on 5 December 1705 and free of the Upholders' Co. by servitude, March 1713/14. [GL, Upholders' Co. records]

Pitt, —, 'The Venetian Curtain', about the middle of London Bridge, facing the Chapel House, London, u (1747–49). [Heal] Possibly Cecil Pitt.

Pitt, Benjamin, Gloucester, cm (1821). Child bapt. at the Church of St Catherine. [PR (bapt.)]

Pitt, Cecil, London, u, appraiser and auctioneer (1754–95). It is possible that he was the Pitt who was trading as a u from an address on London Bridge, 1747–49. At 'The Rising Sun & Fox', five doors from the corner of New Broad St, Moorfields in 1754. A trade card from this period [Leverhulme Coll., MMA, NY] states that he bought and sold 'all manner of Household Goods as Standing Beds & Bedding, Chests of Drawers, Desks & Book Cases, Buroe desks, Card, Dining, Breakfast & Dressing Tables (in Mahogany, Walnuttree or Wainscot) Chairs of all sorts, Sette, and Buroe Bedsteads, Sconces, Pair Chimney & dressing Glasses, with all manner of Upholstery Cabinet & Brasier Goods: new & Old'. The elaborate frame of this trade card is identical with that of Samuel Phene, who was trading in the same area of London at this period, and may suggest some degree of co-operation between the two makers. By the mid 1760s Pitt had changed his trade sign to that of 'The Royal Tent', and gave his address in Moorfields as 'four doors from the corner of New Broad Street and almost facing Bedlam Walk'. When the streets were numbered this address became 10 Brookers Row, Moorfields and directories show him at this location, 1767–75. The number changed to 11 (1775–81), 13 (1782–88), 23 (1790–91) and back to 13 (1792–95). From 1769 the business traded as Pitt & Chessey (late Rodwell). By the mid 1770s there was more than one member of the Pitt family involved and in 1775 the business was known as Pitt, Pitt & Chessey and in 1777 as Pitt, Chessey & Pitt. Cecil Pitt took apps between 1754–75. His trade card [Heal Coll., BM] giving 'The Royal Tent', Moorfields address, states that he dealt generally in household goods, new and secondhand, and made bed furniture and curtains.

Many members of this family were in the upholstery trade in London. A John Pitt, possibly his father, traded at 'The Rising Sun', Moorfields, 1714–26. Another John Pitt was at 25 New Broad St, 1781–84; and a James Pitt traded in the area, c.1760 and 1808–37; and a Pitt & Son, 1813–19. [D; Heal]

Pitt, Cobbett & Son, London(?), japanners (1833). At the Stud House, Hampton Court, Middlx, undertook the japanning of

43 washstands and dressing tables, painted a press in imitation of mahogany, and stained and varnished a large Gothic sideboard. Their bill, dated 30 June 1833, amounted to £25 16s 9d. [Windsor Royal Archives, account bk 1833, 41–P]

Pitt, Francis, Dudley St, Kidderminster, Worcs., cm and u (1835). [D]

Pitt, James, 'The Easy Chair', near Bethlem Walk, between New Broad St and Old Bethlem, no. 7 Old Moor Fields, London, cm and upholder (c.1760). Only known from his trade card [Banks Coll., BM] Appears to have been related to Cecil Pitt and other makers of the same surname in this area of London at this period.

Pitt, James, Moorfields, London, u and cm (1808–37). At 10 Brokers Row, Moorfields, 1808–15, and 25 New Broad St, 1820–37. A John Pitt occupied the New Broad St address 1781–84, and several other members of the family in the area were in the furniture industry. [D]

Pitt, James Thomas, Lower North Gate St, Gloucester, turner and chairmaker (1822–30). [D]

Pitt, John, 'The Rising Sun', Moorfields, London, u (1714–26). Possibly the father of Cecil Pitt, who was trading at the sign of 'The Rising Sun & Fox', Moorfields by 1754. Probably also related to James and John Pitt trading in the same area and in the same trade. [Heal]

Pitt, John, Slough, Bucks., wheelwright and chairmaker (d.1759). His trade label is recorded beneath the seat of a Windsor chair. The address can only be deciphered in part and reads '...LOU .... DSO'. Parish records of Upton cum Chalvey (Slough) record his death on 13 January 1759. [*Furn. Hist.*, 1978, 1979]

Pitt, John, 25 New Broad St, Moorfields, London, upholder (1781–84). [D] James Pitt traded from this address 1820–37. Probably related to Cecil Pitt.

Pitt, Paul, Slough, Bucks., chairmaker (1798). [D] See John Pitt of Slough.

Pitt, Richard, London, upholder, cm, undertaker, later carver and gilder (1778–1809). In 1778 at 5 Princes St, Coventry St, Leicester Fields where he was trading as an upholder, cm and undertaker. He was clearly operating a substantial business for in that year he took out insurance cover of £1,500 of which £1,050 was for utensils and stock. By January 1780 he was, however, bankrupt. Apart from the Princes St address the bankruptcy notice also added 'late of St. Albans-St., Westminster'. By 1784 he had recommenced trading, but possibly lacking the capital to re-enter his old trade, he took up that of carver and gilder. He used the Princes St address in 1784, but then moved to 80 Berwick St where he insured goods for £200. At 20 Gerrard St, Soho, 1790–93, and was at 86 Wardour St, Soho in 1809. [D; GL, Sun MS vol. 262, p. 525; vol. 342, ref. 530335; *Sussex Weekly Advertiser*, 31 January 1780]

Pitt, Richard, Haymarket, London, upholder (1782). [Bailey's list of bankrupts]

Pitt, Richard, London, Looking glass and picture frame maker (1820–29). At 3 Francis St, Brewer St in 1820 and 4 Saville Pl., Lambeth in 1829. [D]

Pitt, Robert, London, cm etc. (1808–28). At Green Walk, Blackfriars as a broker and cm in 1808, and 87 Broad Walk, Blackfriars Rd, 1827. [D]

Pitt, Samuel, Dudley Staffs., carver, gilder, u and bell hanger (1818–30). Trading at High St, 1818–28, and Hall St in 1820. [D]

Pitt, Saul, Dudley, Staffs., cm/u (1822). [D]

Pitt, Thomas, London, upholder and auctioneer (1772–94). Son of George Pitt of East Cheap, Cannon St, London. Free of the Upholders' Co. by redemption, 5 May 1772. Living in Southwark, 1772–78, but by 1778–79 trading at 26 Addle St, Aldermanbury. By 1780 had moved to 26 Red Cross St, Cripplegate, an address at which he was to continue until at least 1794. [D; GL, Upholders' Co. records]

Pitt, Thomas, Egham, Surrey, chairmaker (1794). [D]

Pitt, William, 14 Webber St, Blackfriars Rd, New Cut, cm (1829–39). In 1829 listed as cm but in 1839 as furniture broker. [D]

Pitt & Son, 5 and 6 Broker's Row, Moorfields, London, u and undertaker (1813–19). A substantial enterprise with insurance cover of £1,800 in 1813–14 of which £1,600 was for stock at 6 and £200 for stock at 5 Broker's Row. A James Pitt, probably another member of the family traded at 10 Broker's Row, 1808–15. [D; GL, Sun MS vol. 462, 7 April 1814, ref. 893056] See Cecil Pitt.

Pittaway, John, 47 Baldwins Gdns, London, cm and hardwareman (1803–08). In 1803 took out insurance cover of £900 of which £800 was for utensils and stock. The corresponding figures for 1808 are £1,000 and £600. [GL, Sun MS vol. 427, ref. 747440; vol. 446, ref. 816326]

Pitterd, Samuel, 63 Aldersgate St, London, carver (1775). In 1775 insured his house for £100. [GL, Sun MS vol. 238, p. 238]

Pitts, Carill, London, upholder (1746–54). Member of the Fishmongers' Co. but by trade an upholder. Took as app. James Robinson, 1746–54. [GL, Upholders' Co. records]

Pitts, Ebenezer, Drapery, Northampton, carver and gilder (1830). [D]

Pitts, John, London, plate case maker and cm (1810–20). In 1810 at 5 Hunts Ct, Castle St where he took out insurance cover of £500 which included £200 for utensils and stock. By January 1820 at 3 Upper Castle St, Leicester Sq. Total insurance cover was now £1,600 but of this only £100 covered his workshop behind the dwelling house and £150 utensils and stock. [GL, Sun MS vol. 453, ref. 850680; vol. 483, refs 962578, 96279]

Pitts, John, Cable St, Oldham Rd, Manchester, cm (1836). [D]

Pitts, Joseph, address unknown (1784). Supplied Sir John Griffin Griffin of Audley End, Essex with a 'strong Iron Bound Wains[t.] Chest Lind with green Baise' which was charged at £3 3s. [Essex RO, D/DBy/S42/4]

Pittway, John, London, cm (1803–39). At 47 Baldwins Gdns, 1803–11. In 1811 described as 'mahogany & inlaid case maker'. In 1803 insurance cover was £900 of which £800 was for utensils and stock. The corresponding figures for 1808 are £1,000 and £600. No further references occur to this maker until 1839 when he was at 4 Kirby St, Hatton Gdn, as a cm and u. [D; GL, Sun MS vol. 427, ref. 747440; vol. 446, ref. 816326]

Pivett, Christopher, York, carver and gilder (d.1796). Died on 8 August 1796 at the age of 93. Referred to as 'the well known Mr. Christopher Pivett' and the fact that his death was recorded in a Liverpool newspaper might suggest a more than local reputation, though whether this was for his workmanship or advanced age span is not known. [*Billinge's Liverpool Advertiser*, 22 August 1796]

Pixley, Samuel, 2 Upton Pl., Commercial Rd, Stepney, London, cm and u (1826–28). [D]

Pizzala, Joseph, 84 Leather Lane, Holborn, London, looking-glass manufacturer (1813–39). The directory entry for 1837 is M. Pizzala & Son. [D]

Pizzey, Thomas, London, cm, blind manufacturer and u (1822–40). At 4 Chapel St, Curtain St or Holywell Mkt, 1822–27, but by 1832 at 81 Old St Rd, an address that continued to be used until at least 1840. [D; Shoreditch archives, Rose Lipman Lib., MS 3545, p. 31; GL, Sun MS vol. 575, ref. 1339355]

Pizzie, Alexander, London, upholder and cm (1777–1811). Son of Caleb Pizzie of Albourne, Wilts., farmer. App. to Daniel Hutchinson of the Skinners' Co., 1 April 1777 and free of the Upholders' Co. by servitude, 7 September 1785. At 13 Fenchurch St by July 1786 when he took out insurance cover of £1,000 of which half was for utensils and stock. At this address until 1802 and in that year moved to 2 Cullum St at which he was to continue until 1811. Included in the list of master cabinet makers in Sheraton's *Cabinet Dictionary*, 1803. [D; GL, Sun MS vol. 339, p. 100; Upholders' Co. records]

Pizzie, Thomas, 6 Bath St, Bath, Som., cm, undertaker and auctioneer (1826). [D]

Pizzotti, John, 36 Spear St, Manchester, carver and gilder (1834–40). [D]

Place, Mary, Bedale, Yorks., cm (1823). [D]

Plain, James, Redenhall, Norfolk, cm (1757). In 1757 took app. named Hinchley. [S of G, app. index]

Planner, John, London, u (1768–87). At 61 Bartholomew Close, 1768–1784; 11 Bedford St, Strand in 1784 and Castle St, 1787. Bankrupt 1787. [D; Bailey's list of bankrupts]

Plant, George, 'The Crown & Cushion' in Princes St, opposite the end of Gerrard St, Soho, London, upholder (d.1747). [Heal]

Plant, James, Chesterfield, Derbs., cm and joiner (1793–1822). Recorded at Playhouse Yd, 1818–22. [D]

Plant, James, Pitt St, Manchester, cm (1804). [D]

Plant, James, Templar St, Leeds, Yorks., cm (1822). [D]

Plant, John, 4 Briercliffe Buildings, Salford, Lancs., cm (1804–17). [D]

Plant, Joseph, Liverpool, cm (1827–37). At Elizabeth Ct, Carlton St in 1827 and 2 Springfield St in 1837. [D]

Plant, Thomas, Mill St, Congleton, Cheshire, cm (1818–22). [D]

Plant, William, Baker St, Wolverhampton, Staffs., cm (1770). [D]

Planta, John, Fulneck, near Leeds, Yorks., cm (1764–c.1825). John Planta, born in Jamaica on 16 November 1764, was received into the Moravian community at Fulneck in 1798, where he worked as a cm, the latest *Directory* entry being *Baines*, 1822, although it may allude to his son, another John (b.1802) who was trained in the same trade. Planta specialized in making refined mahogany flax spinning-wheels, often enhanced with crossbanding and ivory fitments; a little drawer below the platform usually contains a printed label: 'Made by JOHN PLANTA, | AT | FULNECK, near LEEDS'. (Fig. 14). Planta's wheels all conform to a distinctive pattern, although he produced utility, standard and de luxe versions, sometimes with extra attachments such as an articulated candle-arm, a cup for holding water or a turned stump to assist in making thread up into hanks. Planta's wheels incorporate an automatic bobbin traverse to ensure even winding, a sophisticated mechanism invented in 1793 by John Antes, a fellow Moravian from Fulneck. Planta received internal payments for various small articles such as bellows, embroidery frames, firescreens, tea-caddies, work-boxes, writing desks, etc., but his label has never been noted on such items. An elegant wheel made by Planta about 1801 for Mrs Rhodes of Armley House, Leeds is now at Temple Newsam; other labelled examples are preserved at the V & A; Cannon Hall, Yorks.; Heath Hall, Manchester and Colonial Williamsburg; over twenty models have been recorded. [Archives at the Church of the United Brethren and the Boys' School, Fulneck; C. G. Gilbert, 'John Planta of Fulneck', *Furn. Hist.*, 1970]
C.G.G.

Plasket, John, Liverpool, cm (1823–37). At 10 Slater St with a shop at 9 Seel St, 1823–29, but from 1834–37 at 52 Duke St. [D]

Plasket, Robert, Newcastle, cm (d. 1801). Will proved on 3 December 1801. [Probate records]

Platt, Edmund, address unrecorded, carver and gilder (1775). Subscribed to Thomas Malton's *Compleat Treatise on Perspective*, 1775.

Platt, John, London, cabinet and chair maker, u (1749–70). In King St in 1749 but his trade card of c.1760 gives the address as Bedford Ct, Covent Gdn. Probably the 'Mr. Platts' who in 1754 subscribed to Chippendale's *Director*. The furniture illustrated on his trade card is very much in the Chippendale tradition. Illustrated are a fine ribband back chair and an elaborate cabinet on stand in the Chinese style. The fine Rococo frame which surrounds the text also supports two Chinese figures. It is no surprise to find that the engravers of this card were Darly & Edwards. One copy of the card is in the Heal Coll., BM, and another amongst the Grimston Papers at the Humberside RO. He may thus have supplied furniture to Kilnwick House, Yorks. and it has been suggested that the Chinese bed at Sledmere might be his work. He was certainly supplying furniture to the 3rd Duke of Ancaster on an extensive scale from 1763. For the period 1763–65 payments amounted to £254 18s and in June 1770 the balance of a bill for £175 for furniture supplied to Richmond House was settled. In June 1771 £410 10s was paid for furniture supplied to the Duke for Grimsthorpe, Lincs, and for his London house in Berkeley Sq. between May 1768 and May 1770. Platt must have died c.1770, for a payment on 3 June 1771 was to his executors Thomas Hearnden and a Mr Middleton. A balance of £108 9s was settled in 1772. [Heal; Westminster poll bk; V&A archives; Lincoln RO, 2 ANC 6/8, pp. 152, 203, 249, 2 ANC 6/13–15]

Platt, Joseph, Leeds, Yorks., journeyman cm (1791). Included in the list of journeymen cm approving of the contents of the *Leeds Cabinet and Chair Makers Book of Prices*, 1791.

Platt, Joseph, Stockwellgate, Mansfield, Notts., cm and joiner (1822). [D]

Platt, Joseph, Priestpopple, Hexham, Northumb., joiner and cm (1827). [D]

Platt, Samuel, Hale, Lancs., cm (1831). In January 1831 the overseers of the poor of the parish of Hale advertised for the apprehension of Platt who had deserted his family and left three children chargeable to the parish. He was said to be about 30 years of age. [*Liverpool Mercury*, 21 January 1831]

Platt, Thomas, 9 Groves Ct, Bolton St, Liverpool, cm (1790). Son of Ralph Platt, shoemaker. Free 20 June 1790. [Freemen reg.]

Platt, Thomas, High St, Wisbech, Cambs., carver and gilder (1839). [D]

Platts, Luke, Chester Rd, Birkenhead, Cheshire, joiner and cm (1834–35). At 70 Chester Rd in 1834 but in 1835 the number was 72. [D]

Plaw, William, Kings Rd, Fulham, London, builder, carpenter and rustic chair maker (1839). [D]

Plaxton, William, Hog Lane, Covent Gdn, London, cm (1749). [Westminster poll bk]

Player, James, Gloucester, cm (1824). Child bapt. in 1824, parish of St John the Baptist. [PR (bapt.)]

Player, Samuel, 9 Artillery Lane, Bishopsgate, London, carver and gilder (1839). [D]

Player, Timothy, Woodmancote, Dursley, Glos., u (1820). [D]

Player, William, Gloucester, cm (1826). Child bapt. in 1826 at St Aldgate's Church. [PR (bapt.)]

Playford, Thomas, Walsingham, Norfolk, cm, chairmaker and joiner (1822–39). [D]

Playle, Richard, Fetter Lane, London, picture frame maker (1768). A freeman of the Merchant Taylors' Co. Licenced in

1768 to employ a non-freeman for three months. [GL, City Licence bk, vol. 6]

Playsted, —, London, u (1793). Subscribed to Sheraton's *Drawing Book*, 1793.

Playstick, Thomas, Cutlers Hall, London, upholder (1781). Free of the Upholders' Co. on 6 June 1781 under the terms of the 1750 Upholders' Act. [GL, Upholders' Co. records]

Pleasant, Stephen, Easthope, Southwell, Notts., cm (1828). [D]

Pleasants, Robert, parish of St Peter Mancroft, Norwich, u (1675–1714). Son of Robert Pleasants snr, and free, 3 July 1675. [Freemen reg.; poll bks]

Pletts, James, St Mary's Chare, Hexham, Northumb., turner and bed post carver (1827). [D]

Plomer, Peter, Canterbury, Kent, cm (1731). [Freemen rolls]

Plowman, George Aram, High St, Wells, Norfolk, cm and joiner (1822–39). [D]

Plowman, Henry, Surrey St, Croydon, Surrey, cm and u (1839). [D]

Plowman, J., 181 High St, Shadwell, London, chair stuffer (1826). [D]

Plowman, M., 5 Gloucester Pl., Commercial Rd, London, cm (1814–20). [D]

Plucknett, John, 21 Mint St, Southwark, London, chair and sofa maker (1826). [D]

Pluckrose, Joseph, 'The Rising Sun', Fleet Ditch, St Brides, London, u (1714–32). Free of the Upholders' Co., 9 February 1714. Took app. James Burley, 1717–23. In February 1724 insured his goods and merchandise at the Fleet Ditch address, which was his dwelling house, for £1,000. [GL, Upholders' Co. records; Sun MS vol. 19, ref. 34824; Heal]

Pluckrose, Robert, 'The Sun and Half Moon', Fleet Ditch, London, u (1718–20). Free of the Upholders' Co., 3 September 1718. In 1720 a fire broke out at his warehouse and he tried to claim for the destruction caused. There was, however, a suspicion that he had caused the fire deliberately. He had insurance cover for £1,000 on the contents of the warehouse, but it was alleged their true value was only £300. He was summoned to appear before the Lord Mayor. [GL, Upholders' Co. records; *Weekly Journal*, 4 and 11 June 1720]

Plukenett, Thomas, High Holborn, London, cm (1750–63). Regularly supplied furniture to the 4th Duke of Bedford for Bedford House, London, Woburn Abbey and the Duke's house at Streatham, London. The furniture appears to have been simple functional items which included wainscot dressing tables, matted chairs, mahogany card tables, chests of drawers and dressing glasses etc. The total cost for the period 1750–59 only amounted to about £300. [D; Bedford Office, London; *Apollo*, January 1956, p. 10]

Plumer, John, Butcher Row, Horsham, Sussex, u and auctioneer (1811–32). [D]

Plumer, Thomas, Horsham, Sussex, upholder (1753–86). In 1753 took app. named Thomas. In 1780 advertised for a further app. At this date Plumer was also trading as a tallow chandler and soap boiler. [D; S of G, app. index; *Sussex Weekly Advertiser*, 20 March 1780]

Plummer, George, Reading, Berks., upholder (1754). [Poll bk]

Plummer, Thomas, address unknown, cm (early 18th century). A cabinet with many drawers is recorded in a private collection with the inscription 'Thomas Plummer me perfeci primo die Decembris 1704'. [V&A archives]

Plumpton, John, 48 Newington Causeway, London, writing desk and dressing case maker (1829). [D]

Plumridge, James, West Wycombe, Bucks., chairmaker (b. c.1784–1841). Aged 57 at the date of the 1841 Census.

Plumridge, John, West Wycombe, Bucks., chairmaker (b. c.1818–41). Aged 23 at the date of the 1841 Census.

Plumridge, William, West Wycombe, Bucks., chairmaker (b. c.1819–41). Aged 22 at the date of the 1841 Census.

Plumtree, George, Hundleby, Lincs., cm and joiner (1835). [D]

Plunkett, Elizabeth, Steep Hill, Lincoln, working u (1826). [D]

Plunkett, Luke, Simpson St, Liverpool, cm (1816). Free 16 June 1816. Freemen rolls]

Plunkett, William, High Holborn, London, cm and broker (1745). On 6 March 1745 married widow Horne at the Church of St George, Bloomsbury. He was described as 'wealthy' and she as 'a gentlewoman of great accomplishments and a very handsome fortune'. A Thomas Plukenett was trading as a cm in High Holborn, 1750–63, and may well have been related. [*General Advertiser*, 8 March 1745]

Pluriet, Clem, Bradford-on-Avon, Wilts., cm (1760). In 1760 took app. named Hunt. [S of G, app. index]

Plush, William, cm (1803). Subscribed to Sheraton's *Cabinet Dictionary*, 1803.

Pluva, John, Queen St, Bath, Som., upholder (1784). [D]

Pochaine, John, Newcastle, barometer and thermometer, looking-glass and picture frame maker (1804). In July 1804 announced his move from the foot of Side to the west side of Dean St. [*Newcastle Courant*, 21 July 1804]

Pocock, A., address unknown, cm (1809–14). Payments to this maker totalling £105 3s were made in 1809, 1812 and 1814 by Nicholas Pearse of Loughton, Essex and London. [Essex RO, D/DHt A1/3, A1/4]

Pocock, John, Hungerford, Berks., cm (1745–59). Took apps named Hoare in 1743, Lynch in 1744 and Heath in 1759. [S of G, app. index]

Pocock, John Wright, 26 Southampton St, London, see William Pocock.

Pocock, L., Ottery St Mary, Devon, cm, chairmaker and auctioneer (1829). Took out a licence as an auctioneer, 10 February 1829. [*Exeter Flying Post*, 12 February 1829]

Pocock, Obadiah, London, cm and u (1808–27). At 43 Eagle St, Red Lion Sq. in 1808 and 80 Charlton St, Somers Town in 1827. [D]

Pocock, W., Leyton, London, cm (1824). Bankruptcy announced, *Brighton Gazette*, 9 December 1824.

Pocock, William, London, cm and u (b.1750–1825). Initially practised the trade of carpenter in London. He was made a member of the Carpenters' Co. by redemption in 1782. By 1786 he was operating a flourishing building business in Essex and it was through this connection that he first became interested in the cabinetmaking trade. From 1801–25 he had showrooms at 26 Southampton St, Strand and the business is described in directories up to 1808 as a cabinet and upholstery warehouse. Later descriptions call the business a patent mattress warehouse. He was joined by his son John by 1809 and the business traded as Pocock & Son 1809–11, and Pocock & Co., 1819–20. Mis-management by the son appears to have contributed to the bankruptcy of the business in February 1825. Only John is cited in the bankruptcy proceedings, and his father may by this date have had no part in its management.

Pocock appears to have had an ingenious mind and the business acumen to satisfy the public interest in furniture displaying novelty or involved mechanical devices. This could be marketed as 'patent furniture' and Pocock did in fact take out a patent in 1805 for an extending dining table, and a number of these tables were sold under the title 'Patent Sympathetic and Self-acting Dining Table'. An engraved brass plate with this description is known on a number of existing examples. The important feature of this table was the ease with which it could be expanded. If one side of the table was pulled towards one the other side automatically receded and a leaf rose from the centre to fill the space. A single person could without assistance effect the expansion or reduction of the table. Trade cards [Banks Coll., BM] show that he had an interest in extending tables from the commencement of the business, and that he also offered library tables with rising tops, to suit both a sitting and standing posture. An example of one of these is known with a label describing it as 'Pocock's Patent Office or Library Table'. A two page advertisement listing an extensive range of such furniture has been located in the Foreign Office papers relating to Spain for 1814. [PRO, FO 185/50] Such patent furniture may have been thought suitable for military personnel posted to the Peninsular. His 'Patent Sofa Beds … suitable either for Camp or Barracks or on Board a Ship' were said to be 'highly approved by distinguished Officers of the Army and Navy'. Pocock also made a particular feature of invalid furniture which included 'The Patent Boethema or Rising Matress' to aid persons to sit up in bed, 'Go to Bed Chairs' to assist infirm persons to get into and out of bed, 'Cradle Beds' which enabled bed linen to be changed without disturbing patients and even 'Invalid Vibrating Pendulem Beds' to give gentle exercise to the bed-ridden or lull them to sleep. Merlin's reading and gouty chairs were also featured. In February 1813 Pocock's 'Reclining Patent Chair' was illustrated in Ackermann's *Repository of Arts*. This item featured an adjustable back, a double footstool which could be extended into a couch, and an adjustable reading desk bedecked with carved classical ornament in the antique taste. 'Treble Reflecting Looking Glasses' were another of the lines that he offered.

In addition to these patent items William Pocock offered 'every article of Cabinet or Upholstery Furniture, from the plain and useful to the most costly and magnificent'. The only recorded patron of Pocock was the 2nd Earl of Rosslyn who in connection with his London house in St James's Sq. settled an account for £33 in 1809. There can be little doubt that the trade was of an extensive nature however. In February 1823 William Pocock took out insurance cover for £3,000, jointly with his son John. [D; Joy, *English Furniture 1800–51*, pp. 206–10; GL, Sun MS vol. 498, ref. 1001603; *Brighton Gazette*, 24 February 1825; Scottish RO, GD 164/Box 41/291/1; *Conn.*, April 1970, p. 68; September 1978, p. 31; Phillips', 15 September 1964, lot 17, 15 June 1971, lot 71; Sotheby's, 19 August 1974, lot 84] B.A.

Pocock, William, 2 Ship St, Brighton, Sussex, cm and u (1814–40). A son and two daughters bapt. at St Nicholas Church, 1814–22. [D; PR (bapt.)]

Podmore, George, Eastgate St, Chester, u and cm (1824–34). Free 16 October 1824. In March 1833 advertised that he was selling off the entire stock of Podmore & Morris 'at prime cost' from the shop at Hotel Row, Eastgate St from which they had traded before the business ceased. He had on offer 'Cabinet Furniture of every description, looking glasses, carpets, druggets, hearth rugs etc'. His involvement in the sale of this trade stock suggests that he was related to William Podmore, one of the partners in Podmore & Morris. [D; freemen rolls; *Chester Courant*, 26 March 1833]

Podmore, James, Bridge St Row, Chester, cm and u (1831–40). Free on 20 April 1831. At Bridge St Row in 1840. [D; freemen rolls]

Podmore, Joseph, Chester, carver and gilder (1827–40). In August 1827 married Miss Mary Gough of Chester. At St Werburgh St in 1828 but in Watergate Row, 1834–40. [D; *Chester Chronicle*, 24 August 1827, 1 May 1840]

Podmore, William, Eastgate St, Chester, u and cm (b.1779–d.1832). Free on 9 December 1809. Claimed to have been employed by Joseph Powell for twenty years in his business in Eastgate St, Chester and to have been for eight years his 'foreman and prime superintendent'. No Joseph

Powell has been traced, but a John Powell was active as an u in Eastgate St at this period, and the incorrect Christian name may have been used. When Powell, his employer, ceased trading in 1815 he set up on his own as a working u and subsequently took three apps: John Simcock in 1820, Samuel Dale in 1827 and Edward Maddocks in 1830. In 1818 he was trading from an address in Eastgate St where in that year he was described as an u but by 1822 the business was an u and cabinet warehouse. His wife Ann died on 21 January 1827 aged 44 leaving a large family, and on 12 April of the same year his youngest daughter Elizabeth also died, aged 12. By this year, however, the business was in a phase of expansion. William Podmore had entered into a partnership with Edward Frodsham Powell and Thomas Powell and they were trading under the style Podmore & Powells. This business was sufficiently respected to be one of the places inspected by the 9th Duke and Duchess of St Albans when they visited the city. *Chester Courant*, 2 October 1829 reported the visit, stating that they inspected in the premises 'a magnificent sideboard exquisitely carved and manufactured' which was being produced to an order from Mr Leche of Carden. This item so impressed the Duke, who had married in 1827, that he placed an order for a similar item promising to forward the dimensions of the recess that it was intended to fit, and a drawing of the family arms to be carved in the centre. Only a month later the partners were advertising for a carver for the business. This enterprise did not endure for long, however, and on 26 June 1829 it was announced that the partnership was dissolved and in September of the same year a sale of the stock was advertised. Powell immediately set up another partnership with a man named Morris, trading as Podmore & Morris from the same address at Hotel Row, Eastgate St. By 21 August 1829 they were advertising their services which included 'Modern and Antique CARVING and GILDING to any pattern by the best workmen in each branch and men sent to any part of the country.' A further partner, George Podmore, possibly William's son was taken into partnership in 1832 and the firm then styled itself as Podmore, Morris & Podmore. They also announced their intention of adding auctioneering and appraising to their activities. On 23 June 1832 William Podmore died after a short illness, aged 53. [D; freemen rolls; app. bks; *Chester Chronicle*, 2 June 1815, 27 April 1827, 1 May 1829, 26 June 1829, 28 August 1829, 28 September 1829; *Chester Courant*, 23 January 1827, 2 October 1827, 26 June 1832; *Liverpool Mercury*, 9 November 1827]

Poile, Samuel, Upper George St, Greenwich, London, carver and gilder (1838–39). [D]

Point, John, Stoke's Croft, Bristol, cm (1793–99). [D]

Pointer, William, Leeds, Yorks., journeyman cm (1791–93). Included in the list of journeyman cm assenting to piece rates laid down in the *Leeds Cabinet and Chair Makers Book of Prices*, 1791. In 1793 subscribed to Sheraton's *Drawing Book*.

Pointon, William, High St, Shifnal, Salop, cm (1840). [D]

Polding, Henry, London, u and cm (1820–25). At 33 Albemarle St, Piccadilly, 1820–23, but in 1825 shown in one directory at 28. Another directory of 1825 lists the address as 26 Duke St, Grosvenor Sq. [D]

Polhill, Edward, 7 Watling St, London, upholder (1756–78). Son of John Polhill of Lydd, Kent, riding officer. App. to David Langton on 27 February 1747 and free of the Upholders' Co. by servitude, 3 June 1756. At Watling St, 1763–78. Succeeded at this address by Lucy Polhill, possibly his widow. [D; GL, Upholders' Co. records]

Polhill, John, Ashford, Kent, upholder (1734). Freeman of Maidstone. [Maidstone poll bk]

Polhill, Lucy, 7 Watling St, London, upholder (1781–83). Successor to Edward Polhill at this address and possibly his widow. [D]

Poll, J. C., Town Green, Wymondham, Norfolk, cm (1839). [D]

Pollard, Austen, Smithy-stale, Halifax, Yorks., cm (1818). [D]

Pollard, Esther & Son, 20 George St, Halifax, Yorks., cm (1837). [D]

Pollard, J. A., London, chair and sofa manufacturer (1817–25). At 36 Castle St East, Oxford Mkt, 1817–19, and 25 Upper Marylebone St, 1825. [D]

Pollard, James, King St, Golden Sq., London, cm (1803). Subscribed to Sheraton's *Cabinet Dictionary*, 1803.

Pollard, James, 3 Howland St, Fitzroy Sq., London, cm, u and chair maker (1825–29). Possibly the J. A. Pollard, chair and sofa maker recorded in Castle St and Upper Marylebone St, 1817–25. [D]

Pollard, James, Chapel Rd, Southampton, Hants., cm (1839). [D]

Pollard, John, parish of St James, Bristol (1774–84). [Poll bks]

Pollard, John, Skeldergate, York, joiner, cm, u and shopkeeper (1823). [D]

Pollard, John, Halifax, Yorks., cm (1818–30). At Silver St, 1818–29, but in 1830 at 2 George St. [D]

Pollard, John, Prospect Pl., Exeter, Devon, cm (1823). Daughter Frances bapt. at St Mary Major, 18 September 1823. [PR (bapt.)]

Pollard, Samuel, Debenham, Suffolk, cm, wood turner and builder (1830). [D]

Pollard, William, 55 Hotwell, Bristol, cm and u (1820–25). [D]

Pollard, William, Oxenhope, near Keighley, Yorks., cm (1822). [D]

Pollard, William, 2 Black Swan Passage, Halifax, Yorks., cm and u (1830). [D]

Pollard, Zaccheus, parish of St Mary, Stamford, Lincs., joiner and cm (1832). [Poll bk]

Pollexfen, James, London, upholder (1707). Free of the Upholders' Co., 2 July 1707. [GL, Upholders' Co. records]

Polly, Richard, Lancaster, cm (1814–16). Named in the Gillow records in connection with a bookcase. [Westminster Ref. Lib., Gillow vol. 344/100, p. 2023]

Polti, Jno., 31 Central Mkt, Leeds, Yorks., carver, gilder and barometer etc. maker (1828). [D]

Polti, Joseph, Kirkgate, Leeds, Yorks., looking-glass and barometer maker (1822–34). At 7 Kirkgate in 1822 but from 1830–34 the number was 72, when he is listed as carver and gilder. [D; Goodison, *Barometers*]

Polti, L., Bristol, picture frame and looking-glass manufacturer (1826–30). At 16 Broad St, 1826–27 and St John's Steps, 1828–30. Bankruptcy announced, *Exeter Flying Post*, 11 March 1830. [D]

Pomeroy, George, Exeter, Devon, carver and gilder (1823–39). At Stepcote Hill in 1823, Pancras Lane in 1827 and Goldsmith St in 1829. A son and two daughters bapt., 1823–29. [PR (bapt.)]

Pomeroy, John, parish of St Sidwell, Exeter, Devon, cm (1821–28). Three sons bapt., 1821–28. [PR (bapt.)]

Poncia, John, 13 St Catherine's Sq., London, picture and looking-glass frame maker (1820). [D]

Pond, Samuel, Colchester and Chelmsford, Essex, u (1820–31). Recorded in the Colchester poll bks in 1820 and 1830–31 and in the Malden poll bk in 1826. Living in Colchester 1820 but in Chelmsford, 1826–31. [Poll bks]

Pond, Uriah, South St, Wincanton, Som., cm and u (1830). [D]

Ponder, Charles, Blackheath Hill, London, cm (1826). [D]

Ponett, William, St Paul and Bradninch, Exeter, Devon, cm (1803). [Militia Census]

Ponking, Francis, Fish St, Wallingford, Oxon., cm and u (1830–40). [D]

Ponsford, William, Exeter, Devon, cm (1816–24). At Fore St Hill, 1816–20 during which period three sons were bapt. at St John's Church. In January 1824 at North St when a further son was bapt. at St Paul's Church. [PR (bapt.)]

Ponsonby, Thomas, London, carver, gilder and glass grinder (1794–1840). Recorded by Heal at 33 Poultney St, Golden Sq. in 1794. At 17 Piccadilly from 1802–19, and then moved to Regent St where the number was 1 from 1820–27 and no. 32 from 1827. From 1806 advertised himself as an English and French plate glass warehouse and in 1825 as 'British plate glass warehouse and carver & gilder to His Majesty, and T.R.H. the Duchess of Gloucester, Princess Augusta & Princess Sophia of Gloucester'. By 1835 the business was trading as T. Ponsonby & Son. The firm used labels to identify some of their manufactures, and items noted include a pier glass in a Queen Anne style, and a small gilt octagonal top table with a painted top, c.1800, which was at Syon House, Brentford.

Their claims to royal patronage are amply documented. In 1807 a chimney glass was supplied for 'Her Majesty's Chinese Drawing Room at Frogmore' which had an enriched gilt frame and cost £170 5s. From 1838 considerable work was undertaken at Buckingham Palace, which included composition mouldings and tablets to picture frames, many new large gilt picture frames, console pier tables and other work. In total the sums were substantial and in December 1839 an account for £1,492 7s 1½d was submitted. Other patrons included Chandos Leigh Esq. who bought frames in 1815–16, costing £29 12s and the 3rd Marquess of Londonderry who used his services in 1820 in connection with the furnishing of Wynyard Hall, Co. Durham. [D; V&A 50–G–6 (1929); Windsor Royal Archives, 25249; Account bk, 1833–41, Box I, item 2; PRO, LC11/100–01, 110; Shakespeare Birthplace Trust, Leigh receipts, DR 18/5; Durham RO, D/LO/E 484]

Pont, Charles & Son, High St, Canterbury, Kent, cm and broker (1824). [D]

Pont, John, 6 High St, Canterbury, Kent, cm and u (1838). [D]

Pontin, Daniel, Devizes, Wilts., cm and u (1822–30). Recorded at Leg of Mutton St in 1822 and Sidmouth St in 1830. [D]

Ponzini, James, 74 Leather Lane, Holborn, London, carver, gilder and looking-glass manufacturer (1839). [D]

Ponzini, John, Leather Lane, Holborn, London, looking-glass manufacturer (1835–39). At 73 Leather Lane in 1835 but the number was 74 from 1837. [D]

Pool, N., Lancaster (1840). [Westminster Ref. Lib., Gillow records]

Pool, Richard, Norwich, chairmaker (1755). On 3 May 1755 his son Richard was declared free on servitude to his father. [Freemen reg.]

Pool, Robert, Haswell Lane, Louth, Lincs., cm/joiner (1822). [D]

Pool, Thomas, Southgate, Market Weighton, Yorks., cm (1830). [D]

Pool, William, Friar Gate and St Mary's Gate, Derby, cm and u (1835). [D]

Pool & Boswell, Brewer St, North Goswell Rd, London, chair and sofa manufacturer (1835). [D]

Poole, George, 6 Charlotte St, St Paul's Bristol, cm (1818). [D]

Poole, George, North St, Leighton Buzzard, Beds., cm and u (1839). [D]

Poole, Henry, 182 High St, Hoxton, London, cm and u (1839). [D]

Poole, Hugh, 10 Birdcage Walk, Hackney Rd, London, looking-glass manufacturer (1826–39). In 1826–28 the address is given as 10 London St, but this is probably a case of the renaming of a road. In 1839 the business was trading as Poole & Son. [D]

Poole, Jacob, London, carver (1760–66). At Beech Lane in 1760 and Barbican, 1765–66. Freeman of the Joiners' Co. Took out licences to employ two or three non-freemen for periods extending to three months in 1760 and 1765–66. [GL, City Licence bks, vols 2, 4 and 5]

Poole, James, How End, Kirbymoorside, Yorks., cm and joiner (1830–34). In 1834 his son was also active in the business. [D]

Poole, James, Gloucester, carver and gilder (1830–39). Listed at College St in 1830 and College Green in 1839. [D]

Poole, Jeremiah, London, upholder (1715). On 17 August 1715 he took as app. Charles Collins, son of John Collins of London, yeoman. [V&A archives]

Poole, John, Little Poultney St, London, upholder (1774). [Westminster poll bk]

Poole, John, near Crown Ct, Chapel St, Soho, London, carver (1778). In 1778 insured a house at 18 Pitt St for £400. [GL, Sun MS vol. 265, p. 190]

Poole, John, Harp Lane, Ludlow, Salop, cm and u (1835). [D]

Poole, Richard, Bromsgrove, Worcs., cm (1793). [D]

Poole, Robert, 3a Cooper St, Manchester, cm and u (1840). [D]

Poole, Thomas, Hoxton, London, cm and u (1826–39). In 1826 at 3 Hoxton Market as a cm, but from 1835–39 at 4 James Pl., Hoxton, as a cm and u. [D]

Poole, Thomas, Broseley, Salop, cm (1835–36). [D]

Poole, William, Liverpool, carver and gilder (1834). Married in May 1834 Miss Mary Lancaster at St Nicholas's Church. [*Liverpool Mercury*, 16 May 1834]

Poole & Jeffs, Nottingham, carvers (1834). Dissolution of partnership announced, *Chester Courant*, 13 May 1834.

Pooley, John, parish of St Julian, Norwich, cm (1830). [Poll bk]

Poolman, James, Market Pl., Frome, Som., cm and u (1839–40). [D]

Poor, W., St James Sq., Newport, Isle of Wight, Hants., cm and u (1839). [D]

Poore, John, Upper St James St, Newport, Isle of Wight, Hants., cm and u (1823). [D]

Pope, Benjamin, 4 Cross Land, Long Acre, London, u (1839). [D]

Pope, Henry, King's Lynn, Norfolk, u (1667–75). His son Henry who was his app. was declared free, 1674–75. He also took as app. Thomas Donne who was free by servitude, 1667–68. [Freemen rolls]

Pope, Henry, 44 Tidy St, Brighton, Sussex, cm and u (1839–40). [D]

Pope, J., 9 Gt Blond St, Gt Dover Rd, London, cm and u (1839). [D]

Pope, John, Maidstone, Kent, upholder (1734–61). In 1735 took app. named Calverley and in 1752, Bartram. [Poll bks; S of G, app. index]

Pope, John, Bristol, cm (1778). Bankruptcy announced, *Sussex Weekly Advertiser*, 28 December 1778.

Pope, John, Blandford, Dorset, cm (1784). Freeman of Bristol. [Bristol poll bk]

Pope, John, Charlotte St, Gt Yarmouth, Norfolk, cm, chairmaker and u (1822–36). In 1832 recorded as John Pope jnr. Bankruptcy announced, *London Gazette*, 23 February 1830. [D; poll bk]

Pope, John, Waterloo Rd, London, writing desk manufacturer (1835). [D]

Pope, Joseph, 26 Dean St, Soho, London, cm and u (1839). [D]

Pope, Joshua, Bristol, cm (1781). [Poll bk]

Pope, Samuel, Liverpool, cm (1840). App. to John O'Neill and free by servitude, 27 July 1840. [Freemen reg.]

Pope, Thomas, Norwich, upholder (1761). Re-admitted a freeman of Norwich on 25 August 1761. [Freemen reg.]

Pope & Maclellan, 'The Pope's Head', corner of Harvey Ct, near Half Moon St, Strand, London, upholstery and paper hanging warehouse (c.1760). His trade card survives [Heal Coll., BM] advertising a 'Great Variety of Paper Hangings and Painted Floor Cloths by the Makers'. *The Craftsman* of 1734 contains an advertisement for Samuel Pope's 'Patent Marbled Papers'. In 1767 Half Moon St became part of Bedford St. [Heal]

Poppleton, Thomas, Low Skellgate, Ripon, Yorks., joiner/cm (1834–37). [D]

Poppleton, William, Skellgate, Ripon, Yorks., cm (1822–37). [D]

Poquet, —, London, cm (1793). Subscribed to Sheraton's *Drawing Book*, 1793.

Porrett, Thomas, Whitehart St, Aylsham, Norfolk, cm and u (1822–30). [D]

Porri, Vecchio & Co., 17 Gt Queen St, Lincoln's Inn Fields, London, carvers, gilders and picture frame makers (1802). Their trade card survives. [D: Banks Coll., BM]

Portal, Gilharm, London, upholder(?) (1693–94). Supplied in 1693–94 large quantities of crimson and blue(?) and gold Genoa silk, also purple and gold Lucca silk for fifteen beds at Hampton Court at a cost of £324 6s 6d. [PRO, LC9/128/4]

Portbury, Edward, parish of Heavitree, Exeter, Devon, cm (1832). [Poll bk]

Portch, Ambrose, 1 All Saint's St, Bristol, carver and gilder (1816–18). In 1817–18 the business is listed as Portch & Davis. In 1818 they had additional premises at 27 College Green and 1817–18 made also swing-glasses. [D]

Porteous, George, 49 Lime St, Liverpool, carver and gilder (1835). Formerly in partnership with Henry Porteous to 1834. [D]

Porteous, George M. & Henry J., Liverpool, carvers and cm (1829–34). At 60 Gloucester St with a shop at 1 School Lane in 1829. The partnership was dissolved in October 1834. Despite this, one directory still lists Henry & George Porteous at 39 Lime St in 1837 and it is possible that they had once again arranged to conduct their business in partnership. [D; *Chester Courant*, 14 October 1834]

Porteous, Henry, Liverpool, cm, carver and gilder (1835–39). In partnership with George Porteous to 1834, and in the following year trading on his own behalf at 37 Richmond Row. In 1839 at 68 Lime St. [D]

Porter, Alfred, London, cm and chairmaker (1826–29). In 1826 at Westminster Rd as a chair and sofa maker and in 1829 at 3 Hatfield Pl., Lambeth as a cm. [D]

Porter, Algernon, St Mary Arches' St, Exeter, Devon, cm (1838). Daughter bapt. at St Olave's Church, 13 October 1838. [PR (bapt.)]

Porter, Mrs Ann, Exeter, Devon, u (1830–33). Widow of Samuel Porter who died in 1830. In that year she moved from St Martin's Lane to more convenient premises in Castle St. [D; *Exeter Flying Post*, 25 November 1830, 26 July 1832]

Porter, Arnold, Leicester, cm (1801). In 1801 bought his freedom as a 'stranger'. Took as app. Joseph Rouse. [Freemen rolls]

Porter, David John, Manchester, chairmaker and broker (1832–39). At 3 Shepley St in 1832 as a chairmaker but from 1836–39 at 20 London Rd. as a furniture broker. [D]

Porter, Edward, Leicester, cm (1832). Free 1832. 4th son of Arnold Porter. [Freemen rolls]

Porter, James, 3 Little St, St Thomas the Apostle, London, upholder (1786–99). Son of Adam Porter of Trowbridge, Wilts. App. to William Cope on 2 April 1761 and free of the Upholders' Co. by servitude, 4 October 1786. Took as app. Henry Dobson, 1790–99. [GL, Upholders' Co. records]

Porter, James, London, cm and u (1825–39). At 19 Stephens St,

Tottenham Ct Rd as an u in 1825; and High St, Camden Town, 1838–39, as a cm and u, no. 166 High St in 1839. [D]

Porter, John, Manchester, cm (1803–25). At 56 Tib St, 1804–06 and 3 Oldham Rd, 1825. Probably the John Porter who subscribed in 1803 to Sheraton's *Cabinet Dictionary*. [D]

Porter, John, High St, Honiton, Devon, cm (1823–38). [D]

Porter, John, London, cm and u (1827–39). At 25 Welbeck St, Cavendish Sq., 1827–29 and 5 Bartholomew Pl., Hertford Rd in 1839. In 1829 the business was described as Porter & Co. invalid chair etc., maker. [D]

Porter, John, Leicester, cm (1827–40). In 1827 at Townhall Lane, and in 1828 at Market Pl. From 1835–39, in High St, where he described himself as an u, cm and paper hanger. [D]

Porter, John Barrick, Cambridge, cm (1834–37). At East Rd, 1834–35 and Eden Terr. in 1837. [Poll bks]

Porter, John, 82 Upper Thames St and Dowgate Dock, London, iron bedstead maker (1839). [D]

Porter, John, Sheridan St, Nottingham, chairmaker (1840). [D]

Porter, Joseph, Chester and Liverpool, u (1747). App. to Griffith Briggins of Chester and free, 14 July 1747. Very shortly afterwards he moved to Liverpool. [Freemen rolls; Chester poll bk]

Porter, Joseph, Brunswick St, Macclesfield, Cheshire, u (1828). [D]

Porter, Lewis, Congleton, Cheshire, cm (1822–34). At Swan Bank from 1822–28 and High St, 1834. [D]

Porter, Samuel, Exeter, Devon, u (b.1789–d.1830). In August 1815 when he married Ann Way at St Mary Major he was foreman in the upholstery branch of Carter & Son. In April 1817, however, he set up his own business from his home in Friernhay St as a working u and stated that 'Paper hangings, Prints, Fringes and other Materials required in furnishing he will shortly be enabled to offer on most reasonable terms by Agency, from the best London Manufacturers'. By 1823 he was trading from 206 High St and in addition to his work as an u he acted as a house and property agent and auctioneer. In April 1828 his bankruptcy was announced and he moved to Martins Lane where he died in 1830 aged 41. His widow Ann continued the business from premises in Castle St. [D; *Exeter Flying Post*, 16 November 1826, 6 August 1829; *The Alfred*, 11 October 1825; 22 April 1828]

Porter, Sarah, High St, St Mary's, Lincoln, cm and u (1828). [D]

Porter, Thomas, London, upholder and cm (1749–68). Son of Thomas Porter of St James, Clerkenwell, Gent. App. to Daniel Woodroffe on 2 January 1739 and free of the Upholders' Co. by servitude, 23 May 1749. His trade card [Heal Coll., BM and Landauer Coll., MMA, NY] gives an address at 'The King's Arms', New Round Ct, Strand, and states that he appraised goods and performed funerals. The style of the chair and pole screen illustrated and the general Rococo character of the frame would suggest that the card probably dates from the 1750s or 60s. It also bears an engraving of the Royal coat of arms, but the significance of this is unclear. From the Strand address he appears to have moved to a property at St Alban's St, Pall Mall, a house held on a Crown lease of fifty years at a rental of £2.50 per annum. In 1768 he announced his intention to quit 'Shop-keeping' and his stock was auctioned by James Christie. Apart from the usual cabinet and upholstery lines it also included 'Useful and Ornamental China, Fire Arms, Plated, Japanned and Pontepool Goods, Marble, Stone and Plaster Busts and Vases, an Eight-day Chime-Clock, a table ditto and Variety of Cutlery and other Articles'. The catalogue lists papier mâché items, 'India dressing boxes', Nankeen 'basons', shagreened knife cases and tortoiseshell items. Porter's new address was given as the corner of Charles St, near Parliament St, Westminster. The only known patron of Thomas Porter is the

4th Duke of Bedford who, between February 1761 and the following year, purchased a number of modest items of furniture which included 'slatt back chairs with matt seats', a wainscot desk and bookcase and a walnut chair. [GL, Upholders' Co. records; Christie's, 14 December 1768; Bedford Office, London]

Porter, Thomas, 7 Beavoir Pl., Kingsland Rd, London, chair and sofa maker (1835–39). [D]

Porter, William, High St, Lincoln, cm and u (1790–1826). [D; poll bks]

Porter, William, 69 Thomas St, Manchester, cm (1825). [D]

Porter, William, London, carver and gilder (1832–35). At Redcross St, Lambeth from 1832–34 and 9 Brokers Row, Southwark in 1835. [D]

Porter, William, Bear St, Exeter, Devon, cm and u (1838–40). [D]

Porter & Radford, Claverton St, Bath, Som., japaners and ornamental painters (1793). [D]

Porters, Thomas, Newington Rd, Dalston, London, chairmaker (1826). [D]

Portovine, John, Nantwich, Cheshire, chairmaker (1803–04). Son John bapt. on 9 July 1803 but died in the April following. [PR (bapt. and burial)]

Portti, James, 2 Queen St, Hull, Yorks., carver and gilder (1818). [D]

Portus, John, Blandford, Dorset, carver (1774). Freeman of Bristol. [Bristol poll bk]

Post, Walter, 14 Clare St, Bristol, carver, gilder and manufacturer of lustres (1809–15). Declared bankrupt May 1810. Also at St James's Pl. in 1810 and Lawrence Hill, 1814–15. [D; *Exeter Flying Post*, 31 May 1810]

Postan, Paul, London, cm and auctioneer (1773–92). In 1773 at 17 Aldersgate St as a u, but in March 1776 declared bankrupt, *Gents Mag*. His address at this date was Bluecoat Buildings, near Christ's Hospital and his trade was listed as cm. In 1792 at 142 Aldersgate St as an auctioneer. [D]

Postell, Andrew, Hull, Yorks., bedstead maker (1803–23). At Little Passage St, Nile St in 1803, 1 Providence St, 1806–10, and Little Passage St again, 1817–23. [D]

Postlethwaite, Isaac, High Hill, Keswick, Cumb., joiner/cm (1828–34). [D]

Postlethwaite, Thomas, Keswick, Cumb., cm/joiner and cartwright (1834). [D]

Postlethwaite, William, Wigan Lane, Lancs., cm (1825). [D]

Postlethwaite, William, Dalton, Westmld, cm (1829). [D]

Postlewhate, William, Whitehaven, Cumb., cm (1753). In 1753 took app. named Johnson. [S of G, app. index]

Potbury, George, Sidmouth, Devon, u (1812–14). In October 1814 were advertised for sale 'five extremely beautiful china jars of very large dimensions which belonged to the Nabob of Arcot'. Interested persons were asked to enquire of George Potbury. [*Exeter Flying Post*, 21 May 1812, 27 October 1814]

Potbury, Gregory, Sidmouth, Devon, cm (1807–22). In June 1807 advertised for two or three workmen who were promised 'constant employment'. Bankruptcy announced in January 1822, but still listed in an 1823 directory. [D; *Exeter Flying Post*, 18 June 1807, 10 January 1822]

Potbury, Gregory, 8 Hereford St, Lisson Grove, London, u (1839). [D]

Pott, Samuel, Buxton, Derbs., cm (1793). [D]

Pott, William, Sandwich, Kent, cm etc. (1784–1807). A partnership listed as Pott & Denne were trading in the town, 1823–29. [D]

Pott & Denne, Market Pl., Sandwich, Kent, cm and u (1823–29). A William Pott was trading as a cm in the town, 1794–1807. [D]

Pottage, Thomas, Northgate, Market Weighton, Yorks., cm (1840). [D]

Pottenger, John, Coombe St, Exeter, Devon, cm (1823). Daughter bapt. on 9 February 1823. [PR (bapt.)]

Potter, —, High Holborn, London, cm (1737). [Heal]

Potter, David, Dayson Lane, Derby, chairmaker and turner (1818–35). Addresses given at Friar Lane, 1818–22; Dayson Lane, 1828–29; and Curzon St, 1829–35. [D]

Potter, David J., 22 Old Inkleys, Birmingham, bedstead and fancy chairmaker and carpenter (1830). [D]

Potter, David John, Manchester, chairmaker (1832–40). Listed at 3 Shepley St, 1832–33; 20 London Rd, 1836–38; and 2 Britain St, Granby Row, 1840. [D]

Potter, Edward, Friar Gate, Derby, chairmaker and turner (1823–29). [D]

Potter, G. A., 10 Bakers Row, Walworth, London, u (1829). [D]

Potter, George, Market Pl., Kirkbymoorside, Yorks., joiner and cm (1823–40). [D]

Potter, Henry, London, cm and u (1826–35). At 11 Bridge St, Southwark, 1826–27 and 2 Hampton St, Walworth in 1835. [D]

Potter, James, London, cm (1793). Subscribed to Sheraton's *Drawing Book*, 1793.

Potter, John, Liverpool, u and auctioneer (1773–d.1791). There were possibly two craftsmen of the same name in Liverpool in this period. A John Potter was declared free on 3 November 1774 by servitude to William Roberts. It is unlikely that he can be identified with the John Potter who in February 1773 declared that he had taken over the business of his former master the late Edward Roberts. This John Potter apart from his service to Roberts also claimed to have been employed 'in London for some Time, & had the pleasure to work in the most Capital Shops'. On 4 November 1774 his marriage to Miss Eaton was announced, and he is probably shown trading from 170 Dale St, 1774–77. He was probably related to Thomas Potter and in June 1782 announced the sale of the stock in trade of the late Thomas Potter and his partner George Cleator. John Potter may well have been the partner of a man named Irving trading from 5 Paradise St in 1790 as Potter & Irving. The death of John Potter was announced on 30 May 1791. [D; freemen reg.; *Williamson's Liverpool Advertiser*, 19 February 1773, 4 November 1774, 17 November 1775, 3 January 1782, 30 May 1791]

Potter, John, Chesham, Bucks., cm (1793). [D]

Potter, Joseph, Barton St, Tewkesbury, Glos., cm, u and chairmaker (1830–39). [D]

Potter, Joseph, High St, Croydon, Surrey, cm and u (1832). [D]

Potter, Richard, 'The Hen & Chickens', Aldersgate St, London, cane chairmaker (1725). On 28 February 1725 took out insurance cover of £500 of which £150 was for stock. [GL, Sun MS vol. 22, p. 122]

Potter, Richard, Godalming, Surrey, u (1838). [D]

Potter, Robert, London, cm (1793). Subscribed to Sheraton's *Drawing Book*, 1793.

Potter, Samuel, Parliament St, Nottingham, cm (1835). [D]

Potter, Stephen, 'The Looking-Glass', Jewin St, Aldersgate St, London, carver, gilder and looking-glass maker (c.1760). His trade card [Banks Coll., BM] states that he made looking-glasses, pier glasses, sconces and dressing glasses.

Potter, Thomas, address unknown, cm (1735–38). On 10 May 1735 he was paid £19 by Sir Justinian Isham for a communion table for Lamport Church, Northants. Amongst the Stourhead, Wilts. bills is one dated 1738 receipted by Kelsey & Potter which was a partnership of this maker with a John Kelsey. [V&A archives]

Potter, Thomas, Liverpool, cm (1761–81). In 1761 petitioned for his freedom. He had served five years as an app. under Thomas Gerrard and had subsequently served Josiah Baxendale. In 1774–81 at 35 Union St, but also shown in partnership with George Cleator at Pool Lane, 1766–81. Thomas Potter probably died in 1781 and on 3 January 1782 the sale of the stock of the business was announced as George Cleator was retiring from the business and leaving Liverpool. Their stock consisted of 'mahogany chairs, tables, desks, chests of drawers, bedsteads, a very good mahogany wardrobe, looking-glasses etc.'. Materials also sold off included 'about seven hundred feet of mahogany in boards & plank & a quantity of very fine veneers; together with some walnut, oak, deal etc.'. At the date of Potter's death the business was trading from 47 Lord St. The business of Potter & Cleator is listed in a directory at this address as late as 1784. [D; freemen's committee bk; *Williamson's Liverpool Advertiser*, 3 January 1782, 10 January 1782]

Potter, Thomas, 1 Warwick Pl., Kingsland Rd, London, carver and gilder (1839). [D]

Potter, William, Lincoln, cm (1793). Subscribed to Sheraton's *Drawing Book*, 1793.

Potter, William, Bath, Som., upholder (1802–05). Bankruptcy announced, *Billinge's Liverpool Advertiser*, 13 September 1802. A directory of 1805 lists him trading at Monmouth St, Bath however.

Potter, William, 2 Green St, Grosvenor Sq., London, u and cm (1820–29). [D]

Potter, William, West Auckland, Co. Durham, joiner and cm (1828). [D]

Potter, William, High St, Amersham, Bucks., chairmaker (1830). [D]

Potter & Irving, 5 Paradise St, Liverpool, cm (1790). Also referred to as Irving & Potter. The Potter involved may have been John Potter who traded from 1774 at 170 Dale St. [D]

Potters, John, parish of St Michael, Bath, Som., carver (1784). Freeman of Bristol. [Bristol poll bk]

Potti, Louis, Bristol, carver and gilder (1830). Bankruptcy announced *Liverpool Mercury*, 12 March 1830.

Pottinger, William, Lower Castle St, Bristol, cm (1824–40). At 14 Lower Castle St, 1824–40 but in 1830 the number was listed as 15. [D]

Potts, Benjamin, Nottingham Rd, Derby, chairmaker and turner (1835). [D]

Potts, George, Hendricks Pl., Chenies St, Bloomsbury, London, upholder and cm (1823). In February 1823 took out insurance cover of £700 on goods in trust. [GL, Sun MS vol. 498, ref. 1001378] See William Potts, snr and jnr.

Potts, George, London, cm and u (1826–39). At 5 Nassau St, Middlx Hospital, 1826–27 and 18 Montague St, Brick Lane in 1839. [D]

Potts, James, London, cm and looking-glass manufacturer (1804–29). At Back Hill, Hatton Gdns, 1804–08, as a looking-glass manufacturer. His trade card [archives dept, borough of Hackney] gives an address at 7 Gloucester St, Curtain Rd however. It advertises that he silvered and polished old glasses, and framed prints. By 1820 he was at 6 Clements Lane, Lombard St where his trade was stated to be cm; the same trade is indicated for the new address at 27 Bennet St, Gt Surrey St in 1826. In 1829 he was at the same address, but his trade was once more that of a looking-glass manufacturer. [D]

Potts, James, Liverpool, cm (1807–37). At 2 Gibralter St in 1807; 20 Cheapside, 1810–14; 7 Torbock St, 1818–27; and 42 Gerard St, 1835–37. [D]

Potts, John, Toddington, Beds. and London, upholder (1761–d.1800). In the 1760s and early 1770s appears to have traded from Toddington, Beds. He undertook the repair of furniture, the renewal of upholstery and the provision of wallpaper and curtains for Woburn Abbey, Beds. and also the parish church in Woburn. A four post painted beech bedstead was provided in 1763; and in August 1768 two wainscot chests of drawers, three wainscot dressing tables and one in mahogany were provided for Elizabeth, Marchioness of Tavistock for Houghton House, Beds. On the death of Francis, Marquis of Tavistock in March 1767, Potts was owed money and £4 10s was paid on 25 March of that year on this account. Potts was, however, more than merely a rural craftsman and for a time maintained a business in London at 'The Black Spread Eagle', Covent Gdn. His trade card from this address [Heal Coll., BM] has its text framed by a fashionable Rococo surround, and engravings of a cabinet, chair, a bed post and tea chest. This states that he also sold paper hangings and cabinet furniture and acted as an appraiser and undertaker. He died at Toddington in May 1800, but his address was listed as King St, Covent Gdn. [Heal; *Cambridge Chronicle*, 25 September 1773; Bedford Office, London; *Gents Mag*, May 1800]

Potts, John, Fore St, Hexham, Northumb., joiner and cm (1827–28). [D]

Potts, John, Norton, Stockton, Co. Durham, cm (1832). [D]

Potts, John, 23 Gt Passage St, Hull, Yorks., cm (1837). [D]

Potts, Joseph, Allendale, Northumb., joiner and cm (1827–34). [D]

Potts, Stephen, 44 Wynatt St, London, japanner (1839). [D]

Potts, Thomas, address unknown, u (1760). In 1760 he was paid £33 14s for a beech bedstead, hangings, pillow, blankets etc. for a bedchamber at Whitney House for John, 4th Duke of Bedford. May have been related to John Potts of Toddington, Beds. and London who was also supplying this family with similar items in the 1760s. [Bedford Office, London]

Potts, Thomas, Broughton, Lancs., cm (1784). [D]

Potts, Thomas, Morpeth, Northumb., cm (1784). [D]

Potts, Thomas, Whitehaven, Cumb., cm (1793–1807). Subscribed to Sheraton's *Drawing Book*, 1793. Probate granted on will, June 1807. [Deanery of Copeland, Cumb., probate records]

Potts, William, Compton St, Soho, London, cm (1776–93). Initially in partnership with Humphry Walton and in 1776 the partners were using not only premises at 11 Compton St (which were insured for £600, half of which was for utensils and stock) but also additional workshops at 4 Peter's Ct, St Martin's Lane, valued at £200 inclusive of utensils and stock. From the following year Potts was trading on his own behalf and only using the Compton St address. This was valued for insurance at £300 inclusive of utensils and stock at £180 in 1777, the corresponding figures for 1782 being £200 and £80 and 1792 £400 and £230. In July 1792 the address was recorded as 14 Old Compton St. He subscribed to Sheraton's *Drawing Book*, 1793. The only known patron was Mrs David Garrick who is recorded purchasing small items of furniture, 1786–87. These included a chimney board, a frame to hold hatboxes and two tea chests. Some repairs were carried out in addition. The total expended came to £5 6s which fits well the modest size of the supplier. [GL, Sun MS vol. 246, p. 436; vol. 248, p. 409; vol. 258, p. 342; vol. 302, p. 485; vol. 389, ref. 602634; Westminster poll bk; V&A Lib., 86.NN.4]

Pott(s), William snr and jnr, London, u and cm (1800–25). At 90 Wardour St, 1800–11, Gresse St, Rathbone Pl. in 1811 and Chenies St, Bedford Sq. from 1811. Initially the business traded as Potts & Son but by 1804 George Croyson Collinson had become a partner and they traded as Potts, Son & Collinson and numerous other variants. In 1803 Potts & Son were listed by Thomas Sheraton in his *Cabinet Dictionary* as one of the leading cm. Fire insurance records indicate that the business was carried on in a substantial manner. On 26

December 1800 took out a policy for £1,000 of which £500 was for utensils and stock. Cover taken out in May 1804 on the Wardour St premises came to £3,100, much of which was on utensils and stock. In 1808 cover was £2,300 and in the following year the same. By 1809, however, the additional premises at Kendricks Pl., Chenies St were also being used and cover here amounted to £3,000. The interest of the Potts family in the business appears to have ended in 1825 and from the following year the firm was trading as Collinson & Son. [D; GL, Sun MS vol. 419, ref. 709893; vol. 431, refs 762272–73; vol. 445, ref. 819322; vol. 448, refs 825886–87] See George Potts of Chenies St and George Croyson Collinson.

Poulton, Charles, Market Pl., Reading, Berks., u (1777–98). Insurance records suggest that this business was substantial. In 1786 cover for £1,000 was taken out, and of this utensils and stock amounted to £720. Subscribed to Sheraton's *Drawing Book*, 1793. [D; poll bks; GL, Sun MS vol. 279, p. 215; vol. 339, p. 219]

Poulton, George, Hull, Yorks., cm, turner and carver (1826–31). In 1826 living at Shield's Ct, Manor Alley and trading as a cm. In 1831, however, the trade was listed as turner and carver, and the Shield's Ct address is no longer given as a residence and may have been used solely as a workshop. His residence in 1831 was at Cook's Buildings. [D]

Poulton, Henry, Torquay, Devon, cm (1837). Bankruptcy announced, *Sussex Agricultural Express*, 22 April 1837.

Poulton, Robert, Chapel Lane, Hull, Yorks., cm and musical instrument repairer (1806–31). In 1806–22 listed in local directories as a cm, but from 1823–31 as a musical instrument repairer or maker. At Hospital Yd, Chapel Lane, 1826–31, but prior to this only Chapel Lane. [D]

Poulton, Roger, London, upholder (1723). Son of Roger Poulton of Overton, Wilts., yeoman. App. to Samuel Kempster on 2 June 1714 and free of the Upholders' Co. by servitude, 4 December 1723. [GL, Upholders' Co. records]

Pounder, Robert, Stokesley, Yorks., joiner and cm (1840). [D]

Pouney, Matthew, 25 Leather Lane, Holborn, London, cm (1781). In 1781 took out insurance cover of £200 of which £30 was in respect of utensils and tools. [GL, Sun MS vol. 296, p. 362]

Poupart, Aubin, London, 'menuisier' (1682). Recorded receiving charitable payments amounting to £2 15s from September to December 1682. [Huguenot Soc., 1949, p. 159]

Pout, Charles, Canterbury, Kent, u and cm (1789–1829). Free 1789. At Hawk's Lane in 1790, but by 1794 at 6 High St which continued to be used for the remainder of the firm's existence. In 1829 described as Charles Pout & Son. The son was John Pout who subsequently took over the business at this address. [D; poll bks; freemen rolls]

Pout, James, parish of St Mary Bredman, Canterbury, Kent, cm (1768–75). Free 1768. In 1775 took out insurance cover of £600, stock accounting for £450 of this. [Freemen rolls; GL, Sun MS vol. 237, p. 340]

Pout, John, High St, Canterbury, Kent, upholder (1784). [D]

Pout, John, 6 High St, Canterbury, Kent, cm, furniture broker and u (1826–39). Son of Charles Pout and assisting his father in the business by 1826. In 1829 the firm was trading as Charles Pout & Son, but by 1832 John Pout was in sole control and trading under his own name. [D; poll bks]

Pout, William, Canterbury, Kent, u (1760–1818). Free 1760. Shown in High St, 1790–94 and 1818; but in 1796 the address is given as the parish of St Mary Bredman. [Freemen rolls; poll bks]

Pout & Son, Canterbury, Kent, upholders (1793). [D]

Pouvreau, Francois, London, 'menuisier' (1682). Between 15 August and 26 September 1682 given six charitable grants totalling £1 10s. [Huguenot Soc., 1949, p. 159]

Povah (or Pover), Daniel, Liverpool, cm (1804–35). At 26 Russia St in 1804 but in the next year the number was 41. From 1807–35 at 12 Richmond Row. Marriage to Miss Peeling reported, *Liverpool Mercury*, 31 January 1812. [D]

Pover, Michael, 15 Ben Jonson St, Liverpool, cm (1827). [D]

Powell (or Powle), Mrs, Three Kings Ct, facing George Yd, Lombard St, London, upholder (c.1753–65). The widow of William Powell who traded at this address. Francis Pyner succeeded her. [Heal]

Powell, —, 27 Winchester Row, Edgware Rd, London, cm (1809). [D]

Powell, Anthony, 341 Oxford St, London, trunk and plate case maker (1784). [D]

Powell, Barnard, London, upholder (1704). Free of the Upholders' Co., 2 August 1704. Dead by 1748. [GL, Upholders' Co. records]

Powell, Benjamin, London, upholder (1713–32). Recorded taking an app. in 1713. In September 1715 his address was 'The Crown', New Southampton St, London in the parish of St Paul, Covent Gdn. From 1724–31 he traded from an address in Wardour St, and in 1732 was at 'The Crown & Cushion', Prince's St, facing Gerard St, Leicester Fields. [S of G, app. index; GL, Sun MS vol. 5, ref. 5852; Heal]

Powell, Charles, London, upholder (1730–56). In December 1730 took out insurance cover of £800 of which £450 was for household goods and stock and the remainder on his dwelling house. This was in Abchurch Lane, parish of St Mary Abchurch. By 1755–56 he was in Basinghall St. [D; GL, Sun MS vol. 32, ref. 52646; *Public Advertiser*, 15 December 1756]

Powell, Charles, Hare Lane, Gloucester, cm and chairmaker (1820–21). Child bapt. in parish of St John the Baptist, 1821. [D; PR (bapt.)]

Powell, Charles, Bridge St, Northampton, chair turner (1830). Successor to John Powell at this address. [D; poll bk]

Powell, Edward, 4 Sparling St, Liverpool, u (1821). [D]

Powell, Edward Frodsham, Chester and Liverpool, u and cm (1824–35). Freeman of Chester, 23 October 1824. Entered into partnership with William Podmore and Thomas John Powell, trading in Chester as u until June 1829 when it was dissolved. In March 1829 Edward Powell was appointed agent to the Palladium Life and Fire Assurance Society of London but he may have continued to live and trade in Chester for a time. In 1835, however, he was in Liverpool trading as an u and cm from an address at 55 Bold St. In 1837 the number had changed to 60 and in 1839 he was at 172. [D; freemen rolls; *Chester Chronicle*, 27 March 1829, 26 June 1829] See William Podmore and Thomas Powell.

Powell, Edward & Thomas, Bridge St Row, Chester, u and cm (1829). A short-lived partnership between Edward Frodsham Powell and Thomas John Powell which traded between the dissolution of the partnership of Podmore & Powells in June 1829 and the disposal of the assets by auction in October 1829. Stock disposed of on 16 October included 'handsome Sofas, Trafalgar Chairs, Sofa Tables, Sideboards handsomely carved, Card and Pembroke Tables, Mahogany Wardrobes, Secretaires, several Chests of Drawers of different sizes, Feather-Beds etc. etc. Likewise Two valuable Piano-fortes'. [*Chester Chronicle*, 2 and 16 October 1829]

Powell, George, 334 High St with workshop at 25 Amrose St, Cheltenham, Glos., cm and u (1839–40). [D; GL, Sun MS ref. 1332227]

Powell, Henry, parish of St John the Baptist, Hereford, cm (1835). [Freemen rolls]

Powell, Hopkin, 24 Castle Green, Bristol, cm (1775). [D]

Powell, James, West Wycombe, Bucks., chairmaker (1798). [Militia Census]

Powell, James, Lichfield St, Birmingham, cm and u (1822). [D]

Powell, James, 5 Chalcroft Terr., New Cut, London, cm (1829). [D]

Powell, James, Stroud Hill, Stroud, Glos., cm (1833). Child bapt. in 1833. [PR (bapt.)]

Powell, James, Kirkbymoorside, Yorks., cm/joiner (1834). [D]

Powell, James, Queen's Row, Pentonville, London, chairmaker (1835). [D]

Powell, John, Wisbech, Cambs., joiner and cm (1749–94). In 1749 took app. named Bourn. Advertised in June 1766 that he had walnut planks for sale and also required a house joiner and a cm. Announced his retirement from business in March 1794. A sale of stock followed. [S of G, app. index; *Cambridge Chronicle*, 7 June 1766, 22 March 1794]

Powell, John, Chelmsford, Essex, u (1778). Bankruptcy announced, *Gents Mag.*, April 1778]

Powell, John, Eastgate Row, Chester, u (1792–1818). In 1792 took as app. John Price. At Eastgate Row in 1814 but by December 1818 was dead and the business wound up. Possibly the Powell who supplied furniture to Erddig, Clwyd, N. Wales, 1807–14 for Simon Yorke. On 20 March 1807 he was paid £200 with a further £100 on 11 April. A further account dated 22 July 1814 was for £75 16s 4½d. [D; app. bk; *Chester Guardian*, 19 December 1818; V&A archives]

Powell, John, Wardour St, Soho, London, chairmaker (1807). Made freeman of York in 1807, but working in London. [York freemen rolls]

Powell, John, Wellington St, Chester, cm (1820–40). Free 18 April 1820. Trading at Wellington St in 1840. [D; freemen rolls]

Powell, John, Bridge St, Northampton, chairmaker (1820–26). In 1826 described as a chair turner. A Charles Powell is recorded at this address in the same trade 1830. [Poll bks]

Powell, John, Harleston, Norfolk, carpenter and cm (1830). [D]

Powell, John, 4 High St, Guildford, Surrey, cm and broker (1838–40). [D]

Powell, John Henry, 38 Duke St, West Smithfield, London, cm and u (1839). [D]

Powell, Joseph, Northampton, chairmaker and turner (1823–30). Listed at Bridge St in 1823 and Bearwood St in 1830. [D]

Powell, Joseph, Bristol, cm, u and undertaker (1824–40). At 3 Unity St, St Philip's, 1824–37, but in 1839 the number is shown as 28 and by 1840 he had moved to Orange St. From 1833–38 referred to as Joseph Powell jnr. [D]

Powell, Joseph, Belgrave Gate, Leicester, chairmaker (1828). [D]

Powell, Joseph, Hereford, carver and gilder (1828–35). At St Owen St in 1830 and Broad St in 1835. Supplied frames and glasses, and gold and bronze ornamental brackets to Capt. N. L. Pateshall, RN, of Hereford in April 1828 and July 1830, the bills amounting to £4 18s 6d and £4 8s respectively. [D; Herefs. RO, F60/105; 221]

Powell, Peter, Benson, Oxon., chairmaker (1774). In April 1774 married, at the age of 55, the 27 year old daughter of John Stevens of Watlington, Oxon. [*Jackson's Oxford Journal*, 16 April 1774]

Powell, Rees, Blandford, Dorset, cm (1771). Came from Wales to settle in Blandford. [Dorset RO, P70/OV12]

Powell, Richard, St Clements, Oxford, cm (1765–77). Born c.1740 and in 1765 took over the business of Richard Shepherd, a cm whose foreman he had been for a number of years. Married at Holywell, Oxford, on 23 April 1773. Fire insurance records suggest that the business was only of a modest size with total cover of £300 of which utensils and stock accounted for £200. His name does appear in connection with a number of Oxford Colleges for which he supplied furniture, and some of this survives. In 1766 he supplied a mahogany orrery case for Queen's College at a cost of £24, and a firescreen for the Common Room of the same College. In 1771 two mahogany tables were supplied to Jesus College. His best known work was, however, for Christ Church. Tables and stools were made for the Library in 1774 costing £16 7s 6d. Two stools made to match a set supplied by Thomas Chippendale in 1764 are believed to be of Powell's manufacture and compare well with those bought from the London maker. In 1773 he was also paid £15 12s for six chairs for the Audit House, and it is possible that these also survive. [Bodleian index of Oxf. marriage bonds; GL, Sun MS vol. 255, p. 182; *C. Life*, 5 January 1945; *Jackson's Oxford Journal*, October 1765]

Powell, Richard, 112 Chapel St, Salford, Lancs., cm (1814–16). [D]

Powell, Robert, Salisbury, Wilts., upholder (1749). In 1749 took app. named Batten. [S of G, app. index]

Powell, Robert, King's Head Yd, Kirkgate, Leeds, Yorks., cm (1817–22). [D]

Powell, T. N., near Deptford Bridge, Greenwich, London, u (1838). [D]

Powell, Thomas, Eastgate St, Chester, u, appraiser and auctioneer (1756–1808). App. to John Bridge of Chester, u and free on 18 April 1756. Shown trading on his own behalf in Eastgate St by 1781. He entered local politics at an early stage and in 1762 was elected a councilman. In 1788 he was elected Alderman and in 1790 became Mayor of the city. The auctioneering side of the business was of some importance, and sales were conducted not only in his own county, but also in north Shropshire. He had agents from whom sale catalogues could be obtained in Whitchurch, Salop, Wrexham, Clwyd and Neston, Cheshire. By 1796 his son had joined him in the business and from thence to 1808 it traded as Thomas Powell & Son. He supplied carpets in July 1796 to Sir John Leicester of Tabley Hall, Knutsford, Cheshire, amounting to £47 10s. [D; poll bks; freemen rolls; Chester RO, names index and Leicester papers; *Chester Chronicle*, 26 April 1782]

Powell, Thomas, 178 St John's St, London, cm and u (1808). [D]

Powell, Thomas jnr, Queen St, Wakefield, Yorks., cm and u (1822). [D]

Powell, Thomas John, Chester, u (1829). Partner with William Podmore and Edward Frodsham Powell in the firm of Podmore & Powells, u of Bridge St Row, Chester. The partnership was dissolved in June 1829. [*Chester Chronicle*, 26 June 1829] See William Podmore, Edward Frodsham Powell and Edward and Thomas Powell.

Powell, Thomas, 16 Slaney St, Birmingham, cm (1835). [D]

Powell, Thomas, 3 Low Ousegate, York, cm (1837). [D]

Powell, William, Three Kings Ct, facing George Yd, Lombard St, London, upholder (1738–d. 1753). A substantial business whose insurance cover in March 1750 amounted to £2,000 of which three quarters was for stock-in-trade and household goods. He died in May 1753 and was described as 'an eminent upholder & cabinet maker'. His widow carried on the business from the same address and was still active in 1765. [Heal, GL, Sun MS vol. 89, ref. 120573; *London Evening Post*, 24–26 May 1753]

Powell, William, Gt Mays Buildings, London, carver and gilder (1775). In 1775 insured his utensils and stock for £300 out of a total cover of £500. [GL, Sun MS vol. 244, p. 55]

Powell, William, 16 Gt Earl St, Seven Dials, London, u and undertaker (1808). [D]

Powell, William, 7 Alfred Hill, Bristol, u (1825–31). [D]

Powell, William, Evelyn Pl., Deptford, London, cm (1823–26). [D]

Powell, William, London, bedstead maker (1826–39). At 2 Mint St, Southwark in 1826 and 3 Cumberland Pl., Newington in 1839. [D]

Powell, William George, Belgrave Gate, Leicester, chairmaker (1827–35). In 1835 listed as a chairmaker and cm. [D]

Powell, William John, Belgrave Gate, Leicester, u and paper hanger (1835). [D]

Powell & Reynolds, Silver St, Lincoln, cm and u (1826–28). [D]

Power, John, address unknown, cm (1803). Subscribed to Sheraton's *Cabinet Dictionary*, 1803.

Power, Michael, 15 Ben Jonson St, Liverpool, cm (1827). [D]

Power & Pavey, Barrack St, Bridport, Dorset, cm (1840). [D]

Powers, Edmund, High St, Leicester, cm, chairmaker, joiner and turner (1746–52). Free 1746 on servitude to John Elliott. In 1752 took app. named Thickpenny. A double topped mahogany tea and games table on cabriole legs, with a frieze decorated with blind Chinese fret is recorded, with this maker's label pasted in the drawer. On this label he claimed to make and sell a wide range of cabinet furniture, tables, chairs, beds and other items applicable to his trade. [Freemen rolls; S of G, app. index; Sotheby's, 2 June 1967, lot 141]

Powers, Richard, Piccadilly, London, carver (1774). [Westminster poll bk]

Powis, William, London, carver and gilder, picture frame and looking-glass maker (1813–26). At 4 St James's Walk, Clerkenwell, 1813–23, but by February 1824 at 18 Arlington Pl., St John St, where he took out insurance cover of £500. At 94 St John St in 1826. [D; GL, Sun MS vol. 497, ref. 1014091]

Powlay, Henry, Keswick, Cumb., joiner/cm (1828–34). [D]

Pownall, Thomas, Manchester, cm (1794–97). At 13 Thomas' St in 1794, but shown in 1797 directories at either Hulme or China Lane. [D]

Pownall, Thomas, Lower Hillgate, Stockport, Cheshire cm (1825). [D]

Poyer, Richard, address unknown, cm (1803). Subscribed to Sheraton's *Cabinet Dictionary*, 1803.

Poynton, Edward, Nottingham, carver (1722–d.1737). One of the craftsmen patronised by the Warwick architect, Francis Smith. Recorded on the lead foundation plate (now lost) at Sutton Scarsdale House, Derbs. dated 1724 as a 'gentleman carver'. He was responsible for the Oak Room of this house (now in the Philadelphia Museum of Art), and also for stone carving. He also worked at Chicheley House, Bucks., 1719–21. In 1722 he undertook an ambitious memorial at West Stockwith, Notts. to William Huntingdon, a 'ship carpenter'. In 1729 he took app. named Watson. He died in 1737, and his will survives (Notts. RO). [Gunnis; *Records of Bucks*, XVII, 1961, pt 1; *C. Life*, 8 June 1961, p. 1326; Beard, *Craftsmen and Interior Decoration in England*, p. 276; S of G, app. index]

Poyntz, William snr, Cannon St, London, upholder (d.1720). Freeman of the Upholders' Co. and father of William Poyntz jnr. He died in 1720 and is buried at Battersea. His second wife was Jane, daughter of Stephen Monteage, a London merchant. Their grand-daughter, Georgiana Poyntz (1737–1814) married in 1755 John Spencer, 1st Earl Spencer of Althorp, Northants. [GL, Upholders' Co. records; Sir John Maclean, *Historical and Genealogical Memoir of the Family of Poyntz*, (1886), pp. 208, 226]

Poyntz, William jnr, London, 'upholder' (1725). Son of William Poyntz snr, and free of the Upholders' Co. by patrimony, 10 December 1725. He is referred to in the Company records as 'esquire' and the prosperous nature of the family might indicate that he did not practice the trade. [GL, Upholders' Co. records]

Pozzi, Charles, Paradise St, Liverpool, looking-glass and picture frame maker (1837–39). Shown in different directories at either 71 or 73 Paradise St in 1837. In 1839 the number was 14. Shown as a carver and gilder in both 1837 and 1839. [D]

Prandi, Francis, Sheffield, Yorks., carver, gilder and looking-glass maker (1822–25). At 11 High St in 1823 when the business is listed as F. Prandi & Co. In 1825 at 32 Church St. [D]

Prankard, John, 'The Golden Ball', Aldermanbury, London, cm (1720). [GL, Sun MS vol. 10, refs 16499–500]

Pratchett, Thomas, Nantwich, Cheshire, cm (1779). Married on 31 August 1779. [PR (marriage)]

Pratchett, Thomas, 49 Angel St, Manchester, cm (1817). [D]

Pratt, —, Kingston, Surrey, chairmaker (1796). On 28 May 1794 invoiced '6 Neat Cottage Chairs with rush seats, moulded japann'd Bamboo' to Mrs Garrick at a cost of 10/- each. [V&A Lib., 86 NN 4 (1)–10]

Pratt, Andrew James, London, upholder (1755). Son of William Pratt of Greenwich, ship carpenter. App. to John Forfar on 4 May 1768 and Richard Walker on 2 December 1772 and free of the Upholders' Co. by servitude, 2 August 1775. [GL, Upholders' Co. records]

Pratt, Benjamin & Attfield, Richard, 19 Lower Brook St, Grosvenor Sq., London, cm and u (1821–22). In November 1821 took out insurance cover of £3,000 but of this only £500 was in respect of utensils and stock. The corresponding figures for October 1822 are £2,000 and £500. [GL, Sun MS vol. 488, ref. 985155; vol. 493, ref. 997007]

Pratt, Charles Thomas, London, fancy cm (1816–39). At 9 Cold Bath Sq., Clerkenwell from 1816–27, and in December 1821 took out insurance cover of £500 at this address. Half of the sum insured was for utensils and stock. At 4 Vineyard Walk, Clerkenwell from 1829–39. Although in both 1829 and 1839 his trade is listed in directories as merely cm or cm and u he appears to have specialised in the manufacture of small items of case furniture such as writing and dressing cases. [D; GL, Sun MS vol. 491, ref. 987214]

Pratt, George, Portsmouth, Hants., cm (1774–98). On 3 December 1774 took out insurance cover for £500 but of this only £100 was for utensils and stock. This policy also covered his house in Hannen St. [D; GL, Sun MS vol. 235, ref. 346987]

Pratt, George, address unknown, u (1803). Subscribed to Sheraton's *Cabinet Dictionary*, 1803.

Pratt, George, Bengeworth, Evesham, Worcs., cm (1818–35). A Joseph Pratt, cm traded in Evesham, 1779–91. [D; poll bk]

Pratt, George, Clifton near Halifax, Yorks., cm (1822). A Joseph Pratt was trading as a joiner and cm from this address in 1834. [D]

Pratt, Henry, 18 Kennington Pl., London, turner and chairmaker (1808). [D]

Pratt, James, Keyford, Frome Som., cm and u (1840). [D]

Pratt, John, London, cm (1763–93). At Bedford Ct in 1763 and 4 Earl's Ct, Leicester Sq., 1790–93. [D]

Pratt, John, Chandos St(?), Grosvenor Sq., London, carver and picture frame maker (1804). Supplied picture frames and framed prints for Mrs Leigh and his account for this work dated 24 September 1804 amounted to £14 os 6d. [Shakespeare Birthplace Trust, Leigh receipts, DR 18/5]

Pratt, John, Hailgate, Howden, Yorks., joiner and cm (1823–28). [D]

Pratt, Joseph, Evesham, Worcs., cm (1779–91). In 1779 took out insurance cover of £1,700 of which £450 was in respect of utensils and stock. Total cover in March 1791 was, however, down to £500. [GL, Sun MS vol. 273, ref. 412167; vol. 374, ref. 581101] See George Pratt of Evesham.

Pratt, Joseph, Priestpopple St, Hexham, Northumb., joiner and cm (1828). [D]

Pratt, Joseph, Clifton, Brighouse, near Halifax, Yorks., joiner

and cm (1834). A George Pratt cm was trading at this location in 1822. [D]

Pratt, Martha, St George's St, Canterbury, Kent, u (1805–09). [D]

Pratt, Michael, Worcester, joiner, carpenter and cm (1760). App. to William Reding, joiner, carpenter and cm and free, 29 December 1760. [Freemen rolls]

Pratt, Philip, Cawood, near Selby, Yorks., grocer and cm (1822–37). [D]

Pratt, Richard, London, cm (1790–1829). At 20 Kirby St, Hatton St, 1790–93 and 29 Greenhills Rents, St John's St, Smithfield 1809–29. In 1817 recorded also as an upholder and in 1827 also as a u. In 1829 listed as a cm, writing desk and dressing case maker. [D]

Pratt, Richard, Riccall, Yorks., cm (1823). [D]

Pratt, Samuel, New Bond St, London, u (1813–30). Supplied eighteen chairs for Kilniddery, Co. Wicklow, Ireland in 1813 at a cost of £75 12s. In April 1830 listed as an upholsterer in the Windsor Castle accounts and owed the sum of £151 6s. [*C. Life*, 21 July 1977; Windsor Royal Archives]

Pratt, Samuel & Henry, London, u, invalid furniture and camp equipage manufacturers (1833–40). Traded from 19 Cockspur St and 47 New Bond St, 1833–35 but may have later concentrated the business solely on the New Bond St address. Their billhead states that they were military equipage makers, upholsterers and writing and dressing case manufacturers to their Majesties. They also featured 'Elastic Beds, Easy Chairs &c. Stuffed with Iron Wire', 'Patent folding Brass Camp Bedsteads', 'Patent Stuffed Recumbent Chairs' and leather trunks and carrying cases of a wide range of different types. The Samuel Pratt, was probably the u recorded in New Bond St, 1813–30. In December 1833 they supplied a chaise longue to Lord Leigh of Stoneleigh Abbey, Warks. at £13 13s and in March 1834 a patent sofa seat at £7. John Arkwright of Hampton Court, Leominster, Herefs. in May and June 1834 purchased goods to the value of £10 which included a set of mahogany french polished drawers costing £6 15s. Furniture supplied to Stafford House, London in 1838 amounted to £228. By 1839 the type of trade carried on by the business may have changed considerably for in a directory of that year they are referred to as 'Antique & Foreign Furniture Dealers'. Samuel Pratt is, however, recorded in the Lord Chamberlain's papers as a trunk maker 1832–45. [D; Shakespeare Birthplace Trust, Leigh receipts, DR 18/5; Herefs. RO, Arkwright papers, A63/161; Staffs. RO, D 593/R/1/26/8]

Pratt, Thomas, Leek, Staffs., cm (1744). In 1744 took app. named Morris. [S of G, app. index]

Pratt, Thomas, Jermyn St, London, cm (1774). [Westminster poll bk]

Pratt, Thomas, Priestpopple, Hexham, Northumb., joiner/cm (1834). [D]

Pratt, Thomas, Cullompton, Devon, cm (1838). [D]

Pratt, Walter, London, upholder (1708–17). Son of John Pratt of Tillington, Sussex, Gent. App. to Philip Mervin on 6 October 1708 and free of the Upholders' Co. by servitude, 1 May 1717. [GL, Upholders' Co. records]

Pratt, Walter jnr, Dover, Kent, u (1830). Freeman of Canterbury. [Canterbury poll bk]

Pratt, William, address unknown (1774). Freeman of Lincoln. [Lincoln poll bk]

Pratt, William, Hull, Yorks., cm (1774–80). [Poll bks]

Pratt, William, Gt Yarmouth and Harleston, Norfolk, cm (1812–39). Freeman of Norwich and living at Gt Yarmouth, 1812–18. Trading at Harleston in 1839. [D; Norwich poll bks]

Pratt, William, Church St, Warwick, cm and u (1822). [D]

Preamer, John, Strutton Ground, Westminster, London, carver (1774). [Westminster poll bk]

Prebble, J., 21 Crown Row, Walworth, London, cm (1829). [D]

Prebble, John, Rathbone Pl., Oxford St, London, u and cm (1830). Bankruptcy announced, *London Gazette*, 10 August 1830.

Prebble, Stephano, Liverpool, carver (1837–39). At 38 Devon St in 1837 and 1 Marble St in 1839. [D]

Predam, William, Lower St, Dartmouth, Devon, cm (1823–30). [D]

Predary, James, Manchester, carver, gilder, picture frame and looking-glass maker (1817–40). At 24 Church St, 1817–22; 13 Oak St, 1825–33; and 17 Oak St, 1838–40. [D]

Preddy, J., Taunton, Som., cm, chairmaker and u (c.1810). Trade label recorded on a three pillar mahogany dining table of c.1810.

Preddy, James, Taunton, Som., cm (1822–39). Listed at East St in 1822 and Upper High St, 1830–39. [D]

Preece, James, 9 Gt Stanhope St, Bath, Som., cm (1833). [D]

Prendergast, Daniel, 25 Bow St, Covent Gdn, London, u and cm (1784–99). In 1784 called in by Edward Gibbon to pack up and forward his belongings from Downing St. Gibbons refers to him as the 'honest cabinet maker'. [D; Heal]

Prenson, Abraham, 5 Cleveland St, Liverpool, cm (1813–14). [D]

Prentice, Richard, 25 Ebury St, Pimlico, London, cm and u (1826–27). [D]

Prentice, Thomas, Little Wild St, Lincoln's Inn Fields, London, cm (1809). [D]

Prentice, William, 12 Little Wild St, Lincoln's Inn Fields, London, cm (1787–1817). A fire at his shop was reported in July 1787 and in 1793 he was declared bankrupt. His address at this period is not known and it is not until 1794 that he begins to be shown regularly in trade directories at the Little Wild St address. In 1793 he subscribed to Sheraton's *Drawing Book*, and is included in the list of master cabinet makers in his *Cabinet Dictionary*, 1803. William Prentice had a son who joined him in the business and an early 19th-century mahogany Pembroke table, the top with rounded corners and reeded edge, on turned tapering legs is known with the trade label of Wm Prentice & Son. [D; *Gents Mag.*, July 1787; Bailey's list of bankrupts; Phillips', 24 August 1965]

Prenton, Thomas, Liverpool, cm (1761). Free 12 March 1761. [Freemen reg.]

Presbury, Philip, Bridge St Row (or Bridge St), Chester, cm and auctioneer (1750–95). Son of Samuel Presbury of Chester, wet glover. His father was dead by 9 March 1750 when Philip was made free. He took as apps John Cooke in 1750, James Green in 1752, Walter Griffith in 1753, John Linney in 1754, John Edwards in 1755, Robert Hooker in 1757, John Crimes in 1759, Thomas Roberts in 1767 and Robert Adams in 1773. In 1767 an application to extend the front of his property forward in line with the two adjacent buildings was granted. He appears to have traded from the first floor of the building and an application made at the same time to build a flight of steps directly from the street was refused. Despite the impressive number of apps taken in the 1750s, soon after the establishment of the business, it appears to have been only of modest size in 1780 with total insurance cover of £400 of which £150 was for utensils and stock. He advertised several auction sales in the period 1777–82 and may have scaled down his cabinet making to some extent to concentrate more on this side of the business. [D; poll bks; freemen rolls; Chester RO, AB/4; GL, Sun MS vol. 110, ref. 145963; vol. 282, ref. 427606; *Chester Chronicle*, 25 April 1777, 15 March 1782, 6 September 1782]

Prescott, James, Hull, Yorks., chairmaker (1814–40). App. in March 1814 to George Thornham, woodturner and chairmaker. At 5 Wincolmlee, 1837–40. [D; Hull app. reg.]

Prescott, Richard, Lord St, Liverpool, carver (1702–d.1747). His wood carvings, of considerable quality, are only known to date within churches, particularly those at N. Meols Church, removed from St Peter, Liverpool. He acted as a joiner for wainscoting at Croxteth Hall (1702) and Woolton Hall (1709), both Lancs. [Preston RO, will (1747); Sir James Picton, *Memorials of Liverpool*, 1875, p. 46; P. Fleetwood-Hesketh, *Lancashire, Architectural Guide*, 1955, pls 84–85; Beard, *Craftsmen and Interior Decoration in England*, p. 277]

Prescott, Richard, Knight Ct, Knight St, Liverpool, cabinet turner (1830). Free 17 November 1820 by patrimony as the son of William Prescott, watch engraver. [Freemen reg.]

Presland, John, Brewer St, Golden Sq., Soho, London, u (1825–26). At 44 Brewer St in 1825 but the following year the number was 46. In 1826 the business was listed as John Presland & Co. and the trade as u and warehousemen. [D]

Presswell, Henry, Exeter, Devon, cm (b.1806–d.1829). Died May 1829 aged 23. [*Exeter Flying Post*, 14 May 1829]

Presswell, Thomas, 5 Little Albany St, Regent's Park, London, cm and u (1839). [D]

Presswell, William snr, Exeter, Devon, cm (1816–33). At Sidwell St in 1816 but by 1822 had moved to 188 Fore St, an address that he was to continue to occupy until his retirement in 1833. In December 1829 his daughter Sarah married R. Anning, grocer, at St John's Church. He also had a son William who traded independently of his father in Fore St from at least 1825. William Presswell snr announced his retirement in September 1833 and his stock was sold by auction on 16 September. This consisted of 'handsome sets of mahogany, zebra and rosewood loo and card tables; sets of dining tables, in 1 set on pedestals, 11 ft. 3 by 4 ft. 8; a set of telescope, 9 ft. 10 by 4 ft. 2; and a set of pillar and claw ditto 6 ft. 6 by 4 ft. 6; sets of mahogany and rosewood dining room chairs; handsome mahogany sideboards, dwarf wardrobes; wash and dressing stands; dressing glasses; cheval glass plate 3 ft. 1 by 1 ft. 9; mahogany Pembroke tables; butlers' trays; mahogany and other 4 — post bedsteads, feather beds, folding straw mattresses etc. etc. — Also several pairs of carved mahogany and other bed pillars; mahogany, rose, satin, and other woods in plank and veneers; working benches, tools, patterns etc.'. Debtors of the business were requested to settle their accounts with William Presswell jnr. [D; *Exeter Flying Post*, 31 December 1829, 12 September 1833]

Presswell, William jnr, Fore St, Exeter, Devon, cm, broker and u (1825–33). In November 1825 announced his move from 136 to 138 Fore St. An 1832 voters list shows him living in the parish of St David. At the time of the retirement of his father from the cabinet making trade in September 1822, William jnr was at 248 Fore St and his father's debtors were requested to settle their accounts with him. [*The Alfred*, 8 November 1825; *Exeter Flying Post*, 12 September 1833; poll bk]

Prestage, John, Savile Row, London, cm and auctioneer (1745–48). In March 1745 supplied the Duke of Gordon with a mahogany table costing £1 7s. A further account for this patron is dated 2 March 1748 and totalled £9 7s. The largest item was two mahogany card tables which together cost £5 5s, the other items being two tea chests, nine tea boards and a dressing glass. Prestage was also paid £4 10s on 25 June 1746 for a mahogany writing table supplied to Benjamin Mildmay, Earl Fitzwalter at Moulsham Hall, Chelmsford, Essex. Prestage combined with William Vile in 1754 in compiling an inventory of furniture for Anthony Chute's house. The Vyne, Hampshire. [Hants. RO, 31M 57/646] He advertised as an auctioneer in *General Advertiser*, 29 March 1750. [Scottish RO, GD 44/51/299, GD 44/51/302; A. C. Edwards, *The Account Books of Benjamin Mildmay, Earl Fitzwalter*, p. 111]

Preston, —, address unknown, cm (1778–79). The Stanhope papers indicate the supply by this maker in the period 1778–79 of 'a pierced commode' for which £4 9s was charged and a 'cabriole couch' which cost £4 4s. [Kent RO, U590 A61/8]

Preston, Charles, 53 Stanhope St, Clare Mkt, London, cm, u, undertaker and appraiser (1827). [D]

Preston, Charles, Emsworth, Hants., cm and u (1830). [D]

Preston, Daniel, parish of St Oswald, Durham, wood carver (1724). Son bapt. on 16 February 1724. Daniel Preston was recorded as 'a stranger'. [PR (bapt.)]

Preston, Francis, 142 Sloane St, Chelsea, London, upholder and undertaker (1817). [D]

Preston, Francis, Nafferton, Yorks., cm (1823). [D]

Preston, Gawen, Newcastle, u (1664). Free 1664. His son Ralph was declared free, 24 November 1703. [Freemen reg.]

Preston, George, Sunderland St, Bishop Wearmouth, Sunderland, Co. Durham, cm (1827). [D]

Preston, James, 4 New Bridge St, Keighley, Yorks., joiner/cm (1828–37). [D]

Preston, John, address unknown, cm (1754). Subscribed to Chippendale's *Director*, 1754.

Preston, John, Liverpool, cm (1761). Son of Josiah Preston and free, 24 January 1761. [Freemen regs]

Preston, John, Lincoln, cm and u (1770–90). The name of this maker appears in the Massingberd accounts 1770–79. In 1770 he was paid £2 13s for a table and picture frame; in 1772 for a joiner's bill, bookcase and clothes press £18 8s; in 1774 for a book press, table etc. £3 12s 6d; and in 1776, 19s for picture frames. His name also appears in the Monson accounts in 1789 where he is described as an u. He was paid £17 3s 2d in December 1789 and £41 0s 9d a year later. [Lincoln RO, MM919, MM9110; Monson 10/1/A/6, pp. 101, 112] See Robert and Thomas Preston of Lincoln.

Preston, John, 349 Rotherhithe St, corner of Prince's St, London, u, undertaker and auctioneer (1781–1825). Son of Lewis Preston of Ludlow, Salop, shipwright. App. to Francis Pyner on 2 May 1781 and free of the Upholders' Co. by servitude, 1 October 1788. Insurance records show him at the Rotherhithe address by August 1782 and insuring properties at 4 and 5 King St, Scots Place, Islington for £300. He is included in the list of master cabinet makers in Sheraton's *Cabinet Dictionary*, 1803. Traded at the Rotherhithe address until at least 1825. [D; GL, Upholders' Co. records; Sun MS vol. 387, p. 508]

Preston, John, Birmingham, cm (1831). [Worcs. poll bk]

Preston, John, Chapel Allerton, near Leeds, Yorks., joiner, builder and cm (1834). [D]

Preston, Joseph, Lancaster, cm (1785–86). Free 1785–86, when stated 'of Kendal'. [Freemen rolls]

Preston, Matthew, Gainford, near Darlington, Co. Durham, joiner, cm and ironmonger (1828). [D]

Preston, Robert, Wisbech, Cambs., upholder (1716–23). Probably the Robert Preston who was app. to Thomas Preston of King's Lynn, Norfolk and free, 1708–09. In January 1720 insured a tenanted house at Upwell, Cambs. Took app. in 1723 named Day. [King's Lynn freemen rolls; GL, Sun MS vol. 5, 8 May 1716; vol. 10, 6 January 1720; S of G, app. index]

Preston, Robert, Lincoln, u (1788). On 22 December 1788 submitted to Lord Monson his account for £19 8s 8½d. [Lincoln RO, Monson 10/1/A/6] See John Preston on Lincoln.

Preston, Thomas snr, King's Lynn, Norfolk, u (c.1701–14). Master of Robert Preston, probably a relative, who was

declared free, 1708–09. Also took as app. his son Thomas jnr who was free, 1714–15. [Freeman rolls]

Preston, Thomas jnr, King's Lynn, Norfolk, u (1714–50). App. to his father Thomas jnr and free 1714–15. Took app. named Springold in 1719 and was also master to Asty Hardwick jnr, who was declared free 1743–44. Thomas Preston jnr's will was proved at Norwich 1750. [Freemen rolls; S of G, app. index; Norfolk Record Soc., index of wills]

Preston, Thomas, High St, Lincoln, u, joiner and cm (1778–93). In 1780 took out insurance cover of £1,000 of which utensils and stock accounted for £800. This would suggest a substantial business by provincial standards and he appears to have regularly supplied furniture to Lord Monson. On 21 January 1779 he received the sum of £44 13s 4d for items supplied from 1 June 1778. Much of this was for upholstery work, carpeting and wallpaper but included was a large sofa at £9 15s. In the year to January 1781 £15 6s was due for work undertaken, being mostly repairs and alterations, but also including a large deal wardrobe at £3 18s and a large marquee at £6 6s. For the following year the total cost was £19 12s 8½ the largest amount being £3 5s for a 'small portable bedstead for Miss Monson'. Payment for the previous year appears to have been made in January of the each year and were for 1783, £14 2s; 1784, £27 0s 6d; 1785, £18 8s 10d; 1785, £43 14s; 1786, £34 10s; and 1787, £30 17s. In 1793 Preston subscribed to Sheraton's *Drawing Book*. His name is recorded stencilled on the sackcloth under a chair of late 18th-century date. [D; poll bk; GL, Sun MS vol. 282, p. 410; Lincoln RO, Monson 11/28, 11/50, 10/1/A/6; *Antique Collector*, February 1956 p. 108] See John and Robert Preston. Probably:

Preston, Thomas, Lancaster and Lincoln, u and cm (1758–86). App. to R. Thorney in 1758 and free, 1785–86. This extended period between the start of his apprenticeship and his freedom is noteworthy as is also the remark in the freemen roll 'of the City of Lincoln'. [Lancaster freemen rolls]

Preston, Thomas, Harrison's Yd, Easingwold, Yorks., joiner and cm (1828–34). [D]

Preston, William, King's Lynn, Norfolk, u (1659–60). [Freemen rolls]

Preston, William, Lancaster and Louth, Lincs. cm (1767). Free 1767–68 and the freemen roll states 'of Louth in Lincolnshire'. Recorded trading in Louth 1777 when he took out insurance cover of £500 which included £40 for his shop. [Lancaster freemen rolls; GL, Sun MS vol. 256, p. 163]

Preston, William snr and jnr, Tower St, Seven Dials, London, cms and brokers (1805–10). In February 1805 took out insurance cover of £500 of which £400 was in respect of utensils and stock. By April 1810 total cover had risen to £650 though stock remained at the same valuation. In 1810 mention is made of a warehouse behind 15 Tower St. [GL, Sun MS vol. 431, ref. 772657; vol. 453, ref. 844485]

Preston, William, Dog Bank, Newcastle, cm, u and furniture broker (1821). In an advertisement of May 1821 he claimed to have been established 'many years'. He stated that he stocked 'a large & elegant assortment of the following articles viz: sofas, couches, secretary desks and bookcases; sets of dining tables; card, pembroke, loo, library & turn-over tables; mahogany chairs, cane & bass bottomed ditto; mahogany & beech bedsteads; wardrobe, mahogoney & other press beds; pier, chimney piece & all sorts of dressing glasses; mirrors; wash stands; mahogony & wainscot case eight day & other clocks; mahogany circular & straight-fronted lobby beds; prime goose feathers; feather beds & bedding; carpeting carpets; staircase & second hand ditto; hair & straw mattresses; chintz & all other descriptions of bed furniture made or in the web'. He stocked kitchen furniture and bought and exchanged second hand items. [*Durham County Advertiser*, 12 May 1821]

Preston, William, 16 Castle St, Long Acre, London, u (1829). [D]

Preswell, Joseph, Southernhay, Exeter, Devon, cm (1814). Son Joseph bapt. on 19 September 1814 at St David's Church. [PR (bapt.)]

Preswell, William, Precinct of Bedford, Exeter, Devon, cm (1803). [Militia Census]

Prett, Mrs, Canterbury, Kent, upholder (1803). [D]

Prett, Walter, Canterbury, Kent, u (1774–1830). The long period involved might suggest more than one maker of this name. [D; poll bks]

Prew, William, John, 7 Walworth Rd, London, cm and u (1839). [D]

Price, Mr, Pall Mall, London, u (1747–48). Heal records him in contemporary newspapers of 1747 as 'near St Alban's Street'. The *General Advertiser*, 28 October 1748, reported that three servants of this 'eminent Upholsterer' were committed for robbing him.

Price, Mr, Oxford Rd, London, cm (1749). His house was robbed in December 1749 and 'Money and Goods to a considerable value' taken. [*Whitehall Evening Post*, 2–5 December 1749]

Price, —, Whitchurch, Salop, chairmaker (1818). In June 1818 his son Joseph was married to Miss Martha Palin of Whitchurch. [*Chester Guardian*, 27 June 1818]

Price, Arthur, 7 Renshaw St, Ranelagh St, Liverpool, u (1804). [D]

Price, Charles, Craw St, Moorfields, London, bedstead maker (1793). [D]

Price, Charles, Red Cross St, Southwark, London, upholder and cm (1813–14). Took out insurance cover of £1,000 on a dwelling house, 'being two houses with offices, Workshop, Horse wheel house, stable with lofts and feather warehouse' and other property in Birdcage Walk Alley. [GL, Sun MS vol. 462, ref. 893049; vol. 462, 7 April 1814] See Thomas Price of Red Cross St.

Price, Charles, 29 New North St, Red Lion Sq., London, billiard table and backgammon board maker (1832). [D]

Price, Edward, Liverpool, cm (1802). App. to Isaac Marsh and free 8 July 1802. [Freemen reg.]

Price, Edward, College Lane, Ludlow, Salop, cm and u (1835). [D]

Price, Elizabeth, London, 'joyner' (1683–86). Widow of Richard Price who died in 1683. She continued his business as a supplier of furniture to the Crown. From 1685–86 supplied furniture for Whitehall and St James' Palaces to the value of £43 6s. The items included three sets of walnut chairs. [PRO, LC9/21/121/28]

Price, Francis, Worcester, cm and joiner (1779). App. to James Twitty and free 10 May 1779. [Freemen rolls]

Price, George, London, cm (1818). Eldest son of Thomas Price of Hereford, joiner. Freeman of Hereford 18 June 1818. [Hereford freemen rolls]

Price, George, Cross St, Oswestry, Salop, cm (1835–36). Successor to Griffith Price at this address. [D]

Price, Giles, on the Bridge, Bristol, u (1715–18). In 1717 took app. named Naish. [Poll bk; S of G, app. index; GL, Sun MS vol. 8, ref. 11351]

Price, Griffith, Cross St, Oswestry, Salop, cm (1822). Succeeded at this address by 1836 by George Price. [D]

Price, Horatio, 3 Church Lane, Church St, Liverpool, carver and gilder (1837). [D]

Price, James, Five Pound Court House, Court St, Whitechapel Rd, London, cm (1802). In November 1802 took out insurance cover for £999 of which £770 was for stock and utensils. [GL, Sun MS vol. 426, ref. 740133]

Price, James, Castle St, Long Acre, London cm and buhl manufacturer (1817). William Lovett records working in the early 1820s in a small shop in Castle St, Oxford Mkt, where repairs to buhl-work, marquetry and antique furniture were carried out. It is very likely that this was the workshop of James Price. [Heal; *Burlington*, June 1980, p. 416]

Price, James, Bradford St, Birmingham, cabinet case maker (1820). [D]

Price, James, 18 Borough Rd, London, cm and u (1822). [D]

Price, James, 59 Cold St, St Lukes, London, cm (1825). [D]

Price, John, 'The Three Chairs & Cabinet', Catherine St, Strand, London, u, undertaker and appraiser (1726–58). Son of Petley Price of Wantage, Berks., Gent. App. to Thomas Money on 7 December 1726 and free of the Upholders' Co. by servitude, 3 March 1735/36. His trade card [Heal Coll., BM and Gardener Coll., Westminster Ref. Lib.] indicates that he made and sold a wide range of upholstery and cabinet goods. These included 'All Sorts of Standing Beds, Feather Beds Mattresses Quilts Blankets Ruggs, Coverlids, Bed Ticks, Goods by the piece, viz. Silk & Worstead Damasks, Camblers Harrateens Chenys, Printed Stuffs and all Sorts of Silk & Worstead Lace Carpets, Tapestry Hangings, Chairs, Cabbinets, Desks, Book-cases, Chests of Drawers, Tea Chests. Mahogany and other Tables Peir and Chimney Glasses Large Gold and other Sconces with all sorts of goods necessary for Funerals'. John Price is recorded as a supplier of cushions, carpets and curtains for the House of Peers and the House of Commons and their Committee Rooms 1754–55. He was responsible for the supply of furniture to Lord Monson 1748–58. The first payment recorded was in February 1748 for £25 but from 1751 the sums were much more substantial. For making chairs, tables, stands and repairs and other work at Burton Hall, Lincoln, 1753–54, £413 8s 4d was charged; and £150 8s 4d was paid in 1751–53 for new furniture and repairs at Broxbournebury. The more substantial items included eight mahogany elbow chairs in June 1752 at £16 16s, twelve mahogany chairs in April 1753 at £18, a walnut sofa frame in March 1754 at £5 12s 5½d and a mahogany one in July at £6 10s. The most expensive item was, however, a 'very large ... Chinese carved and painted frame' for which £23 was paid. The account for £413 8s 4d submitted in 1755 was not fully settled until February 1758. The Strathmore MS [Durham RO] indicates that George Bowes hired a furnished house from John Price, 1755–56. [GL, Upholders' Co. records; PRO, LC9/291; Lincoln RO, Monson 10/3/13a, 10/3/13b, 11/50, 12; Durham RO, D/St/ 325]

Price, John, Liverpool, cm (1761). Free 12 March 1761. [Freemen reg.]

Price, John, Tothill St, London, upholder (1781–88). Son of John Price of Tothill St, Westminster, victualler, and app. to William Rawlins, 7 February 1781. Free of the Upholders' Co. by servitude, 5 March 1788 and at that date living at Mr Askey's in Tothill St. [GL, Upholders' Co. records]

Price, John, Chester, cm (1784–92). App. to John Croughton of Chester, cm and free by servitude, 16 April 1784. His son John Price jnr was app. to John Powell, u in August 1792. [Freemen rolls; app. bk]

Price, John, Southwark, London, looking-glass manufacturer (1804–20). At 1 Queens St in 1804 but by 1813 the number was 81. At 157 Union St, 1815–20. [D]

Price, John & Joseph, London, bedstead and cabinet makers (1804–39). At 4 Crown St, Finsbury 1804–25 an address which is also rendered as Crown Ct, Finsbury Sq. On 13 May 1805 a fire broke out in their premises. In 1825 moved to

59 Crown St, where the business stayed until 1839. In 1835 was listed as J. Price & Son and also in this year and in 1839 as simply Price & Son. In 1839 at Redman's Row, Mile End Rd. Another John Price is shown at 21 Brook St, Holborn in 1839. [D; *Gents Mag.*, May 1805] See Joseph Price.

Price, **John**, Southgate St, Gloucester, cm and u (1822–30). [D]

Price, **John**, Liverpool, cm (1822). In 1822 took app. named William Roscoe Alcock. [App. enrolment bk]

Price, **John**, London, frame maker (1825–37). At 1 Chapter House Ct, St Paul's Churchyard in 1825 as a 'miniature frame maker' but by 1835 he had moved to 17 Ave Maria Lane. He was still at this address in 1837 but was then advertising his trade as a 'miniature frame maker, glass & morocco case manufacturer'. [D]

Price, **John**, Stockport, Cheshire chairmaker (1834). On 9 January 1834 married Miss Mary Lee of Stockport 'after a tedious courtship of three days'. [*Chester Courant*, 14 January 1834]

Price, **John**, Upper Church St, Oswestry, Salop, cm (1835–36). [D]

Price, **John**, 21 Brook St, Holborn Bars, London, bedstead maker (1839). [D] See John & Joseph Price above.

Price, **John**, Liverpool, u (1839). Free 29 July 1839 by patrimony as the son of David Price. [Freemen reg.]

Price, **John**, 147 Bromsgrove St, Birmingham, fancy chairmaker (1839). [D]

Price, **John**, Chester, chairmaker (1840). His only daughter Harriet was married on 3 September 1840 to Mr Thornton of Liverpool. [*Chester Chronicle*, 4 September 1840]

Price, **Joseph**, 4 Crown St, Finsbury Sq., London, bedstead, chair and cabinet maker (early 19th century). Trade card in Landauer Coll., MMA, NY. See John & Joseph Price at this address.

Price, **Lewis**, 5 Brewer St, Golden Sq., London, cm and u (1784–93). Listed in 1784 as a cm and 1790–93 as a u. [D]

Price, **Martha**, 59 Upper Frederick St, Liverpool, u (1837). [D]

Price, **Philip**, Broad Capuchin Lane, Hereford, joiner, cm etc. (1775–d.1779). In August 1775 advertised for a journeyman cm who understood chairmaking, and a joiner. Dead by January 1780, when William Watkins advertised himself as his successor. [*Pugh's Hereford Journal*, 3 August 1775, 27 January 1780]

Price, **Philip**, 2 Spa Pl., Bermondsey, London, cm and u (1839). [D]

Price, **Richard**, St Martin's Lane, London, joiner and u (1670–d.1683). Supplied considerable quantities of furniture to the royal palaces during the reign of Charles II. In 1678 appointed joiner to the Crown, but most of the furniture supplied was in the upholstery branch. His work is often described as having features that are French or Dutch and this seems to indicate that he was familiar with the styles of those two countries, which were having a profound influence on the English furniture making trades at this time. A chair supplied in 1671 was described as 'French turned all over'. Items provided for the Queen, 1671–73 included a 'French Beddsted', at £2 10s, 'Two French folding stools turned all over' at 10s, and for Somerset House a 'large French Beddstead' at £3 2s 6d. Part of the same commission included sixteen 'French stooles turned all over' which cost 5s each. In 1676 Price was at Windsor setting up a bedstead and carving four lion feet for it, and in November 1680 he was back there again 'mending the great winding up Chair' and another chair in the King's Bedchamber. A chair of estate and two French tables also received his attention and he supplied two walnut forms 'wrought wth mouldings and scrowles with great bases on the ffeet and of the dutch form'. Numerous other beds, chairs, stools, tables etc. were supplied, and furniture was produced for Hampton Court, Whitehall and other locations. Richard Price died in 1683 and his wife Elizabeth continued to provide furniture until at least 1685. A caned walnut armchair carved with crowns at Temple Newsam House, Leeds, is stamped five times with the initials 'RP' and may be of his workmanship. [*DEF*; PRO, LC3/56, LC3/61; LC9/271–77; *C. Life*, 10 June 1954, p. 1917; Gilbert, *Leeds Furn. Cat.*, vol. II, p. 72]

Price, **Richard**, London, cm (1793). Subscribed to Sheraton's *Drawing Book*, 1793.

Price, **Richard**, 43 Union St, City Rd, London, cm (1812). In November 1812 took out insurance cover of £300 but of this £270 was cover for his dwelling house and only £30 for a chest of tools kept at 9 George Yd, Lombard St. [GL, Sun MS vol. 455, ref. 875727]

Price, **Richard**, 33 Wardour St, Soho, London, u (1829). [D]

Price, **S.**, 41 Clerkenwell Close, London, chair japanner (1835). [D]

Price, **Samuel**, Chester, chairmaker (1814–40). At Bridge St Row, from 1814–22, and by 1828 at Watergate Row. In 1840 he was back in Bridge St Row and describing himself as a cm and furniture broker. Took as app. James Rowlands who proved to be an unsatisfactory worker and was accused of threatening his master, damaging his reputation by spreading false reports and eventually absconded. In May 1829 he was committed to the house of correction for a month. An S. Price, probably Samuel Price, is recorded in the account book of Josiah Hinckes of Tettenhall Wood near Wolverhampton, Staffs. and on 6 March 1819 was paid £1 0s 8d for mending a chair. [D; *Chester Chronicle*, 22 My 1829; Herefs. RO, Foxley papers, B47/540]

Price, **Thomas**, Worcester, joiner, carpenter and u (1748–49). Free 6 March 1748/49. [Freemen rolls]

Price, **Thomas**, Hereford, cm (1789). Free 1789. [Hereford City Lib., Hopton Coll. 3574]

Price, **Thomas**, Red Cross St, Southwark, London, cm and u (1790–1817). Described as a cm, 1790–1802, and from 1809 as an u. Subscribed to Sheraton's *Drawing Book*, 1793 and included in the list of master cabinet makers in his *Cabinet Dictionary*, 1803. A Charles Price took out insurance cover on property in Red Cross St, which included workshops, 1813–14. A late 18th-century mahogany clothes press is also recorded bearing two labels of Price & Ball, Redcross St, Southwark. They were described as 'Appraisers & Undertakers' and maintained an 'Upholstery & Cabinet Warehouse. [D]

Price, **Thomas Henry**, London, upholder and broker (1808–22). At Rosomon's Building, Islington in 1808 and 1 Castle St, Long Acre, 1820–22. On 14 January 1822 took out insurance cover of £400 on a house and shop at 13 Belmont Pl., Vauxhall which was let to an oilman. [D; GL, Sun MS vol. 489, ref. 987594]

Price, **Thomas**, Gt Dover St, London. See William Pugh.

Price, **Thomas**, Worcester, carver and gilder (1828–40). Listed at Denmark Row, 1828–37, and St Paul's St in 1840. [D]

Price, **Thomas**, Brewood, Staffs., joiner/cm (1834). [D]

Price, **Thomas**, 1 Cumberland Pl., Newington Butts, London, bedstead maker (1835). [D]

Price, **W.**, address unrecorded, cm (1713). A fine japanned bureau cabinet with mirror doors is inscribed on one of the dust-boards 'W. Price, maker, 1713'. [*C. Life*, 13 February 1948]

Price, **William**, London(?), carver (1705). On 8 August 1708 paid £1 5s by Samuel Tufnell of the Middle Temple, London for carving two coats of arms. [Essex RO, D/DTu 276]

Price, **William**, Ipswich, Suffolk, u (1712). In 1712 took app. named Stannard. [S of G, app. index]

Price, William, Bilston, Staffs., cm, grocer and dealer in spiritous liquors (1793). [D]

Price, William, Smallbrook St, Birmingham, cm (1800). [D]

Price, William, Edgcumbe St, Stonehouse, Plymouth, Devon, u and cm (1822). [D]

Price, William, London, cm and furniture broker (1835–37). At 8 New Park St, Bloomsbury in 1835 and 6 Old St, 1835–39. [D]

Price & Ball, see Thomas Price.

Prichard, George, 4 Barrs St, Bristol, furniture broker and u (1833–34). [D]

Prichard, John, 23 Cleveland St, Fitzroy Sq., London, u (1829–39). [D]

Prichard, Richard, St James's Churchyard, Bristol, u (1815–19). [D]

Prichard, Thomas, London, upholder (1704). Free of the Upholders' Co., 24 June 1704. [GL, Upholders' Co. records]

Prichard & Priest, 11 Providence Rd, Finsbury, London, u (1839). [D]

Pricker & Henderson, New Bond St, London, u (1803). An action was brought against this firm by Bogle French Esq. concerning the furnishing of a villa at Dulwich. The plaintiffs were described as 'upholsterers to the circle of fashion'. [Gents Mag., December 1803]

Pricket, Charles, 122 Aldersgate St, London, u and cm (1795–1811). [D]

Prickett, Charles, Clerkenwell, London, cm (1768). Freeman of Oxford. [Oxford poll bk] Possibly:

Prickett, Charles, Foster Lane, London, cm (1793–1802). Freeman of Oxford. In 1793 subscribed to Sheraton's Drawing Book. [Oxford poll bk]

Prickett, Charles Richard, 1 St Ann's Lane, Aldersgate St, London, cm, chairmaker and undertaker (1781–1803). In 1781 took out insurance cover of £300 of which £100 was for utensils and tools. [D, GL, Sun MS vol. 297, p. 388]

Prickett, John, London Rd, Chesham, Bucks., chairmaker (1830). [D]

Pricket(t), John, Rickmansworth, Herts., chairmaker (1838–39). [D]

Prictor, William, 61 Whitehorse St, Stepney, London, cm and u (1839). [D]

Pridham, William, 11 St Martin's Churchyard, London, cm (1808). [D]

Priest, David, Liverpool, carver (1827–39). At 5 Wood St in 1827, 33 Clayton St in 1829, 27 Stanley St, 1834–37 and 19 Stanley St in 1839. [D]

Priest, James, address unknown, cm (1803). Subscribed to Sheraton's Cabinet Dictionary, 1803. A coromandel centre table of late 18th-century date has been recorded stamped 'J.B. Priest'. [Antique Collecting, July 1968, p. 30]

Priest, John, High Wycombe, Bucks., chairmaker and caner (b. c.1791–1841). Six sons and two daughters bapt. between 1815–31. Aged 50 at the time of the 1841 Census. [PR (bapt.)]

Priest, Richard, Castle St, London, chairmaker (1749). [Westminster poll bk]

Priest, Robert, corner of Belton St in Castle St, London, broker and cm (1807). In October 1807 took out insurance cover of £300 of which £260 was for utensils and stock. [GL, Sun MS vol. 440, ref. 806855]

Priest, W., London, auctioneer, appraiser and u (1837–40). A maker whose name is well-known from the large number of items surviving stamped with his name and address, or having his trade labels affixed. The business was trading at 23 Gt Charlotte St, and 17 and 24 Water St, Blackfriars, 1837–39. The Water St address is recorded on some furniture, but labels and stamps bearing the address 1 and 2 Tudor St, Blackfriars

are not infrequently found. The date of the furniture so marked ranges from c.1790 to the mid Victorian period. The labels bearing the Tudor St address describe the business as a 'Furniture Warehouse' and it is probable that Priest was selling secondhand items which he marked before disposal. One form of his label states that he specialised in 'Office & Library Furniture'. [D; V&A archives; Christie's, 23 May 1968, lot 101; Sotheby's, 28 June 1968, lot 123; 29 April 1983, lot 91; Phillips', 15 October 1963, lot 84; Antique Collector, February 1955, p. x; Antique Collecting, November 1979, p. 68; C. Life, 10 October 1970, supplement, p. 40, 1 November 1979, supplement, p. 65; Conn., September 1975, p. 35, November 1979, p. 205]

Priest, William, St Mary St, Bridgwater, Som., cm and u (1822). [D]

Priest & Co., 43 Mill Lane, Shaw's Brow, Liverpool, cm (1839). [D]

Priestland, John, London, upholder (1773–81). Son of John Priestland of Old Broad St, London and app. to Henry Blaxland on 7 July 1773. Free of the Upholders' Co. by servitude, 4 April 1781. [GL, Upholders' Co. records]

Priestley, Joseph, Smithy-door, Manchester, cm (1815). [D]

Priestley, Peter, address unknown, cm (1803). Subscribed to Sheraton's Cabinet Dictionary, 1803.

Priestley, Stephen, Northgate, Wakefield, Yorks., cm (1818). [D]

Priestly, William, Andrew's Hill, Doctors' Commons, St Paul's, London, carver and gilder (1790–93). [D]

Priestman, Robert, High-bridge, Newcastle; chairmaker and turner (1833–38). Recorded at Dean(s) Yd, 1833–34. [D]

Prigg, Cooper, Cambridge, joiner and u (1752–58). Worked for Trinity College where he not only undertook joinery work but supplied blankets, repaired curtains, cushions and tables, supplied green silk lace for cushions and four new walnut chairs. [Trinity College records]

Prigg, Daniel, Ham Lane, Stratford, London, u (1777). In 1777 took out insurance cover of £1,100 on his house. [GL, Sun MS vol. 256, p. 630]

Prihorn, —, address unknown, u (1753–56). Supplier of furniture to Henry Hoare. In 1753 a payment of £74 was made in May and in August £200 was given on account. On 8 January 1754 £109 19s was paid in connection with Henry Hoare's house at Clapham and on 22 January £300 in part payment for furniture at Lincoln's Inn Fields. No further payments are recorded until 14 April 1756 when a part payment of £109 16s was made, followed on 24 April by a further £20 to complete it. [V&A archives].

Prime, George, Swine Mkt, Leicester, cm (1828–29). [D]

Prime, Samuel, London, cm and u (1827–39). At Skinner St in 1827 but at 34 Meredith St, St John's St, Clerkenwell, 1829–39. [D]

Primrose, William Ashton, Bristol, cm (1831–33). At Lower Montague St in 1831 and 4 All Saints' St, 1832–33. [D]

Prince, George, Westminster, London, cm (1749). [Poll bk]

Prince, Godwin, near Durham Yd, Strand, London, carver, gilder and undertaker (1749). His trade card [Heal Coll., BM] states that he also undertook 'cabinet & Upholsterers Work in General'. He bought and appraised goods and sold items on commission. [Westminster poll bk; Conn., June 1981, p. 145]

Prince, John, Newbury, Berks., turner and chairmaker (1798). [D]

Prince, Richard, Nantwich, Cheshire, cm (1832–38). Three sons bapt. between 1832–39. [PR (bapt.)]

Prince, Thomas, Foregate St, Chester, u (1818). Free 13 June 1818. [Freemen rolls]

Prince, Thomas, 13 Leatherseller's Buildings, London, cm and u (1839). [D]

Prince, William, Leeds, Yorks., cm (1822–37). At the back of Hope St in 1822 and at 77 Hope St in 1837. [D]

Prindle, John, Pentonville, London, cm (1798). [D]

Pring, William, parish of St Sidwell's, Exeter, Devon, u (1837). Daughter bapt. on 21 August 1837 [PR (bapt.)]

Pringle, John, 12 Old St Sq., Old St, London, cm (1792). On 5 July 1792 took out insurance cover of £100 on his household goods in his new dwelling house. [GL, Sun MS vol. 388, p. 171]

Pringle, John & Robert, London, u and cm (1784–1829). At 126 Wardour St, Soho, 1784–1825, and 232 Regent St, 1825–29. After moving to Regent St, the premises in Wardour St appear to have been retained. In 1829 the addresses shown are 232 Regent St and 46 Berners St. The business appears to have been mainly concerned with upholstery, although in 1807 the trade is listed as cm and inlayer, and cabinet making is mentioned also in 1820, 1827 and 1829. In 1793 'Pringle' subscribed to Sheraton's *Drawing Book* where he is described as 'Cabinet Maker & Upholsterer to the Duke of Clarence'. Also subscribed in 1803 to the *Cabinet Dictionary* and is included in the list of master cabinet makers contained in that publication. In June 1796 the bankruptcy of John Pringle was announced and a further bankruptcy occurred in November 1802. Robert Pringle is not mentioned in these proceedings. John Pringle snr died in 1816 and the John and Robert Pringle who carried on the business appear to have been his sons. As a Robert Pringle had been a partner in the business as early as its commencement in 1784 this would suggest that there was also a Robert Pringle snr and jnr. In July 1820 premises at 127 Wardour St appear to have been used in addition to those at 126 and were insured for £500 which included £300 for stock and utensils kept there. In August 1823 insurance cover of £1,500 was taken out on 128 Wardour St. The partners were signatories to the prefatory recommendation to P. & M. A. Nicholson's *Practical Cabinet Maker*, 1826. Some documents relating to this business including daybooks, accounts and deeds are preserved at Marylebone Library. In its later years the business is sometimes referred to as Pringle & Co.

Despite the long period of trading few of the firm's clients are known. Alexander Wedderburn made payments to John Pringle between 1784–92 and these were in most cases specified as for his London house. In certain years the sums were substantial with £100 being paid in 1784, £200 in 1785, £100 in 1787, £69 13s in 1788 and £157 4s 3d in 1790. The firm also supplied furniture for Government House, St Johns, Newfoundland in 1829. [D; *Billinge's Liverpool Advertiser*, 6 June 1796, 12 December 1796, 20 November 1797, 8 November 1802; Marylebone Lib., Pringle D Misc./153; GL, Sun MS vol. 483, ref. 970074; vol. 498, ref. 1006384; V&A archives; Scottish RO, GD 157/815, GD 164/Box 20/177/2–3]

Pringle, John, Sunderland, Co. Durham, cm (1832). [D]

Pringle, William, 40 Stephenson St, Newcastle, cm (1834). [D]

Pringle, William, North Shields, Northumb., cm (1834). [D]

Prior, Edwin, Chipping Sodbury, Glos., cm and u (1839). [D]

Prior, John, London, u (1707–14). Employed at St Mary's Church, Walthamstow, London in October 1714. [*London Gazette*, 17 July 1707; *Guide to St Mary's, Walthamstow*]

Prior, John & Robert, High St, Uxbridge, Middlx, rustic chairmakers and turners (1808–38). Directories show John Prior at the London end of Uxbridge High St in 1808, and a panorama of Uxbridge High St, drawn *c.*1810, shows at 101, on the south side, Prior & Son 'Wind. Chair Manufactory'. Listed at Hillingdon End, 1823–38, as Windsor chairmaker in 1832. Robert was a member of the Providence Congregational Chapel and his son William was bapt. here on 13 March 1814. The billhead of J. & R. Prior used from 1818–20

describes the business of 'Windsor Chair-Maker & Turner' and is embellished with a fine engraving of a Windsor Chair. It states that they dealt 'Wholesale, Retail & for Exportation'. They had trading links with London and in September 1818 a consignment of six yew arm chairs for the 3rd Lord Lyttelton's house, Hagley Hall, Stourbridge, Worcs. were first sent to Joseph Bury at 'The Ram Inn', West Smithfield, London. The Priors charged Bury £4 10s for these chairs, but his account to Mr Grove, Lord Lyttelton's agent at Hagley, was for £5 2s and carriage of £1 7s 6d in addition. Another bill of the Priors which survives and is dated 20 March 1820 is only for stakes, poles and pea sticks. A Windsor chair is known with the stamp 'ROBERT PRIOR/MAKER/UXBRIDGE' impressed. [D; Uxbridge Ref. Lib.; Temple Newsam House, Leeds, Exhib. Cat., *Common Furniture*, 1982; Worcs. RO, Lyttelton MS, 5467/705: 658/122(i)]

Prior, Samuel, Cricklewood, Kilburn, London, rustic chairmaker etc. (1839). [D]

Prior (or Pryor), William, Baker St, Enfield, Middlx, carver and gilder (1838–39). [D]

Prisk, Richard, 13 Edgware Rd, Paddington, London, cm (1803–23). Subscribed to Sheraton's *Cabinet Dictionary*, 1803. In October 1823 at Edgware Rd, where he took out insurance cover of £300. [GL, Sun MS vol. 498, ref. 1010017]

Prissick, William, Hull, Yorks., cm and u (1816–40). At 46 Salthouse Lane in 1816 and referred to as William Prissick jnr. In 1817 at 21 Grotto Sq., Mason St; at 16 Worship St, 1823–26; 15 Worship St, 1828–31; 8 Clarence Ct, Princess St; 1835–38, Charlotte St from 1838; and Charlotte St Mews in 1840. [D]

Pritchard, C., 12 Westage St, Bath, Som., auctioneer, appraiser and u to HM (1819). [D]

Pritchard, Edward, Liverpool, cm (d. by 1832). In September 1832 his daughter E. Pritchard was married at St David's Church to Stewart Bond of Armagh, Northern Ireland. The bride's father, Edward Pritchard was already dead by this date. [*Liverpool Mercury*, 21 September 1832]

Pritchard, James, 42 Sir Thomas Buildings, Liverpool, cane and whalebone worker (1823). [D]

Pritchard, John, Long Acre, London, u (1749). [Westminster poll bk]

Pritchard, John, Cross St, Oswestry, Salop, cm and joiner (1828). [D] Successor to Samuel Pritchard at this address.

Pritchard, John, 59 Chisenhale St, Liverpool, joiner and cm (1835). [D]

Pritchard, Richard, 120 Curtain Rd, Shoreditch, London, chair and sofa manufacturer (1826–37). [D]

Pritchard, Robert, Eastgate St Row, Chester, cm (1816–28). Listed in directories at this address in 1816 but admitted freeman on 12 May 1818. In 1822 advertised that he was cm to HRH the Duke of York. [D; freemen rolls]

Pritchard, Robert, Nantwich, Cheshire, carver and gilder (1830–31). Son George bapt. on 28 March 1830 and another, William, on 21 June 1831. [PR (bapt.)]

Pritchard, Samuel, Twickenham, Middlx, carver, gilder and plaisterer (1797–1809). [D]

Pritchard, Samuel, Cross St, Oswestry, Salop, cm and joiner (1822). [D] Succeeded by John Pritchard at this address by 1828.

Pritchard, William, Philip Lane, Aldermanbury, London, cm (c.1760). Known from trade labels on two pieces of furniture at Rousham House, Oxon. These are a mahogany bureau bookcase of c.1760, and a kneehole desk perhaps of slightly later date. Labels have also been noted in items of furniture elsewhere. [*DEF*]

Pritchard, William, Middle St, Brighton, Sussex, u (1837). [Poll bk]

Pritchard, William, 22 Dorset Cresc., New North Rd, London, carver and gilder (1837). [D]

Pritchett, William, London, cm, u and broker (1829–39). At 38 Drury Lane, 1820–29 and 204 High Holborn, 1839. [D]

Pritchitt, John, Worcester St, Birmingham, cm, u and broker (1828–30). Recorded at no. 33 in 1828. [D]

Pritt, Isaac, Cable St, Green Area, Lancaster, cm and u (1822–34). [D]

Pritchard, James, 30 Fishergate, Preston, Lancs., u and paper-hanger (b.1810–d.1833). Son of the keeper of the 'King's Arms Inn', Lancaster. Died on 15 November 1833 aged 23 though still listed in an 1834 directory. [D; *Liverpool Mercury*, 29 November 1833]

Pritt, John, Lancaster and Liverpool, cm (1817–18). Free 1817–18 when stated 'of Liverpool'. [Freemen rolls]

Proctor, Christopher, Lancaster (1754–89). App. to J. Wright in 1754 and named in the Gillow records 1785–89. [App. reg.; Westminster Ref. Lib., Gillow]

Proctor, Christopher, Lancaster and Skipton, Yorks., cm (1789–1814). App. to W. Bruce of Lancaster and free, 1789–90 when stated 'of Skipton'. Trading in Skipton, 1806–14, when he supplied furniture and undertook work at Broughton Hall near Skipton for Stephen Tempest. Four mahogany trunk stands supplied on 4 September 1813 at a cost of £3 4s (16s each) have been identified. Other minor furniture was supplied, jobbing work undertaken and in 1814 together with his son and an employee, John Hall, he carried out extensive alterations to library bookcases. The nine bills in the Tempest Papers for the period 1806–14 amount to £133 19s 10d. [Lancaster freemen rolls; Temple Newsam, Leeds, Exhib. Cat., *Furniture from Broughton Hall*, 1971, p. 24]

Proctor, Christopher, Lancaster, u (1826–38). App. to Edward Lodge in 1826 and free, 28 July 1838. [App. reg.; freemen rolls]

Proctor, George, Lancaster and Skipton, Yorks. (1806–22). Received the freedom of Lancaster, 1806–07, but appears to have immediately moved to Skipton where he was trading at Mount Pleasant in 1822. [D; Lancaster freemen rolls]

Proctor, George, 5 Old Bridge St, Keighley, Yorks. joiner/cm (1833–37). [D; PR]

Proctor, James, Lancaster, cm (1817–18). [Freemen rolls]

Proctor, John, Leeds, Yorks., cm (1752). In 1752 took app. named Howden. [S of G, app. index]

Proctor, John, 1 Pollard's Row, Bethnal Green, London, cm and u (1839). [D]

Proctor, William Grosvenor, London, cm and u (1820–26). Initially probably the manager for Robert & Henry Chipchase but by 1809 had become a partner in the business which traded as Chipchase & Proctor from an address at 27 Albemarle St. The Chipchases had withdrawn from the business by 1818 when it was trading as Proctor & Chadley. William Proctor did not maintain this business connection for long, however, and by 9 October 1820 had broken away and was trading on his own behalf from an address at 29 Argyle St, Oxford St. The Albemarle St premises continued to be occupied by Robert & George Chadley. The move to Argyle St probably resulted in a scaling down in the size of the enterprise, for although Proctor took out insurance cover of £4,500 on the new premises only £1,000 was for utensils and stock. In October 1822 the corresponding figures were £5,900 and again £1,000. [D; GL, Sun MS vol. 483, ref. 970952; vol. 493, ref. 997314]

Proctor & Chadley, 27 Albemarle St, London, cm and u (1818–20). Successors to Chipchase & Proctor at this address. One of the partners was William Grosvenor Proctor, formerly the manager and then a partner with the Chipchases in the former business. There were possibly two persons by the name of Chadley involved, for from 1821 Robert & George Chadley were in possession of the Albemarle St business, then at no. 28. Proctor moved in October 1820 to 29 Argyle St, where he set up on his own in the same trade. Henry Leigh Esq. of Stoneleigh, Warks., whose family had previously patronised Chipchase & Proctor, bought furniture from the new partners in 1818. The major item supplied in February 1818 was a bookcase with 'brass trellis work & rose colour'd silk curtains in the doors' which was charged at £34 13s. Other items supplied from February to April 1818 increased the total to £90. The business was still of substantial size in January 1820 when insurance cover came to £4,000 of which £3,800 was for stock and utensils in the workshops, warerooms and in an open yard. [D; GL, Sun MS vol. 483, ref. 962562; Shakespeare Birthplace Turst, Leigh receipts, DR 18/5]

Proffer, William, Bristol, cm (1774–81). [Poll bks]

Prola, Francis, 23 Cable St, Liverpool, gilder and picture frame maker (1796). [D]

Prosser, Frederick, Worcester, cm and u (1822–30). Addresses given at 2 Pump St in 1822, 36 Bridge St in 1828 and 36 Broad St in 1830. [D]

Prosser, James, Rossbottom St, Staylybridge, Lancs., cm (1825). [D]

Prosser, John, Holborn, London, japanner, painter and gilder (1781–93). At 7 Wharton's Ct, Holborn in 1781 when insurance cover of £300 was taken out of which £100 was for utensils and stock. By 1789 at 220 High Holborn and in the following year the business is shown as Prosser & Bassana. [D; GL, Sun MS vol. 288, p. 413]

Prosser, William, Bristol, cm (1754–84). In 1754 the address is shown as the parish of St Augustine, but in 1775 at 13 Stoney Hill. [D; poll bks]

Proston(?), Sarah, Cambridge, u (1710–12). Worked for St John's College, 1710–12, and supplied new curtains, a quilt and blankets. [St John's College records]

Prother, Hugh, Oxford, cm and u (1693–97). Worked for Pembroke College and in 1693 supplied bedsteads, tables, shelves for two studies at a cost of £2 14s. In 1697 supplied three bedsteads, a table etc. at £13 2s, and in the same year bedding, chairs and a curtain for two chambers at £15. [Pembroke College records]

Prothero, William & Spraggon, City Rd, Moorfields, London, cm and upholders (1791). Bankrupt by September 1791. [*Williamson's Liverpool Advertiser*, 19 September 1791, 4 February 1793]

Proud, William, London, cm (1793). Subscribed to Sheraton's *Drawing Book*, 1793.

Proud, William, Far Bondgate, Bishop Auckland, Co. Durham, joiner and cm (1827). [D]

Proudman, John, London, upholder (1758–66). Son of John Proudman of Queen St in the Park, Southwark, distiller. App. to William Guidott on 16 November 1758 and then Edward Shipman on 6 May 1761. Free of the Upholders' Co. by servitude, 6 March 1766. [GL, Upholders' Co. records]

Prowse, William, 17 Chapel St, Devonport, Devon, carver and gilder (1830). [D]

Pruden, Elizabeth, 2 Western Rd, Brighton, Sussex, u and calenderer (1832). [D]

Prudie & Hinchcliff, 98 High Holborn, London, cm (1794). [Heal]

Prussurot, John, 7 Greese St, Rathbone Pl., London, carver and gilder (1783–90). Employed by order of Mr Garbert at Carlton House, London for the Prince of Wales, 1783–84. He was responsible for carving and gilding '6 girandoles representing an African Marygold flower with 3 branches to each supported by Baskets, Ribbons, Tassels etc.' For this work £38 was charged with an additional £1 4s for putting them up in the Long Gallery. By 1790 Prussurot had undertaken work for the Prince of Wales to a value of £7,057 3s 7d and in that year £433 1s 7d in interest was added in respect of the £6,817 still outstanding. Prussurot was also employed by the 4th Lord Howard de Walden at Audley End, Essex. On 17 April 1785 he charged £6 10s for carving and gilding a large frame with an additional £2 2s for carving an imperial crown and gilding. The total of all work undertaken from 9 July 1785 to 12 January 1786 was £12 16s 6d, but a further account for £10 was submitted in 1786 for making, gilding and repairing frames. [Windsor Royal Archives, RA25054 RA25073, RA25075, RA25088; Essex RO, D/DBy/A44/2 and 10]

Prussurot, Thomas Francis, 7 Greese St, Rathbone Pl., London, carver and gilder (1781). Clearly related to John Prussurot who may have been his successor. In 1781 took out insurance cover of £400 of which half was for utensils, stock, goods and a timber shop. [GL, Sun MS vol. 294, p. 157]

Pryce, William snr, London, upholsterer (1726–d. by 1786). Son of William Pryce of Ipswich and father of William Pryce jnr. App. to Richard Wood on 20 September 1726 and William Jones on 19 June 1729. Free of the Upholders' Co. by servitude, 1 October 1735. [GL, Upholders' Co. records]

Pryce, William jnr, London, upholsterer (1768). Son of William Pryce snr, freeman of the Upholders' Co. William Pryce jnr was admitted freeman of the Upholders' Co. by redemption under the terms of the 1750 Upholders' Act, 27 October 1768. [GL, Upholders' Co. records]

Pryer, Charles, London, cm and u (1789–1803). At 96 New Bond St in 1789 and then traded from 472 Strand, 1790–1803. His trade card [Banks Coll., BM] states that he also had a manufactory at Paradise Row, Chelsea. He appears to have specialised in small cabinet furniture and his card is embellished with engravings of writing and medicine cases, a toilet mirror, a caddy, a backgammon board and a shell inlaid tea tray. He also stocked floor cloth, matting, ivory, Tunbridge-ware, brooms, brushes and turnery goods and undertook funerals. The turnery goods were produced at his own manufactory. [D] Possibly the 'Son' in:

Pryer & Son, opposite Craven St, Strand, London, cm and u (1784). [Heal]

Pryer, Steains & Mackenzie, 30 Brydges St, Covent Gdn, London, u and cm (1810–37). The Pryer appears to have been George Pryer who in 1803 subscribed to Sheraton's *Cabinet Dictionary*. George Pryer and James Steains were already established in Brydges St by 15 August 1810 when they took out insurance cover of £1,100 of which £800 was in respect of utensils and stock. Half of the value of these items was at Brydges St and the other half at a workshop that they used in Denham St, Little Drury Lane. By February 1812 they had been joined by John Mackenzie, and insurance cover had risen to £1,900 of which £1,200 covered utensils and stock at 30 Brydges St and two houses behind, also in Little Drury Lane. By 1817 James Steaines had withdrawn from the business and it traded from this date as Pryer & Mackenzie. By 1837 John Mackenzie had also ceased his involvement, and George Pryer was trading alone. As with a number of other makers in this part of London they were strongly involved in the making and marketing of 'patent' furniture. They could offer 'Patent Brass Screw Bedsteads, Sofa & Chair Beds, Dining Tables, Sideboards &c.'. In common with other 'patent' furniture makers they labelled the furniture they produced. Two beds and a writing table have been recorded with labels. In April 1816 they supplied the 6th Duke of Bedford with six strongly made beech chairs for his stables at a cost of £2 5s. [D; GL, Sun MS vol. vol. 453, ref. 846979; vol. 459, ref. 867633; V&A archives; Bedford Office, London]

Pryner, John, Lombard St, London, u (1778). In 1778 took out insurance cover of £2,200 of which £1,550 covered utensils, stock and goods. [GL, Sun MS vol. 264, p. 580]

Prynn, William, Lichfield, Staffs., cm and u (1818–35). Listed at Butch Row in 1818, Butcher Row, 1826–35, and Dam St, 1828–35. [D; poll bks]

Prynn, William, Burton-on-Trent, Staffs., cm and u (1822–35). Listed at Butcher Row in 1822 and High St, 1834–35. [D]

Puckle, Thomas, London, cm (1692). Supplied William III at Whitehall Palace in 1692 with tablestands and a glass frame 'Japan Lackro' at £32 5s. [PRO, LC9/280]

Puckridge, William, Hosier Lane, West Smithfield, London, carver and gilder (1789–1839). At 24 Hosier Lane, 1789–1802, but the number was 26 from 1804–20 and 17 from 1829–39. In directories he is described from 1789–93 simply as a carver, and his trade card [Heal Coll., BM] confirms that his main interest was in the making of trade signs including 'Bacchus's, Bunches of Grapes'. [D]

Pugh, —, address unknown, carver (1719–39). Employed at Holkham Hall, Norfolk where in 1719 he supplied a large pillar glass and three chimney glasses at a cost of £64. Small commissions in connection with a dressing glass, a walnut frame and re-silvering existing glasses occur in 1727 and 1733 totalling £3 but more substantial work was undertaken in 1739 for the new house at Holkham. Two glasses supplied in this year were charged at £42. He was also responsible for the supply of console tables for the Saloon at Holkham. [V&A archives; *C. Life*, 11 February 1980, pp. 427–31]

Pugh, Edward, Shrewsbury, Salop, u (1707–20). Free 1707. In 1720 took app. named Weden. [Freemen rolls; S of G, app. index]

Pugh, Ellis, address unknown, cm (1766). In February 1766 supplied Sir Gilbert Heathcote with an ebony frame and mended 'a fine amber cabinet'. The total cost was £7 19s. [Lincoln RO, 2 ANC 12/D/27]

Pugh, John, Stroud, Glos., cm and u (1820–37). Trading at High St in 1822 and London Rd in 1830. Children bapt. in 1823, 1825 and 1837. [D; PR (bapt.)]

Pugh, Thomas, High St, Shrewsbury, Salop, carver and gilder, cm and u (1828–35). [D]

Pugh, Thomas B., 14 Gt Dover St, London, carver and gilder (1839). [D]

Pugh, William, Southwark, London, u and cm (1809–25). At 303 Kent St, 1809–19. On 10 October 1810 took out insurance cover of £550 of which £450 was for utensils and stock. In October 1812 total insurance cover had risen to £1,100 but utensils and stock rose only modestly to £500. By March 1814 Pugh had a partner, Thomas Price and they appear to have remained trading together until 1825. In 1817 they were at 10 Gt Dover St and in 1825 25 Gt Dover St. By August 1820 insurance cover had been raised to £1,600 with utensils and stock at £700 and a stock of glass additionally valued at £100. Some insurance records, 1821–24, are in the names of William & Charles Pugh but they do not concern business stock. Charles Pugh was, however, to enter a partnership with William from 1825. [D; GL, Sun MS vol. 449, ref. 848912; vol. 457, ref. 875427; vol. 463, refs 891676–77; vol. 486, ref. 970655; vol. 489, ref. 995574]

Pugh, William & Charles, Blackman St, Southwark, London, u and cm (1825–39). William had successfully operated a similar business at 303 Kent Rd from 1809–14 before going into partnership with Thomas Price at the same address. The partnership lasted until 1825, but from 1817 addresses in Gt Dover St were used. Charles Pugh appears as the joint insurer of property with William, 1821–24, and was probably living at the Gt Dover St address. He may even have been William's son. When the partnership with Thomas Price broke up in

1825 William & Charles Pugh moved to 11 Blackman St and are shown there, 1825–28. By 1837, however, they were at 6 Blackman St and were still at this address in 1839. [D; GL, Sun MS vol. 485, refs 981738, 981790; vol. 489, ref. 995575; vol. 497, ref. 1019484]

Pugh, William, 6 Lower Montague St, Bristol, cm, u, paper hanger and undertaker (1836–40). [D]

Pugh, William, 54 Ashley Cresc., City Rd, London, cm and u (1839). [D]

Pugh & Co., 153 Borough High St, London, carver, gilder and looking-glass manufacturer (1812–15). [D]

Pugin, Augustus Welby Northmore, London, architect, designer and cm (b. 1812–d. 1852). Pugin's career as England's most celebrated Gothic Revival architect is too well known to detain us here; his little known foray into the realm of cabinet making however, is relevant. Pugin was from 1827–29 employed as the designer of a wide range of Gothic Revival furniture for Windsor Castle. This furniture was manufactured to his designs by Morel & Seddon and much of it still survives in situ.

In 1829 Pugin noted in his fragmentary autobiography 'Novr. 23 began business for myself in the carving and joinery line at 12 Hart Street, Covent Garden. At this time I had only the upper loft'. [V&A Lib., L.5204–1969 f. 30] Hart St is now named Floral St. Pugin was also working at this time as a stageman at the nearby Covent Gdn Theatre. His business was a pioneering one for 'In those days great difficulty was felt in finding artificers and carvers capable of doing justice to the execution of designs in the mediaeval style . . . young Pugin now proposed not only to undertake the delineation of working drawings, but also to superintend the execution of work which he designed'. [Ferrey, pp. 64–65]

No bills, accounts or other documents of the firm survive and Pugin's name does not appear in the rate bks, probably because he rented the premises. [Wainwright, p. 5] As shown below only four commissions are documented and only three of these are certainly for furniture. Pugin's firm manufactured carved details as well as furniture and 'Would undertake to supply all the ornamental portions of a building which could possibly be executed apart from the structure and fixed afterwards'. [Ferrey, p. 65] Pugin certainly supplied carved details and possibly furniture to Murthly Castle in 1830 and 1831 [Macaulay, pp. 248–49] which was then being built to the designs of his friend the architect James Gillespie Graham. Pugin almost certainly also designed and possibly furnished the interiors at Murthly: '. . . I designed all the interior decoration of a large mansion for Mr Gillespie Graham . . . in the style of James I, the drawing room in the style of Louis 14th.' [V&A Lib., L.5204–1969 f. 29]

The furniture manufactured by the firm was not only Gothic in the manner of Pugin's Windsor pieces, but Jacobean as at Murthly and at times Tudor also. A considerable number of furniture designs by Pugin survive from this period [Wedgwood, 1977]; how many were executed is unknown. A group of designs in the Gothic and Jacobean styles survive [Wedgwood, 1985] which were certainly executed for Mrs John Gough of Perry Hall. The Pugin letters which accompany them cover the period June 1830–September 1831 and provide more information concerning the activities of his firm than is available from any other source. None of this furniture is known to survive.

The firm was short lived, for in 1831 Pugin '. . . not being brought up as a man of business was incapable of estimating the sufficient profit he attached to labour and materials in order to secure a proper return on invested capital . . . he was sued for non-payment of rent and placed in a sponging house . . . he must have become bankrupt but for the final discharge of his liabilities by Miss Welby his aunt'. [Ferrey, pp. 66–68] In September he wrote to Mrs Gough '. . . I have at length determined to relinquish the execution of work myself altogether to confine myself entirely to my original profession of an architect and designer'. [V&A, Print Dept, E.65–1955] He never again ran a business, only working as an architect for the usual fees.

The history of this short-lived firm is important not only because of Pugin's fame as an architect, but also because of the advanced character of the carving and furniture which it produced. The pieces in the Jacobean and Tudor styles particularly were to be emulated in so many pieces made by other firms in the later 1830s and 1840s. Only two pieces made by this firm are known to survive, that mentioned below and a Tudor style oak table in the V&A which is stamped 'A. PUGIN'. [Wainwright, p. 5] [B. Ferrey, Recollections of A.W.N. Pugin and his father Augustus Pugin, 1861; J. Macaulay, The Gothic Revival, 1745–1845, 1975; A. Wedgwood, Catalogue of the Drawings Collection of the Royal Institute of British Architects the Pugin Family, 1977; A. Wedgwood, Catalogues of Architectural Drawings in the Victoria and Albert Museum, A.W.N. Pugin and the Pugin Family, 1985; C. Wainwright, 'A.W.N. Pugin's Early Furniture', Conn., CXCI, no. 767, 3–11]

PERRY HALL, Warks. (Mrs John Gough). Furniture supplied 1830–31. [V&A]

MURTHLY CASTLE, Perthshire (Sir John Stewart of Grantully). 1830–31. Carved details and possibly furniture. [Macaulay]

WESTON HOUSE, Warks. (Sir George Philips) 1830–31. Furniture and possibly carvings. [Pugin letters noted by Warwick RO in 1932 as in house, now lost]

PRIORY CHURCH OF HOLY TRINITY, Christchurch, Hants. 1831. The altar table, which is still in situ, bears the inscription 'This table was made and presented to this church by Augustus Welby Pugin AD 1831'. The design also exists. [Wedgwood, 1977, p. 43]   C.W.

Pujola(i)s, Henry, Margaret St, Cavendish Sq., London, painter, gilder and carver (1761–63). Fellow of the Society of Arts 1761–63. Painted, varnished and gilded the state coach of King George III, c.1761. [D; J. Harris, Sir William Chambers, p. 220]

Puleston, Edward, 17 Green St, Plymouth, Devon, chairmaker (1836–38). [D]

Pulford, Charles, Harleston, Norfolk, cm (1808). Married in 1808. [Suffolk RO, 50/2/114, p. 67]

Pullan, Jos., Bond St, Hull, Yorks., cm (1803). [D]

Pullan, Thomas, Kettlewell, near Skipton, Yorks., cm (1822). [D]

Pullen, —, 26 Redcliff St, Bristol, cm (1831). [D]

Pullen, H. & R., Farnham, Surrey, chairmakers (1838). [D]

Pullen, James, 5 Charles St, Westminster, London, carver and gilder (1820). [D]

Pullen, John, White's Alley, Chancery Lane, London, cm (1784). Freeman of Bristol. [Bristol poll bk]

Pullen (or Pullan), John, London, billiard table and backgammon board maker (1822–39). In 1822 at Commercial Rd, but by 1832 at 195 Fleet St, and by 1839 at no. 197. [D]

Pullen, Joseph, Little Moorfields, London, upholder (1788–1802). Son of John Pullen of Little Moorfields, Gent. App. to Charles Burrell on 5 March 1788 and free of the Upholders' Co. by servitude, 1 April 1795. [GL, Upholders' Co. records]

Pullen, Robert, Hatfield, near Thorne, Yorks., auctioneer and cm (1822). [D]

Pullen, Robert, Paris St, Exeter, Devon, cm (1838–39).

Daughter bapt. on 7 January 1838 and a son on 30 June 1839 at St Sidwell's Church. [PR (bapt.)]

Pullen, Thomas, Masham, Yorks., joiner and cm (1828). [D]

Pullen (or Pullan), Timothy, High Bridge, Knaresborough, Yorks., cm (1834–37). [D]

Puller, George, Cranbourn St, Leicester Fields, London, u (1766–68). Fellow of the Royal Society, 1766–68.

Puller, Isaac, 'The Golden Plow', South side of St Paul's Churchyard, London, chairmaker (1714). His trade card [Landauer Coll., MMA, NY] states that he made and sold 'Cane-Chairs, Stools and Couches of all sorts: and also Easie Chair-Frames, Chair-Stool Frames both round and square, to cover: and sells Rattan-Canes, whole and split'.

Pullin, William, Atherstone, Warks., cm and chairmaker (1793–96). In November 1796 advertised for an app. [D; *Leicester Journal*, November 1796]

Pulling, William, Upper Main St, Totnes, Devon, cm (1823–38). [D; poll bk]

Pulsford, Robert, Knightsbridge, London, gilder and chaser (1749). [Westminster poll bk]

Punchard, Jeremiah, Norwich, u (1772). On 17 June 1772 his son Robert was made free of the London Upholders' Co. [GL, Upholders' Co. records]

Punchard, Robert, London and Norwich, upholder and auctioneer (1772–d.1798). Son of Jeremiah Punchard of Norwich, u. App. to Nathaniel Spurling in London and free of the London Upholders' Co. by servitude, 17 June 1772. By September 1780 he had returned to Norwich and in 1784 was trading from an address at Elm-hill St. His will was proved at Norwich in 1798. [D; GL, Upholders' Co. records; poll bks; Norfolk Record Soc., index of wills]

Punshon, John, Newcastle, u (1731–56). Free on 11 October 1731, and his son John was free by patrimony on 26 April 1756. He was employed at Gibside, Co. Durham in 1743–44. On 16 April 1744 he was paid £7 8s 3d for blankets and curtain material etc. supplied in the previous year, and on 4 October 1744 a further sum of £2 7s 6d for putting up hangings, matting and baskets etc. He was declared bankrupt, in *Gents Mag.*, September 1746, but in May 1750 was mentioned as living at The Close in an advertisement of Leonard Backwith. [Freemen reg.; poll bk; Durham RO, Strathmore MS, D/St/V. 989; *Newcastle Courant*, 26 May 1750]

Purcell, John, Bristol, upholder (c.1755). Took as app. John Stephens who set up his own business in August 1756 claiming to be his 'late Apprentice'. [*Farley's Bristol Journal*, 28 August–4 September 1756]

Purcell, John, Cross, Stroud, Glos., cm (1820–30). [D]

Purcell, Thomas, 165 Bristol St, Birmingham, cm (1835). [D]

Purchell, Thomas, Winchester, Hants., chairmaker (1730). In 1730 took app. named Peater. [S of G, app. index]

Purden, John, opposite Still Alley, Houndsditch, London, cm etc. (c.1770). [Heal]

Purden, William, Corn Mkt, Warwick, cm and u (1822–31). [D; poll bk]

Purdie, Andrew, London, cm (1785–1811). In 1785 at 2 Little Queen St, Lincoln's Inn Fields where he took out insurance cover of £100 on utensils, stock and goods in trust. By 1790 he had moved to 22 Queen St Holborn, an address previously occupied by a Henry Purdie; but in 1792 was at 98 High Holborn in partnership, trading as Purdie & Hinchcliff. The partnership lasted until 1799 but from 1800 Purdie was trading on his own behalf from the High Holborn address. In 1803 he was included in the list of master cabinet makers in Sheraton's *Cabinet Dictionary*. [D; GL, Sun MS vol. 329, p. 524]

Purdie, Henry, 22 Little Queen St, Lincoln's Inn Fields, London,

cm (1789). [D] By 1790 this address was occupied by Andrew Ourdie.

Purdom, Thomas, 54 John St, Holland St, Blackfriars, London, cabinet carver (1835–39). [D]

Purdy, John, 6 and 7 Greenland St, Gray's Inn Rd, London, bedstead maker (portable, brass and iron) (1839). [D]

Purdy, Richard, Norwich, u (1739). Son of John Purdy. Free 14 July 1739. [Freemen rolls]

Purdy, Robert, High St, New Walsingham, Norfolk, cm (1839). [D]

Purkis, C., Southampton, Hants., u (1834–39). At Bridge St in 1834 but at Pembroke Sq., 1836–39. An advertisement of 1836 states that he also acted as an auctioneer, appraiser, broker, undertaker, paperhanger and house and estate agent. [D] Probably:

Purkiss, Charles, Hanover Buildings, Southampton, Hants., cm (1823). [D]

Purkiss, Robert, 8 Newton St, Holborn, London, carver (1808). [D]

Purnell, James, Cross St, Ryde, Isle of Wight, Hants., cm and u (1839). [D]

Purnell, John, Bristol, cm and u (1817–29). At 5 Mill's Pl. in 1819 but from 1818–29 at 32 Milk St. In 1823 also a grocer. [D]

Purnell, John, Bath, Som., cm, u and appraiser (1819–33). Listed at 8 New King St in 1819 and 7 Chapel Row in 1813. [D]

Purnell, Thomas, Bristol, upholder (1739–54). [Poll bks]

Purnell & Lockier, Wine St, Bristol, u (1792). [D]

Purrier, Thomas, 13 Baldwin St, Bristol, cm (1775–81). [D; poll bk]

Purser, William, Birmingham, cm and u (1828–35). Recorded at 50 New St in 1828 and Paradise St, 1830–35, no. 50 in 1835. [D]

Pursseveill, J. R., 5 Lime St, Leadenhall St, London, frame maker, carver and gilder (1781–82). Claimed to have been app. to John Overlove who traded at 'The Golden Key', 36 Leadenhall St as a frame maker and gilder, 17775–82. Pursseveill's trade card [GL] states that he framed 'Prints, Drawings & Needle-work'. [D]

Purver, James, 258 Tottenham Ct Rd, London, cm and u (1835–39). [D]

Purver & Johnson, 8 Gt Newton St, Soho, London, cm and u (1825–27). [D]

Purves, James, Wool Mkt, Berwick-on-Tweed, Northumb., cm and u (1834). [D]

Purvis, Edward Hutchinson, Bondgate St, Alnwick, Northumb., joiner, cm and u (1828–34). Recorded also at 5 Pottergate, as cm and joiner in 1834. [D]

Putt, —, address unknown, joiner (1662). In 1662 supplied to Salisbury House, London a half headed bedstead for Lord Cranborne's footman at a cost of £3 14s 8d. [Hatfield House MS bills 269]

Pyall, Robert, near 'The Red Cow', Dover, Kent, joiner and cm (1729). In August 1729 advertised that he imported and sold 'all sorts of Deal Planks, Deals, Timber and Spars for Building. Likewise makes all sorts of Joyners or Cabinet-makers goods, as Buroes, Desks, Chests of Drawers, Tables &c. Also Buyes and Sells all sort of second-hand Household Goods.' [*Kentish Post*, 6 August 1729]

Pyatt, Jos., Dudley, Staffs., cm and clock case maker (1838). [D]

Pyatt, Joseph, New Mill St, Dudley, Staffs., cm and u (1840). [D]

Pybus, William, Hull, Yorks., cm (1774–84). Freeman of York. [York poll bks]

Pycock, George, Market Pl., Malton, Yorks., joiner, cm and u (1834–40). [D]

Pye, Brian, Liverpool, joiner and cm (1772–96). In 1772 at

Tythbarn St; in 1744 at 44 Lancelots Hey; in 1787 at Hackins Hey; in 1790 at 12 Lancelots Hey; and in 1796 at 39 Union St. In 1790 described as a household broker and in 1790 also had an auction room at 35 Lancelots Hey. [D]

Pye, Bryan, Liverpool, cm (1780). Son of John Pye, carter. Free 11 September 1780. [Freemen reg.]

Pye, Edward, Lancaster and Preston, Lancs., cm (1801–17). Free of Lancaster, 1801–02, but by this period living in Preston. Returned to Lancaster and is named in the Gillow records, 1804–06, 1808 and 1813–17. His name is signed in pencil under the drawer of a night table at Heveningham, Suffolk and other signed furniture exists at Tatton Park, Cheshire. His signature appears on a Gillow furniture drawing of *c.*1810. [Lancaster freemen rolls; Westminster Ref. Lib., Gillow; V&A archives; *C. Life*, 8 June 1978, p. 1614]

Pye, Thomas, 16 Manor Row, Chelsea, London, cm and u (1823). [D]

Pyecroft, John, Ship St, Brighton, Sussex, u (1837). A Samuel Pyecroft was trading as a cm and u at 27 Ship St from 1839. [D]

Pyecroft, Samuel, 27 Ship St, Brighton, Sussex, cm and u (1839–40). A John Pyecroft was trading in Ship St as an u in 1837. [D]

Pyke, —, Cambridge, u (1688–91). In 1688 mended cushions and supplied matting to Trinity College and in 1691 charged 16s 3d 'for fringe and worke done about yᵉ covering of yᵉ forms' for St John's College. [Trinity and St John's College records]

Pyke, Michael, Coventry St, London, u (1709). [Heal]

Pyke, William, St Martin's Lane, London, u (1707–18). Free of the Upholders' Co., 4 February 1707. By 1709 in St Martin's Lane and in August 1711 his house was said to be at the sign of 'The Black Lyon' on the south side of Cecil Ct, west side of St Martin's Lane. In 1709–11 supplied items to the Heathcote family which in the latter year amounted to £6 os 4⅓d and were feathers and work on bedding. [GL, Upholders' Co. records; Hand in Hand MS vol. 9, p. 214; vol. 8, 27 July 1718; Heal; Lincoln RO, 2 ANC 12/D/4–5]

Pyle, Henry William, Addington St, Margate, Kent, cm (1839). [D]

Pym, Joseph, Bridge St, Belper, Derbs., cm (1835). [D]

Pyman, John, Whitby, Yorks., cm (1798). [D]

Pymm, Hammond, Rochester, Kent, carver (1780). [Poll bk]

Pyner, Francis snr and jnr, Lombard St, London, upholder and cm (1764–93). Francis Pyner snr was app. to William Powle, freeman of the Clothworkers' Co., and made free of the Upholders' Co. under the terms of the 1750 Upholders' Act on 1 November 1764. He is, however, shown taking apps as early as 1762 and may already have been trading at the time he was granted the freedom of the Upholders' Co. This is further confirmed by his name being included in a directory of 1763. He traded from 37 Lombard St, near George Yd, but an early version of his trade card gives the address as 'The Tent' near George Yd, Lombard St. He took over the business of his former master William Powle. This business had been conducted since the death of William Powle in 1753 by his widow. The business operated by Pyner was not in the same premises, however, as his trade card states 'Successor to Mrs Powle from three King Court'.

The items that Pyner claimed to make and sell included 'bedsteads & Furnitures, Window Curtains, Goose & other Feather Beds, Quilts, Blankets, Counterpanes & Coverlids, Damasks, Harrateens, Cheneys & Bed Tickings, Easy Chairs, Wilton Turkey & other Carpets, Mahogany & Wallnut-tree Chairs, with Leather & Matted Seats, Looking Glasses in Carv'd Gilt or Painted Frames, Dressing Glasses in Mahogany or Wallnut-tree Frames, Mahogany or Wallᵗ Book Cases, Chests of Drawers, Writing Tables, Cloaths Presses, Buroes & Dressing Tables, Dining Card & Claw Tables, Night Tables, China Tables, Tea Boards & Brackets with all Sorts of Tea Boards & Tea Chests, Spring Blinds, and all Sorts of Window Blinds'. He also bought and appraised household goods and performed funerals in 'any Part of Town or Country'. From 1765–71 took out licences to employ non-freemen which included permission to employ two to four throughout the year in 1766 and two for the entire year in 1766–69. By 1786 the business was being described as Pyner & Son. The son was Francis Pyner jnr who was app. to his father, 1776–83, and admitted a freeman of the Upholders' Co. by servitude, 2 April 1783. Other apps of Francis Pyner snr were William Burkmire (1762–79), Bartholomew Payne (free 1772), John Loader (1774), John Preston (1781–88) and George Woolley (1783–86). Francis Pyner jnr took over as app. George Wooley who completed his training in 1790. This would suggest that Francis Pyner snr either retired from the business or died in 1786. The firm continued to be listed in London directories until 1793 when the son seems to have given up the trade also. In the following year he is listed in the Upholders' Co. records as F. Pyner Esq. of Cheshunt, Herts. [D; GL, Upholders' Co. records; Heal; GL, City Licence bks, vols 4–6, 9]

Pyner, George, London, upholder, appraiser and undertaker (1749–68). At Little Poulteney St, Westminster in 1749 but by 1768 in Princes St, Soho where he maintained an establishment which he called 'The Blanket Ware-house'. His hand-bill is amongst the accounts of Sir John Griffin Griffin (later 4th Lord Howard de Walden), of Audley End, Essex. On this Pyner listed the extensive range of items that he stocked. These included bedsteads, feather beds, blankets, bed-ticks, quilts, counterpanes, rugs and coverlets, mattresses, carpets and floor cloths. Next door to his upholstery and bedding warehouse, at the sign of 'The Cock and Star' he maintained a wareroom for cabinet furniture and chairs. As an impressive finale to this listing he stated he maintained 'Un Magazin pour Toutes Sortes de Meubles'. [Poll bk; Essex RO, D/DBy/A26/9]

Pyner, George, James St, Westminster, London, chairmaker (1749). [Poll bk]

Pyner, James, Cow Lane, West Smithfield, London, upholder (1778). Free of the Upholders' Co. under the terms of the 1750 Upholders' Act, 2 December 1778. [GL, Upholders' Co. records]

Pynn, William, Butcher Row, Lichfield, Staffs., cm etc. (1834). [D]

Pythian, John, Eccleston, near St Helens, Lancs., joiner and cm (1834). [D]

Q

Quare, Daniel, 78 Houndsditch, London, carver and gilder (1784–1827). [D]

Quartermaine, Abraham, Banbury, Oxon., upholder (1829–31). Named in 1829 regarding one-year lease of a cottage in Banbury in his occupation, as heir of his mother; and in 1830–31 concerning the assignment, lease and release of the cottage. [Oxford RO, Gar I/v/7–12] See Joseph Abraham Quartermaine.

Quartermaine, James, George St, Portman Sq., London, u (1835–39). Recorded at no. 39 in 1835 and no. 32 in 1839. [D]

Quartermaine, Joseph Abraham, Chipping Norton, Oxon., cm (1829). Named regarding one-year lease of a cottage in Banbury in occupation of Abraham and Joseph Quartermaine, as heir of their mother. See Abraham Quartermaine.

Quartermaine, Joseph, New St, Chipping Norton, Oxon., cm and u (1830). [D]

Quarterman, James, High Wycombe, Bucks, chairmaker (b. c.1801–41). Aged 40 at the time of the 1841 Census.

Quarterman, Thomas, James St, Grosvenor Sq., London, cm (1759). Recorded in newspapers in 1759 as selling off his stock. [Heal]

Quay, James, Liverpool, cm (1800–34). Addresses given at 5 North St, Dale St in 1800; 5 Johnson St, Dale St in 1803; Addison St in 1810; 24 Mathew St in 1811; 23 Bispham St in 1827; and Roberts Ct, Edmund St in 1834. Marriage of James Quay jnr at St Nicholas's Church to Miss Mary Ann Jackson of Liverpool on 14 May 1827 reported in *Liverpool Mercury*, 25 May. [D]

Quay, John, Liverpool, carver and gilder (1830). Admitted freeman on 27 November 1830 as son of James Quay, ironmonger. [Liverpool freemen reg.]

Quelch, William, Reading, Berks., auctioneer and u (1833). Named concerning the lease and release of property in Goring, Oxon. Acted as one of three assignees of the estate of William Lewis, bankrupt. [Oxford RO, FIX/263]

Quennell, Robert, address unrecorded. Mentioned in the Monson archive on 30 June 1742 being paid £2 19s 5d for items including 'Three Parsells Bedstids', '2 Casses, 1 Table', 'Trunk Box', and '5 Chear Frame'. Quennell's bill also mentions 'Esq. Watsons', and was receipted by George Read. [Lincoln RO, Monson 12]

Quick, James, Tiverton, Devon, linen-draper and cm (1793–98). Quick, cm of Tiverton, subscribed to Sheraton's *Drawing Book*, 1793. [D]

Quick, James, Barnstaple, Devon, cm (1826–30). Trading at High St in 1830. Notice in *Exeter Flying Post*, 19 January 1826 read: 'Mr. James Quick, Cabinet-maker, of Barnstaple, was lately on his return from Bideford, preserved from robbery and probably being murdered, by the sagacity and courage of his dog, who on two several occasions compelled the ruthless villain to forgo his purpose.' The birth of his son was reported in *The Alfred*, 31 October 1826. [D]

Quick, John, Market Pl., Kimbolton, Hunts., cm etc. (1830–39). Recorded also at High St in 1839. [D]

Quick, Joseph, Liverpool, cm (1824). App. to John Roberts in 1824. [Liverpool app. enrolment bk]

Quiggin, John, Liverpool, cm (1796–1839). Addresses given at 4 Bath St, North Shore in 1796; 38 Queen St, Old Hall St in 1803; no. 23 in 1804; no. 22, 1805–11; no. 18, 1813–14; 29 Mathew St, 1823–27; no. 22 in 1834; no. 28 in 1835; no. 26 in 1837; and no. 30 in 1839. [D]

Quilley, William, Norwich, cm (1826). App. to C. Jones and John Kerry, and admitted freeman on 3 May 1826. [Norwich freemen reg.]

Quilton, Henry, St Ives, Hunts., u (d.1762). Death announced in *Cambridge Chronicle and Journal*, 27 November 1762.

Quin, William, Liverpool, cm and joiner (1741–67). Recorded on Hackens Key in 1747. Took app. named Charnock in 1741. Took out a Sun Insurance policy on 18 September 1747 for £300. Former apps petitioned freedom: William Clarkson in 1760, and Thomas Charnock in 1767. [S of G, app. index; GL, Sun MS vol. 81, ref. 109494; Liverpool freemen's committee bk]

Quincey, Lawrence, Newcastle, u (1713). App. to Simon Webster and admitted freeman on 22 December 1713. [Newcastle freemen reg.]

Quincey, William, St Neots, Hunts., cm (1784). [D]

Quineau (or Quino), Augustinus (or Augustus), St Martin-in-the-Fields, London, master cm (1709–13). Registered in St Martin's poor rate in 1709, as resident in Long Acre. Recorded in 1713 as having taken app. named Isaac, son of Ann Crowdell, widow, for seven years from 2 October 1711 for £5. Took app. on 15 February 1712/13. [PRO, IR/1/2]

Quinnell, Charles, East Hill, Hastings, Sussex, chairmaker and turner (1839). [D]

Quint, Joshua, Lawton St, Liverpool, u (1790). [D]

Quint, William, Ashburton, Devon, cm, u, hardwareman and ironmonger (1778–93). Advertised for one or two journeymen cm in *Exeter Flying Post*, 23 October 1778; and on 5 April 1792 that he had a large house with shop to let, on his removal, with stock of ironmongery, haberdashery and grocery to be taken over. Still trading in Ashburton in 1793. [D]

Quint, William, Plymouth, Devon, cm (1798–1812). Recorded at Woolster St in 1812. Probably the Quint of Plymouth who advertised in *Exeter Flying Post*, 27 September 1798 for sycamore, holly and walnut timber, and an auction sale of household furniture at his repository. [D]

Quintin, Thomas, London, glass-maker (c.1760–1810). Trade card, c.1760, shows him in partnership with Weatherby, Crowther & Windle at 106 East Smithfield, with manufactory at the Green Yard, making glass articles such as chandeliers and candle-shades. In 1781 the firm was styled Thomas Quintin & Co., in 1786, Thomas Quintin & Son, and from 1799–1810, Quintin & Son, the London Plate Glass Co. Quintin gave evidence before the Parliamentary Committee of 1773, stating that he had made very few glass plates, the largest being 84 by 38 ins, and that he had never sold one. He could cast plates, 'but not in the Manner they do in France.' By 1815 the firm had been succeeded by Macnamara & Brett. [Wills, *Looking-Glasses*]

Quinton, John, London, cm (1829–35). Trading at 4 Bacon St, Spitalfields in 1829, and 4 Shepperton St, Upper St, Islington in 1835. [D]

Quinton, Jno., Grosvenor St, Cheltenham, Glos., cm (1839). [D]

Quinton, P. S., London, cm (1818). [Norwich poll bk]

Quinton, William, 6 Garden Row, St George's Fields, London, chair and sofa maker, cm (1817–39). [D]

Quintus, —, London. On 4 March 1723 he was paid 5s for 'a Table Fire Screen for the Committee Room'; and 2s 6d 'for cleaning the Society's Scrutore' at Holy Trinity Church, Marylebone Rd. [SPCK subscription ledger and cash bk, FT9/2] Possibly:

Quintus, Martin, over against Apothecaries' Hall, Blackfriars, London, cm (1713). Took out a Sun Insurance policy on 4 December 1713. [GL, Sun MS vol. 3, p. 83]

Quirk, Henrietta, 20 Harrington St, Harrington, Liverpool, u (1839). [D]

Quirk, Thomas, Milton St, Liverpool, chairmaker (1837–39). Trading at no. 48 in 1837 and no. 61 in 1839. [D]

Quirk, William, Liverpool, carver (1814–29). Trading at 6 Stanley St in 1827; and no. 73 in 1829. App. to John Summer in 1814; petitioned freedom on servitude in 1822, paying 6s 8d; and admitted freeman on 16 October 1827. [D; Liverpool freemen reg. and committee bk]

Quirke, Tom, address unrecorded. Worked at Shardeloes, Bucks. in May 1769 providing two large bookcases 'with open pediment cornices with door framed ovals flat bead and flush. Ditto in pedestal part framed flush two sides and veneered inside fitted with sliding shelves & compartments for writing. No. 16 drawers with brass handles, locks, hinges and compleat.' On 30 May he supplied a mahogany '4-drawer Table, inclosed with neat foulding quadrant doors and carved cornice. 2 mahog. pillasters with carved caps. and fluted fixed with double iron joynts to the ends of the table (for handles)'. [Bucks. RO, Shardeloes papers, D/DR/5/64]

Quy, Thomas, Rochford, Essex, cm, u, ironmonger and auctioneer (1823–49). Will dated 1849. [D; *Wills at Chelmsford*]

R

Rabbit, —, next door to the coachmaker's in Bishopsgate St, London, u (1703). [Harris, *Old English Furniture*]

Rabett, Edward, London, upholder (1699–1714). Recorded at the sign of 'The Blackmoor's Head', Paternoster Row, St Michael's in 1709. Admitted freeman of the Upholders' Co. on 12 March 1699/1700. Took app. named William Ventris, 1704–14. Took out a Hand in Hand Insurance policy on 20 September 1709 for £200 on his house. [GL, Upholders' Co. records; GL, Hand in Hand MS vol. 7, ref. 4914]

Rabjohns, William, bottom of Butcher's Row, Exeter, Devon, carver and gilder (1829). Son William bapt. at St George's on 23 August 1829. [PR (bapt.)]

Rabner, Matthias, Leeds, Yorks., cm, joiner and u (1791–1822). One of the journeymen who signed the *Leeds Cabinet and Chair Makers' Book of Prices*, 1791. Trading on his own account at St James's St, 1814–22. [D]

Race, William, 24 New St, Whitehaven, Cumb., u (1834). [D]

Racey, Joseph, at 'The Crown & Cushion', Milk St, Bristol, cm (1820–23). [D]

Rackell, James, High Wycombe, Bucks., chairmaker (b. c.1806–41). Aged 35 at the time of the 1841 Census.

Rackham, Edward, Bungay, Suffolk, cm (1784–93). [D]

Rackham, James, Norwich, cm (1826). App. to Henry Huggins and admitted freeman on 3 May 1826. [Norwich freemen reg.]

Rackham, John, Heigham, Norwich, cm (1830). [Poll bk]

Rackham, John, White Horse Plain, Gt Yarmouth, Norfolk, u (1830–41). Polled at Norwich in 1830 and Gt Yarmouth in 1841.

Rackstraw, James, Wardour St, Soho, London, cm (1749). [Poll bk]

Rackstraw (or Rackshaw), Philip, Tottenham Ct Rd, London, u and cm (1806–08). [D]

Rackstrow (or Rackstraw), Benjamin, London, cm, sculptor and picture frame maker (c.1720–d.1772). Trade card, c.1720, shows early-Georgian mirror, and gives address at 'The Crown & Looking-Glass', the lower end of the paved stones in St Martin's Lane, and states that Rackstrow 'Makes and Sells all sorts of Cabinet Work, Looking-Glasses, Coach-glasses, Window-Blinds, Picture-frames &c. after the newest fashion and at the most Reasonable Rates. He likewise cleans and repairs all sorts of Cabinet work, Exchanges New Glasses for Old ones and makes Old ones fashionable. NB. He also cleans Pictures in the best manner and takes off Busto's, Basso Releivs and Figures of any Size, in Wax, Metal, or Plaister of Paris'. A second address, at 'Sir Isaac Newton's Head', the corner of Crane Ct, Fleet St, is on a Rococo trade card dated 1738, and signed by the engraver and furniture designer, Henry Copland. It is worded similarly to the preceding card. Rackstrow announced in *Daily Advertiser*, 5 May 1747 that he had 'found out and completed an Apparatus to exhibit that Grand Experiment the Chair of Beatification . . .'. On 14 April 1739 Benjamin Rackstrow submitted a bill to Sir R. Hoare for 'mahogany top to table', costing £1 5s, for Barn Elms House. The *London Magazine* reported the death of Benjamin

Rackstrow on 29 May 1772. It is possible that two men, perhaps father and son, have been confused here. [Banks Coll., BM; Heal; Wills, *Looking-Glasses*; *C. Life*, 7 May 1759, p. 1031; V&A Lib., English Manuscripts, tradesmen's bills to Sir R. Hoare]

Radcliff, Joseph, Notts., carver (1757–60). Recorded at Nottingham in 1757, when he took app. named Bullemer; and at Trentbridge in 1760, when he took another app. [S of G, app. index]

Radcliffe, Albert, 238 High Holborn, London, u (1839). [D]

Radcliffe (or Radclyffe), Edward, London, carver and gilder (1814–39). Addresses given at 49 Brewer St, Golden Sq., 1814–17; and 237 High Holborn, near Little Turnstile from Brewer St, Golden Sq., 1817–39. Three trade cards recorded, one with address in Brewer St, and two with address in High Holborn. Declared bankrupt, *Brighton Gazette*, 11 November 1824. [D; Banks Coll., BM]

Raddon, John, Gattey's Ct, Exeter, Devon, carver and gilder (1838). Daughter Jane bapt. at St Sidwell's on 2 December 1838. [PR (bapt.)]

Radford, John, near the Exe-Bridge, Tiverton, Devon, u, cm and chair manufacturer (1815–38). Recorded at Angel Hill in 1838. Parquetry inlaid mahogany occasional table recorded, with central column with pineapple decoration, and platform base on four scroll feet. Trade label underneath reads: 'J. RADFORD, UPHOLSTERER, Cabinet and Chair Manufacturer NEAR THE EXE-BRIDGE, TIVERTON. London Paper Hangings, Carpet Warehouse, Floor Cloths &c.', with the date, 'March 29th 1822' written by hand. Radford appears in a list of creditors of John Shuckburgh, clerk, of Sampford Peverel in *Exeter Flying Post*, 9 March 1815. Submitted a bill to Thomas Clarke on 5 April 1815 for paper, borders and fixing, including 'satin Paper for two Parlors'; and for repairing 'Venetian Blinds to front Parlor', totalling £28 8s ½d. Notice in *Exeter Flying Post*, 11 December 1834 read: 'Samuel Dearing, an apprentice to Mr. John Radford, cabinet-maker, Tiverton, was a few days since, so burnt, from the bursting and ignition of the contents of a jar, in which he was preparing polish, as to occasion death.' [D; V&A archives]

Radford, Joseph, Birmingham, cm, joiner and upholder (1767–77). Trading at 23 Bull St, 1767–70; as Radford & Field at 43 Edmund St in 1770; and at 14 St Thomas's St in 1777. [D]

Radford, Joseph F., Chard, Som., builder and cm (1793). [D]

Radford, Joseph, 5 Lower Vale Pl., Hammersmith, London, cm (1832). [D]

Radley, Jarvis, address unrecorded. Named in the Chatsworth vouchers in 1786 supplying white serge covers for the Music Room costing £13 12s; and in 1788, 147½ yards of 36″ wide carpeting, costing £26 13s.

Radley, Joseph, Queen St, St Ann's, Manchester, u (1781–88). [D]

Rae, John, Bedford St, North Shields, Northumb., cm and joiner (1827). [D]

Rae, R., 11 Castle St, Long Acre, London, broker and u (1808). [D]

Rafe, Thomas, Bristol, cm (1781). [Poll bk]

Ragge, James, parish of St Mary, Guildford, Surrey, u (1790–94). [D; poll bk]

Ragsdale, Richard, Tothill Fields, London, cm (1749). [Poll bk]

Railton, Joseph, Kendal, Westmld, cm and u (1780). Took out a Sun Insurance policy in 1780 for £400 of which £50 accounted for his workshop. [GL, Sun MS vol. 280, p. 262]

Railton, Thomas, Waterloo Vale, South Shields, Co. Durham, cm and joiner (1828–29). [D]

Railton, William, Leeds, Yorks., journeyman cm (1791). Named in the *Leeds Cabinet and Chair Makers' Book of*

Prices, 1791 with other journeymen in basic sympathy with its contents.

Rainer, Thomas, St Gregory, Norwich, chairmaker (1761). [Poll bk]

Rainer, Thomas, Norwich, chairmaker (1818). [Poll bk] See Thomas Rayner.

Rainey, Edward, Spilsby, Lincs., cm, surveyor and auctioneer (1822). [D]

Rainey, J., 13 Southgate St, Bath, Som., cm and broker (1833). [D]

Rainford, —, 4 Haymarket, Liverpool, cm and bedstead manufacturer (1804). Notice in *Liverpool Chronicle*, 22 February 1804, concerned the resignation of Joseph Bennet, cm, in favour of Thomas Sharples & Rainford. Rainford & Sharples, joiners and cm, were trading in the Haymarket in 1804. [D] See Sharples & Rainford.

Rainford, Thomas, Liverpool, cm (b. *c*.1786–d.1833). Addresses given at Gellings Pl., Duckenfield St in 1806; 16 William St in 1810; no. 17 in 1811; 3 Nash St, 1813–14; 10 Scotland Rd in 1818; and 11 William St in 1821. Admitted freeman on servitude to Thomas Dutton on 5 November 1806. Death aged 47 reported in *Liverpool Mercury*, 26 April 1833. [D; Liverpool freemen reg.] Possibly two tradesmen of the same name.

Rainford, William, 6 Milton St, Liverpool, cm (1805). [D] Presumably the William Rainford of Liverpool who signed the supplement to the *Liverpool Cabinet and Chair Prices*, 1805, on behalf of the masters.

Rainford, William, Liverpool, u (1830–39). Addresses given at 8 Ryley Gdns in 1830; Kirkdale Village, near Liverpool in 1834; 63 Lord St, 1835–37; and 25 Devonshire Pl. in 1839. Admitted freeman on 15 November 1830 as son of Thomas Rainford. [D; Liverpool freemen reg.] Probably of:

Rainford, Stretch & Co., 54 Lord St, Liverpool, cm and u (1839). [D]

Rainy, Edward, Spilsby, Lincs., joiner and cm (1826). [D]

Rairs, A. & D., 70 Gracechurch St, London, u and cm (1808–11). [D]

Raliegh (or Rayley), John, Hull, Yorks., cm (1774–84). [Poll bks]

Ralph, Daniel, Ipswich, Suffolk, cm (1754). Took app. named Cook in 1754. [S of G, app. index]

Ralphs, John, 'Red Lion', Wellow, Notts., chairmaker and victualler ((1832–35). [D]

Ram, —, (1791). See John Jackson.

Ram, John, 5 Queen's Buildings, Knightsbridge, London, u and cm (1835–39). [D]

Ramet (Ramé), Isaac, London, 'tourneur en bois' (1681). Registered at Threadneedle St for relief on 12 October 1681. [Hogarth Soc., 1949, p. 163]

Ramm, Edward, Marshall St, Carnaby Mkt, London, cm (1784). [D]

Ramm, John, Swan Yd, London, cm (1774). [Poll bk]

Ramm, William, White Lyon Ct, White St, London, cm (1778). Took out a Sun Insurance policy in 1778 for £600 of which £500 accounted for utensils and stock. [GL, Sun MS vol. 266, p. 215]

Ramm, William, 14 Brownlow St, Holborn, London, cm and u (1783–99). [D]

Ramsay, John, address unrecorded, cm (1803). Subscribed to Sheraton's *Cabinet Dictionary*, 1803.

Ramsay, Robert, 20 Wells St, Oxford St, London, cm (*c*.1786). Took out a Sun Insurance policy, *c*.1786, for £100, including £60 on household goods. [GL, Sun MS vol. 339, p. 377]

Ramsay (or Ramsey), Robert, Sheffield, Yorks., carver and gilder (1787–1808). Recorded at Back Lane in 1787, 42 High St in 1797, and High St, 1808. [D]

Ramsay, T. G., Church St, Ampthill, Beds, cm (1839). [D]

Ramsay, William, Cockermouth, Cumb., joiner and cm (1793). [D]

Ramsden, Ann, French Gate, Doncaster, Yorks., cm and/or u (1837). [D]

Ramsden, Benjamin, Hull, Yorks., cm (b. *c*.1812–d.1901). [1841 Census; V&A archives]

Ramsden, John, Doncaster, Yorks., cm and u (1834). [D]

Ramsey, —, 37 Assembly Row, Mile End Rd and 83 Poplar, London, cm, u and undertaker (*c*.1830). Mahogany drop-leaf sewing table with turned legs, *c*.1830, recorded bearing stencilled name, trade and address inside drawers.

Ramsey, Isaac & Son, 83 High St, Poplar, London, cm and u (1839). [D]

Ramsey, J. & E., Poplar, London, u (1811). [D] See Ramsey & Carter, and Ramsey & Co.

Ramsey, John, High St, Huntingdon, carver and gilder (1839). [D]

Ramsey, Nathan, Chester-le-Street, Co. Durham, cm and/or joiner (1834). [D]

Ramsey, Peter, Bishop's Stortford, Herts., upholder, shopkeeper and dealer in plate (1778). Took out a Sun Insurance policy in 1778 for £2,300 including £850 on utensils and stock. [GL, Sun MS vol. 267, p. 171]

Ramsey, William, Whiting St, Bury St Edmunds, Suffolk, u, cm and chairmaker (1795). Announced in *Bury and Norwich Post*, 14 October 1795 that he had 'taken out a licence for exercising the business of an AUCTIONEER . . .'.

Ramsey & Carter, 83 High St, Poplar, London, cm, upholders, undertakers, auctioneers and appraisers (1813–28). [D]

Ramsey & Company's Old Established Manufactory of No. 83 High St, Poplar, London, 'Solid Mahogany Furniture on the Newest Principals'. Label recorded on desk, *c*.1800, with rising top for reading and in reverse adjustable mirror and holes for wash bowl and container; reeded edge to top; three drawers and cupboard. Probably for campaigning. See Ramsey, —, Isaac Ramsey & Son, and J. & E. Ramsey.

Ramshaw, John, East and Middle Herrington, Houghton-le-Spring, Co. Durham, victualler, joiner and cm (1827–28). [D]

Ramshaw, William, Bishop Auckland, Co. Durham, cm (1805–34). Trading in Market Pl., 1827–34. Advertised for two journeyman cm in *Newcastle Courant*, 27 July 1805. [D]

Ramuz, Alexander, 17 Frith St, Soho, London, cm, u, undertaker and billiard table maker (1826–46). Named in the Lord Chamberlain's Royal Accounts in 1846. [D]

Ramuz, Henry, 17 Frith St, Soho, London, cm and u (1827–28). [D]

Rance, Richard, King St, Chelmsford, Essex, cm (1838). Named in the Essex jurors' book for Chelmsford Hundred in 1838. [Essex RO, Q/RJ/2/1]

Rand, Charles & Sandell (or Tandell), Samuel, London, upholders (1776–83). Recorded as Rand & Sandell at 1 Compton St, Soho, 1779–80 and 101 New Bond St, 1781–83. Charles Rand and Samuel Tandell at the corner of Greek St in Compton St took out Sun Insurance policies in 1776 for £900 including £500 on utensils, stock and goods; and in 1780 for £4,500, £2,500 on utensils, stock and goods, and £500 on warehouse. [D; GL, Sun MS vol. 246, p. 540; vol. 286, p. 542]

Rand, William, Maidstone, Kent, upholder (1712–19). Took apps named Post in 1712 and Argles in 1719. [S of G, app. index]

Rand, William, Battle, Sussex, u, tallow chandler and soap boiler (1759). Sale on 17 September of the stock in trade and utensils of William Rand 'he having left the trade', announced in *Sussex Weekly Advertiser*, 10 September 1759.

Randall, Edward, St Paul's Sq., Bedford, cm and u (1830–39).

a

Listed at Stonehouse Lane in 1830 and St Paul's Sq. in 1839. [D]

Randall, G., 12 Francis St, Bedford Sq., London, u (1812). [D]

Randall, George, Cranbourn Alley, Leicester Sq., London, cm (1804–08). Randall of no. 6 took out a Sun Insurance policy on 14 May 1804 for £700 on a house belonging to Daniel Woodward. [D; GL, Sun MS vol. 431, ref. 762284]

Randall, George, 2 Chapel St, Bedford Row, London, cm and u (1820–28). [D]

Randall, George, Park St, Cambridge, cm (1837–39). [Poll bks]

Randall, Gladman, 55 The Corner of Talbot Ct, Gracechurch St, London, trunk and plate case makers. 18th-century trade card with delicate Rococo border shows knife-case, small chests, leather jug and bucket, and states that Randall 'Makes & Sells all Sorts of Hair & Black Leather Trunks, Hair & Gilt Leather Nests of Trunks for EXPORTATION. With an Assortment of all Kinds of Travelling and Campaign Trunks ... Cases for Plate, China and Glass. Likewise all Sorts of Leather Ware ...'. [MMA, NY]

Randall, James, Wardour St, London, upholder (1774). [Poll bk]

Randall, James, King St, Golden Sq., London, upholder and cm (1790–93). Recorded at no. 5 when he took out a Sun Insurance policy on 30 August 1792 for £1,200, including £100 on workshop behind with utensils and stock; and £100 on a house in Naylors Yd, Silver St, in tenure of Marley, coachmaker. [D; GL, Sun MS vol. 389, ref. 604256]

Randall, James, 171 Piccadilly, London, u (1796–1808). Named in Sheraton's list of master cabinet makers, 1803. [D]

Randall, James, 52 Dean St, Soho, London, cm (1807–11). [D]

Randall, John, parish of St Luke, London, cm (1768). Took app. named Elizabeth Harding in 1768. [Westminster Ref. Lib., St Martin-in-the-Fields PR, MS 4309, p. 5]

Randall, John, 112 Marylebone High St, London, cm (1809–11). [D]

Randall, John, 14 Merchant St, Bristol, fancy chair and cm, broker (1840). [D; GL, Sun MS vol. 268, ref. 1334076]

Randal(l), Mat(t)hew, London, freeman merchant tailor, upholder and cm (1763–84). Addresses given at Lothbury, 1763–66; Old Broad St, 1767–70; Bishopsgate St, 1774–76; Cullum St, 1777–78; 34 Lime St, 1779–81; and 13 Fenchurch St, 1782–84. Admitted freeman of the Upholders' Co. on 7 November 1765. Employed one non-freeman for three months in 1763; four for six weeks in 1766; six for three months in 1767; and four for three months in both 1770 and 1777. Declared bankrupt, Gents Mag., December 1774, and Sussex Weekly Advertiser, 12 February 1776. Took out Sun Insurance policies in 1779 for £500, of which utensils, stock and goods accounted for £300; and in 1781 with Richard Philp for £100 on utensils and stock in warehouse at 2 Ingram Ct, Fenchurch St. [D; GL, Upholders' Co. records; GL, City Licence bks, vols 5, 6 and 9; GL, Sun MS vol. 276, p. 90; vol. 289, p. 304] Possibly two tradesmen of the same name.

Randall, Robert, 42 Market Pl., Poole, Dorset, cm and furniture broker (1830). [D]

Randall, Thomas, Eagle & Child Alley, Fleetmarket, London, freeman joiner, cm (1760). Employed two non-freemen for three months and six weeks in 1760. [GL, City Licence bks, vol. 2]

Randall, William, 38 Broad St, Soho, London, cm, joiner and u (1809–17). Recorded at Carnaby Mkt in 1811. [D]

Randall, William, Market St, Poole, Dorset, cm, carpenter and joiner (1823–30). [D]

Randall, William, 48 Long Alley, Finsbury, London, bedstead maker and cm (1829). [D]

Randall, William, Broad St, Ely, Cambs., turner and chairmaker (1830). [D]

Randall & Blaxlan, 73 Old Bond St, London, u (1773). [D]

Randall & Hay, 49 Skinner St, Snow Hill, London, u and cm (1814–16). [D]

Randel, —, Thame, Oxon., chairmaker (1836). A van-load of chairs made by Randel was transported in 1836 by Benjamin North, the first recorded pioneer in the business of exporting Wycombe chairs from the locality. [Joy, English Furniture, 1800–1850, p. 240]

Randell, John, North Walsham, Norfolk, cm, u and ironmonger (1822–30). Trading at Market Pl. in 1830. [D]

Randle, Charles, Nuneaton, Warks., cm, chairmaker and turner (1822–28). [D]

Randle & Williams, Plymouth, Devon, u (1808). [D]

Randles, George, Chester, cm (1780). Admitted freeman on 10 June 1780. [Chester freemen rolls]

Ran(s)ford, John, Walbrook, London, u (1768). Declared bankrupt, Gents Mag., October 1768.

Rangecroft, John, Gt Minster St, Winchester, Hants., carver (1839). [D]

Ranger, Charles, address unrecorded, upholder (1773). Son of Solomon Ranger, Gent., of Edmonton, Middlx; app. to Andrew Parker, and admitted freeman of the Upholders' Co. by servitude in 1773. [GL, Upholders' Co. records]

Rankin, John, Newcastle, cm and chairmaker (1754–82). Addresses given adjoining Mr Steel's, Big-market in 1764; and near 'The Black-horse', White-cross, 1778–82. Possibly the John Ranken, cm, who subscribed to Chippendale's Director, 1754. Advertised a long list of goods for sale in Newcastle Courant, 1 February 1764. [D]

Rankin, Richard, 5 Dickinson St, Liverpool, u (1839). [D]

Rannie, James, St Martin's Lane, London, upholder and cm (1754–d.1766). He was Thomas Chippendale's first partner and put up capital to finance an expansion of the business following publication of the Director in 1754. They signed a joint lease on spacious premises in St Martin's Lane in August 1754 and issued a trade card [Westminster City Libraries] about this time. In the subscription list to Chippendale's Director he is described as 'cabinet-maker' and in his will [PRO, Prob. 11/915 c/7021, p. 255] referred to himself as 'upholder and cabinet-maker', but his contribution was probably mainly as a financier and accountant, there being little evidence that he possessed practical knowledge of furniture crafts. In 1758 'Rannie & Co. Upholders' received a premium of £42 for taking John Burrows as app. for 7 years. He owned property in East Lothian and was related to the wine dealers Bell & Rannie of Leith, while his brother Thomas (with whom he owned a share in the ship John & James) was a prosperous Edinburgh merchant — these contacts doubtless explain the firm's early success in attracting Scottish customers. He died in 1766 and was buried in St Martin's Church. His widow was left £200 p.a. for life and small legacies included £100 'to my Book-Keeper Thomas Haig'. Rannie's estate took at least 5 years to wind up and the dissolution of the partnership brought Chippendale to the verge of bankruptcy. [Gilbert, Chippendale]

C.G.G.

Ransford (or Ranceford), Charles, Oxford, carver (d.1737). Probate will granted on 26 September 1737. [Bodleian index of Oxford wills]

Ranshall, John, address unrecorded, upholder (1771–78). Son of John Ranshall, weaver of Christchurch. App. to John Evans, cook and working upholder, on 4 July 1771, and admitted freeman of the Upholders' Co. by servitude on 4 November 1778. [GL, Upholders' Co. records]

Ranshall, John, Bishopsgate Without, London, upholder (1783–96). Recorded at no. 86, 1783–84; no. 83, 1786–96; and also as an auctioneer in 1789. Took out a Sun Insurance policy on 13 July 1786 including £100 on household goods, and £530 on utensils etc. [D; GL, Sun MS vol. 339, p. 77]

Ranshall, John, 48 Shoreditch, London, u (1799–1816). [D]

Ranson, Henry, South St, Eastbourne, Sussex, turner and chairmaker (1823). [D]

Raper, Henry, East Witton, Middleham, Yorks., joiner and/or cm (1834). [D]

Raper, James, Spennithorne, Harnby, Yorks., cm (1823). [D]

Raper, James, 23 Curtain Rd, London, picture frame maker (1826–27). [D]

Raper, John, York, joiner and cm (1816–38). Trading at Feasegate, 1816–17; Starcourt Lane in 1830; and 11 Davygate in 1838. [D]

Raper, Thomas, York, cm (1836). Son of Thomas Raper, stage coachman; app. to John Milner and Thomas Harland, cm, on 9 February 1836. [York app. reg.]

Raper, Thomas, 27 Cross St, Hatton Gdn, London, carver and gilder, looking-glass manufacturer (1835–37). [D]

Rasbury, Stephen, Standish St, Liverpool, carver and gilder (1810–11). Trading at no. 40 in 1811. [D]

Rasbury, Thomas, 114 Tottenham Ct Rd, London, carver and gilder (1808). [D]

Raseigh, John, Redruth, Cornwall, cm (1830). [D]

Rason, Henry, Tunbridge Wells Kent, chairmaker (1832–34). [D]

Ratcliff, John, Stowell St, Newcastle, cm (1833–38). Listed at no. 48, 1833–34, and no. 47 in 1838. [D]

Ratcliff, Thomas, 15 Castle St, Long Acre, London, cm (1808–10). Took out Sun Insurance policies on 4 March 1808 for £150 on his house and goods; and on 14 April 1810 £300, £200 accounting for stock, utensils and goods in trust. [GL, Sun MS vol. 445, ref. 814461; vol. 453, ref. 844488]

Ratcliffe, Edward, 49 Brewer St, London, carver and gilder (1811–12). [D]

Ratcliffe, John, York, cm (1740–67). Recorded at Coney St in 1740; Low Ousegate in 1743; 'next Door to the Sign of the Blue Anchor upon Ouse Bridge' in 1746; and in St Helen's parish, 1759–67. Advertised in *York Courant*, 12 August 1740 as 'John RATCLIFFE from Amsterdam, now living in Coney Street, York, Makes all Sorts of Cabinet-Work after the newest English, French and Dutch Fashions; Likewise Glass and Picture Frames; Pictures clean'd and refresh'd; also all Sorts of English and Dutch Varnish, and Lacquer made and sold by him.' Advertised again on 9 August 1743 as a framemaker in Low Ousegate, who 'Makes all Sorts of gilded or black Frames for Pictures or Prints'; and on 4 March 1746, announced sale at his shop on Ouse Bridge, 'on Wednesday in the Assize week' of 'all Sorts of CABINET WORK ... viz desks with Brass Mountings all other Sorts of Desks, Glasses, Tables and Chairs, &c....'. Probably the JR, cm aged 50, recorded as having been resident for eight years in St Helen's parish in the 1767 Census of Roman Catholics. [*Catholic Recusancy in York*]

Ratcliffe, John, Liverpool, joiner and cm (1799). Admitted freeman on servitude to Robert Tyrer on 3 December 1799. [Liverpool freemen reg.]

Ratcliffe, John, Chester, cm (1812–37). Trading in Foregate St, 1812–19; Britain's Entry in 1826; and Brook St in 1837. Admitted freeman on 10 October 1812. [Chester freemen rolls and poll bks] Notice in *Chester Chronicle, Cheshire and North Wales Advertiser*, 6 November 1829, concerned the 'violent Assault' by Ratcliffe on Mathias Rowlands, when Ratcliffe visited Rowlands's sister 'to demand some clothes which she had taken off his child's back'. Rowlands had attempted to throttle him, and Ratcliffe 'was obliged to cut at them with a large hinge'. The case was settled by Ratcliffe agreeing never to molest Rowlands in future, and paying all expences, including the surgeon's bill.

Ratcliffe, John, Spa Fields, London, corn chandler and cm (1822). Took out a Sun Insurance policy on 20 November 1822 for £500, £400 on his house, and £100 on warehouse, workshop, stock, utensils and goods in trust. [GL, Sun MS vol. 490, ref. 997860]

Ratcliffe, John, Rosemary Lane, Ashton-under-Lyne, Lancs., joiner and cm (1828). [D]

Ratcliff(e), M., New Brentford, Middlx, u and furniture broker (1838). [D]

Ratcliffe, Thomas, Richmond St, Liverpool, cm and merchant (1781–83). [D]

Ratenbury, William, Spilsby, Lincs., cm and joiner (1835). [D]

Rathbone, Charles, 95 Old St, London, carver (1791). Took out a Sun Insurance policy on 18 April 1791 for £100, including £5 on utensils in the workshops adjoining Mr Seddon, cm, in Aldersgate St. [GL, Sun MS vol. 376, p. 227]

Rathbone, John, 24 Linal St, Liverpool, cm (1794). [D]

Rathbone, Phillip, 29 Lowdon St, Ratcliff, London, cm (1775). Took out a Sun Insurance policy in 1775 or £500 of which £350 accounted for utensils and stock. [GL, Sun MS vol. 238, p. 593]

Rathbone, Richard, 3 Dufours Ct, Broad St, Golden Sq., London, carver and gilder (1794–1800). Took out a Sun Insurance policy on 9 July 1794 for £600 on his house, contents and utensils. Recorded at 3 Dufours Pl. in the account books of Edward, Lord Harewood, 1st Earl, and Edward, Lord Lascelles, relating to Harewood House, Yorks., and Harewood House, Hanover Sq., London. Between 19 June 1795 and 25 May 1799 Rathbone was paid a total of £361 4s for unspecified work. On 23 June 1797 he supplied 'a frame for Mrs. Chaloner', costing £4 19s; on 27 October 1798, a picture frame costing £7 2s; and on 14 June 1800 he was paid 12s 6d 'for taking down the great Lanthorn'. [GL, Sun MS vol. 401, ref. 630179; Leeds archives dept, Harewood MS 211–12 and 189–92]

Rathell, Samuel, 8 Devonshire St, Queen Sq., London, upholder (1788–99). [D]

Rathnell, Samuel, 37 Queen Sq., Bloomsbury, London, u (1808). [D]

Rattenbury, William, Spilsby, Lincs., joiner and cm (1826). [D]

Rause, Richard, Oxford, cm (1780). Insured his house and stock for £300 in 1780. [GL, Sun MS vol. 283, p. 262]

Ravald, Ann & Abbott, William, 16 Bedford St, Covent Gdn, London, u (1791). Took out a Sun Insurance policy on 12 March 1791 for £500. [GL, Sun MS vol. 374, ref. 580963] See Ravald & Abbat, and Ravald & Holmes.

Ravald, John, Lancaster and London, u (1767–68). Admitted freeman of Lancaster, 1767–68, when stated of Gt Queen St, London. [Lancaster freemen rolls] Probably:

Ravald (or Ravauld), John, at the Blanket Warehouse, Prince's St, Leicester Fields, London, cm and upholder (1778–84). Took out Sun Insurance policies in 1778 for £600 on his house; and in 1783 with John Morland for £1,500 on utensils, stock and goods. Named with his son, John, in the Preston Guild record of burgesses in 1782 of Princess' St, Soho. Polled at Westminster in 1784. [GL, Sun MS vol. 266, p. 608; vol. 313, p. 365] See Ravald & Morland.

Ravald & Abbat, 16 Bedford St, Covent Gdn, London, upholders (1791–95). [D] See Ann Ravald.

Ravald & Holmes, 16 Bedford St, Covent Gdn, London, upholders (1793–94). Recorded also as Ravald & Co. at this address in 1793. [D] See Ann Ravald.

Ravald & Morland, London, upholders and cm (1779–93). Recorded at 13 Prince's St, Soho, 1780–93. Submitted a bill to Sir John Griffin Griffin of Audley End, Essex, dated

19 January 1779 and totalling £64 7s 9d for items supplied to Sir John's London house in New Burlington St. Items included 'A Set of Carved Cornishes made to your Laths with honeysuckle middles . . .'; 'Covering the above cornishes with your furniture stripe'; thirty-six 'splat back rout Chairs with shaped Matted seats neatly Japand to Match your Stripe'; Wilton carpeting for the ante-room, dressing-room and stairs; and '2 Neat pole stands with turnd Ivory tops for your Screens a Moulding round Ditto and japand to match the rout Chairs'. In 1780–81 Ravald & Morland were paid 4s for repairing a 'Japan Rout Chair' and 'Japan Pole Fire Screen'. The firm was employed at Carlton House, 1783–86, submitting a bill of £513 15s 3d for upholstery work. On 10 August 1784 they charged the Prince of Wales £33 18s for a large mahogany secretaire, the lower part consisting of a desk drawer and three drawers with folding doors, the upper part with a variety of drawers and sliding shelves; a carved scroll pediment, octagonal glazed doors, and two silk curtains which cost an extra £1 12s. Ravald & Morland also provided a mahogany library stool 'stufed & covered w. plain satin haircloth and finished w. best brass nails', costing £3. Bills at Osterley Park, London, include one from Ravald & Morland for £5 10s 8d dated 6 December 1784 to Mrs Child, for cleaning and repairing furniture, hangings, ornaments and pictures throughout the house. Further repairs were carried out in 1787. A receipt for £92 11s dated 1788 is signed by John Morland for furniture delivered 'for self and the Representative of Mr. Ravald Deceased.' [D; Essex RO, D/DBy/A37/4; A39/5; A210–2; RA, 25069; H. Clifford Smith, *Buckingham Palace*; Fastnedge, *Sheraton Furniture*] See John Ravald.

Raven, Edward, Thornton Lane, Leicester, u (1827). [D]

Raven, John jnr, address unrecorded. In 1730 he was paid £1 19s for a chest of drawers and a folding bed supplied to James, Duke of Montrose, for his house at Cley. [Scottish RO, GD 220/6/31/P602]

Raven, John, Wharf St, Leicester, cm (1828). [D]

Raven(s), Thomas, Goswell St, London, cm and bedstead maker (1829–39). Recorded at no. 110, 1820–35, and no. 135, 1837–39. [D]

Ravenhill, George, St Paul's Churchyard, London, upholder and cm (1776–89). Recorded at no. 22, 1782–89. Admitted freeman of the Upholders' Co. on 7 February 1776. Named in Bailey's list of bankrupts, 1788. [D; GL, Upholders' Co. records]

Ravenhill, James, 22 St Paul's Churchyard, London, freeman joiner, cm (1769–83). Employed six non-freemen for three months in 1770; four for three months in 1771; six for six weeks in 1772; and six for six months in 1773. Took out a Sun Insurance policy in 1777 for £1,000 of which £500 accounted for utensils and stock. Trade label recorded on privately owned mahogany card table, datable by style c.1750–60. Label reads: 'James Ravenhill, at the Golden Key against the South door of St. Paul's Church, London: Makers and sellers of coach and looking glasses, chairs and cabinets working at the lowest prices, N.B. merchants may be furnished . . . and other chairs to take to pieces.' [D; GL, City Licence bks, vols 7 and 8; GL, Sun MS vol. 262, p. 120] See Thomas Ravenhill.

Ravenhill, Richard, 44 London Wall, London, cm and u (1822–23). [D]

Ravenhill, Thomas, St Paul's Churchyard, London, cm and upholder (1789). Dividends on bankruptcy announced in *Williamson's Liverpool Advertiser*, 23 November 1789. See James Ravenhill.

Ravenhill, William, 10 North St, City Rd, London, chairmaker (1808). [D]

Ravenhill & Sparrow, 87 Bartholomew Close, London, cm (1790–93). [D]

Ravens, T., 24 New Church St, Edgware Rd, London, cm (1835). [D]

Ravenscroft, James, Nantwich, Cheshire, chairmaker (1810–d.1812). Daughter Mary by wife Ellen bapt. on 14 March 1810. Ravenscroft was buried on 31 January 1812. [Chester RO, PR]

Ravenscroft, John jnr, Nantwich, Cheshire, chairmaker (1788). Married on 4 February 1788. [Chester RO, PR]

Ravenscroft, Samuel, address unrecorded, u (1640–d.1664). Named in the *List of Principal Inhabitants of the City of London in 1640* as Alderman of Vintry Ward. Died in 1664. [Heal]

Ravis, Nathaniel, London, upholder and cm (1807–09). Trading at Three King Ct, Lombard St, 1807–08, no. 6 in 1807; and as Ravis & Rickman at 11 High St, Southwark in 1809. [D]

Ravner, William, 2 Broker's Row, Moorfields, London, upholder, broker and undertaker (1784). [D]

Raw, Christopher, Northallerton, Yorks., cm (1828–29). [D]

Rawbone, Thomas, Snowhill, London, upholder (1773–74). Son of William Rawbone of All Hallows, London Wall; admitted freeman of the Upholders' Co. on 7 April 1773. Declared bankrupt, *Gents Mag.*, January 1774; as Rawhone in February 1774. [GL, Upholders' Co. records]

Rawbone & Rainper, Snowhill, London, upholstery warehouse (1773). [D]

Rawden, Christopher jnr, York, cm (1807–23). Trading at Barker Hill in 1823. Son of Christopher Rawden, brushmaker; app. to William Fawbert, cm, on 18 January 1807. Admitted freeman in 1820. [D; York app. reg. and freemen rolls]

Rawes, Christopher, Lancaster, u (1767–68). [Lancaster freemen rolls]

Rawes, Gerrard, Lancaster, joiner and cm (1738–68). App. to George Haresnape in 1738. Took apps on 22 January 1749, 1 January 1752, 26 January 1756; and 1 December 1762. His son, Christopher, admitted freeman u, 1767–68. [Lancaster app. reg. and freemen rolls]

Rawley, Charles, Beverley, Yorks., cm (1754). Took app. named Walker in 1754. [S of G, app. index] Probably Charles Rawling.

Rawlin, James, Chepping Wycombe Borough, High Wycombe, Bucks., chairmaker (1798). [Militia Census]

Rawling (or Rawlins), Charles, Beverley, Yorks., cm (1756–61). Took apps named Andrew in 1756, Stokes in 1760 and Hunsley in 1761. Named in the Burton Constable vouchers on 6 September 1761 providing 'A Fret Rim Put Round a Large Meogney Board' costing £1.1s. Took app. named Thomas Walker of Hull. [S of G, app. index; C. *Life*, 3 June 1976, p. 1476–80] Probably Charles Rawley.

Rawlings, Ann, Wood St, Walthamstow, London, cm (1826–32). Trading as cm and u in 1832. [D] See George Rawlings.

Rawling(s), Edward, 17 Mount St, London, cm, upholder and broker (1790–93). Took out Sun Insurance policies on 7 December 1790 for £600 including £420 on stock and goods in trust; and on 27 December 1790 for £200 on his warehouse and workshops over stables in North Bruton Mews. [D; GL, Sun MS refs 576726 and 577554]

Rawlings, Edward, 21 Drury Ct, Strand, London, cabinet inlayer (1836). [D]

Rawlings, Francis, High St, Cheltenham, Glos., cm and u (1820–40). Trading at 22 High St in 1820; as cm, u, building surveyor and paper hanger in 1822; and at 76 High St, 1830–39, in 1839 as Rawlings & Son. [D]

Rawlings, George, Wood St, Walthamstow, London, cm (1809–11). [D] See Ann Rawlings.

Rawlings, George, Long St, Sherborne, Dorset, cm and u (1840). [D]

Rawlings, John E., 170 Tottenham Ct, London, u and cm (1829–39). [D]

Rawlings, Philip, 173 Drury Lane, London, turner (1792–93). In partnership with John Smart, as turners and bedstead makers, took out a Sun Insurance policy on 8 October 1792 for £600 of which £300 accounted for goods and stock in trust in their workshop. A Rawlins subscribed to Sheraton's *Drawing Book*, 1793. [GL, Sun MS vol. 389, ref. 605989] See Robert Rawlings and P. & W. Rawlins.

Rawlings, Robert, London, cm and bedstead maker (1775–1823). Addresses given new Holborn, Drury Lane in 1775; 187 Drury Lane in 1783; in Heal as R. Rawlings of Theobalds Rd in 1794, and in directories at no. 50, 1806–23; and at 26 Red Lion Sq., 1826–27. Took out Sun Insurance policies in 1775 for £700, and in 1783 for £500, utensils, stock and goods accounting for £450 and £250 respectively. Probably the Rawlins, bedstead manufacturer of Theobald's Rd who subscribed to Sheraton's *Drawing Book*, 1793. [D; GL, Sun MS vol. 239, p. 482; vol. 313, p. 582] See Philip Rawlings & John Smart, and P. & W. Rawlins.

Rawlings, Thomas, 170 Tottenham Ct Rd, London, cm and chairmaker (1817–28). [D]

Rawlin(g)s (or Rawling or Rawlens), William, London, cm, upholder, appraiser and undertaker (1770–1802). Recorded at 93 Fleet Mkt in 1778; 91 Street Mkt in 1779; Moorfields, 1781–86; 11 Broker Row in 1790; as a member of the Upholders' Co. in Old Bethlem, 1792–94; and as Sir William Rawlins, Knight and Sheriff in Old Bethlem in 1802. Trade card [BM] states: 'Rawlins Cabinet Maker Upholder Appraiser & Undertaker. The Royal Bed & Star No. 12 Broker Row Opposite Bedlam Walk, Moorfields London. Genteel Furniture New & Second hand in great variety.' Son of Simon Rawlins, farmer of Bridgcombe, Berks. App. to Thomas Harris, weaver, on 6 August 1770, and to Samuel Swaine on 25 March 1773. Admitted freeman of the Upholders' Co. by servitude on 6 May 1778. Took app. named John Price, 1781–88. William Rawlins, u and cm of 91 Street Mkt took out a Sun Insurance policy in 1779 for £800 of which £670 accounted for utensils, stock and goods. Successor to Pitt & Chessey at 12 Broker's Row, and formerly James Rodwell. [D; GL, Upholders' Co. records; GL, Sun MS vol. 278, p. 422; Heal]

Rawlins, James, Duke St, Trowbridge, Wilts., cm etc. (1839). [D]

Rawlins, P. & W., 26 Red Lion Sq., London, bedstead manufactory (1802–04). [D] See Robert Rawlings.

Rawlins, Thomas, Westgate, Grantham, Lincs., joiner and cm (1790). Sale of Rawlins's wood and stock in trade on his declining business advertised in *Lincoln, Rutland and Stamford Mercury*, 5 March 1790. Stock consisted of mahogany, walnut, elm and other wood; and 'The Whole of his CABINET STOCK ready made; consisting of a handsome Mahogany Wardrobe; a Desk; Four Sets of Drawers; Five Dining Tables; Three Pembroke Tables; Four Tea Tables; Two Night Tables; Eight Bason Stands; a Number of Tea, Glass and Butlers' Trays; a Wainscot Desk; Two Sets of Drawers; Two Tea Tables, with several Card and Dressing Tables; Twenty Pier and Swing Glasses; Kitchen Chairs; a Number of other Articles in the above Branches entirely new. The above Furniture is worth the Attention of the Public, being finished in a Workmanlike Manner out of fine old-seasoned wood.'

Rawlinson, Anne, Warrington, Lancs., u (1789). [D]

Rawlinson, James, New Rd, Whitechapel Rd, London, u (1780). Insured his house for £100 in 1780. [GL, Sun MS vol. 282, p. 603]

Rawlinson, James, 120 Rosemary Lane, London, u (1780–82). Took out Sun Insurance policies in 1780 for £100, £50 accounting for utensils, stock and goods; and in 1782 for £300, £200 on utensils and stock. [GL, Sun MS vol. 284, p. 264; vol. 303, p. 92]

Rawlinson, James, Artillery St, Wisbech, Cambs., cm and u (1824). [D]

Rawlinson, Stephen, Newmarket, Suffolk, cm or u (1796). Son of William Rawlinson, coachman of Newmarket; app. to Edward and Thomas York of Cambridge, u and cm, for £21 on 26 March 1796. [Cambs. RO, Corp. day bk]

Rawlsham, Richard, Liverpool, cm (1755). Took app. named Hill in 1755. [S of G, app. index]

Raworth, Thomas, 43 Hill St, Newfoundland St, Bristol, cm (1834). [D]

Rawson, Gervas, Watson's Yd, Leylands, Leeds, Yorks., chairmaker (1822). [D]

Rawson, John, Ripon, Yorks., cm and victualler (1798). [D]

Rawson, John, Sheffield, Yorks., cm (1816–34). Trading at Westbarr in 1816 and Woodgrove in 1822. [D]

Rawson, John & Son, Hill Foot, Penistone Rd, Sheffield, Yorks., cm and joiners (1825–33). [D]

Rawson, John, Chapel St, Tadcaster, Yorks., joiner and/or cm (1834–37). [D]

Rawson, Thomas, Manchester, cm (1828–33). Trading at 31 Port St in 1828; 172 and/or 472 Oldham Rd in 1829; and no. 64, 1832–33. [D]

Rawson, Thomas, 15 West St, Leeds, Yorks., u (1837). [D]

Ray, Andrew, Stone Bridgegate, Ripon, Yorks., joiner and cm (1828–29). [D] Possibly Andrew Roy.

Ray, J., Atherstone, Warks., hair and chair seating manufacturer (1796). [D]

Ray, John, 6 Robert St, Liverpool, cm (1811). [D]

Ray, Robert, Linacre Marsh, Liverpool, cm (1839). [D]

Ray, Thomas, address unrecorded, upholder (1710–19). Son of John Ray, Gent. of Gomersal, Yorks.; app. to Thomas Dixon in 1710, and admitted freeman of the Upholders' Co. by servitude on 9 September 1719. [GL, Upholders' Co. records]

Ray, Thomas, Bartholomew Close, Little Britain, London, upholder (1724–34). [D; poll bk]

Ray & Co., Thomas, Raquet Ct, Fleet St, London, upholders (1727). Took out a Sun Insurance policy on 17 May 1727 for £1,200 on stock in house in Raquet Ct occupied by Richard Say. [GL, Sun MS vol. 24, ref. 41759]

Ray, Uriah, Market Drayton, Salop, chairmaker (1822–28). Trading at Horse Mkt in 1822 and Cheshire St in 1828. [D]

Ray, William, Lancaster. Named in the Gillow Records in 1786. [Westminster Ref. Lib.]

Raybold, Richard, St Botolph, Bishopsgate, London, carver (1772). Declared bankrupt, *Gents Mag.*, June 1772.

Rayer, Moses, Worcester, upholder (1798). App. to Abraham Fluke, upholder, and admitted freeman on 1 October 1798. [Worcester freemen rolls]

Rayley, Joseph, Beverley, Yorks., cm and u (1774–99). [D; poll bks]

Rayment, Jeremiah Joseph, The Wash, Hertford, carver, gilder and printseller (1839). [D]

Rayment, William, 137 High Holborn, London, upholder (1790–93). [D]

Raymond, Ann & Co., 48 Wine St, Bristol, upholders (1775). [D]

Raymond, Christopher, Bristol, upholder (1729–39). Polled of Christ Church parish, 1734 and 1739. Took app. named Witchell in 1729. [S of G, app. index]

Raymond, James, 11 Manchester Mews South, London, chair and sofa manufacturer (1829). [D]

Raymond, Mary, 34 Primrose Hill, Liverpool, furniture painter (1839). [D]

Rayner, —, address unrecorded, cm (1803). Subscribed to Sheraton's *Cabinet Dictionary*, 1803.

Rayner, George Thomas, Ramsgate, Kent, cm (1832–39). Addresses given at 9 Plains of Waterloo, 1832–34, and Bellevue Hill, 1838–39. Polled at Sandwich in 1831 and 1832; and as Thomas George Rayner in 1837. [D].

Rayner, Henry, 41 Gt Marylebone St, Cavendish Sq., London, cm (1808). [D]

Rayner (or Raynor), Joseph, Wakefield, Yorks., cm, u and joiner (1814–37). Recorded at Kirkgate, 1814–20, and Westgate, 1822–37. [D]

Rayner, Philip, corner of Brook(e) St, Holborn, London, cm and u (d.1745). Sale of stock in trade on his death advertised in *London Evening Post*, 2–4 May 1745. Stock consisted of 'Mahogany Buroes and Dressing Tables, Chairs ditto, Tables ditto, Walnut Chairs, Leather Easy Chairs and other Chairs, double Chest of Drawers, Sconces and Chimney Glasses, Settee Beds, Four Posted, worsted Damask Curtains . . . N.B. Two India Cabinets and an Eight Day Clock.' Sale announced again in *Daily Advertiser*, 9 May 1745.

Rayner, Thomas snr, Norwich and Cambridge, chairmaker (1757–1830). Thomas Rayner, was app. to William Rayner, chairmaker of Norwich on 3 May 1757. He is recorded in the Norwich poll bks between 1768–1830 as Thomas Rayner, chairmaker of Cambridge and the later references may be to Thomas jnr. As no record of his having a business in Cambridge can be found he presumably remained a journeyman working for one of the firms in Cambridge. With this in mind it is interesting to note that his son, Thomas Rayner jnr was employed by Elliot Smith of Cambridge, so it is quite possible that Rayner snr was employed in the same workshop. The idea is strengthened by the fact that in 1820, Elliot Smith supplied a set of 28 dining chairs to Trinity College, eight of the set being stamped with the chairmaker's initials 'T.R.' (Fig. 38). [Norwich app. reg.; *Furn. Hist.*, 1976]
R.W.

Rayner, Thomas jnr, Cambridge, chairmaker (1816–30). The *Cambridge Chronicle and Journal* reported on 19 April 1816, that 'On Wednesday last Thomas Rayner jun., was committed to the town goal by John Purchas Esq., charged with stealing 6 chairs from a warehouse belonging to his employer Mr. Elliot Smith'. On 25 April he was sent to prison 'for stealing six rush bottom chairs valued at eighteen shillings from his employer'. He is recorded as living in Cambridge in the Norwich poll bk of 1830. [Cambs. RO, Cambridge sessions records, 1808–18]
R.W.

Rayner, Thomas III, Norwich; chairmaker (1812). Son of Thomas Rayner, chairmaker; admitted freeman on 13 June 1812. [Norwich freemen reg.]

Rayner, Thomas, Acre Lane, Clapham, London, carver and gilder (1822–32). [D]

Rayner, W., High St, Newport, Isle of Wight, Hants., chairmaker and turner (1823). [D] See William Rayner of Newport.

Rayner, William, Norwich and London, chairmaker (1735–61). Admitted freeman of Norwich on 3 May 1735, not by apprenticeship. Former app., Thomas Raynor, chairmaker, admitted on 3 May 1757. Of London, polled at Norwich in 1761. [Norwich freemen reg.]

Rayner, William, address unrecorded, cm (1756). Carried out cabinet-makers work for Peter Du Cane snr at Braxted Park, Essex, for which he was paid £4 4s on 31 August 1756. [Essex RO, D/DDc A13, folio 59]

Rayner, William, Moorfields, London, upholder, broker and undertaker (1775–87). Recorded at 2 Broker's Row, 1777–87. App. to Cecil Pitt (?), and admitted freeman of the Upholders' Co. by servitude on 5 April 1775. Trade card gives address at 2, the corner of Old Bethlem and Moorfields, and states Rayner was successor to Henry Shakespear. [D; GL, Upholders' Co. records; Banks Coll., BM; Beavan's *Aldermen of the City of London*, 1908]

Rayner, William, Newport, Isle of Wight, Hants., chairmaker and turner (1777). Took out a Sun Insurance policy in 1777 for £200 of which utensils and stock accounted for £150. [GL, Sun MS vol. 255, p. 552] See W. Rayner of Newport.

Rayner, William, Ferrybridge, Yorks., cm, house carpenter, wheelwright and timber merchant (1822–34). [D]

Raynerd, John, 53 Leather Lane, Holborn, London, carpenter and cm (1808). [D]

Raynes, Francis, the corner of the street, City Rd, London, cm (1791). Took out Sun Insurance policies on 1 January 1791 for £600; and on 18 April 1791 for £1,000 including £400 on his house, and £600 on two adjoining houses in City Rd. [GL, Sun MS vol. 375, p. 88; vol. 376, p. 221]

Raynes, Henry, 11 Lamb's Pl., Kingsland Rd, London, carver and gilder (1837). [D]

Raynes, John Smith, Dorking, Surrey, cm (1839). [D]

Rayns, Robert, near Market Cross, Blandford, Dorset, upholder (1733). Took out a Sun Insurance policy on 6 December 1733 for £300 including £150 on household goods and goods in trust in his house and shop; and £150 on a house mortgaged in Salisbury St, occupied by Robert Taylor, joiner. [GL, Sun MS vol. 38, ref. 62571]

Rayson, —, 14 Gresse St, Rathbone Pl., London, cm (1808). [D]

Rayson, George, York, cm (1739–d. by 1774). Polled in 1758 of Micklegate. Son of Matthew Rayson, joiner; admitted freeman in 1739. [York freemen rolls]

Rayson, Henry, Micklegate, York, cm (1774–84). Son of George Rayson, deceased; admitted freeman in 1774. [York freemen rolls and poll bks]

Rays(t)on, James, Newcastle and London, upholder (1771–77). App. to William Charnley, and admitted freeman of Newcastle on 23 February 1771. Polled at Newcastle of London in 1774 and 1777. [Newcastle freemen rolls]

Rayson, Thomas, 41 Keppel St, Russell Sq., London, carver and gilder (1839). [D]

Rea, John, Worcester, joiner, carpenter and u (1741–49). Took app. named Thomas Price in 1741, admitted freeman on 6 March 1748/49. [S of G, app. index; Worcester freemen rolls]

Rea, John, 26 Gresse St, Rathbone Pl., London, cm (1809–11). [D]

Rea, Thomas, Johnson's Entry, High St, Hull, Yorks., cm (1838–39). [D]

Rea, William, Liverpool, cm (1780). Petitioned freedom on servitude to Richard Hones in 1780, paying 6s 8d. [Liverpool freemen's committee bk]

Reach, Christian, 11 New St, near Broad St, Carnaby Mkt, London, cm (1786). Took out a Sun Insurance policy on 18 March 1786 for £200 including £30 on utensils etc. [GL, Sun MS vol. 335, p. 634]

Read, —, London, u (1787–88). Named in the accounts of C. Blunt, u, in 1787-88, receiving £17 10s. [PRO, C114/164, pt. 1]

Read, Charles, Berwick St, London, cm (1774). [Poll bk]

Read, Charles, Liverpool, cm (1802–d.1830). Admitted freeman as son of Roger Read, cm, on 7 July 1802. Died in February 1830. [Liverpool freemen reg.]

Read, Georgie, Knutsford, Cheshire, joiner and cm (1790). [D]

Read, George, Cheapside, Oldham, Lancs., cm and u (1825). [D]

Read, J., Upper West St, Gloucester, u and auctioneer (1802). [D]

Read, James, Birmingham, carver, gilder, picture frame and looking-glass manufacturer (1816–30). Trading at Bull St, 1816–18, no. 28 in 1816; and 4 Ann St, 1828–30. [D]

Read, James, 43 Worcester St, Birmingham, cm (1839). [D]

Read, John, West St, Oldham, Lancs., cm (1825). [D]

Read, John Parish, Ipswich St, Stowmarket, Suffolk, cm (1839). [D]

Read, Joseph, London (?) and Ely, Cambs., upholder (1759–1802). Recorded at Cannon St, London (?) in 1773, and Ely, 1774–1802. Son of William Read, farmer of the Isle of Ely. App. to Francis Say on 12 June 1759, and admitted freeman of the Upholders' Co. by servitude on 6 April 1768. A Joseph Read took app. named John Southwell, 1778–85. [GL, Upholders' Co. records]

Read, Joseph, London, chairmaker, u and freeman merchant tailor (1771–85?). Receipt dated 11 July 1771 gives address at 'No. 78, Facing the DIAL, FLEET-MARKET', and displays the sign of 'The Chair & Crown'. The receipt was for '2 Compting House Stools from Hors Hair', costing 14s, supplied to a Mr Graham, and signed for Read by John Smith. Read was admitted freeman of the Upholders' Co. on 6 February 1771. Took apps named George Gibson, 1770–74, and possibly John Southwell, 1778–85. [V&A archives; GL, Upholders' Co. records]

Read(e) (Reed or Riade), Joseph, Kuntsford, Cheshire, cm and joiner (1782–1841). Recorded at King St, 1822–41. [D]

Read (or Reed), Robert, Liverpool, chairmaker (1816–d.1830). Son of John Reed, tobacconist; admitted freeman on 10 June 1816. Died on 16 March 1830, and buried at St John's [Liverpool freemen reg.] Possibly Robert Reid.

Read (Reed or Reid), Roger, Liverpool, joiner and cm (1760–1818). Addresses given at 31 Frog Lane, 1769–74; 37 Whitechapel, 1781–84; no. 42 in 1790; no. 37 in 1794; no. 45 in 1796; no. 41, 1800–04; nos 31 and 42 in 1805; no. 49, 1807–10; no. 46 in 1811; no. 48, 1813–14; and no. 49 in 1818. In 1760 as a joiner he petitioned freedom on servitude of seven years to Richard Copeland, joiner and cm; admitted freeman in 1761. Former apps petitioned freedom: James Atherton in 1780; Roger Corles in 1784; and James Ashton in 1812, taken as app. in 1804. His son, Charles Read, cm, born in 1778, petitioned freedom on birthright in 1802, paying 3s 4d. [D; Liverpool freemen's committee bk] Probably two generations of tradesmen of the same name.

Read, Thomas, Penzance, Cornwall, joiner and cm (1777). Took out a Sun Insurance policy in 1777 for £400, of which £100 accounted for workshop, utensils and stock. [GL, Sun MS vol. 254, p. 110]

Read (or Reed), Thomas, Grimsby, Lincs., joiner, cm, u and paper hanger (1819–35). Addresses given at Bull Ring, 1819–22, and High St, 1826–35. [D]

Read, Thomas, 13 Punderson Pl., Bethnal Green, London, cm and u (1839). [D]

Read, William, Chester, u, cm, painted and stained chair manufacturer (1819–34). Addresses given at Northgate St in 1819; Bridge St Row, 1826–34; and 51 Bridge St in 1829. Admitted freeman on 20 October 1819. Notices regarding his bankruptcy appeared in *Chester Courant and Anglo-Welsh Gazette*, on 20 March 1827 concerning dividends; on 11 December concerning his discharge; and on 18 December concerning the deed of assignment to pay off his debts. In *Chester Chronicle and North Wales Advertiser*, 1 May 1829 Read advertised 'DESIRABLE LODGINGS In BRIDGE STREET directly opposite to the opening of NEW BRIDGE. TO BE LET for the RACE WEEK, or a longer period ... Apply to W. Read, upholsterer, Painted and Stained Chair Manufacturer, 51 Bridge-street, Chester.' [D; Chester freemen rolls and poll bks]

Reader, Henry, Liverpool, cm (1790–1827). Addresses given at 4 Davies St, 1790–96; 7 Pepper St in 1818; 14 and 16 Mansfield St in 1827. [D]

Reader, John, Oxford St, London, u (1784). [Poll bk] See Edward, Joseph and Richard Reeder.

Reader, John, Skipton, Yorks., cm (1840). [Holy Trinity PR]

Reader, Thomas, 2 Walton Ct, Cheapside, Liverpool, chairmaker (1821). [D]

Reader (or Reeder) & Doyle, Bridgewater St, Liverpool, u (1821–39). Trading at no. 68, 1821–29; no. 75 in 1835; no. 73 in 1837; and no. 14 in 1839. [D] See Reede & Doyle.

Reading, J. S., 5 Love St, Bristol, cm and undertaker (1834). [D]

Reading, John, Chepping Wycombe Borough, High Wycombe, Bucks., chairmaker (1798). [Militia Census]

Reading, Thomas, Wakefield, Yorks., chairmaker (1814–37). Trading in Northgate, 1818–20, and Kirkgate, 1822–37. [D]

Reading, Thomas, 1 North Mews, Gray's Inn Lane, London, cm (1820). [D]

Re(a)dwin, John jnr, Holt, Norfolk, joiner and cm (1784). Took out a Sun Insurance policy in 1784 for £200 of which £70 accounted for utensils and stock. [D; GL, Sun MS vol. 324, p. 422]

Readwin, Robert, Burnham Mkt, Norfolk, cm and joiner (1830–39). [D]

Ready, John, next the 'Ship & Mermaid', Snowfield, London, cm and broker (1781). Took out a Sun Insurance policy in 1781 for £200, utensils, stock and goods accounting for £130. [GL, Sun MS vol. 289, p. 273]

Ready, John, 1 Cullum St, Fenchurch St, London, cm (1790–93). [D]

Ream, G., 9 and/or 10 Queen St, Seven Dials, London, cm (1804). With Papworth, sawmaker, rented the above properties from Susanna Walmsley, widow, who insured them for £99 on 18 June 1804. [GL, Sun MS vol. 431, ref. 762573]

Reany, Robert, High St, Huntingdon, carver and gilder (1839). [D]

Reany, William & Adam, 5 Todd St, Manchester, cm and u (1834). [D]

Reardon, John, 19 Cannon St Rd, London, chair and sofa maker (1839). [D]

Reason, Thomas, Moor's Yd, St Martin's Lane, London, u (1709). [Westminster Ref. Lib., St Martin's poor rate bks]

Reason, Thomas, Frith St, Soho, London, u (1713). Named in contemporary newspapers. [Heal]

Reason, Thomas Filmer, Sittingbourne, Kent, cm and u (1790–1839). Recorded in High St, 1838–39. Polled at Canterbury in 1790, 1796 and 1818. [D]

Reason, William, London, upholder (1736–54). Recorded at St Martin-in-the-Fields in 1736 when he took app. named Jeffries. Polled at Westminster of Long Acre in 1749. Named in the Royal Household accounts in partnership with Sarah Gilbert, 1736–41; with Sarah Lowys, 1742–44; and alone, 1745–54. Frequently employed in the Royal palaces towards the end of George II's reign. In 1752–53 he re-covered a four-leaved screen with harateen and trimmed it with silk garnished with brass nails 'for Mr. Schroider, the King's Page'; and in the same year there is an item of £66 17s in his bills for Princess Amelia's drawing-room 'hung all over down to the surbase first with fine Linnen then with White Paper over Do Linnen, India Paper over that, neatly finished with Pictures over the Doors & Chimney with Bordering

Compleat...'. The Royal accounts show him providing carpets, curtains and bedding, and covering the King's chair and stools at the palaces of St James, Kensington, Hampton Court and Richmond. Reason was appointed Royal u to George II, but dismissed from his post on account of dishonest practices. [PRO, LC9/289–91; S of G, app. index; *DEF*; *GCM*]

Reay, George, Turnpike Rd, North Shields, Northumb., cm and joiner (1827–33). Declared bankrupt, *London Gazette*, 8 October 1833. [D]

Reay, Robert, Low St, Sunderland, Co. Durham, joiner and cm (1827). [D]

Reay, Thomas, Church Way, North Shields, Northumb., furniture broker and cm (1827). [D]

Reckard, William & John, Church St, Doncaster, Yorks., cm (1818). [D]

Reckards, Ezechiel, King St, St Giles-in-the-Fields, London, upholder (1701–09). Took out Hand in Hand Insurance policies on 11 September 1701 for £100 on his house, and £100 on the house next door. Both policies are endorsed 'Ren'd Do Reckards 31 March 1709'. [GL, Hand in Hand MS vol. 2, refs 2076–77]

Record, John, Norwich and Lakenham, Norfolk chairmaker (1790–1830). Polled at Norwich of All Saints' parish, 1790–1818, and of Lakenham in 1830. John Record, cm, also polled in 1818.

Redding, Arthur, High St, Amersham, Bucks., Windsor chairmaker (1830). [D]

Redding, Edward, Worcester, cm (1780). App. to Richard Morton, cm, and admitted freeman on 15 September 1780. [Worcester freemen rolls]

Redding, Samuel, Worcester, cm (1802). Former app., Henry Mountford, admitted freeman on 12 July 1802. [Worcester freemen rolls]

Reddish, James, George St, Gt Yarmouth, Norfolk, cm and chairmaker (1830–41). [D; poll bks]

Red(d)ish, John, Leeds St, Liverpool, cm (1821–27). Trading at no. 33 in 1821 and no. 38 in 1827. [D]

Redfarn, Daniel, St Giles, Cambridge, cm (b.c.1755–d.1848). Died aged 93 in 1848.

Redfarn (or Redfarm), William Robert, Christopher Alley, Shoreditch, London, chairmaker (b.1785–d.1859). On 27 December 1808 took app. named Lawrence Wright, son of Lawrence Wright, yeoman of Lower East Smithfield, for seven years, full-board. The £5 charge was 'Charity Money paid by yᵉ Trustees of Sir Jnᵒ Cap's Charity'.[Private archive]

Redfearn(e), John, Liverpool, cm (1777–84). Recorded at 2 Brooks Sq. in 1777; no. 9, with cabinet shop at 9 Cooper's Row in 1781; and 9 Brook's St in 1784. [D]

Redfearn, John Samuel, Hull, Yorks., cm (1819–39). Trading at Edward St in 1839. App. to John Dickon in July 1819. [D; Hull app. reg.]

Redfearn & Cary, Jury St, Warwick, u (1822). [D]

Redfern, Charles, Jury St, Warwick, cm and u (1828–35). [D; poll bk]

Redfern, Samuel, Nursery, Sheffield, Yorks., cm (1816–20). [D]

Redford, —, London, cm (1793). Subscribed to Sheraton's *Drawing Book*, 1793.

Redford, Burdus, Dog-bank, Newcastle, joiner and cm (1775–1801). Insured his house for £100 in 1775. [D; GL, Sun MS vol. 237, p. 295]

Redford, Robert, Pilgrim St, Newcastle, cm, joiner and chairmaker (1793–1801). Advertised in *Newcastle Courant*, 21 December 1793, that he had 'commenced business at the SHOP, lately occupied by Mr. Rayne, Surgeon, foot of Pilgrim-street.' [D]

Redhead, William, Lancaster. Named in the Gillow records, 1825–33. [Westminster Ref. Lib.]

Redhope, John, Manor-chaire, Newcastle, chairmaker (1811). [D]

Reding, William, Worcester, joiner, carpenter and cm (1760–73). Former apps admitted freemen: Michael Pratt in 1760; Richard Morton in 1768, and Thomas Wilkes in 1773. [Worcester freemen rolls]

Redknap, Christopher, London, freeman upholder (1723). His son, William Redknap, admitted freeman of the Upholders' Co. by patrimony in 1723. [GL, Upholders' Co. records] Probably Christopher Rednapp.

Redknap, William, London, upholder (1723). Son of Christopher Redknap, upholder of London; admitted freeman of the Upholders' Co. by patrimony on 15 May 1723. Took app. named Edward Grice, 1723–30. [GL, Upholders' Co. records]

Redman, Christopher, Kirby, Kendal, Westmld, upholder etc. (1741). Took apps named Barrow and Pedder in 1741. [S of G, app. index]

Redmayne, Leonard, Lancaster and London, cm, u, book-keeper and later Director of Gillow & Co. (b.1781–d.1869). Son of Joseph Redmayne, house joiner of Lancaster. App. to Richard Gillow, Robert Gillow the elder and younger, and George Gillow on 6 May 1796 as an u. Admitted freeman of Lancaster with Joseph Redmayne, victualler, by invitation, 1799–1800. Marriage on 18 December 1802 to Miss Treasure, daughter of Captain Treasure, reported in *Billinge's Liverpool Advertiser*, 20 December. Leonard Redmayne, book-keeper, acted as witness to the indentures of Thomas Leeming in 1809. In 1816 he was elected a Common Councillor of Lancaster. In the same year his testmonial was used on a circular by James Carter Moon, who was app. to him on 14 August 1817 as a u. Directories list Redmayne, Whitesides & Ferguson (late Gillow) top of Church St, cm, 1814–17; also Redmayne & Co., u, Castle Hill, 1814–25, and Church St, 1834. Redmayne was elected Mayor of Lancaster in 1824, and in 1826 became Chairman of the Directors of Lancaster Joint Stock Bank. Redmayne lived for many years at Madix Hall, near London, supervising the London end of Gillow & Co. business. Took out a Sun Insurance policy on 176 Oxford St, London, in 1840. He retired from Gillows in 1862, dying seven years later. [D; Preston RO, app. indentures and freemen rolls; GL, Sun MS ref. 1339076]

Redmond, Mrs, address unrecorded. In June 1784 she was named in the Massingberd account books receiving £5 9s for a portrait and frame. [Lincoln RO, MM 9/10]

Rednapp, Christopher, at 'The Cock', Wych St, London, u (1697). Named in contemporary newspapers. [Heal] Probably Christopher Redknap.

Redpath, J., Greenwich, London, u (1804). [D]

Redpath, J., Deptford Bridge, London, u (1808–11). [D]

Redpath, James, Woolwich, London, upholder (1802–03). Trading at High St in 1802. [D]

Redsdale, Benjamin, address unrecorded. Label with name and the date, 7 April 1779, found on a carved mahogany sidetable with male mask in centre of apron. [Christie's, 22 November 1974]

Redshaw, George, London, cm and u (1776–1809). Recorded at Sanday St, Bishopsgate St in 1783, and 4 Sandys St, Widegate St, London, 1807–09. Son of William Redshaw, farmer of Skipsea, Yorks. App. to John Phillips on 7 February 1776, and admitted freeman of the Upholders' Co. by servitude on 5 March 1783. Took out Sun Insurance policies on 2 October 1807 including £350 on utensils and goods in trust and workshop; and on 23 October 1809 for £800 of which £450 accounted for stock, utensils and goods in trust and in workshop. [GL, Upholders' Co. records; GL, Sun MS vol. 442, ref. 806903; vol. 443, ref. 836171]

Redshaw, John, Newcastle-under-Lyme, Staffs., cm (1792). [Poll bk]

Redshaw, Jos., London, u and cm (1820–39). Trading at 41 Warren St, Fitzroy Sq. in 1820, and 23 Frederick St, Regent's Park in 1835. [D]

Redshaw, Thomas, Newcastle-under-Lyme, Staffs., u (1790–92). Declared bankrupt, *Williamson's Liverpool Advertiser*, 25 June 1792. [Poll bks]

Redshaw, William, 6 Riding House Lane, Gt Portland St, London, upholder (1809). Took out a Sun Insurance policy on 1 March 1809 for £300, including £250 on household goods in the house of a carpenter, and £50 on stock and utensils. [GL, Sun MS vol. 448, ref. 828516]

Redstone, Jane, Waterloo St, Richmond, Yorks., u (1823–27). [D]

Redward, —, Penton St, Walworth, London, upholder (1808). [D]

Reeby, James, Plymouth, Devon, cm and u (1830–36). Trading at 1 Park St in 1830 and Frankfort St in 1836. [D]

Reed, Andrew, address unrecorded, cm (1754). Subscribed to Chippendale's *Director*, 1754.

Reed, Charles, address unrecorded, cm (1803). Subscribed to Sheraton's *Cabinet Dictionary*, 1803.

Reed, Charles, Sidbury, Worcester, cm and u (1835–40). Listed at Sidbury St in 1840. [D] See Thomas Reed.

Reed, Henry, Newcastle, u (1740–84). Admitted freeman in 1740. Former apps admitted: John Gibson on 3 May 1769; Robert Turnbull on 6 September 1780; and William Donaldson on 20 April 1784. [Newcastle freemen reg. and poll bks]

Reed, Henry, Wickham, Northumb., u (1780). [Newcastle poll bk]

Reed, James, Warren St, Liverpool, cm (1816–18). Recorded at no. 8 in 1816 and no. 10 in 1818. [D]

Reed, John, Newcastle, cm and looking-glass maker (1773–87). Recorded at Silver St, 1776–78 and Pilgrim St in 1782. Advertised in *Newcastle Courant*, 19 June 1773 that he, 'having begun the business of grinding, polishing & silvering plate glass, proposes to serve his friends . . . with the produce of the new Plate Glass Manufactory, at Howdon Pans . . . with looking glasses, jamb dowels, chimney glasses, seeing glasses, sconces &c &c, likewise old glasses silvered and framed with mahogany, white burnish gold or Japan frames . . .'. Announced in the same paper on 18 May 1776 that he was declining business 'on account of his bad state of health', and that he had assigned his estate and effects to Joshua Henzell. His freehold messuages or tenements, warehouses and workshops in Silver St, and his stock of cabinet goods were to be 'disposed of'. Sale of his stock by Thomas Shene, u and appraiser, advertised in *Newcastle Courant*, 1 June 1776. Stock consisted of 'mahogany & beach chairs; mahogany dining, turn-over, card, skreen & dressing tables, drawers, beaureau desks, beds, tea chests, bason stands, and hand boards; a mangle and a large assortment of pier, dressing and other looking glasses, in fashionable white, burnished gold, and mahogany frames.' Reed was still listed at Silver St in 1778. [D] See Robert Reed in Pilgrim St.

Reed, John, Amersham, Bucks., chair and brush block maker (1793). [D]

Reed, John, Prudhoe St and Leazes Lane, Newcastle, cm (1833–38). Recorded at Prudhoe St and Leazes Lane, 1833–34; 33 Prudhose St in 1834; and Stamfordham Pl., 1838. [D]

Reed, John, 9 Fox Lane, Whitehaven, Cumb., cm and joiner (1834). [D]

Reed, John, Newport St, Barton-on-Humber, Lincs., joiner and cm (1835). [D]

Reed, Joseph, Newcastle, u (1729). Admitted freeman by apprenticeship on 18 July 1729. [Newcastle freemen reg.]

Reed, Mat(t)hias, Louth, Lincs., cm and joiner (1826–41). Trading at Kidgate, 1826–28; Aswell Lane, 1831–35; and Walkergate in 1841. [D]

Reed, Ralph, Haydon Bridge, Northumb., joiner and cm (1828–29). [D]

Reed, Richard, Chertsey, Surrey, cm (1793). [D]

Reed, Robert, Pilgrim St, Newcastle, cm (1790–98). [D] Possibly successor to John Reed.

Reed, Robert, Hull, Yorks., cm (1799). [Beverley poll bk]

Reed, Shakespear(e) & Wainwright, George & Charles, Upper East Smithfield, London, plate glass manufacturers, cm, carvers and gilders, frame makers (1821–22). Took out a Sun Insurance policy on 3 December 1821 for £19,450 including £7,000 on glass house at Whites Yd, £1,000 on stock and utensils therein, and £1,400 on glass stock in two private houses. On 29 April 1822 they took out insurance for £1,350 including £350 on their arched warehouse, £650 on glass stock and utensils therein; £120 on gasometer house and apparatus therein; £100 on the smith and millwright shop; £80 on stock and utensils, and £50 on the porter's lodge. A further policy dated 30 December 1822 totalled £20,900, including £1,400 on counting house, warehouses, straw-packing and silvering rooms above arched warehouses; £100 on stock and utensils, and £1,000 on glass stock therein; £350 on the arched warehouse and £650 on glass stock therein; £200 on a private house; £600 on silvering and emery rooms with storeroom, workshops and smoothing shops; £200 on stock and utensils therein; £600 on house, offices and cabinet maker's shop above; £200 on books and plate; and £3,800 on steam engine house and machinery. [GL, Sun MS vol. 489, ref. 985918; vol. 491, refs 991570 and 999503]

Reed, Thomas, Market Pl., South Shields, Co. Durham, u (1802). Announced that he was setting up business in *Newcastle Courant*, 23 January 1802.

Reed, Thomas, Bristol, cm and clock-case maker (1813–30). Addresses given at Lower Montague St, 1813–15; 17 Merchant St in 1817; 95 Old Market St in 1819; 17 Merchant St, 1824–30, also no. 47 in 1825. [D]

Reed (or Read), Thomas, Sidbury, Worcester, cm, u and undertaker (1820–30). Listed at '28 Sidbury' in 1822. Submitted bill dated 14 September 1821 to J. S. Russell of Powick Court, near Worcester, totalling £3 3s 10d for cotton materials and the making of sofa covers. The engraved heading gives address at Sidbury St, and reads: 'T. REED' with '& SON' deleted. Heading shows pedestal sofa table, sabre-legged chair, bow-fronted chest of drawers, library steps and a sofa. [D; Worcs. RO, 2309/705: 380/55 (i)] See Charles Reed of Sidbury.

Reed, Thompson, Whitehaven, Cumb., cm (1834). [D] Probably Thompson Reep.

Reed, William, Harrington St, Liverpool, painter and gilder (1774–81). Trading at no. 45, 1774–77, and no. 41 in 1781. [D]

Reed, William, Castle St, Saffron Walden, Essex, cm (1811). [Population Census]

Reed, William, 90 London Rd, Southwark, London, cm and u (1839). [D]

Reed & Son, 24 Queen St, Whitehaven, Cumb., joiners and/or cm (1829). [D]

Reed & Wilson, 22 Prince's St, Leicester Sq., London, cm (1789–93). [D]

Reede, Henry, 11 Vauxhall Rd, Liverpool, chairmaker (1803). [D]

Reede & Doyle, 11 Bridgewater St, Liverpool, u (1834). [D]

Reeder, —, 392 Oxford St, London, cm and chairmaker (c.1780–1803). Trade card, c.1780, has inscription on fine Neo-classical urn. Subscribed to Sheraton's *Drawing Book*, 1793, and named in the list of master cabinet makers, 1803. Stamp of 'REEDER PATENT OXFORD STREET' recorded on Regency patent extending mahogany dining table with moulded semicircular ends and two leaves, raised on plain central pillar with four reeded well-splayed legs. [Banks Coll., BM; Sotheby's, 17 June 1983, lot 112] See Edward, Joseph and Richard Reeder; and John Reader.

Reeder, Mrs, Lime St, Liverpool, u (1816). [D]

Reeder (or Reider), Edward, 392 Oxford St, London, cm and u (1803–08). Subscribed to Sheraton's *Cabinet Dictionary*, 1803. [D] See Reeder, —; and Joseph and Richard Reeder and John Reader.

Reeder, Henry, 3 Clifford St, Liverpool, cm (1835). [D]

Reeder, Joseph, 392 Oxford St, London, upholder (1788–1803). Named in Sheraton's list of master cabinet makers, 1803. [D] See Reeder, —; and Edward and Richard Reeder; and John Reader.

Reeder (or Reader), Richard, 392 Oxford St, London, upholder and cm (1781–1811). Named in Sheraton's list of master cabinet makers, 1803. [D] See Reeder, —; and Edward and Joseph Reeder; and John Reader.

Reeder, Richmond, London, cm (1784). [Lancaster poll bk]

Reefe, G. C., 13 Charles St, Queen's Elm, London, carver, gilder, etc. (1820). [D] Possibly George Cornelius Reeper.

Reeks, William, Poole, Dorset, cm and joiner (1744–65). Took apps named Verren in 1744, Drew in 1759 and John Trim some time between 1760–65 for seven years. Reeks is recorded in the settlement examination for Trim. [S of G, app. index; Dorset RO, P22/OV21]

Reely, George, 10 Renshaw St, Liverpool, carver and gilder (1796). [D] See George Ryley.

Reep, Thompson, 18 Queen St, Whitehaven, Cumb., cm and joiner (1834). [D] Probably Thompson Reed.

Reeper, George Cornelius, 3 Brindsey Pl., Bridge St, Southwark, London, carver, gilder and paper hanger (1832–34). [D] Possibly G. C. Reefe.

Rees, T., Bristol, carver, gilder and picture frame maker (1835–40). Trading at Bridewell Lane in 1835 and 15 St Augustin's Back, 1836–40. [D]

Reeve, —, Exeter, Devon, cm (1792). Marriage to Miss Clarissa Drusilla Macey of Exeter reported in *Exeter Flying Post*, 8 November 1792.

Reeve, —, Church St, Hackney, London, cm (1808). [D]

Reeve, —, Marlborough and Devizes, Wilts., from London, upholder, auctioneer and undertaker (c.1830). Label recorded in a mahogany dwarf bookcase, c.1830, with one drawer, reeded shelves and side pilasters. Possibly J. Reeve of Marlborough.

Reeve, Ann, Ashford, Kent, cm and distributor of stamps (1823–29). [D] See Lewis Ambrose Reeve(s), and Reeve & Son.

Reeve, Charlotte, 72 High St, King's Lynn, Norfolk, cm and u (1830). [D] See James Reeve.

Reeve, Edmund, 4 Wilmot St, Brunswick Sq., London, u and cm (1820). [D]

Reeve(s), Ham(b)den (or Hampden), Strand, London, u (1704–d.1714). Recorded in rate bks as Hambden in the Strand, 1709; and as Hamden Reeves in 1712 when he took out a Hand in Hand Insurance policy on 19 April for £600 on his house at the sign of 'The Lamb & Lyon', Strand, St Martin-in-the-Fields. Named in the Royal Household accounts, 1704–13, supplying furnishings for the Royal residences and the Houses of Parliament. On Lady Day 1705 he provided 'for Her Majᵗⁱᵉˢ Bedchamber at Kensington . . . a large fine Dimity Bed tick and Bolster covered with White Satin and filled with Seasoned Swans Downe containing ninety pounds of Down in them £18.10.0.' In 1704–05 he supplied forty-eight turkeywork chairs to the House of Commons, three large turkeywork arm chairs and a carpet to the House of Lords, and twenty-four turkeywork chairs for the Lobby at St James's Palace. In 1709–10 he provided a further twelve for the Court of Wards at Westminster. In 1713–14 he was responsible for Queen Anne's bed at Windsor, and upholstered eight matching walnut stools and an elbow chair made by Richard Roberts. Named in newspapers in 1712, and his death was reported in 1714. [GL, Hand in Hand MS vol. 10, ref. 7931; PRO, LC9/282–85; Winterthur, Delaware, Symonds papers, 75x69, 14, p. 13; *Old Furniture*, vol. 2, 1927, p. 80; *Conn.*, vol. 127, 1951, p. 12; *Conn.*, June 1977, p. 141]

Reeve, J., High St, Marlborough, Wilts., cm and u (1839). [D] Possibly Reeve, —, of Marlborough.

Reeve(s), James, High St, King's Lynn, Norfolk, cm and u (1784–d.1829). Will proved at Norwich in 1829. [D; Norfolk Record Soc., index of wills] See Charlotte Reeve.

Reeve, John, address unrecorded, u (1660–69). Provided items for William, 5th Earl of Bedford: on 23 March 1660 'One dove colour cloth bed with cases for the chairs and stools all at £48.0.0.', in the 'new style'; on 17 May 1660, 'Two pieces of fine ten foot drepe hangings — £50.0.0.'; and on 6 July 1669, 'One gold colour damask bed with bedstead, chairs and all things complete to it . . . £100.0.0.' [Bedford Office, London]

Reeve, John, London, looking-glass manufacturer, carver and gilder (1825–39). Recorded at 163 Drury Lane, 1825–29, and 53 High Holborn in 1835. [D] See Richard Reeve.

Reeve, Jonah, High St, Swindon, Wilts., auctioneer, appraiser, cm and u (1830). [D]

Reeve(s), Lewis Ambrose, High St, Ashford, Kent, cm, u, paper hanger and sub-distributor of stamps (1838–39). [D] See Ann Reeve, and Reeve & Son.

Reeve, Richard, Drury Lane, London, carver and gilder, looking-glass manufacturer (1813–25). Recorded at no. 163, 1813–20; no. 169 in 1820; and as Richard & Son at no. 163, 1817–25. [D] See John Reeve.

Reeve, Samuel, Norwich, u (1677–92). App. to William Mason, and admitted freeman on 11 January 1677. Former app., William Edwardes, admitted on 24 February 1692. [Norwich freemen reg.]

Reeve, Sarah, Hadleigh, Suffolk, u and cm (1830–39). Trading at High St in 1830. [D]

Reeve, Thomas, 45 Green St, Bethnal Green, London, carver and gilder (1839). [D]

Reeve(s), William, Poole, Dorset, joiner, cm and u (1793–1840). Recorded at 5 New St in 1830 and Market St in 1840. [D]

Reeve & Son, Ashford, Kent, cm and sub-distributor of stamps (1832–34). [D] See Ann and Lewis Ambrose Reeve.

Reeves, —, Long Lane, London, u (1668–87). The entry in Samuel Pepys's *Diary*, [1976 edition] 15 October 1668 reads: 'After dinner my wife my I & Deb. out by coach to the Upholster's in Long Lane, Alderman Reeves and then to Alderman Crow's, to see variety of Hangings; and were mightily pleased therewith and spent the whole afternoon thereupon; and at last I think we shall pitch upon the best suit of Apostles, where three pieces for my room which come to almost 80£.'. On 16 October Pepys bought 'his second suit of Apostles, the whole suit, which comes to 83£.' These hangings may have been either second hand or imitation tapestries made of painted or stained cloth. The 'Acts of the Apostles' was a favourite design based on cartoons by Raphael and manufactured at Mortlake. A MS survey of London dated 14

March 1686–87 made by Oliver Mills, twenty years after the Great Fire reads 'I sett out a foundation for Mr. Reeves in Long Lane as described below.' [Heal]

Reeves, —, address unrecorded, turner (1768). On 24 May 1768 he was paid £2 13s for six chairs supplied to Nathaniel Ryder, 1st Lord Harrowby, for Sandon Hall, Staffs. [Harrowby MS Trust, Notebooks]

Reeves, —. See Thomas Russell, clockcase maker, who took out a Sun Insurance policy in 1784 on property sub-let to Reeves.

Reeves, Benjamin, 1 Upsdell Row, Kingsland Rd, London, cm and undertaker (1822–27). [D]

Reeves, C. Edward, address unrecorded. On 25 July 1754 he submitted a bill to the 'Hon. Miss Lee' for items including 'A Large Chest with a Lock & Hinges', which cost 16s. [Shakespeare Birthplace Trust, Leigh receipts, DR 18/5]

Reev(e)s, Henry, Devizes, Wilts., cm (1756–59). Took app. named Robert Keevil(l) on 28 October 1756 by indenture for £33; and Nicholas Reevs on 2 February 1759 for £5. [*Wilts. Apps and their Masters*; S of G, app. index]

Reeves, J., Well St, Hackney, London, cm (1808). [D]

Reeves, J., 25 New Union St, Little Moorfields, London, u (1839). [D]

Reeves, Joseph, address unrecorded, upholder (1708). Admitted freeman of the Upholders' Co. on 7 April 1708. [GL, Upholders' Co. records]

Reeves, Richard, London, clock-case maker (1808). Late 18th-century trade label gives address at '11 Little Bandy-Leg-Walk, Southwark', and states that he 'MAKES all Sorts of CLOCK CASES in the neatest Manner, and the . . . Terms, and shortest Notice. N.B. Country Orders carefully executed.' Directories record him at 52 Henry St, Old St in 1808. [A. Smith, *The Guinness Book of Clocks*, 1984, p. 82]

Reeves, Thomas, High Wycombe, Bucks., caner (b. c.1811–41). Aged 30 at the time of the 1841 Census.

Reeve(s), William A., Maidstone, Kent, cm (1820–30). [Poll bks]

Reeves, William Alexander, High St, Cranbrook, Kent, cm and furniture broker (1831–39). Polled at Maidstone in 1831. [D]

Reevs, Nicholas, Devizes, Wilts., cm (1759). App. to Henry Reev(e)s, cm of Devizes, on 2 February 1759 by indenture for £5. [*Wilts. Apps and their Masters*]

Regnart, Philip, 18 Old Cavendish St, Cavendish Sq., London, carver and gilder (1803–08). [D]

Regnier, —, London (?), billiard table maker (1743). [*Daily Advertiser*, 1 July 1743]

Reich, Christian, Meards Ct, Dean St, Soho, London, cm (1780). Insured his house for £100 in 1780. [GL, Sun MS vol. 281, p. 414]

Reid, Charles, London, later Leith, cm (1785). Described as 'late cabinet-maker in London, thereafter residing in Leith' on 3 August 1785. [Scottish Record Soc., Registers of Testaments, Commissariot of Edinburgh, 1701–1800]

Reid, James, 38 Windmill St, London, cm (1778–d.1800). Wrote his will on 11 December 1799. It was proved on 6 March 1800, and mentioned his wife, Mary, son Thomas, chairmaker, and 'all my real estate in North Britain . . .'. His executors were Joseph Parker, timber merchant of Tottenham Ct Rd, and Archibald Currie, cm, of Denmark St. [Holborn Lib., rate bks]

Reid, James, Little Castle St, Oxford St, London, cm (1784). [D]

Reid, James, 6 Wells St, Oxford St, London, cm (1786). Took out a Sun Insurance policy on 3 August 1786 for £800, including £60 on utensils, stock etc., and £600 on two houses in Marylebone. [GL, Sun MS vol. 338, p. 566]

Reid, James, 53 Goodge St, Tottenham Ct Rd, London, cm and u (1839). [D]

Reid, John, William, George, Ann(e) & James, 53 Goodge St, London, cm (1781–1856). John Reid first paid rates on 53 Goodge St in 1781, and died in February 1803. From 1813–23 George Reid is named as the occupier; and in 1824, Anne Reid. After 1824 it is either George or Ann; in 1838, Ann and William Reid; and from 1840–56, James Reid. William and John are named amongst the vouchers for Burton Constable, Yorks. In 1782 they received £34 7s 11½d; and between April and May 1783 they charged £45 10s 2d for dyeing and making up fabrics, and providing 'a neat 3–6 field bed stained Mahogany', £2. In 1784 Reid's supplied for Mrs Constable's Dressing Room and Family Bedchamber '24 sheets of fine India paper White ground Trees & birds at 18/-', for £21 12s; and '10½ doz. of borders "Reed and Ribbon" at 5/-', for £2 16s 3d. The firm's commissions for Mrs Constable's Sitting Room, Breakfast Room and best Apartments totalled a cost of £177 1s 2d. The wallpaper in the Family Bedchamber is still there. Further payments were made in 1794 for £33 16s 2d for decorating and upholstery work; and on 6 December 1788, £34 0s 10d for furnishings. In 1787 the firm supplied Wilton carpets costing £49 7s 10½d and in May 1789 received a further payment of £83 18s 7d. [Holborn Lib., rate bks; Humberside RO, Burton Constable papers]

Reid, John, London, cm (1784–86). Carried out work at Mount Stewart, N. Ireland, receiving £6 12s 4d on 8 October 1784; and £18 7s 5d on 17 December 1786. [Mount Stewart papers, D654/H1/1, pp. 59 and 103]

Reid, John, Liverpool, cm (1790–1811). Addresses given at' Kent St in 1790; 29 Cable St, 1805–10; and no. 30 in 1811. [D]

Reid, Joseph, High St, Bideford, Devon, cm (1823–24). [D]

Reid, R., 71 John St, Tottenham Ct Rd, London, u and undertaker (1813). [D]

Reid, Richard, 42 High St, Marylebone, London, cm, u and undertaker (1817–27). [D] See William Reid.

Reid, Robert, St James's, London, cm (1764–d.1765). Will written on 2 April 1764, and proved on 22 February 1765, left his money, plate, household goods and working tools to his wife and executrix, Ann. [PRO, wills]

Reid, Robert, 48 Whitechapel, Liverpool, cm (1821). [D] Possibly Robert Read.

Reid, Thomas, Moorfields, London, cm (1779). [Heal citing reg. of unclaimed dividends of bank stock]

Reid, Thomas, Windmill St, London, chairmaker (1799–1800). Son of James, cm, and Mary Reid of 38 Windmill St. Mentioned in his father's will, 1799. Paid rates on 6 Windmill St in 1800. [Holborn Lib., rate bks]

Reid, Thomas, 38 Theobalds Rd, London, u (1829). [D]

Reid, William, London, u (1770). Employed by Thomas Chippendale and spent many weeks at Harewood House, Newby Hall and Nostell Priory, Yorks., erecting beds, putting up furniture, and general jobbing. In the summer of 1770 Samuel Popelwell, the Steward at Harewood, recorded in his Day Work Book payments to William Reid for stuffing the chairs in the Billiard Room. These are presumably the upholstered settee and open armchairs referred to in the accounts; and the '6 Mahogany Armed Chairs covered with Red Leather' and 'One Sofa with 2 Bolsters' in that room at the time of the 1795 inventory. The sofa may be identified as the George III mahogany settee sold at Christie's, 1 April 1976, lot 42. [Leeds archives dept, Harewood MS 18/3: M3248; L756]

Reid, William, Orange St, London, cm (1774). [Poll bk]

Reid, William, 13 Castle St, Bloomsbury, London, cm etc. (1820). [D]

Reid, William, 67 Mortimer St, Cavendish Sq., London, cm and upholder (1824–28). Took out a Sun Insurance policy on 15 March 1824 for £350 on workshop behind his house, including £150 on stock and utensils. [D; GL, Sun MS vol. 499, ref. 1014462]

Reid, William, 42 High St, Marylebone, London, cm and upholder (1827–28). [D] See Richard Reid.

Reid, William, 23 Charlotte St, Fitzroy Sq., London, cm (b. c.1779–d.1838). His will, written on 3 April 1838 and proved on 12 June, mentioned no relatives, but referred to workmen, George Newton and William Draper. He also expressed a desire to be buried at St Mary Newington, which he was on 11 April 1838, aged 59. [D]

Reid & Brockbank, New St, Whitehaven, Cumb., joiner and/or cm (1811). [D]

Reid & Caukill, Commercial Ct, Briggate, Leeds, Yorks., cm (1834). [D]

Reiky, John, 71 Long Acre, London, upholder and exchange broker (1792). [D] Probably John Riley.

Reilly, Henry, Gerrard St, Soho, London, u (c.1773). Carried out work in the Glass Drawing Room at Northumberland House, now at the V&A Museum. [*Apollo*, September 1970, pp. 206–09]

Reilly (or Riley), Peter, Gerrard (or Sherrard) St, Golden Sq., London, upholsterer, dealer and chapman (1771–77). As Riley, polled at Westminster in 1774. Declared bankrupt with Henry Walle, *Gents Mag.*, June 1771; and alone, April and May 1776. Supplied drawing room mirrors at Northumberland House, costing a total of £1,465, c.1773. [D; V&A archives]

Reill(e)y, William, Ironmonger St, St Luke's, London, cm, u, Tunbridge-ware and portable desk manufacturer (1832–51). Trading at no. 15, 1832–40; also no. 16, 1839–40; and 8 Finsbury Terr., City Rd in 1844. [D]

Relph, J., address unrecorded, cm (1803). Subscribed to Sheraton's *Cabinet Dictionary*, 1803.

Relph, John, 9 Rupert St, Haymarket, London, cm, u and chairmaker (1823–39). Took out Sun Insurance policies on 2 October 1823 for £1,200; and on 1 December 1823 for £1,000 on goods in his new house, including £900 on stock and utensils in his house and adjoining workshop. [D; GL, Sun MS vol. 498, ref. 1008434; vol. 499, ref. 1010725]

Remington, George, Bloomsbury Sq., London. In 1807 he filed a patent (no. 3090) for enlarging tables and improving couches. [Fastnedge, *Sheraton Furniture*, p. 59]

Remington, Thomas, 138 Bradford St, Birmingham, carver and gilder (1835). [D]

Remington, William, Richmond, Surrey, cm (1798). [D]

Remington & Rew, London, cm and u (1826–35). Trading at 7 Gt Eastcheap, 1826–27, and 1 Gt St Thomas Apostle in 1835. [D]

Remington & Son, 1 Gt St Thomas Apostle, London, u and feather merchants (1839–40). Took out a Sun Insurance policy in 1840. [D; GL, Sun MS vol. 574, ref. 1333988]

Remmington, Alexander, Rugeley, Staffs., cm and u (1828–35). Listed at Horsefair, 1834–35, in 1835 as cm and original spring mattress manufacturer. [D]

Remus, I., 74 Piccadilly, London. Stamp found on a small marquetry commode of Louis XV design, the serpentine front with three drawers, the top, front and sides inlaid with scrolling flowers and leaves, on a walnut ground cross-banded with satinwood. [Christie's, 6 November 1969]

Ren, William, Liverpool, cm (1757–65). App. to Richard Hayhurst on 3 May 1757 for 10s 6d, and petitioned freedom on servitude in 1765. [Liverpool freemen's committee bk]

Renald, William, address unrecorded. Subscribed to Sheraton's *Cabinet Dictionary*, 1803. Probably William Reynolds of 28 Aldermanbury, London.

Render, John, 26 Kirkgate, Leeds, Yorks., cm and joiner (1837). [D]

Rendle, Henry, Plymouth, Devon, cm (1798). [D]

Renno, T., 41 Parker St, Drury Lane, London, iron bedstead maker (1835). [D]

Renshall, John, 86 Bishopgate St Without, London, u (1780–81). Took out Sun Insurance policies in 1780 for £600 including £400 on utensils, stock and goods; and in 1781 for £500 on his house. [GL, Sun MS vol. 285, p. 313; vol. 291, p. 384]

Renshaw, James, Manchester, cm (1816–33). Addresses given at 24 Byrom St, 1816–17; 21 Lower Byrom St in 1817; and 5 Broughton St, Cheetham, 1832–33. [D]

Rentchall (or Reutchall), Jonathan, Chester, joiner, carver and gilder (1688). Took app. named Thomas Shearar in 1688. [Chester app. bks]

Renton, George, St Benedict's, Norwich, u (1768). [Poll bk]

Renton, George, Huddleston St, Sunderland, Co. Durham, joiner and cm (1828–29). [D]

Renwick, Robert jnr, Newcastle, cm, u, joiner and furniture broker (1824–40). Recorded at Dog-bank and Pilgrim St, 1824–34, nos 9 and 50 respectively in 1834; and 79 Pilgrim St, 1838–40. Notice in the *Durham Advertiser*, 8 May 1840 offered thanks for the 'kind favoures' Renwick had received 'during the many years he had been in business'. He stated that 'he continues to manufacture every article connected with his trade of the very best material, & that he has always on hand an assortment of Dining & Drawing Room Furniture, Wardrobes, Bedsteads, with or without hangings, Chamber furniture & Kitchen Requisites of the best workmanship, which he can with confidence recommend, as they are manufactured under his own immediate inspection. R.R. begs further to draw attention to a Sick Table of the most approved principle. EXCELLANT FEATHERS FURNITURE EXCHANGED.' [D]

Requier, —, at 'The Golden Ball', Newport St, Long Acre, London. Rococo trade label states that he sold prints, portraits, paintings, statues, vases, drawing books, '& all sorts of ornaments as Compartments, Mask Faces, Trophies, Ceilings, Chimneys, Patterns of Alters, Organs, Pulpits, Clocks, Looking Glass Frames, Sconces, Tables &c.' as well as artist's materials, and varnish for japanning. [GL, trade card coll.]

Resbury, Stephen, 5 Young St, Manchester, carver and gilder (1808). [D]

Revall, Champ., Mardol, Shrewsbury, Salop, chairmaker (1835). [D]

Revely, Cuthbert, Newcastle, joiner and cm (1760). Took app. named Wardle in 1760. [S of G, app. index]

Reville, George, Southwell, Notts., joiner and cm (1832). [D]

Rew, Charles, London, cm (1787). Subscribed to George Richardson's *A Treatise on the Five Orders of Architecture*, 1787.

Rex, William, St Sidwell's, Exeter, Devon, carver (1837). Daughter Harriet bapt. at St Sidwell's on 14 July 1837. [PR (bapt.)]

Reynell, Charles, 19 Castle St, Oxford St, London, carver and gilder (1820). [D]

Reynell, Richard, 19 Castle St East, London, carver and gilder (1820–27). [D]

Reyner, John, 404 Oxford St, London, cm (1781–83). [D] Probably John Reynor.

Reynier, Charles, address unrecorded, carver (1755–77). On 5 May 1755 he charged Lady Ann Conolly £6 10s 6d for 'a chimney piece carved in wood' at Stretton Hall. [V&A Lib., English Manuscripts, Box II, 86. KK] In 1777 he was paid £20 1s for 'carving shutters, architrave, mahogany doors, chimney pieces' at Shugborough, Staffs. [Staffs. RO, Anson papers, D615 E(H)/2/6]

Reynolds, —, address unrecorded, u (1685). Named in the account books for Gorhambury, St Albans, Herts., in December 1685 receiving £90. [Herts. RO, XI 22]

Reynolds, —, address unrecorded, cm and u (1775). Subscribed to Thomas Malton's *A Compleat Treatise on Perspective*, 1775.

Reynolds, —, address unrecorded, chairman (1805). Named in the account books for Gorhambury, St Albans, Herts., on 9 March 1805 receiving £2 4s 6d. [Herts. RO, XI 77]

Reynolds, —, Collumpton, Devon, cm (1817). Notice in *Exeter Flying Post*, 14 August 1817 concerned sale of a house in Collumpton, to be viewed on application to Mr Reynolds. Possibly James or John Reynolds.

Reynolds, —, 15 Ivy Lane, Hoxton, London, cm and u (1827–28). [D] Possibly Henry Reynolds.

Reynolds, Charles, Coombe St, Exeter, Devon, cm (1820–22). Daughter Mary bapt. at St Mary Major on 24 December 1820, and son Charles on 21 July 1822. [PR (bapt.)]

Reynolds, Francis, London, cm (1749–54). Polled at Westminster of Wych St in 1749. Declared bankrupt, of Holborn, in *Gents Mag.*, December 1754.

Reynolds, George, Oxford Rd, near Dean St, Soho Sq., London, cm, appraiser and undertaker etc. (1754). Subscribed to Chippendale's *Director*, 1754. Trade card bears inscription within cartouche of Rococo scrolls, drapes, putto, flower chains and musical instruments. It states: 'Estates and all Sorts of Household Furniture bought or sold by Commission in TOWN and COUNTRY.' [V&A print dept, trade cards]

Reynolds, Henry, 132 Hoxton, London, bedstead maker, cm and broker (1823–28). Took out a Sun Insurance policy on 30 June 1823 for £450 of which £270 accounted for utensils and stock. [D; GL, Sun MS vol. 497, ref. 1005826]

Reynolds, Henry, 15 Haberdashers Walk, London, u (1835). [D]

Reynolds, James, Collumpton, Devon, cm (1793). [D]

Reynolds, James, High St, Shifnal, Salop, cm and u (1822–28). [D]

Reynolds, James, Silver St, Lincoln, cm (1828). [D]

Reynolds, John, at 'The Crown & Fox', Fleet St, London, u (1692). [Hilton Price, *Signs of Old London*]

Reynolds, John, address unrecorded, upholder (1760). Son of John Reynolds, Gent. of Atherstone, Warks.; app. to Joseph Forfeit, apothecary, and J. Phipps, apothecary. Admitted freeman of the Upholders' Co. on 7 February 1760. [GL, Upholders' Co. records]

Reynolds, John, St Thomas's, Oxford, formerly of London, carver (1778–80). Named in *Jackson's Oxford Journal*, 13 June 1778, in list of prisoners at the Castle intending to take advantage of the Insolvent Debtor's Act. On 7 October 1780 in the same paper he was reported as a runaway, leaving his family chargeable to incorporated Oxford parishes.

Reynolds, John, 2 Smiths Rents, St John's St, London, cm (1783). Took out a Sun Insurance policy in 1783 for £100 of which utensils and stock accounted for £20. [GL, Sun MS vol. 319, p. 39]

Reynolds, John, Bungay, Suffolk, upholder (1784–1802). [D; Norwich bks]

Reynolds, John, Norwich, u (1792). App. to John Marks, and admitted freeman on 17 March 1792. [Norwich freemen reg.]

Reynolds, John, Redcross St, London, cm (1792). [D]

Reynolds, John, Chepping Wycombe Borough, High Wycombe, Bucks., chairmaker (1798). [Militia Census]

Reynolds, John, Hull, Yorks., house, ship, sign and furniture painter (1821–26). Residing at 3 Gt Passage St, with shop at Smith Alley, Castle St in 1821. Recorded at 3 Gt Passage St as master mariner in 1822, and as Gent. in 1823. John Reynolds, painter, is also recorded at Cockpit Yd, 6 Castle St in 1823.

John Reynolds jnr, painter, was trading at Smith's Pl., Castle St, with house at 9 Upper Union St in 1826. [D]

Reynolds, John George, Cross Church St, Huddersfield, Yorks., cm (1822). [D]

Reynolds, John, Fore St, Collumpton, Devon, cm (1830). [D] See Reynolds, — of Collumpton.

Reynolds, John, Manchester St, Liverpool, joiner and cm (1835–39). Recorded at no. 16 in 1835, no. 46 in 1837, and no. 31 in 1839. [D]

Reynolds, Joseph Hisock, Shaftesbury, Dorset, cm and joiner (1790). Took out a Sun Insurance policy in 1790 for £500 including £50 on utensils and stock. [GL, Sun MS vol. 370]

Reynolds, Joseph, Upper Harrington St, Liverpool, cm (1827–29). Trading at no. 12 in 1827, and no. 18 in 1829. [D]

Reynolds, R., Manchester, cm (1838). Declared bankrupt, *Sussex Agricultural Express*, 5 May 1838. Possibly Robert Reynolds.

Reynolds, Ralph, Friar's Lane, Shrewsbury, Salop, cm (1796). [Shrewsbury burgess roll]

Reynolds, Richard, parish of Christ Church, Bristol, upholder (1734). [Poll bk]

Reynolds, Robert, King St, Manchester, cm and u (1822–38). Recorded at no. 10, 1822–39, with house at Hope Cottage, Broomhouse Lane, Pendleton in 1825; and 31 King St, 1834–38. Declared bankrupt, *London Gazette*, 30 October 1832. [D] See R. Reynolds, and Reynolds & Gregory.

Reynolds, Robert, Paris St, Exeter, Devon, cm and u (1837–40). Daughter Betsy Anna bapt. at St Sidwell's on 24 September 1837. Named in the *Exeter Pocket Journal*, 1840. [D; PR (bapt.)]

Reynolds, Samuel, St Martin-in-the-Fields, London, cm (1751–76). On 5 August 1751 the Earl of Burlington 'Paid Mr. Willm Hallett by Saml Reynolds the sum of £8.5.0. for Machine Chair etc.' The entry in the Earl's account book, kept by John Ferrett, is signed by Samuel Reynolds for William Hallett. [Chatsworth, Burlington papers] Reynolds was a signatory to the will, made in 1763, of William Vile, who left him a legacy of £20. [*Conn.*, April 1938] On 13 June 1769 S. Reynolds signed a receipt on behalf of John Cobb for £73 6s paid by the Earl of Coventry, Croome Court, near Worcester. [Worcs. RO, 4025/970.5: 73] In 1776 he insured house and goods 'at W. Cobbs, St. Martin's Lane' for £300. [GL, Sun MS vol. 244, p. 498]

Reynolds, Thomas, St Mary, Bungay, Suffolk, cm (1790–93). Named in the calendar of marriage licence bonds on 11 January 1790. [D; Suffolk RO, FAA: 50/2/108]

Reynolds, Thomas, Dover, Kent, carpenter and cm (1793). [D]

Reynolds, Thomas, address unrecorded, cm (1803). Subscribed to Sheraton's *Cabinet Dictionary*, 1803.

Reynolds, Thomas, Grosvenor Sq., London, painter and gilder (1809). Took out a Sun Insurance policy on 7 June 1809 for £1,300 of which £100 accounted for his workshop, and £200 for stock and utensils. [GL, Sun MS vol. 448, ref. 832369]

Reynolds, Thomas, Chapel St, Pentonville, London, cm (1811–20). Took out a Sun Insurance policy in association with Samuel Pullin on 1 December 1811 for £300 on his house, warehouse, and workshop at 79 Chapel St. Recorded at no. 82 in 1820. [D; GL, Sun MS vol. 449, ref. 854448]

Reynolds, Thomas, Cambridge, chairmaker (1818). [Norwich poll bk]

Reynolds, Thomas, 88 St John's St Rd, London, cm (1826–28). [D]

Reynolds, Thomas, Walsall, Staffs., chairmaker (1839). [D]

Reynolds, Thomas, Conduit St, Bedford, cm and u (1839). [D]

Re(y)nolds, William, 28 Aldermanbury, London, cm and undertaker (1776–99). Took out a Sun Insurance policy in

1776 for £300 of which £80 accounted for utensils, stock and goods. [D; GL, Sun MS vol. 246, p. 169]

Reynolds, William, back of 22 North St, Dale St, Liverpool, chairmaker (1796). [D]

Reynolds, William, High St, Uppingham, Rutland, chairmaker and turner (1835). [D]

Reynolds & Gregory, 10 King St, Manchester, u (1818–21). [D] See Robert Reynolds.

Reynoldson, George, York, u (1695–d.1764). George Reynoldson was one of the most eminent u and cm in York during the 18th century. He was a Catholic and this largely dictated both the path his life followed and, to an extent, the commissions he was given. He had a business in Stonegate and a woodyard on Manor Shore. He was presented as a Papist in St Helen's parish, 1733–35 and 1745 [York City archives, House Book XLI f.170] but moved to St Michael le Belfrey parish c.1743–44. He was a friend of Francis Drake and subscribed to his *Eboracum*, 1736. He is acknowledged in the preface as supplying information about the 'Trade and Navigation of The City'. He married Mary, daughter of Richard Brigham, a wool draper of York and she, too, was a Papist. She was related to many of the country gentry Papist families. They had eight children (although there is speculation that they may not all have been by the same woman). Reynoldson took the freedom of York as an u by redemption, paying £35 in 1715/16. [York City archives, House Book XLI f.170 and *Surtees Soc.*, vol. 102, p.212] He subscribed to Thomas Gent's *History of York*, 1730 and in the same year was Chamberlain of York. However, he was fined £70 in 1741 for avoiding the Sheriffdom, which he probably did on religious grounds. [York City archives, House Book XLIII f.61v] His stock in trade was insured for £300 on 29 September 1728. [GL, Sun MS vol. 26, p. 430] There are no records or accounts of business ventures before 1729. A Mr George Reynoldson, of the City of York was referred to in the *Yorkshire Herald*, 26 October 1731 for having invented a 'Hydrographical Machine' — to do with navigation.

In 1754 Reynoldson subscribed to Chippendale's *Director*. He advertised himself from his Stonegate premises variously as an u, undertaker and appraiser, but never as a cm. On 1 October 1734 he advertised in the *York Courant* as follows: 'George Reynoldson upholsterer, undertaker and sworn appraiser, in Stonegate, York. Makes all sorts of looking glasses and scones, in gilt Mahogany or walnut frames and coach glasses, by wholesale or retail, at the *London* prices; where old glasses are cut, polished and silvered, very reasonably. He also makes and sells all sorts of Beds, of Mohair, Silk and worsted Damasks, Camblets, Harrateers, cheneys and printed stuffs; Feather Beds, Mattresses, Blankets, Quilts, Rugs and Coverlets, *Flanders* and *English* Ticks, Paper Hangings, imbosed, damasked or plain, Tapestry Hangings, Silk, Worsted Bed-Lace, *Turkey*, *Muscate*, *Persian* and *French* carpets, List, Hair or Painted Floor Cloths, *Dutch* and Floor Matts, Wax Candles, Flambeaux, single or double Brass Arms, Gallery Hall or Door Glasses and Lamps, Mahogany and Walnut Desks and Book Cases, Breakfast and Dining Tables, Chamber and Card Tables, Cases of Drawers, scaloped and round Tea Boards, shaving Stands, Night stools, Chairs of all prices, Folding and Fire Screens, gilt or plain etc. He also undertakes Funerals at reasonable rates and in decent manner will perform them to any part of *Great Britain*, when required'.

He advertised in the *York Courant* on various other occasions, often acting as agent for the sale of the contents of houses. Another advertisement in the *York Courant* on 25 December 1750 reads: 'Since the 11th of December instant, there has been taken out of my wood-yard on the

Manor Shore one (or more) dry Mahogany Boards ten feet six inches long and eighteen inches broad. If any such Board or Boards, is or shall be offered for sale, please stop them and give Notice thereof to George Reynoldson, in Blake Street, York, who will pay one Guinea on conviction of the offender; or if any person concerned will give information of his Accomplice, or who bought the same, he shall receive the same Reward, as above.'

Between 1718 and 1762, Reynoldson took ten apps: John Fowler, 25 March 1718; Richard Farrer, 7 November 1722; Martin Sandys, 5 April 1727; Henry Reynoldson, 18 June 1731; John Yates, 26 November 1733; Henry Smith, 29 September 1734; Nicholas Brigham, 7 February 1739; John Glenton, 6 November 1749; Joseph Northouse, 5 November 1755; Michael Dunn, 7 December 1762. [York app. reg.] Richard Farrar also subscribed to Chippendale's *Director* and there are many cases in which it has not yet, in practice, proved possible to separate the work of the pupil from that of his master. A case in point was some of the furniture supplied to William Constable of Burton Constable, Yorks. In *William Constable as patron 1721 to 1791*, Exhib. Cat., Hull, 1970, a walnut armchair and a mahogany chair are ascribed to either one or other cm. However, Reynoldson is known to have supplied various mirrors, gilt candlesticks and a variety of chairs (mostly in walnut) between 1747 and 1763.

There are many accounts which indicate that Reynoldson was patronised by the Yorkshire gentry and evidence shows that the majority of his clients shared his Catholic faith. He also undertook Catholic funerals — of Lady Hungate and the Fairfax children, among others. There is correspondence between himself and the Grimston family of Kilnwick Hall for whom he arranged a funeral. He is presumed to have been paid £20 for this in August 1748. On 22 November 1752, Reynoldson wrote to John Grimston for instruction regarding the wallpapering and curtain making for the drawing room and principal bedrooms of Kilnwick. Between 1729 and 1730 he worked for York Corporation supplying a good deal of furniture to the City House, now the Mansion House, St Helen's Square. No doubt his being Chamberlain in 1730 was instrumental in securing this commission. Reynoldson and another u, Robert Barker, supplied furnishings to the York Assembly Rooms. [York Assembly Rooms, Directors' minute book, 1730–58].

There is no mention of George Reynoldson in the 1758 poll bk and the *York Courant* of 27 September 1764 announced his death. Reynoldson's will dated 5 October 1764, formed a trust 'for the use of my children and grandchildren' [Borthwick Institute of Historical Research, York, Wills 1765, p. 205], and among his trustees were his wife and Thomas Lupton, his 'faithful servant'. His widow received £50 'for mourning' and his gold watch.

Of Reynoldson's children, Henry, Thomas, Joseph and Rowland carried on, for a proportion of their lives, a similar trade to their father. Henry was app. to his father as an u. Joseph, the youngest son, born about 1743, joined his mother to carry on the business when his father died. He was listed as a Papist being resident in St Michael le Belfrey parish in 1767. His house and ware rooms were insured for £1,200 in 1777 [GL, Sun MS vol. 259, p. 111], but in August of the same year the *York Chronicle* mentioned that he gave up his shop and business in Blake St. His name is mentioned in the accounts of Lord Fairfax, but these are mainly for various supplies rather than construction and craftwork. Thomas was an u and took the freedom of York in 1758. He voted in the 1758 poll. His name does not appear in the 1767 census of Papists. It is possible that he turned out badly for in the *York Courant*

24 December 1754, his father announced that he would not be responsible for debts incurred by his son.

On 11 December 1764, the *York Courant* announced that Reynoldson's widow, Mary, was continuing the business which she did with her son, Joseph and two faithful servants, Thomas Lupton and Henry Smith. The accounts, however, suggest a declining business. Mary's death, aged 88, was announced in *York Courant*, 4 March 1788 and Joseph sold his stock to Thomas Allanson, u of Blake St in 1777. [M. E. Ingram, *Leaves from a Family Tree*, 1951; J. H. Aveling, *Catholic Recusancy in the City of York, 1558–1791*, 1970; C. Hutchinson, 'George Reynoldson, Upholsterer of York, fl. 1716–1764', *Furn. Hist.*, 1976; I. Hall, 'New Light on Yorkshire Craftsmen: Furniture', *C. Life*, 3 October 1974; I. Hall, *William Constable as Patron 1721–1791* (Exhib. cat.), Hull, 1970]

TOWNELEY HALL, Lancs. (Richard Towneley). There is an extensive bill dated 25 November 1719 for mending beds, hanging and altering bed curtains and window curtains, covering three chairs, paper hanging, making valances etc. The bill totalled £5 1s 4¾d. [Preston RO, Towneley papers, DDTO Q/10/2]

ALDBY PARK, Yorks. (Henry Darley). Brief account of furniture supplied. [*Furn. Hist.*, 1976]

NEWBY PARK, Yorks. (William Robinson). A household inventory compiled by Reynoldson in June 1762. [Leeds archives dept, Newby Papers: 2789]

GILLING CASTLE, Yorks. (Fairfax family). Reynoldson's name occurs spasmodically during the 1740s to 1760s for trifling amounts. Large bill for £153 2s 4d dated between 1763 and 1764 for 74 items, mainly soft furnishings. [*Furn. Hist.*, 1976]

BRANDSBY HALL, Yorks. (Francis Cholmeley). Between 1745 and 1748 he supplied furniture and furnishings to the value of £113 17s 8½d. Over 80 items including curtains, papers, chairs. A conspicuous absence of cabinet furniture. [*Furn. Hist.*, 1976]

KILNWICK HALL, Yorks. (John Grimston). Reynoldson was paid £20 in August 1748 for arranging funeral. Reynoldson wrote on 22 November 1752 regarding instructions for decorating drawing room and principal bedrooms. [Ingram, op. cit.]

YORK ASSEMBLY ROOMS. Reynoldson supplied numerous items between 1730 and 1758 including 'a glass 30 inches by 27 inches in a gilt frame with two double branches', 'two dozen of chairs . . . with Spanish leather bottoms the seat 21 inches by 10 inches, with brass nailes' and 'four Mahogany card tables . . . at one pound fourteen shillings each'. [York City archives, Assembly Rooms, Directors' minute book, 1730–58]

BURTON CONSTABLE, Yorks. (William Constable). Various mirrors, candlesticks and chairs, mostly walnut, supplied e.g.: '1741 September 24, paid Mr George Reynoldson for 3 swing glasses No 1393 £1.6.6' and '1757 July 27, 6 Walnut chairs, cushion backs and seats . . . £6.0.6'. Also walnut armchair and three mahogany chairs described in a manner typical of Reynoldson's (and Farrer's) terseness and thus in some doubt as to authorship. [Hall, op. cit.]

MANSION HOUSE, York. Bill for £17 8s in 1729 including '12 Walnut matted bottom chairs 13/6 . . . £8 2s; 12 Oake chairs 8/- . . . £4.16s' etc. Bill for £40 12s 3d in same year includes rugs, bankets, curtains, quilts and 'one bed of broad green cheany, . . . an oak foulding bed with curtains sack bottom . . . 2 close stools . . . one large oak Buroe' etc. In 1736 'One Wallnutt framed setee bed with green furniture' at £5 5s was ordered by the Lord Mayor. [York City archives, Mansion House bills]   V.W.

Reynoldson, Henry, Joseph and Thomas, See George Reynoldson.

Reynor, John, Oxford St, London, cm (1784). [Poll bk] Probably John Reyner.

Rhodes, Charles, Fleet St, London, u (1732). Served at St Bride's as Scavenger 'part of the year and then failed'. [GL, MS 6561, p. 55]

Rhodes, Francis, Hull, Yorks., cm and furniture broker (1822–26). Listed as a cm at 92 Mytongate in 1823; but only as a broker, 1822 and 1826; at 13 Castle St in 1826. [D]

Rhodes, George, Harrison Lane, Halifax, Yorks., cm and joiner (1830). [D]

Rhodes, Henry, York, cm (1828). Son of Elizabeth Rhodes, widow of Clifton; app. to George Beal, cm and u, on 31 July 1828. [York app. reg.]

Rhodes, J., 6 Queen St, Hoxton, London, ebony inkstand manufacturer to His Majesty's Stationery Office (1820). [D] See Thomas Rhodes & Sons.

Rhodes, James, 19 Guildford St, Leeds, Yorks., cm (1837). [D]

Rhodes, John, Woodhouse Lane, Leeds, Yorks., cm (1818). [D]

Rhodes, John, Adwalton, near Birstall, Yorks., cm (1822). [D]

Rhodes, John, 3 King St, Westminster, London, cm and u (1827–28). [D]

Rhodes, John, Knaresborough, Yorks., joiner and/or cm (1834). [D]

Rhodes, Joseph, Drighlington, near Bradford, Yorks., cm (1822). [D]

Rhodes, Joseph, 9 Greek St, Leeds, Yorks., cm (1837). [D]

Rhodes, Joseph, 14 Eldon St, London Wall, London, u (1839). [D]

Rhodes, Richard, Back Lane, Otley, Yorks., cm (1822–37). [D]

Rhodes, Robert, Hampton, Middlx, gilder (1833). During the quarter ending 30 June 1833 he carried out work at Hampton Court at the Stud House, repairing picture and looking-glass frames. [PRO, LC11/80]

Rhodes, Thomas, York St, St James's Sq., London, frame maker (1774). [Poll bk]

Rhodes, Thomas & Sons, 1 Vine St, America Sq., London, ebony inkstand manufacturer to His Majesty's Stationery Office (1837). [D] See J. Rhodes.

Rhodes, William, London, u and cm (1754–1804). Addresses given at Knight St in 1768; Ivy Lane in 1771; 127 Holborn, opposite Fetter Lane, 1777–1800; no. 27 in 1778; and Warwick Ct in 1802, no. 7 in 1803. Son of William Rhodes, victualler of Greenwich. App. to Richard Farmer and Nicholas Parkes, draper, on 27 May 1754. Admitted freeman of the Upholders' Co. by servitude on 7 April 1763, and master in 1794. Took app. named William Williams, 1771–78. In 1768 he employed one non-freeman for six weeks. Named in Sheraton's list of master cabinet makers, 1803. Employed to decorate Drayton House, Northants. when it was inherited by Lord George Sackville in 1769. The decoration was done in 1773–74. In 1771 Rhodes also supplied a pair of painted and carved side tables with marble tops costing £72 for either end of the Dining Room, and the chimney piece, costing £130. Possibly the William Rhodes whose death, aged 76, was reported in *Gents Mag.*, November 1816. [D; GL, Upholders' Co. records; GL, City Licence bks, vol. 6; *C. Life*, 3 June 1965, p. 1349; C. Musgrave, *Adam and Hepplewhite Furniture*, p. 125]

Rhodes, William, Berwick St, London, cm (1784). [Poll bk]

Rhodes, William, 27 Southampton Buildings, Chancery Lane, London, upholder, appraiser and undertaker (1808–17). [D]

Rhodes, William, Barton St, Tewkesbury, Glos., cm (1822). [PR (bapt.)]

Rhodes & Goodman, 13 Clerkenwell Close, London, cm

(1801–11). Trading as looking-glass manufacturers in 1804. [D]

Riade, Joseph, King St, Knutsford, Cheshire, cm and joiner (1822). [D]

Ribbins, Mary, 276 Strand, London, u (1826–27). [D]

Riccall, William, Beverley, Yorks., cm (1774). [Poll bk]

Rice, Charles, North Walsham, Norfolk, upholder and cm (1775–86). In May 1775 Rice, u of North Walsham, valued furniture for the Rev. James Woodforde, Rector of Weston Longville. Charles Rice's marriage at Oulton to Mrs Boutell, widow of the late Charles Boutell of Swaffham, Gent., reported in *Norfolk Chronicle,* 3 May 1783. Took out a Sun Insurance policy on 1 September 1786 for £400, including £100 on utensils etc. [*The Diary of James Woodforde,* ed. R. L. Winstanley, p. 193; GL, Sun MS vol. 338, p. 394]

Rice, Henry, Uckfield, Sussex, cm and turner (1839). [D] Possibly Henry Rich of East Hoathly.

Rice, James & Richard, Bradford St, Birmingham, cm, dressing case and portable desk maker (1828–30). [D]

Rice, John, Basingstoke, Hants., u (1762–93). Took app. named Spencer in 1762. [D; S of G, app. index]

Rice, Joseph, St Albans, Wood St, London, upholder (1695). Married Mary Osmond at Holy Trinity Church in 1695. [Westminster Ref. Lib., PR]

Rice, Richard, Ship Alley, Wellclose Sq., London, carver and gilder (1790–93). [D] See William Rice.

Rice, Richard, Hull, Yorks., carver and gilder (1803–10). Trading at Saville St in 1803 and St John's St, 1806–10. [D]

Rice, Richard, Liverpool, cm (1834–39). Addresses given at 4 Brook St, Harrington St in 1834; 1 Clarke St, Toxteth Park in 1835; no. 20 in 1837; and 11 Blair St, Toxteth Park in 1839. [D]

Rice, William, Ship Alley, Wellclose Sq., London, carver and gilder (1790–93). [D] See Richard Rice.

Rice, Zachariah, Norwich, cm (1818–30). Recorded in the parish of St Lawrence in 1818, and Heigham in 1830. [Poll bks]

Rich, Ann, Lincoln's Inn Fields, London, clock-case maker (1808). [D]

Rich, Henry, East Hoathly, Sussex, turner and chairmaker (1839). [D] Possibly Henry Rice of Uckfield.

Rich, Henry, Chapel Rd, Worthing, Sussex, u (1839). [D]

Rich, John, Crown St, Diss, Norfolk, cm and u (1822–39). [D]

Rich, Joseph, address unrecorded, u (1803). Subscribed to Sheraton's *Cabinet Dictionary,* 1803.

Rich, Joseph, 6 Macclesfield St, Soho, London, u (1809–11). [D]

Rich, Philip, 26 Bishopsgate Within, London, u and cm (1793). [D]

Rich, Timothy, Northfield Terr., Cheltenham, Glos., cm and u (1830). [D]

Richard, John, Chapel St, London, cm (1774). [Poll bk]

Richard, Samuel, High St, Tottenham High Cross, London, cm etc. (1823–26). [D] Possibly Samuel Richards.

Richard(s), William, 125 Wardour St, four doors from Oxford St, London, cm and chairmaker (1774–93). Polled at Westminster in 1774 and 1784. Trade card recorded with fine illustration of Chinese Chippendale-style glazed cabinet. Took out a Sun Insurance policy in 1778 for £600 of which £420 accounted for utensils, stock, goods and shop. [D; Banks Coll., BM; GL, Sun MS vol. 267, p. 291]

Richardby, James jnr, Durham, joiner and cm (1805). Declared bankrupt, *Leeds Intelligencer,* 29 July 1805.

Richardby, James, Hall Ings, Bradford, Yorks., cm (1822). [D]

Richardby, Thomas, Durham, joiner and cm (1803–16). Subscribed to Sheraton's *Cabinet Dictionary,* 1803. Notice in *Durham County Advertiser,* 16 March 1816 read: 'THOMAS RICHARDBY of the City of Durham who had

carried on the business of joiner, cabinet maker, builder etc. in that city & its vicinity for more than 40 years, & until within the last seven, when he declined on the prospect of other objects; but circumstances of late having turned out adverse to his expectations, he finds it necessary to resume his former occupations, of which he takes the opportunity of acquainting his friends & the public, & trusting that from his former long experience he will be able to give satisfaction to those who may please to honour him with their commands which it will be his study to do.'

Richards, —, address unrecorded, u and cm. Several payments to Richards in the 1750s are recorded in Henry Hoare's account book of 1749–70. [Wilts. RO, MS 383/6]

Richards, Benjamin, St Giles, Oxford, cm (1802). [Poll bk]

Richards, Benjamin Tapley, Liverpool, cm (1840). Son of Samuel Richards, soapmaker; admitted freeman on 24 July 1840. [Liverpool freemen reg.]

Richards, C. F., 93 Redcliffe St, Bristol, carver and gilder (1825–27). [D]

Richards, Charles, address unrecorded, upholder (1771). Son of Rev. George Richards of West Peckham, Kent. App. to Richard Hearne, and admitted freeman of the Upholders' Co. by servitude on 3 April 1771. [GL, Upholders' Co. records]

Richards, Charles, 2 Myrtle St, Hoxton, London, carver and gilder (1808–20). [D]

Richards, Charles, High St, Hoxton, London, carver and gilder (1815). On 9 June 1815 Maria Gregory is recorded as having had an illegitimate child by Richards. [GL, P83/MPY1/873/(140)]

Richards, Charles, 64 Barbican, London, looking-glass manufacturer (1820). [D]

Richards, Charles, 38 Union Row, New Kent Rd, London, carver and gilder (1832–34). [D]

Richards, Emanuel, Church St, Staines, Middlx, cm/carpenter (1823). [D]

Richards, Frederick, 17 Woodscock St, Oxford St, London, portable desk, dressing case, work box and cabinet case maker (1835–39). [D]

Richards, George, 3 Featherstone St, Bunhill Row Watch, London, chairmaker (1777). Took out a Sun Insurance policy in 1777 for £200 of which utensils and stock accounted for £50. [GL, Sun MS vol. 258, p. 254]

Richards, George, 1 Old Bailey, London, looking-glass manufacturer (1826–27). [D]

Richards, H., 11 Peter St, Bath, Som., cm and broker (1819). [D]

Richards, Hugh, 279 Strand, London, carver, gilder and glass grinder (1784–1827). Trade card reads: 'Richards, Carver & Gilder, at Apollo's Head, No. 279 Strand (Opposite Norfolk Street) Great choice of the most elegant & fashionable Looking Glasses, Girandoles, Picture Frames, Borders and various other Ornaments, for Rooms of exquisite Workmanship, also Paintings, Prints & Variety of all sorts for Exportation and at the lowest Prices. Pictures, Prints & Needle-work framed and Glazed.' A pair of elbow chairs at Brighton Pavilion, c.1800, of carved and gilt beech, with sabre legs, are stamped 'H.R. at Pavilion'. They are similar to chairs at Hartwell House designed by Henry Holland. [D; Landauer Coll., MMA, NY; Royal Pavilion Catalogue, 1966]

Richards, Hugh, Duke St, Chester, cm (b.1772–d.1833). Death aged 61 on 25 July 1833 reported in *Chester Courant and Advertiser for North Wales,* 27 August 1833.

Richards, I. (or J.), London (?), cm (1746). Mahogany corner cabinet recorded, styled with a richly carved cornice above double glazed doors with enriched mouldings, the cupboard below enclosed by panelled double doors, with carved ogee bracket feet. The carcase is impressed 'I. RICHARDS 1746'

Fig. 1). The same stamp without a date recorded beneath a secretaire cabinet of c.1755.

Richards, Jacob, 122 High Holborn, London, cm, u, undertaker and dealer in piano fortes (1817–39). Took out a Sun Insurance policy on 13 February 1822 for £2,200 on his house, £500 on household goods, £100 on china and glass, and £1,200 on utensils and stock in house, shed and open yard. Submitted a bill dated 22 June 1822 to 'Wilson Esq.' totalling £4 7s 6d for 'A Curricle Bugeir Chair staind Rose Wood Carved back & Seat & Cushion to do', and 'An Extra cushion covered with purple Morocco leather'. [D; GL, Sun MS vol. 490, ref. 989259; GL, trade card coll.]

Richards, James, London, Master Sculptor & Carver in Wood, Office of Works (1721–67). Carried out carving work at Kew for Frederick, Prince of Wales, receiving £60 3s in 1731, £150 in 1732, and £130 in 1733. A further payment in 1733, totalling £467 13s 5¾d included carving settees, chairs and frames, chimneypieces and architraves. In 1732 Richards was paid £150 16s 6d for carving work done on the Royal Barge, designed by William Kent, and Kent later employed Richards for carving at the Horse Guards and at Lord Pelham's house at 17 Arlington St. The overmantel in the King's Gallery at Kensington Palace is said to be by Richards to Kent's design of 1726. Colen Campbell, also employed Richards at Burlington House. Richards and his men were employed at Compton Pl., Eastbourne, until 1731, when he received the balance of his bill for £290. The carved work in the Gallery, Dining Room, Library and Great Staircase is all presumably his. [Duchy of Cornwall, Royal Household accounts of Frederick, Prince of Wales, vol. 2, pp. 218, 256–57, 289–91; vol. 3, pp. 261–66; vol. 4, pp. 222, 237–42; Beard, *Georgian Craftsmen*, p. 31; *C. Life*, 1926, C37, and 20 October 1960, p. 791; G. Beard, '18th Century English Woodcarvers', *C. Life Annual*, 1965; *Conn.*, June 1981, pp. 143–44; *Burlington*, December 1975] James Richards worked as a carver at Cleveland House, London, in 1752. [V&A archives] Richards, carver, is recorded in several notable country house archives of the period, and is most probably James Richards. Some of these commissions are noted in *Burlington*, October 1985. In November 1722 he is named in the accounts of Sir John Chester 'for carving ye Tabernacle & ye Frontispiece for ye Hall' at Chicheley Hall, Bucks. This was a niche in the Hall, built to house a painted statue made by William Kent, and described in a letter from Sir John Chester to Massingberd on 29 February 1723/24. [Bucks. RO, D/C/2/36 iii; *C. Life*, 16 May 1936; J. Tanner, 'The Building of Chicheley Hall', *Bucks. Journal*, 1964] The account books of Sir John Dutton of Sherborne House, Glos., refer to Richards, probably of London, on 2 November 1731, being paid £19 for carving, painting and gilding two table frames made by James Moore jnr for a garden banqueting house at Sherborne. He also received £53 8s 6d for supplying six carved and fluted Corinthian columns. [Glos. RO, Sherborne House MS, D678, acc.1790; *Burlington*, March 1969, pp. 148–49] Richards also worked for Earl Fitzwalter of Moulsham Hall, Chelmsford. On 6 March 1740 'Mr. Richards, carver in wood' was paid £12 2s for carving the chimneypiece in the drawing room above stairs in the Earl's Pall Mall house. On 11 December 1749 he received £56 19s, the last payment of his bill for £106 19s. [A. C. Edwards, *The Accounts of Benjamin Mildmay, Earl Fitzwalter*, pp. 76 and 112] Possibly the Richards, carver of London, who in 1767 supplied picture frames to Henry Knight of Tythegston Court, Glam. [*C. Life*, 5 October 1978, p. 1024]

Richards, James, Green St, London, carver (1749). [Poll bk]

Richards, James, Shrewsbury, Salop, chairmaker and turner (1796–1828). Named in the Shrewsbury burgess roll in 1796

at Castlegate(s), and listed in directories there, 1822–28. Trading at Barker St in 1828. [D] See Thomas Richards of Shrewsbury.

Richards, James, 58 Cherry Garden St, Devonport, Devon, bedstead manufacturer etc. (1830). [D]

Richards, Job, 27 Milk St, Bristol, cm (1838–40). [D]

Richards, John, Shrewsbury, Salop, cm and clock-case maker (1730). Inscription 'JOHN RICHARDS — 1730 — SALOP' recorded on a handsomely grained walnut cabinet of exceptionally small size, with central cupboards enclosed by two sham drawer fronts. His signature has also been noted on two long-case clocks. Richards was one of the few recorded cm then working in Shrewsbury. [*C. Life*, 14 June 1962, p. 1420]

Richards, John, Kensington Sq. and Piccadilly, London, cm (1760–d.1773). Took out a Hand in Hand Insurance policy in June 1760 for £300. Inscription 'JOHN RICHARDS, KENSINGTON SQUARE' noted on a piece of furniture reported to Sotheby's in 1970. [GL, Hand in Hand MS vol. 94, p. 24; V&A archives]

Richards, John, 5 Westmorland Buildings, Aldersgate St, London, joiner and cm (1809–11). [D]

Richards, John, 79 Old St, St Luke's, London, cm and u (1827–28). [D]

Richards, John, 83 London Rd, Manchester, cm and u (1829). [D]

Richards, John, Mary's Yd, Exeter, Devon, u (1832). [D]

Richards, Jonathan, Exeter, Devon, cm and u (1803–32). Advertised his removal from The Mint to 163 Fore St in *Exeter Flying Post*, 27 February 1812. Recorded in Fore St, 1812–19; and at no. 162, 1822–32. Notices in the above paper on 1 December 1803 concerned the charge against him by H. Hurford, wheelwright, of pickpocketing and stealing one pound; and on 30 September 1824, the dividends on his estate on bankruptcy. Advertised in *The Alfred*, 24 and 31 October 1820 for 'three good workmen'. Named in the *Exeter Pocket Journal*, 1822–31, and in the Exeter list of voters of St Mary Major in 1832. [D; PR (bapt.)]

Richards, Joseph, 4 Tower St, Seven Dials, London, cm (1789). Took out a Sun Insurance policy in 1789 for £100 on household goods and wearing apparel in the house above of Coward, carver. [GL, Sun MS vol. 363, ref. 555671]

Richards, Joseph jnr, Cowes, Isle of Wight, Hants., cm and u (1823–39). Recorded at High St, 1830–39, and also Union Rd in 1839. Submitted a bill dated 24 February and 20 August 1832 for £2 3s 5½d to J. S. Pakington of High Park, Westwood, Droitwich, Worcs., for cabinet and upholstery work on board the yacht 'Liberty'. Items included a 'New holland blind' and 'Repairs to mahogany sideboard'. J. S. Pakington was earlier known as J. S. Russell of Powick, near Worcester, and later was knighted, eventually becoming 1st Lord Hampton. [D; Worcs. RO, 2309/705:380/56/iv]

Richards, Peachey, High St, Bognor, Sussex, cm (1839). [D]

Richards, Philip, Fore St, Brixham, Devon, cm (1823–30). [D]

Richards, Robert, at 'The Lyon & Lamb', near the Maypole, Strand, London, u (1675). Named in contemporary newspapers. [Heal]

Richards, Sam, Nottingham, joiner and cm (1832). [Nottingham app. list]

Richards, Samuel, Lower Ward, Tottenham, London, u and cm (1839). [D] Possibly Samuel Richard.

Richards, Simeon (or Simon), Hull, Yorks., cm and broker (1814–20). Recorded at 26 Queen St in 1814. [D]

Richards, T., Fore St, Exeter, Devon, u (1816). [*Exeter Pocket Journal*]

Richards, Thomas, Shrewsbury, Salop, cm and chairmaker (1822–35). Trading at Wyle Cop, as cm and fancy chairmaker in 1822; and at Baker St, 1828–35. [D] See James Richards of Shrewsbury.

Richards, Thomas, Church St, Bishops Castle, Salop, chairmaker (1840). [D]

Richards, Tirrell, Holton, chairmaker (1730). Took app. named Stannard in 1730. [S of G, app. index]

Richards, William, Penzance, Cornwall, cm (1758). Took app. named Young in 1758. [S of G, app. index]

Richards, William Richard, Mount St, London, u (1784). [Poll bk]

Richards, William, Coombe St, Exeter, Devon, cm (1827). His son George John bapt. at St Mary Major on 28 December 1827. [PR (bapt.)]

Richards & Macdonald, 3 Somerset St, Portman Sq., London, u and cm (c.1830). Trade card recorded. [Heal]

Richardson, —, Bedford St, Covent Gdn, London, u (1793). [D]

Richardson, —, London, cm (1793). Subscribed to Sheraton's *Drawing Book*, 1793.

Richardson, Anthony, 13 Clipstone St, Fitzroy Sq., London, carpenter and cm (1820). [D]

Richardson, Benjamin, London, joiner and u (b.1699–d.1750). Son of Samuel Richardson, joiner and cm; admitted freeman of the Joiners' Co. by patrimony on 1 September 1724, when the witnesses included John James, joiner of Tower Hill, and John Johnson, joiner of Whitechapel. He was made a liveryman on 8 October 1734. Took apps named William Kiplin on 11 May 1725; John Gibson on 15 August 1727; Robert Dawson on 26 March 1744; and his own son, John, in 1749. Brother of William Richardson, u of St Botolph's, Aldgate.

Richardson, Charles, Crown Pitts, Godalming, Surrey, cm and u (1839). [D]

Richardson, Christopher, Cambridge, joiner (1708–23). In 1711 he supplied a 'Walnutree Table' costing 12s to St John's College. Possibly the Christopher Richardson of Cambridge who married Margaret Nelson in All Saints' Church on 6 June 1708. Will dated 1723. [Univ. Lib., AR2:2S]

Richardson, Christopher, Doncaster, Yorks. (c.1740–67). Took apps named Theakston in 1753, Halley in 1754 and Kidson in 1759. [S of G, app. index] Subscribed to James Paine's *Noblemen's and Gentlemen's Seats*, 1767. Worked under George Platt at Cusworth Hall, near Doncaster, c.1740, as a carver in wood and stone. J. Battie, the owner of Cusworth wrote to John Grimston regarding a picture frame maker: 'his name is Richardson and he lives at Doncaster & is thought to be a very good workman, the round frames cost 5 guineas each and the square ones six'. He offered to have frames made for John, if he would 'have a plan of them sent'. [M. E. Ingram, *Leaves from a Family Tree*, p. 51; Beard, *Georgian Craftsmen*, p. 61] On 12 August 1755 Richardson was paid £42 for six gilt sconces supplied to the Doncaster Mansion House, possibly after a design by James Paine, and all of which remain *in situ*. [Doncaster borough archives, credit bk, 1755–62] Worked for the Duke of Norfolk at Worksop Manor, Notts., during the rebuilding of 1763–67. His bill for carver's work, amongst James Paine's papers relating to Worksop Manor, totalled £336 1s 11½d. [Arundel Castle records, MD18, pt 2] Richardson is also recorded in the V&A archives as having worked at Burton Constable, Yorks.

Richardson, David, Saville Ct, Newcastle, carver and gilder (1795). [D]

Richardson, Edward, London, upholder (1769–1802). Recorded at Fore St in 1794 and Cripplegate in 1802. Son of Thomas Richardson, mason of St Thomas, Southwark. Admitted freeman of the Upholders' Co. on 6 September 1769. Took apps named Jeremiah Bray, 1773–83, and John Williams, 1783–92. [GL, Upholders' Co. records]

Richardson, Edward, Cambridge, cm and u (1820). App. to Thomas Sharpe, cm and u of Cambridge, on 27 April 1820 for £29 18s. [Cambridge app. lists]

Richardson, Elizabeth, 13 Upper Temple St, Birmingham, cm and chairmaker (1835). [D]

Richardson, Francis, Newcastle, carver and gilder (1754–66). Subscribed to Chippendale's *Director*, 1754. Advertised in *Newcastle Courant*, 15 February 1766, that he, '... Having wrought for several Years with the most distinguish'd Artists in London ... has opened a Shop in Pilgrim Street, opposite the Low Bridge End, Newcastle ... executes carving, gilding, sculpture and glass grinding ... marble chimney pieces, gerandoles ... Now employs the most able Artists in the several branches abovenamed'.

Richardson, Francis, Long Acre, London, carver and gilder (1771–75). A memorandum at the end of the 1771 diary of Edward Morant of Brockenhurst Park, Hants., mentions 'Francis Richardson Carver & Gilder in Long Acre 5th door above James Street makes the pillow [pillar?] for 10: a glass'. A memorandum at the end of the 1772 diary reads: 'Francis Richardson, Carver & Gilder in Long Acre makes the pillow Glass for £100.' [Owned by E. Morant, Hants.] Francis and John Richardson, carvers and gilders of 50 Long Acre, took out a Sun Insurance policy in 1775 for £500 of which £250 accounted for utensils and stock. [GL, Sun MS vol. 244, p. 154]

Richardson, Francis, Old Round Ct, Strand, London, cm and u (1775). Rented a house from John Dawes of Canonbury House, Islington, who insured it for £400 on 9 January 1775. Took out a Sun Insurance policy in 1775 for £600, including £490 on utensils, stock and goods. [GL, Sun MS vol. 236, ref. 348496; vol. 239, p. 512] See Jonathan Farlam and James Butler.

Richardson, George, Orange St, Bloomsbury, London, carver and stationer (1784–87). Recorded at 'The Bible & Crown' in 1784 when he took out a Sun Insurance policy for £600, £60 accounting for utensils and stock. On 6 January 1787 he insured three houses with goods and utensils for £1,500. [GL, Sun MS vol. 319, p. 569; vol. 340, p. 497]

Richardson, George, Ferryhill, Co. Durham, cm (1828). [D]

Richardson, George, Bondgate Without, Alnwick, Northumb., cm (1828–34). Recorded as cm and joiner in 1834. [D]

Richardson, George, Sandon Terr., Mill Lane, Shaw's Brow, Liverpool, carver (1834). [D]

Richardson, Harman Henry, 62 Skeldergate, York, cm (1837–40). [D]

Richardson, Henry, Jew Lane, Nottingham, cm (1812). [Poll bk]

Richardson, Henry, Manchester, cm and u (1822–29). Trading at 1 St Anne's Pl, 1822–25, and 1 Police St in 1829. [D]

Richardson, Henry, Ashford, Kent, cm, u and undertaker (1832–39). [D]

Richardson, J., 26 John St, Tottenham Ct Rd, London, carver (1829). [D] See Thomas Richardson.

Richardson, J. & R., Walsall, Staffs., furniture makers (1839). [D]

Richardson, James, Birchin Lane, Cornhill, London, cm and glass grinder (1748). Sale of household goods, stock and utensils of James Richardson, late of Birchin Lane, announced in *General Advertiser*, 10 February 1748. The *Gents Mag.*, April 1748 lists Richardson amongst the 'tenants burnt out by the late fire', and carries an engraving showing his ruined premises. He is also listed among bankrupts in the same issue.

Richardson, James, Suffolk St, Birmingham, cm, u and broker (1828–30). Recorded at no. 50 in 1828. [D]

Richardson, James, Parkes Ct, Upper Temple St, Birmingham, cm and chairmaker (1830). [D]

Richardson, James Christopher, Verulam St, St Albans, Herts., cm and u (1839). [D]

Richardson, John, Durham, cm (1740–93). Recorded at New-Helvit in 1749 and at Ferryhill, 1756–62. Children bapt. at St Oswald's parish, 1740–48. Took apps named Peacock in 1743, Craggs in 1755, Gainford in 1756, Guderick in 1760 and Gainford in 1762. Report in *General Advertiser*, 17 April 1749, stated that he took Richard Taylor as app. under the Sons of the Clergy scheme for a premium of £10. On 2 February 1760 he was paid £7 10s for 'two Mohogany Dressing Tables sent to Gibside' for Mrs Bowes. [D; PR (bapt.); S of G, app. index; Durham RO, Strathmore MS, D/St/V1488–90; V993]

Richardson, John, Newcastle, u (1747). [Newcastle freemen reg.] Possible confusion with:

Richardson, John, Newcastle and London, u (1773–80). App. to John Ridpath, and admitted freeman of Newcastle on 11 October 1773. Polled at Newcastle in 1780. [Newcastle freemen reg.] Possibly:

Richardson, John, Penrith, Cumb., u (1777–80). [Newcastle poll bks] See Nathaniel Richardson, possibly John's father.

Richardson, John, at 'the Duke's Head', Back Lane, Ratcliffe, London, cm (1793). Took out a Sun Insurance policy on 30 December 1793 for £400 of which £200 accounted for utensils and stock. [GL, Sun MS vol. 397, p. 250]

Richardson, John, Fulham, London, u and cm (1808). [D]

Richardson, John and Thomas, High-bridge, Newcastle, joiners and cm (1811). [D]

Richardson, John, High St, Tewkesbury, Glos., cm (1813–20). Trading at no. 30 in 1820 as a chairmaker. [D; PR (bapt.)]

Richardson, John, Retford, Notts., cm and u (1819–35). Trading at New St in 1819; at Carolgate in 1822 and 1835; Chapel Lane in 1830; and Spa Lane in 1832. [D]

Richardson, John, Nether End, Penrith, Cumb., joiner and/or cm, furniture warehouseman (1818–34). [D]

Richardson, John, Lancaster, chairmaker (1822–34). Trading at Church St, 1822–34. Submitted a bill to Charles Gibson of Quernmore Park, Lancs., for work done in March and November 1824, 'repairing 8 satinwood chairs &c' at a cost of £1, 'lining the above & varnishing', for £1 1s, and 'making a stool & stuffing &c' for 13s. [D; Preston RO, DDQ]

Richardson, John, 3 Bowling Alley, Cripplegate, London, cm (1829). [D]

Richardson, John, College St, Northampton, cm (1830). [D]

Richardson, John, Liverpool, carver and gilder (1831). App. to Henry Edward Cashin in 1831. [Liverpool app. enrolment bk]

Richardson, John, St Peter's, St Albans, Herts., cm and u (1832). [D]

Richardson, John, West St, Horsham, Sussex, cm (1839). [D]

Richardson, Jonathan, Market Pl., Otley, Yorks., cm (1822). [D]

Richardson, Joseph, at 'The Unicorn & Sun', near Paternoster Row, Cheapside, London, u (1687). Named in contemporary newspapers. [Heal].

Richardson, Joseph, Old Quay, Whitehaven, Cumb., joiner and/or cm (1811). [D]

Richardson, Joseph, Botchergate, Carlisle, Cumb., joiner and cm (1828–29). [D]

Richardson, Joseph, 23 Mill Hill, Leeds, Yorks., cm and u (1834–37). [D]

Richardson, Joseph, 19 Bowlalley Lane, Hull, Yorks., cm and u (1838–39). [D] See Richardson & Spencer.

Richardson, Joshua, 1 Wellington St, Leeds, Yorks., cm and u (1839). [D]

Richardson, K., Littlehampton, Sussex, cm, u, undertaker etc. (1832–33). Worked for the Earl of Surrey at Littlehampton in December 1832–33 supplying small items of furniture, and carrying out repairs and upholstery work, for which he charged a total of £127 4s 2d. [Arundel Castle records, A1996 and A1999]

Richardson, M., 29 North Audley St, Grosvenor Sq., London, u (1829). [D]

Richardson, Matthias, 31 Guildhall St, Bury St Edmunds, Suffolk, cm and u (1830). [D]

Richardson, Nathaniel, Newcastle and Penrith, Cumb., u (1727–77). Admitted freeman by apprenticeship on 5 September 1727. His son, John, was admitted by patrimony on 13 October 1774. Polled at Newcastle of Newcastle in 1741 and 1777; also of Penrith in 1777. [Newcastle freemen reg.] See John Richardson of Newcastle and Penrith.

Richardson, Richard, Lancaster. Named in the Gillow records, 1790–93. [Westminster Ref. Lib.]

Richardson, Richard, Foulford, Berwick-upon-Tweed, Northumb., cm and u (1827–34). Recorded at Bridge St in 1834. [D]

Richardson, Robert, Doncaster, Yorks., cm (1733–74). Son of John Richardson, fellmonger; admitted freeman of York in 1733. Polled at York of Doncaster in 1758 and 1774. Took app. named Barck in 1738. [York freemen rolls; S of G, app. index]

Richardson, Robert, Hull, Yorks., cm (1747). [Poll bk]

Richardson, Robert, Gt Union St, Hull, Yorks., chairmaker (1817). [D]

Richardson, Robert, Felton, Northumb., joiner, cm and stamp sub-distributor (1828–29). [D]

Richardson, Samuel, London and Derbyshire, joiner and cm (b.c.1650–d.c.1736). His son, the novelist, Samuel Richardson, stated in a letter of 2 June 1753 to Johannes Stinstra: 'My Father's Business was that of a Joiner, then more distinct from that of a Carpenter, than now it is with us. He was a good Draughtsman, and understood Architecture. His Skill and Ingenuity, and an Understanding superior to his Business . . . made him personally beloved by several Persons of Rank, among whom were the Duke of Monmouth and the first Earl of Shaftesbury . . . Their known Favour for him, having, on the Duke's Attempt on the Crown, subjected him to be looked upon with a jealous Eye, notwithstanding he was noted for a quiet and inoffensive Man, he thought proper, on the Decollation of the first-named unhappy Gentleman, to quit his London Business and to retire to Derbyshire; tho' his great Detriment.' The *Universal Magazine*, 1786, described Richardson as '. . . at first a Cabinet-maker, and afterwards a considerable importer of mahogany, in Aldersgate-Street. He had a genius superior to his business, and was, in particular, an excellent Architect.' It is not stated when he was trading, but he was certainly in Aldersgate St, 'next door to the Cock and Bottle, over against the George Inn' in 1680, when he advertised in the *London Gazette*, 31 May to 3 June, as having 'the best and choicest Cedar both for Colour and Scent.' 1680 would be a very early date for Richardson to be a 'considerable importer of mahogany', so the article in the *Universal Magazine* may refer to the business after his return to London from Derbyshire, by 1699, although addresses other than Aldersgate St are then given. His son claimed that Richardson left London due to Monmouth's execution on 15 July 1685, but he appears to have been resident in the Aldersgate area, 1686–87, when his daughter Anne by wife Elizabeth, was bapt. at St Botolphs on 13 February. He had moved to Derbyshire by 1689, when his son Samuel, the novelist, was bapt. at All Saints', Mackworth, near Derby, on 19 August; son William on 8 April 1691; and daughter Sara at

St Alkmund's, Derby, on 5 December 1693. The Richardsons had returned to London by 1699 when their son, Benjamin, was bapt. at St Botolph's, Aldgate, on 4 October. Samuel Richardson's address is then given at Tower Hill. On 6 June 1700 he is recorded as residing in Mouse Alley in the scavenger's assessment list in rate bks of St Botolph's. His son's later correspondence suggests that Richardson was in business at the time of his death, c.1735–36, apparently dealing in timber. The novelist wrote to Lady Bradshaigh on 15 December 1748: 'A Father, an honest, a worthy Father, I lost by the Accident of a broken Thigh, snapt by a sudden Jirk, endeavouring to recover a Slip passing thro' his own Yard.' Other details of Richardson's career have been recorded. He was the son of William Richardson of Byfleet, Surrey, and app. to Thomas Turner, joiner, on 25 June 1667. Admitted freeman of the Joiners' Co. by recommendation of Richard Rogers on 2 July 1678. Took apps named William Cambridge on 13 October 1679, and Humphry Sterling on 13 November 1683, turned over to John Meres, and admitted freeman on 4 April 1693. Richardson assigned Francis Storey from William Pritchard by 11 December 1688. In that year Richardson and his tenant, Charles Hodson, were recorded as in arrears of tax as inhabitant householders; in 1689 in the list of inhabitants and landlords, and in 1693 in the list of householders and stockholders, but no addresses are given. Hodson is recorded alone at Richardson's address, 1692–96, when the latter was in Derbyshire. In 1737–38 Samuel Richardson, 'Householder' is listed in the Joiners' Co. quarterage records as owing 48 quarters, having paid last in 1724–25. Samuel Richardson's son, William, was an u in St Botolph's, Aldgate; and son Benjamin, joiner and u, was admitted freeman of the Joiners' Co. by patrimony on 1 September 1724.   A.E.

Richardson, Stephen, 260 Deansgate, Manchester, u (1832–33). [D]

Richardson, Thomas, Spilsby, Lincs., joiner and cm (1826–35). [D]

Richardson, Thomas, 26 John St, Fitzroy Sq., London, carver and modeller (1826–35). [D] See J. Richardson.

Richardson, Thomas, Lancaster. Named in the Gillow records in 1828. [Westminster Ref. Lib.]

Richardson, Thomas, Hull, Yorks., cm (1814–42). Addresses given at Tan House Lane, 1814–20; Castle St, 1817–22; 6 Cockpit Yd, Castle St in 1823; Smith's Pl., Castle St, 1828–38; and as Thomas & Son, cm etc. at 34 Bond St, 1840–42. [D] See Richardson & Son.

Richardson, Thomas, Trueman St, Liverpool, cm (1821–35). Trading at no. 47, 1821–29; no. 17 in 1834; and no. 15 in 1835. [D]

Richardson, Tim., Thompson's Entry, Salthouse Lane, Hull, Yorks., cm (1838–39). [D]

Richardson, W., 7 Redcross Sq., Cripplegate, London, cm (1835). [D]

Richardson, William, at 'The Star in the East', on Tower Hill, St Botolph's, Aldgate, London, upholder (1716–35). Took out Hand in Hand Insurance policies on his house at 'The Star' in King St, on 29 August 1716 for £400, and on 28 August 1723 for £500. Named in newspapers in 1735. [GL, Hand in Hand MS vol. 16, p. 205; vol. 27, p. 286; Heal] Possibly son of Samuel Richardson and brother of Benjamin.

Richardson, William, at W. Cobb's timbershop, Round Ct, London, cm (1776). Took out a Sun Insurance policy in 1776 for £100 of which utensils and stock accounted for £25. [GL, Sun MS vol. 244, p. 512]

Richardson, William, Wild St, London, cm (1778–80). Took out Sun Insurance policies in 1778 for £800 including £470

on utensils, stock and goods; and in 1780 for £400 on his house. [GL, Sun MS vol. 266, p. 207; vol. 281, p. 410]

Richardson, William, Stanhope St, Clare Mkt, London, cm (1782–87). Insured his house for £600 in 1782. [D; GL, Sun MS vol. 301, p. 77]

Richardson, William, Wakefield, Yorks., upholder and coach maker (1784). [D]

Richardson, William, Newcastle St, Strand, London, cm and u (1789–96). Recorded at no. 10, 1789–91; no. 15, 1792–96; and in 1792 as cm to His Royal Highness the Duke of York. Declared bankrupt, *Derby Mercury*, 29 April 1790, and Bailey's list of bankrupts, 1793. [D]

Richardson, William, Maiden Lane, Covent Gdn, London, cm (1797). [D]

Richardson, William, 18 Mortimer St, London, cm (1799). [D]

Richardson, William, 44 Cannon St, Ratcliff, London, cm (1813). Took out a Sun Insurance policy on 15 November 1813 for £700 on his house, household goods and musical instruments. [GL, Sun MS vol. 462, ref. 887842]

Richardson, William, 45 Stonegate, York, joiner, u and cm (1816–40). [D]

Richardson, William, New Pavement, Pocklington, Yorks., cm and u (1823). [D]

Richardson, William, 3 Bowling Alley, Whitecross St, London, cm and upholder (1827–28). [D]

Richardson & Lyon, Godalming, Surrey, u (1838). [D]

Richardson & Son, 34 Bond St, Hull, Yorks., u (1840). [D]. Richardson & Sons of Bond St supplied furniture costing £11,000 to Burton Constable, Yorks., including an amboyna and purplewood console cabinet. The commission ended in a Chancery suit. [C. *Life*, 17 June 1976, pp. 1622–24] See Thomas Richardson.

Richardson & Spence(r), 19 Bowlalley Lane, Hull, Yorks., cm and u (1840). [D] See Joseph Richardson.

Richars, William, Wisbech, Cambs., u (1729). Took out a Sun Insurance policy on 2 April 1729 for £300 on a house, let. [GL, Sun MS vol. 29, ref. 47314]

Richdale, George, Greenhill, Lichfield, Staffs., cm (1835). [Poll bk]

Richerley, T., Durham, cm (1793). Subscribed to Sheraton's *Drawing Book*, 1793.

Riches, Joseph, Market Pl., East Dereham, Norfolk, u (1839). [D]

Riches, Robert, Norwich, cm (1826–30). Recorded at Heigham in 1830. App. to Samuel Martin, and admitted freeman on 3 May 1826. [Norwich freemen reg. and poll bk]

Riches, Robert jnr, Norwich, cm (1829). App. to Thomas Larter, and admitted freeman on 24 February 1829. [Norwich freemen reg.]

Riches, Robert, Market Pl., Downham Mkt, Norfolk, cm and u (1830–39). [D]

Riches, Robert, Market Pl., East Dereham, Norfolk, cm and u (1836). [D]

Richiardi, J., 73 St Martin's Lane, London, carver and gilder (1826–27). [D]

Richlieu, Robert, Dovecot St, Stockton-upon-Tees, Co. Durham, joiner and cm (1827–29). [D]

Richlieu, Thomas, Stokesley, Yorks., cm and joiner (1828–29). [D]

Richman, John, 22 Greek St, Soho, London, carver and gilder (1791). Took out a Sun Insurance policy in 1791 for £900 including £350 on utensils, stock and glass. [GL, Sun MS vol. 370] See John Richmond.

Richman, John, Bow St, Covent Gdn, London, looking-glass manufacturer (1792). [D]

Richmond, Henry, Lancaster, cm (1784–85). [Lancaster freemen rolls]

Richmond, Henry, Liverpool, cm (1818–21). Trading at 12 Lionel St in 1818 and 2 Weale St in 1821. [D]

Richmond, James, Lancaster, chairmaker (1806–11). Son of James Richmond, late of Nether Wyresdale, now of Lancaster, labourer, deceased; admitted freeman, 1806–07. Took app. on 5 August 1811. [Lancaster freemen rolls and app. reg.]

Richmond, James, 7 Hormans (?) Buildings, St Luke's, London, cm (1809–11). [D]

Richmond, James, Chorley, Lancs., chairmaker, cm and broker (1816–34). Recorded at Market St, 1816–18, and Chapel St in 1834. [D]

Richmond, James, 10 Duncan St East, Liverpool, cm (1837). [D]

Richmond, John, 22 Greek St, Soho, London, carver and gilder (1789). [D] See John Richman.

Richmond, John, Gt Yarmouth, Norfolk, cm (1822–41). Recorded at Charlotte St in 1822 and Howard St, 1830–39. [D; poll bks]

Richmond, John, Thirsk, Yorks., cm and u (1823–40). Trading at Kirkgate in 1823; Market Pl., 1828–29; Chapel Lane, 1834–40; and Chapel St in 1840, as cm/chairmaker. [D]

Richmond, William, Liverpool, furniture painter (1818). Admitted freeman on 11 June 1818. [Liverpool freemen reg.]

Richmond, William, 73 St Martin's Lane, London, cm (1829). [D]

Rickaby, James, St Oswald's, Durham, spinning-wheel maker (1725). Marriage registered on 19 June 1725, and son's baptism on 10 October 1725. [PR]

Rickaby, Thomas, St Oswald's, Durham, spinning-wheel maker (d.1719). Burial registered on 23 January 1719. [PR]

Rickaby, Thomas, St Oswald's, Durham, spinning-wheel maker (1725–d.1729). Marriage registered on 30 November 1725, and death of Thomas Rickaby, wheelwright, on 20 November 1729. [PR]

Rickarby, John, Lancaster. Named in the Gillow records in 1800. [Westminster Ref. Lib.]

Rickard, George, Queen St, Derby, cm and u (1828–29). Listed at no. 36 in 1828. [D]

Rickard, John, Norwich, cm and chairmaker (1780–1802). Recorded at St Peter Hungate, 1780–86; and All Saints' parish, 1796–1802. [Poll bks]

Rickard(s), Ezechiel, London, upholder (1709–15). Recorded at King St, St Martin's parish in 1709; at 'The Golden Fleece', near Bromley St End, Drury Lane, St Giles-in-the-Fields in 1813; and King St, St Giles-in-the-Fields in 1715. Took out a Hand in Hand Insurance policy on 31 March 1709 for £100 on his house and warehouse in King St; a Sun Insurance policy on 15 August 1713 on his goods; and a Hand in Hand policy on 15 March 1715 for £200 on two houses and workshop in King St, and £500 on two houses in Drury Lane. [GL, Hand in Hand MS vol. 7, ref. 2076; vol. 15, p. 481; GL, Sun MS vol. 3, ref. 3274]

Rickard(s), George, Queen St, Derby, cm and u (1823–29). Trading at no. 36 in 1829. [D]

Rickards, Robert, Brownlow Buildings, Drury Lane, London, u (1691). Named in contemporary newspapers. [Heal]

Rickards, Samuel, 211 Oxford St, London, u (1822–35). Took out a Sun Insurance policy on 26 December 1822 for £200 on utensils and stock. [D; GL, Sun MS vol. 498, ref. 999413]

Rickerby, John, Baldock, Herts., cm and u (1838–39). Recorded at White Horse St, also as a paper hanger, in 1839. [D]

Rickett(s), Edward, London, upholder (1783–1815). Recorded at 19 Gt Trinity Lane, Cheapside in 1792; and as an upholstery warehouseman at 14 Brokers Row, Moorfields, 1802–15. Named in Sheraton's list of master cabinet makers, 1803. Probably the Rickett, upholder and cm of 14 Little

Moorgate, Moorfields, whose trade card, c.1820, is recorded. [D; GL, Upholders' Co. records; Heal]

Ricketts, J., Belgrave Gate, Leicester, u (1827). [D]

Ricketts, James, St Catherine St, Gloucester, chairmaker (1822–23). [D]

Ricketts, John, Gloucester, carver (1729). Took app. named Robins in 1729. [S of G, app. index]

Ricketts, John, Snow Hill, Birmingham, u (1828–30). Recorded at no. 16 in 1828; and in 1830 also traded as cm and broker. [D]

Rickman, John, 62 Greek St, Soho, London, carver and gilder (1790–93). [D]

Ricknoll (?), —, address unrecorded, u (1787). Named in the Longford Castle accounts in 1787 receiving £24. [V&A archives]

Ricks, William, Poole, Dorset, cm (1752). Took app. named Trim in 1752. [S of G, app. index]

Riddett, George, Union St, Ryde, Isle of Wight, u (1839). [D]

Riddiough, James, 3 Birkett St, Soho, Liverpool, cm (1829). [D]

Riddle, James & Thomas, 54 Wells St, Oxford St, London, cm, u and chairmakers (1826–40). [D]

Riddle, William, 16 Nottingham Pl., Whitechapel Rd, London, cm (1823). Took out a Sun Insurance policy on 15 January 1823 for £200, including £30 on a chest of tools in Baynes's workshop in Wheatsheaf Yd, Fleet Mkt. [GL, Sun MS vol. 489, ref. 999880] See Matthew Lawther.

Riddles, William, Brighton, Sussex, cm, u and furniture broker (1822–39). Addresses given at Cumberland Pl. in 1822; High St, 1824–31, no. 34 in 1832; and 27 Cavendish Pl. in 1839. Children by wife Mary bapt.: Mary Ann on 22 February 1822; John Alfred on 25 December 1824; and Charles on 27 November 1831. [D; E. Sussex RO, PR (bapt.)]

Riddoch, David, 99 High Holborn, London, cm and upholder (1780). Took out a Sun Insurance policy in 1780 for £600 including £340 on utensils, stock and goods. [GL, Sun MS vol. 284, p. 451]

Riddock, David, corner of Gt Turnstile, Lincoln's Inn Fields, London, cm (1778). Took out a Sun Insurance policy in 1778 for £200 of which £100 accounted for utensils, stock and goods. [GL, Sun MS vol. 268, p. 453]

Riddout, J., 4 Kirkhams Buildings, Bath, Som., cm (1819). [D]

Ride, Thomas, Belper Lane, Belper, Derbs., joiner and cm (1835). [D]

Rider, Francis, Nottingham and Harewood, Yorks., cm (1758–74). Polled at York of Nottingham in 1758, and of Harewood in 1774.

Rider, John, Exeter, Devon, cm (1777). Took out a Sun Insurance policy in 1777 for £200 of which £160 accounted for utensils and stock. [GL, Sun MS vol. 256, p. 34]

Rider (or Ryder), Joseph, Plymouth, Devon, cm and u (1830–38). Trading at 12 Basket St in 1830 and Raleigh St, 1836–38. [D]

Rider, Samuel, Stafford, cm (1801). Took out a Sun Insurance policy on 28 March 1801 for £300 on his new dwelling house and front shop, and on stock in adjoining workshop, timber yard and stable. [GL, Sun MS vol. 39, ref. 716821]

Rider & Milner, 6 Red Lion St, Southwark, London, upholstery warehousemen (1768–72). [D]

Ridge(s), John, London, u (1682–85). In 1682 John Ridge supplied a bed for the Duke of Hamilton's rooms in Holyrood House, Edinburgh, charging £218 10s for 'a crimson & gould velvett bett, loynd with satin with 8 chairs & velvet cases, a feather bed & bolster, quilts, Japanned glass & stands a footstool blankets . . .'. Payment was completed in June 1683 with a memorandum 'That a sett of white feathers for the bed mentioned are to be returned or eight pound in Lieu of them — J. Ridge.' In 1684 the inventory included 'In my Lady's

Bedchamber — One large bedstead with flowered Courtines of red & yellow with covervolet of taffetie three quilts . . . A Japan painted table & two stands with ane looking glass conforme . . . four armed chairs with four other chairs and a footstool all painted conforme to ye tables 9 stands . . .'. [Scottish RO, Duke of Hamilton's archives, 165/1/3, F1/490–1; F2/380/21; *Furn. Hist.*, 1978] John Ridges, u, is recorded in the Royal Household accounts in 1683 providing beds, curtains, two walnut tables and stands, a large inlaid walnut table, and a looking-glass, costing £15. [PRO, LC9/277] John Ridge was named in newspapers in 1685.

Ridge, John, London, u (1754). Subscribed to Chippendale's *Director*, 1754.

Ridge, John, Newark-upon-Trent, Notts., bookseller and u (1796). Marriage to Miss Crafts of Nottingham reported in *Cambridge Chronicle and Journal*, 3 September 1796.

Ridge, Samuel, Market Pl., Newark, Notts., u (1822–35). Recorded as Samuel & John in 1822 and Samuel & Co. in 1835. [D]

Ridge, Timothy, London and Lewes, Sussex, upholder (1780–1802). Recorded at 71 Fleet St in 1791; Phoenix Fire Office in 1794; and Lewes in 1802. Son of Joseph Ridge, surgeon of Lewes. App. to Josiah Phipps on 5 July 1780, and later to William Marston. Admitted freeman of the Upholders' Co. by servitude on 6 April 1791. [GL, Upholders' Co. records]

Ridges, John, near Watling St, London, chairmaker (1729). Named in contemporary newspapers. [Heal]

Ridgeway, Charles, Chester, cm (1789). App. to Samuel Gellion in 1789. [Chester app. bks]

Ridgeway, Hugh, St Julian's Friars, Shrewsbury, Salop, cm (1826). [Shrewsbury burgess roll]

Ridgeway, Thomas, London, upholder, cm, appraiser and auctioneer (1759–81). Trading at Houndsditch, 1759–65; Norton Falgate, 1767–72; as Ridgeway & Rolleston in 1768; and 168 Fenchurch St, 1773–81. Trade card, c.1760–65 gives address at the 'Easy Chair near Gravel Lane in Houndsditch, London' and states that he 'Selleth four post & other Bedsteads & Furnitures ready made, Likewise Feather Beds, Blankets, Quilts, Ruggs Counterpanes & Coverlets, Mattresses, Flock Beds &c, Damasks Harriteens Cheneys, Linceys, Feathers & Flock ticking by y Yard or piece with all Sorts of Cabinet Goods. Chairs Tables, Glasses &c For Sea or Land; Also all Sorts of Paper Hangings, at the Lowest Prices. Funerals Furnishd.' In 1763 he employed four non-freemen for three months when he was described as 'citizen and skinner by trade an upholsterer'. Took app. named James Williams until 1769. Declared bankrupt, *London Gazette*, 13–20 October 1764. [D; Leverhulme Coll., MMA, NY; GL, City Licence bks, vol. 3; GL, Upholders' Co. records]

Ridgeway, William, Foregate St, Chester, u (1819). Admitted freeman on 20 October 1819. [Chester freemen rolls]

Ridgway, William, at the corner of St Dunstan's Hill, Tower St, London, u and appraiser (c.1760). Trade card states that he 'Makes up & Sells all Sorts of Upholstery Goods, in the neatest Manner, & at the Lowest Prices.' [Heal]

Ridgyard, William, 6 Upper Rathbone Pl., Fitzroy Sq., London, carver and gilder (1820). [D]

Riding, James, 22 Chestergate, Macclesfield, Cheshire, cm, u and chairmaker (1816–18). [D]

Riding, William, Preston, Lancs., joiner, cm and timber merchant (1795). Notice of dissolution of his partnership with Richard Salthouse on 11 September 1795 given in *Billinge's Liverpool Advertiser*, 19 October 1795.

Ridler, —, address unrecorded, upholder (1803–15). Named in the Longford Castle, Wilts. accounts receiving payments totalling £384 18s between 1803 and 1815. [V&A archives]

Ridley, S., 234 Strand, London, army furniture and coach trimming manufacturer (1804). [D]

Ridley, Samuel, 46–47 Newgate St, London, upholsterers' warehouseman (1839). [D]

Ridley, William, 27 Ridinghouse Lane, Gt Portland St, London, chair and sofa maker (1839). [D]

Ridley & Son, Saxmundham, Suffolk, furnishers and iron-mongers (1836). [Suffolk RO, ref. 50/22/4.118]

Ridpath, James, Deptford Bridge, London, cm and u (1813–19). [D]

Ridpeth (Ridpath), John, Newcastle, u (1766–73). App. to George West, u, and admitted freeman on 13 June 1766. Former app., John Richardson, admitted on 11 October 1773. [Newcastle freemen reg.]

Ridsdale, Benjamin, address unrecorded. Carved pine sideboard in the Dining Room at Rokeby Park, near Barnard Castle, Co. Durham is signed and dated 7 May 1793 in pencil. In the Neo-classical style, it has fluted, square tapering legs, fluted frieze with paterae at the junctions, and a marble top. Two tables carved with a mask of Hercules draped with the skin of the Nemean lion and bearing a label inscribed in ink: 'Benjamin Ridsdale, April 7th 179–' from the collection of John Aspinall, were sold at Christie's on 22 November 1973, lot 180. [Bowes Museum archive, Barnard Castle]

Ridsdale, Thomas, York, cm (1820). Son of Hannah Ridsdale, widow, of Grimston; app. to Robert Dugelby, cm, of St Peter the Little parish on 18 July 1820. [York app. reg.]

Ridsdales, Ryley & Pearson, 25 Clements Lane, Lombard St, London, wholesale u (1779–83). [D] See George Rigdale.

Rielly, George, 10 Renshaw St, Liverpool, carver and gilder (1800). [D]

Rielly, T., 14 Dean St, Soho, London, chair stainer and cane maker (1829). [D]

Rieusset(t), Peter, London, joiner (1706–16). Recorded at St Ann's, Westminster in 1716. Named in the Royal Household accounts in 1706 providing a wainscot desk for the Office of the Great Wardrobe costing £4 15s. [PRO, LC9/282] Took out a Hand in Hand Insurance policy on 30 December 1716 for £300 on a house in St Lawrence Lane, parish of St Lawrence Jewry. Ralph, Duke of Montagu owed Rieusset £4,860 16s 3½d on his death. [GL, Hand in Hand MS vol. 15, p. 537; Boughton MS]

Rigby, —, Lancaster, carver (1793–1829). [Westminster Ref. Lib., Gillow records]

Rigby, Charles, Liverpool, cm (1780–d. by 1820). Admitted freeman on servitude to George Parker on 12 September 1780. [Liverpool freemen reg.]

Rigby, Charles, Warrington, Lancs., cm (1798). [D]

Rigby, Henry, 5 Reed Ct, Pool Lane, Liverpool, cm (1827). [D]

Rigby, James, Lichfield, Staffs., cm (1753). Took app. named Harrison in 1753. [S of G, app. index]

Rigby, James, Lancaster. Named in the Gillow records in 1797. [Westminster Ref. Lib.]

Rigby, James, Commerce St, Lane End, Staffs., chairmaker (1818). [D]

Rigby, John, 3 Crown Ct, Dean St, Soho, London, cm (1809–11). [D]

Rigby, Michael, Market St, Lancaster, carver (1825). [D]

Rigby, Peter, Mersey St, Liverpool, joiner, cm and victualler (1803–14). Addresses given at no. 6, with joiner's shop at Ridgewater St and Hackins Hey in 1803; 7 Mersey St, 1805–10; no. 5 in 1811; and no. 7, 1813–14. [D]

Rigby, Samuel, Liverpool, cm (1710–d. by 1780). Admitted freeman on 6 December 1710. Took apps named Winstanley in 1718 and Lea in 1720. Samuell Rigby of Liverpool supplied items of glassware to Nicholas Blundell of Crosby Hall, 1720–26, including on 13 February 1720 'a Glass for my little Chariot'; in 1722 a 'Peer Glass & Chimney Glass' costing £7; and on both 23 June and 11 August 1722 'a pair of Glass Scances'. On 18 December 1725 Blundell 'gave Rigby orders to make me a Looking Glass', and in 1726 bought from him other looking-glasses including a dressing-glass for his daughter at £3. [Liverpool freemen reg.; S of G, app. index; *The Great Diurnal of Nicholas Blundell*, vol. 3, ed. Frank Tyrer; Nicholas Blundell's Disbursement Bk, 1702–36, at Crosby Hall]

Rigby, Thomas, Liverpool, cm (1747–d. by 1763). Recorded at Atherton St on 18 September 1747 when he took out a Sun Insurance policy for £300 on various properties including a house in tenure of Catherine Linecar, bread-baker in Phoenix St. Took app. named Becket in 1757. Former app., James Holmes, petitioned freedom in 1760, and Robert Kenyon in 1767. Sale of stock on his death reported in *Williamson's Liverpool Advertiser*, 14 January 1763. Stock consisted of 'Sundry Kinds of seasoned WOOD, for the use of Cabinet makers & Joiners . . .' to be sold on 20 January at Mr Ingram's warehouse in Pool Lane. On 2 February the sale of Rigby's stock of 'Several Kinds of neat HOUSEHOLD FURNITURE of the Newest Fashion' was to take place. Rigby's widow, Mary, intended to carry on the business. [GL, Sun MS vol. 81, ref. 109492; S of G, app. index; Liverpool freemen's committee bk]

Rigby, William, Liverpool, cm (1761). Admitted freeman on servitude to Nicholas Cross on 28 January 1761. [Liverpool freemen reg.]

Rigby, William, Runcorn, Cheshire, cm and builder (1822–28). [D]

Rigdale, George, Clements Lane, London, u (1780). [Heal citing registers of unclaimed dividends of bank stock] See Ridsdale, Ryley & Pearson in Clements Lane.

Rigg, Edward, Liverpool, cm (1750–d.1765). On 21 March 1749–50 the house he occupied in Water St was insured by Thomas Liversley, apothecary, for £250. Took apps named Whitby in 1754 and Mohun in 1761. Advertised in *Williamson's Liverpool Advertiser*, 14 December 1759 as a cm in New-market, near St George's Church, who 'has provided the best Workmen for Grinding, Polishing etc: Looking, Coach, & Chariot Glasses, with a variety of Glass Frames Gilt & Burnished by the best Hands in London, with all sorts of Looking-Glasses, suitable for the African & West-Indian Trade. Mahogany Tubs & Cisterns for Table service made by the best workmen in England; Japanned Toilet Frames; Neat Brass Sconces Chased & Lacquer'd of several sorts; Chamber Lamps, Cut Glass & silver-top Castors, Plain ditto; Backgammon Men & Boxes with or without Tables; Mahogany Tea Chests at 5s per; [sic] Best Leaf Gold 3 Inches & one quarter 6s per 100; Coffin Furniture Gilt & Silver'd by the best Maker in London at as low a Price as the common sorts; Emery . . . & Putty for Glass-grinders & Marble Polishers; Quicksilver & Tin Foyle, variety of Cabinet works in the newest Taste, as well in the Common way, as after the new Designs of Chippendale (now publishing) & the best Masters in London. Merchants, Gentlemen, etc: may be supplied with the above at the lowest Prices, by their most Humble Servant, EDWARD RIGG. N.B. Shopkeepers in Town or Country may be furnished with Looking Glasses, of all sizes, Framed or Plates Silver'd: Old Looking Glasses Silver'd. Any ingenious Cabinet or Chair-makers (several being wanted) may meet with suitable Encouragement & Constant Employ; none but good workman need offer, as no other will be continued. An Apprentice wanted.' Edward Rigg's widow, Ellen, announced in *Williamson's Liverpool Advertiser*, 25 October 1765, her intention of continuing the business 'in the same shop her late Husband did, proposing to

enter in Partnership with John Eden, jun. who has been several Years in some of the principal Shops in London . . .'. She assured 'Gentlemen & Others that have been her late husband's Customers, that she will take Care to accommodate them with the best Goods of all Sorts, & at the lowest Prices having a stock of well season'd wood fit for present use . . .'. [GL, Sun MS vol. 89, ref. 120437; S of G, app. index]

Rigg, Edward, Liverpool, cm (1761–d. by 1780). Admitted freeman on 15 October 1761. [Liverpool freemen reg.]

Rigg, Edward, Liverpool, cm (1784). His son, Edward Rigg, petitioned freedom on birthright in 1784. [Liverpool freemen's committee bk]

Rigg, John, London, carver and gilder (1835–39). Listed at 20 Earl St, Finsbury in 1835 and 111 London Wall in 1839. [D]

Rigg, R., High St, Wigton, Cumb., joiner and/or cm (1811). [D]

Rigg, Thomas, Fleet St, St Bride's, London, chairmaker (1734–49). In 1734 he served as Constable at St Bride's; in 1740 as Questman and Collector for the Poor; in 1741 as Sidesman; in 1744 as Scavenger; and in 1749 as Church-warden. Trade card, dated 1749, records Thomas Rigg, cm of Peterborough Ct, near 'The Globe Tavern', Fleet St. [GL, MS 6561, p. 53; Heal]

Riggins, H. (?), Oxford or London, cm (1751). Supplied items to All Soul's College, Oxford. On 11 January 1751 he was paid £8 11s for three mahogany step ladders, which are probably the three seven-tread sets with pierced side rails which still survive. On 19 October 1751 he was paid £20 10s for tables, desks and steps, which may be the small reading desks each supported by a small pillar on tripod base, in the Codrington Library. [All Souls' College MS DD, a.257]

Right, Thomas, Bristol, cm (1781). [Poll bk]

Righton, John, London, upholder (1704–25). Took his son, Richard Righton, as app. from 1713–25, when he was admitted freeman of the Upholders' Co. Took app. named Abraham Smith, 1704–16. [GL, Upholders' Co. records]

Righton, Richard, London, upholder (1713–34). Recorded at 'The Artichoke', Gracechurch St, 1724–27. Son of John Righton, freeman upholder of London. App. to his father on 9 September 1713, and admitted freeman of the Upholders' Co. by servitude on 3 November 1725. Took app. named John Hodges, 1730–34. Took out a Sun Insurance policy on 15 February for £500, of which £200 accounted for goods and merchandise in his house. Named in newspapers, c.1727. [GL, Upholders' Co. records; GL, Sun MS vol. 19, ref. 34652; Heal]

Righton, Thomas, Bristol, cm (1792–1801). Recorded at St Michael's Churchyard, 1792–95, and St Michael's Hill, 1799–1801. [D]

Riland, —, Oxford St, London, cm (1793). Subscribed to Sheraton's *Drawing Book*, 1793.

Riley, —, address unrecorded, u (1755). Subscribed to Thomas Malton's *A Compleat Treatise on Perspective in Theory and Practice*, 1775.

Riley, —, Preston, Lancs., u (1804). In January 1804 he was commissioned by Charles Towneley of Towneley Hall, Lancs., to supply 'Bed-posts for three old beds in the gallery —a new cornish to the bed in the last room — the bed head of the first room to be painted white and the linings of the vallance to be repaired with white callico. New and complete bedding for the old Ratcliff bed — a Carpet for that room and a complete dressing table — The Cotton for the curtains of the bed and the Window to be sent to Mr. Riley — Bed-posts for the old blue bed in the Kitchin chamber — and a small Commode with writing desk for the Window pier of that Room.' [Preston RO, Towneley papers, DDTO] Possibly John Riley of Preston.

Riley, Edward, Bridge St, Bilston, Staffs., cm (1818–30). [D]

Riley, John, address unrecorded. Signed a chair, c.1770, at Stanmer Park, Sussex, and is recorded in the archives at Goodwood Park, Sussex, as having painted the ceiling of the Neo-classical library. [*Conn.*, June 1969; C. Musgrave, *Adam and Hepplewhite Furniture*, p. 102]

Riley, John, Leeds, Yorks., u (1774–82). In 1774 he advertised stock at his shop near the Market Pl., Leeds, including upholstery fabrics, bedding, carpets, paper-hangings, looking-glasses and cabinet goods, and announced that he had replenished his stock from London. Similar advertisements in *Leeds Mercury*, 14 annd 28 June 1774, 25 May 1779, 21 May and 4 June 1782 gave addresses near Market Pl., or back of the Shambles, Leeds, and stated that he 'Makes & sells all sorts of Beds, such as Damasks, Moreens, Harrateens, Cheneys, Cintzes, Stripe & check & Furniture ditto etc. . . . Paper Hangings . . . Likewise all sorts of Looking Glasses, Cabinet Goods . . .'. In 1775 he appeared as 'John Riley, Upholsterer', son of William Riley, yeoman of Flawith, in the York freemen rolls. Two bills from Riley in the Harewood accounts survive, one dated 1778 for bedside carpets, the other of 1780 for general upholstery materials. [*Furn. Hist.*, 1965]

Riley, John, 71 Long Acre, London, upholder, cm, auctioneer and undertaker (1773–94). Took out Sun Insurance policies in 1778 for £3,700, £2,800 on utensils, stock, goods; in 1779 for £200 on his house, and £200 on a house in Park St, Grosvenor Sq.; in 1780 for £200 on a house; in 1781 for £2,500 on a house; in 1783 for £5,900, £3,100 on utensils, stock, goods, workshops and warehouse; and on 17 October 1792, as upholder at 70 Long Acre, for £5,000 on eleven houses and their contents. Recorded in 1791 concerning the assignment of a lease to Samuel Morsey. [D; GL, Sun MS vol. 263, p. 189; vol. 276, p. 650; vol. 277, p. 130; vol. 284, p. 461; vol. 297, p. 451; vol. 306, p. 484; vol. 389, ref. 607011; Marylebone Lib., MS 154/1] Probably John Reiky.

Riley, John, Broad Ct, Drury Lane, London, upholder (1784). [D]

Riley, John, 1 Clifford St, Burlington Gdns, London, u and exchange broker (1795–99). [D]

Riley, John, Cork St, Burlington Gdns, London, u (1796–1815). Recorded at no. 1, 1796–97, and no. 25, 1801–03. Took out a Sun Insurance policy on 16 January 1801 for £800. Named in Sheraton's list of master cabinet makers, 1803. [D; GL, Sun MS vol. 419, ref. 712715]

Riley (or Ryley), John, 125 Church St, Preston, Lancs., u (1798–1828). Trading as John & Son, 1818–28, at 121 Church St, 1825–28. [D] See Riley, —, of Preston.

Riley, John, Moxon's Yd, Leeds, Yorks., joiner, builder and cm (1830–34). [D]

Riley, Stephen, Oxford St, London, u, cabinet and carpet warehouseman (1785–1811). Recorded at no. 338, 1785–92; in partnership with Fowler there, 1787–96; alone at no. 331, 1809–11; at 77 Swallow St, 1800–08, with Fowler there in 1803; and alone at 333 Oxford St in 1811. Took out Sun Insurance policies on 19 December 1785 for £2,400; and on 8 June 1792 for £450 on household goods and printed books. Probably the S. Riley, u, who submitted a bill to John Gregory in 1804. [D; GL, Sun MS vol. 333, p. 619; vol. 389, ref. 601207; V&A archives] See Riley & Fowler.

Riley, Thomas, York, cm (1740–48). As a master, took apps for seven years: James Wells in 1740, and George Marshe, carpenter and cm, in 1742. Sale by auction of all the household goods and stock in trade of Thomas Riley, cm, next door to 'The Black Swan', Coney St, advertised in *York Courant*, 16 February 1748. It was to take place from 23–26 February, and stock consisted of 'Standing Beds, Feather-Beds, Blankets, Quilts, Chest of Drawers, Tables, Chairs, Looking Glasses, Sconces, and all Sorts of Goods in the Cabinet Trade. Likewise all Sorts of Kitchen Furniture as Pewter, Brass, Ironwork, and other useful Furniture.' [York app. indentures]

Riley, Thomas, Leicester, carver and gilder (1815–42). Trading at Eastgate(s), 1815–28, and Haymarket, 1835–42. [D]

Riley and Batt, address unrecorded. A set of six Regency mahogany dining-chairs recorded, one impressed 'Riley', another, 'Batt'. The chairs have curved panelled toprails carved with roundels, partly upholstered backs with baluster splats, and padded seats on sabre legs. [Christie's, 12 February 1981, lot 75]

Riley & Fowler, London, u and cm (1787–1803). Trading at 338 Oxford St, 1787–96, and at 77 Swallow St in 1803. Bill head dated 7 October 1787 shows Classical female figure by urn on pedestal, and gives address at 338 Oxford St. It states that the firm stocked 'Great variety of Paper Hangings', and furnished funerals. Trade card [Banks Coll., BM] is similar to that of Oakley. Two mahogany Gothic chairs in the Samaria Room, Dean's House, Westminster, bear painted labels, dated 1794. Named in Sheraton's list of master cabinet makers, 1803. [D; V&A archives]

Rim(m)ington, Edward, Liverpool, chairmaker and cm (1783–1810). Addresses given at 5 Haymarket in 1783; nos 4–5 in 1790; no. 6 in 1794; Rose Green, St Anne's with shop at 4 Haymarket, 1796–1801; 5 Haymarket, 1800–03; 16 Bean (or Beau) St in 1805; and 19 Haymarket, 1807–10. Took out a Sun Insurance policy on 29 December 1800 for £1,800 including £300 on house, shop and back buildings in Hays Mkt; £200 on stock and utensils; £500 on a house nearby; and £400 on a house at Everton. Notice from Rimmington's creditors in *Liverpool Chronicle*, 25 November 1807, concerned the payment of his debts. [D; GL, Sun MS vol. 38, ref. 713206]

Rim(m)ington, Edward, Yorkshire St, Rochdale, Lancs., cm and chairmaker (1814–18). [D]

Rimington, Edward, Skinnergate, Darlington, Co. Durham, chairmaker (1828–29). [D]

Rimington, J. & W., Castle-gate, Penrith, Cumb., chairmakers (1811). [D]

Rimington, William, Castle-gate, Penrith, Cumb., chairmaker and/or turner (1829). [D]

Rimmer, George, Jones St, Salford, Lancs., cm (1808). [D]

Rimmer, Henry, Liverpool, cm (1774–1807). Addresses given at 11 Charles St in 1774; 3 Wood St in 1777; 14 St Thomas Buildings, with shop at back of 20 Peter St in 1790; Peter St, 1792–94; 63 Peter St, Whitechapel in 1804; and 21 Pitt St, 1805–07. Took out a Sun Insurance policy on 23 October 1792 for £200 on utensils and stock in his shop at Peter St. [D; GL, Sun MS vol. 391, p. 196]

Rimmer, James, Liverpool, cm (1780). Petitioned freedom on servitude to Thomas Dobb in 1780. [Liverpool freemen's committee bk]

Rimmer, John, 1 Downe St, Liverpool, cm (1834–35). [D]

Rimmer, Joseph, Liverpool, cm (1796–1823). Admitted freeman as son of Timothy Rimmer, roper, on 25 May 1796. Trading at 39 Gerard St in 1823. [D; Liverpool freemen reg.] Possible confusion with:

Rimmer, Joseph jnr, Liverpool, cm (1830–39). Recorded at 27 Jordan St and Down St in 1830, and 17 Springfield St in 1839. Admitted freeman on 15 November 1830 as son of Joseph Rimmer, cm. Marriage to Miss Ann Lobley of Kirkdale at St Phillip's Church reported in *Liverpool Mercury*, 21 February 1834. [D; Liverpool freemen reg.]

Rimmer, Thomas, Liverpool, cm (1780). Admitted freeman on 11 September 1780. [Liverpool freemen reg.]

Rimmer, William, Woodstock St and Collingwood St,

Liverpool, cm (1812). Admitted freeman on servitude to John Mears on 7 October 1812. [Liverpool freemen reg.]

Rimmington, John, Liverpool, chairmaker and grocer (1790–1807). Addresses given at 157 Dale St in 1790; 12 Hunter St in 1794; 4 Vernon St in 1796; nos 3 and 4 in 1800; Richmond Row, St Anne's, 1803–04; no. 25 in 1805; no. 37 and also 93 Dale St in 1807. [D]

Rindell, Nicholas, Queen St, London, u (1784). [Poll bk]

Ring, John, 43 St Paul's Churchyard, London, cm (1769–73). [D]

Ring, John, Basingstoke, Hants., cm, auctioneer, joiner and u (1784–93). Took out a Sun Insurance policy on 25 March 1792 for £1,800 including £700 on his house and adjacent warehouse in Church St, and £800 on utensils and stock. [D; GL, Sun MS vol. 386, p. 160]

Ring, Peter, London, cm (1775–84). Recorded at Cavendish St in 1775, when he took out a Sun Insurance policy for £400 of which £200 accounted for utensils and stock. Trade card of 1781 gives address at 98 Gt Portland St, near Portland Chapel; and another of 1784, at 97 Jermyn St, shows several different pieces of up-to-date furniture, and gives trade as cm, u and inlayer. Directories record him at 97 Gt Portland St in 1784. [D; GL, Sun MS vol. 238, p. 387; Banks Coll., BM]

Ring, Stephen, 128 St John St, London, carver and gilder (1835–39). [D]

Ringer, Mrs Elizabeth, Rampant Horse St, Norwich, cm and u (1839–42). [D] Possibly widow of:

Ringer, James, Norwich, cm and chairmaker (1808–d.1837). Recorded at Rampant Horse St in 1836. Admitted freeman, not by apprenticeship, on 21 September 1808. Former app., James Lancaster, admitted on 24 January 1824. Will proved in 1837. [D; Norwich freemen reg. and poll bks; Norfolk Record Soc., index of wills]

Ringer, James, Ber St, Norwich, cm and chairmaker (1839). [D]

Ringsell, George, High Wycombe, Bucks., chairmaker (1813–15). Sons bapt. in 1813 and 1815. [PR (bapt.)]

Ringsell, Samuel, High Wycombe, Bucks., chairmaker (1837). Son bapt. in 1837. [PR (bapt.)]

Ringshill, Henry, High Wycombe, Bucks., chairmaker (b.c.1819–41). Aged 22 at the time of the 1841 Census.

Ringwell, Samuel, High Wycombe, Bucks., chairmaker (b.c.1816–41). Aged 25 at the time of the 1841 Census.

Riorto, James, London, cm (1718–31). Recorded at St Giles-in-the-Fields in 1718 when he took app. named Abraham Delamere. In 1727 he supplied the Duchess of Montrose with a fire-screen, 'finely carved & gilt', costing £6 6s. Named in the Royal Household accounts of Frederick, Prince of Wales, Duchy of Cornwall, in 1731, receiving £139 1s for preparing a six leaf screen, varnishing a room and gilding the plaster cornice and ceiling. [Boyd's index of IR app. reg.; Scottish RO, GD 220/6/1362/53; Duchy of Cornwall vouchers, vol. 2, pp. 205 and 224]

Ripkey, John, 1 Coalyard, Drury Lane, London, bedstead maker (1839). [D]

Ripley, James, Lancaster, japanner and furniture painter (1784–88). [Westminster Ref. Lib., Gillow records]

Rippin, Richard, 10 Upper East Smithfield, London, broker and cm (1779). Took out a Sun Insurance policy in 1779 for £200 of which utensils and stock accounted for £100. [GL, Sun MS vol. 272, p. 394]

Rippingale, Francis, Newark, Notts., cm (1828). [D]

Rippon, George Calvert, York, carver and gilder (1796–1830). Trading at Minster Yd in 1803, and 37 Stonegate, 1816–30. Son of John Rippon, carver and gilder; app. to Robert Tomlinson, carver and gilder, on 5 April 1796. Admitted freeman in 1803. [D; York app. reg. and freemen rolls]

Rippon, John, Nottingham, carver and gilder (1815–20).

Named in the Nottingham burgess list in 1815, and polled of St James's Yd, Milton St in 1820.

Rippon, Reuben, 8 Tudor St, Sheffield, Yorks., joiner and cm (1822). [D]

Rishforth, Major, 7 Ogle St, Portland Chapel, London, cm (1783). Insured his house for £200 in 1783. [GL, Sun MS vol. 317, p. 435]

Rison, Jos., 14 Gresse St, Rathbone Pl., London, cm (1809–11). [D]

Ritchie, Allan, Main St, Cockermouth, Cumb., joiner and/or cm (1829–34). [D]

Ritchie, Hugh, 14 Brownlow St, Holborn, London, cm and u (1811–13). [D]

Ritson, John, Gt Richmond St, St Anne's, Liverpool, cm (1804). [D]

Ritson, Jonathan, address unrecorded, carver (1816–c.1827). In 1816 he supplied picture frames, including one for his own portrait, in the style of Grinling Gibbons, to Petworth House, Arundel, Sussex, and also worked on the Carved Room there. Supplied further picture frames, c.1827. [C. *Life*, 25 September 1980, p. 1032; Nat. Trust guide to *Petworth*]

Ritson, Jonathan, Main St, Cockermouth, Cumb., cm and joiner (1834). [D]

Ritson, William, Parsonby, Maryport, Cumb., cm (1829). [D]

Rittener, Mrs, London. Recorded in the account book of Edward, Lord Lascelles, relating mainly to Harewood House, Hanover Sq., London, on 21 May 1798 receiving £26 5s for a pair of girandoles. [Leeds archives dept, Harewood MS 191]

Rittener, E., address unrecorded. In February 1794 Rittener provided a pair of girandoles for Francis, 5th Duke of Bedford, at a cost of £19 1s. This may have been part of the furnishing of the south rooms at Woburn Abbey which had been remodelled a few years earlier by Henry Holland for the Duke. [Bedford Office, London]

Rivers, G., Middlx, u (1826). Declared bankrupt, *London Gazette*, 29 April 1826.

Rivers, George, London, cm and u (1822–39). Trading at 32 Judd St, Brunswick Sq., 1822–23; as George Rivers & Co., 1826–27; at 1 Orchard St, Portman Sq., 1827–28; and at London Rd, Twickenham, 1832–39. [D]

Rivers, Joseph, West St, Middlesbrough, Yorks., joiner and cm (1840). [D]

Rivers, Wm, 7 Westgate Buildings, Bath, Som., cm (1833). [D]

Rivett, J., 5 Crown St, Moorfields, London, cm (1816–25). [D] See Samuel and W. Rivett.

Rivett, John, Gt Yarmouth, Norfolk, chairmaker (1777). [Poll bk]

Rivett, Samuel, Crown St, Middle Moorfields, Finsbury, London, cm and bedstead maker (1787–1800). Recorded as Samuel & Son at no. 50 in 1800. On 2 February 1787 his wife Elizabeth, insured their new unfurnished house for £200. [D; GL, Sun MS vol. 343, p. 68] See J. and W. Rivett.

Rivett, W., Crown St, Finsbury, London, cm, bedstead maker and joiner (1807–39). Trading at nos 3 and 4 in 1807, no. 5 in 1820, and no. 50 in 1823. [D] See J. and Samuel Rivett.

Rivett, William, Shipdham, East Dereham, Norfolk, cm (1839). [D]

Rivolta, Anthony, 32 Brook St, Holborn, London, looking-glass, barometer and thermometer maker (1819–45). [D; Goodison, *Barometers*]

Rix, George, Snettisham, Norfolk, cm (1830). [D]

Rix, James, Crown Ct, High St, Southwark, London, cm (1784). [Bristol poll bk]

Rix, Mary, Gaol St, Gt Yarmouth, Norfolk, u (1830). [D]

Roach, Charles, Crown St, Halifax, Yorks., carver and gilder (1818–20). [D]

Roach, Charles, Kirkgate, Wakefield, Yorks., carver and gilder (1822). [D]

Roach, Francis (?), London, cm (*c*.1790–1824). An inlaid and carved satinwood cabinet for gem casts, of superb quality and designed by James Wyatt, bears an ivory plate inscribed 'Roach, Cabinet-Maker, London'. This, and another cabinet attributed to Roach, are in the Hermitage Museum, Leningrad. [Inv. Nos 342 and 344] He might be Francis Roach, who emigrated to America and was active in Baltimore in 1824.

Roach, John, Bristol, chairmaker (1799–1812). Addresses given at Castle Ditch, 1799–1800, Old King St, 1801–10, and Lower Castle St in 1812. [D]

Roads, James, High St, Tewkesbury, Glos., chairmaker (1818–25). [PR (bapt.)]

Roake, Joseph, 20 Gloucester St, Bloomsbury, London, cm and u (1771–72). [D]

Roake, Samuel, 20 Gloucester St, Bloomsbury, London, cm and u (1772). [D]

Roasway, John, Margate, Kent, cm (1794). [D] See John Roffway of Margate.

Robarts, Martin, Shortmead St, Biggleswade, Beds., cm and u (1830–39). [D]

Robarts, Martha, Short Mead St, Biggleswade, Beds., u (1839). [D]

Robarts, Wm. & Jh., 13 Fenchurch St, London, upholders etc. (1788–1800). Trade card, *c*.1800, recorded. [D; Heal]

Robb, John, Liverpool, cm (1797–1806). App. to Edward Lowe in 1797, and petitioned freedom on servitude in 1806, but application rejected. [Liverpool freemen's committee bk]

Robbins, —, 8 Bridge St, Bristol, cm (1785). Sale of stock on 'leaving off the Shop he now occupies in Bridge Street' reported in *Bonner and Middleton's Bristol Journal*, 24 September 1785. Stock consisted of 'a great Variety of handsome Mahogany Chairs, covered over the Rail with Hair seating and Brass nailed; fine Wardrobes, Chests of Drawers; Dining, Pier, Pembroke, Pillar and Dressing Tables; Bason-stands; exceeding good Clock Cases; Pier and swing Looking-Glasses; Four-post Bedsteads, with Mahogany oak post; Dressing Chairs, Windsor ditto; and every Article in the Cabinet Business, the whole of which are made in the best wood . . .'. [*Furn. Hist.*, 1979]

Robbins, —, Abbey Hill, Kenilworth, Warks., builder, cm, u and paper hanger. Probably early 19th-century trade card shows Kenilworth Castle, a bed, bookcase, and Regency chair and sofa. [Heal Coll., BM]

Robbins, Edwin, 19 Stangate St, Lambeth, London, carver and gilder (1839). [D]

Robbins, James, Milk St, Bristol, cm (1792–93). [D]

Robbins, John, London. In 1792 he made a set of four painted and gilt torchères on triangular pedestals in the hall at Sledmere House, Yorks., and a suite of gilt seat furniture in the drawing room. [*Sledmere Guide Book*]

Robbins, Joseph, Norwich, u (1667–92). Admitted freeman on 17 July 1667. Former app., Timothy Ganinge, admitted on 21 September 1692. [Norwich freemen reg.]

Robbins, William, Snow Hill, London, u (1781–94). Recorded at no. 2, 1790–93. Son of William Robbins, Gent. of Grosvenor St. App. to Samuel Braithwaite on 5 September 1781, and admitted freeman of the Upholders' Co. by servitude on 6 December 1788. Marriage recorded in *Gents Mag.*, January 1781. Declared bankrupt, *Derby Mercury*, 30 September 1790. [D; GL, Upholders' Co. records]

Robbs, James, 105 Goswell St Rd, London, cm and u (1839). [D]

Robbs, John, Liverpool, cm (1812). Admitted freeman on servitude to Edward Lowe on 5 October 1812. [Liverpool freemen reg.]

Roberts, Adrian, Oxford, u (1666–1702). Married Bridget Goddard at St Cross, Oxford, on 24 July 1666. In 1675 he is recorded concerning a 99-year counterpart lease for a messuage in Wendlebury, made to Richard Wise, u of Oxon., his wife Elizabeth, and daughters Francis and Katherine. In 1702 Adrian Roberts of Worton, parish of Cassington, sold a copyhold messuage and land for £100 to Richard Wise. [Bodleian index of Oxf. marriage bonds; Oxford RO, Talbot III/i/1; CJ.v/67]

Roberts, Archibald, 5 Kent Sq., with shop at 12 Cornhill, Liverpool, carver and blockmaker (1834). [D]

Roberts, Christopher jnr, The Parade, Tunbridge Wells, Kent, Tunbridge-ware manufacturer (1792). Named in the poor rate for Speldhurst parish. Took app. named William Japp of Speldhurst on 7 May 1792. [Kent RO, P344/11/1; P334/14/23]

Roberts, D., Uttoxeter Heath, Uttoxeter, Staffs., cm (1818). [D]

Roberts, Edward, Liverpool, u (1759–73). Trading in Dale St, 1766–73. Petitioned freedom on servitude to Thomas Hales 1759, paying 6s 8d. Admitted freeman on 18 September 1760, in which year he took app. named Sandbank. [D; Liverpool freemen reg. and committee bk; S of G, app. index]

Roberts, Edward, 147 Hoxton Old Town, London, cm and u (1839). [D]

Roberts, Edward, Egerton St, Chester, u (1840). [D]

Roberts, George, Chester, cm (1818–26). Recorded at Gorst Stacks in 1812, Frodsham St, 1818–19, and Pitt St in 1826. [Poll bks]

Roberts, H., 83 Tottenham Ct Rd, London, cm etc. (1820). [D]

Roberts, Henry, 17 Horseferry Rd, Westminster, London, cm and u (1827–28). [D]

Roberts, Henry, 4 Spitalfields, Liverpool, cm (1837). [D]

Roberts, I. & T., Back Pool Fold, Manchester, cm (1817). [D]

Roberts, J., Frodsham St, Chester, cm (1819). [Poll bk]

Roberts, J. & T., Farnley, Leeds, Yorks., cm (1822). [D]

Roberts, James, 17 Pavement, London, upholder (1801–02). Son of John Roberts, u, of Moorfields. Admitted freeman of the Upholders' Co. by patrimony on 7 October 1801. [GL, Upholders' Co. records]

Roberts, James, Chester, cm (1801–40). Recorded at Gorst Stacks in 1819, and King St in 1840. On 28 February 1801 James Roberts, son of Ann Roberts, widow of Chester, was assigned over from Matthew Holland, cm, to William Faulkener, cm, for three years, the residue of his original term of seven years. [D; poll bk; Chester app. indentures]

Roberts, James, Lancaster, u and cm (1759–d. by 1805). Warerooms recorded 'under the Assembly Room' in 1804; and trading at Market St at his death in 1805. Admitted freeman, 1759–60. The Gillows Ledger, 1763–68, shows a large account with Roberts. Took apps on 14 November 1760, 13 November 1765, 24 February 1773, 5 July 1785, 31 May 1796 and 22 June 1802. Advertised that he was selling off his cabinet stock, but 'means to carry on in the Upholstery business, as usual', in *Lancaster Gazette*, 28 January 1804. Stock consisted of 'High and low wardrobes; Ladies secretaries with bookcase tops; Ladies Writing Tables with nests of drawers; Ditto Dressing Tables, with glass, drawers and boxes; Oval and square card tables, Pembroke tables; Lobby Chests; Commode and Plain Dressing Chests; Gardivines; Night Chairs; Bidets, various forms; Portable Desks; Backgammon Boxes; Sophas; Chairs, brass nailed and loose bottoms; Camp Bedsteads, with white lawn hangings; A Billiard Table of the first make, 12 feet long by 6 feet wide, compleat . . .'. Sale of his upholstery stock, shop fixtures and workroom on his death advertised in *Lancaster Gazette*, 29 June 1805. [D; poll bks; Lancaster app. reg. and freemen rolls]

Roberts, James, Leeds, Yorks., u (1834–37). Recorded at 127 West St as a 'working' u in 1834; and at 33 Templars St in 1837. [D]

Roberts, James, 35 Platt Terr., Somerstown, London, cm and u (1839). [D]

Roberts, John, address unrecorded. Submitted a bill dated 28 August 1725 to Sir John Heathcote for '2 Wainscot Chests of Drawers with 5 locks each & Brass Works', costing £2 4s. The bill was receipted on 3 September 1725. [Lincoln RO, 2 ANC 12/D/15]

Roberts, John, address unrecorded, cm (1754). Subscribed to Chippendale's *Director*, 1754.

Roberts, John, St Giles, London, cm (1755). Took app. named Jos. Clarkson for £10 in 1755. [V&A archives]

Roberts, John, address unrecorded, upholder (1772). Son of Richard Roberts, and possibly father of James Roberts. App. to Samuel Swain, and admitted freeman of the Upholders' Co. by servitude on 1 April 1772. [GL, Upholders' Co. records]

Roberts, John, Cross Lane, Long Acre, London, cm (1774). [Poll bk]

Roberts, John, Chester, cm (1784). Son of Thomas Roberts; app. to Samuel Mercer, cm, 2–4 February 1784. [Chester app. bks]

Roberts, John, near the Silk Mill, Chesterfield, Derbs., cm (1828–29). [D]

Roberts, John, Liverpool, cm (1823–24). Addresses given at 26 St James's St in 1823 and 3 Marshall St in 1824. Took app. named Joseph Quick in 1824. [D; Liverpool app. enrolment bk]

Roberts, John William, Liverpool, cm and u (1827–37). Recorded at 20 Castle Ditch, with house at 20 Torbock St in 1827; Hawke St, with shop at 54 Church St in 1835; and at 4 Hawke St, shop as before, in 1837. [D]

Roberts, John, Cheapside, Birmingham, cabinet, dressing case and portable desk maker (1830). [D]

Roberts, John, 9 Military Rd, Chatham, Kent, carver and gilder (1832–39). [D]

Roberts, John, Liverpool, carver and gilder (1834–39). Trading at 1 Spencer Buildings, Christian St, 1834–35, and at 4 Washington St, Everton, 1837–39. [D]

Roberts, John, 122 West St, Leeds, Yorks., carver, gilder and beer house owner (1837). [D]

Roberts, John, Scotland St, Ellesmere, Salop, cm (1840). [D]

Robert(s), Joseph & John, Falmouth, Cornwall, u (1805–30). Recorded as J. & J. Roberts in 1805, and listed at Market St, also as cm, in 1830. [D]

Roberts, Joseph, Liverpool, cm (1818–39). Trading at 54 Greenland St in 1818 and 69 Stanley St in 1839. Admitted freeman on 12 June 1818, on servitude to William Longworth Walker. Took app. named Joseph Broadbent jnr in 1822. [D; Liverpool freemen reg. and app. enrolment bk]

Roberts, Josiah, London, u (1776–1808). Trading at 13 Fenchurch St in 1784; Bishopsgate St, 1794–97; City Rd in 1802; and no. 9 in 1808. Son of Josiah Roberts, coal merchant of Mile End. App. to John Jenning on 4 September 1776, and admitted freeman of the Upholders' Co. by servitude on 5 May 1784. Declared bankrupt, *Billinge's Liverpool Advertiser*, 13 March 1797. [D; GL, Upholders' Co. records]

Roberts, Josiah, Snow Hill, Birmingham, cm (1777–80). [D]

Roberts, Lawrence, Park St, Chester, cm (1819–26). Admitted freeman in 1819 and polled in 1826.

Roberts, Rice, 16 Bedford St, Harrington, Liverpool, cm (1839). [D]

Roberts, Richard, at 'The Royal Chair', Marylebone St, London, see Thomas Roberts.

Roberts, Richard, Norwich, chairmaker (1741). Admitted freeman, not by apprenticeship, on 15 June 1741, in which year he took app. named Smith. [Norwich freemen rolls; S of G, app. index]

Roberts, Richard, Gorst Stacks, Chester, cm (1812–26). Admitted freeman on 5 October 1812. [Chester freemen rolls and poll bks]

Roberts, Robert, Chester, turner and carver (1752). Took app. named William Collier, turner, in 1752. [Chester app. bks]

Roberts, Robert P., Liverpool, cm (1802–d.1811). Admitted freeman on servitude to Edward Myers, on 7 July 1802. Died on 9 December 1811. [Liverpool freemen reg.]

Roberts, Samuel, Nantwich, Cheshire, cm (1773). Marriage registered on 21 September 1773. [Chester RO, PR]

Roberts, Sarah, Brewer St, London, mantuamaker and upholder (1779). Took out a Sun Insurance policy in 1779 for £100 including £10 on utensils, stock and goods. [GL, Sun MS vol. 274, p. 224]

Roberts, Thomas (1685–1714) and **Richard** (1714–1729), at 'The Royal Chair', Marylebone St, London, joiners, chairmakers and carvers. Thomas Roberts was a carver and joiner, who succeeded Richard Price as the chief supplier of bed frames, seat furniture and fire-screens to the Royal Household in 1686, and who held this important position throughout the reigns of James II, William and Mary, and Anne. His name has become almost synonymous with the elaborate walnut chairs and stools of the period, carved with 'festoons and flowers' or 'mouldings and foldings', as they are often described in the accounts. Their scrolling arms and stretchers, also referred to in the documents as 'horsebone', seem to derive from Flemish and Dutch prototypes in the so-called auricular style, but Roberts was also influenced by contemporary French design. The gilded caryatid frames of the seat furniture in the Venetian Ambassador's Room at Knole, supplied *en suite* with a state bed for James II only a few months before his flight and exile, may have been directly influenced by similar sets sent over from Paris by the carver Peyrard and the u Delobel towards the end of Charles II's reign. [C. *Life*, 9 June 1977] Many references to 'French tables' and 'French beds' are found in his later bills of the 1690s, and the description of that made for 'his Majesty's great Bedchamber at Windsor Castle' in 1697, 16 feet high, with 'a large moulding Ovall Tester and headboard, and ironworks to support the tester and cornices' as well as 'rich carved work' on the tester, cornices, headboard, vases and feet, makes it very likely that he was carrying out the elaborate designs of Daniel Marot, William III's Huguenot architect and *ornemaniste*.

To judge by the vast amount of routine furniture which Roberts made for the use of ambassadors, court officials and military officers, as well as more elaborate items for the sovereigns themselves, he must have had one of the biggest workshops of any London furniture-maker of the period. Like his contemporary, the cm Gerrit Jensen, he is recorded as making models of proposed furniture for William III's own use — for instance 'two Pattern chairs and two stooles made to show the King', and intended for Windsor Castle, in 1697. His bills for 'saffaws' or sofas made for Chatsworth, as well as for the royal palaces, are among the earliest recorded references to this form of furniture, and as well as carved and gilded pieces he could produce exotic finishes such as the 'blue and white Japan' frames for twelve round stools with caned seats sent to Hampton Court in 1693, at a cost of £52 15s.

Thomas Roberts' premises at the sign of 'The Royal Chair', were in Marylebone St, Westminster, as recorded in a policy taken out with the Sun Insurance Co. on 7 November 1713 [GL, Sun MS vol. 3, p. 75] and he was succeeded here by Richard Roberts, almost certainly his son, who also took over as carver and joiner to the Royal Household in 1714. Richard appears in the Sun Insurance Co. records at the same address in 1723 [GL, Sun MS vol. 17, p. 49], when the goods and merchandise in his dwelling house were valued at £150, those in his warehouse at £150, and those in the yard at £200. However, he had moved to Air St, Piccadilly by 1728 when the *London Journal*, 19 October recorded that 'on Wednesday Night some Rogues attempted to break into the Kitchen Windows of Mr. Robert's house, Chairmaker to His Majesty, in Air Street by Piccadilly; but were disturbed by a Maid Servant, who happen'd to be up a Washing; so that the Villains were obliged to make off before they had compleated their Design'. The younger Roberts continued to supply bed frames, firescreens, chairs and stools to the Royal Household until 1729, though with 'bended backs' to the chairs, cabriole legs and hoof feet, showing that he kept up with the latest fashions. The very large debt owed by Sir Robert Walpole to 'Thomas Roberts' for furniture at Houghton in 1729 is puzzling, unless Richard had just died (quite likely in view of his disappearance from the Household Accounts at this time) and the business had been taken over by his brother or son, a second Thomas. To confuse matters still further a 'Mr. Roberts' of St Bartholomew's Close in the City provided chairs for Moulsham Hall in 1730, and there may well have been other London furniture-makers of the same name.

[*Conn.*, vol. 57, 1920, pp. 89–92; *C. Life*, 15 January 1921; *Old Furniture*, vol. 2, 1927, pp. 16, 32, 79, 82–83, 181; *Conn.*, June 1933, August 1933, October 1933, October 1935; *Burlington*, September 1967; *C. Life*, 9 June 1977; *Conn.*, June 1977]

ROYAL PALACES. 1686–1729: Thomas Roberts held the royal warrant as joiner to the Royal Household, providing beds, chairs and firescreens for Whitehall, Kensington, Hampton Court, Windsor Castle, the Treasury, the Great Wardrobe, royal yachts such as the *William and Mary* and the *Charlotte*, as well as furniture for coronations, funerals, embassies and other state occasions from 1686 until 1714. One of his earliest commissions was to supply caned chairs for James II's tent on Hounslow Heath, while in 1687 he provided Mary of Modena with '20 leaves of cedar skreenes to Stand round the bed (in the Queen's Dressing Room at Whitehall) all hinged together and wyred with gold & silver wyre'. Occasionally Roberts seems to have made carcase pieces such as 'a large Cedar Table to fall doune with two drawers in it' (1686) and 'a glass case with shelves in it made of right wainscott to hold books' (1697), but on the whole he was responsible for the moveable pieces, called in France the *courant*, as opposed to the *meublant*, which came within the province of the royal cm Gerrit Jensen. One of the most elaborate of all the items in the accounts is a 'large rich fire skreene, the top piece carved both sides into leaves and cyphers, the pillows (i.e. pillars) into festoons and flowers and two firepotts on top, the two claws into Lyons . . .', made for Windsor in 1697. In the same year he made another screen and set of stools for the long gallery at Kensington Palace.

Among the surviving pieces which can be firmly attributed to Roberts are the bed and matching chairs and stools in the Venetian Ambassador's Room at Knole, upholstered by Jean Poitevin, and made for James II only a few months before he fled to France in 1688, and other chairs in the Brown Gallery and Cartoon Gallery at Knole (also acquired as perquisites by the 6th Earl of Dorset) which closely match descriptions in the royal accounts — e.g. 'chaires of state carved all over very rich with scrowles and leaves and figures in the forefeet and crownes and sceptres in the fore rayles and . . . on the top of the backs', supplied in 1689. For the funeral of Mary II in 1695 he made a state bed of oak, the tester 'with 4 great shields in the 4 corners and 4 crowns', and for the coronation

of Queen Anne in 1702 a 'rich Chaire of state the Top of the back carved with a Lyon and Unicorn and Shields Cypher and Crowne and scepters'. This throne and its accompanying footstool was acquired as a perquisite by the 5th Earl of Salisbury and is still at Hatfield. [*Burlington*, September 1967, p. 66] Three years later Roberts also made for the Queen's use at St James's Palace a 'wallnuttree gout chair frame & footstool to run on wheels, & ironwork fixed to the feet to turn with handles'. [Symonds papers, Winterthur, Delaware, 75x69 pp. 14, 17]

Richard Roberts succeeded Thomas as the chief joiner to the Royal Household, supplying a bed to Queen Anne at Windsor a few months before her death, and another for the Prince of Wales at Hampton Court in 1716, together with window cornices, eighteen walnut stools, a firescreen and two armchairs *en suite*, all with upholstery by Phill and Fletcher. [*Old Furniture*, vol. 2, 1927, pp. 82–83] Peter Thornton [*Conn.*, June 1977] has associated this account with a surviving bed at Hampton Court, and another set of eighteen walnut chairs with 'India backs . . . bended . . . for H.M.'s eating room at Hampton Court' have also been identified with the remainder of a set still at the palace. [*DEF*, III, p. 41] Roberts' name appears in the Lord Chamberlain's accounts for the last time in 1729.

PENSHURST PLACE, Kent (Earl of Leicester). c.1700–01: An elaborate day-bed and matching suite of chairs and stools have been attributed to Roberts because of their similarities with a pair of stools at Hampton Court made by him in 1700–01. [*DEF*, III, p. 41] The Penshurst set, upholstered to match some remarkable wall-hangings in the style of Daniel Marot, may in fact have royal origins, and could well have been acquired as a perquisite by the 5th or 6th Earl of Leicester some time after William III's death.

MOOR PARK, Herts. (Duchess of Monmouth). 1701: Work amounting to £103 19s 5d and including two 'saffaws' (or sofas) with carved frames, and a 'twisted walnuttree foot for a bed', is recorded in account books among the Buccleuch Collection at the Scottish RO. [GD 224/Box 29] Some of the furniture from Moor Park, including chairs in the style associated with Roberts, may well be among the contents of Boughton House, Northants., a seat of the present Duke of Buccleuch.

CHATSWORTH, Derbs. (1st Duke of Devonshire). 1702: From an account of 'Goods bought at London, June 2 1702' in 'Mr Whildon's Account Book' it appears that Thomas Roberts was paid a total of £34 for a variety of items including '14 chair frames Carv'd and Japan'd black for a dineing roome', '8 large Armed Chairs of wallnuttree for a Bedchamber', '6 Banketts of wallnuttree all carved with Mouldings round the seats', and '9 large packing Cases to pack up a Rich Bed and furniture, and all the Chaires and Banketts'. [Chatsworth papers] Roberts may also have made the frame for the earlier state bed at Chatsworth, upholstered by Francis Lapierre in 1697 — whose tester survives as a canopy in the Long Gallery at Hardwick. A pair of armchairs with matching stools in the same room, upholstered with red velvet embroidered with silver thread, also seem to parallel descriptions in Roberts' contemporary Royal Household accounts (e.g. 'a large Chaire of State made to spread out at Top') and may have been acquired by the Duke of Devonshire as perquisites at a later date.

BOUGHTON HOUSE, Northants. (1st Duke of Montagu). 1703: Thomas Roberts supplied 'a feild Bedstead of Walnuttree with 4 posts made to ffold up altogether with ironwork and Springs' at a cost of £14. [MS account book at Boughton] (See also under Moor Park).

WESTMINSTER ABBEY 1727: Richard Roberts supplied four

new lions for St Edward's Throne and 'a rich carved and gilt Footstool Frame for Do' in preparation for George II's Coronation. [*Conn.*, vol. 133 (1954), pp. 80–81]
HOUGHTON HALL, Norfolk (Sir Robert Walpole). 1729: Furniture to a value of £1,420 8s 7½d 'less £200 by cash' is recorded as being owed to Thomas Roberts in Walpole's accounts. [Cambridge Univ. Lib. MS]
MOULSHAM HALL, Essex (Earl Fitzwalter). 1730: A bill of March 10 'To Mr Roberts of Bartolomew Close for 6 Dutch Chairs & packing sent to Moulsham £2'. [A. C. Edwards, *The Accounts of Benjamin Mildmay, Early Fitzwalter*, p. 101]
HARDWICK HALL, Derbs. (see Chatsworth)
HATFIELD HOUSE, Herts. (see Royal Palaces)
KNOLE, Kent. (see Royal Palaces)   G.J.-S.

Roberts, Thomas, address unrecorded, upholder (1716–27). Son of Edward Roberts, yeoman of Mimms, Middlx. App. to John Howard on 4 July 1716, and admitted freeman of the Upholders' Co. by servitude on 2 August 1727. [GL, Upholders' Co. records]

Roberts, Thomas, Chester, cm (1767–1818). Recorded at Northgate St in 1784, and Gorst Stacks, 1812–18. Son of Thomas Roberts; app. to Philip Presbury, cm of Chester, 1 August 1767–13 September 1768. Admitted freeman on 31 March 1784. [Chester app. bks, freemen rolls and poll bks]

Roberts, Thomas, Chester, cm (1790–91). Son of Thomas Roberts; app. to William Henderson, cm, 25 March 1790–21 May 1791. [Chester app. bks]

Roberts, Thomas, Bristol, cm (1793–1809). Trading at Merchant St, 1793–1801; as T. Roberts snr at 4 Bridge St, 1805–07; and Narrow Wine St in 1809. [D]

Roberts, Thomas jnr, Bristol, cm, broker, auctioneer and appraiser (1805–07). Trading at 29 Bath St in 1805 and St James's Back, 1806–07. [D]

Roberts, Thomas, Harper's Hill, Birmingham, cm (1800). [D]

Roberts, Thomas, Manchester, cabinet and chair warehouseman (1804–17). Addresses given at 20 Gt Newton St in 1804 and 19 Oldham Rd in 1817. [D]

Roberts, Thomas, Abelwell St, Walsall, Staffs., cm and u (1818). [D]

Roberts, Thomas, Bridge St, Northampton, cm (1820). [Poll bk]

Roberts, Thomas, Chester, carver and gilder (1824–37). Addresses given at Botany St in 1824; Pitt St in 1826; City Walls, Northgate, 1828–34; and Northgate St Row in 1837. Admitted freeman on 12 October 1824. [D; Chester freemen rolls and poll bks]

Roberts, Thomas, Liverpool, carver (1821–31). Recorded at 23 Pellew St in 1831. App. to John Summer in 1821. Petitioned freedom in 1830, paying 6s 8d, and admitted freeman on 29 April 1831. [Liverpool freemen reg. and committee bk]

Roberts, Thomas, Liverpool, cm (1829–35). Addresses given at 12 Upper Mann St in 1829, no. 20 in 1834; and 5 Warwick St in 1835. [D]

Roberts, Timothy, Duckingpond Alley, Clerkenwell, London, cm (1749–54). Polled at Westminster in 1749. Probably the Timothy Roberts, cm, who subscribed to Chippendale's *Director*, 1754.

Roberts, Timothy, Todmorden, Lancs., cm (1828–37). Trading at Church St, 1828–34, and Market Pl. in 1837. [D]

Roberts, William, Chester, joiner, carver and turner (1702–21). Son of Thomas Roberts, labourer; app. to William Bolland, joiner, carver and turner, 5 March 1702–17 November 1703. Granted a portion of Sir Thomas White's money in 1716. In 1721 he protested to the Co. of Joiners, Carvers & Turners regarding the election of John Brixton who had not served seven years as app. [Chester app. bks. and freemen rolls]

Roberts, William, Chester, cm (1732). [Chester freemen rolls]

Roberts, William, London, u (1735). Son of Ric. of St James West; app. to William Bradshaw, u, of St Ann's for £35 in 1735. [V&A archives]

Roberts, William, address unrecorded, carver (1741–43). Named in the Holkham accounts in 1741 receiving £25 14s 10d, and in 1742, £23 1s 6d for carving frames, £2 9s 3d 'for assisting Mr. Sutton', and £22 9s 6d for carving six picture frames. In 1743 he charged £3 3s for 'carving 3 picture frames for ye Rustick parlour', £1 1s for 'carving festoons etc. for My Lords dressing room', £7 7s for a further three picture frames, and £1 3s 6d for other carving work. [V&A archives]

Roberts, William, Alnwick, Northumb., u and stuccoist (1753). Advertised in *Newcastle Courant*, 10 February 1753, his 'Large & curious assortment of Paper Hangings from London ... Flock or Velvet Paper, Landskip, Stucco or Chintz Patterns of any Sort. Likewise performs the new fashion'd Ceilings & Stair Cases (after the Manner of Stucco Carvings) consisting of large or small circles and Panneling, with Fret Work etc. etc.'

Roberts, William, address unrecorded, picture frame maker (1761). Named in the Raby Castle MS supplying picture frames to Cleveland House, London, in 1761. [V&A archives]

Roberts, William, Liverpool, u (1774). Former app., John Potter, petitioned freedom in 1774. [Liverpool freemen's committee bk]

Roberts, William, address unrecorded, cm (1797). Mahogany secretary with tulipwood banding recorded bearing label which reads: 'This Secretary was finished 3rd August 1797. William Roberts.' Secretary has three secret drawers and a circular watercolour inset in the style of Angelica Kauffmann. [V&A archives]

Roberts, William, Westgate, Wakefield, Yorks., cm (1814–20). [D]

Roberts, William, Bristol, coach, cabinet, chair and ornamental carver (1814–31). Addresses given at Limekiln Lane, 1814–21; 19 College St, 1822–23; Lamb St, near College St, 1825–29; and Lamb St and 5 College St, 1830–31. [D]

Roberts, William John, Liverpool, cm (1816–40). Addresses given at 2 Hawke St in 1816; 22 Torbock St in 1821; 55 Church St and 22 Torbrook St with shop at 9 Clayton Sq. in 1827; 23 Torbrook St with shop at 53 Church St in 1829; 1 Hawke St with shop at 53 Church St in 1834; and 62 Church St in 1839. Admitted freeman as son of John Roberts, blockmaker, on 8 June 1816. Took app. named John Meineke in 1816, admitted freeman in 1829. Took apps named William Maddock Knowles in 1819; John Townson jnr in 1825; Robert Barton Boyd in 1826; David Hawkins in 1827; Henry Molyneux in 1828; Richard Echlers in 1830; Peter Dixon in 1831; William Mills in 1832; Hugh Martin in 1833; William Kermode and Thomas Howarth in 1834; Edward William Whinfield Taylor in 1835; William Mathews in 1836; Thomas Taylor, Edward Howard and John Kelly in 1838; Mark Gardner in 1839; and Francis Livesey in 1840. [D; Liverpool freemen reg., committee bk and app. enrolment bk]

Roberts, William, 13 Phillips Lane, London, cm (?) (1822–23). [D] Possibly:

Roberts, William, 110 Aldersgate St, London, cm (1826–28). [D]

Roberts, William, Ackworth, Yorks., joiner, cm and wheelwright (1837). [D]

Roberts, William, Waterloo Cottage, Exeter, Devon, cm (1837–40). Children bapt. at St David's Church, Exeter: son Joseph on 8 March 1837; James John on 8 August 1838; and daughter Maryanne on 17 September 1840. [PR (bapt.)]

Roberts, William, West St, Southampton, Hants., cm and chairmaker (1839). [D]

Robertson, Adam, 15 Side, Newcastle, carver, gilder, house and ship carver and picture frame maker (1834). [D]

Robertson, Alexander, 393 Strand, London, cm (1780–81). Took out Sun Insurance policies in 1780 for £1,000 of which £800 accounted for utensils, stock and goods; and in 1781 for £600, £410 on utensils, stock, goods and workshop. [GL, Sun MS vol. 286, p. 375; vol. 290, p. 566]

Robertson, Archibald, Liverpool, ship carver and gilder (1823–37). Trading at 6 Vincent with shop at 16 Cornhill in 1823 and 13 Cornhill, 1835–37. [D]

Robertson, Charles, London, u and undertaker (1808–27). Recorded at 15 Hollen St, Soho in 1808; 34 Gt Marlborough St, Oxford St, in 1811; and no. 54, 1813–15. Carried out work at Taymouth Castle, Scotland, for the Earl of Bredalbane, 1813–15. The accounts of 1813 list items supplied, including '4 prs. of curtains, Scarlet cloth Richly ornamented with broad gold silk lace' costing £330 12s; '2 Large Turkish Couches, Black Velvet Fringed', £43 17s; 'A Satinwood Grecian Couch with Eliptic Ends', £24; 'An elegant ebony frame for your glass with Rich Gothic pillars & Gothic leaves', costing £79 12s; and '2 Rich chimney glasses with frames to correspond', £261 15s. In 1815 Robertson charged £105 7s 10d for 'Men's time making 9 Gothic Heads 15 Columns, 15 Caps. & 3 Dome Tops for Tops of bookcases.' [D; Scottish RO, GD112/20/4/12/11, 13 and 14] See S. Robertson.

Robertson (or Robinson), George Valentine, Liverpool, cm (1823–24). Recorded at 13 Russel St in 1823 as Robertson, with house at 37 Seymour St in 1824 as Robinson. [D]

Robertson, George, 14 Ship St, Brighton, Sussex, cm and u (1826–28). Advertised in *Brighton Herald*, 30 December 1826 as 'ROBERTSON (From Wilkinson's Ludgate Hill) Appraiser and Commission Agent, at his new and second-hand Furniture Ware rooms, 15 Ship-street, Brighton. A large assortment of well-manufactured Furniture always ready. Second-hand furniture, bought, sold, exchanged or let on hire.' Announcement in the same paper, 7 June 1828 offered a large assortment of household furniture plus a Broadwood piano, to be sold by 'GEO. ROBERTSON Agent, 15 Ship St.' [D]

Robertson, J. & D., 20 Brownlow Hill, Liverpool, cm (1839). [D]

Robertson, James, parish of St James, Bristol, chairmaker (1774–81). [Poll bks]

Robertson, James, Hawkesbury, Glos., chairmaker (1784). [Bristol poll bk]

Robertson, James, All Saints' parish, Stamford, Lincs., cm (1809–31). [Poll bks]

Robertson, John, 11 Wells St, London, cm (1779). Took out a Sun Insurance policy in 1779 for £100, including £20 on his chest of tools in a timber workshop behind the dwelling house of Messrs. Chipchase & Co., upholders in Beak St. [GL, Sun MS vol. 273, p. 105]

Robertson, John, 7 Rathbone Pl., Oxford St, London, upholder and cabinet manufacturer (1820). [D]

Robertson, Josiah, London, cm (1793). Subscribed to Sheraton's *Drawing Book*, 1793.

Robertson, M. A., 21 Russell Sq., Brighton, Sussex, 'from London', upholsteress (1825). Advertised in *Brighton Gazette*, 8 September 1825 stock of 'French and drapery bed Furniture; dining and drawing room window curtains; chair, cushion, and sofa covers, made up, or altered, in the most fashionable manner.'

Robertson, S., 54 Gt Marlborough St, London, u (1829). [D] See Charles Robertson at this address.

Robertson, Samuel, John St, Dale St, Liverpool, cm (1803). [D]

Robertson, Thomas, Argyle Building(s), London, cm (1774–75). Polled at Westminster in 1774. Took out a Sun Insurance policy on 8 February 1775 for £300 on his house. [GL, Sun MS vol. 236, p. 249]

Robertson, Thomas, 19 Judd St, Brunswick Sq., London, upholder and undertaker (1817). [D]

Robertson, Thomas, 10 Narrowgate, Alnwick, Northumb., cm, u and joiner (1834). [D]

Robertson, William, London, furniture-maker (1769). Advertised in *Aberdeen Journal*, 29 May 1769, that he was visiting that city.

Robertson, William, Richmond, Surrey, cm etc. (1809–38). Recorded at Lower George St in 1822, and George St in 1826 also as a chairmaker. [D]

Robertson, William, South Shields, Co. Durham, cm and/or joiner (1834). [D]

Robertson, & Landbeck, 21–22 Broker Row, Moorfields, London, furniture warehousemen (1807–11). [D]

Robeshaw, Levi, St Sepulchre Gate, Doncaster, Yorks., cm (1822–37). [D]

Robillion, Jan Baptiste, Westminster, London, carver (1752). Declared bankrupt, *Gents Mag.*, January 1752.

Robins, —, address unrecorded, cm and u (1775). Subscribed to Thomas Malton's *Compleat Treatise on Perspective*, 1775.

Robins, —, address unrecorded, cm (1809). The account book of Sir John Geers Cotterell, Bart of Hertford St, London, and Garnons, near Hereford, records payment 'To ROBINS for Furniture in Hertford St.' costing £815 13s, on 30 August 1809. [Herefs. RO, Garnons papers, W69/III/182]

Robins, Charles, Bristol, cm (1775–1807). Addresses given at 24 Milk St in 1775; 12 Bridge St, 1792–93; 25 Milk St, 1793–94; Broad Mead, 1799–1807, and also Milk St in 1801. [D]

Robins, Henry, Gt Piazza, Covent Gdn, London, upholder (1788–94). Trading with John Robins in 1790, and listed as upholder and auctioneer in 1793. [D]

Robins, Henry, St Pancras, Chichester, Sussex, cm and u (1832–39). [D]

Robins, I., Warwick St, Golden Sq., London, u (1802–04). [D] Probably John or Joseph at this address.

Robins, J., Chancery Lane, London, cm (1793–1803). Subscribed to Sheraton's *Drawing Book*, 1793, and *Cabinet Dictionary*, 1803. Probably either John or Joseph Robins.

Robins, James, 2 Hotwells Cresc., Bristol, cm, carpenter, builder and undertaker (1815–16). [D]

Robins, John, parish of St John Maddermarket, Norwich, upholder (1714). [Poll bk]

Rob(b)ins, John, London, u, auctioneer, warehouseman and cm (1776–1828). Addresses given at 28 Chancery Lane, 1776–94, and Warwick House, Beak St, Golden Sq., 1793–1828. He is also listed at 170 Regent St, 1825–28. Took out Sun Insurance policies in 1776 for £1,200 including £200 on shop, utensils and goods; on 9 January 1786 for £400 on a house in Oxford St; on 6 September 1792 for £3,000 on house and offices at 34 Harley St, and coach houses and stables adjoining; on 23 April 1793 for £1,300, including £450 on warerooms and workshops; on 30 November 1800, 9 August 1809 and 30 November 1809 for £5,000 including £1,000 on house, merchandise and workshops, and £4,000 on stock and utensils. A further policy of 9 August 1809 was for £5,400 on various properties; and another of 30 November 1809 was for £3,600 on houses including £350 on 5 Northumberland St, Marylebone; £450 on 25 Beak (or Northumberland) St; £300 on one in tenure; £500 on one at the corner of Oxford St; £400 on one in Titchbourn (or Titchfield) St in tenure; £100 on a house behind; £500 on 8 Weymouth St, and £1,000 on 50 Wimpole St. The same properties were insured on 25 June 1812, with the addition of £1,000 on his house, warehouse and warerooms, and £4,000 on stock and utensils, giving a total of £8,600. Robins was recorded in the 'Liberty of the Rolls, Chancery Lane', when admitted freeman of the Upholders' Co. by redemption on 2 April 1788. Took app. named George Perring, 1789–1803. Named in Sheraton's list of master cabinet makers, 1803, and is probably the John Robins snr, cm, who subscribed to the *Cabinet Dictionary*. His son's death was reported in *Gents Mag.*, February 1806. [D; GL, Sun MS vol. 246, p. 104; vol. 334, p. 261; vol. 387, p. 561; vol. 395, p. 91; vol. 443, ref. 836762; vol. 446, refs 834248–49; vol. 443, refs 836762–63; vol. 457, ref. 871532; GL, Upholders' Co. records] He is probably the John Robins named in the accounts for Croome Court, Worcs. on 27 February 1777 charging £12·10s for 'The use of sett of tables fitted to the parlours with forms to do and the Ball Room coverd with green baze, japaned chairs tables candelstands etc.' [V&A archives] A friend of Sir John Soane, Robins supplied him with a library table and other pieces in 1804, and in 1828 a set of eight mahogany trellis-back chairs costing 24 guineas. He also provided two sideboards and a writing table for the Bank of England, designed by Soane. The table, which cost £32 8s, is fitted with a rising desk in the centre, with antique lion masks with ring handles at the angles, fluted, tapering legs and lion-paw feet. In 1827 Robins made for the Bank 'A large Partner's Chair with high back and sides round stuffed and covered with black Spanish leather tuffed and finished with brass nails for Lobby' costing £9 9s. [Soane Museum, London, Bank of England Bill Bk no. 13; R. A. Woods, *English Furniture in the Bank of England*, 1972, pl. 26; Fastnedge, *Sheraton Furniture*, p. 87, pl. 13; C. *Life*, 3 October 1947; V&A archives] John Robins submitted a bill to J. H. Leigh of Stoneleigh, Warks., dated 13–30 May 1818, totalling £30 15s 6d and receipted by J. Nash. Robins supplied a 'Mahogany enclosed washstand with hinged top in centre rising Glass, Drawers & Door in front fitted up with Wedgwood Ware & Glass tumbler'; 'A High Musicstand formed of East India rosewood three heights of Shelves with a Drawer underneath, turned legs brass knobs socket castors'; and a 'Mahogany Childs Crib with turned stump feet framed Walls strained with ticken lath bottom on brass socket Castors'. Bedding for the crib included 'A Bordered white Irish Mattress filled with Wool & hair tufted'; 'A fine white Swandown Pillow'; 'A white Irish upper Mattress filled with wool & hair tufted'; 'A Pair of fine flannel Blankets bound with white Silk Lace'; and a 'white cotton Marseilles Quilt'. [Shakespeare Birthplace Trust, Leigh receipts, DR 18/5] A late George III mahogany library bookcase recorded, with a dentil cornice and a pair of fifteen-panel glazed doors enclosing adjustable shelves; the projecting lower part with a pair of panelled cupboard doors also enclosing adjustable shelves. The underside of the cornice bears the printed label of 'John Robins cabinet and upholstery manufactory, Warwick House, Regent Street, London', which is addressed to the 'Rt. Hon. Lord Heniker, Mojor House, Stonham, Suffolk'. [Sotheby's, 28 October 1977, lot 114] See I. and Joseph Robins.

Robins, Joseph, London, upholder (1770–1802). Addresses given at Chancery Lane, 1780–94, and Warwick St, Golden Sq. in 1802. Son of William Robins of Gray's Inn Lane. App. to Samuel Braithwaite on 7 November 1770, and admitted freeman of the Upholders' Co. by servitude on 3 May 1780. Took app. named William Fassett, 1787–88. [GL, Upholders' Co. records]

Robins, T., address unrecorded, picture frame maker (1785). Named in the accounts of the Hon. H. Fane on 3 March 1785

receiving £2 0s 6d for picture frames. [Lincoln RO, Fane 7/1, 1783–85, p. 118]

Robins, William, Snow Hill, London, u (1790–93). Notices concerning certificate and dividends on bankruptcy appeared in *Williamson's Liverpool Advertiser*, 27 December 1790, 9 May 1791, and 18 March 1793.

Robins, William, Tabernacle, Blandford, Dorset, cm (1840). [D]

Robinson, —, address unrecorded, carver (1752). Carried out carving work, including a chimney-piece, at Sidney Sussex College, Cambridge in 1752. [C. *Life*, 25 February 1960, p. 382]

Robinson, —, 7 St Anne's Ct, near Wardour St, Soho, London, carver and gilder (1794). Trade card recorded, hand-coloured and of simple design. [Banks Coll., BM] Probably:

Robinson, —, address unrecorded, frame maker (1797–99). Employed at Southill, Beds., supplying frames for which he was paid £6 11s on 26 August 1797, and a further £18 12s 6d in the same year. Payments to Robinson amounted to £20 16s in 1798, and £10 14s in 1799. Charpentier and Goyer also provided frames. [*Southill, A Regency House*, 1951, p. 46; Rep. Gainsborough Exhib., 46 Park Lane (1936), illus. souvenir, p. 67]

Robinson, —, Brigg, Lincs. Subscribed to Sheraton's *Cabinet Dictionary*, 1803. Possibly Francis Robinson.

Robinson, —, Birmingham, carver and gilder (1821). Notice in *Liverpool Mercury*, 2 March 1821 concerned the sale of a 'Genuine Collection of valuable pictures By Mr. Winstanley ... Catalogues may be had of Mr. Robinson, Carver & Gilder, Birmingham ...'. Possibly I.B. or Thomas Robinson.

Robinson, —, Gt Queen St, Lincoln's Inn Fields, London, cm (1829). Fire at premises listed in *Palmer's Indexes of the Times*, 6 August 1829. Possibly George, or R. Robinson & Son.

Robinson, Anthony, King St, Derby, cm (1829). [D]

Robinson, Archibald, 5 Kent Sq. with shop at 15 Cornhill, Liverpool, carver (1829). [D]

Robinson, Benjamin, London, upholder (1712–49). Son of Benjamin Robinson, clerk of London; app. to Thomas Swaine on 25 July 1712. Admitted freeman of the Upholders' Co. by servitude on 11 December 1721, and master in 1749. Took app. named John Huggett, 1725–36. Polled in 1724. [GL, Upholders' Co. records; Heal]

Robinson, Benjamin, Freckleton, Lancs., joiner and cm (1828). [D]

Robinson, C., Lancaster. Named in the Gillow records in 1787. [Westminster Ref. Lib.]

Robinson, Charles, 76 High St, Marylebone, London, u (1802–27). Named in Sheraton's list of master cabinet makers, 1803. [D] See Elizabeth Robinson.

Robinson, Christopher, address unrecorded, upholder (1710–17). Son of John Robinson, yeoman of Lancaster. App. to Richard Bradshaw on 6 September 1710, and admitted freeman of the Upholders' Co. by servitude on 2 October 1717. [GL, Upholders' Co. records]

Robinson, Christopher, Union St, Leeds, Yorks., cm (1791). Took out a Sun Insurance policy on 11 January 1791 for £200 of which £150 accounted for goods in trust in Land's Lane. [GL, Sun MS vol. 375, p. 152]

Robinson, Christopher, Newgate St, Morpeth, Northumb., joiner and cm (1827–34). [D]

Robinson, Cuthbert, Newcastle, cm (1714). Took app. named Colvill in 1714. [S of G, app. index]

Robinson, Eleanor, 32 Bridge St, Manchester, cm and u (1836). [D]

Robinson, Elizabeth, 76 High St, Marylebone, London, u (1809–25). Trading with John Robinson, 1809–11, and listed as u and undertaker in 1817. [D] See Charles Robinson at this address.

Robinson, Francis (or Frank), Bigby St, Brigg, Lincs., cm and u (1819–35). [D] Possibly Robinson, — of Brigg.

Robinson, George, address unrecorded, upholder (1719–24). Son of Henry Robinson, innholder of Carlisle, Cumb. Admitted freeman of the Upholders' Co. by redemption by order of the Court of Aldermen, on 4 March 1718/19. Took app. named John Marsh, 1721–24. [GL, Upholders' Co. records]

Robinson, George, 21 Bridge St, Westminster, with workshop at 30 King St, Westminster, London, cm (1792). Took out a Sun Insurance policy on 2 July 1792 for £100. [GL, Sun MS vol. 389, ref. 602254] Probably:

Robinson, George, London, upholder and cm (1805–11). Trading at 10 Union St, Westminster, 1805–08, and 3 Cannon Row, Westminster, 1809–11. Took out a Sun Insurance policy on 26 July 1805 for £1,000 including £300 on utensils and stock, £180 on goods in trust, and £200 on utensils, stock and goods in trust in workshop over stable and coach-houses in Boar's Head Yd, King St, Westminster. [D; GL, Sun MS vol. 434, ref. 777975]

Robinson, George, London, u (1793). Subscribed to Sheraton's *Drawing Book*, 1793.

Robinson, George, London, upholder, cm and undertaker (1793–1837). Trading at 29 Little Queen St, Lincoln's Inn Fields, 1793–1803; at 2 Gt Queen St, Holborn in 1811; and as George & Son in 1826. Took out a Sun Insurance policy on 8 June 1793 for £1,000 of which utensils and stock accounted for £500. Named in Sheraton's list of master cabinet makers, 1803. [D; GL, Sun MS vol. 395, p. 284] See Bruce & Robinson at this address.

Robinson, George, Liverpool, joiner and cm (1767–95). Addresses given at Cropper St, near Ranelagh Gdns in 1767; 43 Hurst St in 1775; and 35 Park Lane in 1795. Advertised periodically between 1767–95 his methods of destroying upholstery bugs. In *Williamson's Liverpool Advertiser*, 3 July 1767, he claimed 'THAT he is possessed of an Infallible Remedy for the killing & destroying of BUGS which is quite free from any disagreeable smell ... He likewise dresses new Bedstocks for 3s. 6d. which will stand good for Sixty Years. ... N.B. Beware of having your Bedstocks dressed with Liquids, for as soon as the Liquid is dried up its Virtue is gone.' Advertised similarly in the same paper on 2 June 1775 and 9 May 1791; and in *Billinge's Liverpool Advertiser*, 11 May 1795.

Robinson, George, Liverpool, cm and chairmaker (1772–1807). Addresses given at Hale's St, 1772–73; 14 Fontenoy St in 1796; Paradise St in 1802 no. 14, 1803–05; also 23 Rainfords Gdns, Whitechapel, in 1804; 5 Rainfords Gdns, 1807–10, and also 18 Paradise St in 1807. Announcement in *Billinge's Liverpool Advertiser*, 24 May 1802 read: 'GEORGE ROBINSON, CHAIR MAKER etc: (late partner with John & Joseph Robinson) MOST respectfully informs his friends & the Public that he has taken & entered on a large & commodious SHOP, in PARADISE-STREET, next door to the STAR & GARTER TAVERN, where he has ON SALE, STAINED, PAINTED, & WINDSOR CHAIRS, CABINET GOODS, LOOKING GLASSES etc. etc. ... N.B. Ten Journeymen Chair-Makers Wanted.' Notice to the creditors of George Robinson of Paradise St regarding dividends and payment of debts, presumably on bankruptcy, given in *Liverpool Chronicle*, 2 September 1807. [D]

Robinson, George, Dale St, Liverpool, furnishing iromonger, cabinet founder, cutler etc. (1821). Advertised in *Liverpool Mercury*, 13 April 1821, that he had started business, and that his stock included 'Iron Book-cases & chests'.

Robinson, George, 70 High St, Ramsgate, Kent, cm (1826–29). [D]

Robinson, George, Foulford, Berwick-on-Tweed, Northumb., joiner and cm (1834). [D]

Robinson, George, Market Pl., Cockermouth, Cumb., cm and/or joiner (1834). [D]

Robinson, George, Northgate, Darlington, Co. Durham, cm and/or joiner (1834). [D]

Robinson, George, Battle Barrow, Westmld, joiner and/or cm (1834). [D]

Robinson, George, 7 Temple Row, Keighley, Yorks., joiner and/or cm (1837). [D]

Robinson, H., 38 Moorgate St, London, carver and gilder (1839). [D]

Robinson, Henry Sacheverell, 37 Sea Coal Lane, Snow Hill, London, knife casemaker (1781). Took out a Sun Insurance policy in 1781 for £100 of which £20 accounted for utensils and stock. [GL, Sun MS vol. 291, p. 275] Possibly:

Robinson, Henry, 11 Angel Ct, Snow Hill, removed to 18 Cow Lane, London, maker of shagreen and mahogany knife cases, tea caddies etc. (1802). Trade card recorded. [Heal]

Robinson, Henry, Liverpool, cm (1816–35). Addresses given at 8 Thomas' Pl., Hill St in 1816; 13 Warren St in 1821; no. 36, 1823–24; 25–26 Clayton St in 1827; and 24 Hill St, Copperas Hill in 1835. [D]

Robinson, Henry, 37 Clifton St, Finsbury, London, carver and gilder (1826–37). [D]

Robinson, I. B., Bull St, Birmingham, carver and gilder (1805–08). [D] See Robinson, — of Birmingham.

Robinson, Isaac, London, cm (1793). Subscribed to Sheraton's *Drawing Book*, 1793.

Robinson, Isaac, Lancaster. Named in the Gillow records, 1787–1824. [Westminster Ref. Lib.]

Robinson, Isaac jnr, Lancaster. Named in the Gillow records, 1825–35. [Westminster Ref. Lib.]

Robinson, J., 13 Ratcliff Highway, near Wellclose Sq., London, 'Bedstead Manufactory, CARPET BEDDING & FURNITURE WAREHOUSE'. Trade card, *c.*1790, reads as above and shows tallboy, bureau-bookcase, 'lit a la Polonaise', and two square-backed chairs. [Heal]

Robinson, J., 27 Oxford St and 56 Rathbone Pl., London, 'Decorator and Furnisher a l'Antique, IMPORTER OF AND DEALER IN Ancient Furniture, Pictures, Bronzes, Sculpture, Armour, Carvings, Books, China, CURIOSITIES, &c.' (1837?). Submitted a bill to G. Lucy 1837 (?), totalling £91 15s and including a library table at £47 5s. Billhead gives address and trade as above and continues: 'N.B. PART OR WHOLE COLLECTIONS CLEANED, REPAIRED, ARRANGED AND VALUED, BOUGHT, SOLD AND EXCHANGED. Commissions carefully attended to.' [Warwick RO, L6/1114 and 1118]

Robinson, J. S., 122 Old St, London, cabinet and chair manufacturer (1835). [D]

Robinson, J., Dudley, Worcs., cm (1839). [D]

Robinson, James, address unrecorded, upholder (1739). Son of Richard Robinson, farmer, of Enfield, Middlx. App. to William Kemp, and admitted freeman of the Upholders' Co. by servitude on 3 May 1739. [GL, Upholders' Co. records]

Robinson, James, address unrecorded, upholder (1746–54). Son of James Robinson, tinplate worker of Middlx. App. to Carill Pitts, freeman fishmonger, by trade upholder, on 16 March 1746. Admitted freeman of the Upholders' Co. by redemption tn 9 April 1754. [GL, Upholders' Co. records]

Robinson, James, Liverpool, cm (1765–80). Took app. named Dewhurst in 1756, presumably the John Dewhurst, cm, who petitioned freedom as former app. of James Robinson, joiner of Liverpool, in 1767. Other former apps petitioned freedom:

John Howell in 1761 and Edward Taylor in 1780. [S of G, app. index: Liverpool freemen's committee bk]

Robinson, James, Lancaster, joiner and cm (1762–95). App. to R. Thorney in 1762, and admitted freeman, 1779–80, when stated 'of Poulton in the Fylde'. Marriage to Miss Slater, eldest daughter of Mr Thomas Slater, clerk of Lancaster Parish Church, reported in *Billinge's Liverpool Advertiser*, 14 December 1795. [Lancaster app. reg. and freemen rolls]

Robinson, James, Bath, Som., cm (1774–84). Listed at Walcot in 1784. [Bristol poll bks]

Robinson, James, Sawick (?), cm (1784). [Lancaster poll bk]

Robinson, James, Liverpool, cm (1823–29). Addresses given at 22 Beany (?) St, 1823–24, with house at Fleet St in 1824; 8 Bold St with shop at 28 Tarleton St in 1827; and 36 Stanley St in 1829. [D]

Robinson, Jane, 15 Prince William St, Harrington, Liverpool, u (1835). [D]

Robinson, John, Northgate, Wakefield, Yorks., cm (1816–24). See Richard Wright & Edward Elwick.

Robinson, John, Leeds, Yorks., cm (1740). Took app. named Brown in 1740. [S of G, app. index]

Robinson, John, Bear St, London, cm (1749). [Poll bk]

Robinson, John, Hull, Yorks., cm (1774). [Poll bk]

Robinson, John, Barbican, London, cm (1779–93). Recorded at 1 New Ct when he insured his house for £100 in 1779. [D; GL, Sun MS vol. 273, p. 352]

Robinson, John & William, Sheffield, Yorks., chairmakers (1787–97). Trading at New St in 1787 and 14 West Bar in 1797. [D]

Robinson, John, Saffron St, Saffron Hill, London, cm (1787–1813). Recorded at no. 7 on 5 June 1787 when he insured household goods for £300, and at no. 5 in 1813. [D; GL, Sun MS vol. 346, p. 76] See John Rolinson at this address.

Robinson, John, London, Tunbridge-ware manufacturer (1797–1818). Addresses given at 34 Duke St, St James in 1797; next to York House, Piccadilly in 1798; 53 Piccadilly in 1799; and 51 Piccadilly, 5 Margaret St, Cavendish Sq., date unspecified. Trade cards in Banks Coll., BM; and Sprange Coll., Tunbridge Wells Museum. [D; E. Pinto, *Tunbridge and Scottish Souvenir Woodware*, 1970, p. 43]

Robinson, John, Liverpool, chairmaker (1794–1814). Recorded at 23 Mount Pleasant in 1794; 7 Gerard St, Byrom St in 1800; Pleasant St, 1803–04; no. 16 in 1805; no. 17, 1807–14; and no. 18 in 1811. [D] A John Robinson, chairmaker of Liverpool, is recorded in the accounts of lives in leases granted by the Corp. of Liverpool as aged 61 in 1821, and dying before 1833. He is presumably either this maker or:

Robinson, John, Liverpool, cm (1796–1829). Addresses given at 22 Johnson St in 1796; 13 New Fontenoy St in 1811; 2 Scotland Rd in 1816; 21 Crosshall St in 1818; no. 24 in 1821; 108 London Rd in 1827; and 140 London Rd with shop in Commutation Pl. in 1829. [D]

Robinson, John & Joseph, Liverpool, chairmakers and cm (1796–1818). Recorded in partnership with George Robinson at 43 Whitechapel in 1796; as brothers John & Joseph at no. 42 in 1804; and at 43 Whitechapel and 50 Dale St in 1805; at various numbers in Whitechapel and Dale St, 1803–16; and at Statham's Buildings, Lord St in 1818. Advertisement in *Liverpool Chronicle*, 22 May 1805 read: 'TO JOURNEYMEN CHAIR MAKERS WANTED several good workmen, at the different branches of the business, also a BEDSTEAD MAKER, who will have constant employ :- likewise a FOREMAN to the concern — an active, steady man, who perfectly understands the business, to whom a liberal salary will be paid, & may be accommodated with a House to live in, near the Works, at a moderate rent. Apply at J. & J. Robinson's Manufactory, Dale-street, or at their

warehouse, Whitechapel.' Dissolution of the partnership between John and Joseph reported in *Liverpool Mercury*, 5 December 1817. [D] See Joseph Robinson, chairmaker and cm of Liverpool.

Robinson, John, address unrecorded, cm (1803). Subscribed to Sheraton's *Cabinet Dictionary*, 1803.

Robinson, John, & Burton, William, 203 Oxford St, near Orchard St, London, japanned chair and sofa manufacturers, cabinet and upholstery warehousemen (1804–19). Trade card of 1804 recorded in Heal. Took out Sun Insurance policies on 31 January 1805 for £600 of which £400 accounted for utensils, stock and goods in trust; John alone on 13 April 1807 for £800, £400 on utensils and stock; John and William on 18 April 1809 for £1,200 including £850 on stock and utensils in their house and painting room, £150 on Robinson's household goods, and £200 on Burton's goods at 26 Adam St, East Portman Sq. A policy for the same amounts of 14 April 1810 gave Robinson's home address as 2 Jews Harp Fields, Marylebone. On 8 July 1807 Robinson & Burton were paid £11 for chairs supplied to Sir John Geers Cotterell, Bart of Garnons, near Hereford, and Hertford St, London. [D; GL, Sun MS vol. 431, ref. 772347; vol. 440, ref. 802413; vol. 448, ref. 830680; vol. 453, ref. 844406; Herefs. RO, Garnons papers, W69/III/182]

Robinson, John, Preston, Lancs., chair and bedstead maker (1816–42). Trading at Friargate in 1816, 42 Lord St in 1818, and no. 44, 1825–42. [D]

Robinson, John, 33 Wilderness Row, Goswell St, Clerkenwell, London, cm and chairmaker (1817). [D] See Joseph Robinson of Clerkenwell.

Robinson, John, Mile End Rd, Whitechapel, London, cm and chairmaker (1817). [D]

Robinson, John Thomas, 49 Curzon St, Mayfair, London, upholder and cm (1817–39). [D]

Robinson, John, 50 Bunhill Row, Chiswell St, London, cm (1820). [D] See John Rolinson at this address.

Robinson, John, Baildon, Yorks., cm (1822). [D]

Robinson, John, Norton Priory, near Doncaster, Yorks., joiner and cm (1822). [D]

Robinson, John, 30 North St, Brighton, Sussex, Tunbridge-ware manufacturer and perfumer (1822). [D]

Robinson, John, Richmond, Surrey, cm etc. (1822–26). Recorded at Upper Hill St in 1822 and Hill St in 1826, when listed as cm/chairmaker. [D]

Robinson, John, Lartington, near Romaldkirk, Yorks., cm (1823). [D]

Robinson, John, High St, Colne, Lancs., joiner and cm (1824). [D]

Robinson, John, 64 Broad St, Reading, Berks., cm (1826). [D]

Robinson, John, 12 Dorrington St, Cold Bath Sq., London, cm (1826–29). [D]

Robinson, John, High St, Bishop Wearmouth, Sunderland, Co. Durham, u (1827). [D]

Robinson, John Edwin, 37 Old Gravel Lane, Wapping, London, cm and upholder (1827–28). [D]

Robinson, John, Liverpool, u (1826–34). Addresses given at Rupert St, 21 Matthew St in 1827; 9 Rupert St in 1834; and as turner and furniture broker at 39 Stanley St and 21 Matthew St, with turner's shop at 21 Cumberland St in 1837. Marriage at St Thomas's Church to Miss Anne Tate, sixth daughter of Mr Isaac Tate of HM Customs, reported in *Liverpool Mercury*, 30 June 1826. Admitted freeman as son of Thomas Robinson, brushmaker, on 16 October 1827. [D; Liverpool freemen reg.]

Robinson, John, High Wind, Appleby, Westmld, cm (1828–34). [D]

Robinson, John, 10 St Mary's Gate, Derby, chairmaker and turner in wood and metal (1829). [D]

Robinson, John, Hayton and Melay, Aspatria, Cumb., joiner and/or cm (1829). [D]

Robinson, John, Newcastle-under-Lyme, Staffs., cm (1830–39). Trading at Wilmots Row in 1832, and no. 7, 1838–39. [D; poll bks]

Robinson, John, Richmond, Yorks., cm (1833). Child bapt. on 9 August 1833. [PR (bapt.)]

Robinson, John Kendrick, 22 Bath St, Leamington, Warks., carver, gilder and looking-glass manufacturer (1835). [D]

Robinson, Jos., Wolsingham, Co. Durham, joiner and cm (1828–29). [D]

Robinson, Joseph, Cambridge, carver (1732–54). Recorded in the St Edward's parish rate bk carrying out carved work in the Church on 12 August 1732, and 29 January 1732/33. In 1742 he was paid £10 10s for picture frames supplied to Trinity College. Two wills are recorded for Joseph Robinson, carver, one for St Edward's parish dated 1753, the other dated 1754. [Cambs. RO, P28/4/1; AR3:38 and 40]

Robinson, Joseph, Liverpool, chairmaker and cm (1790–1832). Addresses given at 39 Gerrard St in 1794; 30 Lionel St, off Gerrard St in 1796; Dale St and Whitechapel in 1800; 14 Fontenoy St, Dale St, 1803–04; Richmond Row, opposite Comus St in 1805; 77 Richmond Row, 1807–10; no. 79 in 1811; no. 76, 1813–14; no. 82 in 1816; no. 81 in 1818; warehouse at 43 Whitechapel, 1817–21; no. 55, 1824–27, with premises also at 81 Richmond Row in 1824, and 7 Stafford St in 1827. Retired from business at Whitechapel in 1832. Joseph Robinson, letter-case maker of Liverpool was admitted freeman on 24 June 1790. Notice of termination of the partnership with his brother, John Robinson, given in *Liverpool Mercury*, 5 December 1817. Joseph announced that he would continue the business on his own account, and had on sale at his warehouse, 43 Whitechapel, 'an elegant & complete assortment of Chairs, Sofas, & Grecian Couches, of the most approved & fashionable London Patterns; also Cabinet Furniture, in fine Mahogany, Rosewood, etc. elegant Four Post & Camp Bedsteads, of the best workmanship, & on the most reasonable terms. N.B. Merchants & Captains of ships supplied on liberal terms, & at the shortest notice.' Death of his eldest son, George Robinson, aged 28, on 18 October 1823 'at Southwood Lodge, near Nachez', reported in *Liverpool Mercury*, 19 December. Notice regarding the sale of stock of 'CABINET FURNITURE of a VERY SUPERIOR MANUFACTURE' on Joseph Robinson's retirement given in the same paper, 9 November 1832. Stock consisted of 'Bookcase with Glazed Doors, Wardrobes, Chests of Drawers, modern Pedestal Sideboards, several sets of Chairs & sofas in black hair cloth, Pembroke, Loo, Sofa, & Elliptic Pillar Card Tables, Dressing Glasses, Portable Desks, Tea Chests, Caddies etc. in Mahogany, Rosewood etc. A set of Imitation Rosewood Chairs, & a Couch in Canvass, with other Articles. The well-known excellence of Mr. Robinson's Manufacture, as well as the goodness of material & the modern fashion, render these articles well worth the attention of the Public.' [D; Liverpool freemen reg.] See John & Joseph Robinson.

Robinson, Joseph, Liverpool, cm (1809). Admitted freeman on 7 February 1809. [Liverpool freemen reg.]

Robinson, Joseph, Liverpool, cm (1812). Admitted freeman on servitude to William Harvey on 6 October 1812. [Liverpool freemen reg.]

Robinson, Joseph, Preston, Lancs, cm (1799–1802). Signed the *Preston Cabinet Makers' and Chair Makers' Book of Prices*, 1799, on behalf of the masters and also the 1802 edition. Named with his brother John in the Preston Guild record of burgesses in 1802.

Robinson, Joseph, Lancaster, cm (1799–1833). Named in the Gillow records, 1799–1833, as the brother of Isaac. App. to J. Addison in 1806 and admitted freeman, 1806–07. [Westminster Ref. Lib.; Lancaster app. reg. and freemen rolls] Possibly two tradesmen of the same name.

Robinson, Joseph, Clerkenwell, London, cm, chairmaker, auctioneer, appraiser, u, undertaker and bed-pillar carver (1823–39). Recorded at 33 Wilderness Row, Goswell St, 1823–29; and as J. Robinson at 154 Goswell St in 1835. [D] See John Robinson at 33 Wilderness Row, Goswell St.

Robinson, Joshua, Grimshaw St, Preston, Lancs., joiner and cm (1814–18). [D]

Robinson, Leonard, York, cm (1745–66). On 11 October 1745 it was recorded that as a Papist he was required not to travel more than five miles from his house without a licence. Listed in 1766 as a Papist in St John del Pike parish. [York City archives, quarter sessions bk; York Minster Lib., C/IIIa]

Robinson, Mark, Coney St, York, cm and joiner (1776). Advertised in *York Courant*, 4 June 1776, offering thanks for past support, and recommending Christopher Sedgwick, his late servant, who was taking over the business.

Robinson, Nicholas, Hedon, near Hull, Yorks., carpenter, cm and joiner (1826–29). [D]

Robinson, Peter, Leeds, Yorks., journeyman cm (1791). Named in the *Leeds Cabinet and Chair Makers' Book of Prices*, 1791, with other journeymen in basic sympathy with its contents.

Robinson, R. & Son, Gt Queen St, London, trunk and platecase maker, writing and dressing case manufacturer (1819–37). Recorded at no. 54 in 1819, and no. 53 in 1837. [D] See Robinson, —.

Robinson, R. snr and jnr, Barnoldswick, Yorks., cm (1822). [D]

Robinson, Ralph, Lench St, Birmingham, cm (1800). [D]

Robinson, Ralph, New Elvet, Durham, cm and looking-glass silverer (c.1820–d.1880). Recorded at 85 New Elvet, date unspecified; and in the *City Almanac*, 1861. Retired in 1865, and died on 21 March 1880, when his obituary declared that he had 'commenced his business nearly 60 years ago'. Recorded as the maker of a circular oak table on pillar and base, c.1850. [D; Aldridge's, Bath, 8 November 1983, lot 131; Bowes Museum archive, Barnard Castle]

Robinson, Richard, at 'The Flower Pot', Beaufort St, Strand, London, looking-glass maker (1697–1711). Recorded in newspapers in 1697. [Heal] Advertised in *London Gazette*, 14–17 November 1698, his 'Engine for Grinding, Pollishing and Cutting Looking-Glass Plates (for which a Patent is granted by His Majesty) by which Glass is truly ground and pollished with the best black pollish: and also the borders cut most curiously hollow, and with a better lustre than any heretofore done ... There are also sold the new-invented Frames for Coach-Glass Plates, or for windows, of ¾ inch broad, made of metal of a Gold colour.' Robinson supplied looking-glasses to Drayton House, Northants.: in October 1700, a 'great glass' costing 37 guineas; from September 1701 to July 1702 items totalling £46, and including a 'mould frame & a glass head' at £15; and from May to September 1707 items totalling £215, including a 'glass in a carved frame', £35. In partnership with Thomas Howcraft, Robinson supplied looking-glasses to the Earl of Nottingham for Burley-on-the-Hill in 1711. In the previous year he had advertised in the *Tatler*, 19 April, that the 'Engine Looking Glass Wharehouse' was leaving off trade, with 'no more of the Engine-Work to be had after this sale'. The glasses sent to the Earl of Nottingham were probably made prior to this event. [Wills, *Looking-Glasses*; DEF; *The Antique Collector*,

November–December 1947; *C. Life*, 15 February 1930; V&A archives]

Robinson, Richard, St Giles, Cripplegate, London, cm (1718). Named in contemporary newspapers. [Heal]

Robinson, Richard, York, cm (1788–1802). Son of Joshua Robinson, joiner; app. to William Stables, cm on 9 July 1788. Admitted freeman of York in 1802, when stated of Manchester. [York app. reg. and freemen rolls]

Robinson, Richard S., 7 Bold St, Liverpool, u and cm (1825–35). Advertised in *Liverpool Mercury*, 1 April 1825 the opening of his 'NEW UPHOLSTERY & CABINET WAREHOUSE, No. 7, BOLD-STREET (opposite Jowett's London-house)' where 'he trusts several years' practical experience which he has had in some of the first houses in London (since his apprenticeship here) will ensure him a part of their patronage. He now submits to their notice an entire new Stock of Cabinet Furniture, Carpets, Floor Cloths, London Papers, etc: all of which he will warrant to be of the best quality & as reasonable as any house in the trade. N.B. A FOREMAN wanted to the Cabinet Business'. Marriage at St Anne's Church to Agnes, third daughter of Mr Paton, brewer, of Seel St reported in *Liverpool Mercury*, 6 February 1829. [D]

Robinson, Richard, 59 Barr St, Birmingham, fancy box, case and caddy maker (1835). [D]

Robinson, Robert, St Oswald's parish, Durham, spinning-wheel maker (1725–29). Marriage at Simondburn (Simonburn, Northumb.?) registered on 21 October 1725. Daughter bapt. on 16 September 1726. Death of son registered on 10 January 1729. [PR]

Robinson, Robert, address unrecorded, carver (1762). Executed carved work according to designs by Robert Adam for Sir Nathaniel Curzon at Kedleston Hall, Derbs. in 1762. For the breakfast room Robinson carved a pair of giltwood window seats, with turned fluted legs and scalloped aprons ornamented with acanthus leaves; and for the same room, a pair of mahogany tables, their frames with flute and acanthus leaf decoration supported on spiral twist legs. Their scagliola slabs bearing the coat of arms of Sir Nathaniel and Lady Caroline Curzon among a spray of oak leaves, were probably supplied from Florence by L. C. Gori. [*Conn.*, July 1978, pp. 200–01, illus.]

Robinson, Robert, Tamworth, Staffs., cm (1784–98). [D]

Robinson, Robert, North Bar St (Within), Beverley, Yorks., cm (1831–40). [D]

Robinson, S., 18 and 19 Phoenix St, Soho, London, frame maker (1837). [D]

Robinson, Samuel, at 'The Royal Tent', Red Cross St, Southwark, London, bedstead and cm, sworn appraiser and auctioneer (1780). Trade card in Banks Coll., BM, and also on a mahogany chest-on-chest in private ownership. [V&A archives]

Robinson, Samuel, 27 Prince's St, Dale St, Liverpool, cm (1800). [D]

Robinson, Samuel, Prescot, Lancs., cm (1832). Death of his wife, Lydia, aged 72, reported in *Liverpool Mercury*, 6 July 1832.

Robinson, T., London, u (1827). Declared bankrupt, *Chester Chronicle and North Wales Advertiser*, 12 January 1827.

Robinson, Thomas, address unrecorded, upholder (1771). Son of Richard Robinson; app. to Benjamin Dell, and admitted freeman of the Upholders' Co. by servitude on 6 November 1771. [GL, Upholders' Co. records]

Robinson, Thomas, Hosier Lane, Smithfield, London, bedstead maker (1784). [D]

Robinson, Thomas, London, cm (1793). Subscribed to Sheraton's *Drawing Book*, 1793.

Robinson, Thomas, Liverpool, cm (1780). Admitted freeman on

servitude to Joseph Baxendale on 13 September 1780. [Liverpool freemen reg.]

Robinson, Thomas, Liverpool, cm (1790). Admitted freeman on servitude to Edward Lowe on 21 June 1790. [Liverpool freemen reg.]

Robinson, Thomas, Liverpool, cm (1790–96). Addresses given at 10 Haymarket in 1790; 27 Paradise St in 1794; and 35 Lionel St in 1796. [D]

Robinson, Thomas, 7 or 18 Richmond Row, Liverpool, cm (1816). Admitted freeman as son of Charles Robinson, cooper, on 8 June 1816. [Liverpool freemen reg.]

Robinson, Thomas, Liverpool, cm (1819). Marriage at St Anne's Church to Alice Howard, daughter of John Howard, wheelwright, of Gt Crosby, Lancs., reported in *Liverpool Mercury*, 28 May 1819.

Robinson, Thomas, 6 Lower Thurlow St, Liverpool, cm (1823–29). [D]

Robinson, Thomas Baker, Birmingham, carver, gilder, glass grinder, polisher and picture frame maker (1800–35). Recorded at High St in 1800; 64 Bull St in 1803; Temple Row in 1805; at 61 Bull St, 1816–22, and at 64 Bull St, 1828–35, also as a looking-glass manufacturer and restorer of old paintings. [D]

Robinson, Thomas, Hull, Yorks., cm (1803–39). Addresses given at Dock St and Clarence Ct, Princes St in 1803; North St in 1806; Southend, High St in 1810; Cogan St in 1834; Mytongate in 1838; and 3 Daltry's Ct, Mytongate, and William's Pl., Cogan St in 1839. Took apps named William Porter of Hull in September 1804; William Oliver of Owstwick in November 1804; Benjamin Ward of Sculcoates in December 1807; and Benjamin Matson of Sculcoates in June 1808. [D; Hull app. reg.] Possibly two tradesmen of the same name. See William Robinson at William's Pl., Coggan St.

Robinson, Thomas, Salford and Manchester, u (1813–34). Recorded at 18 Gravel Lane, Salford, in 1813; 22 Cable St, Salford, in 1817; 85 Greengate, Manchester in 1825; and 32 Bridge St, Manchester, 1832–34 as cm and u. [D]

Robinson, Thomas, Altofts, near Normanton, Yorks., cm (1822). [D]

Robinson, Thomas Wilkinson, Ironmonger St, Stamford, Lincs., carver and gilder (1828). [D]

Robinson, Thomas, Staindrop, Co. Durham, u, cm and/or joiner (1831–34). Daughter bapt. on 17 August 1831. [D; PR (bapt.)]

Robinson, Thomas, South Shields, Co. Durham, cm and/or joiner (1834). [D]

Robinson, Thomas, High Wycombe, Bucks., chairmaker (b. c. 1811–41). Aged 30 at the time of the 1841 Census.

Robinson, William, Lancaster, joiner and cm (1763–80). App. to R. Thorney in 1763, and admitted freeman, 1779–80, when stated 'of Preston'. [Lancaster app. reg. and freemen rolls]

Robinson, William, address unrecorded. In 1780 he was named in the accounts of Sir John Griffin Griffin of Audley End, Essex, for daywork and materials for repairs to a dressing table and small mahogany flower stand, for which he was paid £2 0s 4d. [Essex RO, D/DBy/A38/3]

Robinson, William, Oxford, upholder (1780–1808). Polled of St Mary the Virgin parish in 1802, and trading at High St, 1805–08. Notice given in *Jackson's Oxford Journal*, 1 April 1780, that John Wood, upholder, had taken William Robinson as partner. Robinson took out a Sun Insurance policy in 1783 for £500 including £400 on utensils and stock. [D; GL, Sun MS vol. 306, p. 667]

Robinson, William, Ribchester, Lancs., cm (1784). [Lancaster poll bk]

Robinson, William, 11 Preston St, Liverpool, cm (1790). [D]

Robinson, William, Hull, Yorks., cm and chairmaker (1806–35). Recorded at Witham, 1806–14, with residence at 1 Prospect Pl., Drypool in 1826; and William's Pl., Coggan St in 1835. [D] See Thomas Robinson of Hull.

Robinson, William, 14 North St, City Rd, London, cm and joiner (1808). [D]

Robinson, William, Gainsborough, Lincs., joiner, cm and u (1816). App. to William Rollett of Gainsborough, Lincs., in March 1816. [Hull app. reg.]

Robinson, William, 2 Leece St, Liverpool, u (1821). [D]

Robinson, William, Bold St, Liverpool, u (1817–24). Addresses given at no. 68 from 1817, with general upholstery warehouse at no. 71 from February 1818; nos 68 and 71 from May 1818; and as William Robinson & Co., general u, at no. 85 in 1821. Advertised the opening of his shop at 68 Bold St in *Liverpool Mercury*, 4 April 1817, 'for the Sale of Feather Beds, Blankets, Carpets, Paper Hangings etc. & having selected an entirely new & elegant assortment of the best articles, now ready for inspection, & which he is enabled to offer on the most moderate terms . . .'. Announced in the same paper on 13 February 1818 that, 'for the greater advantage of carrying on his trade, he has connected himself with a house of the first respectability, & has removed from no. 68 to 71, three doors lower, where business will, in future, be carried on by himself & company. From having laid in an extensive stock of Carpets before the recent advance; importing & preparing their own Feathers; selecting their stock of Paper Hangings from the best London Manufacturers; & have personally opened a communication with the principal houses in *Paris*, in the trade, the Public may rely on being supplied with a greater variety & on more reasonable terms, than by any other house in the trade. From these considerations, W.R. & Co. hope to merit a Continuance of that preference which the house has hitherto so amply experienced. W.R. & Co. have just received, *direct from Paris*, the following beautiful decorations, which, from *execution & richness of colouring*, exceed anything hitherto exhibited:- Cupid & Psyche, Telemachus in the Island of Calypso, Views of the Monuments & Public Buildings in Paris, Views from Captain Cook's Voyages to Otaheita, Views of a Turkish Seraglio, from the shores of the Bosphorus etc: with Suitable Gold & Flock Borders.' Re-opening of the shop at 68 Bold St announced in *Liverpool Mercury*, 1 May 1818 'for the Sale of Paper Hangings only'. The firm also sold 'Feathers, Bedding, Carpets, & every article in the Upholstery Business'. Death of William Robinson's second daughter, Ellen, aged 3, reported in the same paper on 21 March 1823. W. Robinson, u of Liverpool, was declared bankrupt, *London Gazette*, 6 July 1824. [D]

Robinson, William H., 3 Cleaver St, Kennington Cross, London, carver and gilder (1826). [D]

Robinson, William, Catton Village, Allendale, Northumb., joiner and cm (1827). [D]

Robinson, William, 7 Clifton Pl., Bristol, carpenter and cm (1829–30). [D]

Robinson, William Stevinson, Northallerton, Yorks., cm, u and undertaker (1830–40). Trade card shows a typical range of Late Regency furniture beneath flamboyantly arranged curtains. [D; Leeds City Lib., local history dept]

Robinson, William, Market Pl., Pocklington, Yorks., cm (1831–34). [D]

Robinson, William, Hatfield, near Doncaster, Yorks., joiner and cm (1834). [D]

Robinson, William, Thorne, Yorks., joiner and/or cm (1834). [D]

Robinson, William, 4 Green St, Blackfriars Rd, London, cm and u (1839). [D]

Robinson, Wilson, King St, Hammersmith, London, cm (1826).[D]

Robinson, Woodhall (or Wodhull), corner of Red Lyon Ct, Fleet St, St Dunstan's in the West, London, cm and joiner (1714–18). Took out a Sun Insurance policy on 9 October 1714 on goods and merchandise in his house; and a Hand in Hand policy in November 1715 for £450 on his house. Robinson, cm at this address, was named in newspapers in 1718. [GL, Sun MS vol. 4, p. 97; GL, Hand in Hand MS vol. 15, p. 266; Heal]

Robinson & Robson, Welbeck St, London, upholder and cm (1837–39). Recorded at no. 68 in 1837 and no. 63 in 1839. [D]

Robotham, —, address unrecorded. In 1791–92 supplied items to Baron Grey de Wilton, formerly Sir Thomas Egerton, Bart, later 1st Earl of Wilton, for Heaton Hall, Manchester. On 26 November 1791 he received £2 16s for two firescreens; and on 9 July 1792, £7 5s for a music stand and a writing desk. [Preston RO, DDEg]

Robshaw, Levi, Doncaster, Yorks., cm (1834). [D]

Robson, Anthony, Newcastle, u (1741–62). Son Joseph admitted freeman by patrimony on 11 January 1762. [Poll bk; Newcastle freemen reg.]

Robson, Benjamin, Newcastle, joiner, cm, furniture broker and joiner (1811–38). Trading at Scotch Arms Yd, Nun's-gate, 1811–24; and 48 Groat Mkt, 1833–38, also 9 St John's Lane in 1833. [D]

Robson, Christopher, Newcastle, u (1755). [Newcastle freemen reg.]

Robson, David, Castle Yd, Newcastle, cm and carpenter (1778). [D]

Robson, Dawson, Newcastle, joiner and cm (1759). Took app. named Newton in 1759. [S of G, app. index]

Robson, Edward, Lincoln's Inn Fields, London, cm (1780–82). Recorded at Newmans Row in 1780, when he insured stock and utensils for £600 with the Sun Co. Declared bankrupt, *Gents Mag.*, March 1782. [GL, Sun MS vol. 289, p. 77]

Robson, Edward, Blackwellgate, Darlington, Co. Durham, cm and/or joiner (1834). [D]

Robson, James, Blackfriars St, Carlisle, Cumb., cm and/or joiner (1834). [D]

Robson, John, Newcastle, u (1702–41). App. to Robert Webster and admitted freeman on 11 March 1702/03. Notice in *London Gazette*, 26 May 1707 read: 'Whereas the Rt. Hon. the Lord High Chancellor of Great Britain hath referred the Certificate of John Robson, late of Newcastle upon Tine, Upholsterer, unto the Lord Chief Baron Ward and Mr. Justice Powis, in order for them to confirm the same.' Polled in 1741. [Newcastle freemen reg.]

Robson, John, Battle Hill, Hexham, Northumb., joiner and cm (1834). [D]

Robson, John, South Shields, Co. Durham, cm and/or joiner (1834). [D]

Robson, Joseph, Lincoln, carver (1746). [Lincoln RO, subject index — Careers, DAW1/42]

Robson, Joseph, London, u (1774–77). [Newcastle poll bks]

Robson, Matthew, Execution Dock, Newcastle, cm and carpenter (1778). [D]

Robson, Philip, Front St, Brampton, Cumb., joiner and/or cm (1829–34). [D]

Robson, Robert, 64 Northumberland St, Newcastle, cm and u (1838). [D]

Robson, Thomas, London, cm (1793). Subscribed to Sheraton's *Drawing Book*, 1793.

Robson, Thomas, Patrington, Yorks., cm (1798). [D]

Robson, Thomas, Liverpool, joiner and cm, carver and gilder (1835–39). Addresses given at 35 with shop at 38 Parliament St in 1835, and 58 Stanhope St in 1839. [D]

Robson, Timothy, Newcastle, u (1726). Admitted freeman on 22 November 1726. [Newcastle freemen reg.]

Robson, William, Allendale, Northumb., joiner and/or cm (1827–34). [D]

Robson & Hale, London, paper hangers (1833–40). Carried out mostly jobbing work at Kensington, St James's and Buckingham Palaces, including re-gilding of mouldings, and supplying eighteen 'honeysuckle corners for the angles, in old gold', for the King's Closet at St James's. [PRO, LC11/80–110] Supplied furniture to Mount Stewart, Co. Down. [*C. Life*, 13 March 1980, p. 755]

Robson & Spark, Manors, Newcastle, cm (1838). [D]

Roby, Moses, address unrecorded, upholder (1709–10). Admitted freeman of the Upholders' Co. on 1 February 1709/10. [GL, Upholders' Co. records]

Roby, Richard, Chester, cm (1834). His only daughter, Jane's marriage at Trinity Church to Edward Roberts, book-keeper, reported in *Liverpool Mercury*, 23 May 1834.

Roby, Thomas, address unrecorded, upholder (1715–25). Son of Thomas Roby, yeoman of Tamworth, Staffs.; app. to John Houseman on 3 October 1715 and admitted freeman of the Upholders' Co. by servitude on 2 June 1725. [GL, Upholders' Co. records]

Rock, Edward, 28 Moor St, Birmingham, cm (1770). [D]

Rock, John, Charles Ct, Charing Cross, London, upholder (1727). Named in contemporary newspapers. [Heal] See John Rocke.

Rock, Thomas, Canterbury, Kent, cm (1756–d.1780/81). Took apps named Kidder in 1756, Wike in 1759 and Walter in 1762. Death reported in *Gents Mag.*, January 1781. [S of G, app. index]

Rocke, John, address unrecorded, upholder (1713–20). Son of John Rocke, Gent. of Somerset. App. to Henry Lowth on 29 September 1713 and admitted freeman of the Upholders' Co. by servitude on 7 October 1720. [GL, Upholders' Co. records] See John Rock.

Rockliff, Henry, Tadcaster, Yorks., joiner and/or cm (1834). [D]

Rockliff, Thomas, East Tadcaster, Yorks., joiner and/or cm (1837). [D]

Rodbart, Thomas, 9 Curriers Row, Bristow St, Water Lane, Blackfriars, London, cm (1812). Took out a Sun Insurance policy on 26 August 1812 for £150 on household goods and wearing apparel. [GL, Sun MS vol. 455, ref. 873479]

Rodd, H., 17 Air St, Piccadilly, London, carver and gilder (1826–27). [D]

Rodd, John, Topsham, Devon, cm (1797). [D]

Rodd, William, Broad Wall, Southwark, London, cm (1779). Took out a Sun Insurance policy in 1779 for £100 of which utensils, stock and goods accounted for £40. [GL, Sun MS vol. 273, p. 207]

Rodda, Thomas, Launceston, Cornwall, cm, u and glass silverer (1766–67). Announced in *Sherborne Mercury*, 5 and 12 January 1767, that he 'Intends to leave off Business. Any Person inclinable to take the Stock and Fixtures, may have them on reasonable Terms. There is good Beach Benches, a good Stone for silvering on, and every Conveniency for carrying on the three Branches. And there is a good Trade established. There is no other of the Branch here, or within many miles of this Place. There are six Market Towns that have most of their Furniture from here. Who this may suit, may be instructed in Glass silvering and gilding — Letters (Post Paid) punctually answered. N.B. A good Chest of Tools to be sold, Launceston, Dec. 17 1766.'

Roddam, Thomas, Staithes, Yorks., joiner, cm and/or cartwright (1834). [D]

Roddis, John, Wood Hill, Northampton, u (1774). [Poll bk]

Rodds, John, Fore St, Upper Edmonton, London, cm (1838–39). [D]

Roden, Samuel, Hodnet, Market Drayton, Salop, cm (1840). [D]

Rodger, William, Saltergate, Chesterfield, Derbs., cm (1828–35). [D]

Rodgers, Robert, Sheffield, Yorks., cm (1805–22). Trading at Norfolk St, 1805–08, High St in 1817 and West Bar, 1818–22. [D]

Rodgers, Thomas, 24 Campo Lane, Sheffield, Yorks., chairmaker (1797). [D]

Rodick, John, 3 Templer Terr., 11 George St, Liverpool, cm (1839). [D]

Rodman, Richmond, Sign of 'The Crown', Guard House Passage, Maryport St, Bristol, cm (1820–21). [D]

Rodway, John, Edgbaston St, Birmingham, cm, auctioneer, appraiser and importer of goose feathers (1816–18). [D]

Rodwell, James, 'At the Royal Bed & Star the 2nd Door from the Corner of New Broad Street, faceing Bedlam Walk in Moorfields', London, u and sworn appraiser (1743–62). Trade card [MMA, NY] shows a 'lit à la duchesse' within an ornate surround of heavy Baroque acanthus scrolls. Card states that Rodwell 'Buys, Sells & Appraises all manner of Household Goods, New & Old, as Standing Beds & Bedding, Chests of Drawers, Desk & Book-Cases, Bueroe [*sic*] Desks, Card, Dining, Breakfast & Dressing Tables, (in Mahogany, Walnuttree or Wainscot) Chairs of all Sorts, Settee & Bueroe Bedsteads, Sconces, Pier, Chimney & Dressing Glasses, with all other Sorts of Upholstery, Cabinet & Braizery Goods &c.' A later and more elaborate card [BM] is in the Rococo-Chinoiserie style and shows a mid 18th-century bed chamber with a 'lit d'ange'. Card gives same address and details of stock, with the addition of 'All Sorts of Paper Hangings for Rooms, Stair Cases &c. of the Newest Patterns.' Card has a bill on the back for 'a fine Mahogany double chest of drawers with a table in it' and is dated 1756. Rodwell was still in business in 1762 when an app. was bound to him. A receipt dated 1743 [GL], is signed by James Rodwell for the business of William Tomkins, whose trade card is very similar. Rodwell appears to have taken over Tomkins's business by August 1760, and to have been succeeded by John Brown. [Heal; V&A archives]

Rodwell, James, Leeds, Yorks., journeyman cm (1791). Named in the *Leeds Cabinet and Chair Makers' Book of Prices*, 1791, with other journeymen in basic sympathy with its contents.

Rodwell, John, Kirkgate, Tadcaster, Yorks., joiner and/or cm (1837). [D]

Rodwell, William, at 'The Walnut Tree' south side of St Paul's Churchyard, London, window blind and frame maker (1726–32). Heal records him in newspapers of 1726. William Rodwell, near Ludgate, supplied Earl Fitzwalter of Moulsham Hall with 'Two Window Blinds of Canvas, Mosaic Gilt', for which he was paid £4 3s on 9 February 1732. [A. C. Edwards, *The Accounts of Benjamin Mildmay, Earl Fitzwalter*, p. 103]

Roe (or Row), Benjamin Hambling, Norwich, u and paper hanger (1810–42). Addresses given at Colegate St in 1810, St George's Colegate, 1812–22 and St George's Plain, 1830–42. Former app. of Charles Martin and Benjamin Row, George Arnold, upholder, admitted freeman on 27 September 1817. Former app. of Benjamin Hambling Roe, Robert Hare, u, admitted freeman on 3 May 1833. [D; Norwich freemen reg. and poll bks]

Roe (or Rowe), George, Mardol, Shrewsbury, Salop, cm (1835). [Shrewsbury burgess roll]

Roe, Roger, Fillingley, Northants., cm (1754–61). Subscribed to Chippendale's *Director*, 1754. Took app. named James Coleman in 1761 for £10 10s. [V&A archives]

Roe, William, Dursley, Glos., cm (1825). [PR (bapt.)]

Roefe, Samuel, address unrecorded, u (c.1680). Paid £1 5s 6d by Threadneedle St Relief. [*Hogarth Soc.*, 1949, p. 16]

Roentgen, Abraham, cm (b.1711–d.1793) working in London c.1733–38. A celebrated German cm, born at Mühlheim on the Rhine, who learned his trade from Gottfried, his father. He left home in 1731 to work with masters at the Hague, Rotterdam and Amsterdam. About 1733 he moved to London where, according to a private family chronicle, he specialised in 'engraving, making mosaics in wood and producing mechanical devices and was sought after by the most expert masters' one of whom was 'Master Gern at Newcastle House, St. John's Square, Clerkenwell' — clearly a garbled reference to the furniture maker William Gomm of that address. About 1765 he despatched one of his own workmen Michael Rummer 'to stay a year' with his old master. While in London, Abraham joined the Moravian Brotherhood before returning to Germany in 1738. Nothing definite is known about Abraham's London products, but the Anglo-Germanic character of some brass inlaid furniture attributed to the Channon workshop has fuelled speculation that he was associated with this firm. About 1752 Abraham founded a workshop at Neuwied, near Coblenz, which established a European reputation for prodigy furniture. His son, David, who styled himself 'Englischer Kabinettmacher' was the premier continental *ébéniste* of his generation. The workshop closed down about 1795. [H. Huth, *Roentgen Furniture*, 1974; J. M. Greber, *Abraham und David Roentgen*, 2 vols, Starnberg, 1980; *Burlington*, June 1980, p. 395]
C.G.G.

Rofe, Thomas, Liverpool, u and cm (1835–39). Recorded at 120 Mount Pleasant in 1835; no. 124 and also 31 Vauxhall Rd in 1837; and 52 St Anne St in 1839. [D]

Roffway, James, Charlotte Pl., Maidstone, Kent, cm (1839). [D]

Roffway, John snr, All Saints, Canterbury, Kent, cm (1790–93). [D; poll bk]

Roffway, John jnr, Margate, Kent, cm (1818). [Canterbury poll bk]

Rofs, D., 98 Gt Portland St, London, carver and gilder (1814). [D]

Roger, —, address unrecorded, upholder (1792). Named in the Longford Castle, Wilts. accounts in 1792 receiving £4 8s 6d. [V&A archives]

Rogers, —, address unrecorded, u (1710). Named in the accounts for Felbrigg, Norfolk, in June 1710, receiving payments of £45 and £12 8s. [Norfolk RO Felbrigg papers, WKC 6/23, index of payments, 1707–12]

R-gers, —, Houndsditch, London, cm (1770). Notice in *Gents Mag.*, June 1770 read: 'Sunday 27 May. Mr. Venables, a respectable butcher in Whitechapel and Mr. R-gers, an eminent cabinet maker in Houndsditch, were both shot dead by villains who attempted to rob them but were resisted.'

Rogers, —, address unrecorded. In 1783 received payment of £31 11s 6d for a large library bookcase supplied to Brandsby Hall, Yorks. [C. Life, 9 January 1769]

Rogers, Andrew, Nantwich, Cheshire, chairmaker (1806). Daughter Mary Ann by wife Jane bapt. on 16 September 1806. [Chester RO, PR (bapt.)]

Rogers, Charles, Clifton, Bristol, cm, joiner and house carpenter (1819). App. to his father, Daniel Rogers, on 6 September 1819.

Rogers, Daniel, King's Lynn, Norfolk, joiner and cm (1711). Took apps named Cufaud and Giles in 1711. [S of G, app. index]

Rogers, Daniel, Clifton, Bristol, house carpenter, joiner and cm (1819). Took his son, Charles, as app. on 6 September 1819.

Rogers, Francis & Daniel, Love St, Hotwells, Bristol, cm, carpenters and undertakers (1824–26). [D]

Rogers, George, Docks, Gloucester, chairmaker (1839–40). [D]

Ro(d)gers, Isaac, Crosland, near Huddersfield, Yorks., joiner and/or cm (1822–30). [D]

Rogers, James, Sherborne, Dorset, cm (1793). Mentioned as a cm in deeds printed in *Dorset Nat. Hist. and Arch. Proceedings*, vol. LIII, p. 192.

Rogers, James Sampson, Mardyke, Hotwells, Bristol, cm (1817–24). Recorded at 54 Mardyke, 1819–24. [D]

Rogers, John, address unrecorded, u (1725). On 26 March 1725 Rogers was paid 1s. for 'takeing down the Yellow China bed' at Erddig, Denbighshire. This is possibly the state bed delivered in 1720, and still at Erddig. Since no carriage was paid, Rogers was probably a local u. [V&A archives]

Roger(s), John, Hereford, u (1734). [Bristol poll bk]

Rogers, John, Stock's Yd, Mill St, Leeds, Yorks., cm (1822). [D]

Ro(d)gers, Margaret, Liverpool, u (1827–37). Addresses given at 1 and/or 11 Craven St in 1827, no. 25 in 1829; and 10 Greek St, 1834–37. [D]

Rogers, Marmaduke, Gee-Cross, Hyde, near Stockport, Lancs., cm (1825). [D]

Rogers, Richard, near Gt Turnstile, Holborn, London, upholder (1725). Named in contemporary newspapers. [Heal]

Rogers, Richard, Stratford, Essex, carver and gilder (1835–37). [D]

Rogers, Richard, Preston St, Faversham, Kent, cm (1838–39). [D]

Rogers, Robert, Chester, cm (1708–d.1757). Admitted freeman in December 1708. Chosen as almsman to Richard Bird, merchant, 1749–50. [Chester RO]

Rogers, Robert, Preston, Lancs., cm (1732). [Chester poll bk]

Rogers, Robert, Weaverham, Cheshire, cm (1747). [Chester poll bk]

Rogers, Robert, Castle St, Long Acre, London, broker and cm (1804–07). Recorded at the corner of Belton St in 1804 and at the corner of Hanover St in 1807. Took out a Sun Insurance policy on 28 April 1804 for £1,000 including £500 on utensils and stock, and £400 on those in his shop on the south side of Castle St. On 12 January 1807 he insured stock and utensils for £750, and £400 on houses in tenure of a cm and a broker. [GL, Sun MS vol. 431, ref. 762227; vol. 437, ref. 798736]

Rogers, Robert, Plymouth, Devon, carver and gilder (1823–36). Addresses given at 5 Frankfort St, 1823–24; Treville St and Whimple St in 1830; and Lockyer Terr. in 1836. [D]

Rogers, Robert, 73 French St, Southampton, Hants., carver and gilder (1839). [D]

Rogers, Samuel, Sign of 'The Funeral in Procession', George St, near St George's Fields, London, cm (1775). Insured his house for £100 in 1775. [GL, Sun MS vol. 240, p. 406]

Rogers, Samuel, York Buildings, Bridgwater, Som., cm and u (1830). [D]

Rogers, Thomas, at 'The Blew Boar', next door to 'The White Horse Inn', Fleet St, London, u (1675–d.1687). Heal records him in contemporary newspapers. Notice in *London Gazette*, 14 April 1687 reads: 'At the Blew-Boar next door to the White Horse Inn in Fleet Street will be exposed to Sale, the Household Goods of Mr. Thomas Rogers, Upholsterer, lately deceased, viz. Tapistry Hangings, Carpets, and Printed Stuffs, Damask Beds, Mahair Beds and Camblet Beds, lined or unlined, Feather Beds, Rugs, Blankets, pewter and Brass etc. and a collection of Italian and other Pictures. The Sale will begin on Wednesday the 20th Instant.'

Rogers, Thomas, address unrecorded, upholder (1710–18). Admitted freeman of the Upholders' Co. on 5 July 1710. Took app. named Benjamin Adams, 1710/11–1717/18. [GL, Upholders' Co. records]

Rogers, Thomas & Goodwin, Richard, The corner house of Queen St, Bartholomew Close, London, upholders (1713).

Insured goods on 14 January 1713. [GL, Sun MS vol. 2, p. 164]

Rogers, Thomas, Brook St, Ipswich, Suffolk, 'from London', upholder and sworn appraiser (1728). Advertised in *Ipswich Journal*, 27 January 1728 that he had 'taken a Ware House the next Door to the Coach House, in Brookstreet, Ipswich, all Gentlemen, Ladies and Others, may be supply'd with the best of Goods, and have all Sorts of Beds, Window Curtains, Hangings, Chairs, &c. made up and compleatly fixed in the neatest and newest Fashion. N.B. Letters and Parcels are desired to be directed for Thomas Rogers at Mr. Samuel Debnam at the Coach House In Ipswich.'

Rogers, Thomas, Norwich, u (1774). App. to Henry Withers and admitted freeman on 3 May 1774. [Norwich freemen reg.]

Rogers, Thomas, Strand, London. On 7 November 1786 a patent (no. 1568) was granted to Thomas Rogers for 'A new method of ornamenting looking glasses, picture frames & other kinds of furniture, with carved & moulded glass in relief plain or coloured — applicable to many other purposes.' [Wills, *Looking-Glasses*]

Rogers, Thomas, London, upholder (1806–30). Recorded at Paddington in 1830. [Norwich poll bks]

Rogers, Thomas, Ironbridge, Salop, cm (1828). [D]

Rogers, Thomas, Angel Lane, Penrith, Cumb., joiner and/or cm (1828–29). Recorded also at Burrow Gate in 1829. [D]

Rogers, Walter, at 'The White Lyon', Basinghall St, London, cm (d.1738). Sale of stock on his death advertised in contemporary newspapers. [Heal]

Rogers, William, London, upholder and cm (1745–74). Trading at 1 Budge Row, 1765–74, as Rogers & Solly, 1765–70. Son of Richard Rogers, carpenter of Woodford, Essex. App. to Daniel Demee on 4 April 1745, and admitted freeman of the Upholders' Co. by servitude on 13 January 1761. A William Rogers took app. named Robert Brooke, 1765–71. In 1770 he employed seven non-freemen for three months; in 1771, three for six months; and in 1772 one for three months. [D; GL, Upholders' Co. records; GL, City Licence bks, vol. 7]

Rogers, William, London, upholder (1753–1802). Addresses given at Watling St, 1769–72; Bromwell Heath, Harford Bridge, Hants. in 1786; and Old Bethlem, 1794–1802. Son of William Rogers, Gent. of Hackfield, Hants. App. to Michael Bradshaw on 1 March 1753, and admitted freeman of the Upholders' Co. by servitude on 4 March 1762. A William Rogers took app. named Robert Brooke, 1765–71. [GL, Upholders' Co. records]

Rogers, William, parish of St Nicholas, Bristol, cm (1774–81). [Poll bks]

Rogers, William, Swallow St, London, upholder (1785–93). Recorded at no. 30 in 1785 and no. 39, 1790–93. Took out a Sun Insurance policy on 18 June 1785 for £80 on household goods. [D; GL, Sun MS vol. 329, p. 506]

Rogers, William, 23 Gt Pulteney St, London, upholder and undertaker (1791–1819). Took out Sun Insurance policies on 23 June 1791 for £200 of which utensils and stock accounted for £50; and on 6 June 1809 for £300, £100 on stock and utensils. [D; GL, Sun MS ref. 585513; vol. 448, ref. 832638]

Rogers, William, 3 Husband St, Broad St, Carnaby Mkt, London, chairmaker (1809–11). [D]

Rogers, William, Eastgate St, Stafford, cm (1818–22). [D]

Rogers, William, Birmingham, chairmaker (1818–35). Addresses given at Woodcock st, 1816–18; Love Lane in 1822; and 25 Duddeston Rd, 1828–35, in 1835 trading as a 'fancy chairmaker'. [D]

Rogers, William Gibbs, 13 Church St, Soho, London, ornamental carver and collector of antique carvings (1835–39). [D]

Rogers, William, Green Dragon Yd, Finsbury, London, chair and sofa maker (1839). [D]

Rogers, William, High Wycombe, Bucks., chairmaker (b. c. 1811–41). Aged 30 at the time of the 1841 Census.

Rogers & Shimmeld, High St, Sheffield, Yorks., cm (1814). [D]

Rogerson, Edward, 1 Bury St, Manchester or Salford, u (1813). [D]

Rogerson, George, 5 Millgate, Bury, Lancs., cm and u (1824). [D]

Rogerson, John, Ewarts Buildings, 48 Gt Homer St, Liverpool, cm (1835). [D]

Rohleder, George, 158 Kingsland Rd, London, bed and mattress maker (1827–28). [D]

Rokes, George, 247 Half Moon Lane, Southwark, London, upholder and undertaker (1817). [D]

Roles, —, address unrecorded, cm (1803). Subscribed to Sheraton's *Cabinet Dictionary*, 1803.

Roles, Henry, Queen St, Oxford Rd, London, carver (1774). [Poll bks]

Rolf, Samuel, address unrecorded, u (1680–83). In 1680 he was paid £3 for work at St Stephen's, Walbrook, and in 1681–82, £3 18s. In 1683 he received £5 'in full for painting, gilding &c. of the Dial only, for the use of my mother, Mrs. Dorcas, Year.' [*Wren Soc.*, vol. X, pp. 113 and 115; vol. XIX, p. 56]

Rolfe, George, High Wycombe, Bucks., chairmaker (1813–21). Daughters bapt. in 1813 and 1821; twins in 1815; and sons in 1817 and 1819. [PR (bapt.)]

Rolfe, John, West Wycombe, Bucks., chairmaker (b. c. 1801–41). Aged 40 at the time of the 1841 Census.

Rolfe, Joseph, Bream's Buildings, Chancery Lane, London, cm (1796). Declared bankrupt, *Billinge's Liverpool Advertiser*, 6 June 1796.

Rolfe, Robert, West Wycombe, Bucks., chairmaker (b. c. 1818–41). Aged 23 at the time of the 1841 Census.

Rolin(g), Edward, Berwick St, Soho, London, carver and gilder (1808–09). Recorded at no. 83 in 1808 and no. 74 in 1809. Took out a Sun Insurance policy on 2 October 1809 for £430 on household goods, and £70 on stock, utensils and goods in trust. [D; GL, Sun MS vol. 448, ref. 834671]

Rolinson, John, 5 Saffron St, Saffron Hill, London, cm (1816–25). [D] See John Robinson at this address.

Rolinson, John, 50 Bunhill Row, Chiswell St, London, portable desk manufacturer (1820). [D] See John Robinson at this address.

Rollas(t)on (or Rollison), William, Edmund St, Birmingham, fancy chairmaker (1828–35). Recorded at no. 71 in 1828–30; and no. 17 in 1835, as a Windsor chairmaker. [D]

Rollett, William, Gainsborough, Lincs., joiner, cm, u, chairmaker and builder (1815–41). Trading at Market Pl., 1819–41, as William Rollett & Son in 1841; and also listed at Church St in 1835. Took apps named William Maugham of West Halton, Lincs. in March 1815; James Tall and William Robinson of Gainsborough in March 1816; Thomas Tarrey of Market Rasen, Lincs., in August 1817; Samuel Bass of Gainsborough in August 1818; H. Sleight of Kirton-in-Lindsay, Lincs. in August 1819; George Torry of Market Rasen in June 1821; Albert Norman in January 1822; and James Benson of Gainsborough in February 1823. [D; Hull app. reg.]

Rollinson, Richard, Cross Green, Otley, Yorks., cm (1822). [D]

Rollit, Richard, Gt Union St, Hull, Yorks., cm (1834). [D]

Rollo(s), Andrew, London, cm and chairmaker (1809–24). Recorded as Andrew Rollos, cm and bedstead manufactory, 42 Leman St, Goodman's Fields, 1809–11; and as Andrew Rollo at Castle St, City Rd, 1816–24, and 3 Sandys Row, Bishopsgate in 1820. Declared bankrupt, *Brighton Gazette*, 1 April 1824. [D]

Rolls, James, Kennington Lane (late Old Kent Rd), London, furniture japanner and painter (1839). [D]

Rome, David, Liverpool, cm (1800–18). Addresses given at 82 Pitt St, 1800–03; 6 Greetham St, Park Lane in 1804; 26 Pitt St, 1805–10; 7 Greetham St in 1811; no. 21, 1813–14; 21 Cleveland Sq. in 1816; and 17 Pitt St in 1818. [D]

Rome & Turner, Upper Frederick St, Liverpool, cm (1803). [D]

Romney, George, Lancaster, cm (1794–1840). Son of Thomas Romney. App. to Gillows in 1794 and admitted freeman, 1801–02. Named in the Gillow records, 1795–1840. [Lancaster app. reg. and freemen rolls; Westminster Ref. Lib., Gillow]

Romney, Robert, London, u (1777). [Newcastle poll bk] Possibly Robert Rumney, Newcastle, 1774.

Romney, Thomas, Lancaster, carver (1788–1816). Westminster Ref. Lib., Gillow records]

Romsey, —, address unrecorded. In January 1831 received £1 for a table supplied to 3rd Lord Braybrooke for Audley End, Essex, Billingbear, Berks., or his London house. [Essex RO, D/DBy/A361] See William Rumsey.

Ron, John, London, upholder (1708). Took out a Hand in Hand Insurance policy on 20 April 1708 for £100 on a house, east side of Butcher Hall Lane, Christchurch parish. [GL, Hand in Hand MS vol. 6, ref. 15988]

Ronalds, John, Hythe, Kent, cm etc. (1823–24). [D]

Ronchetti, Joseph, 29 Balloon St, Manchester, barometer and looking-glass manufacturer (1817). [D]

Ronchetti, Joshua, Manchester, barometer and looking-glass manufacturer, mathematical, philosophical and chymical instrument maker (1829–40). Addresses given at 4 Cateaton St in 1829, 1 St Anne's St in 1834 and 43 Market St in 1840. Son of Baptist Rocheti [*sic*], weatherglass manufacturer at Warwick St, Oldham St, Manchester, 1802. [D]

Rood, Heal & Co., 28 and 29 Old Compton St and Maiden Lane, Battle Bridge, London, bed and mattress maker (1822–35). [D]

Rooe, John, Stamford, Lincs., cm (1806–d. by 1835). Admitted freeman in 1806 and polled in 1809. John Rooe, paper hanger, polled in 1830. [Stamford freemen rolls and poll bks]

Rook, —, London, cm (1754). Notice given in *Public Advertiser*, 30 March 1754 of 'Auction by Mr. Heath At the Corner of Queen Street, near Storey's Gate Westminster. All the general stock in Trade of a Cabinetmaker, going intirely into another Business, consisting of Mahogany Desk and Book Cases, Buroes, Dining, Dressing, Card and Claw Tables, Picture and Dressing glasses, with variety of Chairs and Sundry sorts of Furniture …'. Notice in same paper, 13 April 1754, gives name as Rook.

Rook, J., 10 Crown St, Soho, London, cm (1819). [D]

Rooker, Thomas, Manchester, cm, auctioneer, sworn appraiser and victualler (1797–1802). Trading at 54 Oldham St in 1797; and at 'The White Hart', Gt Ancoats St in 1800. [D]

Rookes, William, Exeter, Devon, cm (c.1821–32). Recorded at 2 Back Lane, c.1821–26, and Prospect Pl. in 1832. Children bapt. at St Mary Major: Jane on 2 October 1821; Edmund John on 30 March 1823; Elizabeth Ann on 12 February 1825; Ellen on 12 November 1826; and Eliza Catherine on 9 September 1832. [PR (bapt.)]

Rookledge, Francis, Easingwold, Yorks., joiner and cm (1834). [D]

Rooklidge, William, Long St, Easingwold, Yorks., joiner and cm (1828–29). [D]

Room, I., 1 Knightsbridge, London, u and broker (1820). [D]

Roome, Samuel, South St, London, carver (1749–74). [Poll bks]

Roome, Thomas, Bristol, upholder (1781). [Poll bk]

Roope, James, Norwich, cm (1801–03). Recorded at 6 Timberhill St, 1801–02, and 6 Timberland Hill in 1803. [D]

Root, John jnr, Colchester, Essex, cm (1820–31). [Poll bks]

Root, William, Hull, Yorks., cm (1807). App. to Samuel Gear in April 1807. [Hull app. reg.]

Rope, Robert, London, cm (1786). Subscribed to George Richardson's *A Treatise on the Five Orders of Architecture*, 1787.

Roper, —, Deptford, London, turner and chairmaker (1791–93). [D]

Roper, Edwin, Mary St, Bridgwater, Som., carver and gilder (1840). [D]

Roper, Henry, Blackboy Rd, Exeter, Devon, cm (1837). Daughter Maria bapt. at St Sidwell's on 1 October 1837. [PR (bapt.)]

Roper, John, Preston, Lancs., chairmaker (1818–22). Recorded at 18 Shambles in 1818; and in the Preston Guild record of burgesses in 1822 as son of Thomas, deceased. [D]

Roper, John, Haworth, near Keighley, Yorks., cm (1822). [D]

Roper, William, Cambridge, cm and u (1734–d.1783). William Roper is first recorded in the rate bk of St Edward's parish on 12 February 1733/34 with a property in Trumpington St (now no. 14 King's Parade). From 21 February 1750/51 a property in St Edward's Lane is also listed in his name, both these being held until 16 September 1773 when he appears to have retired and moved into the parish of St Mary's the Less. A hand bill of Roper's has survived glued inside the lid of a panelled oak chest in the Cambridge and County Folk Museum, recording his address 'Near the Corner of Saint Edwards Lane, Trumpington Street, Cambridge' with a detailed list of the type of furniture and upholstery that he sold. Edward Yorke, a cm and u, had opened a shop next door to Roper in 1753 and when in 1773 he retired, Yorke took over his premises and occupied both for some years. The *Cambridge Chronicle and Journal*, 1 October 1783 records that 'Yesterday died Mr. William Roper, formerly a cabinet maker of considerable eminence in this town who had retired from business some years'. In his will he left over £1,000 divided between his nieces with a small bequest for his servant and the poor of the parish. [St Edward's parish records, Cambs. RO, P28/4/1; Will WR15:262, University Lib.; *Furn. Hist.*, 1978]

R.W.

Roper, William, 2 Gt Queen St, Lincoln's Inn Fields, London, frame maker, metal border ornaments and saddlers' iron-maker (1780–83). [D]

Rorrs, R. & D., 70 Gracechurch St, London, u (1809–11). [D]

Roschone, John, London, looking-glass manufacturer, carver and gilder (1835–39). [D]

Rose, —, Sheerness, Kent, u (1807). [D]

Rose, Charles, 59 Judd St, Brunswick Sq., London, u (1826–29). [D]

Rose, Charles, Gainsborough, Lincs., cm and u (1831–41). Trading at Silver St in 1831 and Caskgate St in 1841. [D]

Rose, Charles, 2 King St, Holborn, London, cm (1835–39). [D]

Rose, Henry, 1 New North St, Red Lion Sq., London, broker, cm and u (1784). Took out a Sun Insurance policy in 1784 for £300 of which £200 accounted for utensils, stock and goods. [GL, Sun MS vol. 322, p. 477]

Rose (or Rowe(s)), Isaac, Stanley St, Liverpool, cm and household broker (1810–14). Trading at no. 15 in 1810, no. 17 in 1811, and no. 18, 1813–14. [D]

Rose, J., Shipyard, Gainsborough, Lincs., cm and u (1835). [D] See William Rose of Gainsborough.

Rose, John, address unrecorded, upholder (1704–12). Son of William Rose, freeman cooper of London. App. to Thomas Wilcox on 1 December 1704, and admitted freeman of the Upholders' Co. by servitude on 26 August 1712. Took app. on 26 September 1712. [GL, Upholders' Co. records; PRO, app. reg.]

Rose, John, Sheffield, Yorks., cm and u (1821–37). Addresses given at Smith St in 1821; 9 Church St in 1822; Orchard Pl. in 1825; and Anson St in 1837. [D]

Rose, John, 3 Newton's Entry, Salthouse Lane, Hull, Yorks., carver and gilder (1838–39). [D]

Rose, John, 55 High St, Poplar, London, cm, u and undertaker (1839). [D]

Rose, Joseph, Queen Anne St, London, plasterer and frame maker (c.1723–80). Named in Mrs Bowes's accounts on 4 April 1763 receiving £42 2s for four papier mâché frames for glasses intended for Gibside, Co. Durham, and made in 1758. Also worked on ornament for cove in the Drawing Room at Gibside. [Durham RO, Strathmore MS, D/St/Box 199]

Rose, Joseph, St Andrew, Holborn, London, cm (1776). Declared bankrupt, General Mag., February 1776, and Gents Mag., March 1776.

Rose, Josh., Bartlett's Buildings, Holborn, London, freeman joiner, cm (1768–74). In 1768 he employed six non-freemen for three months, and in 1774, six for six weeks. [GL, City Licence bks, vols 6 and 8]

Rose, Robert, High St, Newport Pagnell, Bucks., cm and u (1823–30). [D]

Rose, Robert, St James Sq., Thirsk, Yorks., cm/chairmaker (1840). [D]

Rose, S., 29 Hog Lane, Shoreditch, London, looking-glass maker (c.1790). [Wills, Looking-Glasses]

Rose, Thomas, parish of St Thomas, Bristol, cm (1784). [Poll bk]

Rose, Thomas, Liverpool, upholder (1823–30). App. to Henry Lace in 1823 and assigned to Bartholomew Tyrer in 1824. Admitted freeman in 1830. [Liverpool app. enrolment bk and freemen's committee bk]

Rose, W. H., 3 City Rd, London, u (1826–27). [D]

Rose, William, address unrecorded, upholder (1706–23). Son of George Rose, yeoman of Gadoden Magna, Hertford. App. to Joseph Howard on 5 March 1706, and admitted freeman of the Upholders' Co. by servitude on 2 May 1722. Took app. named David Langton in 1723. [GL, Upholders' Co. records]

Rose, William, Hampstead, London, upholder (1734). [Poll bk]

Rose, William, Cambridge. On 11 June 1768 the Cambridge Chronicle and Journal reported that Rose had eloped from his master, William Rush, cm in Cambridge.

Rose, William, 6 Fontenoy St, Dale St, Liverpool, cm (1800–03). [D]

Rose, William H., London, looking-glass and cm, u and undertaker (1813–29). Trade card, c.1800 [Heal Coll., BM], gives address at 12 Old St. Directories list him there, 1813–19, and at no. 74 in 1820. Recorded at 12, the corner of Golden Lane, Old St in 12 April 1810, when he took out a Sun Insurance policy for £1,300 including £100 on house and workshop, £600 on household goods and utensils, and £600 on stock and utensils at the back of 13 Old St. [GL, Sun MS vol. 451, ref. 844058]

Rose, William, Preston, Lancs., cm (1802–18). Signed the Preston Cabinet Makers' and Chair Makers' Book of Prices, 1802, on behalf of the masters. Recorded at 39 Duke St in 1818. [D]

Rose, William, 33 Ironmonger Row, Old St, London, looking-glass frame maker (1803). Took out a Sun Insurance policy on 1 July 1803 for £500 of which £300 accounted for utensils and stock. [D; GL, Sun MS vol. 426, ref. 750152]

Rose, William, 3 Gt Pulteney St, Golden Sq., London, carver and gilder (1808). [D]

Rose, William, Gainsborough, Lincs., cm (1819–41). Trading at Shipyard, 1819–26, and Silver St, 1822–41. [D] See J. Rose of Shipyard, Gainsborough.

Rose, William, 29 Windmill St, Finsbury, London, cm and upholder (1827–28). [D]

Rose, William, 5 Angel Pl., Islington, London, u (1829). [D]

Rose, William, 6 Regent St, Leamington, Warks., cm and u (1835–37). [D]

Rosedon, John, Hexham, Northumb., u (1780). [Newcastle poll bk]

Rosedon, Joseph, Newcastle, u (1755–79). Admitted freeman in 1755; his son, John, by patrimony on 29 July 1779. [Newcastle freemen reg.]

Rosenburgh, Fred., Rose St, Soho and Stafford Pl., London, carver and gilder (1820). [D]

Rosewassa, Thomas, Richmond, Yorks., cm (1825). [PR (bapt.)]

Rosier, —, address unrecorded. Tradesman employed by Morel & Seddon who signed the frame of a dining chair supplied to Windsor Castle in 1828. [Gilbert, Leeds Furn. Cat., vol. 1, pp. 101–02]

Rosilin, Hugh, Boston, Lincs., chairmaker (1741). Took app. named Burrows in 1741. [S of G, app. index]

Roskell, James, late of Bridgewater St, Liverpool, cm and victualler (1829). Declared bankrupt, Liverpool Mercury, 23 January 1829.

Roskell, John, 34 Pool Fold, Manchester, cm (1838–39). [D]

Roskill, Gilbert, Berry St, London Rd, Manchester, cm (1817). [D]

Roskilly, John, Market St, Falmouth, Cornwall, cm (1840). [GL, Sun MS ref. 1334910]

Ross, Alex, 14 Gt Quebec St, Portman Sq., London, cm (1808). [D]

Ross, Charles, address unrecorded, carver (c.1759). Charles Ross supplied the tables and benches for the premises of the Society of Arts. Designs by William Chambers were approved by the Society on 14 November 1759, and ordered 'to be forthwith made'. They no longer survive. [Journal of the Royal Society of Arts, April 1966, pp. 430–32]

Ross, David, Gt Portland St, London, joiner and composition man, carver and gilder (1786–1815). Recorded at 96 Portland St in 1786, 98 Gt Portland St, 1790–1815, and no. 113, 1790–93. Pretty Neo-classical trade card [Banks Coll., BM] reads: 'ROSS, JOINER, CARVER, GILDER & PICTURE FRAME MAKER At his Composition Ornament MANUFACTORY, No.113 Great Portland Street, PORTLAND CHAPEL'. Took out a Sun Insurance policy on 4 July 1794 for £1,000 on his house, goods, books and workshop. In 1786 he charged Lord Howard of Audley End, Essex, £1 1s 'To Makeing two pedestals Ornamented with Composition for Standing on Terms.' Ross was paid in 1792. [D; GL, Sun MS vol. 401, ref. 630117; Essex RO, D/DBy/A50/6] See James Ross.

Ross, David, 6 Marble St, Manchester, u (1797). [D]

Ross, David, 40 Charles St, Hampstead Rd, London, u and cm (1809–11). [D]

Ross, David, 48 Crosshall St, Liverpool, u (1811). [D]

Ross, Francis, Cottingham, near Hull, Yorks., cm and chairmaker (1804–31). Trading at Hallgate in 1826. App. to Thomas Ross of Cottingham in June 1804. Took app. named John Deggitt in September 1821. [D; Hull app. reg.]

Ross, James, London, carver and gilder (1816–35). Recorded at 98 Gt Portland St, Marylebone, 1816–27, and 35 Charles St, Middlx Hospital in 1835 as James N. Ross. [D] See David Ross of Gt Portland St.

Ross, John, London, cm (1793). Subscribed to Sheraton's Drawing Book, 1793.

Ross, Joseph, Hull, Yorks., cm (1768). [Poll bk]

Ross, Joshua, Bath, Som., gilder and frame maker (1745–c.1765). Subscribed to John Wood's A Description of the Exchange at Bristol, published at Bath in 1745. A printed trade card in Bath Ref. Lib. states that 'Joshua Ross, frame carver and gilder from Mr Pascall's in Long Acre, London' had taken up residence with Thomas Ross, painter in Bath and that he 'Makes and Sells all Sorts of Gold, Silver and Laquer'd Black Pear-Tree and Deal FRAMES; Looking-Glass Frames, Gold & lacquer'd ... N.B. The above shall be performed as well and as cheap as in LONDON'. Mr Pascall was presumably James Pascall, carver and gilder, author of the Temple Newsam long gallery suite.

Ross, Mary, Cottingham, near Hull, Yorks., cm (1823). [D]

Ross, Thomas, address unrecorded, carver (mid 18th century). At Little Haugh Hall, Suffolk, house of the antiquary, Cox-Macro (1683–1767), the carving round the dining room fireplace, and that of both the chimney piece and doorcase in the tapestry room is probably the work of Thomas Ross. [C. Life, 5 June 1958, figs 7, 8 and 9]

Ross, Thomas, Cottingham, near Hull, Yorks., cm and chairmaker (1804–19). Took app. named Francis, son of James Ross, in June 1804; Joseph Carter of Cottingham in February 1806; John Teal in December 1807; of Cottingham, Richard Todd in August 1810, Joseph Westerman in June 1811, and Nicholas Sipling in June 1812; and George Stephenson of Lincs. in August 1819. [Hull app. reg.]

Ross, Thomas, 6 Castle St, Hastings, Sussex, carver and gilder (1839). Trading also as Ross & Mann at this address, and at 34 High St. In 1845 Thomas Mann, carver and gilder, and Thomas Ross, bookseller, stationer and print seller, were listed at 34 High St. [D]

Ross, William, Frith St, London, cm (1784). [Poll bk]

Ross, William, Buross St, Commercial Rd, London, cm, carpenter and wheelwright (1824). Took out a Sun Insurance policy on 8 July 1824 for £600, including £480 on stock and utensils in workshops, open yard, sheds and sawpits. [GL, Sun MS vol. 494, ref. 1017935]

Rossall, Thomas, Liverpool, cm (1835–39). Trading at 14 Basnett St in 1835, 8 Duncan St East in 1837 and 17 Hotham St in 1839. [D]

Rossall & Gradwell, 14 Basnett St, Liverpool, cm (1837). [D] See Russell & Gradwell.

Rossi, George, St Lawrence, Norwich, looking-glass maker (1822–30). [D; Goodison, Barometers]

Rossiter, Henry, Broad St, South Molton, Devon, cm (1830–38). [D]

Rosson, Andrew, Liverpool, u, appraiser and auctioneer (1766–1810). Addresses given at Chapel St, 1766–71; Harrington St in 1769; 1 Dale St in 1772; warehouse at 34 School Lane in 1781; no. 35 in 1787; 62 Oldham St and 42 Chapel St in 1790; at 5 Castle St as Andrew Rosson & Son, 1796–1803; at 46 Chapel St, 1796–1800; and Dale St in 1803; 50 Lord St in 1804; no. 59, 1805–10; no. 52 in 1807; and 9 Christian St in 1810. Notice given in Williamson's Liverpool Advertiser, 26 July 1781, of sale of a client's property in Rosson's capacity as an auctioneeer, and sale of his own wares as an u, consisting of 'Wilton & Kidderminster carpeting, damasks, morines, cheneys, great variety of fringes, & other articles in the upholstery branch...'. Andrew Rosson, presumably jnr and the 'Son' of Andrew Rosson & Son, petitioned freedom on servitude to Lloyd Baxendale in 1792, and was admitted freeman on 10 January 1793. Took app. named James Rosson in 1794, who petitioned freedom in 1806; and Thomas Kirkham in 1805, petitioned in 1812. Probable confusion between Andrew Rosson, snr and jnr. [D; Liverpool freemen's committee bk and reg.]

Rosson, James, Liverpool, u (1806–11). Recorded at 10 Beau St in 1806 and 9 Christian St, 1810–11. Admitted freeman on servitude to Andrew Rosson on 7 November 1806. Described in 1829 as 'now soap boiler'. [D; Liverpool freemen reg.]

Rosson, Richard, Liverpool, upholder (1799–1814). Trading at

8 Earle St, St Paul's in 1800; no. 16, 1803–04; as R. & Son, u and auctioneers at Castle St in 1805; 9 Christian St in 1807; 59 Lord St in 1810; as Richard & James, upholders, appraisers and auctioneers at no. 60 in 1811; and as Richard only at 71 Lord St, 1813–14. Marriage to Miss A. Bushell, daughter of the late Mr J. Bushell, tobacconist, at St Nicholas's Church, reported in Billinge's Liverpool Advertiser, 29 April 1799. Sale of remaining stock in trade of R. Rosson, u and cm in Lord St advertised in Liverpool Mercury, 13 May 1814. Stock consisted of 'a variety of Kidderminster, Venetian & Brussels Carpeting, Oil Cloths, Blankets, Paper Hangings, Chintz Furnitures, Superb Loo & Sofa Tables, elegant Grecian Couches, Sofas in Hair Seating, Cabinets, an upright grand Piano Forte by Clementi, Dining, Card, Pembroke & Quartetto Tables, Wardrobes, Drawers, Chairs etc. etc. Also a quantity of Hair Seatings, Curled Hair, Diaper Web, Brass Work, Bindings etc.' [D] See John Wilson, u, cm and looking-glass manufacturer.

Rostill, William, 90 Hill St, Birmingham, fancy box, case and caddy maker (1835). [D]

Roswell, Samuel, Stall St, Bath, Som., cm and milliner (1733). Took out a Sun Insurance policy on 30 August 1733 for £300 on his house and out houses. [GL, Sun MS vol. 38, ref. 61691]

Rothera, John, Drury Lane, London, cm and upholder (1817–23). Trading at no. 29 in 1817 and no. 25 in 1820. [D]

Rothera, William, address unrecorded, cm (1803). Subscribed to Sheraton's Cabinet Dictionary, 1803.

Rothera, William, 5 and 6 Brokers Alley, Long Acre, London, cm etc. (1820). [D]

Rotherel, James (?), Stockport, Cheshire, u (1781). [D]

Rothery, —, London, cm (1793). Subscribed to Sheraton's Drawing Book, 1793.

Rothery, Joseph, Christiane Alley, Moorfields, London, cm (1801–02). In 1801 Rothery arranged for Abraham Bellamy of Gt Cheverell, Wilts., to borrow money from Samuel Jones, merchant of Limehouse. Bill of 1802 recorded. [PRO, C13, 599/20]

Rothery, John, Lancaster, cm (1788–1802). App. to R. Mashiter in 1788 and admitted freeman, 1801–02. [Lancaster app. reg. and freemen rolls]

Rothwell, —, Manchester, cm and u (1803). Bill for a tent bed for £30 8s 11d noted by Charles Towneley of Towneley Hall, Lancs., in November 1803. [Preston RO, Towneley papers DDTO] Possibly James or John Rothwell.

Rothwell, Mrs, Chapel Walks, Manchester or Salford, u (1808). [D]

Rothwell, Daniel, Liverpool, painter and furniture japanner (1810–14). Addresses given at 5 Gt Crosshall St, 1810–11 and 10 Oxford St, Bevington Bush, 1813–14. [D]

Rothwell, James, Queen St, St Anne's, Manchester, upholder (1773–84). Recorded at no. 12 in 1773. [D] See John Rothwell, and Rothwell & Marsden.

Rothwell, James, St Anne's St, Manchester, u and cm (1815). [D]

Rothwell, James, 15 Bedford Sq. Rd, Brighton, Sussex, cm and u (1839). [D]

Rothwell, John, Manchester, u (1772–1804). Trading at Back Sq. in 1772 and Queen St, St Anne's in 1788. [D] See James Rothwell, and Rothwell & Marsden.

Rothwell, Lydia, 1 Pool Fold and St Anne's St, Manchester, cm and u (1813–16). [D]

Rothwell (or Rotherel), Richard, Stockport, Cheshire, u (1781–1807). Recorded at Little Underbank in 1784 and Underbank, 1805–07. [D]

Rothwell, Thomas, High Wycombe, Bucks., cm (1773). [PR (marriage)]

Rothwell & Marsden, Manchester, u (1800–02). Recorded at 3

Queen St, St Anne's in 1800. [D] See James and John Rothwell.

Rottenbury, Peter, Falmouth, Cornwall, cm (1737). Took app. named Grenfield in 1737. [S of G, app. index]

Roughey, William, Newtown, Whitchurch, Salop, cm (1840). [D]

Roughley, Mary, Butter Mkt St, Warrington, Lancs., u (1834). [D]

Roughton, Henry, High St, Lincoln, chairmaker (1826). [D]

Roughton, William, Pinchbeck St, Spalding, Lincs., woodturner and chairmaker (1826). [D]

Rounce, —, Southwold, Suffolk, 'Carver, Gilder, Looking-Glass & Picture-Frame manufacturer, Plumber, Glazier, House, Sign & Ship Painter, Paper Hanger, etc. . . Imitator of Woods & Marbles'. [Trade card at Grosvenor Antiques Fair, 1985]

Rounce, Thomas, Queen St, Halesworth, Suffolk, carver and gilder, paper hanger (1830–39). [D]

Round, Thomas, Reading, Berks., cm (1826–37). Trading at Upper Friar St in 1826 and Chatham St in 1837. [Poll bks]

Rourke, Patrick, Court, 90 Northgate, Huddersfield, Yorks., cm and/or u (1837). [D]

Rouse, Joseph, 22 Compton St, Clerkenwell, London, cm (1802). [Oxford poll bk]

Rouse, Joseph, 21 Union St, Lambeth, London, cm (1802). Took out a Sun Insurance policy on 9 November 1802 for £400 of which £100 accounted for utensils and stock. [GL, Sun MS vol. 426, ref. 740152]

Rouse, Joseph, Leicester, cm (1826). App. to Arnold Porter, a stranger who bought his freedom in 1801. Admitted freeman in 1826. [Leicester freemen rolls]

Rouse, Richard, Oxford, cm and joiner (1751–1802). In 1751 or 1752 Rouse, cm, was paid £1 0s 10d by All Soul's, Oxford. Announced in *Jackson's Oxford Journal*, 6 June 1767, that he had moved from Eastgate to Carfax, but still kept his workshop in Long Wall. Polled of St Martin's parish in 1768. Of St Peter-in-the-East, took out a Sun Insurance policy in 1775 for £500 including £150 on utensils and stock. Polled at St Thomas's parish in 1802. [GL, Sun MS vol. 239, p. 585]

Rouse, Robert, Summer-Town, Oxford, cm (1830). [D]

Rouse, William, Wickham Mkt, Suffolk, cm (1839). [D]

Rouseau, —, London, upholder (?) (1675). In June 1675 he was paid £60 7s 6d for crimson and white fringe for the Queen's 'crimson figured velvet Bed', at Whitehall, and 'white lace for the cupps and four spriggs for the corners of the bed.' [PRO, LC5/41]

Rousset, Samuel, at the corner of Angel Ct, Long Acre, London, carver (1723). Took out a Sun Insurance policy on 19 July 1723 for £500 on goods and merchandise in his house. [GL, Sun MS vol. 15, ref. 29327]

Rout, William, East St, Gt Coggeshall, Essex, cm (1838–39). Listed in the Essex jurors' bk for Lexden Hundred in 1838. [D; Essex RO, A/RJ/2/1]

Routh, James, Bristol, cm (1792–1805). Addresses given at Christmas St, 1792–94; Christmas St and Thomas St in 1795; 1 Thomas St, 1799–1800, and no. 2 in 1805. [D]

Rouths, James, 12 Scotland Rd, Liverpool, cm (1807). [D]

Routledge (or Rutledge), Christopher, Romsey, Hants., cm (1797). Supplier of furniture to Broadlands, Hants. [*C. Life*, 29 January 1981, p. 288; 5 February 1981]

Routledge, Charles, Romsey, Hants., cm and auctioneer (1792–98). [D]

Routledge, Thomas, Romsey, Hants., cm and auctioneer (1792–93). [D]

Row, Charles John, Little Bridge St, Blackfriars, London, carver and gilder (1839). [D]

Row, James, Petworth, Sussex, cm and u (1798–1826). [D]

Row, John B., Fighting Cock's Yd, with house at Rosemary Lane, Newcastle, joiner and cm (1833). [D]

Rowe, William, Croydon, Surrey, cm (1809–11). [D]

Rowbotham, Richard, Whipp's Ct, Carr Lane, Hull, Yorks., cm (1839). [D]

Rowden, John, Gattey's Ct, Exeter, Devon, carver and gilder (1835). Son John William Burkit bapt. at St Sidwell's on 23 August 1835. [PR (bapt.)]

Rowdon, John, Harcot, Moretonhampstead, Devon, later Exeter, cm (d. by 1818). Notice in *Exeter Flying Post*, 10 September 1818 read: 'On Thursday last, at Harcot, in Moretonhampstead, aged 32 died Mr. Wᵐ Rowdon, youngest son of the late Mr John Rowdon of that place, and late of this city, cabinet-maker.'

Row(e), Charles, London, upholder (1704–34). Recorded at 'The Bed', Knave's Acre, St James's, Westminster in 1714, and St Anne's, Westminster in 1722. Son of Charles Rowe, cook of St Anne's. App. to John Howne (Horne?) on 2 August 1704, and admitted freeman of the Upholders' Co. by servitude on 2 August 1711. Took app. named John Wood, 1720–32. Took out a Sun Insurance policy on 1 January 1714. Declared bankrupt, *London Gazette*, May 1722. Possibly the Charles Rowe of Prince's St, Leicester Sq. recorded by Heal in contemporary newspapers in 1734. [GL, Upholders' Co. records; GL, Sun MS vol. 3, pp. 91, 190 and 221]

Rowe, Charles, 61 Mount St, Davies St, London, cm and upholder (1835–39). [D]

Rowe, Hugh, 3 and 4 Edward St, Gt Surrey St, London, cm and u (1839). [D]

Rowe, James snr, London, upholder (1716–d. by 1736). Took app. named Daniel Wearg, 1716–24. Polled of Broad St, Westminster in 1727. His son, James Rowe jnr, admitted freeman of the Upholders' Co. in 1736. [GL, Upholders' Co. records]

Rowe, James jnr, London, upholder (1718–44). Son of James Rowe snr, upholder of London. Admitted freeman of the Upholders' Co. by patrimony on 1 December 1736. James Rowe, probably both snr and jnr, took app. named William Goff, 1718–44. [GL, Upholders' Co. records]

Rowe, James, Exeter, Devon, cm and u (1814–34). Recorded as a cm at Okehampton St, St Thomas, 1814–17, Alphington St in 1821, and as an u in Sun Lane, 1834. Sons bapt. at St Thomas's Church: William on 20 February 1814, William Matthias on 18 May 1817, and Henry William on 22 April 1821. Daughter Mary Ann bapt. at St Mary Major on 4 June 1834. [PR (bapt.)]

Row(e), John, St Bride's, London, upholder (1715–27). Recorded at Ditch Side in 1715, and at 'The Angel', Fleet Ditch, in 1727. Fined for non-service at St Bride's in 1715. Took out a Sun Insurance policy on 23 September 1727 for £500 on goods and merchandise in warehouse at Kent St, Southwark, belonging to Mr Stone, near 'The White Bear' in Kent St. [GL, MS 6561, p. 1; GL, Sun MS vol. 25, ref. 42584]

Rowe, John, Winwick St, Warrington, Lancs., cm (1834). [D]

Rowe, Robert, Upper Olland St, Bungay, Suffolk, cm and u (1830). [D]

Rowe, T. B., Thorverton, Devon, cm (1832). [Exeter voters list]

Rowe, Thomas, 34 Duke St, Grosvenor Sq., London, cm (1790). Took out a Sun Insurance policy on 19 November 1790 for £300 including £120 on stock in trust. [GL, Sun MS ref. 576129]

Rowe, Thomas, address unrecorded, cm (1803). Subscribed to Sheraton's *Cabinet Dictionary*, 1803.

Rowe, Thomas, Knightsbridge, London, bedstead maker (1837–39). Trading at 13 High Rd in 1837 and 13 Trevor Terr., 1839. [D]

Rowe, William, Medbourne, Leics., chairmaker (1840). [D]

Rowell, George Auguste, Alfred St, Oxford, cm and u (1830). [D]

Rowell, John, 40 James St, Oxford St, London, cm and u (1839). [D]

Rowen, I., 110 Goswell St, London, cabinet manufacturer (1820). [D]

Rower, Thomas, 79 Edgware Rd, Paddington, London, cm (1820). Took out a Sun Insurance policy on 2 August 1820 for £1,300 of which £50 accounted for a chest of tools in workshop of Ferguson & Co., Providence Ct, North Audley St. [GL, Sun MS vol. 483, ref. 970327]

Rowland, David, 43 Shouldham St, Bryanston Sq., London, cm and u (1826–28). [D]

Rowland(s), Edward, Liverpool, u and paper hanger (1821–37). Addresses given at 12 Tessary Pl. in 1821; 21 Bispham St in 1823; 123 Duke St in 1827; 15 Scotland Rd in 1829; 43 School Lane, 1834–35; and 31 Vauxhall Rd with shop at 21 Arcade in 1837. [D]

Rowland, James, 34 Church Rd, St George's East, London, cm, u and undertaker (1839). [D]

Rowland, John, Leeds, Yorks., cm (1834–39). Trading at 44 Mason St in 1837 and 20 Moxon's Yd, Kirkgate in 1839. [D]

Rowland, John, 48 Cornwall Rd, London, cm and u (1839). [D]

Rowland, Joseph, 8 St Mary Ave, London, cm and u (1839). [D]

Rowland, Thomas, parish of St James, Bristol, carver (1784). [Poll bk]

Rowland, Thomas, Richmond, Surrey, carver and gilder (1826–39). Trading at Hill St in 1826, and at Ormond Row, 1838–39, as carver and gilder to Her Majesty in 1839. [D]

Rowland, William, 13 Grenada Terr., Commercial Rd, London, cm, u and undertaker (1829–39). [D]

Rowland, William, Newport, Salop, cm (1836). Child bapt. at St Mary's Church in 1836. [PR (bapt.)]

Rowley, Edward, London, upholder (1765–d.1789). Recorded at 41 Newgate St, 1768–84, as Rowley & Jennings, 1783–84; 'near the Asylum', 1778–86; and 15 Newgate St in 1784. Trade card [Stone Coll., GL] c.1780, gives address at 'the Corner of Queens head Alley, Newgate Street', and trade as u, cm, appraiser and undertaker, who 'Makes & Sells all Kinds of Household Furniture in the Neatest Manner and at the Most Reasonable rates.' Son of William Rowley, farrier of Walham [sic] Green, Middlx. Admitted freeman of the Upholders' Co. by redemption on 9 July 1765. Took app. named James Blissatt, 1766–74. Insured his house at 41 Newgate St in 1776 with the Sun Co. [D; GL, Upholders' Co. records; GL, Sun MS vol. 249, p. 294] Possibly two tradesmen of the same name, or confusion with:

Rowley, Edward, 9 Hercules Buildings, Lambeth, London, upholder (1776). Took out a Sun Insurance policy in 1776 for £500 of which £100 accounted for utensils, stock and goods. [GL, Sun MS vol. 253, p. 622]

Rowley, Francis, 28 Snow Hill, Birmingham, cm and joiner (1767). [D]

Rowley, Joseph, Willenhall, Staffs., cm (1838–39). [D]

Rowley & Jennings, 15 Newgate St, London, upholders (1783–84). [D] See Edward Rowley.

Rowlings, Robert, 26 Red Lion Sq., London, upholder (1808). [D]

Rowling(s), Thomas, Strand, London, carver, gilder and printseller (1779–1820). Recorded at no. 460 in 1779; no. 464, 1784–1820; as frame maker to the Princesses in 1790; and as Rowling & Brown, 'Carvers & Gilders to their R.H. Princess Royal, Augusta and Elizabeth' in 1817. Trade card [Banks Coll., BM] bears the Royal Arms, and reads: 'ROWLING, 464 Strand, London, Carver, Gilder and Frame Maker to T.R.H. the Princess Royal, Princess Augusta,

Princess Elizabeth.' Took out a Sun Insurance policy in 1779 for £500 of which utensils, stock and goods accounted for £200. [D; GL, Sun MS vol. 278, p. 486]

Roworth, —, address unrecorded. 'ROWORTH' is clearly marked under the seats of two of a set of dining chairs, c.1805, with turned legs, a satinwood panel in the back and loose seats; in private ownership. [V&A archives]

Rowsell, Henry, Taunton, Som., cm (1757–61). Took apps named Rowsell in 1757 and Taylor in 1761. [S of G, app. index]

Rowsell, Thomas, adjoining St Stephen's Row, Exeter, Devon, cm (1772). Sale of his house, shop and appurtenances advertised in Exeter Flying Post, 25 September 1772.

Rowson, Thomas, Smith St, Marygate, Grimsby, Lincs., joiner/cm (1822). [D]

Rowton, Henry, High St, Lincoln, chairmaker (1822). [D]

Rowton, William, Spalding, Lincs., chairmaker (1797). [D]

Roy, Andrew, St Mary's Gate, Ripon, Yorks., cm (1822–37). [D] Possibly Andrew Ray.

Roy, William, Burnham Mkt, Norfolk, cm and joiner (1830). [D]

Royal, John, High St, Weymouth, Dorset, cm and u (1830). [D]

Royale, G., 78 Newgate St, 13 Bull-head Ct, London, u, appraiser, auctioneer, undertaker, cm and paper hanger. Trade card continues: 'Estates and Effects sold by Auction or Private Contract. Elegant Fashionable Paper hangings and Ornamental Borders . . . Rout Chairs. Card Tables Let by the Night.' [V&A archives]

Royale, William, High St, Manchester, joiner and picture framer (1788). [D]

Royall, Peter, Filby, Norfolk, cm (1838). [Gt Yarmouth poll bk]

Roybold, —, address unrecorded, chairmaker (1709). Named in the Felbrigg papers in January 1709 receiving £6, and on 12 August 1709, £6 8s. [Norfolk RO, Felbrigg papers, WKC 6/23, index of payments, 1707–12]

Roybould, Edward, London, turner (1714–45). Addresses given 'at the Catherine Wheel, Corner of Richmond Street on the backside of St. Ann's', Westminster, in 1714; the north side of Richmond St, west side of Princes St, St James's, Westminster in 1722; and St James, Westminster and Princes St, St Ann's in 1745. Took out a Sun Insurance policy on 27 March 1714 on his goods; and a Hand in Hand policy in 1722 for £600 on his house. Declared bankrupt, Gents Mag., April 1745. Sale of stock in trade and household furniture of 'Mr. Edward Roybould, a Bankrupt, at his late Dwelling-House, in Prince's Street, St. Ann's' announced in Daily Advertiser, 28 June 1745. Stock consisted of 'all sorts of Upholder's and Cabinet Goods'. [GL, Sun MS vol. 3, ref. 3803; GL, Hand in Hand MS vol. 26, p. 334]

Royboult, Richard, Peter St, Bishopsgate, London, freeman innholder, carver and chairmaker (1771–72). Employed twenty non-freemen for three months in 1771; and thirty for three months in 1772. [GL, City Licence bks, vol. 7]

Royde, George, 78 Newgate St, London, u, auctioneer, appraiser and undertaker (1806–20). Trade card of 1810 gives this address, and also 13 Bull Head Ct. [D; Banks Coll., BM]

Roylance, Ellen, late of Stockport, Cheshire, chairmaker (1825–27). Notice in Chester Chronicle and North Wales Advertiser, 8 June 1827 concerned the case of Ellen Roylance in the Court of Relief of Insolvent Debtors. [D]

Roylance, John, 7 Bamford St, Stockport, Cheshire, chairmaker (1834). [D] Possibly son of:

Roylance, P., Stockport, Cheshire, chairmaker (1816–20). At Bamford St in 1816 and Mealhouse Brow, 1818–20. [D]

Royle, James, 51A Oldfield Rd, Salford, Lancs., cm (1836). [D]

Royle, John, Manchester, cm (1773–87). Trading at Turner St in

1773 and Church St in 1781. Took out a Sun Insurance policy on 15 June 1787 for £200 on utensils and stock. [D; GL, Sun MS vol. 346, p. 113]

Royle, John, 53 Stanley St, Liverpool, u and broker (1821). [D]

Royle, William, High St, Manchester, joiner and picture framer (1788). [D]

Ruckman, J., London, chair manufacturer (1807–15). Trading at 26 Red Cross St, Southwark, 1807–12, and 30 Mint St in 1815. [D]

Ruckman & Winter, 26 Red Cross St, Southwark, London, chair manufactory (1803–04). Named in Sheraton's list of master cabinet makers, 1803. [D]

Rudd, —, England, later Bruges, Belgium, cm (c. 1788). Left England and settled in Bruges, where his son, Jean Baptiste Rudd, was born in 1792 and became the city architect. Table by Rudd described in Hepplewhite's *Guide*, 1788. [*C. Life*, 2 June 1966, p. 1409]

Rudd, Francis, Calvert St, Norwich, cm, u, carver and gilder (1830). [D]

Rudd, John, St Sidwell's, Exeter, Devon, chairmaker (1803). [Militia list]

Rudd, John, Norwich, cm (1830–31). Named on 26 June 1830 as being admitted freeman; also on 2 June 1831, as app. to Joseph Pigg. [Norwich freemen reg.]

Rudd, Thomas, Calvert St, Norwich, carver and gilder (1836–39). [D]

Rudd, William snr, Norwich, cm (1795–1812). Recorded in St Stephen's parish in 1812. Admitted freeman, not by apprenticeship, on 24 February 1795. [Norwich freemen reg. and poll bk] Possible confusion with:

Rudd, William jnr, Norwich, cm (1829–30). Recorded in St Clement's parish in 1830. Admitted freeman on 24 February 1829. [Norwich freemen rolls and poll bk]

Rudd, William, 149 Norfolk St, King's Lynn, Norfolk, carver and gilder (1839). [D]

Rudder, Edmund, Dursley, Glos., cm (1823–25). [PR (bapt.)]

Ruddock, William, Market Pl., Shepton Mallet, Som., cm (1830). [D]

Rudge, Benjamin Johnson, Eastgate St, Gloucester, cm and u (1830). [D]

Rudge, James, Oxbody Lane, Gloucester, cm and chairmaker (1774–1820). [D; Bristol poll bks]

Rudge, John, Stroud, Glos., cm (1827–39). [PR (bapt.)]

Rudge, Thomas, address unrecorded, upholder (1704–12). Son of Thomas Rudge, grocer of Eversham, Worcs. App. to Jonathan Hatley on 14 March 1704, and admitted freeman of the Upholders' Co. by servitude on 1 October 1712. [GL, Upholders' Co. records]

Rudge, Thomas, London, upholder (1727–34). Recorded at Houndsditch in 1727 and Hackney in 1734. [Poll bks]

Rudledge, William, 1 Mount St, Grosvenor Sq., London, cm (1809–11). [D]

Rudyard, Lawrence, London, upholder (1733–58). Son of John Rudyard, Gent. of Winchfield, Southampton. App. to John Hodson on 14 December 1733, and admitted freeman of the Upholders' Co. by servitude on 3 October 1745. Laurence Rudyard, cm of St Anne's, Westminster, declared bankrupt with John Hudson in 1747; and Lawrence Rudyeard, u and cm of Thrift St, St Ann, with Hodson in *London Gazette*, 21–25 November 1758. [GL, Upholders' Co. records] See John Hudson & Lawrence Rudyard.

Rudyerd, Launcelot, St Anne's, Soho, London, u (1745). Heal records him amongst children app. by the sons of the clergy.

Ruffel(l), John, London, cm to His Majesty (1777–84). Trading at 11 New Bird St, Oxford Rd in 1777, and Moorfields in 1784. [D] See John Russell of 11 New Bird St.

Ruffel & Co., 67 St Martin's Lane, Charing Cross, London, cm and u (1814). [D]

Ruffell, John, 21 Church St, Soho London, carver and gilder (1839). [D]

Ruffle, Robert, 17 Princes St, Drury Lane, London, cm and u (1839). [D]

Rule, James, Workington, Cumb., joiner and/or cm (1828–34). Trading at Washington St, 1828–29, and Jane St, 1829–34. [D]

Rullidge, Charles, Norwich and Ipswich, chairmaker (1802–07). Son of William Rullidge, chairmaker; admitted freeman of Norwich on 3 July 1802. Polled at Norwich of Ipswich in 1807. [Norwich freemen reg.]

Rullidge (or Rullege), William, Norwich and London, chairmaker (1780–1802). Polled at Norwich of St Margaret's parish in 1780, and of St Giles in 1784. Former app., Jos. Downing, chairmaker, admitted freeman of Norwich on 3 May 1787; and his son, Charles Rullidge, chairmaker, on 3 July 1802. Polled at Norwich of London, in 1786, 1799 and 1802. [Norwich freemen reg.]

Rumball, Charles, London, u (1781–93). Recorded at 66 Leather Lane, Holborn in 1781, and Islington in 1793. Took out a Sun Insurance policy in 1781 for £400 on utensils and stock. Declared bankrupt, *Williamson's Liverpool Advertiser*, 10 June 1793. [GL, Sun MS vol. 290, p. 194]

Rumball, Charles, Cheshunt, Herts., cm (1826). [D]

Rumball, Charles Wilson, Brighton, Sussex, cm and u (1837–39). Trading at Grenville Pl. in 1837 and 20 Western Rd in 1839. [D]

Rumbal(l), Thomas, London, cm (1773–1817). Recorded at 29 Minories, 1773–86, and 36 Wood St, Cheapside, 1789–1817. Took out Sun Insurance policies on 28 January 1775 for £2,800, £800 on utensils and stock at warehouses in Shepherd Yd, Minories; in 1776 for £3,700, £400 on utensils and stock; in 1779 for £600 on houses; and in 1780 for £4,800, £600 on utensils and stock. Thomas Rumball jnr, upholder of 29 Minories took out a Sun Insurance policy in 1782 for £1,300, £920 on utensils and stock. [D; GL, Sun MS vol. 236, p. 262; vol. 247, p. 262; vol. 279, p. 598; vol. 284, p. 601; vol. 300, p. 471]

Rumball, Thomas, 3 Long Alley, Moorfields, London, bedstead-maker (1782). Took out a Sun Insurance policy in 1782 for £300 of which £100 accounted for shop, utensils and stock. [GL, Sun MS vol. 303, p. 553]

Rumble, William, Windmill St, Finsbury Sq., London, cm, chairmaker, furniture broker and bedsteadmaker (1817–39). Recorded at no. 29, 1817–20, no. 28½, 1826–27, and no. 20 in 1829. [D]

Rumble, William jnr, London, cm and u (1823–29). Recorded at 7 Ballicourt Pl., St John St Rd, 1823–24; 134 St John St Rd, 1826–27; and 53 Myddleton St, St John's Rd, 1829. Took out Sun Insurance policies on 26 February 1823 for £100 on workshop behind his house, with stock and utensils; and on 18 February 1824 for £700, including £200 on stock and utensils in his house, £150 on those in open yard behind, and £200 on those in workshop behind 7 Wood St, Spa Fields. [D; GL, Sun MS ref. 1001815; vol. 495, ref. 1014377]

Rumfitt, William, Clementhorp, York, joiner and cm (1830). [D]

Rumford, C., Arthur's Hill, Newcastle, u (1838). [D] Probably:

Rumford, Cuthbert, 106 Pilgrim St, Newcastle, u, paper hanger and undertaker (1833). [D]

Rumming, William, Calne, Wilts., cm (1830–39). Trading at Wood St in 1830 and High St in 1839. [D]

Rumney, Robert, Newcastle, u (1774). App. to William Charnley and admitted freeman on 4 October 1774. [Newcastle freemen reg. and poll bk] Possibly Robert Romney of London, polled at Newcastle, 1777.

Rumsey, William, address unrecorded. In June 1833 named in the account book of 3rd Lord Braybrooke of Audley End, Essex, receiving £16 for making a wardrobe. [Essex RO, D/DBy/A230]. See Romsey, —.

Runciman, Robert, London, cm (1778–91). Recorded at 58 Silver St, Golden Sq. in 1778, and also as a broker at 19 Berwick St in 1791. Took out Sun Insurance policies in 1778 for £300, £170 on utensils and stock; and on 3 December 1791 for £1,000, including £100 on house, rooms and workshop, and £550 on utensils and stock. [GL, Sun MS vol. 265, p. 540; vol. 382, ref. 392747]

Runnage, William, St Gregory, Norwich, chairmaker (1768). [Poll bk]

Rusbridge(r), Richard, 8 Crown St, Moorfields, London, bedstead and chairmaker (1808–16). [D]

Rusby, U., Micklegate, York, cm and u (1818–20). [D]

Ruse, James, Fore St, Hertford, carver and gilder (1826). [D]

Ruse, James, Crouch St, Colchester, Essex, carver and gilder (1832). [D]

Ruse, James, King St, Chelmsford, Essex, carver and gilder (1839). [D]

Rush, Thomas, Wardour St, London, cm (1749). [Poll bk]

Rush, William, St Clement's, Cambridge, cm and joiner (1768–80). Notice given in *Cambridge Chronicle and Journal*, 11 June 1768, of elopement of his app., William Rose. Will dated 1780. Death of his widow reported in *Gents Mag.*, 1790. [Univ. Lib., Will, WR1S:192]

Rusher, Benjamin Gilson, Chelmsford, Essex, cm (b.1785–1815). Named in the Essex freeholders' bk for Chelmsford Hundred in 1815, aged 30. [Essex RO, Q/RJ1/12]

Rushforth, Isaac, Market Pl., Louth, Lincs., cm and joiner (1835). [D]

Rushforth, Major, London, cm (1784). [York poll bk]

Rushforth, William, Union St, Rochdale, Lancs., cm (1825–34). Recorded also in Cheetham St, 1828–34. [D]

Rushton, John, Red Sq., Jewin St, London, freeman haberdasher, looking-glass frame maker (1762–68). Employed one non-freeman for six months in 1762 and one for three months in 1768. [GL, City Licence Bks, vols 3 and 6]

Rushton, John & Son, 122 Church St, Preston, Lancs., u (1818). [D]

Rushton, Joseph, 13 Northampton Pl., Old Kent Rd, London, cm and u (1839). [D]

Rushton, Samuel, 5 Water St, Preston, Lancs., u (1818). [D]

Rushton, Samuel, Bow St, Lichfield, Staffs., chairmaker (1818). [D]

Rushworth, —, 51 George St, Blackfriars Rd, London, cm and u (c.1790). Trade card recorded. [Heal] See W. Rushworth.

Rushworth, Constantine, Wakefield, Yorks., carver (1798). [D]

Rushworth, James, Manchester, cm and u (1817–40). Recorded at 7 Hanover St, 1817–32; with William Rushworth at 74 Hanover St, 1832–34 and also 52 Long Millgate in 1834; together at 52 and/or 59 Long Millgate in 1836; and James only there, 1836–40. [D] See William Rushworth of 7 Hanover St.

Rushworth, John, Lockwood, Yorks., cm, joiner and carpenter (1828–29). [D]

Rushworth, Thomas, 2 Sloane Sq., Chelsea, London, cm (1826–27). [D] See William Rushworth at this address.

Rushworth, W., North St, Sloane St, London, cm (1820). [D]

Rushworth, W., 51 George St, Blackfriars Rd, London, cm (1835). [D] See Rushworth, —.

Rushworth, W., 1 Wellington Terr., Waterloo Rd, London, cm and u (1839). [D]

Rushworth, William, Cheapside, Halifax, Yorks., cm (1814). [D]

Rushworth, William, 7 Hanover St, Manchester, cm and joiner (1825). [D] See James Rushworth of Manchester.

Rushworth, William, 2 Sloane Sq., Chelsea, London, cm and u (1826). [D] See Thomas Rushworth at this address.

Rushworth, William, New Lenton, Nottingham, chairmaker (1835). [D]

Russ, Robert, 62 Redcliffe St, Bristol, cm (1792–93). [D]

Russel, James, Marsh, Newcastle, Staffs., joiner and cm (1822–23). [D]

Russel, John, Bristol, cm (1803). Subscribed to Sheraton's *Cabinet Dictionary*, 1803.

Russel, Seaton (or Sitton), Windsor, Berks., cm (1794–1824). Trading at Park St in 1824. [D; poll bks]

Russell, —, Upper Moorfields, London, cm (1751). Notice in *General Advertiser*, 5 August 1751 read: '(Friday) night about 9 o'clock Mr. Russell, a Cabinet maker in Upper Moorfields, was attacked by three fellows at the end of Chiswell Street, & robb'd of a gold ring, one guinea & some silver.'

Russell, Alexander, address unrecorded, cm (1803). Subscribed to Sheraton's *Cabinet Dictionary*, 1803.

Russell, Benjamin, Stone Cutter's St, St Bride's, London, cm (1743). Fined for non-service at St Bride's in 1743.

Russell, Charles & Thomas, 18 Barbican, Aldersgate St, London, clockcase makers (1775–1817). Charles recorded alone at 4 Paul's Alley, Red Cross St, Cripplegate on 13 June 1785 when he insured utensils, stock and goods in trust for £40 with the Sun Co.; also alone at Jacobs Well Passage, Barbican on 26 November 1801 when he took out insurance for £300; and at 18 Barbican on 15 November 1810 for £1,300, including £500 on two houses and offices at 11 and 12 Barbican in tenure of Smith, a chinaman, £300 on warehouse over sawpits there, and £50 on stock and utensils there. Charles and Thomas together took out Sun Insurance policies on 9 May 1811 and 20 April 1813 for £400 on four houses in tenure at 5, 7, 8 and 9 Silver St, Charles St, Bridgewater Sq. Heal records trade card of Charles & Thomas Russell, 18 Barbican. [D; GL, Sun MS vol. 329, p. 437; vol. 424, ref. 725308; vol. 449, ref. 850600; vol. 452, ref. 858056; vol. 461; F. J. Britten, *Old Clocks and Watches*, 1922] See Thomas Russell.

Russell, Edward, 9 Old St Rd, London, chair and sofa maker (1839). [D]

Russell, Francis, at 'The Queen's Head', corner of Phoenix Alley, Long Acre, London, cm and glass seller (1727). Took out a Sun Insurance policy on 7 December 1727 for £800 including £600 on household goods, utensils, stock and glass in trade in his front house; and £200 on those in his back house. [GL, Sun MS vol. 24, ref. 43332]

Russell, G., 29 Claverton St, Bath, Som., u (1819). [D]

Russel(l), George, Abington St, Northampton, upholder (1820–26). [D; poll bks]

Russell, George, 14 Goswell Rd, London, cm and u (1839). [D]

Russell, Henry, 89 Golden Lane, London, cm (1790). Took out a Sun Insurance policy on 26 August 1790 for £100. [GL, Sun MS ref. 572938, p. 512]

Russell, Henry, 12 Old St Sq., London, cm and dealer in cloth (1791–94). Took out Sun Insurance policies on 16 July 1791 for £700, £380 accounting for utensils and goods in trust; and on 21 April 1794 for £400. [GL, Sun MS vol. 379, p. 129; vol. 397, p. 494]

Russell, Henry, London, cm, u and undertaker (1801–28). Recorded at 17 North St, City Rd, 1801–13; as Henry Russell & Bruce there in 1812, and at 67 St Martin's Lane in 1817; as Henry Russell & Co. at 67 St Martin's Lane, 1813–23; and 21 Paul St, Finsbury in 1826. Took out Sun Insurance policies on 14 October 1807 for £900 on utensils and stock; on

2 February and 15 November 1813 for £1,000 on stock, utensils and goods in trust in warehouses, open yard and workshop; also on 15 November 1813, £300 on household goods; on 1 May 1820 for £3,000 on stock, utensils and goods in trust or on commission in workshops; on 19 December 1821 for £300 on household goods; on 21 October 1822 on stock and utensils in house, offices and workshops; and on 15 December 1823 for £300 on the same. [D; GL, Sun MS vol. 441, ref. 809040; vol. 462, refs 889945 and 887818–19; vol. 481, ref. 966585; vol. 491, ref. 987275; vol. 490, ref. 997222; vol. 494, ref. 1010988]

Russell, Henry, Cathedral Yd, Canterbury, Kent, carver and gilder (1838). [D]

Russell, Henry, 120 Curtain Rd, London, cm (1840). [GL, Sun MS vol. 576, ref. 1333576]

Russell, Isaac, Long Acre, London, cm (1749–70). Polled at Westminster in 1749. Heal records him in registers of unclaimed dividends of bank stock, 1770.

Russell, Isaac, High Wycombe, Bucks., chairmaker (1839). [PR (bapt.)]

Russell, Jabez, Whittlesey, Isle of Ely, Cambs., cm and joiner (1779). Took out a Sun Insurance policy in 1779 for £200 of which £40 accounted for utensils and stock. [GL, Sun MS vol. 275, p. 591]

Russell, James, London, cm and chairmaker (1811–27). Trading at 136 St Johns St, 1811–13, and 10 Goswell St Rd, Goswell St in 1817. [D]

Russell, James, Alnwick, Northumb., joiner, cm and u (1828–29). [D]

Russell, James, 8 Marchmont St, Brunswick Sq., London, u (1839). [D]

Russell, James, East St, Chichester, Sussex, cm (1839–40). [D]

Russell, John, Market Harborough, Leics., chairmaker (1729). Took app. named Stains in 1729. [S of G, app. index]

Russell, John, Bedford, cm (1730). Took app. named Towyer in 1730. [S of G, app. index]

Russell, John, New Bond St, London, cm and chairmaker (1773–1810). Heal records him in contemporary newspapers.

Russell, John, Panton St, London, cm (1774). [Poll bk]

Russel(l), John, opposite New Broad St, Moorfields, London, u and cm (1775–79). Took out Sun Insurance policies in 1775 for £200 on houses; in 1776 for £1,100, £800 on utensils and stock; in 1778 for £2,000, £1,600 on utensils and stock; and in 1779 for £2,100, £1,700 on utensils and stock. [GL, Sun MS vol. 240, p. 293; vol. 244, p. 538; vol. 271, p. 100; vol. 276, p. 501]

Russell, John, 11 New Bird St, Oxford Rd, London, chairmaker to His Majesty (1775–93). [D] See John Ruffel(l).

Russell, John, Moorfields, London, cm and upholstery warehouseman (1782–99). Trading at 17 and 28 Lower Moorfields, c.1782–93; and 11 and 12 Broker's Row, Moorfields, c.1794–99. [D]

Russell, John, Gt Portland St, Oxford Rd, London, chairmaker (1796). [D] A John Russell, carpenter, at no. 121 took out a Sun Insurance policy on 8 July 1794 for £2,000 on house, contents, workshops and stores. [D; GL, Sun MS vol. 401, ref. 630163]

Russell, John, London, chairmaker, joiner, u and cm (c.1773–1822). Employed by the Crown between 1773 and 1822, and was chairmaker to the King. In 1773 Russell supplied 'for his Majesty's House at Kew' a set of carved mahogany forms which are now in the Royal Collection. [H. Clifford Smith, *Buckingham Palace*] In 1780 he provided for the Prince of Wales's apartment in the Queen's House, St James's Park, '2 large cabriole sophas with compass tops and ends moulded on the edges, carved elbows & fluted stumps;

the feet termed, turned & fluted . . . with oval carved pateras on top of the feet', costing £6 6s each. In 1784 Russell was apparently in partnership with Benjamin Parran, and in that year they sent in a bill together for 'a wainscot Basin stand' for His Majesty's House at Newmarket, and for a writing-table supplied to the Council Office, Whitehall. In 1784 Russell also provided a state canopy, chairs and footstools for the Duke of Dorset, Ambassador to the Court of France; and equipped the funerals of HRH Princess Amelia in 1786, and the Duke of Cumberland in 1790. In 1791 he supplied 'twelve fancy back chairs, very neatly drawn with flowers, painted and japan'd blue, green and white' for the Princesses Mary and Sophia. [BM, Add. MS 33, 342] In 1800 '6 mahogany chair-frames with carved vase and feather backs, moulded feet to match' were obtained from him for St James's Palace at a cost of £9 18s. In 1807 he equipped the Speaker's new Gothic rooms at the Houses of Parliament with '26 large elbow chair frames with back frames for stuffing, caned seats, 4 Gothic sofas to match, 30 Gothic chairs without elbows'. In 1808 he provided the Prince Regent with 'a double-headed couch bedstead richly carved with figures and ornaments, Egyptian heads, gilt leaves, chased honey-suckeles, lyres', for which he charged £209 10s. [*Burlington*, November 1915] Russell continued to supply furniture to the Royal Palaces of St James, Kensington, Hampton Court, Westminster and Whitehall, 1813–18, including on 10 October 1814 a 'rising state canopy', £16 10s; '1 large Grecian elbow state chair frame', £6; and '2 Grecian square stool frames', £7 10s for Lord Stewart, Ambassador to the Emperor of Austria. On 5 January 1815 Russell provided state furniture for George Canning, Ambassador to Portugal, and on 5 January 1818 to the Ambassador to the Netherlands. In 1819 the firm became John Russell, J. Vallance & Sam. Evans, joiners and cm, and appear in the Royal accounts, 1819–22, supplying mainly chairs. [*DEF*; *GCM*; PRO, LC9/320–339; LC11/1–37] Several tradesmen of the same name are recorded at this time, and there is probably confusion in their identities. The one named in the Royal accounts is most likely, however, to be John Russell of 11 Bird St, since he is specified in directories as 'chairmaker to His Majesty'.

Russell, John, at 'The Ship', 28, the corner of Bethlem Walk, Moorfields, London, cm, upholder and undertaker (1792–1803). Trade card [Leverhulme Coll., MMA, NY] states that Russell 'Buys & Sells all sorts of Household Furniture, such as Bedsteads & Curtains, Feather Beds, Blankets & Quilts, Scotch, Wilton & other Carpets, Cabinet & Chair Work in general in the newest Taste. All kinds of Looking Glasses in rich carv'd & gilt, or Mahogany & other Frames. All sorts of Braziery & Iron Work . . .'. [D]

Russell, John, 6 Cross Ct, Drury Lane (or Russell Ct), Covent Gdn, cm and broker (1823–28). Took out Sun Insurance policies on 16 July 1823 for £600 and £500 of which £350 accounted for utensils and stock. [D; GL, Sun MS vol. 498, refs 1005988–89]

Russell, John, Mardyke, Bristol, cm (1835–40). [D]

Russell, John, Old Market Pl., Kirkby Lonsdale, Westmld, joiner and/or cm (1828–34). [D]

Russell, John, West Bromwich, Staffs., joiner and/or cm (1834). [D]

Russell, Joseph snr (?), Newcastle-under-Lyme, Staffs., cm (1790–1802). [D; poll bks]

Russell, Joseph jnr (?), Newcastle-under-Lyme, Staffs., cm (1823–37). Recorded at Bow St in 1832. [Poll bks]

Russell, Jos., 57 Hatton Gdn, London, looking-glass manufacturer (1803). [D]

Russell, Nathaniel, address unrecorded, upholder (1704–30). Son of Richard Russell of Dollington [Dallington], Sussex.

App. to Phillip Merwyn on 30 March 1704, and admitted freeman of the Upholders' Co. by servitude on 4 March 1729/30. [GL, Upholders' Co. records]

Russell, Richard, Nottingham, joiner and cm (1782). Son of John Russell, husbandman of Tollston. Taken as app. in 1782. [Nottingham app. list]

Russell, Robert, Lancaster, cm (1765–84). App. to Blackburn, Bateman & Forrest in 1765, and admitted freeman, 1771–72. Polled at Lancaster, of London, in 1784. [Lancaster app. reg. and freemen rolls]

Russell, Robert, London, upholder (1782–89). Trading at 71 Fleet Mkt in 1789. Son of Robert Russell, Gent. of Greenwich Hospital. App. to Richard Walker on 5 June 1782, and Millicent Walker on 28 January 1785. Admitted freeman of the Upholders' Co. by servitude on 7 October 1789. [GL, Upholders' Co. records]

Russell, Robert, London, upholder (1777–93). Trading at 83 Fleet Mkt, 1787–93. Son of William Russell, shoemaker of Lancaster. App. to J. Russell on 5 September 1777, and admitted freeman of the Upholders' Co. by servitude on 19 December 1787. [D; GL, Upholders' Co. records]

Russell, Robert, 17 Chancery Lane, London, cm (1809–16). [D]

Russell, Robert, 26 Bow St, Covent Gdn, London, upholder and undertaker (1817–28). [D]

Russell, Robert, Lancaster, u (1816–18). App. to L. Redmayne in 1816 and admitted freeman, 1817–18. [Lancaster app. reg. and freemen rolls]

Russell, Robert, Market Pl., Kingston, Surrey, u (1838). [D]

Russell, Robert, Cathedral Yd, Canterbury, Kent, carver and gilder (1839). [D]

Russell, Samuel, High Wycombe, Bucks., chairmaker (1816–23). Sons bapt. in 1816 and 1823, daughter in 1819. [PR (bapt.)]

Russell, Stephen, at 'The Cabinet', Langley St, near Long Acre, London, cm (1716). Insured goods and merchandise in his house on 17 December 1716. [GL, Sun MS vol. 6, p. 88]

Russell, Thomas, Queen St, St Saviour's, Southwark, London, upholder (1767). Took out a Hand in Hand Insurance policy in 1767 for £50, plus £75 on timber. [GL, Hand in Hand MS, vol. 106, p. 134]

Russell, Thomas, 18 Barbican, London, freeman joiner and clockcase maker (1762–1815). Recorded in partnership with Charles Russell throughout this period, but also alone. Employed several non-freemen each year between 1762–87, and as many as thirty throughout 1780. Took out Sun Insurance policies on houses in 1779 and 1780 for £400; and in 1781 for £300. In 1784 insured utensils and stock in warehouse for £400, and houses in tenure of Reeves, cm, for £200; and on 23 October 1809, two houses in tenure at 10 and 11 Little Trinity Lane for £300. On 15 November 1810 took out insurance totalling £700 including £300 on 10 and 11 Little Trinity Lane, and £400 on house and workshop at 54 Barbican in tenure of Cole, silversmith. [GL, City Licence bks, vols 3–6, 9 and 10; GL, Sun MS vol. 277, p. 518; vol. 283, p. 339; vol. 291, p. 510; vol. 321, p. 476; vol. 443, ref. 836117; vol. 449, ref. 850580] See Charles Russell.

Russell, Thomas, Chapel Allerton, Leeds, Yorks., cm (1822). [D]

Russell, Thomas, High Wycombe, Bucks., chairmaker (b. c. 1806–41). Daughters bapt. in 1827 and 1839, son in 1836. Aged 35 at the time of the 1841 Census. [PR (bapt.)]

Russell, W. & I., Bridge St, Southampton, Hants., u and cm (1829–31). Recorded in *Hampshire Advertiser and Royal Yacht Club Gazette*, 25 April 1829, and March 1831.

Russell, Walter, Strand, London, upholder (1774). [Poll bk]

Russell, William, address unrecorded, cm and chairmaker (1728–29). Heal records notice of sale of stock in newspapers of 1728. Harris & Son in *The English Chair*, p. 176, mention that William Russell advertised in October 1728 and January 1729 sale of 'several sorts of chairs in the newest fashion covered with Spanish leather, silk damask, mohair or worsted damask, or uncovered with walnut tree or beech-matted bottom'd chairs from 1s. a peice to 40s. and several easy chairs, dressing chairs, close-stool chairs.' Presumably:

Russell, William, Soho Sq., St Anne's, Westminster, London, cm and chairmaker (1729). Notice in *Daily Journal*, 26 June 1729 read: 'To be sold . . . at the Two Houses on the East Side of Soho Square . . . all the Goods in Trade of Mr. William Russell . . . consisting of new Walnut Tree desks . . . Mahogany desks . . . several fine tables carved and gilt with gold . . . several sorts of fine new Walnut Tree Chairs of the newest Fashion . . . with Walnut Tree or Beech matted Bottom'd Chairs from 1 shilling a piece to 40 . . . Bedding, Quilts, Blankets . . . Eight Day Clocks, Pictures . . . N.B. Lately imported, a large parcel of Turkey, Muscovite and other Fine Carpets.'

Russell, William, address unrecorded, upholder (1751–58). Son of Robert Russell, gardener of Wimbledon. App. to Richard Farmer and Richard Walker Tayler on 5 September 1751. Admitted freeman of the Upholders' Co. by servitude on 2 November 1758. [GL, Upholders' Co. records]

Russell, William, Fetter Lane, London, turner and cm (1754–c.1770). Notice in *Public Advertiser*, 8 February 1754 read: 'Whereas John Clay, about 20, and James West, about 18 years of age, Apprentices to Mr. William Russell of Fetter Lane, Turner and Cabinetmaker, did on Sunday last absent themselves from their said Master's Service, and as it is they are supposed they are entered, or about to enter on board some Ship, this is to caution all Captains and Masters of Ships, not to pay them any wages, as their Masters will be legally entitled to receive the same . . .'. Trade card, c.1770, reads: 'William Russell, Mahogany Turner & Cabinet Maker, Makes & Sells all sorts of Turners & Cabinet Work at the Lowest Prices, Wholesale & Retail, at his Shop in Bonds Stables, Or his House in Fetter Lane, London.' Card illustrates various items of furniture including three-tiered and fall-front tripod tables, a bureau chest of drawers, and a fourteen-scallop tea board. [Heal; C. *Life*, 2 May 1957, pp. 865–66]

Russel(l), William, Strand, London, upholder (1789–96). Trading at no. 70 in 1789, and no. 75, 1790–c.1796. [D]

Russell, William, High Wycombe, Bucks., chairmaker (b. c. 1794–1841). Son bapt. in 1819, daughter in 1824. Aged 47 at the time of the 1841 Census. [PR (bapt.)]

Russell, William & John, Bridge St, Southampton, Hants., cm and u (1830). [D] See W. & I. Russell.

Russell & Gradwell, 25 Basnett St, Liverpool, cm (1839). [D] See Rossall & Gradwell.

Rustland, William, Boston, Lincs., chairmaker (1742). Took app. named Burnett in 1742. [S of G, app. index]

Rutherford, John, 11 Prince's St, Leicester Fields, London, cm and upholder (1792). Took out a Sun Insurance policy on 6 January 1792 for £900 including £500 on utensils and stock. [GL, Sun MS vol. 382, ref. 594482] See Thomas Watson.

Rutherford, Michael Frederick, London, carver and gilder (1808–27). Trading at 5 Little St Andrew St, Seven Dials in 1808, and 21 Greek St, Soho, 1826–27. [D]

Rutherford, Robert, Sewer Lane, Hull, Yorks., cm (1790–99). [D] Probably the Rutherford, cm of Hull, who subscribed to Sheraton's *Drawing Book*, 1793.

Rutherford, William, Newcastle, joiner and cm (1811–27). Trading at Foot of the Side in 1811 and 27 Butcher Bank in 1827. [D]

Rutherford, William, Queen St, Derby, carver and gilder (1818–24). [D]

Rutherford & Watson, Broad St, St Giles, London, cm (1790–93). [D]

Rutledge, Christopher, Romsey, Hants., carpenter, joiner and cm (1784). [D]

Rut(t)ledge, William, Newcastle and London, u and cm (1774–1807). App. to George West, and admitted freeman of Newcastle as an u on 15 October 1774. Polled at Newcastle, of London in 1774 and 1777. Trading at Conduit St, Hanover Sq., London, 1781–c.1786, and Mount St, Grosvenor Sq. in 1790. Of 1 Mount St, took out a Sun Insurance policy on 16 April 1807 for £400, £100 on utensils and stock in trust. [D; Newcastle freemen reg.; GL, Sun MS vol. 440, ref. 802466]

Rutley, —, London (?), cm (1669). In April 1669 Rutley supplied a 'Cabbinet' costing 7s to Giles Moore, Rector of Horsted Keynes, Sussex. Since Moore visited London on 20 April Rutley could be a London craftsman. [R. Bird, *The Journal of Giles Moore*, Sussex Record Soc. (1971), p. 333]

Rutley, R. & Lewis, John, 5 Gt Newport St, Long Acre, London, carvers and gilders (1835–39). [D] Label of 'R. Rutley, Carver & gilder, Great Newport Street, Long Acre' recorded on a large George II-style giltwood pier glass. [V&A archives]

Rutt, Thomas, London, u (1758–1802). Son of Edward Rutt, Mile End, London. App. to Charles Greenwood on 5 August 1772. Admitted freeman of the Upholders' Co. by servitude on September 1779. In partnership about this time with William Elliott at 2 Clements Lane, Lombard St. Noted in 1802 at Dalston or 'King's Arms', Cornhill. [D; GL, Upholders' Co. records]

Rutter, Edward, Dover, Kent, cm and auctioneer (1784–93). Trading at Bench St, 1784–89. Took out a Sun Insurance policy in 1789 for £200 on his house, workshops and storehouses, £50 on household goods, and £200 on utensils and stock in house and yard. [D; Sun MS vol. 362, p. 637]

Rutter, Gascoigne, Norwich, u (1704). App. to Timothy Ganning and admitted freeman on 9 October 1704. [Norwich freemen reg.]

Rutter & Jinnings, Sandwich, Kent, cm (1784–98). [D]

Ryall, Joseph, 57 Red Cross St, Cripplegate, London, cm (1787). Insured household goods for £100 on 3 July 1787. [GL, Sun MS vol. 345, p. 271]

Ryan, Richard, 40 Leeds St, Liverpool, cm (1811). [D]

Ryan, Thomas, 2 New John St, Hull, Yorks., cm (1826–29). [D]

Ryan, Thomas, Stanley St, Sheffield, Yorks., chairmaker (1837). [D]

Rycroft, John, Liverpool, cm (1780–1812). Petitioned freedom on servitude to John Mears in 1780, he was admitted 'on the same terms as R. Fairclough', paying 6s 8d. Recorded separately as being admitted freeman in 1784. His son, John Rycroft jnr, joiner, born 7 August 1787, was admitted freeman on birthright in 1812. [Liverpool freemen's committee bk]

Ryder, Francis, Norwich, cm (1828–30). Polled of the parish of St George Tombland in 1830. App. to Henry Huggins and admitted freeman on 4 December 1828. [Norwich freemen reg.]

Ryder, Herbert, Holsworthy, Devon, cm (1838). [D]

Ryder, J. E., 56 Whitehorse St, Commercial Rd, London, cm (1820). [D]

Rylance, John, St Clement Danes, London, cm (1717). App. to John Berselaer of St Clement Danes on 4 July 1717. [PRO, IRI/5, No. 14]

Ryland, A., address unrecorded. Charged £72 for 'covering a chair, footstool and cushion set on ye throne in Westminster Abbey — for 8 yds. of wich gold and blue brocard at £9.' [V&A archives]

Ryley, —, address unrecorded, cm (c.1775). Supplied furniture to Denton Park, Yorks., totalling £9, c.1775. [*Furn. Hist.*, 1968]

Ryley, George, 10 Renshaw St, Liverpool, carver and gilder (1795). [D]. See George Reely.

Ryley, John, 5 Church St, Clements Lane, Lombard St, London, u (1778). Insured his house for £300 in 1778. [GL, Sun MS vol. 265, p. 78]

Ryley, John, 21 Moorfields, Liverpool, cm and victualler (1810). [D]

Ryley, John & Son, Church St, Preston, Lancs., u (1822). [D]

Ryley, Peter, Gerrard St, London, upholder (1776). Named in Bailey's list of bankrupts, 1776.

Ryley, Robert, Jubbergate, York, cm (1784). [Poll bk]

Ryley, William, Birmingham, cm and u (1800–28). Trading at Union St in 1800 also as a fancy chairmaker; Cherry St, 1805–08; and Union St, 1809–28, no. 28 in 1828. Small advertising pamphlet of William Ryley, cm and u, Union St, Birmingham, survives in Landauer Coll., MMA, NY. [D]

Ryman, James, High St, Oxford, printseller, carver and gilder (1830). [D]

Rymell, Thomas, address unrecorded, cm (1694–1709). Submitted a bill to the Duchess of Norfolk for Drayton House, Northants., dated April to November 1694, and totalling £80. Items included 'a prince wood press', £10; 'mending a mother of perle tea table and making a brass rim to it & lacquering both', £2 5s; and 'making a table & stand of japan', £3. A further bill of 1696 totalled £81 6s; and one of 1701, £28 6s 6d, including 'a large glass in a marvel [*sic*] frame over the chimney' at £18. [V&A archives] Possibly the supplier of tables, stands and firescreen 'for Her Maj[ties] Service', 1708–09. [Symonds papers, Winterthur, Delaware, 75x64, 155. 18.6. p. 53]

Rymer, George, 1 Jones's St, Salford, Lancs., cm (1813). [D]

Rymes, William, Wardour St, London, cm (1749). [Poll bk]

Ryton & Walton, Wolverhampton, Staffs., papier mâché makers (c.1810). Stamp of 'Ryton & Walton, Wolverhampton' recorded on a set of four rectangular papier mâché trays each decorated with a vase of crimson and white irises on a maroon ground, the borders with gilt bunches of grapes. [Sotheby's, 20 January 1967, lot 77] William and Obadiah Ryton who were brothers took over the firm of japanners Taylor & Jones which had been established in 1770, and used their premises at Old Hall Works. Initially they were japanners and decorators of metal domestic wares. Obadiah died in 1810 and William Ryton took as partner Benjamin Walton and the production of papier mâché products commenced. Their main lines were tea trays but they also produced caskets, workboxes, hand screens and inkwells. Did not produce large pieces of furniture. Used artists of quality who had previously been decorating their tin wares. [J. Toller, *Papier Mâché in Great Britain and America*, 1962, p. 38]

S

Sabbarton, Jno., Bagnigge Wells Rd, London, cm (1835). [D]

Sabberton, Joshua, 22 Botolph St, Norwich, cm (1783–84). [D]

Sabine, —, 104 Queen St, Portsmouth, Hants., cm (1795). [V&A archives]

Sabourin, George, London, cm (1799–1820). In 1799 living at Back Lane, Stepney. Trading at 51 Shoreditch in 1808 and 19 Curtain Rd in 1811; but at 39 Paul St, Finsbury Sq., 1814–20.

Probably ceased furniture making after this date but is shown at 4 Commercial Rd as a timber merchant, 1823–27. The trade card of Sabourin & Marchand, cm, upholders and undertakers at 47 Church St, Bethnal Green exists [Heal Coll., BM] and may relate to George Sabourin. [D; PR (bapt.) St George-in-the-East]

Sach, John, Maldon, Essex, u (1784). [D]

Sackham, —, address unknown, upholder (1754). Subscribed to Chippendale's *Director*, 1754.

Sacx, Thomas, parish of St Martin-in-the-Fields, London, carver (1711). In 1711 took out a lease for 21 years on a property on the south side of Long Acre. [Marylebone Ref. Lib., deed 176/17–18]

Sadd, John, Needham Market, Suffolk, looking-glass maker (1685). Probate inventory. [Suffolk RO (Ipswich), FE1/3/81]

Sadgrove, Thomas, Broker's Row, Moorfields, London, cm, u and looking-glass warehouse (1809–17). From 1809 the business traded as Thomas Sadgrove & Son, the latter being William who by 1817 had taken over the business. The address is shown as 20 Broker's Row, 1808–09, but by 1814, no. 21 was also being used. In 1817 Thomas Sadgrove corresponded with the Royal Society of Arts on the uses of mahogany. His address was shown as Mulberry Ct, Wilson St, Moorfields, probably his home. [D; Heal]

Sadgrove, William, London, cm, u and looking-glass warehouse (1817–40). Successor to his father Thomas Sadgrove and continued to use the 20–21 Broker's Row, Moorfields address. One directory of 1820 however lists 18, 20 and 21 Eldon St, Finsbury Circus which is probably the same address. [D]

Sadleir, Thomas, Highgate, London, cm, upholder and undertaker (1823–39). Recorded at High St in 1839. [D]

Sadler, Edward, Hanley, Staffs., cm and u (1828–35). Listed at Tontine St in 1828, Market Sq., 1830–34, Market St in 1834 and Lamb St in 1835. Advertised for an u, *Chester Courant*, 26 January 1830. [D]

Sadler, Francis, 28 Aldgate St, Aldgate, London, upholder etc. (1817). [D]

Sadler, George, 25 Lime St, Liverpool, u (1816). [D]

Sadler, George, Globe Rd, Mile End, London, cm (1826). [D]

Sadler, George, St Giles St, Norwich, u (1836–39). [D]

Sadler, I., Whitchurch, Salop, cm (1797). [D]

Sadler, James, Leeds, Yorks., cm (1834–39). At 107 West St in 1834 and 18 Wellington Lane in 1839. [D]

Sadler, John, Watlington, Oxon., u (1755). In *Jackson's Oxford Journal*, 17 May 1755 advertised that he was continuing the business of the late John Sibley.

Sadler, John, address unknown, cm (1803). In 1803 subscribed to Sheraton's *Cabinet Dictionary*.

Sadler, Richard, 31 Drury Lane, London, upholder (1784). [D]

Sadler, Robert, 30 Wilkes St, Spitalfields, London, chairmaker (1810). In February 1810 took out insurance cover of £400 of which half was for utensils and stock. [GL, Sun MS vol. 449, ref. 841611]

Sadler, Robert snr, 6 Globe Terr., Mile End, Old Town, London, cm and u (1822–39). [D]

Sadler, Slacksle, address unknown (1782). Paid £32 3s by Paul Methuen for new furniture supplied to Corsham Court, Wilts. on 30 April 1782. [V&A archives]

Sadler, William, 24 Little Alie St, Goodman's Fields, London, u and cm (1813–17). [D]

Sadler, William, Liverpool, cm and chairmaker (1834–35). In 1834 shown in one directory at 4 Leece St but in another at 11 Shannon St, an address that he also occupied in 1835. [D]

Saevent, William, 46 Church St, Shoreditch, London, cm and u (1827). [D]

Safreey, Thomas, Norwich, cm (1759). In 1759 took app. named Gosling. [S of G, app. index]

Sagar, Stephen, York, u (1759–84). Son of Robert Sagar of 'Mektham', clerk. App. to Robert Barker, u, on 10 November 1759, and admitted freeman in 1771. At Micklegate in 1774 but in 1784 at Jubbergate. Bankruptcy announced, *Gents Mag.*, July 1776. [App. bk; freemen rolls; poll bks]

Sage, George, Bristol, cabinet turner (1831–40). At 7 St John's Bridge in 1831; 5 St James's Churchyard, 1832–35; Withington Ct, Horse Fair in 1836 and Canon St, 1837–40. [D]

Sage, John, Bristol, furniture japanner, sign and furniture painter (1824–40). At 56 Broadmead, 1824–25; in the yard near 48 Broadmead, 1826–29; and Alden's Ct, Broadmead, 1830–37. After this date the business is listed as J. & T. Sage and traded from 1 Trinity St. [D]

Sage, Samuel, Coombe St, Exeter, Devon, cm (1838–40). Daughters bapt. in 1838 and 1840 at St Mary Major. [PR (bapt.)]

Saggers, John, Saffron Walden, Essex, cm, u and brazier (1778–80). In 1778 insured his stock for £300. His nearness to Sir John Griffin Griffin's house, Audley End, Essex, ensured some patronage of a minor nature. An oak four post bed and bedding was supplied in 1778 at a cost of £7 8s, and in 1780 a 3 ft wainscot desk was the major item on an account which totalled £2 7s. [GL, Sun MS vol. 267, p. 29; Essex RO, D/DBy/A36/6, A38/9]

Sainsbury, Joseph, Tottenham Ct Rd, London, u and cm (1835–40). At 169 Tottenham Ct Rd in 1835 but by 1839 the number was 167. [D]

Sainsbury, Mary, 5 Rosemary St, Bristol, u (1830–40). [D]

Sainsbury, Philip, Audley St, Westminster, London, carver (1749). [D]

Saint, Aaron, New St, The Potteries, Staffs., joiner and cm (1818). [D]

Saint, Gideon, 'The Golden Head', Princes St, near Leicester Fields, London, carver and gilder (b. 1729–d. 1799). Gideon Saint, a London craftsman active in the 1760s and 1770s, is remembered chiefly for his remarkable album or scrapbook of carvers' designs, now at the MMA, NY. Pasted to its inside front cover is an elaborate engraved trade card inscribed 'Gideon Saint Carver & Gilder, at the Golden Head in Princes Street, near Leicester Fields. Makes all sorts of Sconces, Girondoles, Chandeliers, Brackets, Tables, Chimney-Pieces, Picture Frames &c. in the best and most Reasonable manner.'

The scrapbook exemplifies the intimate connection between the French Huguenot community in England and the Rococo style there. Saint appears to have travelled almost exclusively in Huguenot circles. He was born of French Huguenot parents in London in 1729. At age fourteen he was app., for a seven year term, to 'Jacob Touzey of St Martin's fields Midx. Carver.' [PRO, IR 1/17 — September 22, 1743] At the end of his apprenticeship, about 1750, Saint presumably became a journeyman carver and gilder. In 1762 he married Marie Catherine Paisant. The following year he set up as a carver and gilder at 'The Golden Head', Princes St, London, the address on his trade card. As apps he took Richard Giles in 1765 and Geo. Swain in 1766. [PRO, IR 1/24] He carried on his business there until 1779, when he moved to Charles St, Hoxton. Apparently he left the carvers' trade at that time. Sometime after his wife's death in 1791, Saint moved to Groombridge, Kent, where, with the rank of a gentleman, he died in 1799. He had been a warden and overseer of the French Church, Soho (1775) and a director of the Ecole de Charité Française de Westminster (1792).

The 364 numbered pages of Saint's album are divided into twelve sections, each identified by a finger tab marked with the name of one or more related forms of carvers' work: 'House Furniture, Brackets, Shields & Odd Ornaments,

Pannells & Cealings, Signs & Other Outworks, Stands & Clock Cases, Ornaments for Mouldings, Gerandoles, Tables & Slabbs, Ornaments for Chimneys, All Kinds of Glass Frames.' Saint began filling these sections with Régence-style engravings (or drawings after engravings) from French books by Berain, Boulle, Mariette, Pineau, and Roumier. Shortly, however, he switched exclusively to the English engravings in the fully-developed Rococo manner — by Lock, Copland, and Johnson — that comprise the bulk of the illustrations. In addition he made a number of finely executed drawings on the pages of the album itself. Mostly of frames, carved mouldings, and chimney ornaments, they suggest that Saint may have specialized in interior architectural ornament.

Gideon Saint's scrapbook is the most graphic surviving document of how a Georgian craftsman worked. For it, he cut up inexpensive booklets of carvers' designs, trimming off all names and inscriptions, re-arranging the parts by type of object, and numbering them. The result was a library of anonymous designs for his clients to choose from. Examples of Saint's executed work have yet to be identified. [M. Heckscher, 'Gideon Saint: An Eighteenth-Century Carver and His Scrapbook', *Met. Museum Bulletin*, February 1969, pp. 299–311] M.H.H.

Saint, Thomas, Newcastle, u (1761–80). App. to William Charnley and free, 26 March 1761. [Freemen reg.; poll bks]

St George, John, London (?), upholder (1685). In 1685 submitted an account to Lord Petrie of Ingatstone Hall, Essex for furniture, upholstery, embroidery, looking-glasses etc. totalling £555 7s 11½d. [Essex RO, D/DP A164A]

St Quintin, Percy, Queen St, Bank Pl., St George's Tombland, Norwich, mahogany merchant, cm and u (1817–40). App. to Samuel Mathue(?) and free as a cm on 3 May 1817. [D; freemen rolls]

Saitt, Richard, 92 Jermyn St, London, upholder (1791). On 12 July 1791 took out insurance cover of £1,000 on glass in his dwelling house. [GL, Sun MS ref. 586502]

Saker, J., Tonbridge, Kent, chairmaker (1803). [D]

Sale, Joseph, Upper end of St James St, near Portugal St, London, upholder (1712–23). The St James St address is included in an insurance record of 1712. In 1722–23 the address is simply recorded as the parish of St Martin-in-the-Fields. [GL, Sun MS vol. 2, p. 39; Hand in Hand MS vol. 26, p. 133; Heal]

Sale, Phineas, London, upholder (1719–33). Son of William Sale of Bromyard, Herefs., Gent. App. to Nicholas Patrick on 13 January 1719 and free of the Upholders' Co. by servitude, 8 April 1719. Took as apps Timothy Wright, 1719–26, and William Greer, 1720–33. [GL, Upholders' Co. records]

Sale, Robert, 26 Cavendish St, New North Rd, London, cm and u (1839). [D]

Sale, William, 5 and 6 Guildhall St, Bury St Edmunds, Suffolk, cm and u (1830–39). The name 'Saile' recorded on a canvas chair seat probably refers to this maker. [D; poll bk; *Antique Collector*, June 1956]

Salisbury, Charles Pyne, Exeter, Devon (1797). Married Miss Leach, daughter of Capt. Leach of Exmouth. [*Exeter Flying Post*, 9 November 1797]

Salisbury, John snr and jnr, Exeter, Devon, cm and u (1770–1814). John Salisbury snr opened a cabinet and upholstery warehouse at Fore St in October 1770. This appears to have adjoined the French Church. He offered to furnish 'houses for Ladies and Gentlemen at an easy per cent per annum' and stated that he retailed 'mahogany, wainscott, deals, laths etc.'. He also acted as an appraiser and undertook building work. At the time he announced the opening of his warehouse he also advertised for two joiners 'that have been mostly used at the bench' and 'a pair of sawyers that have been used to work for the cabinet and chair branch'. He also had a vacancy for an

app. In March 1784 he advertised for information about John East, cm and chairmaker, possibly one of his apps or workmen, who had absconded to Cornwall 'with money from the illegal sale of John Salisbury's property'. In December 1785 John Salisbury married Mrs Mary Larkworthy, widow of a linen draper and daughter of Capt. Scott of Lympstone, Devon. In 1771 and 1776 he is recorded acting as agent for the sale of furniture and a house which he advertised for disposal.

There appears to have been another John Salisbury, almostly certainly the son of John Salisbury snr. He married in May 1792 Miss Fisher of the parish of St Thomas, and is included in an Exeter Militia List of 1803 living in the parish of St Olave. The date that he took over the business is uncertain, but was possibly sometime in the 1790s. In August 1808 he announced that he had left his residence but was still maintaining his ware-rooms and shops in Fore St. Letters were to be addressed to Mr Stong, baker and flour factor in Fore St. In March 1810 a removal to St Thomas, near the Bridge was advertised. John Salisbury's stock was auctioned off in February 1814, when he indicated that he was giving up the business as he was 'about leaving this country'. This consisted of 'four-post, tent and other bedsteads; feather beds, blankets and counterpanes; handsome mahogany wardrobes; commode and straight front set of drawers; dressing and deception night tables; night, and bason stands; pier and dressing glasses; handsome inlaid secretary and bookcase, with fancy glass doors; mahogany and coromandel wood, card, sofa and Pembroke tables; handsome sideboards, sofas; mahogany and fancy chairs; with a variety of other articles'.

Salisbury used trade labels to mark items he sold, and one has been recorded on a brass bound mahogany wine cooler of c.1780–1800. Trade cards of this firm also survive which indicate that papier mâché ornaments and wall paper were stocked and which also claim that looking-glasses could be polished from the rough. Billiard balls and bowling green and skittle balls could also be supplied. From October 1807 auctioneering was added to the activities of the busines. [D; *Exeter Flying Post*, 26 October 1770, 8 March 1771, 3 May 1776, 5 March 1784, 15 December 1785, 24 May 1792, 27 December 1792, 9 October 1794, 1 October 1807, 25 August 1808, 1 March 1810, 17 February 1814; Heal Coll., BM]

Salisbury, M. A., Exeter, Devon, u (1838–40). At Mint Lane in 1838 and Bartholomew Yd, 1839–40. [D]

Salisbury, Thomas, London, upholder (1729). Son of Thomas Salisbury of the parish of St Martin-in-the-Fields, Gent. App. to William Humphreys on 1 February 1720 and free by servitude, 16 May 1729. [GL, Upholders' Co. records] Possibly:

Salisbury, Thomas, Dyers Ct, Aldermanbury, London, u (d.1767). Death 'at an Inn in Clare-Market' of this 'eminent Upholsterer . . . who had retired from Business and resided in Nottingham' reported in *Public Advertiser*, 30 June 1767.

Salisbury, Thomas, London, carver and gilder (1812–39). In July 1812 at 6 Edward St where he took out insurance cover of £300 which included £100 for china and glass and £50 for utensils and stock. In 1820 at 13 Brokers Alley, Long Acre where he declared his trade as a looking-glass and frame maker. By 1835 at 1 Brokers Alley, Drury Lane as a furniture broker and in 1839 at 2 Brokers Alley when once more his trade was listed as carver and gilder. [D; GL, Sun MS vol. 459, ref. 873097]

Salisbury, William, 2 Cumberland St, Shoreditch, London, looking-glass and frame maker (1835). [D]

Salkeld, James, Wigton, Cumb., chairmaker (1829–34). In 1829 at Meeting House Lane and in 1834 at West St. [D]

Salkeld, John, Penrith, Cumb., chairmaker (1811–34). In 1811 at Dockray and in 1834 in Middlegate. [D]

Salleway, John, 15 Gt Turnstile, Holborn, London, carver (1785). In July 1785 insured his utensils and stock for £40. [GL, Sun MS vol. 330, p. 326]

Sallis, George, Bull Head Ct, Jewin St, London, chairmaker (1749). [Heal]

Sallows, John snr, Colchester, Essex, cm (1780–1812). [Poll bks]

Sallows, John, Gt Yarmouth, Norfolk, cm (1795). App. to John Sewell and free by servitude 1795. Changed his name to Sallows from Aldred. [Freemen rolls; poll bk]

Sallows, John jnr, Colchester, Essex, cm (1806–31). [Poll bks]

Sallows, Richard, Colchester, Essex, cm (1768). [Poll bk]

Salloway, William, 30 Bow St, Covent Gdn, London, carver and gilder (1809). [D]

Sallway, John, 30 Bow St, Covent Gdn, London, carver and gilder (1808–37). [D]

Salmon, Abraham, parish of St Gregory, Norwich, chairmaker (1786). [Poll bk]

Salmon, Charles, 'Five Fields Row near the Flaske', Westminster, London, cm (1784). [Poll bk]

Salmon, Charles, address unknown, carver and gilder (1800–03). Recorded supplying the Crown. On 16 July 1800 he was paid 6s as a carver and gilder. On 5 February 1803 paid £52 8s for rental of a warehouse room for furniture for five years. [Windsor Royal Archives, RA 88863, 88919]

Salmon, George, Oxford St, St Anne Sq., London, chairmaker (1814). In 1814 took app. named James Cudland. [Westminster Ref. Lib., MS E3559 Grinsells charity app. indentures]

Salmon, Henry, London, cm, u and undertaker (1795–1817). At 25 Lamb's Conduit St, 1795–96; 15 Chapel St, Lamb's Conduit St, 1798–1803; but by 1806 the number had changed to 16. Included in the list of master cabinet makers in Sheraton's *Cabinet Dictionary*, 1803. [D]

Salmon, Isaac, Norwich and London, u (1802–06). Freeman of Norwich and living in the parish of St Gregory in 1802. By 1806 living in London. [Norwich poll bks]

Salmon, John, London, upholder (d. by 1720). Freeman and member of the Upholders' Co. His son Thomas was also free of the Upholders' Co. and received his freedom in 1729. [GL, Upholders' Co. records]

Salmon, John, 427 Oxford St, London, japanned chair manufacturer (1803–25). From 1809 traded as John Salmon & Son. The initial of the son was H. The trade label of this firm advertises 'Drawing Room Chairs Settees Sofas etc. in Gold or Colours, BED ROOM CHAIRS TO MATCH, Furniture Paper Hangings &c., Bed & Window-Cornices, Card & Dressing Tables With every Article in the above Business on Reasonable Terms. N.B. Great Allowance to Merchants & Captains. Country Orders Executed with Punctuality.' Included in the list of master cabinet makers in Sheraton's *Cabinet Dictionary*, 1803. [D]

Salmon, Richard, parish of St Giles, Norwich, cm (1806). [Poll bk]

Salmon, Robert, Bristol, cm (1754–c.1785). Shown living in the parish of St Nicholas from 1754–84 and in 1775 at 9 Bristol Back. In 1762 took app. named Williams. In the mid 1780s he was one of the craftsmen who supplied furniture for the new Mansion House. Salmon's contribution was of a minor nature consisting of a 3 ft 4 in. oak bureau at £2 15s and 'a coaco ruler' at 1s. He also supplied, probably for another Corporation building, seven large dining tables at £3 10s each, two mahogany pedestals with vases at £10, two sideboards for the recesses at £1 16s and sixty mahogany brass-nailed chairs at £1 2s each. [D; poll bks; *Furn. Hist.*, 1976]

Salmon, Robert snr, Cambridge, chairmaker (1774). [Poll bk]

Salmon, Robert, parish of St Clement, Cambridge, cm (1819). Child bapt. parish of St Clement. [PR (bapt.)]

Salmon, Robert, Pilgrim St, Newcastle, cm (1824–27). [D]

Salmon, Samuel, Spurriergate, York, carpenter and cm (1778–79). In both 1778 and 1779 insured his utensils and stock for £100. In 1779 total insurance cover was £200. [GL, Sun MS vol. 265, p. 478; vol. 277, p. 378]

Salmon, Samuel, Cambridge, cm, u and broker (1805–40). At Bridge St, 1805–07, and from 1832 at Sidney St. Samuel Salmon, turner, was listed in a directory of 1792. [D; poll bks]

Salmon, Sarah, 106 Pottergate St, Norwich, upholder (c.1803). [D]

Salmon, Thomas, London, upholder (1729). Son of John Salmon, a member of the Upholders' Co. App. to his mother Sarah Salmon on 11 January 1720 and free of the Upholders' Co. by servitude, 3 December 1729. [GL, Upholders' Co. records]

Salmon, Thomas, New Canal, Salisbury, Wilts., cm and u (1822–30). [D]

Salmon, Thomas, 14 Albion St, Cheltenham, Glos., cm and u (1830). [D]

Salmon, William, Cambridge, chairmaker (1774–80). [Poll bks]

Salmon, William, 3 Gt Pulteney St, London, tailor and upholder (1777). In 1777 took out insurance cover of £1,200 of which £500 was for utensils and stock. [GL, Sun MS vol. 255, p. 146]

Salmon, William, High Wycombe, Bucks., chairmaker (b. c. 1821–41). Aged 20 at the time of the 1841 Census.

Salph, Elias, Fisherton Anger, Salisbury, Wilts., cm and u (1830). [D]

Salter, John Henry, Regent Terr., City Rd, London, cm and u (1839). [D]

Salter, Thomas, 40 Greek St, Soho, London, cm (1778). In 1778 took out insurance cover of £400 and of this sum £140 was for utensils and stock and £50 for a timber workshop. [GL, Sun MS vol. 266, p. 371]

Salteri, Ant., 17 Gt Queen St, Lincoln's Inn Fields, London, looking-glass manufacturer (1813–27). In 1825 the business is listed as Salteri & Co. [D]

Salteri & Co., 374 Strand, London, carvers, gilders and looking-glass manufacturers (1815–40). On their trade card [Landauer Coll., MMA, NY] they claimed to have been established in 1815 and were successors to Cattaneo & Co. They also stated that they were carvers and gilders to the late King William IV. The relationship of this business to Ant. Salteri of 17 Gt Queen St, Lincoln's Inn Fields is unknown.

Salthouse, Richard & Riding, William, Preston, Lancs., joiners, cm and timber merchants (1795). Dissolution of the partnership was announced, *Billinge's Liverpool Advertiser*, 19 October 1795.

Saltmarsh, William, 79 Coleman St, Lothbury, London, looking-glass manufacturer (1815–29). From 1819–25 listed as William Saltmarsh & Son. Their label is recorded on a mirror in a private collection and indicates 'Old Glasses polished, silvered carefully framed, in the best manner ladies needlework carefully framed. Prints and drawings framed and glazed. German sheet-glass of the largest dimensions. Funerals decently performed.' [D; V&A archives]

Saltmarsh & Wicking, Edger Terr., Tunbridge Wells, Kent, carvers and gilders (1838–39). In 1839 the business is listed in a directory simply as 'Saltmarsh'. [D]

Saltmire, Rd., Market Pl., Market Weighton, Yorks., cm and joiner (1828). [D]

Saltonstall, William, Leeds, Yorks., u (1710). In 1710 took app. named Woordsworth. [S of G, app. index]

Salvin, Robert, 2 Cross Pl., Sunderland, Co. Durham, cm (1827–32). [D]

Sambach, William, Russell Ct, Drury Lane, London, upholder (1716–24). Took out insurance cover of £175 on his rented house. [GL, Hand in Hand MS vol. 16, p. 634; vol. 28, p. 170]

Samber, Samuel, Long Acre, London, u (1747–49). From September to November 1747 supplied furniture to Alscot Park, Warks. to a value of £20 7s 10d. The most expensive item was a mahogany couch on brass casters 'with a squab stuft in Canvise and quilted' at £7. [Westminster poll bk; V&A archives]

Sammes, James, 53 Russell St, Bloomsbury, London, upholder, cm and undertaker (1764–1808). Undertook work for Elizabeth, Marchioness of Tavistock but most of this occurred in 1768–69 after her death and to the order of her steward George Rawson. In February to March 1768 repairs to a japanned stand and taking down a bed at Bedford House, London cost 15s 6d; and in September of that year £8 9s was paid for the upholstery of a small mahogany chair and a mahogany tea chest. Sammes does not appear in London directories until 1781 and his address before this date is unknown. Included in Sheraton's list of master cabinet makers in his *Cabinet Dictionary,* 1803. [D; Bedford Office, London]

Sammonds, James, High Wycombe, Bucks., chairmaker (b.c. 1811–41). Aged 30 at the date of the 1841 Census.

Sammonds, John, High Wycombe, Bucks., chairmaker (b.c. 1806–41). Two daughters and a son bapt. 1827–35. Aged 25 at the date of the 1841 Census.

Sammonds, Samuel, High Wycombe, Bucks., chairmaker (1830–41). Aged 35 at the date of the 1841 Census. [D]

Sammonds, Tom, High Wycombe, Bucks., chairmaker (1825). [PR (bapt.)]

Sammons, Jer., 12 South St, Lambeth, London, chair and sofa maker (1826). [D]

Sammons, T., 12 Portugal St, Lambeth Walk, London, chair and sofa maker (1826). [D]

Sammons, Thomas, Tunbridge Wells, Kent, chairmaker (1832). [D]

Sample, John, 6 Gt Portland St, London, upholder and cm (1782). In 1782 took out insurance cover of £300 which included £190 for utensils and stock. [GL, Sun MS vol. 299, p. 160]

Sampson, Abraham, Conduit St, London, u (1749). [Westminster poll bk]

Sampson, Nicholas, William St, Bishop Wearmouth, Sunderland, Co. Durham, cm (1827). [D]

Sampson, Thomas, Ashford, Kent, u (1774–93). Freeman of Canterbury. [D; Canterbury poll bks]

Sampson, Thomas, Liverpool, chairmaker (1829–39). In 1829 at 7 Pellew St; in 1834–37 at 63 Bostock St; but by 1839 the number was 30. [D]

Sampson, Thomas, Exeter, Devon, cm (1830–31). Shown in one directory at 1830 at 4 Paris St but in another of 1830–31 at Silver St. [D]

Sampson, William & Richard, parish of St Mary, Woolnoth, London, u (1777). Bankruptcy announced, *Gents Mag.,* July 1777.

Sampson, William, 11 Bostock St, Liverpool, chairmaker (1837). [D]

Sampson & Shaw, York St, Chorlton-on Medlock, Manchester, cm (1840). [D]

Sams, J. & J., London, bedstead makers (1835–39). Shown at 4 Chapel St, Holywell Mt (Curtain Row) and 8½ Charlotte St, Old St. [D]

Sams, James, Down St, Westminster, London, carver (1774). [Poll bk]

Sams, Samuel, Snowfields, Southwark, London, bedstead maker (1809). [D]

Samson, J., 18 York Terr., Borough Rd, London, cm and chairmaker (1835). [D]

Sam(p)son, John, 8 Newington Causeway, London, chair and sofa maker and cm (1820–26). [D]

Samson, Philip, 29 Tooley St, London, wood carver (1775–77). [D]

Sampson, Thomas, Ashby-de-la-Zouch, Leics., u (1791). [D]

Sampson, Thomas, High St, Rye, Sussex, cm, u and paperhanger (1823). [D]

Samuel, George, 118 Golden Lane, London, cm (1822). In November 1822 took out insurance cover of £100 of which £70 was for stock and utensils. [GL, Sun MS vol. 491, ref. 997908]

Samuel, H., 484 Oxford St, London. A number of pieces of furniture of late 18th to early 19th century date are recorded stamped with the name of this firm. Items include a satinwood 'bonheur du jour', a mahogany plate and cutlery stand and a pair of mahogany cheval screens. [Sotheby's, 7 February 1969, lot 131; 16 July 1971, lot 76; 8 September 1978, lot 238]

Samuel, Isaac, 25 Nicholas Lane, Lombard St, London, merchant, looking-glass manufacturer and cabinet manufacturer (1819–25). [D]

Samuel, Isaac, 29 Finsbury Pl., London, cm (1826). [D]

Samuel, James, Peterborough Ct, St Bride's, London, cm (1749–61). Occupied the following parochial offices in the parish of St Bride, Fleet St: Constable 1749, Collector for the Poor 1754, Sidesman and Questman 1755, Scavenger 1759 and Churchwarden 1761. [GL, MS 6561, p. 82]

Samuel, S. J. & P., 39 Leonard St, Shoreditch, London, looking-glass manufacturer and merchant (1817). [D]

Samuel, Simon, Billiter Lane, London, merchant, looking-glass manufacturer and factor (1815). [D]

Samuel, William, Houndsditch, London, upholder (1771). Son of William Samuel of Merioneth, Wales, clerk. Free of the Upholders' Co. by redemption under the terms of the 1750 Upholders' Act, 2 February 1771. [GL, Upholders' Co. records]

Sancroft, Joshua Baker, Norwich and Gt Yarmouth, Norfolk, cm (1826–30). Son of James Sancroft, surgeon. Free of Norwich 20 May 1826 but by July 1830 living in Gt Yarmouth. [Norwich freemen rolls; Norwich and Gt Yarmouth poll bks]

Sanctury, James, Burnham Market, Norfolk, cm (1839). [D]

Sandalands, —, address unknown, cm (1803). Subscribed to Sheraton's *Cabinet Dictionary,* 1803.

Sandall, Thomas, Richmond Green, Surrey, cm (d. by 1753). In August 1753 the sale of the stock in trade, tools and utensils of the late Thomas Sandall was announced. His stock included 'a great variety of exceeding good Cabinet Work, in Walnut-tree & Mahogany, in Cabinets, Bureaus, Commodes, Writing, Dining, Dressing, Card, Claw & Night Tables, Chests, & Chests of Drawers, glasses, Marble Tables on Carv'd Frames, Chairs etc. Two Wainscot Models of Houses, Mahogany Planks & Boards, Cherry Tree Sticks, Veniers etc.' [*Public Advertiser,* 4 August 1753]

Sandaver, Jno., 12 Kenton St, Brunswick Sq., London, cm u and undertaker (1839). [D]

Sandbach, William, Liverpool, u (1767–d. by 1820). App. to Edward Roberts and free 3 December 1767. [Freemen reg.]

Sandbach, William, Northwich, Cheshire, u (1782). In January 1782 advertised the disposal of his stock in trade and offered the house and shop that he had occupied for sale. He claimed to be the only u in Northwich at this time. [*Chester Chronicle,* 11 January 1782]

Sandell, Samuel, 101 New Bond St, London, upholder (1782–96). App. to William Jellicoe, a member of the Skinners' Co.

but by trade an upholder, on 12 January 1768. Already trading on his own account from 101 New Bond St by 1782, but was not admitted a member of the Upholders' Co. until 7 October 1789 and then under the terms of the 1750 Upholders' Act and not by servitude. In January 1793 took out insurance cover of £500 on a property at 11 Orchard St, Portman Sq., possibly his dwelling house. [D; GL, Upholders' Co. records; Sun MS vol. 389, ref. 601836]

Sander, Thomas, Oldbury, Tewkesbury, Glos., cm (1837). Child bapt. in 1837. [PR (bapt.)]

Sanders, Benjamin, Sevenoaks, Kent, cm (1824–29). [D]

Sanders, Daniel, parish of St John, Wapping, London, carver (1736). In 1736 took app. named Cowell. [S of G, app. index]

Sanders, Frances, 9 Hanover St, Bristol, u (1827–32). [D] By 1835 Richard Sanders was trading at this address in the same trade.

Sanders, John, 15 Crown St, Finsbury Sq., London, cm (1802–03). In January 1802 took out insurance cover of £300 of which £200 was for utensils and stock. By December 1803 these figures had risen to £500 and £350 respectively. [GL, Sun MS vol. 424, ref. 727054; vol. 426, ref. 743754]

Sanders, John, 224 Shoreditch, London, cm and carpenter (1808–13). In November 1809 took out insurance cover of £2,100 of which stock and utensils amounted to £1,800. This level of insurance cover was reached by few of the large central London cm working in the fashionable part of the trade and is most unusual for a business in the Shoreditch area [D; GL, Sun MS vol. 447, ref. 836626]

Sanders, John, parish of St John, Exeter, Devon, cm (1832). [Poll bk]

Sanders, Joseph, 1 Budge Row, London, upholder (1789–96). Son of William Sanders of Chertsey, Surrey, linen draper. App. to Gawn Shotter on 1 July 1789 and free of the Upholders' Co. by servitude, 7 September 1796. [GL, Upholders' Co. records]

Sanders, Joseph, Catherine St, London, see Morgan & Sanders.

Sanders, Richard, Hanover St, Bristol, u (1822–40). An R. Sanders is shown in Bristol directories at 4 Hanover St, 1822–24 and 9 Hanover St, 1825–26. Between 1827–32 this address is shown in the occupation of Frances Sanders carrying on in the same trade. No entries appear for the years 1833–34, but from 1835 Richard Sanders is shown at this address. The likely explanation is that there were two Richard Sanders, father and son and that Frances was wife of Richard Sanders snr. [D]

Sanders, Thomas, address unknown, carpenter, joiner and cm (1823). Listed as an insolvent debtor, *The Alfred*, 25 February 1823.

Sanders, William, St Ives, Hunts., cm (1798). [D]

Sanders, William, 8 Rosemary St, Bristol, fancy chair maker (1840). [D]

Sanders & Colbron, address unknown, u (1819–20). Undertook removals, cleaning and repairs at Brighton Pavilion in 1819, and supplied a canopy, chair and footstools for the Duke of Wellington, Ambassador to the Court of France in 1820. [PRO, LC11/29]

Sanderson, —, Green Dragon Yd, Worship St, London, cm (1832). [D] The firm of Bagnall & Sanderson traded from this address.

Sanderson, George, Newcastle, u (1760–87). In 1760 took app. named Sanderson, possibly related. In 1778 at Bigg-market, and in 1782 at 'The Crown', Bigg-market of which he was the publican. In 1787 at Rosemary Lane. [D; S of G, app. index]

Sanderson, George, Sandgate, Berwick-upon-Tweed, Northumb., cm and u (1827–34). Also listed at Foul Ford in 1828. [D]

Sanderson, George, Bridge-gate, Howden, Yorks., joiner and cm (1828). [D]

Sanderson, Henry, Swallow St, London, cm and upholder (1775–79). In partnership with James Paul, February 1775, he took out insurance cover of £500 of which £390 was for utensils and stock. Bankruptcy announced in July 1779 at which date he appears to have been in partnership with Alex. Sanderson. [GL, Sun MS vol. 236, p. 246; *Sussex Weekly Advertiser*, 26 July 1779]

Sanderson, James, 119 Fore St, Cripplegate, London, cm and broker (1775). In 1775 took out insurance cover of £1,200 of which £700 was for utensils and tools. [GL, Sun MS vol. 237, p. 170]

Sanderson, James, Bath, Som., cm (1759). In 1759 took app. named Hambleton. [S of G, app. index]

Sanderson, James & Co., Hedon, Yorks., cm and joiners (1828). [D]

Sanderson, John, 'The Golden Angel', Haymarket, London, upholder (1698–c.1745). App. to Henry Gage, draper, and free of the Upholders' Co. by servitude, 24 October 1698. Trading in Haymarket by 1709, and in 1714 took out insurance cover for his dwelling house at the sign of 'The Golden Angel' in that street. Took as app. William Cooke, 1720–26. A pine side table and oval mirror *en suite* in the Court Room of the Foundling Hospital were made by a John Sanderson c.1745. [GL, Upholders' Co. records; Heal; GL, Sun MS vol. 4, 7 October 1714; V&A archives]

Sanderson, John, Manchester, cm (1742). In 1742 took app. named Hardman. [S of G, app. index]

Sanderson, John, Alnwick, Northumb., cm (1757–76). In 1757 took app. named Atkinson and in 1761, Hunter. A 'Saunderson, Alnwick' is included in a list of furniture makers drawn up c.1776 by the Duchess of Northumberland. [S of G, app. index; Gilbert, *Chippendale*, p. 154]

Sanderson, John, Wood St, York, cm (1779–1818). Recorded in Wood St, 1784–87. His apps taking the freedom of the City included Thomas Kirlew (1779), James Rodwell of Leeds (1784), William Mariner (1790) and William Colbeck (1818). William Mariner is recorded as starting his apprenticeship in 1783, William Colbeck in 1787 and John Shores in 1781. [D; poll bk; freemen rolls; app. bk]

Sanderson, John, Liverpool, carver and gilder (1821–39). At 27 Clarence St in 1821; 12 Head St, 1827; 8 Pomona St, 1829; 111 Mount Pleasant 1834–35; 115 Mount Pleasant, 1837; and 22 Mount Pleasant in 1839. [D]

Sanderson, Joseph, Castlegate, Penrith, Cumb., chairmaker (1834). [D]

Sanderson, William, High-bridge, Newcastle, cm and joiner (1794–1804). On 14 June 1794 he announced the opening of his shop on High-bridge for the sale of cabinet goods. Items stocked included 'Portobello Games Tables, Triamedam ditto. Ladies' and Gentlemen's travelling Shoffaneers'. He is recorded in the cash books for Gibside, Co. Durham as the supplier of two mahogany trays for which he was paid £1 11s on 16 April 1804. [*Newcastle Courant*, 14 June 1794; Durham RO, D/St/V.999]

Sanderson & Gibson, 39 Wardour St, Soho, London, cm (1816). [D]

Sandford, Thomas, Shrewsbury, Salop, u (1752–59). In 1752 took app. named Kent, in 1756 Blakeway and in 1759 Laurance. [S of G, app. index]

Sandford, Thomas, 2 Dean St, Fetter Lane, London, cm (1803–08). In June 1803 took out insurance cover for £300 of which £100 was for utensils and stock. [D; GL, Sun MS vol. 427, ref. 750019]

Sandford, Thomas, Wem, Salop, cm (1822). [D]

Sandford, William, Exeter, Devon cm (1816–25). At 33 Holloway St, 1816–19, 212 High St from February 1820 but by 1821 the number had changed to 209. His trade card

[Johnson Coll., Bodleian Lib., Oxford] from the Holloway St address is illustrated with an engraving of the premises, a double-fronted shop with three storeys above labelled 'Holloway House'. He declared himself to be an 'Upholsterer, Cabinet & Chair Manufacturer, Carpet & London Paper-hanging Warehouse'. He also performed funerals. He travelled regularly to London to select stock and typically in November 1821 advertised his stock of 'Brussels, Persian and Kidderminster carpets and rugs, rich Moreens and London paper hangings selected by himself in London a few days since. He has also selected some of the newest and most tasteful designs in upholstery and cabinet furniture'. In 1819 he stated that one of his London suppliers of stock was W. & A. Copp. He also acted as agent for the sale and letting of property. His retirement was advertised in December 1825 and he disposed of the business to Henry Force. [D; *Exeter Flying Post*, 7 May 1818, 18 March 1819, 25 November 1819, 24 February 1820, 15 March 1821, 24 November 1825; *Western Luminary*, 9 March 1819, 20 July 1819, 29 February 1820; *The Alfred*, 20 November 1821, 27 September 1825, 6 December 1825]

Sandiford, H., 18 Colchester St, Savage Gdns, London, chairmaker (1809). [D]

Sandland, G. & J., Lincoln's Inn, London, cm (1806–09). At 15 Stone-cutter's Building, 1806–07, but by 1808 only James Sandilands appears to have been active in the business and he had moved his address to 15 Tate St. [D]

Sandilands, George, Tweedmouth, Northumb., cm, u, dealer and chapman (1770). In October 1770 his goods including furniture and timber were auctioned on bankruptcy. [*Newcastle Courant*, 6 October 1770]

Sandilands, James, 112 Wapping, London, cm and ship joiner (1802–08). [D]

Sandilands, James, Harrow, Middlx, cm (1839). [D]

Sandland, Robert, Ellesmere, Salop, cm (1779–98). In 1779 took out insurance cover of £300 of which £60 was for utensils and stock. [D; GL, Sun MS vol. 281, p. 1]

Sandland, Thomas, Wem, Salop, cm (1798). [D]

Sandland, William, Chester, cm (1784–1826). App. to Philip Presbury and free by servitude, 7 July 1784. At Bridge St, 1812–19 but in 1826 at Duke St. [Freemen rolls; poll bks]

Sandoe, Anthony, London, cm (1829–39). At 54 Southampton Row, Russell Sq. in 1829 but from 1837–39 the address was 24 King St, Holborn. In 1837 also trading as a fancy stationer. [D]

Sandorby(?), —, address unknown, cm (1801). Named in the Longford Castle, Wilts. archives receiving payment of 10s in 1801. [V&A archives]

Sandover, John, Fore St, Exeter, Devon, carver and gilder (1791). [D]

Sandrino, John Baptist, Liverpool, print seller, carver and gilder (1804–13). In 1804 at 21 Paradise St where he carried on the trade of print seller, looking-glass and picture frame manufacturer. In June of that year he advertised his return from London 'with a choice assortment of English & Foreign Prints, Drawings, Medallions, & Fancy Gold & Coloured Papers of the newest patterns, Drawing Paper etc.'. In February 1805 he announced an impending change of addresses and the consequent selling off of his stock in trade. This included 'an assortment of elegant Pictures, framed & glazed, by eminent masters, Pier Looking Glasses, mahogany box & swing Glasses, Weather Glasses, Prints, Drawings etc: A quantity of Cambric & book Muslin, Flannels, Swansdown & toilenet waistcoating, silk & cotton Handkerchiefs, with some Plate & kitchen requisites'. By early March he was installed in his new premises at 45 Lord St where he stocked a wide range of prints, artists' materials and fancy goods, and continued to offer a service framing and glazing prints and needlework. In September 1805 he married Miss Disley of Croxteth at St Anne's Church. On 9 August 1811 however he advertised that he was selling off his stock in trade as he was 'declining retail business'. By this date he was also including amongst his stock telescopes, barometers and thermometers. A sale of his household furniture followed later in the same month. He does not appear to have entirely given up the business however, for in 1813 he is shown trading as a print seller, carver and gilder from 36 High St, Edge Hill with a shop behind 62 Lord St. From 1804–11 he advertised his name as B. Sandrino and it is only from 1811 that J. B. Sandrino was used. [D; *Liverpool Chronicle*, 6 June 1804; 27 February, 6 March and 18 September 1805; 27 May 1807; *Liverpool Mercury*, 9 and 23 August 1811; 2 October 1811]

Sands, Benjamin, Nottingham, joiner and cm (1783). [Freemen rolls]

Sands, David, Soho, London, upholder and cm (1749–84). At Dean St in 1749 but by 1774 in Greek St. [Westminster poll bks; Heal]

Sands, David, Gt Russell St, Bloomsbury, London, upholder (1782–94). At 12 Gt Russell St in 1782 when insurance cover of £700 was taken out. In 1789 shown at 115 Gt Russell St. [D; GL, Sun MS vol. 301, p. 106]

Sands, John, Hull, Yorks., chairmaker (1826–40). At 7 Waterhouse Lane, 1826–31, 7 Davis St, 1838–40 and Little Albion St in 1839. Described as a fancy chairmaker in 1840. [D]

Sandwell, Henry, London, upholder (1730–46). Son of Hartley Sandwell of Ratcliffe, Bucks., Gent. and brother of Joseph Sandwell. App. to George Tarry on 1 April 1730 and free of the Upholders' Co. by servitude, 5 October 1737. Took as app. his brother Joseph Sandwell, 1740–46. [GL, Upholders' Co. records]

Sandwell, Joseph, London, upholder (1740–48). Son of Hartley Sandwell of Ratcliffe, Bucks., Gent. and brother of Henry Sandwell to whom he was app. on 1 October 1740. On 3 July 1746 he was transferred to William Milward and was free of the Upholders' Co. by servitude, 15 July 1748. [GL, Upholders' Co. records]

Sandwick, Robert, Lancaster, cm (1837). Described in the will of Thomas Walton as his nephew. [Preston RO, DDX 1122]

Sandwick, William, Lancaster, cm (1829–38). Step-son of James Taylor of Lancaster and app. to John Battersby on 1 June 1829. Free 28 October 1837. Nephew of Thomas Walton and mentioned in his will of 1837. Named in the Gillow records, 1836–38. [Preston RO, DDX 1122, app. reg.; freemen rolls; Westminster Ref. Lib., Gillow]

Sandy, Samuel, Bath St, City Rd, London, cm (1821). On 18 July 1821 took out insurance cover of £400 which included £20 for his tools in the workshop of Messrs Seddons of Aldersgate. [GL, Sun MS vol. 484, ref. 981620]

Sandys, Charles, London(?), picture frame maker (1771). In 1771 submitted an account for £1 15s 6d to Sir John Griffin Griffin of Audley End, Essex for '1 H^f Length Picture made into a whole length wth Compass Head frame & Poerter^ge to Bishopsgate'. [Essex RO, D/DBy/A29/10]

Sandys, Martin, York, u (1727–33). Of Myton, Yorks. App. to George Reynoldson of York on 5 April 1727 and free 1733. [App. bk; freemen rolls]

Sandys, William, Bambers Ct, Watkinson St, Liverpool, cm (1790–96). [D]

Sandys, Windsor, London, upholder (1712–27). In 1712 took out insurance cover on a house in Watling St valued at £300 and nine other properties. By 1722 when he was nominated for the office of Sheriff he was living in Hoxton Sq. and continued at this address until at least 1727. [GL, Hand in Hand MS vol. 10, 5 September 1712; Heal]

Saner, Elias Christopher, 34 Water Works St, Hull, Yorks., cm and u (1834–40). A directory of 1835 gives the christian name as Edward but this may be an error. [D]

Sanford, Abel, London, upholder (1709). Free of the Upholders' Co. 2 November 1709. [GL, Upholders' Co. records]

Sanford, John, Exeter, Devon, upholder (1713). In 1713 took app. named Lee. [S of G, app. index]

Sangar, Benjamin, St Augustine's Back, Bristol, cm, u and undertaker (1813–30). From 1816–28 the business is shown as a partnership of Benjamin & James Sanger and from 1821 the number is shown as 13 St Augustine's Back. A directory of 1822 however lists the partners at 33 College Green as Sangars & Co. for this year only. After 1830 the business appears to have been in the sole charge of James B. Sangar, whilst Benjamin Sangar in this year is listed at Exchange Buildings near the Post Office as an auctioneer, and house and estate agent. [D]

Sangar, James B., 13 St Augustine's Parade, Bristol, cm, u and undertaker (1830–40). Partner with Benjamin Sangar in the same trade from 1816–29 at St Augustine's Back (same address). He took sole control in 1830. [D]

Sansbury, Amos, Calthorp, Banbury, Berks., upholder (1683). [Oxford RO, Misc. SU LUI/7]

Sansby, Richard, Hull, Yorks., carver and gilder (1803–40). At 23 Savile St, 1803–26 but from 1831–40 at 10 Grimston St. [D]

Sansby, Robert, 10 Grimston St, Hull, Yorks., carver and gilder (1837). [D]

Sansom, Henry, Church St, Bilston, Staffs., cm (1818–22). [D]

Sansom, Richard, Stockwellgate, Mansfield, Notts., chairmaker (1828–40). [D]

Sansom, Thomas, Rose Ct, Mansfield, Notts., chairmaker (1832–40). By 1835 at Church St. [D]

Sansom, William, Warsop, Notts., chairmaker (1832). [D]

Sant, Aaron, New St, Burslem, Staffs., cm and chairmaker (1818–22). [D]

Santley, Joseph, Liverpool and Bolton, Lancs., u (1828). In 1828 married at Bolton Susannah, daughter of John Grime of that town. Described as 'late of Liverpool'. [*Liverpool Mercury*, 14 March 1828]

Santley, Thomas, Liverpool and Birmingham, cm (d.1817). Death on 21 October 1817 at Birmingham 'after a long illness' reported in *Liverpool Mercury*, 31 October. Described as 'late of Liverpool'.

Santon, Vincent, Market Pl., Bedale, Yorks., joiner/cm (1834). [D]

Sapp, Robert, London, u (1715–39). Son of Edward Sapp of Chelsea College. App. to Joseph Hudson on 6 April 1715 and free of the Upholders' Co. by servitude, 3 February 1724/25. In 1739 supplied furniture, window curtains and carpets to the new Treasury building in Whitehall which was completed 1734–37. Sapp's account dated 28 June 1739 included items for the room of the Secretary to the Treasury who was at this time Stephen Fox (created Earl of Ilchester in 1756). These consisted of a large mahogany writing table at £4 4s, 'a mahogany desk of curious wood' at £5 10s, six walnut chairs 'with compass backs' and matching elbow chairs covered in Spanish leather £22 13s, and three mahogany cupboards 'with compass fronts' at £4 14s 6d. Alterations and additions to a table in the boardroom added £5 15s 6d. None of the furniture at present in the Treasury corresponds to this account. [GL, Upholders' Co. records; *DEF*]

Sapwith, Thomas, Newcastle, cm (1803). Subscribed to Sheraton's *Cabinet Dictionary*, 1803.

Sarbearin, C., 39 Paul St, Finsbury, London, cm (1813). [D]

Sarell, William, Exeter, Devon, cm (1772). On 20 March 1772 published a public apology for assaulting John Salisbury on condition that the latter withdrew from prosecuting him. [*Exeter Flying Post*, 20 March 1772]

Sargeant, Jacob, Market Pl., Trowbridge, Wilts., u (1839). [D]

Sargent, A., 22 Friday St, Cheapside, London, looking-glass manufacturer (1800–01). [D]

Sargent, George, Battle, Sussex, u, cm and undertaker (1823–40). [D]

Sargent, John, 104 Bishopsgate Within, London, cm (1778). In 1778 took out insurance cover of £400 of which utensils and stock accounted for £300. [GL, Sun MS vol. 264, p. 321]

Sargood, Joseph, 17 St Ann's Ct, Soho, London, picture and looking-glass frame maker (1839). [D]

Sarjeant, George, Bishopsgate St, London, u (1779). [Bailey's list of bankrupts]

Sarjeant, John, Etruria, Hanley, Staffs., cm (1834). [D]

Sarratt, Samuel, Lancaster (1800). Named in the Gillow records in connection with the making of tables. [Westminster Ref. Lib., Gillow vol. 344/98, pp. 1545, 1560]

Sarratt, Samuel, Chester, cm and chairmaker (1816–40). At Northgate St, 1816–37 but by 1840 in Watergate Back Row. [D]

Sartain, John Frederick, 5 Charles St, Bristol, cm (1828). [D]

Sartorio, John, 60 Cable St, Liverpool, carver and gilder (1807). [D]

Sarvas, Abraham, 7 Sloane Sq., Chelsea, London, cm and u (1826). [D]

Sarvis, A. W., 174 Sloane St, Chelsea, London, u and appraiser (1820–26). [D]

Sassi, Peter, Wallgate, Wigan, Lancs., carver and gilder (1834). [D]

Satchell, John, Fore St, Exeter, Devon, cm (1838). Daughter bapt. at St George's on 25 December 1838. [PR (bapt.)]

Satterthwaite, Charles, 4 Beech St, Barbican, London, cm (1809). [D]

Satterthwaite, Robert, Lancaster, u (1823–24). [Freemen rolls]

Saul, David, Watergate, Carlisle, Cumb., joiner/cm (1828–29). [D]

Saul, Edward & Co., Liverpool, cm (1774–90). Traded at South Side, South Dock but this address is also rendered as 30 Cornhill. In October 1789 announced that he was giving up the cm side of the business and acting from then on as a glass and timber merchant. His stock in trade of the cabinet side was sold off and consisted of 'Pier & Dressing GLASSES, Mahogany PLANK & BOARD, OAK, MAPLE, & DEAL with a large quantity of choice VINNEARS ... Benches, Chests of Tools'. He still advertised his ability to supply 'Jamaica, Spanish & Honduras Mahogany in Logs, Planks & Boards, Birch, Beach & Maple Timber, with a quantity of Bed Posts, Sides & Ends' as part of his continuing trade. [D; *Williamson's Liverpool Advertiser*, 26 October 1789]

Saul, John, Ipswich, Suffolk, chairmaker (1762). In 1762 took app. named Adams. [S of G, app. index]

Saul, John, 35 Berwick St, Soho, London, cm and u (1839). [D]

Saul, Michael, 58 South Molton St, Oxford St, London, cm and u (1820–35). Loudon's *Encyclopaedia*, 1833 (pp. 652–54) features a combined bookcase, writing desk and clock which may possibly have been designed by this maker. [D]

Saul, Robert, Gt Shaw St, Preston, Lancs., joiner and cm (1814–25). [D]

Saul, W., Belvedere Buildings, Southwark, London, bedstead maker (1835). [D]

Sault, Joseph, Newcastle-under-Lyme, Staffs., chairmaker (1818–37). In 1818 at King St, Nelson Pl. but in 1832 was living in Bagnall St. [D; poll bks]

Sault, Richard, Market Lane, Newcastle-under-Lyme, Staffs., chairmaker (1818). [D]

Saunders, —, 158 Aldersgate St, London, cm. Heal records this maker but with no date or source.

Saunders, —, Cateaton St, London, u (1749). Supplied catalogues for the sale of goods of Joseph Atherton to take place from 3 April. [*General Advertiser*, 21 March 1749] Possibly Abraham Saunders.

Saunders, Mr, address unknown, cm and u (1775). Subscribed to Thomas Malton's *Complete Treatise on Perspective*, 1775.

Saunders, —, New St, Cloth Fair, London, cm (1763). [D]

Saunders, —, Faversham, Kent, cm (1803). [D] Possibly James Saunders of Faversham.

Saunders, Abraham, Cateaton St, London, freeman skinner, by trade an u (1762). Employed three non-freemen for three months in 1762. [GL, City Licence bks, vol. 3] Possibly Saunders, — of Cateaton St.

Saunders, Alfred, St Mary St, Bridgwater, Som., cm and u (1839–40). [D]

Saunders, Ann, upholder (1775). See John Bracken.

Saunders, Edward, St Giles, Oxford, cm (1802). [Poll bk]

Saunders, Edward, Brighton, Sussex, Tunbridge-ware and toy manufacturer and dealer (1839). One directory gives address at 14 Cheltenham Pl., another at 26 New Rd. [D]

Saunders, Elizabeth, address unknown, upholder (1712). Admitted freeman of the Upholders' Co. on 1 October 1712. [GL, Upholders' Co. records]

Saunders, Henry, 'The White Bull', Bradpole, near Bridport, Dorset, victualler and cm (1791). Took out a Sun Insurance policy on 27 October 1791 for £200 of which £80 accounted for utensils and stock. [GL, Sun MS vol. 381, p. 249]

Saunders, Hugh, see Paul Saunders.

Saunders, J., 16 Duke St, St James, London, u (1820). [D]

Saunders, J., Church St, Sidmouth, Devon, cm (1838). [D]

Saunders, James, 175 Bermondsey St, London, cm, broker and chandler (1778). Took out a Sun Insurance policy in 1778 for £200 of which utensils and stock accounted for £100. [GL, Sun MS vol. 263, p. 584]

Saunders, James, Reading, Berks., cm (1782). [Poll bk]

Saunders, James, Faversham, Kent, cm (1811–24). Trading at Preston St, 1823–24. [D] Possibly Saunders, — of Faversham.

Saunders, James, 10 Gt Castle St, Oxford Mkt, London, carver and gilder (1819–25). [D] See Thomas and William Saunders at this address.

Saunders, John, 9 Poland St, London, upholder and broker (1783). Took out a Sun Insurance policy in 1783 for £500 of which £20 accounted for utensils and stock. [GL, Sun MS vol. 319, p. 74]

Saunders, John, 49 Castle St East, London, cm and upholder (1820–35). [D]

Saunders, John, 7 Joanna St, Lambeth, London, chairmaker (1826). [Maldon poll bk]

Saunders, John, Brighton, Sussex, cm, u and joiner (1827–41). John Saunders appears to have continued the family's general upholstery work at Brighton Pavilion after the death of his father, Thomas Saunders, c.1826. The Royal Household accounts, 1827–31, detail his regular employment for 'frequent and sundry jobbing', cleaning, repairing furniture, upholstery work and also providing blinds and carpets. Items supplied included '2 fancy chairs' costing £2 12s on 5 April 1831. His position at the Royal Pavilion appears greatly enhanced after the accession of William IV, and considerable furniture was provided both for their Majesties' rooms and for household and staff apartments.

In 1830–31 lengthy bills cover the furnishing and refurbishing of the stable quarters, HRH Princess Augusta's house, a house at 14 Castle Sq. being prepared for the footman, and new rooms for the cellarman. Furniture supplied included half-tester bedsteads, tent bedsteads, 'chests of Common Draws', washhand stands, Pembroke tables, dining tables, cheval glasses, pillar and claw tables and writing tables, totalling £910 in the quarter to April 1831. John Saunders's bill in October 1830 read: 'Preparing for their Majesties the Pavilion & House, uncovering rooms, throughout cleaning, dusting, repairing Furniture, beating Carpets, preparing the Chapel. Furnishing 2 houses for their Majesties' servants, putting up additional Beds, Window Curtains, Blinds, and putting down Carpets . . . attendance in rooms, cleaning and dusting everyday to the rooms occupied by their Majesties and Sundry jobbing.' Saunders's bill totalled £1,784 16s 1d. In January 1831 Saunders provided a coffin, mourning clothes, hearse, 'best velvet cloth' and 'cambrai sheet' for the funeral of Mr Robinson, last Page to His Majesty, and in the same month he was paid £50 as allowances performed by Mr Saunders as 'Tapissier' for the past quarter.

On 29 September 1832 Saunders supplied to the Royal Pavilion '5 doz. stained rush-bottomed chairs' at £6 10s, two mahogany dining table tops at £9 18s and '6 deal dressing tables', £12 8s. Extensive estimates were submitted by John Saunders in September 1834 and items included Ottomans, sofas, settees, elbow chairs and firescreens for the Music Room Gallery, and six chairs, 'cane seats & backs, japanned black & gold in imitation of bamboo' for the Music Room. The bills for regular work continued after Victoria's accession, and, in fact, until the Pavilion was sold and finally dismantled in 1848. In 1839 Saunders was still supplying the Pavilion with high quality furniture including, on 11 December, '2 Grecian stool Back Chairs with caned seats' and '6 Large elbow chairs bamboo Patterns with cane seats & Backs — with back & seat cushions covered in Morocco.' [PRO, LC11/56–77, 11/95–98; RA, item 17, box 1 (estimates); RA, box 1, item 2; Joy, *English Furniture, 1800–1851*] N.N.T.

Saunders, John, Spa Lane, Retford, Notts., cm and casemaker (1832). [D]

Saunders, John, Ashburton, Devon, carver and gilder (1836). Marriage to Miss Tarr on 15 November 1836 reported in *Exeter Flying Post*, 17 November.

Saunders, John, High Wycombe, Bucks., chairmaker (1836). Son bapt. in 1836. [PR (bapt.)]

Saunders, Jos., near Hillingdon Gate, Uxbridge, Middlx., Windsor chairmaker (1832). [D]

Saunders, Joseph, Southwark, London, upholder and cm (1772–1802). Recorded at 42 Borough High St, 1782–96 and also at no. 112, 1790–96. Son of Joseph Saunders and app. to Benjamin Soundy. Admitted freeman of the Upholders' Co. by servitude on 7 October 1772. [D; GL, Upholders' Co. records]

Saunders, Paul, Soho Sq., London, upholder (b.1722–d.1771), succeeded by **Saunders, Hugh & Bracken, John**, upholders (1774–94). Paul Saunders was a major London u of the 1750s and 1760s supplying the important upper strata of London and country house clients as well as holding the position of Tapestry Maker to His Majesty George III. After Saunders's death in 1771, his firm carried on until 1794 from his last premises in Charlotte (now Bloomsbury) St with his eldest son, Hugh and his clerk, John Bracken forming a partnership.

Paul Saunders, the son of John Saunders, citizen and skinner of London, and his wife Sarah, was christened on 27 January 1722 at St Martin-in-the-Fields. His career began on 7 November 1738 when he was app. for seven years to Michael Bradshaw, citizen and upholder of London. However, a second confusing entry in the records of the

Upholders' Co. states that Saunders 'doth put himself apprentice to Richard Bradshaw, Citizen and Upholder, from the date dated the 7th day of December, 1738 . . .' and a sum of £30 is listed for the Master. Michael and/or Richard are most likely to have been related to William and George Smith Bradshaw with whom Saunders was later to be associated. In 1747 Paul Saunders polled at Hartshorne Lane, Westminster (now Northumberland St), where he insured his household goods, utensils and stock for £500 on 3 March 1749. [GL, Sun MS vol. 89, p. 255] By 1 July 1750 the Sun Insurance policy lists Saunders's address as 'near Slaughter's Coffee house in St Martin-in-the-Fields' and insures household goods and stock for £1,000. [GL, MS Sun vol. 93, p. 271] On 5 December 1751 he was admitted freeman of the Upholders' Co. by servitude, at which time he took his first app. for the sizeable consideration of £60. At about this time, Saunders and George Smith Bradshaw seem to have formed a partnership, probably using the premises of George's relative, William Bradshaw (a possible third member of the partnership), whom they succeeded as rate-payers at 59 Greek St as noted in the 1755 rate bks for St Anne, Soho.

Carlisle House on the east side of Soho Sq. was leased by Saunders and George Smith Bradshaw, described as 'upholsterers of Greek Street', in May 1753. This property extended eastward from the Square along Sutton St and included coach house and stables in Hog Lane (now Charing Cross Rd) where workshops were established in 1754. A notice in *Public Advertiser*, 6 February 1755 gives an idea of the size of the workforce: 'The late unhappy Fire at the Workshop of Mess. Smyth, Bradshaw & Saunders [*sic*], Upholders & Cabinetmakers, Soho, having not only consumed the same, but also the Chests & Working tools of thirty-seven journeymen there employed . . .'. Later in the same year the 2nd Duke of Portland, as ground landlord, granted the partners a reversionary lease of Carlisle House until 1853—the usual fine being remitted as 'His Grace's regard for their loss by the late fire'. [Notts. Univ. lib., Portland MS, Soho lease bk] Saunders and Bradshaw announced the dissolution of their partnership in *London Gazette*, 26–30 October 1756: 'Business will continue to be carried on as usual, by Mr. Bradshaw in Greek Street, Soho, and by Mr. Saunders in Soho Square, the Corner of Sutton Street.' Already on 19 October 1756 Saunders had insured the utensils, goods and stock in workshops and warehouses on these premises for £3,000. [GL, Sun MS vol. 117, p. 410]

The *British Chronicle*, 30 September 1757 announced that 'Mr. Paul Saunders of Sutton Street, Soho is appointed Tapestry Maker to His Majesty and on Thursday was sworn into office' — thus succeeding John Ellys as Yeoman Arrasworker to the Great Wardrobe. Saunders and Bradshaw's partnership had already been engaged in supplying tapestries to Holkham and Petworth, continuing William Bradshaw's established position in this field, although as was typical of most Soho Tapestry makers, the partners were primarily u and cm. The dominant role in the tapestry side of the business seems to have been assumed by Saunders who rose to a position of prominence as a tapestry worker. Known for depictions of Oriental-style landscapes with soft trees and picturesque ruins, his most famous design is 'The Pilgrimage to Mecca' — of which examples survive at Alnwick Castle, Petworth and Holkham. In May 1761 Saunders received a second appointment in the Great Wardrobe as Yeoman Tapestry Taylor, thereafter holding the two positions concurrently until his death in 1771. Both appointments were chiefly concerned with repairing and cleaning royal tapestries, but new hangings were also supplied, and his connections with the Great Wardrobe were undoubtedly partially

responsible for the entry referring to Paul Saunders, undertaker, being paid for the funeral of the Duke of Cumberland in 1765. [PRO, LC9/293] His second appointment coincided with Saunders's removal from the premises which he apparently called 'The Royal Tapestry Manufactury, Soho Square' to the house in Gt Queen St, Lincoln's Inn Fields, formerly occupied by John Vanderbank and John Ellys, and the site of the Great Wardrobe tapestry workshops until 1742.

Carlisle House was leased in April 1760 to Mrs Theresa Cornelys, to whom in May 1761, Paul Saunders's assignees sold the lease of the entire site including the workshops on Sutton and Hog Streets. Samuel Norman, carver and gilder signed an agreement in June 1760 with Saunders enabling him to take over the 'Royal Tapestry Manufactury', Sutton St, whose premises consisted of: 'dwelling house with an apprentices' room; extensive workshops which included tapestry, cabinet-making, upholstery, feather and carpet shops; a gilding shop and a silvering room; a counting house; a timber shed and a 'little drying yard'. [PRO, LC12 1518/16, PRO, C 12 2062/2] Norman also agreed to buy the unwrought stock in trade valued at £2,270 19s 10d by Messrs Hyde, Smith and Evatt, whose detailed list provides a highly important insight into the contents of an 18th-century furniture maker's workshop and tells us that Saunders had '32 cabinet-makers' benches', Unwrought wood valued at £800 (three-quarters of the investment in mahogany), utility hardware valued at almost £100, and forty-six pounds of seasoned down in addition to 480 pounds of feathers'. An elaborate contract outlined the sharing of cabinet, upholstery and funeral orders for a year from June 1760, during which time Norman would supply Saunders with goods needed at trade prices. On 1 July 1760 Paul Saunders, using a Dean St address (where presumably he had temporary premises), had taken out a Sun Insurance policy on utensils, stock, goods in trust (glass excluded) in workshop and warehouse next to Samuel Norman cm in Sutton St, Soho Sq., £2,000. [GL, Sun MS vol. 132, p. 375] A year later a similar policy of Saunders's insured the contents of Samuel Norman's workshops and warehouses in Sutton St, Soho for £1,000. [GL, MS Sun vol. 136, p. 600] Problems developed over Norman's repayment of his debt to Saunders, and in 1762 the Trustees of Paul Saunders filed a suit in the Court of Common Pleas which Norman answered with a Chancery bill against Saunders in 1764. [PRO, C.12, 2062/2]

Throughout his career, Paul Saunders seems to have had a clientèle of extremely important stature — perhaps beginning with early contacts made in William Bradshaw's workshops. The Petworth archives contain a Saunders's letter of September 1748 demonstrating both a high degree of literacy and a familiarity with Petworth and the Duke's health. Although the major identifiable commissions of Saunders (Petworth, Holkham and Uppark) concern tapestry, upholstered seat furniture and bed fittings, the prepared 1760 inventory of his stock-in-trade lists many standard cabinetmaker's items. In connection with Norman versus Saunders [PRO, C.12, 2062/2], an impressive schedule of Saunders's prestigious patrons (i.e. the Duke of Cumberland, the Duke of Norfolk, the Duke of Northumberland, the Earl of Scarborough, Viscount Irwin, Sir Orlando Bridgeman, etc.) and their accounts at the time of Norman's takeover of the Sutton St premises was drawn up.

Paul Saunders took six apps between 1751 and 1770, the first William Davis for a consideration of £60 when he became a freeman in 1751; following on with Thomas Russell in 1755 (£63); Mo. Dignam in 1758 (£50); William Hodgson, 1764 (£100); his son Hugh in 1767; and Charles Elliot for no consideration except orphan duty in 1770. In 1760 the Duke of Bedford called in Paul Saunders and Thomas Woodin to value the 'large glass' in the Blue Drawing Room at Woburn — apparently their valuation was in agreement with Norman's bill. Saunders joined John Trotter in making an inventory of the furniture in the Earl of Guilford's Grosvenor Sq. house in March 1767 for a proposed sale to Lord Sondes, another patron. Saunders's standing in London is shown by his membership in the Royal Society of Arts and his wide-ranging interests by his subscription to Chippendale's *Director*, 1754, and to James Paine's *Noblemen's and Gentlemen's Seats*, 1767. By 1770 he had become a member of the Court of Assistants of the Upholders' Co.

A front-page advertisement in *Public Advertiser*, 28 January 1768 announced Paul Saunders's removal from Lincoln's Inn Field (as the lease had expired on the Gt Queen St property) to a large house on the corner of Charlotte (now Bloomsbury) and Streatham Streets, near Gt Russell St. Saunders probably died in June or July 1771; his will dated 23 April 1770 [PRO, Prob. 11, Trevor 369] was proved on 28 August 1771 and included the following important provisions: 'to John Bracken £100 if living with me either as a clerk or partner' whilst 'the lease of the said dwelling House, workshops, warehouses and premises' were left in trust to his wife Ann Saunders, his eldest son Hugh, and his 'worthy friend' Theodosius Forest ... my children Hugh, John and Mary ... as then under twenty-one or unmarried'. The executors were Ann and Hugh Saunders.

A Sun Insurance policy of 24 June 1761 to Paul Saunders, 'Cabinet maker, Upholder & Tapestry Worker at the corner of Charlotte and Streatham Streets, Bloomsbury' lists 'household goods in dwelling, £250; utensils above goods in trust, workshops and warehouse, £1500; glass therein, £200; stock of timber in timber yard behind, £250' — for a total of £2,200. [GL, Sun MS vol. 206, p. 325] A second policy dated 21 July 1771 covered 'utensils, stock goods in trust in warehouse at the corner of Dyot [*sic*] Street — £500'. [*Ibid.*, vol. 206, p. 523] The Dyott St warehouse would have been behind the workshops at 2 and 4 Streatham St which adjoined the house facing onto Charlotte St. These policies show the value of Saunders's business at the time of his death to have been very similar to that in 1760 when his premises were sold to Samuel Norman. 'Paul Saunders, Upholder', appears as a yearly entry in London trade directories from 1759 until 1774 when the partnership of Saunders & Bracken is first listed.

Hugh Richard Francis, son of Paul and Ann Saunders, was christened in St Martin-in-the-Fields on 30 January 1752, and was app. to his father 'of Great Ivershot, Lincoln's Inn Fields on 2 April 1767 for the Consideration of love and affection'. Hugh received payment from the Duke of Bedford on his father's behalf in November 1769, and after his father's death in 1771, he and his mother issued the firm's bills in the name of the 'Executors of the late Paul Saunders'. At the beginning of 1773, the firm of Saunders & Bracken was formed, the reorganisation coinciding with Hugh Saunders's reaching his majority and with his admission as freeman of the Upholders' Co. by patrimony on 7 April 1773. A Bedford Office lease of 11 February 1773 shows Ann Saunders and her son Paul, the younger [*sic*], taking a lease of a coach-house, stable and warehouse on the north side of Streatham St west, and east side of Dyott St. The Mr Saunders who subscribed to Thomas Malton's *Compleat Treatise of Perspective*, 1775 is most likely Hugh.

The firm of Saunders & Bracken, upholders at Charlotte St, Bloomsbury, was listed annually from 1774 to 1794 in local directories. Little is known of John Bracken: in Paul Saunders's will he is mentioned as clerk and seems to be a

likely future partner. In 1775, the Sun Insurance policy on the work premises was in the name of Ann Saunders and John Bracken. The existing bills of the firm seem to indicate that cabinet making was at least as important to the livelihood of Saunders and Bracken as was upholstery — unlike the emphasis of Paul Saunders's commissions. Nothing is known of the date of the death of either man or of the firm's ceasing to do business. [Heal; *GCM*; *DEF*; W. G. Thompson, *A History of Tapestry*, 1910, p. 159; M. Harris & Son, *Old English Furniture*, p. 27; *Survey of London*, vol. XXXIV, parish of St Anne Soho, London, 1966. Appendix I, pp. 518–20; A. Coleridge, *Chippendale Furniture*; Gilbert, *Chippendale*; H. Hayward and P. Kirkham, *Linnell*]

MANSION HOUSE, London. 1752–53: Employed in the furnishing of the newly-completed Mansion House, 1752–53. [*Conn.*, December 1952, p. 181]

HOLDERNESS HOUSE, London [Earl of Holderness]. 1754–58: Large payments to Paul Saunders for work at Holderness (later Londonderry) House, Old Park Lane: 1754, £500; 1757, £300 and £497, 1758, £315 15s. [BL, vol. CLXXIV, Egerton MS 3497; YAS, Duke of Leeds papers]

HOLKHAM HALL, Norfolk (1st Earl of Leicester). 1755–58: Considerable furniture, tapestry, upholstery fabric and bed furniture supplied to nearly-completed Hall. Furniture delivered in 1757 included '10 elbow chairs with carved & gilt frames and covered with blue Turkey leather — £74.0.4; 2 large sophas, £41.18; do. 12 chairs mahogany frames gilt & stuffed, £39.10.3' — much of this suite still survives in the Sculpture Gallery and Octagon. Saunders provided a 'Model of ye state bed — £13.2.0', bed furniture for the state bed and is felt to have been responsible for the completed state bed and the Canopy of State. 'Tapestries for ye state Bedchamber — £54.5.0' included the well-known 'Pilgrimage to Mecca' tapestry signed 'Paul Saunders of Soho'. [*Apollo*, February 1964, pp. 122–23, 126, figs 1 and 2; *Apollo*, October 1974, p. 299, footnote 34; *Burlington*, December 1975; C. *Life*, 11 February 1980, pp. 427–31]

CLEVELAND HOUSE, London. 1756–60: Raby Castle archives show that Saunders was employed as an u between 1756 and 1760.

PETWORTH HOUSE, Sussex (Duke of Somerset and the Earl and Countess of Egremont). 1748–67; A 1748 letter in the Petworth archives shows Saunders's familiarity with Petworth and its Duke. In 1759 he was paid £111 for unexplained work; then over the next three years, £400 for tapestries. A bill sent after the 1763 death of the second Earl details '14 French Elbow Chairs, the frames richly carved & gilt — £70; 2 Sofas in every respect to match the Chairs — £32; 8 smaller French Elbow Chairs — £40 & 2 Settees to match them — £23.10.0'. [PHA, 6613–6624] Armchairs of both sizes fitting the description survive in the Carved Room and are of advanced French construction with central struts behind the backs, and arm-pads screwed on from below, showing the influence of Parisian meneusiers. A 1767 bill is chiefly devoted to reupholstery and restuffing, but charges for a 'carved claw' which is probably the gilt firescreen with a tapestry panel of a parrot. [PHA, 6613–6624; *Apollo*, May 1977, pp. 364–65, fig. 22; C. *Life*, 14 June 1984; Nat. Trust Guide to *Petworth*, 1981, p. 19]

STOWE HOUSE, Bucks. (Earl Temple). 1760: 'Paid Mr Saunders upholsterer's bill £28'. [Huntington Lib., California, Stowe MS, T3 LL3/2]

UPPARK, Sussex (Sir Matthew Fetherstonhaugh). 1761: On 20 March 1761 Sir Matthew's account bks record £33 0s 6d 'for Tapestry to Mr. Saunders in full'. This entry almost certainly referred to the tapestry coverings on a set of eight gilded open armchairs now in the Saloon, and it seems likely that Saunders also supplied the frames. [*Conn.*, November 1967, pp. 162–63, fig. 10]

WOBURN ABBEY, Beds. and **BEDFORD HOUSE**, London (4th Duke of Bedford until 1771; Gertrude, Executor & Dowager Duchess, 1771–83). 1765–1771: Paul Saunders was paid £150 by John, 4th Duke of Bedford, in 1765 for carver's and cabinet maker's work — and from then until his death in mid 1771, Saunders worked regularly for the Duke, especially at Bedford House, Bloomsbury. From 1767, he presented his account every few months: for Bedford House — 'a rich carved compass sideboard frame with 4 legs & rail gilt in burnished gold for dining room'. — £19 os . . . the quarterly bill to January 1770 totalling £188 os 4d. Saunders's bill of December 1771 is marked 'deceased.' 1772–83. Two bills were presented in 1772 in the name of the 'Executors of the late Paul Saunders', followed in January 1773 by regular accounts from the firm of Saunders & Bracken which continue until 1783 when the bills at the Bedford Office cease. Throughout the Saunders & Bracken period, the Bedford estate was controlled by Gertrude, widow of the 4th Duke, during the minority of her grandson, Francis, and considerably less work was undertaken. However important items delivered in 1772 included: 'a neat canopy with gadrooned cornice, carved middle and corners with pineapple at top — £4.15. & Hangings—£25.12.6'; 'a mahogany double headed couch bed — £8.8.0.' Between April 1778 and March 1780, furniture was ordered from Saunders & Bracken for the Dowager Duchess's niece, Miss Wriothesley, who lived with the Duchess. [Bedford Office, London]

AUDLEY END, Essex and **BURLINGTON ST**, London (Sir John Griffin Griffin). 1765–1772: Furniture, upholstery goods and fine tapestry supplied between February 1765 and June 1772. An account for upholstery goods and other furniture for Audley End and London in 1765–66 came to £177 18s 11d, and in addition, '58 Ells fine Tapestry in two Pieces work'd to your own Designs — £145.' Furniture delivered during this period came to £138. [Essex RO, D/DBy/A24/6 and A/30/6, and account bks D/DBy/202–203]

BAGSHOT PARK, Surrey (Earl of Albemarle). 1769–71: The Bagshot Park account books have several small entries in 1769 and three payments of £50 in Michaelmas Quarter 1771 'to Paul Saunders, Upholsterer'. [Suffolk RO, HA67:461/443]

THORNDON HALL, Essex and **SOUTH AUDLEY ST**, London (the Hon. Mrs Howard, mother of Lady Petre). 1771–80: A series of bills from Saunders & Bracken ending in February 1780 concerned with sundry repairs, the supply of upholstery goods and furniture. The largest account (A 189/7) was for £49 3s 8d for bedhangers' work, and included a detailed listing of removal work, repairs and alterations to curtains, carpets, and bedsteads. Furniture pieces were returned on account, and second-hand items as well as the quality cabinet work was supplied: 'A Neat Mahg. Library Bookcase the upper Part with wire Doors green tammy Curtains . . .'. £12 12s. [Essex RO, D/DP A189/3, 6, 7, 8; A190] N.N.T.

Saunders, Paul & Trotter, John, address unknown, cm (1767). Signed inventory of furniture of the Earl of Guilford at his house in Grosvenor Sq., 14 March 1767. [V&A archives]

Saunders, Peter, Oxford, cm (1812). Recorded concerning the lease and release of property. [Oxford RO, MISC PRU I/9–10]

Saunders, Reuben, 4 Charles St, Brighton, Sussex, u (1822). [D]

Saunders, Richard, Mount St, London. Between 1815–23 supplied furniture for Col. Henry Knight of Tythegston Court, Glam. [*C. Life*, 5 October 1978, pp. 1024–29]

Saunders, Richard, Oxford St, London, carver and gilder (1819–39). Recorded at 48 Wells St, 1819–25 and 31 Foley St, 1826–39. [D]

Saunders, Samuel, Bridge St, Cambridge, cm (1792–1805). Possibly the 'Sam Sanders' who received payment, probably for joinery work, from Trinity College in 1792. Sale of his stock, household furniture, timber, benches, saw pit frame etc. advertised in *Cambridge Chronicle and Journal*, 6 July 1805. [D; Trinity College archives]

Saunders, Samuel, Fore St, Plymouth, Devon, carver and gilder (1822–38). Recorded at no. 101, 1822–30 and no. 22 in 1838. [D]

Saunders, Stephen, High St, Newport, Isle of Wight, Hants., cm and u (1823–30). [D]

Saunders, Thomas, Abingdon, Berks., u (1696). Acted as 6th party in a marriage settlement by way of a release after lease on property in Goring. [Oxford RO, Hen. I/i/8]

Saunders, Thomas, Briton (or Bruton) Mews, London, cm (1749). [Westminster poll bk]

Saunders, Thomas, 11 High St, Sheffield, Yorks., feather merchant, broker and u (1797). [D]

Saunders, Thomas, St Peter's-in-the-East, Oxford, u (1802). Recorded as not voting, Oxford poll 1802.

Saunders, Thomas, 10 Gt Castle St, Oxford Mkt, London, carver and gilder (1817). [D] See James and William Saunders at this address.

Saunders, Thomas, Brighton, Sussex, u (1821–26). Thomas Saunders and his son, John, who continued the family's business through the 1830s, were the upholsterers regularly employed at the Pavilion in Brighton between 1820 and 1840. In this capacity, they were responsible for general jobbing, cleaning, repairing, 'putting-up and taking-down', as well as the supply of routine household items.

Thomas Saunders is almost certainly the Saunders of Saunders & Colbron, upholders (or Upholsterers — *sic*) listed in the Brighton accounts of the Prince Regent for the years 1816–19, in connection with the hire of miscellaneous items of furniture, beds, bedding, chests of drawers, Pembroke tables, chairs, etc. Small upholstery goods, hooks, ribbons, blind lines, tacks, etc., were also supplied. [PRO, LC11/21–24–27] Earlier, the firm Colbron & Co., Brighton upholsterers, had appeared regularly in the Pavilion accounts between July 1801 and January 1804. [Windsor RA 88883 — RA 88919]

Thomas Saunders's name appears in the Brighton accounts for 1821–22 providing upholstery and furniture for the King's Room. [PRO, LC11/33–35] Quarterly entries cover most of the period from late 1823 to 1826 — addressed to Messrs T. & J. Saunders in March 1824, and later to Thos. Saunders & Son. After 1825, they style themselves upholsterers and cabinet-makers. Many of their entries are notated: 'under the superintendence of Mr. Henry Saunders', a person probably related who appears to have been in charge of the accounts at Brighton Pavilion. [Windsor RA 35573, RA 35583, RA 35607 and PRO, LC11/41–47] In the bills listed, no furniture is detailed, but the firm-supplied wood framed covers for furniture, oil cloths, billiard covers, etc.

N.N.T.

Saunders, Thomas, 7 Riding House Lane, Gt Portland St, London, carver and gilder (1835–39). [D]

Saunders, Thomas, Salisbury St, Blandford, Dorset, cm (1840). [D]

Saunders, William, London, turner and gilder (1780–1808). Trading at 10 Charterhouse Lane, 1780–82, 23 Charterhouse Lane, 1783–87 and 10 Gt Castle St, 1792–1808. Took out a Sun Insurance policy on 10 July 1792 for £600 of which £300 accounted for utensils, stock and goods. [D; GL, Sun MS vol. 389, ref. 602654] See James and Thomas Saunders at 10 Gt Castle St. Possibly:

Saunders, William, Cavendish Sq., London, frame maker

(1797). Received £6 5s 6d in payment for 'a half whole length frame for the portrait of Mr. Dundas' (Henry Dundas, later 1st Viscount Melville) by George Romney. [Scottish RO, GD 160/Box 46/Bundle XIV]

Saunders, William, Bridge St, St Ives, Hunts., cm and u (1830). [D]

Saunders, William, St Mary Arches St, Exeter, Devon, cm (1838). His son Joseph Jutson bapt. at St Mary Arches on 2 April 1838. [PR (bapt.)]

Saunders, William, Brighton, Sussex, cm and u (1839–40). Trading at 7 Park St in 1839. Marriage of William Saunders, 14 Broad St, to Susannah King recorded on 29 February 1840. [D; E. Sussex RO, PAR 255/1/3/12]

Saunders & Woolley, 170 Regent St, London, house decorators and u 'By Appointment to the Queen' (1840). In August 1840 supplied Lord Fitzalan with 'A richly carved & gilt chair mounted with customer's own needlework' costing £15 15s. [Arundel Castle records, A1963]

Saunderson, James, Turn Lane, Retford, Notts., chairmaker and turner (1830). [D]

Saunderson, John, Colliergate, York, cm (1758). [Poll bk]

Saunderson, John, Chapel St, Westminster, London, cm (1774). [Poll bk]

Saunderson, William, Watermill, Barton-on-Humber, Lincs., joiner and cm (1835). [D]

Saunier, John Charles, Carnaby Mkt, London, cm, u and undertaker (1801–08). In July 1801 at 15 Marshall St, Carnaby Mkt, where he took out insurance cover of £400, half of which was for utensils and stock. By 1803 at 52 Broad St, Carnaby Mkt, and in 1808 the business trading from the same address was in the names of John & Julia Saunier. [D; GL, Sun MS vol. 419, ref. 721197]

Savage, Cephas, Soresby St, Chesterfield, Derbs., cm (1829–35). [D]

Savage, Charles, 102 St Martin's Lane, London, carver and gilder (1835). [D]

Savage, John, Little Chelsea, London, u (1739). On 24 December 1739 submitted his account to Mr Hoare for a 'settee of Tappistry, 4 chairs D°, 8 D°' at a total cost of £7 4s. These items were for Sir Richard Hoare and supplied in connection with his house at Barn Elms, Barnes, Surrey. [V&A Lib., 86.NN.3]

Savage, John, Lancaster, cm (1772–1826). App. to Jeremiah Sowerby in 1772 and free by servitude, 1779–80. In the freemen rolls he is entered as 'John Savage, otherwise Winter'. In 1799 he was trading from an address at Dam-side. A mahogany chest with four drawers in the bottom, possibly a silver chest, is known with a brass plate let into the lid inscribed in script 'John Savage, Lancaster, 1786'. The name of John Savage also appears in the Gillow records in 1784–85, 1797–1806, 1808–09, 1811, 1814–15, 1818–23 and 1826 and may be the same person. [D; app. reg.; freemen rolls; *Lancaster Guardian*, 29 March 1974; Westminster Ref. Lib., Gillow]

Savage, John, 47 Garden Lane, Salford, Lancs., carver and gilder (1838–40). [D]

Savage, Michael, parish of St Martin-in-the-Fields, London, carver (1710–19). In October 1710 insured six houses at a valuation of £600. [GL, Hand in Hand MS vol. 8, refs 4843–50; V&A archives]

Savage, Michael, Lancaster, cm (1768–80). App. to H. Gibson in 1768 and free by servitude, 1779–80. [App. reg.; freemen rolls]

Savage, Purbeck, St Bartholomew Close, London, upholder (1701–20). Free of the Upholders' Co. on 2 July 1701, and in December 1712 living in Bartholomew Close where he insured his house for £200. Took as app. William Cooke,

1718–20. [GL, Upholders' Co. records; Hand in Hand MS vol. 11, p. 73]

Savage, Thomas, Commercial Rd, London, carver and gilder (1826–39). In 1826 at 23 Commercial Rd but in 1839 at 27 Gt Turner St, Commercial Rd. [D]

Savage, Walter, London, upholder (1723–33). Son of William Savage of Broadway, Worcs., 'practitioner in physick.' App. to Robert Milner on 6 November 1723 and free by servitude, 7 March 1732/33. [GL, Upholders' Co. records]

Savage, William & Co., address unknown, u and picture frame maker (1701–02). On 9 September 1701 issued his account totalling £56 4s to the Earl of Salisbury for textiles supplied to Hatfield House, Herts. Three of the five items were rich pieces of damask. On 27 January 1702 he charged £29 14s for picture framing at Hatfield House. [Hatfield House MS, Bills 395]

Savegnac, Paul, Dover St, Piccadilly, London, u (d.1800). Death by suicide reported in *Gents Mag.*, October 1800.

Savery, Thomas, Bristol, chairmaker (1753). In 1753 took app. named Chambers. [S of G, app. index]

Savile, Thomas, Westminster, London, upholder (1788). [Bailey's list of bankrupts]

Savill, Thomas, 17 Aldgate High St Without, London, u and cm (1771–1808). Son of William Savill of Bocking, Essex. App. to Samuel Walker, draper, and free of the Upholders' Co. under the terms of the 1750 Upholders' Act, 6 February 1771. Despite the location of the business away from the fashionable trade in central London, this Whitechapel business appears to have developed into an enterprise of some magnitude. By April 1791 utensils and stock were valued at £1,000 for insurance purposes. He also took a number of apps including Samuel Legg in 1771; Samuel Waldergrave, 1778–86; James Flower and Edward Brander, 1786–1802; and John Bennett, 1798–1801. He was included in the list of master cabinet makers in Sheraton's *Cabinet Dictionary*, 1803. [D; GL, Upholders' Co. records; Sun MS vol. 376, p. 215]

Saville, Benjamin, Gomersal, Birstall, Yorks., cm and joiner (1828). [D]

Saville, Benoni, Birstall, Yorks., joiner and cm (1830). [D]

Saville, Peter, Sheffield, Yorks., chairmaker (1797–1830). At 40 Barkers Pool, 1814–18, but from 1817 addresses in Fargate are also recorded. The number in this street was 40 in 1817, 37 in 1822, and 68 from 1825–30. In 1821–25 listed as Saville & Co. [D]

Savory, David, Norwich, cm (1802–30). Living in the parish of St Lawrence, 1802–18 and at Heigham in 1830. [Poll bks]

Savory, John, Gloucester, cm (1814). Child bapt. parish of St Catherine in 814. [PR (bapt.)]

Savory, Joseph, Cirencester, Glos., cm (1828). Child bapt. in 1828. [PR (bapt.)]

Sawer, Joseph Philip, Maidstone, Kent, cm and u (1826–38). In Union St, 1826–29 but from January 1832 in County Rd where the address was given as County Pl., 1838–39. [D; poll bks]

Sawer, William, 1 Mount St, Blackburn, Lancs., cm (1824–28). Continued to be listed in directories until 1834 as a joiner. [D]

Sawkill, John, South Shields, Co. Durham, cm/joiner (1834). [D]

Sawkins, K., 12 Castle St, Bloomsbury, London, cm and u (1827). [D]

Sawyer, Charles, High St, Southwold, Suffolk, cm and u (1824–d.1840). Will proved at Norwich in 1840. On 4 February 1832 submitted an account for £11 9s 6d in respect of cabinet goods supplied to Sir Charles Blois of Cockfield Hall, Yoxford, Suffolk. [D; Norfolk Record Soc., index of wills; Suffolk RO (Ipswich), HA30: 312/418]

Sawyer, James (or John), 112 Wardour St, Soho, London, chairmaker and cm (1817–19). [D]

Sawyer, John, St John's St, Golden Sq., London, cm (1744–49). On 12 April 1744 his premises were severely damaged by fire. [*Daily Advertiser*, 13 April 1744; Westminster poll bk]

Sawyer, Thomas, address unknown, framemaker (1728). In 1728 paid £73 in connection with work at Stowe, Bucks. [Huntington Lib., California, Stowe MS ST 82, p. 247]

Sawyer, Thomas, High St, Salford, Blackburn, Lancs., joiner and cm (1818). [D]

Saxon, Samuel, Fore St, Exeter, Devon, u, cm and chairmaker (1764). Stated that he had moved from London and was in occupation of the house where John Stone formerly lived which was the back part of Spencer's printing office, opposite St Martin's Lane. He offered 'Upholstery, Glasses, Cabinets, and Chairs in Mahogany and Walnut'. He also featured billiard tables which he offered at prices from twenty to fifty guineas. [*Exeter Mercury*, 23 November 1764]

Saxon, Thomas, 32 Ironmonger Row, Old St, London, cm (1808–09). [D]

Saxton, Joshua, Listergate, Nottingham, joiner, cm and u (1832–40). [D]

Saxton, Nathaniel, High St, Leicester, cm and u (1785–1828). From 1785 trading in partnership with John Shipley at the High St address. John Shipley died in 1796 and after a brief partnership with Ann Shipley (widow) Saxton continued the business taking his son into partnership by 1824 when the style N. Saxton & Son was adopted. Trading had ceased by April 1828 when the entire stock was advertised for sale at a discount of 20% under cost. The furniture was stated to be 'superior to the generality of furniture made in the country'. The quality of Saxton's work can be assessed as he used trade labels to identify his manufactures. A set of four single chairs and a further set of six mahogany dining chairs in a Regency style are known with the label of 'N. SAXTON High St. Leicester', and a small tripod table with that of N. Saxton & Son. [D; *Leicester Mercury*, 13 November 1795; *Leicester Chronicle*, 19 April 1828]

Saxton, Thomas, Nottingham, joiner, cm and u (1821–40). In 1832 in Chesterfield St but by 1841 at Middle Pavement. Took all his three sons as apps: George in 1821, Henry 1836 and Alfred in 1838. Henry was stated to be 13 years of age on 28 January 1835 and Alfred was born 16 June 1824. [D; app. bk]

Saxton, William, Otley, Yorks., joiner/cm (1834). [D]

Say, Francis, Ludgate Hill, London, u (1738–78). Son of Richard Say, a freeman of the Upholders' Co. who traded from an address in Racquet Ct, Fleet St until his death in 1762. Francis Say was app. to his father on 4 October 1738 and free of the Upholders' Co. by patrimony, 10 October 1745. He was subsequently to take an active part in the affairs of the company becoming Junior Warden in 1772, Senior Warden in 1773 and Master, 1774–75. Francis Say initially traded from an address next to 'The Crown Tavern', Ludgate Hill, subsequently numbered 83. On his trade card he claimed to make and sell 'all sorts of Upholsterers & Cabinet Makers Goods'. He also acted as an appraiser, undertaker and bought and sold 'all Sorts of Goods by Commission or otherwise'. His name first appears in London directories at 83 Ludgate Hill in 1753 and he remained here until 1763. In 1763, however, he took into partnership Quintin Kay and in 1767 the partners moved to 14 Ludgate Hill where they continued to trade as Say & Kay until Francis Say's death in 1778 at 'Hadley' after which Kay continued the business under his sole control from this same address. Evidence suggests that the business was conducted on an extensive scale. As early as 1750 Francis Say was taking out licences to employ six non-freemen for periods extending to six months but by 1753 the number employed had reached twenty. He also was responsible for the training of an impressive list of apps and the premiums commanded suggest that the business was well-respected. His apps included George Good (1745–62), Lynnel Eames, son of John Eames, app. in 1749, premium £50), Peter Davidson (1755–63, premium £100), Joseph Read (1759–68), and Robert Orton, son of William Orton of Hampstead (app. on 10 March 1760, premium £84). Francis Say subscribed to Chippendale's *Director*, 1754.

Francis Say supplied furniture to George Bowes for Gibside, Co. Durham, 1753–60. An account dated 17 July 1753 totalling £33 6s was for '10 Mohog Chairs Stufft back & seat, the frames richley carved in the Chinese manner' at £18 10s, a 'large sopha to match w Bolsters' £10 18s, 'brass Burnished Nails' £2 14s, and packing. Correspondence exists dated 1759 regarding the purchase of a bed and its delivery by sea to Gibside and in the following year payments were made on 1 March 1760 on behalf of George Bowes' late sister (£22 1s) and 19 June for furniture for Gibside (£67).

There is a two page bill of 1763/64 [Isle of Wight RO, JER/WA] from Say & Kay to Mrs Crow totalling £22 14s 4d. Items include 'Advertising your House' and charges for storing furniture during a house move. The partners were responsible for the funeral arrangements for Sir Francis Gosling, the banker, and a detailed account for the costs dated 7 January 1769 exists. In 1770 a desk and a pair of chests of drawers were supplied to Henry Knight of Tythegston Court, Glam., S. Wales. The desk and the original design survive.

A short biography of the Say family was written in 1948 by L. G. N. Horton-Smith with the title *The Old City Family of Say*. [D; Heal; GL, Upholders' Co. records; City Licence bks, vol. 1; S of G, app. index; Durham RO, D/St/309, D/St/243, D/St/V1510; *C. Life*, 5 October 1978, p. 1027] B.A.

Say, Richard, Racquet Ct, Fleet St, London, upholder (1712–d.1762). Son of Hugh Say, freeman and member of the Merchant Tailors' Co. Father of Francis Say. Richard Say was app. to William Humphreys on 5 September 1705 and free of the Upholders' Co. by servitude, 4 February 1712. He was master of the Upholders' Co., 1744–45. Took as app. Daniel Wisker on 15 October 1713 at a premium of £30 and was made free 1722. Other apps were Lawrence Whithorn (1719–30) and his son Francis Say (1738–45). He was Collector for the Poor in the parish of St Bride's, Fleet St in 1720 and subsequently Questman and Scavenger in 1730, Sidesman in 1731 and Churchwarden 1741–42. His eldest daughter Henrietta was married in 1746 to Joseph Partington, an 'eminent apothecary in Fleet St.'. [GL, Upholders' Co. records; MS 6581, p. 28; PRO, IR 1/2; *London Evening Post*, 15–17 April 1746]

Say & Kay, see Francis Say and Quintin Kay.

Sayer, Benjamin, 48 Long Alley, London, cm (1835). [D]

Sayer, James, Alphington St, Exeter, Devon, cm and u (1830–32). In voters' lists, 1831–32 shown at St Mary's Steps. [D; poll bks]

Sayer, John, address unknown (1685). In July 1685 supplied for the 5th Earl of Bedford 'a large press for writing with lock and hinges' at £2 15s and 'a wainscot case and mending the drawers and fitting them in' 15s. [Bedford Office, London]

Sayer, John, Henley-on-Thames, Oxon., chairmaker (1776). On 3 June 1776 married, at Henley, Mary Floyd of that town. At this date he was aged 27. [Bodleian index of Oxf. marriage bonds]

Sayer, John, Tarleton Ct, Stanley St, Liverpool, chairmaker (1824). [D]

Sayer, John, London, bedstead maker (1835–39). At 41 Fashion St, Spitalfields in 1835 and 27 Auction St, Spitalfields in 1837. By 1839, however, the business was trading as John Sayer & Son, furniture brokers from 27 Long Alley, Finsbury. [D]

Sayer, Richard, Dorking, Surrey, upholder (1838). [D] See R. Sayers.

Sayer, William, Stanley St, Liverpool, carver and furniture broker (1837–39). At 15 Stanley St in 1837 but by 1839 the number was 29. [D]

Sayers, James, North St, Chichester, Sussex, cm and auctioneer (1793–d.1825). The death of James Sayers was announced in March 1825 and the business was subsequently conducted by William & Charles Sayers. [D; *Brighton Gazette*, 3 March 1825]

Sayers, John, address unknown, frame maker (1778–87). Worked for George Cooke at Dunham Massey, Cheshire. On 7 November 1778 he was paid £23 1s for making frames and repairing others. On 24 September 1784 £10 14s 6d was paid for frames, and further payments for similar work were made on 17 May 1786, 3 November 1787 and 11 October 1788. [John Rylands Lib., Manchester, George Cooke's accounts]

Sayers, John, 38 Davies St, Liverpool, chairmaker (1839). [D]

Sayers, R., Dorking, Surrey, carpenter and cm (1811). [D] See Richard Bayer.

Sayers, William & Charles, North St, Chichester, Sussex, cm and u (1826–32). [D] Successors to James Sayers at this address.

Scadding, Thomas, Wellington, Som., house joiner and cm (1767). Advertised that 'he performs all the Branches of Business, and Cabinet-Work in the neatest Manner, and in the newest Taste'. [*Sherborne Mercury*, 30 November 1767]

Scaife, Thomas, London, upholder (1747–54). Son of the Rev. John Scaife of Cottenham, Cambs. App. to William Kilpin on 18 June 1747 and free of the Upholders' Co. by servitude, 31 July 1754. [GL, Upholders' Co. records]

Scales, James, Liverpool, cm (1812). Son of William Scales, cm and free by patrimony, 5 October 1812. Probably dead by 1818. [Freemen reg.]

Scales, Samuel, Neptune St, Rotherhithe, London, upholder and undertaker (1817). [D]

Scales, William, North St, Liverpool, cm (1780–96). Free 7 September 1780 and by 1790 trading at 9 North St. In 1796 at back of 26 North St. Father of James Scales who was free 5 October 1812. William Scales was dead by 1820. [D; freemen reg.]

Scaley, T., 37 Cary St, Lincoln's Inn Fields, London, upholder and undertaker (1817). [D]

Scambler, Henry, 5 Market St, Oxford St, London, u and cm (1805–26). The premises used were described as a dwelling house and workshop. Insurance cover in November 1805 was £500 with utensils and stock accounting for £400 of this. In January 1807 the corresponding figures were £500 and £300 and in January 1809 £1,000 and £400. On 9 June 1812 Sir John Geers Cotterell of Garnons, near Hereford and Hertford St, London paid Scambler £1 for a table. [D; GL, Sun MS vol. 434, ref. 781713; vol. 437, ref. 798713; vol. 448, ref. 825833; Herefs. RO, Garnons W69/III/183]

Scamen, Allen, Hull, Yorks., cm (1768–84). [Poll bks]

Scandrett, William, High St, Kington, Herefs., carpenter, joiner, cm and u (1835). [D]

Scanes, Alexander, Bartholomew St, Exeter, Devon, cm (1840). Daughter bapt. on 20 September 1840 at St Mary Arches. [PR (bapt.)]

Scantlebury, John, Campo Lane, Sheffield, Yorks., carver, gilder and looking-glass maker (1814–18). [D]

Scantlebury, Thomas, 69 Campo Lane, Sheffield, Yorks., looking-glass manufacturer (1797–1817). [D]

Scantlebury, Thomas & Co., Thomas St, Bristol, cm (1784). [D]

Scaping, George, 1 East St, Finsbury Mkt, London, cm and bedstead maker (1826). [D]

Scaping, Joseph, 68 Long Alley, Moorfields, London, sofa, couch and bedstead manufacturer (1817–20). [D]

Scaplen, John jnr, Poole, Dorset, cm (1773). [Surrey RO (Guildford), deed BR/T/1020/2]

Scarfe, C. & Lowes, 2 Buckingham Pl., Fitzroy Sq., London, cm and bedstead manufacturers (1820–25). [D]

Scarfe, Charles & Co., Hatter's Lane, Boston, Lincs., chairmaker and turner (1835). [D]

Scarfe, James, South St, Bishop's Stortford, Herts., cm (1823–26). [D]

Scarfe, Samuel, 45 Paddington St, Marylebone, London, u and cm (1826–28). [D]

Scarlet, S., near the Market Pl., Derby, u (1796). In 1796 advertised that he had taken over the shop 'late in the occupation of Mr. Moss upholsterer'. He intended to carry on a business retailing upholstery, cabinet and paperhanging goods and claimed to have a stock of such items. [*Derby Mercury*, No. 3325]

Scarlet, Samuel, Newcastle-under-Lyme, Staffs., u (1794). Bankruptcy announced, November 1794. [*Williamson's Liverpool Advertiser*, 1 December 1794]

Scarlet, Samuel, Piccadilly, Hanley, Staffs., u (1818). [D]

Scarll, William, Lowestoft, Suffolk, u, pawnbroker and furniture broker (1830–39). [D]

Scarrott, Thomas, 48 William St, Birmingham, cm and u (1830–39). [D]

Scarrott & Busswell, Digbeth, Birmingham, cm (1816–18). [D]

Sceats, Joseph, Somerset Green, Redcliffe Hill, Bristol, carpenter, veranda and rustic chairmaker (1817–19). [D]

Scevery, James, 17 Pellew St, Liverpool, carver and gilder (1823–24). [D]

Schade, Andrew F., 14 Kinnerton St, Belgrave Sq., London, cm and u (1839). [D]

Schaeffer, Henry, 46 Castle St East, Oxford Mkt, London, carver and gilder (1808–20). In 1817 the name is listed as Samuel Schaeffer but this may be an error. [D]

Schaw, John, London(?), u (1740–49). Supplied goods to the Duke of Gordon. In 1740 charged £1 12s for 'superfine English blankets' and 1s per day for 32 days work by his servant James Hastie at Gordon Castle 'doing up furniture'. In 1743 supplied a bed and bedding and a tent bed sent by sea to Leith. The following year 'two shoulder knots for your servants' were charged at 9s. The account was settled in full 15 May 1749. [Scottish RO, GD44/51/302/35/36]

Schelton, —, Haymarket, London, u (1734). In 1734 described as 'an eminent upholsterer . . . lately appointed Beadle to the Company of Upholders'. [Heal]

Schiavi, Antonio, Liverpool, carver, gilder and looking-glass manufacturer (1821–37). At 14 Standish St, 1821–23 but at 67 Stanley St, 1824–37. [D]

Schiavi, Francis, Liverpool, carver and gilder (1834–37). At 12 Standish St in 1834, 43 Tenterden St in 1835 and Major Pl., 103 Burlington St, 1837. A William Schiavi is also shown in the same directory at the latter address in 1837. [D]

Schiavi, James, Liverpool, carver and gilder (1827–39). At 13 Copperas Hill, in 1827–29 but by 1839 at 21 Bevington Bush Rd. [D]

Schiavi, Margaret, 26 Stanley St, Liverpool, carver and gilder (1839). An Antonio Schiavi was trading at 67 Stanley St in the same trade in 1837. [D]

Schiavi, William, Major Pl., 103 Burlington St, Liverpool, carver and gilder (1837). Successor to Francis at this address. [D]

Schofield, —, Charlotte St, Rathbone Pl., London, cm (1803). Subscribed to Sheraton's *Cabinet Dictionary*, 1803.

Schofield (or Scholefield), John, Halifax, Yorks., cm (1792). Bankrupt April 1792, but a dividend was declared as late as

September 1798. [*Leeds Intelligencer*, 30 April 1792; *Billinge's Liverpool Advertiser*, 3 September 1798]

Schofield, John, Lower Hillgate, Stockport, Cheshire, cm and joiner (1825–28). [D]

Schofield, William, Goose Lane, Macclesfield, Cheshire, cm (1816–22). [D]

Schofield, William, Butchery, Brigg, Lincs., chairmaker (1826). [D]

Schofield & Russell, Hatton Gdn, London, looking-glass manufacturers (1800–13). At 57 Hatton Gdn, but a directory of 1803 lists the firm as Schofield & Russell & Co. and gives the number as 55. [D]

Scholcroft, Robert, 6 Park St, Preston, Lancs., cm (1818). [D]

Schole, —, address unknown, cm (*c*.1775). Supplied furniture to Denton Park, Yorks. to the value of £206 17s. [*Furn. Hist.*, 1968]

Scholefield, Richard, London, upholder and cm (1793–1802). In 1793 subscribed to Sheraton's *Drawing Book*. Shown at 5 Gt Portland St in 1797 but in 1801 the address was Little Portland St. Bankruptcy announced, *Liverpool Advertiser*, 27 December 1802. [D]

Scholes, Abner snr, Chester, u (1688–1721). Free 2 February 1688. Took as apps Randle Bingley and Samuel Maddock (free 1697) and in 1721 another app. named Williams. [Freemen rolls; app. bk; S of G, app. index]

Scholes, Abner jnr, Chester, u (1722–36). Son of Abner Scholes snr. Free 2 March 1722. Took as app. Harwar Harvie who was free in 1736. [Freemen rolls; poll bk]

Scholes, Benjamin, Birkby, near Huddersfield, Yorks., cm (1785). In *Leeds Mercury*, 22 February 1785 announced the dissolution of his partnership with John Dyson.

Scholes, George, North St, Woodhouse Lane, Leeds, Yorks., cm (1818). [D]

Scholes, Henry, Old Churchyard, Manchester, cm (1840). [D]

Scholes, Richard, Wakefield, Yorks., carver (1798). [D]

Scholes, Robert, Halifax, Yorks., upholder and auctioneer (1784). [D]

Scholes & Askey, White Horse Yd, Leeds, Yorks., cm and dealers in mahogany (1823–34). [D]

Scholes & Grayson, Manchester, u (1828–38). At 6 Port St in 1828, 9 Pall Mall 1829, 29 Pall Mall 1834, and 27 Tib Lane, 1836–38. An 1828 directory lists the business as Scholes & Graham. [D]

Scholey, John, York and Rotherham, Yorks., cm (1733–41). Son of Nathaniel Scholey, cm, and free of York in 1733. In 1741 at Rotherham. [Freemen rolls; York poll bk]

Scholey, John, Loft St, Grimsby, Lincs., cm (1819). [D]

Scholey, Joseph, Grimsby, Lincs., joiner and cm (1809–22). Listed at Bull-ring in 1822. Recorded in the Hull Corp. records as taking the following apps: William Cooke (May 1809), Thomas Peasegood (December 1809), Robert Gooseman (August 1813), John Goforth (July 1814), Samuel Crowder (March 1816) and William Everitt (May 1821). All the apps were from Grimsby with the exception of Everitt who was from Kealby, Lincs. [Hull app. reg.]

Scholey, Nathaniel, York, cm (1733). Father of John Scholey who was free of York as a cm 1733. [Freemen rolls]

Scholey, Robert, 69 Sun St, Bishopsgate, London, carver and gilder (1811–25). [D] See Robert Snell.

Scholey, William & J., Upper St, Islington, London, carvers and gilders (1820–39). The number in Upper St was 16 in 1820, 97 in 1835 and 129 in 1839. [D]

Scholfield, —, Sledwick, near Wakefield, Yorks (*c*.1720). A kneehole writing table with several drawers marked is known. [Sotheby's, 3 May 1974, lot 47]

Scholfield, Abraham, Roomfield, Langfield, Todmorden, Yorks., joiner/cm (1837). [D] See James Scholfield.

Scholfield, Arthur, Manchester, u (1728). In 1728 took app. named Brabin. [S of G, app. index]

Scholfield, James, Roomfield, Langfield, Todmorden, Yorks., joiner/cm (1837). [D] See Abraham Scolfield.

Schorfell, Thomas, Butchery, Brigg, Lincs., chairmaker (1828). [D]

Schouten, William, London, upholder (1720–28). Son of John Schouten of St Martin-in-the-Fields, Gent. App. to James Gronous on 4 May 1720. Free of the Upholders' Co., 5 June 1728. [GL, Upholders' Co. records]

Schultz, Henry James, Eyre St Hill, Cold Bath Fields, London, bedstead maker (1822). In February 1822 took out insurance cover for £200 which included £50 for a workshop behind the house and £50 for utensils and stock kept there. [GL, Sun MS vol. 491, ref. 989402]

Schurrey, William, Wakefield, Yorks., cm (1793). Subscribed to Sheraton's *Drawing Book*, 1793.

Schweitzer, L. F. G., 7 Broad St, Long Acre, London, plate case maker (1825). [D]

Sclater, E., 191 Snargate St, Dover, Kent, carver and gilder (1838–39). [D]

Scobie, James, Peter St, Westminster, London, cm (1774). [Poll bk]

Scoltock, John & Richard, Market Sq., Shrewsbury, Salop, cm and u (1828). [D]

Scoltock, Jonathan & Richard, Shrewsbury, Salop, cm and u (1828–35). Listed at Corn Mkt in 1828 and Market Pl., 1835. [D]

Scorah, Joseph, 32 Lever St, Manchester, cm (1825). [D]

Scorah, William, Retford, Notts., cm (1832). Bankruptcy announced April 1832. A directory of that year gives the address as West Retford but the bankruptcy notice states East Retford. [D; *London Gazette*, 10 April 1832]

Scotford, Thomas, 10 Francis Pl. and 8 Cheltenham Pl., Westminster Rd, London, cm and u (1835). [D]

Scotland, Lawrence, St James, Westminster, London, cm (1774). Bankruptcy announced, *Gents Mag.*, June 1774.

Scott, —, address unknown, carver (1754). Subscribed to Chippendale's *Director*, 1754.

Scott, Adam, Whitehaven, Cumb., joiner/cm (1828–34). At 159 Queen St in 1828, 2 West Strand in 1829 and 3 Tangier St, 1834. [D]

Scott, Alexander, 12 Francis St, Tottenham Ct Rd, London cm (1820–35). [D]

Scott, Alexander, 57 Collingwood St, Liverpool, cm (1835). [D]

Scott, Charles, Little Grosvenor St, London, carver (1774). [Westminster poll bk]

Scott, Charles, Swinegate, York, cm (1794–1802). Son of Mary, wife of William Elston, butcher. App. to John Barber, cm, on 14 October 1794. Free in 1802. [Freemen rolls]

Scott, Charles, 3 Aylesbury St, Clerkenwell, London, Tunbridge-ware manufacturer (1805–20). [D]

Scott, Charles, 4 Silver St, Golden Sq., London, cm (1826). [D]

Scott, Francis & Son, Wakefield, Yorks., cm (1781–84). [D]

Scott, George, Bottle-bank, Gateshead, Co. Durham, joiner and cm (1824). [D]

Scott, James, London, cm (1793). Subscribed to Sheraton's *Drawing Book*, 1793.

Scott, James, Lancaster, cm (1795–97). Free 1795–96. Named in the Gillow records, 1796–97. [Freemen rolls; Westminster Ref. Lib., Gillow]

Scott, James, Ormskirk, Lancs., cm (1822). [D]

Scott, James, East Bank Lane, Southport, Lancs., cm (1828–34). Wife died on 9 January 1828. [D; *Liverpool Mercury*, 18 January 1828]

Scott, John, 'The Plough & Harrow', east side of Bishopsgate St Without, London, upholder (1707–15). Freeman of London.

On 31 December 1707 took out insurance cover of £200 on the property in Bishopsgate St described as 'his dwelling house'. In January 1715 he was still insuring this property at the same valuation but appears to have been living then in Dulwich. [GL, Hand in Hand MS vol. 5, ref. 15137; vol. 13, ref. 15137]

Scott, John, London, upholder (1718–43). Son of John Scott of Chippenham, Wilts., Gent. App. to John Spicer on 3 September 1718 and free of the Upholders' Co. by servitude, 4 October 1743. [GL, Upholders' Co. records]

Scott, John, 'The King's Arms', Cheapside, against Bow Churchyard, London, leather gilder and u (1746). [Heal]

Scott, John, 419 Strand, London, cm and undertaker (1779). In 1779 took out insurance cover of £200 on his utensils and stock. [GL, Sun MS vol. 273, p. 299]

Scott, John, Liverpool, cm (1777–84). At 160 Dale St in 1777 but at 19 Pitt St, 1781–84. In 1777 also a grocer. [D]

Scott, John, Baxtergate, Whitby, Yorks., cm (1787). In March 1787 insured his utensils and stock for £100. [GL, Sun MS vol. 344, p. 330]

Scott, John, Berwick St, Soho, cm, u and undertaker (1793–1835). Shown at 52 Berwick St, though some directories state 50. Probably the John Scott, cm, who subscribed to Sheraton's *Drawing Book*, 1793. A pair of Regency mahogany dining chairs on reeded sabre legs are known stamped 'J. SCOTT'. [D; Heal; Christie's, 25 October 1979, lot 42]

Scott, John, snr and jnr, White Lion St, Norwich, u and paper hanger (1796–1830). His son John participated in the business and in 1822 it is listed in a directory as John Scott & Son. John Scott snr appears to have died between 1822 and 1830 and the son carried on alone. In November 1830 he was declared bankrupt. He may have restarted the business however. Up to 1830 the address was 15 White Lion St (in 1808 White Lion Lane), but a trade card in the Norfolk Local Hist. Lib., which from the furniture illustrated probably dates from c.1840–50, states 19 White Lion St. [D; poll bks; *London Gazette*, 9 November 1830]

Scott, John, Boston, Lincs., cm (1806). Freeman of Lincoln but living in Boston in November 1806. [Lincoln poll bk]

Scott, John, Rickergate, Carlisle, Cumb., carver and gilder (1810–34). [D]

Scott, John, Church St, Clitheroe, Lancs, joiner, housebuilder and cm (1824). [D]

Scott, John, Castlegate, Grantham, Lincs., woodturner and chairmaker (1826). [D]

Scott, John, 28 Gt Titchfield St, London, cm and u (1827). [D]

Scott, John, Middlegate, Penrith, Cumb., joiner and cm (1828). [D]

Scott, John, King's Lynn, Norfolk, cm (1830–39). At Broad St but a directory of 1836 indicates North St. [D]

Scott, John, Berwick-on-Tweed, Northumb., cm and u (1834). Listed at Weston Lane in 1834. [D]

Scott, John, 315 Oxford St, London, upholsterer's warehouse (1835–39). [D]

Scott, Joseph, Fisher St, Carlisle, Cumb., joiner/cm (1828–29). [D]

Scott, Luke, London, cm (1807–09). In June 1807 at 2 Newman St where he took out insurance cover for £300 which included £30 for a chest of tools at Wright & Co., cm, 410 Oxford St. By July 1809 he was carrying on trade as a victualler at 'The Two Chairmen' in Dartmouth St, but also trading as a cm and took out cover of £300 on stock and utensils and a further £25 for a chest of tools. [GL, Sun MS vol. 440, ref. 804296; vol. 448, ref. 834167]

Scott, Michael, London, upholder (1707). Free of the London Upholders' Co., 7 May 1707. [GL, Upholders' Co. records]

Scott, Nicholas, Saville Ct, Newcastle, cm and joiner (1838). [D]

Scott, R., 101 Dean St, Soho, London, 'patent revolving chairmaker' (1835). [D]

Scott, Robert, Lancaster, joiner (1788–1803). Named in the Gillow records. [Westminster Ref. Lib., Gillow vol. 344/94, pp. 351, 429]

Scott, Robert, 'The Fountain', Pipewellgate, Gateshead, Co. Durham, joiner and cm (1802). In January 1802 took out insurance cover of £300 which included £50 for a workshop. [GL, Sun MS vol. 43, ref. 728601]

Scott, Robert, Church St, Gateshead, Co. Durham, joiner and cm (1811). [D]

Scott, Robert, Norwich, cm and u (1822–40). At Lower Westwick St in 1822 but from c.1830 at 18 Charing Cross. From 1836 the business is listed as Robert Scott & Son. The will of a Robert Scott, probably the father, was proved at Norwich in 1842. Robert Scott's trade card [Norfolk Local Hist. Lib.] described the business as a 'Cabinet, Upholstery, Paper Hanging and Carpet Warehouse'. Floor cloth and matting were also stocked. [D; poll bk; Norfolk Record Soc., index of wills]

Scott, Robert Sadler (or Sadley), 61 Blackett St, Newcastle, house and ship carver, gilder (1833–38). [D] See James Hardy at this address.

Scott, Samuel, Norwich, cm and u (1828–40). App. to John Norris and free, 24 February 1828. At Lower Westwick St, 1836–39 but by 1842 had moved to Charing Cross. [D; poll bk; freemen reg.]

Scott, Thomas, London, upholder (1746–54). Son of William Scott of the parish of St Anne's, Blackfriars, tailor. App. to William Cope, 6 November 1746 and free of the Upholders' Co. by servitude 5 December 1754. [GL, Upholders' Co. records]

Scott, Thomas, London, upholder (1758). Son of James Scott of Pateley Bridge, Yorks., mercer. Free of the Upholders' Co. by redemption under the terms of the 1750 Upholders' Act, 11 April 1758. [GL, Upholders' Co. records]

Scott, Thomas, 29 Ludgate Hill, London, upholder (1782–1804). A substantial business. In 1782 insurance cover amounted to £700 of which £600 was for utensils and stock. By 1784 these figures had risen to £2,000 and £1,300 respectively and stock levels remained high being £1,500 in 1785 and £1,400 in the following year. Scott was included in the list of master cabinet makers in Sheraton's *Cabinet Dictionary*, 1803. The death of his wife was recorded in January 1786. Scott is particularly associated with the manufacture of the ingeniously fitted dressing table known as a Rudd. This is illustrated in Hepplewhite's *Guide*, 1784. Examples are known with the trade label of Scott's business. [D; GL, Sun MS vol. 299, p. 571; vol. 322, p. 8; vol. 336, p. 122; vol. 338, p. 45; *Gents Mag.*, January 1786; *Burlington*, May 1968, p. 277; *C. Life*, 12 May 1966, pp. 1174–75]

Scott, Thomas, 9 Tottenham St, Middlx Hospital, London, u (1808).

Scott, Thomas, 12 Dover St, Southwark, London, cm and upholstery warehouse (1820–21). [D]

Scott, Thomas, Little Blake St, York, cm (1823). [D]

Scott, Thomas, Upper Maudlin St, Bristol, u, chair and couch manufacturer (1829). [D]

Scott, Thomas, Bishop Wearmouth, Co. Durham, chairmaker (1840). In 1840 employed at Bishop Wearmouth Iron works. His daughter aged 13 escaped injury after falling in front of a train of laden coal waggons. [*Chester Chronicle*, 25 December 1840]

Scott, Walter, Petergate, York, cm (1784). [Poll bk]

Scott, Walter, 1 Marshall St, London, cm (1792). In June 1792 took out insurance cover on his house and household goods of £100. [GL, Sun MS vol. 389, ref. 601775]

Scott, William, 19 Leicester St, London, carpenter and cm (1781). In 1781 took out insurance cover of £200 which included £75 for utensils and stock. [GL, Sun MS vol. 291, p. 410]

Scott, William, 27 Warwick St, Golden Sq., London, cm (1783). In 1783 insured his house for £300. [GL, Sun MS vol. 306, p. 481]

Scott, William, Newcastle, joiner and cm (1770). In June 1770 advertised his move from the head of Side to 'a new House, near Mr Dagnia's at the Forth'. Apart from undertaking work as a joiner and house carpenter he made 'all sorts of Household Furniture of Mahogany, Walnut-tree, Wainscot, Beech &c.' [*Newcastle Chronicle*, 30 June 1770]

Scott, William, Wakefield, Yorks., cm (1793). Subscribed to Sheraton's *Drawing Book*, 1793.

Scott, William, 2 New Inn Passage, Clare Mkt, London, chairmaker (1808–09). [D]

Scott, William, St Cuthbert's Lane, Carlisle, Cumb., joiner/cm (1829). [D]

Scott, William, Norwich, cm (1830–40). At Ber St, but one directory of 1830 shows an address at Surrey Rd also. By 1842 the business was using addresses at both Ber St and Timberhill St. [D; poll bk]

Scott, William, Newcastle, cm and joiner (1834–38). Trading at Groupe Close in 1834 and Javel-group Close in 1838. [D]

Scott, Wrighton, Yearby, Yorks., joiner/cm/cartwright (1834). [D]

Scott & Boswell, Clerkenwell Green, London, wood japanners (1808). [D; *C. Life*, 23 April 1964, p. 1004]

Scott & Innes, 12 Francis St, Bedford Sq., London, cm and u (1839). [D]

Scotter, Joseph, parish of St James, Norwich, chairmaker (1828–30). App. to Benjamin P. Titter and free by servitude, 24 February 1828. [Freemen reg.; poll bk]

Scowles, Thomas, parish of St Edwin, Bristol, cm (1722). [Poll bk]

Scrace, Charles, West St, Horsham, Sussex, cm and u (1823–26). Marriage to Sarah Hawes reported in *Brighton Gazette*, 12 February 1824. [D]

Scrambler, Edmund, Alcester, Warks., turner, chairmaker and parish clerk (1793). [D]

Screens, Wortly, Stamford, Lincs., cm (1793). Subscribed to Sheraton's *Drawing Book*, 1793.

Scrimshire, Matthew, London, upholder (1704–16). Father of Richard Scrimshire. Matthew was free of the Upholders' Co., 16 May 1704. He took as app. Richard Farmer, 1708–16. [GL, Upholders' Co. records]

Scrimshire, Richard, Suffolk St, Cavendish Sq., London, upholder (1728–d.1793). Son of Matthew Scrimshire, a member of the Upholders' Co. App. to William Scrimshire snr on 1 January 1728, and free of the Upholders' Co. by servitude, 2 August 1738. Master of the Upholders' Co., 1767. [GL, Upholders' Co. records]

Scrimshire, William snr, 'The Woolpack', Bucklersbury, London, upholder (1712–51). Member of the Upholders' Co. and father of William Scrimshire jnr, who was made free of this company by patrimony in 1751. His first app. was John Harris son of John Harris of Preston-on-Wye, Herefs. who was indentured on 19 February 1713 at a premium of £30 but not free until 1744. Other apps were John Harris (1714), Thomas Eyre (1716–23), Samuel Skelton (1719–33), John Tillier (1719), Henry Stonestreet (1722–30), and Richard Scrimshire (1728–38). He remained at the Bucklersbury address until 1745 but in May of that year when his bankruptcy was announced in *Gents Mag*. he was described

as 'late of London'. [D; GL, Upholders' Co. records; Sun MS vol. 2, p. 209; PRO, IR 1/2]

Scrimshire, William jnr, London, upholder (1751–70). Son of William Scrimshire snr and free of the Upholders' Co. by patrimony, 22 May 1751. Clerk of the Upholders' Co., 1770. [GL, Upholders' Co. records]

Scruby, James, Dunmow, Essex, turner and chairmaker (1793). [D]

Scruby, James, Ongar, Essex, turner, chairmaker and cooper (1798). [D]

Scudworth, Rudolph, Broad Sanctuary, Westminster, London, cm (1808). [D]

Scullard, George, London, upholder (1717–27). In February 1717 living on the north side of Hill St, a little above St Saviour's Dockhead, parish of St Olave, Southwark, where he also had a warehouse. By January 1727 in Fenchurch St, where he took out insurance cover of £300 on household goods and stock. [GL, Hand in Hand MS vol. 18, p. 182; Sun MS vol. 24, ref. 43826]

Scullerd, Mary, London, upholder (1712–19). The address given in insurance policies is 'next the EXETER CITY at St. Saviour's Dockhead in the Parish of St. Olave'. This address may possibly be the same as that occupied by George Scullard in 1717. Even if not identical the properties must have been close at hand and the two persons related. [GL, Sun MS vol. 2, p. 78; vol. 9, p. 55]

Sculthorpe, John, Park St, Westminster, London, carver (1749). [Poll bk]

Scum, John, address unknown, cm (1803). In 1803 subscribed to Sheraton's *Cabinet Dictionary*.

Scurfield, Robert, London & Stockton, Co. Durham, u (1762). In *Newcastle Courant*, 22 May 1762 he advertised himself as 'upholsterer from London'. He stated that he sold 'all sorts of upholstery goods at his warehouse at Stockton upon Tease'.

Scutz, Henry, 40 Plat Terr., Islington, London, cm and u (1827). [D]

Scyffert, George, 81 Margaret St, Cavendish Sq., London, cm (1820). [D]

Seaborne, Jno. Henry, 8 York St, Chelsea, London, cm and u (1826). [D]

Seabright, Joseph, St Clements, Oxford, cm (1770). Aged 23 when on 6 June 1770 he married Sarah Linzey at St Clement's, Oxford. [Bodleian index of Oxf. marriage bonds]

Seabright, Mark, Oxford, cm (1769). Aged 21 when on 30 March 1769 he married Ann Butler at the church of St Peter-in-the-East, Oxford. [Bodleian index of Oxf. marriage bonds]

Seabrook, —, 5 Corner of St Paul's, next Cheapside, London, trunk-maker (1840). Amongst the items stocked were writing desks and dressing cases and camp beds. Also had a manufactory at St Martin's Pl., St Martin-le-Grand. [V&A archives]

Seabrooke, Robert, Smithfield, London, upholder (1708–d.1745). Free of the Upholders' Co., 3 March 1707/08. Took as app. John, son of Richard Stockwell, a member of the Barber Surgeons' Co. on 7 November 1711 at a premium of £35. [GL, Upholders' Co. records; Heal; PRO, IR 1/1]

Seabrook, Samuel, 22 Hounsditch, London, u and cm (1757–68). Member of the Turners' Co. Employed non-freemen between 1757–68, and from 1764–67 was taking out licences to employ as many as ten continuously. [D; GL, City Licence bks, vols 2–6; Heal]

Seacombe, Richard, St Clement Danes, London, u (1756). In 1756 took app. named Wilkin. [S of G, app. index]

Seager, George, Watford, Herts., cm (1793). Freeman of Canterbury, Kent. [Canterbury freemen rolls]

Seager, George, Colchester, Essex, cm (1796–1802). Recorded in the poll bks of Canterbury, Maidstone and Rochester, Kent. [Poll bks]

Seager, George, London, cm (1806–09). At 8 Holywell Row, Shoreditch in 1808 and 10 Chapel St, Curtain Rd in the following year. Freeman of Maidstone. It is possible that he is the same George Seager who was living at Watford in 1793 and Colchester, 1796–1802. [D; Maidstone poll bk]

Seager, Stephen, York, upholder (1776). [Bailey's list of bankrupts]

Seager, William, near Morris St, Haymarket, London, upholder (1775). In 1775 took out insurance cover of £200, half of which was for utensils and stock. [GL, Sun MS vol. 238, p. 374]

Seager, William, Westminster, London, cm (1830). Freeman of Rochester, Kent. [Rochester poll bk]

Seagrave, Thomas, 8 New Compton St, Soho, London, chair japanner and varnish maker (1808–39). [D]

Seagrief, John, 39 Cable St, Well Close Sq., London, chairmaker (1808). [D]

Seal, —, Arlington St, St James's, London, u (1725). [Heal]

Seal, John, Paulin St, Hanover St, Westminster, London, cm (1749). [Poll bk]

Seal, John, Little Berrington St, Hereford, cm (1840). His eldest surviving son, Philip George, was free by patrimony in 1849. [D; Hereford Lib., Pilley Coll., 982]

Seal, Josiah, 9 Whitmores Row, Hoxton Fields, London, bedstead maker (1808). [D]

Sealy, Alexander, Tetbury, Glos., cm and u (1830). [D]

Sealy, H. W., St Mary's St, Stamford, Lincs., cm (1819). [D]

Sealy, Henry Wilmot, 26 City Rd, London, u and cm (1837–38). Bankruptcy announced, *Sussex Agricultural Express*, 24 February 1838. [D]

Sealy, Thomas, 37 Cary St, Lincoln's Inn Fields, London, u (1826). [D]

Seaman, Allen, Louth Searge, Lincs. and Hull, Yorks., cm (1774–84). Recorded in the Lincoln poll bk of 1774 and the Hull poll bk of 1780 at Louth; but by April 1784 living in Hull. [Poll bks]

Seaman, William, Market Pl., Gt Yarmouth, Norfolk, u and auctioneer (1780–98). In 1780 took out insurance cover of £700 of which £500 was for utensils and stock. Took jointly with Robert Harley app. named John Kemp who was free in 1787. Seaman also took John Allured, free 1790. [D; poll bks; freemen rolls; GL, Sun MS vol. 285, p. 629]

Seapton, John, Poole, Dorset, cm (1747). In 1747 took app. named Sapp. [S of G, app. index]

Sear, Henry, Bedford, chairmaker and turner (1830–39). Listed at Old Market Pl. in 1830 and Caudwell St in 1839. [D]

Searby & Codlin, Wellington Mart, Hull, Yorks., cm, clock case maker and undertaker (1838–40). Shown at 2 Wellington Mart as Searby & Codlin, 1838–39; but in 1840 Robert Searby was living at 8 Wellington Mart while the business of Robert Searby & Co. was trading from 41 Queen St. [D]

Search, —, probably London, u (1768–69). Supplier to Shelburne House, Berkeley Sq., London and Bowood, Wilts. Between 29 July and 15 October 1768 supplied thirteen bedticks, bolsters, pillows, feathers etc. costing £73 10s 6d. On 7 and 14 January 1769 invoiced three servants' beds and two better beds for Bowood costing £24 17s. [Bowood MS]

Search, Francis, 48 Clerkenwell St, London, bed and mattress maker (1822–27). [D]

Search, William, London, upholder (1767–94). Son of George Search of the parish of St Mary, Whitechapel, Gent. App. to Francis Search, a member of the Merchant Tailors' Co. on 3 June 1767 and then to Henry Ladyman. Free of the Upholders' Co. by servitude, 6 July 1774. In 1777 at 7 Aldgate, Within, where he insured a house for £100. In 1794

at Clerkenwell Green. [GL, Upholders' Co. records; Sun MS vol. 258, p. 117]

Searl, John H., Temple St, Bristol, basket and chairmaker (1809–33). Shown at 7 Temple St in 1809, no. 6 in 1810 and both 6 and 7 from 1813. Was additionally using premises in Gloucester Lane in 1813 and 1 St James's back, 1822–25. [D] See William Searle of Bristol.

Searle, George, 'The Crown & Cushion', the New Road, near the Turnpike, Lambeth, London, upholder (mid 18th century). His trade card [Leverhulme Coll., MMA, NY] states that he was prepared to conduct funerals in 'any Part of Town or Country'. He also stocked 'Coffins & Shrouds of all Sizes Ready Made'.

Searle, Henry, 26 Bishopsgate Without, London, cm, u, appraiser and undertaker (1835–39). In 1839 the business is listed as Henry Searle & Co. [D]

Searle, John, Saffron Walden, Essex (?), cm (1778–93). In 1778 supplied Sir John Griffin Griffin of Audley End, Essex with six looking-glasses and one swing looking-glass at 16s 6d. In 1793 buckram strapping etc. and a wainscot chest of drawers were supplied costing £1 14s. [Essex RO, D/DBy/A36/6, D/DBy/A51/6]

Searle, John, Upper Brook St, Teignmouth, Devon, cm (1793–1838). In *Exeter Flying Post*, 19 December 1793 advertised for an app. who had absconded. Shown at Upper Brook St, 1824–38. [D]

Searle, Nicholas, 2 Gloucester Lane, Bristol, basket and chairmaker (1814–21). [D]

Searle, R. C., Market Pl., Saffron Walden, Essex, u and cm (1815). The sale of his stock in trade and effects was advertised in *Cambridge Chronicle*, 3 February 1815.

Searle, Thomas, Southend St, Ledbury, Herefs., cm (1835). [D]

Searle, William, Chudleigh, Devon cm (1798). Marriage to Miss Susanna Maer, linen draper of Chudleigh, reported in *Exeter Flying Post*, 6 December 1798.

Searle, William, 1 St James's back, Bristol, basket and chairmaker (1818–21). [D] See John H. Searl.

Searle, William, 7 Temple St, Bristol, comb maker and cm (1837). [D] See John H. Searl.

Searle & Phipps, 50 Gracechurch St, London, , u (1825–29). [D]

Sears, William, Bungay, Suffolk, cm (1804). [*Ipswich Journal*, 3 March 1804]

Searson, George, Stamford, Lincs., joiner and cm (1746–d. by 1773). Freeman and Alderman of Stamford. Father of Wortley and William Searson. In 1746 took app. named Gilbert and in 1759, Thickbroom. [S of G, app. index]

Searson, Robert, Stamford, Lincs., cm (1809). [Poll bk]

Searson, William, High St and Ironmonger St, Stamford, Lincs., cm, u and appraiser (1769–76). Son of George Searson and brother to Wortley Searson. Claimed to have worked 'in the principal shops in London' prior to setting up in Stamford in 1769. Free of Stamford by patrimony in 1770, and in 1776 Capital Burgess. Initially associated in business with Wortley Searson and in 1769 opened a shop in the High St and also took over the shop and stock of the late Thomas Williamson, upholder at the corner of Ironmonger St. [Stamford Town Hall Bks, Box 2A/1/3; *Cambridge Chronicle*, 20 May 1769, 4 August 1770]

Searson, Wortley, Stamford, Lincs., cm, u and appraiser (1765–88). Son of George Searson and brother to William Searson with whom he was associated in business. Initially worked in London, and in 1765 was free of Stamford by patrimony. Advertised auction of the contents of a house, *Leicester Chronicle*, 11 November 1775. In 1773 Capital Burgess, in 1787 Alderman and in 1788 Mayor of Stamford. Took as apps William Banks on 17 August 1776 and Henry Flower on 24 June 1783. The premium in both cases was £30.

Supplied furniture to Burghley House, near Stamford. [Stamford Town Hall Bks, 2A/1/3, 2A/1/4; *Cambridge Chronicle*, 20 May 1769, 4 August 1770; V&A archives]

Seath, John, Canterbury, Kent, cm (1755–96). In 1755 took app. named Pout. In May 1796 living in the parish of St Paul. [S of G, app. index; poll bk]

Seath, John, 4 Morden Pl., Maidstone Rd, Rochester, Kent, u (1838). [D]

Seath, William, Faversham, Kent, cm (1790–94). Freeman of Canterbury. [D; Canterbury poll bk]

Seaton, Benjamin, High St, Chatham, Kent, cm, u and undertaker (1823–32). [D] See Joseph Seaton.

Seaton, Frederick, London, carver and gilder (1774–1809). At Great Chapel St, Soho from 1774–1809, the number being 3 in 1809. Also shown at 54 Well St, Oxford St in 1794 and 40 Oxford St in 1809, the latter being in addition to the Chapel St address. In 1794 supplied Lord Howard of Audley End, Essex for his London house at New Burlington St, a gilt picture frame 12 ft by 6 ft 6 ins which together with the lettering on the table was charged at £4 8s 6d. In 1809 also a stationer and paperhanger. [D; Westminster poll bks; Essex RO, D/DBy/A52/6]

Seaton, John, Red Lion Sq., London (1788). [Bailey's list of bankrupts]

Seaton, John, Market Pl., Greenwich, London, cm, u and undertaker (1779–1808). In 1779 took out insurance cover of £300 of which £240 was for utensils and stock. By November 1785 utensils and stock in his house were valued at £315 with £100 extra for similar items in a warehouse; these figures were £515 and £100 by May of the following year. Included in the list of master cabinet makers in Sheraton's *Cabinet Dictionary*, 1803. [D; GL, Sun MS vol. 276, p. 179; vol. 333, p. 365; vol. 337, p. 316]

Seaton, Joseph, High St, Chatham, Kent, upholder and cm (1782–1805). In 1782 took out insurance cover of £800 but only £100 of this was for warehouse and stock. By July 1792 however, out of a total insurance cover of £750 no less than £550 was accounted for by utensils and stock in his house and a workshop behind. He also insured a cottage at Smarden, Kent. In 1805 the business was described as Seaton & Son. [D; GL, Sun MS vol. 300, p. 630; vol. 387, p. 303; vol. 392, p. 176] See Benjamin Seaton. Joseph was possibly father of:

Seaton, Joseph, New Rd, Chatham, Kent, cm, u and undertaker (1824–40). [D]

Sebire, Nicholas, 23 Fenchurch St, London, upholder (1788). Free of the Upholders' Co. by redemption, 4 June 1788. [GL, Upholders' Co. records]

Seccombe, Richard, Craven Ct, London, u (1753). In 1753 married Martha Kemp, the daughter of a Westminster wholesale tobacconist. [*Public Advertiser*, 3 August 1753]

Secker, Thomas, Norwich and London, u (1814–18). Son of James Secker, gardener, and free of Norwich on 8 July 1814. By June 1818 living in London. [Freemen reg.; Norwich poll bk]

Secker, Thomas, 23 Wilson St, Finsbury, London, u (1823–25). [D]

Secret, Samuel, 20 North St, Sculcoates, Hull, Yorks., cm (1839). [D]

Seddon, George, Aldersgate St, London, cm (1753–1868).

The firm of Seddon was the largest furniture-making firm in London in the last quarter of the 18th century when it employed more people, held more extensive stocks and produced a wider range of goods than any other furniture-making business It remained of considerable importance throughout its history, yet few labelled or documented pieces are known so it is not possible to present a stylistic analysis of the output of this major firm.

Family tradition has it that in about 1750 George Seddon, of a Lancashire family of that name, went to London and set up as a furniture maker. [Seddon, *Memoirs*, 1858] It may well be that his great grandson was correct about his origins because there was a George Seddon, cm, who had to buy his freedom of the London Joiners' Co. because he had not been trained by a member of that company. [GL, MS 8046/9, special court 11 June 1754] Other writers have claimed the founder of the Seddon firm as the George Seddon who came from Blacklea and Eccles in Lancashire and was app. to George Clematson of the Joiners' Co. [Heal; Hall and Gilbert, *LAC*, vol. 68, 1971] However, this is contradicted by the entry in the Joiners' Co. app. records which states that the George Seddon who was app. to George Clematson in September 1742 was the son of John Seddon, Clerk, of Warfield, Berks. The premium charged by the master was £16 and it was met by a charitable payment from the 'Stewards of the Sons of the Clergy'. This same George Seddon became a freeman of the Joiners' Co. in 1751. [GL, MS 8051/5]

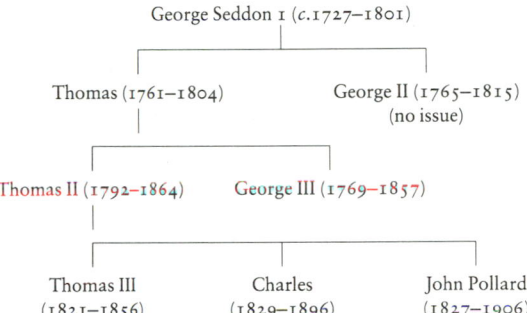

George Seddon I (c.1727–1801)
— Thomas (1761–1804)
— George II (1765–1815) (no issue)
Thomas II (1792–1864)   George III (1769–1857)
— Thomas III (1821–1856)   Charles (1829–1896)   John Pollard (1827–1906)

Whatever his background, the George Seddon who headed the famous firm of that name, had purchased a two-acre site in Aldersgate St which included London House, the former residence of the Bishop of London, by 1753. The choice of site suggests that Seddon intended to establish a large firm from the outset. It remained in Aldersgate St until 1826. Directories gave the address as 158 Aldersgate St until 1770, whereafter re-numbering led to it being 151 and sometimes also 150 Aldersgate St. George Seddon took his first app. in 1753, and bound one per year until 1759. In 1754 he subscribed to Chippendale's *Director*. Despite a comment in 1786 by Sophie Von La Roche that Seddon was always 'creating new forms', the known work of the firm is mostly conventional in design terms and it is possible that, in the early days at least, pattern books such as Chippendale's were used frequently.

The firm expanded fairly rapidly in the 1760s. The number of journeymen regularly employed is not known but Seddon soon took advantage of a licensing arrangement which enabled him to employ craftsmen who were not freemen of the City of London. Between ten and twenty workers were thus engaged in 1760–61. In 1762 and 1763 twenty men worked under licence for Seddon and the number rose to thirty in the years 1764–67. In 1768 and 1769 one hundred non-freemen were employed. A fire at Seddons in 1768 was reported as consuming 'upwards of eighty chests of tools' and it would appear, therefore, that the majority of Seddon workers at that date had not been trained within a London Company. This does not automatically mean that they had been app. outside London but it is likely that some of them were provincially trained.

By 1783, when there was another fire, the firm employed nearly 300 'of the most capital hands' in London while in 1786, Sophie Von La Roche, noted that Seddon was 'foster-father' to 400 'apprentices'. Her figure must have included both journeymen and apps, and it probably also included metal and glass workers whom she stated worked on the premises. Seddon regularly took on apps, all of whom appear to have been bound for the traditional period of seven years. By 1757 there were seven in the firm and there were more than ten at any one time during the years 1766–69. In the 1770s the figures fluctuated between four and nine and in the 1780s between five and ten. In 1790 and 1791 there were ten apps, but the app. records note only one app. taken by George Seddon after then. The Inland Revenue app. records tail off at this time but the fact that there are no further entries for Seddon in the Joiners' Co. records after 1794 suggests that George Seddon did not take on any further apps. Rough ratios of apps to journeymen can be calculated. When the firm was still establishing itself in the late 1760s, it had approximately one app. for every seven workmen but when it greatly expanded its workforce in the 1780s the number of apps did not rise proportionately, with only one app. for every thirty or forty workmen at that time. The expansion of the firm, therefore, was based on the employment of craft-trained journeymen rather than apps.

The improving fortunes of the firm are reflected in insurance and stock valuations. In 1756 and 1757 Seddon's insurance policies gave cover for £500 and included domestic residence, workshops and stock. By 1763–64 household and business goods were insured for £1,000 with the Sun Insurance Office but in 1763 Seddon also had a policy with the Union Fire Office for £1,000. There are a few references to George Seddon insuring with both firms but it is not clear whether this was done on a regular basis. Stock and goods were insured for £3,300 [Sun MS] in 1768 but in the latter year Seddon unfortunately allowed his policy to lapse before a fire did extensive damage to both premises and stock. He claimed losses of £7,700 but the Directors of the Sun Insurance Office only awarded him £500 compensation. He appears to have made good his loss fairly quickly and by 1770 had policies totalling £7,700 for both dwelling house and business. [Sun & Union] By 1787 the sum insured with the Sun Office was £17,500, of which £13,000 related to the business. Such very large sums confirm that George Seddon's business was the largest in London. The DEF states that the firm's stock-in-trade amounted to as much as £118,926 in 1789 (£21,702 for timber, £9,068 for carpets and £3,293 for contents of upholstery warehouse) but it has not been possible to verify these figures.

Sophie Von La Roche's description of Seddon's premises adds flesh to these statistical bones. She recorded that Seddon employed a variety of tradesmen on 'any work connected with the making of household furniture- joiners, carvers, gilders, mirror-workers, upholsterers, girdlers- who mould the bronze into graceful patterns — and locksmiths. All these are housed in a building with six wings. In the basement mirrors are cast and cut. Some other department contains nothing but chairs, sofas and stools of very description, some quite simple, others exquisitely carved and made of all varieties of wood, and one large room is full up with all the finished articles in this line, while others are occupied by writing-tables, cupboards, chests of drawers, charmingly fashioned desks, chests, both large and small, work-and toilet-tables in all manner of wood and patterns, from the simplest and cheapest to the most elegant and expensive. ... Chintz, silk and wool materials for curtains and bed-covers; hangings in every possible material; carpets and stair-carpets to order; in short, anything one might desire to furnish a house; and all the workmen besides and a great many seamstresses; their own saw-house too, where as many blocks of fine foreign wood lie piled, as firs and oaks are seen at our saw-mills. The entire

story of the wood, as used for both inexpensive and costly furniture and the method of treating it, can be traced in this establishment ...'.

It is not surprising to find the partners in such a large and comprehensive firm subscribing to Edward T. Jones, Jones' English System of Book Keeping, Bristol, 1796.

There can be no doubt that all aspects of furniture making were carried out on the premises. Besides this, the firm probably also made some of its own metal work: Von la Roche noted 'girdlers — who mould the bronze into graceful patterns'. She also claimed that 'mirrors were cast and cut' in the workshops. She may have mistaken finishing processes for those of manufacturing but George Seddon had close business connections with glass making. The firm's bill-heads of the 1780s and 90s refer to it as 'Manufacturers of British Large Plate Glass' and George Seddon had dealings with the British Plate Glass Manufacturers. In 1780 Matthew Boulton bought plate glass from this firm which he later found he could not use. He offered it to Seddon who had not only bought it cheaply but prevailed upon the company to lower the price originally asked of Boulton. [Birmingham City Ref. Lib. archive dept, Boulton papers] The evidence suggests that Seddon was a member of the Board and, taken with the evidence of the firm's bill-heads, it seems safe to say that Seddon was financially involved in a firm which manufactured plate glass for both windows and mirror glass. In all probability the large plate glass intended for the Empress of Russia and destroyed in the 1783 fire was made by the British Plate Glass Manufacturers. Whether it was made at Aldersgate St is another matter: one would like confirmation from other sources before stating that Seddon was the only known London furniture maker to branch out into glass making in the late 18th and early 19th century. In 1804 George Seddon's sons, Thomas and George, owed money to a glass company and tried to raise cash by selling glass in New York.

George Seddon was in the same entrepreneurial mould as Matthew Boulton who, in 1781, wished him 'success in your great undertaking'. [Boulton papers, Letter Book M51] This could have referred to Seddon's glass making ventures or to the fact that he bought a copy of James Watt's copying machine. [Letter Book M.72, see also H. W. Dickinson, James Watt, Craftsman and Engineer, Cambridge 1936, pp. 191–97 and Art Union, 1848, p. 193] This was a forerunner of the carving machines which were used commercially by certain furniture makers from the 1840s. It may be that Seddon attempted to use the machine to cut down the cost of roughing out carving which then had to be finished by hand. If so, Seddon again appears as a pioneer; on this occasion in terms of the mechanisation of the production process in furniture making. George Seddon trained his sons within the family firm and bound them through the Joiners' Co. His first born, named George, was app. in 1769 but died sometime before Thomas was bound as a cm from 1775 to 1782. The younger son George was also bound through the Joiners' Co. two years later but he was trained as an u. Although Seddon snr was in an influential position within the Joiners' Co. (he joined the Livery in 1757 and became master in 1795) his son George was forced to become free of the Upholders' Co. in 1787 upon threat of legal action by the company.

George Seddon took his sons into partnership in about 1785. From about 1790–95 his son-in-law Thomas Shackleton, u (who had married Mary, the eldest daughter) was also a member of the firm which then traded as 'Seddon, Sons & Shackleton'. Thomas appears to have shared his father's enterprising spirit, if not his abilities. In the 1790s, at a time when he was working in the family partnership with his father and brother, he started in business for himself. Directories show him at 10 Charterhouse St (1790–97) and at 24 Dover St (1793–1800). He took on two apps, Aveline in 1791 for £105 and Holt in 1793 for £100 and in the former year independently subscribed to Sheraton's *Drawing Book*, giving the Dover St address. He formed a partnership with John Blease about 1802, at a time when he was in great financial difficulties. The latter eventually took over the firm, probably after Seddon's death in 1804, although it appears in directories as Blease & Seddon until the former's bankruptcy in 1811. [PRO, B3/274]

When he retired in 1798, George Seddon passed on the firm to his two sons. He allowed them to use £25,000 remaining in the business at 5% interest and they agreed to pay him £1,000 per annum to rent the Aldersgate St premises. On retirement Seddon made a will, supplemented by a codicil of 1799, to provide for his family after his death. His wife had died in 1788 but he had three daughters, Dorothy, Mary and Lydia who were each left £6,000. In order to assist his sons, to whom he left the residue of this estate, George Seddon specified that the money for the legacies be left in the firm for two years after his death whereupon half should be paid, followed by the other half in a further three years. George Seddon snr died in 1801 and two years later Mary and Lydia pressed for their legacies (Dorothy having died). The brothers found themselves unable to pay. Thomas Shackleton claimed that they had mis-managed the business and it is clear that what had once been a flourishing concern floundered after the retirement and death of its founder.

Despite the production of 'patent' furniture, using a mechanism developed and patented by Day Gunby in 1798 [Patent No. 2248], whereby a small reading desk or nest of drawers and pigeon-holes could be made to rise up from tables, desks and other items of furniture, by means of a system of weights, bolts and springs, the brothers were not successful in business. By 1804, the pair, who were both commissioned as officers in the volunteer army in that year (Thomas as Lieutenant Colonel and George as a Captain of the London (Loyal) 11th Regiment), faced bankruptcy.

The finances are somewhat difficult to disentangle. Some debts went back to the days of Seddon snr, as in the case of John Pollard, Thomas's father-in-law who was owed over £20,000 from the years 1795–1801. Thomas Seddon borrowed over £6,000 from Frank Cappell of Nottingham St (who had also loaned money to Seddon snr) without the knowledge of his younger brother and partner and escaped bankruptcy only by death. George Seddon II claimed in court that his brother had paid him an annuity in lieu of his interest in the family firm but this was not confirmed by anyone else and was probably the desperate claim of a desperate man. He made attempts to raise money to pay the firm's creditors by disposing of furniture and glass as far afield as New York and the Cape of Good Hope. 6s in the pound was paid to creditors in 1805 and an extra 2s in 1806, followed by further sums in 1814. By the time he died in 1815, George Seddon II had not redeemed the family fortunes but he had done sufficient for the family firm to continue.

The records of George Seddon's bankruptcy case reveal a number of tradesmen from whom he bought goods to use in his trade or whose services he used between 1804 and 1815. They included brass founders (John D. Griffith, Birmingham, Thomas Jones and Edward Barker, Birmingham, George Penton, New St Sq., London and Thomas Catherwood, Hoxton); japanners (Smith, Morley & Mason, St John's Sq., John Scott, Pentonville, and Boswell & Scott, Clerkenwell Green); horse hair manufacturers (William Lewis, Old St, and Cabel Welch Collings, Fleet St); carpet manufacturers/

warehousemen (John Lea, James Cole, John Cooper and Henry Talbot, all of Kidderminster, Francis Seward, Wilton, John Clarke, Market Harborough, Thomas Whitty, Axminster, Thomas Willows, Leicester Sq., Robert Richards, Finsbury Sq., Daniel Sutton, Southampton St and Henry Widnell, Holborn); glass manufacturers/glassmen (Thomas Quinton, East Smithfield, Thomas H. Fenton, West Smithfield, William Peckham, Grayston Passage and John Blands, Ludgate Hill); timber merchants (William Fox, Lambeth, Michael Crapping, Lambeth, Joseph Cross, Lambeth, J. McLean French, Marshall St, William Quincey, Albion Wharf, Surrey, James Yerroway, Blackfriars and Thomas L. Carter, Deptford); paper stainers (Benjamin Mind, Beech St and John Hall, Aldermanbury); blanket manufacturers (John Sheppard, Witney and John Henver, Witney); dyers (Joseph Landell, Old Change, Thomas Hughes, Bunhill Row, and James Eve, Rawstorne St); silk mercers (James Brant, Cheapside and John Fearn, Ludgate Hill); leather gilders (John Newberry, Upper Marylebone St and George Footman, West Smithfield); linen drapers (Harry Kemp, Islington Rd, John Waugh & James Reid, Edinburgh and David Greg, Kirkcaldy, Scotland); a glue manufacturer (Stephen Goom, Southwark); a bell hanger (Peter Odell, Goswell St); a furniture printer (J. Hill Darley, Sackville St) and an undertaker (Benjamin Holmes, Cripplegate). [PRO, B3 4464] This list indicates the number and type of manufacturers and suppliers with whom it was necessary to liaise in order to run a large scale furniture-making firm.

In the midst of his financial problems George Seddon II hoped that the firm would be able to continue as a family business after his death. In his will of 1808 he recommended his wife to take a partner who could manage the business and bring at least £8,000 into the firm in the event of financial difficulties after his death. He suggested, however, that if money was not withdrawn from the firm on his death then his wife should continue to run it on her own until their eldest nephew was of age. As it was, Thomas Seddon II, who had been app. to his uncle from 1806–13 and had obtained his freedom of the Upholders' Co. in 1815, took over immediately after his uncle's death in 1815. He was joined by his brother, George III, soon after the latter completed his apprenticeship in 1817 and, together, they ran the family business until the 1850s.

Little is known of the firm between 1815 and 1826 when the brothers signed a prefatory recommendation to P. and M. A. Nicholson's *Practical Cabinet Maker*, 1826. In 1827 George Seddon III went into partnership with Nicholas Morel, who had been chosen by King George IV as furniture maker in charge of re-furnishing Windsor Castle [G. de Bellaigue and P. Kirkham] Morel did not join the Seddon family firm. It was only George Seddon who initially went into partnership with Morel in 1827, although Thomas stood surety for his brother and Morel when they signed a bond with George IV for £10,500 in the same year and joined the partnership in September 1830.

The firm of Morel and Seddon used Morel's address, 13 Gt Marlborough St, but the work was produced at the Seddon workshops in Aldersgate St. Morel needed the co-operation of a large established firm for the Windsor commission, which was eventually to amount to nearly £200,000, and Seddon probably offered the largest workshops in London as well as experienced draughtsmen, managers and skilled workers. Within the partnership, Morel generally took charge of the major artistic decisions while George Seddon ran the business side, negotiating advances and agreeing delivery details with the Treasury and Lord Chamberlain's Office. [G. de Bellaigue and P. Kirkham] Morel and Seddon employed designers who worked with assistants in the 'artists' room' in Aldersgate St. They included Bogaerts; J.-J. Boileau; F.-H.-G. Jacob-Desmalter (furniture and furnishings in the Neo-classical style) and A. W. N. Pugin (furniture and furnishings in the Gothic style).

In June 1830 the Treasury refused to pay more than the balance owing on Morel and Seddon's original estimate of £143,000 rather than the sum of over £200,000 which they by then demanded. The whole question of cost was examined by a Select Committee which reported to the House of Commons in February 1831, but it was not until the end of that year that it was decided to accept a final bill of £179,300 18s 9d.

Apart from a very large commission to supply furniture worth over £15,000 to Stafford House for the Marquess of Stafford in 1830, the work of Morel and Seddon appears to have been restricted to royal work. Windsor Castle was the main commission but work was also done for other royal houses and palaces. Royal patronage continued after George IV's death and the firm altered a rosewood dining table for William IV in 1831. Morel's name disappears from the royal accounts in 1831. The work then passed to George and Thomas Seddon alone although they were not officially given the royal warrant until 1832. [PRO, LC3/60] The delay in payments relating to the Windsor work caused problems and in February 1832 creditors of Morel and Seddon requested the suspension of payments to the firm by the Lord Chamberlain's Office until its affairs were sorted out. [PRO, LC1/16] In August and October 1832 T. and G. Seddon experienced difficulty in extracting payments for royal work and complained of having to meet 'heavy engagements'. The latter may have referred to expenditure involved in a move to Gray's Inn Rd from Aldersgate St which took place at about that time. The decision to move was made after a fire of 1830 did extensive damage to the premises: 100 tool chests belonging to Seddon workmen were destroyed. [*Times*, 11 and 13 August 1830] The new premises were designed by J. B. Papworth, who added large open sheds for drying veneers in 1836. The firm's finances remained in a delicate position. In 1840 a charge of bankruptcy was brought but annulled. [PRO, B4/48.190] The story of the firm beyond this date lies outside the remit of this dictionary, but an interesting glimpse of the family and firm can be found in J. Seddon, *Memoirs*, 1858. [*GCM*; *DEF*; Heal; C. Williams, (trans.), *Sophie in London (1786)*, 1933; G. B. and T. Hughes, *Small Antique Furniture*, 1967; G. Wills, *English Furniture 1760–1900*; H. Spear (ed.), *Memoirs of William Hickey*, 1948, vol. IV, pp. 26 and 365; *C. Life*, 21 October 1933, pp. 415–18; *C. Life*, 27 January 1934, p. 102; *C. Life*, 20 January 1934, pp. 72–73; *C. Life*, 17 January 1947, p. 180; *C. Life*, 21 February 1957, pp. 330–31; *Apollo*, May 1957, pp. 177–81; *Antiques*, October, 1960, pp. 362–63; *C. Life*, 2 June 1966, p. 1400; *Times*, 22 June 1967; *C. Life*, 15 January 1970, pp. 130–31; C. Gilbert and I. Hall, 'New Light on the Firm of Seddon', *LAC*, 1971, 68, pp. 17–19; G. de Bellaigue and P. Kirkham, 'George IV and The Furnishing of Windsor Castle', *Furn. Hist.*, 1972, pp. 1–34]

SAXMUNDHAM, Suffolk (Charles Long). 1766: Bill for mahogany sideboard, £4 13s. 1768: Bill (addressed to Bond St) for chest of drawers, chamber table, walnut kitchen chairs, bottle cistern. [Suffolk RO, HA/18/EC/4 and 14]

HULL, Houses in High St and Charlotte St (Joseph Robinson Pease). 1778: Bill for wardrobe, sideboard, dressing tables, writing table, billiards table, chairs, etc. £221 17s. [V&A Lib., 86 CC 45] 1781 bill. Total £352 13s 10d for drawing room furniture. Reprinted in full in *LAC*, no. 68, 1971, pp. 17–19.

STRETTON HALL, Staffs. (Mr Turner). 1780: Bill for pearl inlay on card tables, repairs, carpet etc. £2 13s 6d signed T. Cobham for George Seddon. 1782: Bill for mounting screen, varnishing chest, £1. [V&A Lib., Box II.86.KK]

TOWNELEY HALL, Lancs. (Charles Towneley). 1780: Payment in account bk to Seddon for Pembroke table £5 10s, writing table £22 10s. [Account bk in possession of Mr Simon Towneley]

CROFT CASTLE, Herefs. (Sir Herbert Croft). c.1780: Combined writing table and filing cabinet known as 'The Croft'. [Nat. Trust Guide, *Croft Castle*, 1982, p. 23 and A. Heal, 'The Croft: an 18th century writing cabinet', *C. Life*, 17 January 1947, p. 80 (features piece with label which states it was manufactured and sold by Messrs. Seddon, Sons & Shackleton]

MRS ELIZABETH MONTAGU. Probably for 22 Portman Sq., London 1782. Seddon probably supplied Mrs Montagu with a piece of furniture ornamented with paintings by Boulton & Co. In that year Matthew Boulton informed George Seddon that 'the paintings' about which he had enquired and which Mrs Montagu wanted could be made fit for the object they were to ornament. [Birmingham City Ref. Lib., Boulton papers, Letter Book I, 912, MB to GS, 10 January 1782]

HON. H. FANE. The entry 'To Siddons for a Bed' in 1783–85 noted in his accounts presumably refers to Seddon. [Lincoln RO, Fane 7/1, April 1783 — £41 5s 0d]

RUSSIA, (Empress of Russia). 1783: Large plate glass intended for Empress destroyed in fire at Seddon's warehouse.

AUDLEY END, Essex (Lord Howard). 1783: Reflecting lanthorn £3 13s 6d. 1786: Wainscot bureau, mahogany chest of drawers, mahogany wardrobe £15 4s. [Essex RO, D/DBy/A41 and 44/10 respectively]

MASTER ROBERT HEATHCOTE, 1786; Account bk of Heathcote's expenses includes 8s 'To Cash Paid Mr. Seddon Cabinet Maker For A Table Writing Desk'. [Lincoln RO, 3ANC 6/20]

HEATON HALL, Manchester (Sir Thomas Egerton, Bt). 1783: Bill to Seddon £18 14s. 1790: Bill to Seddon £4 10s 6d. [Preston RO, Bank deposit and account bks, DDEg. Unpaginated]

WILLIAM CLAYTON. 1787: Bill. Geo. Seddon & Sons. 'Seddon's bill for Mariann's box'. Bill signed by John Jacobs for George Seddon. A satinwood work box and leather cover £13 8s. [*C. Life*, 20 January 1934, pp. 72–73]

BADMINTON HOUSE, Glos. (5th Duke of Beaufort). 1788: Received £93 as 'Seddon & Co.'. 1789: *Ibid.*, Received £42. 1791: *Ibid.*, Received £56 7s. [Badminton papers, 5th Duke of Beaufort's copy of Hoare's bank bk, 1788–91]

CALCUTTA, India (William Hickey). 1791: Billiard table made by Seddon, purchased at price of 1000 sicca rupees (approx. £188). [A. Spear (ed.), *Memoirs of William Hickey*, 1948, vol. IV, pp. 26 and 365]

HAUTEVILLE HOUSE, St Peter Port, Guernsey (D. Tupper). 179–: Bill of Geo. Seddon, Sons & Shackleton for £414 11s 4½ for furniture including 18 painted satinwood elbow chairs which cost 73s 6d each. Three French stools (window seats) were made to match at £15 15s each and a settee for £17 10s. Also supplied were mahogany chairs, a pair of girandoles and screens. [*DEF*, vol. I, p. 301, fig. 241; E. F. Strange, 'Seddon Furniture', *Old Furniture*, 1928, vol. v, pp. 118–20, and M. Harris & Sons, *Old English Furniture*, 1935, pp. 62–63] A window seat resembling those from the set described above was sold at Christie's [*Apollo*, December 1960, p. 225, figs a & b] while a pair of chairs were sold at Sotheby's, 20 November 1970, lot 191. One seat rail stamped 'IP', the other stamped 'WR', twice. Lot 190 was a matching semi-circular card table.

BRIDWELL HOUSE, Dorset (R. Clarke). 1792–93: Bill.

Seddon Sons & Shackleton for furniture £139 os 4d. This included matching satinwood card and Pembroke tables with leather covers, £25 for the three; two white and gold tripods with cut glass, £21; and ten white and gold elbow chairs covered with the owner's own needlework, £46 and a matching sofa, £12. The original bill, together with a letter from the firm, was sold with the 'white and gold tripods' catalogued as 'painted and parcel-gilt, torchères [with] cut-glass drop-hung foliate drip-pans ... 167 cm high' at Sotheby's, 19 June 1981, Lot 109. Later sold through Hotspur Ltd.

NORWAY, Ulefoss Manorhouse, near Posgrunn (Niels Aalls). In 1793 Seddon exported 28 pieces of furniture (mainly mahogany) though several items were 'japanned' i.e. painted white). The bill totalled £73 3s. [*Apollo*, May 1955, p. 144, May 1957, pp. 180–81, figs V–VIII]

WOBURN, Beds. (Francis, 5th Duke of Bedford). 1793: 4 satinwood pillar & claw octagon tables £20. [Bedford Office, London]

MASSINGBERD. 1793: May 23: Mr Siddons 'A Mattress. £3 4s 6d Dº, A Door Rug 2s. — £3 6s 6d'. 'Sept 31: Mattress, Siddons Bill. £3 5s'. These entries presumably relate to a Seddon commission. [Lincoln RO, Massingberd, MM 9110]

SPAIN (King Charles IV). 1793: Cabinet made to order of King Charles IV of Spain. Designed by Sir William Chambers, decorated with panels painted by Sir William Hamilton and made by Seddon, Sons & Shackleton. Name of the main craftsman involved (R. Newham) and date on which it was finished (28 June 1793) inscribed inside. The cabinet was broken up after 1908 when it was shown at the Franco-British Exhibition. [*Conn.*, XVIII, 1907, p. 211; *DEF*, III, pp. 68–69]

PHILADELPHIA, USA (William Bingham). The traveller Henry Wansey noted that the drawing room chairs in Bingham's 'magnificent house' in Philadelphia were from Seddon's in London. They were in 'the newest taste; the back in the form of lyre, adorned with festoons of crimson and yellow silk'. [H. Wansey, *Excursion to the United States of North America in the Summer of 1794*, quoted in C. Montgomery, *American Furniture: The Federal Period*, 1966, p. 42]

KENWOOD HOUSE, London (2nd Lord Mansfield). 1795: Payment noted in bank account of Lord Mansfield to Seddon & Co. £35 10s. [Hoare's Bank]

THE MANOR HOUSE, Lee (Lewisham) (Thomas Baring). 1798: Bill for supplying items including a crib bedstead and repairing and cleaning a dressing table and folding bedstead. The firm charged £1 2s 10d for cutting Baring's own plank of satinwood into veneers (120 feet of them). Total bill £17 19s 10d. [Private archive]

DEVONSHIRE PLACE, London (Lord Deerhurst). 1799: Bill from George Seddon and Sons to Lord Deerhurst, son of the 6th Earl of Coventry, totalled £1,068 12s 11d. It included chairs, dining tables, bedstead, carpet, music stand, cushions, glove stand, repairs, etc. mainly for his London house. [Herefs. RO, Croome Court archive, account 128, 1799] There is a further long bill [account 138.n.d.] which includes stuffing a sofa, laying a carpet, and supplying chimney glasses, a writing table, breakfast table, floor cloth, Pembroke table, dining tables, festoon window curtains, Venetian window blinds, hall chairs and other items which probably also relate to the London house).

LONGFORD CASTLE, Wilts. (3rd Earl of Radnor). 1801: Payment in Longford Castle accounts to Seddon & Co.

GORHAMBURY, Herts. 1807: 5 March. Mr Seddon's Bill for Furniture in the Drawing Room, £75 4s. [Herts. RO, Gorhambury account bk XI, 77]

JOANNA SOUTHCOTT. 1814. Cradle for 'Prince of Peace', the Messiah which Southcott announced she was expecting. It

was reported that her followers subscribed £1,000 towards the cost (which was given by Wheatley as £500) and flocked to see it at London House. [H. B. Wheatley, *London Past and Present*, 1891, vol. 1, pp. 22, 24; *C. Life*, 21 October 1933, p. 417]

STONELEIGH ABBEY, Warks. (Henry Leigh). 1819: rosewood dressing table £24. [Shakespeare Birthplace Trust, Leigh receipts, DR 18/5]

HAMPTON COURT, Leominster, Herefs. (John Arkwright). 1829: Bill for furniture including 'rosewood occasional table £18 and Davenport £21. Total £42 3s. [Herefs. RO, A63/161, Hampton Court Coll., dispersed 1912. NB. see later commission of 1840]

LORD MACARTNEY. 1790: Bill from Thomas Seddon, 24 Dover St. [Heal Coll., BM]

HENRY THOMAS, LORD VISCOUNT FALKLAND. 1794: Thomas Seddon, Dover St. Furnished house for Lord Viscount Falkland who rented the furniture (total value £1,400). [PRO, C12 198/30]

BADMINTON HOUSE(?), Glos. (5th Duchess of Beaufort). 1793: Seddon, Sons & Shackleton supplied a large square mahogany sofa. Received £33 2s 6d. [Badminton papers, The Duchess of Beaufort's red leather account bk]

PRINCE OF WALES and DUKE OF SUSSEX. Blease & Seddon's label on sideboard: 'Upholstery, Cabinet & Carpet manufacturer', Dover St. [Christie's, 15 April 1982, lot 95]

WINDSOR CASTLE. 1827–32: Morel & Seddon, 13 Gt Marlborough St. [See G. de Bellaigue and P. Kirkham]

STAFFORD HOUSE (Marquess of Stafford). 1830: Receipted bill 30 March 1830, £15,410 8s. [Staffs. RO, D 593/R/2/10/6]

ROYAL COMMISSIONS [Royal Warrant, October 1832, PRO, LC3/60)] T. & G. Seddon, 1829–40: work at Brighton Pavilion; Belvedere, St James's Palace; Royal Lodge, Windsor; Kew Palace and Cumberland Lodge. Early work was mainly jobbing and repairs. Other work included: December 1832 (Brighton Pavilion) for Her Majesty's own use. A Spanish mahogany writing table £26 and September 1834 (Windsor, for corridor) 6 square framed scagliola thermes £78 [Windsor Royal Archives, Box 1, Item 17, Estimates] December 1835. 8 wainscot sofas in 'Elizabethan character' very similar to specification for Thomas Turner December 1835) covered in crimson plush £374 [Windsor Royal Archives, Box 1, Item 2] 1839/40: Among bills for 'Extra Expenses for the Accommodation of HRH The Prince Albert' at Windsor prior to his marriage with Victoria is one for a 6' maple 4-post bedstead with richly carved pillars and footboard and elaborately inlaid cornice and centre ornaments £124. [PRO, LC11/107] March 1839: Suite of maplewood bookcases and cabinets inlaid with purple wood statuary £430. December 1840: A rich mahogany and gold cot and two mahogany wash hand stand. Total £300. [Windsor Royal Archives, Box 1, Item 2] [The main references for this royal work are PRO, LC11 and Windsor Royal Archives, account bks, estimates]

GOVERNMENT HOUSE, Prince Edward Island, Canada. 1835: Some of the furniture supplied by Seddon. [Information from Mrs P. Mackenzie, Charlottetown, Prince Edward Island]

HAMPTON COURT, Leominster, Herefs. (John Arkwright). 1840: Bill for a 9' mahogany wardrobe £112. [Herefs. RO, A63/161]

LABELLED/STAMPED PIECES:

SEDDON, SONS & SHACKLETON (labels). Mahogany writing table or 'croft': 20" wide. [Sotheby's, 1 November 1946, lot 156]

Mahogany pedestal writing table, rectangular top. 5'6" × 3'5½". [Sotheby's, 30 May 1975, lot 93]

Dressing table c.1800. Mahogany, inlaid in mahogany, box, satinwood and ebony with painted floral borders on cabinet doors. Glass roll-top in centre enclosing four turned satinwood toilet boxes 58″ × 32¾″ × 16″. [MMA, NY Acc. no. 19.66 (illus. Antiques, October 1960, p. 363)]

THOMAS AND GEORGE SEDDON 1798–1804 (labels). n.d. Mahogany architect's table, rectangular top concealing pigeon holes, rising drawing table 30″ × 33″ (Day Gunby patent) engraved brass tablet PATENT. SEDDON NO. 6.

[Sotheby's 20 July 1951, Lot 180. Illus. C. Life, 21 February 1957, pp. 330–31]

n.d. Writing-cum-Pembroke table, early 19th-century, brass label. PATENT SEDDON NO. 45. [Illus. Heal, p. 260]

n.d. Mahogany mechanical writing desk, brass label engraved PATENT SEDDON NO. 13. Rectangular top concealing double bank of pigeon holes (Day Gunby patent). [Sotheby's Parke Bernet, 27 September 1980 and Christie's, New York, 17 October 1981, lot 159]

n.d. Sofa table with mechanical works, counter balance etc. to convert to writing table or adjustable reading desk (Day Gunby patent). [Conn., June 1950, p. 46]

SEDDON'S UPHOLSTERY & CABINET WAREHOUSE, 24 Dover St, Piccadilly (labels). c.1800. Amboyna and satinwood tea caddy recorded (Figs 19–21).

n.d. satinwood tea-caddy, tulip cross-banding and, yew panels. [Conn., October 1957, p. 97, fig. 10]

BLEASE & SEDDON (c.1802–11), 24 Dover St (label). n.d. Mahogany pedestal sideboard with brass rail and top inlaid with chequered lines. [Christie's, 15 April 1982, lot 95]

T. SEDDON (punched stamp). n.d. 3 single chairs, bird's eye maple and gilt, leaf carved toes on sabre legs and back uprights: stamped T. Seddon. [Advert. Conn., July 1978]

THOMAS & GEORGE SEDDON, London House, Aldersgate St (labels). n.d. c.1825 small writing table. T. & G. Seddon label bears no. 1214. [Heal, p. 260]

n.d. c.1825, rosewood tea caddy, label bears no. 1901. [C. Life, 2 June 1966, p. 1400]

n.d. rosewood in Empire style Davenport, brass mounts. [Randolph advert, n.d.]

n.d. rosewood escritoire, Regency period. [Antiques, May 1953, p. 404]

n.d. rosewood escritoire, Regency period, label bears no. 6048. [Conn., June 1950, p. 45]

THOMAS & GEORGE SEDDON, Gray's Inn Rd. n.d. rosewood writing table on two end supports. Frieze fitted with six drawers. Label no. 2151 inscribed 'Roso' in manuscript. [Christie's, 14 May 1981]

n.d. writing table on two end supports recorded with label no. 2866 inscribed 'H_____ Lowther' in manuscript.

[GL, records of Joiners' Co., Upholders' Co., Insurance Companies and Livery lists; PRO, bankruptcy B3/4464; Inland Revenue app. records (IR) and Lord Chamberlain's Office Records (LCO)) and V&A Lib. (86 M. M. 13. A. W. N. Pugin. Notes for an uncompleted autobiography 1812–31). See also the following newspapers/journals: Annual Register, July 1768; Daily Advertiser, 15 July 1768; Gazetteer and New Daily Advertiser, 18 July 1768; Public Advertiser, 18 July 1768; Newcastle Chronicle, 23 July 1768; Norfolk Chronicle, 8 November 1783; Times, 11, 12, 13, 14 and 16 August 1830]   P.K.

Seddon, Henry, 13 Spitalfields, Liverpool, cm (1781–84). [D]

Seddon, Henry, 85 Byrom St, Liverpool, cm (1829). [D]

Seddon, Henry, Liverpool, cm (1820–30). App. to William Harvey in 1820 and seven years later petitioned for his freedom. Sworn free in 1830. [App. enrolment bk; freemen's committee bk]

Seddon, John, Ditchfield Ct, Long Millgate, Manchester, cm (1834). [D]

Seddon, Richard, Liverpool, cm (1824–37). App. to William Harvey in 1824 and in 1837 trading from 22 Maguire St. [D; app. enrolment bk]

Seddon, Thomas, see George Seddon.

Seddon, Thomas, 29 Howell Croft, Bolton, Lancs., joiner, cm and u (1816–18). [D]

Seddon, William, 5 Chaucer St, Liverpool, cm (1827). [D]

Sedgely, Arthur, Sponstreet Ward, Coventry, Warks., turner and chairmaker (1728). Took out insurance cover of £200 on his timber and merchandise. [GL, Sun MS vol. 26, 3 April 1728]

Sedgwick, Christopher, York, cm (1758–84). Son of William Sedgwick, carpenter and father of William Sedgwick, cm. Free 1758, and in the same year shown at Coney St. In Blake St, 1784–87. [D; poll bks; freemen rolls] See Thomas and William Sedgwick of Blake St.

Sedgwick & Son, John, Eccleston St, Prescot, Lancs., joiner and cm (1814–28). In 1816 the business was listed as John jnr & Thomas Sedgwick, and in 1828 as John Sedgwick only. [D]

Sedgwick, Thomas, Blake St, York, cm (1784). [Poll bk]

Sedgwick, Thomas, York, cm and u (1830–40). At 7 Mint Yd in 1830 and from 1837–40 at 25 Blake St. [D] See Christopher Sedgwick.

Sedgwick, Thomas, Fazakerley St, Prescot, Lancs., joiner and cm (1828). [D]

Sedgwick, William, Blake St, York, cm and u (1783–1838). Son of Christopher Sedgwick, cm, and probably took over his business which was also in Blake St. Free in 1783, and living at Blake St from 1784. Listed at no. 25, 1828–30. Took as app. Robert Watson on 1 May 1821. One directory of 1816 gives his address as Petergate. [D; poll bk; app. reg.; freemen rolls]

Sedman, John, Cliffe Lane, Whitby, Yorks., cm (1823). [D]

Sedwell, William, parish of St Clement Danes, London, upholder (1708–23). Free of the Upholders' Co., 7 July 1708. Took as app. Edward White, 1713–21. In December 1723 insured a house on the south side of the Strand for £250 and another 'near over a passage leading into Fountain tavern' for £300. [GL, Upholders' Co. records; Sun MS vol. 28, refs 32549–50]

Seed, John, Liverpool, cm (1827–39). Shown in one 1827 directory at 2 Gt George Pl., but in another at 153 London Rd. Thereafter the addresses are all in London Rd, the number being 186 in 1829, 180 in 1834, 192 in 1835, 198 in 1837 and 14 in 1839. [D]

Seehausen, —, Covent Gdn, London, cm (1728–30). In 1728 supplied for Holkham Hall, Norfolk, two mahogany tables costing £3 10s the pair. In the following year supplied a further mahogany table at £2 10s. Supplied a frame for a sideboard table to Longford Castle, Wilts. in 1730 at a cost of £5 15s. [V&A archives]

Seekerson, James, Gray Stone St, Dudley, Staffs., cm, u and clock case maker (1840). [D]

Seel, George, 29 Lombard St, Liverpool, chairmaker (1794). [D]

Seel, George, 71 Shudehill, Manchester, chair warehouse (1808–11). [D] See Sarah Seel.

Seel, James, Liverpool, cm and victualler (1805–11). At 17 Smithfield St in 1805, 12 Upper Milk St in 1807 and 7 Upper Milk St, 1810–11. [D]

Seel, Sarah, 82 Shudehill, Manchester, chair warehouse (1802). [D] Possibly succeeded by George Seel.

Seel, Thomas, 37 Cock Gates, Manchester, chairmaker (1794–97). [D]

Seers, Mathew, Dry Bridge, Liverpool, cm (1767). The death of his wife was announced in January 1767. [Williamson's Liverpool Advertiser, 2 January 1767]

Seeth, John, Burgate, Canterbury, Kent, cm (1784). [D]

Sefton, Thomas, Misterton, Notts., joiner and cm (1832). [D]

Sefton, William, Liverpool, cm (1810–34). At 20 Christian St, 1810–11, 5 Springfield St in 1821 and 6 Springfield St, 1824–34. [D]

Segar, Stephen, York, u (1788). Declared bankrupt, *Williamson's Liverpool Advertiser*, 28 January 1788.

Selby, Daniel, Buttermarket, Ipswich, Suffolk, cm (1808). [D]

Selby, Isaac, Hensingham, Whitehaven, Cumb., joiner/cm (1834). [D]

Selby, James, Little Britain, near St Bartholomew's Hospital, London, 'an eminent Picture Frame-maker, and Dealer in Pictures' (d.1773). Death at his house near Little Britain reported in *Public Advertiser*, 6 November 1773.

Selby, James, Ratcliffe, London, cm and broker (1801–21). At 32 Cannon St, Ratcliffe in 1808, but by July 1821 at no. 17. He took out insurance cover on this latter address for £200, half of which was for utensils and stock. [D; PRO, C13/591/31; GL, Sun MS vol. 484, ref. 981652]

Selby, Thomas, corner of Queen St, near Gurney's Bank, Norwich, u (1795–96). Immediately prior to 1795 he had been in partnership with a Mr Punchard, probably Robert Punchard. When this broke up he moved to the Queen St address. He advertised his ability to provide military gentlemen 'with good camp furniture, of which a list may be had at his upholstery warehouse'. [*Bury and Norwich Post*, 10 June 1795; poll bk]

Selby, Thomas, Butter Mkt, Ipswich, Suffolk, cm (1805). [D]

Selby, Thomas, 49 Cannon St, St George's East, London, cabinet, toy and pattern manufacturer (1826). [D]

Selby, Thomas, St Pancras, London, upholder (1830). Freeman of Norwich. [Norwich poll bk]

Selby, William, 16 Sittlewhites Alley, Chancery Lane, London, chair painter (1810). In April 1810 took out insurance cover of £100 of which £60 was for stock and utensils. [GL, Sun MS vol. 453, ref. 844282]

Selden (or Seldon), John, Petworth, Sussex, carver (1688–d.1715). Worked at Petworth House from 1688–97 being paid £10 a quarter in 1689, and later may have had £50 p.a. His work survives in the Chapel and the Hall of State (Marble Hall) in the form of picture frames and cornices. He appears to have been a member of a local family and his burial at Petworth is recorded on 12 January 1715. [*Sussex Arch. Collections*, XCVI (1958), pp. 59, 96; *C. Life*, 4 September 1980, p. 799; Beard, *Georgian Craftsmen*]

Self, James, Norwich, cm (1802–30). Son of Thomas Self, cm and free on 8 May 1802. In 1802 living in the parish of St Margaret but by July 1830 in the parish of St Lawrence. His son Richard Self, a cordwainer was made free on 18 August 1830. [Poll bks; freemen admission reg.]

Self, John, Green St, Bath, Som., carver and gilder (1793). [D]

Self, John, Ship Lane, Wisbech, Cambs., cm and u (1824–30). In 1830 the address was given as Ship Passage. [D]

Self, Robert, Misterley, Essex, cm (1818–30). Freeman of Norwich. [Norwich poll bks] See Thomas Self of Misterley.

Self, Robert, Manningtree, Essex, cm etc. (1832–39). [D]

Self, Thomas Cowell, Norwich and East Dereham, Norfolk, cm (1770–1818). Son of Thomas Self, bricklayer. Free of Norwich on 2 April 1770, and in 1780 shown in the parish of St Andrew. Remained in Norwich until 1797, but by July 1802 at East Dereham where he remained until at least November 1806. By October 1812 back in Norwich. His son James Self, cm, was made free of Norwich on 8 May 1802. [Freemen admission reg.; Norwich poll bks]

Self, Thomas, Hardingham, Norfolk, cm (1799). Freeman of Norwich. [Norwich poll bk]

Self, Thomas James, Baxter Row, East Dereham, Norfolk, cm and broker (1822–39). [D]

Self, Thomas, Misterley, Essex, cm (1830). Freeman of Norwich. [Norwich poll bk] See Robert Self.

Self, W., 6 Crown St, Moorfields, London, u, auctioneer etc. (1820–37). [D]

Sell, John, Heath St, Hampstead, London, cm, u and furniture broker (1839). [D]

Seller, Christopher, Foss Bridge, York, cm (1774). [Poll bk]

Seller, John, Eastgate St, Chester, cm (1801–26). Son of William Seller, gardener and app. for seven years to Richard Gorst, cm, on 1 August 1801. Not free, however, until 19 June 1818. [App. reg.; freemen rolls; poll bks]

Seller, Samuel, Brook St, Chester, cm (1818–19). Free 15 June 1818. [Freemen rolls; poll bks]

Seller, William, Market Pl., Bridlington, Yorks. (1823–34). [D]

Sellers, James, Norton, Malton, Yorks., cm (1823–28). [D]

Sellers, John, Ebenezer St, Bradford, Yorks., cm (1830). [D]

Sellers, Richard, Market Rasen, Lincs., chairmaker (1822–40). Listed also as a wheelmaker in 1822, and trading at Bridge St, 1826–40. [D]

Sellers, Samuel, Exchange, Chester, cm (1816). [D]

Sellick, William, Exeter, Devon, cm (1827–40). Shown at James St, 1827–35, and then Mary Arches St, 1836–40. Three daughters were bapt. at St Mary Major, 1827–35, and a further daughter at St Olave in 1840. [D; PR (bapt.)]

Sellman, Henry, 1 Northampton Ct, Northampton St, London, cm (1802). Freeman of Oxford. [Oxford poll bk]

Sellons, John, Chelmsford, Essex, chairmaker (1790). Daughter Hannah bapt. on 17 December 1790. [PR (bapt.)]

Sells, Stephen, address unknown, cm (1687). On 18 October 1687 received payment of £6 from William, 5th Earl of Bedford for two long tables. [Bedford Office, London]

Selly, William, Yealmpton, Devon, chairmaker (1817). [*Furn. Hist.*, 1976]

Selstone, John, Oxford, cm (1778). Drawn by lot to serve in the militia. [*Jackson's Oxford Journal*, 19 June 1778]

Selway, Thomas & Joseph, Milk Alley, Wardour St, Soho, London, cm and upholders (1785). In 1785 took out insurance cover of £200 on their utensils and stock. [GL, Sun MS vol. 239, p. 619]

Selwood, William, Holborn, London, carver (1777). Bankruptcy announced, *Gents Mag.*, December 1777.

Semfield, Robert, Stockton, Co. Durham, u (1798). [D]

Semper, William, Bath, Som., upholder (1770). Bankruptcy announced, *Gents Mag.*, October 1770.

Sempers, John, Newport, Lincoln, cm (1828–35). [D]

Semple, —, Margaret St, Newcastle, cm (1793). Subscribed to Sheraton's *Drawing Book*, 1793.

Semple, John & Alexander, London, cm and upholders (1803–16). At 78 Margaret St, Cavendish Sq. in 1803, in which year Semple was included in the list of master cabinet makers in Sheraton's *Cabinet Dictionary*. Sheraton was also to design their trade card which features an engraving of a furnished dining room. The Margaret St address is shown in one directory as late as 1808, but from October 1804 John Semple was using an address at 2 Berners St. This was described as a dwelling house, workshop and wareroom and was insured for £700. Alexander is first recorded as a partner in February 1806, by which time total insurance cover had risen to £3,200 indicating a substantial business. Utensils and stock alone accounted for £2,400 of this. As £1,500 of the stock was in an open yard this would suggest substantial timber stocks. Also insured in February 1806 was a house at 10 Grafton St, Fitzroy Sq. which was used in part as a store and valued at £500. The Berners St address was used until at least 1809, but by 1811 the partners had moved to Newman

St, Oxford St. They also acted as house agents, and in 1806 advertised themselves as dealers in mahogany. A sofa table of their manufacture is at Temple Newsam House, Leeds. It was supplied in 1809 to William & Charles Shadbolt of Bankside, and was described as 'a fine Kingwood Sophatable with orangewood border 2 Drawers on solid turned standards & Rich Brass Lions paws' and charged at £22 (Figs 32–34). [D; GL, Sun MS vol. 431, ref. 767664; vol. 437, refs 787045–46; Gilbert, *Leeds Furn. Cat.*, vol. II, pp. 349–51]

Senea, William, Bakewell, Derbs., u (1820). [D]

Seneschal, J., address unknown, u (1786). Undertook work at Audley End, Essex under the direction of Chipchase & Lambert, u. Seneschal charged £35 13s 6d on 8 May 1786 for embroidery on bed hangings, chairs and stools. [V&A archives]

Senhouse, Peter, London, upholder (1774–84). At White Hart Yd, Westminster in 1774 and Queen St, Chelsea in 1784. [Poll bks]

Senhouse, William Minet, Lambeth, London, u and cm (1767–69). The business is recorded in directories as Senhouse & Co., 1767–68. In April 1769, when bankruptcy proceedings were put in hand, only William Minet Senhouse was named. [D; *Gents Mag.*, April 1769]

Senior, George, Carlton, near Barnsley, Yorks., joiner and cm (1837). [D]

Senior, John, Widemarsh St, Hereford, cm and upholder (1837). His billhead indicates that amongst items stocked were 'writing desks, work boxes, dressing cases, music stools, floor cloths, Brussels and other carpets, paper hangings, Indian matts, table covers &c.'. An invoice of this maker survives for goods supplied to a Miss Wood between March and June 1837. The major furniture items included an 'imitation Rosewood Sofa' at £7, seven 'stained Beech chairs with cushions' at 10s 6d each, an 'Ottoman Bed' at £5 10s, a mahogany Pembroke table at £3 and a chiffonier at £5. [Hereford Lib., Pilley Coll., 2305 notebook 3]

Senken, G., High St, Deptford, London, feather bed maker and chairmaker (1838). [D]

Senols, James, London, upholder, appraiser and cabinet warehouse (1757–1817). Son of Henry Senols of the parish of St John, Wapping, tailor. App. to Charles Greenwood on 3 November 1757 and free of the Upholders' Co. by servitude, 6 December 1764. Shown at 23 Fenchurch St, 1783–87 although one directory of 1784 gives the address as 1 Rood Lane. From 1790 at 81 Fore St, Moorgate. The long period of trading might suggest that there may have been a son of the same name involved in the business. James Senols took as app. William Davis, 1784–96. [D; GL, Upholders' Co. records]

Senton, James, Carr St, Ipswich, Suffolk, turner and chairmaker (1830). [D]

Senton, James, Leeds, Yorks., cm (1826–34). In 1826 at Harrison St, in 1830 at 6 North St, and in 1834 at 13 Upper North St. [D]

Senton, John, North St, Leeds, Yorks., cm and u (1828–34). Listed at no. 6, 1828–30, and at 13 Upper North St, 1834. [D]

Senton, Thomas, Wingham St, Roundhay Rd, Leeds, Yorks., cm (1839). [D]

Senton, William, Leeds, Yorks., journeyman cm (1791). Included in the list of those in sympathy with the contents of the *Leeds Cabinet and Chair Makers' Book of Prices*, 1791.

Sergeant, George, London, looking-glass manufacturer (1784–93). At 15 Old Broad St in 1784 and 17 College Hill, 1788–93. In 1790 also listed as a 'pierglass & cabinetmaker'. [D]

Sergeant, James, Low Hill with a house at 1 Prospect St, Liverpool, joiner and cm (1824). [D]

Sergeant, Thomas, Oxford, u (1682). A widower, when on 20 November 1682 he married Alice Cox of St Cross, Oxford at the Church of All Saints. [Bodleian index of Oxf. marriage bonds]

Serjeant, John, 11 Concert St with a shop at 7 Parker St, Liverpool, cm (1834–35). [D]

Servant, Samuel, 7 Leather Lane, Holborn, London, carver and gilder (1839). [D]

Service, Thomas & David, Thomas St, Liverpool, joiners and cm (1834–39). At 4 Thomas St, 1834–37, but in 1839 the number was 5. [D]

Servies, James, 37 Gerrard St, Soho, London, French cm (1820). [D]

Servinshire, William, London, upholder (1719). Freeman of London. On 14 May 1719 took as app. Daniel Collins, son of Daniel Collins, freeman and girdler of London. [V&A archives]

Sessions, James, Palace St, Gloucester, cm and u (1830). [D]

Seth, Isaac, 9 Kings Pl., Commercial Rd, St George's East, London, cm and u (1827). [D]

Seth, William, St Thomas the Apostle (Exeter?), chairmaker (1736). In 1736 took app. named Giles. [S of G, app. index]

Seton, —, Chatham, Kent, upholder (1784). [D]

Setterfield, Thomas, Falcon St, Ipswich, Suffolk, cm and u (1830–39). [D; poll bks]

Settle, John, York, cm (1834). [D]

Settle, William, Whitehorse Yd with house at 22 Portland St, Hull, Yorks., cm (1838–40). [D]

Sever, Matthew, Butcher's Row, Beverley, Yorks., cm (1814–28). [D]

Severn, John, Jermyn St, London, upholder (1761–d.1765). Member of the Society for Arts and Manufactures 1761.

Severn, Samuel, Jermyn St, St James's, London, upholder (1727–30). Freeman of Shrewsbury but living in the St James's area of London by 1727. In December 1730 took out insurance cover on household goods and stock in trade valued at £500 and kept in his house on the south side of Jermyn St. [Shrewsbury freemen rolls; GL, Sun MS vol. 33, ref. 52482] Possibly father of:

Severn, Samuel, Jermyn St, St James's, London, upholder (1734–72). App. to Thomas Arne and free of the Upholders' Co. by servitude, 1734. Shown at Jermyn St in 1749. Took as app. John Allen, 1752–56. By 1769 in partnership with Henry Stuart and in this year they undertook work for Sir Gilbert Heathcote. In August 1769 they were responsible for the funeral of the Hon. Lady Margaret Heathcote. On 8 September they supplied twelve 'strong yoked back chairs with matted seats for the garretts' at 3s each and materials and a bed tick also probably for the servants' quarters. The bill totalled £5 19s 4½d. A much more substantial commission for Sir Gilbert Heathcote in 1771 was in the name of Henry Stuart only and it is possible that the partnership had ended by this date. On 8 February 1772, however, Samuel Severn receipted a bill of Stuart's, after his death, on behalf of Mrs Bridget Catherine Stuart. [GL, Upholders' Co. records; Westminster poll bk; Lincoln RO, 2 ANC 12/D/29, 2 ANC 12/D/28, ANC 8/12]

Severs, Benjamin, 110 Fleet St, London, upholder (1798–1802). Son of Samuel Severs of York, butcher. Free of the Upholders' Co. by redemption, 14 November 1798. [GL, Upholders' Co. records]

Severs, Samuel, York and Grantham, Lincs., u and auctioneer (1780–90). Son of Samuel Severs of York, butcher, and brother to Benjamin Severs. Free of York as an u in 1780, but by 1784 living at Grantham. On 7 May 1785 took as app. Thomas Marples at a premium of £42, and in March 1790 advertised for a further app. [D; York freemen rolls; York poll bk; PRO, IR 1/32; *Lincoln, Rutland and Stamford Mercury*, 5 March 1790]

Sevier, John, Bristol, cm (1815–25). At Pithay from 1815–16, but by 1817 in partnership with Brookshaw. Sevier & Brookshaw traded from an address in All Saint's St, Nelson St, 1817–24, but by 1825 the partnership appears to have ended and Sevier then traded on his own behalf from All Saint's St until 1828. [D]

Seward, —, Teignmouth, Devon, cm (1818). Also acted as agent for the hire of pianofortes and harps in S. Devon supplied through a Mr Pilbrow who maintained the 'Grand Musical Repository' probably in Exeter. [Exeter newspaper, 26 March 1818]

Seward, Henry, Southwark, London, upholder and bed and mattress manufacturer (1829–39). At 15–16 Eltham Pl., Kent Rd in 1829 and 15 Blackman St, 1835–39. [D]

Seward, P., Lancaster, japanner (1827). [Westminster Ref. Lib., Gillow records]

Seward, Thomas, Leicester and Rugby, Warks., u (1826). App. to John Measures of Leicester and free in 1826. In that year living in Rugby. [Leicester freemen rolls]

Seward, William, Exeter, Devon, cm and u (1830–34). In 1832 trading from Cathedral Yd, but in September 1834, when the death of his wife Alice was announced, he was living in Heavitree. [D; poll bk; *Exeter Flying Post*, 25 September 1834]

Seward, William J., Exeter, Devon, u (1830–37). At Old Excise Passage 1830; 218 High St, 1831–32; Sidwell St, 1834–36; and 16 King William Terr., 1837. [D]

Sewell, —, Alnwick, Northumb., (c.1776–93). Included in a list of furniture makers drawn up c.1776 by the Duchess of Northumberland. [D; Gilbert, *Chippendale*, p. 154]

Sewell, —, Hertford(?), cm and u (1794). On 27 April 1794 supplied for Panshanger, Herts. a fire screen costing £4 14s 6d, and on 10 September two stools at £7 15s. Also carried out repairs to church pews etc., charging 14s 3d for this work on 27 June 1794. [Herts. RO, PAN Box 44 Bundle 7]

Sewell, George, address unknown, chairmaker (1756). On 25 May 1756 charged Peter Du Cane of Braxted Park, Essex £3 4s for eight chairs supplied to this house. [Essex RO, D/DDc A13 folio 59]

Sewell, Jacob, Workington, Cumb., joiner/cm (1828–34). At Washington St in 1829 and Pow St in 1834. [D]

Sewell, John, Gt Yarmouth, Norfolk and Bungay, Suffolk, cm (1777–95). Freeman of Gt Yarmouth. At Bungay in 1777 but by June 1790 back in Gt Yarmouth. In 1795 his app. John Sallows, who changed his surname to Aldred, was made free. [Gt Yarmouth freemen rolls and poll bks]

Sewell, Richard, Leadenhall St, London, carver and gilder (1782–93). His trade card [Laundauer Coll., MMA, NY] states that he framed prints, drawings and needlework, cleaned, lined and repaired old pictures and regilded frames. At 171 Leadenhall St in 1784 but by 1790 the number was 121. In 1782 took out a licence to employ three non-freemen for six weeks. [D; GL, City Licence bk, vol. 10]

Sewell, Robert, New Elvet, Durham, cm/joiner (1834). Successor to William Sewell at this address. [D]

Sewell, William, New Elvet, Durham, cm (1817–18). Succeeded at this address by Robert Sewell by 1834. [D]

Sewell, William, West Wycombe, Bucks., chairmaker (1830). [D]

Sewell & Cross, London, linen drapers, silk mercers and u (1837). At 44–45 Old Compton St and 46–47 Frith St, Soho. [D]

Sewter, Robert, Norwich, cm (1780–90). In the parish of St John Maddermarket, September 1780, but by April 1784 in the parish of St Stephen. [Poll bks]

Sexton, Robert H., London, carver (1826–39). At 8 Norman St, St Luke's in 1826 and 18 Cleveland St in 1839. [D]

Sexton, Robert, 9 Upper Charlton St, London, carver (1835). [D] Probably dead by 1839 when Sarah Sexton, possibly his wife, succeeded him.

Sexton, Sarah, 9 Upper Charlton St, London, carver (1839). [D]

Seyer, David, 9 South St, Marylebone, London, picture and looking-glass frame maker (1839). [D]

Seyer, Samuel, London, upholder (1699). Free of the Upholders' Co., 3 October 1699. [GL, Upholders' Co. records]

Seyffret, George, London, cm, u and undertaker (1827–40). At 18 Wells St, Oxford St, 1827–29 but by July 1840 was at 77 Wardour St, Soho. [D; GL, Sun MS ref. 1333631]

Seymour, Charles, St David's Hill, Exeter, Devon, cm (1803–25). Included in a militia roll of 1803. Baptisms of two sons and four daughters at St David's Church recorded, 1813–23. [D; PR (bapt.)]

Seymour, George, 4 Helmet Row, St Luke's, London, chair and sofa manufacturer (1826). [D]

Seymour, George, White Horse St, Baldock, Herts., cm and u (1839). [D]

Seymour, James, High St, Poole, Dorset, joiner and cm (1791–98). In 1791 took out insurance cover of £900. [D; GL, Sun MS vol. 374, ref. 579558]

Seymour, James, Landgate, Rye, Sussex, cm and u (1823). [D]

Seymour, John, 'The Black Lion', Fleet Ditch, London, u (1715–16). Fined for refusing parochial office in the parish of St Bride, Fleet St in 1716. [GL, Sun MS vol. 5, p. 141; MS 6561, p. 9]

Seymour, John, Axminster, Devon, cm (b.c.1738–d.1818). In 1785 arrived in Portland, Maine, USA with his son and set up business as a cm.

Seymour, John, Bartholomew's Yd, Exeter, Devon, carver and gilder (1830). Son John Henry bapt. at St Olave's Church, 22 August 1830. [PR (bapt.)]

Seymour, John, Rye, Sussex, cm (1832–40). At Middle St in 1832 but by November 1839 in High St. [D]

Seymour, Richard, High St, Poole, Dorset, cm and u (1840). [D]

Seymour, Samuel, Pond Pl., Chelsea, London, cm (1808). [D]

Seymour, Thomas, 14 Leaf St, Hulme, Manchester, carver and gilder (1832–33). [D]

Shacklady, Henry, York St, Liverpool, cm (1835–39). The number in York St was 12 in 1835, 11 in 1837 and 10 in 1839. [D]

Shackles, John, Hull, Yorks., cm (1756). In 1756 took app. named Pratt. [S of G, app. index]

Shackles, John, Lowgate, Hull, Yorks., cm and u (1774–99). [D] In 1793 Shackles & Son of Hull subscribed to Sheraton's *Drawing Book*. John is possibly father of:

Shackles, Thomas, Hull, Yorks., cm and u (1796–1834). In 1802 had a residence at Hedon, near Hull, but by 1803 living at Lowgate, probably the house previously occupied by John Shackles. He was still shown at Lowgate in one directory of 1828, although others of 1814–31 give 2 Pryme St. His shop was at Eaton St, 1803–34. Directories also state that from 1823–31 he was additionally a ship-owner. In July 1801 took as app. Thomas Dickson (or Dixon) of Sculcoates, near Hull. Patronised by Sir John Nelthorpe who paid him £6 12s in December 1796 and £6 8s in December 1798. The latter payment may have been for 35½ yds of Scotch carpet and sundries supplied on 7 November 1798 at a cost of £6 8s 2d. [D; app. reg.; Lincoln RO, NEL 14/37/72, 74, 75]

Shackleton, Isaac, Beeton Stansfield, Todmorden, Yorks., joiner/cm (1837). [D]

Shackleton, Thomas, 115 Long Acre, London. In January 1784 he supplied Mrs A. Crow with 'a very neat Mahogany fire screen stand' at £1 12s. [Isle of Wight RO, JER/WA]

Shackleton, Thomas, King's Arms Yd, Westgate, Bradford, Yorks., cm (1834). [D]

Shackleton & Evans, see George Oakley.

Shackleworth, Roger, Swallow St, Westminster, London, cm (1749). [Poll bk]

Shacklock, Francis, Bolsover, Derbs., joiner and cm (1793). [D]

Shacklock, John, Bolsover, Derbs., cm, hardware man and bookseller (1793). [D]

Shadforth, J. B., 5 Seymour Pl., Bryanston Sq., London, u (1835). [D]

Shatford, Samuel, Long Acre, London, cm (1749). [Westminster poll bk]

Shafto, William, New North Rd, Durham, cm, u and turner (1836). Suffered from a fire at his premises on 8 March 1836 and a subscription list was opened in aid of the sufferers. William Shafto received £23 7s 4d from this fund which left him at a considerable loss. He was back trading from the premises again, however, by April 1836. [*Durham Advertiser*, 22 April 1836]

Shakell, Edward, Southampton, Hants., u and cm (1823–39). At 6 Bridge St in 1823; 9 St Michael's Sq. in 1830; 17 Above Bar, 1834–36; but in 1839 the address is simply listed as Bargate. [D]

Shakespear, —, address unknown, cm (1772). On 31 December 1772 received from Peter Du Cane of Braxted Park, Essex £4 4s for a bureau. [Essex RO, D/DDc A22, f. 17]

Shale, William, High St, Bilston, Staffs., cm and u (1822–38). Recorded also at Field Lane in 1835. [D]

Shallis, John, London, cm (1793). Subscribed to Sheraton's *Drawing Book*, 1793.

Shallis, John, Exeter, Devon, cm and broker (1782–d. by 1809). In 1782 insured his utensils and stock for £100. Shown at North St, 1787–1803, but on 1 September 1803 he advertised the sale of his stock 'being about to decline the business'. On 22 August 1809 the auction of a dwelling house at 146 Fore St belonging to 'Mr. John Shallis, Cabinet Maker, deceased' was held. The property does not appear to have found a buyer and was again advertised for sale by private contract on 19 October 1809. [D; GL, Sun MS vol. 302, p. 113; *Exeter Flying Post*, 15 February 1787, 1 September 1803, 3 August and 19 October 1809]

Shallis, William, Exeter, Devon, cm (1824). Daughter and son bapt. at Holy Trinity Church, 5 December 1824. [PR (bapt.)]

Shane, —, address unknown, upholder (1754). Subscribed to Chippendale's *Director*, 1754.

Shannon, Martin, 15 Bolton St, Preston, Lancs., chairmaker (1818). [D]

Shannon, Thomas, Taunton, Som., cm (1761). In 1761 took app. named Bartham. [S of G, app. index]

Shapley, Richard, Exeter, Devon, chairmaker (1741). [Freemen rolls]

Shapley, William, London, upholder (1748–78). Son of Samuel Shapley of the parish of St Olave, Southwark, carpenter. App. to Samuel Walker, freeman and member of the Drapers' Co., 22 March 1748. Free of the Upholders' Co. under the terms of the 1750 Upholders' Act, 4 February 1762. In 1765 trading at the sign of 'The Crown & Cushion', north side of Cornhill and by 1767 at 80 Gracechurch St. He traded here as an upholder and cm until 1772, but by the following year had moved to 26 Bishopsgate Within. In November 1765 a fire broke out in Bishopsgate St which damaged the premises of many tradesmen in the area including those of Shapley. [D; GL, Upholders' Co. records; Heal; *Gents Mag.*, November 1765]

Shararth, Lawrence, London, cm (1793). Subscribed to Sheraton's *Drawing Book*, 1793.

Shard (or Sharp), Robert, Leadenhall St, London, upholder (1715–34). Free of the Upholders' Co., 6 July 1715. [GL, Upholders' Co. records; Heal]

Shardlow, Edward, Leicester, cm (1834). App. to William Johnson and free in 1834. [Freemen rolls]

Share, Elizabeth & Sons, High St, Dudley, Staffs., cm and u (1838–40). [D] Possibly the widow of:

Share, John, High St, Dudley, Staffs., cm and u (1818–35). [D]

Share, Thomas, High St, Dudley, Staffs., cm (1818). [D]

Sharford, Daniel, 83 Tottenham Ct Rd, London, cm (1835). [D]

Shark, John, Allendale, Hexham, Northumb., joiner and cm (1828). [D]

Sharland, William, Tiverton, Devon, cm (1823–38). At Fore St, 1823–30 but in 1838 at Gold St. [D]

Sharman, William, Chester, cm (1698). Free 1 April 1698. [Freemen rolls]

Sharp, —, London, cm (1793–1803). Subscribed to Sheraton's *Drawing Book*, 1793. Probably the Sharp (address not stated) who subscribed to his *Cabinet Dictionary*, 1803.

Sharp, Charles, 2 Berners St, Oxford St, London, upholder and undertaker (1817). Took over this address from John & Alexander Semple and may also have taken over their customers and business stock. [D] Succeeded by:

Sharp, Clement, 2 Berners St, Oxford St, London, cm, u, auctioneer and house agent (1819–27). The business was of a substantial size and in May 1820 cover of £2,000 was taken out on the dwelling house, warerooms and workshops. The policy was issued jointly with the Rev. John Quarrington who may perhaps have been supplying some of the capital. In February 1821, when insurance cover was renewed at £1,500 for the utensils and stock, Sharp was associated in the policy with a William Dudds. A further change had occurred by 1823, for from this date the business is listed in some directories as Sharp & Clark. [D; GL, Sun MS vol. 483, ref. 966642; vol. 488, ref. 976435]

Sharp, Clement, Romsey, Hants., auctioneer and u (1823–30). Recorded at Market Pl. as Clement & Sons, cm and u in 1830. [D; *Southampton Advertiser*, 31 October 1829]

Sharp, Edward snr and jnr, Norwich, cm and chairmaker (1780–1830). In 1783 at 41 Pottergate but in the following year at Back of Inns. From 1818 the address was Heigham. Edward Sharp snr took as app. his son Edward who was free 18 June 1786. A younger son, John, a woollen draper, was also made free, 3 October 1795. Edward Sharp snr also took as app. James Darkin, free 21 September 1799. The Henry Sharp, son of Edward Sharp, who by trade was a tailor and free of Norwich on 28 July 1822, must have been the son of Edward Sharp jnr. As late as July 1830, Norwich poll bks list an Edward Sharp, cm and Edward Sharp jnr, chairmaker, both living at Heigham. [D; poll bks]

Sharp, Francis, High St, Henley-on-Thames, Oxon., cm, u and furniture broker (1830). [D]

Sharp, George, Newton St, Holborn, London, carver (1808). [D]

Sharp, George, Rochester, Kent, cm (1830). [Poll bk]

Sharp, James, High St, Poole, Dorset, cm and u (1840). [D]

Sharp, Job, Easington, Co. Durham, joiner and cm (1828–34). [D]

Sharp, John, London(?), upholder (1696–1731). On 1 August 1696 the Earl of Rockingham paid him 8s for a coffin and on 2 October 19s 2d for four bills. In 1731 paid £9 16s for 98 yds of crimson harateen for Lord Bristol's new bedchamber. [Lincoln RO, Monson 10/1/a/19; *DEF*]

Sharp, John, Liverpool, cm (1765–80). App. to Joseph Brown and in 1765 petitioned freedom. Took as app. Edward Miles who petitioned freedom in 1780. [Freemen rolls]

Sharp, John, Liverpool, cm (1784). Freeman of Lancaster. [Lancaster poll bk]

Sharp, John, Lancaster and Liverpool, cm (1789–90). Free of Lancaster, 1789–90, but then living in Liverpool. [Lancaster freemen rolls]

Sharp, John, Old Meeting St, Birmingham, cm (1793). [D]

Sharp, John, parish of St Peter Hungate, Norwich, cm (1802–06). [Poll bks]

Sharp, John, Shirebrow, Blackburn, Lancs., cm (1828). [D]

Sharp, John, James & Ann, Oldenburgh House, London Rd, Tunbridge Wells, Kent, Tunbridge-ware makers (1807–40). Also print publishers. Trading as early as 1807, and a map of 1808 shows their manufactory on the western side of Culverden Down, a short distance from the property at Oldenburgh House. In 1838 described as turnery manufacturers, but clearly had the capacity to undertake small cabinet furniture for in 1828 they were one of four makers in the town considered to undertake the making of a work and writing table as a gift for the Princess Victoria. In 1839 they claimed the patronage of the Queen. Two card boxes are known decorated with hand-drawn displays of playing cards which incorporate the name of this concern. Both probably date from the period 1810–30. [D; Kent RO, Barrow map (1808), Tithe award map (1838)]

Sharp, Joseph, 31 Gt Carter Lane, Doctors Commons, London, cm and broker (1820–26). In May 1820 took out insurance cover of £500 which included £300 for stock. [D; GL, Sun MS vol. 481 ref. 968089]

Sharp, Peter, Liverpool, carver and gilder (1813–27). In 1813 at 42 Copperas Hill with a shop at 78 Bold St. Later addresses are given as 36 Copperas Hill in 1816; 88 Brownlow Hill in 1821; 79 Sparling St in 1823; 3 Elliott St in 1824; 5 and 10 Elliot St in 1827. [D]

Sharp, Peter, Bold St, Liverpool, u, cm and modeller (1817). Named in insolvency proceedings in January 1817. At first named with two partners, William May and Isabella Wilson, but subsequently only Sharp and May are mentioned. Their stock was sold for the benefit of their creditors in two sales on 20 January and the days following and the residue on 27 February. The earlier of the two sales contained 'a large assortment of modern Paper Hangings with rich flock borders, London Chintz Furnitures, Trimmings, Brussels & Kidderminster Carpets, Oil Cloths, several sets of Drawing-room Chairs, Couches, Cabinets, Sofa, Card & Pembroke Tables, in a variety of fancy woods, excellent Mahogany articles, in a set of Patent Dining Tables, Wardrobes, Drawers, Secretaire & Chairs, Looking Glasses, Bronzed & Gilt Busts, Lamps & various ornaments etc.'. A stock of materials was also offered consisting of 'Choice Mahogany in Veneers, Boards & Planks, Tulip & Rose Wood, a large assortment of modern Brass Work, Plate Glass, Lathe, Benches etc.'. The remaining stock offered on 27 February was of a similar nature, but specially featured was 'a large sized Four-post Bedstead, the feet parts & cornice richly carved & brilliantly ornamented in burnished gold'. [*Liverpool Mercury*, 10 and 17 January, 21 February 1817]

Sharp, Peter jnr, 4 Lime St with shop at Mitchell Pl., Ranelagh St, Liverpool, carver (1829). [D]

Sharp, Richard, 44 Leadenhall St, London, carver, gilder and picture frame maker (1776). Copies of his trade card featuring classical figures exist. [V&A Print Dept, Banks Coll., BM and GL] This card was engraved by William Sharpe (1749–1824). Richard Sharp was a freemen of London and a member of the Loriners' Co. He took out a licence to employ one non-freeman for three months and eight non-freemen for six weeks in 1776. [GL, City Licence bks, vol. 9]

Sharp, Samuel snr and jnr, Norwich, chairmakers (1737–61). Samuel Sharp snr was free on 24 February 1737, but had not undertaken an apprenticeship in the city. His son Samuel, was however formally bound app. to him and was declared free on 3 May 1757. Samuel Sharp snr probably died 1761. A chair stamped 'S. SHARP NORWICH' is in the V&A. [Freemen rolls; Kirk, *American Chairs*, pp. 145 and 190]

Sharp, Samuel, Park St, Worksop, Notts., chairmaker and turner (1832). [D]

Sharp, Samuel, South St, Chesterfield, Derbs., chairmaker (1833). [D]

Sharp, Thomas, Tull St, Nottingham, cm (1835). [D]

Sharp, William, Pottergate St, Norwich, cm (1784–90). [D; poll bks]

Sharp, William, Burgate St, Canterbury, Kent, cm and broker (1800–39). Free 1800. [D; poll bks; freemen rolls]

Sharp, William, Stone Chair Shelf, Rishworth, Yorks., joiner and cm (1837). [D]

Sharp & Redshaw, address unknown, u (1716). Paid 19s in July 1716 by the Earl of Rockingham for three bedsteads etc. [Lincoln RO, Monson 10 A/1]

Sharpe, —, 56 Cornhill, London, manufacturer of portable writing desks, dressing cases, cutlery, pocket books and toys (1804). Took out insurance cover for £1,200 on 1 October 1804. [GL, Sun MS vol. 430, ref. 767154]

Sharpe, C., St John's Lane, Cambridge, frame maker (c.1760). Trade label is in the Johnson Coll., Bodleian Lib., Oxford. A Christopher Sharpe is recorded as a carpenter and joiner at Trinity College in 1766; a Christopher Sharpe, turner, is noted in Cambridge, 1797; and a Charles Sharpe, turner in 1792. [D; Cambridge Univ. Lib., AR3:119]

Sharpe, Frederick George, Nottingham, joiner and cm (1836). In 1836 took as app. William Dyson. [App. reg.]

Sharpe, John, address unknown, cm and chairmaker (1665–66). Recorded in the account books of the Countess of Rockingham. On 19 December 1665 he was paid £1 2s 6d for a chest of drawers 'for my Lord' and on 19 May 1666, £3 6s for sixteen turned chair frames. [Lincoln RO, Monson 10 1/A/18]

Sharpe, John, School Lane, Liverpool, cm. Free 11 June 1764 or 1767. Died between 1818 and 1820. [D; freemen reg.]

Sharpe, John, London(?), cm (1772). Signatory to *The Real State of the Complaints of the CABINET MAKERS as published and signed by their Committee*. [Gents Mag., June 1772]

Sharpe, John, Bath St, Birmingham, cm and chairmaker (1818–22). [D]

Sharpe, John, Straight, Lincoln, carver and gilder (1828–35). [D]

Sharpe, Joseph, Blind Middle St, Gt Yarmouth, Norfolk, cm, u and ironmonger (1783–98). In 1783 insured a house for £100 and on 16 November 1786 household goods, utensils, a workshop and thirteen other properties leased to various traders for £1,300. [D; poll bk; GL, Sun MS vol. 306, p. 565; vol. 341, p. 231]

Sharpe, Joseph, Clements Lane, London, chairmaker (1808–09). In 1808 at 27 Clements Lane but in the following year, when he took out insurance cover of £200, the number was 47. The policy dated 18 July 1809 covered his household goods in the main, only £50 of cover being allocated to stock and utensils. [D; GL, Sun MS vol. 448]

Sharpe, Nathaniel, Oakham, Rutlandshire, cm (1755). In 1755 took app. named Goodall. [S of G, app. index]

Sharpe, Samuel, London, upholder (1720–21). In 1720 at 'The Thistle & Crown', near Fleet Bridge; but in 1721, when he served as a Sidesman for the parish of St Bride's, the address was Salisbury Ct. [GL, Sun MS vol. 12, ref. 18746; MS. 6561, p. 30]

Sharpe, Thomas, Cambridge, cm and u (1805–32). Married on 7 June 1808 when he was living in Petty Cury. Admitted freeman on 7 October 1818, and on 5 March 1819 took his relative Thomas Edward Sharpe as app. On 27 April 1820 took as app. Edward Richardson at a premium of £29 18s. In 1824 at Market St. Probably died in 1832. [D; *Cambridge Chronicle*, 8 June 1805; freemen rolls; app. list; Univ. Lib., WR19:457]

Sharpe, Thomas Edward, Cambridge, cm and u (1827). App. to his relative Thomas Sharpe on 5 March 1819 and free in 1827. [Freemen rolls]

Sharpe, Thomas, Crompton St, Warwick, cm (1831). [Poll bk]

Sharples, George, Liverpool, u (1818–39). At 10 Marlborough St in 1818 but from 1827–29 the number was 17. By 1837 had moved to 14 Lawrence St, and in 1839 his addresses were 40 Lawrence St and 7 Virgil St. [D] See William Sharples of 14 Lawrence St.

Sharples, James, Poulton St, Kirkham, Lancs., joiner and cm (1824–34). [D]

Sharples, James, 19 Worsley St, London Rd, Manchester, cm (1825). [D]

Sharples, John, Liverpool, cm (1805–27). In 1805 at Haymarket, but by 1827 had moved to 5 St John's Rd. [D]

Sharples, John, Shire Brow, Blackburn, Lancs., cm (1824). [D]

Sharples, Richard, Lancaster and Liverpool, joiner and cm (1765–80). App. to W. Ball in 1765 and free, 1779–80. By this period had moved to Liverpool. [App. reg.; freemen rolls]

Sharples, Robert, Lancaster (1835–40). [Westminster Ref. Lib., Gillow records]

Sharples, Thomas, Liverpool, cm and u (1804–34). The business is first recorded as a partnership with a person named Rainford, 1804–05. They traded from 4 Haymarket and advertised themselves as cabinet and bedstead manufacturers. Sharples & Rainford stated that they were successors to Edward Rimmington, and on 8 February 1804 indicated that Joseph Bennett, cm and u formerly of Dale St, had transferred the goodwill of his business to them when he retired from trading. On 7 May 1805 Thomas Sharples married Miss Blackburn of Lancaster at St Peter's Church, and by May 1809 was trading on his own behalf from the Haymarket address. From these premises he was able to offer 'a fashionable assortment of Cabinet Furniture, Chairs, Bedsteads, Looking Glasses etc. etc. of all sizes & descriptions'. He remained at the Haymarket address until 1821, and from 1813 additional premises were used at 79 Fontenoy St described initially as a timber yard. In December 1821 he announced a move to 8 Queen's Sq. which he continued to occupy until 1834. These new premises, described as a 'Cabinet & Upholstery Warehouse' could also be entered from St John's Lane. They were said to have spacious rooms 'with a choice assortment of Household Furniture'. He also sold 'Venetian Shade Blinds, Paper Hangings, Mattresses etc.'. The Fontenoy St address was retained but now called a manufactory. The number was however to change to 96 in 1821–29, and 89 in 1834. One directory of 1827 records 49 Fontenoy St. [D; *Liverpool Chronicle*, 22 February 1804, 22 May 1805, 24 May 1809; *Liverpool Mercury*, 14 December 1821]

Sharples, William, 14 Lawrence St, Liverpool, u (1835). [D] See George Sharples at this address.

Sharrat, Samuel, Liverpool, cm (1818). App. to Edward Belshaw 1803 and petitioned freedom in 1818. [Freemen's committee bk]

Sharren, Robert, Sidling, near Dorchester, Dorset, cm (1790). In December 1790 insured his house for £200. [GL, Sun MS ref. 577527]

Sharrock, George, Liverpool, joiner and cm (1742–62). Freeman of Preston, Lancs. In 1742 listed in the burgess roll together with his son John, who was a joiner. Both men are similarly mentioned in 1762, with the additional information

that George Sharrock had a brother named Thomas of Newborough who was by this date dead. [Preston Guild record of burgesses]

Sharrock, James, 49 London Rd, Manchester, cm and broker (1816). [D]

Sharwood, James, Norwich, cm (1825). App. to W. E. Earle and free, 21 September 1825. [Freemen reg.]

Shatford, Daniel, 83 Tottenham Ct Rd, London, cm and u (1839). [D]

Shatford, Samuel, Long Acre, London, cm (1747–55). In 1747 took as app. Anthony Chivers at a premium of £14 14s. In 1754 subscribed to Chippendale's *Director*. [Poll bk]

Shave, Philip, Long Wyre St, Colchester, Essex, cm and u (1826–39). [D]

Shaw, Daniel, 23 North St, Bristol, cm (1827). [D]

Shaw, Francis J., 84 Dorset St, Salisbury Sq., London, upholder (1801). Son of John Shaw of Clements Inn, Gent. App. to William Chivers and then to John Hux, a member of the Clothworkers' Co., on 3 July 1799. Free of the Upholders' Co. by servitude, 2 December 1801. [GL, Upholders' Co. records]

Shaw, J., 110 Goswell St, London, cm and blind manufacturer (1820). [D]

Shaw, James, London, cm (1793). Subscribed to Sheraton's *Drawing Book*, 1793.

Shaw, James, Liverpool, cm (1809–21). On 15 February 1809 married Miss Mary Owen at Trinity Church. At this date his address was St James's St. By 1810 trading at 2 Frederick St, St James's and from 1811, at no. 6. From 1813–16 the addresses used were 105 St James St with a yard at 6 St James St. In 1821 the address was 118 St James St. [D; *Liverpool Courier*, 16 February 1809]

Shaw, James, Beverley, Yorks., cm and u (1814–18). Recorded at Norwood in 1814 and Toll Gravel in 1818. [D]

Shaw, James, 13 Clifton St, Finsbury, London, cm and u (1822). [D]

Shaw, James, 15 Nevile St, Leeds, Yorks., cm and joiner (1837). [D]

Shaw, James, 12 Wish St, Portsea, Portsmouth, Hants., carver and gilder (1839). [D]

Shaw, James, Lancaster, cm (1791–99). App. to Isaac Greenwood in 1791 and free, 1798–99. Named in the Gillow records. [App. reg.; freemen rolls; Westminster Ref. Lib., Gillow]

Shaw, John, Chester, u (1814–40). Free on 18 September 1818, but by that date had been trading in the city for a number of years. At Bridge St Row, 1814–16; Whitefriars, 1818–26; and Foregate St, 1834–40. [D; freemen rolls]

Shaw, John, 2 Peterborough Ct, Fleet St, London, cm and u (1820–29). The value of the utensils and stock kept at his workshops at Peterborough Ct was £300 in July 1820, £350 in September 1821 and £1,050 in August 1823. The latter figure would indicate a business of some size. The addresses of his dwelling houses were 13 Noble St, Goswell St in July 1820; 22 Dean St, Fetter Lane in September 1821; and 9 Thomas St, Gibson St, Lambeth in August 1823. [D; GL, Sun MS vol. 485, ref. 968819; vol. 487, ref. 983628; vol. 497, ref. 1008009]

Shaw, John, Retford, Notts., cm and u (1819–29). From 1819–22 at Carolgate and in 1829 at Clumber St. [D]

Shaw, John snr, Framwellgate, Durham, cm and joiner (1828–d.1831). In partnership with James Mann. By April 1831 John Shaw snr was dead and the business was carried on by his widow, Mary Shaw. James Mann was no longer involved. [D; *Durham Advertiser*, 29 April 1831]

Shaw, John jnr, Framwellgate, Durham, cm and joiner (1835). Son of John snr and Mary Shaw. John Shaw snr died in 1831 and the business was then conducted by his mother until 1835 when it was handed over to John jnr. [*Durham Advertiser*, 20 February 1835]

Shaw, John, Ivory St, Leeds, Yorks., cm (1837). [D]

Shaw, Joseph, Salterhebble, near Halifax, Yorks., joiner and cm (1822). [D]

Shaw, Joseph, Kirkburton, near Huddersfield, Yorks., joiner/cm (1834). [D]

Shaw, Joseph, 12 Wish St, Southsea, Hants., carver and gilder (1839). [D]

Shaw, Mary, Framwellgate, Durham, joiner and cm (1831–35). Wife of John Shaw snr and mother of John Shaw jnr. Her husband was in partnership with a James Mann but this ended in 1831 with the death of John Shaw snr. His widow carried on the business and advertised in April 1831 that she had 'engaged steady workmen'. She appealed to her husband's former customers for support so that she could maintain herself and 'six helpless children'. The premises were said to adjoin the Artichoke public house. In 1835 Mary Shaw retired leaving the business in the hands of her son, John Shaw jnr. [D; *Durham Advertiser*, 29 April 1831, 20 February 1835]

Shaw, Nicholas, Whitechapel, Liverpool, u (b.1773–d.1806). Directories of 1805 show him variously at 48 and 38 Whitechapel. Died in April 1806 aged 33. [D; *Liverpool Chronicle*, 23 April 1806]

Shaw, Richard, Ashby-de-la-Zouch, Leics. and Burton-on-Trent, Staffs., cm and u (1797–1829). In February 1797 announced that in addition to his business in Ashby he was also commencing trading at Burton. In 1829 his address in Ashby was given as Market St. [D: *Leicester Journal*, 24 February 1797]

Shaw, Robert, Woburn, Beds., cm (1752–58). Thirteen accounts rendered by Shaw to John 4th Duke of Bedford exist. Nearly all are for altering or mending furniture at Woburn, but he also provided dressing-tables, tea tables, Windsor chairs and frames for both mirrors and pictures. Items supplied in 1754 for instance included a cedar tea table at £1 9s and a large picture frame at £12 10s. He also gilded 15½ feet of moulding for 11s 7½d. In 1757 he worked on furniture 'in the Temple in the Evergreen'. Thomas Shaw, who undertook work at Woburn and other commissions for the Dukes of Bedford and the family from 1757, was probably his son. [Bedford Office, London; *Apollo*, January 1956, p. 9]

Shaw, Sophia, Bedford Row, Streatham, London, cm and u (1839). [D] Possibly widow of John F. Shawe.

Shaw, Thomas, Woburn, Beds., joiner, u and cm (1757–1802). He passed his whole career of forty-five years as joiner, u and cm in the service of the Dukes of Bedford. He was born about 1740 and may have been the son of Robert Shaw, cm of Woburn. He began work in 1757 and, it seems, succeeded to the business of Robert Shaw a year later. There is evidence that the Shaws were substantial householders in Woburn for Thomas became an Overseer of the Poor in the parish in 1765. In 1772 he married Ann Norton and bought a house in Woburn. He died about May 1803 in which month his widow rendered his final account to the 6th Duke of Bedford. His place as resident furniture-maker/u was taken by Andrew Gardner.

Thomas Shaw's career may be followed in the one hundred and seventy existing accounts rendered from 1758 to 1803 to the 4th, 5th and 6th Dukes of Bedford and to Duchess Gertrude, widow of the fourth Duke. In these he is described as joiner during his early career, but from about 1770 almost invariably as cm or u. His work was mainly in the repair of furniture and fittings such as floors, windows and blinds, but he also made a good deal of furniture for servants' rooms, for stables and grooms' quarters and for the gardens. He worked mainly at Woburn Abbey but also at houses, churches and farms belonging to the family in Bedfordshire; and in London for Duchess Gertrude at her house in Pall Mall. But the chief interest of the accounts lies in the evidence they give of the furnishing and development of Woburn Abbey under the supervision, successively, of Henry Flitcroft (1747–61), William Chambers (1767–72) and Henry Holland (1787–1802), for which see G. Scott Thomson, *Family Background*, 1949, chapter 1 and G. Blakiston, *Woburn and the Russells*, 1980.

The following are examples of Shaw's work at Woburn:

January 1762: Work and materials to 4 pedestals in the gallery and setting the figures up, £4 6s 4d.

November 1763: Taking up the floor in her Grace's bedchamber to make way for the water closet; many visits about the w.c. and general repair work, £4 13s 10½d.

May 1765: For an arbour in the Grotto Garden and for drawing two designs of arbours, £22 7s.

May 1766: To 8 Windsor stool chairs for the Temple in the garden, 4s 6d a chair ... a new circular Gothic seat for the arbour in the Privy Garden, £5 15s 6d.

April 1769: To a 2 in. wainscot sash door to the new water closet in the Privy Garden, and for the seat and counter seat, £4 15s 5½d.

1768–1771: For general joiner's work, under the direction of William Chambers, in the old building and out-office and in the newly built south wing, £876.

[Executorship account of the fourth Duke of Bedford]

Among work carried out by Shaw 'by order of Henry Holland' the following may be noted:

April–August 1789: For furniture for the grooms' new appartments and for the stables, £49 8s 6d.

December 1791–November 1792: For the tennis court: four sofas covered in brown holland, and window blinds; for the new library: blinds and papering shelves, £128 13s 6d.

June–December 1792: For furniture, bedsteads and upholstery for servants' rooms; and Scotch carpet for the W.C. and the Duke's dressing room in the tennis court, £543 9s 5½d.

December 1792–December 1793: For making and fitting mahogany folding blinds lined with green silk for the drawing-room; mending blinds for tennis court; ten window curtains for the tennis court to draw up into festoons, £102 19s 6d.

April–June 1800: Six low bow-back yew chairs to the sheep shearing house, £3 12s. [Bedford Office, London]

Shaw, Thomas, Carlogate, Retford, Notts., cm (1830–35). [D]

Shaw, Thomas, Eccleston, near St Helens, Lancs., joiner and cm (1834). [D]

Shaw, Thomas, 53 Fontenoy St, Liverpool, u (1837. [D]

Shaw, W. B., 20 New St, Birmingham, carver, gilder, cm and mahogany looking-glass frame maker (1803–08). [D]

Shaw, Waltham, Hall St, Spalding, Lincs., cm and u (1835). [D]

Shaw William, Rose St, Westminster, London, cm (1784). [Poll bk]

Shaw, William, 7 Charlotte St, St George's Rd, Southwark, London, upholder (1786). In August 1786 took out insurance cover for £600. Although his house was valued at £350 only £50 was provided for utensils etc. [GL, Sun MS vol. 339, p. 275]

Shaw, William, 11 George's Ct, Clerkenwell, London, cm (1793). Subscribed to Sheraton's *Drawing Book*, 1793.

Shaw, William, Kirkgate, Wakefield, Yorks., u (1805). [D]

Shaw, William, Foulston, near Huddersfield, Yorks., cm (1822). [D]

Shaw, William, Brook Side, Derby, u and cm (1818–23). [D]

Shaw, William, Manvers St, Tuxford, Notts., joiner, cm and looking-glass dealer (1832). [D]

Shaw, William, 1 Castle St, Long Acre, London, u and furniture broker (1835–39). Listed as a furniture broker in 1835 and an u in 1839. [D]

Shaw, William Henry, Norwich, cm (1830). Son of Henry Shaw, tailor. Free 31 July 1830. [Freemen admission reg.]

Shaw & Son, 34 Hatton St, London, u and cm (1802–04). [D]

Shawe, John, Lancaster and London, cm (1783–84). Free 1783–84, but by then he had moved to London and was living in the parish of St Giles-in-the-Fields. [Freemen rolls]

Shawe, John F., Streatham, London, cm, u, auctioneer and appraiser (1832). In 1839 Sophia Shaw was trading at Bedford Row, Streatham as a cm and u and might be his widow. [D]

Shayler, James, Manchester, u (1781–1811). At Cannon St in 1781 and from 1784–88 shown as 43 Cannon St. At 58 Market St, 1794–1811. [D]

Shearcroft, Robert snr, Colchester, Essex, chairmaker (1689). Probate granted on his will at Chelmsford in 1689. [Wills at Chelmsford]

Sheard, Jaxton & Co., address unknown, upholders (1731). In 1731 paid £18 4s 6d in connection with a commission at Stowe, Bucks. [Huntington Lib., California, MS ST82, p. 33] Possibly Sherrard & Paxton.

Shearer, Thomas, London (1788). Signed seventeen of the twenty plates in *The Cabinet-Makers' London Book of Prices*, published by the London Society of Cabinet Makers in 1788. This volume was a practical manual containing tables of prices to help masters and journeymen calculate the cost of labour in making various representative items of furniture (excluding chairs, carved work and upholstered pieces). The plates, which illustrate objects described in the text, are in a fluent style that bridges the short interval between Hepplewhite's *Guide* and Sheraton's *Drawing Book*. Since the *Book of Prices* was widely used on the workbench, furniture corresponding, often exactly to Shearer's elegant designs, is relatively common. It is likely that he was a journeyman cm rather than a professional designer. It may be relevant that an insurance policy taken out on 19 May 1790 by J. H. Sherwood of 75 Aldersgate St, London [GL, Sun MS ref. 569755] included cover on a dwelling house in 'Little Bartholomew Close' and £100 for stock in the house of Shearer, cabinet maker 'in the said Close'. [R. Fastnedge, *Shearer Furniture Designs from the Cabinet-Makers' London Book of Prices 1788*, 1962; *Conn.*, June 1961, pp. 30–33; *Furn. Hist.*, 1966 and 1982]　　　　　C.G.G.

Shearing, —, High St, Brighton, Sussex, cm (1805). [D]

Shearing, —, Limekiln Lane, Bristol, carver (1833). [D]

Shearman, George, Ipswich, Suffolk and London, cm (1830–31). Freeman of Colchester, Essex but living in Ipswich in 1830 and London by March 1831. [Colchester poll bks]

Shearman, James, 17 Church St, Shoreditch, London, turner and cm (1817). [D]

Shearman, John jnr, Queen St, Market Rasen, Lincs., joiner and cm (1826). [D]

Shearman, Jno., 20 Rawstone St, Goswell St, London, cm and u (1839). [D]

Shears, Ambrose, 6 St George's Cresc., Southwark, London, cm and u (1808). [D]

Shearwood, Paul, Strop Hill, Knottingley, near Ferrybridge, Yorks., cm (1822). [D]

Sheen, Edmund Henry, Norwich and Gt Yarmouth, Norfolk, upholder (1818–30). App. to Charles Martin and free by servitude 20 June 1818. By July 1830 living in Gt Yarmouth. [Freemen admission reg.; Norwich poll bk]

Sheen, James, Newcastle (?), u (1734). On 18 September 1734 paid £26 13s 6d for upholsterer's work in connection with beds and bedding at Gibside, Co. Durham. [Durham RO, Strathmore MS, D/St/v.986]

Sheen, Thomas, Newcastle, u, appraiser and auctioneer (1759–98). In 1759 took app. named Graham. On 1 June 1776 sold the stock in trade of John Reed. Announced on 5 February 1780 his move from Cutter's Entry 'to a house facing the Javel Group, in the Close'. Here he sold both new and second-hand furniture and made Venetian blinds. He also offered for sale 'A large assortment of Men and Boys Beaver and Cloth Hats, Gold and Silver Lace, to be sold greatly under prime cost'. [D, S of G, app. index; *Newcastle Courant*, 1 June 1776, 5 February 1780]

Sheen, William, Tarporley, Cheshire, cm (1828). [D]

Sheers, —, Bond St, London, cm (1718). In 1718 paid £18 for tables, bedsteads, coarse chairs, stool boxes, a chest of drawers etc. supplied to the Duke of Montrose's house in Bond St, London. [Scottish RO, GD 220/6/28/P84]

Sheerwood, —, Newcastle, cm (1793). Subscribed to Sheraton's *Drawing Book*, 1793.

Sheerwood, H. J., 42 Little Bartholomew Close, London, cm (1808–19). [D]

Sheetcliff, Jn, 13 Mitchell St, St Luke's, London, cm and u (1822–27). [D]

Sheffery, George F., Durham, u (1793). [D]

Sheffield, James, Timber Hill, Melton Mowbray, Leics., cm (1835). [D]

Sheffrey, W., 184 Fleet St, London, upholder (c.1790). [Heal]

Sheldon, —, King St, Golden Sq., London, cm (1748). On 5 November 1748 knocked down and robbed by 'three fellows in sailors' habits' near Golden Sq. [*London Evening Post*, 5–8 November 1748]

Sheldon & Benton, New Church St, Birmingham, cabinet case makers (1839). [D]

Shelley, Thomas, 174 High St, Lewes, Sussex, carver, gilder and picture dealer (1823). [D]

Shellye, John, parish of St Nicholas, Colchester, Essex, chairmaker (1660). Probate granted in 1660 at Chelmsford. [*Wills at Chelmsford*]

Shelton, Humphrey, London, upholder (1699–1702). Paid £187 for work at the Royal Hospital, Chelsea, 1699–1702. [*Wren Soc.*, vol. XIX, p. 83]

Shelton, John, Nottingham, joiner and cm (1781–99). Took as apps Jo. Killingley (1781), Samuel Webb (1783), Thomas Hazzard (1786), William Simpson (1789), Thomas Walker (1792) and John Henshaw (1796). In 1782 insured his house for £150. By 1784 had entered a partnership with John Eley and in July of that year advertised for craftsmen. Insurance cover in April 1786 amounted to £600 and of this £120 was for stock and utensils at Friar Lane and £420 for stock in a yard, probably timber. The partnership of Shelton & Eley were one of the makers who endorsed the *Nottingham Cabinet and Chair Makers' Book of Prices*, 1791, and subscribed to Sheraton's *Drawing Book*, 1793. By the late 1790s the partnership appears to have ended and John Shelton is shown trading on his own behalf from Friar Lane, 1798–99. [D; app. bk; GL, Sun MS vol. 302, p. 65; vol. 336, p. 329; *Nottingham Journal*, 31 July 1784]

Shelton, Joseph, St Martin-in-the-Fields, London, chairmaker and cm (1729–49). On 13 January 1728/29 took out insurance cover of £300 on his household goods and trade stock at his house in Hungerford Mkt which bore the sign of 'The Chair & Sash'. By June 1740 he was trading at the sign of the 'Hand and Hall Chair', Hungerford Mkt. Here he acted as an undertaker and sworn appraiser as well as making and selling 'Chair Cabinet & Glass Work, Carpenters & Joyner's Work'. His trade bill in the Scottish RO was used for an invoice dated 24 June 1740 in respect of goods supplied to the

Duke of Gordon. The items were of a minor nature such as lifting handles, screws, hinges and castors, and only amounted to £1 1s. Another bill dated 14 June 1740 for similar items totalled £1 3s 6d. His address was given as York Buildings, St Martin-in-the-Fields in 1746 and Villers St, Strand in 1749. [GL, Sun MS vol. 27, ref. 46678; Scottish RO, GD44/51/465/1/46–47; Marylebone Lib., deed 69/27; Westminster poll bk]

Shelton, Robert, High St, Bedford, carver and gilder (1830–39). Recorded also at Silver St in 1839. [D]

Shelton, Thomas, York, cm (1834). [D]

Shelton, William, Bromsgrove St, Birmingham, chairmaker (1818). [D]

Shemeld, Charles, Charles St, Sheffield, Yorks., cm (1821). [D]

Shenfield, John, Heigham, Norwich, chairmaker (1830). [Poll bk]

Shennan, William, address unknown, cm (1775). In 1775 invoiced to Sir John Griffin Griffin of Audley End, Essex a 'Mahogany oister table' which was charged at £1 19s. [Essex RO, D/DBy/A33/10]

Shenstone, William, Spiceal St, Birmingham, chairmaker (1793–1800). [D] Probably William Shenton.

Shenton, John, London, chairmaker (1779–94). In 1779 at 11 Meards Ct, Dean St which he insured for £100. He moved from this house and was at 27 Wardour St Soho in 1789. He was still at this address in 1793–94 but was then in partnership with William Smith. [D; GL, Sun MS vol. 273, p. 96; Heal]

Shenton, Matthew, near New Rd, The Potteries, Staffs., cm (1818). [D]

Shenton, William, Birmingham, chairmaker (1808–22). Recorded at Spiceall St in 1808 as a fancy and dyed chairmaker; and at Bromsgrove St, 1816–22. [D] Probably William Shenstone.

Sheperd, Jesse, Churchfields, Greenwich, London, cm, upholder and broker (1783). Took out insurance cover of £600 in 1783 and of this £550 was for utensils and stock. [GL, Sun MS vol. 314, p. 504]

Shephard, Thomas, parish of St Oswald, Durham, u (d.1700). Burial registered on 2 April 1700. [PR (burial)]

Shephard, William I, London, upholder (1707–d.1733). Father of William Shephard II. Free of the Upholders' Co. on 3 December 1707. Took apps as early as November 1712. His known apps are William Solby (1719–26), Joseph Mander (1719/20) and Henry Weedon (1726–1733/34). The location of his premises in Leadenhall St is variously described. One insurance policy of 1715 gives it as the west side of the street 'over against Crown Tavern' and another of 1717 at the sign of 'The Unicorn'. A third one, however, locates the business on the north side of the street against 'The Crown Tavern'. At the time of his death in 1733 he was at 'The Rising Sun' in Mark Lane. [GL, Upholders' Co. records; Hand in Hand MS vol. 14, p. 742; vol. 26, p. 64; Sun MS vol. 7, 5 December 1717; Heal; S of G, app. index]

Shephard, William II, Lambeth St (?), London, upholder (1738). Son of William Shephard I. Free of the Upholders' Co. by patrimony, 4 October 1738. Probably the father of William Shephard III. May possibly have been the cm and u who in January 1775 was trading from an address near the church in Whitechapel and who insured his utensils and stock for £200. [GL, Upholders' Co. records; Sun MS vol. 235, p. 622]

Shephard, William III, 61 Barbican, London, upholder (1781). Son of William Shephard whose address was Lambeth St and was possibly William Shephard II. William Shephard III was free of the Upholders' Co. by patrimony, 7 March 1781. [GL, Upholders' Co. records]

Shepheard, —, 1 Sion Cottages, Church St, Brighton, Sussex, cm (1822). [D]

Shepherd, —, London, carver (1774). On 21 December 1774 Ralph Yates, a carpenter of Clerkenwell Close, insured a house in the tenure of Shepherd, carver for £80. [GL, Sun MS vol. 235, ref. 347657]

Shepherd, —, next door to 'The Three Tuns Tavern', West Smithfield, London, u (1746). [Heal]

Shepherd, —, Taunton, Som., cm (1829). Daughter married in 1829. [*Exeter Flying Post*, 16 April 1829]

Shepherd, Beachcroft, 4 Chandos St, Covent Gdn, London, upholder and cm (1793–1816). Subscribed to Sheraton's *Drawing Book*, 1793. By 1800 at 4 Chandos St where he took out insurance cover for £1,600 of which £980 was for utensils and stock. The business remained at this address until 1816. [D; GL, Sun MS vol. 419, ref. 709511] See Hannah Fleming at the same address.

Shepherd, George, Church St, Greenwich, London, cm (1774). On 29 December 1774 insured his household goods and clothes for £200. [GL, Sun MS vol. 235, ref. 348032]

Shepherd, George, 75 Maid Lane, Southwark, London, cm and upholder (1787). On 23 February 1787 insured goods for £100. In 1793 a George Shepherd subscribed to Sheraton's *Drawing Book*. [GL, Sun MS vol. 343, p. 166]

Shepherd, Henry, Meadow St, St Paul's, Bristol, cm (1824–26). [D]

Shepherd, I. and/or J., Orchard St, Southampton, Hants., cm (1834–39). [D]

Shepherd, Isaac, Orchard St, Southampton, Hants., cm and chairmaker (1839). [D]

Shepherd, Jacob, Twisden, Goudhurst, Kent, upholder (1802). Son of John Shepherd of York Pl., Walworth, London, freeman and member of the Upholders' Co. Jacob Shepherd was free of the Upholders' Co. by patrimony, 7 July 1802. [GL, Upholders' Co. records]

Shepherd, John, London, upholder (1722–49). Son of Charles Shepherd of Inkleton, Cambs., yeoman. App. to Richard Farmer on 3 October 1722 and Thomas Nash, freeman and member of the Skinners' Co., 3 February 1724. John Shepherd was free of the Upholders' Co. by servitude, 11 November 1730. He took as app. Charles Westwood, 1738–49. [GL, Upholders' Co. records]

Shepherd, John, 69 Leadenhall St, London, upholder (1770–1802). Son of Richard Shepherd of Maidstone, dealer, and father of Jacob Shepherd who in his turn was a member of the Upholders' Co. John Shepherd was admitted a member of the Upholders' Co., 5 December 1770 under the terms of the Upholders' Act of 1750. By 1775 he was trading from the Leadenhall St address as an upholder and auctioneer. He is recorded here until 1785 but appears in no directories after this date and may have retired from the business. In 1794 he was living at Savile Row, Walworth and in 1802, when he was made Master of the Upholders' Co., he was at York Pl., Walworth. [D; GL, Upholders' Co. records]

Shepherd, John, Haymarket, Sheffield, Yorks., chairmaker and u (1821–37). Probably the son of Malin Shepherd to whom he was successor. In 1837 at 17 Haymarket. [D]

Shepherd, John, Bridgegate, Howden, Yorks., cm and u (1823–28). [D]

Shepherd, John, Hull, Yorks., cm (1823–39). At 10 Roper's Row in 1823 and 1 William's Sq., Upper Union St, 1838–39. [D]

Shepherd, John jnr, Helmsley, Yorks., joiner and cm (1828–40). [D]

Shepherd, Joseph, Bridge St, Chester, cm (1814–16). Listed at Lower Bridge St in 1816. [D]

Shepherd, Malin & Son, Haymarket, Sheffield, Yorks.,

chairmaker (1797–1825). Recorded at 17 Haymarket in 1825. The son was probably John Shepherd who carried on the business in Haymarket. Produced turned chairs and dealt in hardware and household furniture. [D]

Shepherd, Richard, St Clement's, Oxford, cm (1757–d. by 1765). Took apps named Grimshaw in 1757 and Seabright in 1760. In April 1758 advertised that he had a model of a newly devised sash window invented by John Baynes of London, carpenter. In January 1760 advertised for a journeyman. By October 1765 he was dead and Richard Powell, who had been his foreman for a number of years, took over the business from Richard Shepherd's widow Mary. [S of G, app. index; *Jackson's Oxford Journal*, 8 April 1758, 26 January 1760, 14 July 1764, 12 October 1765]

Shepherd, Thomas, Upton, Worcs., chairmaker (1728). In 1728 took app. named Baker. [S of G, app. index]

Shepherd, Thomas, London, cm (1793). Subscribed to Sheraton's *Drawing Book*, 1793.

Shepherd, Thomas, 29 Ormond St, Liverpool, cm and victualler (1821–35). [D]

Shepherd, Thomas Walter, 15 Mason St, Toxteth Park, Liverpool, cm (1822–30). App. to Thomas Croft Huxley in 1822 and petitioned freedom in 1828. Sworn free, 15 November 1830. [Freemen's committee bk; freemen reg.]

Shepherd, Vincent, Alnwick, Northumb., cm and house carpenter (1793). [D]

Shepherd, William, parish of St Antholin, London, bed joiner (c.1710). App. in 1703 to James Denham, bed joiner for seven years and served his term. [GL, P91/LEN/1200/1]

Shepherd, William, Nottingham, joiner and cm (1730–46). Son of Richard Shepherd of Nottingham, carpenter. App. in 1730 and free in 1737. Took app. named Nathaniel Stephenson in 1744. Probate was granted on William Shepherd's will, 12 January 1745/46. [App. reg.; freemen rolls; Notts. RO, probate records]

Shepherd, William, 62 St John St, London, cm and coal dealer (1779). In 1779 took out insurance cover of £200, half of which was for untensils and stock. [GL, Sun MS vol. 270, p. 523]

Shepherd, William, Powis St, Woolwich, London, carver and gilder (1832). [D]

Shepherd & Janson, 11 Lee's Yd, Leeds, Yorks., cm, joiners and carpenters (1826). The Shepherd involved was probably Simpson Shepherd who in September 1807 advertised that he was lately the partner of Samuel Croft as a joiner and carpenter but was now carrying on the trades on his own behalf from premises in Mr Lee's yard, Meadow Lane. [D; *Leeds Mercury*, 12 September 1807]

Shepherdson, George, Middle St, Gt Driffield, Yorks., cm (1823–40). Also u in 1840. [D]

Shepley, William, Birstall, Yorks., joiner/cm (1837). [D]

Sheppard, H. M., Sheppard's Walk, Exmouth, Devon, cm and u (1838). [D]

Sheppard, John & Son, Sheffield, Yorks., chairmakers (1798). [D]

Sheppard, John, High St, Taunton, Som., cm and u (1822–39). [D]

Sheppard, John, Penkhull St, Newcastle-under-Lyme, Staffs., carver and gilder (1832–37). [Poll bks]

Sheppard, Richard, High St, Newcastle-under-Lyme, Staffs., carver, gilder and repository of arts (1835–36). Listed at 43 High St in 1836. [D]

Sheppard, Robert, New St, Wellington, Salop., chairmaker and turner (1840). [D]

Sheppard, T., London, chairmaker (1828). Craftsman employed by Morel & Seddon who signed the frame of a dining chair supplied to Windsor Castle in 1828. [Gilbert, *Leeds Furn. Cat.*, vol. 1, pp. 101–02]

Shepperd, Richard, 14 Broker Row, Moorfields, London, cabinet warehouse (1800). [D]

Shepperd, Richard, New St, Wellington, Salop, chairmaker (1835). [D]

Sherard, W., address unknown, u (1694). Recorded in the accounts for Drayton House, Northants. under the date 6 December 1694 as the supplier of upholstery materials and work to a value of £125 11s. [V&A archives]

Sheraton, N., London, cm (1793). Subscribed to Sheraton's *Drawing Book*, 1793.

Sheraton, Ninian John, New Radford, Nottingham, cm (1817–40). Free 1817. Took as apps William Cope (1819), Samuel Potter (1820) and Edward Stapleton (1820). Recorded also at Hyson Green, Nottingham in 1835. [D; freemen rolls; poll bk; app. reg.]

Sheraton, Ralph, Nottingham, turner, joiner, cm and u (1832–40). At Derby Rd, 1832–35 but by 1841 had moved to Fletchergate. Took as apps John Norman in 1833 and Cephas Dawson in 1840. [D; app. reg.]

Sheraton, Thomas, London (b.1751–d.1806) was the son of a schoolmaster, also named Thomas; he married Margaret Mitchinson at Norton, Co. Durham on 8 February 1779 and was buried in the churchyard of St James's Piccadilly on 27 October 1806. An obituary [*Gents Mag.*, November 1806] states that he was 'a native of Stockton-upon-Tees, and for many years a journeyman cm, but who, since about the year 1793, has supported himself, a wife, and two children, by his exertions as an author'. His early life is obscure, but he clearly received a sound practical training in the cabinet trade and in draughtsmanship; he was also a devout Baptist who published several religious tracts. In *A Scriptural Illustration of the Doctrine of Regeneration* (1782) he described himself as 'a mechanic, and one who never received the advantages of a *collegial* or *academical* education'. Later he confessed to 'Having possessed a strong attachment and inclination for carving, in my youth, I was necessarily induced to make attempts in this art, and was employed in the country occasionally in it'. [*Cabinet Dictionary*, p. 136] Two views of Stockton High St engraved after 'T. Sheraton' were published by a local bookseller in 1785 and 1794.

Although the term 'cabinet maker' occurs on the title page of Sheraton's first pattern book it is most unlikely that he ever owned a workshop, certainly after his move to London around 1790. A trade card [Heal Coll., BM] issued c.1796 announcing that: 'T. Sheraton / Teaches Perspective, Architecture and Ornaments, / makes Designs for Cabinet-makers / and sells all Kinds of Drawings, Books, &c...' gives a fair idea of the nature of his business. In 1791 Sheraton was at 4 Hart St; he is recorded at 41 Davies St in 1793 and in 1795 moved to 106 Wardour St. In 1800 he returned to Co. Durham where he was ordained a Baptist minister before coming back to take up residence at 8 Broad St in 1802. Adam Black, the publisher, who, as a young man, undertook some part time work for Sheraton, has left a description of his employer's dismal house and the following character sketch (1804): 'He is a man of talents, and, I believe, of genuine piety. He understands the cabinet business — I believe was bred to it, he has been, and perhaps at present is, a preacher; he is a scholar, writes well; draws, in my opinion masterly; is an author, bookseller, stationer and teacher.'

Sheraton is remembered today as the author of three pattern books. His distinguished and influential *Cabinet-Maker and Upholsterer's Drawing-Book* was published by subscription in fortnightly numbers, priced 1s between 1791–93, a slightly enlarged second edition appeared in 1794 and a third with trifling alterations in 1802. The subscribers were nearly all practicing tradesmen. The *Drawing-Book* was

Sheraton's finest achievement and has deservedly established his reputation as the foremost late 18th-century furniture designer. Many copies found their way to America and a German edition was published at Leipzig in 1794. Some of the designs were inspired by pieces which the author had seen in the shops of smart London cm, but their consistent character leaves no doubt that he was personally responsible for the majority, rather than merely reporting current London fashions. Sheraton's second furniture book *The Cabinet Dictionary*, 1803, contained 'an explanation of all the terms used in the Cabinet, chair and upholstery branches.' The 79 plates which support the text include designs in a progressive Regency style, while the alphabetically arranged entries provide a wealth of technical and general information about household furnishings and the cabinet trade.

In 1803 Sheraton started work on his last venture *The Cabinet-Maker, Upholsterer, and General Artist's Encyclopaedia*, to be published in 125 parts by subscription. It was a discursive rambling work displaying symptoms of the mental debility that preceded his death in 1806. Only 30 sections covering 'A — Capstan' appeared, supported by engravings of stylish furniture. The Furniture Library at High Point, N. Carolina possesses a unique 'temporary subscription list' for the *Encyclopaedia*, also a rare unbound copy of the *Drawing Book* in which the serial numbers retain their original blue wrappers printed with the prospectus and publishing conditions, plus various items of ephemera sent to subscribers. In 1812 eighty-four of Sheraton's plates were reissued by J. Taylor as a single folio volume titled *Designs for Household Furniture by the late Thomas Sheraton*.

A single manuscript design by Sheraton is extant — a pen and wash drawing for an ornate looking-glass dating from *c.*1790, now in the V&A. He designed several engraved trade cards and supplied a design for an impressive piano built by Messrs Broadwoods in 1796 for Don Manuel de Godoy to present to Queen Maria Louisa of Spain. This instrument is now at the Heritage Foundation, Deerfield, Mass. Although the *Drawing Book* was successful in disseminating sophisticated London taste, relatively few period pieces which exactly translate the engravings are known. A facsimile reprint issued by Batsford in 1895 helped to inspire a Sheraton revival which promoted a demand for slavish copies.

[R. Fastnedge, *Sheraton Furniture*; T. Sheraton, *The Cabinet Dictionary*, reprint ed. and introduction by W. P. Cole and C. F. Montgomery, 1970; T. Sheraton, *Drawing-Book*, reprint, introduction by L. O. J. Boynton, 1970; T. Sowler, 'Thomas Sheraton 1751–1806', *Cleveland and Teesside Local Hist. Soc. Bulletin*, Summer 1977, pp. 10–18]
C.G.G.

Sherborn, Charles, London, cm and u (1829–39). At 43 Leicester Sq. in 1829 and 9 Princes St and 52 Leicester Sq. in 1839. [D]

Shergold, John, High St, Winchester, Hants., turner and chairmaker (1823–30). Trading at no. 25 in 1830. [D]

Shergold, Thomas, Romsey, Hants., turner and chairmaker (1784–98). [D]

Shering, John, London, upholder (1709). Free of the Upholders' Co. on 1 June 1709. [GL, Upholders' Co. records]

Sherlock, George, Liverpool, carver, gilder and keeper of beer shop (1835–39). At 8 Norbury St in 1835, 32 Gloucester St in 1837 and 72 Gloucester St in 1839. [D]

Sherlock, John, 53 New Bird St, Liverpool, picture frame maker (1827–29). [D]

Sherman, —, address unknown, cm (1763). On 20 June 1763 paid £2 11s 6d by Nathaniel Ryder, 1st Lord Harrowby, in connection with Sandon Hall, Staffs. [Harrowbury MS Trust, Notebooks]

Sherman, Abraham & Tothill, John, 38 Allerton St, City Rd, London, cm (1811). In October 1811 took out insurance cover of £300 which included £50 for a workshop and £50 for the utensils and stock kept there. [GL, Sun MS vol. 457, ref. 862990]

Sherman, George, 18 Turner Sq., Hoxton Old Town, London, cm and u (1839). [D]

Sherman, John, London and Hungerford, Berks., upholder (1726–67). Son of Randall Sherman of Cricklade, Wilts., Gent. App. to Andrew Lenn on 14 September 1726 and free of the Upholders' Co. by servitude, 5 March 1734/35. Took as app. William Townsend, 1738–54. In October 1767 Sherman was excused office in the Upholders' Co. on the grounds of ill-health which forced him to retire to the country. From 1778–81 he is shown at Hungerford, Berks. [GL, Upholders' Co. records]

Shernin, Thomas, 67 Gt Queen St, Lincoln's Inn Fields, London, fancy cm and comb maker (1823). In January 1823 took out insurance cover of £800 which included £600 for utensils and stock both at his house and at a shop 62 Burlington Arcade, Piccadilly. [GL, Sun MS vol. 492, ref. 999781]

Sherrard & Co., address unknown, cm (*c.*1760). A bureau bookcase of *c.*1760 is recorded with a plaque on the back bearing the name Sherrard & Co. [*C. Life*, 13 April 1951, p. 1099]

Sherrard & Paxton, parish of St James, Westminster, upholders and broker (1740). Took out insurance cover of £300 in May 1740. [GL, Sun MS vol. 54, p. 481] Possibly Sheard, Jaxton & Co.

Sherratt, Charles, 2 Steelhouse Lane, Birmingham, cm, chairmaker and u (1828–30). [D]

Sherratt, James, 61 London Rd, Manchester, cm and broker (1817). [D]

Sherrat, Samuel, Liverpool, cm (1812–21). At 21 Clayton St, 1813–14, 20 Crosshall St in 1818 and 31 Maguire St in 1821. On 22 November 1812 married Mrs Julia Roberts, widow of William Roberts of Liverpool, painter. [D; *Liverpool Mercury*, 27 November 1812]

Sherratt, Samuel, Tunstall's Ct (or Calvert Sq.), Soho St, Liverpool, cm (1818). Free 11 June 1818. [Freemen reg.]

Sherren, James, Weymouth, Dorset, cm (d.1835). Died in 1835 leaving most of his property to his wife and three sons, Samuel, John and James. [Dorset RO, DA/W/1835/4]

Sherren, Robert, 38 Margaret St, Oxford Mkt, London, cm (1793–1803). Subscribed to Sheraton's *Drawing Book*, 1793 and *Cabinet Dictionary*, 1803. Included in the list of master cabinet makers in the latter work.

Sherren, Robert, 31 Charlotte St, Portland Pl., London, u and cm (1806–12). [D] Possibly:

Sherrer (or Sherran), —, address unknown, u (1803–06). Recorded in the account books of Lady Cotton of Madingley Hall, Cambs. On 21 February 1803 paid £40 on account, and in June 1806 £9 12s 'as per bill'. [Cambs. RO, S88/A45]

Sherrett, —, address unknown, u (1770). Paid £20 3s 6d by Lady Caroline Fleming Leicester of Tabley Hall, Cheshire. [Chester RO, DLT/D46/2]

Sherott, Daniel, 42–44 Ratcliffe Highway, London, cm and u (1809–29). The son of John Sherrott who previously occupied this address. The business was of a substantial size and insurance cover taken out in April 1809 amounted to £3,000 of which £2,100 was for utensils and stock. The three properties at Ratcliffe Highway were interconnected and often referred to simply as 44. By June 1811 insurance cover had risen to £3,800 with £2,600 for utensils and stock but only two inter-connected properties are referred to in the policy probably 43 and 44. [D; GL, Sun MS vol. 447, ref. 830390; vol. 452, ref. 858356]

Sherrott, John snr, 42–44 Ratcliffe Highway, London, cm and u (1776–1809). Initially at 44 only but by 1790 in possession of all three properties. In 1776 insurance cover was £900 of which £500 was for utensils and stock. The business was, however, to expand rapidly with total cover reaching £2,800 by 1781, £3,200 by 1790 and £5,000 by 1809. It was in this year that he appears to have handed over to Daniel Sherrott, his son. There was also another son, John jnr involved with the business from 1809. They were probably active in the business at an earlier stage for in 1808 the business was referred to a Sherrott & Sons. A chest on chest of c.1800 is recorded with the trade label of this maker affixed. On this he described himself as 'Upholsterer, Cabinet and Chair maker, Broker and Sworn Appraiser' and stated that he bought and sold household goods, 'stock in trade, estates by commission. Funerals performed'. [D; GL, Sun MS vol. 248, p. 269; vol. 275, p. 245; vol. 286, p. 107; vol. 292, p. 79; vol. 299, p. 529; vol. 370, p. 263; vol. 447, ref. 830389]

Sherrott, John jnr, 42 Ratcliffe Highway, London, cm (1808–19). Son of John Sherrott snr and brother to Daniel Sherrott. Associated with his father's business by 1808 which was then trading as Sherrott & Sons. In 1809 took over his father's enterprise in partnership with his brother Daniel but by 1811 they had decided to trade independently with Daniel occupying 43–44 Ratcliffe Highway and John jnr no. 42. [D; GL, Sun MS vol. 447, ref. 830389]

Sherwen, William, 24 Queen St, Whitehaven, Cumb., joiner/cm (1828–34). [D]

Sherwin, Ann, Leicester, u (1698–d.1700). Free 1698 but died 1700. Took as app. Edward Caulton. (Freemen rolls)

Sherwin, George, London, cm (1746–d. 1757). At Birchin Lane, Cornhill until March 1748 when his property was destroyed by fire. Then set up at 'the first House in Leadenhall St. next Cornill'. He may have moved back to Birchin Lane for when his death was announced in April 1757 he was described as 'an eminent Cabinet Maker in Birchin Lane, and a Common Council-Man of Cornhill Ward'. Supplied furniture to East India House, Leadenhall St and in September and November 1746 was paid two sums of £25 and £25 2s for chairs and £5 10s for looking-glasses. [*General Advertiser*, 29 March 1748; *Gents Mag*., April 1748; *London Chronicle*, 30 April 1757; *Apollo*, November 1965, p. 405]

Sherwin, J., 32 Little Bartholomew Close, London, fancy cm (1835). [D]

Sherwin, James, 75 Rahere St, City Rd, cm and u (1839). [D]

Sherwin, Thomas, 67 Gt Queen St, Lincoln's Inn Fields, London, portable desk, backgammon table, billiard table, workbox, dressing case and cabinet case maker (1825–39). [D]

Sherwin, William, 'The Hornet', Chichester, Sussex, turner and chairmaker (1823–39). [D]

Sherwood, James, Liverpool, carver (1794–1829). In 1794 at Copperas Hill but in 1829 at 9 Atkinson St and 7 Mansfield St. [D]

Sherwood, James, London, cm (1830). Freeman of Norwich. [Norwich poll bk]

Sherwood, John Hallett, London, cm (1790–1825). In May 1790 took out insurance cover of £200 which included £60 for utensils and stock in the dwelling house of Brock, an optician at 39 Little Bartholomew Close, and £100 for stock in the dwelling house of Shearer, cm (possibly Thomas), 'in the said Close'. John Hallett Sherwood's own address was given as 75 Aldersgate St. From 1795 his address is shown in directories as 42 Bartholomew Close. Included in the list of master cabinet makers in Sheraton's *Cabinet Dictionary*, 1803. [D; GL, Sun MS ref. 569755]

Sherwood, Robert, Southwark, London, cm (1826). Freeman of Maldon, Essex. [Maldon poll bk]

Sherwood, Samuel Oakley, Clapham, London, cm (1778). [Heal]

Sherwood, W., Cattlemarket and Bakers Pl., Sheffield, Yorks. cm and broker (1837). [D]

Sherwood, William, Woodbridge, Suffolk, cm and upholder (1784). [D]

Sherwood, William, 59 Lower Shadwell, London, upholder (1790–93). [D]

Sherwood, William, Hull, Yorks., carver, gilder and looking-glass manufacturer (1834–40). At 37 Bond St in 1834 and from 1835–40 at 37 Waterworks St. Described as cm etc. in 1840. [D]

Shether, Thomas, Northgate St, Canterbury, Kent, cm (1830–39). [D; poll bk]

Shevill, William, Mount Building, South Shields, Co. Durham, cm and joiner (1828). [D]

Shew, A. & E., 1 Gt Quebec St and 38 Upper York St, Bryanston Sq., London, u (1835). [D]

Shew, James, Red Lion Sq., Spitalfields, London, broker and cm (1808–20). At 30 Red Lion Sq. in 1808 but at 48 in 1819–20. [D]

Shew, James, 122 High Holborn, London, auctioneer, cm and upholder (1809–16). [D]

Shew, John, Streatham, London, cm, u and auctioneer (1822–26). [D]

Shewan, Alian, Granby St, Leicester, cm (1840). [D]

Shewell, John & Jos., London, chairmakers (1689). On 23 October 1689 invoiced to the Earl of Lothian twelve 'kain' chairs at £4 4s, twelve other chairs at £3 12s, six arm chairs at £3 and twelve 'matts' at 6s. These were despatched by sea. A further 12s was charged for a packing case 'to put yᵉ virginals'. [Scottish RO, GD40 (Lothian) V 329/2]

Shewring, Daniel, Corn St, Bristol, u (1713–18). In 1713 in association with his wife took app. named Hopkins. Daniel took app. named Rogers in 1717. [S of G, app. index; GL, Sun MS vol. 8, ref. 11231]

Shewring, Hester, 118 Temple St, Bristol, Windsor chair and rocking horse maker (1823–35). [D]

Shewring, Joseph, Bristol, upholder (1734–54). In 1734 living in the parish of St John, but in 1739 at Westerleigh near Bristol and in 1754 the address was Castle Precincts. [Poll bks]

Shewring, Luke snr, Temple St, Bristol, chairmaker (1795–1822). The number in Temple St is shown as 118 from 1814–22. His trade is indicated as Windsor and fancy chairmaker, 1799–1800, Windsor chair and portable cot maker in 1819 and Windsor chair and rocking horse maker in 1822. Hester Shewring, probably his widow, continued the business at the same address, 1823–35. [D]

Shewring, Luke jnr, 118 Temple St, Bristol, fancy chairmaker (1815–22). Occupied the same address as his father. In 1819 described also as a dealer in Dutch & English rushes and in 1820 also as a 'Birmingham & Brass factor' trading additionally from 10 Bath St. Not recorded after 1822. [D]

Shick, William, 43 Brick Lane, London, chairmaker (1813). In June 1812 took out insurance cover of £870 which included £600 for stock and utensils mainly in a workshop behind his dwelling house. [GL, Sun MS vol. 462, refs 883428–29]

Shields, George, Pilgrim St, Newcastle, u (1838). [D]

Shields, John, Sunderland, Co. Durham, cm and joiner (1828–32). In 1828 recorded as Jno. Shields & Co. and trading at Whitburn St. In 1832 at Monk Wearmouth trading as a cm only. [D]

Shields, Thomas, Jewin St, Cripplegate, London (1803). Subscribed to Sheraton's *Cabinet Dictionary*, 1803.

Shiers, Richard Peart, Manchester, u and cm (1808–40). In 1808 at 2 Mount Zion and in 1811 3 Nichols Croft. From 1816–18 the address was 2 Nicholas Croft (no. 4 in 1815), but address thereafter were in Shudehill. The number here was 82 in 1819, 74, 1821–25, 68 in 1828–29 and 84 in 1832–40. [D] Succeeded by Mary Shires at 84 Shudehill.

Shiers, Theophilus, Chapel Allerton, Leeds, Yorks., cm (1822). [D]

Shikins, Edward, Wormgate, Boston, Lincs., chairmaker (1822). [D]

Shillick, William, High St, Guildford, Surrey, cm (1806–07). [Poll bks]

Shilling, Thomas, London, u (1685–88). Recorded in the accounts of C. Blunt, u, receiving various payments amounting to £9 15s 8½ between 1685–88. [PRO C114/164, pt 1]

Shillingford, John, King St, Golden Sq., London, carver (1777). In 1777 insured his house for £200. [GL, Sun MS vol. 258, p. 518]

Shillito, James, Liverpool, cm (1840). App. to Thomas Croft Huxley and free 27 July 1840. [Freemen reg.]

Shillito, John, 30 East St, Red Lion Sq., London, cm (1809). [D]

Shillitoe, Daniel, Wakefield, Yorks., carver (1761). In 1761 took app. named Ward. [S of G, app. index; *Conn.*, June 1981]

Shilstone, Michael & Co., Bristol, cm and u (1805–14). At Broadmead in 1805. By 1807 Michael Shilstone appears to have been trading on his own behalf and from 1810 was in Horsefair, the number being 16 in 1813–14. [D]

Shilton, John, Market Pl., Cockermouth, Cumb., joiner/cm (1829). [D]

Shinglewood, William, parish of St Mary, Colchester, Essex, u (1694). Probate granted at Chelmsford, 1694. [*Wills at Chelmsford*]

Shinn, John, 3 St John St Rd, London, cm and u (1839). [D]

Shipley, Ann, High St, Leicester, cm and u (1796). On the death of her husband John in 1796 continued her husband's partnership with Nathaniel Saxton. [*Leicester Journal*, 1 September 1796]

Shipley, John, Nottingham, cm (1757). [Freemen rolls]

Shipley, John snr, High St, Leicester, cm and u (1753–d.1796). In 1753 took as app. Thomas Spicer. Thereafter regularly took further apps until 1791. In March 1785 took as partner Nathaniel Saxton, and when John Shipley snr died in 1796 his widow Ann continued the business in partnership with Saxton. In 1786 supplied to the 5th Duke of Bedford a swing glass and a dressing glass costing together 9s 6d. The invoice is in a bundle of documents marked 'Grooms accounts etc.' and thus these items may have been for the stables at Woburn. [D; app. bks; *Leicester Journal*, 24 March 1785]

Shipley, John jnr, Leicester, cm (1801). Son of John snr and Ann Shipley. Free 1801. There is no evidence to suggest his involvement with his father's business. When John snr died in 1796 the business was continued by Ann Shipley in partnership with Nathaniel Saxton and later by Saxton on his own behalf and in partnership with his son. [Freemen rolls]

Shipley, Jno., Belgrave Gate, Leicester, chair and sofa maker (1828). [D]

Shipley, L., East Bond St, Leicester, cabinet, chair and cane seat maker (c.1815–40). In 1842 she claimed to have worked as a cane worker for twenty-seven years. [D]

Shipley, Richard, Belgrave Gate, Leicester, chairmaker (1820–22). Listed at Belgrave Gate in 1820 and Humberstone St in 1822. [D]

Shipley, Richard, Sheep St, Market Harborough, Leics., chairmaker (1835). [D]

Shipley, Thomas, Knuckles Alley, Drury Lane, London, cane chairmaker (1709). [Heal]

Shipley, Thomas, North St, Chichester, Sussex, carver, gilder and japanner (1823–40). [D]

Shipman, Coleman, 6 Farmer St, Shadwell, London, cm (1783).

In 1783 insured his house for £100. [GL, Sun MS vol. 317, p. 548]

Shipman, Edward, 94 Watling St, London, upholder (1717–d.1790). Son of Benjamin Shipman a Clerk from Norfolk. App. to George Ellis on 5 February 1717 and free of the Upholders' Co. by servitude, 3 March 1725. Took as apps John Proudman (1761–66), Mathew Bendall (1772–80) and Charles Hallier (1780–88). From 1778–86 living in Watling St. [GL, Upholders' Co. records]

Shipman, James, London, upholder and cm (1781–c.1824). Son of William Shipman of Bishopsgate, tailor. App. to James Stirridge and free of the Upholders' Co. under the terms of the 1750 Upholders' Act, 7 February 1781. At this date he was living at 54 Bishopsgate. Recorded in directories at 15 Rood Lane, Fenchurch St, 1789–97, and at 9 George Yd, Lombard St, 1799–c.1824. Included in the list of master cabinet makers in Sheraton's *Cabinet Dictionary*, 1803. Assisted in his business by his son James jnr who took over the running entirely c.1825. [D; GL, Upholders' Co. records; Heal]

Shipman, James jnr, London, cm and u (1825–39). Son of James snr, and his successor at 9 George Yd, Lombard St. Moved to 29 Gracechurch St, c.1836. [D]

Shipman, John, Bury St Edmunds, Suffolk, cm (1722–58). Took apps named Nieman in 1722, Baxter in 1723 Cole in 1730, Evered in 1744 and Fuller in 1758. [S of G, app. index]

Shipman, John, Little Compton St, London, cm (1777). In 1777 took out insurance cover of £300 of which £200 was for utensils and stock. [GL, Sun MS vol. 255, p. 383]

Shipman, Robert, address unknown, u (1740). In 1740 supplied a square mat for Lady Fitzwalter's China Room at Moulsham Hall, Essex costing £2. [A. C. Edwards, *The Accounts of Benjamin Mildmay, Earl Fitzwalter*, p. 109]

Shipman, Samuel, 24 Watling St, London, u (1784). [D] See Edward Shipman in Watling St, 1778–86.

Shipman, Thomas, 14 Pinnington St, Liverpool, cm (1811). [D]

Shipton, William, Coventry St and Dover St, London, upholder (1775–78). Maintained an upholstery warehouse in Coventry St, St James's, 1775–78, but also trading from Dover St, Piccadilly. In 1777 took out insurance cover of £900 on the Dover St premises of which half was for utensils and stock. Bankruptcy announced, *Gents Mag.*, July 1778, only the Dover St address being used in the proceedings. [D; GL, Sun MS vol. 261, p. 367]

Shires, John, Wilson's Yd, Lower Headrow, Leeds, Yorks., carver, gilder and picture frame maker (1819). Business commenced at this address in 1819. [*Leeds Intelligencer*, 1819]

Shires, Mary, 84 Shudehill, Manchester, u (1836–d. by 1840). Appears to have succeeded Richard Peart Shiers, at this address in 1832–33. The executors of Mary Shires are listed in 1840. [D]

Shirley, William, Westgate, Grantham, Lincs., turner and chairmaker (1819–35). [D]

Shirmer & Bird, 37 Mortimer St, Cavendish Sq., London, u and cm (1835). [D]

Shirridge, J., 7 George Yd, Lombard St, London, cabinet warehouse (1794–97). James Shipman upholder and cm used an address at 9 George Yd, 1799–1839. [D]

Shirt, N. & G., 8 Gt Russell St, Covent Gdn, London, cm and u (1813–19). [D]

Shirst, Sarah, 5 Bridges St, Covent Gdn, London, mattress maker and upholder (1809–27). In January 1809 took out insurance cover of £550 of which £100 was for utensils and stock. By January 1812 these figures had risen to £650 and £200. [D; GL, Sun MS vol. 448, ref. 825867; vol. 459, ref. 864718]

Shirtcliff, J., 13 Mitchell St, Old St, London, cm (1808–29). [D]

Shlescha, Paul, London, cm (1793). Subscribed to Sheraton's *Drawing Book*, 1793.

Shobbrook, —, Exeter, Devon, cm (1776). [Freemen rolls]

Shoebridge, Richard, Colchester, Essex, cm (1791). In July 1791 took out insurance cover of £200. [GL, Sun MS vol. 379, p. 279]

Shoobridge, John, Chelmsford, Essex, upholder and cm (1784). [D]

Shoobridge, Richard, Braintree and Chelmsford, Essex, cm (1755–80). At Braintree, 1755–61. In 1755 took app. named Diss and in 1761, Wood. Probate granted on his will in 1780 by which date he was living in Chelmsford. [S of G, app. index; *Wills at Chelmsford*]

Shoobridge & Phillips, 237 High Holborn, London, cm (1786). In July 1786 Robert Shoobridge & Thomas Phillips took out insurance cover of £400 which included £200 for utensils and stock some of which were kept in a workshop and shed. [GL, Sun MS vol. 339, p. 162]

Shoosmith, Robert, Brighton, Sussex, cm and u (1838–39). At Blenheim Pl. in February 1838 when his daughter Hope Elizabeth was bapt. In August 1839 trading at 54 Union Pl. [D; PR (bapt.)]

Shooter, Edwin, Exeter, Devon, carver (1822–40). At Friernhay St, 1822–32; Preston St in 1833; Bear Lane in 1834; 2 South St, 1836; Little Southern Hay Lane, 1837–38; Market St, 1838; and Trinity St, 1839–40. Two sons and a daughter bapt. parish of St George, 1822–28, and a daughter parish of St Olave, 1840. [D; PR (bapt.)]

Shore, John, 14 Tib Lane, Manchester, cm (1815–17). [D]

Shore, Richard, Wickersley, near Rotherham, cm (1837). [D]

Shore, Robert, Market St, Derby, u (1730–48). In December 1730 took out insurance cover of £300 on his house, warehouse, household goods and stock in trade. [GL, Sun MS vol. 33, ref. 52421; poll bks]

Shore, Roger, 9 Back Quay St, Little St, Manchester, cm (1808). [D]

Shore, William, London, upholder (1751–69). Son of Thomas Shore of Little Eastcheap, cheesemonger. App. to John Iliffe on 5 November 1751 and James Grange, 2 July 1767. Free of the Upholders' Co., 5 July 1769. [GL, Upholders' Co. records]

Shores, Anthony, York, cm (1834). [D]

Shores, Arthur, Micklegate, York, cm and u (1822–40). Traded for most of this period in partnership with Edward Steward. Their address is variously given as either 91 or 92 Micklegate. The partnership was already established by April 1822 when they took as app. Charles John Lund. Other apps taken jointly were William Linfoot on 7 August 1823, John Taylor on 4 August 1825 and James Firth on 23 October 1830. It may have been in 1830 that the partnership was terminated, for one directory of this year shows Edward Steward at Blossom St. Subsequent apps taken, such as Francis Jackson on 13 July 1835 and William Dickings on 5 June 1840, were in the name of Arthur Shores only. [D; app. reg.]

Shorey, Ebenezer, 17 Marygold St, Bermondsey, London, u (1826). Freeman of Maldon, Essex. [Maldon poll bk]

Shorey, Timothy, 21 Butcher Hall Lane, Newgate St, London, u (1824–31). Freeman of Maldon, Essex. On 18 February 1824 insured his house and contents for £100 but only £5 was allowed for utensils. [GL, Sun MS vol. 496, ref. 1014416; Maldon poll bks]

Shortland, Richard Watson, 8 Camden Alley, Portsea, Portsmouth, Hants., carver and gilder (1830). [D]

Shorland, Richard, Cross St, Ryde, Isle of Wight, Hants., carver and gilder (1839). [D]

Short, Edward, 49 Marlborough St, Devonport, Devon, cm (1838). [D]

Short, Edwin, Trinity St, Worcester, chairmaker (1835). [Freemen rolls]

Short, Isaac, 84 Oldmarket, Bristol, cm (1775). [D]

Short, Isaac, Lower West St, Bristol, bedstead and chairmaker, cm (1835–40). [D]

Short, James, London, upholder (1738–46). Son of J. Short of Norwich, woolcomber. App. to James Butterfield on 3 May 1738 and free of the Upholders' Co., 5 June 1746. [GL, Upholders' Co. records]

Short, James, 16 Red Lion St, Spitalfields, London, carver, gilder and looking-glass manufacturer (1779). In 1779 insured his house for £300. [GL, Sun MS vol. 277, p. 316]

Short, James, Ipswich, Suffolk, cm (1768). Married on 4 August 1768. [Suffolk RO, FAA: 50/2/94–104]

Short, James, Wooler, Northumb., cm, joiner and u (1834). [D]

Short, James, 65 Seymour Pl., Bryanston Sq., London, u (1835). [D]

Short, John, Chichester, u (1715–16). In 1715 took app. named Rose. In 1716 an app. named Markes was taken by John Short jnr of Chichester. [S of G, app. index]

Short, John, St Nicholas St, Worcester, fancy chairmaker (1828–37). [D]

Short, Joseph, Waterside, Wisbech, Cambs., cm and u (1824). [D]

Short, Nicholas, Allendale, Northumb., joiner and cm (1827–28). [D]

Short, Robert, Fore St, Cripplegate, London, looking-glass maker and cm (1770). The Fore St premises are described on his trade card [Banks Coll., BM] as a warehouse. He stated that he made and sold 'all Sorts of Looking Glass & Cabinet Work which he Manufactures himself to supply Merchants for Exportation or Home Consumption'. Bankruptcy announced, *Gents Mag.*, May 1770.

Short, Shirley, High St, Wotton-under-Edge, Glos., cm (1824). Child bapt. in 1824. [PR (bapt.)]

Short, William, Sherborne, Dorset, chair and basket maker (1798). [D]

Short, William, 14 Compton St, Brunswick Sq., London, cm (1826–33). Bankruptcy announced, *London Gazette*, 17 September 1833. [D]

Short, William, 13 Cadogan St, London, cm and u (1839). [D]

Shorthose, Joshua, Burton-on-Trent, Staffs., chairmaker (1756). In 1756 took app. named Matthews. [S of G, app. index]

Shortman, Samuel, Newham, Glos., cm (1839). [D]

Shortridge, Christopher, Westgate St, Newcastle, cm (1787). [D]

Shotter, Gawen, London, upholder (1781–1802). App. to Robert Brooke on 5 September 1781 and free of the Upholders' Co. by servitude, 19 November 1788. Trading at 1 Budge Row, Cannon St in 1790, and the business was to continue at this address until its closure. Gawen Shotter is shown living at William St, probably his dwelling house, in 1802. Took as app. William Evans from 1794–1801 who took into partnership on the completion of his apprenticeship and the business traded as Shotter & Evans, 1801–02. [D; GL, Upholders' Co. records]

Shotton, William, Fleshmarket, Newcastle, cm (1778–d.c. 1793). His stock-in-trade consisting of finished furniture and a 'large stock of dry Mahogany, wainscot, beach, deals and other wood' was sold off in May 1793 after his death. [D; *Newcastle Courant*, 11 May 1793]

Shoulden, James, Dover, Kent, cm (1818). Freeman of Canterbury. [Canterbury poll bk]

Shoulder, James, Brighton, Sussex, cm (1830). Freeman of Canterbury. [Canterbury poll bk]

Showbridge, John, parish of St Martin-in-the-Fields, London, cm (1733–d.1740). App. to Mr Bell in St Martin's Lane for seven years and free c.1733. [Westminster Ref. Lib., F/5037]

Showring, Daniel, parish of St Thomas, Bristol, upholder (1722). poll bk]

Shreeve, G. T., Gt Yarmouth, Norfolk, cm (1807). [Poll bk]

Shreeve, William, London, u, appraiser and undertaker (1760–c.1780). In 1760 a person with this surname, probably William Shreeve was at the sign of 'The Cabinet', Within Smithfield Bars. Otherwise he is known only from his trade card, c.1780, which gives an address 'Three doors from Ludgate Hill in the Old Bailey'. He made and sold 'all Sorts of Cabinets, Glasses and Chairs' and claimed to be 'The only Inventor and Maker of Venetian Curtains to Common Windows, to hang in the same form as ye Right Venetian Curtains'. A mahogany kneehole desk of the third quarter of the 18th century, the front carved with blind fret in the Gothic taste, is known with this maker's trade label affixed. [Heal; Christie's NY, 17 October 1981, lot 154]

Shreeve, William, Norwich, cm (1780–1818). In the parish of St Peter Mancroft 1780–82 and in 1782 took out insurance cover on two houses, one valued at £100 and the other at £200. In 1802 in the parish of St Margaret and in from 1807–18 in the parish of St Gregory. [Poll bks; GL, Sun MS vol. 300, p. 230; vol. 301, p. 12]

Shreeves, William jnr, Upper Stone St, Maidstone, Kent, cm (1832–35). The property in Upper Stone St was a house. [D; poll bks]

Shrewring, Jos., Westerleigh, Glos., upholder (1739). Freeman of Bristol. [Bristol poll bk]

Shrewsbury, Thomas, 8 Chapel Pl., Pentonville, London, cm (1808). [D]

Shrigley, —, Lancaster, furniture painter and varnishers (1811–38). Named in the Gillow records 1811, 1814–18, 1820–23, 1825–29 and 1831–38. [Westminster Ref. Lib., Gillow]

Shrigley, Robert, London, upholder (1767–74). Son of John Shrigley of Chignall, Essex, clerk. App. to George Thorne on 13 March 1767 and free of the Upholders' Co. by servitude, 7 December 1774. [GL, Upholders' Co. records]

Shrimpton, John, Marlborough, Wilts., chair, basket and parchment maker and victualler (1790). In August 1790 insured a dwelling and offices adjoining 'The Bear & Castle' for £300 and stock and utensils kept there for a further £200. He also insured for £150 a house, workshop and offices that he was renting which also included stock and utensils. [GL, Sun MS ref. 572986, 26 August 1790] See Thomas Shrimpton.

Shrimpton, Joshua, 38 High St, Poplar, London, cm (1835). [D]

Shrimpton, Thomas, Marsh, Marlborough, Wilts., chairmaker, turner and basket maker (1822–30). [D]

Shufflebotham, Jesse, Custard St, Leek, Staffs., carver and gilder (1818). [D]

Shuffrey, William, London, u and appraiser (1774–1811). App. to Edward Smith on 4 May 1774, but also trained under Mary Phipps, weaver, and from 3 November 1779, Thomas Norris, upholder. Free of the Upholders' Co. by servitude, 5 November 1783 and at this date living at 184 Fleet St. In October 1784 he married Miss Bauman of Aldersgate St. In February 1787 at 1 Silver St, Fleet St and here he insured goods to the value of £500. By 1794 at 36 Aldersgate St, but a directory of 1792 gives the number as 6, possibly an error. At 36 Aldersgate St still in 1797, but the next directory entry, of 1809, gives 19 Butcher Hall Lane. The business, which was now called William Shuffrey & Co., remained at this address until 1811. [D; GL, Upholders' Co. records; Sun MS vol. 343, p. 190; Gents Mag., October 1784]

Shuffrey, William Henry, London, cm and u (1826–39). At 19 Stonecutter St in 1826 as an u and carpetmaker. In 1835 at 5 Budge St, in 1837 at 166 Strand and in 1839 at 160 Strand.

Possibly the son of the William Shuffrey who traded as a u in London, 1783–1811. [D]

Shurray, William, Wakefield, Yorks., upholder (1798). [D]

Shury, Robert, St Aldate's, Oxford, cm (1802). [Poll bk]

Shute, Henry, Leeds, Yorks., cm (1790–1840). At St Peter's Sq., 1790–98, 26 Kirkgate 1821–22 and 96 Kirkgate in 1826. By 1828 the business was trading as Henry & James Shute and in that year is shown first at 96 Kirkgate and in 1830 at 32 Call Lane, also as u. The business was still at this address from 1834–39, but the partnership had changed and the business was now trading as Henry & William Shute, cm and u. [D]

Shuter, Edwin, Exeter, Devon, carver (1831). Daughter Caroline bapt. at St Mary Major, 19 October 1831. [PR (bapt.)]

Shuter, John, Cambridge, u (1662–d.1699). Detailed payments are recorded to John Shuter in the accounts of Trinity College between 1662–91 and St John's College between 1667–90. These include supplying matting, material, upholstery and furniture, a payment by Trinity College in 1675 giving a good indication of the type of work he undertook: 'To Mr Shuter for 24 chairs for the Common Chamber at 11s. 6d. the chair £13. 16d. od., To him for a large Turkey worke Carpet £2. 18. od., For a lesser Turkey work carpet £1 10. od., To him for a large Close stool for ye lodging 13s. 6d.'. He died in Cambridge in 1699. [Archives of Trinity and St John's Colleges; Will WR11:58 University Lib.] R.W.

Shutt, John, Bowling, Bradford, Yorks., cm (1822). [D]

Shuttleworth, —, corner of Orange Ct and Swallow St, Golden Sq., London, cm (1751). [London Evening Post, 15–17 January 1751]

Shuttleworth, Barton, London, upholder (1717–30). Son of Richard Shuttleworth of Lancaster. App. to John Heath on 16 September 1717 and free of the Upholders' Co. by servitude, 7 January 1729/30. [GL, Upholders' Co. records]

Shuttleworth, Charles, Smallbrook St, Birmingham, cm, u and broker (1830). [D] Possibly the C. Shuttleworth of Birmingham declared bankrupt, Brighton Gazette, 10 February 1825.

Shuttleworth, James, Leeds, Yorks., cm (1821–34). In 1821 at 11 Hope St, in 1822 at Back of Park Row and in 1834 at 43 Basinghall St. [D]

Shuttleworth, Richard, London, upholder (1749–56). At Gt Jermyn St in 1749 and Upper Grosvenor St in January 1756. [Westminster poll bk; Public Advertiser, 11 January 1756]

Shuttleworth, Robert, Oxford St, London, upholder (1775). In 1775 insured a house for £500. [GL, Sun MS vol. 239, p. 284]

Shuttleworth, Roger, 116 Oxford St, London, u (1775–77). [D]

Shuttleworth, T., 1 Guinea Lane, Bath, Som., broker and cm (1819). [D]

Shuttleworth, Thomas, Lancaster, u (1728–29). [Freemen rolls]

Shuttleworth, Thomas, Kirkgate, Wakefield, Yorks., cm (1798–1818). In 1814 the business was trading as Shuttleworth & Son. [D]

Sibley, A., 11 Broad St, Golden Sq., London, carver and gilder (1835). [D]

Sibley, James, King St, Hammersmith, London, cm (1826). [D]

Sibley, John, Watlington, Oxon., u (1755). In May 1755 it was announced that John Sibley jnr would be continuing the business of his late father John Sibley snr [Jackson's Oxford Journal, 17 May 1755]

Sibley, John, London, carver, gilder, looking-glass and picture frame maker (1829–37). At 20 Duke's Ct, St Martin's Lane in 1829 and 45 Broad St, Golden Sq., 1835–37. [D] Succeeded by Sarah Sibley, probably his widow.

Sibley, Sarah, 45 Broad St, Golden Sq., London, carver and gilder (1839). [D]

Sibley, William, London, carver and gilder (1820–37). At Castle

St, Leicester Sq. in 1820 and 42 Whitcomb St, Haymarket, 1835–37. His trade card [Johnson Coll., Bodleian Lib., Oxford] gives the Whitcomb St address and also 45 Broad St, Golden Sq., an address also used by both John and Sarah Sibley. The trade card indicates that he made picture and looking-glass frames and dealt in old and new music and musical instruments. [D]

Sibson, William, 3 Providence St, Myton St, Hull, Yorks., bedstead manufacturer (1823). [D]

Sibthorpe, Christopher, 'The Japan Cabinet', Aldermanbury, London, cm and looking-glass seller (1714–d.1730). Described in 1714 as a 'joyner', and in 1719 the Philadelphia goldsmith Francis Richardson noted in his account book an intended visit to 'Cristepher Siphtha, a Looking Glass maker, at the Sign Looking Glass in Aldermondary'. [GL, Sun MS vol. 4, ref. 4219; Wills, *Looking-Glasses*; Heal]

Sicklemore, Henry, Brighton, Sussex, cm and u (1837–40). Living in Trafalgar St on 21 August 1837 when he married Louisa Furner. Trading from 11 West St in 1839 but by 1843 had moved to 65 Upper North St. [D; PR (marriage)]

Sickling, John, Hingham, Norfolk, cm (1795). [Poll bk]

Siday, Elias, 1 Richmond Pl., City Rd, London, chair and sofa maker (1839). [D]

Siddall, John, Upper Bryanston St, Edgware Rd, London, cm and blind maker (1817). [D]

Siddall, Samuel, London, upholder (1711–18). Son of Thomas Siddall of Manchester, callender. App. to Joseph Hulton on 6 June 1711 and free of the Upholders' Co. by servitude, 2 July 1718. [GL, Upholders' Co. records]

Siddelley, James, Lower Hillgate, Stockport, Cheshire, cm and joiner (1828). [D]

Sidebotham, Thomas, 87 Hill St, Birmingham, cm, u and broker (1828–30). Shown also at 28 Essex St in 1830. [D]

Sidey, John, Gt Peter St, Westminster, London, chairmaker (1768). In 1768 took app. named Mary Stanbridge. [Westminster Ref. Lib., MS F4309, p. 2]

Sidgier (or Sidgler), Henry, London, carpenter, cm and u (c.1760–84). His trade card, dated by Heal c.1760, gives an address at 'The Carpenters Arms' in Gt Shere Lane, near Temple Bar. In 1784 shown at Chancery Lane. [D; Heal]

Sidnel, David jnr, parish of SS Philip and Jacob, Bristol, carver (1784). [Poll bk]

Sidney, Benjamin, Soho, London, upholder (1700–07). Known in connection with materials supplied to and work done for the Duchess of Buccleuch. In 1700 paid £16 0s 11d for furnishings at Moor Park, Herts. Material was supplied for 'Her Grace's blue & gold chairs' and linen to line 'Indian silk' hangings, a canopy and chairs. Work undertaken in the following year was for delivery to Scotland. This included rods for the Duchess of Buccleuch's needlework bed and work on the bed and matching stools. From 1702–03 furnishings were made for Her Grace's lodgings in Parliament Close, Edinburgh. These included an easy chair, round stools, window curtains, damask cushions for cane chairs and quilts. Some work continued until 1707. [Scottish RO, GD 224/25/3/3; GD 224/Box 29, GD 224/Box 28]

Sidney, Henry, 30 Baldwin St, City Rd, London, carver, wood, cabinet etc. (1839). [D]

Sidney, Jonathan, parish of St Martin-in-the-Fields, London, cm (1757). In June 1757 reported as a 'fugitive for debt'. [*London Gazette*, 14 June 1757]

Sidwell, William, 103 Micklegate, York, cm and u (1830). [D]

Sigsworth, John, Market Pl., Kirbymoorside, Yorks, cm and joiner (1834–40). [D]

Silbon, William, 3 Providence St, Myton St, Hull, Yorks., cm and bedstead maker (1822–23). In October 1822 took an app. Samuel Ayre and in the following month another named

Joseph Blakley, both of Hull. In September 1823 another app. John Hunter was assigned to him by John Hinsley. [D; app. reg.]

Silcock, Jacob, Norwich, u (1784). Son of Obadiah Silcock, u. Free 18 December 1784. [Freemen reg.]

Silcock, Obadiah, parish of St Saviour, Norwich, u (1753–84). App. to Edward White and free 3 May 1753. His son Obadiah, a grocer, was made free, 22 August 1770 and a further son Jacob, an u, was free on 18 December 1784. In 1754 took app. named Watts. [Poll bk; freemen reg.; S of G, app. index]

Silk, Thomas, London, u and cm (1767–1801). Freeman of London and a member of the Joiners' Co. and Ironmongers' Co. In 1767 he was using an address in Little Carter Lane, but from 1768–71 was at Bell Yd, Doctors Commons. From 1772–1801 at 4 St Paul's Churchyard which was next to 'The Queen's Arms Tavern'. He also acted as an appraiser and undertaker. From 1767–83 he took out licences to employ non-freemen on a regular basis, the number often being six. William Cobett was his app. in the 1770s. In 1772 supplied two mahogany side boards to the proprietors of the Coal Exchange in Lower Thames St at a cost of £3 15s. His name is also recorded as a supplier of furniture to Nathaniel Ryder, 1st Lord Harrowby for Sandon Hall, Staffs. 1773–77. The payments made were £9 11s 6d on 31 July 1773, £2 2s on 23 July 1774, £2 15s 3d on 18 July 1775, £10 2s 3d on 24 July 1776 and £11 on 1 March 1777. The payment of 1773 was for chairs and that of 1777 for chairs for bedrooms and the Little Dressing Room. His trade label has been found on items of furniture of the 1770s including a mahogany secretaire bookcase. [D; GL, Upholders' Co. records; City Licence bks, vols 6–10; Coal Exchange ledger; Harrowby MS Trust, Notebooks, vols 334, 337, 338]

Sill, Lancaster, chairmaker (1811–12). App. to I. Boulton and free by servitude, 1811–12. [App. reg.]

Sillett, George, Market Pl., North Walsham, Norfolk, cm (1830). [D]

Sillitoe, William, Church St, Sudbury, Suffolk, cm (1830). [D]

Sillo & Co., 15 High St, Manchester, picture frame makers and print sellers (1800–02). [D]

Silver, Elizabeth, 45 Broad St, Reading, Berks., cm and u (1840). Successor to James Silver at this address and probably his widow. [D]

Silver, James, Broad St, Reading, Berks., cm (1837). [Poll bk]

Silver, James & Sons, High St, Maidenhead, Berks., cm and u (1840). [D]

Silverlock, Richard, Fareham, Hants., chairmaker (1792). [D]

Silverlock, William, Pile St and South St, Newport, Isle of Wight, Hants, cm and u (1787–1801). In April 1787 insured his utensils and stock at both shops and also his household goods for £300. By March 1801 the total cover had risen to £500, but only the Pile St address is mentioned and stock and utensils there in his shop and dwelling house were valued at £300. [GL, Sun MS vol. 344, ref. 529690; vol. 40, ref. 716534]

Silverlock, William, Lymington, Hants., joiner and cm (1792–93). [D]

Silverton, J., 6 Canning Pl., Old St, London, cm (1835). [D]

Silverton, J., 42 Primrose St, Bishopsgate, London, cm (1835). [D]

Silverwood, Benjamin, Gainsborough, Lincs., cm and u (1730–d.1766). In January 1730 took out insurance cover of £250 which was for utensils, stock and household goods. In 1755 took app. named Silverwood, possibly his son Joseph; in 1761 Watson, and in 1762 a third named Hind. His son Joseph, took over the business in August 1766 following his father's death. At this date the business was in Little Church Lane.

[GL, Sun MS vol. 32, ref. 53122; S of G, app. index; *Cambridge Chronicle*, 9 August 1766]

Silverwood, Joseph, Little Church Lane, Gainsborough, Lincs., cm (1766). Son of Benjamin Silverwood whose business he took over in August 1766. He may not have traded for long, for by December a sale of the stock in trade was advertised by 'widow Silverwood'. Timber stocks of mahogany, Virginia walnut, wainscot and elm were offered together with benches and tools. Mrs Silverwood advertised further sales of stock in August 1767 and May 1769. [*Cambridge Chronicle*, 9 August and 4 October 1766, 27 August 1767, 6 May 1769]

Silverwood, Theodore, Derbs., cm (1803). Subscribed to Sheraton's *Cabinet Dictionary*, 1803.

Silverwood, Thomas, Lancaster (1814). [Westminster Ref. Lib., Gillow records]

Silvester, William, London Rd, Gloucester, u (1839). [D]

Sim, William, 128 Queen St, Whitehaven, Cumb., joiner/cm (1834). [D]

Simcock, James, High St, Margate, Kent, cm (1838). [D]

Simcox, Jane, Birmingham, u (1835–39). Listed at 14 Cannon St in 1835 and 68 Bath St, 1839. [D]

Simcox, William, 10 Snow Hill, Birmingham, u (1830). [D]

Simes, Elias, parish of St Clement (Middlx), London, u (1683–93). In 1693 received judgement against Robert Egdon for £260. [Oxford RO, Su. xii/1; Misc. Coventry III/1]

Simkins, John, Southampton, Hants., cm (1774). [Poll bk]

Simm, James, address unknown, cm (1778–83). In 1778 undertook work for Sir Gilbert Heathcote to a value of £9 os 6d which included supplying on 31 October a double chest of drawers in oak at £5 5s, and a single chest of drawers at £3 3s. In part payment £2 was allowed for a lime, walnut, pear and apple tree. Simm received a payment in 1783. [Lincoln RO, 2 ANC 12/D/32, 3 ANC 6/21]

Simmons, J., opposite the Armory, Stapleton Rd, Bristol, u and paper hanger (1840). [D]

Simmonds, James, Southampton Row, London, u and cm (1804–11). At 33 Southampton Row, 1804–08, but in that year the number changed to 44. Some directories describe the business as an upholstery warehouse. [D]

Simmonds, Richard, 44 Cumberland St, Hackney Rd, London, cm and u (1839). [D]

Simmonds, Thomas, Bristol, cm and upholder (1799–1801). At 2 Broad Wear, 1799–1800, and Horse Fair in 1801. [D]

Simmonds, William & Bonnell, Thomas, parish of St Martin-in-the-Fields, London, cm (1744). Bankruptcy announced, *Gents Mag.*, April 1744.

Simmonds, William, 45 Minster St, Reading, Berks. cm and u (1826–40). [D; poll bk]

Simmonds, William, Catherine St, Salisbury, Wilts., cm and u (1839). [D]

Simmons, —, near Middle Temple Gate, Fleet St, London, u (1745). [Heal]

Simmons, George, Exeter, Devon, cm (1826–32). At Northernhay on 18 June 1826 when his son William Henry was bapt. at St David's Church. Two further children were bapt. between 1828–30 at St Mary Arches and then he was living in Synagogue Pl. By 1832 he appears to have moved once more and was living in the parish of St John. [PR (bapt.); poll bk]

Simmons, George, Leamington, Warks., cm (1828–30). [D]

Simmons, John, London, cm (1774–81). Freeman of Bristol but living in London. At Purpool Lane, Gray's Inn Rd in 1774 and 24 Cady St, Lincoln's Inn Fields in 1779. In the latter year he took out insurance cover on some houses for £1,200. In 1781 at Whitechapel Rd. [Bristol poll bks; GL, Sun MS vol. 274, p. 148]

Simmons, John, 96 Old St, St Luke's, London, u and cm (1808–39). By 1835 had taken a partner named Gregory and the business was to trade as Simmons & Gregory, 1835–39. In 1839 the number was given as 97. [D]

Simmons, John, Portsea, Portsmouth, Hants., cm, u and appraiser (1823–39). Listed at 36 Union St in 1823 and 88 Queen St, 1830–39. [D]

Simmons, John, 26 Penton St, Pentonville, London, u (1826). [D]

Simmons, John, Lower Rd, Islington, London, cm (1835). [D]

Simmons, John, East Hill, Colchester, Essex, chairmaker (1839). [D]

Simmons, Joseph, London St, Reading, Berks., cm (1820). [Poll bk]

Simmons, Richard, Red Lion Sq. London, u (1835–39). In 1835 at 4 East St, Red Lion Sq. and in 1839 at New North St, Red Lion Sq. [D]

Simmons, Samuel, 20 Newington Causeway, London, u (1829). [D]

Simmons, Thomas, North St, Cliffe, Lewes, Sussex, cm and u (1839–40). At North St in November 1839 but by 1845 had moved to High St. [D]

Simmons, William, Barnes, Surrey, cm (1831). Freeman of Sandwich, Kent. [Sandwich poll bk]

Simmons, William, Nottingham, cm and u (1834–40). Trading at Derby Rd in 1834 and Toll House Hill in 1840. [D]

Simms, —, Wych St, London, u (d.1729). His death was reported in *Daily Post*, 5 February 1729. He was a Quaker and at the time of his death was said to be worth £50,000 and 'formerly an upholsterer in Wych St'.

Simms, G., Bath, Som., cm (1819–33). Listed at 5 Kingsmead Terr. in 1819 and 5 New Orchard St, 1833. [D]

Simms, Joseph, 1 Blackman St, London, wholesale u (1767–99). [D]

Sim(m)s, Thomas, 14 Hockennall Alley, Liverpool, chairmaker (1813–14). [D]

Simms, W., parish of St Clement, Oxford, cm (1768). [*Survey of Oxford*]

Sim(m)s, William, 145 High Holborn, London, upholder and cm (1774–1808). Included in the list of master cabinet maker's in Sheraton's *Cabinet Dictionary*, 1803. A mahogany Pembroke table with this maker's trade label affixed has been recorded. [D; Christie's, 16 June 1977, lot 99]

Simms, Harrison & Bradford, 1 Gt Dover St, London, u (1839). [D]

Simner, John, 4 Gilbert St, Liverpool, carver (1811). [D]

Simonds, John, Marlborough, Wilts, cm (1797–98). [D]

Simons, George, Clement St, Leamington, Warks., cm (1828). [D]

Simons, John, 12 Charterhouse Sq., London, looking-glass manufactory (c.1790). [Wills, *Looking-Glasses*]

Simons, William E., Radford, Notts., joiner and cm (1832). [D]

Simons, William, Nottingham, joiner and cm (1836). In 1836 took as app. John Stafford. [App. reg.]

Simonton, Robert, Castle Yd, Newcastle, cm and carpenter (1778). [D]

Simper, Robert, 42 Guildhall St, Bury St Edmunds, Suffolk, cm (1839). [D]

Simpkins, John, parish of All Saints, Southampton Hants., cm (1780–93). In 1784 appointed guardian to Catherine and Sarah Hockley. [D; Hants. RO, SC4/3/823; S of G, Winchester Guardianships]

Simple, John, 2 Berners St, London, upholder and cm (1805). In January 1805 took out insurance cover of £1,200 which included £700 for utensils and stock at his house in Berners St and £140 for similar items at 78 Margaret St described as a house, warehouse and workshop. [GL, Sun MS vol. 431, ref. 769982]

Simpson, Alexander, London, cm and upholder (1777–93). At Tyler St in 1777 where he took out insurance cover of £700 of which £200 was for his workshop and stock. In the following year he was at Little Hermitage St and cover had risen to £1,000 with £800 for utensils and stock. By 1780 at 4 New Bond St, an address that he was to occupy until 1793. Patronised by Sir John Nelthorpe who on 11 June 1783 paid £3 23s 6d for a mahogany dressing table and on 24 April 1798 £1 18s for a mahogany writing desk and a portable music desk. Alexander Simpson was succeeded at the New Bond St address by William Simpson in 1794. [D; GL, Sun MS vol. 255, p. 375; vol. 262, p. 376; vol. 284, p. 460; vol. 306, p. 255; Lincoln RO, NEL 9/5/61, NEL 9/11/17]

Simpson, Arthur, 11 Russell Ct, Covent Gdn, London (1808–09). [D]

Simpson, Benjamin, 96 High Holborn, London, cm (1786–d.1815). From 1794 the business was conducted in partnership with Michael Houghton. Simpson died on 5 January 1815. [D; Heal; *Gents Mag.*, January 1815]

Simpson, Carrington, 4 Canterbury Pl., Lambeth, London, cm and u (1839). [D]

Simpson, Daniel, Tavern St, Ipswich, Suffolk, cm (1805–08). [D]

Simpson, David, Hull, Yorks., cm (1803–14). At Manor St in 1803 but by 1814 at 6 Market Pl. [D]

Simpson, David, Flowergate, Whitby, Yorks., cm (1823). [D]

Simpson, Edward, Cambridge, joiner (1686–90). Payments made to Simpson by Christ's College, 1686–90. Most of these were for general joinery work but in 1690 paid for making forms for the Chapel.

Simpson, Frederick, Townfield Gate, Keighley, Yorks., joiner/cm (1837). [D]

Simpson, George, St Paul's Churchyard, see George Simson.

Simpson, George, Hull, Yorks., cm and joiner (1803–38). At Witham in 1803, 4 Simpson's Ct, North St or 4 North St, Prospect St, probably the same address, 1810–35. The address in 1838 was 32 North St. Subscribed to Sheraton's *Cabinet Dictionary*, 1803. [D]

Simpson, Israel, 19 Frederick Pl., Goswell St Rd, Clerkenwell, London, cm (1819). In 1819 took an app. for child bed linen making. [Westminster Ref. Lib., MS B 1268, entry 239].

Simpson, James, Woodbridge, Suffolk, u (1751–52). Married on 19 October 1751. [Suffolk RO, FAA: 50/2/89–93] Probably:

Simpson, James, Ipswich, Suffolk, upholder (1758). In 1758 took app. named Hayward. [S of G, app. index]

Simpson, James, Southampton, Hants., cm (d.1794). Died intestate 1794. [Hants. RO, letters of administration]

Simpson, James, 11 Hope St, Leeds, Yorks., cm (1822). [D]

Simpson, John, York, u (1715). His son John admitted freeman in 1715. [York freemen rolls]

Simpson, John, near the Hermitage Bridge in Lower East Smithfield, London, chairmaker (1778). Took out insurance cover of £200, half of which was for utensils and stock. [GL, Sun MS vol. 262, p. 376]

Simpson, John, Woolpack Yd, Halifax, Yorks., cm and joiner (1830). [D]

Simpson, John, Ackworth, Yorks., joiner/cm (1837). [D]

Simpson, Jonathan, St Martin's Fields, Chester, cm (1840). [D]

Simpson, Joseph, Broad St, Westminster, London, cm (1784). [Poll bk]

Simpson, M., 16 Chorlton St, Fitzroy Sq., London, cm and u (1839). [D]

Simpson, Martin, East Parade, Colne, Lancs., joiner and cm (1824). [D]

Simpson, Michael, 'The Royal Tent', on the Bridge, Leeds, Yorks., upholder, appraiser and undertaker (1762–70). App.

to Alderman Farrer of York and then moved to London. By January 1762 he had returned from London and set up in business in Leeds. He opened a shop at the sign of 'The Royal Tent' on the Bridge in Leeds to 'serve all Persons with Bedsteads, Feather Beds, Mattresses and Bedding; Silk and Worsted Damasks, Furniture Stuffs, Cottons, Linens and Checks; Carpets, Matting and Matts of all Sorts'. He also dealt in other household goods and furniture and kept 'a great Variety of Paper Hangings, Chimney-Boards, Ornaments for Halls, Staircases, Ceilings etc., and will hang and furnish the same in the Genteelest Taste'. His invoice dated 18 November 1770 exists for materials, hangings, wallpaper and bedding supplied to Temple Newsam House. His trade card [Leeds Local Hist. Lib.] has a fine Rococo surround which is identical except for the trade sign, to that of John Potts an upholder who traded at Toddington, Beds. and London, 1761–1800. [*Leeds Intelligencer*, 26 January 1762; Leeds archives dept, TN EA 12/5]

Simpson, Richard, Sunderland, Co. Durham, joiner and cm (1786–98). In December 1786 advertised that he had entered into a partnership with John Penrith jnr, son of the late John Penrith snr with the intention of taking over the business of the latter. They used the shop formerly occupied by John Penrith snr to carry on their trade of cm and house carpenter. The partnership was still trading in 1798. [D; *Newcastle Courant*, 9 December 1786]

Simpson, Richard, Bristol, cm (1793). Subscribed to Sheraton's *Drawing Book*, 1793.

Simpson, Samuel, London, upholder (1725–81). Son of William Simpson of Stow, Lincs. farmer. App. to William Tyte on 2 March 1725 and free of the Upholders' Co. by servitude, 9 March 1732/33. Took as app. Lewis Ducroy, 1741–50. From 1778–81 living in Kensington. [GL, Upholders' Co. records]

Simpson, Thomas, London, cm (1768). Freeman of Colchester, Essex. [Colchester poll bk]

Simpson, Thomas, Leeds, Yorks., cm (1774). [Poll bk]

Simpson, Thomas, London, cm (1808–39). At Swan Pl., Crown St, Finsbury, 1808–17 but by 1820 had moved to 1 Clifton St, Finsbury. He took out insurance cover of £550 on this address in May 1823 and of this £380 was for utensils and stock. He also insured in November 1823 a house in tenure at 20 Union St, Spitalfields for £500. [D; GL, Sun MS vol. 495, ref. 1003979; vol. 494, ref. 1010443; vol. 495, ref. 1019125]

Simpson, Thomas, Tadcaster, Yorks., cm (1818–22). At Bridge St in 1818 and High St in 1822. [D]

Simpson, Thomas, Boston, Lincs., cm, u and chairmaker (1819–40). Born in 1797. At High St, 1819–22; York St in 1826 but by 1835 had moved to Market Pl. The stamp 'T. SIMPSON BOSTON' has been recorded on the seat edge of a Windsor chair. [D; *Furn. Hist.*, 1978]

Simpson, Thomas, St Nicholas St, Lancaster, chair and bedstead maker (1825–34). [D]

Simpson, Thomas James, 20 Wilson St, Finsbury, London, cm and u (1835–39). [D]

Simpson, Thomas, Chamber's Entry, High St, Hull, Yorks., cm (1838–40). [D]

Simpson, Wharton, 58 Fleece Yd, Leeds, Yorks., cm (1837). [D]

Simpson, William, address unknown, u (1707). On 3 July 1707 he was paid for 'hanging Roomes & Collcuring the chaires' for William Bowes. [Durham RO, Strathmore MS, D/St/V606]

Simpson, William, York and Wakefield, Yorks., carver and gilder (1752–74). Son of William Simpson, carpenter. His father was already dead when on 1 November 1752 he was app. to Charles Mitley of York, carver, gilder and mason. Free of York but by 1774 was living at Wakefield. [York app. bk and poll bk]

Simpson, William, 7 Union St, Oxford St, London, cm (1776–1826). In 1776 insured his house for £100. A directory of 1826 shows a cm of this name at 49 Union St. [D; GL, Sun MS vol. 244, p. 587]

Simpson, William, London, cm (1793). Subscribed to Sheraton's *Drawing Book*, 1793.

Simpson, William, Scarborough, Yorks., cm (1798–1840). At St Helens Sq., 1828–30, no. 3 in 1840. Recorded also as an u in 1828. The long period of trading might suggest that the business was taken over by a son of the same name. [D]

Simpson, William, London, cm and u (1794–1839). Successor to Alexander Simpson and he traded from his address at 4 New Bond St, 1794–1820. In 1820 took a partner called Giblett and the business is referred to as Simpson & Giblett or Simpson & Co. In 1821 moved to 37 Argyle St which they were to occupy until 1825. A further partner joined the firm in 1823 and from this date it is recorded as Simpson, Giblett & Atkins. In 1825 another move was made, this time to 6 Argyle Pl., Regent St. Simpson may have withdrawn from the business in 1826 but Giblett & Atkins were still at 6 Argyle Pl. in 1829. William Simpson appears to have continued to trade and was at 31 Chipstone St, Fitzroy Sq., 1826–27 and 39 Upper John St, Fitzroy Sq., 1835–39. William Simpson was included in the list of master cabinet makers in Sheraton's *Cabinet Dictionary*, 1803. The business was conducted on an extensive scale and in July 1810 insurance cover came to £4,100. Utensils and stock at this date were valued at £800. [D; GL, Sun MS vol. 453, ref. 846709]

Simpson, William, Castle Hill, Lincoln, chairmaker (1819). [D]

Simpson, William, Back Lane, Sleaford, Lincs., joiner, builder and cm (1826). [D]

Simpson, William, Church St, Reading, Berks., carver and gilder (1826). [Poll bk]

Simpson, William, High St, Burton-on-Trent, Staffs., turner and chairmaker (1834). Also listed as turner/cm in that year. [D]

Simpson, William, 1 Mount Ct, 14 Hanley St, Liverpool, chairmaker (1839). The business was also known as Simpson & Duke. [D]

Simpson & Co., 124 Wardour St, Soho, London, carvers and gilders (1820). [D]

Simpson, Offord & Co., 410 Oxford St, London, u (1837). [D]

Sims, David, Watford, Herts., cm (1832). [D]

Sims, George, Thomas St, Bristol, cm (1793–1801). [D]

Sims, James, 2 Ellis St, Chelsea, London, cm and u (1823). [D]

Sims, Richard Littleworth, 33 London St, Reading, Berks., carver and gilder (1826–37). [D; poll bks]

Sims, Robert, 36 Compton St, Clerkenwell, London, looking-glass manufacturer (1839). [D]

Simson, Francis, 12 Globe St, Wapping, London, u, auctioneer etc. (1809–16). Recorded in 1809 as a carpenter and ship's joiner and in 1811 as a dealer in mahogany and deals. [D]

Simson (or Simpson), George, 19 St Paul's Churchyard, London, upholder, cm and undertaker (1780–1839). Son of John Simpson (*sic*) of Chatham, Kent, surgeon and apothecary. App. to Noah Chivers of London on 2 December 1772 and free of the Upholders' Co. by servitude in February 1780. By 1787 had established his own business at the St Paul's Churchyard address at which he was to continue to trade until 1839. The long length of trading might suggest that he was assisted by a son, possibly of the same name, and for the period 1837–39 some directories do list 'Simpson & Son'. In 1793 he subscribed to Sheraton's *Drawing Book* and in 1803 was included in the list of master cabinet makers in the *Cabinet Dictionary*. The business was of substantial size and in June 1792 insurance cover of £1,700 was taken out on utensils and stock. The total insurance cover came to £2,700 and the premises in St Paul's Churchyard were described as

consisting of no fewer than seven properties adjoining no. 19. A house at Peckham was also included in the property covered. Insurance was to remain high reaching £6,000 for stock and utensils alone in October 1808. By August 1822 the total was £10,000 which included £8,200 for stock and utensils, a small quantity of which were kept in a stable building in Little Carter Lane. Earlier, in January of that year, insurance of £1,600 had been taken on 2 Prospect Pl., Chelsea which may have been Simson's dwelling house.

Of Simson's customers little is known. Payments were made to him by the 2nd Viscount Palmerston possibly in connection with Broadlands, Hants. A bill dated 13 February 1809 for £324 16s 10¼d for upholstery goods supplied by Simson is in the accounts for Gorhambury House, Herts. Much of his furniture is, however, known from pieces marked with his trade label. The furniture so marked appears to be in the styles of the last two decades of the 18th century and the early to mid Regency and it is possible that this practice was discontinued in the later years of trading. In its place furniture was marked with a stamp reading 'GEORGE SIMPSON UPHOLDER CABINET MAKER & UNDERTAKER, LONDON'. This stamp has been recorded on a rosewood writing desk dating from the 1830s. The quality of the furniture bearing Simson's label is generally high. On the plainer pieces fine figured mahogany and other timbers such as satinwood and sabicu were used. Marquetry and painted decoration was featured on pieces of late 18th-century date such as a table with Neo-classical decoration including a fine central roundel featuring Venus and Cupid. A labelled Pembroke table with a shaped top is veneered with sycamore and has an inlaid central patera. A pair of Regency calamander and rosewood card tables are embellished with ormolu and brass inlay was used on a mahogany cabinet in the Egyptian taste. A bookcase in the Egyptian style has also been noted. Chests of drawers with Simson's labels are either bow or serpentine fronted and fitted with slides. Items that have been noted with his label range in size from wardrobes and sideboards to a cutlery box and an inlaid two division tea caddy. A fine inlaid secretaire cabinet of *c.*1800 has close resemblances to the style of work used on cabinets sold by Weeks's Museum, Titchborne St (Figs 22–23). It is therefore probable that these fine fitted pieces of furniture supplied through the business of Thomas Weeks were made in Simson's workshops. [D; Heal; GL, Upholders' Co. records; Sun MS vol. 388, p. 81; vol. 444, ref. 821734; vol. 487, ref. 978846; vol. 489, ref. 987506, ref. 995571; Herts. RO, Gorhambury account bks, XI 81; *Antique Collecting*, September 1979; *Antique Collector*, March–April 1946, p. 58; *C. Life*, 10 June 1939, p. lxviii, 10 April 1975, supplement p. 48; 29 January 1981, p. 290; *Conn.*, vol. 104, p. 160, November 1969, p. cxxxviii; V&A archives; Anderson Galleries, NY, 8 December 1921, lot 333; Christie's, 26 January 1984, lot 133; Phillips', 18 May 1976, lot 189; Sotheby's, 26 March 1965, lot 114]   B.A.

Simson, John, 17 Hermitage St, London, carpenter, joiner and cm (1784). In 1784 took out insurance cover of £1,300 of which £700 was for workshop, utensils and stock. [GL, Sun MS vol. 322, p. 25]

Simson, S., address unknown (1782). Supplier of two fire screens to Lord Monson. The entry in the accounts is dated 1 May 1782 and the amount charged was £1 16s. [Lincoln RO, Monson 10/1/A/6]

Sinclair, Edward, Liverpool, cm (1760). App. to James Barton and in 1760 petitioned for his freedom. [Freemen's committee bk]

Sinclair, Samuel, 'Red Cow', Exeter, Devon, cm (1832). Son Thomas bapt. at St Sidwell's Church on 8 February 1832. [PR (bapt.)]

Sinclair, William, Plymouth, Devon, cm (1757). In 1757 took app. named Moyle. [S of G, app. index]

Sindrey, William, 21 Finch Lane, Cornhill, London, u and cm (1820). Took out insurance cover of £500 on 24 August 1820. Of this £440 was for utensils and stock. [GL, Sun MS vol. 487, ref. 970734]

Single, Philip, 17 Fleet St, Liverpool, cm (1839). [D]

Singleton, James, St Anne's St, Manchester, cm and u (1829–40). At 4 St Anne's St, 1829–33, but from 1836–40 at 10 and 12. [D]

Singleton, Jane, Briggate, Leeds, Yorks., working u (1834–37). Recorded at Yard 130 in 1834 and Court 131 in 1837. [D] See Martha Singleton.

Singleton, John, Lancaster, u (1760–84). App. to J. Roberts in 1760 and free, 1767–68. [App. reg.; poll bk]

Singleton, John, Mill Hill, Leeds, Yorks., upholder (1798). [D]

Singleton, Martha, 6 Liddle's Yd, 131 Briggate, Leeds, Yorks., working u (1830). [D] See Jane Singleton.

Singleton, Richard, 4 Clare Ct, Clare Mkt, London, picture dealer and cm (1773). Sale by auction of his household furniture and stock in trade was announced, *Daily Advertiser*, 29 April 1773.

Singleton, Richard, 45 Bartlett's Buildings, Holborn, London, cm, upholder and auctioneer (1778–87). In 1778 insured his utensils, stock and goods for £250 out of a total insurance cover of £400. In July 1787 his utensils, stock and goods were insured £500. [GL, Sun MS vol. 265, p. 561; vol. 346, p. 325]

Singleton, Thomas, Bury St Edmunds, Suffolk, carver (b.1715–d.1792). Son of Robert Singleton of Bury St Edmunds, a noted sculptor. Worked at Barking Hall, Suffolk (1753) the Town Hall, Bury St Edmunds (1775) and the Mansion House, Bury St Edmunds (1789). In 1753 took app. named Termyn. Details of his work as a sculptor are to be found in Gunnis. [S of G, app. index]

Singleton, Thomas, Preston, Lancs., master cm (1799). Assented to the *Preston Cabinet Makers and Chair Makers Book of Prices* on the behalf of his fellow masters.

Singleton, Thomas, Wicker, Sheffield, cm, u and paper hanger (1822–25). At 80 Wicker in 1822 and at 84 in 1825. [D]

Singleton, Thomas, Park-Stile Lane, Kettering, Northants., cm and u (1830). [D]

Singleton, Thomas, Ipswich, Suffolk, cm (1813–39). Married on 5 April 1813 and trading at Brook St, 1835–39. [Suffolk RO, FAA: 50/2/116, pp. 108–09; poll bks]

Singleton, William, High St, Kettering, Northants., cm (1823). [D]

Singleton & Son, near the Market Pl., Sleaford, Lincs., joiners, builders and cm (1826). [D]

Simkenson, Henry, Cambridge and London, cm (1835–40). In 1835 a child was bapt. Parish of St Clement, Cambridge. By 1847 living at Hyde Park Corner, London. [Cambs. RO, P27/1/5; Cambridge poll bk]

Sinnock, Henry, Margate, Kent, cm (1832–39). In 1832 at Cranbourn Alley and in 1839 at 6 Fort Cresc. [D]

Sircom, John, Alfred Pl., Bristol, cm (1795). [D]

Sircom, Richard, Old Market, Bristol, looking-glass manufacturer (1792–d.1807). Death reported, *Gents Mag.*, February 1807. [D]

Sissons, —, Ringshall, Suffolk, chairmaker (c.1800). A chair has been recorded bearing a paper label 'SISSONS/RINGSHALL/3/9'. The chair appears to be of provincial manufacture and in style is of the late 18th century. [V&A archives]

Sitch, Samuel, 17 Oxford St, London, carver and gilder (1839). [D]

Sivill, —, Chiswell St, fronting the Artillery Gate, London, upholder (1725–31). [Heal]

Skardon, James, Exeter, Devon, cm (1830). In January 1830 was wounded, possibly fatally, when a firearm in his pocket was accidentally discharged. [*Exeter Flying Post*, 14 January 1830]

Skardon, James, Bedford St, Plymouth, Devon, cm and u (1830). [D]

Skardon, Joseph, Plymouth, Devon, cm, u and broker (1823–38). At 22 Broad St in 1823 and 28 Bilbury St, 1830–38. Also recorded as Isaac & Skardon. [D]

Skardon, Louisa, Exeter, Devon, u (1830–34). At 128 Fore St Hill, 1830–31 and 35 New Bridge St, 1832–34. [D]

Skardon, W. N., parish of Allhallows, Exeter, Devon, cm (1832). [Poll bk]

Skeat, Henry, The Exchange, Chester, cm (1778–82). Free on 10 June 1778. Took as app. William Skeldon in 1779. [D; freemen rolls; app. bk]

Skeat, Henry, Liverpool, cm and victualler (1787–96). At Cable St in 1787, 64 Peter St in 1790 and 59 Peter St in 1796. [D]

Skeate, William, South Park St, Westminster, London, carver (1774). [Poll bk]

Skeats, Highmore, Salisbury, Wilts., cm (1760–61). In 1760 took app. named Ecton and in 1761, Skeats. [S of G, app. index]

Skeeles, George, Crown St, St Ives, Hunts., u and appraiser (1830–39). [D]

Skeer, Thomas, 7 Willmott St, Gartside St, Manchester, carver and gilder (1840). [D]

Skegg, Edward, 7 John St, Curtain Rd, London, sofa and chair maker (1839). [D]

Skelborne, Peter, Stockport, Cheshire, cm (1752). In 1752 took app. named Clayton. [S of G, app. index]

Skeleton, Joshua, Copperas Hill, Liverpool, carver (1790). [D]

Skelhorn, Eleanor, 26 City Rd, London, chair and sofa manufacturer (1829–35). [D] Successor and possibly widow of:

Skelhorn, John, London, dyed and japanned chairmaker (1808–20). At 111 Goswell St in 1808, but from the following year at 26 City Rd, Finsbury. [D]

Skelhorn, Peter, address unknown, cm (1785). On 5 November 1785 paid £4 10s for twelve rush bottomed chairs supplied to Dunham Massey, Cheshire. [John Rylands Lib., Manchester Univ., George Cooke's accounts]

Skellicorn, Robert, Parker St, Liverpool, cm (1803). Free on 4 August 1803. [Freemen reg.]

Skellington, William, Arnold, Notts., joiner and cm (1832). [D]

Skelton, Arthur, London, upholder (1717–24). Son of Samuel Skelton of Poulner, York, Gent. App. to Remey George on 20 September 1717 and free of the Upholders' Co. by servitude, 4 November 1724. [GL, Upholders' Co. records]

Skelton, Elizabeth, 26 Coppergate, York, u (1830–37). [D]

Skelton, Humphrey, London, u (1698–1734). Free of the Upholders' Co., 1698. At Haymarket from 1709–23, Strand in 1727 and Exeter St, Strand in 1734. In August 1723 a fire broke out at the Haymarket premises 'caused by an experiment which was being carried on to smother bugs'. A Commission of Bankruptcy against him was reported in 1727 but he was still trading in 1734 in which year he was elected Beadle of the Upholders' Co. His portrait after H. Hussing and engraved by J. Faber was first published in 1728. Up to the date of his bankruptcy in 1727 he held three small copyhold farms in the manor of Woodham Walter and Ingatestone in Essex. He worked at Dyrham Park, Glos. and in July 1702 charged for a man sent to put up gilt leather. A gilt leather covered couch was also sent to Dyrham by Skelton. His name also appears in the Monson archives. A payment of £4 10s was made on 15 March 1705 and is listed in the Honble Wrey and Lady Mary Saunderson's house book. [Heal; V&A archives; Lincoln RO, Monson 10/1/A/16; GL, Upholders' Co. records]

Skelton, John, Albion St, York, upholder (1823). [D]

Skelton, Joseph, Villers St, Westminster, London, cm (1749). [Poll bk]

Skelton, Joseph, Holborn, London, cm (1790). Freeman of Lincoln. [Lincoln poll bk]

Skelton, Joseph, Halifax, Yorks., cm (1816–30). At Lord St in 1816 and Lister Lane, 1828–30. [D]

Skelton, Samuel, London, upholder (1719–40). Son of John Skelton, clockmaker, late of London. App. to William Scrimshire, upholder, and Timothy Fortune, a member of the Merchant Tailors' Co., on 13 January 1719. Free of the Upholders' Co. by servitude, 31 May 1733. Took as app. Benjamin Browne 1733–40. [GL, Upholders' Co. records]

Skelton, Thomas, Haymarket, London, upholder (1722). Bankruptcy announced, *London Gazette*, 12–15 May 1722.

Skelton, Thomas, Five Fields, Chelsea, London, picture frame maker (1784). [Westminster poll bk]

Skelton, Thomas, 17 Grape Lane, York, cm and u (1830–37). [D]

Skelton, Thomas, Hinderwell, Yorks., joiner/cm/cartwright (1834). [D]

Skerratt (or Skerritt), Samuel, Manchester, cm and u (1818–29). Listed as Skerratt at 59 London Rd in 1818 and as Skerritt at 16 Charlotte St, 1829. [D]

Skerret, George, 30 Bedford St, Covent Gdn, London, upholder (1790–96). A Thomas Skerrett is also shown trading at this address during this period. [Heal]

Skerrett, Joseph snr, Nantwich, Cheshire, u (1742–d.1756). Six sons and three daughters bapt. between 1742–56. Several of the children died in infancy and the eldest surviving son, Joseph jnr, bapt. 1 May 1745, was to follow his father in the same trade in Nantwich. Joseph Skerrett snr took app. named Liversage in 1754, but died two years later, his burial being on 21 June 1756. [PR (bapt. and burial); S of G, app. index]

Sherrett, Joseph jnr, Nantwich, Cheshire, u and auctioneer (b.1745–d.1832). Son of Joseph Sherrett snr of Nantwich and bapt. on 1 May 1745. Married on 14 June 1775 Margaret Caldwell. His father had died in 1756 when Joseph jnr was still a child, and who was responsible for his training is unclear. It is also unknown if his father's business in the town was maintained until he was of sufficient age to be responsible for it, or whether he set up afresh. He was certainly trading as an u in 1777, and in that year insured his stock for £1,000 suggesting a business of substantial size. In 1780 he insured his house for £700. He regularly advertised auction sales between 1780–84 and had agents from whom catalogues could be obtained at Drayton, Eccleshall, Newport, Ternhill and Woore. In 1789 his address was given as High Town. After 1789 no references to this business have been located, but he was still living in the town at the time of his death on 18 January 1832. He was then aged 87 and had been living in Hospital St for a number of years. [D; GL, Sun MS vol. 261, p. 636; vol. 289, p. 8; PR (bapt. and marriage); Hall, *History of Nantwich*, p. 53; *Chester Chronicle*, 19 May 1780, 16 August 1782, 23 May 1784]

Skerrett, Joseph, Baker's St, Northwich, Cheshire, u and auctioneer (1789). Possibly a branch of the Nantwich business of Joseph Skerrett jnr. [D]

Skerrett, Richard, 18 New St, Covent Gdn, London, upholder (1781). In 1781 insured his house for £100. [GL, Sun MS vol. 294, p. 522]

Skerrett, Samuel, Nottingham, cm (1797). [Freemen rolls]

Skerrett, Thomas, Bedford St, Covent Gdn, London, u (1749–d.1789). In 1758 took as app. John Skerrett. The number in Bedford St is recorded as 30 from 1782. His death was

recorded in January 1789, but despite this entries continue regularly in London directories until 1799 suggesting that the business was still trading. In 1782 supplied furniture to Charles Towneley of Towneley Hall, Burnley, Lancs., and on 10 June of that year £60 was paid on account. Heal records a George Skerret at the Bedford St address, 1790–96. [D; Westminster poll bk; S of G, app. index; *Gents Mag.*, January 1789; Charles Towneley's account bk in private ownership]

Skerrit, Robert, Manchester and Salford, Lancs., cm (1797–1808). At 159 Long Mill Gate, Manchester in 1797 but moved to 194 Chapel St, Salford where he traded 1804–08. In 1804 listed as a 'Furniture & Cabinet warehouseman'. [D]

Skerritt, Horatio, Old Church Yd, Manchester, cm (1834–39). In 1838–39 also a patent mangle maker. [D]

Skerritt, Samuel, Manchester, cm, u and auctioneer (1803–29). Freeman of Nottingham but living in Manchester by 1803. At 12 Timber St in 1813, 59 London Rd in 1818 and 16 Charlotte St, 1828–29. [D; Nottingham poll bks]

Sketchley, Power, Atherstone, Warks., cm (1822). [D]

Skidmore, Sedgley, Staffs., carpenter/cm (1838). [D]

Skidmore, Thomas, Birmingham, cm, u and broker (1816–35). Listed at Bromsgrove St in 1816; Horsefair, 1822–30, no. 42 in 1828; and 55 Edgbaston St in 1835. [D]

Skilbeck, G., address unknown, cm (1784). Supplied two inlaid mahogany tables for Dunham Massey, Cheshire in 1784 and was paid £4 4s for these on 29 October of that year. [John Rylands Lib., Manchester Univ., George Cooke's accounts]

Skilito, Daniel, Wakefield, Yorks., carver (1761). In 1761 took app. named Barkham. [S of G, app. index]

Skillicorn, John, Liverpool, carver and gilder (1818–26). Son of Robert Skillicorn, shipwright. Free on 11 June 1818. At this date he was living at Lisborn Pl., Nash Grove but by 1821 was trading at 11 Silver St, moving to 4 Marshall St by 1823 and 5 Thomas Ct, Milton St the following year. Took as apps Daniel Large Dilworth and George Mathew Porteous in 1823 and Joseph Dugdale in 1826. [D; freemen reg.; app. bk]

Skillicorn, Robert, Liverpool, cm (1795–1810). App. in 1795 to Edward Charles and petitioned freedom in 1803. Trading at 57 Stanley St in 1805 as a cm and household broker, and at 16 Prices St in 1807 as a cm and victualler. In 1810 at 14 Liver St. [D; freemen's committee bk]

Skilton, George, Castle St, Salisbury, Wilts., cm and u (1822). [D]

Skinner, Catherine, Boutport St, Barnstaple, Devon, u (1838). [D]

Skinner, David, Newington Causeway, London, cm (1808–10). At 42 Newton Causeway in 1808 but in the year following stated to be at 43. Bankruptcy announced, *London Gazette*, 24 March 1810. [D]

Skinner, Harry, London, upholder (1726–33). Son of Richard Skinner of Pixley, Herts., Gent. App. to Robert Webb on 3 August 1726 and then to Thomas Dobyns 13 September 1732. Free of the Upholders' Co. by servitude, 3 October 1733. [GL, Upholders' Co. records]

Skinner, James, Southampton, Hants., cm and auctioneer (1783–84). [D]

Skinner, John, 20 King St, Lambeth, London, cm (1808). [D]

Skinner, John, Market Pl., Witney, Oxon., cm and u (1830). [D]

Skinner, Joseph, 240 Whitechapel Rd, London, cm and u (1839). [D]

Skinner, Joshua, High St, Southampton, Hants., cm (1798–1808). [D]

Skinner, Nathaniel, 'The Black Lyon', south side of St Paul's Churchyard, London, cm (1754–62). His trade card indicates that he made and sold 'all sorts of Cain Rush & Coverd-Chairs, and Bed-Chairs & Tables, with all Sorts of

Cabinetwork, & Painted-Window-Blinds, all sorts of Looking-Glasses, Wholesale or Retaile'. Heal dates this card to c.1730 but no documentary evidence of this maker is known before 1754. He was a member of the Drapers' Co., and from 1754–61 regularly took out licences to employ non-freemen. The number in the early years was only two, and these were licenced for part of the year only in most years. By 1760 however, the number had risen to three employed throughout the year, and in the following year five who were licenced for three months, and then a further three licenced for three months. On 29 June 1762 Archdeacon Yardley on behalf of the SPCK paid Skinner £1 18s for a mahogany elbow chair for the Common Room. [Heal; GL, City Licence bks, vols 1 and 2; SPCK cash bk FT9/7]

Skinner, Richard, Fore St, Tiverton, Devon, cm and u (1823–28). In March 1824 it was reported that he had been robbed of a pocket book containing £40 in notes, a fellow passenger being responsible. Declared bankrupt in January 1827, but in January of the following year it was reported that the bankruptcy proceedings against him had been suspended. [D; *Exeter Flying Post*, 4 March 1824, 24 January 1828; *London Gazette*, 23 January 1827]

Skinner, Thomas, Tower St, Bristol, chairmaker (1793). [D]

Skinner, Thomas, Nottingham, carver, gilder and victualler (1793–d.1794). Will proved on 26 May 1794. [Notts. RO, probate records]

Skinner, William, Grimsby, Lincs., joiner, cm and u (1831–40). In 1831–35 at South St, Mary's Gate but by 1841 had moved to Bethlem St. [D]

Skinnor, David, Husband St, Westminster, London, cm (1784). [Poll bk]

Skipper, Abraham, London, u and cm (1814–37). Shown at 19 Broker Row in 1814, but in 1821 the number was given as 15. Also occupied 13 and 14 Eldon St from 1815, and was solely at this address in 1826. [D]

Skipsey & Rutherford (or Skipley & Rutterford), Church Rd (or Way), North Shields, Northumb., cm (1827–34). Listed at 23 Church Way in 1834. [D]

Skull, Charles, High Wycombe, Bucks., chairmaker and japanner (1813–40). Two sons and a daughter bapt., 1813–19. Trading at Temple Pl., 1823–30, in 1823 as u, cm and chairmaker and in 1830 as cm and u. [D; PR (bapt.)]

Skull, Edwin, High Wycombe, Bucks., chairmaker and japanner (b.c. 1811–41). Aged 30 at the tme of the 1841 Census.

Skull, John, High Wycombe, Bucks., chairmaker (b.c. 1806–41). Two sons and two daughters bapt., 1835–40. Aged 35 at the time of the 1841 Census. [PR (bapt.)]

Skull, Thomas, High Wycombe, Bucks., chairmaker (1816–37). Children bapt., 1816–37. [PR (bapt.)]

Skurr, John, Dalston, near Carlisle, Cumb., cm/joiner (1834). [D]

Skurr, William, Keswick, Cumb., joiner/cm (1828–29). [D]

Skurray, John, London, u (1731–49). On 24 April 1731 married Mary Wickes, the sister of the Royal goldsmith George Wickes (1698–1761). Subsequently lived in Gerrard St, Soho and had a son and two daughters. In 1749 living at Prince's St, St James's. [Barr, *George Wickes, Royal Goldsmith*, p. 31; Heal]

Skurray, William, Northgate, Wakefield, Yorks., cm (1784–94). In September 1794 the sale of his stocks of timber, workshop and warehouse was announced. [D; *Leeds Intelligencer*, 22 September 1794]

Skynner, John, London, upholder (1707–34). Son of John Skynner of Wenham Magna, Suffolk, clerk. App. to Joseph Richardson and James Clark on 4 April 1707. Clark was a member of the Drapers' Co. He was then transferred to Thomas Kelsall on 1 August 1710. Free of the Upholders' Co.

by servitude, 13 March 1733/34. [GL, Upholders' Co. records]

Skynner, Thomas, Broad St, Hereford, cm (?) (1778). In June 1778 advertised a raffle for a curious piece of furniture which he claimed to have made. This was a 'CABINET EAGLE, with 5 private drawers in its breast, one set with diamonds, topazes, rubies and other valuable stones. It stands between two book-cases upon a bureau, with a serpentine front. . . . The escutcheon on the breast of the Eagle is made to prevent any person from picking the lock, it being made by so peculiar a method, that no person can move it off the keyhole but the person shuts it up, even though they have seen it opened'. The piece of furniture was valued by Skynner at £63 and tickets were offered at £1 1s. The number of persons prepared to purchase tickets was perhaps not as great as anticipated as the period for sale had to be extended beyond 7 July on which date it was previously announced that the draw would take place. [*Hereford Journal*, 18 June 1778]

Slack, John, 4 Dale St, Oldham St, Manchester, carver and gilder (1840). [D]

Slack, Seth, Standishgate, Wigan, Lancs., cm (1822). [D]

Slade, Henry, Beaminster, Dorset, chairmaker (1779). In 1779 took out insurance cover of £200 which included £55 for utensils, stock and a workshop. [GL, Sun MS vol. 277, p. 74]

Sladen, William, 44 Cannon St Rd, London, cm and u (1822). [D]

Slader, R., near the Market Pl., Sidmouth, Devon (1813). In 1813 advertised for an app. Slader claimed to have had 'a number of years' experience in some of the principal shops in London'. [*Exeter Flying Post*, 19 December 1813]

Slader, Richard, Cheltenham, Glos., cm (1830–40). Recorded at 428 High St in 1830, also as an u, and at Montpellier Arcade in 1839. [D]

Slater, —, Budge Row, London, u (1748). [Heal]

Slater, Abraham, Maryport, Cumb., cm/ joiner (1834). [D]

Slater, Charles, Norwich, cm (1805). Son of William Slater, hotpresser; admitted freeman on 26 July 1805. [Freemen reg.]

Slater, Edward, 24 Upper Beau St, Liverpool, cm (1818). App. to William Smith and free 12 June 1818. A Richard Slater, cm was free on the same day. [Freemen reg.]

Slater, Edward, 22 Queen's Buildings, Knightsbridge, London, u etc. (1826–39). In 1835–39 shown also at 21 and 23 Queen's Buildings. [D]

Slater, Edward, 69 High Holborn, London, cm, u and bedstead maker (1827). [D]

Slater, Gilbert, 5 Carthusian St, London, cm etc. (1809). [D]

Slater, John, parish of St John the Baptist, London, u (d.1766). Will proved on 26 July 1766. Appears to have been reasonably affluent at the time of his death. [Probate records]

Slater, John, Liverpool, cm and joiner (1769–1810). At 8 Water St, 1769–84, but then moved to Dawson St, Whitechapel, where he was listed at no. 8 in 1790, 10 in 1796 and 3, 1800–05. He was also recorded at 8 Seel St, Hanover St in 1804, no. 10 in 1805 and from 1807–10 at no. 12. John Slater was already dead by September 1818 when the death of his son William, also a joiner and cm, was announced, *Liverpool Mercury*, 25 September 1818. [D] See Slater & Dutton.

Slater, John, parish of St Martin at Palace, Norwich, cm (1806–18). [Poll bks]

Slater, John, Yorkshire St, Burnley, Lancs., chairmaker and turner (1816–18). [D]

Slater, John, Bridge St, Bishop's Stortford, Herts., cm and u (1832–39). Listed as u and auctioneer in 1838. [D]

Slater, Joseph, 11 Well St, Manchester, chair bottomer (1797). [D]

Slater, Jos., 9 Northumberland Pl., Commercial Rd, London, u (1826). [D]

Slater, Luke, Church St, Blackburn, Lancs., chairmaker (1816–34). Shown at 40 Church St in 1816 but soon afterwards the number was changed to 44. [D]

Slater, Richard, Lancaster, cm (b.1750–d.1833). App. to R. Thorney in 1765. Named in the Gillow records, 1785, 1787–1807, 1809, 1811, 1825 and 1827. A sofa in a private collection stamped 'GILLOWS LANCASTER' has elsewhere on the frame in pencil 'Richd Slater Aprill 1824'. At the time of his death in October 1833 aged 83 it was said that he had formerly been an employee of Gillows 'where he worked at one bench upward of 50 years'. [App. reg.; Westminster Ref. Lib., Gillow; *Liverpool Mercury*, 25 October 1833]

Slater, Richard, Liverpool, cm (1818). Free 12 June 1818. An Edward Slater, cm, was free on the same day. [Freemen reg.]

Slater, Robert, Woodcocks Yd, Preston, Lancs., cm (1818–40). At Woodcock's Yd in 1818 and still in Preston in 1822. In that year he was stated to be the son of Henry Slater, deceased. By 1842 he was living in Manchester. [D; freemen rolls]

Slater, Robert, Talbot St, Derby, cm (1829). [D]

Slater, Samuel, Blackburn, Lancs., chairmaker (1798). [D]

Slater, William, Lancaster, cm (1795–96). Free 1795–96 when stated 'of Hurst Green'. [Freemen rolls]

Slater, William, Lancaster, cm (1817–18). [Freemen rolls]

Slater, William, 10 Seel St, Liverpool, cm and joiner (1805–d.1818). Son of John Slater and probably in 1805 trading in partnership with his father. Died on 13 September 1818 [D; *Liverpool Mercury*, 25 September 1818] See Slater & Dutton.

Slater, William, Cirencester, Glos., cm (1827). Child bapt. in 1827. [PR (bapt.)]

Slater, William, Knowles Ct, Kensington, Liverpool, cm (1829). [D]

Slater & Co., 40 Oxford St, London, u (1825). [D]

Slater & Dutton, Seel St, Liverpool, cm (1803–14). At 9 Seel St in 1803 and 12/13 in 1805–14. John Slater and his son William were trading from addresses at 8, 10 and 12 Seel St at various dates from 1804–10, and were without doubt involved in this partnership.

Slatter, Gabriel, London and Magdalene Bridge, St Clements, Oxford, cm (1779–d.1780). Gabriel Slatter described himself as a cm 'from London', and in 1779 was in partnership with a William Slatter at 191 High Holborn. In October 1779 announced that he had taken over the shop formerly occupied by the late Mr James (George James). He must have died soon afterwards, for probate on his will was granted on 1 April 1780. [*Jackson's Oxford Journal*, 2 October 1779; Bodleian Lib., index of wills]

Slatter, Thomas, Oxford, cm and joiner (1780). In *Jackson's Oxford Journal*, 8 April 1780 it was announced that Richard Rouse late of St Peter's-in-the-East had given up his business as a cm and joiner in favour of Thomas Slatter of Holywell, who had taken over the shop and yard opposite Longwall.

Slatter, William & Gabriel, 191 High Holborn, London, cm (1779). In 1779 took out insurance cover of £300 of which £80 was for stock and goods. [GL, Sun MS vol. 273, p. 98] See Gabriel Slatter.

Slaughter, Matthew, London, upholder (1705). Free of the Upholders' Co., 1 August 1705. [GL, Upholders' Co. records]

Slaughter, Richard, Princes Risborough, Bucks., chairmaker (1839). [D]

Slaughter, Thomas, Lower Holloway, London, bedstead maker (1809). [D]

Slaughter, Thomas M., London and Sandwich, Kent, cm (1831–37). Freeman of Sandwich and living in the town July 1837. In May 1831, however, he was living in London. [Sandwich poll bks]

Slawin, John, Black Bank, Leeds, Yorks., cm (1822). [D]

Sleat, Robert, New Canal, Salisbury, Wilts., carver and gilder (1839). [D]

Slee, —, area of Water Lane, Fleet St, London, portable desk maker. (1807). In August 1807 his premises were destroyed by a fire which started in an adjacent workshop. [*Gents Mag.*, August 1807]

Slee, Benjamin, 24 Gt New St, Fetter Lane, London, cm and u (1839). [D]

Slee, Joseph, Washington St, Workington, Cumb., joiner/cm (1828–34). [D]

Sleeford, Richard, London, upholder (1698). Free of the Upholders' Co., 29 October 1698. [GL, Upholders' Co. records]

Slevan, John, Cockermouth, Cumb., cm/joiner (1834). [D]

Sliegh, Samuel snr, London, upholder (1743). Freeman and member of the Upholders' Co. Father of Samuel Sliegh jnr. [GL, Upholders' Co. records]

Sliegh, Samuel jnr, Gt Bartholomew Close, u and auctioneer (1743–d. by 1757). Son of Samuel Sliegh snr a member of the Upholders' Co.; admitted freeman of the Co. by patrimony on 7 September 1743. He took as apps William Jole, 1740–50/51; Robert Tabor, 1747–54; and Samuel Martin in 1754. Samuel Sliegh jnr was dead by 1757 when the sale of his household goods and stock in trade was announced, *Public Advertiser*, 23 May. [GL, Upholders' Co. records]

Slight & Robertson, 15 Ship St, Brighton, Sussex, cm and u (1826). [D]

Slinger, Thomas, Lancaster (1799–1800). Named in the Gillow records in 1800 in connection with the manufacture of a bookcase. [Westminster Ref. Lib., Gillow vol. 344/98, p. 1561]

Slinger, Thomas, Burton-in-Lonsdale, near Ingleton, Yorks., joiner and cm (1822). [D]

Slingsby, Thomas, Hull, Yorks., cm (1784). [Poll bk]

Slingsby, William, Hull, Yorks., cm (1834–39). At Witham in 1835 and 1839, but in 1838 shown at Church St, Wincolmlee and described as a joiner and beer house keeper. [D]

Sloan, John, 30 Standish St, Liverpool, cm (1839). [D]

Sloan, Robert, 19 Naylor St with a shop at 12 Hatton Gdn, Liverpool, joiner and cm (1835). [D]

Slocombe, Chas., High St, Shepton Mallet, Som., cm (1839). [D]

Slocombe, Thomas, 'The Crossed Keys', Bridgwater, Som., cm (1793–1801). In December 1801 took out insurance cover of £400 but of this only £90 was for utensils and stock. [D; GL, Sun MS vol. 43, ref. 726261] Probably:

Slocombe, Thomas, Bridgwater, Som., cm and u (1822–40). At Cornhill in 1822 and Fore St, 1830–40. [D]

Slocombe, Thomas, Ilfracombe, Devon, cm and u (1838). [D]

Sloman, Bartlett, 88 Wardour St, Soho, London, u and sofa and invalid chair manufacturer (1835). [D]

Sloman, Benjamin, 26 Ann's Ct, Dean St, Soho, London, chair and sofa maker (1839). Another Benjamin Sloman is recorded at 52 Old Compton St in the same year as a furniture broker. [D]

Sloman, Robert, Worcester St, Gloucester, chairmaker (1830). [D]

Sloman, Samuel, 45 Wardour St, Soho, London, cm and u (1839). [D]

Slurt, Nathaniel, address unknown, cm (1803). Subscribed to Sheraton's *Cabinet Dictionary*, 1803.

Sly, Bannister, London St, Greenwich, London, cm and u (1839). [D]

Sly, Joseph, 44 Church St, Little Minories, London, cm and broker (1802). In April 1802 took out insurance cover of £400. [GL, Sun MS vol. 423, ref. 730478]

Smagg, Peter, Frith St, Soho, London, cm (1730–44). Appears to have been associated with the business conducted by John

Hodson in Frith St, probably a partner. He receipted a number of bills 'for Hodson & self'. His name is found in connection with a payment of £52 16s made in 1730 in connection with Longford Castle, Wilts. On 2 November 1731 Sir John Dutton of Sherborne House, Glos. paid him £22 8s for fourteen painted chairs 'for my Hall at ye Lodge', £1 15s for a mahogany basin stand for 'ye Bed Chamber' and other sundries. [Heal; V&A archives; Glos. RO, D678 account bk]

Smailes, John, 5 Tanner St, Scarborough, Yorks., cm and u (1828–40). [D]

Smale, J., Tything, Worcester, carver and gilder (1837). [D]

Smale, James, 1 Ferry St, High St, Lambeth, London, carver and gilder (1826). [D]

Smale, James, Allhalland St, Bideford, Devon, carver, gilder etc. (1830). [D]

Small, James, Piccadilly, London, u (1782–95). Initially in partnership with Nicholas Phillipson. In 1785 the partners supplied Sir John Nelthorpe with six 'yoke top stain'd chairs' at 3s 6d each and two matching stools at 2s each. The account was receipted by William Arundale on behalf of the partners. By 1786 the partnership appears to have ended and both continued to trade on their own behalf. James Small occupied premises at 189 Piccadilly, 1788–93, but from this latter year the number changed to 190. In January 1791 took out insurance cover of £2,000 which included utensils and stock valued at £1,400. This seems to suggest that the business was of substantial proportions at this period. Subscribed to Sheraton's *Drawing Book*, 1793. A pair of satinwood shield back upholstered chairs which were on the market in 1966 were offered with the original invoice which shows that they were supplied to Robert Buxton on 19 July 1786 at a cost of £6 10s including packing and transport charges. [D; GL, Sun MS ref. 579017, 7 January 1791; Grosvenor House Antique's Fair, 1966, p. 89; Lincoln RO, NEL 9/7/19]

Small, John, Church St, Guisborough, Yorks., joiner and cm (1829–40). Probably successor to Thomas Small jnr, who was at this address in 1823. [D]

Small, L. & S., 8 Narrow Wine St, Bristol, working u (1834). The partners were probably Lydia and Samuel Small. [D]

Small, Lydia, Narrow Wine St, Bristol, u (1819–27). [D]

Small, Samuel, Bristol, fancy chairmaker (1814–23). At 79 Redcliff St, 1814–15, 31 Maryport St in 1816 and 5 Bridewell Lane, 1819–23. [D] See L. & S. Small.

Small, Thomas jnr, Church St, Guisborough, Yorks., joiner/cm/u (1823). The John Small trading at this address from 1829–40 as a joiner and cm was probably his successor. [D]

Small, Thomas Bell, 158 Pilgrim St, with a house at Court 9, Bigg Mkt, Newcastle, wood turner and carver (1827–28). [D]

Small, Thomas, 18 King St, Covent Gdn, papier mâché manufacturer (1833–40). Successor to Henry Clay. In March 1833 the business was trading as Thomas Small & Son, 'Manufacturer of Paper Tea Trays &c.'. The Earl of Surrey was in this month supplied with 'Paper Tea Trays, Waiter, Knife Trays' costing £15 18s. The firm claimed appointment to 'her Majesty & the Royal Family', and on 31 March 1840 supplied the Crown with a japanned circular table 'Rich Gold & Flower Ornament' at £15 5s, a japanned paper inkstand with inlay at £2 10s and a further 'Paper Japan Inkstand Buhl', at £2 2s [Windsor Royal Archives, account bks 1833–41; Arundel Castle records, A2045]

Smallbone, John, London, bedstead maker (1829–39). At 28 Gt Titchfield St in 1829 when the business was merely listed as Smallbones. In 1839 at 23 Cumberland St, Tottenham Ct Rd. [D]

Smallbone, Thomas, Buckingham St, London, chairmaker (1794–95). Paid £15 5s 4d by Lord Howard of Audley End,

Essex for making a set of ten hall seats. These were similar to a pattern seat collected from the studio of Biagio Rebecca and they were painted in accordance with his instructions. When completed they were taken to Rebecca's studio in Charlotte St for 'ornamental painting'. The seats were for the Great Hall at Audley End. [Essex RO, D/DBy/A53/4]

Smalley, John, Northampton, upholder (1820–30). In 1820 living in Bearward St and from 1823–30 in Abington St. [D; poll bks]

Smallhorn, John, 9 Cleveland St, Fitzroy Sq., London, carver and gilder (1839). [D]

Smallman, Edward, Syllaton near Oswestry, Salop, joiner and chairmaker (1782). In November 1782 his death was announced at Syllaton. He was obviously a noted character locally and was known as Dick Spot. Apart from his skill at his own trade he was renowned as a 'Jack of all Trades . . . Planetarian and Conjuror'. [*Chester Chronicle*, 15 November 1782]

Smallman, John, address unknown, cm and u (1771–72). Supplied considerable quantities of furniture to Downton Castle Herefs. for Richard Payne Knight 1771–72. Three invoices are known, the first dated 20 February 1771 was for £118 3s 7¾d and later on 22 August 1771 another was issued for £62 15s 1½d The third invoice dated 14 March 1772 for £50 14s 8d was issued in the names of John Smallman and Thomas Hugh. The five-page bill of 20 February 1771 was in the main for fabrics, papers and paperhanging but also included such items as eleven mahogany stools at 11s each and sixteen mahogany chairs for bedchambers supplied in canvas for 14s each. The August bill again listed many fabrics, papers and work undertaken but included a tent bedstead at £6, three mahogany basin stands at 15s each, a pair of mahogany five drawer chests at £7 and a commode chest of drawers at £9 9s. Furniture supplied in March 1772 included further fabrics and paper, several items of bedroom furniture but also a mahogany sideboard at £6 6s, a mahogany wine tub at £2 5s and fire screens and hall lanterns. [Herefs. RO, T74/413A]

Smallman, Joseph, New St, Hereford, cm and u (1830). [D]

Smallman, Robert, Maidstone, Kent, cm (1830–31). [Poll bks]

Smalls & Hipkiss, Birmingham, papier mâché manufacturers (early 19th century). Japanned papier mâché trays are recorded stamped with the name of this firm under a crown. [*Conn.*, August 1967]

Smallwood, —, 29 Chancery Lane, London, cm (1803). Subscribed to Sheraton's *Cabinet Dictionary*, 1803 See John Smallwood.

Smallwood, Edward, Dale End, Birmingham, cm (1818). [D]

Smallwood, Henry, 3 Meeting House Ct, Drury Lane, London, upholder (1781). In 1781 insured a house for £100. [GL, Sun MS vol. 292, p. 408]

Smallwood, John, London, cm and u (1774–1802). From 1774 at 5 Greenfield St, Fieldgate, Whitechapel which was retained as a manufactory throughout the existence of the business. By 1792, however, an additional address at 40 King St, Covent Gdn was being used and the business was described as J. Smallwood & Co., upholsterers. His son, William, who was free of the Upholders' Co. by redemption in 1797, may have been assisting him by this date. He also had another son, Joseph. By 1803 the business was listed as W. Smallwood & Co. and John may have been no longer active, although his name was included in the list of master cabinet makers in Sheraton's *Cabinet Dictionary*, 1803. A Smallwood also subscribed to this publication and was living at 29 Chancery Lane. This may have been John or either of his sons. After 1802 the Whitechapel premises passed first to William and then Joseph. The King St address does not appear in directories after 1799. [D]

Smallwood, Joseph, 2 Greenfield St, Fieldgate, Whitechapel, London (*c*.1808–39). Son of John Smallwood and ultimately his successor. In 1808 operating the business in partnership with William, his brother. It is likely, however, that he was in sole charge from the next year. In March 1809 insurance cover of £1,000 was taken out which included £200 for a workshop and warehouse to the rear of 2 Greenfield St, £300 for utensils and stock in them and £200 for utensils and stock in a yard. Stock levels had, however, fallen considerably by 1820 and then were only £200 out of a total insured value of £950 with similar figures for 1824. Upholsterers to the East India Co., 1820–37. [D; GL, Sun MS ref. 828222, 13 March 1809; vol. 452, ref. 848155; vol. 485, ref. 974155; vol. 497, ref. 1016111] See John and William Smallwood.

Smallwood, Thomas, New Meeting St, Birmingham, cm (1793–1800). At New Meeting St in 1793 and Dale End, 1800. Patronised by Matthew Boulton. [D; V&A archives]

Smallwood, Thomas, 3 Fazeley St, Birmingham, cabinet case maker (1835). [D]

Smallwood, Thomas, Macclesfield, Cheshire (b.1792–1816). Born at Macclesfield and married in 1815. Trading at Park Green in 1816. Moved to Boston, Mass., USA soon after this date and established himself there in business as a cm and u. [American Antiquarian Soc. Coll., Worcester, Mass.]

Smallwood, William, London, cm and u (1797–1809). Son of John Smallwood and free of the Upholders' Co. by redemption, 5 April 1797. In this year living at 40 King St, Covent Gdn, a property then in use by his father. In *Liverpool Advertiser*, 16 August 1802, declared bankrupt. Traded at Greenfield St, Whitechapel, 1803–09 as W. Smallwood & Co., the number being 5 in 1803 and from 1808, no. 2. This property also had been used by his father John. One directory of 1808 lists the business as William & Joseph Smallwood and from *c*.1809 Joseph appears to have been in sole control. [D; GL, Upholders' Co. records]

Smallwood, William & Co., Bull St, Birmingham, u and cm (1784–1822). In 1784 the business was simply listed as Smallwood, but from 1805–22 as Smallwood & Co. Other addresses given in the directory of 1818 for William Smallwood were Honduras Wharf, Snowhill, possibly a timber yard, and Lady Wood Lane, possibly his house. [D] See Smallwoods & Appletree.

Smallwood, William, Darlington St, Wolverhampton, Staffs., cm and u (1827–35). [D]

Smallwoods & Appletree, 69 Bull St, Birmingham, cm and u (1828). [D]

Smart, Abraham Chubb, Bath, Som., cm (1827). In partnership with Charles Symes when their bankruptcy was announced, *Chester Chronicle*, 2 February 1827.

Smart, C., Alvin St, Gloucester, u (1839). [D]

Smart, Daniel, Mount East St, Nottingham, cm (1835–40). [D]

Smart, David, Castle St, Saffron Walden, Essex, chairmaker (1839). [D]

Smart, E. & H., 10 Titchborne St, Piccadilly, London, carvers, gilders and picture dealers (1835–37). [D]

Smart, Francis, Nottingham, chairmaker (d.1838). Will proved on 7 November 1838. [Notts. RO, probate records]

Smart, George, London, cm (1790–93). In 1790 at 331 Oxford St as a cm and musical instrument maker. By 1793 had moved to 16 Bell Alley, Coleman St and was listed as a cm only. [D]

Smart, Henry, Lewes, Sussex, chairmaker and turner (1835–40). At North St in January 1835, St Mary's Lane in July 1837 and New St in November 1839. [D; poll bks] See William Smart of Lewes.

Smart, James, Liverpool, carver and gilder (1793–d.1813). App. to William Cashen in 1793 and petitioned freedom in 1802. His petition was, however, rejected. Died on 5 June 1813 at

Preston, Lancs. 'after a Tedious illness'. [Freemen's committee bk; *Liverpool Mercury*, 18 June 1813]

Smart, John, 84 Leather Lane, Holborn, London, carver (1779). In 1779 insured a house for £100. [GL, Sun MS vol. 274, p. 341]

Smart, Jonathan, High St, Saffron Walden, Essex, cm and u (1832–39). The 3rd Lord Braybrooke of Audley End, Essex paid to a Smart, u, £4 5s 4d in August 1839, and £7 7s 4d in December 1839. It is likely that Jonathan Smart was the tradesman involved. [D; Essex RO, D/DBy/A363]

Smart, Sarah, Fishergate, Nottingham, chairmaker (1840). [D]

Smart, Susannah, 7 St James's Churchyard, Bristol, u (1775). [D]

Smart, Thomas, Nottingham, chairmaker (1814–32). At Red Lion Sq. in 1814; Butcher St, 1818–22, Red Lion St in 1825 and Fishergate, 1828–32. [D]

Smart, Thomas, Soho, London, carver and gilder (1817–39). At 2 Nassau St, 1817–20 and 53 Greek St, 1835–39. [D]

Smart, William, Lower Moorfields, London, cabinet and upholstery warehouse (1784). [D]

Smart, William, Lewes, Sussex, chairmaker and turner (1823–35). At North St in June 1818 but at 3 Market St, 1823–26. Moved to New St and shown there, 1832–35. [D; poll bks] See Henry Smart of Lewes.

Smart, William, Gloucester (1827–31). Three children bapt. between 1827–31 at St Aldgate's Church. [PR (bapt.)]

Smart, William, Ware, Herts., cm and u (1832–39). Listed at Land Row in 1832, Middle Row in 1838, and High St in 1839, also as an appraiser. Recorded as William jnr, 1832–38. [D]

Smartfoot, Benjamin, West Smithfield, London, cm (1723–25). In February 1723 next door to the 'Three Ton Tavern against the sheep pens', West Smithfield. In this month he took out insurance cover of £500 on his goods and merchandise in his dwelling house. In 1725 at 'The Lion & Lamb' near 'The Ram Inn', West Smithfield. [GL, Sun MS vol. 17, ref. 31132; Heal]

Smathers, Samuel, Chester, cm (1818–19). Free 18 May 1818 and at this date living at Lower Lane. In 1819 at Linenhall St. [Freemen rolls; poll bk]

Smee, Samuel, Norwich, cm (1814). App. to Samuel Tubby and free, 3 May 1814. [Freemen admission reg.]

Smee, William, 1 Artillery St, Bishopgate St, London, broker and cm (1793). In April 1793 took out insurance cover of £200 of which £130 was for utensils and stock. [GL, Sun MS vol. 395, p. 8]

Smee, William, London, cm and u (1806–40). At 5 Pavement, Moorfields from 1806, although by 1838 it had been re-numbered 6 and is referred to as Finsbury Pavement. From 1835 had additional premises at 34 Little Moorfields. In the period 1838–40 referred to as William Smee & Sons. A breakfront mahogany bookcase of *c*.1825 is known marked with the name of this maker. [D; Christie's, 16 April 1970, lot 128]

Smee, William, 6 Devonshire St, Bishopsgate St, London, u (1826–29). [D]

Smeed, James, St Mildred, Canterbury, Kent, cm (1826). [Poll bk]

Smeed, John, St Mildred, Canterbury, Kent, cm (1830–31). [Canterbury and Sandwich poll bks]

Smethhurst, Samuel, Manchester, u (1752–56). In 1752 took app. named Rothwell and in 1756, Ashton. [S of G, app. index]

Smiles, James, Newcastle, working u (1827–38). Recorded at Liverpool Terr., Percy St in 1827 and Liverpool St, 1834–38. [D]

Smiles, John, London, cm (1793). Subscribed to Sheraton's *Drawing Book*, 1793.

Smiles, William, St John's Lane, Newcastle, wood turner and carver (1827). [D]

Smith, Mrs, address unknown, u (c.1720). Supplied a bed for Erddig, Clwyd, N. Wales. [*Apollo*, July 1978, p. 52]

Smith, —, at 'The Chair', Fleet St, London, upholder (1744–48). Described as a widow. Succeeded by William Jellicoe. [Heal]

Smith, —, address unknown, u (1772–73). Supplier to Richard Hoare of Boreham House, Essex. Smith was paid £7 19s on 18 April 1772 and 18s in May 1773. It is likely that Smith traded either in London or Chelmsford. [Essex RO, D/Du 649/2]

Smith, —, London, u (1793). Subscribed to Sheraton's *Drawing Book*, 1793.

Smith, — jnr, Norwich, cm (1793). Subscribed to Sheraton's *Drawing Book*, 1793.

Smith, —, Warwick St, London, u (1794–95). Customer of Kennett & Kidd, u and cm of Bond St, London. [PRO, C114/181]

Smith, —, Black Prince Row, Newington, London, cm etc. (1809). [D]

Smith, Abraham, 'The Three Crowns', St Olave's St, Southwark, London, upholder (1704–20). Son of Abraham Smith, a member of the Feltmakers' Co. App. to John Righton on 3 April 1704 and free of the Upholders' Co. by servitude, 11 April 1716. At St Olave's St, Southwark in 1720. [GL, Upholders' Co. records; Sun MS vol. 12, ref. 18976]

Smith, Alexander, 2 Tottenham Ct Rd, London, cm (1782). In 1782 took out insurance cover of £400 of which £250 was for utensils and stock. [GL, Sun MS vol. 303, p. 134]

Smith, Alexander, 11 Orange St, Red Lion Sq., London, carver and gilder (1823–27). His trade card [Landauer Coll., MMA, NY] states that he made 'Borders for Rooms, Bed & Window Cornices, Old Frames regilt & Modernized, Looking Glasses New Polished & Silvered, Drawings & Needle work carefully mounted and neatly Framed & Glazed, Old Paintings Cleaned, Lined & Repaired'. Insurance records show that he also traded as a librarian and dealer in looking-glasses. In December 1823 he took out insurance cover for £500 of which £300 was for utensils and stock. He was succeeded at this address in 1827 by W. S. Smith. [D; Heal; GL, Sun MS vol. 497, ref. 1010879]

Smith, Andrew, Crown Ct, Little Pulteney St, Westminster, London, cm (1784). [Poll bk]

Smith, Ann(e), Broad St, Ludlow, Salop, cm and u (1828–35). [D]

Smith, Benjamin, Lancaster and Arkholme, Lancs., cm (1773–84). App. to W. Blackburn in 1773 and free, 1783–84. Moved from Lancaster to Arkholme and was living there in April 1784. [App. reg.; freemen rolls; poll bk]

Smith, Benjamin, Palace St, St Martin's Norwich, cm (1802–d.1840). Subscribed to Sheraton's *Cabinet Dictionary*, 1803. Will proved in 1840 and at this date said to be of St Giles, Norwich. [D; poll bks; Norfolk Record Soc., index of wills]

Smith, Benjamin, Halifax, Yorks., cm and u (1814–22). At Cheapside 1814–18, Bull Green in 1818 and Southgate in 1822. [D]

Smith, Benjamin, Butcher Row, Oundle, Northants., cm/and joiner (1823). [D]

Smith, Benjamin, 3 Dean St, Soho, London, picture frame and looking-glass maker (1839). [D]

Smith, Charles, Upper End of Broad St, St James's, London, cm (1746–59). Heal gives an address at Marshall St, Carnaby Mkt derived from a poll bk of 1749. These two locations may be identical. A fashionable maker who received patronage from people of note. In 1746 he received a payment from the Earl of Stair and in this commission appears to have been associated with Campbell & Bruce. On 24 May 1753 he invoiced Gertrude, Duchess of Bedford for a Mahog. Ladys Secretary with a Gothick Top good Brass Locks & wro[t] Handles'. This was charged at £7 7s with 10s 6d packing. His billhead, engraved by Matthias Darly, has a fine engraved Rococo cartouche and illustrations of a Gothick cabinet and ribband back chair. Charles Smith was also probably the cm paid £35 on 9 May 1749 in connection with Panshanger, Herts. In January 1759 Ince & Mayhew advertised that they had 'taken the house of Mr. Charles Smith, cabinet maker and upholsterer in Carnaby Market who has left off that branch of business'. [Heal; *Apollo*, January 1956, p. 10; Scottish RO, GD 135/Box 55/31; Bedford Office, London; Herts. RO, D/EP A2]

Smith, Charles, Portugal St, Lincoln's Inn Fields, London, u and cm (1763–d. by 1767). Possibly the same maker who was trading from Broad St, Carnaby Mkt, 1746–59. If this is so, then Ince & Mayhew, who had taken over his former business in 1759 on the understanding that he was giving up his former trade, would no doubt have been displeased at his re-appearance in the trade. In 1763 he was one of the executors of the will of William Vile. Smith was himself dead by May 1767 when an account settled by Sir Laurance Dundas for a bedstead, bedding, drapery, carpets etc. was receipted by Smith's executors. In March of the following year the balance of his stock was put up for sale. [D; Heal; N. Yorks. RO, ZNK x i/7/75; *Public Advertiser*, 17 March 1768]

Smith, Charles, 40 Ridmaid Lane, Hermitage, London, cm (1781). In 1781 insured a house for £100. [GL, Sun MS vol. 295, p. 568]

Smith, Charles, Lower Grosvenor St, London, u (1781–1825). Charles Smith traded on his own account at 69 Lower Grosvenor St, 1784–90, and by 1790 his firm was claiming to be 'Upholsters to Their Majesties'. By 1791, however, he was in partnership with Robert Donald Smith and the business changed its trading style to Charles Smith & Co. The partnership was still in existence in 1794. By 1803 a new partnership had been formed with George Key and in that year Smith & Key were included in the list of master cabinet makers in Sheraton's *Cabinet Dictionary*. This partnership was dissolved from 1 January 1806 and Charles Smith retained their former premises which by this date had been re-numbered 70. George Key set up his own business at 74 Lower Grosvenor St at which he traded until 1835. By January 1810 a further partnership had been formed, this time with John Bywater, which appears to have lasted until 1825.

In 1783 Charles Smith married Lucy Gilroy. The name Lucy Smith is recorded in the Lord Chamberlain's accounts from the early 1780s to 1805 in connection with furnishings for royal residences and offices. She also fitted out the royal yachts 'Mary' and 'Royal Charlotte'. These commissions may have been undertaken in the name of Charles Smith. She is also known to have receipted an account of 1791 submitted by Charles Smith for chair cases and cushion covers for Lady Ann Conolly. The business grew over the years to a substantial size. Additional premises were used in Grosvenor Mews. These were described in 1791 as a stable and coach house but in 1810 as a warehouse and sawpit. By January 1810 insurance cover totalled £3,500 for the stock and utensils used in the business.

Apart from the Royal commissions, an impressive list of patrons can be drawn up.

AUDLEY END, Essex. In April 1811 the 2nd Lord Braybrooke paid Smith £9 4s 6d. [Essex RO, D/DBy/A376]

DRURY LANE THEATRE, London. Between February 1794 and January 1795 fitted up the boxes of George III and the

Prince of Wales at a cost of £2,011. Henry Holland's accounts of 1794 also show Charles Smith as a supplier of goods to the value of £150. [*Survey of London*, XXXV, p. 54; Booker, *Face of Banking*, 1979 appendix]

HAREWOOD HOUSE, Yorks. The Harewood accounts show regular purchases from Smith between July 1791 and July 1810 amounting to some £1,800. The largest payment was £400 for furniture on 23 April 1801 with a further payment of £200 on 21 July of the same year. A sum of £300 was paid on account on 15 March 1809 and sums of £200 each on 15 July 1806 and 6 April 1807. [Leeds archives dept., Harewood MS 189–92, 211–12]

HEATON HALL, Manchester. Sir Thomas Egerton paid Smith 14s on 10 March 1782. [Preston RO, DDEg. bank deposit and account bks]

SHUGBOROUGH, Staffs. Supplied a suite of fourteen arm-chairs and two large sofas in 1794 at a cost of £296. The two sofas and ten of the chairs survive and are displayed in the Red Drawing Room. Other items of furniture supplied to the house include wardrobes, dressing stools, 'Chamber Tables' for various bedrooms and mahogany chairs and bergères covered in red morocco for the Library. [Staffs. RO, D.615 E (H) 2/6; E. Stuart, 'Seat Furniture by Charles Smith & Co. at Shugborough', *National Trust Studies*, 1980, pp. 80–93]

STRETTON HALL, Staffs. On 14 December 1790 charged Lady Ann Conolly £1 15s 'for mounting needlework screen in gilt frame on carved white & gold stand'. On 18 April 1791 the same patron was charged £1 4s 6d for chair and cushion covers. [V&A Lib., Box II, 86 KK; Heal Coll., BM]

OTHER PATRONS. Patronised by Mrs David Garrick from January–July 1786 when £27 19s 7d was spent on chairs, chair repairs, covers, curtains, stools etc. Six japanned chairs with rush seats were provided at a cost of £3 18s. [V&A Lib. 86N.N41(i)–9] A substantial payment of £184 16s was made to Smith, 1789–90 in connection with a house in Manchester Sq., London but the patron is not indicated. [Scottish RO, GD 157/816] Between 1792 and 1799 Richard Cox of Quarley, Hants., a banker of Pall Mall, London, made substantial payments to Charles Smith. His total payments came to £527 18s but some appear to be to an u at Salisbury, also named Smith. It is possible that the two were related. [D; Westminster poll bk; V&A archives; Heal; *Times*, 12 February 1806; GL, Sun MS vol. 373, ref. 580608; vol. 453, ref. 839731; Lloyds Bank archives, account bk of Richard Cox]

Smith, Charles, Quaker's friars, Bristol, cm (1791–1800). Bankruptcy declared, *Exeter Flying Post*, 23 June 1791. [D]

Smith, Charles, Liverpool, u (1813–21). At 41 Mount Pleasant in 1813–14 which appears to have been his residence. He also maintained a shop in Paradise St, the number of this being 86 in 1813–14, 87 in 1816, 85 in 1818–19 and 91 in 1821. In December 1818 he advertised that he stocked 'East India Carpeting' which was said to be manufactured 'from a vegetable production of the East Indies, particularly adapted from its cheapness & durability for Stair Cases, Halls, Common Sitting Rooms etc.' He offered this in a variety of patterns and appears to have derived his stock from Walker & Everard of Wapping who acted as agents for its distribution. He also maintained stocks of cabinet furniture in his ware rooms and In May 1819 offered 'furniture of Foreign Fancy Wood consisting of Card, Loo, Sofa, Chess, Library & Ladies Work Tables, & Drawing-room Chairs & a great variety of Cabinet work, Bedsteads etc.' In the upholstery line 'carpets, Druggets, Patent Floor-cloths, Paper Hangings, Morine Prints, Fringes' were on offer. His eldest son Charles Ralph Smith, aged 19, died on 3 July 1821. [D; *Liverpool Mercury*, 4 December 1818, 28 May 1819, 13 July 1821]

Smith, Charles, Wrawby St, Brigg, Lincs., cm (1819). [D]

Smith, Charles, Bloomsbury, London, billiard table maker (1835–39). At 3 Market St in 1835 and 3 Charles St in 1839. [D]

Smith, Charles, Exeter, Devon, cm (1837–40). At Preston St in May 1837, James St in May 1839 and Red Cow Village in December 1840. Two daughters bapt. at St Mary Major, 1837–39 and another at St David's in 1840. [PR (bapt.)]

Smith, Chester, High St, Boston, Lincs., cm and u (1835). [D]

Smith, Christopher, Baxter Row, East Dereham, Norfolk, cm (1830). Freeman of Norwich. [D; Norwich poll bk]

Smith, Christopher Hill, 48 St Giles St, Norwich, u and paperhanger (1839–40). [D]

Smith, Daniel, 'The Child's Coat', Steel Lane, Holborn, London, carver and gilder (1723). In November 1723 took out insurance on his dwelling house and shop for £100. [GL, Sun MS vol. 17, ref. 30454]

Smith, Daniel, Windsor, Berks., cm, u, auctioneer, appraiser and undertaker (1780–1830). At Sheet St, 1782–91, Park St in 1798, but by 1824 at St Alban's St. Subscribed to Sheraton's *Drawing Book*, 1793. In 1782 took out insurance cover of £800 of which £600 was for utensils and stock. This would indicate a business of fairly substantial size by provincial standards, but in November 1791 the cover had fallen to £400 of which £100 was for utensils and stock. [D; poll bks; GL, Sun MS vol. 304, p. 504; vol. 381, p. 528]

Smith, Daniel, West Wycombe, Bucks., chairmaker (b.1812–41). Aged 29 at the date of the 1841 Census.

Smith, David, King St, Dudley, Staffs., cm and u (1828–40). [D]

Smith, Edward, London, cm (1746). Undertook work for the Earl of Stair in connection with Campbell & Bruce. [Scottish RO, GD 135/Box 55/31]

Smith, Edward, London, upholder (1757–d.1792). Son of Thomas Smith of the parish of St Ann, Blackfriars, carpenter. App. to Charles Westwood on 7 July 1757 and free of the Upholders' Co. by servitude, 6 June 1765. In 1774, when he took as app. William Shuffrey, he was living in Blackfriars; but listed at St Paul's Churchyard, 1778–92. [GL, Upholders' Co. records]

Smith, Edward, 13 Lombard St, Whitefriars, London, cm (1778). In 1778 insured a house for £100. [GL, Sun MS vol. 266, p. 644]

Smith, Edward, 53 Gracechurch St, London, upholder and auctioneer (1778–94). Free of the Upholders' Co. under the terms of the 1750 Upholders' Act, 4 February 1778. In 1778 took out insurance cover of £1,200 and of this £700 was for utensils and stock. In 1781 insured a house for £900 and in 1787 his utensils, stock and a warehouse for £500. [D; GL, Upholders' Co. records; Sun MS vol. 263, p. 625; vol. 289, p. 552; vol. 341, p. 600]

Smith, Edward, Norwich, cm (1770–1810). Son of Wright Smith, barber. Free 14 March 1770, and in 1810 trading at St Laurence's Steps. [D; freemen admission reg.]

Smith, Edward, Newcastle, joiner and cm (1782–1811). Until 1785 in partnership with Ralph Wardle at Westgate St. The partnership was 'amicably dissolved' in March 1785. Smith indicated that he intended to carry on his trade 'at his shop' at the Head of Finkle St, opposite the Low-Friar Chair. Wardle set up in Pilgrim St. Smith stated that he sold 'all Sorts of Looking Glasses'. Subscribed to Sheraton's *Drawing Book*, 1793. His business continued in Finkle St until 1811 [D; *Newcastle Courant*, 26 March 1785]

Smith, Edward, 1 Bellgates, Salford, Lancs., picture frame maker (1825). [D]

Smith, Edward, Church St, Camberwell, London, carver and gilder (1826). [D]

Smith, Edward, Brighton, Sussex, u (1832–39). At 5 Bond St in

1832 and 36 Gardener St, 1838–39. Daughter Eliza bapt. on 12 September 1838. [D; PR (bapt.)]

Smith, Edward, Arabella Row, Pimlico, London, cm (1834–35). In 1834 took an app. through the means of Grinsell's Charity. [D; Westminster Ref. Lib., MS E 3559]

Smith, Edward, 33 Queen St, Derby, cm and u (1835). [D]

Smith, Ellen, 15 Circus St, Liverpool, u (1821). [D]

Smith, Elliot Macro, see John Smith and successors of Cambridge. Probably:

Smith, Elliot, Sidney St, Cambridge, cm and u (1817–30). The principal furniture supplier to St John's College until 1830 when he gave up the trade. John Swan, his employee for thirteen years, established his own cm and u warehouse in Sidney St, next door to that of Elliot Smith, in October 1831 and took on some of Smith's work and former employees. [*Cambridge Chronicle*, 21 October 1831]

Smith, Fillia, 33 King St, Bristol, Windsor and fancy chairmaker (1836). Successor to William Smith. [D]

Smith, Francis, London, upholder (1719–29). Son of Humphrey Smith of Bardfield, Essex and app. to Joseph Pluckrose on 5 August 1719. Free of the Upholders' Co. by servitude, 3 September 1729. [GL, Upholders' Co. records]

Smith, Francis, Bognor, Sussex, cm (1832). [D]

Smith, G., 4 Bradley's Buildings, Bath, Som., chairmaker and upholder (1819). [D]

Smith, George, London, upholder (1705–24). Father of Henry and John Smith, both subsequently members of the Upholders' Co. George Smith was free of this Co. on 24 July 1706 and took as app. Francis Newbery, 1710–17. Insurance records indicate that Smith owned considerable property, although exactly which addresses he used for his business is uncertain. From 1705–12 he took out insurance cover of £250 on a brick house on the east side of Young St, near the Square, Kensington. In February 1718 he took out cover on a house on the south side of Round Crown between Old and New Gravell Lane, Stepney, and in May 1723 insured no fewer than ten properties for £1,175. One of these was on the south side of Three Crown Court and the west side of Poor Jewry Lane, near Aldgate and was valued at £75. Between 1717 and 1724 he insured a brick house near All Hallows Church, Barking valued at £250, and two other properties close at hand for £150 and £400. [GL, Upholders' Co. records; GL, Hand in Hand MS p. 75, 29 November 1705; vol. 10, ref. 9419; vol. 20, p. 30; vol. 17, p. 76; vol. 27, p. 131; vol. 28, p. 312]

Smith, George, Castle St, Westminster, London, cm (1749). [Poll bk]

Smith, George, 99 New Bond St, London, cabinet and upholstery warehouse (1789). [Banks Coll., BM]

Smith, George, Lutterworth, Leics., turner and chairmaker (1790–1840). From 1835–42 shown at Beast Mkt, Lutterworth. [D]

Smith, George, London, cm and u (c.1786–1826). He is described on the title page of his ambitious and influential pattern book *A Collection of Designs for Household Furniture and Interior Decoration*, 1808, as 'upholder extraordinary to his Royal Highness the Prince of Wales'. The 158 aquatint engravings bear dates from 1804 to 1807 and are important as being the first collection of designs for ordinary furniture in a fully developed Regency style. Advertisements for the book in the *Liverpool Chronicle*, 20 February 1805 and 25 November 1807 disclose that it was issued in three parts over three years, each priced £1 11s 6d plain or £2 12s 6d 'elegantly coloured'. Smith contributed designs for furniture to Ackermann's periodical *Repository of Arts* in January and March 1809 and his *A Collection of Ornamental Designs after the Antique* appeared in 1812.

Directories reveal that Smith traded as an 'upholsterer and cabinetmaker' at 69 Dean St, Soho 1795–97 and as 'upholder etc' at 15 Princes St, Cavendish Sq. 1806–11; his trade card issued from this address [Banks Coll., BM] features the Royal Arms and states he was 'Upholder and cabinet maker to HRH The Prince of Wales, draughtsman in Architecture, Perspective and Ornaments.' It is difficult to estimate his status as a furniture maker owing to a dearth of evidence. In the introduction to his final work *The Cabinet-Maker and Upholsterer's Guide*, 1826, he claimed 'experience of forty years devoted to the study of cabinet making, upholstery and drawing, both in theory and practical application', stating that he had been employed 'by some of the most exalted characters in the country to manufacture many of the Designs.' His career was not without setbacks since two bankruptcies were reported in 1790. [Bailey's list of bankrupts and *Liverpool Advertiser*, 15 July 1793] Some furniture supplied by George Smith of London to Mount Stewart, Co. Down [*C. Life*, 13 March 1980, p. 757] might be from his workshop. In 1826 he still described himself as 'Upholsterer and Furniture Draughtsman to His Majesty' although he was then 'Principal of the Drawing Academy' at 41 Brewer St. He was possibly the father of George Smith jnr, a minor topographical artist. [G. Smith, *Collection of Designs for Household Furniture*, reprint, introduction by C. V. Hershey, 1970]   C.G.G.

Smith, George, Liverpool, cm (1796–d.1802). App. to Samuel Chubbard and free, 26 May 1796. Died in May 1802. [Freemen reg.]

Smith, George, 28 Long Acre, London, carver and gilder (1808–10). At 28 Long Acre in 1808. Probably the craftsman whose name appears in the Longford Castle, Wilts. accounts as the recipient of £3 8s in 1808 and £1 14s in 1810. [D; V&A archives]

Smith, George, Derby, chairmaker and turner (1818–35). At St Peter's St, 1818–29; 1 Court, St Peter's St in 1828–35 and also 2 Court, Sadler Gate in 1829. George Smith jnr, chairmaker and turner, was trading at 31 London Rd in 1834. [D]

Smith, George, Wilton St, Northwich, Cheshire, cm/chairmaker (1834). [D]

Smith, George, St John's Sq., Clerkenwell, London, japanner, cm and upholder (1813–39). At 33 St John's Sq., 1813–25, but from 1826 the number was 35. Listed as a japanner except in 1826 when the trade was u, and in 1827 when it was given as cm, upholder and japanner. [D]

Smith, George, Manchester, cm and u (1834–40). At 47 George St, 1834–36 and 33 Princess St, 1838–40. [D]

Smith, George, Kensington, London, carver and gilder (1823–39). At 31 High St in 1823, no. 54 in 1837, 11 Terrace in 1838 and 20 Young St in 1839. [D]

Smith, Henry, parish of St Michael le Belfrey, York, u (c.1741–67). Son of John Smith of Oulstone, Yorks., yeoman. His father was already dead when on 29 September 1734 he was app. to George Reynoldson. He was a Roman Catholic and this fact was noted by the authorities at various dates from 1745. In 1767 he was living in the parish of St Michael-le-Belfrey and had been there for fifteen years. He was aged 48. [*Catholic Recusancy in York*; York City archives, quarter sessions bk, 1744–56]

Smith, Henry, London, upholder (1751). Son of George Smith, a member of the Upholders' Co. (free 24 July 1706). George Smith was brother of John Smith and father of Edmund Smith, both members of the Upholders' Co. George Smith was made free of the Upholders' Co. by patrimony, 5 December 1751. [GL, Upholders' Co. records]

Smith, Henry, Oakham, Rutland, cm (1755). In 1755 took app. named Jelles. [S of G, app. index]

Smith, Henry, 6 near Shadwell Dock, Shadwell, London, cm (1777–81). In both 1777 and 1782 his insurance cover was £100 of which £20 was for utensils and stock. [GL, Sun MS vol. 256, p. 437; vol. 293, p. 420]

Smith, Henry, 7 James St, Covent Gdn, London, carver and gilder (1817). [D]

Smith, Hilton, Lancaster, u (1801–04). [Westminster Ref. Lib., Gillow records] Probably:

Smith, Hilton Thomas, Lancaster, u (1806–21). Free 1806–07. Possibly Hilton Price who was trading at New St in 1816 and Church St in 1818. Took app. on 11 March 1811, 16 January 1817 and 16 April 1821. [Freemen rolls; app. reg.]

Smith, Hugh, Mason Pl., 5 Blair St, Liverpool, joiner and cm (1837). [D]

Smith, I. & T., Mint Sq., London, furniture warehousemen (1802). [D] See John Smith at Mint St, 1808.

Smith, I., 31 High St, Kensington, London, carver and gilder (1826). [D]

Smith, Isaac, 17 Cheshire St, Bethnal Green, London, bedstead maker (1839). [D]

Smith, Isaac George, London, fancy cm (1829–39). In 1829 at 10 Upper Rosoman St, Clerkenwell where his trade was given as cm. In 1837, however, he was at 21 Ratcliff Terr., Goswell Rd, and in 1839 the address was given as 21 Goswell Rd. In 1839 he was making portable desks, dressing cases, work boxes and other small cabinet goods. [D]

Smith, Isaac, 17 Cheshire St, Bethnal Green, London, bedstead maker (1839). [D]

Smith, J., Haymarket, against Pall Mall, London, u (1730). [Heal]

Smith, J., corner of Surry St, St Stephen's, Norwich, u (1810). [D]

Smith, J., 9 Northumberland Pl., Bath, Som., auctioneer, upholder and broker (1819). [D]

Smith, J., 4 Nassau St, Middlx Hospital, London, u etc. (1820). [D]

Smith, J., 4 Bond St, Brighton, Sussex, working u (1832). [D]

Smith, J., 8 Upper Charlton St, Fitzroy Sq., London, carver and gilder (1835). [D]

Smith, J. A., 7 Bridgewater Sq., London, carver and gilder (1835). [D]

Smith, J. C., 92 Crawford St, London, u (1829). [D]

Smith, Jackson, Howard St, North Shields, Northumb., cm and joiner (1827–34). Recorded at no. 14 in 1834 as a cm and paper hanger. [D]

Smith, James, London, upholder (1721–30). Son of James Smith of Passenham, Northants., grazier. App. to John Howard on 4 October 1721 and free of the Upholders' Co. by servitude, 2 April 1729. In the following year he appears to have been in the employ of Robert North and signed a receipt for Paul Foley for £2 4s 'for the youth of my master Robert North'. [GL, Upholders' Co. records; Herefs. RO, Foley MS, F/AIII/55]

Smith, James, St Paul's, Covent Gdn, London, cm (1744). [Heal]

Smith, James, Broad St, Portsmouth, Hants., upholder (1781–84). In 1781 insured a house for £800, and in 1784 his utensils and stock for £400 out of a total cover of £700. [D; GL, Sun MS vol. 291, p. 524; vol. 321, p. 457]

Smith, James snr, Nottingham, cm (1776–91). Free 1776 and in 1780 living at Weekday-cross. In 1791 signed the Nottingham Cabinet and Chair Makers' Book of Prices on behalf of the masters. [Freemen rolls; poll bk]

Smith, James, London, cm (1793). Subscribed to Sheraton's Drawing Book, 1793.

Smith, James snr, Bristol, cabinet varnisher and cm (1795–1816). In 1795 at Bath St, and from 1799–1801 Narrow Wine St as a cm and varnisher. There is then a gap in directory entries until 1812. At 'Swan', St James's Back, 1812–14 and 'White Lion', Temple St, 1815–16, but the trade is now given as cabinet varnisher. [D]

Smith, James jnr, Nottingham, joiner and cm (1799–1835). At Marygate 1799 and in 1832 the address was given as 45 St Marygate. An address at Broad St is also given for James Smith, cm, in 1835. Took his son James as app. in 1834 and other apps named Samuel Brotherhood in 1816 and James Shore in 1834. [D; app. bk]

Smith, James, Chester, cm (1812–37). Free 15 October 1812. At King St, 1818–26 but in 1837 at Linen Hall St. [Freemen rolls; poll bks]

Smith, James, 13 Prince's Ct, Westminster, London, carver and gilder (1817–20). [D]

Smith, James, 14 Crickets Lane, Ashton-under-Lyne, Lancs., cm and joiner (1818–24). [D]

Smith, James, 35 Tooley St, London, carver etc. (1819). [D]

Smith, James, High Wycombe, Bucks., chairmaker (1826–40). Four daughters and two sons bapt. between 1826–40. [PR (bapt.)]

Smith, James, 14 Hackney Rd Cresc., London, cm and u (1826). [D]

Smith, James, Bullring, Horncastle, Lincs., cm (1826). [D] A James Smith with an address in Horncastle was app. as a cm in Lincoln in 1827 and may be his son. [Lincoln app. reg.]

Smith, James, Yarm, Yorks., joiner and cm (1827). [D]

Smith, James, Sadlers Wells, London, cm (1829–35). At 3 Eliza Pl., Sadlers Wells in 1829, but in 1835 the address was 25 Arlington St, Sadlers Wells. [D]

Smith, James, 20 Court, Hampton St, Birmingham, cm (1830–35). Recorded at 20 Court, Hampton St, also as an u, in 1830; and at 7 Gt Hampton St in 1835. [D]

Smith, James jnr, Bristol, varnisher and polisher (1833–40). In 1833 at 2 Frog Lane as a fancy varnisher but from 1836–40 at Coach & Horses Ct, Broadmead as a French polisher. [D]

Smith, James, 1 St Ann's Terr., St Ann's St, Liverpool, u (1834). [D]

Smith, James, Leicester, cm and u (1835–42). At Market St (or Pl.) in 1835 and Albion St in 1842. [D]

Smith, James, 17 Charlotte St, Blackfriars Rd, cm (1835). [D]

Smith, James, 1 Denmark Pl., Camberwell, London, upholder (1835). [D]

Smith, James, High Wycombe, Bucks., chairmaker (b. c. 1817–41). Married in 1838 and aged 24 at the time of the 1841 Census. [PR (marriage)]

Smith, James, 6 Ann's Pl., Collier St, Hull, Yorks., cm (1838–39). [D] A James Smith was app. to Edward Dickon, cm of Hull in August 1815 and may be this maker, or otherwise;

Smith, James, 7 Finkle Ct, Finkle St, Hull, Yorks., cm (1838–39). [D; Hull app. reg.]

Smith, James, 120 London Rd, London, cm and u (1839). [D]

Smith, James, Hadleigh, Suffolk, cm (1839). [D]

Smith, James, 2 London Rd, St Leonards, Sussex, cm (1839–40). At London Rd in November 1839 but by 1845 at Norman Rd West. [D]

Smith, James, High Wycombe, Bucks., caner (b. c. 1806–41). Aged 35 at the time of the 1841 Census.

Smith, Jane, Gaol Sq., Stafford, chairmaker (1818–22). [D]

Smith, Jane, High St, Berwick-upon-Tweed, Northumb., u (1827–28). [D]

Smith, Jeffrey, Richmond, Yorks., cm (1817). [PR (bapt.)]

Smith, Jeremiah, York, u (1758–71). Son of John Smith, joiner. Free 1758 and in this year living at Coney St. Employed by Richard Farrer, and in partnership with Matthew Browne he took over his former employers' shop in High Ousegate in November 1766. Took Christopher Blackburn as app. jointly with Matthew Hearon on 19 January 1767, and on 24 June

1771 George Bradley jointly with his partner Matthew Browne. [Freemen rolls; app. reg.; *York Courant*, 25 November 1766]

Smith, Job., Hinckley, Leics., u (1822). [D]

Smith, Job, Nottingham, u (1832–35). Recorded at St James St in 1832 and Castlegate in 1835, also as a paper hanger. [D]

Smith, Job, 46 Waterworks St, Hull, Yorks., cm (1840). [D]

Smith, John and successors, Cambridge, joiners cm, u and undertakers (1698–1832). The first record of John Smith is when St John's College made a payment to him in 1698. Regular payments appear in his name from 1719, most are for general joinery work although he was paid in 1734 'for Chairs for ye Audit Room 24 at 18s, 2 at £1 3s: pr Chair'. Trinity College made regular payments to him from 1719, and from 1720 he leased a property from them (on the site of 26 Trinity St) 'late demised to Cornelius Austin joyner', consisting of 'a Hall a Kitchen three chambers a shopp yard & House'. Most payments do not indicate what work was undertaken although in 1743 he was paid for mending and supplying furniture after the appointment of a new Master. His son Thomas, born 1709, had from 1746 leased from Trinity the property next door to his father. By 1748 John Smith, presumably then in his early seventies, appears to have relinquished the business to his son as the payment made by Trinity in that year is to him. However, Thomas Smith died in the same year. After the death of his son it would seem likely that John Smith took control of the business again and trained his grandson Thomas who at the time of his father's death was aged fourteen. Other than one small payment, no reference appears to the Smiths in the accounts of both Colleges until 1752. The payment made by Trinity in 1755 is to Thomas Smith who at the age of twenty-one had no doubt taken control of the family business His grandfather also died in that year leaving two thirds of his property to his grandson. In 1756 Thomas took app. named Cockle. In April 1757 he furnished the rooms of Francis, Marquess of Tavistock, who was an undergraduate of Trinity College. The main items provided were a bedstead complete, a draw table, a dressing glass, a basin stand, twelve walnut matted bottom chairs and a wainscot bureau. Smaller items included waiters, a knife box and a boot jack. The total cost was £28 7s. [S of G, app. index; Bedford Office, London]

From the early 1760s the Smiths became virtually the sole suppliers of furnishings to Trinity and St John's Colleges, a situation that continued until 1832. Although they would also undertake general joinery work payments are recorded for supplying furniture, upholstery, papering, carpeting and gilding etc.

Thomas Smith insured a house for £250 in 1780. [GL, Sun MS vol. 287, p. 638] His oldest son John, born 1763, had followed his father into the business as in 1788 an indenture was made between them. In this it was agreed that in consideration of 'services and assistance' of his son, that from 24 June 1788 for eight years the business would continue under the name of Smith & Son. John was to be paid £160 a year. On the 24 June 1796 Thomas Smith was to relinquish the cabinet making and upholstery side of the business to John but was to continue himself as an auctioneer and appraiser. The materials of the cabinet making and upholstery sides of the business were to be valued and paid for by John. Thomas Smith was to hand over the 'two lease-hold dwellings' for which John was to pay £600. During the period of the indenture Thomas was to keep them in good repair and also provide a capital sum of not less than £2,000. The change over took place in 1796 although Thomas Smith died in the following year. On 8 July 1797 it was reported that 'Mr. John Smith Cabinet-maker was sworn into the office of Unversity Appraiser vacated by the death of his father Mr. Thomas Smith'.

When the renewal of the two leases of the property owned by Trinity College became due in 1797 a plan was taken. This shows the shop and dwelling house with a frontage on to Trinity St of approximately fifty feet and a total depth of just over ninty feet. Behind the house was the yard with a warehouse, a two-storied workshop with a saw pit behind.

In 1803 John Smith took his step-brother Elliot Macro Smith, who was aged twenty-one into the business. 'Smith & Elliot' are recorded in directories, 1805–08, at Trumpington St. In an indenture dated 25 March 1803, John Smith took his brother to be his assistant for a term of seven years. Elliot was to receive 2½ per cent of all money taken, this to be paid twice a year on the settling and signing of the accounts. A few weeks after the indenture was signed Elliot Smith married the daughter of 'Mr. Smith, cabinet-maker of Norwich'. This may indicate there was a family or even a business connection with the various cm and u of that name who are recorded in Norwich during this period. Although in the indenture there is no change of name mentioned, there is one isolated payment recorded by St John's College in 1803 to 'J. & E. Smith Upholsterers'. The period of seven years detailed in the indenture was not completed as Elliot Smith took over the business between July/August 1806. John Smith apparently retiring to Broxbourne, Herts., where he died in 1817.

Under Elliot Smith the business continued to prosper with larger payments being recorded by both Colleges who were refurnishing. It is from this period that much of the surviving furniture supplied to Trinity Master's Lodge can be identified. These include a pair of harewood side tables and a set of mahogany dining chairs supplied in 1795, two suites of a pair of sofa tables and matching Pembroke table supplied c.1803–05, a set of japanned arm chairs in 1807, a state bed in 1811 for HRH William Frederick, Duke of Gloucester the Chancellor of the University, a set of twenty-eight sabre-leg dining chairs (Fig. 37) and a pair of card tables in 1820.

In late September 1831 Elliot Smith announced that his son Elliot was to enter the business and that the furnishing side was to be discontinued as they would be concentrating on the auctioneering, appraising and insurance sides of the business as well as keeping the funeral department. At first the stock was sold at 'very reduced prices', the final sales by auction being held in August and November 1832.

The Smiths would appear to have controlled the largest furnishing business in Cambridge and its closure must have affected the other cm and u in the town. John Swan, who had worked for Elliot Smith for thirteen years, enlarged his shop and engaged several of the Smith's workmen. Samuel Yorke employed one of the paperhangers, and three employees, James Hunt, John Worseldine and Robert Hills, started up businesses of their own. The Smith's firm continued as auctioneers and estate agents and finally insurance agents into the early years of this century. [*Furn. Hist.*, 1976]

R.W.

Smith, John, 'The Three Tents' by Fleet Ditch, near Holborn Bridge, London, u (1709). [Heal]

Smith, John, Doncaster, Yorks., upholder (1719). [GL, Sun MS vol. 10, ref. 15491]

Smith, John, Featherstone Buildings, Holborn, London, upholder (1734). [Heal]

Smith, John, Salisbury Ct, parish of St Bride, Fleet St, London, upholder (1739–42). Served the parish of St Bride as Questman in 1739, Collector for the Poor in 1741 and Sidesman in 1742. [GL, MS 6561, p. 66]

Smith, John, London, upholder (1746). Son of George Smith and brother to Henry Smith, both members of the Upholders' Co. George Smith was free of the Upholders' Co. by patrimony, 3 April 1746. [GL, Upholders' Co. records]

Smith, John, London, u (1753). Assigned property in Ducklington, Oxon. to John Wansell for £30. [Oxford RO, Welch MS, XI/vi/1]

Smith, John, Fleet St, London, u (1753–54). [D]

Smith, John, King's Lynn, Norfolk, u (1754). In 1754 took app. named Bedingham. [S of G, app. index]

Smith, John, London, upholder (1743–57). Son of Thomas Smith of Swindon, Wilts., innholder. App. to Henry Herring on 1 February 1743 and free of the Upholders' Co. by servitude, 8 September 1757. [GL, Upholders' Co. records]

Smith, John, 13 Lad Lane, London, wholesale u (1769–73). In 1769 listed as Smith & Slack, cotton merchants and wholesale upholders. [D] Possibly John Smith & Co. at 7 Gt Eastcheap, 1775–1808.

Smith, John, London, upholder (1772). Son of Joseph Smith and app. to John Stephens. Free of the Upholders' Co. by servitude, 7 October 1772. [GL, Upholders' Co. records]

Smith, John, 1 Wellington Mart, Hull, Yorks., cm and broker (1774–84). [D; poll bk]

Smith, John, Berwick St, Soho, London, bed joiner (1774–1809). In 1808–09 the number in Berwick St was 18. [D; Westminster poll bk]

Smith, John, Bristol, upholder (1774–81). Living in the parish of St Mary Port in 1774 and in the parish of St James in 1781. [Poll bks]

Smith, John & Co., 7 Gt Eastcheap, London, wholesale u (1775–1808). Free of the Upholders' Co. under the terms of the 1750 Upholders' Act, 4 April 1781 but had been trading at the Eastcheap address since 1775. In 1775–76 described as a cotton merchant. From 1799 the business is listed as Smith, Trower & Co. and in 1808 as Smith, Trower & Slater. Some directories of 1802–04 list merely Smith & Co. John Smith was included in the list of master cabinet makers in Sheraton's *Cabinet Dictionary*, 1803. [D; GL, Upholders' Co. records] Possibly John Smith of 13 Lad Lane, 1769–73.

Smith, John, London, upholder (1777). Son of John Smith of Wolverhampton, Staffs., whitesmith. App. to Joshua Wilkinson and free of the Upholders' Co. by servitude, 7 May 1777. At this date he was living in Moorfields. [GL, Upholders' Co. records]

Smith, John, Red Cross St, the Mint, Southwark, London, upholder (1782). In 1782 insured houses for £300. [GL, Sun MS vol. 302, p. 610]

Smith, John, Berwick-upon-Tweed, Northumb., cm (1784–1806). In 1806 trading in the High St. On 5 July 1788 debtors of John Carr were asked to make their payments to John Smith. Subscribed to Sheraton's *Drawing Book*, 1793. [D; *Newcastle Courant*, 5 July 1788]

Smith, John, White Bear Yd, opposite the Infirmary, Manchester, joiner and cm (1788). [D]

Smith, John, 1 Berkeley Sq., London, upholder (1785–93). [D]

Smith, John, Burton-on-Trent, Staffs., u (1791–1822). Listed at High St as a cm and u, 1818–22. [D]

Smith, John, Paradise St, Liverpool, cm (1790–96). At no. 66 in 1790 and no. 69 in 1796. [D]

Smith, John, Leeds, Yorks., journeyman cm (1791). Named in the *Leeds Cabinet and Chair Makers' Book of Prices*, 1791 as a journeyman in basic sympathy with its contents.

Smith, John, 13 Charles St, Grosvenor Sq., London, cm (1794). [Heal] See Smith & Brereton.

Smith, John, High Wycombe, chairmaker (1798). [Militia Census]

Smith, John, 70 Paradise St, Liverpool, cm (1802–03). App. to William Smith and free, 5 July 1802. Trading in Paradise St in 1803. [D; freemen reg.]

Smith, John, London, carver and gilder (1804–27). At 98 Swallow St, Piccadilly from 1804–20 but then moved to 49 Gt Marlborough St. His trade label, which has been found on the back of a picture, states that he was also a looking-glass manufacturer, and 'Picture Frame Maker by Appointment to his Majesty'. This claim is amply supported by evidence in the Royal archives and the Lord Chamberlain's accounts. In 1810 an account for £151 13s 3d was submitted to the Prince of Wales for frames and repairs and for carving a large 'Coronet & Plume of Feathers' for the top of a frame. A payment of £23 16s was made in 1814 by the Lord Chamberlain's Department for a large plain frame for a picture of a horse. Other payments are recorded in 1822 and 1827, the latter to J. Smith & Son. John Smith & Son, carvers and gilders, trading from 137 New Bond St, 1835–37, may be a continuation of this business. [D; Windsor Royal Archives, 25314, 35573, 89524; PRO, LC11/18, 10 October 1814]

Smith, John, Gainsborough, Lincs., cm (1806). Admitted freeman of Lincoln in November 1806. At that date living in Gainsborough. [Lincoln freemen rolls]

Smith, John, London, chairmaker (1806–12). Freeman of Colchester, Essex but living in London. [Colchester poll bks]

Smith, John, Mint St, Southwark, u (1808). [D] See I. & T. Smith at Mint Sq. in 1802.

Smith, John, Johnson's Ct, New Bird St, Liverpool, cm (1812–20). Free 5 October 1812. On 24 October 1818 married Margaret Davies of Neston, Cheshire at St Nicholas' Church. A John Smith of Liverpool, cm, took as app. Thomas Smith in 1820. [Freemen reg.; *Liverpool Mercury*, 30 October 1818; app. bk]

Smith, John, Bradshawgate, Bolton, Lancs., cm and u (1816–18). [D]

Smith, John, 37 Bridge St, Bristol, carver and gilder (1816). [D]

Smith, John, Bordesley St, Birmingham, u (1816–18). [D]

Smith, John, Old St, St Luke's, London, Windsor chairmaker (1816–35). At 20 Old St, 1816–29, but in 1835 shown at 23 Old St and 145 Whitecross St. In 1829 described as a sofa manufacturer. [D]

Smith, John, Berry St, Wolverhampton, Staffs., cm (1816–35). Recorded at Gt Berry St, 1818–34, and in 1833 listed also as a joiner. At Mary Ann St in 1835. [D]

Smith, John, Shales-moor, Sheffield, Yorks., cm (1818). A John Smith of Sheffield subscribed to Sheraton's *Drawing Book*, 1793. [D]

Smith, John, High Wycombe, Bucks., chairmaker (1818–34). Three sons and two daughters bapt. between 1818–34. [PR (bapt.)]

Smith, John, Gt Queen St, Lincoln's Inn Fields, London, cm (1820–29). At 23 Gt Queen St in 1820 but from 1826–29 at no. 20. [D]

Smith, John, Liverpool, cm (1821–22). App. to Charles Pemberton and petitioned freedom in 1821. Sworn 1822. [Freemen reg.]

Smith, John, Pinfold St, Loughborough, Leics., joiner/cm (1822). [D]

Smith, John, East Dereham, Norfolk, cm and furniture broker (1822). [D]

Smith, John, Plymouth, Devon, u (1822–30). At Richmond Hill in 1822, 5 Frankfort Pl. in 1823 and Bedford St in 1830. [D]

Smith, John, Leeds, Yorks., joiner/builder/cm (1826–37). At 13 Water Hall and 8 Western Cresc. in 1826; but at South Market, 1828–30, 21 Meadow Lane, also as an u, in 1830, 28 Front Row, Camp Field in 1834 and Middle Row in 1837. [D]

Smith, John, 15 Paradise Row, Chelsea, London, cm (1826). [D]

Smith, John, 77 Judd St, Brunswick Sq., London, cm and u (1827). [D]

Smith, John, Yarm, Yorks., joiner and cm (1827). [D]

Smith, John Robert, London, cm and u (1827–39). At 25 North

Audley St in 1827 and 1 Guildford St East, Wilmington Sq. in 1839. [D]

Smith, John, Rotton Row, Derby, cm and u (1828–29). Listed at no. 1 in 1828. [D]

Smith, John & William, Nottingham, cm and u (1828–40). Recorded at Denman St in 1828; George St, New Radford in 1832; South Parade, Market Pl. in 1835 (also as paper hangers); and Chapel Bar in 1840. [D]

Smith, John, Bridewell Lane, Bristol, chairmaker (1829–32). [D]

Smith, John, 32 Hunter St, Kent Rd, London, u, chair and sofa manufacturer (1829). [D]

Smith, John, Low Ireby, Wigton, Cumb., joiner/cm (1829). [D]

Smith, John, Broad St, Oxford, cm and u (1830). [D]

Smith, John, Bristol, carver and gilder (1829–40). Recorded as John C. Smith, 1829–33, and listed at 2 Cumberland St, 1829–30, 21 Stoke's Croft, 1831–32 and 16 St Paul's St in 1833. Listed as John Smith at 31 Castle St in 1840. [D] Possibly two tradesmen of the same name.

Smith, John, Barrs St, Bristol, fancy chair and bedstead maker, undertaker (1830–40). At no. 8 in 1838 and no. 9, 1839–40. [D]

Smith, John, De Ligne St, Radford, Notts., joiner and cm (1832). [D] See William Smith at this address in 1832.

Smith, John, Dovecot St, Stockton, Co. Durham, cm and u (1832). [D]

Smith, John Martin, George St, Maidstone, Kent, u (1832–38). [Poll bks]

Smith, John, Love Lane, Sheffield, Yorks., cm (1833). [D]

Smith, John, 2 Narrow Weir, Bristol, cm and broker (1834). [D]

Smith, John, Shiney Row, Houghton-le-Spring, Co. Durham, cm/joiner (1834). [D]

Smith, John, Rutland St, Nottingham, u (1834). [D]

Smith, John, Otley, Yorks., joiner/cm (1834). [D]

Smith, John, 14 Maeshouse Lane, Birmingham, cm (1835). [D]

Smith, John, 17 South Audley St, London, u (1835). [D] See Thomas Smith at this address, 1814–37.

Smith, John, 3 Penn St, Bristol, chairmaker (1837–40). [D]

Smith, Jno., Crossbrook St, Cheshunt, Herts., portable desk maker (1838). [D]

Smith, John, 19 Mosley St, Newcastle, cm, u, joiner, carver and gilder (1838). [D]

Smith, John, 145 Whitecross St, London, chair and sofa maker (1839). [D]

Smith, John, West St, Southampton, Hants., cm and chairmaker (1839). [D]

Smith, John, Humberstone Gate, Leicester, cm (1840). [D]

Smith, Jos., 7 Lloyd's Row, St John's St Rd, London, cm and u (1827). [D]

Smith, Jos, 8 Pitt St, Fitzroy, Sq., London, cm (1829). [D]

Smith, Joseph, London, carver (1739). Freeman of Bristol but living in London in 1739. [Bristol poll bk]

Smith, Joseph, Portsmouth, Hants., u (1776). In 1776 insured his household goods for £700. [GL, Sun MS vol. 246, p. 506]

Smith, Joseph P., London, u (1808–23). At 13 Gt Pulteney St, Golden Sq. in 1808, 61 Davies St, Berkeley Sq., 1809–12, 337 Oxford St, 1815–19 and 200 Oxford St, 1821–23. [D]

Smith, Joseph, Bridge St, Westminster, London, cm and u (1808). [D]

Smith, Joseph & Co., Bristol, cm and u (1808–26). At St John's Bridge, 1806–07 and 29 Wine St, 1809–14. Returned to St John's Bridge, 1816–17 where the business was listed merely as Joseph Smith. This last move may have been connected with the bankruptcy which was declared in August 1814. At 2 Park St as Joseph Smith & Co., 1819–25, but in December 1825 once more bankrupt. [D; *Exeter Flying Post*, 18 August 1814, 22 December 1825]

Smith, Joseph, 13 Castle St, Oxford St, London, cm (1809). [D]

Smith, Joseph, 71 Piccadilly, London, cm (1811). [D]

Smith, Joseph, Vicker's Yd, Briggate, Leeds, Yorks., cm and u (1817). [D]

Smith, Joseph, 29 Gt Waterloo St, Lambeth, London, u (1826). [D]

Smith, Joseph, 8 Pill St, Rathbone Pl., London, cm and u (1827). [D]

Smith, Joseph, Bristol, cm, u and undertaker (1824–27). At 1 Pembroke Ct, Maudlin St, 1824–25 and 7 St John St, 1826–27. [D]

Smith, Joseph, 2 Brokers Row, Redcross St, Southwark, London, bedstead maker (1839). [D]

Smith, Joseph, West Wycombe, Bucks., chairmaker (b.c.1796–1841). Aged 45 at the time of the 1841 Census.

Smith, Joseph, Partney, Lincs., cm and joiner (1835). [D]

Smith, Joshua, Westgate, Dewsbury, Yorks., cm (1822). [D]

Smith, Josiah, Dewsbury, Yorks. (1803). Subscribed to Sheraton's *Cabinet Dictionary*, 1803.

Smith, Lewis, High St, Uttoxeter, Staffs., clockcase maker and cm (1834). [D]

Smith, Lucy, see Charles Smith, Lower Grosvenor St, London and Lucy Gilroy.

Smith, Margaret, 15 Circus St, Liverpool, u (1824). [D]

Smith, Mary, 282 Holborn, corner of Gt Turnstile, London, u (1774–90). Her trade bill of 1774 refers to the business as a 'Carpet, Bedding, and Upholstery Warehouse' but her billhead used in 1790 states 'Wholesale & Retail Carpet, Cabinet & Upholstery Manufactory'. The 1774 trade bill indicates the stock to be 'SEVERAL Bales of Summer made BLANKETS, very white and Thick — CARPETS of entire new Patterns, of the *Turkey*, *Persia*, *Wilton*, *Kidderminster*, and *Scotch* Manufactures, of almost evry size — Rooms covered all over in the compleatest Manner — FEATHER BEDS well seasoned and fit for immediate Use — MATRASSES — QUILTS — Cotton COUNTER-PANES, — *English* and *Flanders* BED TICKS — RUGS and COVERLIDS of all Kinds, Variety of Bedsteads and ready made Furnitures, fine Flowered Cotton Checks, Morine, Harateen Cheney, and Lin'sey, made up in the neatest Manner — with all Kinds of Bedding for Sea or Land'. Mary Smith was declared bankrupt, *Gents Mag.*, February 1781. A bill dated 8 May 1790 for a quilt costing £1 2s survives amongst bills for Stretton Hall, Staffs. [*Conn. Year Bk*, 1960, p. 23; Heal; V&A Lib., Box II, 86 KK, envelope 15]

Smith, Mary, 8 Vine St, London, u (1835–39). [D]

Smith, Matthew, St Martin's St, Leicester Fields, London, chairmaker (1709–17). Small payments were made by the Earl of Northumberland, 1714–17. [Heal; V&A archives]

Smith, Metcalf, Sun St, Keighley, Yorks., joiner/cm (1837). [D]

Smith, Michael Joseph, Sidney St, Cambridge, carver and gilder (1830–39). [D]

Smith, Nathaniel, 30 Chapel St, Shoreditch, London, cm and u (1827). [D]

Smith, Nathaniel Alexander, Crossbrook St, Cheshunt, Herts., fancy cm and u (1839). [D]

Smith, P., address unknown, cm (1803). Subscribed to Sheraton's *Cabinet Dictionary*, 1803.

Smith, P. S., London, u (1807). Freeman of Gt Yarmouth, Norfolk resident in London. [Gt Yarmouth poll bk]

Smith, Peter, Covent Gdn, London, carver (1766). Bankrupt, *Gents Mag.*, April 1766.

Smith, Peter, London, upholder (1716–23). Son of John Smith of Wallingford, Berks. ironmonger. App. to John Lytholl on 4 July 1716 and free of the Upholders' Co. by servitude, 11 July 1723. [GL, Upholders' Co. records]

Smith, Richard, address unknown, cm and frame maker (1738–41). Undertook commissions for Stoneleigh, Warks.

for the Dowager Lady Leigh. On 31 December 1738 a large picture frame, a tea chest and a pillar and claw table in mahogany were supplied at a combined cost of £1 16s. Twenty nine polished frames, a large carved frame and two long tables were supplied in 1739 costing £4 14s 2d. On 17 January 1741 four further polished picture frames and eight chair frames were supplied for £3 3s. [Shakespeare Birthplace Trust, Leigh receipts, DR 18/5]

Smith, Richard, Salisbury, Wilts., upholder, cm and auctioneer (1754–97). On 21 December 1754 Richard Smith took as app. Thomas Hunt at a premium of £30. By 1784 the business was trading as Richard Smith & Son and they may have been the business who between 1793–97 supplied items and undertook work for Richard Cox of Quarley, Hants. to the value of £169 15s 9d. Richard Cox, a banker of Pall Mall, London, spent considerable sums with the London u Charles Smith of Lower Grosvenor St. [D; *Wilts. Apps and their Masters*; Lloyds Bank archives, account bk of Richard Cox]

Smith, Richard, Lancaster, joiner and cm (1784–85). [Freemen rolls]

Smith, Richard, Liverpool, u (b.1780–d.1835). At 9 Mt Pleasant in 1805, 22 Church St in 1810, 8 Crosshall St in 1811 and 1 Pepper St, 1816–18. Aged 41 in 1821 and died on 19 December 1833. [D; Liverpool RO, 352/CON 5/2 K–Z]

Smith, Richard, Lancaster and Blackburn, Lancs., cm (1806–07). Free 1806–07 but by this date living in Blackburn Lancs. [Lancaster freemen rolls]

Smith, Richard, 172 Tottenham Ct Rd, London, chairmaker (1809–11). [D]

Smith, Richard, Padiham, near Burnley, Lancs., cm, joiner and builder (1818–40). In 1834 shown as joiner and builder only. In 1854 at Adamson St with a house at Church St. [D]

Smith, Richard, Duke St, Lincoln's Inn Fields, London, cm and u (1819–27). At 47 Duke St, 1819–24 but 1 Duke St, 1826–27. In March 1824 took out insurance of £800 on his household goods and £800 on six houses in Nobles St, Wellington Sq. and Ann St. His stock and utensils were, however, only insured for £150. [D; GL, Sun MS vol. 499, ref. 1014694]

Smith, Richard, 20 Rolls Buildings, Fetter Lane, London, carver and gilder (1820). [D]

Smith, Richard, Kirkgate, Tadcaster, Yorks., cm (1822–37). [D]

Smith, Richard, Leicester, cm and u (1828–40). Listed at St Nicholas St in 1828; Belgrave Gate, 1828–29; London Rd, 1835–40 and also Southgate St in 1840. [D]

Smith, Richard Clay, High St, Leicester, u and paper hanger (1835). [D]

Smith, Richard, London, carver and gilder (1832–39). At 12 Church St, Blackfriars Rd (alternatively referred to as 12 Church St, Gt Surrey St) from 1832–37, but in 1839 at 16 Bennett St, Blackfriars. [D]

Smith, Richard (or Robert), Little Albion St, Hull, Yorks., cm etc. (1838–40). Some directories give the fore-name as 'Rt.' possibly Robert. [D]

Smith, Richard, King's Lynn, Norfolk, cm (1708–09). Freeman of King's Lynn by patrimony, 1708–09. [Freemen rolls]

Smith, Richard, parish of St Martin-in-the-Fields, London, carver and gilder (1786–93). Married on 22 May 1786 at Ipswich. At 17 Duke St, St Martin's Lane in 1790 and 13 Duke's Ct, St Martin's in 1793, although another directory of the same year repeats in 1790 address. [D; Suffolk RO, FAA: 50/2/107]

Smith, Robert, Liverpool, u, auctioneer and appraiser (1787–1810). At Stanley St in 1787 but in that year moved to Old Hall St where he traded in partnership with John Chew at no. 2. They took over the shop at the bottom of Old Hall St which had formerly been used by Samuel Kirkes, Smith terminated his partnership with Chew in April 1792 retaining premises in Old Hall St. In August 1794 he opened an additional shop at 19 Dorman's Lane for the upholstery side of the business, and at the same time commenced trading as an auctioneer using the large shop in Old Hall St for this purpose. In 1796 at 20 Lord St. By 1800 he had taken his sons into the business which from now traded as Robert Smith & Sons. The business was at 18 Lord St, 1800–03. In 1804 the business was trading as Samuel & Thomas Smith at 19 Lord St. By 1805 the number in Lord St had changed to 21 and an additional address at 67 Christian St is mentioned for the first time. At 68 Christian St only, 1807–10. [D; *Williamson's Liverpool Advertiser*, 2 April 1792, 25 August 1794]

Smith, Robert, 7 Cockspur St, London, carver, gilder and printseller (1794–1820). One directory of 1817 lists at this address Richard Smith and another of 1820 J. Smith. [D]

Smith, Robert, 31 High St, Kensington, London, carver and gilder (1826). [D]

Smith, Robert, Mytongate, Hull, Yorks., broker and cm (1803). [D]

Smith, Robert, 24 Park St, Leamington, Warks., cm and u (1835). [D]

Smith, Robert, Park St, Luton, Beds., u (1839). [D]

Smith, S. F., Cambridge(?), cm (1819). In 1819 married Miss Bains of Peterborough. [*Cambridge Chronicle*, 2 April 1819]

Smith, S., 16 Holles St, Clare Mkt, London, carver and gilder (1839). [D]

Smith, Sam., London(?), cm (1740–43). Recorded in the accounts of Holkham Hall, Norfolk. In 1740 supplied a mahogany dining table and mended another table at a combined charge of £9 18s. In 1743 charged £7 6s for 'mahogany dispensatory weight scales', 11s for mending a table for the 'dining room in London', and £3 10s for a piece of looking-glass 40″ × 20″. [V&A archives]

Smith, Sampson, Sheffield, Yorks., cm (1828–37). At 30 Backfields in 1828, 11 Carver St in 1833 and 27 Carver St in 1837. [D]

Smith, Samuel, Chester, cm (1721). Son of William Smith, sawyer. App. to Edward Twanbrook of Chester, cm and free 21 September 1721. His father was already dead by this date. [Freemen rolls]

Smith, Samuel, address unknown, cm (1739). Subscribed to Robert West's *Perspective Views of all the Ancient Churches . . . in the City of London*, Pt II, 1739.

Smith, Samuel, 'The Inigo Jones Head', Compton Ct, Compton St, Soho, London cm and u (1744–d. by 1771). A Fellow of the Society for Arts and Manufactures 1761–65. Dead by 1771 when his remaining stock was sold by auction by Mr Christie at his Great Room, Pall Mall commencing 4 April. He attracted a number of important patrons. The Earl of Dumfries placed orders with him in 1756 totalling £13 17s. The work involved mending and cleaning tapestries and supplying two tables. A 'neat mahog frett Rim tea table' was charged at £1 1s and a 'mahogany nettwood Breakfast Table with a draw to ditto' £3 3s. The latter survives and closely resembles pl. xxxiii of Chippendale's *Director*, 1754. Smith was considered for other furniture and on 25 August 1757 wrote to the Earl enclosing two sketches 'of Glass frames' which he estimated to cost on completion £25 each. He also mentions in this letter designs for chairs and some table tops that the Earl had ordered. Smith hoped to obtain firm orders when the Earl visited London, but the visit was postponed until 1758–59 and by this date it had been decided to place the orders with Chippendale & Rannie. Smith's name also appears in the account book of Sir Robert Burdett of Foremark Hall, Derbs., and a payment of £6 15s was made on 30 January 1768. [D; *Daily Advertiser*, 26 March 1744; Westminster poll bk; Dumfries House papers, DH34/51,

DH34/63; *Burlington*, November 1969, p. 664; Berks. RO, D/EBU A8/1]

Smith, Samuel, Daventry, Northants., u (1776). In 1776 took out insurance cover of £100 and of this £40 was for utensils and stock. [GL, Sun MS vol. 253, p. 470]

Smith, Samuel, Dorking, Surrey, upholder (1776). Bankruptcy announced, *Leicester Journal*, June 1776.

Smith, Samuel, parish of St James, Bristol, cm (1784). [Poll bk]

Smith, Samuel, address unknown, u (1784–85). Recorded in the accounts of Dunham Massey, Cheshire. On 7 December 1784 he was paid £11 13s for 'striped & white cotton Furniture for Gallery Room. On 3 November 1785 a further bill was settled, this time to Smith & Latterfield. This was for 'Callicoe Furniture' at a cost of £15 8s. [John Rylands Lib., Manchester Univ., George Cooke's accounts]

Smith, Samuel, 38 Beech St, Barbican, London, cm (1790–93). [D]

Smith, Samuel, Liverpool, upholder (1794–1807). At 9 Prices St, 1794–1804, 11 Prices St in 1805 and Wavertree in 1807. [D]

Smith, Samuel & Thomas, 19 Lord St, Liverpool, auctioneers and appraisers (1804). [D] See Robert Smith of Liverpool, 1787–1810.

Smith, Samuel & Co., 5 Castle Ditch, Liverpool, u (1807). [D]

Smith, Samuel, 7 James St, Covent Gdn, London, carver and gilder (1819). [D]

Smith, Samuel, Huntingdon St, Lambeth, London, chair and sofa maker (1826). [D]

Smith, Samuel, Windy Bank, Colne, Lancs., cm (1828). [D]

Smith, Samuel, Otley, Yorks., joiner/cm (1834–37). In 1837 at Kirkgate. [D]

Smith, Sarah, 33 College St, Bristol, u (1837–40). [D]

Smith, Seth, 39 Carey St, Lincoln's Inn Fields, London, carver and gilder (1839). [D]

Smith, Sidney, 64 St Aubyn St, Plymouth, Devon, cm and u (1823). [D]

Smith, T., London, u (1793). Subscribed to Sheraton's *Drawing Book*, 1793.

Smith, T., 16 Cleveland St, Fitzroy Sq., London, carver, gilder and frame maker (*c*.1800). [Heal]

Smith, T., Lant St, Southwark, London, looking-glass etc. manufacturer (1804). [D]

Smith, T., Union St, Lambeth, London, chair and sofa maker (1809–26). [D]

Smith, T., 32 Newman St, Oxford St, London, u and undertaker (1816). [D]

Smith, Thomas, London, upholder (1710–21). Son of Gilbert Smith a member of the Drapers' Co. App. to William Cowthorpe on 7 June 1710 and free of the Upholders' Co. by servitude, 3 May 1721. [GL, Upholders' Co. records]

Smith, Thomas, Gracechurch St, London, u (1723). [Heal]

Smith, Thomas (Captain), corner of Gt Queen St, London, upholder (1725). [Heal]

Smith, Thomas, St Giles Without Cripplegate, London, chairmaker, broker and chapman (1728). Bankruptcy announced, *London Gazette*, 30 July–3 August 1728.

Smith, Thomas, Berkeley, Glos., upholder (1738). Freeman of Bristol. [Bristol poll bk]

Smith, Thomas, Chester and Liverpool, cm (1747). Son of Thomas Smith jnr, sawyer. Free 20 July 1747 by which date his father was dead. In 1747 moved to Liverpool. [Chester freemen rolls and poll bk]

Smith, Thomas, opposite 'The Ship Tavern', Ratcliff Cross, London, cm (1747–48). [Heal; *Daily Advertiser*, 30 April 1748]

Smith, Thomas, Chipping Norton, Oxon., cm (1753). On 14 March 1753 married Sarah Leatherhead, widow, of

Chipping Norton. He was aged 43 and she 30. [Bodleian index of Oxf. marriage bonds]

Smith, Thomas, Cambridge, see John Smith and successors of Cambridge.

Smith, Thomas, Shadwell, London, cm and upholder (1757–86). Son of Thomas Smith of Colchester, Essex, vintner. App. to Stephen Abb on 6 December 1757 and free of the Upholders' Co. under the terms of the 1750 Upholders' Act, 2 May 1765. In 1778 at 218 Shadwell High St where he took out insurance cover of £200 of which half was for utensils and stock. Shown at Star St, Shadwell, 1778–86. [GL, Upholders' Co. records; Sun MS vol. 264, p. 520; Colchester poll bks]

Smith, Thomas, Temple Bar, London, bedding, carpet, blanket and upholstery warehouse (1769). [*Middlesex Journal*, 25 April 1769]

Smith, Thomas, Norwich, cm (1770–1818). At 16 St Giles St, but from 1805–10 this address was listed as St Giles, Broad St. Free on 24 February 1770 but not by servitude. His own apps, Francis Clarke and John Blomfield, were free on 3 May 1813 and 14 July 1818 respectively. In 1775 took out insurance cover of £400 of which £350 was for utensils and stock. By 1778 total cover had risen to £900 and utensils and stock to £850 which suggests a prosperous and expanding enterprise. In 1786 he insured a house on the corner of Goat Lane for £300. [D; poll bks; freemen reg.; GL, Sun MS vol. 240, p. 443; vol. 265, p. 295; vol. 337, p. 429]

Smith, Thomas, Butcher Row, London, upholder (1773). Bankrupt, *Gents Mag.*, June 1773.

Smith, Thomas, 50 Baldwins Gdns, Leather Lane, Holborn, London, cm (1776). In 1776 took out insurance cover of £200, half of which was for utensils and stock. [GL, Sun MS vol. 244, p. 280]

Smith, Thomas, Long Acre, London, u (1778). Bankrupt, *Gents Mag.*, December 1778.

Smith, Thomas, Aldersgate St, London, upholder (1779). [Heal]

Smith, Thomas, Worcester, cm (1780). App. to James Twitty and free by servitude 19 June 1780. [Freemen rolls]

Smith, Thomas, Market Drayton, Salop, cm (1784). [D]

Smith, Thomas, Lancaster (1787–89). [Westminster Ref. Lib., Gillow records]

Smith, Thomas, Liverpool, cm (1790–1814). At back of 22 Pool Lane in 1790; 19 Circus St, Byrom St, 1800–03; 30 Circus St, 1804–05; 30 Dale St in 1813 and 10 Dale St in 1814. [D]

Smith, Thomas, London, cm (1793–1803). Subscribed to Sheraton's *Drawing Book*, 1793. The Thomas Smith, cm, who subscribed to his *Cabinet Dictionary*, 1803, but whose address was not indicated, was probably the same person.

Smith, Thomas jnr, Leominster, Herefs., cm (1796–1811). Shown as an elector, 1796–97. The Smith of Leominster who was paid £4 10s 6d by Mr Dunne of Gatley Park near Leominster on 9 October 1811, was probably the same person. [Poll bks; Herefs. RO, F 76/III/40]

Smith, Thomas, Whitby, Yorks., carver (1798). [D]

Smith, Thomas, Shepherd St, Mayfair, London, upholder and cm (1801–12). Insurance records show him at 6 Shepherd St in April 1807, but directories at 1 Shepherd St, 1807–12. In March 1801 took out insurance cover for £2,000 but only £100 covered utensils and stock. By April 1807 total cover had fallen to £500 with utensils and stock still at £100. [D; GL, Sun MS vol. 419, ref. 715573; vol. 440, ref. 802249]

Smith, Thomas, Holy Trinity parish, Exeter, Devon, u (1803). [Militia Census]

Smith, Thomas, 9 Turnstile Alley, Drury Lane, London, broker and cm (1804). In July 1804 took out insurance cover of

£1,000 but only £250 was in respect of utensils and stock. Also owned 5 Turnstile Alley. [GL, Sun MS vol. 431, ref. 762873]

Smith, Thomas, Gainsborough, Lincs., cm, trunkmaker and furniture broker (1805–31). At Silver St, 1819–22, and Market Pl., 1828–31. Listed as a furniture broker in addition to his trade as cm and trunkmaker, 1826–31. [D]

Smith, Thomas, 38 Broad St, Soho, London, u etc. (1806–09). [D]

Smith, Thomas, 5 Chapel St, Mayfair, London, upholder and cm (1809–13). In March 1809 took out insurance cover of £700 which included £350 for utensils and stock at Chapel St and a further £200 on similar items in a wareroom and cabinet workshop in Ducking Pond Yd. [D; GL, Sun MS vol. 448, refs 828645, 828649]

Smith, Thomas, 67 Charlotte St, Fitzroy Sq., London, upholder and undertaker (1809–14). [D]

Smith, Thomas, 32 Upper Marylebone St, London, carver, gilder and looking-glass manufacturer (1812–26). Shown as a carver and gilder 1812–15, but from 1817 as a looking-glass manufacturer. [D]

Smith, Thomas, 17 South Audley St, London, u etc. (1814–37). [D] See John Smith at this address in 1835.

Smith, Thomas, Plymouth, Devon, cm (1815). In March 1815 he was confined to the prison of St Thomas, Exeter for debt. His case was due for consideration under an Act for the relief of insolvent debtors. Named amongst the creditors were Matthew Madge of Plymouth, cm, William Fry of Plymouth, bedstead maker and Jewel Catear of Plymouth, cm. [*Exeter Flying Post*, 2 March 1815]

Smith, Thomas, Barton St, Tewkesbury, Glos., chairmaker (1815–16). Children bapt. between 1815–16. [PR (bapt.)]

Smith, Thomas, Richmond, Yorks., cm (1816–40). Child bapt. in 1816. Trading in Finkle St in 1840. [D; PR (bapt.)]

Smith, Thomas, Liverpool, cm (1817–37). In 1817 app. to William Smith and free 18 June 1827. At this date shown at 2 Marquis St and Union St North. In 1837 trading at 8 Freemen's Row. [D]

Smith, Thomas, 1 Butt's Head Passage, Wood St, London, carver and gilder (1820). [D]

Smith, Thomas, 42 Gt Guildford St, Southwark, London, carver and gilder (1820–26). [D]

Smith, Thomas, Thomas, 200 Oxford St, London, u and undertaker (1820). [D]

Smith, Thomas, 236 Shoreditch, London, u (1820). One directory lists him also at 12–13 Grey Eagle St, Spitalfields and lists his trade as a 'mattress and sea-bed manufacturer, hair merchant and curler'. [D]

Smith, Thomas & Son, Briggate, Leeds, Yorks., hair seating manufacturers (1822). [D]

Smith, Thomas, Baxtergate, Grimsby, Lincs., joiner and cm (1822–31). [D]

Smith, Thomas, Slingsby, Yorks., cm and wheelwright (1823). [D]

Smith, Thomas & Son, 8 Terrace, Kensington, London, u (1826). [D]

Smith, Thomas, Scarborough, Yorks., carver (1830–31). In 1830 at Porretts Lane but in the following year at Quay St. [D]

Smith, Thomas, Bull Mount, Stafford, chairmaker (1834–35). [D]

Smith, Thomas, Northgate, Market Weighton, Yorks., cm (1834–40). [D]

Smith, Thomas, Brompton Row, London, u, appraiser and undertaker (1835–39). At 42 Brompton Row, 1837–38, but by 1839 the number was 41. [D]

Smith, Thomas, 8 Earl St, Lisson Grove, London, cm (1835). [D]

Smith, Thomas, 18 London Wall, London, carver and gilder (1835). [D]

Smith, Thomas, 12 Denmark St, Soho, London, carver and gilder (1835–39). [D]

Smith, Thomas, 50 Gravel Lane, Southwark, London, carver and gilder (1835–39). [D]

Smith, Thomas, 15 Little Titchfield St, London, cm and u (1839). [D]

Smith, Thomas, Wood St, Swindon, Wilts., cm (1839). [D]

Smith, Thomas, Finkle St, Richmond, Yorks., cm (1840). [D]

Smith, Thomas, Belgrave Gate, Leicester, cm (1840). [D] Successor to William Smith, at Belgrave Gate from 1827–28.

Smith, W. B., Market Pl., Leicester, cm (1818–22). [D] Possibly William Bootham Smith of Leicester.

Smith, W. S., 11 Orange St, Red Lion Sq., London (1827). Successor to Alexander Smith, carver and gilder, at this address. [Heal]

Smith, W., 14 Castle St East, Oxford Mkt, London, carver and gilder (1835–37). [D]

Smith, W. H., 72 Old Broad St, London, u etc. (1835–37). [D]

Smith, Wainwright, 8 New Conduit St, King's Lynn, Norfolk, cm (1839). [D]

Smith, William, London, upholder (1705–15). Son of William Smith, freeman of London and a member of the Feltmakers' Co. App. to John Woodburn on 22 October 1705 and then to William Long, patten maker. Free of the Upholders' Co. by servitude, 6 July 1715. [GL, Upholders' Co. records]

Smith, William, Liverpool, carver (1711). Free 27 August 1711. [Freemen reg.]

Smith, William, parish of St Clement, Oxford, cm (1740). Married Mary Barnes of the same parish at the church of St Clement, 8 April 1740. William Smith was aged 25. [Bodleian index of Oxf. marriage bonds]

Smith, William, Norwich, u (1753). App. to Francis Brooke and free 3 May 1753. [Freemen reg.]

Smith, William, the Side, Newcastle, u (1753–d. by 1755). Named as the agent to Philip Magee, linen cloth bleacher in 1753. Cloth could be left at Smith's shop or given to Caleb Alder 'in the Burnt-house entry, on the Side'. By June 1755 Smith was dead and the business was continued by Bartholomew Kent, his son-in-law and formerly his app. [*Newcastle Courant*, 17 March 1753, 7 June 1755]

Smith, William, Wells, Som., cm (1754). Freeman of Bristol. [Bristol poll bk]

Smith, William, near the end of Chancery Lane, near Gray's Inn Gate, Holborn, carpet, upholstery and bedding warehouse (1763–69). [D; Heal; *Middlesex Journal*, 25 April 1769]

Smith, William, Lancaster, cm (1767–68). [Freemen rolls]

Smith, William, Yorks., chairmaker (1771). Supplied Edwin Lascelles of Harewood House in 1771 with '2 dozen of Elm chairs' and two dining tables at £21 2s. The chairs with fan backs and stuffed-over seats were intended for the Steward's Room and at least ten of these still survive. [Temple Newsam House, Leeds, Exhib. Cat., *Back-stairs Furniture*, 1977 (10)]

Smith, William, near Wapping New Stairs, Wapping, London, cm (1774). In December 1774 a cellar under his dwelling was being used by Mary & Jeh. Parker, beer and wine merchants. [GL, Sun MS vol. 235, ref. 347634]

Smith, William, 46 Turn Stile, Little Tower Hill, London, bed and carpet warehouse (1774). [D]

Smith, William, Carnaby Mkt, London, chairmaker (1779). In 1779 insured his house for £100. [GL, Sun MS vol. 273, p. 96]

Smith, William, Midsomer Norton, Som., cm (1781). In 1781 insured his house for £100. [GL, Sun MS vol. 291, p. 323]

Smith, William, address unknown, joiner (1785). Employed by the Duke of Devonshire at Chatsworth, Derbs. in 1785. He supplied a new oak bedstead at £1 10s, six mahogany stools for the Chapel Gallery at £2 12s, eight mahogany basin stands at 18s, and also undertook architectural carving, joinery work and assisted the upholsterer. The bill, which amounted to £116 18s 11d, was examined by John Carr. [Chatsworth papers]

Smith, William, Liverpool, cm (1784–d.1819). App. to John Darbyshire and free 2 April 1784. At Vernon St in 1787, 33 Dale St and Vernon St in 1790, 34 Dale St in 1796 and 1803, no. 30 in 1800 and 1807–10, no. 33 in 1805, no. 28 in 1804 and no. 37 in 1811. The repeated change of number in Dale St was probably due to Post Office re-numbering. Took as apps Hugh Cannell (1791–1802), John Smith (1793–1802), Edward Slater (1810–18) and Thomas Smith (1817–27). [D; freemen's committee bks and reg.]

Smith, William, Christchurch parish, York, u (1787–98). Son of John Smith, yeoman of Water Fulford. App. to Matthew Browne on 28 February 1787 and free 1798. [York app. reg. and freemen rolls]

Smith, William, York, u (1789). Son of William Smith of Fulford, York. Free 1789. [York freemen rolls]

Smith, William, Bawtry, Yorks., cm (d.1793). Probate granted on his will, 2 May 1793. [D; Notts. RO, probate records]

Smith, William, Birmingham, cm, u and broker (1793–1830). In 1793 at Snow Hill, in 1818 at Gt Hampton St and in 1830 at Bromsgrove St. [D]

Smith, William, 10 Beach St, London, cm (1793). Subscribed to Sheraton's *Drawing Book*, 1793.

Smith, William, Southwark, London, cm (1794–99). In 1794 at Queen St, Mint and in 1799 at Mint Sq. [D]

Smith, William, 27 Wardour St, Soho, London, chairmaker (1794–1817). In 1794 trading in partnership with John Shenton. Listed as a master cabinet maker in Sheraton's *Cabinet Dictionary*, 1803, which he also subscribed to. On 24 July 1803 a fire broke out at his workshop. Also listed in directories as a sofa maker and u. [D; Heal; *Gents Mag.*, July 1803]

Smith, William, Devonport, Devon, cm and u (1798–1825). At Fore St in 1812. Bankruptcy announced, November 1821, and in January 1825 the commissioners for his bankruptcy sold a house in St Aubyn St. [D; *Exeter Flying Post*, 8 November 1821; *The Alfred*, 11 January 1825]

Smith, William, address unknown, cm (1803). Subscribed to Sheraton's *Cabinet Dictionary*, 1803. He may be the William Smith, then at 10 Beach (or Beak) St, London, who subscribed to his *Drawing Book*, 1793.

Smith, William, 1 Jane St, Commercial Rd, London, cm (1807–09). In November 1807 took out insurance cover of £300 which included £130 for stock and utensils. In January 1809 the total cover was £300 with utensils and stock £100. [GL, Sun MS vol. 442, ref. 809882; vol. 443, ref. 825667]

Smith, William, Brewer St, Golden Sq., London, u and paperhanger (1808–29). At 34 Brewer St in 1808 but by 1815 had moved to 7. In 1815 took app. sponsored by Grinsell's Charity. His insurance cover in February 1824 amounted to £1,000 but of this only £200 was for utensils and stock. [D; Westminster Ref. Lib., MS E 3559; GL, Sun MS vol. 499, ref. 1012906]

Smith, William, Petergate, York, cm and u (1809–40). Shown at Low Petergate 1809 but by 1828 listed as 37 Petersgate, also as an undertaker. [D]

Smith, William, High-bridge, Newcastle, joiner and cm (1811). [D]

Smith, William, Shrewsbury, Salop, cm (1811). Trustee to John Smith of Ludlow, Salop for £6,200 in annuities left on the death of Martin Dunne of Ludlow. [Herefs. RO, Gatley Papers F76/IV/82]

Smith, William, Gt Hampton St, Birmingham, cm (1818). [D]

Smith, William, Parke-green, Macclesfield, Cheshire, cm (1818). [D]

Smith, William, 74 Newington Causeway, London, u (1819). [D]

Smith, William, 20 Rolls Buildings, Fetter Lane, London, carver, gilder and picture frame maker (1820). In June 1820 took out insurance cover for £400 of which half was for utensils and stock. [D; GL, Sun MS vol. 486, ref. 968456]

Smith, William, Northampton, chairmaker (1820–30). At Woolmonger St in 1820, St Mary St in 1823 and Mare Fair in 1830, also as a turner. [D; poll bks]

Smith, William, Brighton, Sussex, cm (1821–39). Living at Richmond Buildings in 1821, Cavendish St in 1824 and Jubilee St in 1827. Trading at 72 Edward St in 1822. A son and two daughters bapt. between 1821–27 and his son married in September 1839. [D; PR (bapt. and marriage)]

Smith, William, Broad St, Ludlow, Salop, cm and u (1822). [D]

Smith, William, Hull, Yorks., cm (1822–23). At New Postern Gate in 1822 and Cockpit Yd, 6 Castle St and New John Yd in 1823. [D]

Smith, William, 45 King St, Snow Hill, London, pocket book maker and fancy cm (1822–23). In November 1822 took out insurance cover of £6,900 of which £5,000 was for utensils and stock. He also insured property at 9 Spencer St, Northampton Sq. In March of the following year insurance totalled £6,800 of which £6,000 was for utensils and stock. The business was referred to as William Smith & Co. The reason for the high valuations given to utensils and stock is not clear. [GL, Sun MS vol. 492, ref. 997592; vol. 494, ref. 1003208]

Smith, William, Long St, Tetbury, Glos., cm, u, auctioneer and appraiser (1822–39). [D]

Smith, William, Bristol, Windsor and fancy chairmaker (1823–35). At Middle Ave., Queen Sq. in 1823; 34 King St, St Nicholas, 1824–25; 33 and 36 King St in 1826; and 33 King St, 1827–35. Succeeded by Fillia Smith. [D]

Smith, William, Catterick, Yorks., joiner and cm (1823). [D]

Smith, William, Gt Ancoats St, Manchester, cm (1825). His trade address was 32 Gt Ancoats St and his residence was at no. 28. [D]

Smith, William Bootham, Leicester, cm (1826–27). App. to John Shipley but on his death served the remainder of his apprenticeship under his widow. Free 1826 and trading in Hotel St, 1827. [D; freemen rolls] Possibly W. B. Smith of Leicester.

Smith, William, Leicester, cm (1815–28). At Swine Mkt in 1815 and Belgrave Gate, 1827–28. [D] Succeeded by Thomas Smith at Belgrave Gate.

Smith, William, Market Pl., Grimsby, Lincs., joiner, cm and u (1826–35). [D]

Smith, William, Brunswick St, Stockton, Co. Durham, joiner and cm (1827). [D]

Smith, William, Blackwellgate, Darlington, Co. Durham, cm (1827–34). [D]

Smith, William, King St, South Shields, Co. Durham, cm and joiner (1827–34). In 1828 described as William Smith & Son. [D]

Smith, William, Bromsgrove St, Birmingham, cm and u (1828). [D]

Smith, William, Church St, Colne, Lancs., cm (1828–40). His son Robert is also mentioned in a directory entry of 1834. There were two cm named William Smith trading in Colne at the time of the 1841 Census, one trading in Market St and the other in Piece Hall Yd. [D]

Smith, William, 4 Northampton St, Clerkenwell, London, looking-glass and picture frame maker (1829). [D]

Smith, William, Skipton, Yorks., cm (1829–37). In 1837 at Bird's Buildings. [D; PR]

Smith, William Heldon, 7 Crescent, Cambridge, carver and gilder (1830). [D]

Smith, William, 1 Richmond Row and Kirkdale Rd, Kirkdale, Liverpool, carver (1830). App. to John Summer and free 20 November 1830. [Freemen reg.]

Smith, William, De Ligne St, Radford, Notts., joiner and cm (1832). [D] See John Smith at this address in 1832.

Smith, William, George St, Radford, Notts., chairmaker (1834). [D]

Smith, William, Sheffield, Yorks., cm (1833–37). At 87 Scotland St in 1833 and 8 Workhouse Croft, 1834–37. [D]

Smith, William, Durham/Newcastle area, joiner (1834). Worked at Gibside, Co. Durham and on 29 November 1834 submitted his account for work. This included making and painting a large flower pot stand for the Entrance Hall, a large toilette table, furniture repairs and alterations and putting up glasses and curtains etc. [Durham RO, Strathmore MS, D/St/346/33]

Smith, William, Skelton St, Colne, Lancs., cm (1834–40). Two cm named William Smith were working in Colne at this period. In 1841 at the time of the Census one was in Market St and the other in Piece Hall Yd. [D]

Smith, William, Conisbrough, Yorks., joiner and cm (1834). [D]

Smith, William, 170 Moseley St, Birmingham, cm (1839). [D]

Smith, William, Northwood St, Birmingham, cabinet case maker (1839). [D]

Smith, William, 45 Worcester St, Birmingham, cm (1839). [D]

Smith, William, Chipping Camden, Glos., chairmaker (1839). [D]

Smith, William, Dunmow, Essex, cm, u and turner (1839). [D]

Smith, William, New Conduit St, King's Lynn, Norfolk, cm (1839). [D]

Smith, William & Nephew, 28 Hatton Gdn, London, cm and u (1839). [D]

Smith, William, 252 Tottenham Ct Rd, London, bedstead maker (1839). [D]

Smith, William, 94 York St, Westminster, London, cm and u (1839). [D]

Smith, William, Parkston, Poole, Dorset, cm and u (1840). [D]

Smith, William, Liverpool, carver and gilder (1840). Free 22 July 1840. [Freemen reg.]

Smith, Wright, Norwich, cm (1762–d.1791). Living in the parish of St Andrew, 1768 and the parish of St Peter Mancroft, 1780–90. Trading at Coffee House Ct, Market Pl. 1783 and in the following year the address is simply given as Market Pl. His app., William Elden Earle, was made free 18 June 1762. Will proved at Norwich in 1791. [D; poll bks; freemen reg.; Norfolk Record Soc., index of wills]

Smith, Zachariah, Durham Yd, Strand area, London, u and cm (d. by 1741). Dead by May 1741 when his goods were auctioned off 'within Five Doors of Durham Yard in the Strand'. Goods on offer included 'Four Posted and Harrateen Beds, Settee Bedsteads, fine Quilts and Blankets, Cotton Counterpanes, French Carpets, very Handsome Walnut-Tree Chairs, Spanish Leather Seats, Easy Chairs, Chest upon Chest, Buroes, Sconces and Chimney Glasses, a very good Eight Day Clock, and other goods'. Some small 'India Cabinets' were also specified. In connection with certain items it was stated that 'these Goods are almost new, being made to go abroad, and free from Buggs'. [London Evening Post, 1–4 and 20–22 May 1742]

Smith & Beaumont, Barbican, London, cm (1792–93). At 36 Beech St in 1792 and in one directory of 1793. Another of that year gives King's Head Ct, Barbican. [D]

Smith Bradshaw & Saunders, Soho, London, upholders and cm (1755). In February 1755 a fire was reported in their workshops which not only extensively damaged them but also destroyed the tools and tool chests of thirty seven workers who were employed there. The value of these was said to exceed £300. A subscription list was established and on 2 April it was reported that sufficient had been given to make good the damage. [Public Advertiser, 8 February and 2 April 1755] See Paul Saunders.

Smith & Brereton, Charles St, Grosvenor Sq., London, cm and upholders (1785–93). A partnership between John Smith and William Brereton. At 4 Charles St in December 1785 when utensils and stock were insured for £350. By 1790 at 13 Charles St. In 1794 the business appears to have been in the sole control of John Smith. [D; GL, Sun MS vol. 330, pp. 152, 612]

Smith & Brett, 24 Church St, Spitalfields, London, cabinet etc. manufacturers (1825). [D]

Smith & Campion, Gallowtree Gate, Leicester, cm (1799). In May 1799 a sale of their stock in trade was advertised. [Leicester Journal, 24 May 1799]

Smith & Chipp, address unknown (1775). Supplied to Croome Court, Worcs. 'An Italian chair and harness' which was paid for on 4 July at a cost of £25. [V&A archives]

Smith & Griffith(s), 78 Blackman St, London, u (1803–08). Succeeded by Smith & Sindrey. [D]

Smith & Hollingsworth, 6 Bedford St, Bedford Row, London, u etc. (1808–11). A partnership of Thomas Smith and Samuel Hollingsworth. In September 1808 took out insurance cover for £1,500 of which £1,400 was for utensils and stock. By November 1809 these figures had risen to £2,000 and £1,900 respectively. These high levels of insurance cover indicate a business of substantial proportions. [D; GL, Sun MS vol. 445, ref. 819997; vol. 443, ref. 836743]

Smith & Holmes, Little Queen St, Lincoln's Inn Fields, London, cm (1826). [D]

Smith & King, Bristol, cm, u and japanners (1827–40). At Trenchard St, the number being 1 in 1827–29, 10 in 1830 and 16 in 1831–35. From 1836–40 occupied 2 Park St with premises also in Frogmore St. [D]

Smith & Madgwick, 11 Pavement, Finsbury, London, cm and u (1839). [D]

Smith & Powell, 78 Blackman St, London, auctioneers and u (1826). [D] Successors to Smith & Sindrey at this address.

Smith & Rawlins, 2 Falcon Pl., London, chair japanners (1813). In May 1813 took out insurance cover of £700 which included £200 for utensils and stock in the house and a further £200 for similar items in a workshop behind. [GL, Sun MS vol. 463, ref. 881971]

Smith & Richardson, Hull, Yorks., cm and u (1806–35). At Lowgate 1806–10; 19 Chapel Lane, 1817–23 and 1831; 18 Chapel Lane in 1826 and 19 Bowalley Lane, 1834–35. [D]

Smith & Rose, 38 Broad St, Golden Sq., London, u (1808). [D]

Smith & Sindrey, 78 Blackman St, London, u (1809–25). One directory of 1822 lists the business as Smith, Sindrey & Powell and by 1826 the premises were in the occupation of Smith & Powell. It would thus seem that Powell was a new partner introduced c.1822. From 1803–08 the business had traded as Smith & Griffith(s). Thomas Smith was living at 78 Blackman St and owned houses in other parts of London which he insured for sums of up to £800. In some years this property was jointly insured by John & Thomas Smith. No insurance details have, however, been traced for the Blackman St premises or for trade goods kept there. [D; GL, Sun MS vol. 441, ref. 812547; vol. 462, ref. 881129; vol. 461, ref. 901557; vol. 490, ref. 995698; vol. 495, refs 1010515, 1014369]

Smith & Skegg, London, bedstead and chairmaker (1817–20). At 68 Old St, St Luke's in 1817 and 1820 but in 1819 shown at 65 Bunhill Row. [D]

Smith & Son, See John Smith and successors of Cambridge.

Smith & Son, 82 Holborn, London, carpet manufacturers and upholders (1790–93). [D]

Smith & Son, 8 Terrace, High St, Kensington, u (1826–35). [D]

Smith & Theweneti, 29 Kingsmead St, Bath, Som., cm (1833). [D]

Smith & Turner, Bond St, London, cm (1805). In May 1805 a fire occurred in their warehouse in Grosvenor Mews. [*Gents Mag.*, May 1805]

Smith & Tyler, Boston, Lincs., cm and u (1819–35). Listed at Silver St, 1819, and Pump Sq., 1822–35. The directory of 1835 lists the business as St John Tyler of Boston. [D]

Smithers, —, Deal, Kent, cm (1811). [D]

Smithies, William, Market Pl., Knaresborough, Yorks., cm and u (1822). [D]

Smithson, John, Hotel Yd, Leeds, Yorks., cm and furniture broker (1822). [D]

Smithson, John, Bondgate, Otley, Yorks., joiner, cm and builder (1828–34). [D]

Smithson, Richard, London, upholder (1714–29). Son of William Smithson of London, apothecary. App. to Thomas Kelsall on 6 October 1714 and free of the Upholders' Co. by servitude, 7 May 1729. [GL, Upholders' Co. records]

Smithson, Richard, formerly of St George the Martyr, Middlx, late of St Paul, Shadwell, London, u (1761). Discharged from Debtors' Prison, 15 September 1761. [*London Gazette*]

Smithson, Thomas, 5 Redman's Row, Mile End Rd, London, cm and u (1839). [D]

Smithson, William Stephen, 31 Paddington St, London, carver and gilder (1839). [D]

Smiton, Jane, 9 Little Wild St, Lincoln's Inn Fields, London, cm (1792). Took out insurance cover of £400 in November 1792. [GL, Sun MS vol. 389, ref. 607343] Successor and possibly widow of:

Smiton, Ninien, 9 Little Wild St, Lincoln's Inn Fields, London, cm (1786). In February 1786 took out insurance cover of £200 which included £80 for utensils and stock. [GL, Sun MS vol. 335, p. 359]

Smoothy, John, Clare, Suffolk, cm, u, appraiser and auctioneer (1830–39). [D]

Smyth, James Samuel, Cambridge, cm (d.1817). Died in 1817 at the age of 26. [*Cambridge Chronicle*, 6 June 1817]

Smythe, James, Church Lane, South Molton, Devon, cm (1830). [D]

Smythurst, Robert, Litchfield St, Soho, London, cm (1725). [Heal]

Snaith, William, Northgate, Darlington, Co. Durham, joiner and cm (1827–34). [D]

Snape, John, 48 Upper Rathbone Pl., London, chairmaker (1808–09). [D]

Snape, Joseph, 21 Paul St, Finsbury Sq., London, cm (1808–22). [D]

Snape, Thomas, Birmingham, cm (1816–30). At Temple St and later Smallbrook St in 1816, and 86 Smallbrook St from 1818. Also listed as an u in 1828. [D]

Snelgrove, W. & J., East St, Southampton, Hants., cm (1839). [D]

Snell, Frederick, 3 Myddleton St, Clerkenwell, London, carver and gilder (1839). [D]

Snell, John, West St, Bridport, Dorset, cm (1840). [D]

Snell, Robert, London, looking-glass manufacturer, print seller, carver and gilder (1800–25). In partnership with Robert Scholey, 1800–c. 1811 at 69 Sun St, Bishopsgate. Recorded alone at 98 Holborn Hill, 1808–25. In April 1809 took out insurance of £500 on his premises of which £250 was for utensils and stock. On the same day he also took out insurance on 69 Sun St for £450 with £350 for utensils and

stock. Both addresses were described as his dwelling house. [D; GL, Sun MS vol. 447, refs 830314–15] See Robert Scholey.

Snell, William, London, u (1788–d. by 1839). Traded as William Snell from 1788–1817 although one directory of 1794 lists the business as Snell & Wright. From 1819 the business was William & Edward Snell. At 15 Hanover St, Long Acre from 1788–1821, but by 1823 had moved to 27 Albemarle St. From 1835 premises at 1 Belgrave New Rd were used in addition to those in Albemarle St. William Snell was included in the list of master cabinet makers in Sheraton's *Cabinet Dictionary*, 1803. In February 1792 he took out insurance cover of £300 on his property at 13 Hanover St (possibly an error in the number) and 1 Lower Sloane St. The architect John Buonarotti Papworth was concerned with repairs to 24 Berkeley Sq. for William & Edward Snell from 1822–23 and also with their workshop at Belgrave Rd, 1829–35. By the 1820s the firm was noted for the production of furniture in the French taste and was mentioned in the April 1822 issue of Ackermann's *Repository of Arts* in this connection. The furniture plate for this month was of a secretaire bookcase based on a French design and this may have been supplied to Ackermann by Snell. William Snell was dead by 1839 when a lease on the Albemarle St premises were renewed for twenty one years in the name of Edward Snell.

A number of Snell's customers are known. In 1837 two rosewood whatnots were supplied to Buckingham Palace at a cost of £33 12s. They were described as having 'statuary tops, each with three shelves supported on turned columns, with framed backs and three silvered plates with gilt mouldings'. On 31 December of the same year 'an Easy Chair finished in mat & Burnished Gold in fine canvas' was supplied to Windsor Castle at £7 10s. On the accession of Queen Victoria they rented furniture for use at Kensington Palace prior to the move to Buckingham Palace. Snell's men worked from 20–24 June arranging the Vestibule and Saloon for the Council. Snell also moved a bedstead from Claremont, Surrey, and furniture from Kensington Palace to Buckingham Palace apart from re-decorating the State Apartments between 30 October and 5 November 1837. In addition to work for the Royal Household Snell attracted patrons from the aristocracy and gentry. In July 1797 Sir John Geers Cotterell of Garnons, near Hereford and Hereford St, London paid an upholstery bill of £70 to a Snell, probably this maker. Between 1821–23 Lady O. B. Sparrow expended with 'Snell upholsterer' £324 10s 8d in connection with work at Brampton House, Hunts. [D; GL, Sun MS vol. 382, ref. 596347; Colvin, *Dictionary of British Architects*, p. 619; PRO, C13/433/50; Marylebone Lib., deed 103/4; Windsor Royal Archives, account bks 1833–41; PRO, LC11/98; Herefs. RO, Garnons W69/III/180; Cambs. RO (Huntingdon), DDM 16/5]

Snell, William, parish of St Mary Major, Exeter, Devon, journeyman cm (1803–d.1825). Included in a Militia Census of 1803. Married in January 1808 Miss Salter of Honiton, Devon. In June 1825 drowned as a result of a boating accident and left a widow and several children unprovided for. [*Exeter Flying Post*, 14 January 1808, 16 June 1825]

Snelling, John, Wolborough St, Newton Abbott, Devon, cm (1830). [D]

Snellock, Mordante, London, u (1667). In 1667 responsible for supplying 'a bed of blew Damask and hanging the Bedchambers of our Dearest consort the Queene' for which £112 10s was charged. [PRO, LC5/40]

Snewin, William, Market St, Worthing, Sussex, cm, u, paperhanger and undertaker (1839–40). At Market St in 1839 but in 1845 at 6 Brighton Rd as a builder and undertaker [D]

Snoddon, Joseph, Compton St, London, cm (1784). [Westminster poll bk]

Snook, James, St Paul's Sq., Bedford, cm and u (1830). [D]

Snook, Jane, Rochester, Kent, u (1761). In 1761 took app. named Snook. [S of G, app. index]

Snook, Robert snr, High East St, Dorchester, Dorset, u (1725–d.1747). In May 1725 insured his goods and merchandise for £500. Had six sons and a daughter. His eldest son Samuel traded as an u in the town, the second eldest, Joshua, took up the law; and Robert, the next eldest, also became an u in Dorchester. [GL, Sun MS vol. 20, ref. 35977; Dorset RO, DA/W/1747/24]

Snook, Robert jnr, Dorchester, Dorset, u and appraiser (1775). Son of Robert Snook snr. In 1775 took out insurance cover of £800 which included £400 for his utensils and stock. [GL, Sun MS vol. 239, p. 100]

Snook, Samuel, Dorchester, Dorset, u and appraiser (1755–93). Eldest son of Robert Snook snr. Free 1755 but as this was seven years after the death of his father he may not have been his immediate successor in business. Bankrupt, *Gents Mag.*, November 1766, but re-established his business and in May 1785 drew up an inventory of the household goods of Joseph Hardy of Martinstown, Dorset. [D; Mayo & Gould, *Municipal Records of … Dorchester*, 1908, p. 432; *The Antique Dealer and Collector's Guide*, September 1978]

Snook, Samuel, 82 East St, Manchester Sq., London, u etc. (1820–27). [D]

Snook, William, parish of St Thomas, Bristol, u (1739). [Poll bk]

Snow, John, Salisbury, Wilts., cm (1729–57). On 30 October 1729 John Snow took Stephen Lambert, son of Stephen Lambert, as app. for a premium of £21. Subsequent apps were taken in the names of John and Thomas Snow and included John Hodson in 1755 and Mathew Jay in 1756. In 1756 the business was listed as Thomas Snow & Co. but in the following year as John & Thomas Snow once again. [*Wilts. Apps and their Masters*; S of G, app. index] See Thomas Snow, Salisbury.

Snow, John, Stamford, Lincs., u and cm (1805–08). [D]

Snow, John, 2 Middletown Buildings, Foley Pl., London, cm and u (1827). [D]

Snow, Robert, King St, South Molton, Devon, u and cm (1838). [D]

Snow, Thomas, Salisbury, Wilts., cm (1753–77). Son of John Thomas and in partnership with his father 1755–57 although some commissions as early as 1753 are in his name only. Supplied drawing room chairs, sofa etc. to Longford Castle, Wilts. in 1755 at a cost of £28. His name also appears in the account bks for this house from July 1768 to November 1777. The amounts received over this period totalled £127 1s 6d. Thomas Snow also provided mahogany tables for Henry Hoare for which he was paid £2 12s (?) on 29 September 1753. [*C. Life*, 26 December 1931; V&A archives; Wilts. RO, 383/6] See John Snow, Salisbury.

Snow, Thomas snr, Stamford, Lincs., u (b.1751–d.1813). Freeman of Stamford 1780 and became a Capital Burgess of the Borough 1785 and Alderman in 1801. Took as apps Thomas Wortley on 12 September 1785 and Spencer Marquis on 27 May 1807, the latter paying a premium of £50. Died on 23 December 1813 aged 62 as recorded on a tablet which was formerly in the now redundant church of St Michael. The business was substantial by provincial standards with an insurance cover in 1791 of £1,200 of which £900 was for utensils and stock. Payments for work by a Snow, probably this craftsman, are recorded in the Heathcote account bks, 1795–98. On 12 December 1795 he was paid for a bed and bedding for the groom £20 14s 1d, a further £8 4s 5½d on 29 January 1797 for 'carriage for upholsters work' and £4 14s on

7 December 1798 for a bill. [D; Stamford Town Hall Bks, Box 2A/1/4; GL, Sun MS vol. 375, p. 371; vol. 388, p. 391; vol. 391, p. 385; Lincoln RO, 3 ANC 6/20, 3 ANC 6/380, 3 ANC 6/24]

Snow, Thomas jnr, Stamford, Lincs., u (1805–35). Free 1805 by patrimony as the son of Thomas Snow snr. Still alive in 1835 but it is uncertain to what extent he carried on the trade of upholsterer. He is recorded in a poll bk of 1809 but he may not have taken over his father's business on his death in 1813. [Poll bk; Stamford Town Hall Bks, Box 6/1/1–2]

Snow, Thomas, Birstwith, Yorks., clock and cm (1823). [D]

Snowden, George, London, cm, u and chairmaker (1827–39). At Wellington Pl., Stepney Fields in 1827 and 5 Crown Row, Mile End Rd in 1839. [D]

Snowden, John, Botchardgate, Carlisle, Cumb., joiner and cm (1810). [D] See Thomas Snowden at this address.

Snowden, John William, Stepney Green, London, cm, u and chairmaker (1812–27). In 1812 at 9 Clare Hall Row, Stepney Green but in 1827 the address is listed simply as Stepney Green. In January 1812 took out insurance cover of £300 which included £200 for utensils and stock. At that date appears to have been living in the house of his father. [D; GL, Sun MS vol. 457, ref. 867170]

Snowden, Joshua, Leeds, Yorks., cm (1828–34). Listed at West St in 1828 and 54 George St in 1834. [D]

Snowden, Thomas, Botchergate, Carlisle, Cumb., joiner/cm (1811). [D] See John Snowden at this address.

Snowden, Thomas, Water Lane, Richmond, Surrey, cm/chairmaker (1826). [D]

Snowdon (or Snowden), Robert, near the Church, Northallerton, Yorks., cm (1821–40). In 1840 listed as Robert Snowdon jnr, but an earlier trade label states 'Snowden & Son' suggesting that both father and son named Robert were involved in the business. Appear to have marked their furniture on a regular basis, and a number of items are recorded in early 19th-century styles. These include a sarcophagus-shaped cellaret on lion paw feet, a Davenport with sliding top, a writing box, a washstand (Cannon Hall, Barnsley, Yorks.) a bedside table (Kirklees Museums) and a chest of drawers. All are mahogany items of relatively plain functional form. The Davenport was supplied to a Mr Hayes who apparently lived at Whitby, Yorks. and the invoice dated 21 September 1821 indicates that this item cost £8 8s (Figs 26–28). [D; Sotheby's, 6 March 1970, lot 98; *Antique Dealer and Collector's Guide*, October 1980, p. 15; *C. Life*, 3 October 1974, pp. 932–33; Tennants of Richmond, 29 May 1980, lot 396]

Snowdon, Thomas, West St, Oldham, Lancs., joiner and cm (1825). [D]

Snowdon, Thomas, Haltwhistle, Northumb., joiner and cm (1827). [D]

Snowdon, Thomas, Market Pl., Bishop Auckland, Co. Durham, joiner and cm (1827–28). [D]

Snowdon, Thomas, Butchery Lane, Grimsby, Lincs., joiner and cm (1835). [D]

Snowdon, William, Grimsby, Lincs., cm, u and joiner (1822–35). Recorded at High St, 1822–28 and Bull Ring in 1835. [D]

Snowton & Son, 94 Golden Lane, Barbican, London, cm (1839). [D]

Snoxell, Armini, London, upholder (1752–62). Son of Edward Snoxell of Hampstead, farrier. App. to Timothy Matthew, skinner on 3 March 1752. Free of the Upholders' Co. under the terms of the 1750 Upholders' Act, 7 October 1762. [GL, Upholders' Co. records]

Snoxell, William, London, cm (1793–1802). At 34 Wilderness Lane, Salisbury Ct in April 1793 where he took out insurance of £200 which included £150 for utensils and stock. In May 1802 at 84 and 85 Dorset St, Salisbury Sq., Fleet St, and insurance cover had risen to £500 of which half was for utensils and stock. [GL, Sun MS vol. 395, p. 131; vol. 424, ref. 730945]

Snuggs, J., Minories, Tower Hill, London, upholder and cm (1817). [Heal]

Snuggs, John, 27 Mint St, Southwark, London, cm, u and frame maker (1817–29). In 1829 listed as H. Snuggs but this may be an error. Shown as a cm in 1817 and 1829, but in 1820 and 1826 as a frame maker and looking-glass maker. [D]

Soame, Henry Thomas, Fakenham, Norfolk, u and cm (1839). One directory of 1839 gives the address as Oak St and another as Market Pl. [D]

Soames, Charles, London, cm (1818). Freeman of Gt Yarmouth, Norfolk, working in London. [Gt Yarmouth poll bk]

Soans (or Soanes), William, London, cm (1820–40). Freeman of Gt Yarmouth, Norfolk, living in London. [Gt Yarmouth poll bk]

Soar, George, Derby, chair turner (1800–07). On 4 December 1800 took as app. Ann Hudson. The apprenticeship was annulled in 1807 because of his ill-treatment of the child. [App. rolls]

Soar, Michael, 69 Kingsland Rd, London, cm (1820). [D] Succeeded by:

Soar, Richard, Kingsland Rd, London, cm and u (1821–39). The number in Kingsland Rd was 69 from 1821–29 but 67 in 1839. In December 1821 took out insurance cover of £550 which included £170 for utensils and stock in the house, £80 for a shop behind, £70 for stock kept there and £70 for stock kept in an open yard. [D; GL, Sun MS vol. 490, ref. 987093]

Soath, John, Canterbury, Kent, cm (1759). In 1759 took app. named Castle. [S of G, app. index]

Socket, Jeremiah, King's Lynn, Norfolk, chairmaker (1704–05). Eldest son of Henry Socket and free 1704–05 by patrimony. [Freemen rolls]

Soederberg (or Sonderberg), Thomas, Tottenham Ct Rd, London, cm and 'ebonist' (1789–98). At 16 Tottenham Ct Rd in 1789 but at 19 in 1793–94. Bankrupt, *Liverpool Advertiser*, 14 May 1798. In November 1792 supplied 'inlaid tables' for Francis, 5th Duke of Bedford, for Bedford House, London at a cost of £28. Payments were made to Soederberg in connection with the furnishing of Broadlands, Hants. by the 2nd Viscount Palmerston. [D; Bedford Office, London; *C. Life*, 29 January 1981, p. 290]

Soffe, William, 380, Strand, London, carver and gilder (1839). [D]

Solby, William, London, upholder (1719–26). Son of Samuel Solby of the parish of St Paul, Shadwell, baker. App. to William Shepard on 15 April 1719 and free of the Upholders' Co. by servitude, 6 July 1726. [GL, Upholders' Co. records]

Soldan, Francis, West End, Hampstead, London, cm (1766). [Heal]

Sollicey (or Sollier), Amboise, address unknown, u (1789–92). employed by the Royal Household. On 5 April 1789 he was paid £76 or 146 days work as an u, the amount being declared as his 'salary' to 5 April. He received four further payments of £47 10s each during 1790–91, one for each quarter, suggesting continuous employment on a long-term basis. A further payment of £100 was made in August 1792 followed by another of £35 12s 6d to 'Sollier — Tapassier'. [Windsor Royal Archives, RA 88748, 88756, 88764, 88773, 88812, 88821]

Sollis, John, 21 Frogmore St, Bristol, cm (1830). [D]

Solly, Isaac, London, upholder (1756–73). Son of Thomas Solly of Faversham, Kent, linen draper. App. to Michael Bradshaw on 2 September 1756 and free of the Upholders' Co. by servitude, 2 February 1764. He took as app. Richard Wylde, 1765–73. [GL, Upholders' Co. records]

Solly, William Raymant, Dover and Canterbury, Kent, carver and gilder (1826–39). At Stroud St, Dover in 1826 but from 1829–37 at Snargate St, the number being given as 115 in 1832. Moved to Canterbury either late 1837 or early 1838 and was at 2 Burgate St, 1838–39. [D; Dover poll bks]

Soloman, John, Norwich, cm (1802–25). Son of Philip Soloman, shuttle maker; admitted freeman on 29 May 1802 and his son Joshua Edward Soloman on 22 January 1825. Living in the parish of St Peter Mancroft in 1806 and 1818, but the parish of St Stephen in 1812. [Freemen reg.; poll bks]

Soloman, Samuel, 70 Suffolk St, Birmingham, cm and u (1830). [D]

Solomans, M., 16 Strand, London, carver and gilder (1799). [D]

Solomon, Abraham, Gt Queen St, London, furniture broker (1839). A number of late Georgian pieces of furniture are known with a stamped inscription 'A. SOLOMON 55 Gt. QUEEN St.'. Some record the address as 59 Gt Queen St. No cabinetmaker corresponding to this description can be found in London directories, but an Abraham Soloman was trading at 23 Little Queen St in 1839 as a furniture broker. It is highly likely that furniture so marked passed through his hands and was sold by him as secondhand items. [D; V&A archives; Phillips', 3 March 1964, lot 96; Sotheby's, 14 November 1975, lot 79; 26 March 1976, lot 90]

Solomon, Barnet, 81 Redcliff St, Bristol, cm, u and undertaker (1829–31). In 1831 the business was listed as I. L. & B. Soloman. [D]

Solomon, Elijah, Castle St, Long Acre, London, upholder, broker, appraiser, cm and bedstead maker (1790–1816). A trade card of Soloman & Brown, believed to be c.1800 exists giving this address. In February 1792 Elijah Solomon took out insurance cover of £500 of which £400 was for utensils and stock. No directory entries have been recorded after 1793 except one of 1826 which lists Eliza Solomon at this address. This may be his widow or alternatively a directory error. [D; GL, Sun MS vol. 382, ref. 596343; V&A archives]

Solomon, Eliza, see Elijah Solomon.

Solomon, I. L. & B., Bristol, cm, u and undertakers (1831–32). A continuation of the business commenced by Barnet Solomon at 81 Redcliff St in 1829. The last year of trading at this address was 1831 and the next year the partners were at 7 Corn St. [D]

Solomon, John, Norwich, cm (1825). His son Joshua Edward free 22 January 1825 [Freemen rolls]

Solomon, Joshua Edward, parish of St Peter Hungate, Norwich, cm (1825–30). Son of John Solomon, cm, and free 22 January 1825. [Freemen rolls; poll bk]

Solomon, Lyon, 194 Whitechapel Rd, London, cm and u (1839). Also listed as a furniture broker at 5 Surrey Pl., Newington Butts. [D]

Solomon, Moses, 67 Constitution Hill and 80 Islington, Birmingham, cm and u (1839). Trading as a cm from the first address and u from the latter. [D]

Solomon, Samuel, Norwich and Saffron Walden, Essex, cm (1812–30). Living in the parish of St Peter Mancroft, Norwich in October 1812 but by June 1818 had moved to Saffron Walden where he was still living in July 1830. [Norwich poll bks]

Solomon, Susanna, Bristol, u (1798). Bankruptcy declared, *Exeter Flying Post*, 1 March 1798.

Somerscales (or Summerscales), John, Lincoln, cm and clock case maker (1806). His label, or possibly another Summerscales working in Lincoln at this period, has been found on the case of a long-case clock with a movement by Wilson of

Stamford (1786–99). [Poll bk; Robinson, *The Long Case Clock*, p. 343]

Somerton, William, Aldborough, Yorks., joiner and cm (1830). [D]

Sommers, M., 8 Sussex St, Bedford Sq., London, carver (1835). [D]

Sommers, Thomas, 44 Little Britain, Aldersgate, London, carver and gilder (1817). [D]

Sommervale, Adam, Fircourt, Crosby St, Liverpool, carver (1790). [D]

Somervil, William, London, cm (1803). Subscribed to Sheraton's *Cabinet Dictionary*, 1803. In 1803 George Atkinson and William Somerville published a supplement to the 3rd edition of the *Book of Prices*.

Somerville, John, Chancery Lane, London, cm (1803). Subscribed to Sheraton's *Cabinet Dictionary*, 1803 where his address is given as 22 Chancery Lane. Also included in the list of master cabinet makers in this publication where the address was stated to be 29 Chancery Lane.

Somkins, Jonathan, Portsmouth, Hants., cm (1782). In 1782 insured a house for £300. [GL, Sun MS vol. 301, p. 46]

Sommers, —, Carnaby Mkt, London, cm (d.1751). Death announced, *General Advertiser*, 18 December 1751.

Sone, Thomas, Steyning, Sussex, ironmonger, u and auctioneer (1823). [D]

Soper, —, 30 Richmond Pl., Brighton, Sussex, cm (1824). [D]

Soper, Charles, Salisbury, Wilts., carver (1714). On 30 September 1714 took as app. Henry Jefferys, son of Grace Jefferys by common indenture at a fee of £2. [*Wilts. Apps and their Masters*]

Soper, E., 4 Blenheim Terr., Chelsea Common, London, cm (1835). [D]

Soper, Elizabeth, Bedford Pl., Exeter, Devon, u (1822–25). [D] Probably the widow of:

Soper, Samuel snr, Bedford Pl., Bedford Circus, Exeter, Devon, cm and u (1791–d.1821). From 1791–1816 the address is given as Bedford St. His name was included in a Militia Census of 1803 and he was then living in the parish of St Stephen. He died in October 1821 after a long illness. His wife Elizabeth appears to have carried on the business for a number of years, specialising in the upholstery side and attempting to sell off the cabinet stock and finished furniture. The first of these sales was advertised in March 1822 and on offer were 'mahogany dining tables on different principles, some of large dimensions; handsome loo & sofa tables; card Pembroke & other ditto in mahogany, rosewood & satinwood; several commodious dressing stands & tables; wash-hand stands, & chamber tables; dressing glasses, with box & drawers; swing & other glasses; large pedestal & other sideboard tables, sofa; four-post, camp & other bedsteads; mahogany & painted chairs; children's chairs; swing cotts of large & small dimensions; mahogany wardrobes; sets of dressing & other chests of drawers; bagatelle boards; a new & handsome billiard table 12' × 6' with cues, maces, balls, marking board'. Residual stock was, however, still being advertised as late as August 1824 when a discount of 30% off the original prices was offered. Sufficient furniture still remained however for an auction sale of stock to be held in May 1825 with a further sale of timber and tools in June. [D; *Exeter Flying Post*, 11 October 1821, 21 March 1822, 18 March 1824; 12 August 1824; *The Alfred*, 31 May 1825, 7 June 1825]

Soper, Samuel jnr, Exeter, Devon, cm, u and billiard table manufacturer (1819–40). Did not follow his father in the business at Bedford Pl. but set up on his own at 259 High St. The exact date of establishment is not known but in January 1819, when he moved to Bampfylde House, Bampfylde St

near the Post Office, he indicated that he hoped for 'a continuance of those favours he has so liberally experienced since his commencement in business'. He stayed at the new address until November 1825 when he announced a move back to the High St, this time at 253. He had additional premises at 5 Palace St. In 1832 he is recorded living in the parish of St Sidwell. By 1838 he had moved to Salem Pl. and in 1839 was at Queen's Pl., King William Terr. His wife Elizabeth died in April 1822 after a long illness.

Apart from maintaining a general cabinet and upholstery business he specialised in the manufacture of billiard tables and associated equipment. He was in a position to offer 'A great variety of BILLIARD TABLES, both in number and price . . . which he can render at from Fifty to Seventy Guineas each and upwards; also SMALL PORTABLE BILLIARD TABLES calculated for Parlors.' He made also Troumadame and Bagatelle boards, repaired billiard tables and had on sale 'cues, maces, marking boards & balls'. In November 1830 he announced that he had fitted up a billiard room at 253 High St 'where Gentlemen will find the most genteel accommodation'. [D; poll bk; *Exeter Flying Post*, 21 January 1819, 2 May 1822, 10 November 1825, 18 November 1830; *The Alfred*, 18 March 1823, 9 December 1823, 8 November 1825]

Soper, Thomas, Exeter, Devon, cm (b.1776–d.1814). Died at Exmouth, Devon in August 1814 aged 38. Said to have been 'a very ingenious mechanic much respected and was to have been married in a few days'. [*Exeter Flying Post*, 18 August 1814]

Sopwith, Jacob, foot of Pilgrim St, Newcastle, cm and joiner (1801–24). In 1801 announced that he had moved to new premises at the foot of Pilgrim St facing All Saint's Church. This is possibly the Sopwith, cm of Newcastle, who subscribed to Sheraton's *Drawing Book*, 1793. A J. Sopwith, cm, was concerned in the furnishing of Wynyard Park, Co. Durham for the Marquess of Londonderry from 1820. [D; *Newcastle Courant*, 13 June 1801; Durham RO, Londonderry papers, D/LO/E 484]

Sopwith, James, Dog-bank, Newcastle, joiner and cm (1824). [D]

Sopwith, T. J., Market St, Newcastle, cm, u and joiner (1834–38). [D]

Sopwith, Thomas, Dog-bank, Newcastle, joiner and cm (1787–1811). An entry of 1801 refers to Sopwith & Sons. [D]

Sopwith, Thomas, Dog-bank, Newcastle, joiner and cm (1834). [D]

Sopwith, Thomas, Painter-heugh, Newcastle, cm and mahogany yard (1834). [D]

Soroon, William, 17 Kenton St, Brunswick Sq., London, cm (1810). In November 1810 took out insurance cover of £500 which included £130 for stock and utensils in his workshop behind. [GL, Sun MS vol. 453, ref. 850637]

Sotheby, —, 13 Strand, opposite Hungerford Mkt, London, carver and gilder, picture frame maker and print seller (1774–88). Trade card is in the Banks' Coll., BM. The John Sotherley, carver and gilder, who polled at Westminster of the Strand in 1774 is probably of this firm.

Sotheran & Co., Henry, 36 Piccadily, London, library fitters. Their trade card illustrates revolving bookcases of different sizes priced at from £6 to £7 10s. Offered to fit up and furnish libraries 'in their entirety'. The business survives as a bookseller in Sackville St, Piccadilly. [V&A archives]

Souch, Frederick, Brighton, Sussex, Tunbridge-ware manufacturer (1824–33). At 33 Ship St, 1822–24 but at 113 St James's St, 1832–33. Described as a Tunbridge-ware maker in 1822, a toy dealer in 1823 and a Moravian worker in 1832. [D; rate bk]

Souch, Webster, 50 North St, Brighton, Sussex, cm and u (1839). [D]

Souden, William, High St, Grimsby, Lincs., cm (1819). [D]

Soulard, Alexander, 387 Oxford St, London, cm (1835). [D]

Soulsby, James, Northgate St, Gloucester, cm and chairmaker (1820). [D]

Soundy, Benjamin, 26 Gracechurch St or 5 Clements Lane, Lombard St, London, u and cm (1770–88). Son of Benjamin Soundy of Virginia St, Wapping, Gent. Benjamin Soundy jnr was free of the Upholders' Co. under the terms of the 1750 Upholders' Act, 5 December 1770. His app., Joseph Saunders was free in 1772 and he also took as apps Sterry Marks, 1774–79 and Anthony Batger, 1775–81. His address is variously given as 26 Gracechurch St or 5 Clements Lane, possibly alternative addresses for the same premises. His trade label has been found on the frame of an embroidery completed in 1772. This states that he made and sold 'all sorts of Upholsterers & Cabinet Makers Work in the neatest manner, Vis^t Bedsteads & Furniture with Wind^w Curtains in Damasks, Harrateens, Cheneys, Cottons & Checks; Goose & other feather Beds; Quilts, Blankets, Counterpanes Coverlids & Bed Tickings. Easy Chairs. Wilton, Turkey & other Carpets; Mahogany & Wallnuttree Chairs, Look^g Glasses In Carv'd Gilt & Painted Frames Dress^g Glasses in Mahogany or Wallnuttree Frames; Mahog^y or Wallnut^e Book Cases, Chests of Drawers, Writing Tables, Cloaths Presses, Buroes & Tables of all Sorts. Tea Chests, Teaboards, Brackets &c. Spring & all other Window Blinds. NB. Carving & Gilding in the Newst Taste'. In 1782 took out insurance cover of £600 which included £250 for utensils and stock. [D; GL, Upholders' Co. records; Sun MS vol. 306, p. 231; V&A Lib., T63–1935]

Sourbuts, William, Church St, Ormskirk, Lancs., cm and chairmaker (1825–28). [D]

South, George, Chapel St, Blue Town, Sheerness, Kent, cm (1832–39). [D]

South, Sam., Fulham, London, cm and undertaker (1808). [D]

Southall, Enoch, High St, Dudley, Staffs., cm/u (1818–23). [D]

Southall, John, Beatrice St, Oswestry, Salop, cm (1835–36). [D]

Southall (or Southell), William, Rusholme Rd, Manchester, cm (1825–33). At 27 Rusholme Rd in 1825 and from 1829–33 at no.42. [D]

Southam, Henry, Market Pl., Cirencester, Glos., chairmaker (1839). [D]

Southart, Richard, 8 Leather Lane, Liverpool, chairmaker (1796). [D]

Southee, George, 21 Burgate St, Canterbury, Kent, cm, u and furniture broker (1832). [D]

Southee, John, Canterbury, cm (1778). [Poll bk]

Southel & Wilson, Liverpool (1803). Subscribed to Sheraton's *Cabinet Dictionary*, 1803. See Southwell & Wilson.

Southell, William, Liverpool, cm (1814–21). At 12 Ranelagh St with a timber yard at 7 Gt Charlotte St in 1814. In 1816 at 58 Lime St. By January 1817, however, he was insolvent. He appears to have re-established his business, however, and in 1821 was trading from 97 Mount Pleasant. [D; *Liverpool Mercury*, 31 January 1817]

Southeram, John, London, upholder (1758–65). Son of John Southeram of the parish of Allhallows the Great, London. App. to J. Phillips, joiner on 7 February 1758 and then to George Kemp. Free of the Upholders' Co., 7 February 1765 under the terms of the 1750 Upholders' Act. [GL, Upholders' Co. records]

Southern, George, Bond St, Hull, Yorks., cm and u (1826–40). At 15 Bond St, 1826–34 but from 1835–40 at no. 14. [D]

Southerst, Samuel, Edenfield, Lancs., joiner and cm (1834). [D]

Southey, John, 27 Gt Dover St, Southwark, London, upholstery and cabinet warehouse (1826–27). [D]

Southey, Simon, Bristol, furniture japanner (1809–14). At Callowhill St in 1809, 17 Philadelphia St in 1810 at 1 Old Market St, 1812–14. [D] See W. & S. Southey.

Southey, Simon, 1 and 2 North St, Finsbury Mkt, London, japanner, cm and u (1835–39). Shown as a japanned furniture manufacturer in 1835 and as a cm, u, chair and bedstead maker in 1839. [D]

Southey, Thomas, Market Sq., Warwick, cm (1831). [Poll bk]

Southey, William jnr, Bristol, chair manufacturer (1809–25). William Southey was at 25 Broad St, 1809–17, with additional premises at King St in 1815. The discontinuance of the latter address may have been connected with his bankruptcy which was announced in May 1815. In 1819 at 63 Broadmead, in 1820 at St Michael's Hill, in 1821 at 28 Old Market St and from 1822–25 in All Saints' St. The number in All Saints' St was 1 from 1822–24. [D; *Exeter Flying Post*, 4 May 1815] See Simon Southey with whom he was presumably partnered.

Southey, W. & S., 21 Baldwin St, Bristol, furniture japanners and painters (1805–07). [D]

Southwell, John Aylward, London, upholder (1778–85). Son of J. Southwell of Lombard St, peruke maker. App. to Joseph Read on 6 May 1778 and free of the Upholders' Co. by servitude, 3 August 1785. An A. J. Southwell of London subscribed to Sheraton's *Drawing Book*, 1793. [GL, Upholders' Co. records]

Southwell, Thomas Baker, West Castle St, Bridgnorth, Salop, cm (1840). [D]

Southwell & Wilson, Liverpool, cm and u (1796–1813). William Southwell is shown trading on his own account at 1 Coventry St in 1796. By 1800 he had formed a partnership with a man called Wilson which lasted until 1813. The partners' shop address is variously given as either 11 or 12 Ranelagh St. Initially they traded as cm only, but in June 1806 advertised that they had 'laid in a handsome assortment of fashionable Carpets, Printed Furniture, Papers & Feathers of the best quality, as well as every other article in the Upholstery line'. A timber yard was maintained at Gt Charlotte St and was in their possession by 1810. Some directories give other addresses for William Southwell such as 1 Case St, Clayton Sq. in 1804 and various numbers in Line St, 1810–13. These are likely to be the location of his dwelling house. [D; *Liverpool Chronicle*, 25 June 1806]. See Southel & Wilson.

Southwood, Edward, Rocks (or Rack's) Lane, Exeter, Devon, chair caner (1825–32). In August 1831 a fire was reported at his workshop. [D; *Exeter Flying Post*, 18 August 1831]

Southwood, James, South St, Wellington, Som., cm and u (1839). [D]

Southwood, John A., 13 Fountain Ct, Strand, London, u (1820). [D]

Southwood, Thomas, 40 Castle St, Holborn, London, u (1809). [D]

Southwood & Martin, 8 Lower North St, Exeter, Devon, cm and u (1830). [D]

Southworth, —, Lancaster, caner (1827–34). Named in the Gillow records 1827–28 and 1832–34. [Westminster Ref. Lib., Gillow]

Southworth, John, Liverpool, cm (1742). Free of Liverpool, 9 April 1742. Also shown in the Preston, Lancs. freemen rolls of that year as freeman of that town but living in Liverpool. [Liverpool and Preston freemen rolls]

Sowden, Joshua, Leeds, Yorks., cm (1817–40). At East Lane (or Eastern Lane) in 1817, 31 St George St in 1822, West St in 1830 and 54 St George's St, 1834–40. [D]

Sowden, William, Grimsby, Lincs., joiner and cm (1826–41). Also toy and glass dealer. In High St, 1826–31 but in 1841 at Smith's Lane. [D]

Sowerby, Mr, near Beaufort Buildings, Strand, London, cm (d.1746). Dead by December 1746 when his household furniture and stock were sold by auction 'at his late Dwelling House near Beaufort Buildings'. On offer were 'a large Sortment of Pier, Chimney Glasses and Sconces, in carv'd, gilt and other Frames, variety of Dressing Glasses, Chairs, tables, Beauroes, Chests of Drawers and Cloaths Chests in Mahogany and Walnut Tree, with all manner of useful Household Furniture, Likewise his Silvering Stones and Frames, and other Utensils in the Silvering Trade'. A John Sowerby of London, cm, supplied to a patron, probably the Duke of Montrose a walnut desk, an oval glass and a japanned dressing glass at £5 5s and two further glasses at £2 2s. [General Advertiser, 12 December 1746; Scottish RO, GD 220/6/1238/3, 14]

Sowerby, George, Lancaster, cm (1801–02). [Lancaster freemen rolls]

Sowerby, Jeremiah, Lancaster, cm (1765–1816). Free 1765–66, and between March 1772 and October 1812 took eight apps He operated in the Green Area until November 1802 when he disposed of his premises to Edward Hudson and opened up again at Cross St. By May 1811 he had decided to terminate the business and advertised his premises for sale or to let. The main showroom was 24½ ft by 17½ ft and 9 ft high. Another room used for auctions was 29½ ft by 18 ft and 8 ft high. The attic storey, probably used as workshops, was 80½ ft by 17 ft 3 in. In addition there was a cellar. In September he advertised his furniture stock, tools and timbers to any person desiring to set up in the trade and offered either to take the purchase price in instalments or to take interest on any outstanding balance. His timber stock included 'St. Domingo and Honduras mahogany' and 'american Black Birch planks'. Another address at Chapel St in 1816, however, is given for Jeremiah Sowerby, cm. [Freemen rolls; app. reg.; poll bks; Lancaster Gazette, 20 November 1802, 11 May 1811, 7 September 1811]

Sowerby, Thomas, parish of St Mary Redcliffe, Bristol, cm (1781–84). [Poll bks]

Sowerby, Thomas, 16 Blandford St, Portman Sq., London, u (1809–32). In 1825 trading as Sowerby & Kirkman. Bankruptcy announced, London Gazette, 22 June 1832. [D]

Sowlon, R., 44 Newman St, Oxford St, London, cm and u (1820–27). In February 1820 took out insurance cover of £600 which included £200 for utensils and stock in the house, £100 for a workshop behind and £100 for stock kept there. [D; GL, Sun MS vol. 483, ref. 962851]

Sowman, Richard, Savile St, Malton, Yorks., joiner and cm (1840). [D]

Sowter, J., address unknown (1752–57). Appears in the Holkham Hall, Norfolk accounts. He was paid £2 8s in 1752 for making eight wheel-barrow chairs for the garden and 11s in 1757 for mending chairs. [V&A archives]

Sowter, Robert, parish of St Stephen, Norwich, cm (1794–97). [Poll bks]

Spacey & Wragg, Wicker, Sheffield, Yorks., cm (1814). [D]

Spackman, Thomas, Bradford-upon-Avon, Wilts., cm (1784). Freeman of Bristol. [Bristol poll bk]

Spain, Edmund, 9 Lower St, Deal, Kent, cm and u (1823–39). Freeman of Sandwich, Kent. [D; Sandwich poll bks]

Spain, William, address unknown, cm (1803). Subscribed to Sheraton's Cabinet Dictionary, 1803.

Spane, Thomas, St Giles without Cripplegate, London, carver (1682). [Heal] Probably:

Spanger, —, St Giles without Cripplegate, London, carver (1700). On 5 November 1700 he was paid by the Earl of Bristol for picture frames. He was referred to as 'Dutch'. Probably Thomas Spane above. [Heal]

Spanton, W., Newport St, London, cm (1784). [Westminster poll bk]

Spark, James, 37 Pilgrim St, Newcastle, cm and u (1824–28). [D]

Spark, John, Market Pl. Helmsley, Yorks., joiner and cm (1823–40). [D]

Spark, John, Allendale, Northumb., joiner and cm (1827–34). [D]

Spark, John, Painter-heugh, Newcastle, joiner and cm (1838). [D]

Spark & Brydges, London, cm (1750–54). Supplied furniture and undertook alterations at a house in St James's Sq. for Peter Du Cane of Braxted Park, Essex in 1750 at a cost of £83 17s. A John Spark subscribed to Chippendale's Director, 1754. [Essex RO, D/DDe A/12]

Sparkes, Edward, near Lyons Inn, Witch St, London, u (1685). In December 1685 advertised that Benjamin Jay aged 24, an employee or possibly an app., had absconded with goods valued at £60. A reward of £2 2s was offered for information. [London Gazette, 17 December 1685]

Spark(e)s, John, Welsh Row, Nantwich, Cheshire, cm (1822). [D]

Sparkes, Robert, Exeter, Devon, cm (1803). [Militia Census]

Sparkham, John, Kensington Rd, London, carver and gilder (1826). [D]

Sparkman, Jas., Middle Bridge St, Romsey, Hants., cm and u (1830). [D]

Sparks, Peter, Church St, Wells, Norfolk, cm (1839). [D]

Sparrow, Christopher, King St, Bristol, chair carver (1795). [D]

Sparrow, Mrs Hannah, Lord St, Liverpool, u (1790–1802). The number in Lord St was 44 in 1790, 57 in 1796, 54 in 1800 and 53 in 1802. Successor to and probably the widow of John Sparrow of Lord St. In September 1802 she declared her intention of retiring from the business and an auction of her stock was advertised. This consisted of 'Kidderminster, Brussels & Venetian Carpets, Pier & Dressing Glasses, fancy Paper Hangings & Borders, variety of Fringes, Laces & Tassels, plain, fancy & figured Hair Seating, Oil-cloths & a variety of other articles in the Upholstery line'. [D; Billinge's Liverpool Advertiser, 27 September 1802]

Sparrow, J., High St, Watford, Herts., u and paperhanger (1838). [D]

Sparrow, Jeremiah, Holywell Hill, St Albans, Herts., cm and u (1832). [D]

Sparrow, John, Lord St, Liverpool, u (1777–d.1790). The number in Lord St was 54 in 1777, 46 in 1781–84 whilst in 1790 no. 49 was given. Bankrupt by January 1781 and in March of that year a dividend of 10s in the £ was paid to his creditors. By April 1783 he was back in business again and was advertising new stock which had arrived from London. This consisted of 'Morines Harrateens Cheneys, Bed Ticks, Blankets, & Carpets of all sorts; likewise a very large assortment of the most fashionable Patterns of Paper Hangings'. The death of John Sparrow was announced in July 1790 and the business was continued by Hannah Sparrow, probably his widow. [D; Williamson's Liverpool Advertiser, 18 January 1781, 29 March 1781, 3 April 1783, 5 July 1790] Possibly associated with Sparrow & Blount.

Sparrow, John, Butter Mkt, Bury St Edmunds, Suffolk, u (1783–84). In 1783 married at Wistaston, Cheshire, Miss Alicia Wilson, daughter of the Rev. Mr Wilson, late of Ashbourne, Derbs. [D; Chester Chronicle, 31 October 1783]

Sparrow, John, Butter Mkt, Ipswich, Suffolk, u (1805–08). [D] See William Sparrow at Butter Market, 1824.

Sparrow, John, Bridge St, Chertsey, Surrey, cm and auctioneer (1822). [D]

Sparrow, John, 2 Little Portland St, London, wood and cabinet carver (1839). Two other Sparrows, Christian names not specified, were trading in the Oxford St area as carvers in

1829. One was at 5 Upper Rathbone Pl. and the other at 2 Blenheim Mews, Oxford St. [D]

Sparrow, Joseph, Chertsey, Surrey, cm and u (1793–1827). Took an app. John Richman Webb in May 1811 who remained with him until February 1815. [D; GL, P83/MRYI/873/(122)]

Sparrow, Phillis, Watford, Herts., cm (1839). [D]

Sparrow, Robert, London, upholder (1720–31). Son of Samuel Sparrow of Hopton, Suffolk, yeoman. App. to Daniel Woodroffe on 4 January 1720 and free of the Upholders' Co. by servitude, 2 June 1731. [GL, Upholders' Co. records]

Sparrow, Samuel, London, u (1809–14). At Old Cavendish St, 1809–11 but in that year moved to 12 Store St. One directory of 1813 gives the address as 39 Alfred Pl., Bedford Sq. but it is likely that he was referring to the same premises. In 1803 a Samuel Sparrow, u, subscribed to Sheraton's *Cabinet Dictionary*. [D]

Sparrow, Thomas, 19 Charterhouse Lane, London, cm (1781–93). In 1781 took out insurance cover of £100 which included £20 for utensils and stock. [D; GL, Sun MS vol. 289, p. 330]

Sparrow, William, Smith St, Warwick, carver and gilder (1822). [D]

Sparrow, William, Butter Mkt, Ipswich, Suffolk, cm, u and auctioneer (1824). [D] See John Sparrow at Butter Mkt, 1805.

Sparrow & Blount, Castle Ditch, Liverpool, u (1777). A John Sparrow trading as an u was in Lord St from 1777. [D]

Sparrow & Ravenhill, 87 Bartholomew Close, London, cm (1789–93). [D]

Spaven, Simpson, Old Malton, Yorks., joiner and cm (1840). [D]

Speakeman, John, 1 William St, Olive St, Liverpool, cm (1829). [D]

Speakman, Henry, 10 Pepper St, Liverpool, cm (1818). [D]

Spear, Hugh, address unknown, cm (1754). Subscribed to Chippendale's *Directory*, 1754. Possibly related to John and George Speer whose designs reflect *Director*, plates.

Speare, George, 113 Aldersgate St, London, cm, u, auctioneer, appraiser and undertaker (1835–37). [D]

Speare, James, London, carver (1775). Partner with George Mackery. Used addresses at 16 Princes St, Drury Lane and John St, Golden Sq. At the former address insurance cover was £300 but this included household property as well as utensils and stock. At the latter address no trade stock or tools were covered by the £250 insurance cover. [GL, Sun MS vol. 236, refs 349458, 349460]

Speare, James, 22 St Ann's Ct, Soho, London, cm (1786–1808). In 1786 subscribed to George Richardson's *Treatise on the Five Orders of Architecture*. [D; Westminster poll bk]

Spearing, David, Shaftesbury, Dorset, joiner and cm (1761). In 1761 took app. named Cooper. [S of G, app. index]

Spearing, John, London, cm (1722–23). Paid £1 1s for an oval table for Hicks Hall. [Winterthur, Delaware, Symonds papers, 75x69.29]

Spearing, Perrias, Blandford, Dorset, u (d.1747). Died in 1747 without issue. Reversion to Samuel Marsh of Blandford, u. [Dorset RO, DA/W/1747/5]

Spearman, Mr, Derbeigh St, Spitalfields, London, u (1776). In January 1776 his premises in Derbeigh St were 'entirely consumed' by fire. [*Gents Mag.*, January 1776]

Speck, John, Hessle, near Hull, Yorks., joiner and cm (1826). [D]

Spedding, Snowden, Trinity Buildings, Richmond, York., u (1823). [D]

Spedding, Thomas, 14 High Rd, Knightsbridge, London, u (1838). [D]

Spedding, William, James St, Whitehaven, Cumb., joiner/cm (1811). [D]

Speechly, James, King's Lynn, Norfolk, cm (1774–75). Free 1774–75 by servitude to Thomas West, cm. [Freemen rolls]

Speed, Joseph, London, upholder (1753). Son of Joseph Speed, freeman of London and a member of the Haberdashers' Co. Joseph Speed jnr was free of the Upholders' Co. under the terms of the 1750 Upholders' Act, 22 November 1753. [GL, Upholders' Co. records]

Speed, William, Nantwich, Cheshire, cm (1787). Married on 28 May 1787. [PR (marriage)]

Speer, George, 'The Seven Stars', 2 Gt Tower St, London, cm and u (b.1736–d.1802). Free of the London Upholders' Co., 6 March 1771 under the terms of the 1750 Upholders' Act. Does not appear in London directories until 1777. His trade card states that he made and sold 'Desks & Book Cases, Chests of Drawers, Poureaus & all Sorts of Looking Glass frames. Also Venetian, Spring & all other sorts of Window Blinds, Mahogany, Walnut-tree & other Chairs Breakfast, Dining & Card Tables, Tea Chests, Tea Boards, Waiters &c.'. He also sold carpeting and floor cloth, appraised goods and undertook funerals. Initially he may have been associated with John Speer his cousin, who traded for part of the time at the same address as a joiner and cm. The Rococo frames of the trade cards of these two makers are identical. George Speer died in 1802 though his name appears in Sheraton's *Cabinet Dictionary*, 1803 in the list of master cabinet makers. It is possible that his son, George jnr continued the business.

A bureau cabinet obtained by the V&A Museum in 1980 is believed to have been supplied by George Speer on 30 September 1761 though the original invoice is no longer traceable. This piece of furniture does, however, closely resemble a number of drawings by George Speer which were reproduced in an article by Anthony Coleridge in *Apollo*. A mahogany kneehole desk and a secretaire bookcase with glazed doors are also known with George Speer's trade label attached (Figs 35–36). [D; V&A archives; *Apollo*, October 1970, pp. 274–83, May 1972, p. 419; Sotheby's, 1 February 1980, lot 128]

Speer, John, London, carpenter, joiner and cm (c.1760). Cousin to George Speer. Used two addresses, one of which was 'The Seven Stars' in Gt Tower St which was also used by George Speer. The other address used by John was 'The Lion & Lamb', Fleet Mkt. It is uncertain which is the earlier of the two addresses. The Rococo frame of his trade cards is identical to that used by George Speer. John advertised that he sold 'Mahogany, Walnut-tree & other Chairs, Breakfast, Dining & other Tables, Tea Chests, Tea Boards, Waiters' items that also featured in George's stock. Significantly he did not mention large items of case furniture or mirrors, both of which were specialities of the trade conducted by his cousin. John did, however, state that he undertook turnery work and stocked straw hats, floor cloth and mats. [Heal; *Apollo*, October 1970, pp. 274–83; Banks Coll., BM]

Speer, Thomas, Gerrard St, Soho, London, carver (1749). [Westinster poll bk]

Spefford, William, Gt Chesterford, near Saffron Walden, Essex, cm and u (1826). [D]

Speight, George, 4 or 14 Castle St, Long Acre, London, furniture broker and u (1835–39). One directory lists him in 1839 at 10 Portsmouth St as a furniture broker and he may have moved in this year. Martin Speight, also a furniture broker is shown at 4 Castle St in 1839. [D]

Speight, Jarvis, 86 Long Acre, London, upholder (1778). In 1778 took out insurance cover of £300 which included £150 for utensils and stock. [GL, Sun MS vol. 265, p. 1]

Speight, Jervis, Leeds, Yorks., journeyman cm (1791). Named in the *Leeds Cabinet and Chair Makers' Book of Prices*, 1791 as a journeyman in basic sympathy with its contents.

Spence, Ann, 26 Dock St, Leeds, Yorks., working u (1834). [D]

Spence, Anne & Sons, Simpson's Fold, Leeds, Yorks., cm (1822). [D]

Spence, George, Simpson's Fold, Leeds, Yorks., cm (1798–1817). [D] See Anne and William Spence.

Spence, George, London, cm, u and undertaker (1803–17). Subscribed to Sheraton's *Cabinet Dictionary*, 1803. At Theobalds Rd, 1811–13 and 48 Red Lion Sq., Holborn 1816–17. [D]

Spence, John, Husband St, Carnaby Mkt, London, cm (1774). [Westminster poll bk]

Spence, John, 26 Peter St, Soho, London, upholder (1790–99). Bankrutpcy announced, *Billinge's Liverpool Advertiser*, 14 January 1799. [D]

Spence, John, Axminster, Devon, cm (1793–1823). [D]

Spence, John, Hillgate, Stockport, Cheshire, cm (1816). [D]

Spence, Joseph, Fewston, near Otley, Yorks., cm (1822). [D]

Spence, Richard, 9 Cromer St, Brunswick Sq., London, carver, gilder and looking-glass manufacturer (1826–39). [D]

Spence, Robert, address unknown, cm (1754). Subscribed to Chippendale's *Director*, 1754.

Spence, Thomas, 'The Grasshopper', Charing Cross, London, u (1660). [Heal]

Spence, Thomas, 66 Mulberry St, Liverpool, carver (1834). [D]

Spence, William, Newcastle, u (1768). App. to Thomas Hunt and free by servitude, 13 October 1768. [Freemen reg.]

Spence, William, Crosshall St, Liverpool, joiner and cm (1790–1811). At 49 Crosshall St in 1790 and 50 in 1804–11. [D]

Spence, William, Simpson's Fold, Leeds, Yorks., cm and u (1791–1820). Named in the *Leeds Cabinet and Chair Makers' Book of Prices*, 1791 as a journeyman cm in basic sympathy with its contents. Subscribed to Sheraton's *Drawing Book*, 1793. Trading at Simpson's Fold by 1816, the number being 61 in 1818–20. By 1822 the business at this address was being conducted by Anne Spence & Sons. Anne may have been William's widow. Recorded in one directory of 1816 as Spencer, presumably wrongly. [D] See George Spence at this address.

Spenceley, George, Hull, Yorks., cm and chairmaker (1801–17). At Myton Without or Myton St in 1803, Patrick's Ground Lane, 1806–10, New Dock St, 1814–18 and Staniforth Pl., 1817. Took as apps William Wright of Hull in May 1801 and John Haddon of Hull in January 1804. [D; app. reg.] Possibly:

Spenceley, George, Hedon near Hull, Yorks., cm and organ builder (1826–31). Listed as a cm in 1826 but by 1831 an organ builder also. [D]

Spenceley, James, 18 Goodge St, London, u (1829). [D]

Spencer, Christopher J., Castle St, Carlisle, Cumb., u/feather merchant (1829–34. [D]

Spencer, Edward, Chester, cm (1828). In July 1828 he was accused of drunkenness and assaulting his mother-in-law. [*Chester Chronicle*, 11 July 1828]

Spencer, George & William, 19 Newton St, High Holborn, London, upholders and feather bed makers (1786–1818). In 1786 took out insurance cover of £300 of which £200 was for utensils and stock. [GL, Sun MS vol. 336, p. 357] See John & George and Peter & John Spencer.

Spencer, George, Wellington Pl., Darlington, Co. Durham, u and cm (1827–34). [D]

Spencer, George, 11 Henrietta St, Manchester Sq., London, furniture japanner (1829–39). [D]

Spencer, Henry, Lambs Conduit Passage, near Red Lion Sq., Holborn, London, chairmaker (1722–28). In October 1722 took out insurance cover of £160 on goods kept in his dwelling house, shop and yard. A chairmaker by the name of Spencer appears in the records of Chicheley Hall, Bucks. in

1722 and Holkham Hall, 1728, and may be this maker. In July 1722 he was paid £27 by Sir John Chester in connection with Chicheley and in December 1724 another £8 14s for eight chairs at 18s each and two stools at 15s each. It has been suggested that the important suite of seating furniture now at Montacute, Som. was the subject of these payments made to Spencer but it has been pointed out that another suite provided by a Mr Hodson for the Great Parlour at Chicheley and costing £34 is more likely to be the one involved. Spencer also supplied Holkham Hall, Norfolk with thirteen Windsor chairs in 1728 at a cost of £3 9s 9d and two wheel chairs at £4 8s. These items were listed in the garden expenses. It is not clear that the Chicheley and Holkham items were produced by the same maker. Those for Holkham fit more closely the low insurance cover of the maker in Lambs Conduit Passage. Another possible maker is Samuel Spender of 'The Golden Chair', Aldermanbury. He took out insurance cover of £500 on his goods and merchandise in March 1725, and is named in the insurance records as Samuel Spencer. His trade card, however, clearly gives his surname as Spender. [GL, Sun MS vol. 14, ref. 26533; V&A archives; C. *Life*, 27 February 1975, p. 500; Bucks. RO, Chicheley papers, D/C/2/3 (ii), D/C/2/36 (iii)]

Spencer, J., address unknown, Windsor chairmaker (c.1830). Several chairs which by their construction suggest a North Midland area origin, have the name 'J. SPENCER' stamped on the seat edge. Temple Newsam House, Leeds has one such chair. [*Furn Hist.*, 1978]

Spencer, J., 12 Hodgson's Sq., Sykes St, Hull, Yorks., cm (1838–39). [D]

Spencer, James, Leicester, cm (1753–90). App. to John Shipley in 1753 but not free until 1790. [Freemen rolls]

Spencer, James, 68 Thames St, Windsor, Berks., carver and gilder (1824–30). [D]

Spencer, James, Leicester, u (1827–40). App. to John Measures and free by servitude in 1827. In 1842 trading at Humberstone Gate. [D; freemen rolls]

Spencer, James, Knightsbridge Green, London, carver and gilder (1834–40). Listed at 14 High Rd, Knightsbridge, as a picture frame maker in 1838. Regularly appeared in the Royal Household accounts working at Windsor Castle, Buckingham Palace, Kew Palace, Virginia Water and St James's. The work undertaken was of a routine nature involving repairs, re-gilding and alterations. In March 1839 for instance, fifteen old picture frames were enlarged, new corners and tablets added and the whole re-gilded at a cost of £39 10s. In September 1838 the firm was referred to as Baker & Spencer. [D; PRO, LC11/86, LC11/95–8; Windsor Royal Archives, account bks 1833–41; Item 2 Box I; Joy, *English Furniture 1800–1851*, p. 187]

Spencer, John snr, Basingstoke, Hants., upholder (1720–32). His son John Spencer jnr was admitted a freeman of the London Upholders' Co. in 1732. [GL, Sun MS vol. 10, ref. 16237; Upholders' Co. records]

Spencer, John jnr, London, upholder (1723–32). Son of John Spencer snr of Basingstoke, Hants., upholder. App. to William Hayes on 5 February 1723 and free of the Upholders' Co. by servitude, 7 June 1732. [GL, Upholders' Co. records]

Spencer, John, Peter St, Soho, London, upholder (1796). Bankruptcy declared, March 1796. [*Billinge's Liverpool Advertiser*, 7 March 1796; 2 May 1796]

Spencer, John Liddel, Ulverston, Lancs., cm and u (1828–34). At Queen St in 1828 but by 1834 at Theatre St and Market St. [D]

Spencer, John & George, 18–19 Newton St, High Holborn, London, bedstead makers (1839). [D] See George & William and Peter & John Spencer at this address.

Spencer, John, Clarence Ct, 6 Princess St, Dock St, Hull, Yorks., cm (1839–40). [D]

Spencer, Joseph, King's Lynn, Norfolk, chairmaker (1741). In 1741 took app. named Storey. [S of G, app. index]

Spencer, Joseph, Belgrave Gate, Leicester, u (1788–1826). App. to Mark Oliver of Leicester u, and by March 1788 had opened a shop at Belgrave Gate. Took as app. Thomas Atkins who was free 1826. Joseph Spencer's eldest son was declared free in 1825 but he did not follow his father's trade. [*Leicester Journal*, 22 March 1788; freemen rolls]

Spencer, Joseph, Lister In [*sic*] and 7 Old Market, Halifax, cm (1837). [D]

Spencer, Peter & John, 18–19 Newton St, High Holborn, London, upholders and bed mattress makers (1801–27). Successors to George & William Spencer who were manufacturing in the same trade at 19 Newton St in 1786. Initially the address is given as 19 and 20 Newton St, but the property was re-numbered c.1820 and became 18 and 19 Newton St. In 1824 also listed as wine merchants and in this year took out insurance on 'bottled stock'. General levels of insurance cover were high indicating a large enterprise. In February 1801 cover for stock of utensils was £750, in 1808 £2,000, 1810 £2,000 and £1,000 in 1824. John Spencer was living at 4 Newton St in May 1805 and Peter & John living at Fallow Corner, Finchley, in 1810. The former property was insured for £300 and the latter for £500. Peter & John also took out insurance on 31 Bedford Pl., Bloomsbury in September 1820. Together with the associated coach houses and stables this property was valued at £1,200. Other properties insured included a house at Tiverton near Bath, Som. insured in May 1810 for £100 and one in Worthing insured in December 1822 for £600. Both were let out. The partners were no doubt well satisfied with their precautions against fire risk for in July 1818 a fire was reported at the Newton St premises. [D; GL, Sun MS vol. 434, ref. 775705; vol. 453, refs 844833, 850625; vol. 483, ref. 970911; vol. 488, refs 980108, 980109, 981837; vol. 493, ref. 999094; vol. 499, ref. 1014656; *Gents Mag.*, July 1818]

Spencer, Richard, London, carver and gilder (1809–26). At 70 Titchfield St, Cavendish Sq., 1809–17, 15 Cleveland St, Fitzroy Sq. 1820 and 17 Carburton St, Fitzroy Sq. 1826. [D]

Spencer, Richard, North St, Guildford, Surrey, cm (1830–31). [Poll bks]

Spencer, Richard, Church St, Hereford, carver and gilder (1835). [D]

Spencer, Robert, Newcastle, cm (1803). Subscribed to Sheraton's *Cabinet Dictionary*, 1803.

Spencer, Samuel, parish of St George, Southwark, London, cm (1767). Insured three houses tenanted by others for £600. [GL, Hand in Hand MS vol. 105, p. 145]

Spencer, Samuel, Main St, Keighley, Yorks., joiner/cm (1837). [D]

Spencer, Thomas, London, upholder (1733–41). Son of Thomas Spencer of Wishaw, Warks., innkeeper. App. to John Underwood on 4 March 1733 and free of the Upholders' Co. by servitude, 4 March 1740/41. [GL, Upholders' Co. records]

Spencer, Thomas, Leicester, cm and chairmaker (1753–68). App. to John Shipley in 1753 and free by servitude, 1768. [Freemen rolls]

Spencer, Thomas, Roscoe St and Leece St, Liverpool, carver and gilder (1835–39). At 27 Roscoe St with a shop at 19 Leece St as a carver in 1835. By 1837 the numbers were 28 Roscoe St and 10 Leece St and the trade carver and gilder. In 1839 only 22 Leece St is given. [D]

Spencer, William, Nottingham, joiner and cm (1776). [Freemen rolls]

Spencer, William, 51 Crosshall St, Liverpool, cm (1796–1800). [D]

Spencer, William, 10 Marsden's Ct, Fennel St, Manchester, u (1804). [D]

Spencer, William, 36 Darley St, Bradford Yorks., u (1837). [D]

Spencer & Catesby, 99 High St, Marylebone, London, japanners and gilders (1825). [D]

Spender, Samuel, 'The Golden Chair', Aldermanbury, London, chairmaker (1725). His trade card [Landauer Coll., MMA, NY] states that he sold 'All Sorts of Cain Chairs Couches Round-Stools easy Chairs made Japann'd Cain Sashes for windows'. It may be significant that the insurance records state that his name was Spencer. He may well have been the maker of a set of upholstered seating furniture supplied to Chicheley Hall, Bucks. in July 1722 and other chairs supplied to this house in December 1724 and Holkham Hall, Norfolk, in 1728. The insurance cover of £500 on his goods and merchandise accords rather better with the commissions involved than the £160 maintained by the other possible maker, Henry Spencer. [GL, Sun MS vol. 19, ref. 35108] See Henry Spencer.

Spenseley, Thomas, Bury St Edmunds, Suffolk, upholder (1697–d. by 1709). Common Councillor on 18 September 1697, Chief Burgess on 24 September 1697, Alderman, 1699–1700, but dead by March 1709. [Suffolk RO, index of Corp. Members]

Spice, Allan, 22 Charles St, Middlx Hospital, London, (1826). In 1835 trading as Spice & Pryer from 30 Brydges St, Covent Gdn but in 1839 shown once more trading on his own account from both the 22 Charles St and 30 Brydges St addresses. [D]

Spicer, Arthur, Tower St, London, upholder (1707–34). Son of Arthur Spicer of Peckham, farrier. App. to Christopher Broughton on 17 June 1707 and free of the Upholders' Co. by servitude, 11 July 1716. In 1734 at Tower St. [GL, Upholders' Co. records; Heal]

Spicer, John, London, upholder (1709–d. by 1758). Son of John Spicer of Berkhampsted, Herts., Gent. and father of Mary Spicer. App. to William Burnley on 5 October 1709 and free of the Upholders' Co. by servitude, 7 May 1718. At 'The Golden Angel', Wych St, near Temple Bar, 1724–27, 'The Golden Eagle' in Fenchurch St, 1730–32 and in Old North St, 1734. [GL, Upholders' Co. records; Heal]

Spicer, Lewis, 7 Riding House Lane, Portland St, London, cm (1820). In March 1820 took out insurance cover of £100 on household goods. [GL, Sun MS vol. 483, ref. 964061] Possibly:

Spicer, Lewis, 12 Queen St, Northampton Sq., London, cm (1835). [D]

Spicer, Lewis, 6 Garnault Pl., Spitalfields, London, cm etc. (1835–39). [D]

Spicer, Mary, London, upholder (1758). Daughter of John Spicer, upholder. Free of the Upholders' Co. by patrimony, 2 November 1758. [GL, Upholders' Co. records]

Spikins, Benjamin, 26 Mansfield St, Liverpool, chairmaker (1837). [D]

Spi(l)kins, Edward, Wormgate, Boston, Lincs., chairmaker and turner (1826–35). [D]

Spilkins, Jos., Red Lion St, Spalding, Lincs., wood turner and chairmaker (1826). [D]

Spiller, John, Exeter, Devon, cm (1833–38). At New Bridge St in August 1833 when his son John Frederick Heywood was bapt. at St Edmund's Church. By September 1838 at West St when a further son Philip was bapt. at the Church of St Mary Steps. [PR (bapt.)]

Spindler (or Spindlar), Nathaniel, London, upholder (1703–17). From 1703–17 living in a house in the parish of St Mildred,

Bread (or Broad) St. This may have been the brick house in Harts Honar Alley, south side of Basing Lane which is mentioned in insurance policies. He also insured three or four other properties in the same area. The most valuable of these with a cover of £400 was included in the policy in December 1703 but was no longer there in December 1710. One of the other properties, possibly his dwelling house, was valued at £250 and the others at £125 each. [GL, Hand in Hand MS vol. 2, p. 668; vol. 8, refs 5111–15; vol. 10, ref. 23895; vol. 18, p. 106]

Spinnage, John, London, upholder (1772). Son of William Spinnage of Gerrard St, Soho, u. Free of the Upholders' Co. under the terms of the 1750 Upholders' Act, 3 June 1772. [GL, Upholders' Co. records]

Spinnage, William, Gerrard St, Soho, London, u (1770–77). Traded as Spinnage & Howard, u and paper hangings makers, 1772–77. In February 1770 Lady Caroline Fleming of Tabley Hall, Cheshire paid a Mr Spinnage, u, £47 15s. This is likely to have been William Spinnage. William's son John was free of the Upholders' Co. in 1772. [D; Chester RO, DLT/DM 6/2; GL, Upholders' Co. records]

Spite, Robert, parish of St Mary, Chelmsford, Essex, chairmaker (1732). Son Robert bapt. on 4 November 1732. [PR (bapt.)]

Spittall, Elizabeth, 174 High St, Lewes, Sussex, cm and u (1832). [D]

Spittall, Hannah, 168 High St, Lewes, Sussex, cm and u (1826). [D] Widow of:

Spittall, William, Lewes, Sussex, u (1818–23). Living at Gt East St in 1818 but by 1823 trading from 168 High St. His widow Hannah continued the business after his death. [D; poll bk]

Spitton, Thomas(?), address unknown (1773). Recorded in the Croome Court, Worcs. accounts for the period 29 June to 1 July 1773. He supplied a 'large True Madame table and stand', two brass candlesticks for it and repaired a table at a combined charge of £3 7s. [V&A archives]

Splatt, Francis Townsend, Exeter, Devon, cm, chairmaker, u and undertaker (1821–26). In November 1821 advertised for a good workman and in April of the following year announced that he had commenced trading from premises at 171 Fore St and St Mary Arches St. He stated that he had 'engaged workmen of the first abilities, particularly in the chair line' and that 'a number of pattern chairs of the most exquisite workmanship may be seen at his ware-rooms'. In February 1823 he moved to 92 North St and was again advertising for workmen in October 1823. He was declared bankrupt in March 1826. [D; *Exeter Flying Post*, 1 November 1821, 20 February and 16 October 1823, 2 March 1826; *The Alfred*, 18 February and 18 March 1823, 7 and 14 March 1826]

Spokes, Thomas, Gold St, Northampton, cm (1820–30). [D; poll bks]

Spong, Owen, London, bedstead and chairmaker (1776–85). At 4 Hatton Hall, Hatton Gdn, 1776–79. In 1776 took out insurance cover of £300 of which £200 was for utensils and stock. In 1779 a workshop, utensils, stock and timbersheds were insured for £200. By April 1785 at White Lyon Ct, White Lyon St, Seven Dials with utensils and stock valued at £100 out of an entire insurance cover of £150. [GL, Sun MS vol. 249, p. 591; vol. 277, p. 123; vol. 328, p. 198]

Spong, Thomas, London, bedstead and bedding manufacturer (1789–1813). At 3 Stacey St in 1789 when insurance cover of £200 was taken out of which £100 was for utensils and stock. At Brook St, New Rd, Marylebone, 1806–09 and 17 High St, Bloomsbury, 1811–13. [D; GL, Sun MS vol. 363, ref. 55602]

Spong, William, Market Pl., Wellingborough, Northants., cm (1823). [D]

Spooner, James Henry, Staindrop, Co. Durham, u (1774–77). Freeman of Newcastle. [Newcastle poll bks]

Spooner, Joseph Henry, Newcastle, u (1774). App. to Edward Coates and free by servitude, 11 October 1774. [Freemen reg.; poll bk]

Spooner, Richard F., Day's Ct, Upper Market, Norwich, u (1836–39). [D]

Spooner, Thomas, London, cm (1802–22). At 8 Charles St, St George's Rd in June 1802 when he took out insurance cover of £100. In July 1804 shown at 3 Charles St, St John's Rd. The total insurance cover was £200 and £20 of this was for a chest of tools kept at the premises of Oakley & Co., cm in their workshop communicating with 8 Old Bond St. Subscribed to Sheraton's *Cabinet Dictionary*, 1803. In 1808 shown trading at 3 Charles St, Blackfriars Rd, and in 1820–22 at 22 Chapel St, Paddington, Lisson Grove. [D; GL, Sun MS vol. 423, ref. 732614; vol. 430, ref. 764288]

Spooner & Glover, 19 Northampton Pl., Old Kent Rd, London, cm and u (1839). [D]

Spoor, —, North Shields, Northumb., u (1809). In May 1809 advertised for a journeyman u. [*Newcastle Courant*, 13 May 1809]

Spoor, Amor, Newcastle, cm (1817–38). In June 1817 at Blacket St where he was responsible for the collection of sums due to Devergy Lisle, cm, who had probably recently died. Spoor was at Fighting Cocks' Yd, Bigg-market 1824–34. Addresses also given at Hanover House showrooms, 83 Newgate St and Scotch Arms Yd, Brigg Mkt, 1834 (also as an u), and at Hanover Sq. in 1838, as a cm, u and joiner. [D; *Durham County Advertiser*, 14 June 1817]

Spoor, Michael, King St, South Shields, Co. Durham, u (1827). [D]

Spour, George, Northumberland St, Newcastle, joiner and cm (1824). [D]

Spragg, Richard, London, cm (1778–84). At 27 Newgate St, 1778–81 but in this year moved to 98 Leadenhall St. In 1778 insured his stock and utensils for £250 out of a total cover of £400. In 1781 the total cover was the same but utensils and stock was now valued at £200. [D; GL, Sun MS vol. 264, p. 435; vol. 296, p. 109]

Spragg, T., 24 Union Passage, Bath, Som., billiard table maker (1819). [D]

Spraggon, William, City Rd, Moorfields, London, cm and upholder (1790). Bankruptcy announced, *Williamson's Liverpool Advertiser*, 11 October 1790. See William Prothero & William Spraggon.

Sprague, Daniel, Lower North St, Exeter, Devon, cm (1803–17). Named in the Militia Census of 1803. On 25 December 1817 his daughter Pamela was bapt. at St David's Church. [PR (bapt.)]

Sprague, Daniel, 43 Bedford St, Covent Gdn, London, cm (1810). In April 1810 took out insurance cover of £170 which included £10 for stock and utensils. [GL, Sun MS vol. 453, ref. 844242]

Sprague, John, Sun Lane, Exeter, Devon, chair caner (1825–34). At Sun Lane, 1825–30 and Preston St, 1831–34. [D]

Sprague, Saul, 17 Cumberland St, Shoreditch, London, cm and u (1827). [D]

Sprague, William, Exmouth, Devon, cm (1823–38). Trading at the Strand, Exmouth 1823–30 but by the latter year insolvent. He was imprisoned for debt and in May 1832 was stated to have been 'lately a prisoner in the gaol of St. Thomas the Apostle, Devon'. In 1838, however, he was trading again from premises on the Parade. [D; *Exeter Flying Post*, 5 August 1830, 23 June 1831, 24 May 1832]

Spratley, J., High St, Chesham, Bucks., cm (1839). [D]

Spratley, Thomas, 96 Fore St, London, cm and u (1789–93). [D]

Spratt, Martha, St George's St, Canterbury, Kent, u (1805). [D]

Spray, William, Devonport, Devon, cm and u (1798). [D]

Spreadborough, Richard, 11 Coleshill St, Birmingham, cm, u and broker (1828–30). [D]

Spriggs, William, London, cm, case maker, shagreen case maker (b.1746–1805). Born at Chelmsford in 1746 and app. to John T. Castall of Wood St, Cheapside, London in 1759. Later he established his own business in Old Fish St. A tortoiseshell veneered tea caddy is known in a private collection with a late 19th-century written note attributing it to this maker.

Spriggs, William, London, mahogany knife case maker (1793–1808). At 47 Friday St 1793 and 1 Silver St, 1802–08. [D]

Spring, Adam, 2 Little Portland St, London, u (1821). In January 1821 took out insurance cover of £300 which included £30 for stock and utensils. [GL, Sun MS vol. 488, ref. 976008]

Spring, John, Ballingdon, Sudbury, Suffolk, cm (1830–39). [D; Essex RO, Q/RJ/2/1]

Spring, Robert, 24 Upper Union St, Hull, Yorks., cm (1840). In 1842 appears to have been trading as a grocer. [D]

Spring, T., Grimsby, Lincs., cm (1811). The death of his wife aged 82 was reported in December 1811. He appears to have been still living at this date. [*Gents Mag.*, December 1811]

Spring, Thomas, Loft St, Grimsby, Lincs., joiner and cm (1822–26). [D]

Springall, Cubitt Paul, Norwich, cm (1830). App. to Henry Huggins and free 24 February 1830 according to the freemen admisson reg. The freemen rolls, however, give the name as Cubitt Saul Springate and the date of the freedom as 24 February 1831.

Springweiler, Andrew Barnard, 2 Duke St, West Smithfield, London, cm etc. (1819–39). Variously described as a cm, medicine chest and portable desk manufacturer, u, writing desk and dressing case manufacturer and plate case maker. The surname is also rendered as Springweiter and Spring-weiller. In May and July 1821 insurance cover on utensils and stock was maintained at £500. Bankruptcy announced, January 1824, but the business was again trading by 1826. [D; GL, Sun MS vol. 486, ref. 980843; vol. 484, ref. 981611; *Brighton Gazette*, 8 January 1824]

Sprod, Elizabeth, Bristol, u (1835–40). At 4 Langton St, 1835–37, 4 Cathay in 1838 an 15 Narrow Wine St in 1840. [D]

Spry, Messrs, Barnstaple, Devon, u and cm (1793). [D]

Spry, Charles, 36 Gt Queen St, Lincoln's Inn Fields, London, carver and gilder (1835). [D]

Spry, John, Devonport, Devon, cm (1798). [D]

Spry, William, Devonport, Devon, u (1784–d.1796). In September 1796 his death by drowning after an explosion on the *Amphion* was announced. [D; *Exeter Flying Post*, 29 September 1796]

Spurgen, James, John St, Curtain Rd, London, wood and cabinet carver (1839). [D]

Spurgeon, John, 39 Holywell Lane, Shoreditch, London, bedstead carver (1808). [D]

Spurgeon, William, 12 Charlotte St, Old St Rd, London, carver, wood, cabinet etc. (1839). [D]

Spurling, Nathaniel, London, upholder (1738–72). Son of Robert Spurling of Gravesend, Kent, mercer. App. to Thomas Goddard on 17 October 1738 and free of the Upholders' Co. by servitude, 30 April 1754. Took as app. Robert Punchard who was free 1772. [GL, Upholders' Co. records]

Spurr, Hardwick, Low St, Malton, Yorks., joiner and cm (1840). [D]

Spurr, William, Liverpool, cm (1808–16). In December 1808 married Miss Elizabeth Davey of Liverpool at St Nicholas's Church. In 1813 trading at 64 Fontenoy St, but by 1816 had moved to Williamson St. [D; *Liverpool Courier*, 14 December 1808]

Spurret, William, St James St, London, upholder (1721–45). Son of Thomas Spurret of the parish of St James, Middlx, victualler. App. to Thomas Gamlyn on 4 January 1721 and free of the Upholders' Co. by servitude 13 October 1731. Took as app. Thomas Cooper, 1733–40/41. Undertook work for Benjamin Mildmay, Earl Fitzwalter for his house Moulsham Hall, Chelmsford, Essex or Schomberg House, Pall Mall, London. On 10 October 1739 he was paid £2 12s 6d by this patron for a picture frame for a portrait of 'Old Lord Holdernesse'. Between December 1742 and January 1745 he received four further sums amounting to £64 19s. [GL, Upholders' Co. records; A. C. Edwards, *The Accounts of Benjamin Mildmay, Earl Fitzwalter*, pp. 99–100, 190]

Spurrier, Charles, Bristol, cm, u, carver, gilder and looking-glass manufacturer (1827–40). At 26 St Augustine's Parade, 1827–28 but from 1829–34 at no. 25. In 1835 in addition to this address premises at 2 Frogmore St were indicated. At 1 Hammer's Buildings and 2 Frog Lane, 1836–40. Successor to Thomas Spurrier. [D]

Spurrier, John, 101 Leadhall [Leadenhall?] St, London, u (1777). In 1777 took out insurance cover of £500 of which £300 was for utensils and stock. [GL, Sun MS vol. 261, p. 77]

Spurrier, Thomas, Bristol, cm (1774–93). Living in the parish of St Mary Redcliff, 1774 at 13 Baldwin St, 1775. Later directory entries specify Baldwin St only. [D; poll bks]

Spurrier, Thomas, Bristol, cm etc. (1799–1826). At 11 King St, 1799–1810; Bristol back, 1812–17, the number being specified as 31 in 1814–17; and 26 St Augustine's back, 1819–26. This last address he took over from Nancy Stringer. In 1820 listed in directories as a cm, u, carver, gilder and looking-glass manufacturer. By 1827 he had been succeeded at this address by Charles Spurrier. [D]

Spurrier, William, Bristol, cm (1793–95). At Thomas St in 1793 and 11 King St in 1795. Succeeded at this latter address by Thomas Spurrier. [D]

Spurs, William, Hodgson St, Groves, Hull, Yorks., cm (1838–39). [D]

Squire, William, London, upholder (1718). In 1718 his app. was assigned to another master as Squire had 'abandoned home' and left the app. 'destitute of all necessities'. [GL, Middlx session bk 761, p. 69]

Squire, William, London, cm and u (c.1730). Two different trade cards of this maker are known. One lists an address at 'The Three Tents and Lamb' within Bishopsgate, near Cornhill. [Banks Coll., BM] This states that he made and sold 'all sorts of Upholstery & Cabinet goods as Standing Beds, Feather Beds, Genoa Damask, Silk Worsted, Fine Stuff Do., Harrateens, Cheneys, Linseys, fine Holland & Calico Quilts with Variety of fine Linnens & Chints Patterns, Fine Turkey, Persian & Segadio Carpets with French and English Do. Fine Flanders and English Ticken Swan Goose & other Feathers with Pillows Dimothy & Cheques for Cases, Blankets, Rugs, Coverleds & all sorts of Silk and Worsted Lace. Paper Hangings for Rooms with Cabinets, Buroes, Looking Glasses & all Sorts of Goods in the Cabinet Way'. The other trade card [Landauer Coll., MMA, NY] gives an address at 'The Three Tents and Lamb', in the Poultry. On this card he claimed that he manufactured the paper hangings that he sold.

Squires, —, 7 Hatton Gdn, London, looking-glass manufacturer (1837). [D]

Squires, Samuel, Behind the Hall, St Mary's the Great, Cambridge, u (1840). In 1843–47 the address was given as Sparrows Lane. [Poll bks]

Squires, Thomas, 5 Newman's Row, Lincoln's Inn Fields, London, carver and gilder (1835–37). [D]

Squirrell, Robert, Butter Market, Stowmarket, Suffolk, u and cm (1824–39). In 1830 and 1839 the address is simply given as Market Pl. [D]

Stables, William, York, cm (1774–1802). Living at Skeldersgate in 1774, but in 1798 trading at Micklegate. Took as app. Richard Robinson on 9 July 1788, admitted freeman in 1802. [D; poll bk; app. reg.; freemen reg.]

Stace, Freeguiff, Canterbury, Kent, u (1711). [Canterbury freemen rolls] Probably:

Stace, Freegift, London, upholder (1712). Free of the Upholders' Co., 5 November 1712. [GL, Upholders' Co. records]

Stace, William Hill, London, u (1830). Freeman of Dover, Kent. [Dover poll bk]

Stacey, Joseph, King St, Golden Sq., London, upholder (1774–90). Son of Joseph Stacey of Woolwich, broker. App. to Josiah Peacock on 2 March 1774 and free of the Upholders' Co., by servitude, 17 November 1790. [GL, Upholders' Co. records]

Stack, William, Cambridge St, Westminster, London, cm (1784). [Poll bk]

Staddon, S. H., Alphington St, Exeter, Devon, carver and gilder (1832). [D]

Stafford, John and successors, Bath, Som., upholders and cm (1787–1837). The Bath section of the 1787 *Bristol Directory* lists 'Stafford, John, Broker, Market Place' and 'Stafford, William, Upholder, High-street'. The 1792 *New Bath Directory* lists 'Stafford, John, Upholder, Appraiser & Auctioneer, High-street'. *Billinge's Liverpool Advertiser*, 19 February 1798, lists among bankrupts 'John Stafford, Bath, Upholder, Feb. 27, 28, March, 20, White Lion, Bath, Mr Clarke, Bath'. *Robbin's Bath Directory*, 1800, has 'Stafford, John, Upholsterer and Auctioneer, Market-place'. In 1802 the *Gents Mag.* (LXXII, p. 688) listed the death of 'Mr John Stafford, of Bath, upholder'. In 1805, however, the *New Bath Directory* lists 'Stafford, Mr., 11, Westgate buildings' and in 1812 it has entries for 'Stafford, J., Cabinet-maker and Auctioneer, 12 Westgate-buildings', and for 'Stafford, John, Cabinet-mader and Auctioneer, 8 Westgate-street'. In about 1814, John Stafford published *A Series of Designs for Interior Decorations Comprehending Draperies and Elegancies for the Drawing-Room* (18 coloured plates, designed and drawn by Stafford and engraved by W. Smart, Warren St, Fitzroy Sq., London). In a copious preface Stafford mentioned his own apprenticeship to an unnamed provincial u and claimed to have executed most of the designs 'within the period of the last two years'; he also alluded to the superiority of French taste and bemoaned the lack of design education in England. *A Series of Designs* was published in London by James Barron 'Upholsterers' Brass Founder' who also had premises in Birmingham: the work was also available at Longman, Hurst, Rees, Orme & Brown in London and 'at the author's upholstery warehouse, No. 20 Milsom Street, Bath'. Milsom St was then the finest trading street in the city. The dedication is worth quoting in full: 'To Thomas Hope, Esq. Whose Pure Taste and Classical Erudition have so eminently contributed to swell the tide of national benefaction; whose conspicuous researches into the mystic treasures of ancient lore, have rendered The Graces of Grecian Art subservient to the pleasures of domestic life, and directed his countrymen, by better paths, to the distant dome of Attic elegance; the following designs are respectfully inscribed'. Stafford's designs depict window curtains and pelmets; one commemorates the 'memorable epoch of 1814' in homage to Wellington. The designs are followed by an 'Index' (6 pp.) with detailed technical notes and descriptions. The only known copy of *A Series of Designs* is in the V&A Lib. Twelve of the designs were reprinted on a smaller scale in Ackermann's *Repository of Arts* from March 1819 to July

1820: Stafford was there described as 'an eminent upholsterer of Bath'. The designs not reprinted are nos 2, 6, 7, 10, 11, and 15. In 1823 the Stafford plates from the Repository were reprinted in Ackermann's *Fashionable Furniture* (pls 3–5, 8–16), which was later reissued by M. Nattali as *Modern Furniture*. The introduction stated: 'It will be perceived on inspection that the present series is rich in window-draperies, for which it is chiefly indebted to the acknowledged abilities of Mr Stafford, of Bath, whose exertions to ennoble the science of domestic embellishment deserve the highest commendation: especially as that difficult and important branch of the upholstery art, drapery in general, requires the talents of the draughtsman, combined with professional experience and taste'. In *Gye's Bath Directory* for 1819 is 'Stafford, J, Upholder and auctioneer, 20 Milsom St.'. Stafford continued to be listed at this address (*Keenes' Improved Bath Directory*, 1824, *Keenes' Bath Directory*, 1826 and 1829, 'as auctioneer, appraiser, upholsterer, house-agent, and undertaker', *Pigot's National Directory*, 1830), until 1833 when the entry in *Silverthorne's Bath Directory* changes the title of the business to 'Stafford and Son, Messrs. John'. It is changed again in *Silverthorne's Bath Directory* of 1837 to 'Stafford, Thomas & Son': this directory also includes an entry for 'Stafford, William, of Stafford & Son, 27 Richmond Place'. [Simon Jervis, *Penguin Dictionary of Design and Designers*, London, 1984, p. 459]. S.J.

Stafford, Joseph, Lichfield, Staffs., cm (1747). [Poll bk]

Stafford, Joshua, Sawtry, Hunts., cm, gardener and grocer (1762). [Cambs. RO (Hunts.), trades index]

Stafford, Richard, Market Pl., Boston, Lincs., cm (1822). [D]

Stafford, Robert, Adam St East, Portman Sq., London, u (1839). [D]

Stafford, Thomas, see John Stafford of Bath.

Stafford, William, St Botolph's, Aldgate, London, cm (1746). In 1746 took app. named Cross. [S of G, app. index]

Stafford, William, see John Stafford of Bath.

Stafford, William, 13 Theobald St, New Kent Rd, London, u (1839). [D]

Stain, Samuel, Powells Buildings, Pall Mall, London, cm (1749). In 1745 there was a Stane, cm at the bottom of Haymarket, possibly the same address. [Westminster poll bk; *Daily Advertiser*, 13 July 1745]

Stainer, John, 10 St Thomas' Broadway, London, cm (1823). In February 1823 took out insurance cover of £100 of which £70 was for utensils and stock. [GL, Sun MS vol. 491, ref. 1001793] See William Stainer.

Stainer (or Stanier), John, 17 Webb St, Bermondsey, London, cm, u and undertaker (1826–27). [D]

Stainer, William, 11 Broadway, St Thomas's, London, cm (1824). In February 1824 took out insurance cover of £100 on household goods. [GL, Sun MS vol. 496, ref. 1014425] See John Stainer.

Staines, Richard, Canterbury, Kent, u (1766–96). Free 1766. Living in the parish of St Mary Bredman, 1775–87. In 1775 took out insurance cover of £300 of which £100 was for utensils and stock. By July 1787 the total cover had risen to £500. Living in the High St, 1790–96. [Freemen rolls; poll bks; GL, Sun MS vol. 236, p. 204; vol. 345, p. 431]

Staines & Carpenter, 5 Ironmonger Lane, London, upholstery warehouse (1794–1812). This firm was included in the list of master cabinet makers in Sheraton's *Cabinet Dictionary*, 1803. [D]

Stainrod, Samuel, Nottingham, joiner and cm (1805–28). Took as apps James Sparrow in 1805, John Hayes and Richard Dickinson in 1824, Robert Burton in 1826 and William Bilbie in 1828. [App. reg.] Possibly associated with:

Stainrod & Byfield, Derby Rd, Nottingham, joiners and cm (1832). [D]

Stains, Thomas, Market Pl., Canterbury, Kent, upholder (1784). [D]

Stainton, Nathaniel, 29 Drury Lane, London, cm (1821). In June 1821 took out insurance cover on two properties in tenure to others and valued at £2,500. One was at 1 Warwick Pl., Bedford Row, Bloomsbury and in tenure to Tyrell, a carver and gilder. This was valued at £1,000. [GL, Sun MS vol. 488, ref. 980796]

Staley, Thomas, Youlgrave, Derbs., cm (1790). Marriage announced, *Derby Mercury*, 6 May 1790.

Staley, William, High St, Burton-on-Trent, Staffs., cm and u (1834–35). [D]

Stalker, John, 'The Golden Ball', St James's Mkt, London, maker of japanned furniture (1688). Co-author of *A Treatise of Japanning and Varnishing*, 1688. [Heal]

Stalker, John, Liverpool, cm (1751). Free 16 July 1751. [Freemen rolls]

Stallard, Charles, 5 New St, Brompton, London, cm and u (1839). [D]

Stallard, S., New St, Brompton, London, cm (1838). [D]

Stallard, Thomas, 95 Bartholomew Close, London, cm (1778). In 1788 took out insurance cover of £400 of which £220 was for utensils and stock. [GL, Sun MS vol. 268, p. 116]

Stalley, —, Carnaby Mkt, London, looking-glass and picture frame maker (d.1739). In May 1739 committed suicide by shooting himself with a fowling piece. [*Adam's Weekly Courant*, 9–16 May 1739]

Stallord, James, 103 London Rd, St George's Fields, London, u and cm (1809). [D]

Stalon, John, Duck Lane, Wardour St, Soho, London, carver and gilder (1839). [D]

Stalvies, John, Newcastle-under-Lyme, Staffs., cm (1830–37). In 1832 at Marsh St. [Poll bks]

Stalworthy, Edm., 3 Onslow St, Hatton Wall, London, cm (1809). [D]

Stambury, William, 65 Thomas St, Bristol, cm (1825). [D]

Stamford, J., 2 Goodge St, Tottenham Ct Rd, London, upholder (1794). [Heal]

Stamford, Jeremiah, Windmill St, Tottenham Ct Rd, cm (1749). [Westminster poll bk]

Stamford, Jeremiah, Golden Sq., London, cm (1784). [Westminster poll bk]

Stammers, Joseph, London, cm and u (1821–39). At 35 Bedford St, Covent Gdn, 1821–25. In February 1821 took out insurance cover of £2,200 in association with William Gustave. Stock and utensils included in ths cover were valued at £500. In 1825 the business moved to 5 Jermyn St and was in this year referred to as Stammers & Co. From that year onwards, however, Joseph Stammers appears to have been trading on his own behalf. His bankruptcy was announced in June 1833 and it was probably because of this that when he re-commenced his business in 1835 it was from a new address, 5 Percy St, Tottenham Ct Rd. [D; GL, Sun MS vol. 488, ref. 976092; *Liverpool Mercury*, 14 June 1833]

Stamp, E. & Co., 89 Leather Lane, Holborn, London, carvers and gilders (1809). [D] See Stampa & Son.

Stamp, Samuel, Bristol, cm (1817–33). At 112 Temple St in 1817 and thereafter at 65 Thomas St. [D]

Stamp, William, Wellington Pl., Exmouth, Devon, cm and u (1838). [D]

Stampa, Charles & Co., London, looking-glass makers, carvers and gilders (1802–11). At 125 Holborn Hill in 1802 and 25 Kirby St, Hatton Gdn, 1803–11. [D; Goodison, *Barometers*]

Stampa & Son, 74 Leather Lane, Holborn, London, looking-glass and barometer manufacturers (1804–17). [D; Goodison, *Barometers*] See E. Stamp & Co.

Stamper, John, Malton, Yorks., cm (1752). In 1752 took app. named Newton. [S of G, app. index]

Stanaway, Ann, Liverpool, u (b.1725–1826). Worked for 'upwards of forty-two years' making bed bottoms for Mathew Gregson. Died 28 September 1826 aged 101 in the parish workhouse where she had been living for the past fifteen years. [*Liverpool Mercury*, 6 October 1826]

Stanbury, Philip, Brighton, Sussex, cm (1830–39). At Little East St, 1820–21, Cavendish Pl. in 1823 and Cavendish St from October 1824. The number in Cavendish St was 21 in November 1839. Four sons and four daughters bapt. between 1820–37. [D; PR (bapt.)]

Standage, James, Lincoln's Inn Fields, London, cm and u (1808–22). At 11 Portugal St in 1808 but at 35 Carey St, 1817–20. Shown again at 11 Portugal St in 1822. Business continued by Thomas Standage. [D]

Standage, John, London, cm (1793). Subscribed to Sheraton's *Drawing Book*, 1793.

Standage, Peter, Retford, Notts., chairmaker and turner (1830–32). At Chapelgate in 1830 and Old Sun Yd in 1832. [D]

Standage, T., 8 Little Russell St, Covent Gdn, London, upholder and cm (1796). Named as Standage & Son in a recepted bill of 1796 for goods supplied to the Hon. Jasper Drummond of Perth, Scotland. The items paid for were a mahogany wardrobe at £11 11s, a mahogany Pembroke table at £2 2s and a mahogany portable writing table at £1 5s. [Heal; Scottish RO, GD 160/Box 46/ Bundle XIII]

Standage, Thomas, Portugal St, Lincoln's Inn Fields, London, cm and u (1826–29). Successor to James Standage. At 11 Portugal St in 1826 but in 1829 trading from both 4 and 11. [D]

Standage, William, High Wycombe, Bucks., chairmaker (1813–31). Three sons and four daughters bapt. between 1813–31. [PR (bapt.)]

Standerwick, G., 3 Garden Row, Camberwell, London, cm (1826). [D] See James Standerwick at Garden Row.

Standerwick, James, Finch Lane, Cornhill, London, bedstead warehouse (1793). [D]

Standerwick, James, Garden Row, Camberwell, London, cm and u (1826). [D] See G. Standerwick.

Standing, —, London, cm (1793). Subscribed to Sheraton's *Drawing Book*, 1793.

Standish, William, High Wycombe, Bucks., chairmaker (1822). Daughter bapt. in 1822. [PR (bapt.)]

Stane, —, 'the bottom of Haymarket', London, cm (1745). In July 1745 named as a person from whom an auction catalogue, the sale conducted by a Mr Pinchbeck, could be obtained. Possibly the Samuel Stain who is shown in 1749 at Powells Buildings, Pall Mall. [*Daily Advertiser*, 13 July 1745]

Stanford, Edward, 129 All Saints St, Hastings, Sussex, chairmaker and turner (1839). [D]

Stanford, Jeremiah, King St, Golden Sq., London, cm (1774). [Westminster poll bk]

Stanford, Jeremiah, 2 Goodge St, London, cm and broker (1792). In December 1792 took out insurance cover for £300. [Sun MS vol. 389, ref. 607386]

Stanford, Thomas, London, cm and u (1822–27). At 19 Queen St, Soho in 1822 and 3 Windmill St, Tottenham Ct Rd, 1826–27. [D]

Stanger, James, Sevenoaks, Kent, carvers etc. (1838–39). [D]

Staniforth, —, address unknown, u and chairmaker (1758). Supplied to Holkham Hall, Norfolk in 1758 four rush bottom chairs at £1 1s and quilted two quilts at £2. [V&A archives]

Staniland, Joseph, Church Lane, Selby, Yorks., joiner/cm (1837). [D] Successor to:

Staniland, Robert, Church Lane, Selby, Yorks., joiner and cm (1826–34). [D]

Staniland, Thomas, Blackfriargate, Hull, Yorks., cm (1795). App. to Wm Webster. [*Hull Packet*, 1795]

Staniland, William, Thames St, Abingdon, Berks., cm and u (1822–40). Married Miss Hannah Bloxham of Bodicote at Adderbury, Oxon. on 26 August 1822. Trading in Thames St in 1840. [D; Bodleian index of Oxf. marriage bonds]

Stanion, Thomas, 218 Piccadilly, London, bedstead manufacturer (1789). [D]

Stanley, Bullock, 24 Red Lion Sq., Holborn, London, u etc. (1820). [D]

Stanley, Charles, 40 Water St, Liverpool, u (1767–77). The property in Water St consisted of a dwelling house, shop, cellars and a warehouse. It had a frontage of about ten yards to Water St and one of about fifteen yards to Chorley St or Squire's Garden. There was a yard to the rear. This property was leased by Charles Stanley. In January 1768 he advertised a reward for the recovery of a piece of English chintz window curtain and a piece of Flanders tick stolen from him. His bankruptcy was announced in December 1773 and a sale held of his household goods and upholstery stock consisting of 'Damasks, Moreens, Hareteans, Blankets & Carpeting'. As late as 1777, however, he is still listed trading at this address in Liverpool directories. [D; *Williamson's Liverpool Advertiser*, 4 September 1767, 29 January 1768, 10 December 1773, 24 December 1773]

Stanley, Henry, Lincoln, joiner and cm (1752–1806). Henry Stanley snr was probably well-established as a joiner and cm some time before 1752 in which year he took his son Henry jnr as app. Other apps were Thomas Bitchfield Coates in 1753, William Stanley, another son, in 1755 and Francis Fisher in 1764. The Monson archives record a payment of £1 14s to an H. Stanley in 1766 but it is unclear whether this was due to the father or son. It was payment for 'a mohogney glass case with a frett at top — exclusif of ye glass £1.4s' and 'a staind stool with stufd seat 10s'. Henry Stanley jnr was still living in Lincoln in November 1806. [App. reg.; poll bk; Lincoln RO, Monson 12]

Stanley, Richard, Gloucester, cm (1836). Child bapt. parish of St John the Baptist, 1836. [PR (bapt.)]

Stanley, Richard, Parson's St, Banbury, Oxon., cm and u (1837–41). [D]

Stanley, Thomas, Northgate St, Gloucester, cm, u and chairmaker (1820–39). Child bapt. Church of St Michael, 1830. [D; PR (bapt.)]

Stannage, William, High Wycombe, Bucks., chairmaker (1818). Daughter bapt. in 1818. [PR (bapt.)]

Stannard, Edward, 19 Dean St, Soho, London, cm etc. (1820). [D]

Stannard, Erasmus, 36 Gt Russell St, Bloomsbury, London, u (1813–16). [D]

Stannard, J., 5 St Ann's Ct, Dean St, Soho, London, carver and gilder (1835). [D]

Stannard, R., Elm Hill, Norwich, chairmaker (1818–22). [D; poll bk]

Stannard, Richard, Norwich, cm (1815). Son of Richard Stannard, worsted weaver. Free 9 December 1815. [Freemen reg.]

Stannard, William, London, carver and gilder (1830). Freeman of Norwich living in London. [Norwich poll bk]

Stansall, Thomas, Newark, Notts., cm (1790). [Poll bk]

Stansfield, William, Dunkinfield, near Ashton-under-Lyne, Lancs., joiner and cm (1828). [D]

Stanton, Baxter, High St, Donnington, Lincs., cm and joiner (1826). [D]

Stanton, Edward, London, joiner (?) (1712–16). In 1716 the Duke of Montrose recorded in his household accounts 'marble tables' bought in London from Edward Stanton for his lodging in Glasgow. The Edward Stanton mentioned might be the person of that name trading as a joiner 1712–13 and occupying a house and workshop on the south side of Gilbert St, parish of St Giles-in-the-Fields. [Scottish RO, GD 220/6/1168/21–4; GL, Hand in Hand MS vol. 10, ref. 23631; vol. 12, ref. 25602]

Stanton, Edward, Hall St, Spalding, Lincs., cm and u (1826–40). [D]

Stanton, Hammond, Hall St, Spalding, Lincs., cm and u (1835). [D]

Stanton, James, 30 Leonard St, Shoreditch, London, cm and joiner (1820). A James Stanton was trading as a furniture broker at 28 St John St, Clerkenwell in 1839. [D]

Stanton, James, 25 Crown St, Soho, London, carver and gilder (1839). [D]

Stanton, John, Stafford, chairmaker (1765). [Poll bk]

Stanton, John, Chertsey St, Guildford, Surrey, u (1835). [Poll bk]

Stanton, John, 1 Little Edward St, Seven Dials, London, carver and gilder (1839). [D]

Stanton, Robert, Charlotte St, Gt Yarmouth, Norfolk, cm (1805–08). [D]

Stanton, Vincent, Bedale, Yorks., joiner and cm (1840). [D]

Stanton, William, Bangor Ct, Shoe Lane, Holborn, London (1735). On 28 March 1735 supplied 'two veined Italian marble tables' which were charged at 4s 6d per ft and came to £1 18s 3d. His account survives in the Alscot Park, Warks. archives. [V&A archives]

Stanton & Wilcoxon, 58 Lombard St, London, looking-glass manufacturers (1796–1820). Subscribed to Sheraton's *Cabinet Dictionary*, 1803. In 1817 listed as Stanton & Co. [D]

Stanway (or Stanaway), Henry, Ironmarket, Newcastle-under-Lyme, Staffs., cm, u and appraiser (1822–39). Recorded at 66 Ironmarket, 1822–36, and at 9 High St, 1839. [D]

Stanworth, Richard, 37 Gray St, Webber St, Blackfriars Rd, London, Windsor and garden chair and sofa makers (1826). [D]

Stapells, Charles Robert, Union Terr., St Sidwell's Exeter, Devon, carver and gilder (1827). His son Richard Medhurst was bapt. on 1 July 1827. [PR (bapt.)]

Staplee, Thomas, St Mary's Pl., Stamford, Lincs., cm (1831–35). Recorded as Thomas B. Staplee, cm and u, St Mary's St in 1835. [D; poll bk]

Staples, Edward, 17 Ogle St, Fitzroy Sq., London, cm, u, carver and undertaker (1827). [D]

Staples, J., 9 Lambeth Rd, London, cm etc. (1820). [D]

Staples, John, London, cm, u and mahogany merchant (1784–93). At 9 Hart St, Crutched Friars in 1784 and John St, Minories, 1790–93. A directory of 1790 listed James Staples at the John St address but this is probably an error. [D]

Staples, John, 2 Pleasant Row, Regent's Park, London, cm and u (1827). [D]

Staples, Thomas, London, upholder (1698). Free of the Upholders' Co., 29 October 1698. [GL, Upholders' Co. records]

Staples, Thomas, 143 High St, Chatham, Kent, cm, u and general furniture dealer (1838). [D]

Staples, Thomas, Church Pl., Newington Butts, London, chair and sofa maker (1839). [D]

Stapleton, Ann, 48 Red Bank, Manchester, chair seat maker (1825). [D]

Stapleton, Thomas, 35 Red Bank, Manchester, chairmaker (1794–97). [D]

Stapley, Henry, Tunbridge Wells, Kent, cm and u (1838–39). In 1838 at Russell Pl. and trading as Henry Stapley & Son. By the following year at Mount Sion Rd. [D]

Stapley, John Baker, Tunbridge Wells, Kent, cm (1819–25). Two daughters and a son bapt. between 1819–25. [PR (bapt.)]

Stapley, Michael, Tunbridge Wells, Kent, broker, u, paper hanger and house painter (1813–32). Two sons and two daughters bapt. between 1813–20. [D; PR (bapt.)]

Starche, Richard Henry, 51 London Wall, London, cm etc. (1820). [D]

Starimer, Thomas, Cambridge, cm and u (1826). On 29 December 1826 took as app. James Starimer. [App. reg.]

Stark, Edward, Canterbury, Kent and London, cm (1774–96). Free 1774 of Canterbury. In 1790 living in Shoreditch and in 1796 Hoxton. [Canterbury freemen rolls and poll bk]

Stark, James, 2 Cambridge St, Soho, London, cm (1780). In 1780 insured a house for £500. [GL, Sun MS vol. 280, p. 306] See William Stark at this address.

Stark, Richard, Pulteney St, London, cm (1780). In 1780 insured a house for £400. [GL, Sun MS vol. 280, p. 306]

Stark, William, Poulteney Ct, Golden Sq., London, u (1774). [Westminster poll bk]

Stark, William, 2 Cambridge St, Soho, London, cm (1780–93). In 1780 took insurance cover of £1,000 which included £150 for utensils and stock. In 1786 subscribed to George Richardson's *Treatise on the Five Orders of Architecture,* and in 1793 to Sheraton's *Drawing Book.* [D] See James Stark at this address.

Stark, William, Braddon's Row, Torquay, Devon, cm and u (1830–39). Died in February 1839 aged 48 after a long illness. [D; *Exter Flying Post,* 21 February 1839]

Stark, William, address unknown, chairmaker (1833). On 27 March 1833 charged J. S. Pakington of Westwood House, near Droitwich, Worcs., 13s 6d for an ottoman with a further 5s for packing costs. [Worcs. RO, 2309/705; 380/56/iii]

Starke, James, 20 Stone St, Bedford Sq., London, carver and gilder (1835). [D]

Starkey, Charles, 106 Chapel St, Salford, Lancs., cm (1816). [D]

Starkey, John, 3 Albion St, Windsor, Manchester, cm (1825). [D]

Starkey, John, Lower Town, Altrincham, Cheshire, cm (1828–40). [D]

Starkie, —, address unknown, cm (c.1775). Supplied furniture to Denton Park c.1775 to a value of £2 16s. [*Furn. Hist.,* 1968]

Starkie, Arrowsmith, Chapel St, Liverpool, cm (1766–67). Free of Liverpool, 2 October 1766 but in March of that year had already established his business in Chapel St. He claimed to have been 'lately . . . employed in that Trade with some of the Capital Masters in London'. [D; freeman reg.; *Williamson's Liverpool Advertiser,* 14 March 1766]

Starkie, John, Pembroke St, Liverpool, u (1829–39). At 17 Pembroke St in 1829 but in 1837 the number was 26 and in 1839 it was 19. [D]

Starling, Edward, 16 Dukes Ct, Bow St, Covent Gdn, London, carver (1778–83). In 1778 took out insurance cover of £600 which included £40 for utensils and stock. By 1783 insurance cover had fallen to £400 with only £20 for utensils and stock. [GL, Sun MS vol. 263, p. 437; vol. 306, p. 611]

Starling, Henry, Swan Yd, Westminster, London, cm (1774). [Poll bk]

Starling, James, Birmingham, cm, u and broker (1818–35). At Snow Hill in 1818, Worcester St in 1822 and 21 Edgbaston St, 1828–35. [D]

Starmar, John, St Ives, Cornwall, u (1785). [Bailey's list of bankrupts]

Starmer, Richard, Sidney St, Cambridge, u (1825). Child bapt. at All Saints Church on 17 July 1825. [PR (bapt.)]

Starmer, William, East Harding St, St Bride's, London, cm (1763–78). Fined for declining parochial office in the parish of St Bride, Fleet St in 1763. Subsequently became Collector for the Poor in 1764, Questman and Sidesman in 1765, Questman in 1766 and Churchwarden, 1777–78. [GL, MS 6561, p. 99]

Starr, George, 3 North St, Cheltenham, Glos., carver and gilder (1830). [D]

Starr, Thomas, Cambridge, chairmaker (d.1755). [Cambridge Univ. Lib., AR 3:40]

Start, J., Ashby Rd, Loughborough, Leics., cm (1840). [D]

Start, William, 12 Lambeth Walk, London, cm and u (1827). [D]

Statham, Benjamin, 123 Chapel St, Salford, Lancs., cm (1838). [D]

Statham, Charles, High St, Amersham, Bucks., u (1830). [D]

Staunton, —, Moorfields, London, looking-glass seller (1730). [*British Journal,* 21 February 1730]

Staveley, John, York, carver and gilder, see William Staveley.

Staveley, Thomas, adjoining St Clement's Churchyard, near Fybridge, Norwich, carver and gilder (late 18th century). Worked in London before setting up his manufactory in Norwich. He specialised in the manufacture of metal ornaments for pier and oval glasses, picture frames, chimney pieces and girandoles. He claimed that his processes were 'By the KING'S LETTERS PATENT'. [Symonds, *Seventeenth and Eighteenth Century English Furniture,* p. 158]

Staveley, William, York, carver and gilder (1781–1809). Free 1781 and immediately set up business in Coney St. He took as app. John Staveley 15 December 1781 and by 1793 had formed a partnership with him which was to endure until 1809. Other apps of William Staveley were John Dove who was free in 1800 and James Binnington, free 1808. Soon after the formation of the partnership the business was moved to Stonegate, where directories list them in 1808. Trade card states they could execute 'every Branch of House Carving in the most fashionable taste. Also Glasses & Picture Frames, Girandoles, Firescreens &c. Chimneypieces made & finished with Wood or cast Ornaments. Likewise a new & curious immitation of variagated Marble for Chimneypieces which has a beautiful effect & takes the highest polish. Composition cast ornaments Manufactured'. After the breakup of the partnership in 1809 William Staveley continued to trade for a time on his own behalf. In January 1795 the partners received a payment of £88 14s for picture frames and other items supplied to Swinton, Yorks. Their trade label is recorded on a simple black and gilt wooden picture frame in the Gascoigne Coll., Lotherton Hall, Yorks. [D; freemen rolls; app. reg.; *C. Life,* 14 April 1966, p. 875]

Stayner, Robert snr, East St, Blandford, Dorset, chairmaker (1808–d.1811). In 1808 was in occupation of a recently built workshop and maintained a timber yard. On his death in 1811 these passed to his son James with the proviso that a small part of the workshop should be made available to his daughter Luci for basket-making. He had another son, Robert jnr. [Dorset RO, DA/W/1811/5]

Stayner, Robert jnr, Blandford, Dorset, chair and basket maker (1810–18). Son of Robert Stayner snr. Already established in business before the death of his father in 1811 and it was probably for this reason that his father's workshop passed to another son James. Robert Stayner jnr took as apps his three sons, Charles on 29 September 1810, George on 24 June 1816 and Robert on 4 March 1818, all for seven years. [Dorset RO, B5]

Stayward, Richard, Henley-on-Thames, Oxon., u (1756). In 1756 took app. named Smith. [S of G, app. index]

Stead, John, 150 High St, Southampton, Hants., cm and u (1830). [D]

Stead, John, 54 Jubbergate, York, cm and u (1837–40). [D]

Stead, Joseph, 25 Lands Lane, Leeds, Yorks., cm and u (1834–40). At Chapel St, Hunslet in 1841. [D]

Stead, Robert, Castlegate, Kirbymoorside, Yorks., cm and joiner (1828–40). [D] Listed also at Keldholme in 1840. [D]

Stead, Samuel, Mill Hill, Leeds, Yorks., cm and u (1803–11). In 1803 subscribed to Sheraton's *Cabinet Dictionary*. At this date he may have been living in London, for in July 1806 advertised that he had been employed there 'for a long time'. When advertising his Leeds business in July 1806 he claimed that he had 'engaged excellent workmen' to assist him. In September 1808 he moved his business to 'premises nearly opposite, lately in occupation of Mr. Luccock, Wool Stapler'. In his new warerooms he was able to display an 'enlarged Stock of Furniture' which included 'a very elegant, extensive and modern Assortment of various kinds — comprising Patent Dining Tables, fashionable Drawing-Room and other Chairs, Sofas, Squabs'. The business did not, however, trade beyond 1811 for in October of that year John Kendell announced that he had taken over the premises lately occupied by Stead. [*Leeds Mercury*, 26 July 1806, 3 September 1808, 28 October 1811]

Stead, Thomas, Leeds, Yorks., cm and joiner (1826–34). In 1826 at 5 Bywater Yd, Marsh Lane, an address previously occupied by William Stead, cm and joiner. In 1830 Thomas Stead's address was 168 Marsh Lane and in 1834, 62 York St. [D]

Stead, William, Bull Green, Halifax, Yorks., cm and u (1816–18). [D]

Stead, William, 48 Marsh Lane, Leeds, Yorks., cm and joiner (1817–22). This address was also known as 5 Bywater Yd, Marsh Lane. Thomas Stead was his successor at this address. [D]

Stead & Atkinson, Hope St, Leeds, Yorks., cm (1817). [D]

Steadman, James, Lewes, Sussex, cm (1818–30). At Eastgate Lane in 1818, but by 1830 this road had been renamed Friar's Walk. In 1830 described as a journeyman cm. [Poll bks]

Steadman, John, Appleby, Westmld., joiner and cm (1828). [D]

Steadman, Robert, 21 Holywell Row, Shoreditch, London, carver and gilder (1820). [D]

Steadman, William, address unknown, cm (1803). Subscribed to Sheraton's *Cabinet Dictionary*, 1803.

Steaines, John, address unknown, u (1803). Subscribed to Sheraton's *Cabinet Dictionary*, 1803.

Steains, Cs., 12 Church Row, St Pancras, London, cm, u and undertaker (1827). [D]

Steairns, Mackenzie & Pryor, 30 Brydges St, Covent Gdn, London. See Pryer, Steains & Mackenzie.

Stebbing, John, 24 Ratcliff Highway, London, cm (1808). In February 1808 took out insurance cover for £400. [GL, Sun MS vol. 441, ref. 814246]

Stebbings, T., Watton, Norfolk, cm and joiner (1822). [D]

Stedhall, Hills, High St, Croydon, Surrey, cm and u (1839). [D]

Steadman, James, 42 Mortimer St, London, u and appraiser (1820). [D]

Stedston, William, Long Acre, London, cm (1797). In 1797 took as app. Eliz. Green. [Westminster Ref. Lib., MS F4309]

Steed, George, 1 Elim Pl., Fetter Lane, London, carver and gilder (1808). [D]

Steedham, William, Bramwell's Buildings, Soho, London, cm (1809). Bankruptcy announced, *Sherborne Mercury*, 24 July 1809.

Steedman, James, address unknown, cm (1803). Subscribed to Sheraton's *Cabinet Dictionary*, 1803.

Steedman, John, 30 Cirencester Pl., Tottenham Ct Rd, London, cm and u (1835–39). [D]

Steel, —, 27 Union St, Middlx Hospital, London, carpenter and cm (1820). [D]

Steel (or Steele) & Son, 213 High Holborn, London, japanners and u (1803–14). In 1809 described as chair japanners. [D]

Steel, Fletcher, Sun St, Keighley, Yorks., cm and u (1834–37). [D]

Steel, George, Lewin St, Middlewich, Cheshire, chairmaker (1834). Successor to John Steel at this address. [D]

Steel, John, 208 Oxford St, London, u and cm (1793–1802). From 1796–1800 traded as Steel & Little. A J. Steel, u of London subscribed to Sheraton's *Drawing Book*, 1793. [D]

Steel, John, Lewin St, Middlewich, Cheshire, chairmaker (1828). Succeeded at this address by George Steel. [D]

Steel, John jnr, Liverpool, carver and gilder (1824–34). App. to Charles Cashin in 1824 as a gilder. Trading at Ward St with shop at Wood St in 1834. [D; app. bk]

Steel, Samuel, Stoke Lane, Stoke-on-Trent, Staffs., cm (1818). [D]

Steel, Thomas, 128 Kirkgate, Leeds, Yorks., cm and furniture warehouse (1826–30). A set of six early Victorian mahogany dining chairs have been noted stamped 'T STEEL'. [D]

Steel, William, 44 Miller St, Manchester, chairmaker (1811). [D]

Steel, William, York, u (1807–18). Son of William Lazenby, yeoman. App. to William Smith on 30 May 1807 and free 1818. [App. reg.; freemen rolls]

Steel, William, Middle St, Ripon, Yorks., joiner and cm (1828). [D]

Steel, William, Ingrow Bridge, Keighley, Yorks., joiner/cm (1837). [D]

Steel, William, West Wycombe, Bucks., chairmaker (b. c. 1791–1841). Aged 50 at the date of the 1841 Census.

Steele, —, St Pancras, Chichester, Sussex, broker and cm (1804). [D]

Steele, Charles, Chester, cm (1831). Free 3 April 1831. [Freemen rolls]

Steel(e), George, Shude Hill, Manchester, chairmaker and fancy chair warehouse (1802–25). At 71 Shude Hill, but one directory from 1821–25 gives 62 Shude Hill, and one of 1825, Scotland Bridge. [D]

Steele, Nicholas, corner of Catherine St, Strand, London, cm (1777). In 1777 took out insurance cover of £300 but only £15 was for utensils and stock. [GL, Sun MS vol. 261, p. 148]

Steele, Richard, Bridge St, Sandbach, Cheshire, chairmaker (1834). [D]

Steele, Thomas, Sandbach, Cheshire, chairmaker (1822). [D]

Steele, William, Salford, Lancs. and Manchester, painter, gilder and japanner (1804–13). At 20 Spaw St, Salford in 1804, 85 Chapel St, Salford in 1811 and 74 Water St, Bridge St, Manchester in 1833. [D]

Steens, Thomas, Chester, cm (1818–19). At Watergate St in May and June 1818 and Union Walk in 1819. [Poll bks]

Steeples, John, Leicester, cm (1834). [Freemen rolls]

Steeple(s), Thomas, Birmingham, cm and u (1818–35). At Gt Brooke St in 1818, 30 Worcester St, 1822–30, and 132 Bromsgrove St in 1835. [D]

Steer, Edward, 35 Hawley Croft, Sheffield, Yorks., cm (1833). [D]

Steer, George, Petworth, Sussex, chairmaker and turner (1839–40). [D] Probably successor to:

Steer, James, Petworth, Sussex, chairmaker and turner (1832). [D]

Steere, Alfred George, Kew Rd, Richmond, Surrey, carver and gilder (1839). [D]

Steere, John, Southgate St, Leicester, cm, carpenter and joiner

(1774). In *Leicester Journal*, February 1774 announced that he was taking over the business formerly conducted by the late Mr Jennings, carpenter and joiner.

Steet, George, 25 Gt Ormond St, Queen Sq., London, cm (1823). In August 1823 insured his household goods for £300. [GL, Sun MS vol. 496, ref. 1006910]

Steet, James, 29 Everett St, Russell Sq., London, cm (1835). [D]

Steevens, James, High Wycombe, Bucks., chairmaker (1828–32). Son bapt. in 1828 and a daughter in 1832. [PR (bapt.)]

Steevens, John, Oxford St, Birmingham, cm (1800). [D]

Steevens, John, High Wycombe, Bucks., chairmaker (1828). Son bapt. in 1828. [PR (bapt.)]

Steevens, William Henry, High Wycombe, Bucks., chairmaker (1832). Daughter bapt. in 1832. [PR (bapt.)]

Steffenoni, Joseph, London, looking-glass manufactory, carver, gilder, u and cm (1815–39). At 56 Hatton Gdn in 1815 as a looking-glass manufacturer. At 74 Leather Lane, 1820–35 as a carver, gilder and looking-glass maker. At 142 High Holborn, 1837–39 as an u and cm. [D]

Steinfield, H., Warwick St, Golden Sq., London, cm (1750–59). Described in the accounts of Benjamin Mildmay, Earl Fitzwalter as a 'German Cabinet-maker'. This patron paid him £5 on 18 January 1750 'for a Mahogany Campaign Desk and case to send it down into Moulsham Hall'. On 17 December of the same year he was paid 13s 6d for covering a card table, and a further 13s for similar work in January 1752. The Earl of Ancaster paid him £101 18s on 15 May 1754. [Heal; A. C. Edwards, *The Accounts of Benjamin Mildmay, Earl Fitzwalter*, pp. 112–13; Lincoln RO, 2 ANC 6/7]

Steinnitz, Adam, 30 Gt Earle St, Seven Dials, London, cm (1787). In April 1787 insured his house and household goods for £100. [GL, Sun MS vol. 342, ref. 529906]

Stelling, Robert, Albion Pl., Darlington, Co. Durham, cm and joiner (1828). [D]

Stelves, John, Marsh St, Newcastle-under-Lyme, Staffs., cm and u (1839). [D]

Stenart, —, 315 Oxford St and 115 St Martin's Lane, London, cm. A mahogany table with fluted legs and a folding top has been noted bearing the label of this maker: 'Stenart invent. & patent/315 Oxford St./ 115 St. Martins Lane'. [V&A archives]

Stennett, —, Boston, Lincs., cm (*c*.1800). A mahogany chest of drawers corresponding to plate 52c of Hepplewhite's *Guide* is known bearing the label of this maker.

Stenson, Matthew, London, cm (1793). Subscribed to Sheraton's *Drawing Book*, 1793.

Stephen, Mr, between 'The White Bear' and 'The Golden Sugar Loaf', Long Acre, London, looking-glass maker (1702). [*The Post Man*, 19–21 February 1702]

Stephens, —, Brokers Row, Southwark, London, chairmaker (1835). [D]

Stephens, Edward, London, carver and gilder (1781–1811). In partnership with William Habgood at Gt Portland St, 1781–83. In *Gents Mag.*, May 1783 the partners were declared bankrupt. By 1790 Edward Stephens had re-established himself at 85 Park St, Grosvenor Sq. as a carver, gilder and paperhanger. He remained at this address until at least 1808. By 1811, however, he was at 212 Oxford St. Attracted some prestigious patrons. In 1781–82 Sir John Griffin Griffin purchased from the partners two gilt frames costing £4 11s 3d. A further small commission for gilding a frame in 1782 was charged at 10s 6d and a large frame bought in 1784 cost £4 2s and three smaller ones, £3 10s. In 1787 a Stephens, probably this maker, was supplying items for Blenheim Palace, Oxon. In August of that year two large picture frames 'for their Grace's pictures', two pier glass frames and two

table frames for marble tops were supplied, all in gilt wood. [D; *Billinge's Liverpool Advertiser*, 14 December 1795; Essex RO, D/DBy/A40/3, D/DBy/A40/7, D/DBy/A42/2, D/DBy/A42/5; V&A archives]

Stephens, F., 56 Gee St, Goswell St, London, cm (1829). [D]

Stephens, George, Worcester, upholder (1740). App. to Samuel Bolus and free by servitude, 7 July 1740. [Freemen rolls]

Stephens, George, Brooke House, Brooke St, Holborn, London, cm (d. by 1743). Dead by April 1743 when his stock was sold by auction. This consisted of 'large grand Mahogany Bookcases, Buroes, Desks, and Desks and Bookcases; Mahogany and Walnut-Tree Chests of Drawers, fine large Italian stain'd Marble Slabs on rich Frames, Corner Cubboards, Dressing, Dining and Card Tables...'. In July 1742 a payment of £2 16s was made to a 'Mrs Stevens' cm from the estate of the late Duke of Ancaster. It is possible that either George Stephens was dead by this date or that she was receiving the payment on the behalf of her husband. No evidence of a Mrs Stevens trading on her own behalf at this period can be found. [*Daily Advertiser*, 28 April 1743; Lincoln RO, 5 ANC 8/2/5]

Stephens, H., 3 Queen St, Grosvenor Sq., London, carver, gilder etc. (1820). [D]

Stephens, Henry, London, u (1808–35). At 4 Upper James St, Golden Sq. in 1808, 10 Broad St, Carnaby Mkt, 1808–09 and 84 Titchfield St, Fitzroy Sq., 1811–35. He took out insurance cover of £1,100 on the Titchfield St premises in December 1811 but only £110 of this covered stock and utensils. [D; GL, Sun MS vol. 459, ref. 864473]

Stephens, Hugh, Ilfracombe, Devon, cm (1823–30). [D]

Stephens, James, Castle St, Bristol, cm (1781–95). At Castle St, 1792–95 the number being 53, 1794–95. [D; poll bk] Successor to:

Stephens, John, Bristol, upholder (1756–81). In August 1756 announced that he had opened a shop at Castle St 'where he has a great Assortment of all sorts of Upholstery Goods'. Specially mentioned was a 'curious collection of the newest and genteelest Paper Hangings'. John Stephens explained that he was 'late Appentice to Mr. John Purnell'. In *Gents Mag.*, May 1767 he was declared bankrupt and this may have occasioned a change of address. His trade card [Leverhulme Coll., MMA, NY] states that he traded from an address in Maryport St. Here he sold retail and wholesale 'All Sorts of the Newest & Genteelest Paper-Hangings, Also great Choice of Rugs, Blankets, Quilts, Matresses &c.' The exact date of this card is uncertain. In 1774 living in the parish of St Augustine and in 1781 the parish of St Peter. [*Farley's Bristol Journal*, 28 August–4 September 1756; poll bks]

Stephens, John, London, upholder (1750–93). Son of Thomas Stephens of Windsor, Berks., innkeeper. App. to Charles Gage on 4 October 1750 and free of the Upholders' Co. by servitude, 2 March 1758. Took as app. John Smith who was free in 1772. Traded at 71 Fleet Mkt, 1765–70 and in 1765 was fined for declining parochial office in the parish of St Bride, Fleet St. In 1770 moved to 127 Hounsditch at which address he remained until at least 1773. During this period he took out licences to employ non-freemen with as many as twelve being employed for three months in 1772. Some time after 1773 he left London and is shown living at Romford, Essex, 1778–82, Bedfont, Middlx, 1784–86 and Bath, Som. in 1793. [D; GL, Upholders' Co. records; MS 6561, p. 100; City Licence bk, vol. 7]

Stephens, John, 14 Gt Quebec St, Marylebone, London, cm (1820). A Thomas Stevens is shown at this address in 1822. [D]

Stephens, John snr, St Owen St, Hereford, cm (1822–37). In November 1828 supplied a mahogany teapoy to Capt. N. L. Pateshall of Hereford at £3. On 12 May 1831 supplied furniture to a value of £26 1s 6d to John Arkwright of Hampton Court, Leominster, Herefs. The main items were a mahogany wardrobe at £24 and a frame and stand for a sewing glass £1 13s. [D; poll bks., Herefs. RO, F60/125; Arkwright papers, A63/161]

Stephens, John jnr, St Owen St, Hereford, cm (1837). [Poll bk]

Stephens, John, Plymouth, Devon, cm (1822–38). At Colmer Lane in 1822 but in High St, 1836–38. [D]

Stephens, John, Fore St and Spring Gdns, Brixham, Devon, cm (1838). [D]

Stephens, Joseph, in the City Mews, White Cross St, London, upholder (1778). Son of Samuel Stephens, freeman and member of the Upholders' Co. App. to David Langton but free of the Upholders' Co. by patrimony, 17 July 1778. [GL, Upholders' Co. records]

Stephens, Nathaniel, Bristol, carver and gilder (1799–1840). At Bridewell Lane, 1799–1814, 8 Nelson St, 1815–40 and had additional premises at 4 Beaufort Ct (or Pl.), 1815–28. [D]

Stephens, R. M., 6 Old Park Hill, Bristol, u (1838–40). [D]

Stephens, Ralph, Eastgate St, Chester, u (1818–19). [Poll bks]

Stephens, Robert, Plymouth, Devon, u (1729). On 24 May 1729 took out insurance cover of £400 on his dwelling house and shop and the household goods and utensils and stock kept there. [GL, Sun MS vol. 29, ref. 47770]

Stephens, Samuel, London, upholder (1739–47). Son of Timothy Stephens of Spitalfields, weaver. App. to David Langton on 5 March 1739 and free of the Upholders' Co. by servitude, 6 August 1747. Father of Joseph Stephens, upholder. [GL, Upholders' Co. records]

Stephens, Samuel, London, carver, gilder and later u (1783–1819). At Duke St, St James's in 1783 where he insured his utensils and stock for £200. By the following year at 18 Lower Book St where the business was to remain until 1819. Until 1793 his trade is always declared to be that of carver and gilder but from 1801 it is universally described as u. The business traded as Stephens & Gooch, 1806–09 and as Stephens & Wilson, 1814–15. Another directory lists the business as Thomas Stephens, 1811–16, but in 1819 reverted to Samuel once more. Stephens subscribed to Sheraton's *Drawing Book*, 1793 and was included in the list of master cabinet makers in his *Cabinet Dictionary*, 1803. At the period that Samuel Stephens was trading as a carver and gilder the insurance cover was on a modest scale. His workshop was vaued at £200 in 1784 and cover in 1786 which included his house and household goods as well as the workshop, utensils and stock was £800. From 1801, with the business now trading as an u the cover rose substantially. It was £4,450 in July 1801 with £800 for utensils and stock included in this total. In addition to the 18 Lower Brook St house, workshop and stables valued at £2,000, he also insured number 17 in the same street, described as a house, for £1,500. This level of cover was still being maintained in March 1810. In 1784 supplied a small gilt picture frame to Sir John Griffin Griffin of Audley End, Essex at 8s. The invoice was made out in the name of Messrs. Sam¹ Stephens & Co. In the following year eight gilt picture frames were supplied probably to Sir John Nelthorpe, at £4 4s. Samuel Stephens was already being referred to as an upholder in 1790 when he drew up an inventory of the goods belonging to the Rt Hon. William Grenville. [D; GL, Sun MS vol. 314, p. 207; vol. 321, p. 562; vol. 341, p. 45; vol. 419, ref. 721412; vol. 453, ref. 841528; Essex RO, D/DBy/A42/6; Lincoln RO, NEL 9/1/72; Cornwall RO, Fortescue papers, DDF(4) 11427]

Stephens, Thomas, Knightsbridge, London, cm (1784). [Westminster poll bk]

Stephens, Walter, Westwell St, Plymouth, Devon, cm (1836–38). [D]

Stephens, William, parish of St James, Bristol, carver (1774). [Poll bk]

Stephens, William, Gloucester, upholder (1774–84). Freeman of Bristol. [Bristol poll bks]

Stephens, William, Clipstone St, Marylebone, London, carver (1784). Freeman of Bristol. [Bristol poll bks]

Stephens, William, Piccadilly, London, u and cm (1799–1837). At 217 Piccadilly from 1799 until c.1815 though some directories continue to use this address much later. The business then traded at 213 Piccadilly. A number of directories from 1820 give addresses at 19, 20 and 24 Jermyn St and this may be accounted for by the fact that the Piccadilly premises extended back to Jermyn St. Some directories of 1835–37 give the business as William & John Stephens. William Stephens was included in the list of master cabinet makers in Sheraton's *Cabinet Dictionary*, 1803. The business was of substantial size and in January 1810 insurance cover amounted to £3,000 of which £2,000 was for utensils and stock and the remainder for the 217 Piccadilly premises which communicated with 24 Jermyn St. Cover for utensils and stock had risen to £3,000 by September 1812. The business attracted important and extensive patronage. It was patronised by Edward Lord Lascelles mainly in connection with the furnishing of Harewood House, Hanover Sq. London. An entry in his account book for 14 March 1807 states that he had bought goods from Stephens valued at £91 15s. Nicholas Pearse of Loughton, Essex, who also had a house in Marylebone, bought goods from Stephens over an extended period of time from 1811–24. The sums involved ranged from £12 8s 6d to £592 1s. John, 6th Duke of Bedford, was charged £22 with £2 package and carriage in November 1821 for four mahogany tables 'as before'. [D; GL, Sun MS vol. 451, ref. 839650; vol. 459, ref. 873371; Leeds archives dept, Harewood MS 192; Essex RO, D/DHt a1/3; Bedford Office, London] See John Stevens of 24 Jermyn St.

Stephens, William, Dawlish, Devon, cm (1838). Marriage reported in *Exeter Flying Post*, 26 July 1838.

Stephens & Co., 124 Wardour St, Soho, London, cm (1835). [D]

Stephenson, Adam, the Spital, parish of St John and 23 Trafalgar St, Newcastle, cm (1840). [GL, Sun MS ref. 1345062]

Stephenson, George M., 4 Collingwood St, Newcastle, u, cm and gilder (1822–34). Probably the George Meggison Stephenson, u at 30 St Nicholas Churchyard in 1834. In August 1822 notified the public that he had fitted up in his warerooms 'a very elegant CHINTZ DRAPERY BED, also a handsome FRENCH BED & canopy top'. He was also able to offer 'the very best Kidderminster Carpeting & Paper Hangings, from the first houses in London'. [D; *Durham County Advertiser*, 17 August 1822]

Stephenson, George, Newcastle, cm and joiner (1834–38). At Tallentire's Yd, Groat Mkt in 1834 and 58 Groat Mkt, 1838. [D]

Stephenson, James, London, cm (1784). Freeman of York living in London. [York poll bk]

Stephenson, John, London, cm (1774). Freeman of Hull living in London. [Hull poll bk]

Stephenson, John, Newcastle, cm and carpenter (1778–95). At Long-stairs, 1778–90 but at Carling-croft, 1795. [D]

Stephenson, John, Beverley, Yorks., cm (1790–1814). Trading at Lairgate in 1814. Took as apps John Gawan of London on 13 September 1799; and of Beverley Enoch Long in March 1802; Henry Kempling in May 1802; John Sherwood in June 1802; John May in March 1804; Xerxes Bishoprick in April 1805; John Hide in June 1807; and William P. Arnott in March 1812. [D; poll bks; app. reg.]

Stephenson, Luke, address unknown, cm (1737–39). Patronised by Benjamin Mildmay, Earl Fitzwalter of Moulsham Hall,

Essex and Schomberg House, Pall Mall, London. In June 1737 he paid Stephenson £1 10s 6d and on 24 January 1739 a further 18s for 'a Dressing Glass in the silver frame for the Countess Fitzwalter'. [A. C. Edwards, *The Accounts of Benjamin Mildmay, Earl Fitzwalter*, pp. 99, 107–08]

Stephenson, Moses, Little Horton near Bradford, Yorks., cm (1822). [D]

Stephenson, Robert, Kelgate, Beverley, Yorks., cm (1774–91). Freeman of Hull but working in Beverley. [D; Hull poll bks]

Stephenson, Robert, Brown St, Liverpool, cm (1811–14). At 3 Brown St in 1811 but at no. 5, 1813–14. [D]

Stephenson, Sampsom, 30 Museum St, Bloomsbury, London, u, chair and sofa maker (1835–39). Specialised in reclining chairs and claimed to be the patentee of a 'self acting reclining chair'. [D]

Stephenson, Thomas, High St, Maidstone, Kent, cm (1802–05). [D; poll bk]

Stephenson, Thomas, 19 John St, Tottenham Ct Rd, London, cm (1808). [D]

Stephenson, Thomas, Ashton-under-Lyne, Lancs., joiner and cm (1823–34). At Grey St in 1823 and George St in 1834. [D]

Stephenson, Thomas, High St, Barton-on-Humber, Lincs., joiner and cm (1835). [D]

Stephenson, Thomas, The Spital, parish of St John, Newcastle, cm (1840). [GL, Sun MS ref. 1345062]

Stephenson, Timothy, York, cm (1799). Freeman of Beverley, Yorks. living in York. [Beverley poll bk]

Stephenson, Wilberforce, Millhill, Prospect St, Hull, Yorks., cm (1838–39). [D]

Stephenson, William, address unknown, cm and joiner (1719–21). Undertook jobbing work at Towneley Hall, Lancs. and was probably a local craftsman. His bill of 24 November 1719 totalled £3 14s 6d and included supplying a table, an addition to the dining room chimney, 'gringing' and silvering glasses, mending furniture and supplying a spice box and a large washing tub. A further bill dated 7 January 1721 was again for mending furniture, rental of a chest of drawers, supplying a squab frame and fixing blinds to windows. The bill totalled £2 19s 8½d. [Preston RO, Towneley DDTO Q/10/4]

Stephenson, William, Liverpool, carver (1767–69). In 1767 at the East End of Old Dock but in 1769 at Wolstenhome's Sq. [D]

Stephenson, William, Without North Bar, Beverley, Yorks., cm (1774–91). At Without North Bar, 1791. [D; poll bks]

Stepney, Samuel, Brighton, Sussex, carver and gilder (1839–40). In 1839 moved from 6 Cranbourn St, West St to 25 Western Rd. Here he was able to execute 'Bed and Window Cornices, Gold Bordering for Rooms and every description of Ornamental Gilding, Old Frames Cleaned and Re-gilt — Glasses Re-silvered'. By 1843 he was at 159 Western Rd. His son Walter Robert was bapt. on 23 August 1840. [D; PR (bapt.)]

Sterkey, J., 58 Carver St, Sheffield, Yorks., carver and gilder (1833). [D]

Sterridge, James, see James Stirredge.

Sterry, Benjamin, London, upholder (1773–95). Son of Benjamin Sterry. Free of the Upholders' Co. on 2 June 1773 under the terms of the 1750 Upholders' Act, when he was listed at Cripplegate Buildings. Trading at 46 Fenchurch St as a cm and upholder in 1784. In 1795 at 1 George Ct, Lombard St where the business was described as an upholstery warehouse. [D; GL, Upholders' Co. records]

Sterry, George, High St, Worcester, carver and gilder (1820–40). At 11 High St, 1820–37 and no. 42 in 1840. From 1820–22 trading as Sterry & Amphlett, 'Looking Glass & Picture Frame Manufacturers', who also made window cornices, 'gold borders for rooms', re-gilt old frames, polished and silvered mirrors. Amphlett may be Thomas Amphlett who was trading as a carver and gilder at Spring Gdns in 1830, by which time Sterry was also trading on his own behalf. [D]

Sterry, James, see James Stirredge.

Stevan, John, Main St, Cockermouth, Cumb., cm/joiner (1834). [D]

Steven, Mr, London(?), cm (1795). In 1795 supplied Alexander Wedderburn with a 'Rosewood table SHEFFONIER' at £8 8s. [Scottish RO, GD 164/Box 20/177/2 and 3]

Stevens, Edward, Little East St, Lewes, Sussex, cm (1837). [Poll bk]

Stevens, George, Winchester, Hants., chairmaker (1792). [D]

Stevens, George, Portsmouth, Hants., chairmaker (1798). [D]

Stevens, George, Coombe St, Exeter, Devon, cm (1832). Daughter Mary Ann bapt. on 12 August 1832 at the Church of St Mary Major. [PR (bapt.)]

Stevens, George, 85 Gt Peter St, Westminster, London, carver and gilder (1839). [D]

Stevens, Isaac, Houndgate, Nottingham, joiner and cm (1832). [D]

Stevens, J., Chapel St, Devonport, Devon, cm (1814). [D]

Stevens, James, High Wycombe, Bucks., chairmaker (b.c. 1791–1841). Two sons and two daughters bapt. between 1817–34. Aged 50 at the date of the 1841 Census. [PR (bapt.)]

Stevens, James, High Wycombe, Bucks., chairmaker (1822). Son bapt. in 1822. [PR (bapt.)]

Stevens, John, Ware, Herts., upholder and auctioneer (1784). [D]

Stevens, John, West Wycombe, Bucks., chairmaker (1798). [Militia Census]

Stevens, John, 24 Jermyn St, St James's, London, upholder and undertaker (1817). The property at 24 Jermyn St connected directly with 217 Piccadilly and both were used by William Stephens in his business as an u and cm. John was probably his son, and was his partner from 1835–37. It is not clear whether the directory entry of 1817 is evidence of an independent business. [D]

Stevens, John, High Wycombe, Bucks., chairmaker (1821–30). A son and two daughters bapt. between 1821–30. [PR (bapt.)]

Stevens, John, 42 Thames St, Windsor, Berks., cm (1824–41). Appointed carpenter to Windsor Corporation for the year on 2 January 1837 and 7 January 1841. [D; fifth hall book of the borough of Windsor, pp. 52, 93]

Stevens, John, parish of St Paul, Exeter, Devon, cm (1832). [Poll bk]

Stevens, John, 15 Cleveland St, Fitzroy Sq., London, carver and gilder (1839). [D]

Stevens, John, East St, Taunton, Som., cm and u (1839). [D]

Stevens, Samuel, Reading, Berks., cm and u (1826–40). At Upper Friar St 1826 but from that year at 53 Chatham St. [D; poll bks]

Stevens, Thomas, Southampton, Hants., chairmaker (1793–1811). At 110 High St in 1811. [D]

Stevens, Thomas, 30 St John's St, London, cm (1808). [D]

Stevens, Thomas, London, cm (1809–39). At 17 Wilderness Rd, Goswell St in 1809 and 60 Wellington St, Goswell Rd from 1829–39. [D]

Stevens, Thomas, High Wycombe, Bucks., chairmaker (1822). Son bapt. in 1822. [PR (bapt.)]

Stevens, Thomas, 4 Gt Quebec St, Marylebone, London, cm and u (1822). A John Stephens was at this address in 1820 trading as a cm. [D]

Stevens, William, Norwich and London, cm and chairmaker

(1798–1818). At 14 Maddermarket, Norwich, 1801–02. A directory of 1801 shows him at 13 Maddermarket also as a grocer, and tallow chandler. In 1805 at Duke's Pl., and in 1808, Duke's Palace. Poll bks show him living in the parish of St John Maddermarket, 1802–12. On 7 March 1807 his app. John Alexander was free. By June 1818 living in London. [D; poll bks; freemen reg.]

Stevens, William, St Ebbe's, Oxford, bedmaker (1802). [Poll bk]

Stevens, William, Lewes, Sussex, cm (1816–40). Listed in poll bks as a journeyman cm living at Church St, 1816–18. Living in the High St, 1826 and trading at 95 High St, 1835–39. [D; poll bks]

Stevens, William, Kew Rd, Richmond, Surrey, cm/chairmaker (1822–26). [D]

Stevens, William, High Wycombe, Bucks., chairmaker (1823–29). Two daughters and a son bapt. between 1823–29. [PR (bapt.)]

Stevens, William, Bridge St, Ipswich, Suffolk, cm and u (1839). [Poll bk]

Stevenson (or Stephenson), Ann, Carrington St, Nottingham, u and paper hanger (1834–35). [D]

Stevenson, Charles, 22 Fargate, Sheffield, Yorks., cm (1833–37). In 1837 described as a cm, u and furniture wholesaler. [D]

Stevenson, Daniel, 'The Plough & Harrow', Lower Moorfields, London, upholder (1703). Took out insurance cover of £200. [GL, Hand in Hand MS vol. 2, ref. 4764]

Stevenson, David, address unknown, cm (1754). Subscribed to Chippendale's *Director*, 1754.

Stevenson, G. & S., 13 Upper St, Holborn, London, u (1829). [D]

Stevenson, John, 40 High St, Sheffield, u (1828–37). [D]

Stevenson, John, 46 Queen St, Devonport, Devon, cm and u (1830). [D]

Stevenson, John, 7 Hosia Lane, London, furniture japanner (1835). [D]

Stevenson, John, Lee St, Louth, Lincs., cm and joiner (1835). [D]

Stevenson, John, 10 Francis Pl., Westminster Rd, London, carver and gilder (1837). [D]

Stevenson, Nathaniel, Nottingham, cm (1774–d.1819). At Long Row in 1774 and Sand Hill in 1806. [Poll bks; Notts. RO, probate records]

Stevenson, Richard, St Peter, Canterbury, Kent, cm (1826–30). [Poll bk]

Stevenson, T., Church Gate, Leicester, cm (1815). [D]

Stevenson, Thomas, 6 Brown St, Liverpool, cm (1818). [D]

Stevenson, Thomas, Chesterfield, Derbs., cm (1818–35). At Beetwell St, 1818–29 and Knifesmith Gate in 1835. [D]

Stevenson, Thomas, 5 Mint St, Southwark, London, cm and u (1827). [D]

Stevenson, William, Soho, London, cm and u (1787–1828). At 63 King St in 1787 but by 1794 the number was 62. In June 1787 insurance cover amounted to £100, but by July 1794 this had risen to £400. By April 1801 the business had moved to 43 Greek St and insurance cover was on a much more substantial scale, totalling £1,200 of which £1,000 was for utensils and stock. Included in the list of master cabinet makers in Sheraton's *Cabinet Dictionary*, 1803. By February 1810 had entered a partnership with William Scriven. The partnership did not immediately result in a larger scale of production and insurance cover for this year was still £1,200 of which £600 was for utensils and stock and £450 for similar items in a workshop and open yard. The number in Greek St changed to 46 about 1822. Later insurance valuations suggest a fall in stock levels which in January 1824 were down to £550. [D; GL, Sun MS vol. 342, ref. 531404; vol. 401, ref. 630200; vol. 419, ref. 715880; vol. 453, ref. 841237; vol. 499, ref. 1012377]

Stevenson, William, King St, Covent Gdn, London, u and warehouseman (1825–35). At 33 King St, 1825–26 and 8 King St in 1835. [D]

Stevenson, William, Peter St, Liverpool, cm (1827–39). At 52 Peter St, 1827–29 but subsequently the number was 50 in 1835–37 and 40 in 1839. [D]

Stevenson, William, South Biddick, Houghton-le-Spring, Co. Durham, joiner and cm (1828). [D]

Stevenson, William, 5 Little Chapel St, Soho, London, looking-glass and frame maker (1835–37). [D]

Steventon, John, Shrewsbury, Salop, cm (1722). [Freemen rolls]

Steverson, William, Needham Market, Suffolk, cm and u (1830). [D]

Steveson, John, 27 Porter St, London, cm (1775). In 1775 insured a house for £100. [GL, Sun MS vol. 237, p. 529]

Steward, Edward, York, cm (1817–30). Son of George Steward. App. to Francis Ellis and Hugh Rusby, cm, and free by servitude in 1817. By April 1822 in partnership with Arthur Shores in Micklegate. [App. reg.; freemen rolls]

Steward, Henry, Hogg Hill, Bury St Edmunds, Suffolk, u, cm and auctioneer (1766–70). In October 1766 advertised 'walnut-tree Card Tables, neatly lined at £1.1s each, Mahogany ditto £2.2s'. His auctioneering activities extended some distance from Bury St Edmunds and in August 1767 he advertised a sale of stock at Newmarket, Suffolk. [*Cambridge Chronicle*, 11 October 1766, 8 August 1767, 2 June 1770]

Steward, John, 18 Clifton St, Finsbury Sq., London, cm and chairmaker (1817). [D]

Steward, Richard, Norwich, cm (1824). App. to Edmund Woolterton and free by servitude, 21 September 1824. [Freemen reg.]

Steward, Richard, St Pancras, London, carver (1830). Freeman of Norwich. [Norwich poll bk]

Steward, Richard, 15 College St, Chelsea, London, cm and u (1839). [D]

Steward, Robert, Norwich, cm (1826). Son of Joseph Steward, labourer. Free 15 November 1826. [Freemen reg.]

Steward, William, 15 Spring St, Portman Sq., London, cm (1809). [D]

Steward, William, 16 Cambridge Rd, Whitechapel, London, cm (1829). [D]

Stewart, —, Biggleswade, Beds., joiner and cm (1793). [D]

Stewart, Charles, St Andrew St, London, cm (1776–79). In 1776 took out insurance cover of £400 half of which was for utensils and stock. In 1779 insured a house for £300. [GL, Sun MS vol. 245, p. 430; vol. 279, p. 578]

Stewart, Charles, London, cm (1793–1803). Subscribed to Sheraton's *Drawing Book*, 1793 and *Cabinet Dictionary*, 1803.

Stewart, Charles, 33 Lamb's Conduit St, London, cm and upholder (1808). [D]

Stewart, Charles, London, cm and u (1810–27). At 115 St Martin's Lane, 1816–20 but in 1821 moved to 24 Regent St. In 1810 granted patent 3339 for 'certain improvements in the construction of dining and other tables' and he appears to have made good use of this in connection with his business. A number of expanding dining tables are known bearing brass plates and in one case a printed paper label giving the St Martin's Lane address. Some of these also record an address at 315 Oxford St. One table is known with a brass plate giving the Regent St address. Some of these tables when closed can be used as side or pier tables. [D; *Antique Collector*, January 1975; *Conn.*, November 1961, June 1974]

Stewart, Harriet, 20 Wilson St, Finsbury, London, u, bed and mattress maker (1822–27). [D]

Stewart, James, London, cm and broker (1778–81). At Little St Andrews St, Seven Dials in 1778 and Castle St, Long Acre in

1781. In both of these years he took out insurance cover of £500 of which £200 was for utensils and stock. [GL, Sun MS vol. 265, p. 321; vol. 294, p. 142]

Stewart, James, High St, Putney, London, furniture broker, u and pawnbroker (1832). [D] See Jno. Stewart at this address.

Stewart, James, 16 Nile St, North Shields, Northumb., cm and paperhanger (1834). [D]

Stewart, John, Shoreditch, London, cm (1814–15). At 53 Shoreditch in 1814 and 8 Shoreditch in 1815. [D]

Stewart, Jno., High St, Putney, London, furniture broker, u and auctioneer (1832). [D] See James Stewart at this address.

Stewart, Joseph, 10 Derby St, Liverpool, cm and household broker (1816). [D]

Stewart, Matthew, Bell St, North Shields, Northumb., cm and joiner (1803–27). Subscribed to Sheraton's *Cabinet Dictionary*, 1803. [D]

Stewart, Robert, Bow St, London, u (1749). [Westminster poll bk]

Stewart, William, Wakefield, Yorks., cm and u (1816–37). At Cock & Swan Yd in 1816, Churchyard and Northgate, 1828–30 and Cross St in 1834. In 1837 shown at Northgate only. From 1828 the business is named as William Stewart & Son. [D]

Stewart, William, North Shields, Northumb., cm and joiner (1827–28). At Union Lane in 1827 and Church Rd in 1828. [D]

Stewart, William, Church Gate, Leicester, carver and gilder (1840). [D]

Stickley, John, Lewisham Lane, Greenwich, London, cm etc. (1823–39). Listed at Lewisham Rd in 1826. [D]

Stickley, Thomas, Bridge Pl., Lewisham, London, cm and u (1839). [D]

Stickner, John, 1 Woolpack Yd, Gravel Lane, Southwark, London, cm (1809). [D]

Stidolph, Edward, High St, Tonbridge, Kent, cm and commissioner for taking special bail (1832–39). [D]

Stidolph, George, Tonbridge, Kent, u and cm (1800). In May 1800 an auction was held of the household furniture and stock in trade of this maker conducted by Thomas Wise of Tonbridge. This may have been the termination of George Stidolph's business though a directory of 1803 was still listing it. [D; Tunbridge Wells Museum, Sprange Coll.]

Stidolph, George Lambert, Tonbridge, Kent, cm (1819–29). Living in the parish of Tunbridge in December 1819 when his son George Lambert was bapt. In May 1821 a daughter Elizabeth was bapt. in the same parish. This parish covered not only the town of Tonbridge but also significant parts of what is today Tunbridge Wells. Trading in Tonbridge, 1823–29. [D; PR (bapt.)]

Stidolph, Henry, Dartford, Kent, cm (1824–39). [D]

Stidston, William, 137 Long Acre, London, u (1794–1802). [D]

Stiff, H., 27 Upper Parade, Leamington, Warks., cm and u (1837). [D]

Stiggle, William, Strand, London, carver and gilder (1806–20). At 440 Strand, 1806–14 but by 1820 the number was 443. Took over the premises in the Strand previously occupied by Joseph Norman whose successor he claimed to be. In September 1809 provided for John, 6th Duke of Bedford, 'two handsome gold frames 7 inch moulding carved pot flower & water leaf 33 ft. 6 ins. with plate glasses to do. for 2 drawings by Mr Glover £56'. On the foot of the invoice reminding the Duke of the sum due he added a request for payment 'as I am very much pressed for money at this time'. [D; Bedford Office, London]

Stiles, —, Cambridge, cm (1793). Subscribed to Sheraton's *Drawing Book*, 1793.

Stiles, Alfred, High Wycombe, chairmaker (1830). Son bapt. in 1830. [PR (bapt.)]

Stiles, Arthur, London, cm (1818). Freeman of Evesham, Worcs. living in London in June 1818. [Evesham poll bk]

Stiles, Daniel, Suffolk/Essex border area, cooper or chairmaker (1721). On 3 June 1721 an advertisement was placed in the *Ipswich Journal* asking him to contact Thomas Cole of Dedham, Essex as his mother had died and left him her effects. Stiles probably originated from Dedham but appears to have travelled in search of work. He was said to have been working lately at 'Grunsborough' in Suffolk.

Stiles, George, Bridge St, Cambridge, cm and u (d.1817). Died 1817 and sale of his stock, timber and three work benches was announced, *Cambridge Chronicle*, 25 July 1817. [Cambridge Univ. Lib., Will AR 3:153]

Stiles, Henry, Brighton, Sussex, u (1768). Undertook repairs and alterations such as altering a night-stool, setting up a bed, supplying counterpanes etc. at a cost of £10 17s 6d at the accommodation rented by Elizabeth, Marchioness of Tavistock at Brighton in September 1768. [Bedford Office, London]

Stiles, James, West Wycombe, Bucks., chairmaker (b.c.1811–41). Aged 30 at the date of the 1841 Census.

Stiles, Jos. D., 27 Stanford St, Blackfriars Rd, London, cm and u (1839). [D]

Stiles, Susan, 6 Green St, Blackfriars Rd, London, cm and u (1839). [D]

Stimpson, William, Straight, Lincoln, chairmaker (1822–35). At 'Foot of the Hill' in 1822, and 'Straight', 1826–35. [D]

Stimpson, William, Claypath, Durham, turner and chairmaker (1827). [D]

Stimson, William, Lincoln, chairmaker (b.1747–d.1797). Died suddenly aged 50 in November 1797. Possibly the father of the William Stimpson, chairmaker, trading at the Straight, Lincoln in 1826. [*Gents Mag.*, November 1797]

Stinchcomb, James, Bristol, cm and furniture broker (1826–31). At 10 Sims's Alley in 1826 and 46 Stoke's Croft, 1827–31. In 1830 trade given as furniture broker only. Successor to William Stinchcomb. [D]

Stinchcomb, John, Nelson St, Bristol, broker, salesman and u (1803–24). Declared bankrupt July 1803, but back in business again by 1805 and traded 1805–06 from both Nelson St and Pithay. From 1821 used 68 Broadmead in addition to the Nelson St address. [D; *Exeter Flying Post*, 28 July 1803] His successor, and possibly widow, was:

Stinchcomb, Sarah, 63 Broamead and Pithay, Bristol, cm, u and furniture broker (1826). [D]

Stinchcomb, William, Syms's Alley, Bristol, cm, u etc. (1809–19). The number in Syms's Alley was given as 6 in 1819. Declared bankrupt, *Exeter Flying Post*, 13 December 1810. Succeeded by James Stinchcomb. [D]

Stinson, Handley, 39 Edmund St, Liverpool, cm (1839). [D]

Stinton, —, Moorfields, London, looking-glass maker (1730). [Heal]

Stirling, Thomas jnr, 6 St Ann's Pl., Commercial Rd East, London, patent slate table and furniture manufacturer (1839). [D]

Stirredge, James, London, upholder, cm, auctioneer, appraiser and undertaker (1765–96). Also described as James Sterry and James Sterridge. Member of the Turners' Co. but trading as an u. At Gt Winchester St, 1765–69 at which period he took out licences to employ non-freemen, three men usually being authorised. At 7 George Yd, Lombard St, 1781–96. Took as app. James Shipman. Insurance cover in 1781 was £1,400 half of which was for utensils and stock. [D; GL, City Licence bks, vols 4–6; Sun MS vol. 297, p. 534; Upholders' Co. records] See Benjamin Sterry at 1 George Ct, Lombard St.

Stirrup, James, Warrington, Lancs., cm and u (1825–34). His home was in Butter Market St, 1825–34 but he also traded at Union St, 1825–28 and Bridge St in 1834. [D]

Stivenson, William, 43 Prince's St, Leicester Sq., London, cm, timber merchant and sawyer (1807–08). A substantial business with an insurance cover of £1,500 in August 1807 which by April 1808 had increased to £2,450. Of this latter sum only £400 was in respect of household goods and stock kept in an open yard, presumably timber, was insured for £1,000. [GL, Sun MS vol. 440, ref. 804986; vol. 445, ref. 814930]

Stoakes, William, 19 St Mary's Gate, Manchester, carver and gilder (1794). [D]

Stoakes, William, Liverpool, looking-glass manufacturer, bronze figure manufactory and auctioneer (1801–23). Maintained a shop and manufactory in Church St, the number being 41 in 1804, 48 in 1805, 55 in 1811–13, 57 in 1816, and 62 in 1821. An additional manufactory was maintained in Dover St, 1813–14, the number being 2 in 1813 and 3 in 1814. Further addresses were 13 Newington in 1816 and 7 Shannon St in 1821. The looking-glass manufactory was important throughout but in January 1801 he was also acting as an auctioneer of fine art. On 5 January 1801 he held in his Church St premises a sale of paintings 'many of the choicest productions of ancient & modern Artists'. By 1811 he had added to his production of looking-glasses, the casting of bronze figures. Both of these manufactures continued until 1823 when he was declared bankrupt. A sale of his stock in trade and equipment was held on 1 December 1823. On offer were 'a large & valuable SILVERING TABLE, 7 feet 8 long & 6 feet wide, a Ditto 6 feet 10 by 3 feet 8, with Iron Weights Complete, a large quantity of Molds of Busts, Figures, Urns, Brackets & Pedestals, Composition Molds for Ornamental gilding, unfinished Picture & Looking Glass Frames & small quantity of Fancy Wood. Log & Veneers, two Marble Slabs, a Mahogany Sideboard, Gilders' Benches, & other Articles'. [D; *Billinge's Liverpool Advertiser*, 5 January 1801; *Liverpool Mercury*, 28 November 1823] See George Bullock.

Stoate, Richard, Bristol, cm, u and undertaker (1807–40). At Denmark St, 1807–10; 43 Quay in 1812; 33 Quay, 1813–23; 38 Quay, 1824–33; and 2 Unity St, College Green, 1834–40. From 1830 traded as Richard Stoate & Son. [D]

Stobbs, Robert, Barnard Castle, Co. Durham, cm (1751). In 1751 took app. named Andrews. [S of G, app. index]

Stock, George, Bristol, u and cm (1812–28). Shown at 24 Newfoundland St, 1812–14 and 1816, but the number was 25 in 1815 and 12 from 1817–20. At 43 Redcliff St, 1821–26, 1 Cathay in 1827 and 2 Cathay in 1828. Described as an u, 1812–19 but from 1820 as a cm and u. [D]

Stock, George, Bristol, u (1834–35). At Old Park in 1834 and 1 Terrell St in 1835. [D]

Stock, George, 34 Bristol St, Birmingham, u and paper hanger (1839). [D]

Stock, James, 2 St James's Barton, Bristol, cm, upholder, paperhanger and undertaker (1834). Bankruptcy announced, *Exeter Flying Post*, 5 June 1834. [D]

Stock, Thomas, Churchgate, Retford, Notts., cm and u (1822). [D]

Stockdale, —, address unknown, cm (1803). Subscribed to Sheraton's *Cabinet Dictionary*, 1803.

Stockdale, James England, Hull, Yorks., cm (1829–40). App. to John Megson in January 1822. Trading at 6 Junction Dock St in 1831 but from 1835 the numbers were 25 and 18. [D] Succeeded by:

Stockdale, John England, Hull, Yorks., bedstead and pole manufacturer, furniture broker (1838–40). In 1838 at 25 Humber Dock St and 18 Junction Dock St. In 1839 at 25 New Dock Walls, and in 1840 at 18 Junction Dock Rd as a cm etc. Successor to James England though it is possible that the two traded together at the same address. [D]

Stockdale, Joseph, 11 Waterworks St, Hull, Yorks., chairmaker (1838–40). Also a greengrocer. [D]

Stockdale, Mrs Mary, London(?), upholder (1706). On 6 May 1706 supplied to Boughton, Northants. 'eight green cross stitch Elbow Chaires, black Japand fframes, girts bottoms, linings, fine curld hair, Green silk orris and gilt nails and making eight chaires up with green searge false cases to them'. Each chair cost £10 and another chair *en suite* was charged at £20. [V&A archives]

Stockdale, Thomas, 13 Dansie St, Liverpool, u (1834). [D]

Stocker, John, 29 Shepherd St, Spitalfields, London, cm and u (1827). [D]

Stocker, Joseph, Paris St, Exeter, Devon, cm (1837–38). His first wife, Mary, died on 20 February 1837. On 17 July of the same year he married again at St Edmund's Church. His second wife, Ann, was the youngest daughter of Mr R. Maunder of Cheriton Fitzpaine, Devon, boot and shoe maker. A daughter was bapt. at St Sidwell's Church on 10 June 1838. [*Exeter Flying Post*, 2 March 1837, 27 July 1837; PR (bapt.)]

Stockham, James, Chippenham, Wilts., cm (1736–52). In 1736 took app. named Smithe and on 23 July 1752 Gabriel Cruse at a premium of £10. [S of G, app. index; *Wilts. Apps and their Masters*]

Stockham, Thomas, 26 Wigmore St, London, portable desk, work box and cabinet case maker (1839). [D]

Stocking, John, Norwich, chairmaker (1770). App. to Thomas Durrant, chairmaker and free by servitude, 3 May 1770. [Freemen reg.]

Stocks, Joseph, Leeming St, Preston, Lancs., cm (1814–28). At 17 Leeming St, 1814–18 but the number was 16, 1825–28. [D]

Stocks, Robert, Houndsgate, Nottingham, joiner and cm (1782–99). Took as apps George Walker in 1782, Richard Moore in 1788 and William Hensley in 1791. In 1797 signed the *Nottingham Cabinet and Chair Makers' Book of Prices* on behalf of the masters. At Houndsgate in 1799. [D; app. reg.]

Stocks, Thomas, Retford, Notts., cm and u (1819–40). At Moorgate, 1819–35, Church Gate in 1822 and Church St in 1828. [D]

Stocks, William, Retford, Notts., chairmaker and turner (1822–40). Recorded at Moorgate, 1822–35 and Old Tan Yard in 1830. [D]

Stockton, Elitzer Thomas, Leicester, cm (1754). App. to Michael Clarke and free 1754. [Freemen rolls]

Stockton, James, 2 Wells Yd, Waterworks St, Hull, Yorks., cm (1838–39). [D]

Stockton, John, Fletcher St, Newcastle-under-Lyme, Staffs. (1830–32). In 1832 at Fletcher St and described as John jnr. [Poll bks]

Stockton, William, Lee St, Louth, Lincs., cm and joiner (1835). [D]

Stockwell, C. & Son, 128 Snargate St, Dover, Kent, u (1838). [D] Succeeded by:

Stockwell, Elizabeth & Son, 128 Snargate St, Dover, cm and u (1839). [D]

Stockwell, Stephen, 59 Long Alley, Finsbury, London, upholder (1835–39). [D]

Stockwell, William, Peter St, Bristol, basket and chair manufacturer (1814–29). The number in Peter St was 25 in 1821–29. [D]

Stockwell, William jnr, 20 Peter St, Bristol, basket, chair and sieve maker (1820–32). Shown as W. & E. P. Stockwell in 1830–31 and W. S. Stockwell in 1832. [D]

Stoddard, William, Brighton, Sussex, cm (1837–39). At Church St in 1837 and 12 Jew St, Church St, 1839. In September 1839 a daughter was bapt. and the home address was given as Windsor St. [D; PR (bapt.)]

Stoddart, George, 11 Angel Alley, Little Moorfields, London, cm (1777). In 1777 insured his utensils, stock and goods for £40 out of an entire insurance cover of £100. [GL, Sun MS vol. 255, p. 580]

Stoddart, John, Thursby, Wigton, Cumb., joiner and cm (1828). [D]

Stokehill, George, Old Malton Gate, Malton, Yorks., joiner, cm and vat maker (1840). [D]

Stokell, Nicholas, Union Lane, Sunderland, Co. Durham, joiner and cm (1827). [D]

Stoker, Joseph, 44 Frith St, Soho, London, upholder (1785). In May 1785 took out insurance cover of £190 on household goods and clothes. [GL, Sun MS vol. 327, p. 358]

Stokes, Cornelius, Hull, Yorks., varnisher, japanner and fancy painter (1823–31). At 1 Grimston Ct, Saville St as a varnisher in 1823, Grimston Ct as a fancy painter in 1826 and 43 Saville St in 1831. [D]

Stokes, George, Friar St, Droitwich, Worcs., cm (1835). [D]

Stokes, George, 22 Parliament St, Nottingham, cm (1835). [D]

Stokes, J., 21 Newcastle St, Strand, London, carver and gilder (1789–90). [D]

Stokes, Joseph, London, picture frame maker (1777–79). At 3 Chair Ct, Ship Yard, Temple Bar in 1777 where he took out insurance cover of £100 which included £20 for utensils and stock. In 1779 at 43 Carey St with total insurance cover at £200 half of which was for utensils and stock. [GL, Sun MS vol. 261, p. 453; vol. 273, p. 258]

Stokes, Samuel, Lordsmill St, Chesterfield, Derbs., cm (1818–22). [D]

Stokes, Thomas, Tooley St, Southwark, London, cm and u (1802–27). At 26 Tooley St, 1802–25 but in 1827 the number was 55. Included in the list of master cabinet makers in Sheraton's *Cabinet Dictionary*, 1803. [D]

Stokes, Thomas, West Bromwich, Staffs., joiner/cm (1834). [D]

Stokes, William, Walsall, Staffs., cm (1835–39). Listed at Park St, also as an u, in 1835. [D]

Stokes & Wallington, Cavendish Ct, Houndsditch, London, cm (1790–93). [D]

Stokoe, John, Manor-chair, Newcastle, cm (1790–95). [D]

Stokoe, William, 13 St Saviourgate, York, cm (1834–38). Recorded at Wikeley's Ct, St Saviourgate, also as an u, in 1834. [D]

Stolworthy, Edmund, London, bedstead manufacturer and cm (1796–1839). App. to Samuel Bream of Gt Yarmouth, Norfolk and in 1796 free of that town. Immediately on completion of his apprenticeship he moved to London and by 1806 was trading from 3 Onslow St, Hatton Wall. He remained at this address at least until 1811 but by 1820 the number was 17 Onslow St. By February 1822 at 21 Vine St, Hatton Wall, an address that he continued to occupy until 1839. The business was of a substantial size by this date. The total insurance cover was £1,550, all of which covered trade buildings and stock except £150. The business was listed as Stolworthy & Martin, 1824–27 but by 1829 had reverted once more to trading as Edmund Stolworthy. [D; Heal; Gt Yarmouth freemen rolls and poll bks; GL, Sun MS vol. 490, ref. 989227]

Stone, —, Exeter, Devon, carver (1779). Carved the pillars, pilasters and composite style capitals in the Dining Room at Killerton, Devon in 1779. [Nat. Trust guide to *Killerton*]

Stone, Charles, St Giles, Norwich, cm (1768). [Poll bk]

Stone, Edward, High St, Amersham, Bucks., chairmaker (1823–30). [D]

Stone, Edward, 80 Chapel St, Islington, London, cm (1826). [D]

Stone, Elden, 80 Chapel St, Islington, London, cm (1827). [D]

Stone, G., 57 Chapel St, Islington, London, cm (1820). [D]

Stone, George, Bristol and London, carver and gilder (1774–84). Living in the parish of St John, Bristol in 1774 and the parish of St James in 1781. Moved to London and in April 1784 was at Goodge St, Tottenham Ct Rd. [Bristol poll bks]

Stone, Isaac Francis, London, cm and broker (1831). Leased property at New Thame, Oxon. to a grocer. [Oxford RO, Bir I/iii/6/7]

Stone, J., address unknown, u (1794). Undertook commissions for Mrs Leigh of Leighton House. The bill dated October 1794 came to £50 15s and included striped red and white Manchester furniture for the Drawing Room sofa and chairs and for bed and window curtains. [Shakespeare Birthplace Trust, Leigh receipts, DR18/5]

Stone, James, High Wycombe, Bucks., chairmaker (1837–40). Two sons and a daughter bapt. between 1837–40. [PR (bapt.)]

Stone, John, Exeter, Devon, cm (b.1717–d.1810). In 1745 took app. named Gooding, in 1752 Gordon and in 1759, Bond. Died in 1810 aged 93. [S of G, app. index; *Gents Mag.*, supplement, 1810]

Stone, John, 14 Broad St, St Giles, London, carver (1778). In 1778 took out insurance cover of £200 which included £50 for utensils and stock. [GL, Sun MS vol. 264, p. 500]

Stone, John, Bilston, Staffs., victualler, cm and quarry owner (1793). [D]

Stone, John, Uttoxeter, Staffs., cm (1798). [D]

Stone, John, Exeter, Devon, carver (1803–23). Included in a Militia Census of 1803 which gave his address as The Close. At St Sidwell, 1822–23. [D; election squibs, 1816]

Stone, John, Alliston St, Birmingham, cm (1816). [D]

Stone, John, High Wycombe, Bucks., chairmaker (1839). [D]

Stone, Renard, Monmouth Lane, London, carver (1709). [Rate bk]

Stone, René, Berwick St, Soho, London, frame maker (1749–d. by 1774). His premises in Berwick St were originally identified by his trade sign, 'The Golden Head'. Later this was changed to 'The King's Arms'. The change no doubt took pace soon after January 1761 when he was appointed 'Joyner to His Majesty's Privy Council'. He subsequently advertised the business as 'Frame Maker to His Majesty'. Stone had produced frames for the Crown as early as 1752, however, and in 1772 charged £67 4s for frames 'richly carved & gilded for their Majesties pictures'. René Stone was probably a Frenchman and on 8 June 1750 the baptism of Elizabeth, the daughter of Marquis Pierre de Conty was performed at Stone's house in Berwick St. Stone was dead by January 1774 when his appointment as 'Joyner' passed to Isaac Gossett. Stone's business passed to Duffour. [Westminster poll bk; Heal Coll., BM; PRO, LC3/58, LC5/24–25; *Huguenot Soc.*, vol. XXVIII, p. 7; H. Phillips, *Mid-Georgian London*, p. 221]

Stone, Richard, Exeter, Devon, u (1708). [Freemen rolls]

Stone, Richard, Banks, Bingham, Notts., joiner and cm (1832). [D]

Stone, Samuel, London, cm (1770–93). In 1770 William Tustian of Whitechapel took a booth at the annual Stirbitch Fair held near Cambridge in September. He advertised that he was selling furniture of his own manufacture and also that made by Samuel Stone & Co. In 1782 he was trading from Catherine Wheel Alley, Whitechapel and in that year took out insurance cover of £700 which included £500 for his workshop, utensils and stock. Bankrupt in 1790 but by the following year again trading, now from 127 Hounsditch. Subscribed to Sheraton's *Drawing Book*, 1793. [*Furn. Hist.*, 1978; GL, Sun MS vol. 304, p. 443; vol. 379, p. 132; Bailey's list of bankrupts]

Stone, T., 6 Gibraltar Walk, Bethnal Green, London, backgammon table maker (1821–23). [D]

Stone, Thomas, parish of St Michael, Lewes, Sussex, u (1812–26). [Poll bks]

Stone, Thomas, Gedling St, Nottingham, u (1832). [D]

Stone, William, Worcester, u (1711–41). Took apps named Lingen in 1711 and Joseph Pember, 1723–41. [S of G, app. index; freemen rolls]

Stone, William, Hatton Gdn, London, cm (1726). In 1726 advertised walnut tree matted and stuff bottomed chairs. [Heal; Harris & Son, *The English Chair*, p. 174]

Stone, William S., London, upholder (1802–18). Freeman of Norwich living in London. [Norwich poll bks]

Stonebanks, Robert, North Shields, Northumb., cm and joiner (1827–34). At Toll St in 1827, Bird St in 1828, and 30 Church St in 1834. [D]

Stonehewer, Samuel, Chestergate, Macclesfield, Cheshire, cm and chairmaker (1816–22). [D]

Stonehouse, Ann & Sons, Timble Bridge, Leeds, Yorks., cm (1818). [D]

Stonehouse, George, New Elvet, Durham, cm and joiner (1828). [D]

Stonehouse, Roger, Brotton, Yorks., joiner/cm/wheelwright (1834). [D]

Stonehouse, Thomas, London, cm and chairmaker (1800–04). At 6 Tennis Ct, Middle Row, Holborn in April 1800 when he took out insurance cover of £200. By April 1804 he had moved to 3 Princes St, Little Queen St, Lincoln's Inn Fields where insurance cover was £300, half of which was for utensils and stock. [GL, Sun MS vol. 418, ref. 702399; vol. 431, ref. 760746]

Stoneley, Richard, Newport, Salop, cm (1797). [D]

Stones, D., York, turner and cm (1825). In partnership with T. Ashworth, declared bankrupt, *Brighton Gazette*, 16 June 1825.

Stones, George, York, turner, u, cm, Tunbridge-ware maker, fancy chairmaker and dealer in toys (1795–d.1823). Son of Thomas Stones, mariner. App. to John Lund, hardwood turner on 30 September 1777 and free 1785. Took as apps William Ruddock (1790), William Thornton (1792–1800), William Scafe (1795–1805), William Baines (1795), Thomas Fligg (1796–1820), Christopher Oates (1799–1806), Richard Baynes (1799), John Danby (1803–05), John Bird (1805), David Adams (1805), John Sollitt (1812), William Wilson (1814), George Atkinson (1814), Peter Forbes (1820), Thomas Hardcastle (1820), Ralph Page Fryer (1819) and George Clark (1822). He took as app. chairmakers John Bulmer (1797–1812), Francis Duffield (1805–14) and John Darnby (free 1812). At Spurriergate in 1798 but in March 1816 announced his recent move to Pavement where he remained until his death in May 1823. His widow announced in June 1823 her intention of carrying on the business. [D; app. reg.; freemen rolls; *York Courant*, 18 March 1816; *Yorkshire Gazette*, 24 May 1823, 7 June 1823]

Stones, James, Ashton-under-Lyne, Lancs., cm and joiner (1818–34). At 5 Crickets Lane, 1818–28 but in 1834 at 83 Stamford St. [D]

Stones, James & Thomas, 48 Darwen St and Northgate, Blackburn, Lancs., joiners, cm and builders, timber and raff merchants (1814–34). The Darwen St address was a dwelling house. [D]

Stonestreet, Henry, London, upholder (1722–34). Son of Henry Stonestreet of Eaton Bray, Beds., clerk. App. to William Scrimshire on 7 March 1722 and free of the Upholders' Co. by servitude, 25 March 1730. In 1734 living in Friday St. [GL, Upholders' Co. records; poll bk]

Stoney, Benjamin, Weekday Cross, Nottingham, cm, joiner and carpenter (1784–1804). In July 1784 advertised for craftsmen and in 1791 was one of the masters who endorsed the content of the *Nottingham Cabinet and Chair Makers' Book of Prices*. In 1793 subscribed to Sheraton's *Drawing Book*. Took as apps Sam Sodd in 1799 and William Hutton Cox in 1804. [D; *Nottingham Journal*, 31 July 1784; app. reg.]

Stoney, William, High Pavement, Nottingham, cm and u (1812–40). From 1818–35 the business was in partnership trading as Stoney & Clarke. William Stoney was a cm. [D; poll bk]

Stong, Samuel, Gt George St, Bristol, cm (1795). [D]

Stonier, Hugh, Newcastle-under-Lyne, Staffs., cm (1812). [Poll bk]

Stonier, John, High St, Hanley (or Shelton), Staffs., cm and u (1822–54). Also had a house at Charles St in 1822. Possibly the successor to Thomas Stonier who was trading in the High St as a cm, 1818. [D]

Stonier, John, Ironmarket, Newcastle-under-Lyne, Staffs., chairmaker (1830–35). Listed as a cm and u in 1835. [Poll bks] See William Stonier at this address.

Stonier, Thomas, High St, Hanley, Staffs., cm (1818). Probably succeeded at this address by John Stonier. [D]

Stonier, William, Ironmarket, Newcastle-under-Lyne, Staffs, cm and 1818–34). [D] See John Stonier at this address.

Stonier, William, Liverpool Rd, Burslem, Staffs., cm and u (1834–35). [D]

Stooks, Thomas, Rose & Crown Yd, Leeds, Yorks., cm, appraiser and auctioneer (1775–98). Recorded at Briggate in 1798. Advertised that he could offer 'CABINET GOODS of all sorts made in the genteelest taste' and that he 'appraises & sells all Sorts of Household Furniture, Utensils, Stock-in-Trade, Plate etc'. In 1793 subscribed to Sheraton's *Drawing Book*. An invoice and letter relating to the supply of furniture by this maker to a Mr Kear, attorney-at-law, of Barnsley, Yorks., survive. The items supplied include a mahogany camp bed with sacking bottom, a four post bedstead with reeded posts, a dressing glass, a butler's tray and other trays and totalled £22 6s 1d. Stooks was still urging payment in 1799 a year after the issue of the original invoice. [*Leeds Mercury*, 20 June 1775, 14 May, 28 May, 18 June 1776; Calder Valley Museum, John Goodchild Coll.]

Stopford, William, Hillgate, Stockport, Cheshire, cm (1782–84). [D]

Stoppani, Anthony, Leeds, Yorks., carver and gilder (1828–30). Listed at 4 Leadenhall St in 1828 and 37 Lady Lane in 1830, also as a weather glass, thermometer, barometer etc. manufacturer. [D]

Stopperton, John, 16 Croston St, Liverpool, cm (1829). [D]

Stordy, Thomas, Hungate, Pickering, Yorks., joiner and cm (1840). [D]

Storer, Anthony, parish of St Mary Woolnoth, London, upholder (1683). [Heal]

Storer, Joseph, Digbeth, Birmingham, chairmaker (1816–18). [D]

Storer, Joseph, Kingsley, Frodsham, Cheshire, chairmaker (1837). [D]

Storer, William, Derby(?), cm (1764). At Kedleston Hall, Derbs. there is a library table in mahogany fitted with forty-eight drawers, two reading desks and a cupboard completed by this craftsman on 17 December 1764. [*C. Life*, vol. CLXIII, no. 4205, p. 323]

Storey, Benjamin, St James St, Leeds, Yorks., cm (1822). [D]

Storey, Henry, Hungate, Bedale, Yorks., joiner and cm (1828). [D]

Storey, Matthew, Gateshead, Co. Durham, joiner and cm (1798). [D]

Storey, William, London St, Greenwich, London, cm (1826). [D]

Storey, William, 15 King St, Southwark, London, carver and gilder (1826). [D]

Storey, William, Lintz Green, Tanfield, Co. Durham, victualler, joiner and cm (1828). [D]

Storr, John, Mortlake, Surrey, u (1838–39). [D]

Storr, Paul, 23 Air St, Piccadilly, London, carver and gilder (1809). In partnership with Peter Bogaerts in 1809 when they took out insurance cover of £500 whch included £350 for stock, utensils and models in their workshop at 23 Air St and £150 for stock in a shop behind 22 Air St. [GL, Sun MS vol. 448, ref. 836376]

Storror, William, 59 French St, Southampton, Hants., u and cm (1839). [D]

Storrow, John, Appleby, Westmld, joiner and cm (1828). [D]

Story, James, 2 Snowfields, Bermondsey, London, chair and sofa maker (1839). [D]

Story, Ralph, High St, Tewkesbury, Glos., chairmaker (1825). Child bapt. in 1825. [PR (bapt.)]

Story, William, Newcastle, u (1774). App. to Edward Coates and free by servitude as an u, 5 July 1774. [Freemen rolls]

Stott, John, Yorkshire St, Rochdale, Lancs., cm (1798–1818). In Yorkshire St, 1814–18. [D]

Stout, John, North St, Gosport, Hants., cm (1830–39). Listed as a cm and u at 22 North St in 1830. [D]

Stout, M., 42 Well St, Oxford St, London, cm and chairmaker (1816–25). In 1819–25 also mahogany merchant. [D]

Stout, William, London, chairmaker (1723). In 1723 the Duke of Montrose paid Stout £10 7s for chairs. These were for the Duke's house at Shawfoy. [Scottish RO, GD 220/1236/11]

Stout, William, 147 Whitechapel Rd, London, cm (1808). [D]

Stovald, Sam., Guildford, Surrey, cm and turner (1832–35). At South St in 1832 but in 1835 living in Tunsgate. [D; poll bk]

Stove, George, Bristol, carver and gilder (1781). [Poll bk]

Stovell, George, 3 Lower Grosvenor St, London, u (1792–1829). Subscribed to Sheraton's *Drawing Book*, 1793 and included in the list of master cabinet makers in his *Cabinet Dictionary*, 1803. Upholsterer to the Prince of Wales, 1801–19. In October 1792 took out insurance cover of £600 of which half was for utensils and stock. Also insured other properties in London including 73 Lower Grosvenor St, 1808–22 which was probably his dwelling house, and others in the Hanover Sq. area. These were houses of some quality judging from the valuation placed on the household goods kept there of £300 to £600 each. He also owned a house in Quary St, Guildford which in 1804 was valued at £100 and was then in his own tenure. He also appeared on the Guildford poll in June 1818. The only known commission was in 1793 for Lord Howard of Audley End, Essex. This was for two mahogany cupboards made to order at £2 2s and a mahogany frame 'to hold a Survey of Your Lordship's Estates with lock, hinges & Sundry brasswork' £2 2s. [D; GL, Sun MS vol. 389, ref. 605988; vol. 431, ref. 767074; vol. 440, ref. 802659; vol. 445, ref. 816874; vol. 448, refs 832049, 839104; vol. 45., ref. 867630; vol. 493, ref. 993540; vol. 498, ref. 1001965; Guildford poll bk; Essex RO, D/DBy/A51/6]

Stovin, William, Fluttergate, Grimsby, Lincs., joiner and cm, machine maker and wiremaker (1826–35). [D]

Stow, John, Greenwich, London, cm, upholder, appraiser and auctioneer (1808–24). At Royal Hill, 1808–17 but in 1824 at London St. [D]

Stow, Jonathan, 10 John St, Birmingham, cm, carpenter and joiner (1767–70). [D]

Stow, William, London Rd, Greenwich, London, u, auctioneer, appraiser and undertaker (c.1822–39). In June 1834 claimed to have been in business for twelve years. If this was a correct statement he may not be the successor to John Stow who is shown in a trade directory of 1824 at London St. William Stow's lease expired c.1834 and extensive alterations were made to the premises to enlarge them. This resulted in the neglect of customers' orders for which he apologised in June 1834 when he announced the completion of the work. [D; *West Kent Advertiser*, 7 June 1834]

Stra(c)han, Francis, Manchester, cm (1829–34). At 28 Thomas St in 1829 and Cheetwood in 1834. [D]

Strachan, James, 8 Gerrard St, Soho, London, cm and u (1827–35). [D]

Strackles, John, Hull, Yorks., cm (1755). In 1755 took app. named Seaman. [S of G, app. index]

Strafford, William, Park St, Wakefield, Yorks., cm (1816). [D]

Strahan, Patrick, 'The King's Arms & Ball' by Fleet Ditch, London (1709–41). The combination of his name and his ability to attract Scottish clients suggest that he came to London from Scotland in his youth. He was already in the Fleet area by 1715 and both in that year and in 1717 was fined for declining parochial office in the parish of St Bride. His business was substantial and in February 1722 he took insurance cover for £1,000 on his goods and merchandise at the sign of 'The King's Arms and Ball' which was described as his dwelling house. He entered a partnership with James Strahan and both were declared bankrupt in January 1741. The partnership was already formed by November 1737 when a commission was undertaken for the Duke of Gordon. The earliest known commissions were for the Duke of Montrose. A large walnut desk and glass were supplied in 1709 for £3 16s and in 1714 a large walnut arched glass, eighteen fine matted chairs, two elbow chairs and a wainscot table. These latter items cost £14 12s. In the following year payment of £13 was received for a walnut arched desk and bookcase. A wainscot chest of drawers for which £1 1s was charged in 1726 was probably also for the Duke of Montrose. The order of 1714 was specified for the Duke's office in the Cockpit and was placed at the time that he was Secretary of State. Of the Duke of Gordon's orders, which cover the period from November 1737 to May 1740, several of the items were specified for the Duke's London house and all may have been destined for it. Furniture supplied in November and December 1737 included a walnut strong box at £3 10s, a wainscot desk at £1 8s and a clothes press on a 'frame' at £4 10s. The furniture supplied between December 1738 and May 1739 was mostly of mahogany and included a writing table at £4 10s and a large bookcase with glass doors at £12. An account submitted in April 1738 contains sums for porterage from Pall Mall and conveyance by cart to Wapping with the necessary wharfage possibly suggesting some transfer of furniture to Scotland. Between September 1739 and May 1740 three mahogany sea chests were provided in addition to a strong box. [GL, MS 6561, p. 4, Sun MS vol. 14, ref. 24988; *London Daily Post and General Advertiser*, 26 January 1741; Scottish RO, GD 220/6/1121/3, 1162/2, 1159/7, 1162/45, 1348/17; GD 44/51/465/3/66, 465/4/30, 475, 260, 465/1/36, 465/4/63]

Strahan, William, 3 Whittle St, Manchester, cm (1825). [D]

Straker, Jof., Ballast Hills, Newcastle, cm/carpenter (1778). [D]

Strange, James, Dartmouth, Devon, cm (1793). [D]

Strange, Matthew, High Wycombe, Bucks., chairmaker (b.c. 1802–41). Two sons and two daughters bapt. between 1827–37. Aged 39 at the time of the 1841 Census. [PR (bapt.)]

Strange, Nicholas, Tunbridge Wells, Kent, cm (1835). Son bapt. on 13 August 1835. [PR (bapt.)]

Strange, S. B., Bristol, French polisher (1837–40). Had a workshop at 10 Horse Fair, 1837–38 but from 1839–40 shown at 29 Milk St where the initials are given as S.D. [D]

Strangeway & Taylor, Pall Mall, London (1765). In 1765 supplied to Corsham Court, Wilts., a pair of shagreen and inlaid chests which are now displayed in the Gallery. In 1765 they were described as 'fine India Dressing boxes'. [V&A archives]

Strangeways, Christopher, London, cm (1793). Subscribed to Sheraton's *Drawing Book*, 1793.

Strangeways, James, 150 Whitechapel Rd, London, cm etc. (1808–11). [D]

Stransom, William, London St, Uxbridge, Middlx, cm and u (1839). The same directory also lists this maker as a furniture broker at Hillingdon End. These two addresses are possibly identical. [D] Probably:

Stransum, W., London Rd, Staines, Middlx, auctioneer, appraiser and u (1838). [D]

Strap, John, Liverpool, u (1837–39). At 4 Nash St with a shop at 136 Richmond Row in 1837 but in 1839 shown at 40 Richmond Row. [D]

Stratford, Daniel, 83 Tottenham Ct Rd, London, cm, u and furniture broker (1827). [D]

Stratford, George, Maldon, Essex, cm (1839). [D]

Stratford, Henry, High Wycombe, Bucks., chairmaker (1816). Daughter bapt. in 1816. [PR (bapt.)]

Stratford, John, Gloucester, cm and u (1830–39). Trading at Blackfriars in 1830 and Southgate St in 1839. [D]

Stratford, Samuel, Sherrard St, London, cm (1776). In 1776 insured his utensils and stock for £100. [GL, Sun MS vol. 246, p. 566]

Stratford, Thomas, London, upholder (1722–42). Son of John Stratford of Milton Post, Glos., Gent. App. to George Friend on 4 September 1722 and Ovebury Hale, freeman and member of the Drapers' Co., September 1722. Free of the Upholders' Co. by servitude, 7 April 1742. [GL, Upholders' Co. records]

Stratford, Thomas, St John's Bridge, Bristol, bedstead and chair maker (1823–39). [D]

Stratham, Benjamin, 123 Chapel St, Salford, Lancs., cm (1839). [D]

Stratton, John & Co., 213 Tottenham Ct Rd, London, cm, chairmakers and u (1820–25). In one directory of 1820 the business was listed as Stratton & Waddingham. [D]

Strawbridge, Thomas, London(?), u and chairmaker (1691). Two bills survive in the Stoneleigh Abbey archives, one dated 4 April 1691 and the other 30 August 1691. Both concern goods supplied to Theophilus Leigh by this maker. The earlier bill totals £5 1s but the latter was for a number of very substantial commissions and amounted to £113 15s 10d. In the main the items listed were upholstery materials and twelve days labour but some finished furniture was also included. The most interesting item was a charge of £7 10s for four back stools and two elbow chairs 'black varnished' and upholstered in crimson damask. In a sale of contents from Stoneleigh Abbey in October 1981 a set of four japanned side chairs were offered for sale. These had contemporary polychrome leather coverings but might possibly be the set supplied by Strawbridge. A further set of six chairs of William and Mary period *en suite* with the other but in crimson damask are also possibly by this maker. [Shakespeare Birthplace Trust, Leigh receipts, DR 18/5/1030; Christie's, 15–16 October 1981, lots 100–01]

Strawder, Charles Ward, York, looking-glass maker (1809). App. to David Doeg of York, looking-glass maker 28 May 1802. Strawder was said to be from Sheffield, Yorks. Free of York in 1809. [App. bk; freemen roll]

Streat, William, New Canal St, Salisbury, Wilts, carver and gilder (1830). [D]

Streater, John Sonds, Canterbury, Kent, u (1752). In 1752 took app. named Obree. [S of G, app. index]

Stredder (or Stridder), Edward, High St, Royston, Herts., cm and u (1826–39). Trading also as a confectioner in 1838. [D]

Streemson, John, Gainsborough, Lincs., chairmaker (1720). In 1720 took app. named Tee. [S of G, app. index]

Street, George, West St, Exeter, Devon, cm (1837). Daughter Louisa bapt. at St Mary Major on 3 September 1837. [PR (bapt.)]

Street, Henry, St Sidwell St, Exeter, Devon, cm (1820–25). Children bapt. at St Sidwell's Church, 1820–23. [D; PR (bapt.)]

Street, John, Colyton, Devon, cm (1838). [D]

Street, Joseph, St Nicholas, Colchester, Essex, u (d.1716). Probate granted on will, 1716. [*Wills at Chelmsford*]

Street, Joseph, Southampton, Hants., chairmaker (1789–98). [D; Hants. RO, SC/3/927A]

Street, Richard, Bedford St, Covent Gdn, London, carver, gilder and print seller (1784). Trade card in Dept of Prints, GL. [Westminster poll bk]

Street, Samuel, Canterbury, Kent, cm (1818–30). At Castle St in June 1818 but in 1826 living in the parish of St Mildred. [Poll bks]

Streeter, Charles, High St, Croydon, Surrey, cm (1826–32). Listed also as a chairmaker in 1826 and u in 1832. [D]

Streeter, Sarah, Canterbury, Kent, upholder (1745). In 1745 took app. named Mitchell. [S of G, app. index]

Streeting, Thomas, Northgate, Canterbury, Kent, cm (1826). [Poll bk]

Stretch, Joseph, 3 Ridgefield, Manchester, u (1825). [D]

Stretch & Rainford, 63 Lord St, Liverpool, cm and u (1834–37). Joseph Stretch, one of the partners lived at Kirkdale Rd, Liverpool. The firm claimed to manufacture cabinet furniture and could also offer from stock 'CARPETING consisting of Turkey, Wilton, Brussels, Kidderminster and Venetian as also their stock of PAPER HANGINGS, being regularly supplied from the most respectable Manufacturers'. [D]

Stretton, John, Chester, cm (1818–26). Free 12 May 1818. At George St in 1818, George's Yd in 1819 and Princes St in 1826. [Poll bk]

Stretton, John, Eastbourne, Sussex, cm (1826). [D]

Stretton, Samuel, Fazeley, Tamworth, Staffs., cm and u (1822). [D]

Stribling, William, High St, Barnstaple, Devon, cm and u (1806–40). Also a publican in 1806. His brother Charles Stribling, a schoolmaster, died in July 1840. [D; *Exeter Flying Post*, 23 October 1806, 16 July 1840]

Strickett, George, Pilgrim St, Newcastle, cm/carpenter (1778). [D]

Strickland & Jenkins, 75 Long Acre, London, cm and u (1777–93). Successors to John Cobb. Strickland was the nephew of William Vile and had probably been associated with the business of Vile and Cobb and later with John Cobb after his partner's death in September 1767. A mahogany window seat is known with the signature in ink on the inside of the seat rail 'Strickland September 1st 1763'. Strickland is also named in connection with the supply to Strawberry Hill in 1773 of a plumed bed hung with Aubusson tapestry and a set of white and gold elbow chairs from Paris. On 16 April 1763 John Cobb paid Sally Strickland £64 but no subsequent payments are recorded in Cobb's bank account. John Jenkins was Cobb's foreman. Strickland & Jenkins in addition to their work as cm and u were undertakers and appraisers. Their only known commissions were for Alexander Wedderburn. A payment of £33 16s was made in 1777 to the partners. This was a year before Cobb's death. A further payment of £36 5s was made in 1787. From 1794 John Jenkins traded on his own behalf at 75 Long Acre, his partner having probably retired or died. He is last recorded in 1808. [D; Heal; V&A archives; Banks Coll., BM; *C. Life*, 10 June 1954, p. 1896; Scottish RO, GD/64/Box 20/177/2]

Strickley, John, Blackheath Hill, Lewisham, London, cm and u (1832). [D]

Strife, Joachim, Noel St, Westminster, London, picture frame maker (1749). [Poll bk]

Striling, W., Tiverton, Devon, cm (1828). On 5 August 1828 his daughter Elizabeth married a W. Beck, draper. [*The Alfred*, 5 August 1828]

Stringer, Gabriel, Bristol, u (1721–22). In 1721 took app. named Reynolds. [S of G, app. index; poll bk]

Stringer, Gabriel, Bristol, carver and gilder (1792–1816). In 1792 at Christmas St, 1793–95 at St John's Bridge, and 1799 onwards at St Augustine's back, the number being 26 from 1805. From 1809–15 the business traded as Stringer & Browne but in 1816 Gabriel Stringer was the sole proprietor once again. The business was being carried on in 1817 from this address by Nancy Stringer. [D]

Stringer, J. A., 8 Leather Lane, Holborn, London, carver and gilder (1835–37). [D]

Stringer, John, Chester, u (1749–97). At St Peter's Churchyard 1781–89 but in 1771–84 living at Watergate St. John Stringer was app. to Harwar Harvey, u on 24 August 1749 for eight years. He was free 1 April 1755. Subsequently he took as apps John Davenport in 1764 and Thomas Stringer Latchford who was declared free 1797. [D; poll bks; app. bk; freemen rolls]

Stringer, John, 45 Lever St, Manchester, cm (1804). [D]

Stringer, Joseph, Scotch Common, Sandbach, Cheshire, cm and machine maker (1828–34). Also trading in Sandbach at this period was Stephen Stringer of Wheelock Saw Mills, joiner and sawyer of veneers by circular and other saws. [D]

Stringer, Nancy, 26 St Augustine's back, Bristol, carver and gilder (1817). Successor to Gabriel Stringer at this address and succeeded by Thomas Spurrier. [D]

Stringer, Stephen, Ilminster, Som., upholder (1763). Bankruptcy announced, *Gents Mag.*, January 1763.

Stringer, Stephen, Bristol, carver (1774–81). Living in the parish of St Augustine in 1774 and the parish of St John in 1781. [Poll bks]

Strode, Byslet, 16 Cheapside, Liverpool, u (1781–84). [D]

Strode, Edward & John, London, cm (1715–53). Edward Strode was living in the parish of St Bride, Fleet St by 1715 when his address was given as Ditch Side. In that year he served as Scavenger and in 1716 as Questman and was fined for declining parochial office in 1717 and 1723. In 1720 he was trading at 'The Queen's Head & Ball', Fleet Ditch. His trade card states that he made and sold 'all Sorts of Joyners and Cabinetmakers Goods, viz Cabinets, Scrutores, Desks, and Book-Cases; Chests of Drawers, Cabinet-Beds, Union-Shutes, Glasses, Sconces'. A receipt of this year was, however, signed by John Strode and an insurance policy taken out in July 1722 was in his name also. This provided cover for goods of £500. A John Stroud jnr is recorded in the parish records of the Church of St Bride from 1725, in which year he served as Constable. He also held the position of Collector for the Poor in 1738 and Scavenger in 1745. Edward's surname was also rendered as Stroud in the parish records. John jnr's address was given as Ditch Side. This seems to indicate that the two were closely related. It is, however, not clear whether the John Stroud jnr active from 1725 is identical with the John Strode recorded in 1720 and 1722. Certainly John Strode did not take over the business this early for in April 1727 insurance documents were issued in the name of Edward for a total cover of £1,000 of which £500 was for utensils and stock. John jnr traded until 1753, the year of his death, when the address was rendered as 'The Queen's Head & Sun, in the middle of Fleet Market'. In this year his household furniture and stock in trade was auctioned for the benefit of his widow and children. Two customers of this business are known. In 1720 goods to the value of £1 9s were supplied to Paul Foley of the Temple and Little Ormond St, London and Newport House, Almeley, Herefs. In 1728 a chest of drawers and twelve chairs were supplied to Holkham Hall, Norfolk at a cost of £2 8s. A further chest of drawers supplied in the same year was charged at £1 10s. [Herefs. RO, Foley MS, F/AIII/55; GL, Sun MS vol. 14, ref. 25864; vol. 23, ref. 41326; MS 6561, pp. 5, 14; BM, Burney MS, 4266; V&A archives]

Strong, Francis, Swallow St, Westminster, London, cm (1749). [Poll bk]

Strong, John, Carlisle, Cumb., chairmaker (1829–34). In Blackfriars St in 1829 and Finkle St in 1834. [D]

Strong, William, Brisco, Carlisle, Cumb., joiner/cm (1828–34). [D]

Stroubridge, Nicholas, Russell St, Covent Gdn, London, upholder (1709–16). In August 1712 took out insurance cover of £500 on his house. Supplied 37 yards of light blue calamanco to Elizabeth, Duchess of Bedford in 1709 at a cost of £5 11s. In 1716 supplied a looking glass costing £1 15s to the household of the Duke of Bedford. [GL, Hand in Hand MS vol. 10, ref. 23670; Bedford Office London]

Stroud, John, 72 Kirkgate, Leeds, Yorks., carver, gilder and barometer maker (1837). [D]

Stroud, Joseph, Kilwardby St, Ashby-de-la-Zouch, Leics., turner and chairmaker (1822–29). [D]

Strouts, Thomas, London, upholder (1711). Free of the Upholders' Co. 6 June 1711. [GL, Upholders' Co. records]

Strouts, Thomas, Noce Lane, Canterbury, Kent, u (1723–49). In April 1723 took out insurance cover of £250 on his house, outhouses and warehouse. In 1749 took app. named Varham. [GL, Sun MS vol. 15, ref. 28418; S of G, app. index]

Strudwick, John, Bridge St, Chertsey, Surrey, cm etc. (1822–26). [D]

Strudwicke, Henry, Guildford, Surrey, u (1790–96). Shown in Trinity parish in June 1790 and the High St in May 1796. [Poll bks]

Strudwicke, Henry, 26 Mount St, Lambeth, London, u and estate agent (1820). [D]

Strugnell, Charles E., 63 West St, Smithfield, London, fancy cm, u, portable desk and cabinet case maker (1835–39). [D]

Strugnell, Charles, 145 Long Lane, Southwark, London, cm and u (1839). [D]

Strugnell, James, 14 Cross St, Hatton Gdn, London, cm, u, writing and dressing case, portable desk and cabinet case maker (1829–39). [D]

Strugnell, Joseph, Devizes, Wilts., cm (1793). [D]

Strutt, Benjamin, 119 Aldersgate St, London, portable desk, dressing case, work box and cabinet case maker (1839). [D]

Strutt, Joseph, 3 Newgate St, London, looking-glass manufacturer (1774–82). [D]

Strutton, —, 17 Hollen St, Soho, London, cm (1809). [D]

Stuart, Alexander, 33 Charles St, Hampstead Rd, London, cm (1793–1808). Subscribed to Sheraton's *Drawing Book*, 1793. [D]

Stuart, Charles, Norris St, Westminster, London, cm (1749). [Poll bk]

Stuart, Charles, Salisbury, Wilts., cm (1753). In 1753 took app. named Harwood. [S of G, app. index]

Stuart, Francis, Coventry Ct, Westminster, London, cm (1749). [Poll bk]

Stuart, George, London, carver and gilder (1816–19). Undertook carving and gilding for the Duke of Norfolk at Norfolk House, London, 1816–19. [Arundel Castle records, MD 662]

Stuart, Henry, London, cm, u etc. (1771). In February to May 1771 undertook a substantial commission for Sir Gilbert Heathcote. Some of this work was for his house at North End, Fulham and included dying bed and window curtains, supplying cushions for 'bamboo elbow chairs' and a mahogany card table 'with Marlborough legs'. New bed cornices were produced and a man despatched to Grosvenor Sq. to pack up six Bamboo chairs there. Other work involved hanging a room 'with India Taffity Paper, cutting out Flowers &c and making out and filling up the Pattern' which took two men eight days to complete. Wilton carpets were supplied for Normanton Park. The total cost of the commission came to £155 11s 10¼d. The account was settled on 8 February 1772 but Stuart had recently died and the receipt was given by Samuel Severn on the behalf of 'Mrs Bridget Catherine Stuart administratrix'. Stuart had been in partnership with Samuel Severn from 1769 and the partnership may still have been active at the time of this commission but the account is in Stuart's name only and the payment appears to have been accepted in the name of his wife which may equally suggest that the partnership was terminated by c.1770. [Lincoln RO, ANC8/12, 2 ANC 12/D/28–29] See Samuel Severn.

Stuart, John, Pennington's Yd, Highgate, Kendal, Westmld, chairmaker, u and turner (1828–34). [D]

Stuart, Matthew, Bell St, North Shields, Northumb., cm (1828). [D]

Stubberfield, John, Gabriel's Hill, Maidstone, Kent, chairmaker (1830–39). Freeman of Rochester, Kent. [D; Rochester poll bk; Maidstone poll bk]

Stubbin(g)s, Francis, Moorgate, Retford, Notts., chairmaker (1822–35). Also listed at Church St, 1828. [D]

Stubbins, Thomas, Moorgate, Retford, Notts., chairmaker and turner (1832). [D]

Stubbs, Daniel, Bawtry, Yorks., cm (1714–23). In 1714 took app. named Turner and in 1723, Goodwin. [S of G, app. index]

Stubbs, George & Co., 64 Gt Portland St, London, picture and looking-glass frame makers (1837–39). One directory of 1839 described the business as a cm and u. [D]

Stubbs, James, Sowerby Bridge, Yorks., joiner and cm (1830). [D]

Stubbs, John, City Rd and Old St, London, chairmaker (1779–1814). Although trade cards list both the City Rd and Old St addresses, directory entries refer to the Old St premises only. These were initially at 3 Brick Lane, Old St but from 1800 the address became 20 Old St. From 1812 the business traded as Stubbs & Smith. Their trade card, which has an identical frame and engravings to that of Lock & Foulger and William Webb, states that John Stubbs could supply 'all sorts of Yew Tree Gothic & Windsor Chairs Alcoves & Rural Seats Gardening Machines Dyed Chairs &c.'. He was included in the list of master cabinet makers in Sheraton's *Cabinet Dictionary*, 1803. In 1782 he took out insurance cover of £300 of which £100 was for utensils and stock. In January 1812 insurance cover at 21 Old St was taken out in the name of William Stubbs at £700 for the dwelling house and offices (£400) and household goods only. William, described as a chairmaker, may have been the son of John, living next door and active in the business. [D; Banks Coll., BM; GL, Sun MS vol. 303, p. 251; vol. 455, ref. 864859]

Stubbs, John S., Broker Row, Moorfields, London, u (1814–15). [D]

Stubbs, John, Hunslet, Leeds, Yorks., cm (1817–30). [D]

Stubbs, John, 4 St Cuthbert's Lane, Carlisle, Cumb., cm/joiner (1834). [D]

Stubbs, Joseph, Otley, Yorks., joiner/cm (1834). [D]

Stubbs, Richard, 11 Archer St in Windmill St, Haymarket, London, cm and u (1777). In 1777 took out insurance cover of £200 which included £30 for utensils and stock. This may represent an early stage in his business career. Subsequently he was to issue a trade card with the same address which might

suggest a business of somewhat more substantial proportions. [GL, Sun MS vol. 254, p. 469]

Stubbs, Samuel, Foregate St, Chester, cm (1812). Free 5 October 1812. [Freemen rolls; poll bk]

Stubbs, William, Market St, Worthing, Sussex, cm and u (1823). [D]

Stubs, —, St James's St, Brighton, Sussex, u (1805). [D]

Stuck, Matthew, Coggleshall, Essex, cm (1823–26). [D]

Studholm, R., Bridge St, Caldewgate, Carlisle, Cumb., joiner and cm (1810). [D]

Studholme, John Carlisle, Cumb., joiner/cm (1828–34). At Caldewgate in 1828–29 but in 1834 the address was given as 24 Bridge St. This may, however, be the same location. Probably the successor of R. Studholm who was at this address in 1810. [D]

Studwell, W., Stamford, Lincs., turner, French polisher, cm, u and undertaker (c.1830–40). In 1864 the business was described as W. Studwell & Son and was trading from an address in St John St. W. Studwell claimed to have had thirty four years experience 'as a Practical Workman'. [*Johnson's Household Almanac*, 1864]

Sturdee, William Henry, Broomfield Pl., Deptford, London, carver and gilder (1839). [D]

Sturdy, George, Bell's Ct, Pilgrim St, Newcastle, carver and gilder (1824–38). [D]

Sturdy, John, Southampton, Hants., cm and u (1805–39). At St Michael's Sq. in 1805; 52 French St in 1830; Lansdown Hill, 1834–39, no. 1 in 1839; and Commercial Rd, also in 1839. [D]

Sturdy, Stephen jnr, Middleham, Yorks., joiner/cm (1834). [D]

Sturdy, Thomas, Hungate, Pickering, Yorks., joiner and cm (1840). [D]

Sturge, Harry, 16 Marlborough St, Bristol, cm (1775). [D]

Sturges & Noake, Cheap St, Sherborne, Dorset, cm (1823). [D]

Sturgis, John, 'The Rose & Crown', next door to 'The White Rose Inn', Fleet Mkt, London, chairmaker (c.1750). His trade card states that he was 'apprentice to the late Mr. Williams'. He offered 'All Sorts of Leather & Matted Chairs'. [Heal]

Sturney, James, Weymouth, Dorset, cm and u (1803–13). In 1803 subscribed to Sheraton's *Cabinet Dictionary*. Bankruptcy announced, *Exeter Flying Post*, 19 August 1813.

Sturt, Andrew Valentine, London, upholder (1772–79). Son of Andrew Sturt of the Minories, a servant of the East India Co. App. to Joseph Grannar on 1 July 1772 and free of the Upholders' Co. by servitude, 6 October 1779 at which date he was at Mr William's, upholder, Pavement, Moorfields. [GL, Upholders' Co. records]

Sturton, Arnold, against 'The Red Lion', Holborn, London, upholder (1719). [GL, Sun MS vol. 9, p. 148]

Stuttard, James, 12 Basing Lane, London, cm and u (1839). [D]

Styfield, Thomas, 35 Old Compton St, Soho, London, carver and glass grinder (1790–93). [D]

Style, Edward, London, carver (1783–1802). In 1783 at 116 Fore St, Cripplegate where he took out insurance cover of £100 including £10 for utensils and stock. In 1802 at 16 Old Bethlem where the insurance cover was the same in total. [GL, Sun MS vol. 317, p. 191; vol. 424, ref. 738336]

Style, Thomas, Broad Church Alley, Plymouth, Devon, fancy furniture painter (1822). [D]

Styles, James, 83½ High St, Ramsgate, Kent, cm (1838). [D]

Styles, Thomas, 61 Lower Sloane St, London, cm and u (1835–39). [D]

Styring, George, 22 Leecroft, Sheffield, Yorks. cm (1821–28). Succeeded by Richard W. Styring. [D]

Styring, James, 2 Change Alley, Sheffield, Yorks., u (1833–37). Successor to Robert Styring at this address. [D]

Styring, Richard W. (or William), 13 Lee Croft, Sheffield,

Yorks., cm, broker and paperhanger (1837). Successor to George Styring. [D]

Styring, Robert, Change Alley, Sheffield, Yorks., cm and u (1814–28). At 26 Change Alley in 1817 but in 1825 the number was 2. Initially traded as a paperhanger, u, appraiser and auctioneer but in 1828 listed as a cm and u. Was succeeded at this address by James Styring. [D]

Such, John, 169 Kent St, Southwark, London, chairmaker (1820). [D]

Sudbury, J., High St, Loughborough, Leics., cm (1835). [D]

Sudbury, James, Cockey Lane, Norwich, upholder and cm (1783–1812). The number in Cockey Lane was 5, 1784–1810, but one directory of 1801 indicates 4. James Sudbury lived in the parish of St Peter Mancroft 1797–1812 but a poll bk of 1807 indicates parish of St Stephen. From 1801 the business traded as James Sudbury & Son. James Sudbury took as app. James Colby who was free 5 May 1799. One of his customers was Parson James Woodforde who records several transactions in his *Diary.* On 4 April he took delivery of a sideboard and a mahogany cellaret which had been brought from Norwich by two of Sudbury's workmen, Abraham Seely and Isaac Warren. Woodforde paid £4 4s 6d for these goods on a visit to Norwich on 24 May. Earlier, on 14 May of this year, Woodforde had also paid this maker £5 7s. Sudbury called on Woodforde on 31 May to discuss an order for dining tables and then went on to Weston House 'to look at their furniture'. The new mahogany dining tables were delivered on 10 December and consisted of a centre table and two half round ones that could be added at either end. The cost was £7 7s but an allowance of £2 18s was given on three tables taken in part exchange. On 16 September 1796 Sudbury was putting up window curtains and on 24 April 1797 he called again hoping for orders which did not materialise. [D; poll bks; freemen reg.]

Sudbury, John, Swaffham, Norfolk, upholder and cm (1784). [D]

Sudbury, John, High St, Loughborough, Leics., cm (1835). [D]

Sudbury, William Shipman jnr, Bury St Edmunds, Suffolk, cm (1755). In 1755 took app. named Archer. [S of G, app. index]

Sudbury, William, Swaffham, Norfolk, u (d.1825). Will proved at Norwich in 1825. [Norfolk Record Soc., index of wills]

Suddert, John, Liverpool, cm (1752). In 1752 took app. named Fisher. [S of G, app. index]

Suddorth, John, Liverpool, cm (1760). Took as app. John Highfield who was free 1760. [Freemen bk]

Sudell, Margaret, 21 Everton Gdns, Preston, Lancs., cm (1825). [D]

Sudell, Thomas, 6 Churchgate, Preston, Lancs., carpenter and cm (1722. d. by 1762). Had three sons, Thomas, John and James. In 1722 Thomas jnr was stated to be a carpenter and in 1742 a joiner. Sudell was dead by 1762 in which year the death of his son James, an attorney at law of Liverpool was announced. [Freemen rolls; rate bk]

Sudlow, James, Liverpool, u (1818–37). At 4 Meadow St in 1818 and 17 Mount Pl. in 1837. [D]

Sudlow, John, 7 Taylor St, Manchester, cm (1804–17). [D]

Sudlow, T., Newcastle-under-Lyme, Staffs., u (1782). In July 1782 advertised for an u and also an app. 'with or without a premium'. [*Chester Chronicle,* 12 July 1782]

Sudron, James, West Row, Stockton, Co. Durham, cm (1832). [D]

Suffolk, William, 11 Princes St, Leicester Fields, London, cm and upholder (1778–81). In 1778 insured his utensils and stock for £200 but by 1781 the total insurance cover was £2,000 of which £500 was for utensils and stock. [GL, Sun MS vol. 266, p. 588; vol. 294, p. 148]

Sugden, Abraham, Haworth, Yorks., cm (1822–30). [D]

Sugden, Absalom, Haworth, Yorks., cm (1837). [D]

Sugden, George, Lower St, Deal, Kent, u (1832–39). At 14 Lower St in 1838 but in the following year the number was 9. Freeman of Sandwich, Kent. [D; Sandwich poll bk]

Sugden, Joseph, London, cm (1801–23). At 46 Clipstone St in January 1801 where he took out insurance cover of £150. In December 1823 at 7 Harcourt St, Lisson Green where he took out insurance cover of £1,000. Of this £200 was for a workshop behind his house, £100 for utensils and stock in it and the balance for his new dwelling house and household goods. [GL, Sun MS vol. 419, ref. 712757; vol. 499, ref. 1010786]

Sugden, William, Park Lane, Keighley, Yorks., joiner/cm (1837). [D]

Sugdon, James, Tollgavel, Beverley, Yorks., cm (1831–34). [D]

Sugg, James, Exeter, Devon, cm (1816–38). At Southernhay Lane in August 1822 when his daughter Mary Ann was bapt. at Holy Trinity Church. Traded at Goldsmith St, 1831–34. In February 1831 this was described as a 'chair, Sofa and Cabinet Manufactory opposite the New Market'. Amongst the stock was a 'handsome French pattern BAZAAR TABLE'. In 1838 trading in Lower North St. [D; *Exeter Flying Post,* 24 February 1831]

Suggitt, David, 84 Newborough St, Scarborough, Yorks., cm, u and paperhanger (1834). [D]

Suggle, William, 440 Strand, London, carver and gilder (1815). [D]

Sully, George, 1 Kenton St, Brunswick Sq., London, cm, chair and sofa maker (1839). [D]

Sumeran, Bartholomew, 27 Lisle St, Leicester Sq., London, cm, carver, gilder and looking-glass manufacturer (1826–39). In 1826 described as a cm, in 1835–39 as a looking-glass manufacturer and in 1837 also as a carver and gilder. [D]

Summerland, Thomas, Deritend, Birmingham, joiner and cm (1780). [D]

Summer, John, Liverpool, carver (1806–31). Free 1806. Took as apps George Millne (1813–22), William Quirke (1814–22), William Smith (1818–30), Thomas Bisett (1819–30) and Thomas Roberts (1821–31). [Freemen bk]

Summer (or Sumner), John, Lane End, Staffs., cm and u (1828–35). Listed at Green Dock in 1828 and Flint St, 1834–35. [D]

Summer, John, Liverpool, cm (1839). Born 14 October 1818. Son of Robert Summer, cm and free by patrimony in 1839. [Freemen bk]

Summerfield, John, Bridge St, Worcester, u (1818–40). Free 1818. Recorded at 15 Bridge St, 1828–37. [D; freemen rolls]

Summerfield, Stephen, Chapel St, Cheadle, Staffs., chairmaker, turner and basket maker (1834–35). [D]

Summers, —, London, cm (1793). Subscribed to Sheraton's *Drawing Book,* 1793.

Summers, Claus Herman, Neale's Passage, Earl St, London, cm (1780). In 1780 took out insurance cover of £200 of which £50 was for utensils and goods. [GL, Sun MS vol. 282, p. 286]

Summers, George, Market Pl., Maidenhead, Berks., cm and u (1840). [D]

Summers, I., 13 Chenies St, Bedford Sq., London, carver and gilder (1835). [D]

Summers, J. H., North St, Bishop's Stortford, Herts., auctioneer, u, ironmonger and Agent to the Sun Assurance (1838). [D] Probably:

Summers, James, Hillatt, Bishop's Stortford, Herts., u (1832). [D]

Summers, James, Cambridge, u and cm (1830–39). At Wheeler St, 1830–35 and Bridge St in 1839. [D; poll bks]

Summers, John, Chester, carver and gilder (1787–d.1834). At Nine Houses in 1787, City Walls, 1789–92, and from

1814–16 at Weaver's Lane. Died on 7 February 1823 aged 82. [D; *Liverpool Mercury*, 7 February 1834]

Summers, John, Liverpool, carver (1809–34). Married in December 1809 at St Nicholas's Church Miss Margaret Baynes of Liverpool. In 1827 trading at 13 Basnett St and in 1834 at 18 Greek St. [D; *Liverpool Courier*, 13 December 1809]

Summers, John, 21 King St, Soho, London, chair and sofa maker (1835). [D]

Summers, Ralph, Liverpool, cm (1812–24). Free 7 October 1812 and then living at Baptist St. In 1824 trading from 35 Lace St. [D]

Summers, Robert, Liverpool, cm (1818–37). App. to William Harvey 1810 and petitioned for his freedom 1818. Trading at 6 Cavendish St in 1818 and 1 Northampton St in 1837. [D; freemen bk]

Summers, Thomas, Bridge St, Belper, Derbs., joiner and cm (1834). [D] Possibly Thomas Sumner of Belper.

Summers, William, parish of St James, Bristol, picture frame maker and gilder (1734–39). [Poll bks]

Summers, William, Tottenham Ct Rd, London, bedstead manufacturer, u and cm (1816–39). At 253 Tottenham Ct Rd, 1816–19 but from 1820–29 the number was 153. In 1829 both 152 and 153 are listed. In 1835 the number was 149 and from 1837–39, 2 Tottenham Pl., Tottenham Ct Rd. The trade description varies to some degree from directory to directory. From 1816–25 bedsteads and bedding appear to have been the main items of manufacture and trade. Summers is listed as an u, 1826–37, a cm in 1835 and a furniture broker in 1839. [D]

Summerscale, Thomas, Wakefield, Yorks., cm (1773–98). In 1773 supplied to Kirklees Hall, Yorks. a wainscot bookcase at £8 10s and six splat back chairs at £1 19s. In the next year silk fabric and a bed were among the items totalling £12 14s which were supplied. [D: Huddersfield RO, Kirklees papers]

Summerskill, Charles, Rock St, Bury, Lancs., chairmaker (1834). [D]

Sumner, Daniel, Salford, Lancs. and Manchester, cm (1808–17). In 1808 near Islington St, Salford but from 1813–17 at 4 Silver St, Hulme, Manchester. [D]

Sumner, John, Liverpool, carver (1806–39). Free 31 October 1806. Trading at 29 Crosshall St as a carver and shopkeeper in 1813. In 1816 at 30 Crosshall St, in 1818 at 22 Haymarket and thereafter in Basnett St. The number in Basnett St was 17 in 1824 and 13, 1827–37. In 1834 he was described as a carver, gilder and furniture broker. In 1839 at 23 Basnett St and 15 Gt George St. [D; freemen reg.]

Sumner, Robert, Staines, Middlx, upholder (1719–28). In April 1719 insured goods and merchandise in his dwelling house and in July 1728 houses, brewhouses, stables for £500. [GL, Sun MS vol. 9, p. 182; vol. 26, p. 257]

Sumner, Robert, Windsor, Berks., u (1726–27). Free 18 January 1726/27 on payment of a fine of £8 8s. [Second hall bk of the borough of Windsor]

Sumner, Thomas, Belper, Derbs., cm (1822). [D] Possibly Thomas Summers of Belper.

Sumner, Thomas, Liverpool, carver and gilder (1835–39). At 32 Gt Richmond St in 1835, 158 Islington in 1837 and 4 Islington in 1839. [D]

Sumners, John, Chester, carver and gilder (d.1834). Died on 4 February 1834 at his son's residence, Mount Pleasant, aged 82. He was described as being 'formerly of this city'. [*Chester Courant*, 11 February 1834]

Sumners, John, Liverpool, cm (1839). Free 21 July 1839. [Freemen reg.]

Sumners, Robert, Liverpool, cm (1818–39). Free 11 June 1818. In 1839 trading at 1 Southampton St but formerly at Adelaide St, Blair St and 7 Devonshire St. [D; freemen reg.]

Sumners (or Summers) & Sworder, North St, Bishop's Stortford, Herts., cm and u (1839). [D]

Sunderland, George, Gilbert St, Bloomsbury, London, cm (1818). In 1818 took an app. through the Grinsell's Charity. [Westminster Ref. Lib., MS E3559]

Sunley, William, Regent's Ct, Lower Union St, Hull, Yorks., cm (1839). [D] Probably the William Sunley who was app. in April 1814 to John Dickon of Hull as a cm and chairmaker. [App. reg.]

Sunman, Richard, Savile St, Malton, Yorks., joiner, cm and appraiser (1840). [D]

Surman, Jeremiah, London, cm and furniture broker (1729–35). At Soho Sq., St Anne's where he maintained show and salerooms. In 1734 at York St, Covent Gdn. Bankruptcy announced, *London Gazette*, 7 May 1735. It is debatable whether he actually made furniture. He appears to have held stocks of furniture and also conducted auction sales. In July 1733 he sold by auction the stock of Francis Croxford, chair and cabinet maker. Two receipted bills in the Strafford papers in the BM refer to the supply of a mahogany basin stand on 13 January 1731 for £1 1s and a walnut table on 3 February 1731/32 at £1. Amongst the Holkham Hall, Norfolk accounts is a reference to the supply in 1730 of '2 codrell tables & 2 fire screens' at a cost of £6 12s by 'Surman'. [Heal; *Conn.*, February 1933, pp. 89–94, June 1933, pp. 375–76; V&A archives]

Surrey, John, 32 Garden Row, London Rd, London, cm etc. (1811–12). [D]

Surridge, William, London, upholder (1772–86). Son of James Surridge. Free of the Upholders' Co. by redemption, 7 October 1772 and at 54 Fetter Lane, 1778–86. [GL, Upholders' Co. records]

Sussex, George, 5 Bridgwater Gdns, near Bridgwater Sq., London, chairmaker (1774). In November 1774 took out insurance cover of £400. Of this total £190 was for utensils in his workshops in Cupers Ct, Golden Lane and timber, and a further £190 for utensils and stock in yards and a shed adjoining. [GL, Sun MS vol. 235, ref. 346552]

Sutcliffe, James, Todmorden, Yorks., joiner/cm (1830–37). At Millwood, Todmorden in 1830 and at Lobb Mill, Stansfield township and Salford, Todmorden in 1837. [D]

Sutcliffe, William, Burnley, Lancs., cm, chairmaker, turner and u (1824–40). Shown in one directory of 1824 at New Road End and in another at 7 Market St. At 13 St James St, 1828–34 but in 1838 the number was 12. In 1835 when a 'town committee' was formed from the twenty leading tradesmen in the town William Sutcliffe was included. [D; Bennett, *History of Burnley*, vol. 3] See Sutcliffe & Hartley.

Sutcliffe, William, Heptonstall, Yorks., joiner/cm (1834). [D]

Sutcliffe & Hartley, St James's St, Burnley, Lancs., cm and chairmakers (1822). [D] See William Sutcliffe of Burnley.

Sutheran, George, Smeaton St, Hull, Yorks., cm (1838). [D]

Sutherland, Alexander, Plymouth, Devon, cm (1822–38). At Frankfort St in 1822 and 1838 and George St in 1830 and 1836. [D]

Sutherland, John, Petergate, York, u (1818). [D]

Sutton, C., 15 Surrey Rd, Blackfriars Rd, London, carver and gilder (1808). [D]

Sutton, Charles, 22 Mint St, Southwark, London, bedstead maker (1839). [D]

Sutton, Daniel, Salford, Lancs., cm (1794–1811). At Brown St, 1794–97 and 135 Chapel St, 1800–11. [D]

Sutton, Elizabeth, 135 Chapel St, Salford, Lancs., cm (1808). [D]

Sutton, Henry, 17 Skinner St, Clerkenwell, London, carver and gilder (1835–39). [D]

Sutton, James, 4 Crown St, Preston, Lancs., cm (1818–40).

Trading at Crown St in 1818. Freeman of Preston and had three sons who are all listed on the freemen rolls in 1822 and 1842. [D; freemen rolls]

Sutton, Jehu, Leicester, joiner, turner and cm (1720). Free 1720. Took many apps, including John Brown, to learn the art of silvering glass. [Freemen rolls; app. regs]

Sutton, John, London, upholder (1733–43). Son of John Sutton of Shadwell, London, ballastman. App. to Jonathan Fawconer on 18 February 1733 and free of the Upholders' Co. by servitude, 4 October 1743. [GL, Upholders' Co. records]

Sutton, John, Round Ct, Strand, London, carver (1757). In June 1757 advertised as a fugitive for debt. Described as late of Warwick. [*London Gazette*, 14–17 June 1757]

Sutton, John, Wednesbury, Staffs., cm (1834). [D]

Sutton, Leigh, Mersey St, Liverpool, cm (1757–d.1773). App. to Josiah Baxendale and petitioned for freedom in 1757. Free 12 March 1761. Traded from premises in Mersey St, 1767–73 and took as apps David Beard and John Hind, both free in 1780, and Samuel Biggins, free 1790. All of these apps no doubt completed their apprenticeship under other masters, for Leigh Sutton died 1773. In September of that year his stock of 'well-seasoned MAHOGANY & WALNUT BOARDS, & LOGS' on the Mersey St premises were offered for sale. His completed cabinet goods were offered at reduced prices and persons interested in taking over the house, shop and stock with a view to continuing the business were invited to contact Mrs Sutton in Mersey St, a John Sutton or Zacharias Barnes. [D; freemens reg. and committee bk; *Williamson's Liverpool Advertiser*, 3 September 1773]

Sutton, Richard, 5 Woodcocks Yd, Preston, Lancs., cm (1818). [D]

Sutton, Samuel, North Row, Grosvenor Sq., London, cm, u, chairmaker and undertaker (1835–39). [D]

Sutton, Thomas, Southwark, London, upholder (1706–d.1748). Son of Richard Sutton of Friern Barnet, Middlx, yeoman. App. to Peter Leonard on 14 October 1706 but not free of the Upholders' Co. by servitude until 3 June 1719. This long delay is unexplained but Thomas Sutton was unprepared to await such recognition before commencing his own business. The lack of his freedom obliged him to commence trading in Southwark, and on 30 December 1717 he took insurance cover on goods and merchandise at 'The Angel & Rising Sun' in St Olave's St. On receipt of his freedom he took as app. Thomas Mead who was free 1729. In January 1720 he took out insurance on a new dwelling house identified as at 'The Angel & Crown', Eglinsgate Way, St Olaves St. This may have been little more than a change of trade sign. He was still trading from St Olave's St in 1725 and died in 1748. [GL, Upholders' Co. records; Sun MS vol. 7, 30 December 1717, vol. 10, ref. 16256; Heal]

Sutton, Thomas, Moody St, Congleton, Cheshire, cm (1816–22). Listed as Thomas C. Sutton in 1822. [D]

Sutton, William, Leicester, cm (1754). Eldest son of John Sutton, late of Leicester, cm. [Freemen reg.]

Swaby, Robert, Toll Gavell, Beverley, Yorks., cm (1814). [D]

Swaile, John, London, upholder (1740–56). Son of Thomas Swaile of Moorfields, shoemaker. App. to William Chesson, a member of the Haberdashers' Co., on 6 June 1740 and free of the Upholders' Co. under the terms of the 1750 Upholders' Act, 11 November 1756. [GL, Upholders' Co. records]

Swaile, Joseph, York, Nottingham and Doncaster, Yorks., cm (1758–74). Freeman of York but living in Nottingham in 1758 and Doncaster in 1774. [York poll bks]

Swain, Charles, Moorfields, London, u (1797–98). Bankruptcy announced, *Billinge's Liverpool Advertiser*, 28 August 1797, 16 July 1798]

Swain, Elizabeth, Broker's Row, Moorfields, London, u (1791–94). Probably the widow of Samuel Swain who traded in Broker's Row at an earlier date. Elizabeth Swain occupied number 9, 1791–94 but in the latter year was also using 8 and 10. [D]

Swain, James, 10 Linsley Row, Leeds, Yorks., cm and joiner (1837–40). [D]

Swain, John, Liverpool, cm (1806–15). App. to Isaac Marsh and free 31 October 1806. In November 1815 married Miss Jane Dobson. Died in the period 1818–20. [Freemen reg.; *Liverpool Mercury*, 17 November 1815]

Swain, Luke, Liverpool, cm (1774–77). In 1774 at 21 Ormond St but in 1777 at 14 Tithebarn St. [D]

Swain, Samuel, 9 Broker's Row, Moorfields London, u (1755–d.1790). Son of Samuel Swain of Wandsworth, Gent. App. to James Rodwell, joiner on 18 November 1755, John Steel, draper on 1 July 1760 and Caril Pitt, a member of the Fishmongers' Co. on 9 December 1760. Free of the Upholders' Co. under the terms of the 1750 Upholders' Act, 22 November 1762. Took as apps William Rawlins 1773–78, Samuel Wright 1773–81 and Thomas Moore 1766–78. Alderman of the City of London in 1784 and Master of the Upholders' Co., 1787–88. He traded at the sign of 'The Woolpack' and also that of 'The Lamb'. Apart from 9 Broker's Row he also occupied 10. The address was also given as Bedlam Walk, between New Broad St and Old Bedlam, Moorfields. His trade cards [Leverhulme Coll., MMA, NY and GL] state that he furnished funerals and 'Makes, Buys, Sells and Appraises all manner of Household Furniture'. In 1775 he insured his house for £800. An Elizabeth Swain, probably his widow, carried on the business after his death in 1790. [D; GL, Upholders' Co. records; Sun MS vol. 240, p. 285; Heal]

Swain, Thomas, address unknown, cm (1775–78). Supplied furniture to Dunham Massey, Cheshire. On 10 March 1775 he was paid £4 4s for a dressing table. A further payment of £3 13s 6d was made on 12 July 1777 'for Cabinet makers work' and £6 16s paid on 4 June 1778 for a dressing table and a drawing table. [John Rylands Lib., Manchester Univ., George Cooke's accounts]

Swain, William, 'The Sun', Moorfields, London, u (1716–26). Son of William Swain of Ticehurst, Sussex, Clerk. App. to Richard Wood on 5 September 1716 and free of the Upholders' Co. by servitude, 2 October 1723. In November 1726 took out insurance cover on the Moorfields premises of £800 of which £400 was for utensils and stock. [GL, Upholders' Co. records; Sun MS vol. 23, p. 216]

Swaine, Thomas, Old Jewry, London, upholder (1711–18). The property in Old Jewry was a brick house with a warehouse behind and was insured for £400 both in September 1711 and September 1718. Swaine is recorded taking an app. on 4 August 1712. [GL, Hand in Hand MS vol. 9, p. 279; vol. 19, p. 170; S of G, app. index]

Swaine, William, Liverpool, cm and joiner (1785–d.1813). App. to Robert Tyrer in 1785 and petitioned freedom in 1785. Free on 25 May 1796. Died on 26 October 1813. [Freemen reg. and commttee bk]

Swaine, William, Townhill, Bradford, Yorks., joiner and cm (1818). [D]

Swainsbury, Samuel, 2 Finsbury Mkt, London, cm and u (1839). [D]

Swainson, John, Lancaster, cm (1778–79). [Freemen rolls]

Swainson, John, Lancaster, cm (1789–91). Free 1789–90. Named in the Gillow records, 1791. [Freemen rolls; Westminster Ref. Lib., Gillow]

Swainson, John, London, cm (1803–29). Included in the list of master cabinet makers in Sheraton's *Cabinet Dictionary*, 1803. Recorded in directories at 15 Harp Alley, Fleet St, 1808–29. [D]

Swainson, John, Lancaster, cm (1823–32). Free 1823–24. Named in the Gillow records in 1830 and 1832. [Freemen rolls; Wesminster Ref. Lib., Gillow]

Swainson, Joseph, Lancaster, cm (1784). Son of John Swainson. [Poll bk]

Swale, John, Sackville St, London, see Richard Kerby.

Swale, Samuel, Colton, Yorks., cm (1784). Freeman of York living at Colton in 1784. [York poll bk]

Swallow, James, Water Side, Lincoln, cm and u (1835). [D]

Swallow, Joseph, 25 John St, Ancoats, Manchester, chairmaker (1838–40). [D]

Swan, Clifford, New Pavement, Pocklington, Yorks., wood turner and fancy chairmaker (1823). [D]

Swan, Henry, 18 Water Lane, Sheffield, Yorks., chairmaker (1821). [D]

Swan, James, Wakefield Stairs, Liddell St, North Shields, Northumb., joiner and cm (1828). [D]

Swan, John, Cambridge, cm, u and auctioneer (1769–1811). It was reported in the *Cambridge Chronicle and Journal* of 29 July 1769 that 'lately died . . . in the Indies, Sir William Swan of Madingley in this county. He is succeeded in title and a small estate by his only brother Sir John Swan, a young gentleman about 17 years of age, now apprenticed to Mr. Charles Day, cabinet-maker of this town'. An advertisement appeared in the newspaper for John Swan, u and auctioneer, on 2 October 1784. The *Universal British Directory* records him as an u in 1792. Directories of 1805–11 list him as cm in Bennett St, Cambridge. The same address was given on 17 May 1811, when he announced in the newspaper that 'he has declined the Upholstery and Cabinet Making businesses for the purpose of settling his affairs, he solisits the favours of the public in the Appraising, Auctioneering, Timber Measuring, Valuing and Surveying businesses'. The auction was advertised in the same issue with a detailed list of the stock and 'a very large quantity of fine seasoned Spanish and Hondures mahogany in planks, boards, veneers, dry ash and elm plank, white and black holly, tulip and purple wood, oak and elm boards, cherrytree, sycamore, yew tree, box, elm timber, a large stock of walnut tree planks'. The account book of the Cotton family of Madingley Hall record a payment of £26 6s to Swan in 1800 and one in 1809 for supplying a dressing table and carpeting their church pew. [Cambs. RO, 588/A45]   R.W.

Swan, John, Cambridge, cm, u, auctioneer, appraiser and estate agent (1824–45). Living in Jesus Lane, parish of All Saints, 1824–26 when two of his children were bapt. Trading in Sidney St in 1830, and in October of the following year advertised that he was converting premises next to his own (in Sidney St) into a cabinet and upholstery warehouse. Swan claimed that he had been employed by Elliot Smith for thirteen years and that the latter was 'declining the cabinet and upholstery business'. He also stated that he had taken on some of Elliot Smith's former employees. Some of the furniture that he sold was bought in from other makers but in April 1832 he stated that 'his Mahogany, Rosewood, Pollard Oak and Zebra furniture is principally of his own manufacture'. In November 1832 he advised the public that he had in his employment a first rate u who had for many years been in the workshops of Seddons, the important London maker. He also indicated that he sold Daws & Minter's patent recumbent invalid chairs. From 1832–45 he took over Elliot Smith's position as the main furniture supplier to St John's College and also worked for Trinity College, 1831–33. In the St John's College accounts payments are made from 1839 to Swan & Garner. A copy of George Smith's *Cabinet Maker's and Upholsterer's Guide,* 1826, is known bearing the label 'John Swan, Upholsterer & Cabinet Maker, Sidney Street, Cambridge. [D; PR (bapt.)]; *Cambridge Chronicle,* 21 October 1831, 27 April 1832,

23 November 1832; poll bks; archives of Trinity and St John's Colleges]   R.W.

Swan, John, Library Stairs, North Shields, Northumb., cm and joiner (1827). [D]

Swan, John, 1 Grecian Terr., Everton, Liverpool, carver and gilder (1834). [D]

Swan, Robert, Long Acre, London, cm (1774). [Poll bk]

Swan, Robert, 40 North St, Leeds, Yorks., cm (1826). [D]

Swan, Samuel, 126 St John St Rd, London, u (1829–39). [D]

Swan, Thomas, 70 King St, Golden Sq., London, cm (1786). In August 1786 insured his household goods and clothes for £100. [GL, Sun MS vol. 338, p. 572]

Swan, Thomas, Lancaster, cm (1817–18). [Freemen rolls]

Swan, Thomas, Nuneaton, Warks., chairmaker and turner (1835). [D]

Swan, W. E., 14 Sussex St, Bedford Sq., London, carver etc. (1835). [D]

Swan, William, 45 Long Acre, London, cm and haberdasher (1779). In 1779 took out insurance cover for £200 of which £100 was for utensils and stock. [GL, Sun MS vol. 275, p. 85]

Swan, William, Liverpool, cm (1803–39). At 13 Kent St, 1803–04 but the number was 22/23 in 1805–07. There is then a long gap until 1835 when a William Swan, cm was at 122 Mount Pleasant. In 1839 at 7 Basnett St. [D]

Swan, William, Kings St, Cambridge, journeyman cm (b.1796–d.1819). App. to Thomas Chandler, cm on 15 May 1810 at a premium of £20. His suicide at the age of 23 was reported, *Cambridge Chronicle,* 12 February 1819. [App. bk; poll bk]

Swan, William & Co., Adelaide Buildings, Mount Pleasant, Liverpool, carvers and gilders (1833–34). Claimed to manufacture 'Pier, Chimney & Dressing Glasses, Picture Frames in Gold, Mahogany, Rose, Maple & other Fancy Woods, Gilt Window & Bed Cornices, Black & Gold Mouldings for Rooms etc. etc. Marble Monuments, Chimney Pieces & Pier Tables, Ornamental Designs of Rosettes & Friezes for Architects & Builders. Marble Alabaster & Plaster of Paris Busts & Figures made & repaired'. They also stocked London pianofortes and china and porcelain. [D; *Liverpool Mercury,* 26 April 1833]

Swann, Thomas, Hull, Yorks., cm (1784). Freeman of Beverley, Yorks. but resident in Hull in 1784. [Beverley poll bk] Possibly:

Swan, Thomas, 4 Jews Harp Gdns, Marylebone, London, cm (1790–91). Freeman of Beverley, Yorks. In June 1791 took out insurance cover of £100 on his house. [Beverley poll bk; GL, Sun MS vol. 373, ref. 584728]

Swan, William, Lancaster, cm (1786–1802). App. to J. Wakefield 1786 and free 1801–02. Named in the Gillow records 1794–95. [Freemen rolls; Westminster Ref. Lib., Gillow]

Swan, William, Lancaster, cm (1823–24). Free 1823–24 but by this period living in Liverpool. [Freemen rolls]

Swan, William, Hyson Green, Nottingham, cm (1830). [Poll bk]

Swannell, Robert, 45 Wardour St, London, carver (1780). In 1780 took out insurance cover of £200 of which £40 was for utensils and stock. [GL, Sun MS vol. 287, p. 54]

Swanwick, Joseph, London, upholder (1700). Free of the Upholders' Co., 29 October 1700. [GL, Upholders' Co. records]

Swarbrick, John, 9 Half St, Manchester, cm (1788–97). [D]

Swaysland, Thomas, Southover High St, Lewes, Sussex, cm etc. (1837–40). [Poll bks]

Swearse, James, the Square, Axbridge, Som., cm and carpenter (1840). [D]

Sweet, James, High St, Shaftesbury, Dorset, cm and u (1840). A firm named Child & Sweet were trading in the High St in 1830 and an I. Child in 1840. [D]

Sweet, Richard, Newport, Isle of Wight, Hants., chairmaker (1735 or 1755). In 1735 or 1755 took app. named Lisle. [S of G, app. index]

Sweet, Samuel, Bristol, furniture painter (1831–32). At 10 Rosemary St in 1831 and Stapleton Rd in 1832. [D]

Sweet, Thomas, London, carver and gilder (1809–27). At Gt Castle St in 1809 and George St, Adelphi in 1820. Moved to 32 Frith St, Soho where he traded 1825–26. His successor at Frith St was William Sweet who was at this address by 1835. [D]

Sweet, Thomas, 9 Rathbone Pl., London, carver and gilder (1837–39). [D]

Sweet, William, London, carver and gilder (1835–39). At 32 Frith St in 1835 as the successor to Thomas Sweet. By 1839 at 38 Chancery Lane. [D]

Sweet, Zachariah, 38 Chancery Lane, London, carver, gilder and picture frame maker (1813–27). In January 1824 took out insurance cover of £1,100 in association with Sir Edmond Bacon on Sweet's new dwelling house. In 1839 William Sweet, also a carver and gilder, was trading from this address. [D; GL, Sun MS vol. 499, ref. 1012383]

Sweeting, George, 45 and 46 Winchcombe St, Cheltenham, Glos., cm and u (1839). [D]

Sweetman, Arthur, Blackwall, London, joiner and cm (1808). [D]

Sweetman, George, London, u and cm (1816–39). In 1816 at 9 Essex St, Strand and in 1839 at 25 Bolingbroke Row, Walworth. [D]

Sweetman, George, 7 Pipe Lane, Temple, Bristol, sign and furniture painter (1827). [D]

Sweetman, George, 4 Whitelion Ct, Seven Dials, London, furniture japanner and painter (1839). [D]

Swell, Robert, 69 Sun St, Bishopsgate, London, carver and gilder (1809–16). [D]

Swell, William & Son, 15 Hanover St, Long Acre, London, u (1806–16). [D]

Swesh, Robert, address unknown, cm (1803). Subscribed to Sheraton's *Cabinet Dictionary*, 1803.

Swewison, Richard, Hull, Yorks., cm (1780). [Poll bk]

Swift, John, Eccleston St, Prescot, Lancs., cm and joiner (1818). [D]

Swift, John, Bridge St, Gainsborough, Lincs., cm and u (1835). [D]

Swift, John, Thurgoland, Silkstone parish, Yorks., joiner/cm (1837). [D]

Swift, Joseph, Swan Lane, Bawtry, Yorks., cm (1832–37). [D]

Swift, Robert Gay, London, carver and gilder (1809–39). At 8 Wood St, Old St in 1809 and 40 Holywell Lane, Shoreditch 1826–39. In 1839 also a looking-glass maker. [D]

Swift, W., 10 Norton Falgate, London, carver and gilder (1837). [D]

Swift, William, Stamford St, Ashton-under-Lyne, Lancs., joiner and cm (1828). [D]

Swift, Grant & Hurley, 226 Piccadilly, London, upholders and carpet warehouse (1800–04). Included in the list of master cabinet makers in Sheraton's *Cabinet Dictionary*, 1803. In 1803 a London u, named as Swift & Co., worked for the Duke of Norfolk at Norfolk House. [D; Arundel Castle records MD 473]

Swinburn, Henry jnr, Hall Stile, Hexham, Northumb., joiner and cm (1827–28). [D]

Swinburn, Henry, Liverpool, joiner and cm (1834–37). At 2 Gt Richmond St in 1834 and 13 Birkett St, Soho in 1837. [D]

Swinburn, John, Liverpool, cm and u (1834–39). At 4 King St, Soho 1834–35, 39 Norton St with a workshop at 66 St Ann's St in 1837 and 4 St Ann's St in 1839. [D]

Swinburn, Joseph, address unknown, cm (1803). Subscribed to Sheraton's *Cabinet Dictionary*, 1803.

Swinburn, William, Holy Island, Hexham, Northumb., joiner and cm (1827). [D]

Swinburne, John, Lancaster (1820–26). [Westminster Ref. Lib., Gillow records]

Swinchall, Charles, Market Drayton, Salop, cm (1784). [D]

Swin(e)chatt, Charles, Beast St (or Mkt), Market Drayton, Salop, cm (1835–36). [D]

Swindells, Thomas, London, u and cm (1837–39). At 61 Goswell St in 1837 and 118 Aldersgate St in 1839. [D]

Swinderton, James, 19 Bevington Bush Rd, Liverpool, cm and wood turner (1834). [D]

Swindin, Thomas, London, cabinet and buhl manufacturer (1829–37). At 57 Prince's St, Leicester Sq. in 1829 and 39 Castle St, Oxford Mkt in 1837. [D]

Swindle, John, King's Lynn, Norfolk, cm (1767). In August 1767 came from Derby to King's Lynn to look for work but was imprisoned in the gaol at King's Lynn from which he escaped in December. [*Cambridge Chronicle*, 12 December 1767]

Swindles, R., 18 Gt Sutton St, Clerkenwell, London, u (1835). [D]

Swinehat, Mrs, Atherstone, Warks., cm (1796). Stated to be a widow. [D]

Swinehat, Mrs, Market Drayton, Salop, cm (1797). Stated to be a widow. [D]

Swine(c)hatt, Job, Market Drayton, Salop, cm and chairmaker (1822–28). At Beast Mkt in 1822 and High St, 1828. [D]

Swinley, Alexander, New Bond St, London, upholder (1764–71). Son of Robert Swinley of the parish of St Margaret, Westminster, publican. App. to Jeremy Bullock on 2 February 1764 and free of the Upholders' Co. by servitude, 6 March 1771. [GL, Upholders' Co. records]

Swinn, F., 3 James Pl., John's Sq., New George St, Hull, Yorks., cm (1838–39). [D]

Swinn, John, Spilsby, Lincs., joiner and cm (1826). [D]

Swinnerton, Joseph, 4 Temple Ct, Chorlton Row, Manchester, cm (1825). [D]

Swinnerton, Joseph, 33 Russel St, Liverpool, cm (1829). [D]

Swinnock, George, London, upholder (1734). Freeman of Maidstone living in London. [Maidstone poll bk]

Swinny, Robert, Banchester Rents, Chancery Lane, London, carver, gilder and looking-glass manufacturer (1808). [D]

Swinscon, John, 21 Bishopsgate Within, London, cm (1775). In 1775 insured his house for £100. [GL, Sun MS vol. 240, p. 285]

Swinscow, John, London, cm (1791–1802). At 21 Long Walk, Bermondsey Sq., Bermondsey St in March 1791 when he insured his house and goods for £200. By April 1802 at Walcot Pl., Lambeth where he took out insurance cover of £400 of which £200 was for utensils and stock. In this year his trade was listed as cm and ironmonger. [GL, Sun MS vol. 376, p. 79; vol. 423; ref. 730717]

Swinton, Edward, Market Pl., Alnwick, Northumb., joiner and u (1827). [D]

Swinton, Thomas, Compton, near Ashbourne, Derbs., joiner and cm (1790). In September 1790 a disposal sale of his stock was advertised. This consisted of 'MAHOGANY, MAHOGANY-GOODS, DEAL, VENEERS, and various Articles of HARDWARE'. [*Derby Mercury*, 16 September 1790]

Swinton, William, Hawk St, Sandbach, Cheshire, cm and joiner (1822–34). [D]

Swithenband, John, Bradford, Yorks. (1825). On 31 August 1825 invoiced to G. Wentworth of Woolley Hall, Yorks. a mahogany dressing table, washstands etc. at a cost of £17 15s. [YAS, Wentworth papers, MD 272/2]

Sydenham, George, Kidlington, Oxon., cm (1793). On 5 April

1793 married Sarah S. Biling of the parish of St Cross, Oxford at the Church of St Cross. [Bodleian index of Oxf. marriage bonds]

Sydenham, John, High St, Honiton, Devon, cm and u (1830–38). [D]

Syder, George, Beccles, Suffolk, u (1839). The address is given in one 1839 directory as Newmarket Pl. and in another as New market. [D]

Syer, Edward, Ipswich, Suffolk, chairmaker (1727). [Suffolk RO, HA61: 436/486]

Syer, William, South St, Finsbury, London, cm (1835). [D]

Syers, John, Spring Gdns, Manchester, carver and gilder (1786–89). Supplied picture frames to Dunham Massey, Cheshire, 1786–89. On 17 November 1786 an octagonal gilt picture frame was supplied at a cost of £1 12s 3d and on 11 October 1788 Syers was paid £4 14s 6d for framing pictures. Succeeded by Joseph Syers at this address. [D; V&A archives; *Apollo*, July 1978, p. 22]

Syers, John, 3 Duffours Pl., Broad St, London, cm (1813–27). One directory of 1817 gives his name as Joseph. This may be an error, as John was used in 1813 and 1827 though other entries merely state J. John Syers supplied furniture to Broughton Hall, Yorks. in November 1813 to a value of £95 9s. One of the main items was a pair of mahogany library chairs 'caned back & seats and Cushions . . . finished in purple Spanish leather' which cost £18 18s. These chairs are still in the house. Syers also provided 'an Iron Elbow to swing cover'd with leather and fitted up with Brass apparatus for fixing on Chair & reading Desk'. This was charged at £1 14s 6d. [D; Temple Newsam House, Leeds, Exhib. Cat., *Furniture from Broughton Hall*, item 25]

Syers, Joseph, Manchester, carver, gilder and print seller (1793–1808). Successor to John Syers. At 3 Spring Gdns in 1793–94, 79 Market St Lane, 1797–1802 and 1 Spring Gdns, 1804–08. In January 1793 took out insurance cover of £250 of which £100 was for utensils and stock. In 1803 Charles Towneley of Towneley Hall, Lancs. paid this maker £36 12s for two glasses. [D; Preston RO, DDTO Towneley account bk; GL, Sun MS vol. 392, p. 191]

Sykes, Edmund, Lancaster (1767–97). Free 1767–68. Named in the Gillow records, 1792–94 and 1796–97. [D; poll bk; Westminster Ref. Lib., Gillow]

Sykes, Edward, Lancaster (1792). [Westminster Ref. Lib. Gillow records]

Sykes, Edward jnr, 21 Montague Ct, Spitalfields, London, cm and u (1827). [D]

Sykes, Jonathan, Leeds, Yorks., cm (1821–24). At Temple St in 1821 and 58 Wellington St, 1826–34. [D]

Sykes, Samuel, Pontefract, Yorks., joiner/cm (1834). [D]

Sykes, William, Hertford, victualler and cm (1780–82). In 1780 insured his property for £400 of which £160 was for utensils and stock. By 1782 the total insurance cover had risen to £800 and £460 was the value of the utensils and stock. [GL, Sun MS vol. 282, p. 505; vol. 301, p. 465]

Sym, William, London, u and cm (1831–37). Bankruptcy announced, *London Gazette*, 2 December 1831. At 58 Upper Marylebone St, 1835–37. His trade card states that he also undertook funerals. [D; V&A archives]

Symes, Charles, Bath, Som., cm (1827). In partnership with Abraham Chubb Smart when their bankruptcy was announced, *Chester Chronicle*, 2 February 1827.

Symes, William, Tenterden, Kent, chairmaker (1826). [D]

Symington, John, address unknown, cm (1803). Subscribed to Thomas Sheraton's *Cabinet Dictionary*, 1803.

Symond, John, Exeter, Devon, cm (1829–39). At Synagogue Pl., 1829–32 and then in St Mary Arches St. Three sons and four daughters bapt. at St Mary Arches Church, 1819–39. [PR (bapt.)]

Symonds, Charles, 14 Bugle St, Southampton, Hants., carver and gilder (1823). [D]

Symonds, James, Broad St, Hereford, turner and chairmaker (1777–88). In April 1777 it was announced that Thomas Wood, a brush maker from Bristol, had entered a partnership with Symonds but no later references to this arrangement are known. In 1779 Symonds took out insurance cover of £200 which included £160 for utensils and stock. A James Symonds, chairmaker was admitted a freeman of Hereford in 1784. Sir George Cornewall of Moccas Court, near Hereford employed a Symonds in 1788 bottoming chairs for which he paid £1 12s on 15 April. [*Hereford Journal*, 10 April 1777; GL, Sun MS vol. 273, p. 365; freemen rolls; Herefs. RO, Moccas papers, J56/IV/4]

Symonds, Joseph, Hereford, cm (1818–32). Free 1818 and in 1832 living at Prospect Terr. [Freemen rolls; poll bk] Possibly:

Symonds, Joseph, 5 Hollen St, Wardour St, Soho, London, cm (1826). Freeman of Hereford. [Hereford poll bk]

Symonds, Robert Walter, Truro, Cornwall, cm (1825). [Cornwall RO, B/T 38/4]

Symonds, Philip, Boutport St, Barnstaple, Devon, cm and u (1838). [D]

Symonds, William, parish of St Mary Redcliffe, Bristol, cm (1754). [Poll bk]

Symons, William, Chapel St, Devonport, Devon, cm (1838). [D]

Sympson, Thomas (?), London, joiner (1662–68). In August 1666 provided Samuel Pepys with presses for his books. In total Pepys had twelve of these oak bookcases constructed for his house in York Buildings, London. Pepys bequeathed his collection of books and the bookcases to his old College, Magdalene in Cambridge where they now stand. Sympson carried out other work for Pepys including chimney pieces. Sympson was probably a master joiner employed at the Deptford and Woolwich dockyards. A pair of bookcases similar to those made for Pepys were provided for Dyrham Park, Som. to the orders of William Blathwayt. One of these is now in the V&A and the other in the USA. [Pepys, *Diary*]

Syms, —, Truro, Cornwall, cm and u (1797). [D]

Syms, Charles, 14 Bugle St, Southampton, Hants., carver and gilder (1823). [D]

Syms, Charles, 31 St Mary St, Weymouth, Dorset, carver etc. (1830). [D]

Syms, James, Grosvenor Pl., Weymouth, Dorset, carver and gilder (1840). [D]

Syred, Edward, King's Head Lane, Northampton, chairmaker (1820). [Poll bk]

T

Tabb, Charles, parish of St Andrew, Norwich, cm (1830). [Poll bk]

Tabor, —, 28 King St, Golden Sq., London, carver (1826–27). [D]

Tabor, John, address unrecorded, upholder (1709). Admitted freeman of the Upholders' Co. on 6 April 1709. [GL, Upholders' Co. records]

Tabor, John, near 'White Horse Inn', Fleet St, London, u (d.1725). Death reported in contemporary newspapers. [Heal]

Tabor, Robert, address unrecorded, upholder (1747–54). Son of Edward Tabor, baymaker of Bromtree (Braintree?), Essex.

App. to Samuel Sleigh on 1 October 1747, and admitted freeman of the Upholders' Co. by servitude on 5 December 1754. [GL, Upholders' Co. records]

Tacchi, Anthony, Bedford, carver, gilder and paper hanger (1830–39). Trading at High St in 1830 and St John St, 1839. Barometer recorded bearing name of Anthony Tacchi [D].

Tadman, Henry, Hull, Yorks., cm and u (1826–42). Addresses given at 14 New Dock St in 1826; 22 Anne St, Osborne St, 1831–34 and 1838–40; and 22 Myton St in 1835. [D]

Tagg, Charles, Abingdon, Berks., cm (1768). [Poll bk]

Tagg, Charles, Reading, Berks., u and cm (1780). Declared bankrupt, *Leicester Journal*, 1 January 1780. Polled in September of that year.

Tagg, Thomas, 163 Brick Lane, Spitalfields, London, cm and undertaker (1807–11). Took out a Sun Insurance policy on 1 January 1807 for £350 on two houses in Globe Fields, Bethnal Green, in the tenure of John Saunders & Thornton, weavers. [D; GL, Sun MS vol. 438, ref. 798465]

Tagge, Henry Cowell, Norwich, u (d.1783). Will proved at Norwich in 1783. [Norfolk Record Soc., index of wills]

Tagge, William Little, Walsingham, Norfolk, u (d.1791). Will proved at Norwich in 1791. [Norfolk Record Soc., index of wills]

Tagger, Benjamin, Norwich, carver and gilder (1776). Insured his house for £200 in 1776. [GL, Sun MS vol. 249, p. 532]

Tailor (or Taylor), Thomas, Staindrop, near Barnard Castle, Co. Durham, cm (1824–29). Children bapt. between 1824–29. [Bowes Museum, PR (bapt.)]

Tailor, William, High Wycombe, Bucks., chairmaker (1821). [PR (bapt.)]

Tailors, Mrs, address unrecorded. Named in the accounts of Earl Fitzwalter of Moulsham Hall on 11 September 1725 supplying 'a little screen and Tea-board' costing £1 12s. [A. C. Edwards, *The Accounts of Benjamin Mildmay, Earl Fitzwalter*, p. 100]

Tait, George, New Round Ct, Strand, London, cm (1774–75). Polled at Westminster in 1774. Insured his house for £300 in 1775. [GL, Sun MS vol. 242, p. 73] See John Tait at this address.

Tait(t), Gordon, address unrecorded, u (1774). Worked at Panshanger, Herts., receiving £1 7s 6d on 25 January, and £24 12s 10d and £5 13s 6d in February 1774. [Herts. RO, D/EP A16, pp. 64–65, 74] Possibly Gordon & Taitt.

Tait(t), John and Richard, Swallow St, London. See Gordon & Taitt.

Tait, John, New Round Ct, Strand, London, cm (1784). [D] See George Tait at this address; also John Gordon & John and Richard Taitt.

Tait, Margaret, 41 Cornhill, London, perfumer and cm (?). Printing machine recorded in private possession bearing label which states: 'Supplies Merchants, Captains and Country Traders on the most reasonable terms. N.B. An elegant assortment of pocket-books, Ladies and Gentlemen's Dressing-Cases, etc., writing desks & copying machines manufactured and sold wholesale and retail.' [V&A archives]

Tait(t), Richard, 92 Jermyn St, London, upholder, cm and undertaker (1786–1827). Recorded at no. 93, 1786–87. Took out Sun Insurance policies on 28 January 1786 for £1,000 including £650 on utensils etc.; on 10 February 1787 for £2,300 on household goods, utensils and stock in workshop; and on 23 April 1810 for £3,000 on stock, utensils and goods in trust in his house, warehouse and workshops, all adjoining. [D; GL, Sun MS vol. 335, p. 354; vol. 342, ref. 527536; vol. 453, ref. 844639] Named in Sheraton's list of master cabinet makers, 1803. In the first half of 1791 Taitt supplied items to Gertrude, Dowager Duchess of Bedford, probably for her house at 112 Pall Mall. He charged £2 8s for

four 'horse' bedsteads with sacking bottoms, and £1 18s for 'a black dy'd rush bottom cottage armchair with a footboard & 2 poles with strong iron staples'. [Bedford Office, London] In 1793 he provided curtains for John Pinney of Bristol, at a cost of £43 4s. [Bristol Univ. Lib., J. Pinney's private cash bk] Named in the Royal Household Accounts in 1794 supplying a wardrobe, carpets, upholstery, curtains and pier tables for Prince Edward's apartments at St James's Palace; and in 1810, a bedstead, carpets, fabrics and a dressing glass for Col. Taylor and Mr Nicholls's rooms at Buckingham House. [PRO, LC11/4, 7–11; GCM; Fastnedge, *Sheraton Furniture*] See John Gordon & John and Richard Taitt.

Tait, William, Newmarket, Suffolk, u and cm (1830–39). [D]

Taite, Allen, 29 Charles St, Hampstead Rd, London, cm (1805–07). [D]

Talbert, —, 22 Harcourt St, New Rd, Marylebone, London, u etc. (1826–27). [D]

Talbor, Edward, 24 Bridge House Pl., Newington Causeway, London, u (1826–27). [D]

Talbot, John, Newark, Notts., cm (1793–1822). Listed at Bargate in 1819 and Castle-gate, also as an u, in 1822. [D]

Talbot, Joseph, Gill's Yd, Kirkgate, Leeds, Yorks., cm (1822). [D]

Talbot, Joshua & Crump, Thomas, 6 Duke St, Lincoln's Inn Fields, London, upholders (1785). Took out a Sun Insurance policy on 31 December 1785 on utensils, stock and goods in trust in their warehouses at the Old Playhouse in Portugal St, Lincoln's Inn Fields. [GL, Sun MS vol. 335, p. 129]

Talbot, William, Wisbech, Cambs., cm (1798–d.1806). Death reported in *Cambridge Chronicle and Journal*, 1 March 1806. [D]

Talbot, William, High St, Gateshead, Co. Durham, cm and joiner (1834). [D]

Talbott, John, Winburn (Wimborne), Dorset, joiner, cm and dealer in earthenware (1776). Took out a Sun Insurance policy in 1776 for £200 of which utensils and stock accounted for £150. [GL, Sun MS vol. 248, p. 499]

Talintyre, (or Tallentire), William, 2 Pudding Chare, Newcastle, picture cleaner, picture frame and looking-glass manufacturer (1827–38). [D]

Tall, James, Cambridge, u and cm (1781–88). App. to Edward York, u and cm of Cambridge, on 5 January 1781 for £10. Admitted freeman on 8 January 1788. [Cambridge Corp. common day bk]

Tall, James, Gainsborough, Lincs., joiner, cm and u (1816). App. to William Rollett of Gainsborough in March 1816. [Hull app. reg.]

Tallack, William, Norwich, cm (1810–36). Recorded in St Clement's parish in 1812 and Robinson's Yd, Coslany St in 1836. Son of John Tallock, weaver; admitted freeman on 12 May 1810. [D; Norwich freemen reg. and poll bks]

Tallant, James, Watlington, Oxon., chairmaker (1824). Recorded as participant in a conveyance for a property in South Weston to be converted into a chapel or meeting house for the Society of Methodists. [Oxford RO, Bi II/i/9]

Tallantire, Jonathan, Workington, Cumb., cm and/or joiner (1834). [D]

Tallantire, Thomas, 51 Long Lane, Smithfield, London, cm (1805–07). [D]

Tallentire, John, Harrington, Workington, Cumb., joiner and/or cm (1829). [D]

Talputt, Joshua, 115 Long Acre, London, u (1809–11). [D] See Joshua Tolput(t).

Taman, William, St Clement's, Oxford, cm and u (1830). [D]

Tamset, John, Rye, Sussex, cm, auctioneer and sworn appraiser (1798). [D]

Tandell, Samuel. See Charles Rand.

Tandy, Charles, Edward St, Woolwich, London, cm and u (1832–39). Recorded as C. S. Tandy at no. 4 in 1838. [D]

Tandy, Edward, Edward St, Woolwich, London, cm (1823–24). [D]

Tandy, Robert, Edward St, Woolwich, London, cm (1826–27). [D]

Tanfield, William, Northallerton, Yorks., cm and u (1828–29). [D]

Tankard, William, Liverpool, u (1819–39). Addresses given at 17 Milton St in 1821; Hanley St with shop at 9 Roe St in 1829; no. 8 in 1834; no. 9, 1835–37; 13 Rowe St and 3 Bevington Bush in 1839. Marriage at Chester to Miss Ellen Walker of Liverpool reported in *Liverpool Mercury*, 22 October 1819. [D]

Tankard, William, St John's parish, Lewes, Sussex, cm (1826). [Poll bk]

Tanley, G. B., address unrecorded. Stamp found on a set of Regency dining chairs with curved top-rails, pierced inter-laced splats inlaid with ebony lines, leather upholstered seats, and supported on sabre legs. [Christie's, 27 November 1975, lot 7, illus.]

Tann, Mary, 50 Lower Sloane St, Chelsea, London, cm and u (1823). [D]

Tann, William, Byard Lane, Nottingham, cm (1835). [D]

Tanner, —, Worcester St, Birmingham, cabinet and upholstery manufacturer, undertaker. Trade card, c.1820s, is similar in design to that of Freame of Worcester, showing windows, draped pelmet, and Neo-classical sofa. [Heal Coll., BM] Possibly Richard Tanner of Worcester St.

Tanner, Benjamin, 12 Friar St, Worcester, cm and u (1822). [D]

Tanner, Hannah, Kymbrose, Gloucester, cm and u (1822). [D]

Tanner, Jane, Snowhill, Birmingham, u (1822–28). Listed at no. 98 in 1822 and no. 126 in 1828. [D]

Tanner, Richard, 96 Dale End, Birmingham, upholder, appraiser and undertaker (1800). [D]

Tanner, Richard, Worcester St, Birmingham, cm and u (1816). [D] Possibly Tanner, —.

Tanner, Thomas, Gloucester, cm (1829). Child bapt. at St Nicholas's Church in 1829. [PR (bapt.)]

Tanner, Thomas Alexander, 34 Edgbaston St, Birmingham, cm, u and broker (1828–30). [D]

Tanner, Thomas, 176 High St, Deritend, Birmingham, chair-maker (1839). [D]

Tantum, Joseph, Gravel Lane, Houndsditch, London, cm (1719–d.1743). In 1719 Francis Richardson, a Philadelphia goldsmith, recorded in his account book the purchase of '20 Looking Glasses' from Tantum. [Winterthur, Delaware, Downs MS Lib.] Death of 'Mr. Joseph Tantum, a wealthy cabinet maker, one of the People call'd Quakers', at his house in Houndsditch, reported in *London Evening Post*, 9–11 August 1743. Notice given in *Daily Advertiser*, 27 March 1744 of sale of his entire stock in trade, 'consisting of very neat Bookcases, Walnut-Tree and Mahogany Buroes, a large Pier Glass in a carv'd gold Frame, Sconces ditto, Mahogany card and other Tables, double Chest of Drawers...'; catalogues to be had from 'Mr. Smith's, Upholder, at the Chair in Fleet Street'. Tantum & Walker were listed at Cheapside in *The Complete Guide to ... London*, 1749. [D; Wills, *Looking-Glasses*]

Tape, John, Exeter, Devon, carver and gilder (1814–16). Trading at Guinea St in 1814 and Waterbeer St in 1816. Daughter Charlotte bapt. at St Mary Major on 27 November 1814, and son John on 28 January 1816. [PR (bapt.)]

Taplen, John & William, High St, Portsmouth, Hants., upholders and cm (1805–08). [D]

Tapley, William, 12 Seymour Pl., Camden Town, London, cm (1835). [D]

Tappenden, Rd, 5 Gray's Inn Lane, London, looking-glass and picture frame maker (1835–39). [D]

Tappey, Albert & Alfred, 13 Upper York St, London, carver and gilder (1839). [D]

Taprell, Stephen & Holland, William, London, cm, u, chair and sofa manufacturers (c.1803–35) succeeded by Taprell, Holland & Son (1835–43). This firm trading as Holland and Sons after 1843 (sometimes after 1846 as William Holland and Sons) became one of the greatest furnishing firms of the Victorian period and was active until 1942. Taprell is recorded at St James's, Westminster, 1806–07; 25 Gt Pulteney St, 1815–26 and also at 19 Mary-le-Bonne St, 1817–51 with manufactory at 6 Silver St, 1826–43. He is probably the Stephen Taperell who subscribed to Sheraton's *Cabinet Dictionary*, 1803. [D] On 4 December 1806 he took app. named James Potter jnr for seven years for £48. [PRO, IR 1/40]. Stephen Taprell, the senior partner, remained actively in business until his partner William Holland took over in 1843. Little is known about Taprell, but the existence of a deed relating to land in Chelsea purchased by Henry Holland the architect and his cousin Richard Holland, lodged in the V&A among other documents relating entirely to the furnishing firm, points to family connexion between William Holland and Henry, the Regency architect. Book I of the Holland Records reveals much evidence of a close business relationship between the Taprell-Holland partner-ship and a prosperous building and timber firm: Copland, Rowles and Holland. In that firm, Alexander Copland was a successful builder who had been trained by Richard Holland; Henry Rowles was Henry Holland's nephew and the third partner was originally the architect himself.

It seems not unlikely that out of the speculative develop-ment of Hans Town, East Chelsea between the 1770s and 1790s by Henry Holland (d.1806) and his master builder father, Henry Holland snr (d.1785), came the evolution of the building and timber firm, Copland, Rowles and Holland. As that firm had its own brickworks, sawpits and building tradesmen, it would have been in its own interest to foster a related cabinet making business. The closeness of the relationship is suggested by a later note of 1826 in which a payment of £156 18s 6d was made to Taprell and Holland 'by timber from Messrs Copland, Rowles and Holland'. The need for a furnishing firm may have become apparent when that building firm developed the Albany in 1803–04 as residential chambers for wealthy men who did not require large town houses. One was Henry Holland's bachelor son Henry, who occupied chambers in Albany for many years. The special connection between the building and furnishing firms is further emphasised by the evidence of a bill of 1825 for Taprell-Holland furniture supplied to L. Holland, the architect's second son, Col. Launcelot Holland, being met by a credit of timber from Messrs Copland and Co.

Stephen Taprell died in 1847 aged 73 and was buried in the Holland family vault in Kensal Green Cemetery. A man of some substance, he had owned several properties including 29 Hertford St, 24 Chester Terr. and houses in Maida Vale and Tunbridge Wells. His estate was valued at £3,157. The esteem in which he was held by the Holland family is shown by the fact that William Holland's second son James, who was the senior partner of the firm from 1851–72, named his first two sons Stephen Taprell and George Taprell (Holland). By 1824 Taprell and Holland had achieved a reputation which led to their earliest known major commission, the furnishing of the Athenaeum, 1824–38. [*Furn. Hist.*, 1970] Little more is known of the firm's activities in the period up to 1840 except that they supplied furniture to seven other clubs and some items to Arundel Castle, Harewood House and Ickworth.

Having worked alongside the prestigious firm of Thomas Dowbiggin on their first royal commission at Osborne House and elsewhere from 1845, Holland and Sons took over his premises at 23 Mount St in 1851 and his business in 1853. [Colvin; *Burlington*, November 1969; E. Joy, *Holland and Sons: A Victorian Furnishing Firm*, unpublished typescript in V&A archives; Holland records 1824–1942, 235 volumes in above dept (years 1826–35 missing)]

THE UNION CLUB, London, 1823, dining chairs and dinner tables. [*Furn. Hist.*, 1970] THE ATHENAEUM, London, 1824–38. Before the Athenaeum club house, designed by Decimus Burton, was ready in 1830 Taprell and Holland supplied to the Club's temporary quarters at 12 Waterloo Pl. in 1824 '20 dinner tables and 5 dozen chairs of the same pattern and price as those supplied to the Union Club' and lent other needed items. Burton, working in close association with the Club, provided drawings for some fittingly Grecian style furniture and supervised its production by Taprell and Holland. They continued to supply this and their own stock productions until 1830 and again later, as the Club's needs grew, to a final total of £6,700. The firm's records of the period 1826–35 have been lost but a list of the Athenaeum's furniture is available in the Club's Inventory of 1831. Holland's listings of the pre-1826 furniture suggest characteristic Regency forms. There are dining tables 'on pillars and 3 claws each', Pembroke tables with turned legs, 'sofa tables on Grecian stands', circular tables on pillars and triangular bases; chairs are: 'stained rosewood with tablet tops and caned seats', 'gondola chairs with cushions in blue leather', 'mahogany with tablet tops, seats French stuffed', 'zebra wood chairs with scroll over tops, loose seats French stuff'd w/t best hair covered in crimson and drabstripe' and Grecian couches are specified 'with squabs and bolsters'.

Much furniture was designed specifically for the principal reception rooms where much still remains along with replacements and later additions. A good deal of stock furniture was also supplied for servants' bedrooms. Taprell and Holland also made a gallery, to Burton's design, for the library in 1832 and in 1835 they supplied furniture and worked to convert the Map Room into a second library. [Athenaeum Inventory Book, 1830–39; *Furn. Hist.*, 1970; Holland Records Book, I, 1824–26, p. 56 etc.; Book II 1835–39, pp. 12, 318; Humphrey Ward, *History of the Athenaeum 1824–1925*, 1926; H. Clifford Smith, *An Inventory and Valuation of the Furniture etc. of the Athenaeum*, 1939, typescripts in Libraries of the Athenaeum and V&A]

ICKWORTH, Suffolk, 1826–27: Pair of X frame chairs in East Corridor. [Nat. Trust Guide, 1981, p. 16]

ARUNDEL CASTLE, c.1839–42; Tapule (sic) Holland and Son supplied a 'Mahogany Foldg. Top Tea Table' to Viscount Fitzalan for £2 8s. [Arundel Castle Records, A2095]

The papers of James Brogden, MP, record payments to Taprell & Holland in 1820 of £2 for a 'Mahog. Trafalgar Chair w.t Roll over Tablet Top, Rounded sides loose seat Stuff.d w.t best Hair finish in Red Morrocco leather & brass molding' A note on the reverse of the bill reads: 'The former Chairs were charged covered in Hair seating w.t brass moldings @ 37/. Covering in Red Morrocco leather extra 2/9. The full charge of chair 39/9'.

A Regency rosewood writing table recorded with rounded rectangular top and two drawers in a plain frieze framed by scrolled volutes on panelled trestle ends, bar supports and turned feet; stencilled 'From Tapwell, Holland & Sons, Upholsterers &c., Gt. Pulteney St., Golden Sq., London'. [Christie's, 27 January 1983, lot 147] They left Gt Pulteney St in 1826.

ALL SOULS COLLEGE, Oxford, c.1840: A set of 25 single and 2 arm chairs in heavy mahogany with carved ribbons and two little shields on top rails, backs and seats stuffed and buttoned, turned legs carved with pendant leaves. [Label seen but now missing]

The dates and letters in brackets below refer to volumes of Holland Records in the V&A.

OXFORD AND CAMBRIDGE CLUB (1835–40, O–S; 1846–47, H–Q)
REFORM CLUB (1835–40, O–S; 1843–45, O–T)
UNITED SERVICE CLUB (1836–39, T–Z)
BRITISH MUSEUM (1839–42, A–F)
ARTHURS CLUB (1839–42, A–F)
CLARENCE CLUB (1839–42, A–F)
ALBION CLUB (1839–42, A–F)   P.A.

Tapscott, G., 29 Old Town St, Plymouth, Devon, cm (1830). [D]

Tapscott, Henry, Ditton St, Ilminster, Som., cm and agent to Norwich Union Fire and Life Assurance Co. (1840). [D]

Tapster, Stephen, near Boston Rd, Sleaford, Lincs., joiner, builder and cm (1826–40). Small mahogany writing table on turned legs, c.1840, recorded with pictorial maker's label which reads: 'S. Tapster, Builder, Cabinet Maker, Undertaker, Upholsterer, Paper hanger, Sleaford.' [D]

Tar, George, Bath, Som., u (d.1811). Death on 14 January 1811 reported in *Gents Mag*.

Tara, Innocent, Upgate, Louth, Lincs., carver and gilder (1819–31). [D]

Tarbett, John, 36 Red Lion St, Holborn, London, cm (1805–07). [D]

Tarbuck, Henry, Liverpool, cm (1777–80). Trading at 74 Stanley St in 1777. Admitted freeman on 13 September 1780. [D; Liverpool freemen reg.]

Tarleton, Robert, Liverpool, cm (1784–1812). Admitted freeman in 1784. His son, William Tarleton, cm, petitioned freedom on birthright in 1812. [Liverpool freemen's committee bk]

Tarleton, William, 95 Copperas Hill and Gt Homer Buildings, Gt Homer St, Liverpool, cm (1812). Admitted freeman on 12 October 1812 as son of Robert Tarleton, cm. [Liverpool freemen reg.]

Tarn, William, London, freeman turner, cm (1773–1802). Recorded at Aldersgate St in 1773; with Joseph Tarn at 28 London Wall, 1791–98; and as Tarn & Son there, 1791–1802. In 1773 employed fifteen non-freemen for six weeks. William and Joseph took out a Sun Insurance policy on 1 January 1791 for £900 of which £800 accounted for utensils and stock. Subscribed to Sheraton's *Drawing Book*, 1793. [D; GL, City Licence bks, vol. 8; GL, Sun MS vol. 374, ref. 578096]

Tarone, A. & C., 7 Greville St, London, looking-glass maker (1802–19). [D; Goodison, *Barometers*]

Tarone & Co., 39 Charles St, Hatton Gdn, London, picture and looking-glass frame makers (1839). [D]

Taroni & Luzaghi, 9 City Rd, London, looking-glass manufacturers (1829). [D]

Tarplee, William, 303 Cheapside, Birmingham, chairmaker (1835). [D]

Tarrant, John, London, upholstery and cabinet ware-rooms (1807–11). Trading at corner of Bethlem Wall, 28 Little Moorfields in 1807, and 28 Little Moorgate in 1809. [D]

Tarrant, John, Prince George St, Portsea, Portsmouth, Hants., cm and u (1823–39). Recorded at no.8, 1823–30. [D]

Tarrant, William, London, cm (1806–31). [Colchester poll bks]

Tarrey, Thomas, Market Rasen, Lincs., joiner, cm and builder (1817). App. to William Rollet of Gainsborough, Lincs., in August 1817. [Hull app. reg.]

Tarrone, John B., 20 Goulden's Buildings, Leeds, Yorks., carver, gilder, weather glass, thermometer and barometer manufacturer (1830). [D]

Tarry, George, London, upholder (1704–37). Recorded 'at the Golden Ball in . . . Lyon Mkt. near White Cross St. in the parish of St. Giles Without Cripplegate' in 1713. Admitted freeman of the Upholders' Co. on 7 March 1704/05. Took apps named William Milward, 1722–30, and Henry Sandwell, 1730–37. Took out a Sun Insurance policy on 12 February 1713 on his goods. [GL, Upholders' Co. records; GL, Sun MS vol. 2, p. 189] Probably George Terry of Whitecross St.

Tarte, Frederick James L., St Andrew's Hill and East Pottergate, Norwich, carver and gilder (1839). [D]

Tasker, Charles M., Chester, cm (1812–40). Trading at Duke St in 1819; Thomas Buildings in 1819; Foregate St in 1826; and Queen St in 1840. Admitted freeman on 15 October 1813. [D; Chester freemen rolls and poll bks]

Tasker, Edward M., Thomas Buildings, Chester, cm (1818–19). [Poll bks]

Tasker, George, 11 Castle Ct, Strand, London, cm and u (1827–29). [D]

Tasker, Robert, London, cm (1805–14). Recorded at 7 King St, Lambeth, 1805–07; and 4 Hare Row, Cambridge Heath, Hackney Rd on 9 June 1814, when he took out a Sun Insurance policy for £300 on five adjoining houses in Grove Rd, Cambridge Heath. [D; GL, Sun MS vol. 461, ref. 895142]

Tasker, T., Lancaster, furniture painter, gilder and japanner (1815–23). [Westminster Ref. Lib., Gillow records]

Tasker, William, High St, Banbury, Oxon., looking-glass, barometer and thermometer maker (1813–53). [Goodison, *Barometers*]

Tasscher, Robert, London, joiner and cm (1768). Petitioned freedom on servitude in 1768. [Liverpool freemen's committe bk]

Tat(h)am (Tatan or Tattem), Henry, Stamford, Lincs., cm and u (1772–1808). App. to John Cobb of London, and admitted freeman of Stamford in 1772. In that year he did fealty for a tenement in Butcher Row. His Rococo trade card gives address at 'The Corner of Butcher Row', and trade as cm, upholder and appraiser 'From Mr. Cobb's London', supplying 'Furniture made in the French mode, or any other Taste. Variegated with different Kind of Wood as well executed as in London & on as reasonable terms.' Card shows a china cabinet, French chair, ornate bed and serpentine-fronted desk in the Chippendale style. [Heal Coll., BM] Took apps named John Dawkins for £30 on 1 June 1774; Thomas Boyden on 25 March 1781; James Cerrol for £40 on 15 June 1781; and William Barton from 1 May 1808. A Sun Insurance policy in his name, dated 1777, is for £1,000 on Stamford Town Hall, and he was both Alderman and Mayor of Stamford in 1792. In May 1804 as Alderman, his estimate of £2,200 for building the New Shambles at Stamford was rejected, and he promptly resigned from the committee dealing with this work. Henry Tatham's name appears regularly in the Burghley Estate Day Books between 1773 and 1793, when the 9th Earl of Exeter died. Payments are recorded for goods, mahogany and upholsterer's work and also for work as an architect and builder. His label is recorded on a Pembroke table at Burghley, of ambitious design in marquetry, with an overall trellis pattern 'in the French mode', and carried out mainly in walnut and tulipwood, with free use of ebonized work at edges. Another Pembroke table at Burghley, without a trade label, is clearly from the same workshop, with ebonized work and veneer in parti-coloured wood in complicated patterns, rectangular on the top and herring-boned on the legs. Of Tatam's building work, only his house at Barnhill is now identifiable, built between 1797–1802. He is probably the H. Tatham who subscribed to Sheraton's *Drawing Book*, 1793. [D; Stamford Town Hall Bk, 2A/1/4; GL, Sun MS vol. 262, p. 158; C. *Life*, 3 May 1973, p. 1236] He is likely to be the Tatam, u, named in the account book of Sir Gilbert Heathcote for Normanton Hall, Rutland, between 1797 and 1805 receiving payments totalling £101 19s 4d for 'jobs at Normanton', goods and upholstery. [Lincoln RO, 3 ANC 6/24–25]

Tatam, Thomas, York, carver and gilder (1762). Son of John Tatam, clerk, of Whaplode, Lincs. App. to William Marshall, carver and gilder, on 6 May 1762. [York app. reg.]

Tate, —, Lancaster. Named in the Gillow records in 1796 working on a desk and a bookcase. [Westminster Ref. Lib., Gillow vol. 344/97, p. 1259]

Tate, Adam, Oakwellgate-east-chair, Gateshead, Co. Durham, joiner and cm (1795–1801). [D]

Tate, Alexander, 52 Broad St, Worcester, cm and u (1835). [D]

Tate, Alexander, High St, Hampstead, London, u (1838). [D]

Tate, David, Baxter Gate, Whitby, Yorks., cm (1828–29). [D]

Tate, George, Groat Mkt, Newcastle, joiner and cm (1811). [D]

Tate, George, Carolgate, Retford, Notts., cm (1835). [D]

Tate, J., London, cm (1793). Subscribed to Sheraton's *Drawing Book*, 1793.

Tate, John, York, cm (1743–74). Polled of Tanner Row in 1758 and Aldwark in 1774. Son of Thomas Tate, yeoman of Bramham. App. to Thomas Mann, cm and joiner, on 17 September 1743, and admitted freeman as joiner in 1752. [York app. reg., freemen rolls and poll bks]

Tate, John, Walker's Ct, Knave Acre, London, bedstead maker (1774). [Poll bk]

Tate, John, Pilgrim St, Newcastle, cm (1784–1834). [D] Advertised in *Newcastle Courant*, 8 May 1784, that he had 'moved from his situation at the foot of Pilgrim-street, to a house a little above, on the opposite side of the same street, formerly known by the sign of the Queen's Head, and lately occupied by Mr. Charles Turner . . .'. Subscribed to Sheraton's *Drawing Book*, 1793. Notice in *Durham County Advertiser*, 2 September 1815 read: 'J. TATE, Pilgrim Street, Newcastle-upon-Tyne, declining the Cabinet Business, is now selling off his valuable stock of MAHOGONY consisting of the most rare & curious flecked woods; very fine broad Table Wood; with every other description equally good. Also a quantity of ready made Furniture of the best workmanship.' Still recorded in directories, however, in 1834.

Tate, John, Groat Mkt, Newcastle, cm and furniture broker (1834–38). Listed at no. 48 in 1838. [D]

Tate, John, Honley, Huddersfield, Yorks., cm (1834). [D]

Tate, Peter, Newcastle, cm and furniture broker (1834). [D]

Tate, Richard Seddon, 10 Hart St, Liverpool, cm (1796). Admitted freeman on 27 May 1796, on servitude to John Parry. [Liverpool freemen reg.]

Tate, Richard, 39 Islington, Liverpool, cm (1823). [D]

Tate, Thomas, Curwen St, Workington, Cumb., joiner and/or cm (1829–34). [D]

Tate, Thomas, High St, Bognor, Sussex, cm, u, undertaker, appraiser and broker (1832–45). [D]

Tate, William, 5 Fleur-de-luce St, Norton Falgate, London, cm (1782–90). Trading as mahogany dealer in 1790. [D]

Tateson, John, Market Rasen, Lincs., joiner, cm and builder (1822–26). Trading at Queen St in 1826. [D]

Tatham, George, London, cm and upholder (1829–39). Recorded at 13 Theobalds Rd in 1829 and 115 High Holborn, 1835–39. [D]

Tatham, J., address unrecorded, u (1789). In the first volume of Henry Holland's accounts for work done to his order at Woburn Abbey, 1787–89, Tatham is shown to have received £1 16s 'for upholsterer's work', but no details are given. [Bedford Office, London]

Tatham, Robert, Spring Gdns, Lancaster, chairmaker (1834). [D]

Tatham, Thomas, see Marsh & Tatham.

Tatham, Thomas, Lancaster, cm (1789–90). [Lancaster freemen rolls; Westminster Ref. Lib., Gillow records]

Tatham, Thomas, 20 Cadogan Pl., Sloane St, London, upholder and undertaker (1817). [D]

Tatham & Bailey, Tatham, Bailey & Saunders, see George Elward & William Marsh.

Tat(t)nall, John, London, upholder (1707–40). Recorded at Ironmonger Lane, Cheapside, 1711–40. Admitted freeman of the Upholders' Co. on 26 January 1707/08, and master in 1735. Took app. named Edward Good in 1723. Took out Hand in Hand Insurance policies on 7 April 1711 for £400 on a house in Ironmonger Lane, '3rd house southwards from Church Alley', and £100 on a house in Barkers [?] Lane, St Giles-in-the-Fields; on 4 July 1718 for £400 on his house in Ironmonger Lane; and on 3 June 1720 for £100 on a house in Parcess [?] Lane, St Giles. Heal records him in contemporary newspapers and insurance co. records, 1722–40. [GL, Upholders' Co. records; GL, Hand in Hand MS vol. 8, refs 21323–24; vol. 19, p. 3; vol. 22, p. 72] Father of:

Tatnall, William, London, upholder (1738–81). Recorded in Ironmonger Lane, 1772–81. Son of John Tatnall, freeman upholder of London. Admitted freeman of the Upholders' Co. by patrimony on 2 February 1738/39. [GL, Upholders' Co. records]

Tattersal, —, Pontefract, Yorks., cm (1797–98). [D]

Tattersall, John, Haslingden, Lancs., cm and joiner (1822–24). Listed as John snr in George St, 1824, also as house builder and timber merchant. [D]

Tattersil, Thomas & John, Marsden Sq., Haslingden, Lancs., joiners and cm (1828). [D]

Tattersil, Thomas, Pleasant St, Haslingden, Lancs., joiner and cm (1834). [D]

Tatum, Thomas, 3 Bird St, Grosvenor Sq., London, cm (1805–07). [D]

Taunton, Jacob, Downton, Wilts., chairmaker (1742–93). Son of Jacob Taunton. App. to Richard Honeywell, chairmaker of Downton, Wilts., on 22 March 1742–43 by common indenture and counterpart for five years for £6. [D; *Wilts. Apps and their Masters*] Probably the Taunton, chairmaker, named in the accounts for Longford Castle, Wilts. receiving £2 14s in 1785, and £10 in 1801. [V&A archives]

Tavell, Charles, St Laurence parish, Ipswich, Suffolk, u (1798). [Suffolk RO, calendar of marriage licence bonds, FAA: 50/2/111, p. 209]

Tawney, Robert, Oxford, cm, joiner and carpenter (1748–51). Agreed to complete the presses and bookcases in the gallery of the Codrington Library, All Souls' College, for £372 in 1748, on the failure of Jeremiah Franklin to do so. Recorded in the All Souls' College accounts in 1751 as 'Tawney the Carpenter' receiving £159. [All Souls' College MS DD, a.257]

Tayler (or Taylor), —, address unrecorded, cm and u (1804–26). Named in the account books of 2nd and 3rd Lords Braybrooke for Audley End, Essex, Billingbear, Berks., or their London house. As a cm he received £4 6s 6d in June 1804, and in August 1804, £6 7s 6d. As an u, he was paid varying amounts between 1804–26, the maximum being £55 17s 6d. [Essex RO, D/DBy/A357; A376]

Tayler, James, 20 Lower Brook St, Grosvenor Sq., London, u and cm (1835–39). [D]

Tayler, Joseph, 30 Dunnings Alley, Bishopsgate Without, London, cm and u (1827–28). [D]

Tayler, L., 17 Little New St, Shoe Lane, London, carver and gilder (1820). [D] Possibly Lewis Taylor.

Tayloer, Hector, 21 Cable St, Manchester, chairmaker (1813). [D]

Taylor, —, address unrecorded. Supplied two dressing glasses costing £1 16s to Lord Monson on 22 May 1763. [Lincoln RO, Monson 10, 1/A/5]

Taylor, —, East Smithfield, London, cm (1793). Subscribed to Sheraton's *Drawing Book*, 1793.

Taylor, —, address unrecorded, u (c.1823–34). Named in the accounts of Charles William Vane, Marquess of Londonderry, for furniture supplied for Wynyard Park, Co. Durham. [Durham RO, Londonderry papers, D/LO/E 492]

Taylor, —, address unrecorded. In 1838 supplied 'new furniture' for Stafford House, London, costing £39. [Staffs. RO, D593/R/1/26/8]

Taylor, Acten, Dean Ct, Swan St, Manchester, chairmaker (1817). [D]

Taylor, Ann, Liverpool, u (1807–39). Addresses given at 2 Green Lane in 1807; 13 Dance St in 1810; no. 16 in 1811; 4 Harford St in 1813; no. 8 in 1814; 2 Pleasant St, 1818–37; and no. 3 in 1839. [D]

Taylor, Benjamin & Sons, London, cm and u, chairmaker and undertaker (1805–40). Addresses given at 58 Kent St, Southwark, 1805–23; no. 81 in 1817; Gt Dover St, Southwark, 1821–beyond 1840; Roebuck Pl., Gt Dover St, 1823–29; nos 67 and 68, 1835–39, and no. 6 in 1839. Recorded also at King William St in 1837; and 167 Gt Dover St until 1873. Took out Sun Insurance policies on 23 December 1820 for £1,000 on house and warehouse in Gt Dover St, 'unfinished intended for his occupation'; and as James Benjamin Taylor, u and cm, Gt Dover St, on 24 October 1821, for £2,850 including £1,000 on house, warehouse and workshop, and £1,500 on stock, utensils, goods and glass stock. Recorded as the maker of chairs in private possession, with slim turned back supports and legs, upholstered oval back panel and seat. [D; GL, Sun MS vol. 485, ref. 972505; vol. 486, ref. 985043; V&A archives]

Taylor, Benjamin, Guisborough, Yorks., joiner and cm (1823–40). Recorded at Westgate, 1829–40 and listed as Benjamin jnr in 1840. [D]

Taylor, Brian, Bridge St, Manchester, cm and u (1832–34). Recorded at no. 57, 1832–33 and no. 59 in 1834. [D]

Taylor, Burder, near St Alkmund's Church, Derby, carver (1756). Advertised in *Derby Mercury*, 26 November–3 December 1756, that he 'Carves all Manner of Housework in wood or stone; as Frontispieces, Doorcases, Chimney Pieces, Looking Glass, or Picture Frames, Table Frames &c. And all Sorts of Ornaments for Furniture in the Modern, Chinese, French, or Gothick Taste'. Other Derby cm and joiners had workshops near St Alkmund's churchyard.

Taylor, C., address unrecorded. Name found on close cupboard, c.1660, of unusually small dimensions. [*Antique Dealer's and Collector's Guide*, May 1976, p. 11]

Taylor, Charles, Norwich, upholder (1800–08). Recorded at St Andrew's parish in 1800; 44 London Lane, 1801–02; 13 Queen St, c.1803 and Queen St in 1808. Took out a Sun Insurance policy on 25 December 1800 for £600 on stock and utensils in his new house and shop communicating. Former app. of Thomas and Charles Taylor, Henry Utting, u, admitted freeman on 24 February 1801. [D; Norwich freemen reg.; GL, Sun MS vol. 37, ref. 713105]

Taylor, Charles, 27 Basnett St, Liverpool, cm and upholder (1821–24). Sale of stock on declining business 'on account of ill health' advertised in *Liverpool Mercury*, 14 May 1824. Stock consisted of 'Brussels & superfine Kidderminster & Venetian carpets, London Oil Cloths of various widths, Imperial Hearth Ruggs, Druggets, Bed Furniture, Morines, Fringes, Bell Pulls, Bed Ticking, about 350 dozen of glazed and plain Paper, with Suitable Borders, an elegant large-sized Cheval Glass, in rosewood Frame, Chimney, Pier & Dressing Ditto, Capital Wardrobe, well-made Side-board, handsome

Pier Table, Pillar & Claw, Pembroke, Chamber, Card & Work Tables, Circular & straight front Chests of Drawers, Black Hair Sofas, sets of Trafalgar & other Chairs, Four-post & camp Bedsteads, Tea Caddies, Clothes Horses, Wine Cooler, Bedsteps, Music Stools, Easy Chair, Dressing Tables, Bason Stands etc.' [D]

Taylor, Daniel, London, cm (1790–1813). Trading at Shakespeare Walk, 1790–93; 126 Pearl Row, Blackfriars Rd, 1805–07; and 3 Pear Tree Row, Lambeth Marsh, 1805–13. [D] See David Taylor at 22 Shakespeare Walk.

Taylor, David, Swan Yd, Wardour St, London, cm (1775). Insured utensils, stock and goods for £400 in 1775. [GL, Sun MS vol. 243, p. 543]

Taylor, David, Ratcliff Highway, London, cm (1782–85). Recorded at no. 115 in 1782 and no. 75 in 1785. Took out Sun Insurance policies in 1782 for £100 of which utensils and stock accounted for £60; and on 1 November 1785 for £150 on household goods and £150 on utensils etc. [GL, Sun MS vol. 304, p. 482; vol. 333, p. 332]

Taylor, David, 22 Shakespeare Walk, London, cm (1792–1807). Took out a Sun Insurance policy on 12 July 1807 for £1,600 including £200 on workshops and warehouses, and £1,050 on utensils and stock. [D; GL, Sun MS vol. 388, p. 235] See Daniel Taylor at Shakespeare Walk.

Taylor, David, Windsor, Berks., cm (1794–1806). [Poll bks]

Taylor, David F., Sandwich, Kent, cm (1798). [D]

Taylor, David, Nottingham, cm (1802–12). App. to William Taylor in 1802, and named in the burgess roll, 1812. [Nottingham app. list]

Taylor, David jnr, Wellclose Sq., London, cm (1809–16). Trading at no. 38, 1809–11 and no. 37 in 1816. [D]

Taylor, David, Whitechapel Rd, London, cm (1810–16). Recorded at no. 417 in 1810 and no. 147, 1811–16. Took out Sun Insurance policies on 16 July 1810 for £700 including £600 on stock and utensils; and on 19 September 1811 and 4 November 1812 for £2,400 including £900 on stock and utensils, and £500 on workshop and sheds. [D; GL, Sun MS vol. 452, ref. 845499; vol. 455, ref. 860405; vol. 457, ref. 875490]

Taylor, David, 14 Wardour St, Soho, London, cm, u and chairmaker (1809–23). Took out Sun Insurance policies on 29 December 1809 for £800 of which £500 accounted for stock, utensils and goods in trust; and on 8 June 1812 for £1,500, including £300 on his house and workshop, £770 on stock, utensils and goods in trust; £30 on those in workshop behind a house at 13 Wardour St; and £200 on those in open yard. [D; GL, Sun MS vol. 448, ref. 839165; vol. 459, ref. 871089] Submitted bill to Mrs Leigh dated 19 March–14 June 1813 and totalling £9. Items included laying a carpet, putting up a bed and window curtains, scraping, polishing and mending coromandel chairs, supplying a 'new green window blind', and cleaning a bed and curtains from bugs. [Shakespeare Birthplace Trust, Leigh receipts, DR 18/5] Supplied items to Earl Breadalbane of Taymouth Castle, Perth, 1813–15. His account of 1813 lists several pieces of highly ornate furniture such as 'a very fine Mahogany cabinet Richly ornamented w. front & ends of Angular Pilasters with French Antique heads, Therms, Friezes in brass well chases, gilt & Richly coloured & Rich framed to enclose entablature', costing £99 12s. He charged £42 16s for a 'Very Fine Mahogany Meuble for books, Surmounted with Rich Carved trusses to the underpart with ebony ornaments, fluted pilasters & ebony counter flutes, Ebony beads & moulding & terminations with ebony balustrade to shelves.' An elaborate buhl inkstand cost £49 6s, and he charged £92 12s 6d for a 'Very Rich Cabinet of King & tulip wood in feather bands & panels, Serpentine front & ends with French wrought feet &

ornament in brass. Richly gilt and coloured & highly chased & pilasters of dolphins & dragons surmounted with a cabinet of 2 French fancy Supporters of brass highly chased & Richly gilt & coloured, a balustrade of tulip wood & brass ornament finished to Match the Rest'. A 'Fine Rosewood table', with Kingwood feather banding and Buhl-work cost £43 12s; 'A very Rich florid Gothic clock case' with buhl, ebony and brass-work, £106 12s; and 'A pr. of very elegant encoignures of tulip & Kingwood & very Richly ornamented' with brasswork and '2 porcelain entablatures let in with a Mosaic border . . .' cost £90 14s 6d. In 1814 Taylor provided 'a fine Meuble for books & china', at £48 12s for the Earl of Breadalbane's house in Park Lane. In 1815 he made for Taymouth Castle '2 Magnificent cabinets to Design £580 [?] Ebony pedestal for a clock with buhl friezes & shaft on 4 sides with bronzed ornaments & trusses — to design £65.8.6.'. A long letter from Taylor to the Earl, dated 9 August 1815, explains how to steady a three-sectioned buhl cabinet sent to the Earl. He also requests payment, and describes all the expense, workmanship and materials involved in making the cabinet. [Scottish RO, GD 112/20/4/12/15–8; GD 112/20/Box 1/Bundle 33/10] Successor to John Taylor at 14 Wardour St.

Taylor, David, 26 Berners St, London, cm and u (1821–37). Took out Sun Insurance policies on 18 October 1821 for £4,650 including £1,600 on stock and utensils and £600 on workshop with stock and utensils; on 6 November 1822 for £5,200 including £2,600 on house and workshops and £2,100 on stock and utensils; and on 30 October 1823 for £6,600, £2,950 on utensils and stock. In 1832 Taylor supplied to Hopetoun House, Lothian, a large conversation couch costing £15, and '2 Grecian one arm corner chairs', £14 14s. In 1837 he charged £46 19s for 'a large hunter chair; a large tub chair; a side couch' and 'an angular ottoman'. Taylor & Co. of 26 Berners St worked at Panshanger, Herts. in 1833, charging £27 4s 5d for repairs, regilding, and a mahogany dressing table; and in 1835, £9 2s for items including a 'low seated Double . . . chair Fauteuil (Large) Stuffed back' [D; GL, Sun MS vol. 488, ref. 983859; vol. 493, ref. 997359; vol. 498, ref. 1008799; Scottish RO, Hopetoun Bundles 253–54; Herts. RO, Panshanger papers, Box 56]

Taylor, David, 6 Wellington Pl., Albany Rd, London, u (1835–39). [D]

Taylor, Edward, Liverpool, cm (1780–1818). Trading at 6 Lower Myrtle St in 1818. Petitioned freedom on servitude to James Robinson in 1780, paying 6s 8d, and admitted freeman on 11 September. [D; Liverpool freemen's committee bk and reg.]

Taylor, Edward William Whinfield, Liverpool, cm (1835). App. to William John Roberts in 1835. [Liverpool app. enrolment bk]

Taylor, Edward, Back Lane, Kirkham, Lancs., joiner and cm (1834). [D]

Taylor, Elias, address unrecorded, upholder (1725–46). Son of Elias Taylor, shoemaker of Canterbury, Kent. App. to Jeremiah Peell on 22 February 1725, and admitted freeman of the Upholders' Co. by servitude on 21 October 1746. [GL, Upholders' Co. records]

Taylor, George, Wem, Salop, chairmaker (1729). Took app. named Puliston in 1729. [S of G, app. index]

Taylor, George, address unrecorded, upholder (1735–49). Son of George Taylor, baker of Ipswich, Suffolk. App. to James Bull on 8 May 1735, and admitted freeman of the Upholders' Co. by servitude on 29 June 1749. [GL, Upholders' Co. records]

Taylor, George, North Scarle, Lincs., chairmaker (1764). Married on 19 July 1764. [Lincoln RO, marriage bonds]

Taylor, George, 156 St John's St, Smithfield, London, cm and upholder (1774–77). [D]

Taylor, George, London, cm (1793). Subscribed to Sheraton's *Drawing Book*, 1793.

Taylor, George, Liverpool, cm (1810–37). Addresses given at Primrose Hill in 1810; 10 New Fontenoy St in 1811; 49 Fontenoy St in 1813; no. 52 in 1816; no. 57 in 1827; and 7 Jervis St in 1837. [D]

Taylo(e)r, George, Manchester and Salford, cm, u and chairmaker (1808–40). Recorded at 32 Allum St, Manchester in 1808; Dean's Pl., Shudehill in 1813; 75 Chapel St, Salford, 1815–22; 8 Ridgefield, 1824–33 and 7 Ridgefield, 1836–40. [D]

Taylor, George, Exeter, Devon, cm (1814–36). Children bapt. at St Sidwell's Church: Henry Septimus on 8 December 1814; Charles Vaughan on 23 August 1818; George Henry on 11 March 1829; Emily Frances on 24 April 1831; Frederick on 4 August 1833; and Henry on 22 January 1836. [PR (bapt.)] Possible confusion with:

Taylor, George, Exeter, Devon, u (1827–38). Recorded at Castle St, c.1827–34, and 9 Paris St in 1838. Marriage to Miss Simpson, dressmaker, reported in *The Alfred*, 3 July 1827. Advertised house for sale at Higher Summerland Pl. in *Exeter Flying Post*, 15 May 1828; and one at Stafford Terr., Heavitree, on 13 March 1834. Listed as voter in Exeter election, 1832. [D]

Taylor, George, Gainsborough, Lincs., chairmaker (1826–31). Trading at Casket Lane in 1826 and Beastmarket in 1831. [D]

Taylor, George, Yarm, Yorks., joiner and cm (1827–28). [D]

Taylor, George, 229 Whitechapel Rd, London, cm, u and chairmaker (1827–28). [D]

Taylor, George, 227 Shoreditch, London, cm and u (1839). [D]

Taylor, George, 5 Bury St, Bloomsbury, London, cm and u (1839). [D]

Taylor, George, 50 Tottenham Ct Rd, London, cm, u and fret cutter (1839). [D]

Taylor, Grove(s), 29 Gt Prescot St, Goodman's Fields, London, cm and u (1822–28). [D]

Taylor, Henry, Pulteney St, Windmill St, London, cm (1777). Insured his house for £100 in 1777. [GL, Sun MS vol. 257, p. 283]

Taylor, Hynmers (or Henmers), London, later America, cm and u (1746–94). Recorded at 'The Crown & Cushion', over against Lord Monson's, Piccadilly, 1758–72; 5 Piccadilly, 1768–73; in America, 1775–76 and 1787, but also recorded at Portland St, Oxford Rd, 1778–81, and Oxford Rd, 1786 and 1794. Probably two related tradesmen of the same name are concerned here. A Taylor, upholder 'opposite Lord Monson's, Piccadilly', is named in *Public Advertiser*, 25 January 1759. Billhead gives address at 'The Crown & Cushion' by St James's Church. [Heal] Son of Randolph Taylor of London. App. to Samuel Severn on 7 August 1746, and admitted freeman of the Upholders' Co. by servitude on 9 May 1754. Named in the accounts for Croome Court, Worcs. in 1760 receiving £7 7s for 'A very fine mahogany desk'. [V&A archives] Declared bankrupt, *Gents Mag.*, August 1772. Recorded as working in America by 31 May 1775 when he advertised in *Penn'a Journal*, as 'HYNS TAYLOR, Upholder, Late of St. James, London, Takes this method of informing his friends, and the public, that he had engaged a House in Front-street, between Market and Arch streets, the right hand corner of the passage leading to the Old Ferry, where he proposes to make up all kind of Household Furniture, after the most fashionable taste, and upon reasonable terms. To be Sold, a genteel four post Bed with very fine flowered cotton furniture, fringes and ornamented with a cornice.' Advertised again in *Penn'a Evening Post*, 26

March 1776 and as H. & Amelia Taylor in *Penn'a Packet*, 17 April 1787. [D; GL, Upholders' Co. records]

Taylor, Isaac, Moorfields, London, upholder (1781). Took app. named Isaac Vizard in 1781. [GL, Upholders' Co. records]

Taylor, J. R., 76 Judd St, Brunswick Sq., London, u etc. (1814–15). [D]

Taylor, J., Plough Ct, London, carver and gilder (1825). [D]

Taylor, J. & Major, S., Poole, Dorset, u (1837). Declared bankrupt, *Exeter Flying Post*, 26 June 1837.

Taylor, James, Bristol, cm (1761–84). Recorded at St Stephen's parish in 1774; Clare St, 1775–84; and no. 5 in 1775. Pencilled inscription on top of a mahogany bureau bookcase reads: 'James Taylor & S. Davis Day 1st March 1761.' [D; poll bk; Bristol Art Gallery, research file]

Taylor, James, Nottingham, joiner and cm (1778). Took app. named George England in 1778. [Nottingham app. list]

Taylor, James & William, Nottingham, cm (1781). Insured utensils and stock for £200 in 1781. [GL, Sun MS vol. 289, p. 508]

Taylor, James, Queen St, London, carver and gilder (1784–85). Recorded at no. 4 on 12 March 1785 when he took out a Sun Insurance policy for £100 on household goods and wearing apparel. [Poll bk; GL, Sun MS vol. 327, p. 376]

Taylor, James, 44 Hoxton Sq., London, looking-glass manufacturer (1804). [D]

Taylor, James, Liverpool, cm (1803–12). App. to Thomas Savage Tyrer in 1803, and petitioned freedom on servitude in 1812, paying 6s 8d. Admitted freeman on 7 October 1812. [Liverpool freemen's committee bk and reg.]

Taylor, James, Exeter, Devon, carver and gilder (1803–37). Named in the Exeter Militia list, 1803, and in *Exeter Pocket Journal*, at Cathedral Yd in 1816; High St, 1822; Fore St, 1825–32; New Bridge St, 1834; and Fore St, 1836–37. Son Henry bapt. at St Martin's Church on 21 April 1813. Listed in *The Alfred*, 13 June 1826 as in Court for Relief of Insolvent Debtors. [D; PR (bapt.)]

Taylor, James, 34 Fetter Lane, Holborn, London, carver and gilder (1817–20). [D]

Taylor, James, Wallgate, Wigan, Lancs., carver and gilder (1828–34). [D]

Taylor, Jms, 29 Bedford Ct, Covent Gdn, London, u (1835). [D]

Taylor, James, 4 Gt Earl St, Seven Dials, London, turner and gilder (1835). [D]

Taylor, James, Northgate, Louth, Lincs., cm and joiner (1835). [D]

Taylor, James, Broad St, King's Lynn, Norfolk, cm (1839). [D]

Taylor, John, address unrecorded, upholder (1704/05–12). Took app. named Thomas Taylor, 1704/05–12. [GL, Upholders' Co. records]

Taylor, John, address unrecorded, upholder (1713). Son of Richard Taylor, freeman upholder of London; admitted freeman of the Upholders' Co. by redemption on 2 December 1713. [GL, Upholders' Co. records]

Taylor, John, Maidstone, Kent, u (1711–15). Took apps named Hunter in 1711 and Brothers in 1715. [S of G, app. index]

Taylor, John, Colchester, Essex, chairmaker (d.1721). Probate dated 1721. [*Wills at Chelmsford*]

Taylor, John, Oxford, upholder (1734). [Maidstone poll bk]

Taylor, John, Stepney, London, cm (1759). Took app. named Berry in 1759. [S of G, app. index]

Taylor, John, London, upholder (1757–81). Recorded at Cannon St, 1778–81. Son of John Taylor of St Clement Danes, Westminster. App. to John Slater, skinner, on 6 September 1757, and admitted freeman of the Upholders' Co. on 4 October 1764. [GL, Upholders' Co. records]

Taylor, John, late of King St, St Ann's, Soho, London, cm

(1761). Discharge from Debtors' Prison reported in *London Gazette*, 13 April 1761.

Taylor, John, Broad St, Ratcliff, London, u (1766). Declared bankrupt, *Gents Mag.*, May 1766.

Taylor, John, Rochester, Kent, carver (1771–80). [Poll bks]

Taylor, John, 14 Wardour St, London, cm and broker (1774–1807). Polled at Westminster in 1774. Took out a Sun Insurance policy on 29 December 1785 for £120 on utensils, stock and goods in trust, and £100 on his house. Succeeded by David Taylor at this address. [D; GL, Sun MS vol. 334, p. 29]

Taylor, John, 8 Bentinck St, near Broad St, London, cm (1778). Insured his house for £200 in 1778. [GL, Sun MS vol. 262, p. 464]

Taylor, John, near the Church in Limehouse, London, cm (1778). Insured utensils, stock and goods for £100 in 1778. [GL, Sun MS vol. 265, p. 86]

Taylor, John, Lancaster, cm (1783–84). [Lancaster freemen rolls]

Taylor, John, Manchester, joiner and cm (1788–1804). Addresses given at Shude Hill in 1788; 17 Swan St in 1794; 28 Gt Newton St in 1802 and no. 343 in 1804. [D]

Taylor, John, London, cm (1793). Subscribed to Sheraton's *Drawing Book*, 1793.

Taylor, John, York. In March 1796 supplied a new deal table costing 10s to the Retreat Quaker Asylum at York. Another bill of May 1796 was for simple furniture totalling £1 1s 3d. [Borthwick Inst., York, Retreat MS. H/1]

Taylor, John, Colchester, Essex, carpenter, cm and u (b.1775–d.1845). Trading in High St, c.1805–39, at no. 40 in 1812. [D] John Taylor, carpenter, polled in 1796; cm in 1806 and 1812; alderman in 1820, 1830 and 1831. Advertised in *Ipswich Journal*, 14 November 1812 that he was auctioning the contents of Crescent House, Lexden, listing the best furnishings 'all new within the last sixteen months'. Trade label inscribed 'J. TAYLOR, Cabinet Maker, Upholsterer, APPRAISER & AUCTIONEER, No. 27 High Street, Colchester' recorded on an early 19th-century chiffonier at Colchester Museum. Card shows a double chair, chair and bookcase surrounded by draped curtains. [235.1974] Label also found on a clothes press sold at Sudbury, 1979; and on a circular table and a Pembroke table in the Colchester Museum. [318.1965] Label giving address at 40 High St recorded on a mahogany bow-fronted chest of drawers in private ownership. Card shows eagle perched on draped curtain, with sofa, chair, bookcase, bed post and hangings. Label of J. Taylor, cm, u, appraiser and auctioneer, 27 Fish St, Colchester, recorded on a Gothic rosewood glazed bookcase. [V&A archives] John Taylor died on Christmas Day 1845, aged 70.

Taylor, John, London, cm (1806). [Colchester poll bk]

Taylor, John, Oswestry, Salop, cm (1797–98). Trading with Richard Taylor in 1798. [D]

Taylor, John, Lancaster and Preston, Lancs., chairmaker (1801–17). Admitted freeman, 1801–02, when stated 'of Preston'. Trading at Lord St, Preston, 1816–17. [D; Lancaster freemen rolls]

Taylor, John, Skerton, Lancaster, cm (1822–25). [D]

Taylor, John, London, carpenter and cm, u (1805–37). Recorded at 19 Denmark St, 1805–35; no. 8 in 1825; as I. Taylor at no. 19, 1826–27, and 29 Bedford St, Covent Gdn, 1837. [D]

Taylor, John, Rochdale, Lancs., cm (1814–34). Recorded at Cheetham St, c.1814–18 and Entwistle Pl., 1828–34. [D]

Taylor, John, Chester, cm (1818–19). Polled of Princess St in 1818 and of Foregate St in 1819. Son of John Taylor, cooper; admitted freeman on 8 January 1818. [Chester freemen rolls]

Taylor, John, Northgate St, Gloucester, cm, u and chairmaker (1820–30). Children bapt. at St Michael's Church in 1821, 1823, 1828 and 1830. [D; PR (bapt.)]

Taylor, John, Bedford Ct, Covent Gdn, London, u and furniture designer (1821–29). Recorded at no. 16 in 1824, no. 14, 1826–27 and at 16 Bedford St in 1829. At one time employed in the firm of Oakley, and later had his own business. Published an octavo volume of engraved designs of sofas and chairs from 16 Bedford Ct, c.1822. Several of his designs are shown in Ackermann's *Repository of Arts* between 1821–24, including a drawing room sofa and two chairs, July–December 1824. Receipted a bill for £51 11s 3d to the churchwardens of Mickleham, Surrey, for work done when the church was enlarged and refurbished in 1823. [D; Heal; E. T. Joy, *English Furniture, 1800–1851*; Surrey RO, (G), PSH/MIC/-/-]

Taylor, John, Hawes, Yorks., joiner and cm (1823). [D]

Taylor, John, York, cm, upholder and undertaker (1823–37). Trading at Peter St, 1823–c.1830, and 12 High Ousegate, 1830–34. [D] Five Library bookcases from Sewerby House, Yorks, now at The Bayle, Bridlington, c.1830 are labelled 'Taylors . . . No. 12 High Ousegate, York'.

Taylor, John, York, cm (1825). Son of William Taylor, butcher of Heslington, York; app. to Edward Steward & Arthur Shores, cm, on 4 August 1825. [York app. reg.]

Taylor, John, Grantham, Lincs., turner and chairmaker (1826–41). Listed at Swinegate in 1826, Manford Rd in 1835 and Manthorpe Rd in 1841. Aged 55 at the time of the 1841 Census. Windsor chairs recorded bearing the stamp of 'J. TAYLOR, GRANTHAM', on top of seat toward back. [D; *Furn. Hist.*, 1978, pl. 49C and D]

Taylor, John, Exeter, Devon, carver (1827–34). Addresses given at George's Sq., Stepcote Hill, 1827–29; 60 High St in 1831; Gandy St in 1833; and Bartholomew Yd in 1834. Daughters bapt. at St George's Church: Fanny Maria on 7 October 1827, and Selina on 14 January 1829. [*Exeter Pocket Journal*; PR (bapt.)]

Taylor, John, Staindrop, Co. Durham, joiner and cm (1827–34). [D]

Taylor, John, Liverpool, cm (1829–35). Trading at 6 Rupert St in 1829 and 13 Greetham St in 1835. [D]

Taylor, John H., Radford, Notts., joiner and cm (1832). [D]

Taylor, John, Goosepool, Louth, Lincs., cm and joiner (1835). [D]

Taylor, John, 22 Broad St, King's Lynn, Norfolk, cm (1836–39). [D] See Joseph Taylor at this address.

Taylor, John, 29 Charles St, Hull, Yorks., cm (1838). [D]

Taylor, John, Lancaster, cm (1838). Admitted freeman on 28 July 1838. [Lancaster freemen rolls]

Taylor, John, 31 Gt Ancoats St, Manchester, cm (1838–39). [D]

Taylor, (Major), John, Church St, Greenwich, London, cm (1839). [D]

Taylor, John, Spital, Cheshire, u (1839). Admitted freeman on 30 July 1839. [Chester freemen rolls]

Taylor, Jonathan, Lancaster, cm (1826–32). Admitted freeman, 1826–27. Named in the Gillow records in 1827 and 1832. [Lancaster freemen rolls; Westminster Ref. Lib., Gillow]

Taylor, (or Tayler), Joseph, London, upholder and cm (1771–86). Trading as Tayler & Wright at 157 Fenchurch St, 1772–77; alone there, 1777–84, and at Fishmonger Alley, Fenchurch St in 1786. Trade card of Tayler & Wright, cm, u and appraisers at their carpet warehouse, 157 Fenchurch St, states that the firm succeeded Mr Chesson, who is William Chesson, u at this address, 1753–74. [Heal Coll., BM] Joseph Taylor was the son of J. Taylor of St James's, Westminster, and admitted freeman of the Upholders' Co. by redemption in December 1771. Took app. named John Kemp, 1783–85.

Took out Sun Insurance policies in 1777 for £400 on his house; in 1778 and 1780 for £2,000 including £1,400 on utensils and stock; and in 1782 for £800 and £300 on houses. [D; GL, Upholders' Co. records; GL, Sun MS vol. 254, p. 83; vol. 269, p. 105; vol. 283, p. 59; vol. 299, p. 223, vol. 306, p. 41] See Chesson & Bathurst.

Taylor, Joseph, 28 Poultry, London, upholder and cm (1778). [D]

Taylor, Joseph, All Saints, Oxford, cm (1798–1802). [D; poll bk]

Taylor, Joseph, 8 Sun St, Bishopsgate, London, cm (1809). Took out a Sun Insurance policy on 18 December 1809 for £100 of which £30 accounted for tools in workshop nearby. [GL, Sun MS vol. 446, ref. 139051 or 839051] See Joshua and Matthew Taylor at 8 Sun St.

Taylor, Joseph, Pool Lane, Newcastle-under-Lyme, Staffs., chairmaker, turner etc. (1818). [D]

Taylor, Joseph, Haydon Sq., Minories, London, cm and upholder (1820–21). Recorded at no. 43 in 1821. Took out Sun Insurance policies on 8 November 1820 for £800 of which £300 accounted for stock, utensils, goods in trust and stock of glass; and on 19 December 1821 for £500, £350 on stock, utensils and glass in house, offices and workshop in Sugar Loaf Ct, Goodman's Yd. [GL, Sun MS vol. 487, ref. 972856; vol. 491, ref. 987256] See Joshua Taylor at this address.

Taylor, Joseph, King's Lynn, Norfolk, cm and u (1822–39). Trading at High St in 1822 and 22 Broad St in 1839. [D] See John Taylor at 22 Broad St.

Taylor, Joseph, Birmingham, cm and u (1828–30). Trading at 29 Paradise St in 1828 and 135 Snowhill in 1830. [D]

Taylor, Joseph, 7 Swindon Pl., Cheltenham, Glos., cm and u (1830). [D]

Taylor, Joseph, West Auckland, Bishop Auckland, Co. Durham, cm and/or joiner (1834). [D]

Taylor, Joseph & George, Shelley, Kirkburton, near Huddersfield, Yorks., joiners and cm (1834). [D]

Taylor, Joseph, Wednesbury, Staffs., cm (1839). [D]

Taylor, Joshua, Haydon Sq., Minories, London, cm, u and undertaker (1822–39). Recorded at no. 43, 1822–23; no. 4, 1823–25; no. 42, 1827–35; and 42 Bishopsgate Within and Haydon Sq. in 1837. Two trade cards survive with address at 42 Haydon Sq. One reads: 'Joshua Taylor & Sons, Auctioneers & Valuers, HOUSE & ESTATE AGENTS, FURNISHING UNDERTAKERS'; the other, perhaps later, reads: 'JOSHUA TAYLOR & SONS, Cabinet Manufacturers & Upholsterers, AUCTIONEERS & APPRAISERS, FURNISHING UNDERTAKERS, TO HER MAJESTY'S HON^BLE BOARD OF ORDNANCE', surmounted by the Royal Arms. [D; GL, trade card coll.; E. T. Joy, *English Furniture, 1800–1851*, p. 219, illus.] See Joseph Taylor at this address.

Taylor (or Tayler), Joshua, London, cm and u (1826–35). Recorded at 25 Bolingbroke Row, Walworth, 1826–35, and also 8 Sun St and 3 Dunnings Alley, Bishopsgate in 1835. [D] See Joseph and Matthew Taylor at 8 Sun St.

Taylor, Lewis, 20 Cloak Lane, London, carver and gilder (1839). [D] Probably L. Tayler.

Taylor (or Tayler), Matthew, London, cm, u, chair, sofa and bedstead maker, undertaker (1805–35). Trading at 9 Little Cheapside, Sun St, 1805–07; 9 Long Alley, Moorfields, with workshop at 8 Sun St in 1809; and 8 Sun St, Bishopsgate Without, 1811–35. Took out Sun Insurance policies in 1809 for £300 on workshop and stock at 8 Sun St; and on 10 February 1814 for £800 on stock and utensils, £200 on warehouse, £100 on workshop at Dunnings Alley, Bishopsgate, and £400 on stock and utensils there and in open

yard. Undated bill head with address at 8 Sun St is in GL trade card coll. [D; GL, Sun MS vol. 446, ref. 830903; vol. 463, ref. 891175]

Taylor, Matthew, Otley, Yorks., joiner and/or cm (1834). [D]

Taylor, Michael, Pool Dam, Newcastle-under-Lyme, Staffs., chairmaker (1822). [D]

Taylor, Micah, Sheffield, Yorks., cm (1780). Insured his house for £100 in 1780. [GL, Sun MS vol. 283, p. 555]

Taylor, Nathaniel, Earsham St, Bungay, Suffolk, u and cm (1824–39). [D]

Taylor, O., Clarke St, Bury, Lancs., joiner and/or cm (1816–17). [D]

Taylor, Peter, Stoke, Staffs., cm and u (1818–28). Recorded at Market Pl., 1818–23 and Cliff Bank in 1828. [D]

Taylor, Peter, Great Dunmow, Essex, cm (1823–27). [D]

Taylor, Peter, Gt Homer St, Liverpool, joiner and cm (1837–39). Trading at no. 48 in 1837 and no. 62 in 1839. [D]

Taylor, Ralph, Lincoln, cm and u (1822–35). Trading at 'Bail' in 1822 and Castle Hill, 1826–35. [D]

Taylor, Richard, London, upholder (1713). His son, John Taylor, admitted freeman of the Upholders' Co. in 1713. [GL, Upholders' Co. records]

Taylor, Richard, address unknown. In 1749 app. to John Richardson, cm of New-Helvit (New Elvet), Durham, for a premium of £10 under the Sons of the Clergy scheme. [*General Advertiser*, 17 April 1749]

Taylor, Richard, Oswestry, Salop, cm (1797). [D]

Taylor, Richard, Chester, cm (1802). Son of John Taylor, cooper of Chester. Admitted freeman on 8 January 1802. [Chester freemen rolls]

Taylor, Richard, Bristol, carver and gilder (1822–23). Trading at 8 St Stephen's St in 1822 and 7 Steep St, St Michael's, 1823. [D]

Taylor, Richard, Dudley, Worcs., cm and u (1838–40). Trading at Queen's Cross in 1840. [D]

Taylor, Robert, Market St, St James's, London, cm and broker (1775–81). Took out Sun Insurance policies in 1775 for £700 of which £500 accounted for utensils, stock and goods; and in 1781 for £300 on his house. [GL, Sun MS vol. 239, p. 622; vol. 292, p. 614]

Taylor, Robert, Denmark St, St Giles, London, cm (1789). [Bailey's list of bankrupts]

Taylor, Robert snr, Worcester, upholder (1747–61). His first-born son, Robert Taylor jnr, upholder, admitted freeman on 28 March 1761. [Worcester freemen rolls and poll bk]

Taylor, Robert snr, Exeter, Devon, cm (b.1744–d.1826). Took out a Sun Insurance policy in 1777 for £500 of which £450 accounted for stock and utensils. Listed in *Exeter Pocket Journal*, 1791 and 1796; and in election squibs, 1816. Subscribed to Sheraton's *Drawing Book*, 1793. R. Taylor & Son advertised in *Western Luminary*, 31 August 1819 stating: 'Extensive stock of cabinet furniture to be sold at reduced prices until the unmanufactured stock is disposed of, they being about to decline the Manufactory of Cabinet Furniture. A large stock of well-seasoned mahogany to be disposed of. The upholstery business will be continued as usual in all its branches together with the chair & sofa manufactory, carpets, paper hangings, Bedding, an assortment of furniture, prints & moreens, glasses etc.'. R. Taylor jnr took over his father's business in 1821. Death of Robert Taylor snr at St Sidwell's, Exeter, aged 82, reported in *The Alfred*, 22 August 1826. [GL, Sun MS vol. 258, p. 497] Probable confusion with:

Taylor, Robert jnr, Exeter, Devon, cm and u, undertaker and auctioneer (1814–37). Addresses given at St Sidwell's, 1814–17; 16 St Sidwell's, at the corner of Castle St, 1821–26; 254 High St, 1822–37; and 253 Fore St, 1823–30. R. Taylor jnr, cm, listed in election squibs, 1816. His son, Charles William, was bapt. at St Sidwell's on 29 November 1814, and son Robert on 10 November 1817. Announced in *Exeter Flying Post*, 4 October 1821, that the partnership with his father was dissolved, and he was taking over the business. Advertised stock of well-manufactured goods of the best quality, and well-seasoned mahogany. Robert Taylor jnr's election as one of the 'Forty Guardians of the Poor for the North-Ward of this City' reported in *Exeter Flying Post*, 14 June 1821. Acted as agent in sale of furniture of Mrs Cooke, advertising in the same paper on 17 June 1824. Announced on 30 March 1826 that 'he is about to DISPOSE of the whole of his Extensive STOCK of FLOOR and STAIR CARPETS; consisting of above TWO THOUSAND SIX HUNDRED YARDS of BRUSSELS, superfine KIDDERMINSTER, and VENE-TIANS, and a large Assortment of HEARTH RUGS . . . Also a Large quantity of FLOOR CLOTHS and LONDON PAPER HANGINGS and BORDERS, on the same Low Terms . . . N.B. the UPHOLSTERY, CABINET and CHAIR BUSINESS, carried on as usual, of the best Materials and Workmanship.' Announced sale of the whole of his stock, and his premises to let on 26 May 1836. Stock consisted of 'CABINET and UPHOLSTERY FURNITURE', floor coverings, glasses and paper hangings, mahogany and rosewoood timber. Still listed in directories, 1837. [D; PR (bapt.)]

Taylor, Robert, Uttoxeter, Staffs., clock-case maker and cm (1818–35). Recorded at Church St, 1828–35. [D]

Taylor, Robert, Finkle St, Stockton-upon-Tees, Co. Durham, joiner and cm (1827–32). [D]

Taylor, Sam., 20 Laystock St, London, carver and gilder (1809–11). [D]

Taylor, Samuel, 34 Lees St, Gt Ancoats St, Manchester, u (1817). [D]

Taylor, Samuel, Derby Lane, Coventry, Warks., chairmaker (1822). [D]

Taylor, Samuel, New Rd, Woolwich, London, carver and gilder, plumber and painter (1826–27). [D]

Taylor, Samuel, Bermondsey, London, chair and sofa manufac-turer (1829–39). Trading at 21 Grange Rd in 1829 and 7 Bermondsey New Rd in 1839. [D]

Taylor, Samuel, 14 Cow Green, Halifax, Yorks., u (1837). [D]

Taylor, Saul, 139 Kent St, Southwark, London, chair and sofa manufacturer (1826). [D]

Taylor, T., Atherstone Warks., chairmaker (1796). [D]

Taylor, T., Market Drayton, Salop, chairmaker (1797). [D]

Taylor, T., White Cloth Hall, Leeds, Yorks., carver and gilder (1798). [D]

Taylor, Thomas, address unrecorded, upholder (1704–12). Son of John Taylor, freeman upholder of London. App. to his father on 7 February 1704/05, and admitted freeman of the Upholders' Co. by servitude on 9 October 1712. [GL, Upholders' Co. records]

Taylor, Thomas, Maidstone, Kent, u (1725–27). Took app. named Swinock in 1725. Took out a Sun Insurance policy on 10 April 1727 for £500. [S of G, app. index; GL, Sun MS vol. 23, p. 538]

Taylor, Thomas, Ileats (or Keats?) Cabing, Huntingdon. On 11 June 1745 supplied the Duke of Gordon with 'A Larg Cabineat' costing £7 7s; a chest at £1 18s; a dressing box, £1 1s; and a writing box, £1 1s. He also charged for carriage between London and York. [Scottish RO, GD44/51/299/2]

Taylor, Thomas, St Andrew's parish, Worcester, chairmaker (1747). [Poll bk]

Taylor, Thomas, Nottingham, carver (1757). Will dated 16 August 1757. [Notts. RO, probate records]

Taylor, Thomas, Nantwich, Cheshire, chairmaker (1761–d.1813). Married on 28 Jun 1761. Son Thomas bapt.

on 31 October 1784. Daughter buried on 19 June 1789. Died on 13 December 1813, and buried on 25 January 1814. [Chester RO, PR]

Taylor, Thomas, 25 Hosier Lane, London, gilder (1783). Took out a Sun Insurance policy in 1783 for £200 of which £100 accounted for utensils and stock. [GL, Sun MS vol. 314, p. 146]

Taylor, Thomas Paston, Norwich, upholder (1786–1808). Listed in poll bks 1786–1806. Trading at 4 Pottergate St, 1801–02 and Bridewell Alley, c.1803–08. A former app. of Thomas and Charles Taylor, Henry Utting, u, was admitted freeman on 24 February 1801. [D; Norwich freemen reg. and poll bks]

Taylor, Thomas, 74 Pitt St, with warehouse at Lydia Ann St, Duke St, Liverpool, bed and mattress maker (1803). [D]

Taylor, Thomas, Hunslet, Leeds, Yorks., cm, joiner and u (1817–37). Addresses given at Low Rd, 1834–37 and Society St in 1837. [D]

Taylor, Thomas, Liverpool, u (1827–37). Trading at 6 Comus St in 1827; 19 Richmond Row in 1829; and 6 Myrtle St and 19 Hill St, 1835–37. [D]

Taylor, Thomas, Dog Lane, Coventry, Warks., chairmaker (1828). [D]

Taylor, Thomas, 3 Mason St, Manchester, cm (1834–39). Recorded also at no. 5 in 1838. [D]

Taylor, Thomas, Walsall, Staffs., cm (1828–35). Listed at Digbeth in 1828 and Ablewell St, 1830–35. [D]

Taylor, Thomas, Wednesbury, Staffs., cm (1839). [D]

Taylor, Thomas, Liverpool, cm (1838). App. to William John Roberts in 1838. [Liverpool app. enrolment bk]

Taylor, Thomas, Stalbridge, Dorset, joiner and cm (1840). [D]

Taylor, W., New Cut, Blackfriars Rd, London, u (1809–11). [D]

Taylor, Warnford, 21 Mercer St, Long Acre, London, carver, gilder and grocer (1782). Took out a Sun Insurance policy in 1782 for £200 of which utensils, stock and goods accounted for £100. [GL, Sun MS vol. 304, p. 555]

Taylor, William, Lancaster. App. to R. Coulstone in 1758. [Lancaster app. reg.]

Taylor, William, Derby, carver (1775). [Poll bk]

Taylor, William, Nottingham, joiner and cm (1785–1802). Trading at Long Row in 1799. Took apps named William Woolley in 1785, Henry Richardson in 1787 and David Taylor in 1802. Signed the *Nottingham Cabinet and Chair Makers' Book of Prices*, 1791, on behalf of the masters. [D; Nottingham app. list]

Taylor, William, Cable St, Liverpool, carver (1787). [D]

Taylor, William, 23 Upper East Smithfield, London, upholder (1792). Took out a Sun Insurance policy on 8 June 1792 for £300 incuding £250 on stock and utensils. [GL, Sun MS vol. 387, ref. 601147]

Taylor, William F., Uttoxeter, Staffs., carver (1798). [D]

Taylor, William, 6 Little Windmill St, Golden Sq., London, cm (1805–07). [D]

Taylor, William, Lancaster, cm (1803–12). App. to R. Mashiter in 1803 and admitted freeman, 1811–12. [Lancaster app. reg. and freemen rolls]

Taylor, William, Staindrop, near Barnard Castle, Co. Durham, cm (1815–27). Daughter bapt. on 2 July 1815. [D; Bowes Museum, transcript of PR (bapt.)]

Taylor, William Smith, St Ebbe's, Oxford, cm, u and appraiser (1817–30). Married Maria Freeman of Oxford at St Ebbe's on 20 May 1817. Listed at St Ebe's [*sic*] Lane in 1823 and St Mary Magdalen's, 1830. [D; Bodleian index of Oxf. marriage bonds]

Taylor, William, Liverpool, u and cm (1820–39). Addresses given at 1 Ironmonger Lane in 1824; 40–41 Seel St, 1827–35; also 25 Pool Lane in 1827; with yard at 15 Grenville St in

1834; 47 Seel St, also 23 Greek St and 2 Grenville St in 1837; and 64 Seel St in 1839. App. to George Philander Lyon in 1820, and admitted freeman on servitude paying 6s 8d in 1830. [D; Liverpool app. enrolment bk and freemen's committee bk] Possibly two tradesmen of the same name.

Taylor, William, Newcastle-under-Lyme, Staffs., chairmaker (1822–30). [D; poll bks]

Taylor, William, Newcastle, cm and furniture broker (1824–34). Trading at Dog-bank, 1824–34. [D]

Taylor, William, 26 Low Friar St, Newcastle, u (1827). [D]

Taylor, William, Back Bondgate, Bishop Auckland, Co. Durham, joiner and cm (1827–34). [D]

Taylor, William, London, bedstead maker (1829–39). Trading at 16 Bath St, City Rd in 1829; and 6 Back Rd, St George's Path, in 1839. [D]

Taylor, William, Westgate, Mansfield, Notts., joiner and cm (1822–41). [D]

Taylor, William, Chapel Town, Halifax, Yorks., cm (1837). [D]

Taylor, William, Wray's Ct, Cambridge, cm and u (1837–47). [Poll bks]

Taylor, William, Holderness Ct, Witham, Hull, Yorks., cm (1838–39). [D]

Taylor, William, 15 Boar St, Gravel Lane, Southwark, London, chair and sofa maker (1839). [D]

Taylor & Jenkinson, Halifax, Yorks., cm (1834). [D]

Taylor & Son, Nottingham, cm, joiners and carpenters (1784). Advertised for craftsmen in *Nottingham Journal*, 31 July 1784. See Hallam & Pidlock.

Taylor & Sons, Gt Dover St, London, cm. Name and address stamped on early 19th-century mahogany bookcase in the library at Moor House, Herts. Over 24 feet long, it must have been made for its position, extending the north wall of the library. The bookcase is unusual since the doors to its lattice-fronted shelves have no stiles, necessitating an elaborate arrangement of hinges. [*C. Life*, 2 February 1956, pp. 206–07, pl. 6]

Taylor & Utting, Bridewell Alley, Norwich, u (1810). [D]

Taylor & Walton, 110 Fenchurch St, London, u, cm, auctioneers and appraisers (1820–25). [D] Succeeded by Taylor & Fisher.

Taylour, John, 7 Hatton Wall, Hatton Gdn, London, upholder and undertaker (1817). [D]

Teague, J., Falm[outh], Cornwall. Pencilled inscription on back board of X-banded mahogany serpentine chest of drawers formerly in possession of Avon Antiques, Bradford-upon-Avon, reads: 'J. Teague Falm 1779'. Probably:

Teague, John, Truro, Cornwall, cm (1760s–89). Several children of John and Mary Teague were bapt. at St Mary's, Truro, in the 1760s and 1770s. Square chest of drawers with brushing slide, is signed 'John Teague, Truro, August 1770'. 'John Teague, of the parish of St Clements, Cornwall, Cabinet-Maker' made his will on 20 June 1789. [Cornwall RO, probate records]

Teal, —, Pontefract, Yorks., cm (1797–98). [D]

Teal, James, Pontefract, Yorks., joiner and cm (1834). [D]

Teal, John, Cottingham, near Hull, Yorks., cm (1807). App. to Thomas Ross in December 1807. [Hull app. reg.]

Teale, John, Shipley, Yorks., cm (1822). [D]

Teale, John, Leeds, Yorks., u and cm (1834–39). Recorded at 16 Lowerhead Row, 1834–37. Trading until 1851, and succeeded by John Richard Teale. [D] Successor to:

Teale, Josiah, Leeds, Yorks., cm and u (1791–1830). Referred to in *Industries of Yorkshire*, Historical Publishing Co., 1888, as founder of the firm. Signed the *Leeds Cabinet and Chair Makers' Book of Prices*, 1791, as a journeyman cm. Advertised in *Leeds Intelligencer*, 9 December 1811, that he had recently made alterations to his premises in order to keep

'an extensive assortment of all kinds of Cabinet Goods ... Ladies' work-boxes etc.' Trading as Jos. Teale & Son, 1816–30, and listed at 30 Lowerhead Row, 1816–17, at no. 16, 1826–30. Teal & Sons, Leeds, subscribed to Sheraton's *Cabinet Dictionary*, 1803. [D]

Teale, Thomas, 14 Nile St, North Street, Leeds, Yorks., cm (1822). [D]

Te(a)rnl(e)y, —, 1 Garden Row, near the Obelisk, Lambeth, London, chairmaker (1803). Subscribed to Sheraton's *Cabinet Dictionary*, and named in his list of master cabinet makers, 1803.

Teasdale, Robert, Lancaster and London, cm (1785–1807). App. to William Blackburn in 1785, and admitted freeman, 1806–07, when stated 'of London'. [Lancaster app. reg. and freemen rolls]

Teasdale, William, 12 Lancaster St, Burton Cresc., London, carver (1835). [D]

Teasdale, Webb & Co., 29 Gracechurch St, London, wholesale u (1777–84). [D] See Webb & Lawford.

Teasell, Henry, Upper Main St, Totnes, Devon, cm (1830). [D]

Teasell, Joseph, Totnes, Devon, cm (1823–24). [D]

Tebbott, Robert, London, Carpenter to His Majesty, under-taker, joiner, auctioneer and appraiser (b.1782–d.1850). Recorded at Sheet St, Windsor, 1824–30. Listed in the fifth hall book of the borough of New Windsor, 1828–52, as Bailiff, 1815–17, Chamberlain of the Poor, 1817–18, Alderman in 1827, and Mayor, 1828–29 and 1842–43. [D] Carried out mostly jobbing work and backstairs furniture at Windsor Castle, 1831–41. In 1832 he supplied twenty deal table tops for temporary tables, costing £55, and twenty deal sideboard tops at £42 15s. He also provided drawers and racks for storing furniture, deal tables for the Silver Pantry and the Coal Porter's Room, and deal stools for the Steward's Room in June 1836. [PRO, LC11/77, 92 and 95; Windsor RA, Box 1, items 2 and 17 (estimates)]

Teesdale, Joseph, Boston, Lincs., cm (1761). Took app. named Lincoln in 1761. [S of G, app. index]

Telfer (or Telfor), John, Clipstone St, Marylebone, London, cm and pianoforte maker (1804–11). Recorded at no. 25 in 1804 and 1809–11; and no. 35, 1805–07. Took out a Sun Insurance policy on 28 August 1804 for £100 on household goods, and £50 on a private house at 7 Ogle St nearby. [D; GL, Sun MS vol. 431, ref. 764736]

Telling, Thomas, London, carver, gilder and frame maker (1790–1809). Trading at 13 Piccadilly, 1790–93, and Bridge Rd, Lambeth in 1809. [D]

Tempany, J. or G. (?), 35 Union St, Middlx Hospital, London, carver (1835). [D]

Temperley, John & Ralph, Haydon Bridge, Northumb., joiner and/or cm (1834). [D]

Temperton, Edward, Owston, Lincs., cm and joiner (1835). [D]

Tempest, John, Leeds, Yorks., u (1771). Delivered 'sundry Goods ... as per bill £144.18.0' to Harewood House on 16 November 1771. [*Furn. Hist.*, 1973]

Temple, J., 15 Upper St Martin's Lane, London, bedstead and mattress maker (1820). [D]

Temple, Jacob, London, bedstead and chair manufacturer, u, cm and broker of household goods (1817–39). Recorded at 241 Whitechapel Rd, 1817–28; 8 Bedford Pl., Commercial Rd, 1826–28; and 1 Doran's Row, Commercial Rd in 1839. Took out Sun Insurance policies on 1 November 1821 for £1,400 on his house and goods; and on 20 March 1823 for £700 on his new dwelling house only. [D; GL, Sun MS vol. 487, ref. 985211; vol. 492, ref. 1003198] See T. & J. Temple and Temple & Hancock.

Temple, Jeremiah, Fisher Gdns, Knaresborough, Yorks., joiner, cm and builder (1828–29). [D]

Temple, Jeremiah, Southgate St, Hartlepool, Co. Durham, joiner and/or cm (1834). [D]

Temple, John, London, bedstead and mattress maker, u (1816–23). Addresses given at 17 Little Alie St, Goodman's Fields, 1816–17; 14 and 15 Bloomsbury Mkt, 1820–21; no. 15, 1822–23. Took out Sun Insurance policies on 11 March 1822 for £600 on his house; and on 12 February 1823 for £400 including £200 on stock and utensils in his house. [D; GL, Sun MS vol. 490, ref. 989826; vol. 489, ref. 1001432]

Temple, T. & J., 241 Whitechapel, London, bedstead manufacturers (1813). [D] See Jacob Temple and Temple & Hancock.

Temple, Thomas, London, carver and gilder (1820–39). Recorded at Clipstone St, Fitzroy Sq. in 1820, and 50 Gt Titchfield St, 1820–39. [D] Possibly the Thomas Temple, picture framer, mentioned in the Chatsworth furnishing accounts, 1820–34.

Temple, William, 18 Grafton St, Soho, London, bedstead and mattress maker (1820–29). [D]

Temple & Hancock, 241 Whitechapel, London, bedstead manufacturers (1816–25). [D] See Jacob and T. & J. Hancock.

Tempson, J., Milk St, Shrewsbury, Salop, cm (1786). [D]

Tenlan, Samuel, 22 Nelson St, Greenwich, London, cm and u (1832–34). [D]

Tennant, James, Lancaster, cm (1828–39). App. to L. Redmayne in 1828 and admitted freeman, 1836–37. Named in the Gillow records, 1832–39. [Lancaster app. reg. and freemen rolls; Westminster Ref. Lib., Gillow]

Tennant, Thomas, Long Lane, London, chairmaker (1732). An advertisement in *Daily Post*, 26 October 1732 announced 'all the rich Stock in Trade of Mr. Thomas Tennant an eminent wholesale Dealer in all manner of Household Furniture' (warehouses in Long-Lane) were to be sold during the Winter Season at Surman's Great House in Soho. A list of furniture is cited. [D; *Conn.*, February 1933, pp. 90–93]

Tennant, Thomas, Lancaster. Named in the Gillow records, 1814–38. [Westminster Ref. Lib.]

Tennercliffe, Joseph, York, u (1825). Of Clifton, app. to William Smith, u and cm, 28 February 1825. [York app. reg.]

Tentham, Thomas, 136 Strand, London, carver and gilder (1794). Took out a Sun Insurance policy on 29 May 1794 for £750 including his house and two stables. [GL, Sun MS vol. 401, ref. 628512]

Terret(t) (or Terratt), Jos., Josh., or Joseph, Gt Suffolk St, Southwark, London, cm, u and undertaker (1820–39). Recorded at no. 10, 1820–28; no. 129 in 1829; no. 7 in 1835; and no. 11 in 1839. [D]

Terrey, Timothy, 30 Grafton St East, Fitzroy Sq., London, u (1824). Recorded in George IV's accounts on 29 November 1824 receiving £42 for a mahogany library chair 'recently invented, by being constructed on metallic springs, Handsomely carved and polished, Mounted on French castors, covered with purple morocco, and embellished with Golden Borders.' [Windsor RA 25393; 35584]

Terry, Edward, Kent, cm (1779–96). Of Sandwich, declared bankrupt, *Gents Mag.*, March 1779. Polled at Canterbury of Faversham in 1790 and of Sandwich in 1796.

Terry (or Tarry), George, Whitecross St, London, upholder (1724–34). [Poll bks] See George Tarry.

Terry, George, London, carver and gilder (1826–39). Addresses given at 16 New St, Webber St, New Cut in 1826; and 37 Webber Row, Blackfriars Rd, 1835–37. [D]

Terry, Henry, address unrecorded, upholder (1713). Son of Henry Terry of Horsebridge, Southampton, Hants.; app. to William Simmons, and admitted freeman of the Upholders' Co. by servitude on 13 January 1713. [GL, Upholders' Co. records]

Terry, Henry, London, cm and upholder (1765–d.1804). Trading at 16 Ave-Maria Lane, Ludgate St, 1778–99. Son of John Terry, butcher of Wrotham, Kent. App. to Joseph Merryman on 5 December 1765, and admitted freeman of the Upholders' Co. by servitude on 6 October 1773. Took app. named Henry Gee, 1790–1803. [D; GL, Upholders' Co. records]

Terry, Robert, Bethel St, Norwich, u and paper hanger (1822). [D]

Terry, T., 18 Upper Rathbone Pl., Fitzroy Sq., London, u etc. (1820). [D]

Terry, Thomas, Davygate, York, carver, gilder and looking-glass maker (1830–40). Trading at 8 Davygate in 1830, Davygate in 1838 and 43 Goodramgate in 1840. [D]

Terry, William, Kirkgate, Wakefield, Yorks., carver and gilder (1830–37). Trading at Pincheon St in 1837. [D]

Terveld, Pet., 6 Worcester St, Southwark, London, carver and gilder (1826). [D]

Tervella, James, 6 Worcester St, Southwark, London, carver and gilder (1826–27). [D]

Tesdale, Benjamin & Co., London. In 1709 supplied the Duke of Montrose with a mohair bed, chairs, stools and curtains, at a total cost of £40 16s. Mohair was provided by John Prudom & Co. [Scottish RO, GD 220/6/1122/3]

Testi, A., 30 Leather Lane, London, looking-glass maker (1804). [D]

Testi, Joseph, 10 Leather Lane, Holborn, London, looking-glass and barometer maker (1822). [Goodison, *Barometers*]

Teulon, Samuel, London St, Greenwich, London, cm and auctioneer (1823–39). [D]

Tew, Joseph, Penkhull St, Newcastle-under-Lyme, Staffs., cm (1822–23). [D]

Tew, William, Park St, Warwick, cm (1831). [Poll bk]

Thacker, Benoni (or Bonomi), St Paul's, Covent Gdn, London, cm and carpenter (1726–62). Employed by Sir William Chambers in making furniture for Carrington House, Whitehall, and elsewhere. As a carpenter, subscribed to the first edition of Chippendale's *Director*, 1754. Took apps named Thomas Osborne in 1753 for £20, Sam Foyster in 1760 for £31 10s and Fran Englehart in 1762 for £31 10s. [*DEF*; Heal; V&A archives]

Thacker, Phillip, address unrecorded, upholder (1700). Admitted freeman of the Upholders' Co. on 7 August 1700. [GL, Upholders' Co. records]

Thacker, William, 29 Mount St, Grosvenor Sq., London, cm (1809–11). [D]

Thackery, James, 25 Thayer St, Manchester Sq., London, upholder and undertaker (1817). [D] See John Thackray.

Thackray, —, address unrecorded, cm (1803). Subscribed to Sheraton's *Cabinet Dictionary*, 1803.

Thackray, James, Leeds, Yorks., cm (1817–22). Addresses given at 106 Kirkgate, 1817; Wright's Yd, York St, 1818–20; and Church Lane, 1822. [D] See Joseph Thackray.

Thackray, John, Laizenby Ct, London, cm (1803). Subscribed to Sheraton's *Cabinet Dictionary*, 1803.

Thackray, John, 25 Thayer St, Manchester Sq., London, u (1819–25). [D] See James Thackery.

Thackray, Joseph, 106 Kirkgate, Leeds, Yorks., cm (1828–30). [D] See James Thackray.

Thackray, William, 30 South Molton St, London, broker and u (1805–07). [D]

Thackthwaite, —, St James's, London, cm (1757). Took app. named Bailey in 1757. [S of G, app. index]

Thack(th)waite (or Thacwait), Daniel and William, Westminster, London, cm (1740–49). Took out a Sun Insurance policy on 8 April 1740 for £300. [GL, Sun MS vol. 54, p. 428] Both polled at Westminster, of Marshall St, in 1749.

Thack(th)waite (or Thatch(th)waite), Michael, Marylebone St, Golden Sq., London, cm and upholder (1754–95). Recorded at 'The Easy Chair', Marylebone St in 1767; and 7 Marylebone St, 1774–94 as Thackthwaite & Son, 1791–95. Took out a Sun Insurance policy on 20 June 1792 for £1,200, including £1,000 on his house in Hanover Sq. in tenure of a Mrs Walter, and £200 on buildings adjoining. [D; poll bks; GL, Sun MS vol. 388, p. 122] On 5 February 1767 receipted a bill to Sir Gilbert Heathcote for a mahogany bookshelf costing 14s. Receipt is on the back of his Rococo trade card which shows a Chinese Chippendale-style upholstered armchair, and gives address at 'The Easy Chair'. Card states that he 'Makes & Sells all Sorts of Cabinet Work, Chair Work, & Upholstry Work in General, at Reasonable Rates. N.B. Funerals Perform'd both Public & Private, in a Decent Manner.' [Lincoln RO, 2 ANC 12/D/26] Supplied furniture for the State Bedroom at Erddig, Clywd, c.1775. [C. Life, 6 April 1978, p. 909] In July–August 1786 he inventoried the household furniture of the late Edward, Lord Leigh, at Stoneleigh, Warks., and supplied furniture to Mrs Leigh. His bill, dated 9 June–31 August 1786, totalled £30 16s 4½d, and included 'a Moho.' Bason Stand with a drawer', 'an Elbow Chair Matted Seat Dyed Black', and 'a Moho.' Convenient Corner Chair, Seat Cover'd with Sattin horse hair Brass nailed', with 'White Stone Pan'. He also provided a card rack, a mahogany stand for a screen, 'Wainscot Window Blinds', a '5 foot Wainscot Bedstead on 3 Wheel Casters, Moho.' feet Posts . . .'; and fine cotton and lace bed furniture and window curtains, and blankets. He charged for 'Repairing the Paper on the Staircase and Passage', 'Cleaning Down and Sizing the Wall', and 'Colouring the Wall on staircase and Passage Twice over in Virditor Blue.' [Shakespeare Birthplace Trust, Leigh receipts, DR 18/4/69; 18/5; Stoneleigh sales cat., Christie's, 15–16 October 1981, lot 150] Possibly the Thackthwayt, cm of Marylebone St, near Piccadilly, who as an agent announced in Public Advertiser, 16 August 1754, sale of 'An extraordinary good front for a Shop, consisting of strong outside shutters with compass ends and Modillion Cornice, with Mahogany sashes with Crown Glass. A Press which has been used by a Goldsmith for Plate . . . and several other Fitments of a Shop.'

Thackwray, Joseph, Harrogate, Yorks., joiner and cm (1834). [D]

Thairlwall, George, Hull, Yorks., joiner and cm (1817). App. to Edward Dickon in May 1817. [Hull app. reg.]

Thames, William, Church Fields, Greenwich, London, cm (1826). [D]

Tharp, —, at the end of Dover St, Piccadilly, London, u (1720). Named in contemporary newspapers. [Heal]

Tharrat(t), Thomas, London, cm, u, undertaker and chairmaker (1793–1839). Addresses given at 16 Sheppard St, Hanover Sq., 1805–07; 17 Shepherd St, Hanover Sq./Oxford St, 1809–17; 17 High St, St Giles, Bloomsbury, 1827–29; 21 Queen St, Soho, in 1835; and Rose St, Soho, in 1839. Subscribed to Sheraton's Drawing Book, 1793. [D]

Thatcher, Henry, 3 South Molton St, Bond St, London, cm (1829). [D]

Thatcher, Joseph, 3 St James's Ct, Bristol, cm (1775). [D]

Thatcher, William, 49 Frith St, Soho, London, cm (1793). Took out a Sun Insurance policy on 12 January 1793 for £200 including £30 on utensils and stock. [GL, Sun MS vol. 392, p.151]

Thaw, Henry, 2 Bath Pl., New Rd, London, u (1835). [D]

Theaker, Joseph, Leeds, Yorks., cm, upholder and music teacher (1791–1830). Recorded at St Peter's Sq. with workshop at High Ct Lane in 1791; Kirkgate from 1792–1830, with warehouse at Boar Lane in 1813; 107 Kirkgate in 1814;

no. 106 in 1816–17; no. 44, 1826–30; and 59 Chatham St in 1830. As Joseph snr advertised in Leeds Intelligencer, 20 September and 4 October 1791. Announced in Leeds Mercury, 16 June 1792, his removal from St Peter's Sq. to Kirkgate, stating: 'Harpsichords & Pianofortes repaired & tuned. Pictures neatly framed, Maps Mounted, & Rooms carefully Papered. A neat assortment of Looking-Glasses in Gilt & Mahogany Frames, Tea-Trays, Caddies, etc.' In February, March and June 1795 announced in Leeds Mercury, that he taught music, adding: 'The Cabinet & Upholstery Business carried on as usual'. Notice given in same paper on 4 December 1814 of his removal to the corner of Bank St, Boar Lane, where his warehouse was. [D; Furn. Hist., 1971]

Theakston(e), Christopher, Doncaster, Yorks., carver (1773–74). Polled at York in 1774. Named in the Harewood MS on 17 June 1773 receiving payments for carving feet and pedestals of five mahogany tea tables made by John Walker, a local joiner. A payment was made to Walker on 14 January 1774 for '4 Mahogany Tea Tables' costing £3 18s; and another to Christopher Theakstone was for 'Carving work done at Harewood House for Edwin Lascelles Esq.', detailed as: 'Carving a Set of Feet for round table with Lion feet', 18s; 'A Do with Eagles feet & the Mouldings enriched', £1 10s; 'A Do with Scrole foot a rafled leaf and Moudings enriched', £1 5s; 'A Do with plain Scrole foot & the Moudings enriches', 10s; and 'A Do with Eagles feet & the Mouldings enriched', £1 10s. The first, second and fifth on this list correspond to items sold at Christie's, 1 April 1976, lots 47–49; the third and fourth remain at Harewood. Two full-size working drawings which correspond almost exactly to the two tables still at Harewood in 1976 are almost certainly by Chippendale. [Leeds archives dept, Harewood MS 513; Furn. Hist., 1973, pl. 11A and B; I. Hall, 'Newly discovered Chippendale drawings relating to Harewood', LAC, No. 69, 1971; Beard, Georgian Craftsmen]

Thentsi, —, Lincoln's Inn Fields, London. The Duchess of Northumberland visited his establishment, c.1766, and noted the price of certain wares. [C. Gilbert, Chippendale, p. 153]

Thewler, Samuel, Liverpool, cm (1761). Admitted freeman on 29 January 1761. [Liverpool freemen reg.]

Thickpenny, Thomas, Leicester, joiner and turner (1721). App. to Jos. Smith, and admitted freeman in 1721. Took several apps [Leicester freemen rolls]

Thimbleby, James, 23 Long Alley, Finsbury, London, carver (1835). [D]

Thirkettle, Henry, Harleston, Norfolk, carpenter and chairmaker (1830). [D]

Thirkettle (or Thurkettle), Nathaniel Palmer, Norfolk, cm (1807–31). Polled at Gt Yarmouth, of there, in 1807 and 1812; and of Norwich, 1820–31.

Thirkettle (or Thurkettle), William D., Gt Yarmouth, Norfolk, cm (1826–31). [Poll bks]

Thir(l)well, Robert, 13 Groat Mkt, Newcastle, cm and furniture broker (1834). [D]

Thirnbeck, Richard, Philadelphia, Sheffield, Yorks., cm (1822). [D]

Thirtle (or Thurtle), John, Magdalen St, Norwich, carver and gilder (1822–39). [D; poll bk] See Thomas Thurtle.

Thistleton, Daniel, Liverpool, u (1822). App. to Bartholomew Tyrer in 1822. [Liverpool app. enrolment bk]

Thomas, —, Carpenter St, near Berkley Sq., London, cm (1793). Subscribed to Sheraton's Drawing Book, 1793.

Thomas, —, address unrecorded, upholder (1807–09). Carried out upholstery work at Gorhambury, St Albans, Herts., receiving payments totalling £506 11s between 11 July 1807 and 2 April 1819. [Herts. RO, Gorhambury account bks XI 77 and 81]

Thomas, —, Liverpool, cm and joiner (1820). Notice concerning dividends on bankruptcy given in *Liverpool Mercury*, 17 March 1820.

Thomas, Alexander, 82 Upper East Smithfield, London, chairmaker (1778). Took out a Sun Insurance policy in 1778 for £200 of which utensils and stock accounted for £100. [GL, Sun MS vol. 265, p. 209]

Thomas, Alexander, near Bear Gate, Exeter, Devon, chairmaker (1787). Took out a Sun Insurance policy on 7 March 1787 for £200 on household goods and stock etc. [GL, Sun MS vol. 344, p. 197]

Thomas, Alexander & William, 78 Fore St, Exeter, Devon, cm and chair manufacturers (1812–14). Advertised in *Exeter Flying Post*, 22 October 1812 that they had for sale 'A Great Variety of dyed black Drawing-room Chairs with brass ornaments, of which article they were the first Manufacturers in this city; japan and burnish gold ditto; Library fouteuils, Chairs and Chair Loungers; Sofa and Sofa Beds, with all other articles in the above branches and of the newest patterns.' Advertised again on 28 April 1814 their large assortment of cabinet and drawing-room chairs.

Thomas, Benjamin, 107 High St, Worcester, chairmaker (1835–40). [D]

Thomas, Charles, late of St Martin-in-the-Fields, London, cm (1761). Discharge from Debtors' Prison reported in *London Gazette*, 29 September 1761.

Thomas, Charles, 73 Church St, Manchester, cm (1840). [D]

Thomas, Edward, Bristol and Portsmouth, Hants., cm (1774–81). Polled at Bristol of there, parish of St James, in 1774; and of Portsmouth in 1781.

Thomas, Edward, West Cowes, Isle of Wight, Hants., cm (1784). [Bristol poll bk]

Thomas, Edward, 9 Spencer Buildings, Hunter St, Liverpool, cm (1834). [D]

Thomas, F., Rochester, Kent, cm (1806). [Poll bk]

Thomas, Frances, Halesowen, Salop, cm (c.1810–c.1830). Trading at Pekingham St, c.1830. Metal label of 'F. THOMAS — CABINET MAKER — HALESOWEN', recorded on a brass-inlaid mahogany armchair, c.1810, with upholstered seat, originally of black horsehair, rectangular back with horizontal splat surmounted by pierced squat vase between two scrolls; scrolling arms, and turned front legs. [D]

Thomas, Franklen Matthew, 147 High St, Rochester, Kent, cm and furniture broker (1824–34). [D]

Thomas, George, Chester, cm (1819–40). Trading at Wall St in 1819, Nicholas St in 1826, and King St in 1840. [D; poll bks]

Thomas, Henry, Castle Precincts, Bristol, cm (1774). [Poll bk]

Thomas, Henry Walter, North St, Wolverhampton, Staffs., cm and u (1822). [D] See W. H. Thomas of Wolverhampton.

Thomas, I., King's Rd, Chelsea, London, u (1826–27). [D]

Thomas, I. M., 2 Sussex St, Tottenham Ct Rd, London, cm (1835). [D]

Thomas, J., address unrecorded, cm and u (1806–08). Carried out work for the Dowager Lady Heathcote between 17 July 1806 and 9 May 1807, totalling £20 6s 6d. Work included making up and laying carpets, putting up curtains, cleaning and repairing furniture. He also charged for 'Two Pair of Folding Doors fitted to the Book Cases in the Back Drawing Room the Frames Japanned Black & Yellow, Calico for the Pannels'; 'A Pair of Spring Yellow Calico Blinds for the Dressing Room'; making up bed furniture of green morine, and providing 'A Deal Frame for the top of the Bed'. He also supplied '4 Black Stained Chairs', and 'A Swing Dressing Glass in a Mahogany Frame'; and cut glass for a frame. [Lincoln RO, 2 ANC 12/D/39]

Thomas, James, late of Whitecross St, St Luke's London, grocer,

oilman and cm (1755). Recorded in *London Gazette*, 27–31 May 1755 as a prisoner from debt.

Thomas, James, Holy Trinity, Exeter, Devon, carver (1803). [Exeter Militia list]

Thomas, James, 50 Spear St with house at 1 Thomas Ct, St George's Rd, Manchester, cm (1825). [D]

Thomas, James, York, cm (1828). Son of William Thomas. App. to John Taylor, cm, on 21 July 1828. [York app. reg.]

Thomas, James, 1 Commutation Row, Liverpool, cm and u (1837). [D]

Thomas, John, London, carver (1775–84). Recorded at Queen St, Seven Dials in 1775; and High Holborn, 1783–84, no. 153 in 1784. Insured houses for £300 in 1775, and for £600 in 1783. [D; GL, Sun MS vol. 239, p. 495; vol. 317, p. 111]

Thomas, John C., address unrecorded. Pencilled inscription, 'John C. Thomas creator of this work 4th day of May 1777 for Mr. Addam of the Adelfrey in the Strand, London' found on a painted pinewood chimney piece in Hartwell House, Bucks., during renovation in 1958. [*C. Life*, 12 June 1958, E. Perry, 'The Antique Dealers' Fair']

Thomas, John, Poland St, Oxford St, Golden Sq., London, cm (1790–93). [D]

Thomas, John, 4 Angel Porter Alley, Golden Lane, London, cm (1792). Insured his house for £100 and utensils, goods and stock for £20 on 10 September 1792. [GL, Sun MS vol. 388, p. 585]

Thomas, John, Bristol, knife-case maker and cm (1792–1801). Trading at Narrow Wine St, 1792–95, and Bush St, 1799–1801. [D]

Thomas, John, Shrewsbury, Salop, cm (c.1796–1828). Listed as a cm and turner at St Alkmund's Sq., c.1796, and at Barker St, as a cm and u in 1828. [D]

Thomas, John, Gainsborough, Lincs., builder, cm and upholder (1805–08). [D]

Thomas, John, Truro, Cornwall, u and cm (1805–d. by 1822). Advertised in *Royal Cornwall Gazette*, 2 April 1808 giving address 'Directly opposite Pearce's Hotel, 8 Lemon St.' and offering thanks for 'that distinguished patronage he has uniformly experienced since his first commencement in business'. Stated that he was 'lately returned from London', and having had the opportunity of 'seeing the present mode of furnishing, he will be enabled in future to complete his orders in the furnishing in general, in the very first stile.' He had also purchased paper, chintzes, carpeting, hearth rugs, drawing room and dining chairs etc. Announced in the same paper, 16 July 1808, that he had commenced business as an auctioneer; and on 25 April 1812 that he had again just returned from London 'with an entire assortment of every article' for his 'Fashionable Upholstery & Cabinet Warehouse', 8 Lemon St. 'He most earnestly recommends his assortment of Mahogany, which from its superior quality & great variety, he has no doubt will give much satisfaction, having given that particular branch of his business the most attention, by selecting the very best woods the London markets would produce, & which will be manufactured by most approved workmen. Mahogany in Plank & Veneers. Bed Pillars etc. sold wholesale at the London Prices.' Advertised similarly, still at Lemon St, on 10 April 1819. On 21 October 1815 he took two shares of £25 in the Truro Shipping Co. in order 'to acquire vessels for the coasting trade'. His widow gave notice in *Royal Cornwall Gazette*, 16 March 1822, that the premises in Lemon St, 'where the upholstery & Cabinet business had been carried on for the last 14 years with great success', were to be let. [D; Cornwall RO, AD69]

Thomas, John, Chester, cm (1824–26). Recorded at Eastgate St in 1824 and Watergate St in 1826. Admitted freeman on 19 October 1824. [Chester freemen rolls and poll bk]

Thomas, John, Duke St, Chester, u (1828). [D]

Thomas, John, 19 Upper Thornhaugh St, Bedford Sq., London, cm (1829). [D]

Thomas, John, York, carver and gilder (1830). Son of Robert Thomas, stonemason. App. to Benjamin Evers, carver and gilder, on 8 April 1830. [York app. reg.]

Thomas, John, 99 Rea St, Birmingham, chairmaker (1835). [D]

Thomas, John, 24 Duckinfield St, Liverpool, cm (1837). [D]

Thomas, John Molesworth, 24 Bermondsey New Rd, London, cm and u (1839). [D]

Thomas, Joseph, Shrewsbury, Salop, joiner and cm (1723). Took app. named Lomax in 1723. [S of G, app. index]

Thomas, Joseph, Charles St, Grosvenor Sq., London, cm and u (1800–17). Recorded at no. 13, 1800–07, and no. 15, 1809–17. Took out Sun Insurance policies on 9 October 1800 for £200; on 1 August 1809 for £300 on household goods in 'a cottage called Bellmans on the common', Sunbury, Middlx, in tenure; and on 2 November 1812 for £4,000 on a house at 2 Albemarle St, Piccadilly. Named in Sheraton's list of master cabinet makers, 1803. [D; GL, Sun MS vol. 419, ref. 706841; vol. 448, ref. 828899; vol. 459, ref. 875315]

Thomas, Joseph, Bristol, carver and gilder (1809–37). Trading as Thomas & Tucker at 32 Broadmead, 1809–16; alone there, 1817–24; no. 21 in 1825; no. 25 in 1827; no. 23, 1828–30; 15 Nelson St, 1831–34; and 15 All Saints' St, 1835–37. [D]

Thomas, Joseph, Handbridge, Chester, chairmaker (1818–26). [D; poll bks]

Thomas, Joseph, Egerton St, Chester, cm (1826). Admitted freeman on 20 June 1826. [Chester freemen rolls]

Thomas, Joseph, 55 Thomas St, Shudehill, Manchester, chairmaker (1840). [D]

Thomas, M., 54 Burlington Arcade, Piccadilly, London, writing desk and dressing case maker (1829). [D]

Thomas, Mary, 2 York St, Milk St, Bristol, u (1833–40). [D]

Thomas, Nathaniel, King St, Manchester, u and cm (1828–36). Recorded at no. 47a in 1828–29; 47 in 1829; no. 68 in 1832–34; and 55 Back King St in 1836. Declared bankrupt, Chester Courant and Advertiser for North Wales, 7 February 1832. [D]

Thomas, R. W., 22 Dorrington St, Coldbath Fields, London, cm (1805–07). [D]

Thomas, Richard, Gainsborough, Lincs., joiner and cm (1779–94). Insured his house for £100 in 1779. [D; GL, Sun MS vol. 277, p. 205]

Thomas, Richard, South St, Exeter, Devon, cm and chairmaker (1819). Son Walter bapt. at St George's on 16 February 1819. [PR (bapt.)]

Thomas, Richard, King St, Truro, Cornwall, cm, u and undertaker (1824–d.1848). Recorded at no. 17, 1823–30. [D] In 1833 he received, with seven others, £300 as proceeds from the sale of land called the 'Fairmantle', Truro. It was stated that he was married to Elizabeth Ferris, daughter of Joseph Ferris, the Elder, Gent. of Truro. [Cornwall RO] His widow advertised in Royal Cornwall Gazette, 3 November 1848, offering thanks for 'the constant support so largely afforded' her late husband, and announcing her intention 'to continue the business as heretofore in all its branches. Having had the almost entire management of it during her husband's illness for the last 6 years & assisted by able & experienced workmen, some of whom have been long on the establishment, she hopes by giving prompt attention, as hitherto, to all orders committed to her care, by using only the best materials & well-seasoned woods, her stock of which is unequalled in the county, & by moderate charges, to merit a continuation of that patronage so long enjoyed by her late husband.'

Thomas, Robert, Further Northgate St, Chester, cm (1784). [Poll bk]

Thomas, Robert, Wolverhampton, Staffs., upholder (1798). [D]

Thomas, Robert, Bristol, picture frame maker and printseller (c.1820–40). Trade card, c.1820 in style but backing a certificate dated 1861, reads: 'Robert Thomas, Gilt-Fancy Wood Picture-Frame Manufacturer & printseller, 2 Tower Lane (2 doors from John St. BRISTOL'. Listed in directories at 10 Nicholas St, 1839–40.

Thomas, Rutt, 2 Clement's Lane, London, upholder (1782). [D]

Thomas, S., 147 High St, Rochester, Kent, cm (1839). [D]

Thomas, Samuel, Spitalfields, Liverpool, carver (1794–96). Recorded at back of 10 Spitalfields, Whitechapel in 1796. [D]

Thomas, Samuel, Plymouth, Devon, carver and gilder (1822–30). Trading at 3 Chapel St, Stonehouse, 1822–24, and 19 Market St, Devonport in 1830. [D]

Thomas, Susan S., 7 Canon St, Bristol, upholsteress (1828–29). [D]

Thomas, Thomas, St Sidwell's, Exeter, Devon, journeyman cm (1827). Notices in Exeter Flying Post, 10 May 1827 and 12 July 1827 concerned the committing of Thomas and his wife Eliza to the city prison, for trial at the Sessions, for having stolen from several linen drapers' shops and pawn-brokers in Exeter. Eliza was pronounced guilty, but Thomas was acquitted, having received an excellent character from Charles Nolan.

Thomas, Thomas, 30 Marlborough St, Bristol, house and sign painter, furniture japanner (1823–24). [D]

Thomas, W. H., Wolverhampton, Staffs., cm and u (1818). [D] See Henry Walter Thomas of Wolverhampton.

Thomas, William, Ditch Side, St Bride's, London, cm (1715–22). Served as Scavenger at St Bride's in 1715; Questman in 1716; and fined for non-service in one office in 1722. [GL, MS 6561, p. 5]

Thomas, William, Plymouth, Devon, cm (1743). Took app. named Hoskins in 1743. [S of G, app. index]

Thomas, William, Greek St, Soho, London, cm and upholder (1777–96). Recorded at no. 17, 1784–93. Took out a Sun Insurance policy in 1777 for £900 including £550 on utensils and stock. In 1796 receipted a bill for a 'Japanned India Cabinet' costing £4 4s supplied to the Hon. James Drummond of Perth. [D; poll bk; GL, Sun MS vol. 261, p. 353; Scottish RO, GD160/Box 46/Bundle 14] See Thomas & Flint and Thomas & Wallace.

Thomas, William, Wyle Cop, Shrewsbury, Salop, cm (1796). [Shrewsbury burgess roll]

Thomas, William, St Austell, Cornwall, cm and post maker (1798). [D]

Thomas, William, 'Three Boars' Heads', Horse Fair, Bristol, cm (1815–20). [D]

Thomas, William, Magdalen St, Exeter, Devon, cm (1820). Son Richard bapt. at Holy Trinity Church on 20 August 1820. [PR (bapt.)]

Thomas, William, 8 Blewitt's Buildings, Fetter Lane, London, box and dressing case maker (1820). [D]

Thomas, William, London St, Fitzroy Sq., London, carver, gilder, interior decorator (c.1815–39). Recorded at no. 39, 1826–39. Label recorded on back panel of Regency looking-glass, c.1815, inscribed: 'from W. THOMAS, Decorator and Gilder, LONDON STREET, FITZROY SQUARE'. [D]

Thomas, William, Derby Cottage, Bootle Marsh, Liverpool, with shop at 20 Islington, cm and u (1839). [D]

Thomas, William, 1 Virgil St, Liverpool, cm and beer shop (1839). [D]

Thomas, William, Church Fields, Greenwich, London, cm and u (1839). [D]

Thomas, William, 28 Quay St, Salford, Lancs., cm (1840). [D]

Thomas & Flint, 17 Greek St, Soho, London, cm and u (1792–97). [D] See William Thomas and Thomas & Wallace.

Thomas & Son, Plymouth, Devon, carvers and gilders (1836–38). Trading at Squire Terr., Union Rd in 1836 and 14 Bilbury St in 1838. [D]

Thomas & Steward, 2 Little Stanhope St, London, u (1839). [D]

Thomas & Tucker, 32 Broadmead, Bristol, carvers and gilders (1809–16). [D] See Joseph Thomas at this address.

Thomas & Wallace (or Wallis), Greek St, Soho, London, cm and upholders (1781–90). Recorded at no. 17 in 1789. [D] See William Thomas, and Thomas & Flint.

Thomason, Thomas, 1 Robert St, Liverpool, cm (1827). [D]

Thomequay, —, Moorfields, London, gilt chairmaker (1768). Noted in Matthew Boulton's diary in 1768. [Birmingham City Ref. Lib., archives dept. Boulton MS]

Thompkins, George, Hyde Hill, Berwick, Northumb., cm and u (1828–29). [D]

Thompson, —, St Aldates, Oxford, carver, gilder and picture frame maker. Undated trade card [Banks Coll., BM] shows University and City Arms.

Thompson, —, address unrecorded. In April 1722 provided items to Sir John Chester for Chicheley Hall, Bucks., including 'stuffed damask bed & chairs & easy chairs & quilts etc.', and 'worsted damask bed, 3 quilts, 6 chairs, 2 window curtains, easy chair & carpets', costing a total of £20. [Bucks. RO, ref. D/C/2/36 (iii); *C. Life*, 27 February 1975, p. 498]

Thompson, —, London, upholder (1768). Death 'in Broker's-Alley' on 7 March 1768 reported in *Public Advertiser*, 9 March 1768.

Thompson, —, address unrecorded, u (c.1775). Supplied furniture to Brockenhurst Park, Hants., c.1775. [*Antique Collector*, vol. 25, 1954, p. 134] Possibly James Thompson of Fenchurch St.

Thompson, —, 33 (?) Crooked Lane, Cannon St, London, cm, upholder and undertaker (1793). Trade card [Banks Coll., BM] shows two Chippendale-style chairs, a bookcase, a Venetian blind, a chest of drawers and a funeral procession. Card states: 'Window Blinds & Venetian Shades Made & Repaired in the Latest Manner and on the Most Reasonable Terms.'

Thompson, —, Whitehaven, Cumb., cm (1793). Subscribed to Sheraton's *Drawing Book*, 1793.

Thompson, —, London, u (1833). Notice in *Chester Courant and Advertiser for North Wales*, 22 January 1833 concerned the debt owed Thompson for 'costly furniture' bought from him by a Mrs Wellesly of Bruton St. On her leaving for Calais, a Mr Philips, auctioneer, detained the furniture for a further debt of £4,000 owed him by Mrs Wellesly.

Thompson, Abraham, Otley, Yorks., joiner and cm (1828–34). Trading at Nelson St, 1828–29. [D]

Thompson, Alexander, Gt Hermitage St, Wapping, London, cm (1790–1811). Trading at no. 17, 1805–07. [D]

Thompson, Alexander, Castle Sq., Southampton, Hants., u (1803–08). [D]

Thompson, Ann, Main St, Cockermouth, Cumb., joiner and cm (1828–29). [D]

Thompson, Anthony, Milnthorpe, Westmld, cm (1829). [D]

Thompson, Benjamin, 62 Red Lion St, Clerkenwell, London, dyed chairmaker (1811). [D]

Thompson, Brian Rushworth, Clerkenwell, London, dyed chairmaker (1782–1825). Addresses given at 28 St John's Lane, 1782–89; 62 Red Lion St, 1790–1825, as B. R. Thompson, 1789–1825. Took out Sun Insurance policies in 1782 for £600, of which £450 accounted for utensils, stock and warehouse; and in 1790 for £1,000 on utensils and stock in workshops, yard and warehouse. B. R. Thompson is named in Sheraton's list of master cabinet makers, 1803. Probably

confusion between Benjamin and Brian R. Thompson. [D; GL, Sun MS vol. 302, p. 252; vol. 370]

Thompson, Charles, Cowley, Oxford, cm (1802). [Poll bk]

Thompson, Charles, 14 Prospect Row, Woolwich, London, carver and gilder (1839). [D]

Thompson, Clelland, 13 Dooley St, Toxteth Park, Liverpool, cm (1839). [D]

Thompson, Edward, Cambridge, cm and u (1792–94). Declared bankrupt, *Cambridge Chronicle and Journal*, 8 March 1794. [D]

Thompson, Edward jnr, Cambridge, cm, u and furniture broker (1824–1840). Addresses given at Butcher Row in 1824, and Magdalene St, 1835–40. [D; poll bks]

Thompson, Edward, 9 George's Row, St Luke's, London, cm (1805–07). [D]

Thom(p)son, Edward, Watergate St, Ellesmere, Salop, cm (1828–35). [D]

Thompson, Elizabeth, 45 Fountain St, Manchester, u (1808–13). [D]

Thompson, Francis, at 'The Three Chairs', St John's Lane, near Hick's Hall, London, turner and chairmaker 'from Mr. AYLIFFE, Turner to His Majesty' (c.1750). Trade card shows three cabriole-legged chairs with tall, shaped backs and vertical splats, and states that Thompson 'MAKETH and SELLETH all Sorts of dy'd Beach Chairs, Brushes, Brooms, Mops, and Matting, Wholesale and Retail. Likewise Pails, Washing-Tubs, Iron hoop'd Coal-Tubs, Fire-Screens, Plate-Racks, Shop-Stools, Close-Stools, Coal Boxes, Knife-Boxes, Knife-Wetters, Salt-Boxes, Wainscot and Nottingham Voiders, Comb-Trays, Tin-Plate-Baskets, Tin Scuttles, plain and painted; Iron Dust-Pans, Cradles, Flaskets, Child-bed-Baskets, China Plate Baskets, Work Baskets, Kitchen and Chamber Bellows, Hair Cloth and many other Things too tedious to mention. Painted Floor-Cloths of all Sorts and Sizes, of the newest Pattern, warranted to be done well in Oil, and wear well; and to be sold as cheap as any Advertiser in LONDON. Likewise Ready Money for Bees Wax.' [Heal]

Thompson, Frederick, 24 St John St (or Sq.), Clerkenwell, London, cm (1835–39). [D]

Thompson, George, Argyle St, Golden Sq., London, cm (1797–1808). Recorded at no. 4, 1797–1803 and no. 5 in 1808. [D] See J. Thompson at no. 4.

Thompson, George, York, looking-glass maker (1798–1830). Trading at 4 Judge's Old Yd in 1830. Son of Thomas Thompson. App. to David Doeg, looking-glass maker, on 8 November 1798. Admitted freeman in 1806. [D; York app. reg. and freemen rolls]

Thompson, George, address unrecorded, chairmaker (1803). Subscribed to Sheraton's *Cabinet Dictionary*, 1803.

Thompson, George, West St, Boston, Lincs., cm (1819–22). [D]

Thompson, George, Brunswick Pl., Brompton, London, chair and sofa maker (1826). [D]

Thompson, George, Knaresborough, Yorks., joiner and cm (1828–34). Trading at Church Lane, 1828–29. [D]

Thompson, Guy, Oxford, cm (1768). [Frowde, *Survey of Oxford*] Possibly:

Thom(p)son, Guy, 2 Duke St, West Smithfield, London, cm and ebony inkstand maker (1776–1803). Took out Sun Insurance policies in 1776 for £400, utensils and stock accounting for £300; and in 1782 for £600, £450 on utensils, stock and warehouse. Listed as not having voted in Oxford poll, 1802. [D; GL, Sun MS vol. 248, p. 488; vol. 302, p. 247] Heal records trade card of Guy Thompson, cm and case maker. See Thomson & Fiske at this address.

Thompson, J., 4 Argyle St, Golden Sq., London, cm (1805–07). [D] See George Thompson at this address.

Thompson, J., 2 Brunswick Pl., Brompton Sq., London, chairmaker (1826–27). [D]

Thompson, J., Market Pl., Durham, spinning-wheel maker (1827). [D]

Thompson, James, Norwich, u (1660). App. to Thomas Frost, and admitted freeman on 23 January 1660. [Norwich freemen reg.]

Thom(p)son, James, Oxford, cm (1748–68). Polled of St Mary Magdalene parish in 1768. Took apps named Freeman in 1748 and Smith in 1760. [S of G, app. index]

Thompson, James, Fenchurch St, London, u (1753–75). Recorded at Cullum St, Fenchurch St in registers of unclaimed dividends of bank stock in 1753. Trading at 146 Fenchurch St *c.*1767–70 and no. 133, *c.*1771–75. [D; Heal] Submitted a bill to Lord Monson dated 27 February 1769 'for Mr. Eastland', and receipted on 6 April for 'Mr. Dickerson & Colny'. Bill totalled £3 19s 6d and listed 'A Check Mattress Fill'd with Fine Flocks & Tuffted with Silk', a hammock, blankets, a field quilt, and 'a Tucken Pillow filld with 22 of Season'd Fethers'. [Lincoln RO, Monson 11/50] Mentioned in the notebook of Edward Morant of Brockenhurst Park, Hants., *c.*1771, as 'Mr. Thompson Mr. Long Upholsterer in Fenchurch Street.' [Owned by E. Morant, Hants.] See Thompson, —, who supplied furniture to Brockenhurst *c.*1775.

Thompson, James, Maidenhead Passage, Berwick St, London, cm (1784). [Poll bk]

Thompson, James, 53 Davies St, Berkeley Sq., London, u, cm and appraiser (1814–25). [D]

Thompson, James, Liverpool, cm (1818–39). Addresses given at Tarbuck Sq., Milton St in 1818; 12 Gardner's Row, 1821–23; and 2 Upper Mann St, Harrington in 1839. [D]

Thompson, James, Warwick, cm (1822–31). Trading at Castle St in 1828 and Park St in 1831. [D; poll bk]

Thompson, James, Malton, Yorks., cm and u (1823–40). Trading at Newbiggin in 1823 and Yorkersgate in 1840. [D]

Thompson, James snr, Appleby, Westmld, joiner and cm (1828–29). [D]

Thompson, James, 18 London Wall, London, cm (1829). [D]

Thompson, James, Oxford St, Bilston, Staffs., cm (1833). [D]

Thompson, John, parish of St Peter at Arches, Lincoln, upholder (1720). Took out a Sun Insurance policy on 11 July 1720 on goods and merchandise in his house. Entry mentions 'Mr. Thompson merch! in Crooked Lane'. [GL, Sun MS vol. 12, ref. 18933] See Thompson, —, of 33 Crooked Lane, London.

Thompson, John, Peter St, London, cm (1774). [Poll bk]

Thompson, John and successors, Durham, u, cm, auctioneer and appraiser (1793–1828). [D] John was recorded at Sadler St, 1802–19. Subscribed to Sheraton's *Drawing Book*, 1793 and *Cabinet Dictionary*, 1803. The Ellison papers in Gateshead Ref. Lib. (1805–26) include a bill from Thompson for four wash-hand tables supplied to Cuthbert Ellison of Hebburn Hall, Gateshead, in 1808. [*Furn. Hist.*, 1976, pl. 33c] Advertised in *Newcastle Courant*, 20 March 1802 for one or two hands; stating 'none but good workmen need offer'. Announced on 26 March 1814 that he had taken his sons into partnership, and carried out 'Display of Decoration & Ornaments. Plans of rooms taken and designs of furniture prepared for them.' Notice in *Durham County Advertiser*, 4 September 1819, from John Thompson, offered thanks for the 'many favours conferred upon him by his friends for a period of forty-two years', and announced that 'he has DECLINED HIS PART in the above trade to his sons viz: to WILLIAM HALL THOMPSON, the CABINET BUSINESS; and to JAMES and MATTHEW THOMPSON, the UPHOLSTERY BUSINESS, who, he trusts, will merit a continuance of their future favours.' William Hall and James & Matthew Thompson advertised at the same time that they intended to continue their respective trades in the old shops and warerooms in Saddler St. William Hall, cm, promised 'the strictest attention to manufacture fashionable & useful furniture, made from choice wood of every description, & the utmost approved modern designs'; James & Matthew, u and furnishers in general, that 'from their great connections with the principal houses in London, and the Manufactories, they are enabled at all times to have the first fashions and newest patterns'. Label recorded on octagonal library table with frieze drawers on pillar and four splayed legs. Label is framed by festoon curtain surmounted by an eagle with sarcophagus cellaret below, and reads: 'I. THOMPSON, Upholsterer & Cabinet Maker, Sadler Street, DURHAM, Auctioneer & Appraiser'. [*Antique Collector*, September 1973, p. 28, fig. 1] William Hall Thompson is listed in a directory of 1827–28 at New Elvet and Sadler St.

Thompson, John, Whitehaven Cumb., cm (1798). [D]

Thompson, John, York, cm (1807–23). Recorded as John & Son, cm, joiners and packing box manufacturers, Little Stonegate, with house in Marygate, 1823. John Thompson, jnr, son of Joseph Thompson, coachmaker, deceased, was app. to Hugh Rusby, cm, on 1 December 1807, and admitted freeman as cm in 1820. [D; York app. reg. and freemen rolls]

Thompson, John, Blandford, Dorset, cm (1813). Took his son, Samuel, as app. for seven years on 6 April 1813. [Dorset RO, B5]

Thompson, John & Isaac, 64 St James's St, Liverpool, cm (1813). [D]

Thompson, John, Blackburn, Lancs., joiner and cm (1814–34). Addresses given at Queen St in 1814; top of Salford St in 1816; and 14 Eanam St, 1818–24. [D]

Thompson, John Thomas, 116 Long Acre, London, cm, army u, auctioneer, appraiser, military bed and camp equipage maker to their Majesties, patentee of the light military and travelling bed (1818–40). [D] Advertised in *The Times*, 1 January 1816, and 8 January 1818, his 'PATENT EAST and WEST INDIA WELLINGTON BED — This elegant and portable BED-STEAD is made of Wrought Iron Tubes, plated with brass, thereby rendering it extremely light, not liable to rust, or harbour vermin, by its ingenious and simple construction being only one piece, it forms in two minutes into a most complete bed, weighing only 56 lb, with the bedding complete; and by its portability and very small size into which it folds, will fix to any part of a carriage; to the invalid in particular travelling for health it has been invaluable, as by the elasticity of the sacking turning in bed is rendered less painful and when in a warm climate its use will enable them to enjoy the blessing of sleep, often denied to them in the beds of the country which cannot be kept from vermin. As a spare bed in a house it has been found to be extremely useful, it being soon put up, and also forming an elegant couch; a very extensive assortment of different sizes, fitted up with an entire new pattern of Mosquito-Nets are now on show at the warerooms of the patentee J. T. Thompson 116 Long-acre.' In November 1824 Thompson supplied unspecified goods to the value of £31 to John, 6th Duke of Bedford. [Beds. RO, R399, bill 17] In January 1840 provided Lord Fitzalan with three sets of iron bedsteads, curtains, hair mattresses, feather bolsters, pillows, blankets and quilts, at £11 a set. [Arundel Castle records, A1963]

Thompson, John, 8 Brokers Alley, Castle St, Drury Lane, London, u etc. broker etc. (1820–35). Recorded also at no. 5 in 1835. [D]

Thompson, John, 5 Rigby St, Liverpool, cm (1821). [D]

Thompson, John, Market Harborough, Leics., cm and chairmaker (1822). [D]

Thompson, John, Devonport, Plymouth, Devon, cm and u (1822–38). Recorded as J. & S. Thompson at St Aubyn St in 1822; alone at no. 64, 1823–24; with 'Si' there in 1830; alone at Fore St in 1830; and alone at 18 Cherry Gdn St in 1838. [D] See S. S. Thompson.

Thompson, John, Club Row, Church St, Bethnal Green, London, cm (1822–39). Recorded at no. 24, 1822–28; no. 22 in 1829; and no. 21 in 1839. Took out a Sun Insurance policy on 16 January 1822 for £200 of which £100 accounted for stock, utensils and goods in trust. [D; GL, Sun MS vol. 490, ref. 987699]

Thompson, John Atkinson, York, carver and gilder (1825). Son of Francis Thompson, painter of Hull. App. to William Holmes, carver and gilder, on 11 February 1825. Imprisoned for one month in the House of Correction to hard labour in about January 1826. [York app. reg.]

Thompson, John, Darlington, Co. Durham, cm (1827–34). Trading at Posthouse Weind in 1827 and Skinnergate in 1834. [D]

Thompson, John, Wolsingham, Co. Durham, joiner and cm (1828–29). [D]

Thompson, John, Ferguson's Lane, Carlisle, Cumb., joiner and/or cm (1828–34). [D]

Thompson, John, Egremont, Cumb., joiner and/or cm (1828–34). Recorded with William Thompson in 1834. [D]

Thompson, John, Gardener's Row, Bevington Bush, Liverpool, cm (1829–37). Trading at no. 12 in 1829 and no. 7, 1834–37. [D]

Thompson, John, Bramley, Yorks., joiner and cm (1830). [D]

Thompson, John, Kirkgate, Newark, Notts., cm and chairmaker (1822–41). [D]

Thompson, John jnr, Guildhall St, Newark, Notts., cm, chairmaker and turner (1828–35). [D]

Thompson, John, York, cm (1834). [D]

Thompson, Jonathan, Deepcar, Bolsterstone, Midhope, Yorks., cm (1837). [D]

Thompson, Joseph, Liverpool, cm (1796–1835). Addresses given at 5 Newhall St, Crosbie St in 1796; 8 Lionel St, Gerrard St, 1800–03; 12 Bolton St, Copperas Hill in 1804; 19 Lionel St in 1805; no. 10, 1807–10; no. 47, 1811–27; 6 Nelson Pl., Gt Nelson St in 1829; and Walton Breck in 1835. Death of his wife, Elizabeth, aged 58, after a short illness, reported in *Liverpool Mercury*, 24 October 1828. [D]

Thompson, Joseph, Calverley-cum-Farsley, Yorks., cm (1830–37). [D]

Thompson, Joseph, Skipton, Yorks., joiner and/or cm (1830–37). Recorded at Commercial St, Holy Trinity parish in 1837. [D; PR]

Thompson, Josh., Fore St, Wellington, Som., cm and u (1822). [D]

Thompson, M. jnr, Askrigg, Wensleydale, Yorks., cm (1840). [D]

Thompson, Mark, Pilgrim St, Newcastle, joiner and cm (1811). [D]

Thompson, Marmaduke, Lancaster, cm (1789–96). App. to Gillows in 1789, and admitted freeman, 1795–96. Named in the Gillow records, 1792–96. [Lancaster app. reg. and freemen rolls; Westminster Ref. Lib., Gillow]

Thompson, Mary, 44 Piccadilly, London, carver, gilder and glass-grinder (1805–11). [D]

Thompson, Matthew, Sadler St, Durham, u (1827). [D] Succeeded his father, John Thompson, at this address.

Thompson, Michael, Staindrop, Co. Durham, joiner and cm (1827). [D]

Thompson, Noah, Hammond Beck Bridge, Swineshead, Lincs., spinning-wheel maker (1826). [D]

Thompson, Ralph, York, u (1811). Son of Ann Thompson; app. to Thomas King, u, on 13 February 1811. [York app. reg.]

Thompson, Richard, Rawden, Yorks., cm (1830). [D]

Thompson, Richard, Otley, Yorks., joiner and/or cm (1834). [D]

Thompson, Robert, Hull, Yorks., cm (1730–54). Recorded on the west side of Market Pl. on 4 December 1730 when he took out a Sun Insurance policy for £300 including £100 on stock in trade in his house. [GL, Sun MS vol. 33, ref. 52474; poll bks]

Thompson, Robert, Gt Yarmouth, Norfolk, upholder and salesman (1733). Took out a Sun Insurance policy on 3 December 1733 for £700 on household goods and stock in trade consisting of linen and upholders goods in his house and shop near the bridge. [GL, Sun MS vol. 38, ref. 62551]

Thompson, Robert, Market Lane, London, cm (1774). [Poll bk]

Thompson, Robert, Cannon St, Manchester, upholder (1788). [D]

Thompson, Robert, 46 Lord St, Liverpool, upholder (1796). [D]

Thompson, Robert, Otley, Yorks., cm (1798). [D]

Thompson, Robert, King St, Cambridge, cm (1819). Illegitimate child bapt. at All Saints' Church on 21 March 1819. [Cambs. RO, PR (bapt.)]

Thompson, Robert, Newcastle, joiner, cm and furniture broker (1824–38). Trading with Thomas Thompson at Wellington Pl., Pilgrim St in 1824; and alone at Pilgrim St in 1827, no. 25 in 1833–34 and no. 23 in 1838. [D] See Thomas Thompson at this address.

Thompson, Robert, Liverpool, cm (1838). Son of James Thompson, stonemason; admitted freeman on 25 July 1838. [Liverpool freemen reg.]

Thompson, S. S., St Aubyn St, Devonport, Plymouth, Devon, cm (1830–38). [D] See John Thompson at this address.

Thompson, Samuel, Blandford, Dorset, cm (1813). App. to his father, John Thompson, cm, on 6 April 1813. [Dorset RO, B5]

Thompson, Samuel, Liverpool, cm (1821). App. to William Harrison in 1821. [Liverpool app. enrolment bk]

Thom(p)son, Simpson, Bristol, furniture painter (1822). [D]

Thompson, Stephen, Market Lane, St James's, Westminster, London, joiner and cm (1784–86). Took app. named Lawrence McKenzie in 1786. [Westminster Ref. Lib., reg. of St Margaret and St John, MS E2566, p. 1242; poll bk]

Thom(p)son, Stephen, 8 Denmark St, Bristol, furniture painter (1821–24). Recorded as Stephen Thom(p)son jnr in 1823. [D]

Thompson, Thomas, Oxford, cm (1768). [Frowde, *Survey of Oxford*]

Thompson, Thomas, Manchester, chairmaker (1794–1813). Addresses given at Spring Alley in 1794; Nicholas' Croft in 1800; 2 Elbow St in 1808; and 6 Turner St, 1811–13. [D]

Thompson, Thomas jnr, parish of St Peter of Southgate, Norwich, cm (1799). [Poll bk]

Thompson, Thomas, 41 Fenchurch St, London, frame maker, carver and gilder (1800–15). [D]

Thompson, Thomas, 12 Stephen St, Tottenham Ct Rd, London, upholder (1809–10). Took out Sun Insurance policies on 17 or 27 March 1809 for £700 on his house, goods, china and glass; and on 14 April 1810 for £800, including £100 on stock, utensils and goods in trust. [GL, Sun MS vol. 448, ref. 828833; vol. 453]

Thompson, Thomas, 30 Sir Thomas Buildings, Liverpool, cm (1821–27). Recorded also at 15 Chapel Lane, Brownlow Hill in 1824; and 66–67 Tythebarn St in 1827. [D]

Thompson, Thomas, Newcastle, joiner, cm and furniture broker (1824–38). Trading at Wellington Pl., Pilgrim St in 1824 and 23 Pilgrim St, 1833–38. [D] See Robert Thompson at this address.

Thompson, Thomas, Newgate St, Bishop Auckland, Co. Durham, turner and spinning-wheel maker (1827). [D]

Thompson, Thomas, Middlegate, Penrith, Cumb., joiner and/or cm (1839–34). [D]

Thompson, Thomas, High St, Stockton-on-Tees, Co. Durham, cm (1832). [D]

Thompson, Thomas, Liverpool, cm (1834). App. to Cattrall & Whittingham in 1834. [Liverpool app. enrolment bk]

Thompson, Thomas, 12 Norman St, Liverpool, chairmaker (1835). [D]

Thompson, Thomas, Northallerton, Yorks., cm (1840). [D]

Thompson, W., address unrecorded, u (c.1829–41). Supplied furnishings for Charles William Vane, Marquess of Londonderry, for Wynyard Park, Co. Durham. [Durham RO, Londonderry papers, D/LO/E 484, vol. 1, 1829–41]

Thompson, W. L., 5 Brompton Rd, London, furniture ironmonger (1835). [D]

Thompson, William snr and jnr, Beverley, Yorks., cm, u and auctioneer (1764–1846). Recorded at Wednesday Mkt, 1785–91; Flemingate, 1826–29; North Bar St in 1831; and Beckside in 1840. Recorded as William snr, 1774–90 and as William jnr, 1784–99, but their respective addresses and dates are not clear. Took out Sun Insurance policies in 1775 for £200 on shop and stock; and on 22 April 1785 for £250 on utensils and stock, and £150 on his workshop at Wednesbury Mkt. Subscribed to Sheraton's *Drawing Book*, 1793. Death of his wife reported in *Gents Mag.*, 1807. Commissioned by the Corporation on 3 December 1764 to make 'ten armed chairs and six common chairs' for the Magistrate's Room in Beverley Guildhall, at 25s and 17s each, respectively; also a treble-seated chair at £5 5s, and a pair of dining tables at £7 10s 6d. Still in the Mayor's Parlour, some of the chairs are in the 'Chinese' style of Chippendale's *Director*, 1754. On 13 October 1777 Thompson was ordered to provide 'seven leather-bottomed chairs for the Chambers as previously'; and in 1783 Mr W. Thompson, cm, was elected a 'chamber man'. [D; poll bks; GL, Sun MS vol. 237, p. 185; vol. 328, p. 180; Beverley Guildhall, Corp. minutes; C. *Life*, 3 October 1974, pp. 923–33; I. & E. Hall, *Historic Beverley*, p. 50, illus. p. 72]

Thompson, William, London, upholder (1772–83). Trading at Fleet Mkt in 1783. Son of Henry Thompson, coach harness maker of Langley, Bucks. App. to William Pike, joiner, on 4 February 1772, and Philip Stallard, haberdasher, on 27 January 1773. Admitted freeman of the Upholders' Co. by servitude on 7 May 1783. [GL, Upholders' Co. records] Probably William Tomson, and:

Thompson, William, see William Tomson.

Thompson, William, Denmark Ct, London, cm (1784). [Poll bk]

Thompson, William, Savile Row, London, u (1793). Subscribed to Sheraton's *Drawing Book*, 1793.

Thompson, William, address unrecorded, cm (1803). Subscribed to Sheraton's *Cabinet Dictionary*, 1803.

Thompson, William, 19 Gt Barlow St, Marylebone, London, upholder (1805–07). [D]

Thompson, William, St Clement's, Ipswich, Suffolk, cm (1809). [Suffolk RO, calendar of marriage licence bonds, FAA: 50/2/114, pp. 75–76]

Thompson, William, Deritend, Birmingham, wheelwright and chairmaker (1818). [D]

Thompson, William, Butchery, Brigg, Lincs., cm (1819). [D]

Thompson, William, Burghwallis, near Doncaster, Yorks., cm (1822). [D]

Thompson, William, Welburn, Yorks., joiner and cm (1823). [D]

Thompson, William, 7 Lower John St, Commercial Rd, London, cm (1823). Took out a Sun Insurance policy on 19 November 1823 for £250 including £50 on a chest of tools at Mrs Johnston's, 3 Collet Pl., Commercial Rd. [GL, Sun MS vol. 495, ref. 1010586]

Thompson, William, corner of James St, Salmon Lane, Limehouse, London, cm (1824). Took out a Sun Insurance policy on 3 May 1824 for £400 of which £200 accounted for utensils and stock. [GL, Sun MS vol. 497, ref. 1016757]

Thompson, William, 24 Stepney Causeway, Commercial Rd, London, cm (1826–28). [D]

Thompson, William, 57 Curtain Rd, London, chair, and sofa manufacturer (1829). [D]

Thompson, William C., Horse Mkt, Barnard Castle, Co. Durham, joiner and cm (1827–29). [D]

Thompson, William, Durham, cm (1827–34). Recorded at Sadler St in 1827 and 1834, and at Hall, Flesher Gate, 1828–29. [D]

Thompson, William, Penrith, Cumb., chairmaker and turner (1829–34). Trading at Angel Lane in 1829 and Burrow Gate in 1834. [D]

Thompson, William, High St and St Aldate's, Oxford, printseller, carver and gilder (1830). [D]

Thompson, William, Magdalene St, Cambridge, cm (1830–35). [D; poll bks]

Thompson, William, Cow Fair, Banbury, Oxon, chairmaker (1830–41). [D]

Thompson, William, Billericay, Essex, cm (1832). [D]

Thompson, William, 25 Pipewellgate, Gateshead, Co. Durham, cm and furniture broker (1833). [D]

Thompson, William, Harrogate, Yorks., joiner and cm (1834). [D]

Thompson, William, Egremont, Cumb., cm and/or joiner (1834). [D]

Thompson, William, White Mill St, Liverpool, cm and joiner (1835–39). Recorded at no. 12, with shop at no. 7 in 1835; no. 11 with shop at no. 7 in 1837; and no. 19 in 1839. [D]

Thompson, William, Clapham Common, London, carver and gilder (1838). [D]

Thompson, William, Beckside, Beverley, Yorks., cm (1840). [D]

Thompson, Messrs, St James St, Liverpool, cm (1813). Notice in *Liverpool Mercury*, 24 September 1813, given of dissolution of partnership and sale of their manufactured stock, 'comprising an excellent set of Patent Dining-Tables; several sets of Mahogany Chairs, upholstered over the rail, loose seats etc:- Wardrobes, Chests of Drawers, Night Chair, Sofa, Card, Pembroke, Snap & Work Tables; Book-case with glazed doors, Hat Stands, Portable Desks, Butlers' Trays, Couch, Sofas covered with black hair-cloth, Easy Chairs, Foot Stools, Fire Skreens, Long Post & Camp Bedsteads, Dressing Glasses etc.'. Sale carried out by James Trotter, cm and household broker, recorded at 56 Whitechapel in 1816. [D]

Thompson & Beves, 34 West St, Brighton, Sussex, cm and u (1832). [D] See Beeves & Co.

Thompson & Co., 24 Warwick St, Piccadilly, London, cm (1825). [D]

Thoms, Alexander, Exeter, Devon, chairmaker (1786–1816). Removed to North St in 1795, announcing premises to let adjoining Palace Gate, where Richard Toms was recorded in 1791. Removed to 268 Fore St with manufactory at St Paul's St in 1808; and to no. 78 in 1810. Recorded at no. 77 in 1816. A. Thoms recorded at South St and A. & W. Thoms at Fore St in 1816. Took out a Sun Insurance policy on 7 February 1786 for £40 on household goods and £50 on utensils, stock and goods in trust. Advertised in *Exeter Flying Post*, 5 June 1794 that he made and sold 'all sorts of rush-bottom fancy chairs of yew tree & mahogany — also garden chairs, wholesale & retail'. Announced removal to North St on 12 March 1795; and to 268 Fore St on 29 December 1808, 'where work executed with strictest fidelity and despatch. Chairs of newest patterns, drawing room chairs, sofas, settees, couches &c. in gold or colours. Bedroom chairs in newest taste. Orders received at his manufactory, St Paul's St, adjoining the waggon warehouse.' Notice given on 19 April 1810 of removal of 'fancy chair manufactory' to 78 Fore St, where stock consisted of a 'large, elegant assortment of drawing room goods & various articles of furniture of the newest fashion'. Thoms, cm and chairmakers of 77 Fore St, with workshops at St Catherine's St, advertised sale of stock, mahogany and beech timber in *Western Luminary*, 9 July 1816. [*Exeter Pocket Journal*; GL, Sun MS vol. 334, p. 480]

Thoms, George, 148 Fore St Hill, Exeter, Devon, chairmaker (1816–40). Children bapt. at St George's Church on 7 August 1832: Georgina Clarissa Perring, George Peter Perring, and Reuben Perring Martin. Named in Exeter voters list, 1832. Death on 4 January 1838 of youngest son, Reuben reported in *Exeter Flying Post*, 11 January. [D; *Exeter Pocket Journal*; PR (bapt.)]

T(h)oms, Richard, Exeter, Devon, chairmaker (1791–96). Recorded at Palace Gate in 1791 and North St in 1796. [*Exeter Pocket Journal*]

Thoms, William, 10 High St, Exeter, Devon, cabinet manufacturer (1821). Notice in *Exeter Flying Post*, 22 March 1821, read: 'BRITISH OAK FURNITURE, for Sale and for Inspection, at MR. W. THOMS', Confectioner, No. 10, High Street, nearly opposite Castle Street, Exeter. Wm. THOMS, CABINET MANUFACTURER, (from London) begs to inform the Nobility and Gentry of Exeter, and its vicinity, that he has Manufactured from that noble Tree, the BRITISH OAK, DRAWING-ROOM FURNITURE, which for beauty stands unrivalled to any other woods ever imported to this country. W.T. is the only Manufacturer in this County.'

Thomson, —, Market Harborough, Leics., cm (1822). [D]

Thomson, Alexander, York, u (1780). Insured his house for £100 in 1780. [GL, Sun MS vol. 287, p. 30]

Thomson, Alex, 13 Artillery St, Bishopsgate Without, London, cm, u and undertaker (1827–28). [D]

Thomson, Charles, Chester, joiner and cm (1751–55). App. to Richard Ledsham, joiner and cm, from 24 June 1751 to 29 March 1755. [Chester app. bks]

Thomson, D., 23 Upper Marylebone St, Fitzroy Sq., London, cm (1809–11). [D]

Thomson, Edward, see Edward Thom(p)son, Ellesmere, Salop.

Thomson, James, York House, London, cm (1793–1803). Subscribed to Sheraton's *Drawing Book*, 1793 and *Cabinet Dictionary*, 1803.

Thomson, James, 67 Parsons St, Ratcliffe Highway, London, cm (1809–11). [D]

Thomson, Joseph, 8 Barter St with shop at 2 Poynton St, Liverpool, cm (1835). [D]

Thomson & Fiske, 2 Duke St, Smithfield, London, cm and casemakers (1802–06). Named in Sheraton's list of master cabinet makers, 1803. [D] See Guy Thompson.

Thorburn, Samuel, Liverpool, joiner and cm (1834–39). Trading at 8 Brownlow Hill in 1834 and Adelaide Buildings, Mount Pleasant, 1835–39. [D]

Thorley, James, at 'The Golden Head', against the Church, St Martin's Lane, London, upholder (1748–49). Heal records him in newspapers in 1748. Polled at Westminster, 1749.

Thorley, James, Watercrates, Chester, cm (1816). [D]

Thorley, John, Water-coates, Macclesfield, Cheshire, cm (1818–22). [D]

Thorley, John, King St, Woolwich, London, cm (1823–24). [D]

Thorley, Peter, Hull, Yorks., cm (1781–84). [D]

Thorley, William, Ashton Rd, Salford, Lancs., cm (1817). [D]

Thorn, —, at 'The Beehive & Patten', John St, Oxford Mkt, London, cricket bat, turnery and patten warehouseman (1764). Trade card gives long list of stock including floor cloths, cradles, baskets, butlers' trays, tea boards and chests, spice cupboards, backgammon tables, close stools, 'Chairs of all Sorts', 'Tin'd Fire Screens', 'Japan'd Coal Scoops', bellows and coal tubs, bowls and platters, plate racks, washing tubs and stools, clothes horses, wig stands and boot jacks, shop stools, rocking horses and chairs for children. Thorn was the earliest recorded London maker of cricket bats. [Heal]

Thorn, Benjamin, Bagnigge Wells Rd, London, cm and u (1839). [D]

Thorn, Daniel, 10 Stanhope St, Clare Mkt, London, u (1826–35). [D]

Thorn, Edward, Norwich, cm (1780–d. by 1786). Recorded at St Stephen's parish in 1780 and 4 St Stephen's Churchyard in 1783. [D; poll bks] See Thorne, —.

Thorn, George, 39 Carey St, London, upholder (1786). Took out a Sun Insurance policy on 27 July 1786 for £100 of which utensils, stock and goods in trust accounted for £20. [GL, Sun MS vol. 339, p. 181]

Thorn, Richard, Bristol, cm and clockcase maker (1774–1833). Recorded at Castle Precincts, 1774–84; 13 Milk St in 1801; Newgate St, 1809–12; Barrs St, 1812–13; as Richard James Thorn at Barrs St, 1814–17; as Richard Thorn snr at Stoke's Croft, 1814–17; All Saints' St, 1821–33, no. 10 in 1832. [D; poll bks] Possibly two tradesmen of the same name.

Thorn, Robert, Lambeth, London, cm (1817–35). Trading at 5 Lambeth Walk in 1817; 2 Gibson St in 1826–27; no. 4 in 1829; and no. 5 in 1835. [D] See Thomas Thorne at 2 Gibson St.

Thorn, Robert, High St, Wincanton, Som., cm and u (1830). [D]

Thornborough, Francis, Hull, Yorks., cm (1780–84). [Poll bks]

Thornbury, Nathaniel, Stroud, Glos., cm (1827–35). Recorded at Stroud Mills in 1827. Children born in 1827, 1829, 1831 and 1835. [PR]

Thornbury, William, Coventry, Warks., carver and joiner (1715). Took app. named Orton in 1715. [S of G, app. index]

Thorndick, Charles Kyte, Gt Yarmouth, Norfolk, cm (1836). [Poll bk]

Thorne, —, St Stephen's Churchyard, Norwich, cm (1776–84). Parson James Woodforde, Rector of Weston Longville, Norfolk, mentions Thorne in his diary in June 1776, as supplying the following items: 'a very handsome Mohogany Wardrobe', £9 9s; 'a Ditto new Mohogany dressing chest', £3 13s 6d; 'a D°. swing dressing Glass with Drawers', £1 11s 6d; 'a round Mohogany Table', £1 7s 6d; 'a Mohogany Bason Stand', 10s 6d; 'a D°. Tea Chest', 7s; and 'a Mohogany Beaurou & Book-Case, with some new Mohogany Chairs & a Voider & Cheese-Plate of Mohogany'. Woodforde mentions Thorne again on 27 May 1784 as a cm in St Stephen's Churchyard; and on 30 January 1800 as '. . . Thorne, late a Cabinet-Maker of Norwich & of whom I bought most of my Mohogany-Furniture'. [R. L. Winstanley (ed.), *The Diary of James Woodforde*] Probably Edward Thorn.

Thorne, Edward, Ipswich, Suffolk, cm (1835–39). Recorded at St Margaret's Green in 1839. Listed as a free burgess in Ipswich poll, 1835. [Poll bks]

Thorne, George, London, cm and upholder (1753–74). Trading at 35 Houndsditch, c.1760. Son of Edward Thorne of Farringdon, London. App. to Richard Farmer and I. Hollow, founder, on 22 March 1753. Admitted freeman of the Upholders' Co. on 5 April 1764. Took app. named Robert Shrigley, 1767–74. Trade card, c.1760 [GL, Stone Coll.] reads: 'George Thorne, Upholder, Appraiser, Cabinet-Maker & Undertaker, No. 35 in Houndsditch, London, Makes & Sells all sorts of Upholstery and Cabinet Goods in the Genteelest Taste & at the most Reasonable Rates.' Card shows two chairs, a table and a cornice. [GL, Upholders' Co. records]

Thorne, George, Sherborne, Dorset, upholder (1774–98). [D: Bristol poll bks]

Thorne, John, Sherborne, Dorset, upholder (1734). [Bristol poll bks]

Thorne, Lewis, Twickenham, Middlx, cm etc. (1805–07). [D]

Thorne, Mary, 30 Bridge St, Manchester, u (1804). [D]

Thorn(e), Thomas, Sherborne, Dorset, u (1734–81). Took app. named James Higgens in 1738, and John Hyatt for seven years in 1755. Their indentures record Thorne as Overseer of the Poor. [Dorset RO, P155/OV9, 1731; Bristol poll bks]

Thorne, Thomas, 26 Little Windmill St, Golden Sq., London, cm (1805–07). [D]

Thorne, Thomas, 2 Gibson St, Lambeth, London, cm and u (1822–23). [D] See Robert Thorn of Lambeth.

Thorne, William, Chapel St, Twickenham, Middlx, carpenter and u (1838). [D]

Thorne, William, West St, Wiveliscombe, Som., cm (1839). [D]

Thorne & Yarnold, High St, Worcester, cm (1788). [D]

Thornes, James, 2 Pine St, Manchester, cm and u (1800–02). [D]

Thorney, Robert snr, Lancaster, joiner and cm (1739–d.1791). Admitted freeman as joiner, 1739–40. Between 1742–72 took fifteen apps, describing himself as joiner and cm. Death on 18 March 1791 reported in *Williamson's Liverpool Advertiser*, 28 March. [Lancaster app. reg., freemen rolls, and poll bk]

Thorney, Robert, Liverpool, cm (1761–64). Took apps named Pendleton and Tomlinson in 1761, and Preston in 1764. [S of G, app. index]

Thorney, Robert jnr, Lancaster, cm (1773–84). Admitted freeman, 1773–74. [Lancaster freemen rolls and poll bk]

Thorney, Thomas, Lancaster, cm (1762–63). [Lancaster freemen rolls]

Tho(r)nham, George, 7 Blackfriargate, Hull, Yorks., chair-maker, wood turner and spinning-wheel maker (1803–22). Took app. named James Prescott of Hull in March 1814. [D; Hull app. reg.]

Thornham, John, Lord St, Gainsborough, Lincs., chairmaker (1822–23). [D]

Thornham, Thomas, 30 Blanket Row, Hull, Yorks., cm (up to 1793). Advertised in *Hull Packet*, 1793, that he had sold out to Thomas Peck.

Thornhill, George, Newcastle, chairmaker and cm (1804–38). Recorded at 16 Back Hanover St, 1804–17, Back Row, Westgate in 1834 and 7 Postern in 1838. [D]

Thornhill, Joseph, address unrecorded, upholder (1744). Son of Richard Thornhill, freeman upholder of London. Admitted freeman of the upholders' Co. by patrimony on 2 May 1744. [GL, Upholders' Co. records]

Thornhill, Richard, London, upholder (1717–34). Recorded at Gravel Lane, Houndsditch, 1717–18 and Limehouse in 1734. Father of Joseph Thornhill. Admitted freeman of the Upholders' Co. by order of the Court of Aldermen on 11 March 1717/18. [GL, Upholders' Co. records; poll bk]

Thornhill, William, Nottingham, joiner and cm (1832–35). Recorded at Kidd St in 1832 and Cur Lane in 1835. [D]

Thornton, —, Shrewsbury, Salop, u (1757). The Congreve correspondence at the William Salt Lib., Stafford [47/47/6] states in 1757: 'I went yesterday to see your bed at Thornton's which I hope and I think is made to your directions, it was put up for me to see and I ordered him to take it down again and put it up, in a clean chest, till I heard further from you . . . the bed, 25 yards of blue stuff, 3 doz of silk binding, . . . I could not get the bill for these things.'

Thornton, Christopher, London, looking-glass seller and glass grinder (1707–43). Recorded at 'The Looking-Glass', Peter St, Southwark, c.1707 and at Piccadilly, 1720–23. A handbill of c.1707 states: 'At Christopher Thornton's living, in Peterstreet in the Mint in Southwark, at the Looking-Glass near the Square, are now to be Sold all sorts of Looking-Glasses, Sconces, Chimney-Pieces, Pannel-Glasses, very reasonably, or may change your old Looking-Glasses for new ones, or if you have any old Looking-Glasses that want Silvering, shall be done very reasonably. You may also be furnished with Chests of Drawers, or Looking-Glasses at any price, paying for them Weekly, as we shall agree. Coach Glasses whole Fore-Glass £4. Door-glass £1. a Fore-Glass 8s. Pray take care of this Bill.' Thornton does not suggest that he was actually the maker of either glass or frames, but he seems to have been early in the field for supplying furniture on weekly payments. He probably bought his frames from carvers and gilders, but ground his own glasses. In 1720 a notice in the *Weekly Journal* gave his address as Piccadilly, and later still he was at 'The Cabinet', Germain (Jermyn) St. These might have been the same premises with an entrance to each thoroughfare. He was named in insurance co. records in 1723 as a glass grinder in Piccadilly. Announced in *Daily Post*, 1731, that he was retiring from business. Christopher Thornton, glass grinder, was reported as being committed to prison for debt, *London Gazette*, 17 May 1743. [Wills, *Looking-Glasses*; Symonds, *Furniture Making in 17th and 18th Century England*; Heal]

Thornton, Christopher, Lancaster, cm (1819–37). Son of Christopher Thornton of Ingleton. App. to Leonard Red-mayne on 3 March 1819, and admitted freeman, 1825–26. Between 1826–37 took twelve apps. Trading at Cable St in 1834 also as an u. [D; Lancaster app. reg. and freemen rolls]

Thornton, E. N., 174 Half Moon Lane, Southwark, London, upholder and undertaker (1817). [D]

Thornton, F., 139 High St, Ramsgate, Kent, cm (1838). [D]

Thornton, George, Gomersal, Yorks., cm and joiner (1828–29). [D]

Thornton, Henry, 15 Little Tower St, London, cm and u (1809–11). [D]

Thornton, Henry, 23 Fenchurch St, London, cm, u and undertaker (1809–20). Polled at Canterbury in 1818. [D]

Thornton, James, Trinity parish, Cambridge, chairmaker (1792–1806). Claimed freedom as eldest son of James Thornton, gardener, on 10 January 1792. Named as bailiff in 1806. [Cambs. RO, Corp. day bk]

Thornton, James, High Wycombe, Bucks., chairmaker (1830). Baptism of daughter recorded in 1830.

Thornton, James, High St, Bradford, Yorks., cm (1830–34). Listed at High St in 1830 and 10 Westgate, 1834. [D]

Thornton, John, Blackfriargate, Hull, Yorks., cm (1790–99). [D]

Thornton, John, London, joiner (1812). Carried out work, probably at 2 Hamilton Pl., Piccadilly, the London house of John, 6th Duke of Bedford. His bill, totalling £39 13s 9d, lists repairs to furniture, fitting locks, and supplying the following items: on 23 March 'a new washing stool with 2in. beech top', 6d; on 6 April 'To making a large press complete for the nursery', £11 14s 8½d; and 'a large pillar & claw table with 2 flaps hung with rule joints etc., complete', £6 10s 11d. [Bedford Office, London]

Thornton, John, Lancaster. Named in the Gillow records, 1815–26. [Westminster Ref. Lib.]

Thornton, John, Bradford, Yorks., cm (1822–37). Addresses given at Manningham in 1822; Regent St in 1830; and 10 Westgate in 1837. [D]

Thornton, Joseph, Kirkgate, Leeds, Yorks., cm (1798). [D]

Thornton, Joseph, 20 Market St, St James's, London, cm (1805–07). [D]

Thornton, Joseph, Huddersfield, Yorks., cm (1805–20). [D]

Thornton, Joseph, Halifax, Yorks., cm (1808). [D]

Thornton, Joseph, 2 Hale's Terr., Stepney, London, cm and u (1839). [D]

Thornton, Osborn, address unrecorded, cm and u (1758–70). Submitted bills to James West for Alscot Park, Warks., in 1758 for 'mending, polishing, new working', totalling £32 3s ½d; between 1765–67 for taking down, mending, cleaning and putting up furniture, making beds and curtains and supplying bedding, fabric and fringes. In 1768 he charged £2 8s for 'Altering a Soffa in a bed the seat to lift up with a place linned to hold the bedding'; and on 18 June 1769, £28 10s for '2 very large Soffas Jappand blew and white on strong Casters stuffed in linnen.' He was paid a total of £67 19s 2d on 29 March 1765; and £219 14s on 16 November 1770. [Alscot Park, West papers] An account for furniture supplied by Thornton to Sir Thomas Gascoigne of Parlington Hall, Yorks., 13 February 1768 to 4 May 1769, totalled £371 8s 4d. Items included beds, bedding, curtains, servents' furniture, drawing room and dining room furniture and card tables. The most expensive items were 'three gerandoles, white & burnish gold', costing £24 16s; and 'a glass in a white & burnish gold frame', £23 16s. [Leeds archives dept, unnumbered Parlington papers]

Thornton, Robert, Doncaster, Yorks., cm (1738–43). Took apps named Leake in 1738 and Ambler in 1743. [S of G, app. index]

Thornton, Samuel, Scarborough, Yorks., cm and u (1832–40). Addresses given at Globe St in 1823; Leading Post St in 1828–29; no. 24 in 1831; and 11 Sand Side in 1840. [D]

Thornton, T., 8 South St, Manchester Sq., London, cm (1817). [D]

Thornton, Thomas, Carden St, Worcester, u (1835). Admitted freeman of Worcester on 1 December 1835. [Worcester freemen rolls]

Thornton, William, York, carver (1670–1721). [G. Beard, 'English Woodcarvers', *Conn.*, June 1981, p. 143]

Thornton, William, 6 Turnham Pl., Curtain Rd, London, cm (1809). Took out a Sun Insurance policy on 1 May 1809 for £200 of which stock and utensils accounted for £100. [GL, Sun MS vol. 443, ref. 830542]

Thornton, William, 12 Curzon St, Mayfair, London, u (1829). [D]

Thornton & Pemberton, Preston, Lancs. Signed the *Preston Cabinet and Chair Makers' Book of Prices*, 1799 and 1802, on behalf of the masters.

Thorold, John, London, upholder (1706–d. by 1737). Polled of Old St, 1724–34. Son of Benjamin Thorold, ironmonger of London. App. to Daniel Cooper on 3 July 1706, and admitted freeman of the Upholders' Co. by servitude on 9 March 1714/15. Took app. named Richard Dunckley, 1721–28/29. [GL, Upholders' Co. records]

Thorp, —, London (?), u (1727). Named in the account book of Rebecca Tufnell for work probably carried out in London, on 23 December 1727 costing £3 12s. [Essex RO, D/DTu 280]

Thorp, —, Fish St Hill, by the Monument, London, u (1740–47). Named in contemporary newspapers. [Heal]

Thorp, Bethell, Hull, Yorks., cm (1817–39). Trading at 5 Brook St Ct, Brook St in 1839. App. to Robert Waugh in January 1817. [D; Hull app. reg.] See R. Thorp.

Thorp, Daniel, Austerlands, Saddleworth, Yorks., cm and u (1822). [D]

Thorp, Francis, Aldersgate St, London, upholder (1724–34). [Poll bks]

Thorp(e), George, 21–22 Red Lion St, Clerkenwell, London, clockcase maker and cm (1803–10). Took out Sun Insurance policies on 3 May 1803 for £600 on a house at 45 Cow Cross St; and on 27 April 1809, due Lady Day 1810, in association with George Bonnington, for £1,700, including £950 on house and shop; £200 on Thorpe's goods, clothes, books and plate; and £550 on stock and utensils. [GL, Sun MS vol. 426, ref. 747396; vol. 447, ref. 830361] See George Bonnington.

Thorp, George, Goodman's End, Bradford, Yorks., joiner and cm (1818–20). [D]

Thorp, James, address unrecorded, maker of 'Thorp's Composition' (1783). Issued a catalogue of ornaments, in which he claimed, regarding looking-glass frames: 'Any ornament contained in these designs, will be executed of Composition Fifty per cent, and many of them One Hundred per Cent. cheaper than wood carvings, although in many Respects they are equal in Goodness. Any Gentleman, Architect, Builder, or others wishing to have Ornaments made of this composition to their own Designs, and not to be used for any other Persons, may depend on the strict Honour.' [Symonds, *Furniture Making in 17th and 18th Century England*, p. 158]

Thorp, Johannes (John), address unrecorded. Bill in the Lincoln RO, dated 15 November 1721 and receipted on 16 November, is for a total of 19s 6d for six chairs, two tables and a pound of hog's lard. [2 ANC 12/D/11]

Thorp, Nicholas, 67 Worship St, Finsbury, London, cm and u (1839). [D]

Thorp, R., Hull, Yorks., cm (1838). [D] See Bethell Thorp.

Thorp, Robert, Gloucester St, Red Lion Sq., London, upholder (1724–34). [Poll bks] Probably Robert Thorpe.

Thorp, S., Abberley, Worcs. (?). Two mahogany spinning wheels recorded, c.1790 both bearing lables inscribed 'S. Thorp Abberley'. [*C. Life*, 12 September 1985, supplement, p. 91]

Thorp, W., 21 Wells St, Oxford St, London, u and cm (1820). [D]

Thorp, William, York and Leeds, Yorks., cm (1775–84). Son of Thomas Thorp, tailor, of Easingwold. App. to William Hawkin, cm, on 8 July 1775. Of Leeds, admitted freeman of York as cm in 1784. [York app. reg. and freemen rolls]

Thorpe, Edward, parish of St Stephen, Norwich, cm (1781). [Poll bk]

Thorpe, Joseph, Pall Mall, London, upholder (1725–26). Named in contemporary newspapers. [Heal]

Thorpe, Robert, London, upholder (b.c.1675/76–1769). Recorded on the south side of Theobalds Way, east side of Oracle St, parish of St Andrew, Holborn, in 1722. App. to Thomas Lucas in 1691. Admitted freeman of the Upholders' Co. by servitude on 4 November 1713, and Beadle in 1755. In 1769 he was excused office on account of illness and 'his great age being 93 or 4'. Took apps named Thomas Mountier, 1721–28/29; John Johnson in 1757 (transferred immediately); and Joseph Arnold (jointly), 1785–65. Took out a Hand in Hand Insurance policy in 1722 for £200 on his house. [GL, Upholders' Co. records; GL, Hand in Hand MS vol. 26, p. 141] Probably Robert Thorp.

Thorpe, Richard, 10 Upper Charlton St, Fitzroy Sq., London, chair and sofa manufacturer, cm and u, undertaker (1826–39). [D]

Thorpe, William, Market Bosworth, Leics., turner and chairmaker (1792). Advertised in *Leicester Journal*, 9 November 1792, for a journeyman chairmaker to make 'good white chairs'.

Thorpe, William, Birstall, Yorks., joiner and cm (1830–37). [D]

Thowless, William, 5 Bull St, Birmingham, carver and gilder, straw hat manufactory (1816–18). [D]

Thrape, George, Chester, cm (1772–77). Son of John Thrape. App. to Thomas Woodworth, cm, and assigned over to John Johnson for the residue of his term from 27 January 1772 to 30 January 1777. [Chester app. bks]

Threapland, Rt, 34 St Andrewgate, York, cm (1838). [D]

Threlfall, James, Liverpool, cm (1761–99). Admitted freeman on servitude to Josiah Baxendale on 2 April 1761. Possibly the Threlfall, cm of Liverpool, whose marriage to Miss Berry at St Peter's Church was reported in *Billinge's Liverpool Advertiser*, 7 October 1799. [Liverpool freemen reg.]

Thrinbeck, Richard, Philadelphia Pl., Sheffield, Yorks., cm (1821–25). [D]

Thrisk, Henry, York, carver (1692–1729). Admitted freeman in 1692. In 1729 carved 'four Corinthian capitals at 15s. a pair £3' for the Mansion House, York. [York freemen rolls; York Ref. Lib., Mansion House, Chamberlain's list; Beard, *Georgian Craftsmen*, pp. 24 and 182]

Throp, William, Gomersal, Yorks., cm and joiner (1828–29). [D]

Throssell, William, March, Cambs., carpenter, millwright, wheelwright, joiner and cm. Notice in probably 18th-century Cambridge newspaper, dated 30 June, reads: 'To be SOLD by AUCTION by Charles Cruso. (By order to the Assignee of WM. THROSSELL, the Elder, a Bankrupt) on Monday the 30th day of June inst. and the Five following Days, on the Premises, in March, within the Isle of Ely, and County of Cambridge, All the Timber and Wood, Materials, Tools, Utensils, and Implements, Stock in Trade, and Effects of every kind, belonging and appertaining to the several trades of a Carpenter, Millwright, Wheelwright, Joiner and Cabinet-maker; consisting of a great quantity of oak, ash, elm and fir timber; mahogany and wainscot plank and boards, Norway, Finland, and Petersburgh deals; a variety of articles in the cabinet-making business, such as mahogany and wainscot tables, looking-glasses, &c. and a very capital crane, 37ft between the shoulders, which works with a spur gear and counter, for drawing up the beater . . .'. Sale was to take place at 'The White Bear', Cambridge. [Winterthur, Delaware, Symonds papers, DMMC 75x69.21]

Throtman, Andrew, 71 Tottenham Ct Rd, London, cm (1796). [D]

Throwless, William, 5 Bull St, Birmingham, carver and gilder (1816). [D]

Throwsbridge, —, London, joiner or carver (1694). On 26 June 1694, as a member of the Company of Joyners Carvers of London', he signed a petition presented by that Company to the City of London. [*Furn. Hist.*, 1974]

Thruckley, Thomas, Castle Donnington, Leics., cm (1800). Advertised for journeymen cm in *Leicester Journal*, 25 April 1800.

Thurgood, Thomas, Bishop's Stortford, Herts., cm and u (1832–39). Listed at Potter St, 1832–38 and South St, also as a furniture broker, in 1839. [D]

Thurlby, Richard, Castle Donnington, Leics., cm (1840). [D]

Thurlow, Abraham, Palgrave, Suffolk, cm (1825). [Suffolk RO, HA68:2593/2726–2732]

Thurlow, Aeneas, 2 Brokers Row, Drury Lane, London, cm (1829). [D]

Thurlow, Charlotte, Framlingham, Suffolk, u (1839). [D]

Thurlston, Benjamin, Newcastle, u (1741). [Poll bk]

Thurman, Thomas, Nottingham, cm and u (1825–35). Trading at Middle Hill in 1825 and Finkhill St, 1828–35. [D]

Thurman & Attenborough, Week-day-cross, Nottingham, u (1822). [D]

Thurnam & Son, C., English St, Carlisle, Cumb., carvers and gilders (c.1830). Trade label recorded on back of frame, c.1830. [V&A archives]

Thurnell, —, 28 Goulston Sq., Whitechapel, London, u (1820). [D]

Thurnell, Samuel, 1 Upper Eaton St, Pimlico, London, u and cm (1835). [D]

Thurnell, William, 71 Leadenhall St, London, cm and u (1821–39). Recorded also at no. 69 in 1835; and as 'upholstery warehouse, mattress and feather bed manufacturer and Agency House to the Cabinet Makers' Society', 1823–25. Receipt [GL, trade card coll.] dated 21 March 1825, reads: 'Bot. of W. THURNELL, AT THE LONDON REPOSITORY FOR THE CABINET MAKERS' SOCIETY, At 71, Corner of Leadenhall Street, Opposite Aldgate Pump. Cheap Mattress, Feather Bed, Sea Bed and Palliass Manufactory. A Large Assortment of all kinds of Cabinet Furniture. Apartments and Houses furnished in Five Hours Notice'. Receipt states that the Cabinet Makers' Society was 'Established for the benefit of a number of Cabinet Makers with large families, and as there is no Profit attached to the Goods, further than the bare Journeymen's Wages, it enables their Agent to sell so cheap. The Society return their sincere thanks to the Nobility and Public in general, who have so liberally patronised the undertaking, and as they feel themselves so handsomely supported, beg leave to say that no exertion shall be wanting to merit a continuance of their favors.' Thurnell's receipt was for a French bedstead, two mattresses, and '6 Joyner Chair', totalling £9 17s. Took out Sun Insurance policies on 19 December 1821 for £1,000, of which stock and utensils accounted for £890; and on 18 December 1822 for £1,500 on stock, utensils and goods in trust in his house and warehouses, where no cabinet work was done. [D; GL, Sun MS vol. 491, ref. 987264; vol. 490, ref. 999330 and/or vol. 492, ref. 999121]

Thurnell, William, 6 Union Pl., New Rd, Marylebone, London, cm (1829). [D]

Thurrell (or Thurnel), John, 1 Poland St, Oxford St, London, cm, u and chair manufacturer (1835–39). Recorded at Poland House in 1835. [D]

Thursby, William, Norwich, carver and gilder (1778–79). Advertised in *Norfolk Chronicle*, 7 November 1778, that he 'intends opening his Shop on Monday the 9th Inst. in the Dove Lane, Norwich; makes and sells all Sorts of Oval and Pier Glasses; Carlomoratte, Italian, and bordered Picture Frames; Roman, Grecian, and French Lights; Variety of Lead and Paper Ornaments for friezes, Tablets, Mouldings, Borders and other Enrichments, in as neat and elegant a Manner as in London or elsewhere. Nobility, Gentlemen, Tradesmen, &c. who choose to make Trial, may depend on being served on the most reasonable Terms, and all Orders executed with the greatest Punctuality and Expedition, By their very humble Servant, WILLIAM THURSBY. N.B. Old Glasses bought, silvered, and repaired.' Advertised again, also as a picture frame maker, on 12 June and 18 December 1779.

Thursfield, Edward, at 'The Plow', Russell St, Covent Gdn, London, u (1685). Recorded in contemporary newspapers. [Heal]

Thurston, Horatio, Burton St, Bath, Som., upholder (1805). [D]

Thurston, John, 78 Margaret St, Cavendish Sq., London, cm (1813–16). [D]

Thurston, John, 14 Catherine St, Strand, London, billiard table and backgammon board maker (1822–40). [D] Recorded as 'Superior billiard tables, Cue and Mace Manufacturer by appointment to his Majesty' in 1835. Trade card [Banks Coll., BM] gives address at Waterloo House, and states: 'Portable and other Billiard Tables warranted of the best seasoned Materials and most correct Workmanship. The new constructed handsome Portable Billiard Tables with folding legs, very readily adjustable and most conveniently adapted for the Dining or Drawing Room in sizes of 6 feet, 7, 8, 9 & 10 feet. J. THURSTON having continued applications for good second hand Billiard Tables beyond the possibility of supplying them is at length enabled by a careful Purchase of Materials and Manufacturing many together to offer New and Superior Tables at very little more than the prices demanded for Old ones. He submits to the Nobility, Gentry, Merchants, Captains, &c. an unprecedented variety of Portable and other Billiard Tables from 10 Gns. to 90 Gns. each warranted accurate. Cushions re-stuffed in Town and Country — Tables exchanged. Marking Boards. Maces. Cues. Balls. Spirit Levels &c. Superior Bagatelle Boards to play the 4 Games.' In 1836 John Thurston published the third edition of his translation of Monsieur Mingaud's *The noble game of billiards wherein are exhibited extraordinary and surprising strokes which have excited the admiration of most of the sovereigns of Europe.* A 'new Billiard Table' by Thurston was advertised as part of the furniture of Hearthseath Park, Flintshire, to be sold by Mr Phillips of New Bond St, London. [*Liverpool Mercury*, 24 October 1828] Thurston & Co. continue today, and are the oldest known firm of billiard table makers. The firm's records note a billiard table sent to St Helena and played on by Napoleon Bonaparte. [V&A archives] Several of the firm's commissions are documented. The Leigh papers include a bill from Thurston of 1822 for an ash cue, wooden 'Butts' and a box, costing a total of £3. [Shakespeare Birthplace Trust, Leigh receipts, DR 18/5] Thurston charged Nicholas Pearse of Loughton, Essex, and Marylebone, London, £8 on 7 February 1824 for taking down and repairing a billiard table. [Essex RO, D/DHt A1/3] Thurston submitted a bill to Thomas T. Vernon of Hanbury Hall, near Droitwich, Worcs., dated 30 April 1832, and receipted on 7 May. Totalling £97 4s with £7 4s discount for cash, the bill listed 'An excellent mahogany 12 feet Billiard Table with button ornament mouldings turned and reeded legs the whole of fine Spanish wood', balls, cues and other accessóries; also 'A Man's time going to and returning from Hanbury Hall to fix the Table, Coach Hire and travelling expences.' Bill heading has the motto 'Temperantia et Voluptas', and states 'Foreign orders promptly executed'. [Worcs. RO, Vernon papers, 7335/705:7/8ii, 13–14] John Thurston received Royal patronage, supplying small gaming items costing £24 10s in December 1832; the same for Stud Lodge, Hampton Court and St James's Palace in June 1833; and for Windsor Castle in November 1833. The accounts of 30 September 1838 show Thurston providing 'An elegant Imperial Petrosian 12 feet Billiard Table with Indian rubber cushion, best superfine cloth massive legs turned and reeded, & with adjustable screw feet, moulded frame and cushion, the whole of fine Spanish wood and French polished, including 24 cues, 6 maces, a set of balls 2 inch and another set 1 inch 15/14, a marking board, a long cue, a three-quarter cue, a half bull, a long mace, 2 rests, a spirit-level, a brush, a jick cover with roller, a box-iron, cushion-warmer, and fixing the table at Windsor Castle, 90 gns.' 'A circular rack in mahogany', £3 3s; £1 1s for carriage; with a deduction of £26 5s for the old table. [PRO, LC11/101; Windsor Royal Archives, account bks, 1833–41]

Thurston, John Noel, Bath, Som., u (1829). Declared bankrupt, *Chester Chronicle and North Wales Advertiser*, 23 October 1829.

Thurston, Joseph, Queen St, Ipswich, Suffolk, cm (1839). [D]

Thurston, Samuel, Norwich, cm and u (1805–36). Recorded at Charing Cross, 1805–08 and Duke's Palace in 1836. [D; poll bk]

Thurtle, Thomas, St Magdalen St, Norwich, carver and gilder (1839). [D]

Thwaite, T., Lancaster. Named in the Gillow records in 1820 working on a washstand. [Westminster Ref. Lib., Gillow vol. 344/100, p. 3045]

T(h)waites, Edward, Canterbury, Kent, u and cm (1818–30). Recorded at Knott's Lane in 1818; St George in 1826; and Oaten Hill in 1830. [Poll bks]

Thwaites, George & Co., London, later Australia, cm, u and

undertaker (b.1791–d.1865). Trading at 4½ Cirencester Pl., Fitzroy Sq., 1827–28; 4 Gt Portland Rd, corner of Devonshire St in 1835; and 4 Portland Rd in 1839. Trade cards give addresses at Gothic Hall, New Rd, Marylebone, and 4 Portland Rd. Born at Coatham, Yorks., 15 September 1791, the 4th child of Thomas Thwaites, builder. Married Elizabeth Wilkinson of Stockton, Co. Durham, who bore him three sons: George jnr (1821–97); Thomas Henry (1826–1912), and John (c.1832–1903). Two stencils which survive from his London workshops indicate that they must have been of some size. Trade card advertised that he supplied Rout furniture. Declared bankrupt with Samuel Toplis, *Liverpool Mercury*, 23 December 1831. In 1842 Thwaites and his family emigrated to the settlement of Port Phillip, Melbourne, Australia, where he founded a flourishing cabinet workshop. [D; C. Simpson, 'George Thwaites and Son, Colonial cabinetmakers and their work', *The Australian Antique Collector*]

Thwaites, Henry, Hooper St, Clerkenwell, London, upholder and undertaker (1817–20). Trading at no. 8 in 1817 and no. 2, 1819–20. [D]

Thwaites, Robert, Market Pl., Bedale, Yorks., joiner and/or cm (1834). [D]

Tibats, H., address unrecorded. Numerous fine mid 18th-century card tables recorded with 'H. TIBATS' stamped on the concertina action hinge. [*Furn. Hist.*, 1966, pp. 44–45]

Tibbatts (or Tibbetts), John, Birmingham, cm (1756–93). Recorded at 11 High St, 1767–70 and Summer Hill in 1788. Took app. named Vincent in 1756. [D; S of G, app. index]

Tibbatts, William, 10 Little Queen St, Holborn, London, u (1822). Took out a Sun Insurance policy on 11 March 1822 for £500 including £300 on stock and utensils. [GL, Sun MS ref. 989825]

Tibbatts, William, 24 Chadis Row, Gray's Inn Rd, London, bed and mattress maker (1822–23). [D]

Tibbatts, William, 303 High Holborn, London, u (1823–28). Took out Sun Insurance policies on 6 August 1823 for £700 of which £500 accounted for utensils and stock; and on 21 July 1824 for £1,000, including £318 on goods in his house, where no cabinet work was done, £32 on prints, pictures, china and glass, and £650 on stock and utensils. [D; GL, Sun MS vol. 497, ref. 1006563; vol. 496, ref. 1019215]

Tibbatts, William, 76 Hackney Rd, London, u (1835). [D]

Tibbetts, Samuel, 15 Coldbath Sq., Clerkenwell, London, writing desk and dressing case maker (1829). [D]

Tibbs, Edward, 88 Bartholomew Close, London, carver and gilder (1820). [D] See Samuel Tibbs at this address.

Tibbs, Percival snr, Houndsditch, parish of St Botolph, Aldgate, London, upholder (1714–23). Recorded at 'The Sun & Moon' in 1714 when he insured his house with the Sun Co. on 31 July. Insured his house for £200 with the Hand in Hand Co. in January 1715, and again in 1722. Took his son, Percival Tibbs jnr as app. in 1715, admitted freeman of the Upholders' Co. by servitude in 1723. [GL, Sun MS vol. 4, ref. 4336; GL, Hand in Hand MS vol. 15, p. 300; vol. 26, p. 274; GL, Upholders' Co. records]

Tibbs, Percival jnr, London, upholder (1715–23). Son of Percival Tibbs, freeman upholder of London. App. to his father on 16 July 1715, and admitted freeman of the Upholders' Co. by servitude on 2 October 1723. [GL, Upholders' Co. records]

Tibbs, Samuel, 88 Bartholomew Close, London, carver and gilder, looking-glass manufacturer (1790–1825). [D] See Edward Tibbs at this address.

Tichbourne, Isaac, Paradise Row, Chelsea, London, u (1826–27). [D]

Tichner, William, 10 Spencer Row, Goswell St, London, chair and cabinet manufacturer (1811–25). [D] Probably William Tickner.

Tickel, William, Maryport, Cumb., joiner and/or cm (1811–34). Recorded at High St in 1811 and King St in 1829. [D]

Tickell, John, Globe Lane, Cockermouth, Cumb., cm and/or joiner, machine maker (1834). [D]

Tickner, J., 58 Castle St, Southwark, London, bedstead maker (1829). [D]

Tickner (or Tickler), William, Little Sutton St, Goswell St, London, chair and cabinet manufacturer (1805–11). [D] Recorded at no. 4, 1805–07 and no. 3, 1809–11. [D] Probably William Tichner.

Tidd, Elizabeth, 9 Bath St, City Rd, London, cm (1809–11). [D]

Tidd, Thomas, Old St Sq., London, cm (1769). Named in app. records. [Heal]

Tidd, William, 9 French Row, Old St, London, cm (1805–07). [D]

Tiddeman, J. S. & Co., Crown St, Finsbury, London, cabinet and brass founder etc. (1821). [D]

Tiddiman, George, Nottingham, carver and gilder (1812–41). Recorded at Glasshouse Lane, 1818–25; Union Pl., Clare St, 1822–32; and Glasshouse St, 1841. [D; poll bks]

Tiddiman, Joseph, Union Pl., Glasshouse St, Nottingham, carver and gilder (1835). [D]

Tiddowson, George, 48 St Andrew St, Liverpool, cm (1827). [D] Probably George Tidensor and George Tittenson.

Tideman, —, address unrecorded, cm. Bill at Stourhead, Wilts., 1771–178–?, for a large sum of money. [V&A archives]

Tidensor, George, 49 St Andrew St, Liverpool, cm (1829). [D] Probably George Tiddowson and George Tittenson.

Tidman, Thomas, Northgate St, Ipswich, Suffolk, u and paper hanger (1839). [D]

Tidmarsh, Matt., or Wall, London, upholder (1706–22). Recorded at St Botolph without Aldgate in 1708. Admitted freeman of the Upholders' Co. on 2 October 1706. Took an app. on 30 September 1713; one named Thomas Darby, 1713–20, and Thomas Abbis, 1715–22. Took out Hand in Hand Insurance policies on 14 June 1708 for £50 on a building in Wall's Ct, west side of the Gt Minories near Tower Hill; and £50 on two tenements on the west side of Wall's Ct; and on 5 August 1708 for £100 on the same properties. [PRO, app. reg.; GL, Upholders' Co. records; GL, Hand in Hand MS vol. 6, refs 16365–66]

Tidmarsh, Richard, Coventry St, Stourbridge, Worcs., chairmaker (1818). [D]

Tidmarsh, Thos., 11 Mount Pleasant, Bath, Som., cm (1833). [D]

Tidmarsh, William, 24 Park St, Islington, London, carver and gilder (1839). [D]

Tieldsley, Thomas, late of Birmingham, picture frame maker (1790–91). Notices concerning bankruptcy given in *Williamson's Liverpool Advertiser*, 29 November 1790 and 4 July 1791.

Tieurcono, Caspar, 21 Smithy Door, Manchester, picture, looking-glass etc. dealer (1804–08). [D]

Tiffin, C., 17 Somers Pl., East New Rd, St Pancras, London, u (1829). [D]

Tiffin & Sons, 30 Gt Marylebone St West, London, u and bedding manufacturers (late 18th century). Made a settle at Kiplin Hall, Yorks. [V&A archives]

Tight, William, 21 Gee St, Goswell St, London, carver (1826–27). [D]

Tigou, J., Vauxhall Bridge Rd, London, carver and gilder (1835). [D] Probably of Thomas & John Tijou, Southwark.

Tijou (or Tigou), Michael, London, carver, gilder and looking-glass maker (1802–35). Addresses given at 22 Greek St,

1802–07; no. 16, 1804–11; no. 17 in 1820 and 1823; no. 22 in 1821; and no. 16 in 1825. Recorded as M. Tijou at 14 Brighton Pl., New Kent Rd in 1835. [D] See Tijou & Son.

Tijou, Sophia, 10 Stockbridge Terr., Pimlico, London, carver and gilder (1839). [D]

Tijou, Thomas, Southwark, London, carver, gilder and picture dealer (1811–39). Recorded as T. & J. Tijou at 3 Duke St in 1811; as Thomas & John at 73 Union St in 1820; and alone there, 1820–39. [D]

Tijou & Son, Greek St, Soho, London, looking-glass manufacturers, carvers and gilders (1825–27). Recorded at no. 16 in 1825 and no. 17, 1826–27. [D]

Tilbe(e) (or Tilby), John snr, Maidstone, Kent, cm (1802–35). Polled of Market St, 1834–35. Listed as freeman in reg. of electors, 1834. [Poll bks]

Tilbe, Samuel, Leadenhall St, London, u (1727). Named in contemporary newspapers. [Heal]

Tilbe, Spencer, Canterbury, Kent, cm (1823–30). Recorded at Best Lane, 1823–24; All Saints', 1826; and Westgate, 1830. [D; poll bks]

Tilbury, Mr or Mrs, address unrecorded. In 1769 supplied furniture to the Earl of Albemarle of Bagshot Park costing £10 5s 6d. [Suffolk RO, HA 67:461/443]

Tilbury, John, High Wycombe, Bucks., chairmaker (1838). Daughter bapt. in 1838. [PR (bapt.)]

Tilby, John, High Wycombe, Bucks., chairmaker (1840). Daughter bapt. in 1840. [PR (bapt.)]

Tilby, William, 17 Charlotte St, Fitzroy Sq., London, undertaker and cm (1817). [D]

Tilden, M., Deal, Kent, cm (1807). [Rochester poll bk] Probably:

Tilden, Mathew, London, cm (1790). [Rochester poll bk]

Tildeslay (or Tildesley), Thomas, 45 South Molton St, London, cm and u (1835–39). [D]

Tilford, Thomas, Bristol, cm (1739). [Poll bk]

Tilleard, John, Clerkenwell, London, cm (1777–80). Recorded at 47 Clerkenwell Close in 1777 when he took out a Sun Insurance policy in association with John Hewitt for £300 of which £120 accounted for utensils and stock. [GL, Sun MS vol. 260, p. 73] Named in Bailey's list of bankrupts, 1780.

Tiller, Thomas, South St, Guildford, Surrey, cm (1835–37). [Poll bks]

Tillett, Richard Tallott, Watton, Norfolk, chairmaker (d.1740). [Norfolk Record Soc., index of wills]

Tillett, William, 44 Old St Rd, London, chairmaker (1835). [D]

Tilley, George, Bull Ring, Ludlow, Salop, chairmaker (1828). [D]

Tilley, James, All Saints' parish, Stamford, Lincs., cm (1832). [Poll bk]

Tilley, John, Nottingham, chairmaker (1829). Son of William Tilley of Nottingham; taken as app. in 1829. [Nottingham app. list]

Tilley, Samuel, Bull Ring, Ludlow, Salop, chairmaker (1835). [D]

Tillier, John, address unrecorded, upholder (1719–29). Son of Christopher Tillier, Gent. of London. App. to William Scrimshire on 14 August 1719, and James Clarke, freeman draper, on 1 September 1719. Admitted freeman of the Upholders' Co. by servitude on 6 August 1729. [GL, Upholders' Co. records]

Till(i)er, John, Bedford St, London, u (1749). [Poll bk]

Tilling, Edward, Islington, Liverpool, carver and gilder (1837–39). Recorded at no. 30 in 1837 and no. 65 in 1839. [D]

Tillot, John, at 'The Looking-Glass', the Minories, St Botolph without Aldgate, London, cm (1728). Took out a Sun Insurance policy on 24 June for £300 including £200 on household goods and stock in trade, and £100 on stock of glasses. [GL, Sun MS vol. 27]

Tillott, Henry, Bury, cm (1761). Took app. named Harper in 1761. [S of G, app. index]

Tilly, Thomas, Durham and Newcastle, cm and gilder (1806–34). Recorded at Sadler St, Durham in 1806, and Queen St, Newcastle, with house at Denton-chare, Newcastle, 1833–34. [D]

Tilly, William, address unrecorded, cm (1803). Subscribed to Sheraton's *Cabinet Dictionary*, 1803.

Tilly, William, 30 Redcliff Hill, Bristol, cm (1830–31). [D]

Tillyard, Susan, Market Pl., Norwich, cm and u (1839). [D]

Tilney, George, 29 Booth St, Spitalfields, London, cm and u (1839). [D]

Tilsley, John, Nantwich, Cheshire, cm (1795). Marriage recorded on 25 June 1795. [Chester RO, PR]

Tilson, Robert, Westgate, Grantham, Lincs., chairmaker (1819). [D]

Tilston, John, Chester, carver and joiner (1718). App. to William Phillips in 1718. [Chester app. bks]

Tilt, Samuel, London, cm, upholder and undertaker (1787–91). Recorded at 94 Cheapside, 1787–90, when he moved to Hatton Gdns. Named in Bailey's list of bankrupts, 1790. Bill to a Mr Manfield recorded, dated 4 March 1788, and totalling £4 5s 6d. Items listed are 'a Tea Tray Inlaid' at £1 16s; 'a Waiter to match', £1; '2 pair Bottle Stands', £7; 'an Oval Cadie', 15s; and 'a Cadie Ladle', 6s. Bill heading notes: 'Variety of Paper Hangings'. Research in the Thomas Jefferson Memorial Foundation, Virginia, USA, revealed a table which belonged to Jefferson and was made in London by Samuel Tilt in 1791. It is very similar to Sheraton's 'Universal Table'. [D; V&A archives]

Tiltson, John, Chester, joiner and carver (1696–1708). Son of Modland Tiltson of Gresford, Denbighshire, and pupil of Thomas Davies, joiner and carver of Chester. Admitted freeman on 2 October 1696. Took app. named John Hall, admitted in 1708. [Chester freemen rolls]

Tiltson (or Tylston), Thomas, Chester, carver (1732). Son of John Tiltson, carver of Chester, deceased. Admitted freeman on 12 October 1732. [Chester freemen rolls]

Timbrell, Samuel, 5 Lower Symons St, Chelsea, London, carver and gilder (1826). [D]

Timewell, John, Dover, Kent, u (1832). [Poll bk]

Tim(m)ings, John, Worcester, cm, u and auctioneer (1797–1812). Trading at 94 High St, 1797–98, and still at High St, c.1806. Former apps admitted freemen: William Bushell in 1799; William London in 1802; John Dovey and Henry Insull in 1812. Bill head of firm of D. & W. Cowell states they are 'successors to MR. TIMINGS', in 1832. [D; Worcester freemen rolls]

Timmins, Robert, 3 Old Cock Yd, Preston, Lancs., with house at 2 Jordon St, joiner and cm (1825). [D]

Timothy, David, Barbican, London, cm and u (1827–35). Recorded at no. 30, 1827–28, and no. 31 in 1835. [D]

Tim(m)s, Thomas, Upper Charlotte St, Fitzroy Sq., London, u and undertaker (1811–39). Recorded at 57 Charlotte St, Rathbone Pl., 1811–25; 56 Upper Charlotte St, 1826–27; no. 57 in 1835; and no. 5 in 1839. [D]

Tims, Thomas, address unrecorded, cm (1803). Subscribed to Sheraton's *Cabinet Dictionary*, 1803.

Tims, Thomas, Brook Side, Hereford, chairmaker and turner (1835). [D]

Tindale, Atherlston, Bristol, upholder (1718). Took app. named Nicholas Beaker in 1718. [*Wilts. Apps and their Masters*]

Tindale (or Tindall), George, Scarborough, Yorks., cm (1828–40). Trading at Dumple St, 1828–34, and 13 Leading Post St in 1840. [D]

Tindale, M. F., 84 Broad St, Ratcliffe, London, cm (1835). [D]

Tindall, George, Finkle St, Thirsk, Yorks., cm (1823). [D]

Tindall, Robert, Hull, Yorks., joiner and cm (1835–40). Trading at 18 Trundle St with house at 14 Paradise Pl. in 1838. Still at Trundle St in 1840. [D]

Tindall, Samuel, High St, Lincoln, cm (1790). [Poll bk]

Tinddall, John, Heworth Rd, York, cm (1837). [D]

Tingay, George, Fore St, Hoddesdon, Herts., cm (1839). [D]

Tingle, William, address unrecorded. On 9 February 1719 he was paid 9s 'for Pickture Frames' supplied to Jane, Lady Lindsey. [Lincoln RO, 2 ANC 6/52]

Tinker, Robert, address unrecorded, upholder (1714–15). Son of Thomas Tinker of Windsor. App. to William Farmer, and admitted freeman of the Upholders' Co. by servitude on 9 March 1714/15. [GL, Upholders' Co. records]

Tinker, Uriah, Thurlestone, Penistone parish, Yorks., cm (1837). [D]

Tinkler, John, Lancaster, joiner and cm (1766–84). App. to R. Thorney in 1766, and admitted freeman, 1779–80, when stated 'of Bolton le Moors, formerly of Liverpool'. [Lancaster app. reg., freemen rolls and poll bk]

Tinning, Mary, 6 Hobson's Yd, 49 Briggate, Leeds, Yorks., working u (1830). [D]

Tiplady, Stephen, York, u (1792). Son of Stephen Tiplady of Holme. App. to William Halfpenny, u, appraiser and undertaker, on 20 February 1792. [York app. reg.]

Tip(p)ler, Thomas, Leicester, later Derby, cm (1739–66). App. to Thomas Hand of Oakham, Rutland, in 1739; and to Sarah Groce, cm and widow of Leicester, in 1742. Admitted freeman in 1754. Of Derby, took apps in 1764 and 1766. [Leicester freemen rolls]

Tipper, Nicholas, 35 Union St, Middlx Hospital, London, carver and gilder (1779). Insured his house for £300 in 1779. [GL, Sun MS vol. 273, p. 179]

Tippet, Francis, Bristol, bedstead maker and furniture broker (1820–37). Trading as a bedstead maker at 3 Rosemary St, 1820–22; no. 10, 1823–24; 19 Merchant St in 1825; and 7 St John's Bridge in 1827; as a furniture broker at 13 Merchant St, 1828–36; and no. 12 in 1837. [D]

Tippets, Richard, St Thomas, Crediton, Devon, chairmaker (1741). Took app. named Hancock in 1741. [S of G, app. index]

Tipping, Benjamin, Stamford, Lincs., joiner and cm (1713–c.1727). Took app. named Hewett in 1713. Worked at Burghley House, c.1722–27. [S of G, app. index; C. *Life*, 29 August 1874, pp. 562–64]

Tipping, George, Manchester, cm (1804–25). Addresses given at 23 Booth St, Tib Lane in 1804; 33 Swarbrick St in 1813; 22 Richmond St in 1817; and no. 17 in 1825. [D]

Tipping, George, Wavertree, Liverpool, chairmaker (1829). [D]

Tipping, Isaac, at 'The Millstone Inn', Castle St, Birmingham, upholder and 'dealer in blankets & coverlids' (1760–d.1765). Advertised in *Williamson's Liverpool Advertiser*, 18 July 1760, that he had 'brought to town a large Quantity of Upholstery Goods, at the Sign of the Mill Stone in Castle-street, the Sale to begin the 18th of July Inst. & continue 14 Days & no longer. Blankets from 6s. to £1.15s. per piece; Feather Bed-Ticks of all Sorts; Quilts of all Sorts for Beds; curtains ready made from 16s. to £5 per Suit; beautiful Carpets for Floors; white Cotton Counterpanes; Rugs & Coverlids of all Sorts; & Bed side Carpets'. Death reported, same paper, 29 November 1765.

Tipping, Isaac, Bull-ring, Birmingham, upholder (1770–84). Recorded at no. 2, 1770–80. [D]

Tipping, James Frederick, 32 New Compton St, St Giles, London, French polisher (1834). His son, Frederick Knight Tipping by his wife Sarah, bapt. at Westminster Methodist Chapel on 30 March 1834. [PRO, Non-Conf. reg., RG4/4313]

Tipping, John, Brydges St, Strand, London, chairmaker (1809–11). [D]

Tipping, John, Gloucester, cm (1815–20). Children bapt. at St Michael's Church in 1815, 1816 and 1820. [PR (bapt.)]

Tipping, Josiah, Blundell St and St James's St, Liverpool, cm (1816). Admitted freeman on servitude to William Longworth Walker on 10 June 1816. [Liverpool freemen reg.]

Tipping, Robert, address unrecorded, upholder (1706). Admitted freeman of the Upholders' Co. on 6 July 1706. [GL, Upholders' Co. records]

Tirpane, Noul, address unrecorded, 'French varnisher' (1689). Entry in the diary of 1st Lord Bristol on 11 October 1689 reads: 'Paid then to Noul Tirpane, a French varnisher, in full for 10 chairs, a couch & two taboretts & all other accounts to this day £12.0.0.' [*Burlington*, December 1918, p. 226]

Tisdall, Samuel, 33 Tash St, Gray's Inn Lane, London, carver and gilder (1839). [D]

Tissiman, Peter, Globe St, Scarborough, Yorks., cm and u (1828–30). [D]

Tissitt (or Tissett), Mary, Belvoir St, Leicester, u (1822–42). Listed also as a cm in 1822. [D]

Tissott, L., 3 Old Compton St, Soho, London, carver and gilder (1805–07). [D]

Titford, W. C., 1 Finsbury Pl., London, drapery and furniture warehouseman (1808). [D]

Titherley, J., St Lawrence's, Exeter, Devon, cm (1803). [Exeter Militia list]

Titley, John, 29 South St, Sheffield, Yorks., cm (1837). [D]

Titlow, William, High St, Lowestoft, Suffolk, undertaker and cm (1839). [D]

Tittenson (or Tittensor), George, Liverpool, cm (1821–27). Recorded at 9 Thomas Ct, St Andrew St, 1821–24, and 38 St Andrew St in 1827. [D] Probably George Tiddowson and George Tidensor.

Tittenson (or Tittensor), James, Liverpool, chairmaker and cm (1800–39). Addresses given at 16 Upper Frederick St, 1800–03; no. 60, 1804–10; no. 49 in 1811; no. 62, 1813–14; no. 60, 1816–27; no. 66 in 1829; 3 Surrey St in 1834; and 15 Bold Pl., 1837–39. [D] Probably James Titterson.

Tittensor, Benjamin, Newcastle-under-Lyme, Staffs., cm (1812). [Poll bk]

Tittensor, George, Newcastle-under-Lyme, Staffs., cm (1812–23). Trading at Penkhull St, 1822–23. [D; poll bk]

Tittensor, John, Newcastle-under-Lyme, Staffs., cm (1790). [Poll bk]

Tit(t)ensor, John, Shrewsbury, Salop, cm and u (1828–35). Recorded at Wyle Cop as John & Son in 1828; and alone at St Mary's Pl., 1835. [D]

Tittensor, Samuel, Brown Hills, Burslem, Staffs., chairmaker and turner (1834). [D]

Titter, Benjamin Palmer, London and Norwich, cm and chairmaker (1799–1830). Polled at Norwich of London in 1799; of the parish of SS Simon and Jude, Norwich, in 1807; trading at St Simon's St in 1810; and St Gregory's parish, 1812–18. Recorded as auctioneer and appraiser, Pottergate St in 1830. [D; poll bks] Former app., Joseph Scotter, chairmaker, admitted freeman on 24 February 1828. [Norwich freemen reg.] Brass handle back-plates on high quality Regency mahogany dining table, c.1820, are inscribed: 'THE NEW CONSTRUCTED Occasional Table by B. P. TITTER Inventor and Manufacturer, N.4 St. Simons, Norwich.' Table, when fully extended by three extra leaves to 13 ft, is supported at the ends by round, tapering collared legs with brass cup castors that fold up into the frieze when the table is closed. [Christie's, 22 April 1968, lot 277; *Apollo*, December 1955, p. 299a, June 1967] Another extending mahogany dining table bears brass tablets at the ends,

functioning as backplates to squared loop handles, inscribed: 'B. P. TITTER & COMP. Inventors & Manufacturers. N.32 Pottergate Street, NORWICH'. A further table, extending by five extra leaves to 14 ft 5 ins has brass handle plates inscribed: 'B. P. TITTER & COMP. INVENTORS AND MANUFACTURERS, NORWICH'. [Bonham's, 5 July 1979, lot 31]

Titterson, James, Liverpool, cm (1790–96). Recorded at 69 Frederick St, 1790–96 and 20 Dickenson St in 1794. [D] See James Tittenson.

Tittorsan, Joseph, Liverpool, cm '& one of the ringers at St. Nicholas Church' (1822). Marriage at St Anne's Church to Miss Barker, daughter of Mrs Forshaw, Hackin's Hey, reported in *Liverpool Mercury*, 5 July 1822.

Tizon, T. & I., 3 Duke St, Southwark, London, carvers and gilders (1809–11). [D]

Toakley, John, St Martin's Pl., Birmingham, gilder (1818). [D]

Tobin, Michael, 89 St James St, Liverpool, cm (1839). [D]

Toby, Henry, 3 Glebe Pl., Chelsea, London, cm and u (1823). [D]

Toby, James, Ailesbeer, (*sic*), Devon, cm (1761–62). Took apps named West in 1761 and Reed in 1762. [S of G, app. index]

Toby, James, Guinea St, Exeter, Devon, cm (1832). His son Daniel Culliford bapt. at St Mary Major on 26 August 1832. [PR (bapt.)]

Tod, Thomas, Gt Trinity Lane, London, cm (1747). Named in contemporary newspapers. [Heal]

Todd, —, St Ann's, Soho, London, 'an eminent Upholsterer' (d.1768). Death 'of the Gout in his Stomach' reported in *Public Advertiser*, 18 March 1768.

Todd, Caleb, Gosport, Hants., chairmaker (1749). Took app. named Horsey in 1749. [S of G, app. index]

Todd, George, Chester, cm (c.1793–1812). Son of James Todd; app. to William Henderson on 5 October (1793?). Polled of Cow Lane in 1812. [Chester app. bks]

Todd, James jnr, Frodsham St, Chester, cm (d.1832). Death on 23 June 1832 reported in *Chester Courant and Advertiser for North Wales*, 3 July.

Todd, James, Winslow, Bucks., cm (1839). [D]

Todd, John, York and Nottingham, cm (1758–74). Son of John Todd, joiner; admitted freeman of York in 1758. Polled at York of Nottingham in 1758; and of Stonegate, York, in 1774. [York freemen rolls]

Todd, John, Hull, Yorks., cm (1784–1831). Polled at Beverley, of Hull, 1784–99. Recorded at Leadenhall Sq., Hull, 1806–10; and 6 Wellington Mart in 1831. [D]

Todd, John, address unrecorded, cm (1803). Subscribed to Sheraton's *Cabinet Dictionary*, 1803.

Todd, John, Campfield, Leeds, Yorks., cm (1817). [D]

Todd, John, Cottingham, Yorks., cm (1821). App. to Joseph Carter in June 1821. [Hull app. reg.]

Todd, John, Northgate, Hartlepool, Co. Durham, joiner and/or cm (1828–34). [D]

Todd, John, West St, Wigton, Cumb., cm and/or joiner (1828–34). [D]

Todd, John, 61 Wicker, Sheffield, Yorks., cm (1834–37). [D]

Todd, Jonathan, Workington, Cumb., cm (1809). Recorded in death duty reg. relating to wills proved, in the Deanery of Copeland, Cumb.; entry dated 6 January 1809.

Todd, Joseph, Chester, cm and chairmaker (1826–29). Son of James Todd, cordwainer of Chester; app. to Charles Boulton, cm, for seven years. [Chester app. indentures] Notice under 'Chester Police' in *Chester Chronicle, Cheshire and North Wales Advertiser*, 13 November 1829, stated that Joseph Todd, an apprentice chair-maker, for discharging a loaded pistol in the street, was fined 10s and 2s cost; and would be imprisoned for 6 months 'unless the money be sooner paid'.

Todd, Richard, Cottingham, near Hull, Yorks., cm (1810). App. to Thomas Ross of Cottingham in August 1810. [Hull app. reg.]

Todd, Richard, Hyde Hill, Berwick-upon-Tweed, Northumb., cm and u (1827–34). [D]

Todd, Robert, Northants., gilder (1720–48). Of Tansor, took app. named Bellamy in 1720; of Tittlebrough, one named Page in 1748. [S of G, app. index]

Todd, Robert, address unrecorded, cm (1803). Subscribed to Sheraton's *Cabinet Dictionary*, 1803.

Todd, Robert, Newcastle, joiner and cm (1811–27). Trading at Manor-chare in 1811 and Old Butcher Mkt in 1824. [D]

Todd, Thomas, Silver St, Morpeth, Northumb., chairmaker (1827). [D]

Todd, William, High St, Lincoln, cm (1805–26). Recorded as a chairmaker and wheelwright, 1819–22. [D]

Todd, William, King St, Thorne, Yorks., joiner and cm (1828–29). [D]

Todhunter, Thomas, Bondgate, Darlington, Co. Durham, joiner and cm (1827). [D]

Todner, Ralph, Houghton-le-Street, Co. Durham, cm and joiner (1828–29). [D]

Tofts, William, Butcher Row, Cambridge, cm, u and paper hanger (1830–43). [D; poll bks]

Toggett, William, Fore St, Taunton, Som., carver and gilder, bookseller (1779–82). Took out Sun Insurance policies in 1779 for £200 on his house; and in 1782 for £400 of which utensils and stock accounted for £360. [GL, Sun MS vol. 277, p. 65; vol. 303, p. 474]

Tokard, William, Ipswich, Suffolk, cm (1753). Took app. named Gardiner in 1753. [S of G, app. index]

Tolbot, Michael, Downham Market, Norfolk, joiner, cm and chairmaker (1770). Advertised in *Cambridge Chronicle and Journal*, 18 August 1770, that he was lately returned from London with the best materials and workers; and required a 'frame chair maker' and a 'pin chair maker'.

Tolbott, Thomas, 5 Silver St, Liverpool, u (1818). [D]

Tolfree, James & Son, Basingstoke, Hants., cm and u (1823). [D]

Tolfrey, Samuel, address unrecorded, u (1771–72). Named in the accounts of the Hon. Mrs Howard on 31 December 1771–72, receiving £340 for items including '20 yds. furniture' at £17; and 'Damask for Lord Petre'. [Essex RO, D/DP A189]

Tolley, Richard, Lancaster. Named in the Gillow Records in 1814 working on a jardinière and a sideboard. [Westminster Ref. Lib., Gillow vol. 344/99, p. 1957]

Tolmin, William, 32 Charing Cross, London, u (1839). [D]

Tol(l)put(t), Joshua, Canterbury, Kent and Long Acre, London, u (1784–1816). Admitted freeman of Canterbury in 1784, and polled there, 1790–96. Recorded at 115 Long Acre, 1794–1816. Death of his wife reported in *Gents Mag.*, June 1797. Subscribed to Sheraton's *Cabinet Dictionary* in which he was named in the list of master cabinet makers, 1803. [D; Canterbury freemen rolls]

Tolson, John, Penrith, Cumb., cm (1798). [D]

Tombes, Henry, London, cm or furniture japanner (1718–26). Trading at Bond St in 1718. The Duke of Montrose's accounts for furnishing his house in Bond St record payment to Tombes of £21 for a 'Large Japanned Chest with a Frame'. In 1726 Tombes supplied another 'Japan Chest' costing £16, probably to the Duke. [Scottish RO, GD 220/6/28/p. 84, GD, 220/6/1347/11]

Tombs, Bartholomew, parish of St Mary Woolnoth, London, upholder (1679). [PR]

Tomion, William, 57 Fleet St, London, u (1784). [D]

Tomison, Jackman, Selby, Yorks., cm and u (1826–29). Trading at Micklegate in 1826 and Broad St, 1828–29. [D]

Tomkies, John, 23 and 24 Eldon St, Finsbury, London, cm and u (1827–28). [D]

Tomkies (or Tomkins), Richard, Brokers Row, Moorfields, London, u, appraiser and broker (1805–28). Trading at no. 7, 1805–13; nos 4 and 7 in 1816; nos 4 and 12, 1819–20; no. 3, 1822–23; also as Richard Tomkies snr at 12 Moorfields, 1822–23; 4 and 12 Brokers Row in 1825; and as cm and u at 12 Blomfield St, Moorfields, 1827–28. Trade card states: 'Richd. Tomkies, New & Second Hand Furniture Warerooms, No. 12, Broker Row, near New Broad St, Moorfields. Upholsterer, Appraiser, Auctioneer & Undertaker'. [D; Landauer Coll., MMA, NY]

Tomkins, Edward, Church St, Malpas, Cheshire, joiner and cm (1822). [D] See Edward Tomkinson at this address.

Tomkins, J. F. or J. T., London, frame maker (1790–96). Recorded at 49 New Bond St, 1795–96. In 1790–91 provided Lord Howard of Audley End, Essex, with frames costing £12 18s and in 1793, picture frames costing £2 2s, for his London house in New Burlington St. Tomkins's bill of 1795–96 totalled £6 12s 6d, and listed prints, 'A pair of neat frames for Colin Clout etc.', 'A handsome Burnish Gold frame for Drawing Walden Church', 'A German Glass to Do. and Gildg Border', and 'A neat Burnish Gold Frame for Bishop of London with a Rich Embellish'd Gold and Black Glass'. [Essex RO, D/DBy/A50/4; A51/3; A54/5]

Tomkins, John, address unrecorded, cm (1725). On 22 April 1725 supplied to Temple Newsam House, Leeds, 'a New Wanscot Case of Drawes', costing £1 14s, and charged for brass fittings, oiling a table and erecting a bedstead. [*Furn. Hist.*, 1967]

Tom(p)kins, Jonathan, Portsmouth, Hants., u (1782). Declared bankrupt, *Sussex Weekly Advertiser*, 20 May 1782, and *Leicester Journal*, 23 November 1782.

Tomkins, Philip, Moorfields, London, cm (1776). Insured house and goods at London Wall for £300 in 1776. [GL, Sun MS vol. 245, p. 456]

Tomkins, Samuel, London, upholder (1768–1802). Trading at 20 New Broad St, Moorfields in 1783; and Broad St, 1788–1802, as Samuel & Co. at no. 60, 1788–94. Son of Nicholas Tomkins, freeman joiner of London. App. to Samuel Luck, shipwright, on 3 February 1768, and admitted freeman of the Upholders' Co. by servitude on 19 November 1783. [D; GL, Upholders' Co. records]

Tomkins, William, at 'The Royal Bed', corner of New Broad St, near Little Moorgate in Moorfields, London, u and sworn appraiser (1743–c.1760). Trade cards [GL, and Heal Coll., BM] show 'lit à la Duchesse' with Royal arms on headboard, within a frame of heavy scroll-work. Card states that Tomkins 'Buyeth & Selleth all Manner of Household Goods; as Standing Beds & Bedding, Chest of Drawers, Desks, & Bookcases, Bouroe Desks, Card, Dining, Breakfast and Dressing Tables (in Mohogeny, Walnut-tree or Wainscot) Chairs of all sorts, Settee and Bouroe Bedsteads; Sconces, Pier, Chimney and Dressing Glasses; Turkey Carpets of all sorts, —Tapestry Hangings & Painted Floor Cloths; all Sizes of Bell Metal Mortars, with all manner of Upholdstery, Cabinet & Braziery Goods, New and Old, — at very Reasonable Rates. N.B. All Sorts of Goods Appraised.' Another trade card, in the GL, headed 'The Royal Bed', is elaborately engraved with the Royal 'lit à la Duchesse' within an interior showing Palladian doorcase and panelling, cabriole chairs, kneehole dressing table and looking-glass. An invoice for four Russia leather chairs at 4s 6d, dated 12 May 1743 and signed by James Rodwell for Tomkins, is also in the GL. Rodwell appears to have taken over the business by 1760, and his card closely resembles that of Tomkins. See Jane Tompkins at the same address.

Tomkins, William, 14 Brokers Row, Moorfields, London, upholder and cm (1771–d.1778). Heal records him in directories, and states that he died in 1778.

Tomkins, William, 14 Brokers Row, Moorfields, London, upholder and cm (1779–96). Recorded also at 22 New Broad St, 1780–81, and 14 Moorgate in 1783. [D]

Tomkinson, Charles, Welsh (or Welch) Row, Nantwich, Cheshire, cm/joiner (1822–23). [D]

Tomkinson, Edward, Church St, Malpas, Cheshire, cm and joiner (1837). [D] Possibly the same as, or a relation of, Edward Tomkins at this address.

Tomlin, Joseph, Gainsborough, Lincs., chairmaker (1805–07). [D]

Tomlin, Robert, 61 Hanover St, Liverpool, cm (1820). Sale of stock by Taylor & Pinnington of Church St, on Tomlin's 'going to reside in London', advertised in *Liverpool Mercury*, 7 April 1820. Stock consisted of 'Mahogany Articles of good workmanship, in sets of Chairs, Sofas in Hair Cloth, Chests of Drawers, Card & Pembroke Tables, on pillars & claws, Tea Chests, Caddies, Dressing Glasses, Footstools etc: handsome fancy Oak Card Tables, Calico Curtains for two windows etc: together with the HOUSEHOLD FURNITURE, Kitchen Requisites, a quantity of fine Oak & Spanish Veneers, Mahogany Boards, four Cabinet-makers Benches, & other Effects.'

Tomlin, Robert, 24 Ratcliffe Terr., Goswell St Rd, London, cm and u (1822–23). [D]

Tomlin, Roger, London, u (1709–32). Recorded at 'The Crown & Cushion', over against Stock's Mkt, Gt Lombard St, 1723–26; and at 'The Crown & Cushion', Fenchurch St, near 'The Ipswich Arms', Cullum St, 1726–32. Son of Roger Tomlin, Gent. of East Malling, Kent. App. to Arthur Osbourne and James Gronous on 21 April 1709. Admitted freeman of the Upholders' Co. by servitude on 5 April 1721. Took app. named Henry Lodge in 1724. Took out a Sun Insurance policy on 8 July 1723 for £500 on goods and merchandise in his house. Heal notes him in contemporary newspapers, 1726–32. [GL, Upholders' Co. records; GL, Sun MS vol. 15, ref. 29110]

Tomlin, William, Gainsborough, Lincs., chair turner etc. (b.1760–d.1805). Death aged 45 reported in *Gents Mag.*, October 1805.

Tomlin, William, Shambles St, Barnsley, Yorks., cm and u (1814–37). Recorded at Cheapside in 1816. [D]

Tomlinson, Benjamin, Holywell St, Chesterfield, Derbs., cm (1818–22). [D]

Tomlinson, George, Carter St, Uttoxeter, Staffs., cm (1835). [D]

Tomlinson, George, Norton, near Malton, Yorks., joiner and cm (1840). [D]

Tomlinson, James T., Penny St, Lancaster, chair and bedstead maker (1825–34). [D]

Tomlinson, John, Lancaster, chairmaker (1806–07). [Lancaster freemen rolls]

Tomlinson, Richard, Lancaster, cm (1761–68). App. to R. Thorney in 1761, and admitted freeman, 1767–68. [Lancaster app. reg. and freemen rolls]

Tomlinson, Richard, Lancaster, chair and bedstead maker candlebox maker (1777–1825). Recorded at Penny St, 1818–25. App. to Joseph Tyson in 1777, and admitted freeman, 1785–86. Took app. as chairmaker on 11 June 1818. [D; Lancaster app. reg. and freemen rolls]

Tomlinson, Richard, Bromsgrove, Worcs., cm (1784). [Lancaster poll bk]

Tomlinson, Richard, 107 Shoe Lane, London, upholder (1799–1802). Son of Richard Tomlinson, carpenter of Belper, near Derby. Admitted freeman of the Upholders' Co. by redemption on 2 January 1799. [GL, Upholders' Co. records]

Tomlinson, Richard, London, carver and gilder (1804–12). Trading at 12 Welbeck St, Cavendish Sq., 1804–06; and 9 Cambridge St, Golden Sq., 1809–12. [D]

Tomlinson, Richard, Lytham, Lancs., joiner and cm (1825). [D]

Tomlinson, Robert, York, carver and gilder (1777–1816). Trading at Stonegate, 1798–1816. App. to Robert Blakesley, carver and gilder, on 1 July 1777; later assigned to James Hobden of Gartrop Park. Admitted freeman in 1789. Assigned app. named John Hunsley from Robert Blakesley. [D; York app. reg. and freemen rolls]

Tomlinson, Samuel, Newbridge Lane, Stockport, Cheshire, cm (1825–28). [D]

Tomlinson, Thomas, Calender St, Blackburn, Lancs., cm and joiner (1816–18). [D]

Tomlinson, Thomas, Retford, Notts., cm and u (1828–41). Trading at Market Pl. in 1828, Church St in 1835 and Churchgate in 1841. [D]

Tomlinson, William, 3 Bank St, Norwich, u and cm (1839–42). [D]

Tomlinson & Burgess, Harrogate, Yorks., joiners and/or cm (1834). [D]

Tomlisson, John, Old St, St Luke's, London, cm (1809–11). [D]

Tompkins, Francis, 15 London Wall, Moorfields, London, cm (1817). [D]

Tompkins, Jane, at 'The Royal Bed', corner of Petty France, Moorfields, London, u (1727). Took out a Sun Insurance policy on 16 February 1727 for £200 on her stock in three warerooms in the house of Mr Pitman in Petty France. [GL, Sun MS vol. 25, ref. 44025] See William Tomkins at 'The Royal Bed'.

Tompkins, John, Westgate, Grantham, Lincs., cm and u (1819). [D]

Tom(p)kins, Thomas, London Wall, London, cm, upholder and broker (1800–16). Recorded at no. 17, 1800–03, and nos 15 and 16 variously, 1809–16. Took out a Sun Insurance policy on 25 April 1800 for £630 on his new house, shop, workshop, sawpit and stock, including £100 on a house in tenure at 16 London Wall. Another policy of 24 September 1803 was for £1,400, including £150 on utensils and stock. [D; GL, Sun MS vol. 418, ref. 702310; vol. 426, ref. 752461]

Tompson, —, 19 Everett St, Russell Sq., London, cm (1805–07). [D]

Tompson, Jacob, Norwich, u (1692). Former app., William Harrison, admitted freeman on 24 February 1692. [Norwich freemen reg.]

Tompson, John, 6 Devonshire St, Bloomsbury, London, cm (1805–07). [D]

Tompson, John, 12 Stephen St, Rathbone Pl., London, upholder (1807). Took out a Sun Insurance policy on 19 February 1807 for £500 on his house and goods. [GL, Sun MS vol. 437, ref. 800200]

Toms, James, 21 Rathbone Pl., Oxford St, London, carver and gilder (1805–07). [D]

Toms, William, Upton Slip, Falmouth, Cornwall, cm and u (1830). [D]

Tomson, —, address unrecorded. Supplied items for Hatfield House, Herts., on 7 July 1663, 'paintings and chimney piece in middle room', costing £4 10s, for Lady Cranborne; and on 7 December 1664, a 'new cabinet' at £1 6s, for the Earl of Salisbury. [Hatfield House MS Bills 275]

Tomson, Richard, address unrecorded. Submitted a bill, dated 23 February 1719, to the Rt Hon. Lady Mary Saunderson, totalling £6 10s, and listing a bed, six chairs, a pair of bellows, 'A Pott and Fryin Pan', and 'A Box Iron'. Receipted by John Gillson. [Lincoln RO, Monson 12]

Tomson (or Thompson), William, 57 Fleet Mkt, London, u (1784–97). Notices concerning bankruptcy, dividends and certificates, given in *Billinge's Liverpool Advertiser*, 17 October 1796, 1 May 1797, and 5 June 1797. [D]

Tong (or Tongue), Miss M., Bristol, upholsteress (1837–40). Trading at 4 St Michael's Hill, 1837–38; and as S. & M. Tongue at 8 Old Park Hill in 1840. [D] See Sarah Tong(u)e.

Tonge, R., address unrecorded. Name inscribed on chair of 1770 at Stanmer Park, Sussex. [V&A archives]

Tongue, John, 76 Paul St, Finsbury, London, cm and u (1839). [D]

Tong(u)e, Sarah, Bristol, upholsteress (1831–33). Trading at 4 Jamaica St, St James's, in 1831; Park Pl., St Michael's, in 1832; and 13 Old Park in 1833. [D] See Miss M. Tong.

Tooke, George Theodore, 23 Judd St, London, cm and u (1839). [D]

Tooke, Robert, 2 Claremont Pl., Old Kent Rd, London, cm (1829). [D]

Tooke, William Barber, Norwich, cm (1811–30). Polled of the parish of St Martin at Oak, 1812–18; and at Heigham in 1830. App. to William Mowain (?), cm, and admitted freeman on 5 June 1811. [Norwich freemen reg. and poll bks]

Tookey, William, Chatham, Kent, chairmaker (1748). Took app. named Conchey in 1748. [S of G, app. index]

Tool, J., 5 Charles St, St James's, Bristol, cabinet carver (1834). [D]

Tooley (or Tooly), James, address unrecorded, blind maker (1732). Named in Earl Fitzwalter's accounts for Moulsham Hall on 23 February 1723 charging £7 7s 6d for four window blinds, and receiving £5 5s in part payment. On 7 March he was paid the £2 2s outstanding. [A. C. Edwards, *The Accounts of Benjamin Mildmay, Earl Fitzwalter*, pp. 103–04]

Tooley, William, Northbrook St, Newbury, Berks., chairmaker (1840–42). [D]

Toomes, Mrs, London (?). On 26 May 1731 Mrs Toomes and another, unnamed, person charged £16 5s 6d for an 'Indian Chest' to be sent to Moulsham Hall, Chelmsford. [A. C. Edwards, *The Accounts of Benjamin Mildmay, Earl Fitzwalter*, p. 103]

Toon, John, Gosport, Hants., cm and u (1823–30). Trading at North Cross St in 1823 and Seahorse St in 1830. [D]

Toon, John, 61 Buttersland St, City Rd, London, cm and u (1839). [D]

Toon & Co., 45 Featherstone St, City Rd, London, u (1835). [D]

Toose (or Tooze), John, Honiton, Devon, cm, chairmaker, u and auctioneer (1774–84). Took out a Sun Insurance policy on 21 December 1774 for £400 including £30 on utensils and stock in his house, £100 on workshop and offices, and £100 on utensils and stock there and in yard. A policy of 1783 for £700 included £420 on utensils, stock, goods and workshop. [D; GL, Sun MS vol. 235, ref. 347617; vol. 314, p. 33]

Toose, John, Newcastle-under-Lyme, Staffs., cm (1840). Acted as witness in the case against Matthew Fowles for the murder of Martha Keeling. [*Chester Chronicle, Cheshire and North Wales Advertiser*, 25 September 1840]

Toosey, John, Wardour St, Covent Gdn, London, carver (1749). [Poll bk]

Tootell, Joshua, 7 Birchin Lane, Manchester, u and flour dealer (1825). [D]

Tooth, C., 7 Tottenham St, Fitzroy Sq., London, carver and gilder (1835). [D]

Tooth, Samuel, London, carpenter (1776–1802). Trading at Worship St, Moorfields, in 1776; City Rd, Moorfields, in 1794; and Hoxton Sq., 1802. Admitted freeman of the Upholders' Co. by redemption on 1 May 1776. [GL, Upholders' Co. records]

Toovey, Sampson, High St, Amersham, Bucks., chairmaker (1830). [D]

Topham, George, 19 Copper St, Manchester, chairmaker (1817). [D]

Topham, George, Aldborough, Yorks., joiner and cm (1828–30). [D]

Topham, George, Nantwich, Cheshire, cm (1837). Daughter Mary Anne by his wife Sarah bapt. on 11 August 1837. [PR (bapt.)]

Topham, John, Congleton, Cheshire, cm and joiner (1834–41). Trading at Chapel St in 1834 and Lowther St in 1841. [D]

Topham, William, Ackworth, Yorks., cm (1822–37). [D]

Topliff, W., 2 Plumbers Ct, High Holborn, London, u (1835). [D]

Topliff, William, 27 Little Queen St, Holborn, London, cm and u (1839). [D]

Toplis, James, London, cm, decorative u and auctioneer (1790–1828). Addresses given at 9 Old Broad St in 1798; 1 Godfrey Ct, Milk St in 1802; 22 St Paul's Churchyard, 1811–28; and as James Toplis & Co. at nos 22–23, 1814–20. Son of Henry Toplis, warehouseman of Lamb St, Spitalfields. App. to James Duthoit on 5 January 1790, and admitted freeman of the Upholders' Co. by servitude on 3 January 1798. Destruction of premises at St Paul's Churchyard by fire on 17 May 1810 reported in *Gents Mag*. Took out Sun Insurance policies on 24 October 1814 for £2,000 on stock, utensils, and goods in trust or on commission in his house, workshops, warerooms and lofts, and £500 on those in a warehouse adjoining the Meeting House in Knightrider Ct, Knightrider St. A policy of 18 January 1815 was for £500 on livestock, stock and utensils in warehouse and stable at 11 Little Carter Lane; and one of 14 May 1821, taken out in association with Samuel Chandler, was for £400 on coach house, stable and loft in Red Bull Yd, Bury St, Bloomsbury, in tenure of a chair and brush maker. Mahogany hall chair with carved crest is signed 'Toplis St. Pauls' on the underside, and bears the label of 'Toplis & Sons, Cabinet & Upholstery Warehouse & Manufactory 22 St Pauls churchyard London'. [D; GL, Upholders' Co. records; GL, Sun MS vol. 461, refs 897983–84 and 901570; vol. 484, ref. 980543; V&A archives] See Toplis & Wheeler and Toplis & Woolfitt.

Toplis, Samuel, 4½ Cirencester Pl., Tottenham Ct Rd, London, cm and u (1835–39). [D]

Toplis & Wheeler, 22 St Paul's Churchyard, London, decorative u and auctioneers (1821). [D] See James Toplis at this address.

Toplis & Woolfit(t), 22 St Paul's Churchyard, London, u and cm (1813–20). Advertised in *The Times*, 4 April 1815, offering 'FINE BRILLIANT FRENCH PLATE GLASSES of large dimensions' to be sold 'considerably under the British tarif price'. Being next door to no. 23 this firm may have been connected with the old established business of the Bell family. [D; Heal] See James Toplis.

Toppin, Edwin, 17 Prince's St, Brighton, Sussex cm and u (1839). [D]

Toppin & Son, 109–110 Church St, Brighton, Sussex, cm and u (1839). Trading also as furniture brokers at no. 108. [D]

Topping, Charles, King St, Wigton, Cumb., chairmaker (1834). [D]

Topping, George, King St, Wigton, Cumb., chairmaker (1829). [D]

Topping, George, 38 Annetwell St, Carlisle, Cumb., chairmaker (1834). [D]

Topping, John, address unrecorded. Small mahogany Pembroke table with fluted legs and single divided drawer is pencil-signed on underside of top: 'J.T. 1815', and again, 'John Topping, 1815'. Long in private ownership of a family in the Cumb. and Lancs. area.

Topping, John, 38 Marybone, Liverpool, carver and household broker (1827). [D]

Topping, William, Back St, Poulton-le-Fylde, Lancs., joiner and cm (1828–34). [D]

Torbat, —, 36 Red Lion St, London, celleret maker (1793). Subscribed to Sheraton's *Drawing Book*, 1793.

Torber (or Torbet), John, Strand, London, cm (1779). Declared bankrupt, *Gents Mag.*, January 1779, and dividends announced in *Leicester Journal*, 30 October 1779. Named in Bailey's list of bankrupts.

Torbut, —, 12 Red Lion St, London, cm (1803). Named in Sheraton's list of master cabinet makers, 1803.

Torbutt, Charles, Alverthorpe, near Wakefield, Yorks., cm (1822). [D]

Torr, James, 11 Bedminster Parade, Bristol, chairmaker (1828–30). [D]

Torr, Thomas, Fletcher Gate, Nottingham, joiner and cm (1799). [D]

Torre, della & Barelli, 9 Lamb's Conduit St, London, looking-glasses, barometers, thermometers and prints (1826–33). [Goodison, *Barometers*]

Torrent, George, at 'The Golden Ball', Houndsditch, London, u (1723). Took out a Sun Insurance policy on 9 August 1723 for £500 on goods and merchandise in his house. [GL, Sun MS vol. 16, ref. 29587]

Torry, George, Market Rasen, Lincs., joiner, cm and builder (1821). App. to William Rollett of Gainsborough in June 1821. [Hull app. reg.]

Torry, Thomas, Willoughby St, Gainsborough, Lincs., cm and u (1835). [D]

Tort, Thomas, Nottingham. Signed the *Nottingham Cabinet and Chair Makers' Book of Prices*, 1791, on behalf of the masters.

Tory, George, Hall St, Spalding, Lincs., cm, u, joiner and carpenter (1826–41). [D]

Toswell (or Tosswill), John, Exeter, Devon, carver and gilder (1823–40). Addresses given at South St, 1823–24; 103 Fore St, 1825–33; 98 High St before 1826 and no. 70 afterwards; and no. 18, 1834–40. Notice in *The Alfred*, 15 August 1826 stated that a fire at Evans & Co., druggist, destroyed Tosswill's workshops at 98 High St, following which he moved to no. 70. [D; *Exeter Pocket Journal*]

Tothill, Ann, Hart's Row, Exeter, Devon, u (1825). [*Exeter Pocket Journal*]

Touchet, John, Lancaster. Named in the Gillow records in 1815. [Westminster Ref. Lib.]

Toulmin, Robert, Liverpool, cm (1788–1823). Addresses given at 10 School Lane, 1805–11; no. 11, 1813–14; 8 Leigh St in 1816; 17 Russell St in 1818; and no. 20, 1821–23. App. to W. Blackburn in 1788; and admitted freeman of Lancaster, 1801–02, when stated of Liverpool. Notice of sale of household furniture and stock in trade on bankruptcy given in *Liverpool Chronicle*, 25 June 1806. Stock consisted of 'Mahogany Sideboard, Secretary & Bookcase, Drawers & wardrobe, Tea Tables, Clockcase, Dressing Tables, Hair Cloth, viz. 24 inches to 26 & 16, Horse Hair, Canvas Bags, Brass Work, etc. Paper Hangings, Work Benches; Mahogany Boards & Planks, Veneers of different qualities, Beech & Oak Boards, of different thicknesses. After which will be sold The unexpired TERM of Three Years on the House, subject to the year rent of £25 per annum, with the Workshop now erected in the Yard . . .'. [D; Lancaster app. reg. and freemen rolls]

Toulmin & Kerr, Brokers Row, Finsbury/Moorfields, London, upholstery warehouse (1802–03). Trading at nos 10–11 in 1802, and no. 28 in 1803 when named in Sheraton's list of master cabinet makers. [D]

Touret, Henry, at 'The Gold Frame', middle of Maiden Lane, Covent Gdn, London, carver, gilder and frame maker. Rococo trade card, c.1760, in the GL, states that Touret 'Makes all Sorts of Black and Gold Frames for Paintings, Prints, and Glasses, and all sorts of Ornaments, Carved and Guilded — N.B. Prints varnished in the Best Manner at Reasonable Rates.'

Tousey, Henry, 10 Silver St, Golden Sq., London, carver and gilder (1781). Took out a Sun Insurance policy in 1781 for £200 including £100 on utensils, stock and goods. [GL, Sun MS vol. 296, p. 61]

Tousey (or Touzey), John, London, carver and gilder (1749–81). Polled at Westminster of Wardour St, Old Soho, in 1749. Recorded as 'J. de Tousey of Mary Bone', when declared bankrupt, *Gents Mag.*, 1761. Discharge of John Tousey, 'late of Titchfield Street, St Mary le Born' from Debtors' Prison, reported in *London Gazette*, 26 September 1761. Listed in directories at Bow St, Bloomsbury, 1763–81, and described as cm, u and dealer in plate glass, 1780–81. Probably the Touzy, cm, who supplied a cabinet costing £96 4s to Sir John Hot for Shelburne House, Berkeley Sq., London, in December 1767. John Touzey, carver and gilder, carried out wood carving and gilding picture frames at Croome Court, Worcs., in 1769. [V&A archives] See Towsey, —.

Tovell, Charles, London, upholder (1790). [Ipswich poll bk]

Tovey (or Turvey), John, Stratford, Essex, cm, u and undertaker (1826–32). [D]

Towell, James, Charlton Rd, Dover, Kent, cm (1832–33). [Poll bks]

Towell, Robert, Diss, Norfolk, cm (1762). Took app. named Ancold in 1762. [S of G, app. index]

Towell, Robert, 'near opposite the Harry's Head in Mile End Road', London, cm (1774). Took out a Sun Insurance policy on 14 December 1774 for £400 including £200 on utensils and stock in house, workshop and yard. [GL, Sun MS vol. 235, ref. 34390]

Towell, Thomas, Stanley St, Birmingham, ram-rod maker, broker, cm and u (1828–30). [D]

Towells, Robert, Frog Lane, Ilminster, Som., cm (1839). [D]

Towers, Thomas, Lancaster, cm (1766–67). [Lancaster freemen rolls]

Towers, Thomas, Blackburn, Lancs., cm (1784). [Lancaster poll bk]

Towers, Thomas, Leicester, cm (1826). [Leicester freemen reg.]

Towers, William, Preston, Lancs., cm (1795). Marriage on 29 November 1795 at Kirkham to Miss Ellen Nicholson of Wharton, reported in *Billinge's Liverpool Advertiser*, 14 December.

Towers, William, 66 Upper Shadwell, London, cm and/or u (1814). Took out a Sun Insurance policy on 3 November 1814 for £300 of which £70 accounted for stock and utensils. [GL, Sun MS vol. 463, ref. 899284]

Towle, W., Weekday-cross, Nottingham, u and cm (1818). [D]

Towle, William, Bridlesmithgate, Nottingham, cm (1814). [D]

Towler, James, 25 Greek St, Soho, London, upholder and cm (1796). [D]

Towler, John, Masham, Yorks., joiner and/or cm (1834). [D]

Towler, William, 10 Snowfields, Bermondsey, London, cm and u (1827–28). [D]

Town & Emanuel, 103 New Bond St, London, 'Manufacturers of Buhl Marquetrie, Resner & Carved Furniture' (1830–40). Circular occasional table with porcelain bowl inset in the top, from the Duke of Buccleuch's collection, is noted in the V & A archives as having been sold by Christie's in 1948, bears label dated 183–, and stating: '. . . . Town & Emanuel. Manufacturers of Buhl Marquetrie, Resner & Carved Furniture, Tripods, Screens &c. of the finest & most superb designs of the times of Louis 14th. Splendid Cabinets & Tables inlaid with fine Sèvre & Dresden China &c. Old Paintings & Bronzes, Carvings, Oriental & other China, Jewellery & Curiosities Bought & Exchanged. Buhl & Antique Furniture Repaired. By Appointment to Her Majesty'. Label also recorded on Buhl monopodium games table; and on a small kingwood and tulipwood 'bureau plat' of Louis XV style, with serpentine top inset with red leather panel, frieze with three drawers, chamfered cabriole legs, ormolu handles and mounts. Label bears the Arms of Queen Adelaide. [E. T. Joy, *English Furniture, 1800–1850*; V&A archives; Sotheby's, 23 July 1948, lot 142] In June 1830 Town & Emanuel provided 3rd Lord Braybrooke with a looking-glass costing £8 5s for Audley End, Essex, Billingbear, Berks., or his London house. [Essex RO, D/DBy/A362] In 1838 supplied 'new furniture' for Stafford House, London, at a cost of £12 12s. [Stafford RO, D593/R/1/26/8] In 1839–40 the firm was listed in directories at Town & Co., 'dealers in & Manufacturers of antique furniture, curiosities, & pictures.'

Towne, W., Garlick Hill, London, cm and turner (1835). [D]

Towne, William, 7 Lion St, New Kent Rd, London, cm and u (1839). [D]

Townley, —, London, cm (1793). Subscribed to Sheraton's *Drawing Book*, 1793.

Townley, James, Liverpool, cm and victualler (1827–39). Addresses given at 27 Hanover St with shop at 12 Coopers Row, 1827–37; 28 Hanover St with shop at 10 College Lane in 1829; and 43 Hanover St in 1839. [D]

Townley, Richard, Lancaster, cm (1806–16). Admitted freeman of Lancaster, 1806–07, when stated 'of Liverpool'. Named in the Gillow records, 1814–16, working on a bookcase. [Lancaster freemen rolls; Westminster Ref. Lib., Gillow vol. 344/199, p. 1952]

Townley, Robert, Lancaster, cm (1765–86). App. to J. Padget in 1765, and admitted freeman, 1785–86. [Lancaster app. reg. and freemen rolls]

Townley, Robert, Penwortham, Lancs., cm (1784–96). Polled at Lancaster in 1784, and admitted freeman of there, 1795–96. [Lancaster freemen rolls]

Townley, William, 4 Leonard Sq., Finsbury, London, cm and u (1839). [D]

Townsend, Benjamin, Gloucester, cm (1833–35). Children bapt. at St Michael's Church in 1833 and 1835. [PR (bapt.)]

Townsend, Charles, Preston, Lancs., chairmaker (1822–25). Recorded at Friargate in 1822 and North Rd in 1825. [D]

Townsend, Edward, Melton Mowbray, Leics., cm and chairmaker (1822–35). [D]

Townsend, George, Leeds, Yorks., cm (1791–98). Trading at Kirkgate in 1798. One of the four journeymen who signed the *Leeds Cabinet and Chair Makers' Book of Prices*, 1791. [D]

Townsend, George, Exeter, Devon, cm (1815–26). Recorded at Frog Lane on 12 September 1815 when son Frederick bapt. at St Edmund's Church; and at Milk St when children bapt. at St Mary Arches: Susan on 4 March 1819; Frederick (bapt. privately in 1816), Hannah (born July 1821) and George (born 6 December 1823) all three on 29 February 1824; and Sarah on 27 December 1826. [PR (bapt.)]

Townsend, John, at 'The Cabinet', in the Minories, London, cm (1725). Named in insurance co. records. [Heal]

Townsend, John, High St, Leicester, turner and spinning-wheel maker (1794–d. by 1842). [D]

Townsend, John, London, upholder (1796–1816). Trading at 127 Lower Thames St, 1803–08, and 10 Crane Ct, Fleet St, 1811–16. Son of John Townsend, Gent. of Bermondsey. App. to John Preston on 26 June 1796, and admitted freeman of the Upholders' Co. by servitude on 6 July 1803. [D; GL, Upholders' Co. records]

Townsend, John, New Bridge, Exeter, Devon, cm (1816). Son John bapt. at St Edmund's Church on 11 March 1816. [PR (bapt.)]

Townsend, John, Leeds, Yorks., cm and u (1821–37). Recorded as John snr at 96 Kirkgate in 1821; and as John & Charles at 10 Kirkgate (furniture warehouse) in 1826–30, Castle St, 1828–37, also 15 Kirkgate, 1834–37. [D]

Townsend, John, Melton Mowbray, Leics., chairmaker and turner (1826–35). App. to John Clements, chairmaker of Leicester, and admitted freeman in 1826. [D; Leicester freemen rolls]

Townsend, Joseph, Anchor Yard, Preston, Lancs., chairmaker (1825). [D]

Townsend, Joseph, Southgate St, Gloucester, cm and u (1830–40). Trading at Blackfriars, 1830, and Southgate St, 1839–40. [D]

Townsend, Richard, St Ives, Hunts., joiner and cm (1783). Took out a Sun Insurance policy in 1783 for £200 including £130 on utensils and stock. [GL, Sun MS vol. 314, p. 13]

Townsend, Richard, Blackfriars Sq., Gloucester, cm and u (1822–40). Trading at Westgate St, 1822–30 and Blackfriars Sq., 1839–40. [D]

Townsend, Richardson, St Ives, Hunts., u (1798). [D]

Townsend, Robert, Liverpool, residing in Lancaster, cm (b.1739–d. by 1828). Recorded as aged 82 in 1821 in the account of lives in leases granted by the Corp. of Liverpool and carried out between 1819–22.

Townsend, Samuel, Bungay, Suffolk, later Norwich, carver and gilder (1824–42). Recorded at Bungay in 1824; at Colegate St, Norwich, in 1836; St Stephen's St in 1839; and 24 Bethel St in 1842. [D]

Townsend, Thomas, Southgate St, Gloucester, cm and u (1822). [D]

Townsend, W., 11 St Ann's Ct, Soho, London, carver (1835). [D]

Townsend, William, address unrecorded, upholder (1738–d.1800). Son of Thomas Townsend, yeoman of Wilts. App. to John Sherman on 1 November 1738, and admitted freeman of the Upholders' Co. by servitude on 16 May 1754. [GL, Upholders' Co. records]

Townsend, William, London, upholder (1749–79). Polled at Westminster of Charles St, near Grosvenor Sq., 1749 and 1774. Named in a deed of settlement in 1768. [Marylebone Lib., deed 2497] Insured a house in Welbeck St for £400 in 1779. [GL, Sun MS vol. 278, p. 323]

Townsend, William, Wimpole St, London, u (1792). [D]

Townsend, William, St Martin's, Leicester, cm and u (1835). Also recorded at St Nicholas St. [D]

Townshend, —, address unrecorded, u (1776). Henry Hoare's account book of 1749–70 records payment to Townshend, u, of £13 7s 9d on 27 October 1776. [Wilts. RO, MS 383/6]

Townshend, George, 39 Wardour St, Soho, London, carver and gilder (1809–11). [D]

Townshend, John, London, u (1818). [Canterbury poll bk]

Townshend, John, 24 Row, Gt Yarmouth, Norfolk, carver and gilder (1836–39). [D]

Townshend, R., Lancaster. Named in the Gillow records in 1803. [Westminster Ref. Lib.]

Townshend, Robert, Gt Yarmouth, Norfolk, cm (1830–41). [Poll bks]

Townshend, Samuel, Old Broad St, Gt Yarmouth, Norfolk, cm, u and chairmaker (1822). [D]

Townshend, Samuel, Charlotte St, Gt Yarmouth, Norfolk, carver and gilder (1830). [D]

Townshend, Thomas, Gt Yarmouth, Norfolk, carver, gilder and printseller (1822–32). Trading at Old Broad Row in 1822, and Broad Row in 1830. [D; poll bk]

Townshend, Thomas, Northgate, Bridgnorth, Salop, cm (1840). [D]

Townson, C., Lancaster. Named in the Gillow records, 1784–1818. [Westminster Ref. Lib.]

Townson, John, Lancaster, later London, cm (1777–84). Admitted freeman of Lancaster, 1777–78. Polled at Lancaster of London in 1784. [Lancaster freemen rolls]

Townson, John jnr, Liverpool, cm (1825). App. to William John Roberts in 1825. [Liverpool app. enrolment bk]

Townson, Robert jnr, Lancaster. Named in the Gillow records, 1793–98. A drawing and a sketch of 1795 refer to Bob Townson, and Robert Townson jnr. [Westminster Ref. Lib..]

Townson, Robert, address unrecorded, chairmaker (1803). Subscribed to Sheraton's *Cabinet Dictionary*, 1803.

Townson, Thomas, Lancaster, cm (1804–20). Admitted freeman, 1811–12, and named in the Gillow records, 1804–20. [Lancaster freemen rolls; Westminster Ref. Lib., Gillow]

Townson, William, Norfolk, cm (1755–60). Probably the Townson who supplied furniture to Holkham Hall, Norfolk, between 1755–58. The accounts for 1755 total £10 16s and include '3 Chinese cherry tree chairs for ye attics' and armchair to match; '4 walnut tree chairs', also for the attics; winscot and mahogany tables; a 'mahogany stand for a basin'; a 'walnut tree frame & drawers for an inlaid top for a table'; a model of a chair, and four close stools. In 1757 items supplied totalled £21 8s and included three carved mahogany chairs, a reading desk, and two carved and gilt mahogany chairs. In 1758 Townson charged £1 13s for a mahogany stand for a cistern, lamp stand and close stool. [V&A archives] Took app. named Lancaster in 1760 when he was recorded at Burnham Westgate. [S of G, app. index]

Townson & Gardener, address unrecorded. Four-drawer bow-fronted mahogany commode, c.1810, by this firm, advertised in C. *Life*, 27 April 1978, supplement, p. 489.

Towsey, —, Bow St, Bloomsbury, London. Recorded in a list of furniture makers compiled by the Duchess of Northumberland, c.1776. [C. Gilbert, *Chippendale*, p. 154] See John Tousey.

Toy, Jesse, 2 Norris St, London, cm and turner (1777). Took out a Sun Insurance policy in 1777 for £300 including £200 on utensils and stock. [GL, Sun MS vol. 254, p. 332]

Toyne, John, Milton St, Nottingham, joiner and cm (1832–35). [D]

Tozer, J., 29 Duke St, Grosvenor Sq., London, carver, gilder, looking-glass maker, painter and paper hanger (1835). [D]

Tozer, John, Exeter, Devon, gilder (1831). Marriage to Miss Way, second daughter of Mr Way, cm of Dartmouth, reported in *The Alfred*, 17 May 1831.

Tozer, William, North St, Exeter, Devon, cm and broker (1836–40). [*Exeter Pocket Journal*]

Tozer, William, 29 Duke St, Grosvenor Sq., London, carver and gilder (1837). [D]

Traherne, Edward, address unrecorded, cm (1669). On 3 April 1669 he provided the Royal Household with 'a pair of stands of Jamaica wood for the Kings Closset in the Newe Lodgeings at Whitehall', costing £1 15s. [PRO, LC9/271, p. 140]

Traill, John, London, cm (1786). Subscribed to George Richardson's *Treatise on the Five Orders of Architecture*, 1787.

Tranent, William, Bailiffgate St, Alnwick, Northumb., joiner, cm and u (1828–29). [D]

Tranent & Davi(d)son, Balifgate, Alnwick, Northumb., cm, u and joiner (1834). [D]

Tranter, Joseph, Limpsham, Som., upholder (1774). [Bristol poll bk]

Tranter, S., Brighton, Sussex, u (1801). Named in the Windsor

Royal Archives on 18 July 1801 receiving £60 11s 3d. [RA 88883]

Trapnell, Caleb, College Green, Bristol, cm (1824). Principal designer in the firm, C. Trapnell, founded in 1824. Made general household furniture of all prices, and furnished a number of important Bristol buildings, including the Mansion House. [V&A archives]

Trapnell, Henry, Queen St, Bristol, furniture broker and u (1833–40). Trading at no. 3 in 1833; also as cm from 1836; and carpet warehouseman with manufactory and warerooms in Host St from 1840. [D]

Trapp, Benjamin, High St, Bedford, draper, cm and u (1830–39). [D]

Trappes, Robert, Clitheroe, Lancs. The Broughton Hall, Yorks., papers preserve a letter and account dated 29 December 1834, from Robert Trappes to Charles Tempest of Broughton, concerning antique oak furniture. Trappes wrote: 'I fear you will *really* think you have paid dear for a waggon load of rubbish when you see it yet there is great capability of making it very beautiful and I think it is very cheap.' His account itemized a bedhead, 'Ambry', three chairs, a chest, 'Flowered Ornaments', and a 'Chest without lid', costing a total of £28. The pieces were used to furnish a pannelled 'Elizabethan'-style bedroom at Broughton, and most of the objects (several of which display added embellishment) can still be identified. [Temple Newsam House, Leeds, Exhib. Cat., *Furniture from Broughton Hall*, no. 36; E. T. Joy, *English Furniture, 1800–1851*, p. 121]

Tratt & Attfield, 19 Lower Brook St, Grosvenor Sq., London, cm, u and undertakers (1814–39). Recorded at no. 10 in 1820. [D] Named in the account books of 3rd Lord Braybrooke, supplying items for Audley End, Essex, Billing-bear, Berks., or his London house. In June 1831 the firm was paid £4 5s; in June 1832, £1 9s; and in December 1836, £12 17s. [Essex RO, D/DBy/A358 and A363] The Dunham Massey papers record payment to Tratt & Attfield of £10 6s on 22 May 1838, for 'an oak library steps with handrails varnished on castors lined with Brussels carpet'. [John Rylands Lib., Manchester Univ.] Submitted a bill to Stafford House, London, in 1838, for £123 4s 2d. [Staffs. RO, D593/R/1/26/8] Worked for the Duke of Norfolk, 1840–43. [Arundel Castle records, A2095]

Traverse, John, Fazakerley St, Prescot, Lancs., joiner and cm (1834). [D]

Travis, James, Manchester, cm and bow-string maker (1824). Notice in *Liverpool Mercury*, 19 November 1824, concerned his case in the Lancaster Insolvent Court.

Travis, James, St Luke's Buildings, Roscoe St, Liverpool, cm (1837–39). Recorded at 31 Roscoe St in 1837 and no. 18 in 1839. [D]

Travis, John, Spout St, Leek, Staffs., cm (1835). [D]

Travis, Thomas, Shudehill, Manchester, cm and bow-string maker (1808–25). Recorded at no. 67, 1808–18, and no. 59, 1822–25. [D]

Travis, Thomas, Blakestone, near Bawtry, Yorks., joiner and cm (1822). [D]

Treacher, Daniel, High Wycombe, Bucks., chairmaker (1784–98). Sworn a burgess in 1797. Listed in Militia Census, 1798. [D; L. J. Mayes, *The History of Chairmaking in High Wycombe*, 1960, p. 25]

Treacher, Francis, High Wycombe, Bucks., chairmaker (b. c. 1813–41). Daughter bapt. in 1840. Aged 27 at the time of the 1841 Census. [PR (bapt.)]

Treacher, Henry, High Wycombe, Bucks., chairmaker (b. c. 1820–41). Aged 21 at the time of the 1841 Census.

Treacher, James, West Wycombe, Bucks., chairmaker

(b.c.1781–1841). Named in Militia Census, 1798. Aged 60 at the time of the 1841 Census. [D]

Treacher, John, High Wycombe, Bucks., chairmaker (1798–1830). Named in Militia Census, 1798. Married Mary Buggins of Wootton on 26 November 1805, at Wooton. [D; Bodleian index of Oxf. marriage bonds]

Treacher, Samuel, High Wycombe, Bucks., chairmaker and turner (1782–1844). There were probably three tradesmen of the same name. One is recorded as born in 1769, and one took out a Sun Insurance policy in 1782 for £200 of which utensils and stock accounted for £50. Named in directories and Militia Census, 1790–1844, in Chepping Wycombe. Listed at Oxford Rd, High Wycombe in 1839. Named in the parish accounts in 1790 supplying 'a half part of the wood used in the hall' of the workhouse. Sons bapt. in 1832 and 1834. [D; GL, Sun MS vol. 299, p. 603; L. J. Mayes, *The History of Chairmaking in High Wycombe*, 1960, p. 24; PR (bapt.)]

Treacher, Samuel, Marlow Hill, Bucks., chairmaker (1805). Started chairmaking as a winter occupation for his farm hands. [C. Musgrave, *Regency Furniture*, p. 97]

Treacher, Thomas & Co., High Wycombe, Bucks., chairmaker (1798–1844). Named in Militia Census, 1798. Daughters bapt. in 1822 and 1824, and five sons between 1826–34. Trading at High St, 1839. [D; PR (bapt.)]

Treacher, William, High Wycombe, Bucks., chairmaker (1768–92). Marriage registered on 8 June 1768. Took out a Sun Insurance policy on 4 July 1792 for £400 including £250 on his house in four tenements, and £55 on warehouse and shop. Bill head recorded, stating: 'William Treacher, Windsor, dyed and fancy chairs, opposite the Woolpack Wycombe', bearing the open date 179–. [D; GL, Sun MS vol. 388, p. 157; L. J. Mayes, *The History of Chairmaking in High Wycombe*, 1960, p. 24]

Treacher, William Henry, High Wycombe, Bucks., chair manufacturer (b.c.1791–1848). Sons bapt. in 1815, 1822 and 1824, daughters in 1818, 1820 and 1827. Aged 50 at the time of the 1841 Census. [D; PR (bapt.)]

Treadwell, Humphrey, Southampton, Hants., cm (1798). [D]

Trebilock, Richard, Fairmantle St, Truro, Cornwall, chairmaker (1808). Advertised in *Royal Cornwall Gazette*, 26 November 1808, as '. . . workman to Mr. Carkeet, late of Truro', and announcing that 'he has by him a large quantity of rushes for bottoming chairs & that he makes new, or repairs old chairs, let them be ever so bad, on the shortest notice & the most moderate terms.'

Treble, John, 1 Spring Gdns, Manchester, carver, gilder and print seller to their Majesties (1814–15). [D]

Treble & Syers, corner of Spring Gdns, Market St Lane, Manchester, carvers and gilders to their Majesties (1811). [D]

Tredwell, George, High St, Evesham, Worcs., cm and u (1840). [D]

Tree, Anthony, Knottingley Island, near Ferrybridge, Yorks., cm (1822). [D]

Trees, John, 3 Moreton St, Strangeways, Manchester, and Sandy Lane, Cheetham Hill, cm (1834). [D]

Trefry, John, Cornwall, u (1726). Employed by Lewis Tremayne of Heligan, Cornwall, received £2 8s 2d on 5 September 1726 for 'work and materials (as by bill)', in full. [Cornwall RO, DDT 1315]

Tregerthen, George, Chapel St, Penzance, Cornwall, cm etc. (1830). [D]

Treglohan, Philip, Fish Strand, Falmouth, Cornwall, cm and u (1823–24). [D]

Tregoe, John, at 'The Hand & Chair', the east end of St Paul's, London, cm (1749). Named in contemporary newspapers. [Heal]

Tregonning's Repository, Truro, Cornwall, cm (1810). Adver-

tised in *Royal Cornwall Gazette*, 7 April and 12 May 1810, their '. . . great variety of new & fashionable furniture of prime Mahogany now on Sale' at the Repository, 'Where every article in the Cabinet line is made on the shortest notice with superior taste & neatness from the best London models. Tradesmen supplied with Mahogany plank or veneering. Bed Pillars & other articles connected with the branch.'

Trehern, George, Charlotte St, Rathbone Pl., London, cm and upholder (1816–25). Trading at no. 17 in 1816 and no. 12, 1817–25. Took out a Sun Insurance policy on 14 December 1820 for £400 on an empty house at 6 College St, Camden Town. [D; GL, Sun MS vol. 483, ref. 97322]

Treherne, —, address unrecorded. Stamp recorded on rosewood card table, c.1840.

Treherne, J., 12 Charlotte St, Rathbone Pl., London, cm and upholder (1820). [D]

Treherne, T., 22 Dean St, Soho, London, u (1829). [D]

Treherne, Thomas, 39 Oxford St, London, furniture printers, u and cm (1835–39). [D]

Trelford, James, Liverpool, cm (1754). Took app. named Rigby in 1754. [S of G, app. index]

Tremeere (or Tremeene), James, 17 Lamb's Conduit St (or Passage), Red Lion Sq., London, cm and u (1827–35). [D]

Tremeere, William, 17 Lamb's Conduit Passage, Red Lion Sq., London, cm (1805–07). [D]

Trenaman, Joseph, 25 Upper Maudlin St, Bristol, carver and gilder (1840). [D]

Trencham, William, Bramley's Yd, Lowerhead Row, Leeds, Yorks., cm and joiner (1837). [D]

Trengrouse, Helston, Cornwall, cm (b.1772–d.1854). Invented a 'Rocker Life Saving Apparatus' in 1808, experimenting with it on the Serpentine, London, in 1819. He received a silver medal and 30 gns from the Society of Arts in 1821 for his invention. Advertised in *Royal Cornwall Gazette*, 27 August 1803, for a journeyman; and on 28 April and 5 May 1810, sale of 'a very handsome Mahogany Library writing table, a piece of furniture both ornamental & convenient, well worthy of the attention of any Nobleman or Gentleman. It is perfectly new, being manufactured but last Autumn by Mr. H. TRENGROUSE & is now the property of R. MEWTON of whom particulars may be known & the furniture may be viewed.' Listed as agent for the Eagle Insurance Office, London, in *Exeter Flying Post*, 4 January 1816, 26 March 1818, and 13 January 1820. [D; G. C. Boase & W. P. Courtney, *Bibliotheca Cornibiensis*, 1878, vol. 2, p. 784]

Trenin (Tresin or Trewin), William, Falmouth, Cornwall, cm, joiner and carpenter (1754–62). Subscribed to Chippendale's *Director*, 1754. Took apps named Francis Gervas in 1754 for £35, John Peck in 1761 for £35, and John Parkes in 1762 for £10. [V&A archives]

Trent, John, 21 North St, Bristol, decorative house, sign and furniture painter (1820). [D]

Trent, John, 11 Park Pl., Walworth, London, cm and u (1839). [D]

Trentham, Timothy, Atherstone, Warks., cm (1796). [D]

Trentham, Timothy, Market Drayton, Salop, cm (1797). [D]

Trepass (or Tresspass), James, 3 St Martin's Lane, Charing Cross, London, picture frame maker and gilder (1789–1809). Trade card of 1809 [Banks Coll., BM] shows samples of plain frames. [D]

Tresilian, John, address unrecorded, upholder (1726–d.1746). Son of Nicholas Tresilian, Gent. of Cornwall. App. to William Flaxmore, and admitted freeman of the Upholders' Co. by servitude on 6 April 1726. [GL, Upholders' Co. records]

Trested (Trusted or Trusthead), Thomas, Bury St Edmunds, Suffolk, cane chairmaker (1725–29). Took out Sun Insurance policies on 5 July 1725 for £300 on four tenements in St

Botolph's parish, Colchester; on 3 December 1725 for £300 on a house in St Marie's parish, Bury, exclusive of outhouses formerly called 'The Old Swan'; and on 15 August 1729 for £200. [GL, Sun MS vol. 20, ref. 36241; vol. 21, ref. 37503; vol. 28]

Trestram, John, Canterbury, Kent, cm (1736). Took app. named Somes in 1736. [S of G, app. index]

Trett, Thomas, Mark Lane, near Tower St, London, cm (1741). Sale of entire stock and house to let on leaving off trade announced in *London Evening Post*, 10–12 March 1741. Stock consisted of 'great variety of Looking-glasses, Chairs and Cabinet-Ware of the newest Fashion . . .'.

Trevenen, Henry, 7 Bilbury St, Plymouth, Devon, carver and gilder (1838). [D]

Treves, William snr and jnr, Cornhill, Dorchester, cm, u and auctioneer (1823–40). Will made in 1829 and proved in 1830, left the business to his son, Philip Treves, a friend, John Pett, and his son, William Treves on reaching the age of 21. [D; Dorset RO, DA/W/1830/57] The William Treves listed in directories in 1840 is presumably his son.

Trevethan, J., 13 Everett St, Brunswick Sq., London, u (1835–37). [D]

Trevethan, Joseph, 12 Charlotte St, Rathbone Pl., London, cm and u (1826–28). [D]

Trevethan, Samuel, 1 Leigh St, Burton Cresc., London, u (1835–37). [D]

Trevett, James, Redcross St, Southwark, London, u and furniture broker (1826–39). Recorded at no. 45 in 1826–27 and no. 14 in 1839. [D]

Trevett, Samuel, address unrecorded, upholder (1731–38). Son of William Trevett, chapman of London. App. to James Maudlen on 5 May 1731, and admitted freeman of the Upholders' Co. by servitude on 7 June 1738. [GL, Upholders' Co. records]

Trevett (or Trevitt), Richard, North St, City Rd, London, bedstead maker (1805–11). Trading at no. 5, 1805–07. [D]

Trevillian, George, Quay, Bridgwater, Som., chairmaker (1839). [D]

Trevor, James, Hodnet, Market Drayton, Salop, cm (1840). [D]

Trew, James, 5 Saville Row, Walworth, London, carver and gilder (1839). [D]

Tribe, Thomas, 93 Old St, St Luke's, London, cm, u, sofa, Windsor, garden and japanned chairmaker (1817–39). [D]

Trice, John, East Grinstead, Sussex, basket and chairmaker (1832). [D]

Tricker (or Fricker) & Henderson, 80 New Bond St, London, picture framers and restorers (1814–15). Submitted a bill totalling £94 5s 9d to the Hon. Mrs Leigh, dated 30 July 1814, for cleaning and restoring pictures by Cuyp and Canaletto, regilding frames; and supplying 'four new frames . . . with inrich'd hollows, ornamented Corners & Shells 4 Inch Mould⁵ Gilt in Burnish Gold, Measure 50 feet at 12s per foot', costing £30; and two new frames for portraits of Sir Thomas Leigh and his wife, '6½ Mould⁵ french pattern richly ornamented and Gilt in Burnish Gold measure 16 feet at 28s/ pr. foot', costing £22 8s. Note attached to bill dated 10 January 1815 reads: 'Messrs. Tricker & Henderson would feel happy and obliged if you would favour them with the amount being much pressed for money at this season of the Year.' [Shakespeare Birthplace Trust, Leigh receipts, DR 18/5]

Trigg, John, 76 Shoreditch, London, chair manufactory (1809–11). [D]

Trigg, William Henry, West St, Chichester, Sussex, cm and u (1823). [D]

Triggery, Thomas, 17 Butcher Hall Lane, Newgate St, London, bedstead maker (1820). [D] See John Triggey at Butcher Hall Lane.

Triggey, J. & Sons, 3 Warwick St, Leamington, Warks., cm and u (1837). [D]

Triggey, John, 20 Bacchus Walk, Hoxton, London, chairmaker (1805–07). [D]

Triggey, John, 19 Butcher Hall Lane, Newgate St, London, cm and upholder (1817–27). [D] See Thomas Triggery at Butcher Hall Lane.

Triggey, John jnr, Sheep St, Northampton, cm and upholder (1826–30). Recorded also as John & Sons in 1830. [D; poll bks]

Triggey, Joseph Fielding, Sheep St, Northampton, cm (1826–30). [Poll bks]

Triggs, James, Southampton, Hants., u, cm, appraiser and auctioneer (1826–39). Trading at 25 French St, 1826–36 and 20 High St in 1839. Advertisement in *Southampton Town and Country Herald*, 27 November 1826 gave address at 25 French St and trade as u and paper hanger. [D]

Triggs, Messrs William, Newbury. Label recorded on each of a pair of painted armchairs with oval leaf-carved backs headed by anthemion; padded arms with out-curved terminals and fluted supports; serpentine-fronted, fluted seat-rails, raised on husk-carved and fluted tapering legs; now decorated in Etruscan red and gold on a white ground. [Sotheby's, 28 May 1976, lot 145]

Trilley, William, 5 Star Corner, Bermondsey, London, bedstead maker (1826–29). [D]

Trim, John, Poole and Cerne Abbas, Dorset, cm (c.1770). Examination on his application for settlement in Cerne Abbas stated he was app. to William Reeks of Poole, joiner and cm, for seven years. He then went to sea for four or five years, after which he did journey work before marrying at Cerne Abbas. [Dorset RO, P22/OV21]

Trimmell, C., 19 Westgate St, Bath, Som., u and auctioneer (1819). [D]

Trimmell & Cross, Messrs, Bath, Som., u (1764). In October 1764 they provided a pair of blankets and made a cover for a table for John, 4th Duke of Bedford, at a cost of £3 4s. [Bedford Office, London] Probably Trimnell.

Trimnell, Anthony, Bath, Som., upholder (1749). Took app. named Atwood in 1749. [S of G, app. index]

Trimnell, Charles, Bath, Som., upholder, auctioneer and appraiser (1784–85). Trading in partnership with Thomas Trimnell at Westgate St in 1784 and alone there in 1805. A bill in the Dyrham Park papers is from Charles & Thomas, and dated August to November 1785. Items include '2 fine Canvas Sun Blinds with Lincs & Tassels & putting up do. at dirham', 16s; mending furniture, supplying paper hangings and borders; '6 Cherry tree matted Chairs' at 5s each; 'a Field Bedstead with Sweep Tester & Vases & Base Laths', £1 13s; fabrics and trimmings for 'Making the Furniture of 2 Field Beds & 5 pair of Window Curtains', fine Goose feathers to make pillows and bolsters, bedding and '4 Chairs Gilded'. [D; V&A archives]

Tripe, Thomas, Exeter, Devon, cm and victualler (1827). Report in *Exeter Flying Post*, 19 July 1827, stated that he was declared discharged and entitled to benefit of the Act for Insolvent Debtors.

Tripp, John, Tothill St, Westminster, London, chairmaker (1805–07). [D]

Tripp, William, York St, Westminster, London, cm and chairmaker (1820–39). Trading at no. 17 in 1820; and as a furniture broker at no. 38 in 1839. [D]

Trist, Browse, Fore (or Main) St, Totnes, Devon, cm (1823–38). [D]

Trist, Hore Browse, Guinea St, Exeter, Devon, carver and gilder (1819). Daughter, Mary Chapple, bapt. at St George's on 12 March 1819. [PR (bapt.)]

Trist, Nicholas, Exeter, Devon, cm (b.1773–d.1832). Named in Exeter Militia list, 1803. Recorded at Guinea St, 1814–15, when children bapt. at St Mary Major: Alice on 6 March 1814 and Anthony on 13 August 1815. [PR (bapt.)] Report in *Exeter Flying Post*, 7 June 1832 concerned Trist's arrest for stealing from a Mr Weston, grocer, who had employed Trist in fitting up his new shop in High St. During his hour-long detention in a locked room previous to examination, Trist strangled himself to death. A verdict of insanity was returned at his inquest.

Tristram, Henry, Liverpool, cm (1767). Admitted freeman as son of Tristram, cooper, on 4 December 1767. [Liverpool freemen reg.]

Tristram, Thomas, Liverpool, and Settle, Yorks., cm (1765–98). In 1765 petitioned freedom on birthright as son of William Tristram, cooper, freeborn. Admitted freeman of Liverpool on 9 December 1776. Recorded at Settle in 1798, and died there. [D; Liverpool freemen reg. and committee bk]

Tristram, Thomas, Liverpool, chairmaker (b.1784–1806). Petitioned freedom on birthright as son of William Tristram, saddler, paying 3s 4d. Admitted freeman on 2 November 1806. [Liverpool freemen reg. and committee bk]

Trivett, Samuel, formerly of Pigg St, late of Barbican, London, u (1761). Discharge from Debtors' Prison reported in *London Gazette*, 22 August 1761.

Trollope, George, Parliament St, London, cm and u (1820–39). Recorded in partnership with John Amos Trollope as paper hangers, carvers and gilders at no. 15 in 1820; as J. & G. Trollope, house agents, paper hangers, u, carvers, gilders, house painters and glaziers to His Majesty in Parliament St in 1830; and alone at no. 17 in 1839. George and John Amos took out a Sun Insurance policy on 11 April 1820 for £600 on stock and utensils in his house. John Amos, paper hanger, took out a later policy on his house at 13 Chapel St, Stockwell. [D; GL, Sun MS vol. 483, refs 964985–86] In 1830 J. & G. Trollope submitted a bill, headed by the Royal Arms, to John Arkwright of Hampton Court, Leominster, Herefs., for paper hangings, listing '11 Pcs. Drab chintz stripe', '6 doz Rose Flock border', '10 Pcs. lilac Stripe', '5 doz lilac & Green', '11 Pcs. Rose Sprig', '5 doz flock on Olive', '2 Pcs. Drab stripe', '2½ doz Flock', '10 Pcs. lilac & green' (annotated 'Housekeeper'); '5 doz Flock on Satin', '20 Pcs. Green on Shaded ground' (annotated 'Greenroof'); '9 doz Green flock Rope', '20 ... fine lining paper', 'Packing Canvass' and 'Porterage'. Bill totalled £36 9s 3d. [Herefs. RO, A36/161] Mark of 'G. Trollope & Sons, 15 Parliament St.' recorded on simulated rosewood Davenport with ormolu galleried ledge and sloping leather-lined flap enclosing a well; fitted with slides each side and four drawers on the right; the front inlaid with an oval foliate panel between scrolled brackets on concave-fronted base mounted with foliate border and turned gadrooned feet. [Christie's, 29 June 1978, lot 31, illus.]

Trollope & Sons, address unrecorded. Stamp recorded on pair of Regency painted beechwood and caned armchairs with back bars between uprights painted with Greek figure silhouettes on cream ground, and plain bar below; the painting now blackened, was probably originally dark green; on ring turned legs, with scroll arms. [Bonham's, 4 November 1982, lot 119]

Trolten, John, London, u (1750–56). Named in the Royal Household accounts. [Heal]

Trotman, William, St Mary Magdalen, Oxford, upholder (b.1732–68). Married Elizabeth Hill of St Mary Magdalen on 29 July 1756. Polled in 1768. [Bodleian index of Oxf. marriage bonds]

Trott, Thomas snr, address unrecorded, u (1726). The Temple Newsam papers records payment to Thomas Trott snr on 14 February 1726, of £13 for '10 fine Compis Seete Chaires covered with Morrocko Lether', and 5s for 'a leather Carpet for a Bewrow Table'. [*Furn. Hist.*, 1967]

Trott, Thomas jnr, address unrecorded. The Temple Newsam papers records payment to Thomas Trott jnr on 13 August 1728 for 'making a Old Glass into a Sconce', 18s; 'new Sconce to Match', £2 10s, and '2 pair of Brass Armes', 11s. [*Furn. Hist.*, 1967]

Trott, Thomas, Mark Lane (London?), cm (1740). Took out a Sun Insurance policy on 5 June 1740 for £400. [GL, Sun MS vol. 54, p. 577]

Trotter, —, address unrecorded, u (1721–62). Named in Lady Bowes's accounts on 23 January 1721–22 receiving £5 18s, probably for a funeral; in the tradesmen's accounts on 17 June 1760 receiving £9 15s; and in Mrs Bowes's London Trusteeship accounts on 12 February 1762 receiving £26 19s. [Durham RO, Strathmore MS, D/St/352/2; D/St/v1510; D/St/v1392]

Trotter, George, London, cm (1806). Admitted freeman of Lincoln in November 1806. [Lincoln freemen reg.]

Trotter, George, Butcher Mkt, Louth, Lincs., cm and u (1819–22). [D]

Trotter, Henry, Union Lane, North Shields, Northumb., cm and joiner (1827). [D]

Trotter, James, Liverpool, cm (1803–16). Addresses given at 56 Stanley St, 1803–05; no. 58, 1807–10; no. 56 in 1811; no. 62 and also 38 Byrom St in 1813; and 56 Whitechapel in 1816. [D]

Trotter, James, Hodson St, Liverpool, cm (1814). Sale of 'remaining unmanufactured STOCK in TRADE' on 'declining Cabinet business' advertised in *Liverpool Mercury*, 17 June 1814. Stock consisted of 'Rose, Satin & Mahogany Veneers, dry Planks & Boards, Oak, Ash, Maple & Deal, Bedwood, Benches, Chest & Tools, small quantity of Brass Work etc.'

Trotter, John, 'at Mr. Roubiliac Statuary on the East side of St. Martin's Lane in the Parish of St. Martin in the Fields', London, upholder and cm (1746/47). Took out a Sun Insurance policy on 13 January 1746/47 for £300 on household goods and stock in trade in his apartments; and £400 on utensils and stock in his three timber workshops, partly over Roubiliac's workshop and partly over yard. [GL, Sun MS vol. 79, ref. 107286]

Trotter, John, Frith St, Soho, London, upholder and cm to George II (b. before 1730–99). Originally from Berwickshire, he ran a flourishing cm business in Frith St, and Heal records him in directories and the Royal accounts at no. 43, 1755–92. Trotter was 3rd son of Alexander Trotter of Kettleshiel, Berwickshire and his wife Jean, daughter of Sir Robert Stuart of Allanbank, and probably born in Edinburgh. His father died before 1730, leaving his widow with eleven children, mostly minors. John Trotter is said to have served his apprenticeship in Edinburgh, although he is not named in the published list. A brother, James, was app. to Charles Butter, wright, in Edinburgh, on 25 February 1730. Letters in the National Library of Scotland [MS 20262] show that his mother lent money from her Jointure (which he repaid) to set him up in London as a cm. He flourished and though not the eldest son, became principal trustee of his mother's estate, and aquired Kettleshiel. Trotter married Ann Locke in 1752, and had three sons, one of whom, James (?), succeeded him in the business, and also in the estate he bought in Surrey, Horton Manor. John Trotter became contractor to the Army. In 1774 he took as partner his nephew, John, son of Archibald Trotter of the Bush, Midlothian. This John Trotter bought Dyrham Park, Herts., and was brother of Sir Coutts Trotter, Bart, the banker. Both John Trotters appear in Burke's *Landed Gentry*,

1898. John & Coutts Trotter, upholders, are listed in directories at 43 Frith St, 1790–94, and 406 Oxford St in 1799. There is clearly confusion betwen the two John Trotters. He was noted by J. Boswell in *London Journal*, 17 May 1763, as '... a particular friend ... who is originally from Scotland, but has been here so long that he is become quite an Englishman. He is a bachelor, an honest, hearty, good-humored fellow'. Trotter had dined with Boswell, James Coutts, Coutts's brother and a Mr Cochrane. Since John Trotter is recorded as having married in 1752, this passage perhaps refers to his nephew. Other sources record John Trotter as follows: he was admitted freeman of the Joiners' Co. on 4 February 1745, and named in the livery of the Co. on 29 October 1751. Polled at Westminster in 1749, and subscribed to Chippendale's *Director*, 1754. Named as a Fellow of the Society of Arts and Manufactures in 1771 for one year only. In 1779 he insured houses for £1,500, and his house in Surrey for £900, with the Sun Co. John & Coutts Trotter of Frith St, upholders, took out Sun Insurance policies on 25 June 1785 (when recorded at nos 42, 43 and 44) for £500 on household goods, and £1,000 on utensils, stock and goods in trust; on 7 January 1791 for £2,000 on house, stables and offices in Soho Sq.; and on 4 February 1793 for £3,800 including £2,500 on a house in Soho Sq., and £1,300 on outhouses communicating in Oxford St. Gunnis states that Sir Henry Cheere carved chimney pieces for John Trotter of Soho Sq. [D; GL, Joiners' Co. records; GL, Sun MS vol. 276, p. 634; vol. 278, p. 488; vol. 328, p. 619; ref. 579019; vol. 389, ref. 611372] Several of John Trotter's commissions are documented. Between 1754 and 1758 he carried out refurbishing of the Royal yachts, and worked at the Palaces of St James, Kensington, Hampton Court, and the House of Lords. His largest bill in the Royal accounts totalled £1,069 7s 8d and was for work at Kew, and at the houses of Princes William and Henry in Leicester Sq., 1758–59. [PRO, LC9/291–92] Trotter is named in the Blickling Hall, Norwich papers in August 1762. [Norfolk RO, 17148] John (or Bannister) Trotter supplied items to Henry Knight of Tythegston Court, Glam. in 1767. [C. *Life*, 5 October 1978, p. 1024] John & Coutts Trotter are recorded in the accounts for Blair Castle on 8 June 1787 providing bedding, '2 shooting tents', '2 folding bedsteads', and '26 camp chairs with elbows'; and charging for 'Cartage to Mr. Foot's Adelphi'. [V&A archives] On 5 July 1793 John Trotter supplied campaign furniture and baggage to a Lieut. Long for the 1793 Flanders Campaign, charging £47 17s 4d. [*Soc. Army Hist. Research*, vol. 26, p. 39, RUSI, MM 219, pp. 31–34] A.E.

Trotter, Ralph, Durham, u (1754–93). Took apps named Feathertone in 1754 and Smith in 1757. Trading also as bookseller and stationer, 1784–93. [D; S of G, app. index]

Trotter, Samuel, Lincoln, cm and u (1806–35). Trading at High St, 1819–35. Admitted freeman in November 1806. [D; Lincoln freemen rolls]

Trotter, William, 42 Greek St, Soho, London, upholder (1805). Took out a Sun Insurance policy on 18 December 1805 for £200 of which £25 accounted for utensils, stock and goods in trust. [GL, Sun MS vol. 434, ref. 779972]

Trotter & Magill, 6 Shaw's Brow, Liverpool, cm and auctioneers (1813–14). [D]

Troubridge, John, High St, Salisbury, Wilts., cm and u (1822). [D]

Troughton, John, St Leonards, Shoreditch, London, cm (1754–58). Took apps named John Light in 1754 for £10, John Upton in 1755 for £14 14s and John Brown in 1758 for £16. Subscribed to Chippendale's *Director*, 1754. [V&A archives; GL, Sun MS ref. 223502]

Troughton, Nathaniel, at 'The Lamb', under the Royal Exchange, in Cornhill, London, u (1705). [Hilton Price, *Signs of Old London*]

Troughton, Thomas, Gerard St, Liverpool, joiner and cm (1835–39). Trading at no. 41 with shop at 47 in 1835; no. 44 in 1837 and no. 100 in 1839. [D]

Trowell, William, Long Causeway, Peterborough, Northants., cm and u (1830). [D]

Trower & Slater, 7 Gt Eastcheap, Cannon St, London, wholesale u (1811–20). [D]

Trowless, William, Smithford St, Coventry, Warks., carver and gilder (1835). [D]

Trubshaw, James, Nottingham, u (1765–74). Son of John Trubshaw, yeoman of Wollaton; taken as app. in 1765. Listed as burgess in 1772. Took app. named John Mold in 1773. Will dated 14 May 1774. [Nottingham app. and burgess lists; probate records]

Trubshaw, Richard, Manchester, cm (1808–11). Trading at 62 Little Lever St in 1808 and 23 Thomas St in 1811. [D]

Trubshaw, Richard, Gaolgate St, Stafford, cm and u (1828). [D]

Trubshaw, Thomas, Gaolgate St, Stafford, cm (1822). [D]

Trude, Mary, Sidwell St, Exeter, Devon, u (1838). [D]

True, Rice, Grove St, Boston, Lincs., cm (1826). [D]

Trueman, Jonathan, London, cm (1803–20). Trading at Marga St in 1820. [Nottingham poll bks]

Truman, George, Digbeth, Birmingham, chairmaker (1793). [D]

Truman, Jonah, Laxton's Ct, Long Lane, Southwark, London, looking-glass frame maker (1791). Took out insurance for £200 in 1791.

Tru(e)man, Jonathan, 37 Paternoster Row, London, cm (1800–16). [D]

Trundle, Edmund, Newgate St, London, city furniture warehouse (1805–07). [D]

Truscott, James, 6 Brett's Buildings, Camberwell, London, cm and u (1839). [D]

Truscott, John, 18 Douglas St, Vincent Sq., Westminster, London, cm (1831–37). Son William Henderson Truscott by his wife, Sarah, born in 1831, and bapt. at Westminster Methodist Chapel in July 1837. [PRO, Non-Conf. reg. RG4/4313]

Truss, —, Houndsditch, London, cm (d.1741). Notice in *Daily Post*, 14 October 1741 read: 'On Wednesday last died at his house in Houndsditch, Mr. Truss a wealthy Cabinet-Maker.'

Truss, Thomas, London St, Reading, Berks., cm (1837). [Poll bk]

Trustwell, Joseph, Mount St, Nottingham, joiner and cm (1832). [D]

Tubb, Isaac Harwood, address unrecorded, upholder (1771). Son of James Tubb, peruke-maker of Oxford. Admitted freeman of the Upholders' Co. on 13 November 1771. [GL, Upholders' Co. records]

Tubb, John, London, upholder and cm (1778–83). Trading at Catherine St, Strand, 1778–81; no. 11, 1781–82; and 9 Mount Row, Lambeth in 1783. Took out Sun Insurance policies in 1778 for £1,500 on utensils, stock and warehouse; in 1779 for £4,000, £3,100 on stock and goods; and in 1781 for £400 on a house in Acton. [D; GL, Sun MS vol. 266, p. 224; vol. 279, p. 131; vol. 292, p. 313]

Tubb, Samuel, Norwich cm (1798). [D] Possibly Samuel Tubby.

Tubbs, John, 22 Waterloo Rd, London, bedstead maker (1839). [D]

Tubby, Samuel, 77 St Stephen's St, Norwich cm and chairmaker (1801–22). Admitted freeman, not by apprenticeship, on 24 February 1803. Former app., Samuel Smee, cm admitted on 3 May 1814. [D; poll bks; Norwich freemen reg.] Probably the Tubby, cm of Norwich who subscribed to Sheraton's *Drawing Book*, 1793. Possibly Samuel Tubb.

Tucker, B. B., Pyle St, Newport, Isle of Wight, Hants., cm (1839). [D]

Tucker, Edward, New Market St, Exeter, Devon, carver and gilder (1837–40). Recorded also 'near Gandy Street' in 1838. [D; *Exeter Pocket Journal*]

Tucker, Edwin, 5 High St, Exeter, Devon, carver and gilder (1836). [*Exeter Pocket Journal*]

Tucker, Elias, Exeter, Devon, cm, chairmaker and u (b.1755–d.1835). Recorded as Elias at All Hallows, Goldsmith St in Exeter Militia list, 1803, and at Gandy St, 1809–35. Trading as E. Tucker & Son at Gandy St, 1813–39. Marriage of his daughter to Mr F. A. Fernandez, merchant, reported in *Western Luminary*, 18 May 1813. Named in election squibs in 1816. Advertised in the above paper on 16 March 1819, and *Exeter Flying Post*, 11 March, his 'choice Assortment of MAHOGANY and ROSEWOOD FURNITURE of the best materials and most fashionable make ... on the most reasonable terms'; also mahogany, wainscot, cedar and other foreign woods. Advertised in *Western Luminary*, 23 November 1819 for '2 good cabinet maker workmen, who will have constant employment'. Placed notices in *Exeter Flying Post*, 8 June 1809, 15 March and 19 July 1810; 12 March 1812, and 20 May 1813. Report that his app. had run away given on 16 November 1815. Death of his wife, Elizabeth, aged 68 reported on 2 February 1826; and sudden death of his son and partner, John on 20 March 1834. He advertised the continuation of the business on 27 March. His own death, aged 80 on 9 September 1835, was reported on 17 September 1835, when he was described as 'from an early period in his life, an inhabitant of this city, and one of the older tradesmen in it'. On 24 September 1835 an advertisement stated that the family firm would continue under the foreman, Mr Lloyd. [D; *Exeter Pocket Journal*]

Tucker, Francis, Gloucester, cm (1813–23). Child bapt. at St Aldgate in 1813; children at St Michael's in 1819, 1821 and 1823. [PR (bapt.)]

Tucker, George, 4 Walks, Bath, Som., cm and u (1833). [D]

Tucker, George, 20 College St, Westminster, London, u (1839). [D]

Tucker, J. T., Southampton, Hants., auctioneer and cm (1834–39). Trading at Hanover Buildings in 1834, Orchard St in 1836, and Hanover Buildings and 32 Above Bar in 1839. [D]

Tucker, James, Mary Arches St, Exeter, Devon, cm and u (1838). [D]

Tucker, John, at 'The Angel', Houndsditch, London, upholder (1752–55). Notice in *Daily Advertiser*, 28 February 1752 given of sale of 'Twelve Mahogany French-fashioned Elbow Chairs, on Castors, with Check Cases ...'. Reported as a prisoner from debt in *London Gazette*, 27–31 May 1755. [Harris & Son, *The English Chair*, p. 184]

Tucker, John, St Andrew's, Holborn, London, upholder (1788). His son, Thomas Tucker, admitted freeman of the Upholders' Co. in 1788. [GL, Upholders' Co. records]

Tucker, John, Exeter, Devon, cm (1825–40). Recorded at Sun lane, 1825–28; Mint Lane, 1829–33; 75 South St, 1834–37; and Mary Arches St, 1838–40. Son John bapt. at St Olave's on 28 June 1829, and Henry Alfred on 1 April 1832. [D; *Exeter Pocket Journal*; Exeter voters list; PR (bapt.)]

Tucker, John, West Exe, Tiverton, Devon, cm (1830–38). [D]

Tucker, John Samuel, Back St, Trowbridge, Wilts., cm (1839). [D]

Tucker, Nathaniel, High Wycombe, Bucks., chairmaker (b.c.1811–41). Aged 30 at the time of the 1841 Census.

Tucker, Richard, Gold St, Tiverton, Devon, cm and u (1767–74). Advertised in *Exeter Flying Post* for an app. on 4 September 1767; for a journeyman cm and an app. on 31 July 1772; and for two journeymen cm on 7 January 1774.

Tucker, Richard, Harwood, Devon, cm (d.1832). Suicide reported in *Exeter Flying Post*, 5 April 1832.

Tucker, Thomas, London, upholder (1775–1814). Recorded at 315 High Holborn, 1788–91; Somerset St East in 1792; Holborn in 1794; Hatton St in 1802; no. 24 in 1803; and as u, appraiser and undertaker at 24 Hatton Gdn, 1796–1814. Son of John Tucker, upholder of St Andrew's, Holborn. App. to Samuel Braithwaite on 3 May 1775, and admitted freeman of the Upholders' Co. by servitude on 2 July 1788. With George Lillie, rented house and warehouses in High Holborn, insured by the Rt Hon. Jacob, Earl of Radnor of Portman Sq. for £1,000 in 1789 and 1791. Named in Sheraton's list of master cabinet makers, 1803. [D; GL, Upholders' Co. records; GL, Sun MS vol. 362, p. 336] See Tucker & Bra(i)thwaite, Tucker & Lillie, and George Lillie.

Tucker, W. B. & A., 5 High St, Exeter, Devon, carvers, gilders and picture dealers (1828–32). Announced in *The Alfred*, 24 June 1828, that they had succeeded to the business established by their father, William Wallace Tucker, for nearly twenty-five years. They hoped for a 'continuance of the favours bestowed on him', and also advertised their business in taxidermy. [D; *Exeter Pocket Journal*]

Tucker, Walter, East St, Warminster, Wilts., cm and u (1830). [D]

Tucker, Walter, Lavington, Wilts., cm and u (1839). [D]

Tucker, William, formerly of Brook's Mkt, Holborn, late of Gulstone St, Whitechapel, London, cm (1761). Discharge from Debtors' Prison reported in *London Gazette*, 1 September 1761.

Tucker, William, Preston St, Exeter, Devon, cm (1823). Daughter Emma bapt. at St Mary Major on 21 December 1823. [PR (bapt.)]

Tucker, William Wallace, Exeter, Devon, carver, gilder and picture dealer (1807–d.1848). Described as 'originally at 60 Portland St, Middlesex' in *Exeter Flying Post*. Recorded at Church Yd, 1807–16; Cathedral Yd, 1816–22; 253 High St from 1824 and High St, 1825–28. He died at Fore St Hill, 1848. [*Exeter Flying Post*, 4 June 1848] The William Tucker recorded in St Paul's parish in 1835 and 11 Northernhay Pl. in 1838 was probably his son and successor. Advertised in *Exeter Flying Post*, 12 March 1807 that he was continuing business at his shop near the Post Office, in the Churchyard. Announced sale of pictures on 1 July 1813; and on 14 November 1816 that he had taken on picture restoration. On 19 August 1824 announced his removal from Cathedral Churchyard to 253 High St; and on 7 October 1824 that he was opening a gallery for the exhibition and sale of pictures. His gallery was advertised in *The Alfred* several times during 1825, notably holding an exhibition of 'Carving and Guilding in all their branches, by the most experienced workmen in Devonshire', on 21 June. Advertised in the same paper on 14 September 1824 that he wished to let the whole upper part of 253 High St; and notice on 22 February 1825 stated that the High Sheriff was to 'occupy Mr. Tucker's new & elegant lodgings at the picture gallery'. Report in *Exeter Flying Post*, 5 October 1826, stated that his estate and effects were to be filed in the court for relief of insolvent debtors. Declared bankrupt, *London Gazette*, 23 November 1827. Announced in *The Alfred*, 24 June 1828, that he had removed to London, and the business would be continued by his sons, W. B. & A. Tucker. Son of William Tucker jnr also called William, was bapt. at St Paul's on 2 August 1835. [D; *Exeter Pocket Journal*; election squibs, 1816; PR (bapt.)]

Tucker, William, High St, Amersham, Bucks., chairmaker (1830). [D]

Tucker, William, Old Market St, Teignmouth, Devon, cm and u (1838). [D]

Tucker & Bra(i)thwaite, High Holborn, London, upholders (1767–72). [D] See Thomas Tucker.

Tucker & Lil(l)ie (or Little), 315 High Holborn, London, cm and u (1789–94). [D] See Thomas Tucker and George Lillie.

Tudor, Cornelius, Webster St, Fontenoy St, Liverpool, cm (1812). Admitted freeman on servitude to John Ward Turner on 7 October 1812. [Liverpool freemen reg.]

Tudor, John, 4 Lower Myrtle St, Liverpool, cm (1818). Admitted freeman on servitude to John Ward Turner on 18 June 1818. [D; Liverpool freemen reg.]

Tudor, Robert, Liverpool, cm (1812–21). Trading at 19 Crosshall St in 1821. Admitted freeman on servitude to John Ward Turner on 5 October 1812. [D; Liverpool freemen reg.]

Tudor (or Tydder), Samuel, Shrewsbury, Salop, u and cm (1792–1835). Listed at High St, c.1796 and College Hill, 1822–35. Listed in Shrewsbury burgess roll, 1792. [D]

Tudway, Charles, parish of St Mary Redcliffe, Bristol, turner and cm (1774–84). [Poll bks]

Tuely, —, 33 Lamb's Conduit St, London, cm, u and auctioneer (1805–07). [D]

Tuel(l)y (or Tuley), Charles, 49 Kenton St, Brunswick Sq., London, cm and upholder (1809–20). [D] See Tully & Co.

Tuely, P., address unrecorded, cm (1803). Subscribed to Sheraton's *Cabinet Dictionary*, 1803.

Tuftin, Thomas, Bristol, cm (1774–81). [Poll bks]

Tulk, Henry, Swan Yd, London, cm (1774). [Poll bk]

Tull, Samuel, parish of St Ann's, Westminster, London, upholder (1710). Named in contemporary newspapers. [Heal]

Tull, Samuel, Cirencester, Glos., upholder (1722). Took out a Sun Insurance policy on 24 June 1722 for £500 on goods and merchandise in his house. [GL, Sun MS vol. 14, ref. 26176]

Tulley, John, Blyth, Northumb., joiner and cm (1834). [D]

Tulley, Philip, Blyth, Northumb., joiner and cm (1827–34). Trading at Sussex St in 1827. [D]

Tullock, John, High St, Poole, Dorset, cm (1823–24). [D]

Tully, John, 5 Bond St Row, Brighton, Sussex, cm and u (1832). [D]

Tully & Co., 41 Kenton St, Foundling, London, cm (1825). [D] See Charles Tuelly.

Tumberlick (Timberlake?), James, High Wycombe, Bucks., chairmaker (b.c.1798–1841). Sons bapt. in 1825, 1829, 1830 and 1835; daughters in 1827 and 1831. Aged 43 at the time of the 1841 Census. [PR (bapt.)]

Tunbrell, William, 16 Hall's Buildings, Windmill St, Manchester, cm (1817). [D]

Tunbridge, John, High St, Ashford, Kent, cm, u and furniture broker (1839). [D]

Tune, William, Conisbrough, near Doncaster, Yorks., joiner and cm (1834). [D]

Tunmer, Charles Frederick, White-hart Lane, Ipswich, Suffolk, carver and gilder (1824). [D]

Tunmer, James Robert, Ipswich, Suffolk, cm (1830–39). Trading at St Clement's, Fore St in 1830 and Orwell Pl. in 1835. [D; poll bks]

Tunnadine, William, Lichfield, Staffs., cm and u (1779). Declared bankrupt, *Sussex Weekly Advertiser*, 8 February 1779.

Tunney, Charles, Leicester, u (1766). App. to his father, Thomas, u, in 1766. Brother of Thomas Tunney of Leicester, later Nottingham. [Leicester freemen rolls]

Tunney, Thomas, Norwich, u (1745). Son of Oliver Tunney, blacksmith; admitted freeman on 20 July 1745. [Norwich freemen rolls] Possibly:

Tunney, Thomas, Leicester and Nottingham, u (b.1725–d.1799). Took his son Thomas as app. in 1766. Took app. named William Hammond in October 1772.

Advertised for apps in *Leicester Journal*, 1774 and 1776. Polled at Norwich in 1786. Death at Nottingham, aged 74, reported in *Gents Mag.*, February 1799, when described as 'Formerly an upholsterer at Leicester'. [Leicester freemen rolls]

Tunnicliffe, George, Lane End, Hanley, Staffs., chairmaker and turner (1818–34). Trading at High St, Lane End in 1818; Albion St in 1822; Charles St in 1828 and Pall Mall in 1834. [D]

Tunnicliffe, Robert, Sheep Fair, Rugeley, Staffs., chairmaker (1818). [D]

Tunnicliffe, Robert, Rosemary Lane, Huddersfield, Yorks., cm and joiner (1830). [D]

Tunstall, Anthony, Baldwins Pl., Baldwins Gdns, Leather Lane, London, cm (1777). Took out a Sun Insurance policy in 1777 for £200 of which utensils and stock accounted for £100. [GL, Sun MS vol. 257, p. 473]

Tunstall, George, Post House Wynd, Darlington, Co. Durham (1834). [D]

Tunstall, H., 138 St John St, West Smithfield, London, u (1820). [D]

Tunstall, James, 189 Vauxhall Rd, Liverpool, cm (1829). Admitted freeman as app. to Nathan Newall on 8 October 1829. [Liverpool freemen reg.]

Tunstall, John, Skinnergate, Darlington, Co. Durham, cm (1827–34). [D]

Tunstall, Thomas, Westgate, Wakefield, Yorks., u and cm (1778–79). Took out Sun Insurance policies in 1778 for £400 of which stock accounted for £200; and in 1779 for £300, £240 on utensils, stock and goods. [GL, Sun MS vol. 265, p. 380; vol. 271, p. 516]

Tupe, John, Worcester, cm (1743). Admitted freeman in 1743 on payment of £20. [Worcester Guildhall, Chamber order bk]

Turbett, John, Wych St, London, cm (1774). [Poll bk]

Turbett, Thomas, Liverpool, u (1816–18). Trading at 11 St Vincent St in 1816 and 19 Leigh St in 1818. [D]

Turbitt, Johnson Thomas, Nantwich, Cheshire, u (1806). Married on 17 March 1806. [Chester RO, PR]

Turene, —, London, cm (1709). Named in the accounts for Felbrigg, Norfolk, in April 1709 receiving £6 10s and also £1 15s for a 'Bureau in Compton St.' [Norfolk RO, Felbrigg papers, WKC 6/23, index of payments] Probably Turin, —, William Turing, and/or William Turrin.

Turfrey, John, 37 Montague St, Spitalfields, London, chair and sofa manufacturer (1817). [D]

Turfrey, Joseph, Hackney, London, chair and sofa manufacturer, cm (1828). Joseph Turfrey and James Osborne, cm of Hackney Rd were declared bankrupt, *London Gazette*, 2 December 1828. Turfrey was trading at 22 London Terr., Hackney, in 1829. [D]

Turin, —, London. The accounts of Lady Grisell Baillie at Mellerstain, Berwickshire, record payments to Turin in 1715 of £14 for 'a chimny Glas in one pice 54½ by 22½'; £25 for 'a large Glas in a Glase frame'; and £7 for 'a writting Desk on wheels walnut tree'. Probably Turene, —, and/or:

Turing, William, London, looking-glass and cm (1714–30). His address at 'The Eagle & Child', Bedford St, Covent Gdn, is given among the Coke bills at Holkham Hall, Norfolk. From 1723–26 his address was 'over against the New Exchange' in the Strand. After Michaelmas 1721, Turing appears in the Great Wardrobe accounts in partnership with John Gumley; but in 1729 the employment of Mrs Gumley and Turing 'as cabinet-makers for the Wardrobe', was terminated. His appeal in 1730 for re-employment was rejected. Declared bankrupt, *London Gazette*, 26 January 1723; and announced that he had resumed business in the Strand in *Daily Post*, 13 April 1726. A receipted account from Turing dated 1714, in the Montrose papers is for 'Two Screens Mounted', a large cistern and an 'Indian Chest', costing a total of £30 10s. In 1718 the Duke of Montrose bought items from Turing for his London house in Bond St costing £234 15s. [*Treasury Letter Book*, vol. 18, p. 420; *Calendar of Treasury Papers*, 1729–30; Wills, *Looking-Glasses*; *DEF*; *GCM*; Scottish RO, GD 220/6/1159/44; GD 220/6/28/p. 85] Probably William Turrin.

Turk, John, Meards Ct, Dean St, Soho, London, cm (1775). Insured his house for £400 in 1775. [GL, Sun MS vol. 242, p. 45]

Turlay (or Turley), James, Leeds, Yorks., cm and housebuilder (1822–30). Addresses given at Old Infirmary Yd and 52 Kirkgate in 1822 and 1 Russell St, Woodhouse Lane, 1826–30. [D]

Turlay, Hannah, 1 Russell Pl., Leeds, Yorks., working u (1834). [D]

Turley, —, Lamb's Conduit St, Red Lion Sq., London, cm (1803). Named in Sheraton's list of master cabinet makers, 1803.

Turman, —, address unrecorded, wood-carver (1775). Recorded as having signed two carved 18-inch wood panels, dated 1775. [V&A archives]

Turnadine, William, Lichfield, Staffs., cm (1779). [Bailey's list of bankrupts]

Turnage, Samuel, Broomfield, near Chelmsford, Essex, cm and u (1839). [D]

Turnbull, George, Lambton St, Sunderland, Co. Durham, joiner and cm (1828–29). [D]

Turnbull, John, address unrecorded, cm (1803). Subscribed to Sheraton's *Cabinet Dictionary*, 1803.

Turnbull, John, Crossgate, Durham, joiner and cm (1827–34). [D]

Turnbull, John, Bedford St, North Shields, Northumb., cm and joiner (1827–29). [D]

Turnbull, John, 61 Sawney Pope St, Liverpool, joiner and cm (1829). [D]

Turnbull, Robert, Newcastle, u (1780). App. to Henry Reed, and admitted freeman on 6 September 1780. [Newcastle freemen reg.]

Turnbull, William, Baldwin St, Bristol, carpenter and cm (1814–19). Trading at no. 13 in 1814 and no. 10, 1815–19. [D]

Turnbull, William, New Quay, North Shields, Northumb., cm (1834). [D]

Turnbulls, —, Exchange, Cheltenham, Glos., writing desk and workbox maker etc. Early 19th-century trade card shows interior of shop with Regency-style chairs, workbox on stand, umbrellas etc. [Banks Coll., BM]

Turner, —, at 'The Royal Tent', in Compton St, Soho, London, u (1721). Named in contemporary newspapers. [Heal]

Turner, —, address unrecorded, cm (1732). An account with Child & Co., bankers, in the Strathmore papers records payment to Mr Turner, cm, of £35. [Durham RO, D/St/Box 352/27]

Turner, —, London (?), cm (1749). The account book of the Earl of Ancaster records payment to Mr Turner, cm, in full of £69 17s 6d. [Lincoln RO, 2ANC 6/5]

Turner, —, Dean St, Soho, London, cm (d.1752). Notice in *General Advertiser*, 11 February 1752, read: 'Yesterday died after a lingering illness, at his House in Dean Street, Soho, Mr. Turner, late an eminent Cabinetmaker, who had acquired a plentiful fortune and retired from Business some years.'

Turner, —, address unrecorded, cm (1787–90). Named in the Longford Castle accounts in 1787 receiving £13 4s, and in 1790, £162 0s 6d. [V&A archives]

Turner, —, 21 St Paul's Churchyard, London. See Wilkinson & Turner.

Turner, —, 19 Providence Row, London, upholder and tentmaker (1790–93). [D]

Turner, —, St Pancras, Chichester, Sussex, chairmaker (1804). [D] See Philip Turner at this address.

Turner, —, London, u. A portable folding writing desk bound in brass in the Benaki Museum, Athens is stated to have belonged to Lord Byron (1788–1824). [Museum No. 8277]

Turner, Adam, Sunderland, Co. Durham, cm (1758). Took app. named Weems in 1758. [S of G, app. index]

Turner, Adam, Porter St, London, cm (1784). [Poll bk]

Turner, Ann, Bridge St Row, Chester, cm and u (1834). [D] See Samuel Turner of Chester, who she succeeded.

Turner, Anthony, Lancaster, cm (1799–1807). App. to T. Lister in 1799 and admitted freeman, 1806–07. [Lancaster app. reg. and freemen rolls]

Turner, Anthony, 42 New St, Birmingham, cm, u and broker (1828–35). [D]

Turner, D. S., London, cm and u (1807–37). Recorded at 26 and 27 Brokers Row, Finsbury, 1807–15; 27 Moorfields, 1820–23; and 27–28 Eldon St, Finsbury Cresc. (or Circus), 1825–29. [D] Either Daniel or David Turner.

Turner, Daniel, London, japanned chair and cm, broker and appraiser (1811–23). Trading at 132 Ratcliff Highway in 1811 and 218 Whitechapel Rd, 1817–20. [D]

Turner, Daniel, Horse Fair, Rugeley, Staffs., cm (1818). [D]

Turner, David, London, chairmaker and cm (1820–23). Trading at 27 Brokers Row, Moorfields, in 1820 and 218 Whitechapel Rd, 1820–23. [D]

Turner, Edward, Chester, cm (1778). Son of Thomas Turner; app. to James Abbott, cm, 13 April–16 May 1778. [Chester app. bks]

Turner, Edward, Church St, Whitby, Yorks., cm/chairmaker (1828–40). [D]

Turner, Edward, Eldon St, Finsbury, London, u (1839). [D]

Turner, G., address unrecorded. Undated satinwood vitrine with concave sides and heavily decorated with ormolu, is recorded as signed 'G. Turner'. [V&A archives]

Turner, George, Bristol, upholder (1781–1840). Polled in 1781. Recorded at 22 Horse Fair, 1809–10; Old Park Stile, 1815–19; as George snr, u and clerk of St Thomas's Church, at St Thomas St, 1819–20; at 7 Old Park, 1829–30; Old Park, 1831–33; and again as George snr, u and paper hanger, at 9 Old Park, 1837–40. [D]

Turner, George jnr, Alfred Pl., Kingsdown, Redcliff Parade, Bristol, u etc. (1821–40). Recorded at no. 11 in 1821. [D]

Turner, George, 36 Clock Alley, Manchester, chairmaker (1817). [D]

Turner, George, 34 Gt Titchfield St, London, u and cm (1835). [D]

Turner, Henry, address unrecorded, upholder (1705–14). Admitted freeman of the Upholders' Co. on 9 November 1705. Took app. named Edward Webster, 1705–13/14. [GL, Upholders' Co. records]

Turner, Henry, Green St, Leicester Fields, London, cm (1775). Took out a Sun Insurance policy in 1775 for £400, £25 accounting for utensils and stock. [GL, Sun MS vol. 240, p. 361]

Turner, Henry, 11 Compton St, Soho, London, cm (1777). Took out a Sun Insurance policy in 1777 for £1,400, of which £1,800 accounted for utensils, stock and goods. [GL, Sun MS vol. 258, p. 190]

Turner, Henry, London, upholder and cm (1777–99). Recorded at Frith St, 1777–99 when he took out Sun Insurance policies in association with Thomas Like. Polled at Westminster, 1784. Listed as Henry & Co., cm, upholders and tentmakers, 47 Frith St, Soho, 1788–89; and 132 New Bond St, 1790–99. Took out a Sun Insurance policy on 3 July 1794 for £200 on his house and goods. Probably the Turner, cm to the Duke of Clarence, New Bond St, who subscribed to Sheraton's *Drawing Book*, 1793, since his label reads: '. . . Henry Turner, UPHOLSTERER to his ROYAL HIGHNESS the DUKE of CLARENCE, CABINET MAKER, APPRAISER & UNDERTAKER, at his Carpet, Bedding & Blanket Warehouse, No. 132 New Bond Street. NB: Tents, Marquees, Cotts & with sundry articles for Army or Navy'. Label found on combination desk, cabinet and architect's table offered for sale by Malcolm Franklin Inc., *Antiques*, December 1952, p. 465. [D; GL, Sun MS vol. 401, ref. 630131] See J. & H. Turner, Thomas Turner, Turner & Co., and Turner, Smith & Co.

Turner, Henry, 4 Shude Hill, Manchester, chairmaker (1788–94). [D]

Turner, Henry, Cambridge, cm and broker (1834–43). Henry Turner is first recorded in a poll bk of 1834 when he had premises in King St, but by 1836 he was renting a house and workshop in Bridge St belonging to St John's College where he is listed up to 1843, but after that date the property is in the name of Henry Thompson, cm and broker. Turner is very probably the Henry Turner of Bridge St, who on 26 April 1838 was discommoned (debarred from serving undergraduates) by the Vice Chancellor and eight heads of Colleges for 'having suffered persons in statu pupillari to resort to his house for the purpose of playing at billiards'. There is a mahogany Pembroke table in the Cambridge and County Folk Museum, bearing the label 'H. Turner, Broker, Bridge Street, Cambridge'. Three children bapt. in St Clement's parish, 1837–43. [D; poll bks; archives of St John's College; PR (bapt.); C. H. Cooper, *Annals of Cambridge*, vol. IV, 1852; *Furn. Hist.*, 1978]   R.W.

Turner, Henry, Norwich, carver and gilder (1837–66). Daughters Eliza and Emma bapt. at St Michael's Church, Coslany, Norwich in 1837. Son born in 1838 and married in 1866, when his father was still trading.

Turner, J., address unrecorded. A bill from J. Turner in the Audley End papers, dated 21 August 1786, is for a 'mahogany chest of drawers with brass castors', costing £3 3s. [V&A archives]

Turner, J. H., address unrecorded. In July 1809 supplied camp tables and stools costing £10 0s 8d to the Royal Household. [Windsor Royal Archives, RA 89007]

Turner, J. & H., 139 New Bond St, London, upholders, cm and undertakers (1813–40). [D] See Henry Turner of 132 New Bond St and Thomas & Henry Turner of no. 139.

Turner, J., address unrecorded. The Royal accounts of June 1839 refer to built-in furniture at Buckingham Palace, made by J. Turner at a cost of £188. It consisted of a 'satinwood Press fixed in Anti-Room' with 'scribing pieces'; and other furnishings were as follows: 'the right hand wing to have a wainscot Bedstead, to turn up, the bottom stuffed with hair — the left hand of closet with door to open the whole length — the centre to have a large door to open to the Passage & the ends of the wings enclosed to the door next Passage to be panelled & moulded to match the large door, brass wire panels & silk curtains behind & purplewood introduced in the mouldings and french polished. To fix 2 new quarters round open ends to 4 Ebony Commodes; with 2 Ebony shelves in each wing, new ebony plinths, preparing moulds for brass founders & masons. French polishing and fixing brasswork, 14 plate glass backs'. [Windsor RA, Box 1, Item 2]

Turner, James, Market Hill, Cambridge, cm and u (1767–84). Death of his wife reported in *Cambridge Chronicle and Journal*, 21 March 1767. Insured houses with the Sun Co. for £500 in 1784, in which year the above paper on 2 October advertised sale of his stock in trade on retiring from business. [D; poll bk; GL, Sun MS vol. 321, p. 367]

Turner, James, Pilgrim St, Newcastle, looking-glass maker etc. (1782). [D]

Turner, James, 17 Whitmore Pl., Hoxton, London, chair and sofa maker (1789 or 1839). [D]

Turner, James, 'Globe Tavern', Fleet St, London, upholder (1799). Son of John Turner, Gent. of Ipswich, Admitted freeman of the Upholders' Co. by redemption on 3 April 1799. [GL, Upholders' Co. records]

Turner, James jnr, Chester, u (1816). Admitted freeman on 7 September 1816. [Chester freemen rolls]

Turner, James, Bristol, chair and bedstead manufacturer, cm (1827–30). Trading at Lower West St in 1827, 26 West St in 1828, and 9 Lower West St, 1829–30. [D]

Turner, James, Heigham, Norwich, gilder (1830). [Poll bk]

Turner, James, 68 Walmgate, York, joiner and cm (1830). [D]

Turner, James, York, cm, joiner and looking-glass manufacturer (1830–38). Trading at 33 Jubbergate in 1830 and Little Shambles in 1838. [D]

Turner, James, Wyre St, Colchester, Essex, chairmaker (1832). [D]

Turner, James, High Wycombe, Bucks., chairmaker and caner (b. *c.* 1816–41). Son bapt. in 1838. Aged 25 at the time of the 1841 Census. [PR (bapt.)]

Turner, John, London (?), frame maker (1707). The receipt book of Samuel Tufnell of Middle Temple, London (who bought Langley's, Gt Waltham, Essex, in 1710), records payment to Turner of £2 10s 'in full for 5 frames for ye battles of Alexander' on 30 May 1707. [Essex RO, D/DTu 276]

Turner, John, High Holborn, London, cm (1763). Mentioned in Thomas Mortimer's *Universal Director*, 1763.

Turner, John, Lancaster, cm (1767–68). [Lancaster freemen rolls]

Turner, John, 28 Vine St, Clare Mkt, London, carver and dealer in coals (1782). Took out a Sun Insurance policy in 1782 for £200 of which £100 accounted for utensils, stock and goods. [GL, Sun MS vol. 306, p. 456]

Turner, John, 5 Mercer St, London, carver (1785). Took out a Sun Insurance policy on 18 August 1785 for £20 on utensils, stock and goods in trust, and £50 on his house. [GL, Sun MS vol. 330, p. 469]

Turner, John, Scarle (or Searle) St, Lincoln's Inn Fields, London, upholder and cm (1786–93). Trading at no. 5 in 1786 when he took out a Sun Insurance policy on 29 July for £900 including £100 on household goods, and £650 on utensils etc. [D; GL, Sun MS vol. 338, p. 222]

Turner, John, Beak St, London, upholder (1791). See Robert Lambeth at this address.

Turner, John, The Strand, London, cm (1792). Declared bankrupt, *Derby Mercury*, 25 October 1792.

Turner, John, 12 Berwick St, Soho, London, upholder, broker, cm and auctioneer (1791–1815). Took out Sun Insurance policies on 9 December 1791 for £1,300 including £630 on utensils and stock in his house and stable, and £200 on utensils, stock and goods in warehouse behind Duck Lane; on 11 January 1793 for £35 on household goods at 73 Gt Portland St; and on 5 January 1808 for £1,650, £1,000 on utensils and stock. [D; GL, Sun MS vol. 382, ref. 592789; vol. 389, ref. 610487; vol. 440, ref. 812376]

Turner, John, 16 (Gt) Titchfield St, Cavendish Sq., London, cm, u, appraiser and undertaker (*c.*1780–1828). Listed in directories, 1796–1828. Named in Sheraton's list of master cabinet makers, 1803. Trade label reading: 'J. Turner, Upholder, Cabinet Maker, Appraiser & Undertaker, No. 16 Great Titchfield St., Cavendish Sq. NB. Great variety of Paper Hangings', recorded on a George III mahogany partner's desk, *c.*1780, with nine drawers each side and square brass handles; on splayed bracket feet, with shaped aprons. [D]

Turner, John Ward, Liverpool, cm (1800–d.1826). Trading at Pellew St, 1813–16. Admitted freeman on 3 July 1800 on servitude to Thomas Lloyd. Took apps named Robert Tudor in 1804, Cornelius Tudor in 1805 and Thomas Hidley in 1809 (assigned from Edward Myers after serving two years). All three petitioned freedom in 1812. Took apps named John James in 1810 (assigned from Isaac Marsh after three years service), John Hughes in 1805, Richard Holliwell in 1806 and Robert Morrison in 1809, all four petitioning freedom in 1816. Took Charles O'Neill in 1811, petitioned in 1820; Samuel Waters in 1813, admitted freeman in 1830; and Henry Ball (also app. to James Wainwright, cm) in 1814, petitioned freedom in 1822. John Ward Turner died on 29 May 1826. [D; Liverpool freemen reg. and committee bk] Possible confusion with the various John Turners of Liverpool below.

Turner, John, St Mary Arches, Exeter, Devon cm (1803). [Exeter Militia list]

Turner, John Swanton, Pottergate St, Norwich, cm (1805–07). [D]

Turner, John, 46 Devonshire St, Red Lion Sq., London, cm (1809–11). [D]

Turner, John, Halifax, Yorks., cm and u (1814–37). Trading at Crown St, 1814–20; Lister Lane, 1830–37; and Sunderland's Yd, Lister Lane in 1837. [D]

Turner, John, 11 Roscoe St, Liverpool, with shop at Cornwallis St, cm (1810–11). [D]

Turner, John, Liverpool, cm (1818–d. by 1820). Admitted freeman on 11 June 1818. [Liverpool freemen reg.]

Turner, John, Liverpool, cm (1818–37). Addresses given in 1818 at 58 Sawney Pope St, and Stafford Pl., Richmond Row, and 14 Sidney St. Trading at Stafford Pl., 123 Richmond Row in 1835, and no. 126 in 1837. Took app. named Edward Kendall in 1827. [D; Liverpool freemen reg. and app. enrolment bk] Probable confusion between the various John Turners of Liverpool. See John Ward Turner above.

Turner, John, Gold St, Tiverton, Devon, cm (1823–24). [D]

Turner, John, London, cm (1830). [Gt Yarmouth poll bk]

Turner, John, 46 Bishophill, York, cm (1830). [D]

Turner, John, North St, Guildford, Surrey, common carver (1831). [Poll bk]

Turner, John, Pontefract, Yorks., joiner and cm (1834). [D]

Turner, John, 2 Ridgefield, Manchester, cm and u (1834–40). [D]

Turner, John, Alphington St, Exeter, Devon, chairmaker, cm and u (1838). [D]

Turner, Jonas, Meltham, Huddersfield, Yorks., joiner and/or cm (1834). [D]

Turner, Joseph, Newport, Salop, u (d.1680). Buried at St Mary's Church on 1 January 1681. [PR]

Turner, Joseph, Derby, chairmaker (1752). Took app. named Hankinson in 1752. [S of G, app. index]

Turner, Joseph, Chester, cm (1794). App. to Samuel Mercer, cm of Chester. Admitted freeman on 28 June 1794. [Chester freemen rolls]

Turner, Joseph, 4 Red Cross St with shop at Benn's Gdn, Pool Lane, Liverpool, chairmaker and cm (1800–03). [D]

Turner, Joseph, Horse Fair, Bristol, u (1822–23). [D]

Turner, Joshua, address unrecorded, joiner and chairmaker (1701). Supplied a dozen chairs and two stools to Temple Newsam House, Leeds, in 1701. [*Furn. Hist.*, 1967]

Turner, Josiah, address unrecorded, upholder (1758–66). Son of Josiah Turner, victualler of St Marylebone, London. App. to William Adams on 7 September 1758, and admitted freeman of the Upholders' Co. by servitude on 4 December 1766. [GL, Upholders' Co. records]

Turner, Peter, Rotherhithe, London, cm (d.1760). Sale of stock and house advertised on his death in 1760. [Harris & Sons, *Old English Furniture*, p. 28]

Turner, Philip, St Pancras, Chichester, Sussex, chairmaker (1839). [D] See Turner, —, at this address.

Turner, R., 15 Hemming's Row, St Martin's Lane, London, carver, gilder, glass grinder and silverer (1826–27). Simple trade card in GL states 'Gold or Black Frames at One Day's notice'. [D] See T. P. Turner at this address.

Turner, Ralph, Alnwick, Northumb., joiner and cm (1828–29). [D]

Turner, Richard, 49 Oxford St, London, cm and upholder (1777). Took out a Sun Insurance policy in 1777 for £1,000 of which £800 accounted for utensils, stock and goods. [GL, Sun MS vol. 254, p. 253]

Turner, Richard, 30 Ogle St, London, upholder (1779). Took out a Sun Insurance policy in 1779 for £500 including £200 on utensils, stock and goods. [GL, Sun MS vol. 273, p. 296]

Turner, Richard, Henrietta St, London, u (1781–84). [D]

Turner, Richard, Farnham, Surrey, cm and u (1794). [D]

Turner, Richard, Lancaster, cm (1801–02). Admitted freeman, 1801–02, when stated 'of Ravenglass', Cumb. [Lancaster freemen rolls]

Turner, Richard, Manchester, chair bottomer (1808–13). Trading at 3 Foundry St, Red Bank, in 1808 and 28 Scotland Bridge in 1813. [D]

Turner, Robert, Sunderland, Co. Durham, cm (1781–98). Trading at High St in 1784. [D]

Turner, Robert, York, cm (1825). Son of William Turner, yeoman of Clifton. App. to Joseph Marsh, cm on 29 November 1825. [York app. reg.]

Turner, Robert Conway, 22 Bent St, Liverpool, cm (1830). Admitted freeman on 15 November 1830. [Liverpool freemen reg.]

Turner, Robert, Newington, London, carver (1834). Declared bankrupt, *London Gazette*, 14 March 1834.

Turner, Robert, 77 Goodramgate, York, cm etc. (1840). [D]

Turner, Samuel & Edmund, 68 Holborn, London, cm (1786). Took out a Sun Insurance policy on 7 March 1786 for £500 of which utensils accounted for £350. [GL, Sun MS vol. 334, p. 634]

Turner, Samuel, 15 Gt Ancoats St, Manchester, cm (1797). [D]

Turner, Samuel, 24 Nicholas Lane, London (?), upholder (1799). Son of Samuel Turner, shipbuilder of Harwich, Essex. Admitted freeman of the Upholders' Co. by redemption on 3 July 1799. [GL, Upholders' Co. records]

Turner, Samuel, Chester, u and cm (b.1785–d.1828). Trading at Bridge St (Row), 1816–28. Death on 6 February 1828 aged 43, reported in *Liverpool Mercury*, 13 February 1828. His widow, Ann Turner of 33 Bridge St Row, advertised in *Chester Chronicle and North Wales Advertiser*, 7 August 1829, that she was continuing the upholstery and cabinet-making businesses: '...For the UPHOLSTERY she has engaged a VERY COMPETENT PERSON, late in the employ of MESSRS. GILLOW, LONDON, and from his long experience, she has no doubt of giving satisfaction to all those by whom she may be employed. Persons finding their own materials, may have their orders promptly executed in the most fashionable style; for which purpose they will be waited upon either in town or country. She begs further to state, that she has in her service a person well qualified to execute all orders in the cabinet making line, and who is particularly capable of giving the French Polish to all articles of furniture.' See Ann Turner.

Turner, T., 8 Strand, London, u and cm (1792). [D]

Turner, T. P., 15 Hemmings Row, St Martin's Lane, London, carver and gilder (1820). [D] See R. Turner at this address.

Turner, **Thomas**, address unknown, chairmaker. Mark 'THOMAS TURNER' impressed by stamping under the seat of a Windsor chair. The design and construction resemble chairs made in Slough, Bucks. [*Furn. Hist.*, 1978, pl. 54]

Turner (or **Turno(u)r**), **Thomas**, Long Acre, London, cm (1721–48). Trade card and contemporary newspapers record him at 'The Two Golden Balls', near James St, 1746–48. [Heal] Sale of his entire stock on leaving off trade announced in *General Advertiser*, 19 November 1746. Stock consisted of 'all sorts of very neat Cabinet Work, great Variety of LOOKING GLASSES in gold and other Frames and several large Plates of Glass unframed; CHAIRS of most sorts in Walnut Tree and Mahogany. Together with some Upholstery and other Goods. Also his Stock of Wood, Working Benches, Grinding and Silvering Tools etc. . . .'. Probably the Thomas Turner who provided Richard Towneley of Towneley Hall, Lancs., with two large sconces of 'walnuttree frames with glass arms', a chimney glass, picture frames, a dressing table and copper tea table. His bill, dated 15 August 1721, totalled £28 8s 6d. Thomas Turner of Long Acre sent a bill to Ursula Towneley of Towneley Hall, dated 20 December 1735, for mending and polishing a wallnutree writing desk and supplying a wallnutree dressing glass, costing a total of £2 16s. [Preston RO, Towneley papers, DDTO P/10/2 and 16th–17th Peter Rents, 1739] John Turner, cm of Long Acre, was named on 10 June 1741 in a deed of sale of property in Craggs Ct, Middlx, with Robert Lillyman of Middle Temple. [Derbs. RO, Brookhill Hall deeds, 62/4]

Turner, **Thomas**, Kneetford (Knutsford?), Cheshire, cm (1759). Took app. named Orrett in 1759. [S of G, app. index]

Turner, **Thomas**, Cambridge, cm (1780). Insured his house for £200 in 1780. [GL, Sun MS vol. 287, p. 638]

Turner, **Thomas**, 46 Devonshire St, Red Lion Sq., London, u (1809–11). [D]

Turner, **Thomas**, 139 New Bond St, London, u and cm to their Majesties (1809–40). Recorded in partnership with Henry Turner, 1809–25. [D] In 1816 they together submitted a three-page account and business letter concerning furniture supplied to Sir Henry Carr Ibbetson of Denton Hall, Yorks., costing £144 11s 6d. Some items survive at Constable Burton Hall, near Leyburn, Yorks. Thomas alone sent a bill to Sir Henry for £1 8s in 1821, for 'hire of a black stained Easy Chair' for two months. Bill head shows Royal Arms and reads: 'Thomas Turner, UPHOLSTERER & CABINET MANUFACTURER To His Royal Highness the Duke of Clarence. 139, NEW BOND STREET. Army & Navy Equipage. Pleasure Tents made or let on hire. GOODS APPRAISED. FUNERALS FURNISHED. PAPER HANGINGS & DECORATIONS.' [Calder Valley Museum, John F. Goodchild Coll.] The Royal accounts describe the high-quality furniture Turner supplied, 1830–40. The accounts of the quarter ending 5 April 1831 list items supplied to St James's Palace, including a 'Mahog. deep oval foot tub', at £5 12s, four rosewood chairs, £11 12s, a Pembroke table, £6 12s, and mahogany furniture including a 'berjere dressing chair', £9 5s. For Brighton Pavilion Turner provided '12 Japanned chairs' costing £88 4s, and a mahogany 'Bergere dressing chair w. Brass Moulding', £9 5s. Turner also carried out cleaning and upholstery work at St James's Palace and Brighton Pavilion. For Windsor Castle Turner was ordered on 22 August 1832 to supply four Spanish mahogany dwarf wardrobes with sunk pilaster edges to the doors and small carved paterae in the friezes, costing £77 and delivered on 29 September 1832. Items ordered for St James's, and delivered on 5 June 1833 totalled £285 4s 6d and included a Spanish mahogany washing table with tray top, kneehole dressing table on pedestals, and a square footstool covered in needlework, 'for the Queen's use'; four couch bedsteads, seven Honduras mahogany dwarf tray-top wardrobes costing £102 18s; five mahogany writing tables, the tops covered in purple morocco leather, £52 10s; seven more costing £62 9s 6d; ten plain mahogany writing tables, £60; six mahogany pedestal pot stands with tambour sliding fronts and veined marble tops, £36; and twelve mahogany linen airers on claw feet, £13 4s. Further items from Turner were delivered to Windsor Castle on 29 September 1835; '10 large massive sofas, carved wainscot frames, in English gothic, stuffed backs & seats, each with 3 cushions covered with crimson plush, frames French polished, each £48', totalling £485; six large armchairs and twenty-four single chairs to match, totalling £102; '3 octagonal wainscot loo tables, gothic canted pillars, framed quadrangles in blocks, octagon feet and concealed castors, the top lined brown Morocco with gold border, castors, the top lined brown Morocco with gold border, the edge & rim moulded, the whole French polished', each £22 10s; and '6 wainscot occasional tables, tops in brown morocco leather with embossed gold borders, moulded frame, on shaped Gothic standards, octagon feet, concealed castors, each £15. Turner charged £168 15s for 'lengthening out 25 banqueting stools into seats 6ft. long, each new loose frame stuffed and covered with crimson plush, each £6.15s.', and carried out jobbing work at Windsor and Buckingham Palace until 1840. In December 1835 Turner charged £374 4s for altering ten Gothic sofas 'to Elizabethan character' by enriching them with wainscot, buhl, carved lions' heads, and Stars of the Order of the Bath, and making two new ones, for the Waterloo apartments. In September 1837 Turner supplied a satinwood writing table covered in green Morocco leather, and a 'Single Head Couch' stuffed in striped linen, costing £20 15s. [PRO, LC11/71–77, 80, 86, 89, 95–98; Windsor RA, Item 17, Box 1 (Estimates), item 2; E. T. Joy, *English Furniture, 1800–1850*, p. 187] See Henry Turner, J. & H. Turner, Turner & Co., and Turner & Smith.

Turner, **Thomas**, 51 Richmond St, Manchester, cm (1817). [D]

Turner, **Thomas**, York, cm (1823). Son of Thomas Turner. App. to John Taylor, cm on 27 October 1823. [York app. reg.]

Turner, **Thomas**, 29 Market Pl., Alnwick, Northumb., cm and joiner (1834). [D]

Turner, **Thomas**, Somerset Pl., Ripon, Yorks, joiner and/or cm (1834). [D]

Turner, **Thomas**, Dudley, Worcs., cm and u (1838). [D]

Turner, **Thomas**, Wolverhampton St, Dudley, Worcs., carver, gilder, picture frame and looking-glass manufacturer (1840). [D]

Turner, **Thomas**, Russell St, Chester, cm (d.1840). Death aged 60 on 5 November 1840 reported in *Chester Chronicle, Cheshire and North Wales Advertiser*, 13 November.

Turner, **Thomas**, New St, Wellington, Salop, chairmaker and wood turner (1840). [D]

Turner, **W.**, Manchester, chairmaker (b.1803–1819). Charged with being concerned in committing various robberies in *Chester Guardian and Cambrian Intelligence*, 8 April 1819.

Turner, **W. Lord & Co.**, London. Early 19th-century Regency table sold at Christie's 29 March 1984, lot 65 is stamped 'TURNER, W. LORD & CO LONDON

Turner, **W. R.**, 9 Gt Dover St, Southwark, London, looking-glass manufacturer, carver and gilder (1817–25). [D]

Turner, **William**, Lower Brook St, London, carver and gilder (1774). [Poll bk]

Turner, **William**, Snow Hill, Holborn Bridge, London, carver, gilder and printseller (1784–93). Recorded at no. 38 in 1784 and no. 40, 1790–93. Named in Bailey's list of bankrupts, 1789. [D]

Turner, **William**, Chelmsford, Essex, chairmaker (1786–88).

Son William Richard bapt. on 1 October 1786, and daughter Rebecca Rigby on 11 July 1788. [Essex RO, PR (bapt.)]

Turner, William, Liverpool, cm (1777–94). Addresses given at Duke St, 1777–94 and 21 Stanley St in 1781. [D] Notice concerning the assignment of his estate for his creditors, and sale of stock in trade, given in *Williamson's Liverpool Advertiser*, 25 May 1789. Stock consisted of 'Jamaica, Spanish & Honduras MAHOGANY in logs, boards etc. OAK BOARDS & DEALS – The greatest part of which is a heavy cut for the Cabinet-makers use. Any person in want of one or more apprentices to the business of a Cabinet maker, may be accommodated with any number from one to six, who are already well instructed in the business...'. Dividends on his estate and effects announced in the same paper on 11 April 1791, but still listed in a directory of 1794 at Duke St.

Turner, William, Stone, Staffs., cm (1798). [D]

Turner, William, Liverpool, cm (1802–39). Addresses given at 21 Bent St in 1802; 1 Russell Pl. in 1811; 1 Christian St in 1835; 140 Islington in 1837; and 20 Islington in 1839. Admitted freeman on servitude to Samuel Chubbard on 7 July 1802. Assigned app. named John McComb from Mathew Gardner in 1815 after six years service; McComb petitioned freedom in 1818. [D; Liverpool freemen reg. and committee bk]

Turner, William, Lancaster, u (b.1797–d.1837). Admitted freeman, 1817–18. Took an app. on 4 October 1821; one jointly with John Hodgson on 13 June 1825; and one on 8 May 1830. Notice given in *Lancaster Gazette*, 13 May 1826 of the continuing partnership of Turner & Hodgson. Father of Sir William Turner. Died on 7 March 1837 aged 40, and buried in Lancaster Priory Churchyard. [Lancaster app. reg. and freemen rolls]

Turner, William, Bradford St, Birmingham, cm and u (1818–28). Recorded at no. 55 in 1828. [D]

Turner, William, Huddersfield, Yorks., cm and u (1818–30). Trading at 'Top-o'-th'-Town' in 1818 and King St, 1822–30. [D]

Turner, William, Leeds, Yorks., chairmaker (1822–39). Recorded at 14 Marquis of Granby Yd, Quarry Hill, c.1822–37 and 75 Bridge St in 1839. Also listed at 9 Granby Yd, Quarry Hill in 1830. [D]

Turner, William, Low St, St Peter's, York, fancy chairmaker (1822). [D]

Turner, William, Lymington, Hants., cm (1823–24). [D]

Turner, William, Crane St, Chester, u (1826). [Chester freemen rolls and poll bk]

Turner, William, Magdalen St, Colchester, Essex, chairmaker (1826–39). [D]

Turner, William, Bird St, North Shields, Northumb., cm and joiner (1827). [D]

Turner, William, 15 Vine St, Hatton Wall, London, bedstead maker (1829–39). [D]

Turner, William, York, cm (1834). Son of John Turner, paver of Mint Yd, York. App. to John Milner & Thomas Harland, cm on 23 January 1834. [York app. reg.]

Turner, William Macdonald, Tallow Hill, Worcester, carver and gilder (1835). Admitted freeman on 1 December 1835. [Worcester freemen rolls]

Turner, William, 14 Miller St, Manchester, cm (1836–40). Recorded in one directory at no. 18 in 1840. [D]

Turner, William & Co., Church St, Lancaster, chairmaker (1822). [D]

Turner, William, 59 Bath St, City Rd, London, cm and u (1839). [D]

Turner, William, 2 Hampton St, Walworth, London, cm and u (1839). [D]

Turner, William, 52 Ossculton St, Somerstown, London, cm and u (1839). [D]

Turner, William Henry, Old Park, Bristol, u (1839). [D]

Turner & Co., Newington Butts, London, u etc. (1816–19). Trading at no. 16 in 1816 and at Garden Row in 1819. [D]

Turner & Co., 139 New Bond St, London, u (1826–27). [D] See Henry and Thomas Turner and Turner & Smith.

Turner & Ellis, Tipton, Dudley, Worcs., cm and u (1838–39). [D]

Turner & Gee, 49 Wardour St, London. Subscribed to Sheraton's *Cabinet Dictionary*, 1803.

Turner, Hill & Pitter (or Pither), Strand, London. In 1732 made (or provided materials for) the green velvet state bed at Houghton Hall, Norfolk, for Sir Robert Walpole, at a cost of £1,219 3s 11d. [M. Jourdain, *The Work of William Kent*, p. 84]

Turner & Hodgson, Friar St, Lancaster, cm, u and paper hangers (1825). [D]

Turner & Hullah (or Hulloh), 27 Broker's Row, Moorfields, London, u, cm and auctioneers (1803–06). Named in Sheraton's list of master cabinet makers, 1803. [D]

Turner & Smith, London, u and cm (1796–1808). Trading at 132 New Bond St, 1796–1808. Submitted an account covering thirty-one foolscap pages for furniture supplied between August 1798 and April 1803 to the value of £2,315 19s 1d to Sir Henry Carr Ibbetson, Bart of Denton Hall, Yorks. The bill describes pieces of good quality mahogany furniture including bedroom suites, chairs and Pembroke Tables, which are now preserved at Constable Burton Hall, near Leyburn, Yorks. Named in Sheraton's list of master cabinet makers, 1803. [D; Calder Valley Museum, John Goodchild Coll.; *Furn. Hist.*, 1968] See Henry and Thomas Turner and Turner & Co.

Turner & Watkins, 12 Berwick St, Soho, London, cm and u (1805–07). [D]

Turnley, Isaac, Jarvis's Gallery, Francis St, Hull, Yorks., cm (1838–39). [D]

Turnley (or Turnly), John Samuel, Garden Row, London Rd, Southwark, London, fancy chair and sofa manufacturer, cm and u (1805–29). Recorded at no. 1, 1805–07; nos 1 and 2 in 1812; nos 6 and 34 in 1817; as J. Turnley & Co. at no. 1 in 1820; and as Turnley & Sons at no. 1, 1826–29. Named as Turnly in Sheraton's list of master cabinet makers, 1803. Took out a Sun Insurance policy on 20 November 1822 for £1,100 including £400 on warehouses and workshops, £650 on stock, utensils and goods in trust. Three trade cards survive showing furniture of the 2nd quarter of the 19th century. One in the GL reads: 'I. TURNLEY & SONS, Wholesale Manufactory FOR Solid & Imitation Rosewood, Zebra, Mahogany & other Sofas, Chairs, Bedsteads, Bed Pillars, Mattresses, Writing Desks, Tea Caddies, Looking Glasses & every description of CABINET FURNITURE. GARDEN ROAD, SOUTHWARK, London. Mahogany & Veneer Merchants.' Another trade card adds 'Fancy Drawing Room, Solid Rosewood, Mahogany & other Chairs', and states they import Dutch rushes. The third card [Landauer Coll., MMA, NY] is similarly worded. [D; GL, Sun MS vol. 490, ref. 997858; E. T. Joy, *English Furniture, 1800–1851*, p. 221]

Turnock, Daniel, Derby St, Leek, Staffs., cm (1834–35). [D]

Turpin, Richard, Appleton Gate, Newark, Notts., cm and u (1805–22). [D]

Turpin, Robert, Tyne St, North Shields, Northumb., cm (1827–34). Recorded at no. 34 in 1834. [D]

Turpin, Thomas, Pontefract, Yorks., joiner and cm (1834). [D]

Turpin, William, Blue Bell, Brampton, Cumb. joiner and cm (1828–29). [D]

Turrell, J. W., Somerstown, London, cm (1830). [Gt Yarmouth poll bk]

Turrin, William, Bedford St, Covent Gdn, London, cm and glass grinder (1718). Supplied items for the Duke of Montrose's London house in Bond St in 1718, costing a total of £234 15s. The account lists a walnut writing desk and card table, chimney and pier glasses, sconces and 'Bells to sconces with silvered hook', japanned chairs, settee and card table. [Scottish RO, GD 220/6/1192/17] Probably Turene, —, Turin, —, and/or William Turing.

Turtle, John, London, carver and gilder (1809–39). Recorded at Lombard St, 1809–11; and 22 Upper St Martin's Lane, 1835–39, as a furniture broker in 1839. [D]

Turton, James, Gowthorpe, near Selby, Yorks., joiner, cm and u (1826–37). [D]

Turton, John, Rotherham, Yorks., cm (1828–29). [D]

Turton, Joseph, Snaith, near Selby, Yorks., cm (1822). [D]

Turton, Jos., 'Masbro', Rotherham, Yorks., cm (1830). [D]

Turton, William, London (1771). See Lawrence Fell and William Turton.

Turvin, Samuel, Berwick-upon-Tweed, Northumb., upholder (1741). Took app. named Williamson in 1741. [S of G, app. index]

Tushaine, —, address unrecorded, carver (1706). Recorded in the Castle Howard, Yorks. archives in the Mason's & Carpenter's Book, 1702–08. [Beard, *Georgian Craftsmen*]

Tuson, Robert, probably London, cm and u (1759–75). Supplied furniture to Charles Rogers, a distinguished connoisseur and collector of London. Tuson's name first appears in his accounts on 14 July 1759, 'covering the Reading Chair with Horsehair', for £1 1s; and on 25 October 1759 charging £23 for 'an Amboyna Cabinet, Table, &c.' On 18 September 1760 he supplied a 'large Amboina Slab Table' for £6 18s, and a 'Mohogony Claw reading Table', £1 11s 6d; on 1 July 1767, '28 Mahogany Frames vaneered with Amboina at 7sh each, with Hooks', £10; on 23 December 1772 'a Sarcophagus-like Cabinet', £17 15s, and on 17 January 1775 'a Lion's tail of Mahogony for the Sarcophagus', 17s. The sarcophagus cabinet is now in the Plymouth City Museum and Art Gallery. The doors and sides are carved with serpentine fluting in the manner of certain Roman sarcophagi, and it stands of four ponderous, well-carved paw-feet. Another central support in the form of a lion's tail was later added to the front. [C. Musgrave, *Adam and Hepplewhite Furniture*, p. 127; *Apollo*, December 1960, pp. 196–98] See Thomas Wood, connected with the amboyna cabinet supplied on 25 October 1759.

Tuson, Roger, Dorington St, Brook's Mkt, London, cm (1784). [Bristol poll bk]

Tustian, Thomas, Bett's St, St George's in the East, London, cm (1784). [Bristol poll bk]

Tustian, William, Whitechapel, London, cm (1768–70). Advertised in *Cambridge Chronicle and Journal*, September 1768–70, that he had a booth at the annual Stirbitch (Stourbridge) Fair held in September just outside Cambridge, where he sold mahogany and walnut furniture of his own manufacture 'with proper allowances to those who sell again'. [*Furn. Hist.*, 1978] Declared bankrupt, *Gents Mag.*, August 1770.

Tustin, Thomas, St Thomas's, Bristol, cm (1774–84). Supplied furniture to Rev. Hodges of Glos., costing a total of £26 5s 2d. His bill mentions two sets of chairs, of which a mahogany oval-back chair and two of a set of six elbow chairs painted with red decoration on a white ground, survive in the family. [Poll bks; Bristol Art Gallery files]

Tute, William, Sawney Pope St and Stafford Pl., Richmond Row, Liverpool, cm (1830). App. to John Mears, and admitted freeman on 13 November 1830. [Liverpool freemen reg.]

Tutoft (or Tut(t)op), Charles, Westminster, London, cm and upholder (1749–99). Polled as Tutoft of Broad Way in 1749;

and recorded in directories as Tutop at Tothill St, 1781–99. Subscribed to Chippendale's *Director*, 1754. Took app. named Thomas Bennet in 1756 for £15 15s. Death reported in *Gents Mag.*, September 1785, so his business was presumably continued in his name, or by a tradesman of the same name. [D]

Tutson, —, address unrecorded, cm (d.1746). Notice in *General Advertiser*, 27 June 1746 read: 'On Monday last a Cart being overturned near Great Pandon [Great Parndon] in Essex, the Horse was hung, and Mr. Tutson, a Cabinet Maker who was passing by, endeavouring to disengage the poor Creatures, receiv'd a Kick on the Thigh, which broke it and he died in a very few Hours.'

Tutt, Henry, Market St, Rye, Sussex, cm and paper hanger (1832). [D]

Tutt, John, Rye, Sussex, cm (1830). Declared bankrupt, *London Gazette*, 21 May 1830.

Tutt, Samuel, Chichester, Sussex, turner and bedstead maker (1823–26). Recorded at St Pancras in 1823 and Canal Basin in 1826. [D]

Tutton, James, Broad St, St Giles's, London, carver and gilder (1789). [D]

Tutton, John, address unrecorded, u (1818). Supplied two sets of scalloped-edge book shelves, painted 'mineral green' for Georgina, Duchess of Bedford, at a cost of one guinea in 1818. [Bedford Office, London]

Tuxford, John Lefevere, Church St, Boston, Lincs., cm (1835). [D]

Twaddel, William, Hanover St, Long Acre, London, glass grinder (1769–70). In 1769 supplied eighteen plates of looking-glass, 27¼ × 17½ inches to Robert Adam for use at Kenwood, Middlx. The receipted bill for £19 7s is dated 10 February 1770. [Wills, *Looking-Glasses*]

Twanbrook(e), Edward, Chester, cm (1698–1728). Son of Edward Twanbrook, Gent., late of Wallback, Daresbury. App. to William Ingham, cm of Chester, after 1690, and admitted freeman in March 1698. Took apps named Cottingham in 1717, Joseph Burrowes in 1720, and Thomas Calkin in 1725. Former app., Samuel Smith, admitted freeman in September 1721. Elected councilman in 1720. 1728 complaint was made against Twanbrook for obstructing the shop of R. Hackney, glass grinder, in Fairtime. [S of G, app. index; Chester app. bks, freemen rolls and City records]

Tweddle, Henry, King's Arms Lane, Carlisle, Cumb., carver and gilder (1834). [D]

Tweed, James, London, cm, u, chair and bedstead manufacturer (1820–28). Recorded at 118 Rosemary Lane, 1820–27, Darby St, Rosemary Lane in 1824, as James & Co. in 1825 and at 13 Globe Rd, Mile End Rd, 1827–28. Declared bankrupt, *Brighton Gazette*, 20 May 1824. [D]

Tweedy, Joseph, Whickham, Co. Durham, joiner, carpenter and/or cm (1834). [D]

Twemlow (or Twamlow), John, Congleton, Cheshire, cm (b.1777–d.1830). Trading at Market Pl., 1816–18 and High St, 1822–28. Death aged 53 on 20 March 1830 reported in *Chester Courant and Anglo-Welsh Gazette*, 6 April. [D]

Twemlow (or Twamlow), Ralph, Congleton, Cheshire, cm (1789–93). Trading at High Town, 1789–90. [D]

Twentyman, Daniel, Workington, Cumb., joiner, cm and/or looking-glass silverer (1828–34). Trading at Jane St in 1829 and Washington St in 1834. [D]

Twiddy, George, St Michael at Thorn, Norwich, u (1784–86). [Poll bks]

Twiddy, James, St Michael at Thorn, Norwich, cm (1827–30). Son of James Twiddy, cordwainer; admitted freeman on 5 May 1827. [Norwich freemen reg. and poll bk]

Twigg, William, Uppingham, Rutland, saddler and u (1741). Took app. named Browne in 1741. [S of G, app. index]

Twiggs, Edward, Exeter, Devon, cm and u (1823–40). Trading at Coombe St, 1823–31, and Mint Lane, 1834–40. Sons, both William, bapt. at St Mary Major on 18 May 1823, and 12 October 1831; daughters Frances on 12 January 1827; and Matilda at St Olave's on 7 February 1836. [D; *Exeter Pocket Journal*; PR (bapt.)]

Twiggs, Henry, Exeter, Devon carver and gilder (1829–32). Twiggs, carver and gilder of Theatre St had son Henry bapt. at St Paul's on 20 May 1829. Listed at Coffin's Pl., High St, 1830–32. [D; *Exeter Pocket Journal*; PR (bapt.)]

Twisse, William, Dorchester, Dorset, u (1702). Paid 5s to be admitted freeman of the Borough of Dorchester Co. on 24 September 1702. [Mayo & Gould, *Municipal Records of the Borough of Dorchester*, p. 428]

Twisse, William, London, upholder (1712). App. to his father of the same name in June 1712. [GL]

Twist, John, Devonshire Pl., Commercial Rd, London, cm, u and chairmaker (1823–28). Trading at no. 2, 1823–24. Took out Sun Insurance policies on 20 October 1823 and 19 January 1824 for £450 on stock, utensils and goods in trust or on commission in workshop at the corner of Barossa St, Commercial Rd. [D; GL, Sun MS vol. 494, refs 1008873 and 1012572]

Twist, John, Whitechapel Rd, London, furniture broker, cm and u (1826–28). Trading at no. 181 as a broker, 1826–27, and no. 194 as cm and u, 1827–28. [D]

Twist, Samuel, Burscough St, Ormskirk, Lancs., cm (1825). [D]

Twitty, James, Worcester, cm and joiner (1779–80). Former apps admitted freemen: Francis Price in 1779 and Thomas Smith in 1780. [Worcester freemen rolls]

Twyman, Stephen, 56 High St, Ramsgate, Kent, cm (1838). [D]

Tyler, —, London, cm (1769–86). Supplied furniture and furnishings for a house in Hertford St in 1769 for which he received payments of £17 5s 6d, £145 8s 6d and £16 4s 6d. The patron is not specified. Further small payments were made in 1784–86. [Scottish RO, GD 157/814–5] Possibly Joseph Tyler.

Tyler, Frederick, Potter St, Bishop's Stortford, Herts., carver and gilder (1838). [D]

Tyler, George, The Shambles, Worcester, chairmaker (1820–40). Listed at Bank St, 1820. [D] Succeeded by Mary Tyler, possibly his widow or daughter, at The Shambles.

Tyler, Henry John, London, cm and u (1826–35). Trading at 47 Tabernacle Walk, Windmill St, Finsbury, 1826–27, no. 46, 1827–29, and Brittania Row, Hoxton, in 1835. [D]

Tyler, John, London, looking-glass frame maker (1784–1830). [Colchester poll bks]

Tyler, John, 64 Banner St, Old St, London, cm, upholder and undertaker (1817–29). [D] See Samuel Tyler and Tyler & Son at this address.

Tyler, Joseph, London. The Duke of Gordon's accounts for 1738 record items provided by Tyler for his London houses: 'A chimney glass in a walnut frame', costing £2 19s; and 'A chimney glass in a carved & gilt frame', £6 4s. [Scottish RO, GD 44/51/26] Possibly:

Tyler, Joseph, London, cm, carver and u (1754–84). Recorded at St Anne's, Westminster, 1759–62, Wardour St, Soho in 1763, and no. 54 in 1779. Subscribed to Chippendale's *Director*, 1754. Took apps named William Dixon in 1759 for £40, and John Foster in 1762 for £42. Listed in statements regarding working conditions of journeymen, cm and chairmakers in *Lloyds Evening Post and British Chronicle*, 1761. Subscribed to Thomas Mortimer's *Universal Director*, 1763. Took out a Sun Insurance policy in 1779 for £700 of which £200 accounted for utensils and stock. Polled at

Westminster in 1784. [D; GL, Sun MS vol. 272, p. 47; Lewis notes on Chippendale subscribers]

Tyler, Joseph, Broad St, Bloomsbury, London, cm, u, chair and sofa manufacturer (1815–39). Recorded at no. 58 in 1815, 1820 and 1826–39; and no. 57, 1816–19 and 1825. [D]

Tyler, Joseph, 22 Pithay Bristol, cm and u (1833–35). [D]

Tyler, Mary, The Shambles, Worcester, chairmaker (1835–37). [D] Possibly widow or daughter of George Tyler, who she succeeded.

Tyler, Robert, 30 Castle St, Leicester Sq., London, cm and u (1839). [D]

Tyler, St John, Boston, Lincs., cm (1826). [D]

Tyler, Samuel, 47 Long Lane, West Smithfield, London, cm (1777). Took out a Sun Insurance policy in 1777 for £200 of which utensils and stock accounted for £60. [GL, Sun MS vol. 255, p. 56]

Tyler, Samuel, 64 Banner St, Bunhill Row, London, cm and undertaker (1805–11). [D] See John Tyler and Tyler & Son at this address.

Tyler, William, 22 Chapel St, Paddington, London, cm and upholder (1820). [D]

Tyler & Allchin, 4 Trien St, Theobalds Rd, London, chair and sofa makers (1839). [D]

Tyler & Son, 64 Banner St, Bunhill Row, London, cm, u and undertakers (1820–28). [D] See John and Samuel Tyler at this address.

Tymperon, Robert, Stamford, Lincs., cm (1726–72). Taken as app. in 1739 and admitted freeman in 1749; but also recorded as having taken apps named Manby in 1726, Frisby in 1752 and Girling in 1758, so certainly two tradesmen of the same name are concerned here. Advertised in *Cambridge Chronicle*, 24 December 1762 that he had purchased the stock of the late John Cook, u of Stamford. In 1772 Henry Tatam, cm did fealty for a tenement in Butcher Row, late Robert Tymperon. Both Tatam and Tymperon were employed by the 9th Earl of Exeter. Tymperon appears in the Burghley Estate account books for many years, and supplied an upholstered sofa bed in 1750. Later in the century he received a pension. [S of G, app. index; C. *Life*, 29 August 1974, pp. 562–64; V&A archives] See Henry Tatam.

Tymwoll, Edward, Plymouth, Devon, cm (1711). Took app. named Collins in 1711. [S of G, app. index]

Tyndal(l) (or Turndall), Athelston(e) (or Athelstane), Bristol, upholder (1715–39). Took app. named Raymond in 1717. Polled in 1715; of Christ Church parish in 1722, St John's in 1734 and St Augustine's in 1739. [S of G, app. index]

Tyne, Benjamin, 3 Berry St, Liverpool, u (1827). [D] See Bartholomew and Martin Tyrer.

Tyrer, Bartholomew, Liverpool, u (1810–39). Addresses given at Pitt St, 1811–23; no. 39 in 1824; 3 Knight St in 1827; 1 Berry St, 1827–29; no. 2 in 1834; also 4 Roscoe St, 1827–34; 5 Berry St and 19 Roscoe St in 1835; 3 Berry St and 10 Roscoe St in 1837; and 66 Roscoe St in 1839. Son of Bartholomew Tyrer, tallow chandler. Admitted freeman on 8 November 1810. Took app. named Thomas Little and Edward Marshall in 1810; and Charles Brandreth in 1811 (after two years service with Thomas Savage Tyrer snr), all three petitioning freedom in 1818. Took apps named Nathan Dutton in 1818, Samuel Hughes in 1819, William Pearson in 1821, Daniel Thistleton in 1822, Thomas Rose in 1824, Joseph Peppitt in 1825, James Guy in 1826, John Haigh in 1827, Samuel Kay in 1828, William Swann and Thomas Green in 1830, John Fisher in 1832, and John Bennet in 1835. Took app. named Thomas Savage Tyrer jnr in 1827, admitted freeman in 1835. [D; Liverpool freemen reg., committee bk and app. enrolment bk] See Benjamin Tyne and Martin Tyrer.

Tyrer, George, 57 Fontenoy St, Liverpool, cm (1823). [D]

Tyrer, James, Liverpool, cm (1812–27). Addresses given at Essex St, Toxteth Park in 1812; 20 Hodson St in 1816; 8 Adlington St in 1821; no. 3 in 1824; and 5 Edward St in 1827. Admitted freeman on servitude to Thomas Savage Tyrer snr on 5 October 1812. [D; Liverpool freemen reg.]

Tyrer, John, Ker St, Devonport, Devon, carver and gilder (1838). [D]

Tyrer, Martin, 5 Berry St, Liverpool, cm and u (1835). [D] See Benjamin Tyne and Bartholomew Tyrer.

Tyrer, Richard, Liverpool, cm (1780–1806). Petitioned and admitted freeman on servitude to Richard Tyrer in 1780, paying 6s 8d. His son, James Tyrer, painter, born 1781, petitioned freedom on birthright in 1806. [Liverpool freemen's committee bk]

Tyrer, Robert, Liverpool, joiner and cm (1780–d. by 1795). Recorded at Old Hall St in 1782. Admitted freeman in 1780. His son, William Tyrer, joiner, petitioned freedom on birthright in 1784. Took app. named William Swain in 1785, petitioned freedom in 1796; and John Ratcliffe in 1790, petitioned in 1799. Declared bankrupt, *Williamson's Liverpool Advertiser*, 29 June 1780. Notice given in same paper, 10 January 1782 of the assignment of his estate and effects for his creditors, and sale by auction of the house, workshop and yard in Old Hall St occupied by Tyrer. Notice in *Billinge's Liverpool Advertiser*, 20 July 1795, concerned dividends on the bankruptcy in 1780 of Robert Tyrer, now deceased. [Liverpool freemen's committee bk]

Tyrer, Thomas Savage snr, Liverpool, cm (1796–d.1811). Addresses given at 63 Park Lane in 1804, no. 71 in 1805, no. 72 in 1807, and 28 Stanhope St, 1810–11. Admitted freeman in 1796. Took apps named Thomas Blayney in 1802, James Taylor in 1803, and James Tyrer in 1804, all three petitioning freedom in 1812; and Charles Brandreth in 1809, later assigned to Bartholomew Tyrer and petitioning freedom in 1818. Died in December 1811. [D; Liverpool freemen's committee bk]

Tyrer, Thomas Savage jnr, Berry St, Liverpool, u (1835–37). Listed at 19 Hill St, Harrington, 1837. Admitted freeman on servitude to Bartholomew Tyrer on 2 July 1835. [D; Liverpool freemen reg.]

Tyrer, William jnr, Tyrer St North, Liverpool, cm (1820). Admitted freeman on 7 March 1820. By 1833 a different hand had annotated 'Reverend' and crossed out 'junior' and 'cabinet maker' in the Liverpool freemen reg.

Tyrer, Wilkinson & Co., Lord St, Preston, Lancs., cm (1802–05). Signed the *Preston Cabinet Makers' and Chair Makers' Book of Prices*, 1802, on behalf of the masters. [D]

Tyr(r)ell, George, London, carver and gilder (1821–39). On 21 June 1821 Tyrell, carver and gilder of Warwick Pl., Bedford Row, Bloomsbury, insured a house in tenure from Nathaniel Stainton at 29 Drury Lane. George Tyrrell was trading at 1 Warwick Pl., 1826–27 and 72 Chancery Lane, c.1835–39. [D; GL, Sun MS vol. 488, ref. 980796] See Nathaniel Stainton.

Tyrrell, J., 262 Whitechapel Rd, London, cm and u (1839). [D]

Tyrrell, Robert, address unrecorded, upholder (1700). Admitted freeman of the Upholders' Co. on 7 August 1700. [GL, Upholders' Co. records]

Tyrrell, Timothy, Reading, Berks. and London, upholder (1769–1802). Recorded at Minster St, Reading in 1778; Salisbury Ct, Fleet St, London in 1781; and Queen St, Cheapside in 1786. Son of Timothy Tyrrell. App. to John Underwood snr or jnr, on 7 June 1769, and admitted freeman of the Upholders' Co. by servitude on 3 July 1776. Recorded as a City Remembrancer in 1794 and 1802. In 1761 his father, Timothy Tyrrell snr rented a house in Reading to the father of the architect, Sir John Soane. Timothy jnr was a life-long

friend of Soane, to whom his son, Charles, was articled, 1811–17. [GL, Upholders' Co. records; D. Stroud, *The Architecture of Sir John Soane*, 1961]

Tyrrell, William, address unrecorded, u (1710). Supplied to Hatfield House, Herts., a wainscot bedstead costing £10 10s, six walnut chair frames, £3 3s, and two walnut square stools, 12s. [Hatfield House MS Bills 459]

Tyson, George, 45 West Bar Green, Sheffield, Yorks., fancy chairmaker and earthenware dealer (1822). [D]

Tyson, James, 42 Solly St, Sheffield, Yorks., chairmaker (1830). [D]

Tyson, Joseph, Lancaster, chairmaker and candlebox maker (b.1738–d.1803). Between 1 January 1779 and 6 December 1797 took five app. chairmakers. Polled in 1784. Died on 16 February 1803 aged 65, and buried in Lancaster Priory Churchyard. [Lancaster Ref. Lib.]

Tyson, M., Lancaster. Named in the Gillow records, 1827–29. [Westminster Ref. Lib.]

Tyte, James, 29 Chancery Lane, London, cm and u (1786–94). Took out a Sun Insurance policy on 24 July 1786 for £2,500 including £400 on his house and workshops, and £1,200 on utensils, stock and goods in trust. [D; GL, Sun MS vol. 338, p. 195] Heal records him as James Tysse.

Tyte, Richard, address unrecorded, upholder (1712–19). Son of Richard Tyte, labourer of Stepney, Middlx. App. to George Walker on 3 September 1712 and admitted freeman of the Upholders' Co. by servitude on 9 September 1719. [GL, Upholders' Co. records] Presumably brother of:

Tyte, William, address unrecorded, upholder (1718–33). Son of Richard Tyte, labourer of St Leonard, Shoreditch, Middlx. App. to George Walker on 3 September 1718, and admitted freeman of the Upholders' Co. by servitude on 6 October 1725. Took app. named William Simpson, 1725–32/33. [GL, Upholders' Co. records]

Tytherleigh, Arthur, Harvey's Buildings, High St, Taunton, Som., cm (1830). [D]

Tytler, William, address unrecorded, cm (1803). Subscribed to Sheraton's *Cabinet Dictionary*, 1803.

U

Ubank, (or Ewbank), Thomas, York, u (1721). App. to Barnaby Bawtry, u on 1 August 1721. [York app. reg.]

Ubank, William, Netherend, Penrith, Cumb., cm and/or joiner (1828–34). [D]

Ubsdell, John Talbot, Mount Ephraim, Tunbridge Wells, Kent, Tunbridge-ware manufacturer (1829–34). Named in the Speldhurst rate bks in 1829. [D; Kent RO, P344/11/1]

Udall, C. & Co., Winchmore Hill, London, u and cm (1838). [D]

Udell, Jacob, Friar's Gate, Derby, joiner and cm (1809). [D]

Ullathorne, John, Millgate, Selby, Yorks., cm, joiner (and shopkeeper?) (1822–37). [D]

Ullman, —, corner of Little Wild St, Lincoln's Inn Fields, London, cm (1747). Named in contemporary newspapers. [Heal]

Umfreville, —, Long Acre, London, cm (d. 1753). Notice in *Public Advertiser*, 15 June 1753 read: 'Yesterday died of a Paralytic Disorder Mr. Umfrevill, Cabinet Maker in Long Acre.'

Umphry, —, London, u (1715–21). Trading at 'The Drake', Fleet St in 1715, and moved to the lower end of Drake's Yd, Fleet St in 1721. Named concerning a Sun Insurance policy taken out by Thomas Huxley on 16 April 1715. [GL, Sun MS vol. 4, p. 233]

Umpleby, John, Leeds, Yorks., joiner and cm (1798–1837). Recorded at Ebenezer St in 1798; 3 Green Row, Brewery Field in 1826; Williams Row, Brewery Field, 1828–30; and Saracen's Head Yd, 24 Boar Lane, 1834–37. [D]

Umpleby, John, High St, Knaresborough, Yorks., joiner, cm and builder (1828–34). [D]

Underdown, Philip, 254 Strand, London, cm and chair manufacturer (1789–93). [D]

Underhill, J., 37 Goswell St, London, cm and ironmonger (1794–96).

Underhill, T., 37 Goswell St, London, cm and ironmonger (1800). [D]

Underhill, Timothy, Church Side, Macclesfield, Cheshire, u (1828). [D]

Underhill, William, 11 Henrietta St, Manchester Sq., London, upholder (1801). Took out a Sun Insurance policy on 25 July 1801 for £150. [GL, Sun MS vol. 419, ref. 721470]

Underwood, —, Villiers St, York Buildings, London, cm (1768–74). Notice in *Public Advertiser*, 3 August 1768 concerned 'a Servant of Mr Underwood, a Cabinet-maker in Villiers Street . . .'. Mary Rudyard insured her goods at Mr Underwood's house, no. 5 Villiers St, on 16 November 1774. [GL, Sun MS vol. 235] See Richard and Thomas Underwood.

Underwood, A., 105 Long Alley, Finsbury, London, u (1839). [D]

Underwood, Francis, Liverpool, cm (1823). App. to Cattrall & Whittingham in 1823. [Liverpool app. enrolment bk]

Underwood, Hugh, Scarborough, Yorks., cm (1754–98). Subscribed to Chippendale's *Director*, 1754. Took app. named John Hardy in 1758 for £5 5s. Listed in a directory of 1798. [S of G, app. index]

Underwood, James, Northampton, u (1712). Took app. named Brown in 1712. [S of G, app. index]

Underwood, James, address unrecorded, upholder (1723–32). Son of John Underwood, jeweller of London. App. to Ezra Doughty on 3 April 1723 and admitted freeman of the Upholders' Co. by servitude on 7 June 1732. [GL, Upholders' Co. records]

Underwood, John snr, London, upholder (1714–76?). Son of John Underwood, silversmith of St Martin's le Grand, Middlx. App. to Samuel Abbott on 10 May 1714, and admitted freeman of the Upholders' Co. by servitude on 4 July 1722. Took apps named Nicholas Ham, 1722–29; Thomas Perrott, 1730–37/38; Thomas Spencer, 1733–40/41; Joseph Buckle, 1734–42, and his son, John Underwood jnr, 1741–48. [GL, Upholders' Co. records]

Underwood, John jnr, London, upholder (1741–76?). Son of John Underwood, freeman upholder of London. App. to his father on 6 May 1741, and admitted freeman of the Upholders' Co. by servitude on 2 June 1748. Took app. named Timothy Tyrrell, 1769–76. [GL, Upholders' Co. records]

Underwood, John, address unrecorded, cm (1803). Subscribed to Sheraton's *Cabinet Dictionary*, 1803.

Underwood, John, Mount St, Birmingham, gilder (1818). [D] See Joseph Underwood at this address.

Underwood, John & Son, address unrecorded, cm and u (1816–19). Sent a three-page account to George, 2nd Baron Lyttelton of Hagley Hall, Worcs. for furniture supplied and work done between 1816–19, totalling £226 6s 10¼d. Receipted by William Underwood on 30 September 1819. Items listed are chiefly bedding and upholstery materials and papering, but several pieces of mahogany furniture are listed, including a Pembroke table, £3 3s; six brass-nailed chairs and two matching elbow chairs, £16 13s; a night chair, £2 10s; a six-legged dining table with circle ends, £14 10s; a card table, £3 3s; bureau, £7 7s; and a pillar and claw Pembroke table,

£4 14s. Underwood's also provided '6 Cane Coloured Chairs Cane Seats' for £4 13s; a 'Four Post Bedstead and Cornish', £4 10s 6d; and '2 Grecian Cane Coloured Chairs' with two elbow chairs to match, £3 17s 6d. [Worcs. RO, Lyttelton MS, 5467/705:658/122 (i)]

Underwood, Joseph, Mount St, Birmingham, gilder in general (1805–18). [D]

Underwood, Lau., address unrecorded. Mahogany bow-fronted two-drawer side table recorded with 'Lau. Underwood June 28th 1804' written on the frame.

Underwood, Lawrence, Hadleigh, Suffolk, cm and mason (1824–39). Recorded at High St, 1830–39. [D]

Underwood, Richard, Villiers St, York Buildings, Strand, London, cm (1754–64). A Richard Underwood subscribed to Chippendale's *Director*, 1754. Of Villiers, (or Villars) St, mentioned in Thomas Mortimer's *Universal Director*, 1763; and directories, 1763–64. See Underwood, —, and Thomas Underwood at this address.

Underwood, Thomas, Villiers St, York Buildings, Strand, London, cm (1774). [Poll bk]

Underwood, Thomas, Stonegate, York, cm (1823). [D]

Underwood, William, Stourbridge, Worcs., cm and u (1818–35). Recorded as William Underwood & Son, High St, 1818–22; and alone at Hospital Rd in 1830 and New Rd in 1835. [D]

Unicuna, (or Unicum), Christopher, East Grinstead, Sussex, chairmaker and turner (1823–26). [D]

Unsworth, Edward, 19 Prescott St, Liverpool, cm (1834–37). [D]

Unsworth, Robert, Front St, Gateshead, Co. Durham, joiner and cm (1824–27). [D]

Unthank, William, Priestgate, Darlington, Co. Durham, joiner and cm (1827–34). [D]

Unthank, William, Stockton-on-Tees, Co. Durham, joiner and cm (1827–32). Trading at Church Row in 1827 and High St, 1828–32. Notice regarding dividends of his estate on bankruptcy given in *Durham Advertiser*, 11 March 1831. [D]

Unwin, Charles, Westbar, Sheffield, Yorks., cm and u (1833–37). Trading at no. 43 in 1833 and no. 49 in 1837. [D]

Unwin, George, Bedford Ct, Covent Gdn, London, u (1727). Took out a Sun Insurance policy on 16 March 1727 for £300 on his goods and stock. [GL, Sun MS vol. 434, ref. 41076]

Unwin, John, 'against yᵉ Academy, the upper end of Great Tower Street, London,' cm, sworn appraiser, joiner and chapman (1739–40). Trade card in the Museum of London [A9986] has invoice for £4 10s on the back, dated 23 May 1739. Card reads: 'Makes & Sells all Sorts of Cabinet Goods with Coach & Pier Glasses, Chimney Glasses & Sconces, Brass Arms, Shandiliers & fine Glass Lanthorns all Sorts of Picture Frames Mohogany & Wallnut Chairs, Clocks and Clock Cases also Buys and Sells all Sorts of Household Goods. Funeralls Decently Furnished.' Declared bankrupt, *Daily Post*, 19 May 1740.

Unwin, John, Nottingham, u (b. 1717–54). Named in the Nottingham burgess list, 1737. Married on 10 December 1743, aged 26. Polled of Backside in 1754. [Notts. RO, marriage licence index]

Unwin, Paul, London, carver and gilder (1762). Gillow of Lancaster ordered the following items from Unwin on 17 August 1762: 'two or four carved & gilt sconces, with canopies & side-pieces at 31/6, two walnut sconces shaft inside with carving & gildeg, scrawles, Birds & side pieces at 35s'. [V & A archives]

Unwin, William, Well St, Hanley, Staffs., cm (1818). [D]

Upton, David, Manchester and Salford, u (1829–39). Addresses given at 13 Cross St, King St, Manchester in 1829, no. 22,

1832–33; and 12 New Bailey St, Salford in 1838, also as a cm. Trading with James Upton in 1839. [D]

Upton, James, 12 New Bailey St, Salford, Lancs., cm and u (1839–40). Trading with David Upton in 1839. [D]

Upton, John, 1 King Lane, Tysen St, Church St, Bethnal Green, London, cm (1800). Took out a Sun Insurance policy on 21 April 1800 for £200 on his new house, workshop, warehouse, all communicating, and household goods. [GL, Sun MS vol. 418, ref. 702087]

Upton, John James, 15 Upper Russell St, Brighton, Sussex, cm and furniture broker (1838–39). [D]

Upton, Philip, St George the Martyr, London, cm (1754–56). Subscribed to Chippendale's *Director*, 1754. Took app. named John Reed in 1756 for £15. [V & A archives]

Upton, William, Portsea, Portsmouth, Hants., cm, u and auctioneer (1785–98). Trading at Butcher St on 29 July 1785 when he took out a Sun Insurance policy for £225 on utensils and stock in his workshop and storehouse. [D; GL, Sun MS vol. 330, p. 326]

Upton, William, Brighton, Sussex, Tunbridge-ware manufacturer (1815–62). Addresses given at Trafalgar Pl. in 1815; New Rd, 1818–21; 26 East St and 6 Boyces St in 1823; 5 Somerset Pl. and Pool Lane in 1828; 1 Kensington Pl. in 1834; 94 Gloucester Lane in 1838; and at various addresses until 1862. Daughters bapt. on 14 February 1815 and 29 September 1819; sons, both William, on 20 September 1818 and 28 December 1821. Named in the Brighton poor rate bk, 1 April 1822, and rate bks, 1834–35. [D; E. Sussex RO, PR (bapt.)]

Urch, James, 'Queen Adelaide', 199 Temple St, Bristol, cm and beer retailer (1825–32). [D]

Urch & Seabright, Gloucester Pl., Cheltenham, Glos., cm and u (1839). [D]

Ure, John, London, upholder (1780–95). Trading at St Paul's Churchyard in 1780; with William Ure as bedding & carpet warehouseman at no. 26 in 1783; and alone at Blackman St in 1795. Admitted freeman of the Upholders' Co. on 5 July 1780. [D; GL, Upholders' Co. records]

Urio, John, 14 Hanover St, Bristol, picture frame maker (1814–17). [D]

Urmson, Elizabeth, Warrington, Lancs., later Liverpool, u (1767–88). Sale of her stock in trade and letting of her house and shop on her leaving Warrington advertised in *Williamson's Liverpool Advertiser*, 30 October 1767. Recorded at Derby Sq., Liverpool, 1772–73; 38 Castle St, 1774–77; in partnership with Mathew Gregson, cm and u, there, 1778–81, and Preesons Row, 1787. Gregson worked for her during his apprenticeship to William Litherland, u, and entered into a formal partnership with her in 1778, dissolved in 1788. Together they took out a Sun Insurance policy in 1781 for £900 of which utensils and stock accounted for £800. Probably widow of John Urmson, u, recorded in the Liverpool freemen reg. as having 'died before 1768'. [D; GL, Sun MS vol. 294, p. 120; Liverpool records] See Matthew Gregson.

Urmston, John, Liverpool, u (1750–d. by 1768). Admitted freeman on 13 March 1750. Probably the Urmson, who is recorded as having 'died by 1768', and was succeeded by his widow, Elizabeth. [Liverpool freemen reg.]

Urquart, William, Winchester, Hants., upholder (1784). [D]

Urquhart, Thomas, Lord St, Liverpool, u and carpet dealer (1833–39). Trading at no. 59 in 1833; no. 53 in 1835; no. 65 with shop at no. 54 in 1837; and no. 76 in 1839. Advertised in *Liverpool Mercury*, 4 October 1833, his stock of 'New Patterns in CARPETS', and announced 'that he has added to his Establishment the manufacture of BEDS, MATTRESSES, PAILLASSES, & SEA BEDDING, of every description. His FEATHERS being purified by Steam upon an entirely new

principle, he warrants free from smell, & fit for immediate use. Fore-post, Camp & Tent Beds always on hand ... MORINE, DAMASK, LONDON PRINTED FLOOR CLOTH etc. Upholstery in all its Branches. Export & Ship Orders executed with punctuality & despatch.' [D]

Urry, H. R., High St, Newport, Isle of Wight, Hants., cm and u (1839). [D]

Urry, Thomas, Quay St, Newport, Isle of Wight, Hants., cm, u and military trunk maker (1830). [D]

Urry, William, Bargate, Gt Grimsby, Lincs., joiner and cm (1831). [D]

Ursell, Edward, 35 Piccadilly, Manchester, chairmaker (1832–33). [D]

Urwick (?), Thomas, Bond St, London, u (1790). A long bill from Urwick (?), dated 7 February 1790 and totalling £126 2s 6d, survives in the Lincoln RO. It lists mainly repairs to furnishings and curtains, but also refers to 'a New Mahogany Stool for Hall' costing 6s. [9/18/2]

Usher, James, Shaftesbury, Dorset, chairmaker (1755). Took app. named Ellis in 1755. [S of G, app. index]

Usher, James, Lincoln, cabinet and clockcase maker. Label recorded on longcase, *c.* 1800, in oak with mahogany crossbanding and some inlay, for clock by William Smith of Crowland, Lincs. Other Usher labelled longcases have been noticed containing clocks by different Lincolnshire makers.

Usher, John, North Shields, Northumb., cm and joiner (1827–29). Trading at Camden Lane in 1827 and Bedford Lane, 1828–29. [D]

Usher, Ralph, Liverpool, carver (1818–37). Addresses given at 58 Hurst St in 1821; 13 Tabley St in 1823; 14 Tabley St and 9 Sparling St in 1827; 21 Tabley St in 1835; and no. 14 in 1837. Admitted freeman on servitude to William Folds on 17 June 1818. [Liverpool freemen reg.]

Usher, Robert, Rugby, Warks., chairmaker and turner (1828–35). [D]

Usherwood, John, Liverpool, cm etc. (1834–39). Trading at 10 Church Alley, 1834–37, and Hodgson Ct, 37 Hunter St in 1839. [D]

Usherwood, Samuel, Liverpool, u (1804–39). Addresses given at 1 Hale St, Dale St in 1804; no. 17 in 1807; 43 Cable St, 1810–11; 24 Rainford's Gdn, 1813–18; no. 22, 1821–24; and 10 Church Alley (or Lane), 1827–29. [D]

Uting, Samuel, Quay, Gt Yarmouth, Norfolk, u (1805–08). [D]

Uttering, Samuel, 27 Gun St, Manchester, cm (1808). [D]

Utting, Henry Norwich, u (1801). App. to Thomas & Charles Taylor, and admitted freeman on 24 February 1801. [Norwich freemen reg.]

Utting, James Henry snr, parish of St Andrew, Norwich, upholder (1812–25). Polled in 1812. His son, James Henry Utting jnr, upholder, admitted freeman in 1825. [Norwich freemen reg.]

Utting, James Henry jnr, Norwich, later London, upholder (1825–40). Son of James Henry Utting snr, upholder. Admitted freeman of Norwich on 2 April 1825. Polled at Norwich, of London, in 1830. Of 11 Newman St, Oxford St, London, took out a Sun Insurance policy in 1840. [Norwich freemen reg.; GL, Sun MS ref. 1339920]

V

Vachette, Z., 14 Charles St, Manchester Sq. and 35 Marylebone Lane, London, u and mattress maker (1835). [D]

Vago, Joshua, 12 Oxford St, London, looking-glass and picture frame maker (1835–39). [D]

Vaile, J. P., 32 Warwick St and South St, Worthing, Sussex, cm and u (1823). [D]

Vaisey, Ann, Brittox, Devizes, Wilts., cm and u (1830). [D]

Vaisey, Ann Sadlington, Market Pl., Chippenham, Wilts., u (1830). [D]

Vaisey, John, Brittox, Devizes, Wilts., cm etc. (1822). [D]

Vaisey, Richard, Chippenham, Wilts., cm and u (1822). [D]

Vaizey, John, Devizes, Wilts., cm (1793). [D]

Valentine, T., Bevois St, St Mary's St, Southampton, Hants., carver (1839). [D]

Valentino, Dan., 4 New Inn Yd, Shoreditch, London, bedstead maker (1839). [D]

Valiant (or Vallant), George, Pulham (St Mary), Norfolk, chairmaker (1744–48). Took apps named Barber in 1744 and Lincoln in 1748. [S of G, app. index]

Valinder, John snr, Guildford, Surrey, cm (1796–1835). Recorded at Quarry St in 1796 and High St, 1806–35. [Poll bks]

Vallance, John & Evans, Samuel, address unrecorded, joiners and chairmakers (1823–26). Carried out general jobbing work and supplied some furniture for St James's Palace, Hampton Court, Kensington Palace and for the Houses of Parliament, 1823–26. The Royal accounts for the quarter ending 5 July 1824 list furniture provided for St James's Palace, including a range of deal presses costing £32 8s, two folding deal tables, £3 18s, and a 'strong framed bedstead fitted complete in press', £2 9s. The accounts for the quarter ending 5 April 1825 list a 'rising state canopy', £16 10s, a 'Grecian elbow chair', £6, '2 high square stools', £7 10s, and a footstool, £1 12s 6d. [PRO, LC11/41–50]

Valliant, George, London, frame maker (1711–20). Named in the receipt book of Samuel Tufnell of Middle Temple, London, who in 1710 bought Langley's, Great Waltham, Essex. An undated entry records payment to Valliant of £6 'in full for four black & Gold frames'. On 16 January 1711 he received £1 10s 'in full for a half length Lackerd frame'; on 8 June c. 1714, £3 'in full for a hole length frame'; and on 6 September c. 1714, 10s for packing a picture. [Essex RO, D/DTu 276] He is probably the Valliant, frame maker of London, who charged £31 2s to 1st Duke of Portland for 'what is Due in London for Equipage, Furniture, workmanship &c. to August 1721'. [Notts. RO, Pw B90]

Valois, Gabriel, St James's, Westminster, London, later USA, repairer of carved work, carver and gilder (1768–73). In London, took app. in September 1768 for £2; and app. named David Lorimer on 19 October 1772 for £2. Recorded in USA newspapers in 1773 as a carver and gilder from Paris, late of London. [PRO, IR 1/25 and 27; A. C. Prime, 'The Arts and Crafts in Philadelphia, Maryland and South Carolina 1721–1785. Gleanings from Newspapers', *Walpole Soc.*, 1929]

Van Dem Helm, —, over against Compton St, by St Ann's Wall, Soho, London, Dutch table maker (1711). Named in contemporary newspapers. [Heal]

Vanderbost (or Vanderhorst), C., 38 Skinner St, Bishopgate, London, u (1826–29). [D]

Vandergucht, Gerard, London, carver, gilder and picture dealer (1754–79). Heal records his trade card, 1761, and reference to him, dated 1779, in W. J. Whitley, *Artists and their Friends, 1700–99.* Of St George's, Hanover Sq., Vandergucht took app. named William Nicholls in 1762 for £15; and of St George's, Bloomsbury, Francis Patton, son of Thomas, of St Margaret's, Westminster, in 1763, for £31 10s. Subscribed to Chippendale's *Director,* 1754. [V & A archives]

Vandiso (or Vandiozo), —, address unrecorded, picture frame maker (1685). Supplied picture frames costing £18 and £19 5s to Gorhambury, St Albans, Herts. on 22 May and September 1685. [Herts. RO, Gorhambury accounts bk, XI 22]

Vanerba, Cornelius, London (?), carver (1686). The accounts of Sir William Bruce for Kinfour, dated June 1686, mention money due to Vanerba for work done. See Peter Paull Boyse.

Van Gelden, —, address unrecorded, carver (1790). Recorded in the account book of Sir George Cornewall of Moccas Court, near Hereford, and Stanhope St, London on 5 June 1790 receiving £3 16s 9d. [Herefs. RO, Moccas papers]

Van Haesen, —, Jermyn St, London, cm (1737). Named in contemporary newspapers. [Heal]

Vanhausen, Thomas, London, chair and cm (1739). Notice in *London Daily Post and General Advertiser,* 24 October 1739, read: 'To be sold by Hand . . . all the Genuine Household Goods and Stock in Trade of the ingenious Mr. Thomas Vanhausen, Chair and Cabinet Maker, eminent in his Profession for his many and beautiful designs in the Cabinet Way: consisting of Pictures, large Glass Sconces in carv'd and gilt Frames . . .'.

Vanhegan, Samuel, 39 Thomas St, Liverpool, chair and cm (1796). [D]

Vanhuissen, Francis, London, cm (1683). Admitted 'in the place & quantity of Cabinet Maker in ordinary to His Ma^ty' in 1683. [R. W. Symonds, *Furniture Making in 17th and 18th Century England,* p. 105]

Van Opstal, Louis, London, carver (1652–d. 1683). With John van der Stein carved the throne and dais in St George's Hall, Windsor. Worked at Versailles and Marly, 1681–83. [Information from G. Jackson-Stops]

Van Ruyven, Samuel, at 'The George', south side of St Paul's Churchyard, London, cm (1722–28). Heal records him in contemporary newspapers and insurance co. records.

Vant, Thomas, Coventry St, London, u (1749). [Poll bk]

Varden (or Vardam), Frederick, Clapham, London, cm and u (1776–78). Took out Sun Insurance policies in 1776 for £200 of which utensils, stock and goods accounted for £110; and in 1778 for £500, utensils, stock and goods accounting for £200. [GL, Sun MS vol. 245, p. 512; vol. 262, p. 422]

Vardy (or Vardie), Thomas, London, carver (1751–88). Recorded at Park St, 1762–63. Took apps named John Davis in 1751, John Page in 1756, Aubrey Evans in 1758, John Crake in 1763 and William Farnborough in 1765. Admitted to the Livery of the Joiners' Co. on 3 October 1753, and as a master in 1788. Subscribed to William Chambers's *A Treatise of Civil Architecture,* 1769. Brother of John Vardy, the architect, who designed furniture for Lord Spencer at Spencer House, Green Park and Althorp, Northants. The two brothers may have collaborated in designing and making frames. Thomas is named in his brother's will, dated 13 April 1762, which also left £700 for the apprenticeships of his sons, Edward and John, and to the latter all his books on architecture. An app. of Thomas Vardy, named John Clarke, lived with John Vardy snr in order to assist Thomas in his business; and Clarke continued to do so, later living with John jnr. Thomas is named in the accounts for Cobham Hall, Kent on 11 December 1773, receiving £41 9s 'for the Attic freezes of the chimney pieces at Cobham & two D? for two Doors in Drawing Room'; and £100 for 'work done in other Freezes of chimney pieces &c.' On 22 December 1774 Thomas Vardy was paid £250 for carving work at Cobham. Thomas is named in Henry Holland's notebooks, c. 1770 for supplying two marble chimney-pieces for Lord Hillsborough's house near Westerham, Kent, now called Valence, and largely rebuilt in the 19th century. [D; GL, Joiners' Co. records; H. L. Phillips, *Annals of the Worshipful Company of Joiners,* 1915; A. Coleridge, *Chippendale Furniture,* p. 50; *Conn.,* January 1962, p. 12; PRO, C12 49/48, 7 June 1768, PCC 239,

Rushworth; D. Stroud, *Henry Holland*, p. 25; Wills, *Looking-Glasses*; Colvin; *Dictionary of British Architects*; V&A archives]

Vardy, Thomas, Green St, London, carver (1774). [Poll bk]

Vargur, John, St David, Exeter, Devon, cm (1803). [Exeter Militia list]

Varguitz, Phillip Butz, Exeter, Devon, cm and victualler (1781). Took out a Sun Insurance policy in 1781 for £200 of which £130 accounted for utensils and stock. [GL, Sun MS vol. 295, p. 310]

Varham, Vincent, Ashford, Kent, upholder (1760). Took app. named Grant in 1760. [S of G, app. index]

Varley, Henry, St Helens, near Prescot, Lancs., cm (1802). [Preston Guild record of burgesses]

Varley, John, Gt Yarmouth and Norwich, cm (1818–42). Polled at Gt Yarmouth, 1818–20, of Norwich in 1826; and listed in directories at Surrey St, Norwich, 1839–42.

Varley, John, Slaithwaite, Huddersfield, Yorks., turner and u (1837). [D]

Varley, William, Lancaster, cm (1785–86). [Lancaster freemen rolls]

Varney, Frederick, St Mary Hall Lane, Oxford, printseller, carver and gilder (1830). [D]

Varney, Thomas, High Wycombe, Bucks., chairmaker (b. *c.* 1806–41). Daughter bapt. in 1834, son in 1837. Aged 35 at the time of the 1841 Census. [PR(bapt.)]

Vastell, Edward, Guildford, Surrey, u (1757). Took app. named Smith in 1757. [S of G, app. index]

Vaughan, —, 53 Regent St, Cheltenham, Glos., cm (1839). [D]

Vaughan, Alexander, Paradise St, Liverpool, cm (1790–96). Trading at no. 31 in 1790, no. 28 in 1794, and no. 32, with warehouse at no. 33, in 1796. [D]

Vaughan, Edward, Coventry St, St Martin-in-the-Fields, London, chairmaker (1715). Took out a Hand in Hand Insurance policy with George Vaughan in November 1715 for £150 on house and workshop. In 1715 Edward Vaughan charged £30 for 'a chair lined with blue damask with case and poles to it discharged for my Lady Duchess', probably the Duchess of Montrose. [GL, Hand in Hand MS vol. 15, p. 212; Scottish RO, GD 220/6/19/p. 70] See George and Samuel Vaughan, and Vaughan, Holmes & Griffin, sedan chairmakers of Coventry St.

Vaughan, Edward snr, Lower Castle St, Bristol, cm (1805–12). [D]

Vaughan, Edward jnr, 11 Charles's St, Bristol, cm (1805–07). [D]

Vaughan, Edward, Betrice St, Oswestry, Salop, cm and joiner (1822). [D]

Vaughan, George, London, sedan chairmaker (1728–59). Heal records him in newspapers as Chairmaker to the Prince of Wales in Coventry St, near Haymarket, 1730–47. He was still there in 1749 when H. Purefoy visited him. The V & A archives record from an unspecified, undated source that he displayed goods at 67 New Bond St. Submitted bills to the Prince of Wales, 1728–45 for cleaning, oiling, gilding and repairing sedan chairs; and in 1738 for hiring out mourning chairs. Described as 'Mr. Vaughan, King's Sedan Chairmaker, making a rich sedan for Princess Royal, against her marriage', in *Read's Weekly Journal or British Gazetteer*, 9 June 1733. Notice in *General Advertiser*, 13 October 1748 stated: 'Two curious fine Chairs are making by Mr Vaughan, in Coventry-street, which were bespoke by Count Bentinck, and are to be sent over to Holland for their Serene Highnesses the Prince and Princess of Orange.' Polled at Westminster, 1749. Although at first a Royal chairmaker, Vaughan was later patronized by prominent Whig politicians. He was mentioned in a letter from Sir Robert Walpole to Sir Horace Mann, dated 25 February 1750, as having been dismissed by the Prince of Wales for voting for Lord Trentham: '. . . one of his black caps was sent to tell this Vaughan that the Prince would employ him no more. "I am going to bid another person make His Royal Highness a chair". "With all my heart", said the chairmaker, "I don't care what they make him, so they don't make him a throne."' [*The Purefoy Letters, 1735–53*, ed. G. Eland, pp. 108, 358–59; Duchy of Cornwall archives, Royal Household accounts, Prince of Wales, vols. 1, 2, 5, 6, 8, 11, 12, 14, 18; Harris & Sons, *Old English Furniture*, p. 29; V & A archives] Named in the 1746 London account of the Rt Hon. Earl of Stair, with Messrs Campbell & Bruce, bankers. [Scottish RO, GD 135/Box 55/31] John Forrett's account current with the Rt Hon. Earl of Burlington mentions Mr Vaughan, chairmaker of London, on 24 March 1746, receiving £11 18s; and the tradesmen's accounts for March 1759 note payment to him of £2 3s 6d. This may, however, refer to Samuel Vaughan. [Burlington papers, Chatsworth, folio account bk f. 77 and f. 21] He is probably the Vaughan, chairmaker, named in the accounts for Panshanger, Herts., dated 9 May 1749, receiving £6 10s. [Herts. RO, Book D/EP A2] See Edward and Samuel Vaughan; and Vaughan, Holmes & Griffin of Coventry St.

Vaughan, George, Nantwich, Cheshire, chairmaker (1792–1834). Recorded at Hospital St, 1822–34. Married on 5 August 1792. Daughter Elizabeth by wife Sarah bapt. on 26 January 1794. Children by wife Martha bapt.: Margaret on 8 October 1798, Thomas on 1 September 1802, Mary on 24 August 1805, and George on 26 September, 1809. [D; PR (marriage and bapt.)] Probably father of, and confusion with:

Vaughan, George jnr, Nantwich, Cheshire, chairmaker (b. 1809?–1850). Married Francis Davies on 24 December 1835. Trading at Hospital St in 1850. [D; PR]

Vaughan, Henry, St John's, Worcester, cm and u (1835–40). [D]

Vaughan, John, Prince's St, Leicester Fields, London, upholder (1760–74). Probably the Vaughan at this address noted by Heal in newspapers in 1760. Polled at Westminster, 1774.

Vaughan, Joseph, near 'The Red Lion', Whitechapel Rd, London, cm (1775). Took out a Sun Insurance policy in 1775 for £100 of which £30 accounted for utensils and stock. [GL, Sun MS vol. 245, p. 165]

Vaughan, Mary, 7 All Saints' St, Bristol, chairmaker (1828–35). [D] Succeeded Robert Vaughan, and succeeded by Thomas Vaughan, at this address.

Vaughan, Robert, All Saints' St, Bristol, chairmaker (1820–26). Trading at no. 4, 1820–21, and no. 7, 1823–26. [D] Succeeded by Mary, then Thomas Vaughan.

Vaughan, Samuel, London, sedan chairmaker to their Majesties and the Royal Family (1751–72). Recorded at Piccadilly in 1751 and at Coventry St, Piccadilly, 1763–72. [D] Submitted a bill to Lord Monson dated 26 January 1751 for a total of £63 4s 6d. The Monson papers also record payment to S. Vaughan on 30 January 1770 of £2 2s, and to Samuel Vaughan in 1771 of £17 3s 'for a Sedan Chair 16×16 for Miss Monson & Cypher'. [Lincoln RO, Monson 11/9; 10/1/A/3] The Earl of Ancaster paid Sam Vaughan, chairmaker, £50 4s on 14 May 1755; and £22 15s on 14 May 1761 for work done from 1755 to 1 June 1760. [Lincoln RO, 2 ANC 6/7–8] The Sherborne accounts (7th Lord Digby) note under 1763 a payment to 'Mr Vaughan, Chairmaker £37. 13s.' The Croome Court accounts record payment on 28 September 1764 of £101 3s 10½d for building a lady's sedan chair, the 'ornaments as by Mr. Adam's directions'. A bill, dated 1766 in the Nostell Priory papers, is for a lady's sedan chair costing £48 8s. [V & A archives] In Thomas Bridgeman's account of payments made to creditors of Francis, Marquess of Tavistock after the latter's death in 1767, Vaughan is shown as having received £3 15s on 25 March, but items are not specified. [Bedford Office, London] On 19 March 1770 Vaughan charged Sir Gilbert Heathcote, Bart a total of £6 8s 6d for oiling, cleaning and 'gold lackring all the brass' on a sedan chair, making 'new rich white silk curtains', festooned and with 'a rich silk fringe' and white tassels, and painting the poles. [Lincoln RO, 2 ANC 12/D/29] Supplied chairs to Petworth. [*Apollo*, May 1977, p. 362] See Edward and George Vaughan, and Vaughan, Holmes & Griffin, sedan chairmakers of Coventry St.

Vaughan, Samuel, Broadmead, Bristol, cm, u and furniture broker (1829–40). Trading at no. 4, 1829–34, no. 3, 1835–40, also no. 1 in 1840. [D]

Vaughan, Thomas, Bristol, Windsor and fancy chairmaker (1801–40). Trading at Rosemary St in 1801; Merchant St, 1805–10; 46 Merchant St, 1815–19; and 7 All Saints' St, 1827 and 1836–40. [D] See Mary and Robert Vaughan.

Vaughan, Thomas, 14 Court, Snowhill, Birmingham, cabinet case maker (1830). [D]

Vaughan, Thomas, 66 Constitution Hill, Birmingham, cm (1835). [D]

Vaughan, William, 20 Porter St, Soho, London, cm (1826–27). [D]

Vaughan, Holmes & Griffin, Whitcomb St, Coventry St, Leicester Fields, London, sedan chairmakers (1774–77). Recorded at no. 1 in 1775. [D] See Edward, George and Samuel Vaughan.

Vaut, Thomas, Coventry St, Westminster, London, u (1749). [Poll bk]

Veal, Edwin, 14 Somerset Buildings, Bath, Som., cm (1833). [D]

Veal, J., Bathwick Hill, Bath, Som., cm (1819). [D]

Veal, William, Bristol, cm, chairmaker and undertaker (1799–1840). Recorded at Baldwin St, 1799–1801; 2 King St, 1820–30; no. 12, 1831–39; and 2 Thomas St in 1840. [D]

Veale, Jarvis, Church Sq., Dartmouth, Devon, cm (1830). [D]

Veary, James, West Wycombe, Bucks., chairmaker (b. c. 1816–41). Aged 25 at the time of the 1841 Census.

Veere, Henricke, Gray's Inn Lane, London, cm (c. 1655–66). [*Hogarth Soc.*, 1911, p. 69]

Velin, John, Shambles, Bradford, Wilts., cm and u (1822–30). [D]

Vellum, Henry, Cripplegate Buildings, London, cm (1835). Damage of premises by fire reported in *Gents Mag.*, September 1835.

Venables, James, Chester, cm (1831). Admitted freeman on 25 April 1831. [Chester freemen rolls]

Venables, John, address unrecorded, upholder (1732–70). Son of John Venables, distiller of Southwark, London. App. to Ambrose Pearman on 6 December 1732, and admitted freeman of the Upholders' Co. by servitude on 2 May 1770. [GL, Upholders' Co. records]

Venables, John, 21 Earnest St, Regents Park, London, cm and u (1839). [D]

Venes, Henry, 16 Marshall St, Golden Sq., London, cm and u (1829–39). [D]

Venn, Henry, 6 Dean's Row, Walworth, London, cm and dealer in household goods (1809–11). Took out a Sun Insurance policy on 5 November 1810 for £350, £180 on stock, utensils and goods in trust in his house and workshops; and £120 on workshop behind house, and one nearby in Penton Pl. [D; GL, Sun MS vol. 452, ref. 850392]

Venner, Samuel, 3 Little Queen St, Lincoln's Inn Fields, London, cm (1789). Took out a Sun Insurance policy in 1789 for £100 on household goods and clothes in the house of Mr Price, printseller, at above address. [GL, Sun MS vol. 362, p. 478]

Venning, Edward, London, looking-glass maker (1826–39).

Trading at 8 Coburg Pl., Old Kent Rd in 1826, 1 Cornbury Pl., Old Kent Rd, 1826–27, and 28 Wigmore St in 1839. [D]

Venning, William, 43 Cleveland St, Fitzroy Sq., London, carver and gilder (1835–39). [D]

Venoe, Charles, Falmouth, Cornwall, cm (1757). Took app. named Pascoe in 1757. [S of G, app. index]

Ventris, William, London, upholder (1704–34). Son of Sir Peyton Ventris, Knight of Ipswich, Suffolk. App. to Edward Rabett on 3 May 1704, and admitted freeman of the Upholders' Co. by servitude on 7 April 1714. Took apps named William Fox, 1714–31, and John Berrow, 1718–26/27. [GL, Upholders' Co. records] Documents note that 'since 1711 Ventris and family loged at Strand in houses of Brothers Brydges of St Clement Danes, woollen drapers'; and c. 1723 that he was 'now of the Parish of St. Bridgett in the City of London upholdsterer'. [PRO, C11, 240/43] Heal records him in newspapers at Salisbury Ct, Fleet St, 1724–31, and Essex St in 1734. Of Salisbury Ct, served as Collector for the Poor at St Bride's in 1727; and was fined for non-service in one office in 1731. [GL, MS 6561, p. 46]

Verdier (or Verdur), William Francis, 39 Drury Lane, London, cm and u (1821–23). Recorded also at 136 Long Acre in 1823. Took out Sun Insurance policies on 29 November 1821 for £350 including £100 on household goods and musical instruments in his house at 39 Drury Lane; on 9 September 1822 for £500 on nos 39–40; and on 14 May 1823 for £300. [D; GL, Sun MS vol. 493, refs 985710 and 995701; vol. 498, ref. 1005049]

Vere, Joseph, Dale St, Liverpool, chairmaker (1774–47). Trading at no. 126 in 1774 and no. 35 in 1777. [D]

Veree, Joseph, back of 29 Crosshall St, Liverpool, chairmaker (1790). [D]

Verga, John Marie, Macclesfield, Cheshire, carver, gilder and tea dealer (1828–34). Trading at Market St in 1828 and Mill St in 1834. [Goodison, *Barometers*]

Verhuyck, —, address unrecorded, carver (d. by 1709). Elizabeth Verhuyck claimed £136 in 1709 on behalf of her late husband, for work he had done at Boughton, Northants. and Montagu House, London. [Boughton archives, Executors' accounts, 1st Duke of Montagu; Beard, *Georgian Craftsmen*]

Verhyck (or Verrick), James, Piccadilly, London, carver (1749). [Poll bk]

Verlander, Simon, Colchester, Essex, joiner (1727–37). Admitted freeman in 1727, and described as a joiner in 1731. Children bapt. in 1733 and 1737. Lacquered corner cabinet recorded, inscribed on base: 'Simon Verlander/att Colchester'.

Vermaltte, Charles (?), London, carver (1680?–1682). In 1680(?) a Jean Vermaltte, schoolmaster, arrived from Dieppe with his son, 18, a carver, and sister-in-law, Sichely. They were granted a total of £2 18s Threadneedle St Relief. On 8 March 1681/82, denization was granted to John Vermaltte, his wife, Anna, and a Charles Vermalette, possibly their son. [*Hogarth Soc.*, 1949, p. 185]

Vernal, John, Worcester, cm and u (1796). App. to Robert Crump, cm and u, and admitted freeman on 27 June 1796. [Worcester freemen rolls]

Verney, William, 32 Buross St, Commercial Rd, London, chair and sofa maker (1835). [D]

Vernon, Edward, Long Acre, St Martin-in-the-Fields, London, cm (1709–17). Heal records him in rate bks, 1709. Trading at 'The Hen & Chickens', when he took out a Sun Insurance policy on 10 January 1716/17, on goods and merchandise in his house. [GL, Sun MS vol. 6, p. 120]

Vernon, George, address unrecorded. Stamp recorded on a late George III mahogany piano stool with circular swivelling upholstered seat and four splayed, reeded, tapering legs. [Sotherby's, 9 January 1981, lot 140]

Vernon, Matthew, Ludgate St, London, upholder (1724–34). [Poll bks]

Vernon, Richard, 5 Dean's Pl., Shudehill, Manchester, chairmaker (1813). [D]

Vernon, Thomas, Bishops Waltham, Hants., u (1727). Took out a Sun Insurance policy on 27 March 1727 for £300 on goods and stock. [GL, Sun MS vol. 23, p. 476]

Vernon, Thomas, London, cm (1751). Admitted freeman of Liverpool on 5 September 1751. [Liverpool freemen reg.]

Vernon, Thomas, near Air St, Piccadilly, London, upholder and cm (1776–99). Recorded at 22 Piccadilly in 1779. Named in 1776 regarding a Sun Insurance policy taken out by Robert Kennett, and took out a policy himself in 1778 for £1,200 of which £850 accounted for utensils, stock and goods. Declared bankrupt, *Gents Mag.*, February 1780. Trade card [V & A Print Dept] bears inscription within frame of corn swags, female nudes and foliage scrolls. Card reads: 'VERNON, near AIR STREET, PICCADILLY, LONDON. UPHOLDER, CABINET MAKER, APPRAISER and AUCTIONEER, where designs of every Article in the above Branches are Executed from the Neatest and Plain to the most superb.' [D; GL, Sun MS vol. 263, p. 485]

Vernon, Thomas, 5 Prince's St, Leicester Fields, London, upholder and cm (1782–88). Took out Sun Insurance policies in 1782 for £600, £500 accounting for utensils and stock; and on 1 February 1787 for £300 on a house in Bishopsgate, tenanted by Michael Pearson. Declared bankrupt, *Leeds Intelligencer*, 18 March 1788. [D; poll bk; GL, Sun MS vol. 304, p. 543; vol. 343, p. 55] Possibly T. Virnon.

Verral, —, 99 North St, Brighton, Sussex, u (1805). [D] Possibly Henry or William Verrall of Brighton.

Verall, David, Neckinger Rd, Bermondsey, London, bedstead maker (1839). [D]

Verral(l), George, 'in the Cliff', Lewes, Sussex, u, tallow chandler and auctioneer (1762–85). Advertised sale of brandy in *Sussex Weekly Advertiser*, 27 December 1762; and on 2 December 1771 that he wanted an app. 'to a country SHOPKEEPER'. Advertised auctions in the same paper, 10 September 1781 and 26 May 1783. Took out Sun Insurance policies in 1779 for £600, including £210 on utensils, stock and goods; and on 25 June 1785 for £200 on utensils and stock. [GL, Sun MS vol. 278, p. 571; vol. 329, p. 543]

Verrall, George jnr, Lewes, Sussex, u and auctioneer (1794). [D]

Verrall, George Henry, 18 High St, Cliff, Lewes, Sussex, u, paper hanger, undertaker and furniture broker (1823–41). [D; poll bks]

Verrall, Henry, Brighton, Sussex, cm, u and furniture broker (1820–41). Recorded at Duke St in 1820; New Rd, 1822–36; no. 29, *c.* 1822–27; and no. 33 in 1832. Children by Jane Verrall bapt.: Henry Robert on 21 June 1822; William Edward on 17 November 1826; John on 10 April 1829; George James on 23 February 1831; Emma on 2 November 1833; and Elizabeth Catherine on 22 February 1826. [D; E. Sussex RO, PR (bapt.)]

Verrall, William, 9 Nile St, Brighton, Sussex, upholder and tallow chandler (1793–1800). [D]

Verrall, William, Chapel St, Worthing, Sussex, turner and chairmaker (1832–45). [D]

Verrick, James, Piccadilly, London, carver (1749). [Poll bk]

Verscragen, James, Preston, Lancs., cm (1704). Recorded as a leading cm in Preston who on 5 October 1704 was summoned for failing to give town officials the names of his apps. [Preston exhib. cat., *Polite Society by Arthur Devis*, p. 36]

Verscraggen, John, Preston, Lancs., cm (1702–d. by 1742).

Listed in the Preston Guild record of burgesses, 1702 and 1722. Dead by 1742 when his son John was listed.

Versovile, —, London (?). On 20 June 1747 he was paid £1 16s in full 'for 2 Gilt frames for little Pictures', supplied to Earl Fitzwalter for Moulsham Hall, Chelmsford, or Schomberg House, Pall Mall, London. [A. C. Edwards, *The Accounts of Benjamin Mildmay, Earl Fitzwalter*, p. 192]

Vevers (or Verers), Richard, Halegate, Howden, Yorks., joiner and cm (1834). [D]

Vial, —, Hull, Yorks., cm. Worked at Burton Constable Hall, Yorks. [*C. Life*, vol. CLIX, no. 4118, pp. 1476–78]

Vial(l)(s), Thomas, London, carver, gilder and picture frame maker (1756–d. by 1780). Recorded at Gt Newport St in 1756 and 1763; and polled of Leicester Sq. in 1774. [D] Viall, picture frame makers, Gt Newport St, supplied frames to Longford Castle, Wilts. from 1756. [*C. Life*, 26 December 1931, p. 717] Thomas Vialls, carver and gilder, submitted two bills for work carried out at Wilton House, Wilts., 1758–59, totalling £458 9s 3½d, and in 1759, £12 8s. The bills are concerned mainly with carving in the house interiors, but also mention 'carving a Chimney Glass Frame with Vine Leaves & Grapes', and 'carving a bold rich ovale frame for a Plaster Coat of Arms for over the Hall Chimney'. [V & A archives] Two bills from Thomas Vialls survive in the Bedford Office, London. The first, dated December 1760, is for 'woodwork for the ground glew'd up', and carving a large crest, probably part of the decoration of Woburn Abbey after Flitcroft's rebuilding for John, 4th Duke of Bedford. In March 1767 Vialls was paid 16 guineas 'for a picture of Queen Elizabeth'. This may refer to a frame for the Armada portrait of Elizabeth I by George Gower in the Long Gallery at Woburn. From October 1766 to November 1768 Vials, carver and gilder, supplied to Shelburne House, Berkeley Sq., London, 'Ornaments, Glass and Picture Frames, Gilding Etc.' costing £71 6s. [Bowood MS] On 1 September 1768 Thomas Vialls received payment from the 3rd Earl of Darnley of Cobham Hall, Kent, for picture frames, including one for Dance's portrait of Lady Darnley. [*C. Life*, 10 March 1983, p. 570] The private accounts of Richard Hoare of Boreham House, Essex, record payment to Vialls of £2 8s for a picture frame on 23 March 1776. [Essex RO, D/Du 649/2] Dead by 12 March 1780, when 'The Hon. Gentlemen of the Dilettanti Society's Bill to the Executors of the Late Mr. Viall, Carver' was presented. Totalling £42 8s, it listed 'Two Large Burnished Gold Frames, Carved with Antique Eggs, Ribbons and Water Leaf outside, with a Scrolling Fluted Frett, Rich Ornament Tops, with Shield and Palm Branches, For Pictures Painted by Sir Joshua Reynolds', and included 8s 'to Self and Three Men to Fix up the Two Pictures over the Chimneys'. [L. Cust, *History of the Society of Dilettanti*, 1914, p. 222] Succeeded by:

Vials & Co., Leicester Fields, London, carvers and gilders (1784). [D]

Vialon, John, address unrecorded, cm (1803). Subscribed to Sheraton's *Cabinet Dictionary*, 1803.

Vicarman, Richard, formerly of St James, late of St Giles-in-the-Fields, London, cm and upholder (1761). Discharge from Debtor's Prison reported in *London Gazette*, 16 June 1761.

Vice, John, Truro, Cornwall, cm and chairmaker (1756–68). Took apps named Hoskins in 1765 and Johns in 1759. [S of G, app. index] Notice in *Sherborne Mercury*, 23 May 1768, read: 'John Vice, in Pyder-street, Truro, Begs Leave to acquaint the Public, That they may be supplied with all Sorts of Goods in the Cabinet and Chair Branches, In the neatest Manner, on reasonable Terms: Likewise Looking-Glasses, of various sorts and sizes . . .'.

Vick, Christopher Wren, 132 North St, Brighton, Sussex, carver, japanner, gilder and ornamental painter (1831–41). Recorded also at 148 North St in 1839. Named in the Windsor Royal Archives on 30 June 1833 providing '6 Elbow Chairs —Japanned w. various Chinese devices & twice Varnished', costing £5 8s; on 14 October 1833 a 'Cheval Glass in King's Bed Room — regilt in mat & Burnished Gold', £7; on 31 December 1833, 'Painting a Sideboard in Imitation Bamboo & 3 times Varnished', £2 10s; and on 31 December 1834, supplying '12 Chairs Japanned Bamboo pattern & China characters in Tablet-backs Twice varnished', £4 10s. From 30 June 1835 to 30 June 1841 Vick worked at Brighton Pavilion, on 30 June 1836 receiving £1 4s for 'Painting, graining & twice varnishing two new stools for Chapel': and on 30 June 1839, charging for 'Cleaning, regilding, Painting & Ornamenting Chairs, Sofas, Looking Glass frames and Sundry other jobs; throughout the principal suite of Apartment'. He also revarnished a set of forty-eight bamboo chairs at the Pavilion. Carried out jobbing work at Buckingham Palace, charging £7 1s 4½d, which included '21 days and 7½ hours' work painting and running gild lines on tables for Queen's Drawing Room'. [D; Windsor Royal Archives, account bks, 1833–41, V; PRO, LC11/80, 86 and 100; E. T. Joy, *English Furniture, 1800–1851*, p. 187]

Vickerman, James, Hull, Yorks., cm (1818–39). Trading at 32 New Dock St, 1818–20, and Deighton's Entry, High St, 1838–39. [D]

Vickers, —, Northgate, Blackburn, Lancs., cm (1834). See Wolstenholm & Vickers.

Vickers, J., Cheese Mkt, Oundle, Northants., cm/joiner (1823). [D]

Vickers, Samuel, Sheffield, Yorks., chair turner (1790). [Lincoln poll bk] Possibly:

Vickers, Samuel, Lincoln, chairmaker (1806). Admitted freeman in November 1806. [Lincoln freemen rolls]

Vickers & Rutledge, Conduit St, Hanover Sq., London, upholders, cm and undertakers (c. 1775–80). Trade card states they were 'Successors to Mr. [Thomas] Bailey at their Manufactory, Conduit Street', and is framed by two draped gadrooned bedposts and cornice carved with acanthus scrolls centring on a vase, and palmettes at the ends. Card illustrates a Louis XV dressing table and glass, and later Adam-style armchair with oval back filled with a palmette, stuffed seat, serpentine front and turned legs. The chair is similar to satinwood chairs at Kedleston Hall, Derbs. [Heal; C. Musgrave, *Adam and Hepplewhite Furniture*, p. 128]

Vickerson, Ralph, Pilgrim St, Newcastle, joiner and cm (1782–1801). [D]

Vickery, J. C., Regent St. Stamp recorded on undated boulle matchbox holder. [V & A archives]

Vidale (or Vidall), Counzs, 6 New Lisle St, Leicester Sq., London, carver and gilder (1809). Took out a Sun Insurance policy on 10 February 1809 for £1,700 including £300 on stock, utensils and goods in trust and in workshop. [D; GL, Sun MS vol. 448, ref. 828310]

Vidale & Paget, 6 New Lisle St, Leicester Sq., London, looking-glass manufacturers, carvers and gilders, wholesale and retail coach glasses etc. (1807). [D]

Vidall, William, 97 Wardour St, London, carver, gilder, picture frame and looking-glass maker (1822–39). Took out a Sun Insurance policy on 17 July 1822 for £500 on his house. [D; GL, Sun MS vol. 493, ref. 993596]

Vidler, Joseph, Salisbury, Wilts., upholder (1805–22). Recorded at High St in 1822, also as a cm. [D]

Viel, John, Bath, Som., cm (1785–95). Took out a Sun Insurance policy on 16 April 1785 for £130 on household goods and £200 on utensils and stock. [GL, Sun MS vol. 328, p. 94]

Declared bankrupt with Matthew Viel, *Derby Mercury*, 15 January 1795.

Viel, Matthew, Borough Walls, Bath, Som., upholder and auctioneer (1805). [D] Probably:

Viel, Matthew, address unrecorded (1803–05). Submitted bills for work carried out at Corsham Court, Wilts. in 1803 charging £34 15s 7d, and in 1805, £397 8s 7d. Items listed include '6 Gothic chairs — caned seats & backs', £9, and 'to adding & thickening up the Sideboard making new gothic legs and arches', £6 6s. [V & A archives]

Viels, Messrs. F., Grove St, Bath, Som., cm and auctioneers (1793). [D]

Vierne, John Peter, address unrecorded, cm (1742). Notice in a newspaper of July 1742 reads: 'John Barrett discharged from his apprenticeship with John Peter Vierne, cabinet maker. He alleged that he had served for two years and had been employed in making picture frames, or work of the like kind, and that his master did not make any cabinet maker's work above one piece in a year, "having none to do"; and that his master was frequently so needy "as not being able to buy wood for his work or provisions for the family", so that the petitioner "was obliged to live several meals on bread and water".' [Winterthur, Delaware, Symonds papers, 75×69.29]

Vigers, John, Camberwell Green, London, cm and u (1839). [D]

Vigers, William, Church St, Lane End, Staffs., cm and u (1828–35). [D]

Viggan, —, Silver St, Golden Sq., London, cm (1749–51). See Richard Wiggan.

Vigor, M. G., Old Park, Bristol, cm and paper hanger (1814–17). [D]

Vigor, Matthew, Bristol, cm, undertaker and appraiser (1818–25). Addresses given at 16 and 17 Broad St, 1818–22; no. 17 in 1823; and 2 St John's Bridge, 'from 16 Broad St.', 1824–25. Declared bankrupt, *Exeter Flying Post*, 1 February 1821. [D]

Vigor, William, Bristol, cm, upholder and undertaker (1801–17). Trading at 16 Broad St in 1801, and nos 16 and 17, 1805–17, as William Vigor & Co. in 1805. A drawing in the Bristol Art Gallery of the Mulberry Tree Tavern shows the signboard of 'Wm. VIGOR CABINET MAKER'. [D]

Vilder, Joseph, Salisbury, Wilts., u and cm (1798). [D]

Vile, Joseph, Roslyn St, Hampstead, London, cm and u (1839). [D]

Vile, William, Castle Lane (later 72 St Martin's Lane), London, cm (c. 1700/05–d. 1767). William Vile was born early in the 18th century, probably in Somerset. A search of local records shows the name of Vile in profusion, but it may always elude us as to which William Vile of the many the cm was. The problem will perhaps only be solved by the chance discovery of revealing documentation. The clues which might have been afforded by his father's will are denied through the destruction of all Vile (and other) wills proved in the Taunton Archdeaconry, in Second World War air-raids on Exeter. 24 were listed in 1912. [E. A. Fry (ed.). *Taunton Wills, 1577–1799*, British Record Soc., 1912] It is assumed Vile was born in Somerset as the name is common there (much less so in Dorset) and because Vile in his own will left money to a relative at South Petherton. Its parish registers [Somerset RO, D/P Sea, 2/1/1–5] contain many mentions of various Vile families. There is also a tomb to a Thomas Vile (d. 8 July 1788) near the church entrance at South Petherton.

However, genealogical browsings are not hard evidence, and the first documented appearance of William Vile is on 10 August 1749 when he wrote to George Selwyn. The letter [Castle Howard archives] makes it clear that his 'Master' was William Hallett snr. [*Furn. Hist.*, 1975] Vile was supposedly a journeyman in Hallett's employment. We have no evidence of his apprenticeship, but I believe he and Hallett met in the West country, as Hallett came from a prosperous Crewkerne family (which later settled at Little Dunmow, Essex). Vile married a Sarah (surname unknown but almost certainly Strickland) in the late 1730s. A child, William Waldron Vile, was born to them and bapt. at St Paul's, Covent Gdn on 2 June 1740. [PR] Sarah outlived her husband and was paid money by his surviving partner, John Cobb, in 1767–68. [Cobb's bank account, 1767, f.161, 1768, f.161, Drummonds Branch, Royal Bank of Scotland] The new partnership turned to William Hallett snr to back them with finance when they set up on their own. The rate bks show that they set up in the New St ward of St Martin-in-the-Fields. [Westminster Ref. Lib., F.527] They show for 1751 'William Vile & Co'. By 1752 they were paying rents of £62, £29, £29 and £30 on 4 premises in Castle Lane. On 5 June 1752 William Hallett had left Newport St, and moved to St Martin's Lane. He took the house next door to 'William Vile & Co'. On 4 June 1755 Hallett's name is crossed through [ibid., F.536] and John Cobb took it over, a further indication of Hallett moving into 'retirement'.

In these early years the firm took as apps Thomas Plaistowe on 23 December 1752 for £60; and John Daniel on 27 February 1753 for £63. In the same years John Cobb was taking apps: James Lewis on 13 June 1752 and as 'John Cobb Upr', Martin Freeland, 20 December 1754. Intermeshed activity that led them forward with Hallett's backing. The firm evidence for this is in the bank accounts of Hallett, Vile and Cobb (Drummonds). Vile opened his account in 1758, and Cobb did so in 1759. It might be assumed that as they became successful they started to pay money to the elder Hallett, but some of the entries are for money to Hallett jnr. From 1756 Hallett snr's account shows cash in from Vile and Cobb in amounts of £150 to £300, almost monthly. For example the 1758 account reads:

Jan.	21. from Will Vile.	£200
	26. „ „ „	£200
	28. „ „ „	£200
Feb.	2. rec'd of Jn Cobb	£200
	27. „ „ „ „	£200
March	2. Wm Vile	£319
May	25. Cobb	£300
May	27. Vile	£300
June	10. Vile	£100
	19. Vile	£300
July	1. Cobb	£200
	8. Vile	£200
Sept.	18. Cobb	£200
	23. Cobb	£200
	28. Vile	£100

In 1758 William Hallett jnr received from Vile £100, and on 5 April 1760 his father received 'Cash from Vile £500'. The 1761 payments are heavier: 3 March, £1,000, 26 June, £350, 10 July, £400, 28 December, £600. In 1763 there was a payment on 7 March from Vile of £1,000, but I have noted no further payments. This accords with Vile's own 'retirement' in 1764, and payments out to Hallett & Vile are then only in Cobb's account — for example £500 to Vile on 19 February 1767, and £500 to Hallett 19 November 1768. Money was paid to Mrs Vile by Hallett after her husband's death, in accordance with the terms of his will. Further support for the '& Co' of the title is shown by Samuel Reynolds receiving money for Hallett, and then moving into Vile & Cobb's service.

The furniture that Vile made, in partnership with Cobb, was done between about 1751 and 1764. The large body of

furniture attributed to Vile which is of the 1740–50 period must probably be given to his master, Hallett snr or perhaps to Benjamin Goodison or John Boson (d. 1743). It may well be that the carved foliated ovals which appear on some documented Vile furniture (e.g. the breakfront bookcase, 1762, for Queen Charlotte) was a Hallett characteristic. For example a mahogany secretaire cabinet, of which the breakfront upper part was surmounted by a broken pediment, with a centre portion with carved ovals, Vitruvian scroll, the lower part with three doors centred by an oval from the coll. of the Duke of Buckingham at Stowe (Sotheby's, 28 May 1971, lot 53, illus.) — and which relates to similar cabinets at the V & A, and Portsmouth Museums — must be by Hallett, or are very early Vile in a Hallett style. There are also commodes (formerly St Giles's, Dorset, Christie's, 27 March 1952, lot 75, now V & A Museum, W. 74 — 1962; Coleridge, *Chippendale Furniture*, pl. 9) and a rosewood one (Christie's, 22 October 1953, lot 101) which have been attributed to Vile on stylistic grounds. The whole problem awaits a documented breakthrough: the large literature on furniture attributed to Vile is useful mainly only for the illustrations (e.g. C. *Life*, 7 October 1954, pp. 1154–56). Finally to add some further confusion the foliated oval which, as noted, has become almost inseparable from attributions to Vile appears on the sides of a mahogany table press supplied to Holkham by Benjamin Goodison in 1757 (*Apollo*, February 1964, p. 127, pl. 10). It may be evidence for the use of a specialist carver such as Sefferin Alken supplying them to several makers — I suggested this in 1977 (*Burlington*, July 1977, p. 485).

Vile's royal service (with his partner Cobb) did not begin until 1761 — (warrant dated January 1761) — and his name first appears in the accounts for the quarter ending Lady Day of that year. [PRO, LC 9/306 No. 29] His involvement with several important pieces still in the royal collections has been told often enough [GCM, pp. 51–56; Derek Shrub, V & A *Bulletin*, I, No. 4 (October 1965) pp. 26–35; *Burlington*, July 1977] and the items are listed below. However a careful collation of the surviving archives [PRO, LC 9/306, Nos 29, 30, 54, 71, 75; 9/307, Nos 7, 21, 56, 84; 9/308, Nos 8, 22; 9/309, Nos 10, 35, 54; 9/310, Nos 4, 8, 25, 29, 60, 91] and several in the Royal archives at Windsor [Nos 55476, 55496–98] throw up several problems in respect of these celebrated examples of Vile's fine workmanship.

Vile's royal accounts had been variously signed on his behalf by John Bradburne and William France, but seemingly for the last time on 13 December 1764. [PRO, LC 9/214] On 31 May 1763 the Master of the Great Wardrobe appointed William France 'in the room and place of William Vile and John Cobb discharged'. [PRO, LC 5/57] No reason was given for their discharge when the appointment of France was confirmed on 25 June 1764. In the first quarter of 1763 Vile's account had an entry, 'deduct £75 for over charge in the Japan Room' (in the Queen's House) and his bill was reduced from £858 18s to £783 18s. [PRO, LC 9/308] This however could have had little to do with the matter, but perhaps Cobb's known overbearing manner proved too much for George III and his officers. However the *St James Chronicle* note of Vile's death (below) recorded that he was 'formerly an Upholder . . . but had retired', and this may have been the sole reason for the cessation of the Warrant — a man near 65 years?

We known very little of Vile's private life. His will gives some indication of his style of living, with two houses in 'town and country'. He was made a Fellow of the Society for Arts and Manufactures in 1758, retaining it until his retirement six years later. Apart from Cobb's continuation of their business, Vile's nephew William Strickland joined with Jenkins 'late foreman to Cobb' to set up. Their trade-card [Heal] noted the relationship and employment. The carver and gilder William Beaumont succeeded 'Mr Vialls' whom Heal confused, incorrectly, with William Vile. He was Thomas Vials who worked for Adam at Lansdowne House. [A. T. Bolton, *The Architecture of Robert and James Adam*, II, p. 314]

Vile & Cobb's name first appears in the London directories in 1750, and it is entered until 1765. They are noted at 72 St Martin's Lane, on the corner where it joins Long Acre. Chippendale's premises were near. Most of their bills are headed 'Messrs Vile & Cobb, Cabbtt Makers, Upholders &c. The Corner of Long Acre', (variants occasionally put Cobb's name first, and note their services as undertakers). Cobb occupied the premises after Vile's death (1767) until his own in 1778.

The firm's fire insurance record has been first noted for 1752. [GL, Sun MS vol. 95, ref. 129677]: (a) '. . . on their Household Goods, Utensils and Stock in Trade, and Goods in Trust in their now Dwelling houses, being Three Houses, Land together and in & over the Warehouses & Workshops, only Communicating with the Same, part Timber, situate as aforeside, not Exceeding Seventeen Hundred Pounds. On their Glasses therein only, not Exceeding Three Hundred Pounds. On their Stock in their Yard only, belonging to the Said Dwelling . . . (Total £2,600).' (b) [GL, Sun MS vol. 111, ref. 147043]: 11 June 1755. Insured for £4,500, Glass £500, Stock in Yard £1,000. Total £6,000 — a further policy in the same vol. is ref. 147142. Cobb took out insurance on his household goods in the house he had 'over a gateway, leading into the yard of Messrs Vile & Co in St Martin's Lane' in 1755. [ibid., vol. 110, ref. 147142]

Together with the sculptor (John or Henry) Cheere, Sir William Chambers, James Paine and Ince & Mayhew, Vile & Cobb were directors of the Westminster Fire Office. [E. A. Davies, *An Account . . . of the Westminster Fire Office*]

Vile's will [PRO, Prob. 11/932, f. 357] of 24 August 1763, with a codicil of 9 November 1764, was proved on 23 September 1767. Vile had died on 22 August 1767 [*St James Chronicle*, 22/25 August 1767] He described himself as 'of the parish of Saint Martin in the Fields, Cabinet Maker and Upholder'. He bequeathed to his wife, Sarah, two houses at Battersea Hill, together with all household effects and the sum of £300. His nephew John Strickland was left his gold watch, and his other nephew William Strickland his wearing apparel. Those in his employ 'John Bradburn, Samuel Reynolds and William Eversley' received £20 each. The will continues: 'whereas for many years past I have been and am now engaged with my Copartner John Cobb in very extensive Branches of Trade and not having lately made any sort of stock to enable me to judge with any certainty of the Totall Value of my Estate and Effects, and I having the greatest opinion of the honour ability and Integrity of William Hallett of Cannons . . . and of my friend Charles Smith of Portugall Street . . . Upholder and Cabinet Maker give and bequeath . . . all my Estate Goods Chattels . . . upon the Trust and for the purpose herein declared . . . the trustees being empowered to settle . . . accounts depending between me and the said John Cobb'.

Vile then left smaller legacies to his niece Sarah Strickland, to William Strickland (who was app. to him in 1762), to 'James Humphrey and Sarah Humphrey late of South Petherton . . . Somerset, but now of London, my cousins', to 'William Humphrey of Middle Lambrook . . . Somerset, farmer, my Kinsman', and to 'Betty Hulett, wife of William Hulett of Sherborn . . . Dorset, Brasier' £100 'apiece for the trouble they may have'. The name does appear to be Hulett and not Hallett (a reading which would compound the enigma of the liaison). The codicil stipulated that Bradburn,

Reynolds and Eversley were to be 'my servants at the time of my death' to receive their £20, implying some, or one, of them had quitted Vile's employment. This may refer to the establishment of an independent establishment by John Bradburne, and to his succeeding to the Royal Warrant. A later marginal addition shows that in 1782 Hallett was deceased — he died in December 1781 — but Sarah Vile was still living.

It is a measure of the rigorous training enjoyed in a good apprenticeship that Vile should rise in a comparatively short time to provide fine furniture to the Royal family, and to noble patrons. He may have owed some of this in both training and financial support to William Hallett snr and to his equally talented but imperious partner, John Cobb.

THE VYNE, Hants. (Anthony Chute). 1752–54: 2 accounts for furniture and furnishings, supplied by Vile & Cobb in 1752–53, similarly worded — one for £120 16s 4¾d — the other for £121 13s 4¾d. The first for £121 plus starts on 19 May 1752, 'Due on a bill deliver'd' 19s, and therefore implies earlier work. The bills include the whole range of furnishing provision; carpeting, festoon curtains, beds, bedding, 'neat Mahogany Chairs Stuff'd in linnen'; globe lanthorns on Mahogany fluted pillers; bell Lanthorns on brass Armes'; Chamber, Corner and other tables, a 'wallnuttree Buerow on Castors', and even bellows and hearth brooms. In 1754 (2–5 August) Vile also took an inventory of Mr Chute's effects, assisted by the London auctioneer John Prestage. [Hants. RO, 31, M57, 630/1 and (inventory) M57/646]

CANONS ASHBY, Northants. (Revd Edward Dryden) 1753: Honble. Sir John Dryden Bart Bott. of Messrs Vile & Cobb Cab^tt makers & Upholders at the corner of Long Acre

June 29 For two good mahog Dineing tables to Joyn		£5–15–0
packing etc		8–0
Two mahog. bottle boards		3–0
		6–6–0

June 29 1753
Recd of the Revd Mr Dryden for Vile & Cobb
Samll Reynolds
[Northants. RO, D(CA) 179]

BADMINTON, Glos. (4th Duke of Beaufort). 13 August 1753: Received £48 10s. [Hoare's Bank vouchers, Badminton]

CLEVELAND HOUSE, 19 St James's Sq., London (2nd Duke of Cleveland). 1753–54: Vile and Cobb supplied looking-glasses. The house was being amended by Daniel Garrett 1746 — it was demolished 1895. [*Survey of London*, XXIX, pp. 161–63; accounts at Raby Castle, Durham]

LADY CAROLINE BRIDGES. 1753–55:

6 June 1753.	
To a Neat Mahogy Box with Partitions to hold 21 Cupps & 2 Glass Bottles a Drawer an Ivory Pallat & a Cover at Top	
	£3. 10s
To a Neat Mahogy Dressing Table on Castors with Cuttwork'd Sides & a Glass with Partitions within Side	£6. 6.
For a Case &c to pack Do	7s. 6d.
13 Jan. 1755. For a Japann'd Tea Chest	1. 15.
	£11. 18. 6.

Received May 3 1755 for self & Co. Wm Vile.
The reference to Cuttwork'd Sides' is interesting in view of the Holderness and other cabinets below. [Shakespeare Birthplace Trust, Leigh receipts, DR 18/5]

BRUTON ST, London (Sir William Proctor). 1754: January-October Supplied furniture to value of £130 14s 5d which included 'mahog dressing table with folding top & a cabinet at top with doors & drawers with inside glass to draw forwards', £14 10s. Paid 24 December 1754, less £11 8s abatement. [Norfolk RO, BEA. 305/79] See also 1758–61 below, Langley Hall.

LORD ARCHIBALD HAMILTON. 1754: 20 May (*Public Advertiser*): 'Auction. By order of the Executors. On Tuesday the 23rd inst and the following Days, Sunday excepted, All the entire genuine rich Household Furniture, large wardrobe of Linnen and China, of the Rt Hon Lord Archibald Hamilton, Governor of Greenwich Hospital, deceased, at his late House in the Hospital at Greenwich in Kent: collection of rich Genoa Damask\and other furnishings, in Red and W-CIs, large Pier and Looking Glasses, Mahogany Tables, Chairs etc likewise his Coach, Chariot and Post-Chaise. Catalogues . . . At Messrs Vile & Cobb's Cabinet and Upholstery Warehouse, the corner of St Martin's Lane, Long Acre, and at the Place of Sale.' (Vile & Cobb had presumably supplied much of Lord Archibald's furniture. His pictures were advertised in *Public Advertiser*, 29 June 1754 — catalogues from Vile & Cobb.)

DUKE OF MONTROSE. 1755: Received £24 17s for unspecified work. [Scottish RO, GD 220/6/1418/53]

HOLKHAM HALL, Norfolk (1st Earl of Leicester)

3 May 1755. pd Vile for a Pattern Chair like ye Duke of Devonshire's	08.00.00
to ditto for another pattern chair	6.06.00
to one to match ye Parlour chairs lac'd bottom gilt	5.11.00
for 2 strong cases	1. 9. 6
for a muhogany table with a drawer	2.18.00
Pd for a dome Bed stead & making the furniture, fringe etc & 39 yards of lawn for lining	15.14.00
for 2 mattrasses	4.01.00
for mats, paper, packing, painting, shades	1.03.06

[Holkham, Weekly Departmental Accounts, ending 3 May 1755]

BRITISH MUSEUM, London. 1756: Received £159 for a cabinet after winning the commission by competitive tender — 'to see the Cabinet already finished and to deliver in proposals sealed up.' [Standing Committee Minutes, 5 March 1756, I, p. 70] Minutes, 19 October 1757, II, p. 437: 'that Mr Vile is desired to attend at next meeting of the Committee with patterns of chairs'; p. 443 — 9 June 1758: 'That three dozen Chairs of Virginia walnut-tree be provided by Mr Vile according to the pattern agreed upon with banister-backs, at sixteen shillings each chair'. Minutes, 2 May 1760, III, p. 616: 'Resolved that Mr Vile's Bill for Furniture amounting to eighty-four Pounds & eighteen shillings be paid'.

BRAXTED PARK, Essex (Peter Du Cane). 1756: 8 May 'To Cash pd Vile & Cobb for a Mahogany Frame to a Marble Table etc. £4. 15s. 6d.' [Essex RO, D/DDC/A13, f. 59]

CAME HOUSE, Dorset (Hon. John Damer). 1756–64: One bill is cited in *GCM*, p. 118. [See also *C. Life*, 27 February 1953, p. 572.]

SANDON HALL, Staffs. (1st Lord Harrowby)

23 July 1756. to Vile Cabinet maker a bill	£1. 16. 0.
27 Oct. 1762. To Vile Cabinet maker by Bill	£21. 12. 0.
1 June 1763. To Vile Cabinet maker	£15. 2. 6.
15 June 1763. To Vile for a Commode Table & packing case	£8. 18. 0.
27 Ap. 1764. To Vile Cabinet maker	£8. 9. 6.

[Harrowby MS Trust, Sandon, vols 327 (1756); 330 (1762–64)]

CROOME COURT, Worcs. (6th Earl of Coventry). 1757–72: This was Vile & Cobb's most prestigious contract (apart from work in the Royal palaces) and brought them into contact with Robert Adam. There is an extensive archive (xerox copies, V & A archives, quoted in some detail below). The account opened in May 1757 and continued beyond Vile's death (1767) in Cobb's name. It contained well over 1300 items, and concluded circa July 1772:

(1758) 19 May 1758 For 12 Good Mahogy Chairs, the Seats Stuff'd & Cover'd with Leather and Brass Nail'd 16. 16. –.

For a Good Mahogy Library Table made to take apart, the top Cover'd with Leather 12. –. –.

July 1758 for 8 Neat Bamboo Arm'd Chairs with Can'd Seats and Loose Cushions, Cover'd with Your India Damask, and Check Cases 14. 12. –.

For a Good 4 post Bedsd on Castors, Sacking bottom and Compass Rod 6. 10. –.

For a Sett of Carv'd Cornishes to Ditto 5. –. –.

For 51¾ yards of Green Lutestring to Line your India Damask for Furniture a 4/2d 10. 15. 7½

For 8 yards of Silk fringe a 9/6d 3. 16. –.

For 105 Yards of Silk Lace a 4d 1. 15. –.

For Cloth to Line Lead Cloth and Teaster –. 9. –.

For Stuff to Line the Vallens and Baces –. 7. –.

For Buckram to Ditto –. 10. –.

For Rings, Silk, thread, tape, Glew, paste &c –. 14. –.

For Makeing Your Damask into a Furniture Lin'd and Fring'd & Covering the Cornishes Compleat 4. –. –.

Another bed was provided in blue damask, and a mahogany couch 'with one head Stuff'd and Quilted and Cover'd with Your green Silk Damask and Brass Nail'd' (£8. 5s). 29 July 1758 'For a Handsome Comode Chest of Drawers 12. –. –.' December 1758 'For a man's time 138 Days, 2 hours at Croome Repairing and putting up Furniture a 3/6 24. 3. 6.' In 1758 damask supplied cost £177 6s 9d. Most of it was supplied through Vile by Spencer Morris 'at the White Lyon over against the Church in Ludgate Street'. His blue Genoa Damask was at 13s 6d a yard. Vile's overall bill including damask was £582 13s 5¾d, received on 21 May 1759.

(1759) 29 January, 'For an oval Glass in a Handsome Carv'd and Burnish'd Gold frame 40. –. –.

20 July 'For a Large Handsome Carv'd Table frame Gilt in Burnish'd Gold 17. 10. –.

For a Strong Case to pack the Marble Slabb at Mr Wildsmith's & packing –. 15. –.

(1760) Provided blankets and bedding.

(1761) 8 May. For a Good Mahogy Table on Castors, with folding Tops, like a Card table, the inside Lin'd with blue Leather, part of the under top to lift up, and places under Do for papers, a deep drawer at each End, and Sham Drawers fronts on both sides, with Good Locks to suit your Key, and an Engrav'd Scutcheon. 10. –. –.

25 June. For 7 Handsome Carv'd Mahogy Arm'd Chairs on Castors, Stuff'd and Quilted, & Cover'd with Morrocco Leather, and finish'd Complete, with the best Burnish'd Nailes at 7£ each 42. –. –.

5 July. For 2 Handsome Carv'd Mahogy Sophoys on Castors Stuff'd and Quilted and Cover'd with red Morrocco Leather, and finish'd Complete, with Burnish'd Nailes 36. –. –.

12 July. For White Leather Cases to the 6 Morrocco Leather Chairs, and 2 Sophoys & 4 Bolsters 10. –. –.

6 Aug. For 2 neat Mahogy Horses to air Linnen 1. 8. –.

10 Sept. For 2 neat Mahogy Slabb Frames after the Dorick Order, to fitt yr 2 marbles Tops, enrich'd with Trighffs & Balls, carv'd mouldings & fluted Collums & feet to Do. 18. 10. –.

30 Nov. For men hanging the back Parlour with your blue flock Paper, on Cloth, tacks, paste &c 2. 5. –.

1 Dec. For 149 Yards of Cloth, to hang your Bedchambr and Clossett, and sewing Ditto 1. 8. 7.

For 149 Yards of crimson flock paper to hang Ditto 5. 11. 9.

6. Dec. For 2 Large Oval Glasses, in Handsome Carv'd and part painted, and part Gilt in Burnish'd Gold Frames . . . 173. –. –.

For 2 Handsome Carv'd Table frames, to Stand under the Oval Glasses, part painted, and Gilt in Burnish'd Gold   33.12.–.
[Now at Temple Newsam House, Leeds, Gilbert, *Leeds Furn. Cat.*, No. 452]
(1762) 24 July. For a very good 4 post D'ble Screw'd Wainscott Bedstead on Castors with Mahogy fluted Posts, a fine Sacking & Strong Bright Compass Rod to Do.   7.–.–.
(The bed was made up with crimson silk damask).
(1764) For a Sett of Large Mahogany Book Cases to a Drawing of Mr Adams wood work & all other Materialls Compleate.   260.–.–.
[now V & A Museum]
For 10 Cases to Pack the Book Cases in   5.15.9.
For Altering the Palasters of the Book Case By the Order of the Surveyor, Pannelling, all the faces & putting on the Mouldings & Loose Peices of Carving.   1.14.0.
For 2 Men at Croom 226 Days takeing down the old Book Cases & Putting up the new ones takeing them Down again & Cutting the old Dado & Brick Work & Putting them up a Gain Putting up the new Mouldgs . . . (part of)   39.11.–.
For a Man's Time Packing your Mouldings Brot from Mr Aulkins [Sefferin Alken, q.v.] & portridg to the Bell in Wood Street   –.3.–.
[Money received 16 January 1765] (Vile retired in 1764 and the other bills for Croome are in John Cobb's name — Cobb, q.v.).
EDGECOTE, Warks. (Richard Chauncey). 1758: A large bill from 'a ledger, formerly at Edgecot' and amounting to £1,215 7s 11½d is noted as 'Totl. Bill from Messrs Vile & Co.' [GCM, p. 56]
JERMYN ST, St James's, London. 1758: 'To be sold, (with or without the furniture) large house on N side of Jermyn St . . . (new furnished within these seven years). Details from Mr Spencer, Builder . . . or of Mr Vile, Cabinet-maker.' [*London Chronicle*, 9–11 May 1758]
UPPER BROOK ST, London (Sir Charles Hanbury-Williams). 1758: This bill is headed, unusually, in a reverse order from normal, viz. 'Cobb and Vile, Cabinet-Makers, Upholders etc., The Corner of Long Acre'. It was for £437 19s 6d for furniture supplied between 15 April and 18 December 1758. It was receipted by Cobb. [*C. Life*, 7 June 1956, pp. 1222–23; Coleridge, *Chippendale*, p. 28, n. 2, and text of bill, p. 46] On the strength of this commission some furniture made for Admiral Boscawen of Hatchlands, a friend of Hanbury-Williams, was attributed to Vile — particularly a mahogany secretaire, now at Tregothnan, Cornwall. [*C. Life*, 24 May 1956, p. 1115, pl 7]
LONGFORD CASTLE, Wilts. (1st Lord Folkestone). 1760: The patron protested at Vile's high prices — 'Vile, Cabinet-Maker a bill. N.B. He charged £7. 10s. for two girandoles and £1. 15. for the 4 nozzles and I am to pay him these prices for all I am to have from him. £17. 5s' Further payments are made to the partners to 1767 but no details are given in the account book of the actual furniture. [Longford accounts, xerox copy, V & A archives; Coleridge, *Chippendale Furniture*, p. 28; for attribution of a carved and gilt chest at Longford to Vile see *C. Life*, 7 October 1954, p. 1156, pl. 8. It should however be noted that this cabinet bears a close resemblance to pl. 20 of Ince and Mayhew's *Universal System*, 1759–63]
STRAWBERRY HILL, Middlx (Horace Walpole). 1760: Vile provided a bed for the Holbein Chamber with tasselled purple hangings. [Paget Toynbee (ed.), *Strawberry Hill Accounts*, 1927, p. 122: P. Thornton, *Authentic Decor . . .*, 1984, pl. 220]
NORMANTON PARK, Rutland (Sir Gilbert Heathcote) 1760–61: Two 8 p. bills including the provision of all forms of furniture, but seemingly no lavish items, carpets, picture frames, bedding, repairs and cleaning. Vile received

£123 2s 5¾d 'for self & Co.' on 17 June 1760. William France signed for a second sum of £171 8s 9½d 'for Messrs Vile & Cobb' on 4 June 1762. [Lincoln RO, 2 Anc, 12/D/29. Some of the furniture so described is at Grimsthorpe Castle, Lincs.]
SIR LAWRENCE DUNDAS (Work at Moor Park, Herts., 19 Arlington St, London, and Aske Hall, N. Yorks). 1761: May 5. Wm Vile £100. 1762: September 18. Vile & Cobb £200. 1765: January 29. Wm Vile £60. [Drummonds Branch, Royal Bank of Scotland, Dundas account, cited *Apollo*, September 1967, p. 202] The £360 is part of a much larger account. There is a rough note in Sir Lawrence's hand of expenses for furnishing his three houses — 'Cobb & Vile about £1500'. This document, undated, and c. 1770 is filed N. Yorks. RO, 2 ZNK, X 1/7/72]
ROYAL PALACES. Vile's name, with his partner's, were included in the Great Wardrobe accounts for the first time in the quarter ending Lady Day, 1761. [PRO, LC 9/ 306, No. 29] The accounts for the period 1761–65 are filled with details of their work, some examples of which survive in the Royal and other collections.
1761: Medal Coin Cabinets, two, mahogany, originally forming the ends of a 'Grand Medal Case' made for George III, the centre part of which is lost. It would seem that they relate to the case referred to in the accounts for October 1761. [Collections: V & A Museum, London; MMA, NY] Described in detail by Derek Shrub, 'The Vile Problem', *V & A Bulletin*, October 1965, pp. 26–35. PRO, LC 9/306 No. 29, includes a payment of £80 in 1761 to Vile for '3 Different pieces of work fitted in between the legs of His Majesty's Grand Medal Case with Carved Dooers & ends & a new Subplinth to do on a frame'.
1761: Bureau-Cabinet, mahogany. Made by Vile for Queen Charlotte's Apartments in 1761, (finial crown may be later replacement of original), and it has been suggested that the bowed sides of the lower stage are a modification by John Bradburne in 1767. [G. de Bellaigue, *Buckingham Palace*, 1968] Invoiced, Lady Day quarter, 1762 [PRO, LC 9/307, No. 21] 'For an Exceeding fine Mohogony Secretary with drawers & a writing Drawer, a Sett of Shelves at Top with a Crown carv'd at Top & the Side & Back all handsome Cuttwork £71.0.0.' (Queen's Apartment at St James's). [Royal Collection] The cut-work on this documented cabinet has led to the attribution to Vile of three secretaire cabinets, two of which were made for Robert D'Arcy, 4th Earl of Holderness, Secretary of State 1751–61. These cabinets are described under the appelations, the D'Arcy Cabinet, the Hoffman Cabinet, the B.A.D.A. Cabinet, in *The Antique Collector*, June 1969, pp. 116–19. The D'Arcy Cabinet was sold Sotheby's, 27 June 1974, lot 23, and secondly, 18 November 1983, lot 60. The Hoffman cabinet is in a private American coll; sold Parke Bernet, NY, 14 April 1969, illus. *DEF*, I, p. 151, pl. 58; the B.A.D.A. Cabinet, ex coll. Lady Dudley Ward was acquired in 1964 by Noel Terry from Hotspur. It is in the Terry coll. at Fairfax House, York. [*C. Life*, 5 September 1985, p. 656, illus.]
1761: Jewel Cabinet. Made by Vile in 1761 for Queen Charlotte. Invoiced Quarter ending Christmas Day, 1762. [PRO, LC 9/308] 'For a very handsome Jewel Cabinet made of many different kinds of fine Woods on a Mahogany frame very richly Carv'd, all the Front Ends & Top inlaid with Ivory in Compartments & neatly Engraved, the Top to lift up & 2 doors in front & 2 drawers under the Doors all lined with fine Black Velvet, with fine Locks & the brass work Gilt. £138.10.0.' Royal Collection, by descent; purchased by Queen Mary from her nephew, George, Marquess of Cambridge; illus: *DEF*. I. p.186, pls 44–45; *GCM*, pls 62–63. The 'fine woods' referred to included veneers of

olive, padouk, amboyna, tulip and rosewood. A 'secret' top lifts to show Queen Charlotte's coat of arms in ivory.

1761: Paper cases, two of a set of four. Made for George III's Library, St James's Palace. [PRO, LC 9/306, No. 29] 'A handsome Mahogany Paper Case Richly Carv'd with octagon shaped Glass Doors 62.10.0. '
'3 verry neat Mahogony Paper Cases the Insides full of Slideing Pertitions the outsides Richly Carved, with Exceeding fine Locks & 2 Keys 68.0.0. '
Royal Collection: two of four survive. The interior of each originally had eighteen slides and two shelves which have disappeared; illus. H. Clifford Smith, *Apollo*, May 1935, p. 278, pl. 4.

1762: Writing table. Made for the King's Blue Library, Buckingham House. [PRO, LC 9/307] 'A very good Mohogony Library Table on Castors, the top covered with leather, and exceeding fine locks made to the King's key. £24.10s.' This *may* relate to one of a pair of mahogany writing tables, Royal Collection; normally Palace of Holyroodhouse, illus. Clifford Smith, *op. cit.*, p. 279, pl. VI. However the account only mentions one table, but Clifford Smith noted its similarity to the one made for Richard Chauncey [1758, Edgecote, above]

1762: Bookcase, mahogany. Made for Queen Charlotte. [PRO, LC 9/308] 'A very handsome mahogany bookcase with plate Glass Doors (in) the upper part, and wood doors at bottom, a Pedement head with Pilastres and trusses, the whole very handsomely carved to match the Cabinett in the Queen's Bow Closet in St James's. £107.14.0.' Royal Collection: by descent to George IV; Augusta, Duchess of Cambridge; 1904 to Princess of Wales, later Queen Mary. The locks are marked 'C & C'; illus. *DEF*, I, frontis (colour); *Burlington*, July 1977, p. 483, with detail of left lower door.

1763: Cabinet, mahogany. Altered by Vile for Queen Charlotte in 1763 from an organ-case, probably made *c*. 1735 by Benjamin Goodison. [PRO, LC 9/310, No. 8] 'Queen's Dressing Room/Japan Room'. 'For altering the Organ & upright Harpischord by putting a Mahogany Plynth to the bottom part . . . the whole ornamented with Ovals of Laurels and other Carved Ornaments & Carved Moldings — two large Vinetree Ornaments on the top Ends to make the front Door and all the Ornaments neatly Carved & Gilt in Burnished Gold. £57.'. Royal Collection; H. Clifford Smith, *Buckingham Palace*, 1931, p. 78, pl. 69; Coleridge, *Chippendale Furniture*, pl 15. A set of nine mahogany dwarf-cabinets made to contain organ rolls are attributed to Vile. They have his usual central oval mouldings on the doors. Royal Collection: *DEF*, II, p. 168, pl. 23; *GCM*, pl. 67.

1763: Worktable, mahogany, carved fret. For Queen Charlotte at Buckingham House. [PRO, LC 9/308] 'a neat mahogany work table, with shape legs neatly carved and a scrole on the foot and a leaf on the knee. £9.18.0.' Royal Collection: illus, Clifford Smith, op. cit., pl. 64; *DEF*, III, p. 320, pl. 3.

The following is a small selection of items by Vile noted from the PRO, LC accounts, or the Windsor Royal Archives.
[LC 9/307] 1761: 'For a large Oak Tree Jarendole with two lights gilt £6.6.0. For a Mohogony Stand to serve either for a Tea Kettle Stand or for a high Candle Stand £1.10.0.' 1762. 'For making great alterations in 4 large Book Case (sic) taken from the library at St James's, making them Larger by Adding Palesters with Trusses & an entablature at Top with a Pediment to each & a frame with a Vitruvian Scroll between the Top & Bottom part £142.0.0.' [LC 9/308] 1763: 'King's Library. For a Moh. Couch Fashion'd Library Stool with one head the Seat made to turn up to ansr as a pr of Steps, the whole on a Sett of Triple Wheel Castors 14.10.0.'

Three references to 'Cutt work' [LC 9/309] 1763: 'Fine moh. 2 flat Table on Casters with a Drawer & Shelf & a Cutt work border on the shelf & a neat Black Standish to Stand in the Drawer to take out occasionally 4.4.0. For a neat Mohogony Bookshelf with Cutt Work sides 1.5.0. (similar entry) 2.10.0.'
Augusta, Princess of Wales [RA Windsor 55476] 1762 7 August: 'For altering 2 Doors of Miss Vansittart's Organ by taking out the Pannells & putting in wire instead of them & Green Persian Curtains behind Do. £2.14.0. For a neat Mahogy Bookcase to stand in a recess with Shelves & wire doors to Do at Top & Bottom & Green Lutestring Curtains behind Do. £10.15.0.'

Vile rented a house in 1765 in Sackville St. He had repaired and painted it at the Princess's order in 1763. [RA Windsor, 55496–98]

CHARLES HENRY TALBOT. 9 June 1761: To Vile and Cobb £81. [Hoare's Bank, London, Ledger 64/6]

BLICKLING, Norfolk (3rd Earl of Buckinghamshire). August 1762: Vile & Cobb — cabinet-makers £86.5s.9d. [Norfolk RO, MS 17148] The partners served the Duke's needs, 1762–63, through the Great Wardrobe, when he was appointed Ambassador to the Court of Russia at St Petersburg. [PRO, LC 9/307]

WOBURN ABBEY, Beds. (4th Duke of Bedford). Between 1762–64 Vile and Cobb submitted five bills to the Duke for new furniture, repairs to existing furniture and decoration of state rooms at Woburn after the rebuilding by Henry Flitcroft. The chief pieces provided were: June-July 1763: 'A large double drab sofa on treble-wheeled brass castors with 2 heads and 2 bolsters stuff'd and quilted. £11.10.0.' This was provided with a canopy with carved cornice, both sofa and canopy upholstered in blue damask; and with bedding complete to make a sofa bed. The total cost of this piece was £86 15s.

January 1764. '24 back stool chairs with carved backs and seats, upholstered complete in crimson cofoye [sic], at a total cost of £75.12.0.' This bill of January 1764 also shows that the firm was responsible for much decoration in the new gallery and that 254 days of gilders' and painters' time was expended in the work. All this was in embellishment of the work done by James Whittle & Samuel Norman in 1754 and following years. [Bedford Office, London]

EGREMONT HOUSE, 94 Piccadilly, London (2nd Earl of Egremont). 1762: 10 May 'For an extra Fine Mahog. Library Table — the Top Cover'd with black leather & 14 Draws & a Door under — with upright Partitions for Books the whole on Strong Casters, £14.10s.' The full bill was receipted 'for partner & self' by John Cobb. [W. Sussex RO, Petworth MS 377, vouchers No. 2, September 1763]

CHATSWORTH, Derbs. (4th Duke of Devonshire). When the 1st Duchess of Northumberland was on her tour in the mid 1760s she remarked on a bed by Vile at Hardwick in cut-velvet. Among the Chatsworth Burlington papers in the green vellum folio, Abstract of Tradesmen's accounts 1756–65 is:
f78 'Bills paid to 4th January 1764 Mr Vile & Cobb Upholsterers £277.1s.0d.
f88 (1764) Cabinet maker Cobbe 0.4.0. '
[C. *Life*, 7 February 1974, p. 250]

UPPARK, Sussex (Sir Matthew Featherstonhaugh). 1 January 1765: 'Pd Mr Vile in full £23.6s.6d.' [*Conn.*, November 1967, p. 160]

CANNON HALL, Yorks. (John Spencer). 1766: 30 June. 'Pd Vile and Cobb for a glass for Mr Greene £10.' [Sheffield City Library, archives dept, MS. 60633–19, vol. 3. Spencer visited Cobb's showroom in 1768] G.B.

Villeneau, Charles, Piccadilly, London, upholder (1748–49).

Heal records him in contemporary newspapers at the corner of Duke St in 1748. Polled at Westminster of Portugal St in 1749.

Villeneau, Josias (or Tobias?), Southwark, London, upholder and sworn appraiser (1733–c. 1740). Heal records him in newspapers of 1733 at 'The Golden Leg', near St Thomas' Hospital. Trade card, c. 1740 [Banks Coll., BM] gives address at 'The Golden Leg' over against 'Ye Bull's Head Tavern', and is annotated by hand: 'ye stock of ye sale to continue ten Days'.

Vinall, John, High St, Cliff, Lewes, Sussex, cm and u (1832–45). Recorded at no. 48 in 1832; no. 9 in 1839; and as John Vinall jnr in 1837. [D; poll bks]

Vince, C., Salter, 16 Tavistock St, Covent Gdn, London, carver and gilder (1839). [D]

Vince, John, London, carpenter and cm (1805–11). Trading at 17 Artillery St, Bishopsgate St in 1805–07; and John St, Spitalfields in 1809–11. [D]

Vince, William, 2 Gunpowder Alley, Shoe Lane, London, picture frame maker (1812). Took out a Sun Insurance policy on 26 August 1812 for £100 on household goods in the house of a glass cutter, clothes, books and plate. [GL, Sun MS vol. 455, ref. 873480]

Vincent, Edward jnr, St Thomas's, Oxford, cm (1802). [Poll bk]

Vincent, George Matthew (or George Mathyson), King's Lynn, Norfolk, u (1770–d. by 1823). App. to Robinson Crusoe, u, and admitted freeman on servitude, 1770–71. Took out a Sun Insurance policy on 13 December 1774 for £400 of which £360 accounted for utensils and stock. Dead by 1823 when his son, Riches Vincent, u of London, was admitted freeman by birthright, 1822–23. [King's Lynn freemen's calendar; GL, Sun MS vol. 235, ref. 347361]

Vincent, John, Norwich, carver (1745). Son of Clement Vincent, weaver; admitted freeman on 27 July 1745. [Norwich freemen rolls]

Vincent, John Baptiste & Peter, 3 Wardour St, London, bedstead makers (1810). Took out a Sun Insurance policy on 1 November 1810 for £150 on a house at 9, behind 99 Wardour St, in tenure of Blake, cm. [GL, Sun MS vol. 453, ref. 850441]

Vincent, John, Sherborne, Dorset, cm (1830–40). Trading at Half Moon St in 1830 and Long St in 1840. [D]

Vincent, Riches, London, u (1822–26). Son of George Mathyson Vincent, deceased; admitted freeman of King's Lynn, 1822–23. Polled of that city in 1824 and 1826. [King's Lynn freemen's calendar]

Vincent, Thomas, Ivy Lane, Canterbury, Kent, chairmaker (1790–94). [Poll bks]

Vincent, William, St Peter Hungate, Norwich, cm (1806). [Poll bk]

Vincent, William, Downham Market, Norfolk, cm and chairmaker (1822). [D]

Vincent, William, 20 Epworth St, Low Hill, Liverpool, cm (1839). [D]

Viner, Charles, 5 Broad St, Golden Sq., London, u (1835). [D]

Viner, Henry, address unrecorded, cm (1734). Amongst the Brownshill Court MS of the Palling and Carruthers families, (private ownership) are specifications for a chest of drawers, signed by Henry Viner, maker, and dated 1734. [Historical Manuscripts Commission Report, *Brownshill Court*, 6512, p. 57]

Viner, John, parish of St Stephen, Bristol, picture frame maker (1754). [Poll bk]

Viner, Robert, Clifton, Bristol, cm (1784). [Poll bk]

Viney, Joseph, Thomas St, Bristol, cm, broker and auctioneer (1793–1822). Trading with his son, Joseph Viney jnr, 1807–22, at 139–140 Thomas St, 1814–22. [D] Stamp of 'J.

VINEY' recorded on a mahogany commode, c. 1810, with lifting top, on turned legs; in ownership of the family.

Viney, Joseph jnr, Bristol, cm, u, appraiser, auctioneer and undertaker (1807–29). Trading with his father Joseph at Thomas St, 1807–22; alone at nos 139–140 in 1823; no. 140, 1824–28; and 3 Somerset Sq. in 1829. Declared bankrupt, *Liverpool Mercury*, 20 June 1828. [D]

Vinicomb, —, address unrecorded, cm (1803). Subscribed to Sheraton's *Cabinet Dictionary*, 1803.

Vining, R., 125 Regent St, London, writing desk and dressing case maker (1829). [D]

Vinsen, W., Gt Magdalen St, Thetford, Norfolk, cm and chairmaker (1822). [D]

Vinson (or Venson), William, 16 Henrietta St, Covent Gdn, London, carver, gilder and frame maker (1803–37). [D]

Vipond, Nicholas, London, u (1742–1802). Addresses given at 87 Bartholomew Close, 1759–75; no. 1, 1778–81; Little Britain in 1786; 67 Little Britain in 1794; and 16 Silver St in 1802. Son of Nicholas Vipond, Gent. of Norwich. App. to J. Hill, merchant tailor, on 23 September 1742, and admitted freeman of the Upholders' Co. on 7 April 1757. Took app. named Samuel Martin until 1762. Heal records him in newspapers, 1760–74. Declared bankrupt, *Gents Mag.*, January 1773. [D; GL, Upholders' Co. records]

Virgin, Arthur, London, upholder (1685–86). Named in the accounts of C. Blunt, u, in 1685–86, as 'Arthur Virgin upholder (for Mr. Lapeare'). [PRO, C/14/164, pt 1] See Francis La Pierre.

Virnon, T., address unrecorded. On 2 May 1784 charged £37 7s for a bed supplied to the Hon. H. Fane. [Lincoln RO, FANE, 7/1] Possibly Thomas Vernon.

Virran, John, address unrecorded, cm (1803). Subscribed to Sheraton's *Cabinet Dictionary*, 1803.

Virtue, J., 58 Newman St, Oxford St, London, u (1837). [D]

Vittore & Marone, 93 Market St Lane, Manchester, carvers, gilders etc. (1797). [D]

Vittory, I. & V., 93 Market St Lane, Manchester, carvers, gilders, looking-glass makers etc. (1800–02). [D]

Vitty, George Ascough, Manchester, cm, carver and gilder (1815–36). Trading at 122 London Rd, 1815–29; Edward St, Chorlton Row in 1832–33; 1 Russell St in 1834, and no. 2 in 1836. [D]

Vitty, William snr, Bargate, Richmond, Yorks., spinning wheel and reel maker (1823–27). [D]

Vitty, William (jnr?), Newbeggin, Richmond, Yorks., spinning wheel and reel maker (1823–27). [D]

Vivares, —, address unrecorded. On 31 May 1775 charged £2 9s 'for Gold Frames & glasses' supplied to Sir Richard Hoare. [Hoare's Bank, London, private accounts]

Vivian, —, address unrecorded, cm (1803). Subscribed to Sheraton's *Cabinet Dictionary*, 1803.

Vivian, W., Cat St, Plymouth, Devon, carver and turner (1814). [D]

Vizard, Isaac, address unrecorded, upholder (1781–98). Son of Arthur Vizard, victualler of St Giles, Cripplegate, London. App. to Isaac Taylor, upholder of Moorfields, and admitted freeman of the Upholders' Co. on 7 February 1781. Took apps named Richard Britain, 1790–98, and Thomas Lewis in 1795. [GL, Upholders' Co. records]

Vizer, Robert, Bristol, cm and timber merchant (1809–12). Trading at 11 Charles St, 1809–10, and 7 Lower Montague St. in 1812. [D]

Vobe, John, South St, London, carver (1774). [Poll bk]

Voble, John, Berwick St, Soho, London, coach and house carver (1763). [D]

Vogue, L., 14 Goodge St, London, picture and looking-glass frame gilder and cleaner. Undated trade card reads: 'Having made a valuable discovery by which he is enabled to clean & preserve Gilt Picture Frames, Looking Glass Frames etc. without removing — warrants them to stand for many years & bear washing if required & to look as brilliant as when new Gilt. Likewise cleans pictures without removing them from the room or mansion in which they may now be placed.' [Bodleian Lib., Johnson Coll.; *Furn. Hist.*, 1974]

Voice, John, King's Lynn, Norfolk, cane chairmaker (1717–21). Took apps named Storey in 1717 and Ditchfield in 1721. [S of G, app. index]

Voisey, William, Queen St, St Michael's, Bristol, cm, u and broker (1834–40). [D]

Vokins, John, London, carver, gilder and picture restorer (1820–37). Recorded at 5 Upper Rathbone Pl., Fitzroy Sq. in 1820; 5 John St, Oxford St in 1835; and as J. & W. Vokins at 5 John St in 1837. [D]

Volanteno, J., Fishergate, Doncaster, Yorks., barometer and looking-glass maker (1818). [D]

Vollum, H. jnr, London, cm and u (1835–39). Trading at 9 Cripplegate Buildings in 1835 and 84 Goswell Rd in 1839. [D] Presumably Henry, son of:

Vollum, Henry, London, cm and u (1822–39). Trading at 2 London Wall, 1822–23; 58 Barbican in 1829; and 79 West Side, Goswell Rd, 1835–39. [D]

Vollum (or Volumn), Thomas, High Wycombe, Bucks., chairmaker (1815–27). Daughters bapt. in 1815, 1818, 1824 and 1827. [PR (bapt.)]

Vores, John, Market Hill, Northampton, u (1796). [Poll bk]

Voss, George, 39 St Thomas St, Weymouth, Dorset, cm and u (1840). [D]

Vove, John, at 'The Sun', Long Acre, London, victualler and carver (1785). Took out a Sun Insurance policy in 1785 for £600 of which utensils, stock and goods accounted for £240. [GL, Sun MS vol. 236, p. 331]

Vowles, Elizabeth, 53–54 Worcester St, Birmingham, chairmaker (1830). [D]

Voysey, Alexander, Fore St, Exeter, Devon, carver and gilder (1791–96). [*Exeter Pocket Journal*]

Voysey, William, The College, Exeter, Devon, cm (1837–40). Daughters bapt. at St George's: Eleanor Mary on 11 June 1837; Julia on 14 October 1838; and Mary Ann on 3 May 1840. [PR(bapt.)]

Vulliamy, —, address unrecorded. Signed a torchère, *c.* 1790, with three-sided base carved with spears centring on ribboned wreaths, on three lion-paw feet; base supports a turned stand, carved with sphinxes, lotus leaves and gadrooning. [Sold by H. Blairman & Sons, 119 Mount St, London] Probably:

Vulliamy, Benjamin L., Messrs & Son, London, clockmakers (1807–16). Messrs Vulliamy & Son of 74 Pall Mall, are named in George IV's accounts repairing clocks and chandeliers, and supplying various stands and plinths including in 1807, 'An elegant writing stand made of red Saunders wood inlaid with black ebony & gilt mouldings', costing £21; 'A very large Bronze Chimera legs with human head & face, a lion's skin on the head forming a sort of cap . . . finished in the most masterly manner', at £159. 12s; 'a pair of black ebony Plinths lined w. green cloth', £2; and various purplewood stands covered in Genoa velvet. In 1808 the firm charged £31 10s 'for a very elegant writing Stand made entirely of black ebony of an Antique Egyptian Shape . . . ornamented in the centre with a Bronze figure of Isis kneeling . . .'; and in 1809, 20 guineas for '3 very elegant writing stands made of Rosewood with black ebony mouldings & gilt mouldings round the troughs for pens, mounted with 3 bronze vases each designed from the Antique for Ink, Sponge & Wafers'. In 1811 they provided 'a Chinese Moulding in 2 parts made to fit on a Cabinet made by Mr.

Tatham', costing £30. From 1813–16 Benjamin L. Vulliamy carried out work at Carlton House, repairing candelabra and plinths, and supplying stands and bronze tripods for clocks and vases. The Royal accounts on 10 October 1813 list a pair of 'wainscot circular framed stands with reeded purplewood mouldings, covered with crimson Genoa velvet', costing £4 4s; and on 5 October 1814, 'an oval framed wainscot stand for mounted blue china vase with reeded purple wood edge and covered with crimson velvet', at £1 11s 6d; and 'four mahogany circular stands with very thick black ebony edges lined with green cloth', costing £7. [Windsor RA, 25235; 25241; 25246; 25260; 25275; 25277; 25315; 2533; PRO, LC11/15–21]

Vyning, Lyas, Marshall St, London, cm (1784). [Poll bk]

Vyse, George, Ireland and Newcastle-under-Lyme, Staffs., cm (1830–37). Polled at Newcastle of there in 1830 and 1837; of Ireland in 1832.

W

Wacher (or Wacker), John, London, cm (1778–89). Believed to be of Flemish descent. Can possibly be identified with the John Wacker who took out insurance cover of £200 on his utensils and stock at Wells St in 1778. This low insurance cover does not altogether accord with the prestigious commissions that he undertook for the Prince of Wales and the nobility. It is also surprising that his name is absent from London trade directories. This might suggest a specialist craftsman working in association with established furniture makers. At Carlton House where he worked between 1783–89 he appears to have been under the supervision of Daguerre. Bills over this period amounted to £264. Much of the work charged was obviously of a high quality and in 1783–84 much of it was specified as in purple wood. In this period a large sideboard 12 ft in length and with tambour cylinder and folding doors was charged at £20, a library table with ten drawers, 6 ft long at £17 14s and a circular commode at £12 12s. He is also recorded working at Chatsworth in the 1770s. [H. Clifford Smith, *Buckingham Palace*, p. 109; *Apollo*, October 1972, p. 284; *Burlington*, June 1980, p. 413; Windsor Royal Archives, RA 25050, 25052]

Wachers (or Wackers), Thomas, Soho, London, u and cm (1830–39). Freeman of Canterbury. Living in Soho Sq. in July 1830 and from 1835 at 21 Greek St, Soho. [D; Canterbury poll bk]

Waddilove, James, Gumsford St, Blackfriars, London, upholder (1786). Son of J. Waddilove of the parish of Christ Church, 'Surrey', hatmaker. App. to Bartholomew Payne 4 September, 1776 and free of the Upholders' Co. by servitude 3 May 1786. [GL, Upholders' Co. records]

Waddingham & Co., 6 Midford Pl., Tottenham Ct Rd, London, veneer cutters (1821). [D]

Waddington, J., Melton Mowbray, Leics., cm (1791). [D]

Waddington, John, Cullingworth, near Keighley, Yorks., cm (1822–37). [D]

Waddington, W., Padiham, Whalley parish, Lancs., joiner and cm (1825). [D]

Waddington & Wood, Otley, Yorks., joiners/cm (1834). [D]

Waddle, B., Church St, Chelsea, London, u (1826). [D]

Waddy, Thomas Charles, Leeds, Yorks., u (1838). Bankruptcy announced, *London Gazette*, 3 July 1838.

Wade, Edward, Bayley, Calverley-cum-Farsley, Yorks., cm (1837). [D]

Wade, Frederick, Sheffield, Yorks., cm (1821–37). At Duke Lane in 1821 and 40 South St in 1837. [D]

Wade, George, Nantwich, Cheshire, u, cm, appraiser, auctioneer and undertaker (1819–26). 'Successor to the late Mr. Owen', possibly Richard Owen who is recorded in Nantwich, 1808–14. By February 1819 George Wade was well established at an address opposite the Hospital St End, High Town. Subsequent addresses are given as High Town in 1822 and also in the same year High St, but these designations may be identical. Apart from a wide range of fabrics, blankets, quilts etc., he stocked 'Pier and swing looking glasses, Tea Caddies and Ladies Work Boxes, Chests of Drawers, Bedsteads and Bedsteps, Bidets, Chairs and every other article for furnishing of houses'. A daughter bapt. 6 February 1822 and two sons 28 March 1826. [D; PR (bapt.); *Chester Guardian*, 3 February 1819]

Wade, George, Shrewsbury, Salop, cm and u (1826–35). Free 1826 at which date he was at Castle Foregate. In 1835 at Wyle Cop. [D; freemen rolls]

Wade, James, Calverly-cum-Farsley, Yorks., cm (1830). [D]

Wade, John, Saffron Hill, London, carver (1775–81). In 1775 the address was given as near Peter St, Saffron Hill and in 1781 as 16 Saffron Hill. In both years insurance cover amounted to £200 of which £100 was for utensils and stock. In 1775 Sir James Ibbetson paid Wade, carver, £112 16s 10d for furniture supplied to Denton Park, Yorks. This John Wade may have been the craftsman involved but there was also a John Wade living at Potternewton near Leeds in 1782 who was also a carver. [GL, Sun MS vol. 244, p. 154; vol. 290, p. 172; vol. 304, p. 219; V&A archives] Possibly:

Wade, John, Potternewton, near Leeds, Yorks., carver (1782). In 1782 insured his house for £500. [GL, Sun MS vol. 304, p. 219]

Wade, John Wright, Norwich, chairmaker (1808). Son of Thomas Wade, baker. Free 19 November 1808. [Freemen reg.]

Wade, John, Norwich, cm (1812–30). Living in the parish of St John, Timberhill in October 1812 and the parish of St Stephen, 1818–30. [Poll bks]

Wade, John, Chichester, Sussex, turner and chairmaker (1823–39). At Nag Lane in 1823, and Little London and Priory St in 1839. [D]

Wade, Nathaniel, Bristol, cm, u and undertaker (1827–40). At 13 Under the Bank in 1827; St Augustine's Parade, 1812–34; Orchard St facing Unity St in 1835, and 29 Denmark St facing Unity St, 1836–40. [D]

Wade, Thomas, Harewood, near Leeds, Yorks., cm (1822). [D]

Wade, Thomas, Spencer's Yd, Skipton, Yorks., joiner/cm (1834–37). [D]

Wade, William, Leadenhall St, London, carver and gilder (1784–1839). The number in Leadenhall St was 43 in 1784 but from the following year 86 and was situated on the corner of Cree Church Lane. The extended period of trading suggests that more than one William Wade was involved and it may be significant that by 1827 directory entries are in the name of William John Wade. Two versions of his trade card survive. These inform us that he was app. to John Overlove who traded at 'The Golden Key', 36 Leadenhall St, 1775–82. He was not however Overlove's successor. Wade was also a print seller and offered to frame pictures and needlework. He made and sold girandoles and looking-glass frames, cleaned, lined and restored paintings, re-gilded frames, painted seascapes and landscapes, supplied mouldings, composition ornaments for chimney-pieces and paper hangings and undertook funerals. His trade label has been recorded on the back of a framed David Wilkie print. Insurance cover suggests a business of a substantial size with total cover rising from £400

in 1785 to £600 in 1793 and £1,000 in 1810. Of these, utensils and stock accounted for £350 in both 1785 and 1793, and £700 in 1810. [D; Heal; GL, Sun MS vol. 327, p. 207; vol. 392, p. 131; vol. 451, ref. 839659]

Wade, William, Staindrop, near Barnard Castle, Co. Durham, cm (1815–17). Three daughters bapt., 1815–17. [PR (bapt.)]

Wade, William, Church Lane, Thorne, Yorks., joiner and cm (1822–34). [D]

Wade, William, Somers Town, London, cm (1830). Freeman of Rochester, Kent. [Rochester poll bk]

Wade & Jackson, 40 South St, Sheffield, Yorks., cm (1833). [D]

Wadelton, Charles, 3 James St, Devonport, Devon, u and cm (1838). [D]

Wadsworth, Christopher, Hull, Yorks., cm (1774–84). [Poll bks]

Wadsworth, John, High St, Daventry, Northants., cm and u (1823–30). [D]

Wadsworth, Thomas Rawbone, High St, Warwick, cm (1831). [Poll bk]

Wadworth, P., Doncaster, Yorks., carver (1784). [D]

Wafford, John, 9 Prince's Row, Newport Mkt, London, carver (wood and cabinet etc.) (1839). [D]

Wager, Joseph, address unknown, cm (1803). Subscribed to Sheraton's *Cabinet Dictionary*, 1803.

Wagg, David, 125 Norfolk St, King's Lynn, Norfolk, u and paperhanger (1836). [D]

Wagg, Frederick, 270 Whitechapel Rd, London, cm and u (1839). [D]

Wagg, John, address unknown, cm (1803). Subscribed to Sheraton's *Cabinet Dictionary*, 1803.

Wagner & Cottrell, Birmingham, cabinet, dressing case and portable desk makers (1818–39). At 9 Ann St, 1818–22 but at 14 between 1828–30. In Paradise St, 1835–39. [D]

Wagstaff, Anthony, Redcross St, Southwark, London, bed and mattress maker (1827). [D]

Wagstaff, Anthony, 1 Castle St, Long Acre, London, u (1835). An Elizabeth Wagstaff, furniture broker, is also shown in the directory trading at 1 and 6 Castle St in this year. [D]

Wagstaff, Anthony, 5 Waterloo Rd, London, cm and u (1839). [D]

Wagstaff, Charles snr and jnr, Cambridge, cm, u and brokers (1802–24). Charles Wagstaff (snr) is first recorded in a poll bk of 1802. In an advertisement in the *Cambridge Chronicle and Journal* of 13 September 1806, he describes himself as a Broker 'opposite Shoemaker Row' (later renamed Market St), who had 'new and second hand goods for sale'. An advertisement of 18 September 1812, states 'Charles Wagstaff and Son, Cabinet makers, Upholsterers, Paper hangers, and Manufactures of Household furniture of every description, also Appraisers, Auctioneers and Undertakers', with details of the furniture 'of their own manufactury'. 'Charles Wagstaff jun., (of the firm of Charles Wagstaff and Son)', advertised that 'he has commenced the business of Auctioneer and Appraiser' on 20 January 1817. It was reported on 16 January 1818, that 'Died yesterday after a long illness aged 55, Mr. Charles Wagstaff, Cabinet Maker and Upholsterer of this town'. The auction of 'All the valuable well manufactured stock in trade of Mr. Charles Wagstaff ... deceased', was advertised on 13 March 1818. On the 26 April 'Mrs. Wagstaff, widow of the late Charles Wagstaff' announced that the business would be continued 'by her and eldest son ... the shop and Warehouse will be opened on Wednesday 29 April with new stock ... The assortment made with the greatest care and attention to fashion and strength'. Charles Wagstaff of Sidney St is recorded in Pigot's directory, 1823–24. A mahogany D-ended dining table on turned legs has been noted with the inscription 'C Wagstaff/Maker/ Cambridge/1813' written in ink on the underside of the top.

R.W.

Wagstaff, Thomas, Cambridge, cm, u and broker (1793–1812). The Cambridge Corporation day bks record various entries for Thomas Wagstaff between 1793–1810, during part of which time he was a common councillor. On 27 December 1810 his son Thomas James Wagstaff claimed his freedom of the Corporation as eldest son of 'Mr. Thomas Wagstaff of this town, Broker and Cabinetmaker'. The sale by auction was advertised on 13 March 1812, of 'All the valuable manufactured stock in Trade of Mr. Thomas Wagstaff, declining the Upholstery business in Sidney Street', Wagstaff also announced that 'he intends immediately entering into the Grocery Trade'. [Cambs. RO, Corp. records; *Cambridge Chronicle and Journal*]

R.W.

Waid, —, address unknown, cm (1774–75). Paid £621 17s 9d in 1774–75 for work undertaken for the Earl of Egremont at Petworth House, Sussex. It is likely that this person's name was Wade but the details known, and the substantial nature of the commission make it difficult to locate the craftsman involved with certainty. [V&A archives]

Waight, George, Devizes, Wilts., cm and auctioneer (1793). [D]

Waight, John, 'The Looking-Glass', East Smithfield, parish of St Botolph without Aldgate, London, looking-glass maker (1714). In December 1714 insured goods and merchandise at his dwelling house. [GL, Sun MS vol. 4, ref. 4782]

Waight, Robert, Alresford, Hants., cm (1823–30). In 1830 at East St. [D]

Wain, Richard, Derby St, Leek, Staffs., chairmaker/turner (1834–35). [D]

Wainehouse, Thomas, 38 Hart St, Manchester, cm (1824). [D]

Waines, George, Helmsley, Yorks., joiner and cm (1840). [D]

Waineright, Robert, 175 White Cross St, Islington, London, carver and gilder (1837).

Wainhouse, Edward, Lancaster (1795–1800). Free 1795–96. Named in the Gillow records, 1795–96 and 1800. [Freemen rolls; Westminster Ref. Lib., Gillow]

Wainhouse, John, Lancaster, joiner and cm (1783–99). Free 1783–84. Named in the Gillow records, 1784–87, 1789–91, 1793–95 and 1799. [Poll bk; freemen rolls; Westminster Ref. Lib., Gillow]

Wainhouse, Thomas, Lancaster, cm (1811–12). [Lancaster freemen rolls]

Wainhouse, Thomas, Manchester, carver and gilder (1825–40). At 62 Hart St in 1825 and 45 Portland St, 1832–40. [D]

Wainwright, Alice, Windmill Yd, Manchester, u (1813). [D]

Wainwright, Charles, Hunslet, Leeds, Yorks., cm (1830–40). [D]

Wainwright, Duncan, 4 Naylor St, Liverpool, turner and rosewood stainer (1827). [D]

Wainwright, Edward, 2 Back Irwell St, Manchester, cm (1832). [D]

Wainwright, George, Stockport, Cheshire, cm (1790). App. to Charles Charles of Liverpool and petitioned freedom in 1790. [Liverpool freemen's committee bk]

Wainwright, James, Norfolk St, St James, Liverpool, cm (1800). At 36 Norfolk St in one directory of 1800 and 32 in another of the same year. [D]

Wainwright, James & Son, Liverpool, joiners and cm (1800–16). In 1800–03 occupied a shop at the botton of Prince's St, but from 1800–11 there was also a James Wainwright in the same trade living at Wavertree. By 1813 the business was referred to as James Wainwright & Co. and traded from 1 Tobin St. The addresses in 1816 were 15 Hasford St with a shop at 2 Tobin St. In 1822 a former app. Henry Ball petitioned for his freedom. He had been app.

not only to James Wainwright but also to John Ward Turner. [D; freemen's committee bks]

Wainwright, John, 39 Drury Lane, London, cm and broker (1783–93). In 1783 took out insurance cover of £300 which included £100 for utensils and stock. [D; GL, Sun MS vol. 317, p. 90]

Wainwright, John, Liverpool, cm and victualler (1781–1807). At 3 Lawton St in 1781 but from 1790 all the addresses are in Liver St. The number was 17 in 1790 and 1800, 16 in 1800–05 and 61 in 1807. In July 1790 he insured his dwelling house for £100. Married a Mrs Edmundson at St Peter's Church in January 1797. Possibly the John Wainwright who subscribed to Sheraton's *Cabinet Dictionary*, 1803. [D; GL, Sun MS vol. 370, July 1790; *Billinge's Liverpool Advertiser*, 16 January 1797]

Wainwright, John, Park Lane, Liverpool, cm and victualler (1834–39). At 17 Park Lane, 1834–37 and 35 in 1839. [D]

Wainwright, Joseph, Sheffield, Yorks., cm (1763). In 1763 took app. named Gosling. [S of G, app. index]

Wainwright, Joshua, Law Flat, Midehope, Bolstertone, Yorks., cm (1837). [D]

Wainwright, Richard, Ormskirk, Lancs., cm (1751). In 1751 took app. named Moorcroft. [S of G, app. index]

Wainwright, William, Longworth, Liverpool, cm (1810–39). At 2 White St with a shop at 24 Cornwallis St, 1810–11. In 1839 a William Wainwright was shown at 17 Cockspur St. A William Wainwright was also living in Halewood in 1822 at which date he was aged 54. It is possible that there was more than one William Wainwright in this trade in Liverpool in the early 19th century. [D; Liverpool RO, CLE/CON/5/2]

Wainwright Brothers, 44 Conduit St, Bond St, London, looking-glass manufacturers, wholesale u and cm (1839). Their trade card [Landauer Coll., MMA, NY] indicates that they were also importers of 'Mahogany & Every Other Description of Wood'. [D]

Wait, Henry, Bristol, cm (1832–36). At 7 Lower West St, 1832–35 and Eastern Rd in 1836. [D]

Waite, Ezra, Carlisle, Cumb., carver (1755). Freeman of Carlisle. In 1755 took app. named Patinson. By the mid 1760s he had emigrated to South Carolina where he was working on Miles Brewton House, 27 King St, Charleston, which he may have designed. Associated in Charleston with the English carvers Thomas Woodin and John Lord. [S of G, app. index]

Waite, Ezra, Well-bank St, London, carver (1764). Bankruptcy announced, *Gents Mag.*, May 1764. Possibly the same craftsman who was trading in Carlisle in 1755 and emigrated to the United States. The bankruptcy may have provided the incentive to emigrate.

Waite, James, St Stephen St Norwich, cm and u (1821–30). Free 24 February 1821 and trading in Stephen St, 1822–30. [D; freemen rolls]

Waite, John, 170 Temple St, Bristol, joiner and cm (1775). [D]

Waite, John, Hull, Yorks. and London, cm (1790–99). Freeman of Beverley, Yorks. but living in Hull in 1790 and London in 1799. [Beverley poll bks]

Waite, John, 2 Bishop Gate, Manchester, cm (1813–17). [D]

Waite, Matthew, Merchants Row, Scarborough, Yorks., carver and gilder (1830). Son of John Waite, guard. App. to William Fawcett Dodgson of York on 29 March 1819, and trading in Scarborough in 1830. [D; York app. reg.]

Waite, William, Brown Cow Yd, Meadow Lane, Leeds, Yorks., cm (1822). [D]

Waite, William, 117 Northgate, Huddersfield, Yorks., cm and u (1828–37). [D]

Waithman & Co., 244 Regent St, corner of Little Argyle St, London, furniture printers, damask and carpet manufacturers and u (1830). In May 1830 supplied John Arkwright of

Hampton Court, Leominster, Herefs. with carpets and fabrics to a value of £35 6s 9d. [Herefs. RO, Arkwright A63/161]

Wake, —, Long Acre, London, u (1730). [Heal]

Wake, Anthony, Bedale, Yorks., joiner and cm (1840). [D]

Wake, John, Boston, Lincs., chairmaker (1766–91). In October 1766 advertised for two journeymen chairmakers who could 'turn, frame and bottom' chairs. In July 1787 took out insurance cover of £300 on household goods, utensils and stock and four houses. In 1791 utensils and stock accounted for £50 only out of a total of £200 cover. [*Cambridge Chronicle*, 4 October 1766; GL, Sun MS vol. 345, p. 442; vol. 370]

Wake, John, Lofthouse, Yorks, joiner/cm/cartwright (1834). [D]

Wakefield, James, 9 Brokers Row, Moorfields, London, cm (1809). [D]

Wakefield, John, Lancaster, cm (1763–72). Free 1763–64. Took apps, in partnership with Henry Birkett, in October 1764 and January 1766. Other apps of John Wakefield were Robert Cowper, 19 July 1768 and Edward Binns 21 January 1772. [Freemen rolls; app. reg.; poll bk]

Wakefield, John, Lancaster, cm (1779–1804). Son of William Wakefield who was already dead in 1779–80 when John was made free. Took as apps William Swann 12 June 1786, Thomas Darwen 16 November 1789, Simon Bryham 23 February 1791, Edward Pye 9 May 1801 and William Maychell 4 January 1804. Bankrupt by January 1799 when a dividend on his estate and effects was declared. [Freemen rolls; app. reg.; *Billinge's Liverpool Advertiser*, 28 January 1799]

Wakefield, John, Manchester, cm (1800–25). At 5 Chins Lane 1800–04, 14 Thomas St, 1808–17, 13 Thomas St in 1818 and 5 Marshall St, 1824–25. In 1819 referred to also as a furniture broker. [D]

Wakefield, Richard, Fish St, Worcester, cm and u (1840). [D]

Wakefield, Thomas, Birmingham, u (1781–90). In 1781 took out insurance cover of £600 of which £500 was for utensils and stock. At Church St in May 1787 when he insured six houses, two brewhouses and four shops for £1,000. In 1790 his address was given as High St, but he insured a house and shops adjoining in Great Charles St for £500 and stables for £135. The total insurance cover in this year was once again £1,000. In 1800 at 20 High St. [D; GL, Sun MS vol. 290, p. 469; vol. 345, p. 46; vol. 370]

Wakefield, Thomas, High St, Uttoxeter, Staffs., clock-case maker/cm (1828–35). [D]

Wakefield, Thomas, 19 Green St, Bath, Som., carver, gilder and looking-glass maker (1833). [D]

Wakefield, Thomas, Liverpool, cm (1835–39). In 1835 at Victory Pl., 8 Bottom St and in 1839 at 1 Bridport St. Possibly the Thomas Wakefield who was app. to Cattrall & Whittingham in 1830. [D; app. reg.]

Wakeford, W., London, carver and gilder (1837–39). At Percy Mews, Rathbone Pl. in 1837 and 34 Windmill St, Tottenham Ct Rd in 1839. [D]

Wakeham, James, 18 Fore St, Devonport, u and cm (1822–38). [D]

Wakelin, Daniel, 'The Cabinet', Knave's Acre, near Golden Sq., London, cm and u (1763). Known only from his trade card, copies of which are in the BM and GL. The latter is dated 1763. The card indicates that he made and sold 'all sorts of Cabinets and Upholstery Work; sells Carpets, Blankets, Quilts, Rugs; and likewise buys and sells all sorts of Second-hand Furniture. Funerals performed'.

Wakelin, Henry, Hull, Yorks., cm, chairmaker and joiner (1810–16). Took as apps Charles Bray of Lissington, Lincs. in March 1810, William Bell of Market Rasen, Lincs. in July 1813, and Michael Stephenson of Louth, Lincs. in November 1816. [App. reg.]

Wakelin, Hugh, Dam St, Lichfield, Staffs., cm (1828–35). In 1834 trading at Butcher Row. [D; poll bk]

Wakelin, John, Peterborough, Northants., cm and chairmaker (1796). In June 1796 advertised for a cm. [*Cambridge Chronicle*, 25 June 1796]

Wakeling, Giles, 36 Gerard St, Soho, London, u and cm (1819–39). Also shown at 29 Crown St as Wakeling & Son. His trade card [Heal Coll., BM] indicates that he was 'Upholsterer to the Admiralty' and also undertook funerals. Heal lists a Thomas Wakeling at this address, 1825–32, and Giles Wakeling, 1832–39, but no evidence has been seen to support the existence of Thomas Wakeling. [D; Heal]

Wakeman, Richard, Cambridge (?), chairmaker (?) (1660). Paid £8 18s by Trinity College in 1660 for chairs.

Wakeman, Thomas, St Mildred's Ct, Poultry, London, upholder (1798–1802). Son of Thomas Wakeman of St Mildreds Ct, Poultry. App. to Richard Jones and free of the Upholders' Co. by servitude, 1798. [GL, Upholders' Co. records]

Walbancke, Edward, London, u and undertaker (1772–d. 1784). At 1 Rathbone Pl., Oxford Rd, 1772–82. The address is rendered as 24 Oxford St in 1783 but as the premises were on the corner of Rathbone Pl. and Oxford St this may not represent a change of address. In 1782 took out insurance cover of £1,200 of which £900 was for utensils and stock. By this date he was in partnership with a Benjamin Milward. Died March 1784 aged 52. [D; GL, Sun MS vol. 303, p. 360; *Gents Mag.*, March 1784]

Walbancke & Smith, 4 John St, Oxford St, London, upholders (1790–94). [Heal]

Walbridge, John, London, cm (1751). In May 1751 an auction sale was announced 'next door to the Saracen's Head Inn, within Aldgate' of the household furniture and part of the stock in trade of John Walbridge 'lately gone abroad'. On offer were 'four-post beadsteads, with Harrateen and other furniture, good beds and bedding, Pier Glasses and Sconces, with variety of colour work in Mahogany and Walnut-Tree, some China, Pictures, Turkey carpets, stoves etc. There is a very fine Mahogany Cloaths Chest with Drawers, a Chest upon Chest ditto, and a Dyer's Frame and Pan complete'. [*General Advertiser*, 9 May 1751]

Waldegrave, Samuel, 'Bull Inn', Bishopsgate St, London, upholder (1786). Son of Thomas Waldegrave of Bury St Edmunds, Suffolk, minister. App. to Thomas Savile in 1778 and free of the Upholders' Co. by servitude, 4 January 1786. [GL, Upholders' Co. records]

Waldron, E., Magdalene St, Exeter, Devon, rush chairmaker (1816–25). [D]

Waldron, Thomas, 231 Holborn, London, cm and upholder (1780–83). In 1780 the address was rendered as the corner of New Turnstile, Holborn. In this year he took out insurance cover of £800 of which £610 was for utensils and stock. [D; GL, Sun MS vol. 285, p. 580] Possibly:

Waldron, Thomas, London, u (1784–1803). At 11 Catherine St, Strand, 1784–94. The business was of a substantial size. In 1791 insurance cover was £3,000 of which £1,500 was for stock and utensils in the Catherine St premises and a further £800 his timber stock in a yard in the Savoy. In common with other makers who established business in Catherine St, Waldron was interested in patent furniture. He took out a patent for such articles in 1785 and was able to offer 'Patent bedsteads upon a new and elastic construction'. He subscribed to Sheraton's *Drawing Book*, 1793 and *Cabinet Dictionary*, 1803 and is recorded in the list of master cabinet makers in the latter publication. His bankruptcy was announced in November 1790 but he appears to have continued to trade. After 1794 he is no longer recorded in trade directories and by 1803, when Sheraton's *Dictionary* was published, Waldron was at Broad St, Carnaby Mkt. On 23 February 1791 he was paid £5 13s 3d by Edward, Lord Harewood probably for goods supplied to Harewood House, Yorks. [D; GL, Sun MS vol. 373, ref. 584202; Heal; *Derby Mercury*, 18 November 1790; *Williamson's Liverpool Advertiser*, 22 November 1790, 17 January 1791, 4 November 1793; Leeds archives dept, Harewood MS 212]

Wale, George, 63 Mortimer St, Cavendish Sq., London, u (1825). [D]

Wale, William, Baxtergate, Loughborough, Leics., joiner/cm (1822). [D]

Wale, William, Aldgate St, Leicester, cm (1835). [D]

Wales, George Richard, London, u and cm (1821–35). At 63 Mortimer St, Cavendish Sq., 1821–28 though one directory of 1826 gives the address as 1 Mortimer St. By 1835 at 48 King St, Golden Sq. [D]

Walford, —, address unknown, u (1730–44). Undertook work in connection with the Earl of Leicester's London house but possibly also for Holkham Hall, Norfolk. Supplied a chair at 14s which was paid for in 1730. Paid for making curtains in 1737, a settee bed and another bed and curtains 'for Mr. Jerravis room' in 1740 and for repairing three beds in London in 1742. The sums involved are modest the largest being £22 18s in 1741 for cleaning and making up beds. A mattress for a couch bed and work on other beds in 1742 amounted to £11 19s and beds and two chairs in 1744, £6 9s. [V&A archives]

Walford, C., 93 Park St, Camden Town, London, chairmaker and cm (1838). [D]

Walford, Charles, Tonbridge St, Brunswick Sq., London, chairmaker (1826). [D]

Walford, Jn, 14 Nassau St, Middlx Hospital, London, buhl manufacturer (1822–27). [D]

Walford, Obadiah, 17 St James's Sq., Wolverhampton, Staffs., cm (1802). [Rate bk]

Walford, Samuel, 8 Rosomon St, Clerkenwell, London, u (1826). [D]

Walford, Timothy, Colchester, Essex, upholder, cm and appraiser (1768–1834). Timothy Walford snr traded from an address in the High St. He was trading here by 1784 and was still at this location in 1805. On 8 October 1776 he married Elizabeth Daniel at St Botolph's Church, Colchester. The business was, by provincial standards, of substantial size and utensils and stock were valued at £500 in 1775 and £600 in 1777. His son Timothy jnr was married to Mary Ann Moore in Colchester in 1809. He joined his father in the business which in 1822 was described as T. Walford & Son. At this date it was trading from 19 Head St. In the following year the business was named as Timothy jnr and this may be an indication that the father had retired from active participation. Timothy jnr died in 1828 but his father's death was not announced until 1834. In the early 19th century this business used a trade label to mark at least some of its production. A circular pedestal table of c. 1805–20 in Colchester Museum bears such a label inscribed 'T. WALFORD/CABINET MAKER, UPHOLSTERER/AUCTIONEER & APPRAISER/No 19 HEAD STREET, COLCHESTER/ Paper Hangings — Funerals Furnished'. [D; Colchester and Maldon poll bks; GL, Sun MS vol. 240, p. 625; vol. 261, p. 144; Essex RO, D/P 185/5/1; *Wills at Chelmsford*]

Walford, Thomas, Southgate St, Bury St Edmunds, Suffolk, cm (1830). [D]

Walker, —, Leadenhall St, London, u (1748). [Heal]

Walker, —, Cheapside, London, cm (1749). Partner to a person named Tantum. [*A Complete Guide to . . . London*, 1749]

Walker, Aaron, 33 Wellington Rd, Charleston, near Ashton-under-Lyne, Lancs., joiner and cm (1834). [D]

Walker, Adam, High St, Putney, London, furniture broker and u (1832). [D]

Walker, Andrew, Whitburn St, Sunderland, Co. Durham, joiner and cm (1828). [D]

Walker, Anthony, Seaton, Hartlepool, Co. Durham, joiner and cm (1828). [D]

Walker, Benjamin, Furnival St, Sheffield, Yorks., cabinet case maker and cm (1822–38). Bankruptcy announced, *Sussex Agricultural Express*, 25 August 1838. [D]

Walker, Benjamin, Upper and Lower Wortley, near Leeds, Yorks., joiner and cm (1830). [D]

Walker, Benjamin, Horsforth, Leeds, Yorks., cm (1834). [D]

Walker, Charles, Leeds, Yorks., journeyman cm (1791). Name included in the list of journeymen assenting to the contents of the *Leeds Cabinet and Chair Makers' Book of Prices*, 1791.

Walker, Charles, 12–14 King's Pl., Commercial Rd, London, u, cm and linen draper (1826–35). [D]

Walker, Charles, Bacon St, Lichfield, Staffs., cm (1826–35). [D; polls bks]

Walker, Charles & Beck, William, 46 Fish St Hill, London, looking-glass manufacturers (1780–1804). In 1780 took out insurance cover of £600 on utensils, stock and the house. In 1804 also ironmongers and hardwaremen. [D; GL, Sun MS vol. 281, p. 58]

Walker, Christopher, Lancaster, joiner and cm (1751–55). In 1742 app. to John Lowther, joiner and free as a joiner, 1751–52. Took app. named Hayward on 11 May 1752. Two further apps were taken in 1753 and one named Overend in 1755. [App. reg.; freemen rolls]

Walker, David, London, cm (1793). Subscribed to Sheraton's *Drawing Book*, 1793.

Walker, David, 3 Princess St, Westminster, London, u (1837). [D]

Walker, Edward, Chester, cm and joiner (1792–97). At Eastgate St in 1793 and John's Lane, 1795–97. [D]

Walker, Elizabeth, London, carver, gilder and print seller (1790–1807). In 1790 in partnership with Hannah Heath Abbot at 7 Cornhill. The insurance cover of £2,400 carried by this business was very substantial for this trade. In 1799 the enterprise was still at the Cornhill address, but Elizabeth was at this date in partnership with a William Walker, possibly her son. From 1800 William Walker is listed trading on his own account from 31 Old Bond St, but some directories of 1805–06 shown him still in partnership with Elizabeth at the new address. [D; GL, Sun MS vol. 370] See John Walker, Strand and Cornhill, London.

Walker, Elizabeth, Scale Lane and Saville St, Hull, Yorks., cm (1795–97). Widow of Thomas Walker whose business she continued with the assistance of her son, Robert. In 1795 paid £1 16s 5d for a 'best Mahogany Arm'd Chair' supplied to Burton Constable, Yorks. [*Hull Packet*, 16 December 1794; Humberside RO, Burton Constable vouchers] See Robert Walker of Hull

Walker, Frederick, Rockley, Notts., joiner and chairmaker (1832–40). Born 1793. Was an active member of the Rockley Methodist Society. Maintained a policy of marking his chairs which are stamped on the seat edge 'F. WALKER/ROCK-LEY' (Fig. 2). Considerable numbers of Windsor chairs so marked have been recorded, including large matching sets made for Working Men's Clubs and Mechanics Institutes in Yorkshire. The quality of the chairs varies from those made elegantly in yew to inexpensive elm and beech models. He is first recorded in a trade directory in 1832 and at the time of the 1841 Census was one of five makers active in this hamlet. The long low brick workshop that he occupied adjoined the old chapel on the Retford road and survived until 1970. [D; *Antique Collecting*, February 1974]

Walker, G., 134 St John's Rd, Clerkenwell, London, cm and u (1830). [Heal]

Walker, George, London, upholder (1699–1725). Free of the Upholders' Co., 7 June 1699. Took as apps Richard Tyte, 1712–19 and William Tyte, 1718–25. [GL, Upholders' Co. records]

Walker, George, 11 Charles St, Whitechapel, Liverpool, cm (1803). [D]

Walker, George, 7 Tower St, Seven Dials, London, cm (1805). [D]

Walker, George, 10 Ship St, Brighton, Sussex, cm and u (1833–40). A daughter and two sons bapt., 1833–37. [D; poll bk; PR (bapt.)]

Walker, George, 6 and 7 Promenade, Clifton Rd, Bristol, carver and gilder (1840). [D]

Walker, George Benison, 20 Story St, Hull, Yorks., joiner and cm (1831). [D]

Walker, George Townsend, address unknown, cm (1784). A secretaire cabinet has been recorded with the signature of this maker and the date 7 April 1784. [Christie's, 27 July 1978, lot 162]

Walker, H., Lancaster, cm (1831). Bankruptcy announced, Chester Courant, 12 April 1831.

Walker, Henry, Mortimer St, Cavendish Sq., London, upholder and auctioneer (1797). Bankruptcy announced, Billinge's Liverpool Advertiser, 6 February 1797.

Walker, Henry, Lancaster, cm, joiner and u (1791–1831). A Henry Walker is named in the Gillow records 1791–97, 1799, 1803 and 1806 and may perhaps be identified with the person of the same name who set up in business 'at the top of the New Road, in Church Street' in June 1805. This Henry Walker must have prospered for in May 1813 he was able to announce a move to 'commodious premises upon the Green Area, nearly opposite the end of Chapel Street, and adjoining Messrs. Brockbank's ship-yard'. Directories give this address as Cable St. These premises were described as 'new built and commodious'. Free 1823–24 'on gift of the Bailiff of the Commons'. In March 1831 however he was declared bankrupt and his household goods and stock were auctioned for the benefit of his creditors in a three day sale. Also auctioned were his house and business premises. These were built on land leased from the Lancaster Corporation and consisted of 2 Chapel St, rented to a John Harrison, and 3 and 4 Cable St which Walker himself used, the former being described as a house and shop also fronting Chapel St and the latter as a house. He is however still recorded at Cable St in a directory of 1834. A number of pieces of furniture have been noted with an impressed mark 'HENRY WALKER LANCASTER' which correspond with this maker's period of trading. These include a 'Gillow type' table, a mahogany secretaire chest of drawers, a dressing mirror and an oak clock case. [D; Lancaster Gazette, 1 June 1805, 1 May 1813, 26 May 1831, 4 June 1831; Westminster Ref. Lib., Gillow; freemen rolls]

Walker, Henry, Lancaster, cm (1827–28). Free as a cm 1827–28. Listed as the son of Henry Walker of Lancaster, cm, probably the maker trading at Chapel & Cable St, Green Area at this date. [Freemen rolls]

Walker, J., Warwick Ct, London, carver and gilder (1793). Subscribed to Sheraton's Drawing Book, 1793.

Walker, J. K., 39–40 Drury Lane, London, u and cm (1826–39). [D]

Walker, J., Oriel Bar, Cheltenham, Glos., carver and gilder (1839). [D]

Walker, J. B., 6 Clarence Colonnade, Cheltenham, Glos., carver and gilder (1839). [D]

Walker, Jacob, 6 Gt Pulteney St, Golden Sq., London, chairmaker (1805). [D]

Walker, James, London, u, cm and undertaker (1794–1839). At 122 Jermyn St, 1794–1817; 2 Well St, St James's, 1822–27 and 115 Jermyn St in 1839. [D; Heal]

Walker, James, 76 Chapel St, Salford, Lancs., cm (1808). [D]

Walker, James, Lea Ct, Upper Milk St, Liverpool, cm (1813–14). [D]

Walker, James, Sandwich, Kent, cm (1831–32). [Poll bks]

Walker, James, Hexham, Northumb., joiner/cm (1834). [D]

Walker, James, High St, Margate, Kent, cm (1839). [D]

Walker, Jane, York Rd, Westminster, London, cm and u (1839). [D]

Walker, Jasper, 3 Asylum Pl., Newington Causeway, London, chair and sofa maker (1835–39). Described in 1835 as a japanner etc. [D]

Walker, John, 'The White Lyon', Little Old Bailey, London, u (1725). Took out insurance cover in March 1725 on a house and other buildings at Greenford, Middlx leased to a Joseph Harris and valued at £100. [GL, Sun MS vol. 21, ref. 38151]

Walker, John, Bristol, upholder (1734–39). Living in the parish of St Philip & St Jacob, 1734 and in the parish of St Peter in 1739. [Polls bks]

Walker, John, Chesterfield, Derbs., upholder (1743). Bankruptcy announced, Gents Mag., September 1743.

Walker, John, 'The Angel', Goodramgate, York, u (1745–48). Advertised sales of upholstery goods at 'The Angel', Goodramgate in May 1745, August 1746 and August 1748. Possibly an itinerant tradesman. [York Courant, 21 May 1745, 25 August 1746, 16 August 1748]

Walker, John, address unknown, cm (1725). Recorded as one of the cm employed in furnishing the Mansion House, London. [Conn., December 1952, p. 181]

Walker, John, Liverpool, cm (1745–80). Free 16 July 1745. Took as apps Thomas Foster (free 1767), Robert Kenyon (free 1767) and Edward Huddleston (free 1780). [Freemen rolls]

Walker, John, York and Harewood, Yorks., joiner (1766–75). App. to John Halsey, carver, in 1745 and Edward Griffiths, cm, in 1752. Free of York as a joiner, 1766. Involved in the supply of furniture to Harewood House, Yorks. 1771–75, though he was possibly employed at an even earlier date for there is an isolated bill of 1 August 1767 for cleaning and altering a settee at £1 4s 9d. An account of 25 September 1771 was for two commode chests of drawers at £4 4s and eighteen chairs charged at 4s or 6s each and totalling £4 1s. On 14 January 1774 four 'Handsome Mahogany Tea Tables' were supplied at £3 18s and two large chairs for the north front at £3 3s. Both of these were made to designs supplied to Edwin Lascelles by Thomas Chippendale. Between January 1774 and November 1775 Walker supplied two dressing chests at £2 10s, four mahogany stools at 12s and two ornamental garden chairs at £3 5s. Walker provided assistance on several ocassions to William Reid who was Thomas Chippendale's foreman at Harewood and Walker's plain furniture was enriched with carving by Christopher Theakstone, a decorative carver, employed by Edwin Lascelles. The local firm of Bottomley & Walker, joiners, were employed on joinery work at Harewood and it is likely that John Walker was a partner in this business. [York app. reg.; York freeman rolls; Leeds archives dept, Harewood MS 492, 247, 383, 492; Furn. Hist., 1965]

Walker, John, Lancaster and Liverpool, cm (1779–84). Freeman of Lancaster, 1779–80, but after freedom settled in Liverpool. [Lancaster freemen rolls; Lancaster poll bk]

Walker, John, Liverpool, cm (1780–1807). App. to John Eden and free 11 September 1780. Trading at 11 Charles St, 1790–1803; 55 Renshaw St in 1805; and 30 Lime St in 1807 though another directory of the same year gives 19 Cavendish St. His son William Longworth Walker, cm was made free by patrimony in 1806. John Walker was dead by 1812. [D; freemen reg.]

Walker, John, Hull, York., cm (1780–84). [Polls bks]

Walker, John, London, carver, gilder and printseller (1784–1802). At 148 Strand, 1784–88, but already by 1787 owned property at 7 Cornhill where household goods, utensils and stock to a value of £1,000 were kept. On 2 April 1788 made free of the Upholders' Co. by redemption though he never traded as an u. In 1790 trading from 7 Cornhill and he appears to have used this address until 1802. An Elizabeth Walker in the same trade operated from the Cornhill address, 1790–1807. [D; GL, Sun MS vol. 345, p. 55; GL, Upholders' Co. records]

Walker, John, London, carver, gilder and printseller (1786). His trade card [Banks Coll., BM] is dated 1786. This indicates that he was trading at 28 Haymarket but had moved from Parliament St.

Walker, John, Chester, joiner and cm (1784–d. 1804). Took as app. John Hall, 1787. In 1789 trading at Gen. Printing Office Yd. Died November 1804. At the time of his death he was described as 'A man of the strictest integrity of conduct, of the most peaceable deportment & universally respected by his acquaintances'. [D; poll bk; app. bk; *Liverpool Chronicle*, 21 November 1804]

Walker, John, 246 Shoreditch, London, u and furniture warehouse (1789–93). In 1789 the business was described as a furniture warehouse and in 1793 as an u. [D]

Walker, John, Limekiln Lane, Bristol, carver (1795). [D]

Walker, John, 11 Quay St, Manchester cm (1804). [D]

Walker, John, Gateshead, Co. Durham, joiner and cm (1811). [D]

Walker, John, Hull, York., cm and u (1814–40). At 32 Savile St, 1814–23, though in 1823 shown at both Savile St and Blackfriargate. The number in Blackfriargate is shown as 24 in 1823; 25 in 1826–34; and 24 and 25 in 1835. From 1835 shown with a 'mahogany yard' on the north side of Old Dock. Also shown as paperhanger and in 1823 as agent for the Sheffield Fire Office. Joseph Walker, cm is shown at 25 Blackfriargate in 1821–22. [D]

Walker, John, Lower Temple St, Leeds, Yorks., cm (1822). [D]

Walker, John, Tunstall, Staffs., joiner and cm (1822). [D]

Walker, John, 32 Greek St, Soho, London, u, bed and mattress maker (1825–29). [D]

Walker, John, Dunkinfield, near Ashton-under-Lyne, Lancs., joiner and cm (1828). [D]

Walker, John, Brownhills, Staffs., cm, u, joiner and builder (1834–35). [D]

Walker, John, Driffield, Yorks., cm, u and wood turner (1834–40). In 1834 in Middle St and in 1840 at Market Pl. [D]

Walker, John, 79 Newman St, Oxford St, London, u (1835). [D]

Walker, John, Middleham, Yorks., joiner/cm (1834). [D]

Walker, John, Otley, Yorks., joiner/cm (1834). [D]

Walker, John, Lofthouse, Yorks., joiner/cm/cartwright (1834). [D]

Walker, John, Hungate, Pickering, Yorks., joiner and cm (1840). [D]

Walker, John Smith, Snow Hill, Wolverhampton, Staffs., joiner, cm and builder (1818–38). At 27 Snow Hill in 1822 and 23 Snow Hill, 1830–34. [D]

Walker, Joseph, Liverpool, cm (1766–1800). Initially at Rosemary Lane, but by 1781 at 42 Atherton St. In Water St from 1790. The number was 28 in 1790 and 29, 1794–1800. The death of his wife was reported, *Williamson's Liverpool Advertiser*, 6 June 1791. [D]

Walker, Joseph, High Holborn, London, see Joshua and Joseph Walker.

Walker, Joseph, 25 Blackfriargate, Hull, Yorks., cm (1821–22). A John Walker, cm and u was trading from this address, 1826–35. [D]

Walker, Joshua, 28 Wigmore St, London, u and furniture broker (1829–35). Described as an u in 1829 and a furniture broker in 1835. [D]

Walker, Joshua & Joseph, London, u, bed and mattress makers (1820–39). At 8 Aldgate Within, 1820–22, but from 1822 in High Holborn. The number in High Holborn is shown as 60 and 96 in 1822, but in November of that year a fire broke out in their premises at 60 and thereafter only 96 is shown. In 1829 at 109 and in 1835 at 108 and 109. In 1839 the business was listed as Joshua & Joseph Walker & Co. [D; *Times*, 25 November 1822]

Walker, L. W., Ormskirk, Lancs., cm (1822). [D]

Walker, Lucy, 7 Boyces St, Brighton, Sussex, u (1824). [D]

Walker, Martin, 18 Pitfield St, Hoxton, London, cm (1817). [D] See Michael & Martin Walker.

Walker, Matthew, Skinner St, Snowhill, London, bed and mattress maker (1822–27). Trade directories give the number in Skinner St as 49 but his trade card [GL] states 48. This states that he sold his stock of beds, mattresses, counterpanes, blankets etc. for cash only, and he claimed that his prices were 10% lower than those of his rivals. He sought also wholesale and shipping trade. [D]

Walker, Michael, High Wycombe, Bucks., chairmaker (1818). Son bapt. 1818. [PR (bapt.)]

Walker, Michael & Martin, 18 Pitfield St, Old St Rd, London, cm (1813–20). [D]

Walker, Millicent & Mathew, 71 Fleet St, London, u (1789–1809). Included in the list of master cabinet makers in Sheraton's *Cabinet Dictionary*, 1803. In July 1808 insured utensils and stock for £100 out of a total cover of £300. [D; GL, Sun MS vol. 443, ref. 819443]

Walker, Nicholas, Manchester, cm (1754). In 1754 took app. named Anderson. [S of G, app. index]

Walker, Peter, 57 Friargate, Preston, Lancs., cm (1825). [D]

Walker, R., Prince's St, Wolverhampton, Staffs., joiner and cm (1780). [D]

Walker, R. jnr, 6 Garden Row, Camberwell, London, cm (1835). [D]

Walker, Richard, Ditch Side, Fleet Mkt, London, chairmaker and upholder (1752–85). Father of Robert Walker. Richard Walker was made free of the Upholders' Co. as a 'love brother', 16 November 1752. He was described as a 'Citizen & Bricklayer'. Fined for declining parochial office in the parish of St Bride in 1758 and 1765 but held the offices of Collector for the Poor 1760, Sidesman 1761, Questman 1762 and Church Warden in 1770–71. Took as apps Richard Fowler, 1755–63; John B. Dutton, 1755–63; Thomas Watson to 1772; George Penfold to 1773; Robert Walker, 1771–78; Ralph Woollett, 1772–78; Andrew Pratt 1772–75; George Wilkins, 1779–81, and Robert Russell, 1782–85. [GL, Upholders' Co. records; MS 6561, p. 98]

Walker, Richard, Manchester, cm (1771–1805). Also listed as a looking-glass manufacturer in 1781 and as an appraiser and auctioneer in 1788–1802. At 122 Deangate, 1771–81, but from 1788–1808 at 16 St Mary's Gate. An advertisement of August 1771 suggests that by this date the business was already well established. He had stocks of mahogany which he offered for sale. In November of the same year he featured in an advertisement a stock of mirrors which he had purchased in London 'remarkably cheap'. This 'large and elegant Assortment of Looking-Glasses, in the newest taste' consisted of 'ovals and Piers, in burnished Gold; ovals painted

Green and the ornaments burnished gold; ovals painted white; variety of Japann'd Dressing-Glasses, Sconce-Glasses with Mahogany Frames and gilt Edges, &c.'. Although he was to claim in 1781 to be a looking-glass manufacturer it would seem likely that at this earlier date he had no facilities for his own manufacture. The business must have enjoyed a good reputation locally and attracted patrons of consequence. Commissions were undertaken for Dunham Massey, Cheshire, 1779–86. On 24 June 1779 £15 8s was paid for a bookcase and press and Venetian blinds. A further £16 12s 6d was paid on 3 November 1779 and £23 13s 6d on 18 September 1784. Mahogany timber was purchased by a payment of £1 14s on 29 July 1785 and £2 10s paid on 24 June 1786 was for glass bottles for a lady's dressing table. In 1788 Walker supplied sofas, carpets, window curtains and card tables for the Ball Room and Card Room of the Great Hotel, the Crescent, Buxton, his account being examined before payment by John Carr, the architect. Sir John Leicester of Tabley Hall, Cheshire, also patronised Walker. Between June 1794 and August 1798 three payments totalling £19 9s 9d were made for paint, repairs to Venetian blinds and mahogany stringing etc. [D; *Prescott's Manchester Journal*, 10 August 1771, 9 November 1771; John Rylands Lib., Manchester Univ., George Cooke's accounts; Chatsworth papers, 635; Chester RO, Leicester papers]

Walker, Richard, Workington, Cumb., joiner/cm (1811–34). At Washington St in 1811 but from 1828–34 at Cavendish St. [D]

Walker, Richard, Westgate, Dewsbury, Yorks., cm and joiner (1822–30). [D]

Walker, Richard, 20 Upper Marylebone St, London, cm and u (1827). [D]

Walker, Richard, 37 St Saviourgate, York, joiner and cm (1830). [D]

Walker, Richard, New St, Sandwich, Kent, cm (1831–38). [D; poll bks]

Walker, Richard, 1 Little Queen St, Lincoln's Inn Fields, London, carver and gilder (1835). [D]

Walker, Richard, 19 Queen St, Ramsgate, Kent, cm (1839). [D]

Walker, Richard jnr & Robert, 82 Margaret St, Cavendish Sq., London, cm and u (1837–39). [D]

Walker, Robert, Fleet Mkt, London, upholder (1778). Son of Richard Walker of Fleet Market, upholder. App. to his father on 1 May 1771 and free of the Upholders' Co. by servitude, 3 June 1778. [GL, Upholders' Co. records]

Walker, Robert, Hull, Yorks., cm (1795–1806). Son of Thomas Walker of Hull, cm. His father died in 1794 and he initially assisted his mother Elizabeth to continue the business. In 1795 at Scale Lane, 1798 at Bowlalley Lane and also shown from the late 1790s to 1806 at Salthouse Lane. Undertook commissions at Burton Constable, Yorks., 1796–98. An account dated 23 September 1795 for £24 17s 6d included a mahogany bookcase at £17 17s and sundry repairs. A further sum of £3 10s 9d for the period June to November of the following year was for sundries and an account dated 2 January 1798 for £14 17s 11d was for curtains. This is probably the Robert Walker, cm who in 1803 subscribed to Sheraton's *Cabinet Dictionary*. [D; Humberside RO, Burton Constable Steward's account bk] See Elizabeth Walker.

Walker, Robert, 3 Little Carter Lane, St Paul's, London, u (1805). [D]

Walker, Robert, 17 Bishops Walk, Lambeth, London, u (1809). [D]

Walker, Robert, Newfield, Sheffield, Yorks., cm (1821). [D]

Walker, Robert, Leicester, chairmaker (1834). [Lancaster freemen rolls]

Walker, Robert, Birch Row, New Radford, Nottingham, cm (1835). [D]

Walker, Roger, Whitechapel, London, upholder (d. 1750). Death at Hackney of this 'Upholder of considerable Business in Whitechapel' reported, *General Advertiser*, 7 May 1750.

Walker, Samuel, Aldgate, London, upholder (1763–74). In 1763 trading at 'The Crown' near 'The Three Nunns Inn', Aldgate Without. On 21 March of this year Nathanial Barrell, a New England merchant who had been residing in London, 1760–63, bought furniture from Walker. The total of his purchases was £22 11s and they included six mahogany chairs, the seats covered in crimson damask at £6 12s, a mahogany writing table at £4 4s and a large sconce glass at £4 4s. It is likely that when he returned to York, Maine in late 1763 he took these items with him. From 1770 the address is given as 17 Aldgate and in 1773 the business was trading as Walker & Saville. [D; Barrell papers, private ownership]

Walker, Samuel, Whites Yd, White Cross St, Cripplegate, London, cm (1791–1822). At 2 Whites Yd in February 1791, but by February 1813 at number 6 at which he was to continue. The business was of a very modest size with insurance cover totalling only £100 in 1791 and of this only £50 was in respect of utensils and stock. In the period 1813–22 total cover was £1,000 or £1,100 with utensils and stock accounting for only £200. [GL, Sun MS vol. 374, ref. 580469; vol. 462, refs 891511–12; vol. 462, 28 February 1814; vol. 486, refs 983482–83; vol. 489, refs 989140–41]

Walker, Samuel, West Ardsley, near Wakefield, Yorks., cm (1822). [D]

Walker, T., 10 Hanover St, Long Acre, London, u (1829). [D]

Walker, T., Lancs., cm (1833). On 7 November 1833 was married at Melling, Lancs. to Sophia Grime, the youngest daughter of T. Grime of Wray, Lancs., cm. [*Liverpool Mercury*, 15 November 1833]

Walker, Thomas, Lancaster, cm (1725–d. 1758). Son of Henry Walker of Lancaster, cm. Free as a cm 1725–26 and between 1738–56 took six apps. In February 1749 living in China Lane where he had a house and shop with a cabinet maker's workshop behind. He was at this date trading as a cm and milliner. Total insurance cover came to £1,000 but of this only £200 was for stock-in-trade. A letter of Richard Gillow dated 14 January 1759 records his death 'since this Christmas began'. [Freemen rolls; app. regs.; GL, Sun MS vol. 84, ref. 115337; Westminster Ref. Lib., Gillow letter book 1748 p. 58]

Walker, Thomas, Scale Lane and Savile St, Hull, Yorks., cm (1765–94). App. to Charles Rawlins, cm of Beverley, Yorks.; free in 1765. On his death in 1794 the business was continued by his widow Elizabeth and his son Robert. Thomas Walker subscribed to Sheraton's *Drawing Book*, 1793. He must have moved from Beverley to Hull soon after receiving his freedom, for in December 1774 he was supplying mahogany work to the value of £31 16s 10d to Trinity House, Hull. He subsequently supplied furniture to Hull Corp. on a number of occasions from 1776–83. In 1776 four mahogany chairs were made at £1 5s each and six elm chairs at 7s each. A large mahogany wardrobe cost £7 10s in 1780 and a chest of drawers £6. In 1783–84 pieces of satinwood were supplied and also a satinwood table which was charged at £5 5s. He was also a regular supplier of furniture to Burton Constable, Yorks. In 1776 four mahogany arm chairs were supplied for £5 and in 1787 an invalid wheel chair at £15 15s and two years later one with smaller wheels at £10 10s. Numerous tables were made for the house in the early 1780s. Four tables were supplied in May 1782 to fit into niches in the Billiard Room and cost £12. A major item was an inlaid library table which when supplied in September 1782 cost £15 15s. Other items supplied included fire screens, night tables, candle stands, a bookcase, a bureau, a wardrobe, close stools and pedestals. Furniture supplied by Walker often utilised a form of handle of his own devising. This consisted of wrought iron wire encased in carved mahogany. [D; Beverley app. bk, freemen rolls, and poll bk; Humberside RO, DDCC/2, Burton Constable vouchers; Trinity House accounts bks; Municipal records; *C. Life*, 22 April 1982, p. 1117; vol. CLIX pp. 1476–80]

Walker, Thomas, 14 Cheapside, Liverpool, cm (1790). [D]

Walker, Thomas, Cartmel, Lancs., cm (1793). [D]

Walker, Thomas, Doncaster, Yorks., cm (1818–37). At Silver St in 1818, French Gate, 1822–28 and High St in 1837. [D]

Walker, Thomas, 141 Oxford St, London, cm (1820). In July 1820 took out insurance cover of £1,150 of which £1,000 was for stock and utensils kept in his dwelling house. [GL, Sun MS vol. 483, ref. 970001]

Walker, Thomas, 22 Montagu St, Portman Sq., London, upholder and appraiser (1821). In March 1821 took out insurance cover of £800 of which £700 was for stock and utensils kept at his dwelling house. [GL, Sun MS vol. 487, ref. 978275]

Walker, Thomas, 14 Guilford St, Foundling Hospital, London, u (1821). In October 1821 took out insurance cover of £1,000 of which £900 was for stock and utensils kept at his dwelling house. [GL, Sun MS vol. 484, ref. 983719]

Walker, Thomas, London, cm and u (1821–24). Insurance records give his address as 9 Lime St, 1821–22, and 41 Manchester St, Manchester Sq., 1823–24. He also used rooms above 'The Cape of Good Hope' public house which communicated with the Lime St premises in the period 1821–23. Stock levels were substantial and were £900 out of a total cover of £1,000 in April 1821 and £750 out of £800 in August 1822. Other addresses recorded which appear to have been connected with the business were 3 Mark Lane in 1823, 30 Duke St, Manchester Sq. in April 1824 and 46 York St, Baker St in June 1824. [GL, Sun MS vol. 487, ref. 980301; vol. 490, ref. 995605; vol. 492, ref. 999787; vol. 494, ref. 1008294; vol. 495, ref. 1016444; vol. 495, ref. 1017514]

Walker, Thomas, Hereford, cm (1826). Free 16 June 1826. [Freemen rolls; poll bk]

Walker, Thomas, Liverpool, u (d. 1828). Died 30 January 1828 aged 42. [*Liverpool Mercury*, 8 February 1828]

Walker, Thomas jnr, Hospital St, Nantwich, Cheshire, cm (1838). Married 11 December 1838. [PR (marriage)]

Walker, Thomas & William, 22 Blake St, York, carvers and gilders (1816–30). In 1830 William Walker is shown as the sole proprietor. [D]

Walker, W., Savile St, Hull, Yorks., cm (1798). [D]

Walker, W., 74 Fleet Mkt, London, u and chair stuffer (1809). [D]

Walker, William, parish of St James, Westminster, London, upholder (1714–28). Son of William Walker of Ireland, Gent. App. to Richard Camfield, 2 October 1700 and free of the Upholders' Co. by servitude, 5 May 1714. Bankruptcy announced March 1728. [GL, Upholders' Co. records; *London Gazette*, 19–23 March 1727/28]

Walker, William, Ashton-under-Lyne, Lancs., cm (1740–52). In 1740 took app. named Marther and in 1752, Swindells. [S of G, app. index]

Walker, William, James St, Covent Gdn, London, cm, u and turner (1774–1816). At 7 James St, but directories of 1809 indicate 31 though later ones revert to 7. To *c.* 1800 the trade is indicated as cm and turner (or brush maker) but in the early 19th century upholsterer is added. From 1795–1803 the business is named as Walker & Son before reverting once more in 1805 to William Walker. This might indicate the involvement of two William Walkers, father and son, the father ceasing to be active by 1805. The business was

substantial with total insurance cover of £800 in 1776, £1,100 in 1792 and £1,800 in 1807. Of this utensils and stock amounted to £500 in 1776 and £600 in 1807. In August 1812 Walker took out insurance on a house at 1 Dufours Pl., Broad St, Carnaby Mkt in the tenure of a tailor. A murder was committed by one of his apps in 1773. [D; Westminster poll bk; GL, Sun MS vol. 249, p. 252; vol. 389, ref. 604216; vol. 440, ref. 802289; vol. 459, ref. 873339; *Bristol Journal*, 13 March 1773; GL trade card coll.]

Walker, William, 48 Albemarle St, London, carver and gilder (1793). Subscribed to Sheraton's *Drawing Book*, 1793. A William Walker also subscribed to his *Cabinet Dictionary*, 1803.

Walker, William, Snowhill, Woverhampton, Staffs., cm (1798–1809). [D]

Walker, William, Liverpool, chairmaker (1804–07). Free 6 December 1804 after serving his apprenticeship under William Harper. He was said to have been formerly a sailor. Trading at 3 Chapel Lane, Brownlow Hill in 1804 though his address is also recorded as 15 Copeland Ct, Norfolk St. A directory of 1807 shows 7 Mary Ann St with a shop at 11 Chapel Lane. [D; freemen rolls]

Walker, William, 14 Bridge St, Westminster, London, cm and u (1822). In May 1822 took out insurance cover of £900 which included £600 for stock and utensils. The address is also rendered as 14 Little Bridge St, Westminster. [D; GL, Sun MS vol. 493, ref. 991753]

Walker, William, London, glass and picture frame maker (1800–29). At 31 Old Bond St, 1800–01 and 37 Drury Lane, 1803–19. In 1803 described as a looking-glass maker. [D]

Walker, William, Richmond Yorks., cm (1814–27). At Frenchgate in 1823 and Market Pl. in 1827. [D; PR (bapt.)]

Walker, William, Haswell Lane, Louth, Lincs., chairmaker (1819). [D]

Walker, William, High-Town, near Dewsbury, Yorks., cm (1822). [D]

Walker, William, Tattershall Rd, Horncastle, Lincs., joiner/cm (1822). [D]

Walker, William, Northgate St, Chester, cm (1824). Free 21 October 1824. [Freemen rolls]

Walker, William, Style Barn, Ashton-under-Lyne, Lancs., cm and joiner (1824–34). [D]

Walker, William, St Mark's Lane, Lincoln, cm, u and turner (1828–35). [D]

Walker, William, Liversedge, Yorks., joiner and cm (1830). [D]

Walker, William, 22 Blake St, York, see Thomas & William Walker.

Walker, William, Hartlepool/Seaton, Co. Durham, cm/joiner (1834). [D]

Walker, William, Marylebone, London, cm, chairmaker and u (1835–39). In 1835 at 112 Marylebone High St and in 1839 at 4 Westmoreland St. [D]

Walker, William, 10 Gibraltar St, Sheffield, Yorks., cm and broker (1837). [D]

Walker, William, 21 Roupell St, Cornwall Rd, London, carver and gilder (1839). [D]

Walker, William Longworth, Liverpool and Lancaster, cm (1801–18). Son of John Walker, cm who traded in Liverpool 1780–1807. He trained however at Lancaster and was free 1801–02. Also free of Liverpool, by patrimony, 31 October 1806. In March 1807 announced the commencement of a business in Cornwallis St as a cm, bedstead maker and looking-glass manufacturer. In September of the same year he was married at Ormskirk, Lancs. to a Miss Riddiough. Took as apps Henry Corran, 1808–16, Josiah Tipping 1809–16 and Joseph Roberts 1807–18. A directory of 1807 gives addresses at Charles St with a shop at 24 Cornwallis St and also 14 Charlotte St with a shop at 26 Cornwallis St. [D; Lancaster freemen rolls; Liverpool freemen rolls; app. bks; *Liverpool Chronicle*, 25 March 1807, 16 September 1807]

Walker & Cooke's Repository, Ranelagh Pl., Leamington, Warks., carvers and gilders (1837). [D]

Walker & Gadsby, Derby, joiners and cm (late 18th century). Their trade card [Heal Coll., BM] illustrates a bureau bookcase, canopied day bed, a chair and a Pembroke table in a Sheraton style.

Walker & Jones, St James's St, Liverpool, cm (1835–39). The number in St James's St was 9 in 1835, 11 in 1837 and 23 in 1839. [D]

Walker & Knights, 3 Sweetings Alley, Cornhill, London, Printsellers and frame makers (1812). In November 1812 took out insurance cover of £1,000 which included £400 for stock and utensils kept at Sweetings Alley and a further £200 for similar items kept at 26 Windsor Terr., City Rd described as a dwelling house. [GL, Sun MS vol. 457, ref. 877051]

Walker & Saville, see Samuel Walker, Aldgate.

Walker, Salthouse & Butler, Preston, Lancs., cm and joiners (1828–34). In 1828 at 47 Fishergate. By 1834 the business was trading as Walker & Butler at 50 Mount St. [D]

Walker & Steffanoni, 140 Holborn Hill, London, cm and u (1835). A trade card [GL] of Walker & Co., Holborn Hill Bazaar may refer to this business at a later date. [D]

Walkey, William, Paul St, Exeter, Devon, carver and gilder (1829). Daughter Anne bapt. at St Paul's Church, 12 April 1829. [PR (bapt.)]

Walkington, John, London(?), cm (1754). Possibly the John Walkington who was app. to Richard Wood in York on 25 March 1736. In 1754 he subscribed to Chippendale's *Director* and was described as a cm. He may have been the Walkington involved in the business of Jennings & Walkington who traded at the Vine, Long Acre as upholders and cm.

Walkington, Robert, High Holborn, London, u, cm and chairmaker (1817–27). Variously shown at 214 or 215 High Holborn. A substantial business with insurance cover of £2,000 in May 1823. Of this £1,600 was for utensils and stock. [D; GL, Sun MS vol. 497, ref. 1005212]

Walkington, Robert, 2 Charlotte St, Fitzroy Sq., London, cm and u (1835–37). [D]

Walkins, —, upholder (1809–14). Recorded receiving payments of £6 6s in 1809 and £27 5s in 1814 in connection with Longford Castle, Wilts. [V&A archives]

Walkins, Thomas, 39 Berwick St, Soho, London, (1822). [D]

Wall, Allen, London, japanner and varnish maker (1780–1801). At 3 Castle St, Leicester Fields in 1780 but from the following year in Long Acre. The number was 4 from 1781 to 1793 and 6 thereafter. The business was of a substantial size and in August 1785 insurance cover of £4,000 was taken out. The manufactory was covered for £100 but utensils and stock kept there for £400 further. The warehouse etc. was insured for £400 with stock and utensils at £3,100. Wall was paid £100 0s 6d on 10 October, 1789 for work undertaken for the Royal Household, and in the early 1790s described himself as 'Japanner to Her Majesty and H.R.H. the Prince of Wales'. After 1790 the business traded as Allen Wall & Son. [D; GL, Sun MS vol. 330, p. 472; BM, Banks D2 1348; Windsor Royal Archives, RA 88736]

Wall, John, Cambridge, upholder (d. 1758). [Univ. Lib., AR 3:46]

Wall, Thomas, address unknown, cm (1803). Subscribed to Sheraton's *Cabinet Dictionary*, 1803.

Wall, William, 12 Melina Pl., Westminster Rd, London, chairmaker (1835). [D]

Wallace, Mr, London, 'an eminent Cabinet-maker and Upholsterer in Piccadilly' (d. 1768). Death at his house in Chelsea reported, *Public Advertiser*, 18 July 1768.

Wallace, Charles, Newcastle, cm etc. (1827–38). At Fighting Cocks Yd, 1827–33 but in 1838 at Marlborough St. [D]

Wallace, J., 41 Fenchurch St, London, carver, gilder and frame maker (1796–1804). [D]

Wallace, James, 57 Church Hill, Woolwich, London, bedstead maker (1839). [D]

Wallace, John, 5 Gt Poland St, London, u, cm and paperhanger (1802–25). Included in the list of master cabinet makers in Sheraton's *Cabinet Dictionary*, 1803. A cm named Wallace, living in London, was a subscriber to Sheraton's *Drawing Book*, 1793. [D]

Wallace, John, Durham, cm (1793). [D]

Wallace, William, Little Castle St, Oxford St, London, cm (1784). [D]

Wallace, William, Brampton, Carlisle, Cumb., joiner/cm (1829–34). In 1829 in Back St and in 1834 in Front St. [D]

Wallace, William, Hungate, Lincoln, cm and u (1835). [D]

Walle, Henry & Reilly, Peter, London, u, carver, gilder and cm (1768–86). The partners traded from an address in Gerrard St, Soho though in 1776 the address is given as Vine St. By 1786 Henry Walle was trading on his own behalf from 'The Royal Pavilion', 109 St Martin's Lane as an upholder, carver and gilder. The firm attracted patrons of consequence, and between 1 August 1768 and 17 February 1769 supplied items for Shelburne House, Berkeley Sq. to a value of £120 6s. They dealt in luxury items, some imported from overseas. In common with James Cullen of Greek St they were involved in a conspiracy with Baron Berlendinni, the Venetian Resident, to import furniture on a considerable scale under the protection of the Venetian diplomatic bag to avoid customs duty. The practice was so flagrant that London journeyman cm complained against the abuse and in July 1772 the customs raided a number of premises including those of Walle & Reilly. They seized 'several hundred of chairs and sofas, near a ton of curled hair, a large quantity of brass nails, a great number of marble tables, some very rich slab frames, carved and gilt, silk lace, tapestry etc.'. In June 1771 the firm was declared bankrupt and in July 1772 dividends were issued on bankruptcy. There is no evidence of a suspension of trading however. In June 1773 Peter Reilley was negotiating for the supply of mirrors for the Glass Drawing Room at Northumberland House, London. A price of £1,465 was eventually agreed upon after some haggling and once more an attempt was made to smuggle the glass through the Venetian diplomatic bag. The ruse was detected by the customs and the Duke of Northumberland obliged to pay the 75% duty. Their name was included in a list of furniture makers compiled by the Duchess of Northumberland; c. 1776, and they supplied considerable amounts of furniture in 1768–69 to both Alnwick, Northumb. and Northumberland House, London. Items supplied included 'A Bed a la Polonaise . . . carved and gilt', a 'Compleat Bedstead with its Imperial Dome carved and painted in natural flowers . . . £60 16s' and '8 Cabrioles, carved and painted to match the Bedsted' at £3 10s each. The 'Compleat Bedstead' may be the one at present exhibited in the state apartments at Alnwick. The partners are also recorded receiving a payment of £64 9s in connection with Longford Castle, Wilts. in 1772. [Bowood MS; *Annual Register*, 1772, pp. 100–13; *Apollo*, September 1970, pp. 206–09; Alnwick MS, U.I.42; *Gents Mag.*, June 1771; Gilbert, *Chippendale*, p. 154; Musgrave, *Adam and Hepplewhite Furniture*, p. 128; BM, Banks D2 649; V&A archives; S of G, app. index]

Waller, John, Liverpool and Preston, Lancs., cm (1782). Freeman of Preston but living in Liverpool. Son of Richard

Waller, cm of Liverpool but also a freeman of Preston. [Preston Guild records]

Waller, John, Liverpool, cm (1830). Born 26 March 1810. Son of Fred Walter Waller. Free in 1830 by patrimony. [Freemen's committee bk]

Waller, John, Cley, Norfolk, cm (1830–39). [D]

Waller, John, Printing-office Lane, Bungay, Suffolk, cm and u (1839). [D]

Waller, John, Wood St, Walthamstow, London, cm, u and furniture broker (1839). [D]

Waller, John, High Wycombe, Bucks., cm (1839). [D]

Waller, Richard, Preston, Lancs. and Liverpool, cm (1742–62). Freeman of Preston, but living in Liverpool. His brother Thomas, who lived in Preston, was a clockmaker. Also had a son named George and another brother named John. [Preston Guild records]

Waller, Richard, Liverpool, cm (1761). Free 28 January 1761. [Freemen reg.]

Waller, Samuel, Cley, Norfolk, cm and chairmaker (1822). [D]

Waller, William, Bartholomew St, Newbury, Berks., cm, joiner and appraiser (1770). In October 1770 announced that he had taken over the shop formerly occupied by Edward Hayes near the Church. He asked for the continued favour of the former customers of Mr Hayes and indicated that he could offer 'All Sorts of Tunbridge Wares in the newest and Genteelest Taste from one of the most opulent Manufactories in London'. [Reading Mercury, 8 October 1770]

Waller, William, Liverpool, cm (1812–29). Son of John Waller, cooper. Free 5 October 1812 and at this date living at 11 Pleasant Buildings, Gt Horner St. Trading at 2 Chesney St in 1818, 27 Shelhome St in 1821 and 10 Pinnington St, 1827–29. [D; freemen reg.]

Wallet, Robert, Sudbury, Suffolk, cm (1768). Freeman of Colchester, Essex. [Colchester poll bk]

Walley, Samuel, Nantwich, Cheshire, u (1756). Daughter Sarah bapt. 18 August 1756. [PR (bapt.)]

Walley, Thomas, Paul St, Kingsdown, Bristol, u (1806–10). [D]

Walley, Thomas, Howell Croft, Bolton, Lancs., cm (1818). [D]

Wallin, Richard, at the shop of Mrs Bird, turner, Without Newgate, London, upholder, appraiser and undertaker (1747–54). Known from his trade card which states that he made and sold 'all Sorts of Bedsteads and Furnitures, Feather Beds, Matrasses, Blankets, Quilts, Coverlids & Rugs, Carpets, Cabinet Work, Chairs, Looking Glasses &c.' Also stocked a 'Variety of Paper Hangings'. Heal dates the card to 1724 but in style it would seem to be from the mid 18th century. In 1747 trading in the parish of St Barnard, Paul's Wharf and a member of the Haberdashers' Co. His son Richard jnr was app. to Charles Grange 6 August 1747 and free of the Upholders' Co., 5 September 1754. [Heal; GL, Upholders' Co. records] See also William Bird.

Wallin, Thomas, High Wycombe, Bucks., chairmaker (1821). Son bapt. 1821. [PR (bapt.)]

Walling, —, London, cm (1793). Subscribed to Sheraton's *Drawing Book*, 1793.

Walling, Henry, Lancaster, cm (1779–98). App. to H. Baines 1770 and free 1779–80. Named in the Gillow records 1786–90, 1792, 1794, 1797–98. [App. reg.; freemen rolls; poll bk; Westminster Ref. Lib., Gillow]

Walling, Thomas, High Wycombe, Bucks., chairmaker (1813–21). Daughter bapt. in 1813 and son in 1821. [PR (bapt.)]

Wallington & Exley, Chestergate, Stockport, Cheshire, cm (1825). [D] See William Exley.

Wallis, —, 'the Elephant', opposite the South Door, 66 St Paul's Churchyard, London, cm (1757). [Heal; Wheatley & Cunningham, *London Past and Present*, 1891, vol. 3, p. 54]

Wallis, Charles, 'The Crown & Cushion', New Bond St, London, upholder (1722). In November 1722 insured goods and merchandise in his dwelling house for £500. [GL, Sun MS vol. 14, ref. 26942]

Wallis, Christopher, London, cm (1749–c. 1760). At Dirty Lane (or Charles St) in 1749. His trade card of c. 1760 however gives the address as 'the Blue Flower de Luce, next Drury Lane, Long Acre'. He claimed to make and sell 'all Sorts of Cabinet Work'. He also undertook funerals, acted as an appraiser, dealt in secondhand household goods and had for sale mahogany in logs, planks and boards. [Westminster poll bk; Heal]

Wallis, James, James St, Westminster, London, carver (1749). [Poll bk]

Wallis, James, New St, Manchester, joiner and cm (1794–1802). At 4 New St, 1794–97 but by 1800 at 24 New St. [D]

Wallis, James, Queen St, Market Rasen, Lincs., joiner, cm and builder (1826). [D]

Wallis, James, Birmingham (1835–39). At Cross St, Suffolk St in 1835 and 43 Upper Gough St in 1839. [D]

Wallis, John, 19 St Paul's Churchyard, London, upholder and cm (1784). [D]

Wallis, John, Gt Queen St, 38 Lincoln's Inn Fields, London, upholder (1799). Son of Thomas Wallis of Norton Falgate, Liveryman. App. 2 May 1792 and free of the Upholders' Co. by servitude 5 June 1799. [GL, Upholders' Co. records]

Wallis, John, 15 Stanley St, Liverpool, cm (1816). [D]

Wallis, John, New St, Penzance, Cornwall, cm (1823–30). [D]

Wallis, Robert, corner of Little Russel St, in Duke St, Bloomsbury, London, cm (1775). In 1775 took out insurance cover of £200, but only £15 of this was for utensils and stock. [GL, Sun MS vol. 239, p. 649]

Wallis, Samuel, Hull, Yorks., cm (1821–40). Also described as a shopkeeper or grocer 1821–22, 1835 and 1839–40. At Catherine St, 1821–22; Katharine Sq., 1823; 10 Wincolmlee 1826; New George St in 1831; 23 Sykes St in 1834; and 39 Sykes St, 1835–39. [D]

Wallis, Thomas, 64 Long Acre, London, cabinet and varnish maker (1789). [D]

Wallis, Thomas & Josh., Penzance, Cornwall, cm (1824–30). In North Parade in 1824 and South Parade in 1830. [D]

Wallis, Tim, 41 Gilbert St, Oxford St, London, u (1829). [D]

Walls, Joseph, York, cm (c. 1824–40). Son of Thomas Walls, cm. App. to his father 30 December 1817 as was also his brother John on 1 September 1820. Joseph Walls is recorded taking apps from 1846. [App. reg.]

Walls, Thomas, York, cm and u (1809–40). At 9 Peter Lane, 1816–40, but in 1838 the address is given as 9 Layerthorpe. Took as apps his sons Joseph 30 December 1817 and John 1 September 1820. Other apps were Frederick Mush, 2 January 1809; Nathaniel Fountain, 1 July 1812; William Groves, 14 February 1815; Robert Smithson, 19 February 1817; Joseph Smith, 1 January 1822; Robert Clayton, 15 September 1825; Thomas Linfoot, 28 October 1828; Henry Halliday, 18 December 1826; John Hunton, 27 September 1830; Henry Field (alias Fearby), 18 December 1833; George Hawksworth, 1 September 1833; William Howard, 12 August 1835 and Thomas Harrison, 2 August 1837. Apps continued to be taken until 1852. [D; app. reg.]

Walmesley, Benjamin, Lancaster (1767–68). [Lancaster freemen rolls]

Walmesley, Gilbert, Gresley Row, Lichfield, Staffs., cm (1835). [Poll bk]

Walmesley, William, Preston, Lancs., cm and joiner (1814–25). In Church St, the number being 68 in 1814–18 and 65 in 1825. One directory of 1818 gives Shire Hill however. [D]

Walmsley, James, Gloucester St, parish of St Andrew, Holborn,

London, upholder (1727). In May 1727 took out insurance cover of £500 on household goods and stock in his dwelling house. [GL, Sun MS vol. 24, ref. 41586]

Walmsley, John, Marylebone St, Golden Sq., London, cm (1774). [Westminster poll bk]

Walmsley, Robert, 83 Shudehill, Manchester, chairmaker (1828). [D]

Walmsley & Bowerbank, Preston, Lancs., cm/chairmaker (1802). Signed the *Preston Cabinet Makers' and Chair Makers' Book of Prices*, 1802 on the behalf of the masters.

Waln, Robert, Paradise St, Liverpool, cabinet warehouse (1790). [D]

Walsh, John, 4 Clerkenwell Close, London, upholder (1784). Son of Richard Walsh of Gray's Inn Lane, attorney-at-law. App. to James Grange, 7 November 1770 and free of the Upholders' Co. by servitude, 3 November 1784. [GL, Upholders' Co. records]

Walsh, Lawrence William, Little Marlborough St, Westminster, London, carver and gilder (1774–75). Subscribed to Thomas Malton's *Compleat Treatise on Perspective*, 1775. [Poll bk] See also William Walsh.

Walsh, Robert, Wakefield, Yorks., cm and u (1828–34). At Wood St in 1828 and Sharp's Sq. in 1830. [D]

Walsh, Thomas, Blackburn, Lancs., joiner and cm (1824). [D]

Walsh, William, London, carver and gilder (c. 1760). His trade card [Westminster Ref. Lib.] indicates that he worked in both wood and stone and offered 'all different taste of Ornam'' and 'Hydraulic Figures for Gardens or Banquets'. Possibly the Lawrence William Walsh who was living in Little Marlborough St in 1774.

Walsh, William, Skipton, Yorks., cm (1834–35). [D; PR]

Walsh & Moody, 277 High Holborn, London, upholders and cm (1780–83). [D]

Walsham, William, Market Rasen, Lincs., chairmaker and wheelwright (1822–26). At Willingham St in 1826. [D]

Walshaw, John, Bowling Green Rd, Kennington, Stockwell, London, cm (1805). [D]

Walter, —, Kensington, London, u (1749). [Heal]

Walter, —, Strand, London, cm (1787). Death reported, *Gents Mag.*, October 1787.

Walter, J., Chatham Row, Bath, Som., cm (1819). [D]

Walter, John, 'The White Lyon', Little Old Bailey, London, u (1724). [Heal]

Walter, John, Town's end, Kingston, Surrey, u and paperhanger (1826). [D]

Walter, John, 19 Chariot St, Hull, Yorks., cm etc. (1831). [D]

Walter, John, Chapel St, Bungay, Suffolk, chairmaker (1839). [D]

Walter, Joseph, Westgate St, Bath, Som., cm (1771–93). Advertised his stock in the *Bath Journal*, 2 September 1771 which included sedan chairs. Free 1778. Supplied c. 1771 thirteen rout benches for the Assembly Rooms, and received payment of £240 10s for 16 settees. In 1792–93 he also supplied 6 mahogany Elbow chairs, 4 couches, 6 dressing tables, 6 folding horse firescreens, 2 oval dressing glasses and 4 round basin stands. [D; Bath freemen rolls; Bath City archives, minutes of the furnishing committee, 2 September and October 1771]

Walter, Mathias, Bath, Som., cm (1743–67). In 1743 took app. named Sandemore. Took other apps in 1755, 1760 and 1767. [S of G, app. index; Bath City archives, app. bk]

Walter, Matthew, Bath, Som., cm (1747). In 1747 took app. named Brown. [S of G, app. index]

Walter, Matthew, Keynsham, Som., cm (1755). In 1755 took app. named Harford. [S of G, app. index]

Walter, Michael, Hull, Yorks., fancy rush and cane chairmaker (1831). Traded at 19 Princes St, Mason St and had a residence at Grotto Sq. [D]

Walter, Robert, Town's-end, Kingston, Surrey, u and paperhanger (1822–38). Described as Robert Walter jnr, 1826–38. [D]

Walter, Thomas, Kensington, London, upholder (1776). [Heal]

Walter, William, Southwark, London, upholder (1712–21). In 1712 at the 'White horse and Harr', and in October 1714 in the parish of St George, Southwark. In the parish of St Saviour, 1718–21. Insured various properties in Three Falcons Ct and St Mary's Hill in the borough. [GL, Sun MS vol. 2, p. 25; Hand in Hand MS vol. 13, p. 453; vol. 19, p. 23; vol. 24, p. 182]

Walter, William, parish of St Mary Magdalen, Bermondsey, London, upholder (1720). Freeman of London. In September 1720 insured a house on the east side of Bermondsey St for £200. [GL, Hand in Hand MS vol. 22, p. 232]

Walter, William, 46 Gt Peter St, Westminster, London, cm and u (1827). [D]

Walters, —, 71 New Compton St, Soho, London, carver and gilder (1835). [D]

Walters, David, Grosvenor's Mews, London, cm (1749–55). [Heal]

Walters, Edward, High Wycombe, Bucks., chairmaker (b. c. 1816–41). Aged 25 at the date of the 1841 Census.

Walters, George, Court House St, Hastings, Sussex, cm (1839). [D]

Walters, James jnr, 114 Powis St, Woolwich, London, u and fancy cm (1839). [D]

Walters, John, parish of St Stephen, Bristol, carver and gilder (1781–84). [Poll bks]

Walters, John, Flagon Row, Deptford, London, cm and furniture broker (1824–39). [D]

Walters, Jno., 29 Pancras Pl., King's Cross, London, cm and u (1839). [D]

Walters, Miles, Berry St, Liverpool, carver and gilder (1835–39). Traded at 30 Berry St as Miles Walters & Son, 1835–37, but in 1839 at 7 Berry St and the business was refered to simply as Miles Walters. A William Miles Walters was app. to William Cashin of Liverpool, carver and gilder in 1831. [D; app. bk]

Walters, Thomas, Bristol, sign and furniture painter (1819–22). At 1 Lower College St, 1819–20, St John's Bridge 1821 and 2 Upper Maudlin St, 1822. [D]

Walters, Thomas, High St, Wednesbury, Staffs., u (1822). [D]

Walters, William, London(?), frame maker and gilder (1732–42). Recorded supplying furniture to Moulsham Hall, Essex, 1732–42. On 20 December 1732 £14 was paid for marble slabs for the Drawing Room and Bedchamber. A large looking-glass and gilt frame for the North-east Dining Room was charged at £34 1s and paid for on 16 June 1733. Further frames were provided in 1734–35 and 1741–42 and these included a large commission in 1735 which cost £75 alone. Other furniture included a fine mahogany table in 1734 at £8 5s and sums in 1737 and 1741 for gilding chairs, settees and a large stool. Also paid in 1738 for gilding eight chairs, two settees and a large stool for the London house of the Earl of Leicester. [V&A archives; *C. Life*, 11 February, 1980, pp. 427–31]

Walters, William, Kidderminster, Worcs., u (1808–22). In Worcester St, 1818–22. [D]

Walthall, Hugh, Hanley, Staffs., chairmaker (1818–22). At Market Pl. in 1818 and George St in 1822. [D]

Waltham, B., address unknown, cm (1803). Subscribed to Sheraton's *Cabinet Dictionary*, 1803.

Walton, —, address unknown, cm (1803). Subscribed to Sheraton's *Cabinet Dictionary*, 1803.

Walton, Ann, see James Walton.

Walton, Edward, 180 Livery St, Birmingham, joiner and cm (1839). [D]

Walton, George, Lanchester, Co. Durham, joiner and cm (1828). [D]

Walton, Humphrey, London, cm (1776–78). In 1776 associated with William Potts but in the following year trading on his own behalf near 'The Bull & Butcher' in New Compton St, Soho. He took out insurance cover here for £600 of which £470 was for utensils and stock. By 1778 had moved and was trading as a victualler and cm at 'The Bible', Straw Lane. Here the total insurance cover was £500 and utensils and stock accounted for £280 of this. [GL, Sun MS vol. 257, p. 421; vol. 264, p. 489]

Walton, James, London, u (1776–1802). Free of the Upholders' Co. by redemption, 3 July 1776. His address in this year was given as 106 Old St and this may be the same location as 106 Leadenhall St which was being used in 1777. In this year he was in partnership at the Leadenhall St address with Ann Walton and together they took out insurance cover of £1,000 of which £700 was for utensils and stock. The business continued here for a number of years with insurance cover rising to £1,200 in 1784 of which £900 was for utensils and stock. By this year James Walton was in sole charge. In 1794 however his address was given as Surrey side, Blackfriars Bridge and in 1802 as Clapton. [D; GL, Upholders' Co. records; Sun MS vol. 256, p. 40; vol. 321, p. 323]

Walton, John, Silver St, Halifax, Yorks., cm (1816–18). [D]

Walton, John, Cresser's Yd, Micklegate, York, cm (1823). [D]

Walton, Jonathan, Alston, Cumb., joiner/cm (1834). [D]

Walton, Joseph, 5 Lisle St, Newcastle, cm (1787–1801). [D]

Walton, Peter, address unknown, framemaker (1692). Paid £19 5s by William 5th Earl of Bedford in November 1692 for repairing pictures and glueing and blacking frames. [Bedford Office, London]

Walton, Robert, Newcastle, u (1771). App. to William Charnley and free 31 October 1771. [Freemen reg.] Possibly:

Walton, Robert, Staindrop, Co. Durham, u (1774–80). Freeman of Newcastle. [Newcastle poll bks]

Walton, Thomas, Lancaster, cm (1801). Free 1801–02 but then living in Preston, Lancs. [Lancaster freemen rolls]

Walton, Thomas, Mill Wood, Stansfield township, Todmorden, Yorks., cm (1822–37). [D]

Walton, Thomas, Finkle St, Stockton, Co. Durham, joiner and cm (1827). [D]

Walton & Taylor, 110 Fenchurch St, London, u (1825). [D]

Wand, James, 4, opposite Church Lane, Commercial Rd, London, u and broker (1822). In November 1822 took out insurance cover for £800 but stock and utensils amounted to only £150. He maintained a stove for drying feathers and used a stable and loft over in Mulberry St for storage of utensils and stock. [GL, Sun MS vol. 489, ref. 997636]

Wand, John, address unknown, u (1761). Paid £3 4s 9d on 24 January 1761 for silk and worsted damask, worsted lining for curtains and four days work putting up a bed at Gibside, Co. Durham. [Durham RO, Strathmore MS D/St/V. 994]

Wand, Samuel, 15 Little Queen St, Lincoln's Inn Fields, London, carver and gilder (1782). In 1782 took out insurance cover of £160 of which £100 was for utensils and stock. [GL, Sun MS vol. 298, p. 371]

Wanes, George, Helmsley, Yorks., joiner/cm (1828–34). [D]

Wanless, George, Northumberland Pl., Sunderland, Co. Durham, joiner and cm (1828). [D]

Wanless, John, Stockbridge, Newcastle, joiner and cm (1827). [D]

Wannerton, John, Rosemary Lane, parish of St Botolph, Aldgate, London, cane chair man (1717). [GL, Sun MS vol. 7, 27 October 1717]

Wansell, John, 39 Berwick St, Soho, London, chairmaker (1805). [D]

Want, George S., 55 Skinner St, Snow Hill, London, cm, u and appraiser (1822–27). In December 1822 took out insurance cover of £700 of which £550 was for utensils and stock. The Skinner St property was described as a dwelling house and workshops in 1822 but as a warehouse and workshops in 1824. The insurance cover of £800 taken out in April 1824 on the buildings only was in the name of John Frederick Schilfer, probably the owner. Want was declared bankrupt in September 1824 but remained in London directories until 1827 which may suggest some subsequent trading. [D; GL, Sun MS vol. 493, ref. 999018; vol. 496, ref. 1016542; *Brighton Gazette*, 2 September 1824]

Waples, Sam, 125 Wardour St, Soho, London, bedstead maker and turner (1805). [D]

Wapshott, Robert, Noutners(?), carver (1775). In 1775 took out insurance cover of £500 which included £340 for utensils and stock. [GL, Sun MS vol. 238, p. 279]

Warbrick, Thomas, Lancaster, cm (1829–30). [Lancaster freemen rolls]

Warburton, Henry, High St, Honiton, Devon, cm (1830). [D]

Warburton, John, 20 Cable St, Liverpool, cm (1816). [D]

Warburton, Peter, Frodsham, Cheshire, cm/joiner (1834). [D]

Warburton, Thomas, Garratt Row, Manchester, cm (1839–40). [D]

Warburton, William, London, upholder (1770). Son of Thomas Warburton of the parish of St Andrew, Holborn, vintner. App. to James Thompson, draper, 21 April 1763, and free of the Upholders' Co. by servitude, 3 October 1770. [GL, Upholders' Co. records]

Ward, Abraham, 30 Shudehill, Manchester, cm (1813). [D]

Ward, Benjamin, Hull, Yorks., cm and u (1823–31). Possibly the person of this name from Sculcoates, Hull who was app. to Thomas Robinson of Hull, cm in 1807. Benjamin Ward was trading at 28 Chariot St and had a residence at Syke St, 1823–31. A Benjamin Ward, paper hanging manufacturer at 33 Bond St, Hull, appears in an 1834 directory. [D; app. reg.] See Edward Ward at 28 Chariot St.

Ward, Benjamin, Brook St, Warwick, chairmaker (1835). [D]

Ward, Charles & Co., 3 and 4 Dean St, Soho, London, carver and gilder (c. 1800). [Heal]

Ward, Dymoke (or Dymock), Spilsby, Lincs., cm and joiner (1790–1835). In June 1790 advertised for a journeyman cm. [D; *Lincoln, Rutland and Stamford Mercury*, 11 June 1790]

Ward, Edward, 28 Chariot St, Hull, Yorks., cm (1821–22). Benjamin Ward succeeded him at this address in 1823. [D]

Ward, Edward, Beeston, Notts., carver, gilder and bookseller (1832–35). [D]

Ward, G., Nantwich, Cheshire, u (1818). On 2 June 1818 married a Miss Becket of Middlewich, Cheshire at Middlewich. [*Chester Guardian*, 20 June 1818]

Ward, George, Birmingham, cm (1828). Bankruptcy announced, *Chester Chronicle*, 16 May 1828.

Ward, George, South Town, Gt Yarmouth, Norfolk, cm (1830–36). [D]

Ward, George, George St, Market Rasen, Lincs., joiner, cm and builder. (1822–26). [D]

Ward, George, Birmingham, cm and u (1828–39). At 72 Dale End, 1828–30, where he is named as George R. Ward. Also shown at 82 Steelhouse Lane in 1830. In 1835 at 5 Snowhill. Still in Snowhill in 1839 and in this year is named as George A. Ward. [D]

Ward, J., address unknown, u (1778–81). Recorded in the accounts of the Duke of Northumberland. In 1778 he was paid £100 and in 1781 £6 18s for laying and taking up carpets, repairing tables, sofa, glasses. [V&A archives]

Ward, J. & R., 8 Old Bond St, London, upholders and cm (1825). [D]

Ward, James, Bishopsgate, London, carver, gilder and frame maker (1800–37). At 123 Bishopsgate Without, 1800–07; 83 Sun St, Bishopsgate, 1808; 170 Bishopsgate Without, 1816–17; 95 Bishopsgate Without, 1819–29; and 1 Half Moon St, Bishopsgate 1837. [D]

Ward, James, Tarrant St, Arundel, Sussex, cm, u, paperhanger, undertaker and turner (1823–40). Patronised by the Earl of Surrey for whom he supplied in July 1803 three stump bedsteads and various bedding at £21. In 1831 and January 1832 he supplied to the same patron black rush seat chairs, a Pembroke table and undertook repairs totalling £18 2s 11. A further account for £3 was submitted in December 1839. [D; Arundel Castle records, A1960, A2023, A2077]

Ward, James K., 66 King St, St Anne's, Soho, London, carver, gilder and picture frame maker (1777). His trade card [Heal Coll., BM] indicates that he repaired and cleaned pictures and re-gilded old frames. The accounts of Nathaniel Ryder, 1st Lord Harrowby of Sandon Hall, Staffs. record the payment on 14 July 1777 to 'Ward Cabt Maker' of £17 10s for an inlaid table. This commission may have been supplied through this James Ward. [Harrowby MS Trust, Notebooks]

Ward, John, London, upholder (1727–49). In 1727 at Red Lion Sq. and in 1749 at Crown Ct. In 1741 a creditor in bankruptcy proceedings against a person named Rooke. He claimed £6 for 'a Chase Mare and furniture'. [Westminster poll bks; PRO, C108/19]

Ward, John, Oxford, upholder (1787–94). Eldest son of Richard Ward. Aged 22 when on 17 April 1787 he married Phebe Alexander at the church of St Peter le Bailey. [Bodleian index of Oxf. marriage bonds; Oxford RO, I/27]

Ward, John, Daventry, Northants., cm (1793). [D]

Ward, John, Nottingham, cm (1795–d. 1798). Will proved 4 September 1798. [Notts. RO, probate records]

Ward, John, York, cm (1801). Son of Luke Ward, yeoman. App. to John Barber, cm and turner, 1 August 1794 and free 1801. [York app. reg.; freemen rolls]

Ward, John, address unknown, cm (1803). Subscribed to Sheraton's *Cabinet Dictionary*, 1803.

Ward, John, Walworth, London, u, cm, chairmaker, japanner and Venetian blind manufacturer (1809–39). At 11 Saville Row, Walworth in 1809 but in 1820 the number was 1. Between 1822 and 1826 moved to 24 Garden Row, London Rd. He remained at this address until 1839 when the number changed to 23 and he is shown additionally at 13 Manor Pl., Walworth. His specialism in japanning appears to have developed from the mid 1820s. The Saville Row property was described in February 1813 as a 'dwelling house & warehouse & shop & shed' and was valued at £400 with stock and utensils kept there a further £100 and similar items in an open yard additionally £50. [D; GL, Sun MS vol. 457, ref. 879727]

Ward, John, 125 North St, Brighton, Sussex, u (1822). [D]

Ward, John, Church St, Dewsbury, Yorks., cm (1822–37). [D]

Ward, John, Selby, Yorks., joiner and cm (1828–34). At Broad St in 1828 and Gowthorpe in 1834. [D]

Ward, John, Main St, Kirby Lonsdale, Westmld, chairmaker (1829). [D]

Ward, John, Pocklington, Yorks., cm (1828–34). At Chapel St in 1828, New Pavement in 1831 and Market Pl. in 1834. [D]

Ward, John, East St, Bedminster, Bristol, chairmaker (1832–33). [D]

Ward, John, 1 Pilgrim St, Newcastle, cm, trunk maker and furniture broker (1833). [D]

Ward, Matthew, Lower Brook St, Chorlton-on-Medlock, Lancs., cm (1834). [D]

Ward, Nehemiah, Kirkgate, Wakefield, Yorks., cm (1814–37). [D]

Ward, Philip, parish of St Mary the Virgin, Oxford, u (1741–68). In 1741 took app. named Leverett. Conducted the letting of Castle Mills in April 1762. [S of G, app. index; *Jackson's Oxford Journal*, 3 April 1762; poll bk]

Ward, Richard, Chorley, Lancs., cm (1762). In 1762 took app. named Latham. [S of G, app. index]

Ward, Richard, Kirkham, Lancs., joiner and cm (1824–34). At Preston St in 1824 and Back Lane, 1828–34. [D]

Ward, Sam., Nottingham, turner and chairmaker (1789). In 1789 took as app. Peter Green. [App. reg.]

Ward, Samuel, London, furniture broker and cm (1826–39). At 5 North St, Manchester Sq. in 1826 as a furniture broker and 14 Palace Row, New Road in 1835 in the same trade. Another directory of 1835 gives the number as 11 and describes him as a cm. In 1838 at 8 Palace Row. [D]

Ward, Samuel, Birstall, Yorks., joiner/cm (1837). [D]

Ward, Samuel, St Peter's St, Bedford, cm (1839). [D]

Ward, Stephen, 7 College St, Southampton, Hants., cm (1834–39). [D]

Ward, Thomas, 'The Boar's Head', Cornhill, London, upholder (1690–1712). In July 1712 insured his dwelling house at 'The Boar's Head' for £450. [Heal; GL, Hand in Hand MS vol. 10, ref. 23450]

Ward, Thomas, Liverpool, cm (1767). App. to Josiah Baxendale and free 10 September 1767. [Freemen reg.]

Ward, Thomas, 78 Margaret St, Cavendish Sq., London, cm and upholder (1773–80). A maker of considerable consequence although his name does not appear in London trade directories of the period. The business was also probably substantial in size though insurance records refer only to property. In 1779 he took out cover of £1,200 on houses and in 1781 £1,100. He attracted many patrons of note. On 27 November 1773 Sir Edward Knatchbull, of Mersham-le-Hatch, Kent paid Ward £56 10s. In the same year furniture was supplied to Sherborne Castle, Dorset for the Digby family. A payment of £41 2s was made to Ward for this in 1774. Very substantial commissions were undertaken at Petworth House, Sussex from January 1774 to December of the same year. Items supplied included mahogany commodes, dressing chairs, a sofa and a couch. The total cost came to £621 17s 5d. On 8 June 1775 Ward invoiced three giltwood window seats to the 5th Baron Langdale of Holme near York. These had scroll ends and French cabriole legs and were covered in damask. The cost including packing was £12 11s 1d and this was settled on 19 August. These seats and the original invoice were offered in Sotheby sales in March 1959 and July 1961. There is the possibility that Ward supplied furniture to the Duke of Northumberland as his name is included in a list of furniture makers compiled by the Duchess c. 1776. In October 1779 an inlaid sideboard cistern was supplied to Sir Richard Hoare at a cost of £15 11s 6d. [GL, Sun MS vol. 272, p. 462; vol. 275, p. 210; vol. 282, p. 99; Kent RO, U951 A 19/2; Digby family papers; V&A archives; *Apollo*, May 1977, p. 366; Sotheby's, 13 March 1959, lot 113, 14 July 1961, lot 125; Gilbert, *Chippendale*, p. 154; Hoare's Bank MS]

Ward, Thomas, Red Cross St, Mint, Southwark, London, cm (1786). Bankruptcy announced, *Gents Mag.*, June 1786.

Ward, Thomas, Queen St, Sheffield, Yorks., joiner and cm (1787). [D]

Ward, Thomas, Stanley St, Liverpool, cm (1813–21). At 57 Stanley St in 1813 but in 1821 the number was 60. [D]

Ward, Thomas, Waterworks St, Hull, Yorks., carver and gilder (1814–40). The number in Waterworks St was 29 in 1814–17, 30 in 1817–34 and 27 in 1835–40. Ward was also a victualler and his address was also 'The Grapes Inn'. He trained under James Piotti, an Italian who traded in Hull, 1806–23. Piotti was the mentor of the Lincolnshire school of naturalistic carving. The carver Thomas Wilkinson Wallis (1821–1903) was app. to Ward and assisted him on work at Burton Constable, Yorks. Ward was active here from 1833 when he regilded sixteen cabriole chairs originally supplied by Thomas Chippendale. Ward charged £3 per chair for his work. The commissions undertaken in this house were substantial with payments of £84 2s 4d in 1837–38, £103 2s in 1839 and £152 10s 6d in 1840. [D; *C. Life*, 17 June 1976, pp. 1622–24; *Furn. Hist.*, 1972; Humberside RO, Burton Constable vouchers]

Ward, Thomas, 67 Frith St, Soho Sq., London, draftsman, decorative painter, paper hanger and gilder (1819–36). Active at Nostell Priory, Yorks., 1819–36. In 1819 he supplied bronzed colza oil lamps on large circular marbled plinths for the Dining Room to replace the pedestals and vases designed by Robert Adam in 1773. He also painted the sideboards to resemble mahogany. Other work over the long period that he was active in the house included cleaning ormolu, repainting, varnishing, upholstery work, polishing, etching, marquetry work and French polishing. [D; *Furn. Hist.*, 1974; Nostell Priory archive, C3/1/5/62/8, 9]

Ward, Thomas, Feather Hill, Kirkham, Lancs., joiner and cm (1834). [D]

Ward, Thomas, Ackworth, Yorks., joiner/cm (1837). [D]

Ward, William, Worcester, upholder (1740–71). App. to John Hames (or Harries) and free by servitude, 31 March 1740. In 1747 living in the parish of St Nicholas. Took as apps John Auster(?), free 1761; his own son William Ward jnr, free 1765; and John Huntback, 1762–1771. Patronised by the Lechmere family of Severn End, Hanley Castle, Worcs. in whose accounts a payment to 'MR WARD Upholstere Nine Pounds or thereabouts' is recorded. [Freemen rolls; poll bk; S of G, app. index; Worcs. RO, 1531/705:134/65]

Ward, William, Portsmouth, Hants., upholder (1744). In 1744 took app. named Whiteingstall. [S of G, app. index]

Ward, William, 33 Sun St, Bishopsgate St, London, carver and gilder (1809). A James Ward in the same trade is recorded at 83 Sun St in 1808. [D]

Ward, William, 9 Noel St, Soho, London, carver and gilder (1809). [D]

Ward, William, 29 Paradise St, Tabernacle Walk, London, cm (1814–39). In June 1814 took out insurance cover of £500 but utensils and stock were only covered for £20. [D; GL, Sun MS vol. 462, ref. 895250]

Ward, William, 21 Amelia St, Walworth, London, cm and u (1839). [D]

Ward, William, Braddon, Lostwithiel and Bodmin, Cornwall, cm (1806–45). In September 1809 living at Lostwithiel and aged 30. He had two sons William aged 3 and Henry aged 1. He was still in this town in 1817. In August 1845 he was occupying a dwelling house and shop in North Hill, Bodmin. A document of 1817 refers to him as a carpenter. [Cornwall RO, DD.SHM.379; DD SHM 380]

Ward & Donald, London, u (1781). On 9 June 1781 supplied to the order of the Hon. Mrs Howard probably for Thorndon Hall, Essex, six cabriole chairs painted green and white for which £9 9s was charged. Covering with needlework cost an additional £2 5s and check covers £2 10s 6d extra. [Essex RO, D/DP A190]

Wardale, H., Newcastle, cm (1803). Subscribed to Sheraton's *Cabinet Dictionary*, 1803.

Wardale, Robert, Hull, Yorks., cm (1838–40). Before taking up the trade of cm he appears to have been a grocer and flour dealer and is shown in an 1835 directory in this capacity.

Trading as a cm at 13 St Mark's Sq., Edgar St in 1838 and as a cm and joiner at the same address in 1839. By 1840 had moved to 18 St James St. [D]

Wardell, Gilbert, Norwich, cm (1795). [Poll bk]

Wardell, John, Hull, Yorks., carver, gilder and looking-glass manufacturer (1816–40). At 5 Newgate in 1816 and 5 Lowgate, 1817–20. One directory of 1818 gives 7 Lowgate however. By 1831 at 8 Bowl Alley Lane which was used thereafter. [D]

Wardell, John, King St, The Quay, Bridlington, Yorks., cm and u (1823–34). [D]

Wardell, John, Gigs Hill, Thames Ditton, Surrey, carver and gilder (1838). [D]

Wardell, Matthew, Claypath, Durham, house carpenter, joiner and cm (1819). In December 1819 he advertised that he could construct 'Gothic and Chinese work in the neatest style of workmanship, as also the newly invented self acting air tight doors etc'. [*Durham County Advertiser*, 4 December 1819]

Wardell, Thomas, Durham, cm (1793). [D]

Warden, Frederick & Judson, Farshall, Cecil Ct, St Martin's Lane, London, cm (1763). On 9 May 1763 took out insurance cover for £500 of which £340 was for the two brick houses that they used, household goods and stock. [GL, Sun MS p. 146, ref. 198884]

Warden, William, Silver St, Bedford, cm and u (1823). [D]

Warder, John, Hemmings Row, London, cm (1753). His house in Hemmings Row was mortgaged to a George Langdale, surgeon who insured it for £100. [GL, Sun MS vol. 103, ref. 137616]

Wardill, John, Market Pl., Malton, Yorks., u (1823). [D]

Wardlaw, George, Liverpool, cm (1834–39). At 64 Lord St with a shop at 45 Islington St in 1834–35, at 8 Commutation Row in 1837 and this latter address with a workshop at 1 Bridport St in 1839. [D]

Wardle, John, Pilgrim St, Newcastle, joiner and cm (1811). [D]

Wardle, John, Ashby Rd, Loughborough, Leics., cm (1835). [D]

Wardle, Ralph, Newcastle, joiner and cm (1782–98). Trading in partnership with Edward Smith at Westgate St, 1782–85, and in March 1785 the partnership was dissolved. Wardle moved to 'the foot of Pilgrim-street opposite the Low Bridge' and continued his business from there. [D; *Newcastle Courant*, 26 March 1785]

Wardle, Richard, 73 Newgate St, with a house at Elswick West Cottage, Newcastle, house, sign and furniture painter and glazier (1827). [D]

Wardley, Isaac, Liverpool, cm (1767). App. to Richard Wilcock and assigned later to Thomas Gatliff. Petitioned freedom in 1765 and was sworn free 2 December 1767. [Freemen bk]

Wardley, Isaac, corner of Orange St, in King St, Bloomsbury, London, cm and turner (1776). In 1776 took out insurance cover of £600 of which £290 was for utensils and stock. [GL, Sun MS vol. 246, p. 614]

Ware, Charles, Tottenham High Cross, London, cm and bedstead and chairmaker (1826) [D]

Ware, James, address unknown, cm (1754). Subscribed to Chippendale's *Director*, 1754.

Ware, Robert, Leeds, Yorks., cm (1793). Subscribed to Sheraton's *Drawing Book*, 1793.

Ware, William, 32 Pitt St, Old Kent Rd, London, furniture japanner and painter (1839). [D]

Wareing, Thomas, Preston, Lancs., upholder (1742–62). Son of William Wareing of Preston, innkeeper. Free by 1742. [Freeman rolls]

Wareing, Thomas, 12 Cirencester Pl., Tottenham Ct Rd, London, carver and gilder (1826). [D]

Waren, Joseph, Oxford, cm (1814). Aged 21 when on 20 April 1814 he married Elizabeth Whitlock at the church of St Mary

Magdalen. Both were stated to be of this parish. [Bodleian Index of Oxf. marriage bonds]

Wareup, William, 7 Broker's Row, Moorfields, London, u (1800). [D]

Warffe, Ambrose, 168 Ratcliff Highway, London, cm and u (1781–86). In 1781 took out insurance cover of £1,700 of which £500 was for utensils and stock. In October 1786 advertised for cabinetmakers but warned that 'None belonging to the Society will be employed'. [GL, Sun MS vol. 297, p. 10; *Daily Advertiser*, 10 October 1786]

Warge, George, Ditch Side, St Bride's, London, upholder (1747–54). In 1747 fined for declining parochial office in the parish of St Bride, Fleet St. In 1751 served as the Scavenger, in 1753 as the Collector for the Poor and in 1754 as Sidesman. [GL, MS 6561 p. 81]

Warham, —, Coney St, York, carver and gilder (1805–08). [D]

Waring, Basil, next door but one to 'The White Hart' Brew House in King St, Bloomsbury, London, chairmaker and cm (1740). [Heal]

Waring, Ericus Gilchrist, London, carver and gilder (1800–20). At 68 Margaret St, Cavendish Sq., 1800–07 but in 1808 the number was 69 and in 1809 it was 70. At 20 and 41 Castle St East, Portman Sq., 1813–20. In May 1800 took out insurance cover of £400 on two houses jointly with Henry Hayward jnr of 13 George St, Portland Chapel. A further insurance policy for £400 was arranged in November 1800. In 1803 he subscribed to Sheraton's *Drawing Book*. His trade card [Banks Coll., BM] is stated to be of 1790. [D; GL, Sun MS vol. 418, ref. 702730; vol. 419, ref. 709557] A Mary and a Thomas Waring are shown at 70 Margaret St in 1807 in the same trade.

Waring, James, 7 Lloyd St, Manchester, u (1817). The address was his house. [D]

Waring, James, 14 Dukes Ct, St Martin's Lane, London, u (1826). [D]

Waring, John, Liverpool, cm (1816–39). App. to John Mears 1806 and free 8 June 1816. At this date he was living at Randle Ct, Leeds St. In 1839 trading at Myrtle View, 76 Christian St with a shop at 16 Fontenoy St. [D; freemen bk]

Waring, Mary, 70 Margaret St, Cavendish Sq., London, carver and gilder (1807). In July 1807 took out insurance cover of £1,000 of which £400 was for utensils and stock. A Thomas Waring in the same trade was also shown at this address in 1807 and Ericus Waring was at this number in 1809. [GL, Sun MS vol. 440, ref. 804483]

Waring, Michael, Liverpool, carver (1761). App. to William Mercer and free by servitude 12 March 1761. [Freemen reg.]

Waring, Richard, Liverpool, carver (1761). Free 12 March 1761. [Freemen reg.]

Waring, Thomas, 70 Margaret St, Cavendish Sq., London, carver and gilder (1807). In July 1807 took out insurance cover of £1,000 of which utensils and stock accounted for £400. Identical insurance cover was also taken out by Mary Waring in July 1807 while Ericus Waring in the same trade was occupying this address in 1809. [GL, Sun MS vol. 440, ref. 804483]

Waring, William, 14 Fontenoy St, Liverpool, chairmaker (1824). [D]

Waring & Lansdale, 15 St Anne's St, Manchester, u and cm etc. (1813–17). [D]

Warland, Thomas, South St, Cambridge, cm (1840). [Poll bk]

Warlow, William, Liverpool, u and paperhanger (1829–35). At 9 Greetham St in 1829, 27 Lower Pitt St in 1830–31 and 20 Tarleton St in 1835. His showrooms at Lower Pitt St were stated to be on the corner of Greetham St and the 1829 and 1830 addresses may refer to the same premises. Warlow

emphasised that he priced his stock 'with a mere shade of profit' and emphasised the keenness of his prices. He obtained his stock of wall papers from London and in April 1831 featured his 'SATEN & PLAIN PAPER HANGINGS warranted of the first quality'. He could also offer 'Cushion & Fast-seat Sofas, Hair Mattresses, Paillasses, Bedsteads etc.: constantly on sale & made to order'. [D; *Liverpool Mercury*, 28 May 1830, 1 April 1831]

Warlow, William, 8 Laurel St, Birkenhead, Cheshire, u (1839). Possibly the William Warlow who was trading in Liverpool 1829–35. [D]

Warlter, Thomas & Lovejoy, William, 84 Farringdon St, London, u, auctioneers and appraisers (1835). [D]

Warman, Henry, High St, Ramsgate, Kent, cm (1823–39). Freeman of Sandwich, Kent. At 54 High St in 1826 and 37 High St, 1832–39. [D; Sandwich poll bk]

Warman, John, 4 Great St, Thomas Apostle, London, cm and u (1839). [D]

Warne, Henry, Mere St, Diss, Norfolk, cm and u (1822–30). [D]

Warne, John, 412 Strand, London, oval turner, carver, gilder and frame maker (1795–1825). In the period 1795–1800 traded as Warne & Vinson. [D]

Warner, Henry, parish of St Giles-in-the-Fields, London, upholder (1705–13). In October 1713 insured a house on the north side of Gilbert St, Bloomsbury and another on the south side of Gt Russell St, Bloomsbury over against the east part of Montague House. The cover was for £300. [Heal; GL, Hand in Hand MS vol. 12, p. 179]

Warner, Henry & Ebenezer, 21 Maryport St, Bristol, basket, sieve and chair makers (1805–09). From 1810 Henry Warner traded at this address on his own account. [D]

Warner, Henry jnr, 21 Maryport St, Bristol, basket, seive and chair maker (1810–16). Formerly in partnership with Ebenezer Warner at this address, 1805–09. From 1815 the business is listed as 'Warner's Basket, Seive & Chair Manufactory'. [D]

Warner, John, High St, Guildford, Surrey, cm and turner (1826). [D]

Warner, Joshua, 37 Brunswick St, Blackfriars, London, cm and undertaker (1820). [D]

Warner, R., 37 Charlotte St, Whitechapel, London, u (1826). Freeman of Maldon, Essex. [Maldon poll bk]

Warner, Richard, Moulsham near Chelmsford, Essex, cm and u (1826–39). Freeman of Maldon, Essex. [D; Maldon poll bk]

Warner, Samuel, address unknown, chairmaker (1756). In January 1756 provided one dozen chairs for John 4th Duke of Bedford at a cost of £1 16s. [Bedford Office London]

Warner, William, 22 Poland St, Oxford St, London, carver and gilder (1805). [D]

Warner, William, 36 Eastgate St, Gloucester, u (1839). [D]

Warner & Sudbury, Baxter Gate, Loughborough, Leics., cm (1835–40). [D]

Warnsley, John, 22 Shug Lane, London, cm (1790–93). [D]

Warr, John, London, upholder (1774–81). Freeman of Bristol. At Holywell St, St Clements in 1774 and Eagle St, St James's, Westminster in 1781. [Bristol poll bks]

Warr, John & Son, East St, Beaminster, Dorset, cm (1823–40). In 1830 recorded as John & Richard Warr. By 1840 Richard Warr was in sole charge and was listed as a cm and u. [D]

Warren, —, Palace St, Canterbury, Kent, cm (1809). [D]

Warren, Edward, 'The Ship & Anchor', Houndsditch, London, upholder (1712–17). Freeman of London. Took an app. in June 1712. In 1714 insured his 'timber house' for £150. This was stated to be on the west side of Houndsditch near St Botolph's Church. [S of G, app. index; GL, Hand in Hand MS vol. 13, p. 242; Sun MS vol. 6, p. 147; vol. 33, ref. 53225]

Warren, Edward, 'The Crown', Wych St, London, u (1724–26). [Heal]

Warren, George, address unknown (1749–50). Between 16 September 1749 and,18 March 1750 undertook furniture repairs for Frederick, Prince of Wales at a cost of £7 9s. [Windsor Royal Archives, accounts]

Warren, George, 9 Prince St, Copperas Hill, Liverpool, cm (1837). [D]

Waren, I., 10 Braddons Row, Torquay, Devon, carver and gilder (1838). [D]

Warren, James, London, upholder (1705–14). Son of J. Warren of Norfolk, Gent. App. to Reuben Parke, 9 November 1705 and free of the Upholders' Co. by servitude, 7 July 1714. [GL, Upholders' Co. records]

Warren, John, London, upholder (1707–15). Son of Michael Warren of Bushey, Herts., yeoman. App. to Thomas Dawson 20 June 1707 and free of the Upholders' Co. by servitude, 6 April 1715. [GL, Upholders' Co. records]

Warren, John, 9 Tottenham St, London, chairmaker (1810). In April 1810 took out insurance cover of £150 which included £25 for utensils in the workshop of a chairmaker named George Patten behind 4 Rathbone Pl. [GL, Sun MS vol. 453, ref. 844500]

Warren, John, 22 Little Queen St, Lincoln's Inn Fields, London, upholder and cm (1822). In September 1822 took out insurance cover of £300 which included £170 for stock and utensils. [GL, Sun MS vol. 493, ref. 995702]

Warren, Philip, address unknown, cm (1803). Subscribed to Sheraton's *Cabinet Dictionary*, 1803.

Warren, Richard, Southgate St, Leicester, cm and u (1835–40). [D]

Warren, Stephen, Warminster, Wilts., cm (1760). In 1760 took app. named Gerritt. [S of G, app. index]

Warren, Thomas, Gosport, Hants., turner, basket maker and chairmaker (1792–1823). At 20 High St in 1823. [D]

Warren, Thomas, London, upholder (1710–34). Only known from details of commissions in the Monson archives at the Lincoln RO. The commissions were however frequent and on an extensive scale. They commenced with the supply of '6 fine dutch chayers rush buttums' in December 1710. These together with the repair of a feather bed only amounted to £1 18s. From 1722 however commissions are on a much more ambitious scale. On 20 October 1722 bedding, materials and furniture such as chairs and a table supplied to George and Charles Monson came to £44 11s 2d. A chest of drawers included in the items supplied was specified as 'old'. A 'stove grate compleat, & 2 chimney hooks' were also among the items. A large account dated 6 September 1723 to 'Madam Monson' amounted to £37 8s 2d and she was also charged £53 11s 2d on 26 February 1724. In June 1725 an inventory of the Hon. Lady Monson's goods in her house in Pall Mall was drawn up. Goods supplied and work undertaken from June to December 1725 for the Hon. Sir John Monson came to £9 15s and a bill to 'Madam Monson' from December 1726 to May 1727 amounted to £15 16s 4d. Some of the items supplied to Sir John in April 1727 were specified as for his pew in Broxbourne Church, Herts., while a charge was made for fitting up a field bed in Conduit St. The largest sum expended was detailed on an invoice of 28 June 1729 and came to £100 10s 6d. Chairs and bedding were the main items of cost but two smaller sums were for destroying bed bugs. Important commissions continued until May 1734. [Lincoln RO, Monson 10/5/2, 11/8, 11/50, 12]

Warren, Thomas, Well Close Sq., London, carver (1774). Freeman of Bristol. [Bristol poll bk]

Warren, Thomas, 77 Oxford St, London, chair and sofa maker (1839). [D]

Warren, Thomas, 56 Vauxhall Walk, London, chair and sofa maker (1839). [D]

Warren, William, Bristol, upholder (1769). Bankruptcy announced, *Gents Mag.*, April 1769.

Warren, William, 10 Lower Belgrave Pl., Pimlico, London, cm and u (1826–27). [D]

Warren, William, Holyrood St, Chard, Som., cm (1840). [D]

Warren & Co., London, warehouse for furniture, pictures, china etc., u (1763–1819). At Vine St, Piccadilly in 1763, 4 Coventry St, Piccadilly 1795–1800, 18 Clifford St, Bond St, 1808–10 and 15 Air St, Piccadilly, 1811–19. [D]

Warren & Randall, 18 Coventry St, Haymarket, London, u (1796). [Heal]

Warren & Venson, 9 New Round Ct, Strand, London, turners and carvers of oval frames (1796). [Heal]

Warrick, Joseph, Nottingham, joiner and cm (1756–82). Son of William Warrick, farmer of Arnold, Notts. and app. 1756. Took as apps Thomas Hutchinson 1769, Peter Housley 1770, Thomas Hutton 1775 and Isaac Swindale 1782. [App. reg.]

Warrimer, William, Mitcham, Surrey, picture frame maker (1839). [D]

Warriner, B., Lancaster (1799). Named in the Gillow records in 1799. [Westminster Ref. Lib., Gillow]

Warringer, William, London, looking-glass and picture frame maker (1829–39). At 6 Castle St East, Oxford St in 1829 and 39 Gt Castle St, Regent St in 1839. [D]

Warrington, John, Market Harborough, Leics., chairmaker and turner (1822). [D]

Warrington, Matthew, address unknown, cm (1815–16). Recorded in the tradesmen's accounts for South Durham Estates as the supplier of furniture to a value of £16 18s in 1815. The account was paid on 7 January 1817. [Durham RO, D/St/v612, D/St/200]

Warrock, —, 5 Jermyn St, London, joiner and cm (1793). Subscribed to Sheraton's *Drawing Book*, 1793.

Warwick, E., S. & A., 51 Fleet St, London, writing desk and dressing case makers (1829). [D]

Warwick, Orlando, Jermyn St, London, cm (1784). [Westminster poll bk]

Washington, Samuel, 2 Back Blackley St, Manchester, chairmaker (1808–17). [D]

Washington, Thomas, Leek, Staffs., chairmaker (1797). [D]

Wass, R., 76 Cornhill, London, work box and dressing case maker (c. 1810). A Regency red leather covered writing box of bowed sarcophagus shape is recorded with the trade label of this maker. He also sold copying machines. [Sotheby's, 19 October 1979, lot 136]

Wass & Oram, 39 St Paul's Churchyard, London, writing desk and dressing case makers (1819). [D]

Wassell, John, 3 Coldbath Sq., London, fancy cm and u (1835–39). [D]

Wastell, Edward, Guildford, Surrey, u (1778–84). A substantial business with insurance cover of £1,000 in 1778 and £1,300 in 1781. Of these totals £950 and £750 respectively referred to utensils and stock. [D; GL, Sun MS vol. 264, p. 279; vol. 290, p. 76]

Watchers, Thomas, 52 Dean St, Soho, London, u (1829). [D]

Watehouse (or Waterhouse), Joseph, York, cm (1818). Son of Francis Watehouse, wheelmaker, and app. to John Bellerby, cm and u, 12 August 1809. Free as a cm 1818. [App. reg.; freemen rolls]

Waterhouse, Solomon, Owston, Lincs., cm and joiner (1835). [D]

Water, David, Grosvenor Mews, Westminster, London, cm (1749). [Poll bk]

Waterer, James, Chertsey, Surrey, cm, u and furniture broker (1826–39). A small table with two drawers is recorded with an impressed mark on the drawer edges 'I Waterer & Son, Chertsey'. In style the table is *c.* 1840. [D; V&A archives]

Waterfield, John, Cambridge (1779–80). App. to Edward Yorke and free 20 April 1779. [Freemen rolls; poll bk]

Waterhouse, —, address unknown, cm (1840–41). Mentioned in an account of Edward Bailey as being employed with five other craftsmen at Buckingham Palace, 1840–41. They were employed for a total of 182 days 5 hours. for which £65 7s 4d was charged. [Windsor Royal Archives, Lord Chamberlain's accounts]

Waterhouse, Henry, Tadcaster, Yorks., joiner and cm (1822–37). At New St in 1822 and Chapel St in 1837. [D]

Waterhouse, Joseph, Dean St, Soho, London, carver (1761). Member of the Joiners' Co. In 1761 employed four non-freemen for six weeks under licence. [GL, City Licence bks, vol. 3]

Waterhouse, Joseph, 12 Carey St, Temple Bar, London, cm (1809). [D]

Waterhouse, Joseph, 63 Chapel St, Pentonville, London, cm (1835–39). [D]

Waterhouse, Thomas, 38 Hart St, Manchester, cm (1825). [D]

Waterhouse, William, Morley, Yorks., joiner and cm (1830). [D]

Waterman, William, High St, Poole, Dorset, joiner and cm (1789–1840). At 112 High St in 1830. The long duration of this business would suggest that more than one William Waterhouse, possibly father and son, were involved. In 1789 took out insurance cover of £200 on 'his House in three Tenements and Workshop adjoining' and additionally £50 for utensils and stock kept there. [D; GL, Sun MS vol. 362, p. 372]

Waters, David, address unknown, cm (1754). Subscribed to Chippendale's *Director*, 1754.

Waters, Hudson, Main St, Cockermouth, Cumb., joiner and cm (1829). [D]

Waters, James, Compton St, Westminster, London, carver (1784). [Poll bk]

Waters, John, address unknown, cm (1754). Subscribed to Chippendale's *Director*, 1754.

Waters, Samuel, Liverpool, cm (1830). App. to John Ward Turner and free by servitude, 17 November 1830. [Freemen reg.]

Waters, Thomas, Cranbrook, Kent, carver and gilder (1832–39). [D]

Waters, William, Southwark, London, upholder (1712). In 1712 took an app. [S of G, app. index]

Waters, William, London, frame maker and gilder (1729–42). Undertook work for Benjamin Mildmay, Earl Fitzwalter, 1729–39. Much of this work was for Moulsham Hall, Essex but at least one commission may have been for his London property, Schomberg House, Pall Mall. On 11 April 1729 he paid Waters £2 2s for a gilt frame 'for a Head of the Mareschall Schomberg by Kneller wh. I bought at an auction'. On 20 December 1732 £4 10s was paid for two carved and gilt frames for marble slabs in the Drawing Room and Bed-chamber at Moulsham and an oval frame and glass for the North East room 'below-stairs'. On 16 June 1733 £34 1s was paid for a large looking-glass and gilt frame for the North East drawing room. A payment of £15 15s on account towards a total bill of £28 7s was made on 11 September 1735. The last recorded payment was on 20 April 1739 and was for a gilt frame for 'the Pictures of Childers the running horse'. Waters is also recorded undertaking commissions for Charles Wyndham for Petworth House, Sussex. £10 1s 6d was paid for frames in 1735 and a further £16 4s in 1742. [A. C. Edwards, *The Account Books of Benjamin Mildmay, Earl Fitzwalter*, pp. 104–05, 188–90; *C. Life*, 25 September 1980, p. 1010]

Waters, William, 16 Holiday Yd, Cow Lane, Ludgate St, London, carver and gilder (1781). In 1781 insured a house for £100. [GL, Sun MS vol. 299, p. 13]

Waters, William, 71 New Compton St, Soho, London, carver and gilder (1817–37). [D]

Waterson, —, 13 Wells St, Oxford St, London, cm and chairmaker (1835). [D]

Waterson, Joseph, Wolverhampton St, Dudley, Staffs., cm (1835–40). [D]

Waterson, John, Norwich, cm and chairmaker (d. 1828). Will proved at Norwich in 1828. [Norwich Record Soc., index of wills]

Waterworth, Joseph, 12 Queen St, Liverpool, chairmaker (1818). [D]

Waterworth, Thomas, Doncaster, Yorks., carver and gilder (1793). [D]

Wates, James snr and jnr, 114 Powis St, Woolwich, London, cm and u (1832–38). In 1838 James jnr appears to have been the sole proprietor. [D]

Wathen, John, 102 Gt Portland St, London, cm and u (1808). [D]

Wathnall, Leonard, Morledge, Derby, cm (1829). [D]

Watkin, John, Fore St, Bodmin, Cornwall, u (1823–30). [D]

Watkin, John, Barnby Gate, Newark, Notts., carver and gilder (1828). [D]

Watkin, Robert Smart, High St, Putney, London, furniture broker, u and auctioneer (1832–38). The name is given as Watlin in 1838. [D]

Watkins, —, address unknown, cm (1803). Subscribed to Sheraton's *Cabinet Dictionary*, 1803.

Watkins, Christopher, 2 Charlton Pl., Hotwells, Bristol, cm and billiard table manufacturer (1831–40). [D]

Watkins, E., Bridge St, Southwark, London, u (1835). [D]

Watkins, Ephraim, Hereford, chairmaker (1826). [Poll bk]

Watkins, Henry, London, upholder and auctioneer (1784–94). At 44 Fleet Mkt 1784 and 63 Holborn Hill, 1788–94. [D]

Watkins, James, London, upholder (1733). Son of Robert Watkins of Deptford, esquire. App. to Thomas Gardner on 3 February 1725 and free of the Upholders' Co. by servitude, 6 June 1733. [GL, Upholders' Co. records]

Watkins, James, London, cm, u and undertaker (1809–39). At 59 East St, Marylebone in 1809, 31 Crawford St, Montagu Sq., 1817–27, and 57 Lambs Conduit St, 1835–39. [D]

Watkins, John, Windsor, Berks., cm (1802–06). [Poll bks]

Watkins, John, Cambridge St, Westminster, London, cm (1784). [Poll bk]

Watkins, John, 12 and 14 Crown St, Soho, London, chairmaker and u (1822–35). [D]

Watkins, Joseph, Bull Ring, Kidderminster, Worcs., cm and u (1828–35). [D]

Watkins, Philip, 14 Crown St, Soho, London, chair and sofa maker (invalid and recumbent) (1839). [D]

Watkins, Samuel, Wray's St, Clerkenwell, London, cm (1784). Freeman of Bristol. [Bristol poll bk]

Watkins, Thomas, address unknown, cm (1803). Subscribed to Sheraton's *Cabinet Dictionary*, 1803.

Watkins, Thomas, London, u and cm (1809–29). At 39 Berwick St, Soho, 1809–23, and thereafter at 23 Conduit St, Bond St. [D]

Watkins, Thomas, Hereford, cm and u (1822–35). At St John's St in 1822 and Packer's Lane in 1835. In 1835 was a producer of rustic chairs in addition to his other trades. [D]

Watkins, Thomas, 26 St Thomas St, Weymouth, Dorset, cm and u (1830). [D]

Watkins, Thomas James, 19 Devonshire St, Lisson Grove, London, cm and u (1839). [D]

Watkins, William, Hereford, joiner, cm, u and wood carver

(1780). App. to Philip Price of Hereford and in January 1780, on the death of his master, took over the business. [*Hereford Journal*, 27 January 1780]

Watkins, William, Cotton End St, Warwick, cm (1831). [Poll bk]

Watkinson, Henry jnr, Ormskirk, Lancs., cm (1784–98). [D]

Watkinson, John, Gainsborough, Lincs., cm (1792–1811). [D]

Watkinson, Thomas, Leicester, u and saddler (1735). App. to John Marston, saddler and u, and free 1735. [Freemen reg.]

Watkinson, William John, Redruth, Cornwall, cm (1830). [D]

Watkiss, Richard, Hills Lane, Shrewsbury, Salop, cm and u (1835). [D]

Watling, Thomas, London Rd, Swaffham, Norfolk, cm (1839). [D]

Watlington, Isaac, London, upholder (1737). Son of Isaac Watlington of Shoreditch, Gent. App. to John Mercer 6 May 1730 and free of the Upholders' Co. by servitude 6 July 1737. [GL, Upholders' Co. records]

Watmough, James, Wallgate, Wigan, Lancs., cm, appraiser and auctioneer (1814–34). [D]

Watmough, James, 4 Gt Ducie St, Manchester, cm and u (1834–40). [D]

Watmough, John, Gt Ducie St, Manchester, cm (1832–33). [D]

Watmough, John, Eccleshill, Bradford parish, Yorks., joiner/cm (1837). [D]

Watson, Mr, Fore St, London, cm (1748). Reported as knocked down and robbed of a watch and money 'by two fellows under Cripplegate'. [*London Evening Post*, 15–17 November 1748]

Watson, Mr, Leadenhall St, London, cm (1752). [GL, Sun MS vol. 98, ref. 132724]

Watson, —, London, carver (1767). Payments were made in 1767 by Henry Knight of Tythegston Court, Glam. for picture frames. [*C. Life*, 5 October 1978, p. 1024]

Watson, —, London(?), u (1767). On 20 November 1767 paid £22 by Richard Hoare of Boreham House, Essex. [Essex RO, D/Du 649/2]

Watson, —, 21 Wardour St, Soho, London, cm (1803). Included in the list of master cabinet makers in Sheraton's *Cabinet Dictionary*.

Watson, —, Greenwich Rd, London, (1805). [D]

Watson, —, 3 Holywell Rd, Shoreditch, London, cm (1826). [D]

Watson, Adam, London, cm, joiner and turner (1775–82). In 1775 at 208 High Holborn where he took out insurance cover for £300 of which £230 was for utensils and stock. In 1782 at 1 Princes St, Little Queen St but insurance cover was down to £200 with £90 for utensils and stock. [GL, Sun MS vol. 243, p. 9; vol. 301, p. 522]

Watson, Alfred, High St, Hemel Hempstead, Herts., u (1839). [D]

Watson, Amb., 208 Oxford St, London, cm (1784). [D]

Watson, Bingley, Liverpool, u and cm (1823–26). In March 1823 trading at 74 Church St as a carpet and blanket store. He was not the owner of the business but described himself agent 'for the Yorkshire Manufacturers'. This must have referred to the stock of bedding and cloth. He could offer 'Hearth rugs, Druggets, Blankets, Quilts, Morines, Fringes, Float & Orris Silk Laces, Hair Seatings & every other Article in the general Upholstery line'. He offered cloth wholesale and retail and Scotch, Kidderminster and Venetian carpets. In January 1825 he announced that he had given up this agency and was about to open a shop in Bold St 'in a few weeks'. In the mean time he was trading from his residence at 46 Gloucester St. The shop opened at 96 Bold St but only traded for a short time, for by April 1826 Bingley Watson was dead and his widow Elizabeth offered his stock at reduced prices as 'the period she has to remain on the premises' was short. The residue of the stock was sold by auction in December. Apart from the carpeting and bedding this consisted of 'Room Papers, Table Covering, Fringes etc.: excellent & handsome well made Mahogany & fancy Oak Articles, in a Winged Wardrobe, Circular & Elliptic Loo Tables, Circular Library Tables, Sofa, Pembroke, Card, Work & Snap Tables, Circular Library Tables, Sets of Chairs, Sofas in Hair Cloth & Morine, Hatstands, Supper Trays, Hall Chairs, Bedsteps etc. Rosewood framed Sofas, Painted Chamber Articles etc'. Bingley Watson's brother, G. Watson advertised his own business in the same trade in Lime St in April 1827 hoping to attract his brother's former customers. [*Liverpool Mercury*, 7 March 1823, 28 January 1825, 15 September 1826, 15 December 1826, 22 December 1826, 27 April 1827]

Watson, Charles, 107 Silver St, Hulme, Lancs., cm (1840). [D]

Watson, Christopher, 14 Clipston St, Fitzroy Sq., London, u (1820). [D]

Watson, David jnr, London, cm and u (1774–d. 1810). First recorded living in Westminster in 1774 and by 1777 was trading at 16 Little Bridge St. The business at this date was of modest size and insurance cover in 1781 came to only £200 of which £150 was for utensils and stock. By 1782 the address was 14 Bridge St, Westminster and the business was trading as David Watson & Son. In an insurance policy of 1785 however an address at King St, Westminster is mentioned. Cover on utensils and stock was then £1,000. From 1800 an address at 51 Parliament St, Westminster was in use and this is the one recorded by Thomas Sheraton in the list of master cabinet makers in the *Cabinet Dictionary*, 1803. David Watson died in 1810 and a receipt for a child's cot and bedding supplied to Georgina, Duchess of Bedford for her house at 2 Hamilton Pl., Piccadilly was given on behalf of 'the Executors of the late David Watson'. His firm continued trading at the Parliament St address until about 1812. [D; poll bk; GL, Sun MS vol. 254, p. 319; vol. 257, p. 355; vol. 293, p. 461; vol. 333, p. 162; vol. 431, ref. 762532; *Gents Mag.*, 1810, supplement, p. 660; Bedford Office, London]

Watson, Edward, High St, Boston, Lincs., carver and gilder (1819). [D]

Watson, Edward Dalby, 145 Warwick Rd, Leamington, Warks., cm and u (1826–37). App. to Benjamin Storer Chamberlain of Leicester and free 1826. By this date he had already moved to Leamington and is shown trading at Warwick Rd in 1837. [D; Leicester freemen rolls]

Watson, E. F., 49 Poland St, Oxford St, London, carver and gilder (1837). [D]

Watson, Edward, London, carver and gilder (1774–81). Established his business in Long Acre but in March 1774 declared bankrupt. The bankruptcy does not appear to have disrupted his business career seriously for by 1775 he was trading again from 21 Long Acre and was to remain at this address at least until 1778. Insurance cover at this address was £500 in 1775 with £300 of this for utensils and stock. The corresponding figures for 1778 are £700 and £300. A fire policy of 1777 however gives an address at 91 Long Acre and a much higher cover of £1,800 with £785 for utensils and stock. In 1781 at 219 Piccadilly with insurance cover of £2,000 and £1,500 for utensils and stock. In 1777 he was paid £2 2s by Alexander Wedderburn. [*Sussex Weekly Advertiser*, 21 March 1774; GL, Sun MS vol. 244, p. 55; vol. 246, p. 102; vol. 256, p. 184; vol. 269, p. 470; vol. 290, p. 553; Scottish RO, GD 184/Box 20/177/2–3]

Watson, Edward, Gt Yarmouth, Norfolk, cm (1780). Freeman of Gt Yarmouth. In 1780 his son Gilbert, also a cm but living in Norwich, was made free of Gt Yarmouth by patrimony. [Freemen rolls]

Watson, Elizabeth, London, embroideress (1696–1710).

Although described as an embroideress she conducted business of a much wider scope. In 1706 she offered 'wrought beds from £7 to £40 per bed, with all sorts of fine chain-stitch work'. In 1710 her stock included 'wrought beds, curtains & quilts'. At the Corner House of Cherry Tree Alley on Bunhill by the new Artillery Ground in 1696; 'The Wrought Bed', Sword Bearers' Alley, Chiswell St in 1706; and Crown Ct, Old Change near St Paul's in 1710. [Heal]

Watson, Emanuel, Harper's Yd, Kirkgate, Leeds, Yorks., cm, appraiser and auctioneer (1808–17). Claimed to have had a long experience 'in the First Houses in London'. [D; *Leeds Mercury*, 13 February 1808, 20 February 1808]

Watson, G., Liverpool, cm and u (1824–27). At 15 Lime St in December 1824 when he offered for sale 'elegant Four Post & Camp Beds & every other description of Cabinet & Upholstery Goods'. On 17 June of the following year he announced the opening of new showrooms at the Lime St address but indicated that he had formerly traded in Church St. His brother Bingley had maintained a warehouse in this street as the agent of Yorkshire manufacturers in 1823 and he may have assisted in this venture. At Lime St, G. Watson emphasised the attractiveness of his prices and in March 1826 featured 'Silk Flocks for Beds & Mattresses at 6d per Lb & equal to Hair or Feathers & far more essential to health. Best Bristol Oil Cloths at 4s. 6d the square yard'. In April 1827 his special offers were 'London Imitation Rosewood Chairs from 6s & upwards, Strong Kitchen Chairs from 3s. 6d each'. When his brother Bingley died in 1826 and his widow indicated that she had no intention of carrying on the business, G. Watson invited his brother's former customers to patronise him. [*Liverpool Mercury*, 24 December 1824, 17 June 1825, 17 March 1826, 27 April 1827]

Watson, George, Hull, Yorks., cm and broker (1792–1840). In 1792 at Blanket Row but from 1803 addresses are in Blackfriargate. In that year listed at Wrays Entry, Blackfriargate. Thereafter the numbers are 40 in 1806–10, 31 in 1814–34 and 32 from 1835. No. 16 Blackfriargate appears to have been used additionally, 1826–31. In 1831 had a residence at 7 English St, and in 1823, 7 Castle Row is recorded which may also have been a house. The address 7 Wakefield St is listed in 1835. The business is referred to as Watson & Fox in 1805 and from 1834 entries are in the name of George Bielby Watson. [D]

Watson, George, Liverpool, carver and gilder (1804–37). At Limekiln Lane, Bevington Hill in 1804, 11 Richmond Row in 1821 and 43 Shaws Brow in 1823. From 1827 most recorded addresses are in Lime St, the number being 15 in 1827, 17 in 1829 and both 15 and 17, 1835–37. One directory of 1837 lists 139 Islington however. [D]

Watson, George, London, cm (1814–35). At 36 Fetter Lane, Holborn, 1814–20. His insurance cover in July 1814 was for £400 and of this utensils and stock accounted for £200, half in his dwelling house and half, probably timber, in an open yard. At 19 Mansell St, Goodman's Fields, 1819–35 and in 1835 additionally at 83 Charlotte St, Fitzroy Sq. [D]

Watson, George, 11 Newton St, Gt Ancoats St, Manchester, u (1817). [D]

Watson, George, London, cm (1813–30). Freeman of both Norwich and Gt Yarmouth, Norfolk. Living in Lambeth in 1830. [Norwich poll bk; Gt Yarmouth poll bk]

Watson, George, Sheffield, Yorks., cm (1821–22). In 1821 at 16 Castle Green but in the following year the address was rendered as 18 Castle Green. [D]

Watson, George, 63 Colston's St, Bristol, sign, house and furniture painter (1825). [D]

Watson, George, Hailgate, Howden, Yorks., joiner/cm (1823). [D]

Watson, George & J., 36 Bridge Rd, Lambeth, London, cm, u and furniture warehouse (1822–35). [D]

Watson, Gilbert, Norwich, cm (1780). Son of Edward Watson of Norwich, cm. Free by patrimony 1780. [Freemen rolls]

Watson, Gilbert, 1 Four Dove Ct, St Martin's-le-Grand, London, cm (1809). In July 1809 took out insurance cover of £300 but of this only £70 was for utensils and stock. [GL, Sun MS vol. 446, ref. 832537]

Watson, Hanchett, 40 Dean St, Soho, London, u and cm (1820–29). [D]

Watson, Henry, address unknown, cm (?) (1754). Subscribed to Chippendale's *Director*, 1754.

Watson, Henry, London, u and cm (1803–37). Listed at 14 Bridge St, Westminster in the directory of master cabinet makers in Sheraton's *Cabinet Dictionary*, 1803. This address had formerly been used by David Watson who had moved to 51 Parliament St, Westminster. Henry was probably the son of David Watson and may have been in partnership with him during the period from 1782 when the business was trading as David Watson & Son. The insurance cover was substantial, amounting to £4,400 in April 1807 and £5,100 in April 1809. Of these sums £1,600 and £2,000 respectively were for utensils and stock. After 1820 the business traded as Watson & Walker and in 1837 the address was rendered as 33 Westminster Bridge Rd. [D; GL, Sun MS vol. 440, ref. 800951; vol. 448, ref. 830404; vol. 453, ref. 850468; vol. 453, ref. 844641]

Watson, Henry, Swadforth St, Skipton, Yorks., joiner/cm (1830–37). [D; PR]

Watson, Henry, North Bar St Within, Beverley, Yorks., cm (1834–40). [D]

Watson, J., 14 Green St, Theobalds Rd, London, cm and upholder (1817). [Heal]

Watson, J., Elston, Notts., chairmaker (1832). [D]

Watson, James, Market Pl., Retford, Notts., chairmaker (1822). [D]

Watson, Jarvis (or Gervas), Market Pl., Retford, Notts., chairmaker (1822–35). [D]

Watson, John, 'The Red Lyon' over against the Royal Exchange, Cornhill, London, u (1689–d. 1722). [Heal]

Watson, John snr, London, upholder (1699–d. 1750). Free of the Upholders' Co., 23 February 1698/99. At Wood St, 1727–30, and King St, 1734–49. Took as apps Richard Wilcox, 1719–29; Thomas Cason Jones, 1725–33; and his son John, 1732–43. John Watson snr was master of the Upholders' Co., 1747. Notice in *General Advertiser*, 15 March 1749/50 reads: 'On Tuesday last died Mr John Watson sen. an eminent Wholesale Upholsterer in King-street, one of the Common Council of Cheap Ward; a Person of very fair Character, whose Death is greatly regretted by all his Acquaintance'. [GL, Upholders' Co. records; Heal]

Watson, John jnr, London, upholder (1743–d. 1773). Son of John Watson snr and app. to his father, 5 April 1732. Free of the Upholders' Co. by servitude, 7 December 1743. Master of the Upholders' Co., 1771 and died 1773. [GL, Upholders' Co. records]

Watson, John snr, Newcastle, cm and u (1778–1816). At Rosemary Lane, 1778–82 and Spital, Westgate St, 1787–1811. A Joseph Watson was trading in Westgate St in 1778 as an u and may be related. In April 1816 John Watson snr was in Collingwood St which was described as his house. He announced that he was giving up the manufacturing of furniture and his stock of new items was offered for sale by auction. The stock consisted of 'a Secretary & bookcase, mahogany lobby & dressing chests, of drawers, dining & turn-over Tables, chairs, writing tables, night tables, celerets, wash stands, portable desks, chimney glass pier & dressing glasses, painted wash tables, rush-bottomed chairs etc.'. In 1811 John Watson supplied to Cuthbert Ellison of Hebburn Hall, Gateshead, Co. Durham two 'sideboards, inlaid with brass banding, broad & narrow & black stain ditto' at £24 10s. Subscribed to Sheraton's *Drawing Book*, 1793. [D; *Furn. Hist.*, 1976]

Watson, John, Sleaford, Lincs., chair turner (1798). [D]

Watson, John, London, cm and u (1803–11). At 10 Wardour St in 1803 and 20 Wardour St, 1805–11. [D]

Watson, John, 18 Kingsgate St, London, carpenter and cm (1809–10). In January 1809 insured his dwelling house and workshop for £200, his household goods for £100 and his utensils and stock for £200. In January 1810 the cover was raised by £100 to insure additional utensils and stock kept in a shop in Eagle St, Red Lion Sq. [GL, Sun MS vol. 448, ref. 825893; vol. 453, ref. 839463]

Watson, John, 43 Devonshire St, Queen's Sq., London, cm and u (1809–11). [D]

Watson, John jnr, Westgate St, Newcastle, cm and u (1811–28). Son of John Watson snr. In November 1812 he announced that he had taken into his service Joseph Watson, formerly foreman to Willcox & Son. In 1822–23 supplied window cord and fitted curtains for Cuthbert Ellison of Hebburn Hall, Gateshead, Co. Durham. [D; *Newcastle Courant*, 28 November 1812; *Furn. Hist.*, 1976]

Watson, John, 5 Milton St, Liverpool, cm (1811). [D]

Watson, John, Beverley, Yorks., joiner and cm (1814–34). At Fleming Gate in 1814 and North Bar St Without, 1831–34. [D]

Watson, John, London, cm (1817–40). At 14 Green St, Theobalds Rd, 1817–20; 26 Bethnal Green Rd, 1820; 58 Exmouth St, Spitalfields, 1822; and 24–26 Wands Row, Bethnal Green Rd, 1827–40. In 1840 used additionally an address in Warwick Rd, Clapton. [D; GL, Sun MS vol. 574, ref. 1341671]

Watson, John, Swadworth St, Skipton, Yorks. (1822–37). A Henry Watson, either a cm or a joiner was trading in this street, 1830–37. [D]

Watson, John, Witton-le-Wear, Co. Durham, joiner and cm (1828). One directory of 1828 records him in partnership with a William Watson. [D]

Watson, John, Houghton-le-Spring, Co. Durham, cm/joiner (1834). [D]

Watson, John, Brigg Rd, Barton-on-Humber, Lincs., joiner and cm (1835). [D]

Watson, John, 1 Hulme St, Manchester, cm (1836–40). [D]

Watson, Joseph, Westgate St, Newcastle, u (1778). John Watson snr was trading in this street as a cm from 1778. [D]

Watson, Joseph, High St, Rochester, Kent, cm (1823–29). At 47 High St in 1823 but in 1826–29 the number was 25. [D]

Watson, Joseph, Newland St, Kensington, London, cm (1838). [D]

Watson, Joshua & Joseph, 15 Gt Quebec St, London, cm and u (1835–39). [D]

Watson, Peter, Cowling, near Colne, Yorks., cm (1822). [D]

Watson, Ralph, 211 Piccadilly, London, u (1773–81). [D; Westminster poll bk]

Watson, Ralph E. F., London, carver and gilder (1835–39). At 49 Poland St, Oxford St, 1835–37 and 210 Piccadilly in 1839. [D]

Watson, Richard, Canterbury, Kent, cm (1797–1818). Free 1797. Living at Knott's Lane in June 1818. [Freemen rolls; poll bk]

Watson, Richard, Rawcliffe, near Goole, Yorks., joiner, cm and carpenter (1826–34). [D]

Watson, Robert, Butcher Row, Beverley, Yorks., cm (1826). [D]

Watson, Samuel, Heanor, Derbs., carver (1698–1715). Born at Heanor in 1663 and trained under Charles Okey, a carver of the parish of St Martin-in-the-Fields, London. Employed extensively at Chatsworth, Derbs. from 1698, where he undertook much of the wood carving. His carvings in lime in the Chapel are noteworthy, and he was also responsible for some of the furniture. In June 1704 he was paid for '2 large seats for the Chapel Gallery in peartree' which may be those presently there. For details of his work in stone at Chatsworth see Gunnis. Undertook work at Melbourne Hall, Derbs. and may have been involved at Burghley, Northants. Often worked in association with other carvers such as the London craftsmen Lobb, Young and Davis who were all employed at Chatsworth. Sketches for his work are found in the Chatsworth archives, and the Bodleian and Derbyshire County Council possess a sketchbook by Watson. [V&A archives; Chatsworth account bks; *C. Life*, 25 April 1968, 6 November 1980, p. 1658; *DEF*; D. Green, *Grinling Gibbons*, 1967, p. 119; *Gents Mag.*, July 1830; Gunnis; Beard, *Georgian Craftsmen*, p. 182]

Watson, Samuel, London, carver (1708). Subscribed to the *Five Orders of Columns*, by John James, 1708.

Watson, Samuel, 7 Duckworth St, Liverpool, cm (1839). [D]

Watson, Sarah, Burr St, Aldgate, London, upholder (1775). Daughter of Thomas Sutton(?). Free of the Upholders' Co. by patrimony, 3 May 1775. She was described as a widow. [GL, Upholders' Co. records]

Watson, Thomas, Queen St, Westminster, London, cm (1749). [Poll bk]

Watson, Thomas, St Saviour, Southwark, London, cm (1759). In 1759 took app. named William Bines through Grinsell's Charity. [Westminster Ref. Lib., MS E 3559]

Watson, Thomas, London, upholder (1772). Son of Thomas Watson and app. to Richard Walker. Free of the Upholders' Co. by servitude, 4 March 1772. [GL, Upholders' Co. records]

Watson, Thomas & Rutherford, John, 11 Princes St, Leicester Fields, London, cm and u (1792–93). Trading in partnership. Declared bankrupt, July 1793. [GL, Sun MS vol. 382, ref. 594482; *Williamson's Liverpool Advertiser*, 29 July 1793, 23 June 1794]

Watson, Thomas, 18 Upper Rathbone Pl., London, house agent and u (1805–09). [D]

Watson, Thomas, Skipton, Yorks., cm and u (1822–34). At High St in 1822, Market Pl., 1828–30, but another directory of 1830 gives Sheep St. [D]

Watson, William, London, cm (1782–84). In 1782 at 2 Little Argyle St where insurance cover of £300 was taken out which included £70 for utensils and stock. In 1784 at Cannongate with insurance cover of £1,200 which included £600 for a shop, warehouse, sheds, utensils and stock. [GL, Sun MS vol. 339, p. 157; vol. 324, p. 321]

Watson, William, Abbeygate St, Bury St Edmunds, Suffolk, cm (1824). [D]

Watson, William, High St, Belper, Derbs., joiner, cm and shopkeeper (1829–35). [D]

Watson, William, Liverpool, u and cm (1834–39). Shown in one directory of 1834 at 39 Knight St with a shop at 42 Berry St, but another gives 1 White Mill St. In 1835 at 32 Gloucester St and 38 Knight St, with a shop at 45 Berry St; in 1837 at 3 Sidney St East and 38 Knight St, with a shop at 45 Berry St; and in 1839 at 2 Jubilee St and 37 Berry St. [D]

Watson, William, Witton-le-Wear, Co. Durham, see John Watson.

Watson & Bruce, 39 Alfred Pl., Tottenham Ct Rd, London, cm and u (1816–17). [D]

Watson & Fox, see George Watson, Hull.

Watson & Martin, 12 Bartholomew Close, West Smithfield, London, cm and chairmakers (1789–93). [D; Heal]

Watson & Walker, see David Watson.

Watt, John, Liverpool, cm (1823–35). At 14 Peter's Lane in 1823 and 135 Park Lane in 1835. [D]

Watt, John, Warwick, near Carlisle, Cumb., cm/joiner (1828–34). [D]

Wattleworth, John, Liverpool, carver and gilder (1827–39). Born 8 May 1805. In 1826 petitioned for freedom by patrimony as the son of Charles Wattleworth, sailmaker and sworn free, 17 October 1827. At this date he was living at 20 White Mill St. In 1839 trading at 51 Walnut St. [D; freemen reg.]

Watton, James, 39–40 Aldgate High St, London, cm and u (1792). On 4 May 1792 insured the two houses for £200 and the utensils and stock kept there for a further £200. [GL, Sun MS p. 483, ref. 600014]

Watton, Thomas, Lancaster, cm (1820). Probably an employee of Gillows. A small mahogany table in the Abbot Hall Art Gallery, Kendal has the impressed mark 'Gillow Lancaster' on the drawer edge and a pencil inscription under the drawer 'Thomas Watton, Lancaster 1820'. [V&A archives]

Watts, —, London, cm (1793). Subscribed to Sheraton's *Drawing Book,* 1793.

Watts, —, address unknown, cm (1809). Undertook work for Princess Elizabeth. [PRO, C13 661/29]

Watts, Allen, Bloomsbury, London, cm (1830). Freeman of Norwich. Free 3 May 1829 but in July 1830 living in London. [Freemen rolls; Norwich poll bk]

Watts, George, opposite 'The Half Moon', Broad St, Hereford, joiner and cm (1774). Advertised his commencement of trading in Broad St in August 1774. His eldest son George, a piano maker, was living in London in 1818. He was made a freeman of Hereford by patrimony in that year. By 1818 his father was dead. [*Pugh's Hereford Journal,* 1 September 1774; Hereford freemen rolls]

Watts, George Alexander, 6 Everitt St, London, cm and u (1839). [D]

Watts, Henry, 30 Hoxton Sq., London, cm and u (1839). [D]

Watts, James, 3 Brokers Row, Moorfields, London, upholstery warehouse (1790–93). [D]

Watts, James, Brighton, Sussex, carpenter and joiner (1819–21). Undertook work in connection with the re-building and extension of the Royal Pavilion, Brighton. This was on an extensive scale and on 15 November 1821 £3,000 was due to him. He supplied furniture for the new kitchens in 1819 which included a strong kitchen table at £14 5s, a large table with four drawers on each side for the larder at £17 5s and an additional press for china at £65 18s 5d. [PRO, LC11/27; Windsor Royal Archives, RA 35545]

Watts, John, Compton St, Soho, London, cm and u (1764–79). App. to Ince & Mayhew in 1764, the premium being £105. By 1775 trading in Compton St where his insurance cover was £2,000 of which £1,520 was for utensils and stock. Bankruptcy announced November 1778. In February 1771 he supplied a mahogany exercising chair 'with Gothick Back & Elbows' to John Grimston which was charged at £6 6s with an additional 10s 6d for a deal packing case for its transport to York. In 1778 undertook work for the Earl of Egremont for Petworth House, Sussex. He altered the squab of a large sofa and supplied a new canvas cover at a cost of £3 10s. [*Furn. Hist.,* 1974; GL, Sun MS vol. 239, p. 482; *Gents Mag.,* November 1778; Ingram, *Leaves from a Family Tree,* p. 78; V&A archives]

Watts, John, Hull, Yorks., cm and broker (1803–40). In 1803 at Blackfriargate but from 1821–35 at 4 St Mark's Sq., Humber Bank. Residence given as 2 St Mark's Sq., 1831–39. [D]

Watts, John, Alfred St, Hull, Yorks., cm and joiner (1828–40). In 1840 in the number in Alfred St was 36. [D]

Watts, John, Head St, Toxteth Park, Liverpool, cm (1837). [D]

Watts, Samuel, Pottergate St, Norwich, cm and chairmaker (1822–30). Trading in Norwich from 1822 but not free of the city until 3 May 1825. This freedom was not granted by servitude. [D; freemen rolls]

Watts, Samuel Moses, Norwich, cm (1826–30). App. to John Brunning and free by servitude 19 June 1826. In July 1830 living at Heigham, Norwich. [Freemen reg.; poll bk]

Watts, Stephen, Gloucester, cm (1837). Child bapt. at St Michael's Church, 1837. [PR (bapt.)]

Watts, Thomas, Dean St, Soho, London, carver and gilder (1749–59). At Dean St in 1749. In 1753 a payment of £2 17s was made to 'Watts frame maker' in connection with Felbrigg Hall, Norfolk. Undertook work at Croome Court, Worcs. for which accounts dated 13 November 1758 and 25 May 1759 exist. The work included carving and gilding a pediment for a glass frame to match another, re-gilding picture frames and other similar work and cost £90 14s 2d. [Westminster poll bk; Norfolk RO, WKC 6/37; V&A archives]

Watts, Thomas, Temple St, Bristol, chairmaker (1799–1801). [D]

Watts, Thomas, Dale End, Birmingham, u (1816–18). [D]

Watts, Thomas, Broadway, Stratford, London, cm (1826–35). At Broadway in 1835. [D]

Watts, Thomas, St Clements, Oxford, cm and u (1830). [D]

Watts, William, 16 Union St, Lambeth, London, chair and sofa maker, undertaker (1826). [D]

Watts & Fox, 16 and 37 Blackfriargate, Hull, Yorks., cm and brokers (1803). Other directories record a Watson & Fox in this street in 1805 and also a John Watts in 1803. [D]

Wattson, John, London, upholder (1717). Son of Joseph Wattson of Keswick, Cumb., innholder. App. to George Friend 13 April 1709 and free of the Upholders' Co. by servitude, 6 February 1716/17. [GL, Upholders' Co. records]

Watty, Joseph, Colchester, Essex; Woodbridge and Ipswich, Suffolk, cm (1815–20). Freeman of Colchester, Essex. Living at Melton, Woodridge on 27 January 1815 when he married. In 1820 living in Ipswich, but at Colchester, 1830–31. [Colchester poll bks; Suffolk RO, FAA: 50/2/117]

Waud, John Chapman, York and Newcastle, u (1758). Son of John Waud, merchant tailor. Free of York as an u in 1758, and in December of that year living in Newcastle. [York freemen rolls; York poll bk]

Waugh, James, Bridge St, Workington, Cumb., joiner/cm (1811). [D]

Waugh, James & Co., Trinity House Lane, Hull, Yorks., cm and u (1823–35). At 8 Trinity House Lane in 1823–26 but in 1835 the number was 5. Listed as James Waugh & Co., 1823–26 but in 1835 simply James Waugh. See Robert Waugh trading as cm and u in Trinity House Lane in the same period. [D]

Waugh, Robert, Hull, Yorks., cm and u (c. 1809–40). App. to John Dickon of Hull in October 1802. At this date his address was given as Stoneferry, Hull. Took as apps Francis Wood of Hull (May 1811), Philip Brady (February 1812), James Hoare of Hull (May 1814), Edward Gaines (assigned from George Chapman deceased, 16 May 1816). Bethel Thorp of Hull (January 1817), Thomas Grime of Hull (August 1817), Daniel England (assigned from George Brook December 1817), James Hill jnr (assigned from George Chapman March 1818), William Geogan of Hull (June 1818), Michael Harrison of Hull (October 1818), William Holden (assigned from George Spenceley November 1818), John Worrell jnr of Hull (October 1819), William England of Drypool, Hull (June 1821) and William Wilkinson of Sculcoates, Hull

(August 1823). This large number of apps would suggest a business of some size and it is probably significant that in 1818 the business was described as a wholesale cm and u. At 7 Trinity House Lane, 1817 and 1828–31, but the number was 5 in 1818, and 6 in 1821–22 and 1834–40. Also used an address at 10 King St, in 1838. In 1831 the business was referred to as Robert Waugh & Co. See James Waugh trading in Trinity House Lane, 1823–35 as a cm and u. [D; app. bks]

Waugh, William, Four-Lane-Ends, Manningham, Yorks., joiner/cm (1837). [D]

Wavell, Jonathan, High St, Newport, Isle of Wight, Hants., cm and u (1823). [D]

Wawen, Robert, St Martin-in-the-Fields, London, cm (d. 1686). [PCC Wills, vol. XI, p. 293]

Way, David, 6 Sun St, Bishopsgate, London, u (1839). [D]

Way, John, Bristol, frame maker (1756). In 1756 took an app. named Clement. [S of G, app. index]

Way, John, On-the-Foss, Dartmouth, Devon, cm (1823–35). Death reported March 1835. His second daughter married John Tozer of Exeter, gilder in May 1831 and his youngest daughter Mary a Mr W. Tozer of Charlotte St, Fitzroy Sq., London in September 1835. [D; *The Alfred*, 17 May 1831; *Exeter Flying Post*, 13 July 1826, 26 March 1835, 10 September 1835]

Way, John, Exeter, Devon, cm (1827–32). At Frienhay St in December 1827 when his son John was bapt. at St Olave's Church. At Hicks Ct in December 1832 when his daughters Harriet Susan and Mary Ann were bapt. at St Edmund's Church. [PR (bapt.)]

Way, Joseph, Market St, Dartmouth, Devon, cm and u (1838). Possibly the eldest son of John Way of Dartmouth who was the victim of a robbery in July 1826. [D; *Exeter Flying Post*, 13 July 1826]

Way, Thomas, 51 Redcross St, Southwark, London, carpenter and cm (1826). [D]

Way, William, Exeter, Devon, cm (b. *c.* 1777–d. 1825). Born *c.* 1777 and living in the parish of St Mary Major in 1803 when his name was included in a militia list. In Preston St, 1814–17, and the bapt. of his son George is recorded 13 November 1814 and his daughter Susannah 4 May 1817, both at the church of St Mary Major. By July 1819 living in Idol Lane where he had a four bedroom house with two attics over and a large stable and loft. Some of the property was sub-let. In July 1819 he tried to sell this property by private contract but may not have been successful for he was still at Idol Lane in March 1821. Whilst at this address he had his sons Edward and Henry bapt. at the Church of St George on 26 September 1819 and 29 March 1821 respectively. William Way died in April 1825 aged 48 'after a lingering illness'. [D; PR (bapt.); *Exeter Flying Post*, 29 July 1819, 28 April 1825]

Waylen, Robert, 23 Queen St, Golden Sq., London, cm (1835–39). In 1839 also u. [D]

Waylett, John snr, London, upholder (1719–34). Freeman of London. Took as app. his son John Waylett, 1719–22. John jnr was free of the Upholders' Co., 1733/34. [GL, Upholders' Co. records]

Waylett, John jnr, London, upholder (1734). Son of John Waylett snr, freeman and upholder of London. John jnr was app. to his father 1719–22 and then to Thomas Siwill freeman and draper, from 27 April 1722. Free of the Upholders' Co. by servitude, 6 March 1733–34. [GL, Upholders' Co. records]

Waylett, John, London, upholder (1762). Son of John Waylett jnr of the parish of St Luke, Middlx, upholder. App. to Joseph Fisher, a member of the Drapers' Co. but trading as an upholder, 2 August 1753. John was made free of the Upholders' Co. under the terms of the 1750 Upholders' Act, 1 July 1762. [GL, Upholders' Co. records]

Wayte, Thomas, Westmoreland St, London, cm (1790). Freeman of Lincoln but living in London in June 1790. [Lincoln poll bk]

Waytin, Raphael, Carnaby Mkt, London, mattress maker (1769). Bankruptcy announced, *Gents Mag.*, February 1769.

Weale, Daniel, London, upholder and auctioneer (1776–87). At 50 Snow Hill, 1776–79, and 38 Holborn and 23 Lower Holborn, 1780–87. Bankruptcy announced, *Williamson's Liverpool Advertiser*, 29 January 1787. [D]

Weale, James, 11 Edward St, Portman Sq., London, upholder and auctioneer (1792–1829). Also used a warehouse at Grays Yd, James St, Manchester Sq. and owned houses at 40 Manchester St and 32 Duke St, Manchester Sq. Stock and utensils at the Grays Yd warehouse were valued at £500 in July 1806 and total cover fluctuated between £1,000 in June 1792 and £400 in July 1810. The death of his wife was reported in February 1803. [D; GL, Sun MS vol. 389, ref. 601784; vol. 437, ref. 790752; vol. 453, ref. 846267; *Gents Mag.*, February 1803]

Wealing (or Whally), John, Liverpool, cm (1764). By 1764 had served as app. seven years and petitioned for freedom. [Freemen bk]

Wealy, Matthew, London, upholder (1734–41). Son of Matthew Wealy of Ipswich, ironmonger. App. to John Goodchild, 25 March 1734 and free of the Upholders' Co. by servitude, 1 July 1741. [GL, Upholders' Co. records]

Wean, George, Bondgate, Helmsley, Yorks., joiner/cm (1823). [D]

Wear, Hannah, 26 Mint St, Southwark, London, cm and u (1839). [D]

Wear, John, 23 Alfred Pl., Newington Causeway, London, cm (1835–37). [D]

Wear, Richard, London, upholder (1737–54). Son of John Wear of Canterbury, hop planter. App. to Thomas Nickalls, 1 June 1737 and free of the Upholders' Co. by servitude, 4 July 1754. [GL, Upholders' Co. records]

Weare, Edward, Goodrich, Herefs., upholder (1739–54). [Bristol poll bks]

Weare, Robert, Leeds, Yorks., joiner and cm (1796–1816). His premises were taken over by his brother-in-law, W. Massey in 1816. [*Leeds Intelligencer*, 13 May 1796]

Weare, William, London, upholder (1739–53). Son of Aaron Weare of the parish of St Andrew Holborn, salesman. App. to Jonathan Fawconer, 18 December 1739 and free of the Upholders' Co. by servitude, 1 February 1753. [GL, Upholders' Co. records]

Wearg, Daniel, 'The Three Tents', Lamb and Horse Alley, parish of St Bride, London, u (1724–28). Son of George Wearg of London, turner. App. to James Rowe, 6 February 1716 and free of the Upholders' Co. by servitude, 5 August 1724. In October 1728 at the Lamb & Horse Alley address where he insured his household goods and stock in trade in his dwelling house for £250. Additional stock valued at £50 was kept in a warehouse in Vine Ct. [GL, Upholders' Co. records; Sun MS vol. 27, ref. 45992]

Weatherall, John, London, u and cm (1774–1805). At 26 Haymarket, 1774–94. In 1794 moved to 52 Dean St, Soho where he remained until 1805. His total insurance cover in January 1791 was £1,100 and in June 1794 £1,300. Included in the list of master cabinet makers in Sheraton's *Cabinet Dictionary*, 1803. In November 1787 was paid £4 6s by Gertrude, Dowager Duchess of Bedford for eight mahogany India back elbow chairs (£4 4s) and a small kitchen table (2s). These were ordered for 49 Pall Mall. [D; Heal; GL, Sun MS vol. 373, ref. 579404; vol. 401, ref. 628770; Bedford Office, London]

Weatherall, John, Liverpool, cm (1811–21). At 11 Upper

Harrington in 1811 and 2 Chapel Lane, Harrington in 1821. [D]

Weatherill, George, Flowergate, Whitby, Yorks., cm (1823). [D]

Weatherill, Joseph, Skinner St, Whitby, Yorks., cm (1823–34). [D]

Weatherill, Joseph, Eastbrook St, Bradford, Yorks., cm (1830). [D]

Weatherill, William, Whitby, Yorks., cm (1823–40). At Cliffe Lane in 1823, and Low St and Skinner St in 1840. A Joseph Weatherill, cm was trading in Skinner St, 1823–34. [D]

Weatherill, William, High St, Bishop Wearmouth, Sunderland, Co. Durham, cm (1827). [D]

Weatherspoon, Alex., 1 Orange Ct, Castle St, Leicester Sq., London, cm (1809). [D]

Weatherstone, Thomas, 90 Union St, Southwark, London, cm and u (1829–39). [D]

Weaver, Alfred, 1 Brompton Rd, London, carver and gilder (1835). [D]

Weaver, John, Bristol, carver and gilder (1774–84). Living in the parish of St James 1774 and 1784 but in 1781 in the parish of SS Philip and Jacob. [Poll bks]

Weaver, John, 45 High St, Guildford, Surrey, cm and u (1831–39). [D; poll bks] See Weaver and Whitburn.

Weaver, Samuel, address unknown, cm (1803). Subscribed to Sheraton's *Cabinet Dictionary*, 1803.

Weaver, William, 4 Worship St, Finsbury, London, carver (1826). [D]

Weaver & Whitburn, High St, Guildford, Surrey, cm and u (1822–32). The John Weaver who traded as a cm and u at 45 High St, 1831–39 may have been the successor and possibly a partner in this business. [D]

Webb, —, London, cm (1793). Subscribed to Sheraton's *Drawing Book*, 1793.

Webb, —, Robert St, Blackfriars Rd, London, cm (1809). [D]

Webb, —, 72 Margaret St, Cavendish Sq., London, cm (1832). The business of Baker and Webb traded from the same address. [D]

Webb, Alfred, Church St, Liverpool, u (1820–30). At 30 Church St in January 1820 but by July 1822 the number was 34. Directories of 1823 and 1824 show him additionally at 22 Pleasant St, possibly his dwelling house. He maintained a warehouse for the sale of upholstery items and also undertook the manufacture of a number of the lines that he stocked. In January 1820 his stock included 'Orris Laces, Float Laces, Covered Laces, Bed Laces, Blind Lines, Carpets, Morines, Hearth Rugs, Oil Cloths, Bell Pulls, Tassels, London Qualities Ferrils, Carpet Bindings etc. & every other article in the Upholstery Business'. By July 1822 he had 'commenced manufacturing MOREENS & HAIR SEATINGS in addition to that of FRINGES, GOLD LACE etc'. In May 1827 his advertisement featured his range of 'Brussels, Kidderminster and other carpets' and he claimed to have in stock a thousand pieces of Morines. By April 1830 he had extended his premises and claimed to have 'one of the best selected & most extensive Stocks in the Kingdom'. [D; *Liverpool Mercury*, 21 January 1820, 5 July 1822, 18 May 1827, 26 March 1830]

Webb, Arthur, 19 Broker Row, Moorfields, London, cm and u (1822). [D]

Webb, Charles, parish of St Michael, Bristol, cm (1774–81). [Poll bks]

Webb, Charles, 39 St Martin-le-Grand, London, cm (1777). In 1777 took out insurance cover of £300 which included £150 for utensils and stock. [GL, Sun MS vol. 260, p. 74]

Webb, Charles, 4 Aldersgate St Buildings, Aldersgate St, London, clock case maker and cm (1783). In 1783 insured his utensils and stock for £200. [GL, Sun MS vol. 313, p. 28]

Webb, Charles, Bath, Som., cm (1784). Freeman of Bristol. [Bristol poll bk]

Webb, Charles, 6 Beech St, Barbican, London, cm (1790–93). [D]

Webb, Charles, 8 Old Bond St, London, u and cm (1823). In December 1823 took out insurance cover of £8,000. The property at 8 Old Bond St was described as a 'new dwelling house & warerooms communicating'. Stock and utensils kept here were valued at £3,400 and he also owned 7 Old Bond St which was let to a wine merchant and valued at £1,500. [GL, Sun MS vol. 499, ref. 1012011]

Webb, George, London, upholder and cm (1763–72). At St James St, Bedford Row, 1763–72, but one entry of 1772 gives St Andrew, Holborn. On 29 July 1772 took an app. Stephen Crouch at a premium of £20. The bankruptcy of George Webb was announced in *Gents Mag.*, November 1772. [GL, Sun MS vol. 138, p. 245; S of G, app. index]

Webb, George, Bristol, chairmaker (1775–1819). At 8 Bedminster in 1775, Bedminster Causeway, 1793–95; Redcliffe Hill, 1799; Alfred Pl., 1801; Montague St, 1801–09; 58 Broad Quay, 1817 and 15 Upper Maudlin St, 1818–19. [D; poll bks]

Webb, George, 2 Mint St, Southwark, London, chairmaker (1835). [D]

Webb, Henry, Hammersmith, London, chairmaker (1763–91). Recorded in 1763 in connection with the furnishing of Alresford House, Hants. In 1767 supplied 24 forest stools painted white at £5 8s and 6 German stools similarly painted to Sir John Griffin Griffin at Audley End, Essex. The Croome Court, Worcs. accounts record the supply of a ten foot sofa and four German chairs painted green in July 1769 at a cost of £4 14s 6d. Osterley Park, Middlx received chairs from him in 1782 and 1789 and in 1791 he supplied to Lord Ducie '6 large Fluted back German chairs' at 2s each. These commissions indicate that his main trade was in simple sturdy chairs painted and in the main intended for garden use. In 1775 he took out insurance cover of £400 on a house and shops. The business was continued by Martha Webb. [*C. Life*, 5 January 1978, p. 18; Essex RO, D/DBy/A25; V&A archives; GL, Sun MS vol. 238, p. 373]

Webb, James, Canterbury, Kent, cane chairmaker (1714). In 1714 took app. named Holness. [S of G, app. index]

Webb, James & M., 17 Old Bethlem, London, bedstead maker, cm and carver (1788–93). [D]

Webb, James, High Wycombe, Bucks., chairmaker (1825). Daughter bapt. 1825. [PR (bapt.)]

Webb, John, Berkeley, Glos., upholder (1754). Freeman of Bristol. [Bristol poll bk]

Webb, John, Newbury, Berks., upholder and cm (1781–98). In 1781 took out insurance cover of £500 of which £420 was for utensils, stock and a 'storehouse'. [D; GL, Sun MS vol. 294, p. 194]

Webb, John, Bedminster Causeway, Bristol, Windsor chairmaker (1792). Succeeded at this address by George Webb. [D]

Webb, John, 4 Wood St, Old St Rd, London, cm (1805). [D]

Webb, John, 15 Holywell Rd, Shoreditch, London, bedstead maker (1820). [D]

Webb, John, New St, Wellington, Salop, cm and chairmaker (1822–36). [D]

Webb, John, 175 Regent St, London, cm and u (1826–27). [D]

Webb, John, High St, Towcester, Northants., cm and u (1830). [D]

Webb, John, 15 Wellington Mart, Hull, Yorks., joiner and cm (1838–39). [D]

Webb, John, 8 Old Bond St, London, u and cm (1825–35). Successor to Charles Webb at this address. The business is listed as J. & R. Webb, 1825–39, and in one directory of 1835 at Webb & Cragg. [D]

Webb, Martha, Hammersmith, London, chairmaker (1800–32). Successor to Henry Webb and probably his widow. On 13 February 1800 issued a receipt for £6 5s 6d for garden chairs supplied to Lord Monson. By 1804 had taken a partner named Bunce and this enterprise continued to trade until 1832. On their trade card they claimed that their manufactory of park and garden furniture had been established 'upwards of seventy years'. They stated that their products had been 'Sanctioned by their Majesties, the Prince of Wales, the Dukes of Clarence, Cumberland, Sussex and Cambridge'. Products stocked included 'Cove seats and Portable Chaises, Rustic Hermitages, Chairs, Tables, Bridges, Gates, Windsor Chairs for Kitchen, Studies &c., Camp stools, Chairs, Greecian and German Sofas, Chairs, Stools, Gothic Settees, Chairs &c., Chinese Seats, Pavilions, Awnings, Bath chairs, dog houses, pallings &c.'. In December 1811 insurance cover was for £1,300 of which £1,250 covered the dwelling house and workshop in King St and £50 a workshop at the Creek, Hammersmith. Their address was also rendered as 'Corner of Webb's Lane, Hammersmith' on their trade card and King's Rd, Chelsea and at Hammersmith in directories. By 1832 at Dorcas buildings, Hammersmith. In 1804 Webb & Bunce supplied rustic seats to the Heathcote family. [D; Heal; BM, Banks 132–123; GL, Sun MS vol. 459, ref. 864076; Lincoln RO, Monson 11/18; 3 ANC 6/380]

Webb, Robert, 'The Queen's Head & Three Tents', Bedford St, Covent Gdn, London, upholder (1712–45). Free of the Upholders' Co., 5 November 1712. Took as apps Thomas Dobyns, 1722–30, and Harry Skinner, 1726–32. His own son Robert was free of the Upholders' Co. by patrimony, 7 November 1745. [Heal; GL, Upholders' Co. records; Sun MS vol. 3, ref. 3013]

Webb, Robert jnr, London, upholder (1745). Son of Robert Webb and free of the Upholders' Co. by patrimony, 7 November 1745. [GL, Upholders' Co. records]

Webb, Tesdale, 29 Gracechurch St, London, wholesale u (1770–1800). Traded as Tesdale Webb & Co. to c. 1782 but from that year the business is known as Webb & Lawford. Probably the 'Webb' who supplied chairs to the proprietors of the Coal Exchange, Lower Thames St in 1781 at a cost of £18. [D; GL, Coal Exchange ledger, p. 4]

Webb, Thomas, address unknown (1720). On 4 June 1720 supplied a frame for a marble table top to Temple Newsam House, Leeds at a cost of 6s. [*Furn. Hist.*, 1967]

Webb, Thomas, 6 Bermondsey New Rd, London, cm and u (1822–28). [D]

Webb, Thomas, Ware, Herts., cm and u (1832–39). At Water Row 1832–38 but in 1839 was in the High St. [D]

Webb, William, St George's, Bristol, upholder (1774–81). [Poll bks]

Webb, William, 45 Leman St, Goodman's Fields, London, cm (1783). In 1783 insured a house for £200. [GL, Sun MS vol. 314, p. 158]

Webb, William, near the Turnpike, Newington, London, Windsor and rustic chair maker (1779–1811). His trade card, which uses the same frame and engravings as those of Stubbs and Lock & Foulger, indicates that Webb made and sold 'all sorts of Yew Tree, Gothic and Windsor Chairs, China and Rural Seats, Single and double Alcoves, garden machines & Children's chaises'. Member of the Joiners' Co. Included in the list of master cabinet makers in Sheraton's *Cabinet Dictionary*, 1803. One trade directory of 1791 lists additionally an address in Mile End Rd. A Windsor chair is known with Webb's trade label affixed beneath the seat. In 1803 the firm is recorded as William & Richard Webb. It is

possible that the proprietors of this business were related to the business operated in Hammersmith and Chelsea on the opposite bank of the Thames in the same line successively by Henry Webb, Martha Webb and the partnership of Webb & Bunce. [D; BM, Banks 28–148, 28–230; *Furn. Hist.*, 1978]

Webb, William, St George (Bristol), Glos., upholder (1784). (Bristol poll bk)

Webb, William, 227 Strand, London, cm, u and undertaker (1789–97). [D]

Webb, William, Berkhampstead, Herts., chairmaker (1793). [D]

Webb, William, Westcroft Rd, Hammersmith, London, rustic and garden chairmaker (1826). [D]

Webb, William, Frankfort St, Plymouth, Devon, cm (1836). [D]

Webb & Sampson, London, wholesale u (1759–70). At Threadneedle St, 1759–66 but from 1767 the address is rendered as 1 George St, Mansion House. [D]

Webber, Benjamin, Brandon, Suffolk, cm (1793). [D]

Webber, Miss E., address unknown, u (1837). Married John Kerridge of Exeter in February 1837. [*Exeter Flying Post*, 23 February 1837]

Webber, Frances, Exeter, Devon, u (1825–40). In 1825 she was trading in High St but in 1827–34 at Paul St and 1836–40 at New Buildings. [D]

Webber, James, St James St, Taunton, Som., cm (1822–39). [D]

Webber, James, Dunster, Som., cm and u (1840). [D]

Webber, John, address unknown, cm (1769). On 27 November 1769 supplied to William Constable of Burton Constable, Yorks. a travelling bedstead which he took with him on the Grand Tour in 1770. The bedstead was described as 'complete' but cost the incredible sum of £79. [Humberside RO, Buston Constable vouchers]

Webber, John, London, cm (c. 1781–94). App. to Seddon 1774 and during the period of his apprenticeship lived with him. Became a member of the Joiners' Co. Took as app. George Cottle and in November 1794 John Ball. The latter was described as the son of a victualler from Rotherhithe. The premiums were £5 5s and £15 respectively and both apps lived with Webber. [GL, Joiners' Co. bindings, vol. 7, p. 190; vol. 8, p. 10]

Webber, John, London, cm and u (1794–96). At 21 Poland St, Oxford St, 1794–95 and Gt Portland St in 1796. [D; Heal]

Webber, John Thomas, 6 Bermondsey New Rd, Southwark, London, cm (1809–25). [D]

Webber, Joseph, Pithay, Bristol, cm, u and broker (1810–40). At 21 Pithay, 1810–15; 21 and 22 in 1816–17, and thereafter 22. In 1823 also bedstead maker. [D]

Webber, Peter, 19 Sun St, Bishopsgate, London, cm (1805). [D]

Webber, William, Church St, Camberwell, London, cm and u (1826). [D]

Webber, William jnr, Exeter, Devon, carver and gilder (1833–36). At Gandy St in 1833, 246 High St in 1834 and Waterbeer in 1836. [D]

Webber & Sparrow, 20 Castle Ditch, opposite Lord St, Liverpool, u (1774). In May 1774 announced the opening of their 'Upholstery, Carpet, Blanket & Paper Hanging Warehouse' and indicated that they required an app. [D; *Williamson's Liverpool Advertiser*, 6 May 1774]

Webber & Taylor, East St, Horsham, Sussex, cm (1839). [D]

Webley, John Clouter, Bristol, cabinet and chair carver (1831–40). At 4 Rosemary St, 1831–32, 3 Rosemary St, 1833–38 and 53 Milk St, 1839–40. In 1836 described as an ornamental carver. [D]

Webley, William, address not known, chair painter (1809). [D]

Webster, —, Dockhead, Hull, Yorks., broker and cm (1803). [D]

Webster, Barnabas, 20 Pump Yd, Ratcliffe, London, carpenter and cm (1822–23). In February 1822 insured his stock and utensils for £200. In February 1823 total insurance cover was £500 with stock and utensils kept in his house and in a shed behind £190. Total cover was increased in April of that year to £600 with stock and utensils at £200. In April also stated to be a bedstead maker. [GL, Sun MS vol. 489, ref. 989614; vol. 489, ref. 1003068; vol. 496, ref. 1003569]

Webster, Christopher, Bedale, Yorks., cm, joiner and carpenter (1823). [D]

Webster, Edward, London, upholder (1714–45). Son of Samuel Webster of Abbots Bromley, Staffs., weaver. App. to Henry Turner 9 November 1705 and free of the Upholders' Co. by servitude, 3 March 1713/14. Took as apps Henry Weedon 1733/34–36, Stephen Lawrence Husson 1736–1743/44 and George Good 1743–45. [GL, Upholders' Co. records]

Webster, Edward, St Neots, Hunts., carpenter, joiner, cm and u (c. 1730). Known from a label affixed to a mirror of the William and Mary period. This indicates that he made and sold 'tables, chest of drawers, and buroes, desk-book-cases, chairs, settees, or Tea boards, or Tea Chests either in Wallnut, Mahogany or Wainscot, &c. Also looking glasses of all sorts, in all kinds of frames: and frames for Pictures, with Italian floor-cloths and carpets, paper hangings for rooms, gilt trunks and great variety of maps and pictures. Likewise painting oils and varnishes with all curious and common colours ready prepar'd with brushes, coffin plates of brass or tin, Gilt or lacquer'd castors and all sorts of locks, drops'. He also offered to re-silver looking-glasses and reframe them and stated that he undertook house painting. [V&A archives]

Webster, Elizabeth, Newcastle, u (1768–74). In February 1768 announced that she had just moved from 'Sandhill Corner, below the Cross to the House over Mr. Saint's shop in the Side'. Recently arrived stock included 'a neat assortment of Moreens, Harrateens'. She traded at the sign of the Royal Tent. In November she entered into a partnership with Ralph Brown who had formerly been a journeyman employed by the fashionable London u, William France. Brown claimed to have 'wrought at several of his Majesty's Palaces, and Noblemen's Houses' during the 'considerable Time' that he was employed by France. A trade card issued at this period indicates that the partners made and sold 'Beds of Damask, moreen, chintz' and had 'a compleat assortment of paper hangings, also ... carpets, with other articles in the Upholstery Way'. The partnership was dissolved in February 1772 and on 16 July 1774 Elizabeth Webster announced that she had 'engaged a journeyman capable to carry on the upholstery business' and 'intends to carry it on as usual'. [Newcastle Courant, 6 February 1768, 19 November 1768, 29 February 1772, 16 July 1774; V&A archives]

Webster, George, parish of St Simon & St Jude, Norwich, cm (1780). [Poll bk]

Webster, George, King St, Hammersmith, London, cm and u (1839). [D]

Webster, J., 8 Charles St, Liverpool, joiner and cm (1774). [D]

Webster, J., Water Row, Ware, Herts., u and paper-hanger (1823). [D]

Webster, J. & T., London, furniture warehouse, u and auctioneer (1825–27). At 95, 114 and 147 Whitechapel Rd in 1825–26 but 227 High St, Shoreditch 1826–27. [D]

Webster, James, Hull, Yorks., cm and u (1803–26). At Mushroom Row, John St 1803, 37 St John St 1810–23 but one directory of 1817 gives the number as 38. In 1826 at 30 Dock St with a residence at 8 Grimston St. Described as a carpet and upholstery warehouse, 1814–22. [D]

Webster, James, Manchester and Liverpool, u (1814–34). In 1829 he claimed to have been in business in Manchester for fifteen years. By trade he was a manufacturer of upholsterer's trimmings, fringes, smallwares etc. and had his business at 17 Hanover St, Manchester. In December 1829 he advertised the opening of a manufactory at 12 Williamson Sq. It is possible that the Manchester premises were closed soon after as they are not mentioned in subsequent advertisements. Advertised for apps in December 1829 and January 1834 and in August 1831 indicated that he wanted a journeyman u. In 1834 in addition to his manufacturing of trimmings, fringes and coach lace, he claimed also to make 'furniture' and kept stock of 'damask and morine'. [Liverpool Mercury, 11 December 1829, 5 August 1831, 30 January 1834]

Webster, James, Blackfriargate, Hull, Yorks., cm (1838–40). At 14 Blackfriargate in 1838 and 5 Holme's Ct, Blackfriargate in 1839. [D]

Webster, John, London, u (before 1767). In August 1767 resident in Arch St, near Second St, Philadelphia, USA. He claimed to have arrived from London and to have 'had the honour of working with applause, for several of the nobility and gentry in England and Scotland'. He offered seating furniture, a service to hang walls with fabrics or paper, the manufacture of Venetian blinds and a fluid for destroying bed bugs. [Penn'a Journal, 20 August 1767]

Webster, John, 5 Mercer St, Long Acre, London, cm (1774–75). In 1775 took out insurance cover of £400 but only £60 of this was for utensils and stock. [Westminster poll bk; GL, Sun MS vol. 242, p. 519]

Webster, John, Charles St, Liverpool, joiner and cm (d. by 1776). By November 1776 John Webster was dead and an auction sale of his stock was announced for 5 December. On offer were a quantity of deal, oak and mahogany boards, utensils and implements and 'some very neat Cabinet & Household Goods, mostly new'. The Charles St premises included a 'shop & yard' which in November 1776 were being used by John and William Webster, probably sons of the deceased. [Williamson's Liverpool Advertiser, 29 November 1776]

Webster, John, Lancaster and Cartmel, Lancs., chairmaker (1806). Free of Lancaster 1806–07 but by that date living at Cartmel. [Lancaster freemen rolls]

Webster, John, York, cm (1818). Son of Michael Webster, cordwainer of Flaxton, Yorks. App. to George Beal, cm, on 5 October 1811 and free by servitude, 1818. [App. reg.; freemen rolls]

Webster, John, Upper Hill St, Richmond, Surrey, cm etc. (1822–39). [D]

Webster, John, Warton, near Kirkham, Lancs., joiner and cm (1828). [D]

Webster, John, 5 St Ann's Terr., Liverpool, u (1823–37). App. to William Bickerstaff, 1823, and in 1837 trading at St Ann's Terr. [D; app. bk]

Webster, John & Richard, Bromsgrove, Worcs., manufacturers of coffin ornaments, picture frames and wholesale dealers in Birmingham hardware (1793). [D]

Webster, Mary, 2 Savile St, Hull, Yorks., cm and u (1826–28). [D]

Webster, Peter, Pellmell Ct, Broadley St, Hull, Yorks., cm (1831–39). The number in Pellmell Ct was 11 in 1831 and 10 in 1838. [D]

Webster, Robert, Newcastle, u (1684–1709). Free 1684. His son Thomas was free, 25 July 1701. Robert Webster took as apps John Robson, free 11 March 1702/03, and John Armstrong, free 12 April 1709. [Freemen rolls]

Webster, Robert, Ware, Herts., cm and upholder (1784–1818). Freeman of Norwich. [D; Norwich poll bks]

Webster, Simon, Newcastle, u (1705–13). Free 1705. Took as app. Lawrance Quincey who was free 22 December 1713. [Freemen rolls]

Webster, Thomas, Newcastle, u (1701–09). Son of Robert

Webster of Newcastle, u. Free 25 July 1701. Took as app. William Henderson, free 12 December 1709. [Freemen rolls]

Webster, Thomas, Ulverston, Lancs., cm (1784–98). [D]

Webster, Thomas, 34 Bridport St, Liverpool, u (1818–24). App. to Mathew Gregson in 1784 but when he petitioned freedom in 1818 this was not granted as his former master was not free when Webster was bound and the indenture was lost. Trading at Bridport St in 1824. [D; freemen's committee bk]

Webster, Thomas, Straight, Lincoln, cm (1819). [D]

Webster, Thomas, Grimsby, Lincs., joiner and cm (1822–31). At Loft St, 1822–31, but one directory of 1826 gives Upper Burgess St. [D]

Webster, Thomas, Derby Rd, Nottingham, cm (1835). [D]

Webster, Thomas, Kendal, Westmld, cm and u (1834). [D]

Webster, W., Horsepool St, Leicester, cm (1815). [D]

Webster, William, Kimbolton, Hunts. and Pontefract, Yorks., joiner (1719–59). Subscribed to Chippendale's *Director*, 1754. Took as apps Henry Desbrough, 1719, Jn Beasley, 1742 and Richard Thompson, 1759. [V&A archives]

Webster, William, Blackfriargate, Hull, Yorks., cm (1768–95). Retired 1795 and his former app. Thomas Staniland took over the business. [Poll bks; *Hull Packet*, 1795]

Webster, William, 7 Pulteney Ct, Windmill St, Golden Sq., London, cm and glass paper maker (1792). In March 1792 took out insurance cover of £700 but stock and utensils were only valued at £70. [GL, Sun MS vol. 382, ref. 597858]

Webster, William, 4 Castle St, Long Acre, London, cm and undertaker (1805). [D]

Webster, William, Banbury, Oxon., cm and u (1832–40). At Sheep St, 1832–35 but from 1837 at High St. [D]

Webster & Brown, see Elizabeth Webster.

Webster & Carter, 218 Scotland Rd, Liverpool, u and paperhangers (1837). [D]

Webster & Darling, St John St, Hull, Yorks., cm (1806). [D] See William Darling.

Webster & Witty, Blackfriargate, Hull, Yorks., cm (1790–99). Subscribed to Sheraton's *Drawing Book*, 1793. [D]

Wedd, John, 115 Long Acre, London, cm etc. (1820). [D]

Weddall, John, 292 Deansgate, Manchester, joiner, builder and cm (1825). [D]

Wedderal, William, High St, Sunderland, Co. Durham, cm (1828). [D]

Wedderspoon, A. & R., 1 Castle St, Leicester Sq., London, cm and u (1820–23). [D]

Wedgwood, Aaron, the Potteries, Staffs., carver and gilder (1818–34). In 1818 the address is given as 'Near the Big House, the Potteries'. In 1834 it was New St, Burslem. [D]

Weedon, Henry, London, upholder (1726–50). Son of Joseph Weedon of London, a member of the Armourers' Co. App. to William Shepard, 3 November 1726 and then to Edward Webster, 15 February 1733/34. Free of the Upholders' Co. by servitude, 1 December 1736. Took as app. William Henry Halford, 1737–44/45. Living in Wellclose Sq. in 1750. [GL, Upholders' Co. records, Livery list, 1750]

Weeden, John, High Wycombe, Bucks., chairmaker (1826–28). Daughters bapt. in 1816 and 1828. [PR (bapt.)]

Weeks, —, 14 Pitt St, Fitzroy Sq., London, carver and gilder (1820). [D]

Weeks, John, address unknown, cm (1803). Subscribed to Sheraton's *Cabinet Dictionary*, 1803.

Weeks, John, 23 Sutton St, Clerkenwell, London, clock case maker (1809–26). [D]

Weeks, John, Four-posts, Southampton, Hants., cm (1839). [D]

Weeks, Thomas, Southampton, Hants., cm, u, appraiser and auctioneer (1823–39). At 132 High St, 1823–30. Bankruptcy declared, January 1824, and a sale was held of his stock. Continued trading at this address however and in 1830

charged Lord Willoughby de Broke £1 16s 3d for putting new carpet on two cabin stools and five 'mahogany turned pillows' for berths in a yacht. In 1839 at West St. [D; *Brighton Gazette,* 22 January 1824; BM, Banks 28. 150]

Weighill, Christopher, Osmotherly, Yorks., joiner and cm (1840). [D]

Weight, John, London, cm and u (1786–1839). At Bridge St, Covent Gdn, 1786–87 where he insured utensils and stock for £550 in January 1786 and household goods, utensils and stock in a workshop and warehouse for £700 in January 1787. Subscribed to Sheraton's *Drawing Book*, 1793. At Savoy Steps, Strand in 1796 but from 1804 addresses are in Long Acre. At 37 Long Acre 1804 onwards but in 1821 at 115 Long Acre. A rosewood drum table on a pillar support with four legs terminating in brass paw feet has been noted with the label of this maker inscribed 'Weight, 37 Long Acre'. [D; GL, Sun MS vol. 335, p. 342; vol. 342, ref. 526709; Heal; *Conn.,* February 1969, p. xlvii]

Weight, R. M. jnr, 63 Upper Charlotte St, Fitzroy Sq., London, cm and u (1811–37). [D]

Weightman, Anthony, Micklegate, York, cm (1758). [Poll bk]

Weir, David, Silver Ct, Silver St, London, cm (1803). Included in the list of master cabinet makers in Sheraton's *Cabinet Dictionary*, 1803.

Weir, James, 9 Crown St, Soho, London, cm and u (1839). [D]

Wel(l)beloved, Charles, Denmark St, parish of St Giles-in-the-Fields, London, frame maker (1766–73). His house in Denmark St which was the sixth house from Hog Lane on the north side was insured in 1766 for £300 and a similar amount in December 1773. In 1769 paid £3 4s 9d in connection with the framing in a carved and gilt frame of a picture of a lioness and her young for Burton Constable, Yorks. [GL, Hand in Hand MS vol. 105, p. 104; Humberside RO, Burton Constable vouchers]

Welborn, Joseph, 131 St John St, Smithfield, London, cm (1835). [D]

Welch, —, St Paul's, London, chairmaker (1708–09). Supplied furniture to Felbrigg, Norfolk in 1708 for which £7 was paid and in May 1709 a further payment of £2 14s 6d was made to Welch. [Norfolk RO, Felbrigg WKC 6/23]

Welch, Caleb, London, horse hair weaver and cm (1782–91). At 51 Fleet Mkt in 1782 when he was associated with Richard Joyhnson and Henry Ladyman in an insurance policy for £2,200 of which £2,000 was for utensils and stock. In September 1791 at 119 Fleet St with the same insurance cover but only Caleb Welch is named in the insurance contract. [GL, Sun MS vol. 304, p. 278; vol. 379, p. 547]

Welch, Charles, Hospital St, Nantwich, Cheshire, couch maker (1822). A John Welch in the same trade is also shown in Hospital St in 1822. [D]

Welch, George, Whitchurch, Salop, see George Welsh.

Welch, James, behind 'The Rose & Crown', Broadway, Blackfriars, London, glass grinder and looking-glass maker (1724–56). At 'The Rose & Crown', Broadway in July 1724 when he advertised his ability to supply wholesale or retail a 'great Variety of Peer, Chimney or Sconce Glasses, fine Dressing-Glasses, Coach, Chariot or Chair-Glasses, with Plate Sash-Glasses &c.' He offered to clean and modernise old glasses. At the time of his death in March 1756 he was referred to as 'James Welch Esq' and was declared to be 'the greatest manufacturer of the looking glass trade in the kingdom'. [*Daily Courant,* 29 July 1724; *Gents Mag.,* March 1756]

Welch, James, Ludgate Hill, London, cm (1727–32). In 1727 served as Constable in the parish of St Bride, Fleet St, but in 1732 fined for declining parochial office. [GL, MS 6561, p. 48]

Welch, John, Chester, u (1784). Son of Samuel Welch of

Chester, maltster. Free 3 April 1784 and in that year shown living at Further Northgate St and King St. [Freemen rolls; poll bk]

Welch, John, Nottingham, u (1798). [D]

Welch, John, Hospital St, Nantwich, Cheshire, couchmaker (1822). A Charles Welch in the same trade was also in Hospital St in 1822. [D]

Welch, Joseph, Holywell Lane, Shoreditch, London, upholder (1709–42). Free of the Upholders' Co., 6 April 1709. Took as apps John Whistler, 1720–28, Benjamin Key, 1725–36 and James Day, 1735–42. His house in Holywell Lane which was insured for £150, was on the west side and flanked to the south by a property distinguished by the trade sign of 'The Bricklayers' Arms'. [GL, Upholders' Co. records; Hand in Hand MS vol. 12, p. 623; vol. 23, p. 232; Heal]

Welch, Nathaniel, Holywell St, Shoreditch, upholder (1712). In January 1712 insured his house 'situate on the east side of Holywell Street over against Holywell Lane' for £150. [GL, Hand in Hand MS vol. 9, p. 511]

Weldon, George, Bridgegate, Barnard Castle, Co. Durham, joiner and cm (1827). [D]

Wellard, William, Deal, Kent, cm (1831–37). Freeman of Sandwich, Kent. [Sandwich poll bks]

Wellcome, John, Portsmouth, Hants., joiner and cm (1748). In 1748 took app. named Gloven. [S of G, app. index]

Weller, Henry, Ringmer, Sussex, cm (1839). [D]

Weller, John, East St, Chichester, Sussex, cm, u, auctioneer and estate agent (1777–1826). Frequently advertised auction sales in *Sussex Weekly Advertiser*. In April 1777 the advertisement is in the name of John Weller, but from August 1779 they are in the name of John Weller jnr, suggesting the involvement of both a father and son of the same name in this business. [D; *Sussex Weekly Advertiser*, 14 April 1777, 23 August 1779]

Weller, John, High Wycombe, Bucks., carpenter and cm (b. c. 1804–41). Three daughters and two sons bapt., 1829–40. Aged 37 at the time of the 1841 Census. [PR (bapt.)]

Weller, John, 10 Thomas St, Manchester, chairmaker (1832). [D]

Weller, Samuel, North St, Brighton, Sussex, cm, u and furniture broker (1832–40). At 134 North St, 1832 but by 1839 at 150 North St. [D; poll bk]

Weller, Stephen, Greenwall, Lewes, Sussex, journeyman cm (1826–30). [Poll bks]

Weller, T. & Son, Chichester, Sussex, upholders, u and cm (1793). [D]

Weller, Thomas, East Grinstead, Sussex, basket and chairmaker (1832). [D]

Weller, William, 150 North St, Brighton, Sussex, cm, u and furniture broker (1837–39). Samuel Weller in the same trade was also at 150 North St in August 1839. [D]

Weller & Jones, 8 Charles St, Middlx Hospital, London, upholstery warehouse (1821–23). [D]

Welleson, George, Water Lane, Maidstone, Kent, cm (1838). [D]

Wellings, Richard, 2 Lichfield St, Birmingham, cm (1800). [D]

Wellman, John, address unknown, cm (1803). Subscribed to Sheraton's *Cabinet Dictionary*, 1803.

Wells, Alexander, Liverpool, carver and gilder (1839). Free 23 July 1839 on servitude to William James. Took as app. in 1839 Edward Berry. [Freemen reg.; app. bk]

Wells, Augustus F., 30 Grease St, Rathbone Pl., London, cm, u and furniture inlayer (1839). [D]

Wells, Edward, London, upholder (1725). Son of John Wells, freeman and member of the Upholders' Co. Brother to James Wells. Free of the Upholders' Co. by patrimony, 4 August 1725. [GL, Upholders' Co. records]

Wells, George, 3 Castle St, Long Acre, London, u (1790–93). [D]

Wells, George, Queen St, Hull, Yorks., fancy chairmaker, cane worker and wood turner (1823–35). The numbers in Queen St were 4 in 1823, 34 in 1826, 40 in 1831–34 and 62 in 1835. [D]

Wells, George, High St, Bedford, cm and u (1839). [D]

Wells, Gervase, 38 Piccadilly, London, carver and gilder (1769–91). Bankruptcy announced *Gents Mag.*, November 1775 but continued to trade. The business was of substantial proportions and attracted influential patrons. Insurance cover was £1,500 in 1784 and £2,100 in 1787 but this appears to have been mainly for property, much of which was not utilised in the business. On 14 April 1769 supplied nine picture frames to Alscot Park, Warks. at a cost of £10 19s 6d. Two large frames were supplied to Burton Constable, Yorks. in 1771 for which an account for £16 18s was submitted. Gervase Wells is also recorded as a Venetian blind manufacturer. [Westminster poll bk; GL, Sun MS vol. 324, p. 613; vol. 342, ref. 527913; vol. 373, ref. 580074; V&A archives; Humberside RO, Burton Constable vouchers]

Wells, Henry, Chichester, Sussex, chairmaker (1782). In 1782 took out insurance cover in association with John Gregory, wheelwright, on some tenements valued at £100. [GL, Sun MS vol. 303, p. 288]

Wells, Henry, 51 Limekiln Lane with a shop at Peter Lane, Liverpool, cm (1829). [D]

Wells, J., London, portable desk manufacturer and pocket book maker (1805–25). From 1815 the business traded as Wells & Lambe. At 34 Cockspur St, 1802–04, 44 New Bond St in 1815 and 29 Cockspur St, 1817–25. An Anglo-Indian engraved ivory writing box, the exterior decorated with flowers and a pastoral scene in floral borders is known with the trade label of this business. It names Wells & Lambe at 29 Cockspur St and indicates that they were makers to the Duke of Cumberland. [D; Sotheby's, 11 June 1976, lot 71]

Wells, James, Paternoster Row, London, upholder (1696–1727). Freeman and member of the Upholders' Co. His house in Paternoster Row was insured for £400 in October 1703 and it was stated that it had been in his possession for seven years. Father of James Wells jnr and Edward Wells both free of the Upholders' Co. in 1725. [GL, Upholders' Co. records; Hand in Hand MS vol. 2, p. 615; Heal]

Wells, James jnr, London, upholder (1725–d. 1788). Son of James Wells and brother to Edward Wells. Free of the Upholders' Co. by patrimony, 4 August 1725. [GL, Upholders' Co. records]

Wells, James, 19 Carlisle Pl., Lambeth, London, carver and gilder (1826). [D]

Wells, James, 9 Crown St, Soho, London, cm and u (1839). [D]

Wells, Jeremiah, Long Acre, London, chairmaker (1749). [Westminster poll bk]

Wells, John, 'The King's Head', end of Fetter Lane, Fleet St, London, u (1685–89). In 1686 offered 'Bed furniture' for sale at the Exeter Change in the Strand. [Heal; Harris, *Old English Furniture*, p. 29]

Wells, John, 7 Freeman's Row, with a shop at 69 Paradise St, Liverpool, u (1823–24). In 1824 described as a feather bed and blanket dealer. [D]

Wells, John, Barnby gate, Newark, Notts., u (1828). [D]

Wells, John, Market Pl., Norwich, cm and u (1839). [D]

Wells, John, 210 Regent St, London, cm and u (1839). [D]

Wells, Joseph, Plot St, Nottingham, joiner and cm (1832). [D]

Wells, Joseph, Stodman St, Newark, Notts., u (1835). [D]

Wells, Richard, Fareham, Hants., cm (1777–d. 1799). In 1777 insured his house for £200. Died intestate in 1799. [D; GL, Sun MS vol. 254, p. 398; Hants. RO, probate records]

Wells, Richard, Fareham, Hants., cm and u (1811–30).

Declared bankrupt March 1811, but trading in East St in 1830. [D; *Sussex Weekly Advertiser*, 4 March 1811]

Wells, Robert, 2 Watson Ct, Canning St, Hull, Yorks., chairmaker and cane worker (1838–39). [D]

Wells, Stephen, 8 Collingwood St, Blackfriars, London, cm (1809). In 1809 took app. named Tennant. [Westminster Ref. Lib., MS F4310]

Wells, Thomas, 66 Whitecross St, Chiswick, London, cm (1805). [D]

Wells, Thomas, St John St Rd, London, cm and broker (1809–24). At 5 St John's St, Smithfield in 1809 but 1823–24 at 11 George Pl., St John St Rd. In November 1823 insured a dwelling house and warehouse for £700 but in January 1824 insurance cover was £1,600. This included £1,000 for stock and utensils. At this date he was also using a stable with loft over at 26 King St, Clerkenwell. [D; GL, Sun MS vol. 495, ref. 101584; vol. 494, ref. 1012522]

Wells, Thomas, Queen's Pl., Greenwich, London, cm (1826). [D]

Wells, W. & Penn, J., 31 Richmond Row, Liverpool, u (1837–38). In 1838 their partnership was dissolved. [D; *Chester Courant*, 9 January 1838]

Wells, William, Winchester, Hants., u (1729). Undertook upholstery work at the Duke of Montrose's house at Shawford, Hants. [Scottish RO, GD 220/6/1376/13]

Wells, William, Deansgate, Manchester, cm (d. by 1766). Dead by April 1766 when his stock in trade was disposed of at his shop at 'The Rose & Crown', Deansgate. On offer were 'Dining Tables, Falling Tables, Chests of Drawers of different Sizes, Mahogany, Walnut and Oak Chairs of different Patterns, a Clock in a Mahogany Case, Corner Cupboards, &c.'. [*Manchester Mercury*, 1 April 1766]

Wells, William, Newark, Notts., cm, u and auctioneer (1805–32). At Market Pl., 1805–08, Barnby gate in 1819 and Bargate in 1832. [D]

Wells, William, 4 Ridinghouse Lane, Gt Portland St, London, cm and u (1839). [D]

Wells, William, 12 Hackney Rd Cresc., London, cm and u (1839). [D]

Wells, Wilson, Millstone St, Horncastle, Lincs., joiner and cm (1835). [D]

Wellsman, Henry, Norwich, carver (1830–36). At Surrey St in 1830 and 101 Pottergate St in 1836. [D]

Wellsman, John, Sidbury, Devon, cm (1758). In 1758 took app. named Collins. [S of G, app. index] See Nicholas Welsman.

Wellsman, John, 33 Wardour St, Soho, London, cm and chairmaker (1813–23). One directory of 1820 lists 53 Wardour St but this is probably an error. In February 1813 had also apartments in Berwick St, Soho and additional workshops at Portland Mews. Stock and utensils there and at Wardour St were valued at £950. In March 1821 when stock and utensils were insured for £1,200 workshops were maintained at 3 Hollen St, Soho and these were also mentioned in a policy of January 1822. In October 1823 although total cover was £3,600 only £500 of this was for utensils and stock. [D; GL, Sun MS vol. 457, refs 879734–35; vol. 483, ref. 972642; vol. 483, ref. 972927; vol. 483, refs 974382, 974385; vol. 488, ref. 978149; vol. 493, ref. 987496; vol. 498, ref. 1008797]

Wellsman, Nicholas, 32 Newman St, Oxford St, London, cm and chair manufacturer (1820–27). In December 1820 took out insurance cover of £500 of which £450 was for utensils and stock. In January 1822 the figures were £700 and £650 respectively. [GL, Sun MS vol. 483, ref. 974359; vol. 493, ref. 987821]

Wellstead, John, 102 Mount St, Davies St, London, cm and u (1839). [D]

Wellsted, H., 63 Edgware Rd and Molyneux St, London, upholder and decorator (1812). His trade card states that the business was established in 1812. [V&A archives]

Wellsted, James, Molyneux St, Bryanston Sq., London, cm and u (1820–39). The number in Molyneux St is given as either 39 or 12 and 13. From 1835 additional addresses at Sholdam St and Wellsted Yd, Seymour Pl. were used. In 1839 the address was given as 30 Sholdam St. [D]

Welsby, Jonathan, Eccleston St, Prescot, Lancs., joiner and cm (1828–34). [D]

Welsford, Joseph & Co., 139 Oxford St, London, u (1839). [D]

Welsh, George, High St, Whitchurch, Salop, cm and chairmaker (1828–32). At Bargates in 1828, High St, 1828–32 and Green End, 1835. Insolvent by November 1832. [D; *Chester Courant*, 19 March 1833]

Welsh, Hugh, Queen St, Whitehaven, Cumb., joiner/cm (1811). [D]

Welsh, Jacob, 13 Compton St, Soho, London, japanner (1789–91). In 1789 japanned thirty splat back chairs with rush seats and six long stools for Lord Howard de Walden of Audley End, Essex, at a cost of £4 13s. These were for Lord Howard's London house in New Burlington St. These chairs were japanned black and in 1791 were renovated by Jacob Welsh and two further chairs finished in white and colours at a total cost of 18s. [D; Essex RO, D/DBy/A47/5, D/DBy/A49/3]

Welsh, Jacob, Bedminster Parade, Bristol, cm (1813–15). The number in Bedminster Parade was 13 in 1814–15. [D]

Welsh, John, Chester, joiner and cm (c. 1745–84). Son of John Welsh, yeoman. App. to Thomas Wrench, joiner, 19 March 1735. In 1753 took as app. Richard Barber. Living in Barn Lane in October 1771 and King's St in April 1784. [App. bks; poll bks]

Welsh, Paul, 4 Denzell St, Clare Mkt, London, cm, upholder and undertaker (1817–29). [D]

Welsman, George, Exeter, Devon, cm (1834–40). At Catherine St, 1834–38 and 247 High St, 1838–40. [D]

Welsman, Nicholas, Sidbury, Devon, cm (1796). See John Wellsman trading in this village. [*Exeter Flying Post*, 11 August 1796]

Welsman, Robert, Exeter, Devon, chairmaker (1816). [Poll bk]

Wenborn, Josiah, 131 St John St, West Smithfield, London, cm, u and undertaker (1839). [D]

Wendover, G., Havant St, Portsea, Portsmouth, Hants., cm and u (1839). [D]

Wenman, Joseph, 53 Theobalds Rd, London, cm (1805). [D]

Wenman, Joseph, 14 Webber Row, Blackfriars Rd, London, cm (1809). [D]

Wenman, Thomas, London, upholder (1716). Son of Thomas Wenman of Gt Yarmouth, Norfolk, Gent. App. to Thomas Wilcox, 1 October 1707 and free of the Upholders' Co. by servitude, 11 April 1716. [GL, Upholders' Co. records]

Wensley, Richard, Bristol, u and butcher (1822–40). At 136 Temple St in 1822, West St in 1825 and 1 Earl St, 1837–40. [D]

Wenley, W., Moulsham, Chelmsford, Essex, cm (1826). Freeman of Maldon, Essex. [Maldon poll bk]

Wentworth, Daniel, Cambridge, cm and u (1792–d. 1822). Succeeded by: **Wentworth, Joseph**, cm, u, auctioneer, appraiser and undertaker (1817–1849). Daniel Wentworth is recorded at the corner of St John St, 1792 and in Bridge St, 1805–08. His label is recorded: 'D. Wentworth, Cabinet Maker, St. John's Street, Cambridge', printed on card and tacked to the back of a mahogany bow-fronted chest of drawers. Subscribed to Sheraton's *Drawing Book*, 1793. The *Cambridge Chronicle and Journal*, 10 October 1817 carried the announcement 'D. Wentworth, Upholsterer, corner of St. John's Street' thanks his customers 'for the liberal support he has been honoured with for upward of 30 years' and that he was resigning the business to his son Joseph. The Wentworth family monument in Holy Sepulchre Church records Daniel's death in 1822. Joseph Wentworth 'Upholsterer, Auctioneer, Appraiser' followed his father's announcement in the paper 'that he has succeeded his father in the Businesses of Upholsterer, Undertaker . . . and every article in the Cabinet line made to order'. He became a freeman of the Corporation on 7 October 1818, paying a fee of ten guineas. He is listed in Pigot's *Directories*, 1823–24, 1830 and 1839. From 1832–49 regular payments are recorded in the accounts of Trinity College, that of 1840 listing for the Combination Room 'New Chairs, New Tables etc.', £269 2s 6d. The chairs communion rails and communion table in Holy Sepulchre Church were 'furnished' by Wentworth *c.* 1845. He seems to have covered a wide area in his work as an auctioneer, an example being the sale advertised on 14 October 1831 of the cabinet and upholstery stock of William Edwards in Stamford. Joseph Wentworth also acted as an estate agent and paper-hanger. Wentworth is recorded as taking one app., John Adams from 13 April 1825 for a fee of £15. [D; *Furn. Hist.*, 1978; Cambs. RO, Corp. records; freemen rolls; app. bk; archives of Trinity College; City of Cambridge, Royal Commission on Historical Monuments, 1959]   R. W.

Wentworth, John, Lechlade, Glos., u (1839). [D]

Wentworth, Joseph, Cambridge, see Daniel Wentworth.

Wercombe, William, Exeter, Devon, carver and gilder (1836–39). At Russell St in July 1836 when his daughter Mary Ann was bapt. at St Sidwell's Church, and at Adelaide Pl. in January 1830 when his son Charles Richard was bapt. at the same church. [PR (bapt.)]

Were, James, 13 Chapel St, East Stonehouse, Plymouth, Devon, cm (1838). [D]

Wescombe, —, Exeter, Devon, picture frame maker (1831). In April 1831 summoned for failing to maintain his wife from funds received from the Corporation as poor relief. [*The Alfred*, 12 April, 1831]

Wescome, William, Cullompton, Devon, cm (1823–25). In 1823 trading in Cullompton as a cm but by October 1825 insolvent and described as 'late of Cullompton'. In October 1825 he was described additionally as a grocer, linen draper and shopkeeper. [D; *The Alfred*, 11 October 1825]

West, Mr, Duke St, near Lincoln's Inn Fields, London, frame maker (1748). [*General Advertiser*, 30 March, 1748]

West, Andrew, 24 Banna St, St Luke's, London, cm, u and undertaker (1839). [D]

West, Bryan, Newcastle, u (1747). [Newcastle freemen reg.]

West, C., Foulsham, Norfolk, cm (1839). [D]

West, Charles & Son, 35 Bucklersbury, London, upholstery warehouse (1790–1816). [D]

West, Coleman, Elsing, Norfolk, cm, u and paperhanger (1836). [D]

West, Daniel, 8 York St, Pentonville, London, carpenter and cm (1805). [D]

West, F., 19 South Row, New Rd, St Pancras, London, upholder (1835). [D]

West, George, Newcastle, u (1716–24). App. to John Robson, u, tinplate worker and stationer and free by servitude, 5 March 1716. In 1724 took app. named Pierson. [Freemen reg.; S of G, app. index]

West, George, The Side, Newcastle, u (1741–d. 1767). Took as app. Joseph Kidd in 1759 and he was free, 7 October 1765. Other apps were John Ridpeth, free 13 June 1766, and John Graham and William Rutledge, free 15 October 1774. The two latter apps must have completed their training under a new master, for the death of George West was announced in April 1767. The business was continued by Thomas Brown

who was George West's son-in-law and had been engaged in the management of the business prior to 1767. [Poll bk; freemen reg.; S of G, app. index; *Newcastle Courant*, 18 April 1767]

West, George, address unknown, cm (1754). Subscribed to Chippendale's *Director*, 1754. Possibly the u who was trading in Newcastle, 1741–67.

West, George, Newcastle, cm (1811–27). At the Head of the Side in 1811 and Groat Mkt, 1824–27. [D]

West, George, Market Pl., Stoney Stratford, Bucks., cm (1839). [D]

West, Henry, King St, Gt Yarmouth, Norfolk, carver and gilder (1836). [D]

West, J. H., Wisbech, Cambs., carver and gilder (1824). [D]

West, James, Guinea St, Exeter, Devon, cm (1823). Son John bapt. at St Mary Major, 10 August 1823. [PR (bapt.)]

West, John, address unknown, frame maker (1732). Supplied ten pear tree frames, edges carved and gilt at a cost of £7 10s on 20 May 1732 to Edward Monnington of Sarnesfield Court, near Kington, Hererfs. The account was receipted on 4 December 1732. [Herefs. RO, P94/28]

West, John, Oxford, cm (1739). Married Elizabeth Hart at the church of St Peter in the East on 24 April 1739. At this date he was aged 26. [Bodleian index of Oxf. marriage bonds]

West, John, 'The Cabinet', King St, Covent Gdn, London, cm and u (1743–58). May have used the same property as Thomas Arne, father of the composer, in King St. Arne was murdered on 2 March 1730. If this is the case however West must have changed the trade sign, for that of Arne was 'The Two Crowns & Cushion'. David Garrick lodged with John West in King St, 1743–48, and William Ince, later to partner John Mayhew, was West's app. On the death of John West in 1758 the business was taken over by the partnership of James Whittle and Samuel Norman. [Heal; GL, Sun MS vol. 81, ref. 110689]

A number of West's patrons have been identified and indicate his importance as a maker to the nobility and gentry of the period. He was working at Alscot Park, Warks. and supplying furniture to his patron James West for the house from 1745 until the year of his death in 1758. A set of mahogany chairs, carved and the seats 'Cover'd with black leather and Nailed with brass Nails' supplied in 1745 at £2 2s each may be the set presently in the Hall. The total commission came to £39 13s inclusive of other items. An account for £19 18s was submitted in June 1748, a smaller account for £4 11s 9d which included a neat mahogany breakfast table with fly feet in 1753 and a more substantial commission amounting to £62 4s 9d in March 1758. The major items of furniture in this latter order were a mahogany bedstead at £6 10s and a large mahogany sofa charged at the same amount. Much of the remainder was for fabrics. [West papers, Alscot Park; *C. Life*, 22 May 1958]

The Monson archives at the Lincoln RO indicate patronage on a considerable scale extending from 1745–53. A minor commission amounting to £3 6s in November 1745 was followed in March 1747 by the receipt of two 'neat commode dressing tables of rosewood' costing £15 15s. In May of the same year ten carved mahogany elbow chairs costing £23 10s were part of a much larger commission, mainly fabrics, which totalled £103 9s 6d. A minor commission for a dressing table in August 1747 and a mahogany table in January 1748 were followed by much more significant orders. In December 1752 an account for £68 18s 4d included a 'Chimney in the Chinese taste' £11 15s, 'rich carv'd table frames in paint' £30 and a 'Pier glass neat carv'd Chinese frame in white & gold' £16 10s. An account dated 24 December 1752 totalling £67 13s 6d was mainly for fabrics as were also commissions placed in the next year amounting to £28 11s 4d. The largest sum expended was however in November 1752 when an account for £263 13s 7½d was submitted to Holland Goddard. A set of twelve fan back chairs, six elbow chairs and two sofas were included as well as other chairs, tables, fabrics and carpets. [Lincoln RO, Monson 11/22/24, 11/22/25, 11/50, 12]

Other patrons are known. The Grimston family used John West 1753–54. The wallpapers specified by West came from Thomas Bromwich who traded as a 'Leather Gilder & Paper Merchant at the Golden Lion, on Ludgate Hill'. Apart from these West provided a Turkey carpet at £34, 'A neat Carv'd Ornament in paint to go over the Pier Glass' £1 5s and '15 Yards of Cotton to match the Couch'. In November 1754 he received from Mr Grimston a complaint about a table that he had produced and West agreed to its return. 'I would rather be two or three pounds a looser, than give the least cause of uneasiness to a Gentleman who has confer'd such great & infinite obligations'. At Woburn Abbey, Beds., furniture was supplied between May 1755 and the end of 1758 and the total cost of the commissions was £1,947 14s 9d. The upholstery work and furniture was for the new rooms created by Henry Flitcroft for John, 4th Duke of Bedford. Between April and July 1755 Greek damask hangings were provided for the Drawing Room and ten walnut elbow chairs and two sofas upholstered in green. Three pairs of window curtains in green damask were supplied also. Another set of chairs in walnut consisted of ten single and two elbow chairs with yellow laced seats. In August of the same year a number of gilt pier glasses, a mahogany bedstead and hangings and a large mahogany commode decorated with ormolu were provided. The final bill was not settled until January 1759 and the receipt was given by William Dutton, 'Administrator to the late John West'. A payment of £80 was also made to West in 1756 by the executors of the 4th Duke of Beaufort. [Ingram, *Leaves from a Family Tree*, p. 48; Bedford Office, London; Badminton Muniment Room I/Shelf 2, No. 22]   B.A.

West, John, London, upholder (1765). Son of Samuel West of the parish of St George, Hanover Sq., oilman. App. to Thomas Dobyns, 5 October 1758 and free of the Upholders' Co. by servitude, 5 December 1765. [GL, Upholders' Co. records]

West, John, Lancaster, joiner and cm (1770–80). App. to W. Blackburn 1770 and free, 1779–80. [Freemen rolls]

West, John, Sidmouth, Devon, cm (1778–90). In 1778 took out insurance cover of £100 of which £60 was for utensils and stock. By July 1790 insurance cover had risen to £300. [GL, Sun MS vol. 264, p. 60; vol. 370, July 1790]

West, John, Horsemonger Lane, near the King's Bench, Newington, London, upholder (1775–82). Son of John West of Marylebone, butcher. App. to James Bolton, 1 February 1775 and free of the Upholders' Co. by servitude, 6 February 1782. [GL, Upholders' Co. records]

West, John, Tufton St, Westminster, London, joiner and cm (1789–90). In 1789 submitted an estimate for £2,000 in connection with works for Carlton House. Carved the woodwork for the Chinese Drawing Room, Carlton House. Also engaged in work at Althorp, Northants., where he supplied timber etc. costing £227 0s 2½d. A receipt for £50 was given on 11 November 1790 and a further one for £227 on 28 November. [H. Clifford Smith, *Buckingham Palace*, p. 104; V&A archives]

West, John, 9 King's Bench Walk, Temple, London, upholder (1773–91). Son of John West of Goodman's Fields, Whitechapel, brewer. App. to Joseph Merryman, 3 March 1773 and then to Robert Bevan, a farrier, 6 August 1777. Free of the Upholders' Co. by servitude, 26 September 1791. [GL, Upholders' Co. records]

West, John, 23 Charles St, Westminster, London, upholder (1806). On 1 September 1806 took out insurance cover of three houses in Gt College St, Westminster for £900. [GL, Sun MS vol. 437, ref. 792675]

West, John, St John's St, Newport Pagnall, Bucks., cm (1823–39). [D]

West, Joseph, Newcastle, u (1740–41). Free 1740. [Freemen reg. poll bk]

West, Joseph, High St, March, Cambs., carver and gilder (1830). [D]

West, Joseph, 48 Groat Mkt, with a house at 22 Middle St, Newcastle, cm and furniture broker (1833–34). [D]

West, Joseph Henry, High St, King's Lynn, Norfolk, carver and gilder (1822). [D]

West, Martin, Fore St, Bodmin, Cornwall, u and cm (1823). [D]

West, Robert, High St, Shaftesbury, Dorset, cm and builder (1823). [D]

West, Sephrend (or Sophronia), parish of St Mary, Oxford, u (1724). In September 1724 Sophronia took out insurance cover of £500 on goods and merchandise in her dwelling house. In the insurance records she is described as a widow. In the same year Sephrend West took app. named Ward. [GL, Sun MS vol. 17, ref. 32540; S of G, app. index]

West, Stephen, 'The Leopard', corner of Blackamoor St, Drury Lane, London, upholder (1712–21). On 30 November 1721 was paid £14 3s for blankets and quilts supplied to Lady Bowes. [GL, Sun MS vol. 2, p. 90; Heal; Durham RO, Strathmore MS, D/St/352/2]

West, Thomas, King's Lynn, Norfolk, cm (1774–75). His app. James Speechly was declared free, 1774–75. [Freemen rolls]

West, Thomas, Stanningley, near Leeds, Yorks., cm and joiner (1830). [D]

West, William, Oxford, u (1712). In 1712 took app. named Munday. [S of G, app. index]

West, William, St Phillip's, Bristol, cm (1793). [D]

West, William snr, High St, Stoney Stratford, Bucks., cm and u (1830). [D]

Westacott, Samuel, Newport, Barnstaple, Devon, cm (1830). [D]

Westaway, Messrs, 41 Union St, East Stonehouse, Plymouth, Devon, cm and u (1838). [D]

Westbrook, William, at Mr Smith's, Fleet St, London, upholder (1745). [D]

Westbury, Daniel, 16 Pinnington St, Liverpool, cm (1811). The Pinnington St address was described as a shop. [D]

Westbury, Daniel, Princess Row, Coleshill St, Birmingham, cabinet case maker (1818). [D]

Westby, George August, 9 George St, Portman Sq., London, carver and gilder (1835–39). [D]

Westell, Thomas, parish of St James, Bristol, cm (1754–57). Bankruptcy declared, *Gents Mag.*, May 1757. [Poll bk]

Wester, Thomas, address unknown, cm (1723). Paid £9 in 1723 by Sir Richard Hoare, 1st Bart. [Hoare's Bank MS]

Westerdale (or Westerdell), George, High St, Hull, Yorks., cm (1754–92). [D; poll bks]

Westerman, Joseph, Market Green, Cottingham, near Hull, Yorks., cm (1811–40). App. to Thomas Ross of Cottingham, June 1811. Trading at Market Green by 1831. [D; Hull app. bk]

Westerman, Samuel, Morley, near Leeds, Yorks., cm (1822). [D]

Westgarth, Thomas, Durham, cm (1827–34). At King's Arms Yd, Market Pl. in 1827 and Clay Path Gates, 1828–34. [D]

Westlake, William, High Wycombe, Bucks., cm (1816). Daughter bapt. 1816. [PR (bapt.)]

Westlake, William, Cornwall St, Plymouth, Devon, chairmaker (1836–38). [D]

Westley, John, Northampton, u (1784–98). At Horsemarket in 1784 and Abingdon St in 1790. [D; poll bks]

Westmoreland, Edward, Boar Lane, Leeds, Yorks., joiner and cm (1790). [D]

Westmorland, William, Boar Lane, Leeds, Yorks., joiner and cm (1786). In August 1786 advertised for 'three or four journeymen cabinet-makers, one clock case maker and one chair-maker'. Edward Westmoreland was probably his successor. [*Leeds Mercury*, 29 August 1786]

Weston, Field, Nottingham, joiner and cm (1828). Was joint master of William Smith who was app. 1828. [App. bk]

Weston, George, Nottingham, joiner and cm (1828). Was joint master of William Smith who was app. 1828. [App. bk]

Weston, J., 42 Curzon St, Mayfair, London, u and cm (1808–19). In 1811 supplied for the Prince of Wales at Windsor a rosewood 'Ora' table, four black and gold begère chairs with caned backs and seats and eight elbow chairs to match. The table was charged at £27 6s and the seating furniture at £194. [D; Windsor Royal Archives, RA 25335]

Weston, James, Watergate St, Ellesmere, Salop, cm (1798–1822). A William Weston, cm, was trading in Watergate St in 1840. [D]

Weston, John, Uttoxeter, Staffs., cm (1798). [D]

Weston, John, 6 Penn St, Bristol, u (1819). [D]

Weston, John R., Southampton, Hants., cm and u (1823–39). At 8 Bridge St in 1823, 6 St George's Terr. in 1830, Bernard St in 1834 and 8 Middle St in 1839. One directory of 1839 giving the Bernard St address lists the business as R. J. R. & A. H. Weston. [D]

Weston, John, 4 Nevills Ct, Fetter Lane, London, furniture japanner (1826). [D]

Weston, Jonathan, 3 Red Lion Ct, London Wall, London, cm (1782). In 1782 insured his house for £100. [GL, Sun MS vol. 301, p. 186]

Weston, Jonathan, 101 Golden Lane, London, chairmaker (1810). In December 1810 took out insurance cover of £600 of which £140 was for stock and utensils. [GL, Sun MS vol. 449, ref. 852186]

Weston, Joseph, King St, Belper, Derbs., cm (1835). [D]

Weston, Stephen, Weekday Cross, Nottingham, joiner and cm (1784–d. 1810). In 1791 signed the *Nottingham Cabinet and Chair Makers' Book of Prices* on the behalf of the masters. Advertised for craftsmen in July 1784. Patronised by the Massingberd family and on 19 December 1794 £5 17s was paid to Weston for tables, two stands and a writing box. [D; *Nottingham Journal*, 31 July 1784; Lincoln RO, MM9/10; Notts. RO, probate records]

Weston, Thomas, Bristol, upholder (1781–1823). Living in the parish of St James in 1791. At Philadelphia St, 1794–1801 and 1 Old King St, 1805–23. [D; poll bks]

Weston, William, 22 Davies St, Berkeley Sq., London, carver (1821). In May 1821 took out insurance cover of £1,000. Half of this was for utensils and stock in a workshop behind 20 Chapel St, Grosvenor Sq. where he had formerly lived. He also had goods to the value of £30 in the dwelling house of Williment at 25 Green St, Grosvenor Sq. [GL, Sun MS vol. 488, ref. 980136]

Weston, William, Apple Mkt, Northwich, Cheshire, cm (1822). [D]

Weston, William, Bishops Waltham, Hants., cm, u and auctioneer. (1823–30). In 1830 in the High St. [D]

Weston, William, 6 Bridge St, Southampton, Hants., cm and u (1830). [D]

Weston, William, Watergate St, Ellesmere, Salop, cm (1840). James Weston was trading in this street as a cm, 1798–1822. [D]

Weston & Lodsley, Nottingham (1791). Signed the *Nottingham*

Cabinet and Chair Makers' Book of Prices, 1791, on behalf of the masters.

Westwick, William, West St, Middlesborough, Yorks., joiner and cm (1840). [D]

Westwood, Charles, London, upholder (1749–d. by 1785). Son of Thomas Westwood of Sawbridgeworth, Herts. and father of Thomas Westwood jnr. App. to John Shepherd, 1 February 1738 and free of the Upholders' Co. by servitude, 3 August 1749. Took as apps Edward Smith, 1757–65, and William Coxter, 1760–67. [GL, Upholders' Co. records]

Westwood, James & John, Jamaica Row, Birmingham, cabinet case makers (portable desks, dressing cases) (1822–39). At 9 Jamaica Row in 1822 and at 22 in 1828–30. The business was continued by John alone and in 1835 he was at 21 Jamaica Row and still in this street in 1839. [D]

Westwood, John, Harbone, Birmingham, cm (1816). [D]

Westwood, John, Jamaica Row, Birmingham, see James & John Westwood.

Westwood, Johnson, Watling St, London, upholder (1777–1802). Son of Samuel Westwood to whom he was app., 14 April 1767. Free of the Upholders' Co. by servitude, 1 October 1777. At Watling St, 1777–87 but 1794–1802 living in Hertfordshire. [GL, Upholders' Co. records]

Westwood, Marmaduke, London, u and cm (1793–1811). At 3 White Hart Ct, Lombard St, 1800–02. From 1803 at 32 Crooked Lane. In 1793 subscribed to Sheraton's *Drawing Book* and in 1803 was included in the list of master cabinet makers in his *Cabinet Dictionary*. [D]

Westwood, Obadiah, Camp Hill, Birmingham, manufacturer of coffin furniture, picture frames etc. (1803). [D]

Westwood, Samuel snr and jnr, London, upholder (1755–77). Samuel Westwood snr was an ironmonger formerly of Birmingham but by 1748 living in Watling St, London. He was also a member of the Upholders' Co. by redemption from 4 August 1748. He took his son Samuel jnr as app. from 1748–55 and he was declared free of the Upholders' Co. by servitude, 23 September 1755. Either Samuel Westwood snr or jnr took as app. Johnson Westwood, 1767–77. [GL, Upholders' Co. records]

Westwood, Thomas, 7 Bedford Ct, Covent Gdn, London, upholder (1785). Son of Charles Westwood of Blackfriars. Free of the Upholders' Co. by patrimony, 7 December 1785. [GL, Upholders' Co. records]

Westwood, Thomas, Bedminster, Bristol, nail and chairmaker (1818). [D]

Westwood & Smith, 8 Broadway, Blackfriars, London, u (1773). [D]

Wetdrill, Thomas, London, cm (1793). Subscribed to Sheraton's *Drawing Book*, 1793.

Wetherall, John, 26 Haymarket, London, u and cm (1777–84). In 1777 took out insurance cover for £1,000 of which £500 was for utensils and stock and £200 for workshops. [D; GL, Sun MS vol. 254, p. 390]

We(a)therall, John, 52 Dean St, Soho, London, upholder (1804–05). In July 1804 took out insurance cover of £900 on household goods in a warehouse behind 52 Dean St. In September 1805 cover of £500 was taken on household goods at 2 Chapel Row, Little Chelsea. [GL, Sun MS vol. 431, ref. 762880; vol. 434, ref. 779481]

Wetherell, John, Liverpool, cm (1823). Died 6 November 1823 aged 45. [*Liverpool Mercury*, 7 November 1823]

Wetherell & Wilson, 64 Leadenhall St, London, carvers and gilders (1789–93). Wetherell's forename was John. [D]

Wetherley, Thomas, Dover, Kent, turner and chairmaker (1792–93). [D]

Wetherstone, Alexander, 'The Painted Floor Cloth & Brush', Portugal St, Lincoln's Inn Fields, London, carpenter, joiner and turner (1760–65). Although not strictly a furniture maker he did sell 'Mahogany Cisterns with Brass Hoops, Dish & other Stands, Voiders, hand boards, Tea Boards, Tea Trays, Tea Chests, Back Gammon Tables & Draught Boards' some at least of which he probably manufactured. [Heal]

Wetton, Richard, 32 Upper Seymour St, London, u (1839). [D]

Weyman & Smith, High St, Bewdley, Worcs., cm and u (1835). [D]

Weymouth, William Paul, Penzance, Cornwall, cm (1809). [Cornwall RO, DDX 573/70]

Weymouth, William, Bristol, chairmaker (1823–31). At Portwall Lane, 1823–25, Stoney Hill Cottage in 1826, Portwall Lane, 1827–29 and 73 St Thomas St, 1830–31. [D]

Whaite, Henry, Bridge St, Manchester, carver and gilder, looking-glass and picture frame maker (1828–40). At 75 Bridge St in 1828 but from 1832 the number was 4. [D]

Whaite, James jnr, Diss, Norfolk, cm (1784). There was also a James Whaite snr, carpenter, trading in Diss in 1784 who was probably his father. [D]

Whale, William, 11 Mint St, Southwark, London, bedstead maker (1805–09). [D]

Whaley, Henry, Aswell Lane, Louth, Lincs., cm and joiner (1826–40). [D]

Whaley, John, address unknown, u (1710–25). Payments to this maker are frequent in the accounts of Lady Mary Saunderson. Total payments 1710–25 amount to £173 16s 0½d. In only a few instances are the items concerned described, but mending a bed, making a quilt, altering window curtains, supplying a bed and bedding and supplying upholstery materials are specified as is also many hours of labour. Payments totalling £107 also appear in the account books of the Earl of Rockingham, 1715–22, but again details are lacking. [Lincoln RO, Monson 10 A/1, 10/1/A/16, 12]

Whaley, Matthew, Dukinfield, Staylybridge, Lancs., cm (1825). [D]

Whaley, Whiston, Fenchurch St, London, cm (1765). A member of the Armourers & Brazier's Co. but by trade a cm. In 1765 took out a licence to employ a non-freeman for six weeks. [GL, City Licence bks, vol. 4]

Whaller, Thomas, address unknown, cm (1803). Subscribed to Sheraton's *Cabinet Dictionary*, 1803.

Whalley, Charles, London, upholder (1726–33). Son of George Whalley of Norton, Leics., Gent. App. to Bladwell Peyton, 5 October 1726 and free of the Upholders' Co. by servitude, 5 December 1733. [GL, Upholders' Co. records]

Whalley, John, Liverpool, cm (1767). Free 2 December 1767. [Freemen reg.]

Whalley, John, Poulton St, Kirkham, Lancs., joiner and cm (1815–34). On 29 May 1815 took George Woods, son of James Woods of Kirkham, hatter, as app. [D; Preston RO, DDPr. 1/58]

Whalley, Robert, 15 Marble St, Manchester, cm (1804). [D]

Whalley, Thomas, Rose St, Long Acre, London, cm (1774). [Heal]

Wharton, —, London, u (1767–68). From November 1767 to October 1768 supplied to Shelburne House, Berkeley Sq., London materials such as 'Padua serge, green bays' etc. to a value of £15 19s. [Bowood MS]

Wharton, Charles, 'The Crown & Two Septres', Queen St, Southwark, London, picture frame maker (c. 1750). Offered to supply picture frames 'either in Gold, Lacquered or Black'. Also stocked a 'great Choice of Maps & Prints Ready Framed and a variety of Paintings on Glass'. [Heal]

Wharton, George, Bargate, Richmond, Yorks., joiner and cm (1827). [D]

Wharton, George jnr, Northallerton, Yorks., cm (1840). [D]

Wharton, James, 7 Dickson St, Liverpool, cm (1818). [D]

Wharton, Jeremiah, Main St, Cockermouth, Cumb., cooper/turner/chairmaker (1829). [D]

Wharton, John, Sand Lane, Cockermouth, Cumb., cooper/turner/chairmaker (1829). [D]

Wharton, Robert, Chapel Lane, Hull, Yorks., chair bottomer (1803). [D]

Wharton, Robert & Gee, Richard, Oxford, upholders (1823). In 1823 took as app. Eldridge Fields. [Oxford RO, Misc. Coventry I/1]

Wharton, Robert, Le Gendre Pl. and 208 Chapel St, Salford, Lancs., joiner, builder and cm (1825). [D]

Wharton, Thomas, St Mary Magdalen, Oxford, cm (1802). [Poll bk]

Whatley & Barker, 26 Philip Lane, London, bed and mattress maker (1827). [D]

Whatson, Samuel, Wright's Yd, Leeds, Yorks., cm (1818). [D]

Whatton, James, North St, South Shields, Co. Durham, cm (1827–28). [D]

Whatton, William, Liverpool, joiner and cm (1837–39). At 83 Fontenoy St with a shop at 255 Scotland Rd in 1837 and 34 Fontenoy St with a shop at 2 Ormond St in 1839. [D]

Whayt, Charles, King's Lynn, Norfolk, u (1670–71). Free by patrimony 1670–71. [Freemen rolls]

Wheatland, William, Retford and Rockley, Notts., chairmaker (1821–30). In 1821–22 trading at Beardsall Row, Retford as a joiner and chairmaker. He was an important Methodist, and when he moved to the new village of Rockley soon after, he was concerned to see that a chapel was opened there. To this end he presented in 1827 a small piece of land on which it could be built. Wheatland traded in Rockley as a joiner, wheelwright and chairmaker but in February 1830 was declared bankrupt. A number of Windsor chairs are known stamped on the seat edge or rear of seat 'WHEATLAND ROCKLEY', a child's chair of this type being in the Bradford Museum. Chairmaking was subsequently to become an important local industry and c. 1840 five of the thirteen cottages in Mill Lane were inhabited by chairmakers, four of these being Methodists. [D; *Furn. Hist.*, 1978; *Antique Collecting*, February 1974; Retford Lib., Rockley Methodist Chapel Centenary Souvenir; *Chester Courant*, 23 February 1830]

Wheatley, Edward, Mile End Green, Stepney, London, turner and chairmaker (1726). In October 1726 took out insurance cover of £100. [GL, Sun MS vol. 22, p. 420]

Wheatley, Joseph, Exeter, Devon, u (1740). In 1740 took an app. named Hardy. [S of G, app. index]

Wheatley, Joseph, Liverpool, cm (1835–39). In 1835 at 13 Vine St and in 1837 at 36 Falkener St where he was also listed as a 'Beer shop'. By 1839 the number in Falkener St had changed to 188. [D]

Wheatley, Thomas, Manchester, cm and furniture broker (1828–40). In 1828 listed at 8 Thomas St as a cm, and 85 Shudehill as a furniture broker. Continued in Shudehill, and the number was 52 in 1834 when his trade was again furniture broker, and 50 from 1836–40 when his trade was once more given as cm. [D]

Wheatley, Thomas, 2 Edge St, Oak St, Manchester, cm and u (1836). [D]

Wheatley, William, Nottingham, cm (1791). In 1791 signed the *Nottingham Cabinet and Chair Makers' Book of Prices* on behalf of the masters.

Wheatley & Ridsdales, 25 Clement Lane, Lombard St, London, wholesale u (1759–78). Their trade sign appears to have been 'The Lamb'. In 1768 the firm is listed as Wheatley, Risdales & Bell. Trade card in Banks Coll., BM. [D]

Wheawell, John, Workington, Cumb., joiner/cm (1828–29). At Pow St in 1828 and Priestgate in 1829. [D]

Wheeldon, Benjamin, Manchester, cm and u (1811–33). At 1 Chatham St, 1811–18 but by 1821–29 at 58 King St and by 1832 at 34 King St. Supplied furniture to Sir John Leicester at Tabley House, Cheshire. On 5 January 1824 a pair of mahogany fire screen stands were provided at £2 15s and on 28 January 1825 a mahogany folding fire screen at £2 10s. Bankruptcy declared September 1827. [D; Chester RO, Tabley papers DLT; *Liverpool Mercury*, 5 October 1827]

Wheeldon, William, 28 Tib Lane, Manchester, cm and u (1834). [D]

Wheele, Richard, 30 Snowfields, London, cm (1789). [D]

Wheeler, B., 4 Peter St, Cow Cross St, London, u (1820). [D]

Wheeler, Benjamin, 5 Taylor's Rd, Islington Rd, London, cm (1805). [D]

Wheeler, C., King St, Melksham, Wilts., chairmaker (1839). [D]

Wheeler, Charles, Belmont Village, Birmingham, cm, u and broker (1828–30). [D]

Wheeler, Constable, London, upholder (1703–11). Insured various properties in the Strand, Rose St, and Maiden Lane, a number of which were tenanted. He may possibly have traded at the sign of 'The Dolphin & Crown' in the Strand. [GL, Hand in Hand MS vol. 5, p. 697; vol. 4, p. 107; vol. 6, ref. 17715; vol. 9, p. 162]

Wheeler, Daniel, Calne, Wilts., Havant, Hants., and Winchester, chairmaker (1777). Born 1744. Son of Thomas Wheeler. Lived at Calne, Wilts. from where his father moved to Havant leaving Daniel and his mother. Daniel followed when he was aged 19. In 1777 he was living in the parish of St John-in-the-Soke, Winchester with a wife Mary, three daughters aged 2 to 5 and a 5 month old son. [S of G, St John-in-the-Soke settlement papers]

Wheeler, Emanuel, Cross St, Ryde, Isle of Wight, Hants., cm and u (1830–39). [D]

Wheeler, Felstead, 73 Old Broad St, London, u (1768–70). [D]

Wheeler, George, Gloucester, cm (1784). Freeman of Bristol. [Bristol poll bk]

Wheeler, James, London, upholder (1705). Free of the Upholders' Co., 1 August 1705. [GL, Upholders' Co. records]

Wheeler, James, parish of St Lawrence, Norwich, u (1743–61). Free 21 September 1743 but not by apprenticeship. Living in the parish of St Lawrence, March 1716. [Freemen rolls; poll bk]

Wheeler, James, 1 Lambs Conduit Passage, Red Lion Sq., London, carver and gilder (1809). [D]

Wheeler, James, Upper Mill St, Birmingham, carver and gilder (1830). [D]

Wheeler, James, Bridge St, Greenwich, London, cm and u (1838–39). [D]

Wheeler, John, Dorchester, joiner and cm (1784). In 1784 insured a house for £100. [GL, Sun MS vol. 324, p. 364]

Wheeler, John, address unknown, cm (1803). Subscribed to Sheraton's *Cabinet Dictionary*, 1803.

Wheeler, John, Wimborne, Dorset, u and cm (1840). [D]

Wheeler, Joseph, Barton St, Tewkesbury, Glos., cm (1816). Child bapt. 1816. [PR (bapt.)]

Wheeler, Joseph, 14 Compton St, Soho, London, carver, gilder and looking-glass merchant (1835–37). [D]

Wheeler, Mark, 8 Newton St, Holborn, London, chair and sofa maker (1839). [D]

Wheeler, Michael, 28 Kemp St, Southwark, London, chair manufacturer (1817). [D]

Wheeler, Richard, London, upholder (1770–1800). Son of John Wheeler of Albrighton, Salop, miller. App. to William Jellicoe, skinner, 2 February 1762 and free of the Upholders' Co. by servitude, 3 October 1770. Trading at 26 Ivy Lane by 1780 when he took out insurance cover of £1,200 of which £800 was for utensils and stock. By 1782 these figures had

risen to £1,600 and £1,200 respectively. At 151 Fleet St, 1785–94 but by the latter year was insolvent and his move to 1 Bolt Ct, Fleet St is probably related to this. At 1 Bolt Ct, 1795–1800. [D; GL, Upholders' Co. records; Sun MS vol. 284, p. 105; vol. 303, p. 305; *Williamson's Liverpool Advertiser*, 5 May 1794, 25 May 1795, 7 March 1796, 21 March 1796]

Wheeler, Richard, Bideford, Devon, cm (1793). [D]

Wheeler, Thomas, Little Bell Alley, London, carver (1761). Member of the Joiners' Co. In 1761 obtained a licence to employ a non-freeman for three months. [GL, City Licence bks, vol. 2]

Wheeler, Thomas, Havant, Hants., chairmaker (1763–87). Originally lived at Calne, Wilts. Moved to Havant and was joined there in 1763 by his son Daniel, then aged 19. In 1775 took out insurance cover of £300 of which £10 was for his workshop. In April 1787 the insurance cover was still £300 and this was in respect of his workshop and five dwellings. [S of G, St John-in-the-Soke, Winchester settlement papers; GL, Sun MS vol. 239, p. 188; vol. 344, p. 372]

Wheeler, William, nearly opposite 'The Bell' at Battlebridge, Gray's Inn Lane, London, carver (1782). In 1782 took out insurance cover of £200 which included £20 for his utensils and stock. [GL, Sun MS vol. 300, p. 566]

Wheeler, William, 20 Daniel St, Bath, Som., cm (1833). [D]

Wheeler, William, High Wycombe, Bucks., chairmaker (b. c. 1791–1841). Aged 50 at the date of the 1841 Census.

Wheelhouse, W., Hebden Bridge, Yorks., cm and wheelwright (1837). [D]

Whelpton, John, Gainsborough, Lincs., chairmaker (1826–31). At Church Lane in 1826 and Beastmarket in 1831. [D]

Wheway, James, Nuneaton, Warks., cm and turner (1822). [D]

Whible, T., 18 Brownlow St, Holborn, London, carver and gilder (1835). [D]

Whilbourne, John, 29 Park St, Dorset Sq., London, chair and sofa maker (1839). [D]

Whildon, Joseph, Sheffield, Yorks., joiner and cm (1784). In 1784 took out insurance cover of £300 of which £75 was for his workshop, utensils and stock. [GL, Sun MS vol. 321, p. 466]

Whindley, J., 5 Wellington St, Gt Surrey St, Blackfriars Rd, London, picture and looking-glass frame maker (1835–59). [D]

Whinfield, Joshua, 26 Bridge St, Hull, Yorks., cm (1838–39). [D]

Whinray, Thomas, Lancaster, cm (1817–18). [Lancaster freemen rolls]

Whipp, John, Rochdale, Lancs., cm and chairmaker (1828–34). At Drake St in 1828 and Yorkshire St in 1834. [D]

Whisker, William, Little Port St, King's Lynn, Norfolk, cm and u (1822). [D]

Whistler, John, London, upholder (1728). Son of William Whistler of Hoxton, stocking frame knitter. App. to Joseph Welsh on 4 May 1720 and free of the Upholders' Co. by servitude, 8 May 1728. [GL, Upholders' Co. records]

Whitaker, —, 26 Worcester St, Southwark, London, (1805). [D]

Whitaker, Ann, 19 Castle St, Leicester Fields, London, u (1794). [Heal]

Whitaker, George, Hurdsfield, Macclesfield, Cheshire, cm (1828). [D]

Whitaker, James, Drake St, Rochdale, Lancs., chairmaker (1834). [D]

Whitaker, John, Doncaster, Yorks., cm (1753–56). In 1753 took app. named Oxley and in 1756, Boswell. [S of G, app. index]

Whitaker, John, Noble St, Foster Lane, London, upholder (1778). Son of Robert Whitaker of Bromley, Middlx, distiller.

App. to John Evans, 2 May 1766 and free of the Upholders' Co. by servitude, 4 February 1778. [GL, Upholders' Co. records]

Whitaker, John, 24 Cleveland St, Fitzroy Sq., London, broker and cm (1806). In July 1806 took out insurance cover of £500 which included £100 for the workshop behind 24 Cleveland St and £370 for stock and utensils. [GL, Sun MS vol. 437, ref. 792307]

Whitaker, John, 149 Deansgate, Bolton, Lancs., cm and u (1824–34). [D]

Whitaker, Joseph, London, cm (1793). Subscribed to Sheraton's *Drawing Book,* 1793.

Whitaker, Joseph, 1 Union St, Southwark, London, bedstead maker (1835). [D]

Whitaker, Samuel, Liverpool, cm (1812). App. to Edward Lowe 1802 and free by servitude, 9 October 1812. [Freemen reg.]

Whitaker, Samuel, 11 Skinner St, Bishopsgate, London, cm (1820). [D]

Whitaker, Thomas, Retford, Notts., cm (1795–d. 1804). Supplied small items of furniture valued at £17 15s in 1795 to G. Wentworth of Woolley Hall, Yorks. [YAS, Wentworth MD 272/2; Notts. RO, probate records]

Whitaker, William, Yorkshire St, Rochdale, Lancs., cm (1828–34). [D]

Whitbread, George, opposite St George's Chapel, Portsea, Portsmouth, Hants., cm (1787–98). In 1787 in partnership with Thomas Eastman. Jointly they took out insurance cover of £1,100 which included household goods, utensils and stock and a house in Butcher St. [D; GL, Sun MS vol. 345, p. 413]

Whitbread, W. E., Edward St, Birmingham, chair and Venetian blind maker (1818). [D]

Whitburn, Thomas, High St, Guildford, Surrey, u, cm and auctioneer (1830–40). The number in High St was 47 in 1838 and 45 in 1840. [D; poll bks]

Whitby, James, Nottingham, u (1697). [Nottingham freemen rolls]

Whitby, John, London, joiner (1660–67). Although described as a joiner he appears to have specialised in chair making and was a frequent supplier to the Royal family in the early years of Charles II's reign. The Royal accounts for the year 1660–61 include items for '18 French Chair frames' for which £7 16s was charged, a 'large french bed stead' which cost £2 10s and a number of other chairs, 'back chairs' and a foot stool. Most items were for Windsor though a 'French chair frame for grene damask' was for Hampton Court. Other furniture of a like nature was supplied to Whitehall, the House of Commons, Camden House and the Royal yachts. A 'Chair of state with 2 formes, 2 chairs & six folding stools' were specified as for 'our dearest consort the Queen'. [*Conn.,* January 1934, pp. 19–20; *C. Life,* 5 April 1962, p. 790; 9 June 1977, p. 1620; PRO, LC5/39, 40]

Whitby, John, Nottingham, u (1685–d. 1686). [Notts. RO, probate records]

Whitby, John, Mount St, London, u and cm (1741–57). Recorded in the Holkham Hall, Norfolk accounts, 1741–45. In 1741 supplied two card tables of 'pigeon wood' at £12 12s. For the period 1742–43 twenty chairs were supplied for the 'old House at Holkham' at £16, and four leather chairs at £1 19s each. Further chairs and a table were charged at £19 10s. In 1744 the main items supplied were 24 Windsor chairs 'and 2 Large ones' at £4 6s and twelve rush bottom chairs at £3 12s. A large mahogany dining table cost £4 5s in 1745 and a long table £2 5s. Alterations to three picture frames and re-gilding was undertaken in this year also. Joinery and carpentry work was also specified. The most interesting of Whitby's known commissions is that under-taken in 1756 for the 4th Baron Langdale of Holme Hall,

Yorks. This was for six back stools in mahogany with finely carved cabriole legs and a large settee. The back stools survive and are upholstered in contemporary *gros* and *petit* embroidery with scenes from Ovid's *Metamorphoses.* The seating furniture was invoiced on 14 August 1756 and cost including carriage £18 0s 3d. The five chairs that survive were sold by Christie's, 25 June 1981. Whitby was also employed by Thomas Foley of Stoke Edith near Hereford 1756–57. In November 1756 he compiled an inventory of the contents of Mrs Foley's house in Lower Grosvenor St and from June 1756 to January 1757 undertook repairs and alterations and supplied some minor furnishings for Thomas Foley. The total cost amounted to £50 1s 3d. [Westminster poll bk; V&A archives; Christie's, 25 June 1981, lot 50; Herefs. RO, Foley 18/309; 18/126]

Whitby, John, Liverpool, joiner and cm (1790). App. to Richard Chadwick and in 1790 petitioned for his freedom. [Freemen's committee bk]

Whitby, Joseph, Wolverhampton, Staffs., u (1827–34). In Mitre Walk in 1830, Horsley-Fields in 1833 and Oxford St in 1834. [D]

Whitby, Samuel, Sparling St, Liverpool, u (1787). [D]

Whitby, Samuel, Liverpool, u (1818–29). App. to Solomon Whitby and free by servitude, 13 June 1818. Shown at 14 Drayton Sq. but from 1821–29 trading at 10 Thurlow St. [D; freemen reg.]

Whitby, Solomon, Liverpool, upholder (1780–1818). Free 13 September 1780 and by 1803 trading at Redmund Pl., Circus St. The number in Redmund Pl. was 16 in 1803–04, 14 in 1807, 4 in 1811 and 9 in 1813–14. In 1818 at Thurlow St, but died before 1820. His former app. Samuel Whitby was trading from the Thurlow St address, 1821–29. [D; freemen reg.]

Whitby, Stephen, Nottingham, u (1697). [Nottingham freemen rolls]

Whitby, Thomas, London, cm (1808–09). At 3 Peters Ct, St Martin's Lane in October 1808 when he took out insurance cover of £100 on his household goods and £50 on his utensils and stock. In July 1809 insured household goods valued at £200 at 11 Little Andrew St. [GL, Sun MS vol. 445, ref. 823028; vol. 448, ref. 832669]

Whitby, Thomas, London, cm (1816–26). At 29 John St, Tottenham Ct Rd in 1816, Fitzroy Sq. in 1820 and 90 Charlotte St, Rathbone Sq. in 1826. [D]

Whitcher, W., Butchers Row, Southampton, Hants., carver and gilder (1829). [*Southampton Advertiser,* 25 April 1829]

Whitcomb, John, 'The Crown & Cushion', Prince's St, Soho, London, cm and upholder (1759–84). First recorded in 1759 at Marshall St, Carnaby Mkt, but otherwise the Prince's St address was always used. When the street was numbered his premises were known as 1 Prince's St. He offered a wide range of cabinet and upholstery goods which included bedding, window blinds and wallpapers. Funerals were arranged and goods appraised. In 1780 total insurance cover was £900 of which goods and utensils accounted for £500 but at this point the trading activity may have been in decline for by 1784 these figures had fallen to £200 and £100 respectively. Earlier however much more substantial cover had been taken out on other properties. In 1777 he insured a house and shop at 141 Fleet St jointly with George Blackiston, a grocer, for £800 and two years later 30 Harley St for £1,200. Only one patron of this maker is known. He was William Drake of Shardeloes, Amersham, Bucks. who on 8 April 1776 purchased four post bedsteads and bedding costing around £23. [Heal; Westminster poll bk; GL, Sun MS vol. 258, p. 60; vol. 278, p. 334; vol. 281, p. 510; vol. 322, p. 305; Bucks. RO, D/DR/5/109; *Public Advertiser,* 13 January 1759]

Whitcombe, Arthur, 23 Coventry St, Haymarket, London, carver and gilder (1839). [D]

White, Alexander, 10 Duke St, Portland Pl., London, u (1815–19). [D]

White, Ann, 34 New Montague St, Spitalfields, London, u and undertaker (1805). [D]

White, Benjamin, Butcher Row, Exeter, Devon, cm (1822–25). [D]

White, Bylis, Houndsditch, London, cm (1740–d. 1751). In 1740 trading as White & Hickman. Died May 1751 at his house at Woodford Row. He was stated to be an 'eminent Cabinetmaker . . . Who had acquired a genteel Fortune and retir'd from Business'. [Heal; *London Evening Post*, 14–16 May 1751]

White, Charles, address unknown, cm (1803). Subscribed to Sheraton's *Cabinet Dictionary*, 1803.

White, Daniel, 8 Merchant's Row, Scarborough, Yorks., cm and u (1823–40). [D]

White, David, Bishops Hull, Som., cm (1780). Bankruptcy announced, *Leicester Journal*, 19 February 1780.

White, David, High Wycombe, Bucks., chairmaker (b. c. 1801–41). Three sons and a daughter bapt. 1819–28. Aged 40 at the time of the 1841 Census. [PR (bapt.)]

White, David, Golden Hill, Wiveliscombe, Som., cm and joiner (1839). [D]

White, Dean, Norwich, u (c. 1746–52). Son of Edward White of Norwich, u and app. to his father. Free by servitude, 3 May 1746. Took app. named Elliot in 1752. [Freemen rolls; S of G, app. index]

White, Edward, London, upholder (1721). Son of Thomas White of Berks. App. to William Sedwell, 8 September 1713 and free of the Upholders' Co. by servitude, 1 March 1720/21. [GL, Upholders' Co. records]

White, Edward, parish of St Andrew, Norwich, u (1725–51). Free of Norwich, 24 February 1725 but not by app. Took as app. his son Dean who was free by servitude, 3 May 1746. Also took as app. Obadiah Silcock, free 3 May 1753. Silcock could not however had completed his apprenticeship with White as his master's will was proved 1751 at Norwich. [Freemen rolls; poll bks; Norwich Record Soc., index of wills]

White, Edward, High St, Arundel, Sussex, cm, u, paperhanger and auctioneer (1823–40). Successor to White & Son who were trading in Arundel in 1811. Edward White was probably the son mentioned. In July 1836 undertook work for the Earl of Surrey at Arundel Castle and Surrey House, Littlehampton, Sussex. This involved cleaning, repairing and polishing furniture, upholstery work, laying carpets and making blinds. The total cost of this work was £48 16s 6d. [D; Arundel Castle archives, A1960]

White, Edwin, 59 and 69 Old St, St Luke's, London, bedstead maker and carver (1829–37). [D]

White, Francis, Cartmel, Lancs., chairmaker (1824). [D]

White, Francis, Lower Bridge, Ulverston, Lancs., chairmaker (1829). Possibly the maker who was at Cartmel in 1824. [D]

White, Frederick, St James's St, Brighton, Sussex, Tunbridge-ware manufacturer (1822–24). [D]

White, George, Driffield, Yorks., cm (1823–34). At Burlington St, 1823–28, New Rd in 1831 and Bridlington St, 1834. [D]

White, George, Lord's-mill St, Chesterfield, Derbs., cm (1822). [D]

White, George, Primrose Hill, Liverpool, cm (1835–39). At 14 Primrose Hill, 1835–37 though in 1837 additionally at 1 Villar's Pl. In 1839 at 35 Primrose Hill, Fontenoy St. [D]

White, George Morris, Curtain Rd, Shoreditch, London, upholder (1790–1802). Son of George Morris White of Moorfields, merchant. App. to George Gibson, 2 June 1790 and free of the Upholders' Co. by servitude, 1 December 1802. [GL, Upholders' Co. records]

White, Henry, 'The Hand & Crown', St Paul's Churchyard, London, chairmaker (1715–20). Freeman of the Joiners' Co. His premises were on the east side of St Paul's Churchyard abutting north on St Paul's Schools. In May 1715 this property was insured for £250. In January 1718 he was described as a cane chairmaker and had an additional warehouse in Thames St, near Baynards Castle. Probably the chairmaker who on 26 March 1720 was paid £10 in settlement for chairs supplied to Benjamin and Henry Hoare. [GL, Hand in Hand MS vol. 14, p. 364; Sun MS vol. 7, 25 January 1718; Hoare's Bank, private ledger, Benjamin & Henry Hoare, 1719–25, p. 58]

White, Henry, Sloplatch, Shrewsbury, Salop, cm and u (1822). [D]

White, Henry, 75 Bridge St, Manchester, carver, gilder, looking-glass and picture frame maker (1829). [D]

White, Henry, Town's End, Stroud, Glos., cm (1830). [D]

White, Henry, Market Pl., Faversham, Kent, cm and u (1838). [D]

White, Henry, 4 Bridge St, Manchester, carver and gilder (1840). [D]

White, Henry D., 15 Rotherhithe St, London, carver (1826). [D]

White, Hougham, Harbledown, Kent, cm (1796). Freeman of Canterbury. [Canterbury poll bk]

White, J., 22 Magdalene St, Exeter, Devon, cm (1834–40). [D]

White, J. & Fitsal, 1 Camberwell Row, London, upholders and cm (1805–09). [D]

White, James, London, u (before 1754). In July 1754 he advertised his recent arrival in Philadelphia, USA from London. He claimed to make 'all sorts of furniture for beds, window curtains, either festoon or plain, all sorts of chairs, either French or India backs, sofa's, settees or settee-beds, feather beds, mattrasses, and all other sorts of household furniture, after the newest taste, either in the Chinese or Venetian'. He was trading at 'Mrs Bedford's opposite Mr. Tenant's new Church in Third-street'. In 1754 he subscribed to Chippendale's *Director* and his was probably the earliest copy of this work to reach America. [*Penn'a Gazette*, 4 July 1754]

White, James, Canterbury, Kent, turner, cm and u (1778–1809). In 1778 living in the parish of St Alphege and 1784 at Palace St. In 1805 the business is recorded as James White & Sons and was at Sun St and in 1809 White & Co. was in St George's St. Succeeded by Samuel White. In 1778 took out insurance cover of £900 of which £500 was for utensils and stock. [D; GL, Sun MS vol. 264, p. 67]

White, James, Kennington Lane, London, u (1826). [D]

White, James, High St, Taunton, Som., cm and u (1822–30). Bankruptcy announced, *Liverpool Mercury*, 5 March 1830. [D]

White, James, 48 St Thomas St, Weymouth, Dorset, cm and u (1830). [D]

White, James, Birmingham, cabinet case maker (1830–39). At 75 Bartholomew St in 1830 and 5 Little Charles St in 1835. Still trading in Little Charles St in 1839. [D]

White, James, Norwood, Beverley, Yorks., cm and u (1834–40). [D]

White, James, 15 Vere St, Clare Mkt, London, cm and u (1839). [D]

White, James, 11 Prescot St, Low Hill, Liverpool, cm (1839). [D]

White, Jeremiah, 12 Wardour St, Soho, London, cm, u and undertaker (1781–93). In 1781 took out insurance cover for £900 of which £680 was for utensils and stock. Trade card in Banks Coll., BM. Subscribed to Sheraton's *Drawing Book*, 1793. [D; GL, Sun MS vol. 295, p. 585]

White, John, address unknown, chairmaker (1723). Recorded in the Monson accounts as a supplier of '6 wallnutt matted chairs' at 9s 6d each, '6 Spanish leather chairs' at £1 each and '2 elbow chairs ditto' at £1 5s each. The invoice for £11 7s was dated 30 September 1723. [Lincoln RO, Monson 12]

White, John, Preston, Lancs., u (1732–42). Freeman of Preston and recorded paying poor rates in 1732. In 1740 took app. named Amery. In 1742 his son Henry was also free of Preston as was his brother Henry, a sea captain. [Harris Museum, Regulation of poor tax; S of G, app. index; Preston Guild records]

White, John, London, cm and u (1748–55). His address was given as Long Acre in 1748 but subsequently as near Slaughter's Coffee House in St Martin's Lane. Subscribed to the second edition of Chippendale's *Director*, 1755. [*Daily Advertiser*, 12 March 1748; Westminster poll bk]

White, John, Fleet Mkt, London, bedstead maker (1763–78). Member of the Joiners' Co. In both 1762 and 1763 took out licences to employ three non-freemen for three months and four for three months. In 1778 took out a licence to use two for three months. [GL, City Licence bks, vols 3 and 9]

White, John, Bennet St, Westminster, London, upholder (1774). [Poll bk]

White, John, London, upholder and auctioneer (1782–1827). In 1782 at the corner of Gt Queen St, Dartmouth St, Westminster where he insured his utensils and stock for £1,000 out of a total cover of £1,200. Shown at Queen St until 1789 though one directory of 1788 states Princess St. In 1790 moved to 4 Storey's Gate, Westminster though the list of master cabinet makers in Sheraton's *Cabinet Dictionary*, 1803 states 3 Story's Gate. In 1811 at 12 Poland St and from 1813 at Princes St. From 1820 84 Margaret St, Cavendish Sq. was used additionally. From 1820 cm was used in trade description. [D; Heal; GL, Sun MS vol. 302, p. 181]

White, John & Son, Chichester, Sussex, cm, u and auctioneer (1792–1840). At East St, 1792–1802 where the business traded as John White. A number of pieces of furniture with trade labels attached give this address. Items include a mahogany secretaire chest, a mahogany chest of drawers and two clothes presses. One of these is in mahogany and satinwood, the doors painted with oval rustic scenes and with Neo-classical sprandrel ornaments and a Gothic drip cornice. By 1804 in North St, trading as John White & Son. [D; *Furn. Hist.*, 1976; Christie's, 7 July 1983, lot 100]

White, John, Coventry, Warks., chairmaker and turner (1793). [D]

White, John, Cartmel, Lancs., chairmaker (1793–1829). A Francis White, chairmaker, was in Cartmel in 1824. [D]

White, John, Wyle Cop, Shrewsbury, Salop, u and cm (1819–33). Bankruptcy announced, *Liverpool Mercury*, 28 June 1833. [D]

White, John, London, bedstead maker and cm (1820–29). At 17 Snowfields Rd, Bermondsey in 1820 and 4 Cross St, Newington in 1829. In December 1820 took out insurance cover of £300 of which £90 was in respect of utensils and stock and also covered a store in the yard behind the house. [D; GL, Sun MS vol. 487, ref. 974422]

White, John, 5 St Mary St, Weymouth, Dorset, cm and u (1823). [D]

White, John, 17 London St, Reading, Berks., cm and u (1826–40). Successor to Joseph White. [D; poll bks]

White, John, 16 Castle St, Leicester Sq., London, cm and u (1827). [D]

White, John, 21 Kennington Lane, London, cm and u (1827). [D]

White, John, High Wycombe, Bucks., chairmaker (1830). [D]

White, John, 38 High St, Stonehouse, Plymouth, Devon, cm (1830). [D]

White, John, Exeter, Devon, cm (1833–38). At Bedford St in October 1822 when his son Alfred John was bapt. at St Stephen's Church. By December 1836 at Magdalen St when another son, Frank, was bapt. at Holy Trinity Church. Trading in Magdalen St in 1838. [D; PR (bapt.)]

White, John, Tamworth, Staffs., clock case maker (1834). [D]

White, John, Cock Yd, Swaffham, Norfolk, cm (1836). [D]

White, John, Villars St, Liverpool, u (1837). [D]

White, John, Bridge St, Buckingham, cm (1839). [D]

White, John, Wells St, Buckingham, u (1839). [D]

White, John, 19 St James St, King's Lynn, Norfolk, cm and u (1839). [D]

White, John, New Rd, Driffield, Yorks., cm (1840). [D]

White, John Albin, Clyst Hydon, Devon, cm (1831). In July 1831 married Elizabeth Jane Ladd, only daughter of the late Mr Ladd, perfumer of London. [*Exeter Flying Post*, 7 July 1831]

White, Jonadab, Garden St, Wakefield, Yorks., cm and u (1814–30). [D]

White, Jonadab, Kirkburton, near Huddersfield, Yorks., cm (1822–34). [D]

White, Joseph, Bristol, cm (1739). [Poll bk]

White, Joseph, 17 London St, Reading, Berks., cm (1823). Succeeded by John White. [D]

White, Matthew, Garden St, Wakefield, Yorks., joiner and cm (1830). A Jonadab White was trading as a cm and u in this street, 1814–30. [D]

White, Nathaniel, Holborn, London, cm (1748–50). Known from his trade card c. 1750 which gives the address as 'The Desk & Bookshelf, corner of Thavies Inn Gate, Holborn'. This states that he made 'all sorts of Cabinet Work with Sconces, Pier and Chimney-Glasses, Mahogany and other Tables, Chairs of all Sorts . . . Blinds for Windows, Painted on Canvas, Silk or Wire'. The White, cm, who was trading from an address 'next door to the Cross Keys Tavern, in Holborn' in 1748 is probably the same person. [Heal; Banks Coll., BM]

White, Nicholas, Preston, Lancs., chairmaker (1818–34). At 15 Spring Gdns in 1818 and 3 Pole St in 1834. [D]

White, Peter, 26 Broad St, Golden Sq., London, billiard table and backgammon board maker (1832–39). [D]

White, Ralph, address unknown, chairmaker (1767–68). Supplied a junior garden chair to Cassiobury, Herts. at a cost of £2. [Herts. RO, 8742/11]

White, Richard, 63 Fleet St, London, upholder (1786). Son of Benjamin White of Fleet St, bookseller. App. to Joseph Graham, 3 June 1778 and free of the Upholders' Co. by servitude, 1 February 1786. [GL, Upholders' Co. records]

White, Richard, 76 Oxford St, London, cm and u (1788–95). Possibly the Richard White who was declared free of the Upholders' Co. in 1786. [D]

White, Richard, Fore St, Taunton, Som., joiner and cm (1791–98). In May 1791 took out insurance cover of £200. [D; GL, Sun MS vol. 377, p. 390]

White, Richard, 125 Brick Lane, Spitalfields, London, cm and broker (1809). In February 1809 took out insurance cover of £200 of which £120 was for utensils and stock. [GL, Sun MS vol. 446, ref. 825941]

White, Richard, 48 Worcester St, Birmingham, cm (1835). [D]

White, Richard, High Wycombe, chairmaker (b. c. 1806–41). Aged 35 at the time of the 1841 Census.

White, Robert, Bristol, cm (1745). Subscribed to John Wood's *A Description of the Exchange at Bristol* (Bath 1745).

White, Robert, Market Pl., Faversham, Kent, cm and u (1784–1839). In 1803–07 described as an upholder etc. but from 1811 as a cm. In 1824 named as Robert White & Sons. [D]

White, Robert, 55 Upper Marylebone St, London, cm (1826). [D]

White, Ross, 28 North St, Dale St, Liverpool, chairmaker (1796). [D]

White, S., 13 Frederick Pl., Borough Rd, London, cm and u (1839). [D]

White, Samuel, 8 St George's St, Canterbury, Kent, cm and furniture broker (1826–39). [D] See White & Goulden.

White, Samuel, Stockwellgate, Mansfield, Notts., joiner, cm and u (1832). [D]

White, Samuel, Egerton St, Chester, cm (1839). Free 23 July 1839. [Freemen rolls]

White, Simon, 4 Peter St, Saffron Hill, London, cm, u and broker (1758–77). In 1758 took app. named Nuttal. At this date living in the parish of St Bartholomew-the-Great. In 1777 insured his house at Peter St for £300. [S of G, app. index; GL, Sun MS vol. 257, p. 459]

White, Stephen, Liverpool, u (1811–16). At 12 Derby St in 1811 but by 1813 the number was 11. In 1816 at 2 Silver St with a shop at 20 Paradise St. In December 1816 he was declared bankrupt and in January of the following year his stock was disposed of by auction for the benefit of his creditors. On offer was a 'large assortment of modern Brussels, Venetian, Kidderminster & Patent Carpeting, Hearth Rugs, handsome figured Oil Cloths of various widths, a great variety of Paper Hangings with rich Flock & Plain Borders of the newest Patterns, Morines, Chintz Furnitures, Trimmings, Bed Ticks, Mattings etc: & excellent Mahogany Articles in Dining, & Drawing-room Chairs, Secretaire & Bookcase with glazed Doors, Wardrobes, Chests of Drawers, Sideboard, Dining, Loo, Library, Pembroke, Card, Work & Snap Tables, Bed Steps, Night Chairs, Sandwich Trays, Hat Stands, Music Stools, Guardevins, Cribs, Brassbound Portable Desks, Tea Chests, Caddies, Shaving Cases, Backgammon Boxes etc: Couches, Sofas & Lounging Chairs in black Hair Cloth, Chamber Articles in Japanned Chairs, Tables & Washstands, Mirrors, Pier & Dressing Glasses'. Supplies of horsehair, upholstery materials, mahogany, rosewood and deal, brass work and seven work benches were also on offer. In May 1817 a first dividend of 8s in the £ was declared. [D; Liverpool Mercury, 20 and 27 December 1816, 17 January 1817, 2 May 1817]

White, Stephen, Warrington, Lancs., cm and u (1825–28). At School Lane in 1825 and Dolmans Lane in 1828. [D]

White, T., St James St, King's Lynn, Norfolk, u (1839). A John White, cm and u was trading at 19 St James St in 1839. [D]

White, Thomas, Canterbury, Kent cm/u (1797). [Poll bk]

White, Thomas, Petworth, Sussex, cm (1819–21). Probably the Thomas White who was bapt. at Godalming, Surrey, 18 September 1796. Married the daughter of George Knight of Petworth, cm and innkeeper and living in this town in August 1819 and March 1821 when two of his children were bapt. By May 1823 however he was trading in Godalming as a victualler and was subsequently to become landlord of 'The Ship' at Artington, Surrey (1833) and 'The Three Pigeons' in High St, Guildford (1841 onwards). [PR (bapt.); Census 1841]

White, Thomas, 2 Sun St, Bishopsgate, London, cm and u (1827). [D]

White, Thomas, Bread St, Alresford, Hants., cm (1830). [D]

White, Thomas, Middle St, Driffield, Yorks., cm (1834–40). [D]

White, Thomas, 109 Richmond Row, Liverpool, u and cm (1837–39). [D]

White, Thomas, 28 Store St, Bedford Sq., London, u (1839). [D]

White, Timothy, Wyle Cop, Shrewsbury, Salop, cm (1830–35). [D]

White, W., Claypath, Durham, cm (1825). In October 1825 advertised for 'TWO or THREE clever workmen' and also two or three apps. [Durham Country Advertiser, 8 October 1825]

White, William, London, upholder (1768–81). Son of James White of the parish of St Mary, Whitechapel, publican. App. to John Boulton, 2 April 1768, and free of the Upholders' Co. by servitude, 4 May 1768. At Mile End, 1775–78 and Princess St, Mansion House in 1781. [GL, Upholders' Co. records]

White, William, Bristol, cm (1793–95). Living in the parish of St Philip, 1793–94 and in 1795 at Stapleton Rd. [D]

White, William, Worship St, Moorfields, London, cm (1797). Bankruptcy declared February 1797. [Billinge's Liverpool Advertiser, 13 February 1797]

White, William, Swanage, Dorset, cm (1798). [D]

White, William, London, cm (1805–09). At 12 Poland St, Oxford St 1805, but in 1809 at 18 Great Warren St. [D]

White, William, Jacob St, Bristol, carver and gilder (1815–16). [D]

White, William, Birmingham, cm and u (1800–30). At 11 Dudley St, in 1800; Old Meeting Pl., 1816; Moor St, 1818; and 83 Smallbrook St, 1830. [D]

White, William jnr, New Meeting St, Birmingham, cm (1816). [D]

White, William, 64 Old Market St, Bristol, cm (1817–31). [D]

White, William, 41 Duke St, Spitalfields, London, painter, carver etc. (1820). [D]

White, William, Chapel Walk, 6 Queen St, Sheffield, Yorks., cm (1821–25). [D]

White, William, High St, Lane End, Staffs., joiner and cm (1822). [D]

White, William, Waterloo St, Wells, Norfolk, cm and joiner (1822–30). [D]

White, William, Hull, Yorks., joiner and cm (1826–40). At Hanover Sq. with a residence at Bolton Sq., Manor Alley, 1826–31, and in 1834 shown at 12 Manor Alley. In 1835 shown at 3 Manor Alley with a residence at 7 Neptune St. For 1838 two entries are shown. William White is listed at 6 Neptune St, and William White jnr, a joiner at 3 Manor Alley and a residence at 6 Boulton Sq. Subsequent entries are for William White jnr only at the same address as in 1838 but his trade is indicated as architect and joiner or architect and builder. [D]

White, William, Sadler St, Durham, cm (1826–28). In February 1826 advertised that he had commenced trading on his own account and had opened 'a SHOW ROOM OF FASHIONABLE FURNITURE' in Sadler St. [D; Durham County Advertiser, 11 February 1826]

White, William, Horse Mkt, Barnard Castle, Co. Durham, joiner and cm (1827–28). [D]

White, William, Birmingham, chair and sofa maker (1828–35). At Woodcock St in 1828 and Lawley St in 1835. [D]

White, William, Long Lane, Easingwold, Yorks., joiner and cm (1828–34). [D]

White, William, Radford, Worksop, Notts., cm, u and builder (1828–35). [D]

White, William, 29 Horatio St, Liverpool, u (1829). [D]

White, William, 11 Gyde's Terr., Cheltenham, Glos., cm and u (1830). [D]

White, William, Green, Devizes, Wilts., cm and u (1830–39). [D]

White, William, Swanage, Dorset, cm (1830–40). There was a William White trading in Swanage as a cm in 1798, possibly the father of this maker. [D]

White, William, Leamington, Warks., u (1831). Bankruptcy announced, Chester Courant, 8 February 1831.

White, William, Potter St, Worksop, Notts., cm and u (1832). [D]

White, William, 33 Essex St, London, carver, gilder and looking-glass maker (1837). [D]

White, William & Sons, Woodcock St, Birmingham, chairmakers (1830). [D]

White & Goulden, St George's St and Sun St, Canterbury, Kent, cm and furniture brokers (1826–39). [D] See Samuel White.

White & Son, Arundel, Sussex, u and auctioneers (1811). Succeeded by Edward White. [D]

Whiteacre, Stephen, Widcombe, Som., chairmaker (1730). In 1730 took app. named Wornell. [S of G, app. index]

Whitefield, Francis, 13 Quay St, Salford, Lancs., cm (1804–08). [D]

Whitefield, James, Bristol, u and cm (1781–84). In December 1784 his stock in trade and household furniture were sold off. [Poll bks; *Bonner and Middleton's Bristol Journal*, 4 December 1784]

Whitefield, John, 10 Faberswall Walk, London, portable desk, dressing case, work box and cabinet case maker (1839). [D]

Whitefoot, Phineas, Warwick St, Golden Sq., London, u (1733). [Heal]

Whitehair, Benjamin Hollister, Clifton, Bristol, cm (1774–81). [Poll bks]

Whitehair, H., 1 Hillgrove St, Bristol, u (1809). [D]

Whitehead, Francis, Stamford, Lincs., u (1801–d. by 1835). App. to Samuel Hill on 19 November 1801 for seven years. Free of Stamford 1815 but probably dead by 1835. [Freemen rolls]

Whitehead, John, Manchester, carver and gilder (1797–1811). At New Jerusalem Pl. in 1797 but at 74 Water St, 1800–11. [D]

Whitehead, John, Osmaston St, Derby, carver and gilder (1822). [D]

Whitehead, John, Scot Lane, Doncaster, Yorks., cm and u (1834–37). [D]

Whitehead, Jos., 4 Court, Shadwell St, Birmingham, cm (1835). [D]

Whitehead, Joseph, Cheapside, Liverpool, joiner and cm (1824–29). At 3 Cheapside in 1824. In partnership with a Thomas Whitehead at 2 Cheapside in 1827 and 3 Cheapside in 1829. A Thomas Whitehead was at 2 Cheapside in 1823. [D]

Whitehead, Robert, Cartmel, Lancs., chairmaker (1828–34). [D]

Whitehead, Susannah, Albion St, Leicester, u and paper hanger (1835). [D]

Whitehead, Thomas, Wakefield Yorks., joiner and cm (1798). [D]

Whitehead, Thomas, 39 and 43 Aldermanbury, London, u (1808–27). Shown as cm and u 1820–27. [D]

Whitehead, Thomas, 2 Cheapside, Liverpool, joiner and cm (1823). A Thomas Whitehead was in partnership with Joseph Whitehead at 2 Cheapside in 1827 and 3 Cheapside in 1829. [D]

Whitehead, Thomas, Salford, Lancs. and Manchester, carver, gilder, looking-glass and picture frame maker (1825–39). At 27 Queen St, Salford in 1825 but from 1828 at Bridge St, Manchester. The number in Bridge St was 27, 1828–29 and 1836–39 but between 1832–34 it was 61. [D]

Whitehead, William, 2 Upper Spring St, Portman Sq., London, cm and u (1826–27). [D]

Whitehead, William, Etherington, Birmingham, cm, u and chairmaker (1822–39). At Edmund Row in 1822 but from 1828 at 12 Easy Row. In May 1828 declared insolvent but trading again in 1830. [D; *Chester Chronicle*, 2 May 1828]

Whitehead & Priestley, Northgate, Wakefield, Yorks., cm (1814). [D]

Whitehorne, Richard, 'The Royal Bed', Holborn Bridge, London, u (d. 1740). Late partner of J. Nash and E. Hall. [Heal]

Whitehorne, William, London, cm (1740). A sale of his stock was advertised in 1740. In this he is referred to as 'well known for his curious Workmanship in Mahogany and Walnut-Tree'. [Heal]

Whitehouse, George, Waddams Poole, Dudley, Staffs., cm (1820). A John Whitehouse & Son was trading in Dudley as cm and u in 1838. [D]

Whitehouse, John, London, cm (1793). Subscribed to Sheraton's *Drawing Book*, 1793.

Whitehouse, John & Sons, Dudley, Staffs., cm and u (1838). A George Whitehouse was trading in Dudley as a cm, 1820. [D]

Whitehouse, Joseph, 23 High Green, Wolverhampton, Staffs., u (1802). [Rate bk]

Whitehouse, Joseph, High St, Newport, Salop, cm and u (1822–28). [D]

Whitehouse, Robert Bland, York, cm and u (1823–30). At Coffee Yd, Stonegate in 1823 and 17 St Andrewgate in 1828–30. [D]

Whitehouse, Samuel, Farnham, Surrey, cm (1736). In 1736 took app. named Cook. [S of G, app. index]

Whitehouse, Thomas, North St, Ripon, Yorks., joiner/cm (1837). [D]

Whitelaw, Joseph, 1 Walton Ct, Cheapside, Liverpool, joiner and cm (1821). [D]

Whitelaw, S., 7 Sussex St, Bedford Sq., London, cm and u (1839). [D]

Whiteley, Eward, New Dock Walls, Hull, Yorks., carver and gilder (1821–22). [D]

Whiteley, Edward, 64 Manchester Rd, Huddersfield, Yorks., carver and gilder (1837). [D]

Whiteley, James, Back of 34 Spinning Field, Manchester, chairmaker (1813). [D]

Whiteley, Robert, Top of Town, Huddersfield, Yorks., cm (1814–19). [D]

Whiteley, Thomas, 20 Spinning Field, Manchester, chairmaker (1813–17). [D]

Whiteley, William, Manchester, chairmaker (1813–25). At 4 Marsdens Buildings, Bootle St in 1813, 6 Hall's Buildings, Windmill St in 1817 and 32 Spinning Fields in 1825. [D]

Whitelock, Robert, High Gate, Beverley, Yorks., cm (1790–1831). [D; poll bks]

Whitelock, William, 5 Wellington Pl., Wandsworth Rd, London, cm and u (1826–27). [D]

Whiteman, Joseph, London(?), u (1717). The account book of Rebecca Tufnell records the payment of £3 16s to 'Joseph Whiteman upholster'' for making ten cushions. The entry is dated 1 January 1717. [Essex RO, D/DTu 278]

Whiteside, Edward, Church St, Lancaster, and Oxford St, London, cm (1797–1840). App. to Gillows, 23 December 1797 and named in the Gillow records, 1797–1801, 1803–09, 1828–29 and 1832–40. In Bentham's *Directory*, 1805, listed as 'Redmayne, Whiteside & Ferguson (late Gillow & Co.)' and in 1816 this firm was recorded at the top of Church St. The lack of entries in the Gillow records might suggest a period of independent trading covering the 1810s and most of the 20s. In 1822 his newphew Thomas was app. to Leonard Redmayne and at this date Edward Whiteside was living in Oxford St, London. He must have returned to Lancaster by the late 1820s unless his employment was with the Oxford St side of the Gillow business. [D; app. reg.; Westminster Ref. Lib., Gillow]

Whiteside, Henry, Poulton-le-Fylde, Lancs., cm and joiner (1828–34). Son of John Whiteside of Plumpton in Kirkham, Lancs. husbandman. App. to Richard Gillow, Robert Gillow snr and jnr and George Gillow of Lancaster and Oxford St,

London on 25 March 1795. Named in the Gillow records 1798 and 1800–01. In 1828–34 trading at Poulton-le-Fylde. [D; Preston RO, DDX 1122/1/2; Westminster Ref. Lib., Gillow]

Whiteside, James, Lancaster (1822–25). Named in the Gillow records, 1822–25. [Westminster Ref. Lib., Gillow]

Whiteside, John, 176 Oxford St, London, cm (1840). [GL, Sun MS ref. 1339076]

Whiteside, Thomas, Lancaster (1818–23). Named in the Gillow records, 1818–23. [Westminster Ref. Lib., Gillow]

Whitewood, Arthur, Leicester, cm and u (1827–40). At Haymarket in 1827 but by the following year had moved to Belgrave Gate where he remained until 1840. [D]

Whitfield, Mrs, Hull, Yorks., u (1765–66). Paid £18 18s in connection with a bed supplied to Burton Constable, Yorks. [Humberside RO, Burton Constable vouchers]

Whitfield, David, Wetherby, Yorks., joiner/cm (1837). [D]

Whitfield, James, Wetherby, Yorks., joiner/cm (1837). [D]

Whitfield, Lewis, Claypath, Durham, cm/joiner (1834). [D]

Whitford, John, St Columb, Cornwall, painter, carver and gilder (1798). [D]

Whitford, W., King St, Devonport, Devon, cm (1814). [D]

Whitford, W., 8 King St, Truro, Cornwall, 'Burnish gilder &c' (1819). In January 1819 advertised that he had provided specimens of picture frame mouldings to James & Penberthy of Helston, Best of St Columb, Bennett of St Austell and West Bodmin, all cm who acted as his agents for commissions. Also advertised a transparent varnish for protecting prints and drawings. [*Royal Cornwall Gazette* 23 January 1819]

Witham, Lawrence, Liverpool, joiner and cm (1815). Married to Miss Susannah Parkinson at Everton, May 1815. [*Liverpool Mercury*, 12 May 1815]

Whithorne, Lawrence, London, upholder (1719–30). Son of Lawrence Whithorne of Gloucester, silversmith. App. to Richard Say, 10 August 1719 and free of the Upholders' Co. by servitude, 11 November 1730. [GL, Upholders' Co. records]

Whiting, Richard, Hastings, Sussex, cm and carpenter (1794). [D]

Whiting, Richard, 27 Chain St, Reading, Berks., cm and u (1840). [D]

Whiting, Samuel, London, upholder (1735–60). Son of Noel Whiting of London, merchant. App. to George Friend, 8 August 1728 and free of the Upholders' Co. by servitude, 1 October, 1735. Took as app. Robert Jennings, 1747–60. [GL, Upholders' Co. records]

Whiting, Samuel, Watling St, London, u (d. 1748). [Heal]

Whiting, Samuel Stewart, 140 and 143 Houndsditch, London, cm, u, window blind maker and undertaker (1817–28). In December 1820 took out insurance of £300 on 140 Houndsditch of which £200 was for utensils and stock. [D; GL, Sun MS vol. 484, ref. 974513]

Whiting, Thomas, Reading, Berks., u (1754–80). [Poll bks]

Whitlam, Benjamin, Churchgate (or Church St), Retford, Notts., cm and u (1828–35). [D]

Whitlee, Charles, Bury St Edmunds, Suffolk, cm (1742). In 1742 took app. named Raffe. [S of G, app. index]

Whitley, David, 34 Lane St, Southwark, London, chair and sofa maker (1839). [D]

Whitley, John, London, upholder (1662). Supplied a French bedstead, chairs and stools to Hampton Court in 1662. [V&A archives]

Whitley, Solomon, Thurlow St, Liverpool, u (d. 1818). Died 6 December 1818 'after an illness of several years which he bore with resignation'. [*Liverpool Mercury*, 1 January 1819]

Whitley, Thomas, 29 John St, Tottenham Ct Rd, London, cm and u (1817). [D]

Whitley, William, Stamford, Lincs., u (late 17th century). Freeman of Stamford by purchase. [Freemen rolls]

Whitlock, Robert, Old Gravel Lane, London, cm (1791–1804). At 10 Mount Pleasant, Old Gravel Lane in March 1791 when he took out insurance cover of £300. Of this £90 was for utensils and stock in open sheds and a yard. By March 1804 at 156 Old Gravel Lane with the same total insurance cover but £150 was now allocated to utensils and stock. [GL, Sun MS vol. 376, p. 66; vol. 430, ref. 760299]

Whitmarsh, Charles, 36 Charles St, Tottenham Ct Rd, London, carver (1807). On 6 April 1807 took out insurance cover of £150 of which £25 was for utensils and stock. [GL, Sun MS vol. 440, ref. 800997]

Whitmore, John, London, upholder (1699). Free of the Upholders' Co., 8 February 1698/99. [GL, Upholders' Co. records]

Whitmore, Thomas, Saffron Walden, Essex (?), u (?) (1765). Recorded working at Audley End, in 1765 and submitted various accounts for day work 'making up Furniture etc' for Sir John Griffin Griffin. [Essex RO, D/DBy/A23/10]

Whitmore, William, Brackey, Northants., joiner and cm (1793). [D]

Whitney, Abraham, address unknown, u (1761). On 23 October 1761 charged £6 1s for '2 easy chairs compleat' supplied to Temple Newsam, Leeds. [*Furn. Hist.*, 1967]

Whitroe, Abraham, Peter St, Westminster, London, chairmaker (1749–74). [Poll bks]

Whitrow, George, Westminster, London, chairmaker (1774–1829). Living in Pye St in 1774. From 1805 trading in Gt Peter St the number being 25, though insurance records to 1821 give 20. Insurance cover reached £1,300 in November 1820 but of this £800 covered a dwelling house and stock and utensils was £300 and a workshop behind £200. The business appears to have specialised in japanned and painted chairs and by 1829 were also producing sofas. It also acted as a general furniture japanner. From 1805–29 the business is recorded in directories as a partnership between George & John Whitrow and the 20 Gt Peter St address may have been largely the dwelling house of George Whitrow. [D; GL, Sun MS vol. 448, ref. 834625; vol. 453, ref. 848841; vol. 483, ref. 972636; vol. 488, ref. 980702; vol. 498, ref. 1010030]

Whitrow, John, see George Whitrow.

Whittaker, Ann, Kirkgate, Wakefield, Yorks., carver and gilder (1822). Successor to J. Whittaker at this address and possibly his widow. [D]

Whittaker, Dinah, 8 Arthur St, Hulme, Manchester, cm and u (1840). [D]

Whittaker, J., Kirkgate, Wakefield, Yorks., carver and gilder (1818). An Ann Whittaker, possibly his widow, was trading at this address in 1822. [D]

Whittaker, James, Burnley, Lancs., cm and chairmaker (1816–28). In Yorkshire St, 1816–24 but by 1828 had moved to Basket St. [D]

Whittaker, James, Millgate, Bury, Lancs., cm and u (1824). [D]

Whittaker, John, Church St, Clitheroe, Lancs., joiner, cm and house builder etc. (1824). [D]

Whittaker, Josiah, 24 Gt Newton St, Manchester, joiner and cm (1813). [D]

Whittaker, R., 8 Little Chester St, Grosvenor Pl., London, u (1839). [D]

Whittaker, William, Durham Yd, Strand, London, u (1714). On 11 May 1714 took out insurance cover 'for his Goods in his Warehouse adjoining to Souther's Coast in the said yard'. [GL, Sun MS vol. 3, ref. 3939]

Whittaker, William, Manchester, cm (1804–38). At 36 Shudehill 1804–11, 16 Thomas St, 1825–33, 37 Thomas St, 1836 and 5 Brook St, John St in 1838. [D]

Whittall, James, Chester, u (1826–37). Free 1826 when he was living in Brook St. In 1837 in St Anne's St. [Freemen rolls; poll bk]

Whittall, Joseph, Powell St, Lancaster St, Birmingham, joiner and cm (1800). [D]

Whittall, Thomas, Birmingham, cm and cabinet case maker (1816–35). At 23 Temple St, 1816–18 but from 1830–35 at back of 33 Newhall St. In 1835 listed also as a billiard table maker. [D]

Whittam, John, Retford, Notts., joiner and cm (1777–79). In 1777 took out insurance cover of £250 of which £50 was for utensils and stock. In 1779 the utensils and stock were insured for the same figure but the total insurance cover was reduced to £150. [GL, Sun MS vol. 254, p. 284; vol. 276, p. 507]

Whittam, John, Stanningley, near Leeds, Yorks., cm and joiner (1830). [D]

Whittindale, John, Home Market, Westmld, joiner/cm (1829). [D]

Whittingdale, John, Kirkby Lonsdale, Westmld, joiner/cm (1829–34). At Tarn Side in 1829. [D]

Whittingdale, Thomas, Lancaster and Kirkby Lonsdale, Westmld, cm (1766–1806). App. to H. Baines of Lancaster 1759 and free, 1766–67. Living at Kirkby Lonsdale, 1768–84. Named in the Gillow records 1788 and 1806. [Lancaster app. reg.; Lancaster poll bks; Westminster Ref. Lib., Gillow vol. 344/99, p. 1780]

Whittingham, James, Chester, u, cm and appraiser (1829–40). Son of 'Mr. Whittingham of Flookersbrook Iron Foundary'. He possibly trained in London and was employed for two years by Morel & Seddon and then four years by Dowbiggin & Co. before setting up on his own account in Chester in 1829. When working for Dowbiggin he claimed to have been employed in 'the management of furnishing the houses of different noblemen and gentlemen, both in England and most parts of Scotland, and some in this part of the country'. In Chester he took over the business previously operated by Samuel Davies in Foregate St which he obtained from his widow. It is not clear if he actually traded from Foregate St, and certainly from March 1830 he was established at the corner of New St and Upper Bridge St which from 1833 was recorded as 1 Grosvenor St. He was primarily an u and in 1829 claimed 'a perfect knowledge of the spring stuffing upon the latest improved principle in Easy Chairs, Sofas, Dining Room Chairs, Pillows, Bolsters, Beds, mattrasses etc.' In both 1833 and 1834 he advertised that he had travelled to London and had returned with stocks of the most fashionable paper hangings, upholstery materials and carpets. In 1829 he advertised for an app. [D; *Chester Chronicle*, 28 August 1829, 1 May 1840; *Chester Chronicle*, 9 February 1830, 16 March 1830, 26 March 1833, 8 April 1834]

Whittingham, Thomas, Liverpool, cm (1824–39). At 2 Duckworth in 1824; 5 Clayton St, 1829; 7 Clayton St, 1829–34; 30 Islington in 1837 and 65 Islington in 1839. [D]

Whittingham & Cattrall, Liverpool, cm (1823–35). At 2 Marble St 1823 but at 5 Marble St in 1827. In 1829 the address was 17 Gt Charlotte St and in 1835 21 Gt Charlotte St. [D]

Whittle, James, London, carver and gilder (1731–59). Whittle took three apps in the 1730s: James Griffith in 1731 for £10, Christopher Jackson in 1734 for £5 5s and Peter South in 1738 for £15 15s. [PRO, IRI/12, 14, 15] He took app. named Thomas Ashley for £31 10s in 1743 [IRI/17], a year after he supplied a carved and gilt chimney glass frame in the French taste for £11. [Account bk, Earl of Cardigan] Nothing else is known about him until his work for the Duke of Bedford at Woburn Abbey between 1752–55. This included 'a large glass and frame by a design of Mr. Kents Gilt all over like Mr.

Brands . . .' at a cost of £44 15s and another large Chinese style frame and glass for £43. [Bedford Office, London]

From some time in 1752 until May 1755 James Whittle was in partnership with his only son Thomas. Although working with his father, Thomas subscribed independently to Chippendale's *Director*, 1754. During the partnership, Whittle snr and jnr were responsible for carved stone work at Woburn Abbey, the bill for 1755 amounting to £697 11s 4d. Other work undertaken by the partnership included that at Petworth House. There are payments by the 2nd Earl of Egremont to James Whittle between 1753–59. In June 1753 Whittle was paid £88 9s for gilt frames, and a pier glass exists at Petworth House which is very similar in form to a pair at Holkham attributed to Whittle by Matthew Brettingham. [Jackson-Stops, 1980, fig. 9] The remaining payments totalled £1,332 15s.

Thomas Whittle died on 27 March 1755 and within a month James Whittle had a new partner and son-in-law, Samuel Norman. [Kirkham, 1969]

It was only after the death of James Whittle's only son that William Hallett, friend and fellow furniture maker, wrote to Whittle to ask if his nephew, Samuel Norman, could call on Whittle's daughter Ann with a view to marriage. Norman had pressed his uncle to do this on earlier occasions but Hallett had thought it unwise to do so because Norman was in the same business as Whittle and his son. However, when Whittle lost his son and his business was 'in a state of fateague' Hallett recommended his nephew as an ideal son-in-law and business partner. [PRO, C112/194 PT 11] Norman and Whittle's articles of co-partnership reflect the family tie: Norman was guaranteed half of the stock and goods-in-trade of Whittle and, if Norman's wife should have a child living at her father's death, then one half of Whittle's estate should pass to Samuel Norman. [Kirkham, 1969]

Business appears to have picked up after Norman joined Whittle. From November 1755 they subcontracted carving and gilding work to William Long of Long Acre who probably worked on some of their major commissions. [Kirkham, 1969] A full schedule of Long's work for the firm survives. [PRO, C 1287/20] The partners enjoyed the continuing patronage of the Duke of Bedford and the Earl of Egremont. Whittle and Norman were responsible for carving all the mouldings, door cases, screens of columns and other items of interior woodwork at Woburn Abbey which had not been done by the firm of Linnell. They received £1,065 1s 11d for carved work in 1755 and two years later work began on the gilding which, at times, occupied twelve gilders. Two magnificent carved and gilt oval frames with glasses which hang in the saloon at Woburn today were billed in January 1757. Whittle and Norman continued to work at Woburn until Whittle died in late 1759. After Whittle's death Norman submitted a bill for work done in 1759 which included an 'exceedingly large and grand oval frame with eagles' at £97 10s and a 'grand state bed', the furnishings of which cost £123 9s 7d and the frame £52 13s. [Bedford Office, London]

Lord Egremont paid James Whittle £1,332 15s between 1754–59. There are no surviving bills, but the firms of Whittle and Whittle and later Whittle and Norman clearly supplied a great deal of the carved furniture with which Petworth House was re-furnished, including pier tables and candlestands (which resemble work at Holkham) and the magnificent state bed. [Jackson-Stops, 1977 and 1982; *Rococo Exhib.*, V&A, 1984, L49] The frame for the pier glass in the ante-room at Holkham is believed to have been supplied by Whittle's firm in 1759 [Brettingham], although Lady Leicester ordered extra ornaments from the house carpenter and supplied the old glass which was used. [Cornforth and Schmidt, 1980]

Whittle and Norman also worked for the Earl of Holderness from 1755. In May 1758 he gave Whittle a bond for £250 which was not finally honoured by the Earl until nine years after Whittle's death. [PRO, C12 1299/11] They also supplied items totalling £73 14s including a pair of girandoles at £30 for James West in 1758 which were probably for his house in Covent Gdn. The bill was annotated 'dear', 'very dear' by West but was paid in full. [Warwick RO, Alscot Park MS, Box 42]

In 1759 the partners subscribed to William Chambers' *A Treatise of Civil Architecture*, giving their trade as 'Carvers and Gilders'. The firm of Whittle and Norman specialised in carving and gilding, particularly frames, but from September 1758 expanded into cabinet making and upholstery. [PRO, C12 1299/11] In November of that year they moved from Gt St Andrews St, Soho, and took over the premises of the late John West, cm of King St. They were joined briefly by John Mayhew who was probably brought in to help with the expansion into furniture making proper. Mayhew did not stay long, however, because by 1759 he was in partnership with William Ince who was formerly app. to John West. At the time of the move, an app. William Jackson, was taken on and recorded as bound to James Whittle, 'Citizen and Joiner', for £44. [PRO, IR1/21]

The partnership between Whittle and Norman lasted until Whittle's death on 10 December 1759. Whittle left half of his estate to Ann Norman, presumably because there was no heir, and the other half was put in trust for his grandson, John (son of the late Thomas) then a minor [PRO, Wills, Prob. 11/1759, 851 folio 424] Norman, however, was granted the use of John Whittle's half share of the firm's stock, goods-in-trade and book debts 'at an Appraised value'. [Kirkham, 1969]

Only thirteen days after Whittle's death the King St premises were consumed by a fire from which Samuel and Ann Norman were lucky to escape with their lives. The fire occurred before Richard Evatt and Robert Hyde had completed their inventory and valuation of Whittle and Norman's stock and goods in trade. This, together with the fact that most of the firm's records were destroyed in the fire, meant that it proved very difficult to sort out affairs between Norman and those who represented Whittle's grandson John. Norman was left with virtually no stock but, with the continued patronage of Egremont and others, he managed to re-build the business. [GCM; Heal; DEF; M. Brettingham, *The Plans, Elevations and Sections of Holkham House in Norfolk*, 1761, p. 3; G. Scott Thomson, *Family Background*, 1949; *Burlington*, December 1975; *Apollo*, February 1964; J. Cornforth and L. Schmidt, 'Holkham Hall, Norfolk, IV', *C. Life*, February 1980; G. Jackson-Stops, 'Furniture at Petworth House', *Apollo*, May 1977; G. Jackson-Stops, 'Rococo Masterpiece Restored: The Petworth State Bed', *C. Life*, 14 June 1984; P. Kirkham, 'Samuel Norman: a study of an eighteenth century craftsman', *Burlington*, August 1969]

4th EARL OF CARDIGAN. 1742: James Whittle supplied a carved and gilt chimney glass frame in the French taste costing £11. [MS Account bk, Earl of Cardigan, Deene Park, Northants.]

WOBURN ABBEY (4th Duke of Bedford). James and Thomas Whittle, 1752–55. [Bedford Office, London]

PETWORTH HOUSE (2nd Earl of Egremont). James and Thomas Whittle, 1753–55. [W. Sussex RO, Petworth archives]

WOBURN ABBEY (4th Duke of Bedford). James Whittle and Samuel Norman, 1755–59. [Bedford Office, London]

PETWORTH HOUSE (2nd Earl of Egremont). James Whittle and Samuel Norman, 1755–59. [Petworth archives]

HOLKHAM HALL (1st Earl of Leicester). James Whittle and Samuel Norman, c. 1759. [Brettingham, 1761]

4th EARL OF HOLDERNESS, probably for Hornby Castle, Yorks. James Whittle and Samuel Norman, 1755–59. [PRO, C12, 1299/11 and BM, Egerton MS 3497]

JAMES WEST, probably for his house in Covent Gdn. James Whittle and Samuel Norman, 1758. [Warwick RO, Alscot Park MS, Box 42] See Samuel Norman.   P. K.

Whittle, Peter, 30 Whittaker Row, Preston, Lancs., chairman (1818). [D]

Whittle, R., High St, Barnstaple, Devon, cm and u (1838). [D]

Whittle, Robert, Nantwich, Cheshire, u (d. 1818). [PR (burial)]

Whittle, Robert, London, u (1830–35). Previous to June 1830 he was in partnership with Benjamin Merriman Nias jnr and Whittle's address was given as Berners St, Middlx Hospital. From June 1830 he formed a new partnership with William Jones of Wigmore St, Cavendish Sq., auctioneer and appraiser. Whittle appears to have contributed no capital to the partnership. [PRO, C13/556]

Whittle, Thomas, London, carver (1752–d. 1755). In partnership with his father James Whittle, 1722–25. Admitted a member of the Joiners' Co. by consent 11 June 1754. In the same year subscribed to Chippendale's *Director*. See James Whittle.

Whittle, Thomas, St Paul, Covent Gdn, London, u (1767). In 1767 insured property in Mill St, parish of St Mary Magdalen, Bermondsey for £200. [GL, Hand in Hand MS vol. 106, ref. 22477]

Whittle, Thomas, Preston, Lancs. and London, cm (1802–22). Son of John Whittle, shoemaker. A freeman of Preston by 1802. One directory of 1818 gives his address as 10 Minsprit Weind and another as Tithebarn St and 15 Friargate. By 1822 he was living in London. His son John, also a freeman of Preston, was a portrait painter. [D; Preston Guild records]

Whittroe, William, Bullhead Ct, parish of St Sepulchre, London, chairmaker (1785). In 1785 took as app. James Smith. [Westminster Ref. Lib., MS F4309]

Whitton, Mr, St Margaret's Hill, London, u (1742). In September 1742 his marriage to the widow of Mr Pearman, u, was announced. Whitton was described as 'a reputable upholsterer'. [*Daily Post*, 6 September 1742]

Whitwell, Charles, 17 John St, Meadow Lane and Fisher's Yd, Leeds, Yorks., cm and joiner (1817–30). [D]

Whitworth, Benjamin, 65 Shudehill, Manchester, joiner and cm (1788–1800). In 1804 the business was being conducted by Mary Whitworth, possibly his widow. [D]

Whitworth, George, Market Pl., Bingham, Notts., joiner and cm (1832). [D]

Whitworth, John, Gamston, Notts., chairmaker (2nd quarter of 19th century). Windsor chairs are known stamped 'WHITWORTH GAMSTON'. [*Furn. Hist.*, 1978]

Whitworth, John, Nottingham, joiner and cm (1834). Named as joint master of app. Edward James in 1834. [Nottingham app. bk]

Whitworth, John, see James Yates.

Whitworth, John, Manchester, cm and u (1832–40). At 275 Oxford St, Chorlton Row, 1832–33 but in 1834 the number is shown as 274. In 1836 at 12 Oxford St but by 1840 the business was trading as John Whitworth & Co. at 16 Oxford St. [D]

Whitworth, Mary, 65 Shudehill, Manchester, joiner and cm (1804). Possibly the widow of Benjamin Whitworth who traded at this address 1788–1800. [D]

Whitworth, Thomas, London, upholder (1744). Son of Thomas Whitworth, freeman and clothworker. App. to George Friend on 20 March 1735 and free of the Upholders' Co. by servitude, May 1744. [GL, Upholders' Co. records.]

Whitworth & Greasley, Canal St, Nottingham, cm (1835). [D]

Wholler, Benjamin, address unknown, cm (1776). A mahogany wardrobe, the top enclosed by panelled doors and the lower part consisting of two short and two long drawers is known with the top part containing a description of how to take the wardrobe to pieces for transit. This is signed 'Benjm. Wholler Maker 1776'. This piece of furniture was formerly the property of Admiral Hardy of Portesham House, Dorset. [Sotheby's, 26 May 1961, lot 304]

Whormby, William, Lancaster (1827). [Westminster Ref. Lib., Gillow records]

Whyatt, W. G., Liverpool, carver and gilder (d. 1809). Death aged 60 announced, *Liverpool Courier*, 13 December 1809.

Whytall, T., Upper St, Islington, London, upholder (1839). [D]

Whytall, Thomas, 6 Sun St, Bishopsgate, Cripplegate, London, cm and u (1820–27). [D]

Wiblin, Henry, London (1752). The maker of a fine marquetry table. 'In the Centre is the Son situated with a double Glory, round the Glory is a Circumference of Stars consisting of 1344 Pieces; the upper Corner on the Right-hand is a Representation of the Moon; on the upper Corner of the left hand is the Eye of Providence; on the lower Corner on the Right Hand, is a Rainbow in an Octagon, on the lower Corner on the left hand, it forms again in a Smaller Circumference, hanging in an equilateral Triange, both cut in Geometry; with several other Curiosities; the whole being composed of 4978 Pieces of curious Wood'. In February 1752 it was announced that this table had been purchased by Mr Joseph Wright at 'The Three Cranes', Mile End. Henry Wiblin was said to be the son of the late John Wiblin. [*General Advertiser*, 13 February 1752]

Wick, Cullum, Bishopsgate St, London, upholder (1716–30). Son of James Wicks of Bury St Edmunds, Suffolk. App. to Thomas Paine of London, 29 September 1708 and free of the Upholders' Co. by servitude, 7 March 1715/16. Living in Bishopsgate St in 1727. Took as app. John Finch, 1722–30. [GL, Upholders' Co. records; Westminster poll bk]

Wicker, Nicholas, Exeter, Devon, cm (1803–14). Living in the parish of St Mary Major in 1803 when his name was included in a militia list. At Guinea St in December 1814 when his daughter Elizabeth was bapt. [PR (bapt.)]

Wickes, Thomas, Old Kent Rd, London, cm, u, appraiser and furniture broker (1820–39). At 1 Cumberland Pl. in 1826 and 16 Sussex Pl. in 1839. In 1839 described as a furniture broker only. [D]

Wickes, William, Dover, Kent, cm (1828–35). At 13 Townwall St in 1832 but in 1835 the address was given as Above Wall. [D; poll bks]

Wickham, J. H., 21 Wardour St, Soho, London, carver, gilder and picture dealer (*c.* 1840). Known only from undated trade cards in the Landauer Coll., MMA, NY. These indicate that he carried on a varied trade. He offered to buy or sell on commission 'Old Paintings, Carved Picture Frames, Antique Furniture, Pier Tables, Brackets, Bronzes, Ancient Books, Armour, China &c.' He attended sales in both London and the provinces and was prepared to bid for items on commission and also offered to clear 'Lumber or Store Rooms'.

Wicking, —, Edger Terr., Tunbridge Wells, Kent, carver and gilder (1839). [D]

Wicking (or Wickens), Benjamin, 3 Cumberland St, Curtain Rd, Shoreditch, London, cm, u and musical instrument maker (1823–27). In November 1823 took out insurance cover of £300 of which £200 was for stock and utensils. [D; GL, Sun MS vol. 494, ref. 1010422]

Wicks, Charles, 'The Ship', Snow Hill, London, u (1711–13). In June 1711 insured a house on the corner of Greville St and Brooke St for £300 and in August 1713 insured houses in Beare Alley and Sea Coal Lane for £250. [Heal; GL, Hand in Hand MS vol. 9, p. 49; vol. 12, pp. 6–7]

Wickstead, G., Middlx, cm (1826). Bankruptcy announced, *Liverpool Mercury*, 27 October 1826.

Wickstead, William, Liverpool, u (1840). Son of William Wickstead, cooper. Free 24 July 1840. [Freemen reg.]

Wicksted, John, London, upholder and cm (1754–68). Freeman of Bristol but living in London in 1754. In September 1768 quoted for furniture for William Drake of Shardeloes near Amersham, Bucks., his prices representing a 20% discount on those of John Linnell. [Bristol poll bk; Bucks. RO, Shardeloes papers]

Wicksteed, Edward, Nelson St, Deptford, London, carver and gilder (1839). [D]

Wicksteed, George, London, cm and bedstead maker (1816–39). At 10 Broad St, Golden Sq. 1816–27 but in 1835 at 31 Berwick St, Soho and in 1837–39 at 123 Wardour St. [D]

Widdal, Samuel, Knutsford, Cheshire, joiner and cm (1790). [D]

Widdicombe, M., Bristol, u (1834–*c.* 1840). At 9 Culver St in 1834, 48 College St, 1836–37, and from 1838 at 12 College St. [D]

Widdowson, Benjamin, Wood St, Ashby-de-la-Zouch, Leics., cm and u (1835). [D]

Widdowson, Thomas, Church St, Bingham, Notts., joiner and cm (1832). [D]

Widgington, Samuel, St Mary St, High Wycombe, Bucks., chairmaker (1839–41). Aged 30 at the time of the 1841 Census. [D]

Widgington, Thomas, High Wycombe, Bucks., chairmaker (b. *c.* 1776–1841). Bapt. September 1771 and in 1798 when his name was included in a milita return he gave his trade as chairmaker. In 1805 employed in the winter months by a farmer named Treacher to teach his labourers to assemble chairs from components made by local bodgers. Treacher clearly felt that farm work was insufficient in itself to fully employ them in the slack winter months. In 1809 Widgington took as app. John Briggs, a 'charity boy' of Great Missenden, Bucks. Widgington's son, Thomas jnr was bapt. 1814. At the time of the 1841 Census he declared his age to be 65 and stated his trade as timber merchant. [D; L. J. Mayes, *The History of Chairmaking in High Wycombe*, 1960, p. 25; PR (bapt.); Joy, *English Furniture 1800–1851*, p. 236]

Widgington, William, High Wycombe, Bucks., chairmaker (1798–1819). Included in a militia return in 1798. Sons bapt., 1816–19. [PR (bapt.)]

Wier, Hugh, Windsor, Berks., cm (1796–1804). [Poll bks]

Wierne (or Wiormo?), John Peter, address unknown, cm and frame maker (1736–42). Took as app. James Lynham but in July 1742 he applied for his discharge. He stated that he had been an app. of Wierne for five years and nine months and during this period he had been employed the entire time making picture frames. He had however been app. to learn the trade of cm. He further complained that for several meals in the week he received only bread and water. [Winterthur, Delaware, Symonds papers, 75x69.29]

Wife, Richard, Colchester, Essex and London, chairmaker (1784). Freeman of Colchester but in July 1784 living in London. [Colchester poll bk]

Wifeman & Yolland, 111 Tottenham Ct Rd, London, u (1819). [D]

Wiggan, Richard, Silver St, Golden Sq., London, cm (1749–51). Canaletto lodged at Wiggan's house and exhibited pictures there in 1749 and 1751. [Heal; Westminster poll bk]

Wiggens, John, Linen Hall St, Chester, cm (1826). Free 20 May 1826. [Freemen rolls; poll bk]

Wiggin, Jane, Goalgate St, Stafford, cm and u (1828). [D]

Wiggins, William, 21 Grove St, Commercial Rd, London, bed and bedstead maker (1813). [D]

Wiggins, William, Friar St, Reading, Berks., cm (1837). [Poll bk]

Wigglesworth, Robert & William, 8 King St, Blackburn, Lancs., cm and joiner (1816–34). [D]

Wigham, Richard, Dog-bank, Newcastle, cm and furniture broker (1824–33). [D]

Wight, Timothy, Buckingham St, York Buildings, London, u (1735–55). [*London Daily Post and General Advertiser*]

Wightman, Joseph, London, upholder (1705–29). Son of Joseph Wightman of Lindley, Leics., Gent. App. to Humphrey Skelton, 2 March 1704/05 and free of the Upholders' Co. by servitude, 3 September 1729. [GL, Upholders' Co. records]

Wightman, Ralph, Newcastle, u (1777). App. to John Hudson and free 25 February 1777. [Freemen rolls]

Wightman, Samuel, Framlingham, Suffolk, cm (1822). A letter survives from Lord Henniker to this cm dated November 1822. [*East Anglian Daily Times,* 2 December 1981]

Wigley, Benjamin, Chapel Hill, Belper, Derbs., cm (1829). [D]

Wightman, Thomas, High St, Doncaster, Yorks., carver and gilder (1830–37). [D]

Wightman (or Weightman), William, Nottingham, cm (1795). Son of William Wightman of Oxton, Notts., farmer. Free 1795. [App. bk; freemen lists]

Wignell, John, 'The Three Crowns', Cannon St, London, upholder (1709–12). Free 2 March 1708/09 and in July 1712 took out insurance cover on goods at the Cannon St address. [GL, Upholders' Co. records; Sun MS vol. 2, 20 July 1712]

Wike, Hougham, Canterbury, Kent and London, cm (1768). Freeman of Canterbury but living in London in 1768. [Freemen rolls]

Wikeley, Benjamin, 13 St Saviourgate, York, joiner and cm (1823–30). One directory of 1830 shows a William Wikeley at this address. [D]

Wilbee, William, Maryport St, Devizes, Wilts., cm and u (1822–39). [D]

Wilby, Samuel, Kirkgate, Wakefield, Yorks., cm (1814). [D]

Wilcke, Friedrich, address unknown, (1765–70). Employed by Sir John Griffin Griffin at Audley End, Essex on making furniture 1765–67 and 1770. Details of the work undertaken are not given apart from a reference to 'an organ barrel & setting twelve tunes upon it'. Payment appears to have been made regularly between 1765 and 1767 and in 1770 a further £11 12s was given to him for miscellaneous work. He appears to have been of German origin but his surname was anglicised as Wilke and Wilkie on some documents. [Essex RO, D/DBy/A26/1, D/DBy/A28/4]

Wilcock, Crs., Lancaster (1837–39). Named in the Gillow records in 1837 and 1839. [Westminster Ref. Lib., Gillow]

Wilcock, Edward, Thornhill, near Dewsbury, Yorks., chairmaker (1822). [D]

Wilcock, James, Lancaster (1786–1840). Named in the Gillow records in 1786, 1799, 1815, 1819, 1821, 1827, 1829, 1833 and 1838–40. His son was named in 1834 and 1836. [Westminster Ref. Lib., Gillow]

Wilcock, James, Menwith, near Settle, Yorks., cm (1822). [D]

Wilcock, James, Bentham Low, near Ingleton, Yorks., cm and victualler (1822). [D]

Wilcock, John, Lancaster (1826–33). Named in the Gillow records 1826–29 and 1831–33. [Westminster Ref. Lib., Gillow]

Wilcock, Joseph, Lancaster (1806–40). Named in the Gillow records 1806, 1826, 1829–30, 1839–40. [Westminster Ref. Lib., Gillow]

Wilcock, Joseph, Lancaster, cm (1838). App. to L. Redmayne in 1830 and free 27 October 1838. [App. reg.]

Wilcock, Richard, Liverpool, cm (1756–65). His apps Isaac Wardley and William Fairclough petitioned freedom in 1765. [Freemen committee bk; S of G, app. index]

Wilcock, Richard, Lancaster (1806–17). Named in the Gillow records 1806–13 and 1815–17. [Westminster Ref. Lib., Gillow]

Wilcock, Robert, Thornhill, near Dewsbury, Yorks., chairmaker (1822). [D]

Wilcock, Robert, Lancaster, cm (1839). App. to L. Redmayne 1832 and free 27 July 1839. [App. reg.]

Wilcock, Samuel, Below Stockgill, Ambleside, Westmld, cm (1829). [D]

Wilcock, Thomas, York(?), chairmaker (1729). The York city accounts for 13 January 1729 show a charge due to this maker for 18 chairs at 8s and 6 oak chairs at 3s 6d 'to Walmgate Bar'.

Wilcock, Thomas, Lancaster, cm (1830–40). App. to L. Redmayne in 1830 and free 28 October 1837. Named in the Gillow records 1832, 1835–36 and 1840. [App. reg.; Westminster Ref. Lib., Gillow]

Wilcocks, J., Bridge St, Chester, cm (1833). In February 1833 his stock and household furniture was auctioned for the benefit of his creditors. This included 'a handsome zebra wood circular table, pair of handsome zebra wood card tables, zebra wood pier table, painted dressing tables and wash stands, sets of mahogany chairs, several hearth rugs and carpet covers, a few sets of papers and borders, three platform dressing glasses, two sofas, a mahogany Bergère chair, four cabinet making benches nearly new.' [*Chester Courant,* 19 February 1833]

Wilcocks, Thomas, Gloucester, upholder (1723–46). In April 1723 it was reported that Wilcocks and two others had been set upon by Dragoons of Honeywood Regiment. He was declared bankrupt, *Gents Mag.,* November 1746. [*Gloucester Journal,* 26 April 1723]

Wilcocks, Bath, Som., cm (1823). Bankruptcy announced, *Liverpool Mercury,* 21 December 1832.

Wilcocks, William, Uttoxeter, Staffs., cm (1798). [D]

Wilcocks & Co., 176 Fore St, Exeter, Devon, cm and u (1838). [D]

Wilcockson, Joseph, Louth, Lincs., cm and joiner (1780–87). In 1780 took out insurance cover of £300 which included £240 for his house and workshop. A payment of 16s in the Massingberd account book for March 1787 is recorded for Wilcockson for eight kitchen chairs. [GL, Sun MS vol. 284, p. 109; Lincoln RO, MM9/10]

Wilcox, Edward, Shepton Mallet, Som., cm (1740). In 1740 took app. named Gibson. [S of G, app. index]

Wilcox, Humphrey, Below the Conduit, Exeter, Devon, u (1724–31). In October 1724 he advertised that he had taken over the business previously conducted by Anne Alden. In 1725 he took app. named Davie but Wilcox was declared bankrupt, *Gents Mag.,* April 1731. [*The Post Master,* 23 October 1724; S of G, app. index]

Wilcox, James Morris, Chapel St, Warwick (1834–40). An accomplished carver who undertook a number of major commissions for George Lucy of Charlecote Park, Warks. in the late 1830s. A carved sideboard was charged at £1,600 in 1837 and the total account for the period 1834–37 for woodwork in the library and dining room including mouldings and edges for the bookshelves amounted to £4,982 18s. A receipted bill dated 17 January 1840 exists for completing the library shelves and making an oak table for the dining room. [V&A archives; Warwick RO, L6/1118]

Wilcox, Leonard James, 15 Stacey St, Soho, London, carver (1822–23). Took out insurance cover of £300 in September 1822 and £400 in November 1823 but in both years utensils and stock were valued at £50. [GL, Sun MS vol. 490, ref. 995700; vol. 495, ref. 1010540]

Wilcox, Richard, London, upholder (1729). Son of Robert Wilcox of London distiller. App. to John Weston, 3 March 1719 and free of the Upholders' Co. by servitude, 2 April 1729. [GL, Upholders' Co. records]

Wilcox, Thomas, London, upholder (1710). In 1710 took out insurance cover of £400 each on two houses, one in Duck Lane and the other in St Bartholomew's Close, both in West Smithfield. [GL, Hand in Hand MS vol. 8, refs 20615–16]

Wilcoxon, Harding, Owen & Stanton, London, cm and looking-glass makers (1815–39). At 58 Lombard St, 1815–37 but in 1839 at 1 Monument Lane. Declared their trade as wholesale looking-glass and cabinet manufacturers, 1820–25. [D]

Wild, Daniel, 'The Golden Ball', south-east corner of St Paul's Churchyard, London, cm (c. 1725). Known only from his trade labels affixed to furniture. A walnut table on cabriole legs terminating in pad feet is recorded with his label, as is also a walnut tallboy with secretaire drawer and sunburst in the recessed centre of the lowest drawer. [Heal; Christie's, 19 June 1980, lot 91, 27 January 1983, lot 156]

Wild, Jacob, Hanging Ditch, Manchester, chairmaker (1773–1804). At 52 Hanging Ditch in 1797 but the number was 25 in 1800. [D]

Wild, Jacob, Tib Lane, Manchester, picture frame maker (1773–94). On 17 September 1773 paid £1 11s for fourteen frames for prints supplied to Dunham Massey, Cheshire. In 1794 his number in Tib Lane was 6. [D; John Rylands Lib., Manchester Univ., George Cooke's accounts]

Wild, James, Wharf St, Dukinfield, near Ashton-under-Lyne, Lancs., joiner and cm (1834). [D]

Wild, John, Manchester, u and auctioneer (1794–1833). In 1794 at Cateaton St but from 1797 at 8 Hunt's Bank. [D]

Wild, John, 12 Ranelagh St, Liverpool, carver, gilder and looking-glass manufacturer (1827). [D]

Wild (or Wylde), Nathaniel, Nottingham, u (1692–d. 1731). Recorded in the list of freemen 1692 and 1712. Will dated 4 January 1731 was proved 20 December 1731. [Freemen rolls; Notts. RO, probate records]

Wild (or Wylde), Richard, London, upholder (1773–94). Son of James Wylde of Shepperton, Middlx, farmer. App. to Isaac Solly of London, 7 February and free of the Upholders' Co. by servitude, 6 October 1773. From 1776–81 at 1 Budge Row; in 1786 at 53 Gracechurch St, and from 1792–94 at 57 Bishopsgate St. In November 1792 he took out insurance cover of £200 on goods and a house rented from Wrench, a watchmaker. [GL, Upholders' Co. records; Sun MS vol. 391, p. 415]

Wild, Thomas, Union St, Salford, Lancs., cm (1800–04). At 9 Union St, 1800–02 but in 1804 the number was 10. [D]

Wild, Thomas, 2 Paradise St, Manchester, u (1817). [D]

Wild, William, 25 Red Bank, Manchester, cm (1804). [D]

Wild, William, 53 Cannon St Rd, St George's-in-the-East, London, cm, u and undertaker (1820–35). [D]

Wild, William, Weekday Cross, Nottingham, u (1822–34). [D]

Wild, William, Nottingham, cm (1820–28). At Bridlesmithgate in 1820 and Middle Pavement in 1828. [D; poll bk]

Wilde, James, address unknown, cm (1803). Subscribed to Sheraton's *Cabinet Dictionary*, 1803.

Wilde, Joseph, Manchester, cm and u (1829–40). At 9 Bond St in 1829, 10 Bond St, 1832–34 and 21 Bond St, 1836–39. In 1838–39 trading additionally from an address in Faulkner St which was numbered 67 in 1838 and 157 in 1839. In 1840 at 100 Grosvenor St, Chorlton-on-Medlock. [D]

Wilde, Thomas, Manchester, cm and u (1825–29). At 11 Rutland St, Chorlton Row in 1825 and 5 King St, 1828–29. [D]

Wilde, Walter, 1 Moor Pl., Liverpool, cm (1837). [D]

Wilder, Leonard, Wantage, Berks., cm (1761). In 1761 took app. named Belsher. [S of G, app. index]

Wildey, John, Pelham St, Nottingham, u (1840). [D]

Wildey, Thomas & H., Berwick St, Soho, London, bedstead and cornice makers (1816–39). The number in Berwick St was 25 but from 1820 no. 34 was also used. In 1820 insurance cover of £600 was taken out on 25 Berwick St by Thomas Wildey. Of this £350 covered stock and utensils and a further £100 open workshops and an open yard behind no. 25. A further £300 cover was taken out later in that year in respect of stock and utensils in a stable and lofts over it behind 34 Berwick St. By July 1822 the insurance cover on 25 Berwick St had fallen to £300 of which half was for utensils and stock and £50 on the open workshops and yard. [D; GL, Sun MS vol. 483, refs 970083, 974380; vol. 493, ref. 993859]

Wildgoose, John, North Audley St, Grosvenor Sq., cm (1745). [Heal]

Wildgoose, Joseph, London, upholder (1802). Freeman of Oxford. [Oxford poll bk]

Wildgoose, Joseph, Heaton Lane, Stockport, Cheshire, cm (1825). [D]

Wildin, James, 27 London Rd, Manchester, cm (1834–36). [D]

Wilding, Benjamin, Manchester, cm (1804–08). At 62 Little Lever St in 1804 and 76 London Rd in 1808. [D]

Wilding, Robert, Liverpool, cm (1761). App. to Nicholas Cross and free 13 March 1761. [Freemen rolls]

Wilding, Thomas, Liverpool, cm (1806). In July 1806 married at St Anne's Church to a Miss L. Baldock of Liverpool. [*Liverpool Chronicle*, 23 July 1806]

Wilding, Thomas, Liverpool, cm (1812). App. to Edward Lowe and free 5 October 1812. [Freemen rolls]

Wilding, Thomas, 49 Vernon St, Liverpool, cm (1813–18). [D]

Wildman, Mr, London, joiner or carver (1694). On 26 June 1694 signed a petition as a member of the 'Company of Joyners Carvers' that was presented by that Company to the City of London. [*Furn. Hist.*, 1974]

Wildman, John, Hotwell Rd, Bristol, picture frame maker (1801). [D]

Wildman, Thomas, London, upholder (1681–90). In March 1681 supplied to William 5th Earl of Bedford 10 varnished back chairs at 9s each and 3 armchairs at 13s each. The receipt was signed by Richard Linnell, probably an employee of Wildman. In 1688–90 supplied chairs and stools to the Royal Hospital, Chelsea amounting to £46 15s. [Bedford Office, London; *Wren Soc.*, vol. XIX, p. 85]

Wildridge, John, 6 Matthew St, Liverpool, joiner and cm (1790). [D]

Wildsmith, Benjamin & Riley, 99 High Holborn, London, u and cm (1786–88). By January 1788 in financial difficulties and on the 13th a dividend was advertised for his creditors. A demi-lune card table is known bearing their trade label. [D; *Williamson's Liverpool Advertiser*, 28 January 1788]

Wildsmith, John, near St James's Church, Piccadilly, London, mason and carver (1757–82). His work appears to have been in the main with stone. He did however in July 1759 supply for a pier table in the Tapestry Room at Croome Court, Worcs. a black marble top inset with 176 squares of coloured stones which was charged at £42 10s. He was made bankrupt in 1769 and on 31 July and 1 August of that year a sale was held of the contents of his yard in Piccadilly. He may however have recommenced trading, for in December 1782 a dividend was advertised to the creditors of John Wildsmith of St James, Westminster, carver. [Gunnis; V&A archives; *Leicester Journal*, 28 December 1782]

Wildsmith, William, Worcester St, Bromsgrove, Worcs., chair-maker (1835). [D]

Wiles, John, near King's Stairs, Rotherhithe, London, carver

(1733). In October 1733 insured his household goods, utensils and stock for £300. [GL, Sun MS vol. 38, ref. 62088]

Wiles, Samuel, King St, Norwich, cm and u (1830–36). [D]

Wilkerson, John, High Wycombe, Bucks., chairmaker (1815–24). Three sons and a daughter bapt. 1815–24. [PR (bapt.)]

Wilkerson, Thomas, Burnham, Norfolk, carver (1757). In 1757 took app. named Witherson. [S of G, app. index]

Wilkes, George, London(?), u (before 1737). In March 1737 his widow, said to be 'a lady of about £6,000 fortune', married Richard Browgh, a 'very eminent farmer in Middlesex', at St Mary-hill Church. George Wilkes was said to have been 'an eminent upholsterer'. [*Daily Journal*, 15 March 1737]

Wilkes, John, 7 Pembroke St, Liverpool, cm (1837). [D]

Wilkes, Thomas, Worcester, joiner and cm (1773). App. to William Reding and free 11 January 1773. [Freemen rolls]

Wilkes, Thomas, Lancaster, gilder (1795). [Westminster Ref. Lib., Gillow records]

Wilkes, Thomas, 13 Smithfield St, Liverpool, cm (1818). [D]

Wilkes, Thomas, Broad St, Hereford, chairmaker and turner (1822–35). [D]

Wilkie, Alexander, 10 Duke St, Portland Sq., London, upholder and undertaker (1817–29). [D]

Wilkie, John, see Wilkie & Cochran.

Wilkie, William, London, cm (1793). Subscribed to Sheraton's *Drawing Book*, 1793.

Wilkie, William, 91 Percy St, Newcastle, cm and joiner (1838). [D]

Wilkie & Cochran, London, cm and chairmaker (1817–40). In 1817–18 John Wilkie was trading on his own account from 1 Norfolk St, Fitzroy Sq. but by 1820 he was in partnership with William Cochran at 20 Nassau St, Middlx Hospital. Insurance valuations at this period suggest a business of substantial size. These totalled £2,450 in May 1820, £1,900 in April 1822 and £2,100 in April 1823, the majority being for utensils and stock. Workshops were maintained behind the Nassau St premises. The partnership was still operating in 1840. A Regency bergère chair in rosewood is recorded stamped 'WILKIE AND COCHRAN'. A set of ten single chairs and two armchairs are also recorded marked with the name of John Wilkie. Also known is a trade label of John Wilkie from the 20 Nassau St address endorsed 'LATE WILKIE & COCHRAN'. This would seem to represent a post 1840 situation. [D; GL, Sun MS vol. 483, refs 966639–40; vol. 493, ref. 991422; vol. 498, ref. 1003754; Phillips', 22 March 1983, lot 92; V&A archives]

Wilkin, John, 5 Percy St, Liverpool, cm (1829). [D]

Wilkin (or Wilkins), W. & A., Hope Chapel Hill, Bristol, u (1835–36). [D]

Wilkins, Charles, Robertson's Pl., Stockwell, London, carver and gilder (1839). [D]

Wilkins, George, London, upholder (1773–81). Son of George Wilkins. App. to John Dunn, 1 December 1773 and then to Richard Walker, 3 September 1779. Free of the Upholders' Co. by servitude, 2 May 1781. [GL, Upholders' Co. records]

Wilkins, George, London, upholder (1719). Living at 3 Bride Lane, Fleet St, but by January 1791 mention is made of his new dwelling house in Bear Alley. Insurance cover on the contents of his house amounted to only £100. [GL, Sun MS vol. 327, p. 27]

Wilkins, George, 255 Bermondsey St, London, upholder (1809). In March 1809 took out insurance cover of £150 on household goods. [GL, Sun MS vol. 444, ref. 828283]

Wilkins, John, Palmer St, Frome, Som., cm and u (1839–40). [D]

Wilkins, Robert, Oxford (1765). Described as the carpenter of Christchurch, Oxford. In 1764 Thomas Chippendale supplied a number of stools for the College Library and in the

following year Wilkins made a number of additional ones which, together with tables, he charged at £40 7s 6d. [*C. Life*, 5 January 1945]

Wilkins, Thomas, 9 and 10 Broker Row, London, cm and u (1822). [D]

Wilkins, William, 20 Edward St, Cavendish Sq., London, cm and u (1805–11). [D]

Wilkinson, —, Preston, Lancs., see Tyrer & Wilkinson.

Wilkinson, —, Oxford St, London (1833). According to Loudon had 'extensive collections of Elizabethan and Dutch furniture and carvings, from which a judicious compiler of exteriors might clothe skeleton frames, so as to produce objects of curiosity and interest, at a very triffling expense'. Also mentioned as one of a number of London firms who collected 'curious and ancient furniture, including fragments of fittings-up of rooms, altars and religious houses; and rearrange these curious specimens, and adapt them to modern uses'. [Loudon, *Encyclopaedia*, pp. 1039, 1101]

Wilkinson, Alexander, Skipton, Yorks., cm (1839). [PR]

Wilkinson, Caleb, Nottingham, cm (d. 1719). Probate granted on his will 13 May 1719. [Notts. RO, probate records]

Wilkinson, Charles, 21 St Paul's Churchyard, London, cm, u and chairmaker (1748–93). His marriage to Miss Angelica Parnell, sister to Captain Parnell of Limehouse was announced on 6 January 1748. The marriage took place at Enfield, Middlx. The bride was described as 'a very agreeable Lady of Good Fortune' and the groom as 'an eminent Cabinet Maker in St. Paul's Churchyard'. Wilkinson was a member of the Joiners' Co. and between 1751 and 1774 took out a number of licences to employ non-freemen. The number so employed was substantial, from 1763 amounting to twelve on one occasion and averaging about seven to eight. From 1790 the business traded as Wilkinson & Turner [D; *General Advertiser*, 6 January 1748; GL, Joiners' Co. records, Livery list 1750; City Licence bks, vols 1, 3–8, 11]

Wilkinson, Edward, Thursday Mkt, York, cm (1758). [Poll bk]

Wilkinson, Edward, Peterborough, Northants., u and cm (1766–98). His marriage to a Miss Bates was announced in October 1766 and he was described as 'an eminent upholsterer and cabinet maker'. By March 1777 he was bankrupt but must have resumed business again almost immediately for in the following year he insured utensils and stock for £160 out of a total cover of £200. The total cover was unchanged in 1782 but stock and utensils were only valued at £100. In April 1790 he advertised himself as an upholder and auctioneer and indicated that he stocked both secondhand and new furniture. He offered 'Dining, Tea, Pembroke, and Dressing Tables; Bureaus, Commodes, and Dressing Chests of Drawers; Night Tables; Bason Stands; Knife Cases; Dinner Trays, Tea Boards, Caddies &c.; Sofas, Chairs with Hair Seats; several sorts of Chamber Ditto; Windsor Chairs, &c.; some very Handsome Pier Glasses; also Toilet and Dressing ditto; likewise every article in the Upholstery Line for fitting up beds and Window Curtains in the best Manner; a great variety of Carpets, of the newest Patterns, and best Quality, both for Floors and Staircases; also a fresh Assortment of the most fashionable Spring Patterns of Paper Hangings, with a great Variety of elegant Fancy Borders to them'. He also had on offer a collection of paintings and prints 'by eminent Masters'. His name appears in trade directories as late as 1798 but in July 1802 when the death of his son was announced he was described as the 'son of the late Mr. Wilkinson, Upholder'. [D; *Cambridge Chronicle*, 18 October 1766; *Gents Mag.*, March 1777, July 1802; GL, Sun MS vol. 267, p. 561; vol. 303, p. 513; *Lincoln, Rutland and Stamford Mercury*, 2 April 1790]

Wilkinson, Edward, Colne, Lancs., joiner and cm (1824–34). At

Market St, 1824–28 but in 1834 the address was given as Newhouse Backside. [D]

Wilkinson, George, Nantwich, Cheshire, chairmaker (1812–14). A son John was bapt on 29 April 1812 and a daughter Sarah on 20 July 1814. [PR (bapt.)]

Wilkinson, George, Haslingden, Lancs., cm/joiner (1822–34). At Higher Lane in 1823, High St in 1824 and Queen St in 1834. [D]

Wilkinson, George, Market Pl., Settle, Yorks., joiner and cm (1822–37). [D]

Wilkinson, George, Salford, Lancs., carver, gilder, looking-glass and picture frame maker (1822–36). At 94 Chapel St, 1822–28, but in the following year the number was 93. At 73 Bridge St, 1832–36. [D]

Wilkinson, George snr, Boroughgate, Appleby, Westmld, cm (1828–29). [D]

Wilkinson, George jnr, Boroughgate, Appleby, Westmld, cm (1829–34). [D]

Wilkinson, Henry, High St, Watford, Herts., cm and u (1838–39). [D]

Wilkinson, J., 10 Crawford Passage, London, bedstead manufacturer (1835). [D]

Wilkinson, J., 4 East St, Finsbury, London, cm (1839). [D]

Wilkinson, James, Market St, Bradford, Yorks., cm and u (1793–1830). In 1830 the number in Market St was 61. On 2 January 1801 insured his workshops for £100. [D; GL, Sun MS vol. 37, ref. 713358]

Wilkinson, James, Union Warehouse Yd, Hilton St, Manchester, joiner and cm (1804–08). [D]

Wilkinson, James, Nantwich, Cheshire, chairmaker (1831–40). Married 18 April 1831 and a son James was bapt. 23 April 1834. [D; PR (bapt. and marriage)]

Wilkinson, John, Newcastle, u (1700). Son of Gawin Wilkinson, mariner. Free by patrimony, 17 June 1700. [Freemen rolls]

Wilkinson, John, Nottingham, cm (1713). [Freemen rolls]

Wilkinson, John, London, upholder (1724). Son of Thomas Wilkinson, freeman and member of the Upholders' Co. John Wilkinson jnr was admitted to the Company by patrimony, 16 April 1724. [GL, Upholders' Co. records]

Wilkinson, John, Tarporley, Cheshire (?), chairmaker (1773–74). In 1773–74 made two dozen common chairs, a pair of arm chairs and the President's chair for the Tarporley Hunt Club. He appears to have been a local craftsman. The chairs are still in the possession of the Club. [Minute bks]

Wilkinson, John, Market Pl., Leicester, cm and u (1786). In September 1786 came from London to take over the business of the late James James. [*Leicester Journal*, 9 September 1786]

Wilkinson, John, Highgate Hill, London, upholder and cm (1790). Death announced, *Gents Mag.*, 1790, p. 1154.

Wilkinson, John, 48 Marylebone Lane, London, cm and furniture broker (1826–29). [D]

Wilkinson, John, Thomas St, Manchester, cm, u and furniture broker (1829–40). At 18 Thomas St, 1829–33 but from 1836 the number was 41. [D]

Wilkinson, John, 12 Gt Barlow St, Marylebone, London, cm and u (1839). [D]

Wilkinson, John-Henry, London, wholesale u and cm (1794–99). At 25 Budge Row, 1794–97 and 49 Gracechurch St, 1798–99. [D]

Wilkinson, Joseph snr, Watergate St, Chester, cm (1741–71). Free 1741. Took apps named Prestbury in 1742 and James Habbot in 1752. [Freemen rolls; poll bks; S of G, app. index; app. bk]

Wilkinson, Joseph jnr, Chester, cm (1767–1812). Son of Joseph Wilkinson snr and free 12 December 1767. At Watergate St in 1771, Lower Lane in 1784 and Linenhall St in 1812. [Freemen rolls; poll bks]

Wilkinson, Joseph, London, cm and u (1780–84). Associated with Joshua Wilkinson snr and jnr in the business of Wilkinson & Sons which operated a cabinet and upholstery warehouse in the City and Moorfields area. This business was established by 1778 at 24 Change Alley but a fire at this address forced them to re-locate at 107 Cheapside opposite the Church of St Mary-le-Bow by the following year. A trade bill [GL] indicates the nature of the business. They advertised themselves as a 'Cabinet, Upholstery, Carpet & Looking Glass Warehouse' and indicated that their stock included down, goose and other feather beds; Turkey, Brussels, Wilton, Kidderminster and Scotch carpets; library, writing, ladies' dressing, Pembroke card and tea tables; cabroile, japanned and Windsor chairs etc.'. By 1784 the business had moved again to 7 Lower Moorfields which is also rendered as 7 Brokers Row, Moorfields. Stock and utensils were valued at £300 out of a total insurance cover of £1,500 in 1778 but one policy of 1782 was for £2,100 with stock and utensils £1,400 of this. These figures suggest a substantial enterprise. No references to Joseph Wilkinson have been found subsequent to 1784 and by 1790 the business appears to have been operated by William and Thomas Wilkinson in partnership. [D; GL, Sun MS vol. 270, p. 318; vol. 287, p. 190; vol. 299, p. 341; vol. 300, p. 9]

Wilkinson, Joshua snr, London, upholder, cm and broker (1778–80). Associated with his son Joshua and with Joseph Wilkinson in the business of Wilkinson & Sons (see entry for Joseph Wilkinson). Joshua Wilkinson snr was a member of the Goldsmiths' Co. He is recorded at Change Alley in 1778 in which year he took out a licence to employ twenty non-freemen for three months. A further licence was issued in 1780 to employ the same number of six months. The address then given was Cheapside. These licences might suggest an extensive manufacturing side to the business. His son Joshua jnr was made free of the Upholders' Co. in 1781. [D; GL, City Licence bks, vols 9, 10; Upholders' Co. records]

Wilkinson, Joshua jnr, London, upholder, cm and broker (1781–85). Son of Joshua Wilkinson snr and free of the Upholders' Co. under the terms of the 1750 Upholders' Act, 5 September 1781. His addresses are shown at 107 Cheapside, 1781–84 and 7 Brokers Row, Moorfields in 1785 clearly indicating his involvement in the business of Wilkinson & Sons (for details see entry for Joseph Wilkinson). [D; Heal; GL, Upholders' Co. records]

Wilkinson, Joshua, Leicester, u (1791). In 1791 moved from Market Pl. to Cornwall. [D]

Wilkinson, Lawrence, Bolton St, Chorley, Lancs., cm (1818). [D]

Wilkinson, Lawrence, 18 Peter Lane, Liverpool, cm (1827–39). [D]

Wilkinson, Matthew, Coppergate, York, cm (1784). [Poll bk]

Wilkinson, Matthew, Top of Nile St, Preston, Lancs., cm (1818). [D]

Wilkinson, Peter, address unknown, cm (1803). Subscribed to Sheraton's *Cabinet Dictionary*, 1803.

Wilkinson, Richard, address unknown, cm and u (1750). Paid £2 8s 6d by Mrs Bowes for a mahogany chest of drawers on 26 May 1750. On 29 September of the same year paid a further £1 3s 'for a mahogany and damask chair for the child'. A bill also exists made out to George Bowes and dated 26 May 1750 'for a mahogany dressing-table and packing', £2 8s. [Durham RO, D/St/V1488–90, D/St/327c]

Wilkinson, Richard, 1 Cross St, Hatton Gdn, London, cm (1781). In 1781 insured his house for £200. [GL, Sun MS vol. 295, p. 356]

Wilkinson, Richard, 2 Goodge St, Tottenham Ct Rd, London, cm and broker (1786). In August 1786 took out insurance cover of £500 which included £350 for utensils and stock. [GL, Sun MS vol. 338, p. 560]

Wilkinson, Richard, Thomas St, Wrangling, Blackburn, Lancs., cm (1818). [D]

Wilkinson, Richard, Toll House Hill, Nottingham, joiner and cm (1799). [D]

Wilkinson, Richard, Broadmarsh, Nottingham, turner and chairmaker (1832–40). In 1824 app. to Aaron Boot. Trading at Broadmarsh by 1831 when his trade was declared as chairmaker. [D; app. reg.]

Wilkinson, Robert, 67 Newman St, London, upholder (1780). In 1780 insured a house for £1,000. [GL, Sun MS vol. 286, p. 9]

Wilkinson, Samuel, Nottingham, cm (1722). Freeman of Nottingham. [Freemen rolls]

Wilkinson, Samuel, 3 Christopher St, Hatton Wall, London, cm (1820). [D]

Wilkinson, Stephen, York, joiner (1703–29). Free 1703. On 26 November 1729 charged £6 for 'six oak bedsteads and saking booms to them all got up in my lord Mayor hous beside the common hall'. [Freemen rolls; York City archives]

Wilkinson, Stephen, Bywardle, Nottingham, cm (1720–54). Included in freemen list, 1720. [Freemen rolls; poll bk]

Wilkinson, Thomas, London, upholder (1724). A freeman and member of the Upholders' Co. His son John Wilkinson was made free of this Company in 1724. [GL, Upholders' Co. records]

Wilkinson, Thomas, Lancaster, cm (1754–68). App. to J. Wright in 1754 and free 1761–62. [App. reg.; poll bk]

Wilkinson, Thomas, Stonecutter St, near Fleet Ditch, London, looking-glass maker (1725). [Heal]

Wilkinson, Thomas, Newcastle, joiner and cm (1760). In 1760 took app. named Hedley. [S of G, app. index]

Wilkinson, Thomas, Padon, Newcastle, cm and carpenter (1778). [D]

Wilkinson, Thomas & Co., London, cm and u (1812–28). At 9 Brokers Row, Moorfields, 1814–17, and 7–10 Brokers Row and 1 Finsbury Sq., 1823–28. Successor to William & Thomas Wilkinson. [D; Heal]

Wilkinson, Thomas, Hull, Yorks., cm, u and chairmaker (1823–26). At Stubb's Ct in 1823 when he was described as a cm. In 1826 at Stubb's Buildings, West St and his trade was given as chairmaker and u. [D]

Wilkinson, Thomas, St Margaret's Bank, Rochester, Kent, cm (1824). [D]

Wilkinson, Thomas, Gt Aycliffe, near Darlington, Co. Durham, joiner and cm (1828). [D]

Wilkinson, Thomas, George St, Wakefield, Yorks., u (1830). [D]

Wilkinson, Thomas, Gt Ayton, Durham, joiner/cm (1834). Possibly a directory error and the person recorded was the Thomas Wilkinson shown in another directory working at Aycliffe, Co. Durham in 1828. [D]

Wilkinson, Thomas, Bromyard, Herefs., cm (1835). [D]

Wilkinson, Thomas Jowett, 60 Market St, Bradford, Yorks., cm (1834). [D]

Wilkinson, W., 28 Rood Lane, London, cm etc. (1801). [D]

Wilkinson, W., 20 Somerset St, Aldgate, London, cm (1825). [D]

Wilkinson, W. A., 17 Clifford's Inn, London, u (1829). [D]

Wilkinson, W. & C., Ludgate Hill, London, see William Wilkinson.

Wilkinson, William, Newcastle, u (1750). Free 1750. His son Fenwick was made free by patrimony 6 March 1777. [Freemen rolls]

Wilkinson, William, Liverpool, cm (1760). App. to William Boardman and petitioned for his freedom in 1760. [Freemen's committee bk]

Wilkinson, William, 32 New George St, St George's Rd, London, cm and broker (1779). In 1779 took out insurance cover for £300 of which half was for utensils and stock. [GL, Sun MS vol. 271, p. 311]

Wilkinson, William & Thomas, 9 and 10 Broker Row, Moorfields, London, cm (1790–1811). Successors to Wilkinson & Sons and succeeded by Thomas Wilkinson & Co. Their particular specialism was extending tables and in 1807 they were advertising tables covered 'by the King's patent' and 'absolutely original in their Construction'. They claimed that their dining table occupied when closed 'a space considerable smaller than is necessary for the standing of any other dining table now in use'. It could however 'with utmost facility, be extended to any required length'. Also offered were a 'breakfast Table, of the most desirable dimensions, forms a complete set of Dining Tables for sixteen or eighteen persons; and in firmness, convenience and elegance, cannot possibly be exceeded. The Patent Card Table is equally remarkable for its ornamental effect, and for the singularity of the principles on which it is made'. They claimed to be the sole sellers of such tables, which could be obtained from their manufactory and warerooms at 'No, 10 North side of Moorfields near Finsbury Square'. A number of dining tables made by this manufacturer have been noted. One extending on the 'lazy tongs' principle bears the patent number 523 and another is marked 'PATENT 284 MOORFIELD, WILKINSON, LONDON'. [D; *Brighton Herald*, 3 January 1807; V&A archives; Sotheby's, Rainbow, Torquay, 30 September/1 October 1981, lot 772A]

Wilkinson, William, 18 Charlotte St, Hull, Yorks., cm and joiner (1814–26). Directory listings from 1822 suggest that at this stage he was largely engaged on joinery work. [D]

Wilkinson, William, Leeds, Yorks., cm and u (1814–30). At 31 Upperhead Row (or Upper Row), 1814–17, 90 Kirkgate in 1826 and 15 Kirkgate, 1828–30. [D]

Wilkinson, William, Market St, Chorley, Lancs., cm and joiner (1818). [D]

Wilkinson, William, 14 Ludgate Hill, London, cm and u (1808–40). William Wilkinson had formerly been a partner with Thomas Wilkinson at Brokers Row, Moorfields but the partnership broke up soon after 1807 and by 1808 William was trading on his own account at Ludgate Hill. Thomas continued the business in Moorfields. At the Moorfields address the partners had shown an interest in patent furniture and especially tables. William clearly saw commercial advantage in promoting patent furniture at his new address and in October 1812 advertised patent bedsteads 'which for their utter utility, firmness, and simplicity, surpass everything of the kind ever presented to the public: they effectually exclude vermin, and may be fixed and unfixed in five minutes'. He claimed to have several such beds in his showrooms where also were to be found 'portable mahogany chairs, japanned chairs and portable dining tables and every other article made solid and warranted for any climate'. From its commencement the business was of substantial size and insurance cover in March 1808 was £2,000. In November 1824 Wilkinson was unfortunate to have a fire at the Ludgate Hill premises, possibly in a part used for manufacturing, as the address was given as Evangelist Ct, Ludgate Hill. William Wilkinson had a house at Highbury Grove at the time of his death, aged 70, on 29 May 1833. The business had traded from *c.* 1820 as William Wilkinson & Sons and after the death of their father the sons changed the trading style to William & Charles Wilkinson. Important commissions were received. In 1829 they were commissioned by the architect John Rennie to make a table which he presented to the Earl of Lonsdale at Lowther Castle. From 1833–34 they made furniture for the new

977

Goldsmiths' Hall in London to the designs of the architect Philip Hardwick. Much of this survives in the building. The furniture produced for the Court Room and the Court Dining- Room was of carved mahogany in the Grecian style but the Drawing Room furniture reflected the fact that this was a venue for pleasure with ladies present and the recently revived Rococo was used, the furniture being painted white with the detail gilt. The location of this firm in the City made them an obvious contender for patronage by the City Companies and in 1840 they were invited to tender for furniture and upholstery for the Armourers and Brasiers' Co. In 1826 William Wilkinson & Sons signed the prefatory recommendation to P. & M. A. Nicholson's *Practical Cabinet Maker*.

The firm appear to have adopted a policy of stamping their products and a wide range of furniture in the Regency styles has been noted with this identification. Items so stamped include sofa tables, breakfast tables, extending dining tables, sets of tables, secrétaire bookcases, cabinets, chiffoniers, Davenports, chests of drawers, dining chairs, sideboards, wash stands and music or reading stands. Amongst these items is furniture in the Egyptian taste. Furniture was stamped 'WILKINSON, LUDGATE HILL' to *c.* 1820 then 'WILKINSON & SONS 14 LUDGATE HILL' to *c.* 1830 and 'W & C WILKINSON, 14 LUDGATE HILL' thereafter. Some furniture also had a serial number stamped after the name and numbers so far recorded range from 6585 to 19562. One extending dining table was stamped 'WILKINSON, LATE KAY, 14 LUDGATE HILL, LONDON'. The premises in Ludgate Hill had been occupied by Quintin Kay from 1754 to 1807 and Wilkinson took them over very soon after Kay's death in July 1807. Pieces so stamped almost certainly date from the years immediately following the commencement of Wilkinson's business. [D; *Times*, 1 October 1812, 16 November 1824; GL, Sun MS vol. 441, ref. 814543; *Gents Mag.*, 1824, p. 462, June 1833, p. 571; V&A archives; Joy, *English Furniture 1800–1851*, pp. 77, 151; *Antiques*, April 1952, p. 314; *Collectors' Guide*, November 1947, p. 24; Sotheby's, 24 April '64, lot 195, 10 June '66, lot 195, 24 May '68, lot 128, 19 July '68, lot 161, 30 July '71, lot 203, 29 September '78, lot 142; Parke-Bernet NY, 1 February '69, lot 99; Sotheby's Torquay, 30 September '81; Christie's, 16 April '81, lot 120, 16 July '81, lot 128, 25 February '82, lot 38; Phillips', 27 November '62, lot 103, 17 August '82, lot 21; Bonham's, 21 April '83, lot 127]

Wilkinson & Co., 27 Southampton Buildings, London, u (1819). [D]

Wilkinson & Pearson, 25 Clements Lane, London, wholesale upholders (1786–87). [D]

Wilkinson & Rayson, Hungate, York, joiners and cm (1816–18). [D]

Wilkinson & Turner, see Charles Wilkinson.

Wilks, J., Lancaster, furniture painter (1793). [Westminster Ref. Lib., Gillow records]

Wilks, John, 26 Pembroke St, Liverpool, cm (1839). [D]

Wilks, Thomas, Paradise St, Newcastle-under-Lyme, Staffs., joiner and cm (1822). [D]

Wilks, W., London, cm (1793). Subscribed to Sheraton's *Drawing Book*, 1793.

Wilkson, Macclesfield, Cheshire, cm (1762). In 1762 took app. named Sutton. [S of G, app. index]

Willan, William, Mitchellgate, Kirkby Lonsdale, Westmld, chairmaker (1829). [D]

Willatt, Anthony, Lower Rushall St, Walsall, Staffs., cm (1830–34). [D]

Willcocks, Thomas, Old King St, Bristol, cm, u and auctioneer (1833). [D]

Willcox, —, Under the Bank, Bristol, cabinet carver (1821–23). [D]

Willcox, Elizabeth & Son, Newcastle, u (1803–13). When Bartholomew Kent died in January 1803 his business at the foot of Dean St (also referred to as the Side) was continued by his niece Elizabeth Willcox. Initially she tried to dispose of the business which she described as 'respectable as any House in that line out of the Metropolis'. Either no buyer was forthcoming or Elizabeth Willcox changed her mind for the business continued to trade under her direction. In March 1806 she advertised a stock which included paper hangings, japanned and other chairs, carpeting and Marseilles quilts. In May of the following year her son B. Kent Willcox was taken into partnership. It was claimed that he had just returned from London 'where he has been for some time in one of the first houses in the Metropolis in the Upholstery & Cabinet lines and has made a collection of New and Elegant Drawings'. The partners offered chintzes, fringes and cabinet work and stated that 'Funerals attended at any Distance, with Feathers if required'. The son was used to obtain new stock in London because of his knowledge of the trade there. In May 1809 it was stated that he had recently returned from such a buying trip with 'an entire new assortment of every article'. A journeyman and an app. were advertised for. By January 1813 the business had ceased trading and the premises were taken over by William Preston, a furniture broker of Dog Bank. Amongst the customers of Elizabeth Willcox & Son was Cuthbert Ellison of Hebburn Hall, Gateshead, Co. Durham. [D; *Newcastle Courant*, 5 March 1803, 2 March 1806, 23 May 1807, 27 May 1809; *Newcastle Chronicle*, 2 January 1813; *Furn. Hist.*, 1976]

Willcox, Richard, Liverpool, cm (1761). In 1761 took app. named Prenton. [S of G, app. index]

Willcox & Son, 1 Somerset Buildings, Bath, Som., chair and sofa manufacturer (1819). [D]

Willer, William, St James's, Westminster, London, upholder (1776). Bankruptcy announced, *Leicester Journal*, February 1776.

Willers & Warner, Leicester Sq., London, wholesale upholders (1790–93). [D]

Willerton, Robert, Eastgate, Louth, Lincs., cm and joiner (1835). [D]

Willerton & Roberts, corner of Conduit St, in Old Bond St, London, turner and toyman (1768–75). Turners to the Dukes of Gloucester and Cumberland and Toymakers to the Prince of Wales. They supplied a Backgammon table to Croome Court and other sundries, their account dated 27 September 1769 amounting to £2 19s 6d. For the Duke of Atholl of Blair Castle they supplied a small organ in the same year and in an account dated 4 January 1775 charged £14 10s 6d for an assortment of goods which included a Tunbridge workbox, complete at £1 11s 6d, cutlery, toys and games. [Heal; V&A archives]

Wiles, T. H., King St, Woolwich, London, carver and gilder (1826). [D]

Willett, Anthony, Lower Rushall St, Walsall, Staffs., cm and u (1834–35). [D]

Willet, B., see Willett & Blandford.

Willet, James, Beam St, Nantwich, Cheshire, cm (1826–34). Three sons and a daughter bapt. 1826–34. [D; PR (bapt.)]

Willet, James jnr, Beam St, Nantwich, Cheshire, cm (1839). Married on 7 October 1839. [PR (marriage)]

Willet, John Lucas, London, joiner, carver and bedstead maker (1759–73). A freeman of the Clothworkers' Co. Took out licences to employ non-freemen 1759–65 the number rising to ten throughout the year from 1762 to 65. Bankrupt, *Gents Mag.*, 1766. At this period he was trading from an address at Old Bethlem. By 1772 he had recommenced business as a bedstead maker and in that year and the following one took out further licences to employ three non-freemen. His address was now Redcross St. [GL, City Licence bks, vols 2–4, 8]

Willett & Blandford, London, carvers and gilders (1821–37). In 1820 a B. Willett was trading from 2 West St, Smithfield as a carver and gilder. He must have been one of the partners in the firm of Willett & Blandford who were at the King's Arms Yd, West St, West Smithfield in the following year. The firm remained at this address until at least 1826 but by 1829 had moved to 29 Bouverie St, Fleet St. In addition to being carvers and gilders they also advertised themselves as looking-glass and picture frame makers and oval turners. They catered for the wholesale trade. [D]

Willett & Bonnett, 10 Water St, Arundel St, Strand, London, carvers and gilders (1839). Possibly successors to Willett & Blandford. Their trade card [Landauer Coll., MMA, NY] indicates that they also made picture and looking-glass frames and window cornices. Another card in the same collection gives the address of this firm as Middle Row, Holborn but this may be of post 1840 date. [D]

Willey, Abraham John, Exeter, Devon, cm (1819–40). At Paris St, 1819–29 and then from 1830 in Spiller's Lane. Seven Sons and four daughters bapt., 1819–40 at St Sidwell's Church. [PR (bapt.)]

Willey, John, parish of St Sidwell, Exeter, Devon, cm (1803–16). Included in a militia list of 1803. Two daughters bapt. at Sidwell's Church, 1813 and 1816. [PR (bapt.)]

Willey, John, Elvet Bridge, Durham, cm (1828–34). [D]

Willey, Joseph, St Michael's Hill, Bristol, cm (1815–35). The number in St Michael's Hill was 47 in 1822–25, and 46 and 48 in 1826–35. In 1835 described as a cm, u and undertaker. His successor at this address was Mary Willey, possibly his widow. [D]

Willey, Joseph jnr, 62 Park St, Bristol, cm, u and undertaker (1834–40). [D]

Willey, Mary, 46 and 48 St Michael's Hill, Bristol, cm, u and undertaker (1836–37). Successor to Joseph Willey at this address. [D]

Willey, Richard, New St, Retford, Notts., chairmaker (1828). [D]

Willey, Samuel, Chancery Lane, London, u (1754). Common Council man for the Ward of Farringdon Without. Described as an 'eminent upholsterer'. [*Public Advertiser*, 23 December 1754]

Willey & Hughes, 30 Quay, two doors from Clare St, Bristol, cm, u and undertakers (1832–33). [D]

William, John, High St, Stamford, Lincs., cm and u (1838). Also a paper hanger, auctioneer and appraiser. On 1 November 1838 charged the churchwardens of St Michael's Church £1 18s for making and fixing crimson moreen curtains to the south window of the Church. [Stamford Town Hall Lib., T22]

Williams, —, Glass House Yd, Aldersgate Bars, London, cm (1747). [Heal]

Williams, —, Lancaster, carver (1784–1824). Named in the Gillow records 1784–87, 1791, 1800, 1822–24. [Westminster Ref. Lib., Gillow]

Williams, —, Ipswich, Suffolk, chairmaker (1793). Subscribed to Sheraton's *Drawing Book*, 1793.

Williams, —, 12 Cumberland St, Middlx Hospital, London, carver and gilder (1809). [D]

Williams, —, Market Pl., Plymouth, Devon, cm and u (1814). [D]

Williams, Benjamin, Corbridge, Staffs., joiner, cm and grocer (1822). [D]

Williams, Charles, London, upholder (1709–27). In Leicester Sq. area 1709–13. In March 1713 his address was given as 'next my Lord Sommers in Leicester Fields' and in May of the same year as 'east side of Leicester Square . . . and 4th house northward from Green St'. The latter address valued at £500 had a workshop at the rear. On 26 February 1713 he took an app. By 1717 however he had moved and in July of that year he insured a house described as his dwelling, west side, first passage westwards from Red Lyon St, south side of Ormond St. In 1727 the address was rendered as Red Lion St. [Heal; GL, Sun MS vol. 2, p. 209; vol. 11, p. 580; Hand in Hand MS vol. 17, p. 200; S of G, app. index]

Williams, Charles, Bristol, u (1773–75). Bankruptcy announced *Gents Mag.*, February 1773 and in the following year living in the parish of St Peter. Trading at 6 Dolphin St, 1775. [D; poll bk]

Williams, Charles, Preston St, Exeter, Devon, cm (1821). Son bapt. St Mary Major, 28 January 1821. [PR (bapt.)]

Williams, Charles, Park Row, Stockton-on-Tees, Co. Durham, u (1827). [D]

Williams, Charles, Eign St, Hereford, cm (1832–37). [Poll bks]

Williams, David George, London, upholder (1809–25). One directory shows him at 4 Duke St, Manchester Sq. in 1811 but others give addresses in Gt Marylebone St. The number indicated was 41 from 1809 but one directory of 1814 states 11 while another of the following year lists 44. These may be errors. In 1820 claimed to be u to the Royal Family. [D]

Williams, E., Bristol, u (1814–15). In Clare St in 1814 but in the following year at 42 Wine St. [D]

Williams, Edward, Comus St, Liverpool, u (1818–21). The number in Comus St was 14 in 1818 and 12 in 1821. [D]

Williams, Edward, Frankwell, Shrewsbury, Salop, cm (1838). [Shrewsbury freemen rolls]

Williams, Elijah, Bristol, cm and u (1807–18). At 57 Broad Quay, 1807–10, but in 1812 the number was 77. In 1818 an Elijah Williams, u was trading at 11 Hillgrove St. [D]

Williams, Ellis, Chester, cm (1824–26). Free 1824 and in this year his address was recorded as Love St. In 1826 living in Brook St. [Freemen rolls; poll bk]

Williams, G., 10 Little Rider St, St James's, London, cm and chairmaker (1820). [D]

Williams, George, Adderbury, Oxon., carver (1757). On 27 April 1757 married Elizabeth Harris of Adderbury in that village. He was aged 22. [Bodleian index of Oxf. marriage bonds]

Williams, George, Market St, Devonport, Plymouth, Devon, u (1788–1802). In May 1802 his stock in trade was sold off. This consisted of mahogany chairs, sofas, circular end and other dining tables, pier and swing glasses and a handsome secretaire. [D; *Williamson's Liverpool Advertiser*, 23 February 1789; *Exeter Flying Post*, 27 May 1802]

Williams, George, Mint St, Southwark, London, horsehair manufactory (1804). [D]

Williams, George, 69 King St, Golden Sq., London, cm and u (1805–18). [D]

Williams, George, Lower Lane, Chester, cm (1812). [Poll bk]

Williams, George, 6 Midghall St, Liverpool, cm (1816). [D]

Williams, George C., Manchester, carver and gilder (1826–40). At 3 Princess St in 1836 and 73 Bridge St, 1838–40. [D]

Williams, George, London, cm and u (1805–35). At 9 King St, Golden Sq., 1805–07, 41 Gt Marylebone St, Cavendish Sq., 1809–12, 69 King St in 1817 and 10 Little Ryder St, St James's from 1820. Also recorded as I. & David Williams. [D]

Williams, Griffith, Chester, u (1730). Son of Hugh Williams of Caernarfon, Gwynedd, Gent. and app. to Joseph Parker of Chester, u. Free 25 April 1730. [Freemen rolls]

Williams, H., East St, Southampton, Hants., carver and gilder (1839). [D]

Williams, Harry (or Henry), London, cm, u and undertaker (1817–39). From 1817–27 at 5 York St, Covent Gdn, where in February 1821 he took out insurance cover of £1,000 which included £600 for stock and utensils. At 26 Berners St, 1835–39. Supplied to Dunham Massey, Altrincham, Cheshire on 20 June 1838 a mahogany writing table at £6 6s, a writing chair at £9 9s and twelve 'Japanese bamboo chairs' for which £7 16s was charged. [D; GL, Sun MS vol. 488, ref. 976100; John Rylands Lib., Manchester Univ., Dunham Massey accounts]

Williams, Henry, Long Acre, London, joiner and chairmaker (1717–58). In 1717 he was occupying a brick house and workshop on the south side of Long Acre, abutting the east side of Bagnio Walk. This property he insured for £250. His trade was given as 'joyner' but it is clear that from an early stage he was strongly involved in furniture making. In 1749 his address was simply rendered as Long Acre but his trade was then stated to be chairmaker. A reference of 1737 names him as cm.

He was the successor to Richard Roberts as chairmaker to the Royal Family and his name frequently appears in the Lord Chamberlain's accounts as a regular supplier both of seating furniture and cabinet work. He was also extensively patronised by Frederick, Prince of Wales. Furniture was supplied to Windsor Castle, Somerset House, Kensington Palace, Hampton Court and the Houses of Parliament. For Hampton Court he supplied in 1731 a wainscot bedframe for the State Bedchamber though the upholstery work was undertaken by Sarah Gilbert. In 1736–37 he supplied seating furniture for the Queen's Withdrawing Room at Hampton Court. This included 2 large armchair frames and 24 square stool frames *en suite* at £192. Also provided at the same time were four large settee frames, richly carved and gilt and eighteen square stool frames similarly finished all for the Queen's Gallery. The settee frames were charged at £60 and the stool frames a further £99. These items can perhaps be identified with two arm chairs now at Windsor Castle and existing sets of stools (see *GCM*). Apart from such expensive and rich furniture for state apartments, Williams supplied more mundane items and furniture for servants' rooms. In 1752 a wainscot chest of drawers was supplied 'for the New Page'. He also repaired furniture for the Royal Household and in the case of a set of nine walnut chairs he declared them to be 'much out of Repair' and charged for 'taking them all to pieces, New Jointing them, mending, Scraping and polishing'.

For Frederick, Prince of Wales he supplied in 1729 'a very neat Mahogany Windsor Chair' for the Library at St James's Palace and charged £4 for this. Two further chairs of a similar type were supplied for the Blue room. These latter Windsor chairs were said to be 'richly carved' but were charged at the same rate of £4 each. Williams also made a set of six mahogany 'Forest Chairs carved with scrolls &c' for the Royal establishment at Swinley Lodge in 1739–40. In the household accounts of Prince Frederick are payments to Williams of £16 9s 6d in 1731 and £20 17s in 1732, the latter being for stools, chairs, a wainscot bedstead and a wainscot press. One of the most expensive items of furniture supplied to the Prince of Wales must have been the cradle made in preparation for the christening of his daughter Augusta in August 1737. 'The Inside is white Satin, lac'd with Silver Lace, as are the Curtains. The Covering is Crimson Velvet, with Gold Lace, Fringes and Tassels. The Feet that support it are four Lions, finely carv'd and gilt'. This cradle was said to be valued at £500. In 1757 Princess Caroline was supplied at St James's Palace with 'a Turkey walnut tree easy chair frame

with very large brass socket castors' costing £4 15s. This must have been one of the last of Williams' commissions for from 1759 Catherine Naish becomes the main supplier of chairs and upholstery work to the Crown.

Williams' name appears in connection with commissions for a number of members of the aristocracy and gentry. In 1728 he supplied Sir Paul Methuen with a chair and a large mahogany frame for a marble table top. He is probably the 'Mr. Williams' who on 24 March 1727 charged Sir John Dutton of Sherborne House, Glos. £25 for a large looking-glass with a carved frame for his drawing room. In 1729 a further large glass with a gilt tabernacle frame was supplied costing £30. It is also likely that he was the 'Williams' who supplied a set of eighteen walnut framed leather covered chairs costing £19 11s 6d to Holkham Hall, Norfolk in 1720. In 1738 twelve leather chairs for the Steward's room were supplied but only £2 14s appears to have been charged for these. A Mr 'Williams' from London is recorded supplying the Lodge at St John's College, Cambridge with a gilt leather screen in 1748 at £6 13s. [GL, Hand in Hand MS vol. 17, p. 99; Westminster poll bk; *GCM*; *DEF*; PRO, LC9/288–92; *Old Furniture*, vol. 2 (1927) pp. 183, 185; Household accounts, Frederick, Prince of Wales, Duchy of Cornwall, vol. 1(2) p. 507, vol. III, pp. 242, 248; C. *Life*, 24 May 1962, p. 1242; *Furn. Hist.*, 1979; *Gents Mag.*, August 1737; Winterthur, Delaware, Symonds papers 75×69.15, p. 87; Glos. RO, Sherborne D678, account 1790; V&A archives; St John's College account bks] B.A.

Williams, Henry, Wood St, Walthamstow, London, cm and u (1839). [D]

Williams, Henry, 53 Union St, Southwark, London, chair and sofa maker (1839). [D]

Williams, Hugh, 33 Park Lane, Liverpool, cm (1839). [D]

Williams, I. B., 129 Strand, London, dressing case manufacturer, stationer etc. (1837). [D]

Williams, Isaac, Aldersgate St, London, cm (d. 1804). This business does not appear to have been listed in London trade directories. Isaac Williams was however regarded as a sufficiently important craftsman for his death aged 85 at Walham Green near Fulham to be reported in the *Gents Mag.*, January 1804.

Williams, J., Bristol(?), cm (d. 1806). Death at Hotwells, Bristol, reported, *Gents Mag.*, December 1806.

Williams, J., 124 Thomas St, Bristol, cm and furniture broker (1821). [D]

Williams, J., Union St, Portsea, Portsmouth, Hants., chairmaker (1839). [D]

Williams, James, Canterbury, Kent, u (1680). [Canterbury freemen rolls]

Williams, James, London, upholder (1769). Son of Benjamin Williams of Coate, Oxon., farmer, and brother to Thomas Williams. App. to Thomas Ridgeway, a member of the Skinners' Co. but by trade an u. Free of the Upholders' Co. under the 1750 Upholders' Act, 6 December 1769. [GL, Upholders' Co. records]

Williams, James & Thomas, 12 Ivy Lane, Newgate St, London, upholders, cm, appraisers, auctioneers, undertakers (1770). In January 1770 advertised the opening of a shop in Ivy Lane. [*Public Advertiser*, 17 January 1770]

Williams, James, Hull, Yorks., cm (1801). Father of the James Williams who was app. to William Jarratt in March 1801. [App. reg.]

Williams, James, Nantwich, Cheshire, chairmaker (1803). Married at Nantwich, 21 February 1803. [PR (marriage)]

Williams, James, 1 Bedford's Ct, Long Millgate, Manchester, cm (1817). [D]

Williams, James, Market Pl., Preston, Lancs., chairmaker (1818–25). [D]

Williams, James, 16 Theobalds Rd, London, cm and u (1826–27). [D]

Williams, James, St John's Pl., Hereford, cm and u (1830–40). A bill dated 3 July 1830 for twelve rush seated chairs at 7s 3d each made out to a Capt. Pateshall survives. [D; Herefs. RO, F60/205]

Williams, James, 8 Morford St, Bath, Som., cm (1833). [D]

Williams, James, Market Pl., Chippenham, Wilts., cm (1839). [D]

Williams, James, Madeley, Salop, cm (1840). [D]

Williams, Job, Orange Grove, Bath, Som., upholder and fancy chairmaker (1805). [D]

Williams, Job, 8 Hall's Buildings, Windmill St, Manchester, cm (1817). [D]

Williams, John, Oxford, u (1681–1718). On 3 November 1681 married to Jane Darton of Walcot at the Southampton Chapel, Charlbury. In 1692 supplied a set of twelve oak chairs covered with russia leather to Christ Church, Oxford for £6 with a tall backed armchair for which 15s was charged. Both survive, the leather covered chairs now being in the Chapter House. In 1718 took app. named Whitfield. [Bodleian index of Oxf. marriage bonds; W. G. Hiscock, *Christ Church Miscellany*; S of G, app. index; *C. Life*, 8 December 1944, p. 991]

Williams, John, Chester, cm (1742). Son of Thomas Williams of Preston, Lancs., sailor. Freeman of Preston but in 1742 living in Chester. [Preston freemen records]

Williams, John, Bristol, u (1754–75). In *Gents Mag.*, September 1754 his bankruptcy was announced. In this year he was living in the parish of Christchurch. In 1775 trading at 27 Castle Green. [D; poll bks]

Williams, John, Bristol, carver and gilder (1786–99). In 1787 at Square Lane and on 14 June insured his household goods for £900. A trade card of 1788 [BM, print dept] gives the address as 'opposite the Floating Dock, Hot Well Road'. An address in Hotwell Rd is also recorded 1792–93. In 1795 at St Augustine's Back, and 1799 at 17 Trinity St. In December 1786 he insured two houses in the city of Gloucester and two shops for £200. [D; GL, Sun MS vol. 341, p. 393; vol. 346, p. 120]

Williams, John, 91 Fenchurch St, London, upholder (1788–1802). Son of Samuel Williams of Colebrook, Radnor, Gent. Free of the Upholders' Co., 9 January 1788 and living at 91 Fenchurch St, 1788–1802. [GL, Upholders' Co. records]

Williams, John, 13 Little Bardy Leg Walk, Southwark, London, upholder (1783–92). Son of Joseph Williams of Little Bardy Leg Walk, Southwark, carpenter. App. to Edward Richardson, 2 April 1783 and free of the Upholders' Co. by servitude, 6 June 1792. [GL, Upholders' Co. records]

Williams, John, Preston, Lancs., cm (1802–22). Son of John Williams of Bristol, clockmaker. John Williams snr was a freeman of Preston. John Williams jnr was trading in Preston in 1802 and in that year signed the *Preston Cabinet Makers' and Chair Makers' Book of Prices*, 1802. John jnr was also a Preston freeman. In 1822 he was recorded as 'formerly of Preston' and his three sons were also listed as freemen in that year. [Preston Guild records]

Williams, John, Bristol, cm (1809–20). At Gloucester Rd in 1809, Counterslip in 1813 and 62 Redcliffe St in 1820. [D]

Williams, John, Bristol, cm (1810–31). At Christmas Steps 1810–15; 19 Milk St, 1819–26; 6 Horse Fair 1827–30 and Bridewell Lane in 1831. [D]

Williams, John snr, parish of St Mary Major, Exeter, Devon, cm (1812). His son John jnr was made free 1812. [Freemen rolls]

Williams, John jnr, parish of St Mary Major, Exeter, Devon, cm, (1812–19). Son of John Williams snr and free 1812 by succession. Died in May 1819 aged 38 'after a few days illness'. [Freemen rolls; *Exeter Flying Post*, 20 May 1819]

Williams, John, 232 Whitechapel Rd, London, cm (1813). [D]

Williams, John, High Wycombe, Bucks., chairmaker (1814). Son bapt. 1814. [PR (bapt.)]

Williams, John, Duddeston St, Birmingham, cm (1818). [D]

Williams, John, East St, Horncastle, Lincs., joiner and cm (1819–35). [D]

Williams, John, Sittingbourne, Kent, cm and turner (1839). [D]

Williams, John Powell, Lower Maudlin St, Bristol, carver and gilder (1821). [D]

Williams, Joseph, London, upholder (1712–37). Free of the Upholders' Co., 22 October 1712. Took as app. Sarah Chapman, 1716–37. [GL, Upholders' Co. records]

Williams, Jos., opposite Beaufort Buildings, Strand, London, cm (d. 1760). In 1760 his late dwelling house at Beaufort Buildings was offered for sale. [Harris, *Old English Furniture*, p. 29]

Williams, Joseph, Ker St, Devonport, Devon, cm (1838). [D]

Williams, Joseph, 4 Dartmouth St, Birmingham, bedstead maker and chairmaker (1839). [D]

Williams, Joseph, Cook St, Chester, u (1839). Free 3 June 1839. [Freemen rolls]

Williams, M., Bodmin and Truro, Cornwall, u and cm (1804–10). In January 1804 he announced his move from Bodmin to premises in Lemon St, Truro. Here he stocked 'tables & chairs of all descriptions, Drawers, Pier & other looking glasses, beds, bedding, mattresses, paper hanging etc.'. He offered to hang bells and to take old items in part-exchange. An app. was advertised for and it was indicated that a premium would be expected. By March 1810 Williams had decided to give up the trade and offered his stock at reduced prices for ready money. He also offered to lease his shop and dwelling house for a term of fourteen years. This property was in Lemon St near the back entrance of the New Market place. That stock not already disposed of was advertised for sale by auction in May. On offer were 'several setts of Mahogany chairs, a handsome Pier looking glass, Box & Swing ditto, a large Easy chair, a large Glass Case, also a writing desk & several articles of kitchen furniture'. [*Royal Cornwall Gazette*, 7 January 1804; 24 March 1810, 5 May 1810, 19 May 1810]

Williams, Mary, High St, Bridgwater, Som., cm (1840). [D]

Williams, Morgan, King St, Covent Gdn, London, joiner (1803). Included in the list of master cabinet makers in Sheraton's *Cabinet Dictionary*, 1803.

Williams, Nathaniel jnr, Bristol, cm (1784–1824). Living in the parish of St James in 1784. In 1817 at 62 Redcliff St and in 1824 at Cathay. [D; poll bk]

Williams, Nicholas, South Gate St, Exeter, Devon, joiner (1716). In May 1716 he offered for sale 'all sorts of Chests of Drawers, Hanging Presses, Clock cases, Cabinets, Scrutores, Commode Tables, Desks, Book cases and Looking glasses of the newest fashion and best Fineer'd work in Walnut tree, also Japan'd work with variety of other Household Furniture by wholesale or Retail'. Also offered rooms to let furnished or unfurnished. [*Protestant Mercury or the Exeter Post Boy*, 18 May 1716]

Williams, Nicholas, Penryn, Cornwall, cm (1788). Bankruptcy announced June 1788 and a dividend was offered to creditors in May 1791. [*Exeter Flying Post*, 5 June 1788, 24 July 1788, 26 May 1791]

Williams, Peter, Foregate St, Chester, cm (1812–31). Free 1812. Took his son Thomas as app. in 1831. [Freemen rolls; poll bks; app. reg.]

Williams, Richard, Cucumber Ct, Shipyard, by 'The Ship

Tavern', Strand, London, cm and sedan chairmaker (1749). [Westminster poll bk]

Williams, Richrd snr, Liverpool, carver and gilder (1790–96). At 53 Paradise St in 1790 but 18 Dale St in 1794 and 13 Dale St in 1796. In the latter year he also conducted a confectioner's shop at 12 Dale St. [D]

Williams, Richard jnr, Carson's Ct, Vernon St, Liverpool, cm (1801–12). App. 1801 and in 1812 petitioned for freedom from Edward Lowe. Free 14 October 1812. [Freemen rolls]

Williams, Richard, Irish Lane, Leytonstone, London (1831–40). [Census]

Williams, Robert, London, upholder and cm (1774–93). At Bow St, Covent Gdn, 1774–77. In 1777 he moved to King St, Covent Gdn and was at 28 till 1789 and then 40 from 1790–93. In 1777 he took out two insurance policies with the Sun Office, one was for £2,000 which included stock and utensils valued at £1,000. This was for the 28 King St address. He appears to have been using the Bow St address also in this year for he insured a further £300 value of stock and utensils there. [D; GL, Sun MS vol. 261, pp. 29–30]

Williams, Robert snr, 8 Pitt St, Liverpool, cm (1781). [D]

Williams, Robert jnr, Liverpool, cm (1818–29). App. to Nathan Newall and free 11 June 1818. Dead by 1832. [Freemen reg.]

Williams, Samuel, 'The Golden Lion & Ball', St Paul's Churchyard, London, leather gilder (1709–36). Shown at the St Paul's Churchyard address 1720–36 which was described as his dwelling house. He specialised in the supply of leather covered furniture. In 1709 he sold a six leaf screen 'with Indian figures on a black Japan ground' and a four leaf screen with a black ground to the Duke of Montrose for £6 8s. On 4 June 1718 Richard Towneley of Towneley Hall, Lancs. was invoiced for four gilt leather elbow dressing chairs, a couch bed and gilt leather for a window seat, the whole amounting to £13 18s. He was promptly paid on 6 June. St John's College, Oxford purchased from Williams on 15 April 1736 'twenty black Spanish leather chairs, walnut tree frames' at 14s 6d each with a charge of 5s for packing. These were for the Common Room. [GL, Sun MS vol. 10, ref. 16618; Scottish RO, GD 220/6/1129/8; Preston RO, Towneley DDTO Q/10/4; St John's College, Common Room file]

Williams, Samuel, Hadleigh, Suffolk, cm (1824). [D]

Williams, Samuel, Bristol, cm (1775–94). Shown at 12 Castle Mill St 1775 and Castle Green, 1794. [D]

Williams, Sarah, Gloucester Lane, Bristol, cm (1795). [D]

Williams, Sarah, Pithay, Bristol, cm (1826). [D]

Williams, T., 17 Clarence St, Cheltenham, Glos., cm and u (1839). [D]

Williams, Thomas, Stone Cutter St, St Bride's, London, chairmaker (1734–46). Fined for refusing parochial office in the parish of St Bride, Fleet St, 1734, 1739, 1744 and 1746. [GL, MS 6561, p. 55]

Williams, Thomas, London, cm and u (1756–75). At Bow St, Covent Gdn, 1763, Hermitage Bridge, 1767–68 and 8 Gt Tower St, 1769–75. His trade card giving the Bow St address is Rococo in character and uses engravings of a chair and a cabinet in this style. In 1756 provided furniture to a value of £61 5s 6d to Peter Du Cane for his house, Braxted Park, Essex. The payment of £73 for furniture supplied to Sherborne Castle in 1773 to a 'Mr. Williams' probably refers to this maker. An invoice dated 1770 from Thomas Williams to a T. Thornhill is in the collection of the V&A. [D; Heal; Essex RO, D/DDC/A13 folio 59; Digby family papers]

Williams, Thomas, Aldersgate St, London, carver (1767). A freeman and member of the Joiners' Co. In 1767 took out a licence to employ three non-freemen for three months. [GL, City Licence bks, vol. 5]

Williams, Thomas, London, upholder (1761–86). Son of John

Williams of Coate, Oxon., farmer and brother to James Williams. App. to William Cope and Nicholas Parkes, a draper, 11 September 1761. Free of the Upholders' Co. by servitude, 5 April 1769. At Bennett St, Rathbone Pl. 1778, Maddox St, Hanover Sq. 1781 and Duke St, Manchester Sq. 1786. [GL, Upholders' Co. records]

Williams, Thomas, Ivy Lane, London, u (1773). Bankruptcy announced, *Gents Mag.*, October 1773.

Williams, Thomas, Dudley, Staffs., joiner and cm (1793). [D]

Williams, Thomas, address unknown, cm (1803). Subscribed to Sheraton's *Cabinet Dictionary*, 1803.

Williams, Thomas, 23 New Compton St, St Giles, London, carver and gilder (1809). [D]

Williams, Thomas, Duddeston St, Birmingham, chairmaker (1818). See also John Williams in this street, 1818. [D]

Williams, Thomas, Cheltenham, Glos., auctioneer and u (1827). Bankruptcy announced, *Liverpool Mercury*, 30 March 1827. A T. Williams trading as a cm and u was in business at 17 Clarence St in 1839. [D]

Williams, Thomas, Coffee-house Lane, Bridgwater, Som., cm and u (1830). [D]

Williams, Thomas, 13 Silver St, Liverpool, cm (1839). [D]

Williams, Thomas, Excise Passage, Exeter, Devon, cm (1839). Daughter bapt. at the Church of All Hallows, Goldsmith St, 27 June 1839. [PR (bapt.)]

Williams, Thomas Stephen, 161 Snargate St, Dover, Kent, cm and u (1839). [D]

Williams, William, Crown Ct, Long Acre, London, chairmaker (1749). [Westminster poll bk]

Williams, William, St Martin's Lane, London, u (1749–55). Subscribed to Chippendale's *Director*, 1754. [Westminster poll bk]

Williams, William, parish of St James, Bristol, carver and gilder (1754–85). In 1775 at 30–31 St James's Churchyard. In January 1785 his stock-in-trade and household furniture was offered for sale following on his death. The St James's Churchyard address was described as a dwelling house and the goods on offer from his stock included 'a very neat Assortment of Pier and Swing Glasses, in Gilt and Mahogany Frames, with Girandoles to match; Quantity of Prints and Paintings, with a variety of Glass and Print Frames, with many other Articles in the above Business'. [D; poll bks; *Bonner and Middleton's Bristol Journal*, 8 January 1785]

Williams, William, Bristol, cm (1793–1815). At Thomas St in 1793 and Stoney Hill in 1815. [D]

Williams, William, Gerrard St, Soho, London, paper hanger, carver and gilder (1776). Bankruptcy announced, *Williamson's Liverpool Advertiser*, 27 December 1776.

Williams, William, London, upholder (1778–86). Son of William Williams snr of Deptford, London. App. to William Rhodes 18 April 1778 and free of the Upholders' Co. by servitude, 6 May 1778. At this date he was at 66 Paternoster Row and at this address took out insurance cover of £300 of which £250 was for utensils and stock. At 22 Ludgate Hill, 1784–86. [GL, Upholders' Co. records; Sun MS vol. 267, p. 69]

Williams, William, 5 Kirkman's Buildings, Tottenham Ct Rd, London, cm (1786). In October 1786 insured his house and one adjoining in John St for £400. [GL, Sun MS vol. 341, p. 56]

Williams, William, London, upholder and cm (1790–93). At 13 Berwick St, Soho but in 1793 used also an address at 4 Chapel St, Spitalfields. [D]

Williams, William, 29 Barbican, London, upholder and furniture, bedding and carpet warehouse (1801–20). Son of Richard Williams of the county of Salop, Gent. Free of the Upholders' Co. by redemption, 7 October 1801. Possibly the

William Williams who subscribed to Sheraton's *Cabinet Dictionary*, 1803. [D; GL, Upholders' Co. records]

Williams, William, Pontack Lane, Liverpool, cm (1812). App. to Mathew Gardner and free 5 October 1812. [Freemen rolls]

Williams, William, Newington Butts, London, upholder and undertaker (1817). [D]

Williams, William, Cheltenham, Glos., cm (1818). Freeman of Evesham, Worcs. but living in Cheltenham in June 1818. [Evesham poll bk]

Williams, William, Wyebridge Gate, Hereford, cm and joiner (1822). [D]

Williams, William, 12 Marchmont St, Burton Cresc., London, cm (1829). [D]

Williams, William, Marlborough St, Faringdon, Oxon., cm and u (1830–40). [D]

Williams, William, 11 Leece St and 2 Deane St, Liverpool, cm (1839). [D]

Williams, William, 18 Camden St, Islington Green, London, carver and gilder (1839). [D]

Williams & Gibton, 39 Stafford St, (London?), cm (c. 1830). Maker's label or impressed mark recorded on a mahogany Wellington Chest and a Davenport of c. 1830–40 in style. [Phillips', Greenham Ct, Newbury, sale 3 August 1967]

Williams & James, New Bridge St, Exeter, Devon, cm and u (1816–39). The business is recorded in Williams' name only in 1816 and he is described as a cm. The partnership is recorded in a directory of 1839. [D]

Williams & Needin(?), address unknown (1758–59). Name recorded on an account of 19 March 1758 to Lord Monson for £17 9s 4½d. The work carried out included the repair of a japanned dressing glass frame and the fitting of a glass plate to it for which 18s was charged. The account was paid 25 April 1759 and received by a Richard Harper. [Lincoln RO, Monson 12]

Williams & Woodin, opposite Beauford Buildings, Strand, London, u (1759). Advertised the sale of Chaillot work, Gobelins work, carpets etc. [*Public Advertiser*, 24 December 1759]

Williamson, Ann, Market Pl., Boston, Lincs., cm (1835). [D]

Williamson, Edward, 41 Pembroke Pl., Liverpool, u (1834). [D]

Williamson, G., address unknown (1821). A penwork tripod table is known decorated with a chess board, one square of which is signed 'G ... Williamson, 25th May 1821'. [Sotheby's, 1 March 1974, lot 120]

Williamson, George, York, cm (1796). Said to be of the parish of All Saints, North St when he was app. on 21 September 1789 to Peter Davies, cm of the parish of St Michael-le-Belfry. Free 1796. [App. bk; freemen rolls]

Williamson, George, Rochdale, Lancs., cm and u (1798–1828). At Cheetham St, 1798–1825 but in 1828 at Roach Pl. [D]

Williamson, George, address unknown, cm (1803). Subscribed to Sheraton's *Cabinet Dictionary*, 1803.

Williamson, Henry, Chapel St, Salford, Lancs., cm (1811–13). At 111 Chapel St in 1811 but in 1813 at 112 Chapel St. [D]

Williamson, James, King St, London, cm (1779). Bankruptcy announced, *Gents Mag.*, August 1779.

Williamson, John, Vernon St, Liverpool, chair japanner (1790). [D]

Williamson, John, Bedford Ct, Covent Gdn, London, cm and u (1790–93). In 1793 subscribed to Sheraton's *Drawing Book*. [Heal]

Williamson, John, Market Pl., Boston, Lincs., cm and u (1819–26). [D]

Williamson, Joseph, Darley St, Bradford, Yorks., cm (1822–29). [D]

Williamson, Joseph, Liquorpond St, Boston, Lincs., cm (1835). [D]

Williamson, Martin, Chester-le-Street, Co. Durham, cm and joiner (1828). [D]

Williamson, Nicholas, Nantwich, Cheshire, cm (1839). Daughter bapt. 11 March 1839. [PR (bapt.)]

Williamson, Reuben, York and Hull, u (1793–1811). Son of Henry Williamson, yeoman. App. to Matthew Browne of York, 1 April 1793. Free of York 1811 but at this date living in Hull and recorded trading at 7 Lowgate in 1810. [D; York app. bk and freemen rolls]

Williamson, Reuben, 9 Finsbury Terr., City Rd, London, cm and u (1827). [D]

Williamson, Richard, Nottingham, cm (1813). Will dated 8 September 1813 proved 20 May 1814. [Notts. RO, probate records]

Williamson, Richard, 1 Chatham St, Piccadilly, Manchester, u (1825). [D]

Williamson, Robert, Burnham Market, Norfolk, joiner, cm and u (1822–39). [D]

Williamson, Thomas, Stamford, Lincs., u (1745–d. 1769). App. to Henry Wright, u and free 1745. At the time of his death in 1769 he was trading at the corner of Ironmonger St. His business was taken over in May 1769 by Wortley & William Searson. [Freemen rolls; *Cambridge Chronicle*, 20 May 1769]

Williamson, William, 70 Wells St, London, cm (1780). In 1780 insured a house for £100. [GL, Sun MS vol. 289, p. 181]

Williamson, William, Newark, Notts., chair turner (1790). [Poll bk]

Williamson, William & Sons, Guildford, Surrey, cm and u (1790–1840). At Black Horse Lane, 1790–96 and Chapel St, 1822–40. The number in Chapel St was 16 in 1839 and 13, 14 and 16 in 1840. A considerable number of pieces of furniture of good quality have been noted with their impressed stamp reading 'FROM W. WILLIAMSON & SONS, GUILD-FORD'. Amongst the items so stamped that have been recorded are Pembroke tables, one being in satinwood, a rosewood cross-banded sofa table, writing tables, one in tambour form, a chest of drawers, commodes, cabinets, secretaires, a secretaire bookcase and bow-fronted and serpentine-fronted sideboards. All are in late George III or Regency form. [D; poll bks; Christie's, 18 October 1973, 26 January 1984, lot 100; Sotheby's, 6 March 1964, lot 156; 3 July 1964, lot 184; 10 February 1967, lot 165; 10 March 1972, lot 135; 19 April 1974, lot 69; 14 November 1975, lot 75; 13 January 1978, lots 83, 107; 14 November 1980, lot 67; 4 March 1983, lot 46]

Willingham, John, Burgate, Barton-on-Humber, Lincs., joiner and cm (1819–35). [D]

Willins, John, Smith St, Warwick, u (1831). [Poll bk]

Willis, —, address unknown, u (1724). On 3 November 1724 paid £4 10s for work above the Divinity Schools, Cambridge. [Univ. of Cambridge Lib., Univ. audit bk, 1660–1740, p. 545]

Willis, —, near Fleet Mkt, London, cm (1752). On 2 October 1752 it was reported that one of his servants had fallen from the top of a cartload of furniture near Fulham as he was returning to London and had broken his leg. It is possible that the maker referred to was John Willis of St Paul's Churchyard. [*London Daily Advertiser*, 2 October 1752]

Willis, Benjamin, address unknown, cm (1760). In August 1760 supplied to John, 4th Duke of Bedford a mahogany dining table and a mahogany stand which together with some repairs cost £15 10s. [Bedford Office, London]

Willis, James, St Clements, Oxford, cm (1802). [Poll bk]

Willis, John, St Paul's Churchyard, London, cm and u (1730–d. 1797). The length of operation of this business suggests that there were two John Willis's possibly father and son. In 1730 the address was at the sign of 'The Elephant & Castle',

St Paul's Churchyard and insurance cover of £500 taken out on 7 December included £400 for household goods and stock-in-trade and £100 for glass. In 1754 subscribed to Chippendale's *Director*. The John Willis who in 1761 took out a licence to employ two non-freemen for three months was a member of the Joiners' Co. In 1765 the business was trading at the sign of 'The Feather & Ball' and from 1768 the number 19 St Paul's Churchyard was used. At this period insurance cover was £600 though by 1791 this had risen to £1,000.

The commissions received by this business suggest that it was of some importance and reputation. In 1734 George Bowes of Gibside, Co. Durham paid for furniture received from this maker. A four seater and two three seater Windsor settees and eight single chairs were charged at £5 8s. These were despatched from London on the vessel *Thomas & Francis* and George Bowes records the payment of an additional 2s 6d for 'waterage & drink money to the Ship's Crew'. This maker was probably the John Willis who in 1745 supplied 24 Virginia walnut leather covered chairs and two matching double chair back settees to Emmanuel College, Cambridge. They were covered with black Spanish leather and brass nailed. The chairs were charged at £1 2s each and the settees at £3 6s each and a 14s charge was recorded for carriage. The chairs less their original upholstery survive and are in the Gallery of the College. In 1752–53 John Willis was one of the craftsmen supplying furniture to the new Mansion House in London. [D; GL, Sun MS vol. 33, ref. 52540; vol. 327, p. 500; vol. 375, p. 179; Hand in Hand MS vol. 102, p. 116; City Licence bk, vol. 2; *Gents Mag.*, April 1797; Durham RO, D/St/V1390; Emmanual College archives, BUR. 0.8; *Conn.*, December 1952, p. 181]

Willis, John, Hermitage Bridge, London, cm and u (1768). [Heal]

Willis, John, Bristol, cm, u and undertaker (1797–1840). App. to James Hingston 1797 and free 11 December 1804. By 1806 he was in partnership with a person named Sangar at 31 Broadmead. The firm of Willis & Sangar is last recorded in directories in 1812 and in the following year John Willis was trading on his own behalf from the same address. The reason for this change was no doubt associated with the bankruptcy of John Willis in 1812. He remained at 31 Broadmead until 1820 but from 1821–31 his address was under the Bank and from 1832–40 it was St Augustine's Back. A breakfront bookcase is known with the trade label of John Willis. [D; app. reg. freemen rolls; *Exeter Flying Post*, 31 December 1812]

Willis, John, 29 Rose & Crown Ct, Moorfields, London, u (1805). [D]

Willis, Thomas, 3 Naked Boy Ct, Ludgate Hill, London, upholder (1777). In 1777 insured his house for £100. [GL, Sun MS vol. 260, p. 75]

Willis, William, 40 Upper Shadwell St, London, carpenter and cm (1778). In 1778 took out insurance cover of £200 of which half was for utensils and stock. [GL, Sun MS vol. 270, p. 318]

Willis, William, King St, Moorfields, London, glass grinder and looking-glass maker (1780). In 1780 took out insurance cover of £2,200 of which £430 was for stock and utensils. [GL, Sun MS vol. 281, p. 251]

Willison, Jno., Walton St, Aylesbury, Bucks., cm (1839). [D]

Willmore, Elizabeth, Market Pl., Buckingham, cm (1839). [D]

Willmore, James & Son, Market Pl., Buckingham, cm (1839). A bill exists dated 15–17 December 1839 recording furniture supplied to Stowe amounting to £52 2s 6d. Amongst the items delivered were 24 simulated rosewood chairs with cane seats at £7 4s, six pairs of circular fronted bed steps at £13 16s, 12 towel horses painted white at £3 6s, a rosewood coffee table £2 15s and dressing glasses. [D; Huntington Lib., California, Stowe MS Box 148]

Willmot, Joseph, 38 Church St, Mile End, London, cm (1838). [D]

Willmott, John, 21 Tib St, Manchester, u (1804). [D]

Willmott, John, 232 Whitechapel Rd, London, cm (1809). [D]

Willmott, John, Macclesfield, Cheshire, u and furniture dealer (1828). [D]

Willmott, John, Waterloo Rd, Burslem, Staffs., cm and u (1834). [D]

Willmott, John, 11 Redman's Row, Mile End, London, cm and u (1838–39). [D]

Willmott, Richard, Bartholomew Close, London, japanner (1735). Bankruptcy announced, *General Evening Post*, 24–26 June 1735.

Willmott, Robert, 20 Vine Ct, Spitalfields, London, cm (1822). In November 1822 took out insurance cover of £300 of which half was for stock and utensils. [GL, Sun MS vol. 490, ref. 997863]

Willmott, W., 53 Blackman St, Southwark, London, cm (1794–96). [Heal]

Willmott, William, Kinver, Staffs., chairmaker (1748). In 1748 took app. named Willmott. [S of G, app. index]

Willmott, William, College Pl., Bristol, cm (1819–40). At 4 College Pl., 1819–21 but the number was 3 in 1822–23, 9 in 1824–33 and 8 in 1834–40. [D]

Willmott, William, 47 Old Bailey, London, plate case maker (1839). [D]

Willmott & Son, All Saints St, Hastings, Sussex, u (1823). [D]

Willn, Richard, Atherstone, Warks., cm (1822–35). In 1828–35 the business was named as Richard Willn & Son. [D]

Willoughby, William, High Wycombe, Bucks., chairmaker (1814). Daughter bapt. 1814. [PR (bapt.)]

Willows, Thomas, 29 Compton St, London, upholder and carpet factor (1781–84). In 1781 took out insurance cover of £1,000 of which £800 was for utensils and stock. A Thomas Willows, carpet factor was trading at 59 Watling St in 1774. [D; GL, Sun MS vol. 288, p. 455; Westminster poll bk]

Willows, Thomas jnr, Leicester Sq., London, upholder and carpet warehouseman (1800). In November took out insurance cover of £3,000. [GL, Sun MS vol. 419, refs 709579–80]

Wills, Mr, address unknown, frame maker (1772). On 31 October 1772 paid £1 11s 6d for making two frames for Sir Richard Hoare. The glass was supplied independently by a Mr Gapper. [Hoare's Bank MS]

Wills, Benjamin, Exeter, Devon, chairmaker (1723–28). In June 1723 insured goods and merchandise in his house in Exeter for £500. In 1728 took app. named Williams. In this year he was described as a rush chairmaker. [GL, Sun MS vol. 15, 8 June 1723; S of G, app. index]

Wills, F., South St, Southampton St, Pentonville, London, cm and u. [Heal]

Wills, James, Market Pl., Plymouth, Devon, cm (1784). [D]

Wills, James, Axminster, Devon, cm (1823–36). The sale of his warehouse, workshops and dwelling house was advertised in February 1836. [D; *Exeter Flying Post*, 25 February 1836]

Wills, Jasper, 81 South St, Exeter, Devon, cm and u (1816–25). At 81 South St in June 1825 when he advertised that he had recently returned from London with new stock. He claimed to keep in stock 'Brussell's and other carpets, painted Floor Cloths, Blankets, Quilts and Counterpanes, Wardrobes, Chests of Drawers, pedistal Side Boards, sets of Mahogany Tables etc.' and a 'variety of Paper Hangings and Borders'. [D; poll bk; *The Alfred*, 21 June 1825] See William Wills.

Wills, John, 'The Golden Ball by the Ditch-Side, Holbourn Bridge, London' (mid 18th century). Trade label recorded on a mahogany bureau and also on a board from a drawer botton at Temple Newsam House, Leeds. [V&A archives]

Wills, John, Plymouth, Devon, cm and upholder (1781–d. 1826). In 1781 took out insurance cover of £1,000 on his utensils, stock and workshops which suggest a business of substantial proportions. Last recorded in trade directories 1805. His death occurred in January 1826. [D; GL, Sun MS vol. 296, p. 455; *The Alfred*, 31 January 1826]

Wills, Richard, Fareham, Hants., upholder and cm (1784). [D]

Wills, Robert, Crescent, Bridgwater, Som., cm (1840). [D]

Wills (or Willis), William snr and jnr, 81 South St, Exeter, Devon (1779–1840). In 1779 William Wills snr insured his utensils and stock for £300 but in 1785 this cover had been reduced to £200. A fire occurred at his house in Southgate St in 1780. The address at 81 South St was first recorded in 1791 and was to continue in use throughout the existence of the business. William Wills snr died in 1813 aged 72 and the business was then carried on by Jasper Wills at this address until at least 1825. In 1830 the business was styled Willis & Son but was under the control of William Wills jnr. His marriage to Miss Mary Ann Warren was recorded in March 1826 and he already appears to have been in control of the business then. [D; GL, Sun MS vol. 270, p. 426; vol. 333, p. 40; *Exeter Flying Post*, 29 September 1780, 4 March 1813, 16 March 1826, 30 July 1835; *The Alfred*, 21 March 1826]

Wills, William, Essex, cm (1780). Named with George Coryndon, Gent., as joint mortgagers on a house valued at £300. [GL, Sun MS vol. 285, p. 301]

Wills, William, Maidstone, Kent, chair japanner (1826–38). His trading address was 19 Church St but he was living in Stone St in 1834. [D; poll bk]

Wills, William, 16 Church St, Sheffield, Yorks., carver and gilder (1833). [D]

Wills, William, Cirencester, Glos., cm (1837). Child bapt. 1837. [PR (bapt.)]

Willshen, James, 31 Orchard St, Portman Sq., London, carver (1775–78). In 1775 insured a house for £700 and in 1778 a house in Seymour St for £500. [GL, Sun MS vol. 238, p. 394; vol. 263, p. 329]

Willshire, Leonard, 26 Grafton St, Soho, London, carver and gilder (1826–35). [D]

Willson, —, London, upholder, cm, appraiser and undertaker (c. 1790). His trade card gives an address at 20 Aldersgate St, nearly opposite the Church and indicates that he had moved from Jewin St. He sold keyboard instruments and dealt in coal. Engravings used to illustrate the trade card are of an elegant cabinet chamber organ, a secretaire bookcase, a Pembroke table, a bed and a chair. [Heal]

Willson, —, 125 Tottenham Ct Rd, London, upholder and appraiser (1820). [D]

Willson, George, Water Lane, Maidstone, Kent, cm and u (1839). [D]

Willson, Joseph, 15 Newington Causeway, London, cm and u (1809). [D]

Willson, M. S. C. T., 68 Long Acre, London. Stamp recorded on a George III bow-fronted mahogany sideboard. [Sotheby's, 17 November 1978, lot 228]

Willson, Robert, Lucas St, Rotherhithe, London, cm, carpenter and joiner (1777–82). In 1777 took out insurance cover of £500 on his utensils and stock. In 1782 the total insurance had risen to £2,200 of which £820 was for utensils and stock and £300 for a warehouse, workshops and sawpits. [GL, Sun MS vol. 256, p. 229; vol. 302, p. 333]

Willson, Thomas, 68 Gt Queen St, London, furniture broker, etc. (1799–1854). The impressed mark 'T. WILLSON 68 GREAT QUEEN STREET LONDON' has been found stamped on some late 18th-/early-19th century furniture

(Fig. 9). Directories have yielded the undermentioned information:

1799: Thomas Wilson, auctioneer, Little Queen St.

1802: Thomas Wilson, auctioneer and u, 28 Little Queen St.

1821: Thomas Willson, broker and appraiser, 68 Great Queen St.

Thomas Wilson, 28 Little Queen St.

1822: Thomas Wilson, auctioneer and appraiser, 68 Great Queen St.

1823–25: Thomas Wilson, auctioneer, 28 Little Queen St.

1826: Thomas Wilson, furniture broker, 68 Great Queen St.

1828: Thomas Wilson, furniture appraiser and broker, 68 Great Queen St.

1829: Thomas Wilson, furniture appraiser and broker, 68 Great Queen St.

1830–37: Mary Wilson & Son, 68 Great Queen St.

1838–54: Matthew Wilson/Willson, furniture warehouse/furniture works/u, 68 Great Queen St.

1839: J. Willson, furniture broker, 34 Little Pulteney St, Golden Sq.

Compilers of directories vary in accuracy and there seems to have been a predictable confusion between the surnames Willson and the more familiar Wilson. Available material suggests that the Willsons were likely to have been dealers in good quality second-hand furniture (brokers). Although some of the 1838–54 entries refer to 'Furniture Works', the term may have been employed to described a repair workshop and not necessarily a manufactory. [*Furn. Hist.*, 1974] Pieces of furniture bearing the distinctive stamp range in date over the years c. 1780 to c. 1840, and are of mahogany unless otherwise stated. They include:

Pembroke table, the top of serpentine outline and the supports of tapering turned form with brass cup castors. [*Conn.*, August 1952, p. xxx, advert.]

Chest of drawers, serpentine, top crossbanded with ebonized border and inlaid stringing; four long drawers crossbanded with satinwood and the chamfered angles inlaid with pendent husks. [Christie's, 26 February 1970, lot 91]

Secretaire-chest, serpentine, top with gadrooned border, having three long drawers below a simulated pair that fall to reveal fitted secretaire, the canted angles carved with strapwork entwining foliage and flowers. [Sotheby's, 10 December 1965, lot 157]

Chest of drawers, bow-fronted, three small drawers above four long drawers all with satinwood bandings. [Sotheby's, 18 March 1966, lot 73]

Toilet table, banded in ebony and satinwood. Divided tray top enclosing compartments, with a drawer in the front and tapering legs. [Sotheby's, 18 March 1966, lot 74]

Sideboard, bow-fronted, two deep drawers flanking central shallow drawer over a tambour-fronted cupboard, the drawers cross-banded with satinwood and inlaid with fan ornament and the whole raised on square tapering legs with spade feet. [*Antique Collector*, June 1960, advert.]

Sideboard, Sheraton period, in the Dining Room at Wallington, Northumb.

Davenport, late Regency period. [*Antique Collecting*, August 1972, p. 20, advert.]

Wardrobe, c. 1835 with two narrow hanging compartments flanking six drawers. [G. Wills, *English Furniture 1760–1900*]   G. W.

Wilman, Stephen, Settle, Yorks., joiner/cm (1834–37). [D]

Wilmor, James, Market Pl., Buckingham, cm (1823). [D]

Wilmot, John, St George's Rd, Manchester, cm and u (1822). [D]

Wilmot, Thomas, parish of St James, Bristol, cm (1754). [Poll bk]

Wilmot, William, Bristol, u (1834–35). At Thornhill Pl., Upper Maudlin St in 1834 and Spring Hill, King Sq., in 1835. [D]

Wilmott, Thomas, 16 John St, Oxford St, London, cm, u and undertaker (1800–39). The business was already trading by April 1800 when he advertised a number of items of patent furniture, a line in which he took a particular interest in common with a number of his contemporaries. He offered 'SOFA and CHAIR BEDS on an Improved principle, with a new-invented Brass Hinge' and also 'improved Dining-Tables which will form four different Tables in one minute and dine from 4 to 20 persons conveniently'. From its commencement the business was a substantial size and in March 1801 insurance cover was £2,050 of which £1,300 was for utensils and stock. No fewer than three insurance policies were taken out in 1804 and these refer to a store at 13 John St and further stock and utensils at 'the Globe' as well as his household goods at a dwelling house at 6 Crescent, Minories. He was included by Thomas Sheraton in the list of master cabinet makers appended to his *Cabinet Dictionary*, 1803.

Wilmott may have had an export trade to Scandinavia for a set of chairs at the Palace of Tullgarn in Sweden bear his trade label. These are of a common type with an X-form back below the cresting board and turned front legs. Wilmott adopted a policy of labelling his output and a number of items have been noted bearing his trade label. These include a reading and writing table, a sofa table, a drum table, a music Canterbury, and a birchwood chair. [D; *Times*, 2 April 1800; GL, Sun MS vol. 419, ref. 715599, vol. 431, refs 760755, 764394, 769093; *DEF*; Christie's, 20 September 1979, lot 51; 10 May 1984, lot 148; Sotheby's, 28 March 1969, lot 90; *C. Life*, 16 December 1976, supplement, p. 22]

Wilms, Henry, address unknown, (1791). In November 1791 supplied Gertrude, Dowager Duchess of Bedford with 'two new fashionable fire screen stands of best mahogani' for her London house at 112 Pall Mall. £2 2s was charged for these. [Bedford Office, London]

Wilsea, Samuel, Maddermarket St, Norwich, cm (1801–12). The number in Maddermarket St was given as 10 and 11 in 1801–02. In 1805 he was described as a cm and linen draper. [D; poll bks]

Wilshaw, John, 17 Tottenham Ct Rd, London, cm (1809). [D]

Wilshe, William, Wolverhampton, Staffs., cm (1838). [D]

Wilshed, Daniel, Windmill St, Westminster, London, chairmaker (1749). [Poll bk]

Wilsmore, Edward M., Sudbury, Suffolk, cm (1824). [D]

Wilson, —, Ave Maria Lane, London, cm (d. 1788). Died 24 March 1788. He was Clerk of St Martin's, Ludgate. [*Gents Mag.*, September 1789]

Wilson, —, Laizenby Ct, Covent Gdn, London, cm (1803). Subscribed to Sheraton's *Cabinet Dictionary*, 1803.

Wilson, —, Blyth, Notts., cm (1840–d. 1841). His will is dated 19 July 1840 and he died in the following year. [Notts. RO, probate records]

Wilson, A, address unknown, Windsor chairmaker (c. 1830–40). A chair at Temple Newsam House, Leeds bears the stamp of this maker.

Wilson, Alexander, 87 Queen St, Portsea, Portsmouth, Hants., cm and u (1823). [D]

Wilson, Andrew, 47 Wardour St, Soho, London, chairmaker and cm (1779). In 1779 took out insurance cover of £400 of which £275 was for stock and utensils. [GL, Sun MS vol. 271, p. 352]

Wilson, Andrew, King St, Seven Dials, London, bedstead maker (1782–86). In 1782 took out insurance cover of £300 of which £170 was for utensils and stock. In May 1786 total insurance cover was £500. [GL, Sun MS vol. 302, p. 492; vol. 336, p. 440]

Wilson, Ann, High Wycombe, Bucks., caner (b. *c.* 1800–41). Aged 41 at the date of the 1841 Census.

Wilson, Ann & Edward, Strand, London, see Edward Wilson.

Wilson, Anthony, Bath St, Bristol, bedstead maker (1801). [D]

Wilson, Anthony, Lancaster, cm (1811–12). [Lancaster freemen rolls]

Wilson, Arthur, 22 Fishergate, Preston, Lancs., u (1822). [D]

Wilson, Benjamin, 1 Broker's Row, Moorfields, London, upholder, undertaker and furniture warehouse (1784–1825). Free of the Upholders' Co. under the terms of the 1750 Upholders' Act, 7 January 1784. From this year he was in partnership with a person named Dawes and traded as Wilson & Dawes. The partnership lasted until 1790. From 1791 trading on his own behalf but in 1817 the business was described as B. Wilson & Son. Up to this date he had traded as an upholder but in 1825 the business was described as a furniture warehouse. Benjamin Wilson took as app. Robert Metcalf, 1787–95. [D; GL, Upholders' Co. records]

Wilson, Charles, London, upholder (1714). Son of Edward Wilson of Emswell, Notts. and father of Edward Wilson. Charles Wilson was app. to Edward Wood and was free of the Upholders' Co. by servitude, 13 January 1713/14. [GL, Upholders' Co. records]

Wilson, Charles G., Bondgate, Alnwick, Northumb., joiner, cm and u (1827–28). [D]

Wilson, Christopher, Hull, Yorks., cm and undertaker (1790–1823). At 89 Mytongate 1790–1818 and 5 Hope St, 1821–23. [D]

Wilson, Christopher, Settle, Yorks., joiner/cm (1834). [D]

Wilson, D., 18 Compton St, Clerkenwell, London, cm (1820). [D]

Wilson, Daniel, Market Pl., Carlisle, Cumb., joiner and cm (1810). [D]

Wilson, Edward, London, upholder (1740). Son of Charles Wilson of London, upholder. App. to Abraham Saunders, a member of the Skinners' Co., 3 February 1729. Free of the Upholders' Co. under the terms of the 1750 Upholders' Act, 5 June 1760. [GL, Upholders' Co. records]

Wilson, Edward, 17 Mays Buildings, St Martin's Lane, London, cm (1780). In 1780 insured his house for £100. [GL, Sun MS vol. 281, p. 528]

Wilson, Edward, Strand, London, cm, u, appraiser and undertaker (1775–1824). Successor to and possibly the son of Walter Wilson. App. to M. Pennington of Lancaster 1775 and free 1783–84. Already by this date he was living in the Strand, London and no doubt active in the business of Walter Wilson which traded from 376 Strand. Although the business is referred to as Walter Wilson & Co. as late as 1803 it is possible that Edward took over its management from 1797 when a lease of 49¾ years was taken out on 128 Strand in the name of Edward & Ann Wilson. Ann appears to have been in partnership with Edward and their names are recorded jointly on an insurance policy as early as September 1792. Both 128 and 376 Strand were used by the business and Messrs. Wilson is included under both addresses in the list of master cabinet makers in Sheraton's *Cabinet Dictionary*, 1803. Trade cards of 1799 and 1810 are in the Banks Coll., BM, and these give only the 128 Strand address which was the showrooms. An insurance policy of October 1804 shows that both 128 and 129 were being used and utensils and stock here were valued at £3,000. Lofts, sheds and open yards behind 376 Strand were being utilised and cover here was a further £3,000. Walter may have had some continuing involvement, for directories to 1807 list A., E. & W. Wilson, but later only Ann & Edward are mentioned. Ann was still active as late as 1820. The high stock levels maintained in 1804 indicate an extensive business which must for many years have been profitable. In

August 1823 Edward was living at Wellington St, Strand and in that month took out insurance cover of £16,300 on houses jointly with a William Wilson. He appears however to have extended credit to customers on a lavish scale and in January 1824 was declared bankrupt. Creditors of the business included Lord Lilburne who owed £25,442 7s 6d secured by a mortgage on the Mamhead estate in Devon. [D; Lancaster app. reg.; freemen rolls; Marylebone Lib., deeds 133/2, 133/3, GL, Sun MS vol. 389, ref. 605411; vol. 431, refs 764338, 767809; vol. 498, refs 1006733–36, 1008753; *Brighton Gazette*, 22 January 1824; PRO, B3/5264]

Wilson, Edward, Alphington Rd, Exeter, Devon, carver (1791). [D]

Wilson, Francis, Middle St, Gt Driffield, Yorks., cm etc. (1823–28). [D]

Wilson, George, 32 Frythergate, Preston, Lancs., cm and u (1816–18). [D]

Wilson, George, Lancaster and London, u (1821–40). Son of George Wilson of Lancaster. App. to Edward Lodge, 7 March 1821. In 1847 recorded as an u in London. [App. reg.; Preston RO, DDX 1122]

Wilson, George, Greenwich, London, cm (1838–39). In 1838 at Royal Hill and in 1839 in South St. [D]

Wilson, George, 5 Bond St, Brighton, Sussex, cm and u (1839). [D]

Wilson, George, 30 Judd Pl. West, Somerstown, London, cm and u (1839). [D]

Wilson, George, Silver St, Lincoln, cm and u (1835–40). The number in Silver St was 40 in 1841. [D]

Wilson, H., Exeter, Devon, cm (1816). [Poll bk]

Wilson, Henry, Lancaster and Kendal, joiner and cm (1779). Free of Lancaster 1779–80 but at this date living in Kendal. [Lancaster freemen rolls]

Wilson, Henry, 24 Ranelegh St, Liverpool, cm (1803). [D]

Wilson, Henry, Monk Wearmouthshore, Sunderland, Co. Durham, carver and ship's carver (1827). [D]

Wilson, Henry, Skipton, Yorks., cm (1829). [PR (Holy Trinity)]

Wilson, Henry, Skinnergate, Darlington, Co. Durham, cm/joiner (1834). [D]

Wilson, Henry, 28 North Audley St, London, carver and gilder (1839). [D]

Wilson, Isaac, Cabbage Lane, Halifax, Yorks., cm (1822). [D]

Wilson, Isabella, Liverpool, u (1817). In partnership with William May and Peter Sharp, and named with them in insolvency proceedings in January 1817. [*Liverpool Mercury*, 10 January 1817] See Peter Sharp.

Wilson, J. Weatherall, 64 Leadenhall St, London, carver and gilder (1784–93). [D]

Wilson, J., 3 Walkers Ct, Poultrey St, London, cm (1794). [Heal]

Wilson, J., 19 King St, Seven Dials, London, bedstead maker (1820). [D]

Wilson, Jacob, London, cm and u (1809–39). At 90 Charlotte St, Fitzroy Sq., 1809–16 at then at 6 Welbeck St, Cavendish Sq. until 1839. In 1816 the business was said to be situated on the corner of Welbeck St and Wigmore St, Cavendish Sq. In July 1816 Wilson advertised that he had 'obtained a PATENT for improvements in BEDSTEADS and FURNITURE on an entire new principle, which combines elegance with great utility and convenience: and so constructed, as to suit either large or small rooms, offices, cabins or temporary bed-rooms, and may be put away into a very small space'. Beds constructed on this principle were to be seen displayed in his ware-rooms. His trade cards are in the Landauer Coll., MMA, NY, and the BM. [D; *Times*, 3 July 1816] See James Wilson of Wigmore St.

Wilson, James, Castle St, Westminster, London, cm (1749). [Poll bk]

Wilson, James, London, carver (before 1755). By June 1755 working from the Anthony Hay workshop in Virginia, USA. Claimed to be 'from London'. [*Virginia Gazette*, 20 June 1755]

Wilson, James, London, (1772). In 1772 supplied '3 very neat Japan'd Card Racks' at 4s each to Sir John Griffin Griffin for his London house. [Essex RO, D/D/By/A30/2]

Wilson, James, Angel St, St Margaret's, Westminster, London, u (1784). [Poll bk]

Wilson, James, East Side of High St, south of White Lion Entry, Hull, Yorks., cm (1793). [D]

Wilson, James, address unknown, cm (1803). Subscribed to Sheraton's *Cabinet Dictionary*, 1803.

Wilson, James, 18a (or 19), Wigmore St, Cavendish Sq., London, cm (1817–39). A combined writing and games table of c. 1830 exists with a brass plate indicating the name of this maker at 18a Wigmore St. Another games table with a brass plate affixed gives the name Wilson & Son, Wigmore St and the words 'Patent No. 189'. Heal suggests that there was a connection between this maker and Jacob Wilson of Welbeck St. and a trading relationship seems likely. [D; V&A archives; Joy, *English Furniture 1800–1851*, p. 198]

Wilson, James, 53 Duke St, Leeds, Yorks., joiner, builder and cm (1826). [D]

Wilson, James, Dam Side, Morpeth, Northumb., joiner and cm (1828–34). [D]

Wilson, James, 35 Bridge St, Sheffield, Yorks., cm (1833). [D]

Wilson, James, Huddersfield, Yorks., cm (1834). [D]

Wilson, Jasper, 7 Castle St, Long Acre, London, cm (1835). [D]

Wilson, Jasper, 17 Grosvenor Pl., Pimlico, London, u (1835). [D]

Wilson, Jekyl, High St, Boston, Lincs., cm, u and joiner (1822–26). [D]

Wilson, John snr and jnr, Norwich, u (1710–14). Took apps named Bulwer in 1710, Robins in 1712 and Pitts and Clayton in 1714. [S of G, app. index]

Wilson, John, Hull, Yorks., cm (1747–84). [Poll bks]

Wilson, John, Lancaster, cm (1767–68). [Lancaster freemen rolls]

Wilson, John, Sidneys Alley, Leicester Fields, London, cm (1778). In 1778 took out insurance cover of £100 but only £20 of this was for utensils and stock. [GL, Sun MS vol. 267, p. 361]

Wilson, John, Lancaster, cm (1770–87). App. to W. Bruce 1770 and free, 1779–80. Named in the Gillow records 1784 and 1786–87. [Freemen rolls; poll bk; Westminster Ref. Lib., Gillow]

Wilson, John, Beverley, Yorks., cm (1780). Freeman of Hull but in 1780 living in Beverley. [Hull poll bk]

Wilson, John, St Martin's Churchyard, St Martin's Lane, London, cm (1791). On 3 January 1791 insured household goods for £100. [GL, Sun MS ref. 578336]

Wilson, John, London, cm (1793). Subscribed to Sheraton's *Drawing Book*, 1793.

Wilson, John, 26 Borough High St, Southwark, London, cm (1800–03). In March 1800 a Susanna Boswell complained that she was pregnant by John Wilson. A man by this name living in 'Borough' was a subscriber to Sheraton's *Cabinet Dictionary*, 1803. [GL, P83/MRYI/870/46]

Wilson, John, 70 Gt Queen St, Lincoln's Inn Fields, London, upholder and cm (1805–13). In January 1805 took out insurance cover of £350 on utensils and stock kept at his dwelling house at Gt Queen St. He undertook no work here as he maintained a workshop at 41 Eagle St, Red Lion Sq. valued at £50 which contained utensils and stock valued at £250. No further reference is made to this workshop and subsequently the cover of £350 in 1808 and £400 in 1810 was for stock and utensils at Gt Queen St. [D; GL, Sun MS vol. 431, ref. 769573; vol. 440, ref. 812774; vol. 453, ref. 839772]

Wilson, John, Lancaster, cm (1806–07). [Lancaster freemen rolls]

Wilson, John, London, cm (1806–09). At 20 New Round Ct in May 1806 when he took out insurance cover of £200 on his stock and utensils. In July 1809 at 7 Poland St where total cover was only £100 and of this £20 was specified for a chest of tools, the remainder being for household goods. [GL, Sun MS vol. 437, ref. 790221; vol. 448, ref. 832683]

Wilson, John, Liverpool, cm, u and looking-glass manufacturer (1814–34). In June 1814 announced the opening of his shop at 71 Lord St as the successor to R. Rossen. He claimed to have had experience 'in the first Houses in London'. His stock consisted of 'Elegant Beds, Drawing Room Curtains, Chairs etc. with every other article in the above line'. He also had for sale 'Fine seasoned FEATHERS, by Patent Stoves' and offered to alter 'old Beds & Draperies . . . to the present mode'. An app. was also required. He obtained stock from London and in June 1819 claimed to have returned from there with 'a variety of UPHOLSTERY & CABINET FURNITURE'. He also had a quantity of paper hangings at very reduced prices and five large mahogany bookcases that he thought suitable for a library of 'a Professional Gentleman'. The number of his shop in Lord St was given as 51, by 1827 it was 71 and in 1829, 69. This may be a case of Post Office re-numbering rather than a move of location. By June 1827 he had decided to move to Clayton Sq. where his number is given as 17 though he appears to have occupied 15 and 16 also. It was his intention not to renew his lease at Lord St which expired on 3 October 1827 and the surplus stock kept here he put up for auction in August. On offer were 'Brussels, Venetian & Kidderminster Room & Stair Carpets, Hearth Rugs, brown Lapland Rugs, White Sheep Skin Ditto, London Paper Hangings & Bordering, Dressing Glasses, real Rosewood French polished Card Tables, Silk & Worsted Fringes, Mahogany Portable Water-Closets & Lancaster Night Chairs, Mahogany Cribs etc.'. The move was unsuccessful and already by April 1829 he had determined to close the Clayton Sq. premises and move the business back to Lord St. It would seem likely that he never gave the Lord St premises up when he went to Clayton Sq. The move was however rather contracted and it was not until March 1832 that he announced the final closure of the Clayton Sq. address and the sale of the stock there 'at extremely low prices (for cash) to make room for an entirely new stock at 69 Lord-Street'. His stock of wall papers were, he stated, 'regularly supplied . . . from the first London Houses'. The move and the sale of stock were probably connected with financial difficulties for in May 1834 his bankruptcy was announced. One directory of 1834 shows a new address at 3 Devonshire Pl. Possibly the maker who supplied furniture to Erddig, Clwyd and was paid a balance of £106 19s 10½d on 2 May 1820. [D; *Liverpool Mercury*, 10 June 1814, 18 June 1819, 22 June 1827, 10 August 1827, 10 April 1829, 9 March 1832; *Chester Courant* 6 May 1834; V&A archives]

Wilson, John, Livery St, Birmingham, cm and u (1816–30). At 126 Livery St, 1828–30. [D]

Wilson, John, Stockport, Cheshire, cm and joiner (1816–28). At Hillgate in 1816, Mottram St in 1818, Bamford St in 1822 and Chestergate in 1828. [D]

Wilson, John, Manchester, cm and u (1817–40). In 1817 at 8 Garden St, Chorlton Row and in 1822 at 8 New Bailey St, but from 1824 activity was centred in King St. The number was 3 in 1824–25 but one directory of 1825 gives 8 King St and a home address at 8 George St, Windsor. In 1828 the number in King St was 8, in 1829 it was 48 and 1832–40 it was 36. [D]

Wilson, John, Hospital St, Nantwich, Cheshire, cm (1817–34). Four daughters and two sons bapt., 1817–32. [PR (bapt.)]

Wilson, John, 2 Dale St, Preston, Lancs., cm (1818). [D]

Wilson, John, 20 Ravald St, Salford, Lancs., carver and gilder (1825). [D]

Wilson, John, Grantham, Lincs., wood turner and chairmaker (1826–35). At Westgate in 1826 and Manford Rd in 1835. [D]

Wilson, John, 24 Turner St, Manchester, cm (1828). [D]

Wilson, John, Hungate, Pickering, Yorks., cm (1828–40). [D]

Wilson, John, Spencer's Yd, Skipton, Yorks., joiner/cm (1830–37). [D]

Wilson, John, Exeter, Devon, cm (1832–40). Living in the parish of St Martin in 1832. His address is given as Cathedral Yd, 1836–38. [D; poll bk, *Exeter Flying Post*, 4 February 1836, 9 February 1843]

Wilson, John, Wellington Mart, Hull, Yorks., joiner and cm (1834). [D]

Wilson, John, 51 Duke St, Leeds, Yorks., cm and joiner (1834). [D]

Wilson, John, 1 Milk St, Manchester, cm and u (1836). [D]

Wilson, John, Wellington St, Woolwich, London, cm, u and furniture broker (1838–39). In 1838 at 31 Wellington St. [D]

Wilson, John, Liverpool St, Bishopsgate, London, cm and u (1839). [D]

Wilson, John, High Wycombe, Bucks., caner (b. c. 1791–1841). Aged 50 at the date of the 1841 Census.

Wilson, John Wetherall, 64 Leadenhall St, London, carver and gilder (1783–84). In 1783 took out insurance cover of £400 of which £150 was for utensils and stock. [D; GL, Sun MS vol. 314, p. 325]

Wilson, Jonathan, Liverpool, cm (1804–18). At 23 Havington St, Castle St in 1804 but in the following year at 21 School Lane with a shop in Ranelagh St. From 1807 to 1811 at 4 Clare St but from 1813–18 the address was once more shown as School Lane and Ranelagh St. [D]

Wilson, Joseph, Blackman St, Southwark, London, upholder and appraiser (1802–09). At 58 Blackman St in 1802 and 68 in 1805–09. In July 1802 took out insurance cover of £700 of which £550 was for utensils and stock. [D; GL, Sun MS vol. 424, ref. 735160]

Wilson, Joseph, address unknown, cm (1803). Subscribed to Sheraton's *Cabinet Dictionary*, 1803.

Wilson, Joseph, Leeds, Yorks., cm (1821–34). Shown at 3 Duke St in 1821 but the number was 4 from 1826–34. One directory of 1830 however gives an address at Garland's Fold, Timble Bridge. [D]

Wilson, Joseph, 8 Pennell's Yd, Nottingham, cm (1832). [D]

Wilson, Mary, 126 Livery St, Birmingham, u, bed and mattress maker (1828). [D]

Wilson, Mary, Fleece Lane (or Yd), Leeds, Yorks., u (1830–37). The number in Fleece Lane (or Yd) is given as 45 in 1834 and 46 in 1830 and 1837. [D]

Wilson, Mary, Minster Yd, Ripon, Yorks., joiner/cm (1837). [D] See Thomas Wilson of Minster Yd.

Wilson, Mathias, Soresby St, Chesterfield, Derbs., cm (1829–32). [D]

Wilson, Matthew, Hull, Yorks., joiner and cm (1823–39). At Johnson's Ct, 156 High St in 1823. This appears to have been his residence. From 1826–31 however he was trading from Stewart's Yd. In the period 1834–40 at 50 High St, Market Pl. [D]

Wilson, Nathaniel, Beverley, Yorks., cm (1774–91). In 1778 took out insurance cover of £400 on some houses. [GL, Sun MS vol. 266, p. 326]

Wilson, Newman, 13 Bridgewater St, Liverpool, cabinet turner (1824). [D]

Wilson, Peter, 25 Drury Lane, London, cm and broker (1792). In April 1792 took out insurance cover of £600 of which £500 was for utensils and stock. [GL, Sun MS vol. 382, ref. 599080]

Wilson, Peter, Old Gdns, Shudehill, Manchester, chairmaker (1817). [D]

Wilson, Peter, 64 Exmouth St, Spitalfields, London, cm and u (1822). [D]

Wilson, Richard, Gray's Inn Lane, London, cm (1790–93). Heal records Richard & Robert Wilson at this address, 1790–93. [D]

Wilson, Richard, 182 Gt Ancoats St, Manchester, cm (1825). [D]

Wilson, Richard, 69 London Rd, Liverpool, cm (1827). [D]

Wilson, Robert, Gray's Inn Lane, London, cm and joiner (1783–93). At 7 Little James St, Gray's Inn Lane, 1783–87. In 1783 he took out insurance cover of £300 of which stock and utensils were valued at £112. In January 1787 insured a house in Drury Lane for £100. Directories show him at 93 Gray's Inn Lane, 1789–93. [D; GL, Sun MS vol. 317, p. 35; vol. 340, p. 532] See Richard Wilson.

Wilson, Robert, Mount, Castle-garth, Newcastle, joiner and cm (1811). [D]

Wilson, Robert, Liverpool, cm and joiner (1823–39). In 1823 at 61 Fontenoy St and the following year at 67 Sawney Pope St. Directories of 1827 show either 31 Gerard St or 26 Park St. In 1829 at 23 Johnson St with a shop at 82 Gt Crosshall St. By 1834 at 9 Rose St with a shop at 238 Scotland Rd. The Rose St address is repeated in directories of 1835–37 but the number in Scotland Rd changed to 255. One directory of 1835 however lists a yard and shop at 1 Nash Grove. In 1839 his manufactory was at 11 St John Village. [D]

Wilson, Robert, Skinnergate, Darlington, Co. Durham, joiner and cm (1837). [D]

Wilson, Robert, Lancaster (1831–33). [Westminster Ref. Lib. Gillow records]

Wilson, S. W., Laytons Buildings, Southwark, London, u (1820). [D]

Wilson, Sam., London, (1725). In 1725 supplied to the Duke of Montrose a 'pair of tables and men' at £2 9s. These may have been chess boards and pieces. [Scottish RO, GD/220/6/1346/8]

Wilson, Samuel, Chesterfield, Derbs., cm, toyman and auctioneer (1793). [D]

Wilson, Samuel, Chesterfield, Derbs., cm (1818–22). At Market Pl. in 1818 and Sorsby St in 1822. [D]

Wilson, Samuel, 144 High St, Southwark, London, u and undertaker (1820–23). Heal lists Samuel & W. Wilson at this address. 1825–27. [D]

Wilson, Samuel, Radford, Notts., joiner, cm and chairmaker (1832–34). At Alfreton Rd in 1834 when he was described as a chairmaker. [D]

Wilson, Samuel & Sons, High St, Chesterfield, Derbs., u (1822). [D]

Wilson, T., North St, Exeter, Devon, cm (1816). A Thomas Wilson was trading at Cathedral Yd, 1823–32. [D; poll bk]

Wilson, Thomas, Lancaster, cm (1748–84). App. to A. Baines 1748 and free, 1766–67. [App. bk; freemen rolls; poll bks]

Wilson, Thomas, Furness area, Lancs., joiner (1673–76). Employed by the owners of Swarthwood Hall, Furness, Lancs. to make furniture. He is described in the household accounts as a 'wright'. On 1 November 1673 paid 5s 10d for sawing a tree into boards. A payment made on 24 April 1675 was for five days work making a 'firdale chair' at 2s 4d, and on 11 March 1675/76 a further 2s 6d was paid for the five days work making a Trundle bedstead etc. [N. Penney, *The Household Account Book of Sarah Fell of Swarthmoor Hall*, 1920, pp. 11, 209, 251]

Wilson, Thomas, London(?) (1770). Charged Sir John Griffin Griffin of Audley End, Essex £4 17s 6d for a reading stand 'of Pallemon wood Inlaid with Ebbinoy' and fitted with castors. [Essex RO, D/DBy/A28 (3 or 4)]

Wilson, Thomas, 59 Castle St, Oxford Mkt, London, cm (1778). In 1778 insured a house for £200. [GL, Sun MS vol. 263, p. 325]

Wilson, Thomas, London, upholder (1771–1802). Son of William Wilson of St Margaret's, Westminster, victualler. App. to John Kent, 4 December 1771 and free of the Upholders' Co. by servitude, 1 September 1779. [GL, Upholders' Co. records]

Wilson, Thomas, Liverpool, u (1802). App. to Matthew Gregson and free 5 July 1802. [Freemen rolls]

Wilson, Thomas, Southwark, London, cm and u (1790–1805). Partner with a person named Reed and trading from 20 King St as Wilson & Reed, 1790–93. By 1794 the partners had moved to 102 Borough High St, at which address they operated until 1800. By 1804 however Thomas Wilson was back at 20 King St and trading on his own behalf as a cm. In the following year a Thomas Wilson, upholder was at 125 Tottenham Ct Rd, but it is not certain that this was the same man. [D]

Wilson, Thomas, 22 Cathedral Yd, Exeter, Devon, cm and u (1818–40). In April 1818 he advertised his business as a 'FASHIONABLE UPHOLSTERY, CHAIR AND CABINET WARE-ROOMS'. He stocked Kidderminster, Brussels, Venetian and East India Hemp carpeting, paper hangings obtained from London sources, feathers and mahogany and fancy woods. The business was referred to as Wilson & Co. a style that was to be used throughout the trading life of the concern. The rooms for storing and cleaning feathers were said to have been 'lately completed ... on the same construction as the principal houses in London'. The cabinet furniture offered for sale in March 1819 was declared to be 'of their own manufacture'. In March 1823 their stock was stated to be priced 'suited to the present depressed state of manufacture'. Apart from the manufacture and sale of cabinet and upholstery goods they operated a 'General Agency Office' in the name of Wilson, Patey & Co., surveyors, auctioneers and appraisers. The sudden death of Thomas Wilson was announced on 17 January 1831 but Wilson & Co. continued to trade from the same address. [D; *Exeter Flying Post*, 16 April 1818, 11 March 1819, 19 March 1829; *The Alfred*, 25 March 1823, 17 January 1832]

Wilson, Thomas, 138 Snow Hill, Birmingham, cm and u (1828–30). [D]

Wilson, Thomas, Beddern Bank, Minster Yd, Ripon, Yorks., joiner and cm (1828–34). The Mary Wilson trading at Minster Yd in 1837 may have been his widow. [D]

Wilson, Thomas, Harrington, Workington, Cumb., joiner, cm and ironmonger (1811–34). [D]

Wilson, Thomas, Longtown, Carlisle, Cumb., joiner/cm (1829). [D]

Wilson, Thomas, Pickering, Yorks., cm (1834–40). [D]

Wilson, Thomas, 21 King St, Covent Gdn, London, u (1835). [D]

Wilson, Thomas, Liverpool, chairmaker (1840). Free 24 July 1840 by patrimony, being son of John Wilson, broker. [Freemen rolls]

Wilson, Walter, Lancaster and London, cm (1752–68). App. to G. Rawes in 1752 and free 1767–68. At the time of his freedom said to be living in London and still there in 1768. [App. reg.; freemen rolls; poll bk]

Wilson, Walter, Strand, London, cm and u (1767–c. 1797). The business originated in a partnership between Walter Wilson and William Brown. They traded from 405 Strand, 1767–77, but from 1779 until the termination of the partnership in *c.* 1782 the number was 376 Strand. The business traded as Wilson & Brown and was of substantial proportions. In 1775 the partners took out insurance cover of £2,500 of which £2,200 was for utensils and stock. The business attracted influential patrons who placed orders of substantial proportions. Payments for furniture supplied to Chiswick House amounted to £16 19s 6d in 1780, £382 8s in 1785 and £191 2s 8d in 1787. For Chatsworth, Derbs. a 'Field Bedstead with Dome Tester' was supplied complete with 'choclate strip'd cotton furniture'. This was invoiced on 24 December 1785 and charged at £7 7s with an additional 3s 6d for packing. In 1788 white ground Wilton carpeting was supplied valued at £71 19s 8d and '16 very neat Matted Chairs with Taper feet & upright Splats and very richly Japan'd' at £1 5s each. Two matching elbow chairs cost £3 3s. Between 1790 and 1797 furniture was supplied to Richard Arkwright for Willersley Castle, Cromford, Derbs. In 1791 goods to the value of £1,615 17s 11½d were recorded. A state bed, matching armchairs, chairs and canapés supplied in 1794–96 for this house are now in the Alfred Beit Collection at Russborough, Co. Wicklow. The cost of furnishings supplied in 1794 was £4,413 9s 9½d. The 1792–93 bills included work undertaken for Arkwright at 8 Adam St, London. From *c.* 1783 Walter Wilson was assisted in the business by Edward Wilson and later by Ann Wilson, probably his son and daughter. From *c.* 1797 they were responsible for the running of the business. In the 1790s the business is often named as Wilson & Co. [D; GL, Sun MS vol. 240, p. 377; vol. 290, p. 522; vol. 298, p. 378; Chatsworth papers; Derbs. RO, Arkwright 978M/E3–6, 9–11; Russborough Guide]

Wilson, William, parish of St Mary, Newington, London, carver (1766–67). In 1766 insured several properties, the total cover being £2,800. [Heal; GL, Hand in Hand MS vol. 105, pp. 95, 174]

Wilson, William, Little Windmill St, London, cm (1774). [Westminster poll bk]

Wilson, William, Hoxton Sq., London, upholder (1780–87). Son of William Wilson snr of Hoxton Sq., Gent. App. to Mark Dawes, 4 October 1780 and free of the Upholders' Co. by servitude, 5 August 1787. At this date living in Hoxton Sq. [GL, Upholders' Co. records]

Wilson, William, London, u (1789–1823). Connected with the enterprises of Walter Wilson and Edward Wilson who conducted important businesses as cm and u in the Strand. He was certainly related to these two entrepreneurs and was possibly a brother to Edward Wilson. Like Edward he was trained at Lancaster being app. to A. Bell of that town as an u in 1762. He was not however made free until 1789–90. At the date of his freedom he was stated to be 'of the Strand, London'. In 1793 he subscribed to Sheraton's *Drawing Book.* By the first decade of the 19th century the business at 128 and 367 Strand was trading as Wilsons or Wilson & Co. with Edward and Ann Wilson the main partners. One directory of 1805 however lists the business as A. E. & W. Wilson and it is possible that William Wilson was a partner at this period. The death of William's wife was recorded in October 1810. William was said to be an u of the Strand but was living at Caroline St, Bedford Sq. In August 1823 he insured jointly with Edward Wilson houses valued at £16,300 but in that year was recorded independently trading as a cm and u from 2 Wellington St, Waterloo Bridge. When in the following year the bankruptcy of Edward Wilson was announced, William's name was not connected with these proceedings. [D; Lancaster app. reg.; Lancaster freemen rolls; *Gents Mag.,* October 1810; GL, Sun MS vol. 498, refs 1006733–36, 1008753]

Wilson, William, parish of St Michael, Lincoln, cm (1971). In July 1791 took out insurance cover of £600. [GL, Sun MS vol. 379, p. 239]

Wilson, William, Norwich, cm (1780–1818). Living in the parish of St Laurence 1780, parish of St Peter Mancroft 1784, parish of St Michael at Plea, 1790–96, Hemblington, Norfolk 1799 and the parish of St Peter, Hungate, 1802–07. On 1 July 1812 his son Robert, a carpenter, was made free. [Poll bks; freemen rolls]

Wilson, William, Manchester, cm (1788–1808). At Rook St, 1788, 46 High St in 1797–1802; 29 Piccadilly in 1804 and 27 Piccadilly 1805–08. [D]

Wilson, William, Barton-on-Humber, Lincs., cm (1802). Freeman of Hedon, Yorks. [Hedon poll bk]

Wilson, William, 137 Dale St, Liverpool, u (1823–24). Leased his shop in Dale St from Liverpool Corporation. The shop had a frontage of 6 yds and a depth of 21 yds and was identical with its neighbouring property no. 136. Both properties were put up for sale by auction in February 1824. [D; *Liverpool Mercury,* 30 January 1824]

Wilson, William, Waterloo St, Ironmonger Row, Old St, London, clock case maker (1820–35). Shown at 14 Waterloo St in 1820 and 1835 but in 1824 shown at 14. In 1820 took out insurance cover of £600 which included £250 on stock and utensils 'in shops adjoining & £15 in a small shop opposite'. By May 1824 the insurance cover had risen to £1,200 of which £1,125 was for stock and utensils. [D; GL, Sun MS vol. 481, ref. 968046; vol. 497, ref. 1016784]

Wilson, William, Boroughgate, Appleby, Westmld, cm (1828–29). [D]

Wilson, William, Longtown, Carlisle, Cumb., joiner/cm (1828–29). [D]

Wilson, William, 11 Stonegate, York, cm (1830). Son of William Wilson snr who was a basketmaker of Malton, Yorks. The father was already dead by 24 January 1826 when his son was app. to John Ellison, cm. It would appear that William Wilson jnr did not complete his full apprenticeship, as by 1830 he was trading from 11 Stonegate. [D; app. reg.]

Wilson, William, Kirkburton, near Huddersfield, Yorks., joiner/cm (1834). [D]

Wilson, William, 7 Castle St, Hull, Yorks., cm and gilder (1835–40). [D]

Wilson & Bedford, Bawtry, Yorks., cm and joiners (1828–37). In 1828 at High St, but by 1837 trading additionally at Winter Rd and Church St. [D]

Wilson & Co., Exeter, Devon, see Thomas Wilson, Exeter.

Wilson & Co., Strand, London, see Edward, Walter and William Wilson of London.

Wilson & Dawes, see Benjamin Wilson.

Wilson & Popperwell, Hare St, Hull, Yorks., cm (*c.* 1770). A serpentine commode is known with the trade label of this maker affixed. [V&A archives]

Wilson & Read, Southwark, see Thomas Wilson, Southwark.

Wilson & Read, Prince's St, Leicester Sq., London, cm (1790–93). [D]

Wilson & Son, Wigmore St, London, see J. Wilson, Wigmore St.

Wilson & Son, A., 18 Ogle St, Gt Titchfield St, London, cm and u (1831–39). Paid £24 10s in September 1831 by the 3rd Lord Barybrooke of Audley End, Essex. At 18 Ogle St, 1835–39. [D; Essex RO, D/DBy/A358]

Wilson & Wilkinson, Leeds, Yorks., cm (1816–82). At 42 or 43 Kirkgate in 1816 and in Duke St, 1818. A Joseph Wilson, cm was trading in Duke St, 1821–24. [D]

Withew & Wright, 40 Prince's St, Leicester Sq., London, u (1816). [D]

Wilton, Edward, Queen St, Portsea, Portsmouth, Hants., carver and gilder (1823–30). In 1830 at 56 Queen St. [D]

Wilton, J., London, picture frame maker (1774). Two payments are recorded in the Burton Constable accounts to this maker in August 1774. The first dated 6 August was for £7 7s and the second dated 13 August was for £3 13s 8d. [Humberside RO, Burton Constable vouchers]

Wilton, William, Hedge Lane, Charing Cross and Edward St, Cavendish Sq., London (late 18th century). The son of a plasterer. Imitated the French practice of making papier-mâché ornaments for chimney-pieces and looking-glasses. His workshops were at Edward St. [Wills, *Looking-Glasses*]

Wiltshire, S. C., 1 Ball Alley, Lombard St, London, carver and gilder, paper hangings manufacturer (1820). [D]

Wiltshire, Thomas, London, upholder (1718). Son of Jeremiah Wiltshire of Hatfield Broadoaks, Essex, woolcomber. App. to Thomas Goldsmith, 7 December 1709 and free of the Upholders' Co. by servitude, 5 March 1717/18. [GL, Upholders' Co. records]

Wiltshire, Thomas, Upper Ryde, Ryde, Isle of Wight, Hants., cm (1830). [D]

Wilway, George, Broadmead, Bristol, cm and broker (1791–1801). In 1791–92 supplied furniture to the value of £52 2s for the house of John Pinney at 7 Gt George St, Bristol (now the Georgian House Museum). [D; *Furn. Hist.*, 1796]

Wimble, William, 35 Horse Fair, Bristol, cm (1775). [D]

Wimble, William, Church St, Sculcoates, Hull, Yorks., cm (1834). [D]

Wimbles, William, Manchester, cm (1813–17). At 22 Cockgates in 1813 and 20 Queen St, Salford in 1817. [D]

Wimper, George, address unrecorded (1821). A Regency period japanned chinoiserie cabinet signed 'Made by George Wimper in the employ of Mr Loudon Dec. 6th 1821' sold Sotheby's, 15 November 1985, lot 136.

Wimpenny, William, London, upholder (1699–1714). Son of Thomas Wimpenny of the parish of St Clement Danes, cook. App. to Christopher Broughton, 2 August 1699 and free of the Upholders' Co. by servitude, 5 May 1714. [GL, Upholders' Co. records]

Winch, John, Priory St, Colchester, Essex, cm and u (1839). [D]

Winch, William, High Wycombe, Bucks., cm (1836). Daughter bapt. 1836. [PR (bapt.)]

Winchester, Daniel, West side of Fleet Ditch, London, upholder (1710–21). Both in September 1710 and October 1717 insured his house at Fleet Ditch for £550. In 1721 fined for declining parochial service in the parish of St Bride, Fleet St. [GL, Hand in Hand MS vol. 8, ref. 20732; vol. 17, p. 299; MS 6561, p. 32]

Windale, Michael, Northgate, Darlington, Co. Durham, joiner and cm (1827–34). [D]

Winder, Edward, Lancaster and Liverpool, cm (1806–11). Free of Lancaster 1806–07 and already by this date living in Liverpool. Trading at 9 Robert St, 1811. [D; Lancaster freemen rolls]

Winder, George, Lancaster, cm (1778–86). App. to W. Bruce 1778 and free, 1785–86. [App. reg.; freemen rolls]

Winder, Robert, Duke St, Blackburn, Lancs., cm (1818). [D]

Winder, Thomas, Lancaster, cm (1806–20). Free 1806–07. Named in the Gillow records, 1813–20. [Freemen rolls; Westminster Ref. Lib., Gillow]

Winder, Thomas, Lancaster, cm (1825–26). [Lancaster freemen rolls]

Winder, William, Lancaster, cm (1801–02). [Lancaster freemen rolls]

Winder & Johnson, Preston, Lancs., cm (1799–1802). Signed the *Preston Cabinet Makers' and Chair Makers' Book of Prices*, 1802, on behalf of the masters. See Bray & Winder, Preston.

Windgrave, G. H., address unknown, cm (c. 1840). Trade label noted on a rosewood chiffonier. [Sotheby's, 8 May 1981, lot 218, 11 September 1981, lot 125]

Windham, George, East St, Horsham, Sussex, chairmaker and turner (1832–40). [D]

Windle, James, Water St, Clitheroe, Lancs., chairmaker (1824–28). [D]

Windle, John & Joseph, Chipping, near Preston, Lancs., chairmakers (1834). [D]

Windle, Thomas, Bridgegate, Howden, Yorks., cm (1826–34). [D]

Window, William, parish of St. Catherine, Gloucester, cm (1816). Child bapt. 1816. [PR (bapt.)]

Windscheffell, Christian, London, bedstead manufacturer (1820–26). At 2 Leman St, Goodman's Fields in 1820 and 30 Catherine St, Commercial Rd in 1826. [D]

Windscheffell, D. & J., 10 Radcliffe Highway and 3 New Rd, St George's-in-the-East, London, u and bedstead manufacturer (1816–29). [D]

Windscheffell, W., Drury Lane, London, cm, chairmaker, u and bedstead maker (1820–39). At 54 Drury Lane but some directories show no. 134, 1829–35. [D]

Windsor, John, 5 Berkeley St, Clerkenwell, London, cm and firescreen manufacturer (1820). [D]

Windsor, Richard, 24 Gt Sutton St, London, firescreen manufacturer and cm (1820–39). [D]

Windspere, Edward, 30 Parliament St, Liverpool, cm and shopkeeper (1807). [D]

Winfield, James, Peaseholme Green, York, cm (1758). [Poll bk]

Winfield, R. W., Birmingham and London, metal furniture manufacturer (1839). Maintained showrooms at Cambridge St, Birmingham and his residence was 'The Hawthorns', Ladywood, Edgbaston. Also traded in London from addresses at 11 Belle Sauvage Yd, Ludgate Hill and 26 New Bond St. Manufactured a wide range of goods of iron and brass which included 'metallic military bedsteads' for which he claimed he was 'proprietor of the original patent'. Also produced metal fire screen poles and hat and umbrella stands. His advertisement appears in *Pigot's Directory*, 1839.

Wing, —, Pontefract, Yorks., see Lowcock & Wing.

Wing, Matthew, London, u (1706–08). The maker of a bed including the tester, headboard, cornices and mouldings for the Earl of Salisbury for Dover House. The bed with its furnishings cost £142 10s 2d. [Hatfield House MS, bills 431]

Wingate, James, parish of St Catherine, Gloucester, cm and chairmaker (1813–20). Child bapt. 1813. [PR (bapt.)]

Wingate, William, Gloucester, cm, chairmaker, auctioneer and appraiser (1820–36). At Northgate St, 1820–23 and Lower Northgate St, 1830. A child was bapt. at St Aldgate Church in 1836 and he was then living at Bristol Rd. [D; PR (bapt.)]

Wingate & Whitehead, St Katherine St, Gloucester, chairmakers (1839–40). [D]

Wingfield, Henry, Hastings, Sussex, cm, u, auctioneer and appraiser (1823–40). At 42 High St, 1823–26. A trade card listing a High St address is in the Dept of Prints of the V&A. It is illustrated with engravings of a sabre-legged chair and a Grecian settee. In 1832 at West St and in 1839 at 1 George St. [D]

Wingnett, C., address unknown, cm (1803). Subscribed to Sheraton's *Cabinet Dictionary*, 1803.

Wingyett, Charles, Bartholomew Yd, Exeter, Devon, cm (d. 1809). An inquest was held into the death of Charles Wingyett. On 1 June the verdict that he had cut his throat 'in a fit of insanity' was published. An auction of his stock and workshops was arranged for 3 July 1809. [*Exeter Flying Post*, 1 June 1809, 22 June 1809]

Winks, Henry, Bath St, Ashby-de-la-Zouch, Leics., cm (1829). [D]

Winks, William, Gainsborough, Lincs., cm, u and painter (1826–28). At Bridge St in 1826 and Sevenfoot Lane in 1828. [D]

Winmill, Charles, 6 Pleasant Row, Pentonville, London, cm (1835). [D]

Winn, John, Newark, Notts., cm, u and chairmaker (1793–1819). At Parish St, 1793–1808, but in 1819 at Guildhall St. [D]

Winn, John, Kirkgate, Leeds, Yorks., cm, u, appraiser and furniture broker (1815–28). At 82 Kirkgate 1815–22 but by 1828 the number was 19. [D; *Leeds Intelligencer*, 3 April 1815]

Winn, Matthew, 42 Lumber St, Liverpool, cm (1810). [D]

Winn, Robert, Singer's Hill, Suffolk St, Birmingham, cabinet case maker (1835). [D]

Winn, Thomas, Kemps Row, Chelsea, London, cm (1777). In 1777 took out insurance cover of £400 of which £200 was for utensils and stock. [GL, Sun MS vol. 254, p. 230]

Winn, Thomas, Welbeck St, Cavendish Sq., London, upholder and auctioneer (d. 1785). Death on 19 September 1785 reported in *Gents Mag.*, September 1785.

Winnall, Richard, Bromsgrove, Worcs., cm (1793). [D]

Winnard, William, Wigan and Preston, Lancs., u (1702–29). Admitted a freeman of Preston, Lancs. on payment of a fine of £3 in 1702. His address was given as Wigan. His aim in obtaining the freedom of Preston was to commence trading there. In 1722 he took app. named White and in 1729, Hargreave. He was trading in Preston on both of these dates. [Preston guild records; S of G, app. index]

Winnes, G., Daventry, Northants., joiner and cm (1793). [D]

Winning, John, 58 St Paul's Churchyard, London, u (1771). On 24 June 1771 invoiced to William Constable of Burton Constable, Yorks. a 'fine Turkey carpet 24 feet 9 inches by 19 feet 8 £36'. The receipt was given by John Lowry on behalf of Winning. Lowry had formerly been app. on the Burton Constable Estate and had made Dining Room furniture there. [Humberside RO, Burton Constable vouchers]

Winnpenny, William, Compton St, Soho, London, upholder (1706–14). His house in Compton St was on the north side between Dean St and Frith St and on both 24 July 1706 and 1 March 1714 was insured for £250. [GL, Hand in Hand MS vol. 4, ref. 11234; vol. 12, p. 556]

Winrow, Richard, Leicester, cm (1803–35). Free 1803 but described as a 'stranger'. Directories of 1835 show him at either Southgate St or Regent St. [D; freemen rolls]

Winsby, Thomas, Leyburn, Yorks., cm (1840). [D]

Winscomb, William, 11 Frogmore St, Bristol, builder, carpenter, undertaker, cm and u (1830). [D]

Winskel, Benjamin, Circus St, Liverpool, carver and gilder (1835–39). At 47 Circus St 1835–37 but in 1839 the number was 54. [D]

Winskell, Thomas, 24 Baptist St, Liverpool, carver and gilder (1827–29). [D]

Winslade, William, High St, Guildford, Surrey, u and cm (1790–1807). [D; poll bks]

Winskell, William, 111 Brearley St, Birmingham, cm (1839). [D]

Winslade, William, High St, Guildford, Surrey, u cm and brokers (1784–1807). In 1784 the business was named as William & Hyde Winslade but from 1790 William Winslade appears to have been trading on his own behalf. In High St from 1790. [D; poll bks]

Winsor, John, High St, Gosport, Hants., cm and u (1830–39). At 56 High St in 1830 and 53 in 1839. [D]

Winstanley, John, Liverpool, cm (1740–41). In 1740 took app. named Johnson and in 1741, Marsh. [S of G, app. index]

Winstanley, John, Liverpool, cm (1790–d. by 1829). Free 24 June 1790. In that year trading from 33 Edmund St with a timber yard at 8 Rigby St. In 1796 only the Edmund St address is recorded. [D; freemen rolls]

Winstanley, Richard, London, auctioneer and upholder (1780–1816). Free of the Upholders' Co. by an Order of the Court of Aldermen 5 January 1780. In the next year living in Cheapside and from 1784 at 10 Paternoster Row, Cheapside. [D; GL, Upholders' Co. records]

Winstanley, Robert, 13 Little Wild St, London, carver and gilder (1778). In 1778 insured a house for £100. [GL, Sun MS vol. 269, p. 163]

Winstanley, William snr, 34 Lord St, Liverpool, chimney piece and looking-glass maker (1789). In April 1789 advertised for six or eight journeymen joiners 'for the Chimney piece business'. Only two months later on 22 June however he indicated that he was disposing of his stock as he had entered a partnership in London. He offered 'a large assortment of Chimney Pieces of the newest taste, several thousand feet of Moulding; a large assortment of Looking Glasses, in burnished gold frames & Mahogany; Girandoles etc.'. He indicated however that he would continue to trade in Dutch and French glass as a wholesaler and also sell composition ornaments. [*Williamson's Liverpool Advertiser*, 16 April 1789, 22 June 1789]

Winstanley, William, Wallgate, Wigan, Lancs., coach and furniture painter (1825–28). [D]

Winstanley, William, Southgate St, Hartlepool, Co. Durham, joiner/cm (1834). [D]

Winston, Charles, Lancaster, cm (1806–27). App. to I. Greenwood 1806 and free 1817–18. Named in the Gillow records, 1827. A straight-fronted chest of drawers stamped 'Gillows Lancaster' is recorded with this maker's name on the bottoms of the two small drawers. [App. reg.; freemen rolls; Westminster Ref. Lib., Gillow; V&A archives]

Winston, James, Lancaster, (1829–35). Free 1829–30 and named in the Gillow records 1833 and 1835. [Freemen rolls; Westminster Ref. Lib., Gillow]

Winston, Sibill, address unknown, (1729(?)). A bill exists, undated, but with others of 1729, sent to Paul Foley of the Temple and Little Ormond St, London and Newport House, Almeley, Herefs. The total of £1 6s for items supplied includes £1 1s for a walnut frame and stand for a fire screen. [Herefs. RO, Foley F/AIII/55]

Winter, —, Bunnell Row (Bunhill Row, London?), (1768). Noted in Matthew Boulton's diary in 1768 as a 'gilt chair maker'. [Birmingham Lib., archives dept, Boulton MS]

Winter, —, London, cm (1793). Subscribed to Sheraton's *Drawing Book*, 1793.

Winter, Benjamin, 143 Long Acre, London, cm, joiner, u and undertaker (1799). His trade card [BM] indicates his specialism in small items of furniture. He advertised 'a Great Variety of Portable Reading & Writing Desks with secret Drawers, . . . Dressing Cases. Plate Chests, Ink stands, Tea Chests, Caddies . . . Fire & Candle screens, Frames for needlework, Portable Libraries, Work Tables, Desert frames, Flower stands & Book shelves'.

Winter, Benjamin, 6 Charlotte St, Rathbone Pl., London, u and appraiser (1816–19). [D]

Winter, Benjamin, Long St, Sherborne, Dorset, cm (1830). [D]

Winter, David, 24 Church St, Mile End Newtown, London, cm and u (1827–28). [D]

Winter, David, 112 Church St, Bethnal Green, London, carver and gilder (1839). [D]

Winter, George, Fakenham, Norfolk, cm (1836–39). At York St in 1836 and Tunn St in 1839. [D]

Winter, James, 101 Wardour St, Soho, London, furniture broker, appraiser and undertaker (1823–40). Included because of the large number of pieces marked 'JAMES WINTER 101 WARDOUR ST' or 'JAMES WINTER & SONS/101 WARDOUR ST SOHO LONDON'. The business continued to trade to 1870 and it is unlikely that any of the furniture so marked was made by James Winter. His trade card indicated that he offered 'A Liberal Price for Second hand Furniture in Large or Small quantities'. [D]

Winter, John, Kirk Deighton, near Wetherby, Yorks., joiner and cm (1822). [D]

Winter, John, 69 East St, Manchester Sq., London, cm and u (1827–28). [D]

Winter, John, Haltwhistle, Northumb., joiner and cm (1827–28). [D]

Winter, L., Bristol, u (1833–40). She traded at 2 Montague Hill in 1833, 4 Horse Fair in 1834–35 and 46 Milk St, 1836–40. [D]

Winter, Richard, Bawtry, Yorks., cm (1822–40). The address is given as Spittle, 1822–28, Top St in 1832 but by 1841 at High St. [D]

Winter, Samuel, Lichfield, Staffs., cm (1818–28). At Market St in 1818 but at Beacon St, 1822–28. [D]

Winter, Thomas, Huddersfield, Yorks., cm (1834). [D]

Winter, William, Grosvenor Mews, London, carver (1784). [Westminster poll bk]

Winter, William, Oxford, u (1802–08). In 1802 living in the parish of St Mary-the-Virgin. In 1805–08 trading in the High St. [D; poll bk]

Winter, William, Market St, Lichfield, Staffs., cm and u (1830). Possibly successor to Samuel Winter. [D]

Winterborn, James, London, bedstead maker (1829–39). At 66 Tottenham Ct Rd in 1829 and 48 Upper Rathbone Pl. in 1839. [D]

Winterbotham, George, Church St, Ashby-de-la-Zouch, Leics., cm, u and joiner (1829–35). [D]

Winterbottom, James Blundell, 20 Crosshall St, Liverpool, bedstead maker (1806). Free 31 October 1806. [Freemen rolls]

Winterbottom, James, 4 Gascoyne St, Liverpool, cm (1811–18). [D]

Winterbottom, Thomas, Liverpool, chairmaker (1827–d. 1828). Free 20 October 1827 but died 20 September 1828. [Freemen rolls]

Winterburn, John, Brentwood, Essex, upholder (1768). Freeman of Colchester, Essex but living at Brentwood in 1768. [Colchester poll bk]

Winteringham, William, Westgate, Bridlington, Yorks., cm and u (1793–1828). [D]

Winterton, John, 78 Fleet St, London, u (1765–75). Fellow of the Society of Arts 1766–67 and fined for declining parochial office in the parish of St Bride, Fleet St, 1769. [D; GL, MS 6561, p. 103]

Wintie, George, Hull, Yorks., cm, box and trunk maker (1831–38). At 18 Broadley St in 1831, Jackson's Pl., Posterngate in 1835 and 6 Posterngate, 1838. Only referred to as cm in 1831. [D]

Winton, Henry, Essex House, Strand, London, upholder (d. 1740). [Heal]

Winwood, J., Cheapside, Birmingham, cm and chairmaker (1818). [D]

Wisdom, Phillip, Chipping Norton, Oxon., u (1675). In 1675 took out a 99 year lease on a cottage. [Oxford RO, Misc. Su XVIII/iii/i]

Wise, Christopher, 'The Golden Ball', Little Queen St, Golden Sq., London, upholder (1727–49). In October 1727 took out insurance cover of £600 which included £250 for utensils and stock. [GL, Sun MS vol. 25, p. 282; Westminster poll bk]

Wise, George snr, High St, Tonbridge, Kent, Tunbridge-ware manufacturer (1746–84). Although claims have been advanced that George Wise was producing Tunbridge-wares as early as 1685 there is no foundation for such assertions. He appears to have established his business in Tonbridge in the mid 1740s and by 1784 had taken his son Thomas into partnership. The business did not solely produce Tunbridge-ware and its mixed nature can be seen from a directory description of this year which states that the firm were 'Turners, chair-makers, Dealers in medicenes, Tunbridge Ware, Haberdashers, Cutlery, Silver and divers other wares'. On the death of George Wise snr his widow Elizabeth appears to have taken charge, assisted by Thomas. Her death in 1793 left her son in sole charge. [D; Kent RO, P371/12/4] B.A.

Wise, George jnr, High St, Tonbridge, Kent, Tunbridge-ware manufacturer (1806–40). Had taken over the family business from his uncle Thomas by March 1806. Produced a wide range of work boxes, tea caddies, games and other boxes some of which were decorated with topographical prints which Wise himself published. The titling labels were often stuck inside the box concerned and identify it as a product of Wise's manufactory. Prints of Tunbridge Wells, Tonbridge, Brighton, Hastings, Worthing, Margate, Broadstairs and even Cheltenham are known so marked and indicate the extensive nature of George Wise's trade supplying libraries and fancy goods dealers in the rapidly expanding resort centres. Wise also supplied Rudolph Ackermann's Repository of Arts in the Strand, London and possibly obtained materials for decorating his products from this source. Penwork and gilt borders were used by Wise who was also adept at simulating various timbers on his whitewood boxes. In the 1830s he adopted the new techniques of decorative veneering pioneered in the Tunbridge-ware industry by James Burrows of Tunbridge Wells. By the later years of this decade Wise was using tessilated mosaics to produce topographical views of considerable complexity. He claimed to be a maker 'to their Royal Highnesses the Duchess of Kent and the Princess Victoria' and supplied the latter with items decorated with veneers depicting Windsor Castle.

To expand his sales further he opened a branch in Tunbridge Wells. Initially this was at 11 Calverley Promenade (now Calverley Park Cresc.), a new fashionable development of 1830–35. Wise was established here by 1832 but the shops did not attract the degree of popularity expected by the promotors of the scheme and by 1845 he had moved this branch to the Parade (the Pantiles). Wise never marked his veneered mosaic wares and items bearing the trade label of 'George Wise Jun.' refer to products made by his son from 1862. [D; Tunbridge Wells Museum; Wadmore, *Some Details in the History of the Parish of Tonbridge*, 1906; Ackermann account bks] B.A.

Wise, Isaac, Queen St, Green Sq., London, u (1784). [Westminster poll bk]

Wise, John, Bristol and London, upholder (1774–84). Living in the parish of Christ Church, Bristol in 1774 but in 1784 in St Martin's Lane, London. [Bristol poll bks]

Wise, John, 11 Wilson St, Finsbury, London, carver and gilder (1820). [D]

Wise, Richard, Oxford, u (1675–1702). His first wife was Elizabeth, probably the daughter or sister of Adrian Roberts, another Oxford u. By this marriage he had by 1675 two daughters, Francis and Katherine. He married his second wife Ann Wilmot of the parish of All Saints, Oxford on 8 February 1692/93. At this date he was living in the parish of All Saints. [Oxford RO, Talbot III/i/1; CJ V/67; Bodleian index of Oxf. marriage bonds]

Wise, Richard, London, chairmaker (1760–84). Freeman of Colchester, Essex. [Colchester poll bks]

993

Wise, Thomas, High St, Tonbridge, Kent, Tunbridge-ware manufacturer, auctioneer and distributor of stamps (*c*. 1785–d. 1807). Born 1750. Produced wares such as the 'post puzzle' designed to appeal to travellers on the London to Hastings road who might change horses and seek refreshment in the town. He also sought to exploit the growing markets of Tunbridge Wells and Brighton and prints of both of these towns exist with his imprint and dated between 1800 and 1806. These prints could be used for box decoration. In 1804 he bought the premises just north of the Medway bridge which had formerly been leased. The frontage of these buildings is illustrated in a number of prints published by the Wises and used for box decoration. Thomas Wise died 1807 and the business was carried on by his nephew, the second George Wise (1779–1869). [Tunbridge Wells Museum, Sprange Coll.; Kent RO, CTR 371C, 371E] **B.A.**

Wise, Thomas, 40 Castle St East, Oxford Mkt, London, chairmaker and cm (1817–20). [D]

Wise, William, Hull Yorks., turner and carver (1838–39). At 3 Builder's Ct, Scale Lane in 1838 when his trade was listed as wood turner and carver. In 1839 at 5 Blue Bell Entry, High St and trading as a wood and ivory turner. [D]

Wiseman, —, address unknown (mid 1740s). Supplied furniture to Sir James Dashwood for Kirtlington Park, Oxon. in the mid 1740s. [*Apollo*, January 1980, p. 25]

Wiseman, George, 30 Marchmount St, Brunswick Sq., London, u (1820). [D]

Wiseman & Co., 23 Norton St, Fitzroy Sq., London, cm and u (1827–28). [D]

Wiseman & Yolland, 111 Tottenham Ct Rd, London, u (1805–23). Richard Wiseman was one of the partners. [D]

Wisker, Daniel, London, upholder (1713–22). Son of Daniel Wisker snr a freeman of London and by trade an inn keeper. App. to Richard Say, 15 October 1713 and free of the Upholders' Co. by servitude, 4 April 1722. [GL, Upholders' Co. records]

Wisker, John, Drury Lane, London, cm (1774–84). Freeman of York but living in Drury Lane by 1774. [York poll bk; Westminster poll bk]

Wisker, Robert, York, cm (1823–38). At Coffee Yd in 1823, 100 Goodramgate in 1830 and 11 Goodramgate in 1838. [D]

Wison, Edward, Gibson's Ct, Marylebone, London, cm (1774). [Westminster poll bk]

Wists, George, address unknown, u (1732). Worked at Gibside, Co. Durham and on 12 February 1732 was paid £7 1s 6d 'for a new Bed making and for mattings'. [Durham RO, Strathmore MS D/St/v. 986]

Withall, Caleb, London, upholder (1796–1802). Son of Caleb Withall snr of Butcher Row, Temple Bar, carpenter. App. to R. I. Thurgood, cutler and free of the Upholders' Co., 2 March 1796. In that year his address was recorded as Thouse Yd (?) but in 1802 he was living at 3 Mincing Lane. [GL, Upholders' Co. records]

Withall, Joseph, parish of St Giles-in-the-Fields, London, upholder (1712–13). Free of the Upholders' Co. 3 December 1712. Took an app. 16 March 1712/13. In November took out insurance cover of £250 on a house on the north side of Castle St and the west side of Queen St, Bloomsbury. [GL, Upholders' Co. records; Hand in Hand MS vol. 12, p. 303; S of G, app. index]

Witham, Lawrence, Liverpool, cm (1816–23). In 1816 at 6 Jordan St with a shop at 5 Frederick St, St James' but in 1823 at 50 Hill St, Harrington. [D]

Witham, Thomas, 5 St John's Sq., Clerkenwell, London, knifecase maker (1778). In 1778 took out insurance cover of £100 which included £30 for his utensils and stock. [GL, Sun MS vol. 263, p. 607]

Witherall, John, Old Market St, Bristol, chair and bedstead maker (1839–40). In 1840 the number in Old Market St was 73. [D]

Witherington, Richard, Norwich and Walsingham, Norfolk, u (1714–34). Son of Nicholas Witherington, worsted weaver of Norwich. Free of Norwich, 17 November 1714, and in February of this year living in the parish of St George, Colgate. In 1734 at Walsingham. [Freemen rolls; Norwich poll bks]

Withers, Daniel, Broad St, parish of St Bennet, London, upholder (1717–23). The Broad St address was both his dwelling house and business address. In 1723 supplied furniture for Hicks Hall which at this date was being repaired and enlarged. He was paid £12 for twenty walnut chairs with a further balance of £2 to be paid when the the work was complete. [GL, Sun MS vol. 6, 3 April 1717, ref. 8204; vol. 8, 12 June 1718, ref. 11182; Winterthur, Delaware, Symonds papers, 75x69.29]

Withers, Henry, Norwich, upholder (1768–90). His app. Thomas Rogers was made free 3 May 1774 and further apps Edward Crane on 3 May 1775 and William Custance on 3 May 1788. In 1768 Withers was living in the parish of St Andrew, but in the parish of St John Maddermarket, 1780–86, and in the parish of St Giles, 1790. In 1784 his address was recorded as 7 Little Cockey Lane. [D; freemen rolls; poll bks]

Withers, John, All Saints St, Bristol, carver and gilder (1830). [D]

Withers, Maria, Austin's Ct, Norwich, working u (1836). [D]

Withers, Thomas, London, upholder (1802–30). Freeman of Norwich but working in London. In July 1830 in Islington. [Norwich poll bks]

Withers, William, Cannon St, London, upholder and cm (1782–95). Son of Walter Withers of Norton Falgate, Middlx. App. to John Thurston Deeble on 1 May 1782 and free of the Upholders' Co. by servitude, 6 May 1789. Went into partnership with Deeble, presumably his app., and traded at 83 Cannon St as Withers & Deeble, 1790–91. By 1792 trading on his own account, the number in Cannon St being 85. He was still at this number in 1794 but in the following February his bankruptcy was announced. [D; GL, Upholders' Co. records; *Billinge's Liverpool Advertiser*, 2 March 1795]

Withers, William, 7 Bishopsgate Within, London, u (1796–97). [D]

Withers, William, 4 Little Wild St, London, picture frame maker (1835). [D]

Withers, William, 3 Little Carter Lane, London, cm (1835). [D]

Withers, William Bell, 12 Lambeth Hill, London, cm (1824). In August 1824 took out insurance cover of £250. [GL, Sun MS vol. 497, ref. 1019480]

Withey, Samuel, 53 Leather Lane, Holborn, London, cm (1794). [Heal]

Withington, Samuel, 29 Bishop Lane, Hull, Yorks., cm (1838–39). [D]

Withnell, Richard, Botany Bay, Chorley, Lancs., joiner and cm (1834). [D]

Withnell, William, Bolton St, Chorley, Lancs., cm (1822). [D]

Withy, Hilborne, Coleman St, London, upholder (1717–d. 1780). Son of Robert Withy of Ilchester, Som., baker. App. to Richard Chambers of London, 5 February 1717 and free of the Upholders' Co. by servitude, 8 June 1726. Living in Coleman St by 1750 and in 1775 the number was 69. In that year he insured houses valued at £1,300. [GL, Upholders' Co. records and Livery list, 1750; Sun MS vol. 239, p. 577]

Withy, Susannah, 53 Leather Lane, Holborn, London, carpenter and u (1789). [D]

Witney, George, Windsor, Berks., u and cm (1796–1806). [Poll bks]

Witt, Christopher, 86 Charlotte St, Rathbone Pl., London, cm and u (1786). In January 1786 took out insurance cover of £100 on his utensils and stock. [GL, Sun MS vol. 335, p. 137]

Witt, Isaac, address unknown, u (1803). Subscribed to Sheraton's *Cabinet Dictionary*, 1803.

Wittling, John, 56 Bethnal Green Rd, London, cm and u (1827–28). [D]

Witton, William, 'The Royal Bed', St Margaret's Hill, Southwark, London, upholder (1734–52). Son of Ralph Witton of the parish of St John, Southwark, Scrivener. App. to Ambrose Pearman, 1 May 1734 and free of the Upholders' Co. by servitude, 6 May 1741. His trade card of c. 1750 giving the St Margaret's Hill address states that he 'Makes & Sells all Sorts of Upholstery Goods, Wholesale & Retail viz. Fashionable Standing Beds, Feather Beds, Quilts, Ruggs, Blankets, Coverlets, Flanders & English Ticking. Also Leather, Cane & Matted Chairs'. He took as app. William Birchall, 1746–52. [GL, Upholders' Co. records; Heal]

Witworth, —, Gamston, near Rockley, Notts., chairmaker. A Windsor chair is known stamped 'WHITWORTH GAMSTON'. [*Furn. Hist.*, 1978]

Wix, William, Half Money Alley, Bishopsgate St, London, bedstead maker (1783). Free of the Upholders' Co. by redemption, 2 April 1783. [GL, Upholders' Co. records]

Woakes, James, Hereford, cm and u (1817–22). Admitted freeman of Hereford 'as a Foreigner' 11 November 1817. Trading at Bye St in 1822. [D; freemen rolls]

Woburn, Nixon, address unknown, cm (1803). Subscribed to Sheraton's *Cabinet Dictionary*, 1803.

Wolf, Isaac, Over, near Middlewich, Cheshire, cm (1834). [D]

Wolfe, James, London, upholder (1714–30). Son of Robert Wolfe, freeman and distiller of London. App. to John Mercer, 5 June 1714 and free of the Upholders' Co. by servitude, 24 April 1723. Took as app. Thomas Hart, 1723–30. [GL, Upholders' Co. records]

Wolfe, James, 3 Little John St, Spitalfields, London, chair and sofa maker (1839). [D]

Wolfe, John, Foregate St, Chester, cm (1769–77). Free 12 August 1769. In 1777 in Foregate St, where he took out insurance cover of £600 which included £100 for his utensils and stock. [Freemen rolls; GL, Sun MS vol. 256, p. 519]

Wolfe, Joseph, 331 Strand, London, u (1820). [D]

Wolfenden, John, 33 Port St, Piccadilly, Manchester, cm (1840). [D]

Wolland, John, parish of St Sidwell, Exeter, Devon, cm (1817–19). Sons bapt.: William on 10 June 1817 and Samuel Thorn, 11 November 1819. [PR (bapt.)]

Wollard, Benjamin, 224 Whitechapel Rd, London, cm (1835–39). [D]

Wollard, William, Old St, St Lukes, London, cm and u (1826–39). At 25 Old St only, 1826–27, but from 1839 also used 32 Old St. [D]

Wollaston, —, Long Acre, London, cm (c. 1690–1720). Said to be one of the earliest users of mahogany. It is stated that a Dr Gibbons 'an eminent physician, at the latter end of the seventeenth century' was given some mahogany by his brother who was a captain in the West Indies trade. The timber had been brought over as ballast. At that time Dr Gibbons was building a house in King St, Covent Gdn but his carpenters declined to use this timber declaring that it was too hard to work. Some time later he gave some of it to Wollaston to make him a candle box which was so much admired that the Duchess of Buckingham requested some of the timber and Wollaston was engaged to make a bureau for her. [Heal; *The Book of English Trades and Library of the Useful Arts*, 1823]

Wollen (or Woollen), William, Bristol, cm, u and undertaker (1820–23). At 3 King St, 1820–21 but in 1822 the address was rendered as 'near the Theatre, King St., St. Nicholas'. In 1823 in Frogmore St. [D]

Wollett, Charles, 16 Redcross St, Southwark, London, cm and u (1826–27). [D]

Wollett, Ralph, Redcross St, Southwark, London, cm (1808–11). Took out insurance cover of £500 in March 1808 and £400 in September 1810 and November 1811. Stock and utensils were valued at £100 in 1808, and £200 in 1809 and 1811. A warehouse opposite his dwelling is mentioned as being used. [GL, Sun MS vol. 442, ref. 814639; vol. 451, ref. 848646; vol. 455, ref. 864211]

Wolley, Thomas, Pitt St, Chester, cm (1840). [D]

Wolstencroft, Joshua, Manchester, cm and victualler (1804–13). At 23 Edge St in 1804 but by 1808 the number had changed to 24. In 1813 at 'The Bull's Head', 244 Deansgate where he acted as a victualler in addition to his work as a cm. [D]

Wolstenholme, Francis, York, carver and gilder (1818–40). At 6 Bootham 1818–30 but in 1838 at 4 Clarence Pl., and in 1840 at 13 Lord Mayor's Walk. [D]

Wolstenholme, John, 4 Surrey St, Sheffield, Yorks., cm (1817–22). Also razor strop manufacturer. [D]

Wolstenholme, John, 12 Lord Mayor's Walk, York, carver and gilder (1837–40). [D]

Wolstenholme, Lawrence, Blackburn, Lancs., cm (1818–34). At Chapel St in 1818, 6A Northgate in 1824 and Cannon St, 1828–34. [D] See Wolstenholme & Vickard.

Wolstenholme, Thomas, Gillygate, York., carver and composition manufacturer (1809). [D]

Wolstenholme, William, King St, Blackburn, Lancs., cm, joiner and builder (1834). [D]

Wolstenholme & Vickard, Northgate, Blackburn, Lancs., cm (1834). A Lawrence Wolstenholme, cm, was trading in Northgate in 1824. [D]

Wolverton, Edward, Queen St, Norwich, cm (1810–31). Shown at Queen St, 1810–20. In the Norwich Local History Lib. is an invoice for goods and services supplied to a William Foster between 20 June 1819 and 13 May 1820. This invoice contains a number of items concerned with the repair of furniture but also includes a new set of dining tables at £23 and a large three fold screen at £5 10s. [D; poll bks]

Wombwell, Thomas, South Town, Gt Yarmouth, Norfolk, carver (1839). [D]

Wommels, William, Manchester, cm (1797–1813). At 7 Cock Gates in 1797, Higher Ardwick in 1802, 26 Cock Gates in 1804 and 5 Lever St in 1813. [D]

Wonfor, James, Cambridge, cm, u and furniture broker (1824–39). At Magdalen St in 1824 when the trade was given as cm and u. In 1830 at Castle St as a furniture broker. [D]

Wonnacot, —, Lower Brook St, Tavistock, Devon, cm (1838). [D]

Wonter & Benson, St John St, Clerkenwell, London, japan manufacturers (1803–04). Papiér mâché trays stamped with the name of this maker are recorded. [D; *Conn.*, August 1967, p. 254; Sotheby's, 21 March 1969, lot 68]

Wood, Mr, address unknown (1761). On 25 June 1761 paid £1 10s by Lord Monson for a close stool. [Lincoln RO, Monson 10 1/A/5]

Wood, —, Shrewsbury, Salop, cm (1798). [D]

Wood, Abel, 8 Hotwell Rd, Bristol, cm (1775). [D]

Wood, Alexander, 'The Cabinet', near St Olave's St, Southwark, London, looking-glass maker (1720–23). On 4 December 1723 the interest in a policy issued by the Sun Office became the sole property of Stephen Wood. Formerly Stephen and Alexander had jointly taken out insurance cover on goods and merchandise at this address, their policy being dated 3 April 1720. [GL, Sun MS vol. 11, p. 106] See Stephen Wood.

Wood, Benjamin, Halifax, Yorks., cm (1822–37). At Barum Top, 1822–34, the number being 3 in 1820. In 1837 at 20 Waterhouse St. [D]

Wood, Benjamin, 49 North St, Brighton, Sussex, carver and gilder (1837–39). A billhead in the Brighton Ref. Lib. indicates that he also traded as a plumber, decorative painter, glazier, looking-glass manufacturer and paper hanger. [D; Brighton Ref. Lib., Erredge 2]

Wood, Cary, Alford, Lincs., cm (1793). [D]

Wood, Catherine, London, upholder (1725). Daughter of Edward Wood, freeman and upholder of London. Free of the Upholders' Co. by patrimony, 5 May 1725. [GL, Upholders' Co. records]

Wood, Daniel, Henrietta St, Cheltenham, Glos., cm (1839). [D]

Wood, Edward, London, upholder (1713–20). Freeman and member of the Upholders' Co. His daughter Catherine was made free 1725, but by this date her father was dead. Edward Wood took as apps Charles Wilson, free, 1713/14, and Thomas Booden, 1713–20. [GL, Upholders' Co. records]

Wood, Edward, 'The Royal Bed', Shugg Lane, St James's, Westminster, London (1728–32). In 1728 took out insurance cover of £500 which included £100 for a shop and warehouse and £300 for his stock in trade. [Heal; GL, Sun MS vol. 27, ref. 45778]

Wood, Edward, York and London, u (1740–58). Son of David Wood, barber surgeon. Free 1740 but then moved from York to London where in 1741 he was living in College St, Westminster. By 1758 he had moved back to York and was living in Minster Yd. [Freeman rolls; York poll bks]

Wood, Edward, Norwich, cm (1807). App. to Thomas Norris of Norwich and free, 21 September 1807. [Freemen rolls]

Wood, Edward, Rochester, Kent, carver and gilder (1816–39). Shown at St Margaret's Bank, 1824–39. [D]

Wood, Edward, 23 Old Silver Rd, Old St, London, cm and chairmaker (1817). [D; Heal]

Wood, Elizabeth, 7 North Passage, Leeds, Yorks., working u (1834). [D]

Wood, Frederick, Brighton, Sussex, cm and u (1817–40). At New Steyne St in April 1818, Nile St, 1820–21 and Ship St Gdns, 1837–40. Three sons bapt., 1818–21. [PR (bapt.); poll bks]

Wood, George, 31 Sutton St, Clerkenwell, London, chair carver (1809). [D]

Wood, George, Leylands, Leeds, Yorks, cm (1822). [D]

Wood, George, 36 New Church Pl., Leeds, Yorks., cm (1837–40). [D]

Wood, H. & Co., 5 Henrietta St, Covent Gdn, London, carvers (early 19th century). Traded as the Patent Wood Carving Co. Trade card in the Heal Coll., BM.

Wood, Henry, London, carver and gilder (1758–1801). At Little Stanhope St, Mayfair in 1775 when he insured a house for £100. In 1777 at New St, near 'The Swan', Knightsbridge, where he took out insurance cover of £1,200 on his house. From 1779 shown at Sloane St, Knightsbridge and in February 1792 at 26 Sloane Sq. In 1779 insurance cover was £600 on his house but by February 1792 the total insurance valuation had risen to £2,850. This included £500 for his utensils and stock and £100 for his workshop. Other houses covered by this policy included 4, 5 and 12 Sloane St, and some of these properties may have been used in connection with his business. Also insured was 3 North St in the tenure of a baker. In 1786 subscribed to George Richardson's *Treatise on the Five Orders of Architecture*. In 1758 a Henry Wood supplied three pieces of japanned work to Croome Court, Worcs. costing £38 12s. In 1781 three stools were provided and a price of £9 9s paid 'as per agreement by valuation of Henry Holland Junr.' It cannot be asserted with certainty that the men responsible for these two commissions were the same person and 1758 is a much earlier date than any other known commissions of Henry Wood. This craftsman is however very much associated with the architect Henry Holland. It was Holland who was responsible for the employment of Wood at Woburn Abbey, Beds. where extensive works were carried out for Francis, 5th Duke of Bedford. In 1792 he was paid £381 0s 8d for carving and gilding at Woburn and £191 for picture and mirror frames there. In the same year he produced a looking-glass frame, carved and gilt for the Drawing Room, Oakley House at £10 for John, Marquess of Tavistock. Four chimney pieces in the Breakfast Room and bedrooms there were carved at a cost of £9 16s 9½d. Payments of £438 11s 2d were made between March and July 1793 for work at Bedford House, London, and in the following year Wood was in receipt of £1,047 9s 8d for work undertaken as shown in Holland's accounts. As late as April 1800 Wood was being paid for gilding mouldings on picture frames in the Inner Library at Woburn. Apart from his work in wood, this maker also acted as a sculptor in stone. Gunnis records commissions for Lord Clive at Claremont, Surrey, 1771–72, Lord Craven at Benham 1775, Carlton House 1783–89, Cleveland House for the Duke of Bridgewater in 1796 and Mote Park, Maidstone for Lord Romney in 1801. [GL, Sun MS vol. 239, p. 269; vol. 262, p. 261; vol. 273, p. 297; vol. 382, ref. 596337; V&A archives; Bedford Office, London; Gunnis]

Wood, Henry, Grub St, Cripplegate, London, bestead maker (1820). [D]

Wood, Henry, Jermyn St, London, u (1831). Bankruptcy announced, *Liverpool Mercury*, 11 November 1831.

Wood, Henry, 28 King St, Holborn, London, cm (1839). [D]

Wood, Hugh, Tunstall, Staffs., cm (1818–22). [D]

Wood, J., 21 Holloway, Bath, Som., cm (1833). [D]

Wood, J., Holywell Hill, St Albans, Herts., chairmaker, sadler and harness maker (1838). [D]

Wood, James, Gloucester, cm, chairmaker and wood carver (1802–22). At Lower South St in 1802 and Hare Lane in 1822. [D]

Wood, James, Bristol, cm (1819–27). At Bridewell Bridge, 1819–27, but shown additionally at 1 Stoke's Croft in 1821 and 17 Upper Maudlin St, 1822–27. [D]

Wood, James, 50 Wellington St, Goswell St, London, wood carver (1826). [D]

Wood, James, St George's Pl., Cheltenham, Glos., cm (1830). [D]

Wood, James, West St, Warwick, chairmaker (1831). [Poll bk]

Wood, James, St Faith's St, Maidstone, Kent, u (1834–35). On 11 May 1834 his son James Robert Harrison was bapt. at Tonbridge, Kent. [PR (bapt.); poll bk]

Wood, Jeremiah, Bath Terr., Cheltenham, Glos., cm, u and carver (1822). [D]

Wood, John, London, upholder (1710). Free of the Upholders' Co. 5 April 1710. [GL, Upholders' Co. records]

Wood, John, Shrewsbury, Salop, chairmaker (1721). [Shrewsbury freemen rolls]

Wood, John, parish of St Marylebone, London, joiner (1722–24). His house may have been that situated on the north side of Tyburn Rd (Oxford St) a little to the east of the Market House. This he insured for £125 in March 1722 and £250 in December 1723. He also insured other houses in both years however. He was a freeman of London and by trade a joiner. He did however undertake work on furniture and on 25 February 1723/24 was paid 8s for a large leaf table for the Committee Room of the Society for Propagation of Christian Knowledge. [GL, Hand in Hand MS vol. 27, refs 46222–23, 45023; vol. 28, refs 46222–23, 47698–99; SPCK, FT9/2]

Wood, John, Soho, London, upholder (1720–78). Son of Richard Wood of Notts., yeoman. App. to Charles Rowe of London, 7 December 1720 and free of the Upholders' Co. by servitude, 7 March 1732. At Crown Ct, Wardour St in 1749. In 1750 the address was rendered as 'back of St. Anne's, Westminster' and in 1778 as 'St. Ann's, Soho'. [GL, Upholders' Co. records, Livery list 1750; Westminster poll bk]

Wood, John, Oxford, u (1743–d. by 1780). On 21 October 1743 married Ann Stevens at the Church of St Mary the Virgin, Oxford. He was aged 26. In 1759 he took app. named Harper. Wood may at this date have been in the employ of the University. By January 1759 however he was trading on his own account. Apart from his work as an u he acted as an agent for the letting and sale of property and as an auctioneer. On 12 January 1765 he announced a move of premises from opposite St Mary's Church in the High St 'to a more commodius house two doors above Horseman's coffee house, High St'. By August 1768 John Wood had taken into partnership his only son Thomas who had recently married Molly Langthorne, 'daughter of an eminent London glass grinder'. From this date the business traded as Wood & Son. Thomas was active in local politics and filled a council vacancy in September 1769 and was chosen Chamberlain in September 1772. Between his marriage and 1777 Thomas had five children. These were left orphaned by his sudden death, 'supposed of a fit' in June 1777. John Wood had by this date taken a decision to retire from the business but this family tragedy forced him to take over the enterprise again. He advertised for a partner. By February 1780 John Wood was dead and his house was offered to let. [Bodleian index of Oxf. marriage bonds; S of G, app. index; *Jackson's Oxford Journal*, 6 January 1759, 12 January 1765, 6 August 1768, 30 September 1769, 23 December 1769, 11 August 1770, 30 September and 12 November 1772, 29 March 1774, 21 October 1776, 9 June 1777, 19 February 1780]

Wood, John, address unknown, cm (1748–50). On 8 July 1748 invoiced to James West a solid mahogany tea table at £1 15s with an additional 9s for a packing case. The receipt was signed in December 1750 by Daniel Guinn. [Warwick RO, Alscot Park MS]

Wood, John, Princess St, Westminster, London, upholder (1774). [Poll bk]

Wood, John, London, cm (1802–06). Freeman of Norwich but living in London, 1802–06. Possibly the cm who subscribed to Sheraton's *Cabinet Dictionary*, 1803. [Norwich poll bks]

Wood, John, 92 Long Millgate, Manchester, chair bottomer (1817). [D]

Wood, John, Derby, cm and u (1828–35). At Derwent St, 1828–29 but by 1835 at 3 Silk Mill Lane. [D]

Wood, John, Haworth, Yorks., cm (1830). [D]

Wood, John, Clifford, parish of Bramham, Yorks., cm (1837). [D]

Wood, John, 16 Narrow Wine St, Bristol, cm, buhl and marquetry cutter (1835–40). Advertised that he repaired all sorts of inlaid furniture. [D]

Wood, John, 149 Minories, London, cm (1839). [D]

Wood, Joseph, Cocker Bridge, Cockermouth, Cumb., cooper/turner/chairmaker (1829). [D]

Wood, Joseph, North Hill, Highgate, London, carver, gilder and paperhanger (1839). [D]

Wood, Michael, Horsforth, Yorks., joiner and cm (1830). [D]

Wood, P., 10 Portugal St, Lincoln's Inn Fields, London, writing desk and dressing case manufacturer (1829). [D]

Wood, P. & Co., 214 High Holborn, London, cm (1829). [D]

Wood, Philip, Norwich, upholder (1779–1806). At 8 Cockey Lane, Norwich 1780–86. The business was of a substantial size with utensils and stock valued at £500 in an insurance policy of 1779. By 1799 however he appears to have left Norwich and was living at Walsham le Willows, Suffolk. In 1802 he was living at Wattisfield, Suffolk and in 1806 at Suffield, Norfolk. [D; Norwich poll bks; GL, Sun MS vol. 279, p. 64]

Wood, Richard, 'near the Bagnie in Long Acre', London, upholder (1712). [GL, Sun MS vol. 2, p. 140]

Wood, Richard, Fleet Ditch, London, upholder (1713–30). App. to Francis Baron and Randolph Baron and free of the Upholders' Co. by servitude, 2 December 1713. Living at Fleet Ditch 1724–27. Took apps named Morgan Jones, 1715–29/30, William Swayne, 1716–23, William Gamlyn, 1720–22 and William Pryce, 1726–29. [GL, Upholders' Co. records; Heal]

Wood, Richard, York, carpenter, joiner and cm (1726–72). App. to Thomas Raper, carpenter of York for seven years on 18 October 1721. In 1726 he was admitted a freeman as a carpenter. He traded from an address at Spurriergate from 1738 but in 1759 also had property in the Shambles. Although in July 1738 he described himself as a cm he conducted a varied trade. In 1738 he was advertising for sale 'All Sizes of Crown-Glass, all Sorts of Flint Glass and Glass Bottles . . . at the same Price as at the Glass-House'. Three years later he was offering for sale 'Nails and Hinges, Cheap as from the Maker, Brass and Mortice Locks, Iron rim'd and Wood Stock-Locks, Brass Work, and Locks for Cabinet Work, and all other Sorts of Birmingham and Sheffield Goods'. He did however also mention 'Mahogany and Walnut Tree Cabinet Work, Tables and Chairs of all Sorts &c &c.' In 1754 he subscribed to eight copies of the *Director*. There are other connections between this maker and Thomas Chippendale. William Benson who was app. to Richard Wood in 1740 moved to London to become Chippendale's foreman while another app. John Walkington, who was bound to Wood in 1736, was a subscriber to the *Director*. Other apps of Richard Wood were John Lidgley in 1743, William Brown and George Hornley in 1752 and Samuel Proctor in 1753. In June 1772 his stock was advertised for sale following his death. [*York Courant*, 18 July 1738, 28 July 1741, 12 March 1745, 30 June 1772; app. reg.; freemen rolls; Gilbert, *Chippendale*, p. 4]

Wood, Richard, Carrierrls Inn, Shrewsbury, Salop, cm (c. 1796). [D]

Wood, Richard, Walmgate, York, joiner and cm (1816–18). [D]

Wood, Richard, 2 Fish St, Old Sq., Kirkgate, Leeds, Yorks., cm/joiner (1826–30). [D]

Wood, Robert, address unknown, cm (1803). Subscribed to Sheraton's *Cabinet Dictionary*, 1803.

Wood, Robert, Mill Hill, Leeds, Yorks., cm and u (1817–22). [D]

Wood, Robert, Dukenfield St, Liverpool, cm (1827). [D]

Wood, Sampson, 'Rose & Crown', Aberford, Yorks., victualler, cm and house carpenter (1822–37). [D]

Wood, Samuel, 6 South Molton St, London, u (1821). In November 1821 took out insurance cover of £100 which included £20 for stock and utensils. [GL, Sun MS vol. 488, ref. 985466]

Wood, Stephen, 'The Cabinet', near Bridge Foot, Southwark, London, cm (c. 1725). Known only from his trade card which states that he 'Makes and Sells, all Sorts of Cabinet work, Looking Glasses, Peer Glasses and Sconces'. He altered or repaired old glasses and sought wholesale trade with merchants and 'Country Chapmen'. [Heal]

Wood, Thomas, Oxford, see John Wood.

Wood, Thomas, London(?), cm (1755–57). Supplied furniture to Charles Rogers of Laurence Pountney Lane, London. A payment of £15 was made on 9 July 1755 and £70 on 26 October 1757 for 'two Amboina Cabinets and other work'. The collection of the Plymouth City Museum and Art Gallery contains three amboyna breakfront bookcases which may be the two made by Wood and a further one by Robert Tuson. [*Apollo*, December 1960, pp. 196–98]

Wood, Thomas, Prince's St, Leicester Fields, London, upholder (1780–83). In the period 1780–83 insured a house for £1,000. [GL, Sun MS vol. 289, p. 189; vol. 288, p. 465; vol. 313, p. 73]

Wood, Thomas, 122 Old St, St Luke's, London, bedstead maker (*c*. 1790). Known only from his trade card. A William Wood in the same trade was at this address 1802–04. [D; Heal]

Wood, Thomas, 82 Fore St, Cripplegate, London, cm and broker (1798). [D]

Wood, Thomas, Brigg, Lincs., cm (1799). Freeman of Beverley, Yorks. living at Brigg in 1799. [Beverley poll bk]

Wood, Thomas, Balloon Ct, Nottingham, cm (1804–06). Free 1804 and living at Balloon Ct in 1806. [Freemen rolls; poll bk]

Wood, Thomas, 5 Woods Ct, Salford, Lancs., joiner and cm (1804). [D]

Wood, Thomas, 110 Goswell St, London, bedstead maker (1805–19). [D]

Wood, Thomas, Fazakerley St, Prescot, Lancs., cm (1816). [D]

Wood, Thomas, Hull, Yorks., cm (1817–40). At 5 New Dock St, 1817–22 with a residence at 1 Dagger Lane. In 1823–31 at Woolpack Entry, 35 Mytongate and from 1837–40 at 18 Trundle St. His residence from 1835–38 was 8 Paradise Pl. and in 1839 one directory gives an address at 13 Robinson Row. [D]

Wood, Thomas, Bristol, cm (1829–33). At 136 St Thomas St, 1829–30 and 46 Redcliffe St, 1831–33. [D]

Wood, Thomas, 3 Nile St, Brighton, Sussex, cm (1832). [D]

Wood, Thomas, Cheltenham, Glos., u and cm (1833). Bankruptcy announced, *Liverpool Mercury*, 26 April 1833.

Wood, William, London, upholder (1708–21). A member of the Girdlers' Co. but by trade an upholder. Took as app. William Gough, 1708–21. [GL, Upholders' Co. records]

Wood, William, parish of St Stephen, Bristol, upholder (1754). [Poll bk]

Wood, William, Bristol, cm (1774). [Poll bk]

Wood, William, London, upholder (1770–1802). Son of John Wood snr of Botolph Aldgate, surveyor. App. to J. Evans, 19 April 1770 and free of the Upholders' Co. by servitude, 19 November 1777. In that year he was at 246 Shoreditch, in 1794 at Homerton and in 1802 at Curtain Rd. Took as app. John Durrant, 1790–98. [GL, Upholders' Co. records]

Wood, William, London, cm (*c*. 1800). Known only from his trade card which has the same wording as that of William Webb. [Heal]

Wood, William, 122 Old St, London, bedstead maker (1802–04). A Thomas Wood in the same trade was operating from this address *c*. 1790. [D]

Wood, William, 153 High Holborn, London, carver and gilder (1805). [D]

Wood, William, 5 Denmark St, St Giles, London, carver and gilder (1805). [D]

Wood, William, Gaol Sq., Stafford, chairmaker (1818–22). [D]

Wood, William, 45 Goodge St, Tottenham Ct Rd, London, carver and gilder (1820). [D]

Wood, William, 9 Vicar Lane, Leeds, Yorks., cm and furniture warehouse (1826). [D]

Wood, William, Artillery Lane, London, cm (1830). Freemen of Rochester, Kent, living in London. [Rochester poll bk]

Wood, William, Otley, Yorks., joiner/cm (1834). [D]

Wood, William, Clerkenwell, London, japanner (1835–39). At 33 Gt Sutton St in 1835 and 39 Northampton St in 1839. [D]

Wood, William, 1 Bagshaw's Ct, Shudehill, Manchester, cm and u (1836). [D]

Wood, William, Haworth, Yorks., cm (1837). [D]

Wood, William & Son, Redcliffe St, Bristol, cm (1828–40). The number in Redcliffe St was 43, though one directory of 1830 states 42. From 1838 the business was listed simply as William Wood and in 1840 he was stated to be a 'Cabinet, beer & spirit machine, dial & clock case maker'. [D]

Wood & Lockey, York(?), cm/joiner (1796). Supplied furniture for the Retreat, York, a Quaker asylum, in August, October and December 1796. In August forms and a table were charged at £1 13s 4d and in October and December the bills were for ward furniture. [Borthwick Inst., Retreat MS H/1]

Wood & Son, Oxford, see John Wood.

Wood and Sons, 31 Western Rd, Brighton, Sussex, cm (*c*. 1840). Known from a labelled satinwood Davenport of *c*. 1840. [*C. Life*, 24 September 1964, supplement, p. 26]

Woodall, Edward, 2 Phoenix St, Somerstown, London, cm (1805). [D]

Woodall, John, Knutsford, Cheshire, cm and joiner (1782–1822). [D]

Woodall, Robert, Lancaster, (1784–88). Named in the Gillow records 1784 and 1786–88. [Westminster Ref. Lib., Gillow]

Woodberry, James, 29 Curtain Rd, London, cm (1832). Lease sold 1832. [Shoreditch archives, Rose Lipman Lib., MS M3545, p. 39]

Woodberry, Richard, 5 Ellbroad St, Bristol, fancy and cane chairmaker (1840). [D]

Woodbin, Thomas, St Martin-in-the-Fields, London, upholder (1762), Bankruptcy announced, *Gents Mag.*, August 1762.

Woodbridge, James, Edgar St, Liverpool, cm (1827–29). At 18 Edgar St in 1827 and 21 in 1829. [D]

Woodburn, Allen, 112 St Martin's Lane, London, gilder (1832–40). In 1832 paid £1 11s 6d for gilding the top rods of pictures for Panshanger, Herts. In 1834–35 supplied an 'antique' picture and carved and gilded an oak frame for it for Charlecote Park, Warks. The frame cost £7. [Herts. RO, Panshanger box 56; Warwick RO, L6/1118]

Woodburn, Christopher, Ambleside, Westmld, cm (1834). [D]

Woodburn, John, Above Stockdale, Ambleside, Westmld, cm (1829). [D]

Woodbury, James, 127 Curtain Rd, London, cm and u (1820–29). [D]

Woodcock, William, Preston, Lancs., timber merchant, joiner, builder and cm (1805–27). At Woodcock's Ct, Fishergate with a home address in Charles St, 1816–18. Still trading in Fishergate 1825. On 20 December 1805 a fire occurred at his premises which did damage to the value of £2,400 of which only £1,500 was insured. His bankruptcy was declared, *London Gazette*, 17 July 1827. [D; *Gents Mag.*, December 1805]

Woodcock, William, Lancaster and Preston, Lancs., joiner and cm (1810–11). Free 1810–11 but at this date living in Preston. [Lancaster freemen rolls]

Woodeson, Elizabeth, North St, Bristol, cm and upholder (1794–1800). Successor to Fane Woodeson at this address. [D]

Woodeson, Fane, Bristol, cm (1774–93). Living in the parish of St James, 1774–84. Trading in North St, 1792–93 and succeeded at this address by Elizabeth Woodeson. [D; poll bks]

Woodeson, Thomas, London, u (1813–29). At 20 Dover St, Piccadilly, 1813–19 and 14 Norris St, Haymarket 1820–29. [D]

Woodfield, Henry, Ludgate Hill, Birmingham, cabinet case and ebony inkstand maker (1818). [D]

Woodfield, Samuel, 28 Ludgate, Birmingham, cabinet case maker (1830). [D]

Woodfin, William, Chester, cm (1747). [Poll bk]

Woodfoff, Daniel, Oxenden St, London, upholder (1740). In June 1740 took out insurance cover of £400. [GL, Sun MS vol. 54, p. 589]

Woodford, George, Foregate St, Chester, carver and gilder (1839). Free 3 June 1839. [Freemen rolls]

Woodford, Henry, 26 New St Sq., Shoe Lane, London, cm (1805). [D]

Woodford, J. John, St Paul's Churchyard, London, u (1772). A chair is recorded with the frame inscribed 'J. John Woodford, St. Paul's Churchyard, London, April 17th 1772'. [DEF]

Woodford, John, Back Lane, Nottingham, cm (1835). [D]

Woodford, William, High St, Taunton, Som., cm and u (1839). [D]

Woodgate, Joseph, London, upholder (1712). Free of the Upholders' Co., 3 December 1712. [GL, Upholders' Co. records]

Woodgate, William, 29 Seymour St, Euston Sq., London, u (1835–39). [D]

Woodhall, John, Goosegate, Nottingham, joiner and cm (1832). [D]

Woodham (or Woodhams), John, High St, Hastings, Sussex, cm and u (1823–32). At 44 High St, 1823–26 but in 1832 was at 43. [D]

Woodham, Thomas, Tonbridge or Tunbridge Wells, Kent, cm (1837–39). Son, Thomas bapt., 12 May 1837 and a daughter Mary Anne, 22 March 1839. [PR (bapt.)]

Woodhams, George, Northgate, Canterbury, Kent, cm (1830). [Poll bk]

Woodhams, George, Sandwich, Kent, cm (1837). [Poll bk]

Woodhead, Joseph, Brunt St, Mansfield, Notts., joiner and cm (1832). [D]

Woodhead, William, Campo Lane, Sheffield, Yorks., cm and u (1828). [D]

Woodhouse, Hubert, 5 Court, Smallbrook St, Birmingham, cabinet case maker (1830). [D]

Woodhouse, Hubbard, Dudley St, Birmingham, cm (1816–22). [D]

Woodhouse, Humphrey, 117 Gt Charles St, Birmingham, cabinet case maker (1835–39). In 1835 described as a 'fancy box, case & caddy maker' and in 1839 as a 'manufacturer of ivory & tortoiseshell boxes'. [D]

Woodhouse, I. A., Portsea, Portsmouth, Hants., cm (1830). Freeman of Gt Yarmouth living in Portsmouth in 1830. [Gt Yarmouth poll bk]

Woodhouse, James, Lancaster, u (1801–10). Free 1806–07. Named in the Gillow records in 1801 which might suggest that he was app. to this firm or one of their craftsmen. Subsequently named in the records, 1808–10. A set of four yoke back chairs with reeded front legs and back posts has been recorded, the underside of one seat rail inscribed in ink 'J. Woodhouse 1810'. The signature of some of Gillow's craftsmen has been noted on furniture made by this business. [Freemen rolls; Westminster Ref. Lib., Gillow; V&A archives]

Woodhouse, Richard, Lancaster (1829–31). Named in the Gillow records 1829 and 1831. [Westminster Ref. Lib., Gillow]

Woodin, Mark, address unknown (1736). Undertook 'carpenters work' for Lord Monson, and on 9 April 1736 submitted an account for 4s 6d which included a charge 'for fixing a large table to dine upon'. [Lincoln RO, Monson 12]

Woodin (or Wooding), Thomas, St James's, Westminster, London carver and gilder (1746–c. 1760). In 1746 took as app. Samuel Norman who was subsequently to make his name as one of the leading furniture makers of the early years of George III's reign. Woodin emigrated to South Carolina with his wife Rebecca c. 1760. In June 1767 he advertised in *South Carolina Gazette* that he could teach 'Drawing in all its Branches' and had mahogany and bamboo furniture for sale. He undertook carving work at Charleston. On his death in July 1774 he left his tools to his son John. [Boyd's Index of IR app. regs, vol. 22, p. 4284; Museum of Early Decorative Arts, Winston Salem, biographical indices]

Woodins, Joseph jnr, York St, Chester, cm (1818). Free 17 June 1818. [Freemen rolls]

Woodison, Jane, Stokes Croft, Bristol, cm (1787). In January 1787 took out insurance cover of £300 on a dwelling and goods. [GL, Sun MS vol. 344, p. 29]

Woodland, James, Gt George St, Bristol, chairmaker (1794–95). [D]

Woodland, James, Fitzwilliam St, Cambridge, cm (1832–35). [Poll bk]

Woodland, Samuel, Market Pl., Mildenhall, Suffolk, cm (1830). [D]

Woodlitts & Co., 3 St Paul's Churchyard, London, u and appraisers (1821–28). [D]

Woodman, —, Hurst St, Liverpool, cm (d. 1774). [*Williamson's Liverpool Advertiser*, 22 July 1774]

Woodman, D., 8 Walcot Buildings, Bath, Som., cm and broker (1819). [D]

Woodman, Richard Horwell, 118 Jermyn St, St James's, London, carver and gilder (1840). [GL, Sun MS ref. 1341339]

Woodman, Robert, Fore St Hill, Exeter, Devon, cm (1816–22). [D]

Woodmancey, John, Gt Driffield, Yorks., cm and paper hanger (1831–40). At Market Pl. in 1831, Middle St in 1834 and Prospect Row in 1840. [D]

Woodnut & Butter, 18 Molyneux St, Bryanston Sq., London, cm (1826–27). [D]

Woodnutt, W., 32 Bown St, Bryanstone Sq., London, u (1835). [D]

Woodroffe, Daniel snr and jnr, 'The Cross Keys' over against Serjeant's Inn, Fleet St, London, upholders (1707–49). Daniel Woodroffe snr was a freeman of London and a member of the Upholders' Co. He took as apps Thomas Money, 1707–23, John Brumwell, 1712–23, Robert Sparrow, 1720–31 and his son Daniel jnr, 1718–26. An insurance policy of December 1713 gives the address as 'at the Cross between the Legg and the Horn Tavern in Fleet St', and one of 1722 as 'the north side of Fleet St. . . . being part over gateway into the Lyon Court'. In the latter year the insurance cover was £450. In October 1713 a Daniel Woodroffe took out policies on property in the St James's area of Westminster, this being insured for £1,800. His trade was given as upholder. If, as seems likely, this was the same person it would suggest that he was prosperous. A 'Woodrolf', probably this maker, furnished several rooms at Holkham Hall, Norfolk in 1719 and was paid £440. This also points to his importance in the London furnishing trades of the early years of the 18th century. Daniel Woodroffe snr died in 1724 and the business was carried on by his son.

Daniel Woodroffe jnr was not admitted a freeman of the Upholders' Co. by servitude until 7 September 1726. He must have been responsible for Robert Sparrow after his father's death and took another app., Thomas Parker, 1739–49. Woodroffe died in Panton St in 1749, and the auction of his 'valuable collection of rare *Old China* and *Japan* . . . removed . . . from his late Dwelling-house in Panton Street', held on 3–5 May, was announced in *General Advertiser*, 3, 4 and 5 May 1749. [GL, Upholders' Co. records; Sun MS vol. 3, ref. 3526; Hand in Hand MS vol. 12, p. 211; vol. 26, p. 250; Heal; V&A archives] See Woodrose, —.

Woodroffe, James, Gracechurch St, London, upholder, undertaker and appraiser (1761–66). Traded at 'The Royal Bed & Blanket Warehouse'. His trade card indicates that his business premises were near 'The Spread Eagle Inn'. Here he sold 'all Sorts of Upholstery & Cabinet Goods, four post & other Bedsteads with Damasks, Harrateens, Cheneys, Linceys & Washing Furnitures, feather Beds, Blankets, Quilts, Cotton & Linen Counterpains, Ruggs, Coverlids, Turkey — English & other Carpets; paper Hangings, Mahogony & Wallnut-tree Chest of Draws, Dining Dressing & Card Tables, Mahogony & Wallnut Tree & other Chairs — Looking Glasses &c.'. The reverse of a copy of his trade card records the sale on 19 November 1764 of a number of furniture items including a Turkey carpet and eight elbow chairs at a cost of £7 7s. On 7 May he provided twelve chairs for the Committee Room of the Society for Propagation of Christian Knowledge in Hatton Gdn for £10 16s. A set of chairs of simplified Chippendale form were owned by the Society until their disposal in 1971 and may be the set referred to. He was declared bankrupt, *Williamson's Liverpool Advertiser,* 14 November 1766. In the bankruptcy proceedings he was described as a timber merchant and cm of Tufton St, Westminster. [D; Heal; *DEF;* V&A archives; SPCK cash bk, FT9/7

Woodroffe, John, Uttoxeter, Staffs., chairmaker (1798). [D].

Woodrose, —, 'The Sun', Fleet St, London, u (1702). Possibly Daniel Woodroffe though the trade sign is different from that which he was using in 1722. [*The Post Man,* 12 May 1707]

Woodruff, George, Cambridge, carver (1660–67). Employed by St John's College for carving, 1651–65, and Trinity College for similar work, 1660–67. [College records]

Woodruff, John, Mitre Alley, Portsea, Portsmouth, Hants., cm and u (1830). [D]

Woodruff, Richard, Cambridge, carver (1667). Employed by Trinity College for carving moulds for plaster work in 1667. [College records]

Woodruff, Thomas, Fighting Cocks Yd, Newcastle, joiner and cm (1833–34). In 1833 his house was in Bigg-market. [D]

Woodruffe, George snr and jnr, Lambeth, London, cm and u (1827–30). At 29 Upper Stamford St, Blackfriars in 1827 and 36 Waterloo Rd, Lambeth in 1829–30. Declared bankrupt February 1830 when their trade was stated to be wholesale cabinet manufacturers. [D; *Chester Courant,* 23 February 1830]

Woods, Henry, 1 Lawrence Pl., Lawrence St, Liverpool, joiner and cm (1835). [D]

Woods, I. T., 30 Upper George St, Portman Sq., London, u (1839). [D]

Woods, John, Penn St, Bristol, cm (1795). [D]

Woods, John, 123 Gt Portland St, London, cm (1809). [D]

Woods, John, Chester, chairmaker (1829). In August 1829 found intoxicated 'during the hours of divine service' and placed in the House of Correction. Subsequently fined 5s. [*Chester Chronicle,* 28 August 1829]

Woods, John, 1 Collingwood St, Liverpool, chairmaker (1837). [D]

Woods, Jonathan, Snug Lane, Prescot, Lancs., joiner and cm (1834). [D].

Woods, Joseph, Liverpool, u (1827–39). Son of Charles Woods, shipwright. Free 17 October 1827. In 1827 shown in one directory at 23 Campbell St and in another at Hurst St, though the freemen's roll states 5 Orthes St and directories of 1834–39 also show this address. [D; freemen rolls]

Woods, T., 90 Broad St, Portsmouth, Hants., cm and u (1839). [D]

Woods, Thomas, Bristol, cm (1774–84). In 1784 living in the parish of St Augustine. [Poll bks]

Woods, Thomas, Prescot, Lancs., cm (1814–28). At Fazakerley St, 1814–16 but from 1818–28 in Market St. [D]

Woods, Thomas, Church Parade, Hounslow, Middlx, cm (1839). [D]

Woods, Thomas, 2 Westbourne Pl., Sloane Sq., London, cm (1839). [D]

Woods, William, Liverpool, upholder (1767). App. to Robinson Cooke and Edward Roberts and free by servitude, 8 December 1767. Dead by 1820. [Freemen rolls]

Woods, William, Host St, Bristol, cm (1794). [D]

Woods, William, Blackburn, Lancs., cm and joiner (1816–34). At White Bull Yd in 1816, Darwen St in 1818 and Ainsworth St in 1834. [D]

Woods, William, Gay St, Liverpool, joiner and cm (1821–24). In 1821 at 13 Gay St where he had his shop and yard and 1 and 2 Gay St. In 1824 the numbers were given as 1 Gay St with a house at 11 Gay St. [D]

Woodsend, John & William, Upper Richmond St and Mansfield Rd, Nottingham, cm (1840). [D]

Woodsend & Ellis, St James St, Nottingham, cm (1835). [D]

Woodsin, William, Chester, cm (1747). [Poll bk]

Woodstock, James, Salford, Lancs., cm (1800–13). At 5 Garden Lane, 1800–02, Blacklocks Bank 1804, Hope St 1808 and 9 Sherrat St 1813. [D]

Woodsworth, John, Foregate St, Chester, cm (1787). [Poll bk]

Woodsworth, Thomas, Northgate St, Chester, cm (1784). [Poll bk]

Woodtin, William, Chester, cm (1747). [Poll bk]

Woodward, Christopher, London and Tetbury, Glos., upholder (1772–1802). Son of Daniel Woodward of Bristol, wine merchant. App. to William Fassett, 3 June 1772 and free of the Upholders' Co. by servitude, 3 April 1782. In 1782 living at Chavenage, near Tetbury, Glos., and also noted at Tetbury 1794 and 1802. [GL, Upholders' Co. records]

Woodward, Daniel, 18 Green St, Leicester Sq., London, cm (1807). In September 1807 took out insurance cover of £1,100. [GL, Sun MS vol. 440, ref. 806638]

Woodward, Francis, Cambridge, carver (1701–d. 1710). Worked at Trinity College in 1701 and St John's College, 1703. Probate was granted on his will 1710. [College records; Univ. Lib., W.1710]

Woodward, Francis, Cambridge, carver (1711–14). Worked for St John's College in 1711 and Trinity College, 1714. Possibly the son of the Francis Woodward who worked for these Colleges, 1701–10. [College records]

Woodward, George Robert, London, turner, carver and gilder (1837–39). In 1839 described as a looking-glass manufacturer. [D]

Woodward, J., 121 Borough, Southwark, London, (1816–17). [D]

Woodward, James, Liverpool, joiner and cm (1794). Free 25 October 1794. [Freemen rolls]

Woodward, James, Liverpool, joiner and cm (1785–96). App. to John Horrocks 1785 and in 1796 petitioned for his freedom. [App. reg.; freemen's committee bk]

Woodward, John, London, joiner (1707–18). In October 1707 living at the sign of 'The Cabinet' in Aldermanbury and he insured this house for £300. In December 1718 at the sign of 'The Blackamore's Head', Gt Minories and the insurance cover had been reduced to £150. Possibly the John Woodward of London, cm, whose son John jnr was free of the Upholders' Co. in 1729. [GL, Hand in Hand MS vol. 5, ref. 14575; vol. 19, ref. 7171; Upholders' Co. records]

Woodward, John, Cambridge, carver (1711–28). Employed by

St John's College 1711, 1721 and 1723 and by the University, 1720–28. [College records; Gunnis]

Woodward, John, London, upholder (1721–29). Son of John Woodward of London, cm. App. to John Starr Fitchett, 9 November 1721 and free of the Upholders' Co. by servitude, 2 July 1729. [GL, Upholders' Co. records]

Woodward, John, address unknown, carver (1738–41). Paid substantial sums for carving work at Holkham Hall, Norfolk. In 1738 the amount was £37 13s 6d and in the following year £32 13s 1d. The sum for 1740 was £8 7s 3d and in 1741 £106 8s 3d. [V&A archives]

Woodward, John(?), Trumpington St, Cambridge, carver (1747–d. 1767). Worked for Trinity College 1747, 1757 and 1762. The death of a Mr Woodward, carver of Trumpington St was announced in February 1767. [College records; *Cambridge Chronicle*, 28 February 1767]

Woodward, John, Chester, cm (1747). [Poll bk]

Woodward, John, George St, Worcester, cm (1818–35). Free 1818. [Freemen rolls]

Woodward, Paul, Wooton Bassett, Wilts., cm (1792). In June 1792 took out insurance cover of £200 on his house and a further £100 on his goods and utensils. [GL, Sun MS vol. 388, p. 77]

Woodward, Samuel, Parliament St, Nottingham, cm (1779–91). In 1779 insured some houses for £600. In that year he was trading in Parliament St where his business was still being conducted in 1783. He had thought seriously of setting up business in America but by May 1783 had given up this idea and indicated in an advertisement his intention of carrying on his 'Building, Joinery, and Cabinet Making Business' in Nottingham. In July of the following year he advertised for craftsmen and in 1791 he was one of the masters who signed the *Nottingham Cabinet and Chair Makers' Book of Prices*. [D; GL, Sun MS vol. 279, p. 173; *Nottingham Journal*, 3 May 1783, 31 July 1784]

Woodward, Thomas, Cuppins Lane, Chester, cm (1792–93). [D]

Woodward, Thomas, Water St, Gloucester, cm and chairmaker (1802–22). [D]

Woodward, Thomas, Nottingham, joiner and cm (1813). Possibly the Thomas Woodward, son of Samuel Woodward of Nottingham, joiner, who was app. in 1805. Named as a master in 1813 with app. named James Brown. [App. reg.]

Woodward, Thomas, Blackheath Hill, Greenwich, London, u (1838). [D]

Woodward, William, 'The Crown & Cushion', near Old Bedlam, Moorfields, London, u and appraiser (1757). His trade card [BM] indicates that he was able to offer furniture in 'Mohogany, Wallnutt-tree and Wainscott' which included 'settee and Bowroe Bedsteads'. In 1757 took out a licence to employ a non-freeman for six weeks. [Heal; GL, City Licence bk, vol. 1]

Woodward, William, London, u (1761). Discharged from Debtors' Prison in 1761. His address was given as 'late of London Bridge, St. Magnus'. [*London Gazette*, 25 August 1761]

Woodward, William, Sidbury, Worcester, cm and u (1822–40). A William Woodward of this address was made free in 1831 and may be the son of the tradesman who appears in Worcester directories 1822–40. [D; freemen rolls]

Woodward, William, 3 London Rd, London, cm (1839). [D]

Woodward, William, South St, Bridport, Dorset, cm (1840). [D]

Woodward & Miller, Mint St, Southwark, London, u (1820). [D]

Woodward & Johnsons, Half St, Gloucester, cm and u (1830). [D]

Woodworth, John, Chester, cm (1747). Son of John Woodworth, bricklayer. Free 11 July 1747. [Freemen rolls]

Woodworth, John jnr, Martins Ash, Chester, cm (1771). [Poll bk]

Woodworth, John, Foregate St, Chester, cm (1784). Free 2 April 1784. [Freemen rolls; poll bk]

Woodworth, John, Shudehill, Manchester, joiner and cm (1800–02). [D]

Woodworth, Thomas, Chester, cm (1749–72). App. to Joseph Burrowes, cm, 24 June 1749, and free 3 September 1757. Took as app. in 1772 George Thorpe but five years later he was assigned to John Johnson. [App. reg.; freemen rolls]

Wooff, Emanuel, London, cm and chairmaker (1811–29). At Hoxton, opposite Queens Rd in 1811 and 23 Old St Rd, 1813–29. [D]

Woolby, George, Gt Yarmouth, Norfolk, carver and gilder (1830–39). At Regent St, 1830–39 but one directory of 1830 shows St George St. [D; poll bks]

Woolby, John, George St, Gt Yarmouth, Norfolk, carver and gilder (1836). [D]

Woolcock, John, Camborne, Cornwall, cm (1830). [D]

Wooldridge, James, 13 Edgar St, Liverpool, joiner and cm (1835–37). [D]

Wooles, William, Bristol, carver (1799–1813). At Thomas St in 1799, Gloucester St in 1801, Cross St in 1805, Old Market St, 1806–13, the number being 97 in 1813. In 1812–13 described as carver, undertaker and 'Surveyor to the Pitching & Paving'. [D]

Wooles & Bailey, Quay, Bristol, carver (1792–95). The Wooles may have been William Wooles who is shown trading as a carver on his own behalf in Bristol, 1799–1813. [D]

Woolf, Benjamin, Princess St, near Covent Gdn, London, cm (1688). [*London Gazette*, 14 June 1688]

Woolfall, Robert, King St, Blackburn, Lancs., cm and joiner (1814–34). In 1828 the directory entry is in the name of Esther Woolfall, joiner, and in 1834 Robert's trade was listed as joiner only. [D]

Woolfield, Henry, Ludgate Hill, Birmingham, cm, cabinet case and ebony inkstand maker (1818–23). [D]

Woolfield, Samuel, Birmingham, cabinet, dressing case and portable desk maker (1828–35). At 28 Ludgate Hill 1828 and still trading in this street in 1830. At 8 Bath Row in 1835. [D]

Woolfield, Thomas & John, 69 Church St, Liverpool, manufacturers of portable desks etc. (1827–28). The business commenced in October 1827 and manufactured 'Ladies and Gentlemen's Portable Desks, Dressing Cases, Work Boxes, Bagatelle and Backgammon Boards, Tea Chests &c.'. In July 1828 they claimed to have in stock 3–400 writing desks and dressing cases 'in Rosewood, Mahogany, Leather &c. price from 6 to 18 guineas each'. In addition they stocked French and English jewellery, chimney ornaments, bronzes, ivory chessmen, tortoiseshell combs, brushes, perfumes, travelling trunks and bags. They advertised their business as a 'Fancy Bazar'. Some of the stock was obtained from London and in May 1828 Thomas Woolfield announced his intention of going there and also to Paris. He offered to transact business on the behalf of others on commission. The partners claimed a high degree of public patronage, so much so that in August 1828 they announced the opening of additional showrooms at their Church St premises. The engravings used in connection with their advertisements show writing slopes and brass bound dressing cases typical of the period. [*Liverpool Mercury*, 8 February 1828, 9 May 1828, 4 July 1828, 22 August 1828]

Woolfitt, John, 3 St Paul's Churchyard, London, u (1825). [D]

Woolfitt, John, 170 Fleet St, London, cm and u (1835–39). [D]

Woolford, J. John, St Paul's Churchyard, London, u (1772). [Heal]

Woolford, John, 12 Little Knightrider St, Doctors' Commons, London, u (1775). In 1775 insured his house for £200. [GL, Sun MS vol. 244, p. 180]

Woolford, John, London, upholder (1778). Son of John Woolford of Ipswich, Suffolk, flax dresser. Free of the London Upholders' Co., 4 March 1778. [GL, Upholders' Co. records]

Woolford, John, 5 Old Belton St, Long Acre, London, u (1805). [D]

Woolford, R., Fleur de Lis St, Norton Falgate, London, u (1829). [D]

Woolfryes, William, 18 Crooked Lane, London, cm (1776). In 1776 took out insurance cover of £300 on his house and goods. [GL, Sun MS vol. 246, p. 269]

Wooll, George, 5 High St, Hastings, Sussex, carver and gilder (1823–37). In 1833 also bookseller and stationer. Ceased trading early in 1837. W. Arundale claimed to be his successor. [D]

Woollatt, Joseph, 9 Irongate, Derby, cm and u (1834). [D]

Woolett, Henry, London, cm and u (1817–37). At 33 Fore St, Cripplegate, 1817–20, and 143 Aldersgate St, 1822–37. [D]

Woollett, Ralph, Southwark, London, cm and u (1770–1809). Son of William Woollett of the parish of St Saviour, Southwark, carman. App. to William Shuter, 4 October 1770 and transferred to Richard Walker, 3 June 1772. Free of the Upholders' Co. by servitude, 1 April 1778 and at this date living at Queen St Park, Southwark. In June 1809 living at Red Cross St, Southwark where he took out insurance cover of £300 which included £100 for stock and utensils and £200 on timber in a warehouse opposite. [GL, Upholders' Co. records; Sun MS, 29 June 1809, ref. 832411]

Woollett, Thomas, Broker Row, Mint, Southwark, London, u (1825). [D]

Woolley, George Outram, Piccadilly, London, cm, u, undertaker and auctioneer (1783–1829). Son of John Woolley of Gravesend, Kent, tallow chandler. App. to Francis Pyner snr of London, 5 November 1783 and transferred to Francis Pyner jnr on 1 January 1786. Free of the Upholders' Co. by servitude, 17 November 1790. In 1793 subscribed to Sheraton's *Drawing Book*. Trading from an address at 196 Piccadilly by December 1800 when he took out insurance cover of £1,400 of which £600 was for utensils and stock. He was to remain at this address though the number 193 Piccadilly is given in two directories of the 1820s. The business he established was substantial and important. He is included in the list of master cabinet makers published by Sheraton in his *Cabinet Dictionary*, 1803. By January 1809 insurance cover had risen to £1,550 of which £800 was for stock and utensils. He was at this date using two houses in Piccadilly which had been inter-connected. On his billheads he described the business as a 'Cabinet, Upholstery & Carpet Warehouse' which would seem to imply a tendency to retail ready made goods of which a stock was maintained for immediate sale. Two accounts dated 1814–15 show however that he was prepared to undertake substantial commissions for the gentry. Chandos Leigh received from Woolley an account dated 18 October 1814 which included some goods delivered in the previous year and totalled £234 10s 6d. The largest sums concerned a mahogany octagon library table, the top covered in leather and fitted with eight drawer partitions for which £16 16s was charged and two folding dressing stands for which the same price was asked. A further bill in the following year mentioned an outstanding balance of £100 7s and totalled £132 15s 1d. Both invoices are made out to Chandos Leigh Esq[r]., London and may have been for a London house belonging to the Leigh family rather than

Stoneleigh Abbey, Warks. [D; GL, Upholders' Co. records; Sun MS vol. 419, ref. 712149; vol. 445, ref. 825515; Heal; Shakespeare Birthplace Trust, Leigh receipts, DR 18/5]

Woolley, Rowland, London, upholder (1706). Free of the Upholders' Co., 7 August 1706. [GL, Upholders' Co. records]

Woolley, Samuel, Curzon St, Derby, cm and u (1835). [D]

Woolley, William, Smith St, Warwick, carver and gilder (1828). [D]

Woolnough, George, Beccles, Suffolk, cm (1839). One directory gives Northgate St but another New Market. [D]

Woolridge, James, 28 Edgar St, Liverpool, cm (1827). A James Woodbridge was trading in Edgar St, 1827–29. [D]

Woolsey, William, Beastmarket, Gainsborough, Lincs., cm (1819). [D]

Wooltorton, Edmund, Norwich, cm (1824). On 21 September 1824 his app. Richard Stewart was made free. [Freemen rolls]

Wooltorton, James Poston, Bethel St, St Giles, Norwich, cm (1836–39). [D]

Woolverton, E., Gt Yarmouth, Norfolk, cm (1807). [Poll bk]

Woolverton, Edmund, Gt Yarmouth, Norfolk, cm (1830). [Poll bk]

Woolverton, Edmund, Norwich, cm and u (1796–1836). First recorded in a Gt Yarmouth poll bk of October 1796 and at this date living in Norwich. Living at King St, Norwich, October 1812. Trading at Upper King St in 1830 and Calvert St, 1836. [D; Gt Yarmouth poll bk; Norwich poll bk]

Woolverton, Samuel, Gt Yarmouth and Norwich, Norfolk, cm (1777–96). At Gt Yarmouth in 1777 but living in Norwich, 1795–96. [Gt Yarmouth poll bks]

Wooster, Charles, High Wycombe, Bucks., chairmaker (b. c. 1801–41). Four sons and a daughter bapt., 1823–38. Aged 40 at the date of the 1841 Census. [PR (bapt.)]

Wooster, George, High Wycombe, Bucks., chairmaker (1821–40). A daughter bapt. in 1821 and a son in 1830. [PR (bapt.)]

Wooster, James, High Wycombe, Bucks., chairmaker (1817–40). Children bapt., 1817–19. [PR (bapt.)]

Wooster (or Worcester), James, Bradenham, High Wycombe, Bucks., chair manufacturer (1829–40). Two daughters and a son bapt., 1829. [D; PR (bapt.)]

Wooster, John, West Wycombe, Bucks., chairmaker (1798). [Militia Census]

Wooster, Timothy, High Wycombe, Bucks., chairmaker (1798). [Militia Census]

Wooten, Charles, 23 Hatton Gdn, Liverpool, joiner and cm (1829). [D]

Wootton, James, London, upholder (1762). Son of Thomas Wootton of Reading, Berks., coachmaker. App. to Charles Grange, 7 March 1754 and free of the Upholders' Co. by servitude, 6 March 1762. [GL, Upholders' Co. records]

Wooton, John, 5 Long Acre, London, carver and gilder (1790–93). [D]

Wootton, John, Shorts Gdns, London, carver and gilder (1779). In 1779 took out insurance cover of £200 on his utensils and stock. [GL, Sun MS vol. 276, p. 445]

Wootton, John, 19 Mercer St, Long Acre, London, carver and gilder (1816–20). [D]

Wootton, Thomas, 34 Gt Prescott St, London, cm (1809). [D]

Worboys, G. B., 'The Civet Cat', 62 Wine St, Bristol, cabinet case maker (1838–40). In addition traded as a perfumerer, jeweller, cutler and importer of foreign fancy merchandise. Agent for 'Patent Plated Ware'. [D]

Worden, William, Barley Mkt, Tavistock, Devon, cm (1830). [D]

Worhall, Thurston & Fuller, 6 Catherine St, Strand, London, patent and improved cabinet and upholstery makers (1811–12). [D]

Workham, John, Romford, Essex, cm (1809). [D]

Workman, John, Dursley, Glos., cm (1826–40). Child bapt., 1826. Trading at Long St in 1839. [D; PR (bapt.)]

Worley, Frances, 15 Hackney Rd, London, cm and bedstead-maker (1827–29). Described in 1827 as a cm and in 1829 as a bedstead maker. [D]

Worloch, William, Castle St, Long Acre, carver (1774). [Westminster poll bk]

Wormald, James, 159 High St, Poole, Dorset, carver and gilder (1830). [D]

Wormald, William, King's Arms Yd, Lowerhead Row, Leeds, Yorks., house, sign and furniture painter and gilder (1817–22). Advertised that he was commencing on his own account in April 1817. [D; *Leeds Mercury*, 26 April 1817]

Wormell, Joseph, London, joiner (1718–37). In 1718 declared his trade to be joiner and he was then at 'The Golden Hat', the east end of St Paul's Church, parish of St Faith. His name associated with that of Benjamin Lane Wormell, his son, occurs in the Alscot Park archives, 1736–37, for work carried out to the West's London house in Covent Gdn. Much of the bill for £13 3s was for repair work to furniture but a large wainscot table bed was supplied at £1 12s and twelve chairs at £9 12s. [GL, Sun MS ref. 11697, 4 August 1718; V&A archives]

Wormald, James, George St, Gt Yarmouth, Norfolk, carver and gilder (1836). [D]

Worms, Henry, London, cm, u and furniture broker (1808–13). At 44–45 Nightingale Lane in July 1808 when he took out insurance cover of £550. Of this £300 was for stock and utensils. At 17 Wapping Dock St, 1811–13. [D; GL, Sun MS vol. 446, ref. 819712]

Wormsley, —, Margate, Kent, upholder (1803–07). [D]

Worpell, Henry, Market St, Bishop's Stortford, Herts., cm and u (1832). [D]

Worpell, Henry, Turners Hill, Cheshunt, Herts., u and appraiser (1839). [D]

Worrall, Catherine, Cannon St, Manchester, u (1781). [D]

Worrall, William, Manchester, cm (1772–88). At Ackers Gate in 1772, Acres Ct in 1773 and Gravel Lane, Salford in 1788. [D]

Worrell (or Worrall), James, Warrington, Lancs., cm (1769–98). In 1769 married a Miss Stockley of Warrington. Trading at Horsemarket in 1787. [D; [*Williamson's Liverpool Advertiser*, 12 May 1769]

Worrell, John, 29 Ray St, Liverpool, cm (1818). [D]

Worrell & Holmes, 11 Sewer Lane, Hull, Yorks., turners, carvers and cm (1831). One of the partners was Edward Worrell, a wood turner who was resident at 11 Sewer Lane in 1831. [D]

Worrins, John, address unknown, cm (1803). Subscribed to Sheraton's *Cabinet Dictionary*, 1803.

Worroll, Thomas, Bewdley, Worcs., chairmaker (1831). [Worcs. county poll bk]

Worseldine, John, 19 Rose Cresc., Cambridge, cm and u (1820–40). Three children bapt. in the parish of St Clement, 1826–31. At this period he was employed by Elliot Smith but in February 1832 he advertised that after twelve years with this maker he was establishing his own business at 19 Rose Cresc. In 1837 also undertaker, auctioneer and appraiser. [D; poll bks; *Cambridge Chronicle*, 3 February 1832]

Worsell, Richard, High St, Rye, Sussex, cm (1832–39). [D]

Worsfold, George, 1 Charing Cross, London, portable desk manufacturer and cutler (1820). [D]

Worsley, John, Lower Town, Altrincham, Cheshire, chairmaker (1828). [D]

Worsley, Micaiah, Altrincham, Cheshire, chairmaker (1793). [D]

Worsley, Thomas, Glass House St, London, cm (1790–93). [D]

Worsley, William, Hanging Ditch, Manchester, chairmaker (1772). [D]

Worster, John, 81 Leman St, Goodman's Fields, London, carver and gilder (1839). [D]

Worswick, Richard, Leeds, Yorks., cm and u (1791–1840). Included in the list of journeyman cm in basic sympathy with the *Leeds Cabinet and Chair Makers' Book of Prices*, 1791. Shown trading on his own behalf from 1816. At Vicar Lane, 1816–20, 24 Lowerhead Row, 1821, 3 Barron's Yd, 1826 and Woodhouse Lane 1828 onwards. The number in Woodhouse Lane was 11 and 14 in 1830, 18 in 1834 and 9 from 1837. From 1821 the business traded as Richard Worswick & Son. In 1837 undertook the furnishing of the Oxford Pl. Methodist Chapel and submitted an account for £133 13s 4d in this connection. The invoice dated 15 December 1837 gives a trading address at 10 Woodhouse Lane and indicates that they also acted as appraisers and undertakers. [D; Leeds archives dept, OP/35]

Worth, A. C., 86 High St, Chatham, Kent, cm and chairmaker. A drum table of Sheraton period exists with the trade label of this maker. It indicates that the firm also acted as undertakers, appraisers and auctioneers. [V&A archives]

Worth, Henry, Rose Lane, Ipswich, Suffolk, carver and gilder (1830). [D]

Worth, William, 28 Treville St, Plymouth, Devon, cm and u (1838). [D]

Worthington, Joseph, London, upholder (1777–87). In 1777 at 6 Mercer St, Long Acre which he insured for £100. By 1784 at Litchfield St and in January 1787 at 2 Porter St where he insured household goods and stock for £300. On 1 January 1793 the *Charleston City Gazette* carried an advertisement of Worthington & Kirby, cm and u, who claimed to have been formerly of London. The Worthington may have been Joseph Worthington. [GL, Sun MS vol. 263, p. 34; vol. 342, ref. 526716; Westminster poll bk]

Worthy, John, Hemings Row, Westminster, London, cm (1749). [Poll bk]

Worthy, John, Southgate St, Hartlepool, Co. Durham, joiner/cm (1834). [D]

Worthy, Joseph, Broad St, Canterbury, Kent, u (1818). [Poll bk]

Wortley, William, Whitechapel, London, cm (1774). [Heal]

Wortley, William, Stamford, Lincs., cm (late 17th century). Freeman by purchase. [Stamford Town Hall, box 6/1/1–6/4/2, No. 231]

Woster, Thomas, London, cm (1710–36). See John and G. Coxed & Thomas Woster.

Wotton, C., London(?), upholder (1672). In October 1672 charged for marking printed velvet hangings for the Wrought Bed at Wimbledon House and other items for which £24 18s was asked. The same source refers to work on a Red India Bed at Hatfield House, Herts. and £25 3s was expended on making the tester, head curtains and four large curtains. [Hatfield House MS, Bills 301]

Wouldhave, Michael, Market Pl., Barnard Castle, Co. Durham, joiner and cm (1827–28). [D]

Wrag, John, Greek St, Soho, London, carver (1784). [Westminster poll bk]

Wragg, John, Chesterfield, Derbs., chairmaker (1767). On 21 April 1767 mortgaged a cottage in Brampton to Anthony Gallimore to secure a loan of £15. [Derbs. RO, deeds 46/1]

Wragg, Zachariah, Melton Mowbray, Leics., cm (1826–35). App. to Thomas Burton of Leicester and free 1826. In 1835 trading at Factory Row. [D; freemen rolls]

Wragg & Wigfall, 19 Eyre St, Sheffield, Yorks., u (1837). [D]

Wraight, John, High St, Folkestone, Kent, cm (1789). Rented his house, which was valued for insurance at £300, from Robert Milton of Folkestone, Gent. [GL, Sun MS vol. 362, p. 665]

Wraith, Sarah, Kirkgate, Wakefield, Yorks., cm/u (1837). Successor to William Wraith at this address and possibly his widow. [D]

Wraith, William, Kirkgate, Wakefield, Yorks., cm and u (1816–34). Succeeded at this address by Sarah Wraith, possibly his widow. [D]

Wrapson, James, West St, Havant, Hants., cm and auctioneer (1823–30). [D]

Wrapson, William, Fareham, Hants., cm, u and builder (1823–30). In 1830 in the High St. [D]

Wraughton, Mrs Ann, 'The Blue & White Balls', King St, Covent Gdn, London, (1694). In 1694 advertised for sale 'Indian and Japanned Cabinets'. [Heal]

Wray, Benjamin, Lavender St, Reading, Berks., cm (1837). [Poll bk]

Wray, John, 1 Gibson's Yd, Carr Lane, Hull, Yorks., joiner and cm (1823). Still recorded at this address in 1826 but then described as a broker. [D]

Wray, Joseph, 59 Leonard St, Tabernacle Walk, London, cm (1839). [D]

Wray, Richard, 118 High St, Sunderland, Co. Durham, joiner and cm (1828). [D]

Wray, Thomas, London, chairmaker (1835–39). In 1835 at Darlington Pl., Bridge St, Southwark but in 1839 at 17 Darlington Pl. [D]

Wray, Thomas, Northgate, Market Weighton, Yorks., cm and joiner (1840). [D]

Wren, Thomas, 122 Fishergate, Preston, Lancs., cm (1834). [D]

Wren, Timothy, Preston, cm (1796–1818). Free 4 November 1796 and by 1802 was in partnership with a person named Corry and trading as Wren & Corry. In 1802 they endorsed the contents of the *Preston Cabinet Makers' and Chair Makers' Book of Prices* as masters and in 1803 subscribed to Sheraton's *Cabinet Dictionary*. Wren was trading on his own behalf from Theatre St, 1814–16, but by 1818 was once more in partnership, this time with a person named Ladyman. Wren & Ladyman used the Theatre St address and also 15 Fishergate. Wren also traded as a timber merchant and builder. [D]

Wrenshall (or Wrenshaw), Joseph, Lancaster and Liverpool, cm (1738–90). App. in Lancaster and free, 1783–84. Already by this time he had moved to Liverpool, and was trading at 7 Liver St in 1790. [D; Lancaster freemen rolls and poll bk]

Wride, Peter, 68 Curtain Rd, London, cm (1820–22). In March 1822 took out insurance cover of £400, half of which was for utensils and stock. Successor to William Wride at this address. [D; GL, Sun MS vol. 489, ref. 989663]

Wride, William, 68 Curtain Rd, Shoreditch, London, cabinet manufacturer (1817). Succeeded at this address by Peter Wride. [D]

Wrigg, John, 15 John's Row, St Luke's, London, cm (1809). [D]

Wright, —, Cambridge, u (1688). Paid in 1688 by Trinity College for 'printed stuff'. [College records]

Wright, Mrs, address unknown, u (1752–54). On 20 May 1754 paid £93 17s by the Earl of Ancaster for work carried out over the previous two years. [Lincoln RO, 2 ANC. 6/7]

Wright, —, London, cm (1793). Subscribed to Sheraton's *Drawing Book*, 1793.

Wright, —, Clerkenwell, London, cm (1793). Subscribed to Sheraton's *Drawing Book*, 1793.

Wright, A., 4 Grafton St, Fitzroy Sq., London, u (1835–39). [D]

Wright, Abel, 15 Kenton St, London, u (1829). [D]

Wright, Abel, 9 Wilson St, Finsbury, London, u (1829). [D]

Wright, Abraham (or Adam), 410 Oxford St, London, u (1790–1802). One London directory shows Adam Wright at this address, 1790–1802, while another lists Abraham Wright here, 1793–1800. This maker's trade card unfortunately does not assist as the name of the firm is stated simply as 'Wright'. It states however that the firm were also cm and undertakers. The card is illustrated with a settee, two chairs and a commode. A 'Wright' u subscribed to Sheraton's *Drawing Book*, 1793 and may possibly be this maker. F. & W. Wright was the successor to this business at the Oxford St address. [D; Heal]

Wright, Adam, 51 and 55 Long Acre, London, u (1774–93). At 51 Long Acre by 1781 and in that year took out insurance cover of £800, half of which was for utensils and stock. Directories show him continuing to trade at this address until 1793 but a trade card [BM] gives the address as 55 Long Acre. Regularly supplied Lord Monson and £14 19s 10d was paid on 25 April 1785, £25 3s on 4 May 1786, £35 0s 6d on 30 April 1787, £18 6s on 5 May 1788, £15 17s on 16 May 1789 and £23 13s 5d on 26 April 1790. [D; GL, Sun MS vol. 290, p. 575; Lincoln RO, Monson 10/1/A/6]

Wright, Ann, 4 Bell Alley, Goswell St, London, cm (1839). [D]

Wright, Benjamin, Belgrave Gate, Leicester, chairmaker (1818–40). [D]

Wright, Charles, 8 Broker's Row, Moorfields, London, u (1801–19). Son of Richard Wright of Moorfields, upholder. Free of the Upholders' Co. by patrimony, 4 February 1801 and at this date living at the Moorfields address. Trading at this address on his own behalf 1806–19. [D; GL, Upholders' Co. records] See J. Wright.

Wright, Charles, London, carver and gilder (1809–20). Trading at 11 Charles St, Soho Sq., 1809–16, and in 1820 at 28 Garden Row, London Rd. [D]

Wright, Charles, Northbrook St, Newbury, Berks., cm (1823–30). [D]

Wright, Charles, 28 Norfolk St, Fitzroy Sq., London, cm (1825). [D]

Wright, Charles Britannia, Portsea, Portsmouth, Hants., cm, u, paper hanger and undertaker (1830). In 1830 at 71 Hanover St. A mahogany work box is known with the trade label of this maker affixed to a drawer with an address at 68 Union St. [D]

Wright, Clayton, 18 Fennel St, Manchester, cm (1804). [D]

Wright, D., 72 Margaret St, Cavendish Sq., London, u (1816). [D]

Wright, Daniel, 383 Oxford St, London, cm and u (1804–05). [D]

Wright, Daniel, 74 Ayr St, Piccadilly, London, upholder (1826). [D]

Wright, Daniel, 20 Hanway St, London, u (1829). [D]

Wright, Daniel, 32 Greek St, Soho, London, u (1839). [D]

Wright, David, Church St, Lancaster, joiner and cm (1747–66). Acquired some deals from Robert Gillow in 1747 and again in 1753–54, paying for them with his own labour (an accepted form of barter amongst tradesmen in Lancaster at the time). [Westminster Ref. Lib., Gillow vol. 344/2] Obtained his freedom 2 June 1753 by redemption, for a fee of £6 6s. [Lancaster freemen rolls] In 1753 took Robert Carter of Stalwen as app. joiner and cm. In 1766 he was occupying a house in Church St. [Window tax returns] His son William was made free in 1767/68 as a joiner, but it is not known if he carried on his father's business. A mahogany kneehole desk in the V&A (No. W.8–1942) is inscribed on the bottom of one of the drawers 'Lancaster August 19th 1751 / David Wright / Fecit'. [*DEF*, III, p. 376] D.H.

Wright, David, Leeds, Yorks., chairmaker (1826–39). At Wright's Yd, York St in 1826 but in 1828 the address was rendered as York Tavern Yd. By 1830 at 16 York St, but from 1834–39 at 10 Sykes St. [D]

Wright, Edmund, Cavendish St, Ashton-under-Lyne, Lancs., joiner and cm (1828–34). [D]

Wright, Edward, Cannon St, London, u (1755). In January 1755 advised by advertisement that he was contemplating retirement from the business because of his advanced years. He offered to dispose of his enterprise which was described as 'a Shop of good Business & well situated' to any person having a capital of £400 to £500. [*Public Advertiser*, 24 January 1755]

Wright, Edward, Sheaf St, Daventry, Northants., cm and u (1830). [D]

Wright, Elizabeth, Market Hill Brow, Wigton, Cumb., u (1834). [D]

Wright, Ellis, Reading, Berks., upholder (1754). [Poll bk]

Wright, Francis, 43 Rathbone Pl., London, u and undertaker (1809–19). [D]

Wright, Francis & William, 410 Oxford St, London, u and cm (1803–09). Successors to Adam (or Abraham) Wright at this address. Both of the partners were probably the sons of A. Wright and both subscribed to Sheraton's *Drawing Book*, 1793 giving this Oxford St address. They were included in the list of master cabinet makers in Sheraton's *Cabinet Dictionary*, 1803. They claimed to be 'Cabinet Makers to H. M. Stamp Office'. Supplied furniture and undertook work to the value of £115 for the Earl of Jersey, the bill being signed by W. Wright in March 1805. In 1809 the partnership broke up with William Wright continuing to trade at 410 Oxford St and Francis setting up a separate business at 43 Rathbone Pl. nearby. [D; *DEF*; Heal]

Wright, George, Longtown, Cumb., joiner/cm (1811). [D]

Wright, George, Richmond, Yorks., cm (1816). [PR (bapt.)]

Wright, George, Sheffield, Yorks., chairmaker (1822–37). At 8 Cherry Tree Yd, 36 Gibraltar St in 1822, 64 Westbar Green in 1830 and 9 Workhouse Croft in 1837. [D]

Wright, George, 3 Carteret St, Westminster, London, cm and u (1827). [D] See John Wright at this address.

Wright, George, 31 Newton St, Birmingham, cm and u (1828–30). [D]

Wright, George, 40 Seward St, Goswell St, London, cm (1839). [D]

Wright, George, 17 Dartmouth St, Westminster, London, cm (1839). [D]

Wright, Henry, Ironmonger St, Stamford, Lincs., u (1728–45). In 1728 announced that he could offer at his Ironmonger St premises 'all sorts of Feather-Beds, Tickets, Blankets, Quilts, and all sorts of Bed-lace, and Easie Chairs, and other new-fashion'd Wallnut-Tree Chairs from London'. He indicated that he was prepared 'to work at any Gentlemen's House at a reasonable Rate'. In 1736 took app. named Williamson, and in 1745 Thomas Williamson. [*Stamford Mercury*, 18 April 1728; S of G, app. index]

Wright, Henry, Nottingham, u (d. 1767). Probate granted on his will 11 April 1767. [Notts RO, probate records]

Wright, Henry, London, upholder (1776–81). In 1776 living at Holborn Ct, Gray's Inn. Also at Gray's Inn in 1778 but in 1781 at Old Broad St. Free of the Upholders' Co. by redemption, 3 January 1776. [GL, Upholders' Co. records]

Wright, Henry, Bristol, cm (1792–1812). At Thomas St, 1792–93 and thereafter at 10 Bath St. [D]

Wright, Henry, Chichester, Sussex, cm (b. *c.* 1789–1840). Bapt. 17 January 1790 at Chichester. Married at St Martin's Church 16 August 1814 and from 1815 living in the parish of St Olave. In 1821 his address was given as East St and in 1830 as St Martin's Lane. From 1832 trading in South St as a cm, u, auctioneer and appraiser. [D; PR (bapt. and marriage)]

Wright, Henry, Church Gate, Leicester, chairmaker (1835). [D]

Wright, Henry, 7 Commercial Rd, London, cm (1826). [D]

Wright, I., 12 Hart St, Bloomsbury Sq., London, upholder and undertaker (1820). [D]

Wright, J., 8 Broker Row, Moorfields, London, u (1819). Successor to Charles Wright at this address. [D]

Wright, J., 50 South Molton St, London, u and cm (1823–29). [D]

Wright, James, address unknown, (1803). Subscribed to Sheraton's *Cabinet Dictionary*, 1803.

Wright, James, 6 Redcross St, Southwark, London, u (1826). [D]

Wright, James, Brotherton, Pontefract, Yorks., joiner/cm (1834). [D]

Wright, James, Saxmundham, Suffolk, cm (1839). [D]

Wright, Jeremiah, Birmingham, cm and u (1816–35). At Birchall St, 1816–18 and Bradford St, 1822–35, the number being 224 in 1830–35. [D]

Wright, Jesse, King St, Dudley, Staffs., cm, builder and surveyor (1820). [D]

Wright, John, Nantwich, Cheshire, u (1714). In 1714 took app. named Liversage. [S of G, app. index]

Wright, John, Lancaster, cm (1753–75). Became a freeman by redemption in October 1753 and between 1754–70 took on ten apps. He bought small quantities of deals from Gillows from time to time. Fire insurance records with the Royal Exchange record that his premises in the Green area were covered for £300 and the contents for £200. The same source indicates that in 1775 the building was assigned to Thomas Barrow, solicitor. [Window tax returns; freemen reg.; app. reg.; Westminster Ref. Lib., Gillow records]

Wright, John snr and jnr, York, cm (1738–82). Both were probably Roman Catholics. John Wright snr is first recorded in 1738 when he took as app. Gerwas Swift of Penyfigston, York. In 1754 he subscribed to Chippendale's *Director*. John Wright jnr was probably the person who in May 1767 declared his age to be 37 and stated that he had lived in the parish of St Michael le Belfry for eleven years. Further apps were John Smith in 1760, George Hare on 24 October 1770, Robert Heneage on 10 December 1777 and William Wright, son of John Wright jnr on 12 August 1782. [*Catholic Recusancy in York*; app. reg.]

Wright, John, College Lane, Northampton, u (1768–84). [Poll bks]

Wright, John, Nottingham, cm (1770–86). Freeman of Nottingham. Took apps in 1770 and 1780 and in the latter year was living at Wheelergate. [Freemen rolls; app. reg.; poll bk]

Wright, John, Chatham, Kent, upholder (1778). Bankruptcy announced, *Gents Mag.*, December 1778.

Wright, John, 40 Gt Russell St, Bloomsbury, London, u (1784–1811). In 1794–97 the business traded as Wright & Snell before reverting once more to John Wright's sole direction. This business was included in the list of master cabinet makers in Sheraton's *Cabinet Dictionary*, 1803. [D]

Wright, John, 53 Stretton Ground, Westminster, London, cm (1792). In May 1792 took out insurance cover of £200. [GL, Sun MS vol. 389, ref. 600397]

Wright, John, 26 Leadenhall St, London, carver and gilder (1794–97). Bankruptcy announced, *Billinge's Liverpool Advertiser*, 27 March 1797. [Heal]

Wright, John, 3 Carteret St, Westminster, London, cm (1805–09). A George Wright, cm and u was trading at this address in 1827. [D]

Wright, John, 37 Long Acre, London, cm (1809). [D]

Wright, John, Bartholomew St, Birmingham, u and paper hanger (1816–28). At 16 Bartholomew St, 1816–22, but in 1828 the number was 49. [D]

Wright, John, Exeter Row, Birmingham, cabinet case maker (1816). [D]

Wright, John, 10 King St, Bloomsbury, London, upholder and undertaker (1816–17). [D]

Wright, John, 1 Bowling Green Lane, Clerkenwell, London, cabinet manufacturer (1817–20). [D]

Wright, John, 11 Smith St, Westminster, London, u and undertaker (1817). [D]

Wright, John, Horse Fair, Birmingham, joiner and cm (1818). [D]

Wright, John, Worcester St, Birmingham, cm, u, paper hanger and chairmaker (1818–35). At 16–17 Worcester St, 1828–30 and 16 only in 1835. In 1835 the business was trading as John Wright & Son. [D]

Wright, John, 3 Carpenter St, Grosvenor Sq., London, upholder (1820). In March 1820 took out insurance cover of £300 which included £100 for utensils and stock. [GL, Sun MS vol. 483, ref. 962595]

Wright, John, Drapery, Northampton, upholder (1820–30). [D; poll bks]

Wright, John, Alton, Hants., cm (1823). [D]

Wright, John, 26 Cleveland St, Middlx Hospital, London, u (1826–39). [D]

Wright, John, Butcher Mkt, Louth, Lincs., cm and joiner (1826). [D]

Wright, John, Bilston, Staffs., cm, u, joiner and furniture warehouse (1830–35). At Church St in 1830 and High St, 1834–35. [D]

Wright, John, High St, Wednesbury, Staffs., cm and u (1830). [D]

Wright, John, 3 George St, Nottingham, joiner and cm (1832–35). [D]

Wright, John, Worksop, Notts., cm, u, builder etc. (1832–35). At Leadhill in 1832 and White Hart Yd in 1835. [D]

Wright, John & Son, 1 Wellington St, Leamington, Warks., cm and u (1835). [D]

Wright, John, Dukinfield St, Liverpool, cm (1835–39). At 6 Duckinfield St, 1835–37 but in 1839 the number was 11. [D]

Wright, John, 3 Drummond St, Euston Sq., London, chair and sofa maker (1839). [D]

Wright, John, Lowestoft, Suffolk, cm (1839). [D]

Wright, John Jarvis, 83 Tichfield St, Cavendish Sq., London, chairmaker and cm (1802–39). Insurance cover rose from £500 in 1802 to £1,000, 1812–20. Stock and utensils in the dwelling house and an open shed, a warehouse and workshop behind in some years amounted to over half the sum insured. [D; GL, Sun MS vol. 424, ref. 735454; vol. 437, ref. 792147; vol. 459, ref. 871691; vol. 480, ref. 946720; vol. 487, ref. 970108]

Wright, John Martingale, Carlisle, Cumb., cm (1798). In November 1798 a dividend was paid to the creditors of John Martingale Wright under an order in bankruptcy. [*Billinge's Liverpool Advertiser*, 15 October 1798]

Wright, Joseph, Brokers Row, Moorfields, London, upholder (1777–92). Second son of Richard Wright of Moorfields, London, upholder. Free of the Upholders' Co. by patrimony, 3 September 1777 and then assisted his father in the family business in Moorfields. In 1792 the business was listed as Joseph & Richard Wright. For further details see Richard Wright & Co., Wakefield, Yorks. and Moorfields, London, [D; GL, Upholders' Co. records]

Wright, Joseph, 60 Margaret St, Cavendish Sq., London, cm (1782). In 1782 insured utensils and stock for £50 out of a total insurance cover of £200. Possibly the Joseph Wright who subscribed to Sheraton's *Drawing Book*, 1793 though this may also have been the Joseph Wright of Moorfields. [GL, Sun MS vol. 302, p. 197]

Wright, Joseph, Gateshead, Co. Durham, joiner and cm (1801–11). At Church St in 1801 and Pipewellgate in 1811. [D]

Wright, Joseph, Leeming St, Nottingham, joiner and cm (1832–40). Possibly the Joseph Wright who was app. as a joiner and cm in Nottingham in 1814. [D; app. reg.]

Wright, Joshua, Folly Lane, Liverpool, cm (1775–83). Free 9 May 1775 and trading in Folly Lane in 1783. [D; freemen rolls]

Wright, M., address unknown (1763). On 29 November 1763 Lord Leigh paid M. Wright £73 10s 'for furniture'. [Shakespeare Birthplace Trust, Leigh receipts, DR 18/5]

Wright, M., 4 Bell Alley, Goswell St, London, cm (1835). [D]

Wright, Moses, Dudley, Staffs., cm (1809). [D]

Wright, Richard, Nantwich, Cheshire, u (1661–92). Two sons and three daughters bapt., 1661–74. The burial of Richard Wright occurred on 18 October 1692. [PR (bapt. and burial)]

Wright, Richard, 'The White Lion', Lower Moorfields, London, upholder and appraiser (1738–89). Son of Richard Wright, Caversham, Oxon., joiner; app. firstly to Francis Newberry on 1 February 1738 and secondly to William Powle, 7 May 1745; admitted freeman of the Upholders' Co. by servitude, 3 December 1747 and appointed master of the Upholders' Co., 1776. He took Benjamin Dell as app. in 1749, his own son William in 1766 and Thomas Burrell in 1755. In 1766 he took out insurance with the Hand in Hand Co. on a four storey brick house in Moorfields, renewed in 1773. Richard Wright's trade card ornamented with a lion rampant in a Rococo cartouche [Banks Coll. BM] states that he 'Buys and Sells all Sorts of Household Goods As Standing Beds and Beding, Chest of Drawers, Desks & Bookcases, Bouroe Desks, Card, Dining, Breakfasting and Dressing Tables in Mahogany, Walnutt tree or Wainscot, Chairs of all Sorts, Settee and Bouroe Bedsteads, Sconces, Peir, Chimney & Dressing Glasses and Carpets with all Manner of Upholstery and Braisery Goods, New and Old'. [GL, Upholders' Co. records; GL, Hand in Hand MS vol. 105, p. 5; S of G, app. index]

C. G. G.

Wright, Richard, Canterbury, Kent, cm (1744). In 1744 took app. named Smith. [S of G, app. index]

Wright, Richard & Elwick, Edward, Wakefield, Yorks., upholders (1745–1771); **Elwick, Edward & Son** (1771–d. 1787); **Elwick, John & Robinson, John** (1788–1816). Wright and Elwick of Wakefield became the pre-eminent firm of cm and u in Yorkshire during the second half of the 18th century, enjoying a dominance almost comparable to that achieved by Gillows in Lancashire. A small account sent to Charles Ingram of Temple Newsam House, Leeds in 1758 is written on the back of their only recorded and most informative trade card (Figs 39–40). It announced that 'Wright & Elwick Upholders/from London' were trading 'At the Glass & Cabinet Ware House in Northgate/WAKEFIELD'; their premises in Gill's Yard are still standing. The text states they 'Make & Sell all Sorts of Beds & Beding, Coach & Looking/Glasses, in Burnish or Oil Gold, Cabinet work of ye Newest Fashion,/Together with all sorts of Household Furniture./Mr Wright haveing been in ye direction of ye Greatest Tapestry/Manufactory in England for Upwards of Twenty Years,/UNDERTAKES/To Joyn, repair & Clean Tapestry, Persia, Turky, or any other/Carpets & to make all Carpets lye square & even, draws/for all Sorts of Needle Work for Carpets, Beds/Chairs, Fire Screens & c: Furnishes Ladies with/Printed Patterns and Shades of Silk and Worsted/for such Works in the best and pest/Manner/N.B. Old Glass cut Polished and Silver'd/and all the above perticulars Sold as cheap as in/LONDON'. Richard Wright, who may have directed the Soho tapestry factory before moving from London to Wakefield, is something of an enigma. It was clearly his expertise that enabled the firm to advertise such a wide range of services relating to tapestries, carpets and needlework. Wright subscribed (like his partner) to Chippendale's *Director* 1754, was elected Chief Constable of Wakefield in 1757 and was buried in the parish church on 6 July 1771. Three apps are known: Thompson (1755), Jn. Armitage (1759) and Chas. Hutton (1761). [S of G, app. index]

Edward, son of John Elwick, 'merchant taylor' of York was bapt. 12 January 1721/22. He may have been the Edward Elwick who acquired his freedom in 1758 on servitude to Robert Barker of York who unfortunately neglected to register the indenture. On 3 February 1759 Elwick was appointed one of the Chamberlains of the City for a year; he voted in the York elections of 1758 and 1774 as Edward Elwick, upholder of Wakefield and advertised in *York Courant*, 12 March 1745, 16 December 1746 and 25 July 1775. Fifteen letters written by Elwick to his patron John Grimston of Kilnwick Hall, Yorks. between 1770 and 1782 [Humberside RO, DDGR/42–43, pub. *Furn. Hist.*, 1976] contain much of interest about his commerce and personal affairs. He obliged his client by taking on a local boy Edward Halls as an app. while his own son John was sent away from home on business for the first time to Kilnwick in 1772; furthermore, this archive includes an elegant group of furniture designs which Elwick sent on approval. His offer to 'make some further sketches' implies that he produced his own drawings. Other letters show that Elwick dealt in exotic wares. In 1770 he organised a subscription lottery to dispose of 'fine India Goods', the following year offered to procure 'a Very fine set of Nankeen Table China' and the year after wrote 'I have Got a friend that is gon to China to pick up anything Curious'. On at least three occasions he purchased billiard tables from Gillows. [Westminster Ref. Lib., Gillow records, Waste Books 344/4, p. 135; 344/5, p. 287; 344/12/2539]

Like many provincial tradesmen Elwick was at pains to commend the 'neat plainness' of his furniture to patrons; he pointedly condemned some articles seen at Brancepeth Castle: 'there was a Great deal of Inlaid Expensive work sent from London — but badly Designed the Taste Vulgar & Clumsy'. In 1775 Elwick advertised [*York Courant*, 25 July 1775] for an app. 'in the upholstery Business' at his upholstery and cabinet warehouse in Wakefield. A letter of 12 October 1775 to Charles Hotham of Dalton Hall, Yorks. illustrates how Elwick solicited commissions through personal recommendation. He informed his prospective patron 'I have the Honour to serve most of the Nobility & Gentry in the West and North Rideing' and claimed to have sent 'about £3,000 of Furniture . . . into ye East Rideing . . . some Very Expensive' by water. The emerging pattern of patronage confirms that Yorkshire (with small inroads into North Nottinghamshire and Co. Durham) provided nearly all the firm's commissions. So far only two groups of fully documented furniture have been traced: three ceremonial chairs made for the Masonic Lodge at Wakefield in 1768, and at Burton Constable, Yorks., several lavishly carved and gilt pier glasses, an impressive tester bed and some routine mahogany bedroom pieces all of 1772.

Bailey's *British Directory*, 1784 records Edward Elwick & Son, upholders, in Wakefield. Edward's death was reported in *Leeds Intelligencier*, 3 July 1787; his son John summoned a meeting of creditors on 13 July 1788 and in 1794 the firm was trading as 'Elwick & Robinson', who had jointly subscribed to Sheraton's *Drawing Book* the previous year. John Elwick and John Robinson received a major commission to furnish Woolley Hall, Yorks., between 1794 and 1801. John Elwick is a shadowy figure. He married Sally Wood of West Ardsley on 4 October 1781 and as 'picture dealer and upholsterer' was declared bankrupt in 1816. [*Wakefield and Halifax*

Journal, 5 April] Robinson continued to trade as an u and cm on his own account in Northgate, Wakefield until on 11 June 1824 [*W & H.J.*] he advertised the sale of the business described as 'one of the most genteel and flourishing Concerns in that line in the County of York'. John Robinson died aged 68 in August 1824, before the sale and in October [*W. & H.J.*, 15 October] his widow declined the business in favour of Thomas Powell, u, the Corn Mkt, Wakefield who took her late husband's foreman William Marsden into partnership. [M. E. Ingram, *Leaves from a Family Tree*, 1951; *Furn. Hist.*, 1976; I. Hall, *William Constable as Patron* (Exhib. Cat), Hull, 1970]

WENTWORTH CASTLE, Yorks. (Earl of Strafford). 1746: Bill for sofas, chairs, etc. [excerpt transcribed in Symonds papers, Winterthur, Delaware] In her travel diary the Duchess of Northumberland recorded seeing 'French chairs emb'd with flowers upon Brown by the famous Mr Wright' at this house in 1760 [*C. Life*, 7 February 1974, p. 252] which may relate to a suite of tapestry chairs from Wentworth Castle, one of which is in the V&A (W. 36–1964).

WENTWORTH WOODHOUSE, Yorks. (Marquis of Rockingham). 1748–49: Bill for furniture, specialist upholstery work, India paper, etc. Total £117 15s 7½d. 1784 Giltwood table frame for drawing room pier. [Sheffield archives dept, Wentworth vouchers 1748 bundle & Steward's letters p. 6(111)85, May 17 1784]

OXFORD, Countess of. 1754–55: Paid two bills for unspecified work total £3 4s 9d. [Notts. RO, DD. 5P 14/2]

TEMPLE NEWSAM HOUSE, Yorks. (Viscount Irwin) 1758: Bill for close stools inscribed on back of firm's trade card, Total £2 13s 6d. [Leeds archives dept, TN, EA/12/5] 1761: Bill for brackets, carpets, etc. Total £4 4s 7d. [TN, EA/12/5] 1769: Bill for general household furniture. Total £129 5s 8d. [TN, A/12/6]

CUSWORTH HALL, Yorks. (John Battie). 1762–71: Various ledger payments for chairs, bed, wallpaper. Total £131 6s. [Leeds archives dept, Battie-Wrightson papers A/160, 179, 180]

CANNON HALL, Yorks. (John Spencer). Entries in John Spencer's diary between February 1766 and November 1768 reveal that 'Messieurs Wright & Elwick' were involved in furnishing the new drawing room. [Sheffield archives dept, Spencer-Stanhope MS, JS (3) 60633–19]

WORKSOP MANOR, Notts. (Duke of Norfolk). 1766: 'bespoke of Mr Elwick of Wakefield 6 chairs for the staircase' [Sheffield archives dept, Arundel Castle papers: 'Worksop Manor/System/Proposal for Furnishing the/New Building/May 1766, fol. 23 (unnumbered)]

NOSTELL PRIORY, Yorks. (Sir Rowland Winn). 1767: Chippendale's disparaging allusion to 'the Ingenious Mr Elwick' in his letter of 26 August implies he was employed at this house in some capacity. [Nostell archives C3/1/5/3/5]

MASONIC LODGE, Wakefield, Yorks. 1768: 'To 3 Mahog. Elbow Chairs with high backs', £8 9s 6d'. [Lodge records] All three survive in use at the Lodge; they have plain legs and openwork backs, styled with conventional Rococo carving, headed by glazed roundels featuring Masonic emblems in gold on a blue ground. [*Furn Hist.*, 1976]

SERLBY HALL, Notts. (Viscount Galway). An undated document (c. 1770?) survives headed 'Mr Elwick's Valuation of Furniture &c for East Wing', the schedule amounts to £152 10s 4d. [Nottingham Univ. Lib., Galway MS, H. M1/1:12.702]

KILNWICK HALL, Yorks. (John & Thomas Grimston). 1770–82: Fifteen letters together with seven manuscript designs and two minor bills survive from this commission. [Humberside RO, DD. GR/38/15–42/22–43 and 44] Elwick was engaged to furnish new interiors designed by John Carr and there are records of payments to him amounting to £280 and £150 in 1773–74. The correspondence and four of the drawings were published in *Furn. Hist.*, 1976.

BURTON CONSTABLE, Yorks. (William Constable). 1772: Elwick received a 'considerable order' amounting to £704 9s 8½d. [Hull University Lib., archives dept, Burton Constable papers, 1772 bundle] He fully equipped a bedroom and two dressing rooms: Ivan Hall has identified seven items listed in the account: a luxurious tester bed costing £125, a pair of oval pier glasses 'in the Grecian Taste', another carved and gilt 'transitional' pier glass, a mahogany dressing stool and two night tables. [*Furn. Hist.*, 1976] Several articles which do not survive at the house were embellished 'with wrote Brass gilt Furniture' or 'inlaid in the Grecian taste'.

CROWNEST, near Dewsbury, Yorks. (Samuel Buck). Elwick informed John Grimston in 1772 that he had been 'given orders to furnish throughout'. [*Furn. Hist.*, 1976]

SHELBROOK, near Doncaster, Yorks. (Councillor Perryin). Elwick informed John Grimston in 1772 that the owner had given him instructions for the house 'to be fitted up'. [*Furn. Hist.*, 1976]

WHITWORTH HALL, Co. Durham (Robert Shafto). Elwick told John Grimston in 1772 that he had received a commission from the owner. [*Furn. Hist.*, 1976]

HOUSE AT EAST RETFORD, Notts. (Wharton Emerson). Elwick informed John Grimston in 1772 he had been 'Given orders'. [*Furn. Hist.*, 1976]

SWINTON PARK, Yorks. (William Danby). In 1775 Elwick informed Charles Hotham 'I have just furnish'd ... Mr Danby, Swinton'. [*Furn. Hist.*, 1976]

NORTON CONYERS, Yorks. (Sir Bellingham Graham). In 1775 Elwick informed Charles Hotham 'I have just furnish'd Sir Bell Graham'. [*Furn. Hist.*, 1976]

RISE HALL, Yorks. (William Bethell). This large commission is mentioned in Elwick's letter of 1775 to Charles Hotham (q.v.) and a description of the furnishing scheme he contrived for the Drawing Room is supplied in his letter of 28 January 1779 to John Grimston of Kilnwick. [*Furn. Hist.*, 1976]

NESWICK HALL, Yorks. (Robert Grimston). In 1775 Elwick wrote to Charles Hotham that examples of his work could be seen at this house. [*Furn. Hist.*, 1976]

THORPE HALL, near Bridlington, Yorks. (Godfrey Bosvile). Mentioned in 1775 as an on-going commission in Elwick's letter to Charles Hotham. [*Furn. Hist.*, 1976]

WELTON GRANGE, near Hull, Yorks. (John Williamson). Mentioned in 1775 as a current commission in Elwick's letter to Charles Hotham. [*Furn. Hist.*, 1976]

DALTON HALL, Yorks. (Charles Hotham). In a letter dated 12 October 1775 Elwick offered 'my best services in the Upholstery & Cabinet way'. [Hull University Lib., archives dept, Hotham papers, DD. HO./4/16/1] It is not known whether this unsolicited approach resulted in a commission, but Elwick named ten satisfied customers in the area.

GISBURN, Yorks. (Lord Ribblesdale). 1777: February, 'To Mr Elwick of Wakefield, carver, 2 picture frames', £5. 5s. [YAS, Gisburn papers, Ledger 1750–81 (unnumbered)]

BRANCEPETH CASTLE, Co. Durham (Mr Tempest). Elwick wrote to John Grimston in 1779 that he had taken orders for furnishing the Castle and another Tempest house near Hartlepool. [*Furn. Hist.*, 1976]

CHATSWORTH (Duke of Devonshire). c. 1783: Arbitrated in a dispute between Carr and Gaubert over bills. [*Burlington*, June 1980, p. 410]

KIRKLEES HALL, Yorks. (Sir George Armitage). 1783: Account for chairs, sofa furnishings, etc. Total £212 16s 5d. [*Halifax Antiquarian Soc. Trans.*, 1982, p. 36]

WOOLLEY HALL, Yorks. (Godfrey Wentworth). 1794–1801: Three substantial accounts from Elwick & Robinson survive totalling £919 0s 4d, £80 9s 11½d and £257 19s. [YAS, Wentworth papers, MD. 272/2] The partners were responsible for wallpapers, curtains, carpets, bedding, and alterations, besides supplying a very wide range of furniture. It was all dispersed in 1947. The following workmen are mentioned by name: John Houghs, Billy Middleton, James Robert, Tho. Todd, Geo. and John Whittam.   C. G. G.

Wright, Richard, 63 Charlotte St, Fitzroy Sq., London, cabinet warehouse (1809–17). [D]

Wright, Richard, Castle Donnington, Leics., cm (1829). [D]

Wright, Richard, Brunswick Sq., Southampton, Hants., chairmaker (1830–39). [D]

Wright, Richard, 1 Bell Alley, Goswell St, London, cm (1839). An M. Wright, cm, was at 4 Bell Alley in 1835. [D]

Wright, Robert, 8 Little Britain, London, upholder (1791–98). Son of James Wright of Aldersgate St, sawyer. App. to Thomas Shackleton, 5 January 1791 and free of the Upholders' Co. by servitude, 1798 and in this year living at Little Britain. [GL, Upholders' Co. records]

Wright, Robert, Bond St, Hull, Yorks., cm, u and undertaker (1814–34). At 39 Bond St, 1814–1818 but from 1821 the address is given as 38–39 Bond St. [D]

Wright, Robert, Longtown, Carlisle, Cumb., joiner/cm (1828–29). [D]

Wright, Robert, Newcastle St, Nottingham, carver and gilder (1832). [D]

Wright, Robert, 6 John St, Leeds, Yorks., chairmaker (1834). [D]

Wright, Robert, Cox Lane, Ipswich, Suffolk, cm and u (1839). [D]

Wright, S., 388 Strand, London, carver, gilder and looking-glass manufacturer (c. 1830). His premises were on the corner of Southampton St. [Heal]

Wright, Samuel, 'at Mr. Sharmans', 6 Elder St, Spitalfields, London, upholder (1773–81). Son of Samuel Wright, mariner and app. to Samuel Swaine, 3 November 1773. Free of the Upholders' Co. by servitude, 14 November 1781. [GL, Upholders' Co. records

Wright, Samuel, Rose Pl., Liverpool, joiner, cm and undertaker (1804–29). The number in Rose Pl. was 15–16 in 1805, 16 in 1807–10 and 1813, 13 in 1811, 28 in 1816, 15 in 1818, 17 in 1824–27 and 28 in 1829. [D]

Wright, Stephen, Apple Lane, Lincoln, cm (1790). [Poll bk]

Wright, T., 51 Wigmore St, Cavendish Sq., London, cm and paper hanger (1817–20). [D]

Wright, Thomas, Derby, carver (1710). In 1710 took app. named Whittaker. [S of G, app. index]

Wright, Thomas, Hibaldstow, Lincs., chairmaker (1756). In 1756 took app. named Pearson. [S of G, app. index]

Wright, Thomas, London, upholder (1770–78). Son of Gascoigne Wright of Kirby, Lincoln, Clerk. App. to William Chesson of London, freeman and haberdasher. Free of the Upholders' Co. by servitude, 3 October 1770 and set up business in Fenchurch St, the number being 157 in 1778. The business was not successful and in *Gents Mag.*, June 1778 his bankruptcy was announced. It was in this year that he moved to Cannon St. [D; GL, Upholders' Co. records]

Wright, Thomas, 32 St Swithin's Lane, Cannon St, London, u and cm (1771–72). [D]

Wright, Thomas, Leek, Staffs., joiner and cm (1816–22). At Derby St 1816–22 but one directory of 1818 gives the address as Stockwell St. [D]

Wright, Thomas, 16 Broad Wall, Blackfriars, London, cm (1805). [D]

Wright, Thomas, Bristol, cm (1806–17). At 18 Milk St, 1806–09, 10 Bath St, 1813–14 and 19 Milk St, 1816–17. [D]

Wright, Thomas, 24 Church St, Mile End New Town, London, chair japanner (1809). [D]

Wright, Thomas, South Molton St, London, u (1817–39). At 42 South Moulton St in 1817 and no. 47 in 1839. [D]

Wright, Thomas, 51 Wigmore St, London, u (1821–27). [D]

Wright, Thomas, High St, Garstang, Lancs., joiner and cm (1834). [D]

Wright, Thomas, Leeds, Yorks., cm and u (1834–40). At 2 Quebec St in 1834, 18 Guildford St in 1837 and in that year moved to 16 Briggate. In 1839 at 20 Briggate. [D]

Wright, Thomas, 25 Yardley St, Spitalfields, London, cm (1839). [D]

Wright, Timothy, London, upholder (1719–26). Son of Henry Wright, freeman of London and sadler. App. to Phineas Sale, 1 April 1719 and free of the Upholders' Co. by servitude, 8 June 1726. [GL, Upholders' Co. records]

Wright, Timothy, Duke St, Westminster, London, u (1749). [Poll bk]

Wright, Timothy, York Buildings, Buckingham St, Strand, London, u (1747–50). A freeman of the Upholders' Co. [Heal; Westminster poll bk; freemen rolls]

Wright, Timothy, 24 Little Saffron Hill, London, looking-glass manufacturer (1839). [D]

Wright, W., Bishopsgate St, London, cm (1771). Bankruptcy announced, *Gents Mag.*, 1771.

Wright, William, Bishop's St, London, cm (1770). A freeman of the Joiners' Co.

Wright, William, Lancaster, cm (1767–68). [Lancaster freemen rolls]

Wright, William, Westgate, Peterborough, Northants., joiner, appraiser and u (1770). A mahogany Pembroke table of c. 1780 is recorded with the name 'W. WRIGHT' stamped on the top of each leg. [*Cambridge Chronicle*, 17 February 1770]

Wright, William, Moorfields, London, upholder (1773–81). Son of Richard Wright, freeman and member of the Upholders' Co. App. to his father and free of the Upholders' Co. by servitude, 7 July 1773. At Moorfields 1778–81. [GL, Upholders' Co. records]

Wright, William, Porter St, Newport Mkt, London, cm (1774–93). He can possibly be identified with the William Wright, a freeman of Lancaster who was living in London in April 1784. [D; Heal; Westminster poll bk; Lancaster poll bk]

Wright, William, Seething Lane, London, cm and joiner (1789). Bankruptcy announced, *Derby Mercury*, 5 February 1789.

Wright, William, Gloucester Lane, Bristol, cm (1792–94). [D]

Wright, William, 410 Oxford St, London, u and cm (1809–25). In partnership with Francis Wright at this address, 1803–09, and carried on the business when the partnership was dissolved in 1809. [D]

Wright, William, 6 Norfolk St, Oxford St, London, carver and gilder (1809–25). [D]

Wright, William, 82 Titchfield St, Fitzroy Sq., London, cabinet and chair manufactory (1817–39). [D; Heal]

Wright, William, Fleet St, Coventry, Warks., chairmaker (1822). [D]

Wright, William, 9 Wilson St, Finsbury, London, u (1822–26). In September 1822 insured stock and utensils for £100. [D; GL, Sun MS vol. 491, ref. 995839]

Wright, William, Thornton Watlass, Yorks., joiner and cm (1823). [D]

Wright, William, Westgate, Sleaford, Lincs., joiner, builder and cm (1826). [D]

Wright, William, Castle Hill, Richmond, Yorks., joiner and cm (1827). [D]

Wright, William, Rugby, Warks., u and paper hanger (1835). [D]

Wright, William, Windsor, Berks., u (1835). Named on a bill of

Anna McBean, u under 15 May 1835. [Windsor Royal Archives, accounts 1835–40]

Wright, William, Dongate, Rotherham, Yorks., cm (1837). [D]

Wright, William, 38 London St, Fitzroy Sq., London, carver and gilder (1837). [D]

Wright, William, 2–3 Mount Row, New Kent Rd, London, u (1837). [D]

Wright, William, 9 Junction Dock St, Hull, Yorks., cm (1838–39). [D]

Wright, William, Charlotte St, Gt Yarmouth, Norfolk, cm (1839). [D]

Wright, William, High St, Kimbolton, Hunts., cm (1839). [D]

Wright, William, 11 Palace Row, New Rd, London, cm (1839). [D]

Wright, William Hollands, Bicester, Oxon., joiner and cm (1793–1802). Freeman of Oxford. [D; Oxford poll bk]

Wright, William Thrale, 22 Wardour St, Soho, London, carver and gilder (1837–39). [D]

Wright & Son, 22 Lower Parade, Leamington, Warks., cm and u (1837). [D]

Wright & Stevens, 14 Gt Peter St, Westminster, London, furniture japanners (1835). [D]

Wrighten, Thomas, parish of St Michael, Bristol, cm (1784). [Poll bk]

Wrightson, William, Beverley, Yorks., chairmaker (1740s). Worked at Burton Constable, Yorks. and in the 1740s supplied to this house two dozen walnut chairs at £15 0s 6d. [*C. Life,* 3 June 1976, p. 1476]

Wrigley, Edmund snr, Toad Lane, Rochdale, Lancs., cm (1814–16). [D]

Wrigley, Edmund jnr & Robert, High St, Rochdale, Lancs., cm (1814). [D]

Wrigley, James, Middleton, near Manchester, chairmaker (1825–34). At Water St in 1825, Parkfield in 1828 and Long St, 1834. [D]

Wrigley, James, Dukinfield and Stalybridge, Lancs., joiner and cm (1828–34). At Dukinfield in 1828 and Stalybridge in 1834. [D]

Wrigley, Robert, Cheetham St, Rochdale, Lancs., cm (1816–18). In 1814 in partnership with Edmund Wrigley jnr at High St, but from 1816 trading on his own behalf. [D]

Wring, William, Golden Hill, Wiveliscombe, Som., cm (1839). [D]

Wroe, James, 4 Gray St, Oxford St, Manchester, u (1828). [D]

Wroe, John, Manchester, u (1817–29). At 2 Carpenters' Lane in 1817, 6 James St, Thomas St in 1825 and 4 Gray St, Oxford St in 1829. [D]

Wroe, John, Hulme St, Little Bolton, Lancs., u (1816–1818). [D]

Wroe, Joseph, Manchester, u, paper hanger and smallware dealer (1825–33). At 1 Police St, Chorlton Row in 1825, 4 Gray St, Oxford St in 1829 and 6 Gray St, Chorlton Row, 1832–33. [D]

Wryde, Peter, 68 Curtain Rd, Shoreditch, London, cm and u (1822). [D]

Wyand, John, Debenham, Suffolk, cm and carpenter (1824). [D]

Wyat, Mrs, Wine Office Ct, Fleet St, London, u (1748). [Heal]

Wyate, Richard, Church Side, Macclesfield, Cheshire, cm (1816). [D]

Wyatt, Charles, High St, Maidenhead, Berks., cm and u (1840). [D]

Wyatt, Edward, 360 Oxford St, London, carver and gilder (1784–1840). Edward Wyatt was born 1757 and by 1784 was trading at the Oxford St address. His trade card dating from the early years of his business records his trade as carver, gilder and picture frame maker and he offered 'Looking Glasses, Girandoles, Bordering for Rooms &c.'. Directories of 1803 and 1808 have been noted giving the address as

192 Oxford St. By 1820 he was claiming to be 'Carver & Gilder to his Majesty' and the considerable commissions that he carried out for the Royal Household and its members fully justifies this claim. He died in 1833 and was buried at Merton, Surrey where he owned property. The business continued to trade under his name into the 1840s. At this period the enterprise was probably being directed by his son Edward Wyatt jnr who is named in accounts with his father as early as April 1819. In 1822 the business was referred to as Edward Wyatt & Sons.

In his commissions for the Crown Wyatt undertook work at St James's Palace, Carlton House, Buckingham Palace, The Houses of Parliament and possibly the Royal Pavilion, Brighton. The earliest known commission for the Crown was in 1807 for carving at Carlton House. This involved frames with crowns for the Throne Room and other frames and repairs which amounted to £727 14s. Four panels with the orders of chivalry, carved and gilded, to be placed above the doors in the Throne Room were charged at £300. Further commissions are known in 1810–11 for Carlton House, involving the production of pier glass frames for the small blue Throne Room at £86 10s and twenty four emblematical door panels for the Throne Room at £584. In total work carried out in 1811 amounted to £756. Wyatt and other tradesmen working for the Prince Regent found that payment was often slow in arriving and Wyatt's name is included in a memorial requesting settlement for work at Carlton House drawn up in 1812. Additional frames and repairs and alterations were provided for a number of royal properties including Carlton House in the second and third decades of the 19th century. An entry for £3 11s on 5 April 1816 for repairs to the 'Chinese chairs and sofas in the Bow Room' may refer to the Royal Pavilion. Girandoles were restored for the House of Lords and in 1821 a richly carved mahogany shield provided for the Royal Model Repository at Woolwich which was charged at £64 16s. With the accession of Queen Victoria attention turned to alterations and additional carving work at Buckingham Palace, and bills delivered 1838–40 amounted to £1,614 7s 3d.

Work for other patrons was carried on in various parts of the country. In 1794 Thomas Anson paid Wyatt for work at his London house, Lichfield House, 15 St James's Sq. A large chimney glass frame, two carved and gilt table frames and carving 'Reeds and Ribbons to form pilasters of frames round pannels' were included in the work. The architect involved in this commission was James Wyatt and the family connection brought Edward Wyatt other work at Ashridge, Herts. where £200 was paid for carving in 1815. The 2nd Lord Braybrooke of Audley End paid Wyatt £17 14s 6s in 1803 possibly in connection with his London house; and Wyatt's name is mentioned in connection with carved Gothic chairs in oak and 'laird blackwood' supplied in 1810 through James Newton & Son of Wardour St for Taymouth Castle, Scotland. On 13 August 1814 a richly carved pier glass frame and a chimney glass frame together with the glass plates were invoiced to James Henry Leigh at Stoneleigh Abbey, Warks. The account for these together with carriage charges and the costs of workmen sent to install them came to £450 3s 4d. A Neo-classical stand with yellow marbling and carved enrichments resembling bronze is known made by Wyatt and is from Hinton House, Hinton St George, Som. This was supplied originally to Earl Poulet for this house. A late commission was the work carried out after Edward Wyatt snr's death for Scotney Castle, Kent. Furniture was produced for this house 1835–43 to the designs of the architect Anthony Salvin. A dresser which was carved for the house was charged at £97. The name of Edward Wyatt is also recorded in connection with Hackwood House, Hants. and the Church of St Dunstan-in-the-East, London. The main trade of the business was concerned with wood carving but work in stone was also undertaken by Edward Wyatt snr including carving the entrance gate to St James's Park 'in six pannels, and nine lion-heads with a rich pattern of twenty-four flowers' for which he was paid in 1808. [D; Westminster poll bk; Heal; C. Life, 25 October 1979, pp. 1404–06; DEF; PRO, LC1/5, LC11/18–21, LC11/27, LC11/30, LC11/44–74, LC11/80, LC11/95, LC11/104; Royal Works 5/114, 21/19; Windsor Royal Archives, RA 25233, 25298, 25340, 25384, 35554, Account Bk W, Box I, item 2; Essex RO, D/DBy/A357; Shakespeare Birthplace Trust, Leigh receipts, 18/5; Scottish RO, GD112/20/4/12/4] B.A.

Wyatt, Francis, parish of St Michael, Bristol, cm (1784). [Poll bk]

Wyatt, Frederick, West Cowes, Isle of Wight, Hants., u (1838). Bankruptcy announced, *Sussex Agricultural Express*, 2 June 1838.

Wyatt, G., London, cm (1793). Subscribed to Sheraton's *Drawing Book*, 1793.

Wyatt, J., 18 Kingsgate St, Holborn, London, u (1816). [D]

Wyatt, J., 325 High Holborn, Holborn Bars, London, upholder and cm (1817). [D]

Wyatt, James, 37 Eagle St, Red Lion Sq., Holborn, London, u and cm (c. 1800). Not recorded in London directories of the period. A cabinet veneered with mahogany, satinwood and rosewood, enriched with marquetry, mother-of-pearl and ormolu is known with the label of this maker and addressed to the Hon. Richard Ryder (1766–1832), son of the first Earl of Harrowby. A pair of painted and gilt Neo-classical torchère stands from Broome Park have also been attributed to this maker. [Heal; Sotheby's, 26 May 1967, lot 150; GCM; C. Life, 23 September 1976, supplement, p. 49]

Wyatt, James, parish of All Saints, Oxford, carver and gilder (1802). [Poll bk]

Wyatt, James, St John's St, Wolverhampton, Staffs., chairmaker (1822). [D]

Wyatt, James, High St, Oxford, printseller, carver and gilder (1830). [D]

Wyatt, James, 28 Bedford St, Plymouth, Devon, cm and u (1838). Successor to John Wyatt. [D]

Wyatt, John, Plymouth, u and cm (1805–36). At Broad St, 1805–08, Frankfort Pl., 1814–22, and Bedford St from 1823. The number in Bedford St was 27 in 1823–30 and 40 in 1830. [D]

Wyatt, John, East St, Warminster, Wilts., cm and u (1830). [D]

Wyatt, Joseph, High St, Lane End, Staffs., chairmaker (1822–35). [D]

Wyatt, Matthew, address unknown, carver and gilder (?) (1827–32). In 1832 petitioned for payment for furniture supplied to Windsor Castle for George IV 'nearly five years ago'. [PRO, LC1/1, 30 August 1832]

Wyatt, Samuel, Plymouth, Devon, cm (1824). In August 1824 married to Miss Ann Stevens at St Andrew's Church. [*Exeter Flying Post*, 12 August 1824]

Wyatt, Thomas, parish of St Mary the Virgin, Oxford, cm (1768). [Poll bk]

Wyatt, William, 1 Johnson St, Liverpool, carver and gilder (1810). [D]

Wyatt, William, Piccadilly, Shelton, Staffs., cm and u (1835). [D]

Wybrow & Barnard, 'Queen's Arms', Mount St, Grosvenor Sq., London (1767–70). Between June 1767 and August 1768 supplied carved picture frames to Shelburne House, Berkeley Sq. In 1770 the business was describing itself as Wybrow & Co. and trading from the Mount St address. It claimed to be

'Frame makers & gilders to Her Majesty'. On 8 March 1770 charged David Garrick £5 5s for '2 Carlomarat, picture frames Carv'd of Gilt Burnish Gold by Order of Mr Zoffany'. [Bowood MS; V&A Lib., 86 NN 4(i)]

Wybrow, John, Lambeth, London, chair and sofa manufacturer (1820–29). In 1820 at 52 New cut; in 1823–25 at 14 Milner Pl., New Cut and from 1826–29 at 14 Lower Marsh. [D]

Wyburd & Terry, City Rd, London, japan chair manufactury (1802–04). Included in the list of master cabinet makers in Sheraton's *Cabinet Dictionary*, 1803. [D]

Wyburn, Job., Langport, Som., carpenter, joiner and cm (1830). [D]

Wyburn, Job., High St, Bridgwater, Som., cm and u (1840). [D]

Wyburn, John, Fore St, Bridgwater, Som., cm and u (1840). [D]

Wyburn, Robert, East St, Taunton, Som., cm and u (1839). [D]

Wye, Edward, High Wycombe, Bucks., chairmaker (b. c. 1796–1841). Aged 45 at the date of the 1841 Census.

Wyer, Robert, 372 Oxford St, off Wells St, London, cabinet case maker (c. 1820). Trade label noted on a brass bound writing box of c. 1820. The business was described as the 'Original Military and Naval Trunk Manufacturers'.

Wyld, William, 53 Cannon St, St George's East, London, cm and u (1822). [D]

Wylde, Nathaniel, London, upholder (1701). Free of the Upholders' Co. 9 July 1701. [GL, Upholders' Co. records]

Wyles, William, 2 Mount Row, New Kent Rd, London, u (1839). [D]

Wyman, James, Blackmoor St, near Clare Mkt, London, frame maker (c. 1760). His trade card indicates that he had for offer 'All Sorts of Black Peartree or Deal Frames, for Paintings, after the Dutch, Italian or Common Method, with all Sorts of Carv'd & Gilt Ornaments and Frames for Pictures or Looking Glasses, also Prints neatly framed & Glaz'd'. Also stocked artists' materials. [Heal]

Wyman, William, Bristol, carver, gilder and frame maker (1814–19). Traded from 1799, but up to 1813 advertised himself only as a composition ornament maker. At Frogmore St, 1814–19, the number being 6 from 1815. In 1819 moved to 4 Clare St and from 1820 took additional premises in College Pl. The number in College Pl. was 1 in 1820–22 but from 1824 was given as 18 College St. [D]

Wymark, James, Brighton, Sussex, cm, u and furniture broker (1837–39). At Clarence Pl. in July 1837 but by August 1839 had moved to 36 Western Rd. [D]

Wymot, Thomas, 1 Dorchester St, New North Rd, London, cm (1839). [D]

Wymp, George, 5 Frederick St, Liverpool, cm and victualler (1837) [D]

Wynde, James, Golden Lane, London, upholder (1710–34). Father of John Wynde who was free of the Upholders' Co. in 1751 but traded as an apothecary. James was free of the Upholders' Co., 1 February 1709/10 and in 1734 was living in Golden Lane. [GL, Upholders' Co. records; Heal]

Wyndham, George, 38 Cavendish St, Brighton, Sussex, chairmaker (1826).

Wynn, Francis, Kirkgate, Leeds, Yorks., cm and u (1830). Traded from 82 Kirkgate but also had a warehouse at 19 Kirkgate. [D]

Wynn, James, Wolverhampton, Staffs., chairmaker (1816–18). At St John St in 1816. [D]

Wynn, John, Newark, Notts., cm (1790). [Poll bk]

Wynn, John, 82 Kirkgate, Leeds, Yorks., cm and u (1814–30). Francis Wynn who was trading from 82 and 19 Kirkgate in 1830 was probably his successor. [D]

Wynne, —, London, cm (1767). Payments were made in 1767 to this maker by Henry Knight of Tythegston Court, Glam. [C. Life, 5 October 1978, p. 1024]

Wynne, George, Goss St, Chester, cm (1818). [Poll bk]

Wynne, Joseph, Gorst Stacks, Chester, cm (1818). Free 13 May 1818. [Freemen rolls]

Wyrill, Robert, Bradford, Yorks., cm (1784). Freeman of York but living in Bradford in 1784. [D; York poll bk]

Y

Yabbicom, William H., Lower Castle St, Bristol, cm and u (1818–19). Trading at no. 10 in 1818 and no. 8 in 1819. [D]

Yale, Elihu, London, cm, broker and upholder (1784–99). Addresses given at 119 Newgate St in 1784 and 137 High Holborn, 1791–99. Took out Sun Insurance policies in 1784 for £600 of which £400 accounted for utensils, stock and goods; on 5 February 1791 with William Rayment for £1,400, £1,000 on utensils and stock; and alone on 27 June 1792 for £1,400, £800 on utensils, stock and goods. [D; GL, Sun MS vol. 319, p. 561; vol. 375, p. 415; vol. 384, p. 130]

Yale (or Yate), Elisha, 57 Little Britain, London, upholder (1789–93). [D]

Yallop, Jeremiah, Norwich and Ipswich, Suffolk, cm and chairmaker (1788–1818). Polled at St Mary's, Norwich, 1796–1806: of Ipswich in 1799, South Walsham in 1812, and St Stephen's, Norwich, in 1818. Recorded as Jeremiah Yallop jnr in 1796, and snr in 1818. Admitted freeman of Norwich, not by apprenticeship, on 16 June 1788. His son, Jeremiah Grindley Yallop, was admitted in 1810. [Norwich poll bks and freemen reg.]

Yallop, Jeremiah Grindley, Norwich, cm and chairmaker (1810–42). Recorded at Heigham in 1830 and Lower Westwick St in 1836. Son of Jeremiah Yallop, chairmaker; admitted freeman on 21 July 1810. [D; Norwich freemen reg. and poll bk]

Yallord, John, 111 Tottenham Ct Rd, London, u (1825). [D]

Yandell, Joseph, Cannon St, Bristol, cm (1799–1800). [D]

Yarde, Samuel, Exeter, Devon, u (1664). Fined £6 13s 4d in 1664, and 'afterwards remitted because he married an Alderman's daughter and at the instance of Copston [sic] Bampfeild, Bart'. [Devon and Cornwall Record Soc., Exeter freemen rolls]

Yardley, George, Noble St, London, freeman merchant tailor, carver and gilder (1753). Employed four non-freemen for three months in both 1753 and 1754. [GL, City Licence bks, vol. 1] Rococo trade card states: 'GEORGE YARDLEY, — Carver and Gilder. In Noble Street near Aldersgate, — LONDON. Makes & Sells all manner of Ornamental Frames, as Tables Frames, Slab Frames, Jarendoles, Branches, Trusses, Brackets, &c. wth. all sorts of Picture Frames, either Black or Carv'd & Gilt, Likewise Looking Glasses of all Sorts, from ye Smallest Size to ye Highest, in Carv'd & Painted, Carv'd & Gilt, Walnuttree & Gold. Mahogany & Gold. Jappan'd or in plain frames as Piers, Sconces, & Chimneys, wth. Hanging Glasses, or Dressing Boxes, & Dressing Glasses, also small Glasses in Painted Frames, Hollywood, or Varnish'd wth. all manner of work relating to Carving, Gilding, or Looking Glasses, ye above Articles are made at ye lowest Prices, & finished in ye Newest & Genteelest Taste. NB. Mapps & Prints Fram'd & Glaz'd in ye neatest manner'. [Heal]

Yardley, Samuel, St James's Sq., Wolverhampton, Staffs., cm and joiner (1833). [D]

Yarnall, Richard, Barton St, Tewkesbury, Glos., chairmaker (1820–39). Listed at no. 76, 1820–22. [D]

Yarnall, William, Barton St, Tewkesbury, Glos., chairmaker

1011

64*

and turner (1830–39). One directory lists both William and William jnr at Barton St in 1830. [D]

Yarrow, J., 1 Upper Ogle St, Fitzroy Sq., London, cm (1827–29). [D]

Yarrow, Ridley, 68 Curtain Rd, Shoreditch, London, cm (1826–29). [D]

Yate, Richard, London, chairmaker (1820–21). Of 122 Wardour St took out a Sun Insurance policy on 24 February 1820 for £1,400 including £890 on stock, utensils and goods in trust in his house, workshops and open yard, and £400 on workshops and counting rooms. Of 26 Berwick St took out Sun policies on 30 November 1820 and 2 May 1821 for £1,000, £910 on stock, utensils and goods in trust in his house, workshop, on roof and in open yard. A further policy of 2 May 1821 was taken out with William Harris for £1,600, including £550 on Yate's house, £500 on workshops behind, and £550 on a house at 27 Berwick St in tenure of Bell, a chaser. [GL, Sun MS vol. 483, refs 964024 and 972999; vol. 488, refs 980130–31]

Yate, Simon, 3 Golden Lyons by Fleet Ditch, St Bride's, London, upholder (1713). Insured his goods on 24 February 1713. [GL, Sun MS vol. 2, p. 20]

Yateman, William, London, u, cm, undertaker, sworn appraiser and auctioneer (1779–1811). Addresses given at 94 Leadenhall St in 1786; no. 24, 1789–93; no. 94, 1793–95, and 12 St Paul's Churchyard, 1796–1811. Son of William Yateman, haberdasher of Bishopsgate St. App. to James Senols on 7 April 1779, and admitted freeman of the Upholders' Co. by servitude on 3 May 1786. Took app. named Thomas Oakey, 1786–94. Named in Sheraton's list of master cabinet makers, 1803. Trade cards of 1795 and 1797 [Banks Coll., BM] give address at 12 St Paul's Churchyard, and show a canopied bed and two funeral attendants. Card is similiar to that of Benjamin Winter. [D; GL, Upholders' Co. records]

Yateman, William, High St, Daventry, Northants., cm and u (1830). [D]

Yates, Benjamin, 10 Norfolk St, Sheffield, Yorks., cm (1797). [D]

Yates, Charles, Lime St, Liverpool, carver, gilder and victualler (1816–27). Trading at no. 34 in 1816, no. 25 in 1818, and no. 32 in 1821. [D]

Yates, David & Son, South St, Sheffield, Yorks., furnishing u (1825). [D]

Yates, Edward, London Rd, Manchester, u and cm (1828–29). Trading at no. 107 in 1828–29 and also no. 67 in 1829. [D]

Yates, Henry, Liverpool, cm (1784). Admitted freeman on 2 April 1784. [Liverpool freemen reg.]

Yates, Henry, Liverpool, cm (1818–30). Recorded at 16 Pall Mall, 1818–21; and 8 Bixteth St and Pine Pl., Ford St some time between 1818–30. Admitted freeman on servitude to Thomas Gorton on 11 June 1818. Stated as 'not dead 18 Oct. 1830'. [D; Liverpool freemen reg.]

Yates, Isaac, Nantwich, Cheshire, chairmaker (1768). Son Thomas bapt. on 2 April 1768. [Chester RO, PR (bapt.)]

Yates, James & Whitworth, John, Bordesley, parish of Aston, Warks., coffin furniture, picture and looking-glass frame makers (1779). Insured utensils and stock for £1,200 in 1779. [GL, Sun MS vol. 276, p. 225]

Yates, James, Otley, Yorks., joiner, cm and builder (1828–34). Recorded at Clapgate, 1828–29 and Bridegate in 1830. [D]

Yates, John, York, u (1733–48). Recorded as son of Joanna Yates, widow, app. to George Reynoldson, u, on 26 November 1733; and as son of John Yates, pinner and hosier, admitted freeman in 1739. Notice in *York Courant*, 12 July 1748, stated he was 'Upholder nigh Ouse Bridge, Agent for

John Devenport & Co.; printed paper available for room hanging'. [York app. reg. and freemen rolls]

Yates (or Yeat(e)s), John, St Martin's Lane, St Martin-in-the-Fields, London, cm and chairmaker (1749–55). Polled at Westminster in 1749. Listed as a 'Prisoner for Debt in the Poultry Compter, London' in *London Gazette*, 27 May 1755.

Yates, John, Rotherham, Yorks., cm (1798). [D] A John Yates of Sheffield subscribed to Sheraton's *Drawing Book*, 1793.

Yates, Richard, Horse Mkt St, Warrington, Lancs., cm (1822). [D]

Yates, Richard, London, carver and gilder, cm and u (1826–39). Trading at 55 Judd St, Brunswick Sq., 1826–28, and 7 Charlotte St, Tottenham Ct, Rd, 1837–39. [D]

Yates, Robert, 55 Judd St, Brunswick Sq., London, carver and gilder (1825). [D]

Yates, Sarah, Mount St, Birmingham, u (1828–35). Listed at no. 42 in 1828–30 and no. 43 in 1835. [D]

Yates, Simon, Abingdon, Berks., u (1734). [Poll bk]

Yates, Thomas Smith, Essex, cm (1806–30). Polled at Colchester of 'Weeeligh' (Weeley, Essex?) in 1806, and of Colchester, 1812 and 1830.

Yates, Thomas, Manchester, u, cm, paper hanging warehouseman (1811–34). Addresses given at 21 Deansgate in 1811; 17 Piccadilly, 1813–22; and 3 Hanging Ditch, 1825–34. [D]

Yates, William, 17 Mill Lane, Liverpool, carver and gilder (1813–14). [D]

Yates, William, 20 Princess St, Manchester, cm and u (1832–40). Recorded as William Yates & Co., 1836–40. [D]

Yates & Co., Bradford St, Deritend, Birmingham, 'factors & manufacturers of cabinet brass foundary, coffin furniture, picture frames, looking glasses, composition ornaments, coach & coach harness furniture . . .'. (1800). [D]

Yates, Son & Harper, Bradford St, Deritend, Birmingham, coffin furniture, picture frames, looking-glasses, coach and coach harness furniture, composition ornaments (1803). [D]

Yealman, W., 48 Queen St, Leicester Sq., London, u and appraiser (1820). [D] Possibly William Yeatman of 18 Green St.

Yeamans, Edward, Kirkgate, Wakefield, Yorks., chairmaker, turner and carver (1830–37). [D]

Yearbury, George, 3 Redcliffe Hill, Bristol, carver and gilder (1828). [D]

Yeatman, Elizabeth, 18 Green St, Leicester Sq., London, cm (1807). Took out a Sun Insurance policy on 18 September 1807 for £1,100. [GL, Sun MS vol. 440, ref. 806638] See William Yeatman and Hannah Yeatman at this address.

Yeatman, Hannah & Lack, Thomas, 18 Green St, Leicester Sq., London, upholder (1821). Took out a Sun Insurance policy on 7 March 1821 for £2,000, including £1,250 on a private house called 'Horny Cottage', Teddington, Middlx, £600 on household goods, china and glass, and £150 on stable, coach house and offices. [GL, Sun MS vol. 488, ref. 976770] See Elizabeth Yeatman and William Yeatman at this address.

Yeatman, William, 290 Strand, London, cm and upholder (1782). Took out a Sun Insurance policy in 1782 for £700, £500 accounting for utensils, stock and goods. [GL, Sun MS vol. 300, p. 191]

Yeatman (or Yateman), William, 18 Green St, Leicester Sq., London, upholder, cm and appraiser (1784–1828). Recorded also at no. 19, 1805–28. Took out Sun Insurance policies in 1784 for £600, utensils and stock accounting for £300; on 11 January 1793 for £200 on stock and goods in trust in workshop behind his house; and on 14 May 1804 for £1,100 including £1,000 on the house of Daniel Woodward, and £100 on workshop. [D; GL, Sun MS vol. 322, p. 279; vol. 389, ref. 610806; vol. 431, ref. 762275] Possibly

W. Yealman. See Elizabeth Yeatman and Hannah Yeatman at this address.

Yeaxley, William, Clarance St, Staines, Middlx, carver and gilder (1838–39). [D]

Yeeds, Elizabeth, 14 Jervis St, Liverpool, u (1835). [D] Probably Elizabeth Youd(s), and Younds.

Yeoman, Adam, York, u (1777). Son of William Yeoman, u; admitted freeman in 1777. [York freemen reg.]

Yeoman, J., Verandah Terr., Canal Walk, Southampton, Hants., cm (1734–39). [D]

Yeoman, William, York, u (1731–41). Son of Robert Yeoman, tanner; admitted freeman in 1731. Polled of Coppergate in 1741. [York freemen rolls]

Yewd, William, at 'The Golden Lyon', three doors west from Somerset House in the Strand, London, cm and mahogany turner (1703–69). Directories of 1703 and 1763 and early 18th-century trade card give above address. Card states: 'Makes and Sells all Sorts of Cabinet work Chaire work and Turnery ware. Serves Shopkeepers with all Sorts of Voiders, Tea Trays and boards made in the Best Manner at Reasonable Rates. NB. Funerals Furnished and Goods appraisd'. [Leverhulme Coll., MMA, NY] Named as Fellow of the Society of Arts and Manufacturers, 1761–66. William Yewd, cm of St Mary-le-Strand, had app. named George Gigg, c. 1769. [S of G, St John-in-the-Soke, Winchester settlement papers]

Yewdale, J., Wibsey, Bradford, Yorks., cm (1823). [D]

Yolland, Thomas, address unrecorded, cm (1803). Subscribed to Sheraton's *Cabinet Dictionary*, 1803.

York, John, address unrecorded. Bill dated 16 May 1738 to Lord Leigh of Stoneleigh, Warks., lists 'A large Looking Glass in Gilt Frame', costing £9 9s; 'A large Sconce in a Gilt Frame', £7 7s; and 'A Mohogony dressing Table', £1 1s. Receipted on 1 July 1738 by James York for his father, John. [Shakespeare Birthplace Trust, Leigh receipts, DR 18/5; Christie's, Stoneleigh sale cat., 15–16 October 1981, lots 102 and 110]

York, Richard, address unrecorded, cm (1720). [GL, Sun MS vol. 481, ref. 964877]

York, Richard, 5 Brokers Row, London, cm and u (1822–23). [D]

York, Thomas, Gold St, Northampton, carver and gilder (1830). [D]

Yorke, Bridget Nash, Cambridge, see Edward Yorke.

Yorke, Edward and successors, Cambridge, cm, u and auctioneers (1748–1840). Edward Yorke 'lately apprenticed to Thomas Graves, Alderman, Burgess and Joiner' was made free of the Corporation of Cambridge on 17 January 1755. He appears to have finished his apprenticeship some years before this as he is recorded on 5 January 1753 as paying half a years rates on premises in Trumpington St (next door to William Roper, another cm and u). The firm's bill head dated 1848 also announced 'Established 1748'. When Roper retired from business in 1773, Yorke took over his shop and paid the parish rates on both properties up to 1787, when he rebuilt Ropers old premises (what is now 14 King's Parade). Advertised as auctioneer in *Cambridge Chronicle and Journal*, 8 December 1764, 16 August and 11 October 1766 and 31 October 1767.

Yorke's recorded apps are: John Hazzard, 28 May 1765 for £31 10s, Thomas Burgoyne, 24 April 1776 for £42, James Tall, 5 January 1781 for £10, Thomas Chandler, 26 March 1796 for 10s, and Stephen Rawlinson, 26 March 1796 for £21. The last two are listed in the names of Edward Yorke and his son Thomas. Thomas, b. 1761 and bapt. in St Edward's parish, 28 October, was app. to his father 'for natural love' on 24 August 1778 and made free on 29 September 1785. His death aged 53 was reported in *Cambridge Chronicle and*

Journal, 14 March 1814. Edward Yorke announced in *Cambridge Chronicle and Journal*, 2 April 1799 that he was resigning the business to his son Thomas. The death of Edward Yorke aged 77 was announced on 2 July 1803.

Payments to the Yorkes are recorded in the account books of the Cotton family of Madingley Hall, Cambridge between 1800–01. The *Cambridge Chronicle and Journal* reported on 14 (and/or 18) March 1814 the death of Thomas Yorke; this was followed in the next issue with an announcement by 'B. N. [Bridget Nash] Yorke widow of Thomas Yorke' that 'having engaged proper assistants, till she receive the aid of the Son who is prepairing himself for the purpose' she would carry on the business. The son, Samuel Yorke, announced on 20 March 1818 that he had 'taken the business carried on by his late mother', and he traded at King's Parade (previously Trumpington St), 1832–41. His apprenticeship had been in Norwich, then the main furniture making town in East Anglia, as in an advertisement of 21 October 1831 announcing that he had engaged one of Elliot Smith's best paper hangers, he states 'that he is enabled to Furnish Houses and Rooms with dispatch and taste combined with economy, having had considerable experience during his seven years servitude in the Upholstery connected with the Cabinet Business in one of the first houses in Norwich, besides the general knowledge he has since gained from many of the first-rate Houses in London'. Samuel Yorke was admitted freeman on 7 October 1818 for a fee of £10 10s.

All the directories and poll bks list the Yorkes in the shop in Trumpington St later to be called King's Parade but from c. 1843 the business moved to 6 Benett St. This is the address on a bill head dated 1848 in the names of 'C. & T. Yorke, Auctioneers, Upholderers, Appraisers, Cabinet Makers, Undertakers, House Agents' and receipted by Samuel Yorke for monies 'Received for Sons'. The bill head also includes an illustration of 'Yorke's Registered Revolving Easy Chair'. The last entry to the firm is in Slater's directory of 1850. [Cambs. RO, Cambridge Corp. day bks and app. lists; rate bk of St Edward's parish; poll bks; City of Cambridge, Royal Commission on Historial Monuments 1959; Cambs. RO, account book of the Cotton family, 588/A45; bill head, Cambridgeshire Coll., City Lib; *Furn. Hist.*, 1978. R.W.

Yorke, Samuel, Cambridge, see Edward Yorke.

Yorke, Thomas, Cambridge, see Edward Yorke.

Youd, George, Mill Lane, Potton, Beds., u (1823). [D]

Youd(s) (or Younds), Elizabeth, Jervis St, Liverpool, u (1835–39). Trading at no. 15 in 1834; no. 14 in 1835; no. 15 in 1837; and no. 31 in 1839. [D] Probably Elizabeth Yeeds.

Youen, Richard, High Wycombe, Bucks., chairmaker (b. c. 1826–41). Aged 15 at the time of the 1841 Census.

Youens, James, High Wycombe, Bucks., carver, chair-caner (b. c. 1816–41). Daughters bapt. in 1836 and 1837; son in 1839. Aged 25 at the time of the 1841 Census. [D; PR (bapt.)]

Youens, John, High Wycombe, Bucks., chairmaker (b. c. 1805–41). Aged 36 at the time of the 1841 Census.

Youens, Robert, High Wycombe, Bucks., carver, chair and sofa maker (b. c. 1814–48). Son bapt. in 1838. Aged 27 at the time of the 1841 Census. [PR (bapt.)]

Youle, George, St Giles-in-the-Fields, London, cm (d. 1692) [PCC Wills, 1686–93; Index Lib., vol. 11, 1958, p. 293] Possibly brother of:

Youle, John, London, cm (d. 1694). Recorded in newspapers of 1694 as 'leaving off trade' at 'The Cabinet', Drury Lane. [Heal] Will dated 1694 gives address at St Giles-in-the-Fields. [PCC Wills, 1694–1700, Index Lib., vol. 12, 1959–60, p. 465, f.180]

Young, —, Ironmonger Lane, Cheapside, London, u (1747).

Heal records him in contemporary newspapers. See Young & Fall, Hickman Young and Young & Brooks at this address.

Young, —, London, u and silk mercer (1768). Supplied 'Blue Genoa Damask' costing £88 19s to Shelburne House, Berkeley Sq., between 13 September and 17 October 1768. [Bowood MS]

Young, —, 81 Wells St, Oxford St, London, u (1805–07). [D]

Young, Abraham, Epsom, Surrey, upholder etc. (1794). [D]

Young, Abraham, 6 High St, Newington, London, auctioneer, house agent, undertaker, u and cm (1809–11). [D]

Young, Adam, 3 Chapel St, Lamb's Conduit, London, cm and upholder (1835–39). [D]

Young, Benjamin, 29 Deal St, Salford, Lancs., cm (1836–40). [D]

Young, Edward, address unrecorded, upholder (1708). Admitted freeman of the Upholders' Co. on 13 April 1708. [GL, Upholders' Co. records]

Young, George, 52 Goodge St, London, carver (1808). Took out a Sun Insurance policy on 4 April 1808 for £500 on a house at 261 Oxford St in tenure of a corn chandler, and £350 on a house at 34 Edgeware St in tenure of a turner. [GL, Sun MS vol. 445, ref. 814937]

Young, George, 7 Gay St, Liverpool, cm (1813–14). [D]

Young, George, Hull, Yorks., cm (1831–39). Trading at 6 Dock Office Row in 1831 also as a furniture broker; and at the corner of Christopher St and Francis St, also as a beer house keeper, 1835–39. [D]

Young, George, 10 Westgate St, Newcastle, carver and gilder (1833–34). [D]

Young, George, Southgate, Market Weighton, Yorks., cm (1840). [D]

Young, Godfrey, 6 High St, Newington Butts, London, u (1826–30). Recorded as Young & Godfrey, cm and u, 1827–28. Declared bankrupt, *London Gazette*, 1 June 1830. [D]

Young, Henry, Stone-Cutter St, Fleet Mkt, London, chairmaker (1796–1807). Trading at no. 28, 1805–07. Served as Constable at St Bride's in 1796. [D; GL, MS 6561, p. 123]

Young, Henry, King's Lynn, Norfolk, cm (1813–14). App. to James Oldmeadow, cm, and admitted freeman, 1813–14. [King's Lynn freemen calendar]

Young, Henry, Union St, Maidstone, Kent, cm and u (1832–39). [D]

Young, Hickman, London, u (1753–87). Recorded at 4 Ironmonger Lane, Cheapside, 1753–68; and 51 Hatton Gdn (or St), 1771–87. [D] Heal records Young & Hickman, u, at 51 Hatton Gdn in 1777, possibly wrongly. See Young & Brooks and Young & Fall at these addresses.

Young, I., address unrecorded. Good quality rosewood sofa table, c. 1810–20, recorded stamped 'I. YOUNG'.

Young, James, Piccadilly, London, cm (1749). [Poll bk]

Young, James Mates, Bristol, cm (1782). Declared bankrupt, *Leicester Journal*, 4 May 1782.

Young, James, 2 Queen St, by Marlborough St, London, u (1805–39). Recorded at no. 4 as cm and u in 1839. Took out Sun Insurance policies on 30 June 1806 for household goods and clothes; on 18 June 1807 for £300 including £60 on utensils and stock in trust; and on 23 June 1812 for £500 on his house. [D; GL, Sun MS vol. 437, ref. 790735; vol. 440, ref. 804213; vol. 459, ref. 871463]

Young, James, London, chair manufacturer (1820–23). Recorded at 18 Duke St, Westminster in 1820 and 20 Norfolk St, Southwark, 1821–23. [D]

Young, James, Halifax, Yorks., cm and u (1828–37). Recorded at Crown St, 1828–29; Hall End in 1830; and 46 Swine Mkt in 1837. [D]

Young, James, 2 Francis St, Newington, London, cm and undertaker (1839). [D]

Young(e), John, address unrecorded, u (1660–61). Recorded in the Royal Household accounts, 1660–61 supplying luxurious upholstered furniture. Listed are: 'Turned frames for a couch and a great chair. 9 high stools and a low stool with crimson velvet to line the wings of the couch and back of the chair. Holland quilt, pillows & carpets. 200 fourscore and £3.10.4.'. [PRO, LC5/39] Younge's account from Michaelmas 1660–61 lists: 'a Couch Frame turned & with the best Ironworke to it', costing £1 13s 4d; '3 ells ½ of Crimson taffatae to lyne ye winge of the Couch and backes of all the Chaires att XV', £2 12s 6d; 'for 2500 of large nailes double gilt', £6 5s; 'for 650 gilt Burnishe nailes for the backe of the Chaires, & the wings of ye couch', 9s 9d; 'for double gilding the Iron worke for ye Couch', £2 10s; 'for making the large couch wth baggs of Downe, & borders of Crimson vellvett', £2 6s 8d. [*Conn.*, January 1934, pp. 15–22]

Young, John, Worcester, later London, u (1768–86). Described as 'late of the City of Worcester' on 6 July 1768 when admitted freeman of the Upholders' Co. by redemption. Recorded at High Holborn in 1772, and Kentish Town, 1781–86. [GL, Upholders' Co. records]

Young, John, Peter St, London, cm (1774). [Poll bk]

Young, John Mates, Bristol and London, cm (1781–97). Polled at Bristol of there in 1781, and of St Martin's Lane, London in 1784. Declared bankrupt, *Exeter Flying Post*, 14 December 1797.

Young, John, Broughton, Lancs., u (1784). [D]

Young, John, Morpeth, Northumb., u (1784). [D]

Young, John, 26 Pitfield St, Hoxton, London, carver and gilder (1805–25). [D]

Young, John jnr, High St, Gateshead, Co. Durham, cm and furniture broker (1827). [D]

Young, John, Middle St, Newcastle, cm and furniture broker (1833–38). Recorded at no. 32 in 1834 and no. 33 in 1838 as cm and joiner. [D]

Young, John, 34 Miller St, Long Millgate, Manchester, chairmaker (1840). [D]

Young, Joseph, Carlisle Lane, Castle St, Carlisle, Cumb., joiner and/or cm (1829). [D]

Young, Lake, London, coach and looking-glass manufacturer, glass cutter (1768–1802). Rococo trade card, 1769, gives addresses at 'The Coach and LOOKING GLASS MANUFACTORY ... in James Street, Covent Garden: or at his Warehouse near the Pump in WATLING STREET'. Listed in directories, 1774–1802, at 54 Watling St. Trade card states: 'Merchants, Captains of Ships, country chapmen &c. may be supply'd on reasonable Terms with all Sorts of Looking Glasses, Viz^t. Sconces, Pier & Chimney Glasses, Dressing Boxes & Swingers, in Mahogany, Walnut-tree, & Painted, or in rich Carv'd & Gilt Frames in the neatest Taste & newest fashion. All Sorts of Window Glass, Wholesale and Retail, or for Exportation'. [Heal] Young was a member of the Court of Common Council of the City of London, one of the eight men representing Cordwainer Ward, and was elected in 1768 one of the Commissioners of Sewers, Lamps and Pavements. He is listed in 1769 as one of the twenty-four Directors of the Laudable Society for the Benefit of Widows. [Wills, *Looking-Glasses*; C. *Life*, vol. cxxx, no. 3358, p. 91] Succeeded by Brown, Young & Son, glass cutters.

Young, Mathew, Burgate, Barton-upon-Humber, Lincs., joiner and cm (1835). [D]

Young, Neal, address unrecorded, upholder (1764–76). Son of Donall Young, farmer of Atholl, Scotland. App. to Benjamin Dell on 6 September 1764, and admitted freeman of the Upholders' Co. by servitude on 4 December 1776. [GL, Upholders' Co. records]

Young, Peter, Great Lumley, Co. Durham, joiner and cm (1827–28). [D]

Young, Richard, St Mary Magdalene, Oxford, cm (1768). [Poll bk]

Young, Richard, Holywell, Oxford, cm (1802). [Poll bk]

Young, Richard, St Peter-le-Bailey, Oxford, bedmaker (1802). [Poll bk]

Young, Robert, Church Way, North Shields, Northumb., furniture broker and cm (1827). [D]

Young, Robert, 6 Hamilton Terr., Birkenhead, Cheshire, joiner and cm (1839). [D]

Young, Thomas, London, joiner and carver. In the late 17th century worked at Chatsworth, Derbs. with Davis, Lobb and Watson, acting as master carver until 1692. Young was also employed by Thomas Osborne, 1st Duke of Leeds, at Kiveton, rebuilt 1694–1704. Young also worked at Burghley House, Lincs. [V & A archives; Beard, *Georgian Craftsmen*; F. Thompson, *A History of Chatsworth*, pp. 149–50]

Young, Thomas, Hetling Ct, Bath, Som., cm (1793). [D]

Young, Thomas, Liverpool, chairmaker (1830). Marriage at St Nicholas's Church to Miss Ann Sloan reported in *Liverpool Mercury*, 1 October 1830.

Young, W., address unrecorded, cm. Stamp found on early 19th-century chair with tapering, fluted front legs, sabre back legs, scroll arms, upholstered seat, and simple curved back. [V&A archives]

Young, W., 10 Green St, Bath., Som., cm (1819). [D]

Young, William, address unrecorded, carver (1691–92). Mentioned in the accounts for Sudbury Hall, Derbs., 1691–92, and he may have carved the doorcase at the foot of the stairs leading to the Parlour. He later worked at Chatsworth. [O. Hill & J. Cornforth, *English Country Houses: Caroline*, p. 173; V&A archives]

Young, William, York, cm (1745–58). Polled of Micklegate in 1758. Son of William Young; app. to Francis Ryther, cm, on 1 May 1745. Admitted freeman in 1752. [York app. reg. and freemen rolls]

Young, William, London, cm (1784–85). Polled at York of London in 1784. Described of Queen's Ct, Holborn, when his son, William was admitted freeman of York as cm in 1785. [York freemen rolls]

Young, William, Park St, London, u (1769). Declared bankrupt, *Gents Mag.*, April 1769.

Young, William, King St, Little Sanctuary, London, cm (1774). [Poll bk]

Young, William, 160 Ratcliffe Highway, London, u, broker and cm (1789–93). [D]

Young, Will., 3 Caroline Pl., City Rd, London, upholder and undertaker (1817). [D]

Young, William, Roper St, Whitehaven, Cumb., joiner and/or cm (1829–34). Trading at no. 55 in 1834. [D]

Young, William, Guildhall Passage, Hull, Yorks., joiner and cm (1838–39). [D]

Young & Brooke (or Brooks), 4 Ironmonger Lane, Cheapside, London, u (1769–73). Recorded also at Hatton Gdn in 1770, and no. 51 in 1772. [D] See Young, —, Hickman Young and Young & Fall.

Young & Fall, Ironmonger Lane, Cheapside, London, u (1759–60). Recorded at no. 4 in 1760. [D]

Young & Hobson, Gateshead, Co. Durham, joiner and cm (1824–33). Trading at Front St in 1824 and West St in 1833. [D]

Young & Howard, 14 Oxford St, London, upholders, cm, appraisers and undertakers (1790–93). [D]

Young & Trotter, Frith St, Soho, London. Recorded as the makers of a fine Jamaican mahogany tea table, *c.* 1760, with scalloped corners, supported on pillar and claw feet with

castors. [G. Bernard Hughes, 'Mahogany Claw Tables', *C. Life*, 17 March 1955]

Younger, Edward, 14 Old St Rd, London, cm (1829–35). [D]

Younger, Sarah, 14 Old St Rd, London, cm (1839). [D]

Younghusband, John, Church Lane, Workington, Cumb., joiner and/or cm (1798–1811). [D]

Youse, William, Grove St, Wantage, Berks., wood turner (1840). [D]

Youxfield, Robert, St Mary's parish, Chelmsford, Essex, chairmaker (1669). Child bapt. on 21 August 1669. [Essex RO, PR (bapt.)]

Z

Zandra, George, Spear St, Manchester, carver, gilder, picture frame and looking-glass maker (1811–19). Recorded at no. 51 1811–18, and no. 61, 1817–19. [D]

Zanetti, Joseph, 100 King St, Manchester, barometer and looking-glass maker, carver and gilder (1837–40). Declared bankrupt, *Sussex Agricultural Express*, 4 March 1837. [D]

Zanetti (or Zannette), Vinc(i)ent, Manchester, carver, gilder, looking-glass and picture frame maker, printseller (1804–33). Addresses given at 59 Fountain St, 1804–11; 5 Wrights' Ct, Market St, 1813–25; 10 Blackfriars Bridge in 1829, and 20 Blackfriars, 1832–33. [D]

Zanetti (or Zannette), Vittorie (or Vittorio), Manchester, carver and gilder, looking-glass manufacturer, picture framer and printseller (1804–17). Addresses given at 87 Market St Lane, 1804–11, and 94 Market St, 1813–17. Partnership with Thomas Agnew announced in *Manchester Mercury*, 30 September 1817, stating that Zannetti's 'Repository of Art' at 94 Market St had been established for 'the last 20 years'. In 1817 Vittorio Zanetti supplied to Dunham Massey, Cheshire, 'a frame for a drawing 8′ 7″ @ 3/6 ft.' costing £1 10s, and 'Plate glass for do. 22×18', £2 12s 6d. [D; Dunham Massey papers] In Goodison, *Barometers*, he is recorded as Vincente Vittore Zanetti at 98 Market St Lane, and later at no. 87. Advertisement, headed 'Repository of Arts' is cited, stating that his wares included prints, drawings, paintings, busts of famous men, lamps, sideboards, barometers and thermometers.

Zanetti, Bolongaro & Agnew, 94 Market St, Manchester, carvers and gilders, barometer and looking-glass makers (1816–17). [D]

Zan(n)etti & Agnew, Manchester, carvers, gilders, barometer, thermometer, mathematical and philosophical instrument, looking-glass and picture frame makers, printsellers, publishers, dealers in artist's materials, opticians etc. (1810–40). Addresses given at 94 Market St, 1810–25; 25 Gartside St in 1825; 10 Exchange St, 1825–29; at no. 18, 1832–33 and no. 14, 1836–40. Advertisement in *Pigot and Dean's Directory for Manchester and Salford*, 1824–25, gives address at the 'Repository of Arts', 94 Market St, and announces that they 'are now carrying on the above branches on a more extensive scale and, being the Manufacturers, they are enabled to offer every article on as liberal terms as any house in the Kingdom. They have always on hand a very great variety of PIER and CHIMNEY GLASSES, MIRRORS, LUSTRES, CANDELABRAS ... Upholsterers, Cabinet Makers, Glass Dealers, &c. supplied with Plate Glass of any dimensions; old Glasses polished and silvered; old Frames Repaired, gilt and altered to the present fashions ...'. Zanetti

& Agnew are named in the Dunham Massey papers on 31 December 1822 receiving £274 9s for regilding and cleaning pictures etc. A billiard table by the firm is at Manchester City Art Gallery. [D; Goodison, *Barometers*] See Agnew & Zanetti.

Zanfrini & Gugeri, East St, Blandford, Dorset, looking-glass makers (1830). [D]

Zerbon & Co., 18 Mersey St, Liverpool, carvers and gilders (1807). [D]

Zerboni, Battistessa, Moteni & Guanziroli, London, looking-glasses, barometers and thermometers (1835–36). Recorded at 24 Cross St, Hatton Gdn and 13 Baldwins Gdns in 1835; and 106 Hatton Gdn in 1836. [D; Goodison, *Barometers*]

Zuardri, Joseph, St John's Lane, Smithfield, London, looking-glass frame maker (1840). [GL, Sun MS vol. 576 (?), ref. 1335]

Zuraghi, Felix, 9 City Rd, London, looking-glass, barometer and thermometer maker (1832–34). [D; Goodison, *Barometers*]

Zurn, —, address unrecorded. One of a pair of marquetry commodes at the Vyne, Hants., *c.* 1760–65, attributed to Pierre Langlois, is inscribed 'Zurn', presumably a specialist inlayer. [*Conn.*, vol. 179, 1972, pp. 181–83]

INDEX

This index retrieves the names of tradesmen and apprentices mentioned in the text, most of whom do not have an individual *Dictionary* entry. If the reference is only to a surname it has not been included unless that person was in partnership with others. Alternative spellings of names where not obvious have been listed. The index provides readers with a key for checking thousands of names which would otherwise be buried in the main body of this work.

INDEX OF TRADESMEN AND APPRENTICES

Rostilt, 386
Rotherel, Richard, 767
Rouse, Joseph, 706
Rouse, Richard, 821
Row, 373
Row, Benjamin, 19, 580
Row, Benjamin Hambling, 762
Rowe, Charles, 997
Rowe, George, 762
Rowe, Isaac, 765
Rowe, James, 952
Rowes, Isaac, 765
Rowlands, James, 716
Rowley, 516
Rowley, Edward, 81
Rowling & Brown, 769
Rudd, John, 698
Ruddock, William, 859
Rudyard, 440
Rudyard, Lawrence, 439, 458
Rudyeard, Lawrence, 458
Rullidge, William, 254
Rummer, Michael, 763
Rumney, Robert, 160
Rusby, 276
Rusby, Hugh, 74, 395, 568, 855, 886
Rush, William, 766
Russel, Richard, 469
Russell, 789
Russell, Charles, 773
Russell, I., 773
Russell, J., 773
Russell, James, 305
Russell, John, 677, 773
Russell, R., 49, 310
Russell, Robert, 936
Russell, Thomas, 771, 783
Russell, William, 290
Russell & Bruce, 771
Rutherford, 820
Rutherford, John, 950
Rutherford, Joseph, 154
Rutledge, 31, 923
Rutledge, Christopher, 768
Rutledge, William, 959
Rutt, Thomas, 274
Rutter, Gasgoine, 329
Rutterford, 820
Ryan, 210
Rycroft, John, 599
Ryder, Francis, 460
Ryder, Joseph, 746
Ryder & Scribe, 456
Rylance, John, 68
Rylands, Joseph, 230
Ryley, 747
Ryley, John, 749

Ryther, Francis, 1015
Ryton, Obadiah, 774
Ryton, William, 774

S(?)holl, Thomas, 510
Sabourin & Marchand, 775
Sagar, Stephen, 40
Sage, T., 775
Saint, Thomas, 160
St Quintin, Percy, 586
Saladine, Thomas, 312
Sale, Phineas, 369, 1009
Salisbury, John, 264, 781
Sallows, Aldred, 801
Sallows, John, 801
Salter, John, 482
Salthouse, 939
Salthouse, Richard, 747
Sampson, 954
Samuel, James, 71
Sandell, Samuel, 726
Sanders, 129, 261
Sanders, Frances, 779
Sanders, Joseph, 138, 668
Sanderson, 29, 144
Sanderson, Alexander, 779
Sanderson, Harry, 681
Sanderson, John, 136, 186, 438, 517, 574
Sandford, William, 308
Sands, Daniel, 420
Sandwell, Henry, 873
Sandwell, Joseph, 612
Sandys, Martin, 739
Sangar, 984
Sargeant, James, 438
Sargent, 233
Sargood, 329
Satterthwaite, 257
Saunders, 263, 414
Saunders, Ann, 95
Saunders, Henry, 785
Saunders, John, 785
Saunders, Joseph, 840
Saunders, Paul, 98, 99, 100, 554, 652, 653, 835
Saunders, Richard, 30
Saunders, Thomas, 782
Saunders & Colbron, 785
Saunier, Julia, 786
Savage, Michael, 546
Savage, Purbeck, 194
Savage, Walter, 611
Savile, Thomas, 65, 933
Savill, 136
Savill, Thomas, 306, 536
Saville, 937
Saville, Thomas, 102

Sawyer, 421
Saxton, Alfred, 787
Saxton, George, 787
Saxton, Henry, 787
Saxton, Nathaniel, 811
Say, Frances, 500
Say, Francis, 228, 350, 732
Say, Richard, 730, 969, 994
Scafe, William, 859
Scholefield, John, 788–9
Scholes, Abner, 72
Scholes, Benjamin, 263
Scholey, Joseph, 215, 286
Scholey, Robert, 836
Schouten, William, 376
Scoles, Abner, 407, 569
Scott, 319
Scott, Charles, 38
Scott, George, 637
Scott, Samuel, 654
Scott, Thomas, 198, 637
Scribe, 456
Scrimshire, Matthew, 290
Scrimshire, William, 287, 401, 647, 819, 859, 894
Scriven, William, 855
Seabright, 918
Seabrook, 327
Seager, 200
Seal, Richard, 298
Seaman, William, 11, 399, 504
Search, Samuel, 521
Searson, William, 983
Searson, Wortley, 37, 983
Sebire, 369
Seddon, 75, 252, 282, 435, 721, 766, 808, 867, 970
Seddon, George, 6, 178, 372, 562, 624, 653, 658, 688, 728, 780, 954
Seddon, Henry, 408
Seddon, Richard, 408
Seddon Sons & Shackleton, 643, 699, 794, 796, 797
Sedgwick, Christopher, 759
Sedgwick, John, 798
Sedwell, William, 965
Seely, Abraham, 864
Seller, Christopher, 398
Sellers, John, 358
Semple, Alexander, 802
Semple, John, 802
Senols, James, 233, 369, 1012
Severn, Samuel, 10, 863, 876
Sewell, John, 7, 777
Shackleton, 643, 699, 796, 797
Shackleton, Thomas, 658, 659, 660, 794, 795, 1008
Shadbolt, Charles, 800